Chilton's motorcycle repair manual

president and chief executive officer **William A. Barbour;** executive vice president **K. Robert Brink;** vice president and general manager **William D. Byrne;** editor-in-chief **John D. Kelly;** managing editor **John H. Weise,** SAE; assistant managing editor **Peter J. Meyer;** senior editor **Michael S. Yampolsky;** technical editor **Joseph F. Pellicciotti;** editor **Byron P. Collins;** editorial production **Edna H. Jones,** manager; **Carole L. DeCrescenzo, Richard L. Moore, Sandra J. Purrenhage**

Published in Radnor, Pa., by Chilton Book Company
Chilton Way, Radnor, Pa. 19089 215-687-8200
ISBN: 0-8019-5876-8
Library of Congress Catalog Card Number 74–9342

CHILTON BOOK COMPANY Radnor, Pennsylvania

contents

BMW
INDEX

MODEL IDENTIFICATION

The R50, R50 S, and the R50 US are essentially the same machines except that the US model, depicted here, is ½ in. longer, is fitted with telescopic front forks rather than the Earles type forks which came on the European R50 and R50 S models, and comes equipped with side car mountings. The three machines employ the same basic 490cc engine whose compression ratio is 6.8:1 and which breathes through 24mm carburetors; however the S model is slightly hotter with a compression ratio of 9.2:1 and slightly larger 26mm carbs.

The R60, and R60 US models are basically the same as the R50 line, only larger. The 590cc engines have a compression ratio of 7.5:1 and develop 30 hp @ 5800 rpm.

The R69 S and R69 US have the same engine as the R60 models, but they go faster. The S model employs the same hot cam as the R50 S and both machines come equipped with 26mm carbs and a boosted compression ratio of 9.2:1. Again, the main physical difference is the use of a telescopic fork on the US model rather than the Earles fork on the R69 S.

In 1969 BMW introduced their new line designated by "/5" (i.e. R50/5) which follows the model number. The new models are all lighter, faster, and more nimble than their predecessors, yet retain the characteristic BMW silhouette and their penchant for reliability.

The R50/5, pictured here, is the baby of the line yet produces about 10 horsepower more than the earlier R50 model.
The R60/5 now delivers more to the rear wheel than the old R69 S model which was the hot set-up of the old line.

The all new R75/5 has a 745cc engine which breathes through new 32 mm constant velocity carburetors for smooth high speed touring and super bike performance.

In 1971 BMW redesigned their line once again when they added a lot of brightwork to the tanks and side covers of their usually conservative machines. Pictured here is an R60/5 model which looks like all the rest of the models except that all have their own model designation stamped on the crankcases.

GENERAL SPECIFICATIONS

All figures, unless otherwise noted, in inches

	R50	R50S	R60	R69S
DIMENSIONS				
Curb Weight (lb): Without Sidecar	436	436	436	445
With Sidecar	705	705	705	714
Overall Width: Without Sidecar	26	26	26	28.4
With Sidecar	64	64	64	64
Overall Height	38.6	38.6	38.6	38.6
Saddle Height	28.5	28.5	28.5	28.5
Overall Length: Without Sidecar	83.6	83.6	83.6	83.6
With Sidecar	94.4	94.4	94.4	94.4
Wheelbase: Without Sidecar	55.7	55.7	55.7	55.7
With Sidecar	57.0	57.0	57.0	57.0
Ground Clearance	5.3	5.3	5.3	5.3
ENGINE				
Type	Horizontally opposed four-stroke twin			
Displacement (cc)	490	490	590	590
Bore x Stroke (mm)	68 x 68	68 x 68	72 x 73	72 x 73
Compression Ratio	6.8 : 1	9.2 : 1	7.5 : 1	9.5 : 1
Horsepower @ rpm	26 @ 5800	35 @ 7650	30 @ 5800	42 @ 7000
Lubrication	Combined force-feed/centrifugal, operated by geared pump			
Carburetion (Bing): Left	1/24/45	1/26/71	1/24/125	1/26/69
Right	1/24/46	1/26/72	1/24/126	1/26/70
TRANSMISSION				
Clutch Type	Single-disc, dry plate			
Overall Gear Ratios: Without Sidecar 1st	4.171	4.171	4.171	4.171
2nd	2.725	2.725	2.725	2.725
3rd	1.938	1.938	1.938	1.938
4th	1.540	1.540	1.540	1.540
With Sidecar 1st	5.330	5.330	5.330	5.330
2nd	3.020	3.020	3.020	3.020
3rd	2.040	2.040	2.040	2.040
4th	1.540	1.540	1.540	1.540
Final Drive Type	Universal shaft and spiral bevel gears, fully enclosed			
Final Drive Ratio: Without Sidecar	3.13	3.58	3.13	3.13
With Sidecar	4.33	4.33	4.33	4.33
ELECTRICS				
Ignition Type	Magneto	Magneto	Magneto	Magneto
Lighting and Charging	Generator	Generator	Generator	Generator
Starting	Kick	Kick	Kick	Kick
CHASSIS				
Frame Type	Welded duplex-tube steel			
Front Suspension	Swing arm with multirate springs and dual-action shock absorbers			
Rear Suspension	Swing arm with multirate springs and dual-action shock absorbers			
Trail: Without Sidecar	3.74	3.74	3.74	3.74
With Sidecar	2.40	2.40	2.40	2.40
Tire Size: Front	3.50 x 18	3.50 x 18S	3.50 x 18	3.50 x 18S
Rear	3.50 x 18	3.50 x 18S	3.50 x 18	3.50 x 18S
Sidecar	4.00 x 18	4.00 x 18	4.00 x 18	4.00 x 18

	R50/5	R60/5	R75/5
DIMENSIONS			
Curb Weight (lb)	452	463	463
Overall Length	82.7	82.7	82.7
Overall Width	29.1	29.1	29.1
Overall Height	44.0	44.0	44.0
Seat Height	33.5	33.5	33.5
Wheelbase	54.5	54.5	54.5
Ground Clearance	6.5	6.5	6.5
ENGINE			
Type	Horizontally opposed four-stroke twin		
Displacement (cc)	498	599	745
Bore x Stroke (mm)	67.0 x 70.6	73.5 @ 70.6	82.0 x 70.6
Compression Ratio	8.6 : 1	9.2 : 1	9.0 : 1
Horsepower @ rpm	36 @ 6600	46 @ 6600	57 @ 6400
Torque @ rpm	28.2 @ 5000	35.5 @ 5000	43.4 @ 5000
Lubrication	Combined force-feed/centrifugal, operated by geared pump		
Carburetion (Bing): Left	1/26/113	1/26/111	64/32/4
Right	1/26/114	1/26/112	64/32/3
TRANSMISSION			
Clutch Type			
Overall Gear Ratios: 1st	3.896	3.896	3.896
2nd	2.578	2.578	2.578
3rd	1.875	1.875	1.875
4th	1.500	1.500	1.500
Final Drive Type	Universal shaft and spiral bevel gears, fully enclosed		
Final Drive Ratio	3.56	3.36	2.91
ELECTRICS			
Ignition Type	Magneto	Magneto	Magneto
Lighting and Charging	Alternator	Alternator	Alternator
Starting	Electric/Kick	Electric/Kick	Electric/Kick
CHASSIS			
Frame Type	Welded duplex-tube steel		
Front Suspension	Telescopic fork, hydraulically dampened		
Rear Suspension	Swing arm with multirate springs and dual-action shock absorbers		
Tire Size: Front	3.25 x 19	3.25 x 19	3.25 x 19
Rear	4.00 x 18	4.00 x 18	4.00 x 18

TUNE-UP AND MAINTENANCE

TUNE-UP OPERATIONS

Valve Clearance

Set valve clearances with the engine cold, preferably after having been left sitting overnight.

1. Remove the rocker arm cover securing nuts. One is located in the center of the cover (14 mm) and the other two are located on the side (10 mm).

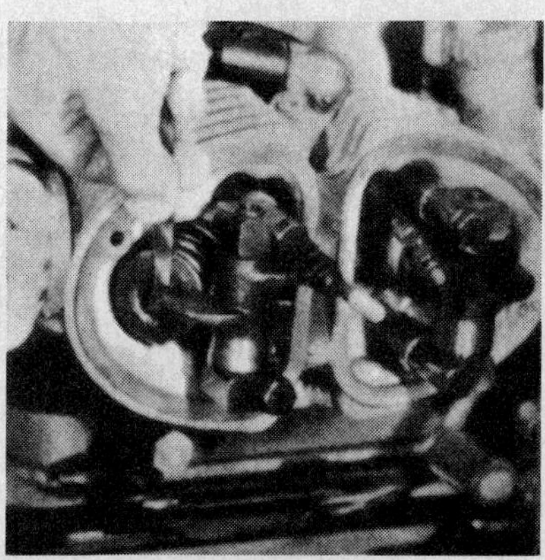

Valve tappet adjustment.

2. Check cylinder head nut and bolt torque. If necessary, tighten them to 25.3 $\pm$ 2.8 ft lbs.
3. Remove the spark plugs.
4. Rotate the engine by turning the alternator rotor bolt with an allen wrench until one cylinder is on its compression stroke (both valves closed).
5. Continue rotating the engine until this cylinder is at top dead center, then slip the appropriately sized feeler gauge between the intake valve stem and rocker arm.
6. If necessary, loosen the adjuster locknut and turn the adjuster until a snug slip fit is obtained. Retighten the locknut.
7. Repeat Steps 5 and 6 on the exhaust valve, then recheck the clearances.
8. Rotate the engine until the other piston is at top dead center (TDC) of its

compression stroke, then repeat the valve adjustment procedure.

Contact Breaker Points

The point set is located behind the dynamo (magneto or generator) cover. To gain access, remove the securing allen screws and disconnect the battery cable (R50/5, R60/5, R75/5).

R50, R50S, R60, AND R69S

NOTE: *Refer to the accompanying illustration while performing the following procedure.*

1. Rotate the engine by turning the alternator rotor bolt with an allen wrench until the points are at their widest gap. This can be detected by watching the breaker cam as it lifts the heel of the movable point.

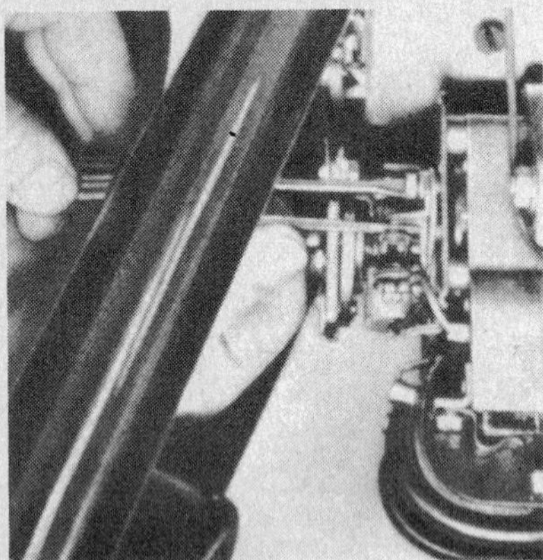

Adjusting breaker point gap (pre-1970 models).

2. Insert the appropriate feeler gauge; it should be a snug slip fit.
3. If the gap requires adjustment, loosen lockscrew (a) just enough to permit movement of the breaker plate.
4. Turn eccentric screw (b) to achieve the proper point gap, then tighten lockscrew (a). Recheck the gap and readjust if necessary.
5. Lubricate the breaker cam felt with Bosch Ft 1 v 4 about every other tune-up.

R50/5, R60/5, AND R75/5

NOTE: *Refer to the accompanying illustration while performing the following procedure.*

1. Rotate the engine by turning the alternator rotor bolt with an allen wrench until the points are at their widest gap. This can be detected by watching the breaker cam as it lifts the heel of the movable point.

CAUTION: *The battery should be disconnected to avoid possible damage to the diode board as you remove the cover.*

2. Insert the appropriate feeler gauge; it should be a snug slip fit.

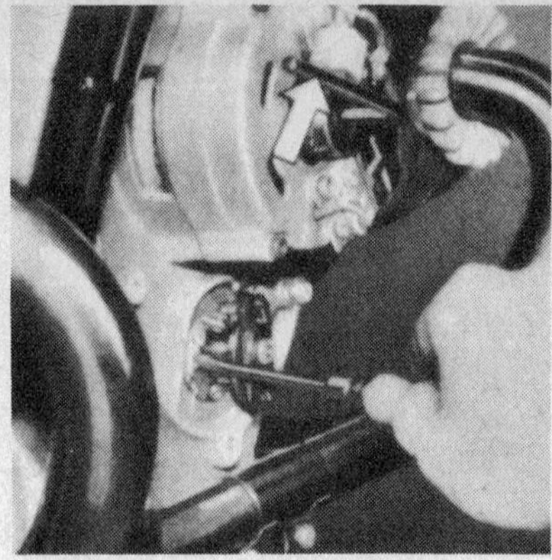

Adjusting breaker point gap (post-1969 models).

3. To adjust the gap, loosen the setscrew slightly, then move the breaker plate by inserting a screwdriver blade between the two little pins and breaker anvil. Retighten the setscrew.
4. Recheck gap and readjust if necessary. Lubricate the breaker cam felt with Bosch grease Ft 1 v 4 every other tune-up.
5. Every other tune-up you should also remove and lubricate the centrifugal advance unit shaft with Bosch grease Ft 1 v 22 or 26. Also check proper spring action.

NOTE: *If the points were oil coated, or if there is evidence of excess oil in the housing, the oil seal must be replaced by driving it into position with a suitable deep socket. Be careful not to hit the spark advance mounting stem as this may result in damage to the camshaft.*

Ignition Timing

R50, R50S, R60, AND R69S

Static Method

NOTE: *Refer to the accompanying illustrations while performing the following procedure.*

1. Disconnect the ignition coil wire (d) from the terminal (c) to protect the magneto from external test lamp current.
2. Connect one lead of the test lamp to terminal (c) and the other one to the ground.

Disconnecting the ignition coil wire (pre-1970 models).

3. Rotate the engine until the flywheel mark "S" is aligned with the reference mark in the engine case inspection hole and one piston is on its compression stroke. This position denotes 9° before TDC, ignition timing fully retarded.
4. At this point, the test lamp should flicker on and off when the flywheel is moved ever so slightly in either direction.
5. If an adjustment is required, loosen the magneto retaining nuts and move the magneto body within the oblong mounting holes. Moving it clockwise advances the ignition; counterclockwise retards the ignition.
6. Tighten the magneto retaining nuts and recheck the timing.
7. Rotate the engine until the other piston is on its compression stroke, then repeat the procedure. The variance in ignition timing for the two cylinders must not exceed 2° of crankshaft rotation.

Dynamic Method

1. Connect the strobe timing light as directed by the manufacturer's instructions.
2. With the engine running, aim the strobe light beam at the engine case inspection hole.
3. At idle (approximately 500–750 rpm), timing mark "S" should line up directly with the inspection hole reference mark. If mark "S" is above the reference mark, the timing is too far advanced. If it is below the reference mark, the timing is too far retarded.
4. Slowly increase the engine's speed. Beginning at approximately 1200 rpm, the "S" mark should rise and disappear from view. At approximately 5800 rpm, the flywheel mark "F" should appear in the inspection hole and line up with the reference mark.
5. Once again, drop the engine speed to idle, then slowly increase it and make sure that the transition from flywheel mark "S" to flywheel mark "F" occurs smoothly and accurately. If not, check the advance mechanism for binding.
6. If an ignition timing adjustment is necessary, loosen the magneto retaining

Safety spark gap (pre-1970 models).

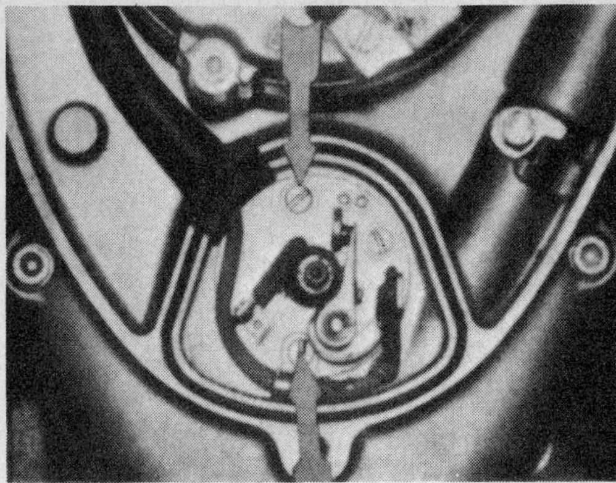

Loosening the magneto mounting nuts.

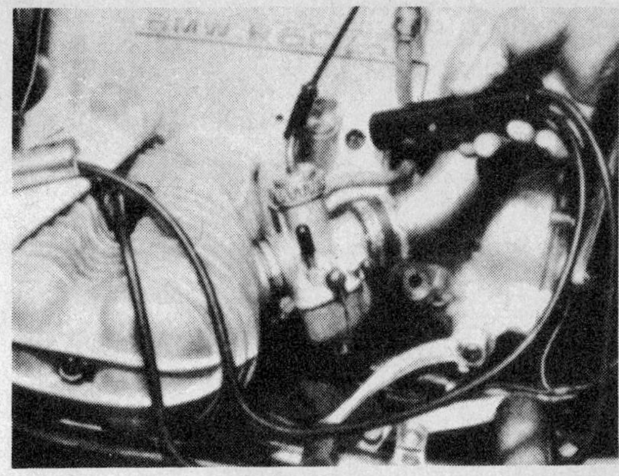

Dynamic ignition timing marks (post-1970 models).

nuts and shift the body as described in "Static Method."

7. When the timing is correctly set, check the safety spark gap. Make sure that the gap in the accompanying illustration is 10–11 mm.

8. Lubricate the breaker cam felt as described in "Contact Breaker Points."

R50/5, R60/5, AND R75/5

Static Method

NOTE: *Refer to the accompanying illustrations while performing the following procedure.*

1. Connect one lead of a timing light to condenser terminal (1) and the other lead to ground (2).

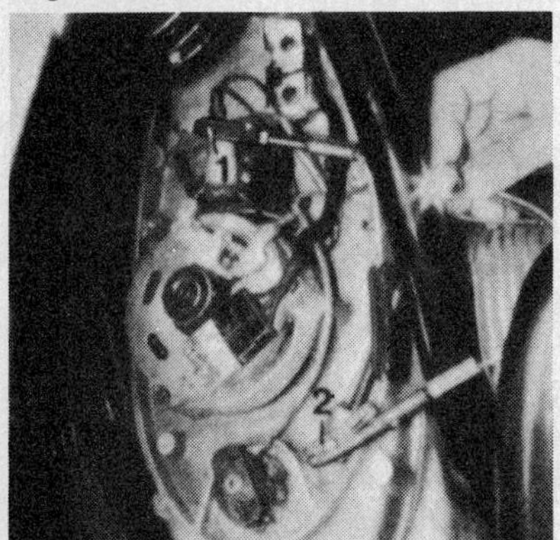

Timing light connections (post-1969 models).

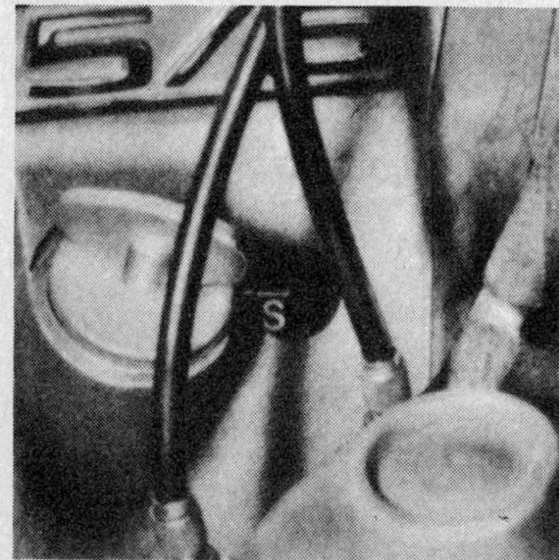

Retarded timing mark (post-1969 models).

2. Rotate the engine until the flywheel mark "S" is aligned with the reference mark in the engine case inspection hole and one piston is on its compression stroke. This position denotes 9° before TDC, ignition timing fully retarded.

3. At this point, the test lamp should flicker on and off when the flywheel is moved ever so slightly in either direction.

4. If an adjustment is necessary, loosen the two slotted screws (1) and rotate the breaker plate clockwise to advance the ignition, and counterclockwise to retard it.

5. Tighten the breaker base plate screws and recheck the timing.

6. Rotate the engine until the other piston is on its compression stroke, then repeat the procedure. Ignition timing between the two cylinders must not vary more than 2° of flywheel rotation.

Dynamic Method

NOTE: *Refer to the accompanying illustration while performing the following procedure.*

1. Connect the strobe timing light as directed by the manufacturer's instructions.

2. With the engine running, aim the strobe light beam at the engine case inspection hole.

3. At idle (Approximately 600–800 rpm) timing mark "S" should line up directly with the inspection hole reference mark. If mark "S" is above the reference mark, the timing is too far advanced. If it is below the reference mark, the timing is too far retarded.

4. Slowly increase the engine's speed. Beginning at approximately 1200 rpm, the "S" mark should rise and disappear from view. At approximately 3000 rpm, the flywheel mark "F" should appear in the inspection hole and line up with the reference mark.

5. Once again, drop the engine speed to idle, then slowly increase it and make sure the transition from flywheel mark "S" to flywheel mark "F" occurs smoothly and accurately. If not, check the advance mechanism for binding.

Breaker plate mounting screws (post-1969 models).

6. If an ignition timing adjustment is necessary, loosen the two breaker plate base screws (1) and turn the base in the direction of normal crank and camshaft rotation to retard the timing, and against the direction of normal rotation to advance the timing.

7. Tighten the breaker base plate screws and recheck the timing.

8.Lubricate the breaker cam felt as described in "Contact Breaker Points."

Carburetor Adjustments

R50, R50S, R50/5, R60, R69S, AND R60/5

Idle Speed and Mixture

1. Set cable free-play at the carburetors to 1 mm (0.04 in.).

Adjusting the throttle stopscrew (pre-1970 models).

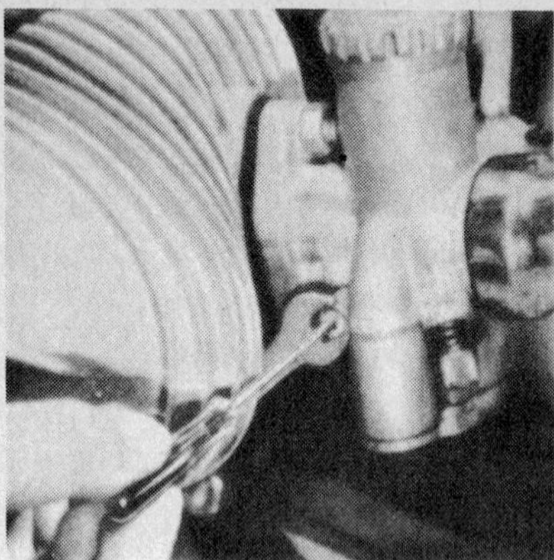

Adjusting idle mixture (pre-1970 models).

2. Set idle speed with the engine running and warmed up to operating temperature. Temporarily disconnect the spark plug lead from one cylinder, then the other. If idle speed is not the same with either lead disconnected, turn "in" the throttle stopscrew of the slower cylinder's carburetor until they are equal.

3. Focus your attention on either the right or left carburetor and slowly turn the pilot air screw in both directions until you find a point where there is a slight increase in engine rpm. At this point, idle mixture is correctly set. Do the same for the other carburetor.

4. The idle speed is now likely to be a little higher than it should be, so back out the throttle stop screws an *equal* amount until the idle is lowered to 600–800 rpm.

Throttle Slide Synchronization

1. Turn the throttle twistgrip slightly so that the engine is running at about 1000 rpm. At this point, the throttle slides are beginning to lift.

2. Disconnect the spark plug lead from one cylinder and note the engine's speed. Now reconnect the lead and disconnect the other one; engine speed should be the same. If it is not, take up a little cable free-play at the slower cylinder's carburetor.

3. Alternately disconnect the spark plug lead from each cylinder and adjust

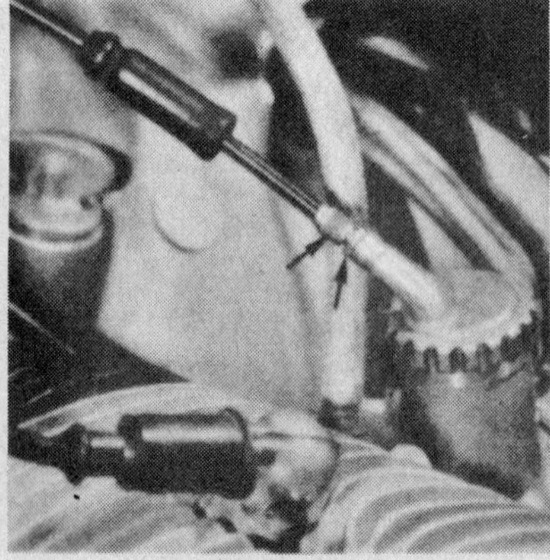

Throttle cable adjustment (pre-1970 models).

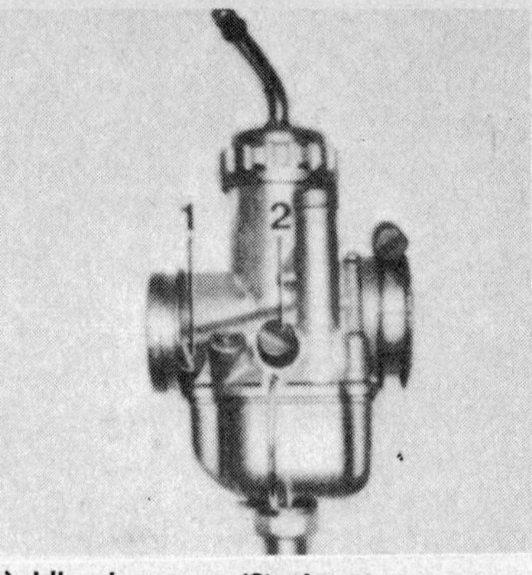

(1) Idle air screw; (2) throttle stopscrew (R50/5 and R 60/5 models).

cable free-play until the engine runs at the same speed with either spark plug lead disconnected.

R75/5

NOTE: *All carburetors should have a "C" stamped on their caps. 1970 and early 1971 models which do not carry this mark should be modified to "C" specifications.*

Idle Speed and Mixture

1. Set butterfly cable free-play at the carburetors to 1 mm (0.04 in.).

2. Set starter jet cable free-play at the carburetors to 0.5–1.0 mm (0.025–0.040 in.). Cable free-play must be exactly the same at both carburetors.

Throttle cable free-play (R 75/5 models).

3. Turn the idle mixture screws "in" until lightly seated, then back them "out" one full turn.

4. Turn the butterfly stopscrews "in" until they just contact the levers, then turn them "in" one full turn.

5. Start and warm up the engine until it reaches normal operating temperature.

6. Focus your attention on either the right or left carburetor and slowly turn the idle mixture screw in both directions until you find a point where there is a slight increase in engine rpm. At this point, idle mixture is pretty close to being correct. Do the same for the other carburetor.

7. Working alternately between carburetors, slowly back "out" the butterfly stop screw, then repeat step six.

8. Disconnect the spark plug lead from one of the cylinders and continue lowering the idle and readjusting the mixture screw until the cylinder cuts out. Reconnect the lead and disconnect the other one. Perform the same procedure on this cylinder and then reconnect the spark plug lead.

9. Start the engine and observe the idle speed. It should be 600–800 rpm but if it isn't, turn the butterfly stop screws "in" or "out" an equal amount until idle speed is correct.

NOTE: *If a suitable adjustment is difficult to attain check the action of the advance mechanism.*

Butterfly Synchronization

1. Turn the throttle twistgrip slightly so that the engine is running at about 1000 rpm. At this point, the butterflies are beginning to open.

2. Disconnect the spark plug lead from one cylinder and note the engine's speed. Now reconnect the lead and disconnect the other one. Engine speed should be the same. If it is not, take up a little butterfly cable free-play at the slower cylinder's carburetor.

3. Alternately disconnect the spark plug lead from each cylinder and adjust cable free-play until the engine runs at the same speed with either spark plug lead disconnected.

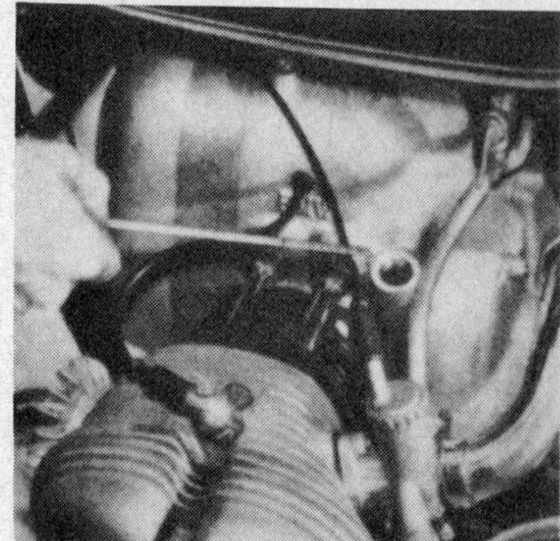

Oil dipstick (pre-1970 models).

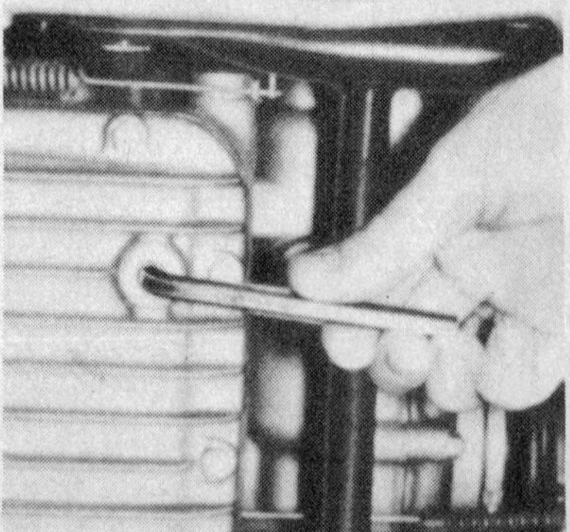

Removing oil drain plug (post-1969 models).

TUNE-UP SPECIFICATIONS

	R50	R50S	R50/5	R60	R69S	R60/5	R75/5
Valve Timing (deg)							
Intake Opens (ATDC)	6	4	6	6	4	6	6
Intake Closes (ABDC)	34	44	47	34	44	47	47
Exhaust Opens (BBDC)	34	44	47	34	44	47	47
Exhaust Closes (BTDC)	6	4	6	6	4	6	6
Valve Clearance (cold)							
Intake (in./mm)	0.006/0.15	0.006/0.15	0.006/0.15	0.006/0.15	0.006/0.15	0.006/0.15	0.006/0.15
Exhaust (in./mm)	0.008/0.20	0.008/0.20	0.008/0.20	0.008/0.20	0.008/0.20	0.008/0.20	0.008/0.20
Breaker Point Gap: (in.)	0.016	0.016	0.016	0.016	0.016	0.016	0.016
(mm)	0.40	0.40	0.40	0.40	0.40	0.40	0.40
Spark Plugs							
Type (Bosch)	W 240 T1	①	W 230 T30	W 240 T1	①	W 230 T30	W 200 T30
Gap (in./mm)	0.024/0.60	0.024/0.60	0.028/0.70	0.024/0.60	0.024/0.60	0.0028/0.70	0.028/0.70
Ignition Timing (deg)							
Static (BTDC)	9	9	9	9	9	9	9
Advance Range	30 ± 2°	30 ± 2°	31 ± 2°30′	30 ± 2°	30 ± 2°	31 ± 2°30′	31 ± 2°30′
Dwell Angle	—	—	110 ± 1°	—	—	110 ± 1°	110 ± 1°
Carburetion				See text procedures			
Cranking Compression (psi)							
Good	140-150	140-150	140-150	140-150	140-150	140-150	140-150
Average	128-140	128-140	128-140	128-140	128-140	128-140	128-140
Poor	125 or less	125 or less	125 or less	125 or less	125 or less	125 or less	125 or less

① W 240 T1 during break-in period; W 260 T1 thereafter.

MAINTENANCE ITEMS

Engine Oil

Change the oil after the engine has been run long enough to be up to normal operating temperature. This ensures the oil being fluid enough to be completely drained and that impurities suspended in the oil only after it has circulated will be removed. BMW recommends that the following lubricants be used:

Below 50° F Outside Temperature	SAE 20, SAE 10W30, SAE 10W50
From 32-86° F Outside Temperature	SAE 30, SAE 20W40, SAE 20W50
Over 86° F Outside Temperature or for High-Speed Riding	SAE 40

Unscrew the stick, clean it with a rag, and reinsert it. Do not screw it back in. Withdraw it again and check the indicated level, then screw it back in. Do not removed or install the dipstick while the engine is running. The amount of oil between the "MIN" and "MAX" marks is approximately 2.1 pints (pt.)

OIL FILTER CARTRIDGE

(R50/5, R60/5, and R75/5)

These models are equipped with an oil filter cartridge, which should be replaced every 3000 miles when changing engine oil.

1. Remove the allen screws securing the filter cover.
2. Remove the center hex head bolt and lay aside the filter cover and O-ring.

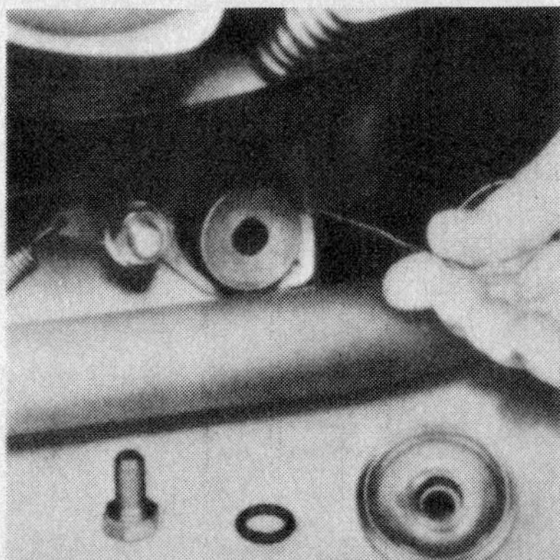

Removing the oil filter cartridge (post-1969 models).

3, Fashion a small hook with a piece of thin wire, then pull out the cartridge and gaskets.

4. Install the new cartridge and gaskets, then the O-ring and cover after checking their condition.

OIL SUMP PAN

The sump pan and filter screen should be removed and thoroughly cleaned at the intervals given at the end of this chapter. Remove any trapped particles, clean the screen in solvent, then blow it dry with compressed air if possible. Use new gaskets when installing the pan.

Removing the sump pan (post-1969 models).

Gearbox

The gearbox oil level can be checked by removing the filler plug located on the left side of the engine case just behind the carburetor. The normal lubricant level is to the bottom thread of the filler plug hole. When changing the gearbox oil, remove both the filler plug and the drain plug, which is located beneath the engine. Drain the oil only after the bike has been running for some time and the lubricant has thinned out enough to allow complete drainage. BMW recommends that a premium-quality hypoid gear oil, SAE 90, be used in both winter and summer.

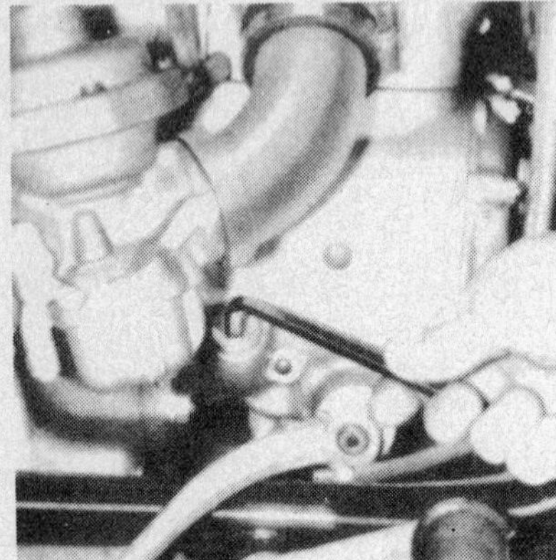

Removing the transmission oil drain plug (post-1969 models).

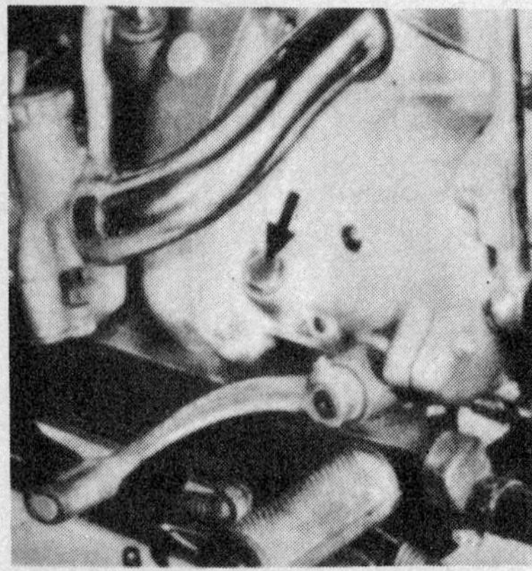

Gearbox filler plug (pre-1970 models).

Driveshaft Housing

Set the machine up on its centerstand, remove the filler plug at the top rear of the driveshaft housing, and insert a thin dowel, or something similar, until it touches the top of the driveshaft. Pull it out and check the indicated oil level. To be exact, the level should be 0.08 inch (in.) above the top of the driveshaft. This is rather difficult to measure, however, so just make sure the top of the shaft is fully immersed.

The drain plug is located at the bottom of the driveshaft housing and must be removed along with the filler plug when changing the oil. Make sure the oil is warmed up to normal operating temperature before draining. BMW recommends that a premium-grade hypoid oil, SAE 90, be used both in winter and summer.

Driveshaft housing filler plug.

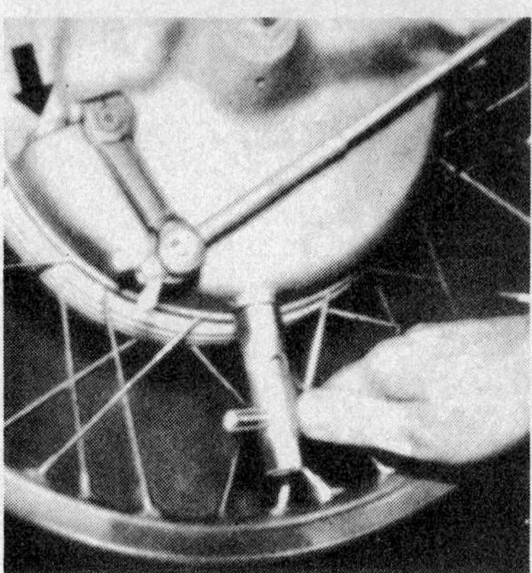

Rear-wheel drive drain and filler plugs.

Rear-Wheel Drive

To check the oil level, remove the filler plug located at the right rear of the wheel hub. The normal level is to the first thread of the filler plug hole.

To change the oil, remove the drain plug located at the bottom of the wheel hub in addition to the filler plug. The oil should be at operating temperature before it is drained. BMW recommends as a premium-quality hypoind gear oil, SAE 90, winter and summer.

Telescopic Fork

1. Set the motorcycle up on its centerstand.
2. Make sure the fork is fully extended, then remove the rubber caps from the bottom plugs of the fork legs.
3. While holding the damper tube end secure with an allen wrench, remove the bottom leg nuts.
4. Remove the caps from the top of the fork legs, using the pin wrench supplied with the machine's tool kit.
5. Pull down both fork legs and let the oil drain into a container.
6. Reinstall the bottom fork leg nuts, then pour the specified amount of oil through the top of each leg. The bottom leg nuts should be torqued to 16.6 ± 2.0 foot pounds (ft lbs). After drainage, add only 265 cc of oil to compensate for oil still clinging to the inside of the tubes.

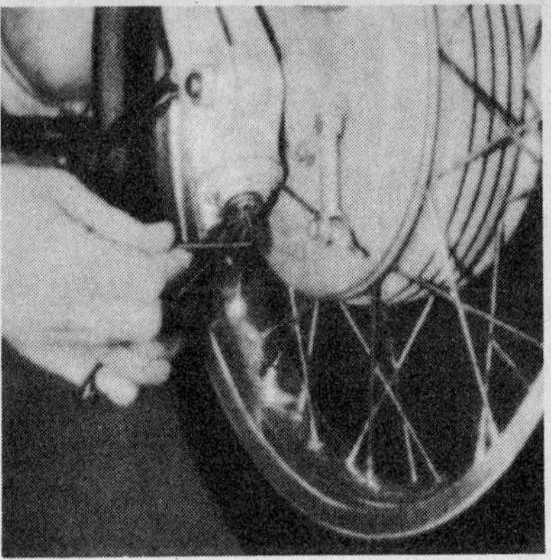

Draining the front fork oil.

BMW recommends that one of the following fork oils be used:

Shell Aero Fluid 4
Shell 4001
Castrol BMW Shock Absorber Oil
BP Olex Hl 2463 (Aero-Hydraulik)

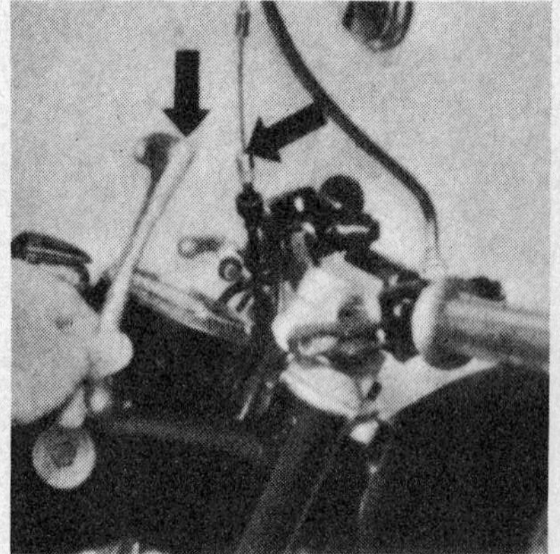

Clutch cable lubrication.

Cables, Levers, and Throttle Grip

Speedometer and tachometer cables can be lubricated in much the same manner except that the lubricant should not be applied to the last few centimeters (cm) of the cable where it enters the speedometer or tachometer head. A moly grease is recommended here.

Disassemble and lubricate the throttle twist grip approximately every 3000 miles. When reassembling, make certain that the slot end (a) in the throttle grip is aligned with the recess (b) in the throttle bracket. Thread the lower cable into the double nipple and insert it, along with the pull chain and throttle cam, into the throttle bracket so that the marks (c) and (d) face each other.

NOTE: *Use the accompanying illustration for reference.*

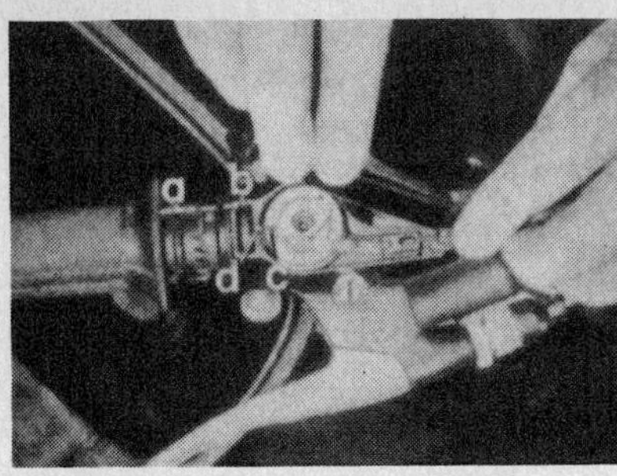

Throttle grip disassembled.

Centrifugal Advance Unit and Breaker Cam Felt

Lubricate these points sparingly whenever a tune-up is performed or at least every 6000 miles. Use Bosch grease Ft 1 v 4 on the breaker cam felt and Bosch grease Ft 1 v 22 or 26 on the centrifugal advance unit.

SERVICE CHECKS AND ADJUSTMENTS

Brakes

R50, R50S, R60, R69S

Front

Front brake cable free-play should be 14–16 mm (0.55–0.63 in.) measured between the lever and the bracket. Adjustment is achieved by loosening the cable adjuster locknut (a milled disc) and turning the adjuster until the desired clearance is obtained. If the proper adjustment cannot be accomplished here, give yourself the necessary extra cable, or take up excess slack, by turning

Front brake cable free-play (pre-1970 models).

the 10 mm nut located at the other end of the cable.

If stopping power is not what it should be, you can immediately suspect that the twin leading shoes are not making contact with the drum simultaneously. This is not an uncommon occurrence. To correct the problem, set the machine on its centerstand with the front wheel held off the ground. Spin the wheel and, while listening at the drum, slowly apply the brake. If both shoes do not make contact with the drum at the same time, turn the brake cam actuating rod with a pair of flat-nose pliers until they do.

Rear

To adjust the rear brake, turn the wingnut on the end of the brake rod to the right until the shoes make contact with the drum, then back it of 4–5 turns.

R50/5, R60/5, R75/5

Front

Front brake cable free-play should be 8–15 mm (¼–½ in.) measured between the lever and bracket. (See accompanying illustration.) Loosen the locknut (2), adjust the knurled screw (1) until the desired clearance is obtained, then retighten the locknut.

Double-leading shoe contact synchronization is achieved in the following manner: (See accompanying illustration for reference)

1. Loosen locknut (2).
2. Turn the adjustment cam (1) to the left with an allen wrench until it is tight.
3. Back off the adjustment cam until the lower front brake lever has a free-play of 4.0 mm before the shoe is fully applied. Free-play is measured at the cable anchor (3).
4. Tighten locknut (2).
5. Adjust the cable by turning nut (4) while holding the sleeve steady, until a free-play of 4.0 mm is obtained at the top front brake actuating lever.

Rear

To adjust the rear brake, turn the wingnut on the end of the brake rod to the right until the shoes make contact with the drum, then back it off 3–4 turns.

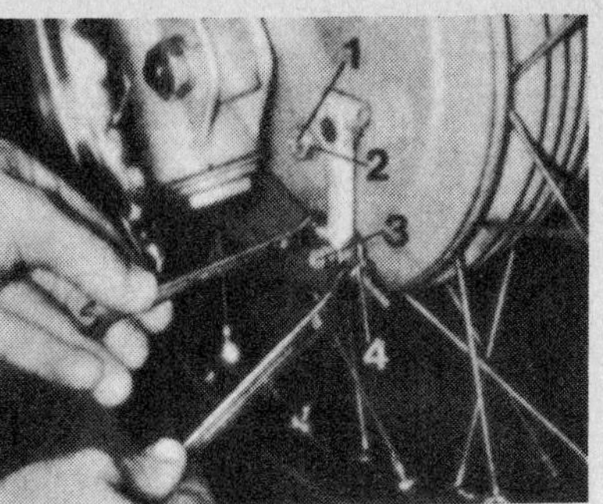

Front brake adjustment (post-1969 models).

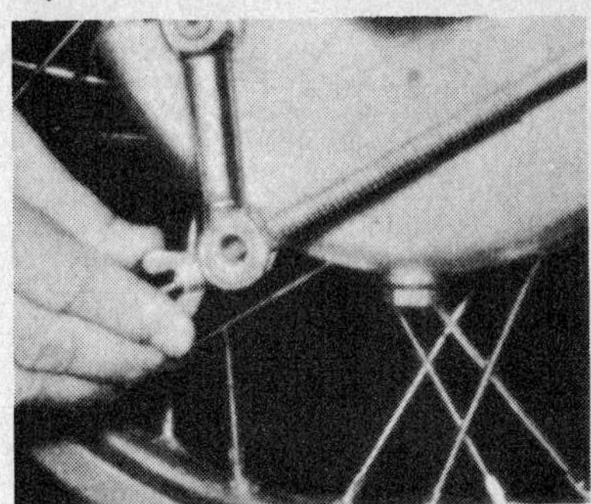

Rear brake adjustment.

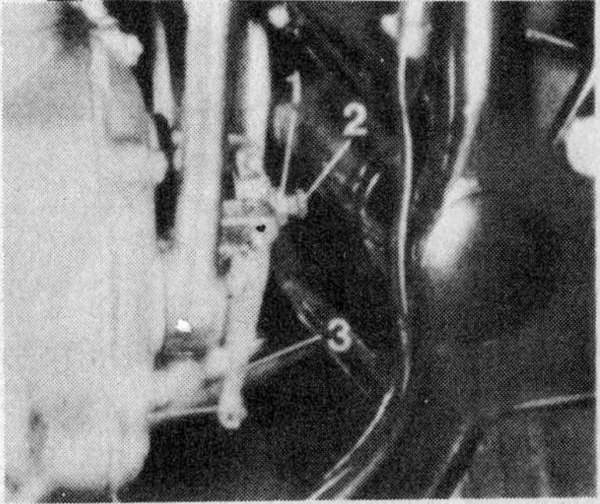

Clutch adjustment.

MAINTENANCE DATA

	R50, R50S, R60, R69S	R50/5. R60/5. R75/5
Fuel Tank Capacity (gal)	4.5	6.3
Fuel Reserve (qt)	2.1	2.0
Engine Oil Capacity (pt)	4.25	4.2
with filter change	—	4.75
Gearbox Oil Capacity (pt)	1.7	1.7
Driveshaft Housing Oil Capacity: fluid ounces	7.0	3.2
cubic centimeters	200	94.7
Rear Wheel Drive Oil Capacity: fluid ounces	5.0	8.0
cubic centimeters	150	237
Front Fork Oil Capacity (each leg): fluid ounces	9.6	9.6
cubic centimeters	280	280
Tire Pressures (psi): solo front	24	27
solo rear	26	30
two-up front	24	30
two-up rear	29	35

MAINTENANCE INTERVALS

R50, R50S, R60, R69S

First 300 Miles
- Change engine oil
- Clean magnetic drain plug (R69S)
- Check cylinder head bolt torque
- Check valve clearances

First 1000 Miles
- Perform the same maintenance as specified at every 4000 miles except lubrication of the centrifugal advance bushing and breaker cam felt, but including the following:
- Remove sump pan and clean oil filter
- Clean magnetic drain plug (R69S)
- Change gearbox oil
- Change oil in rear wheel drive
- Change oil in shaft drive
- Check spoke tension (if equipped with alloy rims)
- Balance wheels (R69S)

Every 2000 Miles
- Change engine oil
- Clean magnetic drain plug (R69S)
- Grease swing arm bearing
- Lubricate cables, levers, hinges, etc.
- Check battery electrolyte level

Every 4000 Miles
- Perform the same maintenance as specified at every 2000 miles in addition to the following:
- Check gearbox oil level and add oil if necessary
- Check rear wheel drive oil level and add oil if necessary
- Change oil in shaft drive
- Change front fork oil
- Clean or replace air filter element
- Check wheel bearing play
- Check swing arm bearing play
- Tighten all loose nuts and bolts
- Adjust cable free-play
- Grease throttle grip control
- Check vibration damper operation (R69S)
- Grease centrifugal advance bushing
- Lubricate breaker cam felt
- Clean carburetors and fuel petcock
- Check cylinder head bolt torque
- Adjust brakes, clutch, etc.

Every 16,000 Miles or Once a Year
- Perform the same maintenance as specified at every 4000 miles in addition to the following:
- Remove and clean sump pan and oil filter
- Change gearbox oil
- Change rear-wheel drive oil
- Repack wheel hub bearings
- Check wheel spoke tension
- Balance wheels
- Remove wheels and inspect brake linings, linkage, etc.
- Replace the air cleaner element
- Clean and check commutator and carbon brushes

MAINTENANCE INTERVALS

R50/5, R60/5, R75/5

First 300 Miles
- Change engine oil
- Replace oil filter cartridge
- Check cylinder head nut and bolt torque
- Check valve clearances
- Check ignition timing

First 1000 Miles
- Change engine oil
- Remove and clean oil pan and screen
- Lubricate swing arm bearings
- Lubricate control levers and throttle grip
- Check battery electrolyte level
- Change gearbox oil
- Change shaft drive oil
- Change rear-wheel drive oil
- Change front fork oil
- Clean air filter element
- Check steering head bearing free-play
- Check wheel bearing free-play
- Adjust brakes
- Adjust clutch
- Adjust control cables
- Clean carburetors and fuel petcock screen
- Check wheel spoke tension
- Tighten all loose nuts and bolts
- Check cylinder head nut and bolt torque
- Adjust valve clearances
- Check contact breaker gap and ignition timing

Every 3000 Miles
- Change engine oil and replace filter cartridge①
- Lubricate control levers and throttle grip
- Check battery electrolyte level②
- Check gearbox oil level
- Check driveshaft housing oil level
- Check rear-wheel drive oil level
- Clean air cleaner element
- Check steering head bearing free-play
- Check wheel bearing free-play
- Adjust brakes
- Adjust clutch
- Adjust carburetor cables
- Tighten loose nuts and bolts

Every 6000 Miles
- Perform the same maintenance as specified at every 3000 miles in addition to the following:
- Grease and check swing arm bearing free-play
- Change gearbox oil③
- Change driveshaft housing oil③
- Change rear-wheel drive oil③
- Change front fork oil③
- Check cylinder head nut and bolt torque
- Check wheel spoke tension
- Balance wheels
- Disassemble and inspect brakes

① At least every six months; 1500 miles or three months in winter
② At least once a month
③ At least once a year

Adjustments pertaining to tuning are not included in the given normal maintenance intervals. Tuning should not be restricted to set intervals, but rather free to be performed whenever deemed necessary.

Clutch

Cable free-play at the transmission clutch actuating lever should be 0.2 in. for the R50, R50S, R60, and R69S and 0.08 in. for the R50/5, R60/5, and R75/5. Make the adjustment by loosening the cable adjuster locknut at the handlever and turning the adjuster until the desired clearance is obtained.

If there is still excess cable slack, or if there is not a sufficient amount of cable, perform the following adjustment at the transmission clutch actuating lever. (See the accompanying illustration for reference)

1. Loosen lever locknut (1).
2. To decrease the amount of cable slack, tighten the adjuster (2). To increase the amount of cable slack, loosen the adjuster (2).
3. Tighten the locknut (1) and readjust cable free-play at the handlever.

ENGINE AND TRANSMISSION

ENGINE SERVICE

R50, R50S, R60 AND R60S

Removal and Installation

1. Remove the transmission as described later in this chapter.
2. Unscrew the carburetor tops and pull out the throttle slides. Tie the slides aside with the cables attached.

Removing the throttle slide (pre-1970).

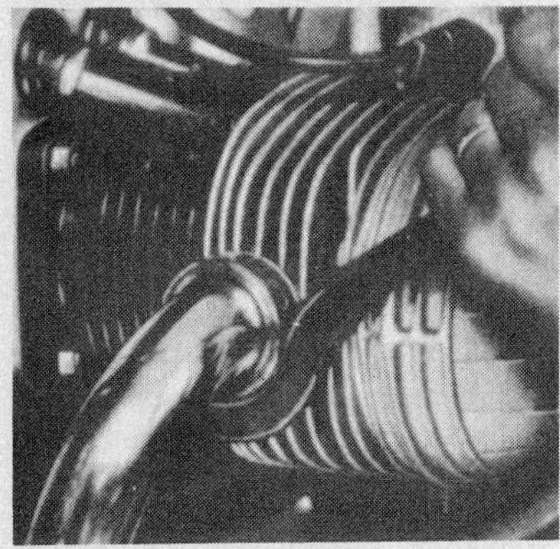

Removing the exhaust pipe ring nut (pre-1970 models).

3. Loosen the header pipe ring's nuts at the cylinder heads

NOTE: *When re-installing, use a new copper seal ring (R50/60) and a light lubricant. Be careful not to cross-thread the collars on the heads, and secure nothing until all hardware has at least been started. The collars must be installed first.*

4. Remove the rear engine mounting bolt nuts, then tap the bolt to the left and remove the footpeg and exhaust pipe clip. Now tap the bolt to the right and remove the other footpeg and exhaust pipe clip.
5. Loosen the rear muffler mountings and remove the entire exhaust system.
6. Disconnect and plug the fuel lines at the carburetors.
7. Remove the securing nuts and the front end case cover.
8. Disconnect, and mark, the following wires from the DC generator:
   a. black wire from terminal 30
   b. red wire from terminal 51
   c. brown wire from ground terminal (a)
   d. black/red wire from ignition coil terminal 2.

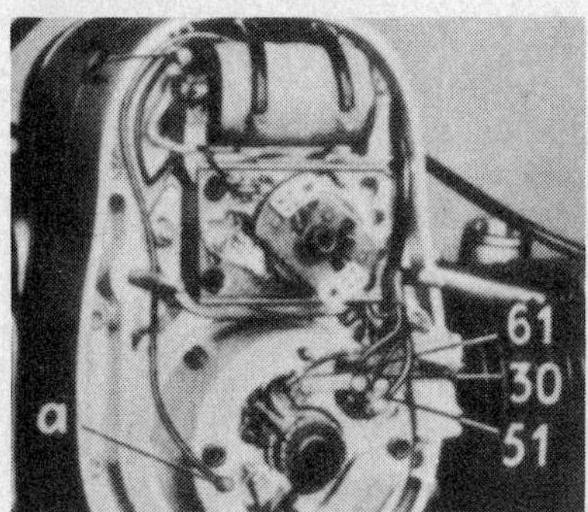

Disconnect these generator wires for engine removal (pre-1970 models).

Jam the brush in place with the spring (pre-1970 models).

9. Lift the brush springs off the generator brushes, then slide the brushes up from the commutator and let the springs hold them in place.
10. Remove the two securing bolts and the generator. Take care not to lose the centering washer, if so equipped.

NOTE: *If you remove the bolts indicated by the arrow in the accompanying illustration, use a gasket compound when re-installing them as they block a breather passage, and oil mist will be blown into the generator housing if a proper seal is not made.*

11. Remove the armature center bolt and replace it with BMW puller 5030 or a suitable substitute. Remove the armature by tightening the puller bolt. Wrap the entire generator assembly and set it aside.
12. Remove the engine housing upper cover and pull the wiring harness out of the housing.
13. Remove the top engine mount, then support the engine with a box or wire basket and remove the bottom rear and front mounting bolts. Don't lose track of the frame spacers which go on the left side of the engine.

Generator securing bolts (pre-1970 models).

Removing the generator armature (pre-1970 models).

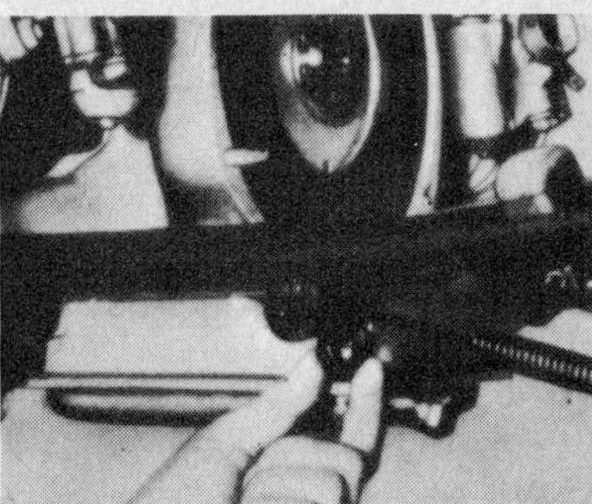

Engine mounting spacer (pre-1970 models).

Removing the engine (pre-1970 models).

14. Tilt the engine rearward, then carefully lift it out the left side of the frame.

NOTE: *The ignition advance unit is in a very vulnerable position when removing the engine. Take care not to let it hit the lower frame tubes.*

15. Installation is a reversal of the removal procedure.

Cylinder Head And Valve Train

DISASSEMBLY

1. Place the engine on a bench or BMW workstand V 5014.
2. Remove the rocker covers and gaskets.
3. Remove the rocker shaft supports, along with the rocker arms, pushrods, and cylinder head.
4. Using a valve spring compressor, compress the springs and remove the split retainer collars and retainers. Lift off the springs and remove the valves.

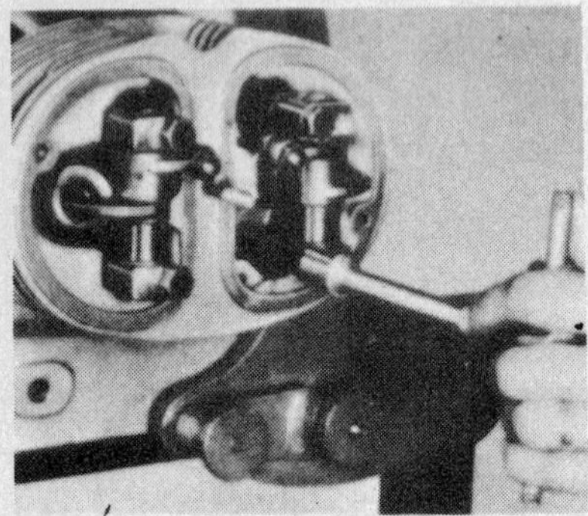

Removing the rocker arm shaft support (pre-1970 models).

Removing the valve spring retainers (pre-1970 models).

INSPECTION AND SERVICE

1. Inspect the cylinder head for cracks, warpage, etc., after having removed any accumulated carbon deposits with a blunt blade.

Grinding down the top of the valve guide (pre-1970 models).

Driving in a new valve guide (pre-1970 models).

2. Examine the rocker arms for cracks, etc., and make sure they turn freely on the rocker arm shafts.
3. Inspect the valve springs and check their free-length and loaded pressure against specifications.
4. Check valve stem-t0-guide clearance and, if necessary, replace the guides in the following manner:

   a. Grind off the top of the old guides down to the snap-ring.

   b. Remove the snap-ring, heat the cylinder head to 356-428° F, then drive the guide inward with BMW drift 5127 or 5128, or a suitable substitute.

   c. Drive the new guides into place while the head is still hot, then, after they have cooled, ream them out to the specified bore.

Reaming out the valve guide (pre-1970 models).

   d. Oversize guides are available, if necessary. The standard interference fit between the guide and cylinder head is 0.0012–0.0020 in.

5. Inspect the valve seats for cracks excessive wear, etc. If replacement or refacing is necessary, it is best to refer the work to a local BMW dealer, as valve seat work is usually beyond the scope of home repair.
6. Inspect the valves for pitting, cracking, or excessive wear. When reinstalling the valves, whether new or reconditioned, they should be lapped into their seats so that a perfect seal will be obtained. To properly lap a valve, first place three small dabs of lapping compound around the valve face. Insert the valve into the guide and using a lapping tool (available at most auto supply stores), rotate the valve back and forth lightly by turning the handle of the lapping tool between the palms of your hands. Reposition the valve every few seconds and examine the valve face and seat surfaces. When they have become smooth and even, with an unblemished finish, the job is completed.

ASSEMBLY

1. Assembly is a reversal of the disassembly procedure. When installing the valve springs, make sure the closed coils are toward the cylinder head. Torque the cylinder head nuts and bolts to the specified value.

Cylinders And Pistons

DISASSEMBLY

1. Remove the four retaining nuts from the cylinder flange, then carefully lift off the cylinder with top and bottom gaskets. It may be necessary to lightly tap the cylinder cooling fins with a rubber mallet to free the cylinder.
2. As soon as there is enough room, stuff some clean lint-free rags into the crankcase hole to prevent dirt from falling into the bottom end. It is also wise to support the piston with a wooden block to protect the connecting rod from sharp case edges.
3. Remove the piston pin circlip with a pointed instrument or narrow straight-slot screwdriver. Make sure it doesn't fall into the crankcase opening.
4. Press the piston pin out with a suitable tool or heat the piston to approximately 110° C and drive it out with a drift.

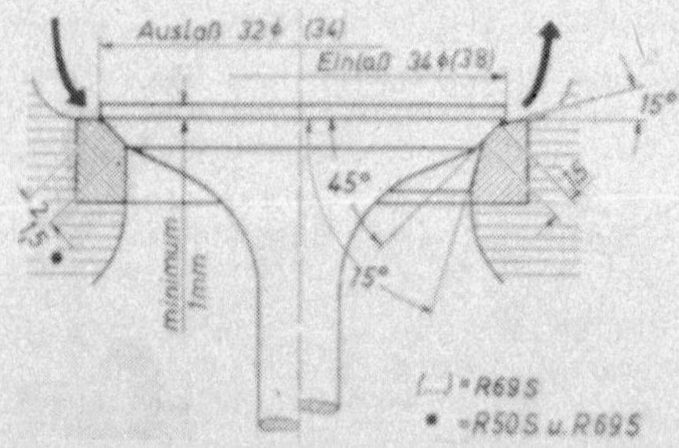

Valve face and seat dimensions (pre-1970 models).

Removing the piston pin circlip (pre-1970 models).

Removing the piston pin with electric heater (pre-1970 models).

Measuring the cylinder bore diameter (pre-1970 models).

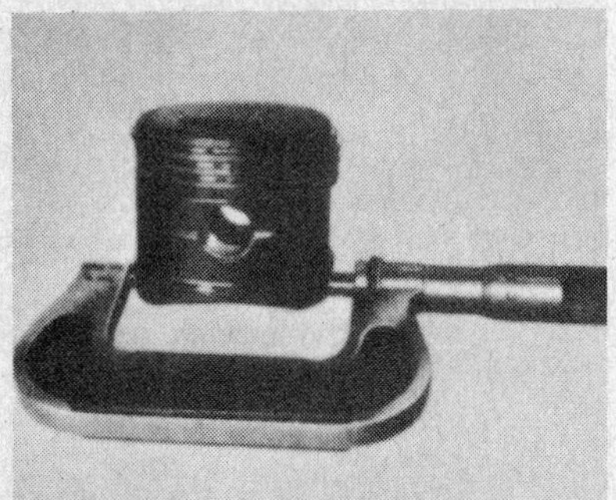

Measuring piston skirt diameter (pre-1970 models).

5. Beginning at the top, carefully spread the piston rings apart and slide them over the piston crown.

INSPECTION AND SERVICE

1. Using a blunt blade so as not to damage the aluminum alloy, remove carbon deposits from the piston crown, cylinder exhaust port, and piston ring grooves. An old broken ring serves as an excellent tool for cleaning the ring grooves.

2. Remove the carbon ridge at the top of the cylinder, then examine it for hairline cracks, etc. Measure the cylinder bore diameter at three points: ½ in. below the top of the barrel, the middle of the barrel, and ½ in. from the bottom of the barrel. Make three more measurements perpendicular to those already made.

3. Inspect the piston for cracks, crown damage, or seizure spots. Measure its diameter at the bottom of the skirt perpendicular to the piston pin, using a micrometer.

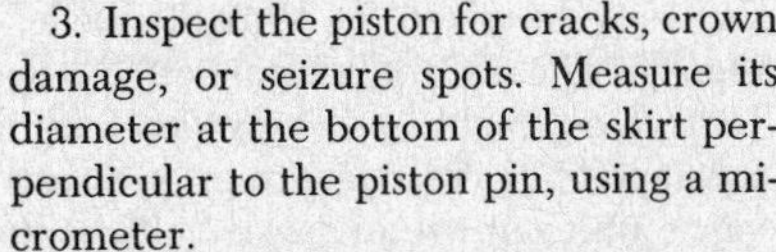

4. Insert the piston pin into the connecting rod small end and make certain there is no noticeable radial play. Examine the pin for center step-wear and make sure its fit in the piston is at least finger-tight. Matching piston pins and pistons are marked with either white or black dots. They are not interchangeable.

PISTON-TO-CYLINDER FIT

When the pistons and/or cylinders are replaced, the cylinder barrel must be bored and/or honed to achieve the correct fit. After having determined the replacement piston diameter, calculate the desired cylinder barrel diameter taking into account the specified piston-to-cylinder wall clearance. Bore the barrel out to just slightly less than this figure, then run a hone up and down the cylinder in a crosshatch pattern.

Since the cylinder is tapered to compensate for heat expansion characteristics, piston-to-cylinder wall clearance must be checked at one spot, approximately at the level of the cylinder flange. Original manufacturing differences from standard are marked on the cylinder flange. The number given, with or without a ± mark, indicates a variance in hundredths of a millimeter (i.e., ±3 means 0.003 mm over standard). A number with a – mark indicates that the cylinder bore is that many hundredths of a millimeter less than standard.

The original piston diameter is stamped in the piston crown. In this case, the entire figure is given (i.e., 67.97 equals 67.97 mm diameter).

For piston-to-cylinder wall clearance specifications see the chart given at the end of this chapter.

ASSEMBLY

1. Slide the piston rings, one at a time, into the cylinder bore and measure their end gaps with a feeler gauge. Although rings should be replaced whenever the engine has been taken down this far, they may be reused if the end gap is not excessive (see specifications).

Measuring ring end-gap (pre-1970 models).

2. Position the piston with the arrow, or word "Vorn" on R50 and R69S models, pointing forward, then heat it and push in the piston pin. Install the retaining circlip.

3. Carefully install the rings on the piston and measure side clearance (between top or bottom of ring and groove). If the rings are new, but the clearance is excessive, the piston is in need of replacement.

4. Install a new cylinder base gasket.

5. Lubricate the piston and cylinder bore with engine oil, then fit a ring compressor over the piston.

6. Slide the cylinder over the piston and, if using your fingers, compress each ring as the cylinder descends over them.

7. Remove the protective wooden block and rags, then slide the cylinder down over the mounting studs.

8. The remainder of assembly is a re-

Measuring ring side clearance (pre-1970 models).

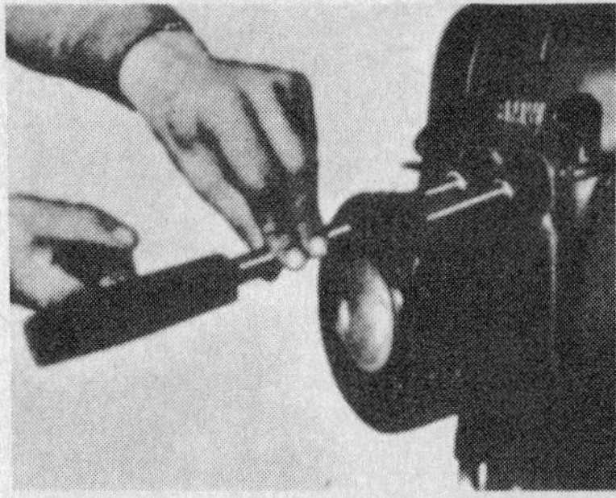

If the push rod tubes leak, tap them a little deeper in their bores with a drift (pre-1970 models).

versal of the removal procedure. Torque the cylinder flange nuts to the specified torque.

Magneto

REMOVAL AND INSTALLATION

1. Remove the centrifugal advance mechanism center bolt and carefully remove the unit.

2. Disconnect the two high-tension cables from the coil terminals.

3. Remove the coil retaining nuts and lift off the coil assembly.

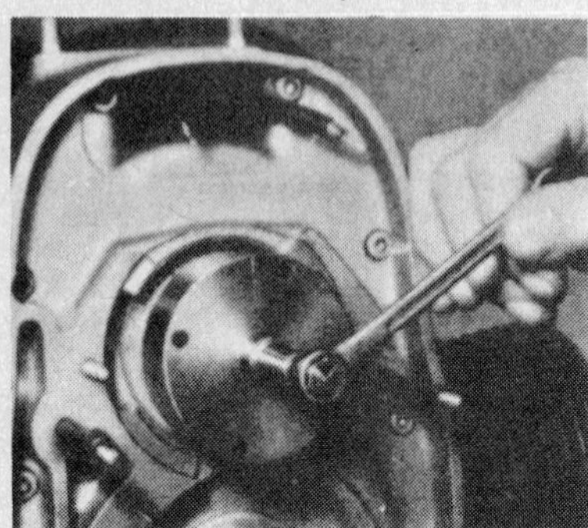

Removing the magneto rotor (pre-1970 models).

Removing the magneto coil and breaker point assembly (pre-1970 models).

Magneto rotor and housing marks (pre-1970 models).

4. Using BMW tool 5030 or a suitable substitute draw bolt, remove the magneto rotor. Wrap the entire magneto assembly carefully, then lay it aside.

5. To reinstall the magneto, perform the following steps.

6. Turn the flywheel until the "S" mark (retarded timing) is in line with the case reference mark.

7. Put a drop of oil on the magneto rotor seal and one on its contact surface, then slide the rotor on the camshaft with the scribed mark pointing upward.

8. Position the coil and breaker assembly on the case, then install and tighten the retaining nuts in the middle of the oblong holes.

9. Lightly lubricate the breaker cam felt with Bosch grease as described in "Maintenance".

10. Lubricate the auto advance unit shaft as described in "Maintenance," then install it and the central bolt loosely.

11. While holding the flywheel from turning, rotate the magneto rotor and advance unit until rotor mark (a) lines up with magneto housing mark (b). (See accompanying illustration.)

12. Tighten the advance unit central bolt to 14.5 ft lbs.

13. Adjust ignition timing as described in "Tune-Up".

Camshaft And Timing Gears

REMOVAL

1. Drain the engine oil.

2. Remove the 12 allen head screws holding the timing cover to the crankcase.

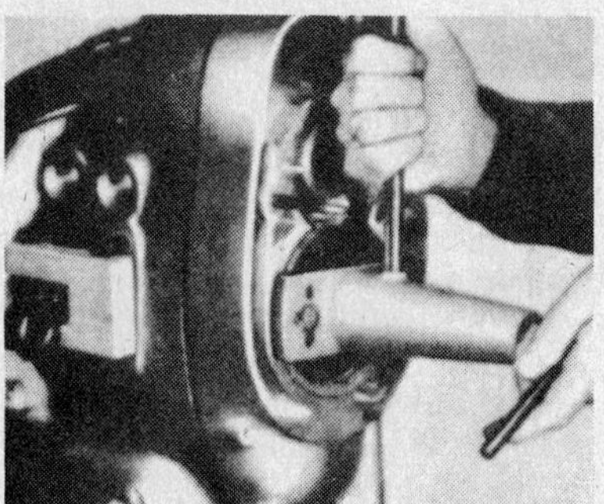

Removing the timing cover (pre-1970 models).

3. Install BMW Matra puller 499 or 536, or a suitable substitute, with the two collar screws over the crankshaft cone. Screw it onto the timing cover, then pull the cover free from the case by turning the extractor bolt, or strike it with a rubber hammer and pull it off by hand.

4. Remove the camshaft gear snap-ring.

5. Remove the breather valve plate with the pressure spring.

6. Remove the four screws that secure the camshaft bearing through the timing gear holes.

7. Install BMW Matra puller tool 355a, or a suitable substitute, on the engine housing. Screw the spindle into the threaded end of the camshaft, then remove the camshaft with bearing and timing gear by turning the extractor bolt.

Removing the camshaft gear snap-ring (pre-1970 models).

Releasing the camshaft bearing bushings (pre-1970 models).

8. If the timing gear or bearing must be replaced, remove the bearing snap-ring and press the bearing out of the bushing.

9. Bend back the oil pump driven gear retaining nut plate and remove the nut.

NOTE: *The oil pump driven gear retaining nut has a left-hand thread.*

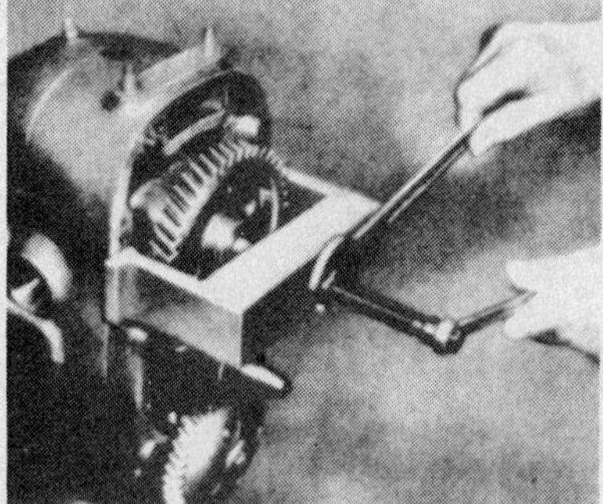

Removing the camshaft gear and bearing (pre-1970 models).

Removing the oil pump drive gear (pre-1970 models).

Removing the crankshaft ball bearing (pre-1970 models).

10. Remove the driven gear from the pump gear shaft, tapping it with a rubber mallet if necessary.

11. Remove the ball bearing from the crankshaft, using two screwdrivers for leverage.

12. Install BMW Matra tool 499, or a suitable substitute, and draw the drive gear off the crankshaft.

INSPECTION AND SERVICE

Inspect the gears for burrs, missing teeth, excessive wear, etc., and replace as necessary. Examine the condition of the ball bearings, clean them thoroughly, and blow them dry with compressed air. Do not spin the bearing until it has been cleaned, dried, and lubricated.

Removing the crankshaft gear (pre-1970 models).

Should the timing gear set require replacement, note the marks on the top of the engine housing, as these indicate the correct set (i.e. ± 2, -3, etc.).

INSTALLATION

1. Heat the crankshaft gear to approximately 300° F, grease the crankshaft cone, install BMW guiding bushing 5040, and slip the gear with sleeve (a) and pressure bushing (b) onto the crankshaft.

2. Screw the spindle (d) of BMW Matra tool 355a into the crankshaft and finish pressing the gear into place with BMW Matra tool 535, or a suitable substitute.

3. Heat the crankshaft ball bearing to approximately 175° F, then press it into position with BMW tool 5039.

CAUTION: *Never strike the bearing or crankshaft with a hammer.*

4. The remainder of the installation procedure is a reversal of the removal instructions. When installing the camshaft, heat the case to approximately 175° F and make sure the alignment marks on the gears match. Also make certain the breather plate is smooth and that it has been liberally lubricated.

Clutch

DISASSEMBLY

1. Remove every other retaining screw on the clutch pressure ring.

2. Install three clamping screws, BMW Matra tool 534, or a suitable substitute, into the holes left by the removed retaining screws.

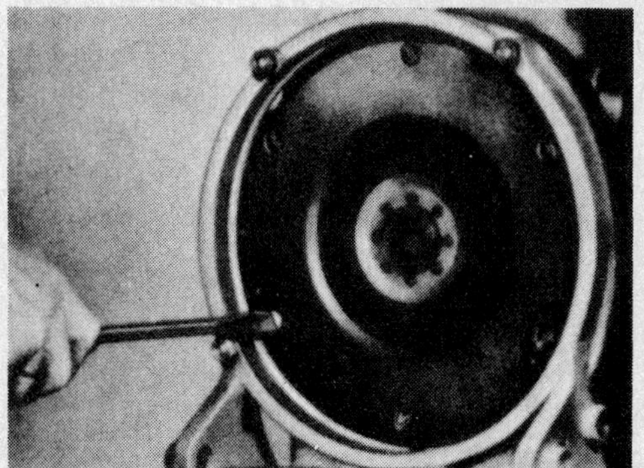

Removing the clutch pressure ring retaining screws (pre-1970 models).

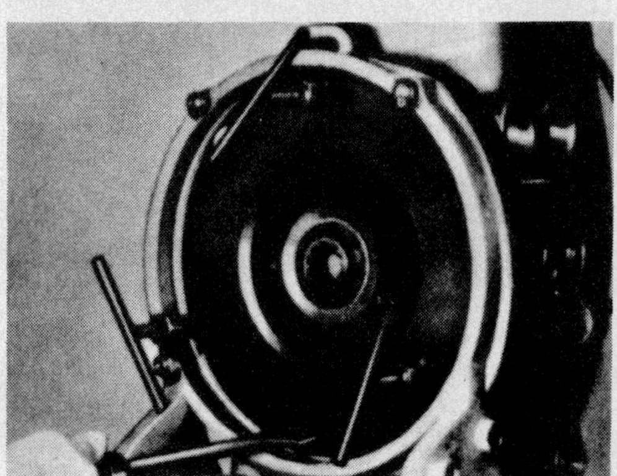

Matra extractor bolts 534 installed on clutch pressure ring (pre-1970 models).

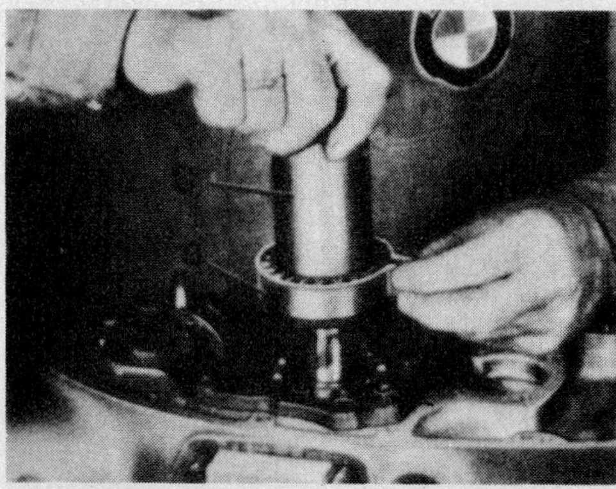

Installing the crankshaft gear (pre-1970 models).

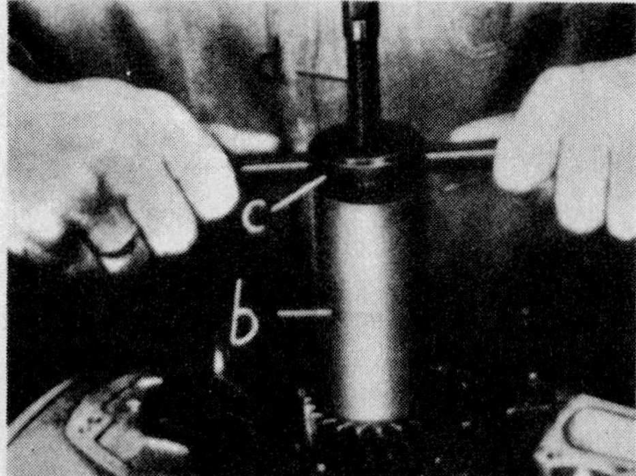

Pressing the crankshaft gear into place (pre-1970 models).

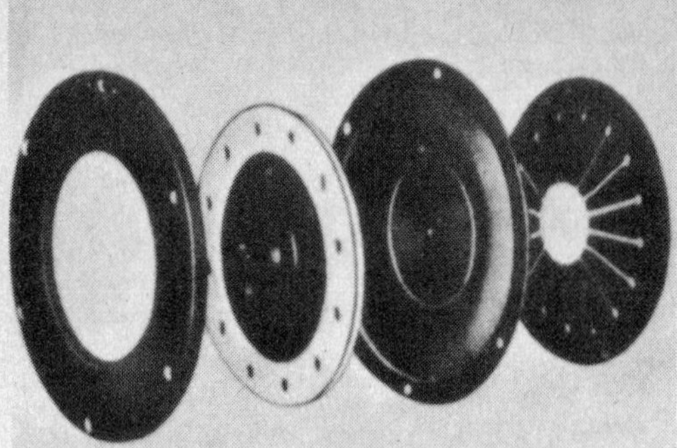

Clutch parts (all models).

Checking pressure plate run-out (pre-1970 models).

3. Remove the three remaining retaining screws, then slowly and evenly loosen the clamping screws until all spring pressure is released.

4. Remove the pressure ring, pressure plate with diaphragm, clutch plate and disc spring.

INSPECTION

Inspect the clutch components for warpage, oil saturation, or excessive wear. Specifications are given at the end of this chapter. Also check pressure plate run-out with a dial indicator, if possible. Maximum limit is 0.02 in.

ASSEMBLY

Assembly is the reversal of the removal procedure. Use BMW Matra tool 529 or a suitable substitute to center the clutch plate.

Flywheel

REMOVAL AND INSTALLATION

1. Lock the flywheel in place, using BMW Matra tool 292 or a suitable substitute.

2. Bend back the tab of the flywheel securing bolt lockwasher, then remove the nut and washer.

3. Install BMW Matra tool 311 on the flywheel and remove the flywheel by turning the extractor bolt.

NOTE: *It may help your efforts to lubricate the extractor bolt threads occasionally.*

4. To reinstall the flywheel, perform the following steps.

5. Make sure the woodruff key is properly installed and that the key groove in the flywheel is clear.

6. Install the flywheel with a new lockwasher and nut.

7. Lock the flywheel in position, then torque the retaining bolt to 123 ft lbs.

8. Bend the tab on the lockwasher against one side of the retaining bolt.

9. Check flywheel run-out with a dial indicator. Maximum allowable run-out is 0.004 in.

Removing the flywheel nut (pre-1970 models).

Torquing the flywheel bolt (pre-1970 models).

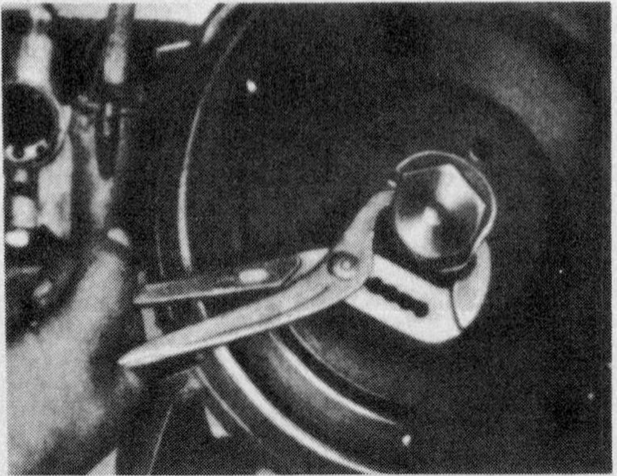

Bending back the flywheel bolt lockwasher (pre-1970 models).

Checking flywheel run-out (pre-1970 models).

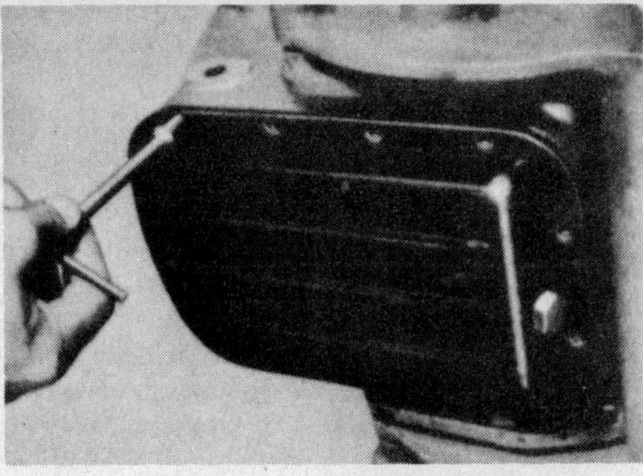

Removing the sump pan (pre-1970 models).

Measuring oil pump gear backlash (pre-1970 models).

Removing the oil sump strainer (pre-1970 models).

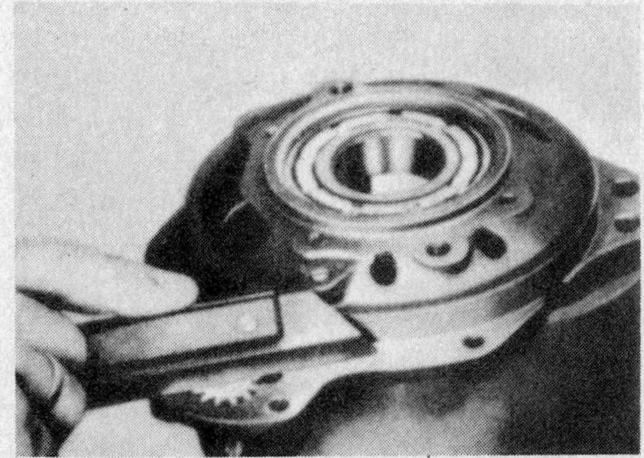

Measuring oil pump gear side-play (pre-1970 models).

Oil Sump, Strainer, And Pump

REMOVAL

1. Drain the engine oil and reinstall the plug.
2. Remove 12 sump pan retaining screws, washers, gasket, and pan.
3. Bend back the locking tab on the strainer securing screws, then remove the screws, gasket, and strainer.

INSPECTION AND SERVICE

1. Thoroughly wash the strainer in solvent, then blow it dry with compressed air.
2. Measure backlash between the oil pump gears and check their general condition. Backlash should be checked with a feeler gauge (0.0012–0.002 in.).
3. Measure the clearance between the oil pump gears and the machined housing surface. Lay a straightedge across the pump housing, then slip a feeler gauge between the gears and the straightedge. Clearance should be 0.0004–0.0016 in.

INSTALLATION

1. Installation is basically a reversal of the removal procedure. Use a new gasket and locktab washer.

Crankshaft And Connecting Rods

REMOVAL

1. Remove the front bearing cover plate securing screws (eight altogether; four long and four short).
2. Install BMW Matra puller 499/1, or a suitable substitute, with the two screws (Matra 499/5) threaded into the cover plate.
3. Draw off the cover plate by turning the special tool extractor bolt.
4. Remove the oil pump gears.
5. Remove the crankshaft spacer ring.
6. If a new front bearing must be installed, a press will be necessary both to remove and install the bearing.
7. Remove the securing screw and the front oil slinger.
8. Heat the engine housing to approximately 180° F, then pull the crankshaft out of the rear bearing seat.

NOTE: *On the R50S and R69S, remove the oil seal and washers, then install guide ring 5048, or a suitable substitute, on the rear journal spherical roller bearing with the flywheel bolt. After heating the case, and the bearing has broken free, remove the guide ring.*

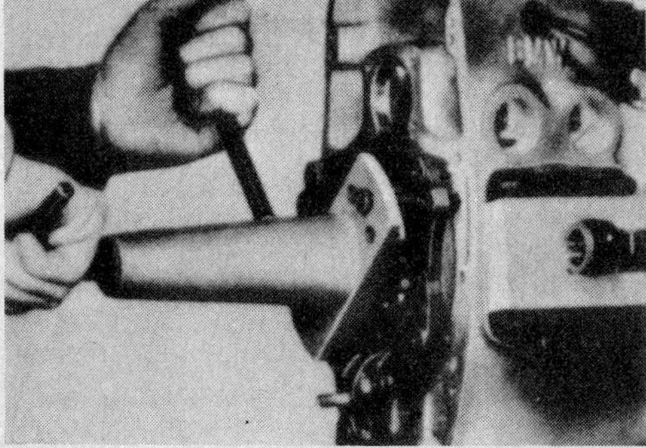

Removing the front crankshaft cover plate (pre-1970 models).

Guide ring 5048 installed (pre-1970 models).

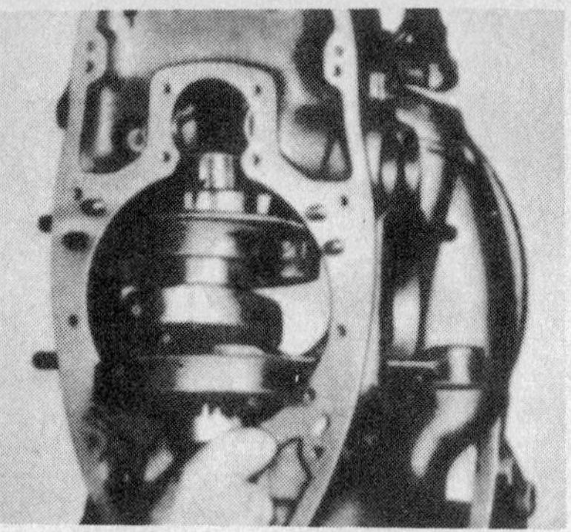

Removing the crankshaft and connecting rod assembly (pre-1970 models).

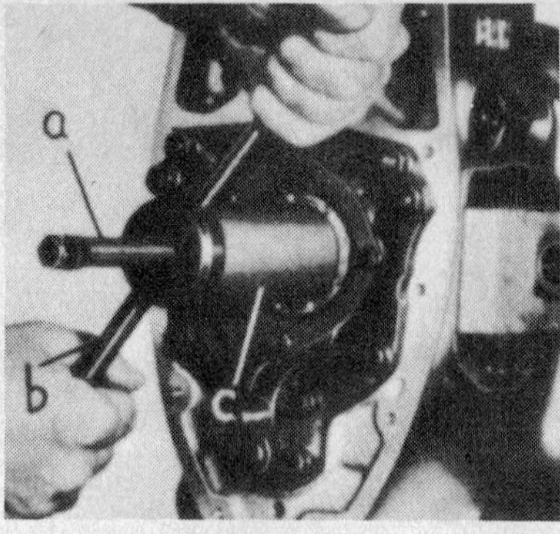

Drawing the crankshaft into the front bearing cover (pre-1970 models).

9. Tilt the front end of the crankshaft downward and lift the rear end through the recess below the camshaft bearing opening.

INSPECTION AND SERVICE

Should there be noticeable play in the connecting rod large end, it is advisable to replace the entire crankshaft/connecting rod assembly. For those who have the experience and the equipment, crankshaft specifications are given at the end of this chapter. Replace all seals and lubricate all parts thoroughly on assembly.

INSTALLATION

1. Heat the engine case to approximately 180° F, then position the crankshaft and connecting rods in the case in the reverse order of removal. Make sure the crankshaft enters completely into the rear bearing seat.
2. On the R50S and R69S, reinstall the guide ring 5048 without the oil retainer plate.
3. Install the oil slinger plate and secure it on the front crankweb with the flat head screw. Secure the screw in place by staking it with a screwdriver or punch.
4. Install the spacer ring with the chamfered edge toward the oil slinger.
5. With the case still warm, install the front bearing cover on the crankshaft journal, making certain that the coned oil pump gear seats in the top bearing opening.
6. Using the illustrated tools (a) Matra 355a, (b) Matra 535, and (c) Matra 5038/1, or suitable substitutes, draw the front bearing cover onto the crankshaft until it is nearly touching the case.
7. Install the bearing cover retaining screws and nuts, then tighten them evenly until the cover touches the case.
8. Continue drawing the crankshaft through the cover until it contacts the inner bearing race.

NOTE: *On the R50S and R69S engines, it is absolutely imperative that the guide ring 5048 be properly installed during this tightening operation.*

9. On the R50S and R69S, remove the guide ring and install the oil retaining washer with the cup-shaped side toward the inner race of the bearing. Install a new oil seal so that approximately 1 mm (0.04 in.) protrudes from the cast surface. BMW tool 5108 can be used for this purpose.

R50/5, R60/5, AND R75/5

Removal And Installation

1. Remove the transmission as described later in this chapter.
2. Turn off the petcock, disconnect the fuel lines at the carburetors, and remove the fuel tank.
3. Remove the left side ignition coil as described in the "Electrical Systems" chapter.
4. Remove the exhaust system as described in the "Chassis" chapter.
5. Remove the right side carburetor assembly.

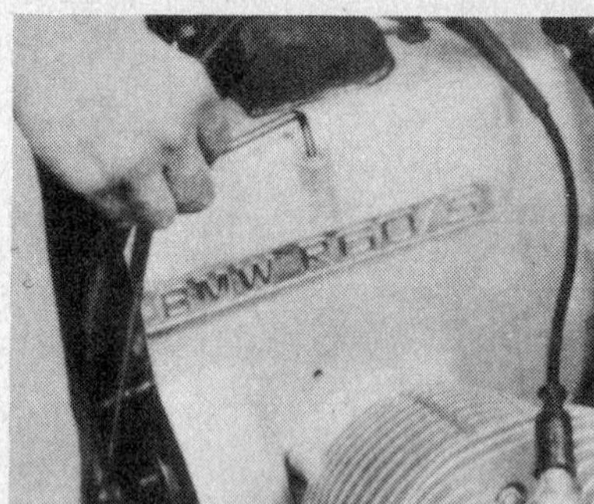

Removing the starter cover

Disconnecting the starter cable

6. Remove the two allen head bolts which secure the starter cover, then remove the cover.
7. Disconnect the starter cable.
8. Loosen the upper horn mounting bolt enough to allow the front engine cover to be removed, or remove the horn entirely. Remove the three allen head bolts which secure the front cover, and remove the cover.
9. Disconnect the alternator and condenser cables, then remove the tach cable securing bolt (4) and withdraw the tachometer cable.
10. Disconnect the two main leads at the diode chassis, then disconnect the remaining lead located on the left side of the diode chassis.
11. Remove the spark plug leads and place them out of the way, then disconnect the lead from the oil pressure sensing switch (5).
12. Remove the front and rear mounting bolts and remove the engine carefully from the frame. Tilting the engine to the left and downward will ease the removal process.

Cover mounting positions

Cable mounting positions

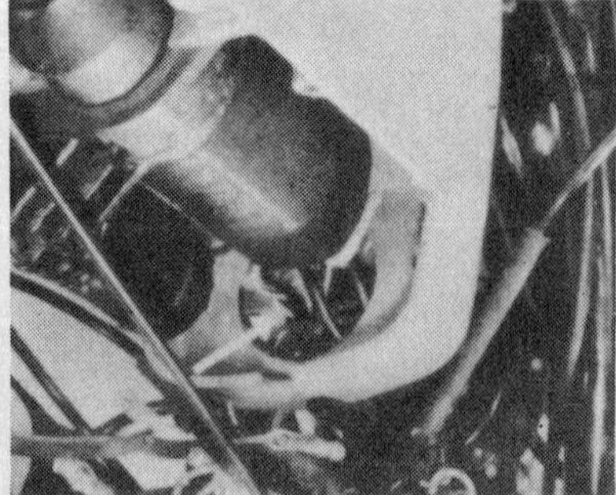

Diode chassis leads

Diode chassis lead

Oil pressure sensing switch

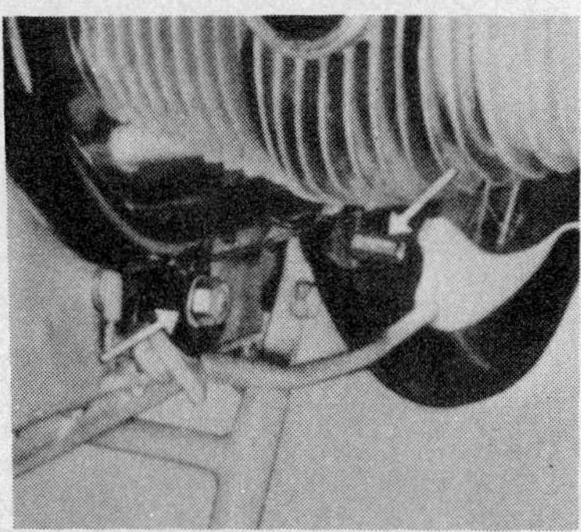
Engine mounting positions

Removing the engine from the frame

13. Installation is in the reverse order of removal. Note the following points;

a. When installing the front engine cover make sure that the ventilating hose is correctly positioned, and is free to perform its function.

b. Place the center stand brackets between the engine housing and the frame on both sides, and position the side stand bracket between the engine and the frame on the left side. Both of these assemblies are secured by the front engine mounting bolt.

c. Position the foot rests and the exhaust pipe clamps so that the rear engine mounting bolt secures them. There should be a spacer between the engine housing and the frame where the rear engine mounting bolt enters.

Cylinder Head And Valve Train

DISASSEMBLY

1. Secure the engine to a bench or to BMW workstand and no. 6000, and secure the workstand (if applicable) to BMW tool 6005/1.
2. Remove the cap nut and the two nuts located on the sides of the rocker cover, then remove the cover and cover gasket.
3. Remove the four nuts which secure the rocker arms, then remove the rockers and withdraw the push rods.
4. Remove the cylinder head in the following manner;

a. Install two shoulder nuts on two diagonally opposed cylinder thru-bolts.

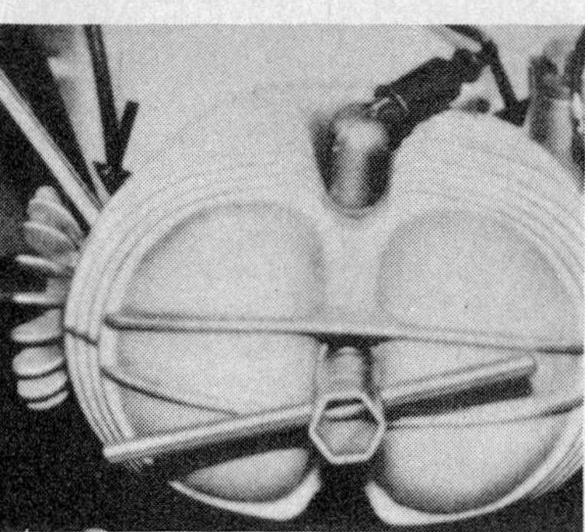
Removing the rocker box cover

b. Install BMW bracket no. 209 or a suitable substitute diagonally across the rocker arm mounting studs as illustrated.

c. Install a suitable nut on the centrally located stud, and turn it down until the cylinder head and cylinder assembly are drawn off of their seat on the crankcase. Cover the crankcase opening with a clean oil soaked rag as soon as there is enough room. This is to prevent foreign objects from entering the crankcase.

Removing the shoulder nuts

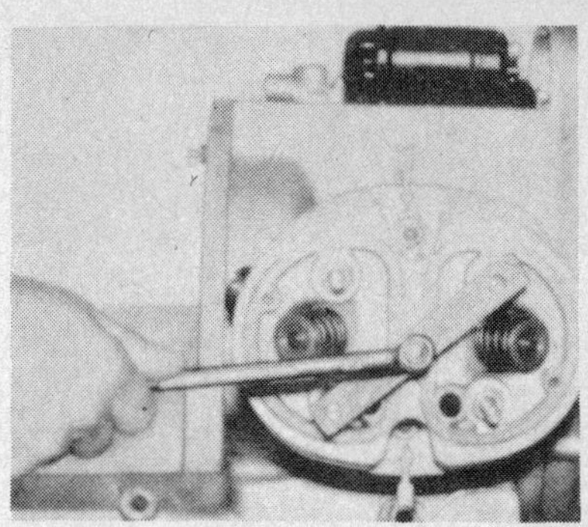
Removing the head

d. Remove the two nuts (indicated by arrows on the above illustration) as soon as the cylinder is clear of the crankcase, then tap on the head with a soft mallet to separate the head from the cylinder.

5. Using a valve spring compressor, compress the springs and remove the split retainer collars and retainers. Lift off the springs and remove the valves.

INSPECTION AND SERVICE

1. Consult the "Inspection and Service" section for the R50, R50S, R60, and the R69S models.

ASSEMBLY

1. Assembly is basically in the reverse order of disassembly.
2. Align the rocker arms with the BMW rocker arm alignment rod no. 200 or a suitable substitute.

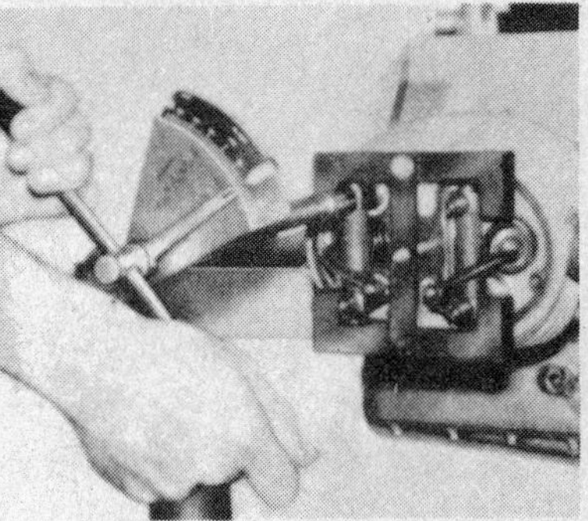
Aligning the rockers and torquing the head

3. Torque the cylinder head bolts down in the order indicated. The first bolt should be torqued to 11 ft lbs, the second to 18 ft lbs, and the third to 25 ft lbs.

CAUTION: *Failure to align the rockers will probably result in noisey engine operation or pushrod damage.*

Cylinders And Pistons

All of the procedures covered in the "Cylinders and Pistons" section for the R50, R50S, R60, and the R60S models are applicable here, except that on the newer models the cylinders are attached

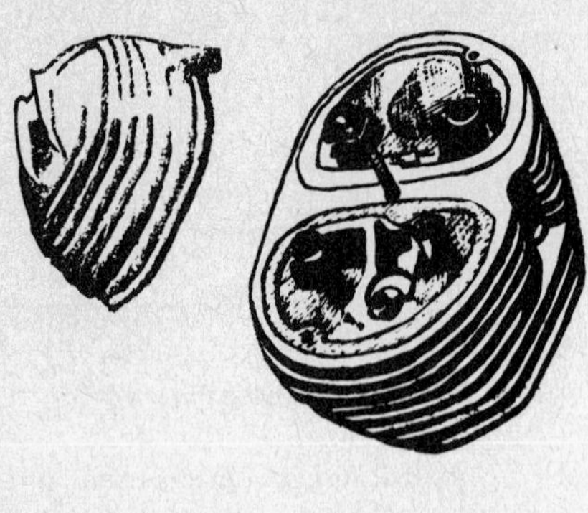

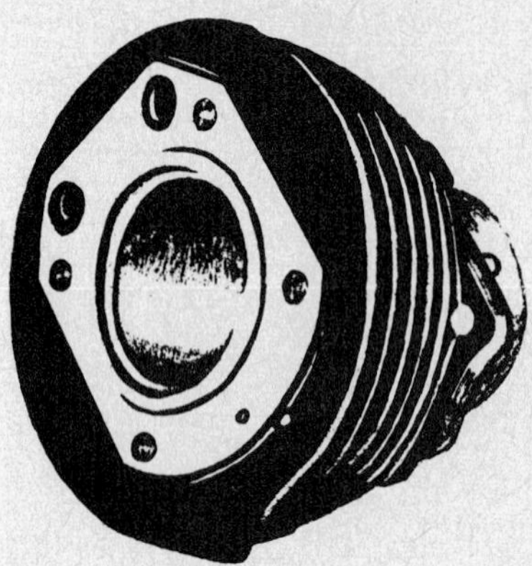

Exploded view of cylinder assembly, including piston

Head torquing sequence

differently to the crankcase. Once the cylinder head has been removed, and the piston has been protected with a wood block, the cylinder can be slipped off of its mounting studs.

Camshaft And Timing Gears

REMOVAL

1. Drain the engine oil into a suitable recepticle.
2. Remove the alternator and automatic advance assemblies.
3. Remove the nine allen head bolts and the three allen head nuts.
4. Assemble the BMW puller tool no. 214 to the alternator mounting holes taking care to install the insert into the crankshaft. A suitable substitute may be used with caution. Remove the cover and the cover gasket.
5. Insert the bearing puller insert into the crankshaft, mount the BMW bearing puller no. 217, or a suitable substitute, on the crankshaft, and remove the bearing.

Removing the cover securing bolts

Pulling the cover

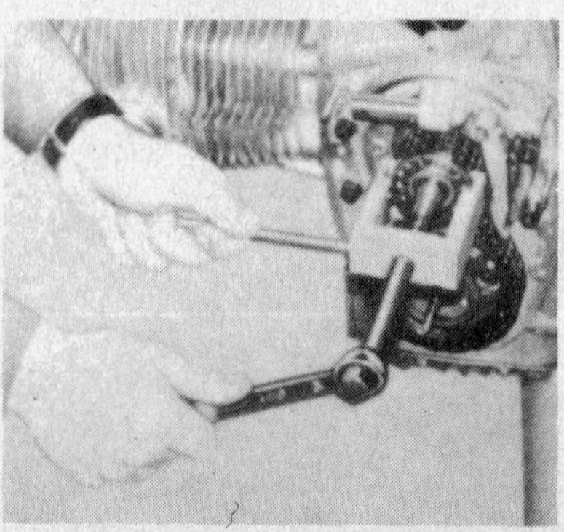

Removing the crankshaft bearing

6. Remove the screws which secure the camshaft bearing, and remove the bearing.
7. Remove the chain tensioner circlip, tensioner, and the tensioner spring.
8. Insert the sprocket puller insert into the crankshaft end, install BMW sprocket puller no. 213, or a suitable substitute, and remove the crankshaft sprocket. Repeat the operation on the camshaft, and remove the camshaft. If you remove the sprockets evenly you will avoid possible damage to both them and the chain.

Removing the camshaft bearing

Tensioner assembly

9. The camshaft sprocket is a press fit on the camshaft, and requires the use of a press to remove it. If a suitable press is not available, take the camshaft to a qualified machinist. If a press is available, proceed in the following manner;

Pulling the crankshaft sprocket

a. Place the camshaft on an anvil tube with an inside diameter of 90 mm (3.54 in.), an outside diameter of 106 mm (4.17 in.), and a length of 225 mm (8.86 in.). The sprocket should lie flat on the top of the tube.

b. Place a BMW sleeve no. 212 on the top of the camshaft, and press off the timing sprocket and the tachometer drive gear at once.

INSPECTION AND SERVICE.

1. Clean all parts in a suitable solvent and blow them dry.

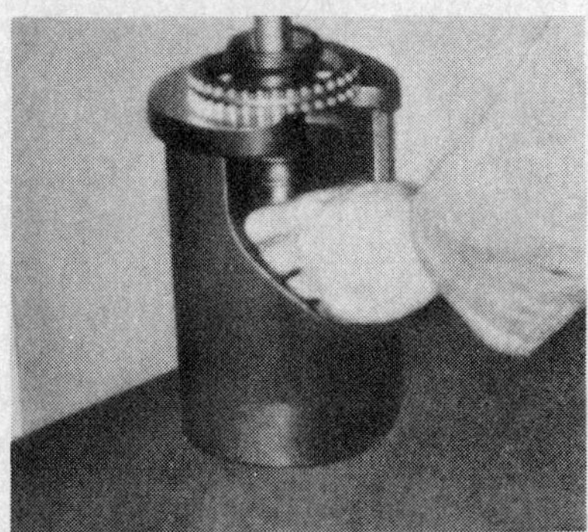

Positioning the camshaft on the anvil tube

Checking bearing endplay

2. Inspect the sprockets and chain for wear, damage, chipped teeth, or a stretched chain and replace them as a set if necessary. If there is any question as to whether they are serviceable or not, they should be replaced. Always replace them as a set.

3. Inspect the covers for a smooth mating surface or a damaged condition and replace them as necessary.

4. Check the camshaft for a worn or damaged condition, and for excessive end play between the bearing and the shaft due to a worn inner bearing, and replace it as necessary. All bearings should be checked for smooth operation and replaced if necessary.

5. Carefully inspect the cover seals for a worn, cracked, or otherwise damaged condition and replace them as necessary.

Drifting out the crankshaft seal

The crankshaft seal can be drifted out and then replaced by drifting in a new one using BMW drift no. 224 or a suitable substitute. Replace the tachometer pinion seal in the following manner;

a. Remove the clamp bolt and withdraw the bushing, then drive the tachometer pinion out with a suitable soft metal drift. The seal will come out with the pinion.

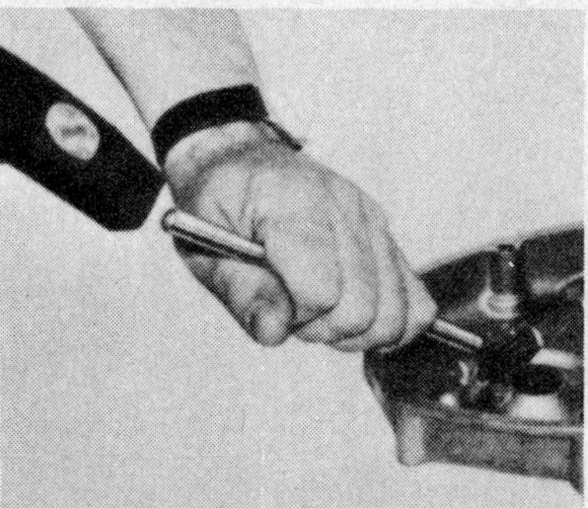

Drifting out the tachometer pinion assembly

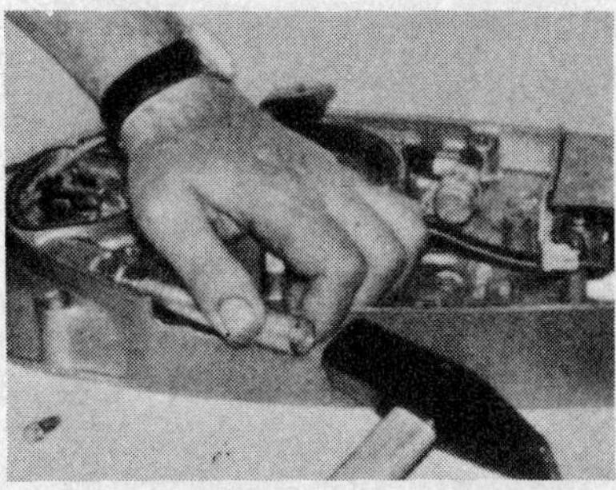

Installing the tachometer pinion assembly

b. Install the tachometer pinion, seal, and bushing by carefully drifting them in with a suitable drift.

ASSEMBLY

1. Assembly is basically in the reverse order of disassembly.

2. Place the inner camshaft bearing on the shaft, press the camshaft sprocket into place, then press on the tachometer drive gear. Installation of the sprocket and gear will be facilitated by a liberal greasing of their bores prior to pressing. Check that the camshaft bearing end play is correct as specified by inserting a feeler gauge between the bearing and the shaft.

Assembling the camshaft

3. Place the engine in a vertical position, place the chain over the camshaft sprocket, insert the camshaft into the crankcase so the mark on the sprocket is pointing straight up and so the end of the shaft seats in the rear bearing bore, and slip the crankshaft gear into the chain so its mark is aligned with the mark on the camshaft sprocket.

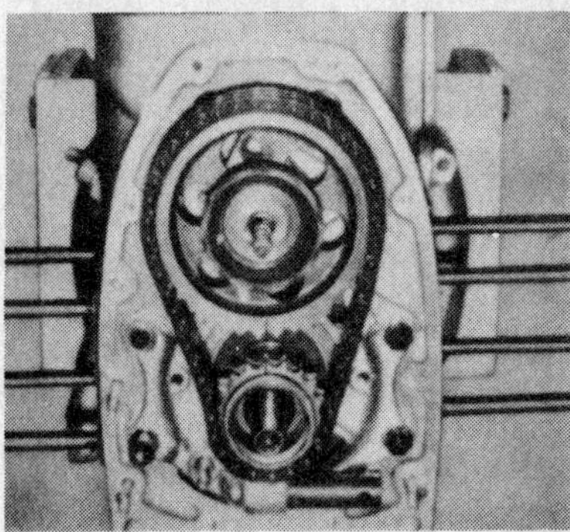

Aligning the camshaft and crankshaft sprockets

4. Lubricate the bore of the crankshaft sprocket to aid in its installation, then push the sprocket on the crankshaft so the key and key groove are aligned. Pull the sprocket fully onto the crankshaft using the BMW fixture sleeve no. 216 and the BMW puller bolt no. 535. Suitable substitutes may be used with caution.

5. Secure the camshaft bearing with

two phillips head screws, using a suitable thread sealing compound.

6. Heat the crankshaft bearing to 170° F and install it flush against its seat.

7. Install the chain tensioner assembly taking care not to deform the spring. Check the contact surface of the tensioner to assure proper operation.

8. With the crankcase in a horizontal position, place a new cover gasket and two sealing strips in their respective positions on the crankcase.

9. Remove the diode chassis and the seal for the advance unit shaft from the cover.

10. Install the BMW guide housing no. 225 into the seal bore for the advance unit shaft.

Positioning the gaskets

Installing the timing case cover

11. Heat the cover to 180° F, position it on the crankcase, then secure it by installing the bolts and nuts finger tight, and then tightening them down from the center out.

12. Complete the assembly in the reverse order of disassembly.

Clutch, Bottom End, Transmission, And Final Drive

Consult the appropriate sections for the older models and follow the procedures given there. These assemblies are quite similar on the new and old models and additional information is not necessary. Consult the Specifications chart at the end of the chapter for the necessary information.

TRANSMISSION SERVICE

ALL MODELS

Removal And Installation

1. Drain the transmission oil and reinstall the drain plug.

2. Remove the rear swing arm as described later in this chapter.

3. Disconnect the battery.

4. Remove the rubber plug, loosen the threaded pin, and disconnect the neutral indicator wire (1). Also disconnect the ground strap from the left cover securing screw (2).

5. Disconnect the clutch cable and remove the return spring.

6. Lift out the cable support bushing from the bottom end of the transmission housing.

7. Loosen the securing screw and disconnect the speedometer drive cable.

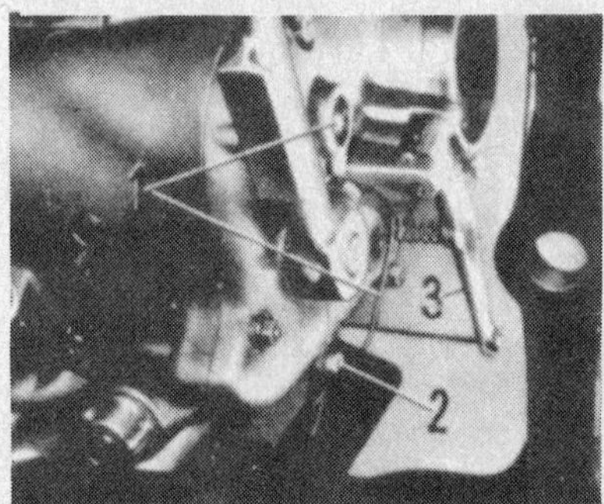

Disconnecting wiring to the transmission (pre-1970 models).

Disconnecting the speedometer drive gear (pre-1970 models).

8. Remove the carburetor air intake tubes from the carburetors and transmission housing.

9. Remove the air filter.

10. Unscrew the four stud nuts that secure the transmission to the engine.

11. Remove the lower securing bolt by pushing it out in the forward direction.

12. Pull the transmission off the engine to the rear, then lift it out the left side of the frame.

13. Installation is a reversal of the removal procedure.

Output Shaft Coupling Flange

REMOVAL

1. Loosen the clamp on the rubber boot at the rear of the transmission and pull off the boot.

2. Remove the cotter pin, retaining pin, and clutch operating lever.

3. Install BMW Matra tool 500 on the coupling flange and unscrew the grooved nut with BMW Matra tool 494/2, or a suitable substitute.

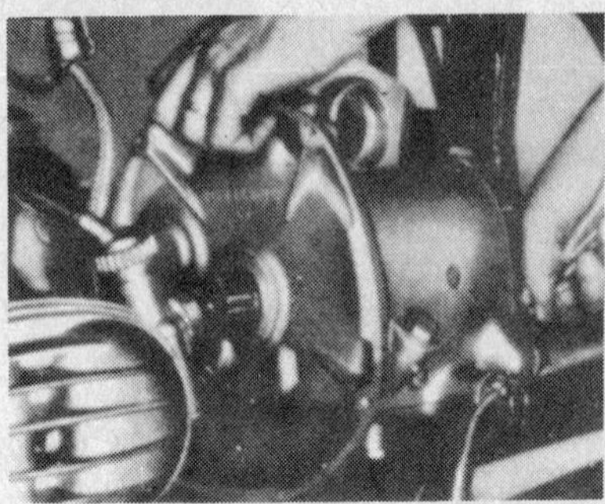

Removing the transmission (pre-1970 models).

Removing the output shaft flange nut (pre-1970 models).

Removing the output shaft coupling (pre-1970 models).

4. Secure BMW Matra tool 501 to the coupling flange, then pull off the flange by turning the extractor bolt.

5. Remove the output shaft oil seal.

INSTALLATION

1. Replace the output shaft oil seal with the lip facing into the housing cover. Install the seal so that approximately 1 mm protrudes from the cover surface.

2. The remainder of the installation procedure is basically a reversal of the

removal instructions. When tightening the grooved nut on the coupling flange, use BMW Matra tool 494/3 along with a torque wrench and tool 500. Tighten the nut to 85–110 ft lbs.

Transmission Shafts

DISASSEMBLY

1. Remove the thrust piece with sealing ring, ball cage, thrust plate, and thrust rod with felt ring from the clutch throwout rod.

2. Remove the seven transmission cover retaining nuts and washers.

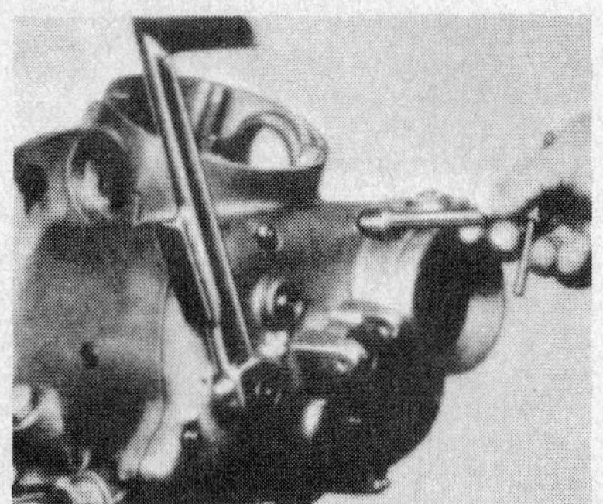

Removing the transmission cover retaining nuts (pre-1970 models).

3. Heat the transmission cover to approximately 180° F, then push down the kick-start lever slightly and tap off the transmission cover with a rubber mallet or wooden stick and hammer. At the same time, tap back the primary shaft ball bearing.

4. Remove the shaft end-play shims.

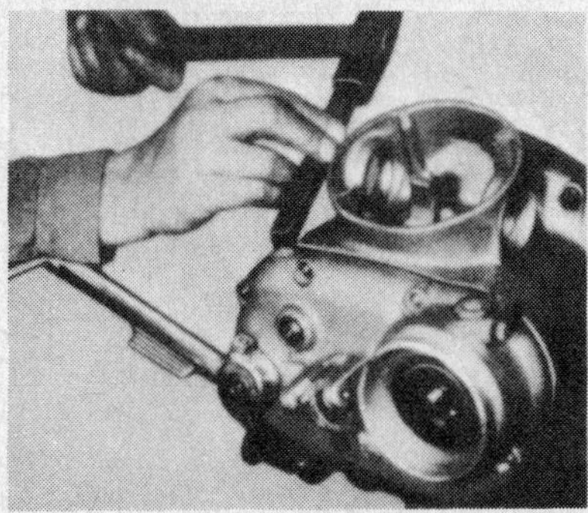

Tapping out the transmission cover (pre-1970 models).

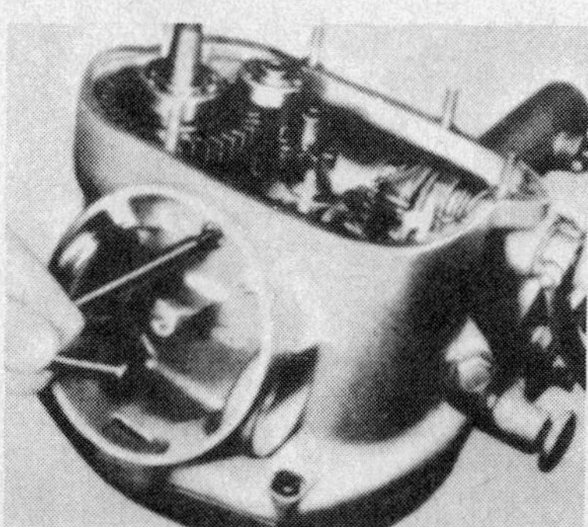

Removing the shift fork retaining plate allen screws (pre-1970 modes).

5. Remove the shift fork retaining plate.

6. Mark the mating shift forks and bushings, then remove the bushings and retaining plate.

7. Remove the transmission cluster together with the shift forks as a unit. If necessary, give the shafts a few taps with a rubber mallet. Remove the oil retainer plate from the primary shaft bearing seat.

Removing the transmission cluster (pre-1970 models).

INSPECTION AND SERVICE

1. Clean all parts thoroughly in solvent, then blow them dry with compressed air.

2. Examine the gear teeth for burrs, nicks, or excessive wear.

3. Inspect the shaft bearing for burrs, etc.

4. Replace gear clusters as complete assemblies, or consult a specialist for individual repairs.

ASSEMBLY

1. Heat the transmission housing to approximately 180–210° F.

2. Install the primary shaft, protecting the oil seal with BMW Matra sleeve 297/1a or a suitable substitute.

3. Tap the shaft into its seat with a suitable drift held against the ball bearing outer race. Do not tap the upper shaft end.

4. Install the oil retainer in the output shaft bearing bore.

5. Install the output and intermediate shafts with the shift forks and mesh the gears with the primary shaft gears.

Tapping the transmission shafts into their bearing seats (pre-1970 models).

6. Tap both shafts into their bearing seats, using appropriate drifts held against the bearing inner races. Be very careful so as not to bend the shift forks.

Measuring transmission shaft end-play (pre-1970 models).

Measuring intermediate shaft end-play (pre-1970 models).

7. Install a new gasket on the transmission housing.

8. If no transmission repairs were performed, the adjustment shims located at the end of each shaft should be the correct size. If repairs were performed, shaft endplay must be reestablished. Standard endplay for all transmission shafts is 0.2 mm (0.008 in.). The intermediate shaft endplay may be as much as 0.4 mm (0.016 in.).

9. Thoroughly lubricate all parts in the transmission case.

10. Heat the transmission cover to 180–210° F and install it on the housing. Depress the kick-starter lever slightly for clearance and make sure the segment gear engages the kick-starter gear on the primary shaft.

11. Install and tighten the transmission cover retaining nuts and washers.

Shifter Mechanism

REMOVAL

(TRANSMISSION DISASSEMBLED)

1. Remove the retaining snap-ring and cam plate.

2. Remove the retaining snap-rings and the sector gear and ratchet plate.

3. Remove the footshift lever nut, lever, and spacer.

4. Remove the interlocking lever with spacer, holder with spring ring, washer, and return spring.

INSTALLATION

1. Assemble the interlocking lever parts in the reverse order of disassembly.

2. Install the interlocking lever so that the return spring ends hold the pilot pin crosswise in the housing.

3. Install the footshift lever with spacer and washer.

4. Slide the sector gear with the interlock gear onto the interlocking lever shaft. The two interlock pawl points, left and right, must be equidistant from the gear sector outer diameter. If necessary, bend the ends of the return spring to achieve this position.

5. Install the ratchet plate on the sector gear and secure it with a new snap-ring.

6. Install a new snap-ring to secure the sector gear on the interlocking lever shaft.

7. Install the ratchet plate return spring on the pin in the housing, then put the ratchet plate on it. Slip on the cam plate so that the second tooth on the sector gear is in line with the mark on the cam plate gear. (See accompanying illustration.)

8. The backlash between the ratchet plate and the detents on the cam plate should be approximately 2.0 mm (0.08 in.) for each gear position. If necessary, adjust by installing washers under the interlocking lever stopscrews.

Kick-Starter Mechanism

REMOVAL

(TRANSMISSION COVER REMOVED)

1. Remove the kick-starter crank cotter screw retaining nut, washer, and washer from the crank.

2. Tap out the cotter screw and remove the kick-starter crank.

3. Pry the segment gear and spring off the transmission cover.

4. Remove the retaining snap-ring and the idler gear.

INSTALLATION

1. Installation is a reversal of the removal procedure. Use flat nose pliers to connect the ends of the return springs.

Speedometer Drive

REMOVAL AND INSTALLATION

(TRANSMISSION COVER REMOVED)

1. Remove the securing lockscrew, then pry the speedo drive bushing out of the case with two screwdrivers.

2. Installation is a reversal of the removal procedure.

Sector gear and ratchet plate (pre-1970 models).

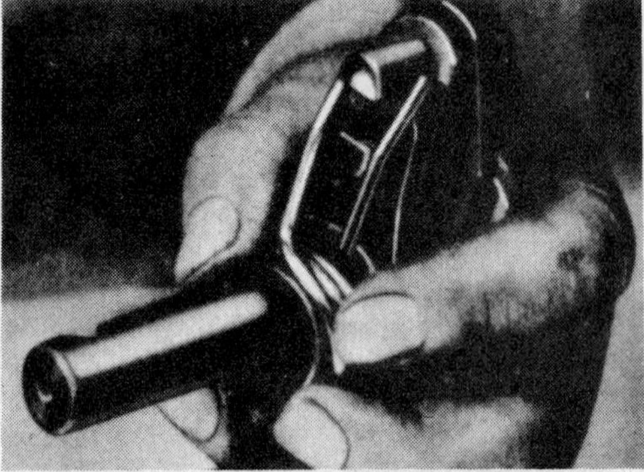

Interlocking lever assembly (pre-1970 models).

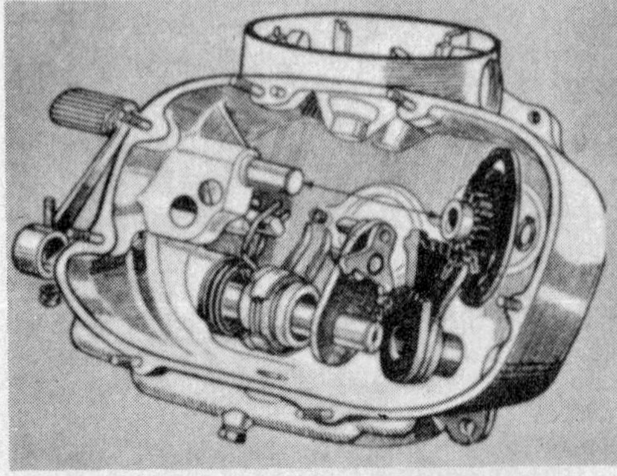

Shifter mechanism cutaway (pre-1970 models).

Sector gear and camplate gear alignment marks (pre-1970 models).

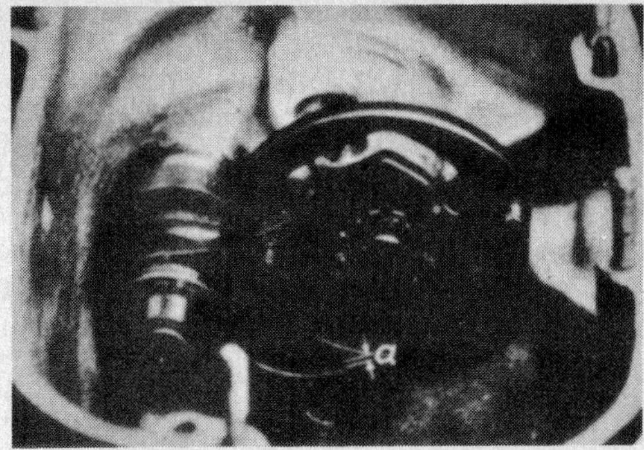

Ratchet plate and camplate backlash (pre-1970 models).

Matra extractor bolts 357 installed (pre-1970 models).

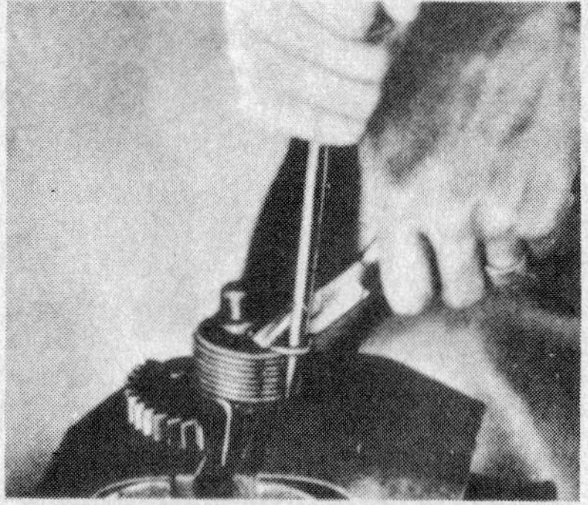

Disconnecting the kick-starter return spring (pre-1970 models).

FINAL DRIVE SERVICE

(All models)

Removal

1. Remove the rear wheel as described in "Chassis."

2. Remove the right bottom shock absorber mounting bolt and washers.

3. Drain the oil from the swing arm and reinstall the plug.

4. Disconnect the brake rod from the brake backing plate.

5. Remove the four swing arm-to-final drive mounting nuts.

6. Remove the final drive from the right swing arm.

DISASSEMBLY

1. Pry up the brake shoe that rests on the flattened washer on the brake cam.

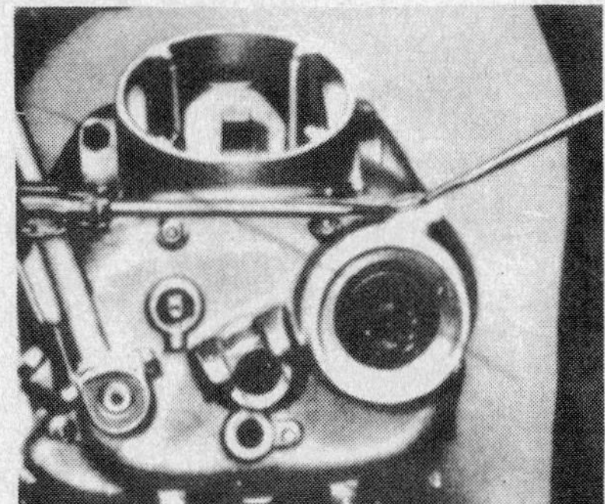

Prying out the speedometer drive bushing (pre-1970 models).

Removing the rear brake shoes (pre-1970 models).

Disconnect the springs, then pry off the other shoe.

2. Remove the brake actuating lever and tap out the brake cam.

3. Remove the six retaining nuts and the final drive cover.

4. Protect the oil seal with BMW Matra sleeve 505 or a suitable substitute, then remove the cover using BMW Matra tools 357a or a pair of suitable extractor bolts.

5. Lift off the cover with the ring gear, bearing inner race and shim.

6. If the housing ball bearing needs replacement, heat the housing to 180° F and tap it out along with the oil seal.

7. Bend back the lockwasher of the drive pinion retaining nut, then install BMW Matra tool 507 or a suitable substitute and remove the nut, washer, and coupler gear.

8. Remove the threaded ring with the oil seal using BMW Matra tool 506a or a suitable substitute, then remove the threaded ring and spacer from the bearing inner race.

Removing the final drive cover (pre-1970 models).

Removing the drive pinion retaining nut (pre-1970 models).

9. Heat the final drive housing to approximately 180° F, then remove the drive pinion with ball bearing, shims, and bearing needles from the outer race left in the housing.

RING AND PINION REPLACEMENT

The ring and pinion gears are selected at the factory in matched pairs and must be replaced as a set. Identification numbers are stamped on the gears so that the proper shims can be installed for gear set positioning.

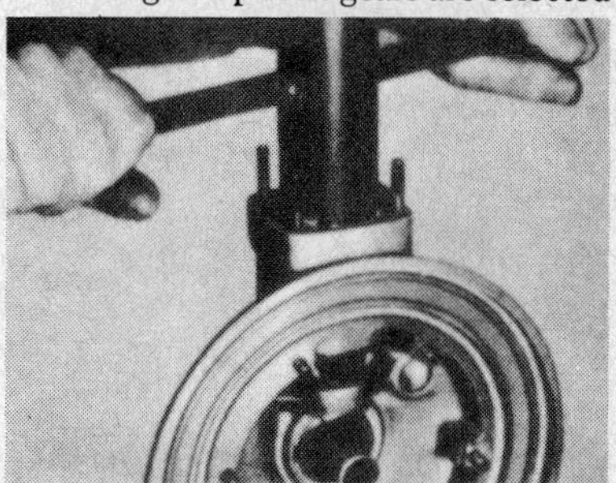

Removing threaded ring with oil seal (pre-1970 models).

The numbers are given, for example, as 314–10, which means that the gear set is of the 314 type with a positioning deviation of −0.10 mm. When installing a new gear set, the proper shims must be chosen so that the positioning deviation is compensated for.

If, for example, the original gear set

Ring and pinion marks (pre-1970 models).

had a deviation of +10, and the new set has a deviation of +30, an additional shim of 0.20 mm must be added between the ball bearing outer race and its seat in the housing.

Measure the backlash between the gears on the ring outer diameter with BMW Matra tool 5042 or a suitable dial indicator. Backlash should be 0.15–0.20 mm (0.006–0.008 in.), and can be adjusted by installing an appropriate shim between the inner and outer race of the needle bearing in the ring gear hub.

CONTACT PATTERN CHECK

Apply Paris blue dye to the ring and pinion, then check the contact pattern. It should be well centered in the drive flank of the pinion, but may be slightly toward the heel. (See accompanying illustration.)

To correct a contact pattern that is too far toward the heel, install a thicker ring and pinion positioning shim and a thinner backlash adjustment shim. To correct a contact pattern that is to close to the toe, install a thinner ring and pinion positioning shim and a thicker backlash adjustment shim.

Ring and pinion contact patterns (pre-1970 models).

NOTE: *Whenever removing or installing the pinion to make these checks, make sure that you first heat the case so as not to disrupt the ball bearing interference fit.*

Make one final check with the Paris blue to make certain the contact pattern is acceptable, then adjust the ring gear sideplay. Using a depth gauge, measure the distance from the ball bearing seat to the machined cover surface. On the final drive housing, measure the distance from the ball bearing on the ring gear to the mating surface gasket.

Correct ring gear side-play is 0.05 mm (0.002 in.). This clearance is obtained by installing the appropriate shims between the ball bearing and its seat. Subtract the second measurement and 0.05 mm from the first measurement and this will give you the correct shim size. Be careful, however, since the gasket on the final drive housing will compress when assembled. Under no circumstances should the ring gear be under pressure.

ASSEMBLY

Assembly and installation are basically a reversal of the removal and disassembly procedures. Note the following:

1. Replace all gaskets and seals.
2. Thoroughly lubricate all parts prior to assembly.
3. When connecting the swing arm shaft to the final drive, engage a gear and turn the engine over with the kick-starter until the coupling is aligned.

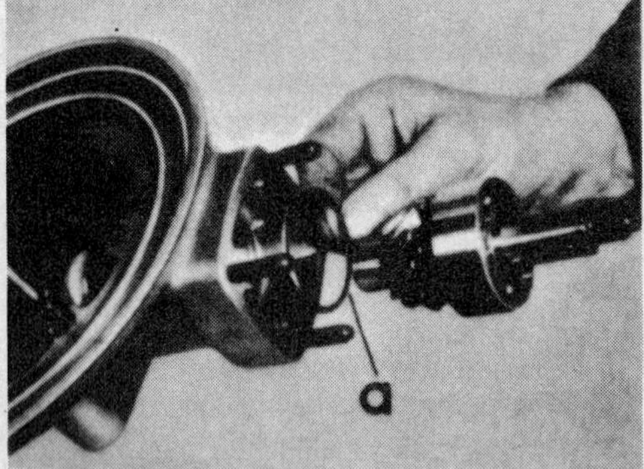

Ring and pinion positioning shim (pre-1970 models).

Gear backlash adjusting shim (pre-1970 models).

Checking for ring gear side-play (pre-1970 models).

ENGINE AND DRIVE TRAIN SPECIFICATIONS

ENGINE

Cylinder Bore	R50, R50S (mm)	R60, R69S (mm)
Standard size	68.000	72.000
1st oversize	68.500	72.500
2nd oversize	69.000	73.000

Machining divergences ±0.01 mm = .0004 in. out of round Taper, not over —0.03 mm = 0.0012 in. (top diameter smaller)

Diameter divergence from correct size marked on cylinder foot

PISTON SKIRT CLEARANCE

	normal (mm)	for authorities and sidecar operation (mm)
R50, R60	0.05-0.06	0.06-0.07
R50S	0.08	——
R69S	0.08-0.09	0.09-0.10
Max total wear of cylinder and piston		①

① 0.12 over piston skirt assembly clearance

CLEARANCES OF PISTON RINGS

Piston ring gap clearance—0.25-0.40 mm

Clearance between rings and sides of grooves in piston:	R50 (5 piston rings) (mm)	R50S, R60, R69S (3 piston rings) (mm)
Piston ring 1 (top)	0.06-0.08	0.07-0.10
Piston ring 2	0.03-0.05	
Piston ring 3 (2) (angular ring)	0.03-0.05	0.07-0.10
Oil rings 4 and 5 (3)	0.03-0.05	0.03-0.05

FIT OF PIN

In piston	0.002 mm (0.00008 in.) tight to 0.004 mm (0.00016 in.) loose. Mating pistons and piston pins are marked with black or white color dots and must not be interchanged.
In connecting rod	0.007-0.026 mm loose
Piston pin arrangement in the piston	
R50, R50S	1.5 mm (0.06 in.) offset. Small side is pressure loaded on working stroke
R60, R69S	central

CONNECTING ROD

Fit of connecting rod bearing on crankpin	No clearance, but must turn freely
Oversize rollers	4.994, 4.996, 4.998, 5.000, 5.002, 5.004, 5.010, 5.020, 5.030 mm in diameter
Diameteral clearance of bearing rollers in roller cage	0.05-0.15 mm (0.002-0.006 in.)
End play of rollers in cage	0.010-0.20 mm (0.004-0.008 in.)
End play of connecting rod on crankpin	0.07-0.10 mm (0.0028-0.004 in.)

CRANKSHAFT AND BEARINGS

Crankpin standard diameter	
R50, R50S	32 + 0.000 mm − 0.018 mm
R60, R60S	36 + 0.000 mm − 0.020 mm
Press power required for fitting crankpin in crankweb	9,000-13,000 lbs
Max. allowable out-of-round on crankshaft journal outer ends, with crankshaft supported on main bearing seats	0.02 mm (0.0008 in.)
Interference fit of main bearings on journals	0.015 mm (0.0006 in.)
Interference fit of crankshaft timing gear	0.013-0.035 mm (0.00052-0.0014 in.) To install, heat gear up to 390°F
Interference fit of ball bearings or spherical roller bearings on crankshaft	0.015-0.025 mm (0.0006-0.0010 in.)
Ball bearing fits in engine housing bearing bushes and in gearcase cover	Slight interference fit. To install bearings, heat engine housing and cover casting up to approx. 176°F
Flywheel clutch face runout (max.)	0.10 mm (0.004 in.)
Max. allowable out-of-round on generator commutator	0.04 mm (0.0016 in.)

CAMSHAFT AND DRIVE

Interference fit of ball bearings on camshaft	0.015 mm (0.0006 in.)
Interference fit of ball bearings in engine housing and bearing bushing, and of bearing bushing in engine housing	0.015 mm (0.006 in.) To install bearings, heat engine housing to approx. 176°F
Max. allowable out-of-round on camshaft front end	0.02 mm (0.0008 in.)
Interference fit of gear on camshaft	To install gear, heat it up to 176°F.

TAPPETS (VALVE LIFTERS) AND VALVES

Diameteral clearance of tappets in bushings	0.02-0.04 mm (0.0008-0.0016 in.)
Rocker arm bushing to rocker shaft clearance	0.01-0.045 mm (0.0004-0.0018 in.)
On R69S needle bearing	playless
Side-play of rocker arms	0.01-0.02 mm (0.0004-0.0008 in.)

	Diameter (mm)	Diameteral clearance in guide (mm)
Valve stem (hard chrome-plated)		
R50, R60 intake and exhaust valves	7 + 0.050 − 0.065	0.040-0.070
R50S intake valve	7 + 0.050 − 0.065	0.040-0.070
R50S exhaust valve	8 + 0.065 − 0.080	0.065-0.095
R69S intake and exhaust valves	8 + 0.050 − 0.065	0.050-0.065

I.D. of valve guide, after shrinking-in, recooling and reaming

R50, R60 intake and exhaust guides	7 + 0.005 mm —0.010 mm (reamer 7K7)
R50 intake guide	7 + 0.005 mm − 0.010 mm (reamer 7K7)
R50S exhaust guide	8 + 0.015 mm 0 mm (reamer 8H7)
R69S intake and exhaust guides	8 + 0.015 mm 0 mm (reamer 8H7)

Valve head diameter	
R50, R50S, R60	
Intake valve	34 mm
Exhaust valve	32 mm
R69S	
Intake valve	38 mm
Exhaust valve	34 mm
Maximum valve face runout (seat eccentricity)	0.03 mm (0.0012 in.)

Interference fit of valve guide in cylinder head	0.03-0.05 mm (0.0012-0.002 in.) To press out and in the guides, heat cylinder head up to 390-490°F.

Valve seat rings (inserts) in cylinder head

Intake valve seat ring	0.18-0.23 mm shrink fit
Exhaust valve seat ring (material Dulenit)	0.13-0.18 mm shrink fit
	To install new rings, heat cylinder head up to 490-550°F.

Valve seat angle	45°
Correction angle, outer	15°
Correction angle, inner	75° (only if required)

Valve seat width in head

R50, R60	
Intake	1.5 mm
Exhaust	2 mm
R50S, R69S	
Intake	1.5 mm
Exhaust	1.5 mm

VALVE SPRINGS

	Inner		Outer	
	R50 R50S R60	R69S	R50 R50S R60	R69S
Wire diameter mm	2.8	3.2	3.8	4.25
Coil outer diameter mm	23.8	28	33.3	38.5
Valve spring free length mm	37.5	42	42.3	43.25
Length, installed mm	30.5	35	34	35
Valve spring load, installed (lb)	16.5	24	41	42.3

TORQUE LIMITS

Cylinder head bolts	25 ft lbs
Flywheel retaining nut	123 ft lbs
Clutch cup spring load, installed	
R50, R60	225-280 lbs
R50S, R69S	341-363 lbs
Generator armature (rotor) on crankshaft	14.5 ft lbs
Ignition magneto rotor on camshaft	14.5 ft lbs

TRANSMISSION

Ball bearings on shafts	Interference fit 0.007 to 0.02 mm (0.00028-0.0008 in.)
Ball bearings in housing	Slight interference fit (To install bearings, heat transmission housing to approx 176°F.)
Diametral clearance of speed gears on bushings	
1st and 3rd gear	0.04-0.09 mm (0.0016-0.0036 in.)
2nd and 4th gear	0.02-0.06 mm (0.0008-0.0024 in.)
Bushings on shaft	
1st and 4th gear	Interference fit 0.00-0.035 mm (0.000-0.0014 in.)
2nd and 3rd gear	Splined bushing only exchangeable together with the shaft
End-play of intermediary shaft	0.2-0.4 mm (0.008-0.016 in.)
End-play of primary and output shafts	0.2 mm (0.008 in.) to be adjusted by means of shims

TORSIONAL TORQUE DAMPER SPRING

Length, installed	1.53 in.
Free length	1.75 in.
Coil diameter, outer	1.35 in.
inner	0.96-0.98 in.
Wire section	5 x 7 mm rectangular
Spring load with 1.53 in. length	235 lbs

FINAL DRIVE

Bearing on pinion	Interference fit 0.015 mm (0.0006 in.)
Pinion bearing in bevel drive housing	Slight interference fit (To install bearings, heat housing to approx. 176°F.)
Ball bearing on ring gear hub	Interference fit 0.015 mm (0.0006 in.)
Needle bearing on ring gear hub	Interference fit 0.012 mm (0.00048 in.)
Ball bearing in cover and needle bearing in housing	Slight interference fit (To install bearings, heat housing to approx. 176°F.)
Backlash between pinion and ring gear (crown wheel) Klingelnberg	0.15-0.20 mm (0.006-0.008 in.)
Ideal setting distance (from ball bearing shoulder on pinion to ring gear axis)	2.93 ± 0.002 in.

ENGINE AND DRIVE TRAIN SPECIFICATIONS

Model	R50/5	R60/5	R75/5
Wrist pin diameter Ø Paint identification white		22 mm 0 −0.003 (0.866 in. 0) 0.00012)	
Wrist pin diameter Ø Paint identification black		22 mm −0.003 −0.006 (0.866 in. −0.00012) −0.00024)	
Wrist pin bore diameter in piston Ø when piston is identified with a "W" (white) on piston head		22 mm +0.003 0 (0.866 in. +0.00012) 0)	

ENGINE AND DRIVE TRAIN SPECIFICATIONS (con't)

Model	R50/5	R60/5	R75/5
Wrist pin bore diameter when Ø piston is identified "S" (schwarz—black) in piston head		22 mm −0.003 0 (0.866 in. +0.00012) 0)	
Wrist pin clearance in piston		0.000-0.006 mm (0.000-0.00024)	
Clearance of wrist pin in wrist pin bushing Identification white		0.015-0.023 mm (0.0006 in.-0.00092 in.)	
Identification black		0.018-0.026 mm (0.00072 in.-0.00104 in.)	
Piston rings: 1st groove (Top ring)① height		1.75 mm +0.060 +0.040 (0.0689 in. +0.0024) +0.0016)	
Ring gap	0.25-40 mm (0.01 in.-0.016 in.)	0.25-0.40 mm (0.01 in.-0.016 in.)	0.30-0.45 mm (0.012 in.-0.018 in.)
Side clearance		0.06-0.07 mm (0.0024 in.-0.0028 in.)	
2nd groove (nose ring)① height		2.00 mm +0.050 +0.030 (0.08 in. +0.002) +0.0012)	
Ring gap	0.25-0.40 mm (0.01 in.-0.016 in.)	0.25-0.40 mm (0.01 in.-0.016 in.)	0.30-0.45 mm (0.012 in.-0.018 in.)
Side play		0.05-0.06 mm (0.0002 in.-0.0024 in.)	
3rd groove (oil scraper ring)① height		4.00 mm +0.030 +0.010 (0.16 in. +0.0012) +0.0004)	
Ring gap	0.20-0.35 mm (0.008 in.-0.014 in.)	0.20-0.35 mm (0.008 in.-0.014 in.)	0.25-0.40 mm (0.01 in.-0.016 in.)
Side play		0.03-0.04 mm (0.0012 in.-0.0016 in.)	
Direction of installation		Writing on ring toward top	
Wrist pin: Wrist pin offset		1.5 mm (0.06 in.)	
Maximum allowable cylinder bore out-of-round		0.01 mm (0.0004 in.)	
Maximum allowable taper of cylinder bore		0.01 mm (0.0004 in.)	
Maximum allowable wear of cylinder and piston		0.12 mm (0.0048 in.)	
Piston: Piston shape		Convex—oval—pitched	

① Not according to German industrial, standards (DIN), BMW's own design

ENGINE AND DRIVE TRAIN SPECIFICATIONS (con't)

Model	R50/5	R60/5	R75/5
Weight selection		+ or − indicated	
Wrist pin selection		W or S indicated	
Standard piston diameter Ø			
A	66.960 mm (2.63 in.)	73.460 mm (2.89 in.)	81.960 mm (3.22 in.)
B	66.970 mm	73.470 mm	81.970 mm
C	66.980 mm	73.480 mm	81.980 mm
1st oversize + 0.50 mm (0.02 in.)			
A	67.460 mm (2.65 in.)	73.960 mm (2.91 in.)	82.460 mm (3.25 in.)
B	67.470 mm	73.970 mm	82.470 mm
C	67.480 mm	73.980 mm	82.480 mm
2nd oversize + 1.0 mm (0.04 in.)			
A	67.960 (2.67 in.)	74.460 mm (2.93 in.)	82.960 mm (3.27 in.)
B	67.970 mm	74.470 mm	82.970 mm
C	67.980 mm	74.480 mm	82.980 mm
Piston clearance		0.035-0.045 mm (0.0014 in.-0.0018 in.) 0.035-0.055 mm (0.0018 in.-0.0022 in.)	
Indication of direction of installation of piston		Arrow with the marking "vorn" (front)	
Bore of connecting rod at big end Ø		52 mm +0.010 0 (2.047 in. +0.0004) 0)	
Bearing insert thickness standard		1.983-1.993 mm (0.078 in.-0.0785 in.)	
Select fit undersize		1.995-2.005 mm (0.0785 in.-0.0789 in.)	
1st undersize		2.108-2.118 mm (0.083 in.-0.0834 in.)	
2nd undersize		2.233-2.243 mm (0.088 in.-0.0885 in.)	
Clearance desired		0.023-0.069 mm (0.00092 in.-0.00276 in.)	
Maximum allowable alignment deviation of connecting rod with bearing inserts installed		0.04 mm (0.0016 in.)	
Maximum allowable torsion deviation of conrod bores		0.015 mm (0.006 in.)	
Permitted weight difference between two connecting rods		± 3g (± 0.105 oz.)	
Cylinder:			
Standard bore diameter			
A	67.00 mm (2.637 in.)	73.50 mm (2.893 in.)	82.00 mm (3.228 in.)
B	67.01 mm	73.51 mm	82.01 mm
C	67.02 mm	73.52 mm	82.02 mm

ENGINE AND DRIVE TRAIN SPECIFICATIONS (con't)

Model	R50/5	R60/5	R75/5
1st oversize + 0.50			
A	67.50 mm (2.657 in.)	74.00 mm (2.913 in.)	82.50 mm (3.248 in.)
B	67.51 mm	74.01 mm	82.51 mm
C	67.52 mm	74.02 mm	82.52 mm
2nd oversize + 1.0			
A	68.00 mm (2.677 in.)	74.50 mm (2.933 in.)	83.00 mm (3.267 in.)
B	68.01 mm	74.51 mm	83.01 mm
C	68.02 mm	74.52 mm	83.02 mm
Cylinder surface finish		2.5-4μm (0.0001 in.-0.00016 in.)	
Bore diameter for front main bearing in main bearing retainer Ø		65 mm +0.019 / 0 (2.56 in. +0.00076 / 0)	
Connecting rod journal diameter Ø		48 mm −0.009 / −0.025 (1.89 in. −0.00036 / −0.001)	
Connecting rod journal diameter select fit oversize		48 mm −0.034 / −0.050 (1.89 in. −0.00136 / −0.002)	
First undersize		47.75 mm −0.009 / −0.025 (1.88 in. −0.00036) / −0.001	
Second undersize		47.50 mm −0.009 / −0.025 (1.87 in. −0.00036 / −0.001)	
Connecting rod journal width		22 mm +0.149 / +0.065 (0.866 in. +0.0595 / +0.0026)	
Maximum allowable dynamic unbalance of crankshaft without flywheel		20 cmp	
Crankshaft end play		0.08-0.15 mm (0.0032 in.-0.06 in.)	
Maximum allowable runout of front crankshaft stub measured with supported at the main bearing journals		0.02 mm (0.0008 in.)	
Maximum allowable wear		−0.20 mm (0.08 in.)	

ENGINE AND DRIVE TRAIN SPECIFICATIONS (con't)

Model	R50/5	R60/5	R75/5
Thrust washer red		2.483-2.530 mm (0.098 in.-0.0995 in.)	
blue		2.530-2.578 mm (0.0995-0.1015 in.)	
green		2.578-2.626 mm (0.1015-0.103 in.)	
yellow		2.626-2.673 mm 0.103-0.105 in.)	
Maximum flywheel clutch fall runout		0.10 mm (0.004 in.)	
Connecting rod: Full length measured from center big end to center small end		135 mm (5.314 in.)	
Connecting rod diameter at wrist pin		24 mm +0.021 0 (0.945 in. +0.00084) 0)	
Connecting rod bushing bore Ø		22 mm +0.020 +0.015 (0.866 in. +0.0008) +0.0006)	
Connecting rod bushing bore Ø		22 mm +0.040 (0.866 in. +0.0015)	
Wrist pin bushing outer diameter		24.060-24.100 mm (0.946 in.-0.948 in.)	
Crankshaft and Bearings: Main bearing journal diameter Ø red		60 mm −0.010 −0.020 (2.362 in. −0.0004) −0.0008)	
blue		60 mm −0.020 −0.029 (2.362 in. −0.0008) −0.000114)	
First undersize red		59.75 mm −0.010 −0.020 (2.352 in. −0.0004) −0.0008)	
blue		59.75 mm −0.020 −0.029 (2.352 in. −0.0008) −0.000114)	
Second undersize red		59.50 mm −0.010 −0.020 (2.342 in. −0.0004) −0.0008)	
blue		59.50 mm −0.020 −0.029 (2.342 in. −0.0008) −0.000114)	

ENGINE AND DRIVE TRAIN SPECIFICATIONS (con't)

Model	R50/5	R60/5	R75/5
Bearing material diameter		2.5 mm +0.003 −0.009 (0.0984 in. +0.00012) −0.00036)	
First undersize	2.75 mm +0.03 −0.009	(0.0108 in. +0.00012) −0.00036)	
Second undersize	3.00 mm +0.003 −0.009	(0.118 in. +0.00012) −0.00036)	
Main bearing clearance	0.029-0.091 mm	(0.0011 in.-0.004 in.)	
Crankshaft journal diameter for alternator bearing Ø	35 mm +0.025 +0.009	(1.377 in. +0.001) +0.00036)	
Bore diameter for alternator bearing in timing case cover Ø	62 mm −0.009 −0.039	(2.44 in. −0.00036) −0.00156)	
Bore diameter for rear main bearing in engine housing Ø	65 mm +0.019 0	(2.56 in. +0.00076) 0)	
Cam shaft:			
Bore diameter for front cam shaft bearing flange	40 mm +0.039 0	(1.575 in. +0.00156) 0)	
Diameter of front cam shaft bearing flange	40 mm 0 −0.016	(1.575 in. 0) −0.00064)	
Cam shaft, bearing flange inner diameter	25 mm +0.021 0	(0.985 in. +0.00084) 0)	
Cam shaft, front bearing journal diameter Ø	25 mm −0.020 −0.041	(0.985 in. −0.0008) −0.00164)	
Cam shaft, rear bearing journal diameter Ø	24 mm −0.020 −0.041	(0.945 in. −0.0008) −0.00164)	
Bore diameter for rear cam shaft bearing Ø	24 mm +0.021 0	(0.945 in. +0.00084) 0)	
Clearance		0.020-0.062 mm (0.0008 in.-0.00248 in.)	
End play		0.1 ± 0.02 mm (0.004 in. ± 0.0008 in.)	
Cam lift	6.198 mm (0.244 in.)	6.198 mm (0.244 in.)	6.756 mm (0.266 in.)
Tappet diameter		22 mm −0.025 −0.045 (0.866 in. −0.001) −0.0018)	
Tappet bore in engine housing		22 mm +0.006 −0.015 (0.866 in. +0.00024) −0.0006)	
Tappet clearance in engine housing		0.01 mm +0.051 (0.0004 in.-0.00204)	
Valve Springs: Wire diameter		4.25 mm (0.167 in.)	
Outer diameter		31.9 mm (1.255 in.)	
Free length		ca. 43.5 (1.71 in.)	

ENGINE AND DRIVE TRAIN SPECIFICATIONS (con't)

Model	R50/5	R60/5	R75/5
Spring load at length		29 Kp/37.6 mm (64 lbs/1.48 in.) 70 Kp/28.5 mm (154.5 lbs/1.125 in.)	
Direction of winding		4	
Number of windings		6	
Installed position		Green painted winding toward cylinder head	
Rocker arm: Rocker arm bore diameter		18 mm +0.059 +0.032 (0.708 in. +0.00236) +0.00128)	
Outer diameter of rocker arm bushing		18 mm +0.030 +0.012 (0.708 in. +0.0012) +0.00048)	
Inner diameter of rocker arm bushing		14.5 mm +0.059 +0.032 (0.57 in. +0.00236) +0.00128)	
Rocker arm shaft diameter		14.5 mm +0.030 +0.012 (0.57 in. +0.0012) +0.00048)	
Clearance of rocker arm shaft		0.002-0.047 mm (0.00008 in.-0.00188 in.)	
Rocker arm clearance		0.002-0.047 mm (0.00008 in.-0.00188 in.)	
Rocker arm side play		No clearance (spring-pre-load)	
Valve seat oversizes		0.2 mm (0.008 in.)	
Valve Guide: Full length		54 mm (2.13 in.)	
Outer diameter		14 mm +0.061 +0.050 (0.551 in. +0.000244) +0.002)	
Inner diameter		8 mm +0.015 0 (0.315 in. +0.0006) 0	
Bore in cylinder head		14 mm +0.018 0 (0.551 in. +0.00072) 0	
Interference fit cylinder head		0.032-0.061 mm (0.00128 in.-0.00244 in.)	

ENGINE AND DRIVE TRAIN SPECIFICATIONS (con't)

Model	R50/5	R60/5	R75/5
Cylinder head Fahrenheit Repair temp		240-260 C (460-500°F)	
Valve guide oversizes		14.1 mm +0.061 +0.050 (0.555 in. +0.00244) +0.002)	
Valve stem clearance: Intake	0.040-0.070 mm (0.0016 in.-0.0028 in.)	0.050-0.080 mm (0.002 in.-0.0032 in.)	0.050-0.080 mm (0.002 in.-0.0032 in.)
Exhaust	0.50-0.080 mm (0.002 in.-0.0032 in.)	0.065-0.095 mm (0.0026 in.-0.0038 in.)	0.050-0.080 mm (0.002 in.-0.0032 in.)
		0.15 mm (0.006 in.)	
Valve actuation:		Ohv through tappets push rods and rocker arms	
Cam/shaft/drive		Duplex chain with chain tensioner	
Cam chain		3/8 x 7/32	
Roller diameter		6.35 mm (0.25 in.)	
Number of links		50	
Exhaust valve shaft diameter	8 mm −0.050 −0.065 (0.315 in. −0.0020) −0.0026)	8 mm −0.065 −0.080 (0.315 in. −0.0026) −0.0032)	8 mm −0.050 −0.065 (0.315 in. −0.0020) −0.0065)
Minimum valve edge thickness Intake Exhaust		 1 mm (0.04 in.) 1 mm (0.04 in.)	
Maximum valve head runout		0.025 mm (0.001 in.)	
Valve Seat: Outer diameter intake	36.2 mm 0 −0.025 (1.425 in. 0 −0.001)	39.2 mm 0 −0.025 (1.544 in. 0 −0.001)	43.2 mm 0 −0.025 (1.7 in. 0 −0.001)
Outer diameter exhaust	36.2 mm −0.050 −0.075 (1.425 in. −0.002) −0.003)	39.2 mm 0 −0.025 (1.544 in. 0 −0.001)	43.2 mm −0.050 −0.066 (1.7 in. −0.002) −0.00264)
Bore diameter for valve seat in cylinder head Intake	36 mm −0.025 0 (1.418 in. −0.001) 0	39 mm +0.025 0 (1.535 in. +0.001) 0	43 mm +0.025 0 (1.694 in. +0.001) 0
Exhaust	36 mm +0.025 0 (1.418 in. +0.001) 0	39 mm +0.025 0 (1.535 in. +0.001) 0	43 mm +0.025 0 (1.694 in. +0.001) 0
Shrink-fit in cyl head: Intake Exhaust To install new seats heat cyl head to 464-500 degrees Fahrenheit	0.15-0.20 mm (0.006 in.-0.008 in.) 0.10-0.15 mm (0.004 in.-0.006 in.)	0.15-0.20 mm (0.006 in.-0.008 in.) 0.15-0.20 mm (0.006 in.-0.008 in.)	0.15-0.20 mm (0.006 in.-0.008 in.) 0.10-0.15 mm (0.004 in.-0.006 in.)
Valve seat angle		45° + 20′	
Valve seat width: Intake		1.5 mm (0.06 in.)	
Exhaust		2.0 mm (0.08 in.)	

ENGINE AND DRIVE TRAIN SPECIFICATIONS (con't)

Model	R50/5	R60/5	R75/5
Valves:			
Length (overall): Intake	103.0—0.4 mm (4.05 in.—0.016 in.)	98.5—0.3 mm (3.88 in.—0.012 in.)	98.8—0.4 mm (3.89 in.—0.016 in.)
Exhaust	102.5—0.4 mm (4.04 in.—0.016 in.)	97.5—0.3 mm (3.84 in.—0.012 in.)	98.8—0.4 mm (3.89 in.—0.016 in.)
Head diameter: Intake	34 mm (1.34 in.)	38 mm (1.495 in.)	42 mm (1.655 in.)
Exhaust	32 mm (1.26 in.)	34 mm (1.34 in.)	38 mm (1.495 in.)
Stem diameter intake	8 mm −0.040 −0.055 (0.315 in. −0.0016) −0.0022)	8 mm −0.050 −0.065 (0.315 in. −0.0020) −0.0026)	8 mm −0.050 −0.065 (0.315 in. −0.0020) −0.0026)
	Engine Torque Specifications (ft lbs)		
Cylinder head nuts 10.8-25.3-25.3 Connecting rod bolts Flywheel bolts	25.3-28.2 34.7-37.6 41.9-44.8	Oil pan lock nut on valve adjustment	8.7 13.0-15.9
Clutch: Type		Single plate dry clutch with diaphragm spring	
Marking (diaphragm spring)	"—"	"+"	without marking
Diaphragm spring pressure, installed (kp)	150-165 (330.75-363.83 lbs)	166-189 (366.03-396.9 lbs)	180-220 (396.9-485.1 lbs)
Height of diaphragm spring, free		17.5 mm ± 0.5 (0.7 in. ± 0.02)	19.0 mm ± 0.5 (0.75 in. ± 0.02)
Testing instruction or diaphragm spring	When placing the diaphragm border upon the measuring plate, the height difference of the spring tongues max. 0.3 mm (0.012 in.) or when placing the spring tongues upon the measuring plate, the vertical runout of the diaphragm border max 0.8 mm (0.032 in.).		
Total thickness of the clutch plate (lamella and lining)		6 mm ± 0.25 (0.24 in. ± 0.01 in.)	
Min. thickness of the clutch plate		4.5 mm (0.18 in.)	
Max. lateral runout of the clutch disc at the outer diameter		0.15 mm (0.006 in.)	
Max. allowable runout of the clutch plate on outer diameter		0.3 mm (0.012 in.)	
Max. runout of the diaphragm driving plate		0.1 mm (0.004 in.)	
Max. allowable unbalance of the clutch plate		6 cmg (0.00834 oz)	
Clutch lever play (cable)		2 mm (0.08 in.)	
	Clutch Torque Specifications (ft lbs)		
	Lock nut for check lever adjusting screw Clutch to flywheel	14.5-16.6 10.8-14.5	
Input shaft end play		0.1 mm (0.004 in.) (adjusted with shims)	
Cluster gear end play		0.1 mm (0.004 in.) (adjusted with shims)	
Output shaft end play		0.1 mm (0.004 in.) (adjusted with shims)	

ENGINE AND DRIVE TRAIN SPECIFICATIONS (con't)

Model	R50/5	R60/5	R75/5
Ball bearing fit in transmission housing		Light prefit, for assembly heat the housing to 180-210° F	
Fit of gears on the bushings			
1st and 4th speed play		0.040-0.085 mm (0.0016 in.-0.00328 in.)	
2nd and 3rd speed play		0.025-0.075 mm (0.001 in.-0.003 in.)	
Fit of bushings on output shaft			
1st speed play		0.005-0.035 mm (0.0002 in.-0.0014 in.)	
4th speed play		0.005-0.047 mm (0.0002 in.-0.00188 in.)	
Bushing for 2nd and 3rd speed has prefit on splines (Bushing can be replaced only together with shaft)		0.005-0.047 mm (0.0002 in.-0.00188 in.)	
Output flange			
Radial runout		±0.05 mm (±0.002 in.)	
Face runout		±0.05 mm (±0.002 in.)	
Power transfer from transmission to rear wheel	Fully enclosed drive shaft in right swing arm tube, provided with a universal joint of the front and a semi-circular tooth coupling in the rear.		
End play of the foot shift lever		0.2 mm (0.008 in.)	
Overshift play measured between shift pawl and shift cam plate in 1st and 4th gear		ca. 2 mm (0.08 in.)	

Transmission Torque Specifications (ft lbs)

Bolts transmission to engine	14.5-16.6	Output flange to output shaft	159.1-173.5
Shift fork bolts	16.6-18.1	Transmission cover bolts	5.8-6.5
Stop ins for interlock pawl	12.3-13.7	Oil filler plug	20.2-23.1
Nut for kickstarter crank	14.5-16.6	Oil drain plug	16.6-18.8

Driveshaft Torque Specifications (ft lbs)

Coupling nut of internally splined bell-shaped gear 173.5-188

Rear Wheel Drive:	R50/5	R60/5	R75/5
Type		Klingelnberg Palloid bevel gears	
Number of teeth	9:32	11:37	11:32
Ratio	1 : 3.56	1 : 3.36	1 : 2.91
Oil recommendation break-in (filled at factory)		Brand name break-in oil SAE 90 Hypoid	
For first oil change and thereafter		Brand name SAE 90 Hypoid	
Capacity		0.25 ltr.	
Backlash		0.15-0.20 mm (0.006 in.-0.008in.)	
End play		No end play (without gasket)	

ENGINE AND DRIVE TRAIN SPECIFICATIONS (con't)

Model	R50/5	R60/5	R75/5
Rear Wheel Drive Torque Specifications (ft lbs)			

Pinion nut	72.3-79.5	Rear drive drain plug	16.6-18.8
Threaded ring (seal retainer)	72.3-86.8	Swing arm filler plug	10.1
Drive shaft coupling nut	173.5-188	Swing arm drain plug	10.1-12.2
Rear drive filler plug	20.2-23.1	Nuts on rear drive cover	13.0-14.2
Swing arm support pins	7.2-8.7	Lock nut on swing arm support pins	72.3-79.5

LUBRICATION SYSTEMS

R50, R50S, R60, AND R69S

Operation

The engine used in these models has pressure-fed and splash lubrication with a wet sump. The pump is of the gear type, driven off the crankshaft via spur gears. It draws oil from the sump through a fine mesh filter, then pumps it through crankcase drillways to the two oil thrower rings on the crankshaft. Centrifugal force throws abrasive particles to the outside of the thrower ring while the clean oil enters the drilled crankpins to lubricate the connecting rod large-end bearings. From here, the oil is splashed onto the cylinder walls, piston, and wristpin. The splash feed oil also passes through a hole behind the tappets into the push rod tubes until it reaches the rocker boxes, where it lubricates the rocker bearings. The oil then drains into cylinder head and cylinder drillways, and returns to the sump.

Oil under pressure is also pumped from the sump to a spray jet for the camshaft spur gears and into a passage around each cylinder. Two holes in each of these passages provide extra lubrication to the cylinder walls and pistons.

A rotary valve type timed breather, driven off the camshaft, is employed to maintain a slight vacuum in the crankcase to help keep the engine oil-tight.

Service

When the engine is disassembled, you should carefully examine the pump gear teeth for any damage caused by abrasive particles in the oil. Also, take the time to blow out all oil drillways in the system to remove any obstructions. The system is very reliable and should never need repair.

R50/5, R60/5, AND R75/5

Operation

The engines used in these models are also lubricated both by pressure and splash, but the layout of the system varies a bit compared to the older models. The oil pump is an Eaton trochoidal type and is driven by the camshaft. It draws oil from the sump through an immersed bell with a perforated screen, and then pumps it through the main oil drillways and into the main flow filter. From here, the oil travels through an annular passage in the camshaft bearing flange to another passage in the main bearing cover, where it then flows, first, through a hole in the left side of the engine case to the rear main bearing, then through two holes leading to the upper tie rod bolts. Passing through these bolts, the oil then reaches the tappet bearing blocks and shafts, where it lubricates the tappet bearings and valve train. Another passage, leading from the same two holes mentioned previously, turns into an annular groove round the cylinders, providing lubrication to the pistons and cylinder walls. The connecting rods receive their oil from the front or rear main bearing grooves via drillways in the crankshaft. The rear camshaft bearing is lubricated by oil under pressure directly from the oil pump, and the remaining internal parts are lubricated by oil splash from the timing chain.

A timed breather is used to maintain a slight vacuum in the engine case, thereby helping to keep the engine oil-tight.

Separate oil splash systems are used to lubricate the transmission, shaft drive, and rear wheel final drive.

Service

The oil pump can be examined either by removing the engine, or by removing the transmission, clutch, and flywheel.

1. Remove the four countersunk securing screws and the oil pump cover.
2. Using a hooked piece of wire, lift out both the outer and inner oil pump rotors.
3. Remove the shaft woodruff key.

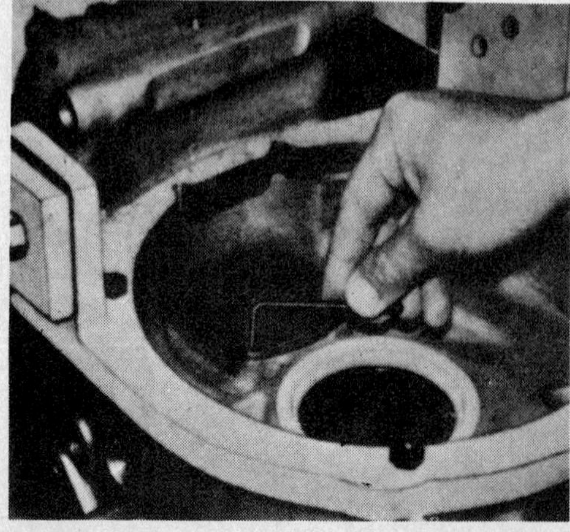

Removing the oil pump cover (post-1969 models).

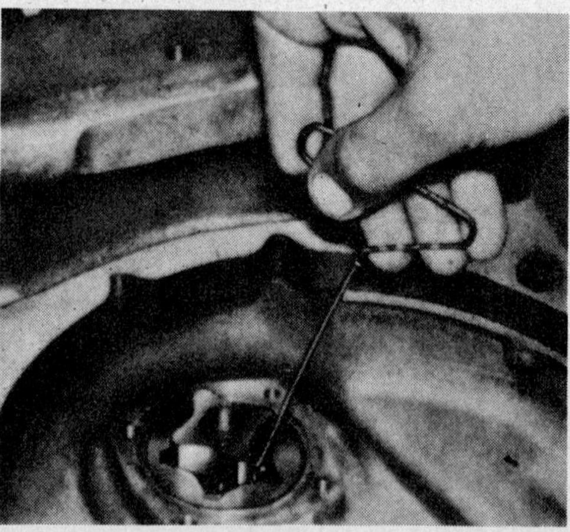

Removing the oil pump rotors (post-1969 models).

4. Examine the rotor surfaces for obvious signs of wear or damage: scoring, burrs, etc.

5. Conduct the following measurements and check them against specifications at the end of this chapter:

a. Using a feeler gauge, check the clearance between the outer pump rotor and the pump housing.

b. Lay a known straightedge over the pump housing with both rotors in place, then measure the clearance between the rotors and straightedge with a feeler gauge.

c. Using a feeler gauge, check the clearance between the inner and outer rotors.

6. Install the shaft woodruff key, inner and outer rotors, and oil pump cover. It's wise to always replace the sealing O-ring.

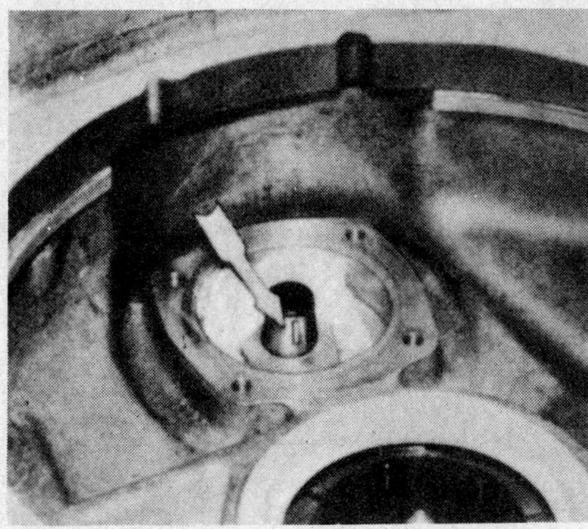

Crankshaft woodruff key (post-1969 models).

Measuring rotor-to-housing clearance (post-1969 models).

OIL PUMP SPECIFICATIONS

	mm (in.)
Type	Rotary, full pressure
Pressure Relief Valve Opens at (psi)	71.0
Pump Output (qt/hr @ rpm)	1480 @ 6000
Outer Rotor Clearance	0.10-0.17 (0.004-0.0068)
Outer Rotor Diameter	57.1 (2.21) wear limit −0.025 (−0.001)
Housing Diameter	57.2 (2.215) wear limit +0.046 (+0.00184)
Rotor Thickness	14.0 (0.551) wear limit −0.016 (−0.00064)
Housing Depth	14.0 (0.551) wear limit +0.025 (0.001)
Clearance Between Housing and Rotor Top	0.050-0.091 (0.002-0.004)
Clearance Between Rotors	0.12-0.30 (0.0012-0.0048)
Maximum Allowable Cover Wear	0.05 (0.002)
Relief Valve Spring Freelength	68.0 (2.68)

Measuring oil pump rotor side-play (post-1969 models).

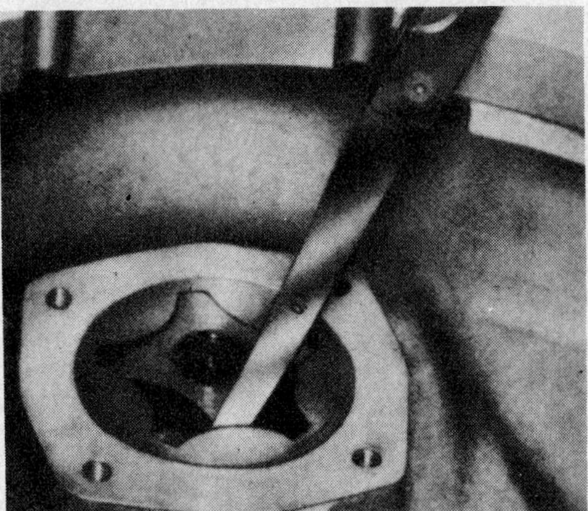

Measuring clearance between inner and outer rotors (post-1969 models).

FUEL SYSTEMS

CARBURETOR

R50, R50S, R60, R69S, R50/5, AND R60/5

Service

1. Unscrew the ring at the top of the carburetor and pull out the throttle slide.
2. Disassemble the float chamber parts and lay them aside in proper reassembly order.
3. Remove all jets and lay them aside also. Ideally, the throttle stopscrew should remain in place.
4. Inspect the throttle slide for scoring along its sides, and replace it if it has enough clearance in the carburetor body to rattle.
5. Inspect the jet needle and needle jet for any nicks or scoring. Make sure the needle jet fits tightly in the carburetor body.
6. Clean all jets in solvent, then blow them out with compressed air. There must be no obstructions.
7. Shake the float to make certain there is no fuel inside and check the general condition of the float needle and seat. Once again, there must be no obstructions, otherwise carburetor flooding will result.
8. Reinstall all jets and make sure they fit tightly in their respective bores. Any air leaks around the jets will cause a lean fuel/air mixture condition.
9. Turn the air screw in until it seats lightly, then back it out the number of turns given in specifications. This will give you the basic setting from which to work. More specific procedures are given in "Tune-Up."
10. The remainder of the assembly procedure is basically a reversal of the disassembly instructions. When reinstalling the throttle slide and ring, make certain to use only hand pressure to tighten the ring. Do not use pliers!

R75/5

1. Remove the attaching screws and the vacuum chamber cover.
2. Remove the jet needle retainer, jet needle, and vacuum piston.
3. Remove the attaching screws, the starter jet housing, and gasket.
4. Remove the attaching screws and the float bowl.
5. Remove the cover screw, main jet, and pilot jet.
6. Turn the carburetor upside down and remove the float pivot pin.
7. Remove the float needle.
8. Remove the needle jet.

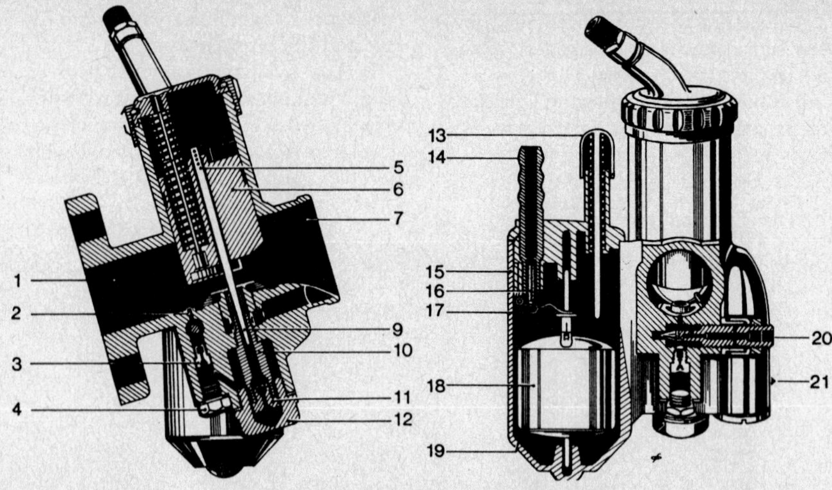

Carburetor construction (pre-1970 models).

1. Inlet tract
2. Inlet tract drilling
3. Slow running jet
4. Sealing screw
5. Jet needle
6. Throttle slide
7. Air intake port
9. Needle taper
10. Needle jet
11. Main jet
12. Main jet cover
13. Priming button
14. Fuel inlet pipe
15. Float chamber
16. Fuel intake valve
17. Lever pivot
18. Float
19. Dampening ring
20. Mixture control screws
21. Throttle slide stop screw

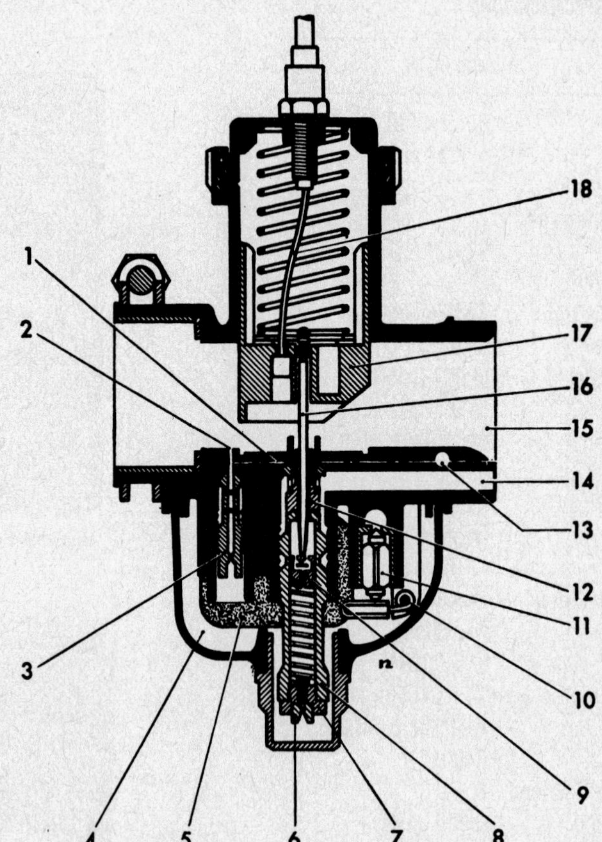

Carburetor construction (R 50/5 and R 60/5).

1. Idle air passage
2. Inlet drilling
3. Idle jet
4. Float bowl
5. Float
6. Main jet
7. Main jet support
8. Lower mixing tube
9. Accelerating pump piston
10. Needle valve coupling
11. Float needle valve
12. Needle jet
13. Idle air screw
14. Air passage
15. Carburetor throat
16. Jet needle
17. Throttle slide
18. Throttle cable

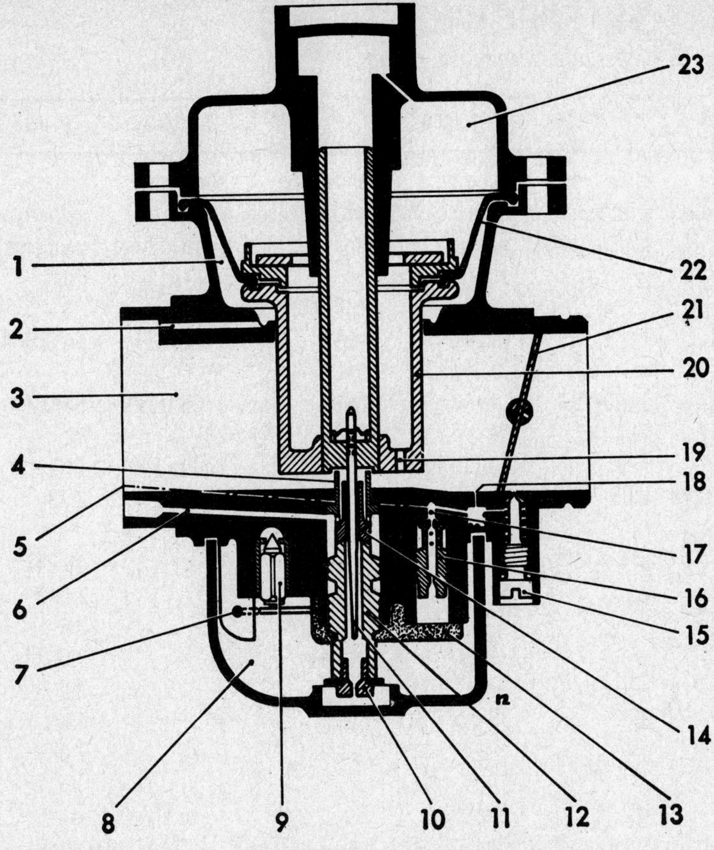

Carburetor construction (R 75/5).

1. Pressure area
2. Intake passage
3. Carburetor throat
4. Pre-atomizer
5. Idle air passage
6. Intake air passage
7. Float tang
8. Float housing
9. Float needle valve
10. Main jet
11. Jet needle
12. Jet holder
13. Float
14. Needle jet
15. Idle mixture screw
16. Idle jet
17. Mixing chamber
18. By-pass passage
19. Vacuum piston passages
20. Vacuum piston
21. Butterfly valve
22. Diaphragm
23. Vacuum chamber

9. Inspect the vacuum piston for scoring along its sides, and replace it if it has enough clearance in the carburetor body to rattle.

10. Inspect the jet needle and needle jet for any nicks or scoring. Make sure the needle jet fits snugly in the carburetor body.

11. Clean all jets in solvent, then blow them out with compressed air. There must be no obstructions.

12. Shake the float to make certain there is no fuel inside and check the general condition of the float needle and seat. Once again, there must be no obstructions, otherwise carburetor flooding will result.

13. Reinstall all jets and make sure they fit tightly in their respective bores.

14. Turn the idle mixture screw in until it seats lightly, then back it out the recommended number of turns given in specifications. Fine adjustment procedures are given in "Tune-Up."

15. Reassemble the carburetor in the reverse order of disassembly. When installing the vacuum piston and diaphragm, make sure the diaphragm locating pin fits in the corresponding recess in the top of the carburetor body. Position the two pressure equalization holes in the vacuum piston near the butterfly valve. Also position the upper diaphragm housing so that the cable adjusting screws are near the butterfly valve.

16. When correctly assembled, the diaphragm should be able to move the entire travel of the guide bore by its own weight.

FUEL PETCOCK

If you experience any fuel delivery problems, first check the gas tank vent, then the fuel petcock. Any sediment, water, etc., in the gas tank will eventually settle in the petcock filter or bowl. Remove the petcocks, disassemble them using the accompanying illustration, wash the filter in solvent, then blow everything dry with compressed air and put them back together.

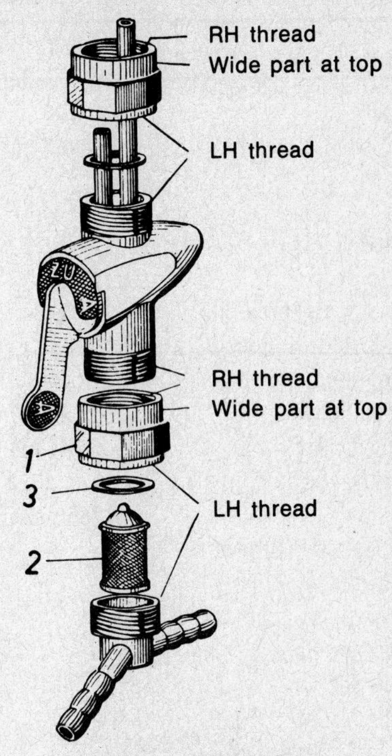

Fuel petcock construction.

ELECTRICAL SYSTEMS

R50, R50s, R60, R69s
COMPONENT SERVICE

Magneto

Troubleshooting Magneto Ignition

If there is no spark, or only a very weak one, check the following possibilities;

1. Improperly engaged ignition key.- This is usually caused by the movable spring in the switch foiling to break contact with the ground terminal. The switch should be replaced, but in an emergency situation you can disconnect the wire at magneto terminal two.
2. Grounded wire between ignition switch and magneto terminal two. The wire should be replaced, but you can juryrig the engine to start by disconnecting the wire at magneto terminal two.
3. Defective ignition cable.
4. Faulty breaker points.
5. A defective condenser, usually indicated by badly burned and pitted points.
6. Check for a binding breaker arm.
7. Worn breaker arm rubbing block.
8. Insufficient magneto safety spark gap can cause a problem. The correct gap is 10–11 mm.

CARBURETOR SPECIFICATIONS

All figures, unless otherwise noted, in mm

	R50	R50S	R50/5	R60	R69S	R60/5	R75/5
Type	slide type with isolated float	slide type with isolated float	slide type with concentric float	slide type with isolated float	slide type with isolated float	slide type with concentric float	constant velocity with concentric float
Model: left	1/24/45 to 149	1/26/71	1/26/113	1/24/125 to 151	1/26/69 to 91	1/26/111	64/32/4
right	1/24/46 to 150	1/26/72	1/26/114	1/24/126 to 152	1/26/70 to 92	1/26/112	64/32/3
Venturi	24	26	26	24	26	26	32
Main Jet	105 to 120	135	130	110 to 125	130 to 135	130 to 140	140
Needle Jet	45-251/1308	45-251/1208	2.68	45-251/1308	45-251/2108	2.68	2.73
Jet Needle	46/255	46/934, no. 4	3	46/255	46/254 to 934, no. 4	4	46-241
Needle Clip Groove	3	2	2	3	2	2	2 or 3
Starter Jets: fuel	—	—	—	—	—	—	0.6
air	—	—	—	—	—	—	2.0
Mixture Bore	—	—	—	—	—	—	2.0
Idle Jet	35	35	35	35	35	40	45
Idle Air Jet	—	—	—	—	—	—	1.0
Idle Air Screw no. turns out	1 to 2½	1 to 2½	½	1 to 2½	1 to 2½	¼ to 1¼	—
Idle Mixture Screw no. turns out	—	—	—	—	—	—	1 to 1½
Bypass Passage	—	—	0.8	—	—	0.8	0.7
Float Needle	—	—	2.2	—	—	2.2	2.5
Float Weight (gram)	7.0	7.0	10.0	7.0	7.0	10.0	10.0
Throttle Slide	22-470 to 542	22-531	22-570	22-470 to 542	22-531 to 542	20-570	—
Vacuum Slide Wt. (gram)	—	—	—	—	—	—	102.0
Idle Passage Bore	—	—	0.8	—	—	0.8	—
Diaphragm	—	—	—	—	—	—	65/811

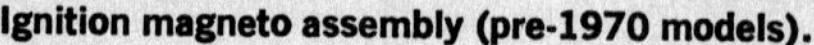

Ignition magneto assembly (pre-1970 models).

DC generator assembly (pre-1970 models).

9. Grounded ignition coil (primary): The coil must not be grounded to any surrounding metal parts. If it is, the malady will be apparent by a jumping spark. The coil must be replaced in this instance, but an emergency remedy can be accomplished by coating the coil and surrounding parts with shellac or a similar nonconductor.

10. Defective ignition coil (secondary):

11. Faulty ignition advance: Disassemble the advance unit, lubricate the shaft, and make certain the unit operates smoothly throughout its entire range.

DC Generator

Quick Output Test

A quick check can be performed to determine the general condition of the DC generator. The only requirement is that the battery is fully charged and all cells are operating normally.

1. Start and warm up the engine.
2. Run the engine up to approximately 2500 rpm, then turn on all the lighting equipment.

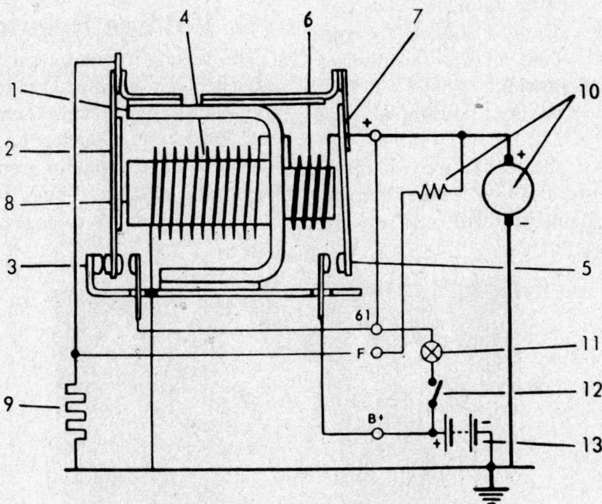

Wiring diagram for RS/ZA voltage regulator.

1. Magnet "U" bow
2. Regulator armature
3. Regulator contact points
4. Voltage regulator coil
5. Contact breaker points
6. Current regulator coil
7. Contact breaker armature
8. Magnet core
9. Regulator resistance
10. Generator
11. Charge indicator lamp
12. Ignition switch
13. Battery

3. Disconnect the battery negative cable and observe the brightness of the lights.
4. The intensity of the lights should increase slightly when the cable is disconnected, and decrease once again when the cable touches the negative terminal. If the lighting does not react, or if it reacts oppositely, the generator should be put on a test machine to check all phases of operation.

No-Load Voltage Check

1. Start and warm up the engine.
2. Run the engine up to approximately 2000 rpm, then disconnect the battery ground cable.
3. Connect a DC voltmeter between terminal D±61 of the voltage regulator and ground.
4. Increase engine speed until the voltmeter indication remains constant. The value should be 7.2–7.9 volts.
5. If the voltmeter indication is less than that specified, the battery is not being charged sufficiently; if it is greater than that specified, the battery is being overcharged.
6. If the voltmeter needle action is erractic; that is, the needle jumps between values, it could be caused by one or more of the following:

   a. Generator brushes too short, dirty, or sticking;
   b. Insufficient brush spring pressure;
   c. Commutator out-of-round;
   d. Defective armature wires;
   e. Damaged voltage regulator.

Cut-In Voltage Check

1. Disconnect the battery ground cable.
2. Connect a DC voltmeter between terminal D±61 of the voltage regulator and ground.
3. Disconnect the wire at voltage regulator terminal 30/51 and connect an ammeter between the terminal and the disconnected lead.
4. Start and warm up the engine.
5. Slowly increase engine speed while closely watching the two meters.
6. As soon as the ammeter needle jumps, take a reading from the voltmeter. It should be 6.4–7.1 volts.
7. If the cut-in voltage is too low, reverse current flows back into the circuit and the battery is rapidly discharged; if it is too high, damage to the regulator contact points may occur.

Load Regulating Voltage Check

1. Connect a voltmeter and a variable resistor between terminal 30/51 of the voltage regulator and ground.
2. Start and warm up the engine, then run it at approximately 1700–2000 rpm.
3. Adjust the variable resistor to the generator wattage value (60 watts) and observe the voltmeter reading. It should be 6.5–7.4 volts.
4. If the load regulating voltage is too high, the generator is overcharging and may roast the armature, or at the very least, shorten the life of the brushes; if it is too low, the battery will not receive sufficient charging current.

Reverse Current Check

1. Disconnect the battery ground cable.
2. Connect a DC voltmeter between terminal D±61 of the voltage regulator and ground.
3. Disconnect the wire at voltage regulator terminal 30/51 and connect an ammeter between the terminal and the disconnected lead. The ammeter must be of the "center zero" type; that is, it must have both positive and negative scales to display forward and reverse current flow.
4. Start and warm up the engine, then increase speed to approximately 2000 rpm and observe the two meters.
5. Slowly decrease engine speed until the ammeter reads zero, then continue slowing down the engine carefully.
6. The ammeter needle should continue its sweep into the negative scale, indicating reverse current flow.
7. When the ammeter needle reaches 2.0–7.5 amps (negative), it should suddenly deflect back to zero, indicating that the contact points in the voltage regulator have broken contact.
8. If the reverse current is too high, the contact points in the voltage regulator tend to stick, which in turn may burn the generator or discharge the battery.

Troubleshooting The DC Generator

Charging Indicator Lamp Will Not Go Out;

1. Faulty generator brushes: Either the brushes are worn or they have seized in their holders.
2. Dirty or oily commutator: Clean the commutator surface with a gasoline dampened rag and remove any brush dust from the mica undercut with a knife blade.
3. Dirty voltage regulator contacts: Clean the contacts by drawing a thin strip of tin between the points. *Do not file the points!*
4. Faulty armature: Have the generator checked out by a qualified service outlet. Chances are the armature must be replaced.

Charging Indicator Lamp Glows Dimly While Riding With Little Or No Lighting Load

1. Discharged battery–Check the specific gravity of each cell, then either recharge or replace the battery.
2. Faulty cable connections–Check the security of all terminal connections and grounds.
3. Faulty voltage regulator points–

Clean the contact points as described previously or, if the problem persists, replace the regulator.

Charging Indicator Lamp Glows Very Brightly And/Or Battery Boils Over. Lighting Bulbs Burn Out Frequently.

1. Inoperative voltage regulator cut-out relay–Examine the relay for any foreign matter that could impede relay operation. Also look for poor grounds.
2. Burned cut-out relay points: Replace the voltage regulator unit. When installing the replacement, polarize the generator by momentarily shorting terminals 51 and 61 on the regulator. Under no conditions apply current to terminal F (DF).

Charging Indicator Flashes On At Regular Intervals

1. This is usually caused by a loose connector or poor ground somewhere in the lighting system. First switch off all the lighting, then check the following wires:
   a. Generator terminal 51 to headlight terminal 51.
   b. Headlight terminal 15/54 to the neutral indicator light.
   c. Horn wiring for short-circuit. If no cause was found, turn on the parking light and check the leads to the taillight, sidecar lighting, parking light, and headlight. If the fault was not located here, switch on the headlight and check its wiring to the bulb.

R50/5, R60/5, R75/5

COMPONENT SERVICE

Alternator

Removal And Installation

1. Remove the engine as described in the "Engine and Transmission" section.
2. Remove the attaching allen head bolts and the front cover.
3. Disconnect the three-prong plug from the alternator stator.
4. Lift the carbon brushes off the commutator and secure them in this position with the brush springs.
5. Remove the stator housing securing bolts.
6. Remove the armature mounting bolt, then install BMW puller bolt no. 5030 or a suitable substitute and press off the armature.
7. Inspect the carbon brushes for wear and the alternator slip rings for scoring. Specifications are given at the end of this chapter.
8. Installation is a reversal of the removal procedure.

Retifier (Diode Chassis)

The diode pack is located just above the alternator behind the front engine cover. Service is by replacement only.

Voltage Regulator

The voltage regulator can be reached after first removing the gas tank and disconnecting the battery negative cable and connector. Specifications for checking the voltage regulator are given at the end of this chapter, though replacement is the accepted way to deal with a faulty unit.

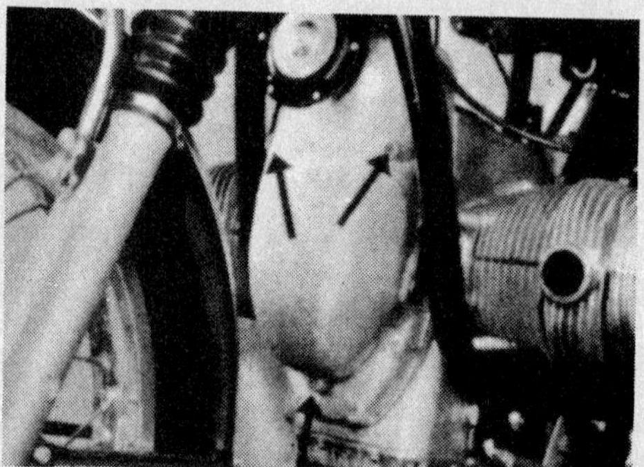

Front cover securing bolts

Carbon brush locked in place with spring

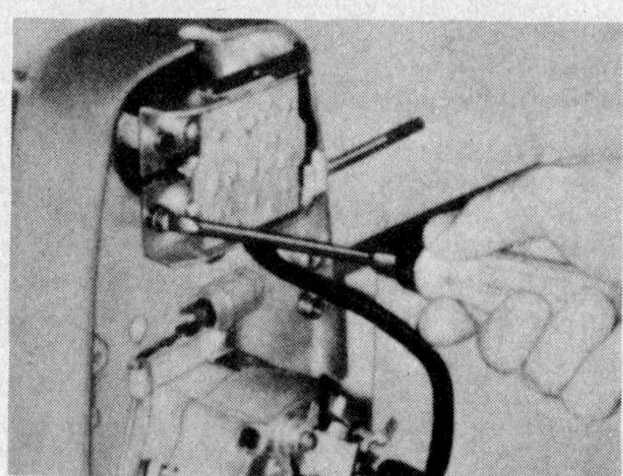

Removing the diode chassis

Removing the armature mounting bolt

Voltage regulator installed

Starter Motor

REMOVAL AND INSTALLATION

1. Remove the air filter element.
2. Loosen nut (1) and bolt (2) in the accompanying illustration, then remove the right air filter housing and breather hose.

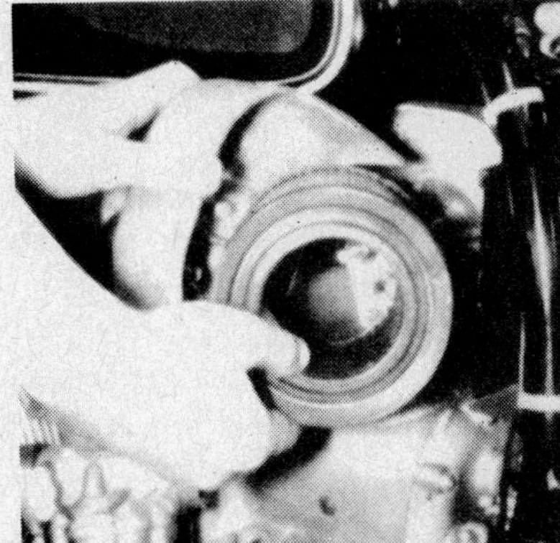

Air filter housing securing nut and bolt

3. Remove the two securing allen bolts and the starter cover.
4. Unhook the retaining straps, remove the battery cover and disconnect the negative cable.
5. Disconnect the starter cables.
6. Remove the starter rear mounting bolts.(See accompanying illustration).
7. Loosen the upper horn mounting bolt.
8. Remove the three securing allen bolts and the front engine cover.
9. Remove the securing bolt indicated by an arrow in the accompanying illustration.
10. Installation is basically a reversal of the removal procedure. Make sure all vent tubes are properly located before installing the front cover and filter housing.

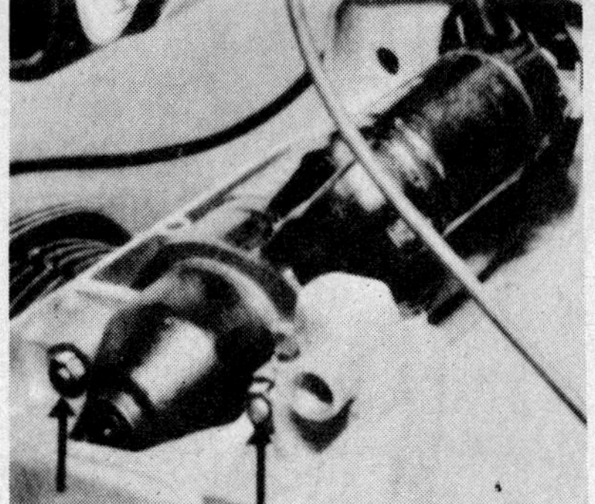

Starter rear mounting bolts

Starter Protection Relay

A starter protection relay is provided to prevent accidental engagement of the motor while the engine is running. It is located underneath the gas tank and can be removed after the tank has been removed and the negative battery cable has been disconnected. For reference, wiring connections are given below:

terminal 97–black wire
terminal 15–green wire
terminal 30–three red wires
terminal 31b–brown/black wire
terminal D$\pm$–two blue wires

Starter securing bolt

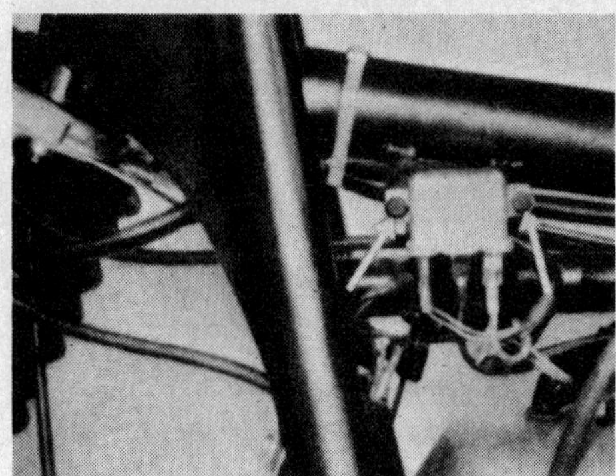

Starter protection relay mounting bolts

Starter motor cables

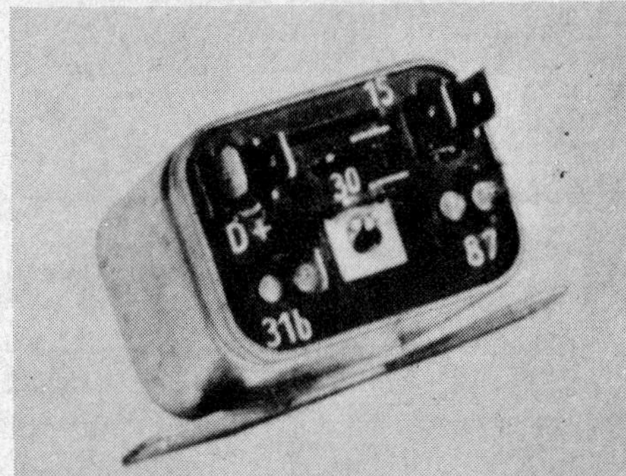

Starter protection relay

STARTER TOUBLESHOOTING

Problem	Possible Causes	Corrective Action
Starter fails to operate when starter button is depressed.	Headlight turned on:	
	a) Lights are dim. Weak battery or dead cell in the battery.	a) Test for specific gravity. Recharge or replace battery as required.
	b) Light is on, but dims upon actuation of starter. Dead battery.	b) Charge battery.
	c) Light is on, but dims as soon as the starter button is depressed. Loose or corroded battery cable terminals.	c) Clean the terminals, apply a light film of petroleum to the terminals after tightening.
	d) Light is normal. Bridge terminals 50 and 30 on the starter. Starter turns. Starter button defect or fauly wiring.	d) Replace starter button, repair open circuit.
	e) Light is normal. Starter solenoid is actuated but starter does not turn. Use auxilliary cable to connect battery positive to terminal 30 on the starter. Starter turns. Solenoid switch contact corroded.	e) Replace solenoid.
Starter does not turn while a cable is connected directly from battery positive to terminal No. 30.	a) Worn brushes. b) Brushes binding. c) Brush spring pressure insufficient.	a) Replace brushes. b) Loosen brushes. c) Replace brush springs.
Starter runs at high RPM but does not turn engine, or turns engine intermittently.	a) Defective starter pinion. b) Broken teeth on flywheel drive gear. c) Starter pinion does not engage.	a) Replace pinion. b) Replace flywheel. c) Repair starter.

BULB SPECIFICATIONS

R50, R50S, R60, and R69S	
Headlight	Bilux lamp (twin filament), 6V, 35/35 watts
Parking light	Pilot lamp, 6V, 2 watts
Neutral indicator	Pilot lamp, 6V, 2 watts
Charging indicator	Pilot lamp, 6V, 2 watts
Speedometer	Pilot lamp, 6V, 1.2 watts
Tail and stoplight	Twin-filament lamp, 6V, 5/18 watts
Turn signals	Tubular lamp, 6V, 18 watts

R50/5, R60/5, and R75/5	
Headlight	Bilux lamp (twin filament), 12V, 45/40 watts
Parking light	Pilot lamp, 12V, 4 watts
Neutral indicator	Pilot lamp, 12V, 2 watts
Charging indicator	Pilot lamp, 12V, 4 watts
Speedometer	Pilot lamp, 12V, 2 watts
Tail and stoplight	Twin-filament lamp, 12V, 5 watts; 12V, 21 watts
Turn signals	Tubular lamp, 12V, 21 watts

ELECTRICAL SPECIFICATIONS (R50/5, R60/5, R75/5)

	R50/5	R60/5	R75/5
STARTER			
Type (Bosch)		DF 12 V 0.5 PS	
Amperage draw maximum (amp)		290	
Power output (hp)		0.5	
Torque (ft lb)		0.885 (6.4)	
Protection relay		Stribel SR 9570	

ELECTRICAL SPECIFICATIONS (R50/5, R60/5, R75/5) (con't)

	R50/5	R60/5	R75/5
ALTERNATOR			
Type (Bosch)		Bosch B 1 14 V 13 A 19	
Drive of alternator		Mounted directly on crankshaft	
Maximum output (w/v)		180/14	
Maximum current output (amp)		13	
Charging begins at RPM		980	
Maximum RPM		10,000	
Max. allowable out-of-round on the slip rings		0.06 mm (0.0024 in.)	
Max. diameter of the slip rings		26.8 mm (1.055 in.)	
REGULATOR			
Type (Bosch)		AD 1/14 V	
Regulated voltage			
without load Volt		13.5-14.2	
with load Volt		13.8-14.8	
DIODE CARRIER			
Type (Bosch)		0 197 002 001 RS 20/1 A 1 A	
IGNITION COIL			
Type (Bosch)		E 6 V	
Starting spark length with 300 sparks/min. and 3 V		8 mm (0.32 in.)	
Operating spark length with 3,600 sparks/min.		13.5 mm (0.54 in.)	
SPARK PLUGS			
Thread		M 14 × 1.25	
Bosch	W 230 T 30	W 230 T 30	W 200 T 30
Beru	230/14/3 A	230/14/3 A	200/13/3 A
Champion		N 7 Y	
Spark plug gap		0.7 mm (0.028 in.)	
IGNITION BREAKER			
Type (Bosch)		Automatic timing advance mounted on camshaft	
Advance begins		800	
Maximum advance at		2500	
Grease for advance unit and breaker cam		Bosch grease Ft 1 v 4	
Grease for breaker cam shaft		Bosch grease Ft 1 v 22 or Ft 1 v 26	
Breaker point gap		0.35-0.40 mm (0.014 in.-0.016 in.)	
Breaker arm spring tension		450	
Dwell angle		110° ± 1°	
Condenser capacitance		0.2 μF − 25%	
Static timing adjustment (for engine assembly)		9° v OT	
Timing range		31° ± 2° 30′	

Torque Specifications (ft lbs)	
Armature mounting bolt	16.6-19.5
Starter motor mounting bolts	34.3
Spark plugs	16.6-21.7

WIRING DIAGRAMS

1. Turnsignal switch
2. Head-light
   a) Turnsignal flasher
   b) High beam
   c) Low beam
   d) Parking light
   e) Connector plug
   f) Ignition and light switch
   g) High beam indicator (blue)
   h) Instrument illumination
   i) Oil pressure warning (amber)
   k) Transmission neutral indicator (green)
   l) Charging indicator (red)
3. Dimmer switch
4. Turnsignal, front right
5. Front brake-light switch
6. Turnsignal, front left
7. Ground to the frame at the ignition coils
8. Starter protection relay
9. Horn
10. Ignition breaker
11. Ignition coils
12. Condensor
13. Transmission neutral switch
14. Oil pressure warning
15. Rear brake-light switch
16. Diode chassis
17. Spark plugs and spark plug caps
18. Alternator
19. Connections on the wiring harness
20. Turnsignal, right rear
21. Tail/stop light
   a) Tail light and license plate illumination
   b) Stoplight
22. Turnsignal, left rear
23. Regulator
24. Battery
25. Ground wire on transmission cover
26. Starter

Identification
BI = Blue
BR = Brown
GE = Yellow
GR = Gray
GN = Green
RT = Red
SW = Black
WS = White

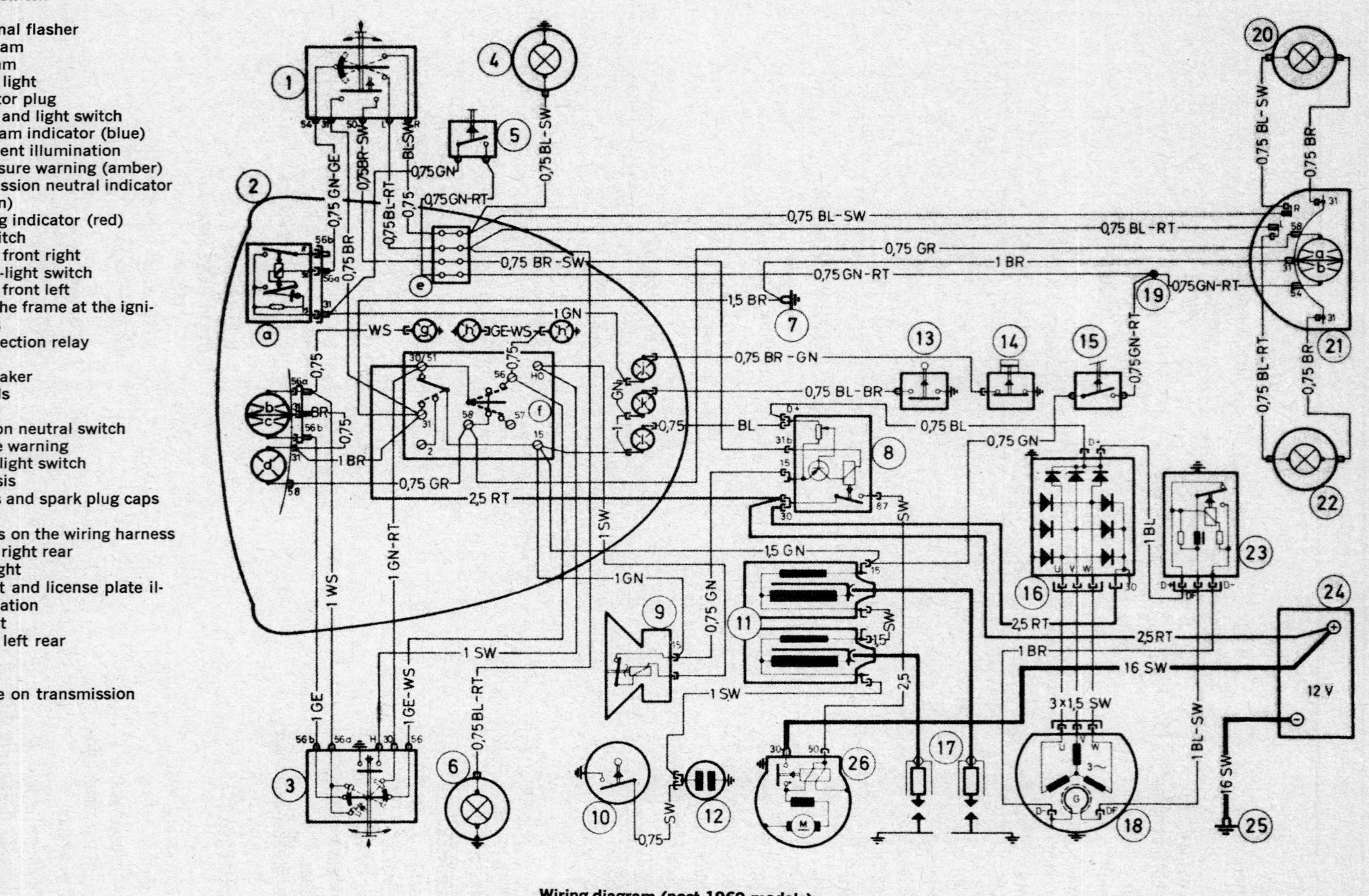

Wiring diagram (post-1969 models).

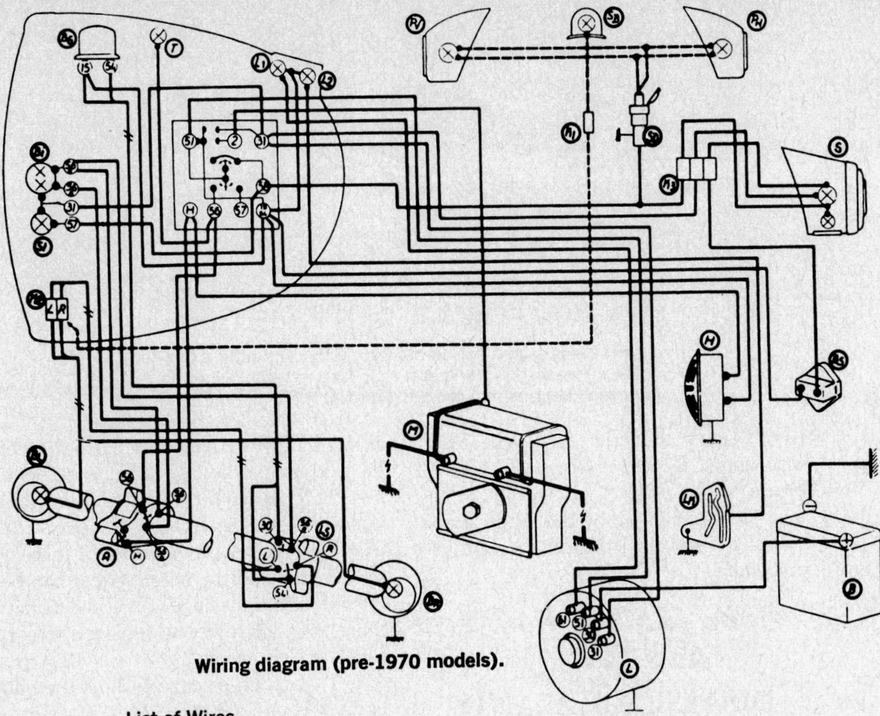

Wiring diagram (pre-1970 models).

A = Dimmer switch
B = Battery
BG = Flasher unit
Bi = Double-filament bulb
BL = Left blinker
BR = Right blinker
BS = Stop light switch
H = Horn
K1 = Cable connector (1-pole)
K2 = Cable connector (2-pole)
K3 = Cable connector (3-pole)
L = Generator (dynamo)
L1 = Charge indicator
L2 = Neutral indicator
LK = Neutral indicator contact
LS = Blinker and headlight-flasher switch
M = Magneto
PH = Rear side light Sidecar
PV = Front side light Sidecar
S = Stop, tail and license plate light
SB = Blinker Sidecar
SD = Electrical jack (socket)
St = Parking light
T = Speedometer light

For sidecar operation, connect the wire, which is shown dotted in the schematic, to cable junction K2 in place of the conductor from right-hand blinker light (BR).

List of Wires

Color	sq. mm.	from	to
black-violet	.75	15 headlamp	31 generator
brown	1.5	31 headlamp	61 generator
blue	.75	charging indi-	2 ignition magneto
black-red	1.5	cator light	51 generator
red	2.5	2 headlamp	horn
black	1.5	30/51 headlamp	horn
black	1.5	15 headlamp	3-pole terminal
black	.75	H headlamp	3-pole terminal
brown	.75	58 headlamp	battery +
black	1.5	31 headlamp	stop light switch
black-violet	.75	30 generator	transmission
black	.75	wire connector	neutral
black	1.5	headlamp,	indicator contact
black	.75	neutral	transmission,
black	3 × .75	indicator	ground
Blinker-System:		battery —	sidecar jack
black	.75	3-pole terminal	(socket)
blue	.75	3-pole terminal	tail light
red	1.0	2-pole terminal	blinker light LH
blue	.75	in headlamp	blinker light RH
black	.75	2-pole terminal	blinker unit,
green	.75	in headlamp	terminal 15
grey	.75	ignition switch,	2-pole terminal
red	.75	terminal 15	in headlamp
		blinker switch RH	2-pole terminal
		blinker switch LH	in headlamp
		blinker switch 54	blinker unit,
		blinker switch 56a	terminal 54
		blinker switch 30	bilux lamp,
		stop light switch	terminal 56a
			blinker unit,
			terminal 15

The 3-pole terminal is situated on battery carrier, at rear.

CHASSIS

WHEEL ASSEMBLIES

Front Wheel

REMOVAL AND INSTALLATION

1. Place the motorcycle on its centerstand and raise the front wheel using a block or wire basket under the oil pan.
2. Remove the cotter pin and unscrew the nut from the brake support arm.
3. Remove the axle nut and washer, loosen the clamp bolt, and withdraw the axle.
4. Installation is a reversal of the removal procedure. Note the following:
    a. Lightly grease the axle before installation.
    b. The axle can be prevented from turning while the nut is being tightened by inserting a bar in the other end.
    c. Work the forks up and down a few times before tightening the clamp bolt to keep the sliders from binding.

Rear Wheel

REMOVAL AND INSTALLATION

1. Place the motorcycle up on its centerstand.
2. Remove the fender brace bolts and

swing the end of the fender up out of the way.

3. Remove the axle nut and washer.

4. Loosen the swing arm clamp bolt and pull out the axle with the bar supplied in the machine's tool kit.

5. Installation is a reversal of the removal procedure. Note the following:

a. Lightly grease the axle before installation.

b. Before tightening the swing arm clamp bolt on the axle, push down on the rear fender or seat several times to operate the rear suspension.

Hubs (R50, R50S, R60 And R69S)

DISASSEMBLY (FRONT AND REAR)

1. Clamp BMW Matra pin wrench 517 or a suitable substitute in a vise, then place the wheel on the wrench and unscrew the sealing cover by turning the wheel.

2. Remove the bearing sealing cover with felt ring retainer, spacer with felt ring, wheel hub plate, and washer.

3. Using a suitable drift or BMW Matra tool 5078, tap out the tapered roller bearings and spaces.

Removing wheel bearing sealing cover.

Tapping out the wheel bearings.

ASSEMBLY (FRONT AND REAR)

1. Inspect the wheel bearings for scoring, or excessive wear. Replace as necessary. Repack the new or old bearings with about 0.7 oz of Shell Retinax A grease.

2. The remainder of the assembly is basically a reversal of the disassembly procedure.

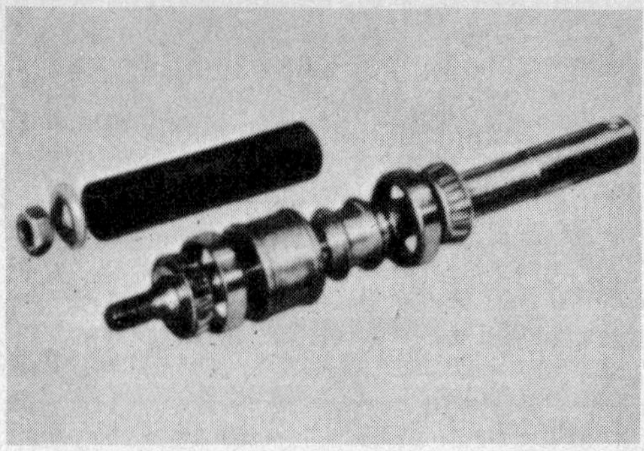

Wheel bearing and axle parts assembly. The only difference between the front and rear hub assemblies is an intermediate bushing provided for the thinner front axle.

Hubs (R50/5, R60/5, And R75/5)

DISASSEMBLY AND ASSEMBLY (FRONT AND REAR)

1. Remove the appropriate wheel(s).

2. Remove the securing bolts, lockwasher, and hub cap.

3. Remove the bearing cover plate with seal and thrust sleeve.

4. Pull out the bearing inner race with cage, spacer ring, and inner spacer sleeve (on the front wheel, first remove the reducing sleeve).

5. Install BMW tool 5074 or a suitable drift into the spacer sleeve on the side of the brake drum and tap out the left bearing outer race, left spacer sleeve, bearings, and right spacer sleeve.

6. Inspect the wheel bearings for scoring, pitting, or excessive wear. Repack the old or new bearings with about 10 grams of Shell Retinax A grease.

7. To check for proper bearing adjustment, assemble all hub components (bearings, washers, spacers, etc.) on the appropriate axle, install BMW tool 553 (front) or 554 (rear) and clamp the whole affair in a vise with something to protect the axle against damage. Secure the bearings together with the axle nut and washer, then check for any freeplay. The bearings are properly adjusted if there is no freeplay and the outer spacer can be moved with light finger pressure. If not, the spacer ring must be replaced to correct the clearance.

8. To install the bearings, heat the hub to 212° F and tap the outer races into place using BMW tool 5079 or a suitable substitute. The remainder of assembly is a reversal of the disassembly procedure.

BRAKE REPLACEMENT

The brake shoes can be removed when the wheel has been removed. Pry up the shoe that rests on the flat portion of the brake cam collar washer. Disconnect the springs, then lift off the other shoe.

SUSPENSION

Shock Absorbers

REMOVAL AND INSTALLATION (EARLES FORK)

1. Set the machine up on its centerstand and raise the front end off the ground using a block or wire basket under the sump pan.

2. Remove the upper and lower mounting bolts and washers, then lift off the shock absorbers.

Removing the top shock mounting bolt (Earles fork).

3. Installation is basically a reversal of the removal procedure. When mounting the shocks, make certain that the top bolt is located in the proper hole for either solo or sidecar operation. The top hole is for solo use, the bottom hole for sidecars.

REMOVAL AND INSTALLATION (REAR)

1. Set the adjusting cam on the solo or lightest spring rate position.

2. Remove the top mounting bolts and washers, then swing the shocks down and remove the bottom mount bolts and washers.

3. Installation is a reversal of the removal procedure.

SERVICE (FRONT AND REAR)

1. Install the pull plate from BMW Matra tool 5094 or a suitable substitute on the shock absorber.

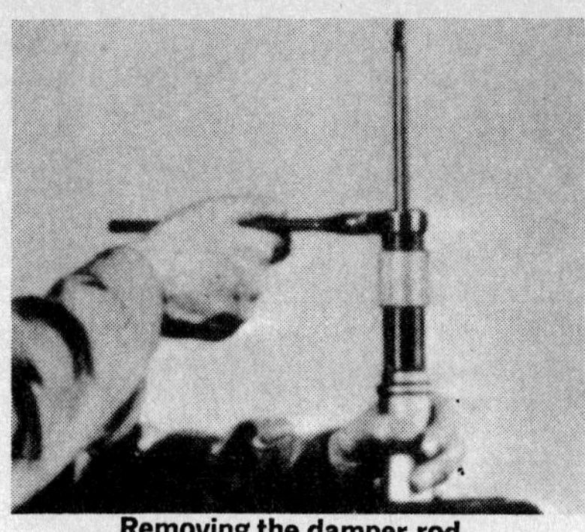

Removing the damper rod.

6. Take care when working with a fully compressed shock. Exerted pressure must not exceed 500 grams or irreparable damage will be done to the internals.

Front Swing Arm (Earles Fork)

REMOVAL

1. Set the machine up on its center-

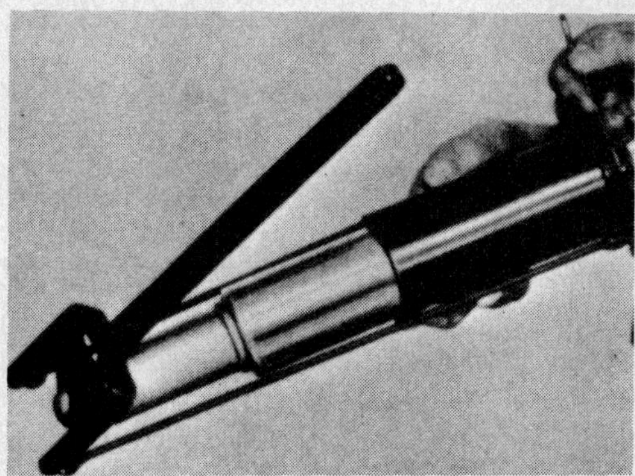

Marta tool 5094 installed on shock absorber.

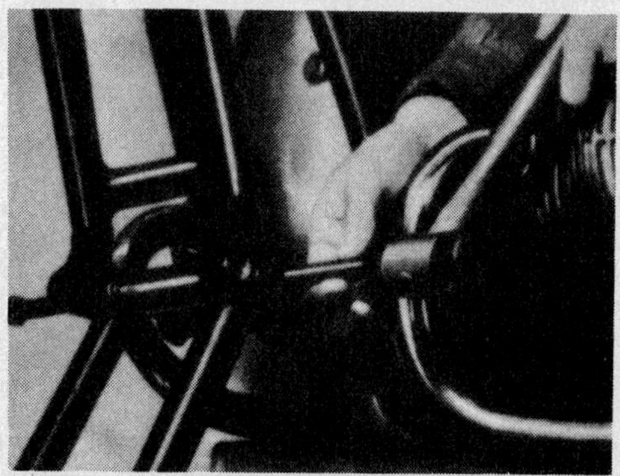

Tapping out the swing arm spindle (Earles fork).

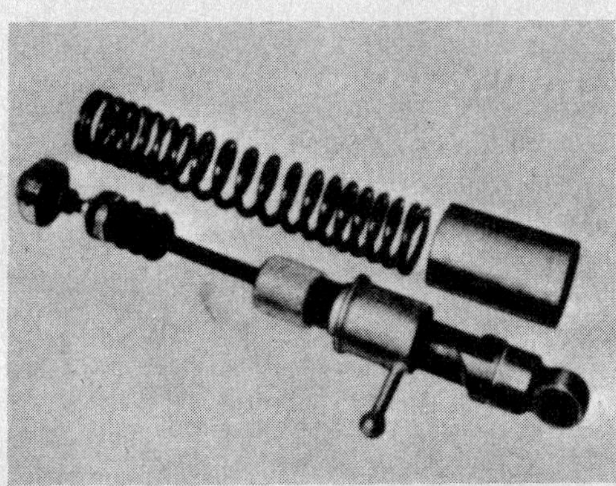

Breakdown of shock absorber parts.

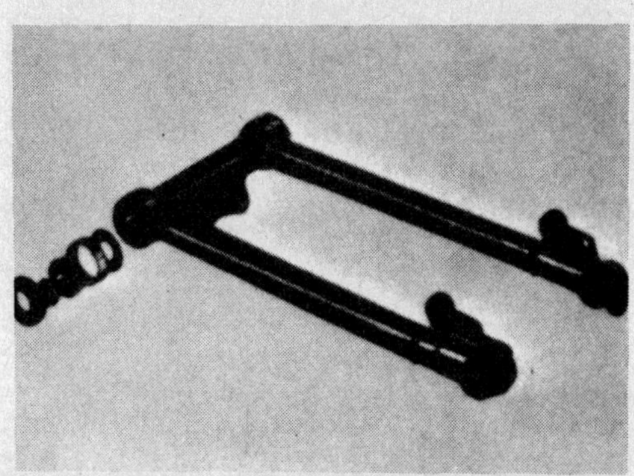

Front swing arm and bearings (Earles fork).

2. Clamp the upper shock eye in a vise, then insert the pin through the pull plate and turn it until the spring is fully compressed.

3. Unscrew the damper rod from the top shock eye with a 9 mm open end wrench.

4. Disassemble and clean all parts thoroughly.

5. Check spring free-length and installed height tension with specifications and replace as necessary.

stand and raise the front end using a block or wire basket under the sump pan.

2. Remove the front wheel.

3. Remove the front fender.

4. Remove the front shock absorber units.

5. Remove the left swing arm spindle nut.

6. Install BMW Matra tool 519 or a suitable substitute by screwing it into the swing arm spindle.

7. Pull or tap out the spindle and tool.

8. Remove the swing arm, taking care to note the number and position of shims on either side of the arm.

9. Remove the bearing seal ring, thrust brushing, and roller bearing inner race and cage on both sides.

10. Remove the bearing outer race only when absolutely necessary, and then do so with a drift inserted in the opposite side of the swing arm.

INSPECTION AND SERVICE

1. Inspect the bearings for pitting, burrs, etc., and replace as necessary.

2. Pack the new or old bearings liberally with Shell Retinax A grease.

INSTALLATION

Installation is basically a reversal of the removal procedure. Note the following:

1. Make sure you install the correct number of shims on each side of the swing arm.

2. When installed, the swing arm should have a maximum side-play of 0.1 mm. If it is greater than this, install appropriately thicker shims.

3. Tighten the swing arm spindle bolt enough so that, with the front wheel removed, the arm will drop slowly about 50° under its own weight.

Installing swing arm spindle (Earles fork).

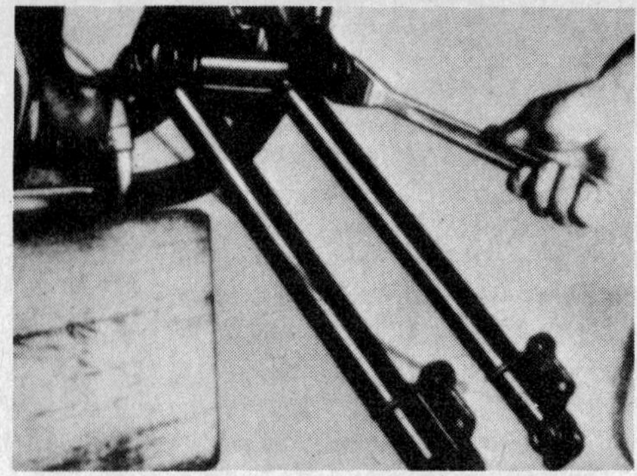
Tightening the swing arm spindle nut (Earles fork).

Front Fork And Steering Stem (Earles Type)

REMOVAL

1. Remove the front wheel, fender, shocks, and swing arm as previously described.

2. On the R50 and R60, remove the steering damper by pulling out the cotter from the bottom of the damper and unscrewing the damper rod. Remove the pressure plate, lockcap, and lockwasher from the bottom of the steering stem. Remove the securing screw and the damper anchor plate with washer and rubber rings.

3. On the R50S and R60S, remove the lock knob and disconnect the coupling lever assembly from the fork and piston rod.

4. Remove the headlight unit.

5. Remove the handlebars. Leave the cables connected and lay the bar aside.

6. Remove the bottom steering stem nut with shims, bearing balls, and races.

7. Remove the fork along with the upper dust cover and bearing balls.

INSPECTION AND SERVICE

1. Inspect the bearings for pitting, scoring, burrs, or excessive wear. Replace as necessary.

2. Pack the new or old bearings with Shell Retinax A grease. There should be 23 balls in each bearing.

INSTALLATION

Installation is basically a reversal of the removal procedure. When the fork has been installed, tighten the steering stem nut and locknut until all free-play is removed, but the fork is free to swing from side to side.

Front Fork And Steering Stem (Telescopic Type)

REMOVAL

1. Remove the front fender.

2. Remove the steering damper.

3. Disconnect the negative battery cable.

4. Remove the upper and lower securing screws from the left switch bracket shown in the accompanying illustration.

5. Remove the cable retaining straps, pull the switch out of the bracket, and remove the switch bracket screw.

6. Remove the switch on the other handlebar in the same manner.

Removing the steering damper rod.

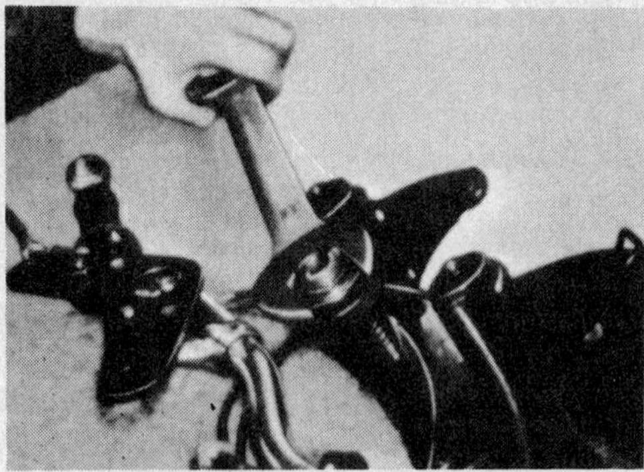
Removing the top steering stem nut.

Removing the steering damper anchor plate.

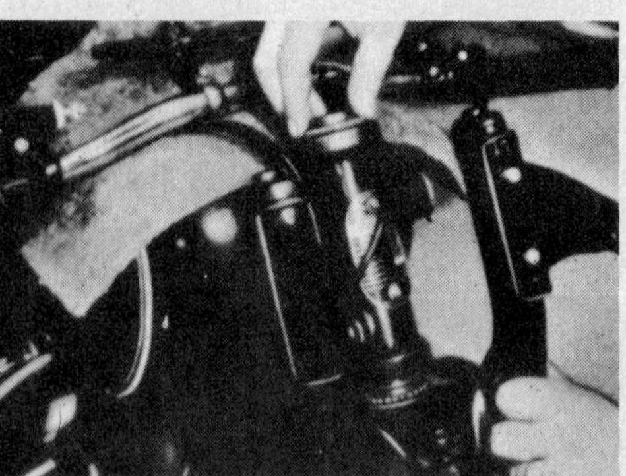
Removing the front fork.

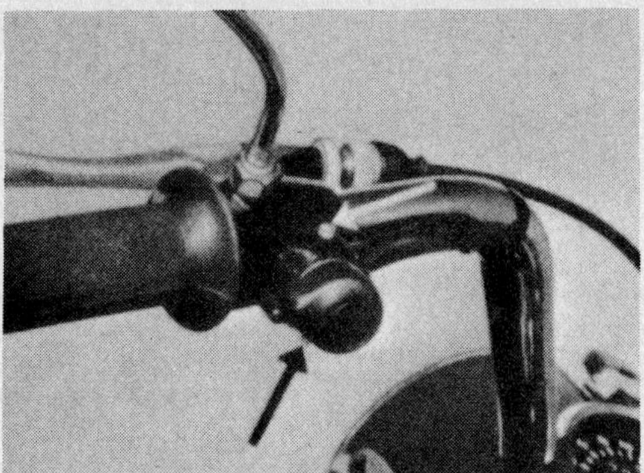

Switch bracket securing screws

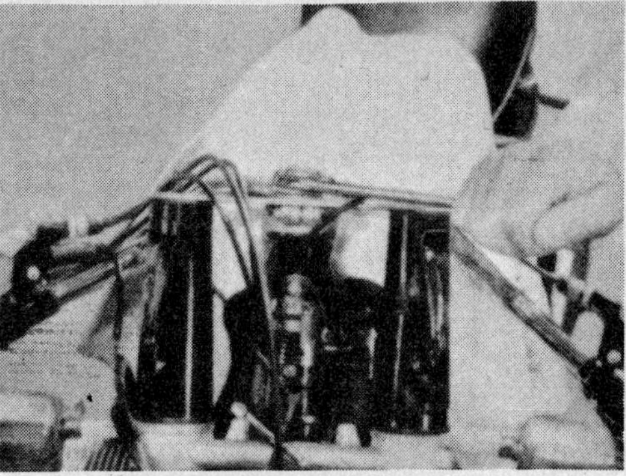

Removing the steering stem nut

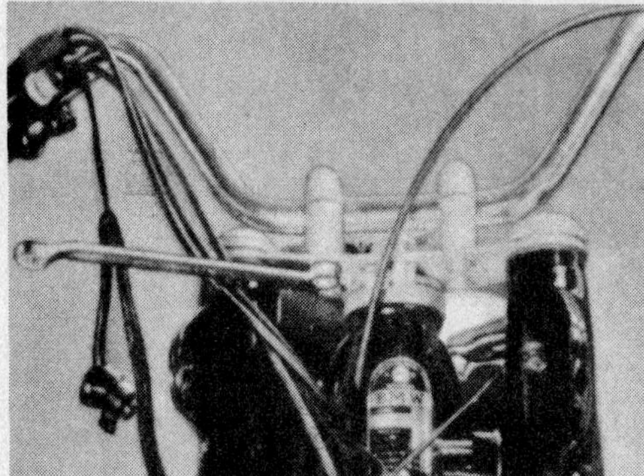

Removing the handlebar brackets

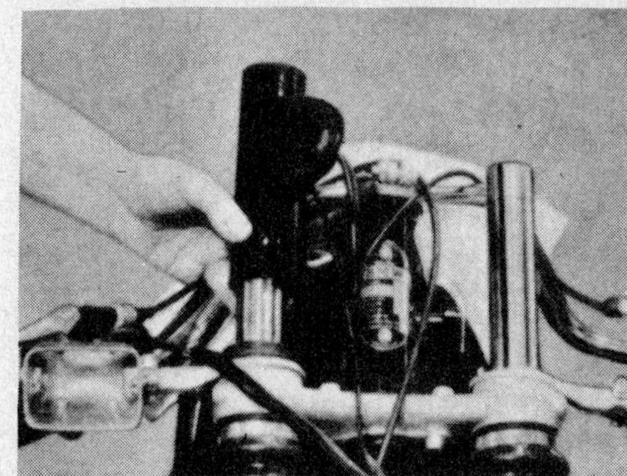

Removing the fork ears

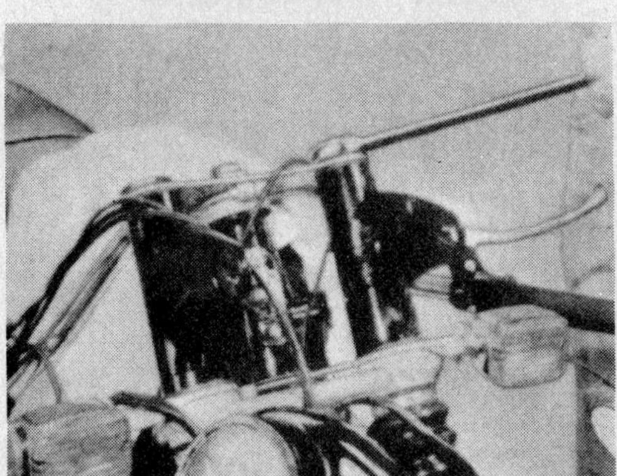

Removing the fork leg caps

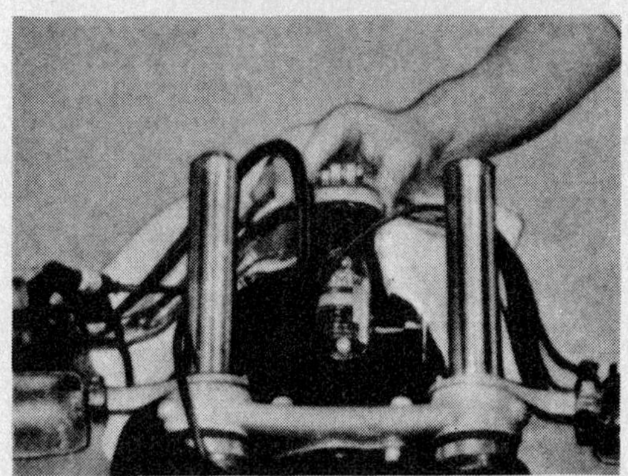

Removing the steering stem clamp

7. Remove the headlight securing bolts and grommets, then carefully lower the headlight and leave it suspended from the wiring.

8. Remove the handlebar brackets, then lay the handlebar on a rag on the gas tank.

9. Remove the fork leg caps with a pin wrench. Also remove the upper spring retainers.

NOTE: *When removing or installing the front fork, it is advisable to place a spacer between the fork stops to prevent accidental damage to the gas tank.*

10. Remove the steering head nut, then lift off the upper fork yoke.

11. If so equipped, remove both turn signal lenses and disconnect the wiring.

12. Remove the fork ears (headlight brackets) with the rubber rings. Pull through the turn signal wiring, if applicable.

13. Remove the allen head steering stem clamp bolt, then remove the clamp.

14. Remove the turn signals and brackets, if applicable.

15. Remove the split ring nut and dust cover.

16. Pull the fork assembly downward,

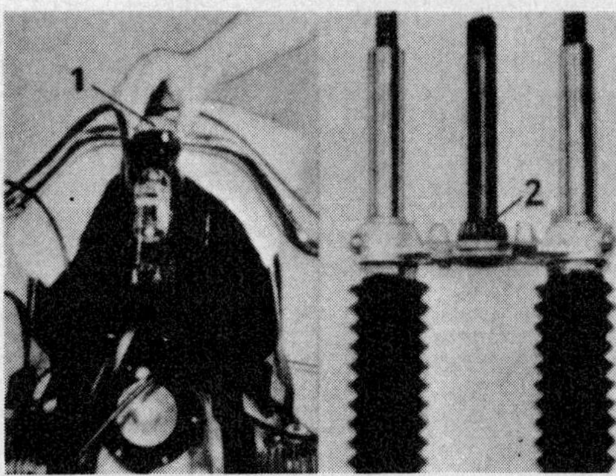

Front fork assembly and steering stem removed

using a rubber mallet if necessary to tap the steering stem. Immediately provide some protection for the tapered steering stem bearings. The outer bearing races remain in the frame.

DISASSEMBLY

1. Drain the fork oil.
2. Providing protection for the alloy parts, clamp the fork in a vise as shown in the accompanying illustration.
3. Loosen the boot clamps and remove the bottom dust covers.
4. Holding the bottom bolt with an allen wrench, remove the shock absorber retaining nuts.
5. Pull out the fork legs.
6. Remove the bottom covers.
7. Remove the gaskets from the bottom shock bolts.
8. Remove the circlips from the bottom of the fork tubes, then remove the oil passage orifice with a pin wrench.
9. Pull out the shock absorber *downward* with the bottoming ring and spring.
10. Remove the springs from the shock absorber by turning them to the right.
11. Loosen the clamping nuts on the lower fork yoke, then install BMW spreading tool 549 and remove the fork tubes (see accompanying illustration).
12. Clamp the hex of the bottom shock absorber retainer in a vise, then unscrew the spring support with the piston rings.
13. Remove the damper valve and spring. To remove the valve at the other end of the tube, unscrew the retainer and remove the ball and spring.

ASSEMBLY

Assembly is basically a reversal of the removal procedure. However, the following points must be considered.

1. If the lower fork yoke is to be replaced, first install the upper and lower yokes in the frame, then adjust the steering head bearings until there is no freeplay, but no more. Insert the fork tubes in the lower yoke and push them up until they are flush with the top yoke. Tighten the clamp bolts and upper spring retainers to the specified torque.
2. When installing the shock absorbers in the fork tubes, use BMW tool 546 or a suitable substitute to compress the scraper rings.
3. Use new seals and gaskets throughout. Tighten all nuts and bolts to the specified torque, if applicable.
4. When installing the rubber fork boots, slide the vent hole over the vent tubes in the lower fork yoke.
5. When installing new fork seals, coat the outer edges with gasket cement and press them into place with BMW tool 547 or a suitable substitute. The metal edge and narrow lip of the seal should face up.

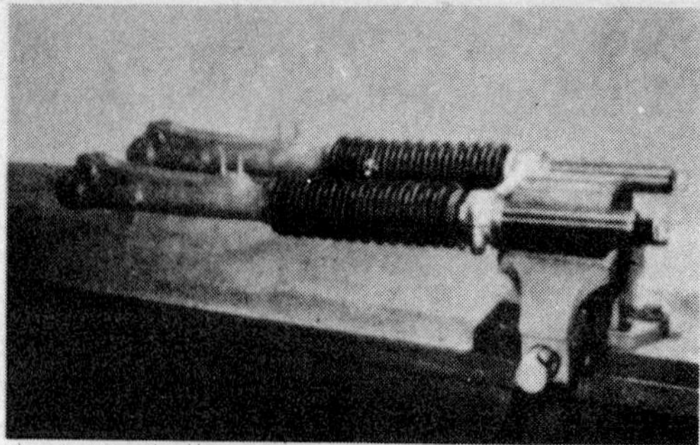

Front fork clamped in a vise for disassembly

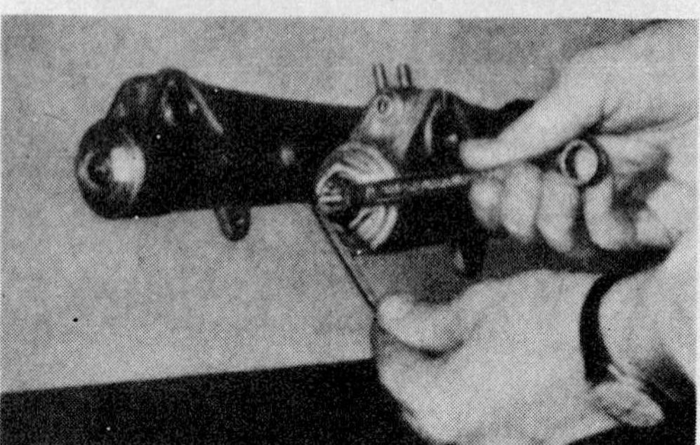

Removing the shock absorber retaining nuts

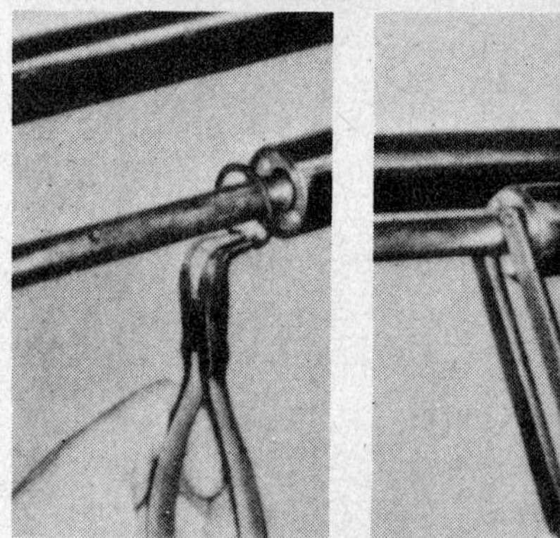

Removing the fork tube circlips and oil orifice

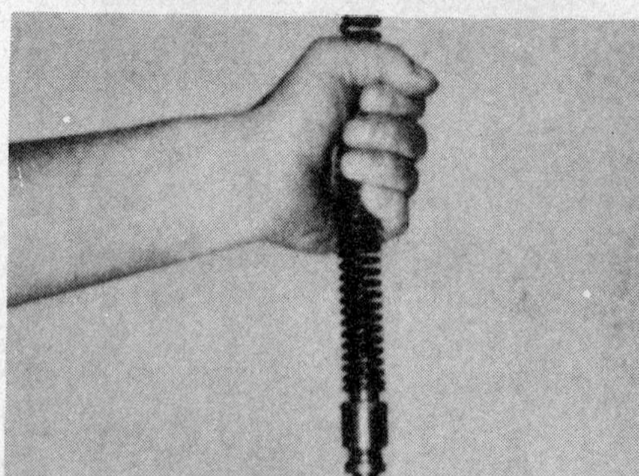

Removing the fork spring

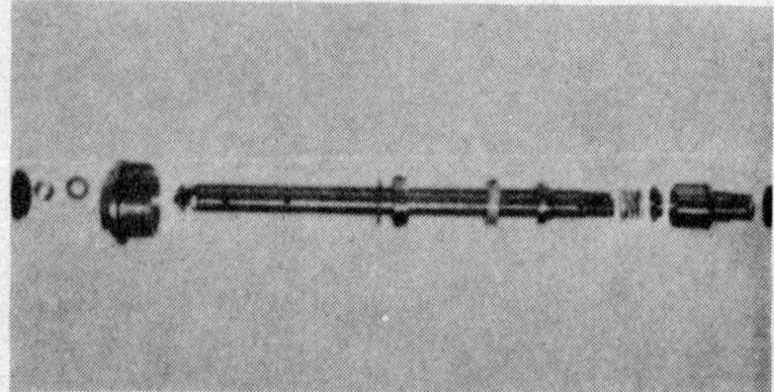

Fork tube parts disassembled

NOTE: *If KACO replacement seals are used, install them without gasket cement and with the open end facing down.*

6. Thoroughly repack the steering head bearings before installation. Tighten the steering stem nut only tight enough to remove play. The fork should be free to fall to either side without binding.

7. The remainder of assembly is a reversal of the disassembly procedure.

INSTALLATION

Installation is a reversal of the removal procedure. Tighten all nuts and bolts to the specified torque, if applicable.

Swing Arm

REMOVAL

1. Remove the rear wheel as directed in the "Rear Wheel Removal and Installation" section.
2. Remove the rear wheel drive box as directed in the "Final Drive Service" section.
3. Remove the battery and rear fender, then remove the right and left side battery brackets.
4. Remove both rear shock absorbers.
5. Remove the clamp which secures the drive shaft boot at the transmission, then fold the boot back as far as possible.
6. Secure the drive shaft using Matra tool 508, or a suitable substitute, then remove the four drive shaft mounting bolts.

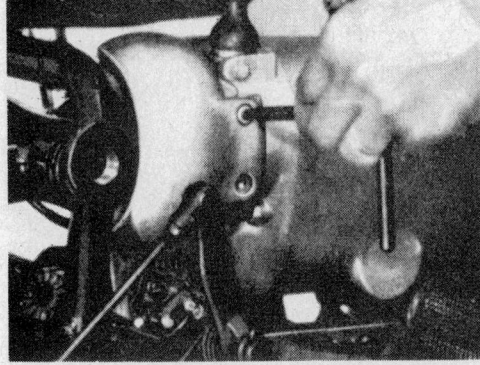

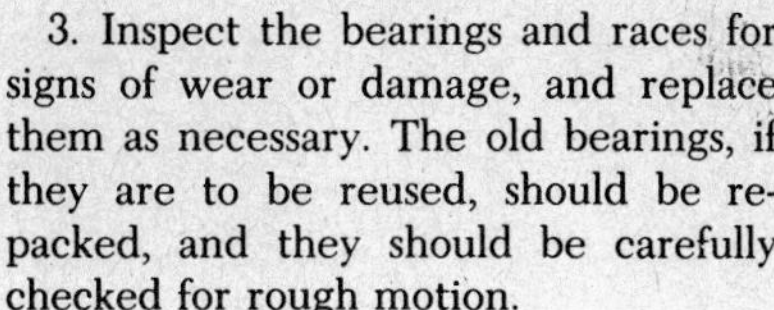

3. Inspect the bearings and races for signs of wear or damage, and replace them as necessary. The old bearings, if they are to be reused, should be repacked, and they should be carefully checked for rough motion.

ASSEMBLY

1. Assembly is basically in the reverse order of disassembly.
2. When installing the pivot pins make certain that the distance (a & c) on both sides is even. Make sure the drive shaft is centered in the swing arm tube so that it won't touch during full swing arm motion. If the shaft touches adjust it so it won't even if this means that the two measurements will be different.
3. Adjust the bearings so that all play has been taken up, then secure them.

2. Replace the standard gearbox cluster for the optional sidecar ratios (R50 and R60). See "General Specifications."
3. Replace the standard speedometer with the corrected sidecar unit.
4. Replace the standard suspension springs (fork and rear shocks) with their beefed up sidecar counterparts.
5. On the Earles type front fork, move the swing arm spindle and bearings to the forward mounting position.
6. Also on the Earles fork, move the front shock absorbers to the lower of the two top mounting holes.
7. Replace the standard brake lever without stopscrew for the lever with the stopscrew. Put the machine up on its centerstand and, while spinning the wheel, turn the stopscrew in until the shoes make positive contact with the drum,

Checking that shaft is centered.

Removing the driveshaft coupling cover.

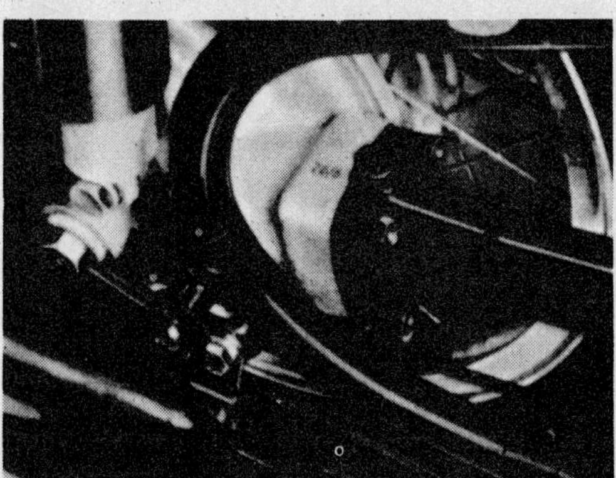

Side-car ring and pinion installed.

7. Remove the dust covers or remove drive shaft coupling cover, at the swing arm pivot points, then loosen the locknuts and remove the pivot pins. The swing arm is now free to be removed. Note the order in which the assembly comes apart.

INSPECTION AND REPAIR

1. Clean all parts in a suitable solvent, then blow dry. All seals should be replaced as a matter of course.
2. Inspect the swing arm for signs of wear, stress, cracks, or other damage, and replace it as necessary.

NOTE: *On pre-/5 models it is important to have the swing arm centered and the studs pre-loaded ⅛ turn before the locknuts are secured. On /5 models the studs should be secured to 8 ft/lbs, and their locknuts to 15 ft/lbs.*

Mounting the BMW Sidecar

1. Replace the standard ring and pinion set in the rear-wheel drive with the optional 4.33 ratio and mark the new gear teeth number 26/6 on the housing.

then back the screw out until the wheel spins freely and tighten the locknut.

8. If possible, replace the standard 25.6 in. handlebar for the 28 in. sidecar bar.
9. If equipped with alloy rims, exchange them for their stronger steel counterparts.
10. Remove the front engine mounting bolt and frame bushing, then install the special BMW ball pin in its place. A special castellated nut is also provided.
11. Install the two eye bolts for the sidecar brace mountings in the eyes on the right frame tube. Tighten the eye bolt nuts to 54 ft lbs.

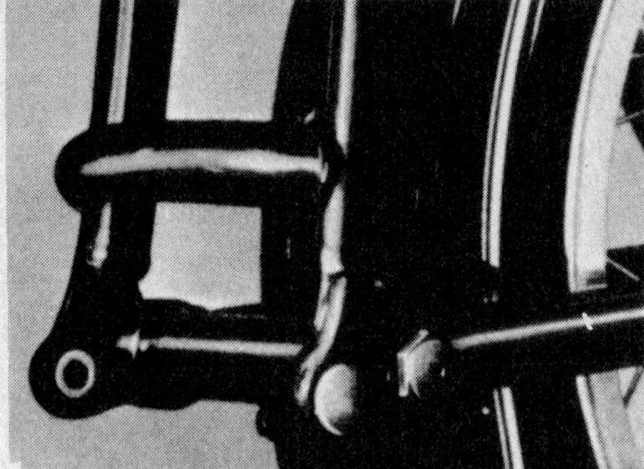

Swing arm and side-car mounting position.

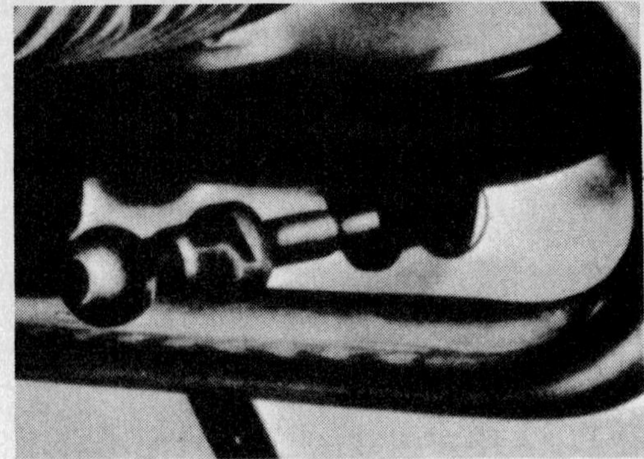

Side-car ball joint installed in engine mounting bolt hole.

Front shock absorbers and side-car mounting position.

Side-car brake eye bolts installed.

Side-car brake lever with setscrew installed.

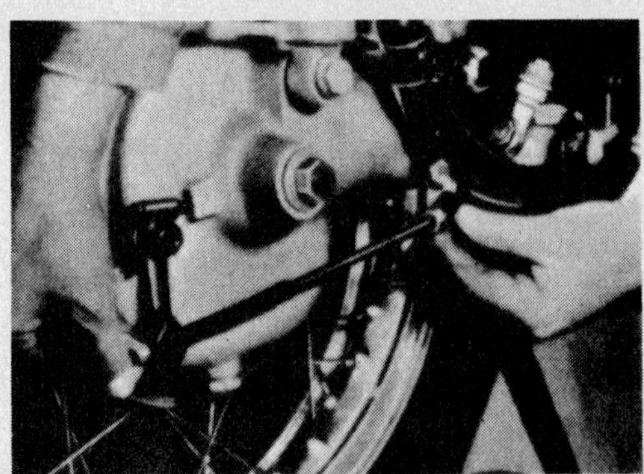

Side-car brake rod installed.

12. Remove the standard brake rod and in its place install the clevis of the brake pull cylinder with the existing pin up front, the new brake rod with washer, and the return spring and lockwasher at the rear. The flat side of the brake rod and the notch in the pin of the new brake lever must point upward. Remove any free-play in the linkage, taking care not to pull the piston in the cylinder off its rest. Make certain the brake cylinder does not touch the frame.

13. Set the motorcycle up on its centerstand and remove the sidecar wheel fender.

14. If installed, remove the sidecar wheel and lightly grease the stub axle. Make sure the wheel hub does not touch the backing plate; if necessary, install a shim.

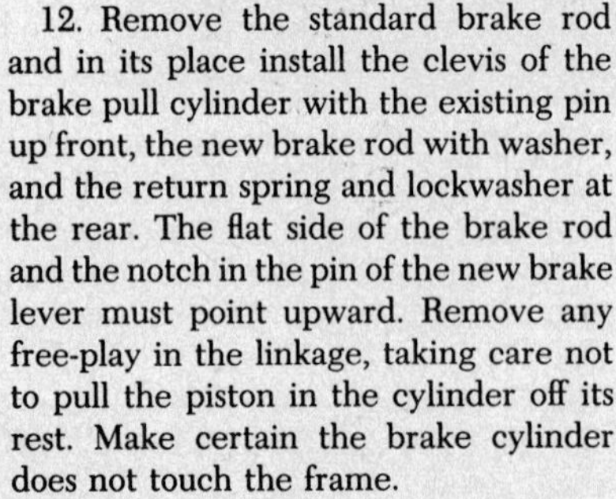

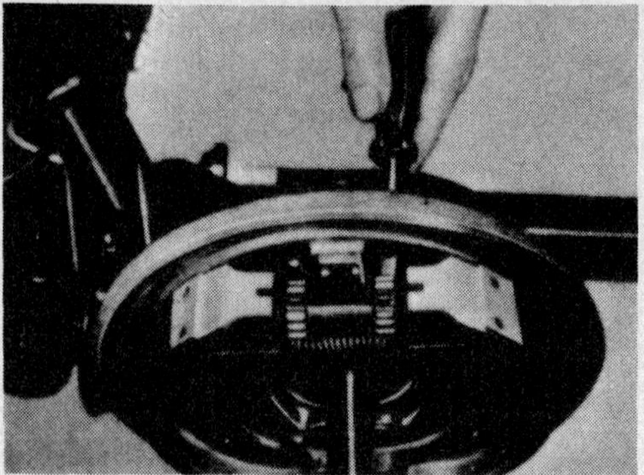

Adjusting the side-car wheel brake.

15. Adjust the sidecar brake by removing the protective rubber plugs and turning the adjuster starwheels with a screwdriver blade until the associated shoe makes contact with the drum, then back off the adjusters until the wheel spins freely.

16. Connect the sidecar frame and constantly rock the motorcycle from side to side in order to seat the ball joints.

When measuring toe-in distance b must be 1.2-1.6 in. less than distance a.

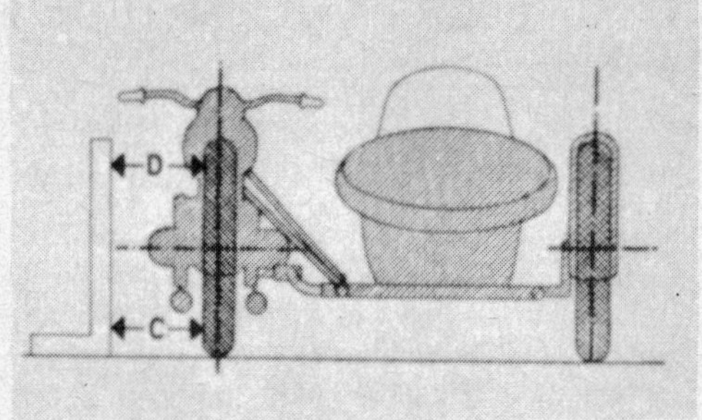

When checking camber with an occupied side-car the difference between C and D should not exceed 3/8-7/16 in. (10mm).

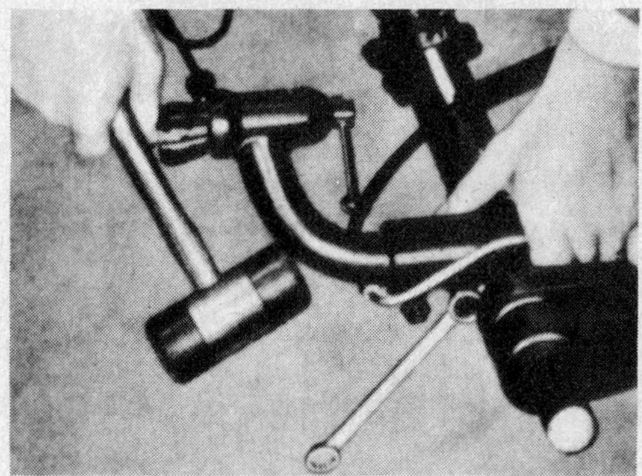

Toe-in is adjusted by moving the coupling arm in the rear cross tube in or out.

Bleeding the hydraulic brake system.

17. Lay some boards along the outside of the sidecar wheel and along the two motorcycle wheels. Adjust toe-in to 1.2–1.6 in.

18. Adjust camber to zero by adjusting the upper rear brace. Make sure the front brace is tension-free. When the sidecar is occupied and there is a rider on the motorcycle, the camber difference (see accompanying illustration) should be approximately ⅜–7/16 in.

19. Connect the hydraulic brake lines, then fill the pull cylinder with ATE blue brake fluid until the level is approximately ½ in. above the cylinder bushing.

20. Bleed the hydraulic brake system in the same way you bleed automotive brakes, then tighten all fittings and check for leaks.

21. Adjust the rear wheel motorcycle brake so that its operation is synchronized with the sidecar brake.

22. Connect the sidecar lighting to the jack provided under the seat of the motorcycle.

23. Take the machine out for a test ride, then make any necessary adjustments so that the car tracks straight and true.

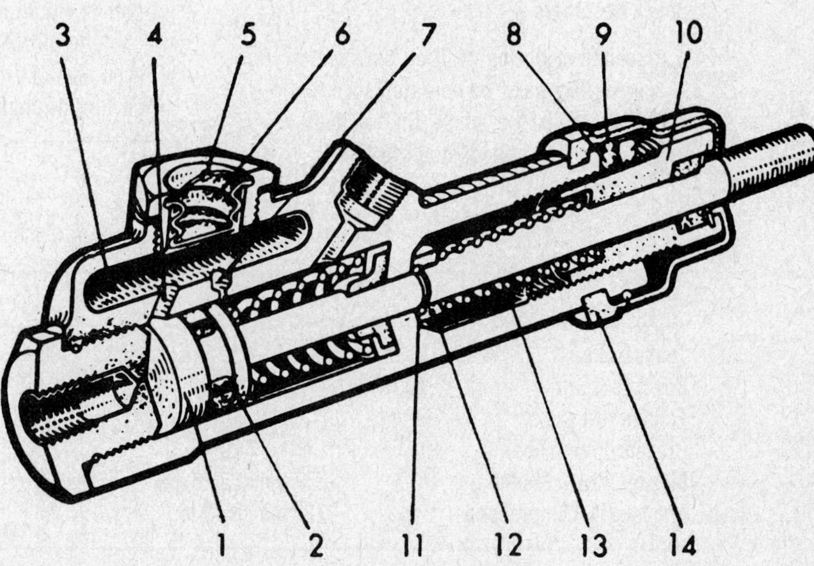

Hydraulic pull cylinder exploded view.

CHASSIS SPECIFICATIONS

	Solo	Sidecar
Rear Wheel Suspension Spring		
Wire dia/Coil outer dia (mm)	7/51	7.6/52.1
Free length (mm)	272.5	271.5
Spring load, installed lbs spring movement (mm)	27/8	33/7
Spring rebound load lbs spring movement (mm)	525/121	661/120
Wire dia/Coil outer dia (mm)	6/48	6.3/48.6
Free-length (mm)	284	273
Spring load, installed lbs spring movement mm	46/26	33/15
Spring rebound load lbs spring movement mm	330/136	396/125

Shock Absorbers

Placed in mounting position the shock absorbers must be operated several times over the whole lift, so that the air may collect itself in the upper part. Shock absorbers should be stored in an upright position.

On examination of the shock absorbers the higher tensile force as well as the lower pressure force should prove to be constant, i.e., motion speed should be invariable over the whole lift. If there are jerking motions this is an indication of worn condition requiring replacement of the shock absorber.

In compressed position no pressure over 1 lb should be exercised on the shock absorber; otherwise interior defects might result.

Hydraulic Steering Damper, cylinder Ø 1.22 in. or (0.95 in.)

Test stroke of test machine (mm)	25 (0.98 in.)	50 (1.96 in.)
Rev rate of test machine (rpm)	100	100
Tensile force (lbs)	66(50)	73(77)
Pressure force (lbs)	66(50)	73(77)
Max length from center of silent-block mounting hole to piston rod end (mm)	9 in. (9.8 in.)	
Min length (mm)	6.7 in. (7.5 in.)	

Test Data for Shock Absorber Test Machine

	Front		Front	
Test stroke	25 mm (0.98 in.)	75 mm (2.95 in.)	25 mm (0.98 in.)	75 mm (2.95 in.)
Rev rate (rpm)	100	100	100	100
Tensile force (lbs)	33	88	44	132
Pressure force (lbs)	11	22	11	44
Max length, extended	337 mm (13.26 in.)		343 mm (13.65 in.)	
Min length, compressed	222 mm (8.73 in.)		243 mm (9.45 in.)	

CHASSIS SPECIFICATIONS (R50/5, R60/5, AND R75/5)

	R50/5	R60/5	R75/5
Wheel bearing lubrication		Multi purpose grease 360° F drip point	
Front wheel caster		ca. 85 mm (3.35 in.) (not adjustable)	
Turning angle of handle bar		approx. 40° to each side	
Turning angle of front fork		46°	
Suspension travel (165 lbs load) Bump travel Rebound travel		214 mm (8.42 in.) 139 mm (5.7 in.) 75 mm (2.95 in.)	
Fork tube installation (measure from the top of the fork tube to the top of the lower fork yoke)		160 mm (6.3 in.)	
Fork tubes		hard chrome plated	
Fork legs		aluminum alloy casting	
Lower fork yoke		drop forged aluminum alloy	
Oil capacity per fork leg		0.28 ltr (0.296 US quarts/ 0.093 Imp quarts)	
Oil brand		Shock absorber oil, Shell 4001, Shell Aero hydraulic 4	
Fork tube outer diameter (hard chrome plated)		36 mm −0.0050 −0.075 (1.417 in.−0.002 in.) −0.003 in.)	
Maximum allowable fork tube runout		0.1 mm (0.004 in.)	
Fork tube (inner diameter)		36 mm +0.025 0 (1.417 in. −0.002 in.) 0)	
Clearance of fork legs on fork tube		0.050 mm bis 0.1 (0.002 in.-0.004 in.)	
Shock absorber piston outer diameter		27.7 mm ± 0.1 (1.09 in. ± 0.004 in.)	
Fork tube inner diameter at shock end		28 mm ± 0.15 (1.1 in. ± 0.006 in.)	
Clearance of shock absorber piston in fork tube		0.05-0.55 mm (0.002 in.-0.01375 in.)	
Length of fork spring Centering nut		540 mm (22.1 in.)	

Front Fork Torque Specifications (ft lbs)

Centering nut	86.8-94	Bottom cover on fork leg	86.8-94
Clamp bolt on clamp ring	7.2-8.7	Nut M 8 x 1 (holding shock absorber to fork leg)	16.6-18.0
Upper spring retainer	86.8	Upper fender brace	16.6
Clamp bolts on bottom fork yoke	23.9-25.3		
Shock absorber bolt bottom and shock absorber piston to shock absorber	18-19.5		

CHASSIS SPECIFICATIONS (R50/5, R60/5, AND R75/5 (con't)

	R50/5	R60/5	R75/5
Turning angle of handlebars		approx. 40° to each side	
		Steering Head Specifications (ft lbs)	
	Allen head clamp bolt on clamp ring	7.23-8.7	
	Centering nut for telescopic fork	86.8	
Front wheel brake		Double leading shoe	
Rear wheel brake		Single leading shoe	
Brake drum diameter		200 mm (7.87 in.)	
Brake lining width		30 mm (1.18 in.)	
Lining area (cm^2)		ca. 107 (16.6 Sq. inches)	
Minimum lining thickness		1.5 mm (0.06 in.)	
Max. allowable run-out of the braking surface to wheel hub		0.02 mm (0.0008 in.)	
Rim type		aluminum alloy drop-center rims	
Rim size front		1.85 x 19	
Rim size rear		1.85 x 18	
Number of spokes per wheel		40	
Radial runout max.		0.5 mm (0.02 in.) measured on the outer rim edge	
Lateral runout max.		0.2 mm (0.008 in.) measured on the outer rim edge	
Tire size front		3.25 S 19	
Tire size rear		4.00 S 18	
Maximum allowable unbalance on the inner rim diameter (cmp) (grams)		170 8-9 (0.28-0.315 oz.)	
Tire pressure			
front wheel		1.9 (27 psi)	
front wheel with passenger		2.0 (27 psi)	
rear wheel		1.8 (26 psi)	
rear wheel with passenger		2.25 (20 psi)	
with tire warm		0.3 more (4 psi additional)	
When driving at maximum speeds for longer periods increase the tire inflation by		0.2 higher (3 psi)	
Wheel bearing grease		Brand name grease with a drip point of 360° F	
Permissible wheel load rear at			
27 psi		178 kg (393 lbs)	
30 psi		270 kg (595 lbs)	
		Wheel Torque Specifications (ft lbs)	
	Axle nuts front and rear	32.5-34.4	

INDEX BSA

MODEL IDENTIFICATION

B25T, Victor Trail 250—247cc; compression ratio: 10:1; Amal 28mm Concentric; dry weight: 287 lbs.

B25SS, Gold Star 250-SS; same as B25T with low front fender, street tires.

B50SS, Gold Star 500-SS—500cc; compression ratio: 10:1; enlarged and improved Victor engine.

B50T, Victor 500-Trail—same as B50SS with raised fender, dirt tires.

B44, Victor Special—441cc; compression ratio: 9.4:1; Amal 30mm Concentric; dry weight: 320 lbs.

A65L (pre-1970), Lightning 650—654cc; compression ratio: 9:1; dual 30mm Amals; 52 hp @ 7000 rpm; chrome tank panels and fenders.

A65T (pre-1970), Thunderbolt 650—same as A65L only with single 28mm carburetor.

A65L, Lightning 650—re-styled with several engine improvements; new frame; oil contained in frame backbone; Ceriani-type front forks; twin leading shoe front brake with air scoop; turn signal indicators; megaphone mufflers.

A65T, Thunderbolt 650—same as A65L with single Amal 28mm carb.

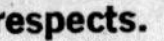

A65FS, Firebird Scrambler 650-SS—654cc; compression ratio: 9:1; dual 30mm Amals; upswept pipes; same as the Lightning in most respects.

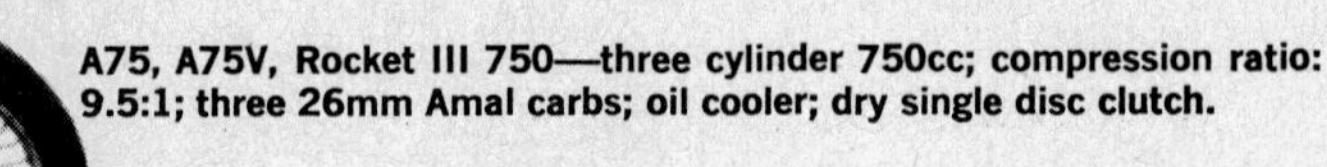

A75, A75V, Rocket III 750—three cylinder 750cc; compression ratio: 9.5:1; three 26mm Amal carbs; oil cooler; dry single disc clutch.

GENERAL SPECIFICATIONS

Model	B25SS	B25T	B44	B50SS	B50T	B50MX	A65T	A65L	A65FS	A75
DIMENSIONS										
Wheelbase (in.)	54.0	54.0	53.0	54.0	54.0	54.0	56.0	56.0	56.0	57.0
Ground clear. (in.)	7.0	7.5	8.0	7.0	7.5	7.5	7.5	7.5	7.5	7.0
Seat ht. (in.)	32.0	32.0	32.0	32.0	32.0	32.0	32.0	32.0	32.0	32.0
O.a. width (in.)	29.0	29.0	27.0	29.0	29.0	33.5	33.0	33.0	33.0	33.0
O.a. length (in.)	85.0	85.0	83.0	85.0	85.0	82.5	87.5	87.5	87.5	88.0
O.a. ht. (in.)	43.5	43.5	42.0	43.5	43.5	43.5	43.0	43.0	43.0	42.0
Dry wt. (lbs)	290.0	287.0	320.0	310.0	298.0	240.0	365.0	365.0	365.0	455.0
ENGINE										
Displace. (cc)	247	247	441	499	499	499	654	654	654	740
Bore & stroke (mm)	67 x 70	67 x 70	79 x 90	84 x 90	84 x 90	84 x 90	75 x 74	75 x 74	75 x 74	67 x 70
Compress. ratio	10 : 1	10 : 1	9.4 : 1	10 : 1	10 : 1	10 : 1	9 : 1	9 : 1	9 : 1	9.5 : 1
Carb. model (Amal)	R.928/20	R.928/20	930/11	R.930/62	R.930/62	R.932/18	R.928/11	930/41 and 930/42	930/41 and 930/42	R.626/28, R.626/30, & L.626/29
H.P. @ rpm	22.5 @ 8250	22.5 @ 8250	N.A.	34 @ 6200	34 @ 6200	38 @ 6200	46 @ 7000	52 @ 7000	54 @ 7250	60 @ 7250
Torque @ rpm	15.8 @ 7000	15.8 @ 7000	N.A.	28 @ 5000	28 @ 5000	35 @ 5000	36.5 @ 5750	39.4 @ 6500	39.4 @ 6500	45 @ 6900
TRANSMISSION										
Clutch type	wet, multi-plate	wet, multi-plate	wet, multi-plate	wet, multi-plate	wet, multi-plate	wet, multi-plate	wet, multi-plate	wet, multi-plate	wet, multi-plate	dry, single disc
O.a. gear ratios										
1st	18.33	19.48	13.62	15.90	17.10	15.04	12.23	12.23	13.60	12.15
2nd	11.35	12.06	8.45	11.84	10.58	11.35	7.80	7.80	8.67	8.42
3rd	8.60	9.14	6.39	7.44	8.03	8.60	5.58	5.58	6.20	6.17
4th	6.92	7.35	5.14	6.02	6.45	6.92	4.87	4.87	5.41	4.98
Sprockets (no. of teeth)										
Engine	23	23	28	28	28	28	28	28	28	28
Clutch	52	52	52	52	52	52	58	58	58	50
Gearbox	17	16	17	16	15	14	●	●	18	19
Rear Wheel	52	52	47	52	52	52	47	47	47	53
CHASSIS										
Front suspen.	two-way dampened hydraulic forks				same	same	same	same	same	same
Rear suspen.	swing arm with hydraulically dampened shocks				same	same	same	same	same	same
Tire: front	3.25 x 18	3.00 x 20	3.25 x 18	3.25 x 18	3.00 x 20	3.00 x 20	3.25 x 19	3.25 x 19	3.25 x 19	4.10 x 19
rear	3.50 x 18	4.00 x 18	3.50 x 18	3.50 x 18	4.00 x 18	4.00 x 18	4.00 x 18	4.00 x 18	4.00 x 19	4.10 x 19
ELECTRICAL										
Syst. volt.	12	12	12	12	12	——	12	12	12	12
Gen. type	alternator	alternator	alternator	alternator	alternator	alternator	alternator	alternator	alternator	alternator
Ignition syst.	battery and coil, with capacitor	battery and coil, with capacitor	battery and coil	battery and coil, with capacitor	battery and coil, with capacitor	E.T.	battery and coil	battery and coil	battery and coil	battery and coil

● 20 tooth sprocket standard, 17 and 18 optional.

TUNE-UP AND MAINTENANCE

TUNE-UP OPERATIONS

Valve Tappet Adjustment

Set valve clearances with the engine cold, preferably after it has been left sitting overnight.

SINGLES

B25

1. Remove the spark plug, rocker inspection caps, and rocker shaft plate.
2. Turn the engine over until the piston is at top dead center (TDC) of the compression stroke.

NOTE: *Make sure that at least one thread of the rocker shafts protrudes beyond the locknut and that the flats milled on the right end of the shafts face each other as shown. If they do not, loosen the rocker box retaining nuts and rotate the shafts with a screwdriver until both conditions are met.*

3. Check the clearance at both valves using the appropriate feeler gauges (see the specifications at the end of the section).

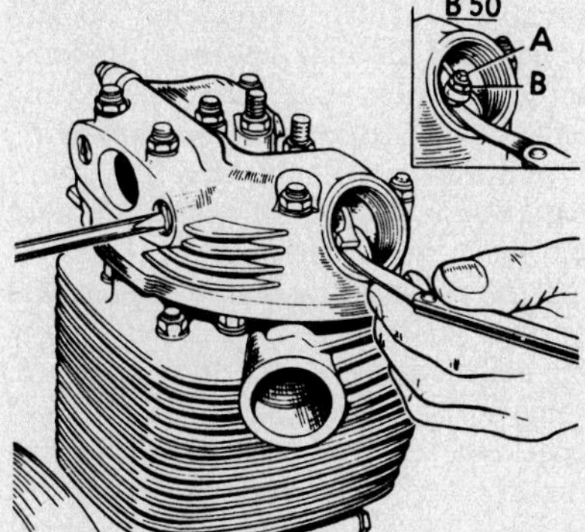

Adjusting the valve clearance. Inset shows the adjuster (A) and locknut (B) on the B50

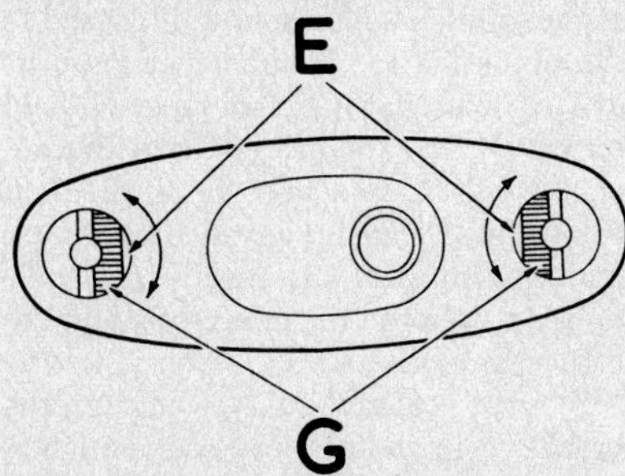

On the B25, the flats (E) of the eccentric rocker shafts must face in (within the shaded area G) for the rocker arm to contact the valve properly

4. If adjustment is necessary, loosen the rocker shaft locknuts opposite the cover plate, and turn the shafts in the required direction until the correct clearance is obtained for each valve.
5. Tighten the locknuts while holding the shafts in position with a screwdriver. Recheck clearance and reinstall the shaft plate, inspection caps, and spark plug.

B44 and B50

1. Remove the spark plug and the rocker box inspection caps.
2. Turn the engine over until the piston is at TDC of the compression stroke.
3. Check the clearance at both valves with the appropriate feeler gauges (see the specifications at the end of the section).
4. If adjustment is necessary, loosen the adjuster screw locknuts at the end of the rocker arms and turn the screws in the required direction until the correct clearance is obtained.
5. Tighten the locknuts while holding the screws to keep them from turning and recheck the clearance. Reinstall the spark plug and inspection caps.

TWINS

The valve clearance on twin-cylinder models is checked and adjusted in the same manner as for the B44 and B50 singles, except that the following sequence for valve adjustment must be used (in place of rotating the piston to TDC as on the singles):

1. Adjust the left exhaust valve when the right exhaust valve spring is fully compressed.
2. Adjust the right exhaust valve when the left exhaust valve spring is fully compressed.

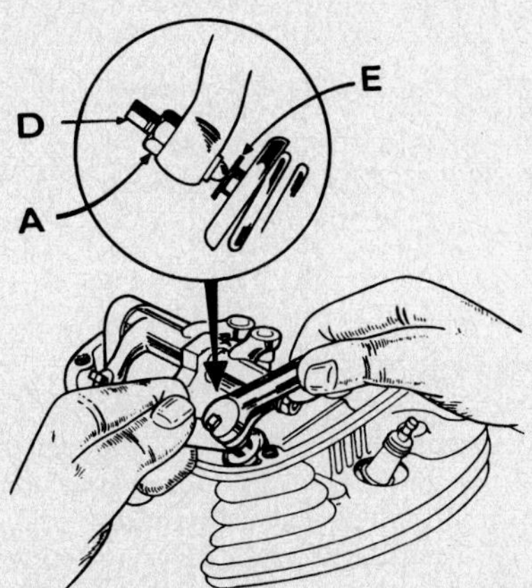

Valve clearance adjustment, showing the adjuster locknut (A), adjuster (D), and feeler gauge blade inserted (E)

3. Adjust the left intake valve when the right intake valve spring is fully compressed.
4. Adjust the right intake valve when the left intake valve spring is fully compressed.

ROCKET 3

Valve clearance on the Rocket 3 is checked and adjusted in the same manner as for the B44 and B50 singles, except that there are three cylinders instead of one. For example, to set the valves for the center cylinder, rotate the engine until the center piston is at TDC of its compression stroke and proceed with valve adjustment for that cylinder. Repeat for the other cylinders. The valve adjusting screw can be turned with the special wrench provided in the tool kit.

Contact Breaker Points

SINGLES

The contact breaker point assembly is located behind the circular cover on the right side of the engine. Observe the following procedures to replace the points.

REMOVAL

1. Remove the breaker point cover.
2. Remove the securing nut, nylon sleeve, and contact breaker lead.
3. Remove the screw that fastens the fixed point of the contact breaker, then lift the unit out.
4. Whenever the points are replaced, it is wise to replace as well the condenser. On later models the condenser is located in the electrical box in front of the engine.

INSTALLATION

Installation is the reverse of the removal procedure. Clean the new points with a nonoily solvent to remove the preservative coating. Do not forget to install the fiber washer that fits between the moving point spring and the fixed point backing plate. Reset ignition timing.

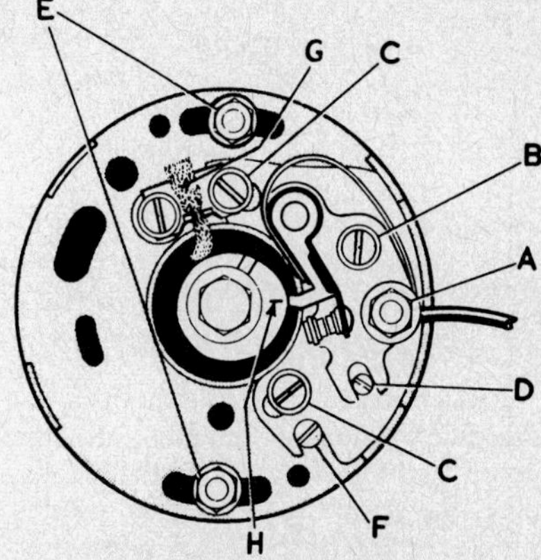

The contact breaker points

A. Contact breaker lead securing nut
B. Contact adjustment screw
C. Baseplate securing screw
D. Eccentric gap adjustment screw
E. Breaker plate assembly securing screws
F. Eccentric base plate adjuster screw
G. Felt oiling wick
H. Breaker cam high point

GAP ADJUSTMENT

1. Put the transmission in gear and rotate the engine by turning the rear wheel until the nylon heel of the contact breaker is aligned with the scribed mark on the breaker cam.

2. Loosen the contact adjusting screw and turn the eccentric screw until a snug slip-fit is obtained with the appropriate feeler gauge.

3. Tighten the adjusting screw and recheck the gap.

TWINS

The contact breaker point assembly is located behind the circular cover on the right side of the engine. Removal, installation, and gap adjustment procedures are the same as for the single-cylinder models, except that there are two sets of points instead of one. The condenser pack in later models is located on a plate below the seat.

ROCKET 3

Like the other models, the contact breaker point assembly on the Rocket 3 is located behind the circular cover on the right side of the engine. Removal, installation, and gap adjustment procedures are the same as for the single-cylinder models, except that there are three sets of points instead of one. The condenser pack is mounted on a plate in front of the battery.

SINGLES

STATIC TIMING

1. Remove the small inspection cover at the front of the primary chaincase to expose the timing pointer and index mark. On engines with two index marks on the alternator rotor, use the mark identified by the number "2." On engines with two pointers, use the one appropriate to your engine as shown in the accompanying illustration.

2. Remove the spark plug and rocker box inspection caps. Rotate the engine until the piston is close to TDC of its compression stroke. Turn the engine back a few degrees so that the timing mark goes past the pointer and then forward again in the normal direction of rotation until the pointer and mark are aligned. This will have taken up any backlash in the contact breaker drive and positioned the engine exactly where the spark occurs under full advance conditions.

3. Connect a test light using an independent battery as shown.

4. With the engine positioned correctly and the test light connected, loosen the baseplate adjusting screws so that the plate can be rotated. To shift the ignition advance unit to the full-advance position, turn the breaker cam counterclockwise until it stops (about 25°) and hold it there. If the points are opening too early or too late, rotate the baseplate in the required direction until the points just begin to open with the advance unit held in the full-advance position.

5. Tighten the plate securing screws and recheck your setting. Reinstall the inspection covers and spark plug.

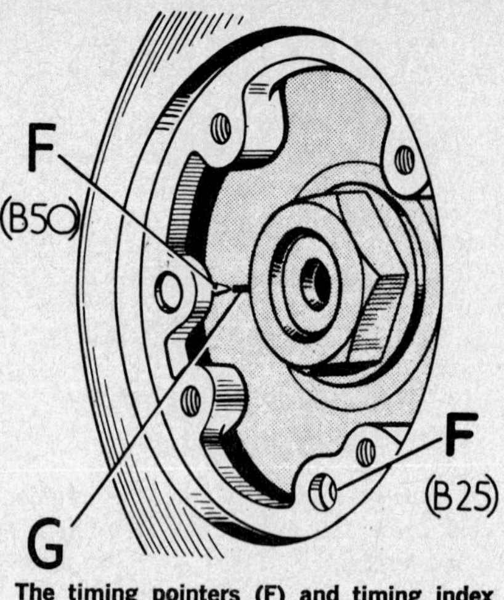

The timing pointers (F) and timing index mark (G)

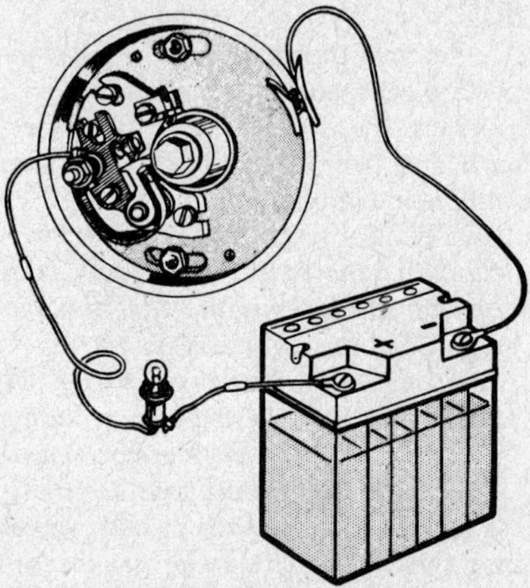

A simple test light

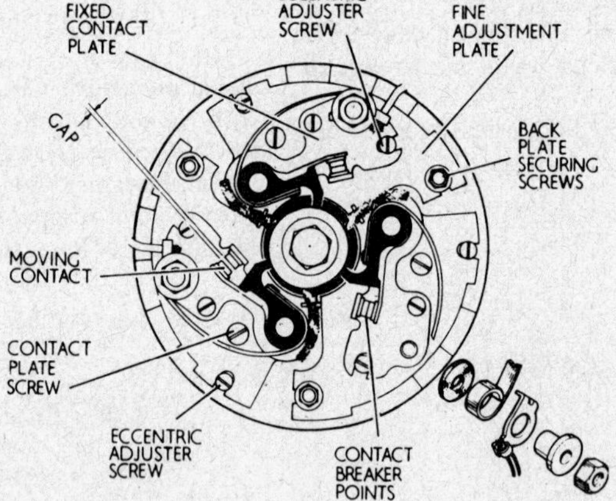

The contact breaker assembly on the Rocket 3

Ignition Timing

It is preferred that the timing be set dynamically (engine running) with the aid of a stroboscopic timing light. However, the static timing method, using a simple test light, can be very satisfactory if done carefully. If for some reason the ignition advance unit has slipped on its taper and the relationship of the crankshaft to the advance unit has been disturbed, or if the advance unit has been removed, refer to "Ignition Timing–When Timing Has Been Lost" in this section.

DYNAMIC TIMING

Observe step 1 in the preceding section on static timing. Connect the stroboscopic timing light according to the manufacturer's instructions, and start the engine. Direct the light toward the alternator rotor and increase the engine speed to above 4300 rpm (B25), or 3000 rpm (B44 and B50). At this point the ignition should be fully advanced and the timing pointer and mark should be aligned. If adjustment is necessary, loosen the screws and rotate the points baseplate in the required direction until the pointer and mark are aligned.

If the advance unit is unsteady or if full advance comes in at a significantly lower or higher speed than that specified, remove the breaker plate assembly and check the advance unit for broken or weak springs and for stiff pivots.

IGNITION TIMING—WHEN TIMING HAS BEEN LOST

The contact breaker cam, which is part of the ignition advance unit, is geared to the crankshaft. It is not keyed onto its driving shaft, but is a plain taper fit, held on by a bolt. Therefore, when the advance unit is removed, or if the bolt comes loose and the advance unit slips, ignition timing is lost because the relationship between the crankshaft and the contact breaker cam has been lost.

So what you have to do is position the breaker cam on its taper close enough to correct ignition timing so that final timing adjustment can be made using the limited range of movement of the contact breaker plate.

NOTE: *If it is necessary to remove the advance unit, remove the retaining bolt and use any bolt that fits the threads inside the cam as a puller, simply by screwing it in.*

To correctly position the advance unit, first follow steps 1, 2, and 3 of the preceding section on static timing. Then lightly fit the advance unit onto its taper and install the contact breaker plate assembly (if removed). Turn the breaker plate as far as possible in the clockwise direction, securing it lightly with the screws. Hold the advance unit lightly against the taper and rotate it counterclockwise until the points just open, as indicated by the test light. Install and tighten the retaining bolt to 6 ft lbs. Finally center the breaker plate so that there is equal adjustment range in both directions, and make the final timing adjustment using either the static or dynamic methods, as described in this section.

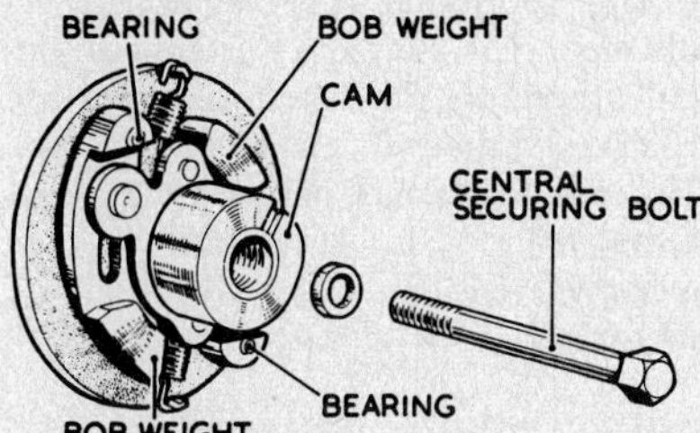

The ignition advance unit, located under the contact breaker plate

TWINS

STATIC TIMING

Static-timing a twin is the same as static-timing a single-cylinder model, except that there are two cylinders with two sets of points which must be timed individually. The following items should be noted:

1. Align the timing pointer with the timing index mark identified by the number 2.

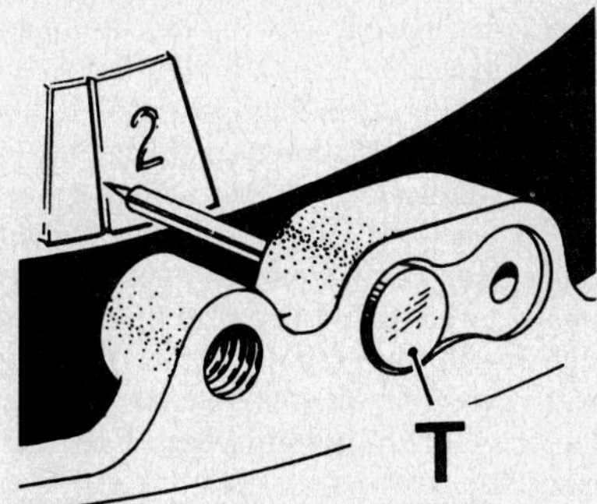

The timing pointer (T) aligned with the timing mark

2. The timing for the left cylinder is set with the lower set of points and the timing for the right cylinder is set with the upper set of points.
3. Either point set may be moved independently of the other by loosening the point baseplate screws and moving the individual point assembly (instead of rotating the entire contact breaker plate).

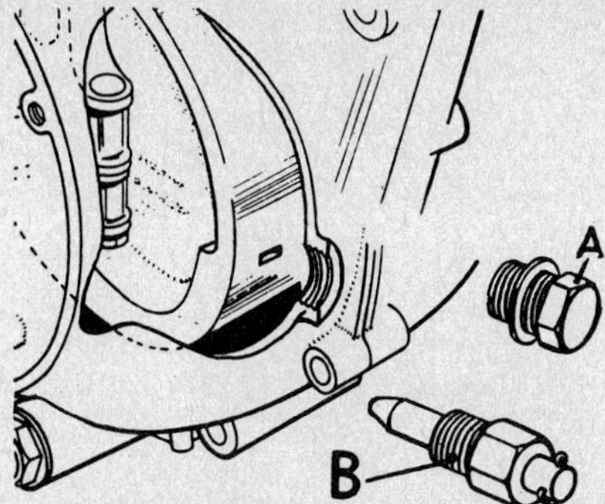

On early models that do not have a timing pointer and mark, the engine can be set at the correct position for timing adjustment (full advance) by locating the flywheel indentation with the special tool (B, tool no. 60-1859) after the crankcase plug (A) has been removed. Alternatively, a degree wheel can be used in conjunction with the timing specifications at the end of the chapter to correctly position the crankshaft.

DYNAMIC TIMING

Follow the procedure given for the single-cylinder models and study the information given in the preceding section on static timing. There is no difference between timing a single or twin-cylinder model, except that you go through the timing procedure twice for a twin and once for each cylinder. Full advance on all the twins comes in after 3000 rpm has been exceeded.

IGNITION TIMING—WHEN TIMING HAS BEEN LOST

Follow the procedure given for single-cylinder models. Note the following points:

1. Either cylinder may be used for this operation. If the left cylinder is used, set the breaker cam so that the lower point set is just opening; if the right cylinder is used, set the breaker cam so that the upper point set is just opening.
2. Align the timing pointer with the index mark identified by the number 2.

ROCKET 3

STATIC TIMING

Static timing the triple is the same as static timing a single, except that three separate adjustments must be made (one for each cylinder). Note the following points:

1. Timing adjustment for the right (no. 1) cylinder is made by moving the point set with the black/white lead wire.
2. Timing adjustment for the center (no. 2) cylinder is made by moving the point set with the black/red lead wire.
3. Timing adjustment for the left (no. 3) cylinder is made by moving the point set with the black/yellow lead wire.
4. The timing mark is located under the small cover plate just below and to the left of the points cover. Replace the lower cover plate screw, which doubles as the timing pointer.

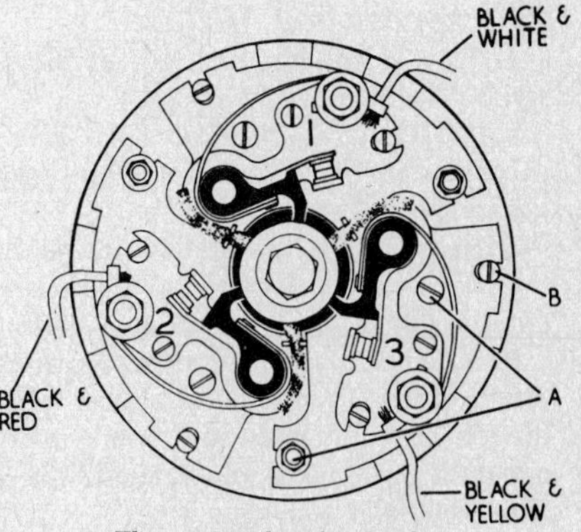

The contact breaker leads

DYNAMIC TIMING

Follow the procedure given for the single-cylinder models and study the information given in the preceding section on static timing. There is no difference between timing a single or three-cylinder model, except that you go through the timing procedure three times on the triple, once for each cylinder. Full advance on the triple comes in after 3000 rpm has been exceeded.

IGNITION TIMING—WHEN TIMING HAS BEEN LOST

Follow the procedure given for the single-cylinder models. Note the following points:

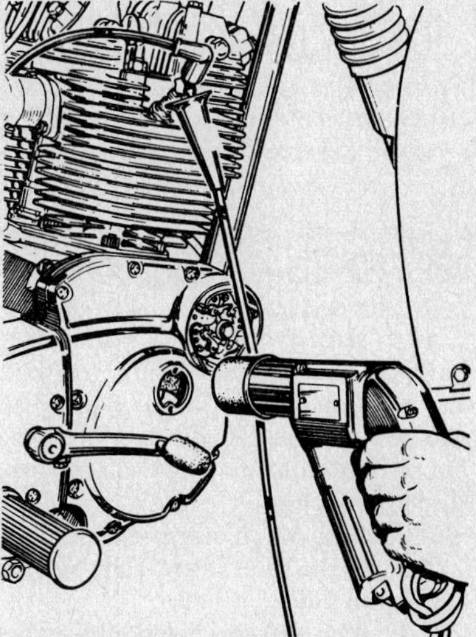

Using a strobe light to check timing

1. Any cylinder may be used for this operation. If the right cylinder is used, set the breaker cam so that the upper point set is just opening; if the center cylinder is used, set the breaker cam so that the left point set is just opening, and if the left cylinder is used, set the breaker cam so that the right point set is just opening.
2. The timing mark is located behind the small cover plate just under and to

the left of the points cover. Reinstall the lower cover plate screw because it also serves as the timing pointer.

Carburetor Adjustments

Idle Speeds and Mixture

1. Turn in the idle mixture (air pilot) screw until it is lightly seated.

CAUTION: *Too much pressure when turning in the adjustment screw will damage the seat.*

2. Back out the idle mixture (air pilot) screw one turn. Later you can readjust it to an exact setting.

3. Start and warm up the engine with the throttle grip completely closed, turn the idle speed (throttle stop) screw in or out until the engine idles smoothly between 800 and 1000 rpm.

NOTE: *On multiple-carburetor models, you can check idle speed synchronization by holding one hand behind each muffler and noting the exhaust pulse frequency. Reset the idle speed (throttle stop) screws until both cylinders are firing alternately and at the same rate. If one side is backfiring or its pulses are erratic, stop the engine; turn both idle speed screws in until lightly seated, then back them out equally a couple of turns (enough to prevent stalling). Start the engine and turn either carburetor's idle speed screw in, then out, and note any increase or decrease in engine rpm. At the position where ½ to one turn does not cause a variation in engine speed, the cylinders should be firing smoothly and at the same rate. The idle rpm may be higher than specified, buy by backing out both idle mixture screws equally it can be lowered to normal.*

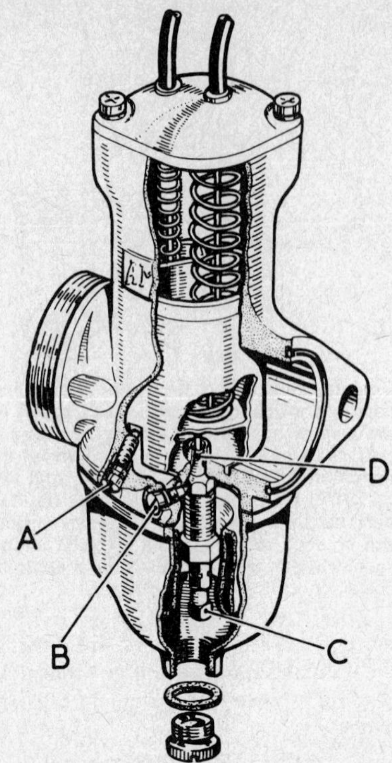

A sectional view of the Amal Concentric carburetor, showing the idle adjusting, or throttle control, screw (A); air pilot, or mixture screw (B); the main jet (C); and the jet needle and tube (D).

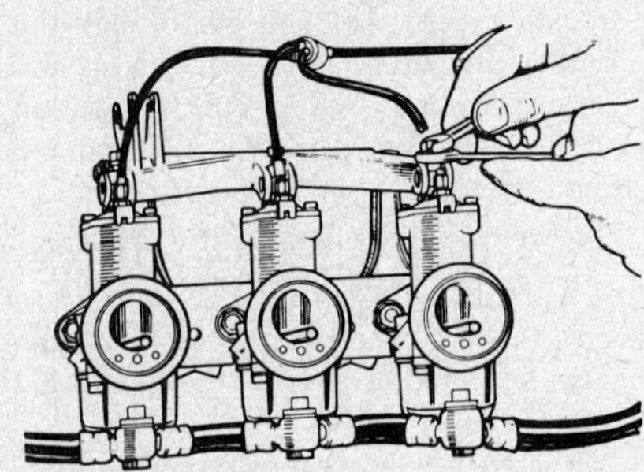

Synchronizing the throttle linkage on the Rocket 3

Multiple-Carburetor Synchronization

After setting ignition timing, points, plugs, idle speed, and mixture, you must also synchronize the throttle slides. This is to ensure that all cylinders are being fed the same amount of fuel at any given throttle opening.

1. Remove the air clearner assemblies.
2. Twist the throttle grip fully open to lift up the slides.
3. Position a mirror behind the carburetors or reach into the carburetor bores with the fingers of your free hand.
4. Slowly close the throttle grip and watch, or feel, the slides as they are being lowered; they should enter their respective bores simultaneously.
5. If the slide positions are unequal, raise or lower one to match the other(s) by turning the adjuster at the top of the carburetor.

NOTE: *The Rocket 3 uses a throttle linkage at the carburetors, operated by a single cable, to open the throttle slides. With this arrangement, the carburetors will be found to stay synchronized longer; however, when synchronization is required, you will find that the job can be done more accurately if the carburetors are removed from the engine.*

Throttle Cable Adjustment

SPLIT-TYPE CABLE

On some twin models, a cable runs from the twist grip to a junction block, where one or more shorter cables are routed to the carburetor top(s). One end of each cable is equipped with an adjustment nut. These are located at the twist-grip cable guide and the carburetor top(s).

Adjust the cable(s) running from the junction block to the carburetor(s) so that there is as close to zero free-play as possible. Adjust the cable between the twist grip and the junction block to have approximately 2 mm free-play.

After setting the free-play at each cable separately, start and warm up the engine, then turn the handlebars from side to side and note any change in idle rpm. If a variation occurs, one of the cables is either adjusted incorrectly (not enough free-play) or is binding somewhere along its routing.

STANDARD TYPE CABLE

Most models are equipped with a one-piece throttle cable. Set cable free-play as close to zero as possible by turning the cable adjuster at the carburetor top. Check the cable(s) for binding as described above.

Carburetor Mixture Adjustment

The fuel/air mixture can be altered at the needle jet and the main jet. The jet needle is adjusted by repositioning its clip in a different groove, and the main jet by replacing it with a different size.

If the plug reading indicated too rich a mixture, install a one-step smaller main jet; if it indicated too lean a mixture, install a one-step larger main jet. Should more than a one-size main jet change be needed, you should also reposition the jet needle clip one groove higher (reading was rich) or lower (reading was lean) to balance out the system. (See "Fuel Systems.")

TUNE-UP SPECIFICATIONS

	B25SS	B25T	B44	B50SS	B50T	B50MX	A65T	A65L	A65FS	A75
VALVES										
Valve Clearance (cold)										
intake (in.)	0.008	0.008	0.008	0.008	0.008	0.008	0.008	0.008	0.008	0.006
(mm)	0.20	0.20	0.20	0.20	0.20	0.20	0.20	0.20	0.20	0.15
exhaust (in.)	0.010	0.010	0.010	0.010	0.010	0.010	0.010	0.010	0.010	0.008
(mm)	0.25	0.25	0.25	0.25	0.25	0.25	0.25	0.25	0.25	0.20
Valve Timing										
intake opens (BTDC)	51°	51°	51°	51°	51°	63°	51°	51°	51°	50°
intake closes (ABDC)	68°	68°	68°	68°	68°	72°	68°	68°	68°	64°
exhaust opens (BBDC)	78°	78°	78°	78°	78°	80°	78°	78°	78°	67°
exhaust closes (ATDC)	37°	37°	37°	37°	37°	55°	37°	37°	37°	47°
IGNITION										
Spark Plug (standard)										
Champion	N3	N3	N4	N4	N4	N3	N3	N3	N3	N3
gap (in.)	0.025	0.025	0.025	0.025	0.025	0.025	0.025	0.025	0.025	0.025
(mm)	0.65	0.65	0.65	0.65	0.65	0.65	0.65	0.65	0.65	0.65
Contact Breaker										
Gap: (in.)	0.015	0.015	0.015	0.015	0.015	0.015	0.015	0.015	0.015	0.015
(mm)	0.38	0.38	0.38	0.38	0.38	0.38	0.38	0.38	0.38	0.38
Timing (full advance)										
piston position (in. BTDC)	0.342	0.342	0.265	0.385	0.385	0.385	0.304	0.304	0.304	0.375
crankshaft (deg BTDC)	37	37	28	34	34	34	34	34	34	38
CARBURETION	see text procedures			see text procedures			see text procedures			

MAINTENANCE ITEMS

Engine Oil

SINGLES

1. On 1971 and later models, remove plug B and filter C, as shown. On earlier models, remove the filter located at the bottom of the oil tank.

2. Clean the filter in solvent. On 1971 and later B25 models, unscrew the oil filter bowl (E) behind the engine and replace the filter element. Clean the filter bowl and reinstall it using a new gasket.

3. Remove the four retaining nuts and the oil sump filter located at the bottom of the crankcase. Wash the filter in solvent and dry it thoroughly.

4. Make sure that the check valve ball is operating correctly by pushing the ball off its seat with a piece of wire and allowing it to drop back. If it will not fall back onto its seat, clean the sludge out of the pipe with gasoline.

5. Reinstall the sump filter with new gaskets, and reinstall the oil tank filter (and frame plug on the later models).

6. Add the recommended oil to the tank until it reaches the correct level mark on the dipstick. Do not overfill; otherwise the excess oil will be blown out the engine breather (F). Before starting the engine, remove the inspection cover from the right side of the rocker box and pour ½ pt of oil into the engine. Turn the engine over until oil is seen at the return pipe just inside the filler neck.

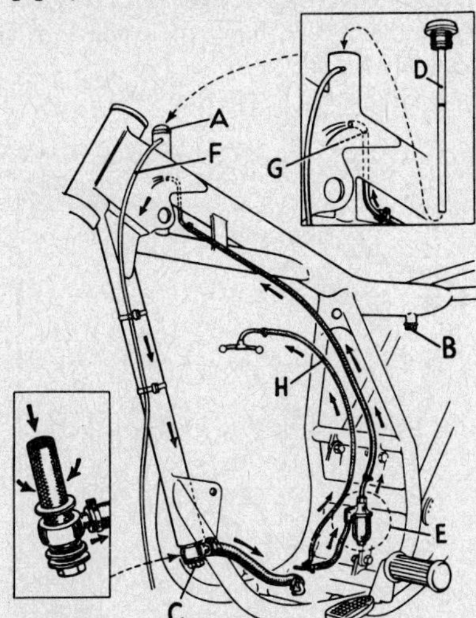

The oil is carried in the frame on 1971 and later models

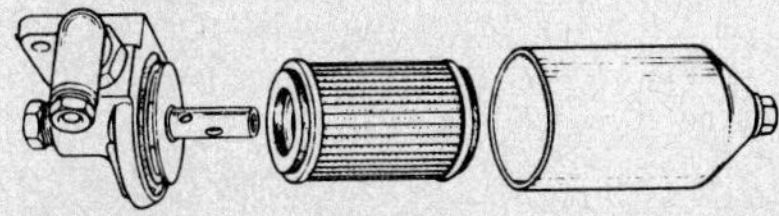
The oil filter assembly used on 1971 and later B25 models

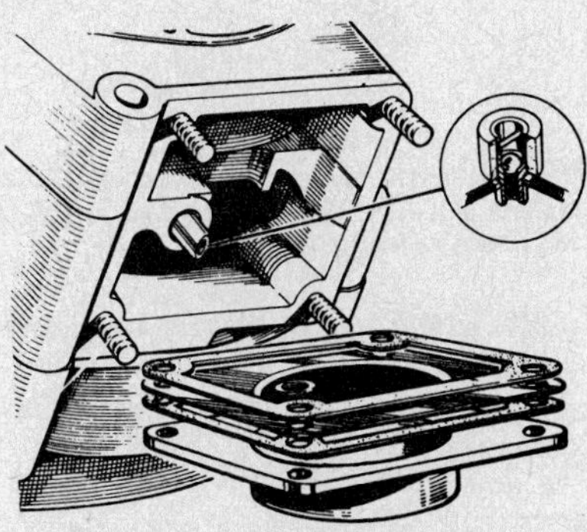
The oil sump filter. Inset shows the construction of the check valve

TWINS

1. On 1971 and later models, remove the plug from the center of the plate at the bottom of the front down-tubes and catch the oil in a container that has a capacity of at least one gallon. After the oil has drained, unscrew the four nuts and remove the plate and filter. On earlier models, remove the filter from the bottom of the oil tank.

2. Unscrew the four nuts and remove the filter from the bottom of the crankcase. Clean both filters in solvent and blow them dry.

3. Reinstall the oil tank filter, using new gaskets where necessary.

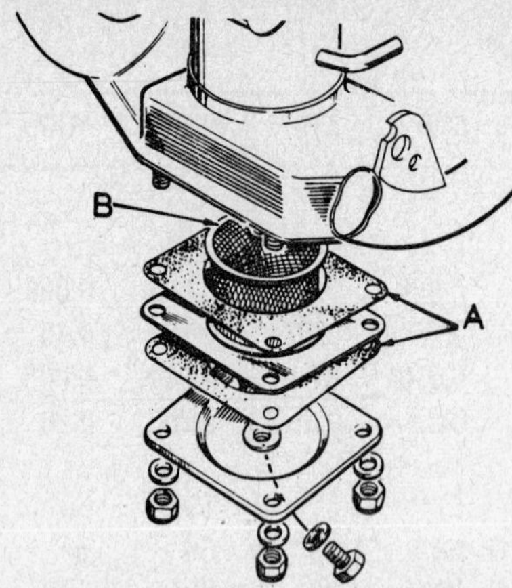

The oil reservoir filter, 1971 and later models, showing the gaskets (A) and filter (B). The drainplug is in the center of the bottom plate

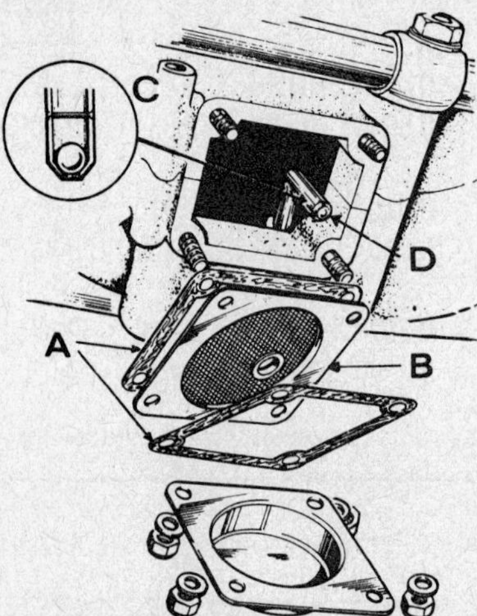

The crankcase (sump) filter, showing the gaskets (A), filter (B), check valve ball (C), and check valve pipe (D)

NOTE: *Self-locking nuts are used to secure the crankcase and oil tank filters (late models only); no other type of nuts must be used at these points.*

4. Before installing the crankcase filter, make sure that the check valve ball is functioning properly by pushing it off its seat with a piece of wire and allowing it to drop back down. If it does not seat fully, clean the sludge from the pipe with gasoline. Install the filter, using new gaskets if necessary.

5. Add the recommended oil to the tank until it reaches the correct level mark on the dipstick. Do not overfill the tank or the excess oil will be blown out the engine breather. Before starting the engine, remove the plug at the front of the timing side crankcase and pour ½ pt of oil into the crankcase to prime the oil pump. Kick the engine over until oil spurts from the return line just inside the oil filler neck.

ROCKET 3

1. Remove the filter from the bottom of the oil tank and catch the oil in a large container.

2. Remove the large cap, situated to the left of the timing cover at the rear of the crankcase, and replace the filter element (4,000-mile intervals). Before reinstalling the retaining cap, make sure that the spring is correctly located and that the gasket is in good condition.

3. Unscrew the four nuts and remove the filter from the bottom of the crankcase.

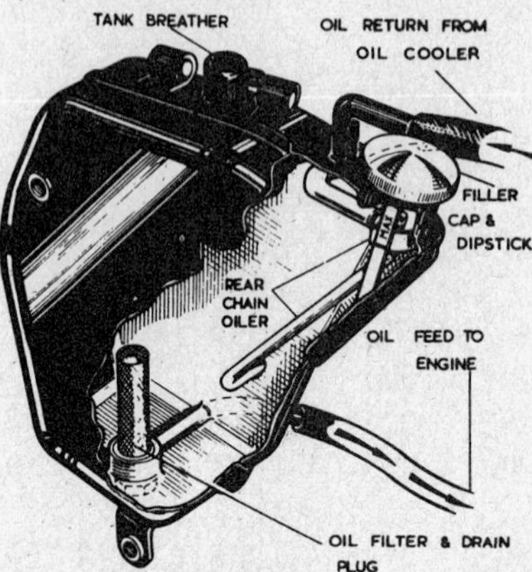

The oil tank

4. Clean the oil tank and crankcase filters in solvent and reinstall them, using new gaskets where necessary.

5. Add the recommended oil to the tank until it reaches the correct level on the dipstick. Do not overfill the tank, otherwise the excess oil will be blown out the engine breather. Before starting the engine, add ½ pt of oil to the engine through either the timing plug at the front of the crankcase or at the rocker box. Kick the engine over until oil spurts from the return line just inside the oil tank filler neck.

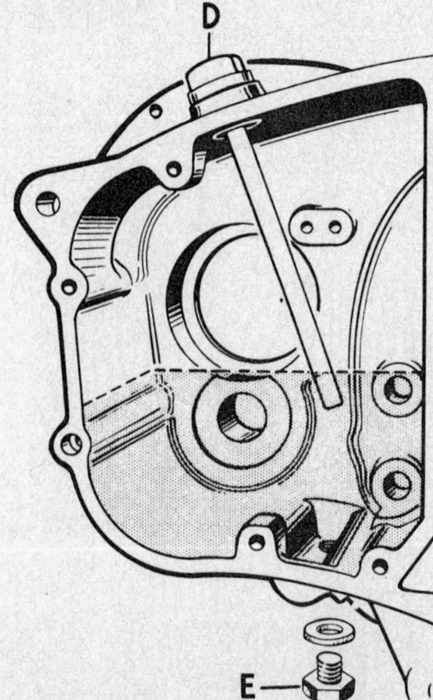

The gearbox oil level, showing the dipstick (D) and the drainplug (E)

Gearbox

All gearbox components, including the shifter and kick-start mechanisms, are lubricated by oil splash. Change the oil after a run when the engine is still warm.

Primary Chaincase

SINGLES

On the B25 and all other pre-1971 models, the oil in the primary chaincase is independent of the engine lubrication system. It is not necessary to check the oil level periodically in the B50 but the oil must be drained at the specified intervals and the primary chaincase refilled before running in order to avoid damage to the primary drive assembly. Do not use oil additives in the primary chaincase because they may cause the clutch to slip.

1. On early models, two of the case retaining screws serve as drain and level plugs. The level screw is painted red and the lower screw next to it is the drain plug. On later bikes, a drain plug is provided at the bottom of the case and a separate level screw is located in the side of the case.

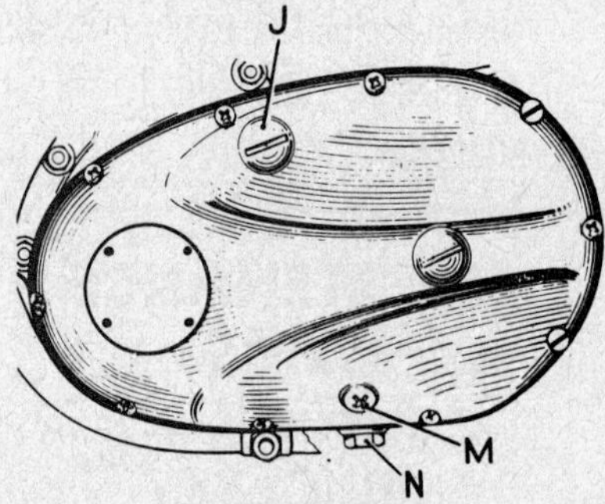

The primary chaincase inspection cap (J), level screw (M), and drainplug (N)

2. Remove the chain inspection cap near the top of the chaincase.

3. Remove the drain plug and level screw, and let the oil drain for about ten minutes. Reinstall the drain plug.

4. Pour oil through the inspection cap hole until it starts to run out of the level screw hole. The bike must be upright on level ground when this operation is carried out or the oil level will be inaccurate.

5. Reinstall the level screw and chain inspection cap.

TWINS

Twin-cylinder models have an independent primary chaincase oil supply. The level should be checked and the oil drained at the recommended intervals.

1. To drain the oil, remove the drain screw and upper inspection cap. Allow the oil about ten minutes to drain.

2. Reinstall the drain plug and remove the level plug in the side of the case.

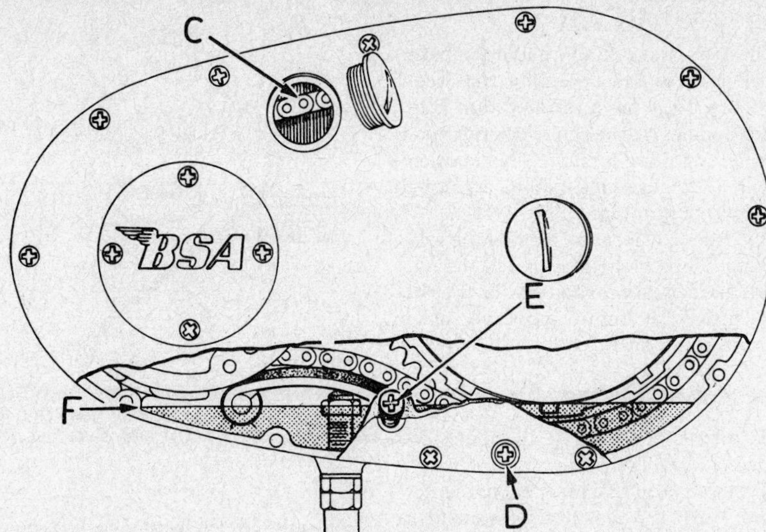

The primary chaincase inspection cap (C), oil level screw (E), oil level (F), and drain screw (D)

3. Add the recommended oil through the inspection cap hole until it flows out the level hole and allow the surplus to run out.

4. Reinstall the level screw and inspection cap.

ROCKET 3

The Rocket 3 primary chaincase is fed from the engine lubrication system through the drive-side main bearing, in the same manner as the B50 models. It is not necessary to check the oil level regularly, but it is necessary to drain and refill the chaincase whenever the engine oil is changed.

1. Remove the drainplug from the bottom of the case and the inspection cap from the side of the case near the top. Allow the oil about ten minutes to drain.

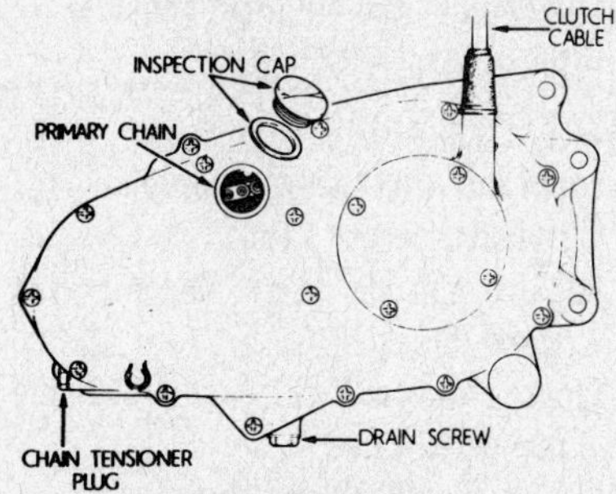

The primary chaincase

2. Replace the drainplug and add ¾ pt of the recommended oil through the inspection cap hole. There is no level hole, so take care to add the correct amount.

3. Reinstall the inspection cap.

Ignition Advance Unit

The ignition advance unit should be lightly lubricated at 2,000 mile-intervals or whenever the contact breaker points are serviced.

1. Remove the contact breaker point cover plate.

2. Scribe a line across the breaker plate and its housing, so that the plate can be replaced in its original position without disturbing the ignition timing.

3. Take out the breaker plate retaining screws and lift the breaker plate assembly away.

4. Apply one drop of oil to the governor weight pivots.

5. Replace the breaker plate assembly in its original position. Apply a drop of oil at this time to the felt wick(s) that rides on the breaker cam and keep it lubricated. Replace the cover plate.

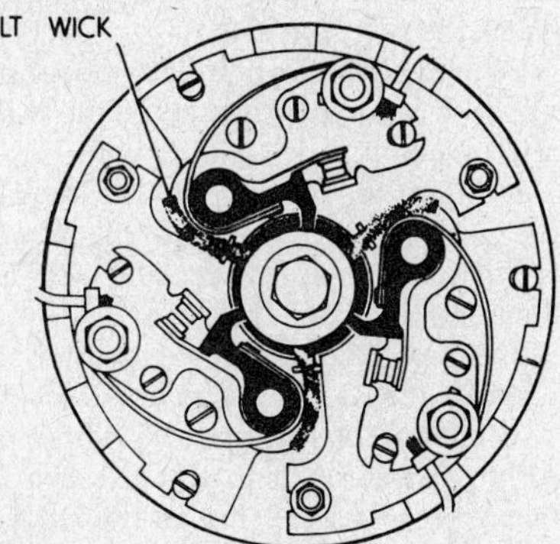

The contact breaker plate assembly (A75 shown)

Front Fork

NOTE: *On the more recent shuttle valve fork, use only automatic transmission fluid.*

1. Remove the small drainplugs at the bottom of each fork leg.

2. Hold the front brake and pump the forks several times to expel all the oil.

3.Remove the fork caps at the top of each leg.

NOTE: *On some machines equipped with a rubber-mounted handlebar, the handlebar will have to be removed to gain access to the fork caps.*

4. Add the specified amount of the recommended oil after installing the plugs, then reinstall the fork caps. If heavier or lighter dampening qualities are desired, choose an appropriately heavier or lighter weight oil.

SERVICE CHECKS AND ADJUSTMENTS

Clutch

SINGLES

1. Remove the primary chaincase inspection cover.

2. Loosen the pushrod adjusting screw locknut.

3.Turn the adjusting screw in until the pressure plate begins to lift. This point can be felt as a sudden increase in turning resistance.

4. Back the screw out one full turn, or until the clutch release lever on the timing cover lies at about 30° to the cover joint. Tighten the locknut.

5. Adjust the clutch cable at the handlever so there is about ⅛ in. free play.

TWINS

1. Completely loosen the cable adjuster at the handlever.

2. Loosen the clutch adjuster locknut and turn the screw in until the pressure plate begins to lift, in the same manner as the singles. Back the screw out ¾ turn and tighten the locknut.

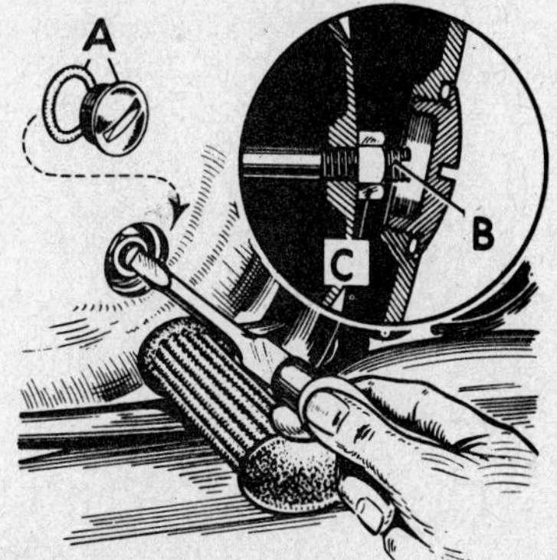

The clutch adjustment point, showing the access cap (A), adjuster screw (B), and locknut (C)

3. Turn the adjuster at the handlever until about ⅛ in. of free-play remains at the end of the lever.

ROCKET 3

The Rocket 3 clutch is adjusted in basically the same manner as the twins. Note the following points:

1. The adjuster is accessible after the primary chaincase inspection plate has been removed.

2. Back the adjuster screw out only ⅛ turn after the pressure plate starts to lift.

3. Adjust the cable at the handlever until 0–1/16 in. free-play remains at the end of the lever.

Brake Adjustment

FRONT

On single-leading shoe brakes, the adjuster is located on the bottom fork leg. Turning the adjuster shortens or lengthens the effective length of the cable, thereby adjusting the position of the shoes in the drum. A locknut secures the adjuster in position. Another adjuster is also provided at the handlever so that cable free-play can be set to suit the individual.

With twin-leading shoe brakes, on 1970 and earlier models, adjustment is made at the handlever. Turning the knurled nut counterclockwise will take up excess cable slack. Cable free-play should be maintained between 1/16 in. (1.5 mm) and ⅛ in. (3 mm). There is no operating rod adjustment on this type of brake because the length of the rod must be preset in order to seat both shoes simultaneously when the brakes are applied. The shoes are also self-centering.

On 1971 and later models with twin-leading shoe brakes and conical hubs, adjustment can also be made at the shoe pivots. Loosen the handlever adjuster and remove the rubber plug from the hub shell. Using a screwdriver, turn one of the adjusters clockwise until the shoe contacts the drum. Back off the adjuster, one notch at a time, until the wheel is just free to rotate. Repeat for the other adjuster and make the final adjustment at the handlever.

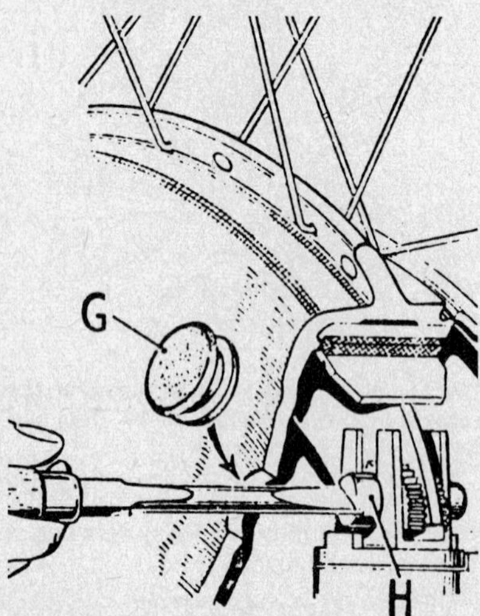

Brake shoe adjustment, 1971 and later models with double leading shoe brakes, showing the rubber plug (G) and adjuster screw (H)

REAR

The rear brake is adjustable for both pedal position and operating rod free-play. The pedal has a serrated cam hole which enables it to be removed and repositioned for rider comfort. This position should be determined before adjusting the operating rod free-play.

Rod free-play is set by turning the self-locking sleeve at the rear end of the rod until there is approximately ½ in. (12 mm) pedal play before the shoes make contact in the drum.

Final Drive Chain

To adjust the chain on all models except 1971 and later singles:

1. Set up the machine on its center stand. The rear wheel must be suspended and not touching the ground.
2. Rotate the wheel slowly until the tightest point on the chain is found, then check total up and down movement in the center of the top or bottom chain run.
3. If the up and down movement is greater than 1 ⅛ in. or less than ¾ in., the chain must be adjusted by moving the rear wheel, either forward to loosen the chain or backward to tighten it.
4. Loosen the rear axle nuts until they can be turned by hand.
5. Loosen the rear-brake adjusting sleeve and the anchor-strap retaining nuts.
6. Turn both chain adjusting nuts exactly the same amount until the correct free-play is achieved.
7. Tighten the anchor strap and rear axle nuts, then adjust the rear brake. Recheck the adjustment.

To adjust the chain on late-model singles with cam-type adjusters on the swing arm pivot:

1. Adjust the chain when the slack on the lower run exceeds about 2 ½ in. with the machine on its center stand (rear suspension fully extended).
2. Release the rear brake adjuster and separate the rod from the brake lever.
3. Loosen the pivot nut D and tap the pivot shaft through to the left side far enough to allow the cam on the left side to clear the peg.
4. Pull the swing arm to the rear and reposition the cam on both left and right sides so that about 2 in. of slack remains at the midpoint of the bottom run of the chain. There must be at least 1 ¾ in. of slack.
5. Make sure that both cams are in the same position so that correct wheel alignment is maintained, then tighten the pivot nut. Fit the brake rod into the lever and adjust the brake.

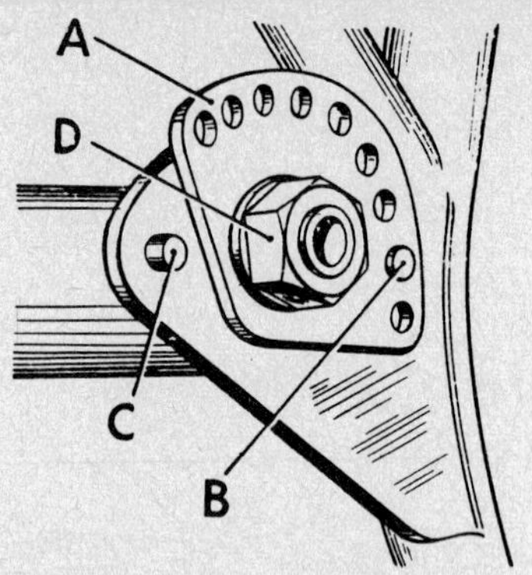

Rear chain adjustment, 1971 and later singles, showing the adjuster cam (A), locating pegs (B and C), and pivot nut (D)

Periodic Maintenance Intervals

DAILY
- Check oil level

EVERY 1,000 MILES
- Check oil level in primary chaincase
- Lubricate throttle linkage (A75)

EVERY 2,000 MILES
- Check oil level in gearbox
- Lubricate rear chain (oil or grease)
- Lubricate center stand and sidestand pivots (oil)
- Grease swing arm
- Lubricate exposed cables and joints (oil or grease)
- Grease clutch cable
- Lubricate brake pedal pivot (oil)
- Lubricate ignition advance mechanism (oil)
- Lubricate contact breaker cam (oil)
- Grease speedometer drive

EVERY 4,000 MILES
- Drain and refill the oil reservoir
- Clean oil reservoir filter
- Replace the oil filter element (B25 and A75)
- Clean crankcase filter and examine pump ball valve
- Drain and refill the gearbox
- Drain and refill primary chaincase
- Grease rear brake cam spindle

EVERY 10,000 MILES
- Drain and refill the front forks
- Clean and repack wheel bearings with grease
- Grease steering head bearings

RECOMMENDED LUBRICANTS

Assembly	Brand: Castrol	Mobil	Shell	B.P.	Esso	Texaco
Engine (and primary chaincase, B50 and A75)	GTX or XL 20/50	Super	Super Motor Oil	Super Viscostatic	Uniflo	Havoline 20W/50
Gearbox	Hypoy	Mobilube GX90	Spirax 90EP	Gear Oil 90EP	Gear Oil GX90/140	Multi-gear 90EP
Primary chaincase	Castrolite	Super	Super Motor Oil	Super Viscostatic	Uniflo	Havoline 10W/30
Front fork	TQF	ATF210	Donax T7	Autran B	Esso Glide	Texomatic F
Wheel bearings Swing arm Steering head	Castrol LM	Mobilgrease MP or Super	Retinax A	Energrease	Multi-purpose H	Marfak All-purpose

Approval is also given to lubricants marketed by companies other than those listed above, provided that they have similar multigrade characteristics and meet the highest A.P.I. Service performance level.

MAINTENANCE DATA

	B25SS	B25T	B44	B50SS	B50T	B50MX	A65T	A65L	A65FS	A75
FUEL TANK										
gallons	2.5	2.5	1.25	2.5	2.5	1.25	3.0	3.0	3.0	3.0
liters	9.0	9.0	7.9	9.0	9.0	4.5	11.5	11.5	11.5	11.5
OIL TANK										
pints	4.75	4.75	4.8	4.75	4.75	4.75	6.0	6.0	6.0	6.0
liters	2.25	2.25	2.3	2.25	2.25	2.25	2.8	2.8	2.8	2.8
TRANSMISSION										
pints	5/8	5/8	0.6	5/8	5/8	5/8	1.0	1.0	1.0	2.5
cubic centimeters	280	280	264	280	280	280	500	500	500	1,150
PRIMARY CHAINCASE										
pints	1/3	1/3	1/3	1/3	1/3	1/3	1/3	1/3	1/3	5/8
cubic centimeters	140	140	142	140	140	140	140	140	140	290
FRONT FORKS (per leg)										
pints	2/5	2/5	2/5	2/5	2/5	2/5	2/5	2/5	2/5	2/5
cubic centimeters	190	190	190	190	190	190	190	190	190	190
TIRE PRESSURE										
front (psi)	22	22	16	22	22	—	21	21	21	22
rear (psi)	24	24	17	24	24	—	22	22	22	28

ENGINE AND TRANSMISSION

ENGINE SERVICE

Singles

REMOVAL AND INSTALLATION

1. Remove the fuel tank. Drain the oil from the engine, transmission, and primary chaincase.
2. Remove the exhaust system by disconnecting the exhaust pipe clamp at the head and removing the two muffler mounting bolts.
3. Remove the right side-cover and unbolt the skid plate from frame tubes.
4. Disconnect the valve rocker oil line from the metal T-connection and disconnect the flexible scavenge line from the crankcase line at the rear.
5. Disconnect the alternator, oil pressure switch (if applicable), and contact breaker point leads from their snap connectors at the electrical box. Disconnect the spark plug wire. Pull the wire off the oil pressure switch at the bottom of the crankcase.
6. Remove the carburetor flange nuts and tie the carburetor out of the way. Leave the rubber connecting hose attached to the air filter housing.
7. Disconnect the top engine mount (at the rocker cover) and disconnect the compression release cable (B50).
8. Remove the chainguard front extension and remove the master link from the chain.
9. Disconnect the clutch cable using a suitable box wrench as a lever on the operating arm.
10. Loosen the footpeg mounting bolt and swing the footpeg down.
11. Remove the remaining engine mount bolts. Note that spacers are installed between the engine and frame at the right side of the front and bottom bolts.
12. Remove the rear engine mounting plate and lift the engine unit out of the frame from the right side.

Installation is in reverse order of removal. Be sure to replace the two spacers correctly. Don't forget to refill the engine, transmission, and primary chaincase with oil; ½ pt should be added to the crankcase to prime the oil pump.

TOP END OVERHAUL

Cylinder Head and Barrel Removal

B25

On the 250 cc models the cylinder head and barrel may be removed with the engine in the frame. The procedure is as follows:

1. Remove the fuel tank.
2. Unbolt the engine steady at the cylinder head and push the bracket up out of the way.
3. Remove the carburetor from the head, leaving it suspended by the throttle cable.
4. Remove the exhaust system by disconnecting the exhaust pipe clamp at the head and removing the two muffler mounting bolts.
5. Remove the spark plug and disconnect the rocker oil feed line.
6. Rotate the engine until the piston is at TDC of the compression stroke.
7. Remove the six cylinder head nuts and, if the head will not move, free it with a rubber mallet.

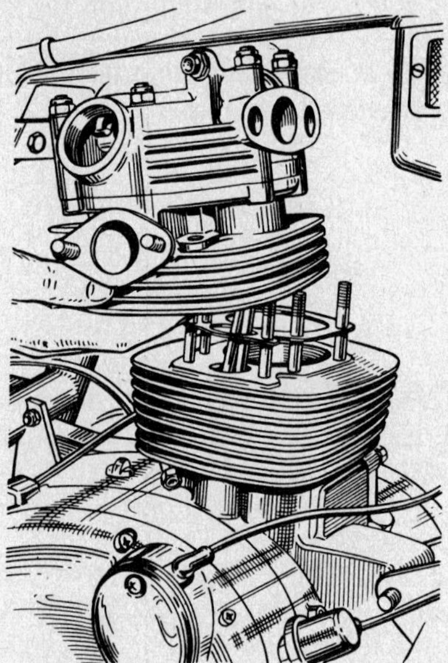

Removing the head with the engine mounted in the frame (B25)

8. Lift the head, rotate it around the pushrods to clear the frame, and remove it from the engine.
9. To remove the barrel, first rotate the engine until the piston is at the bottom of the stroke and then gently lift the barrel off. Steady the piston as the barrel is withdrawn so that it will not be damaged.

B50

Insufficient clearance exists between the cylinder head and frame on the B50 models to allow the head and barrel to be removed with the engine installed. Once the engine has been removed, follow steps 6 through 9 above, for the B25.

Cylinder Head Service

VALVES

Compress the valve springs and remove the split collar. Release tension on the spring and remove the top spring retainer, the springs, and the bottom retainer at each valve.

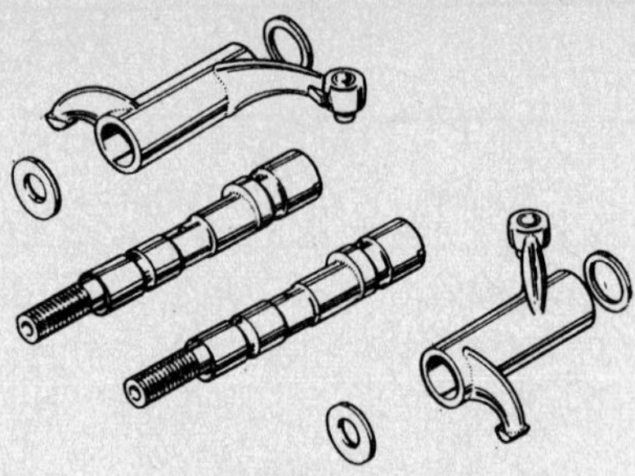

Rocker assembly (B25)

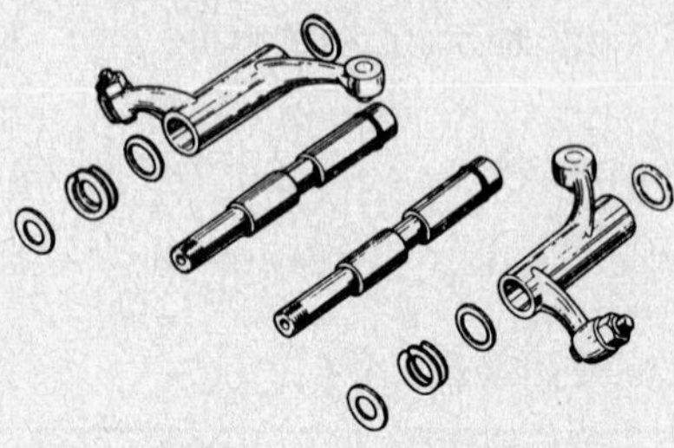

Rocker assembly (B50)

Valve guides can be driven out after the cylinder head has been heated in an oven or immersed in hot water. Install the new guides while the head is still warm. Note that the exhaust valve guide is counterbored at its lower end.

Replace valves that are pitted or burned. Valve seats can be recut, if necessary, using a 45° cutter. If the valve seat area has become pocketed, grind away the metal around the seat as illustrated before cutting.

Remove the carbon from the combustion chamber using a scraper or a small, handheld grinder. Be careful not to scratch the soft metal of the cylinder head. Clean the head in solvent after the carbon has been removed.

CAUTION: *Do not use a caustic soda solution to clean aluminum parts.*

Wether the original valves or new valves are to be used, they should be lapped into their seats. Put three small

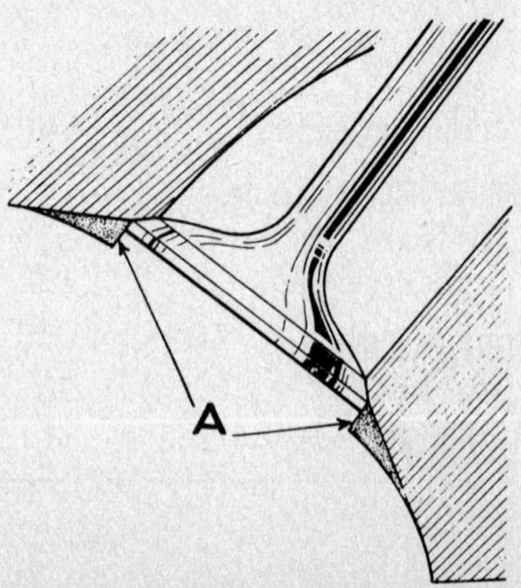

Pocketed valve, showing the metal that should be removed (shaded area A)

Lapping a valve into its seat

dabs of grinding compound around the valve face and, using the valve grinding tool as shown, rotate the valve back and forth. Do not use pressure. Rotate the valve to a new position every few seconds and continue grinding until a smooth, even finish is obtained on the valve and valve seat.

Before assembling the valves, all traces of grinding compound and grit must be removed from the head and valves. Coat the valve stems with fresh oil or assembly lube before installing. Assemble the valve springs and retainers as removed. A small amount of grease will keep the split collar in place as the spring compressor is removed. Make sure the collar is correctly seated by tapping the valve stem with a small, soft hammer.

Cylinder Barrel and Piston Service

Measure the cylinder bore for wear and examine it for scoring. If wear is excessive the cylinder may be bored to accept the 0.020 in. or 0.040 in. oversize pistons that are available. Whether or not the cylinder is to be bored, it should be honed so that the new rings seat properly.

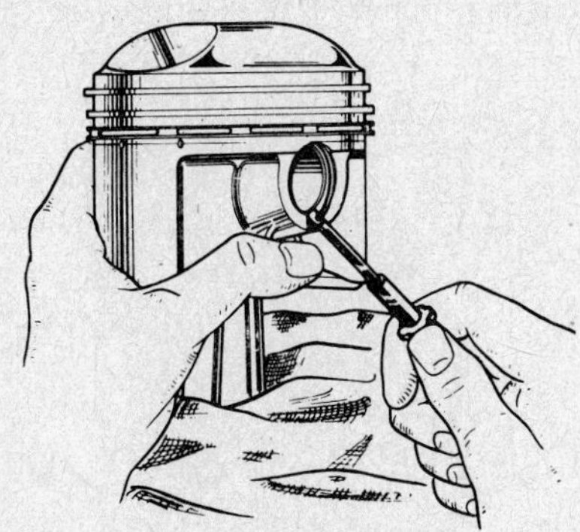

Removing a wrist pin circlip

To remove the piston it will be necessary to heat it slightly to facilitate removal of the wrist pin. First, remove the wrist pin circlips and then use an electric iron against the piston crown. After the piston is warm the wrist pin should slide out rather easily. Mark the front of the piston inside the skirt to facilitate reassembly. Thoroughly but carefully remove all traces of carbon from the piston crown. Remove the old rings, taking care not to scratch the piston.

Break one of the old rings and use the end of it to clean the carbon out of the piston ring grooves. Check the end gaps of the new rings by placing each one into the cylinder bore and measuring with a feeler gauge. End gap should not be less than 0.009 in. (B25) and 0.016 in. (B50). Carefully install the rings onto the pistons. Note that both compression rings on the B50 and the second ring on the B25 are marked TOP and must be installed accordingly. Side clearance of the rings (up and down free movement) should not exceed 0.003 in.

The wrist pin bushing should not need replacement at this time. If necessary, a special tool is available to replace the B50 bushing, BSA part number 61-3653. When replacing the bushing be sure that it is correctly aligned with the oil hole in the connecting rod. The bushing must be reamed to 0.7503–0.7506 in. after installation. The B25 does not have a replaceable bushing; the connecting rod must be replaced, entailing complete engine teardown.

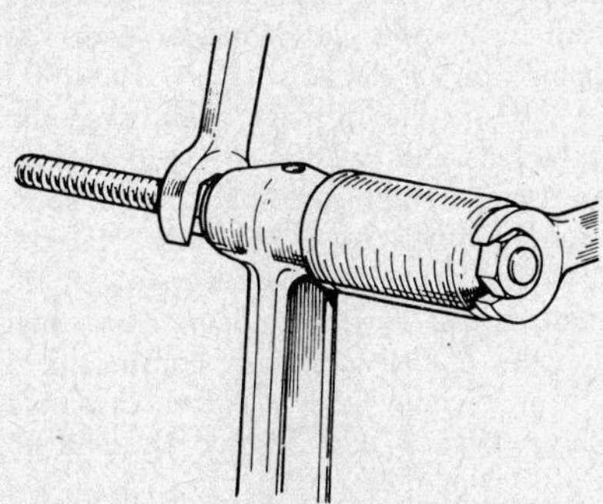

Using service tool No. 61-3653 to remove the small end bushing (B50 only)

Assembly

1. Warm the piston and install it in the correct position on the connecting rod. Insert the wrist pin before the piston has a chance to cool. Install new circlips and make sure that they are seated properly.

2. Install a new cylinder base gasket and support the piston with two pieces of wood approximately ½ in. square by 6 in. long, as shown. Stagger the ring gaps 120° apart, liberally oil the rings, and install a ring compressor. If a ring compressor is unavailable, it is possible to compress the rings by hand, one at a time, as the barrel is slipped over the piston. Slide the barrel over the piston and remove the compressor and wood blocks.

3. Install the two pushrods, noting that the outer one operates the intake valve. The top of the exhaust valve pushrod on the B25 is painted red for identification, as it is slightly shorter than the intake pushrod. The B50 pushrods are identical in length.

4. Install the rocker box on the cylinder head using a new gasket and torque the nuts to 7 ft lb. Install a new head gasket and fit the head onto the barrel.

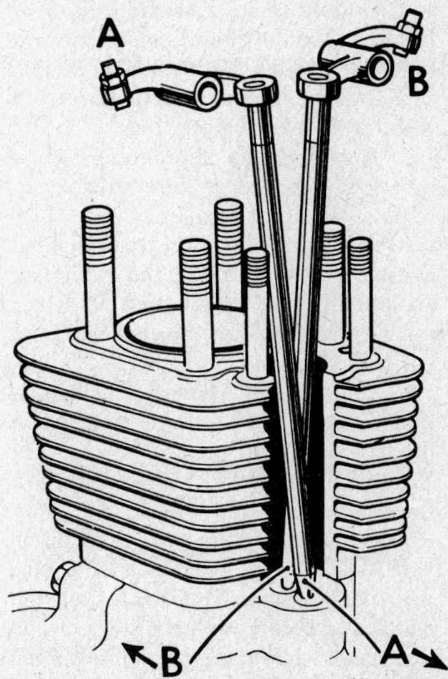

The outer pushrod (A) operates the intake rocker arm (A) and the inner pushrod (B) operates the exhaust rocker arm (B)

5. Place the pushrod ends into the rocker arm ends, making absolutely sure that they are positioned correctly, as illustrated. Keep a light downward pressure on the head and rotate the engine until the piston is at TDC of the compression stroke. Tighten the cylinder head nuts gradually to the figures given in the specifications at the end of the chapter. Install the pushrod inspection cover (B50).

6. If the engine was removed for service, reinstall it in the frame. Reinstall the rocker oil feed line, exhaust system, carburetor, and cylinder head steady. Make sure that the carburetor O-ring and gaskets are in good condition. Check and adjust valve clearances, ignition timing, and carburetor.

CLUTCH AND PRIMARY DRIVE

Clutch Service

DISASSEMBLY

1. If the engine is mounted in the frame, remove the left-side, footpeg, and brake pedal.

2. Drain the oil from the primary chaincase as described, remove the screws, and take off the primary drive cover. It may be necessary to tap the cover with a rubber mallet to break it free.

3. Remove the lockwire (B50 only) from the four-clutch spring retaining nuts and withdraw the pressure plate, springs, and cups.

4. Withdraw the clutch plates.

5. Keep the clutch from turning by wedging a piece of wood between the sprocket and chain or applying the rear brake, and remove the clutch center nut (after the locktab has been bent back).

6. Remove the locktab and spacer and withdraw the clutch pushrod.

7. To remove the clutch completely it is necessary to remove the alternator. To remove the stator (enclosing the rotor), take off the three mounting nuts, pull the alternator lead through the grommet, and pull the stator off the studs. The rotor can be taken off after the crankshaft nut has been removed.

8. Remove the primary chain tensioner, noting that a spacer is installed on the rear stud.

9. Bend back the locktab and unscrew the engine shaft nut. Remove the rotor, wipe it clean, and store it in a clean place.

10. Use a gear puller or special BSA tool (part number 61-3583) to pull the clutch and sprocket off the transmission mainshaft, while at the same time pulling the front sprocket off the engine crankshaft.

INSPECTION

1. The clutch discs should appear to be in good condition. If the thickness of the discs measures less than 0.137 in. they should be replaced.

Removing the clutch hub and sprocket

2. Check that the tabs at the outer edge of the discs are not worn or rounded and that the sprocket slots are not damaged. If there are burrs on the tabs the discs must be replaced.

3. Place the clutch plates on a flat surface such as a plate of glass. If they can be rocked from side to side or evidence any buckling they should be replaced. Also replace the plates if they are scored.

4. To examine the dampers located in the clutch center, remove the four screws adjacent to the clutch spring housings and pry off the retaining plate. The dampers need not be replaced unless they are visibly damaged or worn. It may be necessary to lubricate them when reinstalling; it is recommended that a liquid detergent be used. Do not use petroleum based oil or grease.

5. The clutch center slots should be smooth and undamaged; otherwise, jerky clutch engagement will result. Check clutch spring free length, and if less than 1.65 in., replace the springs.

6. The spring retaining nuts should be replaced whenever they are removed.

ASSEMBLY

If the sprockets or clutch hub have been replaced it will be necessary to realign the sprockets to avoid excessive primary chain wear. To reinstall the clutch:

1. If the clutch sleeve has been removed, smear it with grease and place the twenty-five bearing rollers in position. Slide the sprocket over the rollers and install the clutch center over the splines of the sleeve.

2. Place the primary chain over the sprockets and position the sprockets on the shafts. Make sure that the transmission mainshaft key is correctly located.

3. Install the clutch center spacer. Install a new locktab and apply a small amount of thread locking compound to the mainshaft threads before installing the retaining nut. Torque the nut to 60–65 ft lb.

4. Install the alternator rotor on the crankshaft with the marks facing out, making sure that the key is located correctly. Install a new locktab, apply a drop of thread locking compound to the threads, and tighten the retaining nut to 60 ft lb.

5. Pass the stator lead through the grommet at the front of the crankcase. Fit the stator over the studs and partially tighten the nuts. Check that there is an equal air gap between the rotor and stator at all points using an 0.008 in. feeler gauge. Variations can be corrected by repositioning the stator.

6. To adjust primary chain tension, loosen the rear stator retaining nut and adjust the tensioner to provide ¼ in. freeplay on the top run of the chain midway between the sprockets. Retighten the stator nut.

7. Install the clutch discs and plates alternatively into the clutch housing, beginning with a disc. Insert the clutch pushrod into the mainshaft.

8. Install the pressure plate complete with springs and cups. Make sure the spring cup location pips are seated in the slots in the pressure plate.

9. Install and tighten the four spring nuts until the first coil of each spring is just outside of its cup. Check to see that the springs are tightened evenly by pulling the clutch lever in and kicking the engine over. If any wobble is noticeable at the pressure plate as it turns, tighten or loosen the springs as necessary until it runs true. Lock the spring nuts in position with lockwire (B50 only).

10. Adjust the clutch by means of the screw and locknut at the center of the pressure plate so that the clutch operating lever is angled approximately 30° away from the crankcase/side-cover joint.

11. Clean the crankcase and primary cover mating surfaces, apply a thin coat of gasket cement, and mount the cover using a new gasket. If it is possible to use a torque wrench, tighten the screws to 3.5–4.5 ft lb.

12. Fill the primary chaincase with the correct amount and grade of oil and adjust the clutch lever free-play if necessary.

Primary Drive Service

After the clutch assembly has been removed, the primary drive chain, sprockets, and sprocket hub bearing are free. Sprockets should be replaced if the teeth are rounded, hooked, or worn on

Exploded view of the clutch, showing only one disc and plate

Removing the primary drive

the side. The rear sprocket roller bearing is allowed a light amount of free-play, but if it is excessive the rollers should be replaced.

TRANSMISSION COUNTERSHAFT SPROCKET AND OIL SEAL

To examine or remove the countershaft final drive sprocket, first remove the six screws that retain the plate surrounding the shaft. Pry the plate loose and remove it with its oil seal, taking note of the felt washer that protects the seal from dirt and grit. Check for oil leakage at the back of the plate and replace the plate oil seal if necessary. Install the seal with the lip facing the countershaft sprocket. If the bushing that the seal rides on is worn then it too must be replaced, as it would quickly ruin a new seal.

If the sprocket teeth are hooked or if the sprocket is damaged it should be replaced (along with the drive chain and rear wheel sprocket if it too is worn). To remove the sprocket, bend back the lock-tab, apply the rear brake, and unscrew the retaining nut. Disconnect the drive chain and pull the sprocket off the shaft. Examine the countershaft oil seal at this time. If it shows signs of leakage, remove the circlip, pry out the seal, and replace it with a new one. Coat the new seal with oil to facilitate installation. Examine the sprocket boss for wear, which may have been causing the seal to leak. Lightly oil the boss when installing the sprocket to avoid damaging the seal. Torque the sprocket retaining nut to 100 ft lb. A new felt washer should be used behind the oil seal. Make sure that the small boss cast into the rear of the plate is installed in the four o'clock position or else it will contact the drive chain.

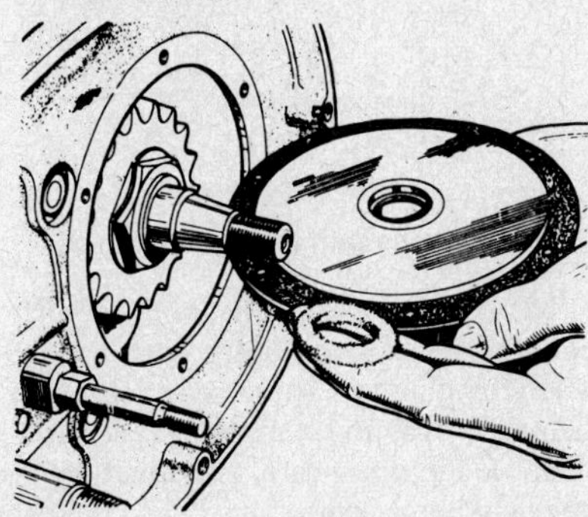

Removing the countershaft sprocket access plate

PRIMARY DRIVE SPROCKET ALIGNMENT

Install the primary sprockets on their shafts, without the chain. The bearing rollers can be held in place with grease. (The crankshaft sprocket spacer used on B25 models must be installed with the chamfered end against the sprocket.) Place a straightedge against the sprockets as illustrated. If the sprockets are aligned properly the straightedge will make contact at three points. Shims of different thicknesses are available for installation behind the crankshaft sprocket to correct misalignment. Refer to the preceding section on clutch service for assembly procedures after the chain and sprockets are installed.

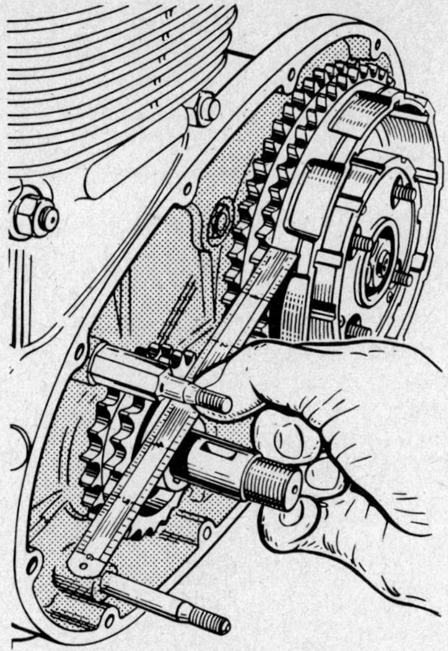

Checking sprocket alignment

TRANSMISSION AND SHIFTER MECHANISM SERVICE

Disassembly

1. If the top end has not been disassembled, position the piston at TDC of the compression stroke to avoid distorting the inner camshaft bushing, due to valve spring pressure, as the inner crankcase cover is removed. Drain the transmission oil at this time.

2. Disassemble the primary drive and clutch assembly as described previously, including the countershaft sprocket. This is necessary to permit the transmission mainshaft to be withdrawn along with the inner crankcase cover at the right (timing) side of the engine.

3. To remove the right-side outer cover, first take off the kick-start and shift levers. Remove the cover retaining screws, noting that the screws are of different lengths and must be replaced in their original positions.

4. Unscrew the kick-start return spring anchor and remove the spring.

5. Remove the contact breaker plate and pull the ignition advance unit off its taper.

6. Take out the remaining inner cover mounting screws and tap the cover with a rubber mallet to break the joint seal. Withdraw the cover, complete with transmission gear cluster. As the cover is removed, exert a slight inward pressure on the end of the camshaft to avoid disturbing the valve timing.

7. Depress the two plungers in the shift linkage quadrant and withdraw the quadrant and spring.

8. Remove the camplate pivot cotter pin from the outside of the cover. Screw one of the small inner cover screws into the pivot and pull the pivot out with a pair of pliers.

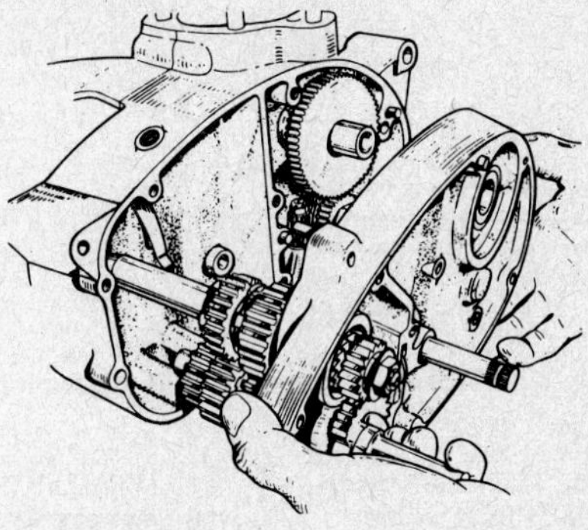

Removing the right-side inner cover and gear assembly

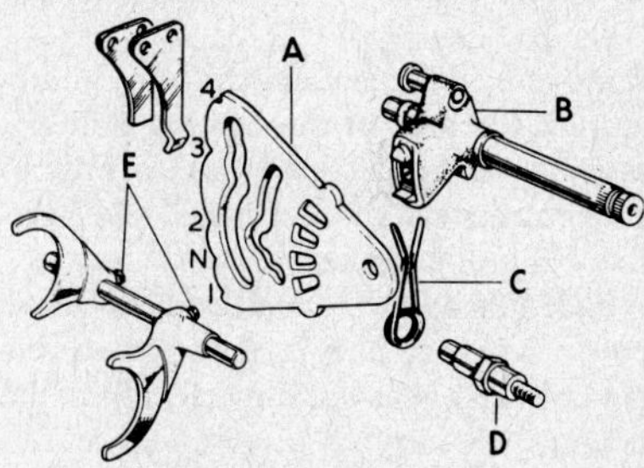

The shifter mechanism

A. Camplate
B. Plunger quadrant
C. Return spring
D. Pivot
E. Shift forks, showing the camplate engagement rollers

9. Remove the camplate, shift forks, and fork shaft.

10. Withdraw the countershaft, complete with gear assembly and mainshaft sliding gear. To remove the mainshaft assembly from the cover, take off the kick-start ratchet retaining nut and remove the ratchet components from the shaft.

NOTE: *When removing the countershaft gears, note that second gear is retained by a circlip.*

11. The two gears remaining on the mainshaft are an interference fit. Remove by clamping the gears in a vice (protected from the jaws with pieces of wood or cloth) and driving the shaft out with a soft metal drift.

12. If it is desired to remove the left-side transmission bearing from the case, drive the pinion out of the bearing and remove the oil seal. The crankcase should be heated with a propane torch before the bearing is driven out to avoid damage to both the bearing and case.

Assembly

1. To reinstall the left-side bearing (if

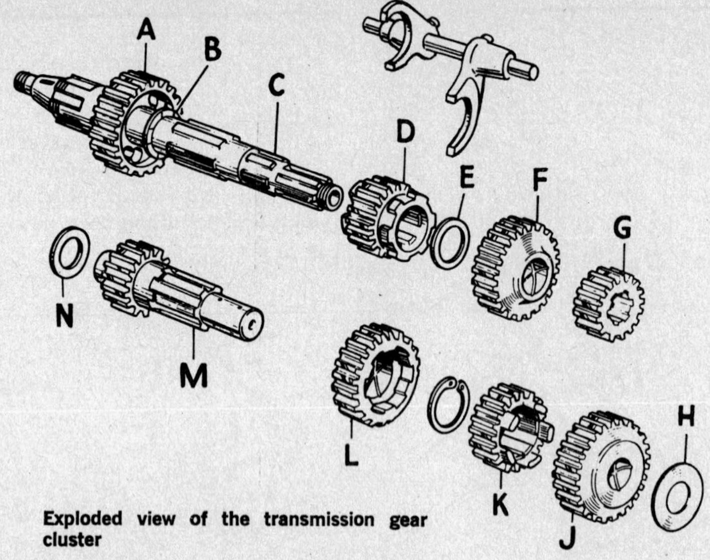

Exploded view of the transmission gear cluster

A. Mainshaft fourth gear
B. Thrust washer
C. Mainshaft
D. Mainshaft second gear
E. Thrust washer
F. Mainshaft third gear
G. Mainshaft first gear
H. Countershaft first gear shim
J. Countershaft first gear
K. Countershaft third gear
L. Countershaft second gear
M. Countershaft
N. Thrust washer

removed), heat the crankcase very gently around the area of the bearing housing, moving the torch slowly and evenly to prevent distortion, and install the bearing. Fit a new oil seal.

2. If necessary, install a new inner cover bearing, having first heated the cover in an oven. Use new oil seals in the cover.

3. Install the camplate with the small mark positioned as shown in the accompanying illustration. Install the camplate pivot and lock in place with a cotter pin.

4. Replace the mainshaft gears on the shaft, fit the shaft into the inner cover bearing, install the kick-start ratchet components, and tighten the retaining nut to 50–55 ft lb. Lock the nut in place with the locktab.

5. Install the kick-start half-gear into the inner cover. Place the cover, with the outside surface down, close to the edge on your workbench so that the half-gear shaft is over the edge but the gear is retained in the cover. Place the countershaft first gear shim over the bearing in the half-gear shaft. Use a small amout of grease to hold it in position.

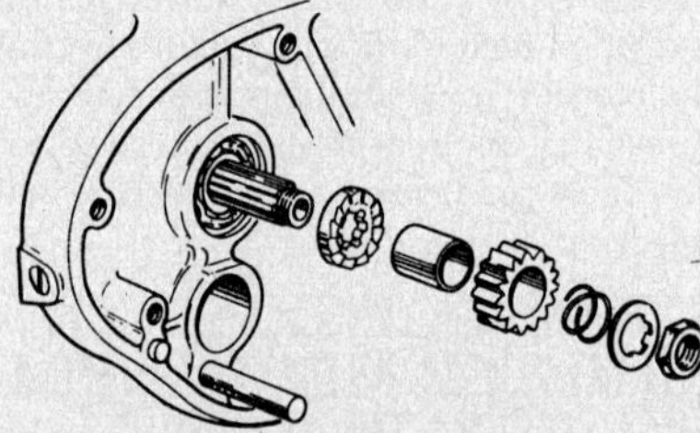

Kick-start ratchet components

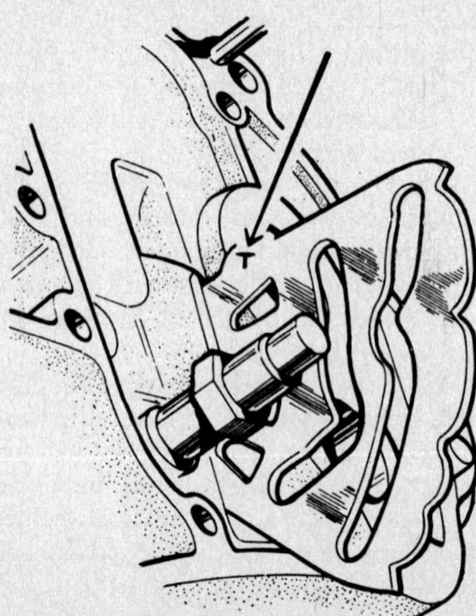

Correct positioning of the camplate

6. Engage the mainshaft and countershaft first gears and fit the shift fork into the countershaft third gear with the machined (flat) side of the fork up. Engage the roller (button) of the fork in the lower camplate track.

7. Fit the mainshaft second gear with its shift fork (machined side of the fork down) and engage the fork roller in the upper track of the camplate.

8. Insert the shift fork shaft through the forks and into the inner cover. Position the countershaft second gear on the shaft and install the countershaft in the inner cover.

9. Place the mainshaft fourth gear thrust washer over the shaft, retaining it with a dab of grease. Install the countershaft thrust washer, making sure that the side with the radius faces the gear.

10. Lubricate all components with motor oil and rotate the shafts to confirm that they are free.

11. If the shift return spring has been removed, it must be reinstalled so that the marked (painted) side of the coil faces the shift quadrant body. If the spring is unmarked, install it in the position in which it appears in the accompanying illustration (in line with the two pins) by trial and error.

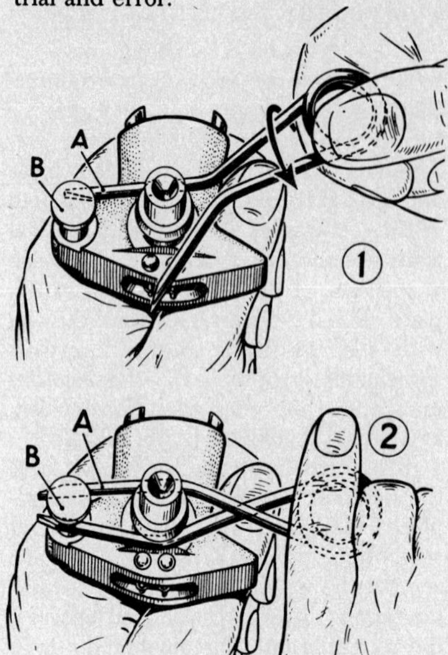

Installing the shift return spring (A)

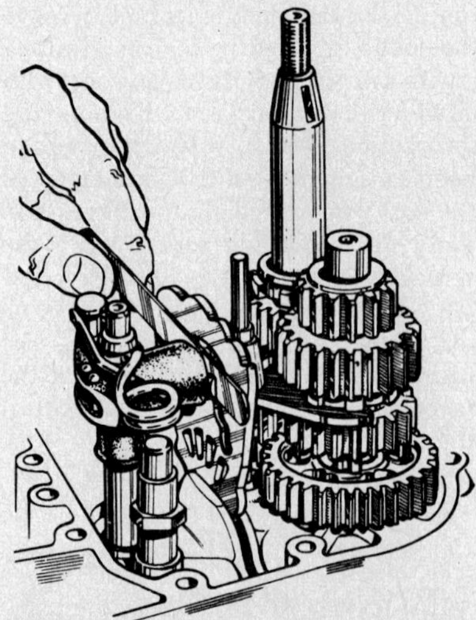

Installing the shift quadrant assembly

12. Install the shift quadrant assembly into the inner cover, using a flat blade to keep the plungers depressed so that they can slide over the camplate, as shown.

13. If the inner case, mainshaft, countershaft, or any gears have been replaced it will be necessary to check end-float of the shafts and adjust if necessary. To accomplish this, mount the inner cover on the crankcase and tighten the screws. Remove the kick-start ratchet assembly and half-gear, and the ends of the mainshaft and countershaft will be accessible. End-float should be just perceptible. If excessive, thrust washers of different thicknesses are available for end-float adjustment.

14. When all components have been

assembled on the inner cover and it is ready to be installed, clean the crankcase and inner cover mating surfaces thoroughly and apply a think coat of gasket cement to one of the surfaces. Lubricate the crankshaft oil seal and camshaft end, and mount the cover on the crankcase. Tighten the screws to 3.5–4.5 ft lb. Check operation of the gears. Loosely replace the ignition advance unit and contact breaker plate.

15. Install the outer cover, cleaning the mating surfaces and applying gasket cement as above. Install the kick-start and shift levers.

NOTE: *Before the cover is installed, the position of the shift linkage quadrant can be adjusted for smoother gear selection (late models only). Loosen the adjuster locknut and select each gear in turn. If the gears do not engage positively, turn the adjuster screw a little at a time until gear selection is satisfactory. Do not turn the screw more than ¼ turn from vertical in either direction. Tighten the locknut when adjustment is complete.*

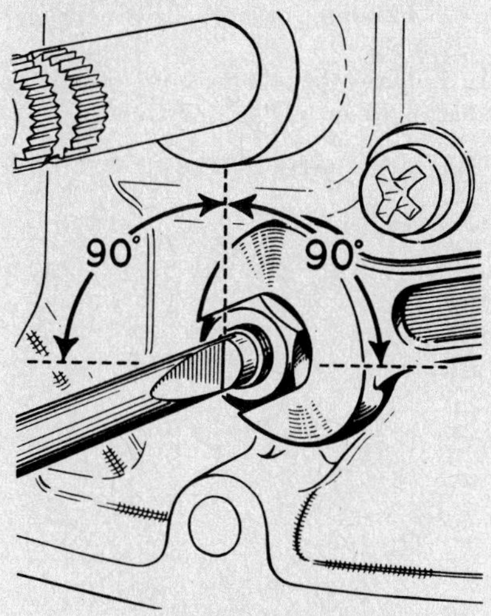

Shift quadrant adjustment

16. Install the primary drive and clutch assembly and refill the transmission and primary case with oil. Adjust the ignition timing before running the engine.

BOTTOM END OVERHAUL

Disassembly

1. Drain the oil from the engine, transmission, and primary case. Remove the engine.
2. Remove the cylinder head, piston, and barrel as described in the top end overhaul section.
3. Remove the primary drive and clutch assembly as outlined in preceding sections.
4. Remove the right-side outer cover and then take off the inner cover, complete with transmission gearset, as described in the preceding section.
5. Note the alignment of the marks on the timing gears and withdraw the upper gear and camshaft, allowing the tappets to fall clear.
6. Insert a bar through the connecting rod small end, place blocks of wood under the bar to protect the crankcase, and unscrew the nut at the end of the crankshaft. The bar will keep the engine from turning over as the nut is broken free.
7. Remove the small timing gear with a suitable gear puller or BSA tool number 61-3773.
8. Take off the nut and remove the oil pump drive gear.

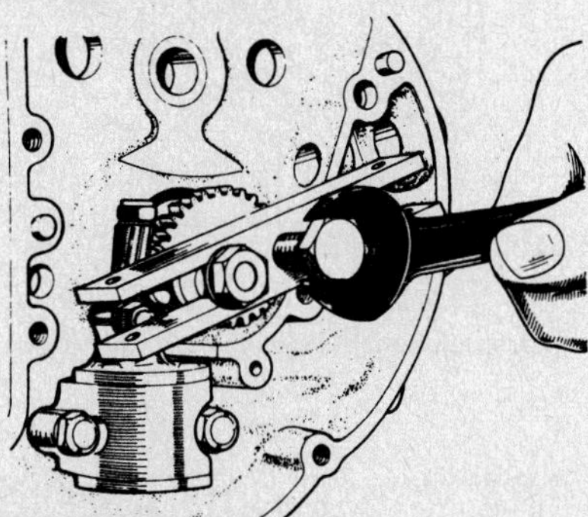

Removing the oil pump drive gear with tool No. 61-3773

9. From the left side of the crankcase, remove the three bolts at the lower front of the case, the two stud nuts at the center of the case, and the remaining two stud nuts at the cylinder base.
10. Remove the woodruff keys from the crankshaft ends and separate the crankcase halves by tapping them with a rubber mallet. Do not pry the cases apart by forcing a tool into the joint, as this will damage the mating surfaces and cause an oil leak. Lift away the right crankcase as shown, and remove the crankshaft assembly. A slight amount of pressure may be necessary to remove the crankshaft on B50 models because of the main bearing arrangement. Note the number of shims used, if any, between the right-side flywheel and main bearing on B25 models.

Main Bearings

B25

The inner and outer races of the left-side roller bearings are separated as the crankcase halves are split. The outer race can be driven out after the case has been heated in an oven. The inner race, remaining on the crankshaft, can be pulled off using a suitable gear puller or BSA tool number 61-3778. The right-side (timing side) ball bearing assembly can be driven out after heating the case.

New bearings can be installed in the cases in the same manner, after the cases have been heated.

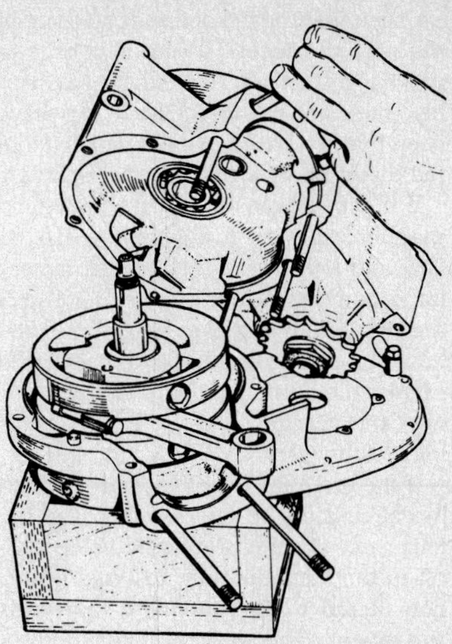

Separating the crankcase halves

B50

To remove the two drive (left) side bearings, the bearing retaining ring—attached to the crankcase by four countersunk screws—must first be taken off. Heat the crankcase and drive out the bearings, spacer, and abutment ring. The timing side bearing can be driven out after the right crankcase has been heated.

Install new bearings in the same manner, after the cases have been heated. Make sure that the abutment ring is correctly located. Apply a drop of thread locking compound to the four retaining ring screws upon installation.

Connecting Rod Bearings and Crankshaft Assembly

B25

The connecting rod can be removed by

Removing the main bearing inner race

simply unbolting the bearing cap. Loosen the nuts alternately, a turn at a time to prevent distortion. To facilitate reassembly, the connecting rod and cap have been marked with a center punch. Note the direction in which the marks face.

If it is necessary to regrind the crankshaft, bearings are available in 0.010, 0.020, and 0.030 in. undersizes. It is very important that the radius at either end of the crankpin is machined to 0.070–0.080 in. when regrinding. Do not attempt to refinish the bearing shells or file the bearing cap mating surfaces to reduce bearing clearances.

If the crankshaft is to be reground the flywheels must be removed. Loosen the four short flywheel retaining bolts (closest to the crankpin) first to avoid distortion. Remove the remaining four bolts and separate the flywheels. It would be a good idea at this time to clean the oil sludge trap, located in the right flywheel. Unscrew the plug and clean the passage with solvent and compressed air.

When reinstalling the flywheels, make sure that the flywheel incorporating the sludge trap is fitted on the right side. Apply a drop of thread locking compound to the threads of each flywheel retaining bolt and tighten evenly to 50 ft lb.

When installing the connecting rod on the crankshaft, make sure that the rod-bearing shells are properly located in the connecting rod and cap. The oil hole should face the drive (left) side flywheel. Lubricate the bearing surfaces with fresh engine oil and install the bearing cap, taking note of the position of the punch marks to ensure that the cap is installed in its original position. It is recommended that new connecting rod bolts and nuts be used as a precaution against breakage. Clean the threads, apply a drop of thread locking compound, and tighten the nuts to 22 ft lb. Using a pressure oil can, force oil into the passage at the right end of the crankshaft until it comes out around the connecting rod bearing.

B50

Replacement of the connecting rod bearing on B50 models entails the use of a press for removal and installation of the flywheels, and a special jig (with dial indicators) for trueing the flywheels after assembly. This work should therefore be left to a qualified specialist.

Camshaft and Tappets

The camshaft lobes and tappet feet should be carefully examined for damage and wear. Replace any part that does not appear to be in perfect condition. Insert the tappets into their guide bores and check to see if they are free to move without binding. Replace if movement is restricted. Oil the tappets before installing.

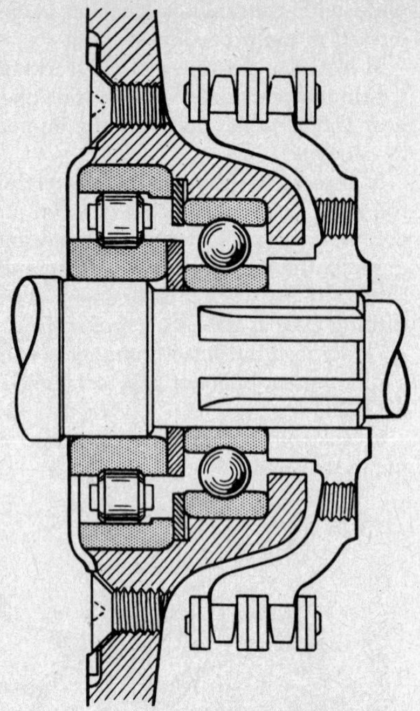

Drive-side main bearing assembly (B50)

Assembly

1. On B25 engines the crankshaft end-float must be checked. Proceed with step 2 below, omitting the gasket cement. Check crankshaft end-float, disassemble the cases again and add or remove thrust washers as necessary between the flywheel and right-side main bearing to adjust end-float to within 0.002–0.005 in. Then start with step 2 again and follow the remainder of the assembly procedure.
2. Place the crankshaft assembly into the drive side crankcase. Clean the crankcase mating surfaces and apply a thin coat of gasket cement to the mating surface of one of the cases. Fit the crankcase halves together and install the three bolts and four nuts. Tighten evenly to 16–18 ft lb.
3. Rotate the crankshaft to make sure that it turns freely. If it does not, the cause of the trouble must be determined and rectified. Look for incorrect main bearing alignment or insufficient crankshaft end-play.
4. Install the small timing gear on the end of the crankshaft, taking care to locate the woodruff key properly. Tighten the retaining nut to 50–55 ft lb.
5. Install the oil pump drive gear on the pump shaft using the special locknut (or a suitable replacement) as originally installed.
6. Place the two tappets into their bores with the thinner end of the tappet foot facing forward. Install the camshaft and timing gear unit, with the timing marks aligned, and fit the thrust washer on the end of the camshaft (late B25 models only).

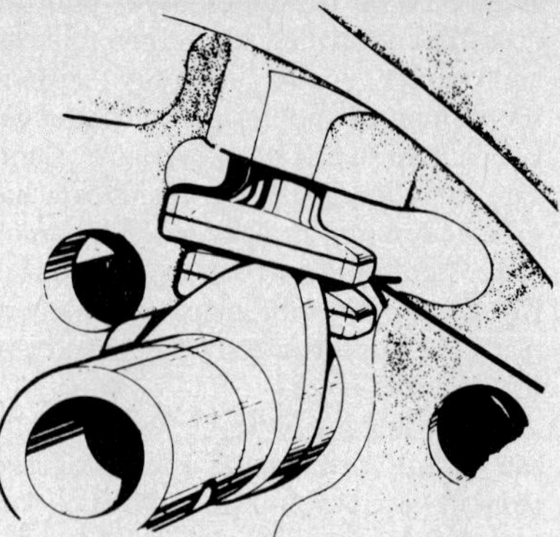

Correct installation of the tappets

NOTE: *On early engines there are two marks on the camshaft timing gear—a dash and a V. On these engines the dash must be ignored and the marks aligned as illustrated. On later engines that do not have the V mark, simply align the dash marks.*

7. Install the right-side inner cover complete with transmission gearset as described earlier, and install the outer cover.
8. Install the primary drive and clutch assembly.
9. Install the cylinder head, piston, and barrel. Refer to Top End Overhaul.

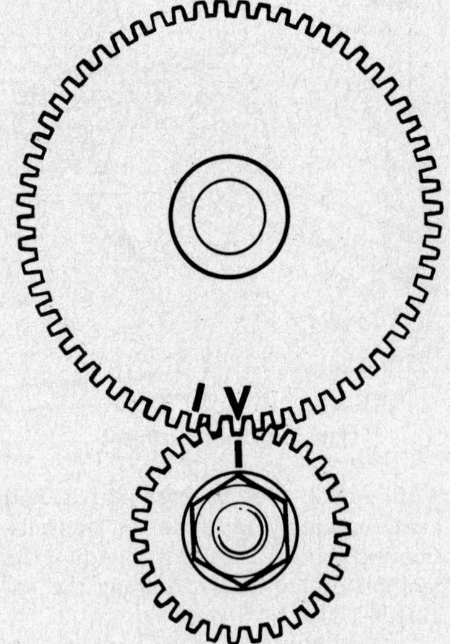

Timing marks—late models

10. Install the engine into the frame. Allow the engine a few hundred miles of gentle running to break in properly, and check valve adjustment, ignition timing, and so on after about 500 miles have been covered.

Twins

REMOVAL AND INSTALLATION

1. Drain the oil from the engine, transmission, and primary chaincase.

2. Disconnect and remove the final drive chain.

3. Remove the front chainguard mounting bolt, loosen the rear one, and lift the chainguard away toward the rear.

4. Disconnect the alternator leads at their connectors behind the engine. Remove the spark plug wires.

5. Remove the fuel tank.

6. Disconnect the rocker oil feedline.

7. Disconnect the carburetors from the engine and tie them to the frame to keep them out of the way.

8. Disconnect and remove the entire exhaust system.

9. Unbolt and remove the left footpeg assembly.

10. Back off the rear brake adjuster to allow the pedal to be depressed as the engine is removed.

11. Back off the adjuster at the handlebar and disconnect the clutch cable from the hand lever. Coil the cable up, leaving it attached to the engine.

12. Disconnect the tachometer cable from the tachometer drive at the front of the timing case.

13. Disconnect the wire from the oil pressure switch and remove the switch to prevent it from being damaged.

14. Unbolt the oil line junction from the bottom of the right-side crankcase. Examine the two O-ring seals at this time to determine if they can be reused.

15. Remove the engine mounting bolts, taking note of the number (if any) and position of the shims on the long front bolt. Remove the engine from the left side, with the aid of a helper.

Installation of the engine is a reversal of the removal procedure. The following points should be noted:

1. Replace any mounting bolt shims in their original positions.

2. Install the chain master link clip with the closed end facing the forward direction of rotation.

3. Make sure that the carburetor O-rings and gaskets are in good condition. Torque the mounting nuts to 10–12 ft lb.

4. Correctly position the interconnecting pipe (on models so equipped) before tightening the exhaust system bolts.

NOTE: *Before starting the engine, ½ pt of oil should be added to the crankcase to prime the oil pump.*

TOP END OVERHAUL

Cylinder Head and Barrel Removal

The cylinder head and barrel can be removed with the engine in the frame. The procedure is as follows:

1. Turn off the fuel taps and disconnect the lines. Raise the seat and remove the screws that secure the tank center strip (late models). Remove the strip and then loosen the tank center retaining bolt. On earlier models, remove the rubber plug to expose the bolt. Lift the tank away, leaving the bolt in position.

2. Unbolt the carburetors from the engine and tie them out of the way.

3. Disconnect the rocker oil feedline, taking care not to lose the filter and fiber washers.

4. Unbolt and remove the cylinder head steady.

5. On models equipped with an exhaust interconnection pipe, loosen the clamps and slide the sleeve to the left side. Remove the entire exhaust system.

6. Remove the four bolts and two nuts that secure the rocker cover. Tap the cover with a soft hammer to break the seal and remove the cover.

NOTE: *On 1970 and earlier engines, the cover is retained by six nuts.*

7. Loosen the two exhaust valve rocker arm adjusting screws until the two pushrods can be removed.

8. Cover the pushrod tunnel with a cloth to prevent parts from falling down inside. Then unscrew the exhaust rocker shaft retaining nut (at the right front side) and drive the shaft out toward the left. The two head bolts under the shaft will now be exposed. The intake valve rocker assembly need not be removed in order to remove the head.

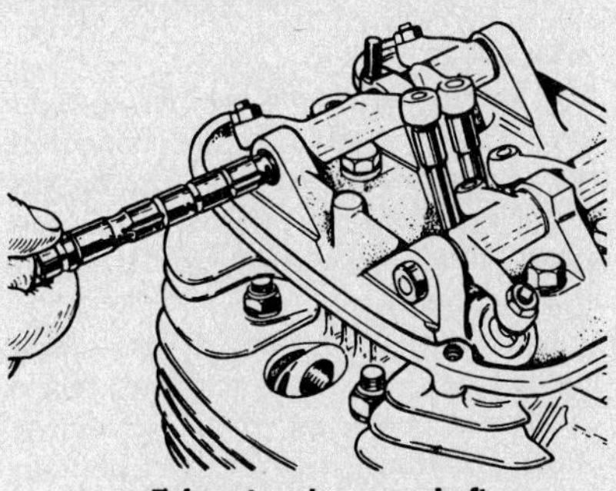

Exhaust rocker arm shaft

9. Remove the spark plugs and disconnect the oil line at the rear of the head.

10. Loosen the intake valve rocker arm screws and remove the pushrods.

11. Loosen the four long head bolts below the rocker shafts and then the center bolt (shown in the illustration). Finally, loosen the four head nuts evenly, a turn at a time, to avoid distorting the head.

Center head bolt

12. When all the nuts and bolts are removed, tap the head with a rubber mallet to break the head gasket seal and lift the head off. To remove the barrel, unscrew and remove the eight cylinder base nuts, turn the engine over until the pistons are at the bottom of the bores, and lift it away.

NOTE: *As the pistons clear the bores, take care to steady them so that they are not damaged on the studs or crankcase flange.*

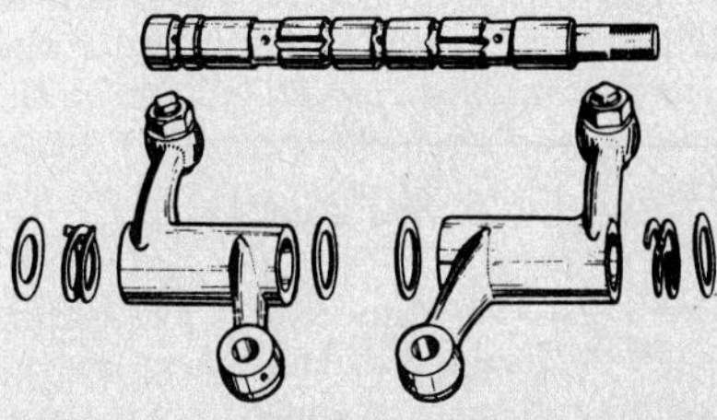

Valve rocker assembly (exhaust side shown)

Cylinder Head Service

VALVE TRAIN INSPECTION

To remove a tappet, drive it out of the block using a soft metal punch on the upper end. Remove the circlip and the tappet can be removed from its guide. Examine both ends for signs of wear or chipping and check that they can move freely in the block. In addition, the camshaft should be inspected for wear if any of the tappets are bad, as it may be damaged in the same way. When reinstalling the tappets, install them into the same guides from which they were removed. Take care not to damage the surface when installing the circlips. BSA tool no. 61-3702 will make the job easier.

VALVES

Compress the valve springs and remove the split collar. Release tension on the springs and remove the top retainer, the springs, and the bottom retainer at each valve.

Valve guides can be driven out after the cylinder head has been heated in an oven or immersed in hot water, using BSA tool no. 61-3382 or a suitably sized drift. Install the new guides while the head is still warm.

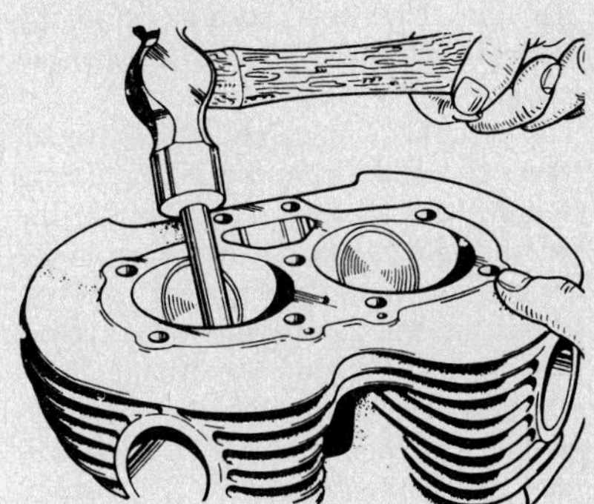

Driving out the valve guide

Replace valves that are pitted or burned. Valve seats can be recut, if necessary, using a 45° cutter. If the valve seat area has become pocketed, grind away the metal around the seat before cutting.

Remove the carbon from the combustion chamber using a scraper or a small, hand-held grinder. Be careful not to scratch the soft metal of the cylinder head. Clean the head in solvent after the carbon has been removed.

CAUTION: *Do not use a caustic soda solution to clean aluminum parts. For valve lapping, consult "singles" cylinder head service.*

Cylinder Barrel and Piston Service

Measure the cylinder bore for wear in both the fore-and-aft and side-to-side directions, about ½ in. down from the top. If wear exceeds 0.005 in. or if scoring is evident, the cylinder may be bored to accept the 0.020 in. or 0.040 in. oversize pistons that are available. Whether or not the cylinder is to be bored, it should be honed so that the new rings will seat properly.

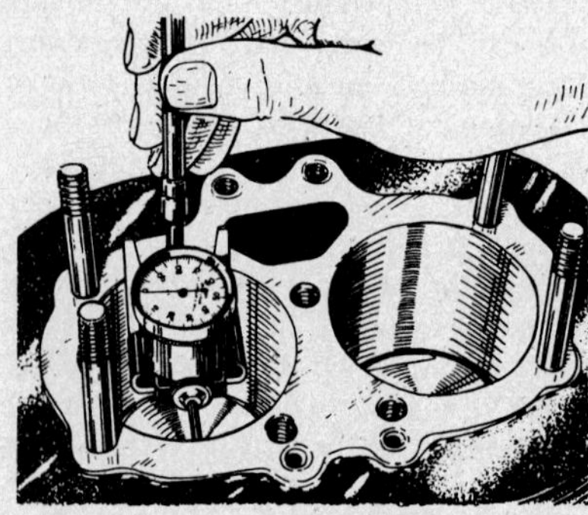

Measuring the cylinder bore

The pistons can be removed after the wrist pin circlips have been removed, the piston crowns heated with an electric iron, and the wrist pins pushed out. Mark the front of the pistons inside the skirt to facilitate correct reassembly. The wrist pin should be a tight push-fit in the connecting rod small end bushing. If clearance is excessive, the bushing should be replaced. When replacing a bushing, make sure that the hole in the bushing is lined up with the oil hole in the connecting rod. The new bushing must be reamed to 0.7503–0.7506 in. after installation.

Thoroughly but carefully remove all traces of carbon from the piston crown. Remove the old rings. Break one of the old rings and use the end of it to clean the carbon out of the piston ring grooves. Check the end gaps of the new rings by placing each one into the cylinder bore and measuring with a feeler gauge. End gap must not be less than 0.008 in. Carefully install the rings onto the pistons. Note that the lower compression ring on each piston is tapered, and the letter T must be facing up when the ring is installed.

Check that the tappets are free to move in the block and that there are not signs of scuffing on the tappet feet. To remove a tappet, drive it out of the block using a soft metal punch on the upper end. As soon as the circlip is released from its groove, the tappet can be removed from the lower end of its guide. If the tappets are damaged, the camshaft should be examined because it may be damaged in the same way. When reinstalling the tappets, install them in the same guides from which they were removed. Service tool no. 61-3702 will make circlip installation easier.

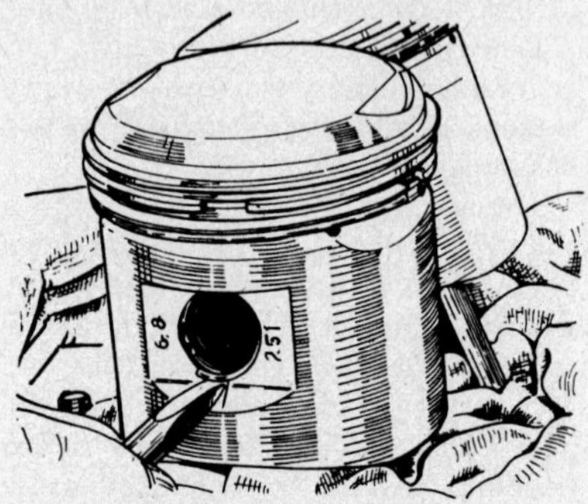

Removing the wrist pin circlip

Assembly

1. Warm the pistons and install them in the correct position on the connecting rods. Insert the wrist pins before the pistons have a chance to cool. install new circlips and make sure that they are seated properly.
2. Install a new cylinder base gasket and support the pistons with two blocks of wood about ½ in. square, as shown. Stagger the ring gaps 120° apart, liberally oil the rings, and install a ring compressor on each piston. If ring compressors are unavailable, it is possible to compress the rings by hand, one at a time, as the barrel is slipped over the pistons. Slide the barrel down over the pistons and remove the compressors and wood blocks. Install and tighten the cylinder base nuts evenly to 28–30 ft lb.
3. Install a new head gasket on top of the barrel. Loosen the intake rocker arm screws completely, and place the head in position on the cylinder barrel.
4. Install the head bolts and nuts. The shortest bolt is installed adjacent to the pushrod tunnel. Tighten the nuts and bolts evenly in the sequence shown, a turn at a time, until each is tightened to 31–33 ft lb.
5. Install the two short pushrods on the outer tappets at the bottom of the pushrod tunnel. Fit the cupped ends of the pushrods under the intake rocker arm ball pins.
6. Assemble the exhaust rocker components and install the two remaining pushrods under the exhaust rocker arms. Apply a pressure oil can to the rocker oil line junction to fill the passages with oil, and connect the line.

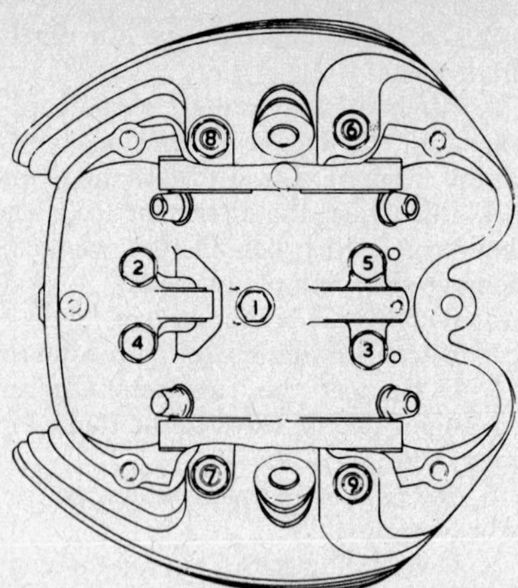

Cylinder head tightening sequence

7. Reinstall the exhaust system, cylinder head steady, and carburetor(s) as removed.
8. Check and adjust valve clearances, ignition timing, carburetor adjustments, and so on. Allow the new components a few hundred miles of gentle running to break in properly.

CLUTCH AND PRIMARY DRIVE

Clutch Service

DISASSEMBLY

1. Remove the left footpeg and the brake pedal.
2. Drain the primary chaincase and remove the case retaining screws. Tap the case with a rubber mallet to break the gasket seal and remove it. Note the positions of the different screw lengths to facilitate installation.
3. Unscrew the three clutch spring retaining nuts.
4. Withdraw the springs and cups, and then take out the pressure plate, friction disc, and plates. If these are the only components that will require attention, the clutch need not be disassembled further.
5. Place a block of wood between the primary sprocket and chain to keep the

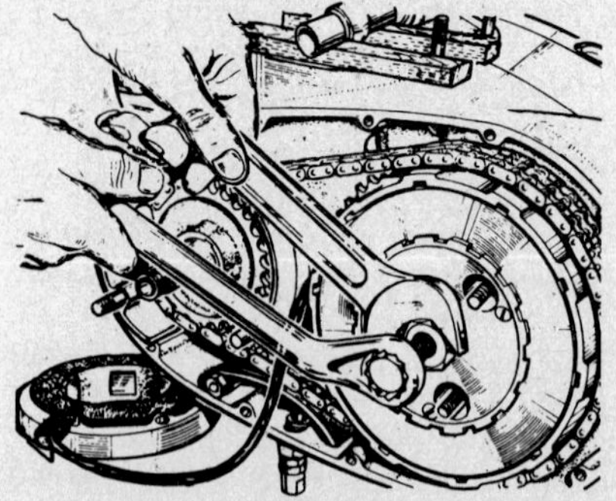

Removing the clutch hub

engine from turning, and unscrew the clutch center nut. Withdraw the spacer, hub, and release pushrod. Removal of the hub will be made easier with service tool 61-3766 or a suitably sized bolt.

INSPECTION

1. The clutch discs should appear to be in good condition. If the thickness of the discs measures less than 0.11 in., they should be replaced.

2. Check that the tabs at the outer edge of the discs are not worn or rounded and that the sprocket slots are not damaged. If there are burrs on the tabs the discs must be replaced.

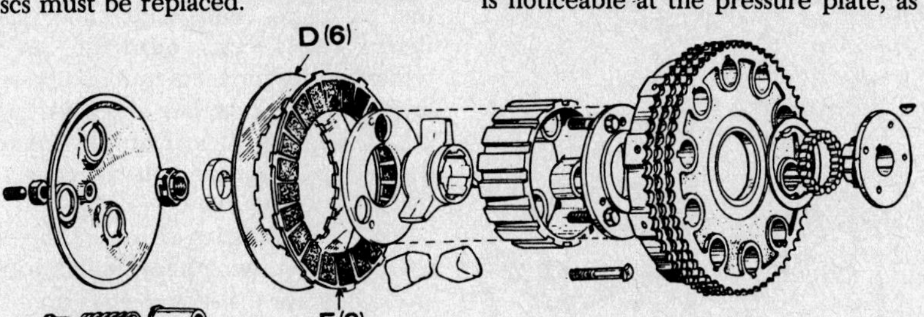

Exploded view of the clutch assembly, showing only one disc and plate (E and D), of which there are normally six

3. Place the clutch plates on a flat surface such as a plate of glass. If they can be rocked from side to side or evidence any buckling they should be replaced. Also replace them if they are scored.

4. If the damper rubbers are to be inspeced, the riveted ends of the three hub retaining bolts will have to be drilled or machined away. (On earlier models it is only necessary to remove the three screws and pry off the retaining plate.) Check the damper rubbers for damage or deterioration, and replace as necessary.

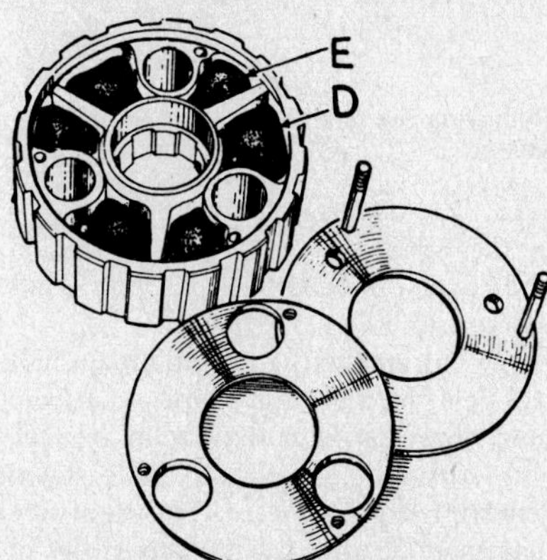

Clutch hub damper rubbers (D and E)

5. If difficulty is experienced when installing the damper rubbers into the hub, lubricate them with soap or any other lubricant that does not deteriorate rubber. Do not use oil or grease. Use new bolts with reassembling the hub on later models, and rivet the ends as originally found. Use thread lock compound to secure the three screws on earlier models

ASSEMBLY

1. Install the clutch hub and tighten the center nut to 60–65 ft lb. Note that the spacer should be installed with the chamfered edge outward.

2. Install the clutch discs and plates, alternatively, into the clutch housing, beginning with a disc. Install the release pushrod into the mainshaft.

3. Install the pressure plate assembly including the springs, spring cups, and nuts. Tighten the nuts evenly. Pull the clutch lever in and kick the engine over while observing the clutch. If any wobble is noticeable at the pressure plate, as it turns, tighten or loosen the springs as necessary until it runs true.

4. Loosen the clutch adjuster locknut and turn the adjuster screw in until the pressure plate begins to lift, indicated by a slight increase in turning resistance. When this point is reached, back the adjuster screw out ¾ turn and tighten the locknut.

5. Adjust cable play at the hand lever so that about ⅛ in. free-play remains at the end of the lever. Operate the clutch lever, taking note of the amount of pressure required. If operating pressure is obviously too great or too small, loosen or tighten the three clutch spring nuts evenly until lever pressure feels right. Then repeat steps 3 and 4, and readjust cable play at the lever.

6. Clean the crankcase and primary cover mating surfaces, apply a thin coat of gasket cement, and mount the cover using a new gasket. Tighten the retaining screws evenly.

7. Refill the primary chaincase with the correct amount and grade of oil, and install the footpeg and brake pedal.

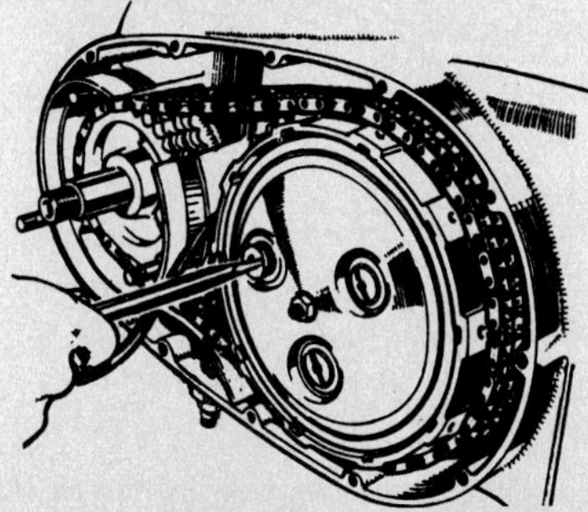

Adjusting the clutch springs

Primary Drive Service

DISASSEMBLY

1. Remove the clutch assembly as described in the preceding section.

2. The alternator must be removed from the end of the crankshaft before the primary drive assembly can be withdrawn. First bend back the locktab on the rotor retaining nut, lock the crankshaft in position by placing a wood block between the primary chain and sprocket, and unscrew the nut from the end of the crankshaft.

3. Remove the self-locking nuts that secure the stator, and pull the stator off its studs. Note that the leads are clipped to the housing and pass through a grommet at the back of the case. They must be replaced exactly as found upon reassembly.

4. Pull the rotor off the crankshaft and remove the woodruff key from the shaft.

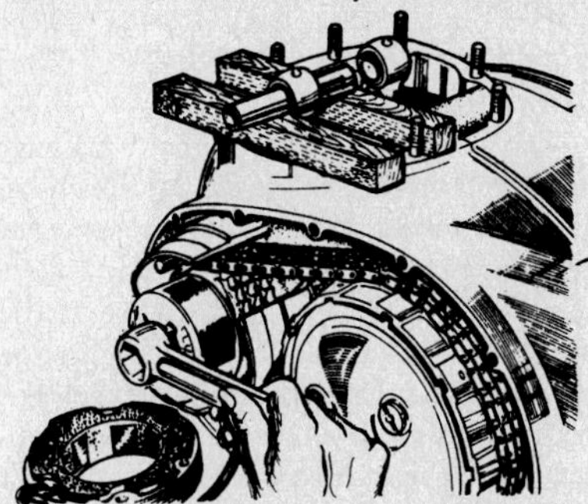

Removing the alternator rotor

5. The primary drive chain and sprocket assembly can be removed as a unit after the chain tensioner is loosened. If necessary, the large sprocket can be broken loose from the transmission mainshaft using service tool no. 61-3676 or a gear puller.

INSPECTION

Sprockets should be replaced if the teeth are rounded or hooked, or if the teeth are worn on the side. To check the rear roller bearing play, temporarily assemble the sprocket, clutch hub, and bearing rollers on the shaft. The bearing is allowed a slight amount of free-play, but if excessive the rollers should be replaced.

Transmission Countershaft Sprocket and Oil Seal

To examine or remove the countershaft final drive sprocket, first remove the six screws that secure the circular plate surrounding the shaft. Pry the plate loose and remove it with its oil seal, taking note of the felt washer that protects the seal from dirt and grit. Check for oil leakage at the back of the plate and replace the seal if necessary. Install the oil seal with the lip facing the countershaft sprocket. If the bushing that the seal rides on is worn, then it too must be replaced, as it would quickly ruin a new seal.

If the sprocket teeth are hooked or if the sprocket is damaged it should be replaced (along with the drive chain and rear wheel sprocket if it too is worn). To remove the sprocket, bend back the locktab, apply the rear brake, and unscrew the retaining nut. Disconnect the drive chain and pull the sprocket off the shaft. Examine the countershaft oil seal at this time. If it shows signs of leakage, remove the circlip (if fitted), pry out the oil seal, and replace it with a new one. Coat the new seal with oil to facilitate installation. Examine the sprocket boss for wear, which may have been causing the seal to leak. Lightly oil the boss when installing the sprocket to avoid damaging the seal, and tighten the sprocket retaining nut to 100 ft lb. Make sure that the gasket between the round plate and case is in good condition, and use a new felt washer behind the oil seal.

Primary Drive Sprocket Alignment

Temporarily install the primary sprockets on the shafts without the chain. Do not forget the crankshaft sprocket spacer. The rear sprocket bearing rollers can be held in place with grease as the sprocket is installed. Place a straightedge against the sprocket sides near the centerline. If the sprockets are aligned properly the straightedge will make contact at three points. Shims of different thicknesses are available for installation behind the crankshaft sprocket to correct misalignment.

ASSEMBLY

Assemble the primary drive components in reverse order of disassembly. Note the following points:

1. Tighten the self-locking alternator stator nuts to 15 ft lb.
2. Tighten the alternator rotor nut to 60 ft lb.
3. Make sure that the stator leads are correctly routed through the case, and seal the grommet with gasket cement.
4. Check that the gap between the stator poles and the rotor is not less than 0.008 in. If necessary, the stator mounting studs can be slightly repositioned to achieve this.
5. Adjust the primary chain tensioner until total movement on the top run of the chain is ⅛–¼ in., and secure it with the locknut and capnut.

TRANSMISSION AND SHIFTER MECHANISM SERVICE

Disassembly

1. Drain the oil from the primary chaincase.
2. Remove the clutch primary drive assembly, and countershaft sprocket as described in the preceding sections.

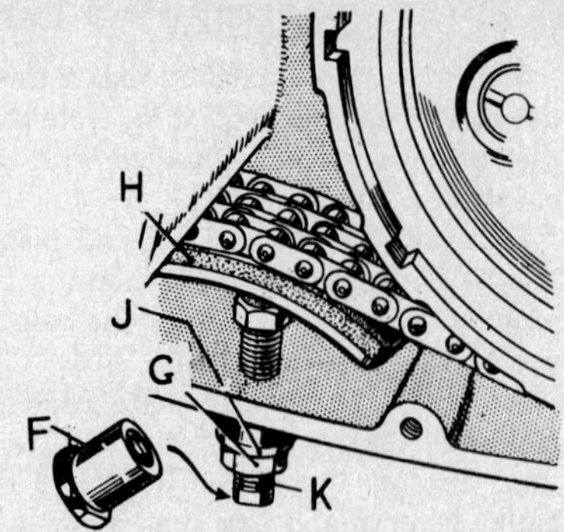

Primary chain tensioner guide (H), washer (J), adjuster bolt (K), locknut (G), and cap (F)

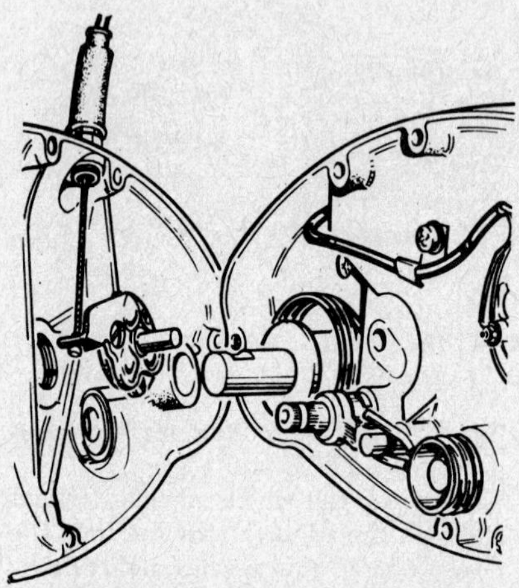

Removing the right-side outer cover

3. Remove the shift lever, kick-start lever, and footpeg. Take out the screws and remove the right-side outer crankcase cover.
4. Remove the contact breaker plate assembly and the tachometer drive. Take out the center bolt and free the ignition advance unit from its taper by screwing in a bolt that fits the threads on the inside of the cam and using it as a puller. Take out the screws and remove the right-side inner cover.
5. Unscrew the five nuts that secure the transmission end cover, and break the cover gasket seal with a rubber hammer.
6. Withdraw the cover complete with gear cluster and shifter mechanism.

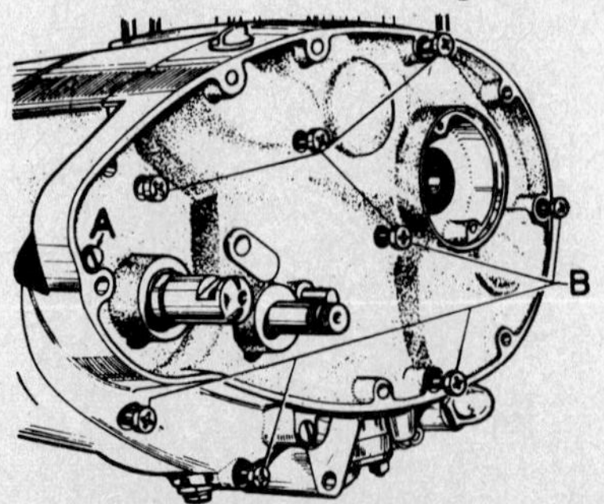

Inner cover securing screws (B). Screw (A) does not need to be removed

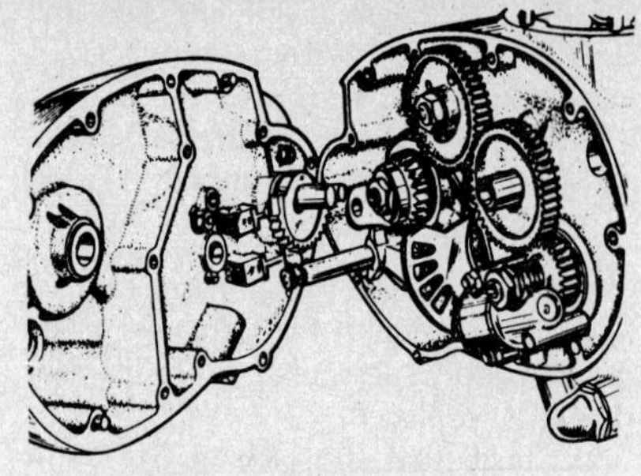

Removing the inner cover

7. Take out the pivot pin and remove the camplate, shift forks, and shaft. Before the selector quadrant can be removed, the plungers must be pressed in to clear the camplate windows.
8. Bend back the locktab and unscrew the kick-start ratchet nut. Remove the ratchet assembly.
9. Drive the mainshaft out of the end cover bearing, using a soft metal drift.
10. Remove the sliding gears from the mainshaft and countershaft. If the two remaining gears on each shaft must be removed for replacement, a hydraulic press must be used to press the shaft out of both gears at the same time. Note that there is a thrust washer installed between the larger gear and the splines.

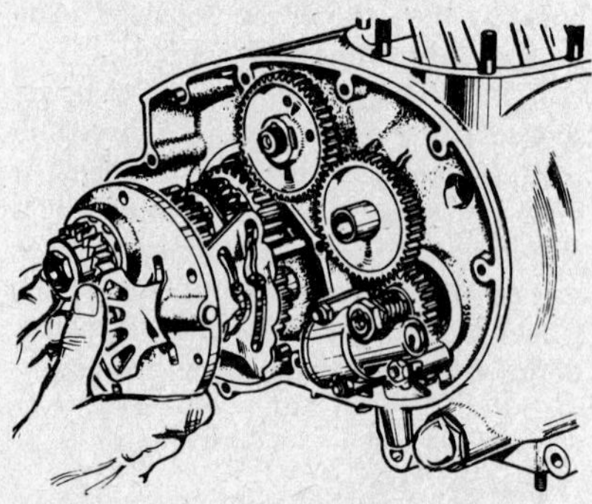

Removing the gear cluster and shift mechanism

11. The countershaft needle bearings in the crankcase and the transmission end cover can be driven out with a soft metal drift.
12. To remove the left-side mainshaft ball bearing, drive the bearing out from inside the case after the circlip, oil seal, and mainshaft top gear have been removed from the case. The right-side mainshaft bearing can be driven out of the end cover after the circlip has been removed.

Inspection

Examine all components for wear and damage. Look for worn camplate tracks, weak springs, sloppy bearings, and worn bushings. Inspect the gear teeth for pitting on the thrust faces and check the dogs for rounding off and breakage. Clearance between the camplate tracks and shift forks should not greatly exceed

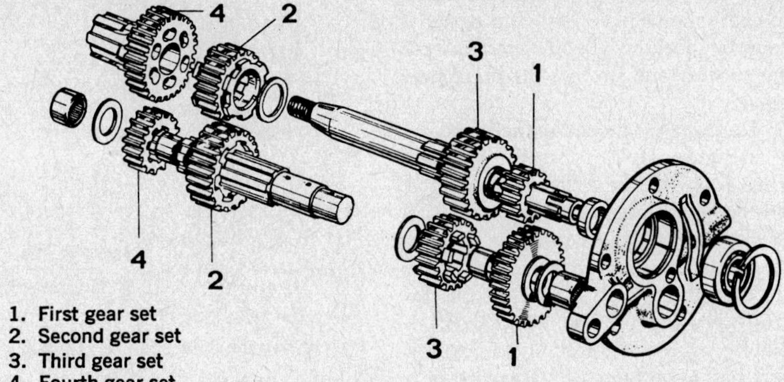

Exploded view of the gear cluster. The upper shaft is the mainshaft, the lower is the countershaft

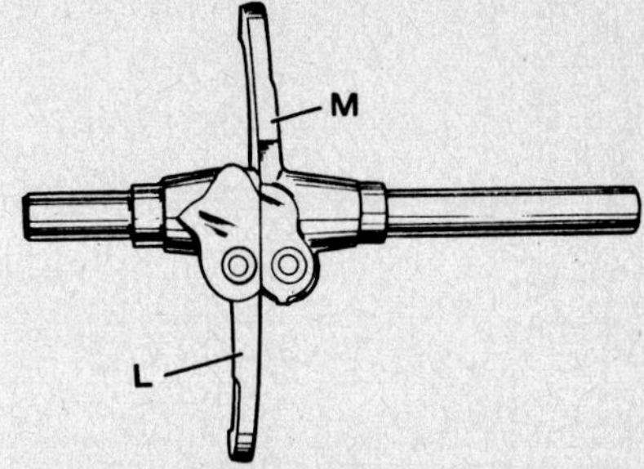

The shift forks assembled onto the shaft. The mainshaft fork (M) and the countershaft fork (L) must be positioned as shown

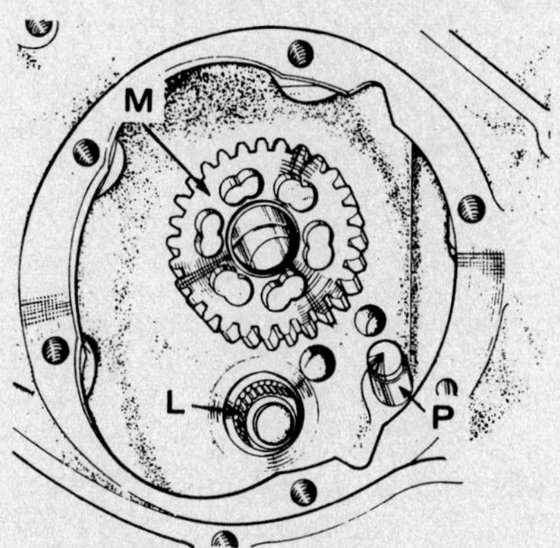

Countershaft needle bearing in the crankcase (L), mainshaft fourth gear (M), and camplate plunger (P)

0.008 in. Check that the camplate windows and notches are not worn or scored. The camplate plunger in the left side of the crankcase should be able to move freely in its housing. The shift quadrant plungers should also move freely and must not be chipped or worn.

If it is necessary to replace any bushings in the aluminum cases, heat the case before pressing a bushing out and then install a new one while the case is still hot. When replacing any oil seals, make sure in all cases that the lip of the seal faces in toward the source of the oil.

Assembly

1. Clean all mating surfaces of pieces of old gasket and gasket cement.

2. Install the sliding gears on the mainshaft, followed by the small spacer. Install the mainshaft in the bearing through the end cover, and install the kick-start ratchet components on the end of the shaft. Tighten the nut to 55–60 ft lb, and secure it with the locktab. Mainshaft end-float is automatically taken up by the starter ratchet assembly.

3. To check countershaft end-float, temporarily assemble the countershaft, complete with sliding gears and thrust washers into the gearbox and install the cover plate. End-float should be just perceptible. If excessive, thrust washers of different thicknesses are available for end float adjustment. Installation of a different size thrust washer must be made at the left (sprocket) end only.

4. After end-float has been checked, assemble the gear cluster onto the end cover. Place one of the standard thrust washers on the inside face of the cover and install the countershaft first gear on the shaft with the plain face against the washer. The sliding gear must be installed on the shaft with the oil hole aligned with a corresponding hole in the shaft.

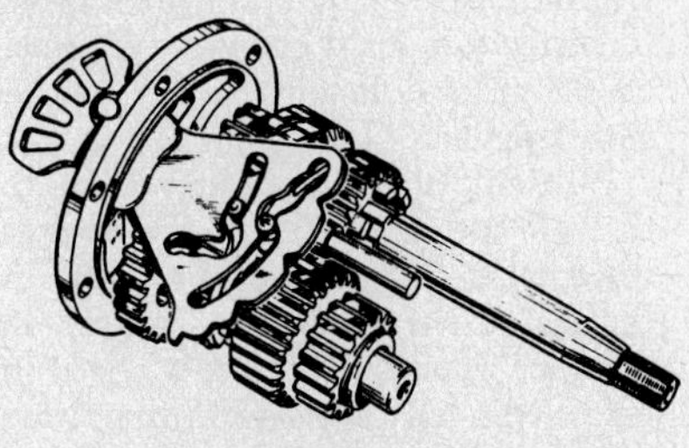

Gear cluster assembled

5. Assemble the shift forks on the shaft as shown in the illustration. Engage the countershaft fork with the countershaft third (sliding) gear, and engage the mainshaft fork with the mainshaft sliding gear.

6. Insert the camplate through the slot in the cover plate, with the long end of the outer track at the bottom, and adjust the positions of the sliding gears until the shift fork rollers engage the tracks in the camplate. Fully insert the shift fork shaft at this point, and install the camplate pivot pin.

7. Install the mainshaft top gear through the mainshaft ball bearing (if this has not already been done), and install the circlip and oil seal.

8. Check that the camplate plunger and spring are in position in the left crankcase, and adjust the camplate and shift forks to the position shown in the illustration. The transmission is now in neutral. Install the remaining thrust washer on the left (drive) end of the countershaft, and install the assembled gear cluster and shifter mechanism unit into the case. Rotate the shafts gently and when the cover plate is seated, install the washers and nuts. Tighten the nuts to 18–20 ft lb. Do not use force in an effort to persuade the cover to seat properly.

9. Insert the selector quadrant shaft into its bearing in the cover plate and engage the plungers in the camplate windows using a thin strip of metal, as shown. Fit the small end of the kick-start half-gear into the bushing in the cover plate, and install the inner cover. Loosely install the ignition advance unit and contact breaker plate. Check that the gasket and O-ring are in good condition, and install the tachometer drive. Make sure that the tachometer drive shaft engages the slot in the oil pump shaft.

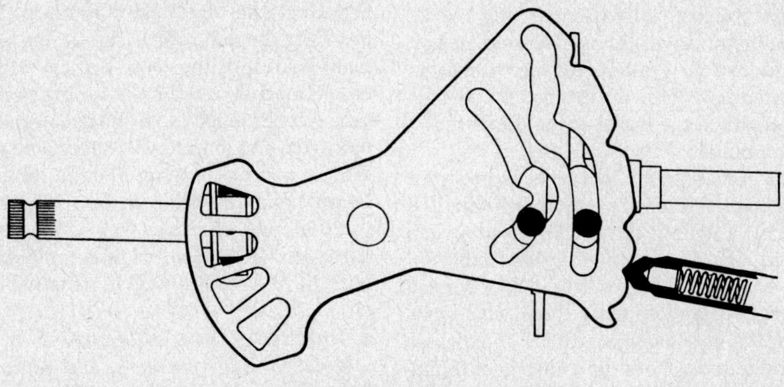

Neutral position

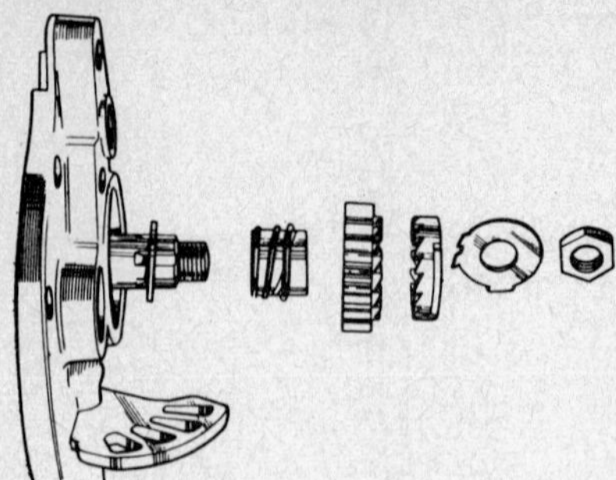

Kick-start ratchet components

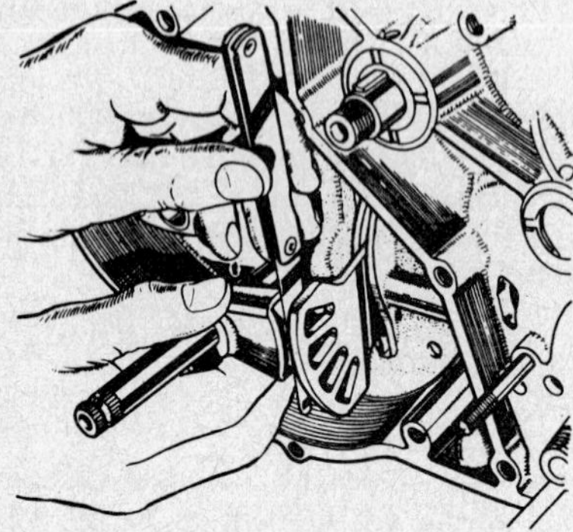

Installing the selector quadrant

10. Install the right-side outer cover, shift lever, kick-start lever, and footpeg. Assemble the clutch and primary drive as described in preceding sections.

BOTTOM END OVERHAUL

Disassembly

1. Remove the engine from the frame.
2. Remove the cylinder head, barrel, and pistons as described in the top end overhaul section.
3. Remove the clutch and primary drive assemblies as described in preceding sections.
4. Remove the shift lever and kick-start lever. Take out the screws and remove the right (timing side) outer crankcase cover. The kick-start return spring, shift lever return spring, and clutch release assemblies will be removed along with the outer cover, and need not be disturbed. Remove the contact breaker plate assembly and the tachometer drive. Take out the center bolt and free the ignition advance unit from its taper by screwing in a bolt that fits the threads on the inside of the cam, using it as a puller.
5. Unscrew the two bolts and remove the tachometer drive unit, including the shaft. Take out the phillips head screws and remove the inner crankcase cover.
6. Install the wrist pins in the connecting rods and support them with wood blocks, as shown. Bend back the locktab and unscrew both the timing gear retaining nut and the worm behind it on the end of the crankshaft. Note that these two components have left-hand threads. The wood blocks will keep the crankshaft from turning and protect the crankcase flange.
7. Unscrew the three nuts and remove the oil pump. Do not lose the ball and spring that will be released from the delivery oil passage in the crankcase when the pump is removed.
8. Before removing the timing gears, note the position of the marks on the gears, as shown in the illustration, to facilitate correct reassembly. Lock the crankshaft in position using the wrist pins and wood blocks as before, bend back the locktab, and unscrew the camshaft timing gear nut. Remove the gear, using service tool no. 61-3676 or any suitable gear puller. Remove the woodruff key from the shaft. The idler gear can be removed from the case without the use of a puller. Pull off the small crankshaft timing gear with an appropriate gear puller.
9. Unscrew the four nuts and remove the crankcase sump oil filter. Remove the crankcase securing nuts and bolts, A, B, and C, as shown in the illustration, and remove the nut at the bridge across the mouth of the crankcase. Remove any woodruff keys still remaining in the shafts, noting their locations. Separate the crankcase halves by tapping them with a rubber hammer. The inner race of the drive side main bearing will remain on the crankshaft and can be removed with a puller.
10. Remove the camshaft from the case. On later models, the timed breather valve and spring may come out with the camshaft. The stationary half of the breather valve is located by a peg at the base of the left camshaft bearing, which must be removed to gain access to that part of the valve. Finally, mark the connecting rods and caps so that they can be replaced on their original journals, unbolt the caps, and remove the rods. The bolts must also be replaced exactly as removed.

Main Bearings

If the drive side roller bearing is excessively sloppy, simply install a new bearing. Heat the case before removing or installing the outer race. The timing side plain bearing is the more critical of the two. If journal wear on the timing (right) side exceeds 0.002 in., or if the journal is damaged, the journal will have to be reground and an undersize bearing fitted. Bearings are available in 0.010 in. and 0.020 in. undersizes, as well as the standard size. If the journal is reground, it must have a 0.050–0.060 in. face radius.

Connecting Rod Bearings

Measure crankpin wear, and regrind the crankpins if wear exceeds 0.002 in. or

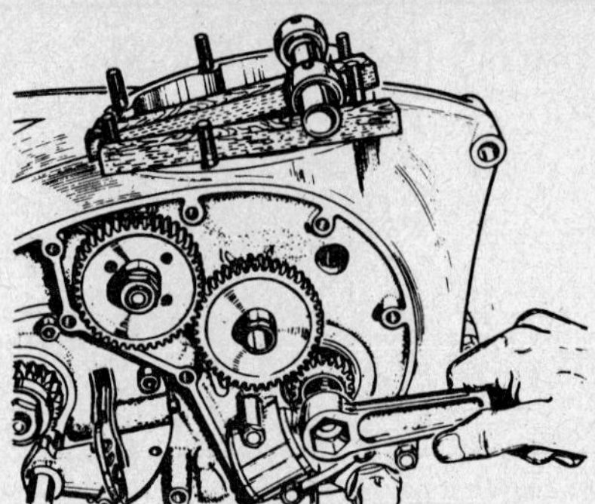

Unscrewing the crankshaft timing gear nut

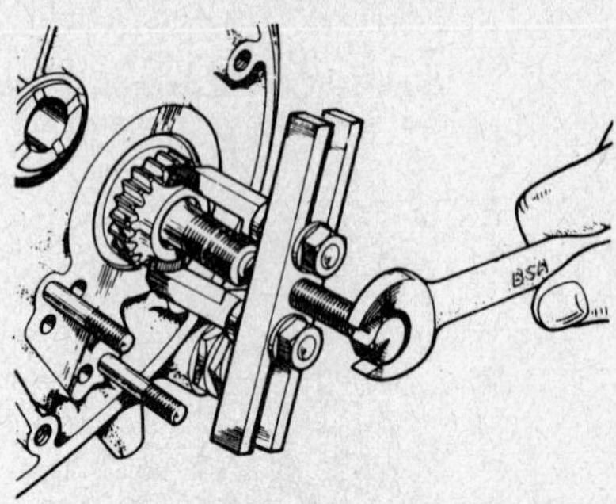

Removing the crankshaft timing gear

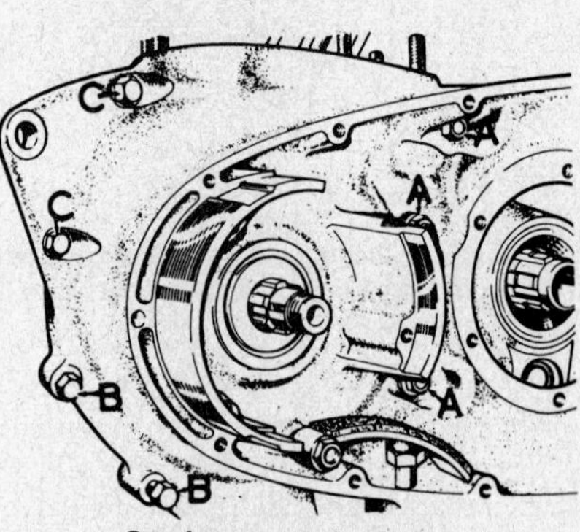

Crankcase securing bolts

if the crankpins are damaged. Bearings are available in 0.010, 0.020, and 0.030 in. undersizes, as well as the standard size. If the crankpins are reground they must have a 0.115–0.120 in. face radius.

Crankshaft Oil Filter and Flywheel

If the crankshaft is to be reground, the flywheel should be removed. Simply unscrew the bolts and slip the flywheel off. It would be a good idea at this time to clean the sludge trap in the crankshaft, which is retained by a plug at the end of the crankshaft and located by one of the flywheel retaining bolts. Clean the filter and crankshaft passage with solvent and dry with compressed air.

When reinstalling the filter, first locate it with the flywheel bolt and then install the plug. Both the plug and the flywheel bolts should be coated with a thread locking compound. The plug should be staked with a punch to keep it from loosening, and the flywheel bolts tightened to 45 ft lb with a torque wrench.

The crankshaft assembly is accurately balanced at the factory and should never need rebalancing. In any case, balancing requires special tools and experience, and should be left to a qualified specialist.

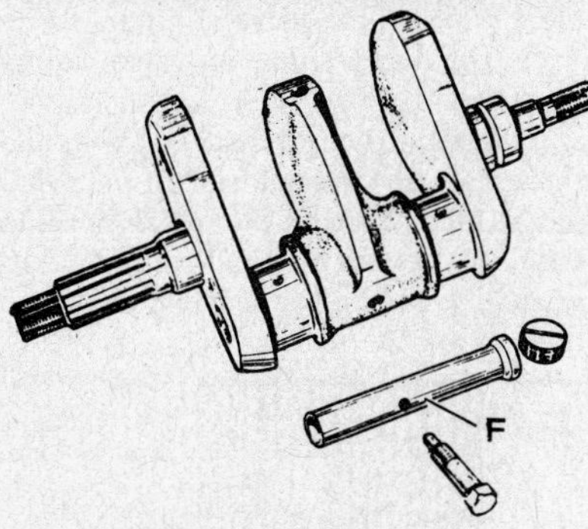

Crankcase sludge trap (F)

Connecting Rods

Bolt the rods and caps together without the bearings and measure the diameter of the bearing seat in perpendicular directions. If ovality exceeds 0.0004 in., the rod and cap should be replaced.

Camshaft

Examine the cam lobes for signs of wear and scoring. Check camshaft dimensions against those given in the specifications section. If damage is visible, the camshaft should be replaced and the tappets carefully checked for the same damage. If the cam bearings are to be replaced, the leftside bearing can be removed after the case has been heated. The new bearings must be line-reamed with the cases assembled to the dimensions given in the specifications at the end of the section.

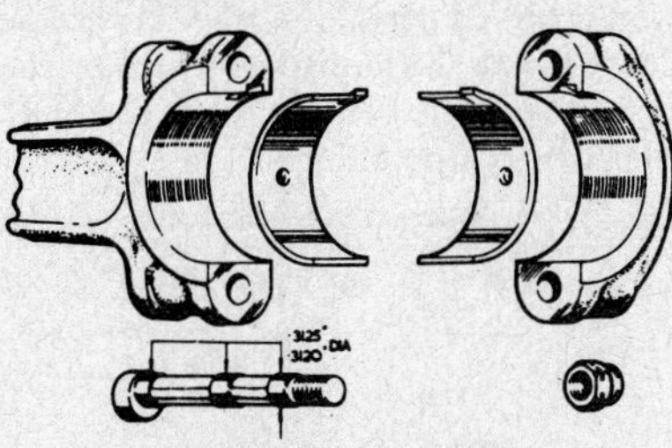

Connecting rod assembly

Assembly

NOTE: *Whenever you replace any oil seals, lubricate the seal before installation and always install the seal with the lip facing in, toward the source of the oil. In addition, make sure that the surface that the lip rides on is not worn, or the new seal will quickly be ruined.*

1. Clean all oil passages and make sure that the oil pump check valve at the base of the crankcase is clean and seating properly.

2. Install the rod bearing shells in the rods and caps and lubricate them thoroughly. Assemble the rods onto their original journals, making sure that the marks on the rod and cap correspond, and that the marks are facing in the same direction as when removed. The rod with the small lubricating hole on each side of the web must be assembled on the left side, as shown. Use new self-locking nuts on the rod bolts, and tighten to 22 ft lb.

3. Crankshaft end-float must not exceed 0.003 in. However, end-float does not have to be measured if the original crankshaft and crankcases are used. Simply use the same shims between the crankshaft weight and roller (main) bearing that were removed during disassembly. Otherwise, the crankcases will have to be bolted together with the crankshaft installed and end-float measured. Minimum allowable end-float is 0.0015 in.

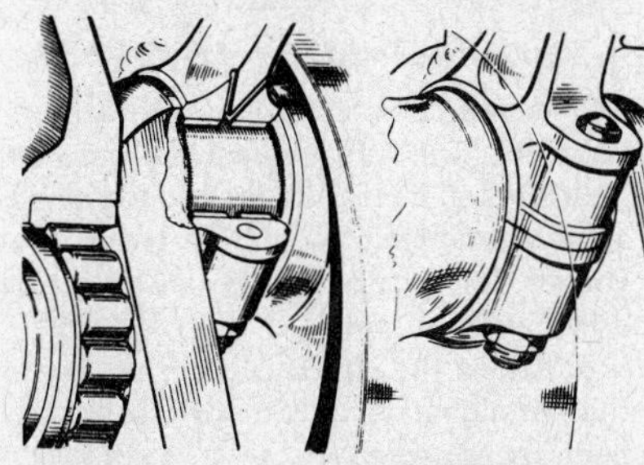

Connecting rods correctly positioned on the crankshaft

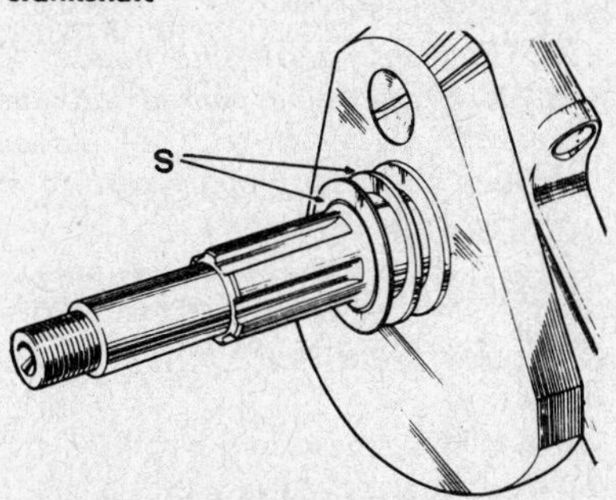

Crankshaft shims

4. Carefully clean the crankcase mating surfaces.

5. Install the crankshaft into the left-side crankcase, making sure that the thrust washers have been placed on the end of the crankshaft. Check that the bearing has entered the outer race and is seated properly.

6. Insert the breather valve disc into the cam bearing with the drive tongues facing toward the inside of the case. Install the spring and then the camshaft, engaging the drive slots in the camshaft with the tongues on the valve.

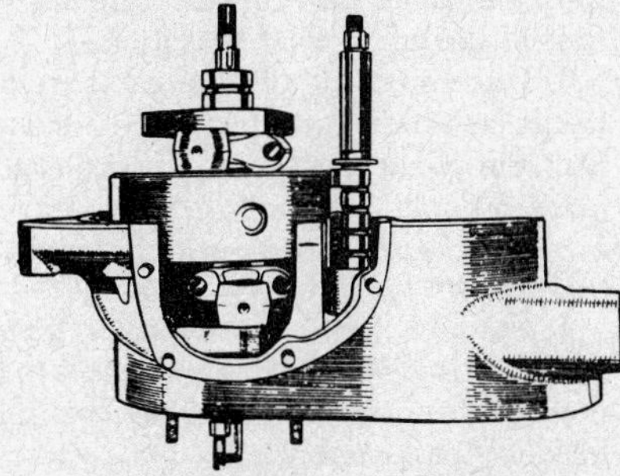

Left-side crankcase assembly

7. Replace the thrust washer in position on the crankshaft, with the oil grooves next to the crank web. Apply a thin coat of gasket cement to the crankcase mating surfaces, lubricate the timing side main bearing, and fit the cases together. Install and tighten the nuts and bolts evenly. Check that the crankshaft and camshaft are able to rotate freely. If not, alignment is incorrect and the cases should be taken apart again and the cause investigated.

NOTE: *Camshaft end-float will automatically be taken up when the gear is fitted.*

8. Install the crankcase oil filter using new gaskets.

9. Fit the woodruff key in the right side of the crankshaft, and install the small timing gear with the mark out. Install the crankshaft spacer, the oil pump (with ball and spring), and the oil pump worm gear (which has a left-hand thread). Install the locktab and tighten the retaining nut (which also has a left-hand thread) on the end of the crankshaft to 35 ft lb. Secure the nut with the locktab.

10. Fit the woodruff key in the camshaft, install the timing gear with the mark facing out, install the locktab, and tighten the nut. Secure the nut with the locktab. Install the timing idler gear so that its marks align with the marks on the camshaft and crankshaft gears.

11. Clean the mating surfaces and install the inner cover over the timing gears, using a new gasket. Make sure that the O-ring and gasket are in good condition, and install the tachometer drive unit. Make sure that the tachometer drive shaft engages with the drive slot in the oil pump shaft.

Timing marks

12. Loosely install the ignition advance unit and contact breaker plate, leaving ignition timing adjustment until after the engine is installed in the frame. Install the outer timing side crankcase cover.

13. Install the clutch and primary drive assemblies.

14. Install the pistons, barrel and cylinder head as described in the top end overhaul section.

15. Install the engine in the frame and perform a complete tune-up. Allow the

engine a few hundred miles of gentle running to break in properly, and check valve adjustment and ignition timing after about 500 miles have been covered.

Rocket 3

REMOVAL AND INSTALLATION

1. Remove the fuel tank.
2. Drain the oil tank and crankcase. Remove the oil cooler. Drain the transmission and primary chaincase.
3. Disconnect the rocker box oil lines, then disconnect the oil supply lines from underneath the rear of the crankcase.
4. Remove the carburetors and exhaust header pipes.
5. Unbolt and remove the right-side footpeg.
6. Unscrew the retaining bolt at the front of the chainguard, remove the lower left-side shock absorber mounting nut, and remove the chainguard.
7. Remove the master link and pull the drive chain off the countershaft sprocket.
8. Disconnect the alternator and contact breaker point leads at their connectors. Remove the spark plugs.
9. Turn the cable adjuster at the clutch lever all the way in until the cable is completely slack. Take out the four-clutch inspection cover retaining screws and disconnect the clutch cable from the release lever.
10. Disconnect the tachometer cable from the tachometer drive at the front of the crankcase.
11. Pull the engine breather tube off at the rear of the inner primary chaincase.
12. Unscrew the pinch-bolt and pull the brake pedal off its shaft.
13. Unscrew the nut from the kick-start lever shaft and drive out the locating pin by tapping on the end of the threads with a small hammer. Remove the kick-start lever.
14. Unscrew the five bolts and nuts from the right-side rear engine mount plate. Unscrew the swing arm shaft nut and remove the plate. It is not necessary to remove the left mount plate.
15. Unscrew the nut from the long engine mount bolt underneath the crankcase and drive the bolt out. Note the position of the spacer between the crankcase and frame lug before removing the bolt.
16. Support the engine and remove the engine mount bolt at the front frame downtube. Raise the engine slightly and remove it from the left side of the frame.

Installation is in reverse order of removal. The following points should be noted:

1. Be sure to reinstall the engine mount spacers and washers in their original positions.

Lifting the engine out of the frame

2. When connecting the oil lines underneath the crankcase, the smaller (delivery) oil line is attached to the small, straight junction pipe, and the larger (scavenge) line is attached to the stepped down junction pipe.
3. Adjust the clutch cable free-play at the handlebar lever after the cable has been reconnected.
4. Adjust the rear brake after the pedal has been installed.

NOTE: *Before starting the engine, ½ pt of oil should be poured into the crankcase. The oil can be added through the timing plug aperture in the right-side case.*

TOP END OVERHAUL

Cylinder Head and Barrel Removal

The cylinder head and barrel on the triple can be removed with the engine in the frame. The procedure is as follows:

1. Turn off the fuel taps and disconnect the lines. Remove the metal strip running down the center of the fuel tank (early models) or the rubber plug at the top of the tank (later models). Unscrew the retaining nut and remove the tank.
2. Loosen the oil line clamps at the oil cooler and pull the lines off their connector pipes. Mark the lines and pipes to facilitate correct reassembly. Do not unscrew the large hexagonal connectors from the cooler. Unbolt the oil cooler bracket from the frame and remove the cooler. Note that the bracket is insulated from the frame with rubber bushings to protect the cooler from vibration.
3. Disconnect the throttle cable from the linkage at the carburetors and disconnect the choke cable at the handlebar lever. Loosen the carburetor-to-intake manifold clamps and remove the carburetors as a unit.
4. Unscrew the exhaust header pipe nuts at the cylinder head. Disconnect the mufflers from the pipes and remove the header pipe assembly.
5. Unbolt and remove the top engine mount (cylinder head steady).
6. Unscrew the two acorn nuts that secure the rocker oil feedlines to the rocker shafts and tie the pipes out of the way. Remove the access covers and completely loosen the valve adjusters to relieve the head studs of valve spring pressure.
7. Remove the two small end bolts and three nuts (at the underside of the cylinder head) that secure the rocker boxes to the head. Loosen the head bolts and nuts gradually, in the sequence shown, and then lift off the rocker boxes.

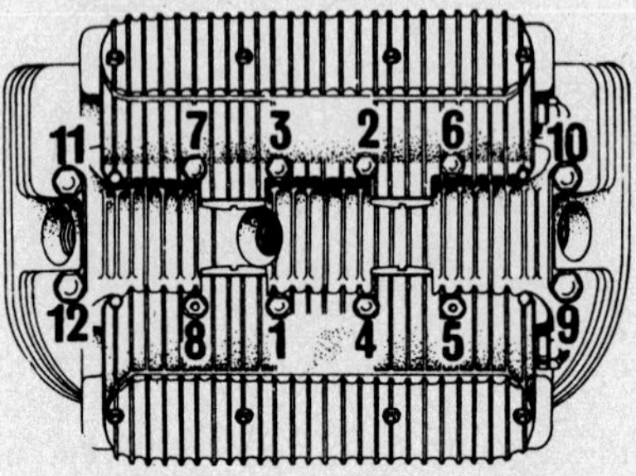

Cylinder head loosening sequence

8. Remove the spark plugs, unscrew the remaining cylinder head bolts, and lift the head carefully off the studs. Remove the pushrod tubes and pushrods.
9. To prevent the tappets from falling into the crankcase when removing the barrel, wrap electrical tape around the top of each tappet.
10. Loosen the cylinder barrel retaining nuts gradually, in the sequence shown, to prevent distortion. Lift the barrel carefully off the crankcase, taking care to support the pistons as they are exposed by the cylinders so that they won't be damaged on the crankcase flange. Mark the tappets so that they can be replaced in their original positions. This is very important.

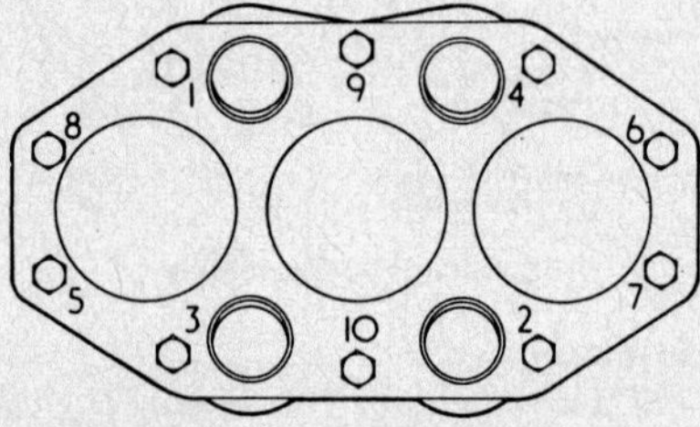

Cylinder barrel nut loosening and tightening sequence

Valve rocker assembly

Cylinder Head Service

VALVES

Using a suitable valve spring compressor, compress each spring and remove the split collar. Release the compressor and remove the springs and retainers.

Mark the valves so that they can be replaced in their original positions.

Valve guides can be driven out after the cylinder head has been heated in an oven or immersed in hot water. Install new guides while the head is still warm.

Valve seats can be recut if the seat is worn or if the seat area has become pocketed. Grind away the metal around the seat before recutting the seat if it has become pocketed. In any case, if valve guides have been replaced, the seats should be recut. Valve seat angle is 45°.

Remove carbon from the combustion chamber using a scraper or small, hand-held grinder. Be careful not to mar the soft metal of the cylinder head. Clean the head in solvent after the carbon has been removed.

CAUTION: *Do not use a caustic soda solution to clean aluminum parts.*

Whether the original or new valves are to be used, they should be lapped into their seats. Put three small dabs of grinding compound around the valve face and, using a grinding tool, rotate the valve back and forth. Do not use pressure. Rotate the valve to a new position every few seconds and continue grinding until a smooth, even finish is produced on the valve face and seat.

Before reassembling the valves, all traces of grinding compound and grit must be removed from the head and valves. Coat the valve stems with engine oil or assembly lube before installing. It would be wise to replace the valve springs with new ones at this time as a matter of course; however, if the spring free-length measures within 1/16 in. of the original specification (given at the end of the chapter), the springs may be reused. Assemble the springs and retainers as removed. When replacing the split collars, you will find that a small amount of grease will hold them in position as the spring compressor is removed. Make sure that the collar is correctly seated by tapping the valve stem with a small, soft hammer.

Cylinder Barrel and Piston Service

Examine the cylinder bores for scoring and measure the diameter in several places to determine wear. If wear exceeds 0.005 in. the cylinders should be rebored. Pistons are available in 0.010, 0.020, 0.030, and 0.040 in. oversizes.

NOTE: *The cylinder liners should protrude from the cylinders 0.002–0.007 in.*

The tappet guide blocks, pressed into the base flange of the cylinder, should not normally need replacement. If it does become necessary to replace them, the dowels must be drilled out and the cylinder heated before the guides can be pressed out. New dowels will have to be used together with the new guides.

Remove the wrist pin circlips and drive the wrist pins out of the pistons. In some cases it may be necessary to heat the pistons before the pin can be removed. Mark the piston inside the skirt so that it can be replaced in its original position. Carefully remove all traces of carbon from the piston crown. Remove the old rings, taking care not to damage the piston.

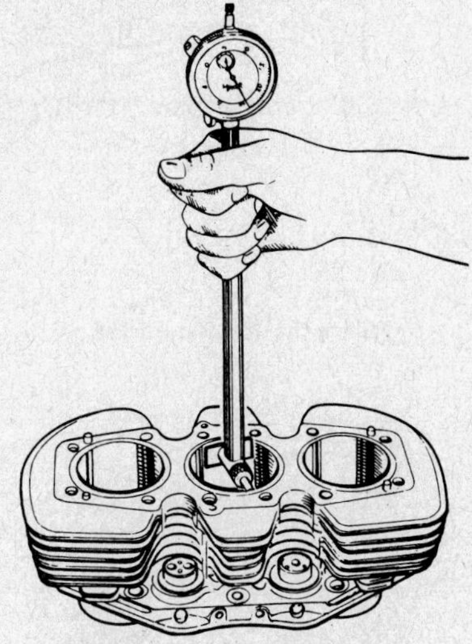

Measuring the cylinder bore

Break one of the old rings and use the end of it to clean the carbon out of the piston ring grooves. Check the end gaps of the new rings by placing each one into its bore and measuring with a feeler gauge. The ring gap should not be less than 0.009 in. or greater than 0.013 in. Note that the compression rings are tapered, and the word "top" must be installed facing up.

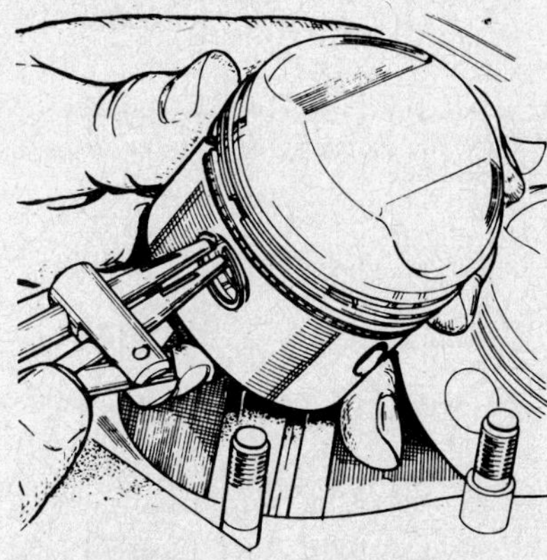

Removing a wrist pin circlip

Assembly

1. Warm the pistons and install them, in their original positions, on the connecting rods. Insert the wrist pins before the pistons have a chance to cool. Install new circlips and make sure that they are properly seated.

2. Install the tappets in their original positions. Wrap a piece of tape around the top of each tappet stem to prevent it

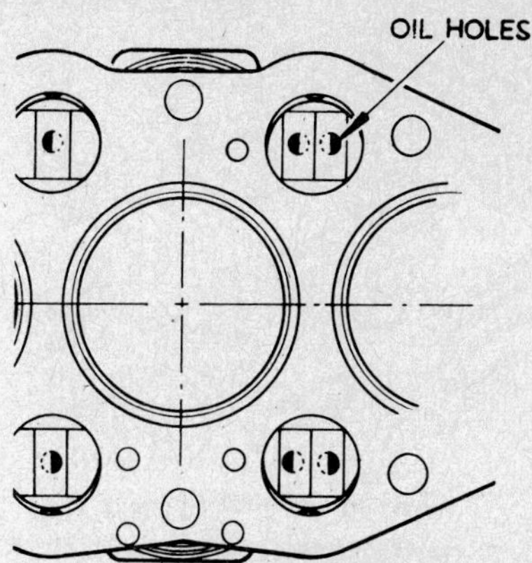

Tappet oil holes

from falling into the crankcase as the cylinder is installed. Make sure that the oil holes in the tappet stems line up with the oil holes in the guide blocks, as shown.

3. Install a new cylinder base gasket on the crankcase flange. Stagger the end gaps of the piston rings 120° apart and oil the rings liberally. Bring the center piston up to TDC and install a ring compressor. Slide the cylinder down over the piston. Raise the outside pistons up as far as possible without accidentally pulling the center piston out of its base. Install ring compressors on the outer pistons and seat the cylinder against the crankcase. Tighten the cylinder retaining nuts gradually, in the proper sequence, to 20–22 ft lb.

4. Remove the tape from the tappets and fit the pushrod tubes over the tappet guides. Make sure that the rubber seals at either end of the tubes are in good condition.

5. Install a new head gasket on the cylinder with the ribs facing down (toward the cylinder). Install the cylinder head carefully over the studs and onto the cylinder. Fit the four outer head bolts loosely. Insert the pushrods onto their tubes. Make sure that the pushrods line up evenly.

6. Install the rocker boxes on the head using new gaskets. Coat only one side of the gaskets with cement. Make sure that the pushrods are properly seated in the rocker arms.

7. Install the remaining eight cylinder head bolts and tighten all twelve nuts and bolts evenly, in the sequence shown, to 18 ft lb. Refit the remaining rocker box mounting bolts and nuts.

8. Reconnect the rocker oil lines using new copper washers. Install the top engine mount and exhaust header pipes.

9. Install the carburetors on the head and connect the throttle and choke cables. Bolt the oil cooler onto the frame, taking care to install the rubber bushings correctly, and connect the oil lines. Install the fuel tank.

10. Check and adjust valve clearances, ignition timing, carburetor, and so on.

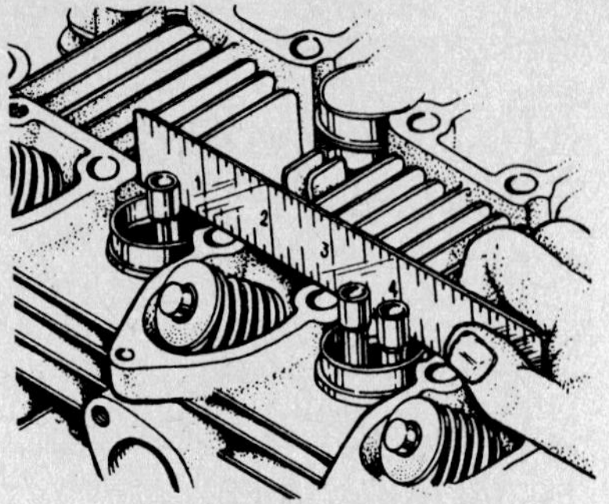

Checking pushrod alignment

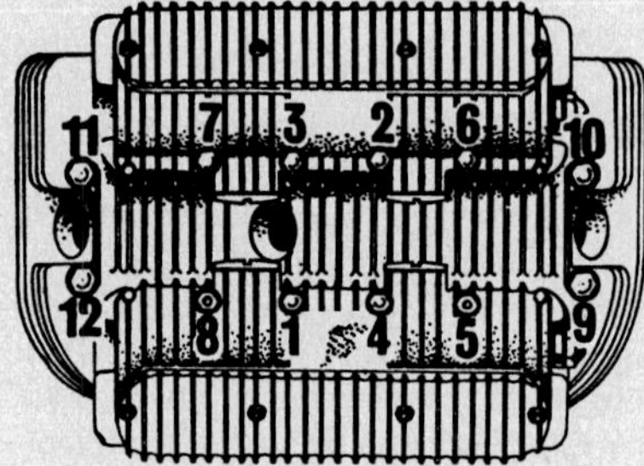

Cylinder head tightening sequence

CLUTCH AND PRIMARY DRIVE

Clutch Service

DISASSEMBLY

1. Drain the oil from the primary chaincase.

2. Take out the four screws and remove the clutch inspection cover. Unscrew the large locknut and the adjuster nut from the end of the clutch release rod.

3. Back off the primary chain adjuster, remove the 14 screws, and pull off the primary cover. Note that the screws are of different lengths; they must be replaced in their original positions.

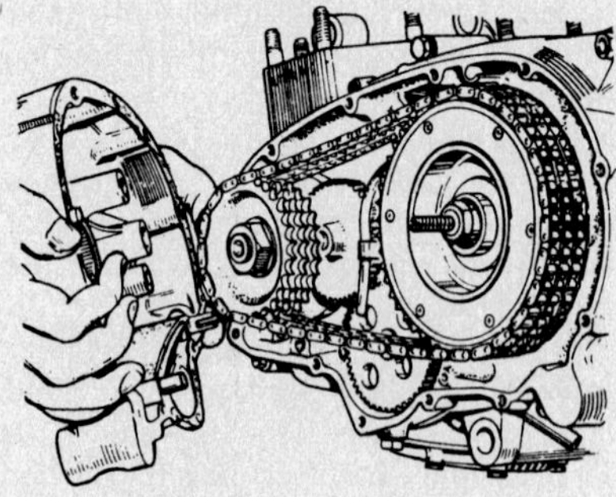

Removing the primary cover

4. Bend back the locktab, install oil seal protector 61–6051, and unscrew the engine sprocket retaining nut. Remove the transmission sprocket (clutch hub) retaining nut and pull both sprockets off together using suitable gear pullers.

5. To remove the inner crankcase (clutch) cover, first take out the screws and bolts that secure the cover, noting their positions to facilitate reassembly.

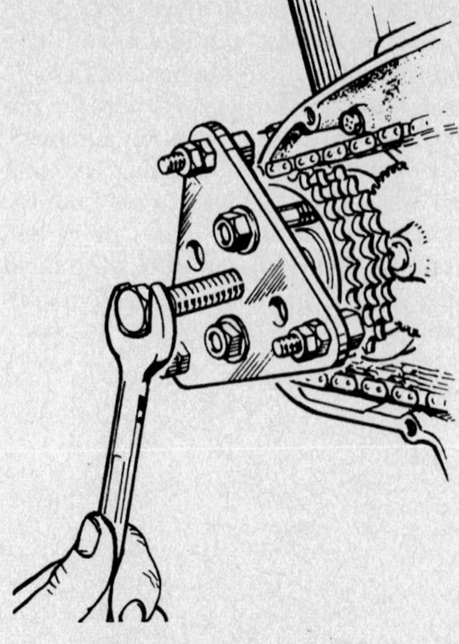

Pulling the engine sprocket

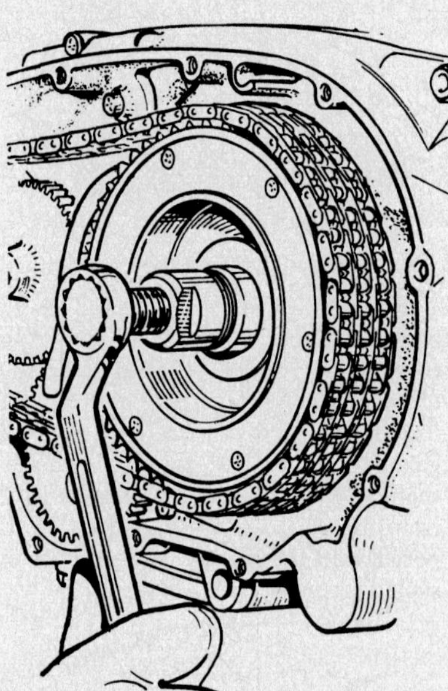

Pulling the clutch sprocket using extractor No. 60-1862

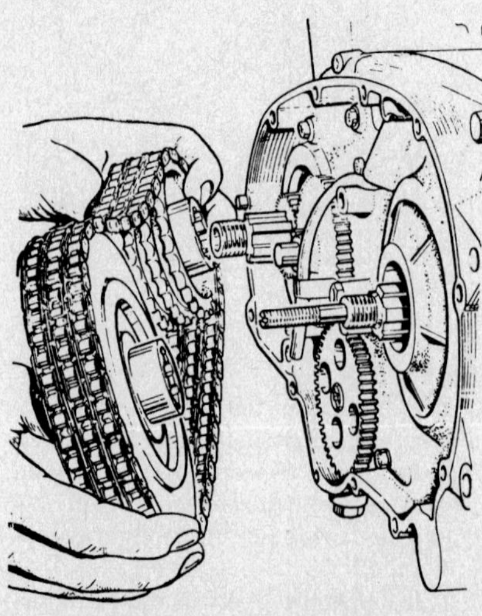

Removing the primary drive assembly

Pull off the inner cover, taking care not to damage or lose the oil pump O-rings.

6. Take off the spacer and pull the clutch unit off the shaft.

7. Mark the relative positions of the clutch cover, drive plate, and pressure plate. Bend back the locktabs on the 12 cover bolts and loosen the bolts gradually, a turn at a time, to prevent distortion of the cover.

8. Separate the clutch components, taking care not to lose the three dowel pins in the cover.

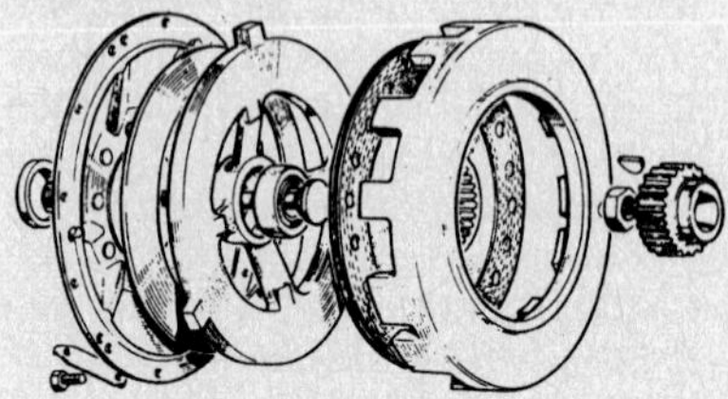

Exploded view of the clutch components

INSPECTION

The clutch unit is extremely simple in operation and construction. The disc is the only component that should require replacement. Examine the drive plate and pressure plate for cracks, scoring, and overheating (extreme blue discoloration). Check that the drive plate slots and pressure plate tabs are not broken or excessively worn. The diaphragm spring may be reused unless it shows signs of being overheated, in which case it may have been weakened. If the bearing is worn and/or the oil seal damaged, replace both components.

ASSEMBLY

1. Apply a small amount of high temperature grease to the sides of the three pressure plate tabs and assemble the pressure plate, disc, and drive plate (aligning the positioning marks).

2. Apply a small amount of grease to the machined ridge on the pressure plate and install the diaphragm on the ridge with the outer edge of the spring upward.

3. Lightly grease the ridge inside the cover and install the cover (in alignment with the drive plate and pressure plate positioning marks) and install the twelve bolts using new locktabs. Tighten finger-tight only.

4. Install centering tool number 61–6042 from the rear of the clutch and tighten the twelve bolts ½ turn at a time, working around the cover, until the cover meets the drive plate. Fully tighten the bolts and lock them with the locktabs.

5. Remove the centering tool, install the release rod, lightly grease the disc splines, and install the clutch on the engine.

6. Install the oil pump O-rings and check the clutch hub needle bearing for

excessive play. Check the oil seal and replace if worn or deformed.

7. Apply gasket sealing compound to the crankcase and inner cover mating surfaces. Install the cover, on the crankcase, using a new gasket, and tighten the screws evenly.

8. Install the twelve damper rubbers and then the outer plate. Apply threadlock compound to the six plate-retaining screws.

NOTE: *Later models use six bolts with locktabs and a modified plate. If the screws on earlier models were found to be in need of replacement, replace the screws and plate with the later components.*

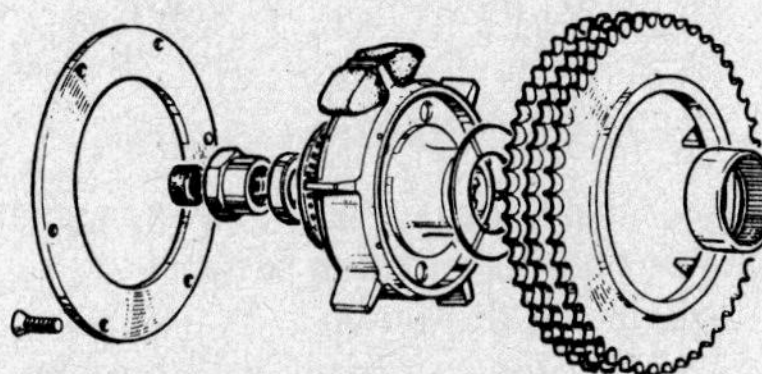

Exploded view of the clutch hub damper

9. Install the thrust washer on the back of the damper hub, fit the primary chain over the sprockets, and install the sprockets on the shafts. Tighten the crankshaft sprocket nut to 60 ft lb and lock in position with the locktab. Install the spacer and tighten the mainshaft sprocket nut to 60 ft lb.

10. Install the thrust bearing and replace the primary cover using gasket cement and a new gasket. Do not forget to use new gaskets at the center retaining bolts.

11. To adjust primary chain tension, bring the engine up on compression and hold it there with the kick-start pedal. Turn the chain tensioner in until there is about 3/16 in. slack on the top chain run and lock it in position.

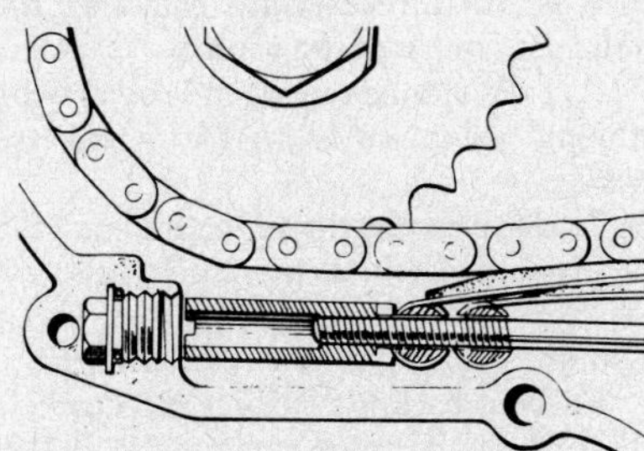

Primary chain tensioner adjuster

12. Install the large clutch adjusting nut, taking care not to damage the oil seal on the release rod threads. Insert an 0.005 in. feeler gauge between the bearing and large nut, and tighten the small locknut while keeping the release rod from turning. Refill the primary chaincase with the correct amount and grade of oil and check the clutch for correct operation.

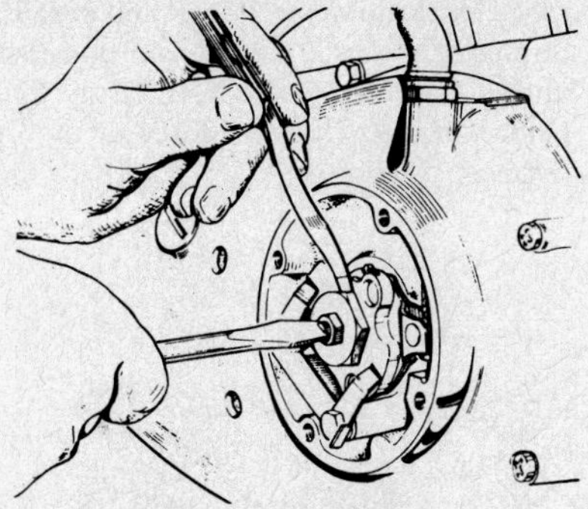

Clutch adjustment

Primary Drive Service

Follow steps 1–4 above for clutch disassembly. Inspect the sprockets for worn and broken teeth. If the sprockets are to be replaced, the chain should be replaced also; otherwise the new sprockets will be ruined in a short time.

TRANSMISSION COUNTERSHAFT SPROCKET

1. Remove the small clutch hub and clutch housing.

2. Remove the clutch hub retaining nut and pull the hub using a suitable gear puller. Do not lose the woodruff key.

3. Remove the clutch housing from the crankcase. Check the oil seal for wear and distortion, and replace if necessary. Unscrew the sprocket nut and then remove the final, drive chain master link. Pull the sprocket off the shaft.

4. To replace the sprocket, install it on the shaft using hardening gasket cement on the sleeve gear splines to prevent oil from leaking between the sprocket and sleeve gear.

5. The remainder of installation is in reverse order of removal.

TRANSMISSION, SHIFTER, AND KICK-START MECHANISM SERVICE

Disassembly

1. Drain the primary chaincase and transmission.

2. Remove the clutch.

3. Take out the five screws and the acorn nut, and remove the transmission outer (right-side rear) cover complete with kick-start assembly and shifter mechanism. The kick-start half-gear is a press fit onto the shaft. If the return spring is to be replaced, load it 1 ¼ turns before slipping the hook over the dowel pin. The starter shaft oil seal is accessible after the kick-start lever is removed.

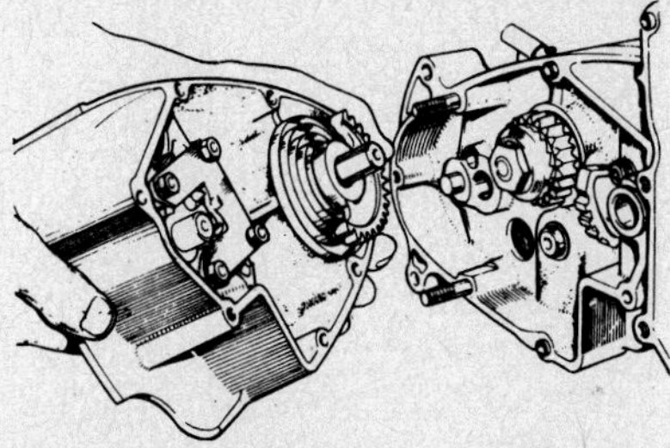

Removing the transmission outer cover

4. To remove the kick-start ratchet and gear, bend back the locktab and unscrew the transmission mainshaft nut. If a new gear is to be installed, use a new spring also. The ratchet need not be removed for removal of the transmission gears.

5. Take out the two screws and bolts and remove the transmission inner cover, complete with selector quadrant and mainshaft assembly. Note the countershaft thrust washer located on the inner face of the cover by a small peg.

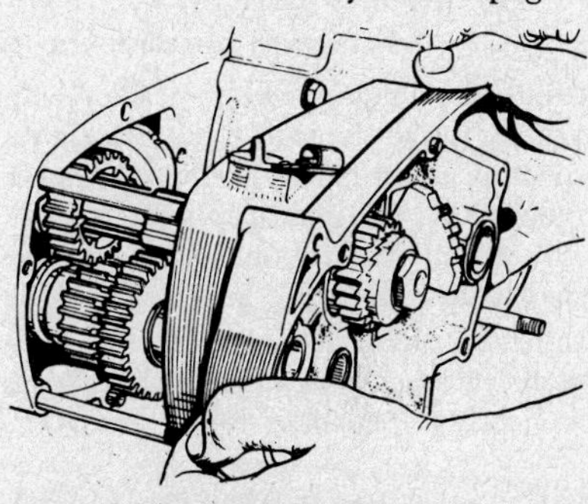

Removing the transmission inner cover and mainshaft assembly

6. Unscrew the plug from the base of the transmission case that retains camplate plunger and spring.

7. Pull out the shift fork shaft and remove the countershaft first gear. Remove the sliding gears and selector forks from the case. Do not lose the fork rollers as the assemblies are pulled away from the camplate.

8. Pull the countershaft assembly out of the case and then remove the shift camplate. The countershaft top gear or sleeve pinion is attached to the final drive sprocket by a large nut.

Assembly

1. Install the high gear into the bearing and then the final drive sprocket into the case.

2. Lubricate and install the camplate shaft into the case.

3. Install the camplate plunger and spring, with retaining plug, under the transmission case. Do not forget the fiber washer.

4. Set the camplate so that the plunger is located in the high gear notch. Install the thrust washer over the inner needle bearing. The grooved surface of the washer should face the countershaft. The washer can be held in place with grease.

5. Lubricate the components and assemble the countershaft and mainshaft gear clusters.

6. Place the camplate rollers on the

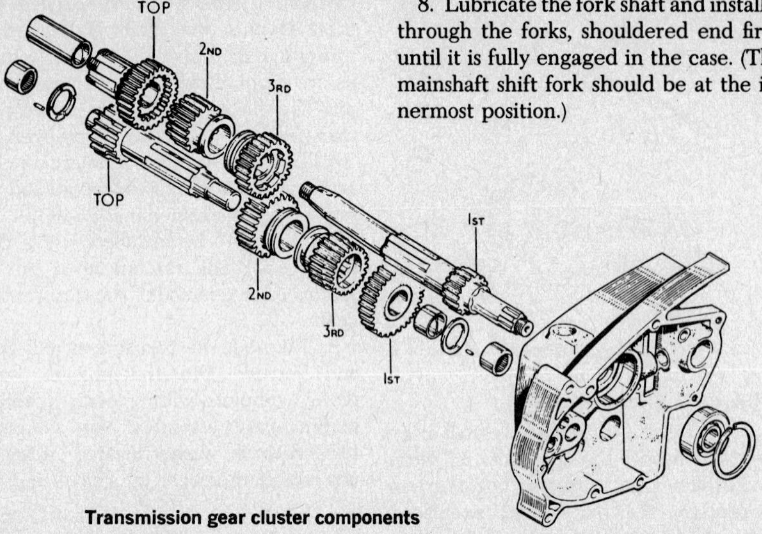

Transmission gear cluster components

shift forks, holding them in position with grease. Install the shift forks in their respective gears. The fork with the smaller radius is for the mainshaft cluster.

7. Install the mainshaft and countershaft gears, align the gears so that the shift fork rollers are located in the camplate tracks, and align the shift fork bores as closely as possible.

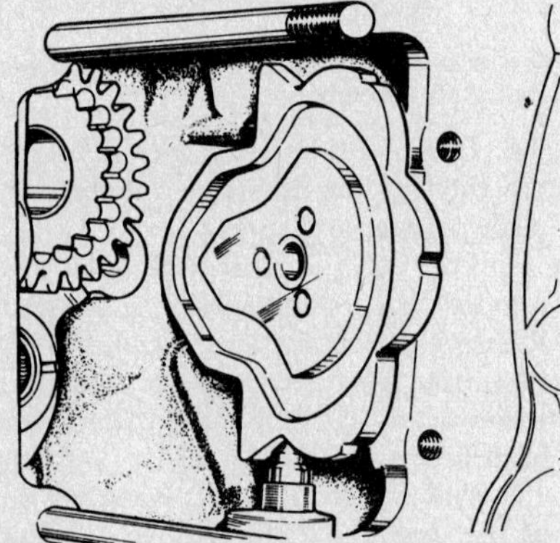

Correct positioning of the camplate and plunger

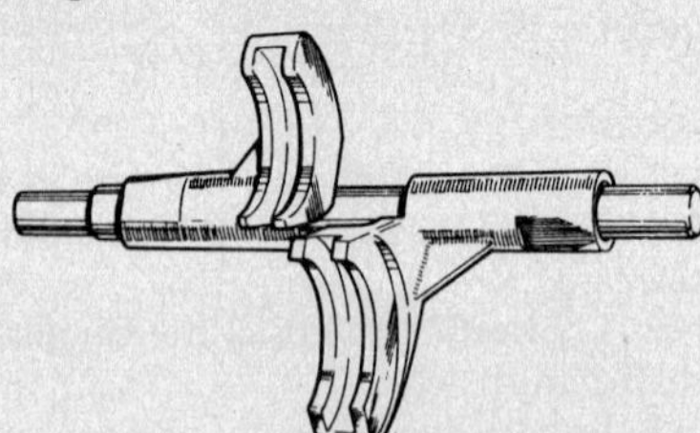

Shift forks assembled onto the shaft

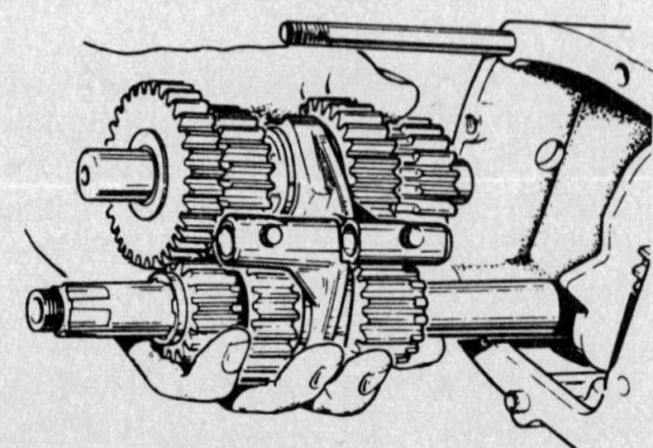

Replacing the gear cluster

8. Lubricate the fork shaft and install it through the forks, shouldered end first, until it is fully engaged in the case. (The mainshaft shift fork should be at the innermost position.)

9. Make sure that the camplate quadrant is able to move freely in the inner cover. Position the countershaft thrust washer over the needle bearing in the inner cover, holding it with grease.

10. Lubricate all the transmission components. Apply gasket cement to the inner cover and transmission mating surfaces, make sure that the two dowel pins are in position, and install the inner cover.

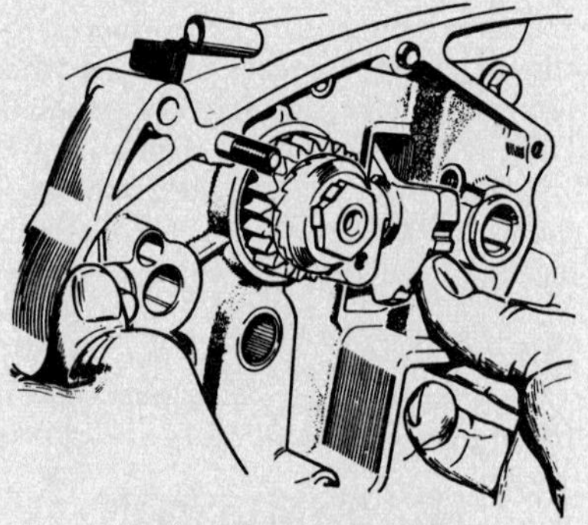

Installing the inner cover

11. Temporarily install the outer cover and check to see that the shift sequence is correct by operating the shift lever while turning the final drive sprocket. If the shift sequence is not correct, remove the inner cover and make sure that the quadrant teeth are accurately engaged with the camplate gear. When reinstalling the inner cover, make sure that the top of the first tooth is on the centerline of the mainshaft.

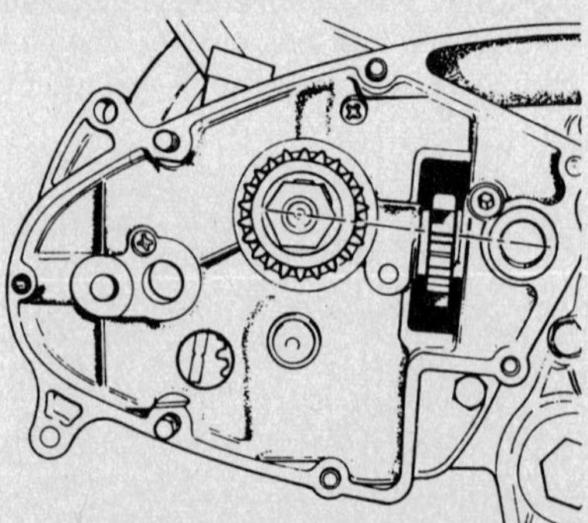

Correct positioning of the selector quadrant

12. Reassemble the kick-shaft ratchet and gear as shown, tightening the nut to 40–45 ft lb. To facilitate this, install the final drive chain, put the transmission in gear, and apply the rear brake.

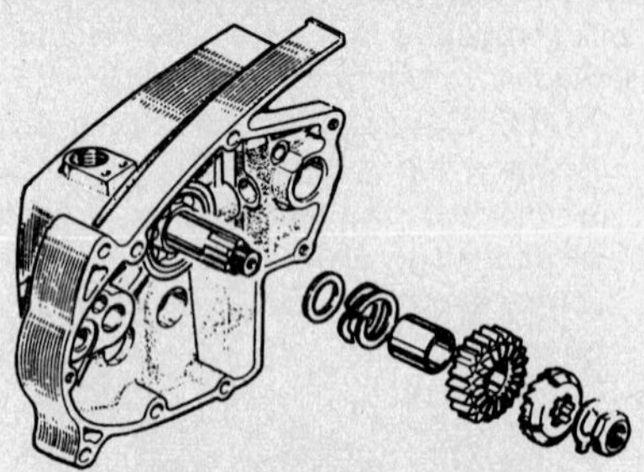

Kick-start ratchet components

13. Install the outer cover using gasket cement on both mating surfaces.

14. Install the clutch.

15. Fill the primary chaincase and transmission with oil.

BOTTOM END OVERHAUL

Disassembly

1. Drain the oil from the crankcase, transmission, and primary drive. Remove the engine.

2. Remove the cylinder head, barrel, and pistons.

3. Remove the primary drive and clutch assembly.

4. Remove the transmission gear cluster.

5. Remove the ignition points cover. Take out the three bolts and remove the breaker plate assembly. Unscrew the bolt in the center of the breaker cam and remove the ignition advance unit with tool no. 60-782, or by screwing in a bolt that fits the threads in the cam until the advance unit is broken loose.

6. Take out the screws and remove the timing gear cover (right crankcase cover).

7. Unscrew the three nuts and pull the alternator stator off the studs. Unscrew the cable sleeve nut (covered by a rubber grommet) and pull the cable through.

8. Bend back the locktab and unscrew the alternator rotor retaining nut. Pull the rotor off the shaft, leaving the key in place to prevent the crankshaft timing gear from turning.

9. Before removing the timing gears, take note of the marks on the gear teeth that will line up if the gears are installed correctly. Pull the crankshaft pinion off using tool no. 61-6019 or a suitable gear puller.

10. Remove the circlip and pull off the idler (center) timing gear and its thrust washer.

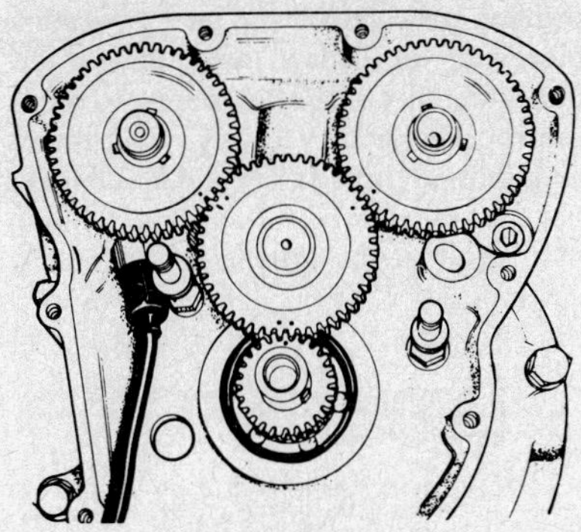
Timing marks

11. To unscrew the two camshaft timing gear retaining nuts, it will be necessary to lock the crankshaft in position by inserting a bar through two of the connecting rods. Take care not to damage the crankcase. Unscrew the nuts, which have left-hand threads, and pull off the camshaft timing gears using tool no. 60-2213 or a suitable gear puller. Remove the woodruff keys.

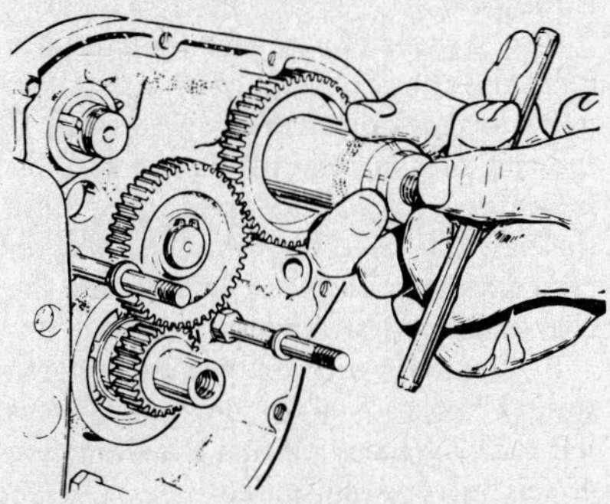
Unscrewing the camshaft timing gear nut which has left-hand thread

12. Take out the three bolts and remove the tachometer drive, located just above the front engine mount.

13. Remove the oil filter from the bottom of the crankcase, held in place by a large brass plug.

14. To separate the crankcases, first take out the hex bolts, allen bolt, and bolts A, B, C, D, and E from the timing side crankcase as shown in the illustration.

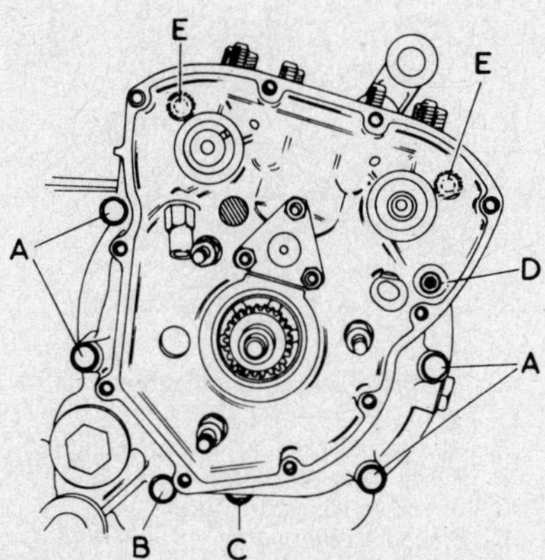

Timing-side crankcase securing bolts

15. Next, remove hex-head bolts F, G, and H, as illustrated, from the drive side crankcase. Tap the drive side crankcase off using a soft metal drift. Place the drift against the lug at the rear of the case, as shown.

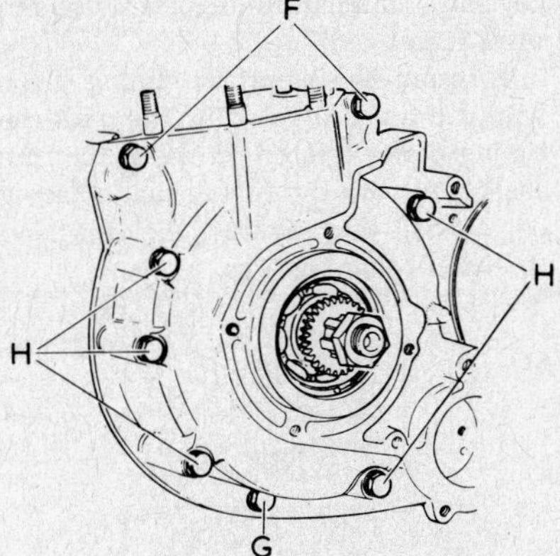

Drive-side crankcase securing bolts

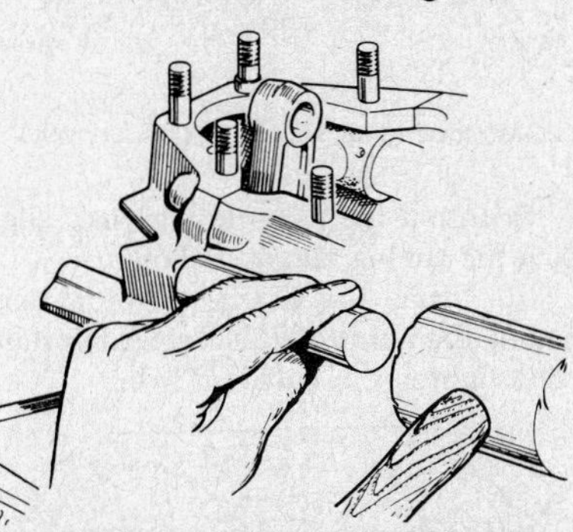
Tapping the crankcase halves apart

Camshafts

Withdraw the camshafts from the timing side crankcase and examine the lobes for wear and damage. Examine the tachometer drive gear on the exhaust camshaft for broken or worn teeth. Replace the camshafts if they do not appear to be in perfect condition.

Crankshaft Removal

1. Remove the retaining screws from the two small oil lines on top of the main bearing journal caps, pull the lines up, turn them away from the caps, and push them down and out of the crankcase.

2. Remove the locknuts from the main bearing caps. To remove the caps, screw the oil line screws, with washers, back into them and pry the caps off the studs with levers.

3. The crankshaft assembly can now be removed.

Center Main Bearings and Connecting Rod Bearings

The crankpins and the two center crankshaft journals run on replaceable plain bearing inserts. Be sure to mark the rods and caps before removal so that they may be replaced in their original positions. It will be necessary to regrind the

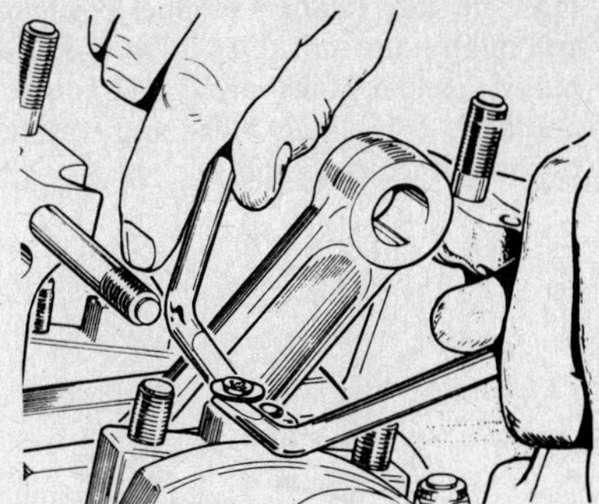
Using the oil line retaining screw to withdraw the main bearing cap

crankshaft if journal or crankpin wear exceeds 0.002 in. or if their surfaces are damaged. Bearings are available in 0.010, 0.020, 0.030, and 0.040 in. undersizes. The crankshaft assembly will not require rebalancing if components are replaced or if the crankshaft is reground.

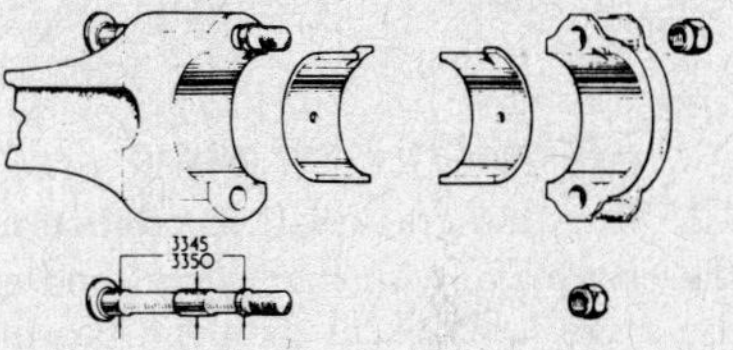

Connecting rod assembly

Outer Main Bearings

The timing side roller and drive side ball bearings should not normally require replacement. If they are to be removed, it will be necessary to remove the circlips on either side of the bearings.

NOTE: *The center of the timing side roller bearing will remain with the crankshaft as the crankshaft is removed.*

Oil seals should be replaced at this time to avoid future trouble. Take care not to damage seals during installation. The flat side of the seal always faces outside.

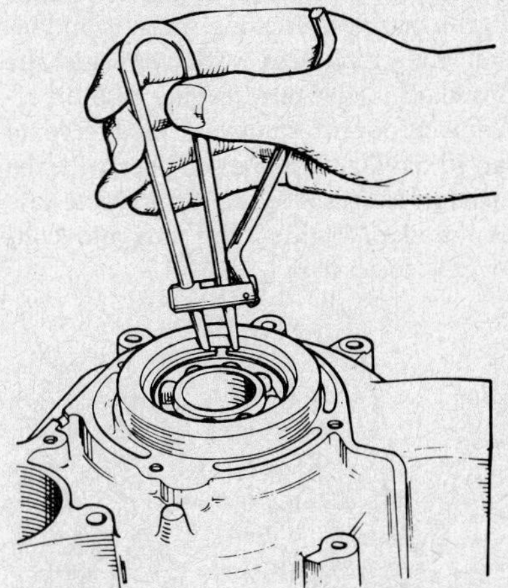
Removing the main bearing circlip

Assembly

1. Fit the rod and main bearing inserts into their seats and lubricate them with fresh engine oil. Install the connecting

rods and caps in their original positions and tighten the nuts to 18 ft lbs. Use new nuts if possible. Make sure that all components are completely clean and well lubricated during assembly.

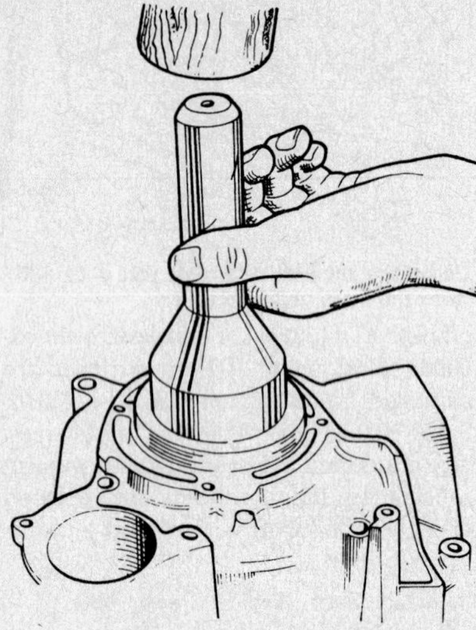

Removing the main bearing

2. Place the crankshaft in position in the crankcase, with the splined end on the drive side. Install the main bearing caps, making sure that the marks on the caps and lower bearing seats correspond. Install the washers and nuts (new nuts should be used) and tighten to 18 ft lb. Check that the crankshaft is free to rotate easily. If it will not, switch the main bearing inserts around, make sure they are seated properly, and reoil them. Too tight a fit will require turning down the crankshaft journals slightly.

3. Install new rubber seals for the tappet oil lines (connecting at the main bearing caps) and install the lines as removed, taking care not to damage the seals.

4. Replace the oil filter O-rings in the center crankcase.

5. Apply a thin coat of gasket cement to the crankcase mating surfaces and install the crankcases (with the camshafts installed in the turning side case) in reverse order of removal. Take care to avoid damaging tappet oil lines with the exhaust camshaft as the turning side case is installed. Tighten the nuts and bolts evenly to 15 ft lb.

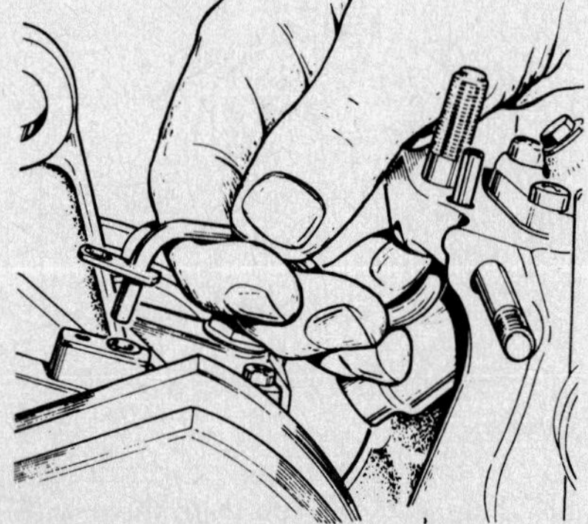

Replacing the tappet oil lines

6. Check that the crankshaft and camshafts are free to rotate freely. If not, alignment is incorrect somewhere and must be corrected.

7. Install the crankshaft spacer on the timing side and then install the special key and crankshaft timing gear (with the mark facing out).

8. Install the camshaft timing gears with the no. 1 keyway (in line with the timing mark) located on the key in the shaft, and with the timing marks facing out. Install and tighten the left-hand threaded retaining nuts.

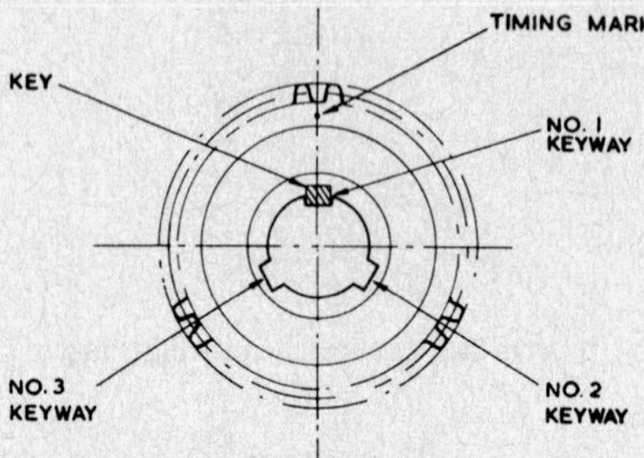

Intake and exhaust camshaft keyways

9. Install the idler timing gear, aligning the timing marks as shown.

10. Install the alternator rotor, tightening the nut to 50 ft lb. Install the stator and tighten the nuts to 8 ft lb.

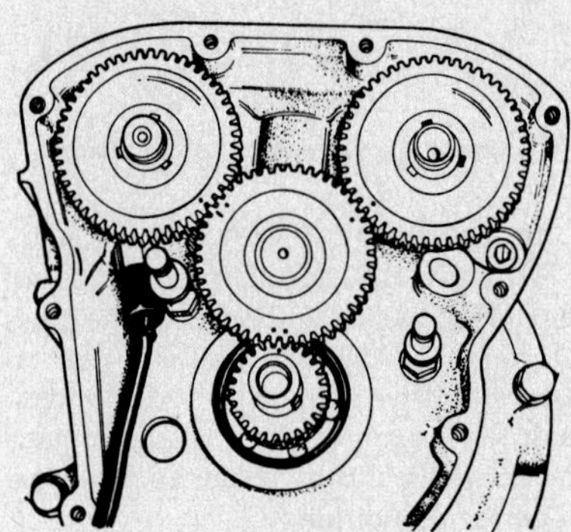

Valve timing marks

11. Loosely install the ignition advance unit and breaker plate assembly. Coat the crankcase and cover mating surfaces with gasket cement and install the timing side crankcase cover using a new gasket.

12. Install the oil filter in the bottom of the engine.

13. Install the tachometer drive unit, coating the gasket with gasket cement on both sides. Tachometer drive components generally do not require replacement unless an obvious fault is visible.

14. Install the transmission gear cluster as detailed earlier.

15. Install the primary drive and clutch.

16. Assemble the top end components as described in preceding sections.

17. Install the engine in the frame.

18. Refill the engine, transmission, and primary case with oil and perform a complete tune-up. Allow the engine a few hundred miles of gentle running to break in properly and check valve adjustment and ignition timing after about 500 miles have been covered. Change the oil and filter again at this time.

LUBRICATION SYSTEMS

SINGLES

SCAVENGE CHECK VALVE

The scavenge check valve is located within the oil return pipe in the engine sump. It's a good idea to check its operation whenever the sump strainer screen is removed.

Poke a piece of wire into the pipe and force the check ball out of its seat. Allow it to drop back down of its own weight. If the ball does not seat itself properly, this indicates a sludge buildup in and around the valve. If necessary, immerse the return pipe in gasoline and let it sit until the check ball operates freely.

If you have a problem with the engine sump filling with oil whenever the bike is left to sit, chances are that a malfunction of this valve is the source.

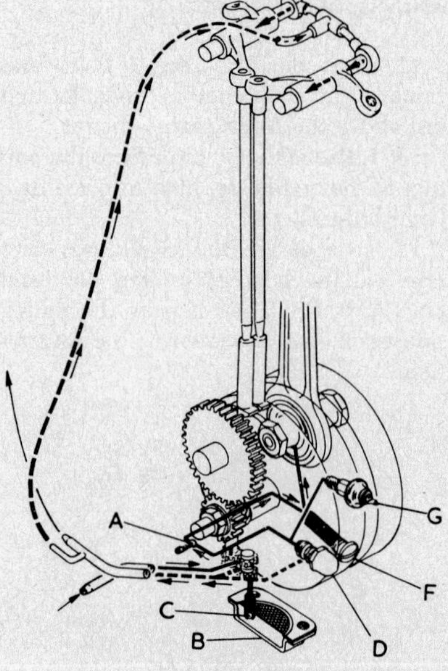

Lubrication system diagram

A. Non-return (check) valve, feed side
B. Sump plate and filter
C. Check valve, return side
D. Pressure relief valve
F. Crankcase sludge trap
G. Oil pressure switch (B25 only)

ENGINE, TRANSMISSION, AND CLUTCH SPECIFICATIONS

B25 Engine

VALVES

Seat angle	45°
Head diameter (intake)	1.450-1.455 in.
(exhaust)	1.312-1.317 in.
Stem diameter (intake)	0.3095-0.3100 in.
(exhaust)	0.3090-0.3095 in.

VALVE GUIDES

Material	Hidural 5
Bore diameter	0.3120-0.3130 in.
Outside diameter	0.5005-0.5010 in.
Length	1.844 in.
Interference fit in head	0.0015-0.0025 in.
Counterbore in exhaust guide	0.323 in.-0.326 in. × 0.12 in. deep

VALVE SPRINGS

Free length (inner)	1.40 in. (35.5 mm)
(outer)	1.75 in. (44.5 mm)
Fitted length (inner)	1.26 in. (32.0 mm)
(outer)	1.37 in. (34.8 mm)

CAMSHAFT

Journal diameter, left and right	0.7480-0.7485 in.
Cam lift (intake)	0.345 in.
(exhaust)	0.336 in.
Base circle radius	0.906 in.
Bush bore diameter, fitted	0.7492-0.7497 in.
Bush outside diameter, left and right hand	0.908-0.909 in.

TAPPETS

Stem diameter	0.3735-0.3740 in.
Clearance in crankcase	0.001 in.

CYLINDER HEAD

Intake port size	1.125 in.
Exhaust port size	1.25 in.
Material	Aluminum alloy LM4 with integral cast iron valve seats

CYLINDER BARREL

Bore diameter (standard)	67 mm
Oversizes	0.020 in. and 0.040 in. (0.5 and 1.0 mm)
Material	Aluminum alloy LM4 with austenitic iron liner

PISTON

Compression ratio	10 : 1 (alternative 8.5 : 1, Fleetstar only)
Clearance (top or skirt)	0.0042-0.0053 in.
Clearance (bottom of skirt)	0.0025-0.0028 in.
Wrist pin hole diameter	0.6884-0.6886 in.
Material	Alum. alloy H.G. 413

PISTON RINGS

Width (top and center)	0.101-0.107 in.
Width (oil control)	0.101-0.107 in.
Depth (top and center)	0.0615-0.0625 in.
Depth (oil control)	0.124-0.125 in.
Clearance in groove (all rings)	0.001-0.003 in.
Fitted gap (all rings)	0.009-0.013 in.
Material (all rings)	Cast iron H.G. 22

CONNECTING ROD AND CRANKSHAFT ASSEMBLY

Connecting rod small end diameter	0..6890-0.6894 in.
Conecting rod big end diameter	1.5630-1.5635 in.
Connecting rod length between centers	5.312 in.
Crankpin diameter	1.4375-1.4380 in.
Regrind undersizes	0.010 in., 0.020 in., 0.030 in. (0.25, 0.50, 0.76 mm)
Journal diameter (left and right)	0.9841-0.9844 in.
Rod bearing running clearance	0.0005-0.0015 in.
Crankcase main bearing (roller, left)	0.875 in. × 2.0 in. × 0.5625 in. (Hoffman R325L)
Crankcase main bearing (ball, right)	0.875 in. × 2.0 in. × 0.5625 in. (Hoffman 325)

CLUTCH

Type	Multiplate with integral cush drive
Number of friction plates	5
Number of plain plates	5
Overall thickness of friction plate	0.167 in. (4.2 mm)

ENGINE, TRANSMISSION, AND CLUTCH SPECIFICATIONS

Free length of springs	1.66 in. (42.0 mm)
Clutch pushrod length	9.0 in. (22.9 cm)
Clutch pushrod diameter	0.1875 in.
Clutch rollers	25, 0.1875 in × 0.1875 in.
GEARBOX	
Type	4 speed, constant mesh
Countershaft bear. (needle roller)	0.5 in. × 0.625 in. × 0.8125 in. (Torrington B108)
Mainshaft bearing (left)	30 × 60 × 16 mm (Hoffman 130)
Mainshaft bearing (right)	0.625 in. × 1.5625 in. × 0.4735 in. (Hoffman LS7)
Countershaft diam. (left and right)	0.6245-0.6250 in.
Mainshaft diameter (left)	0.7485-0.7490 in.
Mainshaft diameter (right)	0.6245-0.6250 in.
Sleeve pinion inside diameter	0.752-0.753 in.
Sleeve pinion outside diam.	1.179-1.180 in.

GEAR RATIOS	
Gearbox	B25SS, B25T
Top	1.00
Third	1.24
Second	1.64
First	2.65
CHAINS	
Primary chain (all models)	
Pitch	0.375 in. (9.53 mm)
Roller diameter	0.250 in. (6.35 mm)
Distance between plates	0.225 in. (5.72 mm)
Length	70 links
Breaking load	3,900 lbs (1770 kg)
Type	Renolds 114 038 Duplex endless
Rear chain	
Pitch	0.625 in. (15.88 mm)
Roller diameter	0.400 in. (10.16 mm)
Distance between plates	0.255 in (6.48 mm)
Length	106 links (B25SS) 107 links (B25T)
Breaking load	5,000 lbs (2268 kg)
Type	Renolds 110 054

B44 Engine

PISTON	
Material	"Lo-Ex" aluminum
Compression ratio	9.4 : 1
Clearance (bottom of skirt)	0.003-0.0035 in. (0.0762-0.0889 mm)
(top of skirt)	0.006-0.0065 in. (0.0524-0.1651 mm)
(both measured on major axis)	
PISTON RINGS	
Material—	
compress. (top) 1968	Brico 8
compress. (top) After 1968	Brico BSS.5004 (chrome-plated)
compress. (center)	Brico 8
Material—scraper	Brico BSS.5004
Width—compress. (top & cen.)	0.0625 in. (1.5875 mm)
scraper	0.125 in. (3.175 mm)
Depth	0.120-0.127 in. (3.048-3.2258 mm)
Clearance in groove	0.001-0.003 in. (0.0254-0.0762 mm)
Fitted gap—(maximum)	0.014 in. (0.3556 mm)
(minimum)	0.009 in. (0.2283 mm)

OIL PUMP	
Body material	Zinc base alloy
Type	Double gear
Drive ratio	1 : 1
Non-return valve spring (free length)	0.5 in. (12.7 mm)
Non-return valve spring ball (diameter)	0.25 in. (6.35 mm)
Oil pressure release valve spring (free length)	0.6094 in. (15.4781 mm)
Oil pressure release valve ball (diameter)	0.3125 in. (7.9375 mm)
CAMSHAFT	
Journal diam. (left-hand)	0.5598-0.5603 in. (14.2189-14.2316 mm)
(right-hand)	0.7480-0.7485 in. (18.9992-19.0119 mm)
Cam lift (inlet)	0.345 in. (8.763 mm)
(exhaust)	0.336 in. (8.534 mm)
Base circle radius	0.386 in. (9.8044 mm)

ENGINE, TRANSMISSION, AND CLUTCH SPECIFICATIONS

CAMSHAFT BEARING BUSHINGS	
Bore diam. (fitted) left hand	0.561-0.562 in. (14.2494-14.2748 mm)
right-hand	0.7492-0.7497 in. (19.0297-19.04238 mm)
Outside diam. (left-hand)	0.719-0.720 in. (18.2626-18.2880 mm)
(right-hand)	0.908-0.909 in. (23.0632-23.0886 mm)
Camshaft clear. (left-hand)	0.0007-0.0022 in. (0.01778-0.05588 mm)
(right-hand)	0.0007-0.0017 in. (0.01778-0.04318 mm)

VALVES	
Seat angle (inclusive)	90°
Head diameter (inlet)	1.535-1.540 in. (38.9890-39.1160 mm)
(exhaust)	1.407-1.412 in. (35.737-35.864 mm)
Stem diameter (inlet)	0.3095-0.310 0in. (7.861-7.874 mm)
(exhaust)	0.3090-0.3095 in. (7.848-7.861 mm)

VALVE GUIDES	
Material	Phosphor bronze
Bore diameter	0.3120-0.3130 in. (7.9248-7.950 mm)
Outside diameter	0.5005-0.5010 in. (12.7127-12.7254 mm)
Length	1.859 in. (47.2186 mm)
Cylinder head interference fit	0.0015-0.0025 in. (0.0381-0.0635 mm)

VALVE SPRINGS	
Free length (inner)	1.500 in. (38.10 mm)
(outer)	1.670 in. (42.418 mm)
Fitted length (inner)	1.218 in. (30.9372 mm)
(outer)	1.312 in. (33.3248 mm)

CYLINDER BARREL	
Material	Aluminum with austenitic iron liner
Bore size (standard)	79 mm
Stroke	90 mm
Oversizes	0.010 in. & 0.020 in. (0.254 & 0.508 mm)

CYLINDER HEAD	
Material	Aluminum alloy
Inlet port size	1.125 in. (28.575 mm)
Exhaust port size	1.25 in. (31.75 mm)

BEARING DIMENSIONS	
Clutch roller (25)	0.1875 × 0.1875 in. (4.7025 × 4.7025 mm)
Con-rod big-end bush (bore)	1.7701-1.7706 in. (44.9605-44.9732 mm)
Con-rod big-end roller (24)	0.250 in. diam. × 0.250 in. (6.35 × 6.35 mm)
Con-rod small-end bush (bore)	0.7503-0.7506 in. (19.0576-19.0652 mm)
Crankpin diameter	1.2698-1.2700 in. (32.253-32.258 mm)
Crankcase bearing (drive-side)	25 × 62 × 17 mm
Crankcase bearing (gear-side)	25 × 62 × 17 mm
Flywheel shaft diameter (drive-side and gear-side)	0.9841-0.9844 in. (24.9961-25.0038 mm)
Gearbox layshaft bearings (drive-side and gear-side)	0.5 × 0.625 × 0.8125 in. (12.7 × 15.875 × 20.6375 mm)
Gearbox layshaft diameter (drive-side and gear-side)	0.6245-0.625 in. (15.8623-15.8750 mm)
Gearbox mainshaft bearing (drive-side)	30 × 62 × 16 mm
Gearbox mainshaft bearing (gear-side)	0.625 × 1.5625 × 0.4375 in. (15.875 × 39.2875 × 11.1125 mm)
Gearbox mainshaft diameter (drive-side)	0.7485-0.749 in. (19.0119-19.0246 mm)
Gearbox mainshaft diameter (gear-side)	0.6245-0.625 in. (15.8623-15.8750 mm)
Gearbox sleeve pinion (internal diameter)	0.752-0.753 in. (19.1008-19.1262 mm)
Gearbox sleeve pinion (external diameter)	1.179-1.180 in. (29.9466-29.9720 mm)
Piston pin diameter	0.750-0.7502 in. (19.05-19.055 mm)

CLUTCH	
Type	Multi-plate with integral cush drive
Number of plates	
Driving (bonded segments)	4
Driven (plain)	5
Overall thickness of driving plate and segments	0.167 in. (4.242 mm)
Clutch springs	4
Free length of springs	1.65685 in. (42.0687 mm)
Clutch push rod (length)	9.0 in. (228.6 mm)
(diameter)	0.1875 in. (4.7025 mm)

CHAIN SIZES	
Primary	Duplex 0.375 in. × 72 links
Transmission	0.625 in. × 100 links

ENGINE, TRANSMISSION, AND CLUTCH SPECIFICATIONS

B50 Engine

VALVES

Seat angle	45°
Head diameter (intake)	1.750-1.755 in.
(exhaust)	1.526-1.531 in.
Stem diameter (intake)	0.3100-0.3105 in.
(exhaust)	0.3095-0.3100 in.

VALVE GUIDES

Material	Phosphor-bronze
Bore diameter	0.3120-0.3130 in.
Outside diameter	0.5005-0.5010 in.
Length	1.859 in.
Interference fit in head	0.0015-0.0025 in.
Counterbore in exhaust guide	0.323-0.326 in. × 0.12 in. deep

VALVE SPRINGS

Free length (inner)	1.50 in. (38.1 mm)
(outer)	1.67 in. (42.4 mm)
Fitted length (inner)	1.22 in. (31.0 mm)
(outer)	1.31 in. (33.3 mm)

VALVE TIMING

Tappets set to 0.015 in. (0.38 mm) for checking purposes only	B50SS, B50T	B50MX
Intake opens B.T.D.C.	51°	63°
Intake closes A.B.D.C.	68°	72°
Exhaust opens B.B.D.C.	78°	80°
Exhaust closes A.T.D.C.	37°	55°

CAMSHAFT

Journal diam., left to right	0.7480-0.7485 iin.
Cam lift (intake)	0.345 (0.355 in. B50MX)
(exhaust)	0.336 (0.355 in. B50MX)
Base circle radius	0.906 in.
Bush bore diameter, fitted	0.7492-0.7497 in.
Bush outside diameter, left and right	0.908-0.909 in.
Tappet clearance (intake)	0.008 in. (0.20 mm)
(exhaust)	0.010 in. (0.25 mm)

CYLINDER HEAD

Intake port size	1.20 in.
Exhaust port size	1.625 in.
Material	Aluminum alloy LM4 with cast iron valve seats

CYLINDER BARREL

Bore diameter (standard)	84 mm
Oversizes	0.020 in. and 0.040 in. (0.5 mm and 1.0 mm)
Material	Aluminum alloy LM4M with austenitic iron liner

PISTON

Compression ratio	10 : 1
Clearance (top of skirt)	0.005-0.007 in.
Clearance (bottom of skirt)	0.0035-0.0045 in.
Wrist pin hole diameter	0.7499-0.7501 in.
Material	Aluminum alloy H.G. 413

PISTON RINGS

Width (top and center)	0.127-0.134 in.
Width (oil control)	0.138-0.145 in.
Depth (top and center)	0.0615-0.0625 in.
Depth (total, oil control)	0.1550-0.1560 in.
Clearance in groove (all rings)	0.001-0.003 in.
Fitted gap (all rings)	0.016-0.024 in. (0.40-0.60 mm)
Material (all rings)	Cast iron H.G. 22

CONNECTING ROD AND CRANKSHAFT ASSEMBLY

Connecting rod small end diam.	0.8115-0.8125 in.
Small end bush bore diameter	0.7503-0.7506 in.
Connecting rod big end diam.	2.0190-2.0195 in.
Big end bush bore diameter	1.8110-1.8116 in.
Connect. rod length betw. centers	6.00 in. (15.24 cm)
Crankpin bearing diameter	1.4957-1.4961 in.
Big end bearing (needle roller)	38 × 46 × 20 mm (R. & M K38-46-20F)
Flywheel shaft diameter (left and right)	0.9841-0.9844 in.
Crankcase main bearings (roller, left and right)	0.875 in. × 2.0 in. × 0.5625 in. (Hoffmann R325L)
Crankcase main bearing (ball, left)	0.875 in. × 2.0 in. × 0.5625 in. (Hoffmann LS9)

CLUTCH

Type	Multiplate with integral cush drive
Number of discs	5
Number of plates	5
Overall thickness of friction plate	0.167 in. (4.2 mm)
Free length of springs	1.66 in. (42.0 mm)
Clutch pushrod length	9.0 in. (22.9 cm)
diameter	0.1875 in.
Clutch rollers	0.1875 in. × 0.1875 in., 25

ENGINE, TRANSMISSION, AND CLUTCH SPECIFICATIONS

GEARBOX	
Type	4 speed, constant mesh
Countershaft bearings (needle roller)	0.5 in. × 0.625 in. × 0.8125 in. (Torrington B108)
Mainshaft bear. (left)	30 × 60 × 16 mm (Hoffmann 130)
(right)	0.625 in. × 1.5625 in. × 0.4735 in. (Hoffmann LS7)
Countershaft diameter (left and right)	0.6245-0.6250 in.
Mainshaft diam. (left)	0.7485-0.7490 in.
(right)	0.6245-0.6250 in.
Sleeve pinion inside diam.	0.752-0.753 in.
outside diam.	1.179 in. × **1.180 in.**
CHAINS	
Primary chain (all models)	
Pitch	0.375 in. (9.53 mm)
Roller diameter	0.250 in. (6.35 mm)
Distance between plates	0.225 in. (5.72 mm)

CHAINS	
Primary chain (all models)	
Length	72 links
Breaking load	3,900 lbs (1770 kg)
Type	Renolds 114 038 Duplex endless
Rear chain	
Pitch	0.625 in. (15.88 mm)
Roller diameter	0.400 in. (10.16 mm)
Distance between plates	0.255 in. (6.48 mm)
Length	106 links (B50MX) 107 (B50T) 108 (B50SS)
Breaking load	5,000 lbs (2268 kg)
Type	Renolds 110 054

A65 Engine

PISTON	
Material	"Lo-Ex" aluminum alloy
Compression ratio	9.0 : 1
Clearance: (bottom of skirt)	0.0039-0.0054 in. (0.0990-0.137 mm)
(top of skirt)	0.0094-0.0109 in. (0.2387-0.2768 mm)
(both measured on major axis)	
Wrist pin hole diameter	0.7500, 0.7502 in. (19.05, 19.055 mm)
Oversizes	+ 0.020, + 0.040 in. (+ 0.5, + 1.0 mm)
PISTON RINGS	
Material	Cast-iron (to British Standard 5004)
Compression rings (lower compression ring is tapered to same dimensions)	
width	0.0615-0.0625 in. (1.562-1.587 mm)
thickness (radial)	0.114-0.121 in. (3.00-3.07 mm)
clearance in groove	0.001-0.003 in. (0.025-0.076 mm)
fitted gap	0.008-0.013 in. (0.203-0.330 mm)

WRIST PINS	
Material	Nickel-chrome high tensile steel
Diameter	0.7500-0.7502 in. (19.05-19.055 mm)
Length	2.368-2.373 in. (60.15-60.27 mm)
SMALL-END BUSHING	
Material	Phosphor-bronze
Outside diam. (before fitting)	0.8775-0.8785 in. (22.289-22.314 mm)
Length	0.940-0.950 in. (23.88-24.13 mm)
Finished bore (fitted)	0.7503-0.7506 in. (19.0576-19.0652 mm)
Interference fit in rod	0.002-0.004 in. (0.0508-0.1016 mm)
CONNECTING RODS	
Length between centers	6.0 in. (152.394 mm)
Big-end bearing type	Vandervell D2 Bimetal
Rod side clearance	0.018-0.024 in. (0.457-0.605 mm)
Bearing diametrical clearance	0.001-0.0025 in. (0.254-0.0635 mm)
Small-end bore diameter	0.8745-0.8755 in. (22.212-22.237 mm)

ENGINE, TRANSMISSION, AND CLUTCH SPECIFICATIONS

A65 Engine

Oil control ring	
width	0.124-0.125 in. (3.15-3.17 mm)
thickness (radial)	0.114-0.121 in. (3.00-3.07 mm)
clearance in groove	0.001-0.003 in. (0.025-0.076 mm)
fitted gap	0.008-0.013 in. (0.203-0.330 mm)
CRANKSHAFT	
Main bearing (gear-side)	
inner diameter (fitted)	1.4995-1.4990 in. (38.077-38.075 mm)
outer diameter (before fitting)	1.6300-1.6285 in. (41.402-41.364 mm)
width	0.940-0.960 in. (23.876-24.384 mm)
Crankpin diameter	1.6865-1.6870 in. (42.837-42.849 mm)
Minimum regrind	−0.010 in. (0.254 mm)
Second regrind	−0.020 in. (0.508 mm)
Third regrind	−0.030 in. (0.762 mm)
Gear-side journal regrind (two only)	−0.010 in. (0.254 mm) −0.020 in. (0.508 mm)
Drive-side shaft size	1.1251-1.1249 in. (28.5775-28.5725 mm)
Crankshaft end float	0.0015-0.003 in. (0.038-0.076 mm)
Stroke	2.9134 in. (74.00 mm)
VALVES	
Seat angle (inclusive)	90°
Head diameter: intake	1.595-1.600 in. (40.51-40.64 mm)
exhaust	1.407-1.412 in. (35.74-35.86 mm)
Stem diameter: intake	0.3095-0.3100 in. (7.86-7.87 mm)
exhaust	0.3090-0.3095 in. (7.85-7.86 mm)
VALVE GUIDES	
Material	Hidural 5
Bore diameter (intake and exhaust)	0.312-0.313 in. (7.9248-7.950 mm)
Outside diameter (intake and exhaust)	0.5005-0.5010 in. (12.713-12.725 mm)
Length (intake and exhaust)	1.96-1.97 in. (49.78-50.04 mm)
Clearance on valve stem	
intake	0.002-0.0035 in. (0.051-0.089 mm)
exhaust	0.0025-0.004 in. (0.0635-0.102 mm)

CRANKSHAFT	
Type	One-piece forging with bolt-on flywheel
Main bearing (drive-side)	Hoffmann RM.11L (roller)
bore	1.125 in. (nominal) (28.574 mm)
outer diameter	2.812 in. (nominal) (71.435 mm)
width	0.812 in. (nominal) (20.637 mm)
TIMING GEAR	
Crankshaft gear	
number of teeth	22
fit on shaft	−0.0005 in. + 0.0005 in. (0.0127 mm)
Camshaft gear	
number of teeth	44
interference fit	0.0000-0.001 in. (0.0254 mm)
Idler gear	
number of teeth	44
shaft dimen., both ends	0.6875-0.6870 in. (17.449-17.463 mm)
bush dimen., both (inside)	0.6885-0.6880 in. (17.475-17.488 mm)
(outside)	0.939-0.940 in. (23.851-23.876 mm)
Shaft working clearance	0:0005-0.0015 in. (0.0127-0.0381 mm)
CAMSHAFT	
Journal diameter: left	0.810-0.8105 in. (20.574-20.586 mm)
right	0.8735-0.874 in. (22.188-22.2 mm)
End float	Nil (spring-loaded)
Cam lift (zero tappet clear.)	0.375 in. (exhaust) (9.52 mm) 0.385 in. (intake) (9.78 mm)
Base circle diameter	0.812 in. (20.624 mm)
CAMSHAFT BEARINGS	
Bore diam., fitted (left side)	0.8115-0.8125 in. (20.612-20.637 mm)
Outside diameter (left)	0.906-0.907 in. (23.012-23.037 mm)
Interference fit in case (left)	0.0018-0.0033 in. (0.046-0.084 mm)
Bore diam., fitted (right side)	0.875-0.876 in. (22.225-22.25 mm)
Outside diameter (right)	1.065-1.066 in. (27.051-27.076 mm)

ENGINE, TRANSMISSION, AND CLUTCH SPECIFICATIONS

A65 Engine

VALVE SPRINGS	
Free length: inner	$1\frac{7}{16}$ in. (36.51 mm)
outer	$1\frac{3}{4}$ in. (44.45 mm)
Fitted length: inner	1.277 in. (32.44 mm)
outer	1.37 in. (34.8 mm)
CYLINDER BARREL	
Material	Cast-iron (close grained)
Bore size (standard)	2.9521-2.9530 in. (74.983-75.0062 mm)
Tappet bore size	0.3745-0.3750 in. (9.512-9.525 mm)
Oversizes	+0.020, +0.040 in. (+0.5, +1.0 mm)
TAPPETS	
Material	20 carbon steel body (stellite tipped)
Tip radius	1.250 in. (31.75 mm)
Tappet diameter	0.3740-0.3735 in. (9.5-9.49 mm)
Clearance in barrel	0.0005-0.0015 in. (0.0127-0.0381 mm)
CYLINDER HEAD	
Material	DTD.424 aluminum alloy (British Standard)
Intake port size (at valve)	$1\frac{1}{2}$ in. (38.1 mm)
Exhaust port size (at valve)	$1\frac{5}{16}$ in. (33.34 mm)
Valve seat	Cast-iron (cast-in)
INTAKE BALANCE PIPE	
Length	4 in. (101.6 mm)
Bore	$\frac{9}{32}$ in. diameter (7 mm)
CLUTCH	
Type	Multiplate with built-in cush drive
Number of plates: discs	6
plates	6
Disc segments	
number	288
overall thickness	0.140-0.145 in. (3.56-3.68 mm)
Clutch springs: free length	3
	$1\frac{13}{16}$ in. (46 mm)
working coils	$7\frac{1}{2}$
spring rate	121 lbs per inch
Clutch sprocket	
number of teeth	58
bore diameter	1.8746-1.8736 in. (47.615-47.590 mm)

CRANKSHAFT BEARINGS	
Interference fit in case (right)	0.002-0.004 in. (0.0508-0.1016 mm)
Material	"Clevite 10" and bronze
bush length (2)	$1\frac{3}{8}$ in. (35 mm)
bush protrusion	$\frac{1}{2}$ in. (12.7 mm)
working clearance	0.0027-0.0042 in. (0.0685-0.1066 mm)
GEARBOX	
Countershaft first gear	
bush diameter (fitted)	0.7495-0.7505 in. (19.0273-19.0627 mm)
working clearance	0.001 in. maximum (0.0127 mm, maximum)
Gearbox shafts	
mainshaft (left end) diam.	0.8098-0.8103 in. (20.568-20.581 mm)
(right end) diam.	0.7495-0.7499 in. (19.047-19.057 mm)
length	$10\frac{5}{8}$ in. (269.875 mm)
countershaft (left) diam.	0.7495-0.750 in. (19.057-19.05 mm)
(right) diam.	0.7495-0.750 in. (19.057-19.05 mm)
length	$6\frac{5}{8}$ in. (168.3 mm)
GEARBOX BEARINGS	
Mainshaft top gear bearing	$2\frac{1}{2} \times 1\frac{1}{4} \times \frac{5}{8}$ in. Ball Journal
Mainshaft bearing (right side)	$\frac{3}{4} \times 1\frac{7}{8} \times \frac{9}{16}$ in. Ball Journal
Countershaft bear. (left side)	$1 \times \frac{3}{4} \times \frac{3}{4}$ in. Needle Roller
(right side)	$1 \times \frac{3}{4} \times \frac{3}{4}$ in. Needle Roller
KICK-START MECHANISM	
Pinion bore diameter	0.937-0.938 in. (23.8-23.82 mm)
Bush (outside diameter)	0.933-0.935 in. (23.7-23.75 mm)
(inside diameter)	0.750-0.751 in. (19.05-19.075 mm)
Outside working clearance	0.002-0.005 in. (0.0508-0.127 mm)
Inner working clearance	0.0001-0.0015 in. (0.0254-0.0381 mm)
Ratchet spring free length	$\frac{1}{2}$ in. (12.7 mm)

ENGINE, TRANSMISSION, AND CLUTCH SPECIFICATIONS

A65 Engine

Clutch hub bearing diameter	1.3740-1.3730 in. (34.9-34.874 mm)
Clutch roller diameter (20)	0.2495-0.250 in. (6.337-6.35 mm)
length	0.231-0.236 in. (5.867-5.99 mm)
PRIMARY CHAIN	3/8 in. triple roller (80 links)
CLUTCH OPERATING ROD	
Length	11 1/8 in. (282.5 mm)
Diameter	7/32 in. (5.5 mm)
GEARBOX	
Mainshaft top gear bush diameter (fitted)	0.813-0.814 in. (20.6502-20.6756 mm)

GEAR SELECTOR QUADRANT	
Plunger diameter	0.3352-0.3362 in. (8.514-8.539 mm)
Housing diameter	0.3427-0.3437 in. (8.7045-8.73 mm)
Working clearance	0.0065-0.0085 in. (0.165-0.216 mm)
CAM PLATE PLUNGER	
Plunger diameter	0.4335-0.4325 in. (11.011-10.985 mm)
Housing diameter	0.437-0.4375 in. (11.0998-11.1125 mm)
Working clearance	0.0050-0.0035 in. (0.127-0.089 mm)
Spring free length	2 1/4 in. (57.15 mm)

1969 and Earlier Twins (Dual Carbs)

PISTON	
Material	"Lo-Ex" aluminum alloy
Compression ratio	9.0 : 1
Clearance (bottom of skirt)	0.0039-0.0054 in. (0.0990-0.137 mm)
(top of skirt)	0.0094-0.0109 in. (0.2387-0.2768 mm)
(both measured on major axis)	
Gudgeon pin hole diameter	0.750-0.7502 in. (19.05-19.055 mm)
PISTON RINGS	
Material	Cast-iron
Compression rings—lower compression ring is tapered to same dimen.	
width	0.0615-0.0625 in. (1.5621-1.5875 mm)
thickness	0.114-0.121 in. (2.9972-3.0734 mm)
clearance in groove	0.001-0.003 in. (0.0254-0.0762 mm)
fitted gap	0.008-0.013 in. (0.2032-0.3302 mm)
Oil control ring	
width	0.124-0.125 in. (3.1496-3.175 mm)
thickness	0.114-0.121 in. (2.9972-3.0734 mm)
clearance in groove	0.001-0.003 in. (0.0254-0.0762 mm)
fitted gap	0.008-0.013 in. (0.2032-0.3302 mm)

CONNECTING RODS	
Length between centers	6.0 in. (152.394 mm)
Big-end bearing type	Vandervell VP/D2
Rod side clearance	0.024 in. (0.6049 mm)
Bearing diametrical clearance	0.001-0.0025 in. (0.0254-0.0635 mm)
Small-end bore diameter	0.8745-0.8755 in. (22.212-22.237 mm)
CRANKSHAFT	
Type	One-piece forged, two-throw crank with bolt-on flywheel.
Main bearing (drive-side)	Hoffmann RM11L (roller)
journal diameter	1.125 in. (28.574 mm)
outer diameter	2.812 in. (71.435 mm)
width	0.812 in. (20.637 mm)
Main bush (gear-side)	
inner diameter	15000-1.5005 in. (38.10-38.113 mm)
outer diameter	1.6245-1.6255 in. (41.262-41.288 mm)
width	0.940-0.960 in. (23.876-24.384 mm)
Crankpin diameter	1.6865-1.687 in. (42.837-42.849 mm)
Minimum regrind	−0.010 in. (0.254 mm)
Second regrind	−0.020 in. (0.508 mm)
Third regrind	−0.030 in. (0.762 mm)
Gear-side journal regrind (two only)	−0.010 in. (0.254 mm)
Crankshaft end-float	−0.020 in. (0.508 mm)
	0.0015-0.003 in. (0.038-0.076 mm)
Crank throw	1.4567 in. (37.00 mm)

ENGINE, TRANSMISSION, AND CLUTCH SPECIFICATIONS

1969 and Earlier Twins (Dual Carbs)

GUDGEON PIN

Material	Nickel-chrome high tensile steel
Diameter	0.750-0.7502 in. (19.05-19.055 mm)
Length	2.368-2.373 in. (60.147-60.275 mm)

SMALL-END BUSHING

Material	Phosphor-bronze
Outside diam. (before fitting)	0.8775-0.8785 in. (22.2885-22.3139 mm)
Length	0.940-0.950 in. (23.876-24130 mm)
Finished bore (fitted)	0.7503-0.7506 in. (19.0576-19.0652 mm)
Interference fit in rod	0.002-0.004 in. (0.0508-0.1016 mm)

VALVES

Seat angle (inclusive)	90°
Head diameter: (inlet)	1.595-1.60 in. (40.513-40.64 mm)
(exhaust)	1.407-1.412 in. (35.737-35.864 mm)
Stem diameter: (inlet)	1.3095-1.310 in. (7.861-7.874 mm)
(exhaust)	1.309-1.3095 in. (7.848-7.861 mm)

VALVE GUIDES

Material	Hidural 5
Bore diam. (inlet & exhaust)	1.312-1.313 in. (7.9248-7.950 mm)
Outside diam. (inlet & exh.)	1.5005-1.501 in. (12.7127-12.7254 mm)
Length (inlet and exhaust)	1.96-1.97 in. (49.784-50.038 mm)
Clearance on valve stem (inlet)	0.002-0.0035 in. (0.0508-0.0889 mm)
(exhaust)	0.0025-0.004 in. (0.0635-0.1016 mm)

VALVE SPRINGS

Free length: (inner)	$1\frac{7}{16}$ in. (36.512 mm)
(outer)	$1\frac{3}{4}$ in. (44.45 mm)
Fitted length (inner)	1.277 in. (33.00000 mm)
(outer)	1.37 in. (34.798 mm)

OIL PUMP

Body material	Zinc-base alloy
Type	Double gear
Drive ratio	1 : 3
Non-return valve spring (free length)	0.8125 in. (20.637 mm)
Non-return valve ball, size	$\frac{1}{4}$ in. (6.35 mm)
Oil pressure relief valve spring (free length)	0.609 in. (15.478 mm)
Oil pressure relief valve ball, size	$\frac{5}{16}$ in. (7.937 mm)
Blow-off pressure	50 lbs per square inch
(1970) Oil pressure relief valve spring (free length)	1.370 in. (34.798 mm)

TAPPET CLEARANCE (Cold)

Inlet	0.008 in. (0.2032 mm)
Exhaust	0.010 in. (0.254 mm)

IGNITION TIMING

(Standard Ignition System)	
Piston position (B.T.D.C.) full advanced	0.304 in. (7.216 mm)
Crankshaft position (B.T.D.C.) full advanced	34°
Contact breaker gap setting	0.015 in. (0.381 mm)

CAMSHAFT

Journal diameter: (left)	0.810-0.8105 in. (20.574-20.586 mm)
(right)	0.8735-0.874 in. (22.188-22.2 mm)
End float	Nil (spring-loaded)
Cam lift	0.306 in. (7.772 mm)
Base circle diameter	0.812 in. (20.624 mm)

CAMSHAFT BEARING BUSHES

Bore diam., fitted (left-hand)	0.8115-0.8125 in. (20.612-20.637 mm)
Outside diam. (left-hand)	0.906-0.907 in. (23.012-23.037 mm)
Interfer. fit in case (left-hand)	0.002-0.004 in. (0.0508-0.1016 mm)
Bore diam., fitted (right-hand)	0.875-0.876 in. (22.225-22.25 mm)
Outside diam. (right-hand)	1.065-1.066 in. (27.051-27.076 mm)
Interfer. fit in case (right-hd.)	0.002-0.004 in. (0.0508-0.1016 mm)
Material	"Clevite 10" and bronze

ENGINE, TRANSMISSION, AND CLUTCH SPECIFICATIONS

1969 and Earlier Twins (Single Carb)

VALVE TIMING (Sports Camshaft)

Tappets set to 0.015 in. (0.381 mm) for checking purposes only:	
inlet opens	51° B.T.D.C.
inlet closes	68° A.B.D.C.
exhaust opens	78° B.B.D.C.
exhaust closes	37° A.T.D.C.

TIMING GEAR

Crankshaft pinion:	
number of teeth	22
fit on shaft	−0.0005 in. +0.0005 in. (0.0127 mm)
Camshaft pinion:	
number of teeth	44
interference fit	0.0000-0.001 in. (0.0254 mm)
Idler pinion:	
number of teeth	44
spindle dimen., both ends	0.6875-0.6870 in. (17.449-17.463 mm)
bush dimen., both (inside)	0.6885-0.6880 in. (17.475-17.488 mm)
bush dimen., both (outside)	0.939-0.940 in. (23.851-23.876 mm)
Spindle working clearance	0.0005-0.0015 in. (0.0127-0.0381 mm)

INTAKE BALANCE PIPE

Length	4 in. (101.6 mm)
Bore diameter	7/32 in. (5.56 mm)

CARBURETOR (Concentric)

Type	Amal R930/34 (right-hand, concentric) Amal L930/35 (left-hand, concentric)
Main jet	190
Pilot jet	20
Needle jet size	0.106 in. (2.6924 mm)
Needle position	1
Throttle valve	3
Nominal choke size	30 mm
Air cleaner type	Dry surgical gauze
Throttle slide return spring	3 in. (free length) (76.2 mm)
Air slide return spring	2 3/4 in. (free length) (69.8 mm)

CLUTCH

Type	Multi-plate with built-in cush drive
Number of plates	
driving (bonded)	6

CYLINDER BARREL

Material	Cast-iron (close grained)
Bore size (standard)	2.9521-2.9530 in. (74.983-75.0062 mm)
Maximum oversize	2.9921-2.9930 in. (75.999-76.022 mm)
Tappet bore size	0.3745-0.375 in. (9.5123-9.525 mm)
Stroke	74 mm

TAPPETS

Material	20 carbon steel body (stellite tipped)
Tip radius	1.250 in. (31.75 mm)
Tappet diameter	0.3735-0.375 in. (9.488-9.5 mm)
Clearance in barrel	0.0005-0.0015 in. (0.0127-0.0381 mm)

CYLINDER HEAD

Material	DTD424 alum. alloy (B.S.)
Inlet port size	1 1/2 in. (38.1 mm)
Exhaust port size	1 5/16 in. (33.337 mm)
Valve seatings	Cast-iron (cast-in)
Working clearance	0.0005-0.002 in. (0.0127-0.508 mm)
Spring free length	2 1/4 in. (57.15 mm)

GEARBOX	Top	Third	Second	First
Internal ratios (std.)	1 : 1	1.144 : 1	1.60 : 1	2.51 : 1
Overall ratios (std.)	4.87 : 1	5.57 : 1	7.79 : 1	12.23 : 1

GEAR DETAILS

Mainshaft top gear	
bush diameter (fitted)	0.813-0.814 in. (20.6502-20.6756 mm)
bush length	3 1/8 in. (79.375 mm)
bush protrusion	31/64 in. (12.3031 mm)
working clearance	0.0027-0.0042 in. (0.0685-0.1066 mm)
Layshaft first gear	
bush diameter (fitted)	0.7495-0.7505 in. (19.0273-19.0627 mm)
working clearance	0.0005-0.001 in. (0.0127-0.0254 mm)
Gearbox shafts:	
mainshaft left-hd. end diam.	0.8098-0.8103 in. (20.568-20.581 mm)
right-hd. end diam.	0.7495-0.7499 in. (19.047-19.057 mm)
length	10 5/8 in. (269.875 mm)
layshaft left-hand end diam.	0.7495-0.750 in. (19.057-19.05 mm)
right-hd. end diam.	0.7495-0.750 in.

ENGINE, TRANSMISSION, AND CLUTCH SPECIFICATIONS

1969 and Earlier Twins (Single Carb)

driven (plain)	6
Driving plate segments	
number	288
overall thickness	0.140-0.145 in. (3.556-3.683 mm)
Clutch springs	3
Free length	1 13/16 in. (46.03 mm)
Working coils	9 1/2
Spring rate	113 lbs per inch
Clutch sprocket	
number of teeth	58
bore diameter	1.8745-1.8755 in. (47.612-47.638 mm)
Clutch hub bearing diameter	1.3733-1.3743 in. (34.882-34.907 mm)
Clutch roller diameter (20)	0.2495-0.250 in. (6.337-6.35 mm)
length	0.231-0.236 in. (5.8674-5.994 mm)
SPROCKETS	
Number of teeth	
engine sprocket	28
clutch sprocket	58
final drive sprocket	20 solo (18 sidecar)
PRIMARY CHAIN	3/8 in. triple roller (80 links)
CLUTCH OPERATING ROD	
Length	11 1/16 in. (280.987 mm)
Diameter	7/32 in. (5.5562 mm)
CAM PLATE PLUNGER	
Plunger diameter	0.4355-0.4365 in. (11.0617-11.0871 mm)
Housing diameter	0.437-0.4375 in. (11.0998-11.1125 mm)

	(19.057-19.05 mm)
length	6 11/16 in. (169.862 mm)
GEARBOX BEARINGS	
Mainshaft top gear bearing	2 1/2 × 1 1/4 × 5/8 in. Ball Journal
Mainshaft bearing right side	3/4 × 1 7/8 × 9/16 in. Ball Journal
Layshaft bearing left side	1 × 3/4 × 3/4 in. Needle Roller
right side	1 × 3/4 × 3/4 in. Needle Roller
KICK-START RATCHET	
Pinion bore diameter	0.937-0.938 in. (13.799-23.825 mm)
Bush outside diameter	0.933-0.935 in. (23.698-23.749 mm)
inside diameter	0.750-0.751 in. (19.05-19.0574 mm)
Outside working clearance	0.002-0.005 in. (0.0508-0.127 mm)
Inner working clearance	0.0001-0.0015 in. (0.00254-0.0381 mm)
Ratchet spring free length	1/2 in. (12.70 mm)
GEAR SELECTOR QUADRANT	
Plunger diameter	0.3352-0.3362 in. (8.514-8.539 mm)
Housing diameter	0.3427-0.3437 in. (8.7045-8.729 mm)
Working clearance	0.0065-0.0085 in. (0.1651-0.2159 mm)

1969 and Earlier Twins (Single Carb)

All specifications are the same as 1969 and Earlier Twins (Dual Carbs) except the following:

CARBURETOR (Concentric)	
Type	Amal R928/2 (right-hand, concentric)
Main jet	230
Pilot jet	20
Needle jet size	0.106 in. (2.6924 mm)
Needle position	1
Throttle valve	3 1/2
Nominal choke size	28 mm
Air cleaner type	Dry surgical gauze
SPARK PLUGS	Champion N4
INTAKE MANIFOLD	
Carburetor port size	1 1/8 in. (28.575 mm)
Cylinder head port size	1 1/16 in. (26.987 mm)

ENGINE, TRANSMISSION, AND CLUTCH SPECIFICATIONS

A75 Engine

VALVES	
Seat angle (inclusive)	90°
Head diameter (intake)	1.528-1.534 in. (38.81-38.96 mm)
(exhaust)	1.309-1.315 in. (33.24-33.4 mm)
Stem diameter (intake)	0.3095-0.3100 in. (7.86-7.874 mm)
(exhaust)	0.3090-0.3095 in. (7.84-7.861 mm)
VALVE GUIDES	
Material	
Bore diam. (intake & exh.)	0.3122-0.3129 in. (7.93-7.947 mm)
Outside diam. (intake & exh.)	0.5005-0.5010 in. (12.71-12.725 mm)
Interference fit in head	0.001-0.003 in. (0.0254-0.0762 mm)
Length	1⅞ in. (47.625 mm)
VALVE SPRINGS	
Free length (inner)	1.468 (37.28 mm)
(outer)	1.600 in. (40.64 mm)
Fitted length (inner)	1.181 in. (30.0 mm)
(outer)	1.229 in. (31.2 mm)
PISTON	
Material	"Lo-Ex" aluminum
Compression ratio	9 : 1
Clearance (bottom of skirt)	0.0018-0.0033 in. (0.0457-0.0838 mm)
(top of skirt)	0.0045-0.0056 in. (0.114-0.142 mm)
(both measured on major axis)	
Wrist pin hole diameter	0.6883-0.6885 in. (17.48-17.59 mm)
CRANKSHAFT	
Type	One-piece forged three-throw crank
Main bearing (drive-side)	Hoffman MS.11 (ball)
Journal diameter	1.1245-1.1248 in. (31.56-31.57 mm)
Outer diameter	2.812 in. (71.42 mm)
Width	0.812 in. (20.6 mm)
Center main bearings	Vandevell VP.3
Journal diameter	1.9170-1.9175 in. (49.69-48.7 mm)
Bearing diametrical clearance	0.0005-0.002 in. (0.0127-0.0508 mm)
Main bearing (gear side)	Hoffman R.125 (roller)
Inner diameter	0.9840-0.9843 in. (24.993-25.00 mm)

PISTON RINGS	
Material—compression (top and center)	Cast-iron (tapered)
oil control	Chrome-plated steel
Width—compression (top and center)	0.0625 in. (1.587 mm)
Oil control	"Apex"
Depth	0.091-0.107 in. (2.31-2.71 mm)
Clearance in groove	0.0015-0.0035 in. (0.038-0.088 mm)
Fitted gap (minimum)	0.009 in. (0.228 mm)
(maximum)	0.013 in. (0.33 mm)
WRIST PIN	
Material	EN.32B
Fit in small-end (clearance)	0.0011-0.0005 in. (0.028-0.012 mm)
Diameter	0.6883-0.6885 in. (17.48-17.59 mm)
Length	2.235-2.250 in. (56.76-57.15 mm)
CONNECTING RODS	
Length between centers	5.749-5.751 in. (146.02-146.07 mm)
Big-end bearing type	Vandervell VP.6
Rod side clearance	0.008-0.014 in. (0.203-0.355 mm)
Bearing diametrical clear.	0.0005-0.002 in. (0.0127-0.05 mm)
Small-end bore diameter	0.6890-0.6894 in. (17.5-17.511 mm)
Finished width of cap	0.903-0.905 in. (22.93-22.98 mm)
CYLINDER BARREL	
Material	Aluminum with Austenitic iron liner
Bore size (standard)	2.6368-2.6363 in. (66.21-66.19 mm)
Maximum oversize	2.6768-2.6763 in. (67.99-67.98 mm)
Tappet bore size	0.3120-0.3125 in. (7.9248-7.9375 mm)
TAPPETS	
Material	High tensile steel with Stellite tip
Tip radius	1.125 in. (28.575 mm)
Tappet diameter	0.3110-0.3115 in. (7.899-7.912 mm)

ENGINE, TRANSMISSION, AND CLUTCH SPECIFICATIONS

A75 Engine

Outer diameter	2.047 in. (51.99 mm)
Width	0.590 in. (14.986 mm)
Crankpin diameter	1.6235-1.6240 in. (41.23-41.25 mm)
Min. regrind (big-end)	−0.010 in. (−0.254 mm)
Second regrind (big-end)	−0.020 in. (−0.508 mm)
Third regrind (big-end)	−0.030 in. (−0.762 mm)
Max. regrind (big-end)	−0.040 in. (−1.016 mm)
Min. regrind (cen. main bear.)	−0.010 in. (−0.254 mm)
Second regr. (cen. main bear.)	−0.020 in. (−0.508 mm)
Third regr. (cen. main bear.)	−0.030 in. (−0.762 mm)
Max. regr. (cen. main bear.)	−0.040 in. (−1.016 mm)
Crank throw	1.375 in. (34.925 mm)
TIMING GEAR	
Crankshaft gear:	
Number of teeth	25
Fit on shaft	−0.0005 in. (0.0127 mm) +0.0005 in.
Camshaft gear:	
Number of teeth	50
Interference fit	−0.0000-0.001 in. (0.0254 mm)
Idler gear	
Number of teeth	47
Idler pinion shaft size	0.6870-0.6875 in. (17.449-17.462 mm)
Idler pinion hole size	0.8745-0.8755 in. (22.212-22.237 mm)
Type of bearing	Torrington B.1110 (needle roller)
CAMSHAFT	
Journal diameter—left (intake and exhaust)	1.0605-1.0615 in. (26.936-26.962 mm)
Journal diameter—right (intake and exhaust)	1.0605-1.0615 in. (26.936-26.962 mm)
Journal diameter—center (intake and exhaust)	1.0605-1.0615 in. (26.926-26.962 mm)
End float	0.007-0.012 in. (0.1778-0.304 mm)
Cam lift (intake)	0.329 in. (8.33 mm)
Base circle diameter	0.406 in. (10.3 mm)
KICK-START MECHANISM	
Pinion diameter (inner)	0.6205-0.6215 in. (15.76-15.786 mm)
Running clearance	0.0015-0.0035 in. (0.0381-0.0889 mm)
Bore diameter (inner cover)	0.623-0.624 in. (15.824-15.849 mm)

Clearance in tappet blocks	0.0005-0.0015 in. (0.0127-0.0381 mm)
CYLINDER HEAD	
Material	DTD.424 aluminum alloy
Intake port size	$1^7/_{16}$ in. (36.5 mm)
Exhaust port size	$1^7/_{32}$ in. (30.9 mm)
Valve seats	Cast-iron (cast-in)
CLUTCH	
Type	Borg and Beck: single dry-plate
Overall thickness of disc	0.262 in. (6.654 mm)
Diaphragm spring (maximum release load)	1,000 lb (approx.) (453.6 kg)
GEARBOX	
Mainshaft top gear	
Bush diameter (fitted)	0.8145-0.8155 in. (20.688-20.713 mm)
Bush length	$2^7/_{32}$ in. (56.35 mm)
Working clearance	0.0042-0.0057 in. (0.1066-0.1447 mm)
Countershaft first gear	
Bush diameter (fitted)	0.8135-0.8145 in. (20.662-20.688 mm)
Working clearance	0.0025-0.0040 in. (0.0635-0.1016 mm)
GEARBOX SHAFTS	
Mainshaft—left end diam.	0.8098-0.8103 in. (20.568-20.581 mm)
right end diam.	0.7494-0.7498 in. (19.034-19.044 mm)
Length	$10^{21}/_{64}$ in. (262.33 mm)
Countershaft—left end diam.	0.6870-0.6875 in. (17.449-17.462 mm)
rt. end diam.	0.6870-0.6875 in. (17.449-17.462 mm)
Length	$6^{31}/_{64}$ in. (164.7 mm)
GEAR SELECTOR QUADRANT	
Plunger diameter	0.4315-0.4320 in. (10.96-10.97 mm)
Housing diameter	0.4325-0.4330 in. (10.98-10.99 mm)
Working clearance	0.0005-0.0015 in. (0.0127-0.0381 mm)

ENGINE, TRANSMISSION, AND CLUTCH SPECIFICATIONS

Pinion diameter (outer)	0.747-0.748 in. (18.973-18.999 mm)
Running clearance	0.003-0.005 in. (0.0762-0.127 mm)
Bush bore diameter	0.751-0.752 in. (19.075-19.10 mm)
Ratchet spring free length	½ in. (12.7 mm)

CAM PLATE PLUNGER	
Plunger diameter	0.4355-0.4365 in. (11.061-11.087 mm)
Housing diameter	0.4370-0.4380 in. (11.099-11.125 mm)
Working clearance	0.0005-0.0025 in. (0.0127-0.0635 mm)
Spring free length	2.65 in. (67.46 mm)

Torque Specifications

Singles

Application	Torque ft lb
Auto-advance unit bolt	6
Carburetor flange nuts	10
Clutch center nut	55-60
Con-rod end cap nuts (B25)	22
Crankcase stud nuts	16-18
Crankpin nuts (B50)	200
Crankshaft pinion nut (B25)	50-55
Crankshaft pinion nut (B50)	55
Cylinder head nuts (B25)	26-28
Cylinder head nuts (B25)	18-20
Cylinder head nuts (B50)	18-20
Cylinder head nuts (B50)	30-33
Flywheel bolts (B25)	50
Kick-start ratchet nut	38-40
Oil pump stud nuts	5-7
Oil pressure release valve	25
Rotor mounting nut (B25)	60
Rotor mounting nut (B50)	60
Rocker box nuts	8
Stator mounting nuts	5-7
Gearbox sprocket nut	100
Timing and primary cover screws	3.5-4.5
Fork leg end cap nuts	15
Fork leg top nuts	50-55
Fork yoke pinch bolts	23-25
Fork stanchion end plug	25
Flasher stanchion to flasher body nut	3

Twins

Application	Torque ft lb
Cylinder head studs in barrel	5
Cylinder barrel/crankcase nuts	28-30
Oil pump worm (L.H.T.)	35
Connecting rod nuts (S.L.)	22
Cylinder head bolts	31-33
Clutch center nut	60-65
Crankcase stud nut	16-18
Flywheel bolts	45
Kick-start ratchet nut	55-60
Oil pump nuts (S.L.)	8-10
Rotor nut	60
Stator nuts (S.L.)	15
Crank pinion nut (L.H.T.)	35
Cylinder head nuts	31-33
Manifold nuts	6
Carburetor nuts (S.L.)	10-12
Gearbox sprocket nut	100
Gearbox end cover nuts	18-20
Oil pressure valve to crankcase	30
Auto-advance unit bolt	6
Front fork cap nuts	50
Engine cover screws (Posidrive yellow)	6.5-7.5
Engine cover screws (Posidrive yellow)	6.5-7.5
Crankcase sump plate nuts	6

L.H.T.—Left hand thread.
S.L.—Self-locking.

Rocket 3

Application	Torque ft lb
Alternator rotor nut	50
Clutch center nut	60
Connecting rod nuts (S.L.)	17½-18½
Crankcase junction bolts	15
Crankcase junction stud nuts	15
Cylinder barrel nuts	20-22
Cylinder head bolts	18
Cylinder head stud nuts	18
Engine sprocket nut	58-63
Fork bottom yoke pinch bolts	23-25
Fork top cap nuts	75-80
Fork top yoke pinch bolt	23-25
Front wheel spindle cap bolt	23-25
Kick-start ratchet nut	40-45
Main bearing cap nuts (S.L.)	17½-18½
Rocker box bolts	6
Rocker box stud nuts	6
Shock absorber nut	75-80
Stator mounting nuts (S.L.)	8
Zener diode nut	2-2.3
Headlamp mounting bolts	10
Gearbox sprocket nut	58

CRANKCASE OIL LINE JUNCTION (1970 And Earlier Models)

The oil line junction is secured to the crankcase with one nut. If a leak has developed at this point, disconnect the oil lines and inspect the O-rings. Replace if necessary.

When reinstalling the junction, note that the oil lines are correctly connected when they are crossed (i.e., outer line from the oil tank to the inner connection of the junction).

OIL PRESSURE RELIEF VALVE

The oil pressure relief valve is located at the front of the crankcase. Should oil pressure exceed a preset limit, the valve routes the excess oil directly back into the sump.

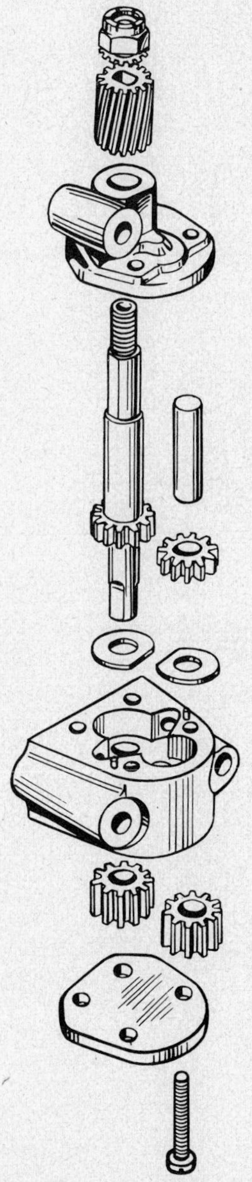

Exploded view of the oil pump

To remove the valve, unscrew the hexagonal plug and withdraw the ball and spring. Inspect them for corrosion, and replace them if necessary. The spring will in time lose its strength, so it is advisable to replace it if the machine has accumulated high mileage. Also replace the fiber washer if it is in less than perfect condition, and tighten the valve to 25 ft lb.

NOTE: *On 1971 and later models, the valve can't be disassembled, and it must be replaced as a unit if it is not functioning properly.*

OIL PUMP

The oil pump is located at the front right side of the engine under the inner crankcase cover.

Disassembly

1. Remove the four screws at the base of the pump and remove the baseplate and top cover.
2. Mark the worm gear for reassembly, then remove the nut and washer that secure the gear and driving spindle to the top cover. Note the position of the thrust washers under the feed gears (B50).
3. Clean all parts thoroughly in solvent and blow them dry with compressed air.

Inspection

Examine the oil pump parts for excessive scoring and damage. If oil changes have been neglected, it will be evident by the damage done to the pump gear teeth and pump body. Small scratches can be ignored, but any more substantial wear calls for parts replacement.

Inspect the pump gears for worn or broken teeth. If formerly sharp edges have become rounded, the gear should be replaced.

Assembly

1. Make sure that all parts are absolutely clean and bathed in engine oil or assembly lube.
2. Insert the driving shaft into the pump top cover.
3. Install the worm drive gear and secure it with the nut and spring washer.
4. Install the driven shaft and gear in the top cover, and install the thrust washers (B50).
5. Install the lower pump gears and baseplate.

NOTE: *Coat the pump housing top and bottom surfaces with a suitable sealing compound before installing the top and bottom plates.*

6. Rotate the shaft and gears to make certain there is no binding, then tighten the four securing screws.
7. Check the joining surfaces of the oil pump to make sure that they are all parallel. If not, the pump may not be free to operate when installed in the engine.
8. When installing the pump, use a new gasket and tighten the self-locking nuts evenly to 5 to 7 ft lb. If self-locking nuts are not used, apply thread locking compound to them to prevent loosening.

TWINS

SCAVENGE CHECK VALVE

The scavenge check valve is located within the oil return pipe in the engine sump. Operation of the valve should be checked at every oil change, or whenever the sump filter is cleaned.

Poke a piece of wire into the pipe and force the check ball off its seat. Allow it to drop back down of its own weight. If the ball does not seat properly, this indicates a sludge buildup in and around the valve. If necessary, immerse the return pipe in gasoline and let it sit until the check ball operates freely.

OIL PRESSURE RELIEF VALVE

The pressure relief valve is located at the front right side of the crankcase under the large acorn nut. If oil pressure exceeds 50 psi, the valve opens and directs oil back into the crankcase until pressure drops to normal.

The pressure valve normally does not need attention or maintenance. If the engine is being rebuilt or has accumulated high mileage, the pressure relief ball should be inspected for war and damage, and spring strength should be checked. Make sure that the fiber sealing washer is in good condition when reinstalling the valve.

NOTE: *On 1971 and later machines, the pressure relief valve cannot be disassembled and must be replaced as a unit if it is not functioning properly.*

OIL PRESSURE SWITCH

On later models with an oil pressure warning light, the oil pressure switch is located at the front of the crankcase near the pressure relief valve. The switch cannot be disassembled and must be replaced if faulty.

OIL PUMP

The oil pump can be removed after the outer and inner right-side crankcase covers have been taken off. The delivery side check valve ball and spring will be released as the pump is removed.

Disassembly

1. Take out the circlip at the shaft end and remove the shaft and thrust washer.
2. Unscrew the four bolts at the base of the pump and remove the baseplate and

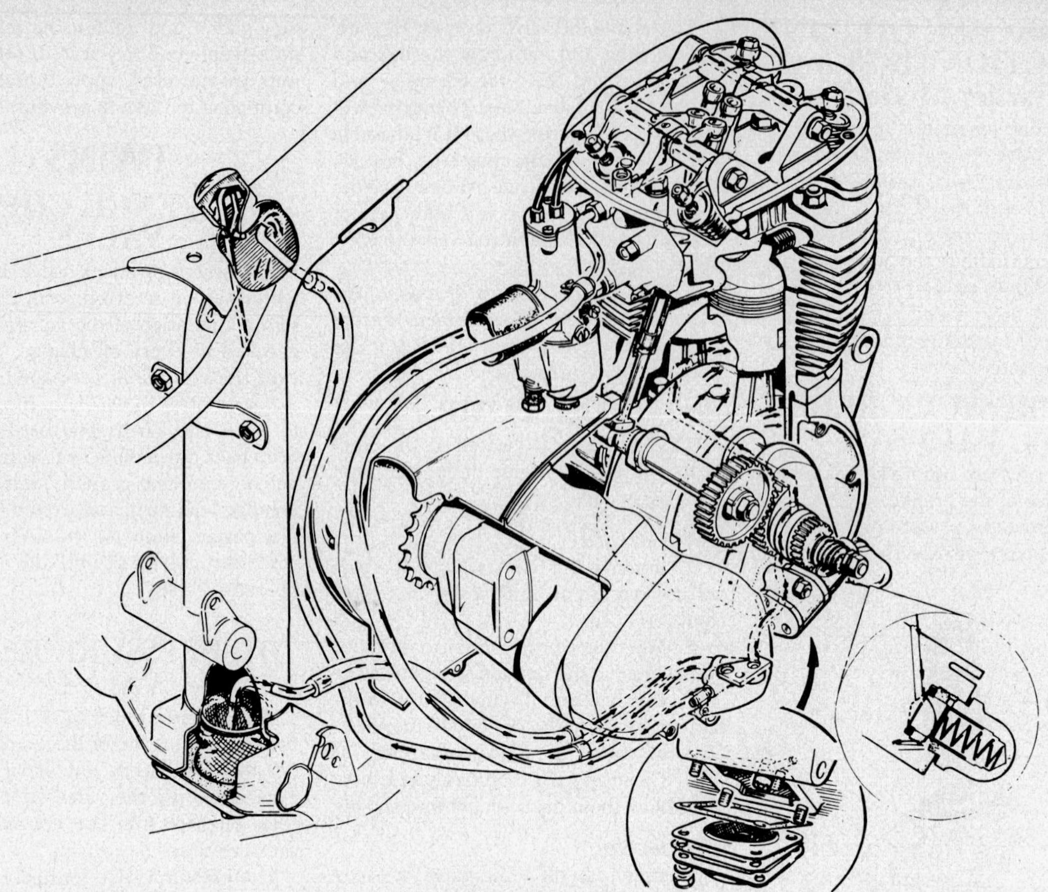

Lubrication system diagram

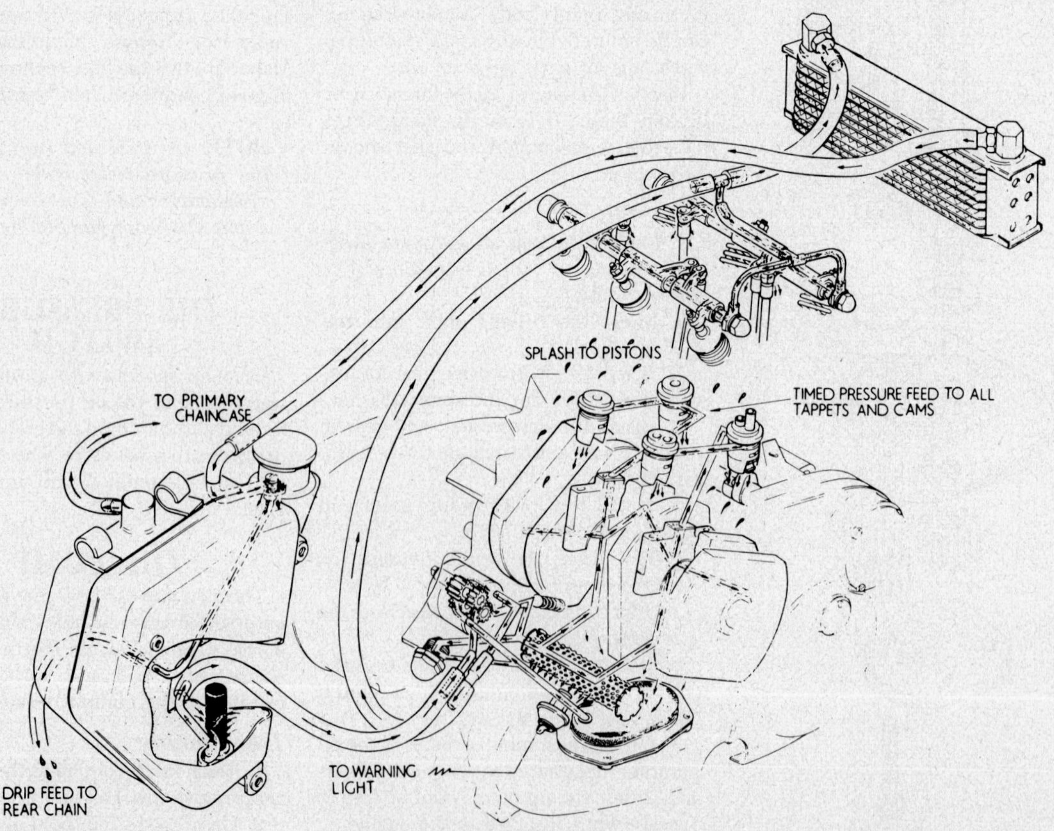

Lubrication system diagram

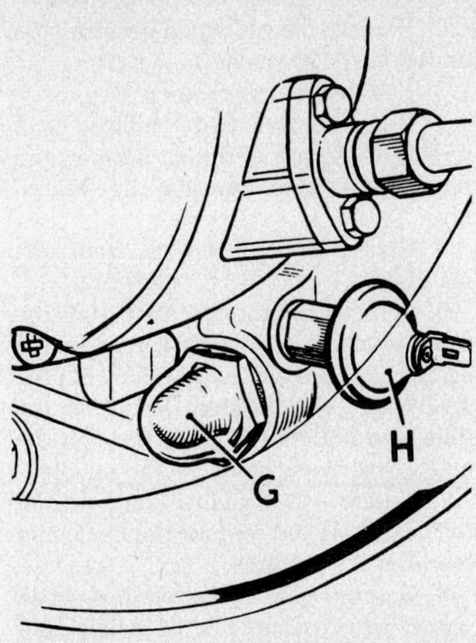

Oil pressure relief valve (G) and pressure switch (H)

housing. Remove the two sets of pump gears, which will be exposed as the housing is removed.

3. Take care not to lose the two dowel pins that are essential for correct pump alignment.

Inspection

Clean all components in solvent and dry thoroughly. Examine the gear teeth for damage and excessive wear, and check the gear recesses in the housing for scoring. Replace parts as necessary. Light scoring or wear is not serious, but heavy damage is indicative of neglected oil changing.

Assembly

1. Coat all parts with fresh motor oil before assembly.

2. Insert the narrow delivery side driving gear into its recess, and install the long shaft (projecting through into the base) and its mating gear.

3. Install the large scavenge gears into the recesses in the other side of the pump housing.

4. Install the plain shaft through the two driven gears until the end of the shaft is flush with the gear.

5. Using a new O-ring, install the baseplate with its machined face inside, and tighten the bolts evenly.

6. Install the driving shaft and check that the gears move freely. If they do, install the thrust washer and circlip.

7. Using a straightedge, make sure that the mating surface of the pump is perfectly flat, or else when the pump is bolted to the crankcase it will be distorted and cause the gears to bind.

ROCKET 3

CHECKING OIL PRESSURE

Normal running oil pressure at 3000 rpm is 75–90 psi, but may rise above that when the engine is cold. Pressure can be checked by installing an oil pressure gauge in one of the blanking plugs at the front of the center crankcase.

If the oil pressure is unsatisfactory, check the following:

1. Faulty or dirty oil pressure relief valve.
2. Insufficient amount of lubricant in the oil tank.
3. Dirty or incorrectly installed oil filters.
4. Faulty oil pump.
5. Obstructed crankcase drillings.
6. Excessively worn main or connecting rod bearings.
7. Leaking crankcase oil line junction O-rings.

OIL PRESSURE RELIEF VALVE

The oil pressure relief valve is located at the rear of the crankcase under the large acorn nut. It requires no regular maintenance, but should be inspected at the time of an engine rebuild. Check the valve and seat for damage, and measure the length of the spring to determine if it has settled. Use a new fiber washer whenever the valve is removed to prevent oil leaks.

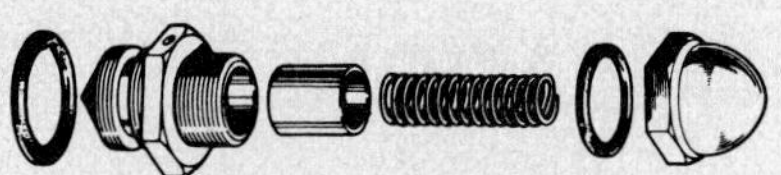
Oil pressure relief valve

OIL COOLER

The Rocket 3 is equipped with an oil cooler mounted below the gas tank on two support brackets. Great care should be taken when handling this component.

Removal

1. Remove the gas tank.

2. Mark both oil lines for reassembly, then disconnect the clamps and pull the lines off the connectors. Do not unscrew the connectors. Take care not to tilt the cooler as it still contains approximately ½ pint of oil.

3. Loosen the top support bracket bolts and remove the bracket insulating rubber.

4. Hold the cooler upright and remove the bracket bolts, nuts, and washers. Note that rubber bushings are used for further vibration insulation.

5. Lift out the cooler, then drain the remaining oil by inverting the cooler over a suitable container.

6. Clean the outside of the cooler with kerosine and a soft-bristled brush. It is not necessary to flush the cooler.

Installation

Installation is a reversal of the removal procedure.

Note the following:

1. The large oil line fittings at the top of the cooler should face rearward when the cooler is installed.

2. When the cooler is properly installed the left oil line fitting should be connected to the oil tank and the right fitting to engine via the rocker feedline.

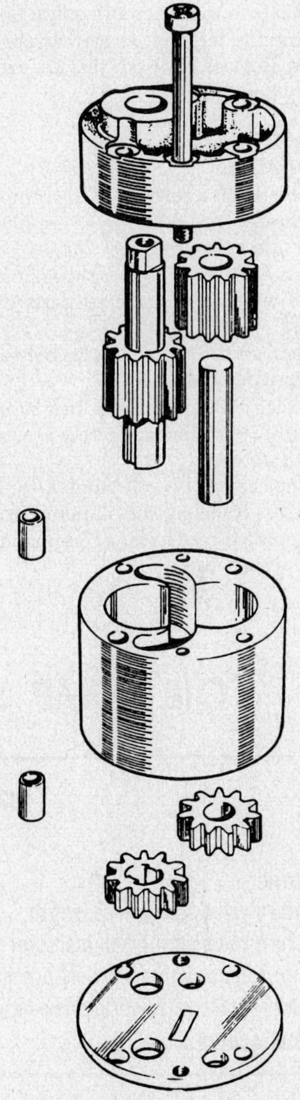
Exploded view of the oil pump

OIL PUMP

The oil pump is mounted in the primary side crankcase. Drive is provided by the crankshaft via reduction gears. Since the pump is immersed in oil, wear should be negligible on all but the feed and scavenge drive gears.

Removal

1. Remove the outer and inner left-side crankcase covers. (Refer to 'Engine and Transmission.'

2. Remove the four large retaining screws and pull out the oil pump assembly.

3. Remove the two remaining screws and separate the pump parts.

4. Drive out the gear shafts, if necessary, with a thin, soft metal drift.

5. Wash all parts thoroughly in solvent and dry thoroughly with compressed air.

Inspection

Examine the gear teeth for scoring or rounded edges. Check the shafts and shaft bores in the gears and pump body. Examine the top and bottom covers for scoring. Replace any parts that are excessively worn.

Installation

Installation is a reversal of the removal procedure.

Note the following:

1. Assemble the pump as shown in the illustration, and lubricate all parts with fresh oil.
2. Replace the gasket that fits between the pump and crankcase.
3. Make certain that the two screws holding the pump body together are sufficiently tightened.
4. Replace the two oil pump O-rings.
5. When installing the oil pump drive gear, apply a thread locking compound to the securing screw.

OIL PUMP SPECIFICATIONS

B25 and B50	
Type	Double gear
Drive ratio	1 : 4
Non-return valve spring free length	0.5 in. (12.7 mm)
Non-return valve spring ball diameter	0.25 in.
Pressure release valve blow-off pressure	80-100 lbs p.s.i. (5.6-7.0 kg/cm²)
Pressure release valve spring free length	1.37 in. (34.8 mm)
Pump body material	Cast-iron

A65	
Pump body material	Cast-iron
Pump type	Double gear
Pump drive ratio	1/3 engine speed
Pump non-return valve spring free length	0.8125 in. (20.637 mm)
Pump non-return valve ball, size	1/4 in. diameter (6.35 mm)
Relief valve blow-off pressure	50 lbs p.s.i. (3.51 kg/cm²)
Oil pressure switch	Smiths PS.5300/1/07

A75	
Pump body material	Cast-iron
Pump type	Double-gear
Pump non-return valve spring (free length)	1.500 in. (38.1 mm)
Pump non-return valve ball size	0.437 in. diam. (1.11 mm) diam.
Oil pressure relief valve spring (free length)	1.500 in. (38.1 mm)
Blow off pressure (oil at 80° C.)	70-90 lb/in² (4.9-6.3 kg/cm²)

FUEL SYSTEMS

CARBURETOR

Service

AMAL CONCENTRIC

The Amal Concentric carburetor was introduced in late 1967 and has become standard equipment on all British motorcycles made since that time. The significant difference between the Concentric and the Monobloc carburetor, which it replaced, is the construction of the float and arrangement of the float bowl. The plastic float is one-piece and semi-circular in shape and it surrounds the main jet, rather than being isolated from or next to it. The float bowl is shaped to accomodate this set-up.

Removal and Disassembly

1. Shut off the fuel taps and disconnect the lines at the carburetors. Drain the float bowls on models equipped with a drain plug.
2. Remove the gas tank if necessary (as on twin cylinder models).
3. Remove the air cleaner.
4. Unscrew the two phillips head screws at the top of the carburetor and remove the cap and throttle slide assembly.
5. Unbolt the carburetor from the manifold.
6. Remove the throttle slide from the cable by compressing the return spring against the carburetor cap, taking out the needle and clip through the top of the slide, and pulling the cable through the hole formerly occupied by the needle.
7. Unscrew the fuel line banjo bolt on the float bowl and remove the banjo and the filter it contains.
8. Unscrew the two phillips head screws which secure the float bowl and remove the bowl, taking care not to mishandle the float and float needle it contains.

Note that the float spindle is press fit in the float bowl and that the float needle is secured in position by the rear, forked end of the float.

9. Unscrew the jet holder, which has the main jet in its lower end, and the needle jet at the other end.
10. Unscrew the pilot jet from the carburetor body.
11. Take out the pilot air screw and the throttle stop screw.

Inspection

1. Clean the filter in the banjo.
2. Check the float bowl for any sediment which may have gotten past the filter. be sure that the fuel passage in the bowl which leads to the pilot jet is clear. The float needle seat should be free of any marks, scoring, or deposits. Place the float bowl on a piece of glass or a known flat surface and make sure the mating surface of the bowl is quite flat. Even out the surface with emery cloth if necessary.
3. The float itself is constructed of nylon, as is the float needle. The float level is not adjustable; therefore the only checks which can be carried out are to make sure that the fork which holds the float needle is in good condition and that the float itself is not punctured and can pivot freely on the spindle. Shake the float to see if there is any gas in it.

The float needle must be able to shut off the supply of gas to the float bowl and to do this, it must form a good seal with its brass seat in the float bowl. A visual check of the needle's sealing ability can be carried out by connecting the fuel line to the float bowl and, keeping the bowl level, turning on the gas.

Be certain to have a rag beneath the float bowl to catch any spilled gas.

The bowl should fill with gas until the float rises sufficiently to close the needle on its seat, when the flow should stop.

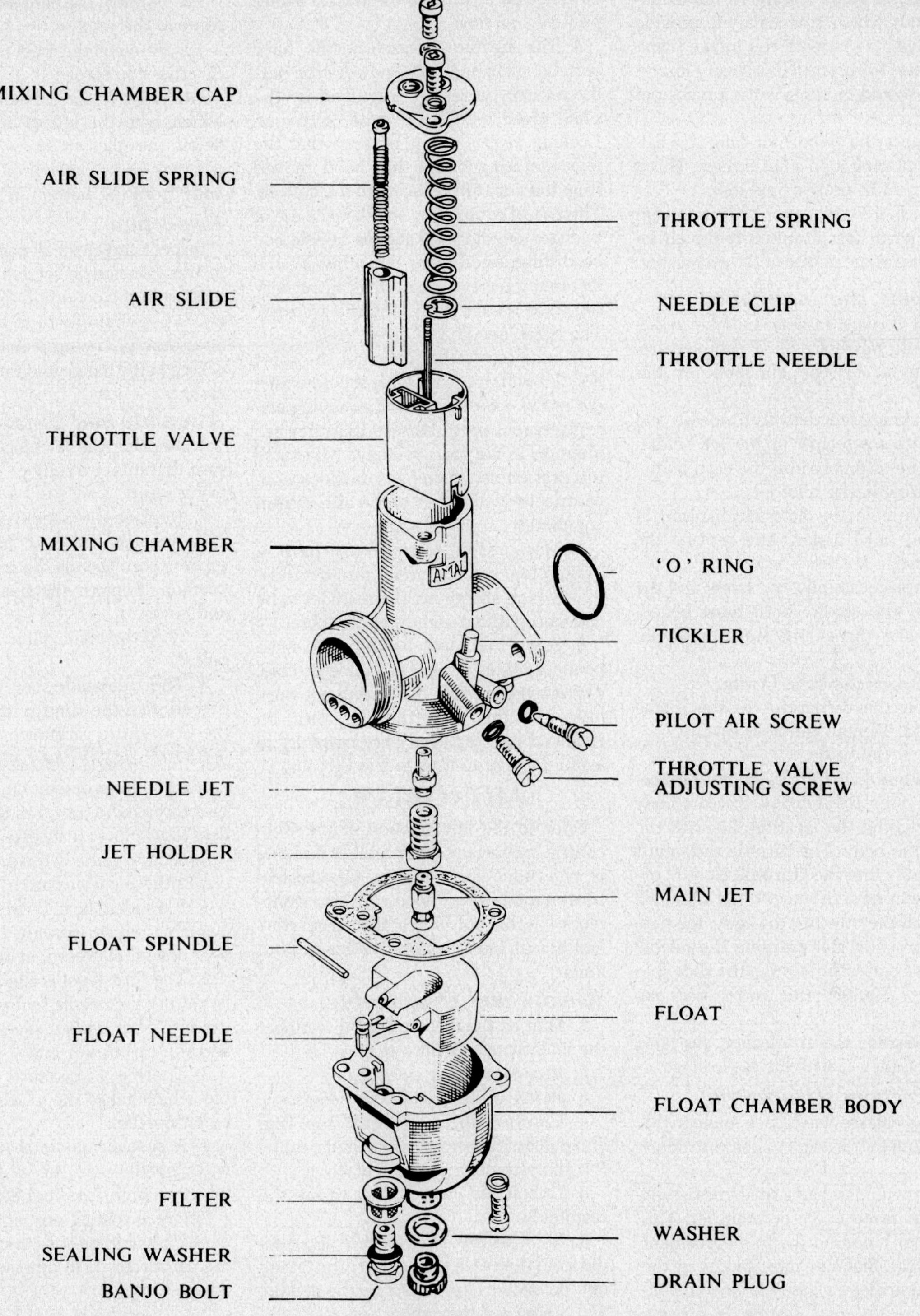

Amal Concentric Carburetor

If the carburetors have not been dismantled, the same check can be made if you have transparent fuel lines. Make sure the float bowl is empty and turn on the gas. The gas should flow through the line for about ten seconds and then stop.

4. The pilot, needle, and main jets can all be cleaned by washing them in a solvent or carburetor cleaning fluid and blowing dry.

5. The needle and needle jet are prone to wear after many miles, since they are usually in contact. This wear will cause a rich running condition noticable in the mid-throttle range. Replace both if this condition is present, assuming that the needle jet is the correct size and the needle is located properly.

Also, check the needle for scoring or nicks along the tapered portion.

6. Make sure that the throttle slide can move effortlessly in the carburetor body. It should not be too loose a fit, however. A hollow sounding clatter at idle may be due to a worn slide. The slide is prone to wear after extended use, especially if the motorcycle has been run without an air cleaner. Minute score marks at the front of the slide may be present caused by abrasive particles in the air.

7. The pilot air screw and throttle stop screw are both fitted with rubber O-rings. These provide an air seal and also keep the adjustment screws from turning while the bike is running. If they can do this, they are probably okay.

There is a larger O-ring on the carburetor body which is necessary to provide a positive air seal with the intake manifold. This O-ring is obviously very important. It should be replaced as a matter of course.

8. Check the carburetor flange for flatness by placing it on a flat surface. This is also critical to proper operation.

9. Wash the carburetor body in solvent paying particualr attention to the air intake holes at the mouth of the carburetor.

Assembly and Installation

1. All O-rings, gaskets, and fiber washers should be replaced. A complete rebuilding kit can be obtained for this purpose.

2. Making sure that both needle and main jets are secure in the jet holder, screw the assembly into the carb body.

3. Screw in the pilot jet.

4. Assemble the float mechanism, fit the float bowl gasket, and replace the float bowl.

5. Replace the pilot air screw and the throttle stop screw. Both must be adjusted with the engine warm and running.

6. Replace the large O-ring.

7. Bolt the carburetor to the intake manifold. Tighten the bolts evenly.

8. Refit the banjo.

9. Assemble the throttle slide and needle and insert the slide into the carb body after aligning the locating tab with the slot in the body. The throttle slide must slip readily into the "throttle closed" position with no resistance. If the slide will not go all the way into the body, the needle is probably not entering the needle jet. Never attempt to force the slide into position. Tighten the carburetor cap screws.

10. Replace the air cleaner, gas tank, and fuel lines. Check for gas leakage.

Modifications (Concentric)

Several changes have been made to the Amal Concentrics since their introduction.

1. Early models had a small mesh-type fuel filter fitted over the main jet. This sometimes hindered the free movement of the float. Since at most places in the U.S., impurities in gasoline are uncommon, and the fuel system is already equipped with filters in the tank and at the carb banjo, the filter on the main jet is really unnecessary and can be removed.

2. A newer type float bowl has been fitted. This has fuel passages for the pilot jet which take the gas near the bottom of the bowl rather than half-way down as before. This was done to assure a positive fuel flow to the pilot jet regardless of variations in fuel level in the float.

3. The jet holder has been changed to thrust the main jet deeper into the float bowl. Once again, the air was to assure positive fuel flow.

4. The needle jet and needle have both been changed. The newer type needle jet can be readily identified by the small bleed hole at the base of the jet. Looking closer, it can be seen that the jet's metering orifice has been moved from the very top of the jet to the bottom. This has, of course, necessitated the use of a longer needle. This longer needle can be distinguished from the other by the fact that it has two small rings at the very top of the needle (above the clip grooves). The other needle has three rings.

It need hardly be said, that the short needles will not work with the new needle jets or vice versa. Before buying any replacement parts, be sure that they are identical to the parts you have. Of course it is preferable, if you have an older Concentric, to switch over to the new system completely.

5. Most recent carburetors have a drain plug incorporated into the float bowl which also allows the main jet to be changed without removing the bowl.

6. Some units will be found to have peening marks around the pilot jet hole. This is to assure that the jet will not work loose. In this case the jet must be removed and replaced very carefully to avoid damage to it or to the threads.

MONOBLOC

Prior to the introduction of the Concentric carburetor, British bikes had one or two Monobloc carbs. An unusual feature on models equipped with two Monoblocs was that only one of the carburetors had a float bowl, which fed gas to both units.

Remove and Disassembly

1. Shut off the fuel taps and disconnect the lines at the carburetors.

2. Remove the air cleaner.

3. Remove the gas tank (if necessary).

4. Unscrew the carburetor top ring and pull out the throttle slide and needle. Put the assembly in a safe place.

5. Unbolt the carburetors from the manifolds.

6. Remove the throttle slide and needle from the cable, if necessary, by taking out the needle clip, removing the needle, and taking out the cable.

7. Unscrew the fuel line banjo bolt and remove the banjo and its filter.

8. Unscrew the needle seating. Be careful as this may have an important washer fitted.

9. Unscrew the three screws for the float bowl cover and remove the cover and gasket.

10. Take out the float, float spindle bush, and needle.

11. Unscrew the main jet cover nut and the jet holder which will be removed with the main and needle jets.

12. Remove the pilot jet cover nut and remove the jet also.

13. Remove the pilot air jet and the throttle stop screw.

14. Remove the jet block fixing screw which is to the left of and just slightly below the pilot air screw. The jet block can now be pushed out of the carburetor body from the bottom of the carb.

Inspection

Inspect and clean all parts as described in the Concentric section. Pay close attention to the condition of all fiber washers. It is preferable to fit a new set after disassembly. The same holds true for the O ring at the flange and for the float bowl gasket.

Assembly and Installation

1. Replace the jet block and, making sure that it is correctly positioned, fit the fixing screw.

2. Replace the needle seating.

3. Replace the float bowl assembly, making sure the needle is in the correct position. Replace the float bowl gasket and cover.

4. Refit the banjo, filter, and the banjo bolt.

5. The remainder of the assembly procedure is the same as that outlined for the Concentric carburetor.

Modifications (Monobloc)

Most of the problems on Monobloc carburetors can be traced to the fuel feed or float level. Several accessories have been produced to remedy the problems inherent in these carburetors.

1. Extended float bowl end caps are available which increase the amount of float bowl fuel present at any given time.

2. The float level is slightly adjustable by raising the needle seating through the use of a fiber washer placed between it and the carburetor body.

3. There is a brass float needle available which takes the place of the stock nylon needle.

4. A special needle seating complete with needle can be obtained which promises increased fuel flow.

Before installing any of these components, it would be wise to make sure that the carburetor is in otherwise good condition.

MODEL IDENTIFICATION

Monobloc

Type	Bore (in.)
375	25/32, 13/16, 7/8
376	15/16, 1, 1 1/16
389	1 1/8, 1 5/32, 1 3/16

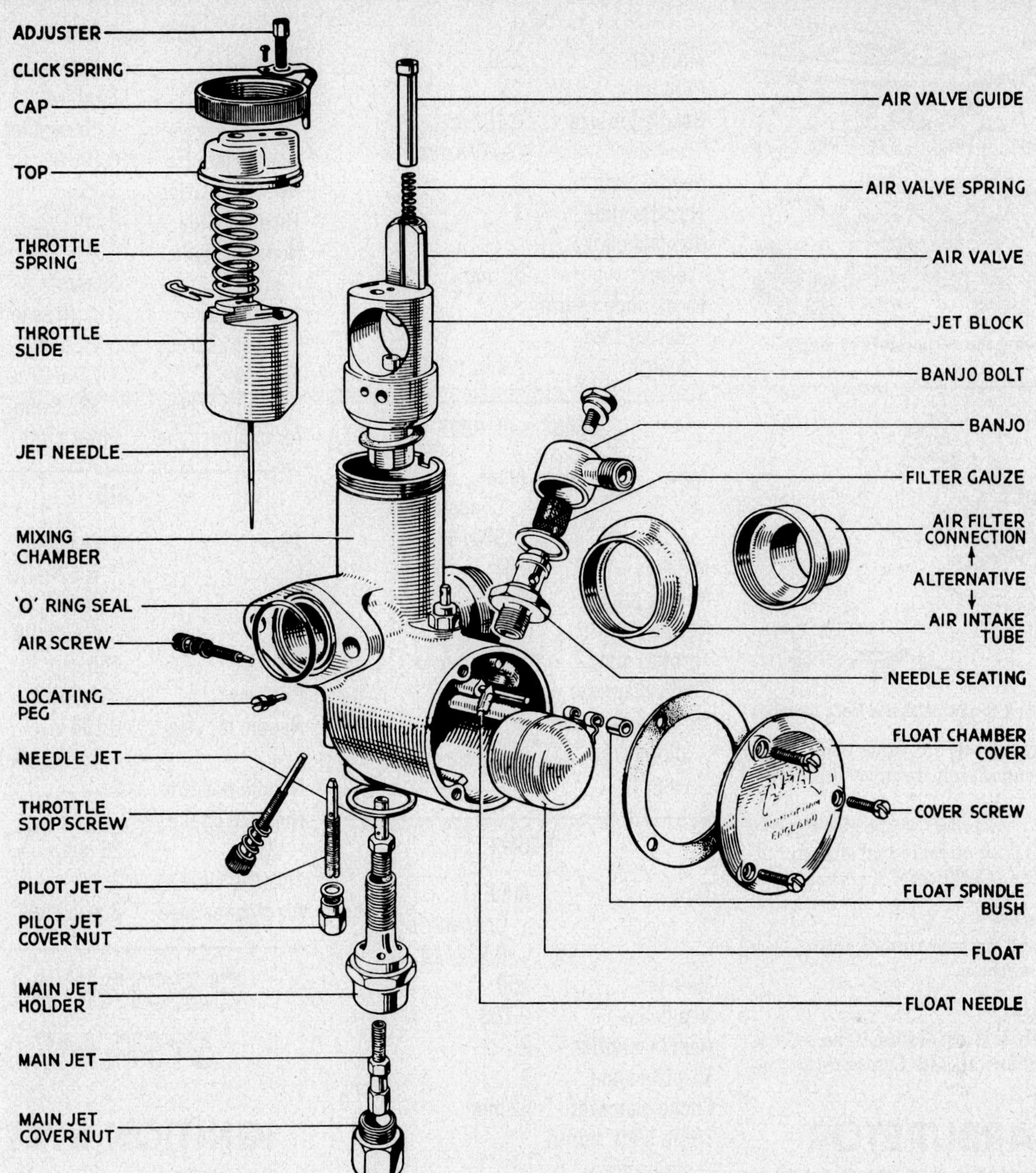

Amal Monobloc Carburetor

Concentric

Type	Bore (mm)	Bore (in.)
622	22	0.865
624	24	0.944
626	26	1.023
928	28	1.118
930	30	1.181
932	32	1.260

SINGLES

The 250 and 500 cc singles are equipped with a single Amal Concentric.

TWINS

Twin-cylinder models are equipped with one Concentric (Thunderbolt) or two (Lightning and Firebird Scrambler) which are identical in construction details to the carburetor used on the singles.

ROCKET 3

The triple is equipped with three Model 626 Concentrics. These units differ from the other Concentric carburetors in that the throttle slide has no conventional spring, but is returned by a scissor spring located on the external throttle linkage.

Removal and Disassembly

1. Remove the side panels and the fuel tank.

2. Disconnect the throttle cable from the throttle linkage and disconnect the choke cable from the handlebar lever.

3. Remove the air cleaner assembly from the left side of the machine.

4. Remove the two screws which secure each carburetor top, then remove the manifold nuts and pull each carburetor back and down, leaving the slide assemblies fastened to the throttle linkage.

5. To remove the carburetor top and slide assemblies, disconnect the slide from the throttle rod and the air valve from its cable. Remove the jet needle retaining clip and compress the throttle rod return spring to free the top retaining plate. Push the bottom nipple of the throttle rod down to clear the throttle slide and compress the air valve spring to free it from the cable end nipple.

Removing the carburetors as a unit

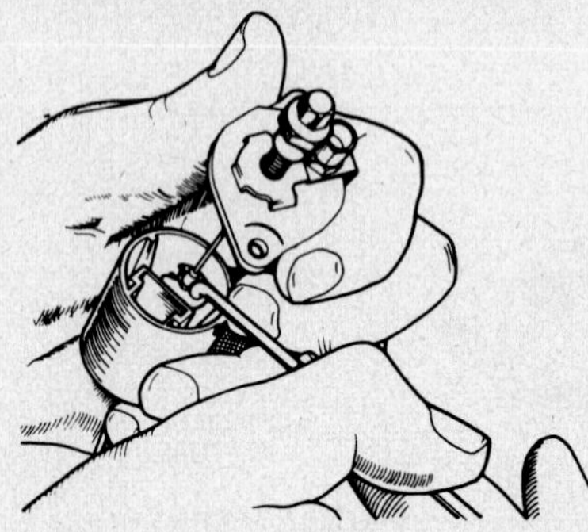

Disconnecting the throttle rod from the slide

6. Unscrew the air valve cable abutment to completely remove the carburetor top.

7. The remainder of the disassembly procedure is identical to that already outlined under "Carburetor Overhaul."

Inspection

Inspect all parts as described in "Carburetor Overhaul."

Assembly

Assembly and installation is the reverse of the "Removal and Disassembly" instructions.

CARBURETOR SPECIFICATIONS

B25SS and B25T

Type	Amal Concentric 928/20
Main jet	200
Needle jet	0.106
Needle position	1
Throttle slide	3½
Choke diameter	28 mm
Throt. slide return spring free length	2.5 in. (6.4 cm)

B44

Type	Amal Concentric 930/11
Main jet	230
Pilot jet	25
Needle jet size	0.107 in. (2.7178 mm)
Needle position	2
Throttle slide	3
Nominal choke size	30 mm
Throt. slide return spring free length	2.5 in. (63.5 mm)

B50SS and B50T

Type	Amal Concentric 930/62
Main jet	200
Needle jet	0.106
Needle position	1
Throttle slide	3½
Choke diameter	30 mm
Throt. slide return spring free length	2.5 in. (6.4 cm)

B50MX

Type	Amal Concentric R.932/18
Main jet	250
Needle jet	0.106
Needle position	2
Throttle slide	3
Choke diameter	32 mm
Throt. slide return spring free length	2.5 in. (6.4 mm)

A65T

Type	Amal R.928/17 (right-hand, concentric)
Main jet	230
Needle jet size	0.106 in.
Needle position	1
Throttle slide	3½
Nominal choke size	28 mm
Air cleaner type	Filter cloth

A65L and A65FS

Type	Amal R.930/42 (concentric) Amal L.930/41 (concentric)
Main jet	Lightning—220 Firebird Scrambler—230
Needle jet size	0.106 in.
Needle position	1
Throttle slide	3
Nominal choke size	30 mm
Throt. slide return spring	3 in. (free length) (76.2 mm)
Air slide return spring	3¼ in. (free length) (82.5 mm)
Air cleaner type	Filter cloth

A75

Type	Concentric R.626/28; R.626/30; L.626/29
Main jet	150
Pilot jet	622/107
Needle jet size	0.106 in. (2.692 mm)
Needle position	2
Nominal choke size	26 mm
Throttle slide	3
Air cleaner type	Zig-zag felt

ELECTRICAL SYSTEMS

IGNITION SYSTEM

Since 1962, most BSA models have, as standard equipment, an alternator and coil ignition system. It operates on AC current provided by the alternator, which is driven off the end of the crankshaft and located in the primary chaincase. The AC current is converted to DC current by a silicon diode rectifier and then supplied to the battery, lights, and, via the contact breaker and ignition coil, the spark plugs.

To determine whether an electrical problem is located in the high-tension circuit (secondary winding to the spark plug) or the low-tension circuit (contact breaker to primary coil winding) perform the following check:

Circuit Test

1970 AND EARLIER MODELS

Singles

1. Make sure that contact breaker

points are clean and correctly gapped. Also make certain that the battery terminals are tight and in good condition.

2. Check the main wiring harness fuse located near the battery.

3. Turn the ignition switch on and slowly turn the engine over while watching the ammeter needle. As the points open and close, the needle should flick between zero and a slight discharge. If it does not, there is a fault somewhere in low-tension circuit.

Twins

1. Check the condition and gap of the contact breaker points and the tightness of the battery terminals.

2. Disconnect the wire that connects to the "SW" terminal of the right ignition coil.

3. Turn the ignition on and slowly turn the engine over while observing the ammeter needle. As the contact points open and close, the needle should flick between zero and a slight discharge.

4. Reconnect the wire to the right coil and disconnect the wire from the "SW" terminal on the left coil. Repeat step 3.

5. If the ammeter needle does not flick in the described manner for both the left and right ignition coils, a fault exists in the low-tension circuit.

Rocket 3

1. Lift up the seat and disconnect the white lead that connects the "SW" terminals of all three ignition coils.

NOTE: *Lucas coils are marked "SW" and "CB." Siba coils are marked "1" instead of "SW" and "15" instead of "CB."*

2. Connect the white lead to one coil at a time and check the ammeter needle movement as described for the other models.

1971 AND LATER MODELS

Singles

1. Make sure that the contact points, battery terminals, and main wiring harness fuse are all in good condition.

2. Connect the negative lead of a 0–15 volt DC voltmeter to the "CB" or "+" terminal of the coil, and connect the positive lead to the ground.

3. Turn the ignition on and turn the engine until the points open. The voltmeter should read battery voltage.

4. No reading indicates a fault in the low-tension circuit. If the points are suspected of being at fault, you can quickly confirm this by disconnecting the points (CB) wire at the coil. If the voltmeter then reads battery voltage, the points are shorted out (usually caused by incorrect assembly of the insulating washers).

Twins

Twin-cylinder models can be tested in the same manner as described for singles. Perform the test twice, once at each coil.

Rocket 3

Perform the test in the same manner as for single-cylinder models, checking at each of the three coils separately.

Low-Tension Circuit Tests

If the above tests showed that the fault exists somewhere in the low-tension circuit, isolate the problem source in the following manner:

NOTE: *On 12V machines, disconnect the zener diode center terminal.*

1. Place a piece of nonconducting material, such as a strip of rubber, between the contact breaker points. Turn the ignition switch on.

2. Using a 0–15 volt DC voltmeter (0–10 volts for 6V machines), make point-to-point checks as described below.

3. Check the battery by connecting the voltmeter between the negative terminal of the battery and ground (frame). No reading indicates a blown main fuse, or a faulty battery lead; a low reading indicates a poor ground.

4. Connect the voltmeter between the ignition coil negative terminal (SW or 1) and ground (one at a time on twins and triples). No reading indicates a faulty lead between the battery and coil terminal, or a faulty switch or ammeter connection.

5. Connect the voltmeter between ground and one ammeter terminal at a time (if applicable). No reading at the "load" terminal indicates either a faulty ammeter or a break in the the blue/-brown lead from the battery; no reading on the battery side indicates a faulty ammeter.

6. Connect the voltmeter between the ignition switch input terminal and ground. No reading indicates a break or faulty terminal along the ignition switch input lead. Check for voltage readings between ground and the input lead terminals at the rectifier, ammeter, and lighting switch (if applicable).

7. Connect the voltmeter between the ignition switch output terminal and ground. No reading indicates a faulty switch. A positive reading at this point, but not in step 4, indicates a break or faulty connection along the white lead.

8. Disconnect the ignition coil lead from the positive (CB or 15) terminal and connect one voltmeter lead in its place (one coil at a time on twins and triples). Connect the other voltmeter lead to ground. No reading indicates a faulty primary coil winding.

9. Reconnect the ignition coil lead(s) and connect the voltmeter across the contact breaker points one set at a time. Leave the rubber insulator in place. No reading indicates a faulty connection, insulation, or condenser.

10. On 12V machines, reconnect the zener diode center terminal and connect the voltmeter to this terminal and ground. The meter should read battery output voltage.

High-Tension Circuit Tests

If the preliminary ignition system checks showed that the problem lay in the high-tension circuit, check the following:

1. Test the ignition coil(s) as described in component tests. If the coils are in satisfactory condition, either the high-tension cables or spark plug cap(s) are at fault.

2. Remove the spark plug cap(s) from the cable(s) and turn the ignition switch on. Hold the cable ⅛ in. away from the cylinder cooling fins and kick the engine over. A bright blue spark should jump across the gap; if not, the cable is defective. If the spark does appear, the spark plug cap is faulty.

Component Tests

IGNITION COIL

1. Check the coil in the machine by removing the spark plug cap and holding the high-tension cable end about ⅛ in. away from the cylinder cooling fins. Turn the ignition on and kick the engine over. Observe the caution given in the "High Tension Circuit Tests."

2. Check primary winding resistance by removing the coil and connecting an ohmmeter to the low tension terminals.

3. Inspect the high-tension cables for any signs of insulation deterioration.

CONTACT BREAKER CONDENSERS

A faulty condenser is usually indicated by burning or arcing of the points. To check the condenser(s), first turn the ignition switch on, then take readings across the contact breaker((s) (open position) with a voltmeter. No reading indicates that the condenser insulation has broken down and that the unit should be replaced.

Capacitor Ignition System–1971 And Later Singles

On 1971 and later singles, a capacitor is installed, along with the legally required battery, to allow you to run the machine with the battery removed for competition purposes. When you remove the battery to run the machine on the capacitor, wrap the end of the negative (brown/blue) battery cable with electrical tape to prevent it from grounding out.

If the engine will not start with the battery disconnected, check the capacitor in the following manner:

1. Disconnect the capacitor.
2. Connect a 12V battery directly to the capacitor (negative to blue/brown terminal, positive to red terminal) for five minutes.
3. Disconnect the battery and let the capacitor stand for five minutes.
4. Connect a DC voltmeter across the capacitor terminals. If the capacitor is functioning properly, the voltmeter will read not less than 9 volts.

To maintain the capacitor in good condition, the machine should be run for a few minutes with the battery disconnected twice a year. Do not run the engine with the zener diode disconnected, or the capacitor will be damaged due to the excessive voltage. If you experience hard starting with the battery connected, disconnect the capacitor to eliminate the possibility of a short circuit.

INSTALLATION

1. The capacitor terminals can be identified as follows:

single terminal—positive (ground) marked with a red dot on the mounting rivet.

double terminal—negative.

2. Install the capacitor in its spring with the terminals facing down. Push the unit into the spring until the last coils fit into the capacitor body groove.
3. Connect the capacitor negative terminal and zener diode to the center (brown/white lead) connector of the rectifier.
4. Connect the positive terminal of the capacitor to the rectifier center ground bolt terminal.
5. Mount the capacitor spring in any convenient spot near the battery carrier.

Before putting the machine into operation, a few precautions should be taken to avoid any damage to the capacitor or wiring system.

1. If the battery is to remain in the machine, it is essential that the negative lead be very carefully insulated to prevent it from shorting to the frame. This can be done either by wrapping the lead in electrical tape or better yet, by replacing the battery fuse with a wooden dowel of similar dimensions.
2. If the capacitor is being used as a back-up system in case of battery failure, take the time to check it occasionally to ensure that it's still operational.
3. Do not run the engine with the zener diode disconnected as the capacitor will be destroyed due to excessive voltage.

TEST

The capacitor has a limited storage life of approximately 18 months at 68° F, or 9 to 12 months at 86° F. Therefore, it would be wise to check its condition regularly if it is not in use.

1. Connect the capacitor to a 12V battery for approximatley 5 minutes. Make sure that the terminal polarity is correct, the capacitor will be ruined.
2. Let the capacitor stand for at least 5 minutes, then connect a DC voltmeter to the terminals. Note the instantaneous reading of the meter. A good capacitor will register at least 9 volts.

CHARGING SYSTEM

The charging system consists of an alternator and a full-wave bridge rectifier that converts the AC pulses in the DC for recharging the battery and powering the lights. Twelve-volt machines are also equipped with a zener diode to absorb any excess charge.

Alternator Output Test

Singles

1. Disconnect the alternator output leads.

NOTE: *Earlier machines have three leads; later machines have two.*

2. Start and run the engine at 3000 rpm.
3. Connect a 0–15 volt AC voltmeter with a 1-ohm load resistor in parallel with each of the alternator leads as described below.
4. Three-lead-type stator:
   a. White/green and green/black leads—minimum voltmeter reading 4.0 volts.
   b. White/green and green/yellow leads—minimum voltmeter reading 6.5 volts.
   c. White/green and green/black with green/yellow leads—minimum voltmeter reading 8.5 volts.
5. Two-lead-type stator:
   a. White/green and green/yellow leads—minimum voltmeter reading 8.5 volts.
6. If low or no readings are obtained, inspect the leads for damage and make sure that they have tight connections. Check the alternator output again, and if the same results are obtained, the difficulty lies in the alternator itself and must be referred to a qualified repair shop.
7. To check for grounded coils within the stator, connect the voltmeter to each terminal and ground. If a reading is obtained, the coil connected to the lead being tested is grounded.

Twins

Test the alternator output as described for the single-cylinder models. Correct output. Readings are given in the chart.

Stator Number	System Voltage	Alternator Output Min. AC Volts @ 3000 rpm A	B	C
47162	6V 12V	4.0	6.5	8.5
47164	6V	4.5	7.0	9.5
47167	6V	7.7	11.6	13.2
47188	6V	5.0	1.5	3.5
47204	12V	N.A.	N.A.	8.5
47205	12V	N.A.	N.A.	9.0

A—Green/White and Green/Black
B—Green/White and Green/Yellow
C—Green/White, Green/Black, and Green/Yellow connected
Note: On machines fitted with two-lead-stator, only test C is applicable.

Rocket 3

Check alternator output for the triple in the same manner as described for the three-lead-stator on single-cylinder models. Correct output readings are given below.

RM 20 Stator
47209 (12 volt)

Alternator Output Minimum AC Volts @ 3000 rpm		
green/white and green/black connected 5.0	green/white and green/yellow connected 8.0	green/white green/black and green/yellow connected 10.0

Rectifier Test

When removing or installing the rectifier, it is very important that the adjustment of the center bolt not be disturbed. Therefore, avoid putting a wrench on the bolt head.

1970 AND EARLIER MACHINES

Singles

1. Disconnect the brown/white lead from the center terminal and wrap the end in tape to prevent a short circuit to ground.
2. Connect a DC voltmeter in parallel with a 1-ohm load resistor between the center rectifier terminal and ground.
3. Start and run the machine at 3000 rpm and observe the voltmeter reading. It must be 7.5 volts minimum. If the reading is higher than specified, check the rectifier ground. If the ground is OK, replace the rectifier. If the reading was zero or less than specified, the problem lies in the rectifier or charging system

wiring. First perform the rectifier bench test.

Twins

1. Disconnect the alternator green/yellow lead and connect it to the rectifier green/black lead with a jumper wire. Make sure that this connection is insulated to prevent a short circuit.

2. Carry out step 3, above, as described for single-cylinder models.

Rocket 3

Check rectifier output on the triple in the same manner as described in the previous section on single-cylinder models.

1971 AND LATER MACHINES

Singles

1. Disconnect the zener diode by removing the straight connector with blue/brown lead from the capacitor in the electrical box.

2. Disconnect the connector for the blue/brown lead running to the electrical box.

3. Connect a DC voltmeter in parallel with a 1-ohm load resistor between the blue/brown lead from the electrical box and ground.

4. Using a jumper wire, connect the white/yellow lead from the electrical box to the negative battery terminal.

5. Start the engine and run it at about 3000 rpm, and observe the voltmeter. If the rectifier is operating properly, the meter will register 7.75 volts. If a higher reading is obtained, the rectifier is either improperly grounded or faulty. If a low reading is obtained, remove and benchtest the rectifier.

Twins

Perform the rectifier output test for 1971 and later twins in the same manner as for 1970 and earlier singles. The voltage reading in this case should be 7.75 volts.

Rocket 3

Perform the test in the same manner as for 1970 and earlier singles.

RECTIFIER BENCH TEST

1. Disconnect and remove the rectifier. Observe the note on handling the unit.

2. Connect the rectifier to a 12V battery and a 1-ohm load resistor.

3. Connect a DC voltmeter in the V_1 position as shown in the accompanying illustration. The meter should read 12 volts.

4. Disconnect the voltmeter and, using the accompanying illustrations for guidance, test each of the diodes with the

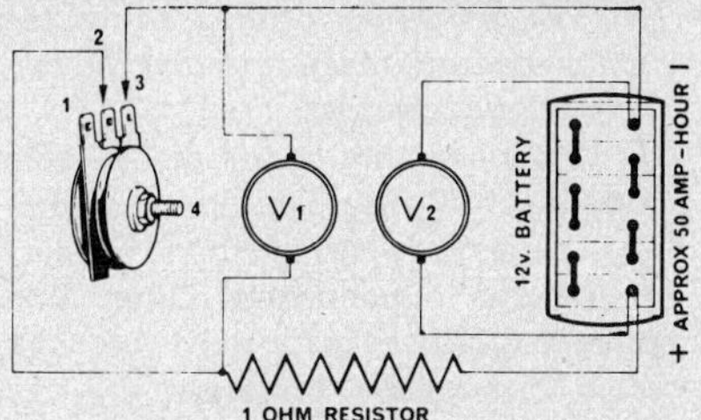

Rectifier bench test set-up

voltmeter leads. Keep the testing time as short as possible so that the rectifier does not overheat. No reading should be greater than 2.5 volts in Test 1, and no reading should be more than 1.5 volts less than the battery voltage in Test 2 (i.e., 10.5 volts minimum).

5. If the rectifier does not meet specifications, it should be replaced.

Charging Circuit Continuity Test

If the rectifier tests did not pinpoint the problem, it must be located somewhere within the charging circuit wiring. For checking continuity, the battery must be in a good state of charge and the alternator leads must be disconnected at their snap connectors

Singles

1. Make sure that there is a power at the rectifier by connecting a DC voltmeter, with a 1-ohm load resistor in parallel, between the center rectifier terminal and ground. The meter should read battery voltage.

2. If there is no voltage at the rectifier, repeat steps 3, 5, and 6 under "Low-Tension Circuit Tests" to isolate the problem in the wiring.

Twins

6 VOLT ELECTRICAL SYSTEMS

1. Repeat steps 1 and 2 given for the single-cylinder models.

2. Connect the green/yellow lead from the main wiring harness (under the engine) to the rectifier center terminal with a jumper cable. Turn the ignition switch to ON.

3. Connect a DC voltmeter, with a 1-ohm resistor in parallel, between the green/white lead at the rectifier and ground. With the light switch in the OFF position, the meter should read battery voltage. If not, the leads to the ignition switch terminals 16 and 18, and the leads to light switch terminals 4 and 5, should be checked.

4. Connect the green/yellow lead from the main wiring harness to the rectifier center terminal with a jumper cable. Turn the ignition switch to the IGN position and the headlight switch to the HEAD position.

5. Connect a DC voltmeter, with a 1-ohm resistor in parallel, to the green/-black lead at the rectifier and ground. The meter should read battery voltage. If not, the leads to ignition switch terminals 16 and 17; and the leads to light switch terminals 5 and 7, should be checked. With the light switch in the PILOT position, there should be no voltage reading between ground and the rectifier green/-black or green/white leads.

12 Volt Electrical Systems

1. Check the battery to make sure that the fuse is intact and that the battery is correctly connected to ground (positive).

2. Check to see that there is voltage at the rectifier center terminal as previously described. If there is not, disconnect the alternator leads at their snap connectors under the engine.

3. Connect a jumper wire between the center and green/yellow rectifier terminals and check the voltage between the snap connector and ground. If there is no reading, the alternator harness lead is faulty.

4. Repeat step 3 for the rectifier green/white lead.

5. If there is voltage at the center rectifier terminal, check the ammeter terminal (if applicable). If it is satisfactory here,

TEST 1 CHECKING FORWARD RESISTANCE

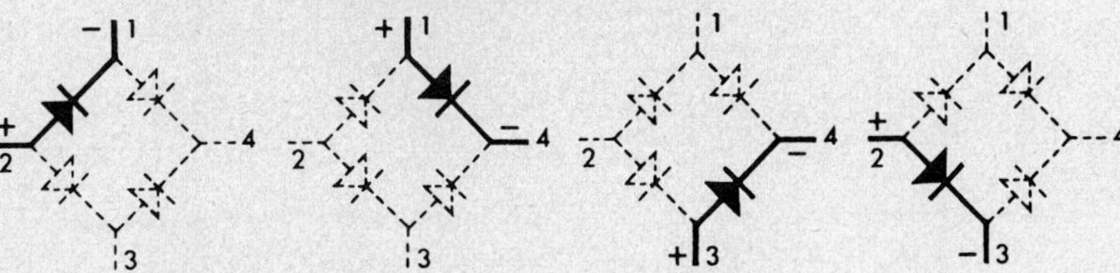

TEST 2 CHECKING BACK LEAKAGE

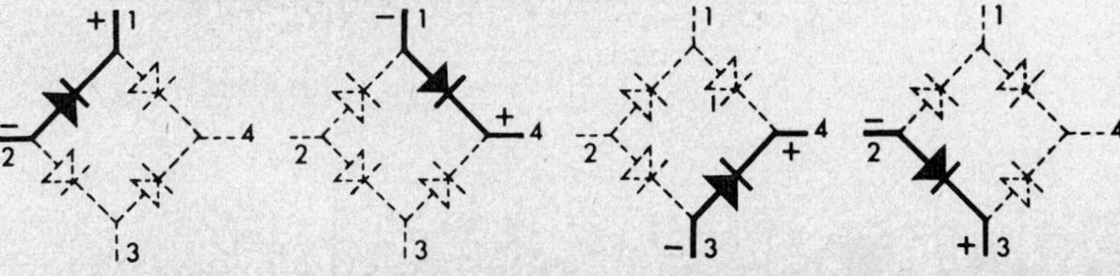

Rectifier diode test sequence

the brown/white lead to the rectifier center connector if faulty.

6. If there is no voltage at either the rectifier or the ammeter, the blue/brown wire from the battery is faulty.

Rocket 3

Perform the charging circuit continuity test for the triple in the same manner as described for the 12V twin-cylinder models.

Zener Diode Test

The zener diode serves the function of a voltage regulator, tapping off excess alternator current output and rerouting it to a heat sink. It is very important that the diode be kept clean and free from obstruction in the cooling airstream at all times. Other than this, if you make sure that the base of the diode and heat sink have firm metal-to-metal contact, the diode is a maintenance free item.

NOTE: *Before performing any of the following tests, make sure that the battery is fully charged.*

1. Disconnect the zener diode cable and connect a 0–5 amp (minimum) ammeter in series between the diode connector and the disconnected cable. The ammeter positive lead must be connected to the diode terminal.

2. Connect a DC voltmeter between the zener diode and the heat sink. The red or positive lead of the voltmeter must be connected to the heat sink, which is grounded to the frame.

3. Make sure that all lights are off, then start the engine and slowly increase its speed while observing both meters.

4. Until the voltmeter reaches 12.75 volts, the ammeter should read zero.

5. Continue increasing the engine speed until the ammeter reads 2.0 amps, at which time the voltmeter should be reading 13.5 to 15.3 volts.

6. If the ammeter registers before the voltmeter reaches 12.75 volts in step 4, or if the voltage is higher than stated in step 5 when the ammeter reads 2.0 amps, the zener diode should be replaced.

Bulb Specifications All Models (12v)

Bulbs	Rating	Type (Lucas)
Headlamp	50/40 watt	370
Stop-tail	21/5 watt	380
Flasher	21 watt	382
Speedometer	6 watt	281 or 643
Tachometer	6 watt	281 or 643
Warning lights	24 v., 2 w.	281
Pilot	6 watt	989

WIRING DIAGRAMS

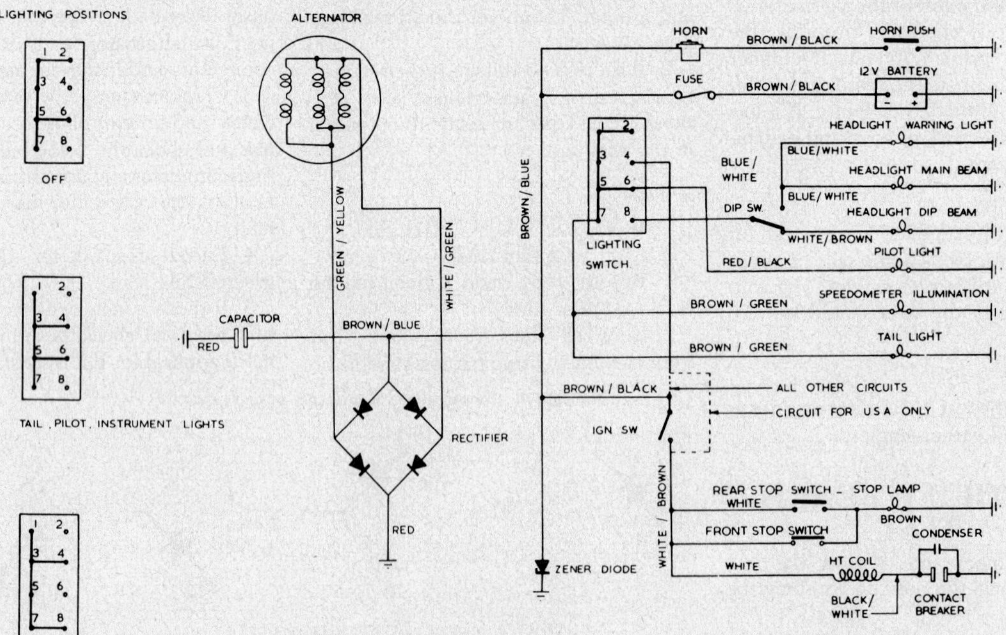

250 models

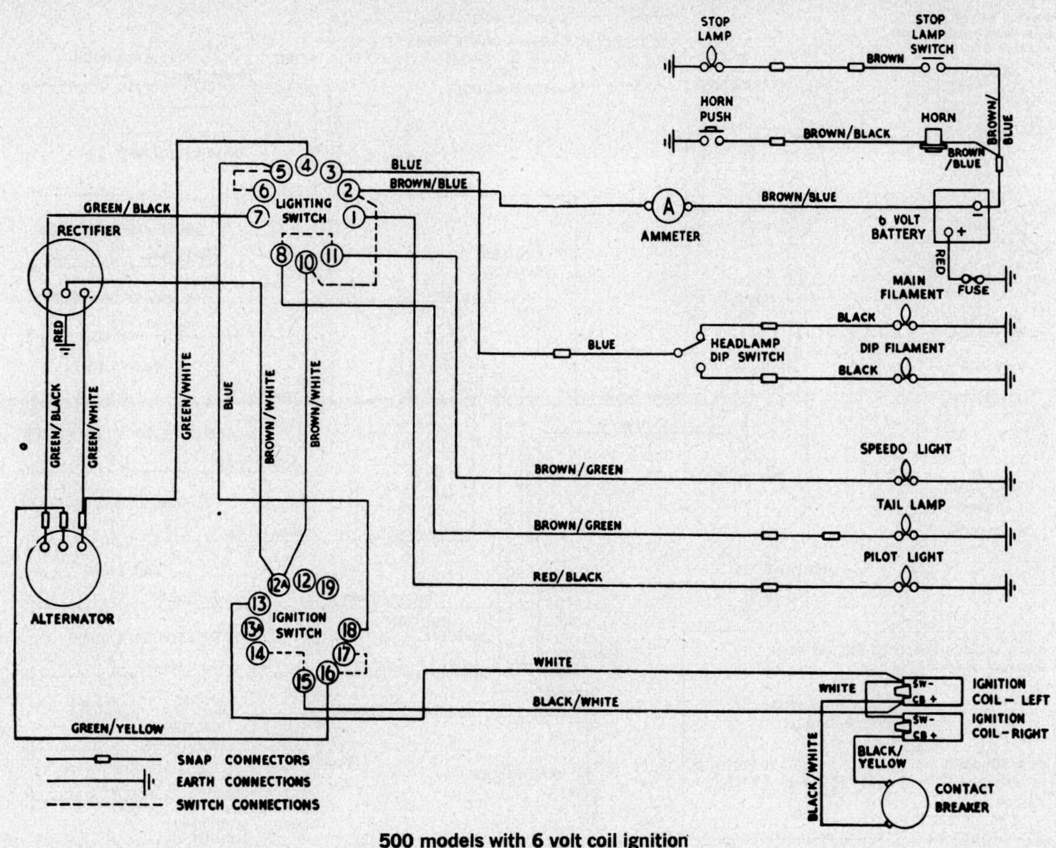

500 models with 6 volt coil ignition

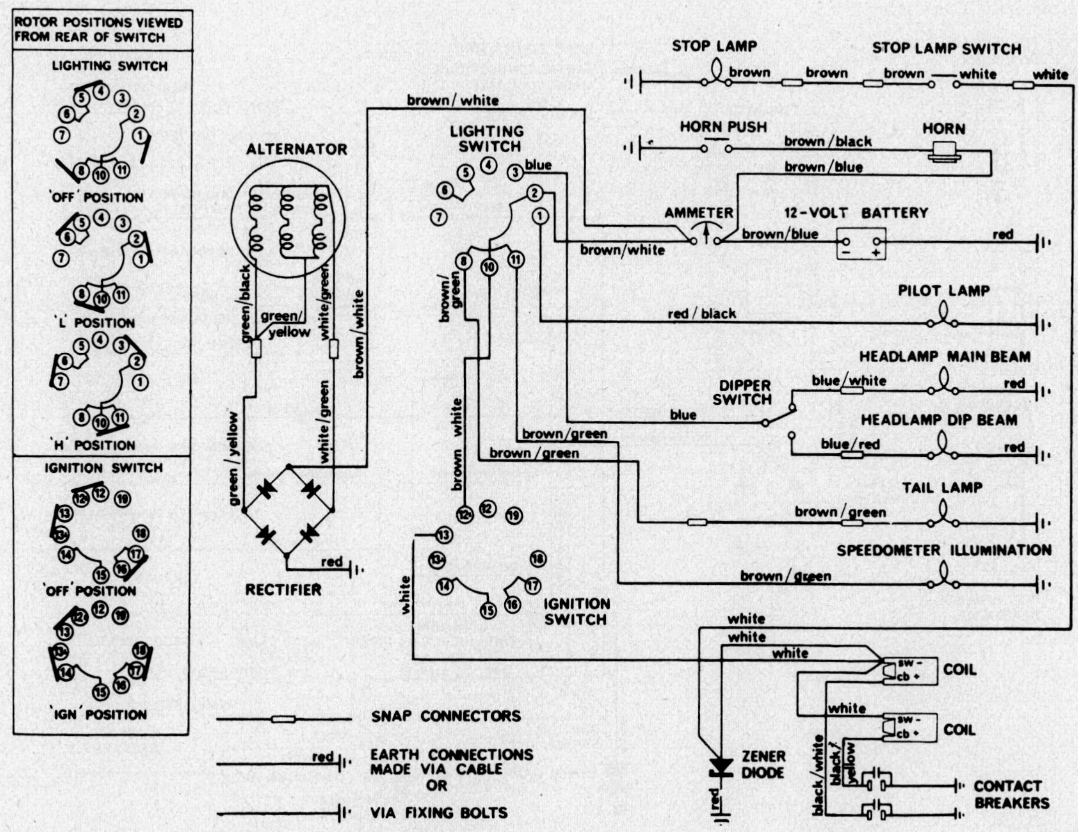

500 models, 12 volt coil ignition with nacelle up to Serial No. H49832

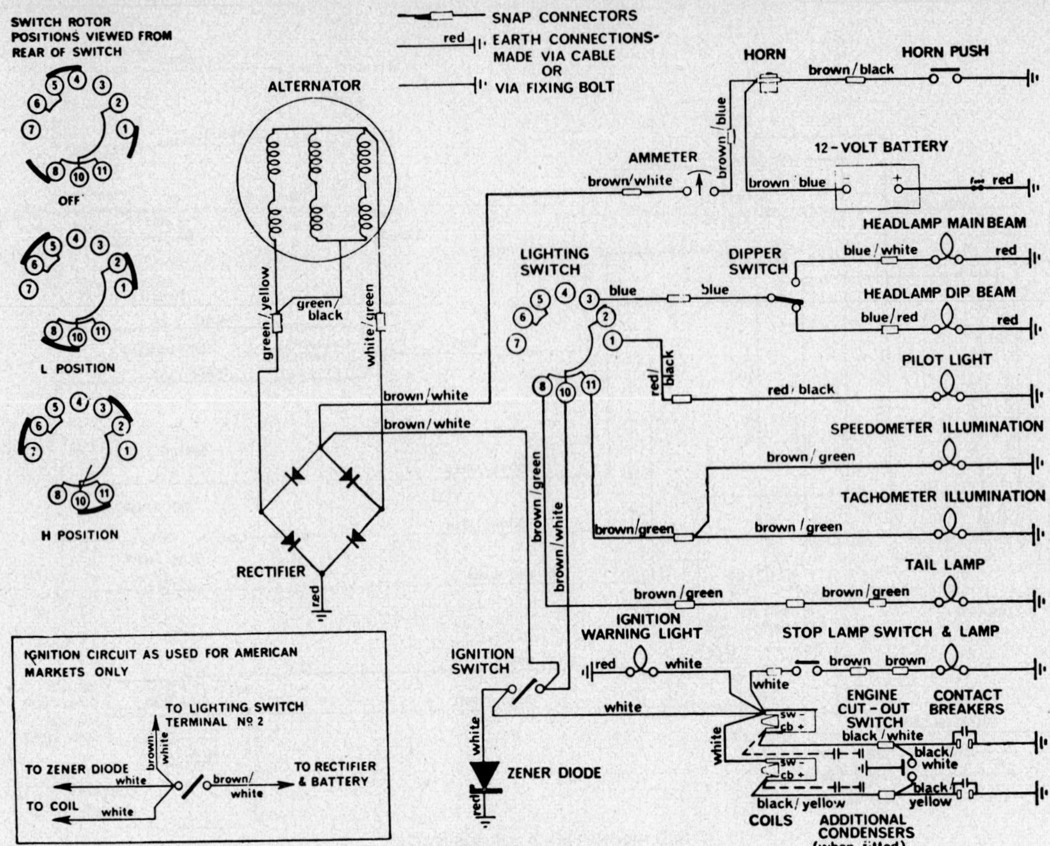

500 models, 12 volt coil ignition without nacelle up to Serial No. H49832

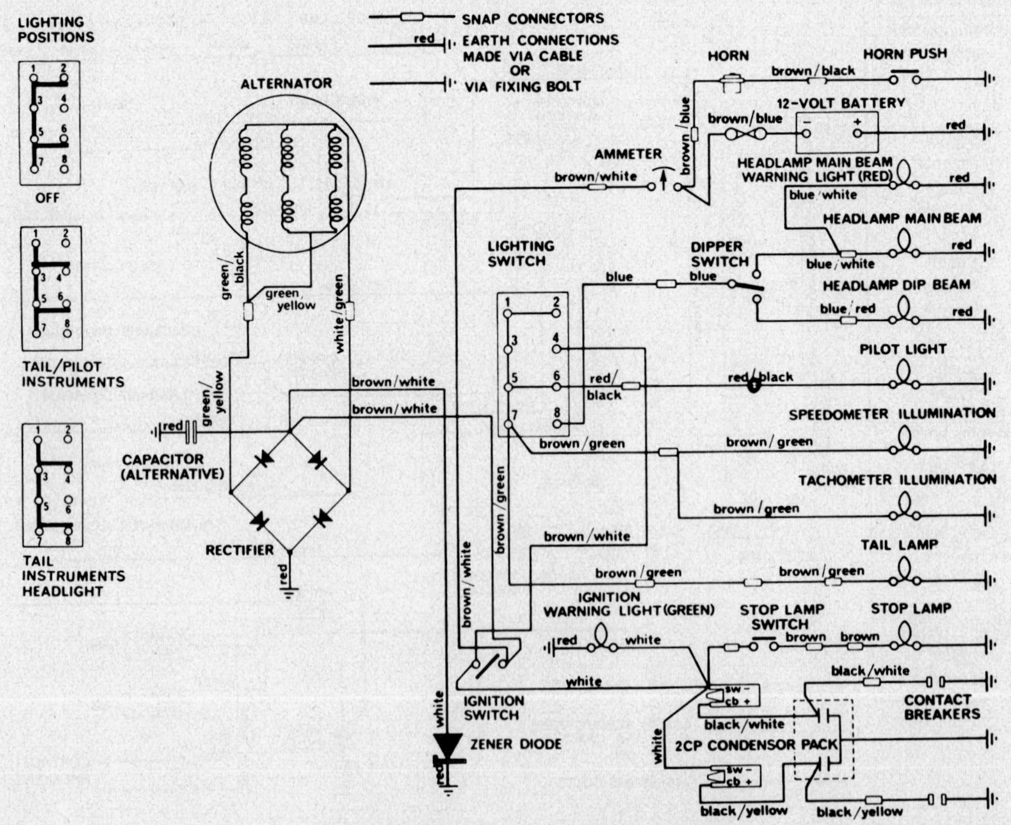

500 models, 12 volt coil ignition with separate headlight after Serial No. H57083

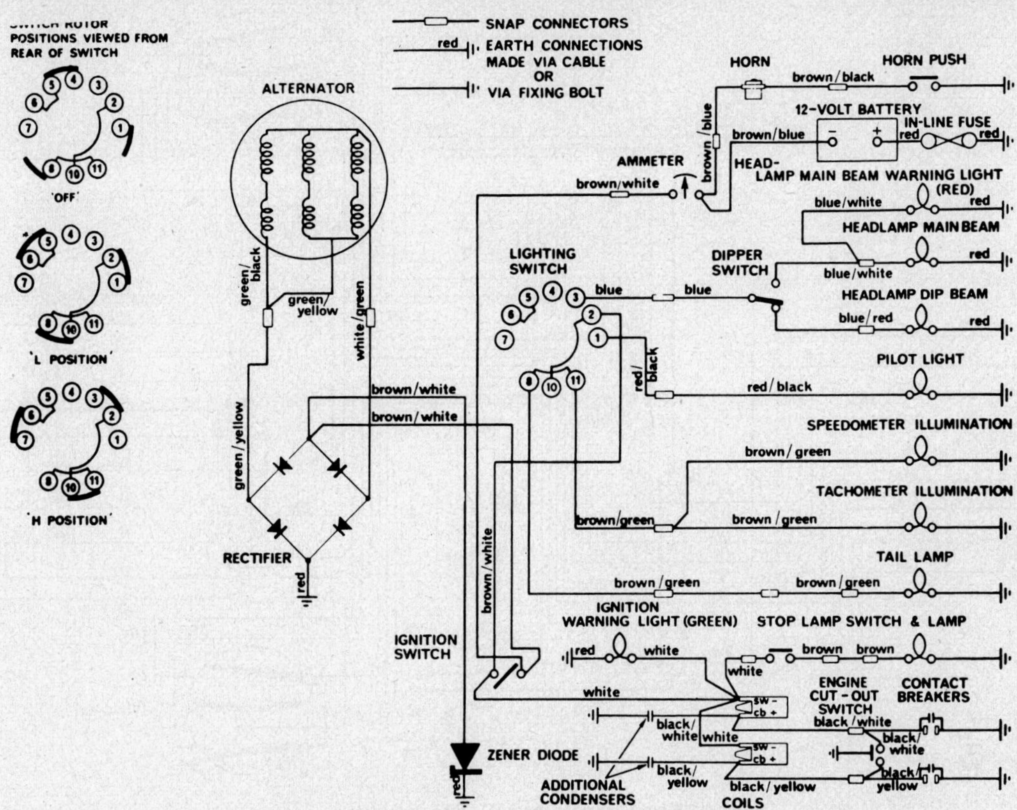

500 models, 12 volt coil ignition with separate headlight between Serial Nos. H49832 and H57083

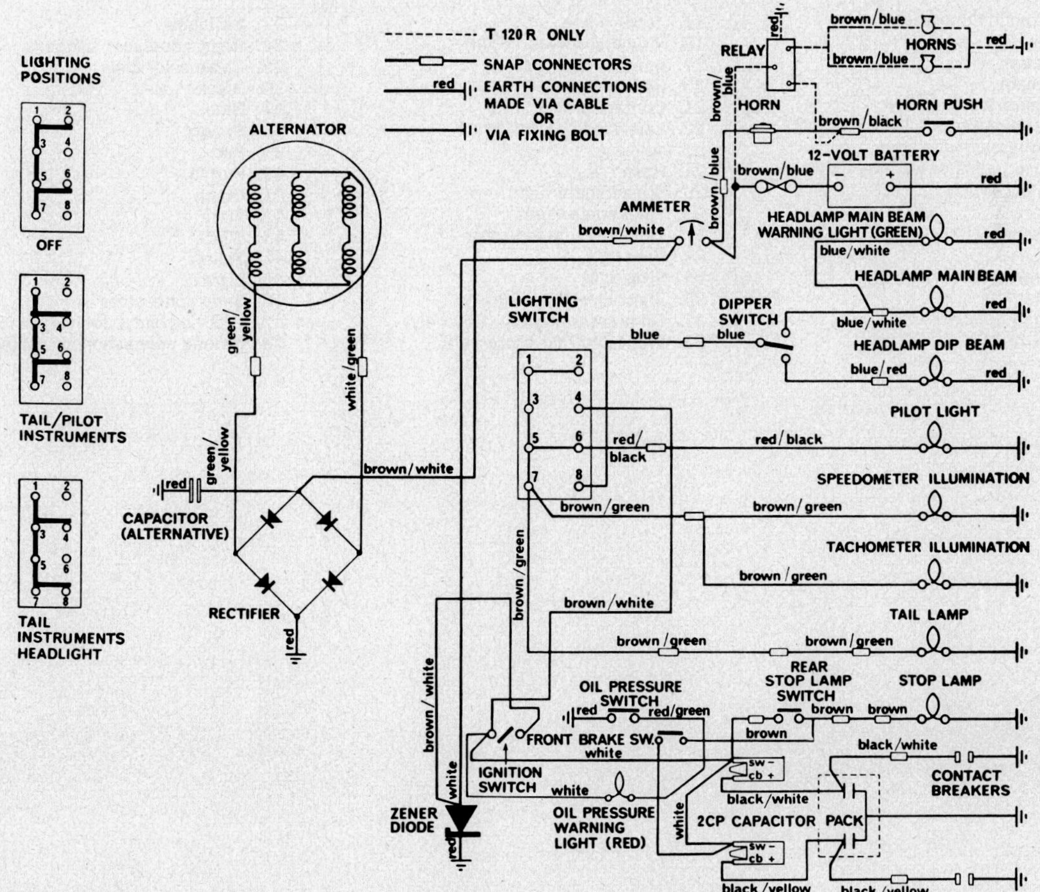

650 models, 12 volt coil ignition

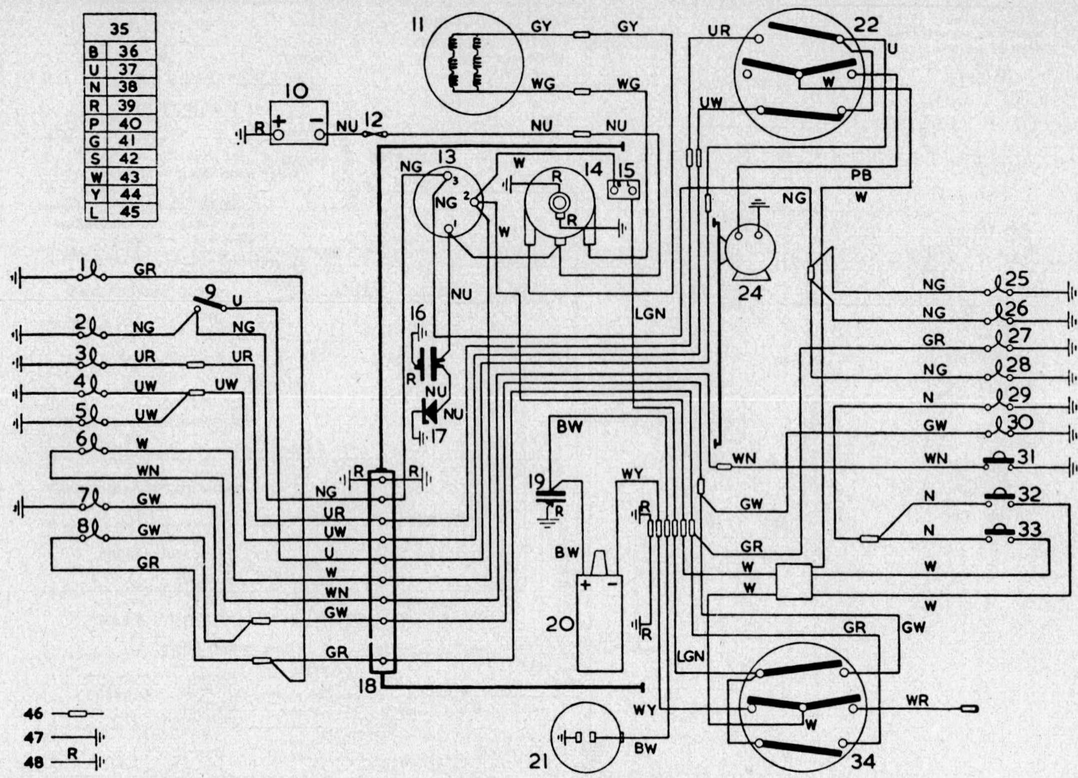

Single-cylinder models, 1971 and later

1. Left direction indicator
2. Parking light
3. Low beam
4. High beam
5. High-beam warning light
6. Oil pressure warning light (250 only)
7. Right direction indicator
8. Direction indicator warning light
9. Headlight switch
10. Battery
11. Alternator
12. Fuse
13. Ignition/light switch
14. Rectifier
15. Direction indicator unit
16. Capacitor (2.M.C.)
17. Zener diode
18. Plug and socket (9 pin)
19. Ignition capacitor
20. Ignition coil
21. Contact breaker
22. Left handlebar switches
23. ——
24. Horn
25. Speedometer light
26. Tachometer light
27. Left direction indicator
28. Rear light
29. Stop light
30. Right direction indicator
31. Oil pressure switch (250 only)
32. Front and rear brake light
33. Switches
34. Right handlebar switches
35. Cable color code
36. Black
37. Blue
38. Brown
39. Red
40. Purple
41. Green
42. Slate
43. White
44. Yellow
45. Light
46. Snap connectors
47. Ground connection via cable
48. Ground connection via fixing bolt

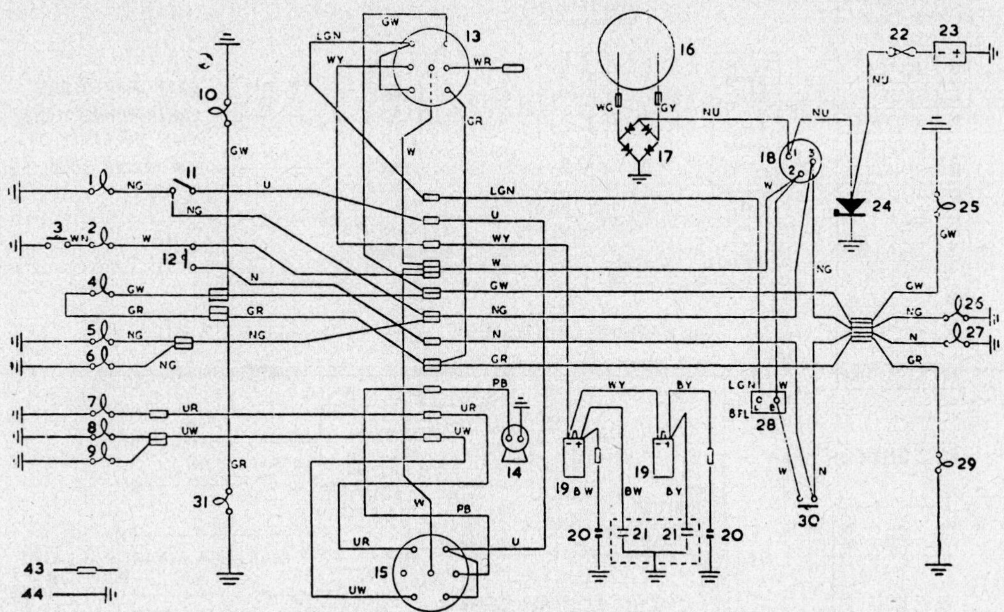

Twin-cylinder models, 1971 and later

1. Parking light
2. Oil pressure warning light
3. Oil pressure switch
4. Direction indicator warning light
5. Speedometer light
6. Tachometer light
7. Low beam
8. High beam
9. High-beam warning light
10. Right direction indicator light (front)
11. Switch
12. Front brake light switch
13. Right handlebar switches
14. Horn
15. Left handlebar switches
16. Alternator
17. Rectifier
18. Ignition/lighting switch
19. Ignition coils
20. Contact breakers
21. Condensers 2CP
22. Fuse
23. Battery
24. Zener diode
25. Right direction indicator light (rear)
26. Taillight
27. Stop light
28. Direction indicator unit
29. Left direction indicator light (rear)
30. Rear brake switch
31. Left direction indicator light (front)

Cable color code

- B. Black
- U. Blue
- N. Brown
- R. Red
- P. Purple
- G. Green
- S. Slate
- W. White
- Y. Yellow
- L. Light

43. Snap connectors
44. Ground connections via fixing bolt

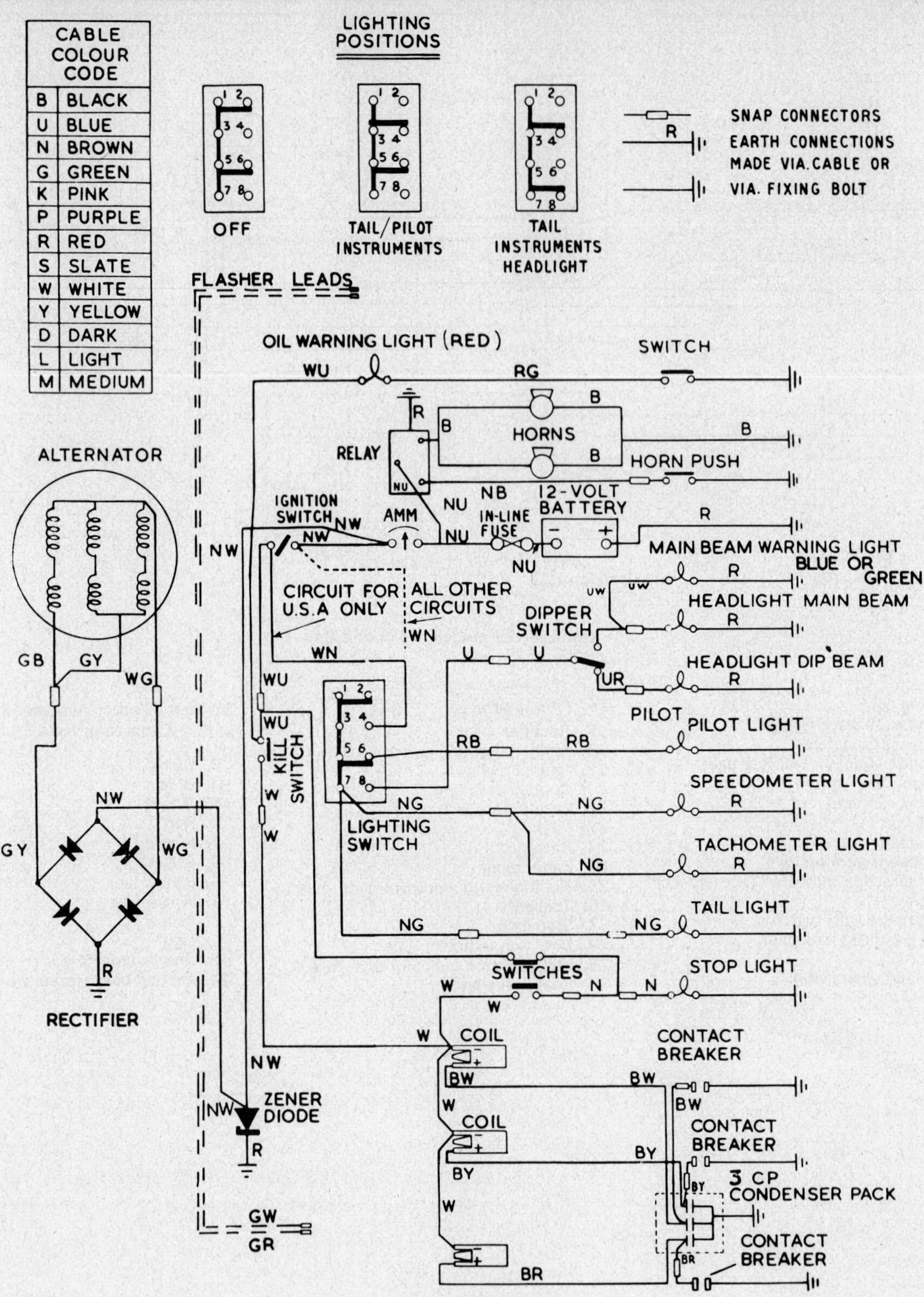

Rocket 3, 1968-1970

CHASSIS

FRONT WHEEL AND HUB

Singles

1970 AND EARLIER MODELS

Removal And Disassembly

1. Support the bottom of the engine with a wooden box or wire milk basket, positioning the bike so that the front wheel is about 6 in. off the ground.

2. Loosen the front brake cable at the handlebar adjuster, then disconnect it at the brake backing plate.

3. Remove the two axle securing nuts, slide the axle through the hub, and remove the front wheel assembly.

4. Separate the front anchor plate from the wheel and remove the right retainer with BSA service tool no. 61–3694 or a suitable substitute.

NOTE: *The retainer ring has left-hand threads.*

5. Remove the right wheel bearing by driving it out from the left side with the axle used as a drift.

6. Remove the backing ring and the inner retainer disc.

NOTE: *On machines equipped with double leading shoe brakes, the backing ring and retainer disc are replaced by a single part.*

7. Remove the left wheel bearing circlip and drive the bearing (with retaining plates) out from the right side with the axle.

8. Remove the brake backing plate center nut and withdraw the brake shoe assembly.

9. On machines equipped with double leading shoes, lift up the edge of one shoe until it is free of the backing plate. Disconnect one end of each brake return spring and then remove the second shoe. Remove the pivot pin cotter key at each end of the lever adjustment rod and lift out the pivot pin. Remove the brake cam securing nuts and washers and disconnect the return spring from the front cam. Pry off the levers one at a time and remove the brake cams.

10. On machines equipped with single leading shoes, turn the brake operating lever to relieve the pressure of the shoes against the drum, then pull out the brake and backing plate assembly. Slowly release the operating lever until the return springs can be removed, then remove the springs and the brake shoes as shown in the accompanying illustration. Remove the operating lever securing nut and washers, then remove the lever and cam spindle.

11. Thoroughly clean all parts (except brake shoes) in solvent and blow them dry with compressed air. Do not spin the bearings until after they have been completely dried and lubricated.

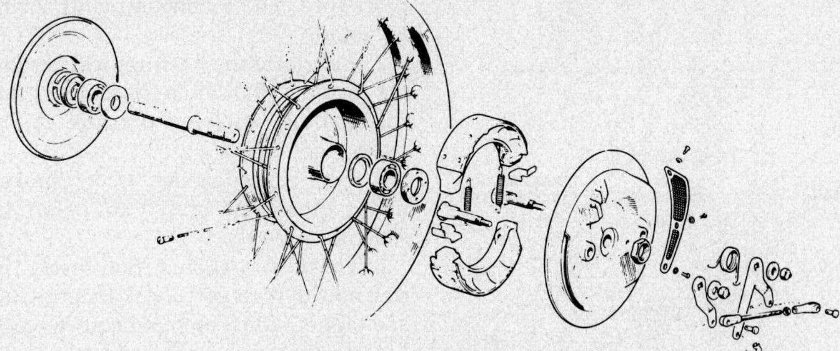

250, 441, and 500 front wheel assembly (double leading shoe brake)

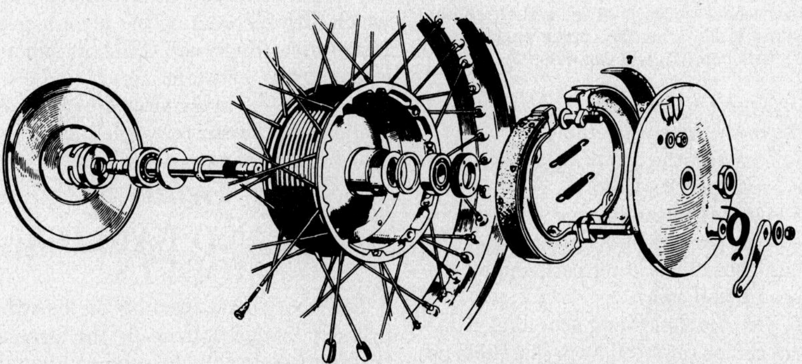

250, 441, and 500 front wheel assembly (single leading shoe brake)

Inspection

Examine the ball bearings for any signs of pitting or excessive wear. Replace them both if there is any doubt as to their condition.

Inspect the anchor plate for any cracks or signs of distortion, particularly in the area of the brake cam housing. Check the return springs for general condition and signs of fatigue. Measure the drum diameter in several places and check for scoring, etc. If drum diameter is 0.010 in. greater than specified, replacement is in order.

Check the condition of the brake shoes. If oil-soaked, cracked or badly scored, or if the lining has worn down to the rivets, replace the shoes.

If possible, check wheel rim run-out on a wheel stand. Tighten any loose spokes.

Assembly And Installation

1. On machines with single leading shoes, install the operating lever, cam spindle, and pivot pin. Fasten the return springs to their respective hooks on the brake shoes, then position the shoes over the cam and pivot pin. Snap the shoes in place by pressing on the outer edges of the shoes. Position the operating lever in a counterclockwise location, then connect the return spring.

2. On machines with double leading shoes, first lubricate the spindles lightly, then install both cams—wedge shape out. Install the outside return spring on the front cam, then reinstall both brake cam levers and secure them with washers and nuts. Install the abutment plates on the anchor plate with the tag side toward the anchor plate. Position the shoes with the radiused end toward the pivot pin and connect the return springs. This is most easily accomplished by installing one shoe, connecting the springs, and snapping the other shoe into place.

3. Coat the wheel bearings and retainers liberally with the recommended grease, then install the left inner retainer, the bearing, and the outer dust cap. Install the retaining circlip and then drive the bearing up against the circlip, using the shouldered end of the axle as a drift.

4. Install the right retainer disc and backing ring (one piece on machines with double leading brakes).

5. Using the shouldered end of the axle as a drift, drive the right bearing into place, then install the left-hand thread retainer ring.

6. The remainder of the assembly and installation procedure is in reverse order of the removal instructions.

7. Adjust the front brake.

1971 AND LATER MODELS

Removal And Disassembly

1. Support the bottom of the engine

with a wooden box or wire milk basket, positioning the bike so that the front wheel is about 6 in. off the ground.

2. Unscrew the bolt securing the brake anchor to the right fork leg. Loosen the brake cable at the handlever and disconnect it at the backing plate.

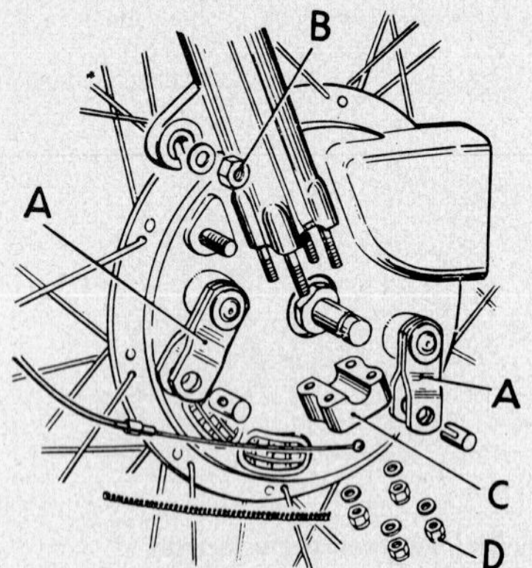

Front wheel removal (8 in. brake), showing the brake arms (A), brake anchor nut (B), fork cap (C), and cap nuts (D)

3. Unscrew the fork cap nuts and remove the wheel assembly.

4. Unscrew the center nut and remove the brake plate assembly

5. On single-leading shoe brakes, turn the brake cam about 90° to disengage the shoes from the locating slots, and lift the shoes up and away.

6. On double-leading shoe brakes the shoes can be removed by prying them up and away at the pivot points.

7. Remove the right-side wheel bearing retainer (which has a left-hand thread) and remove the bearing by tapping the left end of the axle shaft with a rubber hammer. Remove the axle shaft and right-side inner grease seal.

8. Take out the circlip and outer grease seal and drive out the left-side wheel bearing.

Inspection

Thoroughly clean all parts (except the brake shoes) in solvent and blow dry with compressed air. Do not spin the bearings until after they have been completely dried and lubricated. Examine the ball bearings for any signs of pitting or excessive wear. Replace them both is there is any doubt as to their condition.

Inspect the anchor for any cracks or signs of distortion, particularly in the area of the brake cam housing. Check the return springs for general condition and sign of fatigue. Measure the drum diameter in several places and check for scoring and damage. If the drum diameter is 0.-010 in. greater than specified, replacement is in order.

Check the condition of the brake shoes. If oil-soaked, cracked, or badly scored, or if the lining is more than half-worn, replace the shoes. If the original shoes are to be reused, replace them in their original positions.

If possible, check wheel rim runout on a wheel stand, and tighten any loose spokes.

Assembly And Installation

Reverse the removal and disassembly procedure. The following points should be noted:

1. Lubricate the bearings with a suitable grease and drive them squarely into the housing, applying pressure to the outer race only.

2. On single-leading shoe brakes, lightly grease the brake cam before installing the shoes.

3. On double-leading shoe brakes, install new O-rings and check that the cam and tappet slide freely in the pivot block. Lightly grease the cam and install the shoes in the fully retracted position. Do not forget to install the abutment pads, which prevent wear on the pivot blocks. Install the springs with the short end adjacent to the adjusters.

4. Adjust the brake after the wheel assembly has been reinstalled and the brake cable connected.

Twins

1970 AND EARLIER MODELS

The front wheel assembly on the twin-cylinder models is basically the same as that used on the singles, and can be serviced in the same manner.

1971 AND LATER MODELS

All 1971 and later BSAs use the same front wheel and hub assemblies (except for the off-road singles). Refer to the preceding section on 1971 and later single-cylinder models.

Rocket 3

1970 AND EARLIER MODELS

The front wheel assembly on the twin-cylinder models is basically the same as that used on the singles, and can be serviced in the same manner.

1971 AND LATER MODELS

Refer to the preceding section on 1971 and later single-cylinder models.

REAR WHEEL AND HUB

Singles

1970 AND EARLIER MODELS

Removal And Disassembly

1. Disconnect the speedometer drive cable (if applicable), then remove the securing nut and the rear axle.

2. The spacer that fits between the hub and the swing arm should drop out when the axle is removed, thereby facilitating wheel removal.

3. Remove the speedometer drive unit and unscrew the end cover.

4. Withdraw the wheel, leaving the brake hub assembly fastened to the swing arm.

5. Remove the left-side bearing retainer.

NOTE: *This bearing retainer has left-hand threads.*

6. Using a drift slightly under ¾ in. diameter, drive out the hollow hub spindle. This will release the right bearing, inner collar, and washers.

7. Drive out the left bearing and thrust washer from the right side. Do not disturb the bearing oil seal unless it must be replaced.

8. To remove the brake hub assembly from the swing arm, disconnect the final drive chain and unscrew the brake adjusting rod sleeve. Remove the axle nut and disconnect the torque arm at the hub. Lift out the brake assembly.

9. The brake assembly can now be disassembled and inspected as previously described for the front brakes.

10. To remove the brake hub bearing, first drive out the hollow spindle from the left side and remove the bearing circlip. The bearing can then be driven out with a suitable drift.

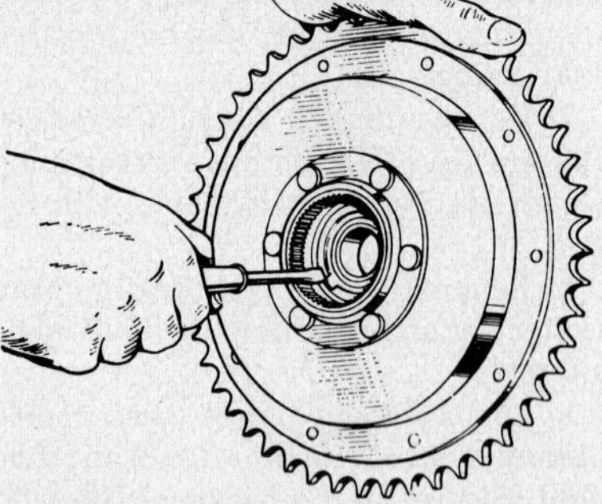

Removing the rear hub bearing circlip (250 and 500)

11. Do not disturb the chain sprocket unless it must be replaced. To remove it, bend back the locktabs and remove the six securing bolts.

12. Thoroughly clean all parts (except brake shoes) in solvent and blow them dry with compressed air. Do not spin the bearings until they have been completely dried and lubricated.

Inspection

Examine all parts as previously described for the front wheel and hub. Replace the chain sprocket if the teeth have become hooked or rounded.

Assembly And Installation

1. Assemble the brake hub in reverse

order of disassembly. Liberally grease the bearings. Be sure to install the steel washer that fits between the bearing and circlip, otherwise the bearing will not seat properly.

2. Install the hub assembly, complete with brake shoes, on the swing arm. Readjust the final drive chain.

3. Assemble the wheel hub in reverse order of disassembly. Liberally grease the bearings. Note that the bearings should be driven in place by applying pressure to the outer bearing race only. Install the hollow spindle with the short end on the left-hand side, and install the bearing seals facing outward.

4. Install the wheel and hub assembly in the reverse of the removal procedure. Do not forget the spacer between the swing arm and hub. If the brake hub assembly was not removed, it will not be necessary to readjust the chain.

1971 AND LATER MODELS

Removal And Disassembly

1. Disconnect the brake operating rod, speedometer cable, and torque strut.

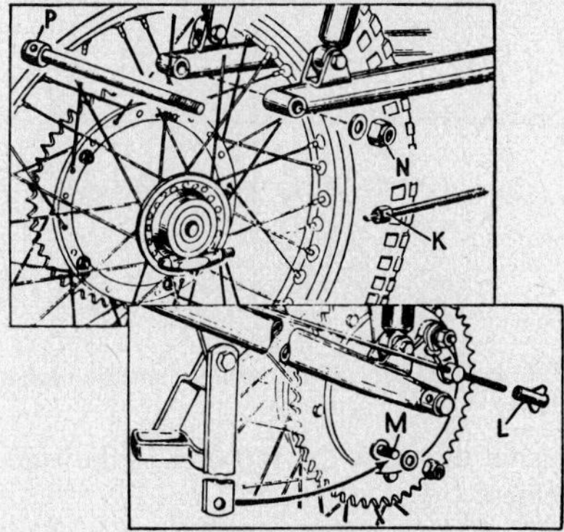

Removal of the rear wheel, showing the speedometer cable (K), brake rod adjuster nut (L), torque link anchor (M), rear axle nut (N), and axle (P)

2. Remove the master link to uncouple the drive chain.

3. Remove the axle nut and withdraw the axle. Withdraw the wheel assembly, and remove the speedometer drive and spacer.

4. The brake assembly may be removed from the hub after the wheel has been removed. Disassemble and inspect the brakes as previously described for the single leading shoe front brake.

5. Unscrew the speedometer drive flange, which has a left-hand thread.

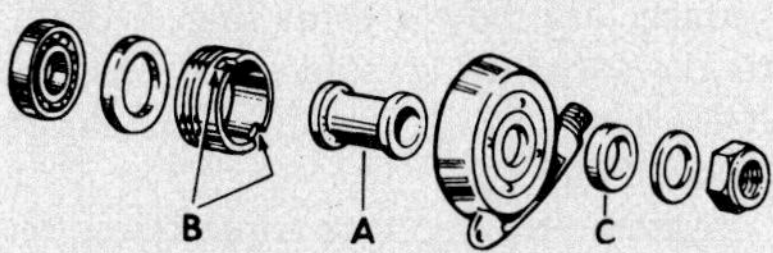

Speedometer drive assembly, showing the spacer (A), drive ring slots (B), and collar (C)

6. Unscrew the left wheel bearing retainer and drive out one of the bearings, using a drift having a diameter slightly larger than ¾ in., applying the driving force to the spacer.

7. Remove the inner abutment ring or grease seal, and use the spacer to drive out the remaining bearing. Take care not to damage the spacer.

8. Remove the remaining grease seal.

Inspection

Examine all parts as previously described for the front wheel and hub. Replace the chain sprocket if the teeth have become hooked or rounded.

Assembly And Installation

1. Install the left wheel bearing abutment ring. Liberally grease the bearings and drive the left bearing into position.

2. Install the lockring on the left side and insert the spacer from the right.

3. Locate the grease seal and drive in the right-side bearing. Make sure that the bearings are installed squarely into the housing. Apply pressure to the outer bearing race only during installation.

4. Grease the operating cam lightly and install the brake shoes. Install the speedometer drive and spacer.

5. When reinstalling the wheel assembly on the swing arm, the axle must be inserted from the left side. Replace the drive chain master link with the closed end of the clip facing in the direction of forward rotation. Don't forget to readjust the chain and brake.

Twins

1970 AND EARLIER MODELS

NOTE: *Twin-cylinder models are equipped with either standard or quickly detachable rear wheels.*

Removal And Disassembly (Standard)

1. Disconnect the rear brake adjuster and the final drive chain.

2. Loosen the front securing bolt and swing the chainguard up out of the way.

3. Disconnect the torque arm at the hub.

4. Disconnect the speedometer cable.

5. Loosen the axle nuts and slide off the wheel assembly.

6. Unscrew the backing plate retaining nut and withdraw the brake assembly. Service the brake assembly as described in the "Singles" section.

7. Remove the wheel spindle, complete with speedometer drive, out the right side.

8. Remove the screw that locks the left bearing retainer ring in place.

9. Remove the retainer ring, noting that it has left-hand threads.

10. To gain access to remove the left bearing, drive the central spacer from the left side until the grease retainer collapses. The bearing can now be driven out from the right side, using a suitable soft drift.

11. Remove the backing ring, collapsed grease retainer, and central spacer.

12. Drive out the right bearing and dust cap with a drift approximatley 1 ⅝ in. in diameter.

13. Thoroughly clean all parts (except brake shoes) in solvent and blow them dry with compressed air. Do not spin the bearings until they have been completely dried and lubricated.

Inspection

Examine all parts carefully as described in the "Singles" section.

Assembly And Installation

1. Liberally grease the bearings and retainers.

2. Drive in the right grease retainer (new or straightened) and bearing. Install the dust cap after making sure that the bearing and the cavitites on either side of the bearing are filled with grease.

3. Install the spacer, right grease retainer, and right bearing. Make sure that everything is well packed in grease.

4. Bring the spacer in line with the axle, then install the threaded (left-hand) retainer ring.

5. Install the retainer screw.

6. The remainder of the assembly and installation procedure is a reversal of the removal and disassembly instructions. Don't forget to readjust the rear brake and final drive chain.

Removal And Disassembly (Quickly Detachable)

1. Disconnect the speedometer cable.

2. Unscrew the axle from the right side

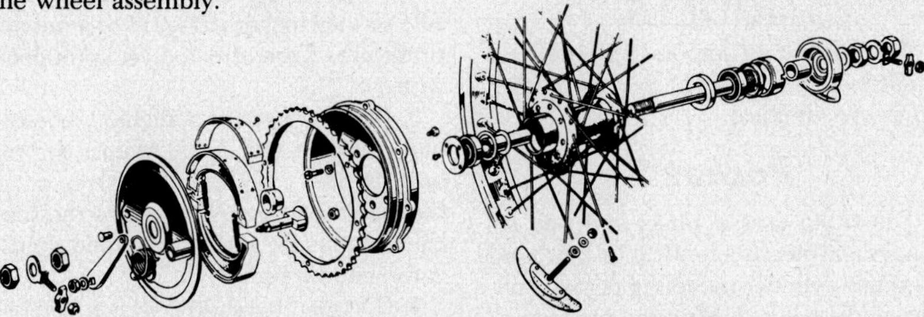

Standard rear wheel assembly (500 and 650 models)

of the machine and pull out the spacer.

3. Pull the wheel clear of the engaging splines and withdraw it out the back of the machine.

4. Remove the locknut on the right side of the axle sleeve and lift off the speedometer drive unit.

5. Disassemble the wheel hub and bearings as previously described for the standard rear wheel.

6. Disconnect the final drive chain, brake operating rod, and torque arm, and then remove the axle sleeve nut.

7. Disassemble the brake components as previously described in the "Singles" section.

8. Press out the axle sleeve, then remove the bearing circlip located in the brake drum.

9. Pry out the retainer and felt washer and drive out the bearing with a suitable drift.

10. Thoroughly clean all metal parts in solvent, then blow them dry with compressed air. Do not spin the bearings until they have been completely dried and lubricated.

FRONT FORK

Singles (Shuttle Valve Type)

1970 AND EARLIER MODELS

Unit-construction BSAs are equipped with either rod damper or shuttle valve type front forks. In general, the shuttle valve type can be identified by its longer and narrower spring and by its overall slimmer appearance.

The front fork seldom requires service other than the recommended oil changes. If the seals develop a leak, or the fork has sustained accidental damage, however, disassembly, inspection and any necessary parts replacement should be performed.

Removal

1. Drain the fork oil.
2. Remove the front wheel and fender.
3. Slide the boots clear of the top fork shrouds.

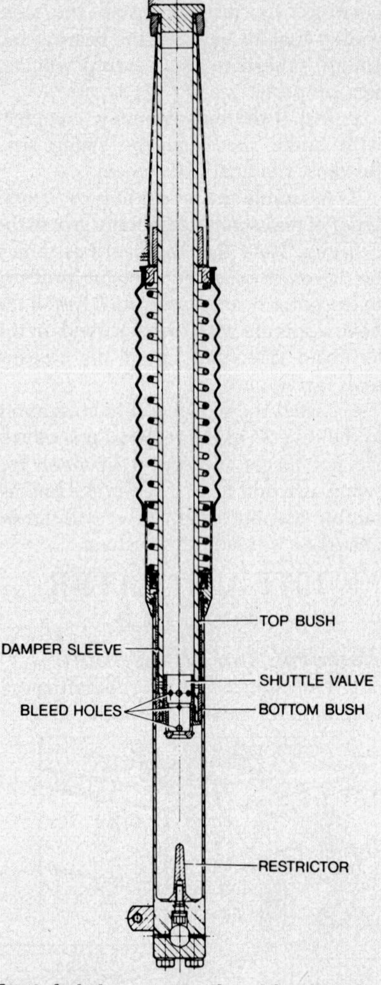

Front fork leg construction (shuttle valve type)

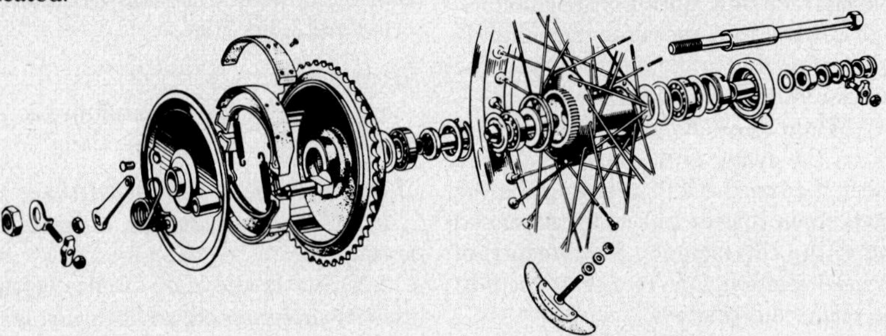

Quickly detachable rear wheel assembly (500 and 650 models)

Inspection

Examine all parts as previously described and make any necessary replacements.

Assembly And Installation

Assembly and installation is a reversal of the removal and disassembly instructions. If brake work was performed and the hub was removed from the swing arm, it will be necessary to readjust the rear brake and the final drive chain. Make sure that the bearings and retainers are thoroughly packed with grease and remember to soak the felt washer in oil before reassembly.

1971 AND LATER MODELS

Refer to the section on 1971 and later single-cylinder models. Service procedures are identical.

Rocket 3

The triple uses a wheel and hub arrangement nearly identical to that used on single-cylinder models of corresponding model years. Follow the procedures previously outlined.

4. Remove the fork leg caps together with cable brackets.

5. Loosen the bottom triple clamp pinch-bolts and screw BSA service tool no. 61-3824 or a suitable substitute into the top of the fork stanchion.

6. Hit the tool sharply with a mallet and the stanchion taper will be freed of the top clamp.

7. The fork legs can now be removed.

8. After removing the fork legs, lift off the boots and mainsprings.

Disassembly

1. Wrap a piece of rubber around the fork leg and clamp the leg in a soft-jawed vise.

2. Remove the oil seal holder, using BSA service tool no. 61-6017 or a suitable substitute. Turn the tool counterclockwise.

3. Firmly grasp the stanchion tube and move it back and forth against the top bushing until the bushing is driven out of the lower fork leg. At this time the stanchion, complete with busings and shuttle valve, can be removed.

4. To free the shuttle valve, remove the bottom retaining circlip and let the valve slide out the top end of the stanchion.

5. Do not disturb the bottom bushing unless it is to be replaced. If it is, then remove the bottom bearing retaining nut and drive the bushing out with a hammer and chisel. Take care not to slip and damage the stanchion tube.

6. If it is necessary to remove the restricter at the bottom of the leg, unscrew the bolt in the spindle cutaway.

7. To remove the oil seals from their holders, take out the loose backing washer from the trheaded end of the holder, and drive the seal out through the exposed slot. Note the O-ring in the threaded end of the seal holder.

Inspection

Check the stanchion tubes for straightness by rolling them along a known flat surface. Any bow greater than 5/32 in. requires that the stanchion be replaced. If less than 5/32 in., the stanchion may be straightened.

Examine the top fork triple clamp for cracks and then insert the fork legs (if true) and tighten them down with the top caps. Take several measurements to

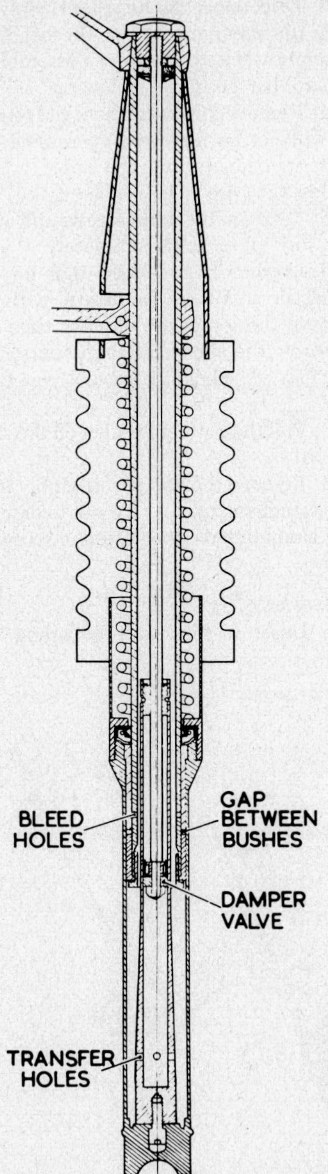

Front fork leg construction (rod damper type)

ensure that the legs are parallel to each other and perpendicular to the top yoke. Check the bottom triple clamp in the same manner, but make sure that at least 6 ½ in. of the fork legs protrude above the clamp. The bottom clamp is made of malleable metal and, therefore, can be easily straightened if need be.

Examine the bottom fork legs for any damage. Insert the stanchion tubes (with new bottom bushing) and note the amount of free-play of the bushing within the bores of the bottom legs. If excessive, or any restriction of movement is noted, the bottom legs should be replaced.

Check bottom fork leg and front axle alignment by installing the axle and measuring their inclusive angle with a square. Check one leg at a time, then both simultaneously.

Inspect the condition of the top and bottom bushings, and measure their inside or outside diameters (see specifications). Excessive wear, or too great a clearance between the bushing and its mating surface, indicates that the bushings should be replaced.

Check the main springs for any stress cracks and measure their freestanding height. Both springs must be within ¼ in. of their original dimension.

Assembly

Assembly is basically a reversal of the disassembly procedure. Note the following:

1. Make sure that the new bottom bushing is correctly seated before installing the retaining nut.
2. Note that the large end of the shuttle valve fits into the stanchion.
3. Thoroughly lubricate all parts in the fork before reassembly.
4. Replace the oil seals and apply locking compound to the holder threads.

Installation

1. Slide the fork leg boots over the oil seal holders and install the main springs.
2. Insert one leg through the bottom and top triple clamp bores and place the BSA service tool no. 61-3824 on the top of the stanchion. Install the collar and nut and tighten the nut until the stanchion is firmly locked in its taper.
3. Tighten the bottom clamp pinch bolts and then remove the special tool
4. Slide the top of the fork boot over the shroud and secure in place.
5. Repeat the previous steps for the remaining fork leg.
6. Install the front wheel and fender.
7. Fill the fork legs with the recommended lubricant as specified in 'Maintenance Items.' Adjust the front brake.

Singles (Rod Damper Type)

Removal

1. Drain the fork oil
2. Remove the front wheel and fender.
3. Slide the fork boots off the top shrouds and loosen the bottom triple clamp pinch bolts.
4. Unscrew the fork leg caps and raise them high enough to loosen the damper rod locknut.
5. Remove the fork leg caps from the top of the rod damper.
6. Install BSA service tool no. 61-3350 or a suitable substitute into the top of one fork leg.
7. Hold the bottom of the fork leg firmly, then strike the special tool sharply with a mallet. This will free the fork leg from its taper in the top clamp.
8. Remove the other fork leg in the same manner.
9. Remove the fork boots and mainsprings.

Disassembly

1. Clamp the fork leg in a soft-jawed vise at the axle lug.
2. Slide BSA service tool no. 61-3005 over the main tube and engage the dogs at the bottom of the oil seal holder.
3. While applying pressure to the end of the tool, turn counterclockwise and free the seal holder.

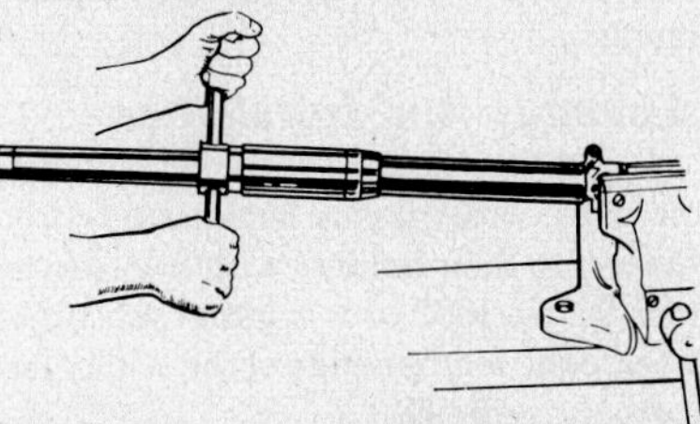

Removing the oil seal holder (rod damper type)

4. Remove the special tool and slide the seal holder to the end of the tube. Do not attempt to entirely remove the seal holder because damage may result.
5. The main tube assembly and lower sliding leg can now be separated.
6. Clamp the unmachined portion of the tube in a soft-jawed vise and remove the large nut at the base of the shaft. Remove the bushings, spacer, and oil seal assembly.
7. Remove the allen screw that secures the damper tube to the lower portion of the fork leg.
8. Remove the two circlips at the top of the damper tube. This will free the damper rod with valve and bushing.
9. Remove the nut that secures the damper valve to the rod. Do not disturb the sealing washer and special retainer located just below the nut unless they require replacement.
10. If an oil seal requires replacement, position the holder with the bottom edge on a wooden block and drive out the seal with BSA service tool no. 61-3007 or a suitable substitute.

Inspection.

Examine all parts as generally de-

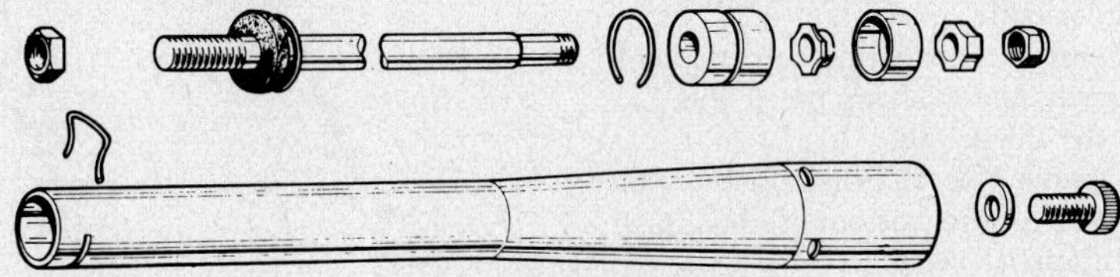

Rod and damper assembly

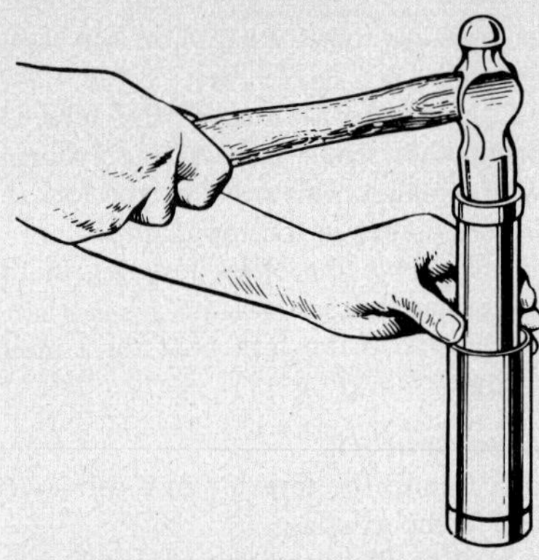

Removing the oil seal (rod damper type)

scribed for the shuttle valve type fork. Compare measurements with those given in specifications at the end of this chapter and make any necessary replacements.

Assembly And Installation

1. Coat the outside of the replacement oil seals with gasket sealer and drive them into their holders with BSA service tool no. 61-3007 or a suitable substitute. Grease the feather edge of the seal before further assembly.

2. Make certain that all parts are completely clean, then reassemble the remaining parts in reverse order of disassembly.

NOTE: *When tightening down the oil seal holders, it's a good idea to wrap a piece a no. 5 twine around one of the last threads. This will provide additional protection for the seals.*

3. BSA service tool no. 61-3350 must be used to set the fork leg in its taper, and tool no. 61-3765 must be used to raise the damper high enough in the tube to screw on the fork leg cap.

Twins And Rocket 3

These machines are equipped with fork assemblies almost identical to those used on the singles. Disassembly, inspection, and assembly procedures remain the same, but the removal and installation instructions vary slightly to suit various instrument arrangements and the use of a steering damper.

Removal And Installation

1. Drain the fork oil.
2. Remove the front wheel and fender.
3. Remove the headlight assembly.
4. Disconnect throttle, choke, and front brake cables.
5. Disconnect any instrument or diode wiring, or both.
6. Remove the steering damper knob and loosen the top clamp pinch bolt. Unscrew the sleeve nuts.
7. Remove the steering damper anchor plate at the bottom of the frame head (if applicable.).
8. Remove the handlebar mounting bolts and swing the handlebar out of the way. It may or may not be necessary to disconnect the contols.
9. Hold on to the fork and then give the underside of the top triple clamp a good swat with a mallet. This should free the fork legs for further disassembly.
10. Installation is a reversal of the removal procedure. Service tool no. 61-3824 must be used to seat the fork leg in its top clamp taper.

All Models

1971 AND LATER

Removal

1. Unscrew the handlebar clamp nuts and lay the bar across the tank, which should be protected with a piece of cloth.
2. Unscrew the fork cap nuts, taking care to support the speedometer and tachometer (if fitted). Withdraw the springs.
3. Disconnect the headlight wires (inside the shell) and unbolt the headlight assembly. Note the order of assembly of the rubber bushings, and so on.
4. Remove the front wheel and fender. It will not be necessary to remove the fork stanchions from the triple clamps unless they are to be replaced.
5. Take out the drain screws and allow the fork oil to drain completely.
6. Engage BSA service tool no. 61-6113, or a suitable substitute, with the slots in the top of the damper tube and unscrew the allen bolt at the bottom of the fork while holding the tool from turning.
7. Pull the bottom fork leg off the stanchion.
8. Remove the damper assembly from the stanchion, taking care not to damage the aluminum damper when unscrewing it.

Disassembly

1. Unscrew the valve retaining nut

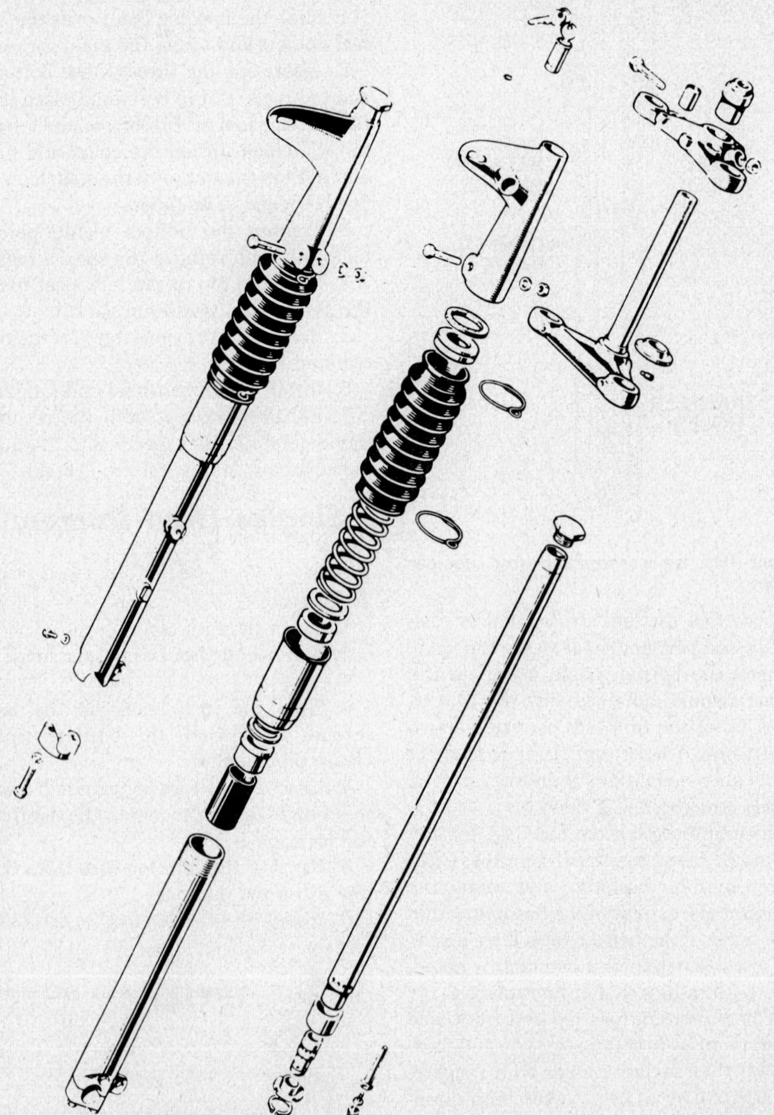

Front fork assembly (500 and 650 models)

and remove the valve and shuttle washer.

2. If it is desired to remove the stanchions, first loosen the triple clamp pinch-bolts. Then reinstall the fork cap nuts loosely and smack the cap nuts with a soft hammer or a piece of wood to break the stanchions free.

3. Place the bottom fork leg in a vice (protected with soft wood or cloth) and collapse the seal inward with a chisel or screwdriver (after the small boot is removed). Then pry the seal out.

CAUTION: *Be extremely careful not to damage the fork leg when removing the seal.*

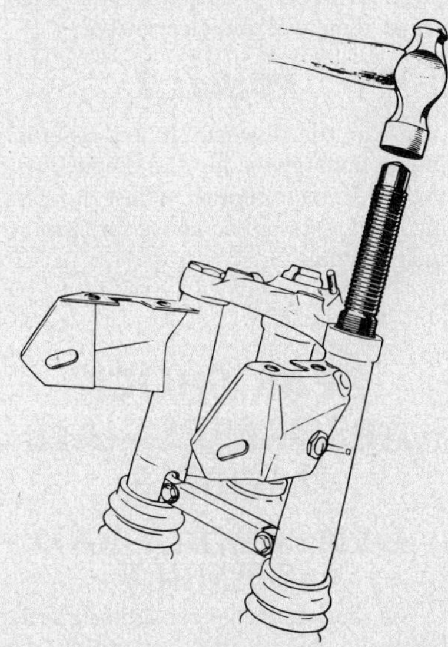

Removing the fork leg stanchion (Rocket 3)

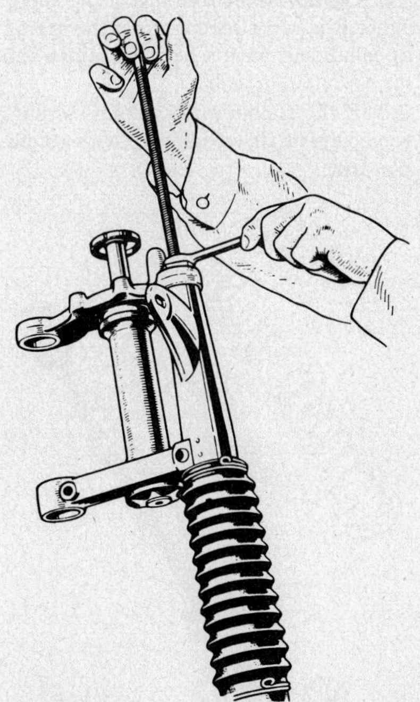

Installing the fork leg with tool No. Z161 (500 models)

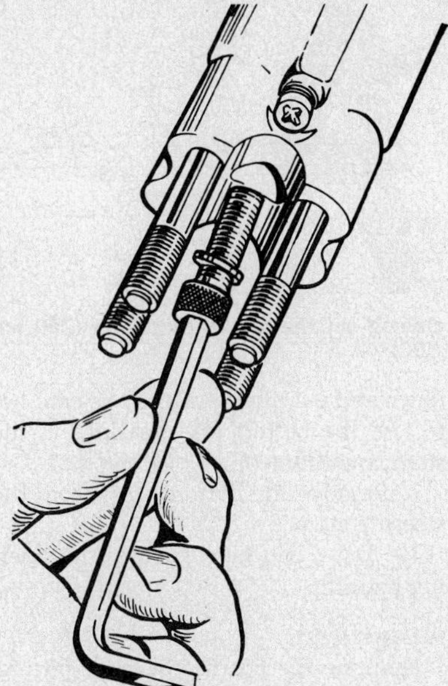

Removing the allen bolt

Inspection

Check the stanchions for straightness by rolling them along a known flat surface. Examine the top fork triple clamp for cracks. Check the bottom fork legs for damage and check the damper components for damage and wear. Measure the free length of the springs and compare with the dimension given in the specifications chart at the end of the chapter. The springs should be free of stress cracks and other damage and measure within ¼ in. of the original dimension

Assembly And Installation

Assemble the forks in reverse order of disassembly. The following points should be noted:

1. All seals and O-rings should be replaced as a matter of course. When installing a new seal the lip should face toward the inside of the fork leg. Press or drive it in squarely, taking care not to damage it.

2. The damper valve should be installed with its plain face against the retaining nut. Do not forget the shuttle washer.

3. Lubricate the main seal before fitting the bottom fork leg over the stanchion, and take extreme care to avoid damaging the edge of the seal.

4. Apply thread lock compund to the threads of the socket screw before installation.

5. After installation, fill the forks with the correct amount and grade of oil and tighten the fork cap nuts to 50 ft lb.

FORK ALIGNMENT

Forks that have sustained minor damage can be checked and aligned in the following manner:

1. Remove the front wheel and fender.

2. Reinstall the front axle shaft.

3. Using BSA service tool no. 61-6025 or a steel plate that has been machined flat, check the alignment of the bottom fork leg as shown in the illustration.

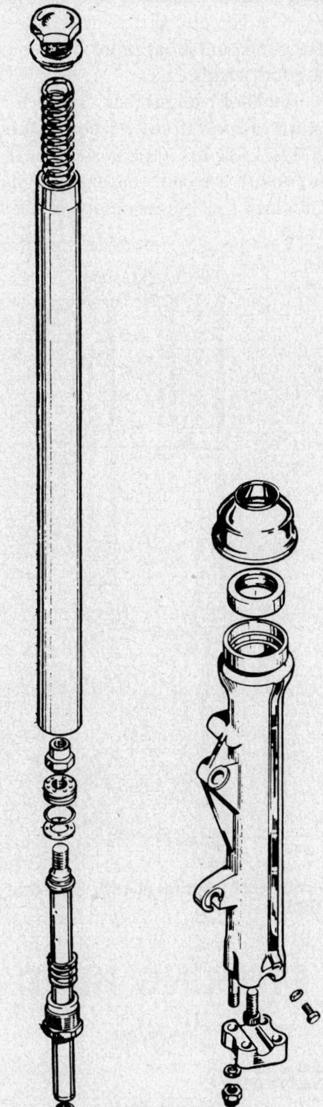

Exploded view of the fork leg

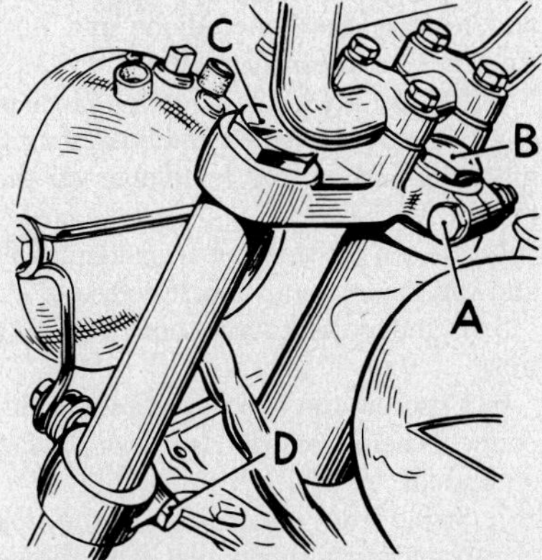

Top triple clamp pinch-bolt (A) and steering head adjuster bolt (B), 1971 and later models. Also shown is the top filler bolt (C), and the left-side lower triple clamp pinch bolt (D)

4. If the tool does not make contact at all four points, loosen the bottom triple clamp pinch-bolts and the top steering stem pinch-bolt. If the tool does not make contact at point A, give point C a sharp smack with a hammer and soft metal drift. Conversely, if the tool does not make good contact at point B, give point D a good whack.

5. Recheck alignment and if the amount of rock at any corner of the tool exceeds 1/32 in., repeat step 4. If any components are badly damaged, it should be obvious that replacement is the only answer.

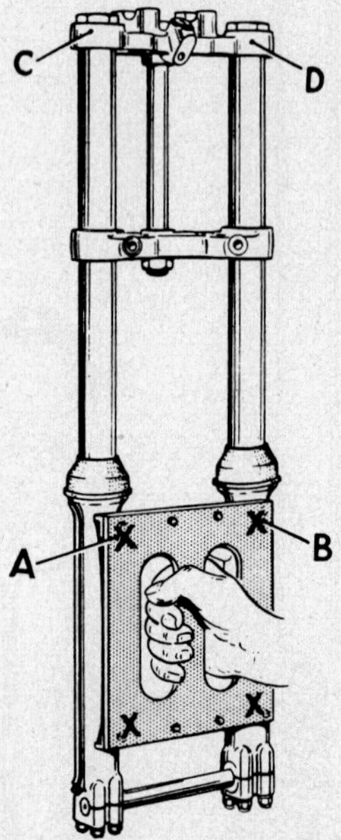

Checking fork alignment with BSA tool No. 61-6025

STEERING HEAD

Singles

Disassembly

1. Remove the headlight assembly and instruments.

2. Disconnect the front brake cable and remove the zener diode and heat sink (1970 and earlier models).

3. Protect the gas tank with a piece of cloth, then remove the handlebar mounting bolts and lay the handlebar on the tank.

4. Loosen the steering head clamp bolt and top triple clamp pinch bolt.

5. Remove the steering head adjusting nut.

6. Unscrew the fork leg caps and disconnect them from the damper rod (if so equipped).

7. Strike the underside of the top clamp sharply with a mallet. This should free the fork legs from their tapers in the clamp.

8. Locate the top clamp somewhere out of the way, then pull steering stem down and out of the head. Take care not to lose the bottom ball bearings as the stem is withdrawn.

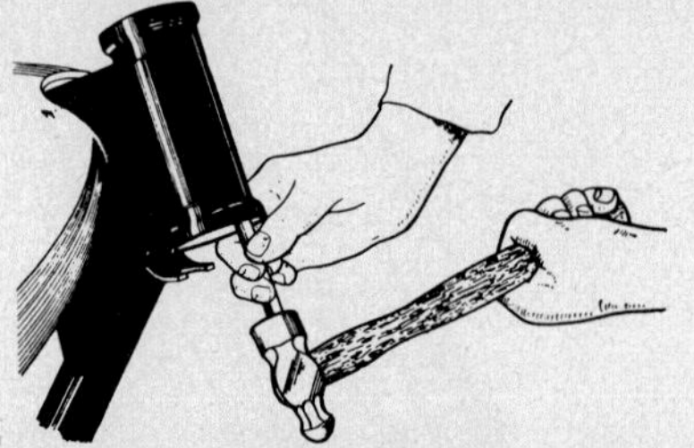

Driving out the top bearing cone (250 and 500)

9. Remove the bottom cone from the steering stem.

10. Drive out the cups from the steering housing.

Inspection

Examine the bearing balls for pitting, scoring, or flat spots and if necessary, replace the bearings, cups, and cones.

Clean out the steering housing bore and remove any burrs with a fine file or emery cloth. Also clean and inspect the stem itself.

Assembly

1.Install the bearing cups by driving them into position with a suitable drift. Make sure that the cups are squarely seated in their housings. Install the cone on the steering stem.

2. Liberally grease the bearing races with the recommended lubricant and install the lower bearing balls.

3. Slide the stem back into the head and assemble the top bearing and dust cover.

4. Install the top triple clamp and screw on the adjuster cap. The remainder of assembly is a reversal of the removal procedure.

5. Adjust the steering head as described below.

Adjustment

1. Place a strong support under the engine so that the front wheel is about 6 in. off the ground.

2. Standing in front of the bike, attempt to rock the front fork back and forth. If there is any play, an adjustment will be necessary.

NOTE: *It is very difficult to distinguish between steering head play and front fork bushing wear, so a more accurate method of determining whether or not an adjustment is necessary is by having a helper hold the fingers of one hand on the top head bearing race while the fork is being rocked. Any play will be easily detected by the helper.*

3. Turn the fork side to side through its full travel. The movement should be free of any binding. A "lumpy" feeling when turning the fork indicates that the bearings and races need replacement.

4. If an adjustment is necessary, loosen the steering head clamp bolt and the top triple clamp pinch bolt.

5. Turn the adjuster bolt until there is no rocking free-play. Make sure the bearings aren't too tight by centering the front fork and giving it a slight push to one side. The fork should fall freely until it reaches the steering lock.

Twins

Follow the disassembly and assembly instructions given for the singles, with the following exception: steering head adjustment is achieved by loosening the top clamp steering stem pinch-bolt and turning the sleeve nut until the bearings are at their working clearances.

Rocket 3

Follow the disassembly and assembly instructions given for the singles, with the following exception: adjust the steering head as described above for twin-cylinder models.

REAR SHOCK ABSORBERS—ALL MODELS

DISASSEMBLY AND ASSEMBLY

The shock absorber consists of a sealed hydraulic damper unit, coil spring, dust covers, and rubber end bushings.

1. Position the cam ring or adjusting ring in its lowest (light load) setting.

2. Clamp the bottom lug of the shock in a soft-jawed vise, compress the spring by hand, and have a helper remove the spring retaining collars.

3. If the rubber end bushings require replacement, drive them out with a suitable drift.

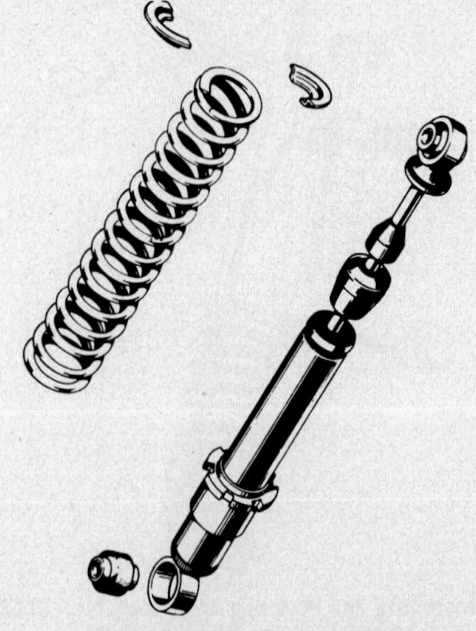

Latest type shock absorber

4. Inspect the damper unit for any signs of oil leakage, bending of the plunger rod, or similar damage. Replace it if necessary. Examine the coil spring for any stress cracks, then measure its freestanding height and compare with specifications.

5. Assembly is a reversal of the disassembly procedure. If installing new end bushings, smear them with soapy water to aid assembly.

SWING ARM

Singles

1970 AND EARLIER MODELS

Removal And Disassembly

1. Remove the rear wheel, chainguard, shock absorbers, and rear brake pedal.
2. Disconnect the brake light switch connectors and remove the switch with its bracket.
3. Remove the large shaft nut and washer on the right side of the machine
4. Drive the shaft out of the swing arm bore with a suitable drift and mallet.
5. Tap the left side of the swing arm down and the right side up, using a mallet. This will free the swing arm from the frame plates.
6. Each swing arm bushing consists of two steel sleeves bonded together with rubber. The inner sleeves are slightly longer than half the width of the swing arm and are locked together, thereby putting the rubber under tension when the arm swings through its arc.

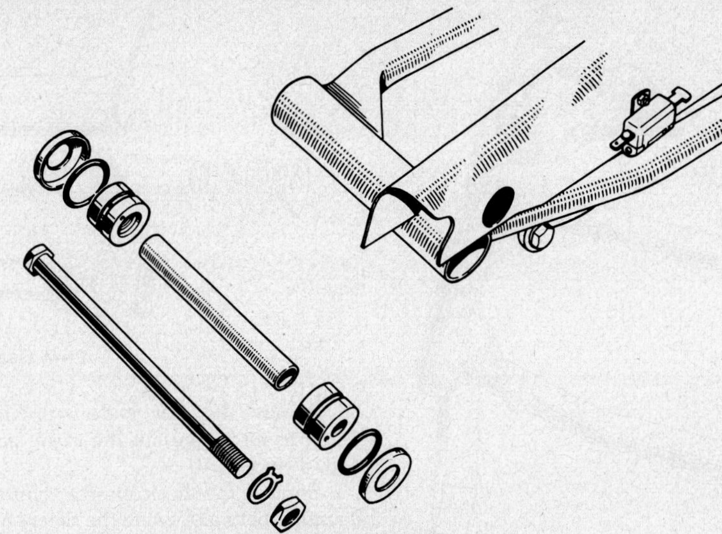

Swing arm construction (650 and 750 models)

If it is necessary to replace the bushings, the rubber must first be burned out to facilitate removal. This can be done with a thin rod or strip of metal heated until cherry red.

7. When enough rubber has been removed, drive out the inner sleeves and then the outer sleeves.

Assembly And Installation

Assembly and installation is a reversal of the removal and disassembly procedure. Do not tighten the swing arm shaft nut until after the shock absorbers have been installed.

Twins And Rocket 3

Removal And Disassembly

1. Disconnect the chain and rear brake torque arm, then remove the brake rod adjuster.
2. Loosen the rear axle nuts and remove the rear wheel.
3. Remove the two long and two short bolts that secure each of the rear engine mounting plates.
4. Loosen the rear chainguard bolt and remove the front chainguard bolt.
5. Disconnect the stoplight wiring connectors and remove the chainguard.
6. Remove the bottom shock absorber mounting bolts.
7. Disconnect the oil scavenge line from the oil tank for clearance if necessary, then remove the swing arm shaft locknut.
8. Unscrew the shaft until it is free to be withdrawn.

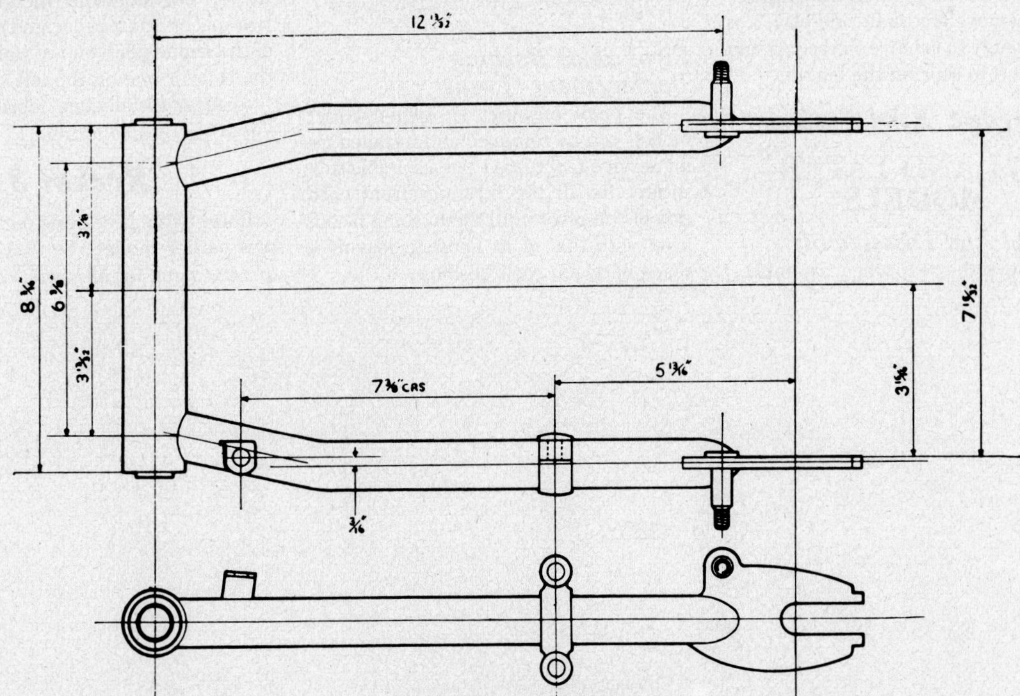

Swing arm construction (250)

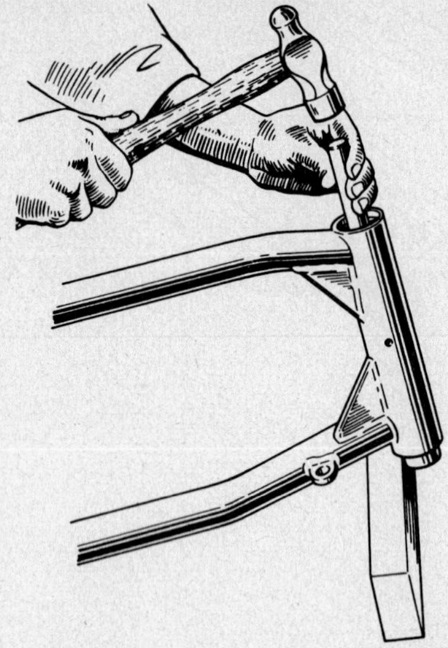

Removing a swing arm bushing (650 and 750 models)

9. Remove the swing arm assembly and separate it from the end plates, outer sleeves, and spacers.

10. Drive out the swing arm bushings with a suitable, shouldered drift.

Assembly and Installation

1. Install new swing arm bushings as previously described for single-cylinder models.

2. Thoroughly lubricate all parts with grease, then assemble them in the order shown in the accompanying illustration. Tighten the shaft bolt until the swing arm just moves under its own weight.

NOTE: *If the swing arm shaft is replaced, make sure that the new one has the same thread pitch as the original.*

3. To remove any shaft side-play, it is necessary only to remove the spacer and file one end to shorten the length.

Singles And Twins

1971 AND LATER MODELS

Removal And Disassembly

1. Remove the rear wheel assembly.

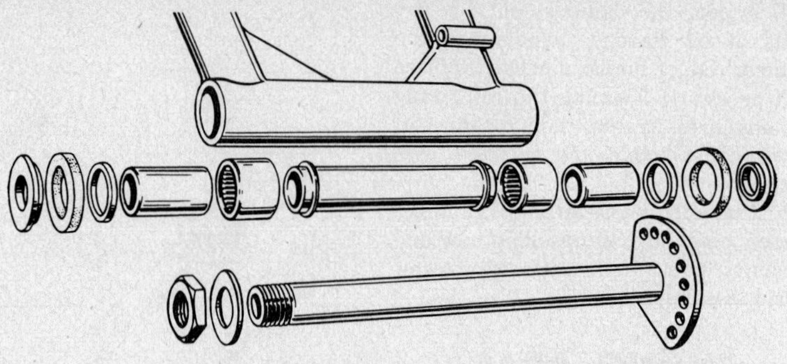

Pivot assembly—Singles

2. Remove the brake pedal to provide clearance for taking out the swing arm shaft, if necessary.

3. Remove the shock absorber bottom mounting bolts and swing the shocks out of the way.

4. Unscrew the pivot shaft nut and drive the shaft out, using a suitable drift.

Pivot Shaft Bearing Replacement (Singles)

Caged needle bearings are used to support the swing arm pivot shaft on single-cylinder models. The oil seals and spacers can be pulled out by hand, and the inner bushings can be withdrawn using pliers. Take care not to damage the bearing surface of the bushings if they are to be replaced. The bearings can then be driven out using a suitable drift. When installing the bearings, use a drift of the correct size to avoid damaging them, and install the bearings squarely in the housing. Assemble the pivot components using the accompanying illustration as a guide.

Pivot Shaft Bushing Replacement (Twins)

The pivot bushings on twin-cylinder models can be removed and installed using service tool 61-6117 or a suitable substitute. Install the bushings from each side of the pivot until the bushing face is level with that of its housing, leaving a space between each bushing.

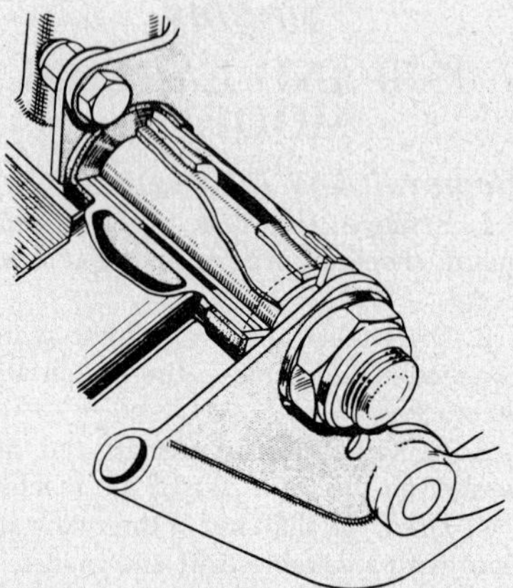

Sectional view of the pivot assembly—Twins

Assembly And Installation

Proceed in reverse order of the removal and disassembly instructions. Note the following points:

1. Thoroughly coat all pivot components with grease before installation.

2. Use new oil seals.

3. The shaft should be inserted from the left side. On twins, the thinner of the two spacers must be located on the inside of the frame plate on the right side, with the thicker one on the left side.

4. After installation, lubricate the pivot at the grease fitting.

Rocket 3

Refer to the preceding section on 1970 and earlier models. Service procedures are the same for all years.

CHASSIS SPECIFICATIONS

Singles

FRONT FORKS

Type	Coil spring, hydraulically damped	
Steering head bearings	Taper roller (Timken LM 11949L)	
Springs	Main Spring	Recoil Spring
Free length	19.5 in. (48.2 cm)	0.94 in. (23.8 mm)
Spring rate	21 lbs/in.	242 lbs/in.
Number of coils	63	4½
Shaft diameter	1.3610-1.3605 in.	
Sliding tube diameter	1.363-1.364 in.	

SWING ARM

Bearings	Needle roller (Torrington B1616)
Housing diameter	1.2505-1.2495 in.
Shaft diameter	0.800-0.801 in.

REAR SUSPENSION UNITS

Type: Girling coil spring hydraulically damped

	B25, B50SS, T	B25 Fleetstar	B50MX
Ext. length (bet. cent.)	12.9 in.	12.9 in.	12.9 in.
Comp. length (bet. cent.)	10.3 in.	10.3 in.	9.9 in.
Springs: Fitted length	8.4 in.	8.4 in.	8.4 in.
Spring rate	100 lbs/in.	100 lbs/in.	70-100 lbs/i
Color ident.	Green/green/green	Green/green/green	Green/pink/green
Spring part No.	64543708	64543708	64543626
Part No. (compl. unit)	64052483	64052453	64052487

BRAKES

	B25SS, B50T B50MX	B25, B50SS
Front		
Diam. and type	6 in. single leading shoe	8 in. twin leading shoe
Width	0.875 in.	1.5 in.
Rear		
Diam. and type	7 in. single leading shoe	7 in. single leading shoe
Width	1.125 in.	1.125 in.
Lining area, in.² (cm²)		
Front	9.8 (63.3)	22.5 (145.4)
Rear	17.4 (112.4)	17.4 (112.4)

Twins

SWING ARM

Bush type	Glacier (butt joint)
Bush bore	1 in. nominal (25.4 mm)
Bush outside diameter	1⅛ in. nominal (28.57 mm)
Sleeve outside diameter	0.9984-0.9972 in. (25.359-25.328 mm)
Sleeve bore	0.628-0.626 in. (15.951-15.900 mm)
Housing diameter	1.1250-1.1260 in. (28.575-28.600 mm)
Shaft diameter	0.625-0.619 in. (15.875-15.723 mm)

REAR SUSPENSION UNITS

Type	Coil-spring hydraulically damped
Springs: Free length	9.48 in. (241 mm)
Fitted length	8.44 in. (214 mm)
Rate	88 lbs per in.

FRONT FORKS

Type	Coil-spring hydraulically damped
Springs: Free length	19.80 in. (503 mm)
Fitted length	18.5 in. (470 mm)
Rate	25 lbs per in.
Number of coils	68 (66 working)
Shaft diameter	1.3610-1.3605 in. (34.569-34.557 mm)
Outer member bore diameter	1.3634-1.363 in. (34.646-34.620 mm)

BRAKES

Front (two leading shoes)	
Diameter	8 in. (203.2 mm)
Shoe, complete with lining	Lockheed 4523-166
Lining area, in.²	23¼ (150 cm²)
Rear: Diameter	7 in. (177.8 mm)
Width	1⅛ in. (28.6 mm)
Lining thickness	3/16 in. (4.7 mm)
Lining area, in.²	15.5 (100 cm²)

Material for all linings—Ferodo AM14.

CHASSIS SPECIFICATIONS

Rocket 3

SWING ARM	
Bush type	Glacier WB.1624
Housing diameter	1.0012-1.000 in. (25.43-25.4 mm)
Shaft diameter	0.810-0.811 in. (20.574-20.599 mm)
Spacer tube diameter (inner)	0.812-0.817 in. (20.624-20.651 mm)
(outer)	0.9972-0.9984 in. (25.328-25.359 mm)

SWING ARM	
Spacer tube clearance (swinging arm spindle)	0.001-0.007 in. (0.0254-0.1778 mm)
Clearance in bush	0.0016-0.0040 in. (0.0306-0.1016 mm)
Bush diameter (inner)	1.000-1.0012 in. (25.4-25.43 mm)
(outer)	$1^1/_8$ in. nominal (28.5 mm)

REAR SHOCK ABSORBERS	
Type	Coil spring, hydraulically damped
Springs: Fitted length	9.4 in. (238.76 mm)
Spring rate	110 lbs/in.
Color identification	Red/white

FRONT FORKS	
Type	Coil spring, hydraulically damped
Springs: Free length	9.75 in. (247.6 mm)
Spring rate	32.5 lbs/in.
Number of coils	17
Color identification	Yellow/green

FORK BUSHINGS	
Material	Sintered bronze
Outer diameter (top)	1.498-1.499 in. (38.49-38.074 mm)
(bottom)	1.4935-1.4945 in. (35.648-35.674 mm)
Inner diameter (top)	1.3065-1.3075 in. (33.185-33.21 mm)
(bottom)	1.2485-1.2495 in. (31.7-31.73 mm)
Working clearance (top)	0.0035-0.0050 in. (0.0889-0.127 mm)
(bottom)	0.0035-0.0065 in. (0.0889-0.1651 mm)
Length (top)	1 in. (25.4 mm)
(bottom)	0.870-0.875 in. (22.098-22.225 mm)
Shaft diameter	1.3025-1.3030 in. (25.463-25.476 mm)
Sliding tube diameter	1.498-1.500 in. (38.049-38.1 mm)

REAR WHEEL SPROCKET	
Number of teeth	52
Chain size	$^5/_8$ in. × $^3/_8$ in. × 108 pitch (15.875 × 9.525 mm)

BRAKES	
Diameter (front)	8 in. (203.2 mm)
(rear)	7 in. (177.8 mm)
Width (front)	$1^5/_8$ in. (41.275 mm)
(rear)	$1^1/_4$ in. (31.7 mm)
Lining thickness (front)	$^3/_{16}$ in. (4.7 mm)
(rear)	$^3/_{16}$ in. (4.7 mm)
Lining area (front)	12.8 sq/in. (82.5 sq/cm)
(rear)	7.875 sq/in. (50.7 sq/cm)

INDEX
BULTACO

MODEL IDENTIFICATION

The Sherpa T comes in two sizes, a 250 cc and a 350 cc model, and both use the same frame and running gear

The Alpina comes in four sizes, a 125 cc, a 175 cc, a 250 cc, and a 350 cc model, and all use the same frame and running gear

The Pursang comes in the same four sizes as the Alpina and, like the rest of the line, all of the models use the same frame and running gear

MODEL LISTING

Street Legal Models

Mercurio
- 125
- 175
- 200

El Tigre
- 200
- 250

Campera
- Mk 1 (4-speed)
- Mk 2 (5-speed)

Matador
- Mk 1, 200 (4-speed)
- Mk 2, 250 (4-speed)
- Mk 3, 250 (5-speed)
- Mk 4, 250 (5-speed)
- Mk 5, 250
- "SD" 250

Metralla
- Mk 1, 200
- Mk 2, 200
- Mk 3, 250

Lobito
- Mk 1
- Mk 2, 100/125
- Mk 3, 100/125
- Mk 4, 125/175
- Mk 5, 125/175

El Montadero
- Mk 1
- Mk 2

Sherpa T
- Mk 1
- Mk 2
- Mk 3
- Mk 4

Alpina
- 125
- 175
- 250
- 350

Racing Models

Lobito
- AK 100

Sherpa S
- Mk 1
- Mk 2
- Mk 3, S100
- Mk 3, 125
- Mk 3, 175
- Mk 3, 200

Pursang
- Mk 1, 250
- Mk 2, 250
- Mk 3, 250
- Mk 4, 250 "A" and "E"
- Mk 5, 125/250/350
- Astro, 250

El Bandito
- Mk 1, 350
- Mk 2, 350
- Mk 3, 360

TSS
- Mk 1, 125/250
- Mk 2, 125/250/350

Astro
- 250

TUNE-UP AND MAINTENANCE

TUNE-UP OPERATIONS

Ignition Timing

BREAKER POINT IGNITION

1. Remove the kickstarter. Unscrew the four allen bolts which secure the left side engine case, and take off the case.
2. Remove the spark plug and, in its place, install a dial gauge.
3. Rotate the magneto flywheel until one of the windows is at twelve o'clock and the other is at ten o'clock.
4. Turn the flywheel slightly in either direction until piston Top Dead Center is indicated by the dial gauge.

If a dial gauge is not available a thin, non-metallic object (such as a pencil) can be inserted into the plug hole to find the highest piston position. Scribe a mark on the pencil even with the top thread of the spark plug hole. Another mark must be scribed above the first corresponding to the correct ignition timing for each machine. Refer to accompanying chart. Note that most models fire 3.0–3.25mm BTDC.

	All BTDC mm
Lobito	
100 cc	3.00-3.25
Metralla	
200 cc	3.00-3.25
Mercurio	
125 cc	3.00
175 cc	3.00-3.25
Campera	
175 cc	3.00-3.25
Matador	
200 cc	3.00-3.25
Sherpa S	
125 cc	3.25
175 cc	3.25
200 cc	3.25
TT Scrambler	
250 cc	3.85-4.10
Motocross Scrambler	
250 cc	3.85-4.10
Matador	
250 cc	3.85-4.10
Pursang MK IV	
250 cc	2.75-2.95

Test light properly connected with a dial gauge in place in the spark plug hole

This applies to models with conventional breaker point ignitions.

5. Connect a test light or continuity tester with a self contained power source to the ignition points circuit. One lead is connected to the black wire going from the electrical junction box to the points. The other is grounded to the engine as shown in the accompanying illustration. On five-speed models, the ground lead must hold the exposed end of the green wire against the engine case.
6. The continuity test light should be on at this point. Rotate the flywheel clockwise. The points should begin to open (and the test light will go out) when the piston is at the proper distance before top dead center. This value will be indicated by the dial indicator or by the second scribed line on the pencil.
7. Measure the point gap with the appropriate feeler gauge. Point gap for all models should be 0.015in.

Checking the point gap

8. If adjustment is necessary, remove the flywheel nut and pull off the flywheel with the special Bultaco tool No. 132-015 (or Tool No. 11-32-015 for engines with the large taper shaft).
9. To adjust the timing, loosen the three screws on the stator disc and rotate the disc clockwise to increase, or counterclockwise to decrease, the gap.
10. Before rechecking the timing, ensure that the flywheel nut has been torqued to the correct value (75 ft lbs).

FEMSATRONIC IGNITION

1. Remove the spark plug.
2. Remove the left side engine case.
3. Fit a dial gauge into the spark plug hole and rotate the engine until the gauge shows a maximum reading. The piston is now at top dead center. Rock the piston back and forth several times to ensure that it is correctly positioned. Zero the gauge at this point.
4. The rotor has a pin hole in it. The 2mm pin should be inserted in this hole and the rotor turned in a clockwise direction until the pin aligns with, and will slip into, the hole in the left-hand corner of the upper coil. The pin will be approximately in the "9 o'clock" position.
5. With the rotor aligned as described, the dial gauge should have indicated a total piston movement of 3.0–3.25mm.
6. If adjustment is necessary, remove the rotor with the special tool and loosen the three screws which secure the stator plate.
7. Replace the rotor, but not the rotor nut. Leave the 2mm pin in position.
8. Rotate the rotor and stator until they are in the correct timing position, as indicated by the dial gauge (3.0–3.25mm BTDC).
9. Remove the rotor carefully, assuring that the stator does not move, and tighten the stator screws securely.
10. Replace the rotor and rotor nut. Tighten the nut, and recheck the timing as described.

Spark Plugs

The correct gap for all models is 0.020 in. Recommended plugs for individual models are given in the following chart. Note that the best heat range for each motorcycle may vary according to how the machine is used.

RECOMMENDED SPARK PLUGS

Model	NGK Plug
Lobito	
100 cc	B7H or B7HC
Metralla	
200 cc	B7EC
Mercurio	
125 cc	B7HC
175 cc	B7EC
Campera	
175 cc	B7EC or B77EC
Matador	
200 cc	B7EC or B77EC
250 cc	B77EC or B8EN
Sherpa S	
100 cc	B8EN-B10EN
125 cc	B8EN-B10EN
175 cc	B8EN-B10EN
200 cc	B8EN-B10EN
Scrambler	
250 cc	B9EN or B10EN (Dual plug B9EN and B10EN)*
Motocross Scrambler	
360 cc	B9EN or B10EN (Dual plug B9EN and B10EN)*

* Dual Plugs—The hotter plug on the carb. side; other on exhaust side

Carburetor Adjustment

1. Start the engine and allow it to warm up.

2. Screw in the pilot air screw until it bottoms against its seat and then back it out ¾ turn. This is an average setting.

3. Adjust the throttle stop screw so that the engine will idle as smoothly and steadily as possible.

4. Screw the pilot air screw in or out in small increments until the engine runs the smoothest.

Amal Monobloc carburetor

MAINTENANCE ITEMS

Lubrication

TRANSMISSION OIL

The oil in the transmission and primary chaincase should be changed at least twice a year, or more often depending on use.

1. When the transmission oil has reached operating temperature, remove the drain plug from the bottom of the case and drain off the oil.

2. Refill with 500 cc of 90 weight gear lube.

3. Drain the oil in the primary chaincase in the same manner. Refill with 250 cc of SAE 10W or 20 W oil.

FRONT FORKS

The oil should be changed twice a year on street machines, once a month on competition bikes.

1964–67 Mercurio, 1964–67 Metralla, 1965 Sherpa S, and 1964–65 Matador

To change the oil in the forks on the above models, it is necessary to remove the sliders, pour out the old oil, add the new oil to each slider, and reassemble. The capacity of each slider is 85 cc of oil.

1. Compress the forks and unscrew the two stanchion plugs from the stanchion tubes.

2. Loosen the locknut at the bottom of the stanchion plug.

3. Support the machine so that the front wheel is off the ground and then disconnect the front brake cable and the brake anchor.

4. Remove the axle nut. On the Metralla and Matador, loosen the four axle clamp bolts. Withdraw the axle and remove the wheel.

5. Remove the front fender. Remove the dust covers from the sliders, if fitted.

6. Press upward on each slider and remove the stanchion plug and washer. Pull off the slider.

7. Drain and refill each slider with 85 cc of oil. The correct grade is SAE 20W or 30W.

8. Reassemble in the reverse order of disassembly. Refer to the "chassis" section for assembly procedures.

1965–66 250 cc Scrambler, 1966–67 Matador, and 1966–67 Sherpa S

1. Remove the drain plug at the bottom of each fork leg and drain the oil. Pump the forks up and down a few times to ensure that all of the oil has been removed.

2. Replace the drain plugs and remove the cap at the top of each fork leg.

3. Add 160cc of 20 or 30W and oil to each fork leg.

4. Torque the stanchion plugs to 100 ft lbs (250 cc Scrambler) or 50 ft lbs (1966–67 Matador and 1966–67 Sherpa S).

5. Work the forks up and down. If any oil escapes from the valve holes in the stanchion plugs or if you can hear air reentering the valve when the forks are rebounding, the ball bearings in the stanchion plugs will have to be reseated.

6. To reseat the bearings, remove the screw from the top of the plug and insert a magnet to lift out the spring. Insert a 3/16 in. drift into the valve hole so that the drift bears against the ball. Tap the drift lightly to reseat the ball. Reinstall the spring and screw and retest the forks again to make sure that the ball is seated.

1966–67 Campera and 1963–64 Sherpa S 4-Speed

To change the fork oil, it is necessary to remove the fork sliders.

1. Unscrew the stanchion plugs from the tubes. On the Sherpa S, the allen bolt must first be removed from the top of each stanchion plug.

2. Compress the forks and loosen the locknut at the bottom of the stanchion plugs.

3. Remove the front fender. Disconnect the brake cable and the brake anchor.

4. Remove the lower clamp from the fork boots (if fitted) and push the boots up off the slider legs.

5. Remove the axle nut, pull out the axle, and remove the front wheel.

6. Press up on the slider and unscrew the stanchion plug from the damper rod (Campera).

7. Remove the sliders from the fork tubes.

8. Hold the fork spring in a vise (Sherpa S). Unscrew the spring carrier, using pliers, and push the spring down and away from the carrier locknut. Put a wrench on the locknut and remove the carrier with pliers.

9. Remove the fork springs and carriers from the slider legs (Campera).

10. Turn the slider legs upside down and pump the damper rod to expel the oil.

11. Refill each slider with 85cc of SAE 20W or 30W oil. Work the damper rod up and down until the oil has been sucked into the cylinder and the unit is working satisfactorily.

12. Reassemble in the reverse order of disassembly. Refer to the "chassis" section for reassembly procedures.

1966–67 Lobito

1. Remove the slotted drain plug near the bottom of each fork leg.

2. Work the forks up and down to expel the oil from the legs.

3. Remove the handlebars and unscrew the two stanchion plugs.

4. Add 70cc of SAE 20W or 30W oil to each fork leg.

5. Loosen the fork tube clamp bolts on the lower triple clamp. Screw the stanchion plugs into the tubes and torque them to 50 ft lbs. Tap the top and bottom of each side of the lower triple clamp with a mallet to relieve any strain.

6. Torque the clamp bolts to 15 ft lbs.

FORK LEG CAPACITIES

Model	Quantity Each Leg cc	SAE #
Lobito "K"		
100 cc	70	20*
Lobito Trail		
100 cc	70	20
Mercurio		
175 cc	85	20
Campera		
175 cc	85	20**
Matador		
200 cc	85	30-50
Sherpa S 4-speed		
125 cc	85	20-50
175 cc	85	20-50
200 cc	85	20-50
TT Pursang		
250 cc	160	10-30
Motocross Pursang		
250 cc	160	10-30
Matador Mk II, Mk III		
250 cc	160	10-30
Lobito 5-speed		
100 cc	80	30
125 cc	80	30
Campera 5-speed		
175 cc	80	30
El Tigre		
250 cc	85	30
200 cc	55	30
Sherpa S 5-speed		
100 cc	80	20
125 cc	150	20
175 cc	150	20
200 cc	150	20
Bandido Scrambler		
360 cc	160	20
El Montadero		
360 cc	160	20
Metralla		
250 cc	85	20

* 30 or 40 optional
** 30 or 50 optional

Service Checks and Adjustments

BRAKES

1. Remove the wheels periodically and check the shoes and drums for excessive wear or glazing. Remove any surface glaze with emery cloth or fine sandpaper and replace the linings if they are worn down near the rivets or show signs of oil penetration.

2. The front brake can be adjusted at either end of the brake cable. Adjust the cable so that actuation occurs after about 1 in. of free-play is taken up.

3. The rear brake is adjusted by turning the adjusting nut on the brake cam actuating lever. Pedal free-play should be about 1 in. If the machine is equipped with lights, make sure that the stoplight switch is adjusted so that the stoplight comes on when the brakes begin to bite.

CLUTCH

Always maintain clutch lever free-play at approximately ½–¾ in. Cable play can be adjusted by turning the screw at the handlebar end of the cable.

FINAL DRIVE CHAIN

To check chain adjustment, put the bike on its stand and move the chain up and down at the midway point of the run. If total movement exceeds about 1 in., the chain must be readjusted.

Loosen the rear axle nut and turn the two adjusting screws at each swing arm end in an equal amount until the chain has about ½–¾ in. freeplay. Retighten the axle nut and check the play again.

STEERING HEAD

To check steering head bearing condition, put the bike on its center stand or place blocks under the frame to lift the front wheel and swing the forks slowly through their full steering travel. Movement should be smooth, light, and free from any binding. Check for play in the bearings by grasping the bottom of the fork legs and trying to rock them back and forth in line with the motorcycle. Play can be removed by tightening the steering head main nut. *Tighten no more than necessary to remove play.* If steering movement remains unsatisfactory after adjustment, the bearings should be replaced.

SWING ARM

The swing arm should be checked for bushing side-play periodically. There should be absolutely no play and the swing arm must not be bent or weakened by cracked welds.

ENGINE AND TRANSMISSION

FOUR SPEED MODELS

Engine Removal

1. Unscrew the plastic cap from the top of the carburetor and pull out the slide.

Carburetor securing points

2. Unscrew the fuel line banjo capscrew and remove the banjo, fuel filter, and washer. Unscrew the retaining nuts and remove the carburetor.

3. Unscrew the gearbox and primary case filler plugs. Using a 19 mm wrench, remove the drainplug from the bottom of the primary chaincase, catching the oil in a suitable container.

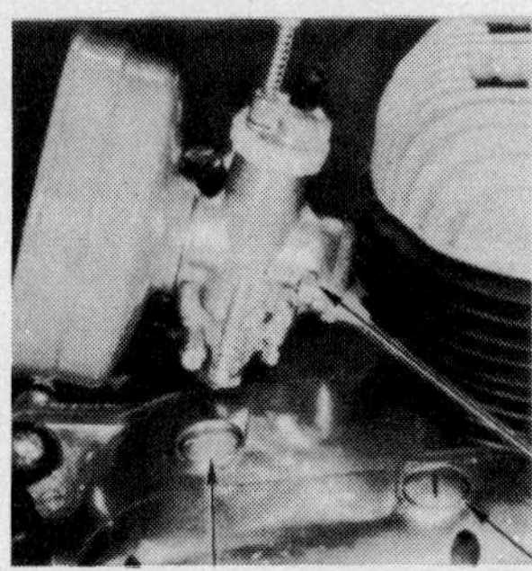

Gearbox (left) and primary case (right) filler plugs

Crankcase drain plug

4. Remove the kickstart lever and then unscrew the four allen bolts which secure the left side engine case.

5. Engage First gear in the transmission and, while a helper holds the rear brake on, unscrew the nut which secures the flywheel to the crankshaft. A magnet can be used to remove the two flat washers and one lockwasher from the end of the crankshaft.

Kickstarter lever and case securing bolts

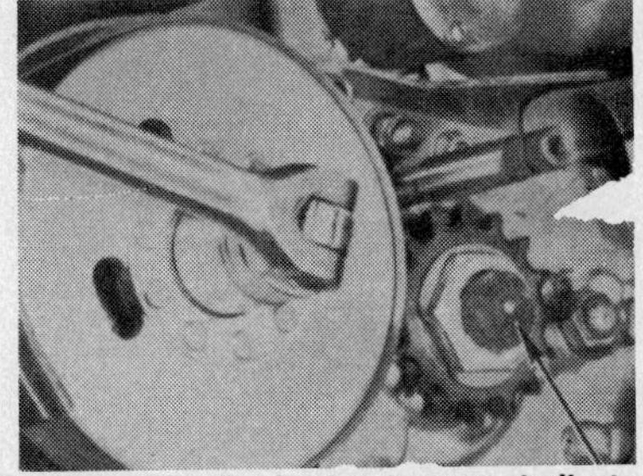

Removing the flywheel nut; arrow indicates the clutch pushrod and felt washer

6. Turn Bultaco tool 132-015 (or Tool No. 11-32-015 for engines with the large taper shaft) completely into the flywheel center. (Use a small amount of grease on the end of the crankshaft and make sure that the center bolt is screwed all the way out so that the tool seats fully.) Tighten the center bolt until the flywheel pulls free of the crankshaft. Remove the woodruff key from the crankshaft.

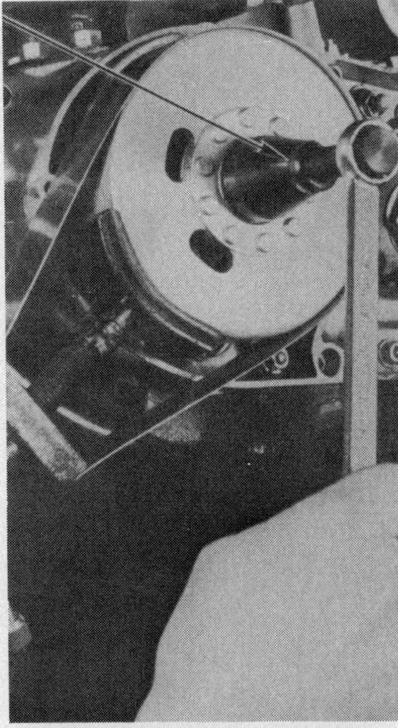

Pulling the flywheel with the special tool

Mark the position of the stator disc and remove the screws

7. Mark the original position of the stator disc in relation to the engine case, as shown (for convenience when reassembling the engine). Pull the wires from the connector block, and unscrew the three screws and remove the stator disc assembly. Pull out all electrical wires leading to the frame through their rubber grommet.

Crank seal cover bolts

8. Remove the six bolts which hold the crankshaft seal cover and remove the cover and gasket.

9. Bend back the tabs of the lockwasher which holds the countershaft nut and again, holding the rear brake on, unscrew the nut.

10. On early models unscrew the three countersunk screws which retain the countershaft seal holder and remove the holder, gasket, and spacer. On mid-1964 and later engines, the triangular plate has been relocated inside the transmission case. These later series engines use a larger countershaft ball-bearing assembly which has the same part number as the main bearings. If this bearing operates roughly or is worn, it should be replaced after the crankcases have been split.

Removing the countershaft nut

Removing the pipe flange nut

11. Unbolt the rear exhaust pipe bracket. While supporting the pipe, unscrew the flange nut at the cylinder head using a pin wrench, as shown.

12. Unscrew and completely remove the shift lever securing bolt and slip the lever off of the selector shaft. Unscrew the seven allen bolts and remove the right side engine cover.

13. Remove the safety wire on the clutch tension nuts. Gradually and evenly loosen the nuts, and then remove the springs, pressure plate, and clutch discs. Remove the clutch rod thrust pin.

Clutch safety wire (left); engine sprocket flywheel on models with duplex chain (right)

14. Bend back the tabs of the clutch hub retaining nut (some models use a star washer) and, using the clutch tool to stop the clutch from turning, remove the nut. Use the same procedure to remove the inner hub nut. To remove the inner clutch hub and engine sprocket flywheel, screw two of the tension nuts to studs on opposite sides of the inner clutch hub and use two hooked pry bars against the other clutch hub to remove it. Also take care not to misplace the woodruff keys.

15. Remove the clutch sprocket and engine sprocket together, using gear pullers if necessary. Use pry bars to pull the inner clutch hub spacer off of the transmission shaft. Remove the O-ring after the spacer and woodruff key has been removed.

16. Unscrew the six bolts from the crankshaft seal cover. Before the cover can be removed from 250 cc scramblers and engines with duplex primary chains, it will be necessary to pry off the spacer in the same manner as described in the previous step. After removing the spacer and its O-ring, the seal cover can be pulled off.

Removing the clutch hub and engine sprocket

NOTE: *On some models there is a notch in the seal holder. Upon reassembly, this notch must fit into the cylinder stud which extends down from the top of the case.*

17. Unscrew and remove the speedometer cable from the speedometer drive at the engine.

18. For assembly convenience, measure and record the end-play of the transmission mainshaft using a dial indicator or vernier caliper, as shown.

19. Pull off the cap and remove the sparkplug. Remove the drive chain master link and remove the chain. Unbolt and remove the *chainguard.*

20. Unscrew the three (four on recent models) engine mounting nuts and withdraw the bolts. Lift the front of the engine while lowering the rear until all of the frame flanges have been cleared, and remove the engine.

Engine Disassembly

1. Loosen the six cylinder heat nuts, 3 ft lbs at a time, in reverse sequence of that shown in the illustration. Lift the head off of the cylinder head studs.

2. Loosen and remove the seven nuts which hold the cylinder to the crankcase. The two nuts below the intake flange can be removed after the cylinder has been lifted up slightly. Remove the cylinder, taking care not to let the piston and connecting rod hit the case as they are withdrawn.

3. Pry out the wrist pin circlips as shown, using a small screwdriver. A cloth placed around the crankcase opening will prevent them from falling down inside. Do not attempt to save the clips. New ones should always be used.

Head nut tightening sequence

4. Before attempting to remove the wrist pin, carefully remove any burrs that may be present around the circlip grooves using a sharp scraper. Using a drift that is slightly smaller in diameter than the wrist pin, heat the piston push the pin out of the piston while supporting the connecting rod with your other hand.

5. Remove the three countersunk screws in the speedometer drive cover and remove the small setscrew from the side of the speedometer drive housing. The drive cover can be removed by screwing a nut (or bolt on some models) onto the end and using this as a leverage point in order to pry the cover off.

NOTE: *The speedometer drive cover need not be removed at this point except on 125 and 155 cc Mercurios and*

Removing the piston pin circlip

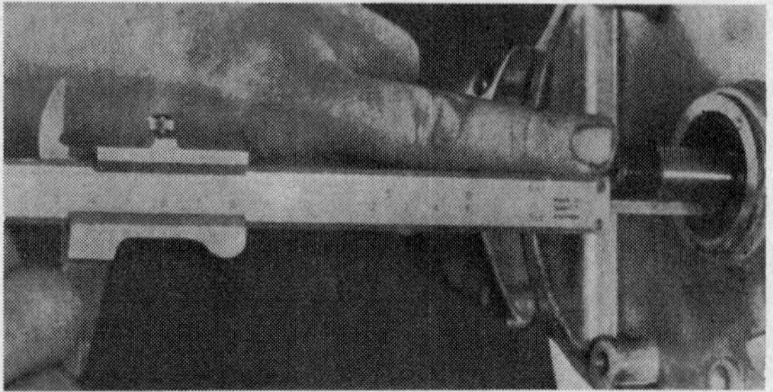

Measuring mainshaft end-play

Removing the crankshaft spacer

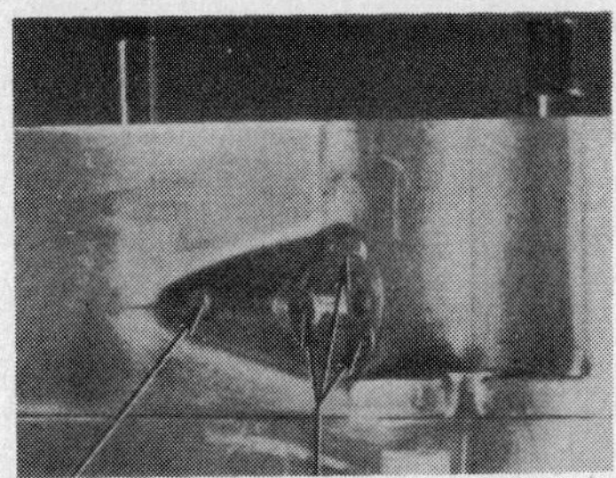

Speedometer drive bushing setscrew and cover screws

200 cc Matadors. In addition, it will be necessary to remove the speedometer drive bushing on these models. This can be accomplished by splitting the bushing and replacing it with a new one on assembly, or removing it with Bultaco tool 132-069 (which can also be used to extract the speedometer drive cover). On all other models, the cases can be split without removing the speedometer drive and bushing, but these parts must be removed before the cases can be reassembled.

6. It is not necessary to remove the kickstarter spring or shaft in order to split the cases. However, if the spring or shaft are to be replaced, remove the spring at this time using a T-bar with a hook on one end or a screwdriver to force the spring end away from its retaining stud. Allow the spring to unwind around the shaft, then slip the kickstart lever onto its shaft and rotate it clockwise until the part of the spring that passes through the shaft if vertical. Then force the spring up until the end is clear of the hole in the shaft and pull it off of the shaft.

7. Unscrew the 12 nuts that secure the crankcase studs and remove the flatwashers and lockwashers. Remove the allen bolt and lockwasher located behind the front engine mounting flange.

8. The crankcases are now ready to be separated. Before attempting this, heat the engine to approximately 300°F.

If the Bultaco crankcase puller (Tool No. 132-043) is not available, place the engine, magneto side down, on a bench. Grasping the cylinder studs of the uppermost crankcase half, with the engine placed as described, lift the engine a few inches off of the bench; with a soft-faced mallet, carefully tap around the circumference of the crankcase assembly on the joint until the cases begin to separate.

Removing the kickstarter return spring

Removing the allen bolt and lockwasher behind the front engine mounting flange; crankcase nuts are also shown

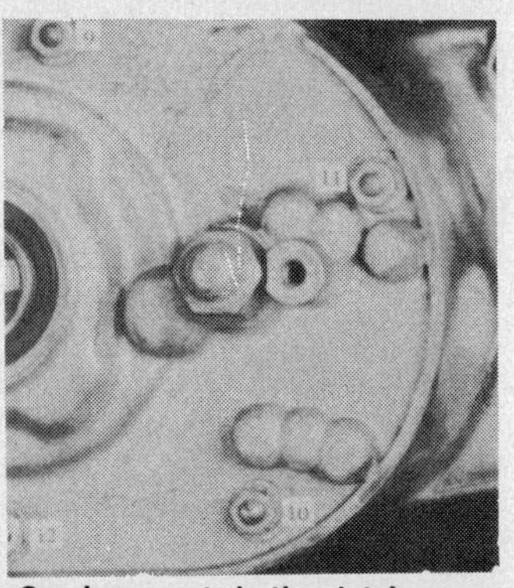

Crankcase nuts in the clutch case

Separating the crankcase

Transmission

MODEL VARIATIONS

NOTE: *The mainshaft gears are interchangeable among engines in all street machines and the Matador. The first, second, and third gears on the countershaft are interchangeable on all models except the 125 and 155 cc Mercurios and the Matador, which have a one-piece countershaft with non-removeable gears. The first and second gears in the Sherpa S have different ratios from those in other models (close ratio). Bandido gears are not interchangeable with any other model.*

All of the gears in the transmission were redesigned early in 1965, the new gears differing in both size and shape. The new style gears can be used to replace the old ones, providing that they are replaced in mating pairs.

The following procedures apply to all models except the 250 Scrambler. If you are working on a 250 Scrambler transmission, note these constructional variations:

a. The internal shifting pattern is different. When shifting from First to Second gear, the 1st/3rd sliding dog moves out of engagement with the 1st gear idler and stops in a neutral position between the First gear idler and Third gear idler. The 2nd/4th sliding dog moves over to engage the Second gear idler.

In all other transmissions, the 1st/2nd sliding dog is located between the First gear idler and Second gear idler on the mainshaft. When shifting from First to Second gear, the 1st/2nd sliding dog moves out of engagement with the First gear idler (mainshaft) and continues its travel until it has moved into engagement with the second gear idler.

b. The dogs and their engaging slots are different. Care must be taken not to interchange one type of sliding and engaging dog with the other.

Differences in the dogs and slots

c. The pattern of the shifting cam plate in the 250 Scrambler is different and cannot be interchanged with other models.

d. The 250 scrambler uses a forged steel cam plate support bracket which can be used as an improved replacement part in other models if trouble is experienced with the forged aluminum bracket.

e. The 4th gear driving sprocket is wider than that used on other models. The wider sprocket necessitates the use of a different countershaft with a repositioned snap-ring groove.

GEARSHIFT SELECTOR ADJUSTMENT (4-Speed Models)

On all models except the 250 Scrambler and Sherpa T, the selector mechanism can be adjusted with the engine in the frame.

1. Remove the shift lever from its shaft. Unscrew the three allen bolts and remove the triangular selector mechanism cover. (Hold down the cover until the bolts are removed or the selector fork spring will push it out with sufficient force to bend one of the screws.

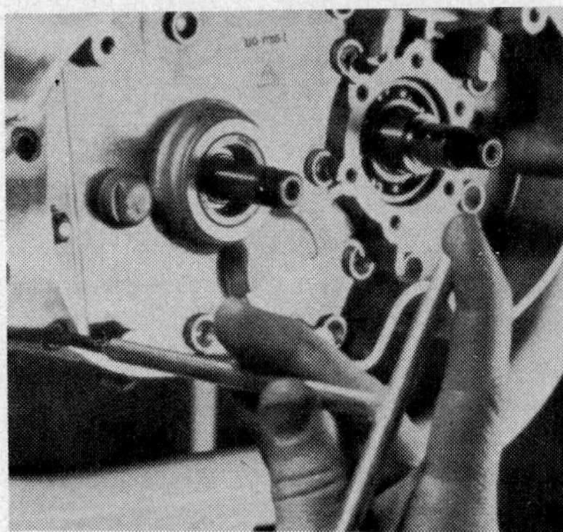

Removing the selector cover

2. Check for a bent selector shaft by checking it with a straightedge at several places around its diameter. A bent selector shaft can cause binding and erratic operation of the shift lever.

3. Note the machined aluminum surfaces in the engine case just above and below the selector shaft. These are the selector shaft stops which limit the movement of the shift lever when shifting gears. The selector shaft is supposed to hit its stop at the same instant the spring-loaded cam plate plunger comes to rest in a notch in the cam plate.

If the selector shaft hits its stop too soon or too late, the cam plate will not be rotated far enough (or will be rotated too far) for maximum engagement of the corresponding idler gear and sliding dog. The result will be either a false Neutral or jumping out of gear. To find out if the selector shaft is hitting the stop at the right time, proceed as follows:

4. Make sure the selector shaft thrust washer is in place. Install the selector cover while holding the selector shaft in position (A small amount of grease will hold the gasket in place.) Make a special tool from a plunger sleeve nut, no. 111-020 (no. 11-11-020 for the 250 Scrambler). Drill a 6 mm hole in the outside end of the sleeve nut to enable the plunger spring to stick out. Install the sleeve nut, substituting it for the regular one, and push the protruding spring in with one hand. Shift gears in both directions with your free hand; you will be able to feel the exact position of the plunger at the moment the selector shaft hits its stop. If the selector shaft hits its stop too soon, you will not feel the plunger slide into its notch in the cam plate. If it hits too late, you'll feel the plunger slide into its notch and then be forced out again.

Selector shaft cover removal

5. Remove the shift lever and the cover again. To remove the selector shaft, rock the splined end up and down while pushing forward and inward. This will free both ends of the selector hairpin spring from its anchor pin. (Do not remove the locknut from the spring anchor pin.) Withdraw the selector assembly.

6. If the top or bottom of the selector shaft extension is not hitting its stop soon enough, the extension will have to be built up through brazing and filed smooth. Only trial and error can show how much added metal is necessary. If the shaft extensions hit too soon, grind a *small* amount of metal off and retest it.

7. If the thrust surfaces of the selector fork fingers have become rounded (shown in illustration), replace the fork with a new one.

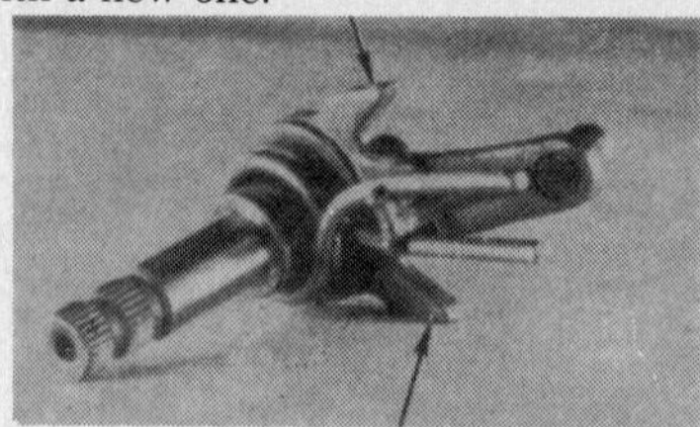

Top and bottom extensions

8. If the selector fork, shaft, or return spring have been replaced, several other checks will have to be made.

a. First, check to see if the shift lever sticks as you shift into or out of Second gear (Third gear on 250 Scramblers). If it does, remove the selector mechanism and grind the ends of the selector fork fingers. Remove no more than ½ mm of material and follow the original curves. Do not overheat the metal or it will lose its hardness. Reassemble and test the selector; continue this operation until the shift lever returns easily to the central position.

b. If the gearshift works stiffly or not at all, the selector fork is probably hanging up on its thrust peg. To remedy this, dress off any burrs or high spots that are interfering with the pivoting of the selector fork.

c. If you experience trouble shifting up into Third or down into Second gear, it is likely that the hairpin return spring is not adjusted correctly. If the problem is in shifting up from Second to Third, bend both legs of the spring up about 2 mm. If the gearbox will not shift from Third to Second, bend both legs down about 2 mm. Both legs must be bent the same distance in order to keep them parallel.

TRANSMISSION COMPONENTS

Removal and Installation

1. Lift out the countershaft cluster, taking care not to lose the thrust washer on each end.

2. Withdraw the shift fork shaft. Rotate the cam plate to the second gear position, then pivot the upper shift fork clockwise and remove it. Rotate the cam plate to the third gear position and remove the remaining shift fork in the same manner.

3. Remove the spacer from the starter shaft. Using both hands, remove the mainshaft and the kickstart gear from the case together.

4. Clean all components thoroughly and check for wear and damage. Any part with a thrust surface that has turned blue should be replaced, as the blueing indicates that overheating has occurred.

5. Installation is in the reverse order of disassembly.

Inspection

1. Using the amount of mainshaft end-

Selector fork fingers

Removing the countershaft gear cluster

Removing the mainshaft and the kickstarter gear

play you recorded when disassembling, make a temporary spacer of the same thickness with a 14 mm hole in the center. Install the spacer onto the end of the mainshaft that slides into the sleeve gear. Reinstall the mainshaft assembly with the spacer in place. Also reinstall the selector forks and shaft in the left side engine case. With the cam plate in the first gear position, measure the gap between the first gear sliding dog and the first gear idler. (Take care not to deflect the selector fork shaft, which is normally supported by the right side engine case.) Record the measurement and repeat the operation for second, third, and fourth gears (with the cam plate in the appropriate positions). If any measurement amounts to more than 30% of the length of the engagement pegs, observe the following procedures.

a. Measure the width of the machined surface on the selector fork. It should not be less than 2.85 mm. The width of the groove in the sliding dog should not be greater than 3.2 mm. Replace any part that is worn beyond specification.

b. Measure the clearance between the shift fork cam plate follower and the slot in the cam plate. If greater than 0.65 mm, either or both parts should be replaced.

c. Check the end-play between each idler gear and its lock ring. If necessary, place a shim between the ring and idler. Do not reduce clearance to less than 0.2 mm. If you are able to rotate a lock ring with your fingers, it should be replaced with a new one. If the lock ring grooves are not at least 0.3 mm deep, or if their edges have become rounded, the mainshaft should be replaced.

d. Check the straightness of the mainshaft by placing it in V-blocks, or between lathe centers, and rotating it while measuring with a dial indicator. If runout exceeds 0.04 mm, the mainshaft should be replaced.

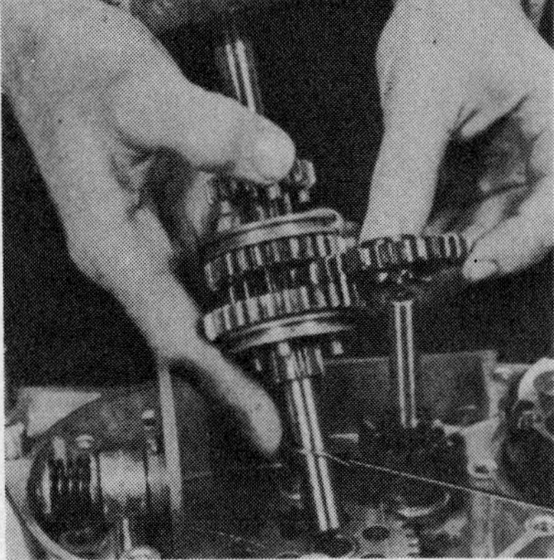
Temporary spacer

Measuring the gap between the first gear sliding dog and the first gear idler

Measuring the width of the machined surface on the selector fork

Shift fork-to-camplate follower clearance

2. Bend back the locktabs and unscrew the four bolts which secure the cam plate bracket. Rock the cam plate back and forth until it is freed from its dowel pins. Check the straightness of the cam plate using an engineers square, as shown. The bracket can sometimes be bent due to harsh shifting, and it should be replaced if not in proper alignment.

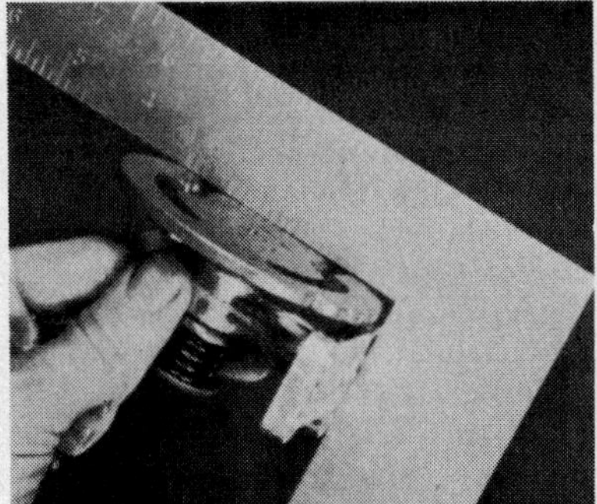
Checking camplate warpage

3. If the countershaft or either of its two ball bearings are replaced, the end-play must be checked and adjusted. First, measure the distance between the two countershaft bearings in the crankcase halves. To accomplish this, measure the distance between the ball bearing inner face and the inner edge on each crankcase half and add the two figures. Add 0.4 mm to the result to compensate for gasket thickness. Next, install the two thrust washers on either end of the countershaft and measure the distance from the outside edge of one thrust washer to the outside edge of the other. Subtract this figure from the preceding one; the remainder is the countershaft end-play. If at least 0.2 mm end-play does not exist, file the thrust washers evenly until the desired amount is obtained.

4. Having already removed the kickstart return spring, you can now remove

Checking mainshaft runout

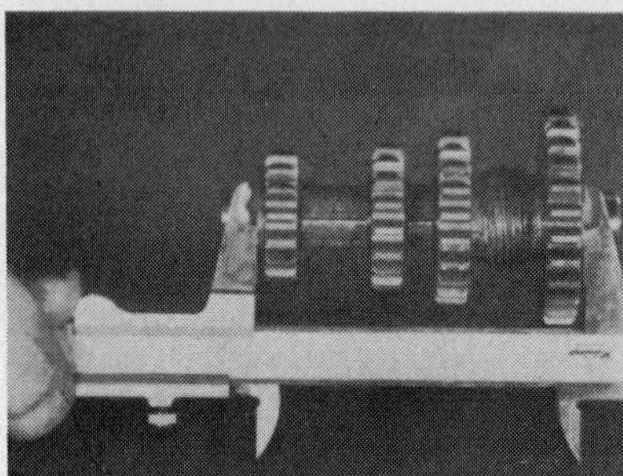
Calculating countershaft end-play

the kickstart shaft, the ratchet, the ratchet spring, and the washer. These components can be removed by rotating the kickstart shaft clockwise from the outside of the crankcase half and lifting the assembly from the case.

5. If the crankstop in the left crankcase half is bent (a common occurrence in early 1964 models), it can be replaced with the later improved one. The stop is secured by the chamfered nut behind which the kickstart return spring is hooked.

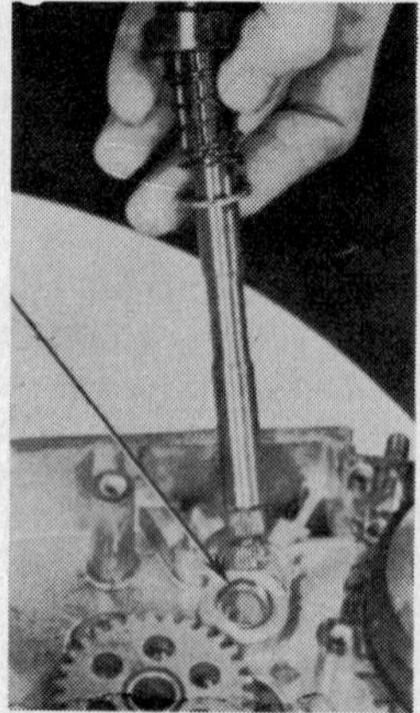
Kickstarter crankstop

6. Tap out the sleeve gear with a rubber hammer and inspect its support bearing for looseness or rough operation. Remove the O-ring located between the support bearing and the spacer, and drive out the seal and sleeve from inside the case. Thoroughly clean the exposed countershaft bearing. If it is necessary to replace the countershaft bearing, remove the three screws from the retaining plate and lift off the plate. Heat the case to 300° F. and the countershaft bearing and crankshaft assembly will drop out of the case.Install the new bearing while the case is still hot.

Removing the sleeve gear

The Crankshaft Assembly

The transmission components need not be removed in order to work on the crankshaft. To remove the crank, heat the engine case to 300° F. While holding the gear clusters with one hand, tap the magneto end of the crankshaft with a rubber mallet until it is free.

1. Whenever connecting rod bearing failure has occurred, the first thing to suspect is crankcase pressure leakage. Check the crankshaft seals. If stiff, scratched, or rough, they must be replaced. Leaky seals can cause main bearing failure and piston seizure due to insufficient lubrication.

2. Check connecting rod side play with a feeler gauge between the thrust washer and the cheek of the flywheel. This value should be about 0.016 in. for 100 and 125cc engines; 0.018 in. for 175, 200, and 250 cc bikes, and 0.020 in. for the 326 and 360 cc machines. Values in excess of these will necessitate the replacement of the rod and bearing.

3. On engines with a solid crankpin assembly, the crankshaft can be pressed apart after a careful cleaning. On some 175 and 200 cc machines, the crankpin is hollow. Before pressing these assemblies apart, drill through the solid end of each expansion plug in the crankpin ends with a 5/16 in. drill and knock out the plugs with a drift. (When reassembling a hollow crankpin assembly, do not press the expansion plugs into the crankpin until the crankshaft assembly has been perfectly aligned.)

4. To reassemble the crankshaft halves:

a. Press the crankpin into one of the crankshaft halves until the pin is flush with the outer surface of the flywheel. Install one of the thrust washer on the crankpin.

b. Pack the bearing cage with light grease and place a roller in each window of the cage.

c. Place the caged bearing on the crankpin and push each opposite pair of rollers inward until they touch the crankpin, then slip the connecting rod over the cage and put the other thrust washer on the crankpin.

d. Using a straightedge as a guide, press the other crankshaft half onto the crankpin until the outer surface of the flywheel is flush with the end of the crankpin. Insert the proper feeler gauge (0.016, 0.018, or 0.020 in.) between a thrust washer and flywheel, and press the crankshaft assembly together until the feeler gauge is a tight fit.

e. Place the crankshaft assembly in V-blocks or between lathe centers and check runout using two dial gauges against the bearing surfaces. Check whether the needles swing in unison or out of phase, and whether they move the same amount. If the needles neither swing the same distance nor start and end their swings at the same time, the crankshaft halves are both eccentric and non-parallel.

Checking crankshaft runout

To correct the eccentric condition, rotate the crankshaft until the drive side dial gauge reaches the point of maximum travel. Draw an imaginary line between the ends of the dial gauge shafts and make a chalk mark on the rim of the drive side flywheel at the place where the imaginary line would cross it. Remove the crankshaft assembly and, holding it on the magneto side, hit the chalk mark on the rim of the drive side flywheel with a bronze or lead hammer. This will rotate the flywheel slightly on the crankpin to bring it into alignment with the magneto side flywheel. Repeat this procedure until the gauge needles begin and end their swings at the same time.

To correct the non-parallel condition, rotate the crankshaft assembly until the dial gauge needles reach the high point of their travel. If the crankpin lies along an imaginary line drawn between the

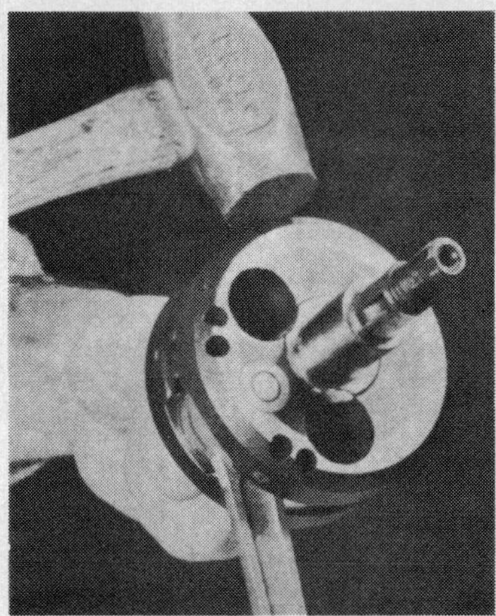

Aligning the crankshaft assembly

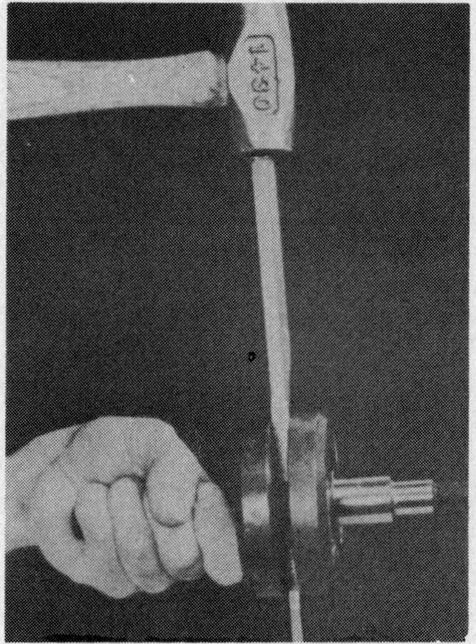

Aligning the flywheels

ends of the two dial gauge shafts, the flywheels are pinched together opposite the crankpin. To correct this, rotate the crankshaft until the crankpin is at the bottom. Insert a wedge at the top of the flywheels and spread them slightly by tapping the wedge with a hammer. Check the alignment again; the assembly has been aligned properly if neither gauge needle travels more than 0.025 mm. (0.001 in). If necessary, continue this operation until this requirement is met.

If, in the above paragraph, the crankpin did not lie on or near the imaginary line between the dial gauge shafts but was opposite this line, the flywheels have been spread apart. To correct this, draw a chalk line on a flywheel (to match the imaginary line) from the driveshafts to the outer rim. Hold the assembly by the crankpin and lay the portions of the flywheels on the other side of the driveshafts flat on the bench with the chalk mark up. Hit the upper flywheel on the chalk mark with a mallet to bring the flywheels closer together. Retest, and continue this operation until neither dial gauge moves more than 0.025 mm (0.001 in.).

Aligning the flywheels

5. After completing crankshaft alignment, the expansion plugs can be inserted into the hollow crankpin (if applicable). Press the plugs in until they are flush with the ends of the crankpin. Take care to install the plugs straight; if they go in crooked, the end of the crankpin may split. After installing the plugs, recheck and correct, if necessary, flywheel parallelism

6. Recheck connecting rod side play as described earlier. If side play is less than the prescribed amount, press the flywheels apart just enough to restore proper end-play.

Piston Size Information

1. Oversize pistons have the oversize number stamped on the crown. Four over-sizes are available: 0.25mm, 0.50mm, 0.75mm, and 1.0mm.

2. Pistons are stamped with a "+" or "−" on the crown to indicate different machining tolerances.

Piston crown markings

The accompanying chart shows dimensions for "+" and "−" pistons up to 250cc. In all cases, however, the cylinder must be bored to match the particular piston which will be fitted.

To properly fit a piston, the following dimensions must be obtained: cylinder barrel taper, concentricity, piston clearance, and piston ring end gap. These measurements are obtained as follows. Refer to the specifications chart for correct operating tolerances.

3. Wash the cylinder in hot, soapy water and rinse thoroughly. Allow it to stand for two hours at room temperature. Measure the diameter of the cylinder bore, from front to back, at the lowest point of piston travel. Measure the diameter of the piston on an axis perpendicular to the wrist pin on the lower portion of the piston. Subtract the piston diame-

PISTON-CYLINDER SPECIFICATIONS

	100 cc	125 cc	175 cc	200 cc	250 cc	326 cc	360 cc
Max allowable bore taper	0.0015 in.	0.0015 in.	0.0015 in.	0.002 in.	0.002 in.	0.0025 in.	0.0025 in.
Max. out or round before rebore	0.0012 in.	0.0012 in.	0.0012 in.	0.0012 in.	0.0015 in.	0.0015 in.	0.0015 in.
Max. ring end gap	0.020 in.	0.020 in.	0.030 in.	0.030 in.	0.035 in.	0.045 in.	0.045 in.
Max. piston clear	0.0055 in.	0.0057 in.	0.0065 in.	0.0065 in.	0.007 in.	0.0083 in.	0.0098 in.
Piston clear. (New)	0.001 in.	0.001 in.	0.0015 in.	0.0015 in.	0.002 in.	0.002 in.	0.0035 in.
Trail-Enduro-Trials	0.002 in.	0.002 in.	0.0025 in.	0.0025 in.	0.003 in.	0.0035 in.	0.0045 in.
Competition	0.0015 in. 0.0025 in.	0.0015 in. 0.0025 in.	0.0017 in. 0.003 in.	0.0017 in. 0.003 in.	0.0025 in. 0.0035 in.	0.0025 in. 0.0037 in.	0.0035 in. 0.0045 in.

ter from that of the bore to determine piston clearance. Check the value obtained with the correct value shown in the specifications chart.

4. To obtain the bore taper, take two measurements in the same plane across the bore. The first is taken ½ in. below the top of the bore, the other just below the intake port.

5. Check for bore concentricity, or out-of-round, with two measurements, at an angle of 90° apart, ½ in. below the top of the cylinder; two measurements at 90° in the area of the exhaust port, and two measurements at 90° below the intake port.

6. Piston ring end gap is obtained by inserting the ring into the top of the cylinder and using the piston to push it down about 1 in. into the bore. Measure the end gap with a feeler gauge.

In all cases, values for the above dimensions should be within the specified tolerances shown in the chart.

7. After boring or honing a cylinder, it is necessary to bevel all of the port edges in the bore. A chamfer of 5° (.5mm radius) is correct.

Bevel the port edges

8. If piston damage has occured, it is important to check the cylinder liner for cracks, especially in the area of the lower transfer port cutouts in the portion of the liner below the cylinder barrel.

Installing A New Cylinder Liner

1. To remove the old liner, support the cylinder upside down in an oven so that the liner is free to drop out of the cylinder after reaching a temperature of 700° F. Do not exceed 800° or the aluminum alloy will be damaged.

2. The new liner can be inserted in the cylinder immediately after the old one has been withdrawn if the inside of the cylinder is very clean. If cleaning is necessary, reheat the cylinder before installing the new liner. Support the bottom fins of the hot cylinder so that the liner will not touch anything when it is in place. Insert the new liner and align the ports as closely as possible with the cylinder ports. Place a weight on the liner flange to keep it from shifting while cooling, or clamp it into position by fastening the cylinder head to its studs and torqueing the nuts to half the specified value.

3. Measure the outside diameter of the bottom of the new liner and the inside diameter of the crankcase opening to see if the new liner will fit in the crankcase. If not, the liner will have to be turned down. Before doing this, remove the connecting bridges at the bottom of the lower transfer ports in the liner with a hacksaw. Next, blend the edges that were sawed with a file. Then mount the cylin-

CYLINDER MACHINING TOLERANCES

Engine Displace. and Model	Standard Piston mm +	−	1st O.S. Piston mm +	−	2nd O.S. Piston mm +	−	3rd O.S. Piston mm +	−	4th O.S. Piston mm +	−
125 cc										
TSS	51.535	51.525	51.785	51.775	52.035	52.025	52.285	52.275	52.535	52.525
Sherpa S	51.525	51.515	51.775	51.765	52.025	52.015	52.275	52.265	52.525	52.515
Mercurio	51.525	51.515	51.775	51.765	52.025	52.015	52.275	52.265	52.525	52.515
	51.515	51.505	51.765	51.755	52.015	52.005	52.265	52.255	52.515	52.505
155 cc										
Mercurio	57.025	57.015	57.275	57.265	57.525	57.151	57.775	57.765	58.025	58.015
	57.015	57.005	57.265	57.255	57.515	57.505	57.765	57.755	58.015	58.005
175 cc										
Sherpa S	60.945	60.935	61.195	61.185	61.445	61.435	61.695	61.685	61.945	61.935
TSS	60.935	60.925	61.185	61.175	61.435	61.425	61.685	61.675	61.935	61.925
Mercurio	60.935	60.925	61.185	61.175	61.435	61.425	61.685	61.675	61.935	61.925
	60.925	60.915	61.175	61.165	61.425	61.415	61.675	61.665	61.925	61.915
200 cc										
Metralla	64.525	64.515	64.775	64.765	65.525	65.515	65.275	65.265	65.525	65.515
	64.515	64.505	64.765	64.755	65.515	65.505	65.265	65.255	65.515	65.505
Matador	64.525	64.515	64.775	64.765	65.525	65.515	65.275	65.265	65.525	65.515
	64.515	64.505	64.765	64.755	65.515	65.505	65.265	65.255	65.515	65.505
Sherpa S	64.545	64.535	64.795	64.785	65.045	65.035	65.295	65.285	65.545	65.535
	64.535	64.525	64.785	64.775	65.035	65.025	65.285	65.275	65.535	65.525
TSS	64.545	64.535	64.795	64.785	65.045	65.035	65.295	65.285	65.545	65.535
	64.535	64.525	64.785	64.775	65.035	65.025	65.285	65.275	65.535	65.525
250 cc										
Metisse	72.060	72.050	72.310	72.300	72.560	72.550	72.810	72.800	73.060	73.050
	72.050	72.040	72.300	72.290	72.550	72.540	72.800	72.790	73.050	73.040

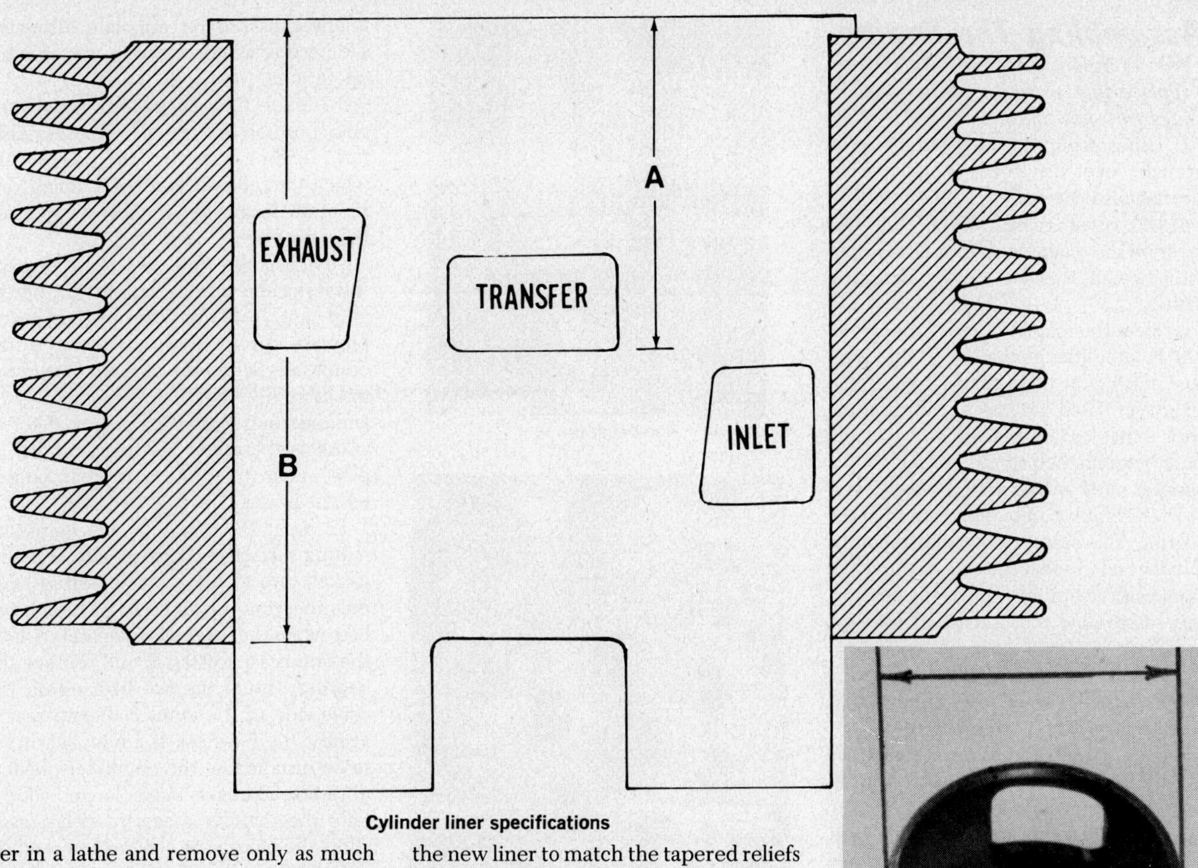

Cylinder liner specifications

der in a lathe and remove only as much metal as necessary from the outside of the liner for it to fit into the case. The liner must be machined to the specifications shown in the accompanying illustration.

4. Follow the instructions in the preceding section to fit a new piston to the new liner. The liner must be bored to the proper specifications for piston clearance.

5. Match the ports in the liner with those in the cylinder by filing the port entrances in the liner until they form smooth extensions to the ports in the aluminum cylinder. After matching the ports, carefully chamfer the edges of the ports with an 0.5 mm radius until they are smooth and round.

6. On 125cc machines there are two 10 mm rectangular reliefs in the bottom of the cylinder bore. Blend the holes in the new liner to match the tapered reliefs in the cylinder to provide clearance for the swing of the connecting rod. Remove metal from the bottoms of the holes in the liner until the taper of the cylinder reliefs is continued in the liner holes; then file the edges until they are smooth and straight.

7. Finally, wash the cylinder in hot, soapy water, then rinse and dry with compressed air. Coat the cylinder bore with oil to protect it from rust.

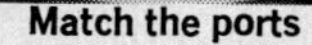

Match the ports

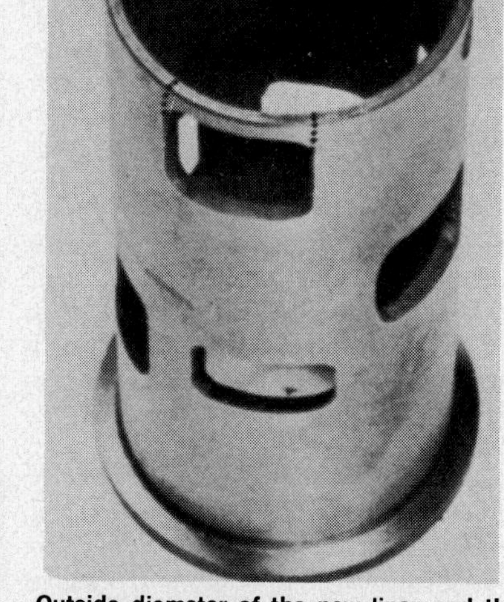

Outside diameter of the new liner and the connecting bridges

CYLINDER LINER SPECIFICATIONS

Measurement	Model	Measurement mm	In.
"A" Bottom of transfer to top of sealing lip	350 cc and 360 cc	64.0	2.520
	100 cc	51.5	2.028
	125 cc to 327 cc	60.0	2.362
"B" Base of cylinder to top of sealing lip	350 cc and 360 cc	96.7	3.807
	100 cc	90.0	3.543
	125 cc to 327 cc	95.8	3.772
Clearance between bottom of head and top of cylinder	All	①	0.020

① Minimum clearance 0.5

Assembling The Engine

NOTE: *Before reassembling the cases, replace any worn transmission bearings with new ones.*

1. Using an appropriately sized pipe or wrench socket, drive out the oil seal from the magneto side seal cover; then remove the seal cover gasket. Install the seal cover on the magneto side crankcase half with two of the seal cover mounting screws.

2. Heat the magneto side crankcase to 400° F. and slide the crankshaft into position, butting the main bearing against the seal cover. Hold the assembly in position until it has cooled enough to seize the main bearing, then allow it to cool for five minutes more and remove the seal cover. Turn the crankshaft to make sure that the bearing still rotates freely and smoothly. If it does not, reheat the case, remove the crankshaft assembly, replace the bearing, and reassemble the crankshaft into the case.

3. While the case is still hot, fit the sleeve gear into its bearing. If necessary, tap the gear lightly to seat it.

4. Reassemble the kickstart assembly by sliding the kickstart shaft, thrust washer, ratchet spring, and ratchet, as an assembly, into the kickstart shaft boss. Slide the ratchet onto the six large splines on the kickstart shaft so that when the ratchet is against its stop, the return spring hole in the shaft is as near horizontal as possible with the engine in its normal position. It may take several times before you get the ratchet aligned properly.

5. Install the cam plate bracket on its dowel pins and secure it with the four bolts and locktabs. The short tab plate should be under the two bolts that are at the top of the bracket when the engine is in its normal position. Torque the bolts to 5 ft lbs and lock them in place with the tabs.

6. Remove the homemade spacer from the transmission mainshaft and, while holding the kickstart gear in place, slip the mainshaft assembly into position. Install the kickstart shaft spacer.

7. Hold the 1st/2nd gear sliding dog up against the first gear idler on the mainshaft and, with your other hand, fit the countershaft assembly into its ball bearing in the crankcase. Make sure a thrust washer is fitted at each end of the layshaft (except engines with solid countershaft clusters).

8. Rotate the cam plate to its third gear position (one position back from the clockwise limit of rotation as viewed from the crankshaft side). Install the shift fork with the longer cam plate follower into the 3rd/4th gear sliding dog, holding it so that the side toward which the follower is offset if facing the base of the cam plate bracket. Pivot the shift fork so that its follower fits into the cam plate, lifting the sliding dog as necessary to perform the operation.

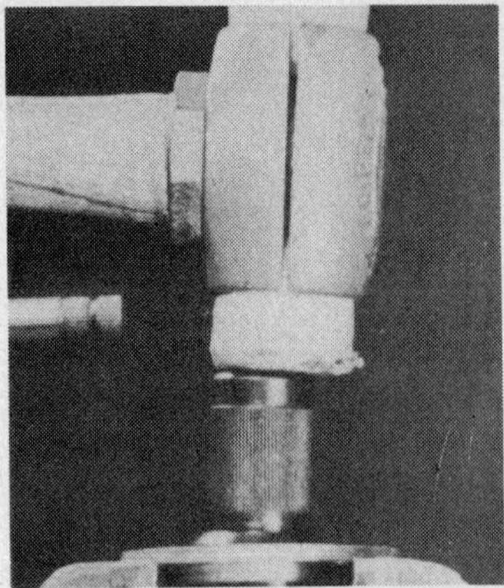

Removing the seal

Kickstarter assembly in position

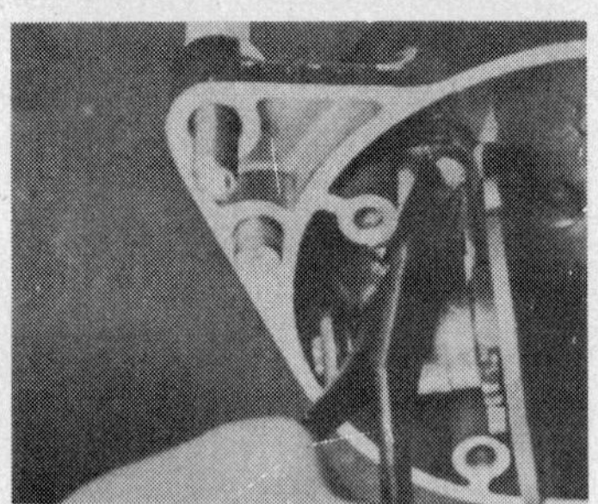

Camplate bracket bolt lockcaps

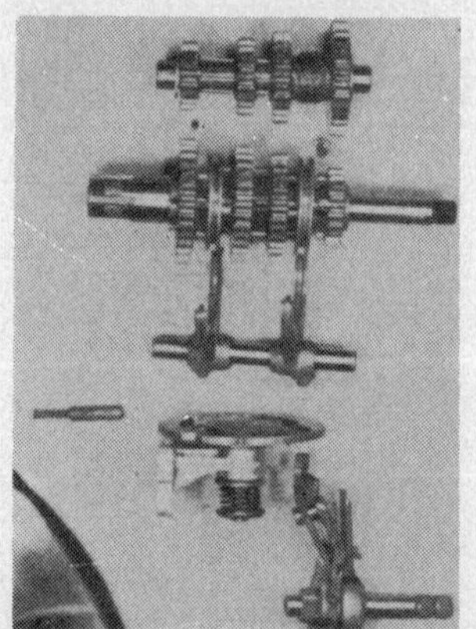

Transmission components

9. Rotate the cam plate to the second gear position and install the other shift fork, holding it so that the side toward which the follower is offset is facing you. Pivot the fork so that the follower fits into the cam plate.

10. Push the shift fork shaft through the forks and into its support in the engine case. Install the cam plate plunger, plunger spring, and washer into the crankcase. Screw the plunger sleeve nut in. Liberally oil the transmission gears and bearings. Make sure that the two crankcase locating dowel pins are in place near the front and rear engine mount bosses.

11. Coat the magneto side crankcase mating surface with grease and fit a new gasket into position. If the drive side main bearing remained in the crankcase boss when the cases were separated, heat the crankcase to 400° F. and remove the bearing. Install the hot bearing on the drive side of the crankshaft and seat it against the flywheel. If a new bearing is to be installed an the crankshaft, heat it until the oil begins to smoke and slide it onto the shaft as above. In either case, allow the bearing to cool for ten minutes before proceeding further.

The magneto side crankcase ready for the drive side case to be installed

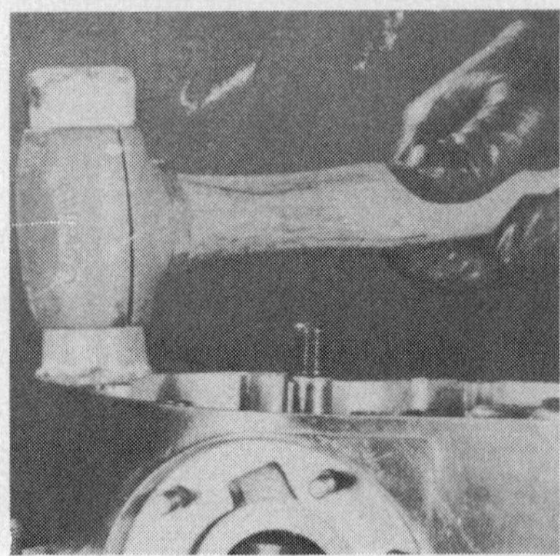

Seating the case halves

12. Prop the magneto side crankcase on the bench so that the crankshaft end is not touching the surface. Heat the drive side crankcase to 400° F. and mate it quickly to the drive side case, with the case studs started in their holes. While

the case is still hot, tap it on each end with a rubber hammer to seat the ball bearing assemblies.

13. Install the twelve lockwashers and nuts on the crankcase studs and tighten them in the sequence shown, in 1 ft lb increments, to 5 ft lbs. Use a thread locking compound on the nuts and studs to prevent the nuts from loosening due to vibration. Install the allen bolt and lockwasher just behind the front engine mount.

Crankcase nut tightening sequence

14. It is possible, when reassembling the crankcases, to disturb the crankshaft alignment. If the case was not hot enough and did not seat fully before cooling and contracting around the main bearing, the flywheels will have been forced together as the cases were drawn tight. For this reason it is necessary to check crankshaft runout at this point. Make up brackets to hold the dial gauges and install a gauge on both sides of the engine, as shown, so that the gauge shaft will contact a smooth, unbroken portion of the crankshaft. Rotate the crankshaft and watch the gauges. If the flywheels have been squeezed together, both needles will be at their highest point of travel when the connecting rod is at the bottom of its travel. If runout exceeds 0.025 mm (0.001 in.), rotate the crankshaft and stop at the point where the gauge needles are at their highest point of travel. Insert a wedge between the flywheels at top center and spread them until the needles move back to about half their original travel. If you overdo it, the flywheels can be closed up by hitting both ends of the crankshaft. Recheck runout and repeat this procedure until alignment is within specification. It is important to align the crankshaft perfectly for accurate ignition timing and for long life of the main bearings and crankcase seals.

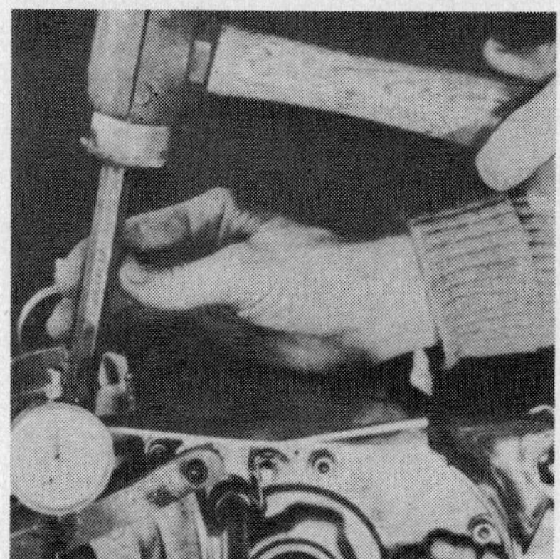
Measuring crankshaft runout

15. Remove the seal cover from the magneto side crankcase that you installed earlier to position the crankshaft assembly correctly. Remove the old seal from the other seal cover. To install a new seal in the cover, place the cover on the jaws of a vise. Position the jaws so that they are opened slightly wider than the diameter of the seal. Start a new seal into the cover with the open side up. Oil the seal lightly to ease installation. Use a piece of pipe or wrench socket that is slightly smaller than the outside diameter of the seal to drive it into the cover. Take care to start the seal squarely and make sure it bottoms in the seal cover. Oil the seal lips and crankshaft ends with oil. Coat one side of each seal cover gasket lightly with grease and place the gaskets on the seal covers. Slide the seal covers over the crankshaft ends with the open side of the seals facing in. (The larger crankshaft seal on the 250cc Scrambler goes on the drive side.) Install and tighten the bolts until they just contact their star washers; then progressively tighten each opposite pair of bolts until a torque of 5 ft lbs is reached.

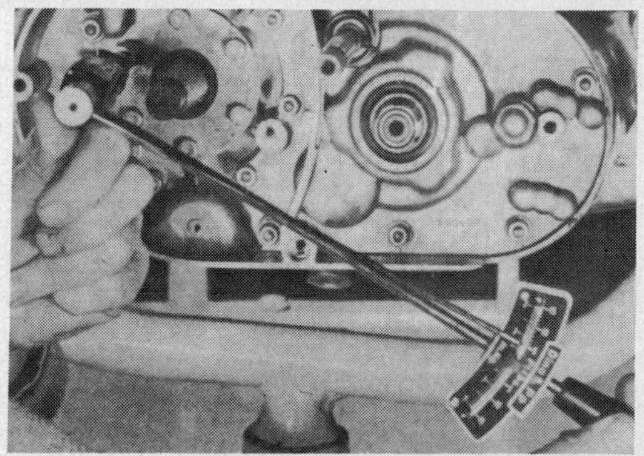
Installing the seal cover

16. Turn the kickstart shaft counterclockwise until it hits its stop in the crankcase. Install the kickstart return spring on the shaft, starting with the hook side first. Slide the kickstart lever on the shaft so that the lever is parallel with the spring mounting hole in the shaft; both should be horizontal at this time. Rotate the kickstart lever clockwise until it is pointing straight down, then install the straight end of the return spring in the hole drilled in the shaft. Grab the curved end of the spring with a hooked instrument and wind it around counterclockwise until it can be anchored behind its stop.

17. Install a new O-ring on the end of the countershaft on the magneto side of the engine. Install a new oil seal on the shouldered countershaft sprocket spacer and put the spacer, shouldered end first, on the countershaft. Using an appropriately sized pipe or socket, drive the seal in until it is flush with its housing.

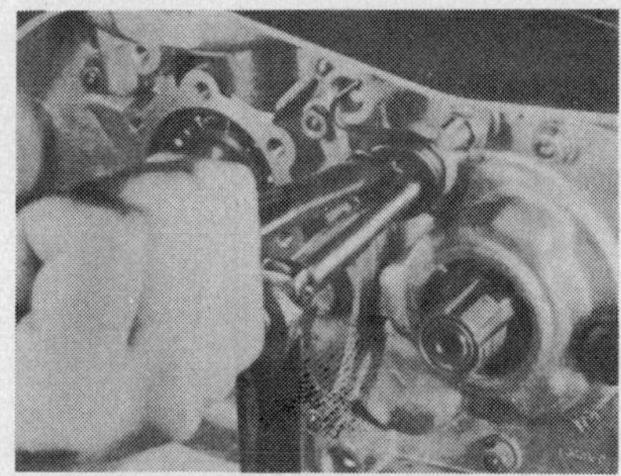
Installing the kickstarter return spring

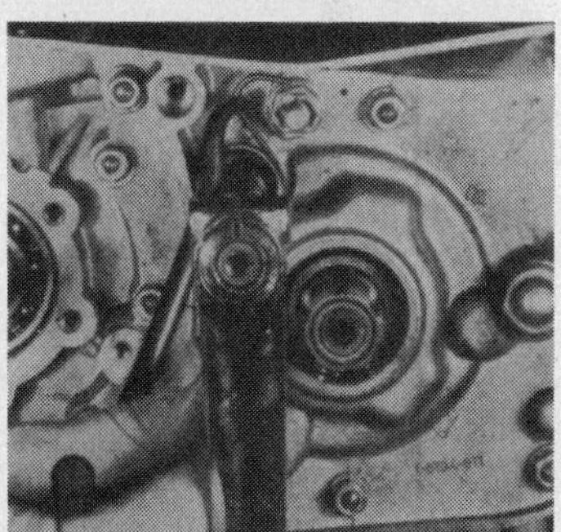
Anchoring the kickstarter return spring

18. Install the woodruff key in the slot in the drive side of the crankshaft. If the key is loose in the slot or is damaged, a new one should be used. Install new O-rings on the drive side crankshaft and transmission mainshaft and fit the shoul-

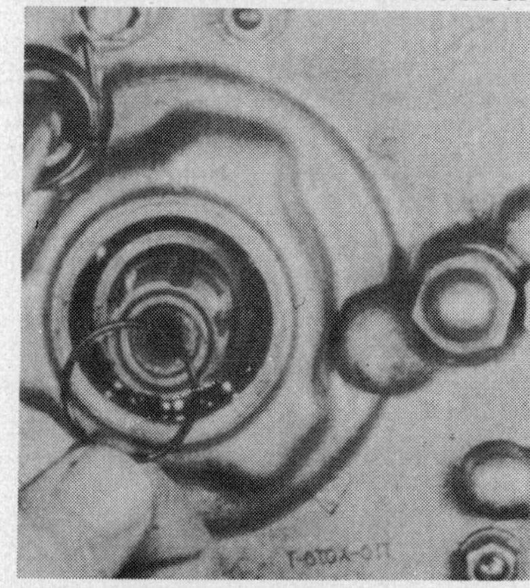
Left side countershaft O-ring

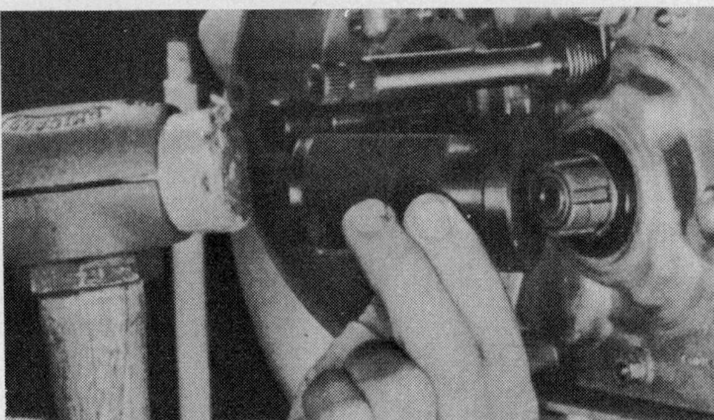
Installing the seal

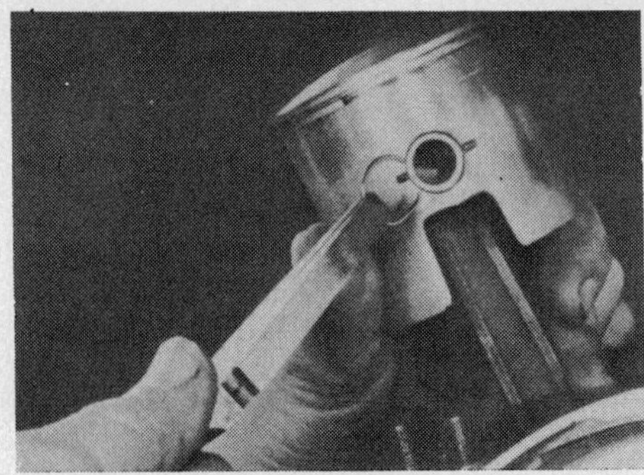
Installing the circlip

Left side countershaft oil seal

dered spacers on the shafts. Install the woodruff key on the mainshaft.

19. Check the length of the clutch springs and replace any that measure less than 22 mm. Install the primary chain over the outer clutch housing and the engine sprocket. Slide this assembly onto the crankshaft and mainshaft, as a unit, taking care not to knock the woodruff keys out of place.

20. Hold the outer clutch housing bushing tight against the woodruff key and, with your other hand, slide the inner clutch hub onto the mainshaft and start the inner hub on the woodruff key. Then holding the outer clutch housing centered on the mainshaft, push the inner clutch hub through the bushing and up against the spacer. A slight tap may be necessary to seat the hub. Install the nuts and washers on the mainshaft and crankshaft and run them up finger tight. Torque the nuts after the engine has been reinstalled in the frame.

21. Install the magneto side crankshaft woodruff key into its slot. Lightly lubricate the felt lubricating pad attached to the stator disc with distributor cam grease. Install the stator disc (magneto backing plate), taking care to align the marks that you made when disassembling. If the stator is loose on its bosses, place strips of stiff paper, cut 5 mm wide, between the disc and bosses. The strips should be thick enough to take up the slack and you should barely be able to rotate the stator disc when the strips are in place and the mounting screws are loose. Finally, tighten the mounting screws.

22. Tie up the condenser-to-contact breaker points wire with a piece of strong string. If the wire drops too low it can rub against the points cam boss in the flywheel and be worn through. Carefully slide the magneto flywheel onto its shaft, taking care not to hit the contact breaker follower or the lubricating pad with the points boss on the flywheel. (Avoid this by sighting through one of the windows in the flywheel as you slide it on.) Install the one or two flat washers, the lockwasher, and the nut on the crankshaft. Tighten the nut to 75 ft lbs.

23. Secure the electrical junction box to the crankcase, just below the flywheel. Securely tighten the mounting screw. Plug the black wire from the contact breaker points into the top left side of the junction box. Plug the yellow wire from the lighting coil into the bottom left socket in the box.

The Top End

1. Clean and inspect the piston and piston rings. Check for hairline cracks in the piston at the top edges of the transfer cutaways. Use a new piston if any are found.

2. Remove the carbon from the piston crown, taking care not to scratch the soft aluminum alloy. The thin, hard bottom layer of carbon should be left alone.

3. Break an old piston ring in half and use it to clean the ring grooves. Insert the unbroken end into the ring groove and push the ring around the piston until the carbon deposits have been removed. Finally, use the end of a sharp knife to remove the thin band of carbon remaining between the top edge of the top groove and the top edge of the piston.

4. Take one of the piston rings and roll it around the top ring groove. If the ring sticks even slightly at one point, dress the top and bottom of the groove at that point with a 1 mm thick flat file until the ring no longer sticks. Repeat this for the bottom ring groove.

5. Check the piston ring end gap as directed in a preceding section.

6. Oil the wrist pin bearing assembly and place it in the connecting rod. If any of the needles are loose enough to fall out, the bearing should be replaced. It is always a good idea to stuff a rag into the crankcase opening to catch any parts that are dropped during assembly.

7. Heat the piston in a container of light oil to 100° F. or wrap it in rags soaked in hot water. Remove the piston from the oil and insert the wrist pin slightly beyond the first boss. Place one of the thrust washers inside the piston on the protruding wrist pin.

8. Holding the piston so that the shorter skirt faces the intake port, fit the piston to the connecting rod and push the wrist pin halfway through its bearing. Hold the other thrust washer in place between the connecting rod and the other piston boss and push the wrist pin through until it is centered. If the piston has cooled during this interval, wrap it with hot rags once more before inserting the wrist pin.

9. To install a snap ring, hold it firmly along its center section with a pair of broad-nosed pliers, as shown, and push it into its groove at the angle shown in the illustration. Take care to compress both sides of the ring evenly; do not attempt to hold it at one end and push the other end into the groove or you will bend it. When the ring has been pushed in far enough so that it won't pop out, use the blunt end of the pliers to shove it in until it snaps into its groove. If, after installation, you are able to rotate the ring with only slight pressure, it should be replaced with a new one.

10. Install a new cylinder base gasket on the crankcase with the printed side down. If the gasket overhangs the transfer port cutouts in the crankcase, tap the gasket lightly at the edges with a small ball-peen hammer. Remove the gasket and trim away the excess gasket with a razor.

Installing the thrust washers and wrist pin

Transfer port cutouts

Piston ring compressor in use

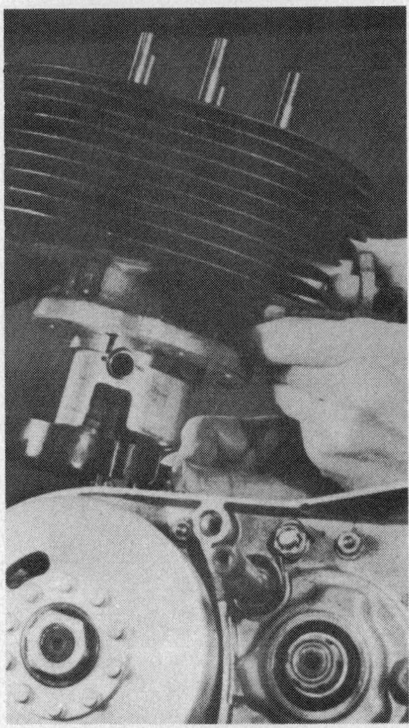
Installing the barrels

11. Install the rings on the piston and position them so that their ends are butted against the small dowel pins. Check to see that the dowel pin reliefs in the ends of the rings are deep enough so that the ring ends can touch when the ring is compressed. Deepen the reliefs, if necessary, using a small file.

12. Liberally oil the rings and the piston, and coat the cylinder with oil. Install a ring compressor around the piston and gently lower the cylinder over it until the rings are inside the cylinder. Remove the compressor and continue to lower the cylinder, keeping it aligned with its studs on the crankcase. Install a star washer and nut on each of the studs and progressively tighten each opposing pair of nuts.

13. Rotate the flywheel until the piston is at top dead center (TDC.) The top edge of the top piston ring should be just below the top of the cylinder. If it protrudes even slightly, remove the cylinder, match a second cylinder base gasket to the first, and reinstall the cylinder with both gaskets in place. Install the cylinder head onto the cylinder and place a flat washer on each of the studs. Install and tighten the nuts lightly. Torque the nuts gradually and evenly, 2 ft lbs at a time, to 12 ft lbs. Tighten the nuts diagonally (opposing pairs), beginning with either of the two closest to the intake flange.

14. Set the ignition timing as described in "Tune-Up and Maintenance."

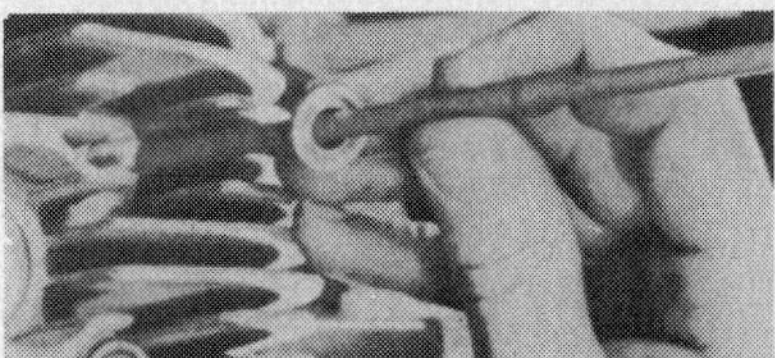
Installing the cylinder head nut washers

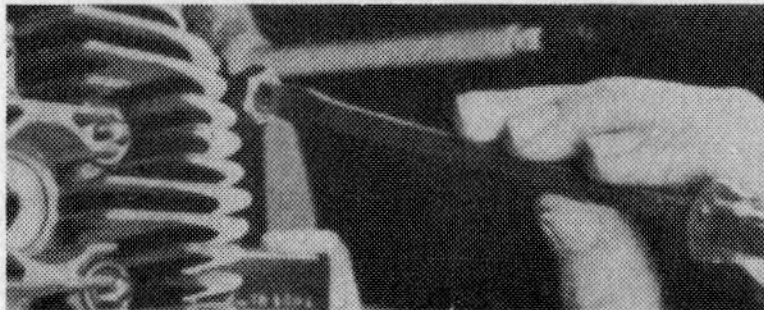
Starting the head nuts on the studs

INSTALLING THE SPEEDOMETER DRIVE

1. If the speedometer drive bushing was removed during disassembly, insert it in its mounting boss. The end of the bushing farthest from the set screw hole should be inserted first.

2. Carefully drive the bushing into its mounting boss until the set screw holes in the bushing and mounting boss are aligned. Use the end of a file or a scribe to align them exactly. Install and tighen the set screw with its fiber washer.

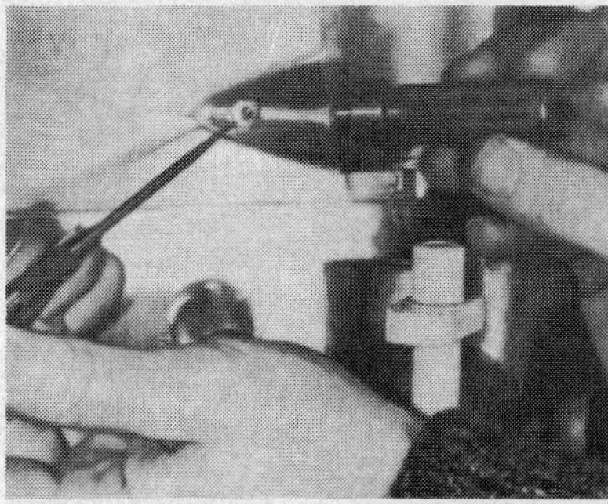
Aligning the holes in the bushings and mounting boss

3. Install the speedometer drive seal to the cable driving end of the drive shaft, with the open end of the seal butted up against the shoulder of the shaft. Slide the drive assembly, splined end first, into the bushing until you can feel the splines mesh with the drive spindle on the countershaft. Tap the oil seal into the boss until it is about 2 mm past the edge of the hole.

4. Lightly grease and install the thrust washers. Install the triangular cable mounting plate with its gasket. Tighten the screws and center-punch them at the edge of the slot to lock them in position.

Installing The Engine

1. Fit the engine into the frame and secure it with the three mounting bolts. Torque the bolts to 35 ft lbs.

2. Grease the clutch pushrod and insert it in the mainshaft, flat end first.

3. Install the countershaft sprocket. Fit the drive chain over the rear wheel sprocket and the countershaft sprocket and join the ends with the master link. Using a new locktab under the nut, tighten the countershaft securing nut to 75 ft lbs while holding the rear brake on. Secure the nut with the locktab.

4. Push the electrical wires through the grommet in the magneto side engine case. Plug the black or red ignition wire into the upper right socket in the junction box under the flywheel. Plug the yellow wire (if applicable) into the lower right socket.

5. Install the magneto side engine cover, fitting the two long screws to the top and bottom of the cover and the two short screws to the front and rear of the cover. Do not mix up the screws or the clutch will not function properly.

6. Slide the kickstart lever onto its shaft and secure it with the bolt. Locate the kick start lever at about 10 o'clock. The lever should contact the peg before hitting the internal stop to avoid the chance of breaking the cases.

7. Apply the rear brake to keep the engine from turning over and torque the clutch sprocket nut to 75 ft lbs and the engine sprocket nut to 90 ft lbs.

8. If your model has steel clutch plates, insert alternately into the clutch assembly a driven plate (with rounded inner-drive tabs) and a drive plate (with holes in its thrust surface). The last plate installed will be a driven plate.

9. If the clutch plates have neoprene surfaces, first install the only driven plate with one bonded side and one plain side. The bonded side goes in first. Then insert alternately a bonded drive plate and a plain driven plate. The pressure plate is the last driven piece in this type of clutch.

10. Early engines have a short clutch rod and a clutch mushroom with loose ball bearings between the clutch rod and pressure plate. On this type, first install the mushroom. Then align the stud holes in the pressure plate with the studs on the inner clutch hub and install the pressure plate.

11. Later model engines have a long clutch rod and a pressure plate with a ball bearing thrust cover. Remove the thrust cover, pack the bearing with high temperature grease, and reinstall the cover. Fit the pressure plate on the clutch assembly, taking care not to let the thrust cover fall off and the bearings fall out before the thrust cover contacts the clutch rod.

12. The latest engines have the pressure plate thrust cover retained by a snap-ring. Squirt a few drops of 10 weight oil into the thrust cover cup. Align the tabs and slots and try fitting the pressure plate to the clutch assembly. It has been fitted properly if the inner clutch hub studs are centered in their holes in the pressure plate. If not, remove the pressure plate, rotate it clockwise until the next set of tabs and slots are aligned, and install it again. If the studs are still not centered in the holes, repeat the process until you can push the pressure plate fully into position on the clutch assembly.

13. Install the spring cups on the inner clutch hub studs protruding through the pressure plate, then fit the clutch springs and nuts. Tighten each nut until the spring bottoms, then loosen each nut four full turns (three turns on the 250 Scrambler).

14. Pull in the clutch lever on the handlebar and turn the engine over with the kickstarter while observing the rotation of the pressure plate. If the pressure plate is not parallel with the drive plate, it will wobble while rotating.

15. While the clutch is stationary, operate the clutch lever several times while watching the pressure plate. One side of the plate might be pushed out farther than the other side. If so, level the pressure plate by slightly tightening the clutch spring nuts nearest the high side of the plate. Repeat the testing and adjusting until the plate is dead-level with the friction plates when the clutch lever is pulled to the handlebar grip.

Safety wire in place in the clutch nuts

16. After adjustment is complete, safety wire the clutch spring nuts using 1 mm diameter stainless steel wire. Pull the wire through the hole in each nut, taking care not to tighten or loosen the nut in the process. When the wire is threaded through all the nuts, twist the ends together.

17. Coat the crankcase side of the primary case gasket lightly with grease and place it on the crankcase. Install the primary case and secure it with the seven allen bolts.

18. Loosen the clutch lever adjuster knob at the handlebar. Remove the slotted clutch adjustment cover cap from the magneto side case and loosen the locknut. Screw in the slotted clutch rod adjustment screw until the clutch lever has about 4 mm free-play. Check to see if you can still pull the clutch lever all the way to the grip. If not, loosen the setscrew on the cable-clamping nipple. Move the nipple back toward the end of the cable and retighten the setscrew. Adjust the clutch rod screw inside the magneto cover again and check for full travel at the clutch lever. When you have obtained the correct adjustment, tighten the clutch rod adjusting screw locknut and replace the slotted cover cap in the magneto cover. Whenever you remove a clutch cable from its clamping nipple, this clutch rod adjustment procedure must be followed.

Clutch cable clamp nipple

19. Install the carburetor on the cylinder and fit the slide in the carburetor. Replace the fuel line.

20. To install the exhaust system, align the rear mounting flange with its bracket on the frame and align the pipe with is mount in the cylinder. While holding the system in place, start the ring-nut into the cylinder, taking care not to cross-thread the cylinder threads. use a pin-wrench to tighten the ring-nut securely. Install the bolts at the rear mounting flange. Do not force the rear mounting flange into place against the bracket or you run the risk of distorting the cylinder. Instead, bend the flange or enlarge the holes so that the bolts can be tightened without putting a strain on the exhaust system.

21. On racing machines, safety-wire the exhaust ring-nut to the frame down-tube.

22. Check the gearbox drainplug for tightness and pour 500cc of SAE 90 gear lube into the gearbox filler hole. Reinstall the filler plug with its rubber gasket.

23. Check the drainplug for tightness and pour 250cc of SAE 10W or 20W oil into the primary drive case through the filler hole.

CAUTION: *Never use ATF in any engine with neoprene clutch plates, as the fluid will deteriorate the neoprene.*

24. Install a spark plug of the correct heat range, tightening it sufficiently to compress the gasket. Do not overtighten. Fit the high tension lead onto the plug.

FIVE SPEED MODELS

Disassembly and repair of five-speed Bultaco engines is similar to the basic four-speed engine. The major differences are:

1. The five-speed engine does not employ cylinder base nuts; instead, the cylinder is spigoted to the cases and held in place by the four head nuts on through-studs.
2. The drive side crankshaft half has two main bearings butted against each other. The engine sprocket flywheel is shaped differently and the inner and outer clutch hubs are larger and stronger.
3. The shift forks are operated by a shift drum instead of a cam plate.
4. The gears and sliding dogs are arranged differently on the mainshaft and countershaft, but their operation is the same as in the four-speed engine.

Because of the similarities in the four and five-speed engines, this section will deal only with the variations in the five-speed engine. Use this section in conjuction with the preceding section on four-speed models.

Engine Removal

REMOVING THE MAGNETO SIDE COMPONENTS

Refer to the "Engine Removal" section on four speed models.

1. Remove the carburetor. Drain the primary case and the gearbox.
2. Remove the kickstart lever and unscrew the allen bolts from the magneto case.
3. Unscrew the magneto flywheel nut and remove the flywheel.
4. Mark the magneto backing plate and remove it. Pull back the wires and pull the wires and pull the wire connectors apart.
5. Remove the seal cover and its gasket.
6. Bend back the locktab and unscrew the countershaft nut.
7. Remove the exhaust system.

REMOVING THE PRIMARY DRIVE COMPONENTS

1. Remove the outer gearshift linkage after taking off the right footpeg.

2. Unscrew the 10 mm nut from the fork that connects the shift lever with the selector shaft. Remove the fork from the shaft.

3. Unscrew the eight allen bolts from the primary case and remove the case.

4. Remove the clutch plates.

5. Take off the engine sprocket nut.

6. To remove the inner clutch hub, first unscrew the inner clutch hub nut and remove the washer. Insert two prybars behind the outer hub ½ in. away from the engine case to avoid straining the primary chain. If the engine sprocket binds, use a gear puller on it and alternate between prying the outer clutch hub and engine sprocket until each one has moved ½ in. on its shaft.

7. Push the outer hub and the engine sprocket back against the engine case together.

8. Insert two prybars between the outer hub and inner hub and remove the inner hub from the mainshaft.

9. Remove the engine sprocket and outer hub.

10. Remove the spacer and O-ring from the crankshaft.

11. Remove the seal cover from the crankshaft.

DISASSEMBLING THE SELECTOR MECHANISM

1. Lift out the selector shaft.

2. Bend back the locktabs behind the wide, slotted selector lever fixing cap bolt. Use a screwdriver with a wide bit to unscrew the bolt.

3. Lift off the selector lever with its welded pin.

4. Remove the three screws from the selector cover and remove the cover.

5. Remove the pawl carrier (trigger housing) with the two spring-loaded pawls from the shift drum.

ENGINE REMOVAL

1. Remove the spark plug.

2. Uncouple the master link and remove the drive chain.

3. Unscrew the four engine mounting bolts. Lift up the rear of the engine until the crankcase boss clears the frame mounting flanges. Lift up the front of the engine and work the engine up higher until it can be lifted out from the left side.

Removing The Piston

1. Mount the engine on the bench in its normal position.

2. Consider the front of the engine as 12 o'clock on the face of the clock and loosen the four head studs in the following sequence: 2 o'clock, 8 o'clock, 10 o'clock, and 4 o'clock. Loosen the nuts gradually and evenly, 3 ft lbs at a time.

3. Take off the nuts and remove the cylinder head.

4. Lift the cylinder off of the crankcase, taking care not to let the piston and rod fall against the crankcase flange as they are freed.

5. Remove the two circlips from the piston. Before removing the wrist pin, check to see that the clips did not burr the piston. Use new clips upon reassembly. Push out the wrist pin and remove the piston from the rod. Remove the cylinder base gasket.

Splitting The Crankcases

If you wish to remove the kickstart return spring, refer to the section on four-speed models. It is not necessary to do this in order to split the cases.

1. Unscrew the twelve 10 mm nuts on the magneto side of the engine.

2. Unscrew the allen bolt near the front of the cases.

3. Refer to the four-speed engine section for details on separating the cases. The standard Bultaco crankcase splitter, Tool No. 132-043, will have to be modified to fit the five-speed engine. To accomplish this, fit the base of the tool to the right side engine case. Notice that on the right (more sharply angled) leg of the base, the lower mounting hole is not aligned with the primary case mounting hole. Elongate the hole in the tool base ⅛ in. Elongate the lower mounting hole in the left leg of the tool ⅛ in. also.

Component Inspection and Repair

TRANSMISSION COMPONENTS

1. To disassemble the transmission, remove the shift drum, shift fork assembly, countershaft assembly, and kickstarter gear assembly as a unit.

2. Remove the gears from the mainshaft. Two snap-rings must be removed to facilitate this; do not reuse the snap-rings.

3. Remove the gears from the countershaft, noting the warning in the previous step.

4. Clean and dry the components. Inspect them for wear, damage, and discoloration on their thrust surfaces. Replace any part showing a blue color at any thrust surface. This indicated that its temper has been lost due to heat.

5. If you have been experiencing shift indexing problems, examine the slot in the arm of the selector shaft and the pin on the selector lever.

6. Another factor that can cause the transmission to jump out of gear is excessive play between the sliding dogs and idler gears. Measure the thickness of the thrust surface (that bears against the sliding dog) on each shift fork. This measurement should be between 4.50–4.74 mm. Measure the width of the thrust groove in the sliding dog, at the widest part of the groove. Groove width should be between 4.80–5.20 mm.

7. Install the short shift drum follower of the largest shift fork into the bottom groove (nearest the detent cam) of the shift drum. Insert a wire feeler gauge between the follower of the fork and the side of the groove and test the fit at several points along the groove. A 0.65 mm gauge is the largest that you should be able to stick between the follower and the groove.

8. Install the small, hooked shift fork in the top groove in the shift drum and repeat the measurement.

9. Install the third shift fork in the middle groove and test again. If any of the shift fork followers has excessive play, replace the shift drum and/or the shift fork. The follower pegs should be 5.50–5.80 mm in diameter. The slots in the shift drum should be 5.90–6.30 mm wide.

10. Check the snap-ring grooves on the mainshaft. Test the trueness of the mainshaft as described in the four-speed section.

11. To inspect the sleeve-gear (or countershaft) bearing, remove the kickstart return spring, the kickstart shaft, and the ratchet. Knock out the sleeve gear and remove the bearing. Test it for smooth operation. If it must be replaced, remove the bearing cover.

The Crankshaft Assembly

1. If it is necessary to service the crankshaft, remove it from the magneto side engine case.

2. Inspect the seals, seal cover gaskets, centercase gasket, and the connecting rod bearing as described in the four-speed section.

3. Before disassembling the crankshaft, remove the main bearings from the driveshafts. If the left side main bearing is still on the shaft, remove it with the main bearing extractor (Tool No. 132-067) or press it off.

4. To remove the outer main bearing from the right side shaft, fit the two halves of a knife-edge gear puller between the two bearings. Tighten the connecting bolts of the puller to force it into position between the bearings. The puller will force the outer bearing free of its interference fit. Be careful not to draw the edges of the puller toward each other enough to mar the shaft.

5. Remove the inner main bearing on the right side shaft with extractor No. 132-067 or with a press.

6. Drill out the expansion plugs in the crankpin as described in the four-speed section.

7. Press out the crankpin.

8. Reassemble and align the crankshaft assembly in the same manner as for the four-speed models.

Piston Size Information

Refer back to this same section under the four-speed engine heading. The five-speed pistons are marked in the same manner.

Cylinder Machining Information

Again, refer back to this same section under the four-speed engine heading. When determining the proper cylinder diameter for an overbore, use the data for the Metisse in the tolerances chart.

When installing a new cylinder liner, it is important to be aware that the fit of the liner in the five-speed crankcases is particularly important. There must not more than 0.25 mm (0.001 in.) clearance between the outside diameter of the liner and the inside diameter of the crankcase mount.

Engine Assembly

INSTALLING THE CRANKSHAFT

1. Before reassembling the cases, replace any badly worn transmission bearings.

2. Remove the crankshaft oil seal and the cover gasket from each seal cover. Install the smaller seal cover on the left side engine case.

3. Clean the main bearings with a solvent. If any dirt remains in the chamfers of the inner races, the seal surfaces of the shafts will be scored if the bearings are ever removed again and the seals will leak.

4. To install the unsealed main bearing on the left side driveshaft, heat the bearing on a hotplate until the oil begins to smoke, then drop the bearing into position on the shaft.

5. Heat the left side engine case and install the crankshaft assembly in it.

6. Install the sleeve gear in the left side case.

7. If the kickstart assembly was removed, it should be installed at this point. In the five-speed engine, the kickstart assembly is fitted with a spacer between the thrust washer and the ratchet spring on the splines of the kickstart shaft.

CONSTRUCTIONAL DIFFERENCES IN THE FIVE-SPEED TRANSMISSION

In the five-speed gearbox, the simplified selector mechanism rotates a shift drum instead of a cam plate. The drum performs the same function as the cam plate, moving the shift forks back and forth along their shaft.

To save space, some of the driving sprockets are located on the mainshaft and others on the countershaft in the five-speed box. Each sprocket is splined to its shaft. Three of the sprockets have built-in sliding dogs and are positioned by the shift forks. Two of these are located on the mainshaft and the other is on the countershaft.

Starting from the clutch side, the gears on the mainshaft are laid out as follows:

1. 4th gear idler
2. 1st gear drive sprocket (with 4th gear sliding dog attached)
3. 2nd gear idler
4. 3rd gear drive sprocket (with 5th/2nd gear sliding dog)

The mainshaft fits inside the countershaft. The sleeve (countershaft) gear is mated with the transfer gear on the end of the countershaft, but the 5th/2nd gear sliding dog couples the sleeve gear directly to the mainshaft in 5th gear to provide direct drive.

Starting from the clutch side, the five gears on the countershaft are arranged as follows:

1. 4th gear drive sprocket
2. 1st gear idler
3. 2nd gear drive sprocket, with 1st/3rd gear sliding dog
4. 3rd gear idler
5. Countershaft transfer gear

TRANSMISSION ASSEMBLY

1. Install the 25 tooth 2nd gear idler on the mainshaft by sliding the dished side of the gear on the unthreaded end of the mainshaft. Butt the gear against the raised splines of the mainshaft.

2. Install a snap-ring in its groove on the mainshaft next to the 2nd gear idler. Besure that the pierced ends of the ring are beneath the sliding dog engaging holes in the 2nd gear idler. Grind down the ends of the snap-ring if necessary. The ring must be tight enough on the shaft so that you can't rotate it with your fingers.

3. Hold the mainshaft with the threaded end pointing up. Drop the 1st gear driving sprocket (19 teeth), with the 4th gear sliding dog attached, onto the mainshaft with the shift fork groove pointing down.

4. Install a second snap-ring on the mainshaft in the groove about 1 in. above the 1st gear drive sprocket. Check the fit and positioning of the ring as in Step 2.

5. Hold the mainshaft with the unthreaded end facing up. Install the 28 tooth 3rd gear drive sprocket, with the 5th/2nd gear sliding dog attached, on the unthreaded end of the mainshaft, with the shift fork groove facing down. Hold the gear in position.

6. Turn the mainshaft over so that the threaded end is pointed up again and install the 30 tooth 4th gear idler on the threaded end of the shaft with the dished side of the gear facing down.

7. Install a snap-ring in the groove in the countershaft that is closest to the midpoint of the shaft.

8. Install the 28 tooth drive sprocket, with the 1st/3rd sliding dog attached, between the snap-ring grooves in the countershaft splines so that the shift fork groove faces the snap-ring that has been installed.

9. Install a snap-ring in the other groove in the countershaft.

10. Holding the countershaft so that the sliding dog groove in the sliding dog gear is facing up, put the 19 tooth 3rd gear idler on the shaft from the top with the dog-engaging slots of the gear facing down. Rotate the idler gear and make sure that the pierced ends of the snap-ring lie beneath the engaging slots; if not, grind down the ends of the ring.

11. Install the thick spacer on the countershaft so that it butts against the 3rd gear idler.

12. Install the 16 tooth transfer gear on

Assembling the third gear drive sprocket

Assembling the fourth gear idler

the countershaft so that it butts against the spacer.

13. Fit the thin spacer and butt it against the transfer gear. Coat the spacer with heavy grease to keep it from falling off. (Late Metrallas use a wider transfer gear that fits flush with the end of the splines. There is no thin washer.)

14. Turn the countershaft upside down, holding the gears and the spacer to keep them from falling off. Install the 28 tooth 1st gear idler with the dog engaging slots facing down. Fit the 17 tooth 4th gear drive sprocket on the countershaft with the flat face of the gear facing down.

15. Hold the countershaft in a horizontal position. Pick up the mainshaft and mesh the gears on the two shafts, with the threaded end of the mainshaft at the same end as the 4th gear drive sprocket on the countershaft. All of the gears should mesh except for the transfer gear on the mainshaft which will mesh with the sleeve gear on the countershaft. The shafts will be parallel if the gears have been assembled correctly.

16. Mesh the 28 tooth kickstart with the 1st gear drive sprocket (4th gear sliding dog attached), with the ratchet teeth on the kickstart gear facing the unthreaded end of the mainshaft. Fit the unthreaded end of the mainshaft into the countershaft and fit the kickstart gear to the kickstart shaft simultaneously.

17. Hold the countershaft with the transfer gear facing the countershaft bearing. Rotate the countershaft gears, so that they mesh with the mainshaft gears, and fit the countershaft into its bearing, taking care not to dislodge the thin spacer from the splines of the transfer gear.

18. Unscrew the detent plunger capscrew from the other side of the engine case until the plunger is flush with its boss. Install the shift drum into its mounting boss. One of the notches on the detent cam at the rear of the drum is shallower than the others; rotate the drum so that the shallow notch is aligned with the detent plunger. Retighten the detent plunger capscrew. The shift drum is in neutral at this point; assemble the transmission with the drum in this position.

19. Install the largest shift fork (the 2nd/5th gear fork) on the 2nd/5th gear sliding dog gear on the mainshaft next to the sleeve gear, with the follower peg on the fork pointing toward the shift drum. Pivot the fork until its follower peg engages with the rear cam groove (nearest the detent cam) on the shift drum.

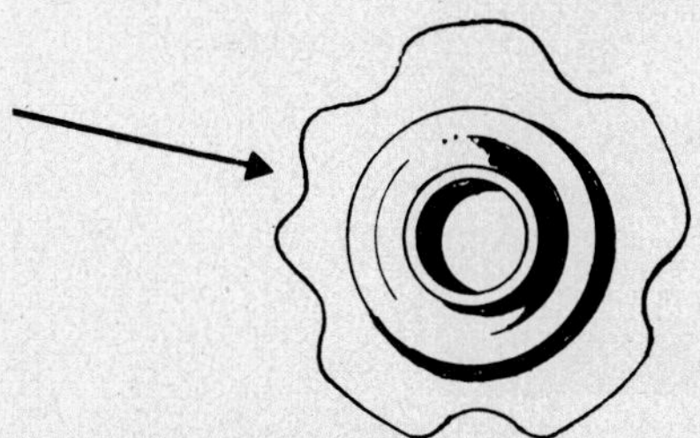

The shallow (neutral) notch

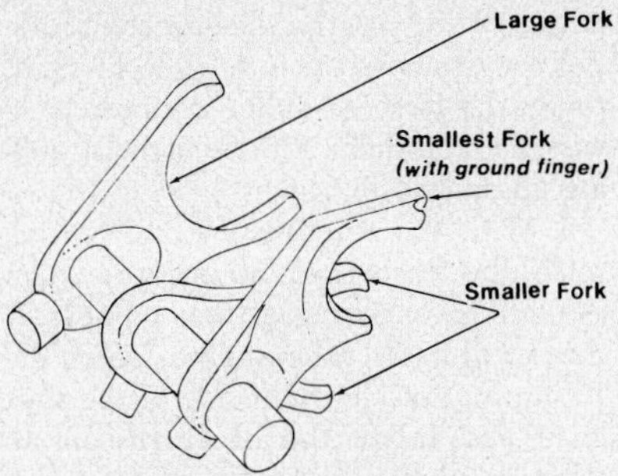

The order of shift fork assembly

Fig. 91–92

20. Pick up the shift fork that has not had part of one of its fingers ground away and install it on the sliding dog gear on the countershaft, with the follower peg of the fork pointing toward the shift drum. Engage this 1st/3rd gear shift fork's follower peg in the middle cam groove of the shift drum.

21. Install the 4th gear shift fork on the 4th gear sliging dog, nearest the threaded end of the mainshaft, with the follower peg pointing toward the shift drum. Engage the peg in the front cam groove in the drum.

22. Insert the shift fork shaft through the holes in the forks and push it into the mounting boss in the engine case.

ASSEMBLING THE CRANKCASES

1. Heat the two remaining main bearings until the oil begins to smoke. Drop the unsealed bearing on the drive side crankshaft and allow it to cool for ten minutes. Install the sealed bearing on the shaft so that it butts up against the first bearing and allow it to cool for the same amount of time. The cooling process can be speeded up with compressed air. Make sure that you install the center gasket before the cases are mated.

2. Heat the right side case and install it onto the left side case. Install and tighten the case-stud nuts to 5 ft lbs. Fit the allen bolt just behind the front engine mount boss.

3. After the cases have been mated, check the flywheel alignment as described in the four-speed section under "Crankshaft Assembly."

4. Remove the magneto side seal cover from the engine. Install new seals in the magneto and drive side seal covers, fit new gaskets to the covers, and install them on the engine.

5. To install the kickstart spring, align the spring mounting hole in the kickstart shaft and fit the end of the spring into it. Hook the other end of the spring over the anchor nut.

6. Install a new O-ring on the countershaft and then mount the countershaft spacer and oil seal.

7. Insert the two shift selector pawls, round end first, into the slots of the pawl carrier. If the square ends of the pawls appear to have been hand filed, insert the rounded ends of the pawls into the slots of the carrier so that the filed edge of the square corner of each pawl faces up.

8. Compress the pawls downward. Holding the pawl carrier as before, with the flats on the shaft in a vertical position, fit the carrier into the shift drum. Neither pawl will drop into a slot in the rim of the drum.

9. Install the selector cover gasket on the inner face of the cover. Fit the cover to the shaft of the pawl carrier, with the semi-circular notch in the cover facing down. Install the three mounting screws.

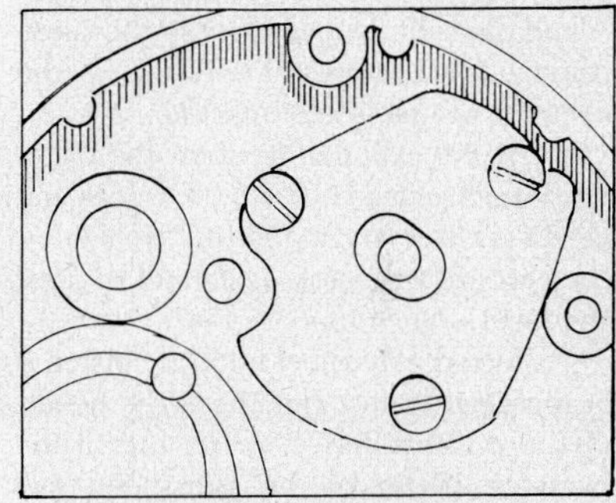

Selector cover installed

10. Using pliers, rotate the pawl carrier shaft clockwise, until one of the pawls drops into a slot.

11. Install the selector lever on the pawl carrier shaft, with the arm of the lever facing the rear of the engine and the pin facing away from the engine. Bend down the tabs on the lever capscrew washer. Fit the washer to the pawl carrier shaft, install the capscrew, and tighten it. Bend up the tabs of the washer to lock the capscrew in place.

12. Install the selector shaft, with its arm facing up, into its mount beneath the selector cover. Adjust the selector lever so that its pin goes into the slot on the arm of the shaft. Press the hairpin spring on the rear of the selector shaft arm so that the spring legs snap over the pin in the engine case underneath the lever. Install the thrust washer on the selector shaft with its chamfered side facing the engine.

13. Install the spacers, with new O-rings, on the crankshaft and mainshaft.

14. Fit the woodruff keys on the primary side crankshaft and mainshaft. Check the length of the clutch springs as described in the four-speed section.

15. Fit the primary chain over the engine sprocket and outer clutch hub. Install the assembly on the mainshaft and crankshaft. Install the inner clutch hub and then replace the mainshaft and crankshaft nuts and washers. Torque the

nuts after the engine has been reinstalled in the frame.

ASSEMBLING THE MAGNETO SIDE ENGINE COMPONENTS

Refer to the four-speed section. The procedures for five speed models are the same.

INSPECTING AND INSTALLING THE PISTON

Refer to the four-speed section.

INSTALLING THE CYLINDER

1. Fit a ring compressor over the piston rings. Install the cylinder base gasket.
2. Install the cylinder over the four studs and gently lower it over the piston. When the cylinder has covered the rings, remove the compressor and bottom the cylinder against the crankcase.
3. Fit the cylinder head on the cylinder. Attach a head nut at 2:00 o'clock and at 8:00 o'clock. Torque the nuts to 3 ft lbs, then unscrew the nuts again and remove the head.
4. Turn the flywheel until the piston is at top dead center and check the height of the piston relative to the top of the cylinder. (Refer to the four-speed section.)
5. Install the head again and fit a washer and nut on each of the studs. Tighten the nuts to 3 ft lbs in the following sequence: 2:00 o'clock, 8:00 o'clock, 10:00 o'clock, and 4:00 o'clock. Repeat the sequence in 3 ft lb increments until 12 ft lbs has been reached.

Engine Installation

Refer to the four-speed section. The following notes apply to the five-speed models:

1. Insert the wires that are dangling from the frame up through the grommet in the bottom of the engine beneath the flywheel. Join the yellow wire to the yellow wire, the green to the green, and the red wire to the black wire. Slide the insulators down over the exposed clips. Position the wires against the engine case beneath the flywheel and tighten the wire clamp screw to secure them.
2. Install the two long primary case allen bolts in the holes beneath the gearshift and the "O" in BULTACO on the case.
3. Install the gear selector fork on the splined selector shaft so that it faces to the rear of the bike and lies parallel with an imaginary line drawn between the footpeg and the selector shaft.
4. After the shift lever and footpeg have been installed, engage the lever with the selector fork. Pull up on the lever to make sure that it can't slip out of engagement with the selector shaft fork. If it does, remove the fork from the shaft, rotate the fork one spline counterclockwise, and reinstall it. Check again by pulling up on the shift lever.
5. With the transmission in Neutral, rotate the rear wheel and press down on the shift lever to engage Second gear. If the lever hits the exhaust pipe, loosen the 13 mm nut on the front side of the shift lever and rotate the eccentric pin to reposition it.

ENGINE TORQUE SPECIFICATIONS

	ft lbs
Flywheel Retaining Nut	75
Countershaft Sprocket Nut	75
Clutch Hub Nut	75
Engine Sprocket	90
Head Bolts	12
Case Half Nuts	5
Seal Retainer Screws	5
Primary & Mag. Cover Screws	5
Engine Mounting Bolts	35

FUEL SYSTEMS

AMAL CARBURETORS

Tuning The Carburetor

The following changes can be made to tune the carburetor to meet various requirements:

1. Changing the size of the main jet.
2. Changing the position of the jet needle in the slide.
3. Changing the needle for one of a different taper.
4. Changing the throttle slide for one of a different cutaway.
5. Changing the size of the needle jet.

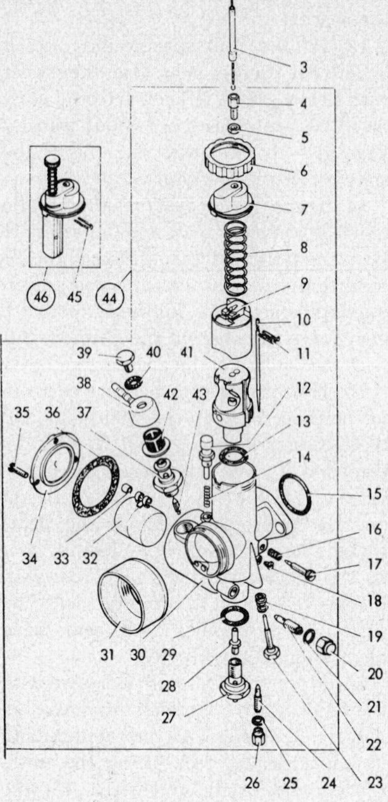

Exploded view of the Amal Monobloc carburetor

Before making any changes in the carburetor, make sure that there are no air leaks and that the ignition system is in perfect condition. To check the points gap and ignition timing, refer to the "Tune-Up" section. To check for an air leak, bottom the low-speed air screw against its seat and back it out ¾ turn. If the engine then revs much faster than a normal idle speed, your problem is caused by an air leak, not by the carburetion.

The carburetor metering systems should be checked in the following sequence:

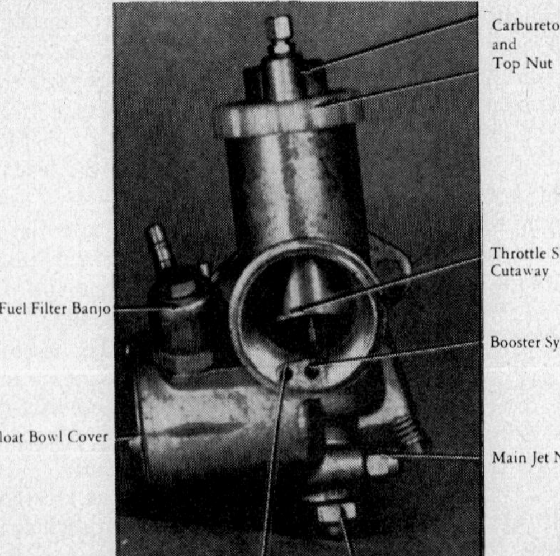

1. Warm up the engine. On level ground, run the engine up to peak rpm in Second gear. Slowly back off the throttle until it is closed. While backing off, listen for a pinging sound which indicates a lean mixture. Check also for four-stroking (engine firing every other stroke), which indicates a rich mixture. Try to determine the throttle openings at which the problem is noticeable.

2. If the engine was pinging between ¾–full throttle, install a larger main jet. If the engine was running too rich, fit a smaller main jet. Road test the machine again to make sure you have solved the problem.

3. If the engine was pinging between ½–¾ throttle, raise the jet needle one notch in the slide. If it was four-stroking, lower the needle one notch.

4. If the engine was pinging between ¼–½ throttle, install a slide with a smaller cutaway. If the engine was four-stroking, fit a slide with a higher cutaway.

5. Between ¼ and closed throttle, if the engine was pinging, fit a larger needle jet. If the engine was four-stroking, fit a smaller jet.

After changing any components, run through the following fine-tuning sequence.

1. Ride the motorcylce for at least ¼ mile with the throttle halfway between the closed and ¼ open. Push the kill button and, at the same instant, pull in the clutch. Hold the clutch in, coast to a stop, and remove the spark plug. It should be dry and malt brown in color at the end of the porcelain insulator surrounding the center electrode. If it is white, the mixture is still too lean. If it is black and oily, the mixture is too rich. Change the needle jet to correct the condition.

2. Perform a plug check in the same manner as Step 1 after having ridden the bike for at least ¼ mile at between ¼–½ throttle. If the mixture is not perfect, as indicated by the color of the plug, change the throttle slide as necessary.

3. Perform a plug check again, this time riding with the throttle open between ½–¾. If necessary, raise or lower the needle in the slide to get the correct spark plug reading.

4. Finally, ride the bike at least ¼ mile with the throttle wide open and check the plug again after pulling the clutch in and shutting the engine down cleanly. If necessary, change the main jet.

AMAL MONOBLOC

Disassembly

1. Unscrew and remove the air cleaner.

2. Remove the fuel line from the fuel line banjo on the carburetor.

3. Unscrew the two carburetor mounting nuts and remove the carburetor from the engine.

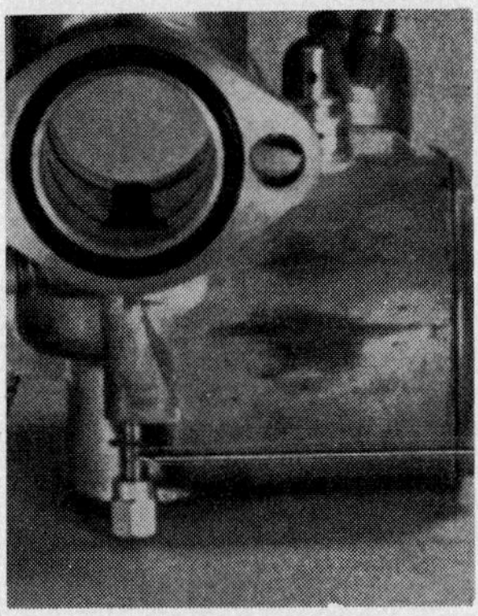

Pilot fuel jet

4. Unscrew the plastic cover nut from the carburetor body, take off the carburetor top, and withdraw the slide from the carburetor body. Take off the needle retaining clip and remove the needle from the slide.

5. Hold the slide and carburetor top in one hand. Press them together to compress the slide return spring, and remove the throttle cable fitting from its slot in the top of the slide. Remove the cable from the slide and the carburetor top.

6. Take off the three mounting screws from the float bowl cover and remove the cover. Remove the float pivot spacer, the float, and the float needle from the carburetor.

7. Remove the tickler assembly from the top of the float bowl. Push the tickler assembly apart; it consists of the tickler button, the spring, and the crown-screw.

8. Remove the float needle jet holder (the float valve seat) from the top of the float bowl.

9. Unscrew the main jet cover nut and remove the main jet with a screwdriver.

10. Unscrew the pilot jet cover nut and then remove the pilot jet.

Removing the jet block

11. Remove the needle jet holder; catch the jet block as it falls out of the slide barrel.

12. Remove the needle jet from its holder. Remove the O-ring from the carburetor mounting flange.

Inspection And Reassembly

1. Separate the gaskets and plastic parts from the metal parts. Wash the metal parts in carburetor cleaner or other solvent, then blow dry with compressed air.

2. Fit a new jet block gasket (Part No. 815-132) to the bottom of the jet block and insert the block into the slide barrel of the carburetor. Make sure that the locating screw is in place.

3. If the bike is more than six months old or has covered more than 4,000 miles, replace the needle jet with a new one of the same size. Mount the needle jet in its holder and tighten it.

4. Install a new needle jet holder gasket (Part No. 815-130) to the needle jet holder.

5. Insert the needle jet holder into the bottom of the carburetor and screw it into the bottom of the jet block.

6. Fit a new gasket to the main jet (Part No. 715-089) and screw the jet into its seat firmly. Install and tighten the main jet cover nut.

7. Fit a new gasket to the pilot jet (Part No. 715-024) and screw the jet into its seat. Install and tighten the pilot jet cover nut.

8. Install and tighten the float needle jet holder into the top of the float bowl. Turn the carburetor upside down and, from the inside of the float bowl, drop the nylon float needle, pointed end first, down into the jet. Fit the float mounting bracket to the float pivot shaft with the narrow side of the bracket pressing against the float needle. Fit the pivot spacer to the float pivot shaft.

NOTE: *If carburetor flooding has been experienced, it is a good idea to replace the float needle and seat assembly. Also, check to see if the float has a hole in it by shaking it. If so, replace it. A few of the carburetors have float pivot spacers that are too thick, causing the lip of the float bowl cover to bind against the spacer and the float. To check for this, first measure the distance that the float bowl cover lip protrudes beyond its gasket. Then measure the distance from the edge of the float chamber to the top of the float pivot spacer, as shown. The first distance measured must be less than the second distance. If not, file the end of the float pivot spacer to provide the clearance.*

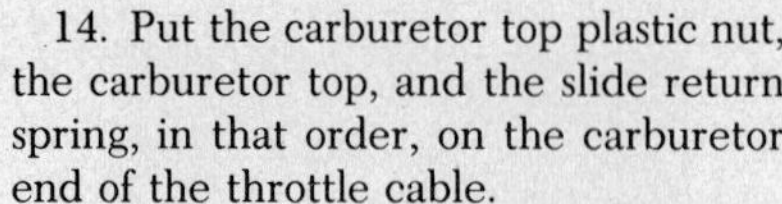

14. Put the carburetor top plastic nut, the carburetor top, and the slide return spring, in that order, on the carburetor end of the throttle cable.

15. Measure the diameter of the slide at several points around its circumference with a vernier caliper. If the slide has worn oval more than ½ mm (0.20 in.), replace it.

16. Compress the slide return spring against the carburetor top so that a portion of the inner throttle cable protrudes past the end of the return spring.

17. Put the fitting on the end of the inner cable down into the hole in the top of the slide and work the cable back to the blind end of the slot. On the underside of the slide top is a round notch to accept the cable fitting. Allow the cable fitting to seat in this notch. Release the return spring.

18. Slide the notched end of the needle up into the rounded portion of the slot in the center of the top of the slide.

19. Fit a new needle clip to the center notch on the needle. Put the slide into the carburetor barrel, being careful to fit

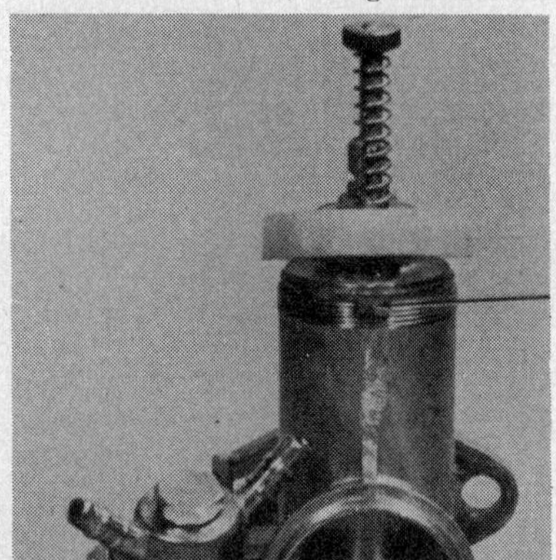

Installing the carburetor cap

Measuring the float axle spacer

9. Install a new gasket and fit the float bowl cover to the float bowl.

10. Put the open end of the tickler button into its mounting hole at the top of the float bowl. Fit the spring and crown screw to the button.

11. Smear a small amount of grease on a new O-ring and press it into its groove in the carburetor mounting flange.

12. Examine the nylon fuel filter. If there are any tears in the mesh, replace the filter element. Install the filter in its mounting spigot and place the banjo over the filter. Fit a new banjo screw gasket (Part No. 815-029) and tighten the screw.

13. Fit the throttle stop screw spring to the throttle stop screw. Turn the screw into its mounting boss.

the needle into its hole in the center of the jet block. If the carburetor is equipped with a choke slide, make sure that the choke is positioned in its slot in the slide. Push the slide down into the barrel. It may be necessary to rotate the slide slightly so that the ridge inside the slide can find and enter the notch in the jet block. Push the slide all the way to the bottom of the barrel.

20. Hold the carburetor top pressed against the top of the barrel and start the plastic top nut on its threads in the barrel. Make sure that the tooth on the bottom of the carburetor top is fitted into its slot in the top of the barrel. Tighten the plastic nut.

21. Look into the carburetor mouth and watch the action of the slide as you open and close the throttle twistgrip. Be sure that the slide is raised and lowered freely, with no binding, as you work the throttle.

22. Check to see that the O-ring is still in place on the mounting flange, and install the carburetor on the engine. Tighten the two nuts just enough to keep them from loosening from engine vibration. If they are overtightened, the mounting flange may be warped.

23. Install the air cleaner.

24. Position the fuel filter banjo so that the fuel line can make an easy sweep from the tank to the fitting, and connect the fuel line.

25. Again tighten the needle jet holder on the bottom of the carburetor.

AMAL CONCENTRIC

Disassembly

1. Shut off the fuel tap and disconnect the fuel line at the carburetor.

2. Lift up the rubber cover and remove the carburetor cap, lifting out the throttle slide assembly.

3. To dismantle the slide assembly, compress the return spring against the cap and take out the needle and clip. Remove the cable from the slide.

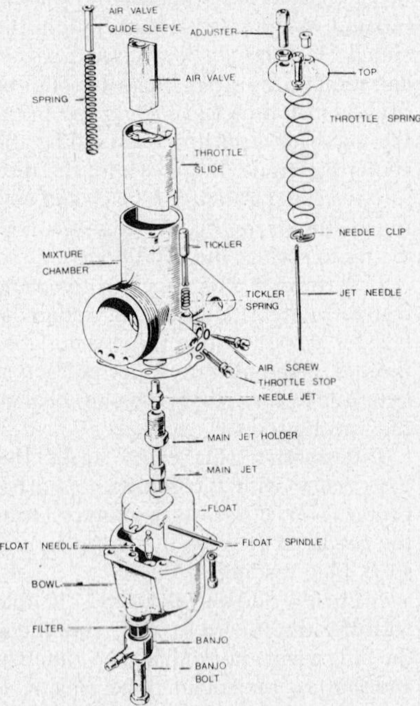

Concentric carburetor

4. Disconnect the air cleaner hose and unbolt and remove the carburetor from the engine.

5. Remove the float bowl banjo bolt.

6. Unscrew the float bowl screws and remove the float bowl.

7. Lift out the float, complete with float needle and spindle.

8. Remove the throttle stop and pilot air screws from the carburetor body.

9. Remove the filter screen (if fitted) from the main jet. The main jet alone can be unscrewed from the jet holder, or the jet holder may be unscrewed which will affect the removal of both the main and needle jets. Both these jets may be cleaned while in place in the jet holder.

10. Unscrew the pilot fuel jet with a small screwdriver.

Inspection

1. All rubber O-rings must be in good condition. This is especially true of the carburetor flange O-ring. Replacement of the O-rings and float bowl and banjo gaskets is advised after disassembly.

2. The fuel passages in the float bowl must be clean. The needle seat in the float bowl must be clean and free of deposits of any kind.

3. Check the float for leaks or punctures. The float needle must be in good condition.

4. Make sure that all jets are clear. Soak in solvent and blow them dry if necessary.

5. Soak the carburetor body in a solvent and blow it dry, paying close attention to all fuel and air passages.

6. Check the flange surface for warpage. Slight imperfections may be removed by grinding on a flat surface.

7. Check the fuel filters.

8. Inspect the throttle slide. It should be free from wear or scratches.

9. The metering needle should be smooth and without signs of wear. The needle and the needle jet should both be replaced after many miles have been covered.

Assembly

Assembly is the reverse of the disassembly procedure. Note that the carburetor flange O-ring should be seated in its seat.

It is important that the flange bolts be tightened evenly and not overtightened.

If a plastic float banjo is used, care should be taken when tightening the banjo bolt. Leakage of gasoline at this point may be due to the bolt being too tight.

IRZ CARBURETORS

Description

1. In the IRZ plot metering system, air enters the carburetor through the larger of the two holes beneath the carburetor. Fuel for the pilot metering system enters the pilot jet directly; the jet protrudes down into the float bowl.

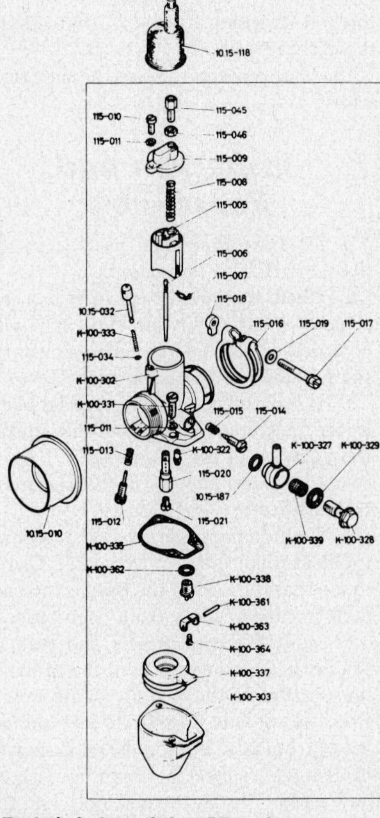

Exploded view of the IRZ carburetor showing parts numbers

2. The slide in IRZ carburetors is grooved. The groove rides on the end of the slide stop to keep the slide positioned correctly.

3. In the IRZ, the spray nozzle is the upper part of the needle jet. The needle jet is stamped with two sets of numbers, indicating the size of the jet (three digits) and the size of the air holes in the jet (two digits).

4. The IRZ slide has its cutaway height marked in millimeters. A slide marked "75" has a cutaway height of 7.5 mm.

5. The air intake for the booster system in the IRZ carburetor is through the smaller hole beneath the mouth of the carburetor. The air is fed directly into six holes drilled into the needle jet body.

Disassembly

1. Loosen the air filter clamps and remove the hose from the mouth of the carburetor.

2. Remove the fuel line from the fuel filter banjo at the carburetor.

3. Loosen the mounting sleeve clamp and remove the carburetor from the intake manifold.

4. Take out the slotted screw from the carburetor top and remove the top. Withdraw the slide from the barrel.

5. Holding the slide and carburetor top as shown, push the slide and top toward each other to compress the slide return spring. Unhook the throttle cable fitting from the slot in the slide. Remove the slide, the spring, and the carburetor top from the cable.

6. Remove the needle clip from the slide.

7. Unscrew the bolt from the fuel filter banjo and remove the banjo, the washer, and the filter element.

8. Unscrew and remove the low-speed air screw.

9. Take off the two screws and remove the float bowl.

10. To remove the float, press against the end of the pivot shaft that protrudes

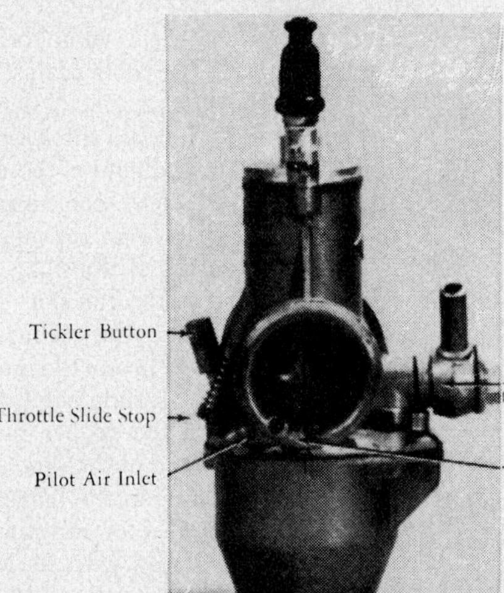

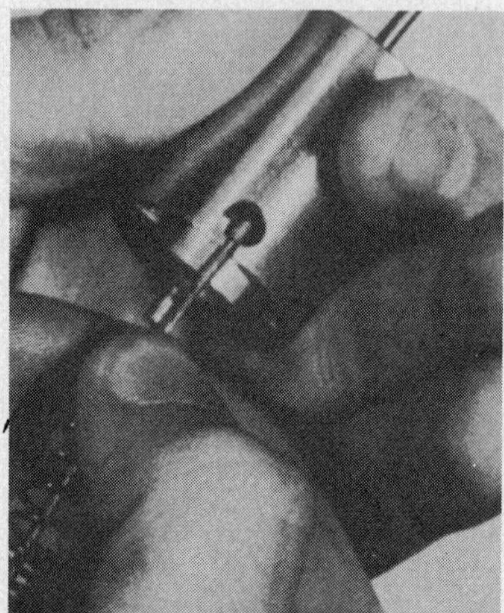
Removing the throttle cable from the slide

Removing the float needle assembly

from the slotted ear of the mounting bracket and remove the shaft.

11. Unscrew and remove the pilot jet from the bottom of the carburetor.

12. Unscrew the needle jet from the jet block in the bottom of the carburetor. Using a screwdriver, unscrew the main jet from the needle jet.

13. Using a pair of pliers with wide, smooth jaws, gently unscrew the float needle assembly by holding it on its center ridge.

14. Twist the mounting clip on the tickler button with a pair of pliers and remove the clip. Remove the tickler button and its spring from the other side of the carburetor body.

15. Unscrew and remove the slide stop screw.

Inspection and Reassembly

1. Separate the metal parts from the plastic parts and the gaskets.

2. Clean the metal parts in carburetor cleaner or other solvent. Blow dry with compressed air, taking care to clear all the fuel and air passages.

3. Install the needle jet in the jet block in the bottom of the carburetor. Install the main jet in the needle jet.

4. Install the pilot jet in the bottom of the carburetor.

5. Tighten the small screw that secures the float pivot mounting bracket. Check to see that the ears of the bracket are not bent toward or away from each other.

6. Hold the float needle and seat assembly in your fingers, with the protruding portion of the needle facing down. Press the needle up into its seat and release it quickly. If it binds, or is slow to drop down, replace the assembly. Using a new gasket, install the assembly into the bottom of the carburetor with the ridge facing away from the carburetor. Tighten it with pliers, taking care not to distort the ridge (which could cause the needle to bind).

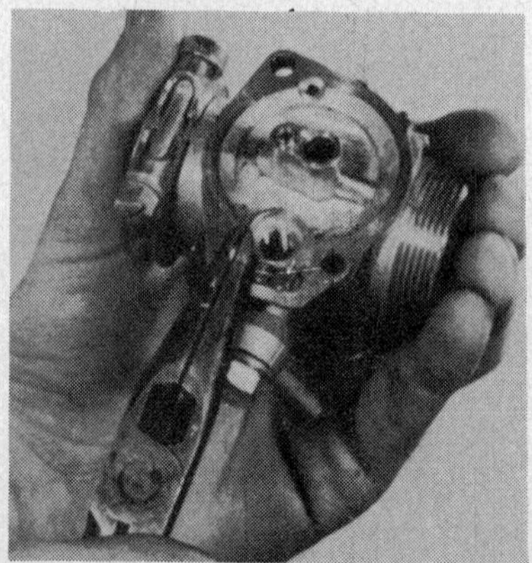
Straighten the float bracket ears as necessary

7. Check to see if the float has a hole in it by shaking it. Leaking floats must be replaced.

8. Position the pivot arm of the float between the ears of the float mounting bracket. The float should be positioned so that the flat side of the pivot arm presses against the bottom of the float needle. Insert the pivot shaft into the plain ear of the mounting bracket. Press against the shaft to force it into the slotted ear of the bracket. Press it far enough so that each end protrudes the same amount.

9. Fit the tickler button to its mount and work it up and down. If it has a tendency to bind, either the tickler button or its mount are bent. Sight down through the tickler mount to determine where the bend is and straighten it or replace the bent part.

10. Fit the spring to the tickler button and insert them into the mount from the top of the carburetor. Install the clip in the groove in the button.

11. Install the float bowl on the carburetor, using a new gasket. Put a lock washer on the two mounting screws and tighten them.

12. Fit the spring on the low-speed air screw and install it. Bottom the screw gently and then back it out one turn.

13. Fit a new washer (Part No. K-100-329) to the banjo mounting bolt. Install the screen on the bolt so that the screen covers the two fuel-feed holes. Fit the banjo to the bolt and install the small washer (Part No. 10.15-187) on the bolt. Install the bolt and run it down finger-tight.

14. Install the rubber cable adjuster cover on the outer throttle cable with the small end of the cover pointing away from the end of the cable.

15. Thread the inner throttle cable through the cable adjuster on the carburetor top. Fit the slide return spring on the inner cable, and compress the spring against the top so that a short portion of the inner cable protrudes from the spring.

16. Fit the cable into the slot in the top of the slide and butt the cable against the blind end of the slot so that it is connected to the slide. Release the spring.

17. Insert the grooved end of the needle in the hole in the bottom of the slide. Align the center groove in the needle with the slot in the top of the slide, and insert the needle clip into the slot.

18. Install the slide in the carburetor barrel with the cutaway facing the mouth of the carb. Rotate the slide slightly in either direction until the groove mates with the positioning end of the slide stop screw. Bottom the slide in the barrel.

19. Install the carburetor top on the barrel. Mount the screw with its lockwasher.

20. Fit the carburetor to the intake manifold. Rotate it until it is aligned (ver-

tically) with the cylinder, and then tighten the clamp screw.

21. Position the air cleaner hose on the mouth of the carburetor and tighten the clamp.

22. Position the banjo so that the fuel line can make a clean sweep from the tank to the connection, then tighten the banjo bolt and install the line.

ZENITH CARBURETORS

Description

1. In the pilot metering system of the Zenith carburetor, air enters the left hole of the three small holes beneath the mouth of the carburetor. The air travels through the pilot metering jet and along a passage to the pilot mixing chamber. Fuel is drawn from the float bowl through a hole drilled in the needle and main jet holder. The fuel travels through a passage to the pilot (fuel) metering jet and is then sucked into the mixing chamber. The mixture then travels to the pilot mixture metering jet, through which it enters the carburetor bore.

2. The slide has an extra large cutaway. The cutaway directs incoming air toward the mouth of the pilot mixture passage and prevents the flow of fuel from the pilot jet from increasing too rapidly. The Zenith carburetor provides outstanding low-speed throttle control because of the overlap between the first and second metering systems.

3. The size of the needle jet is given in letters because the flow capacity of the jet is determined by both its length and the number of holes drilled in it. The higher the letter, the more fuel the jet is capable of passing.

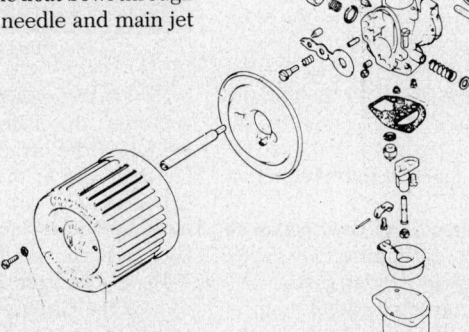

Exploded view of the Zenith carburetor showing parts numbers

4. The number stamped into the bottom of the throttle slide represents the number of degrees from horizontal of the cutaway angle.

5. As the needle passes the halfway point, the movement of the slide is greatly increasing the volume of air taken into the engine. A booster system is used to speed up the flow of fuel out of the spray nozzle. Air enters the center hole of the three small holes beneath the carburetor mouth and is led to an air chamber surrounding the needle jet. The air is sucked into the needle jet through holes drilled in its shank. The mixing of fuel with air is begun in the needle jet, and the rate of fuel flow increases.

6. The Zenith carburetor is equipped with a choke to aid cold starting.

Disassembly

1. Remove the bottom of the fuel line from the fuel filter banjo.

2. Loosen the carburetor mounting clamp and remove the carburetor from the intake manifold.

3. Take out the two screws from the top of the carburetor. Remove the carburetor top and pull the throttle slide out of the barrel.

4. Holding the slide upside down pull the return spring down and away from the slide. This will allow the brass cable protector cup, which normally covers the top of the slide, to fall away. Move the throttle cable over to the enlarged end of the slot and remove the cable fitting from the slide.

Pilot Mixture Jet
Needle Jet Mount
Float Bowl
Pilot Fuel Jet

5. Do not remove the nut from the top of the slide unless you wish to change the needle setting in the slide. If you wish to disassemble the slide, wrap a thick piece of leather around it and clamp it in a vise. Unscrew the top nut and lift out the needle.

6. Remove the brass cup, the slide return spring, and the carburetor top from the throttle cable.

7. Remove the retaining bolt from the fuel filter banjo. Remove the banjo, washer, and filter element.

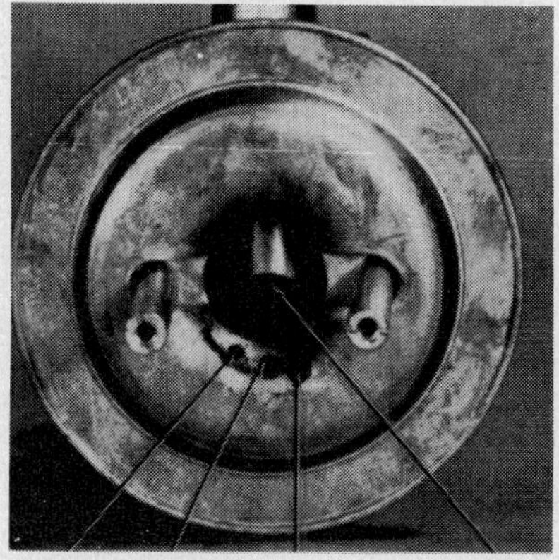

Removing the float needle assembly

8. Take out the throttle stop screw, its spring, and thrust washer from the carburetor.

9. Remove the float bowl mounting screws and remove the bowl.

10. Press the end of the float pivot shaft that protrudes from the slotted ear of the mounting bracket and remove the shaft and float.

11. Remove the clip from the bottom of the tickler shaft. Remove the tickler shaft and its spring.

12. Remove the screw from the float pivot mounting bracket and take off the bracket.

13. Insert a 1/16 in. drill bit shank into each of the two holes in the brass float needle assembly. Insert a screwdriver blade between the two bits, perpendicular to them. Turn the drill bits counterclockwise to unscrew the assembly from the carburetor body.

14. Unscrew the main jet from the bottom of the jet carrier.

15. Take out the screw from the base of the jet carrier and remove the jet carrier from the bottom of the carburetor.

16. Push the needle jet out through the bottom of the jet carrier.

17. Unscrew the two small jets remaining in the bottom of the carburetor. The mixture metering jet (with the larger number) is closest to the carburetor mounting flange, and the pilot fuel metering jet (stamped with the smaller number) is closest to the float needle assembly.

18. Take out the two screws from the front of the air cleaner.

19. Strike the air cleaner with the heel of your hand to separate it from the front of its carburetor mounting plate.

20. Unscrew the two slotted posts that secure the mounting plate to the carburetor and remove the plate.

21. Remove the choke lever mounting screw and its spring. Remove the choke lever. The choke lever spring is molded into the carburetor body; don't attempt to remove it.

22. Remove the unmarked jet from the center hole of the three small holes beneath the mouth of the carburetor.

Inspection and Reassembly

1. Separate the metal parts from the plastic ones and the gaskets.

2. Clean the metal parts in carburetor cleaner or other solvent and blow dry with compressed air. Take care to clear the passageways carefully.

3. Wash the air filter element in clean gasoline and dry it with compressed air. Spray the inside and the louvers on the outside of the element with an aerosol chain lubricant.

4.Install the pilot fuel metering jet (smaller number) in the threaded hole in the bottom of the carburetor nearest the float needle mount.

5. Install the pilot mixture metering jet (larger number) in the hole in the bottom of the carburetor nearest the mounting flange.

6. Test the movement of the float needle in its seat to make certain that it moves freely without binding. If it binds even slightly, replace it.

7. Install the float needle and seat assembly, using a new gasket, in the same manner as it was removed.

8. Insert the needle jet into the unflanged end of the jet holder. Bottom the flange of the needle jet against the jet holder.

9. Screw the main jet into the bottom of the jet holder.

10. Install a new float bowl gasket to the bottom of the carburetor. The gasket also serves as the jet holder gasket.

11. Fit the protruding end of the needle jet through the gasket and into the brass tube cast into the carburetor, and butt the jet holder against the bottom of the carburetor.

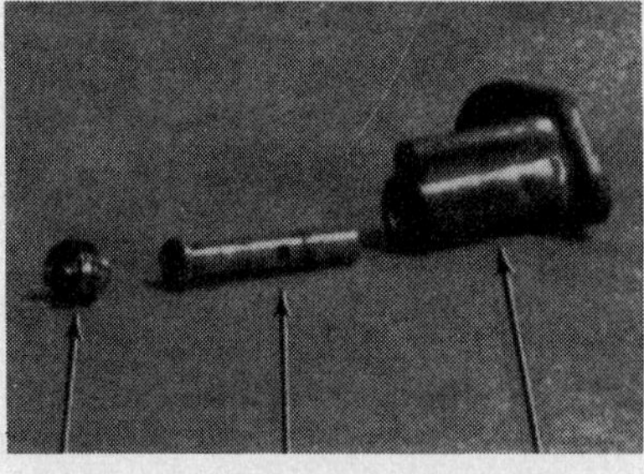

Main Jet — Needle Jet — Jet Holder

Float

Main Jet

12. Align the mounting screw holes in the jet holder and carburetor. Install the screws.

13. Tighten the main jet.

14. Position the float pivot mounting bracket over its mount, so that the side of the base with the cut in it is next to the float needle and seat assembly. Secure the bracket with the self-tapping screw.

Mounting bracket cut

15. Fit the spring to the tickler shaft and insert the shaft into its mount from the top of the carburetor body. Depress the shaft and fit the clip to the groove. Crimp the clip with a pair of pliers. Release the tickler and allow it to spring back to make sure it is properly seated.

16. Position the float against the bottom of the carburetor body so that the ridge on the float pivot arm presses against the float needle. Insert the pivot shaft into the non-slotted ear of the mounting bracket and push it through the pivot arm of the float. Press the shaft into the slotted ear of the bracket; if it goes in too easily, crimp the slot in the ear. Align the float pivot shaft so that it protrudes an equal distance at each end.

17. Holding the carburetor so that the bottom faces down, push the float up against the bottom of the carburetor body and release it quickly. If it binds, spread the ears of the mounting bracket with needle-nose pliers.

18. Install the float bowl and tighten the two mounting screws.

19. Install a new gasket on the banjo mounting screw. Insert the screw into the side of the banjo with the smaller hole, and insert the filter screen between the screw and the banjo. Install the banjo, but don't tighten the screw fully at this point.

20. Fit the spring and washer to the throttle stop screw and install the screw.

21. Position the choke lever on the carburetor with the lever handle facing the rear of the carburetor. Install the choke screw spring on the screw, and insert the screw through the pivot hole in the choke lever. Install the assembly on the carburetor.

22. Install the unmarked jet in the center hole of the three holes beneath the mouth of the carburetor.

23. Fasten the air cleaner mounting plate to the carburetor with the two slotted posts.

24. Fit the air cleaner and its cover to the mounting plate and install the two screws.

25. Pry the old rubber O-ring out of the manifold sleeve at the rear of the carburetor and install a new one.

26. Thread the inner throttle cable through the cable adjuster on the carburetor top. Fit the slide return spring to the inner cable, and then install the brass cup so that its dome fits up into the return spring.

27. Force the cup and spring back against the carburetor top so that an inch of cable protrudes from the cup.

28. Insert the cable end into the slot in the top of the slide and move the cable over to the blind end of the slot. Release the spring.

29. Position the slide above the barrel of the carburetor so that the cutaway faces the mouth. Install the slide in the barrel, rotating it slightly to mate the groove in the slide with its location peg. Bottom the slide in the barrel and install the carburetor top and its two mounting screws.

30. Install the carburetor on the intake manifold. Bottom the manifold against the rubber seal at the rear of the mounting sleeve.

31. Rotate the carburetor so that it is aligned vertically with the cylinder. Tighten the mounting clamp.

32. Position the banjo so that the fuel line makes a clean sweep from the tank to the connector, and install the line.

ELECTRICAL SYSTEMS

In almost all tests of the electrical system described in this chapter it will be necessary to use a multimeter (volts/ohms/amps meter). You will be measuring ohms (resistance) and voltages. To measure resistance with the multimeter, plug the black test wire into the jack marked "common" or "−" on the meter. Plug the red test wire into the jack marked "+", and rotate the AC-DC switch to +DC.

NOTE: *From about 1966 to 1971 Bultaco purchased its headlight and taillight assembly from Lucas. Replacement parts for these pieces may be purchased from British bike dealers.*

For every resistance reading except from the secondary (high voltage) coil of the high tension coil, rotate the large center switch to the position marked "RX1". Read the resistance from the top scale on the dial.

For resistance readings from the secondary coil of the high tension coil, rotate the center switch to the position marked "RX100". Read the resistance from the top scale and multiply the number by 100.

Before taking a resistance reading, clip the test wires together and adjust the knob marked "zero ohms" until the meter needle is on the 0 mark on the top scale of the dial. The ohmmeter is meant to be used for taking resistance readings only when there is no current flowing in the system.

NOTE: *Never rotate the magneto flywheel when you have the meter attached to the electrical circuits to read resistance, or you will burn out the meter.*

To read voltage, leave the test wires plugged into the same jacks. Rotate the AC-DC switch to AC. You will be using the 2.5, 10, and 50 volt positions on the center switch. Read the voltage, when the center switch is positioned for 2.5 volts, on the lower red scale marked "2.5 V.A.C. ONLY". If you are using the 10 volt position of the center switch, read the figures just above the upper red scale. When using the 50 volt position, read the figures just above the upper red scale.

BUILDING A CREST VOLTAGE ATTACHMENT

A crest voltage (or peak to peak) attachment is necessary for testing the Femastronic generator output. It is easy to build, and the materials cost only about five dollars. This attachment will absorb up to 700 volts; correct rated voltage will show on the scale of the meter.

1. You will need two capacitors of 350 volt, 2 microfarad capacity (Mallory Part No. TT350Z2). Two of these connected in series result in 1 microfarad, with 700 volts capacity.

2. You will also need an 800 volt diode (Mallory Part No. SK3032). The arrow on the diode must point toward the meter side of the accessory.

3. Solder the components together as shown and use the plastic box the capacitors came in as a case. Use two tip jacks for receptacles for the test leads. Use two phone tops to allow the accessory to be plugged into the meter.

4. Using your crest voltage attachment, the Femastronic generator should show at least 100 volts on crank speed and 400 to 420 volts at 7,000 rpm. Plug the attachment into the positive and negative sockets in the meter, then plug the probe wires into the accessory sockets. After it has been checked out, you can insulate the accessory by pouring the box full of fiberglass resin. Be sure to first coat the ends of the jacks with wax to prevent them from becoming plugged with resin.

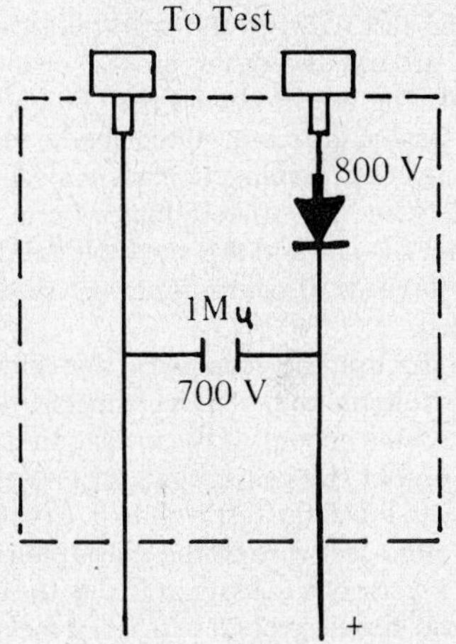

Capacitor wiring diagram

The arrow on the diode must point toward the meter side of the attachment

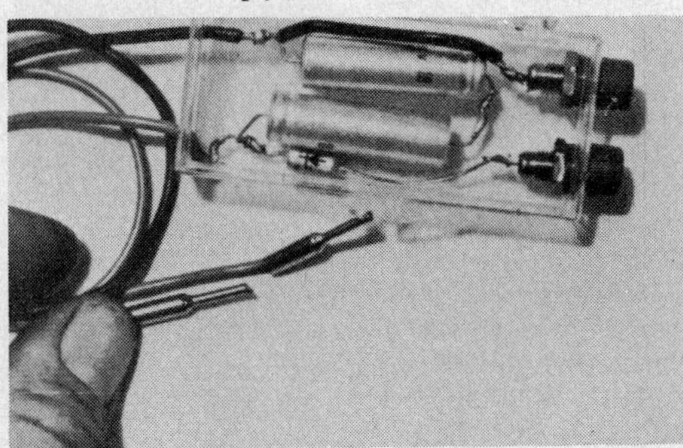

The completed attachment

BULTACO RACING MODELS IGNITION SYSTEM CHART

Model	Magneto Generator	Magneto Coil	Femsatronic Generator	Femsatronic Coil
Lobito				
AK-100	VAJ6-8	19.20-002		
Sherpa S	VAR-VAF	320-002		
1963 through to Mk-II	Specify Model			
Mk-II	42-20-001	42-20-061		
Mk-III S100			GEB1-3	ELA1-1
Mk-III 125, 175 and 200			GEA1-2	ELA1-1
Pursang				
Mk-I and Mk-II	VAR. 41-11	320-002		
Mk-III	1101-001-1	42.20-001 OR	GEA1-2	ELA1-1
Mk-IV			GEA1-2	ELA2-4
El Bandido				
Mk-I and Mk-II			GEA1-2	ELA2-4
TSS				
125-250 cc	VAF-VAK	320-002		
	Specify			
1964 through Mk-I	Model			
TSS				
125 Mk-II			GEB1-1	ELA1-1
250 Mk-II			GEB1-2	ELA1-1
350 Mk-II			GEA1-2	ELA2-4

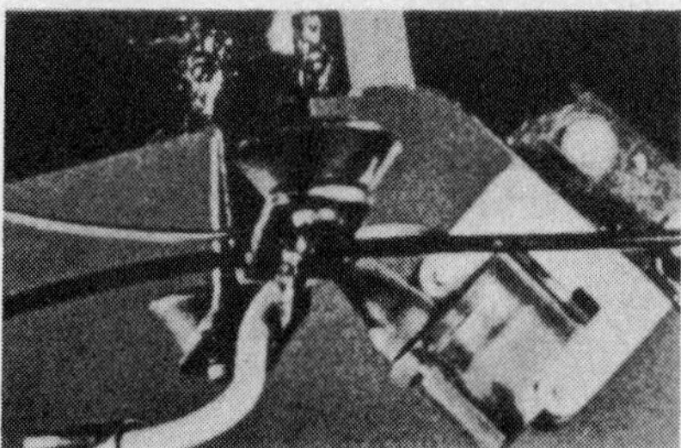

The coil is mounted on the frame under the tank

Magneto coils and points

RACING MODEL IGNITION SYSTEMS

Magneto Ignition System

TESTING THE MAGNETO IGNITION SYSTEM

The following tests are to be performed to determine whether the individual components of the magneto system are functioning properly.

High Tension Coil

1. Adjust the multimeter to read resistance (ohms). Zero the needle. Attach one of the test wires to the sparkplug cable and ground the other on the cylinder head. The needle should read 30 on the top scale of the meter. If the needle reads infinity, then a connection has come loose or a wire has broken somewhere between the coil and the spark plug. If the needle reads 30, continue on with the testing.

2. To test the secondary side of the high tension coil, remove the gas tank and scrape enough of the insulation from the end of the coil ground wire so that you can touch the test wire to it. Connect the other test wire to the spark plug cable. If you get a reading of 25–30, the coil is good but the ground wire is not making good contact with the frame. If you get an open circuit reading the coil is defective and must be replaced.

3. To check the primary side of the coil disconnect the black wire from the small junction box taped to the frame near the coil. Connect the meter to the black wire and the spark plug cable. If you get an open circuit reading the coil is defective. If the meter reads 30, the coil in functioning. Check for full output by adjusting the meter to 2.5 volts AC. Disconnect the red wire from the junction box. Connect the test wires to the red wire and ground. If you get less than 2.0 volts, replace the coil.

NOTE: *If the coil is OK and you still have no spark, it would be a good idea at this point to make sure the kill button on the handle bar is not short-circuiting. You can do this by simply bypassing the button using a jumper wire.*

Low Tension Coil

1. Rotate the AC-DC switch on the meter to the AC position. Turn the center switch to 2.5 volts.

2. Ground one of the test wires on the engine. Disconnect the black wire from the junction box under the gas tank and connect the other test wire to the black wire.

3. Turn the engine over with the kickstarter and watch the meter. If it reads 2.0–2.5 volts, the coil is good. If it does not read 2.0 volts, then either the coil or the magnet in the flywheel is bad.

Points and Condenser

1. Remove the magneto flywheel. Take out the big screw that mounts the points to the magneto backing plate and remove the points. Disconnect the two black wires from the points.

2. Switch the meter to the +DC position and turn the center switch to the Rx 10,000 notch. Zero the needle. Connect one of the test wires to the magneto backing plate. Watch the meter as you clip the other test wire to the end of the black wire from the condenser. The needle should immediately jump to 150 on the top scale and then go back to infinity. If it does not, the condenser is defective.

3. To doublecheck the condenser, run the same test again with the meter switched to 2.5 volts. You should get the same results.

4. To check the points, rotate the center switch on the meter to the R x 1 position and zero the needle. Connect the test wires to the points mounting bracket and the bracket where the electrical wires were mounted to the points assembly. The needle should read 0 (short circuit). Open the points. The needle should read infinity (open circuit). If both of these conditions are not met, replace the points.

NOTE: *If the low-tension (ignition) coil, points, and condenser test out OK,* *check the wires on the magneto backing plate. It is possible that one of them has been rubbed by the flywheel or crimped when the backing plate was mounted.*

Femsatronic Ignition

TESTING

Preliminary Checks

1. Set the multimeter to read resistance and connect the test leads to the spark plug cable and ground. The needle should swing from infinity toward the other end of the scale if the unit is in working order, as this indicates a closed circuit. The meter should read 3.5K ohms when it is set on the 100K ohm scale. If you fail to get these readings, proceed with the next step. If it reads correctly, go on to Step 3.

NOTE: *Make sure that the spark plug cap is securely connected to and making good contact with the spark plug wire.*

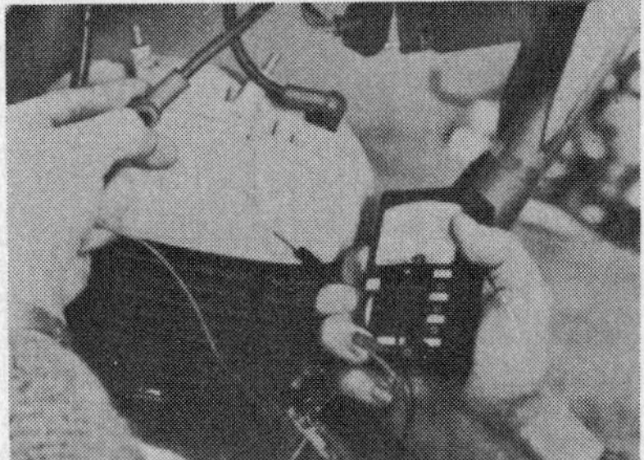

The flywheel has dragged on the coils and burned them out as a result of looseness

2. Connect the test leads to the spark plug wire and the metal body of the coil. If you now get a closed circuit reading, the ground is bad between the coil and the frame at the mounting point. If the circuit is still open, the coil unit must be replaced.

3. Check to make sure that there is a good connection between the plug-in clip and the three-pronged plug that connects the coil to the Femsatronic generator in the flywheel. The connections should be clean and show no signs of discoloration from arcing. If necessary, clean the prongs with emery paper.

4. Pull the rubber cover back from the female portion of the plug and check for broken wires or for any water or other foreign material that could cause a short circuit.

5. Remove the left side engine cover and check to see if there is any play in it. Looseness can mean that it is coming loose from the hub or that the main bearings are worn. In either case, weak or erratic firing can be the result.

Testing the Components

1. Check the condenser loading voltage by running the engine while a voltmeter with a peak to peak circuit (see the introduction to this chapter) is attached. Slide back the rubber covering from the female portion of the connector plug and check the voltage from the green wire to ground. (If there are two green wires, connect the test wire to both of them.) Start the engine and check the voltage. It must not be more than 400 volts or less than 300 at 5,000 or more rpm, or it will burn out the coil. The generator should put out at least 250 volts below 5,000 rpm. A reading lower than 300 volts at high rpm means that either the flywheel is de-magnetized or there is an open circuit in the generator coils. In either case, replace the generator feeder and/or flywheel. (The flywheel should lift one half of its weight if the magnets are in good shape.)

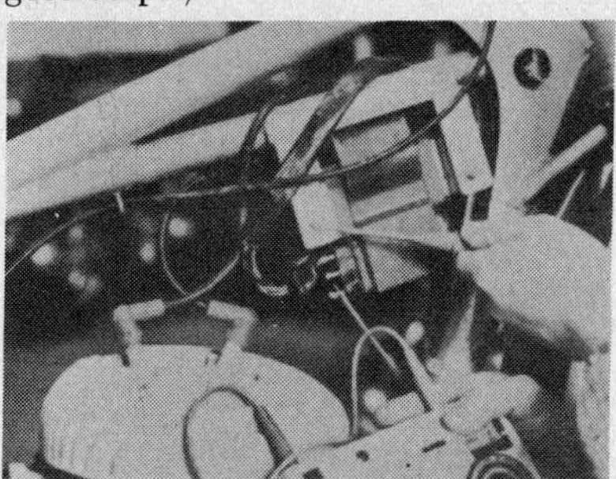

Checking condensor loading voltage

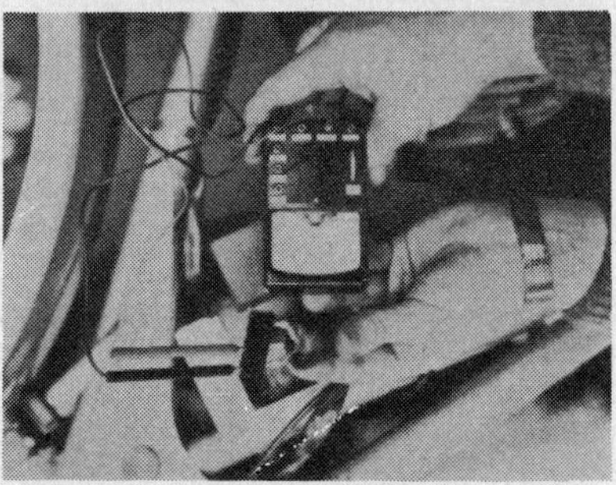

Checking continuity between two cables

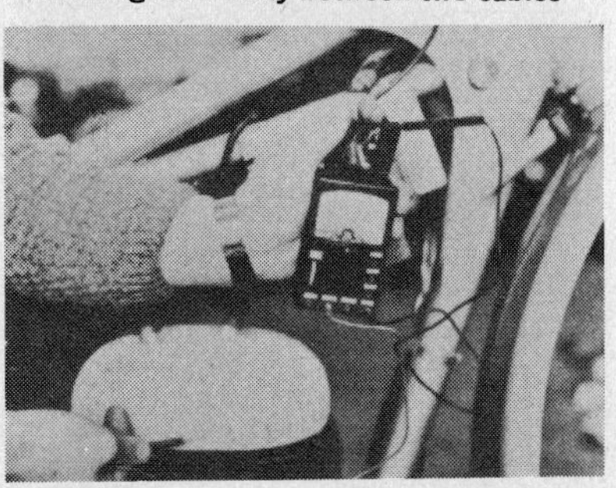

Checking continuity between a cable and ground

2. The generator should show at least 120 volts as the engine is kicked through. If it produces this voltage but will not spark, the coil is faulty. If it shows no voltage, the generator should be replaced.

Feeder Circuit Tests

If the engine will not run, the faulty component can be located without removing anything from the bike. Check the circuits with the meter set to read resistance; all tests will be made at the point where the generator wiring harness plugs into the coil (generator feeder). In the accompanying illustration the feeder on the right is typical of the unit used on bikes equipped with lights, while the feeder on the left has ignition coils. Refer to the chart to determine the correct feeder model for circuit testing.

GAC TYPE FEEDER

1. GAC6-1 feeder:
   a. Check continuity between the green cable and the green cable. The ohmeter should read about 870, plus or minus 60 ohms.
   b. Check continuity between the red cable and ground. The reading should be about 1 ohm.
2. GAC-3,5,6, and 7 feeders:
   a. The continuity between the two green cables will be 1,900, plus or minus 200 ohms.
   b. The continuity between the red cable and ground will be about 1.5 ohms.

GEA TYPE FEEDERS

1. Check the continuity between the green cable and ground. The meter should read 450, plus or minus 35 ohms.
2. Check continuity between the red and black cables. The reading should be about 0.35 ohms.

GEB TYPE FEEDERS

1. Check continuity between the green and yellow cables. The reading should be about 235, plus or minus 30 ohms.
2. Check the continuity between the red and black cables. The reading should be about 0.25 ohms.

GED TYPE FEEDERS

1. Check the continuity between the green cable and the green cable. The reading should be about 1,800, plus or minus 200 ohms.
2. Check continuity between the red cable and ground. The reading should be about 3 ohms.

Testing the Femsatronic Coil With the Engine Off

To check the coil units the wiring har-

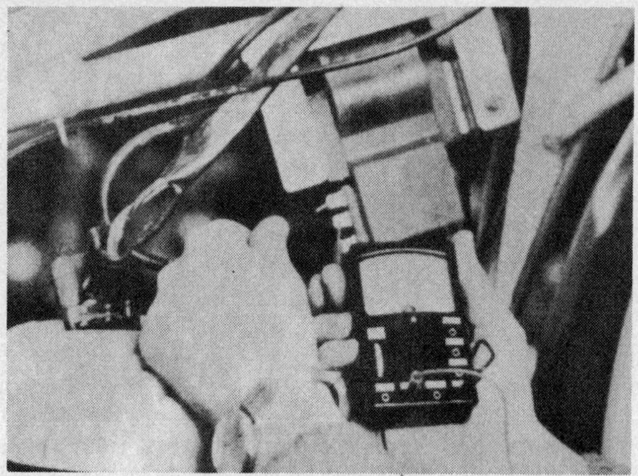

Checking ohm value between terminals two and three

Checking ohm value between terminal one and ground

ness must be unplugged from the coil. Be sure that the positive and negative probes are attached in the manner described below, as the diodes in the circuit are designed to pass electricity in one direction only.

The terminals are identified as follows: No. 1—the terminal furthest from the central one, No. 2—the central terminal, No. 3—the terminal closest to the central one.

If either coil or the generator fails the above tests, it must be replaced.

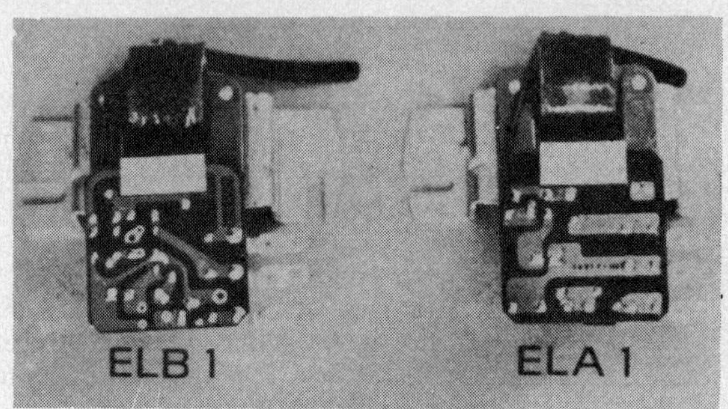

The two basic types of Femsatronic coils

FEMSATRONIC COIL TEST DATA

The ELA Type Coil

Positive Test Point on	Negative Test Point on	Set Ohmmeter on Scale Below ①	Correct Reading ①	Incorrect Reading ①
1	Ground	100K Ohms	Infinity	Less than infinity
Ground	1	100K Ohms	Infinity	Less than infinity
2	3	100K Ohms	Infinity	Less than infinity
3*	2	100K Ohms	40K Ohms	Less than infinity or less than 40K Ohms
High Tension Lead	Ground	10K Ohms	3.5K Ohms	Infinity or less than 3.5K Ohms

The ELB Type Coil

Positive Test Point on	Negative Test Point on	Set Ohmmeter on Scale Below ①	Correct Reading ①	Incorrect Reading ①
2 or 3	3 or 2	100K Ohms	Infinity	Less than infinity
2	Ground	100K Ohms	Infinity	Less than infinity
3	Ground	100K Ohms	Infinity	Less than infinity
Ground**	2	100 Ohms	Approx. 80	0 or infinity
Ground**	3	100 Ohms	Approx. 80	0 or infinity
1	Ground	100K Ohms	Approx. 40K	Infinity or 40K
Ground	1	100K Ohms	Infinity 3.5K	Infinity or 40K
High Tension	Ground	10K Ohms		Less than infinity or less than 3.5K

① K=1000
* Values may vary from 40K ohms due to other components included in the circuit.
** Check for continuity is satisfactory regardless of meter reading.

FEMSATRONIC TYPE IDENTIFICATION CHART

Models	Generator	Coil Unit
El Bandito		
Mk-I and Mk-II	GEA1-2	ELA2-4
Campera		
Mk-II	GAC6-5	ELB1-2
Lobito		
Mk-III 125 cc	GAC6-5	ELB1-2
Matador		
Mk-III	GAC6-7	ELB1-2
El Montadero		
Mk-II	GAC6-6	ELB2-7
Pursang		
Mk-III and Mk-IV	GEA1-2	ELA2-4
Sherpa S		
100	GEB1-3	ELA1-1
125, 175 and 200 Mk-II	GEA1-2	ELA1-1
TSS		
125	GEB1-1	ELA1-1
250	GEB1-2	ELA1-1
350	GEA1-2	ELA2-4

STREET MODEL IGNITION SYSTEMS

Magneto Ignition System

The Bultaco magneto systems are the same for racing and light-equipped models except that the stoplight has been included in the ignition system, and a kill switch is also part of the system. Refer to the racing model section for testing procedures.

Femsatronic Ignition System

All Femsatronic-equipped machines with lighting systems have the same ignition and circuitry as the Femsatronic type racing bikes. Refer to the racing model section for test procedures.

LIGHTING SYSTEM

Magneto Models

The Bultaco lighting system is fed by a lighting coil in the magneto, which operates in the same way that the ignition coil works.

If you are experiencing problems with bulbs burning out rapidly, it is recommended that you install a zener diode in the system. Zener diode kits are available at Bultaco dealerships. The diode will absorb the excessive voltage produced by the lighting coil and high rpm, and help to stabilize the lighting system. In addition, Bultaco dealers carry a sealed beam headlight kit and an improved type of tail light assembly that uses a heavy duty bulb.

IGNITION-LIGHTING CHART FOR BULTACO MACHINES EQUIPPED WITH LIGHTS

Model	Magneto Generator	Magneto Coil	Femsatronic Generator	Femsatronic Coil	Accessories
All Models up to 1965	VAF	320-002			Abril
Mercurio					
175 cc	VAR 41-11	320-002			Abril-Femsa
200 cc	VAR 41-11	320-002			Lucas-Femsa
El Tigre					
200 cc	VAR 41-11	320-002			Lucas-Femsa
Campera					
Mk-I	VAR 41-11	320-002			Abril-Femsa
Mk-II			GAC6-5	ELB1-2	Lucas
Matador					
Mk-I 200	VAR 41-11				Abril-Femsa
Mk-II-III	4920-001	320-002			Femsa-Lucas
Mk-III			CAC6-7	ELB1-2	Lucas
Metralla					
Mk-I 200	VAR 41-21	320-002			Abril-Femsa
Mk-II 200	2620-001	220-002			Femsa-Lucas
Mk-III			GAC6-5	ELB2-7	Lucas
Lobito					
Mk-I	VAJ 6-8	19.20-002			Femsa-Lucas
100 cc, 125 cc, Mk-II	VAJ 6-8	19.20-002			Lucas
Mk-III			GAC6-5	ELB1-2	Lucas
El Montadero					
Mk-I & Mk-II			GAC6-6	ELB2-7	Lucas
Sherpa T					
Mk-I	VAR 125-4	320-002			Femsa
Mk-II	VAR 41-9	320-002			Femsa
49 Series					
Mk-III	49.20-001	320-061			Femsa

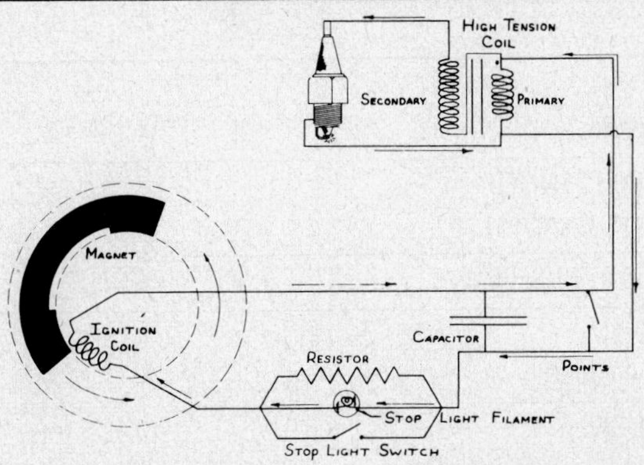

Wiring diagram for magneto ignition bikes equipped with lights

Femsatronic Models

The power supply for battery equipped models comes from the Femsatronic generator. This type of generator is easily identified from the earlier magneto type because it is totally encased in resin.

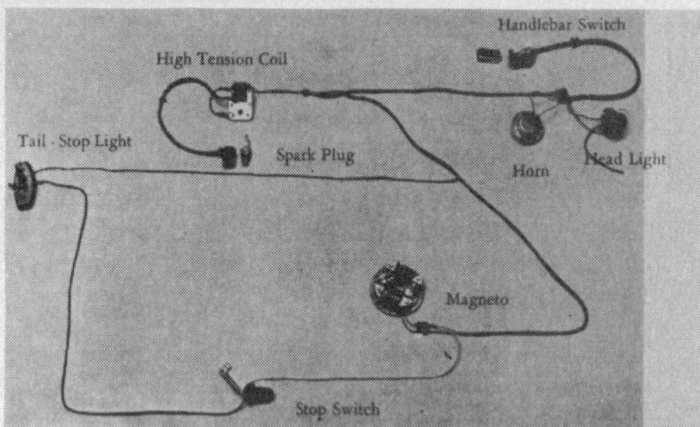

Wiring circuitry for Femsatronic ignition with lights

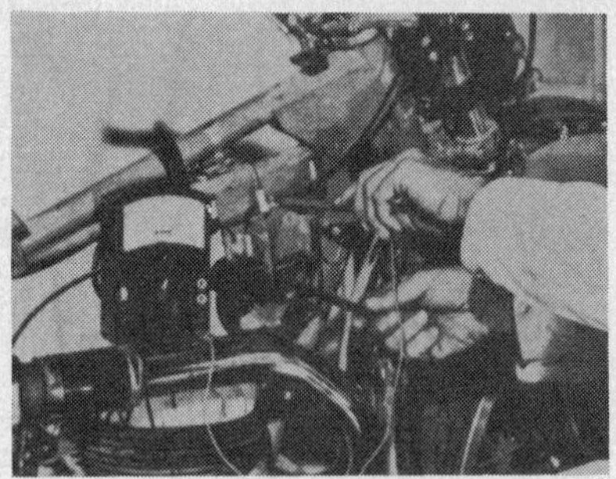
Testing the rectifier

CHECKING GENERATOR OUTPUT

Remove the four allen bolts from the timing side of the engine so that the wiring harness. Use a sharp probe to pierce the insulation on the blue wire, and connect a voltmeter to the blue wire and ground. Start the engine; the meter should read 18 or more volts AC. Perform the same test using the black wire. If improper voltage is obtained, the generator must be replaced.

CHECKING THE RECTIFIER

The rectifier is the unit located on the frame, under the fuel tank. It functions to convert the AC produced by the generator to DC.

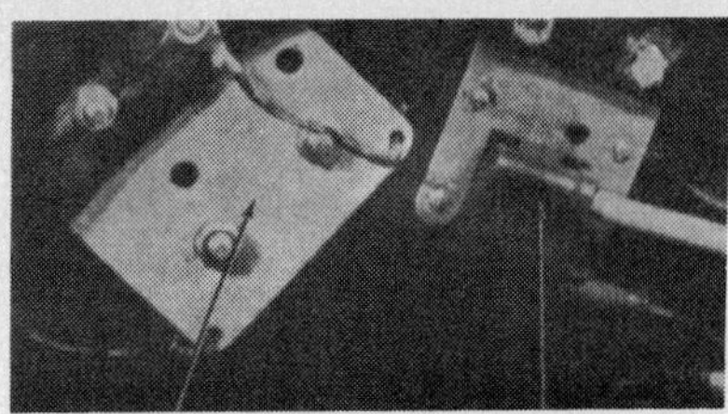
Zener diode assembly (left) and high tension coil (right)

The rectifier has four plugs; refer to the accompanying illustration when making the following tests.

1. Set the multimeter on R x 1 ohms. Place the negative probe on terminal 1 and the positive probe on terminal 4. You should get a continuity reading. Reverse the probes and test from number 4 to number 1. You should read continuity again. If the meter reads infinity in either case, the diode has failed and the rectifier unit must be replaced.

2. Place the negative probe on terminal 2 and the positive probe on terminal 3. You should get a continuity reading. Reverse the probes as above. The meter needle should not move. If it shows continuity the second diode is faulty and the rectifier must be replaced.

MAGNETO IGNITION TROUBLESHOOTING

	Probable Cause										
	Bad Spark Plug Replace	Coil Wire Burn-Back	Poor Grounding or Shorted	Primary Coil Shorted	Secondary Coil Shorted	Breaker Points Worn or Improperly Gapped	Condenser Shorted	Bad Main Bearings Causing Point Gap Wander	Tail-Stoplight System Open	Carburetion Problem	Engine Out of Time
PLUG CHECK Shows no Spark	X	X	X	X	X	X	X		X		
CYCLE CAN BE PUSH STARTED Has 100 lb Min. Compression		X	X			X			X		
ENGINE MIS-FIRES AT HIGH RPM	X	X	X			X		X		X	X
COIL OUTPUT OK Section but no Spark			X	X		X	X				
SECONDARY COIL OK But no Spark			X	X							
BREAKER POINT BADLY PITTED Engine Mis-fires						X	X	X			
ENGINE MIS-FIRES AT ALL RPM'S							X	X		X	X
ENGINE LOADS UP										X	
ENGINE OVER HEATS	X									X	X

FEMSATRONIC IGNITION TROUBLESHOOTING

Probable Cause

	Bad Spark Plug Replace	Coil Wire has Open Circuit	Poor Grounding or Shorted Wiring	Start Windings Burned Out	Generator Coil Burned Out	Spark Unit Secondary Coil Burned Out	Kill Button System Grounded	Flywheel Dragging on Coils	Generator-Feeder Coil Shorted	Flywheel Magnets Weak	Secondary Coil Shorted Spark Coil	Kill Button Ignition Switch Malfunction
PLUG CHECK Shows no Spark	X	X	X	X	X	X	X	X	X	X		X
CYCLE WILL PUSH START (Engine has Minimum 100 lbs. Compression)	X	X	X	X					X	X		
ENGINE RUNS WITH ERRACTIC FIRING (Engine will kick start)	X	X	X					X	X		X	X
PEAK METER TEST SHOWS PROPER VOLTS		X	X	X							X	
PEAK METER TEST SHOWS IMPROPER VOLTS			X					X	X	X		
CYCLE HARD TO START Spark Weak		X	X	X			X	X	X	X	X	
CYCLE HARD TO START Spark Strong	Check Compression for 100 lbs Minimum Check Carburetion											
ENGINE LOADS UP	Check Carburetion Check for Carbon Restriction in Exhaust System											
ENGINE OVER-HEATS	Check Engine Timing Check Carburetion								X			

MAGNETO MK-III AND FEMSATRONIC MK-IV ACCESSORY TROUBLESHOOTING

Probable Cause

	Battery Malfunction	Broken or Shorted Wiring	Bulbs Burned Out	Rectifier Malfunction	Dimmer Switch Malfunction	Generator Output Too High or Too Low	Bad Brake Light Switch Para	Bad Contacts in Bulb Socket	Horn Needs Replacement	Ignition Switch Malfunction	Current Stability Malfunction
NO LIGHTS FUNCTION Engine Off (Battery Equipped Models Only)	X	X	X							X	
NO LIGHTS FUNCTION Engine on or off		X	X	X		X				X	

MAGNETO MK-III AND FEMSATRONIC MK-IV ACCESSORY TROUBLESHOOTING

	Probable Cause										
	Battery Malfunction	Broken or Shorted Wiring	Bulbs Burned Out	Rectifier Malfunction	Dimmer Switch Malfunction	Generator Output Too High or Too Low	Bad Brake Light Switch Para	Bad Contacts in Bulb Socket	Horn Needs Replacement	Ignition Switch Malfunction	Current Stability Malfunction
NO HEADLIGHT Others OK		X	X		X			X			
NO TAILLIGHT Others OK		X	X					X			
HEADLIGHT WORKS ON ONE BEAM ONLY		X	X		X			X			
NO HIGH BEAM INDICATOR LIGHT		X	X								
BATTERY WILL NOT STAY CHARGED	X			X		X					
BATTERY GOES DRY VERY RAPIDLY						X					
NO HORN WITH CHARGED BATTERY		X							X		
NO BRAKE LIGHTS		X	X				X	X			
BRAKE LIGHTS WON'T GO OFF		X					X				
LIGHT BULBS BURN OUT FREQUENTLY						X					X

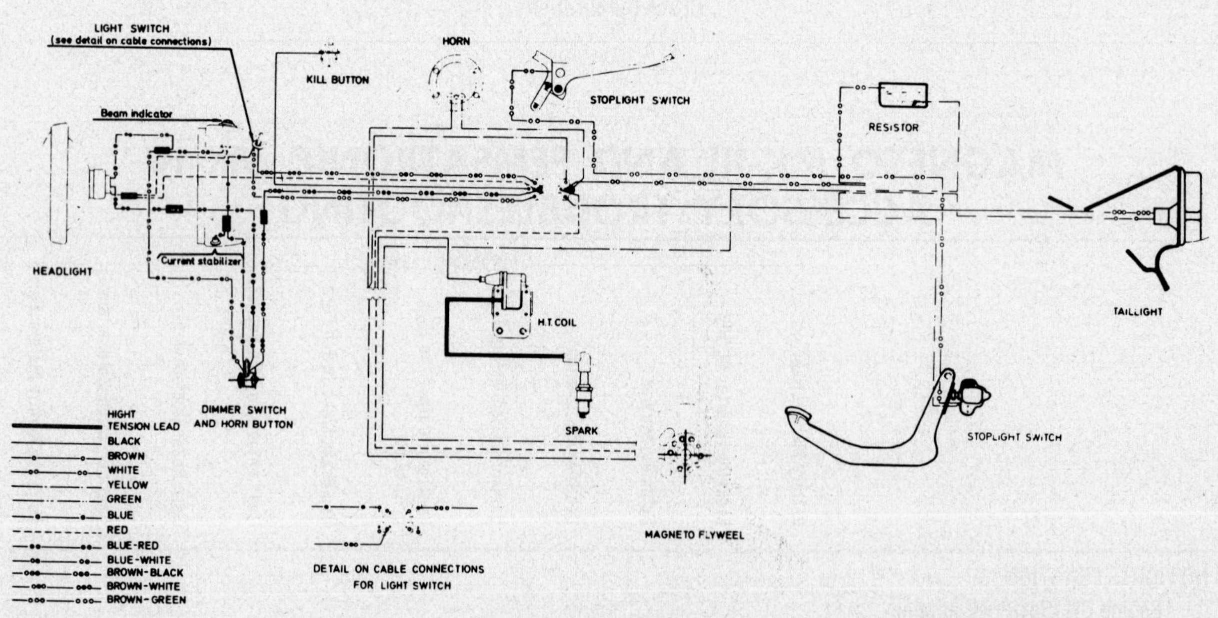

Magneto ignition models

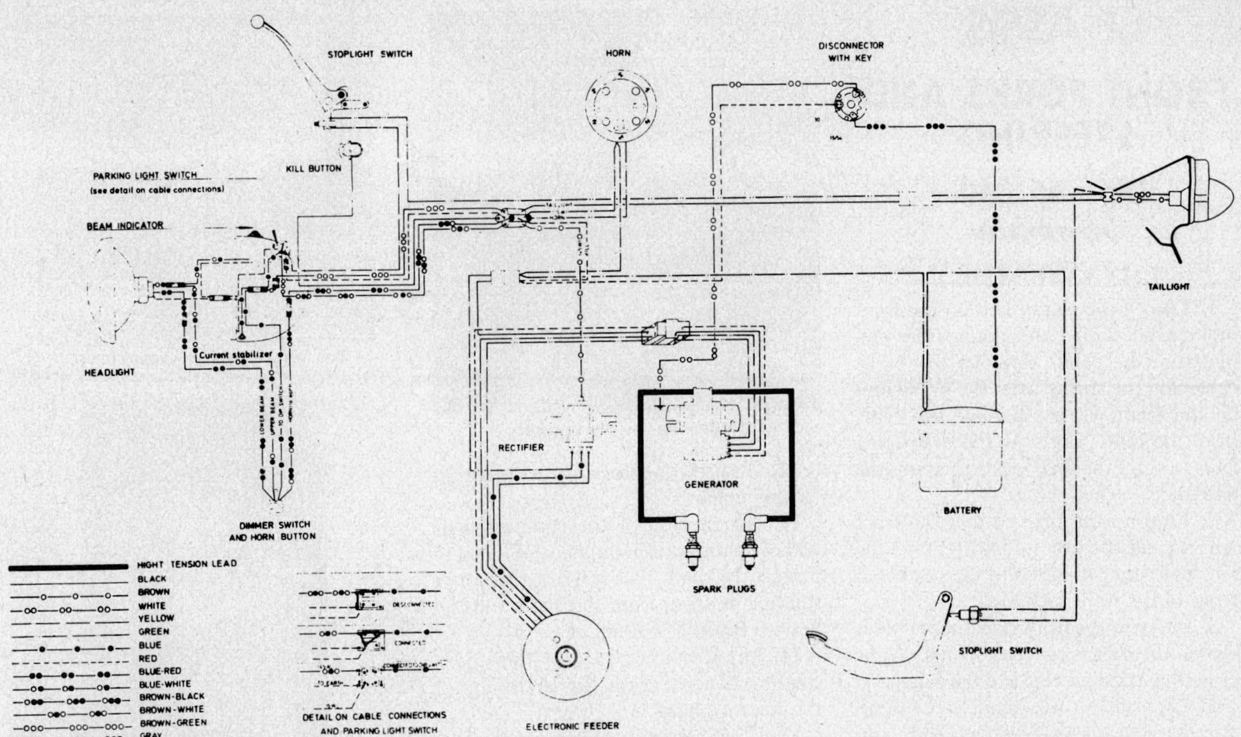

Femsatronic ignition models

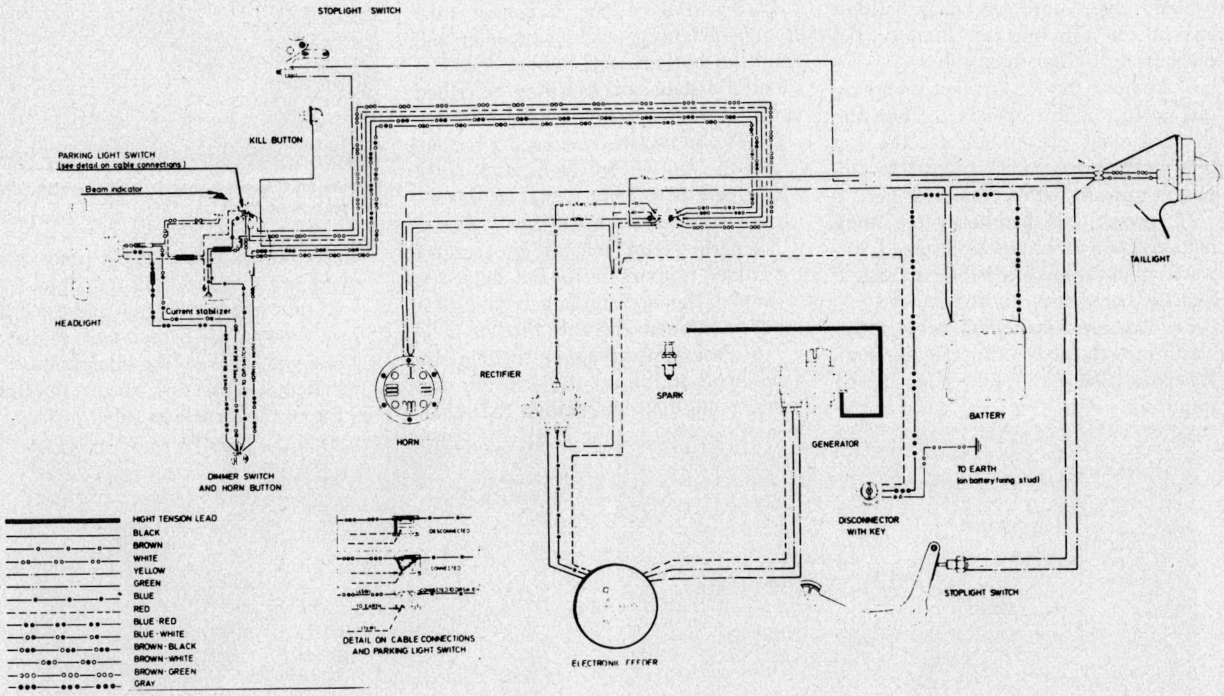

Femsatronic ignition models

CHASSIS

FRONT FORKS AND STEERING

1965-66 250cc Scrambler

DISASSEMBLY

1. Loosen the clamp bolt on the front brake cable nipple and remove the nipple from the cable. Remove the brake cable and the spring from the brake arm on the front wheel. Remove the cable from the forks. Unscrew the drain plug from each of the fork legs and pump the oil out.

2. Prop up the bike so that the front wheel is off the ground and remove the two bolts that mount the brake anchor strap to the right fork leg.

3. Unscrew the front axle nut and then loosen the two axle clamp nuts. Withdraw the axle and remove the wheel.

4. Take off the two fender mounting clamps from the slider legs. Slide the front fender down the forks to remove it.

5.Using a 28mm socket, rotate each stanchion plug five turns to loosen it.

6. On early models with steel top and bottom brackets, loosen the two clamp bolts on each bracket.

7. On late models with a forged alloy top bracket, loosen the four clamp bolts on each bracket.

8. Loosen the stanchion tubes in the top bracket by hitting each plug with a rubber mallet until the plug bottoms against the top bracket. Remove the plugs from the stanchion tubes.

9. Remove the top bracket mounting nut on top of the bracket. Loosen the steering shaft clamp bolt on the top bracket. Remove the top bracket by tapping it upward with a rubber mallet.

10. Loosen the handlebar mounting bolts and pull each stanchion tube downward out of the top bracket far enough so that the handlebar can be removed.

11. Tap each stanchion tube downward through the steering damper stop. When the tube is free of the stop it can be removed.

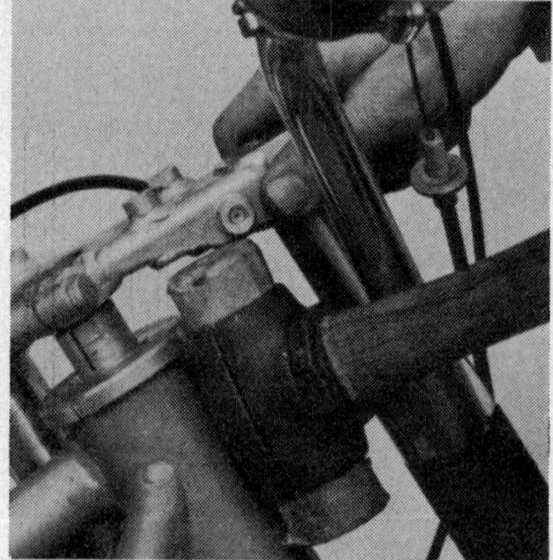

Removing the top bracket

12. Unscrew the steering head bearing locking collar.

13. Hit the top of the steering shaft with a hammer, using a piece of wood to protect the shaft. This will free the upper steering bearing from the shaft and the bottom bracket will fall off.

14. Lift the inner race of the upper steering head bearing out of the top of the steering head.

15. If it is necessary to remove the bottom steering bearing, clamp the bottom bracket upside down in a vise and hammer alternately on the two protruding portions of the dust shield with a hammer and drift.

16. If you wish to remove the outer races of the steering bearings, insert a drift from the opposite end of the steering head and drive them out squarely. Take care in this; if they come out at an angle you can distort the steering head.

17. To remove the stanchion tube from its slider leg, unscrew the allen bolt from the bottom of the slider leg. The slider and stanchion can then be pulled apart.

NOTE: *Sometimes the components inside the leg will rotate with the allen bolt, and it will not loosen. If this occurs, perform the following:*

a. Drill a ⅛ in. hole into the damper cylinder support inside the slider leg through the oil drain hole, taking care not to chew up the hole threads.

b. Pack some grease on the end of a thin drift and insert the drift into the drain plug hole to remove the metal chips. Repeat this as many times as is necessary to remove all the chips.

c. Insert the drift again and use it to hold the damper components in place while you unscrew the allen bolt.

18. Remove the fork spring through the top of the stanchion tube.

The outer bearing races remain

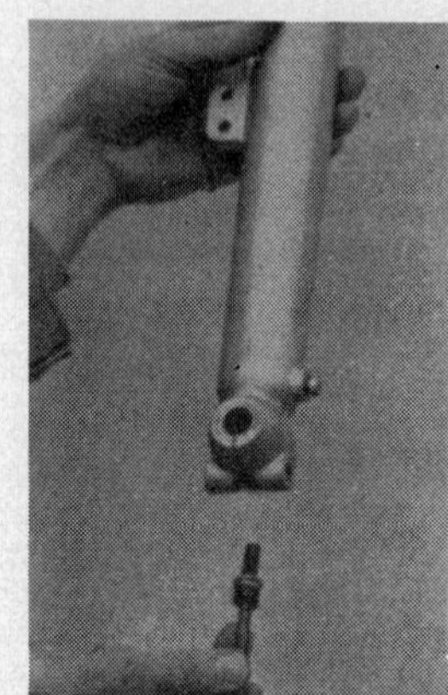

Removing the allen bolt from the bottom of the fork leg

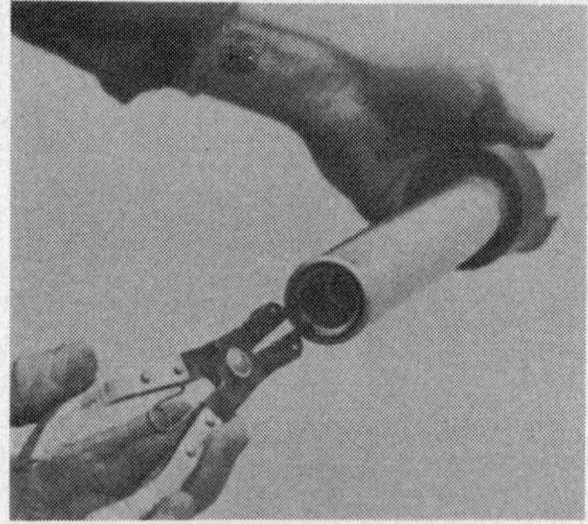

Removing the snap-ring from the bottom of the stanchion tube

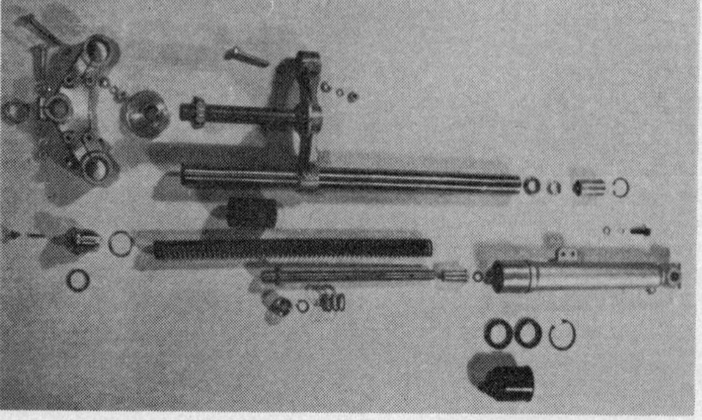

The front forks and steering head disassembled

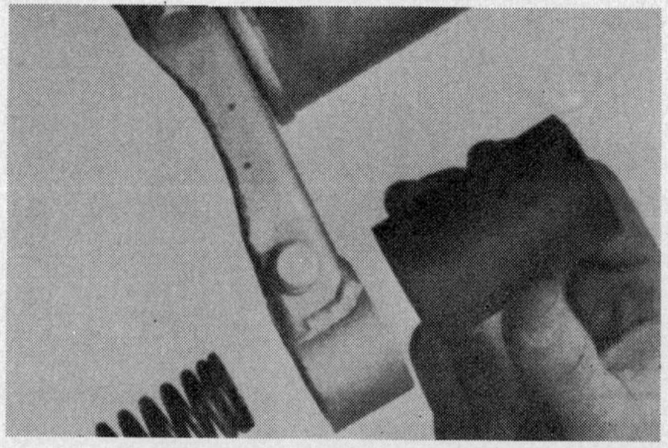

Removing the stanchion tube

19. Turn the stanchion tube upside down and the valve tube assembly will fall out. If the damper cylinder support sticks in the bottom of the tube, screw the allen bolt back into the bottom of the tube a few turns and tap it with a hammer to free the support.

20. Remove the snap-ring from the bottom of the stanchion tube.

21. Insert a squared off broomstick into the top of the stanchion tube and push out the remaining damper components.

22. Remove the rubber dust guard and the snap ring from the top of the slider leg. Pry out the oil seals with a blunt screwdriver, taking care not to gouge the soft walls of the slider leg.

INSPECTION

1. Measure the length of the fork springs. If they are less than 17 11/16 in. long, or are unequal in length, they should be replaced.

2. If you have found that the springs were bottoming regularly, make up two 1 in. spacers and fit them between the top of each spring and the bottom of the stanchion plug.

3. If the distributor ring spring washer on the valve tube has broken or lost its tension, replace it.

4. Examine the threads of the allen bolt and the threads in the bottom of the fork leg where the allen bolts screw in. If worn, replace the bolt and the valve tube.

5. Each time the forks are disassembled, the following components should be replaced:

 a. Oil seals (4);
 b. O-ring (2);
 c. Dust guard (2);
 d. Oil drain plug washer (2);
 e. Stanchion plug O-ring (2);
 f. 30mm internal snap-ring (2);
 g. 16mm external snap-ring (2);
 h. Rubber damper cylinder support washer (2).

6. To compensate for normal wear, the following components should be replaced once a year:

 a. Distributor ring assembly (2);
 b. Damper piston (2);
 c. Valve washer (2);
 d. Valve support cylinder (2).

REASSEMBLY

1. Thoroughly clean all steering head and damper components before reassembly.

2. Install the upper and lower outer steering bearing races in the steering head. Drive them in squarely, using a piece of pipe with an outside diameter slightly smaller than the inside diameter of the steering head. Check often to make sure that the races are going in straight.

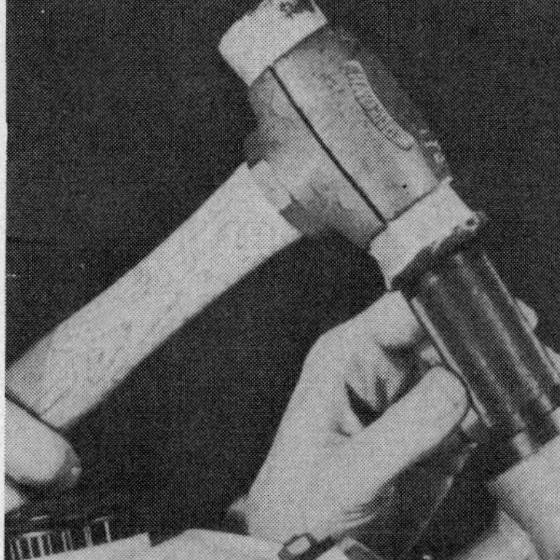

Installing the steering head bearing races

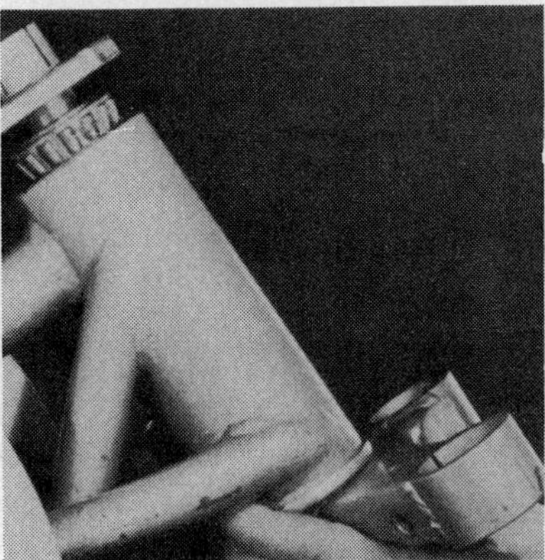

Installing the locking collar

3. Install the inner race of the lower steering bearing on the steering shaft, with the smaller end up, using a suitably sized pipe. Before driving the race into position, fit the bottom dust cover to the shaft with the dished edge facing up and the three drain holes facing the rear of the bottom bracket.

4. Grease the inner races of both bearings with wheel bearing grease.

5. Insert the steering shaft in the steering head from the bottom.

6. Screw the locking collar onto the steering shaft and tighten it until the inner race of the upper bearing is forced into its outer race. When the collar has been tightened enough, you will need to give the bottom bracket a gentle push to rotate it from lock to lock. If you feel any roughness or binding while moving the bracket, there is probably dirt in the bearings and they will have to be removed and cleaned.

7. After adjusting the locking collar, rap the top of the steering shaft with a hammer (protecting it with a piece of wood). If the effort required to move the bottom bracket from side to side remains the same as it was before, the bearings are fully seated and properly adjusted. If the bottom bracket has loosened, readjust the locking collar again.

8. Install the top bracket on the steering shaft.

9. Screw the top nut on the steering shaft down finger-tight.

10. Coat the inner surfaces of the steering damper stops with light oil or liquid detergent so they will slide down the stanchion tubes easily. Lay the stops and the handlebars near the front end of the bike.

11. Insert a stanchion tube from the bottom of the bottom bracket. Fit a rubber stop to the top of the tube and work it down in the tube.

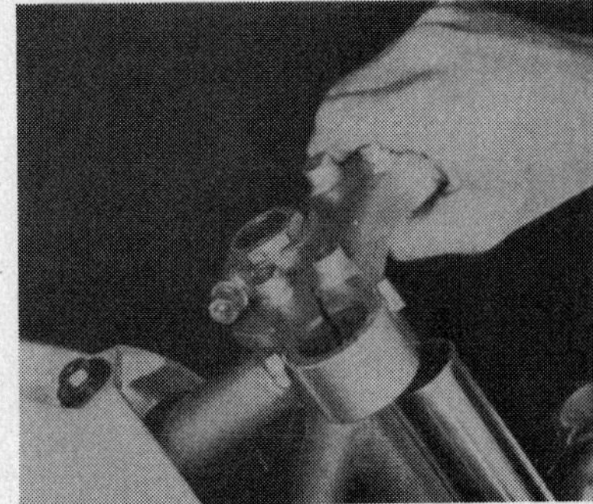

Inserting a stanchion tube

12. Fit a handlebar to the stanchion tube. Seat the tube in the top bracket by bumping the bottom of the tube lightly with a rubber mallet. Install the other tube in the same manner.

13. Tighten the stanchion tube clamp bolts on the top bracket enough to hold the tube in place while the damper components are installed.

14. Fit the damping piston on the end of the valve tube away from the flange. The recessed end of the piston should face away from the flange. Butt the piston against the flange on the valve tube.

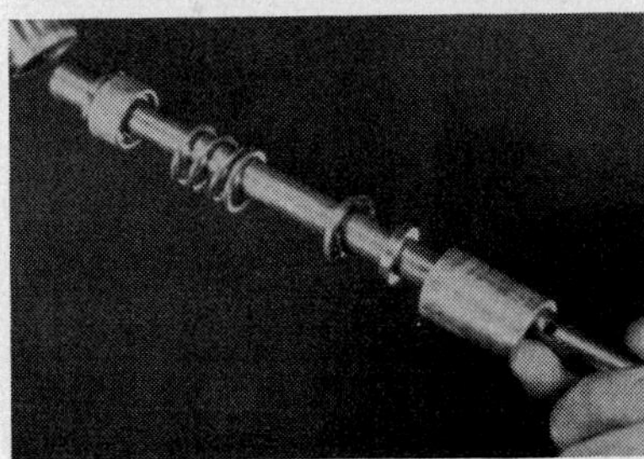

Installing the damping components

15. Spread the 16mm snap ring just enough so that it can be slid along the valve tube into its groove next to the piston.

16. Put the valve tube retaining spring on the valve tube and butt the spring against the piston.

17. Put the distributor ring assembly on the valve tube with the spring washer facing away from the valve tube retaining spring. Butt the distributor ring assembly against the spring.

18. Put the valve spacer on the valve tube. Butt the spacer against the spring washer.

19. Put the valve support cylinder on the valve tube so that the washer fits into the counterbored end of the cylinder. Assemble the other valve tube assembly in the same manner.

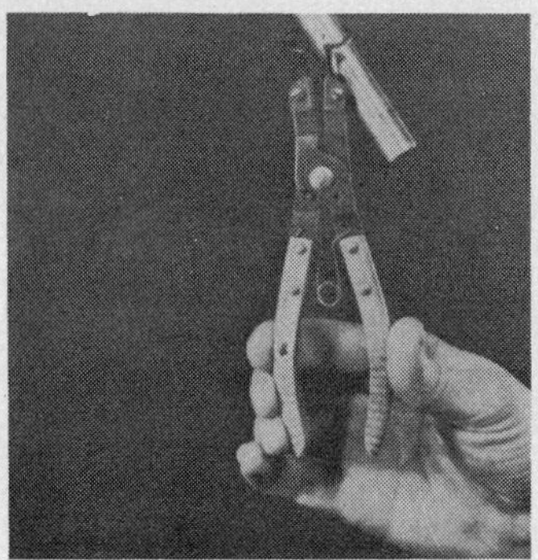

Installing the snap-ring

20. Insert the flanged end of the valve tube into the bottom end of a stanchion tube, while holding the damper components in place.

21. Push the valve tube up into the stanchion tube. The distributor ring will seat against a machined lip near the bottom of the stanchion tube, and the valve support cylinder will come to rest against the distributor ring. Install the 30mm snap ring in its groove in the bottom of the tube. The ring should be installed with the sharp edge facing the bottom of the stanchion tube; make sure that the ring is seated perfectly in its groove. Fit the damping components to the other stanchion tube in the same manner.

22. Install the spring into the top of each stanchion tube. Fit the washer to each stanchion plug and install the plugs finger-tight in the top of the tubes.

23. Smear the oil seal with grease and install it, open end down, into the slider leg. Install the seal squarely. Fit the other seal in the same manner, until it butts up against the first seal. Install the snap ring in the mouth of the leg.

24. Install the two seals in the other slider leg in the same manner.

25. Fit the dust guards to the slider legs.

26. Pry out the old O-ring and install a new one in the damper cylinder support.

27. Fit the damper cylinder support to the bottom end of the valve tube, which is sticking out of the bottom end of the stanchion tube. If the support won't stay in position, smear grease on it and reinstall it.

28. Thoroughly coat the dust guard and seals with light oil. Fit the slider leg to the stanchion tube and move it up until the damper cylinder support reaches the bottom of the inside of the leg.

29. To bottom the support in the leg; you may need to guide the nipple of the support into the anchor screw hole of the leg by fitting a thin drift into the hole and centering the nipple.

30. Hold the slider leg in position and install the flat washer, lockwasher, and allen bolt in the anchor hole. Tighten the bolt securely.

31. Install the other slider leg on its stanchion tube in the same manner.

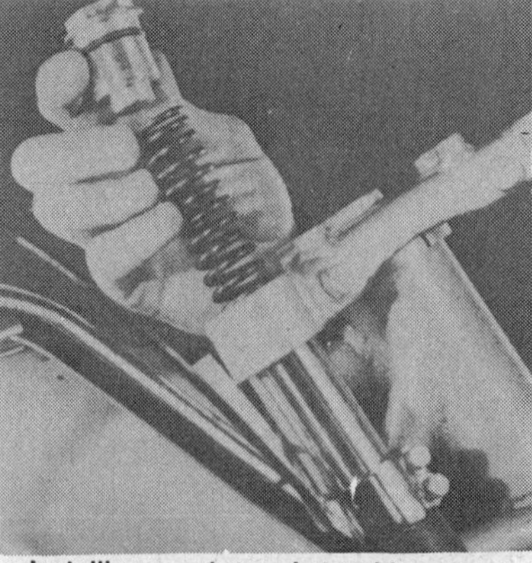

Installing a spring and stanchion plug

32. Install the fork oil drain plugs, using new washers.

33. Fit the rubber fender tab guards to the slider legs and slide the fender up the legs into position. Tighten the fender clamps finger-tight.

34. Position the handlebars and tighten the clamps securely. The clamp bolts must be tightened alternately, a little at a time, in order to secure each handlebar effectively.

35. Check to see that the flanged spacers are still pressed into the wheel bearing oil seals in the front wheel. Position the wheel between the forks and insert the axle from the left side. Fit the flat washer and lockwasher, and run the nut up finger-tight.

36. Align the two mounting holes in the brake anchor strap with the holes in the lug on the right slider leg. Install and tighten the brake anchor nuts and bolts.

37. Straddle the front wheel, holding it between your knees, and work the handlebars to align the wheel with the forks.

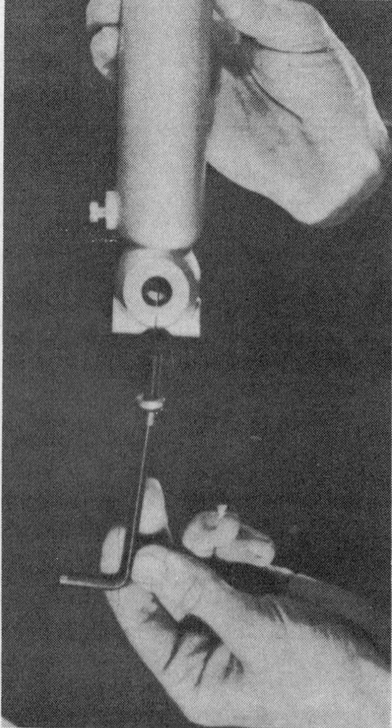

Installing the allen bolt

38. Thread the inner brake cable through the outer cable stop on the right slider leg. Retract the cable adjuster on the front brake handlebar lever into its mount.

39. Install the coil spring on the inner brake cable. Fit the cable through the slot in the brake arm and install the cable nipple on the inner cable.

40. Using pliers, force the nipple up the cable to lift the brake arm until the brake doesn't quite drag when you spin the front wheel, then tighten the nipple clamp bolt.

41. Remove the stanchion plugs and pour 160cc of SAE 20 or 30W oil into each stanchion tube. Install the washers on the plugs and tighten them to 100 ft lbs.

42. On early models with steel top brackets, tighten the top and bottom clamp bolts to 15 ft lbs.

43. On late models with alloy top brackets, tighten the top and bottom clamp bolts to 6 ft lbs.

44. Torque the steering shaft top nut to 35 ft lbs.

45. Torque the steering shaft clamp bolt on the top bracket to 15 ft lbs.

46. Snug down, but do not fully tighten, the two front axle clamp nuts. Tighten the front axle nut until it is compressing its lockwasher, then torque the two clamp nuts to 60 ft lbs.

47. Finally, tighten the front fender mounting clamps.

NOTE: *It is very important to follow the sequence of tightening and observe the torque specifications given above. Proper fork operation depends upon this.*

1966-67 Matador and 1966-67 Sherpa S

DISASSEMBLY, INSPECTION, AND REASSEMBLY

Refer to the previous section on the 250cc Scrambler. Procedures are the same, except that:

1. When reassembling the stanchion tube and slider leg assemblies, insert a stanchion tube from the bottom of the bottom bracket. Slide the tube up through the bracket and fit a handlebar to the top of the tube. Seat the tube in the top bracket by tapping it with a rubber mallet.

2. Be sure to observe this final tightening sequence:

    a. Stanchion plugs—50 ft lbs
    b. Top bracket fixing nut—tight
    c. Steering shaft clamp bolt on top bracket—15 ft lbs
    d. Front axle nuts—30 ft lbs
    e. Front axle clamp bolts—6 ft lbs
    f. Stanchion tube clamp bolts on bottom bracket—15 ft lbs

1964-67 Mercurio, 1964-67 Metralla, 1965 Sherpa S, and 1964-65 Matador

DISASSEMBLY

1. With the bike off its stand, sit on the tank to compress the forks. Unscrew the two stanchion plugs from the stanchion tubes.

2. Loosen the locknut at the bottom of the stanchion plug.

Unscrewing a stanchion plug

Loosening the locknut at the bottom of the plug

3. Prop the bike so that the front wheel is off the ground.

4. Loosen the front brake cable nipple and remove it. Disconnect the brake cable and its spring from the brake arm, and remove the cable from the front forks.

5. On the Metralla and Matador, unscrew the two bolts securing the brake anchor strap to the front forks.

6. Remove the front axle nut.

7. On the Metralla and Matador, loosen the four axle clamp bolts.

8. Withdraw the front axle and remove the front wheel.

9. Take off the bolts and nuts and remove the front fender. Loosen the clamps and work the dust guards off the slider legs (Matador).

10. Press upward on a slider leg and remove the stanchion plug and washer. Pull the leg down off its stanchion tube

Removing the stanchion plug and washer

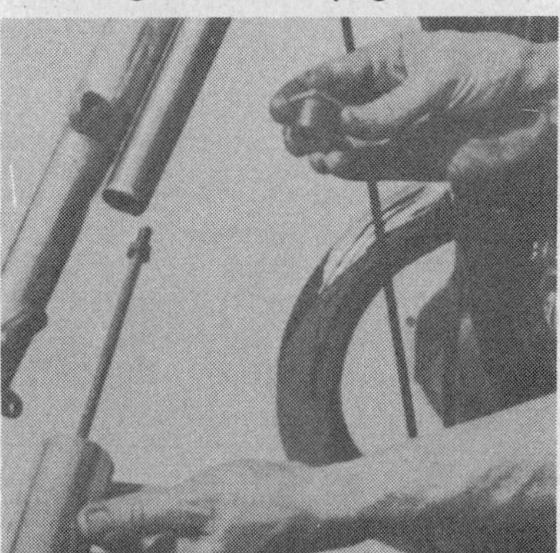

Removing a slider leg

and remove it. The fork spring will fall off the tube. This completes the partial disassembly necessary for changing the fork oil.

11. Remove the allen bolt from the bottom of the slider leg. If the damper rod assembly rotates with the bolt, preventing the bolt from loosening, slide a deep 16mm socket down the damper rod and fit it to the nut down inside the leg. Hold the socket and unscrew the allen bolt.

12. To disassemble the damper rod assembly remove the nut from the top of the cylinder, and remove the rod from the cylinder.

13. Wash the piston at the bottom of the damper rod in solvent and examine it for wear. If it is worn badly, replace the entire damper rod assembly.

14. It is very important that the piston is tightly attached to the damper rod. If it is loose, back off the locknut and tighten the piston until the ball bearing, visible through the bottom of the piston, is seated tightly against the rod. Then, loosen the piston ⅛ in. and tighten the locknut.

15. To remove the oil seal, it is necessary to make a special tool. Procure a length of 1 in I.D. water pipe, with a tapered thread on one end. Squeeze the threaded end in a vise until it is oval, 36mm across the widest part. Thread the pipe into the oil seal in the slider leg, and clamp the other end in a vise. Insert a bar in the axle hole in the slider leg and yank the bar to pull the leg free of the oil seal.

16. Loosen the two stanchion tube clamp bolts in the bottom bracket. On the Matador, it is also necessary to loosen the two mounting bolts on each handlebar and to unscrew the two allen bolts from the headlight brackets and remove the headlight.

17. Turn each stanchion plug ¾ of the way down its tube. Hit the plug with a hammer (protecting the plug with a piece of wood) until it bottoms on the top bracket. Catch the stanchion tube as it falls away. (It may be necessary to pry open the clamps on the bottom bracket to free the tubes.)

18. Take out the three screws and remove the dust guard. If necessary, pry out the rubber suspension stop from the top of the guard.

Tapping a stanchion tube out

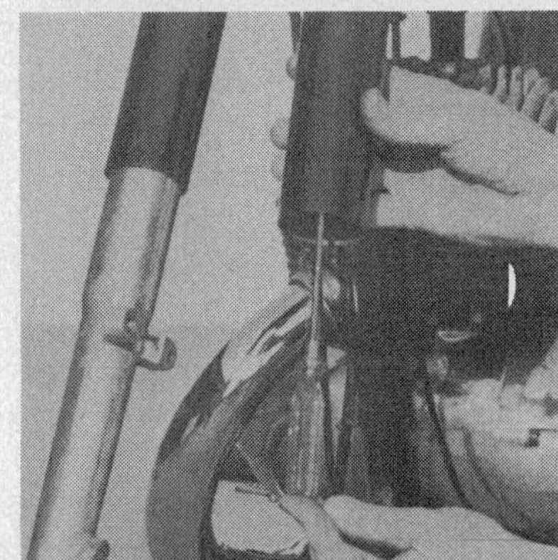

Take out the three screws to remove the dust guard

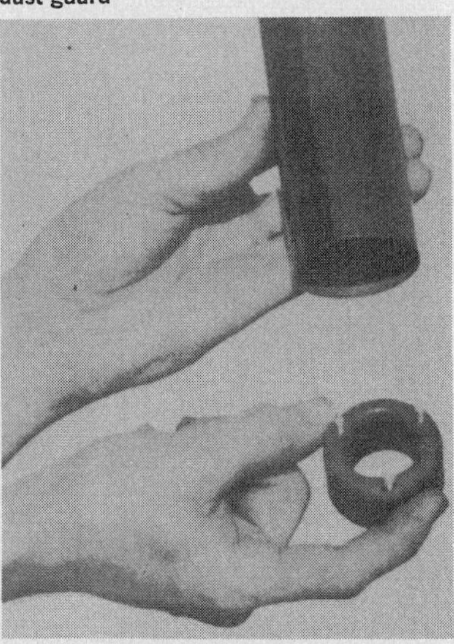

Dust guard and rubber suspension stop

19. Unscrew the steering damper knob and lift it out. Remove the spacer from the top bracket. Remove the two washers and the steering damper anchor from beneath the bottom bracket. On the Metralla and Mercurio, remove the handlebar and let it hang by the cables.

20. Unscrew and remove the top bracket securing nut.

21. Loosen the steering shaft clamp bolt on the top bracket. Tap the bracket up and off of the steering head.

22. Loosen the steering bearing locking collar and unscrew it from the shaft.

Unscrewing the top nut

Removing the top bracket

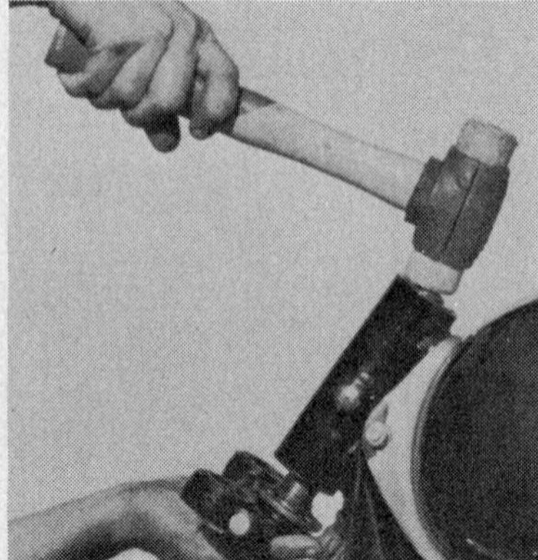

Tapping out the steering shaft

23. Remove the headlight assembly from the Metralla and Mercurio at this point.

24. Spread a cloth beneath the steering head to catch the bearings, and rap the top of the steering shaft with a rubber mallet to drive the bottom bracket out. Catch it as it falls.

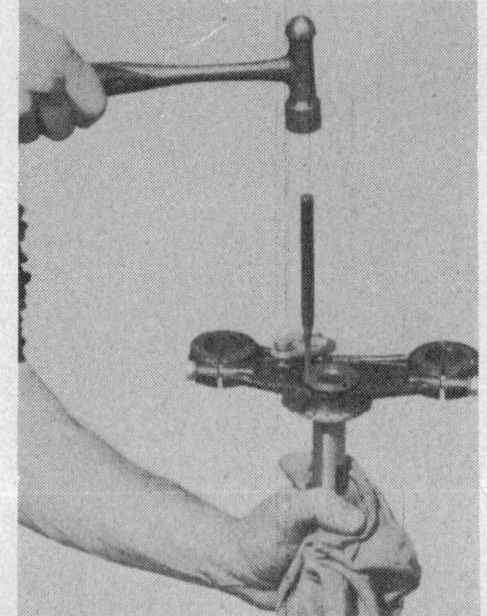

Drifting out the inner race of the lower bearing

25. Lift off the inner race of the upper bearing. Remove the ball bearings from the outer race of the upper bearing, and the inner race of the lower bearing. Wash the bearing components in solvent and dry them. There should be 22 balls per bearing. If any of the races or balls show pitting or wear, the entire bearing assembly must be replaced.

26. If it is necessary to remove the inner race of the lower steering bearing, insert a drift in one of the holes in the steering shaft, as shown, and tap the race out squarely, moving the drift back and forth between the two holes. If you need to remove one of the outer races, drift it evenly out of the steering head.

INSPECTION

1. Measure the fork springs. If one is shorter than the other, or they are less than 7 9/16 in. long, replace them.

2. Replace any damper components that are damaged or worn.

3. Each time the forks are disassembled, the following components should be replaced:

   a. Rubber dust guards (Matador only);
   b. Oil seals;
   c. O-rings;
   d. 8 mm lockwashers;
   e. Brake cable rubber grommet;
   f. 6 mm lockwashers.

4. Replace the following parts at yearly intervals:

   a. Dust guard clamps (Matador);
   b. Front suspension stops;
   c. Damper rod assemblies;
   d. Fork springs;
   e. Suspension stop springs and washers;
   f. The 6 mm nuts;
   g. Steering head bearing assemblies;
   h. Fiber washers in the steering head;
   i. Handlebar bolts.

REASSEMBLY

1. Install the outer steering head bearing races in the steering head using an appropriately sized pipe to drive them in. Take care to install them squarely.

2. Install the inner race of the lower bearing in the bottom bracket. Place the bracket on a bench so that the shaft is pointing up, and fit the race with its dished face up and the three drain holes facing the rear of the bracket (the clamp bolts for the stanchion tubes are at the rear of the bracket).

3. Place the inner race of the lower steering bearing on the steering shaft with the small end of the race facing up.

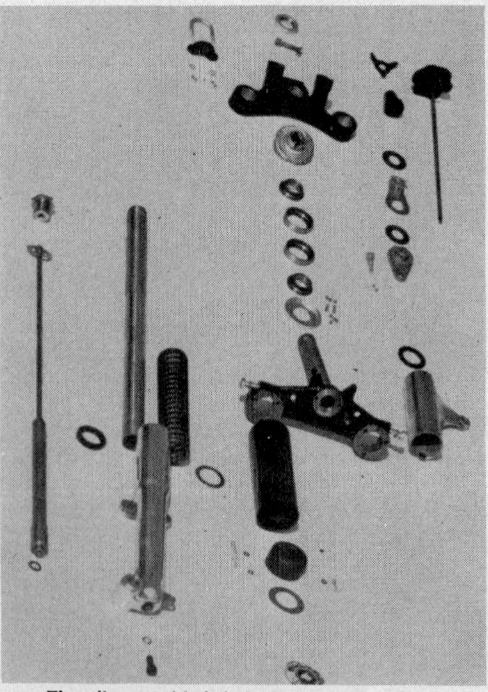

The disassembled fork and steering head components

Drive the inner race and the dust cover down the shaft until they butt against the bracket.

4. Cover the outer race of the upper bearing in the steering head with a layer of wheel bearing grease. Put 22 balls in the race and cover them with another layer of grease. Place the inner race on the balls.

5. Coat the inner race of the lower bearing on the bottom bracket with a layer of grease and place 22 balls on the race. Cover the balls with another layer of grease.

6. Work the steering shaft up into the steering head as far as it will go, holding down the inner race of the upper bearing to prevent the balls from coming loose.

7. Start the locking collar on the steering shaft and tighten it until the balls on the lower inner race are tight against the outer race. As the collar is tightened, guide the bottom bracket so that none of balls in the lower bearing are shaken out.

8. Continue tightening the locking collar until the bottom bracket, when centered, will just swing away to either side under its own weight.

9. On the Mercurio, position the headlight assembly on the bottom bracket and place a rubber gasket on top of each headlight bracket. On the Metralla, fit a headlight bracket gasket to the counterbored bottom of each of the two bracket spacers, and position the two spacers on the bottom bracket. Install the headlight on top of the spacers, and place a gasket on top of each bracket.

10. Place the top bracket on the steering shaft.

11. Mount the dust guards (or supports) on the bottom of the bottom bracket. Insert a rubber suspension stop into a dust guard, with the flat end of the stop going in first. Align the mounting holes in the stop with those in the guard and position the three screws. (Use a thread locking compound on the screws to keep them from loosening.)

12. Position the guard beneath the bottom bracket and mount the three screws to the bottom bracket. Do not overtighten the screws.

13. Fit one end of a rubber boot to the short metal dust guard (Matador). Tighten the clamp, and mount the other boot in the same manner. Position the handlebars on the bracket so that they can be mounted on the stanchion tubes before the tubes are inserted in the top bracket.

14. Check the cables and electrical wires to make sure that they will be routed correctly after the tubes are installed.

15. Start the top bracket securing nut on the steering shaft; run it down finger-tight.

16. Insert a stanchion tube from the bottom of the bottom bracket.

17. On the Metralla and Mercurio, slide the stanchion tube up through the headlight bracket and into the top bracket. On the Matador, fit the handlebar to the stanchion tube and slide the tube up into the top bracket.

18. Tap the bottom of the tube to start it into its taper in the top bracket.

19. Tighten the tube clamp bolts on the bottom bracket only enough to hold them in place while the damper components are installed.

20. Install the damper oil seals in the slider legs with the open end of the seal facing in. Coat the seal with oil before inserting it; drive it down so that it seats against its flange.

21. Insert the damper rod, piston end first, into the damper cylinder. Tighten the damper cylinder nut into the top of the damper cylinder.

22. Install a new O-ring on the bottom of the damper rod.

NOTE: *If the damper rod assembly is not machined at the bottom to accept an O-ring, it is recommended that this early type (6 mm diameter) assembly be replaced with the later type (8 mm) assembly. The later type is much stronger.*

23. Install the allen screw in the bottom of the slider leg and tighten it firmly.

24. Pour 85cc of oil into each slider leg. Use SAE 20 or 30W oil.

25. Work the damper rod up and down until the oil has been sucked down into the damper cylinder.

26. Fit the slider leg to the stanchion tube; the fork spring goes outside and the damper rod goes inside the tube.

27. Pull up the damper rod and run the stanchion plug locknut down to the bottom of the threads on the damper rod. Pull the rod over to the side of the tube and hook the stanchion plug locknut on the top edge of the top bracket.

28. Screw the stanchion plug to the damper rod and run it down until it bottoms. Lift the stanchion plug so that its locknut no longer bears against the top bracket, and tighten the nut against the bottom of the plug.

29. Screw the plug into the stanchion tube until the plug bottoms against the top bracket.

30. Assemble the other slider leg in the same manner after adding the required amount of oil.

31. Work the bottom of the rubber fork boots down over the slider legs on the Matador and tighten the clamps.

32. Tighten the top bracket securing nut securely (75 ft lbs).

33. Mount and secure the handlebars.

34. Install the front fender.

35. Check to see that the flanged spacers are still pressed into the oil seals, and position the front wheel between the forks.

36. Insert the front axle from the left side and start the axle nut on it.

37. Install and tighten the two front brake anchor straps on the Metralla and Matador.

38. Install the front brake cable, connecting it to the brake lever and the brake arm. Retract the handlebar lever cable adjuster into its mount. Fit the cable nipple to the bottom end of the inner cable. Using pliers, pull the nipple up the cable so that it moves the brake arm up; when you reach the point where the front brake does not quite drag when you spin the wheel, tighten the cable nipple clamp bolt.

39. Tighten the front axle nut finger-tight. Straddle the front wheel with your knees pressed against it and work the handlebars to align the wheel with the forks.

40. Tighten the stanchion nuts securely (50 ft lbs).

41. Torque the steering shaft clamp bolt at the rear of the top bracket to 6 ft lbs.

42. Tap the top and bottom of the bottom bracket on both sides of the stanchion tube clamp bolts using a hammer and piece of wood. It is important that this is done at this point to avoid placing strain on the top bracket.

43. Torque the two stanchion tube clamp bolts on the bottom bracket to 15 ft lbs.

44. Tighten the front axle nut until it has just compressed its lockwasher, then torque the four axle clamp nuts to 6 ft lbs. (Metralla and Matador).

45. Torque the front axle nut to 30 ft lbs.

46. Reassemble the steering damper components in the following sequence:

a. Place the plastic spacer on the top bracket.

b. Swing the damper adjuster away from the bottom of the steering shaft.

c. Fit the damper anchor (bent prongs down) to the gusset on the frame downtube. Press the circular portion of the anchor up against the fiber washer on the bottom bracket. Position the other fiber washer against the bottom of the anchor.

d. Swing the adjuster into alignment beneath the fiber washer, and insert the damper into its spacer and down through the steering head. Screw the damper into the adjuster.

1966-67 Campera and 1963-64 Sherpa S

DISASSEMBLY

1. Unscrew the stanchion plugs from the tubes (Campera).

2. Remove the allen bolt from the top of each stanchion plug (Sherpa S), and unscrew the plugs from the tubes.

Loosening the stanchion plug locknut (Campera)

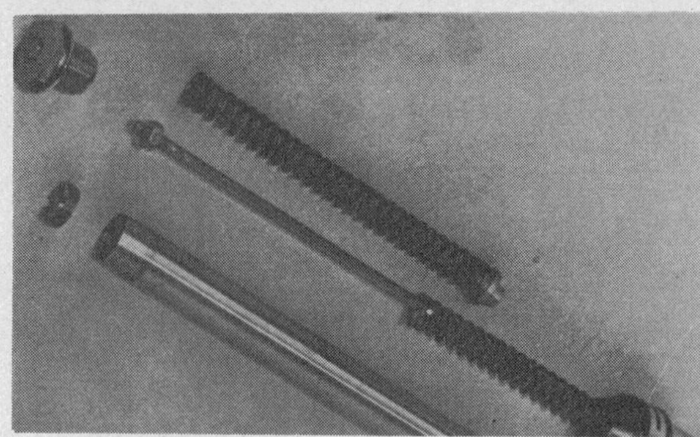
Fork springs and adjustable tensioners (Campera)

3. Sit on the gas tank to compress the forks (Campera) and loosen the locknut on the bottom of the stanchion plugs.

4. Remove the front fender and take off the front brake anchor strap nut.

5. Remove the nipple from the brake end of the front brake cable. Remove the cable from the front forks.

6. Remove the lower clamp from the rubber boots (Sherpa S) and push the boots up off the slider legs.

7. Prop the bike so that the front wheel is free and remove the front axle nut.

8. Withdraw the axle and remove the wheel.

9. On the Campera, press up on the slider leg and unscrew the stanchion plug from the damper rod.

10. Pull the slider legs off the stanchion tubes.

11. Hold the fork spring in a vise (Sherpa S). Unscrew the spring carrier using pliers, and push the spring down and away from the carrier locknut. Put a wrench on the locknut and remove the carrier with pliers.

12. Remove the fork springs and carriers from the slider legs (Campera).

13. Turn the slider leg upside down and pump the damper rod to expel the oil.

14. Unscrew the allen bolt at the bottom of the slider leg. If the damper rod assembly rotates with the bolt, preventing it from loosening, slide a 16 mm deep socket down the damper rod and fit it to the nut. Hold the socket and unscrew the bolt.

15. Remove the damper rod assembly from the leg. Remove and discard the O-ring in the groove in the cylinder.

16. Remove and discard the fiber washer from the damper cylinder (Sherpa S).

17. Take out the two O-rings that are supposed to be on the outside of the damper cylinder. They may be inside the slider leg.

18. Unscrew the damper cylinder nut and remove the cylinder from the rod (Campera).

19. Clamp the round damper cylinder nut in a vise, grab the bottom of the cylinder with vise-grips, and unscrew it from the nut (Sherpa S).

The two fork springs and carrier (Campera)

Removing the damper cylinder from the damper rod (Campera)

20. Wash the piston at the bottom of the damper rod with solvent and dry it. Check it for wear. If it is worn badly, the damper rod assembly should be replaced.

NOTE: *(Sherpa S)—It is very important that the piston be tightly attached to the damper rod. If it is loose, back off the damper piston locknut and tighten the piston on the rod until the ball, visible through the bottom of the piston, is seated tightly against the end of the rod. Back the piston off ⅛ in. down the threads of the rod and tighten the locknut against it. (Don't clamp the piston in a vise or mar its friction surface.)*

NOTE: *(Campera)—It is very important that the piston be tightly attached to the damper rod. If it is loose, back off the damper piston locknut and tighten the piston on the damper rod until the ball, visible through the bottom of the piston, is seated tightly by the end of the rod. Leave it that way; the ball is not supposed to operate as a check valve in the Campera. Tighten the locknut against the piston.*

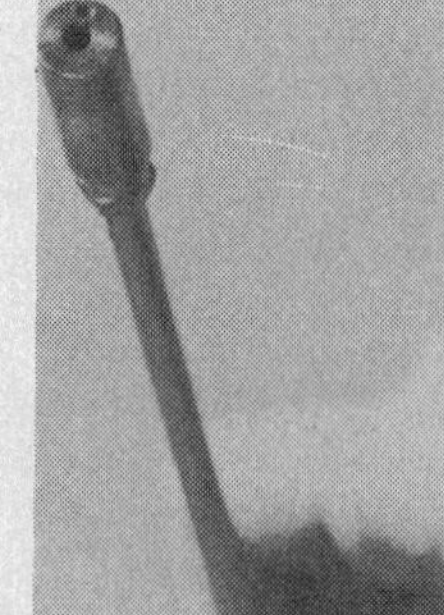
Piston and damper rod (Campera)

21. To remove the oil seal from a slider leg on the Campera, first loosen and remove the dust guard from the mouth of the slider leg.

22. To remove an oil seal from the slider leg of either model, it is necessary to make up a special tool. Refer to the "Disassembly" section for the Mercurio and Metralla, Step 15. The procedure is the same for the Campera and Sherpa S.

23. If you wish to disassemble the steering head, refer to the previous section on the Mercurio and Metralla. The Campera and Sherpa S use the same assembly.

INSPECTION

1. The following components should be replaced each time the forks are disassembled:

Campera—damper cylinder O-rings, dust guards, stanchion plug O-rings, suspension stop O-rings, clamp bolt star washers, and slider leg oil seals.

Sherpa S—slider leg oil seals, damper cylinder O-rings, and clamp bolt star washers.

2. The following components should be replaced once a year:

Campera—top fork springs, damper rod assemblies, dust guard clamps, and bottom fork springs.

Sherpa S—damper cylinder assemblies, rubber suspension stops, fork springs, fork boots, førk clamps, suspension stop screws and washers, and the axle clamp nuts and bolts.

3. The Campera stanchion tubes are fitted with adjustable fork spring tensioners. These tensioners allow you to compensate for weakened springs or varying riding conditions. Normally, the tensioners should be positioned 35 mm below the top edge of the stanchion tubes.

4. If you have found, when the forks are rebounding (Campera), that oil escapes from the small hole in the stanchion plug cap screw (or you can hear air escaping), reseat the ball in the plug as follows:

a. Remove the cap screw.

b. Remove the spring and ball, and clean the ball with solvent. Replace the ball in the stanchion plug.

c. Insert a thin drift so that it rests against the ball, and tap it lightly several times to reseat the ball on its valve seat.

d. Reinstall the spring and cap screw.

Stanchion plug ball and spring

REASSEMBLY

1. If you took apart the steering head, reassemble it as described in the Metralla/Mercurio section.

2. Install new oil seals in the slider legs, with the open side facing in, after the seals have been coated with oil. Drive each seal onto its flange in the leg.

3. Fit the rubber dust guard to the mouth of each slider leg and tighten the clamp.

4. Campera—Insert the damper rod, piston end first, into the damper cylinder. Be sure that the piston spring is located between the damper cylinder nut and the piston on the damper rod. Screw the cylinder nut tightly into the damper cylinder; if necessary, hold the bottom of the cylinder with vise-grips.

5. Sherpa S—Insert the damper rod into the damper cylinder, piston end first. Tighten the damper cylinder nut as described above for the Campera.

6. Install a new O-ring in the groove at the bottom of the damper cylinder.

7. Install the two O-rings on the lower part of the damper cylinder, beneath the holes drilled in the face of the boss (Campera).

8. Install a new fiber washer on the bottom of the damper cylinder (Sherpa S).

9. Insert the damper rod assembly into the slider leg and install the allen bolt in the bottom of the leg.

10. Pour 85cc of SAE 20 or 30W oil into each slider leg. Work the damper rod up and down until the oil has been sucked down into the cylinder and the unit is working satisfactorily.

11. Put the fork spring on the damper rod and screw the spring on the top of the damper cylinder (Sherpa S).

12. Connect the two fork springs to their carrier and fit them to the damper rod (Campera).

13. Fit the slider leg to the bottom of the stanchion tube and work the slider leg up.

14. Campera—Pull the damper rod up and hold it with a pair of pliers. Fit the locknut to the damper rod and screw it down to the bottom of the threads. Put the stanchion plug washer on the rod and then install the plug, turning it down until it bottoms. Hold the stanchion plug and tighten the locknut up against it. Gently release the pliers and screw the plug into the tube until it bottoms.

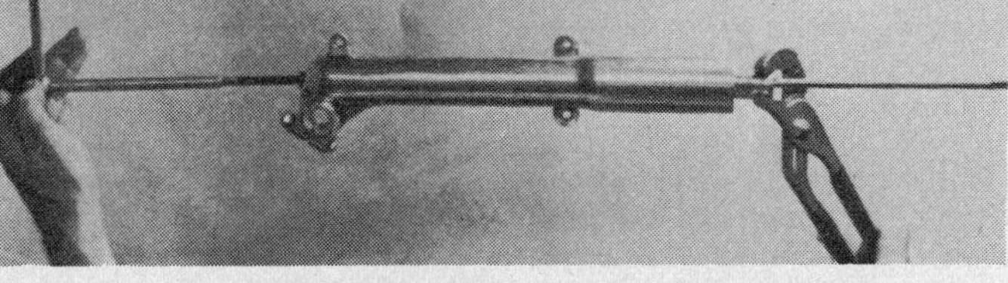

Installing the allen bolt in the slider leg

15. Sherpa S—Pull up the damper rod and hold it with pliers. Screw the spring carrier to the damper rod and run the plug down until it bottoms. Tighten the locknut against the bottom of the spring carrier. Release the pliers and hold the spring so that the slider leg won't fall. Hold the leg down slightly and insert the stanchion plug into the tube. Tighten the plug and push the slider leg back up so that the spring carrier is held against the plug. Insert the allen bolt and lockwasher into the plug and tighten the bolt securely.

16. Pull the bottom of the boot down over the slider leg and tighten the clamp (Sherpa S).

17. If you disassembled the steering head, turn back to the Metralla/Mercurio section and complete the assembly of the front end under the "Reassembly" heading, steps 32-45. If the steering head was not disassembled, continue with this section.

18. Install the front fender (the shorter length faces the rear).

19. Check to see that the flanged spacers are still in place in the front wheel oil seals. Align the wheel with the forks and insert the axle from the left side. Install and tighten the axle nut until it just begins to compress its lockwasher.

20. Position the brake anchor plate and the right fender brace against the lug on the right slider leg. Install and tighten the two fender bolts and nuts, and tighten the anchor plate nut on the brake plate.

21. Connect the brake cable to the brake arm and handlebar lever. Fit the nipple to the inner brake cable and pull the nipple up the cable so that it lifts the brake arm until the brake does not quite drag when you spin the front wheel. Tighten the nipple clamp bolt.

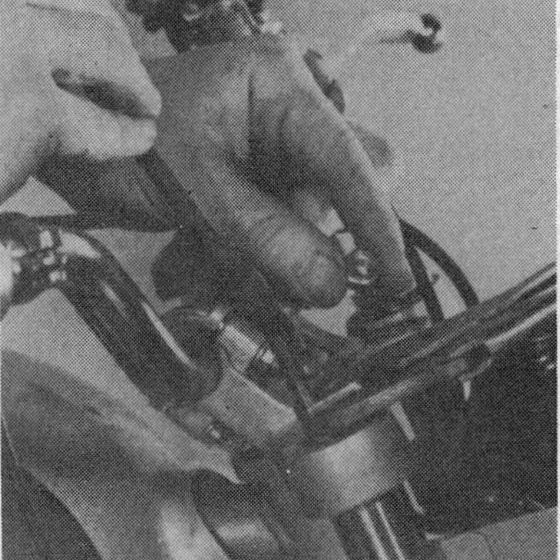

Installing the locknut on the damper rod (Campera)

22. Align the front wheel so that it is parallel with the forks.

23. Tighten the four axle clamp nuts to 6 ft lbs (Campera).

24. Torque the axle nut to 30 ft lbs.

25. Tighten the stanchion plugs securely (50 ft lbs).

26. Rap the top and bottom of the bottom steering bracket on the side of each stanchion tube clamp bolt, using a hammer and piece of wood. Torque the two stanchion clamp bolts to 15 ft lbs.

Stanchion plug wrench (Sherpa S)

Lobito

DISASSEMBLY, INSPECTION, AND REASSEMBLY

The Lobito forks are similar in design to the forks on the 1965-66 250 Scrambler. Refer to that section for fork repair procedures. If it is necessary to strip the steering head, refer to the Mercurio/-Metralla section, as these models use the same type of steering head bearings as the Lobito. Perform the following checks on the fork components after disassembly:

1. Check the top bracket for cracks. If you find any, the bracket must be replaced.
2. Measure the fork springs. Minimum spring length is 5 in. for the bottom spring, 7 ¾ in. for the top spring.
3. Each time the forks are disassembled, these components should be replaced: oil seals, damper cylinder O-rings, rubber boots, oil drain plug washers, stanchion plug O-rings, and all snap-rings.
4. Replace these components at yearly intervals: distributor ring assemblies, damper pistons, valve washers, and valve support cylinders.
5. Front fork seal leaks on Lobito models Mk I through Mk III may be rectified in the following manner:
    a. Replace the old seals with stock items in which the seal springs have been removed and replaced with a rubber O-ring about 1 ⅛ in. Inside Diameter and 3/32 in. thick.
    b. Grease the seals well before installation.
    c. Check and clean the ball check valves in the stanchion plugs (if fitted).

Topping out of the forks on 1972 models (indicated by a clanking noise when the front wheel leaves the ground) may be remedied by increasing the amount of oil in the fork legs. This may be increased to about 195cc of oil in each leg.

Brake Service

FRONT BRAKE INSPECTION

Remove the front wheel and pull the brake panel off the drum. Examine the drum for scoring and excessive wear. Normally, the drum will not become scored unless the brake lining has been worn completely away. If necessary, replace the drum.

Measure the thinnest part of both brake linings. When any part of the lining has worn to less than 0.080 in. (2 mm), both shoe assemblies should be replaced. If any of the brake shoe return springs are stretched, replace them also. Lightly grease the shoe cam and pivots upon reassembly.

REAR BRAKE INSPECTION

The rear brake shoes should be replaced when the brake operating lever moves over-center as the brake is applied. The brake shoes can be replaced after the rear wheel has been removed. Refer to the preceding section for additional information.

ADJUSTMENT

Front and rear brake adjustment is covered in the "Tune-Up and Maintenance" section.

Brake squeal from the Matador Mk IV rear unit can be corrected by slipping a section of rubber tubing 30 mm long and with an 18 mm Outside Diameter and 9 mm Inside Diameter over the brake return spring. The tubing must touch the brake shoe cam.

Rear Suspension

SHOCK ABSORBER AND SPRING REPLACEMENT

The spring/shock absorber unit can be removed after the upper and lower mounting bolts have been taken out. To remove the spring, compress it slightly by hand and remove the retainers. To check the effectiveness of the shock, compress and extend the unit by hand. More resistance should be encountered on the extension stroke if the shock is operating correctly. Replace it if it is leaking or if damping is unsatisfactory.

Swing Arm Service

DISASSEMBLY

1. Remove the muffler (if applicable).
2. Remove the rear wheel.
3. Take off the shock absorber units.
4. Remove the swing arm pivot nut and withdraw the pivot shaft. The swing arm can now be removed from the frame.

INSPECTION

Check the swing arm carefully for cracks and distortion. It is very important that the swing arm is aligned properly and in perfect condition. It is also very important that the pivot shaft and bushings are not worn or damaged. Replace the bushings as necessary; replace the shaft if it is bent or damaged in any other way.

ASSEMBLY

Installation is in reverse order of removal. Observe the following points:

1. Liberally grease the pivot shaft before installing.
2. Lubricate the swing arm pivot at the grease fittings after it is assembled, and make sure that no more than 0.02 in. (0.5 mm) of free-play exists at the pivot. The swing arm pivot bolts should be torqued to 75 ft lbs.

CHASSIS TORQUE SPECIFICATIONS (1972 MODELS)

	ft lbs
Front Forks	
Stanchion Plugs	100
Axle Clamp Bolts	6
Axle Nut	30
Top Bracket Fixing Nut	30
Top Bracket steering shaft clamp	15
Bottom Bracket stanchion tube clamp	15
Rear Suspension	
Swing Arm Pivot Bolts	75
Rear Axle Nut	30
Sprocket Bolts	20

INDEX HARLEY-DAVIDSON SINGLES

MODEL IDENTIFICATION

The M-50, shown here, was introduced in 1965 and is powered by a 50cc two-stroke engine. In 1966 the M-50S, a sport version with a more traditional gas tank configuration, was added to the line.

Shown here is the Rapido, a 125cc trail machine, which was first introduced in 1969. It is the present day version of the Model 125 which, in 1947, started off the entire Harley-Davidson two-stroke line.

In 1967 the M-50 and M-50S models were boosted to 65cc and became known as the M-65 and M-65S. The M-65 is very similar in appearance to the M-50; the sport model pictured here and known as the Leggero, looks very much like the M-50S.

This is the Model 165 (ST), which was first introduced in 1953, the forerunner of the present day Pacer model which appeared in 1960.

The Baja 100, a 100cc two-stroke trail bike, was first offered in 1971 and comes as shown here, ready to race.

In 1966 the Bobcat, a 175cc two-stroke, was introduced, but its popularity was short-lived as it was dropped from the line the following year. What is interesting about this model is that its tank, seat base, and rear fender are all made of Cycolack, a flexible plastic material.

Pictured here is the 250cc Sprint H which first appeared in 1963 to replace the Sprint C, the original four-stroke single of the present line. There is also a Sprint SS version which is a trail bike and features an upswept exhaust pipe.

Here is the Sprint SX, a 350cc competition bike based on the 350cc Sprint SS which first came out in 1969.

MODEL COVERAGE

50 cc	M-50, M-50S
65 cc	M-65, M-65S (Leggero)
100 cc	MSR (Baja)
125 cc	B (Hummer), ML (M-125), MLS (Rapido)
165 cc	ST (Mod. 165), STU (Mod. 165), BTF (Ranger), BT (Super-10), BTU (Pacer)
175 cc	BT (Pacer), BTH (Scat), BTH (Bobcat)
250 cc	C (Sprint), H (Sprint), SS (Sprint)
350 cc	SS (Sprint), SX (Sprint)

GENERAL SPECIFICATIONS—M MODELS

	Model Year	M	MS	ML and MLS	MSR	MC
DIMENSIONS (in.)						
Wheel Base	1965-66	44.1	44.1	—	—	—
	1967-68	44.4	44.8	44.6	—	—
	1969-71	—	44.8	47.2	51.1	—
	1972 and later	—	44.8	48.0	51.1	39.2
Overall Length	1965-66	71.4	67.8	—	—	—
	1967-68	68.9	69.8	72.0	—	—
	1969-70	70.0	69.5	73.8	77.7	—
	1971	70.0	71.0	73.8	77.7	—
	1972 and later	—	71.0	77.0	77.7	56.1
Overall Width	1965-71	25.6	25.6	28.3	33.4	—
	1972	—	33.5	35.6	33.4	32.5
Overall Height	1965-66	38.2	38.2	—	—	—
	1967-68	38.2	38.2	38.2	—	—
	1969-71	—	37.5	40.9	43.3	—
	1972 and later	—	37.5	40.9	43.3	37.4
Saddle Height	1965-71	29.1	28.5	29.0	34.0	—
	1972	—	28.7	30.5	34.0	26.6
Road Clearance	1965-68	5.5	—	—	—	—
	1969-70	4.3	4.7	5.1	11.7	—
	1971	—	5.0	6.3	11.7	—
	1972	—	5.0	6.3	11.7	5.7
Weight (lbs)	1965-66	112.0	116.0	—	—	—
	1967-71	116.0	122.0	179.5	212.0	—
	1972	—	140.3	211.5	212.0	126.0

GENERAL SPECIFICATIONS—M MODELS (con't.)

CAPACITIES					
Gas Tank (total volume in U.S. gallons)	1.6	2.5	2.5, 2.4	2.5	1.4
Reserve (in U.S. pints)	1.0	1.0	0.6, 2.0	2.0	3.5
Transmission Oil (in U.S. pints)	1.0	1.0	1.25, 1.3	1.0	1.0

ENGINE	M and MS	ML and MLS	MSR	MC
Type of Engine		Two-Stroke Single Cylinder		
Model Designation	M-50	M-65	M-100	M-125
Taxable Horsepower	0.94	1.20	1.55	1.95
Bore (in./mm)	1.528/38.8	1.732/44.0	1.968/50.0	2.205/56.0
Stroke (in./mm)	1.65/42.0	1.65/42.0	1.97/50.0	1.97/50.0
Piston Displacement (cu in./cc)	3.03/49.6	3.89/63.86	5.98/98.12	7.53/123.5
Compression Ratio	10 : 1	8.75 : 1	9.5 : 1	7.65 : 1

TRANSMISSION	M and MS	ML and MLS	MSR	MC
Type		Constant Mesh		
Speeds	3	4	5	3
Primary Drive Gear Teeth	13	19	19	18
Clutch Shell Gear Teeth: 1965	60	—	—	—
1966-72	59	61	61	54
Transmission Gear Ratios:				
1st 1965-66	3.18 : 1	—	—	—
1967-72	3.083 : 1	2.50 : 1	2.06 : 1	3.08 : 1
2nd 1965-66	1.78 : 1	—	—	—
1967-72	1.78 : 1	1.40 : 1	1.33 : 1	1.78 : 1
3rd 1965-67	1.17 : 1	—	—	—
1966-72	1.17 :	0.92 : 1	0.92 : 1	1.17 : 1
4th 1969	—	0.072 : 1	0.75 : 1	—
5th	—	—	0.58 : 1	—
Transmission Sprocket:				
Teeth 1965	13	—	—	—
1966-71	14	14	12-15	—
1972	14	13	12-15	12
Rear Wheel Sprocket:				
Teeth 1965	28	—	—	—
1966	27	—	—	—
1967-68	24	42	—	—
1970				
(Standard)	—	50	—	—
(Trail)	—	62	72	—
1971	26	—	—	26

OVERALL GEAR RATIOS	1st	2nd	3rd
M and MS			
1965	31.48 : 1	17.67 : 1	11.67 : 1
1966	29.85 : 1	16.76 : 1	11.06 : 1
1967-70	23.99 : 1	13.83 : 1	9.13 : 1
1971-72	25.98 : 1	14.98 : 1	9.89 : 1

ML and MLS	1st Standard/Trail	2nd Standard/Trail	3rd Standard/Trail	4th Standard/Trail
1968-69	24.0 : 1 —	13.5 : 1	8.9 : 1	6.9 : 1 —
1970-71	28.7 : 1 35.5 : 1	16.1 : 1 19.9 : 1	10.6 : 1 13.1 : 1	8.3 : 1 10.3 : 1
1972	30.8 : 1 38.3 : 1	17.3 : 1 21.4 : 1	11.4 : 1 14.1 : 1	8.9 : 1 11.1 : 1

GENERAL SPECIFICATIONS—M MODELS (con't.)

OVERALL GEAR RATIOIS		1st	2nd	3rd	4th
MSR	Number of Sprocket Teeth	12	13	14	15
	1st	39.7 : 1	36.6 : 1	34.0 : 1	31.7 : 1
	2nd	25.6 : 1	23.6 : 1	21.9 : 1	20.4 : 1
	3rd	17.7 : 1	16.3 : 1	15.2 : 1	14.1 : 1
	4th	14.5 : 1	13.3 : 1	12.4 : 1	11.5 : 1
	5th	11.2 : 1	10.3 : 1	9.6 : 1	8.9 : 1
MC		20.0 : 1	11.5 : 1	7.6 : 1	

GENERAL SPECIFICATIONS—S AND B MODELS

	Model Year	ST and STU	B	BT	BTU	BTH	BTF
DIMENSIONS (in.)							
Wheel Base	1959-61	51.5	51.5	51.5	51.5	——	——
	1962	——	——	51.5	51.5	51.5	51.5
	1963-66	——	——	52.0	52.0	52.0	51.5
Overall Length	1959-61	81	81	81	81	——	——
	1962	——	——	78.5	78.5	76.0	76.0
Overall Width	1963-66	——	——	79.0	79.0	81.0	76.0
	1959-61	28.5	28.5	28.5	28.5	——	——
	1962	——	——	28.5	28.5	30.5	30.5
	1963-66	——	——	30.5	30.5	30.5	30.5
CAPACITIES							
Fuel Tank (total volume	1959-61	1.75	1.87	1.87	1.87	——	——
in U.S. gal.)	1962-66	——	——	1.87	1.87	1.87	1.87
Reserve Tank (in quarts)	1959-61	1	1.5	1.5	1.5	——	——
	1962-66	N.A.	N.A.	N.A.	N.A.	N.A.	N.A.
Transmission	1959-66	1.25	1.25	1.25	1.25	1.25	1.25

	ST and STU	B	BT	BTU	BTH	BTF
ENGINE						
Type of Engine	Two-Stroke Single Cylinder					
Taxable Horsepower	2.25	1.7	2.25	2.25	N.A.	N.A.
Bore (in./mm)	2.37/60.3	2.01/52.39	2.37/60.3	2.37/60.3	2.37/60.3	2.37/60.3
Stroke (in./mm)	2.28/57.94	2.28/57.94	2.40/61.11	①	2.40/61.11	2.28/57.94
Piston Displace. (cu in./cc)	10.1/165	7.6/124.87		②	10.7/175	10.1/165
Compression Ratio	6.6 : 1	6.6 : 1	7.63 : 1	③	7.63 : 1	7.63 : 1
TRANSMISSION						
Type	Constant Mesh					
Speeds	3	3	3	3	3	3

	ST and STU	B	BT	BTU	BTH	BTF/BTH Trail
Number of Sprocket Teeth						
Engine	15	12	15	15	15	15
Clutch	31	33	31	31	31	31
Transmission	14	N.A.	④	④	15	12
Rear Wheel	49	43	49	49	49	84
Gear Ratios 1st						
1959-60	21.1 : 1	26.5 : 1	21.1 : 1	21.1 : 1	——	——
1961-66	——	——	19.8 : 1	19.8 : 1	19.8 : 1	43.3 : 1/ 42.2 : 1

GENERAL SPECIFICATIONS—S AND B MODELS

2nd						
1959-60	12.2 : 1	15.4 : 1	12.2 : 1	12.2 : 1	—	—
1961-66	—	—	11.4 : 1	11.4 : 1	11.4 : 1	24.4 : 1/ 24.5 : 1
3rd						
1959-60	7.21 : 1	8.45 : 1	7.21 : 1	7.21 : 1	—	—
1961-66	—	—	6.7 : 1	6.7 : 1	6.7 : 1	14.5 : 1/ 14.5 : 1
Transmission internal Ratio (1962 and later models)	1st 2.92 : 1 2nd 1.69 : 1 3rd 1.00 : 1					

① Stroke
1962 and earlier models 2.28/57.94
1963 and later models 2.40/61.11

② Piston Displacement
1962 and earlier models 10.0/165
1963 and later models 10.7/175

③ Compression Ratio
1962 and earlier models 6.6 : 1
1963 and later models 7.63 : 1

④ Number of transmission sprocket teeth
1960 and earlier models 14
1961 and later models 15

GENERAL SPECIFICATIONS—SPRINT MODELS

	C	H	SS (1971)	SS (1972)	SX
DIMENSIONS (in.)					
Wheel Base	52.0	53.3	53.7	56.3	56.3
Overall Length	76.3	80.7	85.7	85.5	86.3
Overall Width	30.0	31.6	32.7	32.7	35.0
Saddle Height	29.0	31.0	32.3	32.1	31.3
Road Clearance	5.0	6.0	8.5	6.7	8.5

CAPACITIES	C	H (1966) and earlier)	H (1967)	SS (1967)	SS/SX (1968-71)	SS/SX (1972)
Gas Tank (total volume in U.S. gal.)	4.0	2.6	5.1	2.9	2.6	3.1
Reserve Tank (quarts)	1.4	0.6	1.0	1.0	1.0	1.6
Crankcase (quarts)	2.0	2.0	2.0	2.0	2.0	2.0

ENGINE

Type of Engine		Four-Stroke, Single-Cylinder
Horsepower	Model C	18 bhp @ 6700 rpm
	Model H and SS (1968 and earlier)	21 bhp @ 7250 rpm
	Model SX and SS (1969-72)	25 bhp @ 7000 rpm
Taxable Horsepower (NACC rating)	1966 and earlier	2.7
	1967-68	3.2
	1969-72	3.4
Weight (lbs)	C	261
	H	271
	SS (1968 and earlier)	281
	SS (1969-71)	311
	SX (1971-72)	309
	SS (1972)	325
Bore (in./mm)	1966 and earlier	2.5984/6
	1967-68	2.835/72
	1969-72	2.913/74

GENERAL SPECIFICATIONS—SPRINT MODELS (con't.)

ENGINE

Stroke (in./mm)	1966 and earlier	2.835/72
	1967-68	2.410/61
	1969-72	3.150/80
Engine Displacement (cu in./cc)	1966 and earlier	15/246.2
	1967-68	15.15/248
	1969-72	21/344
Compression Ratio	9.4 : 1	(1968 and earlier models)
	9.0 : 1	(1969-72 models)

TRANSMISSION

Type	Constant Mesh
Speeds	4
Primary Drive Gear Teeth	26
Driven Gear Teeth	65
Transmission Internal Ratios	
1st	2.91 : 1
2nd	1.76 : 1
3rd	1.27 : 1
4th	1.00 : 1
Transmission Sprocket Teeth	
Model C (1961-62)	16
Model C (1963 and later models)	17
Models H and SS (1962-67)	17
Models H and SS (1968)	15
Models SS and SX (1969-72)	14
Rear Wheel Sprocket Teeth	
1961-67	38
1968	46
1969-72	35

Gear Ratios	1st	2nd	3rd	4th
Model C (1961-62)	17.28 : 1	10.45 : 1	7.54 : 1	5.94 : 1
Model C (1963 and later models)	16.27 : 1	9.84 : 1	7.10 : 1	5.59 : 1
Models H and S (1962-67)	18.44 : 1	11.15 : 1	8.09 : 1	6.33 : 1
Models H and SS (1968)	19.69 : 1	11.91 : 1	8.64 : 1	6.76 : 1
Models SS and SX (1969-72)	18.20 : 1	11.00 : 1	7.98 : 1	6.25 : 1

TUNE-UP AND MAINTENANCE

TUNE-UP OPERATIONS

Valve Tappet Adjustment

Valves must be adjusted with the engine completely cold.

1. Remove the rocker arm or tappet covers.
2. Rotate the engine until either rocker arm is at the bottom of its travel (valve open). The opposite valve is now closed and may be adjusted.
3. Insert a feeler gauge between the valve stem and the rocker arm pad to measure clearance. A slight drag while removing the gauge indicates a correctly adjusted valve.
4. Loosen the adjusting screw locknut to adjust the tappet.
5. Rotate the tappet screw clockwise to reduce clearance or counterclockwise to increase it. Secure the locknut while holding the screw steady with a screwdriver, and recheck the clearance.
6. Rotate the engine until the opposite valve is closed and repeat the above procedure.
7. Secure the cover, taking care not to damage the cover gasket.

1. Adjustment Screw (2)
2. Locknut (2)
3. Feeler Gage
4. Wrench
5. Screwdriver

Adjusting the tappets

Contact Breaker Points Replacement and Ignition Adjustment

M MODELS

Contact Point and Condenser Replacement

When points become excessively worn, uneven, burned, or pitted, they must be replaced in the following manner:

1. Remove the crankcase side cover as described in the "Starter" section.
2. Remove the rotor nut, washer, and rotor. The rotor may be pulled with Puller Tool (H-D part no 97344–65P) or (97302–70M) for MSR models, or a suitable substitute.
3. Remove the contact point screw, retaining clip, and washers to free the points.
4. Replace points in the reverse order of disassembly, making sure that the point mating surfaces seat evenly against one another.

Replace the condenser while replacing the points. The condenser leads must be soldered to the magneto coil. Consult the appropriate wiring diagrams for the correct connections.

5. Secure the lockscrew when the points are correctly set. Consult the specifications chart for proper setting.
6. Recheck the gap to make sure that tightening the lockscrew did not affect the adjustment.
7. Apply a few drops of engine oil to the felt cam follower oiler.

Ignition Timing Adjustment

The "A" mark on the rotor indicates the proper rotor position for timing the engine and the "O" mark indicates top dead center.

1. Adjust the contact points as described in "Contact Point Adjustment."
2. Rotate the rear wheel; the rotor may be moved to align the timing mark on the crankcase with the rotor "A" mark. The points just begin to open at this position causing spark to occur.
3. Static-time the engine using a timing light, a buzz box, or some similar device which indicates the moment the points open.
4. Rotate the engine in the direction indicated by the arrow on the rotor until the timing marks align. At this point, the bulb should glow dimly or flicker rather than glow brightly as it will when the points are closed. If it does not become dim, remove the rotor as described in "Contact Point and Condenser Inspection and Replacement" and perform the following operations:
   a. Loosen the base plate securing screws and shift the magneto base plate to the right to advance the timing or to the left to retard it.
   b. Inserting a piece of cellophane between the points and tugging gently on it while moving the base plate will help find out when the points begin to open since the cellophane will be released at the proper position.
   c. Secure the base screws and check to see that the point gap has not changed. Reset the gap and repeat the timing procedure if the gap has been affected.
5. Strobe-time the ignition with the engine operating at its normal operating temperature at a fast idle.
6. Aim the light at the timing marks and note whether they appear in alignment. Correct advanced or retarded timing in the same manner as described in step four.

B MODELS

Contact Point and Condenser Replacement

Replace points in the following manner:

1. Remove the sprocket and magneto-generator cover screws, then shift the cover out of the way.
2. Remove the point pivot and lockscrews from the ignition and stop light contact points.
3. Disconnect all contact point leads from their respective terminals and remove the point assemblies.
4. Replace the points in the reverse order of disassembly, making sure that the point mating surfaces seat evenly against one another.

1. Contact breaker points
2. Lock screw
3. Adjusting slot
4. Timing mark "A"
5. Piston top center mark "O"
6. Crankcase match mark
7. Rotor
8. Base screws (3)
9. Cam
10. Felt

Contact breaker and timing marks

Contact Point Adjustment

1. Disconnect the spark plug and remove the crankcase side cover as described in the "Starter" section.
2. Rotate the engine until the points open to their farthest travel.
3. Insert a feeler gauge and check the gap. Gap is correctly set when there is slight drag on the gauge when moved in and out.
4. If adjustment is necessary, loosen the lockscrew and pry at the adjustment slot with a screwdriver to open or close the points as required.

Contact Point Adjustment

The cam felt oiler should be kept lightly lubricated with engine oil.

1. Disconnect the spark plug and remove the magneto cover.
2. Rotate the engine until the cam follower is at the cam's highest point. Check the gap by inserting a 0.018 in. wire feeler gauge between the points. There should be a slight drag on the gauge when removing it.
3. If the points are in need of adjustment, do so in the following manner:
   a. Rotate the engine until the cam

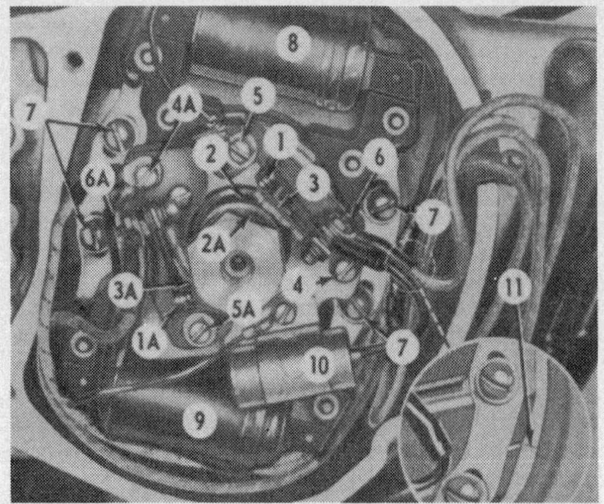

Contact breaker for all B models except the Ranger (BTF)

1. Contact breaker points (Ignition)
2. Contact breaker cam (Ignition)
3. Fiber cam follower and felt oiler (Ignition)
4. Contact breaker assembly pivot screw (Ignition)
5. Contact breaker assembly lockscrew (Ignition)
6. Contact breaker assembly terminal (Ignition) (Condenser and spark coil wires connected here)

1A. Contact breaker points (Stoplight)
2A. Contact breaker cam (Stoplight)
3A. Fiber cam follower and felt oiler (Stoplight)
4A. Contact breaker assembly pivot screw (Stoplight) (Spark coil and ignition-stop light coil wires connected here)
5A. Contact breaker assembly lockscrew (Stoplight)
6A. Contact breaker assembly terminal (Stoplight) (Stop lamp wire connected here)

7. Magneto-generator mounting screws (4)
8. Head lamp and tail lamp lighting coil
9. Ignition-stop light coil
10. Condenser
11. Timing marks on magneto-generator base and crankcase, indicating original factory timing

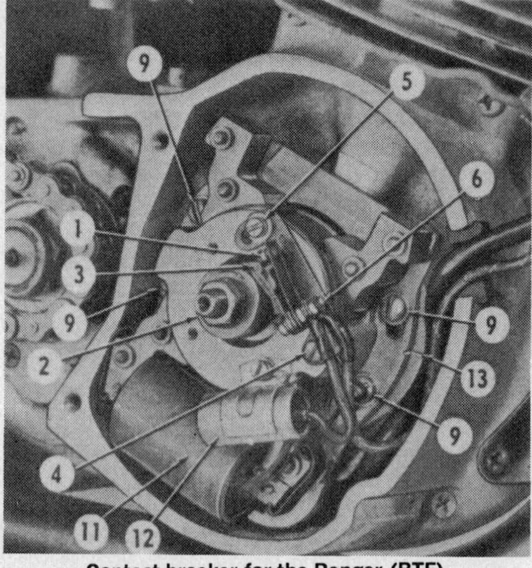

Contact breaker for the Ranger (BTF)

1. Breaker points
2. Breaker cam
3. Fibre cam follower and felt oiler
4. Pivot screw
5. Lock screw
6. Condenser and spark coil terminal
9. Mounting screws (4)
11. Ignition coil
12. Condenser
13. Timing marks

follower is at its highest point on the cam.

b. Loosen the pivot screw slightly and then the lockscrew enough to allow the point base to shift when tapped.

c. Tap the point base at the lockscrew until a gap of 0.018 in. is obtained and then secure the lock and pivot screws.

d. Check the gap by inserting gauges of one size over and under the correct size to serve as a comparison.

Procedure for stop light points adjustment:

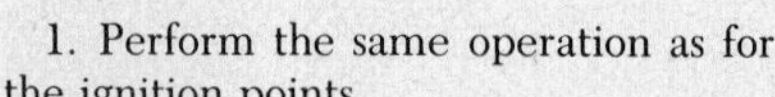

1. Perform the same operation as for the ignition points.

Ignition Timing Adjustment

The timing marks are located on the magneto base and crankcase and serve as a guide when using a timing light.

1. Remove the magneto cover and cylinder head. The cylinder may be secured in poisition by placing a stack of washers on the cylinder studs to approximate the thickness of the cylinder head, and then securing them with a stud nut.

2. Adjust the contact point gap as described in the previous section.

3. Rotate the engine until the piston reaches its highest point of travel (top dead center) then measure the distance from the top of the piston to the top edge of the cylinder bore, taking care not to move the piston.

4. Rotate the engine backward 7/32 in. from the point found in step three.

5. Loosen the base mounting screws and shift the base until the timing marks are in alignment. Clockwise movement will retard the timing and counterclockwise motion will advance it. Secure the base screws.

6. Check and reset the point gap, if necessary, and repeat the timing operation if the gap has changed.

7. A test light can be used as described in the Model M "Ignition Timing Adjust-

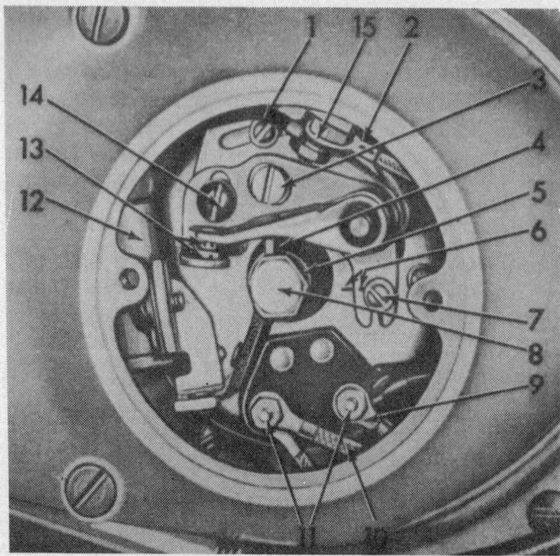

1. Lock screw
2. Wire to coil
3. Eccentric adjusting screw
4. Fiber cam follower
5. Cam
6. Timing marks
7. Lock screw
8. Cap screw
9. To "Gen." terminal of voltage reg.
10. To "F" terminal of voltage reg.
11. Generator terminals
12. Condenser
13. Breaker points
14. Lock screw
15. Contact breaker plate terminal

Contact breaker for the Model 165

ment" section, except that the timing is retarded when the base is moved clockwise. This method should be used if the base has been replaced and the timing marks are no longer accurate.

8. Secure the cylinder head and the magneto cover.

MODEL 165

Contact Point and Condenser Replacement

1. Remove the condenser lead from the contact point plate terminal.
2. Remove the spring lever and point from the terminal.
3. Remove the lockscrew and lift the remaining point and support plate free.
4. Replace the points in the reverse order of disassembly making sure the spring and lever notch are secured by the terminal screw between the nut and the condenser lead.
5. Bend the breaker plate, if necessary, to seat the point mating surfaces squarely against one another.

Contact Point Adjustment

The fiber cam follower should be lightly oiled with engine oil whenever the points are adjusted.

1. Remove the contact breaker cover; rotate the engine until the cam follower is at its highest point on the cam.
2. Check the point gap with a 0.020 in. wire feeler gauge. If the gap is in need of adjustment, do so in the following manner:
   a. Loosen the point lockscrew and rotate the eccentric adjusting screw until the points are open exactly 0.020 in. when the follower is at its highest point on the cam.
   b. Secure the lockscrew and check the gap. There should be a slight tugging on the gauge when trying to remove it. Check the gap by comparing the fit of the next size over and under gauges.
   c. Replace the breaker cover.

Ignition Timing Adjustment

The following method is not dependent on the factory timing marks and should be performed whenever the points are replaced or at least once annually.

1. Steps 1–3 as given for the B Models.
2. Rotate the engine backward 13/64 in. from the point found in step three.
3. Loosen the point lockscrews and shift the point base so the follower is approaching the highest point of the cam and the points are just beginning to open.
4. Use a test lamp as described in the Model M "Ignition Timing Adjustment" section. The leads are connected to ground, the positive terminal, and to the black timer wire from the generator frame.

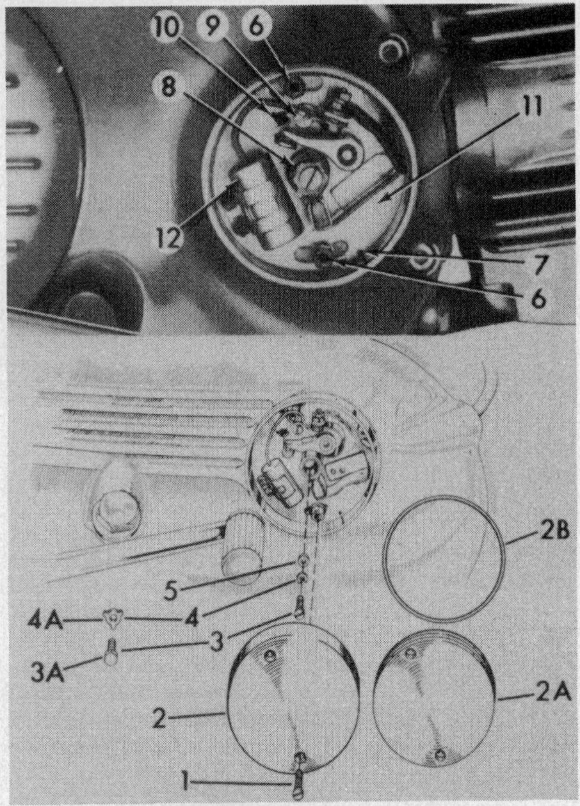

Contact breaker for the Sprint models

1. Contact breaker cover screw (2)
2. Contact breaker cover (1971 and earlier SS)

2A. Contact breaker cover (1971 & later SX, 1972 & later SS)
2B. O-ring (1971 & later SX, 1972 & later SS)

3. Cam screw

3A. Cam screw (1962 & later)

4. Cam lockwasher

4A. Cam lockwasher (1962 & later)

5. Cam washer (1961)
6. Hex screw (2)
7. Timing marks
8. Cam
9. Lock screw
10. Notch to support screw driver
11. Contact breaker plate
12. Condenser

5. Secure the lockscrews and recheck the point gap. If the gap has changed, it must bereset along with the timing.
6. Secure the breaker cover and the cylinder head.

SPRINT MODELS

Contact Point and Condenser Replacement

1. Remove the contact breaker cover screws. Remove the cover by screwing 5 mm screws in the cover holes until the cover is forced off. Screws are available from your dealer (H-D part no. 2863P).
2. Remove the lockscrew and the lead to the points to remove the points from the pivot stud.
3. Replace the points in the reverse order of disassembly.
4. Bend the point contact plate to seat the point faces squarely against one another.

Contact Point Adjustment

Apply a small daub of High-Temperature Lubricant (H-D part no. 99862–72) to the cam follower taking care to avoid excessive lubrication. Engine oil or another high-quality grease may be substituted but will probably require renewal more often.

1. Remove the circuit breaker cover as described in the previous section.
2. Rotate the rear wheel until the points are fully open.
3. Insert a wire feeler gauge set at 0.018 in. between the points. If the gap is in need of adjustment, do so in the following manner:
   a. Loosen the lockscrew.
   b. Pry at the prying notch to shift the fixed contact until a gap of 0.018 in. is attained. There should be a slight tugging on the gauge when trying to remove it.

c. Secure the lockscrew and recheck the gap by inserting the next over and undersize gauges and then comparing them.

d. Replace the breaker cover.

Ignition Timing Adjustment

If the base plate has been removed or if the factory timing marks are no longer valid for any reason, static-time the engine. If a strobe light is available, a more accurate adjustment can be attained. If the timing marks are not valid, new ones may be scribed by static-timing the engine and making arbitrary marks on the base plate and crankcase.

Strobe timing 1971 and later models

STATIC TIMING PROCEDURE:

1. Clean and adjust the contact points as described in the above section.
2. Set the advance mechanism in the advance position in the following manner:
   a. Remove the breaker plate hex screws and plate.
   b. Loosen the cam lockscrew
   c. Insert a wedge to spread the advance weights or place a Timing Washer (H-D part no. 97334–62 for 1968 and earlier) or a suitable substitute under the cam screw and secure the cam. This will hold the weights in the advance position.
3. Attach a test light in the following manner:
   a. If the engine is installed in the frame, connect one lead to the black coil wire at its terminal and ground the other on the engine.
   b. If the engine is out of the frame, connect a ground lead from the engine to the battery negative terminal and another from the points wire stud screw to the test light and from the test light to the battery positive terminal.
   c. With the engine in the chassis, the light will dim as the points open and glow brightly when they close. With the engine removed from the frame, the light will glow when the points open and dim when they close.
4. Place the transmission in high gear and rotate the rear wheel until the left flywheel timing mark is in the center of the access hole. (1971 and later models), or find top dead center (TDC) with the aid of a dial gauge or by removing the head and rotating the engine until the piston is just approaching the highest point of its travel.
5. If the top dead center method is being used, consult the B Models section for measuring instructions. The piston position should be:

1961–66	13/32 in. (0.406 in.) BTDC;
1967 (original factory specification)	11/32 in. (0.350 in.) BTDC;
1967–68	1/4 in. (0.250 in.) BTDC;
1969–70	7/32 in. (0.219 in.) BTDC.

6. Rotate the engine in the direction of normal operation to note whether the light comes on before this position is reached. If the light comes on too early, the timing is too advanced and the base plate must be rotated clockwise. If it comes on late, the timing is too retarded and the base plate must be rotated counterclockwise. Secure the plate screws and recheck the timing. Make sure you release the advance weights before replacing the breaker cover.

STROBE LIGHT TIMING PROCEDURE (1970 And Earlier Models)

1. Remove the breaker and tachometer drive covers from the right and left sides of the crankcase respectively.

Model Year	*Advance (BTDC @ 4500 rpm)*	*Retard (BTDC @ 800 rpm)*
1961	41°	21°
1962–66	41°	5°
1967–68	35°	5°
1969–70	28°	7°

2. Install a Crankshaft Degree Indicator Tool (H-D part no. 95860–67P) in the end of the left-hand threaded generator armature and an indicator bracket on one of the crankcase screw holes. A standard degree wheel can also be used.
3. Locate TDC as described in the above section.
4. Adjust the indicator or degree wheel until 0° is in line with the indicator. Rotate the engine to make certain that 0° will be indicated when the piston is at TDC. Since the crankshaft will move in either direction a few degrees before the piston begins to move, 0° should be set halfway between the points at which the piston begins to move.
5. Connect the strobe leads to ground, the spark plug terminal, and the ignition coil negative terminal or as directed by the strobe manufacturer.
6. With the engine running at normal operating temperature, observe the degree indication of the strobe light on the degree wheel. The engine was on the exhaust stroke rather than the compression stroke if the 0° reading is 180° off the indicated bracket mark position, and the degree wheel must be loosened and reset on the compression stroke.
7. With the engine operating at 4500 revolutions per minute (rpm) for advanced timing or 800 rpm for retarded timing, observe the indicated degree of crankshaft rotation and shift the breaker base until the proper position is attained.
8. Secure the breaker base and recheck the timing.

STROBE LIGHT TIMING PROCEDURE (1971 And Later Models)

1–2. Same as above

3. Rotate the engine until the flywheel timing mark is aligned in the inspection hole.
4. Set the degree wheel so the indicator reads 28°, and secure the wheel. This relates to the flywheel timing mark which is also at 28° advance.
5. Secure the inspection hole cover to avoid oil spray.
6. Operate the engine at normal operating temperature at an idle speed of 1200–1500 rpm and observe the indicated timing with the strobe light as directed in the above section. Retarded timing should be at 7° BTDC.
7. Operate the engine at 5000 rpm to check advance timing which should be from 26–30°.
8. Adjust the breaker base as described in the above section to correct timing.
9. If repeated attempts to adjust ad-

vanced timing fail, inspect the advance unit or replace it.

Carburetor Adjustments

M-50 AND M-65 CARBURETORS

1. Check to see that the throttle and choke are fully closed and adjust the throttle cable if necessary by loosening the carburetor control locknut and adjusting nut, and increasing or decreasing the cable length as required.
2. Adjust the idle with the throttle fully closed.
3. On 1966 and later models, adjust the pilot air screw to get the smoothest idle at low speeds. Avoid excessively low speeds at this will cause hard starting.
4. Adjust the mixture by altering the position of the needle in its clip. Raising the pin will richen the mixture and lowering it will make the mixture leaner. The middle groove is for normal operation.

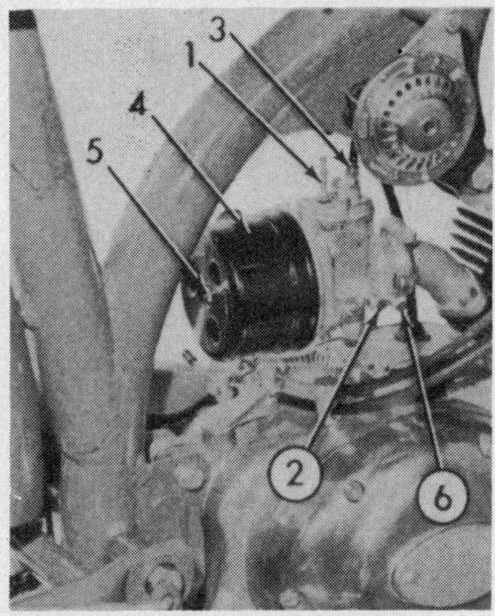

Carburetor adjusting points—shown is a 1966 and later M-50 or M-65

1. Choke
2. Throttle slide stop screw
3. Cable adjusting nut
4. Air cleaner silencer
5. Screw
6. Pilot screw

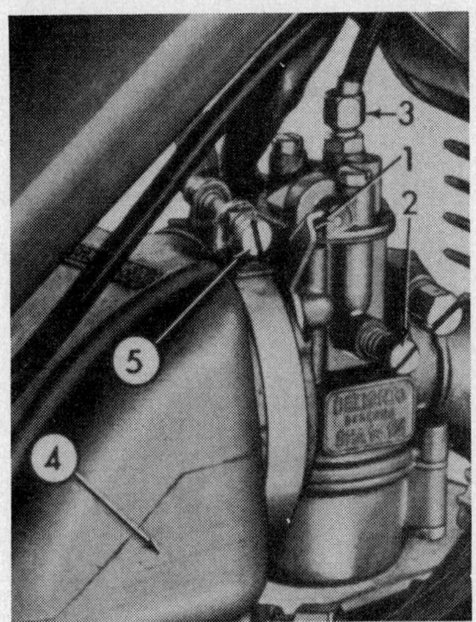

Carburetor adjusting points—shown is a 1965 M-50

1. Choke
2. Throttle slide stop screw
3. Cable adjusting nut
4. Air cleaner silencer
5. Screw

Carburetor adjusting points—shown is a M-100 or M-125

1. Choke
2. Throttle slide stop screw
3. Cable adjusting screw
4. Air cleaner cover
5. Fastener
6. Pilot screw
7. Throttle slide cap
8. Float pin
9. Fuel filter screen

5. If additional mixture adjustments are necessary, the mainjet should be replaced.
6. If the engine still runs irregularly due to the carburetor, disassemble the carburetor and clean it thoroughly in a suitable solvent and blow all passages clear.

M-100 AND M-125 CARBURETORS

1. Adjust the idle speed by manipulating the throttle slide stop screw. Loosen the lockscrew and turn the stop screw clockwise to raise the idle speed and counterclockwise to decrease it, then secure the lockscrew. Readjust the throttle cable if necessary to remove any excess play or tension.
2. Adjust the idle mixture by manipulating the idle pilot screw. The normal setting is ¾ turn off its seat but may be adjusted richer by turning it counterclockwise. If the engine runs irregularly adjust it slightly leaner.

3–6. Same as for the M-50 and M-65.

MODEL 165 CARBURETOR

1. Adjust the idle speed by loosening the adjusting sleeve locknut and turning the adjusting sleeve up to increase idle speed and down to decrease it. Secure the locknut.
2. The mixture is regulated by the position of the needle in the needle retainer. There are four positions available. The normal setting is in the second groove from the top. A richer mixture can be attained by lowering the clip; a leaner mixture can be attained by raising the clip.
3. To adjust the needle remove the cap, spring, and throttle slide from the carburetor body. Reposition the needle clip as desired.
4. When replacing the cable, take care not to bend the retainer.

5–6. Same as for the M-50 and M-65.

B-MODEL CARBURETOR

1. Screw the idle mixture adjusting screw gently in to its seat then back it out ¾ turn.
2. Screw the main mixture adjusting screw gently in to its seat then back it out one full turn.
3. Open throttle halfway and hold it so the engine runs at a constant speed. Slowly turn the main adjusting screw in until the engine speed begins to decrease. Slowly back out the screw until optimum speed and power is attained. This should require no more than ⅛–¼ turn.
4. Check to see that the throttle cable allows the throttle to close fully, then adjust the throttle speed slightly higher than usual by turning in the throttle stop-screw.
5. Slowly turn the idle mixture adjust-

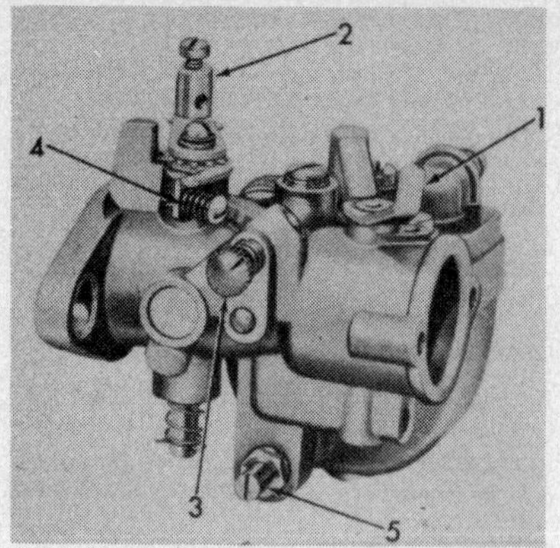

Carburetor adjusting points—B models

1. Choke lever (open position)
2. Throttle lever
3. Idle mixture adjusting screw
4. Throttle stop screw—with which closed throttle idling speed is adjusted
5. Mixture main adjusting screw

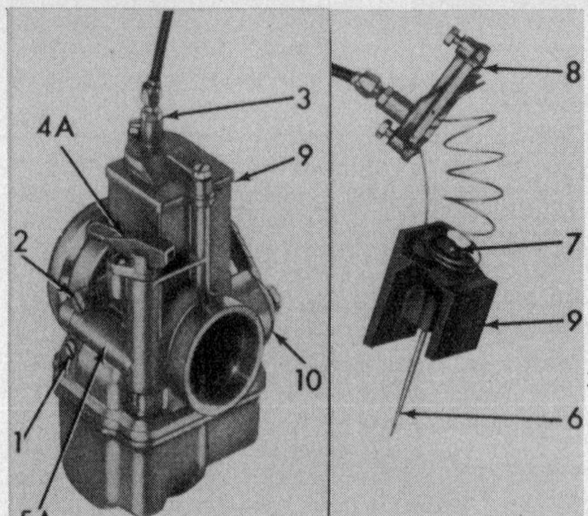

1. Pilot fuel adjusting screw
2. Throttle slide stop screw
3. Cable adjustment
4A. Starting jet lever
5A. Starting passage
6. Needle
7. Clip
8. Mixing chamber cap
9. Throttle slide
10. Carburetor filter screen

Carburetor adjusting points—1969 and later Sprint models

ing screw clockwise until the engine speed begins to decrease. Slowly back out the screw until engine operation is its smoothest. This should require no more than ⅛ turn.

6. Back out throttle stopscrew until a satisfactory idle speed is achieved. Turning the screw in raises the idle speed; backing it out reduces it.

7. If the engine still runs irregularly due to the carburetor, disassemble the carburetor and clean it thoroughly in a suitable solvent and blow all passages clear.

SPRINT CARBURETORS

1. Adjust the idle speed by loosening the locknut (1968 and earlier models) and turning the throttle slide stopscrew. Turning the screw clockwise raises the idle speed; counterclockwise reduces it. An idle speed of 1,200 rpm will prove most satisfactory.

2. Loosen the cable adjustment screw locknut and adjust the cable to remove excessive tension or slack, then secure the locknut.

3. Turn the pilot fuel adjusting screw gently in to its seat, then back it out ¾ turn for 1968 and earlier models and 1¾ turns for 1969 and later models. If the engine runs irregularly at low speeds, the mixture is probably too rich. Turning the screw counterclockwise on 1968 and earlier models, and clockwise on 1969 and later models, will lean out the mixture.

4–6. Same as for the M-50 and M-65.

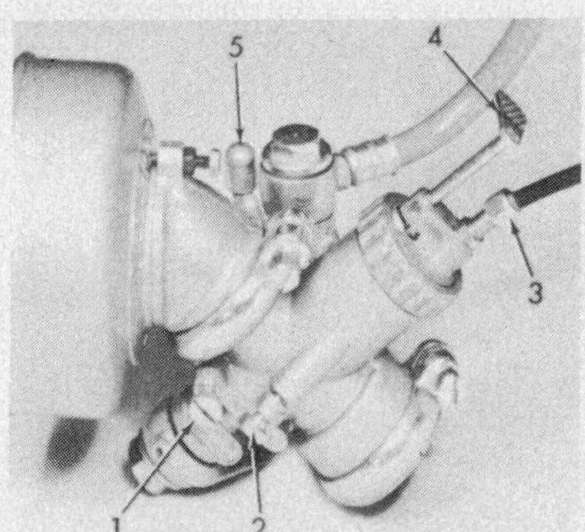

Carburetor adjusting points—1968 and earlier Sprint models

1. Pilot air adjusting screw
2. Throttle slide stop screw
3. Cable adjusting screw
4. Choke
5. Float pin

SPARK PLUG CONVERSION CHART

Heat Range	NGK Standard Type	NGK Projected Type	Champion Y—Projected Type	AC S—Projected Type	Auto-Lite	Bosch	KLG P—Projected Type	Lodge Y—Projected Type
Hot	B-4H	BP-4H	L14, UL15Y, L10	46FF, 46FFS, 45FFS, 45FF	AE52, AE6	W95T1, W145T1	F20, F50 F55P	B14, BN, CNY, CN, CC14
	B-6HS	BP-6H	L90, UL12Y, L83, L86, L85, L95Y	45F, M45FF, 44FFS, 44FF, M43FF	AE4, AE42	W175T1, W175T7	F70, F65P	
	B-7H	BP-7HS	L7, L87Y, UL87Y, L81, L82Y, UL82Y	44F, 43F, 43FFS, 42F, 42FF, 42FS	AE3, AE32, AE2, AE22	W200T7, W200T35, W225T1, W225T35	F75	HN, H14, HH14
	B-7HZ		L5	M42FF, MC42F		W225T7	F80	2HN
	B-7HC							

SPARK PLUG CONVERSION CHART

	B-77HC	L62R			W240T1, W240T16	F100	3HN
	B-8H	L4J, L64Y, L66Y			W260T1		
	B-8HC	L60R		AE903	W270T16		
	B-9H						
	B-9HC	L57R		AE603	W310T16		
Cold	B-10H	L54R					

TUNE-UP SPECIFICATIONS

	M-50	M/MC-65	M/MSR-100	M-125	165	B-Models	Sprint
IGNITION TIMING							
Breaker point setting (gap) (in.)	0.018	0.018	0.016	0.016	0.020	0.018	0.018
Ignition timing (retarded)	27° (0.115) BTDC	①	20° (0.073) BTDC	②	30° BTDC	32° (0.21) BTDC	③
Ignition timing (advanced)							
1961-67	—	—	—	—	—	—	41° (0.406) BTDC
1968	—	—	—	—	—	—	35° (0.250) BTDC
1969-72	—	—	—	—	—	—	28° (0.234) BTDC
SPARK PLUGS							
Gap setting (magneto ign.)							
1965 (in.)	0.020-0.025	0.020-0.025	0.020-0.025	0.020-0.025	—	0.040-0.045	—
1966-72 (in.)	0.025-0.030	0.025-0.030	0.025-0.030	0.025-0.030			
Gap setting (battery ign.) (in.)	N.A.	N.A.	N.A.	N.A.	0.025-0.030	N.A.	0.020-0.025
Heat range (average use)					no. 4	no. 4	no. 5-6
1965	no. 7 or 5-6	no. 7 or 5-6	no. 7 or 5-6	no. 7 or 5-6			
1966-69	no. 6 or 5-6	no. 6 or 5-6	no. 6 or 5-6	no. 6 or 5-6			
1970	no. 5-6	no. 5-6	no. 5-6	no. 5-6			
TAPPET ADJUSTMENT							
Tappet clearance	N.A.	N.A.	N.A.	N.A.	N.A.	N.A.	④
CARBURETOR ADJUSTMENT	Consult the "Carburetor Adjustment" section						

① Ignition timing (retarded)—M-65
(deg/in. BTDC)
1970 and earlier 23/0.073
1971-72 22.5/0.080

② Ignition timing (retarded)—M-125
(deg/in. BTDC)
1969 and earlier 23/0.073
1970-72 20/0.073

③ Ignition timing (retarded)—Sprint
(deg/in. BTDC)
1961 21/0.109
1962-68 5/0.015
1968-72 7/0.015

④ Tappet clearance
Model C intake (cold) 0.004 in.
exhaust (cold) 0.004 in.
1966 and earlier Model H intake (cold) 0.003 in.
exhaust (cold) 0.005 in.
1967-68 Model H and SS
intake (cold) 0.002 in.
exhaust (cold) 0.002 in.
intake (hot) 0.006 in.
exhaust (hot) 0.006 in.
1969-72 Model SS and SX
intake (cold) 0.002 in.
exhaust (cold) 0.002 in.
intake (hot) 0.007 in.
exhaust (hot) 0.009 in.

MAINTENANCE ITEMS

Lubrication

TWO-STROKE MODELS-ENGINE OIL

When mixing the oil, on all models other than the M-100, use a ratio of one part oil to 25 parts gas (5 ounces–oz–oil to one U.S gallon–gal). This comes to about three measuring cupfuls (the oil cup attached to the gas tank cap)to one gallon of gas.

When mixing oil for the M-100, do so in a ratio of one part oil to 20 parts gas (6½ ox to one U.S. gal) or about four cupfuls to one gallon.

SPRINT MODELS-ENGINE OIL

1. Run the engine until its normal operating temperature is reached, remove the drain plug, gasket, and the inner and outer oil filters or the oil cap assembly (1972 and later models), and allow the oil to drain into a suitable receptacle. The filter stop spring may drop off so be aware of its location.
2. Slowly kick the engine through several times with the ignition turned off to remove the last traces of oil which remain in the crankcase.
3. Clean the filters in a suitable solvent, then blow them dry. If the filter screens are clogged or damaged, they should be replaced.
4. Inspect the condition of the drain plug gasket, filter stop spring, oil filter cap, and cap O-ring for a damaged condition and replace them as necessary.
5. On 1963 and earlier models, remove the scavenger pump filter magnetic plug, plug gasket, and the filter screen, and allow the oil to drain into a suitable receptacle. Lean the bike over to the left to make sure that all the oil drains out.
6. Clean the filter screen and magnetic cap in a suitable solvent and blow them dry.
7. Inspect the condition of the screen, gasket, and cap for a worn, clogged, or damaged condition and replace them as necessary.
8. Replace the drain assemblies taking care to seat the filter stop spring against the closed end of the outer filter. The inner filter closed end seats against the closed end of the outer filter, and the O-ring goes between the outer filter and the filter cap. Make sure there is no grit on the plug threads, then install and tighten them securely.
9. Add 2 qt of Harley-Davidson oil, or a suitable substitute, check the level, secure the filler cap, and kick the engine through a couple times with the ignition turned off before starting the engine.

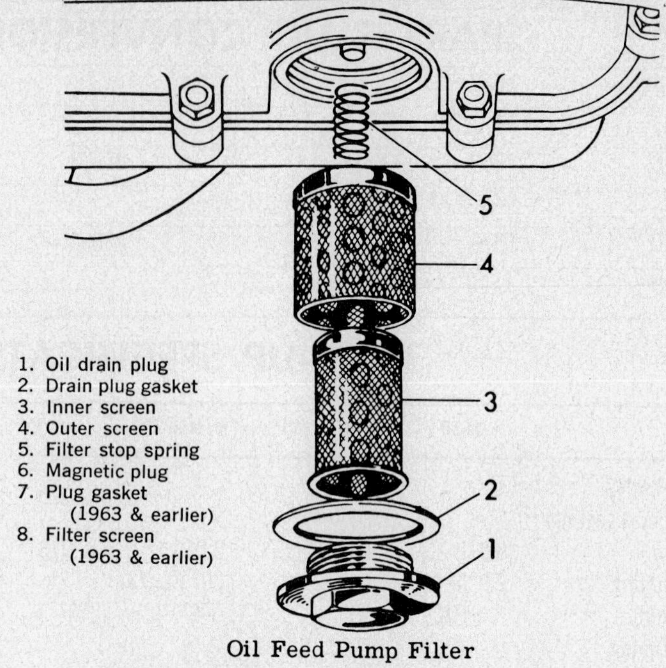

Oil Feed Pump Filter

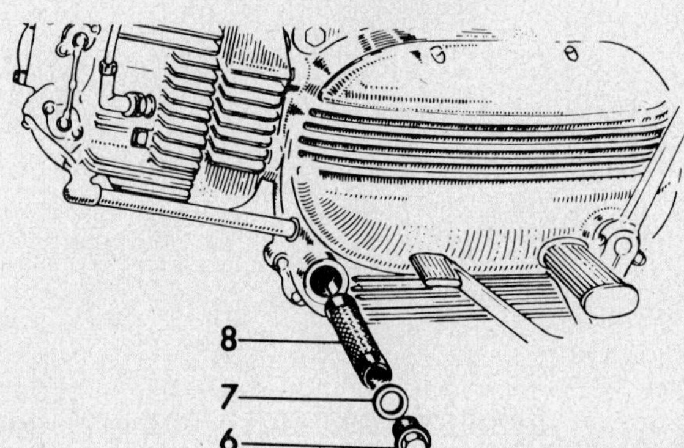

The oil feed and scavenger pump filters

When changing the oil, replace it with an oil of the grade of which is compatible with the lowest temperature expected before the next oil change. Use Harley-Davidson grade 58 oil for use in temperatures below 40 degrees Fahrenheit (40° F), grade 75 oil for temperatures above 40° F, and grade 105 oil for touring or high-speed operation in hot weather. Any high-grade detergent oil may be substituted if Harley-Davidson oil is not available, as long as the viscosity of the oil is compatible with the climate.

TRANSMISSION OIL

All of the two-stroke Harley-Davidson models covered in this guide have separate transmission compartments, for which the state of lubrication requires periodic attention. The Sprint models have a common oil supply for the engine and transmission assemblies.

The M Models use Harley-Davidson two-cycle oil but a high-quality substitute may be used. Drain the oil after riding the bike by removing the transmission filler plug, placing a suitable receptacle beneath the vertical, hex-shaped drain plug located beneath the transmission gear section of the crankcase, and removing the drain plug. Agitate the machine to remove the remaining oil and replace the drain plug. Take care not to remove the angled plug by mistake since this holds the shifting index ball inside the transmission. Fill the transmission to the lower rim of the filler hole with the machine standing perfectly vertical on a flat surface.

The Model 165, Hummer, Super-10, Scat, Pacer, Ranger, and Bobcat transmissions use Harley-Davidson no. 75 (medium heavy) Oil when the temperature is 32° F or higher, and no. 58 (Special Light) Oil when the temperature is 32° F or lower. The oil is drained, after the machine has been ridden, by removing the filler plug located on the left crankcase in front of the cylinder on the Model 165 and Super-10, or on the left crankcase behind the cylinder as on the Hummer. Place a suitable receptacle beneath the drain plug, and remove it to allow the transmission to drain. Shake the machine to remove the remaining oil, then replace the drain plug. Add oil until the level is up to the upper mark on the dipstick for the Hummer model, or until it begins to overflow through the filler hole on the other models. Make sure the machine is standing perfectly vertical on a flat surface when replenishing the oil supply.

CHANGING FORK OIL

All of the fork models except the Tele-Glide fork used on the Model 165, Hummer, Super-10, Scat, Pacer, Ranger, and the Bobcat have a filler cap located at the top of each fork leg, and a drain plug located at the bottom of each leg. The Tele-Glide model has only a filler plug located in the center of the large hex-head cap screw into which the oil is poured. Harley-Davidson Sprint Fork Oil is recommended for use in all but the Tele-Glide forks which use Harley-Davidson Chain-Saver or engine oil. Engine oil may be used in any fork, but due to its effect on rubber, it may damage the oil seals.

Change the fork oil on all of the models, except those equipped with Tele-Glide forks, in the following manner:

1. Remove the fork filler caps, place a suitable receptacle beneath the fork leg drain plugs, remove the drain plugs, and allow the oil to drain out. Hold the front brake on and pump the forks to remove the last of the oil. On 1969 and earlier ML and MLS Models, remove the upper fork plug, invert the forks, and let them drain.

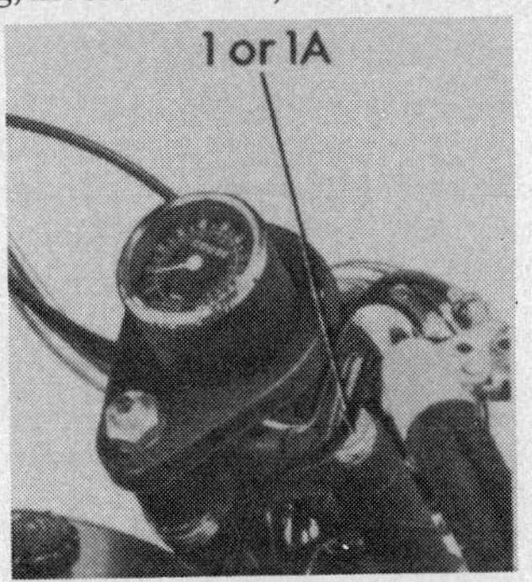

1. Fill plug
1A. Rubber plug
2. Drain plug

Front fork lubrication—shown are ML and MLS models

2. If it is necessary to flush the forks to remove traces of an incompatible oil or foreign particles, fill the fork with kerosine, pump them several times, and drain them out again.
3. Replace the drain plugs and pour in the following quantities of oil, plus 10 cc to compensate for the oil which will remain in the filler device, or ½ oz if the forks have been taken down and are perfectly dry:
   a. Pour 2¼ oz of fork oil into the forks on the models M and MS.
   b. Pour 3¾ oz of fork oil into the forks on the 1969 and earlier models MSR, ML, and MLS, and 4½ oz for 1970 and later models.
   c. Pour 4½ oz of fork oil into the forks on all of the Sprint models.
4. Replace and secure the filler caps and check the forks for smooth operation.

The Tele-Glide type forks don't require fork oil changes. Instead, the fork oil is replenished every 750 miles with one tube cap oil plug full of oil. The tube cap oil plug is located in the center of the tube caps.

AIR CLEANER

The metal, mesh filter elements can be cleaned in clean gasoline or a suitable solvent. Dip the element in clean, light-viscosity engine oil and allow it to drain thoroughly before installing it. Take care to place the filter gasket beneath the element when assembling the filter assembly.

The dry, corrugated paper element is cleaned by tapping the element to shake the dirt free and blowing on it with compressed air. If the element is exceptionally dirty, it may be cleaned in clean gasoline to remove oil or soot deposits. The element must be replaced at least every 10,000 miles, or more often if used in dusty conditions. Replace the element if it is ever immersed in water. This also applies to the cartridge elements (H-D part no. 29037–61) except they should be replaced every 2,500 miles.

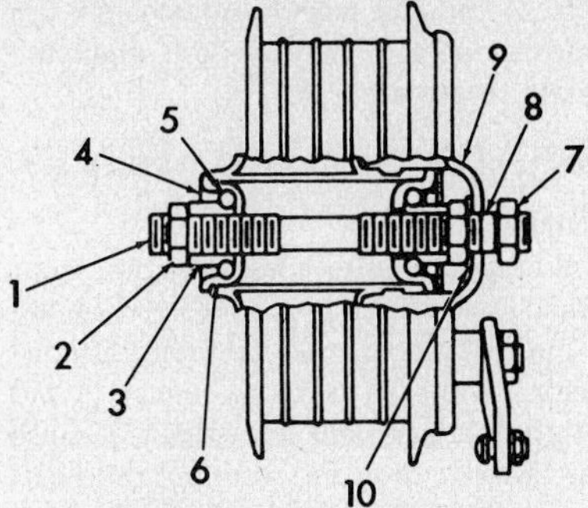

Cone type wheel hub bearings

1. Axle
2. Locknut
3. Bearing cone
4. Dust cover
5. Ball bearings
6. Bearing cup
7. Outer locknut, brake side
8. Outer spacer, brake side
9. Brake sideplate
10. Inner washer, brake side

Adjustments

ADJUSTING CONE TYPE WHEEL HUB BEARINGS

Bearings such as these (found on some of the M and MS models) must be adjusted every 1,000 miles to keep the wheel spinning freely on the axle with only the smallest amout of drag.

Adjust the bearings in the following manner:

1. Remove the front wheel as described in the "Chassis" section.
2. Loosen the wheel bearing cone lock-nut with a 11/16 in. wrench while holding the flat sides of the cone with a 15 mm open-end wrench or a suitable adjustable wrench.
3. Rotate the cone toward the wheel until it seats snugly against the bearing, then back it off ¼ turn so there is slight play when the axle is moved sideways.
4. Secure the cone locknut when the adjustment is correct, while holding the cone to prevent it from moving.

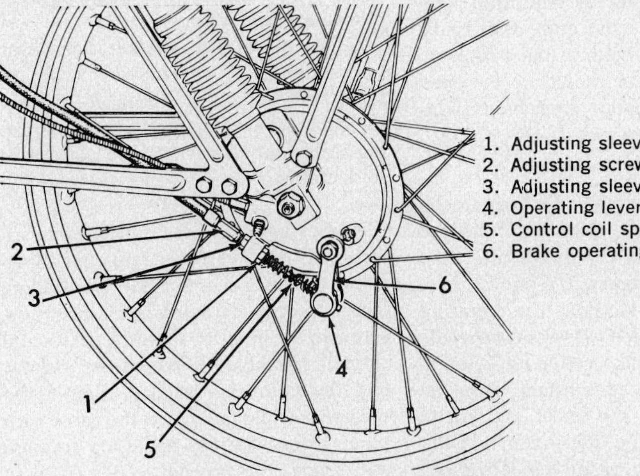

1. Adjusting sleeve lower locknut
2. Adjusting screw
3. Adjusting sleeve upper locknut
4. Operating lever slotted clevis pin
5. Control coil spring
6. Brake operating lever

Front wheel brake adjustments—S and B models

5. Mount the wheel and recheck the adjustment as it may be lost when the axle nuts are secured.

BRAKE ADJUSTMENTS

Front Brake

When properly adjusted, the front brake lever will move about ⅛ (¼ on the S and B Models) of its total distance before the brake begins to engage. Avoid a tighter adjustment since this will cause the brake to drag and wear out the shoes faster. Raise the wheel, spin it to check for drag, and readjust it as necessary.

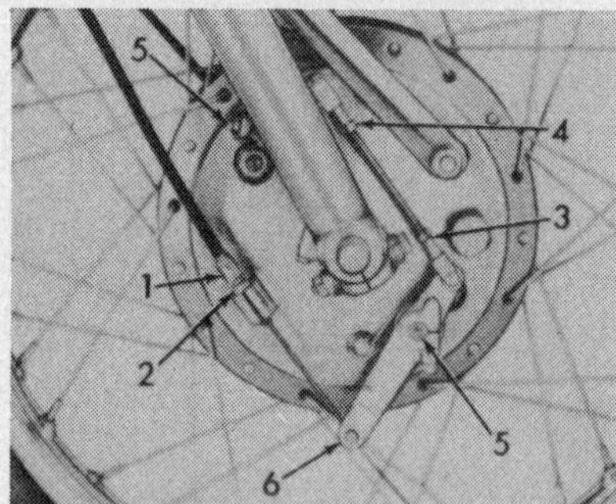

Front wheel brake adjustment—1970 and later Sprint models

1. Adjusting screw
2. Locknut
3. Lower clevis adjustment
4. Upper clevis adjustment
5. Brake camshaft Grease fittings
6. Cable block

Loosen the adjusting screw locknut and rotate the adjusting screw clockwise to increase the free movement of the handlever; counterclockwise to decrease its motion. If it becomes necessary to adjust the cable length, do so by loosening the cable setscrew or clamp stud and nut, and then pulling on the cable. Always take care to secure the adjusting apparatus after the adjustment is completed.

Whenever new shoes are installed on 1970 or later Sprint models, they must be equalized to make sure that both shoes contact the drum at the same time. Perform this operation by adjusting them both at their respective ends of the brake rod clevis while holding the brake on. The clevis adjuster should be loosened before the brake is operated, and retightened before it is released.

Rear Brake

Adjust the rear brake by turning the knurled nut, or the adjusting nut, until the brake begins to engage after the brake lever is depressed ½ in. (¾–1 in. for the S and B Models). The adjusting nut has a notch which sits against the clevis pin in the brake actuating lever to keep the adjustment constant. Turn the nut in to tighten the brake, and out to loosen it. After the adjustment is complete, raise the wheel and spin it to check for drag, and readjust it as necessary.

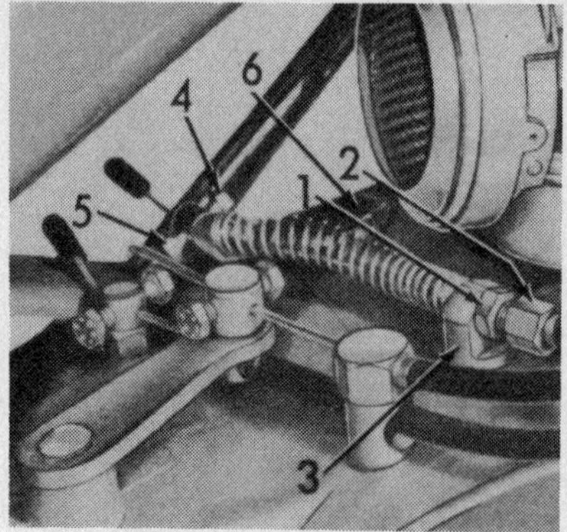

Clutch adjustment—M models

1. Clutch control cable screw locknut
2. Clutch control cable adjuster screw
3. Crankcase anchor
4. Clamping block setscrew
5. Clamping block setscrew
6. Clutch release lever

Rear wheel brake adjustment—cable type brake actuator shown

1. Knurled nut
2. Cable adjusting stud
3. Coil adjusting nut
4. Coil adjusting screw

CLUTCH ADJUSTMENT

M-Models

All adjustments for these clutches are performed at the cable. If the clutch fails to hold and release properly after being adjusted, it will have to be taken apart to determine the reason.

Adjust the cable so the handlever moves ⅛–¼ of its total movement before the clutch begins to disengage. Loosen the cable screw locknut, turn the adjusting screw out to increase the play, or in to decrease it, and then secure the locknut.

If you run out of room at the cable adjuster, if the cable clamp has been removed, or if a new cable is installed, loosen the two clamping block setscrews, screw in the adjuster so there are several threads remaining between the locknut and the crankcase anchor, tighten the setscrews while pulling on the cable with pliers to provide the necessary tension, and repeat the procedure described in the above paragraph.

S And B Models

These clutches are adjusted by turning an adjusting screw which places tension directly on the push rods. The adjusting screw regulates the play in the clutch cable which should be about ¼ of its total movement before there is a noticeable increase in tension. Adjust the clutch by loosening the adjusting screw locknut, turning the adjusting screw counterclockwise one full turn to be certain that the clutch is fully engaged, and then turning the screw clockwise until you feel the release rod contacting the release disc. At this point the clutch is beginning to disengage and there will be an increase of tension on the adjusting screw. From this point, turn the screw counterclockwise ¼ turn and secure the locknut while holding the screw steady with a screwdriver. If the clutch still fails to hold and release properly, it should be taken apart to determine the cause.

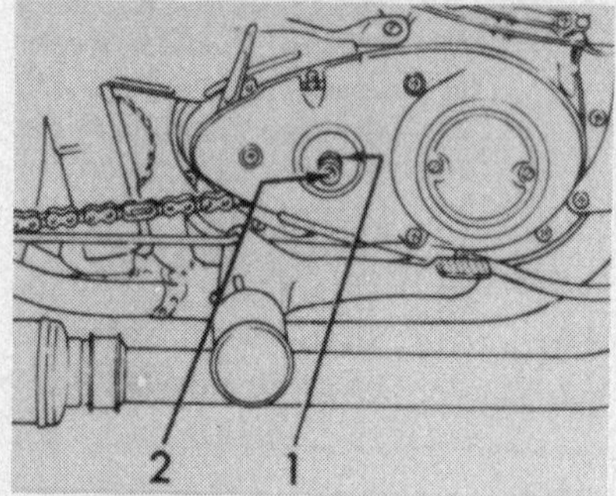

Clutch adjustment—S and B models

1. Clutch adjusting screw locknut
2. Clutch adjusting screw

Sprint Models

All adjustments for these clutches are performed at the cable. If the clutch fails to hold or release properly after being adjusted, it should be taken apart to determine the reason.

There should be play of between ⅛–¼ of the total movement of the handlever before the clutch begins to disengage.

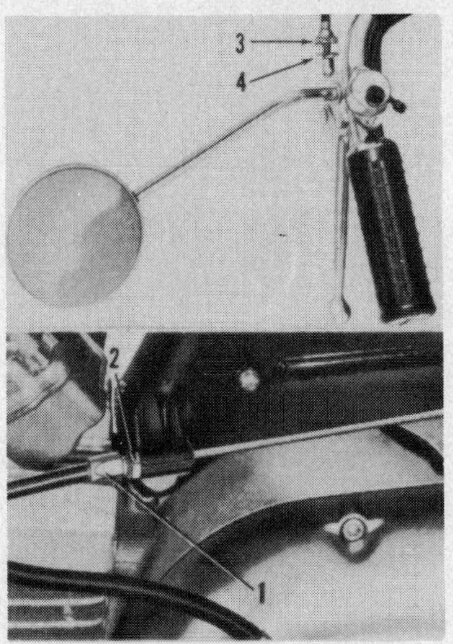

Clutch adjustment—Sprint models

1. Cable adjuster screw
2. Cable adjuster screw locknut
3. Hand lever adjuster
4. Hand lever adjuster locknut

M-125

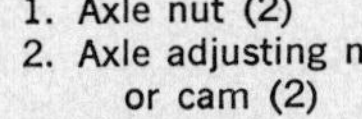

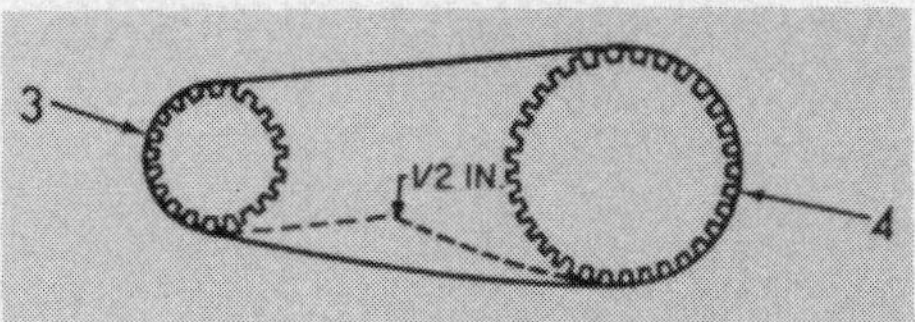

1. Axle nut (2)
2. Axle adjusting nut or cam (2)
3. Drive sprocket
4. Rear wheel sprocket

Drive chain adjustment—models M-50, M-65, M-100, and M-125

Adjust the cable at the cable adjuster screw located at the crankcase. Loosen the locknut and turn the screw clockwise, for increased play, or counterclockwise, for less play, then secure the locknut. Minor adjustments can be made at the handlever knurled nut.

CHAIN ADJUSTMENT

Models M-50 And M-65

Loosen the axle nuts, then alternately rotate each of the adjusting nuts until there is ½ in. free-play in the middle. The chain at its tightest point. Each of the adjusting nuts must be in the same position to align the rear wheel. The wheel should be directly in the middle of the rear forks and the chain should be aligned with the rear wheel sprocket. Secure the axle nuts and adjust the rear brake when the chain is properly adjusted and aligned.

Models M-125 And M-100

These models are the same as the above two, except that the adjustment is made with a cam. The cam is operated by tapping on its ear. Make sure the two sides are kept even.

S And B Models

These models are adjusted in the same manner as the previous models except that the adjusting nuts are located in front of the axle nut.

Sprint Models

These models are adjusted in the same manner as the previous models. The locknut must be loosened before and tightened after the adjustment procedure.

PERIODIC SERVICE SCHEDULE

SERVICE

Interval	*Operation*
Every 1,000 miles	Clean and gap spark plugs Clean air filter element Clean the oil pump filters Adjust the drive chain Adjust the brakes Check the transmission oil Change the engine oil Check the battery Check the tire pressure Tighten all the nuts and bolts
Every 2,000 miles	Contact point condition, gap, and timing Adjust the clutch Adjust the tappets Gas filter
Every 5,000 miles	Change the transmission oil Decarbonize Replace spark plug Check the fork bearings Check the wheel spokes Check generator brushes and commutator Check the shock bushings
Every 10,000 miles	Clean and adjust the carburetor

OIL

Every 1,000 miles	Drive chain Front forks
Every 2,000 miles	Clutch handlever and gearshift control Clutch handlever Brake handlever Brake cable Clutch cable Gearshift cable Saddle hinge assembly (1965 and earlier) Contact breaker felt oilers Brake control joints

GREASE

Every 2,000 miles	Speedometer drive unit Tachometer drive unit Front brake operating shaft Rear brake pedal Rear brake operating shaft Rear fork pivot bushings Contact breaker cam
Every 5,000 miles	Throttle grip Wheel bearings Speedometer cable Tachometer cable
Every 10,000 miles	Repack steering head bearings

MAINTENANCE DATA

Model	Engine Oil Capacity (qts)	Gearbox Oil Capacity (pts)	Fork Oil Capacity (oz)	Gas Tank Capacity (gal)	Reserve Tank Capacity (qts)
M-50 (M, MS)	N.A.	1	2.25	③	—
M-65 (M, MS)	N.A.	1	2.25	③	⑤
Baja (MSR)	N.A.	1	②	2.5	1
Hummer (B)	N.A.	1.25	one capful	1.5	1.5
M-125 (ML)	N.A.	1	②	2.5	—
Rapido (ML, MLS)	N.A.	①	②	2.4	1
Model 165 (ST, STU)	N.A.	1.25	one capful	1.75	—
Super-10 (BT, BTU)	N.A.	1.25	one capful	1.87	—
Pacer (BT, BTU)	N.A.	1.25	one capful	1.87	—
Scat (BTH)	N.A.	1.25	one capful	1.87	—
Ranger (BTF)	N.A.	1.25	one capful	1.87	—
Bobcat (BTH)	N.A.	1.25	one capful	1.87	—
Sprint (C)	2	N.A.	4.50	4	⑥
Sprint (H)	2	N.A.	4.50	④	⑥
Sprint (SS)	2.1	N.A.	4.50	④	1

① Gearbox Capacity (pt)
ML—1.0
MLS—1.3 (1970 and later models)

② Fork Oil Capacity (oz)
3.75 (pre-1970 ML, MLS, and MSR)
4.50 (post-1969 ML, MLS, and MSR)

③ Gas Tank Capacity (gal)
M—1.6
MS—2.5

④ Gas Tank Capacity (gal)
Model H—2.64 (1966) and earlier models)
5.1 (1967 and later models)
Model SS—2.9 (1966 and earlier models)
2.6 (1967 and later models)

⑤ Reserve Tank Capacity (qt)
1—1970 and later Leggero models only

⑥ Reserve Tank Capacity (qt)
Model C—2 (1961 only)
1.4 (1962-65)
1 (1966 and later)
Model H—0.62 (1963-65)
1 (1966 and later)

TIRE SPECIFICATIONS

Model	Front (in.)	Front Pressure (psi)	Rear (psi)	Rear Pressure (psi)
M (1965)	2.00 x 18	23	2.00 x 18	35
M, MS (1966-70)	2.00 x 17	23	2.00 x 17	35
ML (1968)	2.50 x 17	21	2.50 x 17	28
MS (1971)	2.50 x 17	22	2.50 x 17	30
MS (1972)	2.50 x 17	25	3.00 x 16	21
MLS (1968-69)	2.50 x 17	21	3.00 x 17	28
MLS (1970-71)	3.00 x 18	22	3.50 x 18	22
MLS (1972)	3.00 x 19	18	3.50 x 18	18
MSR (1970-72)	3.00 x 21	18	3.50 x 18	22
MC (1972)	3.00 x 10	18	3.00 x 10	22
Model 165, Hummer, and the 1960 Super-10	3.50 x 18	12	3.50 x 18	14
Super-10 (1961)	3.50 x 16	12	3.50 x 16	14
BT, BTU (1962-66)	3.50 x 16	12	3.50 x 16	14
BTH, BTF (1962-66)	3.50 x 18	12	3.50 x 18	14
Sprint C	3.00 x 17	20	3.00 x 17	24
Sprint H	3.00 x 18	18	3.50 x 18	18
Sprint SS	3.25 x 19	18	3.50 x 18	22
Sprint SX	3.50 x 19	18	4.00 x 18	18

ENGINE AND TRANSMISSION

TWO-CYCLE ENGINE SERVICE

Engine Removal And Installation

MODELS M, MS, AND MC

1. Disconnect the spark plug lead and remove the spark plug.
2. Turn off the petcock.
3. Disconnect the fuel line at the tank.
4. Remove the chain guard.
5. Disconnect the drive chain master link and remove the chain.
6. Remove the engine mounting nuts but do not remove the bolts.
7. Disconnect the clutch cable at the release mechanism.
8. Remove the exhaust manifold ring nut and gasket at the cylinder, and shift the pipe out of the way.
9. Remove the carburetor intake manifold nuts and carburetor assembly from the engine, block the intake port with a clean cloth, and support the assembly out of the way.
10. Disconnect the wires at the terminal block.
11. Drift the front upper mounting bolt free.
12. Support the cylinder head while drifting the rear upper engine mounting bolt free. Gently lower the front end of the engine onto something soft.
13. Support the engine from below and remove the rear mounting bolt. The engine is now free to be removed.
14. Install the engine in the reverse order of removal.

MODELS ML, MLS, AND MSR

1. Disconnect the spark plug lead.
2. Shut off the petcock.
3. Disconnect the fuel line at the tank.
4.Disconnect the drive chain master link and remove the chain.
5. Remove the exhaust manifold ring nut and gasket at the cylinder, and shift the pipe out of the way.
6. Remove the rear muffler mounting bolt and the exhaust assembly.
7. Remove the carburetor air cleaner assembly.
8. Remove the carburetor throttle piston cap, remove the piston, and disconnect the throttle calbe.
9. Disconnect the wires at the terminal block.
10. Disconnect the clutch cable at the release mechanism.

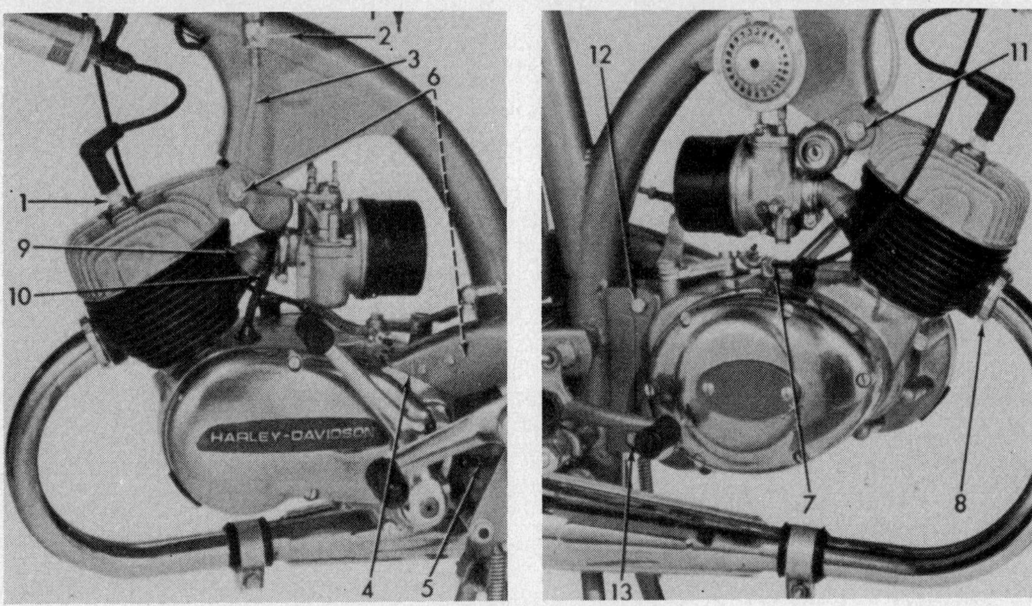

Engine removal points—shown is a MS model

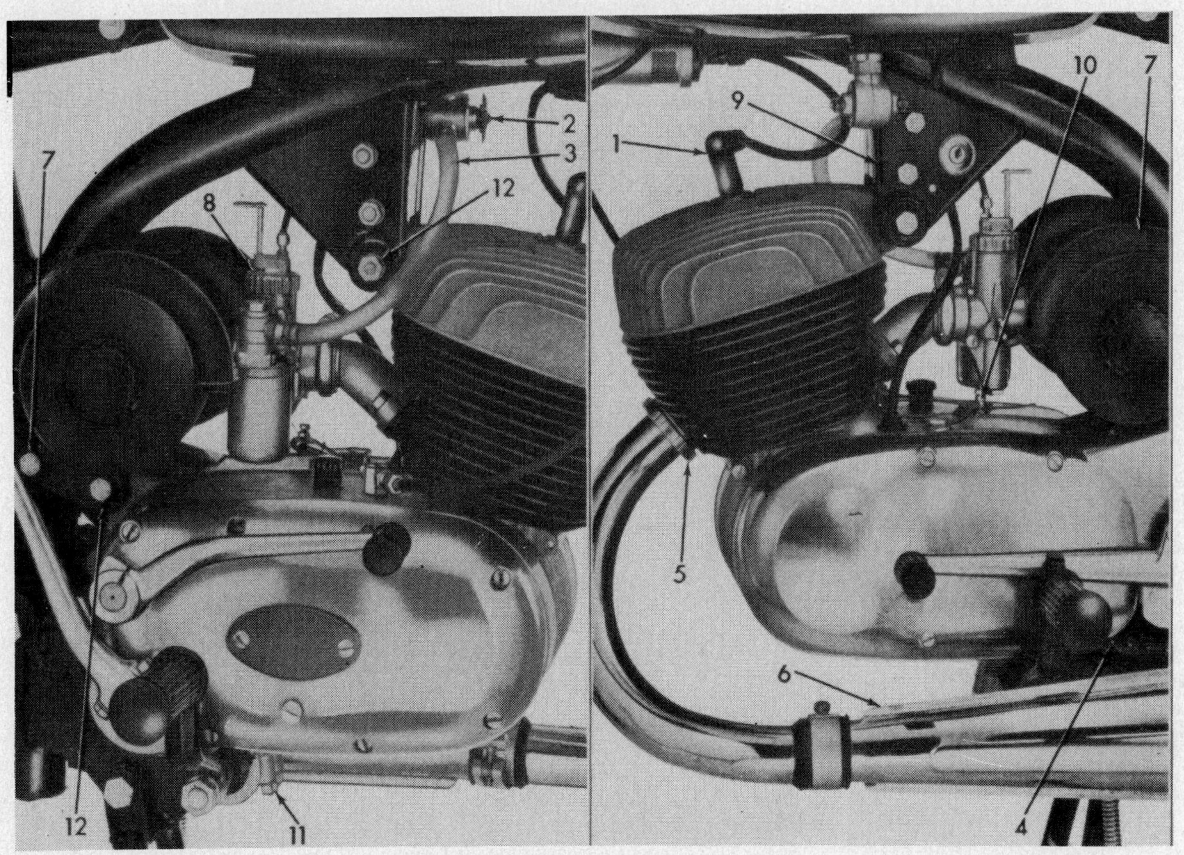

Engine removal points—shown is a ML model

11. Remove the bottom mounting cap nuts and washers.

12. Remove the rear and top engine mounting bolt nuts, lockwashers, and bolts. Be prepared to support the engine in case it tips forward.

13. Carefully support the engine in the front, pry under the bottom of the crankcase rear end to free the engine from the rubber mount, and lift the engine free.

14. Install the engine in the reverse order of removal.

MODEL 165

1. Disconnect the yellow generator lead and the black and white ground wire from the regulator terminals.

2. Remove the exhaust manifold clamp, muffler support bolt, and the exhaust assembly.

3. Remove the chain guard screws and slide the chain guard from the rear of the frame.

4. Disconnect the drive chain master link and remove the chain.

5. Remove the carburetor cover bolts and covers.

6. Remove the crankcase cover screws and cover. It is not necessary to disconnect the clutch cable and housing.

7. Disconnect the spark plug lead, and remove the spark plug and fuel line at the carburetor and tank.

8. Disconnect the throttle cable at the carburetor.

9. Disconnect the black wire from the rear fender terminal and the green wire from the fuse container, then remove the fuse and disconnect the "bat" and "gen" leads from the regulator terminal.

10. Disconnect the remaining battery lead and loosen the battery retaining strap nut until the strap, cover, and battery are free to be removed.

11. Remove the battery holder and regulator as a unit after removing the flat head screw under the battery and the top rear motor mount.

12. Remove the remaining engine mounting bolts and then the engine from the left side of the frame.

13. Install the engine in the reverse order of removal, consulting the wiring diagram for the proper electrical connections.

B-MODELS (Consult The Model 165 Illustration)

1. Consult the above section steps two, three, four, six, and seven.

2. Disconnect the throttle cable at the carburetor.

3. Disconnect the red magneto wire at the stop light switch, and the yellow and green magneto leads from the ignition coil.

4. Disconnect the red lead from the magneto to the ignition switch from its connection at the magneto, and remove the insulating tube (all models except BTF).

5. Disconnect the black wire from the magneto to the handlebar kill button (BTF models).

6. Remove the engine mounting bolts and the engine from the left side of the frame.

7. Install the engine in the reverse order of removal, and do the following:

a. Replace the red magneto-to-ignition switch and insulating sleeve with new ones. Soaking the tube in lacquer thinner to make it pliable will ease installation. Consult the wiring diagrams to complete all connections.

b. Tape the wires to the frame tube located beneath the crankcase.

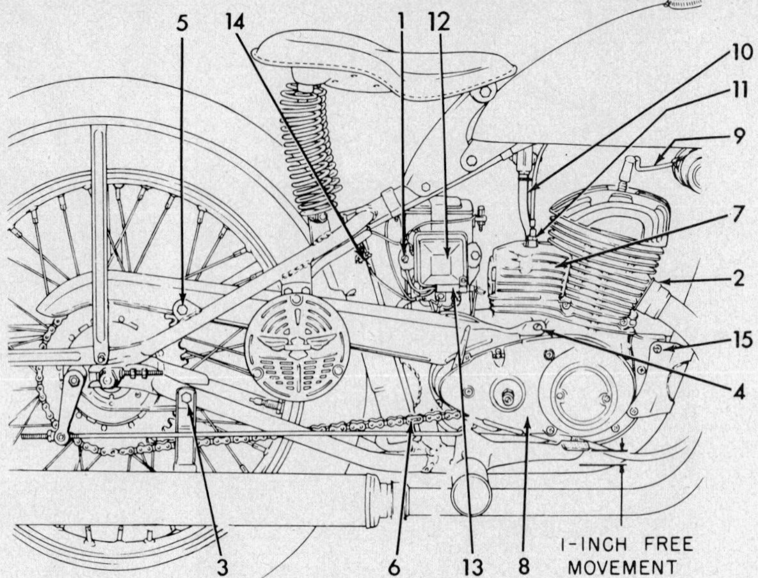

Engine removal points—shown is a Model 165

1. Regulator ground terminal
2. Exhaust pipe clamp
3. Muffler support bolt
4. Front chain guard screw
5. Rear chain guard screw
6. Rear chain master link
7. Carburetor cover (2)
8. Crankcase cover
9. High tension lead
10. Gasoline line
11. Carburetor cap, control housing and cable
12. Voltage regulator
13. Fuse
14. Rear fender terminal
15. Engine mounting bolts (4)

Cylinder And Piston

Disassembly

M MODELS

1. Thoroughly clean the crankcase around the cylinder and blow it dry to prevent any foreign objects from falling into the crankcase.

2. Disconnect the spark plug lead, and remove the spark plug, carburetor silencer, air cleaner, exhaust pipe screw nut, and remove or shift the exhaust pipe out of the way.

3. Turn off the petcock, disconnect the gas line at the tank, and remove the carburetor at the manifold.

4. Remove the cylinder head nuts, washers or lockwashers, cylinder head, and head gasket (if applicable). Loosen the head if necessary by tapping gently with a wooden block and hammer.

5. Carefully work the cylinder free of the cylinder studs far enough to allow a clean, oil-soaked rag to be inserted over the crankcase opening to prevent foreign objects from falling into the crankcase. Lift the cylinder free and remove and discard the base gasket.

6. Remoe the piston ring or rings by prying one end free of the piston grooves, then freeing the other end, and removing the rings while keeping them spread wide enough to clean the piston.

7. Using a sharp, pointed instrument, pry one of the piston pin circlips (lockring) free.

8. Press or gently tap the piston pin free by hand while firmly supporting the piston. Remove the piston and remaining circlip.

S AND B MODELS

1. Perform all the steps in the preceding section. It will be necessary to raise the tank to provide sufficient clearance for cylinder removal. There is a cylinder spacer used on 1962 BT and BTH models.

ALL MODELS

Inspection and Repair

1. Clean all parts in a suitable carbon and gum-dissolving solvent and blow them dry.

2. Inspect the piston pin for a pitted, grooved, or damaged condition, and replace it as necessary.

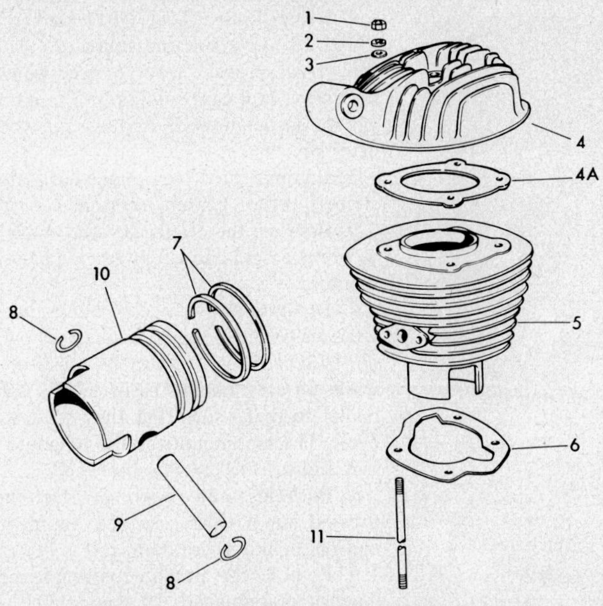

Cylinder and piston assemblies—shown is a M-50

1. Nut (4)
2. Lockwasher (4) (M-50, M-65)
3. Plain washer (4)
4. Head

4A. Head gasket (1967 and later)
5. Cylinder
6. Gasket
7. Rings (2) MSR (1 or 2)
8. Lock ring (2)
9. Piston pin
10. Piston
11. Cylinder stud (4)

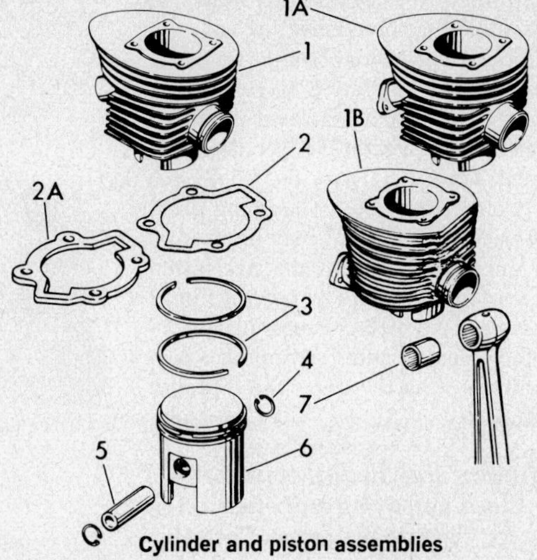

Cylinder and piston assemblies

1. Cylinder (165 model)

1A. Cylinder (Hummer model)

1B. Cylinder (Super 10 model)

2. Gasket

2A. Spacer (1962 BT, BTH)

3. Set piston rings
4. Piston pin lock ring (2)
5. Piston pin
6. Piston
7. Piston pin needle roller bearing

3. Inspect the piston pin fit in the connecting rod for excessive play. Pin fit should be 0.000–0.0001 in. loose for M Models and 0.0002–0.0012 in. loose for the B Models. Consult the "Connecting Rod Needle Roller Bearing Replacement" section for bearing removal procedures if necessary due to wear, pitting, or damage.

4. Inspect the piston pin for excessive clearance in the piston. At room temperature, the fit should be 0.0001 in. tight.

5. Replace the circlips whenever they are removed from their grooves in the piston. If the grooves become damaged, the piston must be replaced.

6. Inspect the piston and cylinder for cracks, burrs, gouges, grooves, or burn spots–especially on the piston crown. Replace the piston if worn or damaged and refinish the cylinder as described in "Cylinder Refinishing" or replace it.

7. Inspect the piston ring locating pins for a secure fit, and replace the piston if they are not tight.

8. Check the connecting rod for excessive end play while the piston is removed.

a. On M Models the connecting rod, bearings, crank pin, and thrust washers (if applicable) must be replaced as an assembly if vertical play or side shake exceeds the limits set forth in the "Engine and Transmission Specifications Chart."

b. On the B Models, the lower connecting rod bearings must be replaced if the vertical play exceeds 0.002 in. total movement.

9. Inspect the connecting rod for damage or misalignment. If necessary, consult the "Crankcase" section for replacement procedures.

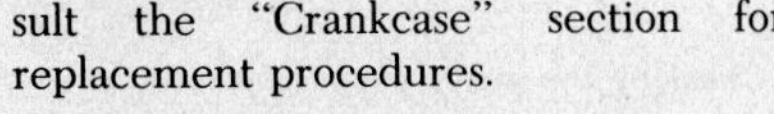

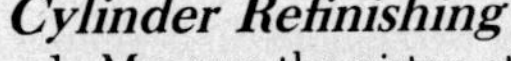

Cylinder Refinishing

1. Measure the piston at a point ½ in. up from the bottom of the piston skirt (measured from front to rear) and 90° from the piston pin center line.

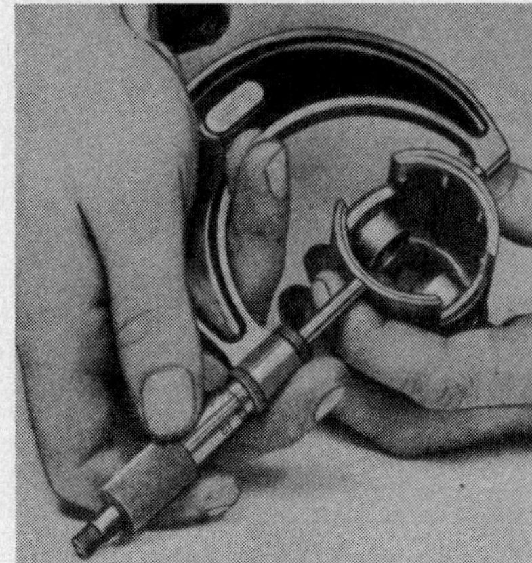

Measuring the piston

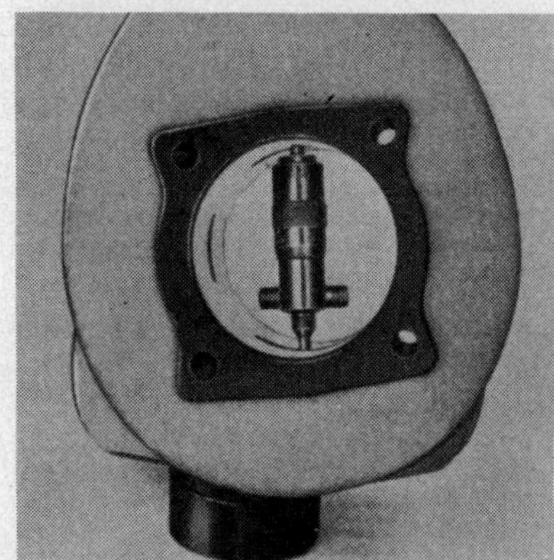

Measuring the cylinder

2. Use an inside micrometer to measure the cylinder bore, front to back and then side to side, at a point ¼ in. above the exhaust port (measured from front to rear).

3. Subtract the figure obtained for the piston from that of the bore to arrive at piston-cylinder clearance.

4. Oversize refinishing is not necessary if the bore is not scored or damaged, and the wear is less than 0.001 in. for the M Models or 0.002 in. for the S and B Models. Install a standard size of piston, or one which will provide standard clearance if the cylinder is oversize, if the clearance is no greater than 0.002 in. for M Models or 0.007 in. for the B Models.

5. If the cylinder is worn less than 0.001 in. for the M Models, or 0.002 in. for the S and B Models, the original piston may be reused if it and the cylinder are not damaged. Always install new rings when the engine is taken down.

6. Oversize pistons are available in 0.008 in., 0.016 in., and 0.024 in. sizes for the M Models and in 0.0005 in., 0.010 in., 0.020 in., 0.030 in., and 0.040 in. sizes for the B Models. A 0.050 in. piston is available for the Hummer only.

7. Refinish the cylinder to the size of the piston to be used, plus the desired clearance. If this necessitates reboring in excess of 0.025 in. for M Models, 0.040 in. for the 165, or 0.050 in. for the Hummer, the cylinder will be overstressed and should be replaced instead.

Connecting Rod Needle Roller Bearing Replacement

1. When bearings are worn or damaged, and replacement becomes neces-

sary, either the crankcase must be disassembled so the connecting rod may be supported (a means of support must be devised if the operation is to be performed while the bottom end is still assembled) or the Piston Pin Needle Roller Bearing Tool (H-D part no. 95971–52) and Connecting Rod Clamping Tool (H-D part no. 95952–33 may be used.

2. Since there is only one size piston pin, appropriate oversize bearings must be used to take up any excess play. Consult the "Engine and Transmission Specifications Chart" for the proper clearances.

Cylinder and Piston Assembly

1. Check piston ring gap before assembling the rings on the piston. The cylinder bore must be thoroughly cleaned.

2. Place the ring squarely in the cylinder bore about ½ in. from the top of the cylinder and check the gap with a feeler gauge. Then check the ring side-clearance against the specifications chart. If the clearance is excessive, replace the piston assembly.

3. If the cylinder is not worn more than 0.001 in. or M Models or 0.002 in. on the B Models, install standard size rings. If wear exceeds these figures, install the appropriate oversize rings. Never try to file the ring ends of rings meant for larger pistons to achieve a correct fit.

4. Install rings with a piston ringer or ring expander taking care not to break, twist, or bend the rings, or damage the finish on the piston. The top two rings are identical (on models with three or more rings) and may be interchanged. The rings must be staggered to keep compression at a maximum.

5. Thoroughly clean the cylinder and crankcase mating surfaces, apply a suitable gasket sealer to a new cylinder gasket, and position the gasket.

6. Lubricate the upper connecting rod bearing with engine oil.

7. Place the piston in position on the connecting rod so the arrow on the crown faces forward. Apply heat to the piston crown in a circular motion with a blow torch. Repeatedly attempt to install the piston pin by hand until it will slide in without undue force. Lightly oiling the pin may help but heat is to be mainly relied on.

8. After the piston cools, insert new circlips with the flat side (if applicable) facing out.

9. Liberally lubricate the cylinder walls, piston, and rod assembly. Slowly lower the cylinder over the piston while squeezing shut first the top two rings and then the bottom one.

10. Replace the cylinder head gasket and install it in place after afpplying a suitable gasket sealer. On the Super-10, which uses no head gasket, apply a coat of aluminum paint to the head and cylinder mating surfaces.

11. Place the cylinder head on the cylinder mounting studs, then assemble the washers tighten the nuts finger-Tight, and secure the head nuts evenly in diagonal pairs.

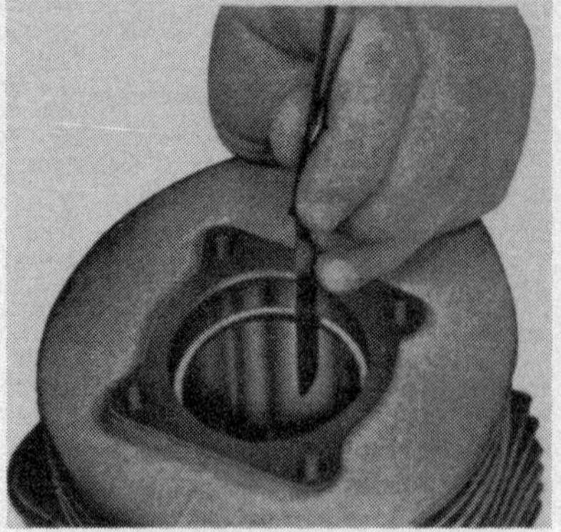

Checking the piston ring gap

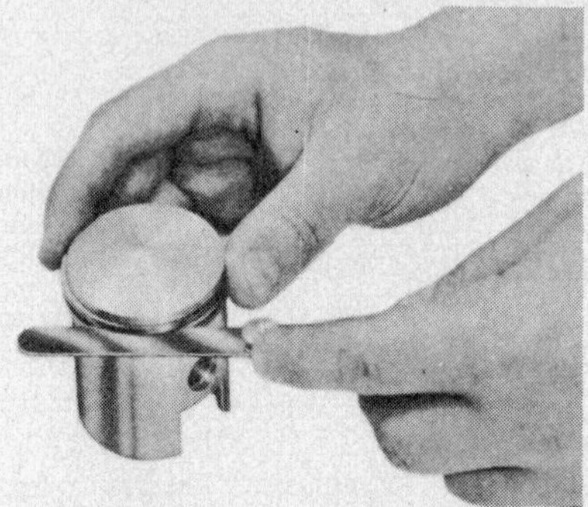

Checking the piston ring side-clearance

Crankcase

Disassembly

MODELS M-50 AND M-65

1. Remove the engine from the frame as described in the engine "Removal and Installation" section, and disassemble the top end as described in the "Cylinder and Piston" section.

2. Remove the left side cover assembly as described in the "Starter" section.

3. Remove the magneto-generator assembly as described in the "Magneto-Generator" section.

4. Using Puller Tool (H-D part no. 97292–61), or a suitable substitute, pull the drive sprocket free. A gear puller may be used if care is taken not to damage the sprocket teeth. Remove the woodruff key.

5. Remove the drive pinion gear as described in the "Clutch" section.

6. Remove the crankcase studs which secure the right and left crankcase halves together.

7. Separate the crankcase halves with Crankcase Disassembly Tool (H-D part no. 97326–65), or a suitable substitute, while tapping on the cases with a soft mallet to make sure that they separate evely. The tool mounts on the magneto's seat and presses on the crankshaft.

8. Bushings and bearings may be pressed out if worn, cracked, rough in motion, or otherwise damaged.

9. Remove the clutch actuating lever; if worn or damaged, by removing the shaft lockscrew (Model M-65 only) and then pulling the lever straight out.

10. Remove the crankshaft assembly from the crankcase.

MODELS M-100 AND M-125

1. Remove the right side cover and clutch assembly as described in the "Clutch" section, and disassemble the top end as described in the "Cylinder and Piston" section.

2. Remove the shifter pawl carrier as described in the "Transmission" section.

3. Remove the magneto generator as described in the "Magneto-Generator" section.

4. Using a suitable gear puller remove the drive sprocket. Remove the woodruff key.

5. Remove the drive pinion nut and pinion as described in the "Clutch" section.

6. Remove the crankcase studs which secure the crankcase halves together, then use Crankcase Disassembling Tool (H-D part no. 97347–68P), or a suitable substitute, while tapping the cases with a soft mallet to separate the crankcase halves. The tool mounts on the left crankcase pad and presses on both the crankshaft and countershaft.

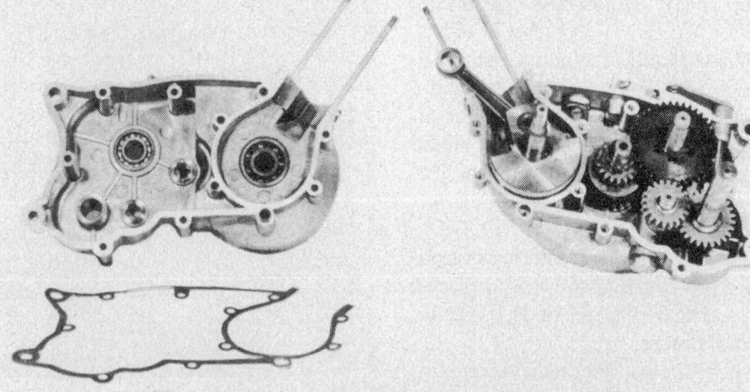

The separated crankcase halves—shown is a M-50

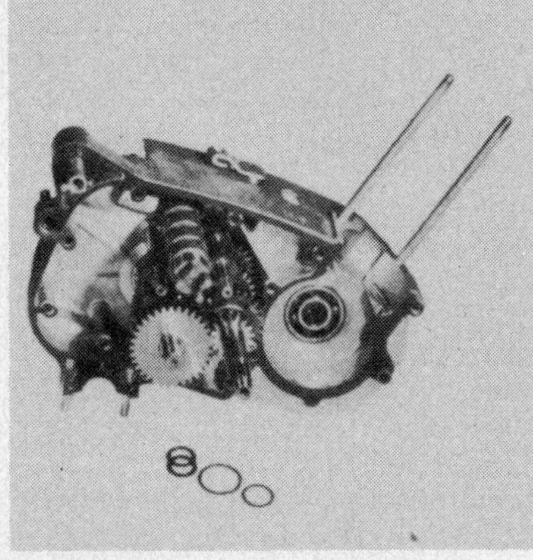

The separated crankcase halves

7. Bushings and bearings may be pressed out if worn, cracked, rough in motion, or otherwise damaged. Blind bearings may be pulled free with Snap-On Puller (H-D part no. CG-40A) or a suitable substitute.

8. Continue as described in steps 9 and 10 in the previous section.

Inspection and Repair

ALL MODELS

1. Clean all parts in a suitable solvent and blow them dry.

2. Inspect all parts for excessive wear or damage and replace if necessary. Parts with worn or broken threads or surfaces must be replaced.

3. If the connecting rod, crankpin roller bearing, or the crankpin are in need of replacement, replace the entire assembly–including the thrust washers.

4. Remove and replace the oil seals.

5. Inspect the main bearings for wear, excessive play, or rough motion, and replace if necessary by pressing them in and out with an arbor press and a suitable size plug.

6. Press replacement bushings in flush, then lap them with a suitably sized lapper. Avoid removing excess metal.

Crankcase Assembly

MODELS M-50 AND M-65

1. Assembly is in the reverse order of disassembly.

2. Use Crankshaft Assembling Tool (H-D part no. 97342–65P), or a suitable substitute, to pull the right crankshaft assembly into the right case ball bearing.

3. Assemble the transmission components as described in the "Transmission" section.

4. Install the left crankcase half on the crankshaft using the same tool as in step two, taking care not to damage the oil seal.

5. Measure the crankshaft end-play between the two main bearings with a dial indicator by shifting the crankshaft all the way to one side then shifting it all the way to the other side while positioning the indicator in such a way as to allow the plunger to measure the distance the crankshaft moves. Add more or less shims to the right crankshaft until play is within 0.004–0.008 in.

6. Complete assembly in the reverse order of disassembly.

MODELS M-100 AND M-125

1. Assembly is in the reverse order of disassembly.

Assembling the right crankcase

2. Assemble the transmission components as directed in the "Transmission" section, taking care to remove the shifter cam stop before assembling the cases.

3. Install the left case over the left crankshaft using Crankshaft Assembling Tool (H-D part no. 97342–65P) or a suitable substitute, taking care not to damage any oil seals while pulling the shaft into the ball bearing.

4. Using Crankshaft Assembling Tool (H-D part no. 96110–68P) or a suitable substitute, assemble the right shaft into the right bearing.

5. Measure the crankshaft end-play between the two main bearings with a dial indicator by shifting the crankshaft all the way to one side then shifting it all the way to the other while positioning the indicator in such a way as to measure the distance the crankshaft moves. Add more or less shims to the left shaft until play is within 0.002–0.004 in. Crankshaft Assembling Tool (H-D part no. 96110–68P) can be used to shift the crankshaft from left to right.

6. Complete assembly in the reverse order of disassembly.

S AND B MODELS

Disassembly

1. Remove the engine from the frame as described in the engine "Removal and Installation" section, and disassemble the top end as described in the "Cylinder and Piston" section.

2. Remove the generator (Model 165) as described in the "Generator" section, or the magneto-generator (Hummer, Super-10, etc.) as described in the "Magneto-Generator" section.

3. Remove the transmission mainshaft sprocket and the outer gear shifter indicator arm as described in the "Transmission" section.

4. Remove the clutch cover, drain the transmission oil, and remove the engine

Assembling the right crankcase

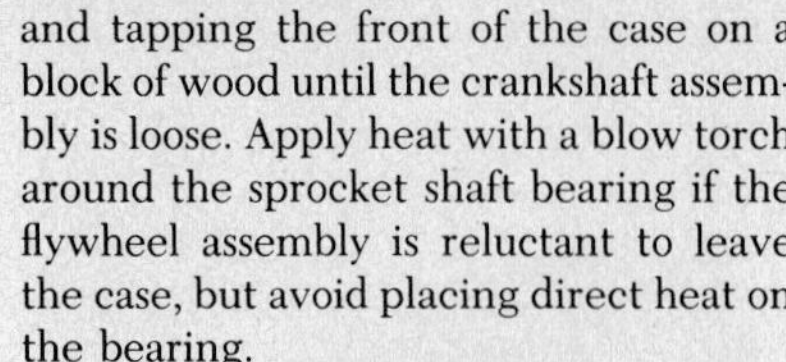

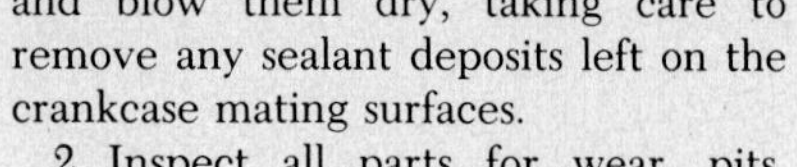

sprocket, primary chain, and clutch assembly as described in the "Clutch" section.

5. Remove the starter assembly as described in the "Starter" section.

6. Remove the oil seal screws and star washers, pry the oil seal from the crankcase side, and remove and discard the gasket.

7. Remove all the crankcase securing screws.

8. Separate the crankcase halves by inserting two engine-frame mounting screws as depicted, then alternately strike each screw with a soft mallet while supporting the crankcase with pliers. Apply heat with a blow torch to the cases around the magneto-generator or generator shaft, and around the locating dowel pins if the cases are difficult to separate.

9. If the crankshaft bearing remains in the case, it may be drifted out at this time with a suitably sized drift.

10. Remove the transmission as described in the "Transmission" section.

11. Remove the crankshaft assembly by holding the case with the shaft down and tapping the front of the case on a block of wood until the crankshaft assembly is loose. Apply heat with a blow torch around the sprocket shaft bearing if the flywheel assembly is reluctant to leave the case, but avoid placing direct heat on the bearing.

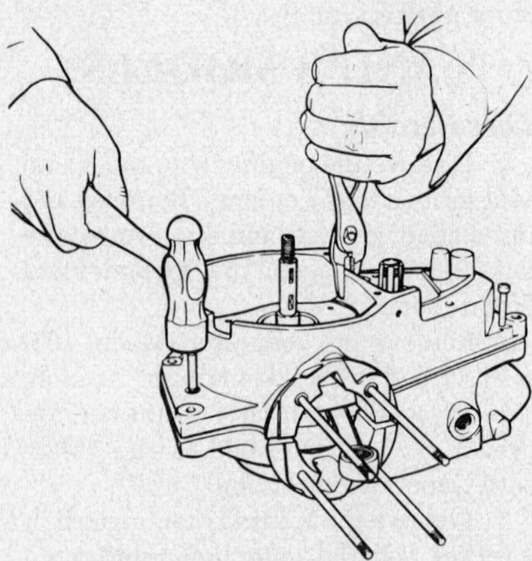

Separating the crankcase halves

12. Remove the shaft bearings. If the bearings will not come free easily, then a puller bar must be fabricated for use with Wedge Puller (H-D part no. 95637–46) or a suitable substitute. You'll need the following items:

a. A piece of flat stock ½ in. thick and 1½ x 4 in. for the puller bar with 7/16 in. wide by 1 in. deep slots at the edges.

b. A puller screw from a Harley-Davidson puller or one with ½ x 18 thread.

c. A pair of 4½ in. long cap screws with ⅜ x 16 thread.

d. A ½ in. hex nut.

Secure the shaft in a copper or wood-jawed vise and use the puller to remove the bearing, then invert the crankshaft and pull the other bearing. Place the ½ in. hex nut between the end of the shaft and the puller screw to protect the shaft while pulling the bearing from the generator or magneto-generator shaft.

13. Drift the sprocket shaft inner and outer bearings free of the case with a suitably sized drift. The oil seal and retainer will come out with the bearings. There are two spacing shims between the inner bearing and the flywheel on 1964 models and one shim on 1965 models. Apply heat with a blow torch to the case around the outer bearings if they are difficult to remove.

Inspection and Repair

1. Clean all parts in a suitable solvent and blow them dry, taking care to remove any sealant deposits left on the crankcase mating surfaces.

2. Inspect all parts for wear, pits, grooves, or damage, and replace if necessary.

3. Inspect the flywheel recesses for a grooved or shouldered condition where the bearings ride. If necessary, the recesses can be lapped out and oversize bearings installed.

4. On 1962 and later models, the rod and bearing set must be replaced if either is worn or damaged.

5. Inspect the shaft bearings for excessive shake, play, or rough motion, and replace them if necessary.

6. Inspect the bearing fit in the crankcases and on the shafts for proper clearances. The fit in the crankcase should be from 0.0005 in. tight to 0.0005 in. loose, and the fit on the shafts should be 0.0001–0.0007 in. tight. Excessive clearance in the generator or magneto-generator shaft bearing can be taken up by installing an oversize bushing in the right case in the following manner:

a. Secure the case in a suitable manner, such as screwing it to a board or work table with wood screws through the mounting screw holes.

b. Ream the crankcase with a suitably sized reamer by rotating the reamer clockwise until it bottoms on the mounting apparatus. Continue to rotate the reamer while withdrawing it.

c. Clean all metal chips from around the crankcase.

d. Slip the knurled end of the oversize bushing onto the shouldered end of the Right Crankcase Bearing Sleeve Tool (H-D part no. 95935–48) or a similar driver. Lightly oil the bushing with engine oil.

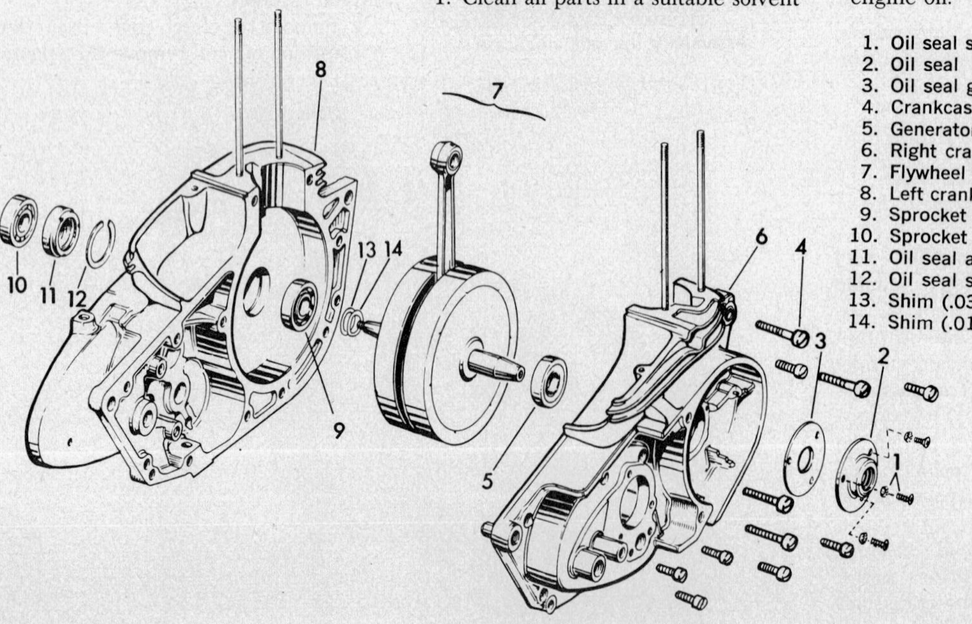

1. Oil seal screw and washer (3)
2. Oil seal
3. Oil seal gasket
4. Crankcase screws (11)
5. Generator-magneto shaft bearing
6. Right crankcase side
7. Flywheel and connecting rod assembly
8. Left crankcase side
9. Sprocket shaft bearing—inner
10. Sprocket shaft bearing—outer
11. Oil seal and retainer
12. Oil seal spring ring
13. Shim (.036) 1964 or (.060) 1965
14. Shim (.014) 1964

Crankcase assembly

e. Hold the bushing over the crankcase bearing boss so the bushing slot and the crankcase oil hole are in alignment.

f. Press the bushing into the case until the knurled end is in the case recess and the smooth end is flush with the outside of the case.

7. Replace the oil seals if worn, damaged, or if the seal retaining springs are damaged. It is always a good idea to replace the seals whenever the bottom end is taken down since any air leaks will adversely affect carburetion.

Crankcase Assembly

1. Support the flywheel assembly on two 5 in. blocks and lightly press the bearings onto their respective shafts until they bottom. The 1964 and earlier models have two spacers between the sprocket shaft bearing and the flywheel. Use a piece of pipe ¾ in. in diameter and 4½ in. long as a sleeve for pressing the bearing in place.

2. With the left crankcase clutch side up on a workbench, install the oil seal spring ring, lubricate the oil seal and retainer with engine oil, and drift or press it into place with the slotted side facing in.

3. Invert the case and assemble the transmission as directed in the "Transmission" section.

4. Place the flywheel tapered spacer which comes in the Tool Set around the lower connecting rod bearing to prevent the flywheels from closing during installation. Anything which will keep the flywheels aligned, and which will fit snugly between the two, may be substituted.

5. Assemble the flywheel assembly in the left case. The sprocket shaft bearing should seat against the oil seal retaining ring. Apply heat to the case around the bearing bore with a blow torch if the bearing will not readily slip into the case. Take care not to damage the oil seal.

6. Apply a suitable sealer to the crankcase mating surfaces and carefully assemble the right case to the left case, making sure that the inner gear indicator arm and the gear shifter ratchet yoke are properly engaged. Apply heat to the dowel pin holes, and around the bearing bore if the bearing will not readily slip into the case. Test for a positive engagement of the indicator arm then secure the crankcase screws.

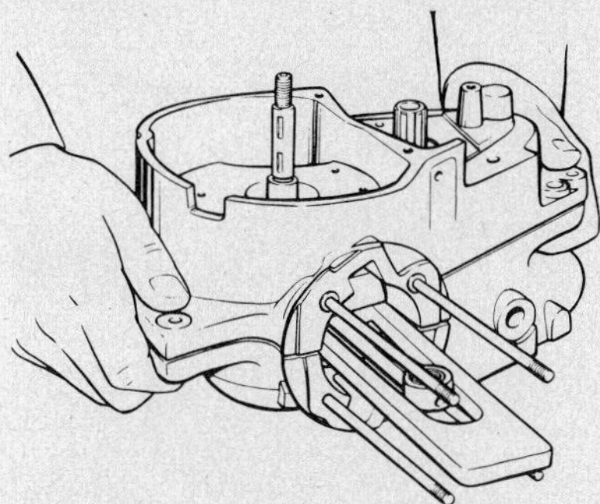
Assembling the crankcase halves

7. Assemble the transmission mainshaft oil seal, drive sprocket, and outer gear indicator arm as described in the "Transmission" section.

8. Apply a suitable gasket sealer to a new oil seal gasket and assemble it and the oil seal to the right case.

9. Remove the flywheel tapered spacer.

10. Install the generator on the Model 165 as described in the "Generator" section.

11. Install the magneto-generator on the B models as described in the "Magneto-Generator" section.

12. Place the engine clutch side up and install the starter assembly as described in the "starter" section.

13. Install the countershaft sprocket, primary chain, and clutch assembly as described in the "Cluth" section.

14. Install the top end as described in the "Cylinder and Piston" section.

15. Install the clutch and magneto side covers, and install the engine in the frame as described in the "Engine Removal and Installation" section.

16. Adjust the ignition timing as described in the "Tune-Up" section.

Clutch

M-50 AND M-65

Disassembly

1. Place a drip pan beneath the clutch cover, remove the cover screws, cover, and cover gasket.

2. Compress the clutch springs with Clutch Spring Compressor (H-D part no. 97345–65P) or a suitable substitute and pry the lockring free.

3. Rem(ve the spring plate, spring caps, springs, pressure plate, clutch discs and plates, and the clutch release pin.

4. Remove the clutch hub nut by holding the clutch steady with Clutch Holding Tool (H-D part no. 97431–65P) and then removing the nut. Any means of holding the hub steady, such as wedging a wooden door stop between the hub gear teeth and the side of the case, will work.

5. Pull the hub with Clutch Hub Puller (H-D part no. 97343–65P) or a suitable gear puller.

6. Remove the bearing assembly, thrust washer, and spacer.

7. Secure the clutch shell assembly with Clutch Shell Gear Holding Tool (H-D part no. 97340–65P) or any substitute means such as the one described in step four and remove the drive pinion gear nut, then remove the pinion gear with Primary Drive Pinion Puller (H-D part no. 97346–65PA FOR THE M-50, and 97348–68P for the M-65) or a suitable gear puller.

Removing the clutch lockring

Removing the clutch hub nut

8. Lift the clutch housing free, and remove the clutch housing gear nuts and bolts to free the gear if so desired.

Inspection and Repair

1. Clean all parts other than the fabric-covered clutch discs in a suitable solvent and blow them dry. Soak the friction discs in clean gasoline, blow dry, then soak them in clean engine oil.

2. Inspect the clutch springs for a collapsed or damaged condition and replace them as necessary. Springs which are less than 0.984 in. long should be replaced. Springs should be replaced as a complete set.

3. Inspect the clutch plates and discs for a warped, worn, scored, or burned condition, and replace them if necessary. Press your fingernail into the fabric of each disc and replace them if no mark remains. Plates and discs should be replaced as complete sets. Remove burrs from the plate's teeth with a file but avoid removing excess metal.

4. Inspect the clutch shell and pinion gears for a worn or damaged condition and replace as a set if necessary.

5. Inspect the shell gear bearings for a worn, damaged, or pitted condition, and replace as a set along with a new thrust washer if necessary.

Assembly

1. Assembly is in the reverse order of disassembly.

2. Grease the clutch hub thrust bear-

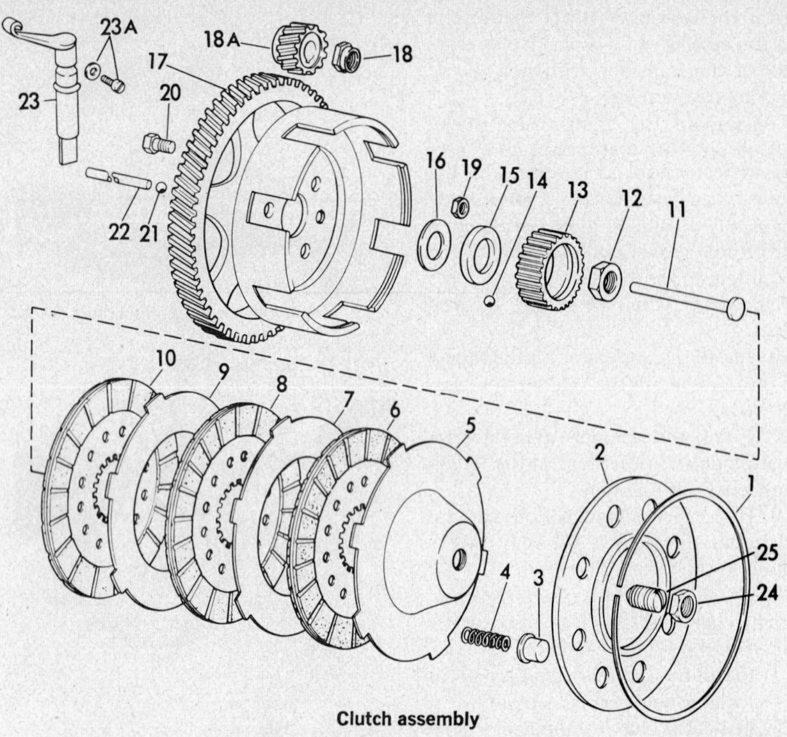

1. Lock ring
2. Spring plate
3. Spring cap (6/M-50) (8/M-65)
4. Spring (6/M-50) (8/M-65)
5. Pressure plate
6. Drive plate (lined)
7. Drive plate
8. Drive plate (lined)
9. Drive plate
10. Drive plate (lined)
11. Clutch release pin
12. Nut
13. Clutch hub
14. Ball bearings (19)
15. Thrust washer
16. Spacer (variable thickness)
17. Clutch shell gear assembly
18. Pinion gear nut

18A. Pinion gear

19. Nut (6)
20. Bolt (6)
21. Ball
22. Release pin
23. Release lever assembly

23A. Retainer screw (M-65) and washer

24. Release adjusting screw nut
25. Release adjusting screw

Clutch assembly

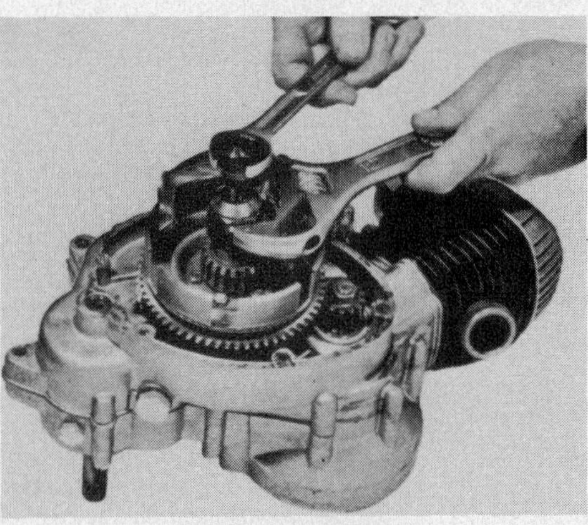

Removing the clutch hub

Removing the drive pinion gear nut

ing balls with Harley-Davidson Grease-All or a suitable substitute.

3. Once the clutch hub nut is secured, check the end-play of the clutch shell gear. End-play should not exceed 0.001–0.004 in. and can be adjusted through judicious use of the variable-thickness spacer which seats against the clutch shell.

4. Replenish the oil supply and adjust the clutch as directed in the "Maintenance Items."

M-100 AND M-125

Disassembly

1. Place a drip pan under the clutch cover and remove the shift lever, kick-start lever, cover screws, cover, and cover gasket.

2. Remove the stud nuts by loosening them one turn each so undue pressure is not placed on the pressure plate.

3. Remove the springs, spring cups, pressure plate, clutch plates and discs, and clutch release pin. The discs and plates are easily removed with a piece of wire which can be used to lift and slide them free, or by tipping the machine over on its side to let them slide out.

4. Remove the clutch hub nut by holding the clutch steady with the Clutch Holding Tool (H-D part no. 97237–68P), or a suitable substitute, and then removing the nut. Any means of holding the clutch steady, such as wedging a wooden door stop between the hub gear teeth and the side of the case, will work.

5. Remove the nut lock, clutch hub, thrust washer, clutch shell gear, and the variable-thickness spacer.

6. Secure the clutch with Clutch Holding Tool (H-D part no. 97237–68P) and remove the pinion gear nut and nut lock.

7. Pull the pinion gear with Puller (H-D part no. 97348–68P) or a suitable gear puller.

Removing the clutch hub nut

Removing the drive pinion gear nut

Removing the drive pinion gear

2. The lined side of the last disc should face the crankcase wall.

3. Once the clutch hub nut is secured, check the end-play of the clutch shell gear. End-play should not exceed 0.002–0.004 in., and can be adjusted through judicious use of the variable-thickness washer which sits against the clutch shell.

4. Replenish the oil supply and adjust the clutch as directed in the "Maintenance Items."

Clutch Cable Replacement

1. Loosen the clamping block setscrews, remove the cable block from the end of the cable, and pull the cable and housing free of the adjusting screw.

2. Disconnect the cable at the handlebar lever by aligning the adjusting screw and nut slots so the cable is free to pass through.

3. Remove the cable and housing from the frame clamps.

4. The old cable can now be pulled through the housing and a new one can be installed. Before replacing the cable, lubricate it thoroughly.

5. When replacing the cable and housing, attach the cable to the handlever first and turn the adjusting screw into the lever. Run the cable through the right side of the fork, through the upper and lower brackets, down through the control guide near the horn, through the cable adjuster screw and cable block, and then seat the cable block against the release lever.

6. Tighten the cable block setscrew and adjust the clutch as described in the "Maintenance Items."

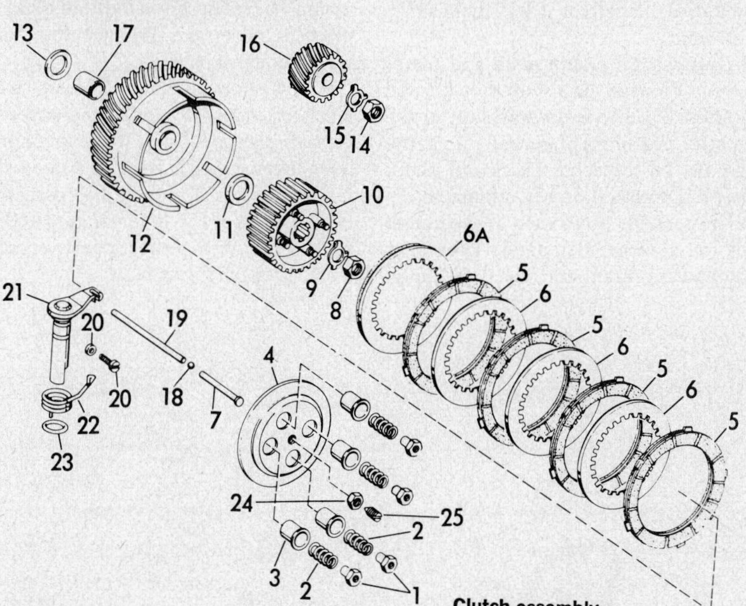

Clutch assembly

1. Stud nut (4)
2. Spring (4)
3. Spring cup (4)
4. Pressure plate
5. Friction (lined) disc (4)
6. Drive (unlined) disc (3)
6A. Back disc (lined on one side)
7. Release pin
8. Hub nut
9. Nut lock
10. Hub
11. Thrust washer
12. Shell gear
13. Spacer (variable-thickness)
14. Pinion gear nut
15. Pinion gear nut lock
16. Pinion gear
17. Shell gear bushing
18. Ball
19. Release rod
20. Release lever retainer screw and washer
21. Release lever
22. Release lever spring
23. Release lever washer
24. Release adjusting screw nut
25. Release adjusting screw

8. Remove the clutch shell gear from the shaft.

9. Remove and release lever retainer screw and washer, release lever, and the lever spring if the crankcases are to be split.

Inspect and Repair

1. Consult the M-50 and M-65 "Inspection and Repair" section.

2. The clutch spring free-length for these models is 1.62 in. If any of the springs are shorter than this, they should be replaced as a set.

Assembly

1. Assembly is in the reverse order of disassembly.

S AND B MODELS

Disassembly

1. Place a drip pan under the clutch cover, remove the shift lever, kick-start lever, clutch cover screws, clutch cover, and the cover gasket.

2. Screw two Clutch Release Disc Studs (H-D part no. 37902–47) through the thrust plate and into the releasing disc, then compress the clutch springs by tightening two Compression Nuts (H-D part no. 7675) down on the studs and against the thrust plate. Studs and nuts with the appropriate size threads may be substituted.

3. Pry off the clutch thrust plate spring ring and remove parts 2–5 (as listed in the illustration) as an assembly. If disassembly of these components is necessary, remove the clutch release disc studs and separate the thrust plate from the releasing disc.

4. Remove the clutch plates and discs from the shell by lifting them with a wire and pulling them free, or by tilting the machine over and allowing them to slide out.

5. Remove the clutch release rod and install the Clutch Lock Plate (H-D part no. 95930–48) or fabricate some means of securing the clutch. Remove the left-hand, threaded clutch hub nut and the engine sprocket nut which has a right-hand thread, then remove the locking device.

6. Pull the clutch hub using the Clutch Hub Puller (H-D part no. 95960–48) or a suitable gear puller. Take care not to lose any of the clutch ball bearings. If any bearings are lost, they should be replaced as a complete set.

7. Loosen, but do not remove the engine sprocket using Engine Sprocket Puller (H-D part no. 95910–48) or a suitable gear puller.

8. Remove the clutch shell, primary chain, and engine sprocket as an assembly.

9. Remove the clutch bushing, bush-

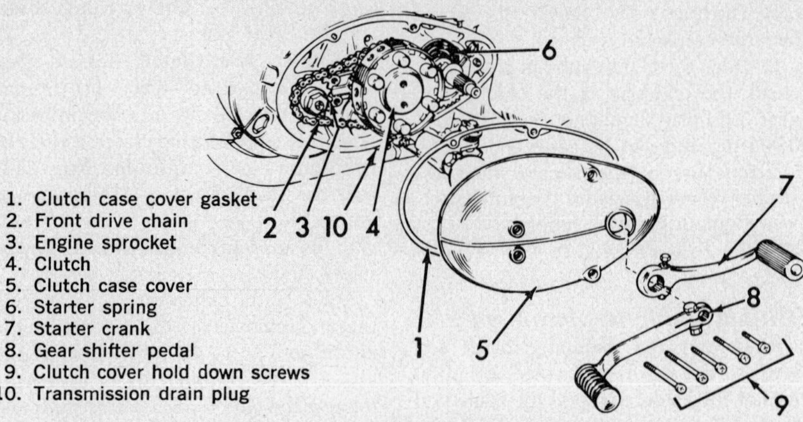

Removing the clutch cover assembly

ing thrust washer, engine sprocket bearing shims, and the engine sprocket key.

10. Pry the starter spring collar lockring from its groove and remove the starter ratchet gear, ratchet spring, and the spring collar.

11. Disassemble the release mechanism, if so desired, in the following manner:

a. Remove the sprocket cover screws and cover, disengage the clutch cable from the clutch release lever, disengage the release lever spring, and loosen the clutch adjusting screw locknut.

b. Remove the adjusting screw, dust cover, and release lever.

c. Drift the release rods free with an appropriately sized drift.

Inspection and Repair

1. Clean all parts other than the clutch friction discs in a suitable solvent and blow them dry. The fabric-covered discs can be cleaned by soaking in clean gasoline, blowing dry, and then soaking in clean engine oil. Carefully scrape any sealer or shellac deposits left from the gaskets with a blunt blade, taking care not to remove any excess metal.

2. Replace the clutch thrust plate spring ring if warped or damaged.

3. Replace the clutch springs if collapsed or damaged, or if less than 13/16 in. in length.

4. Inspect the clutch discs and plates for wear, damage, or a scored or burned condition. If there is no mark left in the fiber after pressing a fingernail into it, the disc must be replaced. Discs and plates should be replaced as a complete set.

5. Inspect the inner face of the clutch shell for a worn, damaged, scored, or scratched condition and install a Clutch Disc Back Plate (H-D part no. 38015–49) in addition to the regular plates and discs if such a condition exists.

6. Inspect the ball bearings and races for wear, pitting, or rough motion, and replace them as a set if necessary. Replace the clutch bushing if there is appreciable play between it and the clutch sprocket hub.

7. Inspect all gears for worn or chipped teeth, and replace them as necessary. The clutch and engine sprockets should be replaced as a set along with the primary chain if it appears to be worn. The clutch sprocket and sprocket hub are removed by removing the rivets which secure them to the clutch shell. When reassembling, the rivets are fed from the outside of the shell (as positioned on the motorcycle) in, and are set flush to no more than 0.047 in. above the clutch shell face. If the clutch sprocket and starter gear have 12 teeth they should be exchanged for the current type which have six teeth.

8. Inspect the starter ratchet spring and clutch bushing thrust washer for a damaged, worn, or—in the case of the spring—a collapsed condition, and replace as necessary. Replace the starter spring collar lockring.

9. Inspect the clutch release worm lever for excessive play in the cover and replace it as necessary. If the lever or release lever spring is worn or damaged, or if the spring is stretched, the parts must be replaced. If the lever fingers and the cable end fit together poorly, replace whichever part is at fault.

1. Clutch thrust plate spring ring
2. Clutch thrust plate
3. Clutch releasing disc
4. Clutch spring (6)
4A. Clutch spring shim washer (6) 1962 and later BTH
5. Clutch spring cup (6)
6. Clutch disc—with fabric lining (3)
6A. Clutch disc—with lining (3) 1962 to early 1964 BTH
7. Clutch disc—steel (2)
8. Clutch release rod—left
9. Clutch hub nut
10. Engine sprocket nut
11. Clutch hub
12. Clutch steel ball (15)
13. Engine sprocket
14. Clutch shell
15. Front chain
16. Clutch bushing
17. Clutch bushing thrust washer
18. Sprocket shaft bearing shim—.007 in.
19. Sprocket shaft key
20. Starter ratchet gear
21. Starter ratchet spring
22. Starter ratchet spring collar
23. Starter spring collar lock ring
24. Clutch sprocket hub
25. Clutch sprocket
26. Clutch sprocket rivet (6)

A Disc, plate, spring assembly

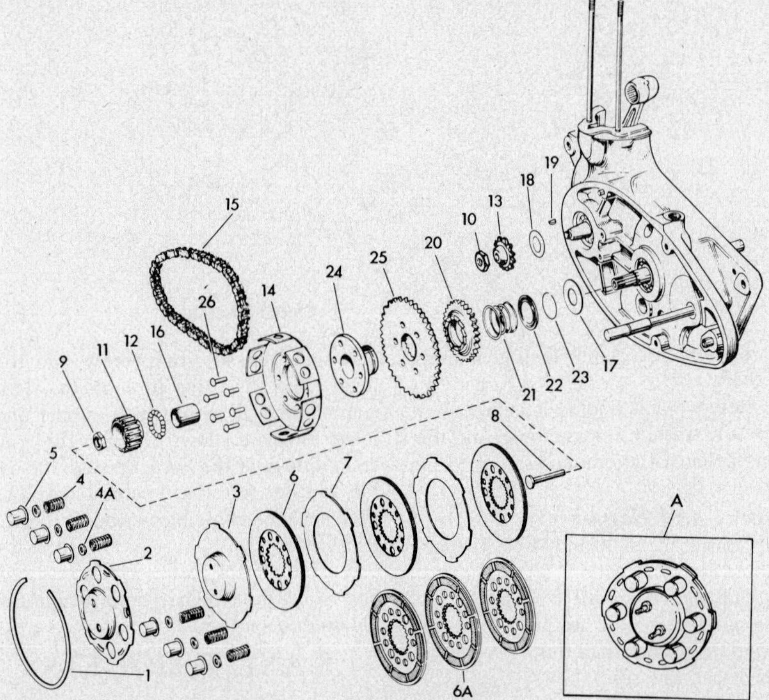

Figure following name of part indicates quantity necessary for one complete assembly.

Clutch assembly

10. Inspect the release rod tips for a worn, damaged, or scored condition and replace them as necessary.

Assembly

1. Lubricate the pushrod tips with engine oil, then insert them in the mainshaft—the short rod first—from the right side of the motorcycle.
2. Assemble the release lever and spring to the sprocket cover, then the adjusting screw, locknut, and the worm cover loosely into the release worm.
3. Check to make sure that the lever action is smooth; lubricate it if necessary. Secure the cable end in the cover slot and lever fingers, and install the cover.
4. Place the starter ratchet gear on the clutch shell and sprocket assembly so the shell and gear teeth mesh.
5. Seat the large end of the starter ratchet spring in the indention on the starter ratchet gear, place the ratchet spring collar over the spring and compress the spring until a new spring lockring can be installed. Rotate the ratchet gear several times to make sure it operates freely.
6. Place the engine sprocket and sprocket nut on the shaft but do not permanently secure them. Using a screwdriver for leverage, press the flywheel assembly as far to the left as it will go. Measure the clearance between the back of the sprocket and the face of the ball bearing mounted in the case. Clearance should not exceed 0.003–0.012 in., and may be adjusted by inserting the appropriate number of 0.007 in. thick shims (H-D part no. 6760) behind the engine sprocket and then rechecking the clearance.
7. Secure the engine sprocket key, slip the clutch bushing thrust washer on the transmission mainshaft, engage the engine and clutch sprockets teeth in the primary chain, and install the two sprockets on their respective shafts. Secure the engine sprocket nut which has a right-hand thread.
8. Lubricate the clutch bushing with grease and install it in the clutch shell.
9. Assemble the clutch bearings in the shell, using grease to hold them in place.
10. Carefully drive the clutch hub onto the mainshaft with a suitable drift.
11. Block the motion of the clutch with Lock Plate (H-D part no. 95930–48), or a suitable substitute, and install and secure the left-hand threaded hub nut to 70 ft lbs torque. Remove the blocking device.
12. Slip the Clutch Disc Back Plate (H-D part no. 38015–49) into the shell if necessary as described in the "Inspection" section. Slip on a fabric disc, then a steel plate, and so on until there are three discs and two plates installed other than the back plate.

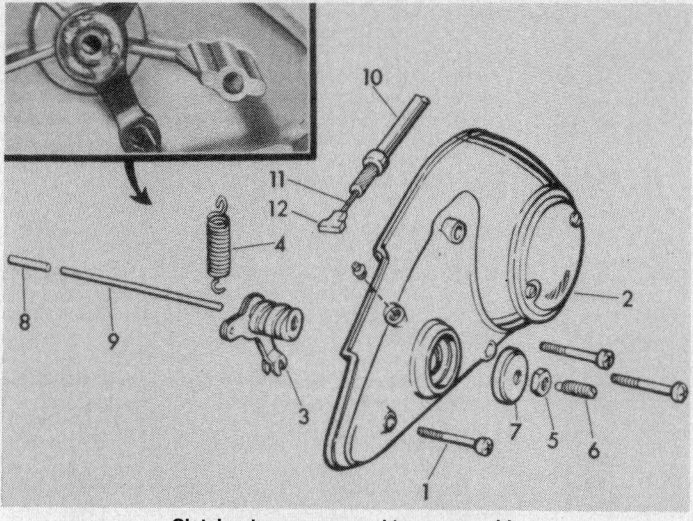

Clutch release worm and lever assembly

1. Sprocket cover screws (3)
2. Sprocket cover
3. Release worm and lever
4. Release lever spring
5. Clutch adjusting screw locknut
6. Clutch adjusting screw
7. Clutch release worm cover
8. Clutch release rod—center
9. Clutch release rod—right
10. Cable (outer)
11. Cable (inner)
12. Cable end

13. Lubricate the tip of the release rod in engine oil and insert it in the mainshaft.
14. Assemble the clutch releasing disc, clutch springs, spring cups, and thrust plate together, then secure the assembly with release disc studs and compression nuts. Slip the entire assembly in place and secure it with the spring ring. Once the assembly is secured, remove the compression studs and nuts.
15. Continue the assembly in the reverse order of disassembly.
16. Replenish the transmission oil supply and adjust the clutch as described in the "Maintenance Items."

Clutch Cable Replacement

1. Pull the cable downward toward the coil after removing the cotter pin, washer, and hollow pin from the clutch handlever.
2. Remove the sprocket cover screws and cover, and disengage the cable from the release lever. Remove the cable from the top of the coil after cutting off the bottom of the cable.
3. Lubricate a new cable thoroughly at installation with engine oil, a wax-based chain lubricant, grease, or some other suitable lubricant.
4. Assemble the pin so the narrow slot straddles the cable, then assemble the washer and cotter pin.
5. Pull the cable taut from the bottom of the coil, making sure it is properly seated at the handlever. At a point 3¾ in., from the end of the coil, install a cable end in the following manner:
   a. Spread and solder the individual strands of the cable to the cable end.
   b. Cut off the extra strands and grind so the cable end is flat.
6. Install the sprocket cover and adjust the clutch as described in the "Maintenance Items."

TRANSMISSION SERVICE

MODELS M-50 AND M-65

Removal and Installation

1. Remove the engine from the frame as described in the engine "Removal and Installation" section.
2. Separate the crankcase halves as described in the "Crankcases" section.
3. Installation is in the reverse order of removal.

Preliminary Inspection

1. Inspect the gear teeth for a worn, damaged, pitted, or scored condition.
2. Inspect the gear dogs for a worn or damaged condition.
3. Inspect the mainshaft, countershaft, transfer shaft, and starter shaft for a pitted, grooved, warped, or worn condition especially at the bearing surfaces.
4. Inspect the shifter finger for a grooved, damaged, warped, or worn condition.
5. Once the necessary repairs have been determined, proceed to disassemble those assemblies which are to be repaired. Gears should be replaced in sets because when a countershaft gear is damaged all those gears which have been in contact with it have been affected and, therefore, require attention.

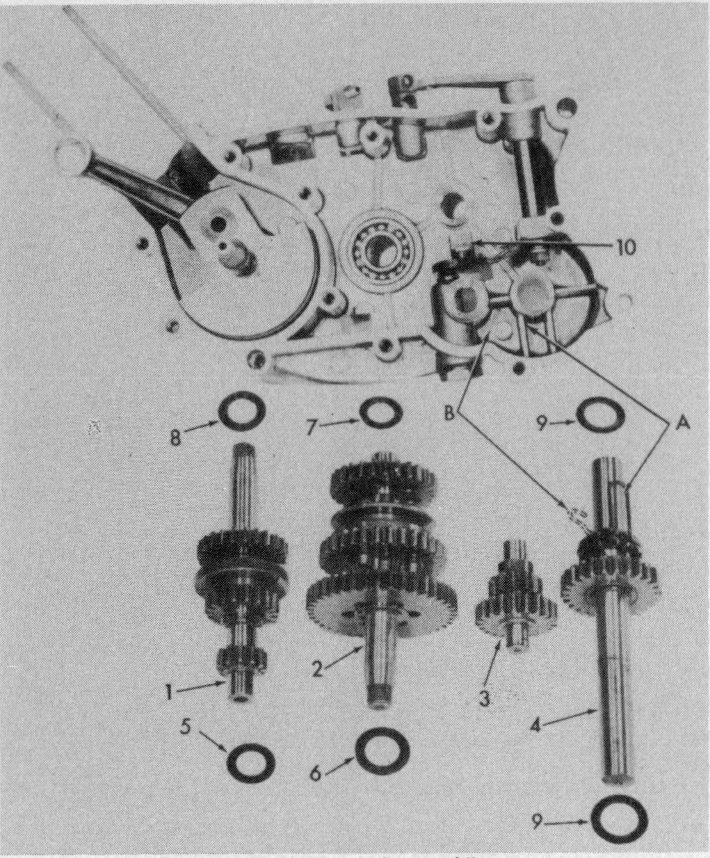

Transmission gear shaft assemblies

1. Mainshaft
2. Countershaft
3. Transfer shaft
4. Starter shaft
5. Spacer washer
6. Spacer washer
7. Spacer
8. Spacer washer
9. Spacer washer
10. Shifter finger

Disassembly

1. Place the transmission in third gear, then remove the transfer shaft, countershaft, and spacer washer.

2. Remove the countershaft lock and thrust washers, and the first, second, and third gears from the countershaft.

3. Remove the mainshaft assembly from the crankcase. Remove the mainshaft spacer washer, pull third gear from the shaft with a suitable gear puller, and slip the mainshaft second gear from the shaft.

4. Remove the shift lever locating guide, gasket, lever ball, and ball spring.

5. Remove the shifter shaft nut, lockwasher, spacer, lever, spacer, and O-ring from the shaft, and pull the shaft from the crankcase. Remove the shifter finger from the shifter lever.

Inspection and Repair

1. Clean all parts in a suitable solvent and blow them dry.

2. Inspect all parts for a worn or damaged condition and replace them as necessary. Don't reuse any part if its life expectancy is dubious.

Assembly

1. Assembly is basically the reverse order of disassembly.

2. Secure first gear on the countershaft with the spacer and lockring, then mount the remaining countershaft gears. Make sure that the smaller side of the third gear clutch holes are facing the second gear lugs.

3. Slip the mainshaft second gear in place on the shaft then press first gear into place.

4. Assemble the mainshaft and countershaft assemblies to the right crankcase half, taking care to engage the shifter finger and the mainshaft second gear collar into the countershaft second gear groove.

5. Engage the starter clutch spring in the crankcase recess as shown in the Transmission Gear Shaft Assemblies illustration. On models before engine no. 65M3539, engage the spring at "A", and for later models engage the spring at "B."

6. Replace the spacer washers in their original locations if no new gear or shaft parts have been incorporated. Where new parts are used determine the correct spacer thickness in the following manner:

a. Install the mainshaft with a 0.6 mm washer in the right crankcase half.

b. Install the countershaft with an 0.8 mm washer in the right crankcase half.

c. Manipulate the shifter lever so the transmission is in third gear, and insert a 0.004 in. thickness gauge between the countershaft second and third gears to determine whether there is at least that much clearance between them.

d. Shift the transmission and repeat the above measuring sequence on the countershaft first and second gears.

e. Check the clearance between the mainshaft first and second gears, with the transmission in first gear, and use the appropriate size washer to bring the clearance to at least 0.004 in.

f. Assemble the appropriate spacer washers to the mainshaft, countershaft, and starter shaft to bring the clearance to within 0.004–0.006 in. for the mainshaft, and to within 0.004–0.008 in. for the other two shafts. This is also a good time to check the crankshaft end-play.

g. Assemble the two crankcase halves with all the components installed, then check the various shaft end-plays with a dial indicator by shifting the shaft to one side and then to the other side. A soft mallet may be necessary to stimulate the shafts into motion.

h. Seperate the crankcase halves and install the appropriate size spacer to correct the end-play, then repeat step "g".

7. Complete the assembly process in the reverse order of disassembly and replenish the oil supply.

Handshift Cable Adjustment and Installation

1. Place the transmission in neutral and loosen both upper and lower cable adjuster locknuts.

2. Turn the knurled adjuster nuts counterclockwise to reduce the cable slack, taking care not to make the cable too taut, then secure the locknuts.

3. If the adjuster runs out of thread space or if the cable clamps have been removed, proceed in the following manner:

a. Loosen the upper and lower clamping block setscrews.

b. Place the transmission hand control in the neutral position.

c. Adjust the cable adjusters so there are several threads left between the locknut and cable coil.

d. Shift the shift lever position to make sure the transmission is in neutral. Moving the lever toward the left will place the transmission in first. One step to the right should be neutral and the rear wheel should rotate freely with the clutch in or out.

e. Secure the upper and then the lower cable clamping block setscrews while pulling on the cable to provide the necessary tension. The upper cable housing must be seated on the crankcase anchor.

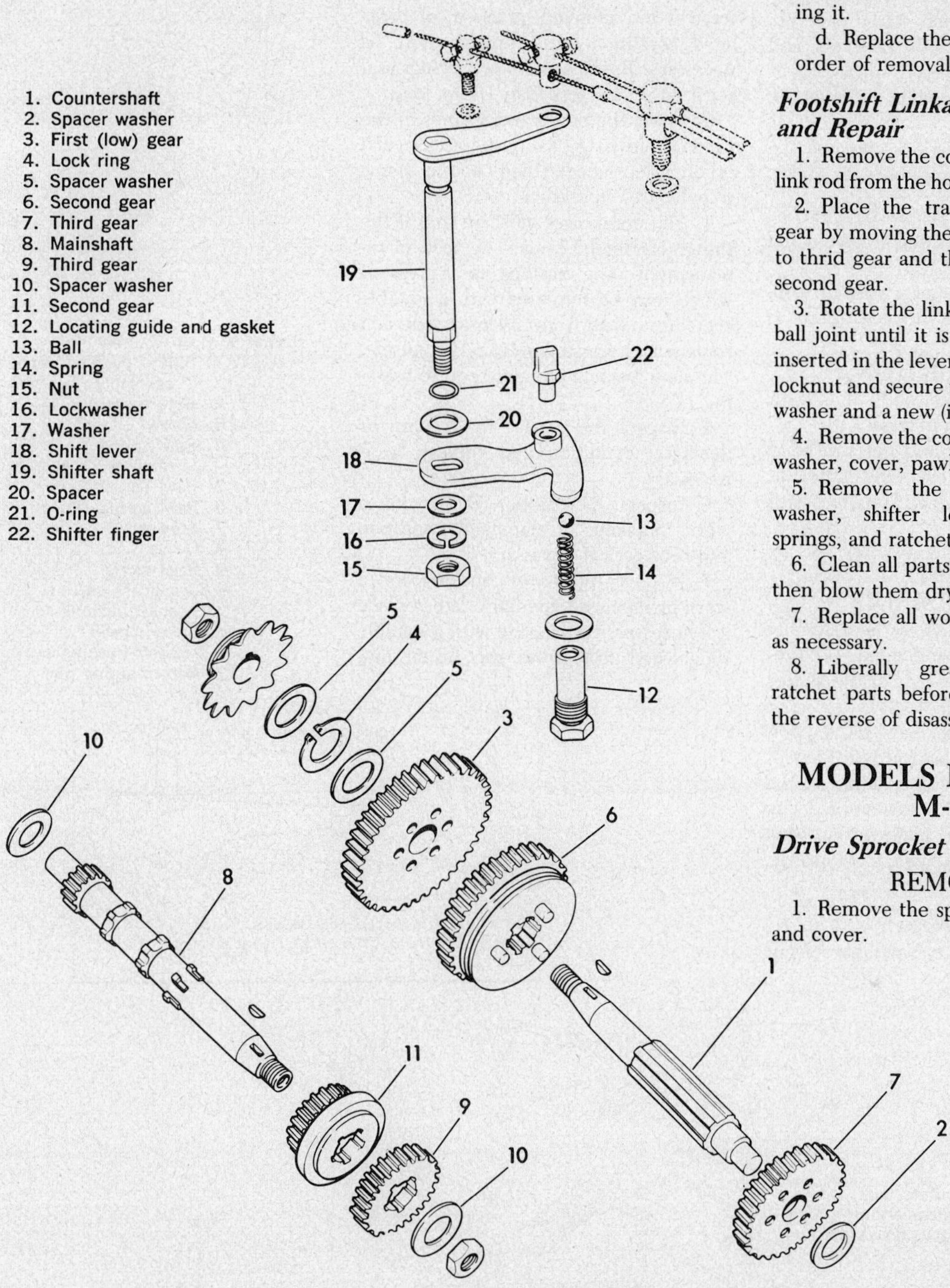

1. Countershaft
2. Spacer washer
3. First (low) gear
4. Lock ring
5. Spacer washer
6. Second gear
7. Third gear
8. Mainshaft
9. Third gear
10. Spacer washer
11. Second gear
12. Locating guide and gasket
13. Ball
14. Spring
15. Nut
16. Lockwasher
17. Washer
18. Shift lever
19. Shifter shaft
20. Spacer
21. O-ring
22. Shifter finger

Transmission assembly

4. Adjust the cable as described in steps one and two. When correctly adjusted, the engine will run while the hand indicator is on neutral without slipping into first or second gear.

5. Install the cable in the following manner:

a. Loosen the housing clamp screw located near the control cables and slip the handgrip off the handlebar.

b. Slip the cables through the housing slots.

c. Inspect all parts for a worn or damaged condition and replace them as necessary. Always grease the cable or lubricate it with engine oil or a chain lubricating compound before replacing it.

d. Replace the cable in the reverse order of removal.

Footshift Linkage Adjustment and Repair

1. Remove the cotter pin, washer, and link rod from the hole in the shifter lever.
2. Place the transmission in second gear by moving the shift lever clockwise to thrid gear and then back one step to second gear.
3. Rotate the link rod in the threaded ball joint until it is aligned so it can be inserted in the lever hole. Secure the rod locknut and secure the link arm with the washer and a new (if possible) cotter pin.
4. Remove the cover screw, acorn nut, washer, cover, pawl spring, and pawls.
5. Remove the shifter lever nut, washer, shifter lever, spring cups, springs, and ratchet.
6. Clean all parts in a suitable solvent then blow them dry.
7. Replace all worn or damaged parts as necessary.
8. Liberally grease all pawl and ratchet parts before assembly which is the reverse of disassembly.

MODELS M-100 AND M-125

Drive Sprocket

REMOVAL

1. Remove the sprocket cover screws and cover.

Removing the drive sprocket

2. Secure the sprocket with Transmission Sprocket Wrench (H-D part no. 97305–68P, for 14 tooth sprockets, and no. 97297–68P for 15 tooth sprockets), or a suitable substitute, then remove the sprocket nut.

3. Remove the nut lock and pull the sprocket free with a suitable gear puller.

INSPECTION AND REPAIR

Clean all parts in a suitable solvent and blow them dry.

2. Inspect all parts for a worn or damaged condition and replace them as necessary.

INSTALLATION

1. Place the sprocket on its shaft with the hub facing the crankcase.

2. Secure the lock and nut and bend the locktab against the flat side of the nut.

3. Replace the cover and secure it with the cover screws.

Shifter Pawl Carrier

DISASSEMBLY

1. Remove the pawl carrier assembly from the crankcase, and remove the return spring from the rear of the shifter carrier.

2. Check the shifter pawl movement. If the movement is awkward or if any of the components are visibly damaged, the assembly must be disassembled by removing the spring plate screw, pawl spring retainer plate, pawls, pawl springs, and the shifter lever stop pin.

Inspection and Repair

1. Cclean all parts in a suitable solvent and blow them dry.

2. Inspect the shifter pawls and springs for a worn, grooved, cracked, or damaged condition, and replace them as necessary. Replace the pawl springs as a set if either are less than 1.5 in. long.

3. Insert the pawls and springs in the carrier holes so the flat portions face each other, then check their action for a smooth, free operation.

4. The crankcases must be split if the shifter carrier bushing is in need of replacement. The bushing is a press fit which may be removed with a suitable shouldered drift from the inside out, and replaced by pressing in from the outside. The new bushing will not require reaming.

5. Inspect the carrier for a worn or damaged condition and replace it as necessary.

6. Inspect the rubber O-ring for a worn, cracked, or damaged condition and replace it if necessary.

7. Inspect the cover bushing for a worn or damaged condition and replace it if necessary by pressing with a suitable shouldered drift from the inside out.

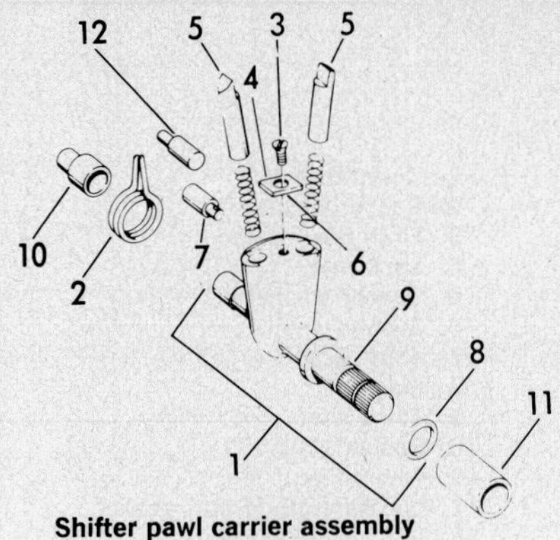

Shifter pawl carrier assembly

1. Shifter pawl carrier assembly
2. Return spring
3. Screw
4. Pawl spring retainer plate
5. Pawl (2)
6. Pawl spring (2)
7. Stop pin
8. O-ring
9. Pawl carrier
10. Crankcase carrier shaft bushing
11. Cover carrier shaft bushing
12. Return spring pin

1. Cotter pin
2. Washer
3. Link rod
4. Link rod locknut
5. Bell crank bolt nut
6. Bell crank bolt nut washer
7. Bell crank bolt
8. Bell crank
9. Shifter bracket footrest nut
10. Shifter bracket extension nut
11. Shifter bracket extension washer
12. Cover screw
13. Cover nut
14. Cover washer
15. Cover
16. Pawl spring
17. Pawl (2)
18. Shifter lever nut
19. Shifter lever washer
20. Shifter lever
21. Spring cup (3)
22. Spring (3)
23. Ratchet
24. Shifter foot lever
25. Lock ring (2)
26. Retainer (2)
27. Return spring
28. Bolt (2)
29. Washer (4)
30. Nut (2)
31. Shifter bracket
32. Shifter housing
33. Extension stud
34. Footrest support
35. Ball socket ring

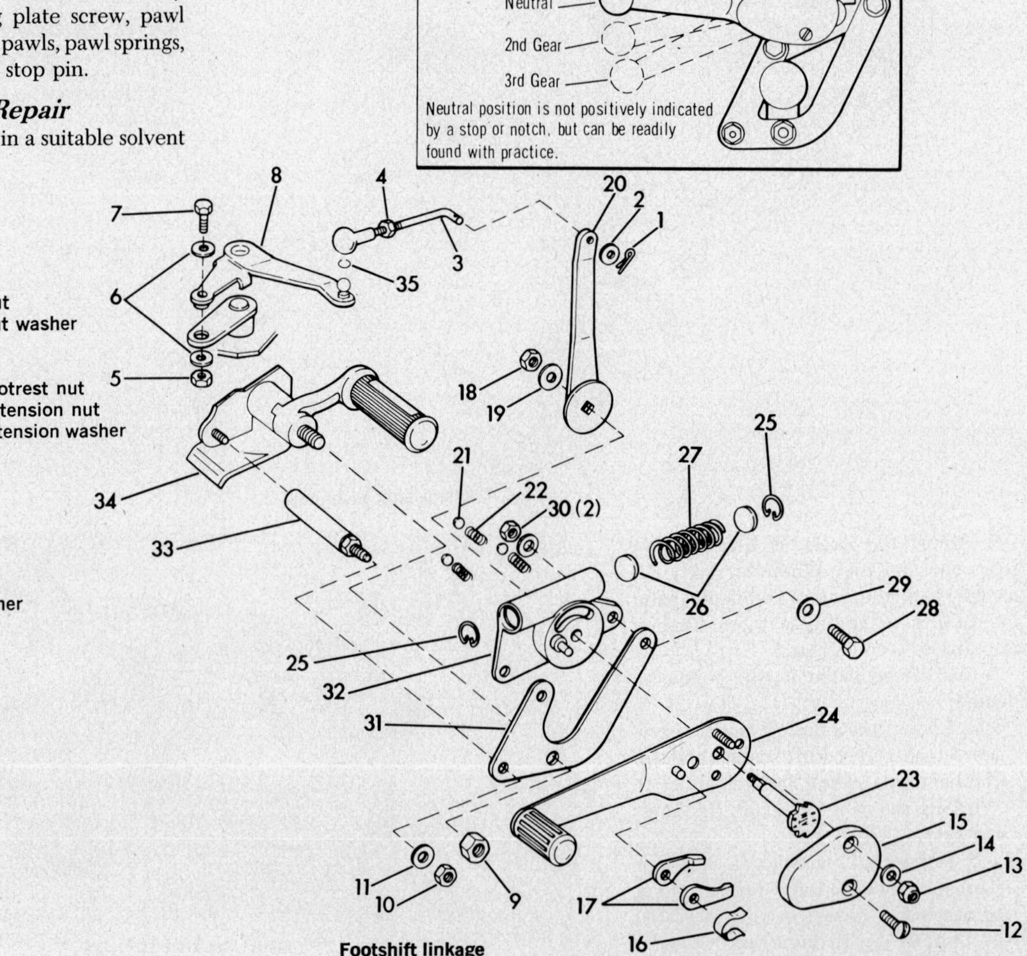

Footshift linkage

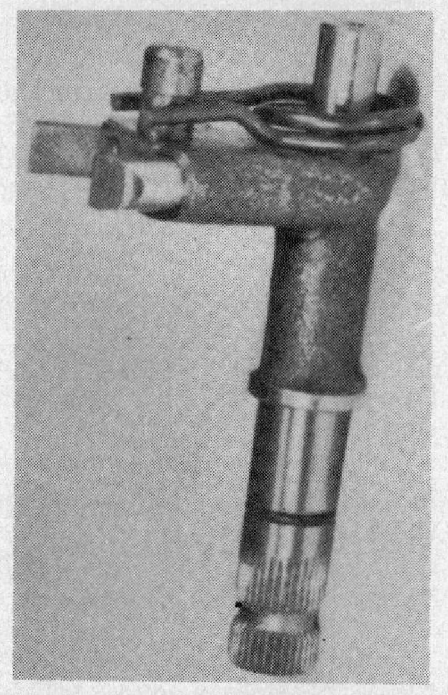

Positioning the return spring on the carrier

When installing the new bushing, make sure the chamfered side is facing in. Press the bushing from the outside in until flush with the bushing boss. Reaming this bushing will not be necessary.

ASSEMBLY

1. Slip the pawl springs into the pawls, then install the pawls into the carrier so the flat portions are facing each other.
2. Press down on the pawls, slip the pawl spring retainer plate down against the carrier, insert the stop pin with its hole facing upward, and secure the assembly with the screw which goes through the carrier and into the stop pin.
3. Slip the return spring on the carrier with the offset portion facing the crankcase and the stop pin between the spring arms.
4. Secure the rubber O-ring in its groove on the carrier shaft.
5. Slip the carrier assembly into the case and engage the return spring on the return spring pin. When the spring is properly engaged, the shaft should not turn.

MODELS M-100 AND M-125

Removal and Installation

1.Remove the engine from the frame as described in the engine "Removal and Installation" section.

2. Remove the magneto-generator as described in the "Magneto-Generator" section.

3. Disassemble the shifter cam stop parts 1–4 (as listed in the exploded view illustration) from the crankcase.

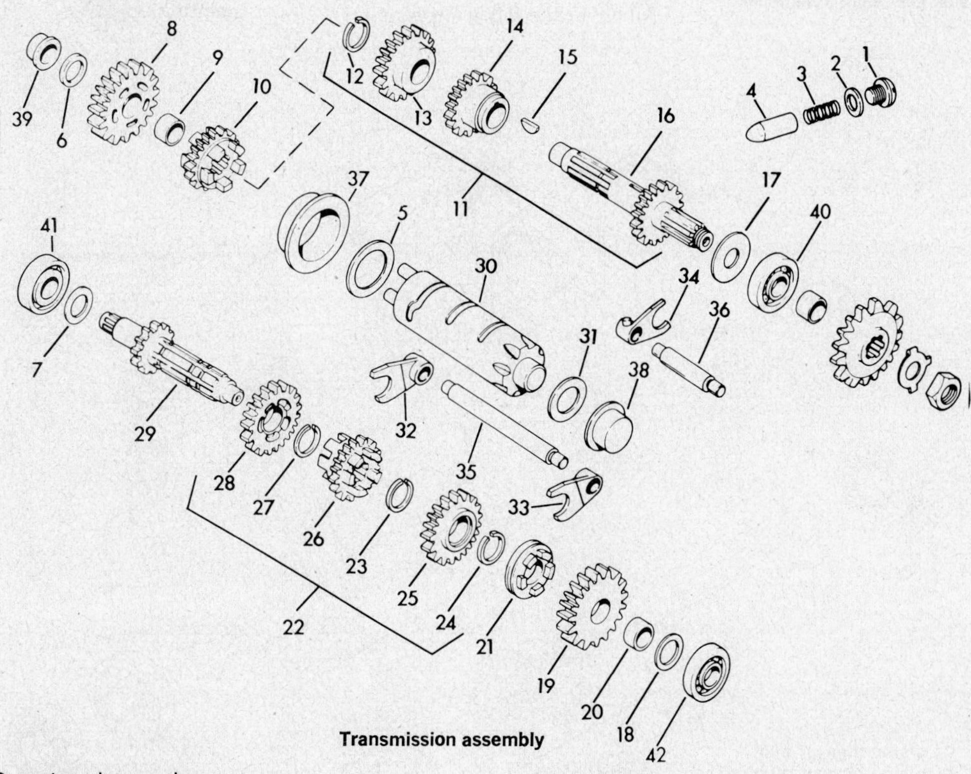

Transmission assembly

1. Cam stop plunger plug
2. Cam stop plunger plug washer
3. Cam stop plunger spring
4. Cam stop plunger
5. Shifter cam spacer washer (variable-thickness)
6. Countershaft spacer washer (variable-thickness)
7. Mainshaft spacer washer (variable-thickness)
8. Countershaft first (low) gear (35T.)
9. Countershaft low grear bushing
10. Countershaft fourth gear
11. Countershaft and gear assembly
12. Lockring
13. Countershaft second (sliding) gear (28T.)
14. Countershaft third gear (24T.)
15. Key
16. Countershaft
17. Counter spacer washer (variable-thickness)
18. Mainshaft spacer washer (variable-thickness)
19. Mainshaft fifth gear
20. Mainshaft fifth gear bushing
21. Mainshaft fifth gear shifter clutch
22. Mainshaft and gear assembly
23. Lockring
24. Lockring
25. Mainshaft third gear (26T.)
26. Mainshaft second gear (20T.)
27. Lockring
28. Mainshaft fourth (high) gear (29T.)
29. Mainshaft
30. Shifter cam
30. Shifter cam assembly
31. Shifter cam spacer washer (variable-thickness)
32. Shifter fork
33. Shifter fork
34. Shifter fork
35. Shifter fork shaft
36. Shifter fork shaft
37. Shifer cam right crankcase bushing
38. Shifter cam left crankcase bushing
39. Countershaft right crankcase bushing
40. Countershaft left crankcase ball bearing
41. Mainshaft right crankcase ball bearing
42. Mainshaft left crankcase ball bearing

Shifter fork cotter pin (2)

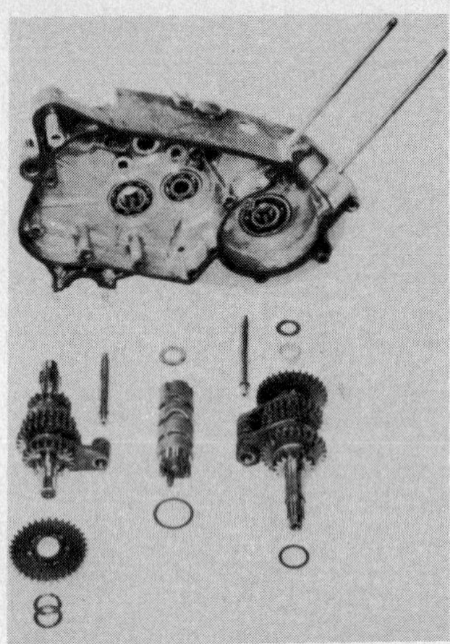

Transmission gear shaft assemblies

4. Separate the crankcase halves as described in the "Crankcases" section.

5. Replacement is in the reverse order of removal.

Disassembly

MODEL M-100

1. Place the left crankcase on the work bench with the gear assemblies pointing up.

2. Remove the variable-thickness shifter cam, countershaft, and mainshaft spacer washers.

3. Hold the countershaft gears together while tapping on the countershaft splined end with a soft mallet, lift all three assemblies free, and remove the left-side washers. Note the positions of the shifter forks in the sliding gears for replacement purposes.

4. Disassemble the countershaft assembly in the following manner:

a. Slip the countershaft first gear and bushing free from the shaft.

b. Remove the countershaft fourth gear from the splined shaft.

c. Remove the lockring, second gear, third gear—with the aid of a suitable gear puller, and the countershaft key (if replacement is necessary).

5. Disassemble the mainshaft assembly in the following manner:

a. Remove the mainshaft fifth gear, bushing, and the fifth gear shifter clutch.

b. Remove the lockring, third gear, second gear, the fourth gear lockring, and fourth gear.

6. Remove the shifter cam, shifter forks, and shifter fork shafts.

MODEL M-125

1.Place the right crankcase half on a work bench so the gear assemblies are pointing up.

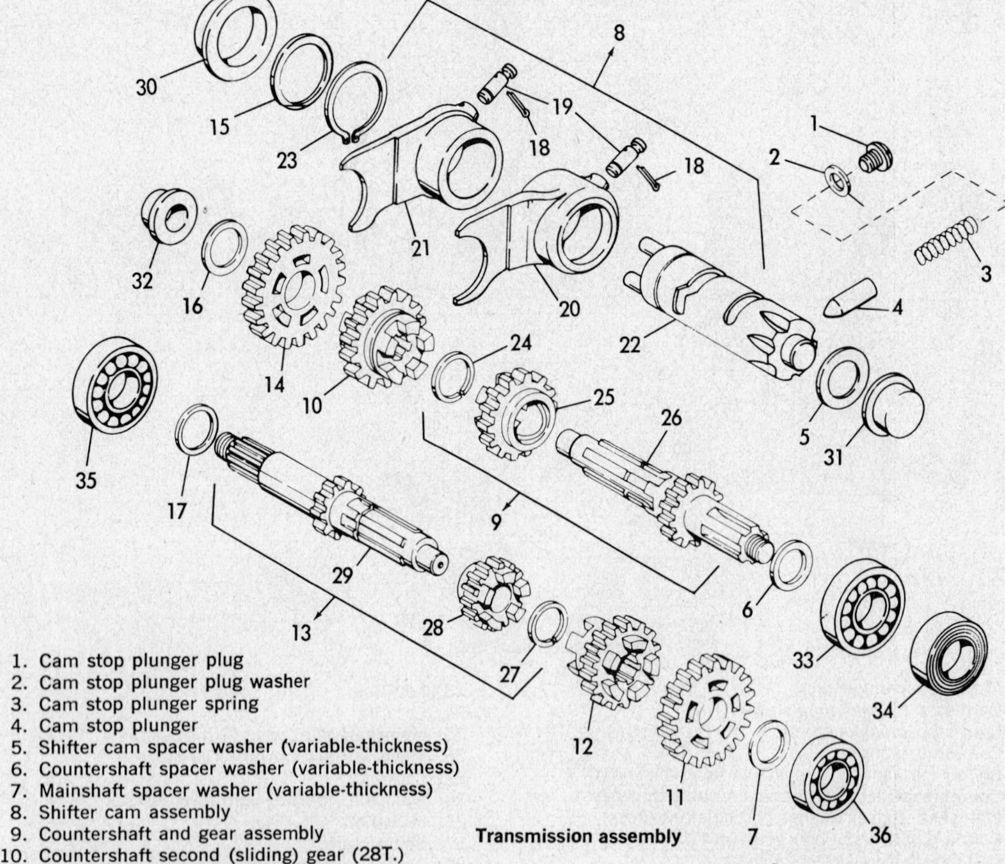

Transmission assembly

1. Cam stop plunger plug
2. Cam stop plunger plug washer
3. Cam stop plunger spring
4. Cam stop plunger
5. Shifter cam spacer washer (variable-thickness)
6. Countershaft spacer washer (variable-thickness)
7. Mainshaft spacer washer (variable-thickness)
8. Shifter cam assembly
9. Countershaft and gear assembly
10. Countershaft second (sliding) gear (28T.)
11. Mainshaft fourth (high) gear (29T.)
12. Mainshaft third (sliding) gear (26T.)
13. Mainshaft and gear assembly
14. Countershaft first (low) gear (35T.)
15. Shifter cam spacer washer (variable-thickness)
16. Countershaft spacer washer (variable-thickness)
17. Mainshaft spacer washer (variable-thickness)
18. Shifter fork cotter pin (2)
19. Shifter fork pin (2)
20. Countershaft second gear shifter fork (male)
21. Mainshaft third gear shifter fork (female)
22. Shifter cam
23. Shifter cam lockring
24. Lockring
25. Countershaft third gear (24T.)
26. Countershaft
27. Lockring
28. Mainshaft second gear (20T.)
29. Mainshaft
30. Shifter cam right crankcase bushing
31. Shifter cam left crankcase bushing
32. Countershaft right crankcase bushing
33. Countershaft left crankcase ball bearing
34. Sprocket oil seal
35. Mainshaft right crankcase ball bearing
36. Mainshaft left crankcase ball bearing

2. Remove the variable-thickness shifter cam, countershaft, and mainshaft spacer washers.

3. Remove the shifter cam and countershaft assemblies, and the mainshaft fourth and third gears all at once. Take careful note of the shifter fork positions in relation to the sliding gears for replacement purposes.

4. Remove the mainshaft assembly by tapping on the end of the shaft with a soft mallet.

5. Remove the variable-thickness shifter cam, countershaft, and mainshaft spacer washers.

6. Remove the countershaft first gear, second gear, lockwasher, and third gear.

7. Remove the shifter fork cotter pins, pins, forks, and cam. Take note of the position of the countershaft fork to the mainshaft fork and the locations of the shifter fork pins in the cam grooves for reassembly purposes.

8. Remove the mainshaft lockring and second gear.

Inspection and Repair

1. Clean all parts in a suitable solvent and blow them dry.

2. Inspect all parts for a worn, scored, warped, or otherwise damaged condition and replace them as necessary.

3. Inspect the gear dogs, dog slots, and shifter fork grooves for a chipped or damaged condition and replace them as necessary.

4. Pay special attention to the gear teeth. If one gear is damaged and is to be replaced, it is a good practice to replace the other teeth which mesh with it.

5. Inspect the shifter cam for grooved or worn slots at the various gear positions.

6. Inspect the shifter forks and fork pins for a warped or damaged condition, and for grooves worn into the fork fingers, then replace them as necessary.

7. Inspect the shifter cam stop plunger and spring for rough motion or a worn or damaged condition, especially on the plunger face, and replace them as necessary. The spring must be replaced if shorter than 1.535 in.

8. Inspect the bushings and bearings for excessive side or radial (up-and-down) play, pitting, damage, or rough motion; and replace them as necessary. Do not remove any bearing or bushing which doesn't require replacement.

9. Press the mainshaft and countershaft bearings out from the outside-in. The mainshaft left side bearing is blind and must be pulled with Bearing Puller (H-D part no. CG-40A) or a suitable bearing extractor.

10. Remove the left-side sprocket gear oil seal, then press the bearing free from the outsie-in.

11. Ream the left and right shifter bushings after installation, using Large Bushing Reamer (H-D part no. 97322–61P) and Small Bushing Reamer (H-D part no. 97318–61P) or suitable substitutes.

Assembly

1. Press in all bearings until they are firmly seated.

2. Use the same number and size of spacers as were removed. Any corrections will have to be made after the end-play has been determined.

3. Make the preliminary assembly without the flywheel assembly so that the most accurate mainshaft, countershaft, and shifter camshaft end-plays can be achieved.

MODEL M-100

1. Assemble the mainshaft group, then insert it and the left-side spacer washer into the left crankcase half.

2. Assemble the countershaft second and third gears to the shaft, then insert the shaft through the left side spacer washer and into the left crankcase half, tapping gently with a soft mallet if necessary. Assemble the countershaft fourth and first gears.

3. Position the left-side shifter cam spacer then assemble the shifter cam to the left crankcase half.

4. Assemble the fifth gear shifter fork to the shifter clutch so the cam pin on the back of the fork pivot section rides in the lower, left-side cam slot. Assemble the second gearshifter fork into the mainshaft second gear groove so the cam pin rides in the upper, right-side slot in the shifter cam.

5. Install the shifter fork shaft, taking care not to disturb the positions of the forks.

6. Install the countershaft shifter fork into the groove in the countershaft fourth gear so the cam pin rides in the middle slot in the shifter cam, and install the shifter fork shaft.

MODEL M-125

1. Slip the shifter forks in position on the shifter cam so the male fork is assembled into the female fork. Secure the forks in their respective grooves by inserting the shifter fork pins and securing them with cotter pins.

Checking the mainshaft end-play

2. Assemble the countershaft gears to the shaft so the mainshaft third gear shifter fork engages the countershaft second gear groove, and the countershaft second gear shifter fork engages the mainshaft third gear groove.

3. Install the above assembly in the right crankcase half along with the mainshaft and countershaft assemblies and their respective spacer washers. Make sure that the flat face of the countershaft first gear is toward the countershaft second gear, and the flat face of the mainshaft fourth gear is facing the mainshaft third gear.

4. Place the appropriate spacer washer on the end of each of the three shafts, and rotate the shifter cam until the transmission is in the neutral position.

5. Temporarily assemble the crankcase halves and secure them together with at least two screws directly opposite one another.

6. Assemble the cam stop plunger, plunger spring, washer, and plunger plug so the plunger engages the middle of the three grooves located sideways on the cam stop end of the shifter cam.

Checking The Transmission Shafts End-Play

1. With the crankcase halves assembled, mount a dial indicator on one side, then shift the shaft to be measured to the extreme opposite side and then back to the extreme other side. Use a screwdriver to aid in shifting the shafts, but remove the screwdriver before taking a reading.

2. Disassemble the crankcase halves and install the appropriate size spacer washer on the shaft ends to bring the endplay to within the specified limits. Rather than just using one larger washer, use two slightly smaller ones to maintain the proper balance.

3. If the crankshaft assembly has been worked on, check the crankshaft end-play.

4. Reassemble the crankcases and recheck the end-play. Repeat the above operations until the end-play is correct. The shifter cam end-play should be within 0.-008–0.012 in.; the countershaft end-play should be within 0.002–0.006 in., and the mainshaft end-play should be within 0.-002–0.006 in. Consult the following chart for the appropriate size washer.

TRANSMISSION SHIM WASHER SIZES

Size mm	Size In.	Right Side Shifter Cam (Large)	Right Side Counter Shaft	Right Side Main Shaft	Left Side Shifter Cam (Small)	Left Side Counter Shaft	Left Side Main Shaft
0.2	0.008				X		
0.3	0.012	X		X		X	
0.4	0.016		X	X	X	X	X
0.5	0.020	X	X	X		X	X
0.6	0.024		X	X	X	X	X
0.7	0.028	X	X	X		X	X
0.8	0.032		X	X	X	X	X
0.9	0.035	X	X	X	X	X	X
1.0	0.039	X	X	X	X	X	X
1.1	0.043	X	X	X	X	X	X
1.2	0.047	X	X	X	X	X	X
1.3	0.051		X				X
1.4	0.055		X				X
1.5	0.059		X				X

S AND B MODELS

Removal and Installation

1. Remove the engine from the frame as described in the "Engine Removal and Installation" section.

2. Separate the crankcase halves as described in the "Crankcases" section.

3. Replacement is in the reverse order or removal.

Drive Sprocket Removal and Installation

1. Remove the clutch release rod.

2. Bend back the mainshaft sprocket nut lockwasher ear from the mainshaft sprocket nut and oil seal, then remove the nut (which has a left-hand thread) and lockwasher.

3. Remove the mainshaft drive sprocket with a suitable gear puller.

4. Remove the main drive gear collar, oil seal screws, oil seal, and the oil seal gasket which should be replaced every time it is removed.

5. Clean all parts in a suitable solvent and blow them dry.

6. Inspect all the parts for a worn or damaged condition and replace them as necessary.

7. Assembly is in the reverse order of disassembly. The replacement gasket should be coated on both sides with a suitable gasket sealer before assembly.

Disassembly

1. Place the left crankcase on the work bench with the gear assemblies pointing up.

2. Remove the countershaft assembly and disassemble the countershaft gear thrust washer, sliding gear, and first gear.

3. Remove the mainshaft sliding gear then drift the shaft out of the left bearing with a suitable drift.

4. Slip the mainshaft into the main drive gear and check for excessive clearance, wear, or damage which would necessitate the removal of the gear. If necessary, tap the gear and its bearing free of the case with a soft mallet. The bearing and bushing need not be removed unless worn, damaged, or excessively loose in the case.

5. Inspect the left mainshaft bearing for excessive play, wear, damage, or rough motion before removing it. Remove the inner and outer spring rings and drift the bearing free with a suitable drift if replacement is necessary.

6. Remove the countershaft gear from the shaft with a suitable gear puller if replacement is necessary. The gear is a press fit on the shaft.

7. Drift the gear shifter shaft from the case with a suitable drift, pry the pawl retaining ring free from its groove in the shaft, and remove the shifter pawl spring and spring cover.

8. Disassemble the ratchet assembly in the following manner:

   a. Remove the ratchet spring key, spring collars, spring, and the gear shifter ratchet.

   b. Bend back the tabs on the ratchet bracket bolt lockwashers, remove the cap screws, and remove the gear shifter ratchet bracket and spring pin.

9. Inspect the ball retainer and retainer washer for a worn or damaged condition, loose fit in the case, or the ball remaining in the depressed condition when pressed down into the retainer. Drift them free with a suitable drift from their press fit position in the case if replacement is necessary.

10. Remove the inner arm of the gear indicator from the case with pliers if replacement is necessary.

Inspection and Repair

1. Clean all parts in a suitable solvent and blow them dry.

2. Inspect the mainshaft sprocket nut and oil seal and the inner oil seal for a worn, cracked, or otherwise damaged condition which might cause leaks, and replace them as necessary. The sprocket nut seal must be pried free.

3. Inspect all the gears for a worn, chipped, damaged, or excessively loose fit on their respective shafts and replace them as necessary.

4. Inspect the gear dogs and slots for wear or damage at the thrust points and replace the gears as necessary.

5. Inspect all points on which the bearings ride for excessive wear, pitting, grooving, or scoring, and replace them as necessary.

6. Inspect the fit of the main drive gear and its bushing for play in excess of 0.-0025 in. and replace them if necessary by drifting them out with an appropriate size drift or by threading a tap into the

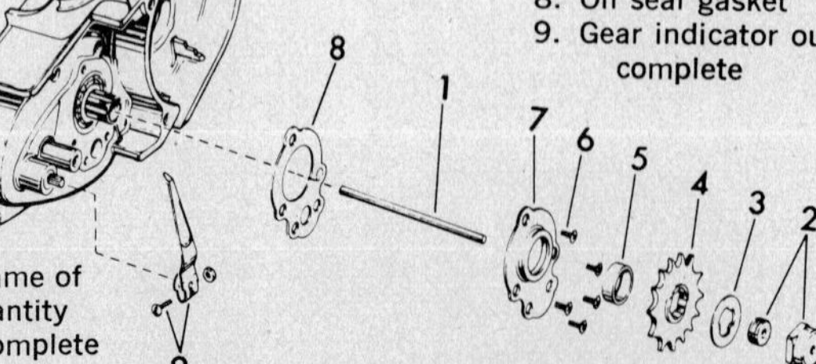

1. Clutch release rod
2. Mainshaft sprocket nut and oil seal
3. Mainshaft sprocket nut lock washer
4. Mainshaft sprocket
5. Main drive gear collar
6. Oil seal screw (5)
7. Oil seal
8. Oil seal gasket
9. Gear indicator outer arm complete

Figure following name of part indicates quantity necessary for one complete assembly.

Drive sprocket and oil seal assembly

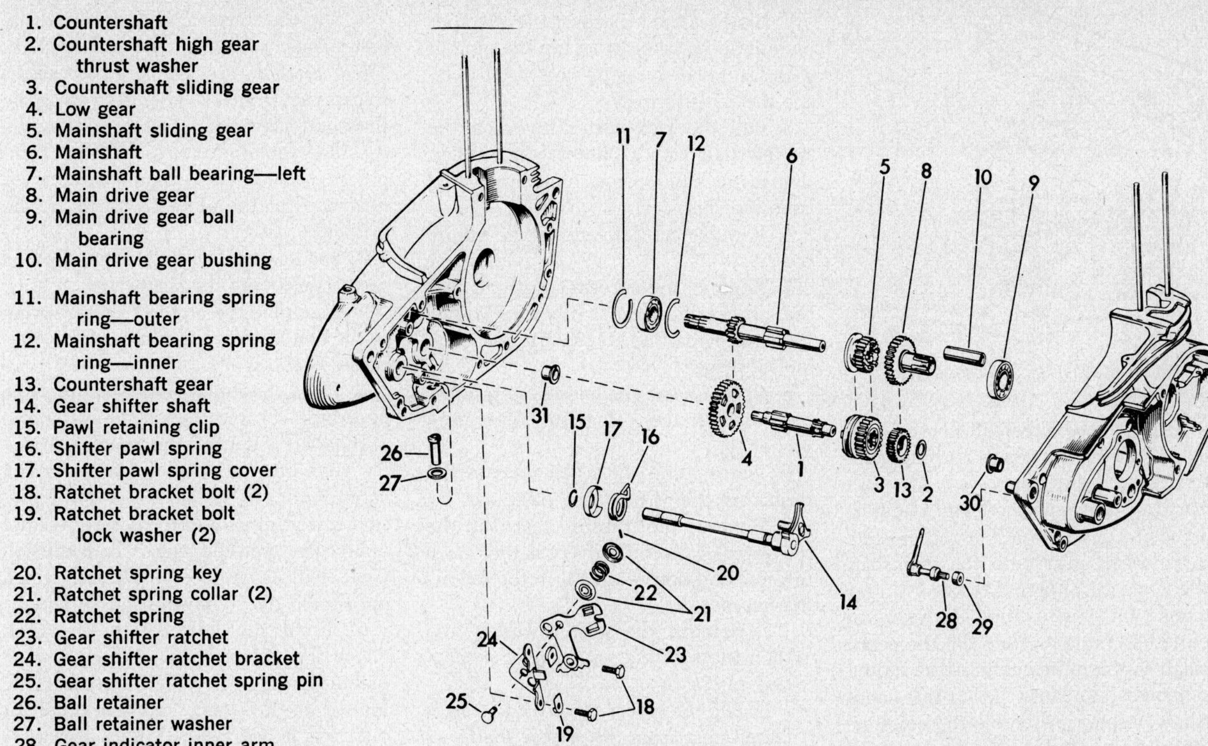

Figure following name of part indicates quantity necessary for one complete assembly.

Transmission assembly

bushing then drifting it free from the opposite side. Ream a new bushing with Reamer (H-D part no. 95924-48) or a suitable substitute.

7. Inspect the mainshaft bearings for wear, damage, pitting, excessive clearance, or rough motion and replace them as necessary with a suitable drift.

8. Inspect the countershaft bushings for excessive play by measuring the shaft side-movement from the end opposite the bushing to be inspected. If the clearance is correct (0.0005–0.0015 in.) there will be 1/64–1/32 in. side-motion. When the motion exceeds these limits by 1/16 in. or more, the need for replacement is indicated. Replace the bushings in the following manner:

a. Drift the bushings out with a suitable drift.

b. Press in the new bushings, taking care to align the bushing shoulder oil slot which should be pointed upward.

c. Securely assemble the crankcase halves to check for proper alignment. It may be necessary to heat the cases around the dowel pin holes to make them come together.

d. Line-ream the bushings using Reamer (H-D part no. 95924-48) or a suitable substitute. Use the bushing opposite the one to be reamed as a guide, then switch and ream the other bushing. Continue to rotate the reamer clockwise while withdrawing it.

9. Inspect the pawl claws of the gear shifter shaft and the mating surfaces of the gear shifter ratchet for a worn or damaged condition which may cause sloppy gear changes, and replace them as necessary.

10. Replace the pawl retaining clip, and inspect the shifter pawl spring for a worn or damaged condition. Replace it as necessary. It is a good idea to replace this spring since, if it fails, the shift lever will not automatically return to a ready position and will have to be manipulated by hand.

11. Inspect the ratchet spring and gear shifter ratchet spring pin for a worn or damaged condition and replace them as a set if either is in need of replacement.

12. Inspect the gear shifter ratchet and ratchet bracket for a worn or damaged condition and replace them as necessary. Do not attempt to straighten out either part.

13. Inspect the ball retainer and washer as described in "Disassembly" step nine.

14. Inspect the tip of the gear indicator inner arm for a worn or damaged condition and replace it if its condition is questionable since failure of this part will immobilize the transmission.

Assembly

1. Place the left crankcase on a work bench with the transmission compartment facing upward.

2. Press the ball retainer and washer into the crankcase, if they have been removed, taking care to align the retainer slot with the crankcase joint face.

3. Assemble the gear shifter ratchet spring pin, ratchet bracket, ratchet, spring collar, spring, and spring key, in that order, then secure the bracket with the bracket bolt lockwashers and cap screws. Fold the tabs of the washers up and engage the ratchet teeth with the ball retainer.

4. Assemble the pawl retaining clip, shifter pawl spring cover, pawl spring, and the gear shifter shaft, taking care to install the spring on the shaft so the end of the spring is as far from the pawl as possible so the spring ends will properly engage the shifter bracket lug.

5. Slip the shaft and pawl assembly into the left case half so the pawl claws extend halfway over the ratchet plate. The ratchet plate should be able to be pushed far enough forward for the pawl to clear the plate in either of its extreme positions. Place the transmission in second gear before continuing.

6. Install the outer mainshaft bearing spring ring, then press the left-side mainshaft bearing into the case from within until seated against the spring ring. Install the inner bearing spring ring in its groove in the case.

7. Press the main drive gear bearing and the drive gear into position in the right crankcase.

8. Lightly oil the mainshaft with clean engine oil then press it into the left-side mainshaft bearing until flush with the outer face of the bearing.

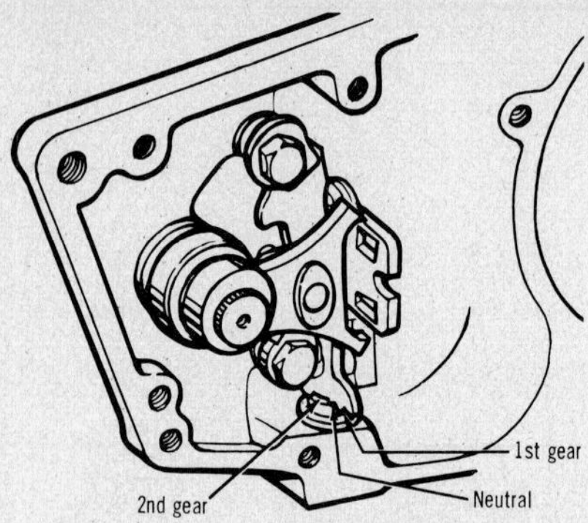

Shifter mechanism in second gear

9. Place the countershaft first gear on the left-side countershaft bushing with the flat side facing up.

10. Hold the mainshaft and countershaft sliding gears in mesh together, slide the mainshaft gear onto the mainshaft and engage the fingers of the gear shifter ratchet while maintaining the gears in the meshed position, then slip the countershaft through the countershaft sliding and first gears and into the left-side countershaft bushing. Assemble the countershaft third gear and the third gear thrust washer to the shaft.

11. Install the gear indicator inner arm and oil seal if it has not yet been done.

12. Lubricate the gears thoroughly with clean engine oil, then shift the gears several times to make sure the transmission will operate smoothly and accurately.

13. Complete the reassembly procedure in the reverse order of disassembly and replenish the transmission oil supply.

Kick-Starter

MODELS M-50 AND M-65

Disassembly

1. Remove the engine from the frame as described in the engine "Removal and Installation" section.

2. Remove the kick-starter lever taper pin nut and washer, then tap the pin out with a soft mallet, taking care not to damage the pin's threads.

3. Pull the kick-starter lever off the starter shaft with a suitable gear puller, then remove the spring shield and spring from the shaft.

4. Remove the left-side cover assembly.

5. Remove the sprocket nut and pull the sprocket from the shaft with Two-Jaw Puller (H-D part no. 97292–61) or a suitable substitute.

6. Remove the magneto-generator as described in the "Magneto-Generator" section.

7. Disassemble the crankcases as described in the "Crankcase" section.

8. Remove the transfer gear, slip the starter shaft assembly free of the transmission, and disassemble it in the following manner.

a. Remove the spacer washer and then the lockring with a pair of snap-ring pliers.

b. Slip the spacer washer and starter clutch gear from the starter shaft.

c. Slip the starter clutch and friction spring free of the shaft.

Inspect and Repair

1. Clean all parts in a suitable solvent and blow them dry.

2. Inspect the starter clutch gear, clutch, and the transfer gear for a worn or damaged condition, paying special attention to the gear teeth. If any of the gears is in need of replacement, they should all be replaced as a set since they all mesh in one way or another.

3. Inspect the remaining components for a worn, pitted, gouged, warped, or otherwise damaged condition and replace them as necessary.

Assembly

1. Assembly is essentially the reverse of disassembly.

2. Slip the starter clutch gear and the first spacer washer on the starter shaft. These washers are available in various thicknesses from 0.2–0.8 mm to bring the shaft-end play clearances to within the specified range of 0.004–0.008 in. Temporarily install the original spacers or new ones of the same thickness as the originals.

3. Secure the lockring, then slip the next spacer onto the shaft.

4. Assemble the clutch friction spring to the clutch, then slip this assembly into place on the shaft.

5. Place the inner spacer washer, one of at least 0.4 mm thickness, on the end of the shaft and insert the shaft and transfer gear into the left crankcase taking care to properly insert the ear of the friction spring in its correct position in the crankcase (consult the "Transmission Gear Shaft Assemblies" illustration which appears in the "Transmission" section).

6. Install the left side cover, then check the starter shaft end-play with a dial indicator by moving the shaft in the limit of its movement, and then pulling it out so it depresses the indicator's plunger. Avoid exerting pressure on the shaft while taking a reading, and make sure the indicator is absolutely motionless. Repeat this procedure several times to make sure the reading arrived at is accurate.

7. Disassemble the assembly once again and correct the clearance to specifications by using the appropriate spacers.

8. Once the end-play has been corrected, mount the kick-starter lever and secure it with the tapered pin, washer, and nut.

MODELS M-100 AND M-125

Disassembly

1. Remove the starter lever nut, washer, and tapered pin by tapping it out with a soft mallet, taking care not to dam-

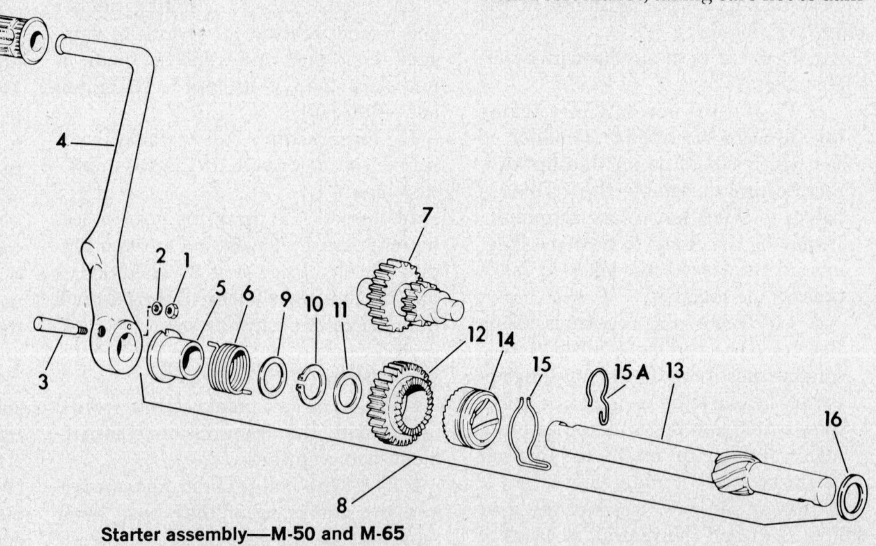

Starter assembly—M-50 and M-65

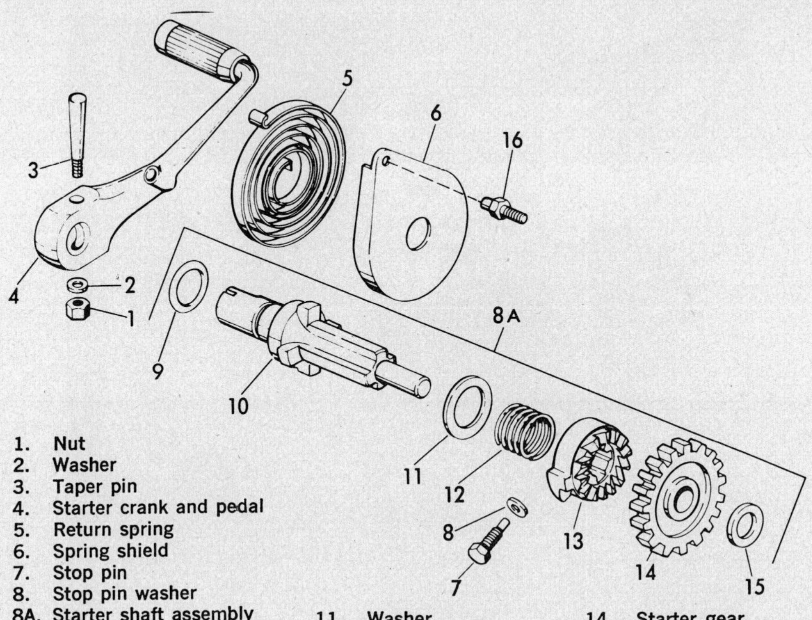

1. Nut
2. Washer
3. Taper pin
4. Starter crank and pedal
5. Return spring
6. Spring shield
7. Stop pin
8. Stop pin washer
8A. Starter shaft assembly
9. O-ring
10. Starter shaft
11. Washer
12. Clutch spring
13. Starter clutch
14. Starter gear
15. Thrust washer
16. Return spring stud

Starter assembly—M-100 and M-125

age its threads. Pull the lever off with a suitable gear puller.

2. Remove the gear shifter lever, clutch cover screws, and the clutch cover. Gently tap on the sides of the cover with a soft mallet to aid in removing it.

3. Remove the return spring and spring shield from the return spring stud.

4. Remove the stop pin and washer, and slip the starter shaft assembly free of the case.

5. The starter shaft assembly components freely slip off the shaft to complete the disassembly procedures.

Inspection and Repair

1. Clean all parts in a suitable solvent and blow them dry.

2. Inspect the gears for a worn or damaged condition, especially the gear teeth, and replace them as a set if necessary.

3. Inspect the remaining components for a worn or damaged condition and replace them as necessary. Take note of the condition of the rubber O-ring and replace it if age cracks are present.

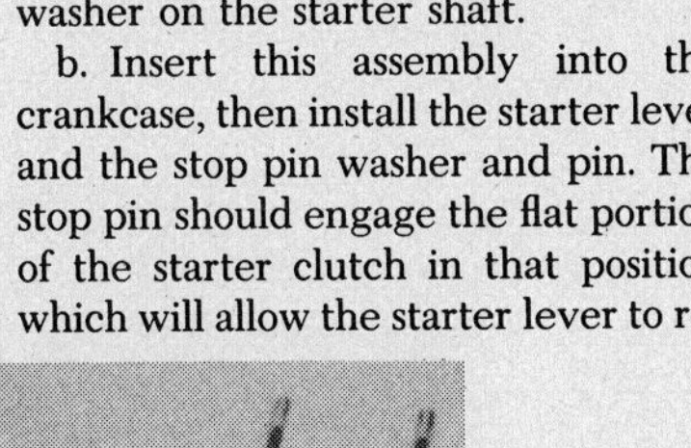

Assembly

1. The correct position for the starter lever is determined by the position of the starter clutch on the splined starter shaft. Locate this position in the following manner:

a. Assemble the crankcase side thrust washer, starter gear, starter clutch, clutch spring, and the thrust washer on the starter shaft.

b. Insert this assembly into the crankcase, then install the starter lever and the stop pin washer and pin. The stop pin should engage the flat portion of the starter clutch in that position which will allow the starter lever to remain in the correct position when not in use.

2. Remove the starter lever and install the spring cover on the return spring stud.

3. Install the return spring in one of the two shaft end grooves, then rotate it to the right to bring it to the correct tension, then engage the spring end on the return spring stud.

4. Install the clutch cover, gearshift lever, press the starter lever onto the shaft, and secure it with the tapered pin, washer, and nut.

1. Taper pin 2. Stop pin

Positioning the starter lever

The clutch spring installed

S AND B MODELS

Disassembly

1. Remove the clutch cover, clutch assembly, primary chain, primary drive gear, starter ratchet gear, ratchet spring, ratchet collar, and the ratchet lockring as described in the "Clutch" section.

2. Remove the shaft thrust washer, starter shaft, sector gear, starter spring, starter spring plate, shaft spring washer, and the shaft shim.

3. Rotate the starter shaft while exerting a gentle pulling pressure on it. When the starter spring tension is relieved, the shaft assembly will be free for removal. Take care not to drop any parts into the crankcase.

4. Remove the shaft shim, spring washer, spring plate, and the spring. If these parts were not on the shaft, they may have fallen into the crankcase and therefore the cases may have to be separated to retrieve them.

5. The sector gear is a light press fit on the starter shaft and need not be removed unless inspection indicates the need for replacement.

Inspection and Repair

1. Clean all parts in a suitable solvent and blow them dry.

2. Inspect the ratchet and starter sector gears for a worn or damaged condition, especially at the gear teeth, and replace them as a set if necessary.

3. Inspect the engaging teeth of the ratchet and clutch sprocket gears for a

worn or damaged condition and replace them as a set if necessary, as described in the "Clutch" section.

4. Inspect the ratchet spring, starter spring, and the shaft spring washer for a collapsed or damaged condition and replace them as necessary.

5. Replace the ratchet lockring regardless of its condition.

6. Inspect the shifter shaft oil seal for a worn, cracked, or damaged condition and replace it if necessary.

7. Inspect the remaining components for a worn or damaged condition and replace them if necessary. If the shifter shaft is warped or damaged in any way it can be replaced as directed in the "Transmission" section.

Assembly

1. Mount the starter sector gear on the starter shaft with the shoulder of the gear away from the shoulder of the shaft. The gear is a light press fit on the shaft.

2. Slip the starter spring onto the shaft so the spring rests against the sector gear, and is coiled clockwise from the center as viewed from the crankcase side.

3. Install the starter spring plate, spring washer, and the shaft shim, using a small daub of grease to hold the parts temporarily in place.

4. Lightly grease the shifter shaft oil seal, then slip the shaft assembly over the shifter shaft and engage the end loop of the starter spring with its slot in the crankcase. Take care not to allow the shim and washer to fall out of position during this operation.

5. Rotate the starter shaft slightly less than one full turn and then carefully push it in until seated against the crankcase. The sector gear should rest against its stop which keeps the assembly from rotating and therefore releasing the spring tension.

6. Slip the shaft thrust washer onto the shaft, thenmanipulate the starter shaft to make sure its motion is smooth and positive.

7. Continue the assembly process in the reverse order of disassembly.

Engine removal points—shown is a Model C

FOUR-CYCLE ENGINES (Sprint Models)

Engine Removal and Installation

1. Disconnect the battery ground wire (−) and the spark plug lead, then remove the spark plug.

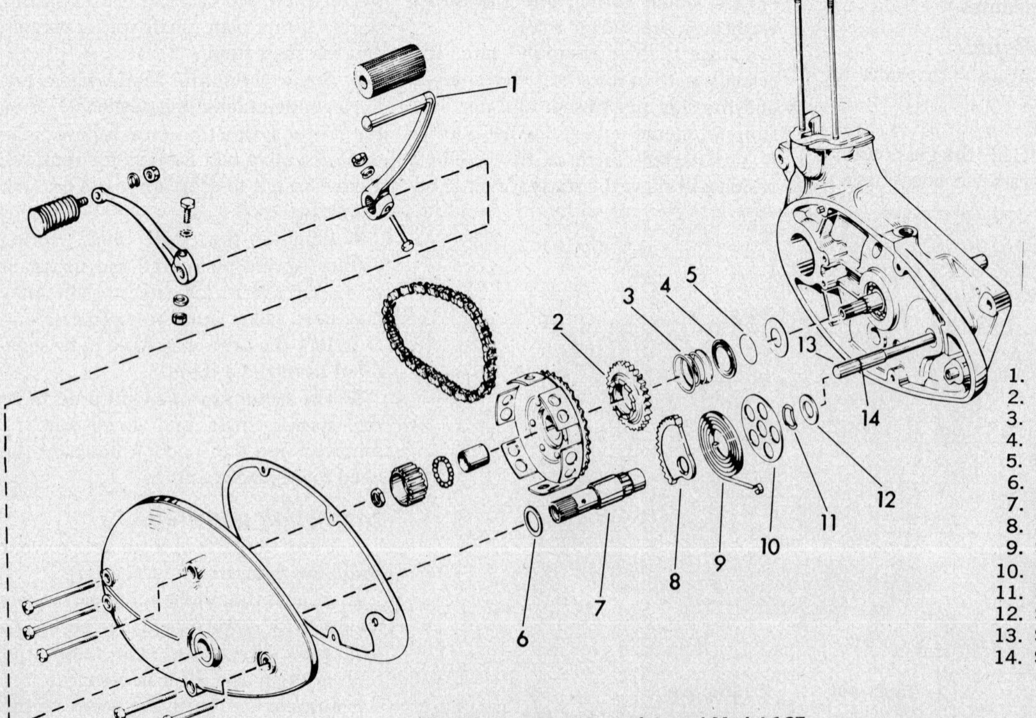

Starter assembly—B models and Model 165

2. Close the petcock, remove the fuel line fitting at the carburetor, release the fuel tank hold-down spring, tilt the tank forward to unhook the front mounting, and remove the tank.

3. Unhook the footbrake lever-return spring and remove the left footrest.

4. Remove the left crankcase cover securing screws and the cover.

5. Disconnect the generator wires at the generator and pull them free from the frame compartment.

6. Disconnect and remove the drive chain.

7. Remove the upper mounting bolt nuts but do not remove the bolts.

8. Rotate the clutch release lever forward and disconnect the clutch cable.

9. Remove the contact breaker cover, disconnect the contact breaker leads, and pull the wires free of the case.

10. Remove the nuts and washers from the exhaust manifold clamp, remove the rear footrest and muffler support, and lift the entire exhaust assembly free.

11. Remove the intake manifold nuts, on early-model carburetors, plug up the intake port with a clean rag, and place the carburetor out of the way without disconnecting the throttle cable.

12. On late-model carburetors, pull back the rubber boot, unscrew the coil control adjusting screw (the screw the cable runs through), lift the throttle piston clear of the carburetor body, and plug the top with a clean rag.

13. Remove the shifter lever screw and pry, or use a wheel puller, to remove the lever from its splined shaft.

14. Drift the front upper engine mounting bolt free.

15. Carefully support the cylinder head so the engine won't drop, and remove the rear upper mounting bolt.

16. Gently lower the front of the engine onto something soft, support the rear of the engine, and remove the right footrest.

17. Install the engine in the reverse order of removal, taking note of the following:

a. Connect the condenser and contact point leads to the contact breaker wire stud screw.

b. Connect the red wire at the generator DF terminal and the white wire at the D+ (D plus) terminal.

c. Replace the drive chain before replacing the left side cover.

d. Clean the oil filters and replenish the oil supply before attempting to turn over the engine.

Top End Service

CYLINDER HEAD

Removal

1. Remove the head on 1966 and earlier models in the following manner:

a. Remove the feed line connector, washers, cylinder head nuts, and washers.

b. Remove the cylinder head assembly, push rods, rocker arm oil return pipe, and the push rod housing rubber gasket. Tap gently on the head with a soft mallet if it is reluctant to come off.

c. Cover the cylinder with a clean, oil-soaked rag.

2. Remove the head on 1967 and later models in the following manner:

a. Remove the feed line connectors, washers, rocker arm oil line, rocker arm cover nuts or bolts, washers, rocker arm cover, and gasket.

b. Remove the cylinder head nuts, collars, O-rings, hose clamp (if applicable), head assembly, and head gasket. Tap gently on the head with a soft mallet if it is difficult to remove.

c. Remove the oil return pipe and O-rings, loosen the hose clamps (if applicable), and remove the hose.

d. Remove the push rod housing rubber gasket, and cover the cylinder with a clean, oil-soaked rag.

Disassembly

1. Disassemble the 1966 and earlier cylinder head in the following manner:

a. Remove the rocker arm oil feed pipe connections, washers, and the rocker arm oil line taking care not to bend the oil line.

b. Remove the tappet cover screws, washers, cover, gasket, and all mounting screws to the intake and exhaust rocker arm covers, gaskets, valve and shaft side rocker arm support flange covers, and gaskets.

c. Remove the intake manifold assembly by removing the nuts, washers, bushing, manifold, and insulator bushing.

d. Remove the rocker arm assembly if necessary by removing the rocker arm set screw, tapping the rocker shaft free of the head, and lifting the rocker arm free. It is not necessary to disassemble the rocker arms to remove the valves.

e. Continue as described in step three.

Engine removal points—shown is a Model H

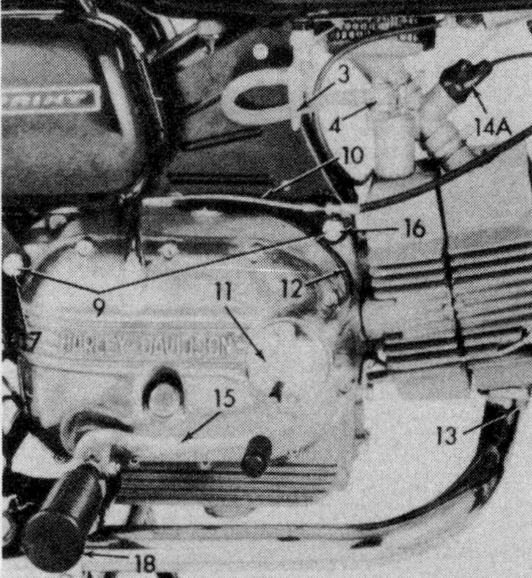

Engine removal points—shown is a Model SS

1. Spark plug cover
2. Spark plug
3. Fuel supply valve
4. Fuel line fitting
5. Brake footlever spring
5A. Tank spring
5B. Tank
5C. Tank front mounting
6. Left footrest
7. Left crankcase cover
8. Generator wires
9. Upper engine mount bolt nuts
10. Clutch control wire
11. Circuit breaker cover
12. Circuit breaker wires
13. Exhaust pipe mounting nuts & washers
14. Intake manifold mounting nuts
14A. Carburetor boot
15. Shifter lever
16. Front upper engine mounting bolt
17. Rear upper engine mounting bolt
18. Right footrest
19. Tachometer cable

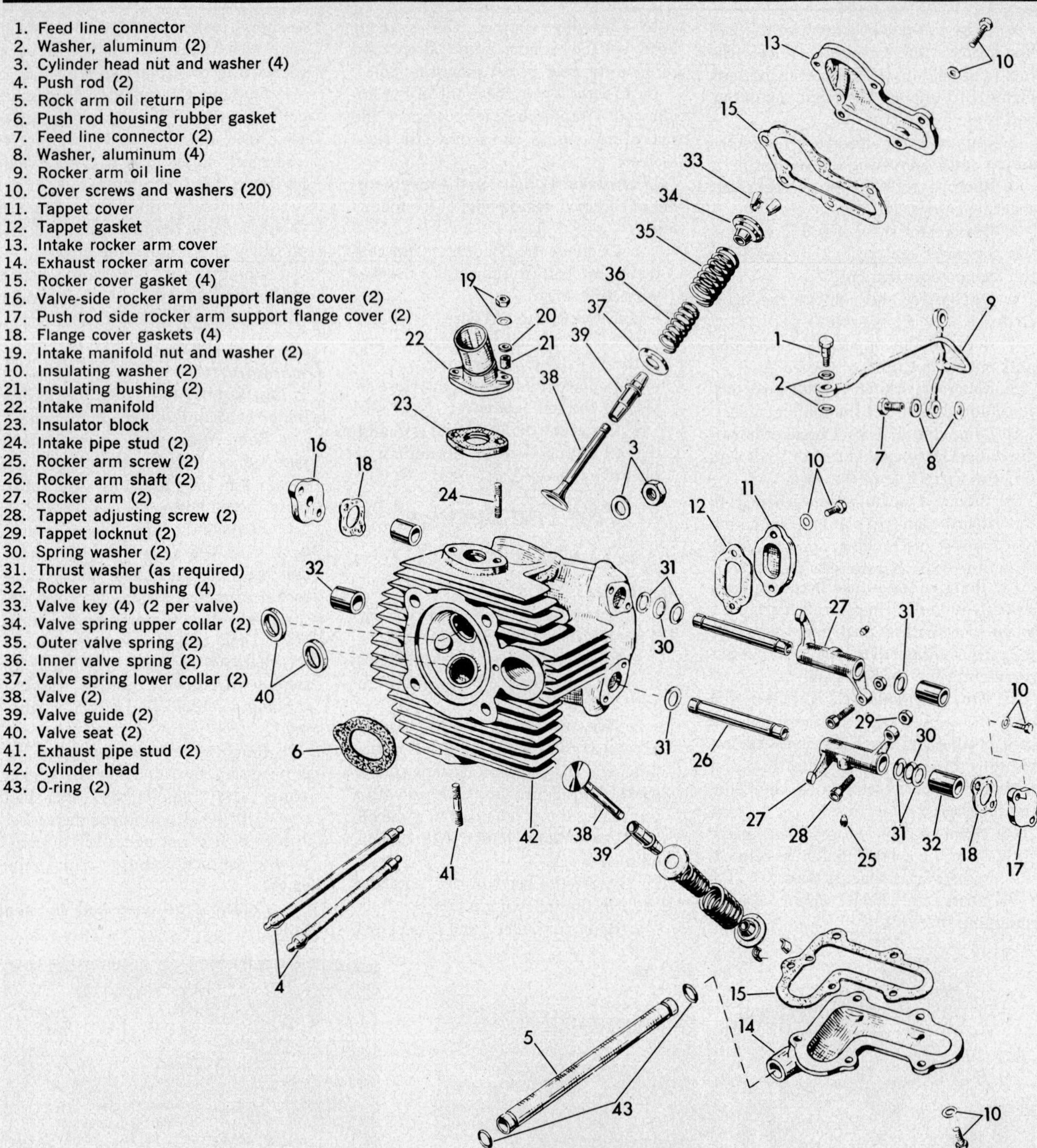

1966 and earlier Sprint cylinder head assembly

2. Disassemble the 1967 and later cylinder head in the following manner:

a. Remove the rocker arm oil feed pipe connections, washers, and the rocker arm oil line, taking care not to bend the oil line.

b. Remove the intake manifold assembly by removing the screws, washers, manifold, and insulating block.

c. Remove the rocker arm assemblies if repair of the valves or rocker arms is necessary, by removing the clamping bolt and lock, tapping the shaft free of the head, and lifting the rocker arm free.

d. Continue as described in step three.

3. Disassembly continued for all models

a. Each rocker arm assembly has a spring washer among thrust washers on one side and thrust washers only on the other. For reassembly purposes make a note of the number and placement of said devices.

b. Remove the valves by compressing them with Valve Spring Compressor (H-D part no. 97290–61P), or any suitable compressor or means of compressing the valves spring long enough to remove the valve keys.

c. Remove the valve spring upper collar, inner and outer springs, lower spring collar, and valve, and keep all the parts separate for reassembly in their original locations.

d. Remove the valve seats and guides only if replacement is necessary as described in the "Inspection and Repair" and the "Refacing and Replacing Valve Seats" sections.

Inspection and Repair

1. Clean all parts in a suitable gum and carbon-dissolving solution and blow them dry, taking care to blow all passages clear.

2. Inspect and repair the rocker arm, shaft, and bushing if worn or damaged in the following manner:

a. Remove any burrs from the rocker shaft with a hone.

b. Inspect the rocker arm pads for an unevenly worn, pitted, or damaged condition. If possible, inspect a new pad, then grind the damaged one until a similar contour is attained.

c. Replace the bushings if loose or damaged by heating the head to about 250° F with a blow torch and then driving or pressing the bushing free using a shouldered drift with a 0.469 in. pilot.

d. Drill a 0.118 in. oil hole in the intake left bushing.

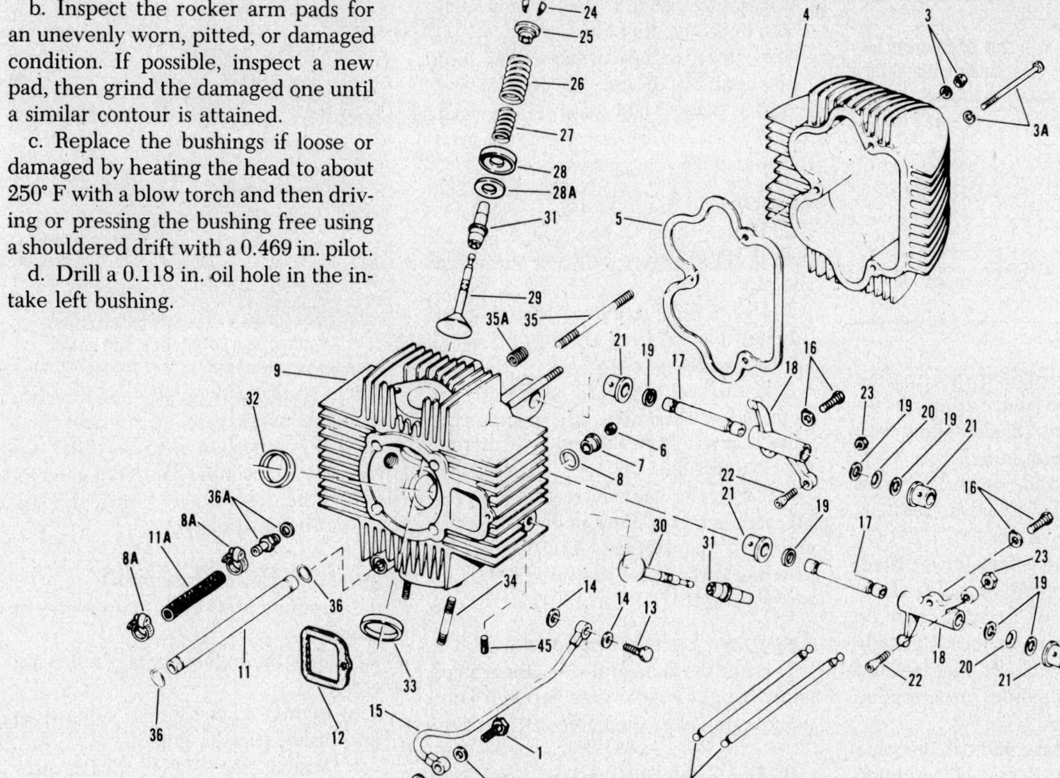

1967 and later Sprint cylinder head assembly

1. Feed line connector
2. Washer, aluminum (2)
3. Rocker arm cover nut and washer (3)
3A. Bolt and lockwasher (late 1970) (3)
4. Rocker arm cover
5. Rocker cover gasket
6. Cylinder heat nut (4)
7. Collar (4)
8. O-ring seal (4)
8A. Hose clamp (1969 SS)
9. Cylinder head
10. Push rod (2)
11. Oil return pipe
11A. Oil return hose (1969 SS)
12. Push rod housing rubber gasket
13. Feed line connector
14. Washer, aluminum (4)
15. Rocker arm oil line
16. Rocker arm clamping bolt and lock (2)
17. Rocker arm shaft (2)
18. Rocker arm (2)
19. Thrust washer (as required)
20. Spring washer (2)
21. Rocker arm shaft bushing (4)
22. Tappet adjusting screw (2)
23. Tappet locknut (2)
24. Valve key (4) (2 per valve)
25. Valve spring upper collar (2)
26. Outer valve spring (2)
27. Inner valve spring (2)
28. Valve spring lower collar (2)
28A. Exhaust valve spring lower collar shim
29. Valve (intake)
30. Valve (exhaust)
31. Valve guide (2)
32. Valve seat (exhaust)
33. Valve seat (intake)
34. Exhaust pipe stud (2)
35. Rocker arm cover stud (3)
35A. Helicoil (late 1970) (3)
36. Oil return pipe O-ring (2)
36A. Oil return hose fitting and gasket (1969 SS)

e. Press the new bushing into the head after heating the head as described above. Line-ream the bushing with Reamer (H-D part no. 97414–61P) or a suitable substitute, and check to see that the oil hole is not blocked.

d. Replace the rocker arm adjusting screw ball sockets if worn or elongated.

e. Replace any springs or thrust washers in questionable condition.

3. After the head has soaked long enough to soften any deposits, clean the outside thoroughly with a wire brush. Scrape the combustion chamber and valve port areas with a blunt blade, taking care not to gouge or scratch the head's face as this may cause combustion leakage.

4. Reclean the head as described in step one.

5. Inspect the valve spring length and tension with a Valve Spring Tester (H-D part no. 96797–47) or a suitable substitute. Springs must be replaced with ⅛ in. or more shorter than a new spring or if the tension is 5 lbs or more below the specifications listed in the "Engine and Transmission Specifications" charts.

6. Valve stem and head carbon deposits can be removed with a blunt blade or a wire wheel. Once all deposits have been removed, polish the stem with a fine grade emery cloth or steel wool. Replace any valves which are severely scored, pitted, warped or bent. Consult the "Refacing and Replacing Valve Seats" section for directions on how to clean pitted, burned, or corroded valves.

7. Inspect the valves stems and guides for an excessively loose fit, worn, or damaged condition, and replace in the following manner:

a. Consult the "Engine and Transmission Specifications Chart" for the proper fit.

b. Remove the guides by heating the head with a blow torch to about 250° F and then drifting the guide free from the chambered side with an appropriately sized, shouldered drift.

c. Choose the necessary size of oversized guide until a very tight press fit is achieved. Make sure you don't mix the guides as they are not interchangeable.

Valve Guide Outside Diameter Oversize (in./mm)	No. of Grooves on Outside Diameter
0.001/0.025	1
0.002/0.050	2
0.003/0.075	3
0.004/0.100	4
0.006/0.150	5
0.008/0.200	6

d. Replace the guide by heating the head as described above, then arbor-press the guide into place, taking care to seat the guide squarely.

e. Ream the guides using a Valve Guide Reamer (H-D part no. 97310–61) or a suitable reamer.

8. Inspect the valve face for a pitted, burned, or worn condition. The face, which should be 5/64 in. wide, may be repaired as described in the "Refacing and Replacing Valve Seats" section, but only after the valve guides are attended to.

9. Inspect the intake and exhaust pipe bolts or studs for a damaged condition and replace them if necessary.

10. On 1966 and earlier models, make sure that the rocker cover oil hole is clear.

11. Inspect any gaskets you wish to reuse for a damaged or collapsed condition and replace them as necessary.

Replacing Valve Seats

Replace the valve seat insert in the following manner:

a. Using progressively larger reamers, bore out the old insert.

b. Heat the head with a blow torch to about 540° F and press the new insert in place. Make sure you are using the correct insert as they are not interchangeable.

Grinding Valve Seats

1. If the valve guides are to be replaced, do so before refacing the valves and seats.

2. Use a valve grinding tool to grind the seat to a 45° angle so that the seat is 1/16 in. wide.

3. If the seat is greater than 1/16 in. wide, it may be narrowed by grinding the valve seat relief at a 15° angle with a suitable cutting stone.

4. Grind the valve faces to 45°, applying pressure only long enough to clean and true the surface. Avoid excessive grinding and replace the valve if the face is worn too thin.

Lapping Valves and Seats

1. After the faces and seats are ground, apply a light coat of fine lapping compound and insert the valve in the guide.

2. Rotate the valve several times with a grinding tool while applying light pressure at the face and seat by pulling on the valve stem. This may also be done by hand by placing a length of fuel line over the valve stem, holding the head so the stem is up, and rotating the fuel line back and forth several times.

3. To check for a well-seated valve, clean the valve and seat thoroughly and insert the valve. Apply light pressure to the seat and face by pulling on the valve, then pour some gasoline on the valve from the combustion chamber side. If it takes several seconds (10–15 is a good indication) before leakage occurs, the lapping has been successful.

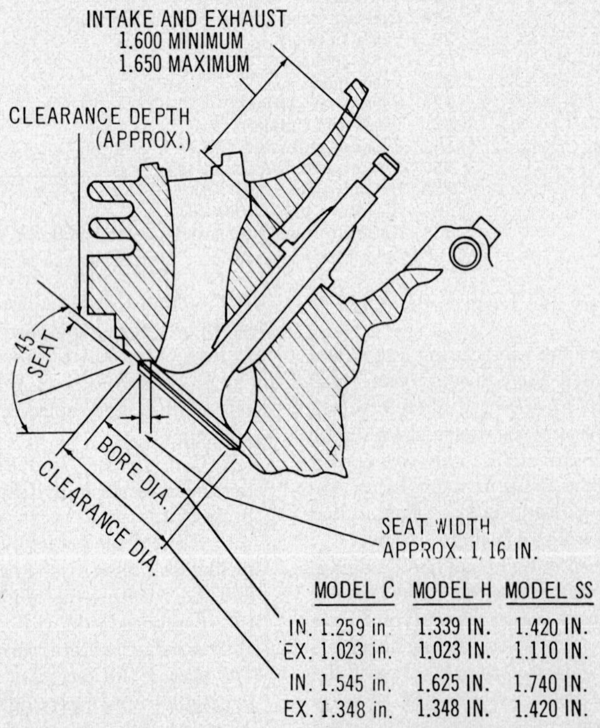

Valve seat specifications

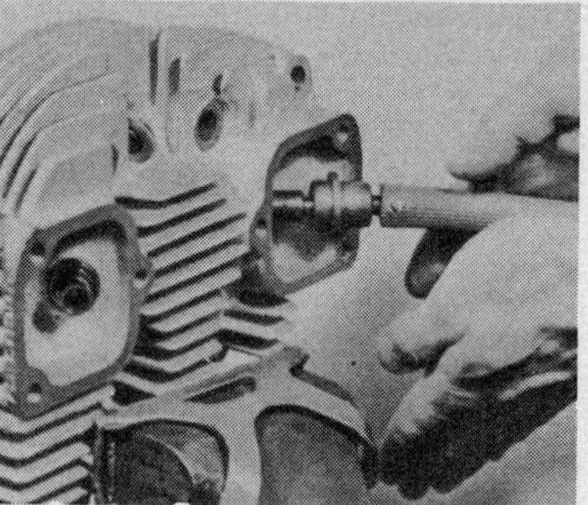
Lapping in a valve face and seat

Cylinder Head Assembly

1. Assembly is basically the reverse of disassembly.

2. Install the valves in the following manner:

a. Lightly oil the intake valve stem and insert it in the guide.

b. Secure the Valve Compressor Tool (H-D part no. 97290–61P), or a suitable substitute, in a vise so the movable parts are on top, then hold the head in place so the intake valve head is in contact with the compressor's stationary jaw.

c. Assemble the lower collar, inner spring, outer spring, and upper collar in place over the valve stem.

d. Compress the springs with the compressor until there is enough room to install the keys. Place a dab of grease on the tip of a screwdriver to easily handle the keys, and always install them with the narrow part down.

e. Release the compressor and remove the head.

f. Perform the above operations on the exhaust valve. Late models have a shim which fits under the lower collar.

3. Install the rocker arm assemblies in the following manner:

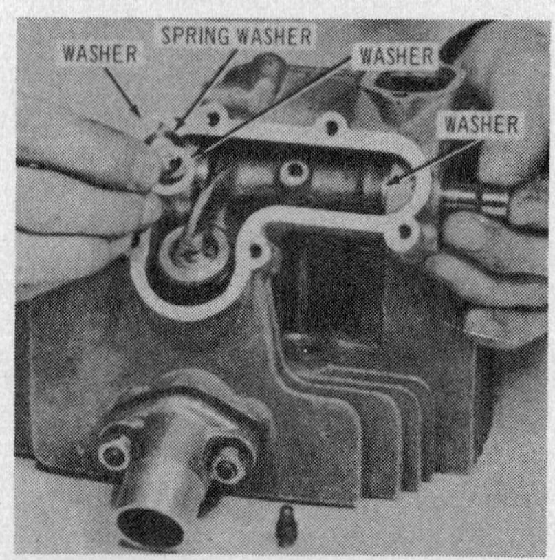

Installing the rocker arm assemblies—shown is the intake valve

a. Place the intake rocker arm in the head and slip the rocker arm shaft into the bushing on the push rod side until it can be seen between the bushing and the arm.

b. Place the appropriate number of thrust and spring washers in position.

c. Push the shaft through the washers and into the arm until the flat portion or hole is visible through the hole in the rocker arm. Position the rocker arm pad on the valve stem by increasing or decreasing the number of washers.

d. Secure the setscrew or bolt and lock.

e. Perform the above operations on the exhaust rocker arm assembly.

Cylinder Head Installation

1. Assembly is basically the reverse order of disassembly.
2. Make sure the mating faces of both the head and cylinder are perfectly clean.
3. Replace the oil return pipe oil seals on 1966 and earlier models, and insert the pipe in the left crankcase oil return hole.
4. Place the intake push rod in the push rod housing closest to the flywheel assembly. When the head is installed, the intake push rod will be above the exhaust push rod.
5. Install the exhaust push rod in the outer push rod housing. The exhaust rod is 0.040 in. longer than the intake rod on 1967 and later models.
6. Install the push rod housing rubber gasket over the push rods.
7. Slip the head in position over the mounting studs, leaving sufficient space to allow needle-nosed pliers to be inserted between the head and cylinder to grasp the push rod.
8. Rock the rocker arm down so the tappet adjusting screw can engage the appropriate push rod ball end. Repeat this procedure on the other push rod.
9. Slide the head down until it comes in contact with the cylinder mating surface.
10. Secure the head nuts until finger-tight, then diagonally torque them to 30 ft lbs.
11. Assemble the rocker arm oil line to the cylinder. Position the line on 1966 and earlier models so the crankcase connection end is between the cylinder head and rocker arm housing, and so it runs between the cooling fins along the lower right side of the cylinder and head. Place an aluminum washer on both sides of the connections, and install the connectors with the longest feed line connector in the crankcase. Wait until you are certain that all three connectors are properly aligned before securing the connectors.
12. Adjust the tappets as described in the "Tune-Up Operations."
13. Assemble the remaining components in the reverse order of disassembly. Take care not to overtighten the tappet cover screws on 1966 and earlier models as damage will result.

CYLINDER AND PISTON

Disassembly

1. Remove the cylinder head as described in the cylinder head removal section.

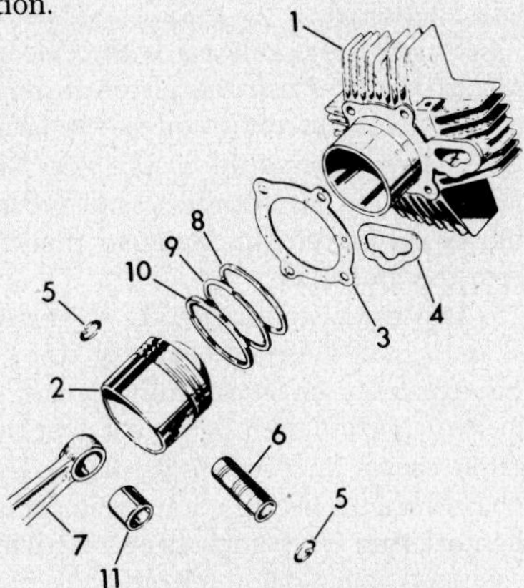

Cylinder and piston assembly

1. Cylinder
2. Piston
3. Cylinder base gasket
4. Push rod gasket
5. Piston pin lock ring
6. Piston pin
7. Connecting rod
8. Upper compression ring
9. Lower compression ring
10. Control ring
11. Piston pin bushing

2. Thoroughly clean the crankcase around the base of the cylinder to prevent dirt or any other alien particles from falling into the crankcase.
3. Lift the cylinder enough to allow a clean, oil-soaked rag to be placed over the crankcase opening.
4. Remove the cylinder from the mounting studs.
5. Pry the circlips free with a sharp, pointed instrument or remove them with snap-ring pliers.
6. Heat the piston to about 250° F with a blow torch, then drift the piston pin free with a suitable drift while supporting the piston.
7. Using snap-ring pliers, remove the piston rings.

Inspection and Repair

1. Clean all parts in a suitable carbon and gum-dissolving solution. Carefully clean the ring grooves with a piece of broken ring.
2. Inspect the piston pin for a pitted or grooved condition and replace it if necessary.
3. If piston pin fit in the connecting rod upper bushing has play in excess of 0.002 in., both parts must be replaced. The pin should be a light, hand press in the bushing with play not in excess of 0.001 in.
4. Inspect the piston and cylinder for cracks, burrs, gouges, grooves, or burned spots on the piston crown, and replace them if necessary.

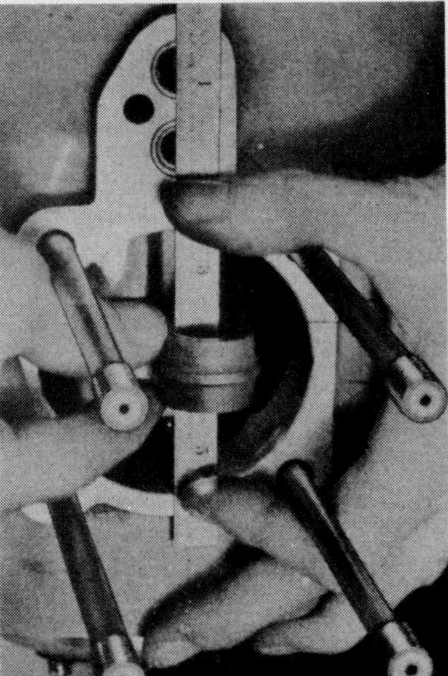

Checking the connecting rod for lower end bearing shake

5. If the connecting rod has vertical or side shake (as measured at the top of the connecting rod) in excess of 1.16 in., the need for a new bottom end bearing and rod assembly is indicated. Consult the "Crankcase" section for additional information.
6. Replace the circlips, piston rings, and gaskets.

Cylinder Refinishing

1. Using a micrometer, measure the piston from front to rear at the base of its skirt.
2. Using an inside micrometer, measure the cylinder bore from front to rear and from side to side at a point ½ in. from the top. Repeat this procedure at various points in the middle and bottom of the ring travel area to determine whether or not the cylinder is still round.
3. Subtract the piston measurement from the cylinder measurement to arrive at the overall clearance.
4. If the cylinder is not damaged, scored, grooved, or worn 0.0025 in. or more, it need not be refinished oversize. If the clearance is not excessive, quieter operation can be achieved with standard sized pistons or the appropriate oversize pistons to fit the already oversize cylinders. If the clearance is excessive, the cylinder may be refinished to the next oversize and fitted with corresponding oversize pistons.

5. Add the desired clearance to the size of the piston to arrive at the appropriate oversize piston measurement. Pistons are available in 0.008 in. gradations from 0.008–0.032 in. oversize.

6. Hone or bore the cylinder to the piston size. If a cylinder requires reboring which will make it 0.036 in. or more oversize, it should be replaced.

Connecting Rod Bushing Replacement

1. When the connecting rod bushing and the piston pin have clearance in excess of 0.002 in., the clearance must be eliminated by one of the following methods:

   a. Ream the bushing out until the proper clearance can be attained by fitting a 0.004 or 0.008 in. oversize piston pin, and reaming the piston bosses to fit.

   b. Replace the bushing and ream it to fit a standard size piston pin unless the piston has already been fitted with an oversize pin.

2. If the engine has been taken down and the connecting rod has been removed, a suitably sized press may be used to remove and install the bushing. Always press the bushing in so the oil holes are aligned.

3. If the bushing is to be replaced during a top-end job, proceed in the following manner:

   a. Secure the connecting rod to prevent damage to it and the lower bearing.

   b. Remove the old bushing with Piston Pin Bushing Tool (H-D part no. 95970–32A) or by heating the rod with a blow torch and then carefully pressing the bushing free.

   c. Install the new bushing with the same tool or a suitable substitute, taking care to align the oil holes while pressing the bushing into place.

4. After the bushing is installed in the rod it must be reamed to provide the necessary 0.0006–0.0012 in. piston pin clearance. Use Expansion Reamer (H-D part no. 94810–65), or a suitable substitute, to perform this operation.

5. Remove the rod from whatever has been securing it and visually check the rod alignment. If the rod has been bent, it should be replaced since bending fatigues metal and one doesn't want a tired rod.

Assembly

1. Select the appropriate size piston ring by adding the desired piston-to-cylinder clearance to the piston measurement and then subtracting that figure from the measurement of the cylinder bore. The result is the size of the necessary ring. Rings are available in 0.008 in. gradations from 0.008–0.0032 in. oversize. Do not use oversize pistons in a standard bore.

2. Check ring gap by holding the piston in the cylinder, in an inverted position, laying the ring on top of the piston skirt, and measuring the gap. The gap must be within 0.010–0.016 in. If the gap is too small, it may be increased by filing with a fine-cut file.

3. Install one of the piston circlips with snap-ring pliers, heat the piston with a blow torch, and lubricate the piston pin, upper rod bushing, and piston pin bosses with engine oil.

4. Cover the crankcase with a clean, oil-soaked rag. Place the piston in position on the connecting rod so the large relief valve is facing the intake side, slip the piston pin into position, and secure the remaining circlip. Remove the rag from the crankcase.

5. Dip the piston and rings in engine oil and install the piston rings by using a ring expander, or by carefully spreading the ring by hand then slipping it over the piston crown and then into place. The top ring is a plain-type compression ring, the next ring is a compression ring with a stepped inner diameter, and the bottom ring, which is installed first, is a slotted oil ring. Stagger the ring gaps but avoid having gaps on the thrust faces of the piston.

6. Check the ring side-clearance for 0.-001–0.002 in. end-play. If the ring is too loose, the ring groove is probably worn and the piston must be replaced. If the ring has been installed and then removed, it still may be used since rings break rather than bend.

7. Place the cylinder base gaskets in position over the mounting studs.

8. Rough up the cylinder bore with no. 150 carborundum emery paper or a no. 300 hone if the cylinder wasn't refinished. This will provide a surface conducive to efficient ring seating and lubrication.

9. If a ring compressor is to be used assemble it now. Lubricate the cylinder walls with engine oil, and rotate the engine until the piston is at its lowest point of travel.

10. Carefully start the cylinder on the mounting studs until about 1½–2 in. of the studs is covered. Gently rotate the engine until the piston is aligned with the cylinder bore. Compress the first ring by hand and insert the piston into the bore by rotating the engine slightly. Continue to insert the piston until it is entirely in the cylinder.

11. Lower the cylinder onto its crankcase mating surface while holding the push rod housing rubber gasket in place.

12. Complete assembly in the reverse order of disassembly as directed in the section on the cylinder head.

Crankcase

Disassembly

1. Remove the engine from the frame as described in the engine "Removal and Installation" section.

2.Remove the generator as described in the "Generator" section.

3. Remove the starter clutch as described in the "Starter" section.

4. Remove the drive sprocket as described in the "Transmission" section.

5. Remove the cylinder head as described in the "Cylinder Head" section.

6. Remove the cylinder and piston assembly as described in the "Cylinder and Piston" section.

7. Remove the gearcase cover, camshaft, tappet assemblies, oil pump, pinion shaft gears, and the pinion shaft bearing lockring and spacers as described in the "Transmission" and "Lubrication" sections.

8. Remove the clutch assembly as described in the "Clutch" section for 1968 and earlier models.

9. Check the crankshaft end-play with a dial indicator in the following manner:

   a. Mount Crankshaft Tool (H-D part no. 97295–61P) on the right crankcase and the dial indicator on the left crankcase.

   b. Push the crankshaft as far to the left as it will go.

   c. Remove the tool and mount Crankshaft Tool (H-D part no. 97297–61P) in its place.

   d. Pull the shaft all the way back to the right.

   e. End-play is regulated by the number of spacer washers used. Washers are available in 0.05 and 0.10 mm sizes or may be replaced with two spring washers (which is the recommended technique).

   f. If the tools are not available the crankshaft may be manipulated with hand tools.

10. Drift the dowel pins free with a suitably sized drift and remove the three allen screws and seven bolts and washers which secure the crankcase halves. If the dowel pins are difficult to remove, heat the case around each pin with a blow torch.

11. Separate the crankcase halves with Crankshaft Tool (H-D part no. 97295–61P) or a suitable substitute. The tool mounts on the right case over the flywheel pinion shaft and presses the cases apart by exerting pressure on the flywheel assembly. Tap on the mainshaft with a soft mallet while using the tool and make sure the cases remain parallel during the entire operation.

12. Remove the transmission as described in the "Transmission" section

13. Remove the pinion bearing lockr-

Measuring the crankshaft end-play

Removing recessed allen screw from the left crankcase half

Separating the crankcase halves

The separated crankcases

ing with snap-ring pliers, then press the pinion shaft bearing from the crankcase. Bearing damage can be avoided by covering the bearing with a flat plate before pressing. Remove the crankshaft orifice plug (if applicable).

14. Press the flywheel assembly from the left case using Crankshaft Tool (H-D part no. 97295–61P) or a suitable substitute.

15. The countershaft ball bearing may now be removed with a puller if so desired.

16. Remove the generator shaft bearing oil seal and press the bearing free.

Inspection and Repair

1. Clean all parts in a suitable solvent and blow them dry, taking care to clear the oil passages in the right flywheel and crankpin.

2. Check the main bearings for a pitted, worn, or damaged condition, excessive play, or rough action, and replace them as necessary by removing the seals and lockrings and pressing the bearings in and out. Heating the case around the bearing boss will aid in installation.

3. Inspect the pinion shaft cover bushing for a worn or damaged condition or excessive play and replace it as necessary.

4. Inspect the camshaft support plate for a worn or damaged condition and replace it as necessary.

5. Inspect the connecting rod, connecting rod bearing set, crankpin, and flywheel thrust washers for a worn, damaged, or loose condition, and replace them as an entire assembly.

Assembly

1. Press all bearings, bushings, and oil seals which have been removed back into the crankcase. Heating the case with a blow torch will aid in installing the bearings and bushings.

2. Install the pinion shaft bearing lockring.

3. Secure the left flywheel shaft in a copper or wood-jawed vise. Lightly oil the pinion shaft and position the right case on it.

4. Assemble the Crankshaft Tool (H-D part no. 97297–61P), or a suitable substitute, to the pinion shaft and draw the flywheel assembly through the right case, taking care not to damage the generator frame stud. Secure the pinion shaft bearing lockring in its groove.

5. Install the transmission as described in the "Transmission" section.

6. Assemble the cases in the following manner:

a. Place Oil Sleeve Installing Tool (H-D part no. 95629–63), or a suitable substitute, on the flywheel shaft to avoid damaging the oil seal lip while assembling the case.

b. Secure the crankcase and engine stud boss gaskets to the right case with a suitable sealer, using new gaskets only.

c. Slide the cases together and rotate the main drive gear to test for positive meshing of the transmission gears.

d. Draw the cases evenly together while tapping with a soft mallet using Crankcase Tool (H-D part no. 97295–61P) or a suitable substitute.

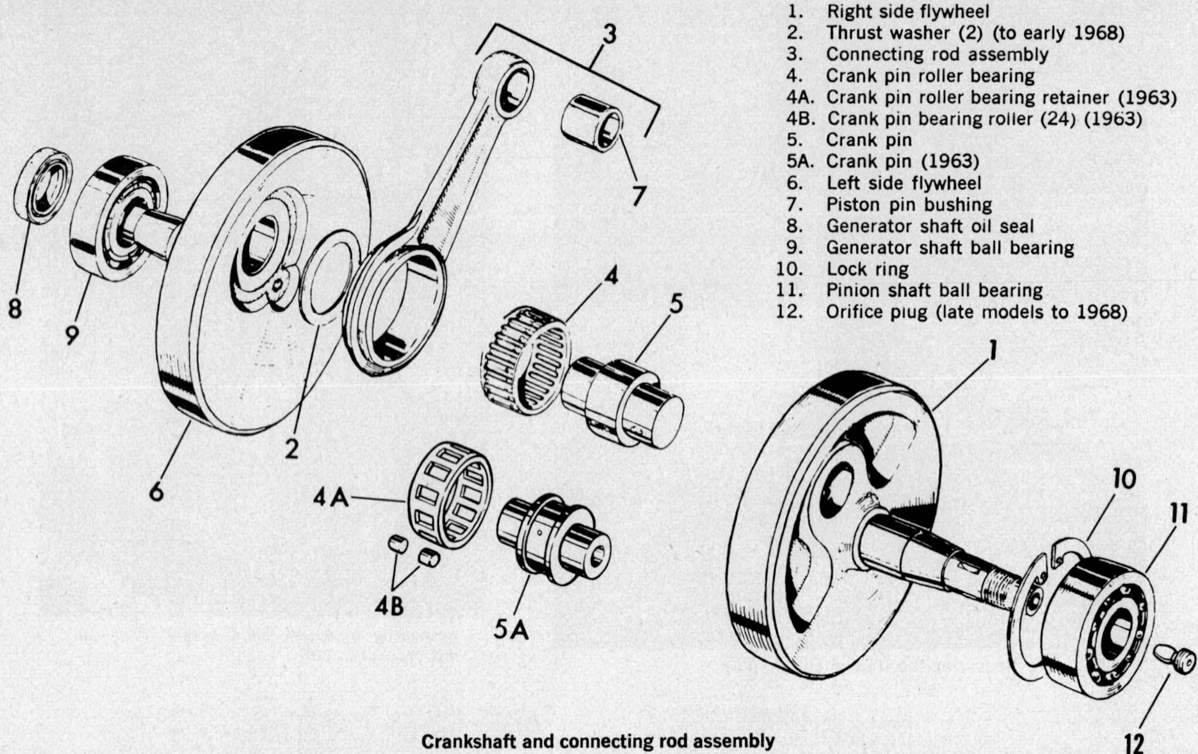

Crankshaft and connecting rod assembly

e. Tap the cases so the dowel pins fit into their receptacles once the case mating surfaces have seated against one another. Secure the remaining seven bolts, washers, nuts, and three allen screws.

7. Install the oil filter screens as described in the "Maintenance" section.

8. Install the gear shifter pawl carrier assembly, pinion shaft gears, and tappets and camshaft assemblies as described in the "Gearcase" section.

9. Install the oil pump as described in the "Lubrication" section.

10. Install the clutch assembly as described in the "Clutch" section.

11. On all Sprint H and 1963 Model C models, use a wood block to tap in a new crankshaft orifice plug, then use a piece of wire or a no. 53 (0.0595 in.) drill to make sure the oil hole is clear and of the proper size (if applicable).

12. Install the gearcase cover as described in the "Gearcase" section.

13. Install the piston, cylinder, and cylinder head as previously described in the "Top End" section.

14. Install the drive sprocket and cover as described in the "Transmission" section.

15. Install the starter clutch assembly as described in the "Starter" section.

16. Install the generator as described in the "Electrical" section.

17. Install the engine in the chassis as described in the engine "Removal and Installation" section.

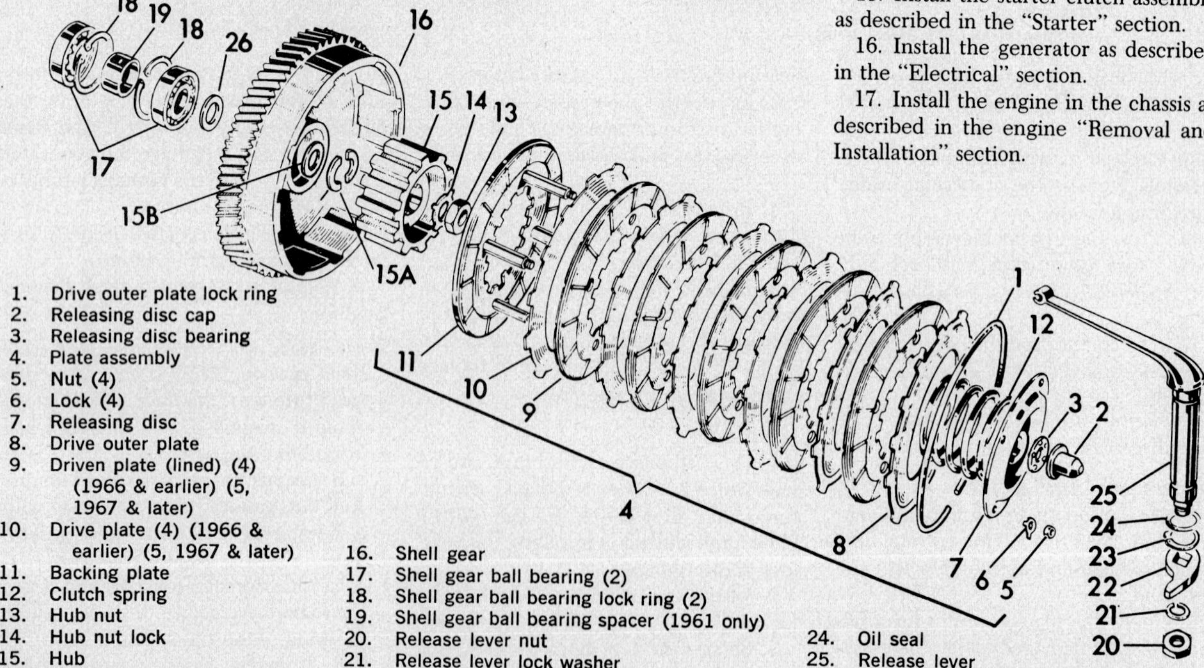

Clutch assembly—1968 and earlier models

Clutch

1968 AND EARLIER MODELS

Disassembly

1. Place a drip pan beneath the right side clutch cover, use a wrench to rotate the release lever forward, disengage the cable from the lever, and remove the foot shift lever, cover screws, cover, and cover gasket. Cover all gear case openings with a clean, oil-soaked towel.

2. Compress the clutch spring with Clutch Spring Compressor (H-D part no. 97293–61P) or a suitable substitute. The compressor's end bolts screw into the gearcase cover holes. When the spring is compressed enough, pry the drive outer plate lockring free and remove the compressor.

3. Remove the releasing disc cap, bearing, and the entire clutch plate and disc assembly. A piece of wire can be used to lift each disc and plate to slide them out, if so desired, once the backing plate nuts and washers have been removed. The machine can also be tilted over far enough to let the plates and discs slide out.

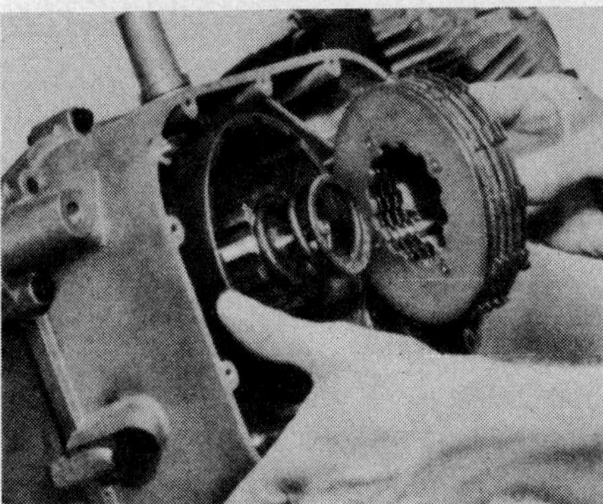

Removing the clutch plate assembly

4. Remove the clutch spring from the clutch hub and assemble the Clutch Holding Tool (H-D part no. 97291–61PA) or substitute some means of securing the clutch, such as blocking the clutch gear with a wooden door stop. Remove the clutch hub nut and lock, then pull the hub from its splined shaft with Crankshaft Pinion Gear and Clutch Hub Puller (H-D part no. 97294–61B) or a suitable gear puller. The mounting studs fit in the tapped holes in the hub. Remove the hub keys and spacer shim.

5. Pull the clutch shell gear free with a suitable gear puller. Pull the clutch shell gear inner bearing free if it remains on the shaft with Puller (H-D part no. 95960–48) and Two-Claw Puller (H-D part no. 97292–61P) or a suitable substitute which will grab the notches in the puller body. Remove the spacing shim if applicable.

Inspection and Repair

1. Clean all parts other than the friction discs in a suitable solvent and blow them dry. The friction discs may be cleaned in clean gasoline, blown dry, then soaked in clean engine oil.

2. Inspect the clutch spring for a collapsed or damaged condition. If the spring measures 3/32 in. less than the standard 129/32 in. or if it is damaged, it must be replaced.

3. Inspect the clutch plates and discs for a warped, scored, or heat-damaged condition, and replace if necessary. If the friction discs are not damaged, and if a mark remains after a fingernail is pressed into the friction material, they may be reused. When replacing clutch plates and discs, it is a good practice to replace them as a set. Burrs may be filed off the teeth of the discs.

4. Examine the clutch hub, clutch shell gear, and the primary drive gear for worn or damaged teeth and replace them if necessary. The shell and primary gears must be replaced as a set.

5. Inspect the clutch shell bearings for excessive side or vetical play, wear, or rough motion, and replace if necessary in the following manner:

a. Press the bearings out from opposite sides, then remove the shell bearing lockrings and spacer (1961 Model C) if so desired.

b. When installing the new bearings, first install the lockrings and spacer, then press the bearings in until seated against the lockrings.

6. Inspect the clutch releasing disc, disc bearing, and disc cap for a worn or damaged condition or rough bearing motion and replace them if necessary. The bearing action must be free and the disc cap must be free on the transmission mainshaft.

Release Lever Removal and Installation

1. Remove the contact breaker wires from the clutch cover.

2. Remove the release lever nut, lockwasher, operating cam, lockring, and release lever.

3. Inspect the oil seal for a worn or damaged condition and replace it and any other worn or damaged components as necessary.

4. Assemble the lever assembly in the following manner:

a. Slip the oil seal in place on the release lever and install the lever in the cover.

b. Secure the lever with the lockring which seats in a groove in the lever.

c. Position the operating cam on the release lever so the lever points to the center and the cam is to the rear of the engine when the cover is installed.

d. Secure the assembly to the cover with the release lever lockwasher and nut.

Assembly

1. Assembly is in the reverse order of disassembly.

2. Proceed as follows for units equipped with a drive take-up gear:

a. Slip the clutch shell gear onto the transmission mainshaft far enough to engage the shell and take-up gear teeth.

b. Rotate the clutch shell gear clockwise to rotate the take-up gear counterclockwise. When the take-up gear has advanced three teeth on the clutch drive gear, press the shell the remaining distance to engage the drive gear completely.

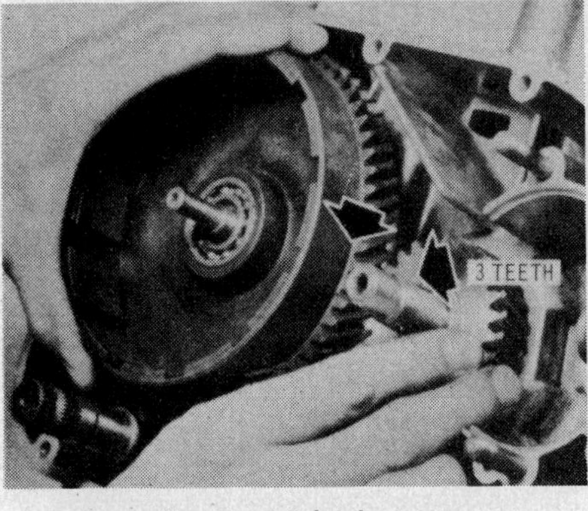

Preloading the clutch take-up gear

3. On units with a single-piece drive gear, merely press the shell onto the mainshaft until it engages the teeth of the drive gear.

4. Install the spacer shim and hub keys if applicable. Select the appropriate shim which will reduce shell end-play to a minimum when the keys are installed.

5. Assemble the clutch hub so the small hole faces out. Hold the hub in the same manner as in step four of the "Disassembly" section while installing the hub nut.

6. Install the clutch plates and discs with a steel plate on the inside against the backing plate then a friction disc and so on until six steel plates and five friction discs have been installed.

7. Slip the releasing disc on the backing plate studs so the spring seat is facing in toward the clutch plates, then secure the stud locks and nuts.

8. Slip the clutch spring into the clutch hub and then position the clutch plate and disc assembly onto the hub, pressing in until seated.

9. Place the drive outer plate over the clutch plate assembly so the shouldered side faces out.

10. Assemble the releasing disc bearing and cap on the releasing disc and assemble the Clutch Spring Compressor (H-D part no. 97293–61P), or a suitable substitute, to compress the spring.

11. When the plates and discs are properly aligned with the hub and shell, secure the entire assembly with the drive outer plate lockring which seats in a groove in the shell. Remove the compressing device and install the clutch cover and shift lever.

Clutch Cable Replacement

1. Rotate the release lever forward with a wrench and disengage the clutch cable.

2. Loosen the cable block screws and remove the cable block from the cable.

3. Disengage the cable and housing from the cable adjusting screw.

4. Align the slots in the handlever adjusting screw and nut, and free the cable at the handlever.

5. The cable may now be slipped out through the top of the coil or the cable and coil may be removed from the frame.

6. Grease the cable or lubricate it with a chain lubricating compound or engine oil while slipping it back into the coil. The coil is run through the right fork brackets and down through the guide near the horn.

7. Secure the cable at the handlever and adjust the adjusting screw and nut in as far as they will go. (On 1961–62 C models, the cable end button short end goes into the lever first.)

8. Slip the adjusting screw assembly on the cable end and run the cable through, and secure it to the cable securing block, and position it so the shoulder of the cable block seats on the release lever.

9. Adjust the clutch as described in the "Maintenance Items".

1969 AND LATER MODELS

Disassembly

1. Remove the footshift lever, clutch cover screws (from the smaller cover located on the front of the right crankcase cover), and the clutch cover.

2. Diagonally loosen the clutch spring nuts, so there is even pressure exerted against the pressure plate at all times, with Clutch Releasing Disc Nut Wrench (H-D part no. 94670–66P) or a screwdriver. Using a screwdriver may damage the nuts; they should be replaced if removed in this manner.

3. Remove the springs, cups, pressure plate, clutch plates and discs, and the steel-lined backing plate.

4. Secure the clutch hub with Clutch Lock Tool (H-D part no. 97177–69P) or by jamming a wooden door stop between the shell gear and the crankcase. Remove the hub nut and lock, then pull the hub free with a gear puller.

5. Remove the clutch hub O-ring, bend back the ears of the clutch shell nut lock, and remove the shell nut with Clutch Shell Nut Wrench (H-D part no. 97235-66P) or a suitable substitute. Remove the nut lock.

6. Remove the clutch shell, washer, clutch drive gear, clutch gear needle bearings, and the gear spacer washers.

Inspection and Repair

1. Clean all parts other than the friction discs in a suitable solvent and blow them dry. The friction plates can be cleaned in clean gasoline, blown dry, then soaked in clean engine oil.

2. Check the clutch springs for a collapsed or damaged condition and replace them if necessary. The free-length of a new clutch spring is 119/32 in.; any spring which is shorter by 3/32 in., or more, should be replaced. Springs should be replaced as a complete set whenever possible.

3. Inspect the clutch plates and discs for a warped, scored, burned, or damaged condition, and replace as necessary. If the friction discs are not damaged, and if a mark remains after a fingernail is pressed into the friction material, they may be reused. When replacing clutch plates and discs, it is a good practice to replace them as a set. Burrs may be removed from the disc teeth with a file.

4. Examine the O-ring for a cracked, rough, warped, or damaged condition and replace it if necessary. If a new O-ring is available, it should be used.

5. Examine the lip seal of the crankcase for a worn or damaged condition and replace it if necessary.

6. Inspect the clutch hub studs for a loose, stripped, or damaged condition and replace them if necessary by drilling out the old stud with a 5/16 in. drill and riveting in a new stud.

Release Lever Removal and Installation

1. Remove the left crankcase cover screws then tap on the cover with a soft mallet while pulling on the kick-starter lever.

2. Remove the release lever nut, lockwasher, operating cam, retaining screw, lock, and release lever.

3. Inspect the oil seal and all other parts for a worn or damaged condition and replace them as necessary.

4. Assemble the release lever assembly in the following manner:

a. Slip the oil seal on the release lever and install the lever in the crankcase cover.

b. Position the operating cam on the release lever so the lever points to the center and the cam is to the rear of the engine when the cover is installed.

c. Secure the assembly with the clutch lever lockwasher and nut, then install the retaining screw and lock.

Clutch Release Push Rod Removal and Installation

1. Remove both crankcase covers.

2. Loosen the push rod adjusting nut and remove the adjusting screw from the clutch pressure disc.

3. Push the two rods and balls out with a piece of wire or a spare rod.

4. When installing the rods again, be sure that the rounded end of the left-side push rod seats against the clutch lever operating cam.

Clutch Cable Replacement

1. Consult the "Clutch Cable Replacement" section for the 1968 and earlier models.

Transmission

If it becomes necessary to take down your transmission, you may as well go over the entire machine and overhaul the top and bottom ends since they will have to be dismantled in the process.

Removal and Replacement

1. Remove the engine from the frame as described in the engine "Removal and Installation" section.

2. Separate the crankcase halves as described in the "Crankcase" section.

3. Replacement is in the reverse order of removal.

Disassembly

1. Place the right crankcase on a work bench so the gear assemblies are pointing up.

2. Remove the small shifter cam spacer, the countershaft thrust washer, the shifter fork cotter pins, the shifter fork pins, and the mainshaft first gear lockring (if applicable).

3. Mount Clutch Spring Compressor (H-D part no. 97293–61P) or a suitable substitute to the outer portion of the crankcase and press the mainshaft assembly free of the right-side mainshaft bearing, then remove the shifter fork connected to the mainshaft from the shifter cam.

4. Drift the countershaft assembly free of the right-side countershaft bearing, and remove the shifter fork, which is connected to the countershaft, from the shifter cam.

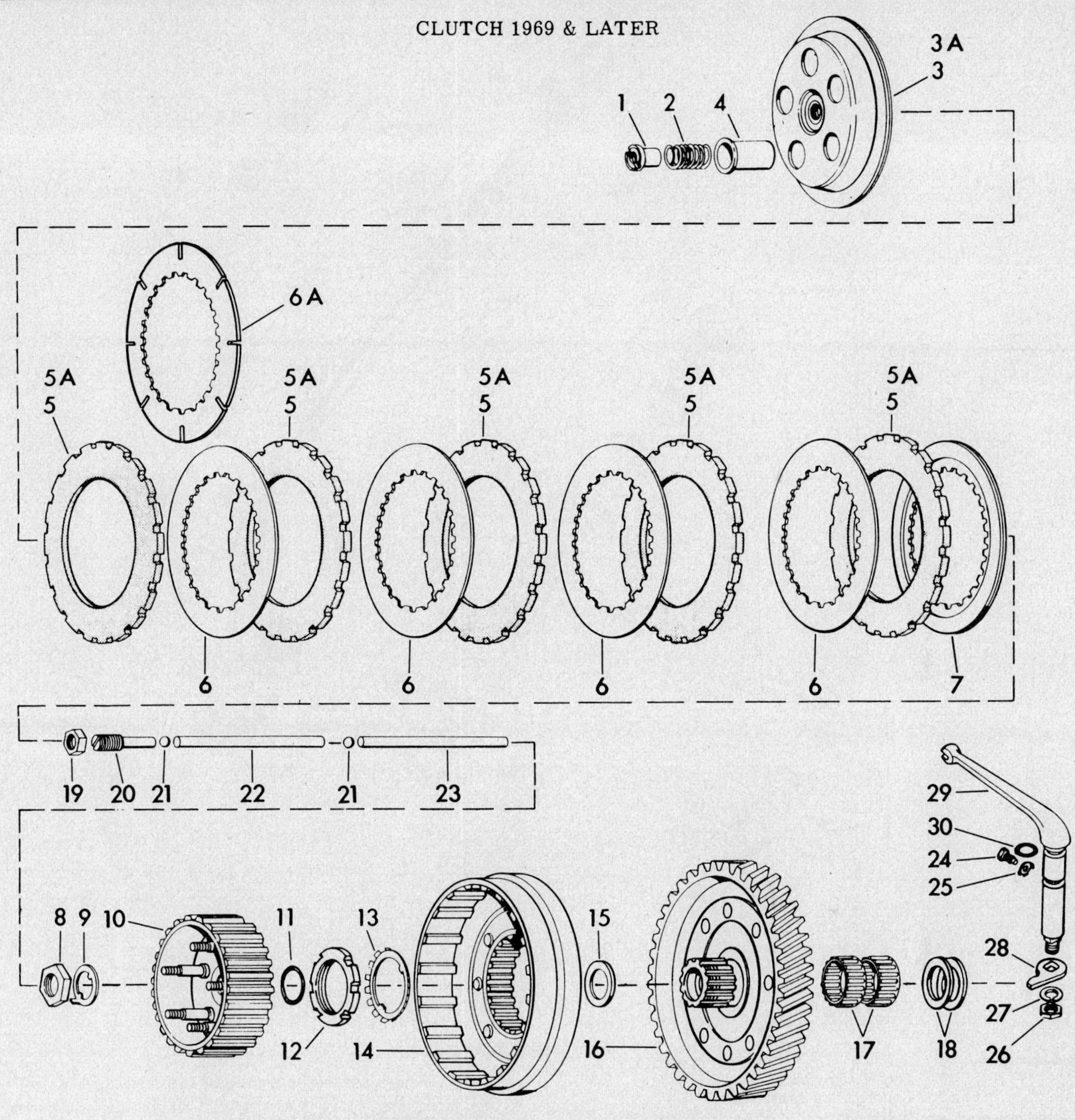

Clutch assembly—1969 and later models

1. Clutch spring nut (5)
2. Clutch spring (5)
3. Clutch pressure disc
3A. Pressure disc (1971 & later)
4. Clutch spring cup (5)
5. Friction (drive) plate (5) (1969-70)
5A. Friction (drive) plate (steel core) (1971 & later)
6. Steel (driven) plate (4 below 3C116752H2) (3 above 3C116752H2)
6A. Steel (driven) plate (dished) (above 3C116752H2)
7. Steel lined (backing) plate
8. Clutch hub nut
9. Clutch hub nut lock
10. Clutch hub
11. Clutch hub O-ring seal
12. Clutch shell nut
13. Clutch shell nut lock
14. Clutch shell
15. Washer
16. Clutch drive gear
17. Clutch gear needle bearing (2)
18. Clutch gear spacer washer (variable number)
19. Push rod adjusting screw nut
20. Push rod adjusting screw
21. Ball (2)
22. Push rod, right side
23. Push rod, left side
24. Clutch lever retaining screw
25. Clutch lever retaining screw lock
26. Clutch lever nut
27. Clutch lever lockwasher
28. Clutch lever operating cam
29. Clutch lever
30. Clutch lever O-ring

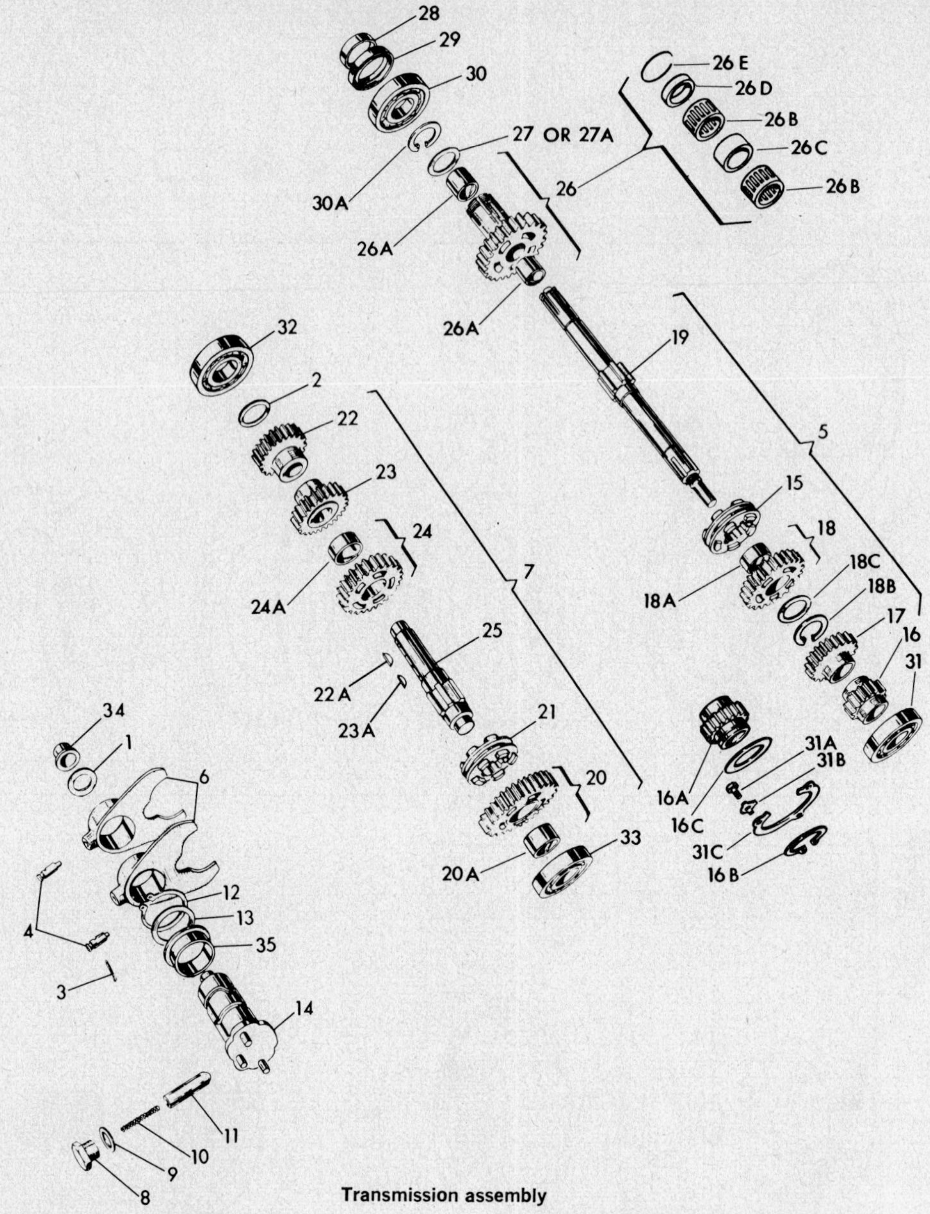

Transmission assembly

1. Shifter cam spacer (small)
2. Countershaft thrust washer
3. Cotter pin (2)
4. Shifter fork pin (2)
5. Mainshaft assembly
6. Shifter fork (2)
7. Countershaft assembly
8. Cam stop plunger plug
9. Cam stop plug washer
10. Cam stop plunger spring
11. Cam stop plunger
12. Shifter cam lockring
13. Shifter cam spacer (large)
14. Shifter cam
15. Shifter clutch
16. Mainshaft first (low) gear 17T.
16A. Mainshaft first (low) gear 17T. (late 1962)
16B. Mainshaft first (low) gear lockring (late 1962)
16C. Shim (variable-thickness) (late 1962)
17. Mainshaft second gear 23T.
18. Mainshaft third gear 27T.
18A. Bushing
18B. Mainshaft third gear lockring (1969)
18C. Mainshaft third gear washer (1969)
19. Mainshaft
20. Countershaft first (low) gear 33T.
20A. Bushing
21. Shifter clutch
22. Countershaft fourth (high) gear 16T.
22A. Key, C/S fourth gear (1971 and later)
23. Countershaft third gear 23T.
23A. Key, C/S third gear (1971 and later)
24. Countershaft second gear 27T.
24A. Bushing
25. Countershaft
26. Sprocket gear 24T.
26A. Bushing (2) (1968 and earlier)
26B. Needle bearing (2) (1969 and later)
26C. Needle bearing spacer (1969 and later)
26D. Bushing (1969 and later)
26E. Bushing lockring (1969 and later)
27. Sprocket gear spacer
27A. Sprocket gear spacer (variable-thickness) (late 1963)
28. Mainshaft sprocket spacer
29. Sprocket gear oil seal
30. Left mainshaft bearing
30A. Left mainshaft bearing retainer (late 1963)
31. Right mainshaft bearing
31A. Right mainshaft bearing retainer bolt (late 1962)
31B. Right mainshaft bearing retainer lock (late 1962)
31C. Right mainshaft bearing retainer (late 1962)
32. Left countershaft bearing
33. Right countershaft bearing
34. Left shifter cam bushing
35. Right shifter cam bushing

5. Remove the cam stop plunger plug, plug washer, plunger spring, plunger, shifter cam lockring, large shifter cam spacer, and the shifter cam.

6. Further work on the transmission should be carried out by your local dealer or by a qualified machinist.

Inspection and Repair

1. Clean all parts in a suitable solvent and blow them dry.

2. Inspect all the gears for wear, damage, chipped dogs, battered dog slots, pits, and grooves, and replace them as necessary. Those gears which mesh together should be replaced in sets.

3. Inspect the mainshaft and countershaft for a warped, worn, pitted, grooved, or excessively worn condition, especially at the bearing surfaces, and replace them as necessary.

4. Inspect all bushings for wear, damage, or an excessively loose fit and replace them as necessary by drifting them in and out with a suitably sized drift. Ream the mainshaft third gear, countershaft first gear, and the countershaft second gear bushings with Reamer (H-D part no. 94806–64) or a suitable substitute, and the sprocket gear bushings with Reamer (H-D part no. 94806–63) or a suitable substitute.

5. Inspect the sprocket gear needle bearings and shaft (1969 and later models) for a worn, pitted, warped, or damaged condition, or for rough bearing motion, and replace them as necessary.

6. Inspect the shifter clutches for worn or damaged dogs and shifter fork grooves, and replace them as necessary.

7. Inspect the shifter cam for grooved or worn cam slots in the running gear positions and replace it if necessary.

8. Inspect the shifter forks for a worn, warped, or grooved condition at the fork fingers. Do not try to save the forks by bending them straight since this will merely tax the metal and cause them to fail before too long.

9. Inspect the shifter fork pins, the shifter cam stop plunger, and the plunger spring for a worn or damaged condition, especially on the plunger thrust face, and for free plunger and spring movement, and replace them as necessary. The spring free-length should be 1.535 in., and must be replaced if collapsed to a shorter length.

10. Inspect the bushings and bearings for wear, pitting, damage, excessive play, or rough motion and replace them as necessary in the following manner:

a. Using a suitable drift, press out the right-side mainshaft, countershaft, and shifter cam bearings from the right crankcase half. The right-side mainshaft retainber bolt, lock, and retainer (if applicable) will have to be removed before the bearing can be removed.

b. Use a suitable puller device to remove the blind left-side countershaft bearing.

c. Press the left-side shifter cam bushing from the outside-in using a suitable drift.

d. Pry out the left-side sprocket gear oil seal then press the left-side mainshaft bearing from the outside-in using a suitable drift.

e. Line-ream the right-side shifter cam bushing with Right Bushing Reamer (H-D part no. 97322–61P), or a suitable substitute, and the left-side shifter cam bushing with Left Bushing Reamer (H-D part no. 97318–61P) or a suitable substitute. Always rotate the reamer clockwise, even when withdrawing it.

Assembly

1. Press the replacement oil seals into place if they have been removed.

2. Install the right mainshaft bearing retainer bolt, lock, and retainer (if applicable).

3. Slip the shifter cam into place in the right crankcase, then install the shifter cam lockring, cam stop plunger, plunger spring, plug washer, and the plunger plug which must be snugly tightened down.

4. Install the countershaft assembly in the following manner:

a. Position the shifter fork so the fork fingers engage the shifter clutch shoulder closest to the second gear.

b. Slip the shifter fork onto the shifter cam while installing the countershaft with the first gear seating in the rightside countershaft bearing, tapping the shaft with a soft mallet if necessary.

5. Determine the size of the appropriate large shifter cam spacer in the following manner:

a. Install the shifter fork pin and cotter pin into the shifter fork mounted on the shifter cam.

b. Place the transmission in the Neutral position.

c. Use a feeler gauge inserted between the shifter cam bushing and the shifter cam lockring (the gauge designated by "A" in the accompanying illustration) to raise the cam by increasing the number of the feeler gauge blades. Use a second feeler gauge (designated by "B") to measure the distance between the first gear and the shifter clutch, and the shifter clutch and the second gear. Increase the size of "A" until the two distances measured by "B" are exactly equal.

d. Subtract 0.003 in. (the correct amount of end-play for the shifter cam) from the measurement of "A" to arrive at the appropriate size large shifter cam spacer. Spacers are available in 0.012, 0.020, 0.028, 0.036, 0.040, and 0.044 in. sizes. Use the spacer which comes closest to the measurement arrived at.

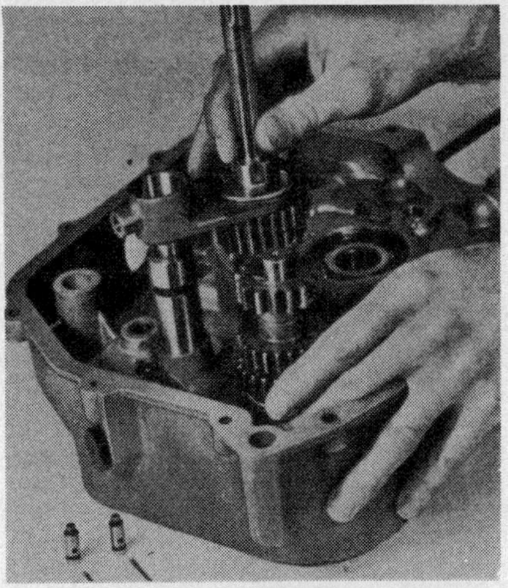
The countershaft and mainshaft assemblies

Determining the correct shifter cam spacer thickness

e. Remove and disassemble the shifter cam assembly, insert the large shifter cam spacer, and reassemble and install the shifter cam.

6. Rotate the shifter cam until the shifter fork pin holes align with the appropriate grooves in the cam. Secure the fork pins and install new cotter pings.

7. Temporarily assemble the original small shifter cam spacer and countershaft thrust washer on their respective shafts.

8. Insert the two sprocket gear bushings into the sprocket gear (if applicable) or install the bearings and bushings used in 1969 and later models. On the 1968 and earlier models where bushings are exclusively used, the bushings must be reamed with Sprocket Gear Bushing Reamer (H-D part no. 94806–63) or a suitable substitute if a new sprocket gear, gear bushings, or mainshaft is to be installed.

9. Insert the mainshaft sprocket spacer into the sprocket gear oil seal.

10. Place the sprocket gear spacer on the splined end of the gear, secure it with the left bearing retainer (if applicable),

and install the assembly in the left mainshaft bearing.

11. Select appropriately sized spacers to take up the shaft's end-play in the following manner:

a. Remove the flywheel from the left crankcase half as described in the "Crankcase" section, and check all bearings to make sure they are completely seated.

b. Install the crankcase gasket and assemble the crankcase halves with at least two bolts.

c. Mount a dial indicator to one of the crankcase halves so the plunger rests on the end of one of the shafts.

d. Shift the shafts to the end of their travel opposite the dial indicator and remember to tap the sprocket gear down, in addition to the mainshaft.

e. Shift the shafts all the way toward the dial indicator so the indicator's plunger is depressed by the shaft. Place no pressure on the shaft when reading the indicator, and repeat the operation for each of the shafts several times to be sure you have arrived at an accurate reading.

f. The end-play specifications are as follows:

1. The shifter cam end-play is measured on the right side and must be within 0.004–0.008 in. The shim is assembled on the left end of the shaft. The cam can be moved with the aid of a pair of pliers, or measured with a feeler gauge.

Checking the shifter cam end-play

2. The countershaft end-play is measured on the right side and must be within 0.004–0.008 in. The shim is assembled on the left end of the shaft. The countershaft may be shifted with the aid of a long screwdriver inserted through the cylinder base opening and under the countershaft fourth gear, or measured with a feeler gauge.

3. The mainshaft end-play is measured on the left side of the crankcase and must be within 0.008–0.010 in. The shim is assembled on the right side of the shaft. The mainshaft can be shifted with the aid of two screwdrivers as indicated in the illustration, and measured with a dial indicator or a feeler gauge.

Checking the countershaft end-play

g. If the end-play exceeds the set limits, it can be corrected by inserting the appropriate size of shim washer which will reduce the play the necessary amount. Consult the chart of available shims.

13. Disassemble the crankcases and insert the correct size shims. Reassemble the cases once more and recheck the end-play. The crankshaft end-play can also be corrected at this time if so desired.

TRANSMISSION SHIM WASHER SIZES (1971 AND LATER SX, 1972 AND LATER SS)

Size		Right Side			Left Side		
mm	In.	Shifter Cam	Counter Shaft	Main Shaft	Shifter Cam	Counter Shaft	Main Shaft
0.10	0.004					X	
0.20	0.008			X	X	X	
0.25	0.010			X			
0.30	0.012	X		X		X	
0.35	0.014			X			
0.40	0.016			X	X	X	
0.50	0.020	X				X	
0.60	0.024				X	X	
0.70	0.028	X				X	
0.80	0.032				X	X	
0.90	0.036	X			X		
1.0	0.040	X			X		
1.1	0.044	X			X		
1.2	0.048	X			X		

14. Install the crankshaft, then reassemble and install the engine in the frame in the reverse order of disassembly. Remember to replenish the transmission oil supply as well as the engine oil before attempting to turn the engine over.

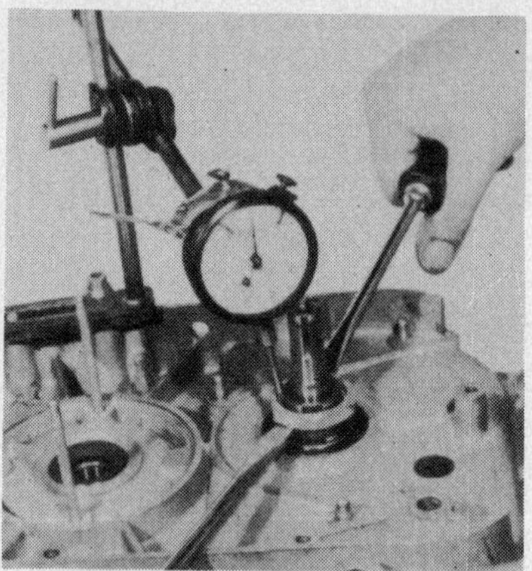

Checking the mainshaft end-play

DRIVE SPROCKET

Removal

1. Remove the left side cover by removing the cover screws then tapping on the sides of the cover with a soft mallet while pulling on the kick-start lever.

2. Remove the starter gear assembly as described in the "Starter" section.

3. Remove the sprocket cover nuts, washers, and cover.

4. Hold the sprocket with the Sprocket Holding Tool (H-D part no. varies with the number of sprocket teeth), or some other means of immobilizing the sprocket, then remove the sprocket nut with a suitable wrench.

5. Remove the lock and pull the sprocket from the sprocket gear. It may be necessary to use a gear puller.

Removing the drive sprocket

Inspection and Repair

1. Clean all parts in a suitable solvent then blow them dry.
2. Inspect all parts for a worn or damaged condition and replace them as necessary.

Assembly

1. Slip the sprocket on the sprocket gear with the shouldered side facing the crankcase.
2. Install the lockwasher and nut in the reverse method of removal.
3. Complete the assembly process in the reverse order of disassembly.

GEARCASE TIMING GEARS

Gearcase Cover Removal and Installation

1. If the engine is to be removed from the chassis, do so as directed in engine "Removal and Installation."
2. If the engine is to remain in the chassis, the motorcycle must be tipped over on the left side, at an angle which is sufficient to keep the oil from draining out, or a drip pan should be placed under the gearcase.
3. Disconnect the clutch cable at the release lever on 1968 and earlier models by rotating the lever forward with a wrench and then freeing the cable from the lever.
4. Remove the footshift lever, contact breaker cover screws, cover, contact breaker cam screw, the clutch assembly on 1969 and later models (as described in the "Clutch" section), the eleven cover screws, the crankcase dipstick, the cover gasket, and the cover. On 1968 and earlier models, the release lever must be rotated forward to remove the cover. As soon as the cover is removed, place a clean, oil-soaked rag over all open holes to prevent foreign objects from entering the crankcase.
5. Before installing the cover, make sure the O-rings from the shifter pawl carrier shaft and the cover pad hole recess are correctly positioned.
6. Make sure the automatic spark advance is correctly located on the camshaft as described in the "Contact Breaker" section.
7. Mount and temporarily secure the cover gasket and cover by inserting, but not tightening, the cover screws.
8. Insert the crankcase dipstick in the cover but do not secure it.
9. Evenly tighten down all of the cover screws until the cover is uniformly secure. Tighten down the dipstick after checking the oil level.
10. Secure the shifter cam assembly.
11. Mount the engine in the frame if it has been removed as described in the engine "Removal and Installation" section.
12. Install the contact breaker cover with the smaller hole on the bottom, and secure the cover screws.
13. Engage the clutch cable in the release lever. Rotate the lever forward using a suitable wrench on 1968 and earlier models.
14. Adjust the clutch as described in the "Maintenance" section.
15. Install the shift lever so the arm is just below the contact breaker cover.

CAMSHAFT AND TAPPETS

Removal

1. Remove the camshaft support assembly nuts, locks, and assembly on 1968 and earlier models.
2. Remove the camshaft assembly from the camshaft bushing or bearing, then remove the thrust washer and free the tappets from the tappet bushings. Teh tappets must be kept separate for reassembly in their original positions. The inner tappet is the intake tappet; the outer one is the exhaust.

Inspection and Repair

1. Clean all parts in a suitable solvent and blow them dry.
2. Inspect the camshaft for a worn, pitted, rough, or damaged condition and replace if necessary.
3. Inspect the cam gear for a worn or damaged condition, and, if replacement is necessary, press it from the camshaft, install an new key in the shaft, and press a new gear into place with the recessed side facing out. Blow the shaft oil passages clear to make sure they haven't been clogged.
4. Inspect the camshaft bushings and bearing for excessive wear, play, pitting, damage, or rough motion, and replace as necessary in the following manner:
   a. The camshaft bushings come in two varieties. Any 1963 or earlier models have a plain bronze bushing which is pressed directly into the crankcase; 1964 and later models have a steel bushing mounted in the case into which a needle bearing is pressed. To replace either type, the crankcases must be separated as described in the "Crankcase" section. The bearing or bushing is pressed out with a suitable,

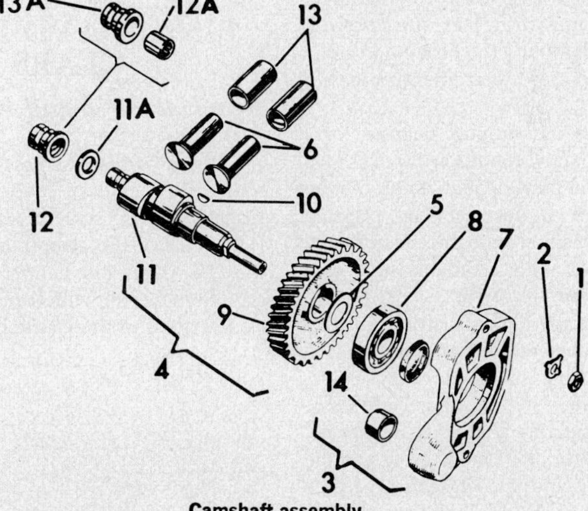

Camshaft assembly

1. Nut (2) (1068 & earlier)
2. Lock (2) (1968 & earlier)
3. Support assembly (1968 & earlier)
4. Camshaft assembly
5. Thrust washer
6. Tappets (2)
7. Support
8. Support ball bearings
9. Gear
10. Key
11. Camshaft

11A. Camshaft washer, variable thickness (1964 & later)
12. Camshaft crankcase bushing (1963 & earlier)
12A. Camshaft crankcase needle bearing (1964 & later)
13. Tappet bushing (2)
13A. Needle bearing bushing (1964 & later)
14. Pinion shaft bushing

shouldered drift from the inside, and pressed in from the outside in a similar manner.

b. Line-ream the camshaft bushings with Camshaft Bushing, and Shifter Cam Left Crankcase Bushing Reamer Set (H-D part no. 97318–61P) or a suitable substitute. The pilot can be mounted on the camshaft support.

5. Inspect the tappets and their bushings for a worn or damaged condition, or for play in excess of the specified 0.0002–0.0005 in. clearance. If the tappets are worn on the cam follower faces, they must be replaced. Ideally the tappets and their bushings should be replaced as sets although individual replacement components are available. Check the bushings for excessive wear by inserting a new tappet and then checking the play.

bushing using a tap holder if the reamer is not equipped with a handle.

Installation

1. Lightly oil the tappets with clean engine oil and slip them into the appropriate tappet bushing.

2. Install the crankshaft assembly in the crankcase bushing, taking care to align the cam gear timing mark with the pinion gear timing mark.

3. Place the cam gear thrust washer and support assembly onto the camshaft (1968 and earlier models), then tap the support assembly into place by placing a piece of tubing or a socket on the support bearing inner race.

4. Install the locks and nuts to secure the assembly.

4. Remove the oil pump drive gear as described in the "Lubrication" section.

5. Remove the pinion shaft nut in the following manner:

a. Assemble the Clutch Lock Tool (H-D part no. 97175–61P), or some other means of securing the clutch—such as jamming a wooden door stop between the clutch gear teeth and the crankcase—to the clutch shell to prevent the pinion shaft from rotating while the shaft nut is removed.

b. Secure the clutch hub with Hub Holding Tool (H-D part no. 97291–61PA), or a suitable substitute, and secure the wrench by placing a bolt in the crankcase mounting stud hole as illustrated in the accompanying illustration.

c. Remove the pinion shaft nut with

Aligning the timing marks—1968 and earlier models

Aligning the timing marks—1969 and later models

6. Tappet bushings must also be replaced if loose in the case. The bushings are a press fit and are pressed from the outside of the case with a shouldered, .472 in. (12 mm) drift. Heat the case with a blow torch around the bushing to aid in the removal and replacement process if necessary.

7. Inspect the support bearing for a worn or damaged condition, for excessive side or radial play, or four rough motion and replace as necessary by pressing from the outside of the cover (1969 and later models) with a suitable drift or a block of wood.

8. Inspect the pinion shaft bushing for a worn or damaged condition and replace in the following manner:

a. Remove the bushing with Bushing and Bearing Puller (H-D part no. 95760–69 or 96729–63) or a suitable substitute, and a 2 in. length of pipe with a ⅞ in. inside diameter as a support sleeve.

b. Press the new bushing into the camshaft support or cover and install the cover or support on the right crankcase but do not secure the mounting screws or nuts as yet.

c. Line-ream the bushing with a suitably sized reamer and pilot which can be inserted through the crankshaft ball bearing mounted in the case. Once the reamer is installed securely, tighten the support or cover and ream the

5. Install the gearcase cover as described in the "Gearcase Cover Removal and Installation" section.

PINION AND DRIVE GEARS

Removal (1968 and Earlier Models)

1. Remove the gearcase cover as described in "Gearcase Cover Removal and Installation."

2. Remove the assemblies covered in the "Camshaft and Tappets" section.

3. Remove the clutch plates assembly as described in the "Clutch" section.

a suitable socket wrench, then remove the lock.

6. Remove the clutch shell and gear assembly as described in the "Clutch" section.

7. Pull the pinion gear free with Two Jaw Puller (H-D part no. 97292–61P) or a suitable substitute.

8. Mark the keyway in which the key is mounted (there are three keyways but only one takes a key) with a small punch mark, and then remove the key.

9. Remove the thrust washer, drive take-up gear, and the take-up gear spring (if applicable).

10. Secure the clutch hub with Hub

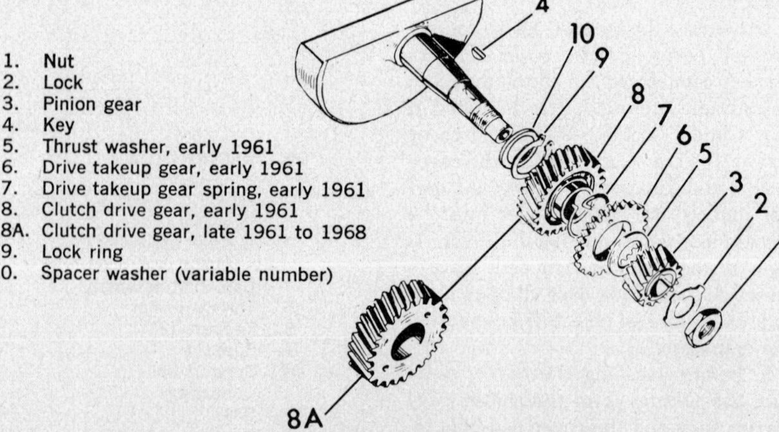

1. Nut
2. Lock
3. Pinion gear
4. Key
5. Thrust washer, early 1961
6. Drive takeup gear, early 1961
7. Drive takeup gear spring, early 1961
8. Clutch drive gear, early 1961
8A. Clutch drive gear, late 1961 to 1968
9. Lock ring
10. Spacer washer (variable number)

Pinion gear assembly

Pinion gear nut removal and installation

Removing the clutch drive gear

Removing the pinion gear

Marking the correct keyway

Holding Tool (H-D part no. 97291-61PA), or a suitable substitute, then pull the clutch drive gear free with Drive Gear Puller (H-D part no. 97294-61P) or a suitable substitute.

Removal (1969 and Later Models)

1. Remove the clutch assembly as described in the "Clutch" section (1969 and later models).
2. Remove the gearcase cover as described in the "Gearcase Cover Removal and Installation" section.
3. Remove the camshaft thrust washer and camshaft as described in the "Camshaft and Tappets" section.
4. Remove the oil pump drive gear as described in the "Lubrication" section.
5. Remove the pinion shaft nut in the following manner:
   a. Disassemble the top end as described in the "Top-End" section.
   b. Slip a cross-shaft through the connecting rod piston pin hole to freeze the motion of the engine.
   c. Remove the pinion shaft wrench with a suitable socket wrench then remove the nut lock.
6. Pull the pinion gear free with Two-Jaw Puller (H-D part no. 97292-61P) or a suitable substitute.
7. Mark and remove the key as directed in the 1968 and earlier models "Removal" section.

Inspection and Repair

1. Clean all parts in a suitable solvent and blow them dry.
2. Inspect all gears for a worn or damaged condition and replace as necessary. If the clutch drive or pinion gears are replaced, those gears with which they mesh must also be replaced.
3. Inspect the take-up spring for a worn, collapsed, or damaged condition, and replace as necessary. As long as you've taken everything apart, you may as well replace the spring if possible just to be sure.
4. Inspect the thrust washer (if applicable) for a worn or damaged condition which would indicate that the clutch drive gear is slipping on the pinion shaft and that the pinion shaft or the gear or both are in need of replacement. Replace the thrust washer if necessary.
5. Inspect the pinion shaft and gear for a worn or damaged condition and replace as necessary by consulting the "Crankcase" section.

Installation (All Models)

1.Replace the spacer washers, spring washers, and the lockring, with the spring washers between the pinion shaft bearing mounted in the crankcase, and the primary drive gear. The dished outer diameters of the washers should face each other, and therefore reduce the crankshaft end-play to nothing.
2. Inspect the tapers on the pinion shaft and drive gear for a clean, burr-free condition before going any further.
3. Install the drive gear on the pinion shaft, slip the drive take-up gear spring over the shaft so it seats in the gear, slip the take-up gear on the shaft, and slip the thrust washer in place (1968 and earlier models).
4. Insert a new pinion shaft key in the marked keyway. If the mark has been obliterated or if you have failed to correctly mark the appropriate keyway, do the following:
   a. Situate the pinion shaft flywheel so the piston is at TDC (or so the crank pin is).
   b. Insert the key in the forward (top center) keyway for 1963 and earlier, and 1969 and later models
   c. Insert the key in the bottom (seven o'clock) keyway for 1964-68 models.
   d. Insert the key in any keyway which has been designated by a grind mark on the face of the gear at one of the keyway positions.

5. Install the pinion gear with the timing mark in the forward position as indicated in the illustration in the camshaft and tappet "Installation" section, then mount and secure the lock and nut to finger-tightness. If the lock is new, one tab may be bent up to engage the groove on the gear. The valve timing is controlled by the proper positioning of the gear and key and must be as shown in the following chart.

	Crank Angle		
	Opens*	Closes**	Lift (in.)
Intake Valve			
1969	36°	67°	0.361
1967 and later	13°	50°	0.296
1966	15°	45°	0.296
Exhaust Valve			
1969	70°	20°	3.50
1967 and later	54°	9°	0.292
1966 and earlier	55°	4°	0.292

6. Complete assembly in the following manner for all 1968 and earlier models:

a. Install the clutch shell gear and hub using Clutch Lock Tool (H-D part no. 97175–61P) or an alternative method as described in the "Removal" section. Secure the clutch hub with Clutch Hub Holding Tool (H-D part no. 97291–61PA), or a suitable substitute, and block the handle with a bolt inserted in one of the crankcase holes. Using a suitable wrench, secure the pinion gear nut to 35 ft lbs torque, then complete the clutch assembly procedures as described in the "Clutch" section.

b. Install the oil pump drive gear as described in the "Lubrication" section.

c. Install the cam gear and support plate as described in the "Camshaft and Tappets Assembly" section.

d. Install the gearcase cover as described in the "Gearcase Cover Removal and Installation" section.

7. Complete assembly in the following manner for all 1969 and later models:

a. Freeze the motion of the engine by inserting a rod through the connecting rod piston pin hole, then secure the pinion gear nut to 35 ft lbs torque.

b. Install the oil pump drive gear, camshaft, camshaft thrust washer, and the primary drive gear as described in their respective sections.

c. Complete the clutch assembly procedures as described in the "Clutch" section.

d. Install the gearcase cover as described in the "Gearcase Cover Removal and Inspection" section.

SHIFTER PAWL CARRIER

Disassembly

1. Remove the gearcase cover as described in the "Gearcase Cover Removal and Inspection" section.

2. Remove the clutch assembly on 1968 and earlier models as described in the "Clutch" section.

3. Remove the shifter pawl carrier thrust washer.

4. Remove the assembled shifter pawl carrier assembly from the case, then remove the return spring from the assembly.

5. Check the motion of the shifter pawls for a smooth and free operation, and a damage-free condition. If the pawls are in need of attention, disassemble them as follows:

a. Remove the spring retainer plate screws, plate, pawls, and pawl springs.

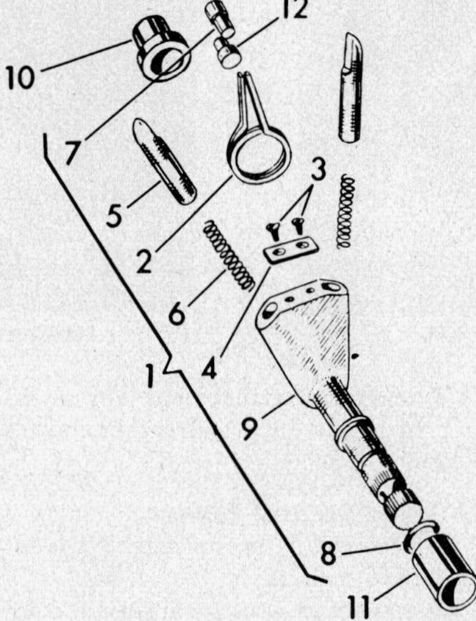

Shifter pawl carrier assembly

1. Shifter pawl carrier assembly
2. Return spring
3. Screw (2)
4. Pawl spring retainer plate
5. Pawl (2)
6. Pawl spring (2)
7. Stop pin
8. O-ring
9. Pawl carrier
10. Crankcase carrier shaft bushing
11. Cover carrier shaft bushing
12. Return spring pin

b. If further inspection indicates the need for replacement of the stop pins, they may be pressed free out from the carrier.

Inspection and Repair

1. Clean all parts in a suitable solvent and blow them dry.

2. Inspect the pawls for a worn, grooved, cracked, or damaged condition and replace them as necessary.

3. Inspect the pawl springs for a collapsed or damaged condition and replace as necessary. The springs must be replaced if they are less than 1½ in long.

4. Insert the springs and pawls into the carrier and check their motion for smooth and free operation. If the springs and pawls are in good condition and the motion is rough, replace the carrier. If the carrier is worn or damaged or its other surfaces, it must then be replaced also.

5. Inspect the crankcase carrier shaft bushing for a worn or damaged condition and replace as necessary by removing the engine from the frame as directed in the engine "Removal and Inspection" section and then separating the crankcase halves as directed in the "Crankcase" section. The bushing may then be pressed out from the inside with a suitable, shouldered drift, and then pressed in from the outside with the same drift.

6. Inspect the shifter carrier rubber O-ring for a cracked or damaged condition and replace as necessary.

7. Inspect the cover carrier shaft bushing for a worn or damaged condition and replace as necessary by pressing it out from the inside of the cover with a suitable shouldered drift and then back in with the chamfered side first until flush with the bushing boss.

Assembly

1. Insert the pawl springs into the pawls, and then slip the pawls and springs into the carrier so the flat portions of the pawls face each other.

2. Install the retainer plate and secure it with the plate screws while holding the pawls down.

3. Press new stop pins into place in the carrier so that the flat portions of the pins are parallel with the retainer plate.

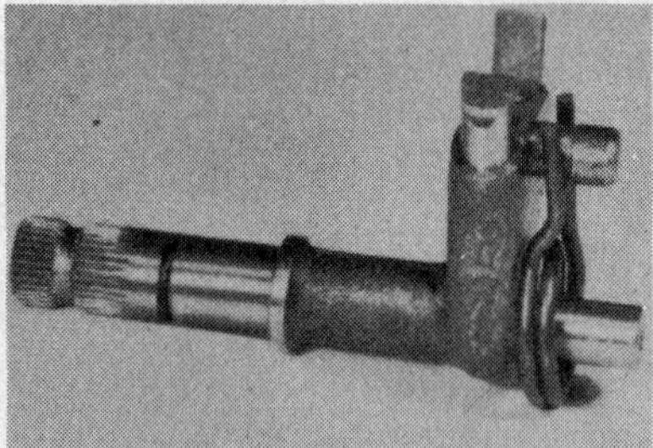

Shifter pawl carrier with the spring mounted

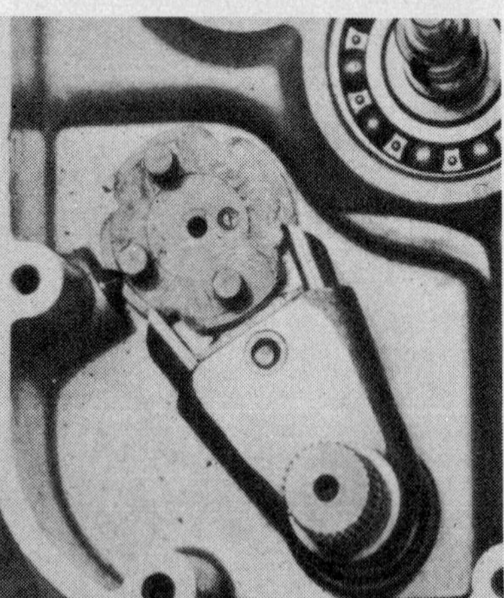

Positioning the carrier assembly in the crankcase

4. Assemble the return spring to the assembly so the offset portion of the spring is toward the crankcase, and so the stop pin is between the spring arms.

5. Slip the rubber O-ring into position in its groove in the carrier shaft.

6. Install the carrier in the crankcase and engage the return spring on its pin as illustrated. If the spring is properly engaged the shaft will not be able to turn.

7. Install the clutch assembly on 1968 and earlier models as described in the "Clutch" section.

8. Install the gearcase cover as described in the "Gearcase Cover Removal and Installation" section.

Kick-Starter

Disassembly

1. Remove the left side cover screws and remove the cover by tapping on its sides with a soft mallet while pulling on the starter crank.

2. Remove the starter crank nut, bolt, the crank and pedal assembly, and the crank clevis (if applicable).

3. Remove the crank gear shaft support bolts, washers, and the support, then remove the stop stud acorn nut and washer (1971 and later models).

4. Secure the crank gear's shaft in a wood or copper-jawed vise, then rotate the cover to relieve the spring tension while removing the crank gear stop bumper and stud from the cover.

5. Carefully release the spring tension and remove the cover assembly from the vise.

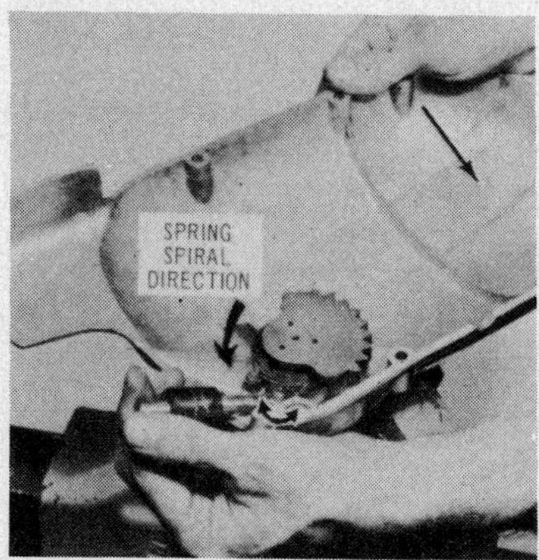

Removing the crank gear stop stud

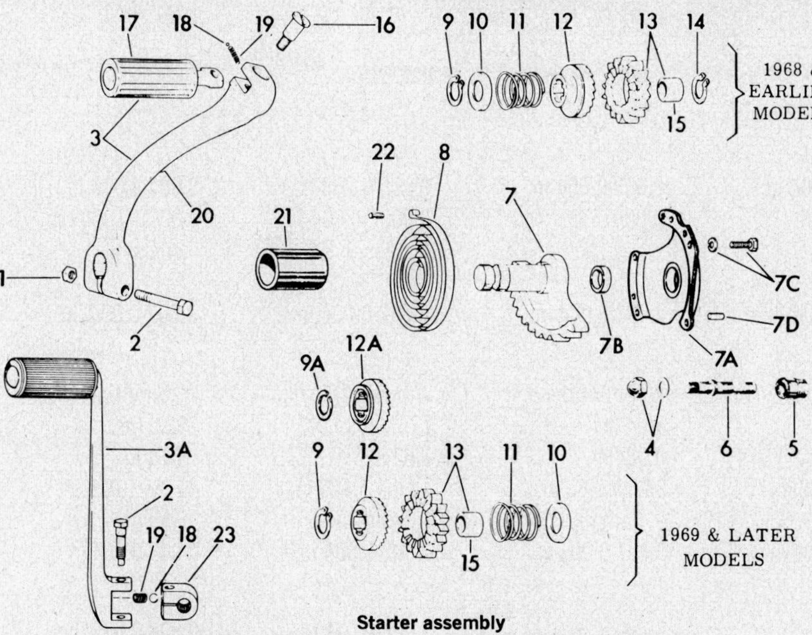

Starter assembly

1. Crank nut (1968 and earlier)
2. Crank bolt
3. Crank and pedal assembly (1968 and earlier)
3A. Crank and pedal assembly (1969 and later)
4. Stop stud acorn nut and washer
5. Crank gear stop bumper
6. Crank gear stop stud
7. Crank gear
7A. Crank gear shaft support (1971 and later)
7B. Crank gear shaft support bushing
7C. Crank gear shaft support bolt and l.w. (5)
7D. Crank gear shaft support dowel pin (2)
8. Spring
9. Clutch gear lockring
9A. Clutch gear lockring (late 1970)
10. Clutch spring collar
11. Clutch spring
12. Clutch
12A. Clutch (late 1970)
13. Clutch gear assembly
14. Clutch gear lockring
15. Clutch gear bushing
16. Crank pedal screw (1968 and earlier)
17. Crank pedal
18. Crank pedal ball
19. Crank pedal spring
20. Crank (1968 and earlier)
21. Crank gear shaft bushing
22. Spring dowel pin
23. Crank clevis (1969 and later)

6. Remove the crank gear and the starter spring from the cover.

7. Remove the clutch gear lockring, using snap-ring pliers, or press the clutch against the clutch spring and pry the outer ring free (late 1970 models).

8. Remove the clutch spring collar, spring, clutch, clutch gear assembly, and the gear lockring. Carefully examine the illustration since there are discrepancies in the order of assembly for the 1969 and later models.

Inspection and Repair

1. Clean all parts in a suitable solvent and blow them dry.

2. Inspect the crank gear, clutch, and the clutch gear assembly for wear, damage, or chipped or battered teeth, and replace them as a set if necessary. Crank gears since late 1961 have had 10 teeth rather than eight, and replacement should be with the newer variety.

3. Inspect the clutch gear bushing for a worn, loose, or damaged condition and replace it as necessary with a 0.570 in. shouldered drift. This bushing will not need to be reamed.

4. Inspect the starter clutch spring for a collapsed or damaged condition and replace it as necessary. The spring must be replaced if it has become shorter than 0.984 in.

5. Inspect the lockrings for a worn, warped, or damaged condition and replace them as necessary.

6. Inspect the crank gear shaft bushings for a worn, excessively loose fit with the core or shaft, or a damaged condition, and replace them as necessary. The bushings may be pressed out with a shouldered drift having a small diameter of 0.669 in. and a large diameter of 0.866 in. When replacing the bushings, press them in until flush with the bushing boss, and so the chamfered side is to the inside of the cover. These bushings will not need to be reamed.

7. Inspect the starter spring for a worn, collapsed, or damaged condition, and replace it as necessary.

8. Inspect the crank gear stop bumper and the stop stud for a worn or damaged condition and replace it as necessary. Pay special attention to the metal sheath around the bumper and replace the bumper if it is damaged.

9. Inspect the spring dowel pin for a worn or damaged condition and remove it only if replacement is necessary. The pin is a press fit into the cover.

10. Rotate the crank pedal in both directions and check to see if it locks in both extreme positions. If it fails to lock, the pedal spring should be replaced.

Assembly

1. Assemble parts 9–15 (as listed in the illustration) to the mainshaft in the re-

verse order of disassembly. The clutch gear bushing is pressed into the gear.

2. Position the starter spring on the crank gear so the spring is wound counterclockwise from the center when viewed from the cover side.

3. Install the crank gear in the gear shaft cover bushing, taking care to secure the loop of the spring on the spring dowel pin.

4. Secure the crank gear shaft in a wood or copper-jawed vise, rotate the cover until the spring is properly tensioned, unwind the cover 1–1½ turns, and then mount the crank gear stop stud and bumper to the cover. Remove the cover assembly from the vise, and secure the stop stud acorn and washer.

5. Secure the crank gear shaft support assembly (if applicable).

6. Assemble the crank and pedal assembly or the crank clevis and then the crank and pedal assembly (if applicable). Before securing the assembly with the crank bolt and nut, and the cover to the crankcase, make sure the crank is so positioned on the shaft splines as to allow the crank to be operated without smashing your shin or the crank against the footrest while kicking the engine over.

ENGINE AND TRANSMISSION SPECIFICATIONS

M Models

	M-50	M-65	M-100	M-125
PISTON ASSEMBLY				
Fit in cylinder (loose)	0.0005-0.0010 in. (1965-67)	0.002-0.0025 in. (1967 and later)	0.002-0.0027 in. (1970 and later)	0.002-0.0027 in. (1967 and later)
Ring side-clearance	①	②	0.004-0.006 in.	0.003-0.0045 in.
Ring end-gap	0.008-0.014 in.	0.008-0.014 in.	0.008-0.014 in.	0.008-0.004 in.
Piston pin fit in piston	Light hand press at 70° F	Light hand press at 70° F	Light hand press at 70° F	Light hand press at 70° F
Pin fit in rod bearing (loose at 70° F)	0.0001 in.	0.0001 in.	0.0001 in.	0.0001 in.
CONNECTING ROD				
End play between crank throws	0.002-0.004 in.	0.002-0.004 in.	0.006-0.008 in.	0.004-0.006 in.
Fit on crank pin bearing	0.00015 in.	0.00015 in.	0.0002-0.0004 in. (loose)	0.0002-0.0004 in. (loose)
CRANKSHAFT				
End-play	0.002-0.004 in.	0.002-0.004 in.	0.002-0.004 in.	0.002-0.004 in.
CLUTCH				
Type	Wet-multiple disc	Wet-multiple disc	Wet-multiple disc	Wet-multiple disc
Operating spring pressure	25.1 lbs	33.4 lbs	175.0 lbs	132.0 lbs
Spring free-length	0.984 in.	0.984 in.	1.62 in.	1.614 in.
Spring set up	24 lbs 0.66 in. (length)	24 lbs 0.66 in. (length)	44 lbs 1.025 in. (length)	44 lbs 1.025 in. (length)
Shell gear end-play	0.001-0.004 in.	0.001-0.004 in.	0.002-0.004 in.	0.002-0.004 in.
TRANSMISSION				
Shifter cam end-play	—	—	0.008-0.012 in.	0.008-0.012 in.
Mainshaft end-play	0.004-0.006 in.	0.004-0.006 in.	0.002-0.006 in.	0.002-0.006 in.
Countershaft end-play	0.004-0.008 in.	0.004-0.008 in.	0.002-0.006 in.	0.002-0.006 in.
Starter shaft end-play	0.004-0.008 in.	0.004-0.008 in.	0.004-0.008 in.	—

① Piston ring side clearance (in.)
1965 models
Upper ring 0.002-0.004
Lower ring 0.001-0.004
1966 and later models
Both rings 0.002-0.004

② Piston ring side clearance (in.)
1965 models
Upper ring 0.002-0.004
Lower ring 0.001-0.004
1966 and later models
Both rings 0.002-0.004

ENGINE AND TRANSMISSION SPECIFICATIONS (con't.)

S and B Models

	165, Hummer and Super-10	BT, BTU, BTF, and BTH
PISTON ASSEMBLY		
Fit in cylinder	0.0025-0.0035 in.	0.0045-0.0055 in.
Ring end-gap	0.012-0.020 in.	0.008-0.019 in.
Ring end-clearance	①	0.006-0.008 in. (top ring) 0.002-0.004 in. (bottom ring)
Piston pin fit	0.0001 in. interference fit at 70° F	0.0001 in. interference fit at 70° F
CONNECTING ROD		
Piston pin fit	0.0002-0.0012 in. loose	0.0002-0.0012 in. loose
End-play between flywheels	0.011-0.017 in.	0.011-0.018 in.
Fit on crank pin	0.0010-0.0013 in. loose	②
FLYWHEEL ASSEMBLY		
Sprocket shaft	Must resist a turning torque of 75 ft lbs in flywheel	
Generator shaft	Must resist a turning torque of 75 ft lbs in flywheel	
Flywheel maximum run-out	0.009 in.	0.009 in.
Mainshaft maximum run-out	0.002 in.	0.002 in.
End-play in crankcase	0.003-0.012 in.	0.003-0.012 in.
CRANKCASE ASSEMBLY		
Main bearing fit in case	0.0005 in. tight—0.0005 in. loose	0.0005 in tight—0.0005 in. loose
Main bearing fit on shaft	0.0001-0.0007 in. loose	0.0001-0.0007 in. loose
Generator armature commutator maximum run-out	0.003 in. (model 165 only)	——
Cam maximum run-out	0.005 in.	0.005 in.
Minimum air gap at pole piece	0.002 in. (except model 165)	0.002 in.
CLUTCH		
Type	Bonded fabric disc wet clutch	Bonded fabric disc wet clutch
Torque capacity	35 ft lbs	35 ft lbs
Clutch disengagement	0.056-0.064 in.	0.056-0.064 in.
CHAIN		
Type	3/8 in. single strand pitch chain	3/8 in. single strand pitch chain
MAINSHAFT GROUP		
Bearing fit in bore	0.0005 in. loose—0.0005 in. tight	0.0005 in. loose—0.0005 in. tight
Bearing fit on shaft	0.0001 in. loose—0.0005 in. tight	0.0001 in. loose—0.0005 in. tight
Drive gear fit on mainshaft	0.001-0.0025 in. loose	0.001-0.0025 in. loose
Mainshaft end-play	0.000-0.022 in.	0.000-0.022 in.
COUNTERSHAFT GROUP		
Bushing fit on shaft ends	0.0005-0.0015 in. loose	0.0005-0.0015 in. loose
First gear fit on shaft	0.0007-0.0022 in. loose	0.0007-0.0022 in. loose

① Ring end-clearance
165 and Hummer models (top and bottom rings) 0.004-0.005 in.
1960 Super-10 (top and bottom rings) 0.009-0.011 in.
1961 Super-10 (top ring) 0.009-0.011 in.
1961 Super-10 (bottom ring) 0.004-0.005 in.

② Connecting rod fit on crank pin
BTU 0.0010-0.0013 in. loose
BT, BTF, and BTH 0.0013-0.0025 in. loose

Sprint Models

PISTON ASSEMBLY	
Fit in cylinder (1968 and earlier)	0.002 in. loose
(1969 and later)	0.004 in. loose
Compression rings end-gap	0.010-0.016 in.
Compression rings side-clearance	0.001-0.002 in.
Oil control ring end-gap	0.010-0.014 in.
Oil control ring side-clearance	0.001-0.002 in.
Piston pin fit in piston	Light hand press at 70° F
Piston pin fit in upper connecting rod bushing	0.0006-0.0012 in. loose
CONNECTING ROD	
End-play between flywheels (1968 and earlier)	0.004-0.008 in.
(1969 and later)	0.006-0.010 in.
Fit on crankpin bearing	0.0005-0.001 in.
VALVES	
Fit in guide (exhaust)	0.002 in. loose
Fit in guide (intake) (1968 and earlier)	0.0015 in. loose
(1969 and later)	0.001 in. loose

VALVE SPRINGS

	Free-Length Spring	Valve Position	Compressed Length	Poundage	Part No.
All C Models and 1968	1.64	Open	0.98	44.0	18205-61P
and Earlier Models	Inner	Closed	1.28	25.0	(Inner)
H and SS	1.77	Open	1.14	88.0	18206-61P
	Outer	Closed	1.42	50.0	(Outer)
1962-63	1.64	Open	0.98	48.0	
	Inner	Closed	1.30	28.0	18203-61P
Model H Only	1.77	Open	1.10	105.0	(Inner)
	Outer	Closed	1.42	55.0	
1969-70	1.64	Open	1.00	45.1	
	Inner	Closed	1.36	18.0	18204-61P
350 cc	1.77	Open	1.14	97.9	(Outer)
Model SS	Outer	Closed	1.49	41.8	

ROCKER ARMS	
Shaft fit in bushings	0.0005-0.0015 in.
End-play	Select those spacer washers which are needed to compress the spring washer.
OIL PUMP	
Minimum pressure measured at 25 mph in fourth gear	3 psi
GEARCASE	
Camshaft in crankcase bushing	0.0005-0.0015 in.
Camshaft end-play	0.001-0.004 in.
FLYWHEEL ASSEMBLY	
Mainshafts run-out	0.001 in. maximum
End-play in crankcase	0.0005-0.0025 in.
Mainshaft fit in camshaft support plate bushing	0.0005-0.002 in.
CLUTCH	
Type (1968 and earlier)	Wet-multiple disc
(1969 and later)	Dry-multiple disc

Sprint Models

Capacity	1966 and earlier 1800 lbs/in. 1967-68 2250 lbs/in. 1969 and later 2040 lbs/in.
Spring free-length	1.90 in.
Spring set up	1963 223 lbs @ 1.12 in. 1964-68 265 lbs @ 1.12 in. 1969 and later 220 lbs @ 1.12 in.
PRIMARY DRIVE	
Type (1968 and earlier)	Helical gears with provision for automatic backlash take-up on early 1961 models.
(1969 and later)	Helical gears in the crankcase.
GEARBOX	
Gear shifter cam end-play in cases	0.004-0.008 in.
Gear shifter cam clearance in right-side cam bushing	0.0005-0.0015 in.
Gear shifter cam clearance in left-side cam bushing	0.0005-0.0015 in.
Shifter fork clearance on gear shifter cam	0.001-0.0015 in.
Shifter pawl carrier shaft in cover bushing	0.0005-0.0015 in.
Shifter pawl carrier shaft in crankcase bushing	0.0005-0.0015 in.
MAINSHAFT GROUP	
Sprocket gear on mainshaft	0.0005-0.0015 in.
Mainshaft third gear on mainshaft	0.001-0.002 in.
Mainshaft end-play	0.008-0.010 in.
COUNTERSHAFT GROUP	
Countershaft first gear on countershaft	0.001-0.002 in.
Countershaft second gear on countershaft	0.001-0.002 in.
Countershaft end-play	0.004-0.008 in.

LUBRICATION SYSTEMS

Oil Pump

DISASSEMBLY

1. Drain all the engine oil as described in "Maintenance items."

2. Remove the gearcase cover as described in the "Gearcase" section and plug up all the openings into the crankcase.

3. On 1968 and earlier models remove the camshaft support assembly as described in the "Gearcase" section.

4. Remove the drive gear locknut and lock while holding the pinion gear steady.

5. Remove the drive gear using Two-Jaw Puller (H-D part no. 97292–61P) and Cap (H-D part no. 95652–43A), or suitable substitutes, taking care not to damage the threads that the cap protects.

6. Remove the scavenger line connection and both washers from 1963 and earlier models.

7. Remove the pump bolts and locks, then remove the entire pump assembly from the gearcase.

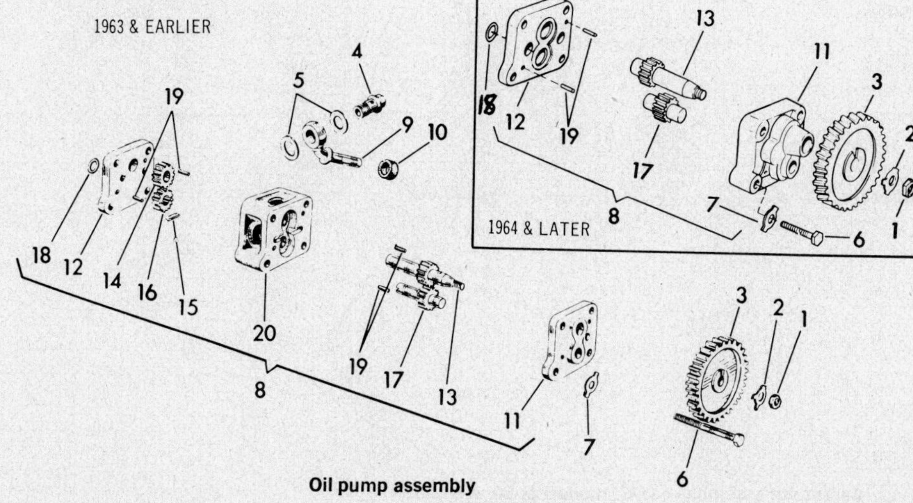

1. Nut
2. Drive gear lock
3. Drive gear
4. Scavenger line connection
5. Copper washer (2)
6. Bolt (4)
7. Pump body lock (4)
8. Pump assembly
9. Scavenger line
10. Scavenger line gasket
11. Outer cover
12. Inner cover
13. Gear
14. Feed idler gear
15. Key
16. Feed gear
17. Idler gear
18. O-ring
19. Dowel pin (4, 1963) (2, 1964)
20. Pump body

Oil pump assembly

Removing the oil pump drive gear

8. Remove the scavenger line and gasket from 1963 and earlier models.

9. Remove the inner and outer covers, the upper gear (when looking at the pump body from the outer cover side), the feed idler gear, the feed driving gear key and gear, and the idler gear.

10. Remove the O-ring from the inner cover, inspect the dowel pins for a worn or damaged condition, and remove them only if necessary.

INSPECTION AND REPAIR

1. Clean all the parts in a suitable solvent and blow them dry, remembering to blow all the oil passages clear.

2. Inspect all the gears for a worn or damaged condition and replace them as necessary. Gears should be replaced in sets.

3. Inspect the remaining components for a worn or damaged condition and replace them as necessary.

ASSEMBLY

1. Assembly is basically the reverse order of disassembly.

2. Lightly oil all moving parts with clean engine oil before assembling them.

3. Press the new dowel pins into the pump body (if applicable).

4. Proceed in the following manner for all 1963 and earlier models:

a. Slip the upper gear and idler gear shafts into the upper hole on the outer cover side of the pump body.

b. Assemble the feed gear and key onto the idler gear shaft, and the feed idler gear shaft onto the scavenger gear shaft.

c. Assemble the inner and outer covers onto the pump body, then install the O-ring to the inner cover.

d. Position the scavenger line gasket then install the scavenger line.

e. Place the oil pump into position in the crankcase, making sure that the O-ring remains in position in the inner cover.

f. Hold the copper gaskets in place on either side of the scavenger line connection to the pump body without securing it.

g. Install the pump body bolts and new locks, then tighten them finger-tight before securing them in diagonal pairs.

5. Proceed in the following manner for all 1964 and later models:

a. Insert the upper and idler gear shafts into the outer cover, then position the inner cover over the shafts, taking care to correctly register the dowel pins.

b. Install the O-ring on the inner cover, and mount the pump in the crankcase with the pump body bolts and new locks.

6. Wipe the gear shaft and drive gear tapers clean, then install and secure the drive gear to the shaft with a nut and a new lock. The shaft can be kept from rotating by pressing down on one side of the driving gear.

7. Install the gearcase cover as described in the "Gearcase" section.

FUEL SYSTEMS

CARBURETORS

Service

MODELS M-50 AND M-65

Disassembly (1965 Model)

1. Close the petcock and remove the fuel line at the carburetor.

2. Loosen the clamp screw and remove the silencer, clamp, air filter, and the filter gasket.

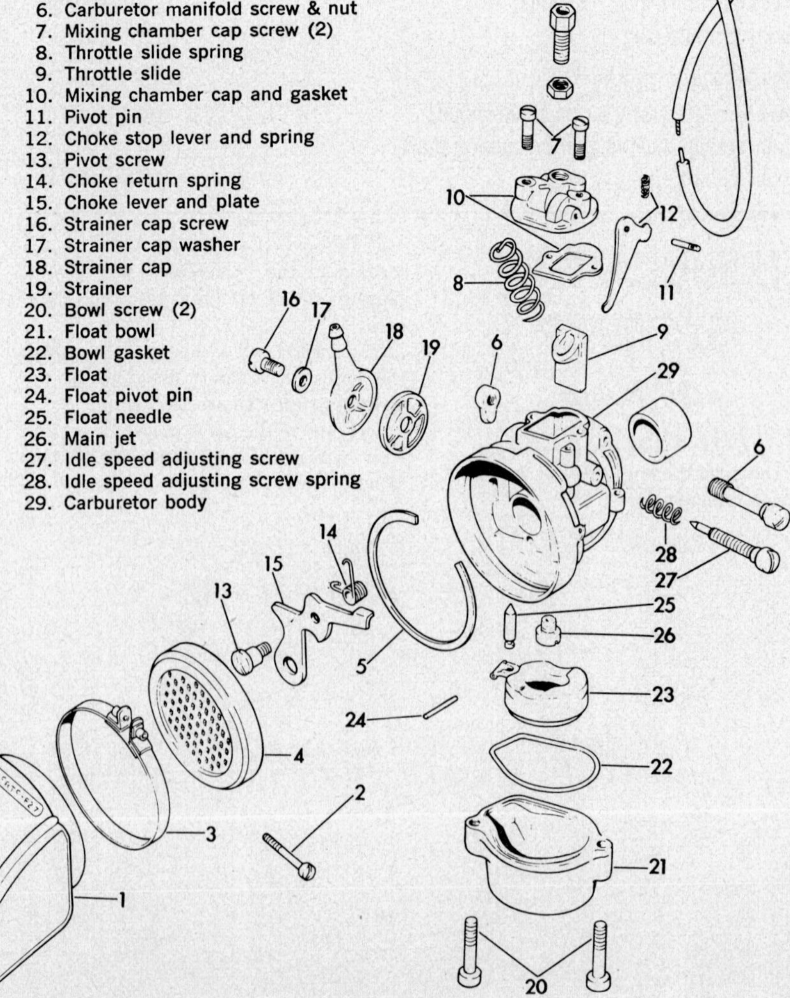

1. Silencer
2. Screw
3. Clamp
4. Air filter
5. Gasket
6. Carburetor manifold screw & nut
7. Mixing chamber cap screw (2)
8. Throttle slide spring
9. Throttle slide
10. Mixing chamber cap and gasket
11. Pivot pin
12. Choke stop lever and spring
13. Pivot screw
14. Choke return spring
15. Choke lever and plate
16. Strainer cap screw
17. Strainer cap washer
18. Strainer cap
19. Strainer
20. Bowl screw (2)
21. Float bowl
22. Bowl gasket
23. Float
24. Float pivot pin
25. Float needle
26. Main jet
27. Idle speed adjusting screw
28. Idle speed adjusting screw spring
29. Carburetor body

Carburetor assembly—1965 models M-50 and M-65

3. Remove the intake manifold clamp screw and pull and twist the carburetor free of the intake port.

4. Remove the mixing chamber cap screws, close the throttle, compress the throttle slide spring by hand, disengage the throttle cable from the throttle slide, then remove the pivot pin and the choke control lever and spring.

5. Remove the pivot screw and choke return spring, then remove the choke plate.

6. Remove the gas strainer cap screw, washer, and the strainer cap.

7. Remove the bowl cover screw, bowl, and bowl gasket. The float can now be removed by first removing the float lever pin and float needle.

8. Unscrew the main jet, then remove the idle speed adjusting screw and spring.

1966 AND LATER MODELS

Disassembly

1. Close the petcock and remove the fuel line at the carburetor.

2. Remove the silencer mounting screw, silencer, spacer and spring, air filter, and the silencer gasket but only if inspection of the gasket indicates that it should be replaced.

3. Loosen the manifold clamp screw and pull and twist on the carburetor until free.

4. Loosen the mixing chamber cap screws and pull the cap and throttle slide assembly free of the carburetor body.

5. Close the throttle, compress the throttle slide spring by hand, disengage the throttle cable from the slide cable fastener, unscrew the fastener from the piston, and remove the needle and retainer clip.

6. Remove the choke plate from the choke pin, push out the choke pin retainer clip, and remove the pin and pin spring.

7. Inspect the throttle cable adjusting screw and nut, and remove and replace them only if necessary.

8. Remove the gas strainer cap screw, cover, large and small strainer gaskets, strainer, bowl cover screws and washers, and then separate the cover from the gasket.

9. Remove the float retainer clip, float pin, pin spring, and float.

10. Unscrew the needle jet plug, remove the plug gasket, and remove the needle jet.

11. Remove the pilot jet, main jet carrier, main jet, idle-speed adjusting screw and spring, throttle slide adjusting screw and spring, and the insulating bushing, only if it requires replacement.

Inspection and Repair

1. Clean all parts other than the gaskets and the float in a suitable solvent and blow them dry, taking care to blow all passages clear. Do not use metal on any of these parts.

2. Replace all gaskets which are worn or damaged.

3. Inspect the fuel strainer for holes or built-up deposits and replace it as necessary.

4. Inspect the inlet valve for wear or damage and replace it as necessary.

5. Invert the carburetor body to check to make sure that the float needle closes, inspect the condition of the needle,

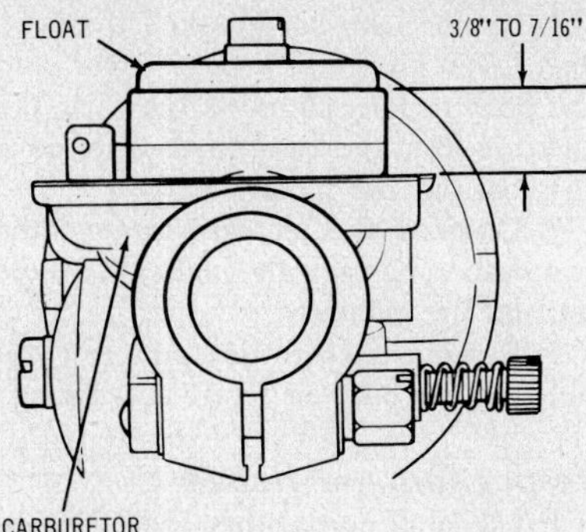

Checking the float level—M-50 and M-65

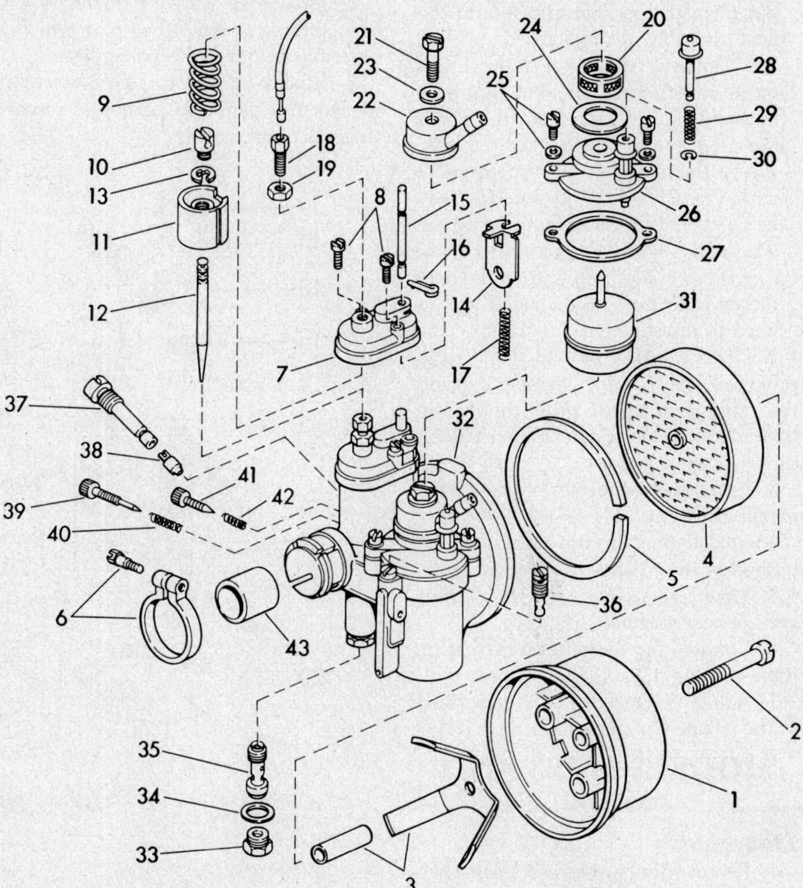

Carburetor assembly—1966 and later models M-50 and M-65

1. Silencer cover
2. Screw
3. Spacer and spring
4. Air filter
5. Gasket
6. Carburetor manifold clamp and screw
7. Mixing chamber cap
8. Screw (2)
9. Throttle slide spring
10. Cable fastener
11. Throttle slide
12. Needle
13. Retainer clip
14. Choke plate
15. Choke pin
16. Retainer clip
17. Choke pin spring
18. Cable adjusting screw
19. Cable adjusting nut
20. Gas strainer
21. Screw
22. Strainer cover
23. Strainer gasket (small)
24. Strainer gasket (large)
25. Bowl cover screw and washer (2)
26. Bowl cover
27. Bowl cover gasket
28. Float pin
29. Float pin spring
30. Retainer clip
31. Float
32. Main body
33. Needle jet plug
34. Needle jet plug gasket
35. Needle jet
36. Pilot jet
37. Main jet carrier
38. Main jet
39. Idle speed adjusting screw
40. Idle speed adjusting screw spring
41. Throttle slide adjusting screw
42. Throttle slide adjusting screw spring
43. Insulating bushing

check the valve for leakage by sucking on it, and replace it if necessary.

6. Inspect the float for a damaged or fuel-saturated condition and replace it as necessary.

7. Inspect the jet passages for a clogged condition and clear them out or replace them as necessary.

Assembly

1. Assembly is basically the reverse order of disassembly with the following exceptions, which pertain to the 1965 model:

   a. Position the float needle in the carburetor body, then insert the pivot pin through the float and mount the float assembly in the body.

   b. Hold the carburetor so the float is up and resting on the float pin, then measure the distance from the float's top ridge to the bowl seat.

   c. If the above measurement is not within ⅜–7/16 in., the situation may be corrected by carefully bending the float tang slightly. If this doesn't correct the problem, the float or the needle or both may be damaged and in need of replacement.

2. Open the throttle and engage the cable coil in the mixing chamber cap and the cable itself to the piston body, and then mount the mixing chamber cap on the carburetor body.

3. Install the carburetor on the intake manifold.

4. Adjust the throttle cable as described in the "Tune-Up" section.

5. Mount and secure the air cleaner and silencer assemblies.

6. Connect the fuel line to the carburetor and fuel tank.

7. Adjust the carburetor as described in the "Tune-Up" section.

MODELS M-125 AND M-100

Disassembly

1. Remove the air cleaner assembly.

2. Close the petcock and disconnect the fuel line at the carburetor.

3. Close the throttle, depress the choke, unscrew the mixing chamber cap nut, and pull the throttle assembly free of the carburetor body.

4. With the throttle closed, compress the throttle slide spring, disengage the throttle cable from the slide, remove the needle retainer clip, needle, and the throttle slide spring.

5. Inspect the cable adjusting screw, nut, and the choke rod hair pin spring and remove them only if they are in need of replacement.

6. Remove the gas strainer cap, gas line fitting, strainer gaskets, strainer, bowl cover screws and washers, and carefully pull the bowl straight down and away from the carburetor body.

7. Remove the bowl gasket, the float, float lever pivot screw, float lever, and the float needle. Remove the float pin lockring from the bowl cover to remove the float pin and spring.

8. Unscrew the jet cap, remove the cap washer, unscrew the main jet, needle jet, and the pilot jet.

9. Remove the throttle stop screw and nut, and the pilot air screw and spring.

Inspection and Repair

1. Clean all parts, other than the gaskets and the float, in a suitable solvent and blow them dry.

2. Replace all worn or damaged gaskets, springs or any other part which is obviously in need of replacement.

3. Inspect the throttle slide assembly for worn or damaged parts and replace them as necessary.

4. Inspect the fuel strainer for holes or built-up deposits and replace it as necessary.

5. Insert the float needle in its seat, invert the cover so the valve closes, and check the valve for leakage by sucking on it.

6. Inspect the float for a distorted, damaged, or fuel-logged condition and replace it if necessary.

7. Inspect the jets for deposits or a clogged condition which might hinder the fuel flow, and clear them out with compressed air.

Assembly

1. Assembly is basically the reverse order of disassembly, but take note of the following exceptions.

2. Install the pilot jet in the carburetor body before installing the needle and main jets.

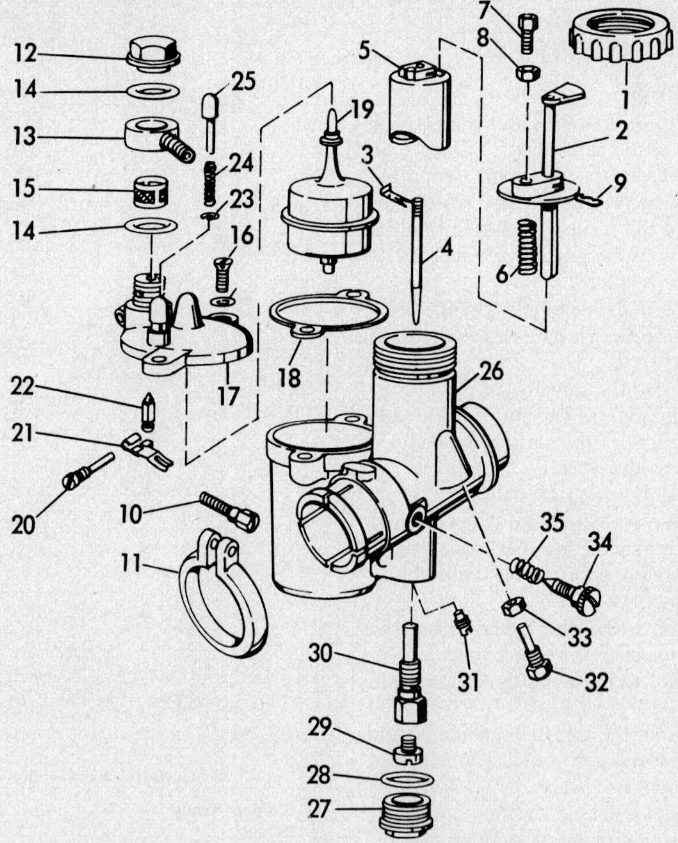

Carburetor assembly—M-100 and M-125

1. Mixing chamber cap nut
2. Mixing chamber cap and choke assembly
3. Needle retainer clip
4. Needle
5. Throttle slide
6. Throttle slide spring
7. Spring adjusting screw
8. Spring adjusting nut
9. Choke rod hairpin spring
10. Intake pipe clamp screw
11. Intake pipe clamp
12. Gas strainer cap
13. Gas line fitting
14. Gas strainer gasket (2)
15. Gas strainer
16. Bowl cover screw and washer (2)
17. Bowl cover
18. Bowl gasket
19. Float
20. Float lever pivot screw
21. Float lever
22. Float needle
23. Float pin lock ring
24. Float pin spring
25. Float pin
26. Body
27. Jet cap
28. Washer
29. Main jet
30. Needle jet
31. Pilot jet
32. Throttle slide stop screw
33. Throttle slide stop screw nut
34. Pilot air screw
35. Pilot air screw spring

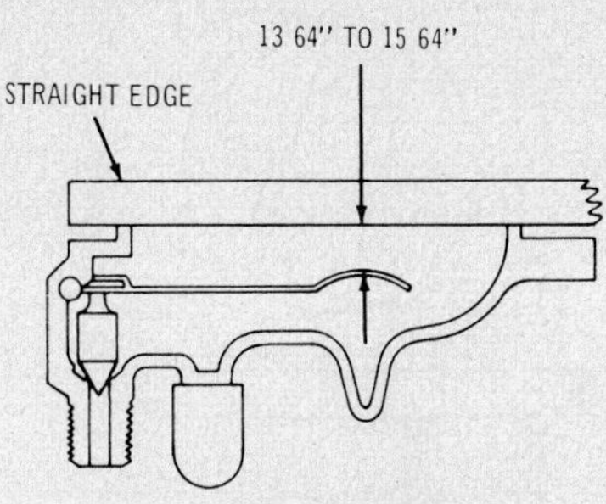

Checking the float level

3. Install the float needle in the bowl cover, engage the fingers of the float lever in the slot provided in the neck of the float needle, and insert the pivot screw through the pivot hole in the end of the float lever and into the bowl cover.

4. Check the float level in the following manner:

a. Invert the bowl cover and lay a straightedge across its face.

b. Measure the distance from the highest point of the float lever to the straightedge. Carefully bend the lever if necessary to bring the measurement within 13/64–15/64 in.

c. If repeated attempts to correct the level fails, either the lever, valve, or float are at fault, and one or more of these items will have to be replaced.

5. Assemble the float pin lockring and the pivot screw, engage the float with the float lever, and mount the assembly in the bowl, taking care to insert the float shaft on the bottom of the float in the hole provided for it in the bottom of the bowl.

6. Assemble the choke rod hairpin spring, cable adjusting nut, cable adjusting screw, and the mixing chamber cap nut on the cap and choke assembly.

7. Insert the needle in the throttle slide and use the retainer clip to secure the needle in the desired groove. Unless abnormal carburetion is required, use the middle groove. Consult the "Tune-Up" section for additional information.

8. Slip the cable through the adjusting screw, then position the throttle slide spring on the cable.

9. Press down on the choke slide and position the throttle slide assembly on it. The cable can be secured in the slide once the spring is compressed by hand.

10. Mount the carburetor on the intake manifold.

11. Open the throttle handgrip and slip the throttle assembly in place in the carburetor body taking care to align the piston cap lug with the carburetor notch. Install and secure the cap nut.

12. Mount the fuel line and the air cleaner assembly.

13. Adjust the carburetor as described in the "Tune-Up" section.

MODEL 165

Disassembly

1. Remove the carburetor cover and air cleaner assemblies.

2. Shut the petcock and disconnect the fuel line at the carburetor inlet connection.

3. Unscrew the carburetor cap and pull on the throttle cable to remove the slide cap, spring, slide needle retainer, and the needle as an assembly.

4. Close the throttle at the handgrip, squeeze the slide and cap together, and disengage the cable from the slide by carefully prying it free with a small, flat screwdriver. The assembly is now free to be disassembled.

1. Throttle slide cap
2. Throttle slide spring
3. Throttle slide
4. Needle retainer
5. Needle
6. Mounting screw
7. Carburetor insulator
8. Carburetor to cylinder bushing
9. Carburetor gasket
10. Jet holder
11. Jet holder gasket
12. Needle jet
13. Main jet
14. Bowl cover screw (2)
15. Float bowl cover
16. Carburetor float
17. Float needle
18. Float needle seat
19. Float primer pin
20. Float primer spring
21. Float primer cotter pin
22. Throttle slide guide screw
23. Carburetor body

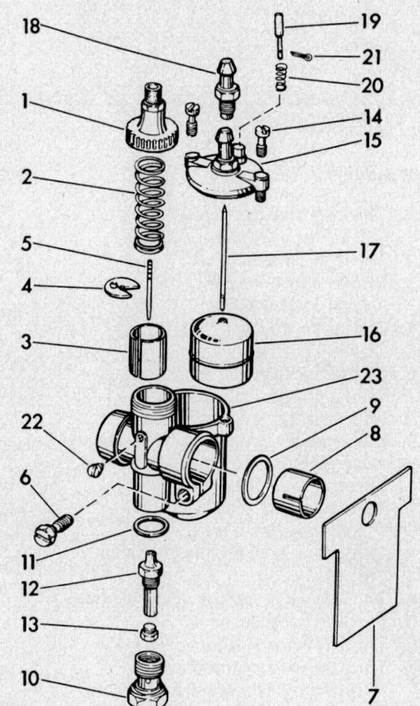

Carburetor assembly—Model 165

5. Loosen the mounting screw and remove the carburetor body from the intake manifold along with the carburetor gasket, bushing, and insulator.

6. Remove the jet holder, needle jet and gasket from the bottom of the carburetor body using a suitable socket or open-end wrench only. If inspection indicates the need for replacement or special attention, the main jet can be removed from the holder with a suitably sized screwdriver.

7. Remove the bowl cover screws, cover, float, and also remove the float needle from the float.

8. Inspect the float needle seat as described in the "Inspection and Repair" section. Remove and replace it only if necessary.

9. Remove and replace the float primer cotter pin, and remove the float primer spring, and the primer pin if inspection indicates the need for replacement.

10. The throttle slide guide screw can be removed from the carburetor if so desired.

Inspection and Repair

1. Clean all parts other than the float and gaskets in a suitable solvent and blow them dry.

2. Inspect the gaskets and the float for a worn, damaged, or gas-logged condition and replace them as necessary.

3. Inspect the throttle assembly for worn or damaged parts and replace them as necessary. Inspect the spring for a collapsed condition and replace it as necessary, especially if the throttle return action has been slow.

4. Inspect the jets for worn, damaged, or clogged condition and replace them if necessary. The passages may be cleared with compressed air.

5. Assemble the float needle seat and needle, invert the cover, and apply sucking pressure to check the valve for leakage, and replace them as necessary.

Assembly

1. Assembly is basically the reverse order of disassembly, with certain exceptions.

2. Insert the float needle in the float and install the assembly in the float bowl.

3. Mount the bowl cover on the carburetor body so the primer pin is away from the slide cap. The float needle should seat in the needle seat.

4. Position the carburetor gasket, bushing, and insulator on the carburetor body and mount the carburetor to the carburetor mounting flange. The slotted end of the bushing should be up and toward the cylinder.

5. Slip the needle retainer into the proper groove in the needle. Consult the "Tune-Up" section for information concerning groove selection.

6. Complete the assembly of the throttle components and adjust the carburetor as described in the "Tune-Up" section.

B-MODELS

Disassembly

1. Remove the air cleaner assembly (if applicable), disconnect the throttle cable at the carburetor, shut the petcock, disconnect the fuel line at the carburetor, and remove the carburetor from the cylinder mounting flange.

2. Remove the thin and heavy carburetor-to-cylinder gaskets, the bowl cover screws and lockwashers, and the bowl cover and gasket.

3. Free the float by pressing the float pin free of the cover, then remove the inlet needle, seat, spring, and gasket with a screwdriver that has a thick blade.

4. Unscrew the main adjusting screw and remove the packing nut and packing.

5. Remove the idle, adjusting screw, spring, idle tube, nozzle, and the nozzle gasket, which may have to be pried out and replaced.

6. Inspect the throttle shaft and bearing assembly for signs which would indicate the need for replacement, and remove them if necessary in the following manner:

a. Pry the throttle shaft retaining clip free of its groove on the shaft and remove the shaft spring, seal, shutter screw, and shutter. The shaft is now free to be removed from the carburetor body.

b. If the choke shaft is to be removed take care not to lose the friction pin and spring by holding your thumb over them while withdrawing the shaft.

Inspection and Repair

1. Clean all parts other than the gaskets and float in a suitable solvent and blow them dry, taking care to blow all the passages clear.

2. To inspect the idle mixture discharge ports, the welch plug will have to be removed by carefully punching a small, shallow hole in the plug at a point near the rim, and then prying the plug free. When installing a new plug, do so with a suitably sized drift, taking care to make it a tight fit.

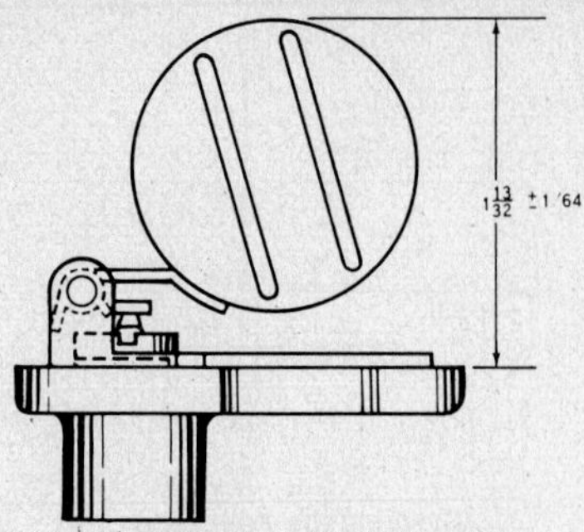

Checking the float level—B models

3. Inspect all the parts for a worn, scored, grooved, or otherwise damaged condition, and replace them as necessary. If the tip of the inlet needle is not in good condition, the fuel level will not be correct. If the throttle or choke shaft bearings are worn or damaged, air leakage will occur which causes rough idling.

4. Inspect the gasket and float for a worn, damaged, or gas-logged condition, and replace them as necessary.

5. Check the float level in the following manner:

a. Assemble the float lever pin, float, inlet needle, spring, seat, and gasket to the bowl cover.

b. Invert the float bowl so the lever tang rests on the seated inlet needle.

c. Measure the distance from the edge of the cover (without the cover gasket) to the top of the float with a straightedge ruler or a depth gauge.

d. Correct the measurement to 1 13/32 in. if necessary by removing the lever pin and carefully bending the float tang as required. Bend the tang evenly so the float sits squarely in the bowl.

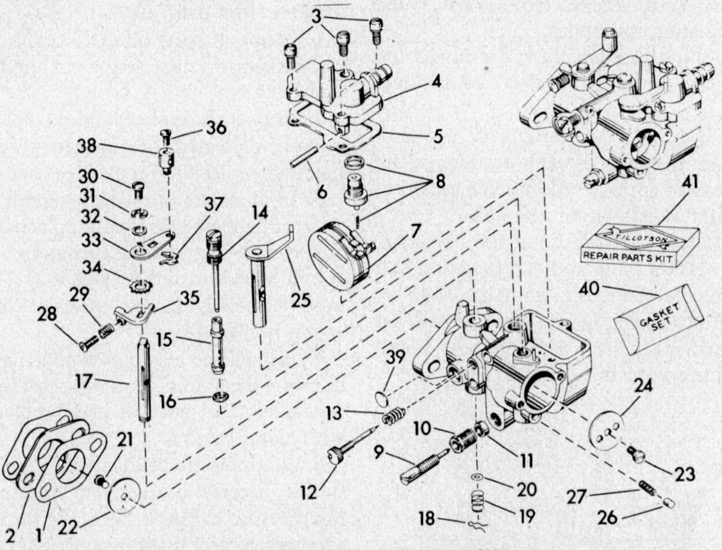

Carburetor assembly—B models

1. Carburetor to cylinder gasket—thin (2)
2. Carburetor to cylinder gasket—heavy
3. Bowl cover screw and lock washer (3)
4. Bowl cover
5. Bowl cover gasket
6. Float lever pin
7. Carburetor float
8. Inlet needle, spring, seat and gasket
9. Main adjusting screw
10. Main adjusting screw packing nut
11. Main adjusting screw packing
12. Idle adjusting screw
13. Idle adjusting screw spring
14. Idle tube
15. Carburetor nozzle
16. Nozzle gasket
17. Throttle shaft
18. Throttle shaft retaining clip
19. Throttle shaft spring
20. Throttle shaft seal
21. Throttle shutter screw and lock washer
22. Throttle shutter
23. Choke shutter screw and lock washer
24. Choke shutter
25. Choke shaft and lever
26. Choke friction pin
27. Choke friction pin spring
28. Idle speed regulating screw
29. Idle speed regulating screw spring
30. Throttle lever retaining screw
31. Throttle lever retaining lock washer
32. Throttle lever retaining washer
33. Throttle lever
34. Throttle lever spring lock washer
35. Throttle stop lever
36. Throttle wire retaining screw
37. Throttle wire connection retaining clip washer
38. Throttle wire connection
39. Channel welch plug

Assembly

1. Assembly is basically the reverse order of disassembly, with the following exceptions.

2. Make sure the idle tube is securely tightened down during the installation procedure.

3. Check the float for free-motion and the correct level.

4. Secure the throttle shutter to the shaft after the spring and clip are installed.

5. Insert the friction spring and then the friction pin into the choke channel and hold them temporarily in place with a daub of grease, a match, or any suitable device which will hold them while the choke shaft is moved into place.

6. Place a thin gasket on either side of the thick gasket when mounting the carburetor on the cylinder mounting flange.

7. Complete the assembly procedure and adjust the carburetor as described in the "Tune-Up" section.

SPRINT MODELS

Disassembly

1. Remove the gas tank on 1967 and later models, then remove the air filter assembly or the hose.

2. Shut the petcock, disconnect the fuel line at the carburetor, push down on the choke (if applicable), open the throttle handgrip, slide the rubber boot up the cable, unscrew the mixing chamber cap or cap screws and washers, and pull the throttle assembly from the carburetor body.

3. Loosen the intake pipe clamp screw and pull and twist the carburetor from the manifold.

4. Disassemble the throttle assembly in the following manner:

   a. Close the throttle at the handgrip and remove the throttle cable from the throttle slide while compressing the spring by hand.

   b. Remove the needle retaining clip and pin from the throttle slide, then remove the throttle spring from the piston.

   c. Remove the spring adjusting screw, nut, friction spring, and the choke rod hairpin spring if so desired.

5. Disassemble the float bowl assembly on 1968 and earlier models in the following manner:

   a. Remove the gas strainer cap, gaskets, and the strainer.

   b. Remove the bowl cover screws and also the cover and gasket.

   c. Remove the float, float lever pivot screw, lever, and float needle.

   d. Remove the float pin lockring, then remove the float pin and spring.

   e. Remove the bowl connection cap, bowl, and the fiber washers.

6. Disassemble the 1969 and later-model float bowl by removing the bowl nut, the main jet, and the nut gasket, then remove the bowl and the O-ring gasket.

7. Disassemble the carburetor body on 1968 and earlier models in the following manner:

   a. Remove the main jet, needle jet, and the pilot jet.

   b. Remove the throttle slide stop screw, nut pilot air screw spring, and the insulating bushing and washer.

8. Disassemble the 1969 and later-model carburetor in the following manner:

   a. Remove the float lever pivot pin, float, and the float needle.

   b. Remove the needle jet pilot and starting jets, starting jet O-ring, starting valve and lever assembly screw, assembly, inlet fitting screw, washer, fitting, and inlet screen.

   c. Remove the throttle slide stopscrew, the pilot air screen and their respective springs.

Inspection and Repair

1. Clean all parts, other than gaskets and the float, in a suitable solvent and blow them dry, taking care to blow all passages clear.

2. Inspect the gaskets and float for a worn, damaged, or gas-logged condition, and replace them as necessary.

3. Inspect the throttle assembly components for a worn or otherwise damaged condition and replace them as necessary.

4. Invert the bowl cover and insert the float needle so the valve is closed. Check the valve for leakage by sucking on its seat, and replace it as necessary.

5. Inspect the fuel strainer for a clogged or damaged condition and replace it as necessary.

6. Inspect the jets for a clogged condition and blow them free.

Assembly

Assembly is basically the reverse order of disassembly with the following exceptions:

1. Install the pilot jet, needle jet, and the main jet, in that order, on 1968 and earlier models.

2. Insert the float needle into the bowl cover, and engage the fingers of the float lever with the neck of the float needle, then slip the pivot screw through the pivot hole in the float lever and insert the

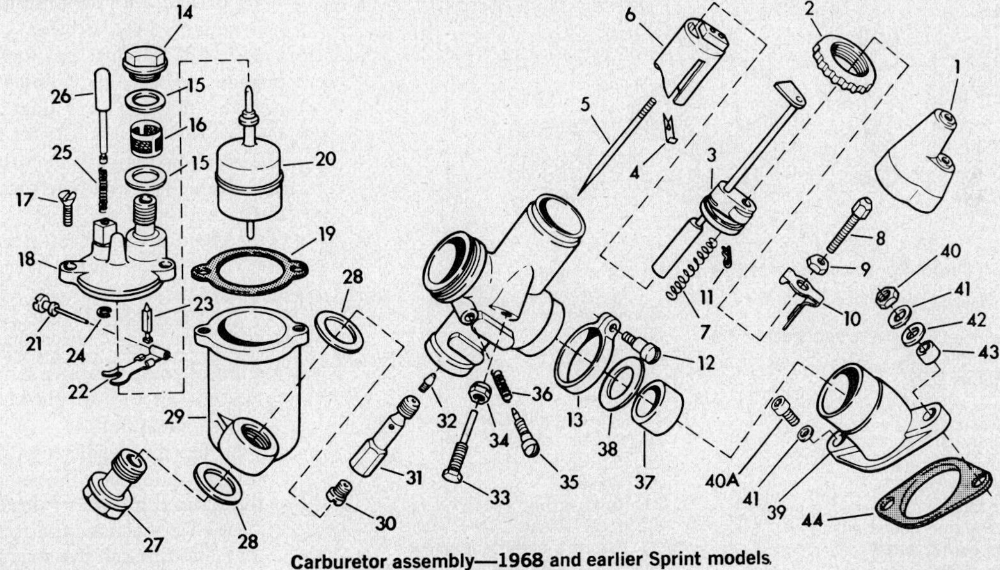

Carburetor assembly—1968 and earlier Sprint models

1. Boot
2. Mixing chamber cap nut
3. Mixing chamber cap and choke assembly
4. Needle retainer clip
5. Needle
6. Throttle slide
7. Throttle slide spring
8. Cable adjusting screw
9. Cable adjusting nut
10. Friction spring
11. Choke rod hairpin spring
12. Intake pipe clamp screw
13. Intake pipe clamp
14. Gas strainer cap
15. Gas strainer gasket (2)
16. Gas strainer
17. Bowl cover screw (2)
18. Bowl cover
19. Bowl gasket
20. Float
21. Float lever pivot screw
22. Float lever
23. Float needle
24. Float pin lockring
25. Float pin spring
26. Float pin
27. Bowl connection cap
28. Fiber washers (2)
29. Float bowl
30. Main jet
31. Needle jet
32. Pilot jet
33. Throttle slide stop screw
34. Throttle slide stop screw nut
35. Pilot air screw
36. Pilot air screw spring
37. Insulating bushing
38. Insulating washer
39. Manifold
40. Nut (2) 1966 and earlier

40A. Screw (2) 1967 to 1968

41. Washer (2)
42. Insulator washer (2)
43. Insulator bushing (2)
44. Manifold gasket

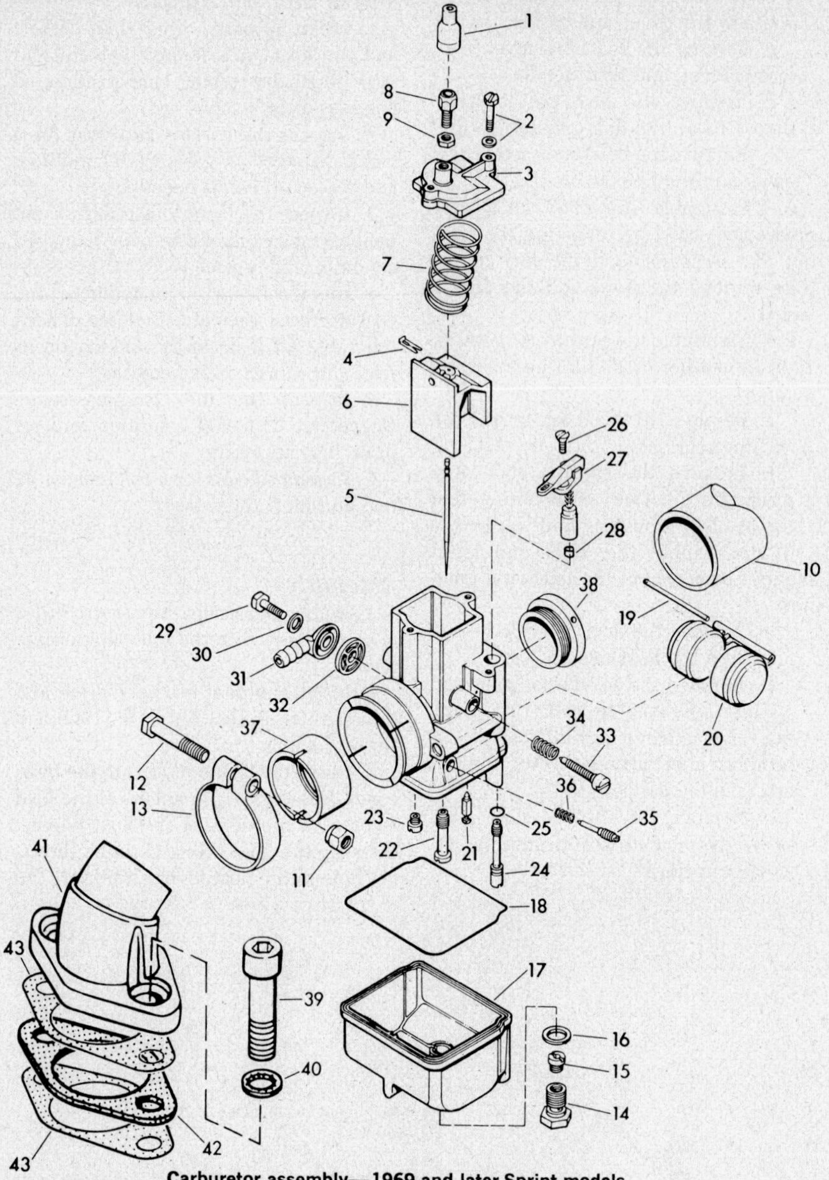
Carburetor assembly—1969 and later Sprint models

1. Boot
2. Mixing chamber cap screw and washer (2)
3. Mixing chamber cap
4. Needle retainer clip
5. Needle
6. Throttle slide
7. Throttle slide spring
8. Cable adjusting screw
9. Cable adjusting nut
10. Air cleaner hose
11. Intake pipe clamp screw nut
12. Intake pipe clamp screw
13. Intake pipe clamp
14. Bowl nut
15. Main jet
16. Gasket
17. Bowl
18. O-ring gasket
19. Float lever pivot pin
20. Float
21. Float needle
22. Needle jet
23. Pilot jet
24. Starting jet
25. O-ring
26. Screw
27. Starting valve and lever assembly
28. Rubber plug
29. Screw
30. Washer
31. Inlet fitting
32. Inlet screen
33. Throttle slide stopscrew
34. Throttle slide stopscrew spring
35. Pilot fuel adjusting screw
36. Pilot fuel screw spring
37. Insulating bushing
38. Intake hose adaptor
39. Manifold screw (2)
40. Washer (2)
41. Manifold
42. Manifold gasket

screw and lever into the bowl cover, on 1968 and earlier models.

3. Check the float level on 1968 and earlier models in the following manner:

a. Invert the bowl cover and lay a straightedge across the cover's face.

b. Measure the distance from the straightedge to the highest point on the float lever.

c. If the distance is not within 13/64–15/64 in., the lever can be bent to compensate for the difference if care is taken to bend it evenly. If repeated attempts to get within the specified limits fail, either the lever or the needle is faulty and must be replaced.

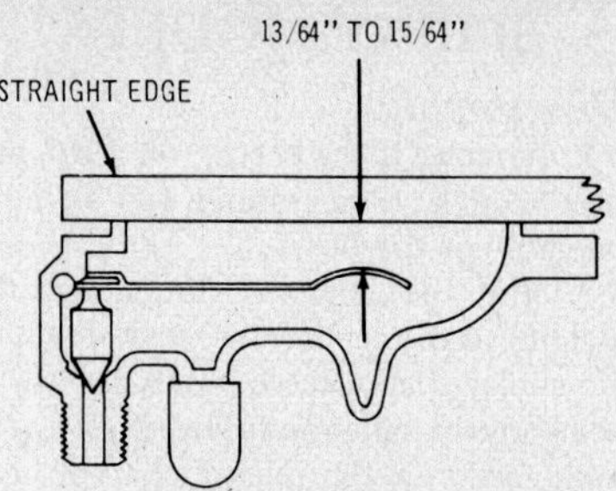

Checking the float level—Sprint models

4. Check the float level on 1969 and later models in the following manner:

a. Measure the distance from the top of both of the floats to the gasket surface when the inlet valve is seated. The distance should be 31/32 in. and is best measured with Carburetor Float Gauge (H-D part no. 94751-69) although substitute gauges may easily be made from cardboard or balsa.

b. If the distance is not within specifications, place the float on a flat surface and bend the ear up or down as necessary.

c. Check to see that both floats are at an even height by seeing whether both are parallel with the pin support when resting on a flat surface.

5. Install the float pin lockring, then engage the float lever fingers with the neck of the float lever fingers with the neck of the float and mount the float in the bowl, taking care to make sure the float shaft sits in the hole provided for it in the bottom of the bowl.

6. Assemble the throttle assembly on 1968 and earlier models in the following manner:

a. Mount the choke rod hairpin spring, friction spring, throttle cable adjusting nut, adjusting screw, and the cap nut on the mixing chamber cap and choke assembly.

b. Slip the needle into place in the throttle slide, place the retainer clip on the desired groove as directed in the "Tune-Up" section, and run the throttle cable through the rubber boot adjusting screw, and throttle slide spring.

c. Push down on the choke slide, mount the throttle slide assembly on the slide, compress the spring by hand, and mount the throttle slide onto the cable.

7. Assemble the throttle assembly on 1969 and later models in the following manner:

a. Slip the needle into the throttle slide, and engage the retainer clip in the desired groove of the needle as directed in the "Tune-Up" section. The

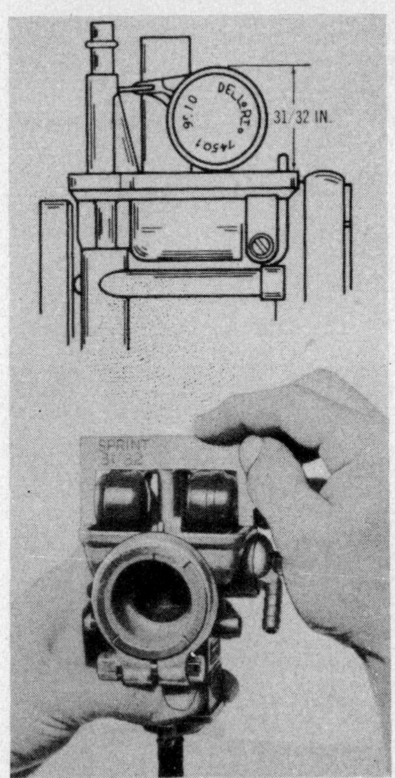

Checking the float level—Sprint models

middle groove is the one used for normal operation.

b. Run the throttle cable through the rubber boot, adjusting screw, and throttle slide spring, then compress the spring by hand and insert the cable into the throttle slide.

8. Mount the intake manifold on the cylinder, then mount the carburetor on the manifold. On 1968 and earlier models, make sure the float bowl is absolutely level to prevent the float from hanging up.

9. Open the throttle at the handgrip and insert the throttle slide assembly in the carburetor body. Make sure the piston is free and operating smoothly before securing the cap.

10. Mount the fuel line and air cleaner assembly, then adjust the carburetor as described in the "Tune-Up" section.

ELECTRICAL SYSTEMS

COMPONENT SERVICE

Magneto-Generator

M MODELS

Disassembly

1. Remove the left crankcase side cover as described in the "Starter" section.

2. Remove the rotor shaft nut and washer, then pull the rotor free with Magneto Rotor Puller (H-D part no. 97344-65P or 97302-70M for the MSR models) or a suitable substitute.

3. Remove the coil screws and washers, disconnect the coil leads at their terminals, and remove the coils.

4. Remove the condenser screw and washer, then remove the condenser.

5. Remove the retaining clip and washers, the contact breaker assembly, the stator plate screws and washers, and the stator plate.

Inspection and Repair

1. Clean all parts other than the coils in a suitable grease-dissolving solvent and blow them dry. The coils may be cleaned with a clean cloth dipped in clean, white gasoline.

2. Inspect all parts for a worn or damaged condition and replace them as necessary.

Assembly

1. Assembly is in the reverse order of disassembly.

2. Check the moving parts for a smooth, free operation.

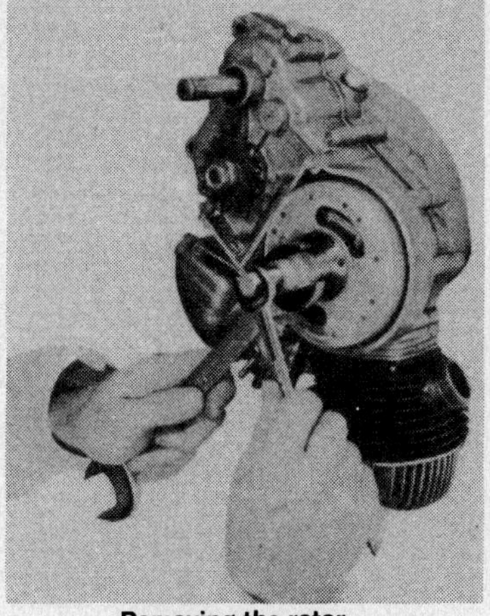

Removing the rotor

Generator

MODEL 165

Disassembly

1. Remove the generator cover.

2. Remove the brush spring clips, springs, insulators, and the frame mounting screws, and pull the frame clear of the armature.

3. Remove the armature mounting screws and lockwashers, and remove the contact breaker cam by tapping gently on its sides with a soft mallet.

4. Remove the armature from the flywheel shaft using Generator Armature Puller (H-D part no. 95900-48) or a suitable substitute. Remove the sprocket shaft key from the flywheel shaft.

5. Disconnect the red and green wires in the cable from the fiber terminal block.

6. Disconnect the brush leads and remove the brushes, then disconnect the black wire at the contact point terminal.

7. Remove the contact breaker and condenser if so desired.

8. Inspect the pole shoes and field coils for a worn or damaged condition and remove them only if replacement is necessary. The shoes may be removed by

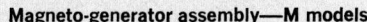

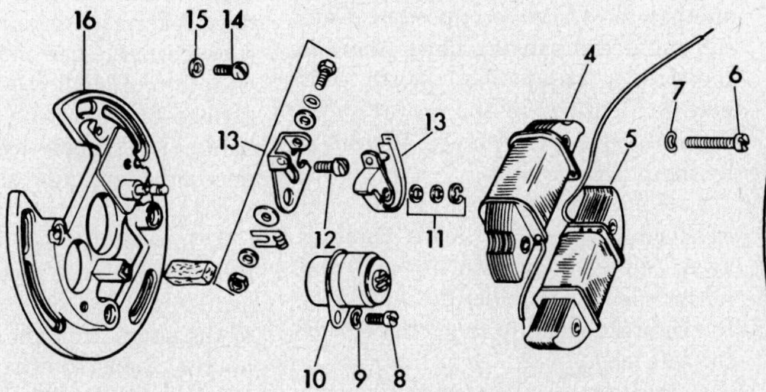

Magneto-generator assembly—M models

1. Rotor
2. Nut
3. Washer
4. Coil
5. Coil
6. Screw (4)
7. Washer (4)
8. Screw
9. Washer
10. Condenser
11. Retaining clip, washers
12. Screw
13. Contact breaker assembly
14. Screw (3)
15. Washer (3)
16. Stator plate

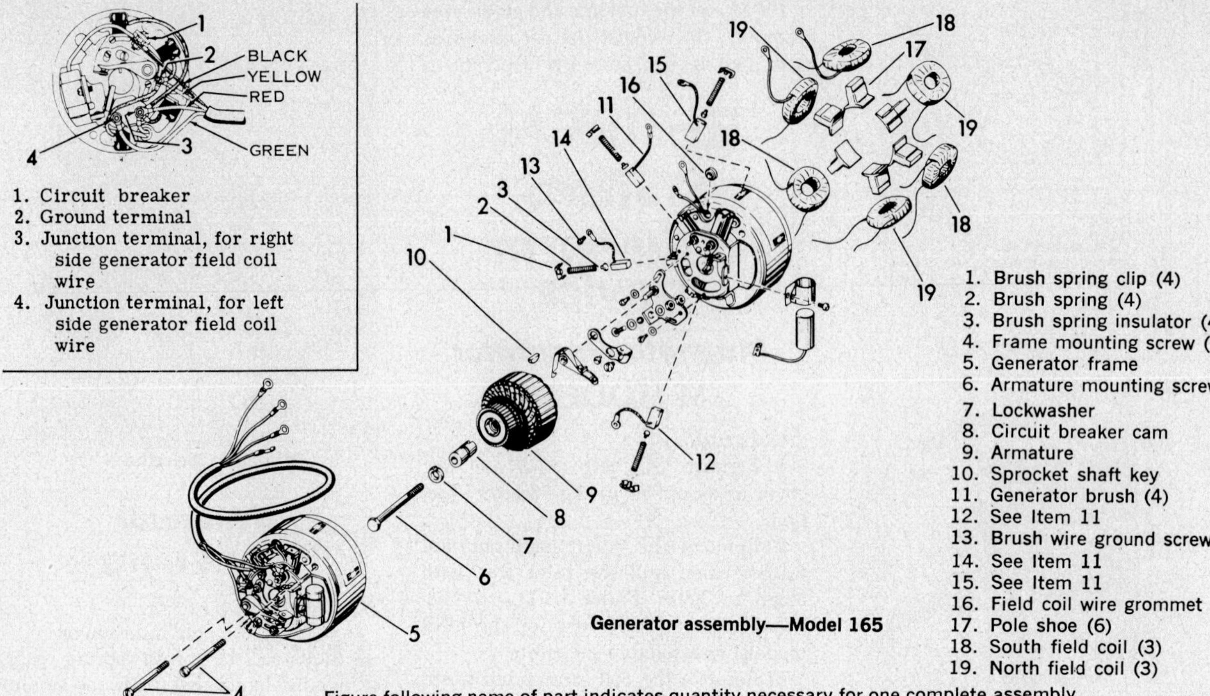

Generator assembly—Model 165

Figure following name of part indicates quantity necessary for one complete assembly.

sharply striking the portion which extends through the generator frame with a hammer. The shoes may be reused if there is enough of the peening material left after they have been removed.

Inspection and Repair

1. Clean all parts other than the armature, field coils, and brushes in a suitable grease-dissolving solvent and blow them dry. Clean the remaining components by wiping them with a clean cloth dipped in clean, white gasoline and then blow them dry.

2. Inspect the insulators, armature windings, field coil wrappings, and the surfaces of the pole shoes nearest the armature for a worn or damaged condition and replace them as necessary.

3. Inspect the brushes for a worn or damaged condition and compare them with new brushes, if possible, to determine their wear. Replace them if necessary.

4. Inspect the brush holder plate for a warped, burned, loose, or otherwise damaged condition and replace them if necessary in the following manner:

a. Remove the heads by chiseling off the plate rivet heads and drifting the rivets free.

b. Remove the brush holder plate from the generator frame.

c. Drill four holes in the new plate using a no. 20 bit, then tap four corresponding holes into the frame with an 8/32 in. tap.

d. Mount and secure the new plate to the frame with four screws and lockwashers (H-D parts no. 2626 and 7115) or suitable substitutes.

e. Take care not to damage the pole shoes and not to allow the screws to contact the shoes. If necessary, use additional lockwashers to keep the screws away from the shoes.

5. Inspect the cam fiber follower for a worn or damaged condition and replace it if necessary by knocking out the old part and riveting in a new one. Always keep the felt portion clean and lightly oiled with clean engine oil.

6. Inspect the coils for a worn or damaged condition and replace them as necessary in the following manner:

a. When installing the field coils, there must be a north ("N") coil to the left of the coil lead hole in the generator frame when the frame is held so the engine side is up and the coil lead hole is to the near side of the frame. Coils are mounted in opposite pairs of "N" and "S," and the coils adjacent to one another must also be opposites. (Consult the accompanying illustration for the proper positioning.) North coils may be identified by the white swatch of paint. South coils may be identified by their red marking.

b. Hold a south coil with the concave side up and the leads pointing away. Slip a yellow insulator over the left-side lead then solder the wire tip of the right-side lead to the connector of the left lead.

c. Perform the above operation on a north coil in the same manner except that the insulator and connector are on the right-side lead.

d. Place the south coil to the right of the generator frame coil lead hole.

e. Place a north coil ,without an insulator or connector, with a shoe in the frame shoe slot directly to the right of the south coil of step "d."

f. Continue to install coils in an alternating order (the next one will be a south coil) so the last coil–the north coil prepared in step "c"–sits to the left of the generator frame coil lead hole.

g. Place insulation under the coils where the frame mounting screws pass so they don't short out against the frame; use the mounting screws as guides.

7. Secure a length of 2 ¼ in. outside diameter (OD) pipe horizontally in a vise, then slip the generator frame, complete with coils and shoes, over the pipe as far as is necessary to completely support the frame shoes.

8. Tap the frame down around the shoes with a ¼ in. chisel ground to a dull edge until it bottoms on the shoe shoulders. After each shoe is seated, stake the shoe corners over the generator frame with the chisel, then peen the entire shoe surface of each shoe with a ball peen hammer. Use only as much force as is necessary, and use a light hammer to avoid using excessive force.

9. Inspect the fit of the armature in the frame. If the clearance is less than 0.014 in. (0.007 in. per side) check to see that all of the shoes are well seated. If this was not the problem, the shoes will have to be carefully bored until the clearance is correct.

10. Check each coil for proper current draw and ground as described in the "Component Testing and Repair" section of this chapter before twisting the coil ends together, then connect the coils

in one of the following manners:

a. Twist the adjacent leads together, clip them off at a point ½ in. beyond the edge of the generator frame, and fuse the wires together with a blow torch. (This is the preferred method.)

b. Scrape the coil leads until the varnish is removed, twist the adjacent leads together, and solder the connections.

11. Bend the coil leads back between the coils taking care to keep them from touching the generator frame. Install a rubber grommet over the leads and press them all into the frame hole.

12. Slip the coil leads onto their respective terminal posts mounted on the insulated terminal strip, taking care not to cross any of the leads.

13. Perform the final field coil polarity test in the following manner:

a. Connect wires from the positive terminal of a 6 V battery to the south coil post, and from the negative terminal to the north coil post.

b. Hold a compass outside the generator frame near the pole shoe of the coil to be tested and observe the reaction of the compass. The south needle of the compass will swing toward the pole shoe if the coil is a south coil.

Assembly

1. Assembly is basically the reverse order of disassembly.

2. Secure the sprocket shaft key and install the armature.

3. Gently tap the contact breaker cam until it begins to seat, then secure it with the lockwasher and armature mounting screw.

4. Mount a dial indicator to the crankcase and check the armature run-out. If the run-out exceeds 0.002 in., the brushes will act erratically at high speeds, causing excessive heat and the damage that is associated with it. The run-out may be reduced by drifting the armature with a small hammer and a suitable brass drift, then recheck the run-out.

5. Check the breaker cam run-out at the portion of the cam nearest the armature (the concentric portion). If the run-out exceeds 0.002 in., it may be reduced by drifting it as you did the armature. Recheck the run-out after drifting the cam.

6. Place a small daub of grease on the cam, and lightly oil the felt cam follower with a small drop of clean engine oil, then assemble the generator frame.

7. Install the brush spring insulators, springs, and spring clips, reconnect the wires as depicted on the wiring diagrams, time the engine as described in the "Tune-Up" section, and install the generator and sprocket cover.

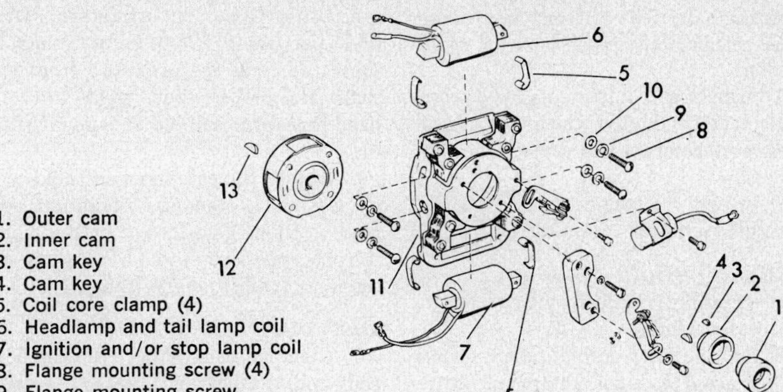

1. Outer cam
2. Inner cam
3. Cam key
4. Cam key
5. Coil core clamp (4)
6. Headlamp and tail lamp coil
7. Ignition and/or stop lamp coil
8. Flange mounting screw (4)
9. Flange mounting screw lockwasher (4)
10. Flange mounting screw flat washer (4)
11. Flange
12. Rotor
13. Rotor key (See item 4)

Figure following name of part indicates quantity necessary for one complete assembly.

Magneto-generator assembly—B models

Magneto-Generator

B MODELS

Disassembly (All Models Other Than The BTF)

1. Remove the right side cover.

2. Carefully pry off the outer and inner cams with a small screwdriver, then remove the cam keys.

3. Disconnect the coil leads from the terminals, pry the large ends of the coil core clamps from the cores, and remove the headlight and ignition coils.

4. Remove the flange mounting screws, lockwashers, flatwashers, and the flange.

5. Pull the rotor using All Purpose Claw Puller (H-D part no. 95635-46) or a suitable substitute. If necessary, grind down the bottoms of the claws to make it fit properly. Remove the rotor key after the rotor is out.

6. Consult the "Tune-Up" section for additional information concerning removing and replacing the breaker point assemblies.

Disassembly (BTF Models)

1. Remove the right side cover.

2. Pry off the cam with a small screwdriver and remove the key.

3. Disconnect the coil leads from the terminals, then pry the large end of the coil core clamps from the cores and remove the flange.

4. Remove the rotor and key as described in the above section.

Inspection and Repair

1. Clean all parts, other than the coils, in a suitable grease-dissolving solvent and

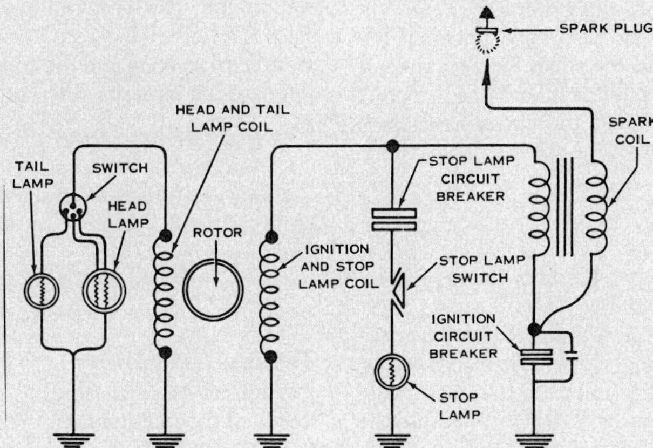

Magneto-generator circuit for the B models other than the Ranger

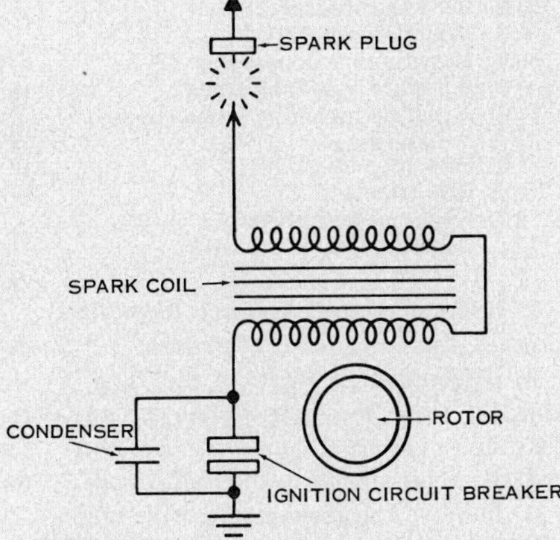

Magneto-generator circuit for the Ranger (BTF) models

blow them dry. The coils may be cleaned with a clean cloth dipped in clean, white gasoline.

2. Inspect all components for a worn or damaged condition which may impair their performance, and replace them as necessary.

3. Inspect the connection of all wires, and their terminals, for a secure fit.

Assembly (Both Models)

1. Assembly is basically the reverse order of disassembly.

2. Pull the rotor onto the shaft, taking care to avoid jarring it as this could cause it to lose its magnetic properties, by using the cams as drive collars and by turning the shaft nut onto the shaft until the rotor seats itself.

3. Press the coil core clamps into position by applying pressure to the curved portion. Never hammer or tap them into place.

4. Apply a daub of grease to the cam and a small drop of clean engine oil to the fiber cam follower. Reconnect the wires by consulting the wiring diagrams and time the engine as described in the "Tune-Up" section.

Generator

SPRINT MODELS

Disassembly

1. Remove the left side cover screws and then the cover by tapping on its sides with a soft mallet while pulling on the kick-starter lever.

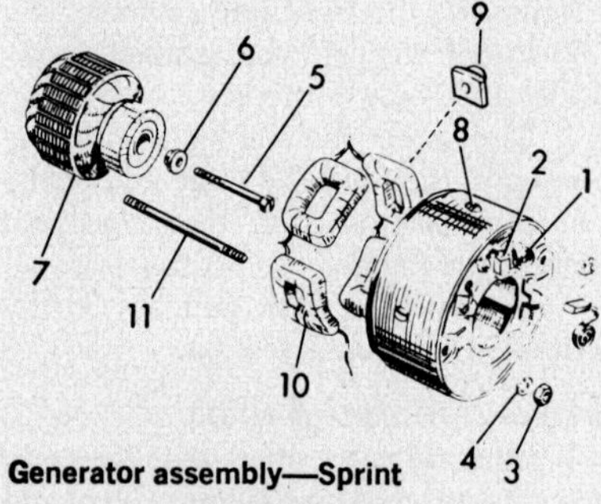

Generator assembly—Sprint

1. Brush spring (2)
2. Generator brush (2)
3. Mounting nut (2)
4. Mounting nut lockwasher (2)
5. Armature mounting screw
6. Armature mounting screw spacer
7. Armature
8. Pole shoe screw (4)
9. Pole shoe (4)
10. Field coil (set of four)
11. Generator frame stud (2)

2. Remove the brush springs from the brushes, then remove the brushes.

3. Disconnect the wires at the "D+" and "DF" terminals, remove the generator mounting nuts and lockwashers, then pull the generator from the frame studs.

4. Remove the tachometer drive unit (if applicable), the armature mounting screw, and the screw spacer.

5. Using Generator Armature Puller (H-D part no. 97296-61P), or a suitable substitute, pull the armature from the shaft. The tool has both right- and left-hand threads to suit either type of armature.

6. Inspect the pole shoes and field coils for a worn or damaged condition, and remove them if necessary by removing the pole shoe screws which will allow the shoes and coils to come free.

Inspection and Repair

1. Clean all parts, other than the field coils and brushes, in a suitable grease-removing solvent and blow them dry. The coils and brushes may be cleaned with a clean cloth dipped in clean gasoline.

2. Inspect all components for a worn or damaged condition and replace them as necessary, paying particular attention to the insulators, armature windings, field coil wrappings, and the surfaces of the pole shoes nearest the armature. If possible, compare the brushes with new ones, and replace them if it appears that they may interfere with the normal operation of the generator.

NOTE: *On models after serial no. 3672, the armature and tapered shaft have been altered. Make sure to use the correct replacement parts if replacement is necessary.*

3. Replace the field coils in the order depicted in the illustration. The lead on each end coil is marked with a colored insulating sleeve. The red sleeve is connected to the generator "D+" terminal and the yellow lead goes to the "DF" terminal. Use the Generator Pole Shoe Arbor (H-D part no. 97302-61), or a suitable substitute, to force the coils into position in the frame.

4. Check the twisted connections between the adjacent coils for a positive connection, scrape the leads free of varnish, solder the twisted connections, clip ½ in. off each connection beyond the generator frame, and bend the leads back between the coils, taking care not to touch them to the generator frame.

5. Check the clearance between the armature and the shoes for clearance. If the clearance is less than 0.014 in. (0.007 in. per side) and the shoes have been properly seated, the shoes will have to be bored to fit.

Assembly

1. Assembly is basically the reverse order of disassembly.

2. Secure the armature with the armature mounting screw spacer and screw, then check the armature run-out for run-out in excess of 0.002 in. Consult the "Generator (Model 165)" section for additional information.

3. Slip the generator frame onto the frame studs and secure it with the lockwashers and nuts.

4. Install the brushes and springs, reconnect the wiring as depicted in the wiring diagrams, and mount and secure the left crankcase cover.

COMPONENT TESTING AND REPAIR

Magneto-Generator

M AND B MODELS

On 1969 and earlier M models the brake light circuit is tied into the ignition circuit. In normal operation the brake light switch is closed, providing the necessary ground. When the brake is applied, the switch opens and the light filament provides the ground. If the machine stalls out when the brake pedal is operated, the problem is probably in the brake light bulb or wiring. After replacing the bulb or fixing the wiring, recheck the ignition for spark as previously described. If you still haven't located the source of the problem, it's probably in the lower coil of the magneto-generator.

Testing for a Grounded Coil

1. Remove the rotor and disconnect both of the leads from the coil in question.

2. Connect a taillight bulb in series with a 6 V battery, then connect one lead of the test circuit to one of the coil leads and ground the other to the generator frame.

3. Wrap the remaining coil lead to insulate it, or place it in such a way that it is not touching the frame.

4. If the test light comes on, the coil is grounded or faulty. Inspect the coil windings for a worn, frayed, or damaged condition and replace as necessary.

Testing for a Shorted Coil

There is no accurate method of testing for a shorted coil without elaborate test equipment. The best method is to replace the bulbs which are in circuit with the coil in question and the coil, and then compare the intensity with another bulb.

Testing for an Open Coil

1. Remove the rotor and coil, and connect both test leads of a taillight bulb in series with a 6 V battery to the two coil leads.

2. If the bulb doesn't light, the coil has an open circuit and must be replaced.

Testing the Rotor

When all other tests fail to reveal the source of the malfunction, the rotor may be considered. If damaged or roughly handled, the rotor may lose some of its magnetic properties. The only test is to compare the strength of the magnets with a new rotor, and replace the rotor if the tests prove it to be low in magnetic energy.

Generator

MODEL 165

Testing the Charging System

1. Disconnect the red wire at the voltage regulator "gen" terminal and connect one lead of an ammeter to the red wire and the other lead to the terminal. Turn on the headlight, then start and run the engine until the normal operating temperature is reached. Open the throttle until the engine is running at a speed equivalent to 20–25 miles per hour (mph) road speed. (This may be done by blocking the machine up so the rear wheel spins freely and then running the engine in high gear until the speedometer indicates the appropriate speed.) The ammeter should indicate a charge under these circumstances, but if it doesn't, go on to the next step.

2. If the above procedure fails to produce a charge on the ammeter, disconnect the green wire at the regulator "F" terminal (without disconnecting the test circuit) and ground it on the crankcase while observing the ammeter. If the ammeter records a charge of five or more amps, either the voltage regulator is not properly grounded or it is defective. Check to see that the regulator is properly grounded before going on to the next test.

3. Compare the regulator connections to the wiring diagrams to make sure everything is properly connected. Flash the regulator "gen" and "bat" terminals by momentarily touching a piece of wire to both of them. This will correctly polarize the generator to keep it charging and to keep the relay points from arcing and burning. Run the engine after polarizing the generator and see if the generator charges as in step one. If the generator fails to charge, go on to the next step.

4. Disconnect the test circuit ammeter lead from the "gen" terminal and connect it to the positive (+) battery terminal, then ground the wire from the "F" terminal on the crankcase. Run the machine as described in step one and read the ammeter. If the ammeter doesn't record a charge, the trouble is within the generator.

5. Inspect the brushes and brush springs for a worn or damaged condition and replace them if necessary. At least clean them with trichloroethylene or a suitable solvent such as clean white gasoline. Polish the commutator with no. 00 sandpaper and blow the assembly clear. Recheck the output as in the above step and proceed to disassemble the generator as described earlier in this chapter if the generator still is not working properly, and go on to the next section.

Testing the Field Coils

Perform the following tests with the generator frame in place after disconnecting the red and green wires from the regulator terminals, and removing the positive brushes which are connected to the same terminal as the red wire. If the ammeter is connected to a short circuit, it will overload and be damaged. If the needle starts to go off the range, the contact should immediately be broken. For this reason it is advisable to momentarily touch the ammeter leads to the terminals or leads to check for a short before securing them.

1. Connect a fully charged 6 V battery and an ammeter in series with the red and green leads and consult the ammeter. The correct reading should be 2 amps. If it is not, go on to the next step.

2. If the above test results in a reading which is higher or lower than the specified amount, or if the test reveals a short circuit, disconnect the red and green wires and the field coil leads from the terminals. Connect the test circuit to the field coils and repeat the test described in step one before going on to the next step.

3. If the reading in step two is correct, inspect the condition of the red and green wires for wear or damage and replace them as necessary. If the wires are all right but a short was discovered in the first step, check to see that the frame terminals are insulated from each other and from the generator frame as well. Inspect the positive brush holders also to make sure they are fully insulated from the generator frame.

4. If tests of the field coils, independent of all terminals and leads, fail to provide the correct reading, the generator frame must be thoroughly cleaned before proceeding to the next step.

5. If an open (no reading) or low reading is arrived at after cleaning the frame, inspect all the connections of the coil leads and of the twisted connections between the coils before proceeding to the next step.

6. If everything checked out in the previous step, cut off the fused portion between the coils and separate them for individual testing. Each coil may be tested with a fully charged 2 V battery instead of the 6 V used in the first step. A correct reading for individual coils is about 3.3 amps.

7. An alternate method to step six is to replace the 6 V battery as the power source for the circuit tester, wire a taillight bulb into the test circuit, and then connect one test lead to the generator frame, and use the other to individually test each coil by touching one coil lead while observing the test light and ammeter responses. If the light lights, the coil is grounded. If there is no reading, the coil is open. If the reading is high the coil is shorted. In any of these cases the coil must be replaced as described in the "Generator (Model 165)" section.

Testing the Armature

Remove the armature from the generator as described in the "Generator (Model 165)" section. Connect a taillight in series with a 6 V battery, then touch one lead to the commutator surface and the other to the armature core. If the light comes on, replace the armature.

Repairing the Commutator

If a lathe is available, the commutator may be turned down enough to remove the rough surface. Armature Commutator Turning Arbor (H-D part no. 96170-50) may be used since it easily mounts in the lathe chuck, but any suitable substitute may be used. Once the commutator is turned down (never remove more metal than necessary), it may be finished with some no. 00 sandpaper. Emery cloth should not be used since the particles will embed themselves in the mica and cause an electrical malfunction.

The mica between the commutator segments will have to be cut to a depth of 0.025 in. if the commutator has been turned or worn down. The cutting may be done with an under-cutting tool or with a piece of hacksaw blade that has been thinned to the appropriate size. Try to make the surface of the mica as flat and as even as possible. Smooth the commutator with no. 00 sandpaper after everything is done, and recheck the armature as described in the above section before installing it.

If all of the above sounds too complicated or if no lathe is available, the commutator may be cleaned by hand, using no. 00 sandpaper. Always make sure that the armature is perfectly clean before reinstalling it.

SPRINT MODELS

Checking the generator means checking the charging system, or the circuit between the generator and the battery, and everything in between. This is done by eliminating the components one at a time until the source of the trouble is isolated by one of the following methods.

Testing the Charging System

1. Compare the regulator wiring to the wiring diagram located at the end of this chapter to make sure it is correct.

2. Disconnect the two white wires at the voltage regulator no. 61 terminal, then connect the negative lead of an ammeter (0–15 amp DC type) to the no. 61 terminal and the positive lead to both of the white leads. Turn on the headlight,

then start and run the engine until normal operating temperature is reached. With the engine running at a speed equivalent to 20–25 mph, the ammeter should register some charge. The bike may be blocked up and run in high gear to approximate the moving speed. Go on to the next step if the ammeter fails to register a charge.

3. Remove the red wire from regulator "DF" terminal if the ammeter didn't register, and briefly touch the wire to the crankcase without disconnecting the test circuit. If the ammeter indicates a charge of five or more amps, the generator is healthy and the problem lies in the voltage regulator or any of the charging system wiring. Inspect the wiring for bad connections, breaks, or a poor grounding of the battery negative terminal or regulator base.

4. Polarize the generator with the battery by momentarily connecting a jumper wire between the battery positive terminal and the regulator no. 61 terminal or the generator "D+" insulated brush (depending on which component or wiring has been worked on). Do this before running the engine as otherwise the relay points may be burned. Repeat step one and go on to step five if the generator does not charge.

5. Remove the wire from the regulator "DF" terminal (after turning off the bike) and place it so it can't make contact with the terminal. Disconnect the negative ammeter lead from the no. 61 terminal and start and run the engine as described in step one. While the engine is running, connect the negative lead of the ammeter to the positive terminal of the battery, and connect the red regulator wire to the regulator base or any other ground on the motorcycle. Observe the ammeter and keep these connections in place only as long as is necessary to get a reading or the battery will discharge through the generator since these connections completely bypass the regulator. If the ammeter shows either no charge or one which is erratic and very low, the trouble is in the generator.

6. Inspect the brushes for a worn or damaged condition and replace them as necessary. At least clean them with trichloroethylene or a suitable solvent such as clean white gasoline. Polish the commutator with no. 00 sandpaper and blow the assembly clear. Recheck the output as in the above step and proceed to disassemble the generator as described earlier in this chapter if the generator is still not working properly, and go onto the next section.

Testing the Voltage Regulator

Perform the following tests to make sure the regulator is operating correctly. All tests should be made with the engine

BULB CHART

Model	Lamp Description	Candle Power (cp) or Wattage (w)	H-D Part Number
M-50, M-65 1965-69, 1970 and later	Headlight	20 w	67716-65
	Taillight	5 w	68165-47
	Stoplight	18 w	68165-47
	Headlight	20/20 w	67717-70PA
M-125 1968-69, 1970 and later	Headlight	28/28 w	67716-68P
	High-Beam Light	1.5 w	71093-67P
	Speedometer Light	1.5 w	71093-67P
	Taillight	5 w	68165-57
	Stoplight	18 w	68165-47
	Headlight	20/30 w	67716-68
MSR	Headlight	30/30 w	67716-68
	Taillight	5 w	68160-69P
	Stoplight	18 w	68160-69P
MC	Headlight	20/20 w	67717-70PA
	Taillight	5 w	68160-69P
	Stoplight	18 w	68160-69P
165	Headlight	21/32 cp	67750-59
	Taillight	3 cp	68165-47
	Stoplight	21 cp	68165-47
	Speedometer Light	1.5 cp	71090-47
	Parking Light	3 cp	68165-15
	Fender Light	2 cp	68462-49
B Models	Headlight	21/21 cp	67751-47
	Taillight	3 cp	68165-47
	Stoplight	21 cp	68165-47
Sprint 1969 and earlier,	Headlight	40/45 w	67717-59
1970 and later	Headlight	30/30 w	67716-68
	Taillight	3 cp	68165-47
	Stoplight	21 cp	68165-47
	Generator Light		
1968 and earlier	High-Beam Indicator Light	5 cp	67291-61P
1963 and earlier	Speedometer Light	5 cp	67291-61P
	Model SS Instrument Panel Lights	3 w	71093-67

at its normal operating temperature and all the lights and accessories turned off. If the regulator proves to be defective in these or in the previous "Generating System" tests, it must be replaced.

1. Connect the voltmeter positive lead to the regulator's "B+" terminal, and ground the negative lead.

2. Run the engine at about 3500 revolutions per minute (rpm) or about 30 mph road speed, with the regulator cover in place, and read the voltmeter.

3. A properly operating regulator will read 7.0–7.5 V.

4. An overactive regulator will read above 7.5 V and will damage the battery by overcharging it.

5. A tired regulator will read below 7.0 V and will constantly allow the battery to discharge.

Testing the Field Coils

Perform the following tests with the generator frame in place after disconnecting the red and white wires from the regulator terminals, and removing the positive brush (the brush connected to the same terminal as the white wire) from the generator frame. The testing procedures are the same as in the "Generator (Model 165)" section earlier in this chapter, except that the complete field circuit should draw 4.4–4.8 amps for 1961–62 C models at 6 V and 2.0–2.2 amps at the same voltage for 1963–66 C models and 1962 and later SS models. In step six, the reading should be the same as those given here instead of being different as they are for the Model 165.

Testing the Armature

Consult the "Generator (Model 165)" section.

Repairing the Commutator

Consult the "Generator (Model 165)" section.

Wiring Diagrams

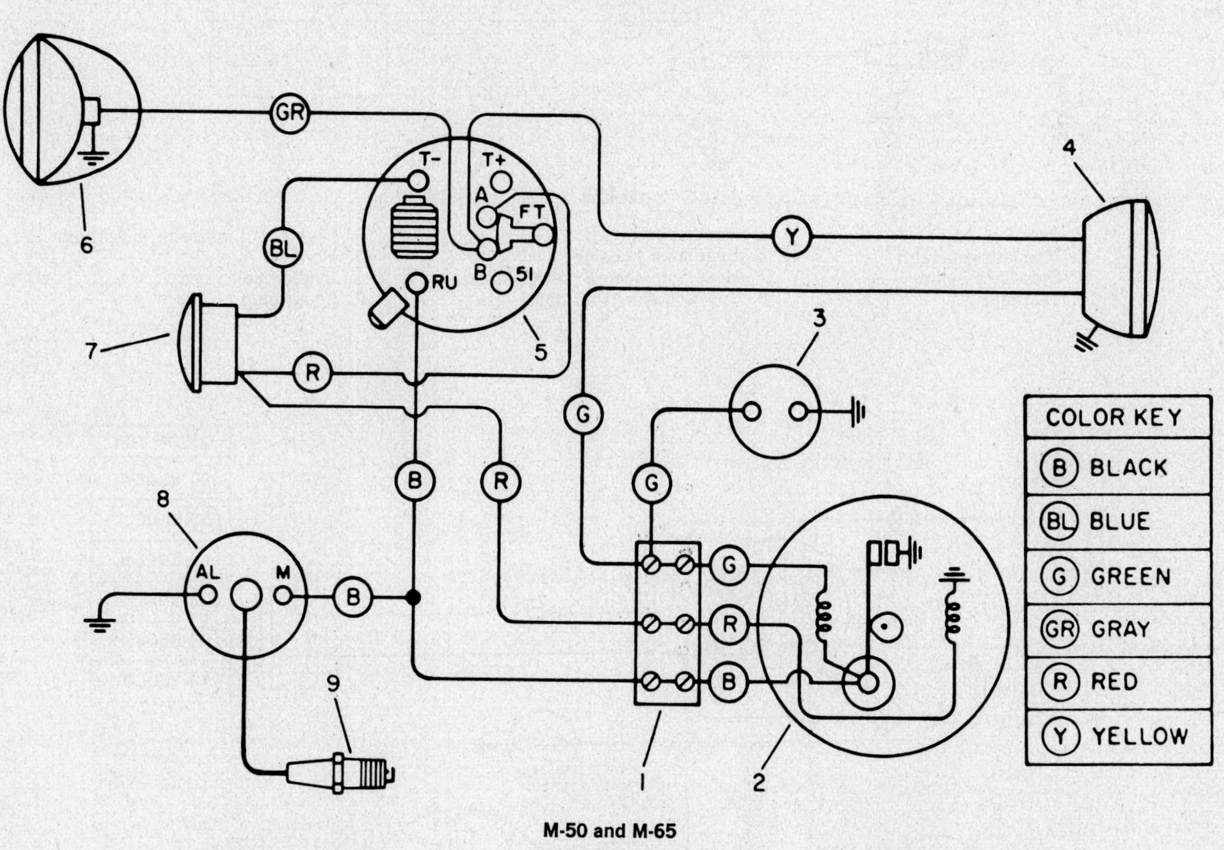

M-50 and M-65

1. Terminal plate
2. Magneto-generator
3. Stop-light switch
4. Tail light
5. Handlebar switches
6. Head lamp
7. Horn
8. Ignition coil
9. Spark plug

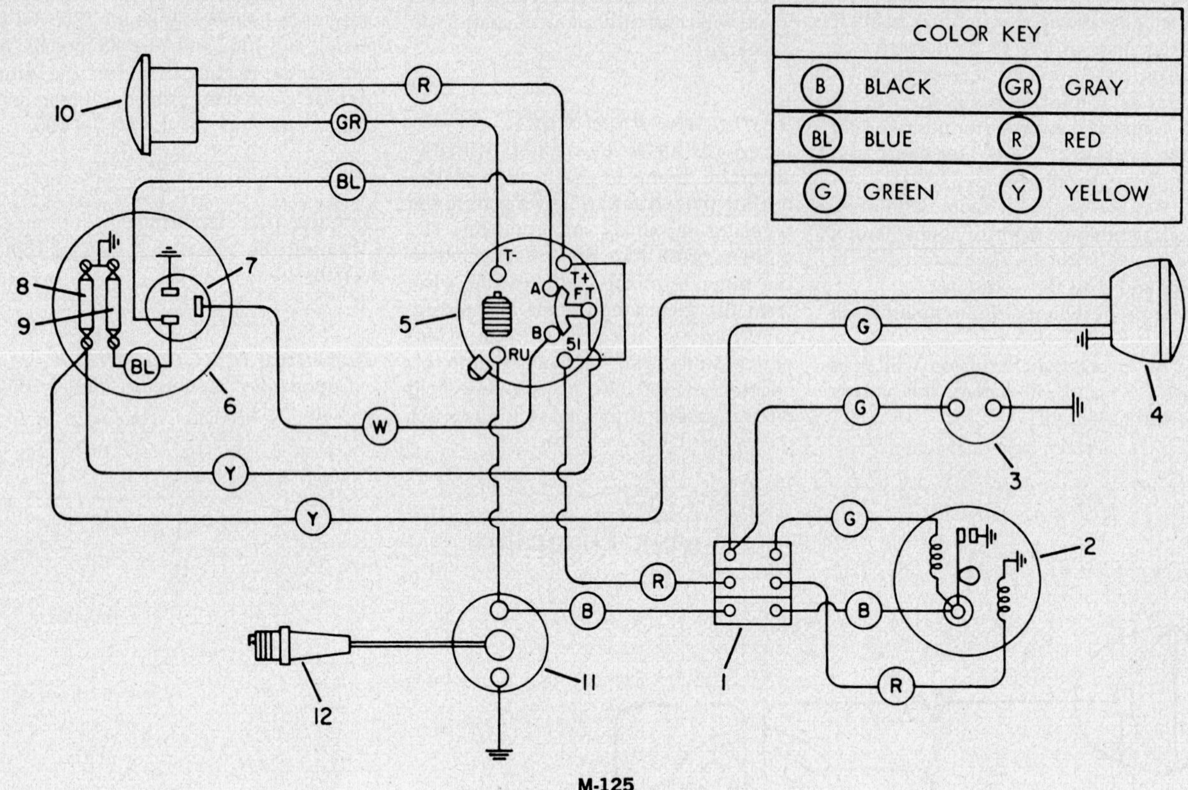

M-125

1. Terminal board
2. Magneto generator
3. Stop-light switch
4. Tail light
5. Handlebar switch
6. Headlamp housing
7. Headlamp sealed unit connector
8. Speedometer lamp bulb
9. High beam indicator lamp bulb
10. Horn
11. Ignition coil
12. Spark plug

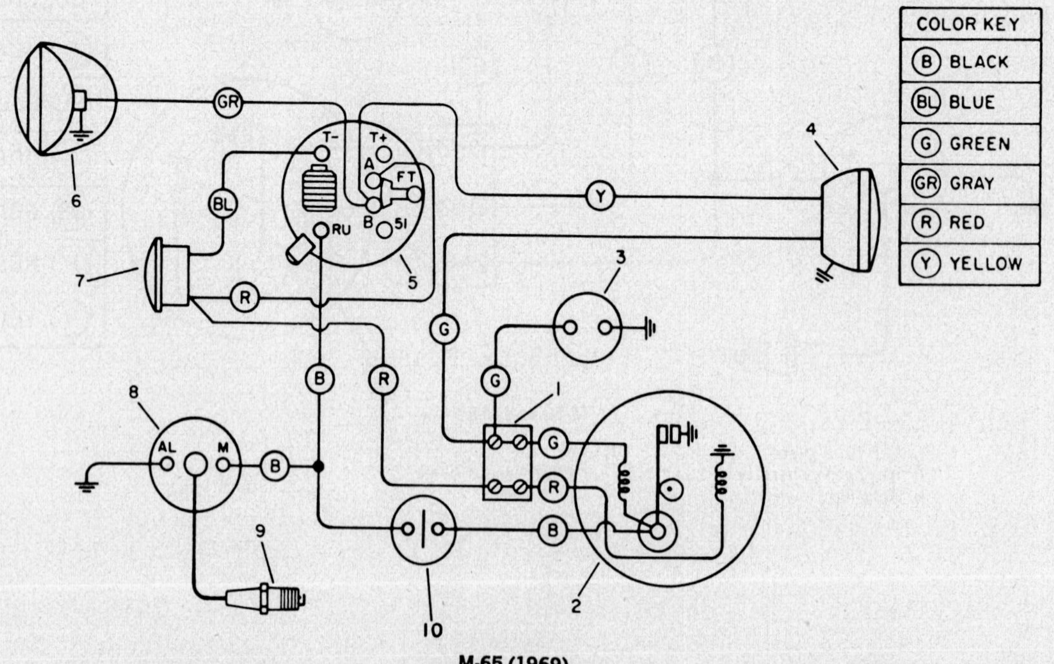

M-65 (1969)

1. Terminal plate
2. Magneto-generator
3. Stop-light switch
4. Tail light
5. Handlebar switches
6. Head lamp
7. Horn
8. Ignition coil
9. Spark plug
10. Ignition switch

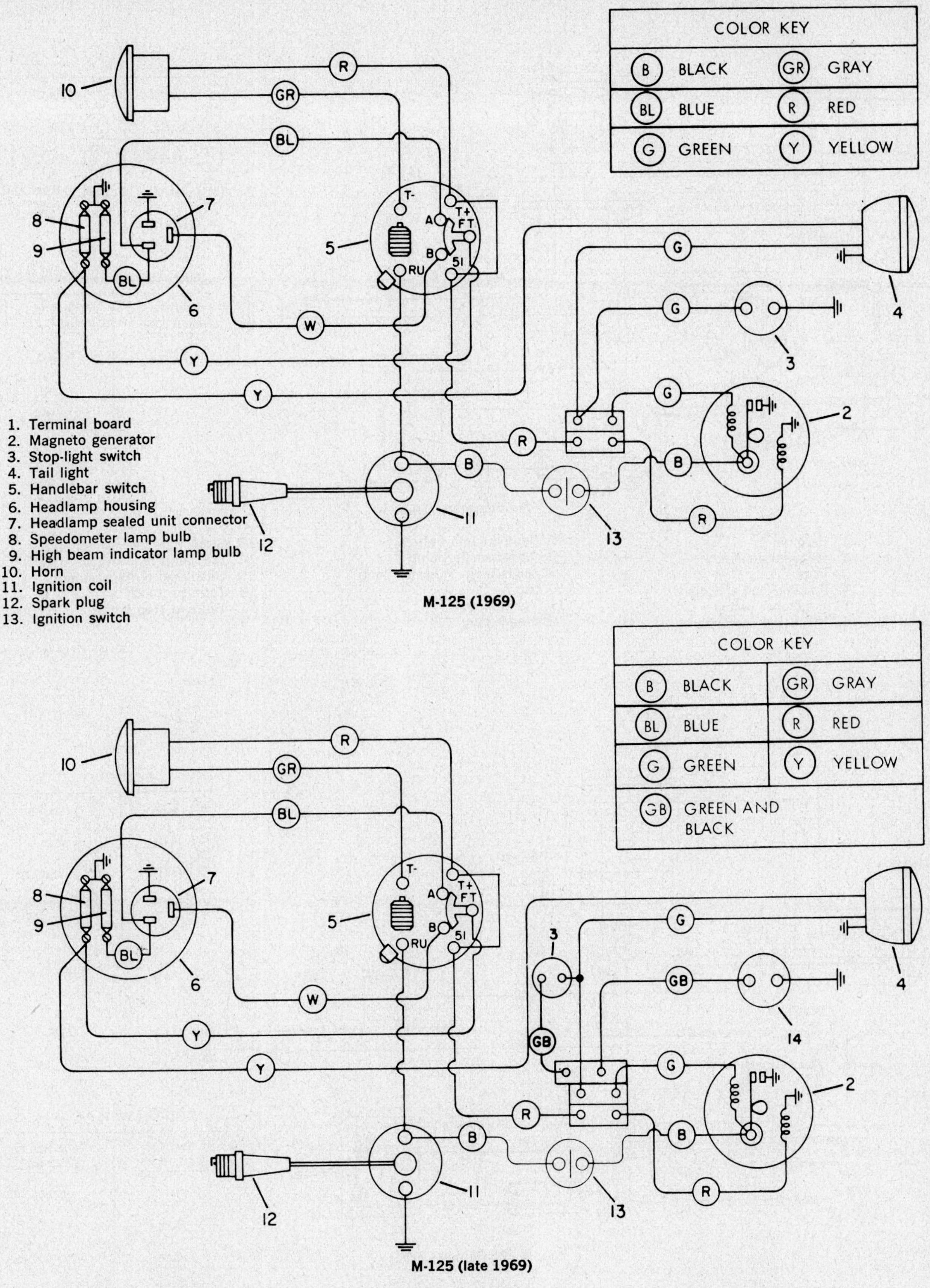

M-125 (1969)

M-125 (late 1969)

1. Terminal board
2. Magneto generator
3. Front stop light switch
4. Tail light
5. Handlebar switch
6. Headlamp housing
7. Headlamp sealed unit connector
8. Speedometer lamp bulb
9. High beam indicator lamp bulb
10. Horn
11. Ignition coil
12. Spark plug
13. Ignition switch
14. Rear stop light switch

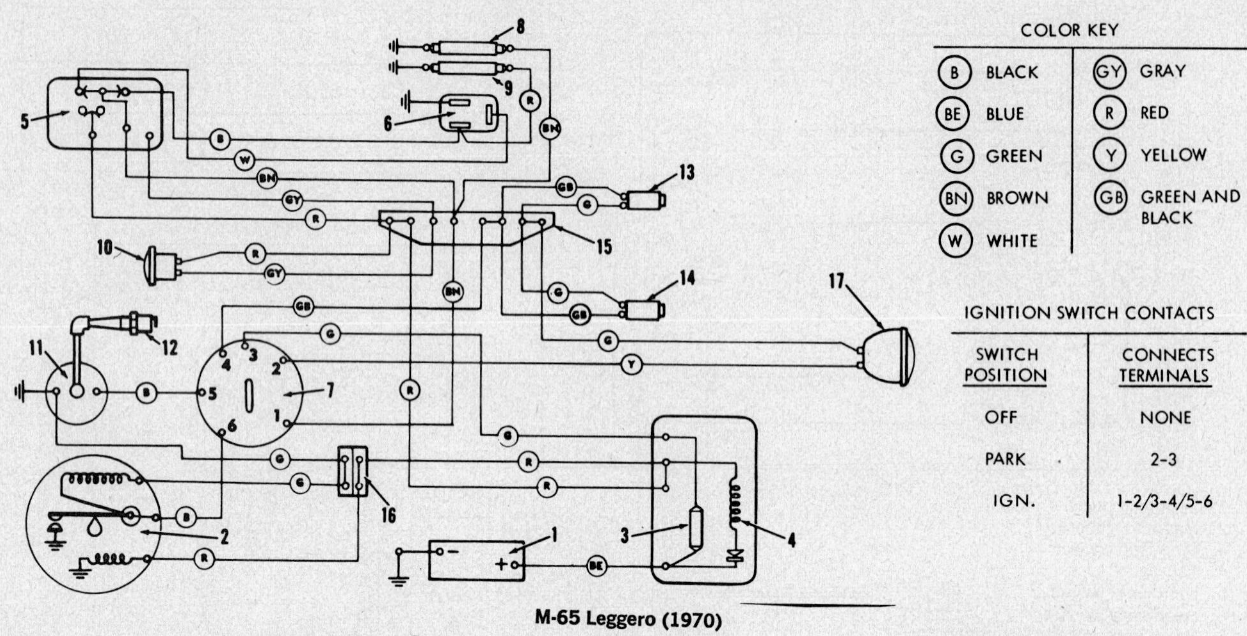

COLOR KEY

B	BLACK	GY	GRAY
BE	BLUE	R	RED
G	GREEN	Y	YELLOW
BN	BROWN	GB	GREEN AND BLACK
W	WHITE		

IGNITION SWITCH CONTACTS

SWITCH POSITION	CONNECTS TERMINALS
OFF	NONE
PARK	2-3
IGN.	1-2/3-4/5-6

M-65 Leggero (1970)

1. Battery
2. Magneto generator
3. Fuse
4. Rectifier coil and diode
5. Handlebar switch
6. Headlamp connector
7. Ignition-light switch
8. Speedometer lamp
9. High beam indicator lamp
10. Horn
11. Ignition coil
12. Spark plug
13. Stoplamp front switch
14. Stoplamp rear switch
15. Headlamp terminal board
16. Terminal block
17. Tail and stop lamp

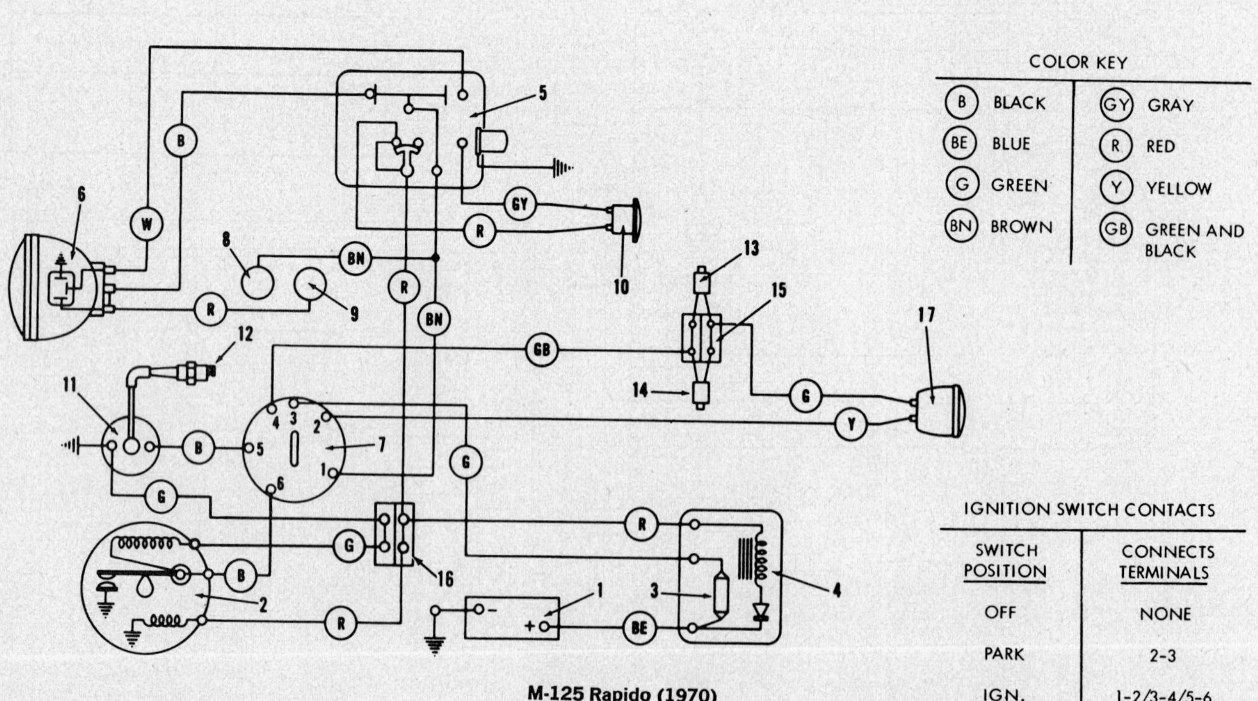

COLOR KEY

B	BLACK	GY	GRAY
BE	BLUE	R	RED
G	GREEN	Y	YELLOW
BN	BROWN	GB	GREEN AND BLACK

IGNITION SWITCH CONTACTS

SWITCH POSITION	CONNECTS TERMINALS
OFF	NONE
PARK	2-3
IGN.	1-2/3-4/5-6

M-125 Rapido (1970)

1. Battery
2. Magneto generator
3. Fuse
4. Rectifier coil and diode
5. Handlebar switch
6. Headlamp
7. Ignition-light switch
8. Speedometer lamp
9. High beam indicator lamp
10. Horn
11. Ignition coil
12. Spark plug
13. Stoplamp front switch
14. Stoplamp rear switch
15. Terminal block
16. Terminal block
17. Tail and stoplamp

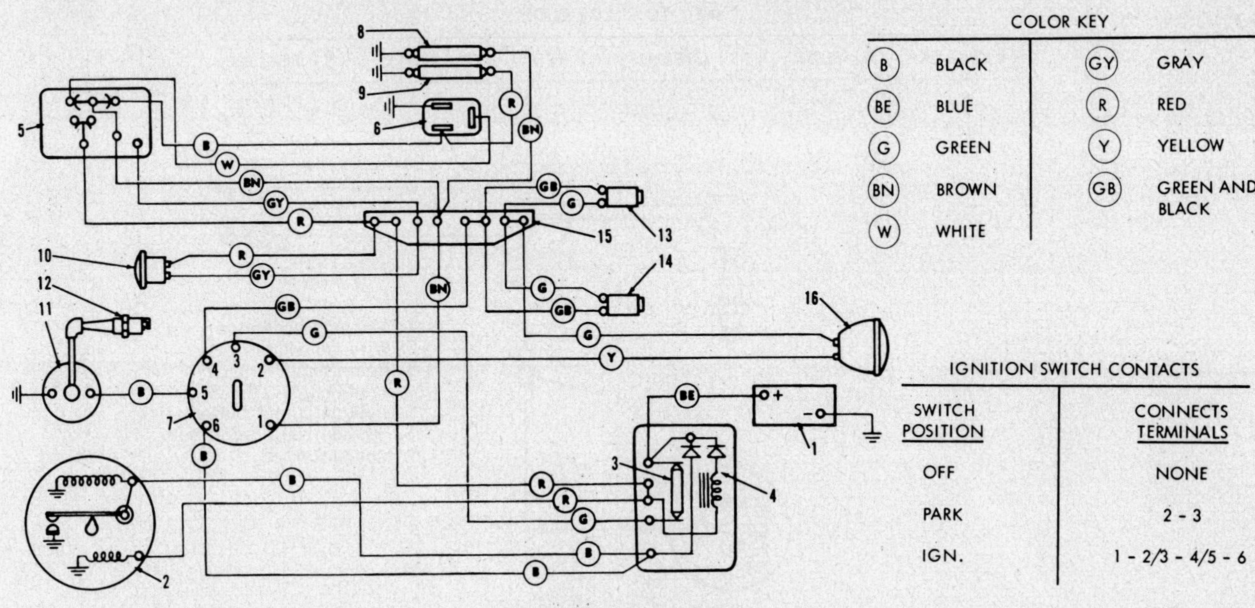

M-65 Leggero (1971)

1. Battery
2. Magneto
3. Fuse
4. Rectifier coil and diode
5. Handlebar switch
6. Headlamp connector
7. Ignition-light switch
8. Speedometer lamp
9. High beam indicator lamp
10. Horn
11. Ignition coil
12. Spark plug
13. Stoplamp front switch
14. Stoplamp rear switch
15. Headlamp terminal board
16. Tail lamp

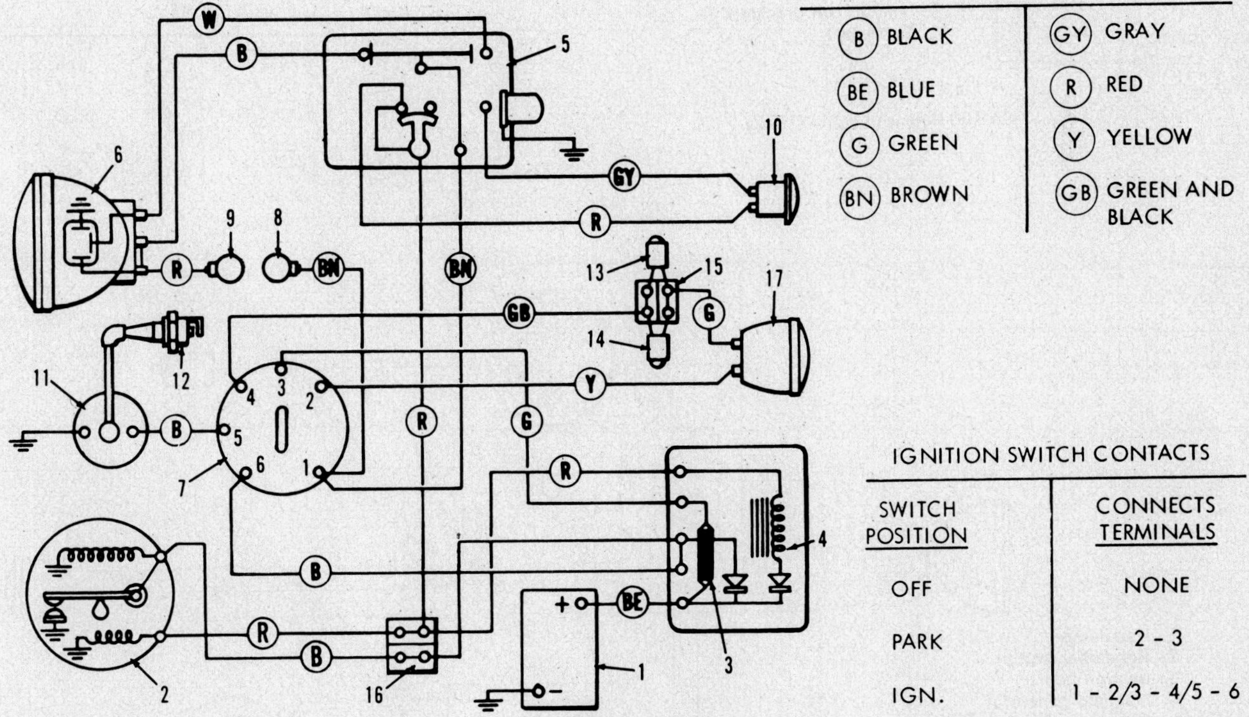

M-125 Rapido (1971)

1. Battery
2. Magneto generator
3. Fuse
4. Rectifier coil and diode
5. Handlebar switch
6. Headlamp
7. Ignition-light switch
8. Speedometer lamp
9. High beam indicator lamp
10. Horn
11. Ignition coil
12. Spark plug
13. Stoplamp front switch
14. Stoplamp rear switch
15. Terminal block
16. Terminal block
17. Tail lamp

KEY TO COLOR CODE

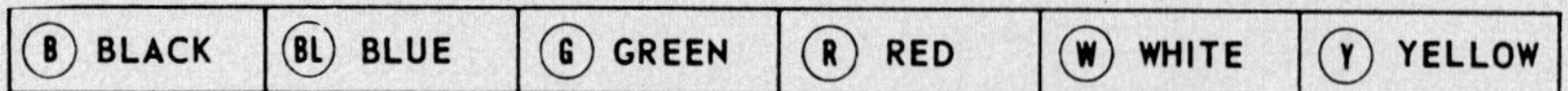

(B) BLACK	(BL) BLUE	(G) GREEN	(R) RED	(W) WHITE	(Y) YELLOW

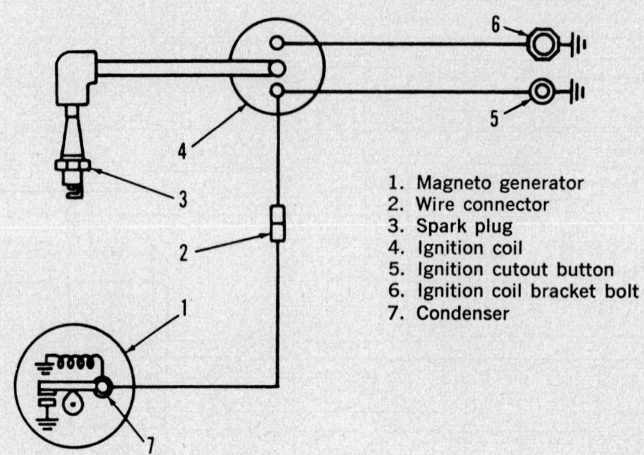

MSR-100 Baja (1970-1971)

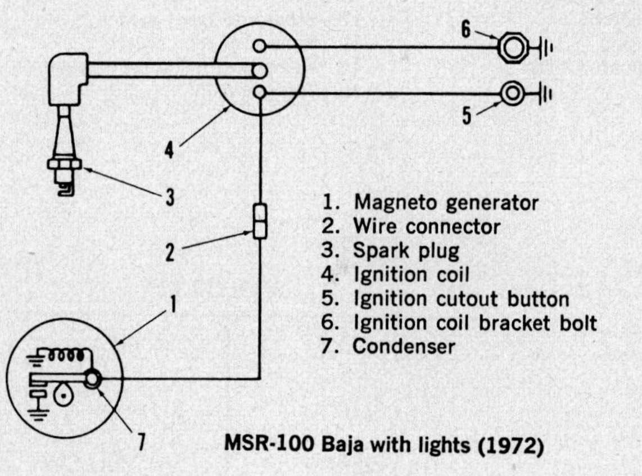

MSR-100 Baja with lights (1972)

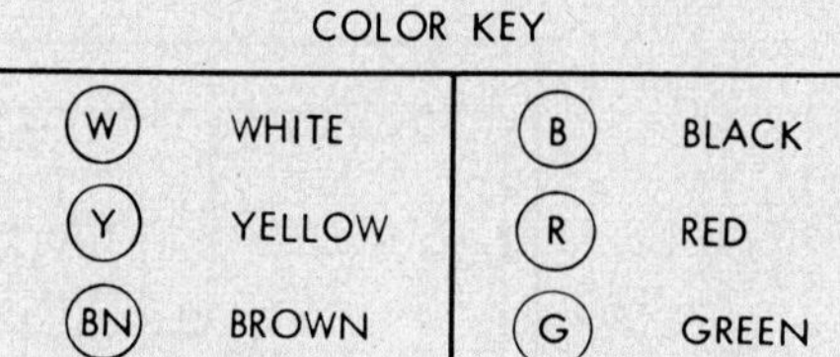

COLOR KEY

(W)	WHITE	(B)	BLACK
(Y)	YELLOW	(R)	RED
(BN)	BROWN	(G)	GREEN

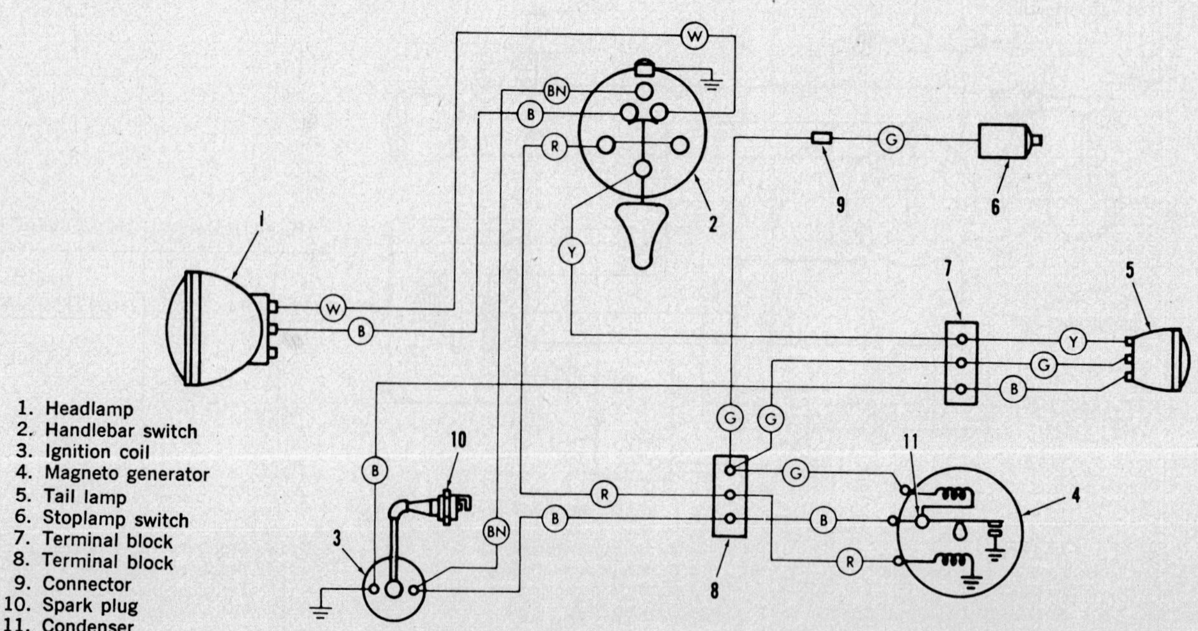

MSR-100 Baja without lights (1972)

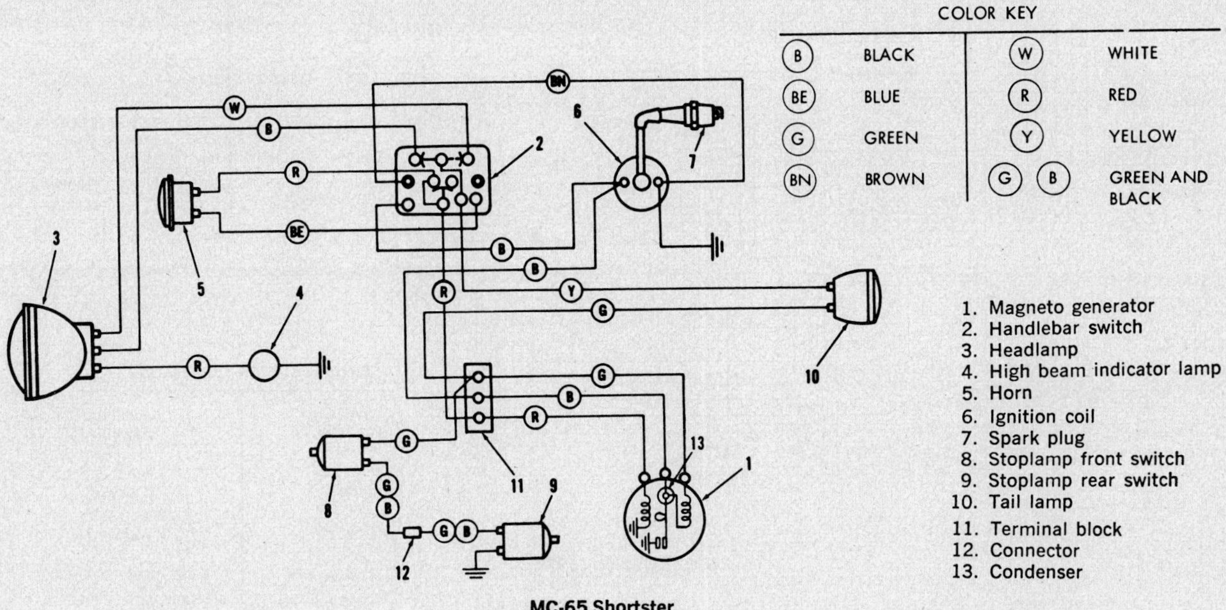

MC-65 Shortster

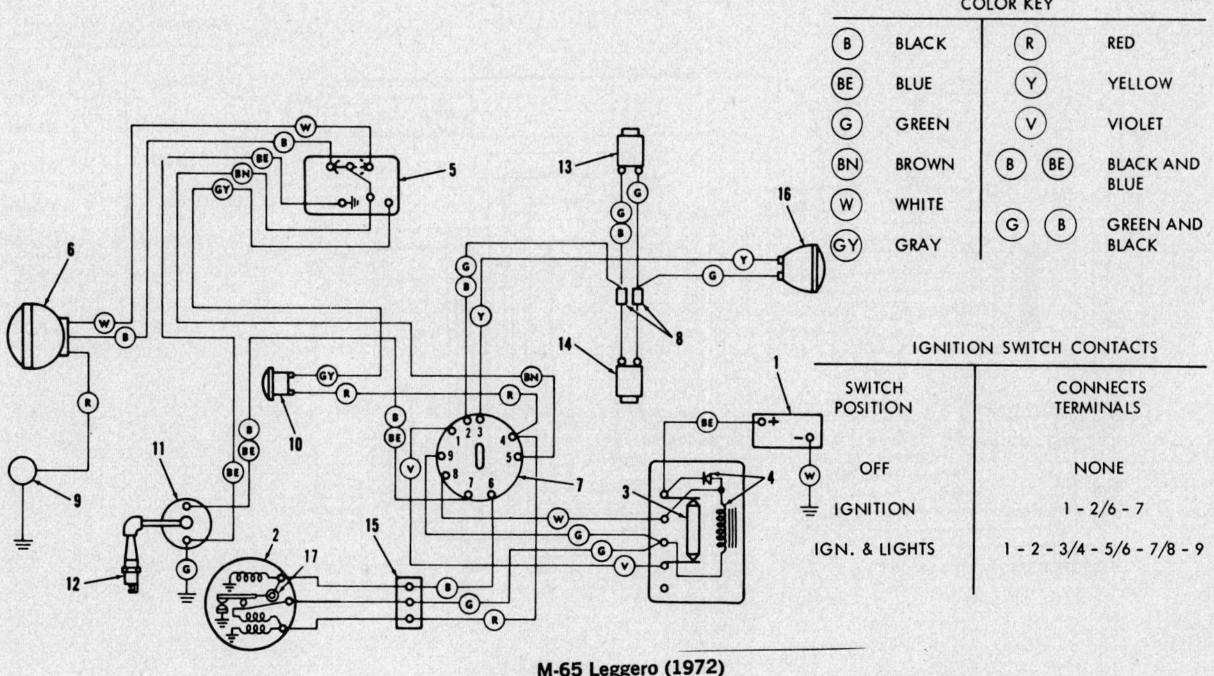

IGNITION SWITCH CONTACTS

SWITCH POSITION	CONNECTS TERMINALS
OFF	NONE
IGNITION	1 - 2/6 - 7
IGN. & LIGHTS	1 - 2 - 3/4 - 5/6 - 7/8 - 9

M-65 Leggero (1972)

1. Battery
2. Magneto generator
3. Fuse
4. Rectifier coil and diode
5. Handlebar switch
6. Headlamp
7. Ignition-light switch
8. Connector (2)
9. High beam indicator lamp
10. Horn
11. Ignition coil
12. Spark plug
13. Stoplamp front switch
14. Stoplamp rear switch
15. Terminal block
16. Tail lamp
17. Condenser

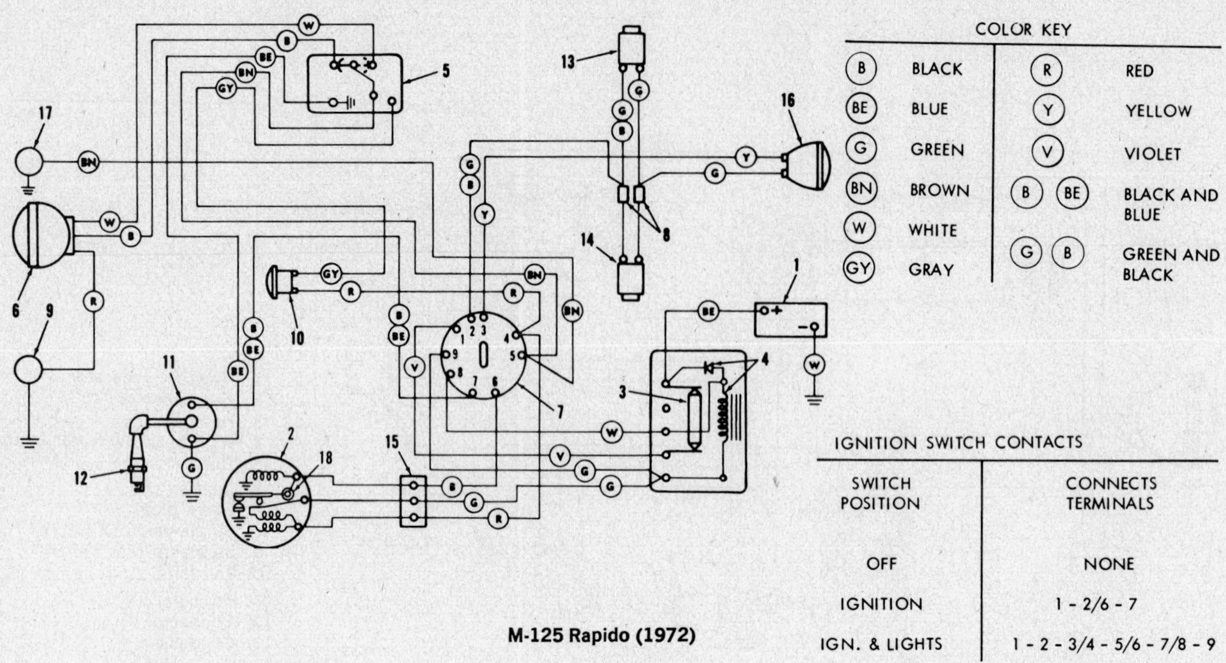

IGNITION SWITCH CONTACTS

SWITCH POSITION	CONNECTS TERMINALS
OFF	NONE
IGNITION	1 - 2/6 - 7
IGN. & LIGHTS	1 - 2 - 3/4 - 5/6 - 7/8 - 9

M-125 Rapido (1972)

1. Battery
2. Magneto generator
3. Fuse
4. Rectifier coil and diode
5. Handlebar switch
6. Headlamp
7. Ignition-light switch
8. Connector (2)
9. High beam indicator lamp
10. Horn
11. Ignition coil
12. Spark plug
13. Stoplamp front switch
14. Stoplamp rear switch
15. Terminal block
16. Tail lamp
17. Speedometer lamp
18. Condenser

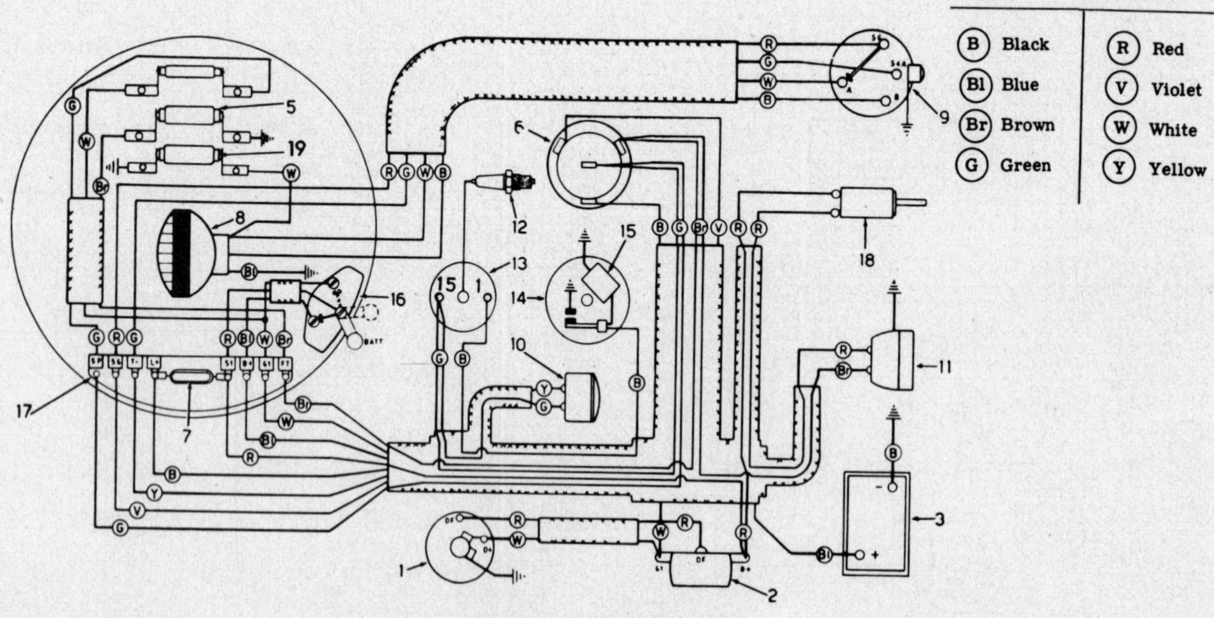

Sprint C and H (1964-1966)

1. Generator
2. Regulator
3. Battery (6v.)
4. Warning lamp (1.5 watts)
5. Speedometer lamp (3 watts)
6. Ignition-light switch
7. Fuse (20 A)
8. Headlamp unit
9. Headlamp dimmer and horn switch
10. Horn
11. Tail and stop lamp
12. Spark plug
13. H.T. ignition coil
14. Circuit breaker
15. Condenser
16. Emergency starting switch (1964 & earlier)
17. Terminal board
18. Stoplight switch
19. High beam indicator lamp (late 1966)

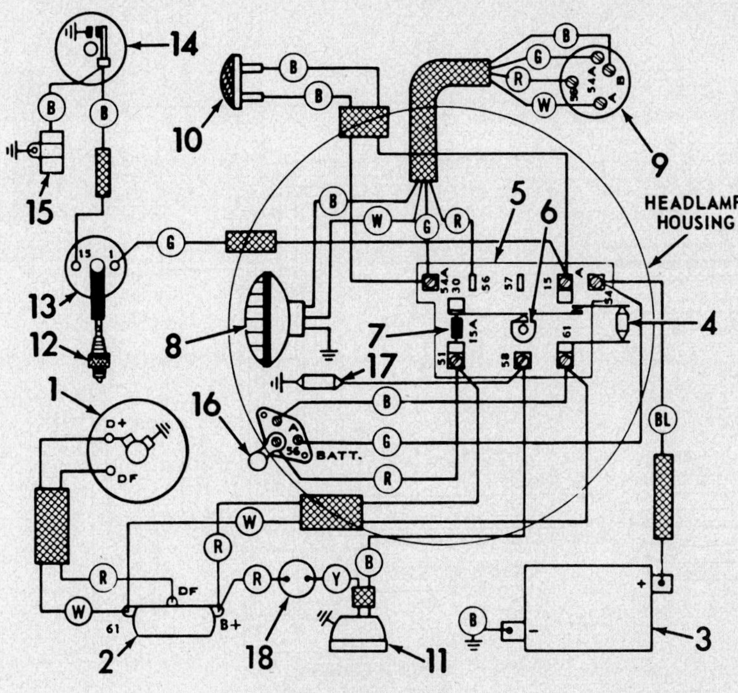

Sprint (1961-1962)

1. Generator
2. Regulator
3. Battery (6v.)
4. Warning lamp (1.5 watts)
5. Ignition-light switch board
6. Ignition-light switch
7. Fuse (20 A)
8. Headlamp unit
9. Headlamp dimmer and horn switch
10. Horn
11. Tail and stop lamp
12. Spark plug
13. Ignition coil
14. Circuit breaker
15. Condenser
16. Emergency starting switch
17. Speedometer lamp
18. Stoplight switch
19. Terminal board

B	BLACK
BL	BLUE
G	GREEN
R	RED
W	WHITE
GR	GREY
BR	BROWN
Y	YELLOW

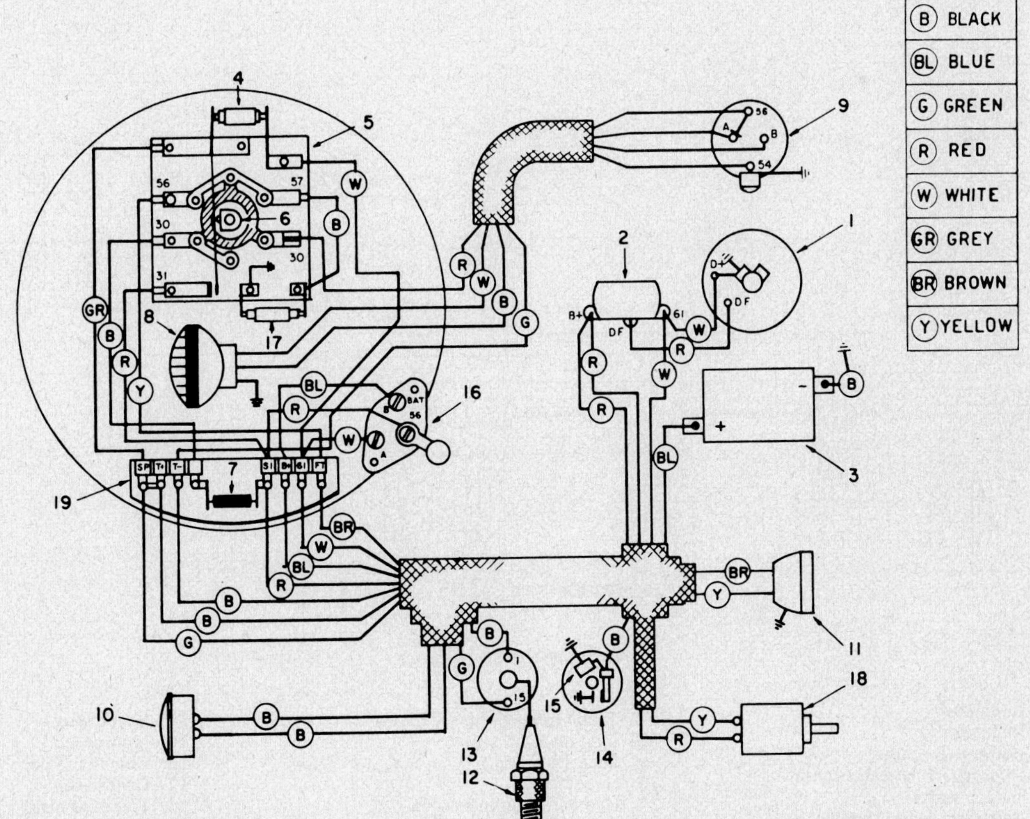

Sprint H (1962), Sprint C and H (1963)

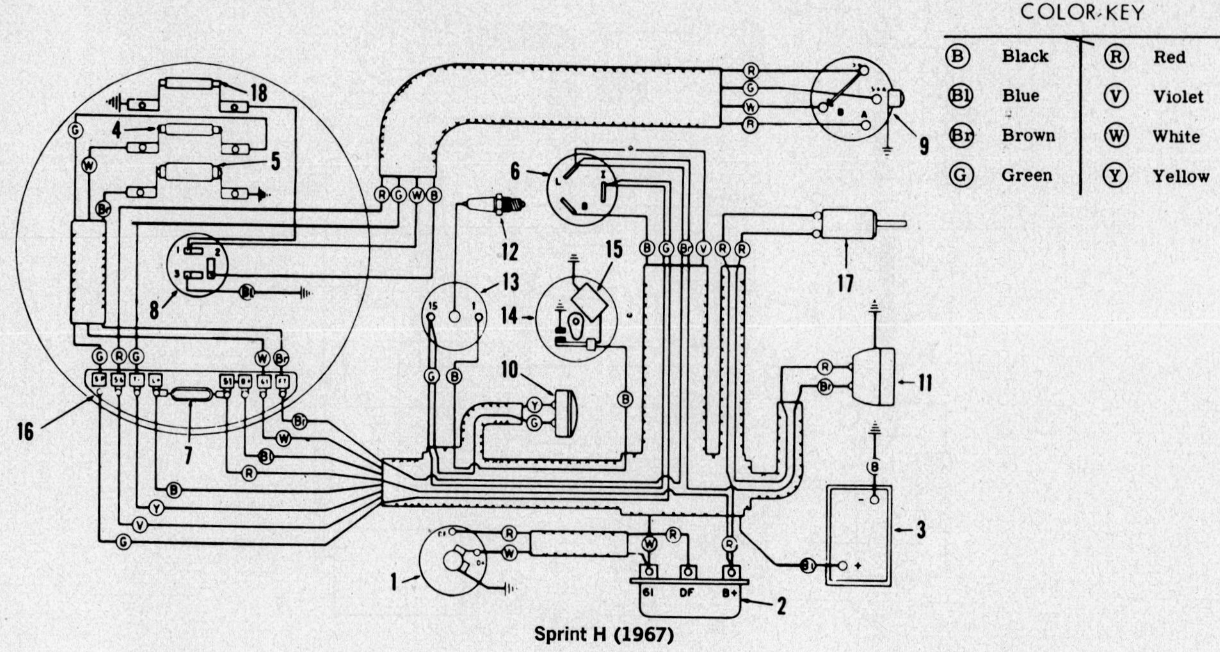

Sprint H (1967)

1. Generator
2. Regulator
3. Battery (6 volt)
4. Warning lamp (1.5 watts)
5. Speedometer lamp (3 watts)
6. Ignition-light switch
7. Fuse (20 A)
8. Headlamp unit
9. Headlamp dimmer and horn switch
10. Horn
11. Tail and stop lamp
12. Spark plug
13. H.T. ignition coil
14. Circuit breaker
15. Condenser
16. Terminal board
17. Stoplight switch
18. High beam indicator lamp (1.5 watt)

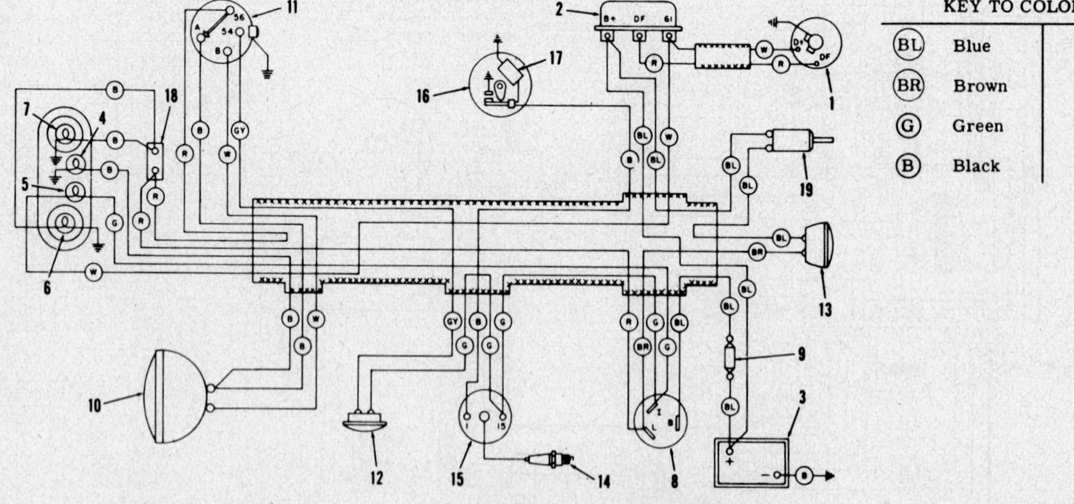

Sprint SS (1967-1968)

1. Generator
2. Regulator
3. Battery (6 volts)
4. High beam indicator lamp (1.5 watts)
5. Generator warning lamp (1.5 watts)
6. Speedometer lamp (3 watts)
7. Tachometer lamp (3 watts)
8. Ignition-light switch
9. Fuse (20 amp.)
10. Headlamp
11. Headlamp dimmer and horn switch
12. Horn
13. Tail and stop lamp
14. Spark plug
15. Ignition coil
16. Circuit breaker
17. Condenser
18. Terminal strip
19. Stoplight switch

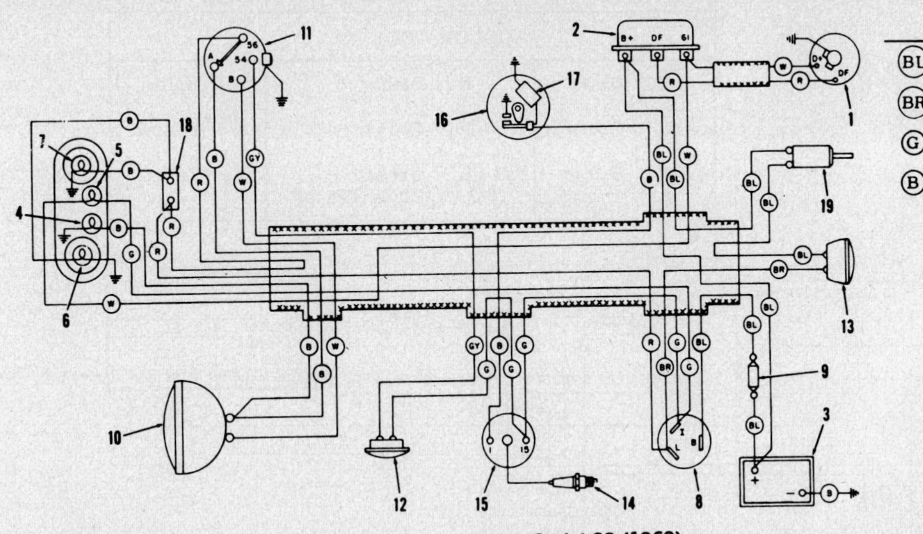

KEY TO COLOR CODE

BL	Blue	GY	Gray
BR	Brown	R	Red
G	Green	W	White
B	Black		

Sprint SS (1969)

1. Generator
2. Regulator
3. Battery (6 volts)
4. High beam indicator lamp (1.5 watts)
5. Generator warning lamp (1.5 watts)
6. Speedometer lamp (3 watts)
7. Tachometer lamp (3 watts)
8. Ignition-light switch
9. Fuse (15 amp.)
10. Headlamp
11. Headlamp dimmer and horn switch
12. Horn
13. Tail and stop lamp
14. Spark plug
15. Ignition coil
16. Circuit breaker
17. Condenser
18. Terminal strip
19. Stoplight switch

COLOR CODE KEY					
BL	Blue	B	Black	W	White
G	Green	R	Red	Y	Yellow
BR	Brown	G B	Green Black Tracer	V	Violet

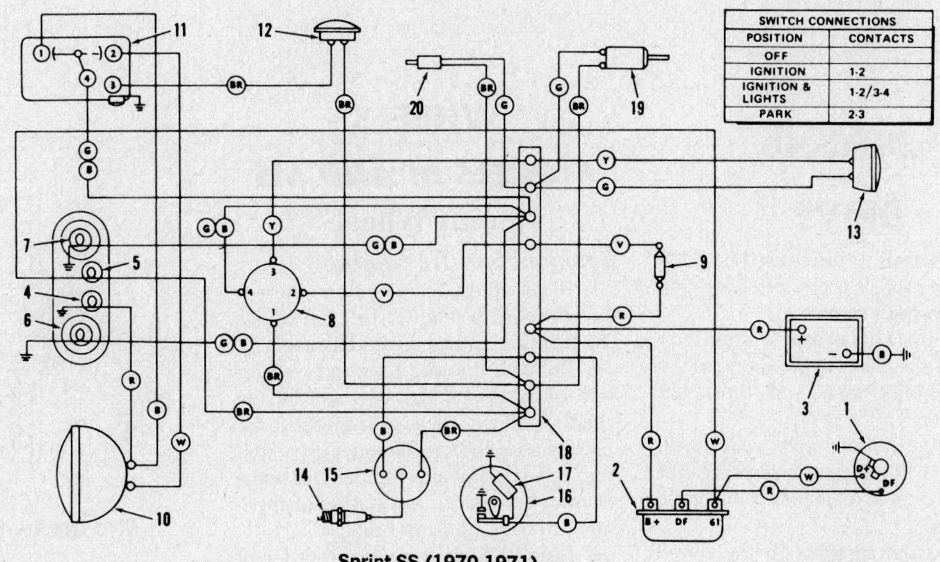

Sprint SS (1970-1971)

1. Generator
2. Regulator
3. Battery (6 volts)
4. High beam indicator lamp (1.5 watts)
5. Generator warning lamp 1.5 watts)
6. Speedometer lamp (3 watts)
7. Tachometer lamp (3 watts)
8. Ignition-light switch
9. Fuse (15 amp.)
10. Headlamp
11. Headlamp dimmer and horn switch
12. Horn
13. Tail and stop lamp
14. Spark plug
15. Ignition coil
16. Circuit breaker
17. Condenser
18. Terminal block
19. Stoplight rear switch
20. Stoplight front switch

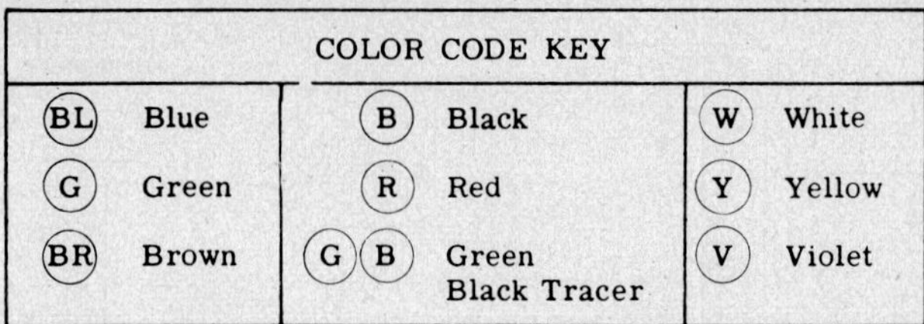

COLOR CODE KEY					
(BL)	Blue	(B)	Black	(W)	White
(G)	Green	(R)	Red	(Y)	Yellow
(BR)	Brown	(G)(B)	Green Black Tracer	(V)	Violet

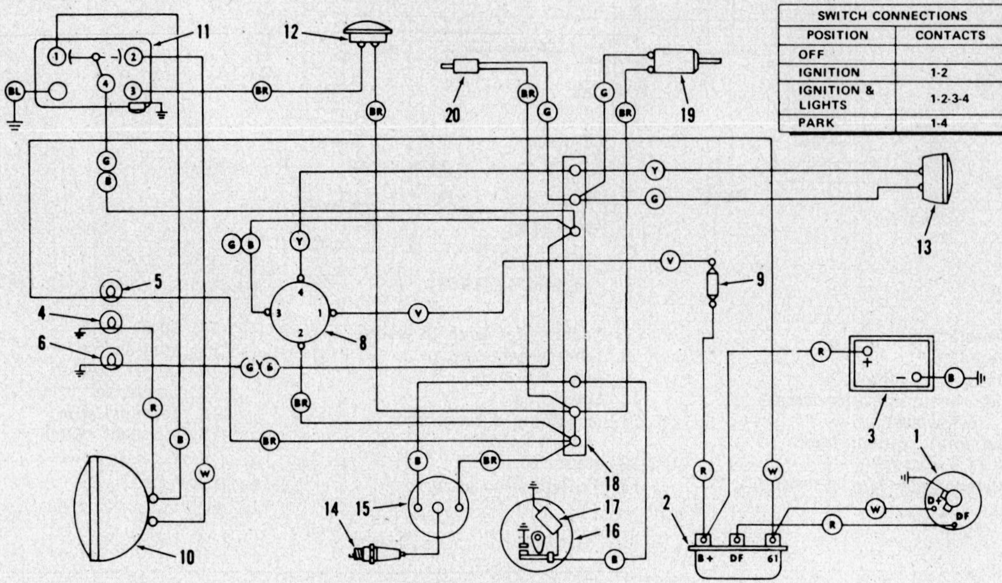

SWITCH CONNECTIONS	
POSITION	CONTACTS
OFF	
IGNITION	1-2
IGNITION & LIGHTS	1-2-3-4
PARK	1-4

Sprint SX (1971-1972), Sprint SS (1972)

1. Generator
2. Regulator
3. Battery (6 volts)
4. High beam indicator lamp (1.5 watts)
5. Generator warning lamp (1.5 watts)
6. Speedometer lamp (3 watts)
7.
8. Ignition-light switch
9. Fuse (15 amp.)
10. Headlamp
11. Headlamp dimmer and horn switch
12. Horn
13. Tail and stop lamp
14. Spark plug
15. Ignition coil
16. Circuit breaker
17. Condenser
18. Terminal block
19. Stoplight rear switch
20. Stoplight front switch

CHASSIS

DRIVE

The large trail sprocket used on 1970 and later M Models is put into operation in the following manner:

1. Disconnect the master link and wire the ends of the chain to the frame so the chain does not come off the front sprocket.
2. Remove the four bolts which hold the sprocket dowel pins in place against the standard sprocket and disconnect the drive chain.
3. Rotate the sprocket so the dowel pins seat in their respective holes in the standard sprocket, and secure the four bolts.
4. Add a short length of chain to the standard chain and secure the master link.
5. Adjust the chain and rear brake as described under "Maintenance Items".

WHEELS

MODELS M AND MS

Front Wheel

Removal and Installation

1. Block up the motorcycle so there is enough room to remove the front wheel. The machine must be well balanced.
2. Remove the axle nuts and washers from both sides of the axle, and let the wheel slip down and away from the forks.
3. Remove the speedometer drive unit from the axle and also remove the brake securing nut, spacer, and washer (if applicable) to free the front brake.
4. Installation is the reverse order of removal, taking care to have the sideplate slot straddle the fork side anchor boss.
5. Install the speedometer drive unit, then mount the wheel in the fork and secure it with the washers and nuts, taking care to seat the axle correctly in the fork side slots.

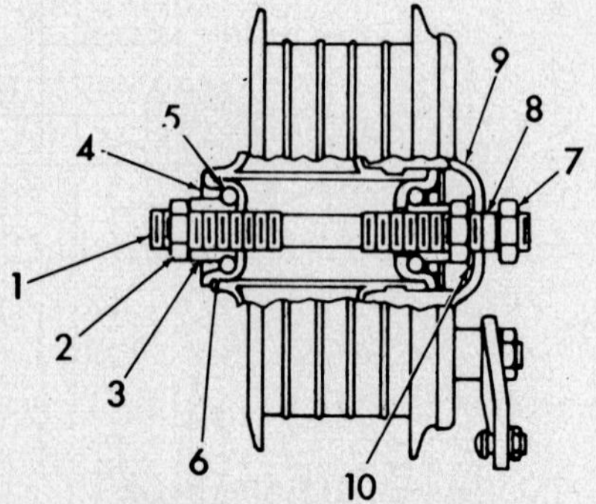

Cone type bearing assembly

1. Axle
2. Locknut
3. Bearing cone
4. Dust cover
5. Ball bearings
6. Bearing cup
7. Outer locknut, brake side
8. Outer spacer, brake side
9. Brake sideplate
10. Inner washer, brake side

6. Adjust the front brake and check the axle nuts for tightness. A light application of a thread sealant isn't a bad idea since those axle nuts are all that's holding the front wheel on.

Front Hub Disassembly

CONE TYPE BEARINGS

1.Remove the front wheel as described in the above section, loosen the locknut and bearing cone, and slip the axle from the hub.

2. Remove both sets of bearings, inspect the bearing cups for a worn, scored, or damaged condition, and, if they are in need of replacement, tap them out.

3. Inspect the dust covers for a worn or damaged condition and remove them only if in need of replacement.

RETAINED BALL TYPE BEARINGS

1. Remove the locknut, spacer, brake side-plate, and inner spacer to free the axle, and remove the axle with the left-side locknut, dust shield, and spacer.

2. Carefully pry the felt seal retainers from the hub with a suitable screwdriver, and remove the felts and washers.

3. Tap the bearings out from their respective opposite sides, and remove the bearing spacer.

grease, install the bearings (11 to a side), and install the dust cover.

2. Slip the axle into place, and replace the bearing cones and locknuts.

3. Adjust the bearings as described under "Maintenance Items."

RETAINED BALL TYPE BEARINGS

1. Install the spacer in the hub, then press the bearings into the hub until the outer races bottom on the hub shoulders.

2. Assemble the seal washers, felts, and the felt seal retainers to the hub. When tapping in the retainers, take care to do so evenly to avoid damaging them.

3. Continue the assembly procedure in the reverse order of disassembly.

Rear Wheel

Removal and Installation

1. Block up the rear wheel of the motorcycle so there is enough room to allow removal of the rear wheel. Make sure the machine is well balanced.

2. Disconnect the drive chain master link and wire the chain to the frame to keep it from coming off the front sprocket.

3. Remove the brake rod adjusting nut and disconnect the brake rod from the brake actuating lever.

1. Axle, front wheel
2. Locknut (2)
3. Spacer, sideplate outer
4. Brake sideplate
5. Spacer, sideplate inner
6. Washer, left side
7. Dust shield
8. Spacer, left side
9. Retainer, felt seal (2)
10. Felt seal (2)
11. Seal washer (2)
12. Ball bearing (2)
13. Spacer
14. Hub, front wheel

Retained ball bearing assembly

Inspection and Repair

1. Clean all parts in a suitable solvent and blow them dry.

2. Inspect all parts for a worn or damaged condition, paying particular attention to the cones, cups, and bearings. If any of the bearings are in need of replacement or if any are lost, they must be replaced as a complete set. Always repack the bearings in fresh grease before reinstallation in the hubs.

3. Inspect the brake shell and shoes for a worn, damaged, or glazed condition, and repair or replace them as directed in the "Brakes" section.

Front Hub Assembly

CONE TYPE BEARINGS

1. Carefully tap the bearing cups into place in the hub, pack them with fresh

4. Loosen the axle nuts and slip the wheel out and back of the frame along with the adjusting mechanism.

5. Install the wheel in the reverse order of removal, making sure that the wheel is aligned in the fork, and that the chain and rear brake are adjusted.

Rear Hub Disassembly

1. Consult the "Front Hub Disassembly" section.

2. Flatten the tab washer and remove the four nuts and bolts to remove the rear sprocket.

Inspection and Repair

1.Consult the "Front Hub Assembly" section.

Rear Hub Assembly

1. Consult the "Front Hub Assembly" section.

2. When replacing the sprocket, use a new tab washer.

MODELS ML, MLS, AND MSR

Front Wheel

Removal and Installation

1. Block up the motorcycle so there is enough room to remove the front wheel, making sure the machine is well balanced.

2. Remove the axle nut and washer, loosen the axle pinch bolt located on the left fork leg, and tap on the right side of the axle with a soft mallet to get the axle started out. Pull the axle the rest of the way out while holding the wheel steady with one hand.

3. Remove the speedometer drive unit from the left side and slip the wheel down and out of the forks.

4. Remove the brake side-plate and the wheel hub spacers.

5. Installation is basically the reverse order of removal.

6. Position the brake side-plate so the side-plate slot engages the fork leg anchor boss.

7. Slip the stepped spacer on the speedometer drive unit side and the thinner spacer on the brake side. Poisition the brake side-plate and the speedometer drive unit on the hub and slip a thin washer between the drive unit and the fork leg.

8. Juggle the wheel assembly into place as deftly as possible, and insert the axle from the left side. Secure the axle washer and nut on the right side, remove the bike from the blocks, and pump the forks up and down to center the fork legs.

9. Secure the axle pinch bolt and adjust the brake as described in the "Maintenance" chapter.

Front Hub Disassembly

1. Consult the "Model MC Front Hub Disassembly" section.

Inspection and Repair

1. Consult the "Model MC Inspection and Repair" section.

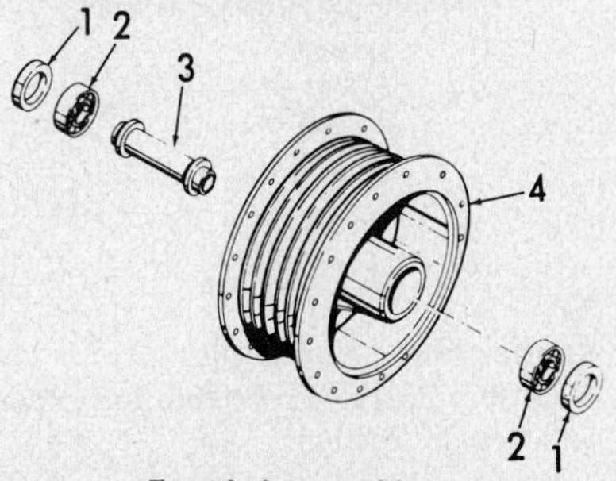

Front hub assembly

1. Dust cover (2)
2. Ball bearing (2)
3. Bearing spacer
4. Wheel hub

2. Inspect the felt seals on the inside of the dust covers for a dirty, worn, or damaged condition and replace them as necessary.

Front Hub Assembly

1. Consult the "Model MC Front Hub Assembly" section.

Rear Wheel

Removal and Installation

1. Block up the motorcycle so there is enough room to remove the wheel, making sure the machine is well balanced.
2. Remove the drive chain master link and wire the chain ends to the frame to keep the chain from coming off the front sprocket.
3. Remove the brake adjusting nut and remove the cable from the actuating lever.
4. Remove the axle nut, washer, adjusting cam, axle, and wheel. The axle may be tapped out with a soft mallet.
5. Installation is in the reverse order of removal.
6. Slip the shorter spacer into place between the brake side-plate and the right-side wheel bearing, and the longer spacer between the axle clip and the left-side wheel bearing. The brake side-plate slot must engage the fork anchor stud.
7. Secure the axle washer and nut and adjust the chain and brake as described under the "Maintenance items."

Rear Hub Disassembly

1. Consult the "Front Hub Disassembly" section.

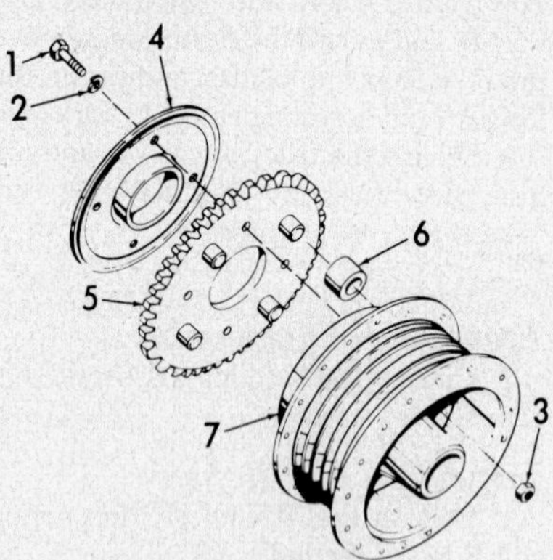

Rear hub and sprocket assembly

1. Bolt (4)
2. Lock washer (4)
3. Nut (3)
4. Outer disc
5. Sprocket
6. Rubber bushing (4)
7. Wheel hub

Inspection and Repair

1. Consult the "Front Hub Inspection and Repair" section.

Rear Hub Assembly

1. Consult the "Front Hub Assembly" section.

Rear Sprocket

Removal and Installation

1. Remove the rear wheel as described in the rear wheel "Removal and Installation" section.
2. Remove the hub bolts, lockwashers, nuts, and outer disc, and pull the sprocket and rubber bushings from the hub.
3. Clean all parts in a suitable solvent and blow them dry, then install the sprocket in the reverse order of removal.
4. Position the rubber bushings in the hub, place the sprocket in place so the dowel pins engage the bushings, position the outer disc, and secure the assembly with the nuts, lockwashers, and bolts.
5. Install the wheel and adjust the chain and brake as described under "Maintenance Items."

S AND B MODELS

Front Wheel

Removal and Installation

1. Block up the motorcycle so there is enough room to remove the front wheel, making sure the machine is well balanced.
2. Remove the cotter pin, washer, and clevis pin from the front brake lever, then remove the lower locknut and withdraw the cable.
3. Remove the speedometer drive grease fitting and pull the housing free of its socket to remove the cable. Do not lose the speedometer drive gear which is a slip fit on the speedometer cable and may come out with the cable.
4. Remove the axle nut and lockwasher, loosen the pinch bolt on the left side, tap out the axle with a soft mallet, and remove the wheel.
5. Repack the wheel bearings with fresh grease before replacing the wheel which is done in the reverse order of removal.
6. Make sure the brake side-plate torque pin engages the fork anchor stud.
7. Lubricate the speedometer drive unit and adjust the front brake as described under "Maintenance Items."

Front Hub Disassembly

1. Remove the front wheel as described in the above section.
2. Remove the bearing grease retainer, retainer felt seal, bearing inner race, and unscrew and remove the bearing locknut.
3. Carefully drift out the bearing with a suitable drift from the opposite side of the hub, if necessary, and remove the bearing spacer.
4. Invert the hub and drift out the needle bearing from the opposite side of the hub using a suitable drift.

Inspection and Repair

1. Clean all parts in a suitable solvent and blow them dry.
2. Inspect the bearings for a worn, pitted, burned, or damaged condition, excessive side or radial play, or rough motion and replace them as necessary.
3. Inspect the brake shell and shoes for a worn, scored, glazed, or otherwise damaged condition and replace or repair them as described in the "Brakes" section later in this chapter.
4. Inspect the speedometer drive gear for wear or damage, especially to the gear teeth. The Speedometer drive gear can be removed for replacement with Sprocket Shaft Extension Puller (H-D part no. 96015-56) or a suitable substitute, and the plug must allow sufficient clearance so the gear can move over it. Press the gear flush with the face of the hub when replacing it.

Front Hub Assembly

1. Pack the ball bearing in fresh grease and carefully press it into place in the hub until seated against the hub shoulder.
2. Install the bearing locknut, slip the bearing spacer into place, and press the needle bearing into place until seated against the remaining hub shoulder. When pressing on the bearing make sure only to press on the printed side.
3. Grease the bearing and insert the inner race, then install the grease retainer felt seal and the retainer.

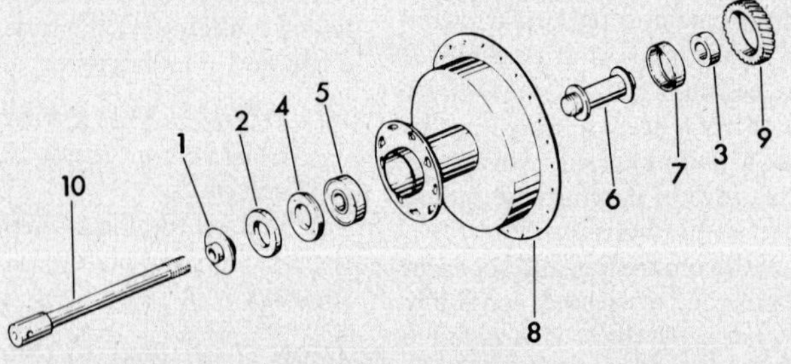

Front hub assembly

1. Bearing grease retainer
2. Grease retainer felt seal
3. Bearing inner race
4. Bearing locknut
5. Ball bearing
6. Bearing spacer
7. Needle bearing
8. Front wheel hub
9. Speedometer drive gear
10. Front wheel axle

4. Mount the wheel and adjust the brake as described in the front wheel "Removal and Installation" section.

Rear Wheel

Removal and Installation

1. Block up the motorcycle so there is enough room to remove the rear wheel, making sure the machine is well balanced.

2. Disconnect the master link and wire the chain to the frame to prevent it from running off the front sprocket.

3. Loosen the rear wheel adjusting stud nuts on both sides, disconnect the brake rod at the lever, loosen the right-side axle nut until the adjusting studs can be removed from their slots in the sides of the frame, and remove the rear wheel.

4. Remove the axle nuts, lockwashers, adjusting studs, the right side spacer (1963 and later models), and the brake sideplate.

5. Installation is in the reverse order of removal.

6. Repack the wheel bearings before replacing the wheel. To do this, the felt seals will have to be removed.

7. Make sure the brake side-cover slot engages the fork leg anchor stud, and adjust the chain and brake as described in the "Maintenance" section after the wheel is mounted.

Rear Hub Disassembly

NOTE: *The Model 165 hub is not interchangeable with the hubs used on the B Models.*

1. Remove the rear wheel as described in the above section.

2. Remove the bearing grease retainer and the left and right felt seals, then screw off the bearing locknut.

3. Drift out the left and right ball bearings (only the Model 165 has a right-side bearing), if necessary, from the opposite sides of the hub, and drift out the needle roller bearing, inner race, and washer on Hummer and Super-10 models.

Inspection and Repair

1. Consult the front wheel "Inspection and Repair" section.

Rear Hub Assembly

1. Pack the left-side bearing with grease and carefully press it into place against the hub shoulder until seated, and secure it with the bearing locknut.

2. Slip two washers onto the sprocket side of the rear axle, and slip the axle into place in the hub.

3. Pack the left bearing or the needle bearing (whichever is applicable) with grease and press it into place in the hub until seated.

4. Mount the felt seals and the felt seal retainer, then install the rear wheel as described in the "Rear Wheel Removal and Installation" section.

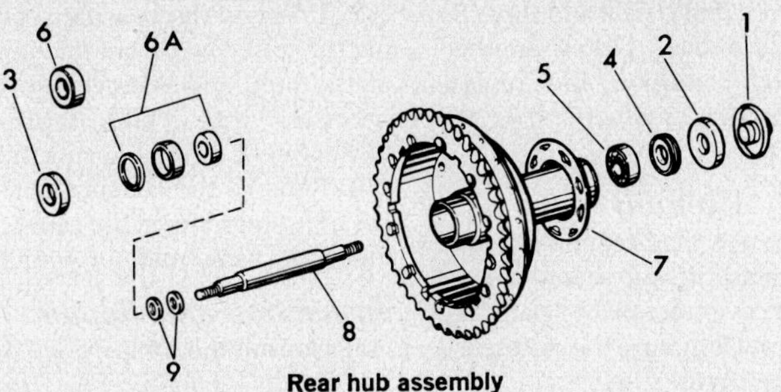

Rear hub assembly

1. Grease retainer
2. Grease retainer felt seal—left
3. Grease retainer felt seal—right
4. Bearing locknut
5. Ball bearing—left
6. Ball bearing—right (165 only)
6A. Needle roller bearing, inner race and seal washer
7. Rear wheel hub
8. Rear wheel axle
9. Bearing spacer washer (2)

Rear Sprocket

REMOVAL AND INSTALLATION

1. Remove the wheel from the bike as described in the "Rear Wheel Removal and Installation" section.

2. Center-punch the rivet heads from the outside sprockets face, then drill them out. Punch the rivets out and install the new sprocket using the bolts which come with the replacement kit. Drilling is not necessary.

3. Install the wheel and adjust the chain and brake as described in the "Rear Wheel Removal and Installation" section.

SPRINT MODELS

Front Wheel

Removal and Installation

1. Block up the front end of the bike so there is enough room to remove the front wheel, making sure the machine is well balanced.

2. Remove the axle nut and washer from the left side, and loosen the pinch bolt on the right side.

3. Remove the anchor arm nut and washer from the anchor stud, then remove the upper arm cap screws and remove the anchor arm.

4. Tap the axle out with a soft mallet while supporting the wheel with one hand, then remove the speedometer drive unit from the hub and allow the wheel to slip down and out of the forks.

5. Remove the brake side-plate and the thick and thin spacers from the hub.

6. Installation is in the reverse order of removal.

7. Position the thin spacer on the brake side of the hub, and the thicker spacer on the speedometer drive side. Mount the brake side-plate and the speedometer drive unit on the hub, and slip the axle into position from the right side.

8. Position the anchor arm on its stud and secure it with the anchor arm nut and washer, then tighten the upper anchor arm capscrews.

9. Position the axle washer on the axle with the chamfered side facing out and secure the axle nut. Remove the bike from the blocks and vigorously pump the forks to align the fork legs, then secure the pinch bolt.

10. Adjust the front brake as described under "Maintenance Items."

Front Hub Disassembly

1. Remove the front wheel as described in the above section.

2. Drift out the dust cover from the opposite side of the hub, then pull the bearing out with Puller (H-D part no. 96729-63) or a suitable substitute, but only if replacement is necessary.

3. Remove the bearing spacer, invert the hub, and remove the other dust cover and bearing in the same manner.

Inspection and Repair

1. Clean all parts in a suitable solvent and blow them dry.

2. Inspect the bearings for a worn, pitted, or damaged condition, or rough motion, and replace them as necessary. Always repack the open type bearings before installing them. (Late models have sealed bearings which require no attention.)

3. Inspect the dust seals inside the dust cover for a worn, dirty, or damaged condition, and replace them as necessary.

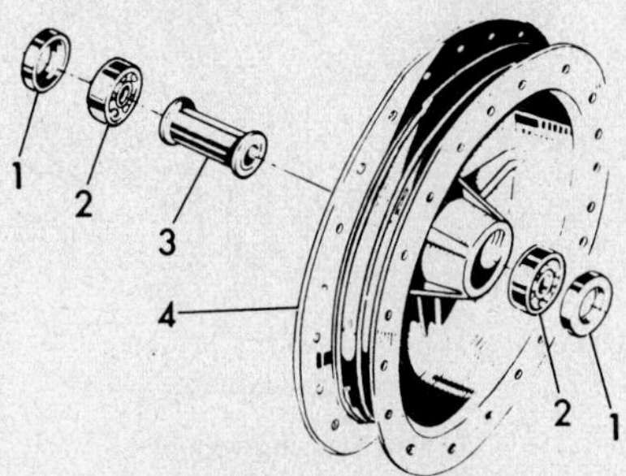

Front wheel hub assembly

1. Dust cover (2)
2. Ball bearing (2)
3. Bearing spacer
4. Wheel hub

4. Inspect the brake shell and shoes for a worn, scored, grooved, glazed, or otherwise damaged condition and replace them as necessary as described in the "Brakes" section.

Front Hub Assembly

1. Press the new bearing in place until it is seated against the hub shoulder, then press the dust cover into place against the bearing, after making sure the dust seal is in place in the cover.

2. Invert the hub and install the bearing spacer, then press the remaining bearing into place until seated against the spacer, and press the dust cover into place until seated against the bearings in the same manner as the first.

3. Mount the wheel and adjust the brake as described in the front wheel "Removal and Installation" section.

Rear Wheel

Removal and Installation

1. Block up the motorcycle so there is enough room to remove the rear wheel, making sure the machine is well balanced.

2. Disconnect the drive chain and wire in to the frame to prevent it from coming off the front sprocket.

3. Remove the brake adjusting nut and disengage the brake rod from the actuating lever, remove the brake anchor arm nut and washer, then slip the arm from the brake side-plate stud.

4. Remove the axle nut and washer, then tap out the axle with a soft mallet while holding the chain adjuster against the swing arm to prevent it from binding the axle. Allow the wheel to fall down between the forks and roll it clear.

5. Remove the brake side-plate and spacer.

6. Installation is in the reverse order of removal. Make sure the spacer washer is properly positioned between the side-plate and the hub.

7. Adjust the brake and chain as described under "Maintenance Items."

Rear Hub Disassembly

1. Remove the wheel as described in the above section.

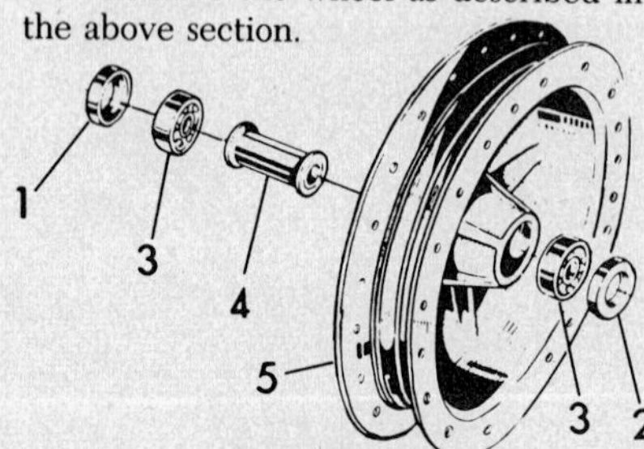

Rear hub assembly

1. Left bearing retainer
2. Dust cover
3. Ball bearing (2)
4. Spacer
5. Wheel hub

2. Unscrew the bearing retainer, drift out the dust cover from the opposite side of the hub, and remove the bearing if necessary with Puller (H-D part no. 95760-69) or a suitable substitute.

3. Remove the bearing spacer, invert the hub, and remove the remaining bearing in the same manner as the first.

Inspection and Repair

1. Consult the front wheel "Inspection and Repair" section.

Rear Hub Assembly

1. Press a new bearing into place until seated against the brake-side hub shoulder, then press the dust cover into place after making sure the dust seal is in place in the cover.

2. Invert the hub, insert the bearing spacer, press in the remaining bearing until seated against the spacer, and screw down the bearing retainer.

3. Install the rear wheel as described in the rear wheel "Removal and Installation" section.

Rear Sprocket

REMOVAL AND INSTALLATION

1. Remove the rear wheel as described in the rear wheel "Removal and Installation" section.

2. Remove the nuts, lockwashers, outer disc, and the sprocket, and then remove the rubber bushings, spacers, inner disc (if applicable), and bolts from the sprocket.

3. Clean all parts in a suitable solvent and blow them dry.

4. Assembly is in the reverse order of disassembly.

BRAKES

M MODELS

Disassembly

1. Remove the wheel as described in the front wheel "Removal and Installation" section of this chapter.

2. Disconnect the brake return springs and pull the shoes off at right angles to the side-plate.

3. Remove the operating shaftnut, washer, operating lever, and operating cam if so desired.

Inspection and Repair

1. Clean all parts other than the brake shoes in a suitable solvent and blow them dry.

2. Inspect the brake shoes for a worn, glazed, oil soaked, cracked, or otherwise damaged condition, and replace them as necessary. The shoes may be reused if only slightly glazed. Rough up the glazed surface of the shoes and drum with some medium grade sandpaper and blow them clean before reusing.

3. Inspect the remaining parts for a worn or damaged condition and replace them as necessary.

Assembly

1. Install the operating cam and lever, and then secure them with washer and nut.

2. Hook the return springs into the shoe holes so that the spring hooks are facing the opposite direction on the same shoes, then fold the shoes and mount them on the operating shaft and pivot studs and press down on the shoes to unfold them onto the side-plate. Use a screwdriver if additional leverage is required.

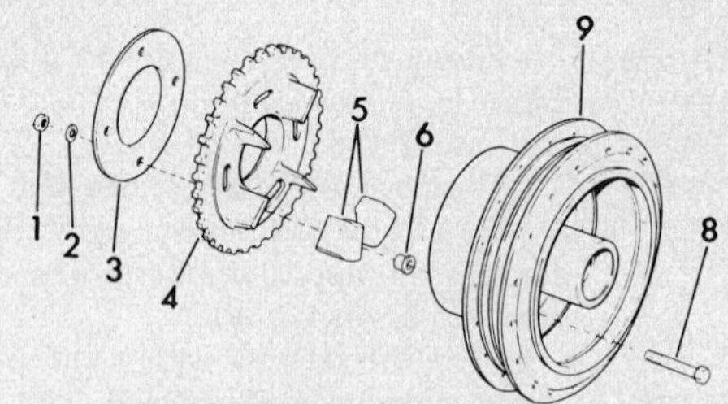

1. Nut (4)
2. Lock washer (4)
3. Outer disc
4. Sprocket
5. Rubber bushing (8)
6. Spacer (4)
8. Bolt (4)
9. Wheel hub

Drive sprocket assembly—1970 and later models

5. Insert the bolts through the hub, mount the inner disc on the hub bolts, insert the rubber bushings and spacers into the sprocket, mount the sprocket on the hub bolts with the shouldered side toward the hub, position the outer disc on the hub bolts with the chamfered side out, and secure the whole assembly with the hub bolts nuts and lockwashers.

6. Install the wheel as described in the rear wheel "Removal and Installation" section.

3. Mount the wheel as described in the appropriate section of this chapter.

Rear Brake Crosshaft

Disassembly and Assembly

1. Remove the brake adjusting knurled nut, lockbar, and brake rod spring, then remove the cotter pin and washer to free the rod from the brake pedal.

2. Remove the footlever mounting nut and washer, and pull the lever from the

shaft. Both footrests are also mounted on the shaft and can be removed at this time by pulling the shaft free of the frame.

3. Inspect the footlever bushings for a worn or damaged condition and replace them as necessary.

4. To assemble the cross-shaft, insert the shaft and both footrests, lightly grease the right-side end of the shaft, and mount the footlever.

5. Position the footlever so it's under the foot rest, then secure the assembly with the washer and nut.

6. Install the brake rod assembly and adjust the brake as described under "Maintenance Items."

S AND B MODELS

Disassembly

1. Remove the appropriate wheel as described in the appropriate wheel "Removal and Installation" section of this chapter.

2. Remove the operating shaft nut, lockwasher, and lever.

3. Pry the return springs from the shoes and remove the operating shaft and spring washer from the brake side-plate.

Inspection and Repair

1. Consult the M Models "Inspection and Repair" section.

2. New linings may be riveted onto the shoes as described in the Sprint "Inspection and Repair" section.

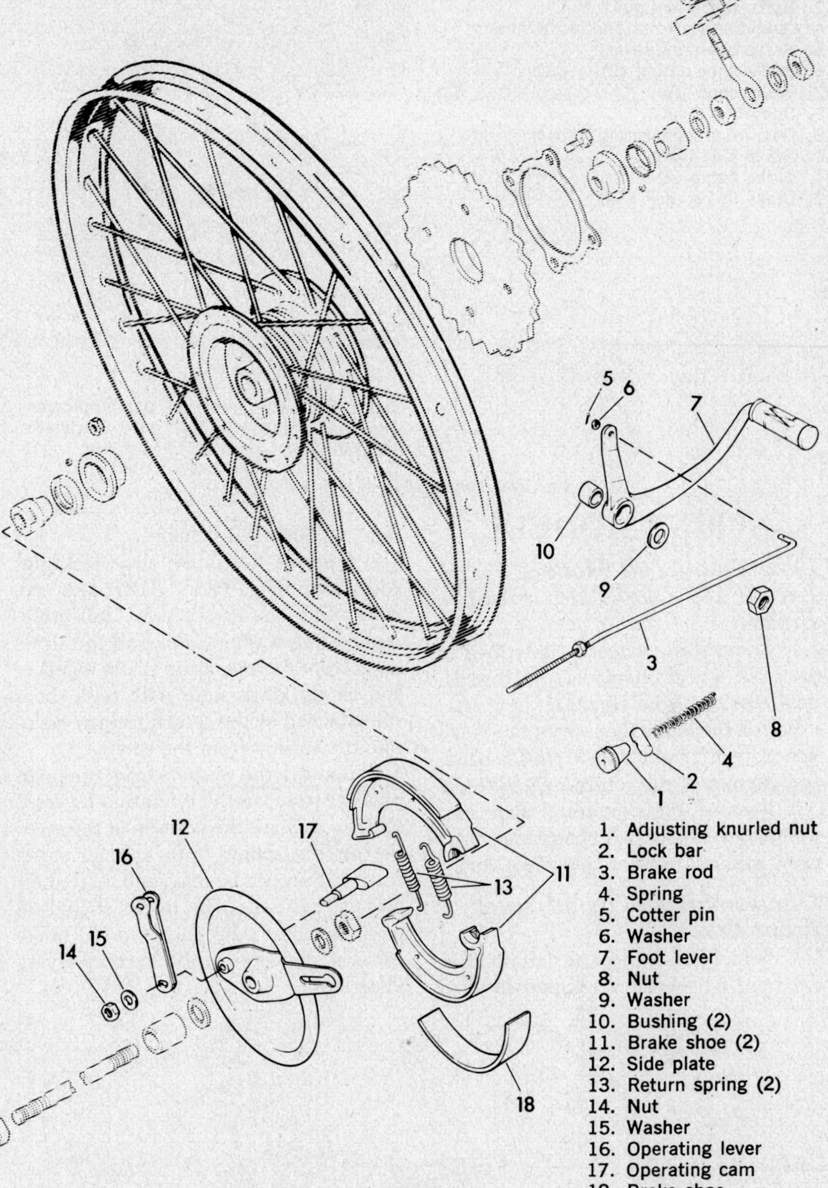

Brake and cross-shaft assembly

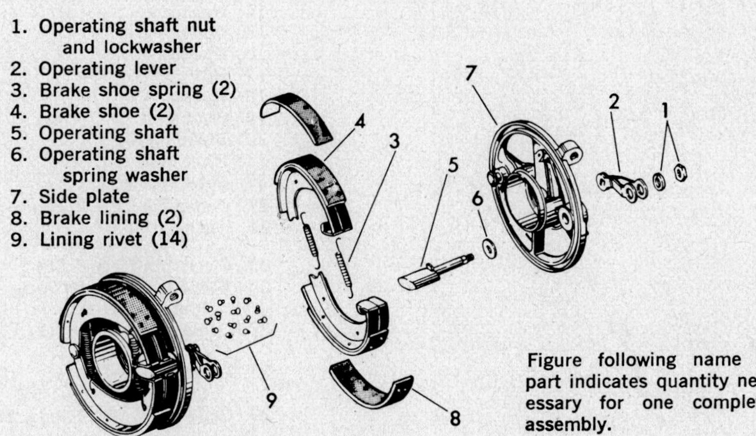

Figure following name of part indicates quantity necessary for one complete assembly.

Front brake assembly—S and B models

Assembly

1. Lay the brake side-plate on a bench with the outside face facing down.

2. Position the operating shaft spring washer on the shaft so the raised portion of the shaft seats against the shaft shoulder, and then insert the shaft into the side plate.

3. Place the shoes on the side-plate, connect them with the spring located nearest the pivot post, and attach the remaining spring.

4. Invert the side-plate and install the operating lever, lockwasher, and shaft nut.

5. Mount the wheel as described in an earlier section of this chapter, and lubricate the brakes as described under "Maintenance Items."

1. Brake rod adjusting nut
2. Rear brake rod
3. Brake rod clevis pin
4. Operatingshaft nut and lockwasher
5. Brake operating lever
6. Brake shoe spring (2)
7. Brake shoe (2)
8. Operating shaft
9. Operating shaft spring washer
10. Brake side plate
11. Brake lining (2)
12. Brake lining rivet (14)

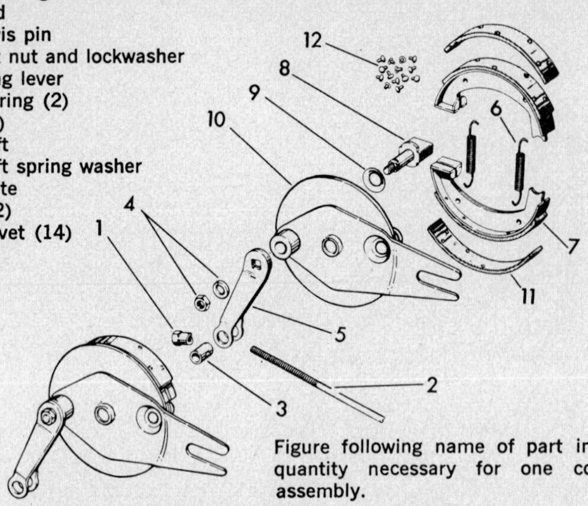

Figure following name of part indicates quantity necessary for one complete assembly.

Rear brake assembly—S and B models

SPRINT MODELS

Disassembly (All Models Except 1970 and Later Front Brakes)

1. Remove the wheel as described in the front wheel "Removal and Installation" section of this chapter.

2. Pull the brake shoes from the brake side plate at a right angle from the plate, and disconnect the return springs.

3. Remove the operating shaft nut, washer, lever, and shaft, then remove the pivot stud nut, washer, and pivot stud.

Disassembly (1970 and Later Front Brakes)

1. Remove the wheel as described in the front wheel "Removal and Installation" section of this chapter.

2. Remove the brake shoe lockrings with Snap-Ring Pliers (H-D part no. 96215-49) or a suitable substitute, remove the washers, and pull the shoes away from the operating shafts together and off the pivot studs with both shoes still attached by the return springs. Separate the springs from the shoes.

3. Remove the washers from the pivot pins and remove the operating levers if so desired. Mark the position of the lever slot on the splines with a small chisel mark so they can be reassembled in their original positions. The levers should be parallel and at right angles to the brake cable as depicted in the accompanying illustration.

Inspection and Repair

1. Consult steps 1–3 of the M Models "Inspection and Repair" section.

2. If the brake shoes are serviceable but the linings are shot, new linings can be riveted to the shoes, or new shoes with the linings already attached can be purchased.

3. Replace the brake linings in the following manner:

a. Install the center rivet first and then alternate the remaining rivets so the next one goes to the right of the first, to the left of the first, to the right, etc., so the lining is drawn down evenly.

b. The rivets may be set by hand or machine, and the end of the lining should be beveled in either case. The rivets should seat the linings tightly against the shoe.

Assembly (All Models Except 1970 and Later Front Brakes)

1. Insert the pivot stud into the side-plate and secure it with the washer and nut.

2. Slip the operating shaft into the side-plate, mount the operating lever onto it so the large flats of the shaft and lever are at right angles to one another, secure the assembly with the washer and nut, and position the lever so it's pointing away from the anchor stud.

3. Attach the return springs to one of the shoes so the spring hooks are facing in the opposite direction from each other.

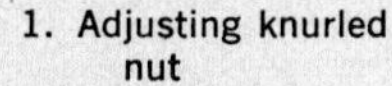

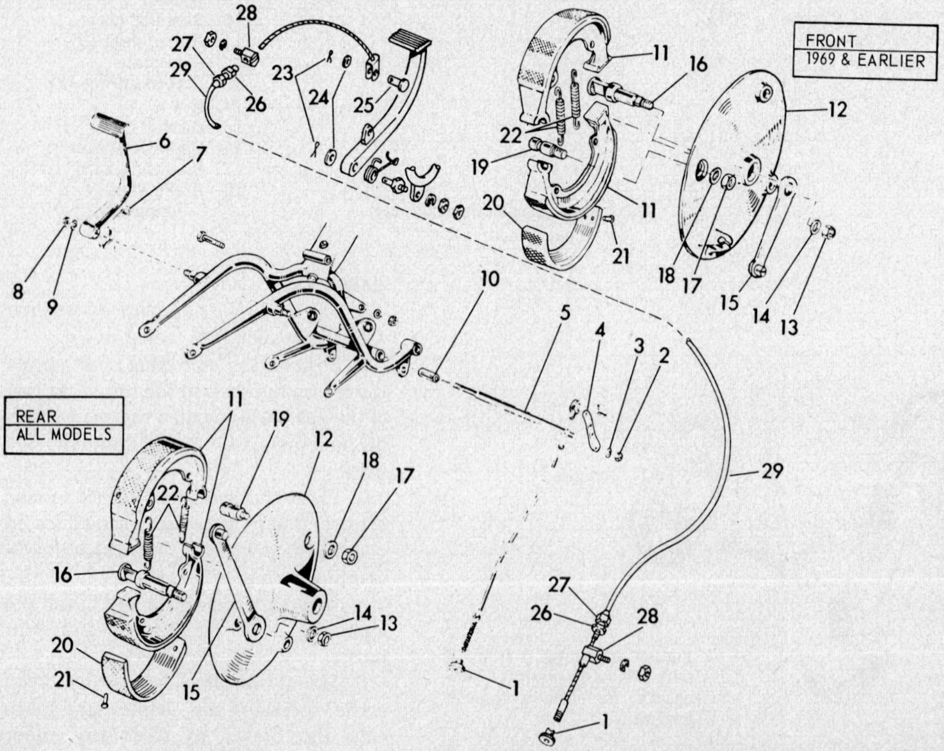

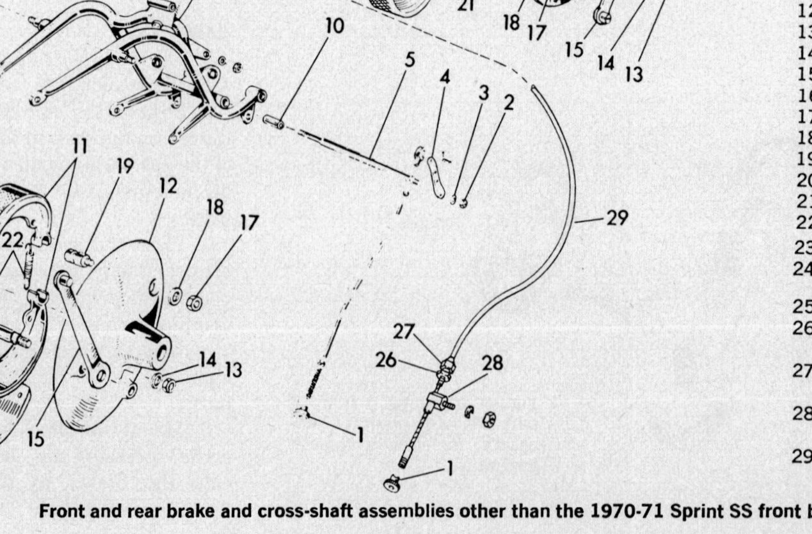

1. Adjusting knurled nut
2. Nut
3. Washer
4. Shaft lever
5. Crossover shaft
6. Foot lever
7. Lever spring
8. Nut
9. Washer
10. Crossover shaft bushing (2)
11. Brake shoe and lining (2)
12. Side plate
13. Nut
14. Washer
15. Operating lever
16. Operating shaft
17. Nut
18. Washer
19. Pivot stud
20. Brake lining (2)
21. Rivet (16)
22. Shoe spring (2)
23. Cotter pin (Model SS)
24. Washer (Model SS)
25. Clevis pin (Model SS)
26 Cable coil adjuster lock nut (Model SS)
27. Cable coil adjuster (2) (Model SS)
28. Cable coil frame fitting (2) (Model SS)
29. Cable assembly (Model SS)

Front and rear brake and cross-shaft assemblies other than the 1970-71 Sprint SS front brake

4. Connect the shoes together with the springs then fold and mount them on the operating shaft and pivot studs, then press down on them to make them unfold onto the side-plate. Use a screwdriver to gain the added leverage that may be necessary.

4. Mount the wheel as described in the appropriate rear wheel "Removal and Installation" section.

Assembly (1970 and Later Front Wheels)

1. Assembly is basically in the reverse order of disassembly except for the shoe assembly.

2. Mount the shoes after lightly greasing the pivot pin and operating shaft ends. Position the shoes without attaching the return springs, then engage the springs using a screwdriver to gain the necessary leverage.

3. Install the wheel as described in the appropriate rear wheel "Removal and Installation" section.

Rear Brake Cross-shaft

(ALL MODELS EXCEPT THE SS)

Disassembly and Assembly

1. Remove the brake rod knurled adjusting nut, the cross-shaft lever nut and washer, then tap on the shaft to remove the lever.

2. Pull the footlever and shaft assembly clear of the frame, then remove the brake lever spring, securing nut and washer, and remove the shaft from the lever.

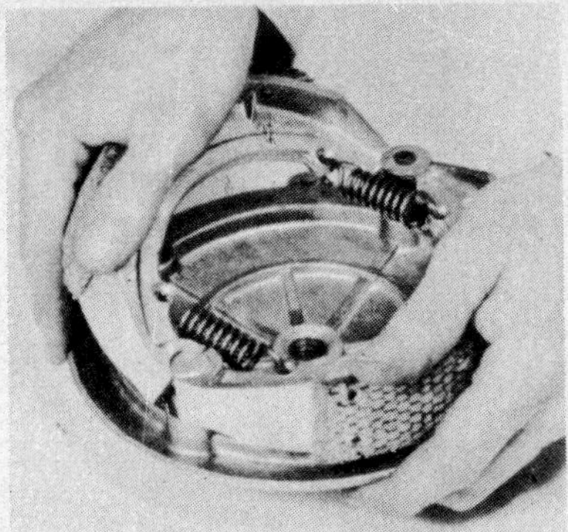

Installing all 1969 and earlier type brake shoes

3. Clean all parts in a suitable solvent and blow them dry. Inspect all the parts for a worn or damaged condition, especially the fit of the shaft in the frame bushings, and replace any parts as necessary.

4. Lightly grease the frame tube, assemble the footlever to the threaded end of the shaft so the notches engage, mount the spring to the shaft so it will support the lever from beneath, and insert the shaft into the frame tube.

5. Mount the crossover shaft lever to the shaft while holding the footlever in its normal position, and draw the shaft lever into position by screwing on the mounting nut and washer.

6. Attach the footlever spring to the lever and secure the lever with the mounting nut and washer.

7. Adjust the brake as described under "Maintenance Items."

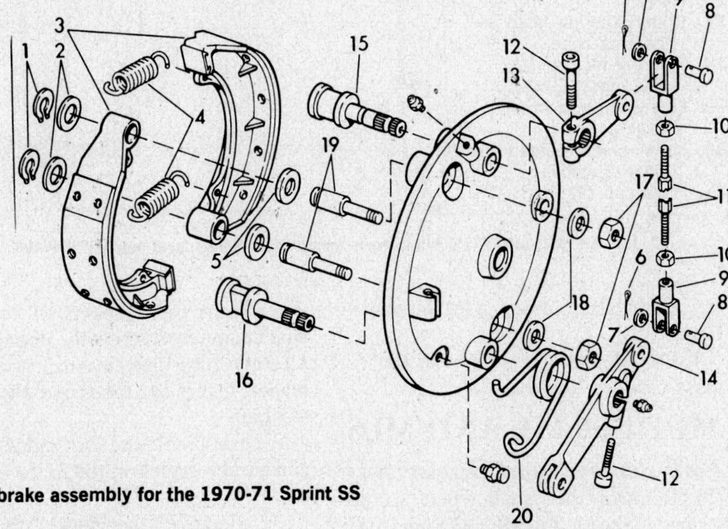

Front brake assembly for the 1970-71 Sprint SS

1. Lock ring (2)
2. Washer (2)
3. Brake shoe (2)
4. Brake shoe spring (2)
5. Washer (2)
6. Cotter key (2)
7. Washer (2)
8. Pin (2)
9. Clevis (2)
10. Nut (2)
11. Control rod
12. Clamp screw (2)
13. Upper operating lever
14. Lower operating lever
15. Upper operating shaft
16. Lower operating shaft
17. Pivot pin nut (2)
18. Pivot pin washer (2)
19. Pivot pin (2)
20. Lever return spring

SUSPENSION

Front Forks

MODELS M AND MS

Fork Removal and Disassembly

1. Remove the front wheel as described in the Models M and MS front wheel "Removal and Installation" section.

2. Remove the front fender and drain the fork oil as described in the "Maintenance" section.

3. Loosen the lower bracket bolts and remove the legs by wedging a screwdriver into the bracket slot and pulling and twisting on the main tubes.

4. Disassemble the fork leg in the following manner:

a. Remove the oil seal from the top of the leg, then remove the fork spring, spacer, lower spring, and the lower cover.

b. Pull the main tube from the slider assembly by sharply jerking them apart.

c. Remove the damper lockring, damper assembly, and the tire assembly tube seal.

5. Remove the headlight mounting bolt and allow the light assembly to hang down on the fork bracket.

6. Remove the speedometer drive unit from the end of the cable and remove the cable from the left fork, upper cover, cable loop, then remove the brake cable locknut and ferrule, and slide the cable out from the right fork upper cover cable loop.

7. Loosen the fork stem nut enough to relieve the tension on the upper fork bracket.

8. If the fork side is to remain assembled, loosen the fork plug several turns so the fork cover can be removed from the bracket assemblies. This will also allow the rubber ring and cap to be removed.

9. The covers are installed in the reverse order of removal.

Inspection and Repair

1. Before tearing into a fork because the action is poor, change the oil to eliminate the possibility of water contamination which might be the cause.

2. If this doesn't appear to be the problem, or if the fork leaks or is damaged, disassemble it as described in the above section, clean all parts in a suitable solvent and blow them dry, and inspect all the parts for a worn or damaged condition and replace them as necessary. Replace the slider if there is any appreciable play in the fit of slider and tube.

3. Inspect the fork stem and bracket, and the upper bracket for a damaged or misaligned condition. They must be replaced as directed in the "Fork Stem and Bracket Assembly Removal" section.

4. Check the fork tubes for a warped or out-of-round condition by first rolling them on a perfectly clean and flat surface to check for warping, and then slip them into a new slider if possible and work them up and down several times. If the tube is in serviceable condition, it will not bind at any point.

5. Tubes can be straightened unless they are severely bent. Take them to your dealer or a qualified machinist. Your dealer can probably recommend one to you. If the stem and bracket assembly or a slider is damaged, it must be replaced.

Fork Stem and Bracket Assembly Removal

1. Disassemble the forks as described in the "Fork Removal and Disassembly" section, then remove the fork upper covers.

2. Remove the handlebar clamp nuts, washers, spacers, U-bolts, and pads, then lift the entire handlebar assembly with the cables and levers still attached and place it out of the way. Try to avoid bending the cables any more than necessary.

3. Remove the fork stem nut and upper washer to free the upper bracket, remove the upper steering head cone while supporting the fork stem and bracket assembly, then remove the stem and bracket assembly while taking care not to lose any of the bearings. There are 23 bearings in each of the cups.

4. Remove the lower steering head bearing cone from the stem and bracket, and remove the head cups if necessary by tapping them out with a piece of bar stock inserted through the steering head. The cups should be removed only if worn, pitted, or otherwise damaged. If any of the bearings are lost, they must be replaced as an entire set.

Fork Stem and Bracket Assembly Installation

1. Assembly is basically the reverse of disassembly.

2. Pack the bearings in fresh grease in the head cups.

3. Tighten up the upper steering head bearing cone and then back it off a turn at a time until the steering action of the forks is as desired. The action of the head should be smooth and free.

4. Continue the assembly process as described in the following section.

Fork Assembly and Installation

1. Assemble the upper covers and forks in the reverse order of disassembly.

2. Wedge apart the fork bracket by inserting a screwdriver in the bracket slot, and force the fork side up through the brackets by twisting, pushing, and tapping with a soft mallet on the bottom of the leg.

3. When the upper tube is flush with the top of the bracket, fill the fork with oil

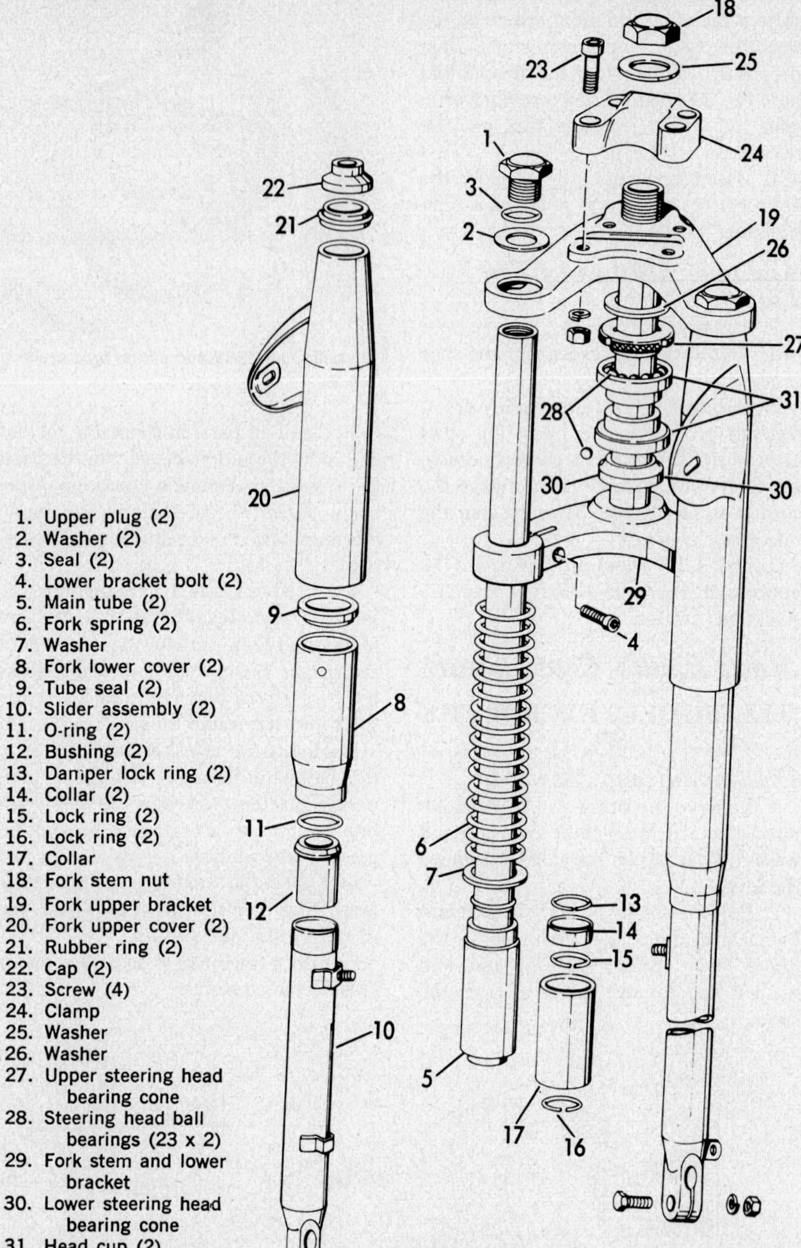

Models ML and MLS front fork assembly—1969 and earlier models

as described under "Maintenance Items."

4. Complete the assembly in the reverse order of disassembly.

MODELS ML AND MLS

Fork Removal and Disassembly

1. Remove the front wheel as described in the Models ML, MLS, and MSR front wheel "Removal and Installation" section.

2. Remove the front fender and the upper plug and washer.

3. Loosen the lower bracket bolt and remove the legs by wedging a screwdriver into the bracket slot and then pulling and twisting on the main tubes to free them from the brackets. If tbe tubes won't come free, screw the upper plug in a couple turns and tap on it with a soft mallet. Invert the tubes and allow them to drain.

4. Disassemble the fork slides on 1969 and earlier models in the following manner:

a. Remove the fork spring and spring washer.

b. Secure the reinforced portion of the fork lower cover in a copper or wood-jawed vise and rotate the slider to the left to remove it. Slip the axle through the axle hole and use it as a lever to aid in removal.

c. Remove the main fork slide tube

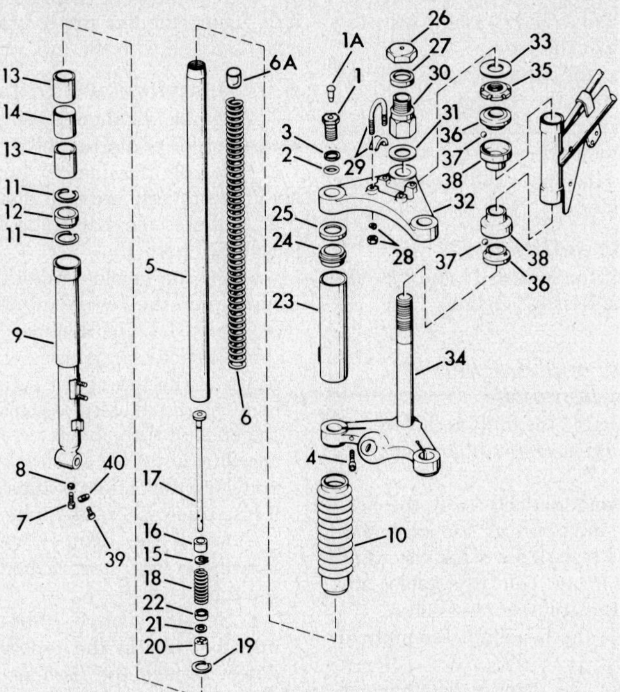

Model MLS front fork assembly—1970-1971 models

1. Upper plug (2)
1A. Upper plug rubber (2)
2. Upper plug washer (2)
3. Upper plug O-ring seal (2)
4. Lower bracket bolt (2)
5. Main tube (2)
6. Fork spring (2)
6A. Fork spring spacer (2)
7. Slider to tube screw (2)
8. Slider to tube screw gasket (2)
9. Slider assembly (2) (left and right)
10. Boot (2) (1970)
11. Lock ring (4)
12. Slider seal (2)
13. Slider bushing (4)
14. Slider bushing spacer (2)
15. Damper piston lock ring (2)
16. Damper piston (2)
17. Damper (2)
18. Buffer spring (2)
19. Damper valve lock ring (2)
20. Damper valve body (2)
21. Damper valve washer (2)
22. Damper valve spacer (2)
23. Upper cover (2) (1970)
24. Upper cover rubber ring (2) (1970)
25. Upper cover cap (1970)
26. Fork stem cap nut
27. Fork stem washer
28. Handlebar U-bolt nuts and lockwashers
29. Handlebar U-bolts and seats
30. Fork stem nut
31. Fork stem nut washer
32. Upper fork bracket
33. Upper fork bracket washer
34. Fork stem and bracket
35. Fork stem cone nut
36. Fork stem cone (2)
37. Fork stem bearing balls (23x2)
38. Head cup (2)
39. Drain screw
40. Drain screw washer

from the slider assembly by yanking on it sharply.

d. Remove the tube oil seal, O-ring, and the lower bushing, only if the need for replacement is indicated.

e. Remove the damper lockring, collar, upper and lower lockrings, and then press the collar from the tube to complete the damper assembly.

5. Disassemble the fork slides on 1970–71 models in the following manner:

a. Remove the fork spring and spacer (if applicable), the slider-to-tube screw and gasket, pull the slider assembly from the tube, and remove the boot (if applicable).

b. Invert the tube and tap on its surface with a soft mallet to free the damper valve assembly and buffer spring.

c. Disassemble the damper valve assembly by removing the lockring from the groove in the bottom of the damper tube.

d. Remove the valve components by slipping the damper tube assembly back into the fork tube, inserting a long rod into the tube, and tapping the rod with a hammer to force the valve assembly from the tube.

e. Remove the damper piston by removing the lockring with a pair of lockring pliers.

f. If the slider seal is in need of replacement, remove the upper lockring with a pair of snap-ring pliers and pry the seal from the slider.

g. If the slider bushing is in need of replacement, cut it carefully with a hacksaw blade, pry the bushing away from the slider wall with a suitable chisel, and grab the bushing with pliers and pull it out. There is a spacer between the two bushings which will also have to be removed.

6. Remove the headlight mounting bolt and allow the light assembly to hang down on the fork bracket.

7. Remove the speedometer drive unit from the end of the cable and remove the cable from the left fork, upper cover, cable loop, then remove the brake cable locknut and ferrule and slide the cable out of the right fork, upper cover, cable loop.

8. Loosen the fork stem nut enough to relieve the tension on the upper fork bracket.

9. If the fork side is to remain assembled, loosen the fork plug several turns so the fork cover can be removed from the bracket assemblies. This will allow the rubber ring and cap to be removed.

10. The covers are replaced in the reverse order of removal.

Inspection and Repair

1. Consult the Model M and MS "Inspection and Repair" section.

2. If the sliders have any appreciable play on 1969 and earlier models, inspect the inside of the slider bushings, the outside of the collar, and the inside of the slider.

Fork Stem and Bracket Assembly Removal

1. Disassemble the forks as described in the "Fork Removal and Disassembly" section.

2. Remove the handlebar clamp screws and the clamp, then lift the entire handlebar assembly with the cables and levers still attached, and place it out of the way. Try to avoid bending the cables any more than necessary.

3. Remove the fork stem nut and upper washer to free the upper bracket, remove the upper steering head cone while supporting the fork stem and bracket assembly, then remove the stem and bracket assembly while taking care not to lose any of the bearings. There are 23 bearings in each of the cups.

4. Remove the lower steering head bearing cone from the stem and bracket, and remove the head cups if necessary by tapping them out with a piece of bar stock inserted through the steering head. The cups should be removed only if worn, pitted, or otherwise damaged. If any of the bearings are lost, they must be replaced as an entire set.

Fork Stem and Bracket Assembly Installation

1. Assembly is basically the reverse order of disassembly.

2. Pack the bearings in fresh grease in the head cups.

3. Tighten up the upper steering head bearing cone and then back it off a turn at a time until the steering action of the forks is as desired. The action of the head should be smooth and free.

4. Continue the assembly process as described in the following section.

Fork Assembly and Installation

1. Assemble the upper cover and forks in the reverse order of disassembly.

2. Wedge apart the fork bracket by inserting a screwdriver in the bracket slot, and force the side up through the brackets by twisting, pushing, cursing, and tapping with a soft mallet on the bottom of the leg.

3. When the upper tube is flush with the top of the bracket, fill the fork with oil as described under "Maintenance Items."

4. Complete the assembly in the reverse order of disassembly.

MODEL MSR AND 1972 MODEL MLS

Fork Removal and Disassembly

1. Remove the front wheel as described in the Models ML, MLS, and MSR front wheel "Removal and Installation" section.

2. Remove the headlight and bracket assembly (if applicable).

3. Remove the cap screws or anchor nuts to remove the front fender and brake side-plate anchor strap.

4. Loosen the fork bracket pinch bolts and pry a screwdriver upward into the bracket slot.

5. Remove the fork plug, washer, and seal, then screw the Fork Tool (H-D part no. 97305-61), or a suitable substitute, into the upper tube and strike it with a copper or lead mallet to drive the fork leg out of the brackets. Make sure the tool has seated before striking it, in order to protect the threads, and take care to keep foreign particles from falling into the tube.

6. Disassemble the fork slider tube in the following manner:

a. Remove the fork spring from the top of the tube, invert the tube, and drain the fork oil from it.

b. Remove the axle pinch bolt and the damper tube screw and its washer from the bottom of the slider assembly, then sharply pull the slider from the tube. Invert the tube to slide the damper out.

7. Disassemble the main tube in the following manner:

a. Slip a 24 in. rod with a ⅛ in. diameter through the bottom of the tube until it engages the buffer spring, then push the buffer spring out of the tube.

b. Remove the damper valve body lockring. It may prove necessary to notch the tube with a sharp instrument to get under the ring so that it may be pried from its groove in the tube.

c. Insert a 24 in. rod with a ⅝ in. diameter into the tube until it seats on the damper valve washer, then strike the top of the rod with a hammer to drift the valve body from the tube. The damper valve and washer will also come free at this time.

8. Remove the damper piston lockring and piston from the damper tube.

9. Remove the fork boots, pull the slider free, and remove the tube seal lockring and the upper and lower oil seals from the slider.

Inspection and Repair

1. Consult the Models M and MS "Inspection and Repair" section.

Fork Stem and Bracket Assembly Removal

1. Disassemble the forks as directed in the "Fork Removal and Disassembly" section.

2. Disconnect and lift away the handlebar assembly with all the cable still attached and place it out of the way while taking care not to bend the cables any more than is absolutely necessary.

3. Remove the headlight assembly (if applicable).

4. Remove the damper assembly on MSR models by removing the steering damper lower nut, spring washer plate, spring washer, rod lock, anchor plate, friction disc, and the fork stem nut and washer.

5. Remove the fork upper bracket by placing a block of wood under the bracket and drifting the bracket up and off of the fork stem and bracket, then push the stem and bracket down through the upper bearing cone until the lower cone bearings are accessible for removal.

6. Remove and separate the bearings for replacement in their original positions. If any of the bearings are lost, or if the sets are mixed, both sets will have to be replaced.

7. Slip the stem and bracket down the rest of the way and remove and separate the upper bearings and cone, then remove the lower cone.

8. Remove the head cups if necessary by drifting them out with a piece of bar stock inserted through the steering head.

Fork Stem and Bracket Assembly Installation

1. Assembly is basically in the reverse order of disassembly.

2. Pack the bearings in fresh grease in the bearing cups.

3. Remove the play from the steering head cones by tightening the fork stem nut until the play is gone but the steering action is still smooth and free.

4. Check the steering action once the bike has been completely reassembled by blocking the front wheel off the ground and rotating it from side to side. Loosen the fork upper bracket bolt until the steering is the way you like it. There should be no appreciable play left in the fork. Secure the fork upper bracket bolt when satisfied with the fork motion.

Fork Assembly and Installation

1. Assemble the slider assembly in the reverse order of disassembly.

2. Assemble the damper tube assembly in the reverse order of disassembly.

3. Assemble the main tube in the following manner:

a. Slip the smaller end of the buffer spring into the lower end of the tube until past the tube shoulder.

b. Position the damper valve in its recess at the top of the damper tube body, place the valve washer on top of the body so the valve is covered, then carefully insert the washer end of the body into the bottom of tube and press it into place against the tube shoulder.

c. Install the damper valve body lockring in its groove in the bottom of the tube.

d. Slip the damper tube assembly into the tube at the top so it drops down through the damper valve assembly. Shaking the tube will help it find its seat.

e. Slip the fork spring into position, then install the Fork Tool (H-D part no. 97305-61) in the top of the tube. Clean the tube thoroughly then insert the tube into the slider and compress the two until the damper tube snaps into position. Install and secure the damper tube screw and washer in the bottom of the slider.

4. Install the fork side in the brackets in the following manner:

a. Install the Fork Tool then slip the tube and tool up through the brackets and pull the tube into place.

b. Add the fork oil as described under "Maintenance Items," install the fork plug washer, seal, and plug, then secure the lower fork bracket pinch bolt.

c. Complete the assembly in the reverse order of disassembly.

5. Install the steering damper (if applicable) in the reverse order of disassembly. The damper star washer should be dished side up on the damper rod assembly.

S AND B MODELS

Fork Removal and Disassembly

1. Remove the front wheel and brake assemblies as described in the S and B Models front wheel "Removal and Installation" section, then remove the front fender, headlight, and fork panel assemblies.

2. Remove the fork tube pinch bolts, headlight bracket, and fork outer tube caps, then wedge a screwdriver into the bracket slot.

3. Loosen the fork boot clamps and

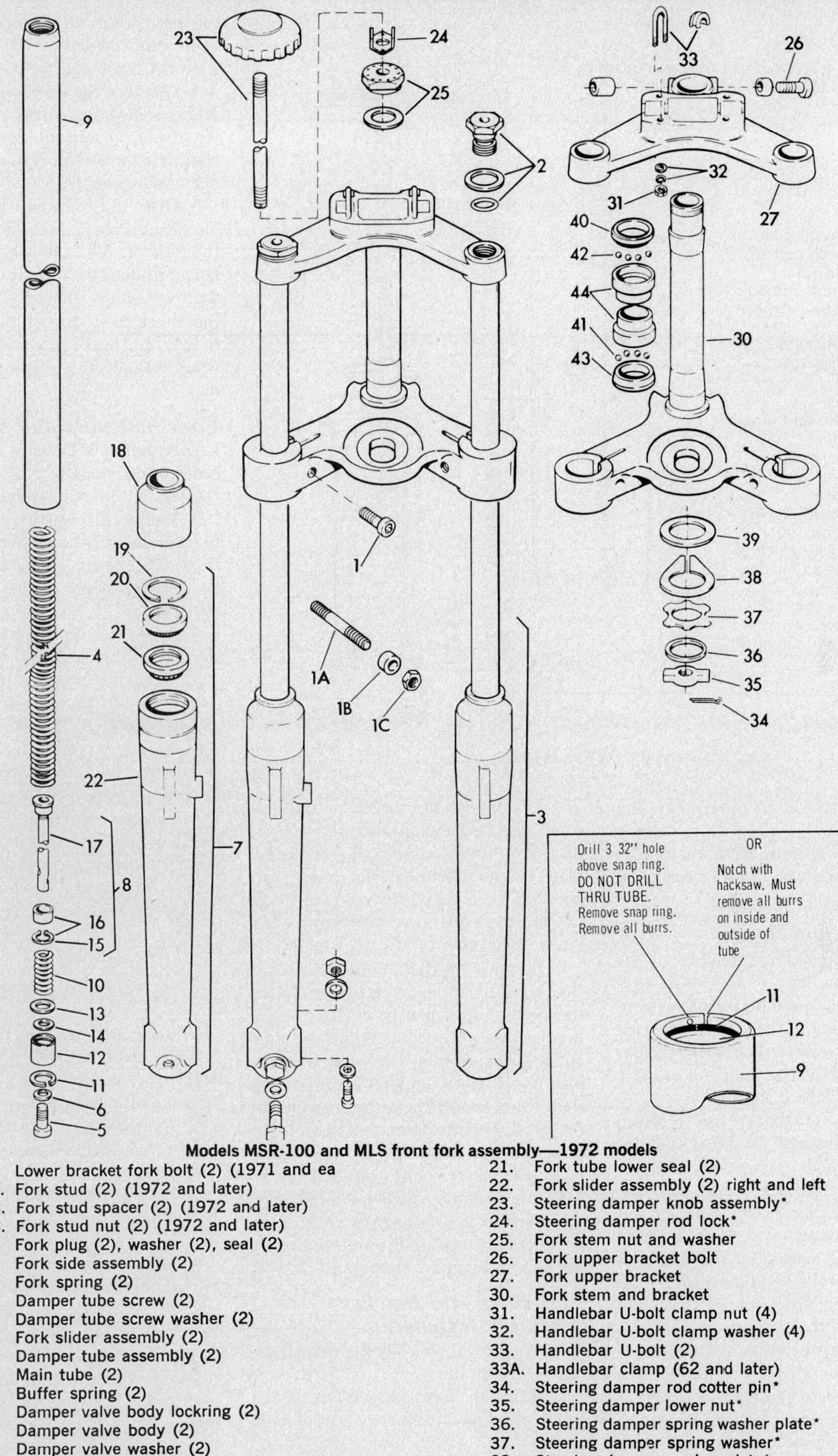
Drill 3 32" hole above snap ring. DO NOT DRILL THRU TUBE. Remove snap ring. Remove all burrs.
OR
Notch with hacksaw. Must remove all burrs on inside and outside of tube

Models MSR-100 and MLS front fork assembly—1972 models

1. Lower bracket fork bolt (2) (1971 and ea
1A. Fork stud (2) (1972 and later)
1B. Fork stud spacer (2) (1972 and later)
1C. Fork stud nut (2) (1972 and later)
2. Fork plug (2), washer (2), seal (2)
3. Fork side assembly (2)
4. Fork spring (2)
5. Damper tube screw (2)
6. Damper tube screw washer (2)
7. Fork slider assembly (2)
8. Damper tube assembly (2)
9. Main tube (2)
10. Buffer spring (2)
11. Damper valve body lockring (2)
12. Damper valve body (2)
13. Damper valve washer (2)
14. Damper valve (2)
15. Damper piston lockring (2)
16. Damper piston (2)
17. Damper tube (2)
18. Fork boot
19. Tube seal lockring (2)
20. Fort tube upper seal (2) (1971 and later)
21. Fork tube lower seal (2)
22. Fork slider assembly (2) right and left
23. Steering damper knob assembly*
24. Steering damper rod lock*
25. Fork stem nut and washer
26. Fork upper bracket bolt
27. Fork upper bracket
30. Fork stem and bracket
31. Handlebar U-bolt clamp nut (4)
32. Handlebar U-bolt clamp washer (4)
33. Handlebar U-bolt (2)
33A. Handlebar clamp (62 and later)
34. Steering damper rod cotter pin*
35. Steering damper lower nut*
36. Steering damper spring washer plate*
37. Steering damper spring washer*
38. Steering damper anchor plate*
39. Steering damper friction disc*
40. Upper steering head bearing cone
41. Lower steering head ball bearings (25)
42. Upper steering head ball bearings (25)
43. Lower steering head bearing cone
44. Head cup (42)

*Used only on MSR

Figure following name of part indicates quantity necessary for one complete assembly.

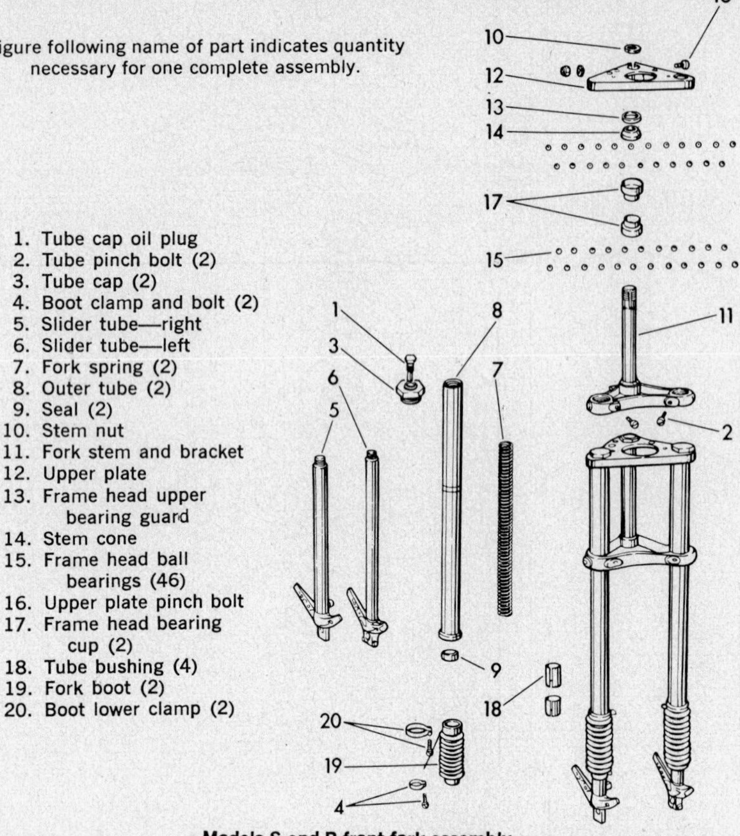

Models S and B front fork assembly

bolts and pull the sliders and springs from the outer tube.

4. Pry the oil seals from their seats with a screwdriver if replacement is necessary.

Inspection and Repair

1. Clean all parts in a suitable solvent and blow them dry.

2. Inspect the condition of all the components for wear or damage and replace them as necessary. The fork springs should be 12 21/64 in. long and must be replaced if collapsed shorter.

3. Inspect the sliders for a worn, scored, or damaged condition and replace them as necessary. If there is appreciable play between the tube and the slider bushing, the bushing and oil seal must be replaced using Fork Bushing Tool Set (H-D part no. 97030-54), or a suitable substitute, and then reamed until the bushing groove aligns with the flanged end of the fork tube.

4. Inspect the bearings and cups for a worn, pitted, or otherwise damaged condition and replace them as necessary. If any bearings are lost, or if bearing sets are mixed, the whole set must be replaced.

Fork Stem and Bracket Assembly Removal

1. Disassemble the fork sides as directed in the "Fork Removal and Installation" section.

2. Disconnect the speedometer cable from the speedometer head, and free the head from the head from the fork upper plate, then disconnect the handlebars and shift them out of the way taking care to bend the cables no more than is absolutely necessary.

3. Remove the fork stem nut, loosen the upper pinch bolt, then carefully tap the stem and bracket from the steering head with a soft mallet. While the stem and bracket assembly is coming free, the fork upper plate, upper bearing guard, stem cone, and the bearings may also be removed. On the Hummer model, the ignition wires leading to the fork upper plate will have to be disconnected.

4. The head cups may be removed if replacement is necessary by inserting a piece of bar stock up through the opposite cup and tapping them out.

Fork Stem and Bracket Assembly Installation

1. Assembly is basically the reverse order of disassembly.

2. Mount the head cups and install the bearings along with a heavy coat of fresh grease.

3. Slip the fork stem into position, then install the fork stem cone and upper bearing guard. The fork upper plate can be tapped into place on the stem with a soft mallet.

4. Tighten down the fork stem nut on the stem until all appreciable play has been removed, and so the motion of the stem is smooth and free.

5. Connect the ignition wires (Hummer models only), install the speedometer head, connect the cable, and complete the assembly in the reverse order of disassembly.

6. Once the front end has been completely assembled, recheck the motion of the forks. Loosen the upper plate pinch bolt and adjust the fork stem nut until the desired result is attained and then secure the pinch bolt. Install the fork panel, mount the headlight, and connect the wires as shown in the appropriate wiring diagram.

Fork Assembly and Installation

1. Assembly is basically in the reverse order of disassembly.

2. Install the outer tube oil seal.

3. Wedge a screwdriver in the fork bracket slot, slip the tubes into place until flush with the top of the bracket, install the tube caps, and secure the fork tube pinch bolts.

4. Install the fork boots and secure them with the clamps.

5. Screw the springs onto the threaded ends of the fork sliders, heavily grease the springs, and insert the sliders and springs into their appropriate fork tubes. Turn the sliders counterclockwise if necessary to properly align the slider fender attaching brackets. Secure the fork boots with the boot clamps and bolts.

6. Complete the assembly and lubricate the front end as described under "Maintenance Items."

SPRINT MODELS

Fork Removal and Disassembly

1. Remove the front wheel as described in the Sprint front wheel "Removal and Installation" section.

2. Remove the cap screws to remove the front fender and brake side-plate anchor strap.

3. Loosen the lower fork bracket pinch bolt or stud nuts, and wedge a screwdriver into the bracket slot.

4. Remove the upper fork plug, screw Fork Tool (H-D part no. 97305-61) or a suitable substitute all the way into the tube until seated, taking care not to allow foreign particles to fall into the tube, and strike the tool with a copper or lead hammer to drive the tube from the brackets, or pull the fork leg out through the bottom.

5. Disassemble the fork side in the following manner:

a. Remove the fork spring from the top of the tube, then invert the tube and allow the fork oil to drain out.

b. Remove the axle pinch bolt and

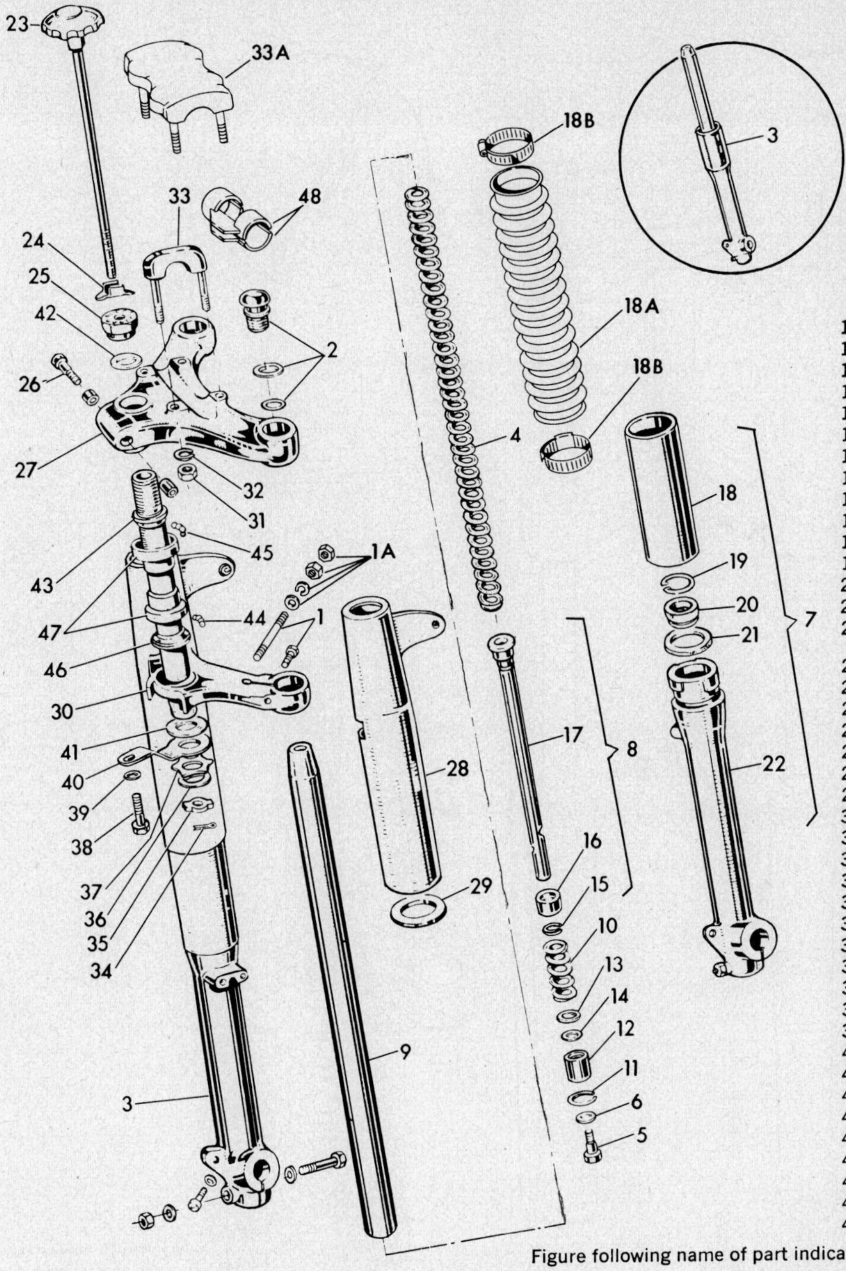

1. Lower bracket fork bolt (2) (C Models)
 Lower bracket fork stud (2) (63 and later H Models)
1A. Stud nuts, washers and lockwashers (63 and later H Models)
2. Fork plug (2) washer (2) seal (2)
3. Fork side assembly (2)
4. Fork spring (2)
5. Damper tube screw (2)
6. Damper tube screw washer (2)
7. Fork slider assembly (2)
8. Damper tube assembly (2)
9. Main tube (2)
10. Buffer spring (2)
11. Damper valve body lockring (2)
12. Damper valve body (2)
13. Damper valve washer (2)
14. Damper valve (2)
15. Damper piston lockring (2)
16. Damper piston (2)
17. Damper tube (2)
18. Fork lower cover assembly (2) (C Models)
18A. Fork boot (H and SS Models)
18B. Boot clamp (2) (H and SS Models)
19. Tube seal lockring (2)
20. Fork tube upper cover seal (2)
21. Fork tube lower cover seal (2)
22. Fork slider assembly (2) right and left
23. Steering damper knob assembly
24. Steering damper rod lock
25. Fork stem nut
26. Fork upper bracket bolt
27. Fork upper bracket
28. Fork upper cover assembly (2) right and left
29. Fork upper cover rubber ring (2)
30. Fork stem and bracket
31. Handlebar U-bolt clamp nut (4)
32. Handlebar U-bolt clamp washer (4)
33. Handlebar U-bolt (2)
33A. Handlebar clamp (62 and later)
34. Steering damper rod cotter pin
35. Steering damper lower nut
36. Steering damper spring washer plate
37. Steering damper spring washer
38. Steering damper anchor plate bolt
39. Steering damper anchor plate washer
40. Steering damper anchor plate
41. Steering damper upper friction disc
42. Fork stem nut washer
43. Upper steering head bearing cone
44. Lower steering head ball bearings (25)
45. Upper steering head ball bearings (25)
46. Lower steering head bearing cone
47. Head cup (2)
48. Handlebar rubber mounts (2) (62 and later)

Figure following name of part indicates quantity necessary for one complete assembly.

Front fork assembly—1970 and earlier Sprint models

the damper tube screw and washer, then separate the tube from the slider with a sharp jerk.

c. Invert the tube and allow the damper assembly to slide out.

6. Disassemble the main tube in the following manner:

a. Slip a 24 in. rod with a ⅛ in. diameter through the bottom of the tube until it engages the buffer spring, then push the buffer spring out of the tube.

b. Remove the damper valve body lockring. It may prove necessary to notch the tube with a sharp instrument to get under the ring so that it may be pried from its groove in the tube.

c. Insert a 24 in. rod with a ⅝ in. diameter into the tube until it seats on the damper valve washer, then strike the top of the rod with a hammer to drift the valve body from the tube. The damper valve and washer will also come free at this time.

7. Remove the damper piston lockring and piston from the damper tube.

8. Remove the clamps securing the fork boots on H Models. Rotate the fork lower cover ¼ turn counterclockwise, pull off the fork slider, and remove the lockring and oil seal on C Models.

9. Remove the fork upper cover assembly in the following manner:

a. Disconnect the headlight and allow it to hang down on the fork bracket.

b. Remove the speedometer drive unit from the cable end, and slip the cable out through the loop on the left fork cover. Disconnect the brake cable at the handlebars and slip the cable out through the loop on the right fork cover.

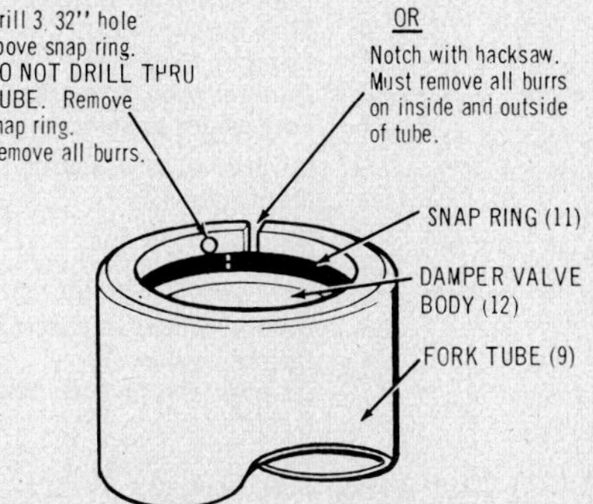
Drill 3/32" hole above snap ring. DO NOT DRILL THRU TUBE. Remove snap ring. Remove all burrs.
OR
Notch with hacksaw. Must remove all burrs on inside and outside of tube.
SNAP RING (11)
DAMPER VALVE BODY (12)
FORK TUBE (9)

Removing the damper valve body snap-ring

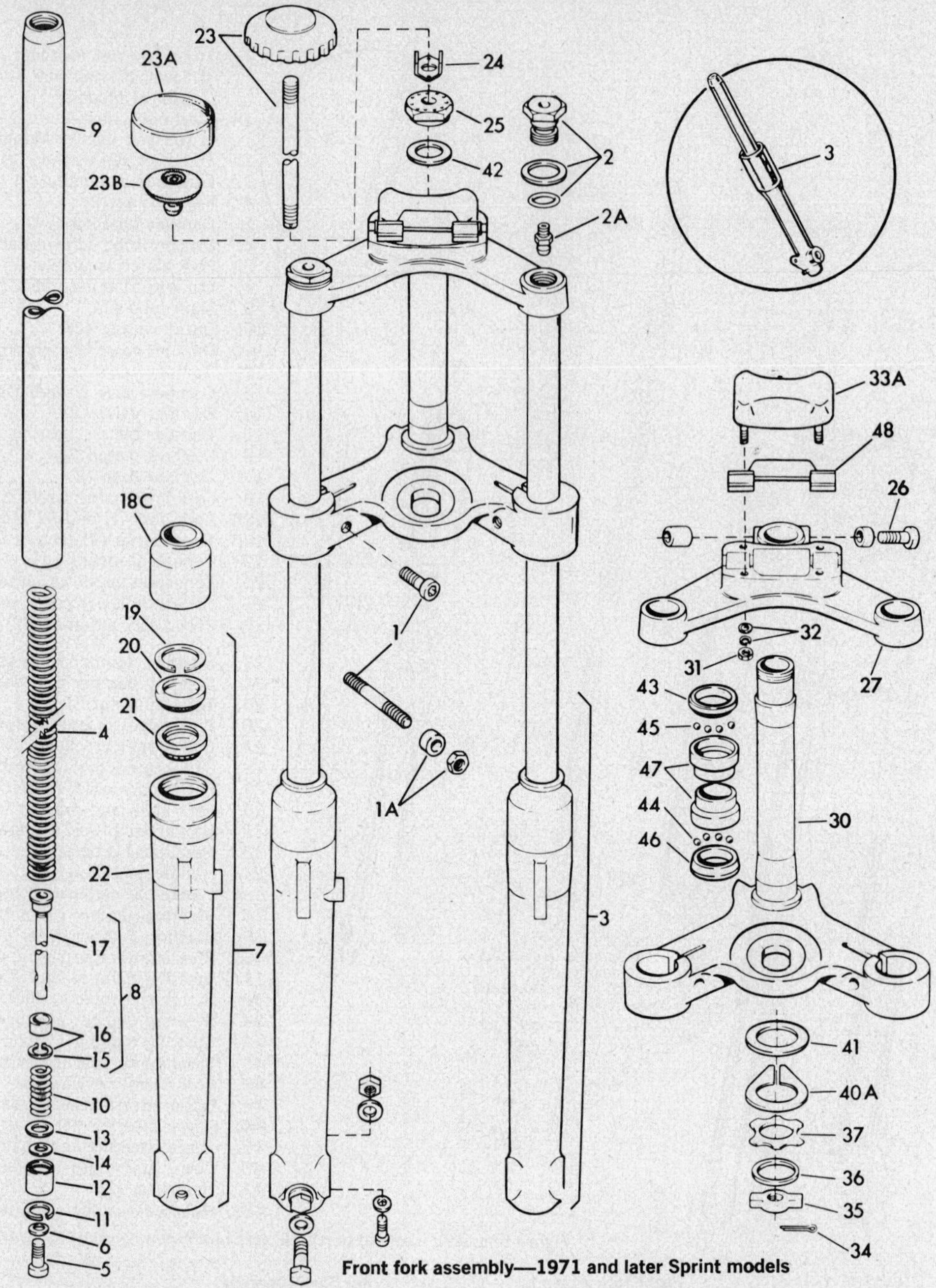

Front fork assembly—1971 and later Sprint models

1. Lower bracket fork bolt (2) (SS)
   Lower bracket fork stud (2) (SX)
1A. Stud nut and spacer (2) (SX)
2. Fork plug (2), washer (2), seal (2)
2A. Fork plug valve (2)
3. Fork side assembly (2)
4. Fork spring (2)
5. Damper tube screw (2)
6. Damper tube screw washer (2)
7. Fork slider assembly (2)
8. Damper tube assembly (2)
9. Main tube (2)
10. Buffer spring (2)
11. Damper valve body and lockring (2)
12. Damper valve body (2)
13. Damper valve washer (2)
14. Damper valve (2)
15. Damper piston and lockring (2)
16. Damper piston (2)
17. Damper tube (2)
18C. Fork boot (2)
19. Seal lockring (2)
20. Fork seal (2)
21. Fork tube lower cover seal (2)
22. Fork slider assembly (2) (right and left)
23. Steering damper knob assembly
23A. Fork plug cap
23B. Rubber pad
24. Steering damper rod lock
25. Fork stem nut
26. Fork upper bracket bolt
27. Fork upper bracket
30. Fork stem and bracket
31. Handlebar clamp nut (4)
32. Handlebar clamp nut washer (4)
33A. Handlebar clamp
34. Steering damper rod cotter pin
35. Steering damper lower nut
36. Steering damper spring washer plate
37. Steering damper spring washer
40A. Steering damper anchor plate
41. Steering damper upper friction disc
42. Fork stem nut washer
43. Upper steering head bearing cone
44. Lower steering head ball bearings (25)
45. Upper steering head ball bearings (25)
46. Lower steering head bearing cone
47. Head cup (2)
48. Handlebar rubber mounts (2)

c. Loosen the steering damper knob until the tension is taken off of the damper rod lock, then loosen the fork stem nut and upper bracket bolt several turns each.

d. If one fork side is to remain assembled, loosen its fork plug.

e. Place a piece of wood under the upper bracket, and carefully drift the upper bracket up until the cover and rubber ring assembly is free to be removed.

Inspection and Repair

1.Consult the Models M and MS "Inspection and Repair" section.

Fork Stem and Bracket Assembly Removal

1. Consult the Model MSR and 1972 Model MLS "Fork Stem and Bracket Assembly Removal" section. Models SS and SX are equipped with steering dampers.

Fork Stem and Bracket Assembly Installation

1. Consult the Model MSR and 1972 Model MLS "Fork Stem and Bracket Assembly Installation" section.

Fork Assembly and Installation

1. Install the fork cover in the reverse order of disassembly, making sure the rubber ring and O-ring are held in place as the cover assembly is slipped into place.

2. Assemble the fork slider in the reverse order of disassembly.

3. Assemble the damper tube in the reverse order of disassembly.

4. Assemble the main tube and fork side as described in steps three and four of Model MSR and 1972 Model MLS "Fork Assembly and Installation."

5. On 1970 and later SS models (from serial no. 12216) and on 1971 and later SS and SX models, a vent valve and baffle assembly is used. If these parts require replacement, or if there is oil leakage from the fork sides on older models, a replacement kit is available which may be installed. Use all of the parts in the kit rather than only those which appear to be in need of replacement.

Rear Suspension

M MODELS

Shock Absorber Disassembly and Assembly

1. Remove the shock absorber locknuts (if applicable), then remove the mounting bolts and their associated apparatus, and pull the shock off of the upper and lower mounting studs.

2. Disassemble 1969 and earlier shocks by compressing them in a vise. The lower cover's lip should seat on the edge of one vise jaw, and the top mounting eye should seat on the other jaw. Cover the top cover to protect it, then compress the spring while holding the upper cover. When the spring is sufficiently compressed, remove the split retainer ring.

3. Disassemble 1970 and later shocks by using Shock Compressor Tool (H-D part no. 97010-52A) and a suitable washer. Remove the split retaining ring when the spring is suitably compressed. If the tool is not available, the shock can be disassembled by having one person compress the spring while another removes the retainer ring.

4. Remove the lower cover (if applicable), the spring washer, the spring, and the upper cover (if applicable).

5. Replace the shock unit and any other components which are worn or damaged, then reassemble the shock in the reverse order of disassebly, taking care not to catch the lower cover in the split ring groove as this will cause the cover to bend.

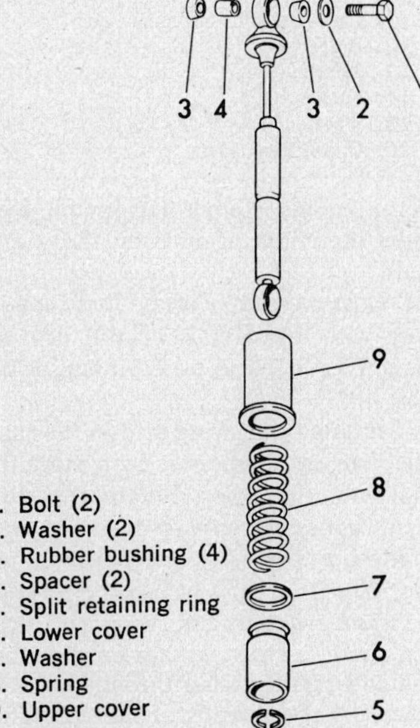

Rear shock absorber assembly

Rear Swing Arm Removal

1. Remove the rear wheel as described in the rear wheel "Removal and Installation" section.

2. Remove the rear shock absorber as described in the above section.

3. Remove the pivot bolt nut, washers, and bolt on all M, MS, MC models.

4. Remove the rear brake lever and spring, then unscrew the pivot bolt and remove the bolt nut and washers on all MLS and MSR models.

Inspection and Repair

1. Clean all parts in a suitable solvent and blow them dry.

2. Inspect the fit of the pivot bolt in the fork bushings for excessive play and replace the bushings if necessary by drifting them out and pressing them back in.

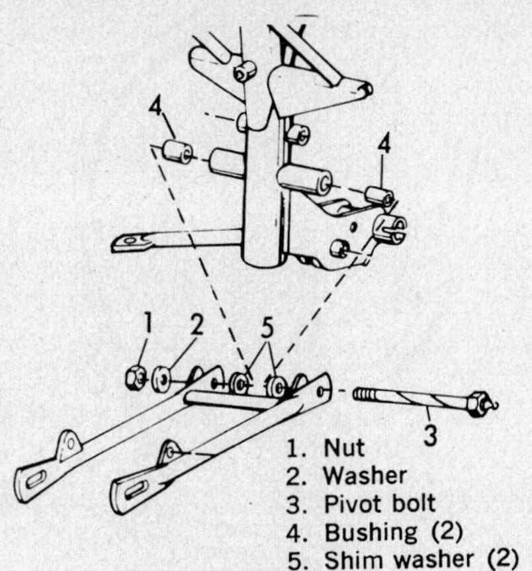

Rear swing arm for M-125 models

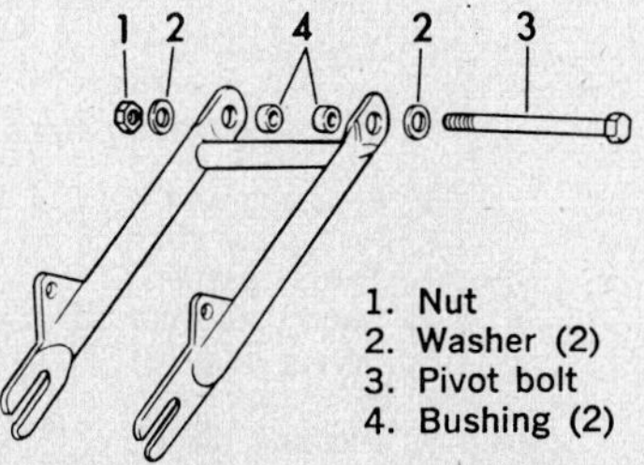

Rear swing arm for M-50 and M-65 models

3. If the swing arm itself appears to be bent or damaged, it must be replaced since bending it back into shape may cause metal fatigue.

Rear Swing Arm Installation

1. Install the swing arm in the reverse order of removal.

2. Adjust swing arm side-play on M and MS models by loosening the pivot bolt locknut and tighten the pivot bolt until the play is minimal. Secure the locknut and lubricate the bushings with engine oil. The bushings should be lubricated every 1,000 miles.

3. Adjust the side-play on ML and MLS models by adding or removing the necessary amount of variable-thickness washers, which come in various thicknesses from 0.3 to 1.0 mm. Grease the pivot bolt at the grease fitting after the swing arm is assembled.

S AND B MODELS

Swing Arm and Spring Disassembly

1. Remove the muffler and its support tube, disconnect the rear brake rod, and remove the rear wheel as described in the rear wheel "Removal and Installation" section.

2. Remove the plug and nipple assemblies then drift the shaft out with a brass drift and hammer. Since shaft is secured in the frame with Grade C Locktite, the frame may have to be heated to loosen the Locktite.

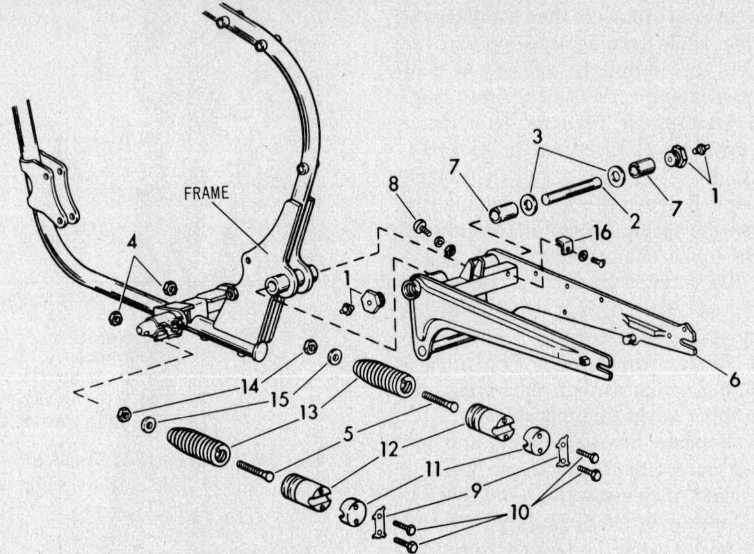

Rear swing arm assembly—S and B models

1. Plug and nipple (2)
2. Fork pivot shaft
3. Thrust washer (2)
4. Spring stud nut (2)
5. Spring stud (2)
6. Rear fork
7. Bushing (2)
8. Bumper
9. Lockwasher (2)
10. Capscrew (4)
11. Cap (2)
12. Body (2)
13. Spring (2)
14. Locknut (2)
15. Washer (2)
16. Chain pad

3. Remove the thrust washers from between the fork and frame, then remove the spring stud nuts and pull the swing arm free.

4. Disassemble the swing arm springs in the following manner:

a. Pry the lockwasher ears to free them, remove the capscrews and caps, then slip the spring assembly free.

b. Remove the spring stud adjusting nuts from the studs, then remove the stud locknuts and washers.

c. Secure the cap on the cap body and place a rod through the hole between them to twist the spring off the cap body.

Inspection and Repair

1. Clean all parts in a suitable solvent and blow them dry.

2. Check the bushings and shaft for wear, damage, or excessive play and replace them as necessary. Bushings are pressed in and out, then reamed with a ¾ (0.7500 in.) diameter expansion reamer.

3. Inspect all parts for a worn or damaged condition and replace them as necessary. If the swing arm is bent, sprung, or otherwise damaged, it must be replaced.

Swing Arm and Spring Assembly

1. Assembly is basically the reverse order from disassembly. All parts which are to be coated with Locktite must be thoroughly cleaned in an oil-free solvent.

2. Assemble the fork spring in the reverse order of disassembly.

3. Position the swing arm in the frame so the rubber stop is facing up, then screw the adjusting nuts on the spring studs.

4. Coat the center of the fork support shaft with Grade C Locktite, leaving about 1 ½ in. clean on each end of the shaft.

5. Position the swing arm so the shaft holes are in alignment, then start the shaft into the holes. Before the shaft passes from the frame to the swing arm, position a thrust washer between the two. When the shaft has passed through the frame, washer, and swing arm, position another thrust washer on the other side and pass the shaft through it.

6. Coat the threads of the end plugs with Grade C Locktite before assembling them. Grease the swing arm through the plug nipples immediately after the plugs are installed to displace any Locktite which may have gotten on the bushings.

7. Complete the assembly in the reverse order of disassembly.

8. Adjust the spring tension by loosening the adjusting nut to decrease spring tension and by tightening it to increase the tension.

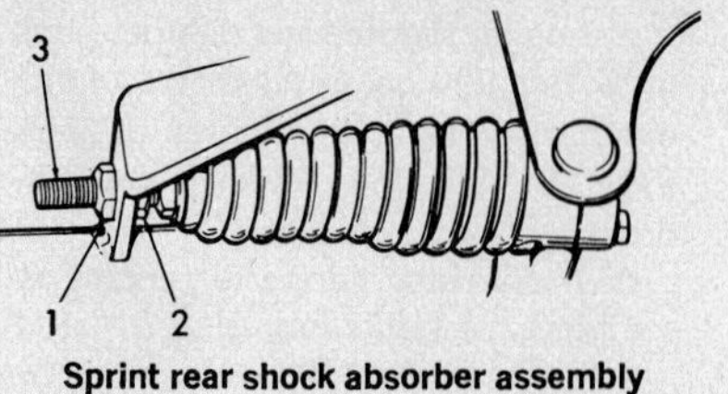

Sprint rear shock absorber assembly

1. Nut 2. Nut 3. Stud

SPRINT MODELS

Shock Absorber Disassembly and Assembly

1. Consult the "Shock Absorber Disassembly and Assembly" section for M models. The Sprint shocks are disassembled like the 1969 and earlier shocks.

Rear Swing Arm Removal

1. Remove the rear wheel as described in the rear wheel "Removal and Installation" section.

2. Remove the rear shocks as described in the above section.

3. Remove the crossover shaft nut and washer on models C and H, then tap on the shaft end with a soft mallet until the brake operating lever is free of the shaft.

4. Bend back the pivot bolt lockwasher ear and remove the pivot bolt nut and lockwasher, then tap out the bolt with a brass drift.

5. Remove the swing arm assembly and the thrust washers from between the frame mounting ears.

1. Nut (2)
1A. Bolt (2) (Models H & SS)
1B. Lockwasher (2) (Models H & SS)
2. Stud washer (2)
3. Rubber bushing (4)
4. Retainer Ring (2)
5. Lower cover (Model C)
6. Seal ring
7. Spring
8. Upper cover (Model C)
9. Shock absorber
10. Spring guide, Upper H & SS)
11. Spring guide, Lower (Models H & SS)

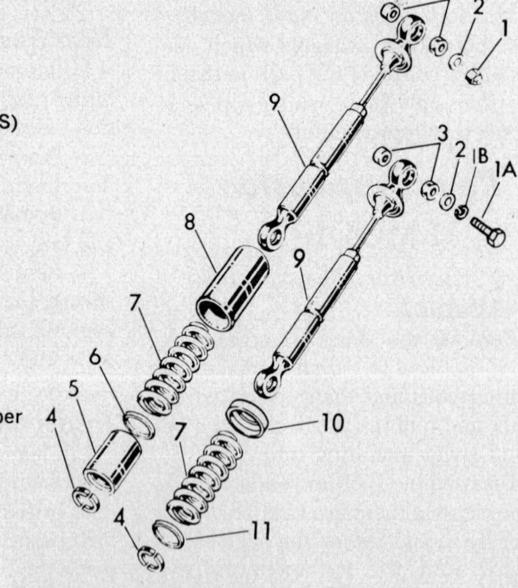

Sprint rear shock absorber assembly

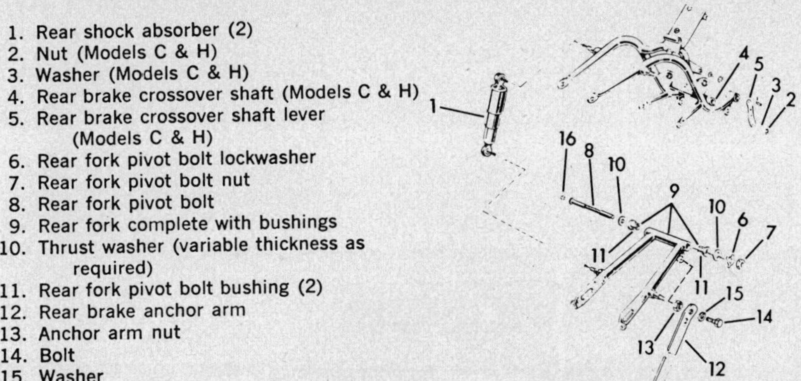

Sprint rear arm assembly—S and B models

Inspection and Repair

1. Clean all parts in a suitable solvent and blow them dry.

2. Inspect all parts for a worn or damaged condition and replace them as necessary. If the swing arm is bent or damaged, it must be replaced.

3. Inspect the fit of the pivot bolt and the swing arm bushings for excessive play and replace them as necessary. Replace the bushings by drifting them out and pressing in the replacements. Ream new bushings with Reamer (H-D part no. 94810-65) or a suitable substitute.

Rear Swing Arm Installation

1. Install the anchor arm nut, bolt and washer but do not tighten them down until the rear wheel has been installed and aligned.

2. Position the swing arm between the frame mounting ears with the anchor arm on the right side of the frame. Make sure the chain is over the swing arm and not behind it.

3. Hold the left-side thrust washer in place between the frame and swing arm, and slip the pivot bolt into position part way. Hold the right-side thrust washer in place and push the pivot bolt the rest of the way through.

4. Rotate the pivot bolt until the locating lugs on the pivot bolt's left end are in alignment with the mounting ear notches, then position the lockwasher so the bent prong seats in the groove in the frame, and mount and secure the pivot bolt nut. Secure the nut by bending the lockwasher ear up against the nut.

5. Check the motion of the swing arm for excessive play or too tight a fit which is indicated by binding, and adjust the play by adding or removing the spacer washers. Variable-thickness thrust washers are available in assorted sizes from 0.6–1.2 mm.

6. Lubricate the swing arm assembly by greasing the pivot bolt grease fitting until grease comes out from both bushings.

7. Mount the brake crossover shaft lever on the crossover shaft and secure it with a nut and lockwasher.

8. Mount the shock absorbers, carefully mounting the right shock so the brake rod is on the inside.

9. Mount the rear wheel as described in the rear wheel "Removal and Installation" section.

INDEX

HARLEY-DAVIDSON TWINS

MODEL IDENTIFICATION

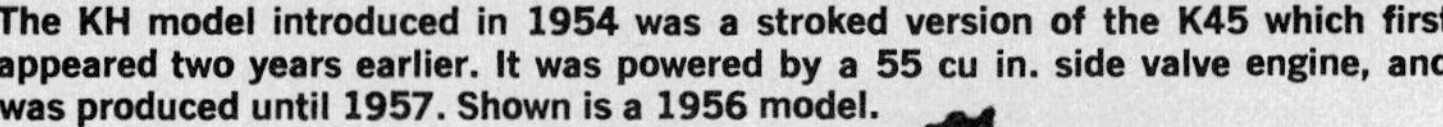

The KH model introduced in 1954 was a stroked version of the K45 which first appeared two years earlier. It was powered by a 55 cu in. side valve engine, and was produced until 1957. Shown is a 1956 model.

The Servi-Car, first introduced in 1932, is the last of the big twin side valve models. Powered by a 45 cu in. flat head, the Servi-Car has long been used as an all purpose vehicle by police departments, garages, etc.

The 1000cc XLCH shown here first came out in 1972. The most noticeable difference between this model and the earlier 900cc models is the side cover configuration which says 1000 on it.

The XLCH pictured here has its roots in the XL 55 which was the first of the OHV Sportster type machines. It can be differentiated from the XLH because it has a kick starter to turn over its 900cc engine.

The XLH is basically a Sportster with an electric starter and no kick starter. First introduced in 1967, the XLH models have a different gas tank and a starter button located on the right handgrip assembly.

Here is the 1000cc version of the XLH. It too has redesigned side covers, and the alternator makes itself known by the conspicuous bulge on the right side cover.

Shown here is an old model 74 complete with springer front end and rigid frame. You'll notice that the engine's exterior appearance has changed very little over the years. The first OHV 74 came out in 1941, became the Hydra-Glide in 1949 with the advent of a hydraulically damped front end, was changed to the Duo-Glide in 1959 when rear shocks were added, and became known as the Electra-Glide in 1965 when an electric starter was added.

Shown here is a modern day Electra-Glide equipped as a "Dresser".

The Superglide, depicted here, was first introduced in 1971, and is intended to be the sport version of the big 74.

Here we have the 1972 model of the Electra-Glide with the new hydraulic disc brake. At last a 74 that can be hauled down from highway speeds with comfort and assurance.

GENERAL SPECIFICATIONS

SERVI-CAR
Models: G, GA, GE
(electric starting—1964 and later)

DIMENSIONS (in.)	
Wheelbase	61
Overall length	100
Overall width	48

CAPACITIES	
Fuel tank	3.4 U.S. gallons
Oil tank	3.5 quarts
Transmission	0.75 pints

ENGINE	
Model design.	G, GE
Number cyl.	2
Type	45 degree, V-type, 4 cycle
Horsepower	21 bhp at 4400 rpm
Bore	2.75 in. (69.85 mm)
Stroke	3.1825 in. (96.8 mm)
Piston displace.	4528 cu in. (742 cc)
Torque	30 ft lbs at 2400 rpm
Compress. ratio	4.75—1

TRANSMISSION

Type: Constant mesh—hand shift

Gear ratios	
first gear	14.4—1
second gear	9.7—1
third gear	5.85—1
reverse	12.45—1

Number of sprocket teeth	
Engine sprocket	22
Clutch sprocket	59
Countershaft	17
Rear wheel	37

TIRE DATA	Size
1968 and earlier	5.00 x 16
1969 and later	5.10 x 16

SPORTSTER
Models XL, XLH, XLCH

	XL, XLH	XLCH	XLH, (1000 cc)	XLCH
DIMENSIONS (in.)				
Wheel base	①	57	58½	58½
O.a. length	②	83¼	87¼	87¼
O.a. width	34	③	33	32
O.a. height	40½	42	40½	42
Road clear.	④	⑤	6¾	6½

CAPACITIES	XL, XLH	XLCH	XLH, XLCH	(1000 cc)
Fuel Tank (gal)	4.0	2.2	4.0	2.2
Oil tank (quarts)	3	3	3	3
Transmiss. (pints)	1½	1½	1½	1½
ENGINE				
No. cyl.	2	2	2	2
Type	45°	V-type	4 cyl.	O.H.V.
Weight (lbs)	204	188	—	—
Horsepower	⑥	⑦	⑧	⑨
Bore	3.00 in. (76.2 mm)		3.188 in. (81 mm)	
Stroke	3.8125 in. (96.8 mm)			
Piston displace.	(883 cc) 53.9 cu in.		(997.5 cc) 60.9 cu in.	
Torque	⑩	52 ft lbs at 3800 rpm		
Compress. ratio	⑪		9.0—1	

① Wheel base (in.)
1966 and earlier: 56½
1967 and later: 58½

② Overall length (in.)
1966 and earlier: 87
1967-1972: 89

③ Overall width (in.)
1966 and earlier 29½
1967-1972: 34

④ Road clearance (in.)
1966 and earlier: 2½ (minimum)
1967 and later: 5½

⑤ Road clearance (in.)
1966 and earlier: 4⅛ (minimum)
1967 and later: 6⅞

⑥ Horsepower
XL: 42 bhp at 5500 rpm
XLH: 55 bhp at 6300 rpm
XLH (1970-71): 58 bhp at 6800 rpm

⑦ Horsepower
XLCH (1969 and earlier): 55 bhp at 6300 rpm
XLCH (1970-71): 58 bhp at 6800 rpm

⑧ Horsepower
XLH (1972 and later): 61 bhp at 620 rpm

⑨ Horsepower
XLCH (1972 and later): 61 bhp at 6200 rpm

⑩ Torque
XL: 48 ft lbs at 3600 rpm
XLH: 52 ft lbs at 3800 rpm

⑪ Compression ratio
XL: 7.5—1
XLH: 9.0—1

TRANSMISSION

Type: Constant mesh—foot shift

GEAR RATIOS

	1966 & Earlier XL, XLH 1967 XLH, XLCH (Optional)	XL, XLH 1972 XLCH (Standard)
first gear	10.63—1	11.16—1
second gear	7.69—1	8.08—1
third gear	5.82—1	6.11—1
fourth gear	4.21—1	4.42—1

	1970-71 XLCH
first gear	11.74—1
second gear	8.50—1
third gear	6.43—1
fourth gear	4.66—1

NUMBER OF SPROCKET TEETH

	1966 & Earlier XL, XLH 1967 XLH, XLCH (Optional)	XL, XLH 1972 XLCH (Standard)
engine	34	34
clutch	59	59
countershaft	21	20
rear wheel	51	51

	1970-71 XLCH
engine	34
clutch	59
countershaft	19
rear wheel	51

TIRE DATA

	Front	Rear
XL, XLH (To 1966)	3.50 x 18	3.50 x 18
XLH (1967-1969)	3.25/3.50 x 19	4.00 x 18
XLCH (To 1969)	3.25/3.50 x 19	4.00 x 18
XLH (1970-1972)	3.75 x 19	4.25 x 18
XLCH (1970-1972)	3.75 x 19	4.25 x 18

GLIDE MODELS
Models: FL, FLP, FLH, FX

DIMENSIONS (in.)

	FL, FLP, FLH (To 1969)	FLP, FLH (1970 on)
Wheel base	60.0	61.5
O.a. length	92.0	89.0
O.a. width	35.0	38.5

	FX
Wheel base	62.7
O.a. length	92.0
O.a. width	33.0

CAPACITIES

Fuel tank (small)	3.5 U.S. gal.
(large—1965 & later)	5.0 U.S. gal.
Reserve tank (small)	1.0 U.S. gal.
(large)	1.2 U.S. gal.
Oil tank	4 quarts
Transmission	1.5 pints

ENGINE

Model Desig.	FL, FLP, FLH, FX
No. cyl.	2
Type	45 degree, V-type, 4 cycle O.H.V.
Horsepower:	
FL, FLP	57.0 bhp at 5200 rpm
FLH	66.0 bhp at 5200 rpm
Bore	$3^7/_{16}$ in. (87.3 mm)
Stroke	$3^{31}/_{32}$ in. (100.8 mm)
Piston displace.	73.66 cu in. (1207 cc)
Torque:	
FL, FLP	62 ft lbs at 3200 rpm
FLH	65 ft lbs at 3200 rpm

COMPRESSION RATIOS

FL, FLP 7.25—1
FLH 8.00—1

TRANSMISSION

Type: Constant mesh band or foot shift Gear ratios (internal)

	4 forward	3 forward, 1 reverse
first gear	3.00—1	2.71—1
second gear	1.82—1	1.50—1
third gear	1.23—1	1.00—1
fourth gear or reverse	1.00—1	2.66—1

NUMBER OF SPROCKET TEETH

Models: FL, FLP, FLH, FX (three and four speed models)

Clutch	37
Transmission	22
Rear wheel	51

ENGINE SPROCKET

	FL, FLP	FLH, FX	Sidecar FL, FLH
Four spd. transmiss.	23	24	22
Three spd. transmiss.	23	24	22

OVERALL GEAR RATIOS (final drive)

Four Speed Transmissions

	FL, FLP	FLH, FX	Sidecar FL, FLH
First gear	11.19	10.74	11.69
Second gear	6.79	6.50	7.09
Third gear	4.59	4.39	4.79
Fourth gear	3.73	3.57	3.90

Three Speed Transmissions

	Solo FL, FLH	Solo FLH	Sidecar FL, FLP	Sidecar FLH
First gear	10.01	9.69	12.20	10.57
Second gear	5.60	5.36	6.75	5.84
Third gear	3.73	3.57	4.50	3.90

TIRE DATA

	Front	Rear
Solo		
FL, FLP, FLH	5.00 x 16	5.10 x 16
FX	3.75 x 19	5.10 x 16
With passenger		
FL, FLP, FLH	5.00 x 16	5.10 x 16
FX	3.75 x 19	5.10 x 16
Sidecar pass.	5.00 x 16	5.10 x 16
FL, FLP, FLH	5.10 x 16	

TUBES: 5.00 x 16 with 5.00 x 16 tire
5.00/5.10 x 16 with 5.10 x 16 tire
3.25 x 18/19 with 3.75 x 19 tire

TUNE-UP AND MAINTENANCE

TUNE-UP OPERATIONS

Contact Breaker Points

SINGLE CONTACT BREAKER WITH MANUAL ADVANCE

This system has one pair of points which regulate the spark in both cylinders simultaneously. The narrow lobe of the cam times the front cylinder and the wide lobe times the rear cylinder. Both cylinders operate from a single ignition coil which fires both spark plugs, but at different stages of the combustion cycle. If the front cylinder is firing, the rear is dormant, since no combustible mixture is present during the exhaust stroke. Manual rotation of the circuit breaker base provides advanced or retarded timing.

Contact Point Adjustment

1. Loosen the point lock screw.
2. Rotate the eccentric adjusting screw until the points open far enough to insert a wire feeler gauge of 0.020 in.
3. Secure the lock screw and check gap against any movement which may have occurred when securing the screw.

SINGLE CONTACT BREAKER WITH AUTOMATIC ADVANCE

This type of contact breaker works the same way as the manual advance type, except that the spark is automatically advanced through the action of flyweights in the contact breaker base as the engine speed increases.

Contact Point Adjustment

The points on the automatic advance type are set in the same manner as on the manual advance type.

DOUBLE CONTACT BREAKER

This system has individual contact point sets and coils for each cylinder. The single lobe cam on the timer shaft has a single mark which aligns with the fiber cam follower for each set of points when the points are open to their fullest travel. Therefore, the cam opens each set of points once every crankshaft rotation.

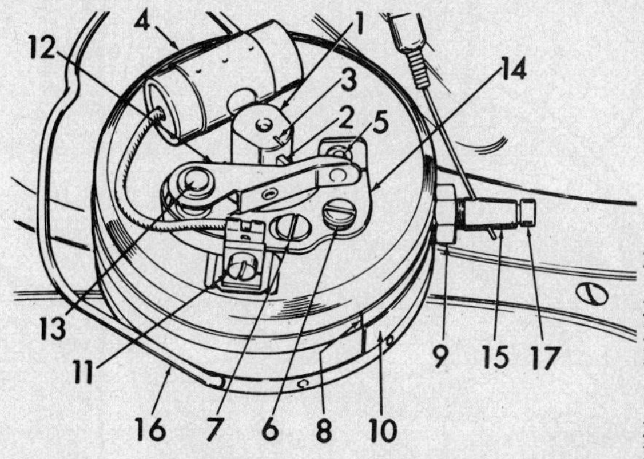

1. Breaker cam
2. Fiber cam follower
3. Cam timing mark
4. Condenser
5. Contact points
6. Lock screw
7. Eccentric adjusting screw
8. Timing mark
9. Adjusting stud lock nut
10. Timing adjusting stud plate
11. Wire stud screw
12. Circuit breaker lever
13. Pivot stud
14. Contact point and support
15. Timing adjusting stud
16. Cover retainer
17. Control wire lock screw

Single contact breaker with manual advance

1. Breaker cam
2. Fiber cam follower
3. Cam timing mark
4. Condenser
5. Contact points
6. Adjustable point lock screw
7. Eccentric adjusting screw
8. Timing marks (1965 model)
9. Circuit breaker head nut (2)
10. Circuit breaker head
11. Wire stud screw
12. Circuit breaker lever
13. Pivot stud
14. Contact point and support
15. Stem clamp nut
16. Stem clamp

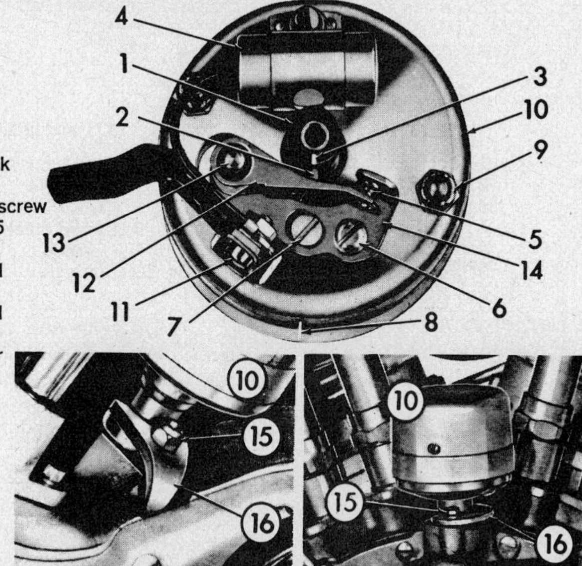

Single contact breaker with automatic advance

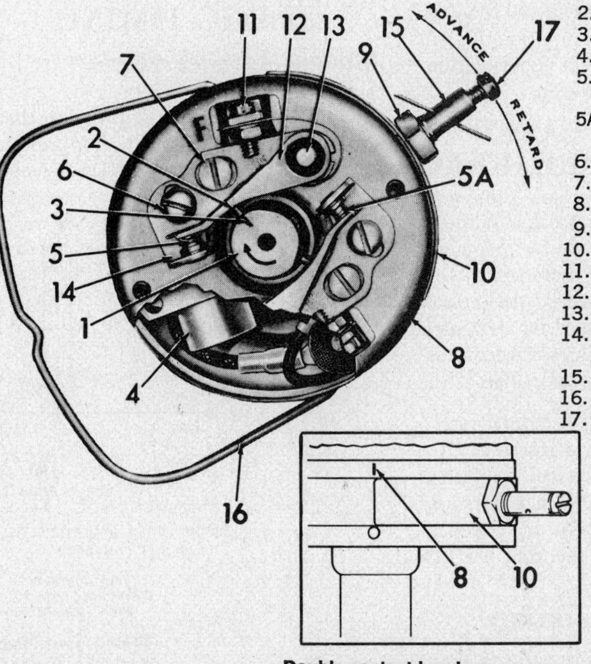

1. Cam
2. Fiber cam follower
3. Cam timing mark
4. Condenser
5. Front cylinder contact points

5A. Rear cylinder contact points

6. Lock screw
7. Adjusting screw
8. Timing mark
9. Adjusting stud lock nut
10. Timing adjusting plate
11. Wire stud screw
12. Circuit breaker lever
13. Pivot stud
14. Contact point and support
15. Timing adjusting stud
16. Cover retainer
17. Control wire lock screw

Double contact breaker

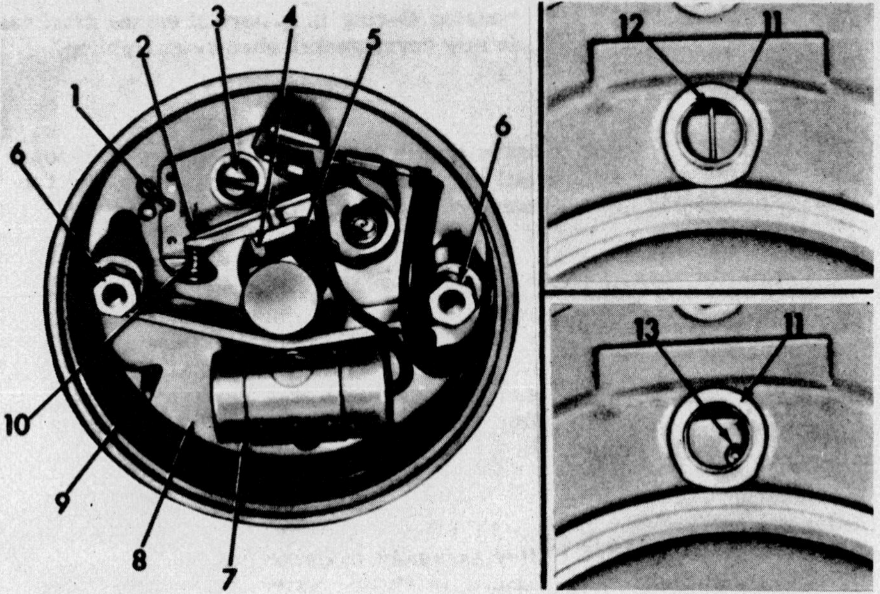

1971 and later contact breaker

1. Contact point adjusting notch
2. Moving contact point
3. Stationary contact point lock screw
4. Cam follower
5. Breaker cam
6. Circuit breaker plate screw (2)
7. Condenser
8. Circuit breaker plate
9. Circuit breaker plate adjusting notch
10. Contacts
11. Timing inspection hole
12. Advance (35°) timing mark on flywheel
13. Retarded (5° B.T.C.) position of piston top center mark on flywheel

Contact Point Adjustment

1. Loosen the front cylinder (indicated by an "F" on the breaker base) breaker point lock screw.
2. Set the front points to 0.022 in. by manipulating the eccentric adjusting screw until the proper gap is obtained. Check the gap with a wire feeler gauge.
3. Secure the lock screw and check gap against possible movement caused by securing the lock screw.
4. Follow the above procedure on the rear set of points.
5. Check ignition timing any time the rear set of points are adjusted as this will affect the timing. Consult "Ignition Timing" section for procedures.

1971 AND LATER CONTACT BREAKER

This type of circuit breaker is the same as the "Single Contact Breaker With Automatic Advance." If, during point gap setting procedures, a discrepancy of 0.004 in. or more is discovered, the breaker cam must be checked for eccentric travel. Consult the "Electrical Systems" section for additional information.

Contact Point Adjustment

1. Loosen the point lock screw.
2. Rotate the eccentric adjusting screw until a gap of 0.018 in. is obtained.
3. Secure the lock screw and check for movement caused by securing the lock screw.

Ignition Timing

Telescoping the front pushrod cover will allow the valve motion to be observed. When the valve adjusting mechanism comes all the way up, the valve is closed. The piston comes up for the compression stroke just after the front intake valve closes.

Remove the crankcase view plug and replace it with a Timing Mark View Plug (H-D part no. 96295-65). This is absolutely necessary if a strobe-light is to be used, otherwise oil will be thrown through the view plug port.

STATIC TIMING

Manual Advance Single Contact Breaker

1. Rotate the engine slightly less than one-half revolution past the compression stroke until the front cylinder flywheel timing mark is centered in the view port in the left crankcase.
2. Check to make sure that the contact breaker base timing mark aligns with the timing adjusting plate mark.
3. Rotate the contact breaker head counterclockwise against its stop by turning the left handlebar grip forward. This is the fully advanced position.
4. Check to see that the cam lobe timing mark is aligned with the fiber cam follower. Loosen the adjusting stud locknut and shift the breaker head until alignment is obtained. Secure the locknut. The breaker base timing mark will no longer be aligned with the timing adjusting plate.
5. With the contact breaker base in its fully advanced position and a timing light hooked up, rotate the engine until the

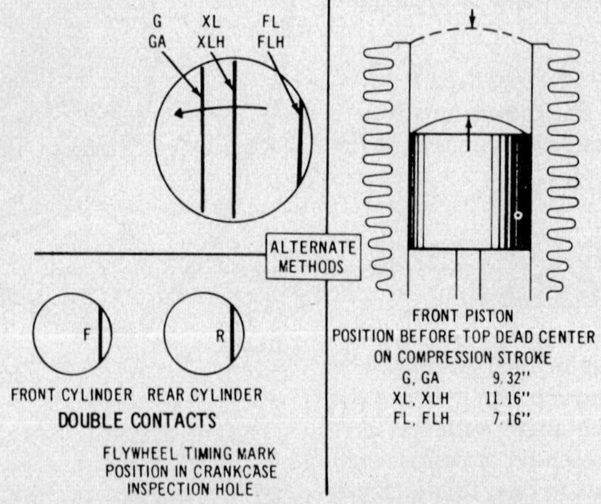

Timing mark position for all models with manual advance contact breakers

lamp goes out and the flywheel timing mark is in position.

6. Rotate the engine backward slightly, with the spark retarded, to see if the light comes back on.

7. If the light stays on, the timing is retarded and must be adjusted by loosening the adjusting stud locknut and rotating the breaker base counterclockwise until the light flickers or goes off in the fully advanced position.

8. If the light goes off before the fully advanced position is reached, the timing is advanced and must be adjusted by loosening the adjusting stud locknut and rotating the breaker base clockwise until the light flickers or goes off in the fully advanced position.

9. Secure the locknut and shift the breaker head from the retard to the advance position to see if the points begin to open when the breaker cam reaches the advance stop. The flywheel must be positioned correctly during the entire operation.

10. It is not necessary to time the rear cylinder as this operation times both.

Manual Advance, Double Contact Breaker

1. Time the front cylinder (marked "F" on the breaker base) in the same manner as for a single contact breaker, manual advance unit. There is an "F" marked on the flywheel for the front cylinder.

2. The rear cylinder is timed in the same manner except that the flywheel mark will be "R" instead of "F," and the test lamp must be attached to the coil for the rear cylinder.

3. If the contact points remain closed in the fully advanced position, the timing is late and the points should be set slightly further apart.

4. If the contact points begin to open before the cam is in the advanced position, the timing is early and the points should be set closer together. These adjustments will result in a setting different from the original 0.022 in.

5. There is no flywheel mark for the rear cylinder on 1961 Duo-Glide models before engine number 61FLH 7987 and piston position must be used instead.

6. A spark timing gauge (H-D part no. 95885–61), which screws into the spark plug hole, can be used to indicate piston position. If such a gauge is unavailable, top dead center can be found by inserting a screwdriver into the spark plug hole and rotating the engine until the highest point of the piston travel is located. By observing valve movement, the compression stroke can be determined.

Automatic Advance Contact Breakers

The main difference in adjusting this

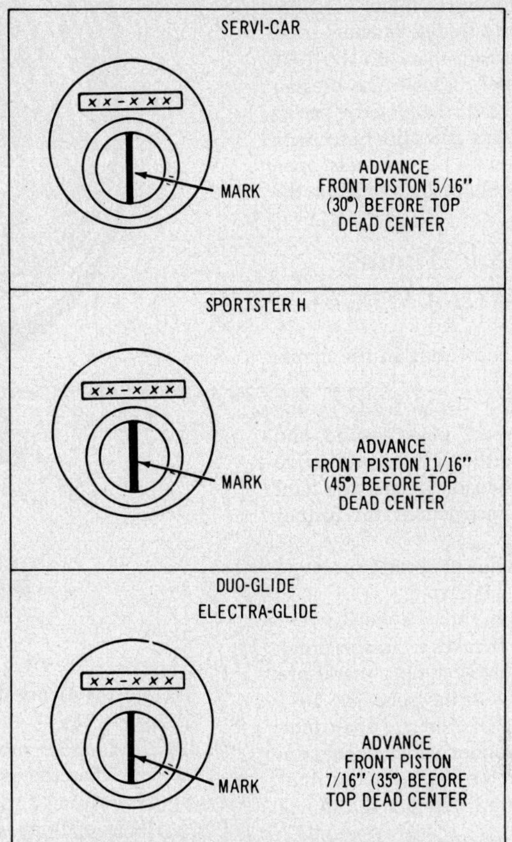

Timing mark positions for all models with automatic advance contact breakers

type of contact breaker is that there is no adjusting screw for advancing the timing. Timing is advanced by a set of flyweights on the cam and therefore the cam must be turned clockwise until the flyweights rest against their stops. This advanced position must be maintained while checking and adjusting the timing. Remember that the cam engages the flyweights on the camshaft in two positions which are 180 degrees apart. Only one of these positions will provide correct timing.

1. Prepare the machine for timing as for the manual advance contact breakers, rotating the engine until the flywheel timing mark is properly aligned in the inspection hole and the cam mark aligns with the cam follower.

2. The cam must be turned clockwise, with the flyweights against their stops, and held in this position during the timing procedure.

3. If the cam follower and the cam timing mark do not align, the contact breaker head must be shifted until alignment is obtained in the following manner:

a. A limited adjustment is available on 1965 and earlier models due to slotted holes in the timer plate in which the base studs ride. Loosen the contact breaker head nuts and shift the base by prying between the plate lip and the base stud with a screwdriver.

b. If this is not enough, the entire shaft must be loosened, lifted free, and rotated a couple of teeth until the follower and the cam mark are in alignment. This will cause the base timing marks to go out of alignment.

c. When the cam and fiber align, while in the fully advanced position, secure the timer plate nuts. Overtightening will cause distortion of the timer base plate and affect timing.

d. On 1966 and later models, there is a clamp on the contact breaker base which allows for adjustment over a 360 degree arc.

e. Loosen the clamp nut or bolts, and shift the head until the cam and fiber are aligned. Shifting the head clockwise will retard the spark and counterclockwise will advance it.

4. The ignition is timed in the same manner as on manual-advance-type contact breakers. Since there is a certain amount of end-play in the contact breaker drive-gear, the timing will always be slightly retarded. To arrive at a truly accurate setting, a strobe light should be used with the engine running since end-play is taken up with the engine in operation.

1971 and Later Case-Mounted Contact Breakers

1. Timing procedures are the same as

for automatic advance contact breakers.

2. Timing is set by the flywheel mark rather than the cam mark on the 1970 and earlier models. Loosen the breaker base screws and shift the plate by prying at the breaker plate adjusting notch with a screwdriver until the contacts open when the flywheel mark is aligned in the inspection hole.

Dynamic Timing

(TIMING WITH A STROBE LIGHT)

1. Install the view plug in the crankcase view port.

2. Connect the strobe leads to the front cylinder spark plug, ground, and the red lead to either a battery terminal or the point hot lead. Consult the light manufacturer's instructions for further information.

3. Run the engine at normal operating temperature at 2,000 rpm.

4. Aim the light into the view port.

5. Adjust the breaker as in the previous sections until the timing marks are lined up properly in the port. The 1971 and later models have a single dot to indicate the rear cylinder which should appear on or near the mark for the front cylinder while viewed under the timing light.

6. Once the engine is turned off, the timing will retard 30 degrees automatically.

NOTE: *For points replacement refer to "Contact Breaker" section in "Electrical Systems."*

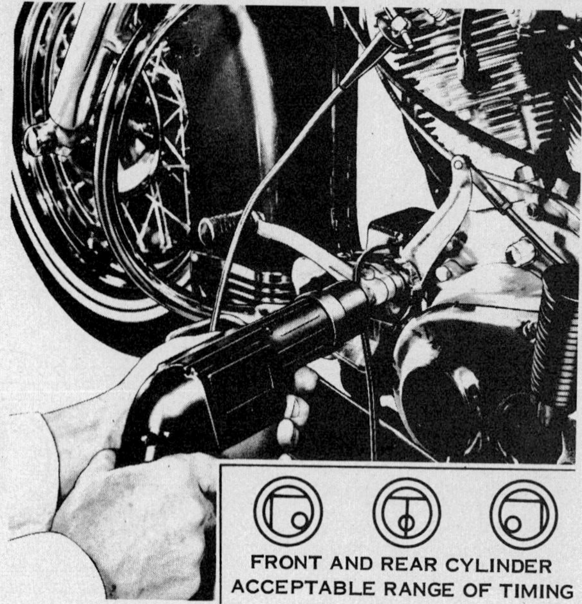

Timing with a strobe light

Sportster XLCH Magneto

The magneto is a generating system composed of a rotor, an induction coil with primary and secondary circuits, a condenser, a contact breaker cam, and contact breaker points. High-voltage discharge is produced and directed to each spark plug twice in a 360 degree cycle, because the magnetic field must be collapsed twice so each plug will fire on its given power stroke. The magneto is shut off by a grounding circuit controlled by a "kill" button.

On 1964 and earlier models, the magneto is fixed so only advanced spark timing is produced. The 1965 and later models have a mobile mounting plate which allows the spark to be retarded for easier starting. This adjustment is made by a twist grip on the left side of the handlebar.

ADJUSTING CONTACT BREAKER POINTS

1. The points should be examined for proper gap and surface 1,500 miles after installation and then at intervals of 2,000 miles.

2. Remove the carburetor, air cleaner, and magneto cover.

3. 1963 and earlier models have a ⅜ in. safety gap when the cover is installed. Gap can be set using a spare cover with a 1 ¼ × 1 ½ in. opening, and a ⅜ in. rod. Never bend the points as they are prepositioned to ensure a correct gap.

4. 1964 and later models have no safety gap.

5. Rotate the engine in its normal running direction until the cam follower is on either high point of the cam.

6. Clean the points with either a point file or fine metal sandpaper before setting, and blow clean.

7. Check the gap with a feeler gauge (preferably a wire-type gauge set at 0.015 in.).

8. Adjust the points by loosening the pivot and adjustment screws and rechecking them.

SETTING IGNITION TIMING

Ignition is timed with the spark advanced and is correctly set when the forward piston is 45 degrees (11/16 in.) before top dead center. This corresponds to the flywheel timing mark position when it is in the center of the inspection hole.

Prior to 1965, magnetos were of the fixed-position variety. The 1965–1967 models have an adjusting screw which, when turned clockwise, advances the timing. A counterclockwise adjustment retards the timing. Applying mild pressure to the magneto housing will cause it to follow the movement of the adjusting screw. The correct amount of spark retardation is obtained by backing off the setting stop screw until there is a distance of 3/16 in. between its head and seat. Adjust the screw only one turn; more will affect retarded timing.

Late 1967 XLCH models have a slot and pin in the base plate which serves the same function as the adjustment screw.

1. Remove the magneto cover, timing inspection hole plug, and spark plugs. Telescope or remove the front intake pushrod cover so that valve motion can be observed.

2. Place the transmission in high gear and put the motorcycle on its center stand so that the engine can be turned by rotating the rear wheel.

3. Set the contact points. (See "Adjusting Contact Breaker Points.")

4. Turn the engine until the exposed valve closes (travels to its highest point). Slowly rotate the engine in its normal running direction until the timing mark is aligned in the center of the inspection hole.

5. Align the timing marks on the magneto base and mounting plate (if applicable—1964 and earlier).

6. If the narrow cam lobe is not located counterclockwise from the cam follower and the breaker points aren't beginning to open, the magneto must be adjusted. Be sure the spark is fully advanced.

7. On 1965 to early 1967 models, an adjustment can be made with the magneto advance stop screw.

8. If alignment, which will not interfere with the air cleaner, cannot be made through adjustment of the screw, or if it is a fixed-position magneto, lift up the magneto until its drive gears become unmeshed. Turn the cam the amount it was out of position and replace the magneto. Repeat this until the proper point timing is obtained and then secure the magneto.

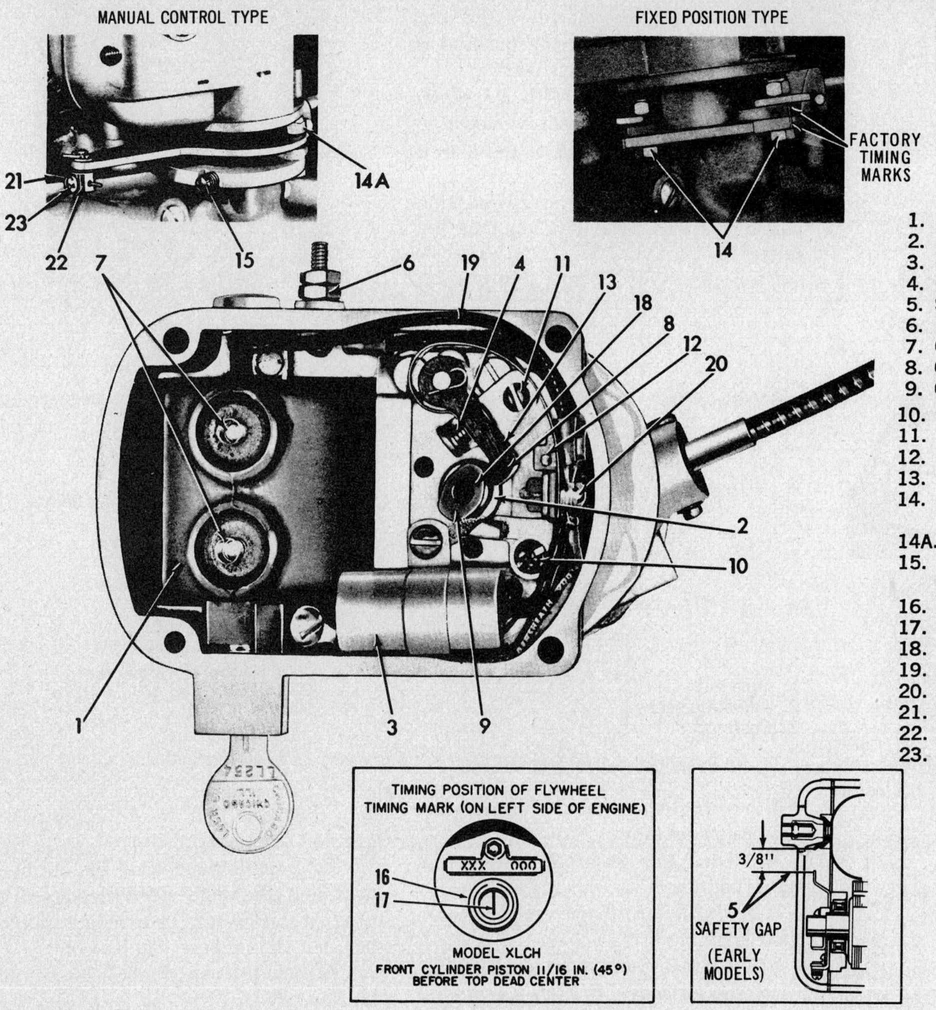

MANUAL CONTROL TYPE

FIXED POSITION TYPE

FACTORY TIMING MARKS

TIMING POSITION OF FLYWHEEL TIMING MARK (ON LEFT SIDE OF ENGINE)

MODEL XLCH
FRONT CYLINDER PISTON 11/16 IN. (45°) BEFORE TOP DEAD CENTER

3/8"
5 SAFETY GAP (EARLY MODELS)

1. Induction coil
2. Rotor
3. Condenser
4. Circuit breaker points
5. Safety gap points (1964 & earlier)
6. Ignition cut-out terminal post
7. Coil secondary terminal spring
8. Cam follower
9. Cam
10. Pivot screw
11. Adjustment screw
12. Adjustment stud
13. Cam oiler felt
14. Magneto mounting bolts & nuts (1964 & earlier)
14A. Magneto Mounting Bolts (1965)
15. Magneto advance stop screw (1965 to early 1967)
16. Timing inspection hole
17. Timing mark
18. Narrow cam lobe
19. Coil lead wire
20. Breaker point terminal post
21. Control wire (1965)
22. Swivel block (1965)
23. Control wire set screw (1965)

Magneto assembly with timing marks

9. A timing or continuity light is one accurate means of determining when the points begin to open. Attach one test lead to the terminal post or point leaf spring and the other to a ground. When the points break contact the light will go out. Never turn on the key if a continuity light with a self-contained power unit is being used as this will blow the light's bulb. An emergency method is to place cellophane between the points and to tug gently on it. When the points begin to open, the cellophane will be released.

10. A strobe light provides the most accurate setting since it is done with the engine running. This takes up any endplay and automatically advances the timing. Leads are attached to the front plug, ground, and the positive battery terminal. Timing view plug, part HD (no. 96295–65), must be used to prevent oil spray. The engine should be operating at between 1,500 and 2,000 rpms.

11. Recheck ignition timing, always rotating the engine in the direction or normal operation. Never overtighten the coil lead wire as this may damage insulators and cause a short circuit.

Valve Tappet Adjustment

Valve tappets must be adjusted with the engine cold or when no heat can be felt when your bare hand is placed on the cylinders.

SERVI-CAR MODELS

1. Unscrew the valve spring covers with the Valve Cover Wrench (H-D part no. 94521–31).
2. Rotate the engine until one of the intake tappets (those closest to the carburetors) is completely closed.
3. Loosen the tappet adjusting screw locknut.
4. Insert a thickness gauge set at 0.006 in.
5. Turn the tappet adjusting screw until a gentle tugging on the gauge is required to remove it. The gauge should be able to come free easily but with some slight drag.
6. Secure the locknut while holding the adjusting screw nut with a wrench so the adjustment isn't altered.
7. Check adjustment again. It may help to secure the locknut with the gauge still in place.
8. Rotate the engine until the other intake valve is closed and adjust it in the same manner.

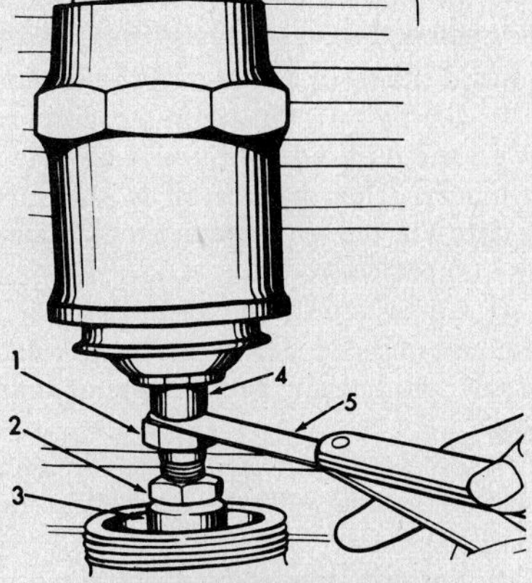

Servi-Car tappet adjustment

1. Tappet adjusting screw
2. Tappet adjusting screw lock nut
3. Tappet body
4. Valve stem
5. Thickness gauge

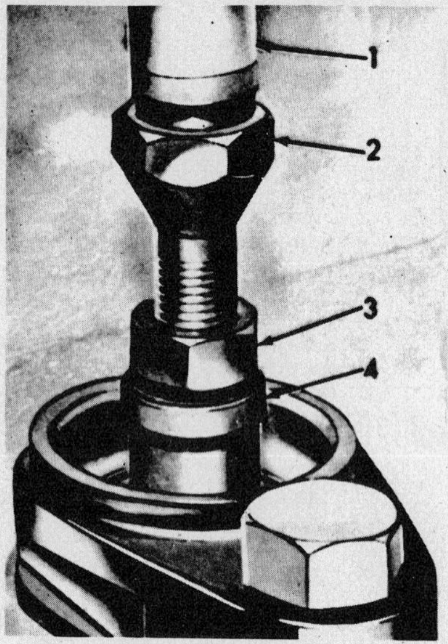

Sportster tappet adjustment

1. Push rod
2. Tappet adjusting screw
3. Tappet adjusting screw lock nut
4. Tappet body

9. Adjust the exhaust valves (those furthest from the carburetor) in the same manner to a setting of 0.010 in.

10. Examine the valve cover and guide gaskets; replace if necessary.

11. Secure the valve spring cover.

SPORTSTER

1. Press down on the pushrod cover retaining spring and remove the cover spring keeper.

2. Block up the telescoped cover so it doesn't slip down.

3. Rotate the engine until the valve that is to be adjusted is at its lowest position.

4. Loosen the tappet adjusting screw locknut and turn the adjusting screw into the tappet body until the pushrod is free and will shake slightly. Hold the pushrod just below the cylinder head and shake it toward the front and rear of the engine.

5. Gently turn the adjusting screw toward the pushrod until nearly all play is removed. Then back it off ¼ turn and secure the tappet screw locknut against the tappet body.

6. Check adjustment again for a slight amount of shake and the ability to rotate freely without any rough spots or binding.

7. Both ends of the valve covers must seat on the cork washers during reassembly.

8. Perform the above operations on the remaining three valve tappets.

GLIDE MODELS

1. Prepare for tappet adjustment as on Sportster models.

2. Loosen the tappet adjusting screw locknut and turn the adjusting screw into the tappet body so that the pushrod is shortened and will shake slightly.

3. Hold the pushrod with a wrench and turn the adjusting screw down to lengthen the rod until all of the play is taken up.

4. Mark the adjusting screw position with chalk and turn it down four full turns.

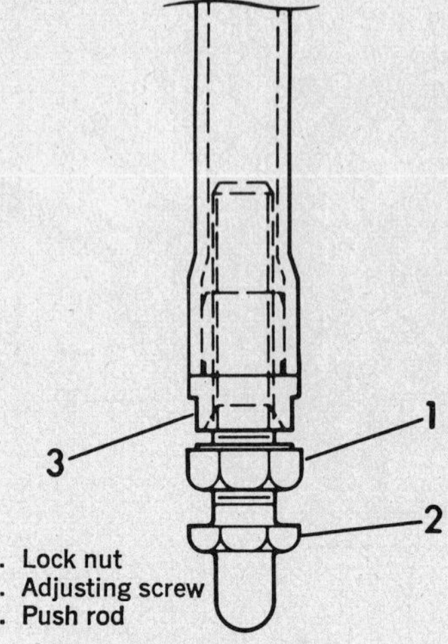

Glide models tappet adjustment

5. Secure the locknut while holding the pushrod steady.

6. Secure the pushrod cover-spring cap retainers.

7. Perform the above operations on the remaining three valves.

8. Use new gaskets whenever possible. Clean the surfaces with a safe solvent but keep the gaskets dry. Grease-soaked gaskets adhere to joint surfaces and may cause damage when removed.

Carburetor Adjustment

LINKERT MODEL "M" CARBURETOR

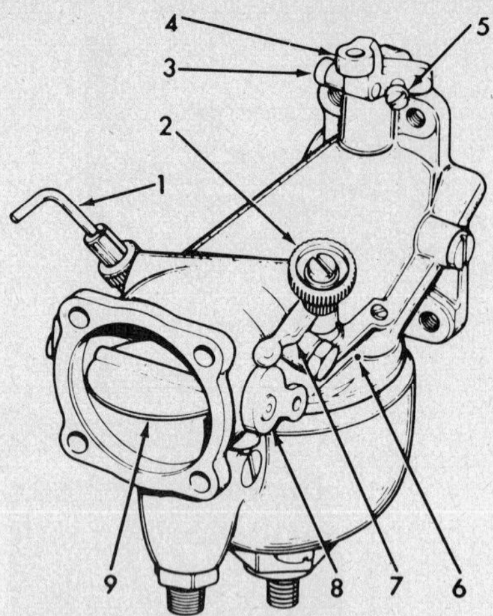

Model M carburetor adjusting points

1. High-speed needle
2. Low-speed needle
3. Throttle lever lock screw
4. Throttle lever
5. Throttle stop screw
6. Carburetor bowl vent
7. Low-speed needle lift lever
8. Choke lever
9. Choke disc

1. Screw both needles in until they meet their seat, but do not apply pressure.

2. Back the low-speed needle out five turns and the high-speed needle two turns. At this setting the machine should start, but the mixture will be rich.

3. Advance the spark all or almost all the way.

4. With the throttle closed and the engine at idle (idle can be set slightly high to ensure against stalling by turning throttle stop screw clockwise), turn the lowspeed needle in until the engine breaks up (runs erratically). Back the needle out 5–10 turns until a smooth idle is achieved.

5. Adjust the idle to the desired speed

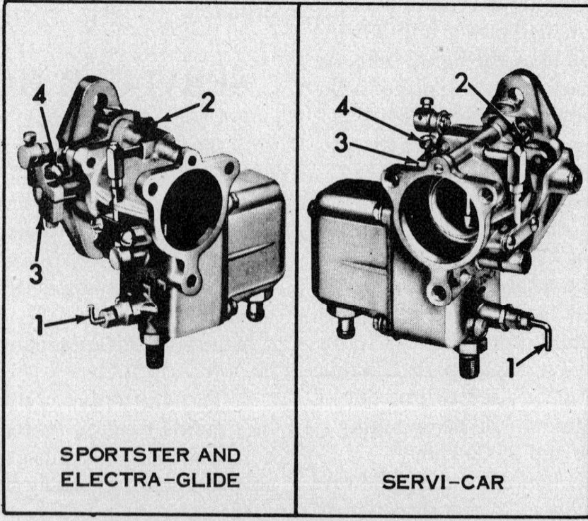

Model DC carburetor adjusting points

1. High-speed needle
2. Low-speed needle
3. Throttle lever
4. Throttle stop screw

with the throttle stop screw. Avoid very slow idle speeds as this causes premature bearing wear, excessive oil consumption, and poor low-speed acceleration.

6. Make a fine adjustment of the low-speed needle until the engine runs its smoothest. A slightly rich adjustment will provide the best all around performance and starting.

7. With the carburetor properly set, the engine should continue to idle more slowly but still smoothly, even when the spark is completely retarded.

8. The high-speed needle can be adjusted to compensate for high altitudes or prolonged high-speed operation.

LINKERT MODEL "DC" CARBURETOR

1. Check the cable adjustment to be sure that the throttle opens and closes fully. Run the engine until the normal operating temperature is reached.

2. Turn the low- and high-speed needles gently to their seat, and back the low-speed needle out 1 ½ turns so that the engine will start. You may wish to turn the idle stop screw clockwise to raise the idle speed slightly.

3. With the choke in the fully opened position and the spark fully advanced, turn low-speed needle in slowly until the engine misses and runs irregularly. Turn the needle out counterclockwise until the engine runs smoothly with the throttle closed. A slightly richer mixture, obtained by turning the needle in, will aid starting and overall performance.

4. Adjust the throttle stop screw until the desired idle speed is obtained. Avoid an idle speed that is too slow, since this causes bearing wear, excessive oil consumption, and poor low-end performance.

5. After adjusting the idle, slight readjustment of the low-speed needle may be required.

6. Turn the high-speed needle ¾–1 ¼ turns off its seat and run the machine at various speeds from 20 mph up, with the spark fully advanced. If the engine runs roughly, make small adjustments until you are satisfied. There should be uniform smoothness throughout the speed range.

7. Once a proper setting is arrived at, further readjustment should require no more than ⅛ turn of the low-speed needle and ¼ turn of the high-speed needle.

TILLOTSON MODEL "HD" CARBURETOR

1. Loosen the cable adjustment so that the throttle lever will open and close fully in response to handlebar manipulation.

2. Turn both the low and intermediate-speed needles in to their seats and then back out about ⅞ turn. This adjustment will allow the engine to start but will cause it to run too richly.

3. When the engine reaches normal operating temperature, open the choke all the way and fully advance the spark.

4. Set the throttle stop screw so the engine idles at about 2000 rpm.

5. Turn the intermediate needle in both directions until the engine runs at its smoothest, with no surge, and with a constant rpm pulse. When the optimal setting is achieved, back the needle out ⅛ turn so the mixture is slightly rich.

6. Adjust the idle stop screw so the engine runs at about 900–1,000 rpm.

7. Adjust the idle needle in the same manner as the intermediate needle.

8. Recheck both needle adjustments.

The idle mixture is made richer by turning the adjusting screw to the right and is made leaner by turning it to the left. The main nozzle provides a richer mixture when the screw is turned to the left and leaner when turned to the right.

TILLOTSON MODEL 'MD' CARBURETOR

1. Gently turn the adjusting screws in until they reach their seats then back main needle out 1 ½ turn and back the idle needle out ¾ turn.

2. Make sure that the cable allows the throttle to close fully.

3. With the engine idling at normal speed and temperature, and the throttle closed, adjust idle to desired rpm. Turning the screw to the right will increase the idle speed and turning it to the left will decrease it. Avoid excessively slow idle speeds.

4. Make idle mixture fine adjustment.

5. Road test the motorcycle at various speeds and make a fine, main needle adjustment until the engine operates smoothly throughout its range.

BENDIX MODEL 16P12 CARBURETOR

The low-speed needle is turned clockwise for a leaner mixture or counterclockwise for a richer mixture.

1. Gently turn the low-speed mixture needle clockwise to its seat, then back it out ½ turn. The engine should start at

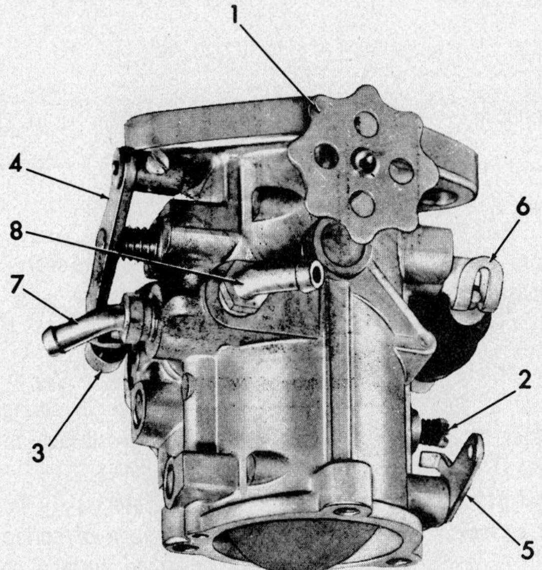

Model HD carburetor adjusting points

1. Low-speed needle
2. Intermediate speed needle
3. Throttle stop screw
4. Throttle lever
5. Choke lever
6. Accelerating pump
7. Inlet fitting
8. Vent fitting

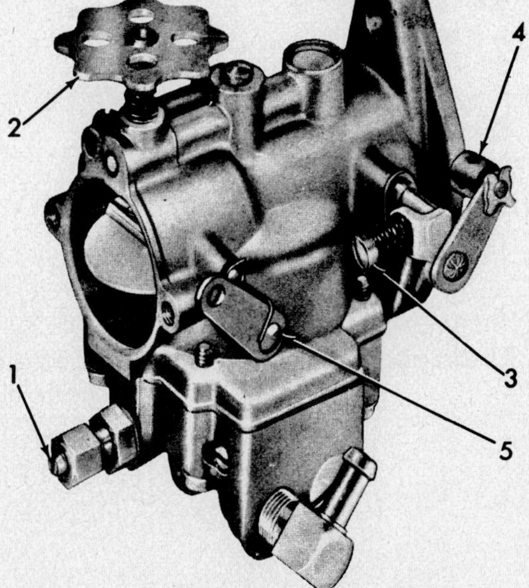

Model MD carburetor adjusting points

1. Main mixture adjusting screw
2. Idle mixture adjusting screw
3. Idle speed stop screw
4. Throttle control lever
5. Choke lever

this setting but will run too richly.

2. Make sure the cable allows the throttle to close fully.

3. With the engine at normal operating temperature, set the throttle stop screw to the desired idle speed. Avoid excessively slow idle speeds, as this will make starting difficult, waste oil, and will burn bearings.

4. Readjust the low-speed needle to the point where the engine runs at its smoothest and at its highest rpm.

5. Reset idle to 700–900 rpm.

6. If the exhaust system is modified or if the machine is to be operated at high altitudes, one of the following main jets may be substituted: nos. 90, 95, 100, 105, 110, 115, 120, and 125.

7. Late 1971 and later pump shafts are adjustable. The bottom hole provides the richest setting and the top hole provides the leanest.

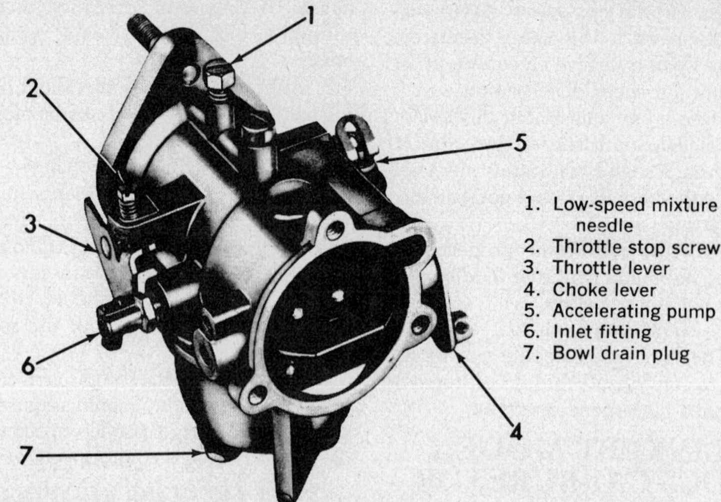

Model 16P12 carburetor adjusting points

TUNE-UP SPECIFICATIONS

	Servi-Car	Sportster	Glide Model
IGNITION TIMING			
Breaker point setting (gap)	0.020 in.	battery ignition: 1970 & earlier: 0.020 in. 1971 & later: 0.018 in.	1971 & earlier: 0.020 in. 1972 & later: 0.018 in.
Dwell	90° at 1000 RPM	1971 & earlier: 90° at 2000 RPM 1972 & later: 140° at 2000 RPM	
Ignition timing (retarded)	1963 & earlier: 26° (9/32 in.) BTC 1964 & later: 0° T.C.	1971 & earlier: 15° (5/64 in.) BTC 1972 & later: 10° (1/32 in.) BTC	5° (1/64 in.) BTC
Ignition timing (advanced)	30° (5/16 in.) BTC	1971 & earlier: 45° (11/16 in.) BTC 1972 & later: 40° (17/32 in.) BTC	35° (7/16 in.) BTC
SPARK PLUGS			
Spark plug gap setting (magneto ignition)	—	0.020 in.	—
Spark plug gap setting (battery ignition)	0.025-0.030 in.	0.025-0.030 in.	0.025-0.030 in.
Spark plug heat range (average use)	#3	#4	#3-4
TAPPET ADJUSTMENT			
Tappet clearance (cold)	0.010 (EX)	0.006 (in.) 1/4 turn loose from a no lash position	1/8 (4 turns) from seat
CLUTCH ADJUSTMENT			
Clutch Spring Adjustment	11/32 in. from releasing disc to outer disc	1970 & earlier: 3/16 in. from inner surface of spring tension plate to outer surface of spring cup flange. 11/32 in. from outer drive plate surface to releasing disc outer surface.	1967 & earlier: 31/32 in. from edge of spring collar to surface of outer disc. 1968 & later: 11/32 in. from edge of spring collar to surface of outer disc.
CARBURETOR ADJUSTMENT			
See "Carburetor Adjustment" section			

MAINTENANCE ITEMS

Oil Changes and Lubrication

CHANGING ENGINE OIL

1. Run the engine until normal operating temperature is reached.
2. Secure the motorcycle so it will stand straight up or lean slightly to the right.
3. Remove the oil tank drain plug and oil filler cap, and allow the oil to drain into a suitable receptacle. Kicking the engine through a couple of times will remove any remaining oil from the sump, however the crankcase need not be drained since it never retains more than five ounces.
4. Replace the drain plug, pour a quart of kerosine into the oil tank, and agitate the machine.
5. Repeat step no. 3.
6. Clean the oil filters thoroughly and blow them dry.
7. Replace the plug and add the specified quantity and grade of oil.

Harley-Davidson Oil	Grade	Air Temperature
Special Light	58	Below 40° F
Medium Heavy	75	Above 40° F
Regular Heavy	105	Demanding usage at high temperatures

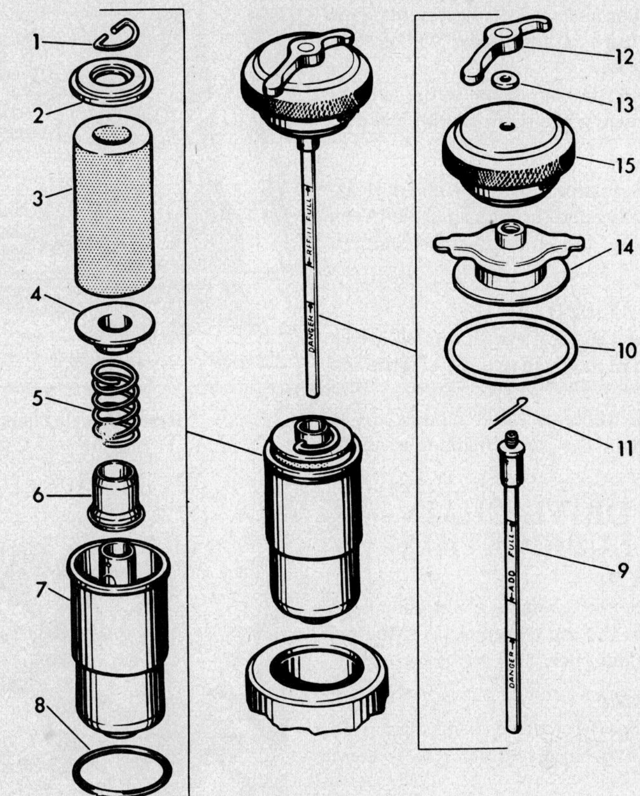

Oil tank filter assembly

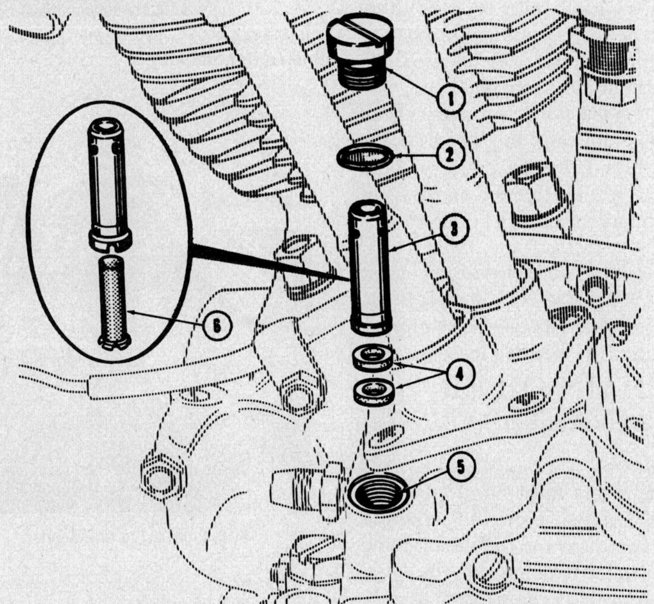

Hydraulic pushrod screen assembly

CHANGING TRANSMISSION OIL

1. Stand the motorcycle upright and remove the oil level plug from the chaincase bottom.
2. Fill the transmission through the large screw hole in the chaincase cover with engine oil until overflow begins from the oil level plug hole.
3. Secure both plugs when overflow ceases.
4. Change oil annually or every 5,000 miles.

NOTE: *Change oil immediately if the gearbox is ever immersed in water.*

CHANGING FORK OIL

1. Remove the fork drain plugs from the bottom of each slider and allow the fork oil to drain into a suitable recepticle. Pump the forks several times to insure complete drainage.
2. Install the drain plugs and remove the filler caps from the top of each fork tube.
3. Fill each tube with 6 ½ oz of Harley-Davidson fork oil (7 oz if the forks have just been taken down and cleaned) or some suitable substitute such as hydraulic brake fluid.
4. Gently pump the forks to expell any air which may be trapped inside and then secure the fork filler caps.

PRIMARY CHAIN LUBRICATION

Servi-Car

1. Loosen the oiler screw locknut and turn the adjusting screw to the right to decrease oil flow, and to the left to increase it.

2. Never make large adjustments since a small turn of the screw will greatly affect oil flow.

3. Hold the adjusting screw with a screwdriver while securing the locknut.

Sportster

The Sportster's primary chain is automatically oiled through a port between the chain and transmission compartments.

Glide Models

1. The 1964 and earlier models are lubricated in the same manner as is the Servi-Car.

2. The 1965 and later models are lubricated in the same manner as is the Sportster.

DRIVE CHAIN LUBRICATION

Servi-Car

The Servi-Car drive chain oiler is adjusted in the same manner as is the primary chain oiler.

Sportster

The Sportster drive chain oiler is adjusted in the same manner as is the Servi-Car.

Glide Models

1. Some early models have no provision for drive chain oiling. In this case, the chain should be lubricated with Harley-Davidson "Chain Saver" or a similar product every 1,000 miles or more often if operated in dusty conditions. Light viscosity engine oil may also be used, although it is not as effective.

2. 1964 models with a primary chain guard oiler lubricate the dirve chain through a hose from the primary oiler. Therefore, the only attention necessary is to the primary chain oiler and to the hose.

3. The oil return bleed-type oiler found on 1964 and earlier models is adjusted like the primary oiler. The normal screw setting is ¼ turn off its seat.

CHAIN OILER MAINTENANCE

Servi-Car

Servi-Car oilers must be attended to every 2,000 miles. Turn the adjusting screw out two turns and run the machine for several miles to flush out the lines. Secure the primary oiler screw at 1 ⅛ turns, and the drive oiler at ½ turn off the screw's seat for normal operation.

Sportster

The sportster primary oiler needs no attention. The drive chain oiler requires flushing every 2,000 miles in the following manner:

1. Back off locknut as far as possible.

2. Count the number of turns it takes before the screw reaches its seat.

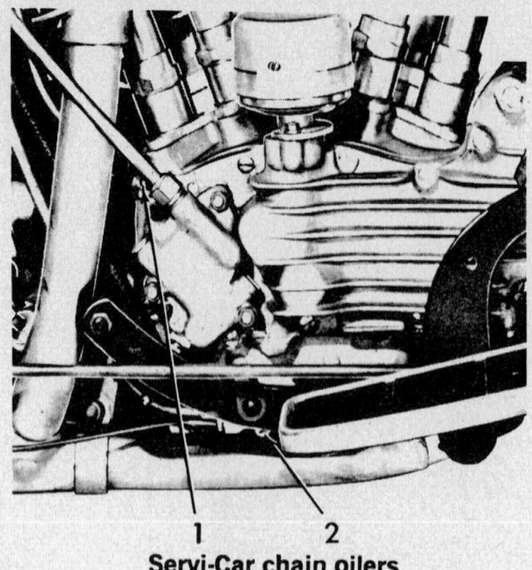

Servi-Car chain oilers

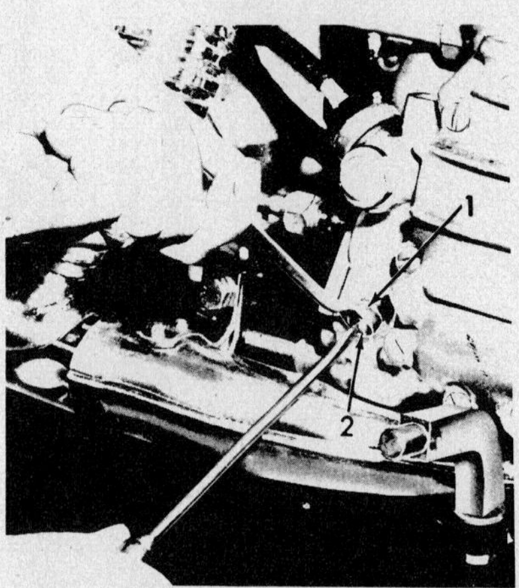

Glide model primary chain oiler—(1963 and earlier models)

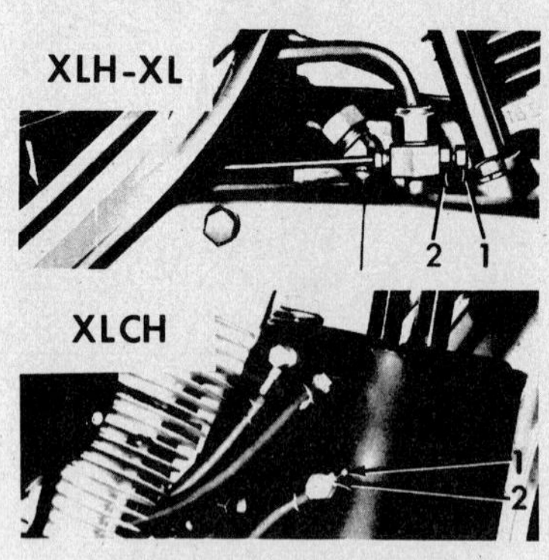

Sportster drive chain oiler

3. Remove the screw and blow the line clear of any deposits.

4. Replace the adjusting screw. Normal operating setting is ¼ turn open for 1968 and earlier models, and ¾ turn for 1969 and later models.

Glide Models

Glide primary oilers are handled in the same manner as Servi-Car oilers except that the normal setting is 1 ¼ turns. The 1965 and later models have a supply port at the pump which may be blown clear after the port screw and washer are removed. The drive chain oiler is handled in the same manner as is the Sportster drive chain oiler, with the screw set ¼ turn open.

CABLE AND FRAME LUBRICATION

Cable and frame lubrication is done by a grease gun at the lubrication points indicated in the periodic service schedule. Grease the brakes sparingly or the shoes may become greasy. One application of the grease gun will usually be sufficient.

Cleaning

FUEL STRAINER

The "M" type carburetor has a strainer under the float bowl which should be cleaned every 2,000 miles or as often as necessary. Remove the strainer by closing the petcock and removing the lower knurled cap. The cap should be finger-tight.

Other carburetors have no internal strainer and the fuel is strained at the petcock. To clean this type, the tank must be emptied and the petcock must be removed. Make sure any dirt lying at the lip of the hole is also removed. Perform this every 2,000 miles or whenever necessary.

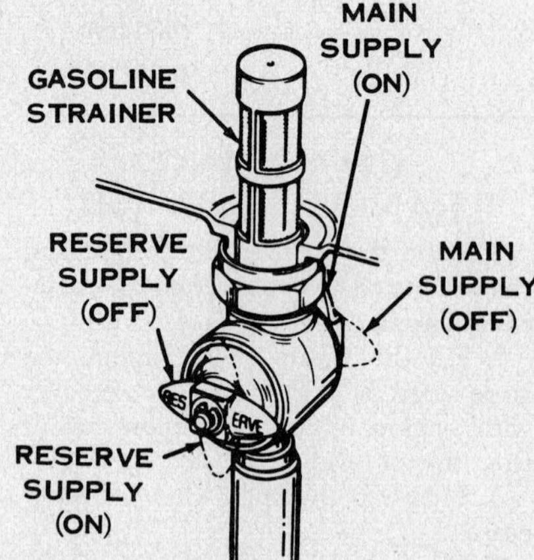

Fuel strainer on diaphragm type petcock

AIR CLEANER

The metal mesh-type filter need never be replaced, but should be cleaned every 1,000 miles in a safe solvent and saturated with engine oil. For *extremely* dusty conditions, this should be performed every 100 miles or at least once a day.

The corrugated paper-type element should be blown free of dirt every 1,000 miles, or more often in dusty conditions. If the surfaces are oily or sooty, the element can be cleaned with a safe solvent. When the element ceases to come clean, it must be replaced. Never coat it with oil.

The plastic foam-type element uses oil in the same manner as the metal mesh air cleaner and requires service at the same intervals. A sooty surface is normal but when the surface pores become clogged or the surface becomes mottled, cleaning is necessary. Remove the filter from the screen and wash it in a nonflammable solvent or detergent. When completely dry, soak it in engine oil, work the oil in until it is an even color, and allow the excess to drain off. The filter is now ready to be replaced.

Routine Checks and Adjustments

CABLE LENGTH ADJUSTMENT

Cables stretch over a period of time and it is necessary to make adjustments periodically. It is important to leave some play in the cable to avoid snapping off the ferrule or breaking the cable in two. On cables with adjusting devices, make sure you leave some play and that the locknut is securely fastened. On cables without these devices (i.e., throttle cables) adjust by loosening the cable clevis and pulling the cable through until the desired play is left. Make sure that the loose operations of any other parts.

CLUTCH ADJUSTMENT

Servi-Car

RELEASE MECHANISM ADJUSTMENT

1. Remove the inspection hole cover and loosen the adjusting screw locknut.
2. Turn the adjusting screw clockwise to decrease play and counterclockwise to increase play. Adjust so that the lever has at least ⅛ in. free-play before disengagement begins.
3. Hold the adjusting screw in place and secure the locknut.
4. Adjust the clutch control cable at the clevis until there is 1/16 in. clearance between the lever and the cover stud when disengaged.

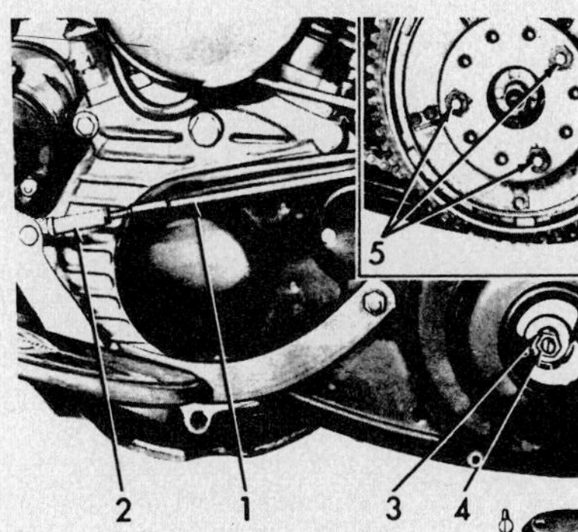

Servi-Car clutch adjustment

CLUTCH SPRING ADJUSTMENT

1. If the clutch drags or slips after the release mechanism is properly adjusted, the tension springs must be adjusted.
2. Tighten the tension adjusting nuts evenly ½ turn at a time to correct clutch slippage. When correct, the clutch will hold while the engine is being cranked.
3. Loosen the adjusting nuts in the same manner if the clutch drags.
4. At no time should there be less than ⅞ in. between the inner edge of the pressure plate shoulder and the face of the release disc. This distance should be 1 1/32 in. on a new clutch and progressively less as wear increases.
5. If the clutch will not hold at ⅞ in. gap, it must be disassembled and inspected.

Glide Models

FOOT CONTROL ADJUSTMENT

1. Remove the chainguard clutch cover (1964 and earlier models), or chain housing cover (1965 and later models).
2. Place the foot pedal in the fully engaged position (toe down).
3. Loosen the pushrod adjusting screw locknut, and turn the adjusting screw until the end of the clutch release lever has about ⅛ in. free-play before the clutch disengages. Turning the screw to the right will decrease the movement and to the left will increase the movement.
4. Secure the locknut while holding the adjusting screw with a screwdriver and recheck the adjustment.
5. On 1964 and earlier models, the release lever will strike the transmission cover. The 1965 and later models should have ¼ in. between the lever and the starter drive housing.
6. The foot pedal should clear the bearing cover to prevent the rod from bending.

HAND CONTROL ADJUSTMENT

1. Loosen the adjusting sleeve until there is about ¼ in. free movement at the hand lever before disengagement begins (½ in. on 1972 models).
2. Turn the sleeve to the right for less lever play, or to the left for more, and secure the locknut.
3. If the above steps fail to correct the problem, or if the sleeve has already been adjusted all the way out, go on to the following steps.
4. Move the clutch release lever until all the slack in the actuating mechanism has been taken up. You will notice a difference in lever motion.
5. If, at this point, there is not ⅜–⅞ in. between the lever and the starter motor, take the following steps.
    a. Loosen the sleeve locknut and turn the sleeve to the right until it is resting against the locknut.
    b. Remove the clutch cover and loosen the pushrod locknut. Turn the adjusting screw clockwise to move the release lever backward, or counterclockwise to move it forward.
    c. Secure the locknut while holding the adjusting screw with a screwdriver when the lever is about ½ in. from the starter motor.
    d. Secure the clutch cover using a new gasket and a gasket sealer.
6. Repeat steps 1 and 2 to complete the adjustment.

HAND LEVER CABLE REMOVAL AND INSTALLATION

1. Turn the adjusting sleeve to the right until it seats against the locknut.
2. Remove the cable by lifting the ferrule clear of the anchor pin and sliding it through the slot.
3. Replace with the pin slot toward the inside.
4. Replace pin-type assemblies with the open end facing down.

HAND CLUTCH BOOSTER CONTROL ADJUSTMENT

The routine adjustment that is made to maintain the correct amount of hand lever play is done in the following manner:

1. Loosen the control-coil adjusting sleeve locknut and turn the adjusting sleeve to the right until there is one or more inches of play at the hand lever.
2. Loosen the bellcrank adjusting screw locknut and turn in the adjusting screw until the bellcrank will no longer cross top dead center when shifted by hand.
3. Loosen the upper adjuster nut which controls the tension of the clutch booster spring. Loosen it all the way.
4. Slowly turn out the bellcrank adjuster screw and repeatedly check the release position that the crank will assume —moving it by hand—until it remains over top dead center. The crank should reach the end of its travel at about ⅛ in. over top dead center. Secure with the locknut.
5. Adjust the clutch rod until the release lever has about 1/16 in. play, and secure the locknut.
6. Back off the adjusting sleeve until

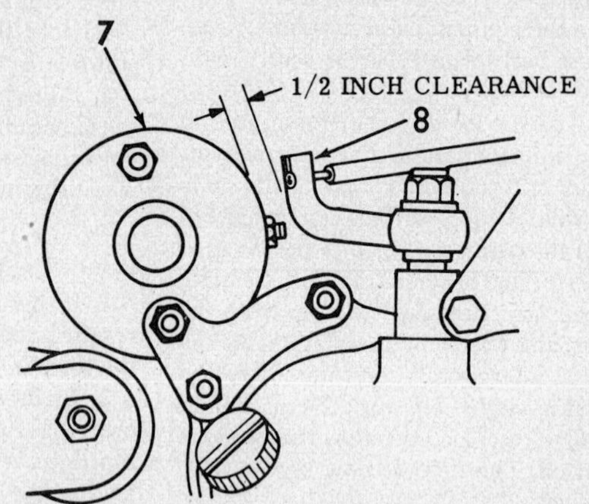

1. Clutch cable adjusting sleeve
2. Sleeve lock nut
3. Bracket
4. Clutch push rod adjusting screw lock
5. Clutch adjusting screw
6. Clutch spring adjusting nuts
7. Starter motor
8. Clutch release lever

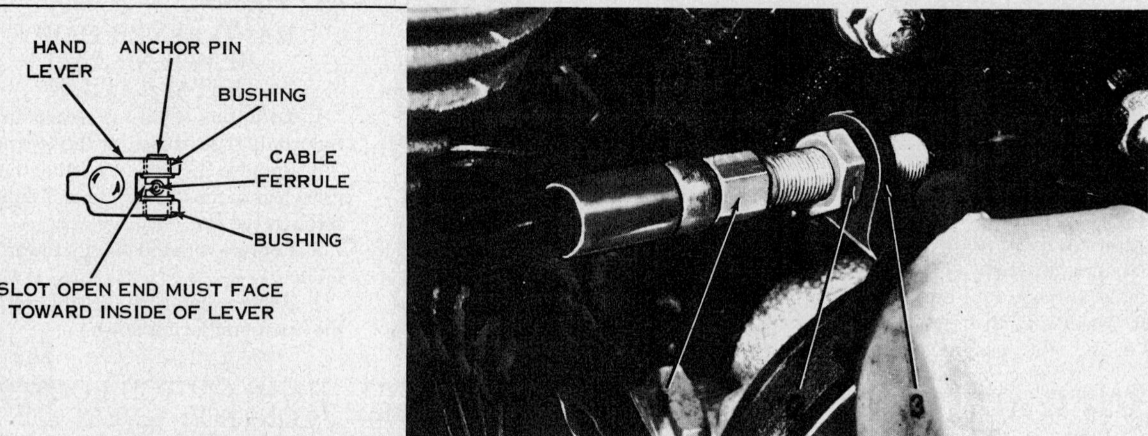

Hand clutch adjustment

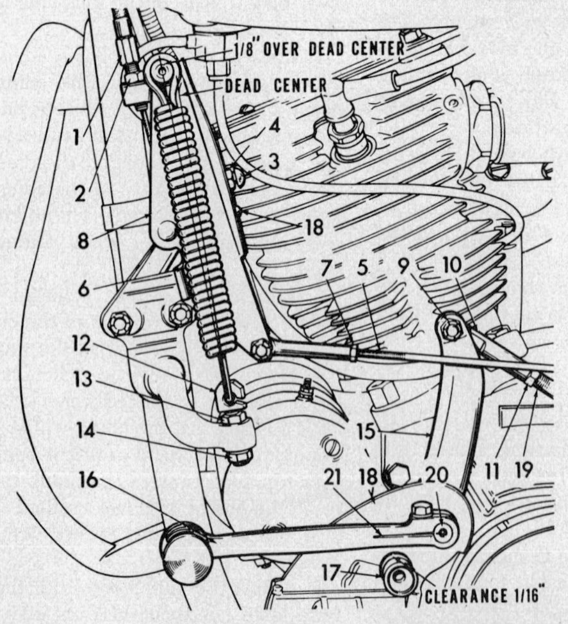

1. Control coil adjusting sleeve
2. Control coil adjusting sleeve lock nut
3. Bell crank adjusting screw
4. Bell crank adjusting screw lock nut
5. Clutch lever rod
6. Clutch control booster spring
7. Clutch lever rod lock nut
8. Clutch control booster bell crank
9. Shifter rod end bolt
10. Shifter rod end
11. Shifter rod end lock nut
12. Clutch booster spring tension adjuster
13. Clutch booster spring tension upper adjuster nut
14. Clutch booster spring tension lower adjuster nut
15. Gear shifter lever
16. Gear shifter foot lever and rubber pedal
17. Foot lever cover mounting stud (1964 & earlier models)
18. Grease gun fittings (2)
19. Shifter rod
20. Foot lever positioning mark
21. Foot lever clamping slot

Hand clutch booster control adjustment

the clutch hand lever has about ½ in. play before the clutch begins to release and then secure the locknut.

7. Pull in the clutch hand lever to its stop and tighten the lower adjuster nut for the booster-spring tension until the had lever remains in. Slowly loosen the nut until the lever returns to the fully extended position.

8. Secure the upper adjuster nut which controls the tension of the booster spring.

The following procedure may help to eliminate hand lever stiffness, failure of the bellcrank to resume its position, or slipping or dragging of the clutch.

1. Back off the clutch lever rod locknut and adjust the rod until the actuating lever has about ½ in. of play.

2. Move the actuating lever forward until all slack is take up.

3. The 1964 and earlier models require about 4 ¼ in. between the lever slot and the shifter housing.

4. The 1965 and later models require about ¼ in. between the chain housing and the clutch lever rod.

Sportster

CLUTCH CABLE AND RELEASE MECHANISM ADJUSTMENT

1. Loosen the locknut on the sprocket cover.

2. Insert a screwdriver and turn the clutch adjusting screw counterclockwise.

3. Placing the hand lever in the fully extended position should seat the releasing worm inside the sprocket cover.

4. Check the cable for binding within its housing if the hand lever doesn't fully return to its seat.

5. Turn the cable adjusting sleeve at the hand lever until the worm almost reaches its stop.

6. Turn the adjusting screw clockwise until there is play in ⅛ of the hand lever's total movement. This is indicated by slightly increased tension on the lever as it approaches the released position.

7. While holding the adjusting screw steady, secure the locknut. Test-ride the motorcycle to check for slipping or dragging.

CLUTCH SPRING ADJUSTMENT

1. Disconnect the battery ground wire from the negative terminal on XLH models.

2. Remove the left footrest and rear brake lever from their splined shafts.

3. On 1966 and earlier models, remove the stoplight switch from its mount, without disconnecting the wires, and place it out of the way.

4. Place a drip pan under the chain cover and remove the cover and gasket.

5. Remove the clutch cover screws, retainers, cover, and gasket. Tap the cover gently to remove it, but do not pry on it as this may warp it and cause leaks.

6. Tighten the adjusting nuts, one-half turn at a time, making sure that they seat in their locked position against the adjusting plate after each turn. The nuts have hex-heads of 7/16 and ½ in. sizes.

7. When properly adjusted, the pressure plate should be uniformly 3/16 in. from the outside of the spring cup flanges.

8. If tightened beyond 7/64 in. clearance, the clutch will not release. The necessity of such an adjustment would indicate worn or oily clutch plates. Excessive tightness will damage the clutch release rods.

1971 AND LATER SPORTSTER CLUTCH RELEASE MECHANISM ADJUSTMENT

1. Remove the access plug of the release mechanism adjusting screw.

2. Adjust the hand lever for free-play before the clutch starts to release by observing the motion of the adjusting screw.

3. If play is present, loosen the adjusting screw locknut and turn the screw inward until increased pressure is felt, then back it out ¼ turn. Secure the locknut while holding the screw with a screwdriver.

4. If no play is present, remove the chaincase cover and check to make sure that the three balls return to their bottom position when the release ramp and lever are released.

5. Loosen the coil adjusting sleeve locknut.

6. Turn the sleeve in until there is no cable slack when the balls are seated in their bottom position.

7. Secure the case cover and adjust the release rod screw as previously described.

1. Sprocket cover bolt (2)
2. Sprocket cover
3. Control cable end
4. Clutch release worm and lever
5. Clutch release worm and lever spring
6. Clutch adjusting screw lock nut
7. Clutch adjusting screw
8. Clutch release worm cover
9. Clutch release rod—left
10. Clutch release rod—right
11. Clutch release rod—right center
12. Clutch release rod—left center
13. Sprocket cover roll pin
14. Clutch cable felt seal retainer
15. Clutch cable ferrule (2)
16. Clutch cable felt seal

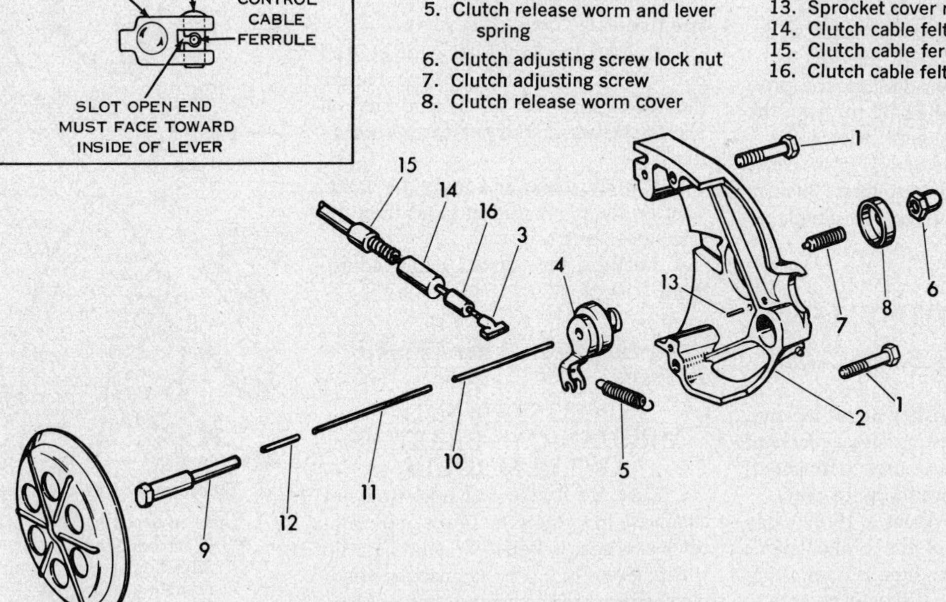

1970 and earlier clutch release mechanism

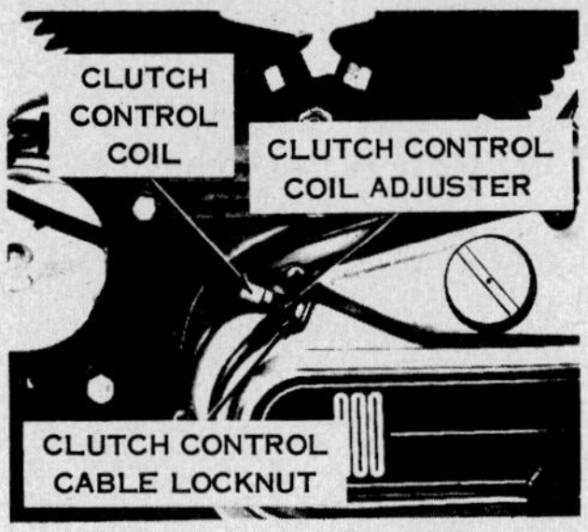

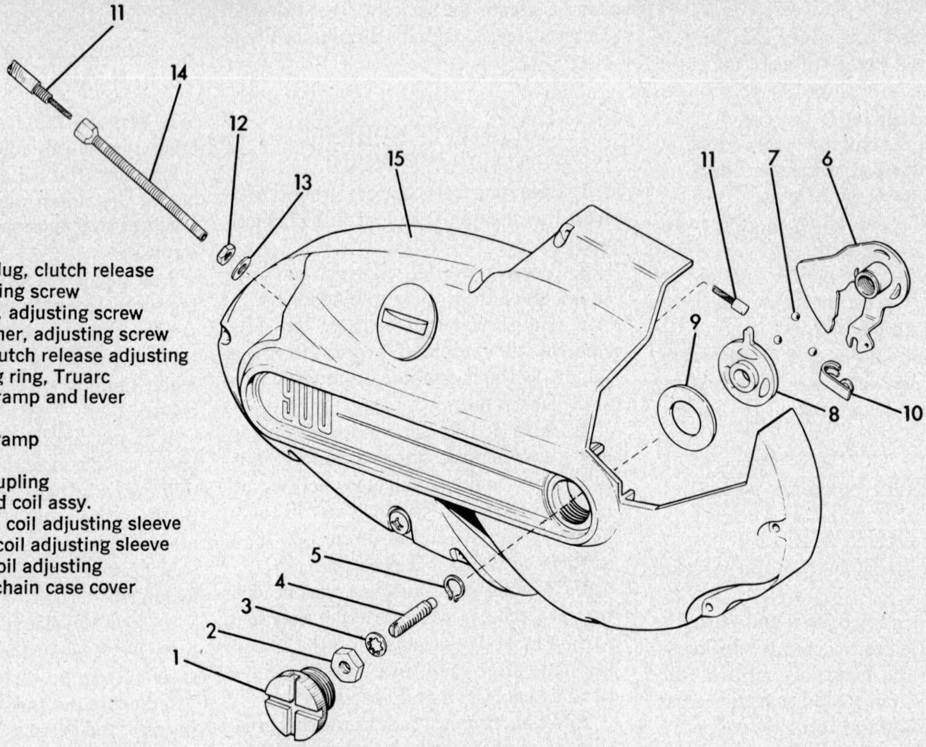

CLUTCH CONTROL COIL
CLUTCH CONTROL COIL ADJUSTER
CLUTCH CONTROL CABLE LOCKNUT

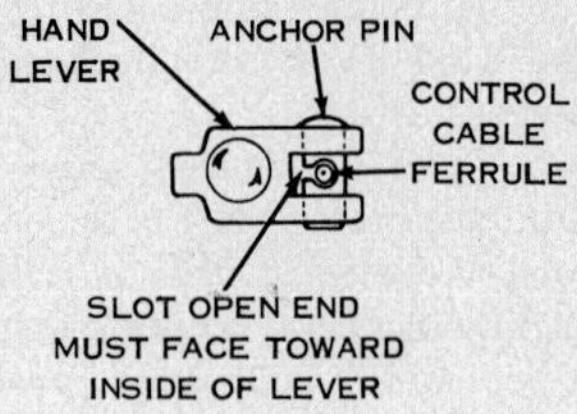

HAND LEVER
ANCHOR PIN
CONTROL CABLE FERRULE
SLOT OPEN END MUST FACE TOWARD INSIDE OF LEVER

CLUTCH ADJUSTING SCREW LOCKNUT
CLUTCH ADJUSTING SCREW

1. Access plug, clutch release adjusting screw
2. Lock nut, adjusting screw
3. Lockwasher, adjusting screw
4. Screw, clutch release adjusting
5. Retaining ring, Truarc
6. Release ramp and lever
7. Ball (3)
8. Release ramp
9. Washer
10. Cable coupling
11. Cable and coil assy.
12. Lock nut, coil adjusting sleeve
13. Washer, coil adjusting sleeve
14. Sleeve, coil adjusting
15. Primary chain case cover

1971 and later clutch release mechanism

1971 AND LATER SPORTSTER CLUTCH SPRING ADJUSTMENT

1. This procedure is the same as described in the "Sportster" section.

2. When properly adjusted, the pressure plate should be 11/32 in. from the outer surface of the outer drive plate.

3. If tightened beyond 5/16 in. clearance, the clutch will not release. Such an adjustment will damage the clutch release rods.

BRAKE ADJUSTMENT

Adjusting Front Brake Cable (All Models)

1. Loosen the adjusting sleeve locknut.

2. Turn the adjusting sleeve locknut clockwise for less play (free movement) and counterclockwise for more play.

3. When there is about 3/16 in. cable play, or when ¼ of the brake lever's movement is free, tighten the adjusting sleeve nut. The wheel should be able to spin freely; it if doesn't, the shoes must be centered (adjusted).

Adjusting Front Brake Shoes (All Models)

1. Raise the front wheel so it may rotate freely.

2. Loosen the brake shoe pivot stud nut and sleeve nut. (Substitute "brake shoe pivot stud" for "pivot stud nut" on Sportsters. Loosen this but do not remove it).

3. Spin the wheel and apply the brake. Tighten the pivot stud nut and then the axle sleeve nut.

4. Recheck for correct cable adjustment.

Adjusting Rear Wheel Brake Linkage

SPORTSTER AND MECHANICAL BRAKE 45 AND 74 MODELS

1. Turn the brake rod adjusting nut clockwise to tighten the brake and counterclockwise to loosen it. The nut has a lip which serves as a stop against the clevis pin in the operating lever. Using a screwdriver as a lever against the brake operating lever, pry it forward, and turn the

Front brake cable adjustment

1. Front wheel brake hand lever
2. Brake adjusting sleeve
3. Adjusting sleeve lock nut
4. Adjusting sleeve nut
5. Brake shoe pivot stud nut
6. Brake shoe pivot stud
7. Axle sleeve nut

adjusting nut. This saves wear on the nut's lip.

2. There should be ¼ in. of play in the brake pedal before the brakes begin to operate. If the brake still drags, center the shoes.

HYDRAULIC BRAKE (SERVI-CAR)

1. Back off the brake rod clevis locknut until the brake rod clevis is disconnected from the master cylinder operating lever.

2. Shift the lower end of the lever forward until the lever top touches the master cylinder piston clevis.

Sportster rear brake linkage adjustment

1. Brake rod adjusting nut
2. Brake rod
3. Operating lever
4. Brake shoe pivot stud nut
5. Rear wheel axle nut

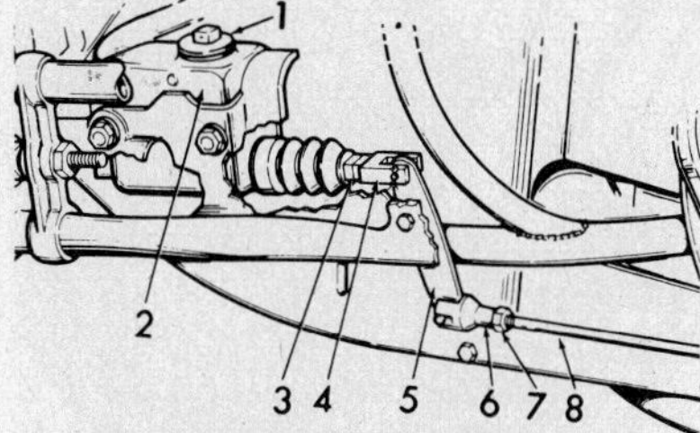

Servi-Car brake linkage adjustment

1. Master cylinder filler plug
2. Master cylinder
3. Connecting link rod clevis lock nut
4. Connecting link rod clevis
5. Master cylinder operating lever
6. Brake rod clevis
7. Brake rod clevis lock nut
8. Brake rod

3. Shift the lower end of the lever backward 1/16 in. to assure clearance between the piston clevis and lever.

4. Adjust the brake rod clevis so the clevis pin can be inserted wihtout further lever movement.

5. If the lower end touches the frame when the pedal is released, the lever must be adjusted up at the piston clevis.

6. If pedal play is less than the prescribed amount, excessive master cylinder wear will result.

HYDRAULIC BRAKE (GLIDE MODELS)

1. Expose the piston pushrod link by

Glide model rear brake linkage adjustment

1. Brake pedal
2. Piston rod
3. Lock nut
4. Plunger
5. Rubber boot

sliding the rubber boot away from the master cylinder.

2. Adjust the piston rod so the foot pedal moves freely about 1 ½ in. before the brake begins to operate.

3. Back off the locknut and turn the plunger clockwise to shorten the pushrod, and counterclockwise to lengthen it.

4. Test for free movement and secure the locknut when satisfied.

Adjusting Rear Brake Shoes

SPORTSTER AND MECHANICAL BRAKE 45 AND 74 MODELS

1. Loosen the brake pivot stud and axle nuts but do not remove the stud.

2. Rotate the rear wheel and operate the pedal while the wheel is spinning.

3. Tighten the pivot stud nut and then the axle nut.

4. Recheck for correct pedal adjustment.

HYDRAULIC REAR BRAKE

1. Rotate the adjusting nut for the front shoe cam in a counterclockwise direction while spinning the wheel until the shoe begins to contact the drum (slight drag will occur).

2. At this point, on Servi-Cars, turn the cam nut clockwise to tighten the shoe.

3. Rock the wheel back and forth to center the shoe (all models).

Glide models rear brake shoe adjustment

1. Leading brake shoe adjusting cam nut
2. Trailing brake shoe adjusting cam nut

4. On Servi-Cars, the cam must be backed off about 1/32 in. (2 in. of wrench movement at the tire) until the wheel spins freely.

5. On Glide models, turn the cam nut clockwise until the wheel spins freely.

6. Repeat this procedure for the rear cam nut, turning the cam in the opposite direction to the front cam nut.

Servi-Car rear brake shoe adjustment

1. Front shoe adjusting cam nut
2. Rear shoe adjusting cam nut

7. On Servi-Cars, repeat the entire process on the other wheel.

8. On sidecars, remove the wheel and brake drum assemblies, and repeat the entire process. Up until 1958, all side cars had rod-actuated mechanical brake units and all sidecars since have a Glide-type hydraulic brake actuated by a line which is connected directly to the rear brake cylinder. If there is no air in the line, both brakes should operate simultaneously.

PRIMARY CHAIN ADJUSTMENT

Servi-Car

The 1963 and earlier models are adjusted by moving the transmission. Loosen the three transmission mounting nuts and the lower clamp bolt of the starter crank brace. Turn the transmis-

Servi-Car primary chain adjustment—(1964 and later models)

1. Front chain adjusting shoe
2. Shoe support bracket
3. Support bracket cap screw (2)

sion adjusting screw clockwise to tighten the chain and counterclockwise to loosen it. Secure the transmission when there is ½ in. play at the center of the chain. Adjust the rear chain, gear shifter, and clutch linkage.

On 1964 and later models, remove the footboard and chaincase cover. Loosen the support bracket cap screws and manually raise or lower the adjusting screw until there is about ½ in. of play at the center of the chain. Secure the cap screws and reassemble the cover and footboard.

Sportster

Sportster primary chains are adjusted in the same manner as are the 1964 and later Servi-Cars. There are three bolts on the XLH and two on the XLCH. A cold chain is adjusted to ⅝–⅞ in. of play and a warm chain is adjusted to ⅜–⅝ in.

Glide models primary chain adjustment

1. Chain adjusting shoe
2. Chain adjusting shoe bracket
3. Bracket backplate
4. Backplate center bolt
5. Outer plate
6. Support bracket
7. Primary chain oiler
A. Adjustment holes
B. Adjustment holes

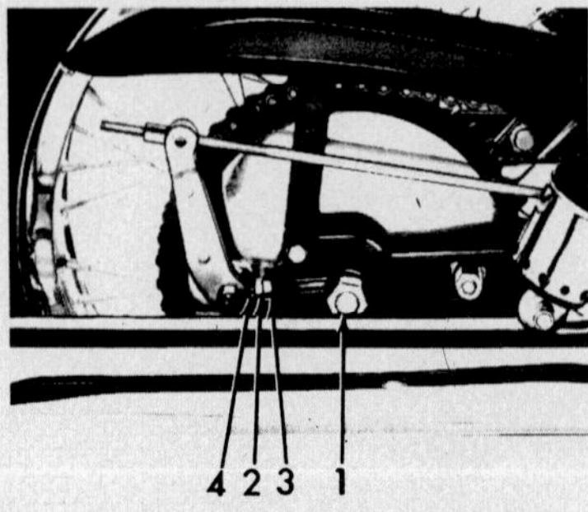

Sportster drive chain adjustment

1. Rear axle nut
2. Adjusting stud lock nut
3. Adjusting stud nut
4. Adjusting stud

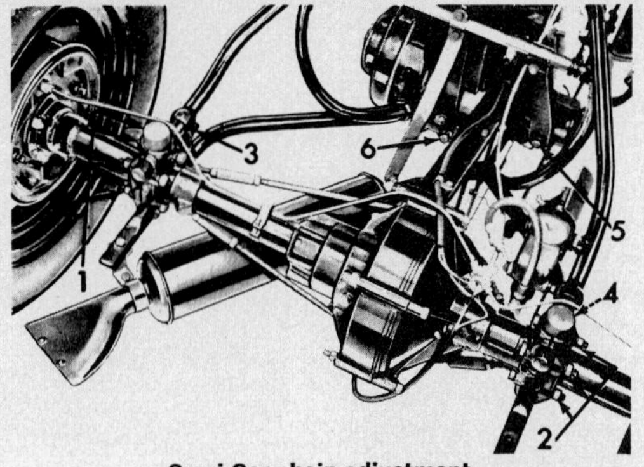

Servi-Car chain adjustment

1. Left frame clamp
2. Right frame clamp bolt nuts (4)
3. Left axle adjusting screw
4. Right axle adjusting screw
5. Starter brace bolt
6. Transmission adjusting screw

Glide Models

On 1964 and earlier models, adjust the chain as directed for 1963 and earlier Servi-Cars.

On 1965 and later models, adjust the chain as directed for Sportsters. The chain bracket has two sets of chain attaching holes so the assembly can be inverted to accommodate various chains or sprockets.

DRIVE CHAIN ADJUSTMENT

Servi-Car

1. Loosen the right and left, frame, clamp bolt nuts until the clamps will slide freely.
2. Loosen the right and left axle adjusting screws.
3. Turn the adjusting screws until all but ½ in. of chain slack is taken up at the chain's tightest point.
4. Measure the distance between the axle housing frame clamp and the adjusting screw on both sides to check alignment.
5. Secure the clamp bolt and adjusting screw locknuts.
6. Recheck adjustment and alighment.

Sportster

1. Loosen the axle nut.
2. Loosen the right and left adjusting stud locknuts.
3. Turn both adjusting stud locknuts clockwise the same number of turns to tighten the chain and counterclockwise to loosen it. While loosening the chain, tap the axle forward with a soft mallet.
4. Secure the locknut against the adjusting nut and measure the distance from the locknut to the outer end of the adjusting stud. Both should be the same to ensure correct alignment.
5. Spin the wheel and look for wobbling of the sprocket which would indicate poor alignment.
6. The chain should have ½ in. of play midway between the mainshaft and the rear wheel sprocket.
7. Secure the axle nut and adjusting stud locknut. Adjust the brake rod if necessary.

Glide Models

1. Remove the axle nut and washer from the right side and loosen the brake sleeve nut, brake anchor stud nut (left side), and adjusting screw locknuts.
2. Proceed as described in the "Sportster" section.

Glide models drive chain adjustment

1. Brake sleeve nut
2. Wheel adjusting screw lock nut
3. Wheel adjusting screw
4. Brake anchor stud nut

BATTERY CHARGING RATE

CAUTION: *When charging, hydrogen gas is formed which will explode on contact with an open flame or an electrical spark. Be careful.*

12 volt 53 ampere hour battery—
10 amperes
12 volt 32 ampere hour battery—
4 amperes
6 volt 51 ampere hour batttery—
3 ½ amperes
6 volt 22 ampere hour battery—
1 ½ amperes
6 volt 10 ampere hour battery—
½ ampere

2—6 volt 8 ampere hour batteries (Series connected—12 volts)—½ ampere

TIRES

The following information is based on rider and passenger weights of about 150 lbs. Increase front tire pressure 1 lb, and rear tire 2 lbs per 50 lbs of weight increase. Proper tire pressure will provide maximum road adhesion and will increase tire life. Pressure may be increased by several lbs over the required pressure if constant, heavy-load touring is to be done.

	Front Tire Size	Front Tire Pressure (lbs)	Rear Tire Size	Rear Tire Pressure (lbs)
SERVI-CAR				
1968 and earlier	5.00 x 16	12	5.00 x 16	18
1969 and later	5.10 x 16	20	5.10 x 16	24
SPORTSTER				
1966 and earlier XL, XLH	3.25/3.50 x 19	14	4.00 x 18	18
1967 and later XL, XLH	3.50 x 18	14	3.50 x 18	18
1969 and earlier XLCH	3.25/3.50 x 19	16	4.00 x 18	18
1970 and later (all models)	3.75 x 19	18	4.25 x 18	30
GLIDE MODELS				
Solo	5.10 x 16	20	5.10 x 16	24
	5.00 x 16	12	5.10 x 16	18
	3.75 x 19	18	5.10 x 16	24
Rider and one passenger	5.10 x 16	20	5.10 x 16	26
	3.00 x 16	12	5.10 x 16	20
	3.75 x 19	18	5.10 x 16	26
Rider, one sidecar passenger or	5.10 x 16	22	5.10 x 16	26
150 lb load	5.00 x 16	12	5.00 x 16	20
Sidecar wheel	5.10 x 16	20		
	5.00 x 16	14		

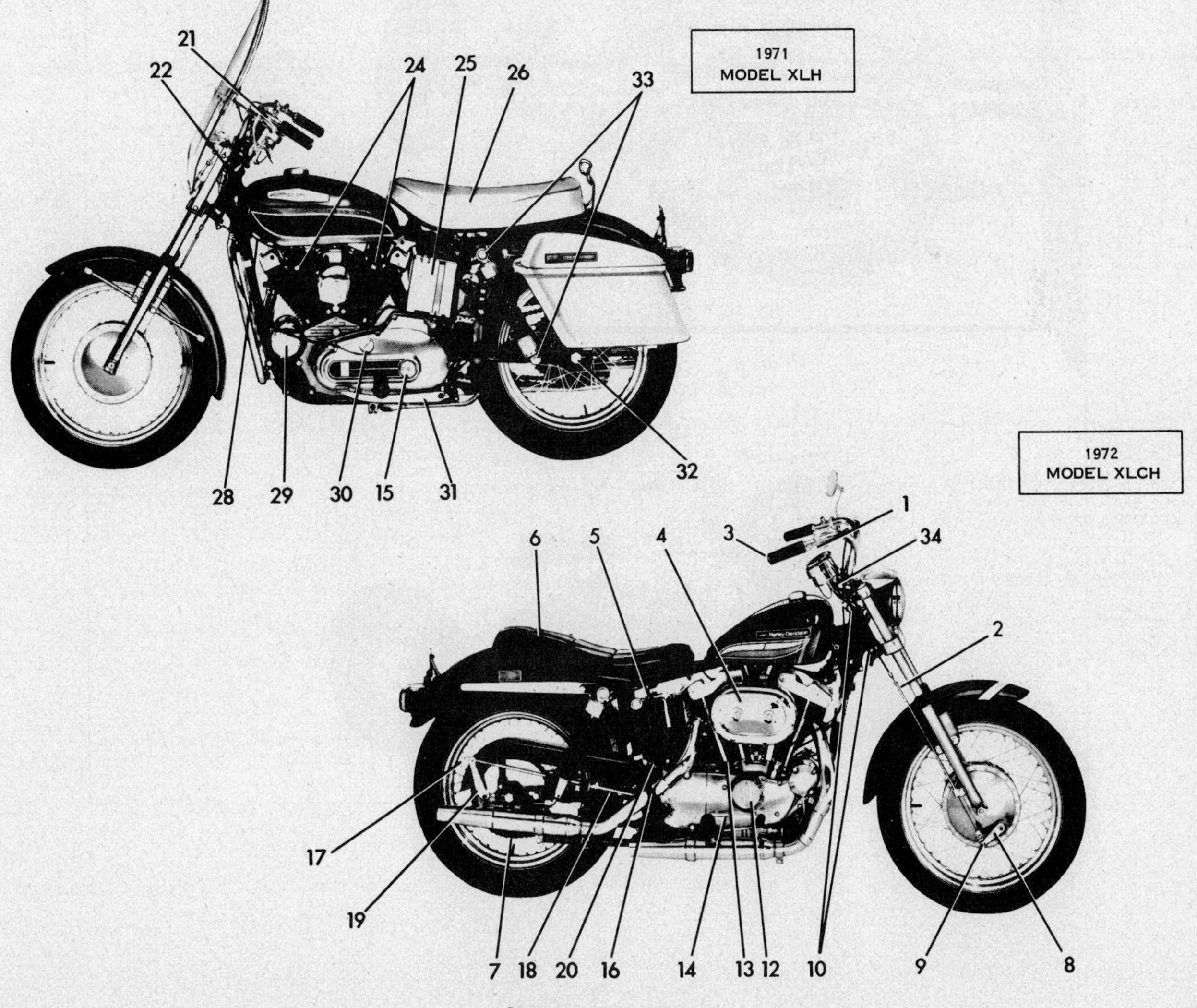

Sportster service points

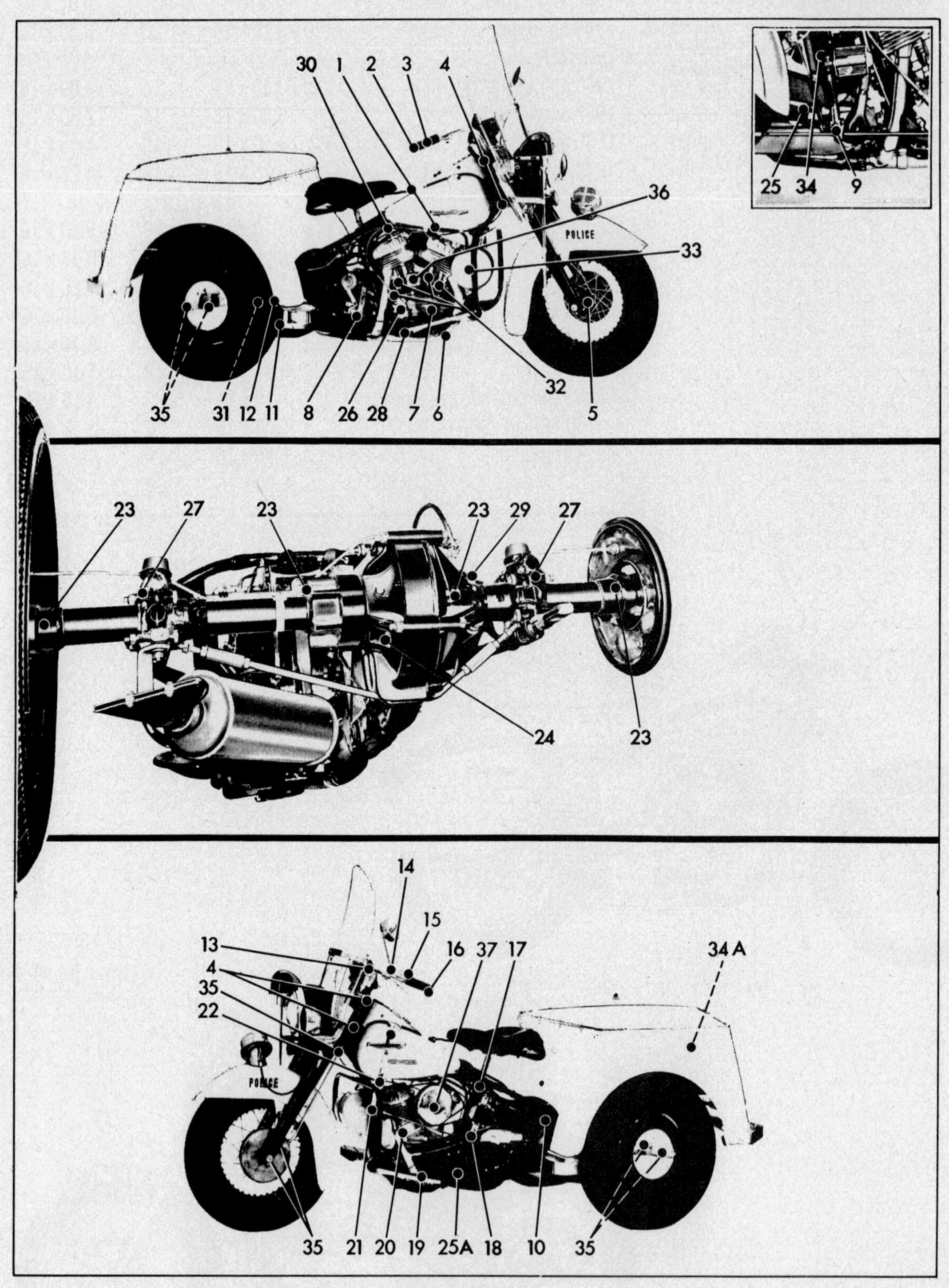

Servi-Car service points

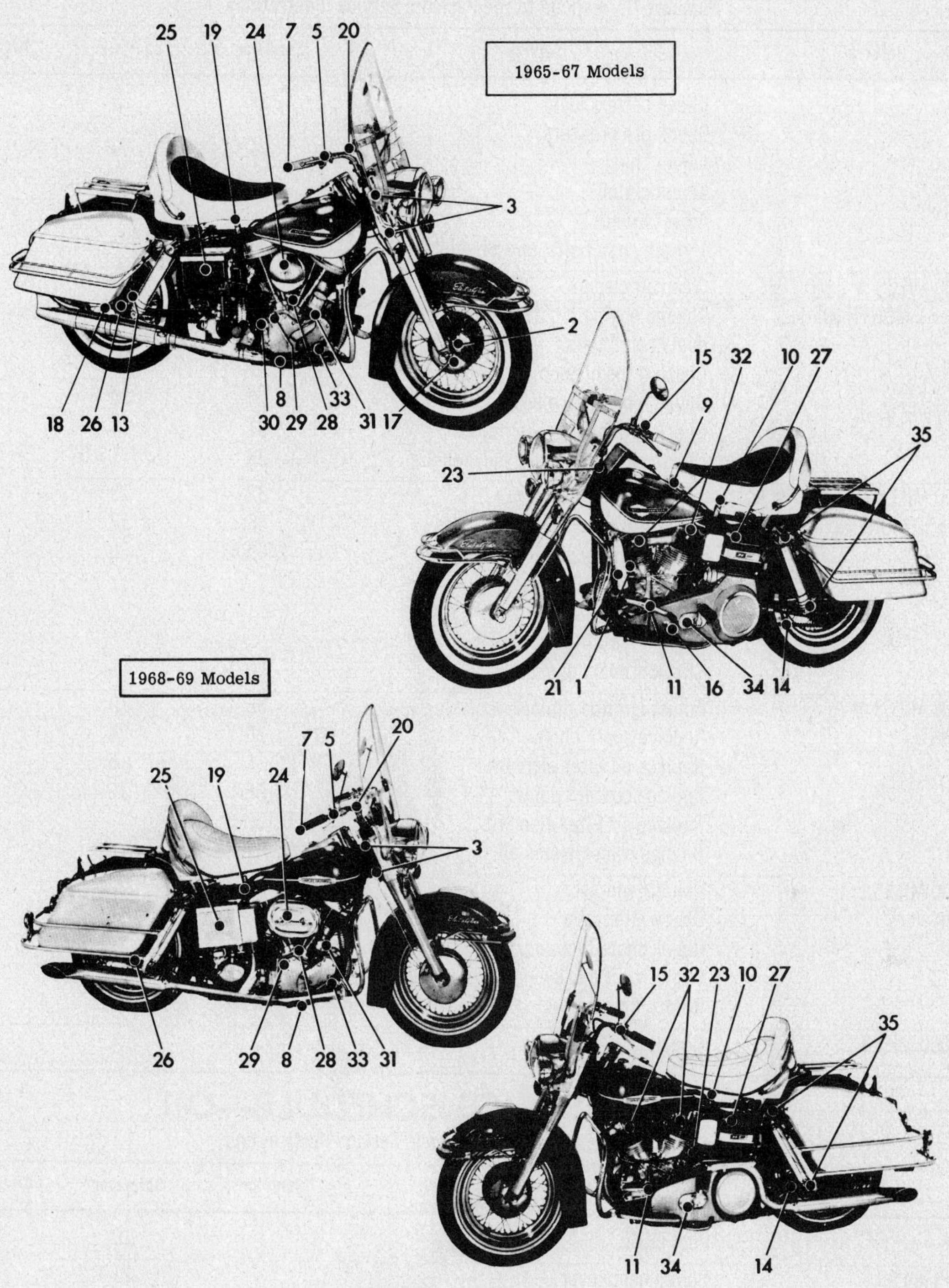

Glide model service points

PERIODIC SERVICE SCHEDULE—GENERAL

Numbers Correspond to the Periodic Service Illustrations

Interval	Service	Servi-Car	Sportster	Glide Models
WEEKLY	Check battery level	34	25	25
	Check tire pressure			
	Adjust chain	27	7	26
	Adjust clutch			
	Adjust brakes			
	Tighten nuts, bolts, and wheel spokes	35		
Every 1,000 MILES or 2 MONTHS (summer) or 1 MONTH (winter)	Clean air cleaner	37	4	24
	Change engine oil (during winter or dusty conditions			
	Check transmission oil			
	Check rear chain oiler	28	20	
	Check hydraulic brake fluid	31		33
	Check alternator drive belt tension	33		
Every 2,000 MILES or 4 MONTHS (summer) or 2 MONTHS (winter)	Adjust tappets	32	13	
	Clean and adjust contact points	36	12	31
	Adjust primary chain	25-25A	30	34
	Clean tappet oil screen			29
	Change engine oil			
	Change fuel filter			28
	Check primary chain oiler	26		30
Every 5,000 MILES or 12 MONTHS	Adjust ignition timing	36	12	31
	Replace spark plugs	30	24	32
	Replace oil filter element		5	27
	Replace contact points	36	12	31
	Replace air filter element	37		
	Change transmission oil			
Every 5,000 MILES or 12 MONTHS	Check generator		29	4
	Check alternator	33		
	Check shock bushings		33	35
	Check front and swing arm bearings		10	
	Rotate tires			
Every 10,000 MILES	Check oil pressure			

PERIODIC SERVICE SCHEDULE—OIL

Numbers Correspond to the Periodic Service Illustrations

Interval	Oil	Servi-Car	Sportster	Glide Models
WEEKLY	Rear chain		10	14
Every 2,000 MILES	Clutch hand lever		21	15
	Brake hand lever		1	5
	Clutch control cable		22	23
	Front brake cable		2	20
	Throttle cable		28	7
	Spark cable		11	12
	Clutch booster lever rod clevis			21
	Shifter lever linkage			
	Rear brake rod clevis		17	
	Front brake cable clevis		9	
	Saddle post bearing		26	19
	Generator bearing		29	4

PERIODIC SERVICE SCHEDULE—GREASE

Numbers Correspond to the Periodic Service Illustrations

Interval	Grease	Servi-Car	Sportster	Glide Models
Every 2,000 MILES	Front brake shaft		8	
	Front wheel hub	5		17
	Rear brake shaft		19	
	Rear brake crossover shaft		31	
	Rear wheel hub		32	18
	Swing Arm pivot bearing			22A
	Body frame bearing	10		
	Clutch release worm		15	
	Clutch release cable housing	18		
	Clutch push rod bearing	8		
	Clutch booster bearing			1
	Clutch pedal bearing	19		
	Foot shift lever		14	11
	Rear brake pedal bearing	6		8
	Kick starter shaft	9	16	
	Master cylinder lever	12		
Every 2,000 MILES	Rear axle bearing	23		
	Saddle bearing and post	17	6	9-10
	Tachometer drive gear			
	Speedometer drive	29		
Every 5,000 MILES	Throttle control spiral	2	3	7
	Spark control spiral	16	23	6
	Speedometer cable		34	
	Tachometer cable		34	
	Contact breaker camshaft and advance unit	36	12	31
	Compensating sprocket			16
	Sidecar wheel hub			
	Rear axle differential	24		
	Generator bearing	20	29	4
	Front wheel hub		27	2
	Rear wheel hub			13
Every 10,000 MILES	Repack rear fork pivot bearing		18	22
Every 50,000 MILES	Repack steering head bearings	4	10	3

ENGINE AND TRANSMISSION

REMOVAL AND INSTALLATION

Servi-Car

For cylinder work with the engine still in the frame, complete the following steps:

1. Remove the spark plugs.
2. Disconnect the battery ground wire.
3. Disconnect the throttle cable at the carburetor.
4. Drain the gas tank, remove the air cleaner assembly, carburetor, and manifold.
5. Drain the oil tank and sump, disconnect the oil feed line at the pumps and bend it clear.
6. Remove the rear chain oiler.
7. Remove the right footrest.
8. Loosen the front muffler clamp beneath the kick-starter.
9. Disconnect the rear brake rod at the pedal.
10. Disconnect the rear frame muffler clamp.
11. Remove the exhaust pipe.
12. Remove the cylinder head bracket bolt.
13. Telescope the valve covers.

Perform the following steps to remove the engine crankcase from the frame:

1. Disconnect the oil return line at the scavenger pump.
2. Remove the oil breather tube from the gearcase.
3. Remove the spark cable from the contact breaker and free the cable from the frame clamp.
4. Remove the oil pressure switch wire.
5. Remove the left footrest.
6. Remove the primary chaincase cover.
7. Remove the primary sprocket and chain.
8. Remove the drive chainguard.
9. Remove the left rear footrest stud.

10. Remove the green lead from generator "A" terminal.
11. Remove the black contact breaker lead from the coil.
12. Remove the engine base stud nuts and lift the engine clear through the right side of the frame.

Sportster

1. Remove the seat, drain the gas and oil, and remove the gas tank.

The following steps pertain to the right side of the machine:

2. Remove the air cleaner assembly.
3. Disconnect the throttle and choke cables at the carburetor.
4. Remove the top center engine support bolt, taking note of the number and placement of the spacer shims.
5. Remove the exhaust assemblies.
6. Disconnect the spark plug cable from the contact breaker or magneto.
7. Remove the generator and horn mounting screw (1964 and earlier XLH).
8. Remove the starter crank and spring.
9. Place the transmission in fourth gear and remove the right footrest and the shifter lever.
10. Remove the transmission sprocket cover. Disconnect the clutch cable.
11. Remove the drive chain from the countershaft sprocket.
12. Remove the oil return line.
13. Remove the oil vent and oil feed lines.
14. Remove the clutch cable and oil pressure switch.
15. Disconnect the speedometer cable. The following steps pertain to the left side of the machine:

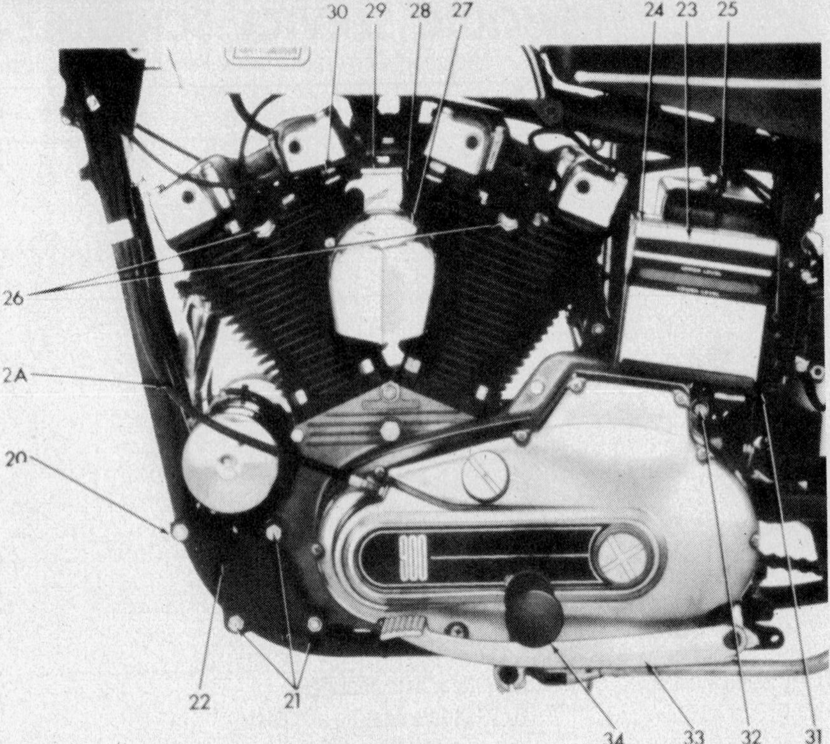

Left side view—1971 XLCH

20. Top front end mounting bolt
21. Engine mounting bolts
22. Safety guard bolt hole
23. Battery
24. Battery carrier
25. Ground wire
26. Spark plugs
27. Horn cover
28. Wire
29. Support bracket and choke control
30. Support bracket bolt
31. Ground strap
32. Engine mounting bolt
33. Foot lever and spring
34. Left footrest

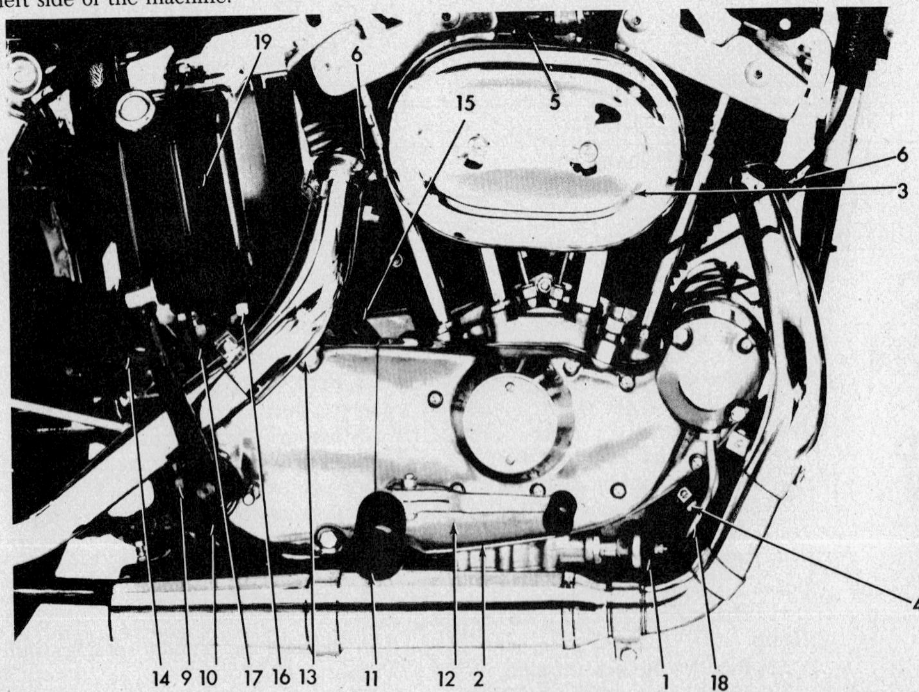

1. Oil pressure switch wire
2. Clutch control cable (1970)
2A. Clutch control cable (1970 & later)
3. Cleaner assembly
4. Clip
5. Engine support bolt location
6. Exhaust pipe port clamp (2)
9. Starter crank clamp bolt
10. Starter spring
11. Footrest
12. Foot shift lever
13. Cover bolt (2)
14. Rear chain
15. Oil return line
16. Oil vent line
17. Oil feed line
18. Breather pipe
19. Oil tank

Right side view—1972 XLCH

16. Loosen, but do not remove, the top front engine mounting bolt.

17. Remove the remaining three, front engine mounting bolts.

18. Remove the tool box (1966 and earlier XLH).

19. Remove the battery tie rod support (1966 and earlier XLH).

20. Disconnect the battery ground wire (XLH) and the spark plug cables.

21. Remove the horn cover and power pack but do not disconnect the wire from the trumpet bracket (1964 and earlier XLH).

22. Remove the horn and engine support bracket (1964 and earlier XLCH; 1965 and later XLCH and XLH).

23. Disconnect the throttle cable and support bracket at the carburetor.

24. Remove the battery cover and disconnect both terminal leads on XLH models.

25. Remove the oil vent line at the crankcase (1966 and earlier models).

26. Disconnect the contact breaker-to-coil lead.

27. Loosen the battery tie rod support (1964 and earlier XLH).

28. Remove the battery, battery carrier, and oil tank (1967 models).

29. Remove the regulator ground strap and the two, top rear, engine mounting bolts.

30. Remove the rear brake lever and return spring on all models, and the stop switch on 1966 and earlier models.

31. Remove the left footrest.

32. Remove the two, lower rear, engine mounting bolts.

33. Remove the battery, generator, and oil switch wires (1964 and earlier XLH).

34. Remove the top front engine mounting bolt.

35. With the engine tilted forward, lift it up and out of the left side of the frame.

Glide Models

For cylinder work with the engine still in the frame, complete the following steps:

1. Remove the instrument cover mounting base screw and pry off the cover side plate.

2. Remove the seat.

3. Remove the shift lever bottom bolts to remove the gas tank on hand-shift models.

4. Drain the gas tank and remove it.

5. Remove the cylinder head bracket, taking note of the number and position of the spacers for reassembly.

6. Remove the spark plugs and disconnect the battery ground wire.

7. Remove the horn cover, power pack, and mounting brackets (1964 and earlier models).

8. Remove the carburetor manifold clamps and the air cleaner assembly.

9. Disconnect the throttle and choke cables from the carburetor, then remove the fuel and vent lines, carburetor, and its support bracket.

10. Remove the horn trumpet on 1964 and earlier models. Disconnect the exhaust pipes at the cylinders. Disconnect and reposition the regulator without removing it. Follow the steps below to remove the engine crankcase from the frame:

11. Remove the left footrest, primary chaincase cover, compensating sprocket, or shaft nut. Remove the chain adjuster mounting bolt (1965 and later models) and clutch assembly.

12. Remove the engine sprocket shaft chain cover. Loosen the transmission base mounting bolts (1965 and later models). Remove the inner chainguard-to-transmission mounting bolts.

13. Remove the clutch hub, shaft key, starter housing chainguard nuts, solenoid wire, inner chainguard from mainshaft, chain oiler hose at oil pump, and the remaining hoses.

14. Disconnect the coil leads, generator wires, and oil switch wire.

15. Drain the oil tank and remove the oil lines at the oil pump. Remove the crankcase breather tube (1965 and later models).

16. Remove the right footrest and the brake master cylinder assembly.

17. Remove the exhaust system.

18. Remove the spark cable at the contact breaker (1964 and earlier models).

19. Remove the front and rear engine mounting bolts. The engine may now be lifted clear of the frame through the right side.

CYLINDER HEAD AND VALVES

Servi-Car

REMOVAL

1. Remove the cylinder head bolts and washers, taking note of bolt positions for replacement.

2. Tap the base of the head with a soft mallet until it is loose and lift the head free. Lightly oil the piston crown and the cylinder bore.

CYLINDER HEAD INSPECTION AND REPAIR

1. Inspect the exhaust valve and seat for a worn, warped, or pitted condition. The 1/16 in. seat must be smooth and shiny.

2. Decarbonize the cylinder head and piston crown surfaces by gently using a blunt scraper, taking care not to gouge or scratch the surfaces.

3. Brush the piston and valve heads with a wire brush and blow them clean. Take care not to allow any dirt to fall into the engine.

4. Clean the head in a suitable solvent and blow it dry.

VALVE AND CYLINDER DISASSEMBLY

In order to work on Servi-Car valves, valve guides, valve springs, spring covers, or any part of the piston assembly, the cylinders must be removed. This can be accomplished with the engine still in the frame.

1. Strip the motorcycle as described in "Engine Removal," following steps 1–13.

2. Remove the cylinder head as described in the Servi-Car section, "Cylinder Head Removal."

3. Rotate the engine until the piston is at its lowest position.

4. Remove the cylinder base stud nuts and lift the cylinder free of the piston. Cover the crankcase opening immediately with an oily rag.

5. Remove the valve keys by compressing the valve 96589–30) using Valve Spring Compressor (H-D part no. 96589-30) or another suitable compressor.

6. Remove the spring collars, springs, covers, and valve guide oil seals. The valves are now free to be lifted from their guides.

7. Valve guides are a press-fit and may be arbor-pressed out if examination indicates replacement is necessary.

VALVE INSPECTION AND REPAIR

1. Consult the valve information under the Sportster section, "Cylinder Head Inspection and Repair."

INSTALLATION

1. It is advisable to replace the head gasket, but it may be used again if it is in good condition.

2. Assemble with the gasket dry, taking care to line up all of the bolt holes.

3. Install the bolts and secure them evenly to 65 ft lbs torque. The long bolt goes between the intake valve and the cylinder.

Sportster

REMOVAL

1. Strip the motorcycle as described in "Engine Removal" following steps no. 1–6, 8, 22, 23, and 24.

2. Remove the air cleaner assembly, carburetor support bracket, carburetor, manifold clamps, and manifold.

3. Remove the oil line nuts and rubber sleeves.

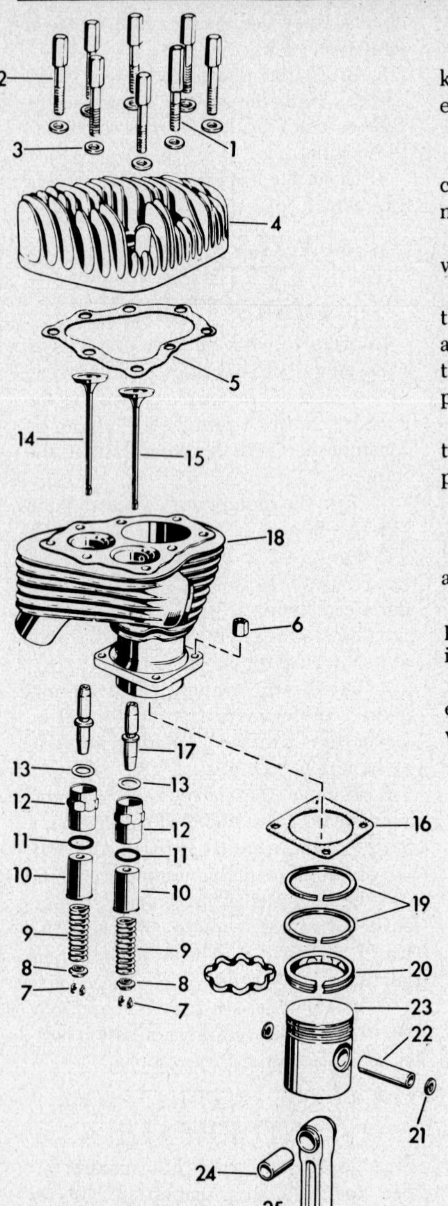

Servi-Car cylinder head and cylinder assembly

1. Cylinder head bolt (1¾ in.)
2. Cylinder head bolt (1 19/32 in.) (7)
3. Head washers (8)
4. Cylinder head
5. Cylinder head gasket
6. Cylinder base stud nut (4)
7. Valve key (2)
8. Valve spring collar (2)
9. Valve spring (2)
10. Upper valve spring cover (2)
11. Valve cover seal (2)
12. Lower valve spring cover (2)
13. Valve guide oil seal (2)
14. Exhaust valve
15. Intake valve
16. Cylinder base gasket
17. Valve guide
18. Cylinder
19. Compression ring (2)
20. Oil control ring and expander
21. Piston pin lock ring (2)
22. Piston pin
23. Piston
24. Piston pin bushing
25. Connecting rod

Figure following name of part indicates quantity necessary for one complete assembly.

4. Remove the spark plugs.
5. Remove the pushrod cover spring keepers while holding the spring retainers down.
6. Telescope the valve covers.
7. Rotate the engine until there is clearance at both tappets. The valves are now closed.
8. Remove the cylinder head bolts and washers.
9. If necessary gently tap the base of the head with a soft mallet to loosen it and lift the entire assembly free through the left side of the frame. Lightly oil the piston crown and cylinder.
10. Separate the pushrods and mark them for replacement in their original positions.

DISASSEMBLY

1. Remove the rocker arm cover bolts and washers.
2. Remove the rocker arm cover, tapping it gently with a soft mallet to loosen it if necessary.
3. Inspect the rocker arm surfaces, for excessive wear, where they contact the valve stems and pushrods.
4. Check the rocker arm shaft and bushings for excessive play.
5. If replacement of the above items is necessary, remove the rocker arm shaft, O-ring, acorn nut, and washer.
6. Drift the shaft from the cover and remove the rocker arm spring, arm, and spacer, and separate them for replacement in their original positions. It is not a good idea to mix parts since this will affect clearances and since some parts are not interchangeable.
7. Compress the valve springs using Valve Spring Compressor (H-D part no. 96600–36), or any suitable spring compressor and remove the valve keys, spring collar, springs, and valves. Separate the parts for replacement in their original positions.

INSPECTION AND REPAIR

1. Clean all parts in a suitable solution and blow them dry, taking care to blow all passages clear.
2. Replace the oil line nut rubber sleeve and the gaskets if worn. Replace the shaft O-ring.

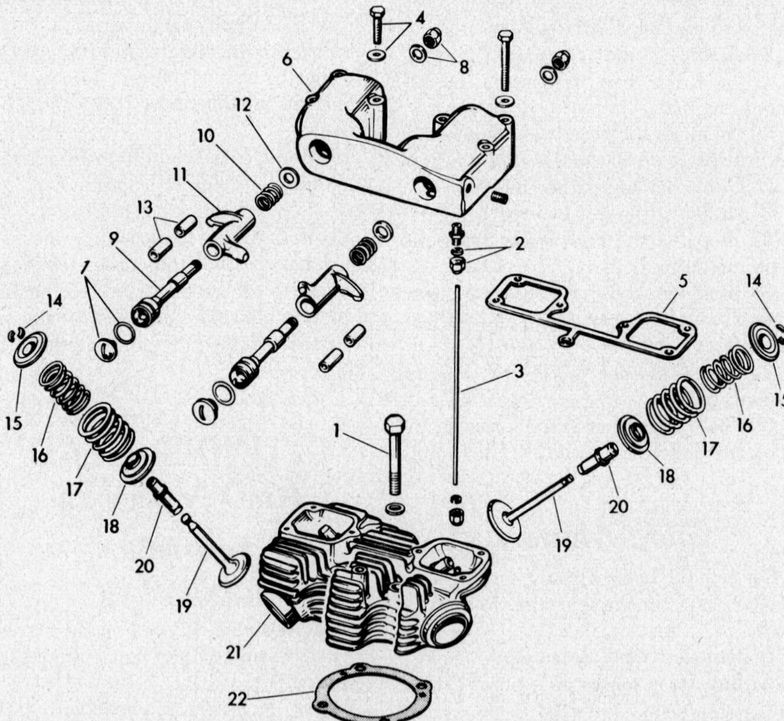

Sportster cylinder head assembly

1. Cylinder head bolt and washer (4)
2. Oil line nut and rubber sleeve (2)
3. Rocker arm cover to crankcase oil line
4. Rocker arm cover screw and washer (7)
5. Rocker arm cover gasket (2)
6. Rocker arm cover
7. Rocker arm shaft screw and "O" ring (2)
8. Rocker arm shaft acorn nut and washer (2 each)
9. Rocker arm shaft (2)
10. Rocker arm spring (2)
11. Rocker arm (2)
12. Rocker arm spacer (2)
13. Rocker arm bushing (4)
14. Valve key (4)
15. Valve spring upper collar (2)
16. Inner valve spring (2)
17. Outer valve spring (2)
18. Valve spring lower collar (2)
19. Intake and exhaust valve
20. Intake and exhaust valve guide
21. Cylinder head
22. Cylinder head gasket

3. Inspect the rocker arm and shaft for wear and replace them if necessary. Rocker arm pads may be ground free of pitting or uneven wear.

4. Replace shaft bushings if play exceeds 0.002 in. Bushings are a press-fit and must be drifted out from the acorn nut side. Inserting a ⅝-11 thread tap will aid in the drifting procedure. Line-ream the new bushing with Reamer (H-D part no. 94804–57) or a suitable substitute.

5. Soak the head in a suitable solvent until all of the carbon deposits are soft, then gently scrape it clean and brush it with a wire brush, taking care not to scratch the head face.

6. Blow the cylinder head and passages clear and clean again in a suitable solvent.

7. Inspect the valve and valve seat for a pitted or corroded condition which may adversely affect seating. Consult "Valve and Valve Seat Refacing" for procedures or replace. Seats which are cracked or loose must be replaced as described in "Valve Seat Insert Replacement."

8. Remove the valve head and the stem carbon deposits with a wire wheel or blunt knife, taking care not to scratch or nick the surface. The stem may be polished with fine emery cloth or steel wool. Warped, bent, or otherwise damaged valves must be replaced.

9. Intake valve guides may be cleaned up with a 5/16 in. reamer and the exhaust valves with a 11/32 in. reamer.

10. Inspect the guides for excessive stem clearance. Consult "Engine Specifications" for proper measurements.

11. Replace the pushrods if warped, bent, or flattened at the ball ends.

12. Inspect the valve springs and check for proper tension and length. Springs which are more than ⅛ in. shorter or which have 5 lbs less tension than listed in "Engine Specifications" must be replaced. A Valve Spring Tester (H-D part no. 96797–47), or a suitable substitute, may be used. If the springs are still their original length, they may be used even if their strength isn't checked.

PUSHROD REMOVAL AND INSTALLATION

1. Rotate the engine until the tappet is at its lowest position.

2. Turn up the adjusting screw locknut until it is seated against the adjusting screw.

3. Turn down the adjusting screw, into the tappet body, until it reaches its seat.

4. Pry the pushrod up and to the side, taking care not to bind the upper end in the rocker housing, and remove the rod and cover assembly.

5. Install new cork cover washers in the rocker cover and tappet guide, taking care not to damage them. Install a new cork washer in the pushrod cover also, taking care to seat all washers.

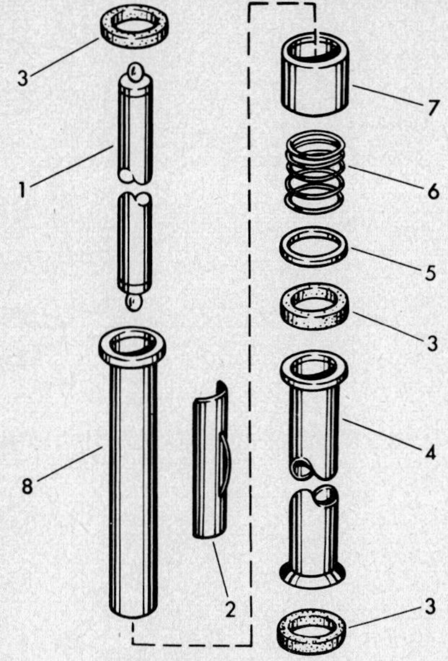

Push rod assembly
1. Push rod
2. Cover spring keeper
3. Cover cork washer (3)
4. Lower cover
5. Cover screw washer
6. Cover spring
7. Spring retainer
8. Upper cover

6. Assemble the pushrod assembly in the reverse order of disassembly and adjust tappets as described in "Valve Tappet Adjustment."

ASSEMBLY

Assemble in reverse order of disassembly. Note the following:

1. Lightly oil the valve seats and stems.

2. Place the lower valve spring collar over the guides, taking care to seat it properly.

3. Install the springs and upper collars, and use a compressor to replace the valve keys. Keys are easily handled by placing a dab of grease on a screwdriver tip, and can be temporarily secured until the springs are released by greasing the key grooves.

4. Install the rocker arm spacer, spring, and arm.

5. Lightly oil the rocker arm shaft and install it so that the spring ends are flush with the spacer and arm.

6. Secure the shaft O-ring, shaft screw, acorn nut washer, and acorn nut. Check arm action for binding.

7. Check to see that the cylinder head and rocker arm surfaces are still clean and apply a thin coat of aluminum paint to the head face if a cover gasket is not to be used.

8. Carefully install the cover gasket, if applicable, and install the cover in either case.

9. Turn the screws to a snug fit and then turn each ⅛–¼ turn at a time until the cover is secure.

INSTALLATION

Install in the reverse order of dissassembly. Note the following:

1. Cylinder and head faces must be absolutely clean.

2. Lightly oil or grease both sides of a new head gasket and align it on the cylinder.

3. With the valve tappets in their lowest position, install the head assembly. Pushrods must seat in the tappet screw and pushrod sockets.

4. Insert the oil line in the head and crankcase fittings.

5. Secure the cylinder bolts in the same manner as the rocker cover bolts and torque them to 65 ft lbs.

6. Position the rubber, oil line nut sleeves and secure the nuts.

7. Install the intake manifold and replace the rubber O-rings before installing the carburetor. Correct alignmnet of these units is critical as air leaks adversely affect performance. The cylinder may have to be shifted slightly to provide proper manifold alignment.

8. Adjust the tappets as described in "Valve Tappet Adjustment."

9. Assemble the remaining parts in the reverse order of disassembly.

Glide Models

REMOVAL

1–7. Same as for Sportster. Oil lines are present on 1963 and later models. Follow steps number 1–10 in "Engine Removal" section.

8. Remove the head bolts and washers from beneath the cooling fins.

8–9. Same as for Sportster.

DISASSEMBLY

1965 and Earlier

1. Remove the rocker arm cover reinforcing screws, cover, and cover gasket. Remove the cover pad only if replacement is necessary.

2. Remove the rocker arm bearing stud nuts.

3. Remove the intake valve oiler and rocker arm bearing halves and rocker assembly.

4. Remove the exhaust valve stem (if applicable) and remove the valves as described in Sportster "Cylinder Head Disassembly."

1966 and Later

1. Remove the cylinder head stud nuts and rocker arm cover.

2. Consult Sportster "Cylinder Head Disassembly" for additional procedures.

INSPECTION

1. Consult Sportster "Cylinder Head Inspection."

2. On 1965 and earlier models, check rocker arm fit in the bearing when dry

and replace it if play exceeds 0.002 in.

3. Bearing faces, with dowel pins removed, may be sanded with emery cloth to reduce clearances. A suitable reamer (such as Reamer HD part no. 94804–57) may be used to line-ream the bearing.

4. Gently strike the edges of the bearings, while assembled, to align parts before checking fit.

5. Continually sand, clean, check clearances, and repeat until the desired fit is obtained.

ASSEMBLY AND INSTALLATION

Assemble in reverse order of disassembly. Note the following:

1. Assemble the valve assemblies as described in Sportster "Cylinder Head Assembly."

2. Install a new intake valve oiler on 1965 and earlier models. The oiler must seat on the rocker arm bearing housing with the tube 3/32 in. from the arm.

3. If the rocker arm is not free, the lifters will not fill with oil.

4. Replace the rocker arm cover, using a new gasket on 1965 and earlier models. Use aluminum paint on the cover faces of 1966 and later models, unless the model is equipped with a gasket as on 1971 and later models.

5. Raise the valve end with a screwdriver when the cover is installed to prevent rocker arm jamming on 1966 and later models.

6. See Sportster "Cylinder Head Installation" for torquing and carburetor assembly procedures.

7. Adjust the tappets as described in "Valve Tappet Adjustment."

8. Assemble remaining parts in reverse order of disassembly.

Valve Guides and Seats

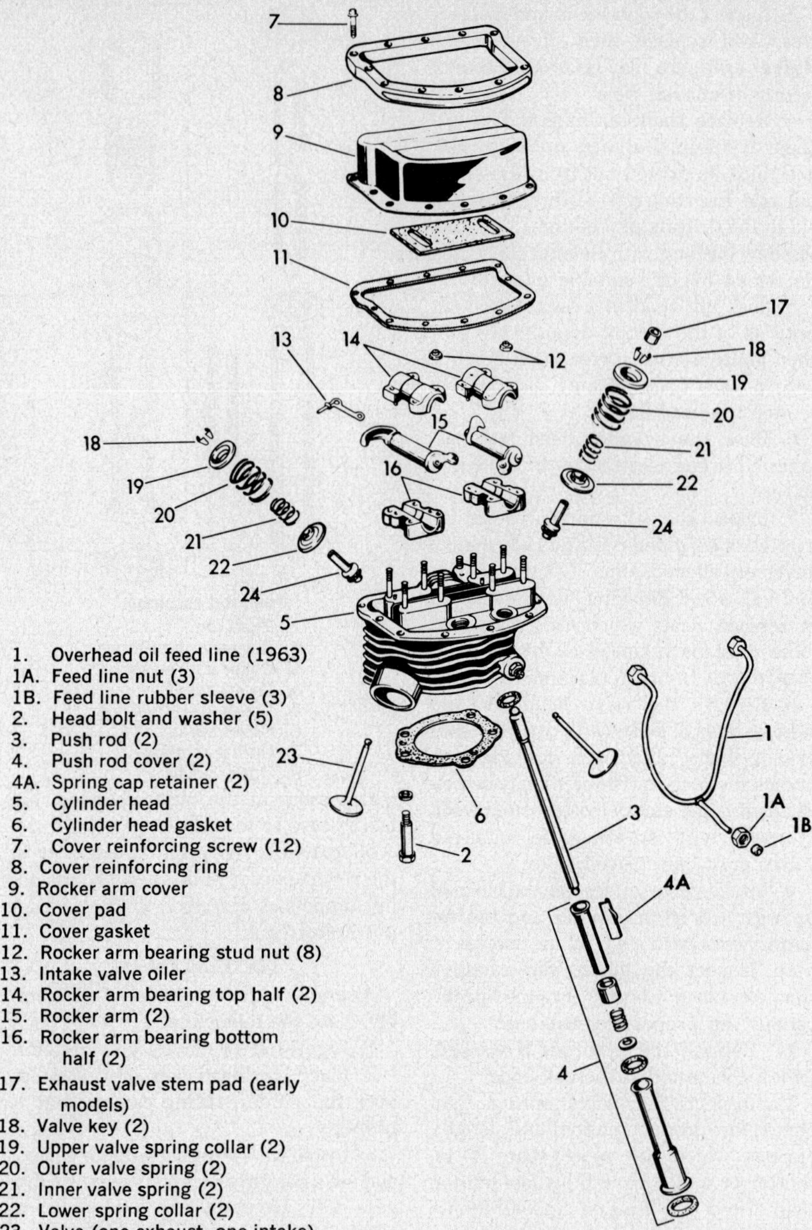

1. Overhead oil feed line (1963)
1A. Feed line nut (3)
1B. Feed line rubber sleeve (3)
2. Head bolt and washer (5)
3. Push rod (2)
4. Push rod cover (2)
4A. Spring cap retainer (2)
5. Cylinder head
6. Cylinder head gasket
7. Cover reinforcing screw (12)
8. Cover reinforcing ring
9. Rocker arm cover
10. Cover pad
11. Cover gasket
12. Rocker arm bearing stud nut (8)
13. Intake valve oiler
14. Rocker arm bearing top half (2)
15. Rocker arm (2)
16. Rocker arm bearing bottom half (2)
17. Exhaust valve stem pad (early models)
18. Valve key (2)
19. Upper valve spring collar (2)
20. Outer valve spring (2)
21. Inner valve spring (2)
22. Lower spring collar (2)
23. Valve (one exhaust, one intake)
24. Valve guide (one exhaust, one intake)

1965 and earlier cylinder head assembly

Figure following name of part indicates quantity necessary for one complete assembly.

REPLACEMENT VALVE GUIDES

Servi-Car

Perform this operation before refacing the valve seats and faces.

1. Valve guide clearance must be within 0.003–.005 in. Guides must be replaced if play exceeds 0.002 in.

2. Using a shouldered drift or an arbor press, remove the valve guides from the valve head side.

3. Carefully tap the new guide squarely into place and ream it with a suitable reamer to remove any possible high spots.

4. Replacement guides are available in 0.001 and 0.002 in. oversizes, if standard guides are not a heavy press fit.

5. Reface the valve seats to assure a concentric fit with the guides and the correct alignment of valve faces and seats. Consult "Refacing Valve Faces and Seats."

Sportster

1. Same as steps 1–3 for the Servi-Car.

2. Ream the guides, with a 5/16 in. reamer for the exhaust guides, and a 11/32 in. reamer for the intake guides, to assure a smooth and perfectly round fit. 1972 and later models require Valve Guide Reamer (H-D part no. 94830–47) or another suitable reamer.

Glide Models

1. Same as steps 1–3 for the Servi-Car.

2. Exhaust valve guide clearance must be within 0.004–0.006 in. Intake valve guide clearance must be within 0.002–0.004 in. Guides must be replaced when play exceeds 0.002 in.

3. Oversize guides are available in 0.-001–0.006 in. oversizes.

4. Ream out the guides with Valve Guide Reamer (H-D part no. 94830–47) or a suitable substitute.

Valve Seats

Cylinder heads may be returned to the factory to have new seats installed. Consult your local dealer for additional information.

REFACING VALVES AND SEATS

1. If the valve guides are to be replaced, do so before refacing the valves and seats.

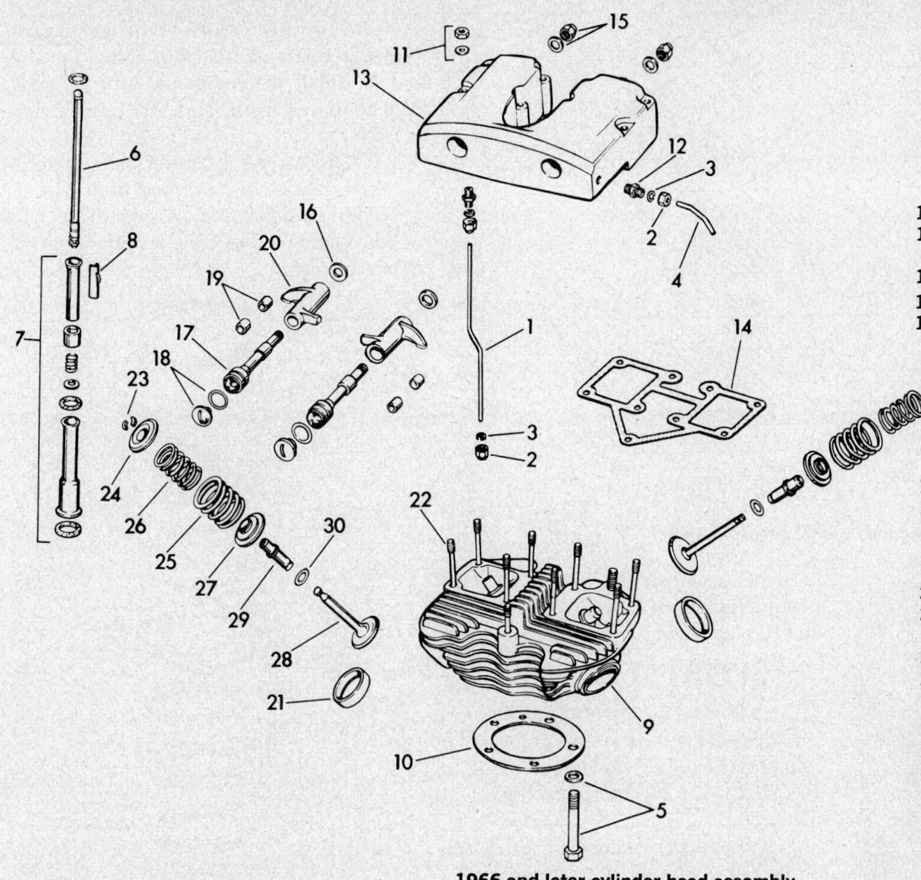

1. Overhead oil feed line
2. Feed line nut (3)
3. Feed line rubber sleeve (3)
4. Cylinder interconnecting oil line
5. Head bolt and washer (5)
6. Push rod (2)
7. Push rod cover (2)
8. Spring cap retainer (2)
9. Cylinder head
10. Cylinder head gasket
11. Rocker housing nut and washer (5)
12. Oil feed line nipple
13. Rocker arm housing
14. Rocker housing gasket
15. Rocker arm shaft acorn nut and washer
16. Rocker arm spacer (2)
17. Rocker arm shaft (2)
18. Rocker arm shaft screw and O-ring (2 each)
19. Rocker arm bushing (4)
20. Rocker arm (2)
21. Valve seat insert (one exhaust, one intake)
22. Rocker housing stud (8)
23. Valve key (2)
24. Upper valve spring collar (2)
25. Outer valve spring (2)
26. Inner valve spring (2)
27. Lower spring collar (2)
28. Valve (one exhaust, one intake)
29. Valve guide (one exhaust, one intake)
30. Valve guide gasket (2)

1966 and later cylinder head assembly

2. Use Valve Grinding Tool (H-D part no. 96550–36) or one of the many commercial grinding tools available.

3. Grind the seat to a 45 degree angle so that the seat is 1/16 in. wide.

4. If the seat is wider than 1/16 in., it may be narrowed by grinding the valve seat relief at a 15 degree angle.

5. Grind the valve to 45 degrees and only long enough to clean and true the surface. Avoid excessive grinding. Replace the valve if it is excessively pitted or warped, or if it is sharp at the face edges.

6. The valve stem end may be turned on a grinding wheel.

LAPPING VALVES AND SEATS

1. After the valve faces and seats are ground, apply a light coat of fine lapping compound and insert the valve in the guide.

2. Rotate the valve several times with a grinding tool while applying light pressure at the face and seat by pulling on the valve stem. This may also be done by hand. A good way is to put a piece of gas line over the stem and hold the head so the stem is up. Rotate it several times and then check as described below.

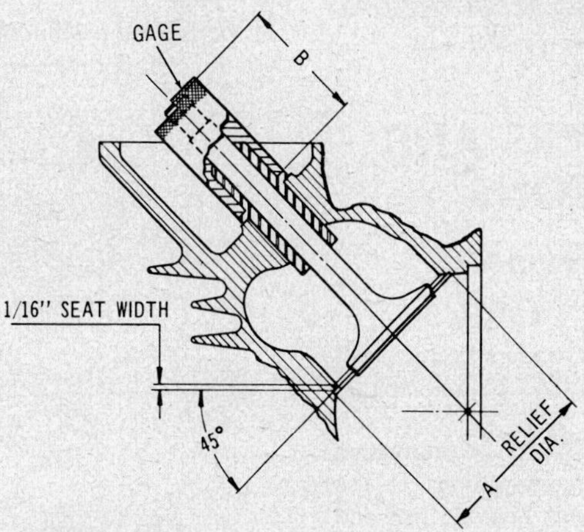

Model	Valve	Relief Dia. A	B Max.	B Min.
XL	Int.	1.75	1.420 (all)	1.375 (all)
	Exh.	1.62		
XLH	Int.	1.87		
	Exh.	1.62		

Sportster valve seat tolerances

3. To check for a well-seated valve, clean the seat and face thoroughly and insert the valve. Apply light pressure to the seat and face, then pour some gasoline on the valve from the combustion chamber side. If it takes several seconds (10–15 is a good indication) before leakage occurs, lapping has been successful. To be absolutely certain, assemble the valve spring collars and keys, and allow the assembly to sit overnight with gasoline on the combustion chamber side. If no leakage occurs, you know you've done an excellent job.

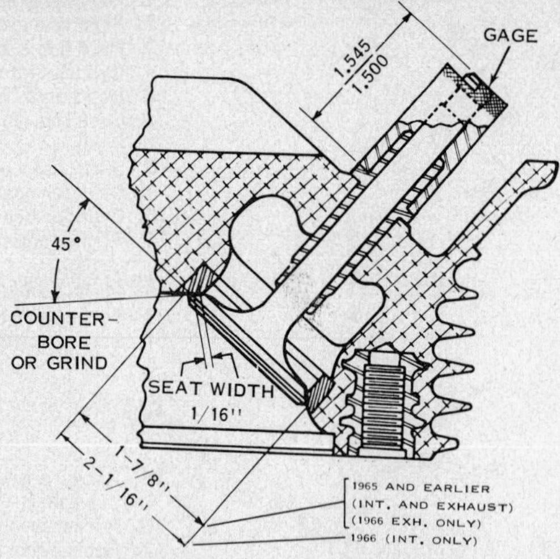

Glide models valve seat tolerances

Lapping valve faces and seats

CYLINDERS AND PISTONS

Disassembly

SERVI-CAR

1. Remove the cylinders as described in "Servi-Car Valve and Cylinder Disassembly."

2. Remove the piston compression rings with a ring expander. Rings can also be removed by prying one end free and blocking the other end, or by pulling both ends free of the grooves and then lifting them free of the piston. If the rings will not clear the piston completely, work them off slowly, taking care not to scratch or nick the piston surface.

3. Pry the piston pin circlips free and discard them.

4. Drift the piston pin from the piston until it can be removed. Separate the pistons for reassembly in the original cylinders.

5. Remove the piston pin bushing, if necessary, using Piston Pin Bushing Tool (H-D part no. 95970–32A), and connecting rod clamping tool (H-D part no. 95952–33) or remove the connecting rod and support the rod around the piston bore then and drift it free. Consult "Connecting Rod Small End Bushing Removal and Replacement."

SPORTSTER AND GLIDE MODELS

1. Strip the motorcycle as described in "Engine Removal" following steps no 1–6, 8, 22, 23, 24 (Sportster), and 1–10 (Glide).

2. Remove the cylinder head as described in "Cylinder Head Removal."

3. Clean the crankcase thoroughly at the cylinder base.

4. Remove the cylinder base nuts and raise the cylinder high enough to place a clean, oily rag over the crankcase to prevent foreign objects from falling in.

5. Rotate the engine until the piston is at its lowest point and lift the cylinder free.

6. Discard the cyclinder base gasket.

7. Continue as described in Servi-Car "Cylinder and Piston Disassembly."

9. Glide models have a lipped, piston pin lock ring.

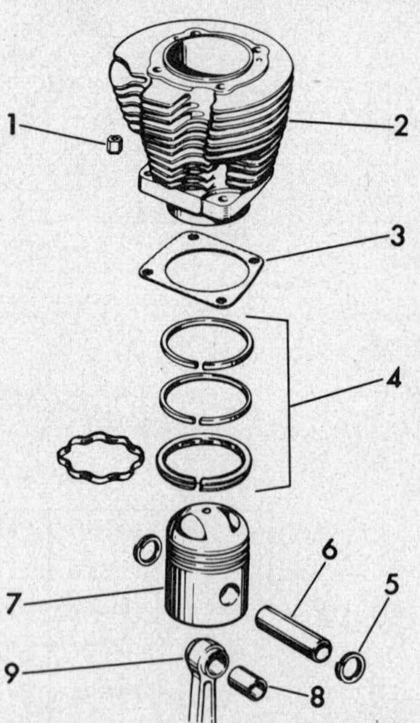

Sportster cylinder and piston assembly

1. Cylinder base nut (4)
2. Cylinder
3. Cylinder base gasket
4. Set piston rings
5. Piston pin lock ring (2)
6. Piston pin
7. Piston
8. Piston pin bushing
9. Connecting rod

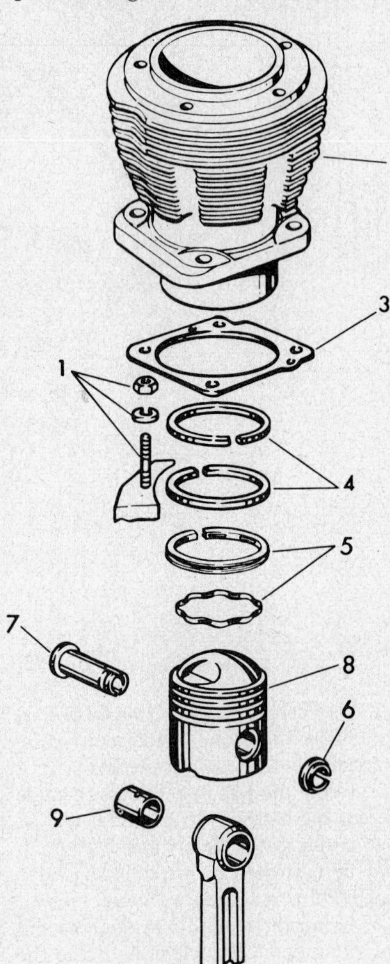

Glide models cylinder and piston assembly

1. Cylinder base stud nut and washer (4)
2. Cylinder
3. Cylinder base gasket
4. Piston rings (2 compression)
5. Oil control piston ring and expander spring
6. Piston pin lock ring (2)
7. Piston pin
8. Piston
9. Piston pin bushing

Inspection and Repair

SERVI-CAR

1. Clean the cylinders and pistons in a suitable solvent until carbon deposits begin to flake off. Scrub with a wire brush if necessary.

2. Clean all parts in a suitable solvent and blow them dry. The piston ring

grooves may be cleaned with a sharpened piece of old ring.

3. Inspect the piston pin and pin bushing for a pitted, scored, or loose condition and replace if necessary. Pins are a hand-press fit with about 0.001 in. clearance. If the pin and pin bushing fit is more than 0.002 in. loose, replace worn parts as described.

SPORTSTER AND GLIDE MODELS

1. Consult Servi-Car "Cylinder and Piston Inspection."

2. On Sportsters, the front rod must have no more than 11/64 in. axial or radial play and no more than 3/64 in. for the rear before lower bearing replacement is indicated.

Assembly

SERVI-CAR

Assemble in reverse order of disassembly. Note the following:

1. Rings should be replaced if they have been removed. Gaps must be staggered around the piston.

2. Install the pistons so that the piston boss web is to the right side of engine or in the original position. The web is a small ridge underneath the piston.

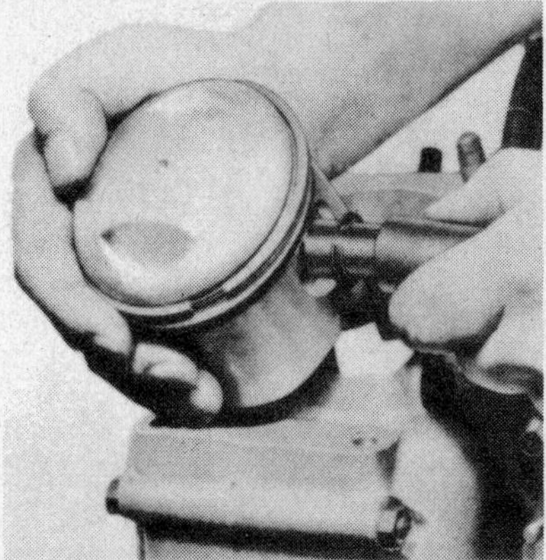

Inserting piston pin circlip

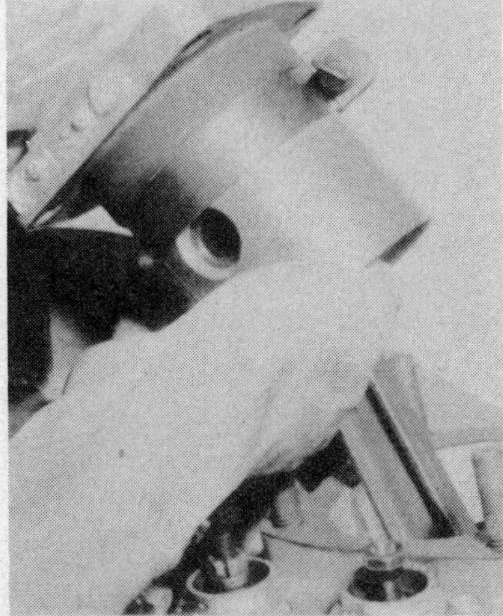

Installing cylinder with the aid of a ring compressor

3. Insert the left-side circlip before assembling the piston to the rod. Pre-heat the piston for easier assembly. Lock Ring Tool (H-D part no. 96780–58) may be used as an aid in assembly. Replace any circlip that fits loosely.

4. Lubricate the cylinder walls, pistons, pins, and bushings.

5. Assemble the cylinders using a ring compressing device if so desired.

6. Secure the cylinder head nuts evenly.

7. Adjust the tappets as described in "Valve Tappet Adjustment," and complete assembly.

SPORTSTER AND GLIDE

1. Consult Servi-Car "Cylinder and Piston Assembly."

2. Use Lock Ring Tool (H-D part no. 96780–58A) on Sportsters and (H-D part no. 96780–32A) on Glide models.

Cylinder Bore Refinishing

ALL MODELS

1. Measure cylinder bore by taking measurements from front to rear and side to side with an inside micrometer at both ½ in. from the top of the cylinder. Repeat at the bottom of ring travel to determine cylinder roundness.

2. Measure piston diameter from front to rear at the base of the piston skirt to check for roundness.

3. Subtract the piston diameter from the cylinder bore to arrive at a clearance measurement.

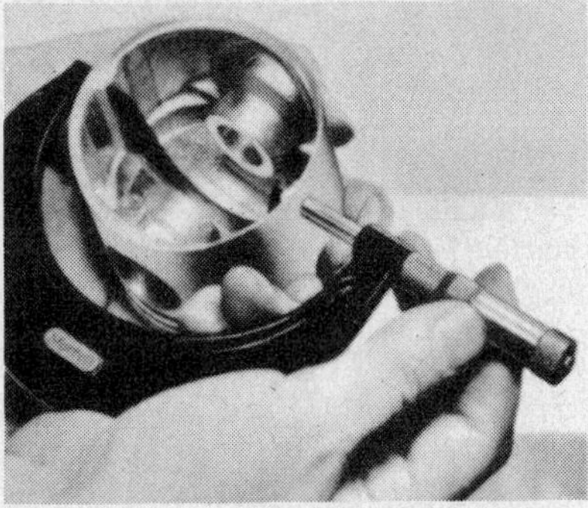

Measuring piston diameter

4. Refinishing is necessary if the cylinders are scuffed, scored, or worn greater than 0.002 in.

5. Oversize pistons can be used to take up excessive clearance when cylinder wear is greater than 0.002 in.

6. If wear exceeds 0.002 in., the cylinders must be bored to the next standard oversize and fitted with suitable pistons and rings.

7. Oversized pistons and rings are available in 0.005, 0.010, 0.020, 0.030, 0.040, 0.050, 0.060, and 0.070 in. oversizes.

8. When it becomes necessary to exceed the 0.070 in. oversize, new cylinders are required.

9. Pistons may be used over again if the cylinders are not worn in excess of 0.002 in. and if damage does not make boring necessary. Replace the rings and rough up the cylinder walls with no. 150 carborundum emery cloth.

10. Refinish the cylinders with a hone or boring bar, and then with a finishing hone. If the cylinders are not badly scored or worn, a hone alone should suffice.

11. Bore to slightly less than the nearest oversize if badly worn or scored, and then finish with a hone to the exact size.

Piston Ring Assembly

1. Replace the rings even if the same pistons are to be used.

2. Rough up the cylinder walls with carborundum emery cloth to facilitate ring seating.

3. The top two ring grooves are for the compression rings. The lowest groove is for the oil control ring.

Measuring ring side clearance

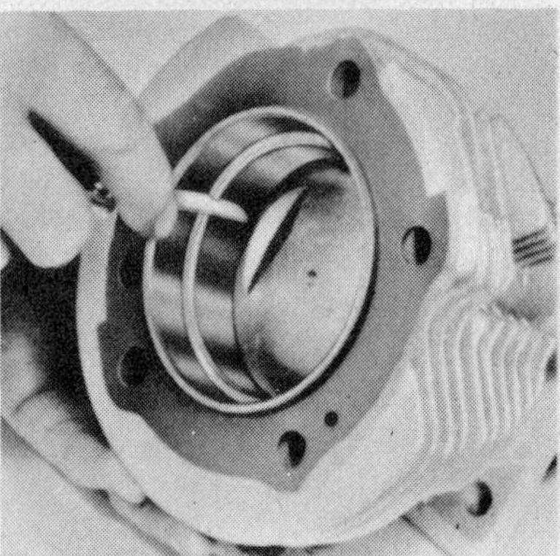

Measuring ring end-gap

4. Consult "Engine Specifications" for ring and piston fit and gap specifications.

5. Ring gap is determined with the piston crown ½ in. (¾ in. on Servi-Cars) from the top of the cylinder. Lay the ring to be checked on top of the piston and check the gap with a feeler gauge.

6. Use standard size pistons and rings in standard bores or match oversize rings and pistons in oversized bores. Oversized rings are available in 0.010 in. gradations from 0.010–0.070 in. (A 0.005 in. is available for Servi-Cars.) Regardless of the oversize, the proper gap is the standard gap. A smaller gap may cause ring failure. If necessary, increase gap with a fine-cut file.

7. Using a ring expander, slip the oil ring in place and then the two compression rings. Rings are fit with the chamfered or dotted side up. On the "U"-Flextype Servi-Car oil rings, damage to any portion of the ring makes replacement necessary.

8. Stagger ring gaps before assembling the piston in the cylinder.

Connecting Rod Small End Bushing Replacement

1. Bushings are a hand-press fit and must be tight in the rod.

2. If the pin clearance exceeds 0.002 in., there are two possible methods of correction:

a. Ream the bushing oversize and use an oversize pin.

b. Install a new bushing and ream it to fit a standard pin. This is the preferred method.

3. Remove bushings by either of the following methods:

a. Remove the rod and support it around the bushing bore then drift the bushing free.

b. Assemble piston pin Bushing Tool (H-D part no. 95970–32) and Connecting Rod Clamping Fixture (H-D part no. 95952–33), and drive the bushing free.

4. Replace the bushings with the oil slot aligned with the rod oil slot.

5. Using Reamer (H-D part no. 94800–26) or a suitable replacement, ream the bushing to size, or ream it nearly to size and finish with a hone. This is the preferred method.

6. The bushing should now afford 0.-001 in. pin clearance.

VALVE TAPPETS AND TAPPET GUIDES

Servi-Car

REMOVAL

1. Remove the cylinder head and cylinder assemblies as previously described.

2. Remove the tappet guide screws, washers, and rubber O-ring.

3. Loosen the tappet adjusting screw locknut and turn the screw out of the tappet body.

4. Remove the tappet guide with Tappet Guide Puller (H-D part no. 95727–38) or find a nut which will screw on the guide sleeve, then use a standard gear puller to remove the guide. Cam gears must be in place during this operation or damage to the camshaft bushings will result.

5. Remove the tappet body and guide gasket.

6. Keep the tappet assemblies separate for reassembly.

5. Turn the adjusting screw and nut into the tappet and insert the tappet in the guide.

6. With the guide screw holes aligned, insert the guide into the crankcase and tap gently with a soft mallet until the guide is seated.

7. Secure the assembly and recheck for free tappet movement.

8. Adjust the tappets as described in "valve Tappet Adjustment."

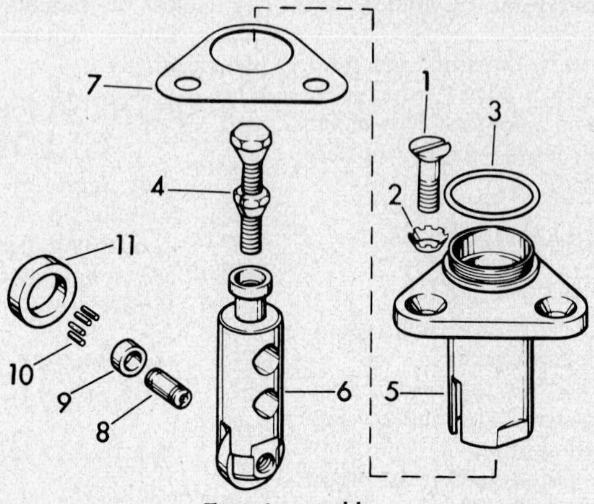

Tappet assembly

1. Tappet guide screw (2)
2. Tappet guide screw lock washer (2)
3. Valve cover-guide gasket
4. Tappet screw with nut
5. Tappet guide
6. Tappet
7. ~~Roller~~ guide gasket
8. Roller pin
9. Roller race
10. Needle rollers (25 small) or (20 large)
11. Roller

Sportster

REMOVAL

NOTE: *Consult the "Timing Gear" section for a tappet assembly illustration.*

1. Remove the tappet guide screw and tappet adjusting screw.

2. Remove the tappet guide with Tappet Guide Puller (H-D 95724–57) or a suitable gear puller. Cam gears must be in place during this operation or damage to the camshaft bushings will result.

3. Remove the tappet guide O-ring, tappet body, and the tappet and roller assembly.

4. Separate the tappet assemblies for reassembly.

Servi-Car and Sportster

INSTALLATION

Assemble in reverse order of disassembly. Note the following:

1. Lightly lubricate the tappet assembly with engine oil before assembly.

2. The roller must seat correctly on the cam and in the guide.

3. Block up the tappet, at its limit of travel, to keep it from falling into the crankcase during installation.

4. Place the O-ring and guide gasket on the guide.

Glide Models

The Glide models have hydraulic tappets which operate under compression force from the valve springs. The tappet roller follows the surface of the cam as do the mechanical units.

The hydraulic unit contains a piston, cylinder, and a ball check valve which maintains a self-adjusting, no-play condition throughout the valve train.

Clicking noises are to be expected until normal operating temperature is reached. A correctly functioning unit should then become quiet.

DISASSEMBLY

1. Remove the pushrod cover spring cap retainer and telescope the covers if the cylinder head is still assembled.

2. Back off the pushrod adjusting screw until the rod can be lifted free of the ball socket.

3. Remove the tappet guide screws and hydraulic units.

4. Gently tap the guides with a soft mallet to loosen them. The tappets and guides can be removed together by pressing the tappet tops against the guide sides with thumb and forefinger, and then by lifting them clear. Do not allow the tappets to fall into the gearcase

through the tappet guide mounting holes.

5. Remove the pushrod cork washers from the guides.

6. Remove the tappet from the bottom of the guide.

7. Remove the guide gasket.

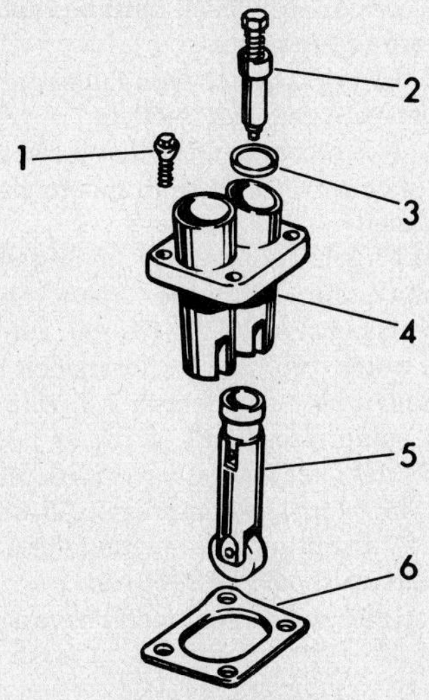

Tappet assembly

1. Tappet guide screw (4)
2. Push rod hydraulic unit (2)
3. Push rod cover cork washer (2)
4. Tappet guide
5. Tappet and roller assembly (2)
6. Tappet guide gasket

Figure following name of part indicates quantity necessary for one complete assembly.

INSPECTION AND REPAIR

1. Clean all parts except the gaskets and hydraulic units in a suitable solvent and blow dry. Do not mix parts.

2. Remove the hydraulic piston and spring from the cylinder, wash them in a suitable solution, and blow them dry.

3. Clear all of the oil passages with compressed air or a piece of wire.

4. Inspect all parts for a worn or damaged condition and replace where necessary.

5. Inspect the cam condition through the gearcase guide ports.

6. Replace the entire tappet as a rule, but roller assemblies only may be replaced, if necessary, by drilling or pressing out the roller pin and installing a roller replacement kit. Rollers should have 0.005–0.001 in. play on the bearings and about 0.008 in. sideplay.

7. Replace worn parts if the tappet fit in the guide exceeds 0.002 in. (Servi-Car), or 0.001 in. (Sportster and Glide Models).

8. The guide is press-fit into the crankcase and must be replaced if play exceeds 0.0005–0.001 in.

9. If the tappet adjusting screw is worn hollow due to pushrod action, it must be replaced to ensure accurate adjustment.

10. Replace the rubber O-rings and gaskets if necessary.

CHECKING PUSHROD OPERATION

1. Check to make sure that the ball valve and seat are clean and dry.

2. Insert the piston in the cylinder.

3. Holding the piston in a vertical position, press down until the spring begins to seat on the cylinder. The cylinder base hole should not be covered.

4. Maintain this pressure for six seconds and then release. The piston should bounce back.

5. If the piston fails to return, repeat steps 3 and 4 while covering the hole. If the piston does not bounce back, replace the unit. If the piston does bounce back, the ball is not seating and the unit must be replaced.

6. Check for a clogged oil screen beneath the large cap screw near the rear tappet guide before replacing the units. If the tappet operates correctly without the screen in place, the problem was not in the hydraulic units. Consult "Gearcase Disassembly" for screen removal procedures.

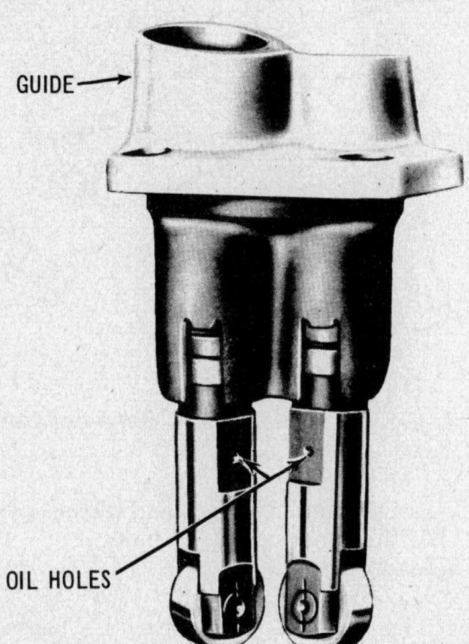

Assembling tappets in guides

ASSEMBLY

Assemble in reverse order of disassembly. Note the following:

1. Insert the tappets into the guides so that the flat surfaces with oil holes are toward the center of the guide.

2. Place a dry guide gasket in position and insert the guide into the gearcase while holding the tappets with the thumb and forefinger. Secure the guide screws.

3. Assemble the cork washers and hydraulic units.

4. Adjust the tappets as described in "Valve Tappet Adjustment."

CLUTCH

Servi-Car and Glide Models

DISASSEMBLY

1. Remove the chainguard and tensioner screw (1964 and later models).

2. Remove the pushrod adjusting screw locknut and place a ⅛ in. thick washer of 1 ¾ in. diameter, with a ⅜ in. hole, over the adjusting screw.

3. Secure it with a locknut and tighten until the spring guide stud nuts are free.

4. Remove the stud nuts and slip out the releasing disc, springs, pressure plate, adjusting screw, and adjusting screw locknut as an assembly.

5. Slide out the friction and steel discs.

6. Loosen the starter motor to provide clearance for removing the clutch sprocket and chain (1964 and later models).

7. Remove the engine sprocket nut with Sprocket Nut Wrench (H-D part no. 94545–26) or a suitable substitute and pull the sprocket off the shaft. A 1.0 in. socket can also be used.

8. Lift the primary chain so that it is free from the clutch sprocket and remove the clutch sprocket.

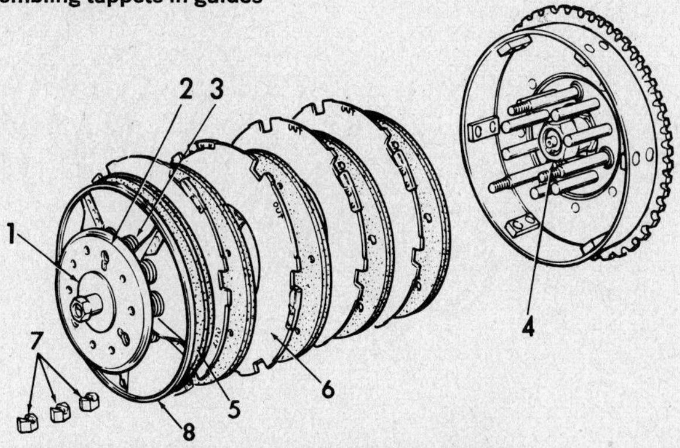

Removing clutch plates

1. Flat washer
2. Spring collar
3. Spring
4. Clutch hub nut
5. Friction discs (5)
6. Steel discs (4)
7. Spring tension adjusting nuts (3)
8. Outer disc

9. Remove the clutch gear nut and washer using clutch gear nut tool (H-D part no. 94545–26), or a hexagonal, 1 in. socket.

10. Pull the clutch hub with Claw Puller (H-D part no. 95960–41A). Most small gear pullers will also work.

11. Remove the bearing plate springs from the hub pins.

12. Remove the bearing retainer from the hub.

INSPECTION AND REPAIR

1. Clean all parts in a suitable solvent and blow them dry.

2. Examine all parts for wear and replace any friction disc linings that are glazed, grooved, worn down to the rivets, oil-impregnated, cracked, or chipped.

3. Glazed friction discs can sometimes be salvaged by soaking them in white gas for several hours and roughing them with a medium grade sandpaper. Make certain that all traces of gas are removed before reinstalling. This is not a recommended practice but will serve temporarily.

4. Steel discs can be reused unless they are burned or grooved, or if buffer balls do not snap back when depressed.

5. Replace the clutch hub roller bearing if, after cleaning and repacking, it sticks or fails to revolve smoothly.

ASSEMBLY

1. Assemble the springs on the releasing disc and place the pressure plate on them, taking care to seat each spring properly.

2. Turn the pushrod adjusting screw into the releasing disc.

3. Lay the washer, as described in "Clutch Disassembly," loosely over the adjusting screw and secure it with the pushrod adjusting screw locknut.

4. Before securing the locknut, check spring alignment and correct if necessary, using a ⅜ in. rod as an aligning tool.

5. Place the hub on the gear shaft with the splines engaged, and secure it with the lockwasher and gear nut. Set the washer in one of the nut's slots with a punch.

6. Slide the clutch sprocket and key ring on the hub.

7. Lightly grease the ball bearings.

8. Slide the clutch discs on in the order and quantity shown in the illustration. The disc which is closest to the hub should be a friction disc, then a steel disc, and so on with buffers staggered in different spline ways. Steel discs are installed with the "out" stamp facing out.

9. Slip the releasing assembly on the hub studs, and secure it with the spring guide stud nuts as described in "Clutch Spring Adjustment."

10. Adjust the clutch control and release lever.

NOTE: *Consult the Servi-Car sections for clutch disassembly, inspection and repair, and for assembly. Below are some variations which apply only to Glide models.*

1. During disassembly, use H-D Clutch Hub Nut Wrench, part no. 94645–41. This nut has a left-hand thread, and the tool is best used in conjunction with a soft mallet. Any socket which fits the nut properly can also be used.

2. 1964 and earlier models use a push rod cork oil seal which must be replaced before reassembly.

3. Use H-D Clutch Hub Puller part no. 95960–41A on Glide models.

4. It is recommended that if the bearing race is worn, the hub should also be replaced.

5. Clutch springs may be tested for compression with the Valve Spring Tester, part no. 96797–47 or an automotive tester. 1967 and earlier models have springs whose free length is 1 31/64 in. and compresses to 42–52 lbs. at 1 ⅛ in. 1968 and later models have a free length of 1 45/64 in. and compress to 30–38 lbs. at 1 ¼ in. Springs not meeting these specifications should be replaced.

6. 1964 and earlier models have a push

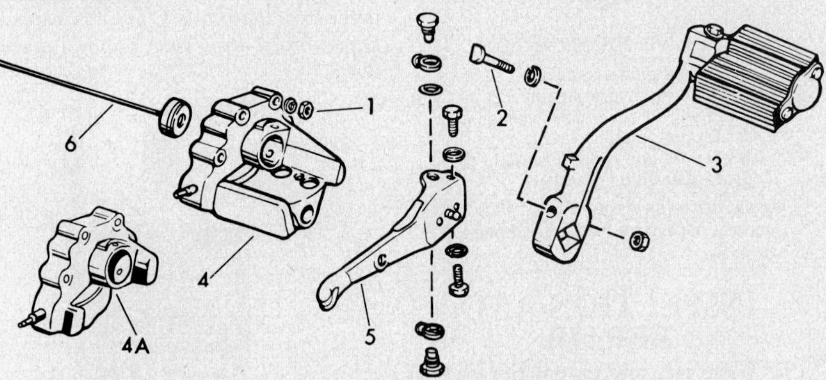

Servi-Car clutch release mechanism

1. Sprocket cover nut and washer (4)
2. Starter crank clamp bolt
3. Starter crank
4. Sprocket cover (1963 & earlier)
4A. Sprocket cover (1964 & later)
5. Clutch release lever
6. Clutch push rod

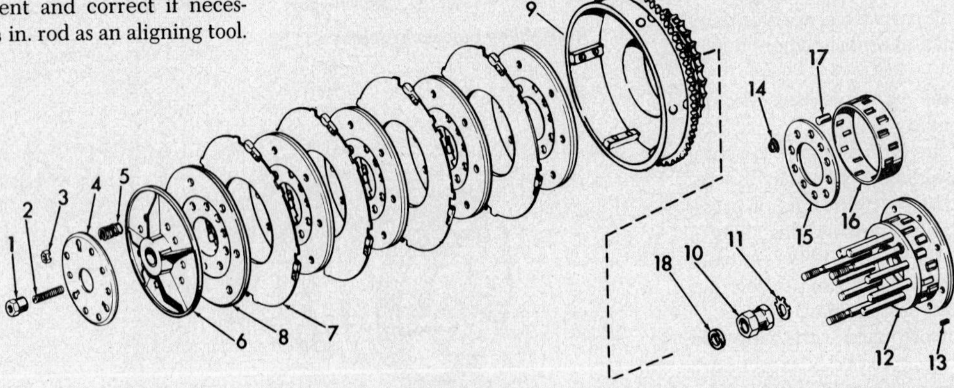

Clutch assembly

1. Push rod adjusting screw lock nut
2. Adjusting screw
3. Spring tension adjusting nut (3)
4. Spring collar
5. Springs (10)
6. Outer disc (pressure plate)
7. Steel disc (4)
8. Friction disc (5)
9. Clutch shell
10. Clutch hub nut
11. Hub nut lock washer
12. Clutch hub
13. Clutch hub key
14. Bearing plate spring (3)
15. Bearing plate
16. Bearing retainer
17. Bearing roller
18. Hub nut seal

rod oil seal spring located inside the hub nut. It should return to its original position immediately after being released by fingertip pressure.

7. When reassembling, the back of the pressure plate to the front of the clutch releasing disc is 31/32 in. for 1967 and earlier models, and 1 1/32 in. for 1968 and later models.

RELEASE BEARING REMOVAL

NOTE: *Consult 'Starters' section for illustrations of Glide Model release bearings.*

1. Remove the clutch control cable from the clutch release lever.
2. Remove the sprocket cover securing nuts and washers.
3. Remove the transmission oil filler plug. This will come loose more easily when the engine is warm.
4. Remove the starter crank clamp bolt and crank on 1963 and earlier models.
5. Remove the sprocket cover and clutch release lever together by prying or tapping them gently with a soft mallet to free the cover from the studs.
6. Remove the clutch release bearing and pushrod from the transmission shaft.

RELEASE BEARING INSPECTION

1. Clean all parts in a suitable solvent and blow them dry.
2. If excessive play is present in the release bearing, the pushrod will wear rapidly. Replace as a unit if it is worn. A bad bearing will cause grinding and whirring noises when the clutch is released.

RELEASE BEARING INSTALLATION

1. Repack the bearing liberally with grease.
2. Insert the pushrod and bearing into the transmission shaft hole as a unit.
3. Install and secure the sprocket cover.
4. Connect the clutch control cable.
5. Adjust the cable mechanism.

CLUTCH CONTROL CABLE AND HOUSING REPLACEMENT

1. Remove the kick-start lever, front cylinder exhaust pipe and muffler, right footrest, and transmission sprocket cover bolts.
2. Loosen the adjusting screw locknut and back off the adjusting screw.
3. Lightly tap the cover with a soft mallet while working it free of the kick-starter shaft.
4. If only the cable is to be replaced, the end may be cut at the lever and the cable may be withdrawn through the top of the housing after being freed from the hand lever.
5. Push the worm lever forward until about 1 in. of cable remains in the cover.
6. The housing will come free by pressing it in and down toward the oil pump.
7. Remove the housing from the left front frame, and lift the ferrule free at the hand lever. This will free both the cable and housing for removal.
8. A new housing should be about 47 ¾ in. long for use with "Speedster" bars, and about 51 1/16 in. long for "Buckhorn" bars.
9. Before installing the upper and lower ferrules, the housing should be stripped of ⅝ in. upper end insulation, and 1 ¼ in. from the lower end.
10. Slip an oiler into place after removing ¼ in. of insulation from the housing at a point 7 in. from the hand lever.
11. Lubricate the new cable while inserting it in the housing from the upper end.
12. Secure the ferrule in the hand lever, with the pin slot facing in, or the open end facing down on the older, slotted-end types.
13. Slip the felt seal retainer and seal on the cable bottom, and secure them with the cable end pieces.
14. Secure the cable end with hard solder after spreading some strands in the fitting countersunk hole.
15. Assemble the remaining parts in reverse order, taking care to properly seat gaskets, replace oil, and adjust the release mechanism.

Sportster

RELEASE MECHANISM

Disassembly

1. Follow steps 1–4 in the "Clutch Control Cable and Housing Replacement" section.

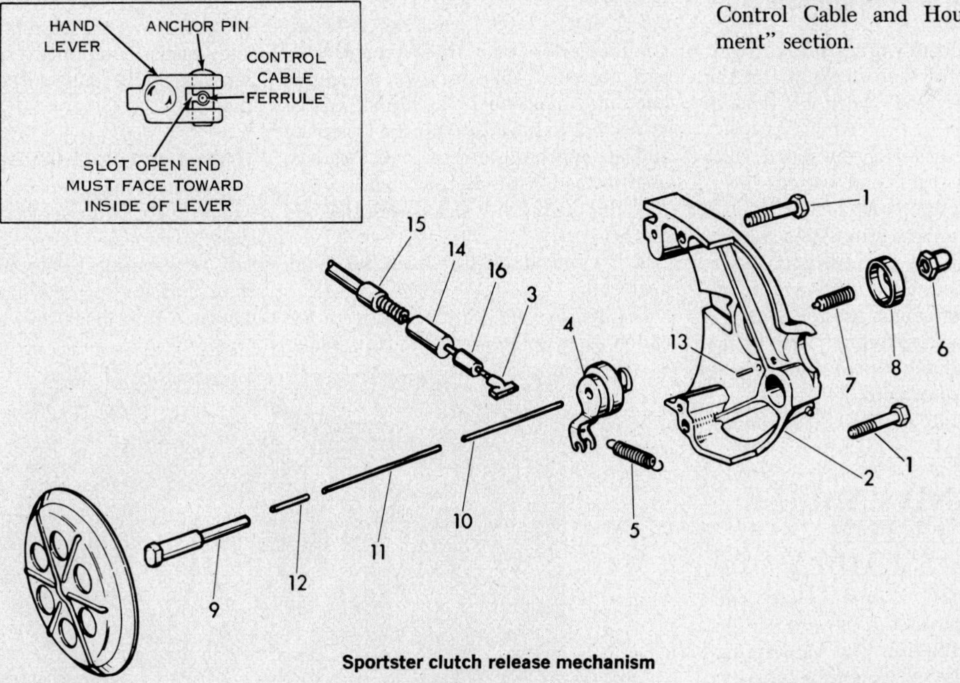

Sportster clutch release mechanism

1. Sprocket cover bolt (2)
2. Sprocket cover
3. Control cable end
4. Clutch release worm and lever
5. Clutch release worm and lever spring
6. Clutch adjusting screw lock nut
7. Clutch adjusting screw
8. Clutch release worm cover
9. Clutch release rod—left
10. Clutch release rod—right
11. Clutch release rod—right center
12. Clutch release rod—left center
13. Sprocket cover roll pin
14. Clutch cable felt seal retainer
15. Clutch cable ferrule (2)
16. Clutch cable felt seal

2. Remove the worm and lever spring, adjusting screw locknut, adjusting screw, and worm dust cover.

3. Remove all clutch parts labeled 1–10 in the illustration to remove the clutch release rods.

4. The left clutch release rod will slip out and the other three must be drifted out from the clutch side.

5. The roll pin is a press-fit and should not be removed.

Inspection and Repair

1. Clean all parts with a suitable solvent and blow dry.

2. Inspect the worm for wear and replace if necessary. Excessive wear will cause clutch drag.

3. Examine the fit of the lever fingers with cable end, and replace if not firm.

4. The correct length of the lever spring is 1 25/32 in. and must be replaced if worn or damaged.

5. Examine the tips of the clutch release rods for wear, roll the rods on a flat surface to check for warping, and replace if necessary.

Assembly

Assemble in reverse order of disassembly. Note the following:

1. Dip the rod ends in oil before installing.

2. Slip in the left release rod from the clutch gear end, and slip in the left center, right center, and right release rods from the sprocket side.

3. Assemble clutch parts 10-1 (see illustration) as described in the "Clutch Assembly" section.

4. Assemble the worm, spring, cover, adjusting screw, and locknut to the sprocket cover and check for smooth movement.

5. Place the cover on the starter shaft and engage the cable end with the lever; secure the cover.

6. Lubricate the worm with a suitable grease through the worm fitting.

7. Check the motion of the worm and be sure it seats against the roll pins.

8. Install the remaining parts as described in "Clutch Cable and Release Mechanism Adjustment."

9. Adjust the clutch release mechanism.

1970 AND EARLIER CLUTCH DISASSEMBLY

1. Remove the chain and clutch covers, and all associated hardware.

2. Remove the hub stud nuts, spring-tension adjusting plate, spring cups, and releasing disc.

3. Slide out the fourteen clutch plates and backing plate by tipping the engine or lifting them out with a hooked piece of wire.

4. Remove the primary chain adjuster brace cap screws and brace.

5. Use a Sprocket Locking Link Tool (H-D part no. 97200–55), if available, to prevent the clutch and compensating sprocket from turning while pulling the hub. A wooden door stop wedged in below the compensating sprocket or a suitable air impact driver are alternatives which will also work.

6. Bend the ears of the hub nut lockwasher away from the hub and remove the left release rod.

7. Using a Clutch Lock Plate (H-D part no. 97175–53) and a Hub Wrench (H-D part no. 94647–52), remove the clutch hub nut. An old steel clutch plate can be drilled out to substitute for the lock plate and an appropriate size socket can be used instead of the hub wrench.

8. Pry the hub nut lockwasher free and discard it.

9. Pry the oil seal free from the clutch gear end.

10. Remove the clutch hub from the clutch gear splines with a Hub Puller (H-D part no. 95960–52) or suitable gear puller.

11. On 1967 XLH models, remove the O-ring from its groove in the clutch gear.

12. Remove the gear shaft nut by using the Compensating Sprocket Shaft Wrench (H-D part no. 94557–55), and remove the clutch shell, primary chain, and engine sprocket. As an alternative method, punches can be inserted in the sprocket holes, and levered with a screwdriver.

13. Remove the clutch hub spacer.

Clutch hub nut removal

1. Front chain adjuster brace and cap screws
2. Front chain adjuster
3. Sprocket locking link tool
4. Clutch lock plate
5. Clutch hub
6. Clutch shell
7. Clutch hub nut wrench
8. Front chain
9. Compensating sprocket

14. Remove the clutch gear extension and O-ring by tapping it with a soft mallet. This applies only to 1966 and earlier models.

Inspection and Repair

1. Inspect the clutch cover for damage which might cause leaks and use a new gasket for reassembly.

2. New springs have a free-length of 1 ⅝ in. and any spring which is too short, damaged from heat, or worn, should be replaced.

Removing clutch hub

1. Clutch hub puller
2. Compensating sprocket shaft wrench

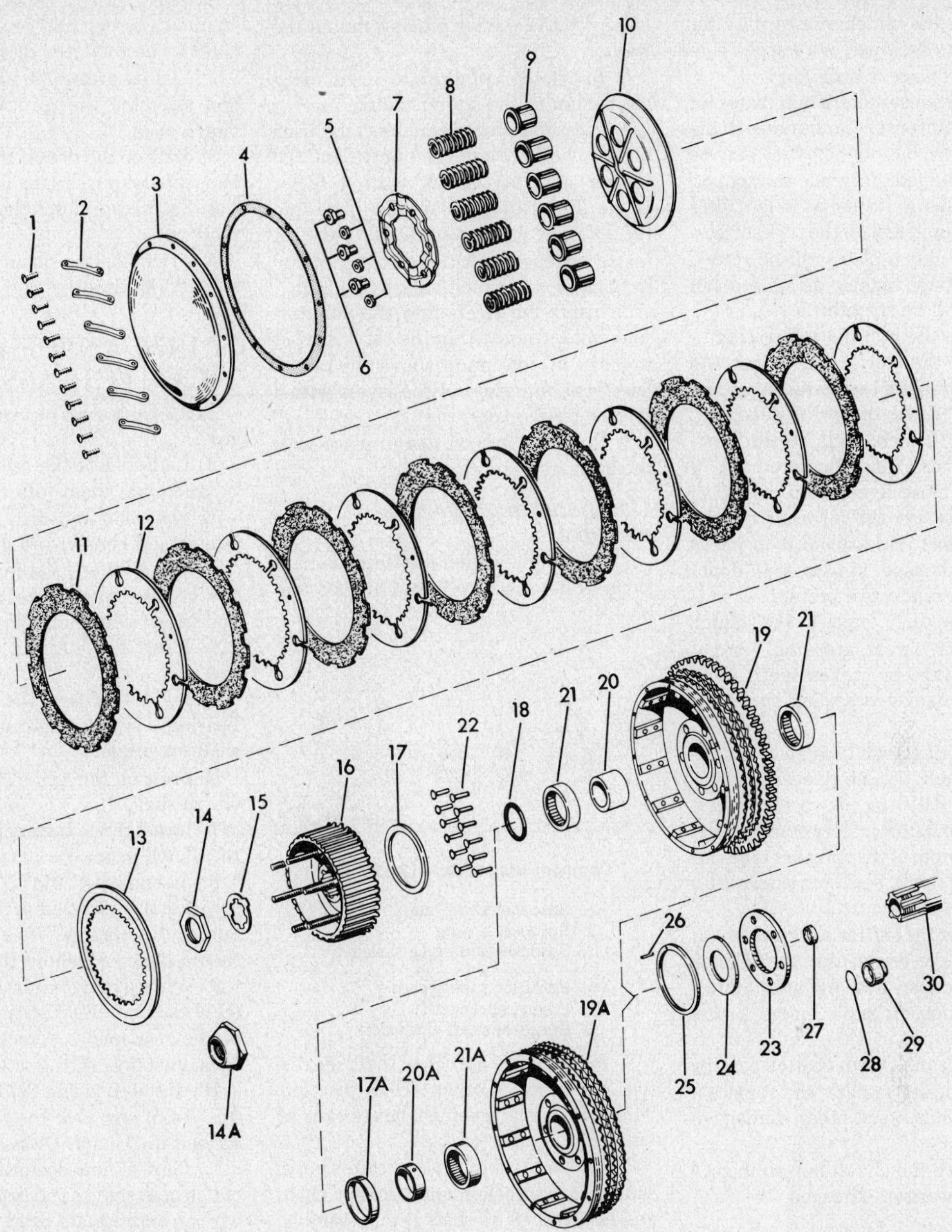

Clutch assembly

1. Clutch cover screw (12)
2. Clutch cover screw retainer (6)
3. Clutch cover
4. Clutch cover gasket
5. Hub stud nut (3)
6. Hub stud nut—long (3)
7. Pressure plate
8. Clutch spring (6)
9. Backing plate cup (6)
10. Releasing disc
11. Friction drive plate (7)
12. Driven plate (7)
13. Backing plate
14. Hub nut (1967 XLH)

14A. Hub nut (1966 & earlier)

15. Hub nut lock washer
16. Clutch hub assembly
17. Clutch hub oil seal (1967 XLH)

17A. Clutch hub oil seal (1966 & earlier)

18. Clutch hub O-ring (1967 XLH)
19. Clutch shell (1967 XLH)

19A. Clutch shell (1966 & earlier)

20. Clutch hub spacer (1967 XLH)

20A. Clutch hub spacer (1966 & earlier)

21. Needle bearing (2—1967 XLH)

21A. Needle bearing (1—1966 & earlier)

22. Sprocket rivet (12)
23. Starter clutch
24. Sprocket bearing washer (variable-size)
25. Sprocket hub washer
26. Sprocket hub washer pin
27. Clutch gear (push rod) oil seal
28. Clutch gear extension O-ring (1966 & earlier)
29. Clutch gear extension (1966 & earlier)
30. Clutch gear

Figure following name of part indicates quantity necessary for one complete assembly.
Note: 1966 and earlier parts also used for 1967 XLCH.

3. Inspect the clutch release disc for grooves, excessive wear, or a warped condition, and replace if necessary.

4. Inspect the clutch friction plates for wear, grooves, or oil saturation. If the plates are worn but not oily, they may be cleaned with medium grade sandpaper. Replace plates if no mark is left after pressing a thumb nail on the cork surface.

5. Driven clutch plates can be reused if they are only slightly discolored but they must still be smooth.

6. Replace the hub nut lockwasher.

7. Inspect the clutch hub spacer and needle bearing for excessive play and wear. Replace the spacer, if necessary, and consult "Clutch Shell Needle Bearing and Starter Clutch Replacement" if the bearing must be replaced.

8. Carefully pry the oil seal from the clutch sprocket and expand it to check for wear or damage. Replace if in doubt or if hairline cracks are present.

9. Examine and replace the clutch shell if excessive wear, grooving, worn or loose keys, worn or broken teeth, loose rivets, or a damaged sealing surface is present.

10. Loose rivets can be replaced if this is the only fault. Set the rivets until they are flush to 0.010 in. above the starter clutch face or 0.080 in. between the rivet head and bottom of the sprocket tooth for key securing rivets. Seal both sides with a solvent-proof sealer.

11. Inspect the starter clutch teeth for wear or damage, and consult the "Clutch Sprocket Needle Bearing and Starter Clutch" section for replacement procedures.

12. Inspect the clutch gear oil seal, by expanding the seal surface, and replace it if hair line cracks or other damage is present.

13. Replace the clutch hub rubber O-ring, if it is worn or damaged.

Clutch Sprocket Needle Bearing and Starter Clutch Replacement

1. Remove the oil seal and sprocket rivets to gain access to the clutch sprocket needle bearings, washers, and starter clutch. Bearings and the sprocket hub washer pin are a press-fit.

2. Replace the bearing by pressing from the inside on the bearing's printed side to a depth of 0.025–0.029 in. from the shell's inner face to the bearing's lip.

3. Press the roll pin until it extends 0.08 in. from the sprocket face.

4. On 1967 XLH models, the two bearings are pressed in the same way. The first seats to 1.010–0.015 in. from the shell to the bearing's inner face, and the second is pressed from the starter clutch side until it is flush with the first.

5. Align the hub washer countersunk hole with the washer pin and mount the washer.

6. Insert the appropriate sized variable washer in the starter clutch.

7. With the starter clutch on the back plate, check clearance between the washer and the clutch with a feeler gauge. Exert pressure on the plate and try different washers until 0.001–0.0021 in. clearance is arrived at. Washers come in thickenesses which vary by .002 in.

8. Insert the rivets into the countersunk holes from within the shell and set to 0.010 in. maximum above the clutch face. Seal both sides of the rivets with a solvent proof sealer.

9. Press the hub oil seal in place with the lip facing into the shell.

Compensating Sprocket Removal

1. Loosen the clutch shell and primary chain as described in "Clutch Disassembly."

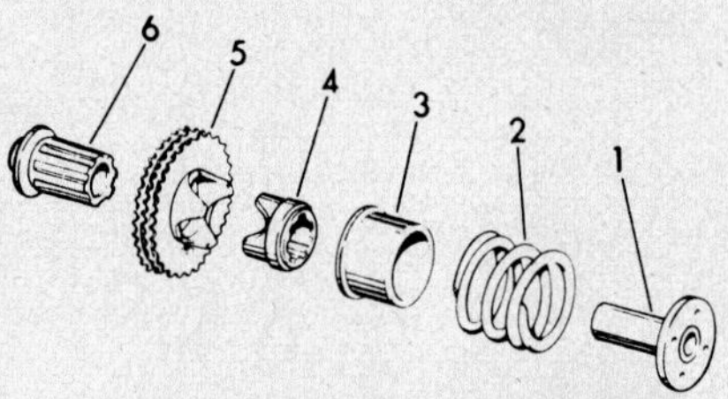

Compensating sprocket assembly

1. Sprocket shaft nut
2. Sprocket spring
3. Sprocket sliding cam sleeve
4. Sprocket sliding cam
5. Engine sprocket
6. Sprocket shaft extension

2. Remove the sprocket shaft nut using Shaft Nut Wrench (H-D part no. 94557–57), or a one-inch hex socket or wrench.

3. Slip the spring, sliding cam sleeve, sliding cam sprocket, and primary chain and clutch shell off shaft as an assembly. Use Sprocket Shaft Extension Puller (H-D part no. 96015–56) or a suitable substitute to remove the shaft extension if desired.

Inspection and Repair

1. Clean all parts with a suitable solvent and blow them dry.

2. Inspect the sprocket teeth, shaft splines, and sliding surfaces for excessive wear or damage, and replace if necessary.

3. The cam and extension must be a matched set, so replace both or neither.

4. If the spring is damaged there will be primary chain noise even when the chain is properly tensioned. Replace it if this is the case.

Installation

1. Set the shaft extension with Sprocket Shaft Bearing Tool (H-D part no. 97081–54) as described in the "Crankcase Assembly" section. A socket can also be used as a drift.

2. Lightly grease the extension splines and assemble the sprocket, chain, and clutch shell.

3. Slide on the sleeve, spring, shaft nut, and cam, taking care to align the splines.

4. Secure the clutch shell and sprocket shaft nut.

5. Assemble the chain cover and associated hardware.

1970 AND EARLIER CLUTCH ASSEMBLY

1. All parts must be clean, dry, and oil-free.

2. Lightly coat the release rod tips in oil and slide them into the clutch gear with the right rod first, then the right center, left center, and left rod last.

3. On 1966 and earlier models, press the gear extension into the clutch gear and seal it with aluminum paint.

4. Insert the hub nut O-ring and oil seal.

5. Lightly grease the needle roller bearings and compensating sprocket shaft extension.

6. Press-fit the roller bearing in the clutch shell.

7. Install the hub spacer and O-ring on the clutch gear.

8. Assemble the compensating sprocket as described in "Compensating Sprocket Assembly." The chain adjuster should be loose behind the chain.

9. With Clutch Hub Installing Tool (H-D part no. 97170–55) install the hub on the gear splines. A socket can be used in conjunction with a soft mallet.

10. Install Locking Plate (H-D part no. 97175–55) and lock the sprocket as described in "Clutch Disassembly" step 5.

11. Slip a new lockwasher over the clutch gear splines and install the hub nut with an appropriate sized wrench or special Wrench (H-D part no. 94647–52). Seat the nut to at least 150 ft lbs torque by striking the wrench handle with a soft mallet.

12. Bend the washer ear against the hub nut.

13. Check to make sure that the hub runs free on the shaft and check clearance between the starter clutch gear and starter clutch as described in the "Starter Assembly" section.

14. Adjust the primary chain tension as described in the "Primary Chain Adjustment" section.

15. Remove the hub locking tools.

16. Install the backing plate against the back of the hub with the grooved side out.

17. Assemble the clutch plates starting with a steel plate, then a friction plate and so on. The last plate should be a friction plate and all should move freely.

18. Install the releasing plate on the hub with the studs centered in the cup holes. The larger of the two grooves on the rim should line up with the hub's notched tooth.

19. Assemble the cups, springs, and pressure plate with the raised surface facing out.

20. Place the ½ in. long nut on the longer studs and tighten them evenly until the shorter studs are available. Start the 7/16 in. nuts on their studs.

21. Tighten all six nuts evenly until the inside of the pressure plate is 3/16 in. from the cup flanges. This is the proper distance for new clutch plates.

22. Assemble the new cover gasket with the graphite side facing out. Do not use sealer.

23. Assemble the clutch cover, screws and screw retainers. Lightly stake the retainers to the screws.

24. Install a new chain cover gasket and apply sealer to both sides. Mount and secure the chain cover.

25. Mount and secure the rear brake pedal, stoplight switch, and footrest.

26. Prop up the motorcycle so it is straight and remove the oil filler cap and oil level plug. Fill with the recommended oil until overflow comes out of the oil level plug. When overflow stops, secure the plug and cap.

1971 AND LATER CLUTCH

Disassembly

1. Remove the chaincase cover as described in "Clutch Spring Adjustment."
2. Remove the retainer nuts and retainer.

Clutch retaining parts

1. Retainer nut (6)
2. Retainer (6)
3. Adjusting nut (beneath retainer) (6)
4. Clutch releasing disc

3. Install the Clutch Spring Compressing Tool (H-D part no. 97178–71) if available. The new clutch has a center spring configuration rather than the traditional six springs. The pressure on the releasing disc won't bend the disc if the spring tension nuts are loosened diagonally, one turn at a time and then removed.

4. Remove the releasing disc, inner and outer springs, and Compressing Tool (if used).

5. Remove the retaining ring from the clutch shell groove and pull all of the clutch plates free as a unit by pulling on the pressure plate studs.

6. Consult "1970 and Earlier Clutch Disassembly" to complete disassembly.

Compressing clutch spring

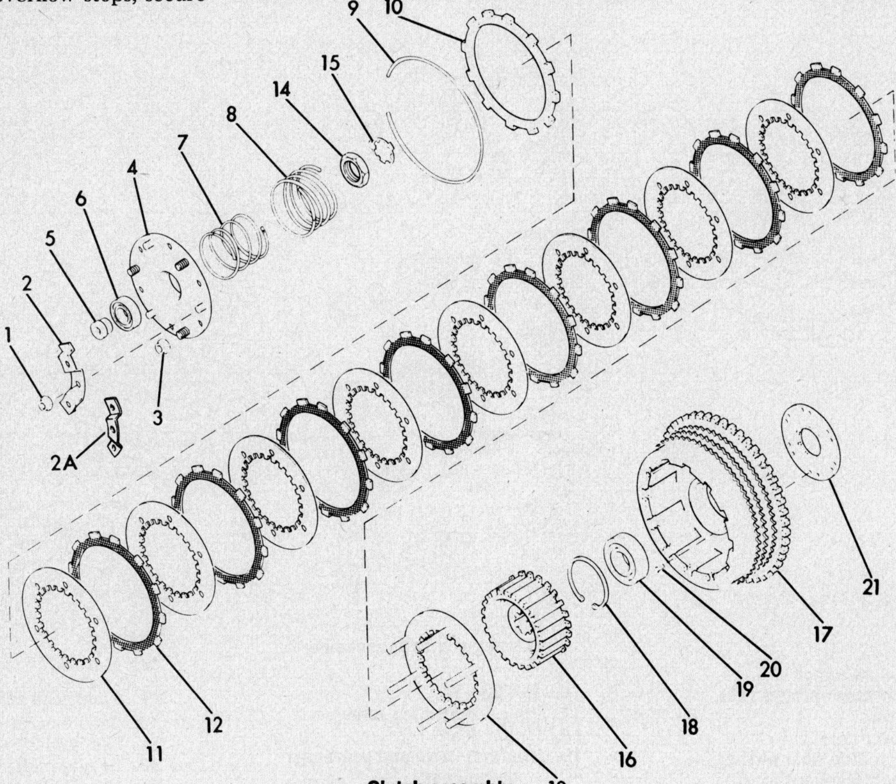

Clutch assembly

1. Nut, retainer (3) (Early 1971) (6) (Late 1971)
2. Retainer (3) (Early 1971)
2A. Retainer (6) (Late 1971)
3. Nut, spring tension (6)
4. Releasing disc
5. Releasing disc collar
6. Releasing disc bearing
7. Spring, inner
8. Spring, outer
9. Retaining ring, outer drive plate
10. Outer drive plate
11. Driven plate (8)
12. Drive plate (8)
13. Pressure plate
14. Hub nut
15. Hub nut lockwasher
16. Clutch hub assy.
17. Clutch shell
18. Retaining ring, clutch shell bearing
19. Bearing, clutch shell
20. Rivet, starter clutch (12)
21. Starter clutch

Inspection and Repair

1. Inspect the clutch springs for heat damage and replace any spring under the following free-length limits: inner springs are to be 2 5/16 in., 1970–71 outer springs are to be 1 ¾ in., and 1972 and later outer springs are to be 2 ½ in.

2. If the clutch shell bearing action is rough or has excessive play, it may be replaced by arbor-pressing it in and out after the retaining ring is removed with snapring pliers.

3. Check the releasing disc bearing action for roughness or excessive play and replace if necessary.

4. Consult "1970 and Earlier Inspection" for additional procedures.

1971 and Later Clutch Assembly

1. Consult "1970 and Earlier Clutch Assembly."

TIMING GEARCASE

Servi-Car

DISASSEMBLY

1. Remove the oil pumps as described in the Lubrication Systems chapter and drain the oil.

2. Remove the contact breaker as described in "Contact Breaker Removal and Assembly."

3. Remove the generator as described in the Electrical System chapter.

4. Remove the tappet assemblies as described in "Tappet Disassembly."

5. Remove the oil pressure switch.

6. Remove the gearcase cover screws and remove the cover by tapping it with a soft mallet. Remove the gasket.

7. Remove the idler gear stud fiber washer and camshaft steel washers if they don't come off as the cover is removed.

8. Remove the front exhaust cam gear, rear intake cam and timer gears, front intake cam gear, rear exhaust cam gear, and the steel washers. Separate all parts, including washers, for reassembly in their original positions.

9. Remove the pinion shaft plug screw and pinion gear using Pinion Gear Puller and Installer (H-D part no. 96830–51). A standard gear puller can be used if precautions are taken not to damage any gear teeth. A suitable size piece of pipe can be used as a dirft during installation.

10. Remove the breather valve and scavenger pump drive gear, right seal ring spring, and right bearing ring spring from the gear shaft.

11. Remove the idler gear stud screw and shaft.

INSPECTION AND REPAIR

1. Clean all of the parts except the cover gasket in a suitable solvent and blow them dry.

2. Clean the inside of the gearcase, taking care to keep the solvent from soaking through into the crankcase.

3. Inspect all parts for wear or damage and replace as necessary. Bushings need not be removed unless wear or damage makes replacement necessary.

4. Inspect the crankcase oil screen for a clogged condition and clean or replace as necessary. Probe the screen hole with a hooked piece of wire to check for foreign objects.

5. Replace the idler gear bushing or shaft if worn.

6. Replace the gear assemblies when excessive lash is present, the teeth are damaged, or the cams are worn or pitted.

7. Blow the crankcase relief pipe clear with compressed air.

8. Inspect the breather oil separator seal ring for free action.

9. Inspect the cover and case bushings for wear and excessive play. Shaft play

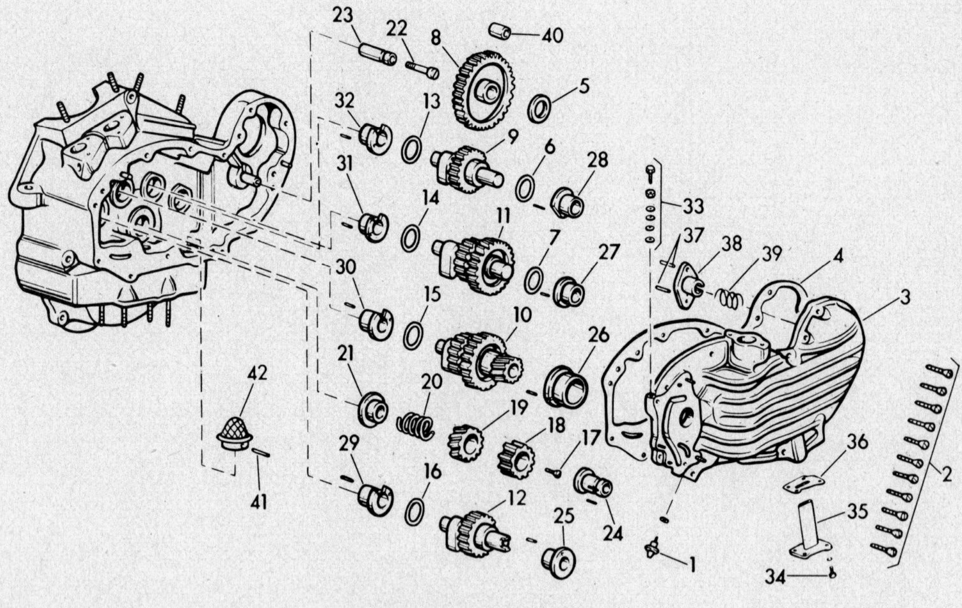

Timing gearcase assembly

1. Oil pressure switch
2. Gearcase cover screws (11)
3. Gear cover
4. Gear cover gasket
5. Idler gear stud fiber washer
6. Cam shaft steel washer (6)
7. See item 6
8. Idler gear
9. Front exhaust cam gear
10. Rear intake cam and timer gear
11. Front intake cam gear
12. Rear exhaust cam gear
13. See item 6
14. See item 6
15. See item 6
16. See item 6
17. Pinion shaft plug screw
18. Pinion gear
19. Breather valve and scavenger pump gear
20. Right seal ring spring
21. Right bearing seal ring
22. Idler gear stud screw
23. Idler gear stud shaft
24. Cam cover gear shaft bushing
25. Cam gear cover bushing
26. Cam gear cover bushing
27. Cam gear cover bushing
28. Cam gear cover bushing
29. Crankcase cam gear bushing (4)
30. See item 29.
31. See item 29.
32. See item 29
33. Chain oiler screw
34. Crankcase relief pipe screw (4)
35. Crankcase relief pipe
36. Relief pipe gasket
37. Seal ring retaining pin
38. Breather oil separator seal ring
39. Seal ring spring
40. Idler gear bushing
41. Oil strainer retaining pin
42. Crankcase oil screen

greater than 0.002 in. indicates the need of bushing replacement.

10. Remove the gearcase cover bushings with Crankcase Cam Gear Shaft Bushing Remover (H-D part no. 96760–36), (H-D part no. 95760–69), or a suitable substitute.

11. Drift the crankcase bushings out from the flywheel side with a suitable drift, or use the above special tool if the crankcase is still assembled.

12. Press the front cylinder exhaust bushing into the gearcase cover with the oil hole toward the rear of the cover. Place a flat plate over the flange to protect it, and press until the flange sits flush on the mating surface. Drill, with a no. 31 drill, ⅛ in. deep. Secure the pin slightly below the bushing and peen the bushing around the pin. Using the bushing boss hole as a guide, drill a 5/32 in. oil hole through the bushing.

13. Press the front and rear cylinder intake bushings into the gearcase cover with the narrow section of the flange pointing downward. Repeat the above drilling operation.

14. Press the rear cylinder exhaust bushing flush with the oil feed pump seat from the outside. Repeat the above dowel pin installation, but do not peen the bushing.

15. Press the pinion gear shaft bushing into the cover with the oil hole pointing 30 degrees forward of its vertical centerline.

16. Arbor-press the crankcase side bushings in place, with the crankcase disassembled, from the gearcase side with the flange notch pointing upward. Repeat the above pin securing procedures.

17. To line-ream the cam gear and timer bushings, insert the Camshaft and Timer Shaft Bushing Reamer (H-D part no. 94803–37) "T" portion through the right crankcase from the flywheel side without turning the reamer and assemble the larger portion of the tool. Start the larger portion in the timer shaft bushing and assemble the gearcase cover. Always secure the cover with at least four screws when reaming and always turn the reamer to the right until bottom is reached, then withdraw it while still turning to the right. A suitable substitute reamer may be used if care is taken.

18. Line-ream the pinion shaft bushing with Pinion Shaft Bushing Reamer (H-D part no. 94812–37) or a suitable substitute. The cover must be assembled and a guide bushing must be used.

19. Ream the rear cylinder exhaust cam gear bushings with Oiler Shaft Bushing Reamer (H-D part no. 94811–36) or a suitable substitute. Work from the gearcase cover side.

20. Using only the smaller reamer of the Cam Shaft and Timer Bushing Reamer (H-D no. 94803–37) or a suitable substitute, line-ream the front cylinder exhaust and intake bushings, taking care not to remove more metal than necessary.

BREATHER VALVE TIMING

1. Rotate the engine until the flywheel timing mark is aligned in the crankcase inspection hole.

2. Install the scavenger pump.

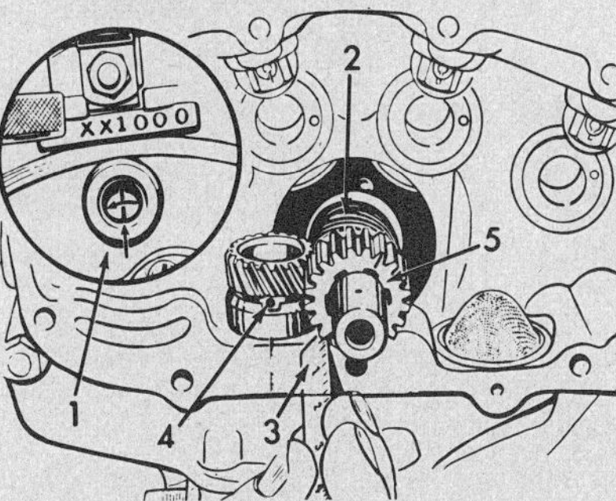

Breather valve timing

1. Flywheel timing mark
2. Oil pump drive gear (spiral gear)
3. Measurement
4. Timing hole in breather sleeve gear
5. Pinion gear

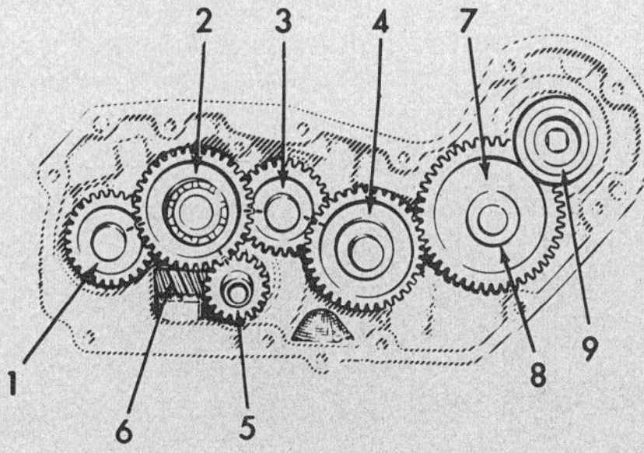

Timing gear alignment

1. Rear exhaust cam gear
2. Rear intake cam gear
3. Front intake cam gear
4. Front exhaust cam gear
5. Pinion gear
6. Crankcase breather sleeve gear
7. Intermediate gear (has no timing mark)
8. Intermediate gear fiber washer
9. Generator drive gear

3. Slip the spiral gear on the splined pinion shaft until it is seated. At this point the breather sleeve gear timing hole will be aligned in the center of the breather housing slot.

4. Assemble the pinion gear with Gear Puller and Installer Tool (H-D part no. 96830–51) or gently tap in place with a hammer and suitably sized drift. If the special tool is used, the locating collar will reach the gearcase face at a point which will leave 5/16 in. between the gear and gearcase face.

This gap must be provided for if an alternate method of assembly is used.

ASSEMBLY

Assemble in reverse order of idsassembly. Note the following:

1. Cam gear marks must be aligned during assembly.

2. Place a 0.006 in. steel shim behind each cam gear and outside the two front cylinder cam gears. The same number of 0.005 or 0.007 in. washers found in disassembly should be used, then more can be added or removed until end play of 0.-001–0.006 in. is arrived at.

3. Install the rear cylinder exhaust cam, front cylinder intake cam, rear cylinder intake cam, and front cylinder exhaust cam—in that order.

4. Gears should rotate freely and move in and out of mesh freely, but not loosely. Check for excessive play by holding one gear steady and trying to rotate the others. There should be no play.

5. With the crankcase on its left side, pour ¼ pt of engine oil over the gear train.

6. Install the idler gear shaft fiber washer on the cover side.

7. Install a new cover gasket.

8. Tap the cover in place over the dowels with a soft mallet.

9. Rotate the engine and check for binding. Too many shims will cause excessive drag. Cam gear end-play can be checked with a feeler gauge inserted through the tappet guides.

10. Assemble and secure the cover gasket with a non-hardening sealer.

11. Assemble the remaining items and adjust tappets as described in "Valve Tappet Adjustment."

12. If shaft clearance in the bearings exceeds 0.0005–0.0025 in., bearing replacement is necessary.

13. Inspect the cam gear plates for wear or damage and replace if necessary.

14. Replace the pinion gear if clearance is present, since any lash will cause noisy operation.

15. Oil separator bushings must have free-play and 1/16 in. running clearance with the generator oil slinger washer.

16. Remove the cam gear needle bearings with Needle Bearing Puller (H-D part no. 97270–60) or disassemble the crankcase as described in "Crankcase Disassembly" and arbor-press them out. Press on the printed side only when replacing, taking care to press the bearing in absolutely straight. Laying a flat plate over the bearing will protect it. Press until flush with mating surface.

17. Remove and install the cover and case bushings in the manner described in Servi-Car "Gearcase Inspection and Repair."

18. Line-ream all but the idler gear bushings in the manner described in Servi-Car "Gearcase Inspection and Repair." Always turn the reamer in to the right until it bottoms and then withdraw it while continuing to turn it to the right. Avoid removing an excessive amount of metal.

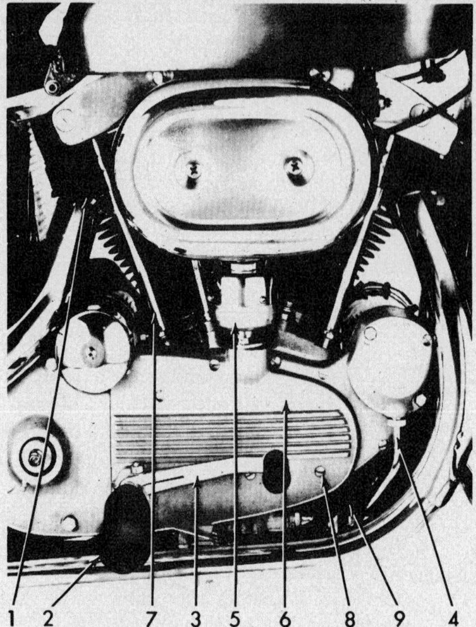

Removing gearcase cover on 1970 and earlier models

1. Exhaust pipe port clamp (2)
2. Footrest
3. Gear shift foot lever
4. Breather pipe
5. Circuit breaker
6. Gearcase cover
7. Push rod (4)
8. Gearcase cover screw (11)
9. Clutch cable

Removing gearcase cover on 1971 and later models

1. Exhaust pipe port clamp (2)
2. Footrest
3. Gear shift foot lever
4. Breather pipe
5. Circuit breaker
6. Gearcase cover
7. Push rod (4)
8. Gearcase cover screw (11)

19. Ream the idler gear bushings with Reamer (H-D part no. 94806–57) or a suitable 9/16 in. substitute.

20. Line-ream the contact breaker shaft cover bushing with Reamer (H-D part no. 94803–37) or a suitable substitute. Use the crankcase bearing opposite to the bushing to support the reamer as described in Servi-Car "Gearcase Inspection and Repair" step no. 17.

Sportster

DISASSEMBLY

1. Remove the exhaust pipe assemblies, footrest, shift lever, breather pipe, contact breaker or magneto, as described in "Contact Breaker Assembly" or "Magneto Removal," and pushrods as described in "Pushrod Removal and Installation."

2. Drain the oil, remove the gearcase cover screws, and remove the cover from its dowel pins by tapping it with a soft mallet or hammer and wood block where the cover projects beyond the gearcase. Remove the cover gasket.

3. Remove the tappets and guides as described in "Tappet Disassembly."

4. Disconnect the clutch cable.

5. Remove the rear cylinder exhaust, rear cylinder intake, front cylinder exhaust, and front cylinder intake cam gears and cam gear plates. Gear lobes are numbered from 1–4 to designate their positions from the back to the front of the gearcase. Remove and separate the gear shaft shims for replacement in their original positions.

6. Remove the idler gear and its fiber washer.

7. Remove the pinion gear with Pinion Gear Puller (H-D part no. 96830–51) or a suitable substitute (see Servi-Car "Gearcase Disassembly" step no. 9).

8. Remove the oil pump drive gear.

INSPECTION AND REPAIR

1–8. Same as for Servi-Car.

9. If shaft clearance in the cover bushings exceeds 0.0005–0.001 in. by 0.001 in. or more, bushing replacement is necessary. Replace the bushings also if the flanges are worn.

10. If the shaft clearance in the bearings exceed 0.0005–0.0025 in., bearing replacement is necessary.

11. Inspect the cam gear plates for wear or damage and replace if necessary.

12. Replace the pinion gear if clearance is present, since any lash will cause noisy operation.

13. Oil separator bushings must have free play and 1/16 in. running clearance with the generator oil slinger washer.

14. Remove the cam gear needle bearings with Needle Bearing Puller (H-D part no. 97270–60) or disassemble the crankcase as described in "Crankcase Disassembly," and arbor press them out. Press on the printed side of the bearing only when replacing, taking care to press the bearing in absolutely straight. Laying a flat piece of metal over the bearing will protect it. Press until flush with the mating surface.

15. Remove and install the cover and case bushings in the manner described in Servi-Car "Gearcase Inspection and Repair."

16. Line ream all but the idler gear bushings in the manner described in Servi-Car Gearcase Inspection and Repair. Always turn the reamer in to the right until it bottoms and then withdraw it while continuing to turn it to the right. Avoid removing excessive amounts of metal.

17. Ream the idler gear bushings with Reamer (H-D part no. 94806–57) or a suitable 1/16 in. substitute.

18. Line-ream the contact breaker shaft cover bushings with Reamer (H-D part no. 94803–37) or a suitable substitute. Use the crankcase bearing opposite to the bushing to support the reamer as described in 'Servi-Car Gearcase Inspection and Repair' step no. 17.

19. Line-ream the front exhaust, front intake, and rear exhaust cam gear shaft cover bushings in the same manner as above.

20. Line-ream the pinion gear shaft cover bushing in the above manner by inserting Reamer (H-D part no. 94812–37A) or a suitable substitute through the pilot bushings.

BREATHER VALVE TIMING

Consult Servi-Car "Breather Valve Timing."

ASSEMBLY

1. Consult Servi-Car "Gearcase Assembly."

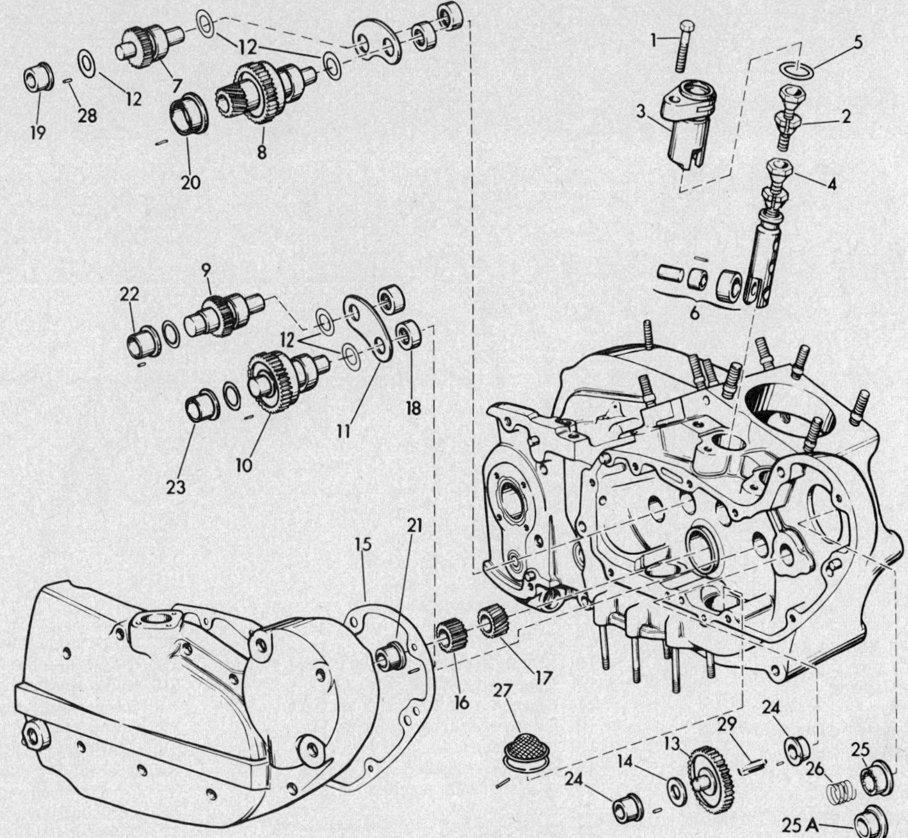

Gearcase and tappet assemblies

1. Tappet guide screw
2. Tappet screw with nut
3. Tappet guide
4. Tappet and roller
5. Tappet guide "O" ring
6. Tappet roller kit
7. Rear cylinder exhaust cam gear
8. Rear cylinder intake cam gear
9. Front cylinder intake cam gear
10. Front cylinder exhaust cam gear
11. Cam gear plate (2)
12. Cam shaft washer—0.005, 0.007 in.
13. Idler gear
14. Idler gear shaft fiber washer
15. Gearcase cover gasket
16. Flywheel shaft pinion gear
17. Oil pump drive gear
18. Cam gear needle roller bearing (4)
19. Rear exhaust cam gear shaft bushing
20. Cam gear and timer shaft bushing
21. Pinion gear shaft bushing
22. Front intake cam gear shaft bushing
23. Front exhaust cam gear shaft bushing
24. Idler gear shaft bushing (2)
25. Oil separator bushing assembly (1962 & earlier)
25A. Oil separator bushing (1963 & later)
26. Breather oil separator seal ring spring (1962 & earlier)
27. Crankcase oil strainer, retaining pin and gasket
28. Gearcase cover bushing pin (7)
28. Idler gear shaft

2. Place the cam gear plates over the bearings with the beveled side facing the cam.

3. Tilt the back end of the generator down as it is inserted in the gearcase to lift the oil slinger over the intermediate gear. Then lift up slightly to mesh the generator drive gear with the intermediate gear.

Glide Models

DISASSEMBLY

1–3. Same as for Sportster.

4. Remove the generator.

5. Remove the oil screen cap, gasket, screen body, screen, and screen seal (if applicable).

6. Remove the idler gear and contact breaker gear spacers, and separate for reassembly.

7. Remove the cam gear, spacer shim, and thrust washer.

8. Remove the breather valve spacer shim, breather gear, contact breaker gear, and idler gear.

9. Remove the left-hand threaded pinion gear shaft nut with Gear Nut Socket Wrench (H-D part no. 94555–55) or vise grips.

Removing pinion gear

10. Remove the pinion gear with Pinion Gear Puller and Installer (H-D part no. 96830–51) or a gear puller, taking care to protect the gear teeth.

11. Remove the pinion gear key, spring, spacer, oil pump pinion shaft gear, and pump gear key.

12. Remove the breather screen and separator from the crankcase pocket.

13. Remove the oiler drive gear spring ring, oiler drive gear, and drive gear key.

14. Remove the oil pump if necessary.

INSPECTION AND REPAIR

1–6. Same as for Servi-Car. Glide models have two screens to be attended to.

7. Assemble the pinion gear, cam gear, and gearcase cover, but do not include the cam gear end spacer. If the gears and bushings are still good, there should be no

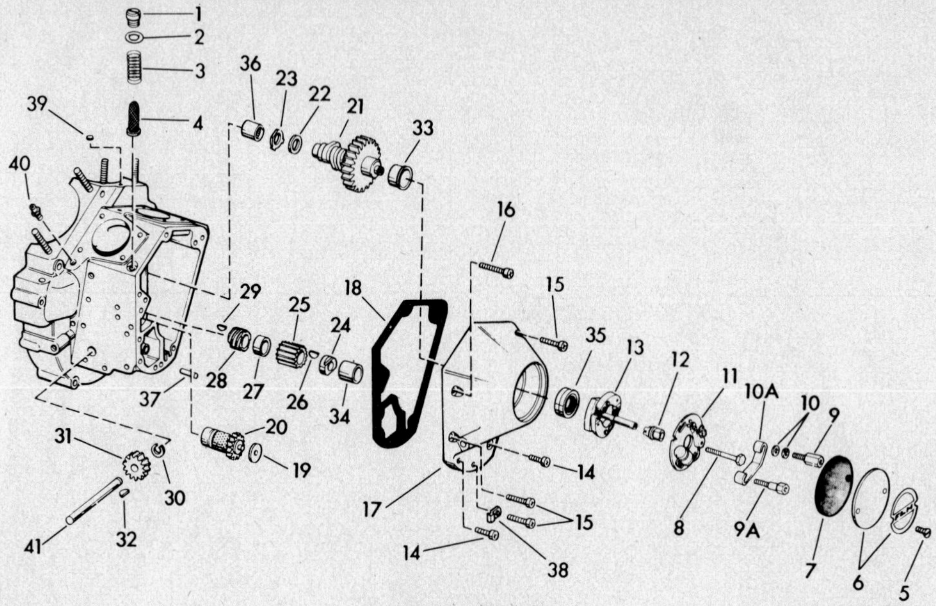

Gearcase assembly

1. Oil screen cap
2. Cap seal
3. Oil screen spring
4. Oil screen
5. Circuit breaker cover screws (2)
6. Circuit breaker cover
7. Circuit breaker cover gasket
8. Circuit breaker cam assy. bolt
9. Circuit breaker plate screw (2) (1970)

9A. Circuit breaker plate screw (1971 & later)

10. Circuit breaker plate screw lock-washer and washer (1970)

10A. Retainer (1971 & later)

11. Circuit breaker plate assy.
12. Circuit breaker cam
13. Circuit breaker advance assy.
14. Gear cover screw, 1 in. (2)
15. Gear cover screw, $1\frac{1}{4}$ in. (3)
16. Gear cover screw, $1\frac{3}{4}$ in. (1)
17. Gear cover
18. Gear cover gasket
19. Breather gear washer
20. Breather gear
21. Cam gear
22. Cam gear spacing washer
23. Cam gear thrust washer
24. Gear shaft nut
25. Pinion gear
26. Pinion gear key
27. Pinion gear spacer
28. Oil pump pinion shaft gear
29. Oil pump pinion shaft gear key
30. Oil pump drive gear lock ring
31. Oil pump drive gear
32. Oil pump drive gear key
33. Gear cover camshaft bushing
34. Gear cover pinion shaft bushing
35. Camshaft oil seal
36. Camshaft needle bearing
37. Cover dowel pin (2)
38. Wire clip
39. Welch plug
40. Oil line fitting
41. Oil pump shaft

appreciable play and the cam gear's movement along the shaft should be free.

8. Inspect the needle roller cam shaft bearing for excessive wear, damage, or shaft play in excess of 0.003 in., and replace if necessary. Remove the needle bearing with Puller Tool (H-D part no. 95760–69) or disassemble the crankcase as described in "Crankcase Disassembly," and arbor-press it out. Press on the printed side only when replacing with the Bearing Tool (H-D part no. 97270–60) or arbor-press it into place. Laying a flat plate over the bearing will protect and guide the bearing straight in. Press until it is flush with the mating surface.

9. Inspect all bushings for excessive wear, pitting, grooving, and shaft play in excess of 0.001 in. Replace if necessary.

10. Remove the pinion and camshaft cover bushings with Puller Tool (H-D part no. 95760–69) or a suitable substitute. Install and secure a new bushing in the same manner described in Servi-Car "Gearcase Inspection and Repair" step no. 12. The pinhole must be 3/16 in. deep before pressing the bushing into place, then continue to drill until the hole is 9/32 in. deep.

Timing gear alignment

11. Line-ream the pinion and camshaft cover bushings as described in Servi-Car "Gearcase Inspection and Repair," using Pinion Shaft Bushing Reamer (H-D part no. 94805–57) or a suitable 9/16 in. substitute on the pinion bushing, and Cam Gear Shaft Bushing Reamer (H-D part no. 94802–36) or a suitable substitute on the cam bushing.

12. Remove and install the contact breaker and idler gear bushing with a suitable drift and an arbor press. Press until flush with mating surfaces.

ASSEMBLY

Assemble in reverse order of disassembly. Note the following:

1. Check for shaft end-play by assembling the breather gear, a new dry cover gasket, and a spacing shim. Lay a straightedge across the gearcase at the shim and measure the gap between the two with a feeler gauge. Subtract 0.006 in. for gasket compression. Correct end play with breather valve and rear spacing shims to within 0.001–0.005 in. Shims are available in 0.115, 0.120, and 0.125 in. thicknesses.

2. Install the thrust washer, spacing shim, cam gear, and gear cover. Measure play between the cover bushing and cam

gear by inserting a feeler gauge through the tappet guide hole. Correct the end-play with spacer shims to within 0.001–0.005 in.

Shims are available in 0.005 in. gradations from 0.050–0.070 in.

3. Assemble the gears with the timing marks aligned.

4. Pour ¼ pt of engine oil over the gear train and check for free motion.

5. Secure the gasket with a non-hardening sealer and secure the cover.

CRANKCASE

Servi-Car

DISASSEMBLY

1. Remove the engine from frame as described in "Engine Removal".

2. Remove the cylinders and pistons as described in "Cylinder and Piston Disassembly".

3. Remove the oil pumps as described in the "Lubrication Systems" section and drain the oil.

4. Remove the contact breaker as described in "Contact Breaker Assembly Removal".

5. Remove the generator and starter.

6. Remove the tappets as described in the "Valve Tappets and Guides" section.

7. Remove the crankcase bolts, one stud nut from each stud, and studs. The top and two bottom studs must be drifted out.

8. Tap the mounting lugs with a block of wood and a hammer to separate the cases.

9. Remove the sprocket shaft bearing washers and the bearing assemblies intact and separate. Sets must be replaced if mixed.

10. Remove the thrust collars.

11. With the sprocket shaft secured in a wood or copper jawed vise, remove the crank pin locknut, and the crank pin using crank pin nut wrench (H-D part no. 94545–26) or any suitable 1 in. socket or wrench.

12. Strike the rim of the right flywheel with a soft mallet at a point about 90 degrees from the crank pin hole to loosen it, then remove the connecting rods.

13. Remove and separate the rod bearing set.

14. Repeat step 11 on the left flywheel and remove the shaft and keys. Striking the end of the crank pin with a soft mallet will free it from the flywheel.

15. Remove the remaining parts as desired.

INSPECTION AND REPAIR

1. Clean all parts in a suitable solvent and blow dry. Blow the oil drillways clear.

2. Inspect all shafts and bearing races for wear, pitting, or damage. Shafts with a shoulder worn 0.005 in., or more, at the sides of the roller path, must be replaced.

3. Inspect all parts for cracks, breaks, grooves, or wear and replace if necessary.

4. Replace all washers and bearing rings if necessary, or if condition is doubtful.

5. Main bearing bushings may be pressed out if replacement is necessary. Beating the cases around them facilitates removal. Remove the lock screws by the right bushing. New bushings are arbor-pressed in. Place a flat steel plate on the bushing lip to avoid damage.

6. Lap the new or used bushings with lapping arbor (H-D part no. 96710–40) or a suitable substitute, in the following manner:

a. Assemble the stripped crankcase halves with at least three registering stud bolts.

b. Assemble the 1 ⅜ in. lapping arbor to the tool's handle.

c. Assemble the guide sleeve to the sprocket shaft bearing bushing (left side).

d. Guide the lapping shaft through the pinion shaft bearing bushing (right side) and into the guide sleeve.

e. Use a length of 5/32 in. rod to tighten the arbor expansion collars until the lap is snug and begins to drag. A snug fit is critical for proper truing.

f. Withdraw the lap enough to

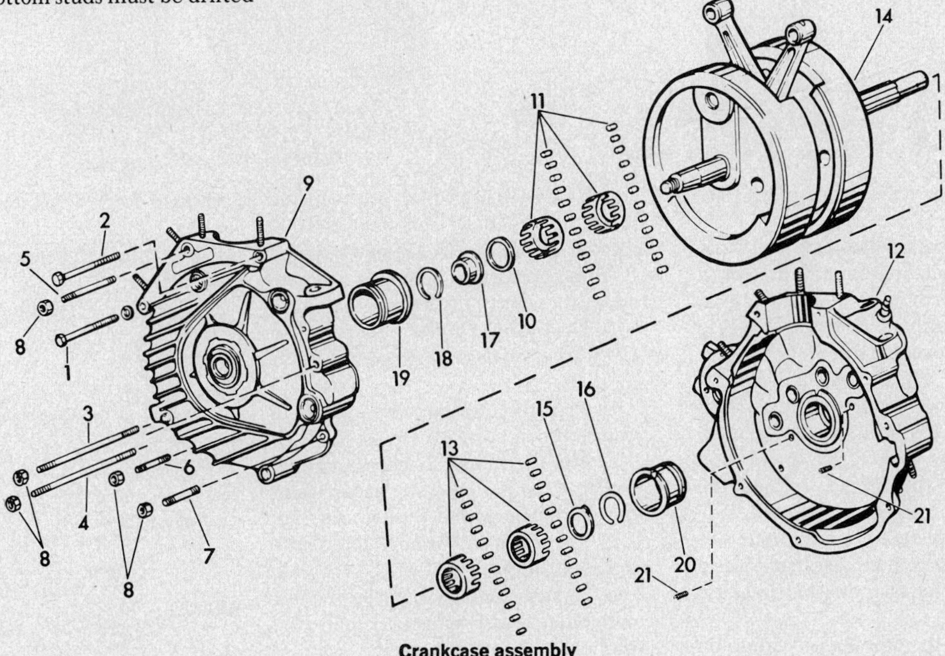

Crankcase assembly

1. Crankcase bolt (2-3/4 in.) (2)
2. See item 1
3. Crankcase stud (5 in.) (2)
4. See item 3
5. Crankcase stud (4-1/2 in.)
6. Crankcase stud (1-5/8 in.) (2)
7. See item 6
8. Crankcase stud nut (10)
9. Left crankcase
10. Sprocket shaft bearing washer
11. Left bearing
12. Right crankcase
13. Right bearing
14. Flywheel assembly
15. Right bearing washer
16. Pinion shaft bearing ring
17. Sprocket shaft bearing end
18. Sprocket shaft bearing ring
19. Left roller bearing bushing
20. Right roller bearing bushing
21. Lock screw (2)

Figure following name of part indicates quantity necessary for one complete assembly.

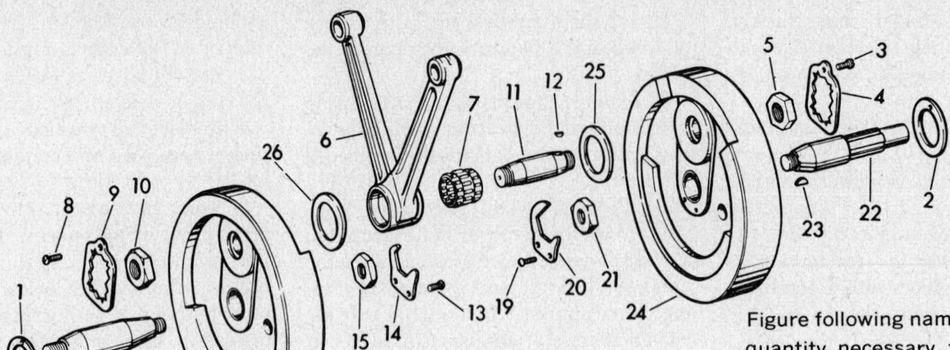

Flywheel assembly

Figure following name of part indicates quantity necessary for one complete assembly.

1. Thrust collar (.066 to .102 in. in steps of .004 in.) (2)
2. See item 1
3. Lock washer screw (4)
4. Crank pin nut lock (2)
5. Crank pin nut (2)
6. Connecting rods
7. Connecting rod bearing set
8. See item 3
9. See item 4
10. See item 5
11. Crank pin
12. Shaft key (3)
13. See item 3
14. Gear and sprocket shaft nut lock (2)
15. Gear and sprocket shaft nut (2)
16. Sprocket shaft
17. See item 12
18. Left flywheel
19. See item 3
20. See item 14
21. See item 15
22. Pinion shaft
23. See item 12
24. Right flywheel
25. Flywheel washer (2)
26. See item 25

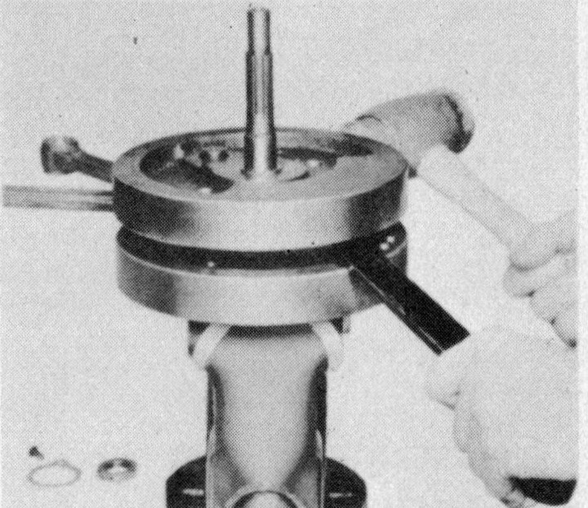

Removing the right flywheel

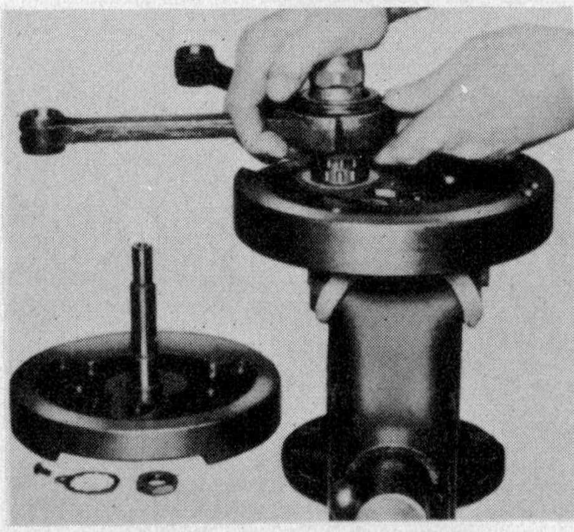

Removing the connecting rods

lightly coat it with fine lapping compound.

g. Slide the lap back into the bushing and begin to rotate and work it back and forth at a moderate speed. Cover the entire race surface evenly to avoid an uneven condition.

h. Several times during the lapping operation, the lapper should be withdrawn, cleaned in a suitable solution, and blown dry. Fresh compound should then be applied. Clean the bushing also and check progress. Lapping is completed when the race surface changes from a smooth and glossy finish to one which is dull and and satin like.

i. Repeat the lapping procedure on the sprocket bearing bushing. The lapping tool should be cleaned thoroughly before storage.

7. Select the proper size bearings to fit the shaft and its respective bushing. Check for a correct plug fit by allowing the shaft to slip through the assembled bearing by itself. Now choose a roller one half the specified clearance for a correct running fit. Oversize rollers are available in 0.002 in gradations from 0.0002–0.001 in. Never mix roller sizes in one bearing.

8. Replace worn or damaged flywheel trust washers in the following manner:

a. Drill a hole slightly deeper than the washer on its outer edge using a ⅛ in. drill.

b. Pry the washer free with a pointed tool.

c. File the staked flywheel material smooth with emery paper and thoroughly clean the washer seat.

d. Insert a new washer taking care to seat it fully.

e. Secure the washer by center punching the flywheel around the washer.

9. Lap worn connecting rod races until there is no wear on the shoulder and both rods will accept the same size rollers. The lapping tool must fit in the bearing race snugly before compound is applied. Connecting rod lapping arbor (H-D part no. 96740–17), or a suitable substitute, used at 150–200 rpm in a lathe, will provide the best results. Use a smooth motion back and forth across the length of the lapper.

10. Fit the rod bearings in the following manner:

a. Assemble the thoroughly cleaned sprocket and pinion shafts to the

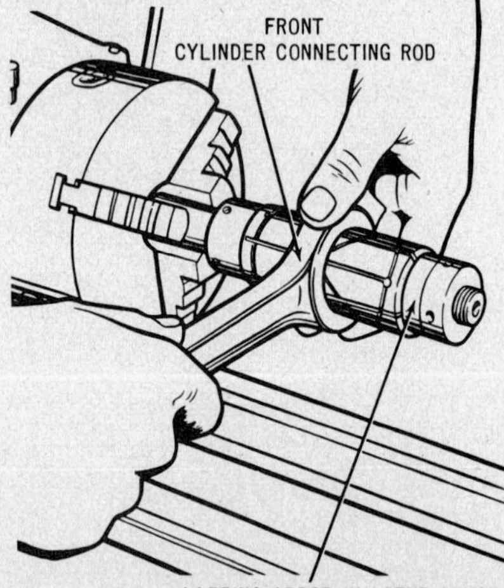

Lapping the connecting rods

flywheel. If the lockwasher screw holes won't line up, increase the tightness of the shaft nut.

b. Secure the crank pin in the left flywheel.

c. Secure the flywheel and sprocket shaft with the crank pin in a vertical position in a copper or wood-jawed vise.

d. Install a connecting rod bearing set on the crankpin and check for a plug fit of both rods. If necessary, lap the tighter of the two rods until both are even.

e. Check for correct fit by subtracting one half the specified running clearance from the roller size.

f. The upper end rod furthest from the flywheel should have side shake of 1/32–3/64 in. Bearings must not extend beyond the rod edges.

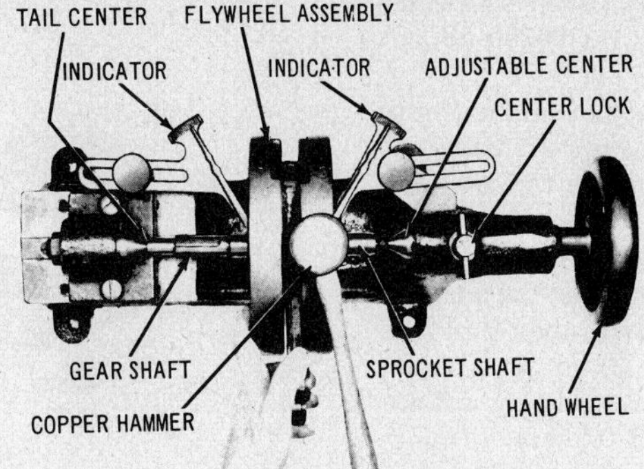

Truing the flywheels

ASSEMBLY

1. Secure the thoroughly cleaned left fly wheel and sprocket shaft in a copper or wood-jawed vise and assemble the crank pin and right flywheel.

2. Check flywheel alighment with a straight edge. Alternately tighten the crank pin nut slightly and recheck alignment until secure. A soft mallet can be used to aid alignment. This method generally provides alignment to within 0.002 in.

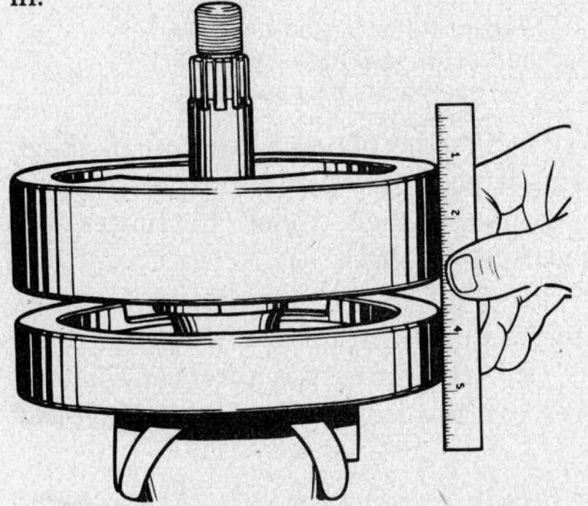
Aligning the flywheels

3. Press one rod against the flywheel thrust washer and measure play between the opposite rod and washer with a feeler gauge. Check for the following if play is less than 0.006 in.:

a. Flywheels and crank pin tapers were oily during assembly, allowing crankpin nuts to be overtightened

b. Flywheel thrust washers are improperly seated

c. Flywheel tapered holes are worn to excessive clearance

d. Cracks at the flywheel tapered holes

4. If play is greater than 0.010 in., wait until the flywheels are trued before correcting.

5. True the flywheels with a truing device (H-D part no. 96650–30) in the following manner:

a. Place the flywheel assembly in the device and adjust until the centers are snug.

b. Rotate the flywheels and mark the high point with chalk. Loosen the device slightly and align using the three following methods.

NOTE: *(A) or (B) should be done before (C).*

(A). A C-clamp can be used on the rims directly opposite the crankpin along with moderate blows to the rim at the crank pin with a soft mallet.

(B). A hardwood wedge can be driven between the wheels directly opposite the crankpin. Moderate blows with a soft mallet are the safest way to perform this operation.

(C). Strike the wheel, at about 90 degrees from the crank pin, with a firm blow with a soft mallet.

c. Repeat steps (A) and (B) above. If truing procedures were effective, shaft play should be 0.001 in. or less. The factory device has 0.002 in. gradations. Check for a cracked flywheel, enlarged tapered hole, or worn sprocket or pinion shafts if repeated truing attempts fail.

d. Secure the crank pin nuts tightly when the flywheels are true, then recheck on device. Minor adjustments may be made without loosening the crankpin nuts.

6. An alternate method is to use a dial indicator, and a lathe or some other means of rotating the flywheels on a steady plane.

7. Continue assembly in the reverse order of disassembly.

8. Assemble the case halves with the top and bottom-most registering studs.

9. Hand-press the flywheel assembly toward the case gear and measure the

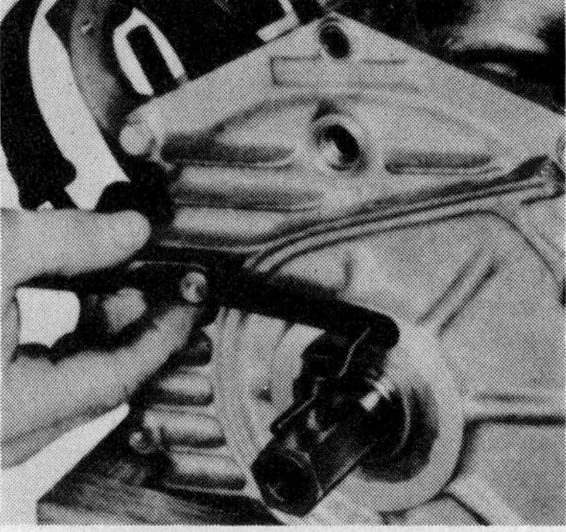
Checking crankshaft end-play

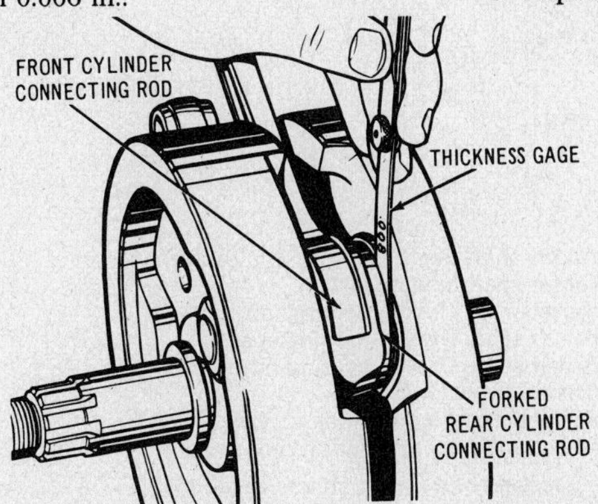

Checking the connecting rod side-play

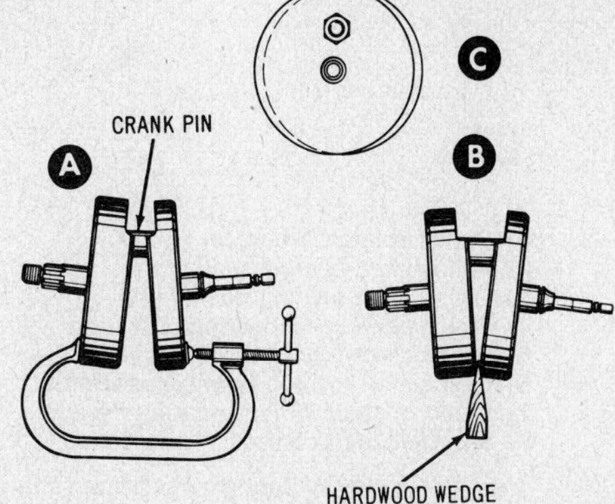

Flywheel truing methods

flywheel end-play with a flywheel end-play gauge (H-D part no. 96700–38) on the sprocket shaft.

10. Adjust the gauge pin until it gently touches the case. Push the shaft to the left and measure the clearance with a feeler gauge.

11. A dial indicator can also be used by securing the indicator so that the plunger gently contacts the shaft, then shift the shaft and measure as above.

12. Adjust flywheel end-play within the crankcase to 0.009–0.013 in. by using the appropriate steel thrust collar. Collars are available in 0.004 in. gradations from 0.066–0.102 in.

Sportster

DISASSEMBLY

1–6. Same as for Servi-Car.

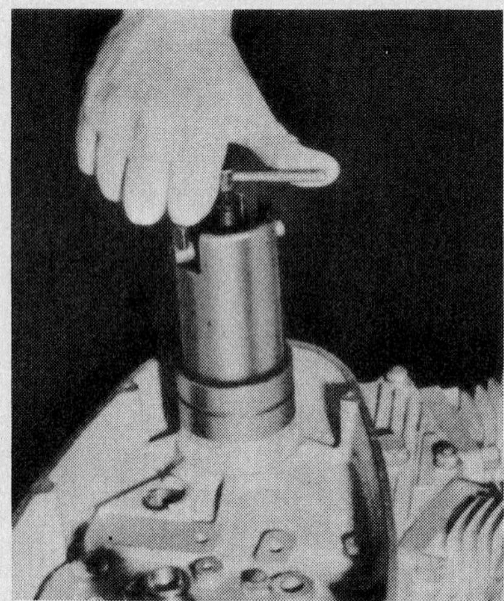

Removing the sprocket shaft extension

7. Remove the sprocket shaft extension with a sprocket shaft extension puller (H-D part no. 96015–56) or a suitable substitute. Solid sprocket models can be removed with a claw puller.

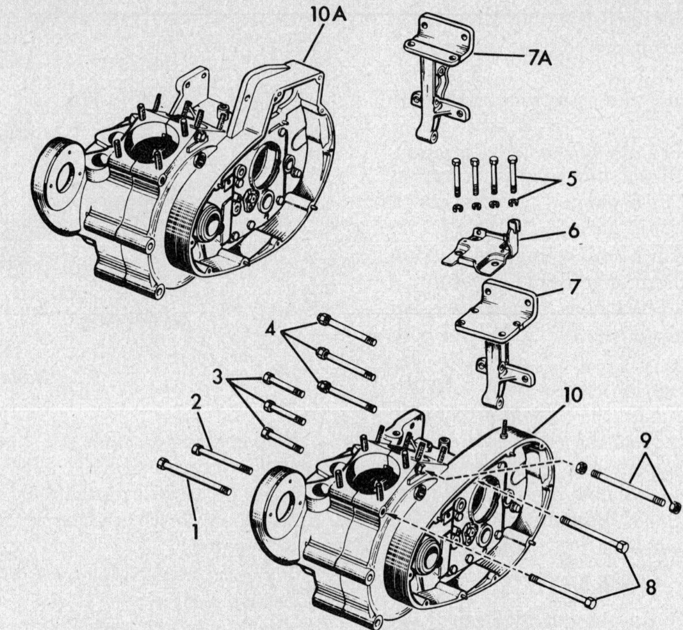

Crankcase assembly

1. Crankcase mounting bolt 5/16 x 4-7/16″
2. Crankcase mounting bolt 5/16 x 4-1/16″
3. Crankcase mounting bolt 5/16 x 2-3/8″ (3)
4. Crankcase rear mounting stud and lock nut (3)
5. Engine rear mounting bolt and lock washer (4) (1966 and earlier), (2) (1967)
6. Battery carrier (1966 and earlier)
7. Engine rear mount (1966 and earlier)

7A. Engine rear mount (1967)

8. Crankcase bolt (2)
9. Crankcase stud and lock nut (center)
10. Crankcase (1966 and earlier)

10A. Crankcase (1967)

Figure following name of part indicates quantity necessary for one complete assembly.

8. Remove the speedometer drive unit, right crankcase bolts, stud lock nuts, rear mount bolts, battery carrier or oil tank bracket, rear engine mount, and top center crankcase stud.

9. Loosen the top of the crankcase by tapping it with a soft mallet and separate the cases.

10. Pry the pinion bearing shaft snap-ring from the shaft and remove the shaft bearing washer, roller bearings, and bearing retainers.

11. Remove the transmission as described in "Transmission Disassembly".

12. Arbor-press the sprocket shaft to remove the flywheel assembly from the

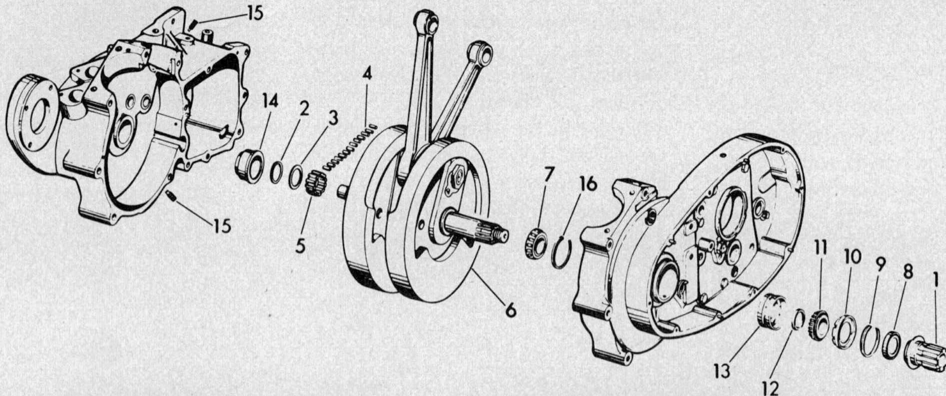

1. Sprocket shaft extension
2. Pinion shaft bearing snap ring
3. Pinion shaft bearing washer
4. Pinion shaft roller bearing (13)
5. Pinion shaft roller bearing retainer
6. Connecting rod and flywheel assembly
7. Sprocket shaft Timken bearing right half
8. Sprocket shaft oil seal
9. Sprocket shaft bearing spring ring (outer)
10. Sprocket shaft bearing spacer
11. Sprocket shaft Timken bearing left half
12. Sprocket shaft Timken bearing spacer
13. Sprocket shaft Timken bearing outer race
14. Pinion shaft bushing
15. Pinion shaft bearing bushing screw (2)
16. Sprocket shaft bearing spring ring (inner)

Figure following name of part indicates quantity necessary for one complete assembly.

Crankcase and flywheel assembly

left case. If drifted free, flywheel alignment will be lost.

13. Remove the Timken bearing right half with a sprocket shaft bearing puller (H-D part no. 96015–52) or a suitable substitute if flywheel is to be disassembled or if the bearing is to be replaced.

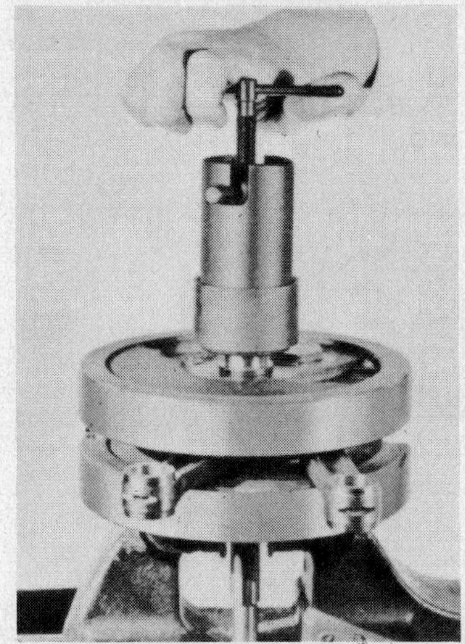

Removing the bearing

14. Pry free the sprocket shaft oil seal and spring with a pointed instrument and replace both.

15. With the crankcase clutch side supported by parallel bars, place the right half of the bearing on the left and arbor-press out the bearing spacers, left half, and outer race.

16. With the pinion shaft secured in a copper or wood-jawed vise, remove the lock plate screw, lock plate, and crankpin nut.

17. Loosen the left flywheel by striking its rim at a point 90 degrees from the crankpin with a soft mallet and remove the flywheel.

18. Separate the connecting rods from the crankpin bearing by holding the bearing with a suitably sized piece of pipe and lifting the rods free.

19. Remove and separate the bearing for reassembly.

20. Remove the lock plate screws, lock plates, and sprocket and crank pin lock nuts.

21. Tap the flywheels with a soft mallet to loosen the sahfts and remove the shafts and keys.

INSPECTION AND REPAIR

1. Clean all parts in a suitable solvent and blow dry. Blow all oil holes clear.

2. Inspect all parts for a worn, pitted, or damaged condition and replace if necessary.

3. Replace the rods, bearing, and crankpin as an assembly if parts are excessively worn.

4. Inspect the pinion shaft bushing and shaft for wear or damage and replace if necessary.

5. Inspect the sprocket shaft bearing assembly for wear or damage. Timken rollers must be replaced in sets.

6. Replace the flywheel washers as described in Servi-Car "Crankcase Inspection and Repair.

7. Lap the connecting rod races as described in Servi-Car "Inspection and Repair" using a connecting rod lapping arbor (H-D part no. 96740–36).

8. Secure the pinion shaft to the right flywheel making sure all parts are completely clean.

9. Secure the pinion shaft key.

10. Secure the pinion shaft in a copper or wood-jawed vise and tightly secure the pinion shaft nut with a crankpin and flywheel nut wrench (H-D part no. 94546–41) until the lock palte notches line up with the nut edges. Do not use additional leverage as damage will result.

11. Secure the crankpin and nut in the above manner.

12. Consult Servi-Car "Crankcase Inspection and Repair" for rod bearing assembly procedures.

13. Replace the pinion shaft bushing and bearing as described in Servi-Car "Crankcase Disassembly". Place the arbor guide sleeve (H-D part no. 96728–56), or a suitable substitute, through the Timken bearing from the inside of the case, and fit the bearings to a running clearance of 0.0008–0.001 in. A slightly looser fit is recommended for sustained high speed driving.

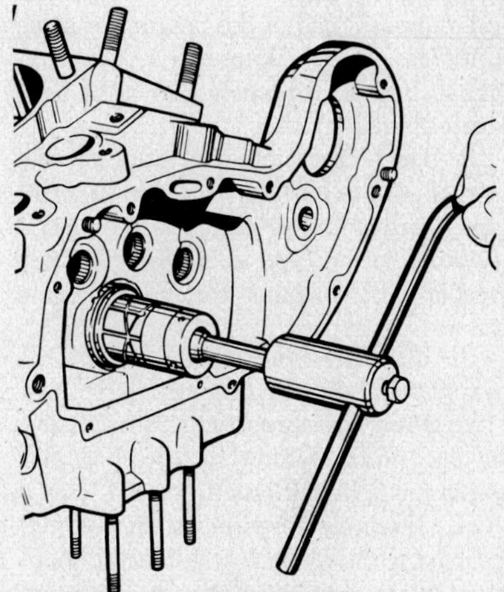

Lapping the pinion shaft bearing race

ASSEMBLY

1. Assemble and true the flywheel as described in Servi-Car "Crankcase Assembly".

2. Replace the sprocket shaft bearing inner spring ring.

3. Support the left crankcase, crankcase side up, on an arbor press and press the Timken bearing outer race in until it seats on the spring ring. Sprocket shaft bearing tool (H-D part no. 97081–54) or an arbor press may be used for all of these operations.

4. Secure the flywheel assembly in a

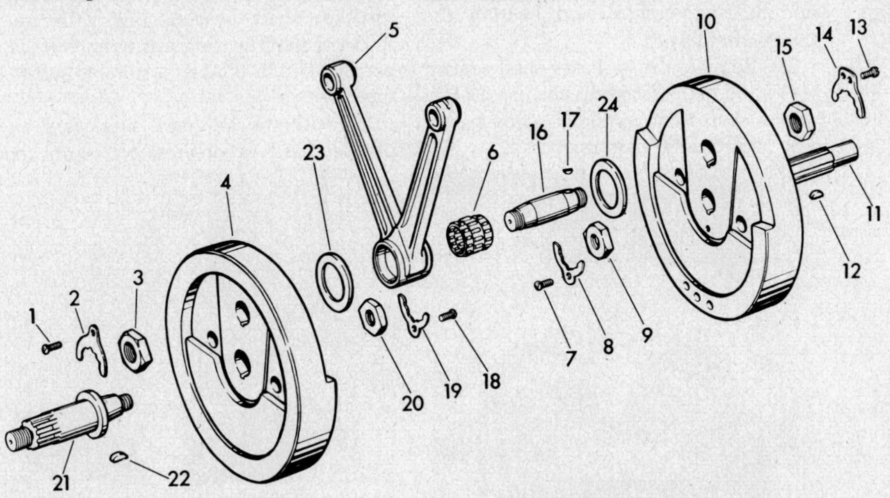

Flywheel and connecting rod assembly

1. Crank pin lock plate screw
2. Crank pin nut lock plate
3. Crank pin nut
4. Flywheel (left)
5. Connecting rods
6. Crank pin roller and retainer set
7. Pinion shaft lock plate screw
8. Pinion shaft nut lock plate
9. Pinion shaft nut
10. Flywheel (right)
11. Pinion shaft
12. Pinion shaft key
13. Crank pin lock plate screw
14. Crank pin nut lock plate
15. Crank pin nut
16. Crank pin
17. Crank pin key
18. Sprocket shaft lock plate screw
19. Sprocket shaft nut lock plate
20. Sprocket shaft nut
21. Sprocket shaft
22. Sprocket shaft key
23. Crank pin boss washer (left)
24. Crank pin boss washer (right)

copper or wood-jawed vise with the sprocket shaft up.

5. Install a flywheel support plate (H-D part no. 96137–52) or a suitable substitute between the flywheel halves.

6. Press the bearing right half on the shaft with a 1 in. I.D. (inside diameter) × 6 in. steel tube until the bearing seats on the shaft shoulder.

7. Slip the sprocket shaft bearing spacer in place and lubricate the bearing with engine oil.

8. Insert the sprocket shaft through the bearing outer race in the left and press the left half of the bearing in place until it is seated, taking care not to damage it. Both bearing halves must be tight against their spacers.

9. Place the notched side of the sprocket shaft bearing spacer on the shaft and gently press it into place or use a suitable screw type extractor until the spacer is tight against the outer bearing race.

10. Install the outer spring ring and oil seal with the lipped side in.

11. Press the sprocket shaft extension in place until seated with the shaft and extension splines aligned.

12. Assemble the pinion shaft bearing, bearing washer, and a new bearing snap-ring, taking care to seat the snap-ring in the shaft groove.

13. Consult Servi-Car "Crankcase Assembly" for flywheel end-play checking and correcting procedures.

14. Assemble the remaining parts in the reverse order of disassembly.

15. Assemble the transmission as described in "Transmission Assembly".

16. Coat the crankcase joint faces with a non-hardening sealer.

17. Apply engine oil to the pinion shaft bearing; assemble and secure the crankcase halves.

18. Install the battery carrier, rear engine mount, speedometer drive unit, transmission mainstaft sprocket, starter, and clutch assembly.

19. Replenish the transmission oil.

20. Install the oil pump, timing gears, gear case cover, tappets, generator, pistons, clylinders, contact breaker or magneto, cylinder heads, and install the engine in the frame.

Glide Models

DISASSEMBLY

1–6. Same as for the Servi-Car.

7. Remove the gearcase assembly as described in "Gearcase Disassembly".

8. Remove the ⅜ × 3 ¼ in. crankcase bolts, 5/16 × 5 in. studs, breather stud and chain oiler, 5/16 × 6 in. stud, and 11/32 × 5 13/16 in. studs.

9. With the gear case side up, tap the crankcase with a soft mallet and remove the crankcase right half, spiral lock ring, and bearing washers and bearing retainer assembly.

10. Remove the sprocket shaft spacer (1968 and earlier models) and secure the pinion shaft in a copper or wood-jawed vise with the left case up.

11. Remove the left-hand threaded sprocket shaft bearing nut with the sprocket shaft bearing nut wrench (H-D part no. 97235–55A) or a suitable substitute.

12. With the left case supported on parallel bars, arbor-press the sprocket

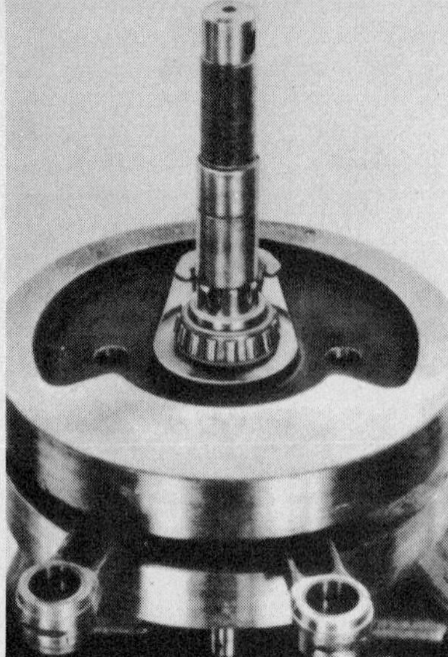

Installing the right half of the bearing and the bearing spacer

Installing the sprocket shaft spacer

Assembling the left crankcase to the flywheel

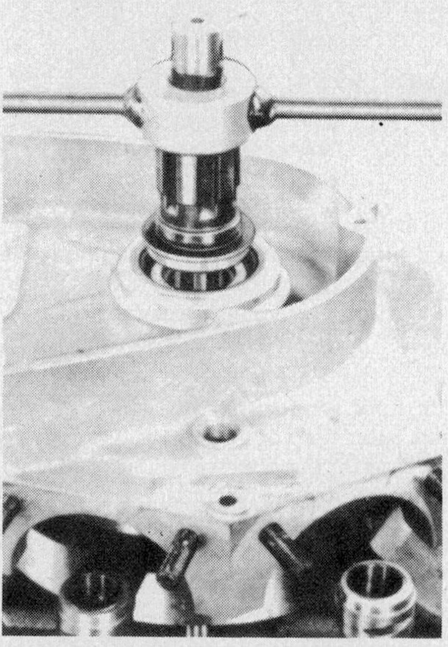

Installing the sprocket shaft extension

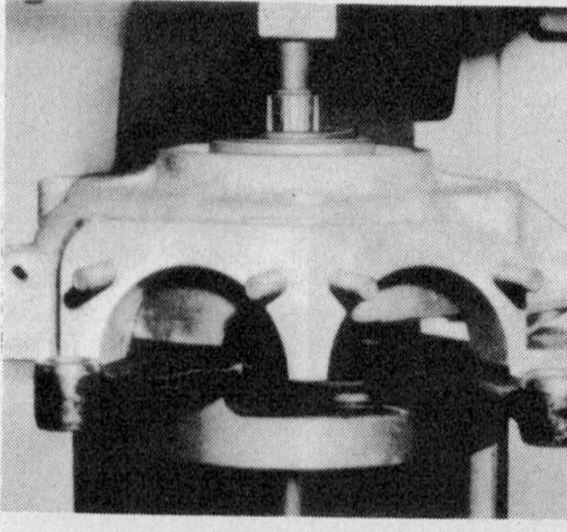

Pressing the flywheel out of the crankcase

Pressing the bearing races out of the crankcase—(1968 and earlier models only)

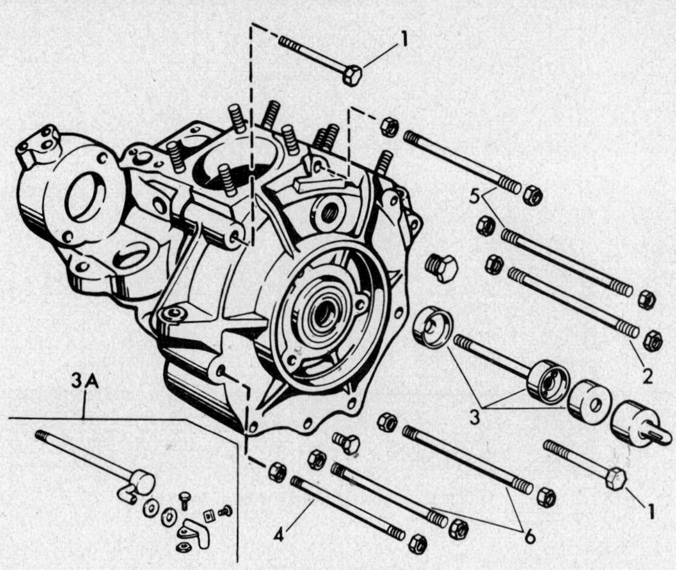

Crankcase studs

1. Crankcase stud bolt, 3/8 x 3-1/4 in. (2)
2. Crankcase stud, 5/16 x 5 in. (right center)
3. Crankcase breather stud and chain oiler (1963 and earlier)
3A. Crankcase breather stud and chain oiler (1964)
4. Crankcase stud, 5/16 x 6 in. (left center)
5. Cankcase stud, 5/16 x 5-7/16 in. (2) (top and top right)
6. Crankcase stud, 11/32 x 5-13/16 in. (2) (left and right bottom)

Figure following name of part indicates quantity necessary for one complete assembly. Locations are as viewed from left side of engine.

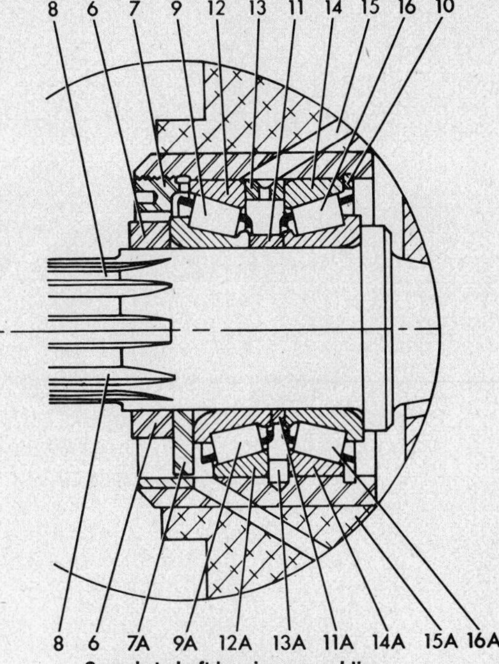

Sprocket shaft bearing assemblies

1968 AND EARLIER PARTS

6. Sprocket shaft bearing spacer
7. Sprocket shaft bearing nut
8. Flywheel and rod assembly
9. Sprocket bearing outside half
10. Outer race lock ring
11. Bearing inner race spacer
12. Bearing outer race
13. Bearing outer race spacer
14. Bearing outer race
15. Left crankcase half
16. Sprocket bearing inside half

1969 PARTS

6. Sprocket shaft bearing spacer
7A. Bearing shield washer
8. Flywheel and rod assembly
9A. Sprocket bearing outside half
11A. Bearing inner race spacer
12A. Bearing outer race
13A. Bearing outer race lock ring
14A. Bearing outer race
15A. Left crankcase half
16A. Sprocket bearing inside half

NOTE: The "A" number suffix indicates part change for 1969.

1. Right crankcase half
2. Spiral lock ring
3. Bearing washer (2)
4. Bearings and retainer
5. Bearing washer (see item 3)
6. Sprocket shaft spacer
7. Sprocket shaft bearing nut
7A. Sprocket shaft bearing seal washer (1969)
8. Flywheel and rod assembly
9. Sprocket bearing half
9A. Sprocket bearing half (1969)
10. Outer race snap ring (1968 & earlier)
11. Bearing inner spacer
11A. Bearing inner spacer (1969)
12. Bearing outer race
12A. Bearing outer race (1969)
13. Bearing outer spacer
13A. Outer race snap ring (1969)
14. Bearing outer race
14A. Bearing outer race (1969)
15. Left crankcase half
15A. Left crankcase half (1969)
16. Sprocket bearing half
16A. Sprocket bearing half (1969)
17. Pinion shaft bearing race lock screw (2)
18. Pinion shaft bearing race

Note: Keep parts 9, 11, 12, 13, 14 and 16 as a set. Do not transpose or interchange parts. Figure following name of part indicates quantity necessary for one complete assembly.

NOTE

Letter Suffix "A" indicates new part for 1969 Models

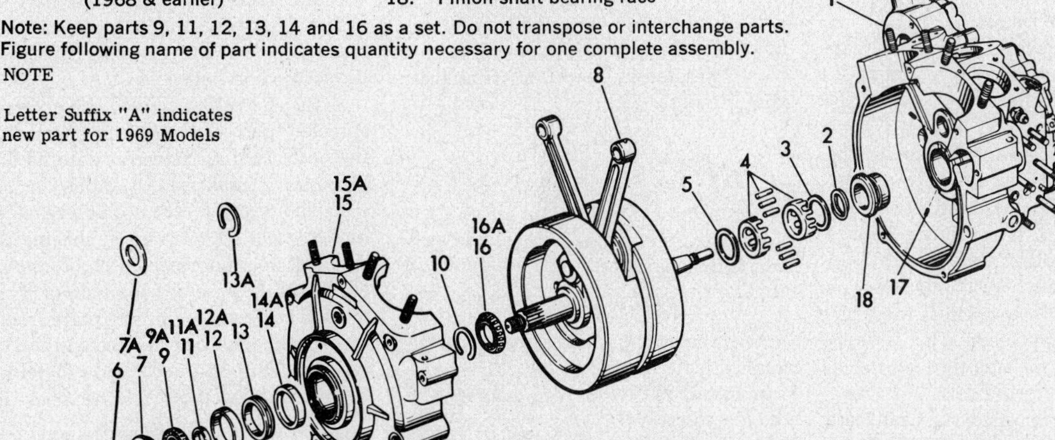

Crankcase assembly

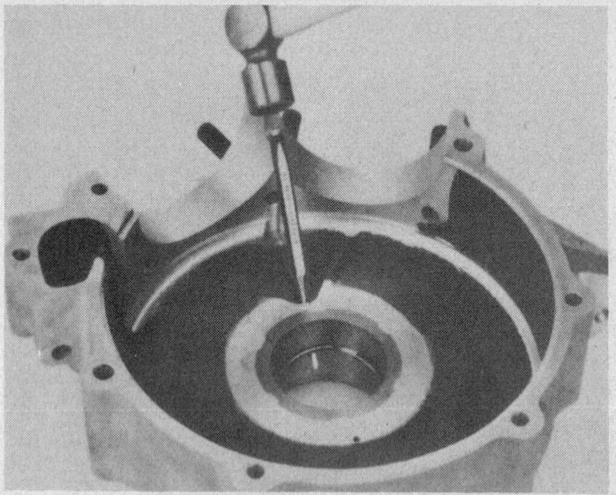

Removing the lockring—(1969 models)

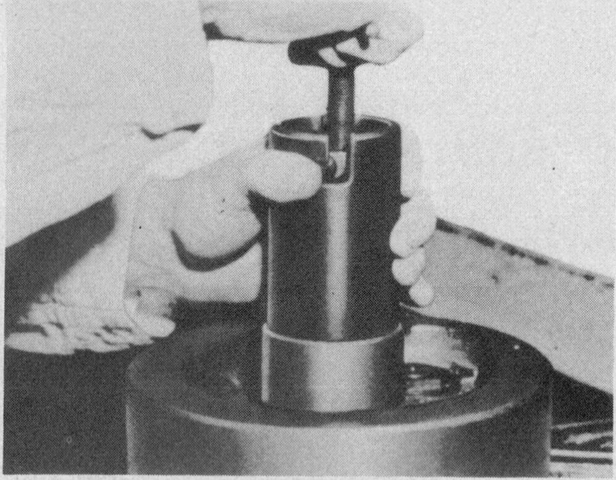

Pulling the bearing from the sprocket shaft

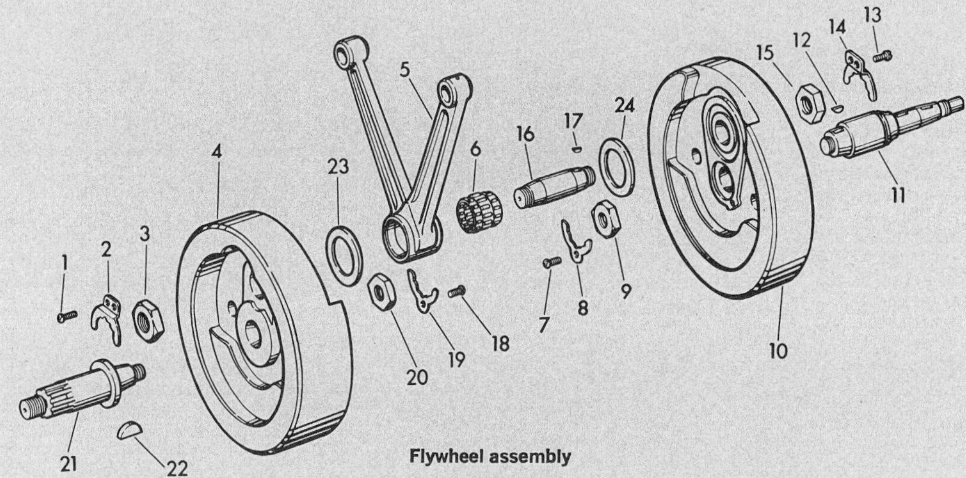

Flywheel assembly

1. Lock plate screw (4)
2. Lock plate (2)
3. Crank pin nut (2)
4. Left flywheel
5. Connecting rods (one forked, one single end)
6. Bearing rollers and retainers
7. Lock plate screw (see item 1)
8. Lock plate (2)
9. Gear shaft nut (2)
10. Right flywheel
11. Pinion shaft
12. Pinion shaft key
13. Lock plate screw (see item 1)
14. Lock plate (see item 2)
15. Crank pin lock nut (see item 3)
16. Crank pin
17. Crank pin key
18. Lock plate screw (see item 1)
19. Lock plate (see item 8)
20. Sprocket shaft nut (see item 9)
21. Sprocket shaft
22. Sprocket shaft key
23. Flywheel washer (2)
24. Flywheel washer (see item 23)

Figure following name of part indicates quantity necessary for one complete assembly.

shaft until the flywheel assembly comes free and remove the sprocket bearing half, washer, and spacer.

13. Pry the flywheel side outer snap-ring free (1968 and earlier models).

14. Arbor-press the bearing outer race press plug (H-D part no. 97194–57) or a suitable drift to prevent damage to the races (1968 and earlier models).

15. Using a suitably sized brass drift and hammer, tap the bearing race free from the opposite side. Remove the outer race snap-ring with a ⅛ in. punch or any suitable pointed instrument if the bearing set is to be replaced. This is easily done by tapping the ring through the oil hole (1969 and later models).

16. Consult Sportster "Crankcase Disassembly" for sprocket bearing inner half removal instructions. Use a bearing puller (H-D part no. 96015–56). Leave the assembly in the vise.

12. Insert a 5 × ½ in. rod through the flywheel holes to secure them. Disassemble as directed in Servi-Car "Crankcase Disassembly".

INSPECTION AND REPAIR

Consult Sportster "Crankcase Inspection and Repair".

ASSEMBLY

Assemble in the reverse order of disassembly. Note the following:

1. Install the outer race snap-ring in the left case.

2. With the case supported on parallel bars, press the bearing outer races and snap-ring into the crankcase bushing. Use an outer race press plug (H-D part no. 97194–57) or a suitable drift to press them in, one at a time, until sealed with the wider end out.

3. Install the bearing and spacer on the sprocket shaft, with the shaft in case and the outer bearing halves as described in Sportster "Crankcase Assembly."

4. The bearing must not be preloaded (under excessive tension). If shaking the case half does not reveal a slight amount of play in the case bearing half, or if the flywheel assembly will not rotate freely, the bearing must be removed and a 0.003 in. shim (H-D part no. 23741–55) added to spacers. Assemble and recheck for play.

5. Slip the inner bearing washer, bearings, and outer washer in place on the

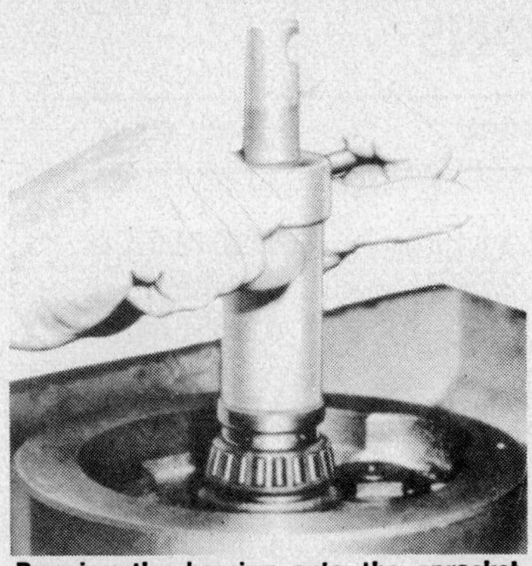
Pressing the bearing onto the sprocket shaft

pinion shaft and secure a new spiral lock ring in the shaft groove.

6. Apply a non-hardening sealer to the joint surface and secure the cases with the 5/16 × 6 in. and the 11/32 × 5 13/16 in. studs.

7. Consult Servi-Car "Crankcase Assembly" for flywheel end-play checking and correcting procedures.

8. Secure the case halves.

9. Secure the sprocket shaft bearing nut (1968 and earlier models).

10. Install the sprocket shaft spacer or seal washer, sprocket or sprocket shaft extension, and sprocket nut.

11. If the sprocket and the rear wheel sprocket are out of alignment, consult the "Drive" section.

12. Complete reassembly by reversing "Engine Removal" procedures.

TRANSMISSION

Servi-Car

SHIFTING LINKAGE ADJUSTMENT

1. Place the transmission in neutral and disconnect the shifter rod from the hand lever.

TRANSMISSION SPECIFICATIONS

	Servi-Car	Sportster	Glide Models
CLUTCH			
Type	Dry multiple disc	①	Dry multiple disc
Capacity (torque)	1344 in./lbs	1900 in./lbs	②
Spring Pressure (total)	290 lbs	③	④
Bearing fit (loose)	0.001-0.004 in.	0.005-0.002 in.	0.002-0.003 in.
Clutch release rod reply movement	1/8 in.	1/8 in.	3/8-5/8 in.
CHAIN			
Primary (type)	3/8 in. pitch, double	3/8 in. pitch, triple	1/2 in. pitch, double
Slack	1/2 in.	5/8-7/8 in. (cold) 3/8-5/8 in. (hot)	5/8-7/8 in. (cold) 3/8-5/8 in. (hot)
STARTER			
Minimum clearance between starter clutch gear teeth and clutch	—	0.040 in. (crank in up position)	—
Crankshaft end play	—	0.001-0.007 in.	—
GEAR BOX			
Shifter mechanism	—	Free operation in all positions	—
Cam end play	0.005-0.0065 in.	—	0.005-0.0065 in.
MAIN AND COUNTERSHAFT GROUPS			
Clutch gear end play (loose)	0.003-0.007 in.	0.001-0.002 in.	—
Clutch gear outer bearing (loose)	0.005-0.002 in.	0.0001-0.0017 in.	—
Clutch gear inner bushing	0.0015-0.0025 in.	—	—
Clutch gear ball bearing	—	0.0001 in. (loose) 0.0009 in. (tight)	—
Low gear bushing (on shaft)	0.0005-0.0015 in.	0.0005-0.00016 in.	0.000-0.0015 in. (loose)
(in gear)	0.002-0.005 in. (press)	—	0.0005-0.0025 in. (loose)
(end play)	0.003-0.007 in.	0.004-0.009 in.	—
Low gear end bearing			
(loose)	—	—	0.005-0.002 in.
(end play)	—	—	0.008-0.012 in.
(in housing)	—	⑤	—
(on shaft)	—	⑥	—
(housing in case)	—	⑦	—

TRANSMISSION SPECIFICATIONS

	Servi-Car	Sportster	Glide Models
Second gear bushing			
(on shaft)	0.0005-0.0015 in.	0.001-0.0025 in. (loose)	0.000-0.0015 in. (loose)
(in gear)	0.002-0.005 in. (press)	—	0.0005-0.0025 in. (loose)
(end play)	0.003-0.007 in.	—	0.003-0.017 in.
Third gear bushing			
(on shaft) (loose)	—	0.002-0.003 in.	0.001-0.002 in.
(in gear)	—	—	press fit
(end play)	—	0.015-0.025 in.	0.000-0.017 in.
Reverse gear and bearing			
(mainshaft)	0.0005-0.002 in.	—	—
(countershaft)	0.001-0.002 in.	—	—
Reverse gear bushing			
(on shaft)	0.0015-0.0025 in.	—	—
(in gear)	0.002-0.005 in. (press)	—	—
High gear end bearing (inner)	0.0015-0.0025 in.	—	—
Drive gear (on shaft)	—	0.0005-0.003 in. (loose)	—
roller bearing (loose)	—	—	0.0005-0.002 in.
inner bearing	—	—	0.002-0.003 in.
end play	—	—	0.003-0.013 in.

① Clutch type
1970 and earlier: dry multiple disc
1971 and later: wet multiple disc

② Clutch capacity
1970 and earlier: 284 ft lbs
1971 and later: 206 ft lbs

③ Spring pressure
1970 and earlier: 150 lbs
1971: 234 lbs
1972 and later: 257 lbs

④ Spring pressure
1970 and earlier: 475 lbs
1971 and later: 315 lbs

⑤ Low gear end bearing in housing
1970 and earlier: snug fit
1971 and later: 0.0015 in. (loose)-0.0001 in. (press)

⑥ Low gear bearing on shaft
1970 and earlier: light press
1971 and later: 0.0001 in. (loose)-0.0010 in. (press)

⑦ Low gear end bearing housing in case
1970 and earlier: light press
1971 and later: 0.0005 in. (loose)-0.0010 in. (press)

2. Rock the shifter rod back and forth until the point at which the shifter cam spring plunger reaches its seat can be determined.

3. Adjust the length of the shifter rod by backing off the rod locknut and by turning the rod end until the rod end and hand lever mounting holes line up.

4. Check to see the hand lever is still in neutral, secure the lever to the rod, and secure the rod locknut.

5. If the transmission still jumps out of gear, the shifter clutches should be attended to.

CLUTCH GEAR OIL SEAL

Removal

1. The transmission mainshaft must still be in the gearbox if the Clutch Seal Tool (H-D part no. 9568–42) is to be used.

2. Remove the chaincase cover, compensating sprocket, primary chain, and clutch hub assembly as described in "Clutch Disassembly."

3. Assemble the oil seal puller guide on the clutch gear until it bottoms.

4. Place the puller body over the guide, with the arm down, and rotate it clockwise until the body reaches its stop.

5. Punch-mark the oil seal through each of the three body holes.

6. Remove the puller body and guide, and drill 3/32 in. holes through the seal face at the punch marks.

7. Assemble the body and guide, and secure the self-tapping screws into the seal through the body holes.

8. Remove the seal by pulling the T-handle puller screw clockwise through the body holes.

9. If the above tool is unavailable or if the procedure is too much hassle, pry the seal loose with a screwdriver, taking care not to damage the case.

Installation

1. Smooth the oil seal recess surface of all burrs and nicks.

2. Lightly grease the inner surface of the seal to prevent damage during installation.

3. Insert the counterbored end of the oil seal puller sleeve through the closed side of the seal and place the sleeve and seal onto the gear. The lipped side of the seal should face into the transmission.

4. Start the puller guide onto the clutch gear.

5. Place the puller body over the guide and press the seal upward against the gearbox.

6. Screw the T-handle puller screw to its seat without moving the body away from the seal.

7. Place the guide nut on the guide and unscrew the T-handle until the seal is pressed into place. Do not continue to turn the handle after the seal bottoms since this will cause damage.

8. Remove the tool and center-punch the seal at three evenly spaced points to prevent it from rotating. Do not do this at places where it was done before.

9. The above procedure can be eliminated by carefully drifting the seal into

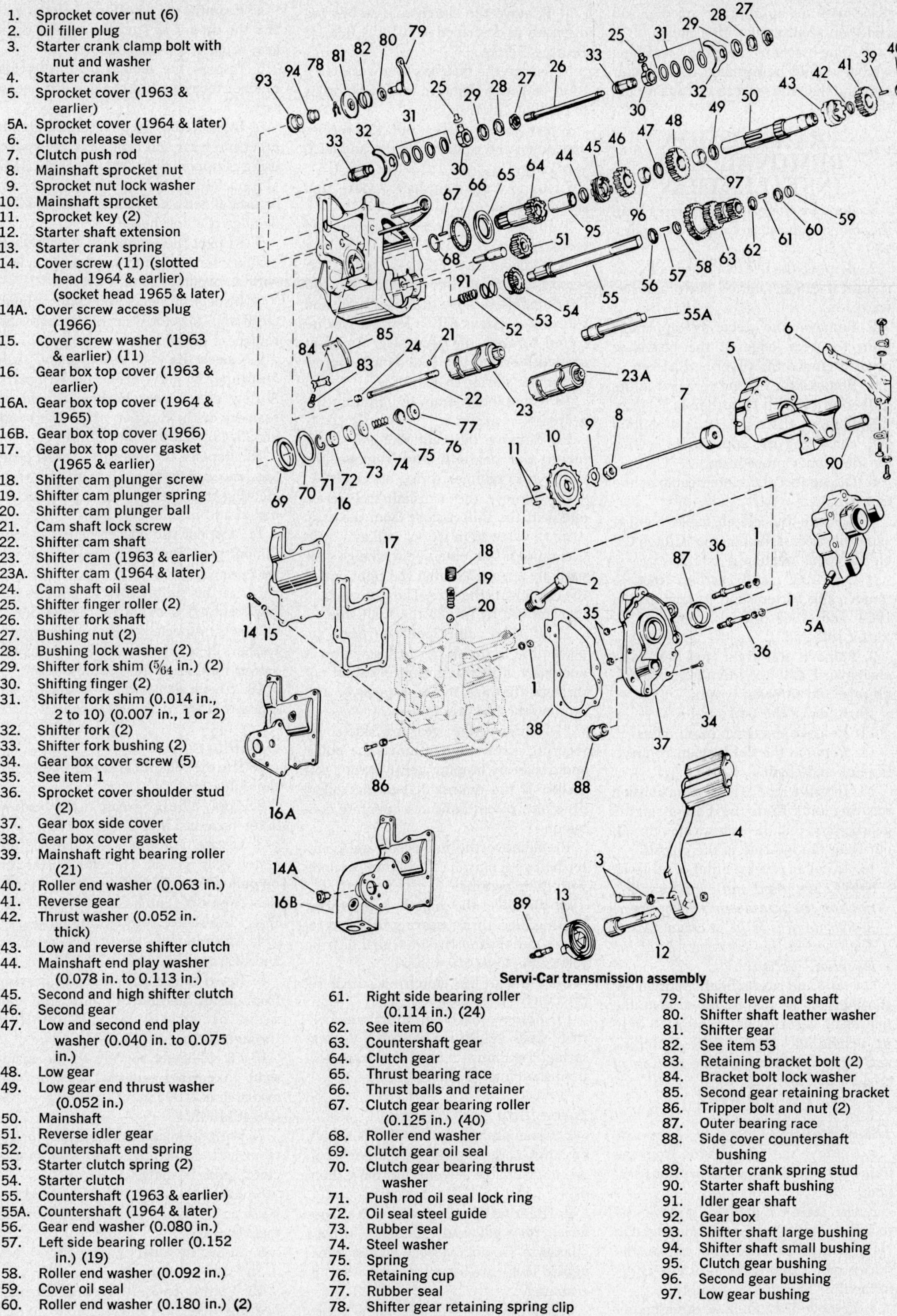

Servi-Car transmission assembly

1. Sprocket cover nut (6)
2. Oil filler plug
3. Starter crank clamp bolt with nut and washer
4. Starter crank
5. Sprocket cover (1963 & earlier)
5A. Sprocket cover (1964 & later)
6. Clutch release lever
7. Clutch push rod
8. Mainshaft sprocket nut
9. Sprocket nut lock washer
10. Mainshaft sprocket
11. Sprocket key (2)
12. Starter shaft extension
13. Starter crank spring
14. Cover screw (11) (slotted head 1964 & earlier) (socket head 1965 & later)
14A. Cover screw access plug (1966)
15. Cover screw washer (1963 & earlier) (11)
16. Gear box top cover (1963 & earlier)
16A. Gear box top cover (1964 & 1965)
16B. Gear box top cover (1966)
17. Gear box top cover gasket (1965 & earlier)
18. Shifter cam plunger screw
19. Shifter cam plunger spring
20. Shifter cam plunger ball
21. Cam shaft lock screw
22. Shifter cam shaft
23. Shifter cam (1963 & earlier)
23A. Shifter cam (1964 & later)
24. Cam shaft oil seal
25. Shifter finger roller (2)
26. Shifter fork shaft
27. Bushing nut (2)
28. Bushing lock washer (2)
29. Shifter fork shim (5/64 in.) (2)
30. Shifting finger (2)
31. Shifter fork shim (0.014 in., 2 to 10) (0.007 in., 1 or 2)
32. Shifter fork (2)
33. Shifter fork bushing (2)
34. Gear box cover screw (5)
35. See item 1
36. Sprocket cover shoulder stud (2)
37. Gear box side cover
38. Gear box cover gasket
39. Mainshaft right bearing roller (21)
40. Roller end washer (0.063 in.)
41. Reverse gear
42. Thrust washer (0.052 in. thick)
43. Low and reverse shifter clutch
44. Mainshaft end play washer (0.078 in. to 0.113 in.)
45. Second and high shifter clutch
46. Second gear
47. Low and second end play washer (0.040 in. to 0.075 in.)
48. Low gear
49. Low gear end thrust washer (0.052 in.)
50. Mainshaft
51. Reverse idler gear
52. Countershaft end spring
53. Starter clutch spring (2)
54. Starter clutch
55. Countershaft (1963 & earlier)
55A. Countershaft (1964 & later)
56. Gear end washer (0.080 in.)
57. Left side bearing roller (0.152 in.) (19)
58. Roller end washer (0.092 in.)
59. Cover oil seal
60. Roller end washer (0.180 in.) (2)
61. Right side bearing roller (0.114 in.) (24)
62. See item 60
63. Countershaft gear
64. Clutch gear
65. Thrust bearing race
66. Thrust balls and retainer
67. Clutch gear bearing roller (0.125 in.) (40)
68. Roller end washer
69. Clutch gear oil seal
70. Clutch gear bearing thrust washer
71. Push rod oil seal lock ring
72. Oil seal steel guide
73. Rubber seal
74. Steel washer
75. Spring
76. Retaining cup
77. Rubber seal
78. Shifter gear retaining spring clip
79. Shifter lever and shaft
80. Shifter shaft leather washer
81. Shifter gear
82. See item 53
83. Retaining bracket bolt (2)
84. Bracket bolt lock washer
85. Second gear retaining bracket
86. Tripper bolt and nut (2)
87. Outer bearing race
88. Side cover countershaft bushing
89. Starter crank spring stud
90. Starter shaft bushing
91. Idler gear shaft
92. Gear box
93. Shifter shaft large bushing
94. Shifter shaft small bushing
95. Clutch gear bushing
96. Second gear bushing
97. Low gear bushing

Figure following name of part indicates quantity necessary for one complete assembly.

place with an appropriate sized socket and then securing it with a punch.

10. The roller bearing retaining washer should be installed in the outer race and then the seal can seat against the race.

TRANSMISSION REMOVAL AND INSTALLATION

1. Remove the cables and wires from the solenoid and starter motor (if applicable).
2. Remove the left footboard or loosen it until it can be shifted down and forward.
3. Remove the securing apparatus from the rear edge of the chaincase cover. Remove the cover and gasket.
4. Remove the engine sprocket as described in "Clutch Disassembly."
5. Remove the regulator and ignition coil, consulting the appropriate section for the proper procedures.
6. Disconnect the clutch cable at the foot pedal.
7. Remove the clutch cable housing and cable as described in the "Clutch Cable Removal" section.
8. On 1963 and earlier models, remove the battery and its carrier. On 1964 and 1965 models, remove the starter solenoid.
9. Remove the right and left, rear chainguard, and free them from the differential and sprocket covers.
10. Remove the brake rod.
11. Remove the drive chain oiler.
12. Remove the drive-chain connecting link and chain.
13. Remove the three transmission securing nuts from the bottom of the gearbox and pull the transmission up and out from the left side of the chassis.
14. Install in reverse order of removal.

NOTE: *On 1963 and earlier models, position the transmission in the frame so that there is ½ in. of chain slack as described in the "Primary Chain Adjustment" section.*

On 1964 and later models, position the transmission in the frame so that the mainshaft vertical centerline is 10 3/16 in. behind the engine shaft centerline and adjust the primary chain to ½ in. of slack.

GEARBOX

Disassembly

1. Remove the transmission from the frame as described in the previous section.
2. On 1964–65 models, remove the starter motor, shaft, and housing. On 1966 and later models, remove the starter motor and drive assembly as described in "Starter Disassembly."
3. Remove the clutch as described in "Clutch Disassembly."
4. Remove the clutch release bearing assembly as described in "Clutch Release Bearing Removal."
5. Secure the gearbox to a work table by at least two mounting points in order to facilitate disassembly.
7. Pry the sprocket nut lockwasher ears down and remove the nut and lockwasher.
7. Remove the mainshaft sprocket and sprocket keys.
8. Remove the starter extension and crank spring.
9. Remove the gearbox top cover screws, gasket, and cover. On 1966 and later models, remove the access plug and remaining screws with a screwdriver inserted through the plug hole. An offset screwdriver may be needed for the screw under the starter shaft boss.
10. Completely drain the oil from the gearcase.
11. Remove the cam plunger screw, invert the gearbox, and remove the shifter cam plunger spring and ball.
12. Remove the camshaft lock screw and drift the shifter shaft from the case. A spare valve stem works well as a drift. Clearance is best obtained with high gear partially engaged so that the right end of the cam clears the boss. The cam also can be removed by prying the shaft free.
13. If shim adjustment or parts replacement in the shifter fork assembly is necessary, drift the shifter fork shaft out through the hole in the side-cover and remove the fork assemblies.
14. Remove the gearbox side-cover securing screws and remove the cover and gasket by tapping gently with a soft mallet. If the mainsahft bearing rollers drop out, place them in a separate container.
15. Remove the mainshaft and countershaft gear clusters as assemblies, along with their bearings.
16. Remove the clutch gear, thrust bearing race, thrust bearing balls and retainer, and the fourth clutch gear bearing rollers. Separate the roller.
17. Remove the clutch oil seal if replacement is necessary.
18. Remove the pushrod oil seal lockring, steel guide, rubber seal, washer, spring, retaining cup, and rubber seal from the clutch gear's splined end.

Inspection and Repair

1. Clean all parts, except rubber seals, bushings, cork gaskets, and leather washers, in a suitable solvent and blow them dry.
2. Examine all parts and replace those which may adversely influence proper operation. Do not overlook washer thicknesses. These are best checked with a micrometer.
3. Replace the races and rollers if they are worn, pitted, or in any way damaged.
4. Examine the gearbox case for cracks and the mounting stud threads for damage; replace if necessary.
5. Inspect the second gear retaining bracket for wear and replace it if necessary.
6. Inspect the tripper bolt heads for excessive wear and replace, if necessary, using Tripper Bolt Nut Wrench (H-D part no. 9467–14). Needle-nose pliers can be used if extreme caution is taken not to damage the bolt heads.
7. Inspect the side-cover countershaft bushing for excessive wear and replace with an arbor press or a drift.
8. Inspect all gears and shifter clutch teeth and dogs for wear or damage, and replace if necessary.
9. Check the gear bushings and shaft for proper fit, and replace all worn parts. A new clutch gear bushing should be reamed with Reamer (H-D part no. 94829–42) or a suitable substitute.
10. Replace the mainshaft thrust bearing race if it is pitted, rough, or worn. Heating the case will make the race removal and installation easier.
11. Inspect the shifter cam and cam pinion gear for wear, and replace if necessary.
12. If the shifter fork assemblies are disassembled, take note of the position of all parts, especially where the spacer washers fit between the shifter finger and shifter fork, as an aid in reassembly.
13. Check all clearance against the tolerances given in specifications.

Assembly

1. Slip the roller bearing end washer in the outer race.
2. Apply a heavy grease to the bearing outer race and install the rollers.
3. Grease the inner surfaces of the clutch gear oil seal. The clutch gear can be pulled through with the oil seal guide sleeve (part of Clutch Gear Oil Seal Tool). Insert the sleeve through the oil seal.
4. Assemble the thrust ball, retainer, and bearing race on the clutch gear.
5. Insert the gear through the bearing from inside and secure it to the tool sleeve or guide it in. Push the shaft through the oil seal.
6. Fit adjusting spacers to the mainshaft to correct end-play. Spacers are available in 0.005 in. gradations from 0.-078–0.113 in.
7. With the spacer washers only on the mainshaft, insert the shaft end in the clutch gear bushing.
8. Assemble the thrust washer and Reverse gear on the opposite end of the mainshaft.
9. Insert the roller bearing end washer in the side-cover race.
10. Lightly grease the mainshaft right bearing roller race and assemble the rollers.

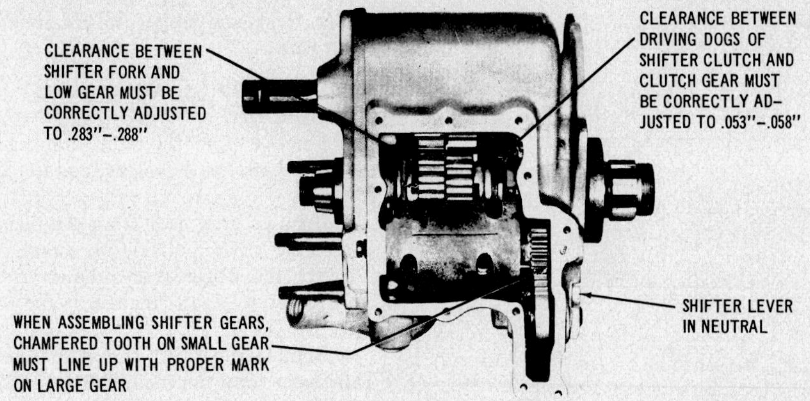
CLEARANCE BETWEEN
SHIFTER FORK AND
LOW GEAR MUST BE
CORRECTLY ADJUSTED
TO .283"–.288"
CLEARANCE BETWEEN
DRIVING DOGS OF
SHIFTER CLUTCH AND
CLUTCH GEAR MUST
BE CORRECTLY AD-
JUSTED TO .053"–.058"
SHIFTER LEVER
IN NEUTRAL
WHEN ASSEMBLING SHIFTER GEARS,
CHAMFERED TOOTH ON SMALL GEAR
MUST LINE UP WITH PROPER MARK
ON LARGE GEAR

Shifter fork adjustment

11. Apply sealer to the case side of the gasket; mount and secure both it and the side-cover.

12. Measure the amount of shaft end-play and correct to 0.003–0.007 in. by adding spacers as needed. An End Play Gauge (H-D part no. 96700–38) or a dial indicator can be used.

13. Lay aside the mainshaft and remove the selected spacer for the moment.

14. Select a spacer washer which will bring the end-play between the face of the second gear bracket and the case cover bearing race to 0.003–0.007 in.

15. Install on the left end of the mainshaft the first gear end thrust washer, First gear, first and second gear end-play washer, and Second gear.

16. On the mainshaft right end, assemble a thrust washer and Reverse gear.

17. Apply sealer to the cover gasket; then mount and secure both the gasket and the cover.

18. Check the end-play between Second gear and the bracket. Disassemble the mainshaft.

19. Assemble the main and countershafts as depicted in the accompanying illustration.

20. Assemble the countershaft gear assembly first and then the mainshaft gear assembly.

SHIFTER FORK ASSEMBLY

1. Insert the shifter shaft into the hole in the right side of the case after mounting the shifter fork bushings on it.

2. Engage the shifter forks with the grooves in the shifter clutches.

3. Install the shifter lever and gear in the following manner:

a. Place the starter clutch spring between the hub side of the large shifter gear and the case bushing.

b. Slip the leather washer between the shifter lever and the outside of the case.

c. With the lever in a vertical position, and the shifter gear teeth facing the shifter cam gear, install the gear on the squared portion of the lever.

d. Secure the gear with the retaining spring clip.

5. Locate the shifter fingers and rollers in the shifter cam slots.

6. Rotate the cam so that the beveled tooth of the pinion gear registers with the notch between the shifter gear teeth.

7. Install the shifter cam.

8. Rotate the shifter cam until the highest points of the Third gear driving dogs overlap about ⅛ in. This is the Neutral position.

9. Check to make sure that the clearance between the shifter clutch dogs and the clutch gear is 0.053–0.058 in. Check to see that there is 0.283–0.288 in. between the shifter fork and the side of the first gear. Correct by adjusting the number of shims that are either 0.007 in. or 0.014 in. thick.

10. Pour ¾ pt of engine oil over the completed gear assemblies, then seal and secure the gasket and top cover. There is no gasket on 1966 and later models so plastic gasket from a tube should be used.

11. Assemble the sprocket assembly on the mainshaft and install the pushrod seal assembly in the clutch gear. Install the clutch assembly.

12. Assemble the remaining parts in the reverse order of disassembly and install the engine in the chassis as described in "Transmission Removal and Installation."

Sportster

CRANKCASE AND TRANSMISSION DISASSEMBLY

This section only applies if such work as overhauling the crankcase or flywheel is to be done. Otherwise the transmission can be serviced through the access cover.

1. Disassemble the crankcase as described in "Crankcase Disassembly."

2. Remove the first gear washer and first gear from the countershaft.

3. Free the assembled mainshaft.

4. Remove Second gear.

5. Remove the gear shifter cam cap screw and retainer ring, and then the shifter mechanism will come free of the access cover.

6. Remove the First gear washer, Third gear, and the shifter fork from the countershaft, and remove the assembled countershaft.

7. For further information, consult "Shifter Mechanism Disassembly" and "Mainshaft and Countershaft Disassembly."

Transmission Access Cover Removal

1. With a drip pan under the clutch, remove the footrest, stoplight switch, brake pedal, chaincase cover, clutch, primary chain, and compensating sprocket assembly by consulting the "Clutch Disassembly" section.

2. Loosen the front cylinder exhaust pipe and muffler; remove the starter crank assembly, right footrest, and shifter lever. Remove the sprocket cover, starter crank gear, starter clutch gear, and starter crankshaft as described in the "Starter" section.

3. Loosen the mainshaft nut.

4. Remove the drive-chain master link and remove the chain.

5. Remove the mainshaft nut, lockwasher, sprocket, oil seal retainer screws and lockwashers, oil seal, seal retainer, and gasket from the mainshaft. If the sprocket requires assistance from a claw puller, make certain that at least two teeth are grasped by the puller or else damage will result.

6. Remove the access cover cap bolts.

7. Pry the clutch gear oil seal free and replace it.

8. Remove the hub nut rubber O-ring from the groove in the clutch gear (if applicable).

9. Pull the access cover free with Transmission Access Cover Puller (H-D part no. 95560–57) or an appropriate sized gear puller.

Shifter Mechanism Disassembly

1. Remove Second gear from the mainshaft, cap screw, retainer ring, and washer. Using snap-ring pliers, remove the cam retaining ring and slide it off the camshaft thrust washer.

2. Remove the gear shifter cam, pawl carrier, pawl carrier support, and pawl carrier support shims (if applicable). Remove the pawl spring and shifter pawls.

NOTE: *On 1972 models, remove the retaining rings to free the pawls, spacers, and springs from the pawl carrier. To free the shifter forks and finger rollers, first remove the countershaft assembly.*

3. After removing the lever arm shaft, fork shaft, cam follower retainer ring, follower retainer, and follower spring, the

Access cover

1. Access cover
2. Access cover cap screws (4)
3. Clutch gear oil seal
4. Hub nut rubber "O" ring (XLCH, 1966 & earlier XLH)

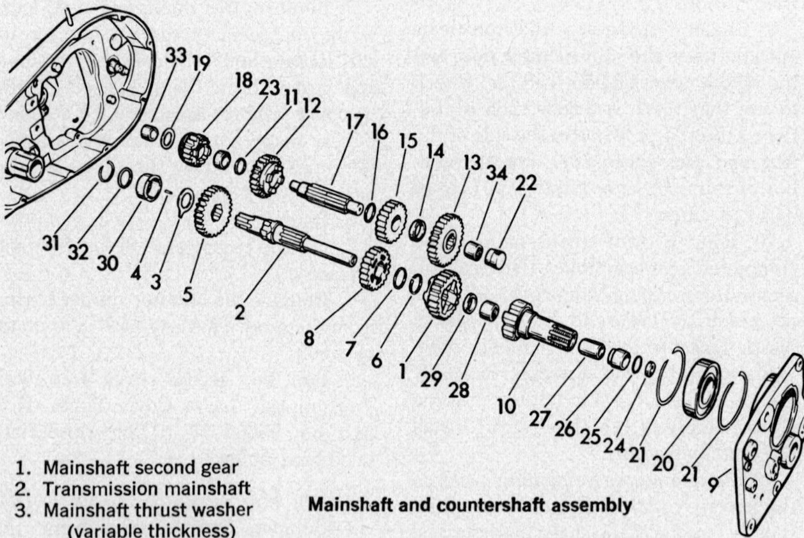

Mainshaft and countershaft assembly

1. Mainshaft second gear
2. Transmission mainshaft
3. Mainshaft thrust washer (variable thickness)
4. Transmission mainshaft roller (23)
5. Mainshaft low gear
6. Mainshaft third gear retainer ring
7. Mainshaft third gear washer
8. Mainshaft third gear
9. Access cover
10. Clutch gear
11. Countershaft low gear washer
12. Countershaft third gear
13. Countershaft drive gear
14. Countershaft gear spacer
15. Countershaft second gear
16. Countershaft second gear thrust washer
17. Transmission countershaft
18. Countershaft low gear
19. Countershaft low gear washer (variable thickness)
20. Mainshaft ball bearing
21. Mainshaft ball bearing snap ring (2)
22. Countershaft oiler plug
23. Countershaft low gear bushing
24. Clutch gear oil seal (1970 only)
25. Clutch hub nut "O" ring (1970 only)
26. Clutch gear oil seal extension (1970 only)
27. Clutch gear bushing
28. Clutch gear needles roller bearing
29. Mainshaft thrust washer
30. Mainshaft roller bearing race
31. Mainshaft roller bearing retainer ring
32. Mainshaft roller bearing washer
33. Countershaft bearing—closed end
34. Countershaft bearing—open end

shifter forks and finger rollers should come free.

Mainshaft and Countershaft Disassembly.

1. Remove from the right crankcase the mainshaft, thrust washer, and the 23 rollers.
2. Remove First gear from the mainshaft using a claw puller if necessary.
3. Pry the Third gear retainer ring from its groove in the mainshaft and replace it.
4. Remove the Third gear washer and Third gear from the mainshaft.
5. With the access cover on an arbor press, press the clutch gear free from its bearing.
6. Remove the First gear washer and Third gear from the countershaft, and remove the gear spacer, Second gear, and the thrust washer.
7. Remove the countershaft low gear and washer.
8. Drift the oiler plug free from inside the access cover.

Transmission Sprocket and Shifter Mechanism Inspection and Repair

1. Clean all metal parts in a suitable solvent and blow dry.
2. Inspect the mainshaft sprocket for worn or damaged teeth and splines; replace if necessary. Replace the oil seal and gasket if necessary.
3. Replace the gear shifter cam retaining ring. Inspect the shifter cam for worn or grooved thrust points which cause irregular shifting and replace if necessary.
4. Inspect the shifter pawl carrier for grooves or wear at the fingers. Inspect the pawl carrier support for breaks or cracks.
5. Check the bearing for excessive play by loosely assembling the shifter cam, pawl carrier, support, and shims (if applicable. Replace any worn or pitted parts.
6. Replace the pawl carrier springs with fourteen or sixteen cadmium plated or coil springs, or fourteen to sixteen black phosphatized springs. Spring free-length should be 2 25/32 in. when new.
7. Check pawl spring operation by inserting the springs in the carrier holes. Spring free-length should be 1 7/32 in. when new. Replace any worn, grooved, or cracked parts.
8. Inspect the finger rollers and shifter forks for warping, wear, or grooves.
9. Check the shifter cam follower and spring for freedom of movement and replace if worn. Free-length of a new spring should be 1 19/32 in. for models up to 1969, 1 7/32 in. for 1970–71 models, and 1 ¾ in. between the hooks for 1972 models.

10. Remove the shifter fork shaft only if it is to be replaced. The shaft is press-fit and aligned at the factory, and therefore should be replaced together with a new cover. Check the shaft for warping or damage by observing shifter fork movement on the shaft. The shaft may only be replaced by pressing out the old and pressing in the new, taking care to keep it perpendicular to the cover face.

11. Inspect the gear shifter lever arm for warping or damage.

12. Check the bushings for excessive play by inserting and rotating the shaft. Bushings must be pressed in with the gearcase cover and oil seal removed. Drift from the right side. Remove any high spots with a ½ in. reamer and replace the oil seal.

Mainshaft and Countershaft Inspection and Repair

1. Clean all metal parts in a suitable solvent and blow them dry.

2. Inspect, and replace if necessary, all gears, pinions, and dogs for a worn, chipped, or otherwise damaged condition—especially if the transmission frequently jumped out of gear.

3. Inspect the mainshaft and countershaft for excessive wear on the splines and bearing surfaces, and replace if necessary.

4. Slip the gears into position on their shafts and check for excessive play and replace if necessary. Specifications are listed in the "Transmission Specifications" chart.

5. The low gear bushing is a press-fit. If replaced, check for high spots and ream it until round.

6. Remove the clutch gear oil seal extension with cloth or leather-covered vise grips in order to remove the clutch gear bushing and needle roller bearing.

7. Drift out the clutch gear bushing and drift out the needle roller bearing and thrust washer from the opposite end of the gear.

8. Press a new bushing into the clutch gear shaft, insert the mainshaft and rotate the gear to check for high spots and free-movement. If there is not 0.001–0.002 in. play, ream the bushing to size (H-D Reamer, part no. 94829–42).

9. Press on the printed side of the needle roller bearing to install the bearing and thrust washer.

10. Seal the oil extension with aluminum paint.

11. Install a new oil seal and O-ring.

12. Test the main shaft and countershaft for alignment with a dial indicator and replace if warped 0.003 in. or more.

13. Check the play between the mainshaft ball bearing, clutch gear, and access cover. Replace if play exceeds specifications listed in "Transmission Specifications."

14. Remove the mainshaft ball bearing snap-ring and press the bearing free on an arbor press from the outside in. If the bearing is drifted out, it should be replaced.

15. Inspect the mainshaft rollers and bearing race and replace if pitted, scored, or worn beyond specifications. Pack with grease before assembly.

16. Remove the race by removing the retaining ring and washer. Heat the case around the bearing and drift from the outside in. Press in a new race until its shoulder seats. Check clearances against those listed in "Transmission Specifications" and replace if necessary. Replace the snapring.

17. Check the countershaft needle roller bearings against the proper specifications listed in "Transmission Specifications." Drift free only if replacement is necessary, pressing on the printed side. The access cover must be 5/64 in. from the side.

18. Replace the oiler plug after the shaft clearances are established and replace with the oil hole up.

TRANSMISSION ASSEMBLY

1. Install the cam follower retainer ring and retainer in the access cover.

2. Seat the pawl carrier springs against the pawl carrier support.

3. Assemble the shifter pawls and springs in their respective sockets with the top engaging grooves facing one another.

4. Depress the pawls with a knife blade and assemble the cam, carrier, support, and shims (if applicable).

5. Install the camshaft thrust washer and a new retaining ring, using snap-ring pliers.

6. Depress one pawl at a time with a knife blade and rotate the shifter cam to ensure free cam movement.

7. Use shims to adjust the height of the cam as shown to ensure proper shifter fork operation.

NOTE: *On 1972 models, assemble the pawls on the carrier using spacers (one on outside, one underneath) to align the spring hooks and holes. Secure the pawl retaining ring and spring. Depress one pawl at a time while inserting the shifter cam in the pawl carrier. Assemble the carrier into the support so that the carrier ear seats between the springs.*

8. Arbor-press the clutch gear into the mainshaft bearing.

9. Assemble the Second gear thrust washer, Second gear, Second gear spacer, and the drive gear on the countershaft, making sure that Second gear rotates freely. Install the assembly in the access cover.

10. Install the mainshaft second gear, countershaft third gear, and shifter forks on the fork shaft with the finger studs pointed toward the access cover and the fork finger in the running groove of the gear. Install the finger rollers.

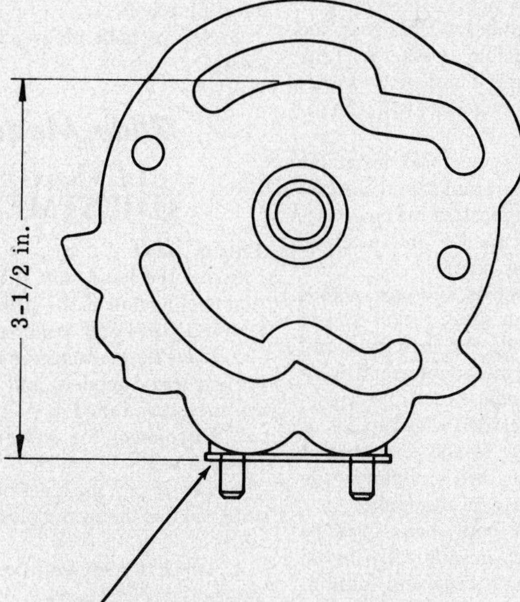
3-1/2 in.
Rotate cam to 3rd gear position and shim as required using quantity of .010 thick shims (7A, fig. 4D-19) necessary to obtain 3-1/2 in. dimension measured to cam surface as shown.

Shimming dimensions for pawl carrier support

11. Install the cam follower and follower spring in the follower retainer. Check to make sure that the follower is free in the retainer.

12. Secure the shifting assembly to the access cover with the cap screw and retainer ring while engaging the shifter fork finger rollers in the shifter cam slots.

13. Assemble First gear, Third gear, the Third gear washer, and a new retainer ring on the mainshaft. The ring is easily inserted with Retainer Ring Sleeve (H-D part no. 96396–52), but snap-ring pliers will also work.

14. Slide Second gear and the clutch gear onto the mainshaft.

15. Place the thinnest, First gear, variable washer against the countershaft shoulder.

16. Slide First gear on the shaft and check the clearance between the faces of it and Third gear. Try different First gear washers until a clearance of 0.038–0.058 in. is obtained. (Washers are available in thicknesses of 0.065, 0.075, 0.085, and 0.100 in.).

17. Assemble all parts to the access cover except for the mainshaft thrust washer, countershaft first gear washer, mainshaft rollers, roller bearing washer, and bearing retainer ring. Shift through the gears several times to ensure proper operation. With the transmission in Neutral, check to see if gear face clearances are between 0.038–0.058 in. Replace the shifter forks if clearance is not obtained.

Mainshaft and Countershaft End-Play

1. Install the thinnest First gear and Third gear variable washers. Temporarily secure the Third gear washer with a dab of heavy grease, with the ear pointing down.

2. With all parts assembled, install the access cover on the crankcase. Take care to align the dowel pins, tap the cover into place with a soft mallet, and secure it with the cover cap screws.

3. Check mainshaft end-play with a dial indicator from the sprocket side of the shaft by shifting the shaft back and forth. Repeat on the countershaft from the access cover side.

4. Wedge a discarded wheel spoke, or something similar, in the countershaft end hole and measure end-play while pulling and pushing on the spoke.

5. End-play for both shafts must be within 0.003–0.009 in. Adjust by installing larger mainshaft thrust and countershaft First gear washers. Washers are available in 0.005 in. gradations from 0.050–0.075 in., and countershaft washers of 0.020, 0.030, and 0.040 in. are also available.

6. Center the lever arm shaft so it will engage the pawl carrier support when the cover is in place. Lightly rotate the shaft to ensure correct engagement before securing the cover.

7. Grease the mainshaft bearing race and assemble the rollers. Secure the roller with the bearing washer and retaining ring.

Mainshaft Sprocket, Starter, and Clutch Assembly Installation

1. Temporarily install the foot-shift lever and place the transmission in Fourth gear.

2. Install the oil seal gasket, seal, retainer, lockwashers, and screws, but do not secure them yet.

3. Temporarily place the sprocket on the mainshaft to correctly position the retainer.

4. Remove the sprocket and secure the screws.

5. Assemble the sprocket, lockwasher, and nut. Secure the washer ear against the nut.

6. Install the rod end and drive chain.

7. Consult the "Starter" section for starter installation procedures.

8. Consult the "Clutch" section for clutch installation procedures.

9. Lubricate the transmission as described in the following section.

Transmission Lubrication

1. Stand the motorcycle upright and remove the oil filler plug from the chaincase top and the oil level plug from the chaincase bottom.

2. Fill the transmission with engine oil until the overflow begins from the oil level plug hole.

3. Secure both plugs when overflow ceases.

Glide Models

LINKAGE ADJUSTMENT

Hand Shift

Adjust the hand shift if the transmission is moved or if the primary chain is adjusted (1964 and earlier models).

1. Place the transmission in Third gear on four-speed models, and Second gear on three-speed models.

2. Disconnect the shifter rod at the shifter lever.

3. Gently shift the lever back and forth until you feel the spring plunger reach its seat.

4. Adjust the clevis until the rod can be attached without moving the lever.

Foot Shift

Adjust the shifter rod when the transmission is moved if wear necessitates adjustment or if the primary chain is adjusted (1964 and earlier models).

1. Align the shift lever clamping slot with the foot lever shaft notch.

2. On 1964 and earlier models, adjust the length of the rod so that 1/16 in. clearance remains between the lever and the cover mounting stud when fully depressed. Disconnect the lever from the rod and adjust the rod end as desired. Secure the locknut and connect the rod and lever.

TRANSMISSION REMOVAL

1. Disconnect the battery ground wire from the negative terminal.

2. Remove the footrest, chain cover, compensating sprocket (if applicable, consult "Clutch" section), or shaft nut (nut is removed by striking a 1 ⅝ in. wrench with a hammer).

3. Remove the chain adjuster mounting bolt and the starter shaft thrust washer (1965 model only).

4. Remove the clutch, clutch hub, drive sprocket, and primary chain as described in the "Clutch" section.

5. Remove the rear chainguard on 1964 and earlier models.

6. On 1965 and later models, loosen the five transmission mounting bolts and remove the chainguard and oiler.

7. Remove the starter solenoid terminal wires.

8. Remove the battery, carrier, and regulator ground strap from the right side of the transmission. Remove the right rear footrest bracket.

9. Remove the starter motor bracket and pull the starter motor out of the left side of the frame. Remove the kickstarter lever (if applicable).

10. Loosen the locknut at the clutch foot control or booster, and turn the rod out until it can be slid free of the clutch release lever.

11. Remove the shifter rod.

12. Disconnect the speedometer cable and housing from the transmission.

13. Remove the Neutral indicator switch.

14. Remove the transmission as a unit.

MAIN DRIVE GEAR OIL SEAL

Consult the transmission as described in "Transmission Removal."

SHIFTER COVER REMOVAL

1. Remove the transmission as described in "Transmission Removal."

2. Remove the twelve securing screws and pull the cover free from the two dowel pins.

HAND SHIFTER COVER

Disassembly

1. Remove the shaft lock screw and drift the shaft free with a discarded valve stem or something similar.

2. Remove the shifter cam.
3. Remove the shifter lever cotter pin.
4. Pry the shifter gear from the shaft by tapping a screwdriver between the gear and the inside of the cover.
5. Remove the shifter lever and leather washer.
6. Remove the cam plunger cap screw, ball spring, and plunger ball.

Inspection and Repair

1. Clean all metal parts in a suitable solvent and blow them dry.
2. Inspect the shifter lever bushing for excessive wear—indicated by excessive lever play—and replace if necessary. Screw a ⅝ in. tap into the bushing. Remove the tap and heat the case to about 300 degrees. Screw in the tap, clamp it in a vise, and tap the cover with a soft mallet until the cover comes free.
3. Inspect the teeth on the shifter gear and cam pinion for wear or damage and replace if necessary.
4. Inspect the plunger ball seat and cam track for excessive wear and replace if the edges are not sharp.
5. The oil seal and cover gasket should be replaced but may be used again if in good condition.

Assembly

1. Hold the shifter gear spring in place inside the cover and place the shifter gear on it so the gear hub is inside the spring. The gear must have the timing mark on the gear tooth facing the shift lever cover port.
2. Slip the leather washer onto the shifter lever and insert the lever through the case and spring so that it meshes with the shifter gear. The lever should be pointed toward the left.
3. Secure the assembly with the lever shaft cotter pin.
4. Insert the cam in the cover so that the pinion gear timing mark aligns with the shifter gear mark.
5. Place the oil seal on the camshaft and insert it through the case and cam. Secure it with the shaft lock screw.

Hand shifter cover assembly

6. If cam end-play is greater than 0.-0005–0.0065 in., install shims as necessary. If play is too little, the cover can be filed as necessary.

FOOT SHIFTER COVER

Disassembly

1. Remove the shifter lever screws, lever, dust shield, and long cover screws.
2. Remove the short cover screw nut from the back of the adaptor plate, withdraw the short cover screw, and remove the pawl carrier cover, gasket, pawl carrier, pawls, pawl springs, and pawl carrier springs.
3. Remove the adaptor plate bracket screw, washer, adaptor plate, and plate gasket.
4. Disconnect the neutral indicator switch from the cover.
5. Bend back the cam follower retainer washer ear to remove the retainer, washer spring, and cam follower,
6. Remove the camshaft lock screw and drift the camshaft from the cover, using an old valve stem, or something similar, as a drift.
7. Remove the shifter shaft cotter pin, gear, spring, and shaft from the cover.

Inspection and Repair

1. Consult "Hand Shift Shifter Cover Inspection and Replacement."
2. The Neutral switch should be cleaned only with Gunk or similar solvent.
3. Depress the neutral indicator switch plunger and observe whether or not it returns freely. If the plunger binds, the panel lamp will not light and the switch must be replaced. Do not run current through it without the panel lamp neutral indicator in series so the circuit is completed.
4. If the pawl carrier hole has been worn until it is oversized, replace the press-fit pawl carrier bushing.

Assembly

1. Hold the shifter gear spring in the cover and place the shifter gear on it so the gear hub is inside the spring. The gear tooth timing mark must face the cover.
2. Slide the shifter shaft through the cover until it meshes with the gear. The timing mark should be in line with the squared side of the shaft and slightly to the left of the last ratchet tooth on the shaft.
3. Gently tap the shaft and gear together; secure them with the shaft cotter pin.
4. Place the oil seal on the wider of the two camshaft end grooves.
5. Place the shifter cam in the cover and hold it in position where the cam pinion timing mark aligns with the shifter gear timing mark.

Aligning shifter gear timing marks

6. Secure the cam with the camshaft and secure the camshaft with the lock screw.
7. Slip in the cam follower and spring and secure them with the retaining washer and retainer.
8. Secure the neutral indicator switch and check to make sure that the plunger contacts the shifter gear.
9. Secure the cover in a vise with the shifter mechanism end pointing up.
10. Place the adaptor plate gasket on the case.
11. Attach the cover screw nut to the back of the adaptor plate with a dab of heavy grease and place the adaptor plate on the gasket.
12. Loosely screw the adaptor plate bracket screw and washer into the hole above the end of the shifter gear.
13. Place the gearshift cam in any gear, other than Neutral, and rock the cam back and forth to be sure that the cam follower is seating properly in one of the indexing notches.
14. Rotate the adaptor plate until the

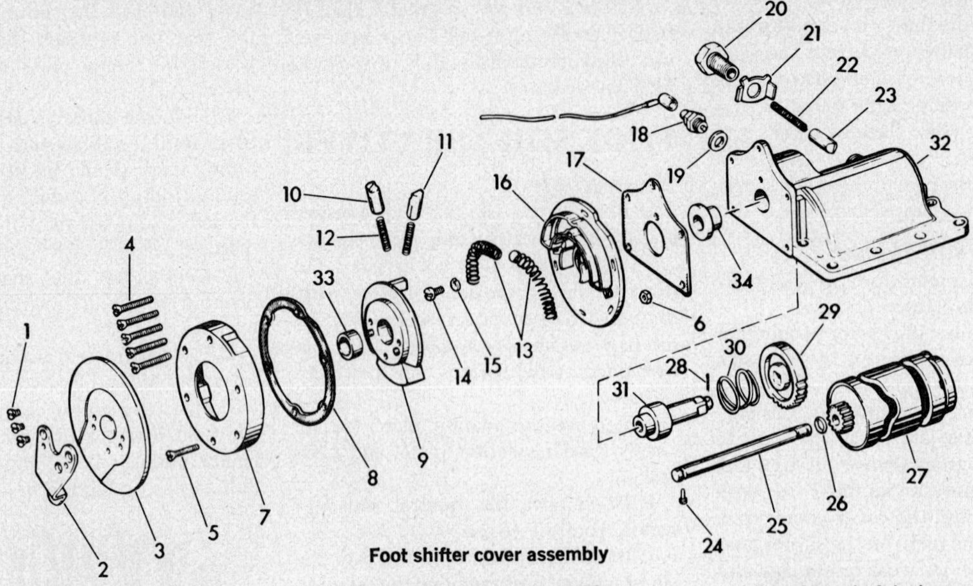

Foot shifter cover assembly

1. Shifter lever screw (3)
2. Shifter lever
3. Dust shield
4. Shifter cover screw (5)
5. Shifter cover screw (short)
6. Cover screw nut
7. Pawl carrier cover
8. Cover gasket
9. Pawl carrier
10. Pawl (right)
11. Pawl (left)
12. Pawl spring (2)
13. Pawl carrier spring (2)
14. Adapter plate bracket screw
15. Adapter plate bracket screw washer
16. Adapter plate
17. Adapter plate gasket
18. Neutral indicator switch
19. Washer
20. Cam follower retainer
21. Cam follower retainer washer
22. Spring
23. Cam follower
24. Cam shaft lock screw
25. Cam shaft
26. Oil seal
27. Shifter cam
28. Cotter pin
29. Shifter gear
30. Shifter gear spring
31. Shifter shaft
32. Shifter cover
33. Pawl carrier bushing
34. Shifter shaft bushing

Aligning shifter adapter plate timing notches

plate timing notch lines up between the two bottom teeth of the shifter gear. Secure it with the adaptor plate bracket screw.

15. Lightly grease the pawl carrier springs and place them in the slots on the adaptor plate.

16. Lightly oil the pawls and check to see that they move freely in the pawl carrier holes.

17. Install the pawl springs and pawls so that the end face notches face each other.

18. Place the pawl carriers on the shifter shaft so that the carrier lug seats between the pawl carrier springs.

19. Lubricate the pawl carrier back.

20. Assemble the cover gasket and cover. Apply Locktite (H-D part no. 99619–60) or a suitable thread-sealing compound to the cover screws and insert them. The short screw should seat in the cover screw nut. Secure all screws.

21. Place the dust shield over the pawl carrier dowel pins and set the shifter lever over the dust shield dowl pins. Secure it with the shift lever screws.

Installation

1. Apply sealer to the shifter cover and secure it to the gearbox.

2. Place the assembled shifter cover over the gearbox and secure it with the twelve securing screws. The two longer screws go in holes near the bulge over the shifter gear. The vented screw goes nearest the locating dowel pin on the gearcase right side. Apply a thread sealer to all but the vented screw.

SHIFTER FORK

Removal

1. Remove the shifter cover as described in "Shifter Cover Removal."

2. Disassembly is not necessary if the shifter fork assemblies are not damaged or worn and shifter clutches are not to be replaced.

3. Remove the shaft lock screw and drift out the shaft.

4. Separate the shifter fork assemblies upon removal; do not mix parts during replacement.

Disassembly

1. Remove the finger rollers.

2. Free the bushing nuts by bending back the washer ears and remove both nuts and washers.

3. Remove the remaining parts, taking note of their positions as an aid in assembly.

Inspection and Repair

1. Clean all metal parts in a suitable solvent and blow them dry.

2. Replace bent or worn forks. Do not use forks which have been bent and then straightened.

3. Check the shifter fork bushings for excessive play and replace if necessary. Check new bushings on the shaft and determine if the shaft bushing contact surface is worn.

4. If the bushings bind, they can be lapped by coating the shaft with valve-grinding compound and then spinning the valve in the bushing until movement is free. Clean both parts again thoroughly.

Assembly

1. Assemble in reverse order of disassembly,taking care not to mix any parts. If parts are mixed, if would be better to replace both assemblies than guess which went where.

2. Place Fork Shifter Gauge (H-D part no. 96384–39) on the shifter cover. Align the tool gauge blocks with the straight cam slots by laying the ⅜ in. gauge rod

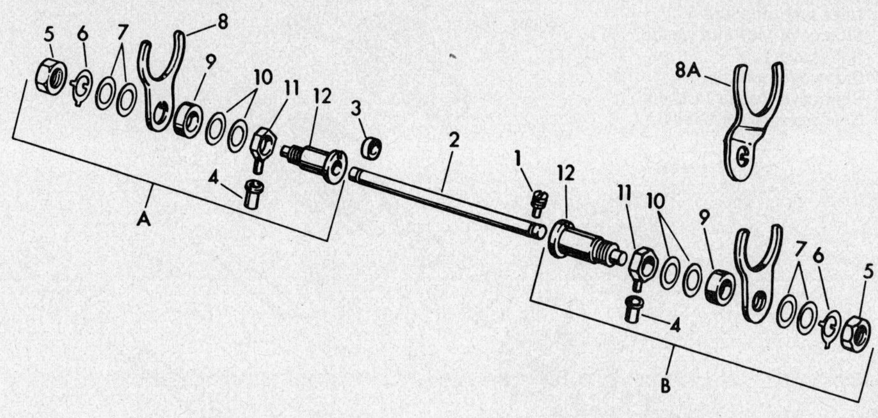

1. Lock screw
2. Shifter fork shaft
3. Rubber oil seal
4. Shifter finger rollers (2)
5. Nut (2)
6. Lock washer (2)
7. Spacing shim (variable number) (0.007 in.) (0.014 in.)
8. Shifter fork (1 or 2)
8A. Shifter fork (3-speed, reverse only)
9. Standard spacing shim (2)
10. Spacing shim (variable number) (0.007 in.) (0.014 in.)
11. Shifting finger (2)
12. Shifting fork bushing (2)

Shifter fork assembly

through both. Secure the blocks with thumb screws.

3. Place the tool on the transmission case so that the shifter finger rollers engage the tool slots.

4. Check that the shifting clutches are centered by inserting a thickness guage on both sides of the clutch.

5. Increase or decrease the number of variable shims, (0.014 or 0.017 in. shims are available), between the fork and finger to center the clutches.

6. First and Second gears should have 0.075 in. clearance on both sides.

7. Third and Fourth gears should have 0.100 in. clearance on both sides.

8. Reverse gear should have 0.055 in. clearance between gear teeth.

9. If the gears have engaging dogs, rotate the gears so that the dogs on the gear and clutch overlap by about ⅛ in. before checking clearance.

10. Secure the shaft nut with a thread-sealing compound. Avoid overtightening.

11. Install the forks in the gearbox and secure them with the shaft. The narrowest fork is for the high gear shifter clutch. Secure the shaft lock screw. Install the shifter cover as described in "Shifter Cover Replacement."

FOUR-SPEED GEARBOX DISASSEMBLY

1. Remove the transmission as described in the "Transmission Removal" section.

2. Remove the clutch as described in the "Clutch Disassembly" section.

3. Remove the starter assembly and clutch as described in the "Starter Disassembly" section.

4. Remove the shifter cover and shifting forks as described in "Shifter Cover Removal" and "Shifter Fork Removal" sections.

Countershaft Disassembly

1. On 1964 and earlier models, remove the end cap screws, washers, end cap, and end cap gasket from the gearcase.

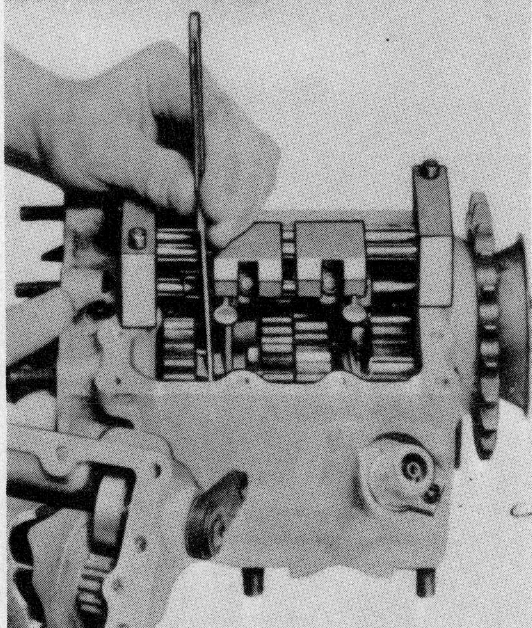

Checking shifter clutch clearances

2. Bend the lockwasher ear away from the countershaft nut and remove both.

3. Drift the countershaft out of the case from left to right.

4. Remove First gear, the First gear bushing, First gear bearing washer, and shifter clutch off the splined countershaft gear.

5. With snap-ring pliers, remove the spring lockring, gear retaining washer, countershaft, Second gear, and Second gear bushing.

6. Remove the roller bearing rollers and roller retainer washer. Do not mix the roller sets; replace entire sets rather than individual rollers.

7. Pry the lockring free and remove the roller thrust washer, rollers, retainer washer, and lockring from the gear end of the countershaft gear.

8. Remove the speedometer drive housing screw, washer, speedometer drive unit, and drive unit gasket.

9. Remove the idler gear shaft, spacer washer, and idler gear on three-speed and reverse-type transmissions. Inserting a ¼–20 tap screw into the shaft will provide a grip for pulling the shaft free. Apply 300° of heat to the case of the shaft will not move.

Mainshaft Disassembly

1. Remove the bearing housing retaining screws, oil deflector, and retaining plate.

2. Using a soft mallet, drive the mainshaft toward the right side of the case, until the mainshaft bearing or bearing housing is free from the case.

3. Pry the mainshaft second gear lockring free of its groove and slide it onto the mainshaft splines.

4. Pull the assembled mainshaft as far as it will go to its right.

5. If the bearing housing does not come off with the bearing, slide the gear through it as far as it will go, clear the gear of the case, and drive the mainshaft out. This should free the housing.

6. Remove Third gear, the retaining washer, lockring, and shifter clutch off

1. End cap screw (4)
2. End cap screw washer (4)
3. End cap
4. End cap gasket
5. Countershaft nut
6. Lock washer
7. Lock plate
8A. Countershaft
8B. O-Ring
9. Countershaft gear end washer
10. Low gear
10A. Countershaft reverse gear
11. Low gear bushing
12. Low gear bearing washer
13. Shifter clutch
14. Spring lock ring
15. Gear retaining washer
16. Countershaft second gear
16A. Countershaft low gear (3-speed and reverse
17. Second gear bushing
18. Bearing rollers (22)
19. Roller retainer washer
20. Lock ring
21. Roller thrust washer
22. Roller bearing (22)
23. Retaining washer
24. Lock ring
25. Countershaft gear
25A. Countershaft gear (19-tooth for 3-speed and reverse)
26. Speedometer drive housing screw
27. Washer
28. Speedometer drive unit
29. Drive unit gasket
30. Idler gear shaft
30A. Spacer washer
31. Idler gear
32. Countershaft mounting collar (starter side)
33. Countershaft mounting collar (clutch side)
34. Idler gear bushing
35. Side cover nut and washer (9)
36. Side cover
37. Side cover gasket
38. Side cover upper bushing
39. Side cover lower bushing

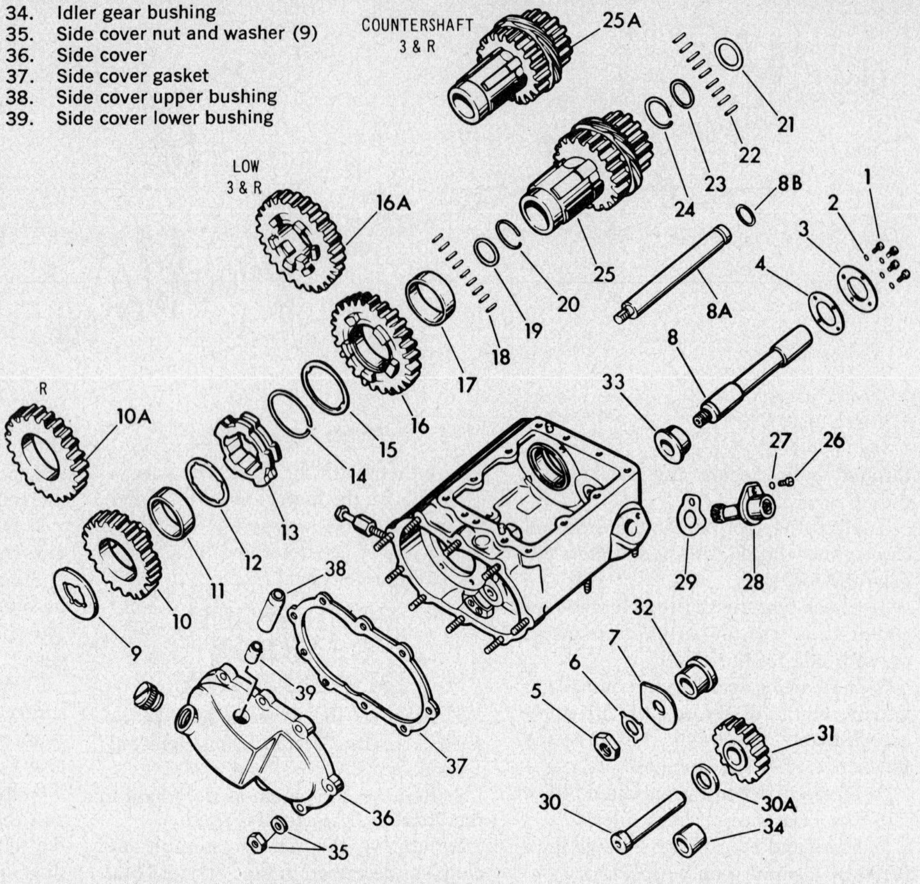

Four-speed transmission assembly

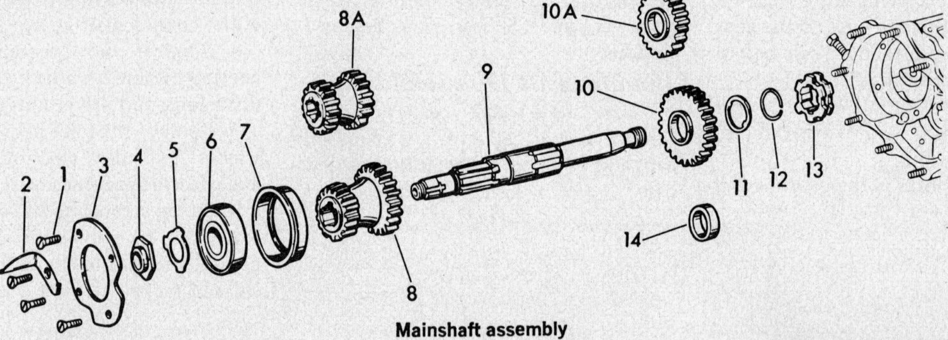

Mainshaft assembly

1. Bearing housing retaining plate screw (4)
2. Oil deflector
3. Retaining plate
4. Ball bearing nut
5. Ball bearing washer
6. Mainshaft bearing
7. Mainshaft bearing housing
8. Low and second gear
8A. Low and reverse gear (hand-shift)
9. Mainshaft
10. Third gear
10A. Mainshaft second gear (hand-shift)
11. Retaining washer
12. Lock ring
13. Shifter clutch
14. Third gear bushing

the mainshaft and lift them out of the case.

7. Remove the mainshaft through the right side of the case.

8. If repair is necessary, disassemble the mainshaft gear and bearing assembly.

9. Secure the mainshaft in a copper or wood-jawed vise. Bend the lockwasher ear away from the shaft nut and remove both. Pull the bearing and then the gear from the shaft with a claw puller (H-D part no. 95635–46) of press them off. Protect the shaft end if a puller is to be used (with H-D part no.95636–46).

MAIN DRIVE GEAR

Disassembly

1. Secure the gearbox in a vise or to a work bench. Secure the chain sprocket by laying a length of chain over its teeth and nailing the chain ends to the bench.

2. Bend back the washer ear and remove the locknut (which has a left-hand thread) and washer.

3. Remove the oil deflector and chain sprocket.

4. Push the main drive gear into the case and lift it and the thrust washer out.

5. Remove the forty-four rollers and place them where no mix-ups or lost bearings will occur. Bearings must be replaced as an entire set.

6. Remove the drive gear oil seal, shaft seal, or main drive gear spacer only if worn or damaged. Consult the "Main Drive Gear Oil Seal Replacement" section for procedures.

Inspection and Repair

1. Clean all metal parts in a suitable solvent and blow them dry.

2. Inspect all of the gears for damage

1. Sprocket lock nut
2. Sprocket lock washer
3. Oil deflector
4. Chain sprocket
5. Main drive gear
5A. Main drive gear shaft seal (1965)
6. Thrust washer
7. Roller bearings (44)
8. Main drive gear oil seal
9. Oil seal cork washer
10. Main drive gear spacer
11. Main drive gear spacer key
12. Bearing race retaining ring
13. Bearing race
14. Gear box
15. Main drive gear bushing

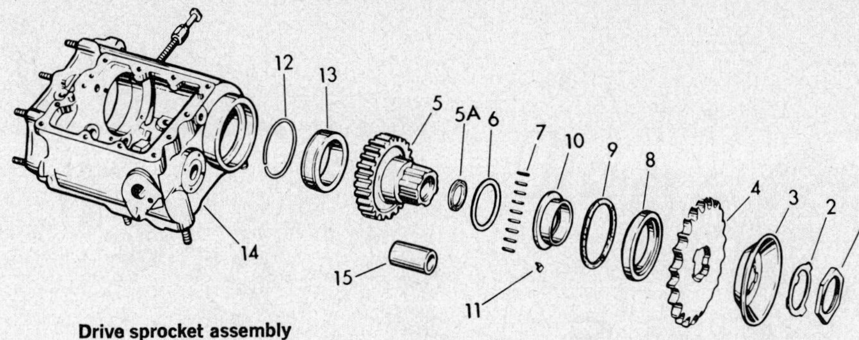

Drive sprocket assembly

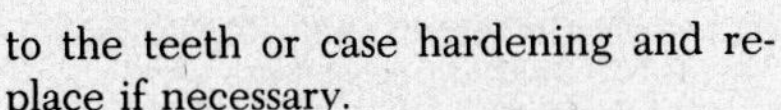

to the teeth or case hardening and replace if necessary.

3. Inspect all bushings, bearings, and shafts for wear and excessive play; replace if necessary.

4. The main drive gear bearing race can be pressed in and out. Heating the case to about 300 degrees will facilitate removal. Press a new bearing in until the flange seats on the case. Replace the race retaining ring.

5. Replace the cork washers and oil seals. Apply sealer to the gear end recess when replacing the shaft seal.

6. Replace the shifter clutches and gear engaging dogs for wear or damage, and replace if necessary. Edges should be sharp rather than rounded.

7. Check bearings for smooth operation and proper fit in their races. Specifications are listed in the "Transmission Specifications" chart. Rollers are available in 0.0004 and 0.0008 in. oversizes and must be replaced as a set.

Assembly

1. Assemble the main drive gear oil seal, cork washer, and gear spacer in the case.

2. Install and grease the bearing race and install the rollers.

3. Assemble the main drive gear thrust washer on the main drive gear and slip the gear into the bearing race, taking care not to displace any rollers.

4. Install the main drive gear spacer key in its slot in the outer edge of the gear spacer, with the long section in any gear splineway.

5. Slip the sprocket, with the flat side away from the case, onto the gear splines. Assemble the oil deflector and lockwasher; secure the locknut.

6. Using a dial indicator, check end-play as listed in the "Transmission Specifications" chart.

MAINSHAFT ASSEMBLY

1. Assemble First and Second (or First and Reverse gear depending on the model) gears on the splines, mainshaft bearing housing, bearing, bearing washer, and the bearing nut to the mainshaft.

2. Press the bearing housing over the mainshaft ball bearing, press onto the shaft, and secure with the lockwasher and nut. Bend the washer ear against the nut.

3. Insert the shaft into the gearbox and install the mainshaft Thrid gear (Second gear on three-speed models), thrust washer, lockring, and shifter clutch with the "high" side facing the drive gear.

4. Seat the lockring in its groove on the shaft.

5. Gently tap the shaft assembly into the case with a soft metal hammer or brass drift until the bearing housing flange seats against the case.

6. Install the Reverse idler gear on three-speed models.

7. Assemble and secure the retaining plate, oil deflector, and retaining plate screws.

COUNTERSHAFT ASSEMBLY

1. Insert the lockrings and bearing retainer washers in the countershaft gear.

2. Apply grease to the inside of the countershaft gear and assemble both roller sets.

3. Install the bearing thrust washer in the gear end.

4. Temporarily install the shaft to check bearing end-play and motion. Consult the "Transmission Specifications" chart for necessary information.

5. Apply a dab of heavy grease to the gear end washer and mount it, and the gear, in the case.

6. Check gear end-play by inserting a thickness gauge between the gear and washer. Consult the "Transmission Specifications" chart for proper clearance and adjust with the appropriate number of washers. (0.074, 0.078, 0.082, 0.085, 0.090, 0.095, and 0.100 in. washers are available.) When the correct amount of washers is arrived at, set aside the shaft, gear, and gear end washer.

7. Assemble the Second gear bushing, gear, thrust washer, and gear lockring on the countershaft gear.

8. Assemble the shifter clutch, thrust washer, first gear bushing, and gear on the countershaft gear.

9. Apply a dab of heavy grease to the countershaft gear end washer and place it on end of the gear.

10. Hold the assembly in the case and insert the countershaft. Secure the bearing lockwasher and nut, and bend up an ear of the washer.

11. Install the end cap gasket, end cap, washers, and end cap screws on 1964 and earlier models.

12. Install the drive unit gasket, drive unit, washer, and screw.

13. Consult the "Shifter Cover Replacement," "Starter," and "Clutch Assembly" sections for completion procedures.

14. Install the transmission and follow the procedures given in "Transmission Removal" section.

STARTERS

Clicking noises from the starter gears are an indication of trouble. This will occur with the engine running and the starter crank in its proper position, and is caused by the starter clutch teeth. Tightening down the starter shaft nut on the crank gear camplate will often solve the problem.

Slipping, or partial engagement of the starter crank during its cycle, indicates either broken or worn starter clutch teeth, a damaged clutch spring, sticking of the clutch gear on the sprocket spacer, or a worn brass fitting.

Sportster

DISASSEMBLY

1. Loosen the front cylinder and exhaust pipe.

2. Remove the starter crank clamp bolt and pry the crank free of the shaft.

3. Apply pressure to the end of the starter spring and pry it free of the shaft.

4. Remove the sprocket cover bolts and lightly tap off the cover with a soft mallet while pulling it from the shaft.

5. Push the clutch lever forward and disengage the cable.

6. Remove the clutch as described in the "Clutch Disassembly" section.

7. Free the starter clutch gear, sprocket spacer, and clutch spring by rotating the crank gear.

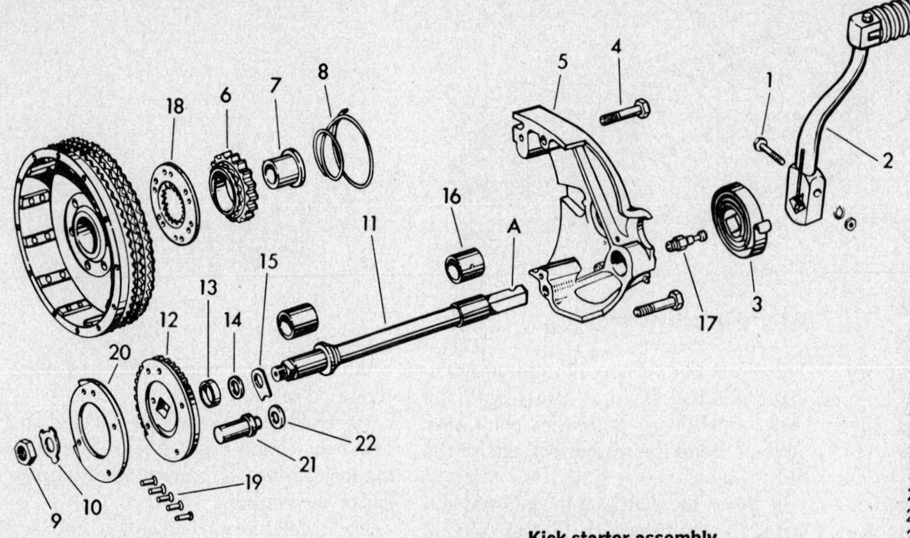

Kick starter assembly

1. Crank clamp bolt, lock washer and nut
2. Crank and pedal assembly
3. Crank spring
4. Sprocket cover bolt (2)
5. Sprocket cover
6. Starter clutch gear
7. Clutch sprocket spacer available (long or short)
8. Clutch spring
9. Shaft nut
10. Crank gear lock washer
11. Crankshaft
12. Crank gear
13. Crank oil seal
14. Crankshaft shim—0.007 in.
15. Shaft thrust plate
16. Shaft bushing (2)
17. Spring stud
18. Starter clutch
19. Crank gear cam plate rivet (5)
20. Crank gear cam plate
21. Crank gear stop pin
22. Crank gear stop pin washer

8. Remove the shaft nut and crank gear lockwasher.

9. Loosen the starter crankshaft from the crank gear by tapping the shaft end with a soft mallet.

10. Slide out the crankshaft, oil seal, shims, and thrust plate.

INSPECTION AND REPAIR

1. Clean all parts with a suitable solvent, except for the cover gasket if it is to be reused, and blow them dry.

2. Inspect the starter clutch and starter clutch gear for worn or damaged teeth, and replace if necessary.

3. Spin the clutch gear on the spacer and check for binding. Replace any damaged parts.

4. Replace the starter clutch spring if the length is under 1 in., in a free state, or if it is extremely fatigued.

5. Check the starter crankshaft for distortion. Check for excessive wear on the surfaces of the bearing and on the faces of the thrust washer and shaft collar. Replace if necessary.

6. Temporarily mount the following assembly in the left crankcase: crankshaft, oil seal, thrust plate, crank gear, lockwasher, and shaft nut, checking all parts for wear and replacing as necessary.

7. Spin the shaft and measure for excessive end-play with a dial indicator. End-play must be within 0.001–0.0007 in. Shims wiich are 0.007 in. thick are available (H-D part no. 6802).

8. Inspect the starter crank gear for wear or damage and replace if necessary.

9. Inspect the crank gear camplate for wear or damage, especially to the ears. The camplate can be replaced independently of the crank gear.

10. Check to make sure that the camplate rivets are all secure.

11. Replace the bushings if excessive end-play is present but the shaft is not worn. Press the old bushing out and the new one in taking care to align the bushing hole with the grease-fitting channel.

12. Only inspect or replace the gear stop pin and washer if the engine is not in the chassis. These parts rarely need service. The pin is a press fit and the washer is secured by peening the pin end.

ASSEMBLY

1. Insert the oil seal into the crankcase.

2. Slide the thrust washer onto the countershaft with the flat side up.

3. Assemble the shim on the shaft (if applicable) and insert the shaft in the crankcase so that the thrust washer notch lines up with the stop pin.

4. Rotate the crank until the notch on the outer end of the shaft is pointing up.

5. Place the starter gear on the shaft end with the recessed portion of the camplate facing down. The slot should seat against the stop pin. Check to make sure that the thrust washer has not shifted out of place.

6. Install the lockwasher over the shaft so that its prong engages the hole in the crank gear face, and secure it with the flat side of the shaft nut against the washer.

7. Slip the spacer into the starter gear so that the grooved side of the gear bushing seats on the spacer lip.

8. Align the clutch spring small end in the gear bushing groove.

Starter crankshaft installation

1. Starter crankshaft shim—0.007 in.
2. Starter shaft thrust plate
3. Starter crank gear stop pin washer

9. Press the starter gear into mesh with the starter clutch, and rotate the crank gear so that the clutch gear and crank gear also mesh. The spring will hold the assembly in place once the cover is installed.

10. Rotate the crank gear to its original position. By taking a strip of metal and drilling holes to match the cover screw securing holes, the strip can be mounted to temporarily hold the spring in position until the cover is mounted.

11. When replacing a sprocket spacer, make sure that you use one of the same length. If new gears are used, the clearance between the teeth must be checked in the following manner:

a. Measure the distance from the spacer collar to the top of the clutch gear teeth.

b. Measure the distance from the top of the clutch gear teeth to the sprocket washer.

c. Subtract the answer of "b" from that of "a" to get the proper clearnace.

d. Use a long spacer if the result is less than 0.040 in. after a small spacer has already been used.

12. Install the clutch as described in the "Clutch Assembly" section.

13. Secure the clutch cable end in the release lever, and mount and secure the sprocket cover, exhaust pipe, and muffler.

14. Place the crank spring on the shaft end with the spring end pointing upward. Secure the spring on the spring stud by prying with a screwdriver.

15. Mount and secure the starter crank.

Glide Models

DISASSEMBLY

1. Place a drip pan under the transmission.

2. Remove the clutch lever rod from the release lever, cover nuts and washers, and pull the cover and release lever assembly free from the mounting studs.

3. The clutch release bearing should come off with the cover, but may bind on the starter clutch. Do not attempt to pry it from the cover, but it may be pried free from the clutch.

4. Pull the pushrod free of the mainshaft.

5. Secure the crank with a vise or vise grips which are blocked against movement.

6. Bend the lockwasher ear from the crank nut and remove both the nut and the washer.

7. Pull the starter gear with a claw puller or remove the vise and drive the crank free with a soft mallet. Block the crank and cover against swinging when the shaft is free from the gear.

8. Pull the crank out of the cover and the crank spring, thrust washer, crank bushings, and oil seal will all come free.

9. Remove the release lever nut and lockwasher, and pull the release lever free with a claw puller.

10. Remove the release finger and thrust washer by removing the cotterpin and washer; pull the shaft free.

INSPECTION AND REPAIR

1. Clean all parts with a suitable solvent and blow them dry.

2. Check play between the starter crankshaft and the cover bushing, and replace if play is excessive. Press new bushings in until they are flush with the outer surface.

3. Replace the oil seal if the transmission was leaking through the starter crank.

4. Check for play in the release lever shaft. Replace the shaft if play is excessive.

5. Inspect the pushrod bearing for wear and replace it if the action is not smooth or is excessively loose.

6. Inspect the crank gear camplate and gear pin for wear. This is all assembled on the starter crank gear and is probably worn if the bushings were worn.

ASSEMBLY

1. Assemble the release lever shaft, lever bushing, release finger, thrust washer, lever bushing, washer, and cotter pin on the starter cover.

2. Press the crank bushing and oil seal in the cover after lightly greasing the seal.

3. Assemble the crank spring and the thrust washer (with beveled side facing spring), and insert the crank after lightly greasing the shaft.

4. Block the crank with a vise and wind the spring by rotating the cover clockwise.

5. With the crank held in normal position, install the crank gear so that the gear will maintain normal crank position.

6. Secure the crank with the lock-

1. Starter cover nut (9)
2. Plain washer (9)
3. Clutch release bearing
4. Push rod
5. Starter crank nut
6. Eared lock washer
7. Starter gear
8. Crank
9. Thrust washer
10. Starter crank spring
11. Starter cover
12. Release lever nut
13. Lock washer
14. Release lever
15. Release lever shaft
16. Cotter pin
17. Plain washer
18. Release finger
19. Thrust washer
20. Starter crank bushing (2)
21. Oil seal
22. Release lever bushing
23. Release lever bushing
24. Starter cover gasket
25. Starter clutch nut
26. Starter clutch washer
27. Starter clutch
28. Starter clutch key (2)
29. Starter mainshaft gear
30. Starter clutch spring
31. Mainshaft gear bushing

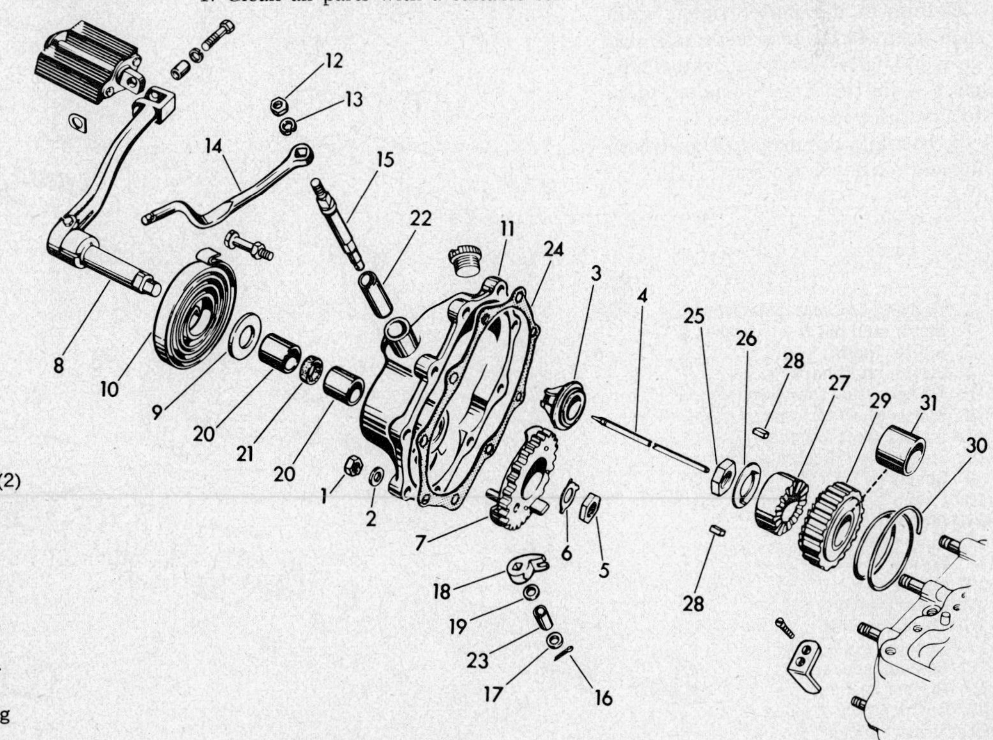

Kick starter assembly

washer and nut, bending the washer ear against a flat side of the nut.

7. Install a new gasket on the case studs after applying gasket sealer or silver spray.

8. Install the clutch release bearing into the cover so that the slot in the bearing race engages the clutch release lever finger.

9. Slide the pushrod's narrow end into the bearing.

10. Slide the cover into place making sure the pushrod enters the main shaft.

11. The starter clutch ball plunger and the groove in the release bearing inner race must be aligned.

12. Secure the cover.

13. Fill the case with 1½ pts of oil of the same viscosity as that used in the engine.

STARTER CLUTCH

Disassembly

1. Remove the starter clutch cover assembly as described in the "Starter Disassembly" section.

2. Bend the lockwasher ear free of the clutch nut and remove both parts.

3. Pull the starter clutch from the mainshaft with Starter Clutch Puller (H-D part no. 95650–42), or a suitable substitute, taking care not to damage the clutch teeth.

4. Remove the starter clutch keys, mainshaft gear, and clutch spring.

Inspection and Repair

1. Clean all parts in a suitable solvent and blow them dry, except for the cover gasket if it is to be reused.

2. Inspect the starter clutch, mainshaft gear, starter gear teeth, mainshaft gear, and starter clutch ratchet teeth. Replace if the teeth are rounded, mushroomed, chipped, or cracked.

3. Examine the mainshaft gear bushing and replace if necessary.

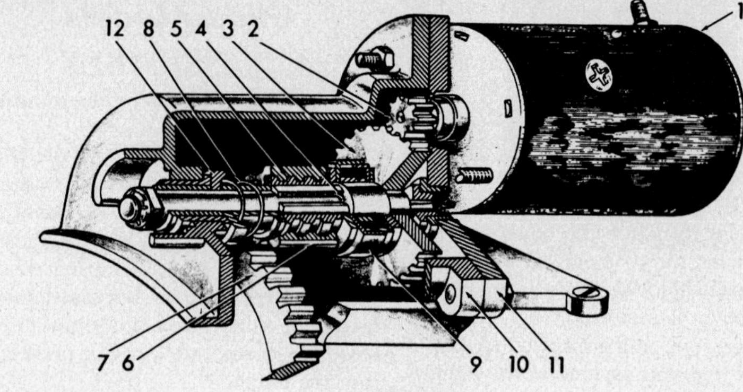

Starter drive

1. Starter motor
2. Armature pinion
3. Drive gear
4. Starter shaft spline
5. Worm sleeve
6. Worm pinion
7. Clutch ring gear
8. Anti-drift spring
9. Cushion
10. Drive housing
11. Transmission cover flange
12. Pinion stop

Assembly

Assemble in reverse order of disassembly. Note the following:

1. Replace the gasket if possible. Apply sealer to the case side of the gasket and position it on the case.

2. Rotate the mainshaft gear to ensure free motion and ream the bushing if necessary.

3. Drive the keys into the slots.

4. Secure the starter clutch nut and bend the lockwasher ear against a nut flat side. The top of the starter clutch must never be less than ⅝ in. above edge of the gearbox. If overtightened, the starter clutch may crack, causing damage to the bearing.

Electric Starter Drive

1964–65 SERVI-CAR

Starter Drive Shaft and Housing Disassembly

1. Using a 1 ⅛ in. wrench, remove the solenoid from the transmission top cover. Note the number and position of spacer washers to ensure correct reassembly.

2. Support the motor.

3. Remove the housing bolts, lockwashers, motor stud nuts, and lockwashers.

4. Disengage the starter shaft and housing as an assembly.

5. Secure the motor to the transmis-

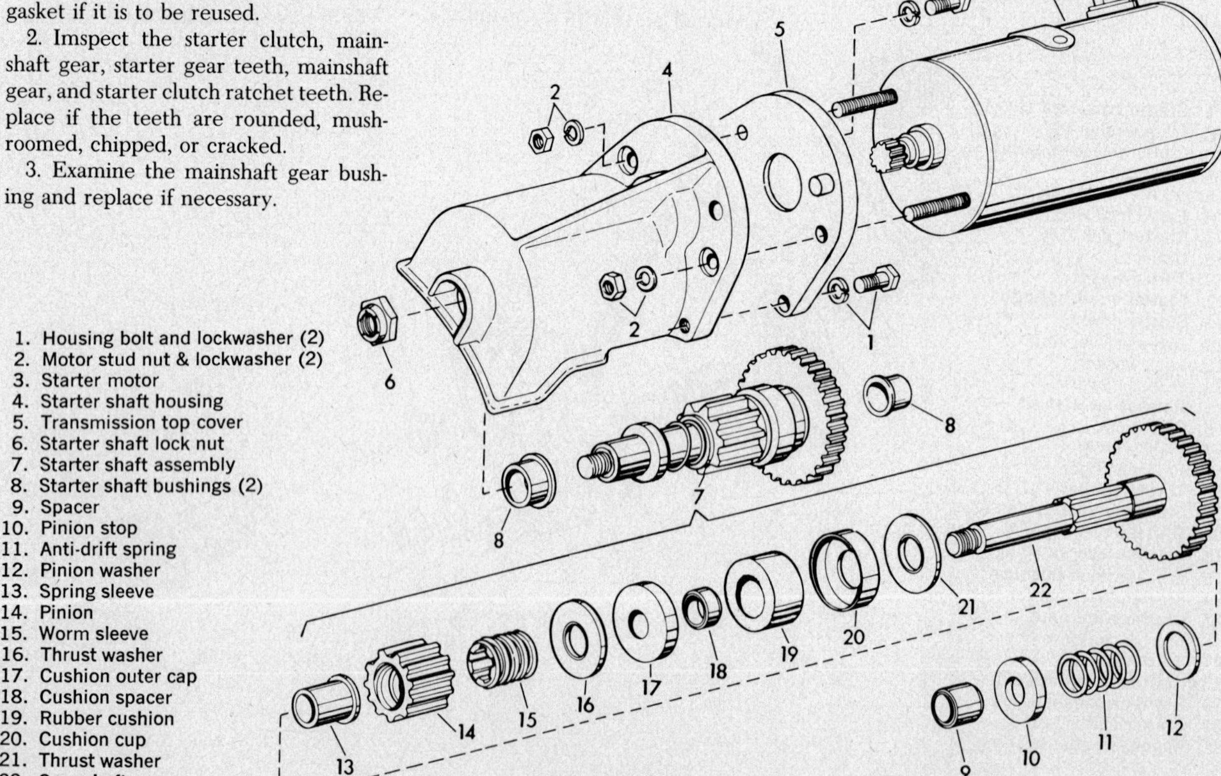

1. Housing bolt and lockwasher (2)
2. Motor stud nut & lockwasher (2)
3. Starter motor
4. Starter shaft housing
5. Transmission top cover
6. Starter shaft lock nut
7. Starter shaft assembly
8. Starter shaft bushings (2)
9. Spacer
10. Pinion stop
11. Anti-drift spring
12. Pinion washer
13. Spring sleeve
14. Pinion
15. Worm sleeve
16. Thrust washer
17. Cushion outer cap
18. Cushion spacer
19. Rubber cushion
20. Cushion cup
21. Thrust washer
22. Gear shaft

Starter assembly

sion top cover with the stud nuts and lockwashers.

6. Remove the starter shaft locknut and withdraw the shaft assembly.

7. Slip the spacer, pinion stop, anti-drift spring, pinion washer, and spring sleeve from the gear shaft.

8. Slide the worm pinion and worm sleeve from the shaft splines, and unscrew them from each other.

9. Slip the thrust washers, cushion outer cup, rubber cushions, cushion cup, and thrust washers from the gear shaft.

Starter Drive Shaft Inspection and Repair

1. Clean all parts in a suitable solvent, except for the rubber cushion, and blow them dry. This may correct problems in which the motor operates, but the engine doesn't start, such as dirt between the pinion and pinion sleeve which prevents ring gear and pinion engagement.

2. Examine the shaft bushings for wear and replace them if necessary.

3. Inspect all gear teeth for wear and replace them if necessary. Complete gear shaft assemblies are available as well as individual parts.

4. Lightly lubricate the shaft bushings with heavy grease. Do not lubricate the worm, sleeve, or shaft since grease picks up dirt which will interfere with worm pinion operation.

5. Consult the "Starter Motor" section for starter motor servicing instructions.

Starter Drive Shaft and Housing Assembly

Reassemble in the reverse order of disassembly. Note the following:

1. Assemble the gear shaft according to the accompanying exploded view, making sure that the worm sleeve thread faces the cushion assembly.

2. Bushings are a press fit in the housing, with the collars flush on the inside.

3. Insert the shaft into the housing and secure it with the locknut.

4. Remove the motor stud nuts and lockwashers, and support the motor.

5. Loosely mount the transmission top cover to the shaft housing with the housing bolts and lockwashers, and the motor stud nuts and lockwashers.

6. Check to make sure that the armature pinion and drive gear are properly meshed, and secure all of the mounting apparatus.

7. Mount the solenoid, taking care to install the correct number of spacing washers in their proper places.

1966 AND LATER SERVI-CAR, SPORTSTER, AND GLIDE MODELS

Solenoid and Starter Drive Shaft Disassembly

1. Disconnect the battery ground wire from the negative terminal post.

2. Remove the nuts and lockwashers from the solenoid terminals and disconnect the wires.

3. Remove the drive housing end cover bolts, lockwashers, and end cover.

4. Press on the solenoid shaft pin retainer cup, and remove the shaft retainer pin and the plunger shaft spring.

5. Remove the solenoid securing bolts, lockwashers, spacer bar, and solenoid assembly.

6. Remove the solenoid boot, plunger, and plunger spring.

7. Remove the pinion shifter lever screw and lift the lever free.

8. Remove the starter drive shaft assembly.

9. Place the drive gear in a wood or copper-lined vise and remove the shaft nut. This must be done with rubber or cloth between the jaws of a vise grip, or something similar, so that nut is not marred or distorted. The nut has a left-hand thread.

10. Slip the pinion gear and shifter collar from the shaft.

11. Using snap-ring pliers, remove the shift collar retaining ring and separate the pinion gear from the shifter collar.

12. Slip the spacer from the shaft.

13. Bushings are a press fit and should be removed only if they are to be replaced.

Solenoid Starter Drive Shaft Insepction and Repair

1. Clean all parts in a suitable solvent and blow them dry.

2. Inspect all parts for excessive wear and replace as necessary. Pay special attention to all gear and pinion teeth. Complete assemblies are available as well as individual parts.

3. Check the bushings for excessive play and replace if necessary.

4. Repack the needle bearings with grease and press-fit them until they are flush with the outside of the housing (Sportster and Glide Models).

5. Replace, if possible, the collar retaining ring if it has been removed.

6. Consult the "Starter Motor" section for starter motor servicing instructions.

Solenoid and Starter Drive Shaft Assembly

Assemble in reverse order of disassembly. Note the following:

1. Lightly lubricate the bearings with heavy grease.

2. Secure the shaft nut with a thread-locking sealer.

3. Spin the assembled shaft in the bearings to check for free movement. This will indicate whether or not the shaft nut was distorted during removal.

5. Stake the starter shaft housing washer.

6. Secure the battery cable and two red wires to the solenoid "top" terminal. Consult the "Wiring Diagram" section if in doubt.

ENGINE SPECIFICATIONS

	Servi-Car	Sportster	Glide Models
VALVES			
Fit in guide (EX) (loose)	0.0035-0.0055 in.	0.0025-0.0045 in.	0.004-0.006 in.
Fit in guide (IN) (loose)	0.0035-0.0055 in.	0.0015-0.0035 in.	0.002-0.004 in.
Spring (outer): valve closed	50-60 lbs at $2\frac{3}{16}$ in.	52-62 lbs at $1\frac{9}{32}$ in.	
valve open	90-100 lbs at $1\frac{7}{8}$ in.	155-165 lbs at $1\frac{5}{16}$ in.	①
Spring (inner): valve closed	——	30-35 lbs at $1\frac{3}{32}$ in.	②
valve open	——	75-85 lbs at $\frac{3}{4}$ in.	③
Spring free length	$2\frac{37}{64}$ in.	$1\frac{1}{2}$ in. (outer) $1\frac{23}{64}$ in. (inner)	

ENGINE SPECIFICATIONS

	Servi-Car	Sportster	Glide Models
ROCKER ARM			
Fit in bushing (loose)	—	④	0.0005-0.002 in.
End clearance	—	0.0003-0.0005 in.	0.004-0.025 in.
PISTON			
Fit in cylinder (loose)	0.0015-0.002 in.	0.0025-0.003 in.	0.001-0.002 in.
Ring gap	0.010-0.020 in.	⑤	0.010-0.020 in.
Compression ring side clearance	0.0035-0.005 in.	⑥	0.004-0.005 in.
Oil ring side clearance	1/4 in overlap	0.003-0.005 in.	0.003-0.005 in.
Piston pin fit	Light hand press at 70 degrees Farenheit		
CONNECTING ROD			
Piston pin fit (loose)	0.0008-0.0012 in.	0.00008-0.0012 in.	0.0008-0.0012 in.
End play between flywheels	0.006-0.010 in.	0.006-0.010 in.	⑦
Fit on crank pin	0.005-0.0015 in.	⑨	⑧
OIL FEED PUMP PRESSURE			
Minimum	8 psi at 20 mph	6 psi at 20 mph	25 psi at 20 mph
TAPPETS			
Guide fit in crankcase (press)	0.0005-0.001 in.	0.0005-0.001 in.	0.002 in. (tight) 0.002 in. (loose)
Fit in guide (loose)	0.0005-0.001 in.	0.0005-0.001 in.	0.001-0.002 in.
Roller fit	0.001-0.0015 in.	0.005-0.001 in.	0.0005-0.001 in.
Roller end clearance	0.008-0.010 in.	0.008-0.010 in.	0.008-0.010 in.
GEAR CASE			
Intermediate gear shaft in bushing	—	0.0005-0.001 in.	—
Intermediate (idler) gear on shaft (loose)	0.001-0.0015 in.	—	0.001-0.0015 in.
Cam gear shaft in bushing	0.0005-0.001 in.	0.0005-0.002 in.	0.001-0.0015 in.
Cam gear shaft in needle bearing	—	0.0005-0.0025 in.	0.0005-0.003 in.
Cam gear shaft end play	0.001-0.005 in.	—	0.001-0.005 in.
Cam gear backlash	—	0.0002-0.005 in.	—
Timer gear end play	—	—	0.003-0.007 in.
Idler gear end play	—	—	0.003-0.020 in.
Breather gear end play	—	—	0.001-0.005 in.
Oil pump drive shaft (crankcase bushing)	—	—	0.0008-0.0012 in.
FLYWHEEL ASSEMBLY			
Gear shaft nut torque	85-125 ft lbs	⑩	⑪
Sprocket shaft nut torque	85-125 ft lbs	⑫	⑬
Crankpin nuts torque	60-100 ft lbs	150 ft lbs	⑭
Runout (flywheels) (at rim)	—	⑮	0.003 in. maximum
Runout (mainshafts)	0.002 in. maximum	⑯	0.001 in. maximum
End play in crankcase	0.009-0.013 in.	—	
SPROCKET SHAFT BEARING			
Cup fit in crankcase (press fit)	—	0.005-0.0025 in.	0.0015-0.0035 in.
Cone fit on shaft (press fit)	—	0.0002-0.0012 in.	0.0002-0.0015 in.
End play	—	0.001-0.010 in.	0.005-0.006 in.
Shaft fit in bearing (loose)	0.0005-0.001 in.	—	—
Fit in oil return bushing	0.006-0.007 in.	—	—

ENGINE SPECIFICATIONS

	Servi-Car	Sportster	Glide Model
PINION SHAFT BEARING			
Shaft fit in roller bearing (loose)	0.0005-0.0015 in.	⑰	0.0004-0.0008 in.
Shaft fit in cover bushing (loose)	0.0005-0.001 in.	⑱	0.0005-0.0012 in.

① Spring (outer)
FL Model
valve closed: 55-65 lbs at 1 13/32 in.
valve open: 110-120 lbs at 1 1/16 in.
FLH Model
valve closed: 105-115 lbs at 1 3/8 in.
valve open: 180-190 lbs at 1 in.

② Spring (inner)
FL Model
valve closed: 25-35 lbs at 1 1/4 in.
valve open: 70-80 lbs at 29/32 in.
FLH Model
valve closed: 20-30 lbs at 1 3/16 in.
valve open: 70-80 lbs at 51/64 in.

③ Spring free length
FL Model: 1 13/16 in. (outer)
1 15/32 in. (inner)
FLH Model: 1 31/32 in. (outer)
1 25/64 in. (inner)

④ Fit in bushing (loose)
1971 and earlier: 0.0005-0.002 in.
1972 and later: 0.001-0.0025 in.

⑤ Ring gap
1971 and earlier: 0.010-0.020 in.
1972 and later: 0.015-0.025 in.

⑥ Compression ring side clearance
1971 and earlier: 0.025-0.004 in.
1972 and later: 0.0035-0.005 in.

⑦ Fit on crank pin (loose)
1971 and earlier: 0.0008-0.001 in.
1972 and later: 0.0005-0.001 in.

⑧ End play between flywheel
1971 and earlier: 0.006-0.010 in.
1972 and later: 0.005-0.025 in.

⑨ Fit on crank pin
1959 and earlier: 0.001-0.0015 in.
1960-1971: 0.0006-0.001 in.
1972 and later: 0.001-0.0015 in.

⑩ Gear shaft nut torque
1971 and earlier: 100 ft lbs
1972 and later: 150 ft lbs

⑪ Gear shaft nut torque
1971 and earlier: 100 ft lbs
1972 and later: 170 ft lbs

⑫ Sprocket shaft nut torque
1971 and earlier: 100 ft lbs
1972 and later: 150 ft lbs

⑬ Sprocket shaft nut torque
1969 and earlier: 100 ft lbs
1970-1971: 170 ft lbs
1972 and later: 400 ft lbs

⑭ Crank pin nuts torque
1971 and earlier: 175 ft lbs
1972 and later: 200 ft lbs

⑮ Runout (flywheel at rim)
1971 and earlier: 0.002 in. maximum
1972 and later: 0.003 in. maximum

⑯ Runout (mainshafts)
1971 and earlier: 0.002 in. maximum
1972 and later: 0.001 in. maximum

⑰ Shaft fit in roller bearing (loose)
1971 and earlier: 0.0008-0.001 in.
1972 and later: 0.005-0.0015 in.

⑱ Shaft fit in cover bushing (loose)
1971 and earlier: 0.0005-0.0012 in.
1972 and later: 0.0005-0.0015 in.

LUBRICATION SYSTEMS

OIL PUMP

Sportster and Glide models have both feed-type and scavenger gear-type pumps incorporated in one pump body, while Servi-Cars have two separate pumps.

Oil pumps are long-life units which seldom require repair. Therefore, one should check all related possibilities which might contribute to a "light-on" or "no-pressure" situation before disassembling the pump.

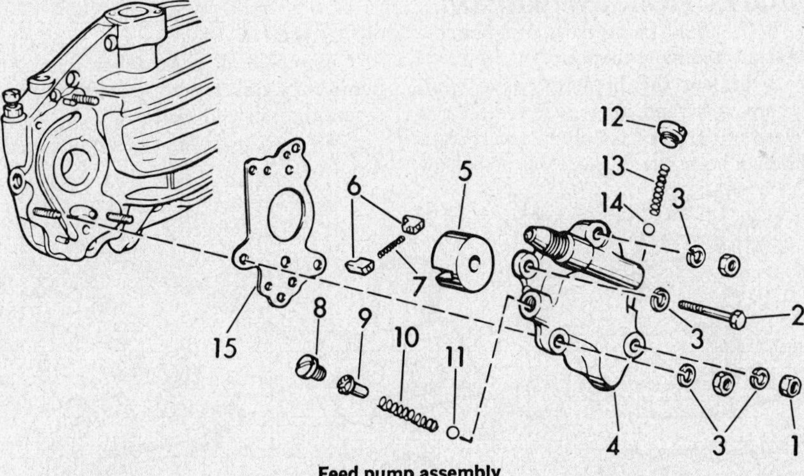

Feed pump assembly

1. Oil pump mounting stud nut (3)
2. Oil pump mounting stud bolt (2)
3. Lock washer (4)
4. Oil feed pump body
5. Vane holder
6. Pump vane (2)
7. Vane spring
8. By-pass valve cover screw
9. By-pass valve adjusting screw
10. By-pass valve spring
11. By-pass valve ball
12. Check valve spring cover screw
13. Check valve spring
14. Check valve ball
15. Oil feed pump gasket

Servi-Car

FEED PUMP DISASSEMBLY

1. Disconnect the oil feed line from the pump body.
2. Remove the oil pump mounting stud nuts, stud bolts, and lockwashers.
3. Remove the pump from the gearcase cover studs.
4. Hold the pump vanes and the vane springs in place, in the vane holder, and slip the assembly out of the pump.
5. Remove the by-pass valve cover screw, adjusting screw, spring, and ball.
6. Remove the check valve cover screw, spring, and ball.
7. Remove the feed pump gasket.

INSPECTION AND REPAIR

1. Clean all parts, other than the gasket, in a suitable solvent and blow them dry.
2. Replace the vane springs if their free-length is less than 1/32 in., the by-pass spring if less than 2 1/16 in., and the check valve spring if less than 1 5/16 in.
3. Replace all worn, rusted, or damaged parts.
4. Inspect the ball valve seats for a clean and smooth condition, and replace the pump body if necessary.
5. Replace the valve balls if they are ringed or are not perfectly smooth. The balls are interchangeable.

ASSEMBLY

1. Assemble in the reverse order of disassembly.

2. All of the components must be completely free of dirt.

3. Set the by-pass valve adjusting screw so that the top of the head is exactly ⅜ in. below the surface of the pump body.

4. Install a new pump gasket.

SCAVENGER PUMP AND BREATHER VALVE

DISASSEMBLY

1. Disconnect the oil return and rear chain oiler lines from the pump body.

2. Remove the pump mounting nuts and lockwashers.

3. Remove the pump and breather assemblies, pump body gasket, and the pump screen from the crankcase mounting studs.

4. Remove the pump cover screws, washers, pump cover, and the cover gasket.

5. Remove the split retaining washer, idler gear and shaft, pump gear, and the gear key.

6. Remove the breather valve from the pump body.

7. Remove the chain oiler adjusting screw, nut, and washer.

INSPECTION AND REPAIR

1. Clean all metal parts in a suitable solvent and blow them dry.

2. Inspect the breather valve gear, pump gear, and idler gear teeth for a worn or damaged condition and replace them if necessary. If there was no oil flow from the return line in the tank and if exhaust smoke was excessive, give special attention to the condition of the pump drive-gear key.

3. Inspect all parts for a worn or damaged condition and replace as necessary.

4. Replace both gaskets.

ASSEMBLY

1. Assemble all parts other than the pump body gasket, pump screen, and the mounting nuts and washers.

2. All parts must be absolutely free of dirt.

3. The breather valve must be a free fit in the pump body.

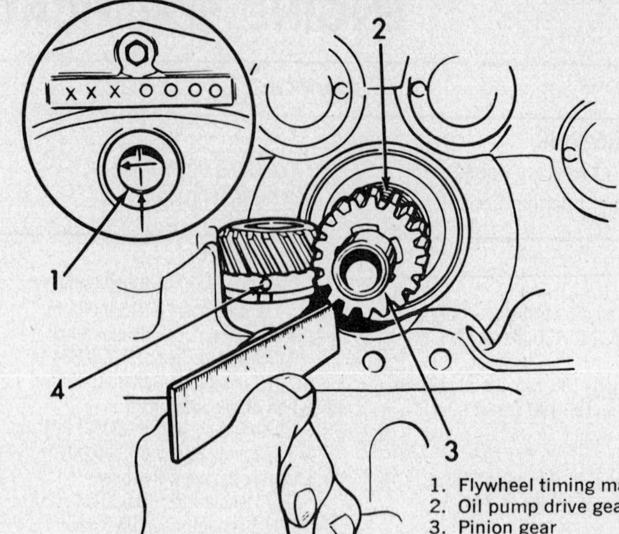

Timing the crankcase breather

TIMING CRANKCASE BREATHER

1. Remove the gearcase cover as described in "Gearcase Disassembly."

2. Rotate the engine until the flywheel timing mark is aligned in the crankcase view port as described in "Ignition Timing."

3. Position the breather gear so the valve hole aligns with the pump body hole.

4. Shift the breather gear two teeth to the right.

5. Place the breather screen and pump gasket in position.

6. Install the pump carefully on the mounting studs and the breather gear will then assume the correct timing position.

7. Check to be sure that the breather valve hole and the pump body hole are aligned. The flywheel timing mark must still be correctly aligned.

8. Assemble and sécure the gearcase cover and pump.

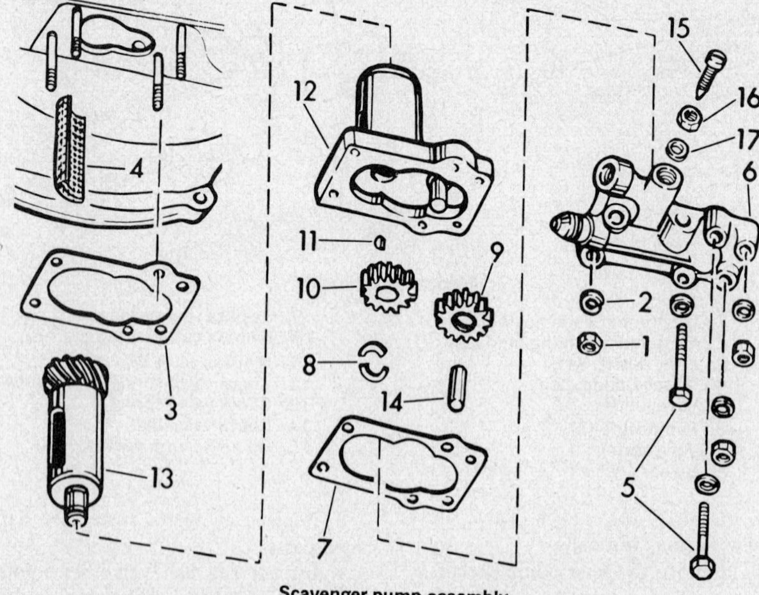

Scavenger pump assembly

1. Scavenger pump mounting nut (4)
2. Lock washer (6)
3. Oil scavenger pump gasket (2)
4. Scavenger pump screen
5. Pump cover screw (2)
6. Pump cover
7. Oil scavenger pump gasket (see item 3)
8. Split retaining washer
9. Pump idler gear
10. Pump gear
11. Pump gear key
12. Scavenger pump body
13. Breather valve
14. Idler gear shaft
15. Chain oiler adjusting screw
16. Oiler adjusting nut
17. Washer

Sportster

OIL PUMP CHECK VALVE

DISASSEMBLY

1. Clean the pump surface and its surrounding area thoroughly with a suitable solvent and blow it dry.

2. Disconnect the oil pressure switch wire and remove the switch, oil pump nipple, check valve spring, and ball valve.

INSPECTION AND REPAIR

1. Clean all parts in a suitable solvent and blow them dry. Blow out the nipple oil passage and the spring guide.

2. Inspect the nipple and spring for free-motion, wear, and damage, and replace if necessary. Spring free-length should be 1 15/64 in.

3. Inspect the nipple threads and replace them if they are worn or damaged.

4. Replace the valve balls if they are ringed or are not perfectly smooth.

5. Inspect the ball valve seat for a clean and smooth condition. Slight pitting or striation marks can sometimes be removed by gently tapping with a suitable drift. Replace the pump body if such defects can not be corrected.

ASSEMBLY

1. Assemble in the reverse order of disassembly.

2. All of the parts must be absolutely clean.

3. Lightly oil all of the moving parts.

4. Check for free ball action and seating.

OIL PUMP

DISASSEMBLY

1. Remove the engine from the frame as described in "Engine Removal."

2. Clean the pump surface and its surrounding areas thoroughly with a suitable solvent and blow it dry.

3. Remove the crankcase stud nuts and the assembled pump. Tap with a hammer on a piece of brass or wood, held on the breather sleeve, to loosen it if necessary.

4. Disassemble the check valve as described in "Oil Pump Check Valve Disassembly."

5. Remove the oil pump body plate and the body plate gasket.

6. Remove the retaining rings with snap-ring pliers (or split-ring if applicable) and slip the scavenger gears free.

7. Remove the breather valve key.

8. Remove the oil pump cover and breather valve assembly.

9. Remove the oil pump and the idler gears.

10. Pry the oil pump seal free.

11. Punch-drive the lockpin free from the oil-pump breather valve gear. Remove the gear from the pump cover only if it is necessary.

12. Remove the breather valve screen.

13. Press the idler gear shaft free only if replacement is necessary.

INSPECTION AND REPAIR

1. Clean all of the parts in a suitable solvent and blow them dry. Blow all passages free.

2. Replace all gaskets, the retaining ring, lockpin, and the oil seal. Homemade gaskets must be avoided since the proper thickness and proper passage holes are essential.

3. Replace all worn or damaged parts.

4. Inspect the pump body for wear or damage.

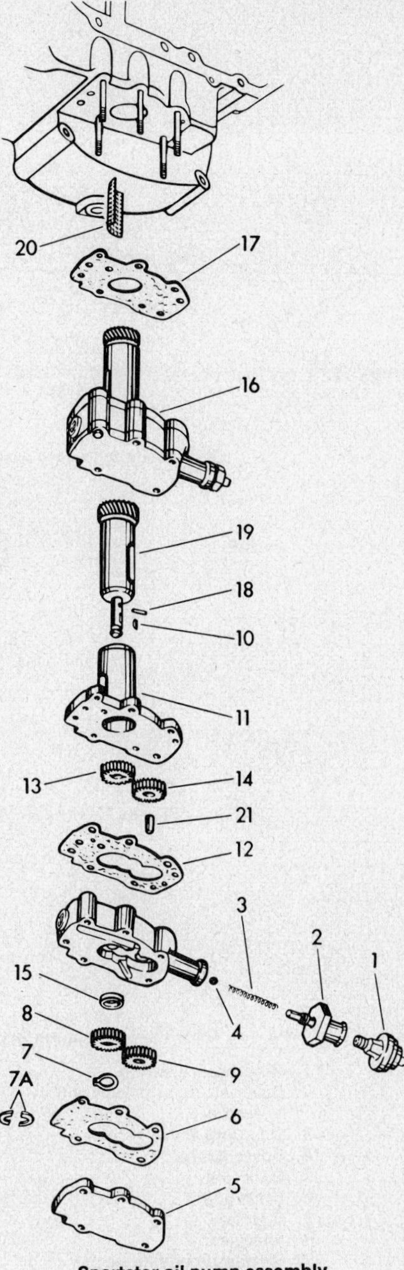

Sportster oil pump assembly

1. Oil pressure switch
2. Oil pump nipple
3. Check valve spring
4. Ball valve
5. Body plate
6. Body plate gasket
7. Retaining ring

7A. Retainer (2) (Half ring)

8. Scavenger pump gear
9. Scavenger pump idler gear
10. Breather valve key
11. Oil pump cover
12. Body cover gasket
13. Pump gear
14. Pump idler gear
15. Oil pump seal
16. Oil pump body
17. Body gasket
18. Drive lock pin
19. Breather valve gear and shaft
20. Crankcase breather valve screen
21. Idler gear shaft

5. Inspect all of the gears for worn or damaged teeth and replace them as necessary.

6. Replace the breather valve key if it is worn or loose.

7. Inspect the breater valve and pump for wear and damage.

8. Check that the valve is a free fit.

ASSEMBLY

1. Assemble in the reverse order of disassembly.

2. Lightly oil all of the moving parts.

3. Assemble the check valve as described in "Oil Pump Check Valve Assembly."

4. Place the breather valve screen in position and secure it with a daub of grease.

5. Assemble the breather valve in the oil pump cover and secure it with a lockpin.

6. Press a new scavenger-pump idler gear shaft into the pump body if the old one has been removed.

7. Assemble the pump gears to the pump body.

8. Secure the body gasket using a non-hardening sealer. The gasket must be carefully aligned to permit free oil passage.

9. Assemble the assembled breather valve and cover to the pump body.

10. Place a thin strip of acetate tape over the groove in the breather valve shaft. Install a new oil seal flush into the pump body counterbore with the seal's lip facing the body. Remove the tape.

11. Install the breather valve key and scavenger pump gears, and secure them with a retaining ring (or retainer, whichever is applicable).

12. Install a new body plate gasket using a non-hardening sealer. The gasket may be flattened if necessary by soaking it in water before sealing it.

13. Slide the oil pump and the body plate onto the crankcase studs, and evenly secure the studs.

14. Check for free-motion of the gears. If the gears bind, the pump may be slightly out of alignment. Remedy this by loosening the stud nuts and gently tapping the pump with a soft mallet until the correct alighment is attained.

15. Time the breather valve as described in the Servi-Car "Timing Crankcase Breather" section.

16. Assemble the engine to the frame as described in "Engine Removal and Replacement."

Glide models

OIL PUMP

DISASSEMBLY (With Engine In Frame)

1. Disconnect the oil switch, feed, and scavenger lines from the pump body.

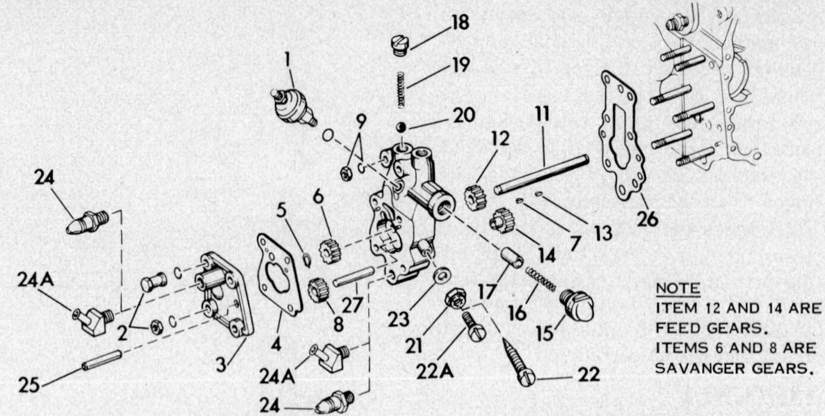

NOTE
ITEM 12 AND 14 ARE
FEED GEARS.
ITEMS 6 AND 8 ARE
SAVANGER GEARS.

Glide model oil pump assembly—1967 and earlier models

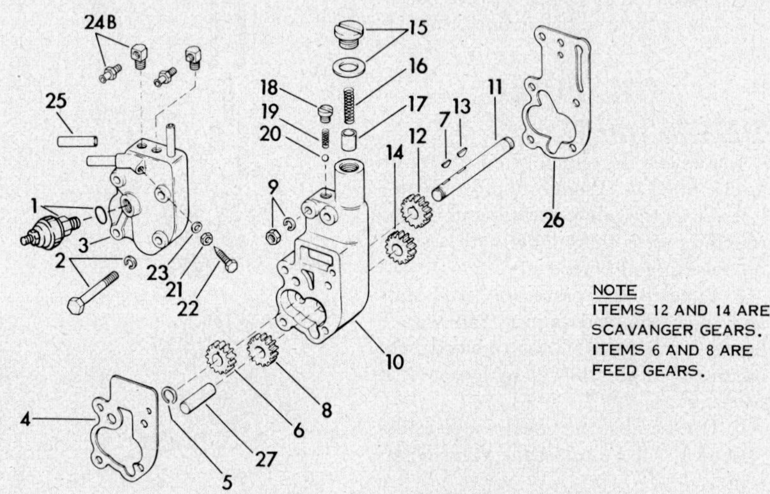

Glide model oil pump assembly—1968 and later models

1. Oil pressure switch
2. Cover stud nut or bolt and washer
3. Oil pump cover
4. Cover gasket
5. Lock ring
6. Drive gear
7. Gear key
8. Idler gear
9. Oil pump body mounting stud nuts and washers (2)
10. Oil pump body
11. Oil pump gear drive shaft
12. Drive gear
13. Gear key
14. Idler gear
15. By-pass valve plug
16. By-pass valve spring
17. Check valve spring cover
18. Check valve spring cover screw
19. Check valve spring
20. Check valve ball
21. Chain oiler adjusting screw
22. Chain oiler adjusting screw
22A. Chain oiler screw (1965-67)
23. Chain oiler adj. screw washer
24. Oil line nipple (2) (1964 and earlier)
24A. Oil line nipple (2) (1965)
24B. Oil line nipple (2) (1968)
25. Chain oiler pipe
26. Body gasket
27. Idler gear shaft

Figure following name of part indicates quantity necessary for one complete assembly

2. Remove the cover stud nuts or bolts and their washers.
3. Slip the oil pump cover and the cover gasket from the gearcase studs.
4. Remove the driveshaft snap-ring with snap-ring pliers, and then remove the drive gear, gear key, and idler gear.
5. Remove the stud nuts which mount the oil pump body and then remove the body.
6. Remove the oil pump gear driveshaft.
7. Remove the scavenger (1968 and later) or the feed (1967 and earlier) drivegear, gear key, and the scavenger idler gear and key.
8. Remove the bypass valve plug, spring, and spring sleeve.
9. Remove the check valve cover screw, spring, and ball valve.
10. Loosen the chain oiler adjusting screw locknut (if applicable) and gently seat the adjusting screw while counting the number of turns necessary to seat it. Remove the adjusting screw and washer. The screw must be replaced in the same position during assembly.
11. Remove the chain oiler screw on 1965–67 models.
12. Remove the oil pump nipples.
13. Do not mix any gears or keys.

DISASSEMBLY (With Engine Removed From Frame)

1. Remove the engine from the frame as described in "Engine Removal and Replacement."
2. Remove the gearcase cover securing screws, cover, and cover gasket.
3. Remove the left-hand threaded pinion gear nut from the pinion shaft using the Gear Shaft Nut Socket Wrench (H-D part no. 94555–55); vise grips may be substituted.
4. Remove the pinion gear with Pinion Gear Puller (H-D part no. 96830–51) or a suitable, standard gear puller.
5. Remove the pinion gear key, spring, spacing collar, and the oil pump pinion shaft gear.
6. Remove the pump drive-gear shaft spring-ring, drive gear, and shaft key.
7. Remove the pump body nuts and bolts, then slip the assembled pump and pump gear driveshaft from the gearcase.
8. Disassemble the pump as described in the previous section.

INSPECTION AND REPAIR

1. Clean all of the metal parts in a suitable solvent and blow them dry.
2. Blow all of the passages clear.
3. Inspect the valves and seats for pitting and wear, and replace the pump if its seats are damaged.
4. Inspect the keys and key seats for damage or excessive clearances—especially the pump gear shaft key if oil does not return to the tank, or the driveshaft key if oil is not being circulated.
5. Inspect all gears for wear or damage, and replace them if necessary.

ASSEMBLY

1. Assemble in the reverse of disassembly.
2. All the gears and keys must be replaced in their proper locations.
3. Replace gaskets and lockrings. Only factory approved gaskets should be used.
4. Secure the bolts and nuts evenly to no more than 4–5 ft lbs torque or damage to the gasket and pump will result.
5. If leaks persist, replace the gaskets again. A small amount of non-hardening sealer may be used if great care is taken not to clog any passages.
6. Replace the oil hose clamps and squeeze them tight with Hose Clamp Tool (H-D part no. 97087–65). Worm-type automotive hose clamps may be used and will require no special tools.
7. See "Gearcase Timing Gears" for breather information.

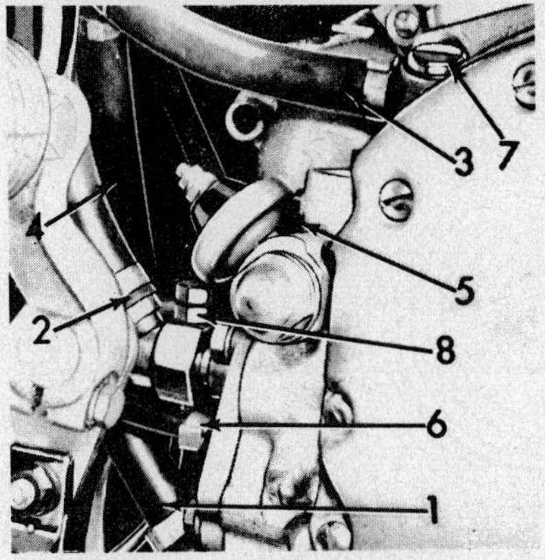

Oil lines—1965-67 models

1. Oil supply line from tank
2. Oil return line to tank
3. Vent line to oil tank
4. Vent line to chain housing
5. Return line from chain housing
6. Front chain oiler line to chain housing
7. Overhead and tappet oil screen plug
8. Rear chain oiler adjusting screw

Oil lines—1968 and later models

1. Oil supply line from tank
2. Oil return line to tank
3. Vent line to oil tank
4. Vent line to chain housing
5. Return line from chain housing
6. Front chain oiler line to chain housing
7. Overhead and tappet oil screen plug
8. Rear chain oiler adjusting screw

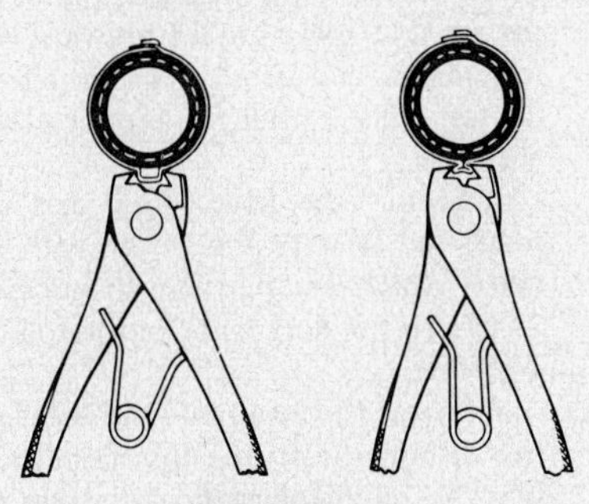

Hose clamps

OIL PUMP MINIMUM PRESSURE RATINGS

Servi-Car	8 psi at 20 mph
Sportster	6 psi at 20 mph
Glide models	25 psi at 20 mph
	35 psi at 30 mph

FUEL SYSTEMS

CARBURETOR

Linkert Model M

REMOVAL

1. Remove the air cleaner cover, element, and back plate.
2. Close the petcock and disconnect the fuel line and strainer at the carburetor.
3. Disconnect the throttle cable.
4. Remove the carburetor support from the top center crankcase bolt.
5. Remove the choke lever stud nut and washer. Twist the choke lever off the rod and remove the rod.
6. Remove the four securing bolts and pull the carburetor out—to the right.

DISASSEMBLY

1. Remove the bowl locknut, gasket, main nozzle retainer spring, main nozzle, bowl, and bowl cover gasket.
2. Remove the float seat valve and gasket.
3. Remove the float lever pin, slip float, float lever, and float valve.
4. Loosen, but do not remove, the throttle-stop lock screw and slip the throttle lever off the throttle shaft with the throttle lever arm and the throttle shaft spring.
5. Remove the throttle shaft screws, slip the throttle disc out of the slot in the throttle shaft, and pull out the throttle shaft.
6. Remove the low- and high-speed needle valves.
7. Remove the needle valve lever screw, needle valve lever, lever spring, and the lever spring collar.
8. Remove the air intake shaft nut and washer, air intake shaft stop, friction ball, and friction spring.
9. Remove the air intake disc screws and the air intake disc, and then pull out the air intake shaft.
10. Remove the idle hole body plug, two idle passage plug screws, and the carburetor fixed jet.

INSPECTION AND REPAIR

1. Clean all of the parts, other than the gaskets and float, in a carbon and gum-dissolving solution such as Gunk Hydro-Seal (which is recommended by the factory). Rinse thoroughly and blow them dry.
2. Clear all of the carburetor barrel passages with compressed air. Do not scrape the carbon deposits with any steel instrument.
3. Check the throttle shaft for play and replace the throttle shaft bushings if excessive play is present. Drift the bushings out and press in replacements, then ream with a 0.250 in. drill.
4. Examine the venturi and replace it if it is pitted or extremely loose.
5. Check the float valve and float valve seal as indicated below:
   a. Assemble, in reverse order the labled parts 12–7 in the illustration, to the bowl.
   b. Suck on the bottom of the float valve seat, with the bowl inverted, so the float valve closes. Replace the valve

CROSS SECTION OF CARBURETOR BOWL SHOWING FLOAT MECHANISM AND FLOAT SETTING

TOP VIEW OF CARBURETOR BOWL SHOWING FLOAT MECHANISM AND OFFSET OF FLOAT

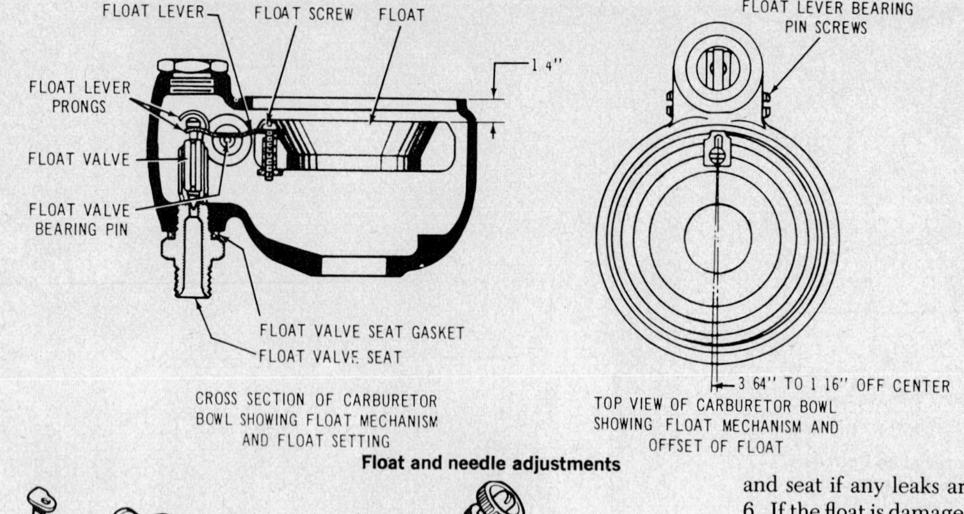

Float and needle adjustments

1. Bowl lock nut
2. Lock nut gasket
3. Main nozzle retainer spring
4. Main nozzle
5. Bowl
6. Bowl cover gasket
7. Float valve seat
8. Float valve seat gasket
9. Float lever pin
10. Float
11. Float lever
12. Float valve
13. Throttle stop lock screw
14. Throttle lever
15. Throttle lever arm
16. Throttle shaft spring
17. Throttle shaft screw (2)
18. Throttle disc
19. Throttle shaft
20. Low speed needle valve
21. High speed needle valve
22. Needle valve lever screw
23. Needle valve lever
24. Needle valve lever spring
25. Lever spring collar
26. Air intake shaft nut and washer
27. Air intake shaft stop
28. Friction ball
29. Friction spring
30. Air intake disc screw (2)
31. Air intake disc
32. Air intake shaft
33. Idle hole body plug
34. Idle passage plug screw (3)
35. Fixed jet
36. Throttle shaft bushing (2)
37. Venturi (1 5/16 in.)

Model M carburetor assembly

Figure following name of part indicates quantity necessary for one complete assembly.

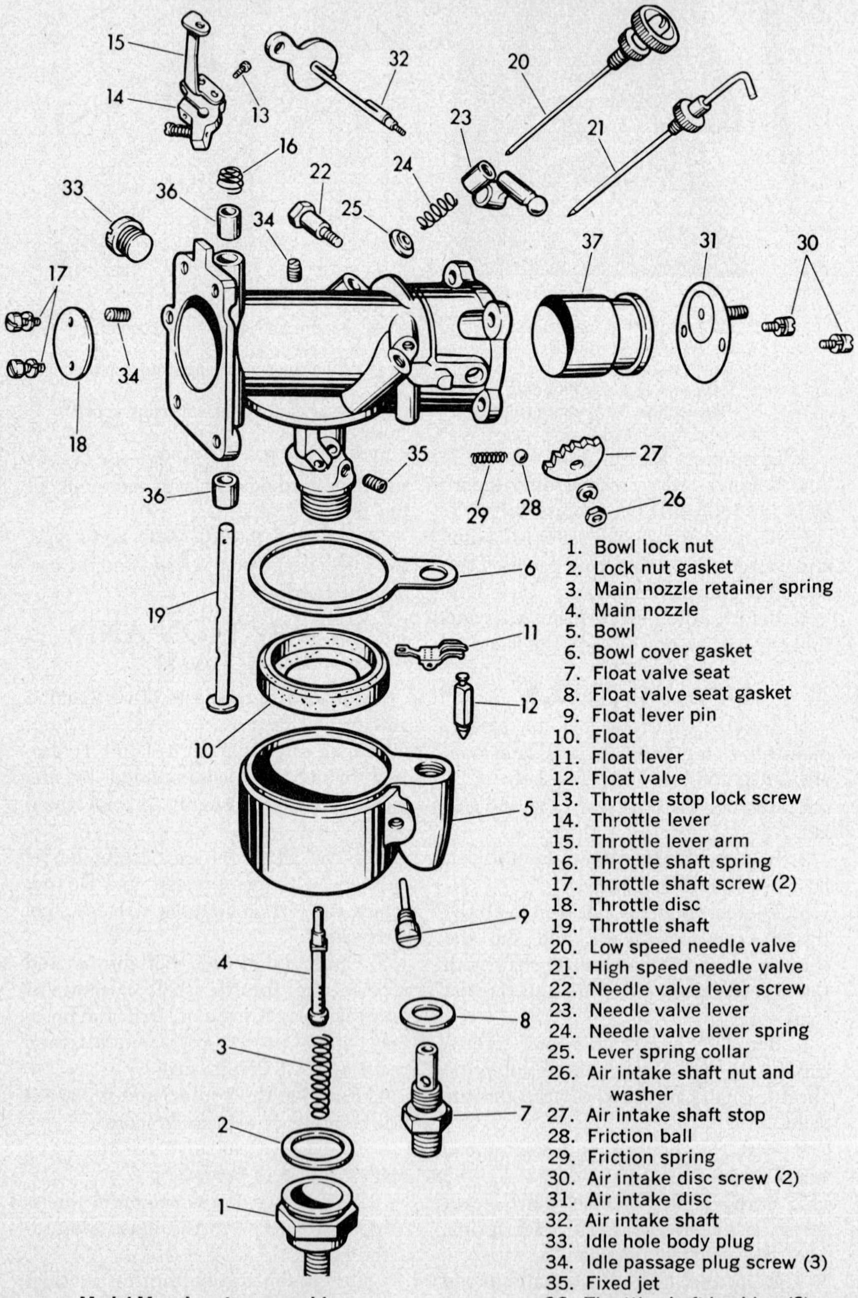

and seat if any leaks are discovered.

6. If the float is damaged or gas-logged, replace it in the following manner:

a. Remove the float from the float lever by cutting the cement seal.

b. Remove the float screw and assemble a new float to the lever without securing the screw.

c. Holding the bowl in its position when mounted (with gasoline inlet on the far side), slide the float toward you to its stop, and about 1/16 in. left of center. This is vital for proper clearance.

d. Secure the float screw and cement the float to the screw with an epoxy which is impervious to gasoline.

7. Check the float lever in the following manner:

a. Invert the float bowl and measure the distance from the lip of the float bowl to the top of the float directly opposite the float lever. This should measure ¼ in.

b. If an adjustment is necessary, remove the float and lever, and bend the lever as required. Do not attempt to bend the lever while it is still in the bowl.

c. Check the fit of the float valve head in the float lever to ensure a free fit with about 0.003 in. clearance. Do this by holding the valve against its seat with a small screwdriver, so that float movement isn't impeded, and then by moving the float up and down to observe play between the valve head and the float lever.

8. If the throttle disc is to be replaced, use only a disc that has the same identification number on its face.

ASSEMBLY

1. Assemble in the reverse order of disassembly.

2. Make sure that the venturi is installed with the choke end (small end) facing out.

3. Install the throttle shaft—which comes from the carburetor bottom—with the notches facing left, as seen in the illustration.

4. Align the throttle shaft screw holes with the throttle disc by manipulating the throttle and insert the throttle shaft screws without securing them.

5. Shift the disc until it seats evenly in the throttle throat and tighten the screws. If its movement isn't free, back off the screws and reposition the disc.

6. With both the throttle disc and lever in a wide-open position, secure the the throttle-stop lock screw.

7. The lever and shaft should operate with a slight drag. Looseness can be adjusted for by loosening the stop lock screw and compressing the shaft parts by hand while securing the screw.

8. Adjust the carburetor.

Model DC

REMOVAL

1. Remove the air cleaner cover, element, and back plate.

2. Disconnect the fuel line at the carburetor.

3. Remove the carburetor bracket (if applicable).

4. Remove the two carburetor securing bolts and pull the carburetor out and off.

DISASSEMBLY

1. Remove the three throttle body screws, lockwashers, body gasket, idle hole body plug, low-speed needle valve, washer, and the needle valve spring from the throttle body.

2. Free the throttle disc from the shaft by removing the throttle shaft screws and lockwashers.

3. Remove the stop screw and spring from the throttle lever, then remove the throttle lever clamping screw from the lever. Remove the spring, washer, and shaft from the throttle body.

4. Remove the carburetor bowl, by tapping it gently, after having removed the four bowl attaching screws.

5. Carefully separate the bowl gasket from the bowl.

6. Free the float by removing the float rod and unscrewing the flat speed nut.

7. Lift the float valve and seat assembly free.

8.Remove the float lever and bracket assembly by removing the float lever screw, lockwasher, and float washer.

9. Remove the support bracket (if applicable), lockwasher, and nut.

10. Removing the bowl nut and gasket reveals the idle tube which should remain in the body. Do not attempt to remove it from the bowl nut, but, if it remains in the body after the bowl nut is removed, it must be removed by tugging gently at the plug end.

11. Remove the nozzle using a screwdriver with a clean, flat head to ensure that no damage is done to the jet orifice.

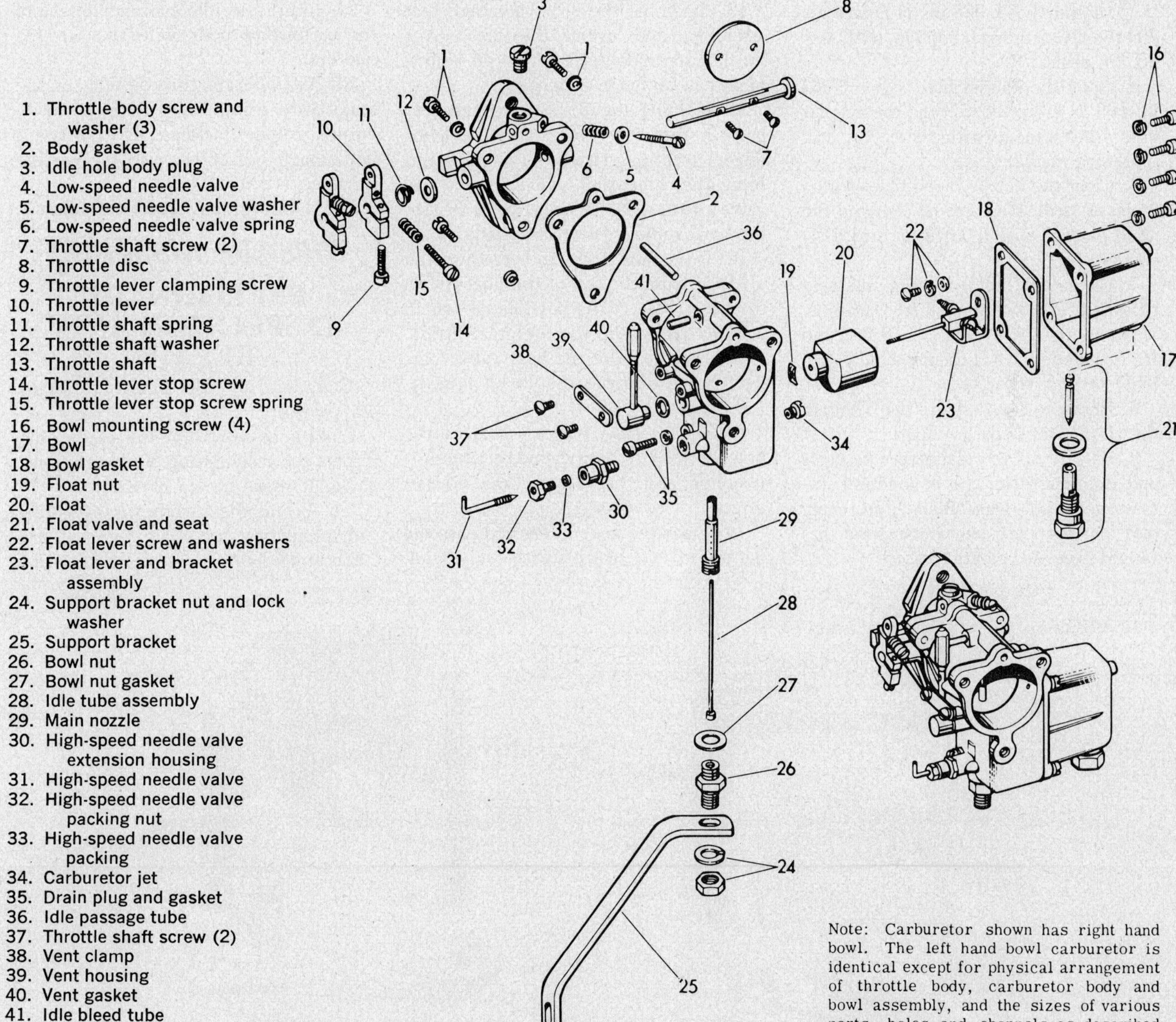

Note: Carburetor shown has right hand bowl. The left hand bowl carburetor is identical except for physical arrangement of throttle body, carburetor body and bowl assembly, and the sizes of various ports, holes and channels as described in text.

Figure following name of part indicates quantity necessary for one complete assembly.

Model DC carburetor assembly

12. Free the high-speed needle valve, packing nut, and packing by removing the high-speed needle valve extension housing.

13. Remove the jet which is located directly across from the high-speed needle valve hole.

14. Free the idle passage tube by removing the drain plug and gasket.

15. Remove the vent housing, gasket, and idle bleed tube by removing the clamp and securing screws.

INSPECTION AND REPAIR

1. See model M section on inspection and repair.

2. Replace the throttle shaft if there is more than 0.002 in. play noticeable at the bearing.

3. Clean out the idle port holes in the throttle body with a drill, if necessary, taking care not to increase the hole size. The proper drill size for models DC–1, IL, 1M, and 10 is 0.028 in. (H-D size no. 70); the DC–2 uses a 0.0465 in. (H-D size no. 56) drill.

4. Open the idle jet hole with a 0.043 in. drill (H-D size no. 57) and the angular hole which it meets with a 0.0635 in. drill (H-D size no. 52).

6. Clear the nozzle bleed holes with a 0.055 in. drill (H-D size no. 54) and the main passage with a 0.073 in. drill (H-D size no. 17).

7. Clean the high-speed needle seat holes with a 0.052 in. drill (H-D size no. 55) for models DC–1, 1L, 1M, 10, 6, 7, and 12. For model DC–2, use a 0.028 in. drill (H-D size no. 70).

8. Check to see that the two vents in the carburetor body are open.

9. Be sure not to enlarge any passages and examine all of the connecting surfaces for possible leaks. Replace any leaky part or any part on which wear has caused excessive clearances.

ASSEMBLY

1. Assemble the vent housing assembly, gasket, idle bleed tube, clamp, and screw in the carburetor body.

2. Slip the tubes into their holes and tap the housing into place.

3. Secure the clamp just tight enough so that the outer ends will touch the body bosses.

4. Assemble the drain plug, gasket, and high-speed jet on the carburetor body.

5. Back out the needle valve before installing this assembly in the main body so that the point will not enter the valve hole when the two units are secured together.

6. Position the needle valve so it doesn't jam into the seat hole and cause damage.

7. Assemble the nozzle.

8. Locate the idle tube in the body hole and press it in until about 1/32 in. extends out from the nozzle hole.

9. Install the bowl nut and gasket; this should hold the idle tube in place.

10. Assemble the float valve and seat assembly, and install the float lever bracket screw loosely so that an adjustment can be made if necessary.

11. Holding the float valve and seat halfway into the bowl, align the lever fingers with the groove in the valve and bring them together while turning the valve into its seat. This must be done with the bowl removed from the body.

12. Invert the bowl and measure the distance from the top of the float rod to the outer edge of the bowl flange which is directly opposite the fuel inlet fitting. At the point where the float valve seats lightly, the distance should be 1 in. $\pm$ 1/64 in.

13. Adust the slotted float lever bracket until the proper measurement is obtained and then secure the bracket screw.

14. Place the float on the rod with the flat side up and secure it with a speed nut.

15. Mount the bowl to the carburetor main body, taking care not to crush the gasket.

16. Insert the throttle shaft so that the screw seats align with the screw holes on the throttle disc and then loosely mount the throttle disc, with the identification number facing out.

17. Rotate the disc and note whether it binds anywhere. When a position is obtained where movement is free, secure the disc and recheck its movement.

18. Install the throttle lever stop screw and spring.

19. Install the throttle lever, throttle shaft spring, and washer, and position them so that slight end-play exists when the lever is clamped tightly. Place the disc and lever in an open position and secure the throttle lever clamping screw.

20. Install the low-speed needle jet, washer, and spring, taking care not to bevel the seat with excessive pressure.

21. Secure the idle hole body plug.

22. Insert the idle passage tube into the carburetor body with the beveled end out.

23. Assemble the throttle body on the main body, using a new body gasket to ensure proper thickness. Do not use a homemade gasket because the correct thickness is critical.

24. Mount the carburetor and adjust it.

Tillotson Model HD

PRELIMINARY INSPECTION AND REPAIR

(Complete all tests before replacing any parts.)

1. Without removing the carburetor, inspect the accelerating pump as follows:
   a. Remove the air clearner.
   b. Prime the carburetor by gently manipulating the diaphragm with a toothpick which can be inserted

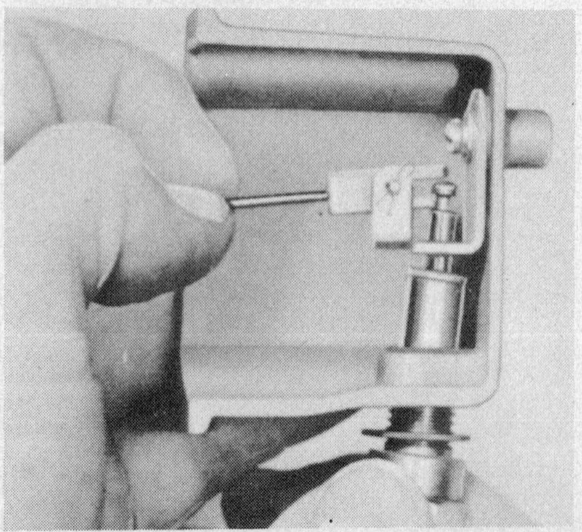

Engaging the float lever in the valve stem groove

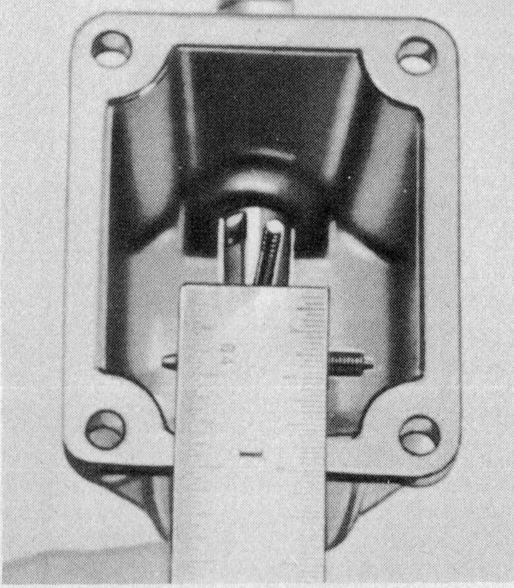

Checking the float setting

through the small hole in the bottom of the plastic pump cover.

c. Twist the throttle several times, slowly and then rapidly, with the petcock in the open position. Observe the action of the pump and note whether a constant jet of fuel is delivered with each stroke. Replace the diaphragm valves and/or pump plunger if the desired result is not obtained.

2. Clean the high, intermediate, and low-speed passages in the following manner:

a. Remove the high-speed screw plug from the rear of the carburetor and gently seat the intermediate needle.

b. Apply a maximum of 90 lbs of air pressure to the high-speed channel.

c. Open the intermediate and idle needles by three or four turns and apply air pressure again.

d. Adjust the carburetor and determine whether or not the performance has been enhanced.

3. Test the inlet needle and seat for air leaks in the following manner:

a. Secure all plastic cover screws firmly.

b. Use Bulb Tester (H-D part no. 94750–68) to pressure-check the needle and seat. With a tester installed in the carburetor inlet fitting and with the vent fitting plugged with a finger, apply 1–1 ½ lbs of pressure. A moist needle should hold about 3–5 lbs and is a better indicator than a dry one.

c. If a tester is not been applied, the tip will appear slightly flattened and the seat will be beveled.

4. Remove the carburetor and inspect the intermediate adjustment needle and spring for binding which will prevent it from realizing its true seat.

a. Shorten each end of the spring with a grinder and test it for proper seating by applying blue dye to the end of the needle taper. Screw the taper lightly down into its seat and check to see if the blue has been disturbed.

5. Test the main nozzle ball check valve for leakage in the following manner:

a. Seal one end of the main jet port in the venturi with your finger and insert an appropriate size rubber tube into the opposite end of the venturi. Apply alternate vacuum and pressure. Pressure should cause the ball to seat and vacuum pressure should release the ball from the nozzle assembly.

b. Replace the main nozzle check valve assembly if any leakage is present.

c. Remove the welch plug by punghing it off center with an appropriate punch. Drift it into the venturi gently, using a soft mallet and an appropriate drift.

d. Replace the new check valve using a drift. Drift (H-D tool no. 96962–68) is available for these operations.

6. Examine the idle needle and seat for damage.

Pressure checking the inlet needle and seat for leakage

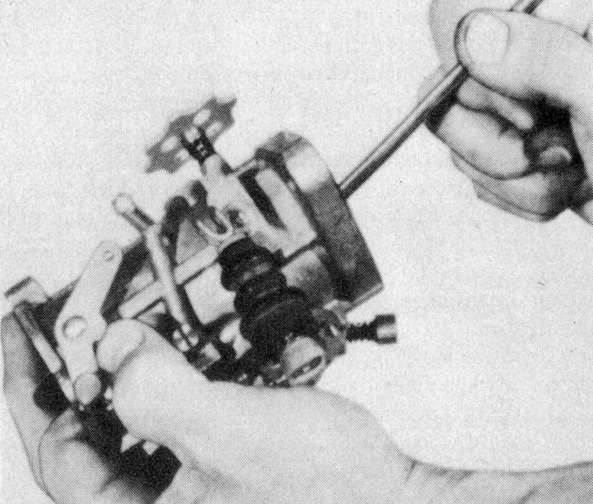

Testing the main nozzle ball check valve for leakage

Removing the welch plug

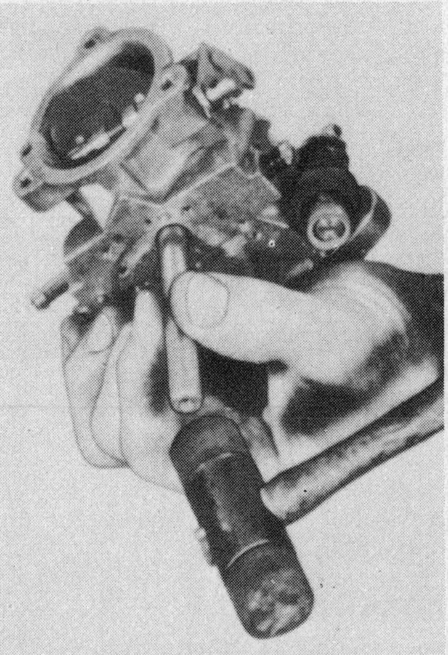

Removing the main nozzle

Installing the main nozzle

Testing the economizer check valve for leakage

7. Examing the choke relief disc (upper half of the choke shutter) for damage.

8. Remove the diaphragm cover and examine the accelerator pump leather and spring for wear or damage.

9. On late 1968 models, examine the accelerator-pump outlet, check-valve ball for freedom of movement.

10. Inspect the gasket and diaphragm for damage and replace them if their surfaces are not uniform. The gasket should adhere to the body.

11. Check the diaphragm washer and the diaphragm for excessive movement, and replace if drag is not present.

12. Check the inlet needle linkage with a bulb tester as described in step 3b. The valve on the tester should be closed and pressure should be asserted on the inlet port. Open and close the bulb valve about ten times while applying pressure to be sure that it isn't sticking closed.

13. The inlet lever should lie flush with the floor of the carburetor and it must be replaced if it doesn't. If it is not equipped with a shackled needle, substitute with kit no. 27588–66 and torque the seat to 45 in. lbs.

14. Check the economizer ball for proper operation in the following manner:

a. Using a rubber tube of the appropriate size, seal off the economizer welch plug hole and apply mouth pressure both in and out. If the ball does not release each time it is tested, replace it.

b. Inspect the welch plugs by attempting to move them in the body. Since they are a press-fit, they should not move. Replace any leaky or loose plug; never reuse a welch that has already been removed.

c. If the leak is due to a damaged seat, replace the plug and apply a small amount of seal-all or epoxy around the edges of the seat.

DISASSEMBLY

1. Remove the idle and intermediate fuel adjusters.

2. Remove the throttle butterfly mounting screws and the throttle butterfly. Note the position of the butterfly as an aid in reassembly.

3. The throttle shaft assembly may be slipped out of the body when the retaining screw is removed.

4. Remove the throttle shaft spring, washers, dust seals, accelerating pump assembly, diaphragm cover plug screw, metering diaphragm, and metering diaphragm gasket. Note that the gasket is mounted next to the body.

5. Remove the inlet control lever screw, inlet control lever pin, inlet control lever, and lever control tension spring.

6. Remove the inlet needle, seat, and needle gasket, taking note of proper positioning for replacement.

7. Remove the main jet plug screw, jet, and gasket.

8. Remove the main jet welch plug by drilling a shallow hole off-center with a ⅛ in. drill and then prying it free with a small punch. If you go too deep, the jet will probably be damaged.

9. Remove the remaining three welch plugs in the same manner and the economizer ball will then come free.

10. Remove the choke butterfly securing screws and the lower half of the choke butterfly.

11. Remove the choke shaft and then the upper half of the butterfly, the spring, choke friction ball, and the friction ball spring will all come free.

12. Slide the choke shaft dust seal off the shaft.

INSPECTION AND REPAIR PRIOR TO REASSEMBLY

1. Remove all plastic parts and gaskets then clean all of the metal parts in a solvent. Hydroseal solvent is recommended.

2. Blow all passages clear with compressed air. Never use wire to poke the passages free as this causes burrs or increases the port diameters.

3. Inspect all parts for wear and replace any parts which were either found defective in tests or appeared to be excessively worn.

4. If the inlet control lever does not rotate freely on its pin or if the forked end does not firmly engage the needle, it must be replaced.

5. Replace the inlet control lever tension spring if it appears to be stretched or damaged.

6. If the inlet needle point is worn or damaged or if the contact end does not provide a snug fit, they must be replaced.

ASSEMBLY

1. Examine all parts for small particles of dirt which can clog the small passages and blow them clean.

2. Assemble in reverse order of disassembly.

3. Seat the welch plugs with the recommended tool, or with a flat end drift of a diameter slightly smaller than that of the welch. A flat (rather than concave) surface is a good indication of a well-seated plug.

4. Mount the metering spring on the stud on the lever and seat it in the indentation on the body casting.

5. Torque the inlet seat assembly to 40–45 in. lbs and torque the accelerating pump channel plug to 23–28 in. lbs.

PERFORMANCE MODIFICATIONS FOR TILLOTSON MODEL HD CARBURETOR

1. Moving the cover of the air cleaner out will improve air flow. This is easily accomplished by using two, ½ in. Harley-Davidson windshield spacers and two, longer, air cleaner bolts.

2. Replacing the stock back plate will improve air flow even more than the above method. Various companies market such replacement units that still use

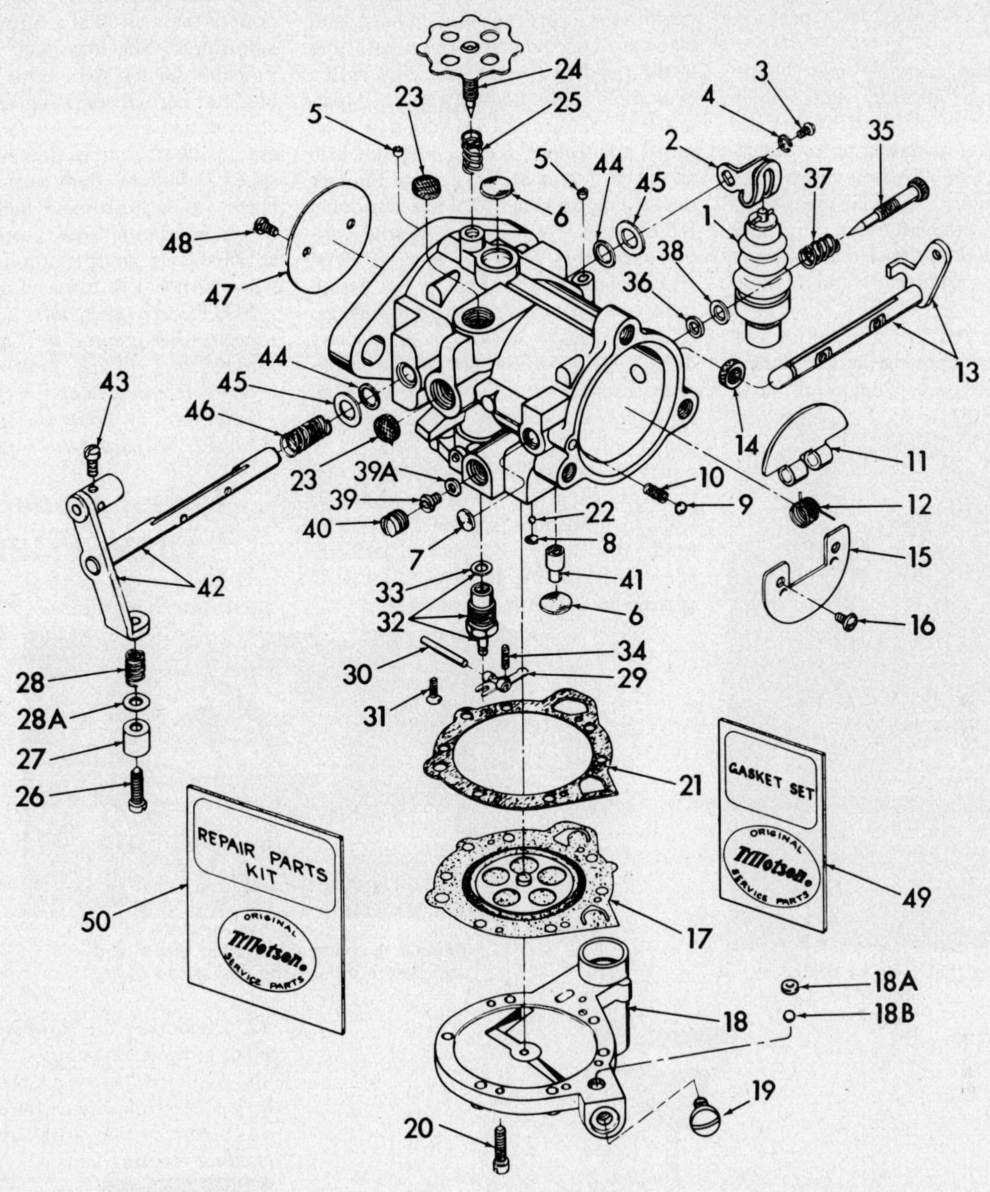

Model HD carburetor assembly

1. Accelerating pump
2. Accelerating pump lever
3. Accelerating pump lever screw
4. Accelerating pump lever screw L.W.
5. Channel plug (2)
6. Welch plug
7. Welch plug
8. Welch plug
9. Choke shaft friction ball
10. Choke shaft friction spring
11. Choke shutter (top)
12. Choke shutter spring
13. Choke shaft assembly
14. Choke shaft dust seal
15. Choke shutter (bottom)
16. Choke shutter screws
17. Diaphragm
18. Cover

18A. Accelerator pump check ball retainer

18B. Accelerating pump check ball

19. Diaphragm cover plug screw
20. Diaphragm cover screws (6)
21. Diaphragm cover gasket
22. Economizer check ball
23. Fuel filter screen (2)
24. Idle adjustment screw
25. Idle adjustment screw spring
26. Throttle stop screw
27. Throttle stop screw cup
28. Throttle stop screw spring

28A. Throttle stop screw spring washer

29. Inlet control lever
30. Inlet control lever pin
31. Inlet control lever screw
32. Inlet needle and seat
33. Inlet needle seat gasket
34. Inlet control lever tension spring
35. Intermediate adjusting screw
36. Intermediate adjusting screw packing
37. Intermediate adjusting screw spring
38. Intermediate adjusting screw washer
39. Main jet

39A. Main jet gasket

40. Main jet plug screw
41. Main nozzle check valve
42. Throttle shaft assembly
43. Throttle lever wire block screw
44. Dust seal (2)
45. Washer (2)
46. Throttle shaft spring
47. Throttle shutter
48. Throttle shutter screws
49. Gasket overhaul set
50. Overhaul repair kit

one of the available H-D air cleaner elements and covers (i.e., H-D part no. 29030–56).

3. The choke assembly may be replaced with a "tickler" unit which mounts outside the plastic carb cover and uses the existing mounting screws. Starting should not be adversely affected by this modification. The choke shaft holes must be filled with plastic aluminum filler and then sanded smooth. Do not attempt this while the carburetor is mounted on the machine.

4. A more even fuel distribution can be attained by removing the vent fitting and drilling the passage behind it out to ¼ in. Remove the plastic carb cover and diaphragm to prevent any damage, and take care not to damage the vent fitting or the needle valve threads. Now drill a ⅛ in. hole in the booster venturi. Measure 1 ¾ in. from the air inlet side (low-speed adjustment needle side) and drill on the casting seam. Use a scribe to mark the drilling position 2/3 of the way down the booster venturi to the desired position of the hole. Tap and insert a 8/32 in. screw in the outside hole in the carburetor body to prevent vacuum leakage. Check to make sure that the screw doesn't enter the airstream in the carburetor throat. Turn this work over to an experienced machinist unless you feel competent.

The vent fitting that is to be drilled out to ¼ in.

5. You will probably want to change the high-speed jet. Jets are available in 0.002 in. gradations from 0.055–0.063 in. from your dealer. For super performance, an adjustable, high-speed jet (H-D part no. 27295–66R) is available.

6. Seat both needles and then back both of them off ⅞ of a turn as an initial adjustment. The low-speed needle will probably be too rich. With the engine idling at normal operating temperature, at about 2,000 rpm, adjust the intermediate needle to that position at which idle speed is highest, then turn it counterclockwise ⅛ turn. The high-speed jet should be adjusted with the engine idling at 900–1100 rpm. It is properly adjusted when turned 1 ¼ turns off its seat.

NOTE: *We gratefully acknowledge permission granted by TRM Publications, Inc., to use information contained in* Street Chopper, *"Tips for the Tillotson," by Brian Brennan, Vol. 3, No. 11, November 1971, pp. 46–49.*

Linkert Model MD

DISASSEMBLY

1. Remove the air cleaner cover, element, and back plate.

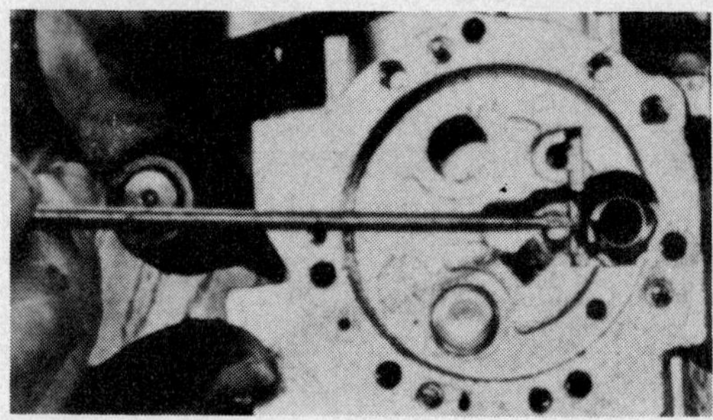

Remove the plate, diaphragm, needle, and seat before drilling the passage to ¼ in.

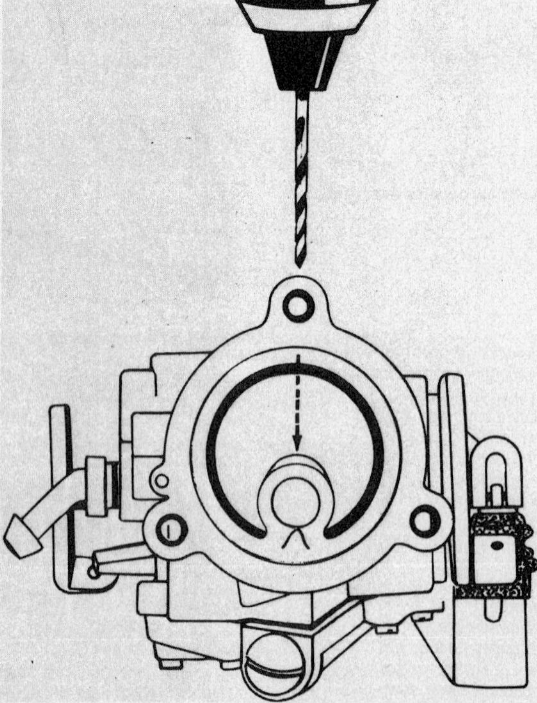

Drill a hole in the booster venturi from the outside in at a point on the seam 1¾ in. from the top.

2. Disconnect the throttle and choke cables at the carburetor.

3. With the petcock closed, remove the gas line from the carburetor nipple.

4. Remove the carburetor intake manifold securing bolts.

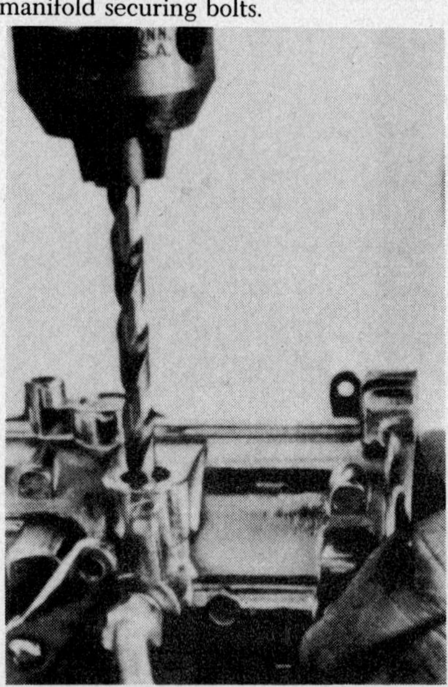

With the vent fitting removed, drill the passage out to ¼ in.

5. Remove the manifold gasket, gasoline elbow, inlet screen, main mixture screw, packing nut, packing, gland, and the packing screw gland gasket.

6. Remove the bowl screens, lockwashers, bowl, and bowl gasket.

7. Remove the float lever pin screw and the float bowl plug screw. The float is now free to be removed.

8. Using Carburetor Inlet Seat Tool (H-D part no. 94816–62), remove the inlet needle valve, spring, seat, and gasket. Needle nose pliers may also be used. Do not try to grab the needle or the spring.

9. Remove the small float bowl plug screw.

10. Remove the idle mixture screw, screw spring, carburetor idle tube and gasket, main nozzle channel plug screw, and the main nozzle.

11. Only remove the throttle shaft if it is excessively worn. Remove the idle speed screw, spring, throttle stop retaining screws and lockwashers, throttle stop lever, throttle shaft friction spring, throttle stop, lockwasher, shaft retainer clip, shaft seal, throttle disc screws, lockwashers, disc, and the shaft with its seals and bushings.

12. Remove the choke shaft only if it is excessively worn. Remove the choke disc screws, lockwashers, disc, shaft retainer clip screw, lockwasher, retainer clip and the shaft with the spring.

INSPECTION AND REPAIR

1. Clean all parts, other than the gaskets and the float, in a carbon and gum-dissolving solution such as Gunk Hydro-seal (which is recommended by the factory), rinse thoroughly, and blow them dry.

2. Blow all of the fuel and air passages clear.

3. If the idle is rough, remove the welch plug by punching and prying. Next, clear the ports and install a new plug.

4. Blow all of the nozzles and needles clear.

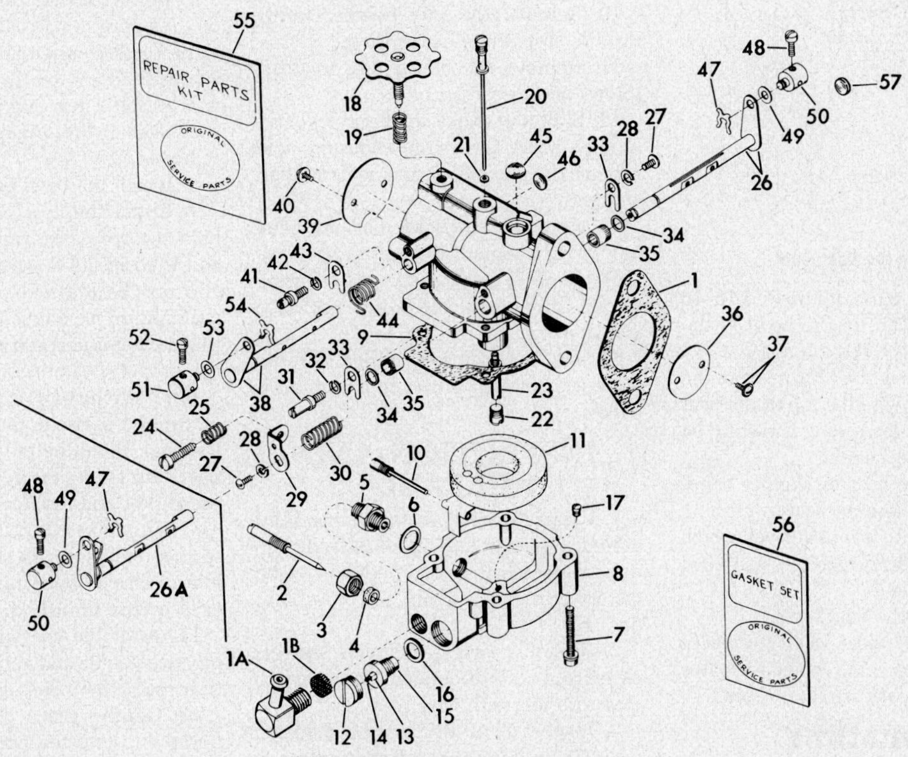

Model MD carburetor assembly

1. Carburetor to manifold gasket
1A. Gasoline line elbow
1B. Inlet screen
2. Main mixture screw
3. Main mixture screw packing nut
4. Main mixture screw packing
5. Main mixture screw gland
6. Main mixture screw gland gasket
7. Bowl screws and lockwashers (4 each)
8. Carburetor bowl
9. Body gasket
10. Float lever pin-screw
11. Float
12. Float bowl plug screw (large)
13. Inlet needle valve
14. Inlet needle valve spring
15. Inlet needle valve seat
16. Inlet needle valve gasket
17. Float bowl plug screw (small)
18. Idle mixture screw
19. Idle mixture screw spring
20. Carburetor idle tube
21. Idle tube gasket
22. Main nozzle channel plug screw
23. Main nozzle
24. Idle speed screw
25. Idle speed screw spring
26. Throttle shaft and lever (to late 1963)
26A. Throttle shaft and lever (late 1963)
27. Retaining screw (2) (to late 1963)
28. Lockwasher (2) (to late 1963)
29. Throttle stop lever (to late 1963)
30. Throttle shaft friction spring
31. Throttle stop
32. Throttle stop lockwasher
33. Throttle shaft retainer clip
34. Throttle shaft seal
35. Throttle shaft bushing
36. Throttle disc
37. Throttle disc screws and lock washers (2 each)
38. Choke shaft and lever
39. Choke disc
40. Choke disc screws and lock-washer (2each)
41. Choke shaft retainer clip screw
42. Choke shaft retainer clip lock-washer
43. Choke shaft retainer clip
44. Choke shaft spring
45. Body channel welch plug
46. Choke shaft bearing welch plug
47. Wire connection retainer clip washer
48. Throttle wire retainer screw
49. Throttle wire connection lock-washer
50. Throttle wire connection
51. Choke wire connection
52. Choke wire retainer
52. Choke wire retainer screw
53. Choke wire connection lock-washer
54. Wire connection retainer clip washer
55. Repair parts kit
56. Gasket set
57. Throttle shaft bearing Welch plug (late 1963)

5. Inspect the main mixture screw, idle mixture screw, inlet needle valve, valve spring, valve seat, and valve gasket for wear and proper seating, and replace as necessary.

6. Replace the float if it is leaky or gas-logged.

7. Replace all of the gaskets and the mixture screw packing.

8. Check the throttle and choke shafts for excessive wear to the bushing surfaces and replace the bushings if necessary.

9. If a repair kit is to be used, use all of the parts.

10. Replace any worn or pitted parts.

11. Check the float level in the following manner:

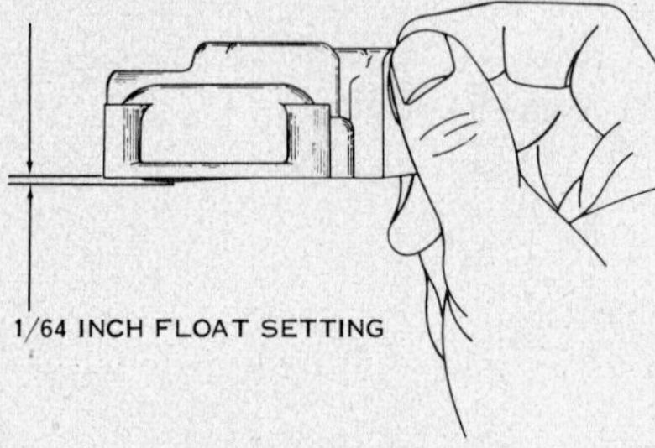

Setting the float level

a. Assemble parts, numbered 16–10 in the illustration, to the bowl in the reverse order.

b. There should be 1/64 in. from the edge of the bowl to the top of the float when the float lever tang is resting on the seated inlet needle.

c. Adjust the float by slightly bending the lever. Raise the float by pushing on the tang with a screwdriver which can be inserted through the float bowl plug screw hole.

d. Recheck the float level.

12. Suck on the float valve seat, with the bowl inverted, and replace the valve and seat if any leaks are discovered.

ASSEMBLY

1.Assemble in the reverse order from disassembly.

2. Be sure that the idle tube is secure.

3. Make sure that the throttle shaft identifying mark is visible through the manifold port.

4. Make sure that the throttle disc mark is pointing to the carburetor bore base.

5. Secure the throttle disc after the stop and clip are secure.

6. Make sure that the choke shaft spring is in its proper position on the shaft and lever.

7. Adjust the carburetor as described in the adjustment section.

Bendix Model 16P12

DISASSEMBLY

1. Remove the air cleaner cover, element, and the back plate.

2. Close the petcock and disconnect the fuel line.

3. Disconnect the choke and throttle cables at the carburetor.

4. Remove the accelerating pump lever screw, lever and pump assembly, and remove the pistion by rotating the pump lever 90 degrees while compressing the piston shaft spring.

6. Remove the idle tube, tube gasket, main jet and tube assembly, fiber washer, rubber O-ring, float bowl, and bowl drain plug.

7. Press the float pin through the float ears.

8. Lift the float, float spring, and float valve free from the bowl.

9. Remove the bowl gasket.

10. Remove the idle needle, spring throttle stop screw, and spring.

11. Remove the choke disc securing screws and disc.

12. Slide the choke shaft and lever assembly free from the housing and remove the plunger, spring, seal retainer, and seal.

13. Remove the choke shaft cup plug only if replacement is necessary.

14. Remove the throttle disc securing screws, disc, shaft and lever assembly, and shaft spring.

15. Do not remove either throttle shaft seal retainer unless replacement is necessary.

INSPECTION AND REPAIR

1. Clean all metal parts in a carbon and gum-dissolving solution such as Gunk Hydroseal (which is recommended by the factory), rinse thoroughly, and blow them dry.

2. Blow all passages, channels, and jets clear from both directions. Do not try to clear the jets with wire or a drill.

3. Inspect all of the parts for damage, wear, or a pitted condition and replace as necessary.

4. Use all of the parts in the repair kit if such a kit is used.

ASSEMBLY

1. Assemble in reverse order of disassembly.

2. With the throttle return spring in place on the shaft, slip the shaft into the seal retainer and seal.

3. Install the shaft from the nipple side of the carburetor and secure the seal and retainer on the shaft hole boss on the opposite side of the carburetor bore.

4. Install the throttle disc on the flat side of the shaft with disc screws. Operate the shaft rapidly several times to center the disc and then secure the screws.

5. Install the choke shaft seal and retainer in the shaft hole and position the starter retainer by using a small punch.

6. Install the shaft through the housing on the opposite side of the throttle lever. Center and secure it in the same manner as was used for the throttle disc.

7. Install a new cup plug in the choke shaft hole if the original plug has been removed.

8. Install the bowl gasket.

9. Install the float valve in the bowl, hold the spring between the float ears, and then install the float pin. The valve clip must be attached to the float tab with a minimum clearance of 0.010 in. Bend the clip if it is necessary in order to attain the proper clearance.

10. With the bowl inverted, slip a 3/16 in. drill bit between the bowl gasket and the float. Bend the tab with needle-nose pliers until the bit is in contact with both the gasket and the float.

11. Install the throttle stop screw and spring, and turn it in slightly. The no. 2 idle discharge hole must not be uncovered by the throttle disc.

12. Assemble the spring on the idle mixture needle and gently screw it in until it seats, then back it out 1 ½ turns.

13. Gently place the accelerating pump cup into the pump well and seat the pump boot around the top of the pump boss.

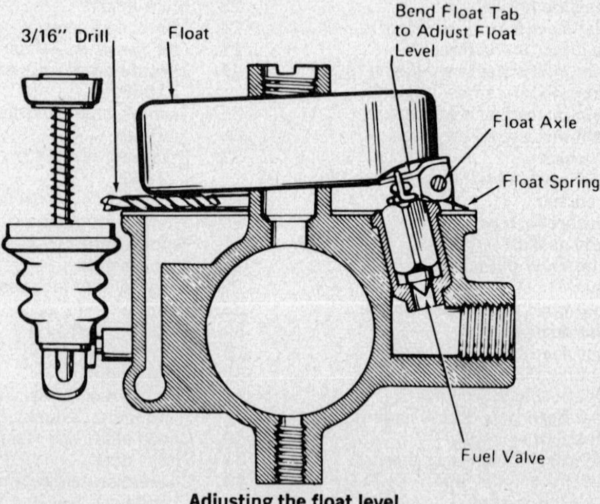

Adjusting the float level

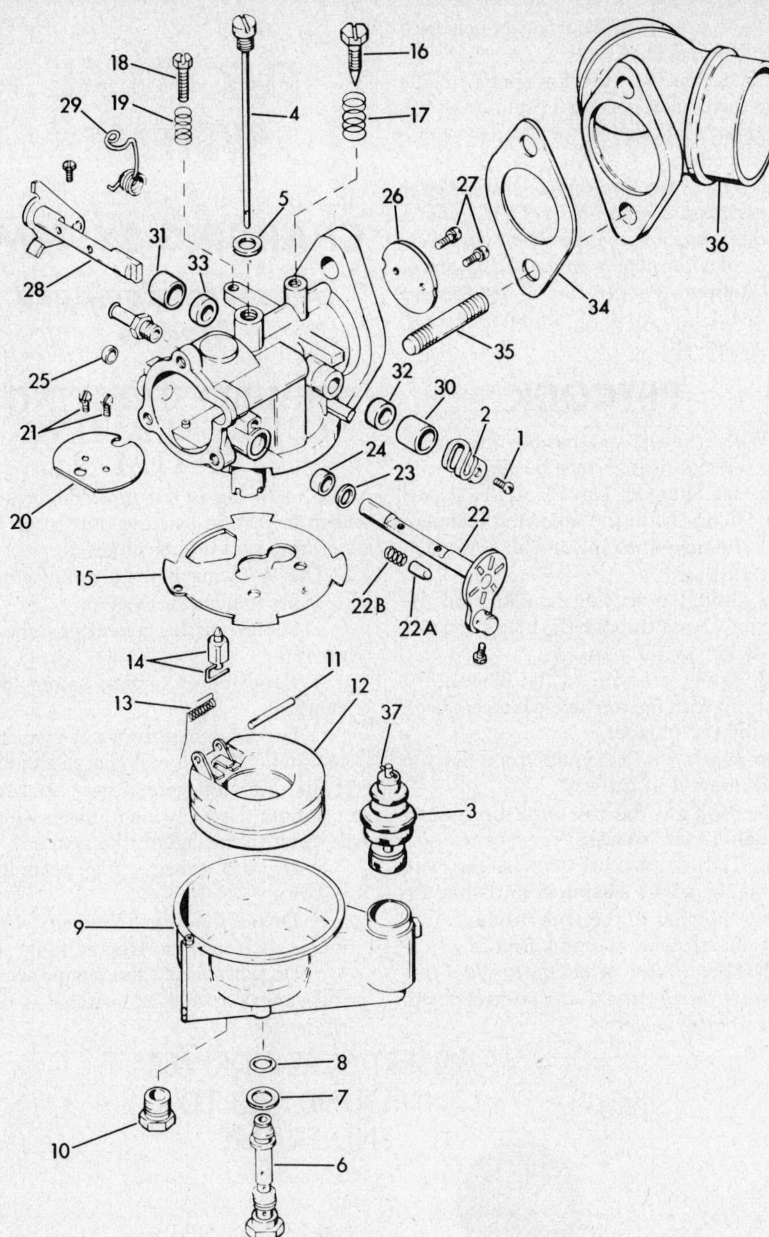

Model 16P12 carburetor assembly

1. Accelerating pump lever screw
2. Accelerating pump lever
3. Accelerating pump
4. Idle tube
5. Idle tube gasket
6. Main fuel jet and tube assembly
7. Fiber washer
8. O-ring
9. Bowl
10. Bowl drain plug
11. Float pin
12. Float assembly
13. Float spring
14. Float valve
15. Bowl gasket
16. Idle mixture needle
17. Idle mixture needle spring
18. Throttle stop screw
19. Throttle stop screw spring
20. Choke disc
21. Choke disc screw (2)
22. Choke shaft and lever
22A. Plunger
22B. Spring
23. Choke shaft seal retainer
24. Choke shaft seal
25. Choke shaft cup plug
26. Throttle disc
27. Throttle disc screw (2)
28. Throttle shaft and lever
29. Throttle shaft spring
30. Throttle shaft seal retainer
31. Throttle shaft seal retainer
32. Throttle shaft seal
33. Throttle shaft seal
34. Manifold gasket
35. Manifold stud (2)
36. Intake manifold
37. Accelerating pump shaft pin

14. Assemble the fiber washer and rubber O-ring on the main jet. The O-ring must seat in the groove near the end of the tube.

15. Check to make sure that the accelerating jet fits properly in the throttle body.

16. With the carburetor inverted and the long end of the spring against the float, install the float bowl. The long end of the spring should seat against the side of the bowl.

17. Loosely install the main jet and secure the drain plug in the bottom of the bowl.

18. Install the idle tube gasket and the tube end in the discharge tube. Secure the idle tube and the main jet.

19. Assemble the accelerating pump lever to the pump and throttle shaft.

PERFORMANCE MODIFICATIONS FOR BENDIX MODEL 16P12 CARBURETOR

1. Make sure that the choke arm isn't being held slightly open by the air cleaner back plate. Many bikes come this way from the factory but can be fixed by adjusting the choke arm for more clearance.

2. Install a three-position accelerator pump shaft (H-D part no. 27762–71A) if the present shaft has only one position. Late 1971 and later models are already modified.

3. Check to be sure that the accelerator pump nozzle is correctly aligned, so that the gas is sprayed directly into the airstream, in the following manner:

   a. Operate the pump while looking into the choke venturi.

   b. If the gas does not pass straight through the choke disc slot, the nozzle must be repositioned.

   c. Gently turn the nozzle, with needle-nose pliers, until the fuel passes through the choke disc slot.

4. Replacing the stock air filter will increase air flow considerably.

5. Placing two, ½ in., Harley-Davidson windshield spacers on two, longer, air cleaner bolts will move the cover out ½ in. and will provide an air flow which is increased by nearly ten percent.

6. Change the float level from ⅛ in. to 3/16 in. and adjust it in the same manner as described in the assembly section.

7. Check the float movement. Float ear holes must be loose enough to allow free movement without sticking or wobbling.

8. Removing the float spring will improve acceleration. If the spring is retained, make sure that it seats properly because if it is crimped between the carburetor body and the float bowl, it will cause the float to hang up.

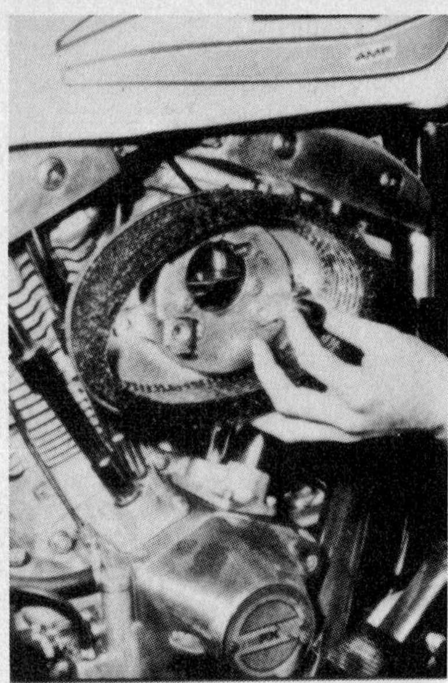

Using windshield spacers to move the air cleaner cover out

9. Use a size 1.00 high-speed jet.

10. Enlarge the idle tube housing notches, using a small file, to twice their normal size.

11. Mark both the jet base and the bowl so the ports can be aligned when the bowl is secured. Shim the jet if the bowl will not mount in such a way as to make it flush.

12. Lightly grease the jet tip O-ring before installation.

13. Replacing the idle jet with a two-hole jet (H-D part no. 27725–71) or cross-drilling the old jet with a 0.038 in. drill will enhance low and middle-range performance.

Enlarging the ports provides increased gas flow

Holes near the base of the jet must be aligned with the float bowl stub slots or the fuel will not enter the jet

14. Carefully drill out the jet hole with a 9/16 in. drill.

15. Open only the low-speed needle one turn when making a preliminary adjustment if you've performed these modifications.

NOTE: *We gratefully acknowledge permission granted by TRM Publications, Inc., to use illustrations and technical information contained in* Street Chopper, *Bendix Lives," by Richard Bean, Vol. 3, No. 9, September 1971, pp. 46–49.*

PETCOCK

When the left tank has been repaired, the petcock fittings must be aligned with the Gas Shut-Off Valve Tool (H-D part no. 96365–42) in the following manner:

1. Remove the tank and all of the petcock fittings.

2. Shift the spacing handle until the aligning bar is through the hole which has been left by the petcock.

3. Apply pressure to the bar until it lines up with the top hole which has been left by the plunger.

4. Insert the T-handle from the top and screw it in halfway.

5. Back out the bar until the spacing handle reads "spacing."

6. Tighten the bar and handle, and strike them with a hammer until they are perpendicular to the tank fitting.

7. Reassemble the tank fittings.

NOTE: *Before installing the fuel petcock, the threads should be coated with a suitable sealer.*

ELECTRICAL SYSTEMS

CHARGING SYSTEM

Generator-Equipped Models

TROUBLESHOOTING THE GENERATING SYSTEM

The following is the most direct approach to take in locating the source of generating system difficulties:

1. The following items are indicators of a faulty generating system:

a. Failure of the generator light to operate.

b. Repeated or sudden battery discharging.

c. Excessive battery water evaporation indicating an overcharged state.

2. In testing the generating system, do not commit the following mistakes which will result in damage to the system:

a. Do not reverse the generator polarity.

b. Do not short or ground any wires unless specifically instructed to do so.

c. Do not operate the engine while the generator output terminal is disconnected.

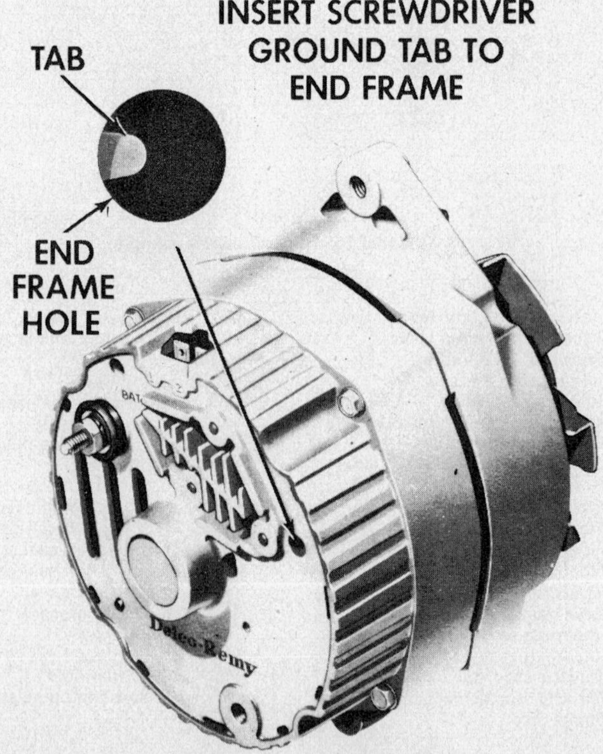

Grounding the generator field winding

d. Always connect positive to positive and negative to negative when connecting a charger or booster to the battery.

3. Check for a faulty generator light in the following manner:

a. If the ignition switch is turned off and the light is on, disconnect the generator 1 and 2 leads at their terminals. If the light stays on, check for a short between these two leads. Replace the rectifier bridge if the light goes out. Failure to remedy this situation will result in a discharged battery.

b. If the generator light doesn't go on when the ignition switch is turned on, check for a short between leads 1 and 2. If the light still doesn't come on, reverse the two leads. If the light still hasn't come on, check for an open circuit in the following manner:

(A) Connect the two leads of a voltmeter to ground and the no. 2 generator terminal, and check for a reading. Go on to the next step if a reading is obtained. No reading indicates an open circuit between no. 2 terminal and the battery. Correct this, then see if the light goes on when the ignition is turned on.

(B) Either connect or disconnect both no. 1 and 2 generator leads, turn the ignition switch on, and momentarily ground no. 1 terminal lead only. If the light does not come on, check for a burned out bulb, blown fuse, faulty bulb socket, or an open condition between no. 1 terminal and the ignition switch. Remove the ground from no. 1 terminal if the light comes on, and with no. 1 and 2 terminals connected, ground generator by inserting a screwdriver into the generator test hole.

(C) If the light still hasn't come on, check for open circuits between the wiring harness and the no 1 terminal, generator brushes, slip rings, and field windings.

(D) If the light came on in the first step and there was a voltmeter reading, replace the regulator.

(E) Consult the next section if the light stays on when the motor is running.

4. Locate the reason for an undercharged battery in the following manner:

a. Make sure the reason the battery keeps going down is not because the accessories have been left on without the engine running.

b. Check the drive belt for proper tension.

c. Check the battery for shorting with a voltmeter or hydrometer indicated by one or more dead cells.

d. Inspect all wiring for loose or poor connections.

e. Connect the leads of a voltmeter from ground to the generator "BAT" terminal, then the no. 1 terminal, then the no. 2 terminal. No reading indicates an open condition between the battery and the voltmeter connection.

5. Check the generator in the following manner if the problem hasn't yet been discovered:

a. Disconnect the battery ground wire, connect an ammeter so the current will pass through it from the generator "BAT" terminal to the lead was connected to the "BAT" terminal, and reconnect the battery ground wire.

b. Turn on all of the accessories and attach a carbon pile across the battery terminals. Operate the engine until maximum current output is obtained.

c. If generator is good, amperage output will be within 10 percent of output stamped on generator frame. Go back and recheck the previous steps.

d. Ground the generator by inserting a screwdriver through the generator test hole if amperage isn't within 10 percent of its normal rating.

e. Recheck with a carbon pile as described above. If the reading is still not within 10 percent, the regulator must be replaced.

f. Recheck with a carbon pile and overhaul the generator if the reading still isn't within 10 percent of its rated amperage.

6. Locate the reason for an overcharged battery in the following manner:

a. Check the state of battery charge with a voltmeter or hydrometer.

b. Connect the leads of a voltmeter to ground and generator no. 2 terminal to check for an open reading (zero). The voltage, in any case, should not exceed 16.0 volts at 0° F. Discrepancies in measurements taken in cold and hot conditions are to be expected.

7. If the above test proves that the circuit is good and excessive water evaporation still indicates an overcharged battery, separate the generator end frames and check the field windings for a shorted condition in the following manner:

a. Connect the leads of an ohmmeter from the brush lead clip to the end frame and then reverse the connections. The ohmmeter must be set on its lowest range scale.

b. If both readings are zero, check for a grounded brush lead. This is probably caused by a missing or damaged insulating washer or insulating screw sleeve.

c. If, after replacing the insulating elements, both readings are still zero, the regulator is defective and must be replaced.

TESTING GENERATOR OUTPUT

1. Remove the wire from the generator "F" terminal and connect a jumper wire from the "F" terminal to ground.

2. Remove wire(s) from "A" terminal and connect the positive lead to a 0–30 amp ammeter.

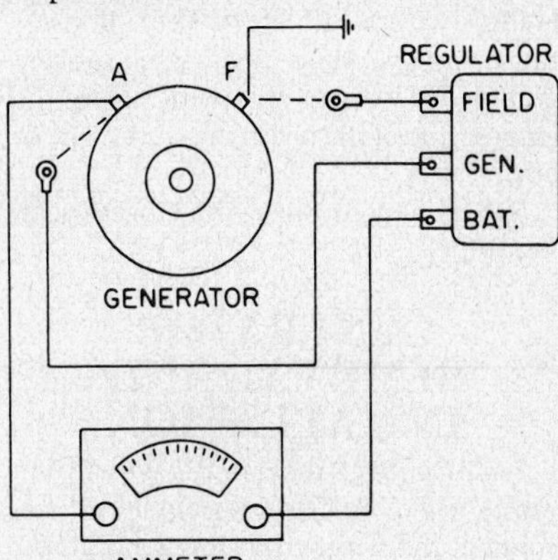

Wiring the diagram for generator output test

3. Run the engine at 2,000 rpm (40 mph in fourth gear) and briefly connect the negative lead of the ammeter to the positive battery terminal.

NOTE: *Avoid running the engine for long periods with the generator field grounded, and always disconnect the ammeter lead from the battery before stopping the engine so the battery doesn't discharge through the generator.*

CAUTION: *Disconnect the wires from the regulator before grounding the regulator "F" (XLH) OR "BT" (XLCH) terminals to check output, or regulator will be damaged.*

4. If the ammeter reads 15 or more amps for a 6 volt generator or 10 amps for a 12 volt generator, the generator is good and the trouble is in the voltage regulator or wiring circuit.

5. When installing generators or batteries and whenever the generator or regulator wires have been disconnected, flash the field coils to make sure the generator has correct polarity. Do this by briefly touching a jumper wire between "BAT" and "GEN" terminals on the regulator before starting the engine and after connecting all of the wires. The momentary surge of current from the battery to the generator will correctly polarize the generator.

NOTE: *If generator output findings are negative, consult the following section before removing the generator for further testing.*

CLEANING AND INSPECTING GENERATOR BRUSHES

1. Remove the commutator end cover nuts, washers, and frame screws.

2. Pry or gently tap off the commutator end cover from the frame and armature shaft.

3. Remove the brush holder mounting plate from the frame and disconnect the brush wires and generator positive brush cable from the brush holder terminals.

4. Remove the brushes and clean the holders with a suitable solvent. Replace the brushes when they are broken, gummy, or worn to the point where the longest side of the brush measure ½ in. or less.

5. Seat new brushes with a brush seating stone.

GENERATOR REMOVAL AND INSTALLATION

1. Disconnect the "BAT" wires from the voltage regulator terminal and disconnect the wires from the generator.

2. Take out the two long generator mounting screws and remove the generator from the left side of the bike.

3. Install the generator in the reverse order of removal.

GENERATOR DISASSEMBLY AND COMPONENT TESTING

Testing Field Coils

An ammeter will react to an overload by sending its needle beyond the range of the calibrated scale. A direct short causes the needle to swing violently to the end of its travel. In both cases, damage will result to the ammeter if contact is not instantly broken. In testing field coils, first make sure there is no short present by making brief contact before securing the test lead. Try to work on a non-conductive surface and never touch the test points together.

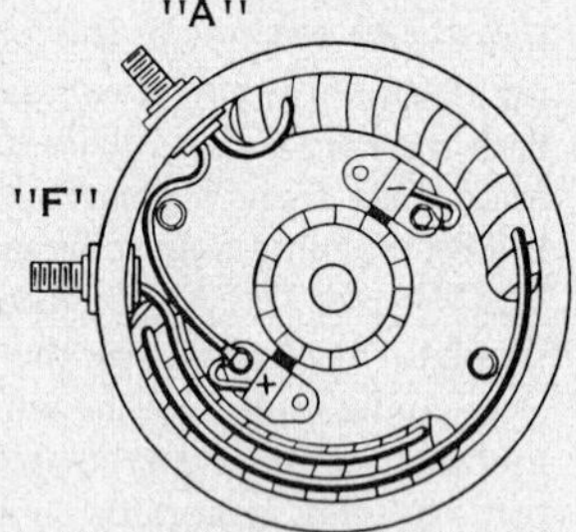

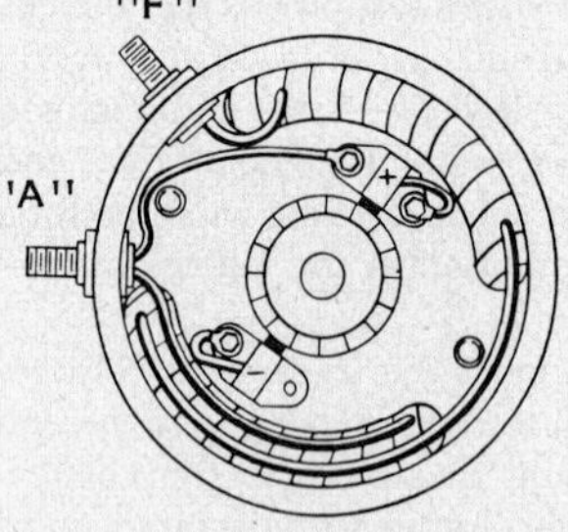

1965 MODEL 65-12V.
1964 MODEL 64-12V.
1958 - 1964 MODELS 58 & 61-6V.

1966 MODEL 65A-12V.

Internal connections of the brushes to the field terminals

The test is made by linking together an ammeter and a battery in series, with the components to be tested connected to leads. Use the 12 volt battery with a 6 volt generator. All 12 volt generators have "12V" following the frame number.

1. Remove or insulate the brushes from armature.

2. Touch one test lead to "F" terminal and ground the other to the generator frame. There should be no reading.

3. Touch one test lead to "A" terminal and ground the other. If there is a reading for either, there is a grounded terminal or else the field coil is grounded to the frame.

4. Check terminal-to-ground contacts. No reading means that the terminals are properly insulated. If there was a reading in steps 2 or 3, but there is not now, the trouble is probably a grounded field coil.

5. Remove the generator drive gear using a gear puller. (H-D puller is part no. 95715–19A.)

6. Press the armature out of the ball bearings with an arbor press. This can be done cheaply at any machine shop or by placing the generator frame between the copper jaws of a vice and tapping the gearshaft end with a soft mallet.

7. Disassemble the terminals and remove the field coil leads. Examine all of the terminal components for wear and damage, especially all of the insulators. Replace any that are worn. Assemble all components except the field coil leads.

8. Touch one test lead to the field coil lead and the other to the ground on the generator frame. Check the other coil lead. A reading means that the coil is grounded and that the two coils must be separated by cutting the wire which connects them.

9. Test each field coil as above. A reading means that there is a grounded coil which must be replaced.

10. Test the field coils by touching the test leads to the coil lead terminals. The 6 volt double coils should produce a reading of 0.2 amps; 12 volt double coils lead. The 6 volt coils should produce a 4 should produce a reading of 0.95 amps (1964 models) or 2.3 amps (1965 models). No reading means an open coil. A higher reading means a shorted coil.

11. Strip back the insulation and scrape the wire clean where the two coil leads are joined. Attach one test lead at this point and the other at either coil

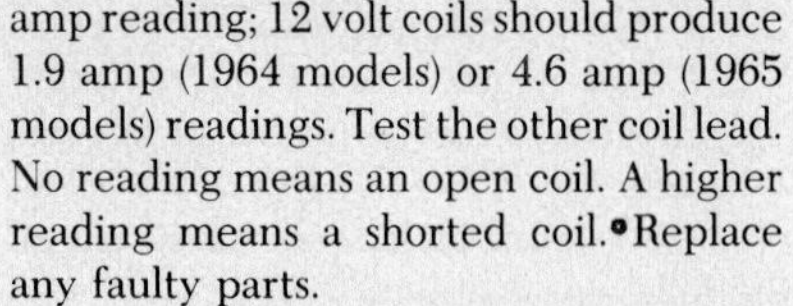

amp reading; 12 volt coils should produce 1.9 amp (1964 models) or 4.6 amp (1965 models) readings. Test the other coil lead. No reading means an open coil. A higher reading means a shorted coil. Replace any faulty parts.

12. Touch one test lead to the brush holder mounting plate and the other to the positive (insulated) brush holder. A reading indicates a shorted holder. Clean, check, and replace the plate if necessary.

13. Check the negative brush holder to see that it is securely mounted and well grounded.

14. If the problem hasn't yet been located, it is probably the armature.

Testing The Armature

Check for electrical continuity between the armature core and the commutator. If continuity exists, the armature is defective and should be replaced.

Repairing Commutator

The commutator can be turned down on a lathe or sanded with fine "00" sandpaper. Never use emery paper since particles will embed, causing arcing. The mica insulation must be 0.025 in. below the surface of the sections and can be reduced to this point with a hacksaw blade if care is taken to keep the slot bottoms square.

Disassembly

1. Remove the gasket, gear shaft nut, and washer.

2. Remove the drive gear with a gear puller (H-D part no. 95715-19A) and slip the drive end oil deflector off the shaft.

3. Remove the brush cover strap and the end nuts and washers, then pull the screws out of the frame.

4. Loosen and remove the end cover with a soft mallet.

5. Remove the brush holder mounting plate and securing apparatus.

6. Press the armature out of the bearing with an arbor press, which can be found in any machine shop, or by clamping the generator in a copper-jawed vise and striking the shaft end with a soft mallet.

7. Remove the terminal screws, nuts, washers, insulator, and positive brush cable.

8. Remove the end plate by tapping gently and remove the bearing retainer with needle nose pliers.

9. Press the armature bearing out of drive end plate and remove the bearing retainer.

10. Press the armature oil seal out of the drive end plate from drive-gear side.

11. Remove the two pole screws with a large screwdriver and remove the pole shoes and field coils (only if replacement is necessary).

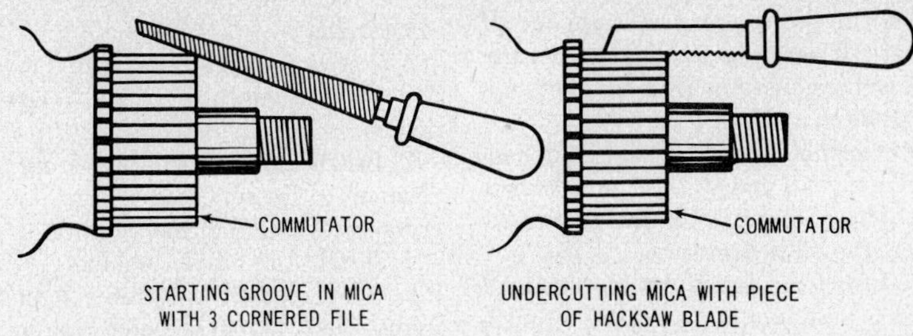

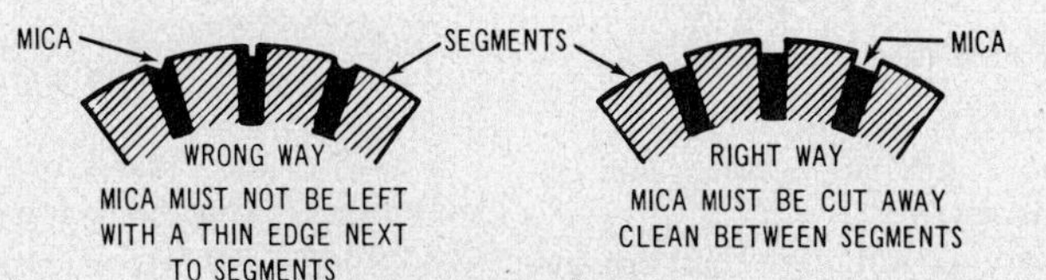

Recessing mica separators

Inspection and Repair

1. Clean all parts except the armature, coils, and brushes in cleaning solvent, and wipe all other components with a cloth and white gasoline.
2. Inspect all parts for excessive wear, especially the insulators, armature windings, coil wrappings, and pole shoe surfaces.
3. Replace the oil seal if the armature looks oily.
4. Replace any part of the brush holder mounting assembly which is bent. Disassemble the parts in the order shown in "Generator Assembly" illustration.
5. Check for excessive play of the armature shaft in the end cover bushing or roller bearing.
6. Bushings can be removed best with a bushing puller (H-D part no. 97250–58)

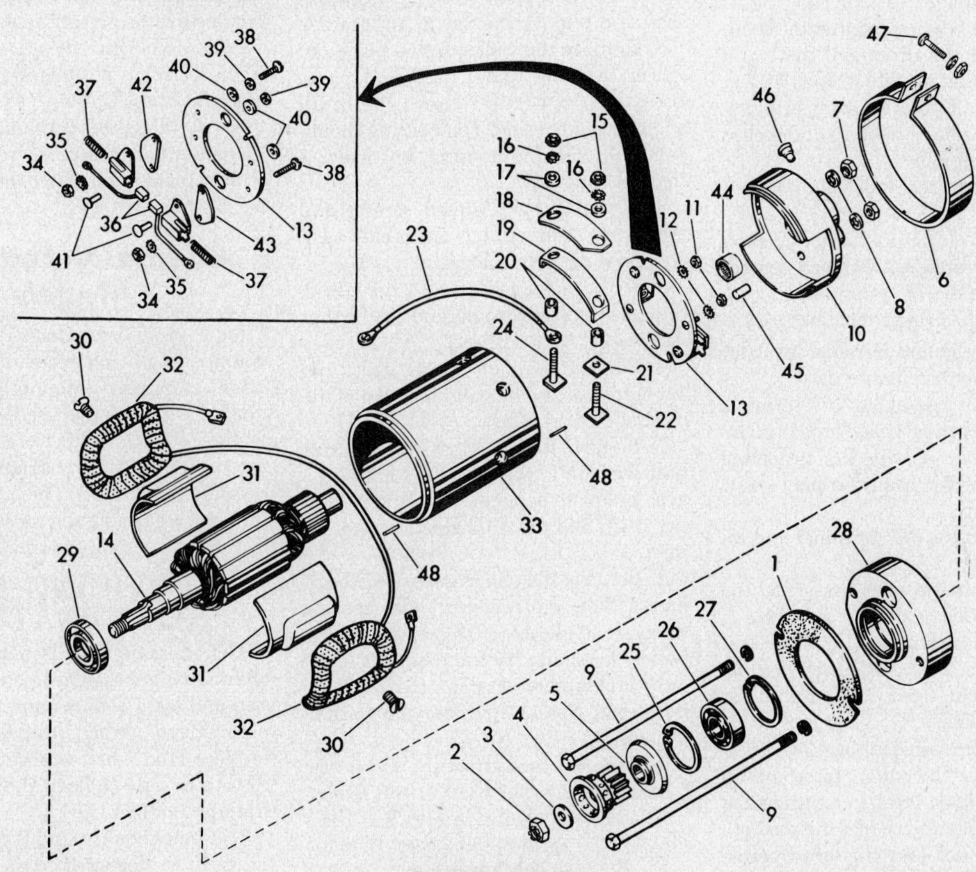

Generator assembly

1. Mounting gasket
2. Gear shaft nut
3. Gear shaft washer
4. Drive gear
5. Drive end oil deflector
6. Brush cover strap
7. Commutator end cover nut (2)
8. Commutator end cover washer (2)
9. Frame screw (2)
10. Commutator end cover
11. Brush cable nut (2)
12. Brush cable washer (2)
13. Brush holder mounting plate
14. Armature
15. Terminal screw nut (2)
16. Terminal screw lockwasher (2)
17. Insulating washer (2)
18. Terminal insulator
19. Terminal bolt clip
20. Terminal screw bushing (2)
21. Bracket insulator
22. Terminal screw (2)
23. Positive brush cable
24. Terminal screw (see item 22)
25. Bearing retainer
26. Armature bearing
27. Bearing retainer
28. Drive end plate
29. Armature oil seal
30. Pole shoe screw (2)
31. Pole shoe (2)
32. Field coil (2)
33. Frame
34. Terminal screw nut (2)
35. Terminal screw lockwasher (2)
36. Brush (2)
37. Brush spring (2)
38. Brush holder plate screw (2)
39. Brush holder plate screw washer (2)
40. Brush holder plate screw washer (3)
41. Brush holder plate rivet (2)
42. Brush holder insulation
43. Brush holder spacer
44. End cover bearing
45. Generator oil wick
46. Commutator end cover oil cup
47. Brush cover screw, lock washer and nut
48. End locating pin (2)

and an arbor. Be sure that the new bushing seats firmly in the bearing recess in the generator drive end plate.

7. To remove an arbor from the generator case, insert a screwdriver to assist in twisting it out.

8. Roller bearings are removed by pressing and new bearings should be pressed in until the bearing end is flush with the end cover.

9. Replace ball bearings if play is present. Always pack the bearings with a suitable grease.

Assembly

1. Assemble all related parts to the brush holder mounting plate.

2. Place the pole shoes in the field coils and insert into the frame. Tighten the pole shoe screws with a large screwdriver and vise grips until the shoes align themselves in the frame.

3. Place the bearing retainer in the inner groove of the drive end plate and press the bearing in until it finds its seat on the retainer. Compress the bearing retainer with needle-nose pliers and secure it in the outer groove.

4. Press the oil seal into the drive end plate.

5. Insert the armature drive end shaft and press it in until it is properly seated.

6. Assemble the "A" terminal coil lead, positive brush cable, terminal screw bushing, bolt clip and terminal insulator on the positive terminal screw.

7. Insert the assembled "A" terminal through the terminal frame hole from inside and secure it with the insulating washer, lockwasher, and terminal screw nut.

8. Assemble the "F" terminal and secure it from the inside out.

9. Slip the frame over the armature, taking care to locate the pin in its hole in the drive end plate.

10. Draw the loose end of the positive brush cable out from the commutator end of the frame.

11. Push the brushes back in their holders to clear the commutator and install the assembled brush mounting plate over the commutator so that the pin lines up with the slot and the brush cable passes through the opposite slot.

12. Secure the positive brush cable and lead to the insulated terminal. Secure the negative brush to the grounded terminal.

13. Place the commutator end cover over the end of the shaft so that the frame pin and notch are aligned.

14. Install the internal lockwashers on the frame screws by feeding them through the generator drive end and secure them from the outside.

15. Check to see if the armature is stuck or if the core strikes the pole shoes, by rotating the shaft. The shaft should turn evenly when pressure is applied. If the core strikes the pole shoes, either the shoes or the generator ends are not properly situated.

16. Assemble the drive end oil deflector, drive gear, and washer on the shaft and tighten them until the gear seats against the oil deflector.

17. Install the brush cover strap and install a new mounting gasket, using a suitable sealer.

FAN COOLED GENERATOR

Disassembly

1. Remove the fan housing and associated hardware.

2. Remove the armature shaft nut and washers. Use a gear puller (H-D part no. 95635–46) to separate the fan from the shaft and remove the key (if applicable).

3. Remove the baffle screws, plate, fan spacer, housing spider, and end plate. Use a gear puller to remove the brush and bearing housing. The bearing should come off with the housing, but leave it there if it doesn't.

4. Remove the terminal screws and the brush and spring assemblies will come out of their holders.

5. If the field coils are to be tested, they are now accessible and no further disassembly is necessary.

6. Drive the clutch spring collar pin out of the collar (Duo-Glide), or out of the oil slinger (Servi-Car).

7. Remove the clutch spring and drive gear from the armature shaft and use a gear puller to separate the clutch from the shaft. Slip the oil deflector from the shaft.

8. Remove the end frame with a bearing, gasket, oil retainer, and bearing shims (if applicable). This can be done best by loosening the frame screws about ¼ in. and tapping on them to unseat the frame end. Note the number and position of shims.

9. Remove the armature from the frame with an arbor press or soft mallet.

10. Remove the drive end ball bearing, spring ring, and felt grease retainer.

11. Remove the brush holders only if tests prove that the positive terminal is shorted, or if they are damaged. This can be done after the negative brush holder screws and terminal screw nuts are removed.

12. If the pole shoes or field coils are to be replaced, they can be removed by loosening the retaining screws and tapping their heads.

13. Remove the air intake shields.

Inspection and Repair

Refer to the preceding "Inspection and Repair" section for the standard generator. Procedures are the same.

Assembly

Assemble the generator in reverse order of disassembly. Note the following points:

1. Install the field coils, armature, felt retainer, spring ring, and bearing. Use an arbor press to install the bearing.

2. Install the brush holders on the frame end and fit the frame over the frame. The end may be drawn on by tightening the frame screws.

3. Route coil leads 1, 2, and 3 through the smaller frame opening, and lead 4 through the larger opening.

4. Run lead 1 behind and around the field coil terminal.

5. Twist leads 1 and 3 together and secure them to the field coil terminal with the terminal screw.

6. Install the positive brush. Twist leads 2 and 4 together and secure them to the positive brush terminal.

7. Assemble the negative brush only when lead 3 is positioned correctly behind the frame screw.

8. Assemble the commutator end of the generator in reverse order of disassembly making sure that the same number of shims are used.

Alternator Equipped Models

Bikes produced before 1971 that are equipped with an alternator, use a separate, externally mounted regulator, much the same as that used with DC generators. Bikes manufactured after 1970 use an alternator that has a transistorized regulator built into it. The built-in regulator is not adjustable and must be replaced if it is not operating correctly.

SERVICING THE ALTERNATOR

The alternator should not need much attention other than inspection for ocrrosion and loose connections at the terminals, frayed wiring, proper alignment, tension of the V-belt, or secure mounting. Always be sure to keep the connections from grounding.

The belt should require 8–10 pounds pressure to deflect it ¼ in. at its midpoint. This should be checked every 1,000 miles or 200 miles after a new belt is installed. Tension should be placed on the stator lamination rather than either end frame.

Removal and Disassembly (1970 and Earlier)

1. Remove both covers and mounting apparatus.

2. Remove the V-belt, alternator, drive bracket, bolts, and gasket.

3. Remove the driveshaft sheave nut, sheave, seal, and bearing. Tighten the shaftnut to 50–60 lbs when reassembling.

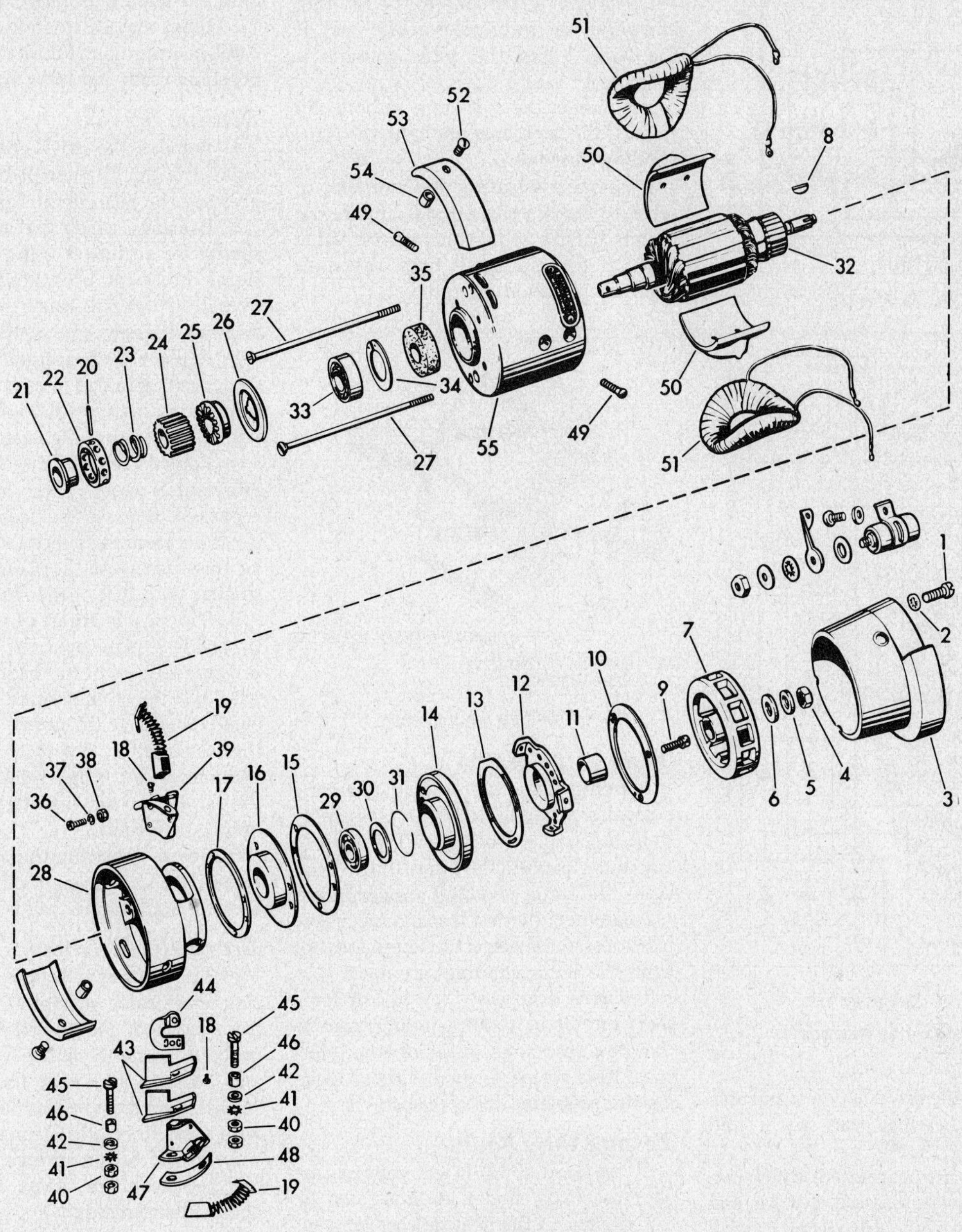

Fan cooled generator assembly

1. Fan housing screw (3)
2. Internal lock washer (3)
3. Fan housing
4. Armature shaft nut
5. Armature shaft lock washer
6. Armature shaft plain washer
7. Fan
8. Armature shaft key (used 1961 and earlier)
9. Fan baffle plate screw (3)
10. Fan baffle plate
11. Fan spacer
12. Fan housing spider
13. End plate
14. Brush end bearing housing
15. Drive end cover gasket
16. Inner oil retainer
17. Commutator end bearing shim (0 to 3)
18. Terminal screw (3)
19. Brush and spring (2)
20. Clutch spring collar pin
21. Clutch spring collar
22. Oil slinger
23. Clutch spring
24. Drive gear
25. Clutch
26. Drive end oil deflector
27. Frame screw (2)
28. Frame end
29. Armature bearing
30. Armature spacing shim (0.020 in.)
31. Bearing plate spring ring
32. Armature
33. Armature bearing
34. Drive end spring ring
35. Felt retainer
36. Negative brush holder screw (2)
37. Lock washer (2)
39. Brush holder screw nut (2)
39. Brush holder (negative)
40. Terminal screw nut (2)
41. Terminal screw lock washer (2)
42. Terminal screw insulating washer (2)
43. Field coil terminal insulator (2)
44. Field coil terminal
45. Terminal screw (2)
46. Terminal screw bushing (2)
47. Brush holder (positive)
48. Brush holder insulation
49. Pole shoe screw (4)
50. Pole shoe (2)
51. Field coil (2)
52. Air intake shield screw (2)
53. Air intake shield (2)
54. Spacing bushing (2)
55. Generator frame

Figure following name of part indicates quantity necessary for one complete assembly.

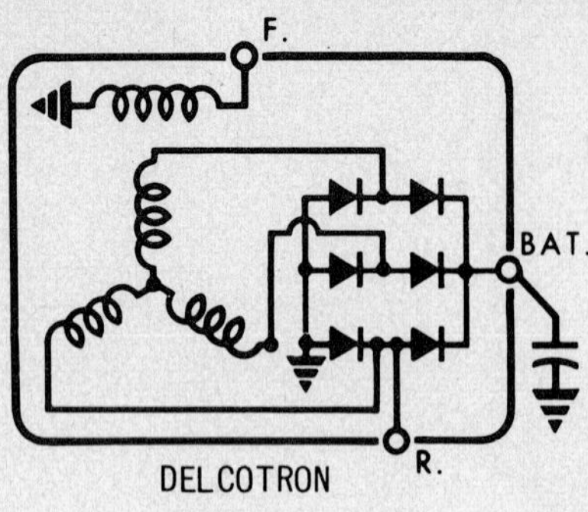

1970 & Earlier

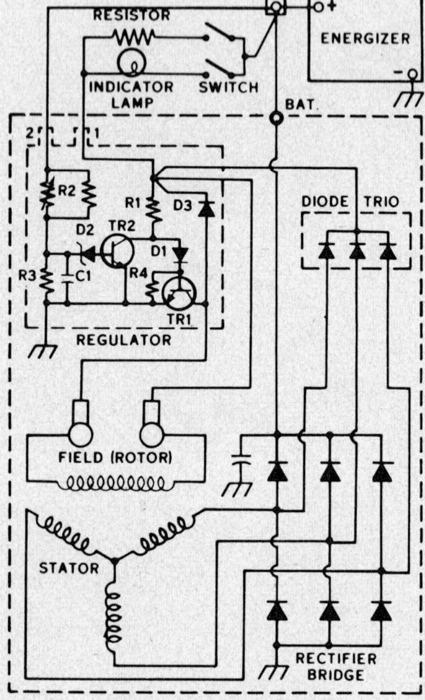

1971 & Later

Delcotron wiring diagrams

4. Remove the driveshaft gear nut and press off the bearing, gear, spacer, and washer.

5. Replace any bearings for which motion is not smooth; the seal, if worn, and sheaves with wear on drive faces. Pack all bearings with grease before installing.

6. Remove the thru-bolts and pry (at the stator slot) the drive end frame and rotor from the stator. Mark the parts so the original position of each can be duplicated during reassembly.

7. Separate the stator from the frame.

8. Use pressure-sensitive tape to protect the slip ring end frame bearing and shaft on the slip ring end from dirt. Do not use friction tape, as it will leave a deposit.

9. Place the rotor in a vise with wooden jaws (or use rags to protect the shaft) and tighten it just enough to remove the shaft nut. Over tightening will distort the shaft surface. Torque to 50–60 ft lbs when replacing the nut.

10. Slip off the washer, pulley, fan, and collar from the shaft.

Testing the Rotor

1. Connect a test lamp to the slip ring and either the rotor poles or the shaft. If the lamp lights, the rotor winding is grounded.

2. Connect the test lamp to both slip rings. If the lamp does not light, the rotor windings are open.

3. Connect a battery and ammeter in series to the two slip rings. Compare the meter reading with the alternator value table. If the reading is high, the rotor windings are short-circuited.

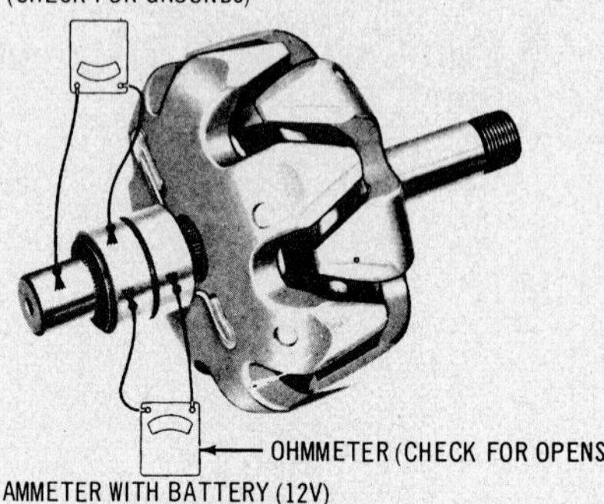

Wiring for testing rotor

Testing the Stator

1. Remove the stator lead attaching nuts and separate the stator assembly from the frame. Connect a test light to any stator lead and the frame. If the lamp lights, the stator windings are grounded.

2. Connect the test leads to successive pairs of stator leads. If the lamp does not light, the stator windings are open.

3. There is no easy way to test for a short circuit in stator windings due to their low resistance, but if all other electrical tests are performed without locating the problem, this is probably it.

Testing the Diodes

A test lamp of 12 or less volts can be used to check diodes. A diode can be tested while in the heat sink by connecting one lead to the heat sink and the other to the diode lead. Test the flow in both directions by reversing the leads. If the lamp lights, or doesn't light, in both directions, the diode is defective. A good diode will light the lamp in one direction but not in the other.

Replacing the Diodes

1. Remove the diodes by supporting the heat sink or end frame and pressing the diode out. Never strike a diode as the shock may damage the others.

2. Replace the diode with a special tool designed for diode installation while supporting the frame or heat sink.

Slip Ring Service

1. Always work on slip rings while they are spinning in order to prevent flat spots.

2. Polish the rings clean with 400 grain, or finer, polishing cloth.

3. Rings may be trued in a lathe set at 0.002 in. maximum. Finish with 400 grain polishing cloth and blow away the dust.

Bearing Service

1. Remove the drive end bearing by detaching the retainer plate screws and pressing the bearing out.

2. Bearings which are to be reused should be repacked using only Delco-Remy lubricant no. 1960373. Do not overfill as this will cause excessive heat and rapid wear.

3. Replace the bearings by pressing in, using a suitable size of collar or tube. Install a new retainer plate if the felt seal has hardened or is damaged.

4. Replace the slip ring bearing if its lubricant is spent. These are not to be repacked. Remove the bearing by pressing them from the outside in, using a collar or tube with a diameter slightly smaller than that of the frame.

5. Slip ring bearings can be replaced by laying a plate over the bearing and pressing it in until the bearing lies flush with the lip of the frame. In order to avoid damage to the frame, support it on the inside with a hollow cylinder. If the cylinder is not properly aligned, excessive stress on the bearing or misalignment may occur.

6. Before replacing the felt seal, saturate it in SAE 20 weight oil. Reassemble the seal and retainer plate.

Brush Replacement

1. The brushes will come off as the slip ring end frame assembly is separated from the rotor and end frame. They will probably come in contact with the shaft and become greasy. If they are to be reused, they must be thoroughly cleaned with a soft, dry cloth. Clean the shaft also.

2. Check brush springs for damage and replace them if you are in doubt about their condition.

3. Inserting a wire or pin into the holes in the brush holder bottom will retain the brush springs until reassembly. Leave part of the wire protruding from the frame to facilitate removal.

ALTERNATOR SERVICE (1971 and later)

Removal and Disassembly (1971 and Later)

1. Disassemble the engine as described in "Engine and Transmission" until the alternator is exposed.

2. Pull the alternator rotor free from the sprocket shaft.

3. Remove the stator securing screws and wire plug, then remove the stator from the engine.

Installation is in the reverse order of removal. Note the following points:

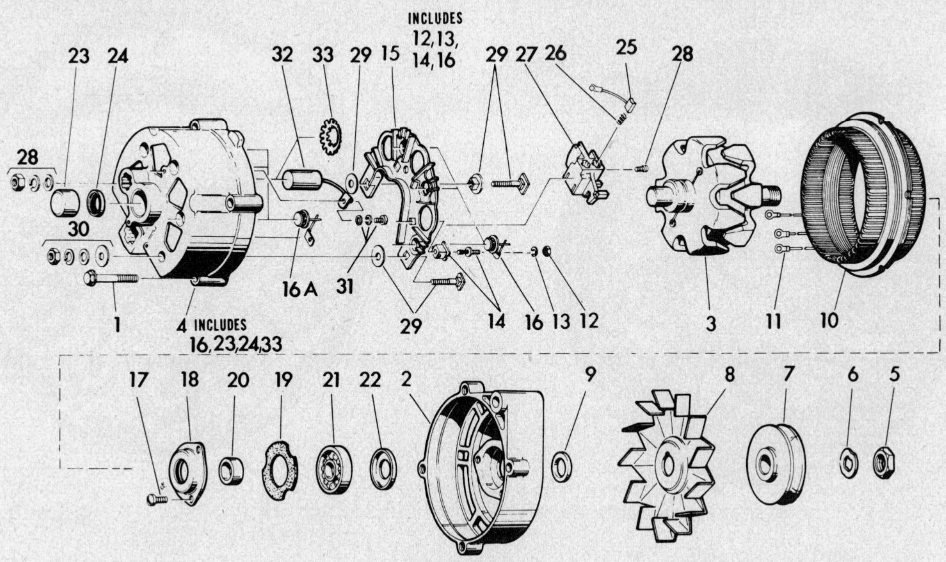

Delcotron assembly

1. Thru bolt (4)
2. Drive end frame
3. Rotor
4. Stator
5. Shaft nut
6. Shaft nut washer
7. Pulley (sheave)
8. Fan
9. Fan spacer washer
10. Stator coil
11. Stator coil terminal (3)
12. Junction terminal nut (3)
13. Junction terminal lockwasher (3)
14. Junction terminal and insulator
15. Heat sink
16. Diode (3) positive
16A. Diode (3) negative
17. Bearing retainer screw (3)
18. Bearing retainer
19. Gasket
20. Spacer
21. Ball bearing
22. Ball bearing shield
23. Needle bearing
24. Needle bearing seal
25. Brush (2)
26. Brush spring (2)
27. Brush holder
28. Brush holder screw
29. Terminal bolt and insulator (2)
30. Terminal nut and insulator (2)
31. Capacitor mounting screw and washers
32. Capacitor
33. Capacitor retaining spring

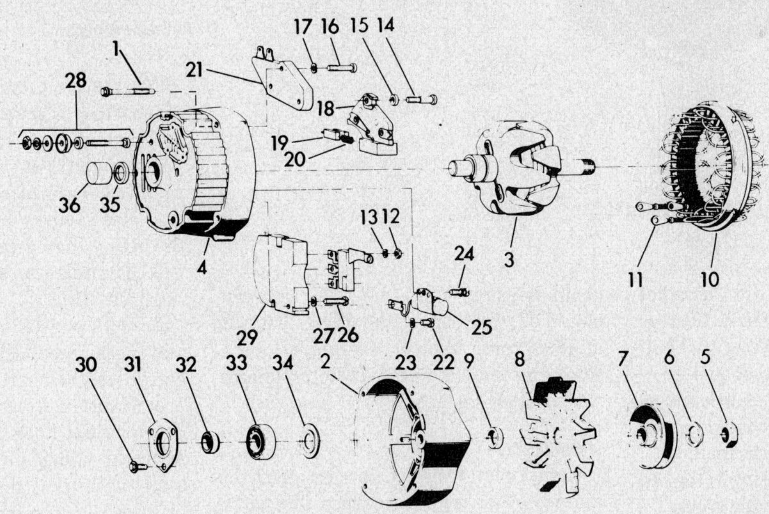

1971 and later Delcotron assembly

1. Thru bolt (4)
2. Drive end frame
3. Rotor
4. Stator
5. Shaft nut
6. Shaft nut washer
7. Pulley (sheave)
8. Fan
9. Fan spacer washer
10. Stator coil
11. Stator coil terminal
12. Nut (3)
13. Washer (3)
14. Screw
15. Insulator
16. Screw (2)
17. Washer (2)
18. Brush holder
19. Brush (2)
20. Spring (2)
21. Regulator
22. Screw
23. Washer
24. Screw & lockwasher
25. Condenser & bracket
26. Screw
27. Washer
28. Battery terminal parts
29. Rectifier bridge
30. Retainer screw (3)
31. Ball brg. retainer
32. Ball brg. seal spacer
33. Ball bearing
34. Ball brg. shield
35. Needle brg. spacer
36. Needle bearing

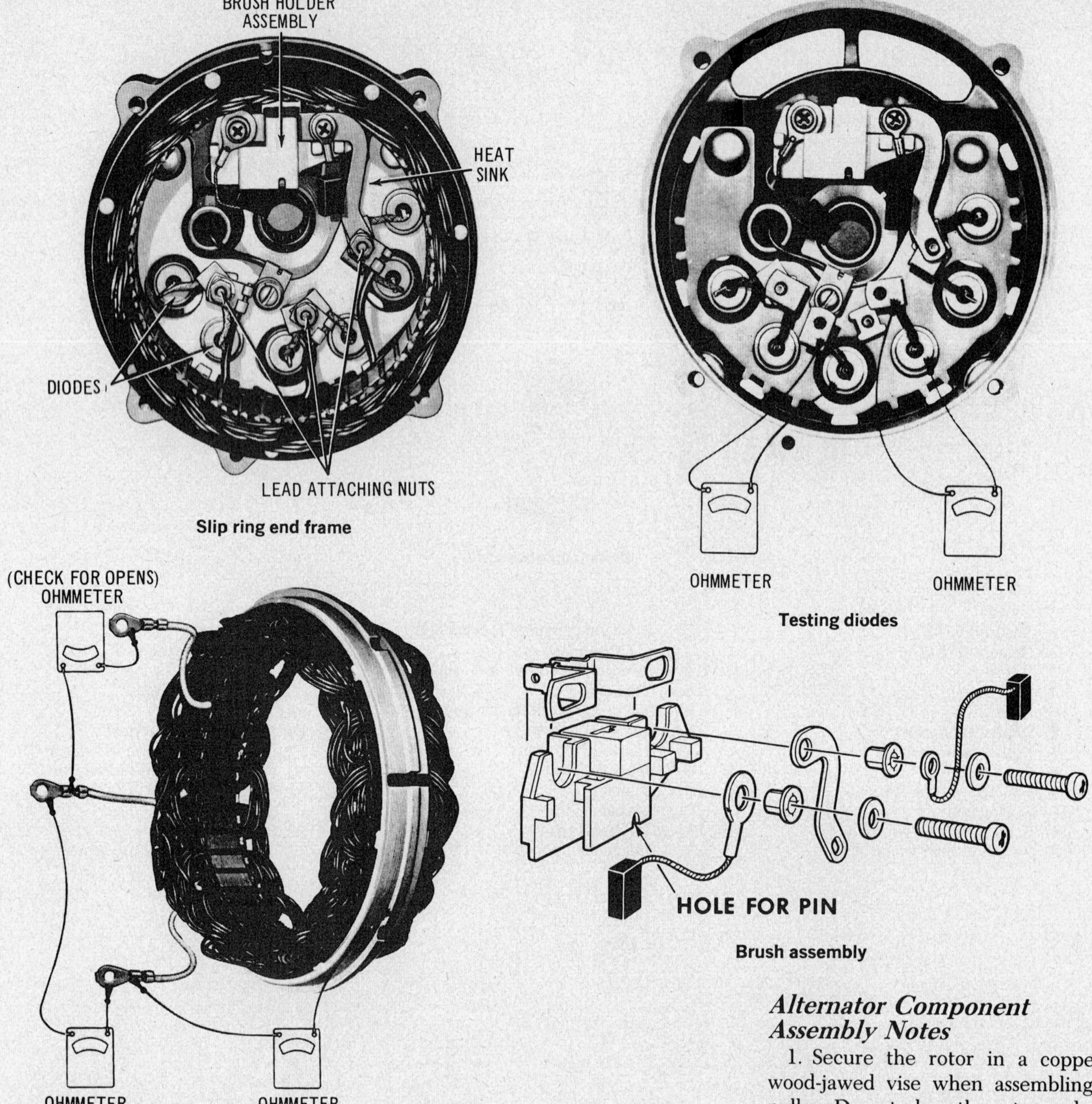

Slip ring end frame

Testing diodes

Brush assembly

Wiring for testing stator

1. Press the rotor onto the sprocket shaft using the Sprocket Shaft Bearing Tool (H-D part no. 97225–55) until it bottoms firmly against the seal spacer.
2. Apply thread-locking compound to the transmission shaft bearing recess in the chain housing and to the shaft.
3. After the bearing housing is tapped into place, pack the race with grease.
4. Use aluminum paint on the chain housing and transmission surfaces where the two meet.
5. Replace the chain housing O-ring in the engine crankcase groove.
6. Replace the cover gasket.
7. Secure the transmission base mounting nuts only after the engine and transmission are secured to the chain housing.
8. Use a vacuum gauge (H-D part no. 96950–68) to check the vacuum in the chain housing. With the vent tee hose closed off, the reading should be 20 in. Hg at 1500 rpm. A lower reading is indicative of an air leak at the gasket, solenoid, starter shaft, or hoses.

Testing

Component testing is carried out in the same manner as for the earlier alternator. If any of the diodes are bad, the diode pack must be replaced.

Brush Holder and Regulator Replacement

1. Remove the attaching nuts, stator, diode trio screw, and brush holder retaining screws.
2. Do not interchange the screws or replace the insulating sleeves on the screws with which they came.
3. All regulators are interchangeable.

Alternator Component Assembly Notes

1. Secure the rotor in a copper or wood-jawed vise when assembling the pulley. Do not place the rotor under undue stress when tightening the vise or distortion may result.
2. Tighten the shaft nut to between 50–60 ft/lbs.
3. Remove the tape from the bearing and shaft, and check to see if any dirt has gotten on the shaft or in the bearing.
4. Insert a straight wire through the brush holder holes to retain the brushes. After the alternator is completely assembled, withdraw the wire to allow the brushes to come in contact with the slip rings.

Rectifier Bridge Check

1. Connect an ohmmeter to one of the three bridge terminals and to the grounded heat sink.
2. Reverse the above. Replace the bridge if both readings are the same. One should read high and one should read low.
3. Perform the test on the other two terminals.

4. If the bridge is in the frame, connect an ohmmeter and press it down onto the flat metal connector rather than onto the stud.

5. Remove the attaching screw, "BAT" terminal screw, and the capacitor lead before replacing. Remember to replace the insulated washer between the frame and insulated heat sink.

Alternator Output Check

Consult the Alternator Check Chart for test specifications and connect the test equipment as shown in the illustration. Make sure that the negative battery terminal is grounded to the frame. The load rheostat can be adjusted to obtain the correct voltage output. On 1971 and later models, use the Delco-Remy test procedures.

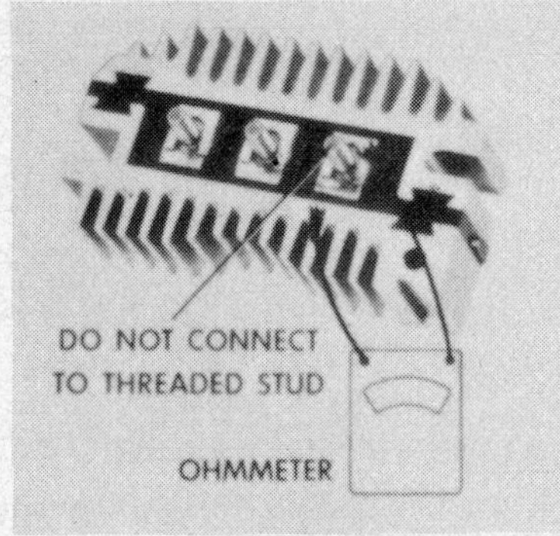

Testing rectifier bridge

Regulators

The Bosch and Delcotron regulators used are not reparable and must be replaced if they are malfunctioning. If a Delco-Remy regulator is suspected of improper operation, check the following:

1. Regulator points dirty, oily, pitted, or oxidized. Points may be cleaned with a point file or fine metal sandpaper. Do not try to restore to a like-new condition, replace if doubtful.

2. Adjust the contact relay air gap and contact point gap according to the Regulator Test Specifications Chart.

3. The ground wire (braided wire between regulator base and mounting bracket) may be broken.

4. Fuse may be blown (fuse holder near regulator).

5. Corrosion of internal components causing malfunction.

If you have a charging system problem and the alternator or generator output check shows that the regulator is probably at fault, the easiest way to verify this is to install a new regulator and recheck the output. The Delco-Remy regulator is adjustable, but in many cases adjustment will not repair it and you can waste a lot of time trying to make it work. Test specifications are provided at the end of the chapter for those who have the equipment to perform the tests and adjustments.

1. Clean the contact point surfaces with a point file and remove oil by running a strip of hard paper, soaked in gasoline, between them.

2. Be sure the points are properly aligned. If in doubt about point condition, replace them.

3. Replace points by removing the terminal screw and fulcrum pin snap-ring, and by lifting the breaker lever from the pivot stud. Remove the stationary circuit breaker contact.

4. Install points in the reverse order of removal and set the gap (refer to chapter 3). Do not overtighten the condenser wire.

5. Apply a light coat of grease to the breaker cam whenever the points are replaced or every 5,000 miles. Do not lubricate excessively. The condenser should be replaced whenever the points are replaced.

Magneto

SPORTSTER XLCH

REMOVAL

1. Remove the air cleaner and carburetor.

2. Disconnect the spark plug leads and the kill switch terminal wire at the magneto terminal.

3. Remove the tachometer drive assembly (if applicable) and loosen the control wire set screw.

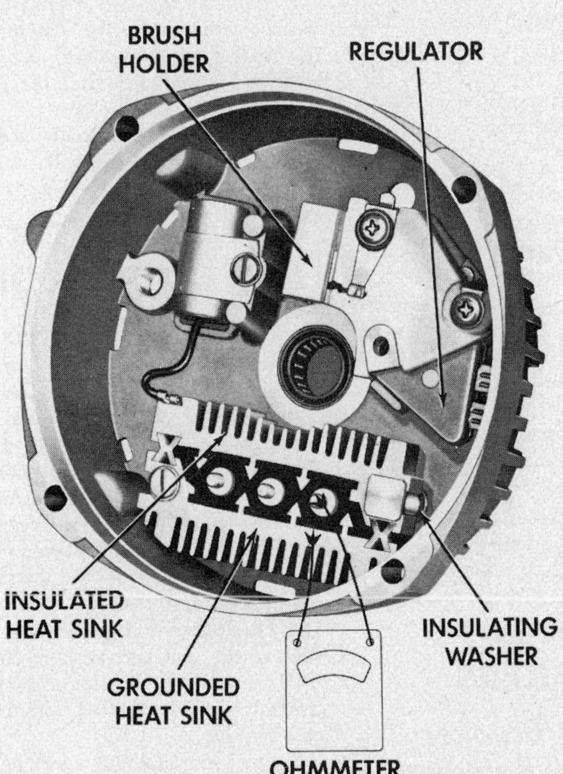

Checking rectifier bridge

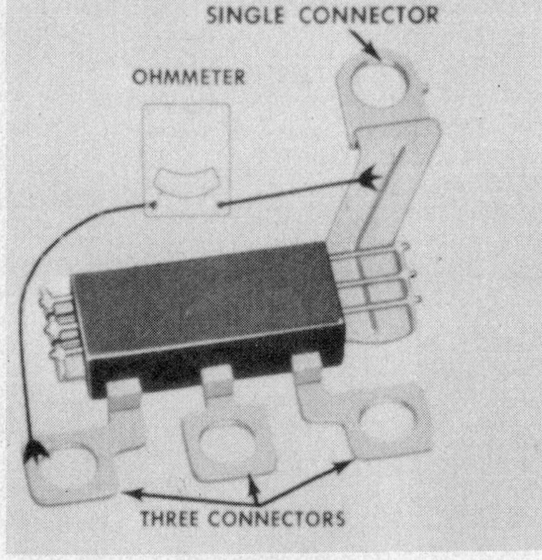

Testing diode trio

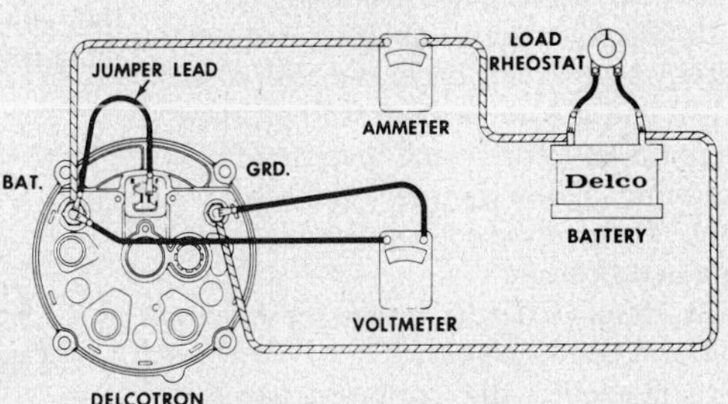

Wiring for testing output

4. Remove the mounting apparatus and lift the shaft and housing clear of the gearcase.

MAGNETO SPARK CHECK

1. Hold the end of the spark plug lead, with the plug cap removed, about ⅛ in. from the spark plug terminal. When the engine is running a blue spark should appear twice in every 360° rotation of the engine between the end of the lead and the plug terminal. If the spark is constant, the engine should not misfire. Do this on both plugs.

2. To test for spark with the engine off but the ignition on, hold the lead not more than ¼ in. from the plug terminal while kicking the engine over. Perform this on both plugs.

3. An easier test method is to remove the plug, reconnect the wire, and ground the plug tip against the cylinder head. Rotate the engine and watch for a blue spark at the plug tip.

4. If no spark is present, the kill button should be checked for a grounded condition before the magneto is removed for service.

DISASSEMBLY AND ASSEMBLY

1. Remove the end cap screws, end cap, and gasket.

2. Remove the spark plug leads. Remove the plug lead terminal by sliding up the lead protector and prying the terminal off with a screwdriver.

3. Remove the condenser mounting screw, washer, breaker arm terminal screw, condenser, and bracket.

4. Remove the point mounting screws, lockwashers, cam fiber and holder, and stationary contact point.

5. Remove the bearing support screws, safety gap (if applicable), and bearing support. Pry the rotor drive and grease retainer washer free, and remove the rotor cam end bearing.

6. Remove the rotor drive-gear pin by filing one end off and then punching it out.

7. Slip the rotor drive-gear from the off the shaft.

8. Remove the housing screws and slip the housing off the shaft.

9. Remove the O-ring and retainer washer, and drive out the bushing from within the housing (if applicable).

10. Remove the rotor drive and seal outer washer, rotor drive end seal, rotor drive, and grease retainer washer, then force the rotor drive-end snap-ring from the rotor shaft and remove the rotor.

11. Remove the rotor drive-end snapring and bearing.

12. Remove the coil bridge set screws, coil, and coil lead springs.

13. Remove the primary ground switch terminal and terminal switch wire.

14. Remove the vent cover screws, cover washers, cover, and screens.

15. Assemble in the reverse order of disassembly, taking care not to severely jar the rotor since this could cause damage.

GROUND SWITCH LOCK

Disassembly

1. Remove the end cap.

2. Remove the retainer clip between the insulating block and housing. This is best done by depressing the retainer clip with a knife, using the key in the switch as a lever, and pulling the key out to exert pressure while turning slightly to pull the lock out of the housing.

3. Remove the ground lock spring and lock ball from the ground-switch insulating block screw hole.

Assembly

1. With the retainer clip on top of the inside switch housing, insert the ground switch lock into the housing.

2. Depress the body retainer clip and push the ground lock switch into the housing, with a knife, so the clip engages the housing.

3. Loosen the condenser screw so the ground switch insulating block screw can be removed.

4. Replace the block screw and switch wire.

5. Replace the lock ball and lock spring.

6. Replace the switch insulating block wire and screw, and tighten the condenser screw.

7. Assemble the magneto in the reverse order of disassembly.

Installation

1. Set the oil seal ring and gasket (if applicable) in place on the gearcase.

2. Mount the magneto adaptor plate.

3. Install the magneto adaptor bolts from inside and tighten the assembly screws.

4. Manual retard magnetos must have the adaptor plates (47A and 47B) installed together.

5. Insert the rotor shaft into the gearcase and secure the magneto on the adaptor plate.

6. Manual retard magnetos must have the control arm installed before the mounting bolts can be replaced

CONTACT BREAKERS

Contact Breaker Assembly Removal

1. Before attempting to remove the contact breaker assembly, thoroughly clean the crankcase area around the unit as well as the contact breaker itself. To make sure that no dirt falls into the crankcase, have a clean oil soaked cloth handy to hold around the crankcase as the shaft is withdrawn.

2. On manual advance units, remove the contact breaker cover and cover retainer, then disconnect the spark control wire from the contact breaker cover.

3. On automatic advance units, remove the screw and lockwasher from the contact breaker cover and then remove the cover.

1964 AND EARLIER SPORTSTER AND 1963 AND EARLIER SERVI-CAR MODELS

1. Remove the contact breaker base and retainer exposing the two screws securing the shaft and housing assembly to the gearcase cover.

2. Remove the screws and lift the shaft and housing from the gearcase cover.

1965 AND LATER SPORTSTER AND 1964 AND LATER SERVI-CAR MODELS

1. On 1965 models, remove the nuts and washer which secure the contact breaker base to the stem and remove the base.

2. Remove the two screws and the washer which secure the shaft and housing to the gearcase cover, and lift the shaft and housing free from the gearcase cover.

3. On 1966 automatic-advance types, remove the stem clamp bolts and clamp to free the entire unit clear from the crankcase.

DUO-GLIDE MODELS

1. On models prior to 1962, remove the front cylinder head from the engine to provide sufficient clearance for the removal of the contact breaker assembly.

2. The two securing screws can best be removed with the Circuit Breaker Wrench (H-D part no. 94501–56). Once these have been removed, the unit can be lifted from the gearcase cover.

3. On manual-advance types, slip the base and retainer from the housing and then lift the unit free.

4. On 1965 automatic-advance types, remove the nuts and washers, then slip the base from the housing. Now the entire unit is free to be lifted from the gearcase housing.

5. On 1966 automatic-advance types, upon removal of the stem clamp nut and clamp, the entire unit is free to be lifted clear of the gearcase cover.

1970 AND LATER CASE-MOUNTED CONTACT BREAKER

1. Remove the contact breaker and gasket by removing the cover screws.
2. Remove the wire terminal and wire from the breaker points.
3. Remove the contact breaker cam bolt, breaker plate bolts, lockwashers, and washers or screw retainer (whichever is applicable).
4. Remove the breaker assembly and free the contact assembly from the breaker plate by removing the breaker contact screw. Free the condenser lead and flat spring from the breaker contact terminal post. Remove the condenser screw, lockwasher, and condenser.
5. Remove the breaker cam and advance assembly.
6. Free the flyweight spring hooks from the pivot pin grooves and slip the flyweights from the pivot pins. Springs need not be removed unless replacement is necessary. Flyweight roll pins are a press fit and need not be removed unless replacement is necessary.

Inspection and Repair

Before inspecting any parts, the entire contact breaker should be cleaned with a cloth and white gasoline.

If the fiber follower is badly worn, the points should be replaced. If the points are excessively burned or pitted, and cannot be cleaned to serviceable state, they should be replaced. A good rule of thumb is: replace when in doubt.

Always use a clean, fine-cut contact point file when cleaning points; never use emery cloth or rough sandpaper. Never use your point file on any other type of metal and always clean it before use if it is dirty or oily. If absolutely necessary, fine-grade metal sandpaper can be used. If residue is left on the point surfaces, particles will be embedded causing arcing and rapid burning of the points.

Using a spring guage, determine whether the point pressure is within 14–18 oz. If not, replace, since excessive pressure causes rapid wear of fiber, cam, and point surface, while insufficient pressure causes high-speed point bounce which leads to arcing, burning, and engine miss. Be sure also that the point faces seat evenly. If not, adjustment can be made by bending the contact plate.

PROCEDURES

1. Loosen the wire stud screw, lift off the condenser wire and connection, and lift away the contact breaker lever. Remove the lock screw and contact point support.
2. Lubricate the breaker cam with a trace of grease, taking care not to overlubricate, which would cause point burning, and lubricate the shaft with light grease (i.e., Delco-Remy no. 1960954). Take care to replace the cam in the same position on the shaft. This should be done every 500 miles.
3. Assemble the points in the reverse order: brass washer, condenser wire end, and stud screw, with the lever notch aligning.
4. Adjust the point gap and ignition timing.
5. Check the contact breaker advance flyweight action (if applicable) by moving the cam until the weights reach their stop. Releasing the cam should bring it back to a fully retarded position due to spring action. Replace weak springs as necessary.
6. Check to see if the flyweight ears, which engage slots in the cam, are worn or if the cam is loose on the spindle, and replace if necessary.
7. If either the base pivot stud or the base is worn or damaged, replace it. The base should turn freely but not loosely. If the base has excessive stem clearance, the gap will vary.
8. The condenser cannot be repaired. If a faulty condenser is suspected, observe for an open or short circuit. An open circuit will cause excessive arcing at the points and a shorted circuit will result in no noticeable spark. Replace the condenser if it is defective and note whether or not performance is improved.
9. Inspect the coil-to-contact breaker low-tension wire, wire stud insulator, and fiber washer for a brittle or cracked condition. Replace if defective.
10. To disassemble the advance mechanism, pry the clips loose from the stem plate. Inspect the teeth and worm gear for wear or damage. Check for excess side and end-play (in excess of 0.008 in.) as this will affect timing and allow oil seepage onto the points.
11. If the timer stem is to be rebushed, drive out the old bushings and replace them. Spacer washers of 0.062 in., 0.066 in., 0.072 in., or 0.076 in. can be used to obtain 0.001–0.007 in. of shaft end-play.
12. When assembling the shaft in the stem, secure the gear and spacer washers to the shaft with a new steel pin riveted in place. Make sure that the shaft moves freely in the stem.

Installing Contact Breaker

1964 AND EARLIER DUO-GLIDE MANUAL ADVANCE

1. Remove the spark plugs, put the machine in high gear on its center stand, remove the screw plug from the timing inspection hole, and telescope the front push rod.
2. Rotate the engine until the "F" mark on the flywheel is in position.
3. Place the breaker base on the shaft and stem assemblies, and wrap the point cable clockwise around the shaft.
4. Install the base retainer over the cable.
5. Align the breaker base timing mark with the end of the adjusting stud plate.
6. Install a new contact breaker gasket using a suitable gasket sealer. Affix the worm gear to the shaft end.
7. Turn the shaft counterclockwise, approximately 60°, from the point where the cam timing mark aligns with the fiber follower.
8. Insert the breaker assembly into the crankcase with the screw holes lined up with the mounting holes in the crankcase. The front points ("F" on base) fiber should align with the mark (double-point-type).
9. Turn the base counterclockwise to the fully advanced position. If the fiber and cam mark don't align, lift the shaft clear and turn the gear, one tooth at a time, until the correct alignment is obtained.
10. Adjust the ignition timing.

1963 AND EARLIER SERVI-CAR; 1964 AND EARLIER SPORTSTER MANUAL ADVANCE

1–3. Consult the previous section.

4. Install the new breaker gasket using a suitable gasket sealer.
5. Insert the breaker shaft and stem assembly into the gearcase with the cable inserted in the hole of the stem flange.
6. Before engaging the driving gear, turn the shaft 60° counterclockwise from the position of the mark and fiber alignment.
7. Temporarily secure the base on the shaft and stem assemblies in the fully advanced position.
8. Adjust the gear position until the cam mark and fiber align by turning the gear one tooth at a time. Secure the crankcase screws.
9. Wrap the cable around the shaft clockwise and install the base retainer over the cable. Engage the cover by moving the base retainer with a screwdriver until the notches align with the cover retainer ends.
10. Adjust the ignition timing.

1965 ELECTRA-GLIDE AUTOMATIC ADVANCE

1–2. Consult the previous section.

3. Lubricate the cam end of the shaft and stem assembly, and install the

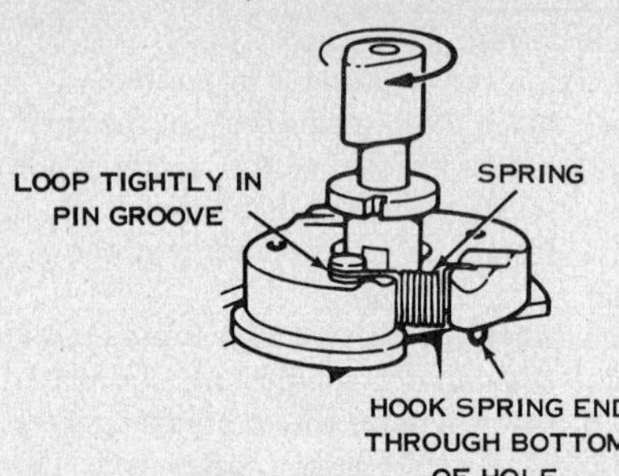

Advance unit spring assembly

breaker cam on the shaft so that the notches in the cam engage with the flyweights.

4. Place the breaker base on the stem and shaft assembly and temporarily secure it.

5. The stem and base can only mount correctly in one way due to the stud positions. Check by aligning the base timing marks.

6. Install a new breaker rubber seal.

7. Turn the shaft counterclockwise 60 degrees from the position at which the cam mark and fiber align.

8. Temporarily insert the stem into the gearcase with the timing base marks away from the engine.

9. Align the flywheel timing mark in the fully retarded position.

10. Adjust the gear engagement, one tooth at a time, untilthe fiber and the cam mark align and secure the assembly to the gearcase.

11. Adjust the ignition timing.

1964 AND LATER SERVI-CAR AND 1956 SPORTSTER AUTOMATIC ADVANCE

1–5. Consult the previous section.

6. Install a new circuit breaker gasket using a suitable gasket sealer. Secure the worm gear to the shaft end.

7. Insert the shaft and stem assembly into the gearcase cover with the cable inserted into the hole of the stem flange. The stem should be positioned with the base timing marks toward the outside of the engine.

8. Before engaging the drive gear, turn the shaft 60 degrees from the position where the fiber and cam mark line up, and temporarily secure the assembly to the gearcase.

9. With the flywheel timing mark in position, note whether the cam mark and fiber align. Lift the shaft and adjust the gear engagement, one tooth at a time, until alignment is obtained. Secure the assembly to the gearcase.

10. Position the base assembly on the shaft with the base timing marks in alignment, and secure the base.

11. Adjust the ignition timing.

1966 AND LATER ELECTRA-GLIDE, SPORTSTER, AND SERVI-CAR AUTOMATIC ADVANCE

1–4. Consult the previous section.

5. Install a new rubber seal.

6. Before installing, turn the shaft to approximately align the cam mark with the fiber follower.

7. Insert the breaker into the gearcase with the cable toward the rear of the engine. This will position the points to the outside of the engine to facilitate adjustment.

8. Align the flywheel timing mark in the center of the insepction hole and observe the position of the cam mark and fiber.

9. Lift the assembly and turn the shaft gear, one tooth at a time, until the cam mark and fiber align. Install the stem clamp and secure the assembly to the gearcase.

10. Adjust the ignition timing.

1970 AND LATER CASE-MOUNTED CONTACT BREAKER

1. Consult the previous section.

2. Assemble in the reverse order of disassembly.

3. Lubricate the cam with a light application of High Temperature Grease (H-D part no. 99862–72) during assembly, and thereafter at every 5,000 miles, or use any heavy grease if the aforementioned product is unavailable.

4. Seat the advance assembly squarely and firmly on the camshaft end.

5. Adjust the point gap as described in "Contact Point Adjustment." The gap must be within 0.016–0.020 in. for both cams if damage is to be averted. Loosen the breaker cam bolt and rotate the advance mechanism toward the points, at their widest setting, to equalize the gap settings.

STARTING SYSTEM

Troubleshooting

If the engine doesn't start after 30 seconds of operating the starter motor, let the starter cool for no less than two minutes before operating it again.

1. If the starter motor doesn't turn at all, the trouble is either a dead battery or, more likely, a disconnected wire. Check the mounting and wiring connections of the starter first, and then check the battery and return circuits. The solenoid switch should be mounted firmly. All connections must be clean and secure for effective operation.

2. Check the battery for charge by noting the brightness of the headlamp or by using a hydrometer. If the battery is charged and the wiring is good, the problem is either the starter, the switches, or the engine itself.

3. If the battery is charged, the problem may be in the switches. This can be checked by bypassing each switch with a jumper.

4. If the engine oil viscosity is too great, or if the bearings or pistons are too tight, the engine may not turn over. If the engine can be kicked over with the normal amount of effort but the starter won't turn it over (assuming the battery is charged), the starter motor is probably faulty.

Delco-Remy Starter Motor

DISASSEMBLY

1. Remove the thru-bolts, nuts, and lockwashers. The bolt which lies nearest the field coil has a vinyl insulating sleeve which must be removed carefully.

2. Remove the commutator end frame and drive end frame. If they don't slide off, tap them gently with a soft mallet.

3. Press or tap the armature from the drive end of the frame.

4. Remove the pole shoe screws, terminal nuts, lockwashers, insulating washers, terminal screw, field coils, and pole shoes.

5. If the brushes are grounded or the holders are defective, remove the brush holders by drilling out the rivets. If done carefully, a cold chisel can be used.

6. Remove the brush springs by turning them clockwise after compressing one side with a screwdriver until the springs leave their seats.

7. Remove the insulated brush by cutting off the lead where it joins the field coil wire.

ASSEMBLY

Refer to the following section on Prestolite starter motors. Procedures are the same.

TESTING THE FRAME AND FIELD ASSEMBLY

1. Test for an open circuit with a test lamp connected to the terminal screw and insulated brush. An open circuit will keep the lamp from lighting.

2. Test for a grounded field circuit with a test lamp lead on the terminal or on each insulated field coil brush, and the other lead grounded to the frame. If the lamp lights, the circuit is grounded.

3. Check each insulated brush holder for a grounded condition by using a test lamp. Replace any for which the lamp lights.

4. Replace the field coils if a short is suspected and note whether performance is enhanced.

TESTING THE ARMATURE

1. Connect a test light or voltmeter between the commutator and armature core.

2. If the light comes on (or the meter responds), the armature coil is grounded and the armature should be replaced.

ARMATURE REPAIR

1. Place the armature in a lathe and turn down the commutator if it is worn, out of round, or if the mica insulation protrudes above the segments. This should only be done by an experienced mechanic.

2. Undercut the mica 1/32 in. with an undercutting machine or a hacksaw blade. Be sure that the mica surface is flat and even, and is kept free of dirt and copper dust.

3. Lightly sand the commutator with "00" sandpaper to ensure a smooth surface.

4. Examine the bearing, bushing, and thrust washer for damage and wear (i.e., excessive play), and replace if in doubt.

5. Information concerning armature testing may be obtained through Delco-Remy, but replacement is advised over repair.

BRUSH REPLACEMENT AND REPAIR

1. Complete replacement sets are available for brushes, grounded holders, and insulated holders.

2. Prepare to replace the insulated brush by cleaning the coil lead end with a file or grinder.

3. Prepare the surface for soldering with rosin flux or use a flux-based solder. Only remove varnish from the leads in the area to be soldered.

4. Solder the coil lead to the back side of the coil, taking care not to use excessive amounts of solder. Solder must never contact the armature. Overheating the brush lead will cause the solder to run onto the wire strands, making the lead inflexible.

5. When replacing the grounded brush, peen the brush holder mounting screws with a hammer so that the nuts won't vibrate loose.

Prestolite Starter Motor

DISASSEMBLY

1. Remove the thru-bolts, washers, lockwashers, and commutator end cover.

2. Insert a tube the diameter of which exceeds that of the commutator. This will keep brushes in place and allow the armature to be replaced without touching the brushes.

3. Remove the armature, drive end cover, and bearing as one assembly. The bearing may have to be pressed out.

TESTING THE FRAME AND FIELD ASSEMBLY

1. Coils can only be tested for an open circuit; any type of coil failure requires replacement of the frame and field assembly.

2. Touch one test lamp lead to the frame and the other to each field coil brush. The lamp should light on each brush; failure to do so indicates an open circuit.

BRUSH REPLACEMENT AND ARMATURE REPAIR

Same as for Delco-Remy starter motor.

ASSEMBLY (all models)

1. If the brushes and springs have been released, clamps can be used to hold them in place while reinstalling the armature.

2. Align the end cover mark to the motor terminal.

3. Align the brush holder positioning notch with the motor terminal insulator.

4. Align the commutator end head with the motor terminal.

5. Install the thru-bolts, washers, and lockwashers, and mount entire unit on engine.

IGNITION SYSTEM

Ignition Coil

If, after checking the battery, plugs, points and condenser, you can't get any spark, it's time to replace the coil. Before doing so, a new coil can be hooked up to see if the problem has been eliminated.

When replacing the cable, warm the coil, so that the sealing compound will

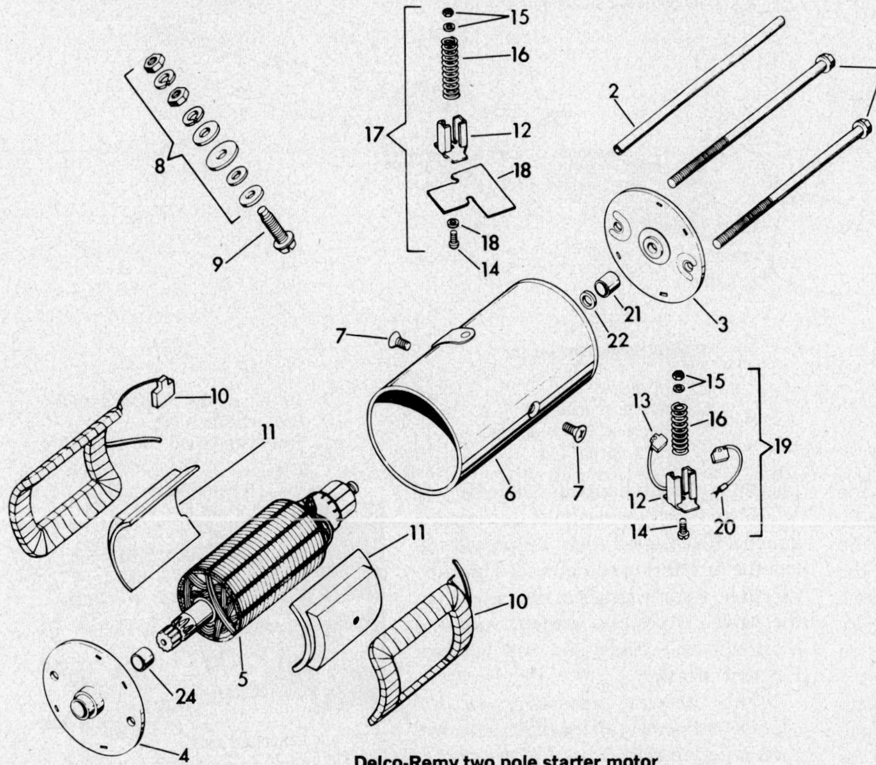

Delco-Remy two pole starter motor

1. Thru-bolt (2)
2. Insulating sleeve
3. Commutator end frame
4. Drive end frame
5. Armature
6. Frame and field assembly
7. Pole shoe screw (2)
8. Terminal nuts, lockwashers and insulating washers
9. Terminal screw
10. Set of field coils with insulated brush
11. Pole shoe (2)
12. Brush holder (2)
13. Grounded brush
14. Brush holder mounting screw (2)
15. Brush holder mounting nut and lockwasher (2)
16. Brush spring (2)
17. Insulated brush holder set
18. Insulator
19. Grounded brush holder set
20. Insulated brush
21. Bushing
22. Thrust washer

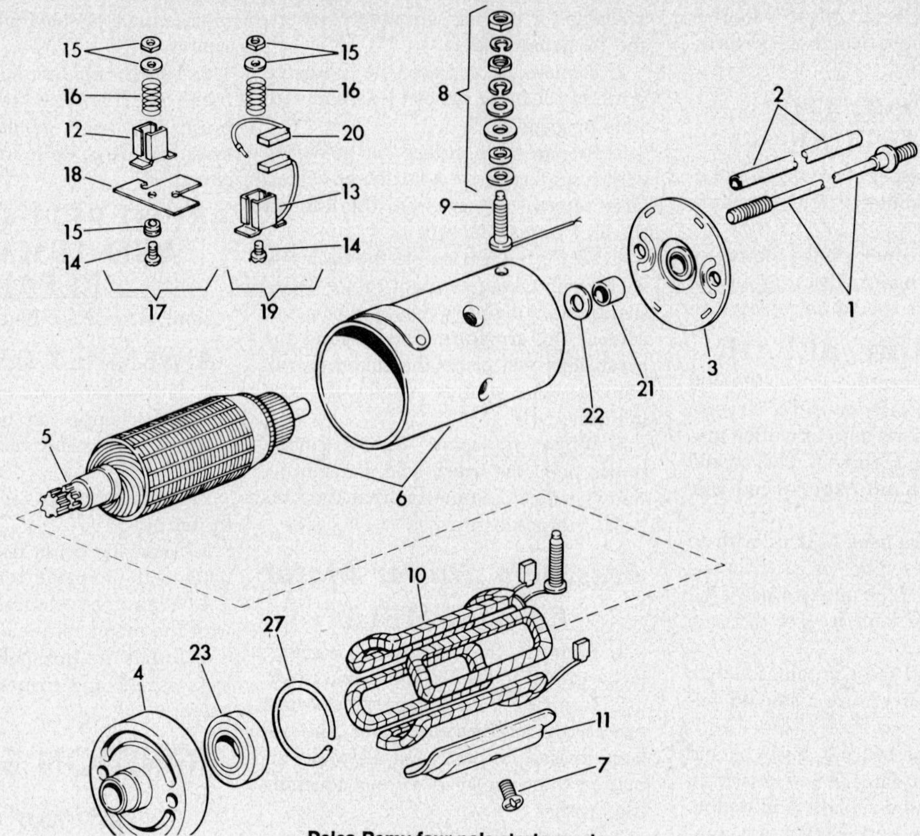

Delco-Remy four pole starter motor

1. Thru bolt (2)
2. Insulating sleeve
3. Commutator end frame
4. Drive end frame
5. Armature
6. Frame and field assembly
7. Pole shoe screw (2 or 4)
8. Terminal nuts, lockwashers and insulating washers
9. Terminal screw
10. Set of field coils
11. Pole shoe (2 or 4)
12. Brush holder (2 or 4)
13. Grounded brush and holder (1 or 2)
14. Brush holder mounting screw (2 or 4)
15. Brush holder mounting nut and lockwasher (2 or 4)
16. Brush spring (2 or 4)
17. Insulated brush holder set
18. Insulator
19. Grounded brush holder set
20. Insulated brush (1 or 2)
21. Bushing
22. Thrust washer
23. Ball bearing
24. Bearing retainer

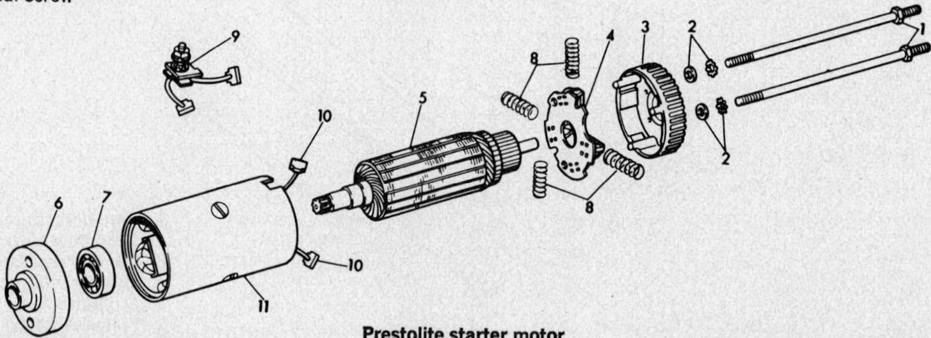

Prestolite starter motor

1. Thru bolt
2. Washer and lockwasher (2)
3. Commutator end cover
4. Brush plate and holder assembly
5. Armature
6. Drive end cover
7. Drive end ball bearing
8. Brush spring (4)
9. Terminal and brush assembly
10. Ground brush (2)
11. Frame and field coil assembly

soften, by turning on the key with the points closed. Prepare the new cables by rounding the ends so they will follow the holes left in the compound and dip the end in light oil. As soon as the old cable is removed, replace it with the new, applying sufficient pressure to skewer it on the brass pin at the cable base.

Be careful not to overheat the compound because the holes will close too quickly and will interfere with the replacement. If this happens, allow the coil to cool and then open a hole, by inserting a tube with a jagged edge, which will collect the interfering compound. This tube should be slightly larger in diameter than the cable. If positive contact with the brass pin isn't made, the coil will not function properly.

NOTE: *Service procedures for the point, condenser, spark plugs, etc., will be found in the "Tune-Up" section.*

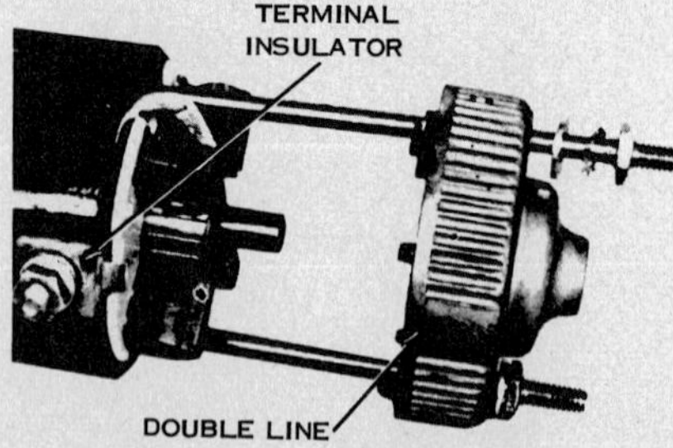

Aligning starter motor cover

ALTERNATOR CHECK CHART

Component	Connection	Reading	Result
Rotor	Ohmmeter from slip ring to shaft	Very low	Grounded
	110 volt test lamp from slip ring to shaft	Lamp lights	Grounded
	Ohmmeter across slip rings	Very high	Open
	110 volt test lamp across slip rings	Lamp fails to light	Open
	Battery and ammeter to slip rings	Observe ammeter reading	1.9 to 2.3 amp
Stator	Ohmmeter from lead to frame	Very low	Grounded
	110 volt test lamp from lead to frame	Lamp lights	Grounded
	Ohmmeter across each pair of leads	Any reading very high	Open
	110 volt test light across each pair of leads	Fails to light	Open
Diodes	12 volt (or less) test lamp across diode, then reverse connections	Lamp fails to light in both checks	Open
		Lamp lights in both checks	Shorted
1970 and earlier Output	Run under load, adjust rheostat across battery to 14 volts and read ammeter	Ammeter	Rated @ 32 amp 18 amp @ 2000, 28 amp @ 5000 (minimum)
1971 and later Output	Run under load, ground field, adjust rheostat across battery to 14 volts and read ammeter	Ammeter	Rated @ 37 amp 22 amp @ 2000 32 amp @ 5000

DELCO-REMY REGULATOR TEST SPECIFICATIONS CHART

Regulator Part Number: Manufacturer's Number	Regulator Part Number: Harley-Davidson	For Testing Procedure See Delco-Remy Service Bulletin Number	Regulator Type	Adjustment and Range: (Amps) Current Regulator Setting	Adjustment and Range (Volts): Cutout Relay Closing Voltage	Adjustment and Range (Volts): Voltage Regulator Setting	Used with Harley-Davidson Generator and Motorcycle Models
74511-51	1118 388	1R 116	3 Unit Current & Voltage	18	6.6	7.5	1950-1951 model 48, 2-brush fan-cooled generator. (Superseded by 74511-51A for parts order)
74511-51A	1118 707 1118 707B 1118 707C 1118 707D	1R 116 1R 118 1R 118 1R 118A	3 Unit Current & Voltage	20 (17.5-20.5)	6.6 (5.9-6.7)	7.5 (7.2-7.5)	Model 51, 2 brush fan-cooled generator
74511-58	1119 187C 1119 187D	1R 118 1R 118A	3 Unit Current & Voltage	15 (13.5-16.5)	6.6 (5.9-6.7)	7.4 (7.2-7.5)	Model 58 Generator
74510-47	118 307	1R 116	2 Unit Voltage		6.4	7.0 7.4	Models 125-165 Generators Model 52K Generator Regulator superseded by 74510-47A for parts order

DELCO-REMY REGULATOR TEST SPECIFICATIONS CHART

Regulator Part Number Manufacturer's Number	Regulator Part Number Harley-Davidson	For Testing Procedure See Delco-Remy Service Bulletin Number	Regulator Type	Adjustment and Range: (Amps) Current Regulator Setting	Adjustment and Range (Volts): Cutout Relay Closing Voltage	Adjustment and Range (Volts): Voltage Regulator Setting	Used with Harley-Davidson Generator and Motorcycle Models	
	1118 794	1R 116	2 Unit Voltage		6.4	7.0	Models 125-165 Generators	Regulator superseded by 74510-47A for parts order
						7.4	Model 52K Generator Model 58 & 61 Generator	
74510-47A	118 995	1R 116	2 Unit Voltage		6.4 (6.9-6.7)	7.2 (7.0-7.3)	Model 52K, 58 & 61 Generators Model 125-165 Generators	
74510-59	1118 989	1R 116	2 Unit Voltage		5.5 (5.0-6.0)	6.7 (6.5-6.8)	Model 58 and 61 Generators	
74510-64	1119 614	1R 119A	3 Unit Current & Voltage	10 (9.0-11.0)	12.4 (11.8-13.0)	14.3* (13.9-14.5)*	Model 64 and later 12V Generator (*Upper contact operation Operation on lower contacts must be 0.1 to 0.3 volt lower)	
74510-65	1100 687	1R 262	2 Unit Voltage		12.5 (11.5-13.5)	14.4* (13.5-14.9)*	Delcotron Alternator	
All 6-Volt Regulators	Current regulator air gap 0.075 in. Voltage regulator air gap 0.075 in.				Cutout relay point opening 0.020 in. Cutout relay air gap 0.020 in.			
All 12-Volt Regulators	Current regulator air gap 0.075 in. Voltage regulator air gap varies with setting				Cutout relay air gap and point opening 0.020 in. Voltage regulator point opening 0.016 in.			

Bosch Regulators

Harley-Davidson	Manufacturer's Number	Relay Cut-in Voltage	Regulator Voltage No Load	Regulator Voltage Load	Used with Harley-Davidson Generator and Motorcycle Models
74511-65	TBA 130-150/12/2	12.4-13.1	13.8-15.4	12.7-14.5 @ 10 amp	1965 Model 65 Generator for 1965-66 Sportster XLH and 1965 and Later XLCH

BULB CHART

Model	Lamp Description	Bulbs Rqd	Candle Power or Wattage 12 V	Candle Power or Wattage 6 V	Harley-Davidson Part Number 12 V	Harley-Davidson Part Number 6 V
DUO-GLIDE ELECTRA GLIDE	HEADLAMP	1			67717-64	67717-48B
	Hi Beam		50 Watts	45 Watts		
	Lo Beam		45 Watts	35 Watts		
	TAIL AND STOP LAMP	1			68165-64	68165-47
	Tail Lamp		4 CP	3 CP		
	Stop Lamp		32 CP	21 CP		

BULB CHART

Model	Lamp Description	Bulbs Rqd	Candle Power or Wattage 12 V	Candle Power or Wattage 6 V	Harley-Davidson Part Number 12 V	Harley-Davidson Part Number 6 V
	INSTRUMENT PANEL					
	Generator Signal Light	1	2 CP	2 CP	68462-64	68462-49
	Oil Pressure Signal Light	1	2 CP	2 CP	68462-64	68462-49
	Speedometer Light	1		1.5 CP	71090-64	71090-47
	Generator Signal Light (Special Radio)	1		2 CP		68462-49
	Neutral Indicator Light	1	2 CP	2 CP	68462-64	68462-49
	High Beam Indicator	1	2 CP		68462-64	
	ACCESSORIES					
	Spot Lamp (Bulb Type)	1	32 CP	32 CP	68715-64	68715-49
	(Sealed Beam Type)	1	30 Watts	30 Watts	68726-64	68726-62
	Parking Lamp	—	3 CP	3 CP	68166-64	68165-15
	Turn Indicator Lamps	4	32 CP	21 CP	68572-64A	68572-50
	Turn Indicator Pilot Lamps	2	1.5 CP	1 CP	71090-64	71090-47
SPORTSTER	HEADLAMP	1				
	Hi Beam		50 Watts	45 Watts	67717-64	67717-59
	Lo Beam		45 Watts	35 Watts		
	TAIL AND STOP LAMP	1				
	Tail Lamp		4 CP	3 CP	68165-64	68165-47
	Stop Light		32 CP	21 CP	71090-65	71090-59
	INSTRUMENT PANEL					
	Generator Signal Light	1	4 CP	3 CP		
	Oil Pressure Signal Light	1	4 CP	3 CP	71090-65	71090-59
	Speedometer Light	1	2 CP	1.5 CP	68462-64	71090-47
	High Beam Indicator	1	2 CP		68462-64	
	ACCESSORIES					
	Spot Lamp (Bulb Type)	1	32 CP	32 CP	68715-64	68715-49
	(Sealed Beam Type)	1	30 Watts	30 Watts	68726-64	68726-62
	Parking Lamp	—	3 CP	3 CP	68166-64	68165-15
	Turn Indicator Lamps	4	32 CP	21 CP	68572-64A	68572-50
	Turn Indicator Pilot Lamps	2	1.5 CP	1 CP	71090-64	71090-47
SERVI-CAR	HEADLAMP	1				
	Hi Beam		50 Watts	45 Watts	67717-64	67717-48B
	Lo Beam		45 Watts	35 Watts		
	TAIL AND STOP LAMP	1				
	Tail Lamp		4 CP	3 CP	68165-64	68165-47
	Stop Light		32 CP	21 CP		
	INSTRUMENT PANEL					
	Generator Signal Light	1	2 CP	2 CP	68462-64	68462-49
	Oil Pressure Signal Light	1	2 CP	2 CP	68462-64	68462-49
	Speedometer Light	1	1.5 CP	1.5 CP	71090-64	71090-47
	High Beam Indicator	1	2 CP		68462-64	
	ACCESSORIES					
	Spot Lamp (Bulb Type)	1	32 CP	32 CP	68715-64	68715-49
	(Sealed Beam Type)	1	30 Watts	30 Watts	68726-64	68726-62
	Parking Lamp	—	3 CP	3 CP	68166-64	68165-15
	Turn Indicator Lamps	4	32 CP	21 CP	68572-64A	68572-50
	Turn Indicator Pilot Lamps	2	1.5 CP	1 CP	71090-64	71090-47

WIRING DIAGRAMS

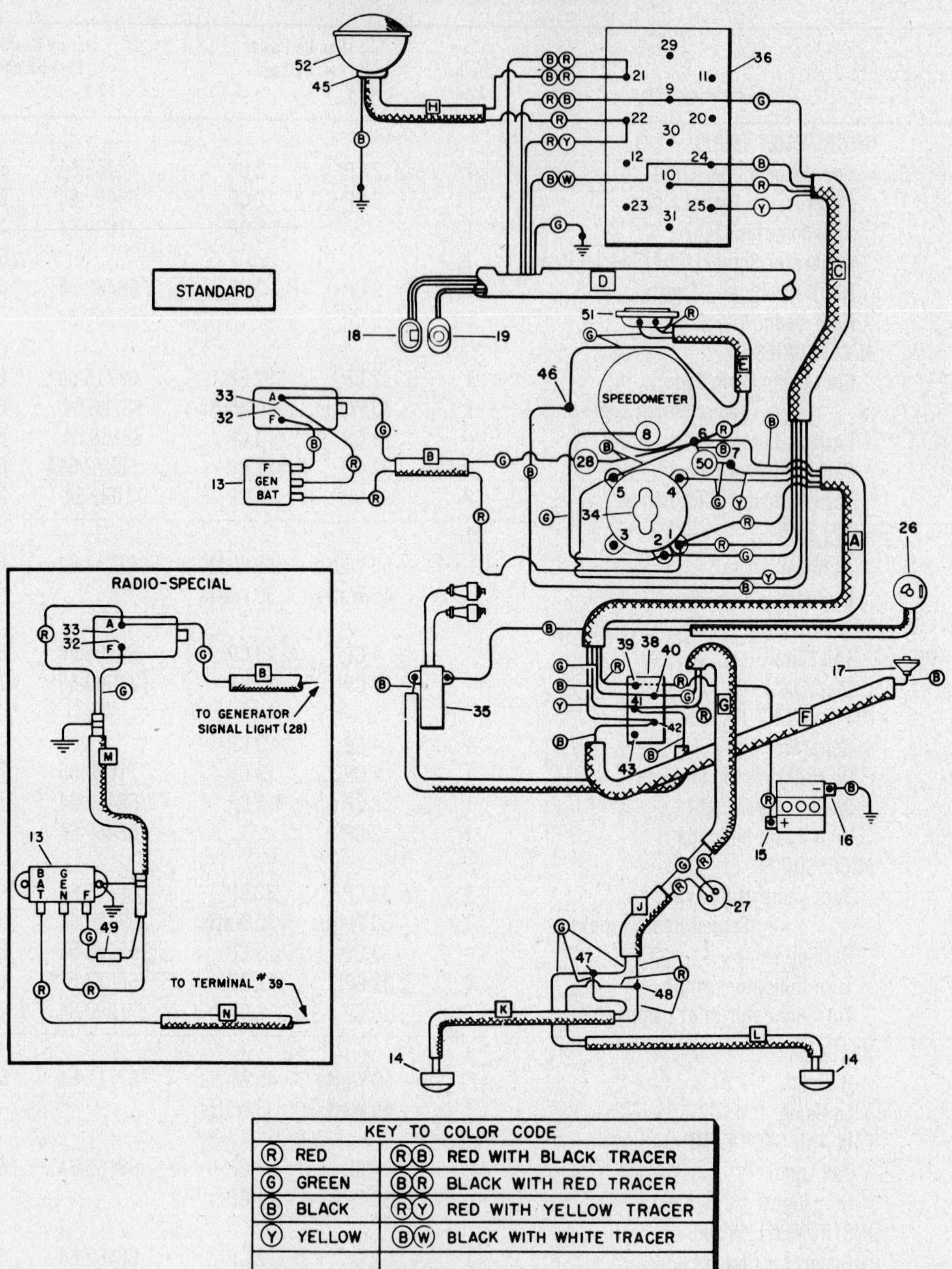

KEY TO COLOR CODE	
(R) RED	(R)(B) RED WITH BLACK TRACER
(G) GREEN	(B)(R) BLACK WITH RED TRACER
(B) BLACK	(R)(Y) RED WITH YELLOW TRACER
(Y) YELLOW	(B)(W) BLACK WITH WHITE TRACER

1959 and earlier Servi-Car

STANDARD

A. Conduit (four wires)—Red, green, black and yellow
B. Conduit (two wires)—Red and green
C. Conduit (four wires)—Red, green, black and yellow
D. Handlebar (loose wires)—Red with black tracer, black with red tracer, red with yellow tracer, black and green
E. Conduit (two wires)—Red and green
F. Conduit (one wire)—Black
G. Conduit (two wires)—Red and green
H. Conduit (two wires)—Red and black
J. Conduit (two wires)—Red and green
K. Conduit (two wires)—Red and green
L. Conduit (two wires)—Red and green

1. Switch terminal—3 red wires
2. Switch terminal—2 green wires
3. Switch terminal—Not used with standard wiring
4. Switch terminal—Green wire
5. Switch terminal—Black and yellow wires
6. Junction terminal—4 black and 1 red wire
7. Junction terminal—Yellow and green wires
8. Speedometer light—Green wire
9. Terminal—Green wire and red with black tracer
10. Terminal—Red wire
11. Terminal—Not used with standard wiring
12. Terminal—Not used with standard wiring
13. Regulator—2 red and 1 black wire
14. Tail and stop lamps—Red and green wires
15. Battery positive terminal—Red wire
16. Battery negative terminal—Black wire
17. Oil signal switch—Black wire

1959 and earlier Servi-Car

18. Handlebar headlamp switch—Black with red tracer, red with yellow tracer, red with black tracer
19. Horn switch—Black and green wires
20. Terminal—Not used with standard wiring
21. Terminal—2 black with red tracer
22. Terminal—Red with yellow tracer and red wire
23. Terminal—Not used with standard wiring
24. Terminal—Black wire with white tracer and black wire
25. Terminal—Yellow wire
26. Ignition circuit breaker—Black wire
27. Stop lamp switch—2 red wires
28. Generator signal light—Black and green wires
29. Terminal—Not used on standard model
30. Terminal—Not used on standard model
31. Terminal—Not used on standard model
32. Generator "F" terminal—Black wire
33. Generator "A" terminal—Red and green wires
34. Ignition light switch—See terminals 1, 2, 3, 4 and 5
35. Ignition coil—2 black wires
36. Terminal plate—See terminals 9, 10, 21, 22, 24 and 25
38. Terminal box—See terminals 39, 40, 41 and 42
39. Terminal—2 red wires
40. Terminal—2 green wires
41. Terminal—2 black wires and red wire
42. Terminal—Black and yellow wires
43. Terminal—Not used with standard wiring
45. Head lamp bracket—Black wire
46. Junction terminal—Black and green wires
47. Terminal—3 green wires
48. Terminal—3 red wires
50. Oil signal light—Black and green wires
51. Horn—Red and green wires
52. Headlamp—Red and black wires

RADIO—SPECIAL

Servi-Car wiring for radio equipment is the same as standard wiring except for regulator and generator connections.

- M. Cable (two wires)—Red and green
- B. Conduit (one wire)—Green
- N. Conduit (one wire)—Red
- 13. Regulator—2 red wires and green wire
- 32. Generator "F" terminal—Green wire
- 33. Generator "A" terminal—Red and green wires
- 49. Fuse

1960-63 Servi-Car

STANDARD

- A. Conduit (four wires)—Red, green, black and yellow
- B. Conduit (two wires)—Red and green
- C. Conduit (four wires)—Red, green, black and yellow
- D. Handlebar (loose wires)—Red with black tracer, black with red tracer, red with yellow tracer, black and green
- E. Conduit (two wires)—Red and green
- F. Conduit (one wire)—Black
- G. Conduit (two wires)—Red and green
- H. Conduit (three wires)—Black, white and yellow
- J. Conduit (two wires)—Red and green
- K. Conduit (two wires)—Red and green
- L. Conduit (two wires)—Red and green

1. Switch terminal—3 red wires
2. Switch terminal—2 green wires
3. Switch terminal—Not used with standard wiring
4. Switch terminal—Green wire
5. Switch terminal—Black and yellow wires
6. Junction terminal—4 black and 1 red wire
7. Junction terminal—Yellow and green wires
8. Speedometer light—Green wire
9. Terminal—Green wire and red with black tracer
10. Terminal—Red wire
11. Terminal—Not used with standard wiring
12. Terminal—Not used with standard wiring
13. Regulator—2 red and 1 black wire
14. Tail and stop lamps—Red and green wires
15. Battery positive terminal—Red wire
16. Battery negative terminal—Black wire
17. Oil signal switch—Black wire
18. Handlebar headlamp switch—Black with red tracer, red with yellow tracer, red with black tracer
19. Horn switch—Black and green wires
20. Terminal—Not used with standard wiring
21. Terminal—2 black with red tracer
22. Terminal—Red with yellow tracer and red wire
23. Terminal—Not used with standard wiring
24. Terminal—Black wire with white tracer and black wire
25. Terminal—Yellow wire
26. Ignition circuit breaker—Black wire
27. Stop lamp switch—2 red wires
28. Generator signal light—Black and green wires
29. Terminal—Not used on standard model
30. Terminal—Not used on standard model
31. Terminal—Not used on standard model
32. Generator "F" terminal—Black wire
33. Generator "A" terminal—Red and green wires
34. Ignition light switch—See terminals 1, 2, 3, 4 and 5
35. Ignition coil—2 black wires
36. Terminal plate—See terminals 9, 10, 21, 22, 24 and 25
38. Terminal box—See terminals 39, 40, 41 and 42
39. Terminal—2 red wires
40. Terminal—2 green wires
41. Terminal—2 black wires and red wire
42. Terminal—Black and yellow wires
43. Terminal—Not used with standard wiring
45. Terminal plate top—Mounting screw (ground)
46. Junction terminal—Black and green wires
47. Terminal—3 green wires
48. Terminal—3 red wires
50. Oil signal light—Black and green wires
51. Horn—Red and green wires
52. Headlamp—Black, white and yellow wires

RADIO—SPECIAL

Servi-Car wiring for radio equipment is the same as standard wiring except for regulator and generator connections.

- M. Cable (two wires)—Red and green
- B. Conduit (one wire)—Green
- N. Conduit (one wire)—Red
- 13. Regulator—2 red wires and green wire
- 32. Generator "F" terminal—Green wire
- 33. Generator "A" terminal—Red and green wires
- 49. Fuse

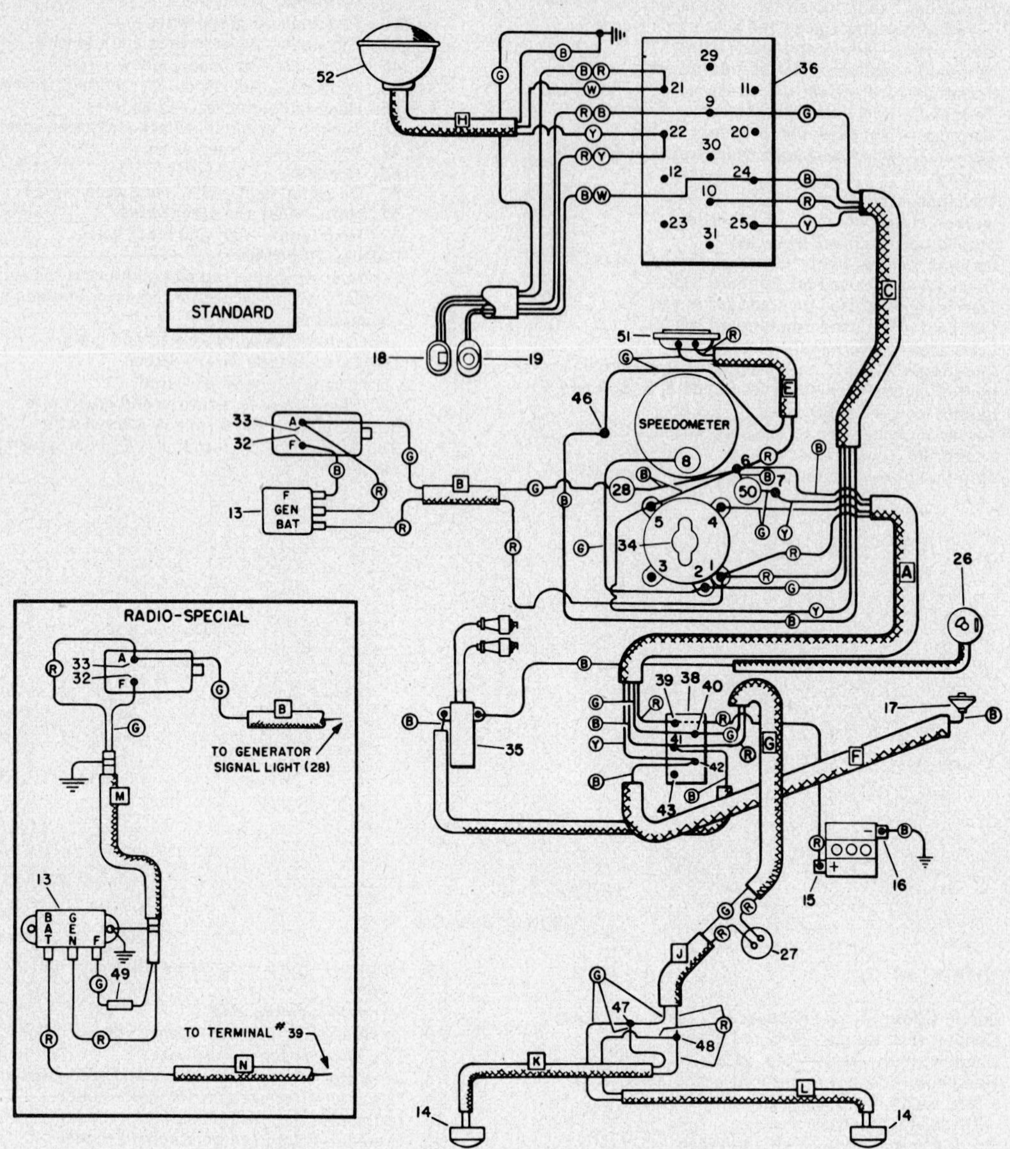

KEY TO COLOR CODE			
(R)	RED	(R)(B)	RED WITH BLACK TRACER
(G)	GREEN	(B)(R)	BLACK WITH RED TRACER
(B)	BLACK	(R)(Y)	RED WITH YELLOW TRACER
(Y)	YELLOW	(B)(W)	BLACK WITH WHITE TRACER
(W)	WHITE		

1960-63 Servi-Car

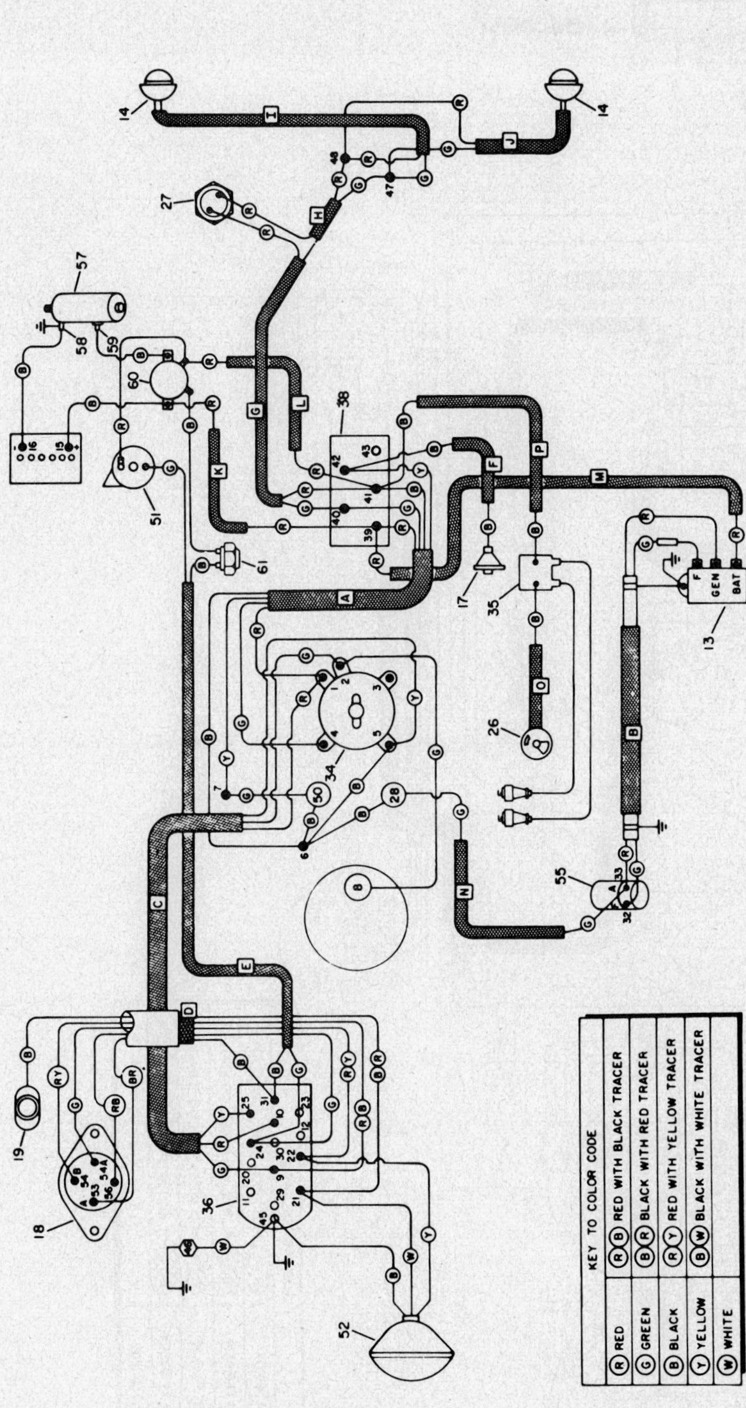

KEY TO COLOR CODE
(R) RED
(G) GREEN
(B) BLACK
(Y) YELLOW
(W) WHITE
(R)(B) RED WITH BLACK TRACER
(B)(R) BLACK WITH RED TRACER
(R)(Y) RED WITH YELLOW TRACER
(B)(W) BLACK WITH WHITE TRACER

1964-65 Servi-Car

A. Conduit (four wires)—Red, green, black and yellow
B. Conduit (two wires)—Red and green
C. Conduit (three wires)—Red, green and yellow
D. Handlebar (five wires)—Red with black tracer, black with red tracer, red with yellow tracer, black and green
E. Conduit (two wires)—Black and green
F. Conduit (one wire)—Black
G. Conduit (two wires)—Red and green
H. Conduit (two wires)—Red and green
I. Conduit (two wires)—Red and green
J. Conduit (two wires)—Red and green
K. Conduit (one wire)—Red
L. Conduit (one wire)—Red
M. Conduit (one wire)—Red
N. Conduit (one wire)—Green
O. Conduit (one wire)—Black
P. Conduit (one wire)—Black
1. Switch terminal—2 red wires
2. Switch terminal—2 green wires
3. Switch terminal—Not used with standard wiring
4. Switch terminal—Green wire
5. Switch terminal—Black and yellow wires
6. Junction terminal—3 black wires
7. Junction terminal—Yellow and green wires
8. Speedometer light—Green wire
9. Terminal—Green wire and red with black tracer
10. Terminal—Red wire
11. Terminal—Not used with standard wiring
12. Terminal—Not used with standard wiring
13. Regulator—2 red and 1 green wire
14. Tail and stop lamps—Red and green wires
15. Battery positive terminal—Black wire
16. Battery negative terminal—Black wire
17. Oil signal switch—Black wire
18. Horn and headlamp switch—Black with red tracer, red with yellow tracer, red with black tracer and green wires
19. Starter switch—Black wire
20. Terminal—Not used with standard wiring
21. Terminal—Black with red tracer and white wires
22. Terminal—Red with yellow tracer and yellow wire
23. Terminal—Not used with standard wiring
24. Terminal—2 green wires
25. Terminal—Yellow wire
26. Ignition circuit breaker—Black wire
27. Stop lamp switch—2 red wires
28. Generator signal light—Black and green wires
29. Terminal—Not used with standard wiring
30. Terminal—Not used with standard wiring
31. Terminal—2 black wires
32. Generator "F" terminal—Green wire
33. Generator "A" terminal—Red and green wires
34. Ignition light switch—See terminals 1, 2, 3, 4 and 5
35. Ignition coil—2 black wires
36. Terminal plate—See terminals 9, 10, 21, 22, 24, 25 and 31
38. Terminal box—See terminals 39, 40, 41 and 42
39. Terminal—3 red wires
40. Terminal—2 green wires
41. Terminal—2 black wires and 2 red wires
42. Terminal—Black and yellow wires
43. Terminal—Not used with standard wiring
45. Terminal plate top mounting screw (ground)—Black and white wires
46. Right handlebar clamp bolt white wire
47. Terminal—3 green wires
48. Terminal—3 red wires
50. Oil signal light—Black and green wires
51. Horn—Red and green wires
52. Headlamp—Black, white and yellow wires
53. Horn and headlamp switch terminal (marked A)—Black with red tracer
54. Horn and headlamp switch terminal (marked B)—Red with yellow tracer
54A. Horn and headlamp switch terminal—Green wire
55. Generator—2 green and 1 red wires
56. Horn and headlamp switch terminal—Red with black tracer
57. Starting motor—2 black wires
58. Starting motor thru bolt—Black wire
59. Starting motor terminal—Black wire
60. Starter solenoid switch—3 black and 3 red wires
61. Starter transmission switch—Two black wires

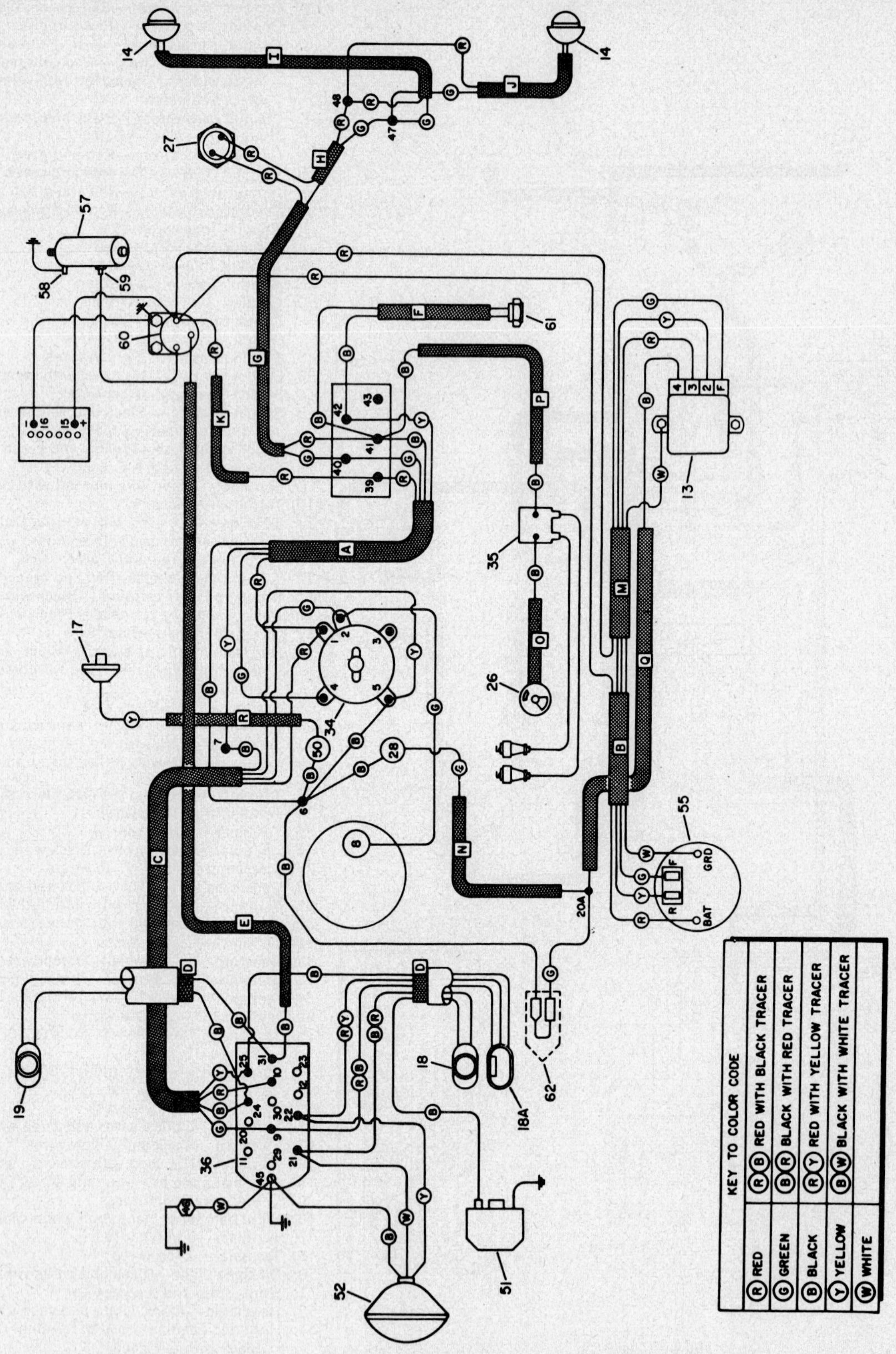

1966 Servi-Car

A. Conduit (four wires)—Red, green, black and yellow
B. Conduit (four wires)—Red, green, yellow and white
C. Conduit (three wires)—Red, green, yellow and black
D. Handlebar—Left side (five wires) red with black tracer, black with red tracer, red with yellow tracer, and 2 black. Right side (two wires) black
E. Conduit (one wire)—Black
F. Conduit (two wires)—Black
G. Conduit (two wires)—Red and green
H. Conduit (two wires)—Red and green
I. Conduit (two wires)—Red and green
J. Conduit (two wires)—Red and green
K. Conduit (one wire)—Red
L. Conduit (one wire)—Red
M. Conduit (four wires)—Red, green, yellow and white
N. Conduit (one wire)—Green
O. Conduit (one wire)—Black

1966 Servi-Car

P. Conduit (one wire)—Black
Q. Conduit (one wire)—Black
R. Conduit (one wire)—Yellow
1. Switch terminal—2 red wires
2. Switch terminal—2 green wires
3. Switch terminal—Not used with standard wiring
4. Switch terminal—Green wire
5. Switch terminal—Black and yellow wires
6. Junction terminal—3 black wires
7. Junction terminal—Yellow and green wires
8. Speedometer light—Green wire
9. Terminal—Green wire and red with black tracer
10. Terminal—Red wire
11. Terminal—Not used with standard wiring
12. Terminal—Not used with standard wiring
13. Regulator—Green, yellow, red, black and white wires
14. Tail and stop lamps—Red and green wires
15. Battery positive terminal—Black wire
16. Battery negative terminal—Black wire
17. Oil signal—Yellow wire
18. Horn switch—2 black wires
18A. Headlamp switch—Black with red tracer, red with yellow tracer, red with black tracer
19. Starter switch—2 black wires
20. Terminal—Not used with standard wiring
20A. Junction terminal—3 wires
21. Terminal—Black with red tracer and white wires
22. Terminal—Red with yellow tracer and yellow wire
23. Terminal—Not used with standard wiring
24. Terminal—2 green wires
25. Terminal—Yellow wire
26. Ignition circuit breaker—Black wire
27. Stop lamp switch—2 red wires
28. Generator signal light—Black and green wires
29. Terminal—Not used with standard wiring
30. Terminal—Not used with standard wiring
31. Terminal—2 black wires
32. Generator "F" terminal—Green wire
33. Generator "A" terminal—Red and green wires
34. Ignition light switch—See terminals 1, 2, 3, 4 and 5
35. Ignition coil—2 black wires
36. Terminal plate—See terminals, 9, 10, 21, 22, 24, 25 and 31
38. Terminal box—See terminals 39, 40, 41 and 42
39. Terminal—3 red wires
40. Terminal—2 green wires
41. Terminal—2 black wires and 2 red wires
42. Terminal—Black and yellow wires
43. Terminal—Not used with standard wiring
45. Terminal plate top mounting screw (ground)—Black and white wires
46. Right handlebar clamp bolt—White wire
47. Terminal—3 green wires
48. Terminal—3 red wires
50. Oil signal light—Black and yellow wires
51. Horn—One black wire
52. Headlamp—Black, white and yellow wires
53. Horn and headlamp switch terminal (marked A)—Black with red tracer
54. Horn and headlamp switch terminal (marked B)—Red with yellow tracer
54A. Horn and headlamp switch terminal—Green wire
55. Alternator—Red, yellow, green and white wires
56. Horn and headlamp switch terminal—Red with black tracer
57. Starting motor—2 black wires
58. Starting motor thru bolt—Black wire
59. Starting motor terminal—Black wire
60. Starter solenoid switch—3 black and 3 red wires
61. Starter transmission switch—Two black wires
62. Diode and resistor assembly—Green and black wires

Late 1967 Servi-Car

A. Conduit (four wires)—Red, green, black and yellow
B. Conduit (four wires)—Red, green, yellow and white
C. Conduit (four wires)—Red, green, yellow and black
D. Handlebar—Left side (five wires)—Red with black tracer, black with red tracer, red with yellow tracer, and 2 black. Right side (five wires)—Green, brown, red and two black.
E. Conduit (one wire)—Black
F. Conduit (two wires)—Black
G. Conduit (two wires)—Red and green
H. Conduit (two wires)—Red and green
J. Conduit (one wire)—Red
K. Conduit (one wire)—Red
M. Conduit (four wires)—Red, green, yellow and white
N. Conduit (one wire)—Green
O. Conduit (one wire)—Black
P. Conduit (one wire)—Black
Q. Conduit (one wire)—Black
R. Conduit (one wire)—Yellow
S. Conduit (two wires)—Red and green
T. Conduit (two wires)—Red and green

1. Switch terminal—battery
2. Switch terminal—headlight
3. Switch terminal—accessory lamp
4. Switch terminal—ignition
5. Switch terminal—tail lamp
6. Junction terminal—instrument panel
7. Junction terminal—instrument panel
8. Speedometer light
9. Terminal—fork panel
10. Terminal—fork panel
11. Terminal—fork panel
12. Terminal—fork panel
13. Regulator
14. Tail and stop lamps
15. Tail and direction lamps
16. Battery positive terminal
17. Battery negative terminal
18. Oil signal switch
19. Horn switch
20. Terminal—fork panel
21. Terminal—fork panel
22. Terminal—fork panel
23. Terminal—fork panel
24. Terminal—fork panel
25. Terminal—fork panel
26. Ignition circuit breaker
27. Stop lamp switch
28. Generator signal light
29. Terminal—fork panel
30. Terminal—fork panel
31. Terminal—fork panel
32. Headlamp switch
33. Starter switch
34. Ignition light switch—see terminals 1, 2, 3, 4 and 5
35. Ignition coil
36. Terminal plate—see terminals 9, 10, 11, 21, 22, 23, 24, 25, 31 and 43
37. Terminal box—see terminals 38, 39, 40, 41 and 42
38. Terminal
39. Terminal
40. Terminal
41. Terminal
42. Terminal
43. Terminal plate top mounting screw (ground)
44. Right handlebar clamp bolt
45. Terminal—box plate stop lamp
46. Terminal—box plate tail lamp
47. Terminal—box plate right dir.
48. Terminal—box plate left dir.
49. Oil signal light
50. Horn
51. Headlamp
52. Junction terminal—instrument panel
53. Alternator
54. Overload circuit breaker
55. Starting motor
56. Starting motor through bolt
57. Starting motor terminal
58. Starter solenoid switch
59. Starter transmission switch
60. Diode and resistor assembly
61. License plate lamp
62. Direction signal switch
63. Direction signal flasher
64. Right front direction signal lamp
65. Right direction signal pilot lamp
66. Left front direction signal lamp
67. Left direction signal pilot lamp
68. Cable connectors
69. High beam indicator lamp

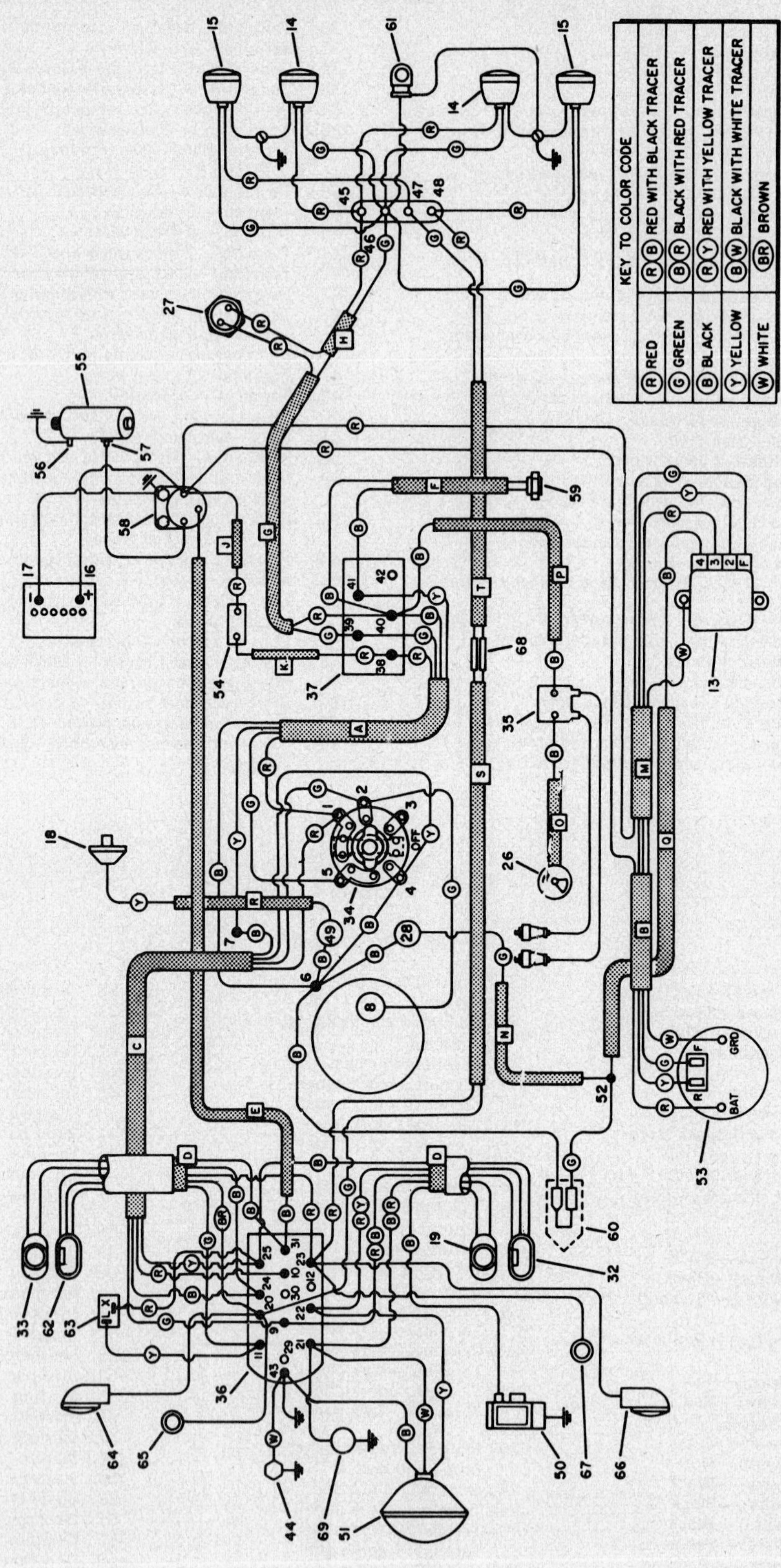

Late 1967 Servi-Car

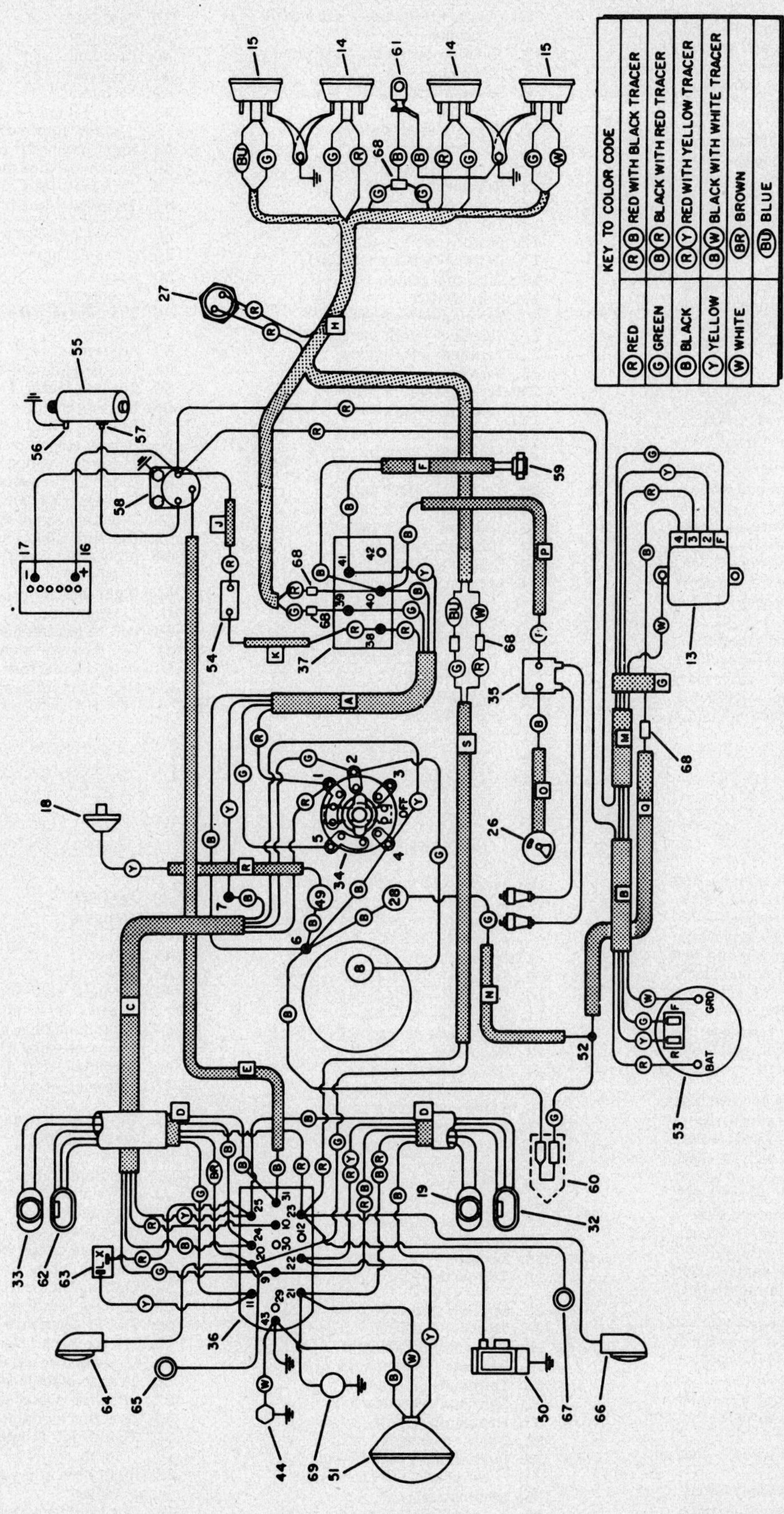
KEY TO COLOR CODE
R RED
G GREEN
B BLACK
Y YELLOW
W WHITE
RB RED WITH BLACK TRACER
BR BLACK WITH RED TRACER
RY RED WITH YELLOW TRACER
BW BLACK WITH WHITE TRACER
BR BROWN
BU BLUE

1969 Servi-Car

1969 Servi-Car

A. Conduit (four wires)—Red, green, black and yellow
B. Conduit (four wires)—Red, green, yellow and white
C. Conduit (four wires)—Red, green, yellow and black
D. Handlebar—Left side (five wires)—Red with black tracer, black with red tracer, red with yellow tracer, and 2 black. Right side (five wires)—Green, brown, red and two black.
E. Conduit (one wire)—Black
F. Conduit (two wires)—Black
G. Conduit (five wires)—Red, green, yellow, black and white
H. Conduit (four wires)—Red, green, white and blue
J. Conduit (one wire)—Red
K. Conduit (one wire)—Red
M. Conduit (four wires)—Red, green, yellow and white
N. Conduit (one wire)—Green
O. Conduit (one wire)—Black
P. Conduit (one wire)—Black
Q. Conduit (one wire)—Black
R. Conduit (one wire)—Yellow
S. Conduit (two wires)—Red and green

1. Switch terminal—battery
2. Switch terminal—headlight
3. Switch terminal—accessory lamp
4. Switch terminal—ignition
5. Switch terminal—tail lamp
6. Junction terminal—instrument panel
7. Junction terminal—instrument panel
8. Speedometer light
9. Terminal—fork panel
10. Terminal—fork panel
11. Terminal—fork panel
12. Terminal—fork panel
13. Regulator
14. Tail and stop lamps
15. Tail and direction lamps
16. Battery positive terminal
17. Battery negative terminal
18. Oil signal switch
19. Horn switch
20. Terminal—fork panel
21. Terminal—fork panel
22. Terminal—fork panel
23. Terminal—fork panel
24. Terminal—fork panel
25. Terminal—fork panel
26. Ignition circuit breaker
27. Stop lamp switch
28. Generator signal light
29. Terminal—fork panel
30. Terminal—fork panel
31. Terminal—fork panel
32. Headlamp switch
33. Starter switch
34. Ignition light switch—see terminals 1, 2, 3, 4 and 5
35. Ignition coil
36. Terminal plate—see terminals 9, 10, 11, 21, 22, 23, 24, 25, 31 and 43
37. Terminal box—see terminals 38, 39, 40, 41 and 42
38. Terminal
39. Terminal
40. Terminal
41. Terminal
42. Terminal
43. Terminal plate top mounting screw (ground)
44. Right handlebar clamp bolt
45. Terminal—box plate stop lamp
46. Terminal—box plate tail lamp
47. Terminal—box plate right dir.
48. Terminal—box plate left dir.
49. Oil signal light
50. Horn
51. Headlamp
52. Junction terminal—instrument panel
53. Alternator
54. Overhead circuit breaker
55. Starting motor
56. Starting motor through bolt
57. Starting motor terminal
58. Starter solenoid switch
59. Starter transmission switch
60. Diode and resistor assembly
61. License plate lamp
62. Direction signal switch
63. Direction signal flasher
64. Right front direction signal lamp
65. Right direction signal pilot lamp
66. Left front direction signal lamp
67. Left direction signal pilot lamp
68. Cable connectors
69. High beam indicator lamp

Late 1969 Servi-Car

A. Conduit (four wires)—Red, green, black and yellow
B. Conduit (four wires)—Red, green, yellow and white
C. Conduit (four wires)—Red, green, yellow and black
D. Handlebar—Left side (five wires)—Red with black tracer, black with red tracer, red with yellow tracer, and 2 black. Right side (five wires)—Green, brown, red and two black
E. Conduit (one wire)—Black
F. Conduit (two wires)—Black
G. Conduit (five wires)—Red, green, yellow, black and white
H. Conduit (four wires)—Red, green, white and blue
J. Conduit (one wire)—Red
K. Conduit (one wire)—Red
M. Conduit (four wires)—Red, green, yellow and white
N. Conduit (one wire)—Green
O. Conduit (one wire)—Black
P. Conduit (one wire)—Black
Q. Conduit (one wire)—Black
R. Conduit (one wire)—Yellow
S. Conduit (two wires)—Red and green
T. Conduit (two wires)—Red and yellow
U. Conduit (one wire)—Red

1. Switch terminal—battery
2. Switch terminal—headlight
3. Switch terminal—accessory lamp
4. Switch terminal—ignition
5. Switch terminal—tail lamp
6. Junction terminal—instrument panel
7. Junction terminal—instrument panel
8. Speedometer light
9. Terminal—fork panel
10. Terminal—fork panel
11. Terminal—fork panel
12. Terminal—fork panel
13. Regulator
14. Tail and stop lamps
15. Tail and direction lamps
16. Battery positive terminal
17. Battery negative terminal
18. Oil signal switch
19. Horn switch
20. Terminal—fork panel
21. Terminal—fork panel
22. Terminal—fork panel
23. Terminal—fork panel
24. Terminal—fork panel
25. Terminal—fork panel
26. Ignition circuit breaker
27. Stop lamp switch
28. Generator signal light
29. Terminal—fork panel
30. Terminal—fork panel
31. Terminal—fork panel
32. Headlamp switch
33. Starter switch
34. Ignition light switch—see terminals 1, 2, 3, 4 and 5
35. Ignition coil
36. Terminal plate—see terminals 9, 10, 11, 21, 22, 23, 24, 25, 31 and 43
37. Terminal box—see terminals 38, 39, 40, 41 and 42
38. Terminal
39. Terminal
40. Terminal
41. Terminal
42. Terminal
43. Terminal plate top mounting screw (ground)
44. Right handlebar clamp bolt
45. Terminal—box plate stop lamp
46. Terminal—box plate tail lamp
47. Terminal—box plate right dir.
48. Terminal—box plate left dir.
49. Oil signal light
50. Horn
51. Headlamp
52. Junction terminal—instrument panel
53. Alternator
54. Overload circuit breaker
55. Starting motor
56. Starting motor through bolt
57. Starting motor terminal
58. Starter solenoid switch
59. Starter transmission switch
60. Diode and resistor assembly
61. License plate lamp
62. Direction signal switch
63. Direction signal flasher
64. Right front direction signal lamp
65. Right direction signal pilot lamp
66. Left front direction signal lamp
67. Left direction signal pilot lamp
68. Cable connectors
69. High beam indicator lamp
70. Stop lamp front brake switch

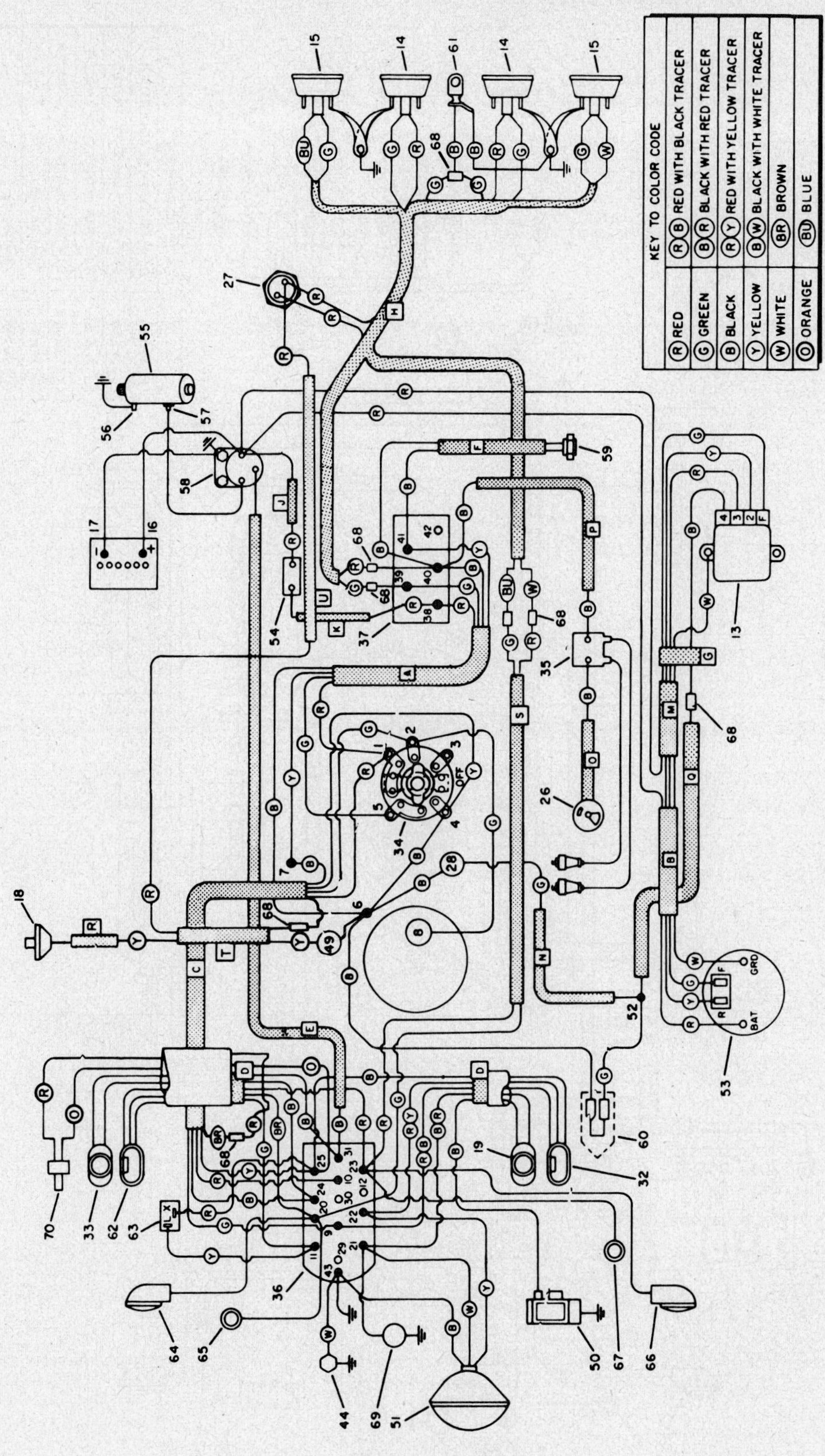

KEY TO COLOR CODE
R RED
G GREEN
B BLACK
Y YELLOW
W WHITE
O ORANGE
R B RED WITH BLACK TRACER
B R BLACK WITH RED TRACER
R Y RED WITH YELLOW TRACER
B W BLACK WITH WHITE TRACER
BR BROWN
BU BLUE

Late 1969 Servi-Car

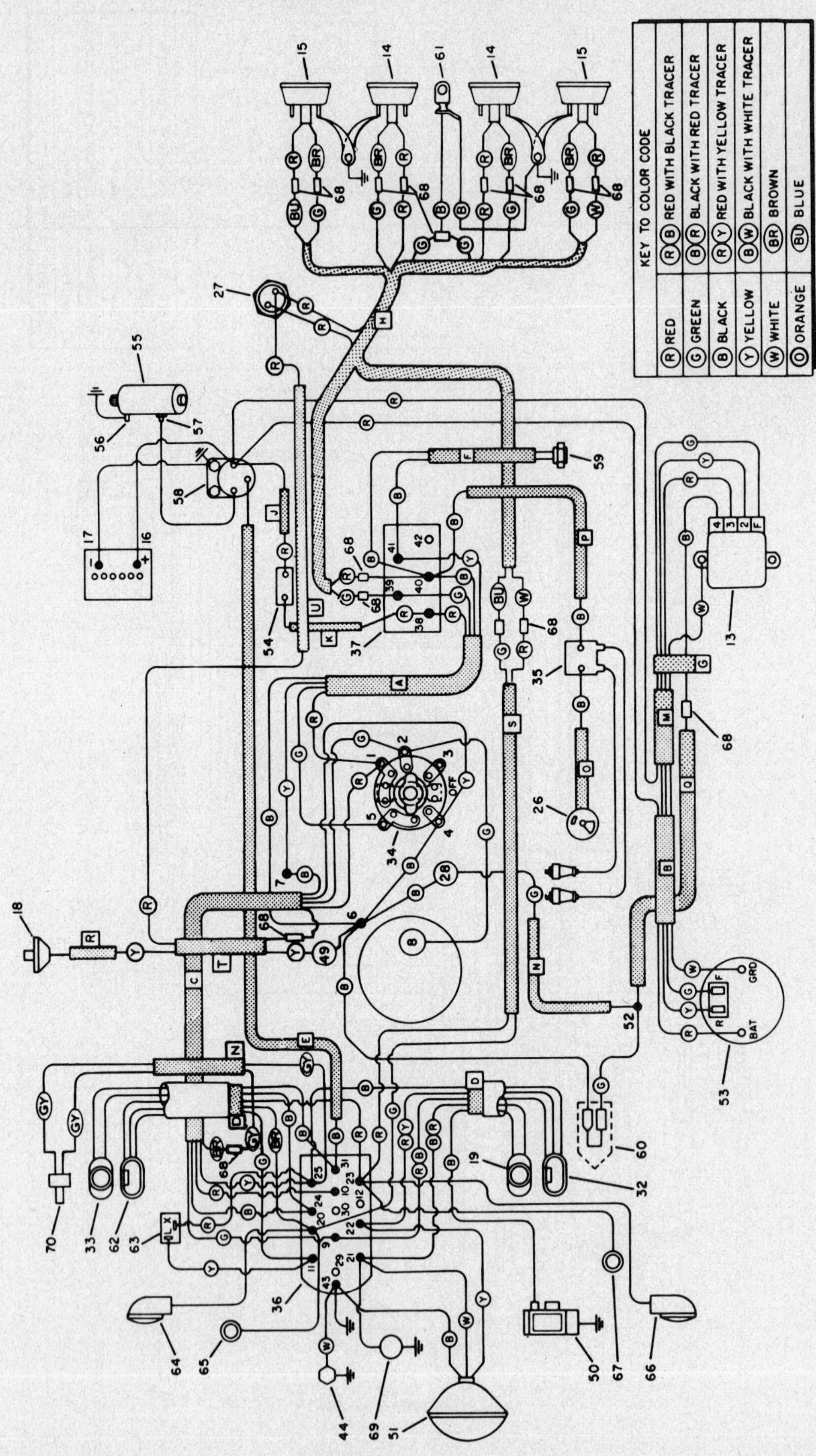

Late 1969 and 1970 Servi-Car

Late 1969 and 1970 Servi-Car

A. Conduit (four wires)—Red, green, black and yellow
B. Conduit (four wires)—Red, green, yellow and white
C. Conduit (four wires)—Red, green, yellow and black
D. Handlebar—Left side (five wires)—Red with black tracer, yellow tracer, and 2 black. Right side (five wires)—Green, brown, red and two black
E. Conduit (one wire)—Black
F. Conduit (two wires)—Black
G. Conduit (five wires)—Red, green, yellow, black and white
H. Conduit (four wires)—Red, brown, white, green and blue
J. Conduit (one wire)—Red
K. Conduit (one wire)—Red
M. Conduit (four wires)—Red, green, yellow and white
N. Conduit (one wire)—Green
O. Conduit (one wire)—Black
P. Conduit (one wire)—Black
Q. Conduit (one wire)—Black
R. Conduit (one wire)—Yellow
S. Conduit (two wires)—Red and green
T. Conduit (two wires)—Red and yellow
U. Conduit (one wire)—Red

1. Switch terminal—battery
2. Switch terminal—headlight
3. Switch terminal—accessory lamp
4. Switch terminal—ignition
5. Switch terminal—tail lamp
6. Junction terminal—instrument panel
7. Junction terminal—instrument panel
8. Speedometer light
9. Terminal—fork panel
10. Terminal—fork panel
11. Terminal—fork panel
12. Terminal—fork panel
13. Regulator
14. Tail and stop lamps
15. Tail and direction lamps
16. Battery positive terminal
17. Battery negative terminal
18. Oil signal switch
19. Horn switch
20. Terminal—fork panel
21. Terminal—fork panel
22. Terminal—fork panel
23. Terminal—fork panel
24. Terminal—fork panel
25. Terminal—fork panel
26. Ignition circuit breaker
27. Stop lamp switch
28. Generator signal light
29. Terminal—fork panel
30. Terminal—fork panel
31. Terminal—fork panel
32. Headlamp switch
33. Starter switch
34. Ignition light switch—see terminals 1, 2, 3, 4 and 5
35. Ignition coil
36. Terminal plate—see terminals 9, 10, 11, 21, 22, 23, 24, 25, 31 and 43
37. Terminal box—see terminals 38, 39, 40, 41 and 42
38. Terminal
39. Terminal
40. Terminal
41. Terminal
42. Terminal
43. Terminal plate top mounting screw (ground)
44. Right handlebar clamp bolt
45. Terminal—box plate stop lamp
46. Terminal—box plate tail lamp
47. Terminal—box plate right dir.
48. Terminal—box plate left dir.
49. Oil signal light
50. Horn
51. Headlamp
52. Junction terminal—instrument panel
53. Alternator
54. Overload circuit breaker
55. Starting motor
56. Starting motor through bolt
57. Starting motor terminal
58. Starter solenoid switch
59. Starter transmission switch
60. Diode and resistor assembly
61. License plate lamp
62. Direction signal switch
63. Direction signal flasher
64. Right front direction signal lamp
65. Right direction signal pilot lamp
66. Left front direction signal lamp
67. Left direction signal pilot lamp
68. Cable connectors
69. High beam indicator lamp
70. Stop lamp front brake switch

1970 Servi-Car

A. Conduit (four wires)—Red, green, black and yellow
B. Conduit (four wires)—Red, yellow, green and white
C. Conduit (four wires)—Brown, red green, yellow and black
D. Handlebar—Left side (five wires)—Black (red tracer), red (black tracer), red (yellow tracer) and two black Right side (five wires)—Green, brown, red and two black
E. Conduit (one wire)—Black
F. Conduit (one wire)—Black
G. Conduit (five wires)—White black, red, yellow and green
H. Conduit (ten wires)—White, blue, two red and six green
J. Conduit (one wire)—Red
K. Conduit (one wire)—Red
M. Conduit (two wires)
N. Conduit (two wires)—Gray
O. Conduit (one wire)—Black
P. Conduit (one wire)—Black
Q. Conduit (one wire)—Black
R. Conduit (one wire)—Yellow
S. Conduit (two wires)—Red and green
T. Conduit (two wires)—Yellow and red
U. Conduit (one wire)—Red
V. Conduit (two wires)—Red and green

1. Switch terminal—battery
2. Switch terminal—headlight
3. Switch terminal—accessory lamp
4. Switch terminal—ignition
5. Switch terminal—tail lamp
6. Junction terminal—instrument panel
7. Junction terminal—instrument panel
8. Speedometer light
9. Terminal—fork panel
10. Terminal—fork panel
11. Terminal—fork panel
12. Terminal—fork panel
13. Regulator
14. Tail and stop lamps
15. Tail and direction lamps
16. Battery positive terminal
17. Battery negative terminal
18. Oil signal switch
19. Horn switch
20. Terminal—fork panel
21. Terminal—fork panel
22. Terminal—fork panel
23. Terminal—fork panel
24. Terminal—fork panel
25. Terminal—fork panel
26. Ignition circuit breaker
27. Stop lamp switch
28. Generator signal light
29. Terminal—fork panel
30. Terminal—fork panel
31. Terminal—fork panel
32. Headlamp switch
33. Starter switch
34. Ignition light switch—see terminals 1, 2, 3, 4 and 5
35. Ignition coil
36. Terminal plate—see terminals 9, 10, 11, 21, 22, 23, 24, 25, 31 and 43
37. Terminal box—see terminals 38, 39, 40, 41 and 42
38. Terminal
39. Terminal
40. Terminal
41. Terminal
42. Terminal
43. Terminal plate top mounting screw (ground)
44. Stop lamp front brake switch
45. Terminal—box plate stop lamp
46. Terminal—box plate tail lamp
47. Terminal—box plate right dir.
48. Terminal—box plate left dir.
49. Oil signal light
50. Horn
51. Headlamp
52. Junction terminal—instrument panel
53. Alternator
54. Overload circuit breaker
55. Starting motor
56. Starting motor through bolt
57. Starting motor terminal
58. Starter solenoid switch
59. Starter transmission switch
60. Diode and resistor assembly
61. License plate lamp
62. Direction signal switch
63. Direction signal flasher
64. Right front direction signal lamp
65. Right direction signal pilot lamp
66. Left front direction signal lamp
67. Left direction signal pilot lamp
68. Cable connectors
69. High beam indicator lamp

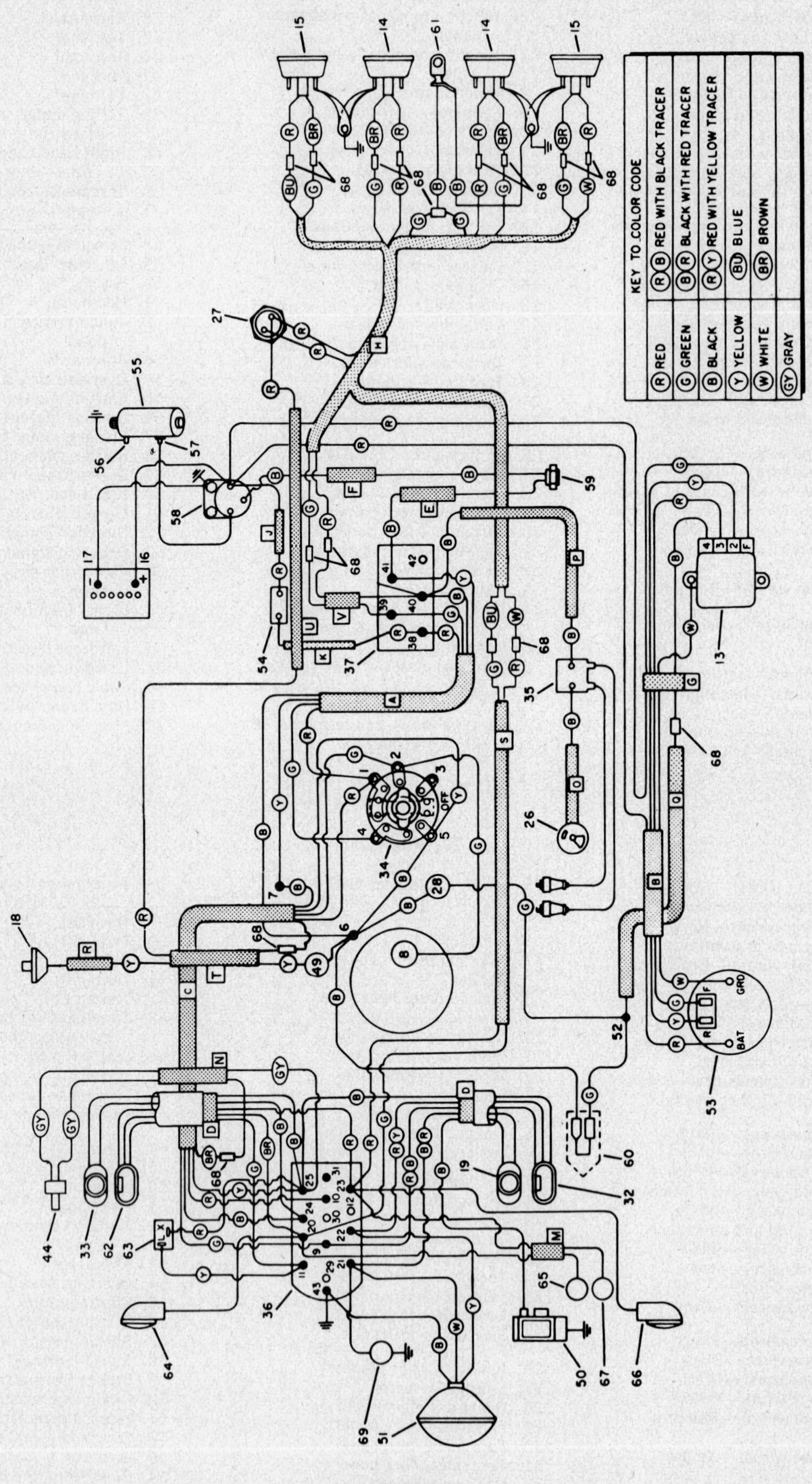
KEY TO COLOR CODE
R RED
G GREEN
B BLACK
Y YELLOW
W WHITE
GY GRAY
RB RED WITH BLACK TRACER
BR BLACK WITH RED TRACER
RY RED WITH YELLOW TRACER
BU BLUE
BR BROWN

1970 Servi-Car

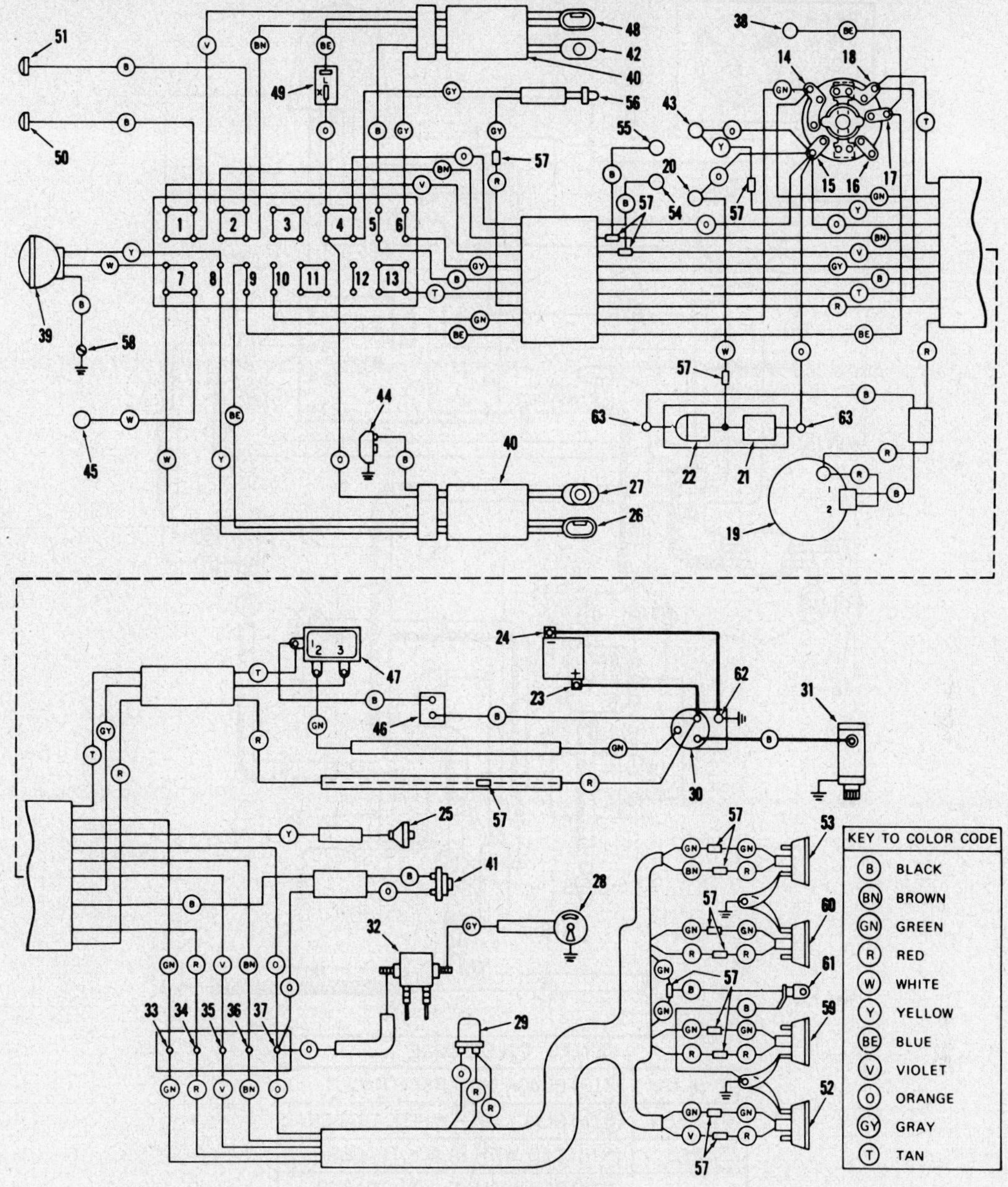

1971 and 1972 Servi-Car

1. to 13. Front terminal board terminals
14. Switch tail lamp terminal
15. Switch ignition terminal
16. Switch terminal (not used with standard wiring)
17. Switch headlamp terminal
18. Switch supply terminal
19. Alternator
20. Generator light
21. Resistor
22. Diode
23. Battery positive terminal
24. Battery negative terminal
25. Oil pressure signal switch
26. Handlebar headlamp switch
27. Horn switch
28. Ignition circuit breaker
29. Stop lamp switch—rear
30. Starter solenoid
31. Starter motor
32. Ignition coil
33. Rear terminal board terminal—top
34. Rear terminal board terminal
35. Rear terminal board terminal
37. Rear terminal board terminal—bottom
38. Speedometer light
39. Headlamp
40. Handlebar
41. Neutral switch
42. Starter button
43. Oil signal light
44. Horn
45. High beam indicator lamp
46. Overload circuit breaker
47. Starter relay
48. Direction signal switch
49. Direction signal flasher
50. Left front direction lamp
51. Right front direction lamp
52. Left rear direction lamp
53. Right rear direction lamp
54. Left direction signal pilot lamp
55. Right direction signal pilot lamp
56. Stop lamp switch—front
57. Connector
58. Terminal board mounting screw
59. Left tail and stop lamp
60. Right tail and stop lamp
61. License plate lamp
62. Solenoid upper mounting bolt
63. Junction terminal

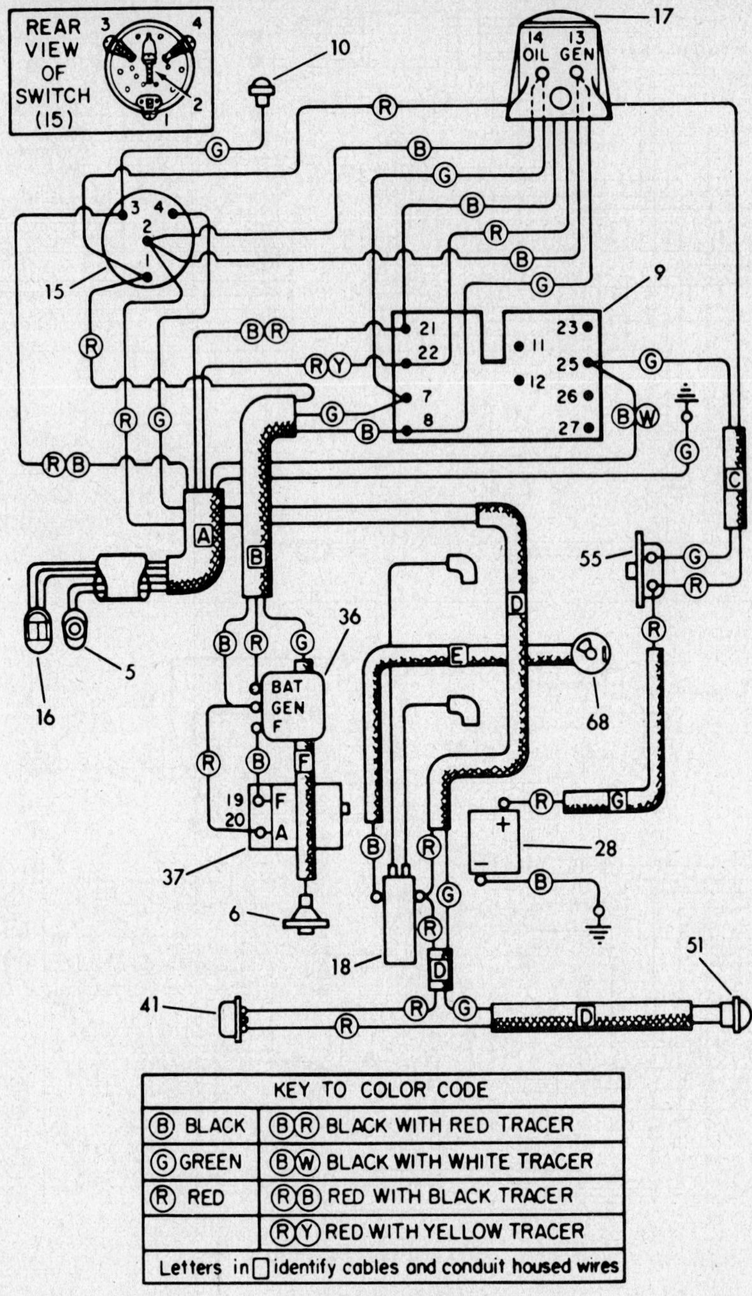

1959-64 Sportster H

A. Handlebars—Red wire with black tracer, black wire with red tracer, red wire with yellow tracer, green wire and black wire with white tracer
B. Conduit (three wires)—Green, red, and black wires
C. Conduit (two wires)—Red and green wires
D. Conduit (two wires)—Red and green wires
E. Conduit (one wire)—Black wire
F. Conduit (one wire)—Green wire
G. Conduit (one wire)—Red wire
H. Conduit (two wires)—Black and red wire
5. Horn switch—Green wire and black wire with white tracer
6. Oil terminal light switch—Green wire
7. Terminal—Two green wires
8. Terminal—Black and green wires
9. Terminal plate
10. Speedometer light—Green wire
11. Terminal—Not used with standard wiring
12. Terminal—Not used with standard wiring
13. Generator signal light—Green and black wires
14. Oil signal light—Green and black wires
15. Ignition-light switch—Terminal #1 two red wires, terminal #2 red wire and two black wires, terminal #3 green wire, and red wire with black tracer, and terminal #4 green wire
16. Headlamp switch—Red wire with black tracer, and red wire with yellow tracer
17. Headlamp—Black and red wires
18. Ignition coil—Two red wires and black wire
19. Generator "F" terminal—Black wire
20. Generator "A" terminal—Red wire
21. Terminal—Black wire with red tracer and black wire
22. Terminal—Red wire with yellow tracer and red wire
23. Terminal—Not used with standard wiring
25. Terminal—Black wire with green tracer and green wire
26. Terminal—Not used with standard wiring
27. Terminal—Not used with standard wiring
28. Battery—Red and black wires
36. Regulator—"B" terminal, red wire; "G" terminal, black and red wires; "F" terminal, black wire
37. Generator
41. Stop light switch—Two red wires
51. Tail lamp—Green and red wires
55. Horn—Green wire and two red wires
68. Ignition circuit breaker—Black wire

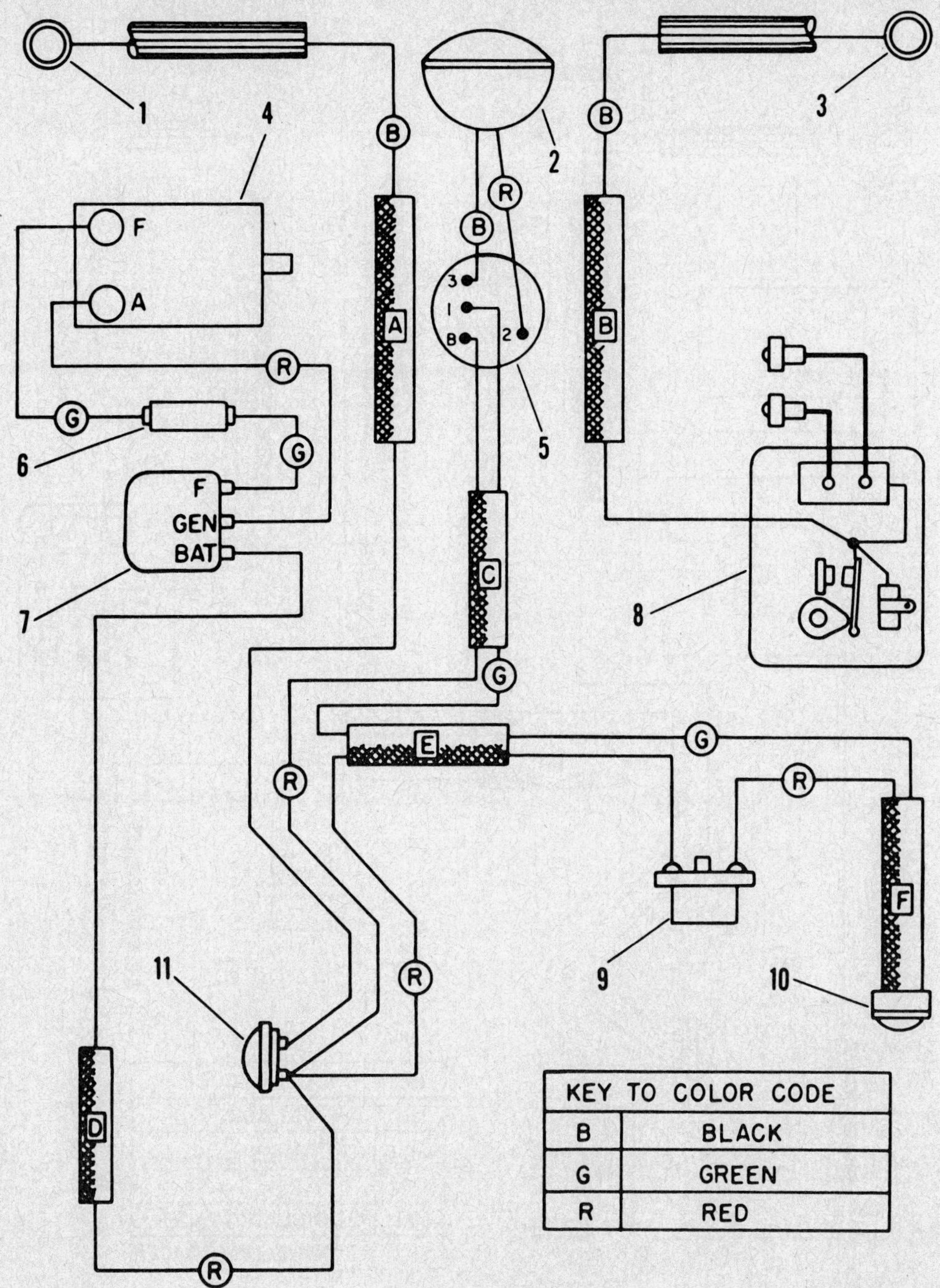

1959-62 Sportster CH

A. Conduit (one wire)—Black wire
B. Conduit (one wire)—Black wire
C. Conduit (two wires)—Red and green wires
D. Conduit (one wire)—Red wire
E. Conduit (two wires)—Red and green wires
F. Conduit (two wires)—Red and green wires
1. Horn switch—Black wire
2. Headlamp—Black and red wires
3. Ignition cutout switch—Black wire
4. Generator—"F" terminal one green wire; "A" terminal one red wire
5. Headlamp switch—"B" terminal one red wire; terminal #1 one green wire; terminal #2 one red wire; terminal #3 one black wire
6. Fuse—Two green wires
7. Voltage regulator—"F" terminal one green wire; "GEN" terminal one red wire; "BAT" terminal one red wire
8. Magneto—Black wire
9. Stoplight switch—Two red wires
10. Tail and stop switch—Red and green wires
11. Horn—Upper terminal one black wire; lower terminal three red wires

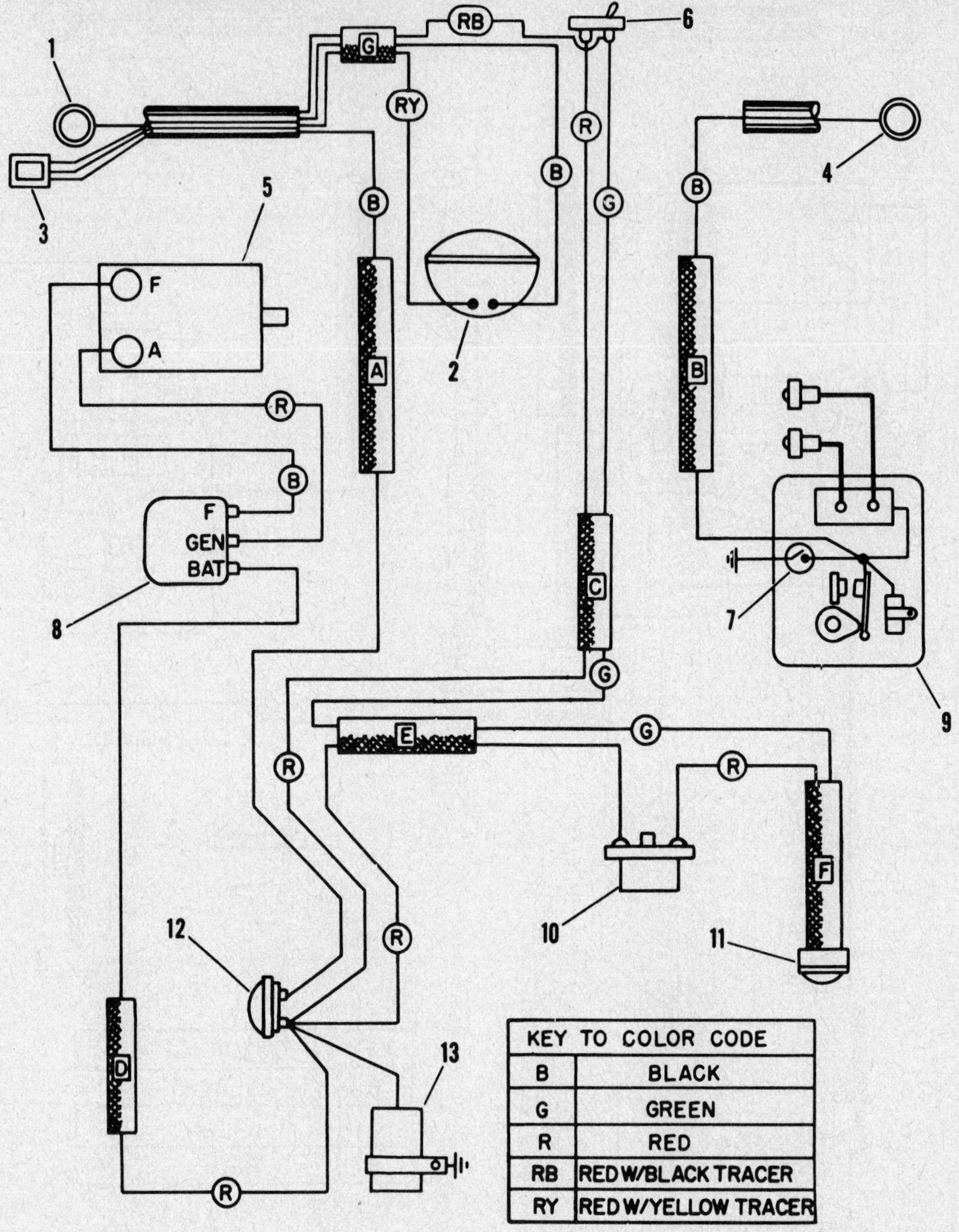

1963-64 Sportster CH

A. Conduit (one wire)—Black wire
B. Conduit (one wire)—Black wire
C. Conduit (two wires)—Red and green wires
D. Conduit (one wire)—Red wire
E. Conduit (two wires)—Red and green wires
F. Conduit (two wires)—Red and green wires
G. Conduit (three wires)—Two red and one black wires.
1. Horn switch—Black wire
2. Headlamp—Black and red wires
3. Dimmer switch—Two red and one black wires
4. Ignition cut out switch—Black wire
5. Generator—"F" terminal one black wire; "A" terminal one red wire
6. Light switch—Two red wires and one green
7. Ignition ground switch lock
8. Voltage regulator—"F" terminal one black wire; "GEN" terminal one red wire; "BAT" terminal one red wire
9. Magneto—Black wire
10. Stop light switch—Two red wires
11. Tail and stop lamp—Red and green wires
12. Horn—Upper terminal one black wire; lower terminal three red wires and capacitor wire
13. Capacitor

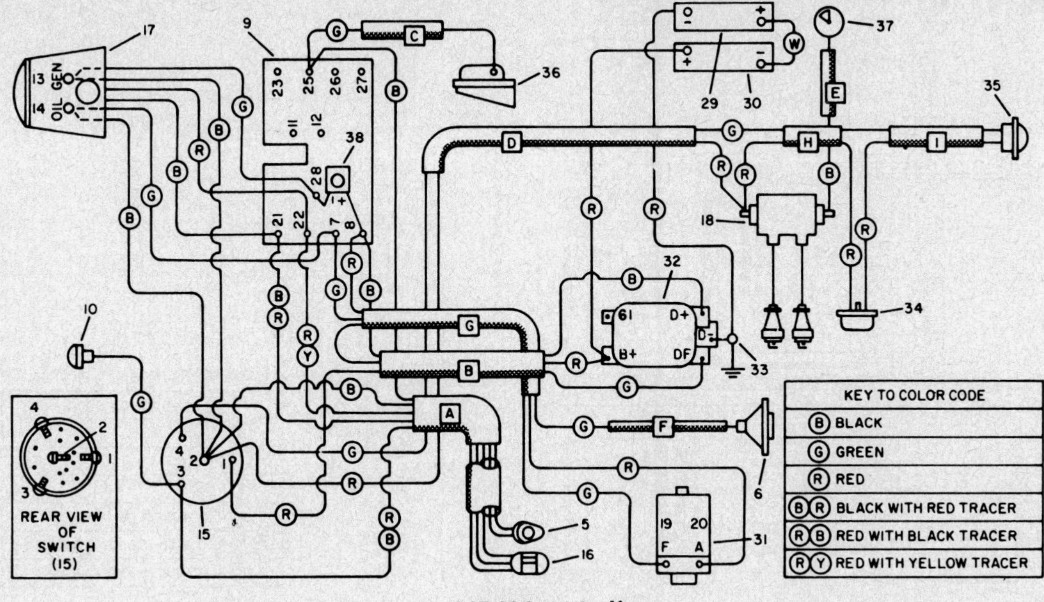

1965-66 Sportster H

A. Handlebars—Red wire with black tracer, black wire with red tracer, red wire with yellow tracer, two black wires
B. Conduit (three wires)—Green, red, and black wires
C. Conduit (one wire)—Green wire
D. Conduit (two wires)—Red and green wires
E. Conduit (one wire)—Black wire
F. Conduit (one wire)—Green wire
G. Conduit (three wires)—One red and two green wires
H. Conduit (two wires)—Black and red wires
5. Horn switch—Two black wires
6. Oil signal light switch—Green wire
7. Terminal—Two green wires
8. Terminal—Black and red wires and rectifier positive terminal
9. Terminal plate
10. Speedometer light—Green wire
11. Terminal—Not used with standard wiring
12. Terminal—Not used with standard wiring
13. Generator signal light—Green and black wires
14. Oil signal light—Green and black wires
15. Ignition-light switch—Terminal #1 red wire; terminal #2 red wire and three black wires; terminal #3 green wire and red wire with black tracer; terminal #4 green wire
16. Headlamp switch—Red wire with black tracer, black wire with red tracer, and red wire with yellow tracer
17. Headlamp—Black and red wires
18. Ignition coil—Three red wires and black wire
19. Generator "F" terminal—Green wire
20. Generator "A" terminal—Red wire
21. Terminal—Black wire with red tracer and black wire
22. Terminal—Red wire with yellow tracer and red wire
23. Terminal—Not used with standard wiring
25. Terminal—Black wire and green wire
26. Terminal—Not used with standard wiring
27. Terminal—Not used with standard wiring
28. Terminal—Green wire and rectifier negative terminal
29. Front battery—Negative terminal black wire; positive terminal white wire
30. Rear battery—Positive terminal red wire; negative terminal white wire
31. Generator—See terminals 19 and 20
32. Regulator—B+ terminal two red wires; DF terminal green wire; D+ terminal black wire; Gnd terminal black wire; G1 terminal not used with standard wiring
33. Terminal, frame screw—Two black wires
34. Stoplight switch—Two red wires
35. Tail lamp—Red and green wires
36. Horn—Green wire
37. Circuit breaker—Two black wires
38. Rectifier—Positive terminal (painted red) to terminal #8; Negative terminal to terminal #28

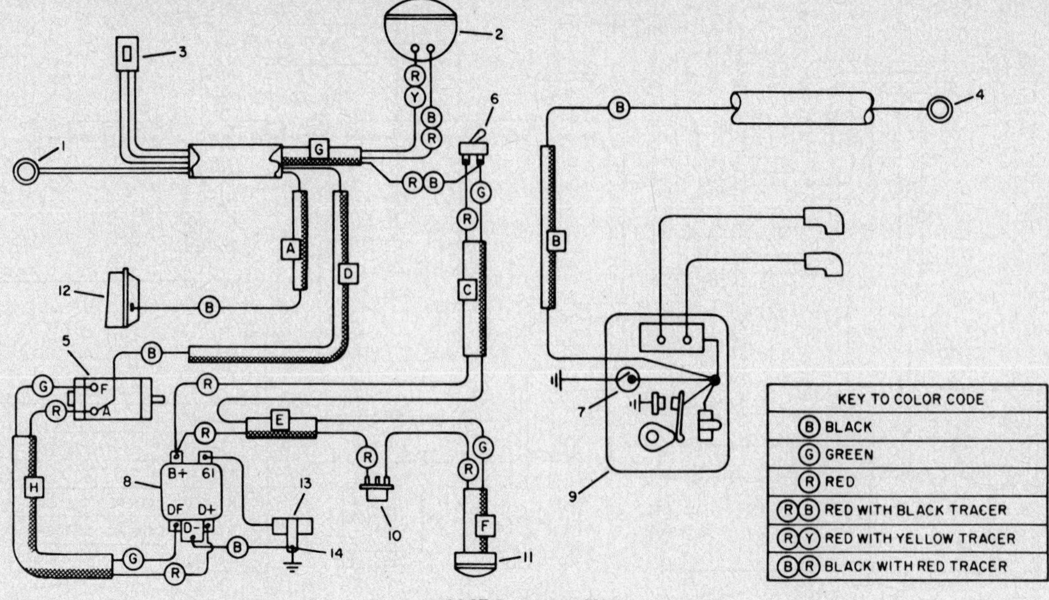

1965 Sportster CH

A. Conduit (one wire)—Black
B. Conduit (one wire)—Black
C. Conduit (two wires)—Red and green
D. Conduit (one wire)—Black
E. Conduit (two wires)—Red and green
F. Conduit (two wires)—Red and green
G. Conduit (three wires)—Red wire with black tracer, red wire with yellow tracer, black wire with red tracer
H. Conduit (two wires)—Green and red

1. Horn switch—Two black wires
2. Headlamp—Black wire with red tracer and red wire with yellow tracer
3. Dimmer switch—Red wire with black tracer, red wire with yellow tracer, black wire with red tracer
4. Ignition cut-out-switch—Black wire
5. Generator
   "F" terminal—Green wire
   "A" terminal—Red and black wires
6. Light switch—(3 wires)—Red, green and red with black tracer
7. Ignition ground switch lock
8. Voltage regulator—
   "61" terminal—Condenser black wire
   DF terminal—Green wire
   D+ terminal—Red wire and condenser wire
   B+ terminal—Two red wires
   Gnd terminal—Black wire
9. Magneto—Black wire
10. Stop light switch—Two red wires
11. Tail and stop lamp—Red and green wires
12. Horn—Black wire
13. Capacitor—Lead connected to regulator "61" terminal
14. Grounding screw—Black wire and condenser ground strap

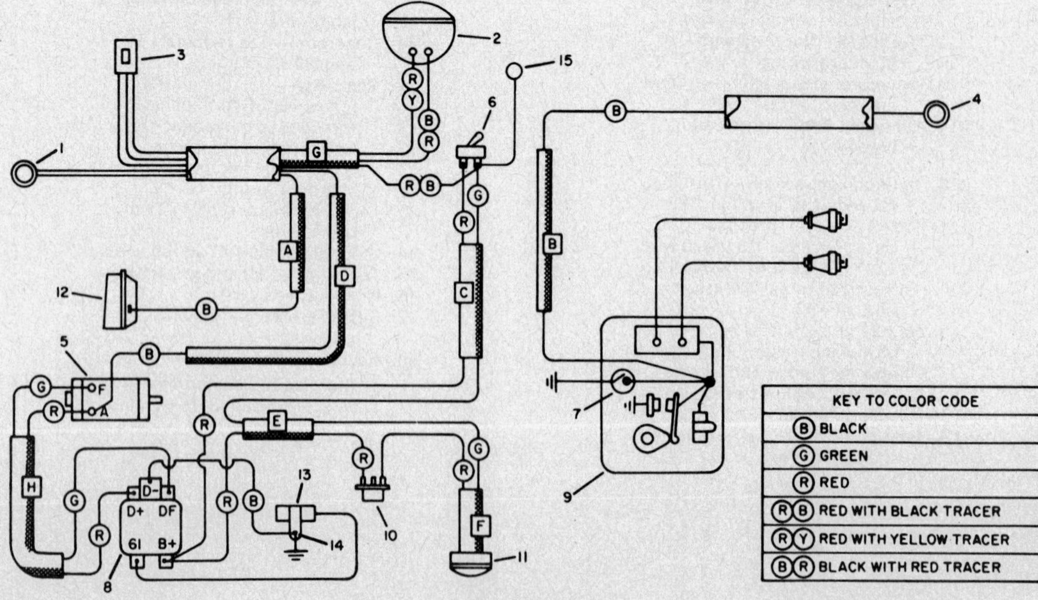

1966 Sportster CH

1966 Sportster CH

A. Conduit (one wire)—Black
B. Conduit (one wire)—Black
C. Conduit (two wires)—Red and green
D. Conduit (one wire)—Black
E. Conduit (two wires)—Red and green
F. Conduit (two wires)—Red and green
G. Conduit (three wires)—Red wire with black tracer, red wire with yellow tracer, black wire with red tracer
H. Conduit (two wires)—Green and red

1. Horn switch—Two black wires
2. Headlamp—Black wire with red tracer and red wire with yellow tracer
3. Headlamp dimmer switch—Red wire with black tracer, red wire with yellow tracer, black wire with red tracer
4. Ignition cut-out-switch—Black wire
5. Generator
   "F" terminal—Green wire
   "A" terminal—Black wire
6. Light switch—Red, green and red with black tracer wires
7. Ignition ground switch lock
8. Voltage regulator—
   DF terminal—Green wire
   D+ terminal—Red wire and condenser wire
   B+ terminal—Two red wires
   "61" terminal—Black wire
9. Magneto—Black wire
10. Stop light switch—Two red wires
11. Tail and stop lamp—Red and green wires
12. Horn—Black wire
13. Capacitor—Center black wire connected to regulator "61" terminal
14. Grounding screw—Black wire
15. Speedometer lamp

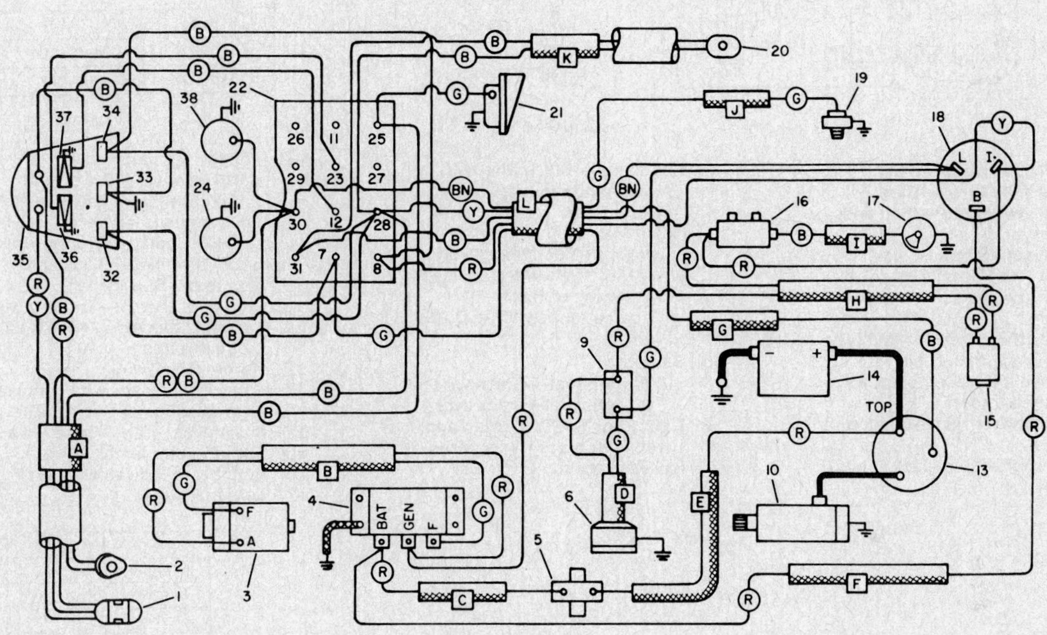

1967 Sportster H

A. Handlebar (five wires)—Red wire with black tracer, black wire with red tracer, red wire with yellow tracer, and 2 black wires
B. Conduit (two wires)—Green and red
C. Conduit (one wire)—Red
D. Conduit (two wires)—Red and green
E. Conduit (one wire)—Red
F. Conduit (one wire)—Red
G. Conduit (one wire)—Black
H. Conduit (two wires)—Red
I. Conduit (one wire)—Black
J. Conduit (one wire)—Green
K. Conduit (two wires)—Black
L. Conduit (five wires)—Brown, yellow, black, red and green

1. Headlamp dimmer switch
2. Horn switch
3. Generator "F" and "A" terminals
4. Regulator
   "BAT" terminal
   "GEN" terminal
   "F" terminal
5. Overload circuit breaker
6. Tail lamp
7. Terminal
8. Terminal
9. Junction terminal board
10. Starter motor
11. Terminal—Not used with standard wiring
12. Terminal
13. Starter solenoid
14. Battery
15. Spotlight switch
16. Ignition coil
17. Circuit breaker
18. Ignition—light switch
19. Oil signal light switch
20. Starter button
21. Horn
22. Terminal plate
23. Terminal
24. Speedometer light
25. Terminal
26. Terminal—Not used with standard wiring
27. Terminal—Not used with standard wiring
28. Terminal
29. Terminal—Not used with standard wiring
30. Terminal
31. Terminal
32. Oil signal light
33. High beam indicator light
34. Generator indicator light
35. Headlamp
36. Left direction signal pilot lamp
37. Right direction signal pilot lamp
38. Tachometer light

KEY TO COLOR CODE

B	Black
Y	Yellow
BN	Brown
G	Green
R	Red
B R	Black with Red tracer
R B	Red with Black tracer
R Y	Red with Yellow tracer

Caution: Disconnect ground cable at battery (—) terminal to prevent accidental starter operation when servicing motorcycle.

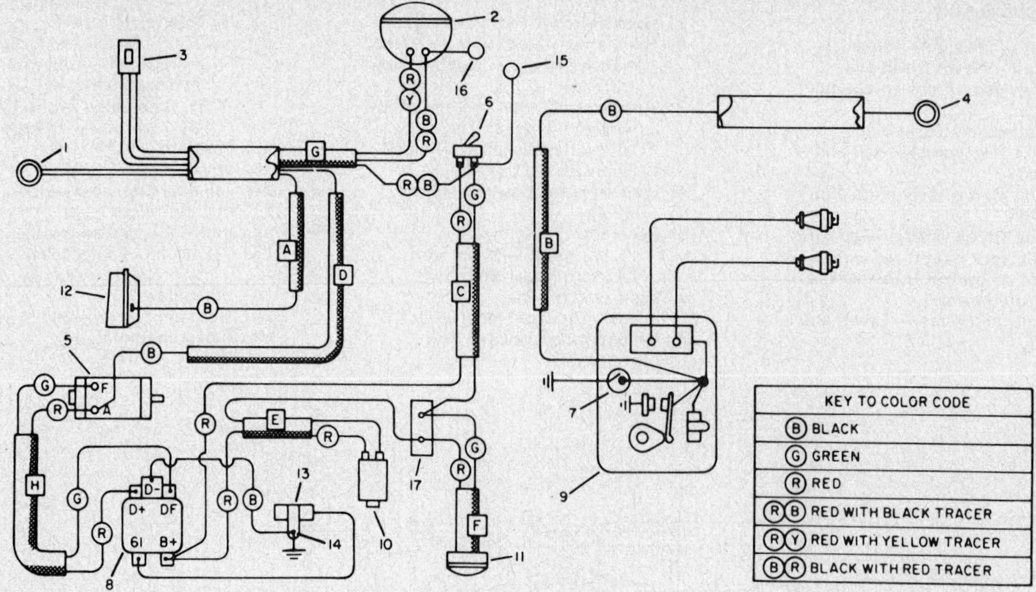

1967-69 Sportster CH

A. Conduit (one wire)—Black
B. Conduit (one wire)—Black
C. Conduit (two wires)—Red and green
D. Conduit (one wire)—Black
E. Conduit (two wires)—Red
F. Conduit (two wires)—Red and green
G. Conduit (three wires)—Red wire with black tracer, red wire with yellow tracer, black wire with red tracer
H. Conduit (two wires)—Green and red

1. Horn switch—Two black wires
2. Headlamp—Black wire with red tracer and red wire with yellow tracer
3. Headlamp dimmer switch—Red wire with black tracer, red wire with yellow tracer, black wire with red tracer
4. Ignition cut-out-switch—Black wire
5. Generator
   "F" terminal—Green wire
   "A" terminal—Black wire
6. Light switch—Red, green and red with black tracer wires
7. Ignition ground switch lock
8. Voltage regulator—
   DF terminal—Green wire
   D+ terminal—Red wire and condenser wire
   B+ terminal—Two red wires
   D− terminal—Black wire
9. Magneto—Black wire
10. Stop light switch—Two red wires
11. Tail and stop lamp—Red and green wires
12. Horn—Black wire
13. Capacitor—Black wire connected to regulator D− terminal
14. Grounding screw—Black wire
15. Speedometer lamp
16. High beam indicator lamp
17. Terminal strip

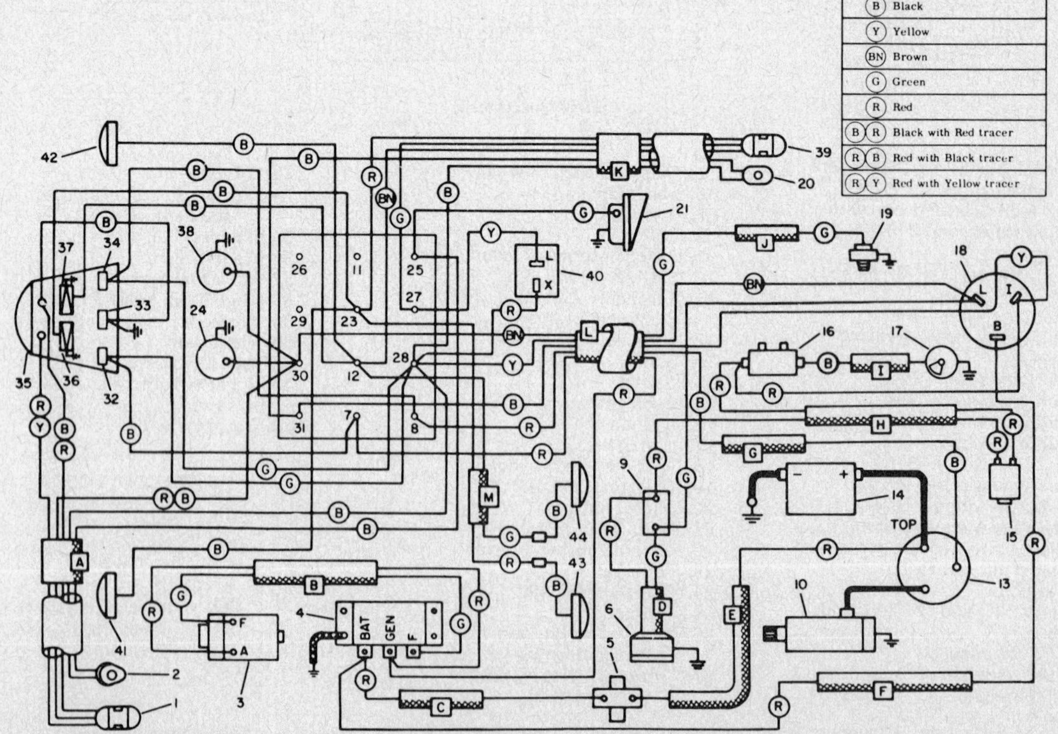

1968-69 Sportster H

1968-69 Sportster H

A. Handelbar (five wires)—Red wire with black tracer, black wire with red tracer, red wire with yellow tracer, and two black wires
B. Conduit (two wires)—Green and red wires
C. Conduit (one wire)—Red wire
D. Conduit (two wires)—Red and green wires
E. Conduit (one wire)—Red wire
F. Conduit (one wire)—Red wire
G. Conduit (one wire)—Black wire
H. Conduit (two wires)—Red wires
I. Conduit (one wire)—Black wire
J. Conduit (one wire)—Green wire
K. Handlebar (five wires)—Red, brown, green, and two black wires
L. Conduit (five wires)—Brown, yellow, black, red, and green
M. Conduit (two wires)—Red and green wires

1. Headlamp dimmer switch
2. Horn switch
3. Generator "F" and "A" terminals
4. Regulator "BAT", "GEN", and "F" terminals
5. Overload circuit breaker
6. Tail lamp
7. Terminal
8. Terminal
9. Junction terminal board
10. Starter motor
11. Terminal—Not used with standard wiring
12. Terminal
13. Starter solenoid
14. Battery
15. Stoplight switch
16. Ignition coil
17. Circuit breaker
18. Ignition—light switch
19. Oil signal light switch
20. Starter button
21. Horn
22. Terminal plate
23. Terminal
24. Speedometer light
25. Terminal
26. Terminal—Not used with standard wiring
27. Terminal—Not used with standard wiring
28. Terminal
29. Terminal—Not used with standard wiring
30. Terminal
31. Terminal
32. Oil signal light
33. High beam indicator light
34. Generator indicator light
35. Headlamp
36. Left directional signal pilot lamp
37. Right directional signal pilot lamp
38. Tachometer light
39. Direction signal switch
40. Direction signal flasher
41. Left front direction lamp
42. Right front direction lamp
43. Left rear direction lamp
44. Right rear direction lamp

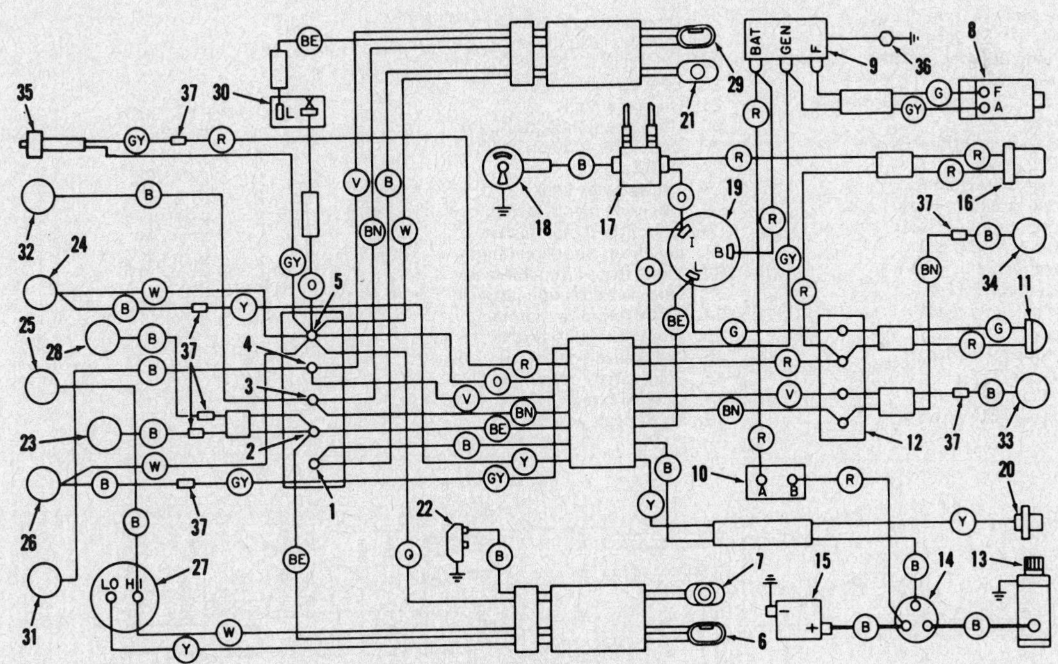

1970-71 Sportster XLH

No's 1 thru 5. Fork terminal board terminals
6. Headlamp dimmer switch
7. Horn switch
8. Generator "F" and "A" terminals
9. Regulator
   "BAT" or B terminal
   "GEN" or D
   "F" or DF terminal
10. Overload circuit breaker
11. Tail lamp
12. Junction terminal board (4 terminals)
13. Starter motor (XLH)
14. Starter solenoid (XLH)
15. Battery
16. Rear stoplight switch
17. Ignition coil
18. Ignition circuit breaker
19. Ignition—light switch
20. Oil signal light switch
21. Starter button (XLH)
22. Horn
23. Speedometer light
24. Oil signal light
25. High beam indicator light
26. Generator indicator light
27. Headlamp
28. Tachometer light
29. Direction signal switch
30. Direction signal flasher
31. Left front direction lamp
32. Right front direction lamp
33. Left rear direction lamp
34. Right rear direction lamp
35. Front stoplight switch
36. Crankcase bolt
37. Connector
38. License lamp
39. Starter relay (XLH)

KEY TO COLOR CODE

B	BLACK
W	WHITE
O	ORANGE
R	RED
G	GREEN
Y	YELLOW
V	VIOLET
BE	BLUE
BN	BROWN
GY	GRAY

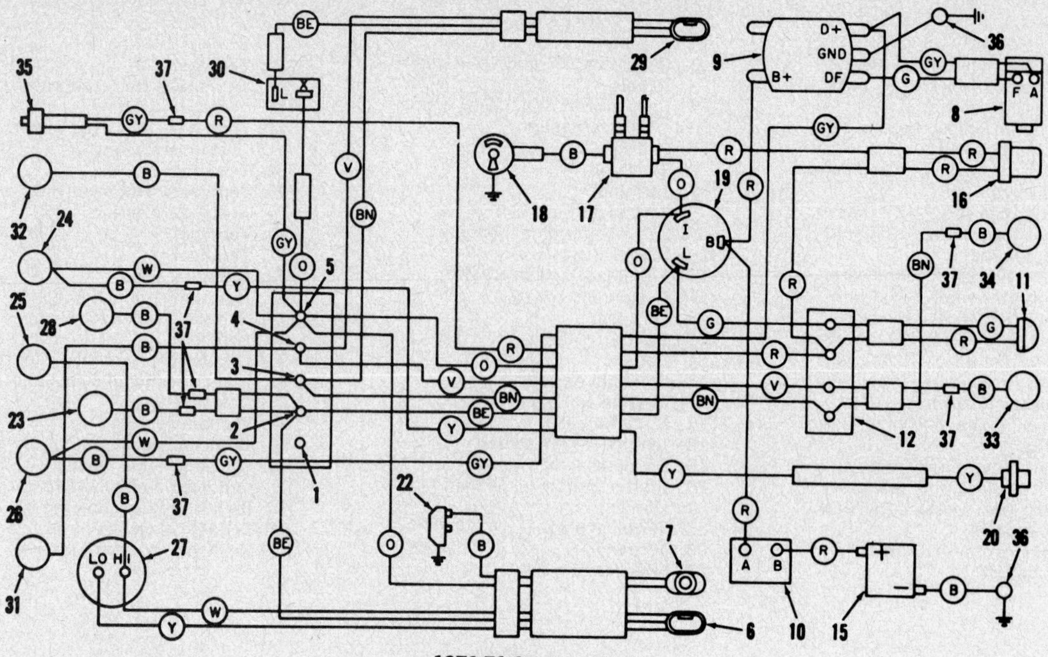

1970-71 Sportster XLCH

No's 1 thru 5. Fork terminal board terminals
6. Headlamp dimmer switch
7. Horn switch
8. Generator "F" and "A" terminals
9. Regulator
"BAT" or B terminal
"GEN" or D
"F" or DF terminal
10. Overload circuit breaker
11. Tail lamp
12. Junction terminal board (4 terminals)
13. Starter motor (XLH)
14. Starter solenoid (XLH)
15. Battery
16. Rear stoplight switch
17. Ignition coil
18. Ignition circuit breaker
19. Ignition—light switch
20. Oil signal light switch
21. Starter button (XLH)
22. Horn
23. Speedometer light
24. Oil signal light
25. High beam indicator light
26. Generator indicator light
27. Headlamp
28. Tachometer light
29. Direction signal switch
30. Direction signal flasher
31. Left front direction lamp
32. Right front direction lamp
33. Left rear direction lamp
34. Right rear direction lamp
35. Front stoplight switch
36. Crankcase bolt
37. Connector
38. License lamp
39. Starter relay (XLH)

KEY TO COLOR CODE

B	BLACK
W	WHITE
O	ORANGE
R	RED
G	GREEN
Y	YELLOW
V	VIOLET
BE	BLUE
BN	BROWN
GY	GRAY

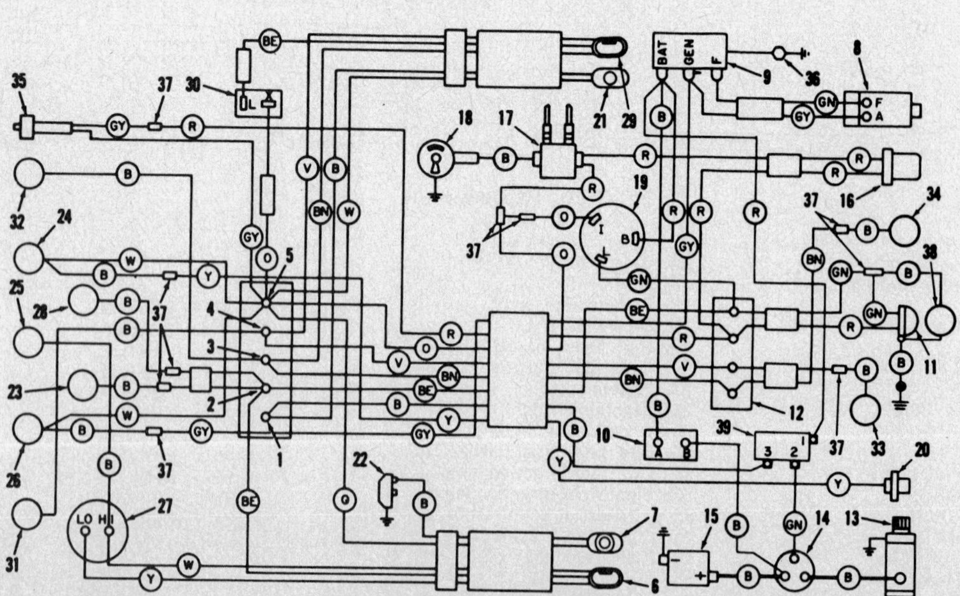

1972 Sportster XLH (standard seat)

1972 Sportster XLH (standard seat)

No's 1 thru 5. Fork terminal board terminals
6. Headlamp dimmer switch
7. Horn switch
8. Generator "F" and "A" terminals
9. Regulator
   "BAT" or B terminal
   "GEN" or D
   "F" or DF terminal
10. Overload circuit breaker
11. Tail lamp
12. Junction terminal board (4 terminals)
13. Starter motor (XLH)
14. Starter solenoid (XLH)
15. Battery
16. Rear stoplight switch
17. Ignition coil
18. Ignition circuit breaker
19. Ignition—light switch
20. Oil signal light switch
21. Starter button (XLH)
22. Horn
23. Speedometer light
24. Oil signal light
25. High beam indicator light
26. Generator indicator light
27. Headlamp
28. Tachometer light
29. Direction signal switch
30. Direction signal flasher
31. Left front direction lamp
32. Right front direction lamp
33. Left rear direction lamp
34. Right rear direction lamp
35. Front stoplight switch
36. Crankcase bolt
37. Connector
38. License lamp
39. Starter relay (XLH)

KEY TO COLOR CODE

B	BLACK
W	WHITE
O	ORANGE
R	RED
G	GREEN
Y	YELLOW
V	VIOLET
BE	BLUE
BN	BROWN
GY	GRAY

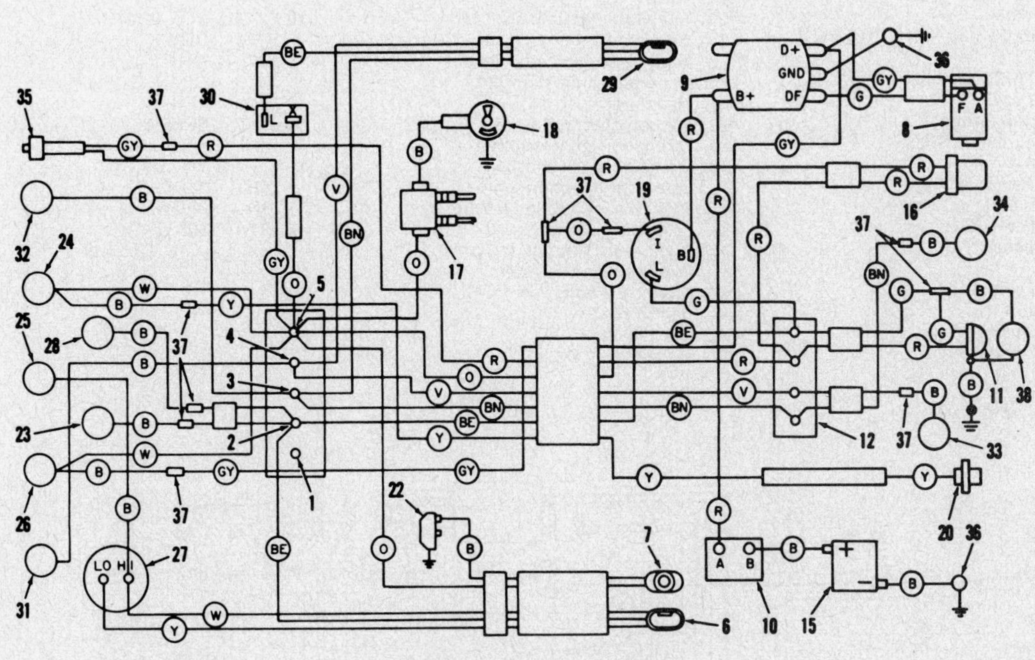

1972 Sportster XLCH (low seat)

No's 1 thru 5. Fork terminal board terminals
6. Headlamp dimmer switch
7. Horn switch
8. Generator "F" and "A" terminals
9. Regulator
   "BAT" or B terminal
   "GEN" or D
   "F" or DF terminal
10. Overload circuit breaker
11. Tail lamp
12. Junction terminal board (4 terminals)
13. Starter motor (XLH)
14. Starter solenoid (XLH)
15. Battery
16. Rear stoplight switch
17. Ignition coil
18. Ignition circuit breaker
19. Ignition—light switch
20. Oil signal light switch
21. Starter button (XLH)
22. Horn
23. Speedometer light
24. Oil signal light
25. High beam indicator light
26. Generator indicator light
27. Headlamp
28. Tachometer light
29. Direction signal switch
30. Direction signal flasher
31. Left front direction lamp
32. Right front direction lamp
33. Left rear direction lamp
34. Right rear direction lamp
35. Front stoplight switch
36. Crankcase bolt
37. Connector
38. License lamp
39. Starter relay (XLH)

KEY TO COLOR CODE

B	BLACK
W	WHITE
O	ORANGE
R	RED
G	GREEN
Y	YELLOW
V	VIOLET
BE	BLUE
BN	BROWN
GY	GRAY

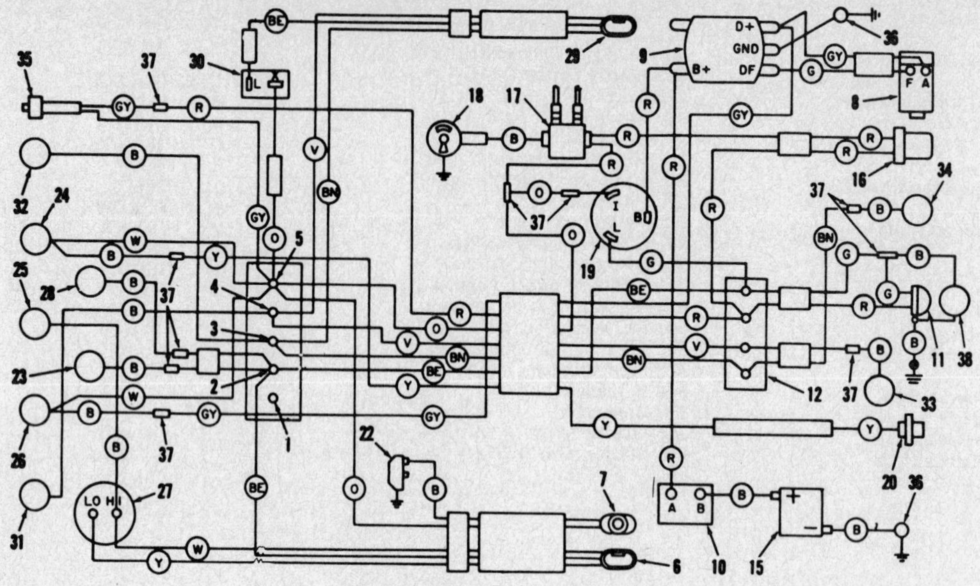

1972 Sportster XLCH (standard seat)

No's 1 thru 5. Fork terminal board terminals
6. Headlamp dimmer switch
7. Horn switch
8. Generator "F" and "A" terminals
9. Regulator
   "BAT" or B terminal
   "GEN" or D
   "F" or DF terminal
10. Overload circuit breaker
11. Tail lamp
12. Junction terminal board (4 terminals)
13. Starter motor (XLH)
14. Starter solenoid (XLH)
15. Battery
16. Rear stoplight switch
17. Ignition coil
18. Ignition circuit breaker
19. Ignition—light switch
20. Oil signal light switch
21. Starter button (XLH)
22. Horn
23. Speedometer light
24. Oil signal light
25. High beam indicator light
26. Generator indicator light
27. Headlamp
28. Tachometer light
29. Direction signal switch
30. Direction signal flasher
31. Left front direction lamp
32. Right front direction lamp
33. Left rear direction lamp
34. Right rear direction lamp
35. Front stoplight switch
36. Crankcase bolt
37. Connector
38. License lamp
39. Starter relay (XLH)

KEY TO COLOR CODE

B	BLACK
W	WHITE
O	ORANGE
R	RED
G	GREEN
Y	YELLOW
V	VIOLET
BE	BLUE
BN	BROWN
GY	GRAY

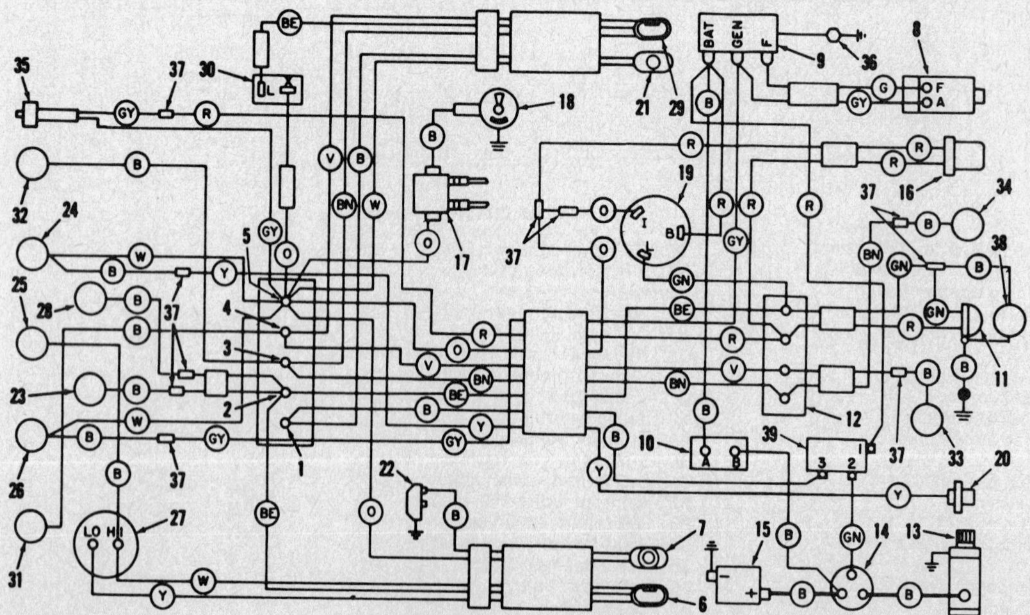

1972 Sportster XLH (low seat)

1972 Sportster XLH (low seat)

No's 1 thru 5. Fork terminal board terminals
6. Headlamp dimmer switch
7. Horn switch
8. Generator "F" and "A" terminals
9. Regulator
   "BAT" or B terminal
   "GEN" or D
   "F" or DF terminal
10. Overload circuit breaker
11. Tail lamp
12. Junction terminal board (4 terminals)
13. Starter motor (XLH)
14. Starter solenoid (XLH)
15. Battery
16. Rear stoplight switch
17. Ignition coil
18. Ignition circuit breaker
19. Ignition—light switch
20. Oil signal light switch
21. Starter button (XLH)
22. Horn
23. Speedometer light
24. Oil signal light
25. High beam indicator light
26. Generator indicator light
27. Headlamp
28. Tachometer light
29. Direction signal switch
30. Direction signal flasher
31. Left front direction lamp
32. Right front direction lamp
33. Left rear direction lamp
34. Right rear direction lamp
35. Front stoplight switch
36. Crankcase bolt
37. Connector
38. License lamp
39. Starter relay (XLH)

KEY TO COLOR CODE

B	BLACK
W	WHITE
O	ORANGE
R	RED
G	GREEN
Y	YELLOW
V	VIOLET
BE	BLUE
BN	BROWN
GY	GRAY

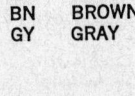

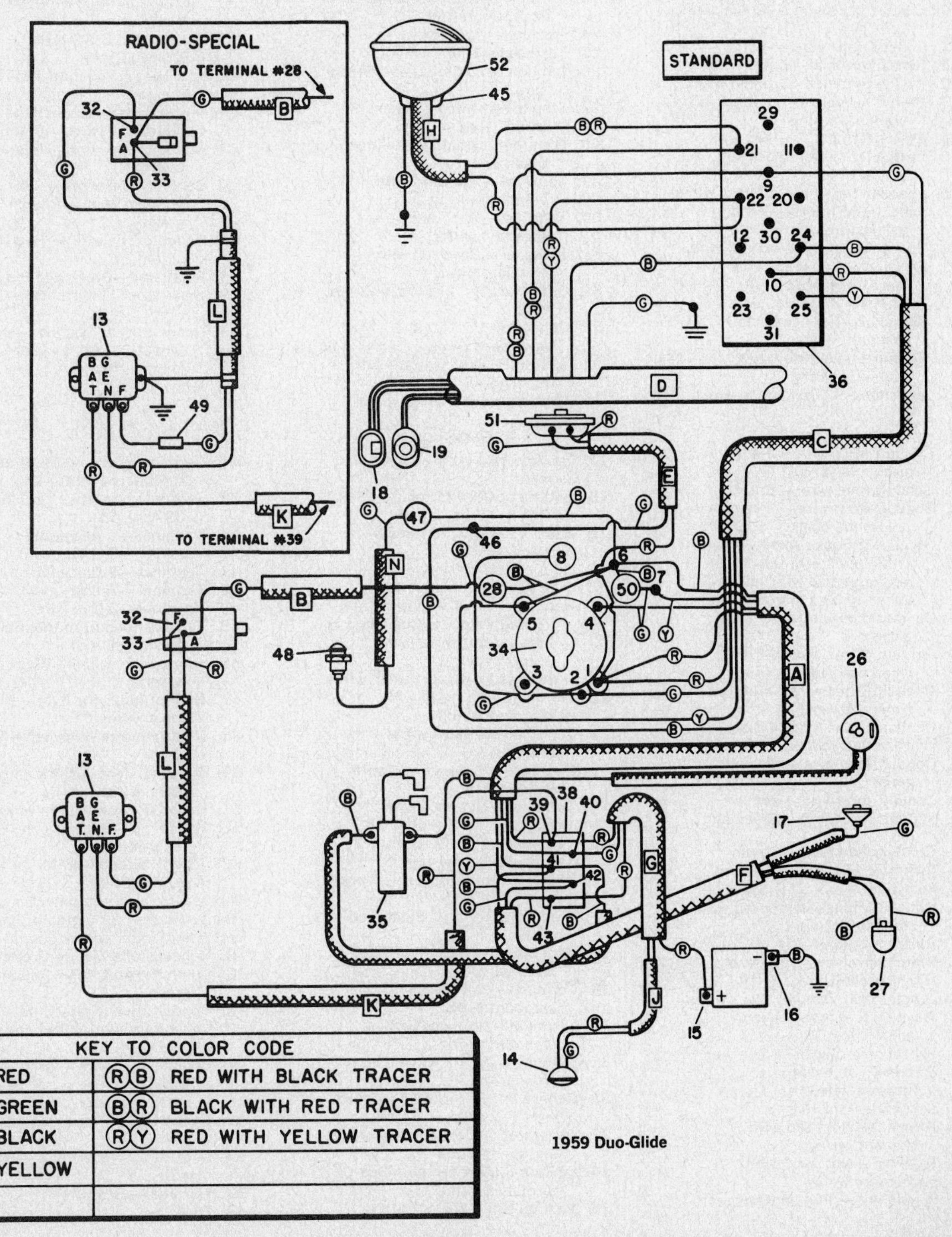

KEY TO COLOR CODE

(R) RED	(R)(B) RED WITH BLACK TRACER
(G) GREEN	(B)(R) BLACK WITH RED TRACER
(B) BLACK	(R)(Y) RED WITH YELLOW TRACER
(Y) YELLOW	

1959 Duo-Glide

A. Conduit (four wire)—Red, green, black and yellow
B. Conduit (one wire)—Green
C. Conduit (four wire)—Red, green, yellow and black
D. Handlebar (loose wires)—Red with black tracer, black with red tracer, red with yellow tracer, black and green
E. Conduit (two wire)—Red and green
F. Conduit (three wire)—Black, green and red
G. Conduit (three wire)—Red, green and red
H. Conduit (two wire)—Black with red tracer and red
J. Conduit (two wire)—Red and green
K. Conduit (one wire)—Red
L. Conduit (two wire)—Green and red
N. Conduit (one wire)—Green
1. Switch terminal—3 Red wires
2. Switch terminal—2 Green wires
3. Switch terminal—Not used with standard wiring
4. Switch terminal—Green wire
5. Switch terminal—Black and yellow wires
6. Junction terminal—5 Black wires
7. Junction terminal—Green, yellow wires
8. Speedometer light—Green wire
9. Terminal—Red with black tracer, green wire
10. Terminal—Red wire
11. Terminal—Not used with standard wiring
12. Terminal—Not used with standard wiring
13. Regulator—2 Red, green wires
14. Tail and stop lamp—Green, red wires
15. Battery positive terminal—Red wire
16. Battery negative terminal—Black wire
17. Oil pressure signal switch—Green wire
18. Handlebar headlamp switch—Red with black tracer, black with red tracer, red with yellow tracer
19. Horn switch—Black, green wires
20. Terminal—Not used with standard wiring
21. Terminal—2 Black wires with red tracer
22. Terminal—Red wire, red with yellow tracer
23. Terminal—Not used with standard wiring
24. Terminal—2 Black wires
25. Terminal—Yellow wire
26. Ignition circuit breaker—Black wire
27. Stop lamp switch—Black, red wires
28. Generator signal light—Green, black wires
29. Terminal—Not used with standard wiring
30. Terminal—Not used with standard wiring
31. Terminal—Not used with standard wiring
32. Generator "F" terminal—Green wire
33. Generator "A" terminal—Red and green wires
34. Ignition—Light switch—See terminals 1 thru 5
35. Ignition coil—2 Black wires
36. Terminal place—See 10 and terminals 20 thru 24
38. Terminal box—See terminals 39 thru 43
39. Terminal—3 Red wires
40. Terminal—2 Green wires
41. Terminal—3 Black wires
42. Terminal—Yellow, green wires
43. Terminal—2 Red wires
45. Headlamp bracket—Black wire
46. Junction terminal—Black, green wires
47. Neutral indicator light—Black, green wires
48. Neutral indicator switch—Green wire
50. Oil signal light—Black and green wires
51. Horn—Red and green wires
52. Headlamp—Red wire black with red tracer

KEY TO WIRING DIAGRAM (RADIO-SPECIAL)

Wiring with radio equipment is unchanged except for regulator, generator and battery connections.

B. Conduit (one wire)—Green
G. Conduit (two wire)—Red and green
K. Conduit (one wire)—Red
L. Cable (two wire)—Red and green
M. Conduit (one wire)—Red (not shown
13. Regulator—Green and red wires
32. Generator "F" terminal—Green wire
33. Generator "A" terminal—Red wire
39. Terminal—Red wire
49. Fuse

1960 Duo-Glide

A. Conduit (four wire)—Red, green, black and yellow
B. Conduit (one wire)—Green
C. Conduit (four wire)—Red, green, yellow and black
D. Handlebar (loose wires)—Red with black tracer, black with red tracer, red with yellow tracer, black and green
E. Conduit (two wire)—Red and green
F. Conduit (three wire)—Black, green and red
G. Conduit (three wire)—Red, green and red
H. Conduit (three wire)—Black, white and yellow
J. Conduit (two wire)—Red and green
K. Conduit (one wire)—Red
L. Conduit (two wire)—Green and red
N. Conduit (one wire)—Green
1. Switch terminal—3 Red wires
2. Switch terminal—2 Green wires
3. Switch terminal—Not used with standard wiring
4. Switch terminal—Green wire
5. Switch terminal—Black and yellow wires
6. Junction terminal—5 Black wires
7. Junction terminal—Green, yellow wires
8. Speedometer light—Green wire
9. Terminal—Red with black tracer, green wire
10. Terminal—Red wire
11. Terminal—Not used with standard wiring
12. Terminal—Not used with standard wiring
13. Regulator—2 Red, green wires
14. Tail and stop lamp—Green, red wires
15. Battery positive terminal—Red wire
16. Battery negative terminal—Black wire
17. Oil pressure signal switch—Green wire
18. Handlebar headlamp switch—Red with black tracer, black with red tracer, red with yellow tracer
19. Horn switch—Black, green wires
20. Terminal—Not used with standard wiring
21. Terminal—2 Black wires with red tracer
22. Terminal—Red wire, red with yellow tracer
23. Terminal—Not used with standard wiring
24. Terminal—2 Black wires
25. Terminal—Yellow wire
26. Ignition circuit breaker—Black wire
27. Stop lamp switch—Black, red wires
28. Generator signal light—Green, black wires
29. Terminal—Not used with standard wiring
30. Terminal—Not used with standard wiring
31. Terminal—Not used with standard wiring
32. Generator "F" terminal—Green wire
33. Generator "A" terminal—Red and green wires
34. Ignition—Light switch—See terminals 1 thru 5
35. Ignition coil—2 Black wires
36. Terminal place—See 10 and terminals 20 thru 24
38. Terminal box—See terminals 39 thru 43
39. Terminal—3 Red wires
40. Terminal—2 Green wires
41. Terminal—3 Black wires
42. Terminal—Yellow, green wires
43. Terminal—2 Red wires
45. Terminal plate top mounting screw (ground)
46. Junction terminal—Black, green wires
47. Neutral indicator light—Black, green wires
48. Neutral indicator switch—Green wire
50. Oil signal light—Black and green wires
51. Horn—Red and green wires
52. Headlamp—Red wire black with red tracer

KEY TO WIRING DIAGRAM (RADIO-SPECIAL)

Wiring with radio equipment is unchanged except for regulator, generator and battery connections.

B. Conduit (one wire)—Green
G. Conduit (two wire)—Red and green
K. Conduit (one wire)—Red
L. Cable (two wire)—Red and green
M. Conduit (one wire)—Red (not shown)
13. Regulator—Green and red wires
32. Generator "F" terminal—Green wire
33. Generator "A" terminal—Red wire
39. Terminal—Red wire
49. Fuse

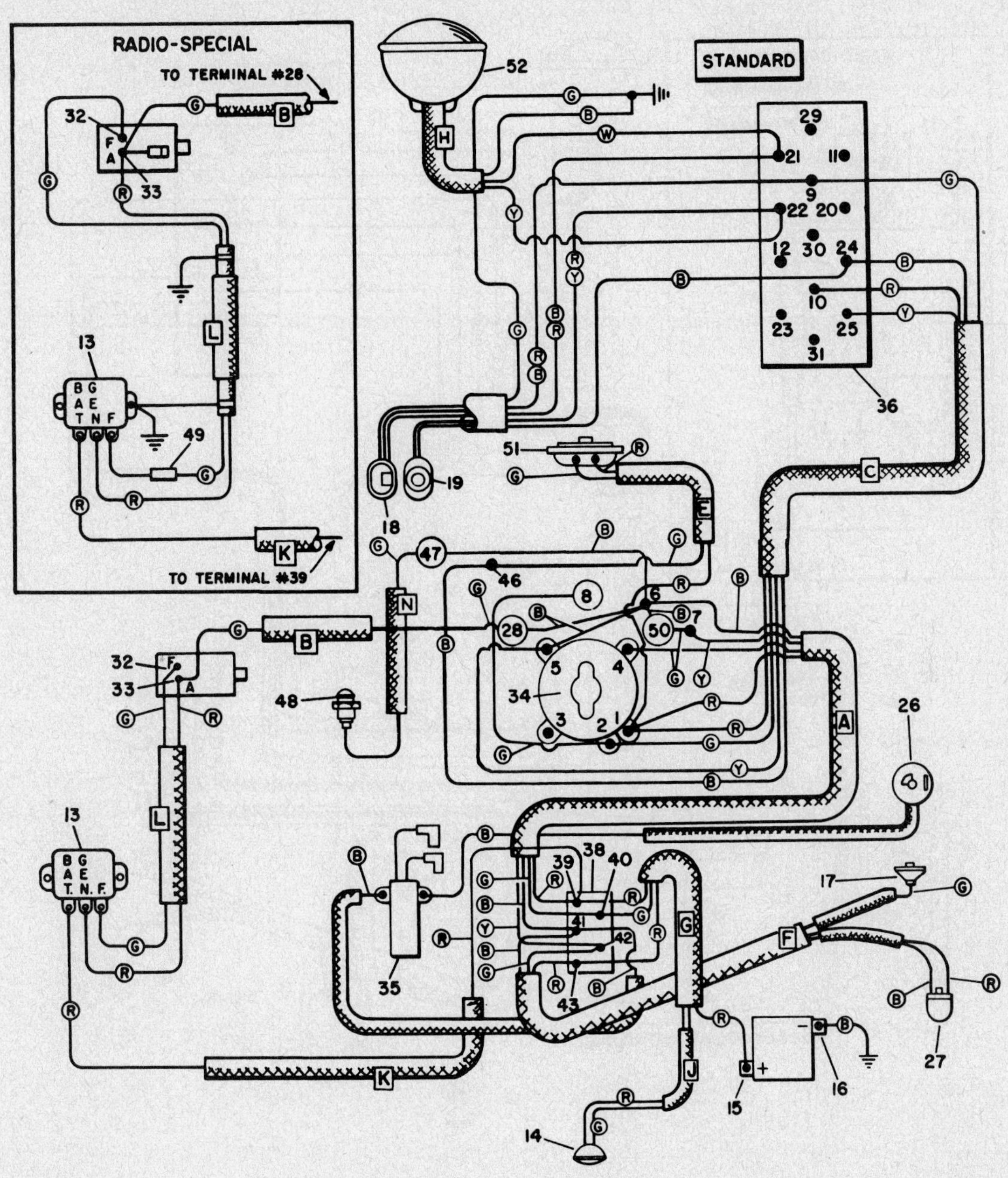

KEY TO COLOR CODE	
Ⓡ RED	ⓇⒷ RED WITH BLACK TRACER
Ⓖ GREEN	ⒷⓇ BLACK WITH RED TRACER
Ⓑ BLACK	ⓇⓎ RED WITH YELLOW TRACER
Ⓨ YELLOW	
Ⓦ WHITE	

1960 Duo-Glide

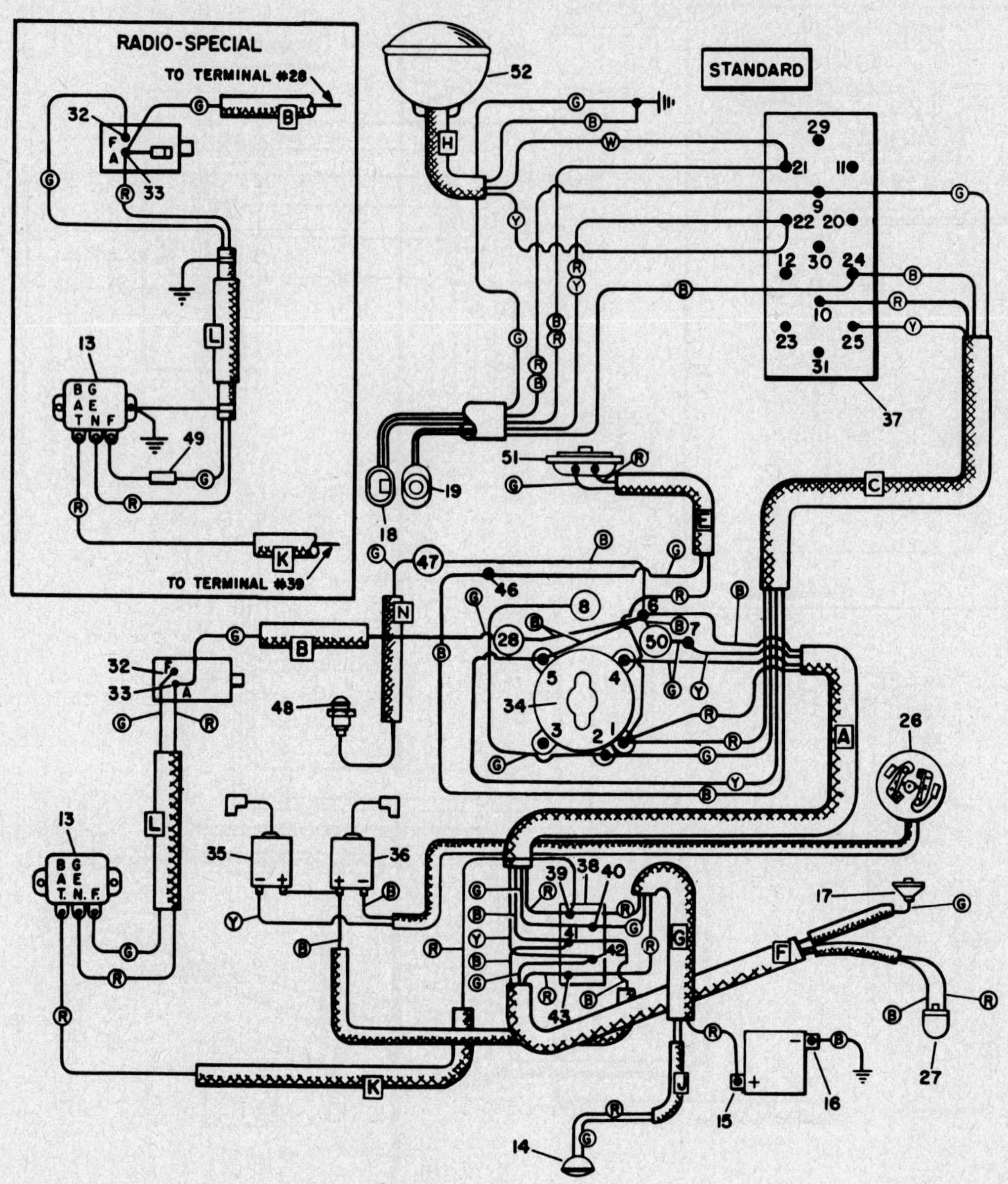

KEY TO COLOR CODE	
(R) RED	(R)(B) RED WITH BLACK TRACER
(G) GREEN	(B)(R) BLACK WITH RED TRACER
(B) BLACK	(R)(Y) RED WITH YELLOW TRACER
(Y) YELLOW	
(W) WHITE	

1961-64 Duo-Glide

A. Conduit (four wire)—Red, green, black and yellow
B. Conduit (one wire)—Green
C. Conduit (four wire)—Red, green, yellow and black
D. Handlebar (loose wires)—Red with black tracer, black with red tracer, red with yellow tracer, black and green
E. Conduit (two wire)—Red and green
F. Conduit (three wire)—Black, green and red
G. Conduit (three wire)—Red, green and red
H. Conduit (three wire)—Black, white and yellow
J. Conduit (two wire)—Red and green
K. Conduit (one wire)—Red
L. Conduit (two wire)—Green and red
N. Conduit (one wire)—Green
1. Switch terminal—3 Red wires
2. Switch terminal—2 Green wires
3. Switch terminal—Not used with standard wiring
4. Switch terminal—Green wire
5. Switch terminal—Black and yellow wires
6. Junction terminal—5 Black wires
7. Junction terminal—Green, yellow wires
8. Speedometer light—Green wire
9. Terminal—Red with black tracer, green wire
10. Terminal—Red wire
11. Terminal—Not used with standard wiring
12. Terminal—Not used with standard wiring
13. Regulator—2 Red, green wires
14. Tail and stop lamp—Green, red wires
15. Battery positive terminal—Red wire
16. Battery negative terminal—Black wire
17. Oil pressure signal switch—Green wire
18. Handlebar headlamp switch—Red with black tracer, black with red tracer, red with yellow tracer
19. Horn switch—Black, green wires
20. Terminal—Not used with standard wiring
21. Terminal—2 Black wires with red tracer
22. Terminal—Red wire, red with yellow tracer
23. Terminal—Not used with standard wiring
24. Terminal—2 Black wires
25. Terminal—Yellow wire
26. Ignition circuit breaker—Black, yellow wires
27. Stop lamp switch—Black, red wires
28. Generator signal light—Green, black wires
29. Terminal—Not used with standard wiring
30. Terminal—Not used with standard wiring
31. Terminal—Not used with standard wiring
32. Generator "F" terminal—Green wire
33. Generator "A" terminal—Red and green wires
34. Ignition—Light switch—See terminals 1 thru 5
35. Ignition coil front cylinder—Yellow wire
36. Ignition coil rear cylinder—2 Black wires
37. Terminal plate—See 10 and 20 through 24
38. Terminal box—See terminals 39 thru 43
39. Terminal—3 Red wires
40. Terminal—2 Green wires
41. Terminal—3 Black wires
42. Terminal—Yellow, green wires
43. Terminal—2 Red wires
45. Terminal plate top mounting screw (ground)
46. Junction terminal—Black, green wires
47. Neutral indicator light—Black, green wires
48. Neutral indicator switch—Green wire
50. Oil signal light—Black and green wires
51. Horn—Red and green wires
52. Headlamp—Red wire black with red tracer

KEY TO WIRING DIAGRAM (RADIO-SPECIAL)

Wiring with radio equipment is unchanged except for regulator, generator and battery connections.

B. Conduit (one wire)—Green
G. Conduit (two wire)—Red and green
K. Conduit (one wire)—Red
L. Cable (two wire)—Red and green
M. Conduit (one wire)—Red (not shown
13. Regulator—Green and red wires
32. Generator "F" terminal—Green wire
33. Generator "A" terminal—Red wire
39. Terminal—Red wire
49. Fuse

1965-67 Electra-Glide

A. Conduit (four wire)—Red, green, black and yellow
B. Conduit (one wire)—Green
C. Conduit (four wire)—Red, green, yellow and black
D. Left handlebar (loose wires)—Red with black tracer, black with red tracer, red with yellow tracer, 2 black wires
E. Right handlebar (loose wires)—2 Black wires
F. Conduit (two wire)—2 Red wires
G. Conduit (one wire)—Yellow
H. Conduit (three wire)—Black, white and yellow
J. Conduit (two wire)—Red and green
K. Conduit (one wire)—Red
L. Conduit (two wire)—Green and red
M. Conduit (one wire)—Black
N. Conduit (one wire)—Black
O. Conduit (one wire)—Black
P. Conduit (two wire)—2 Black
Q. Conduit (one wire)—Red
1. Switch terminal—Switch supply
2. Switch terminal—Headlamp
3. Switch terminal—Not used with standard wiring
4. Switch terminal—Tail lamp
5. Switch terminal—Ignition coil
6. Ignition—Light switch—See terminals 1 through 5
7. Junction terminal
8. Junction terminal
9. Terminal
10. Terminal
11. Terminal—Not used with standard wiring
12. Terminal—Not used with standard wiring
13. Regulator
14. Tail and stop lamp
15. Battery positive terminal
16. Battery negative terminal
17. Oil pressure signal switch
19. Horn switch
20. Terminal—Not used with standard wiring
21. Terminal
22. Terminal
23. Terminal—Not used with standard wiring
24. Terminal
25. Terminal
26. Ignition circuit breaker
27. Stop lamp switch
28. Generator signal light
29. Terminal—Not used with standard wiring
30. Terminal—Not used with standard wiring
31. Terminal
32. Generator "F" terminal
33. Generator "A" terminal
34. Starter solenoid
35. Starter motor
36. Ignition coil
37. Terminal plate
38. Terminal box—See terminals 39 through 43
39. Terminal
40. Terminal
41. Terminal
42. Terminal
43. Terminal
44. Speedometer light
45. Terminal plate top mounting screw (ground)
46. Headlamp
47. Neutral indicator light
48. Neutral switch
49. Starter button
50. Oil signal light
51. Horn
52. Circuit breaker

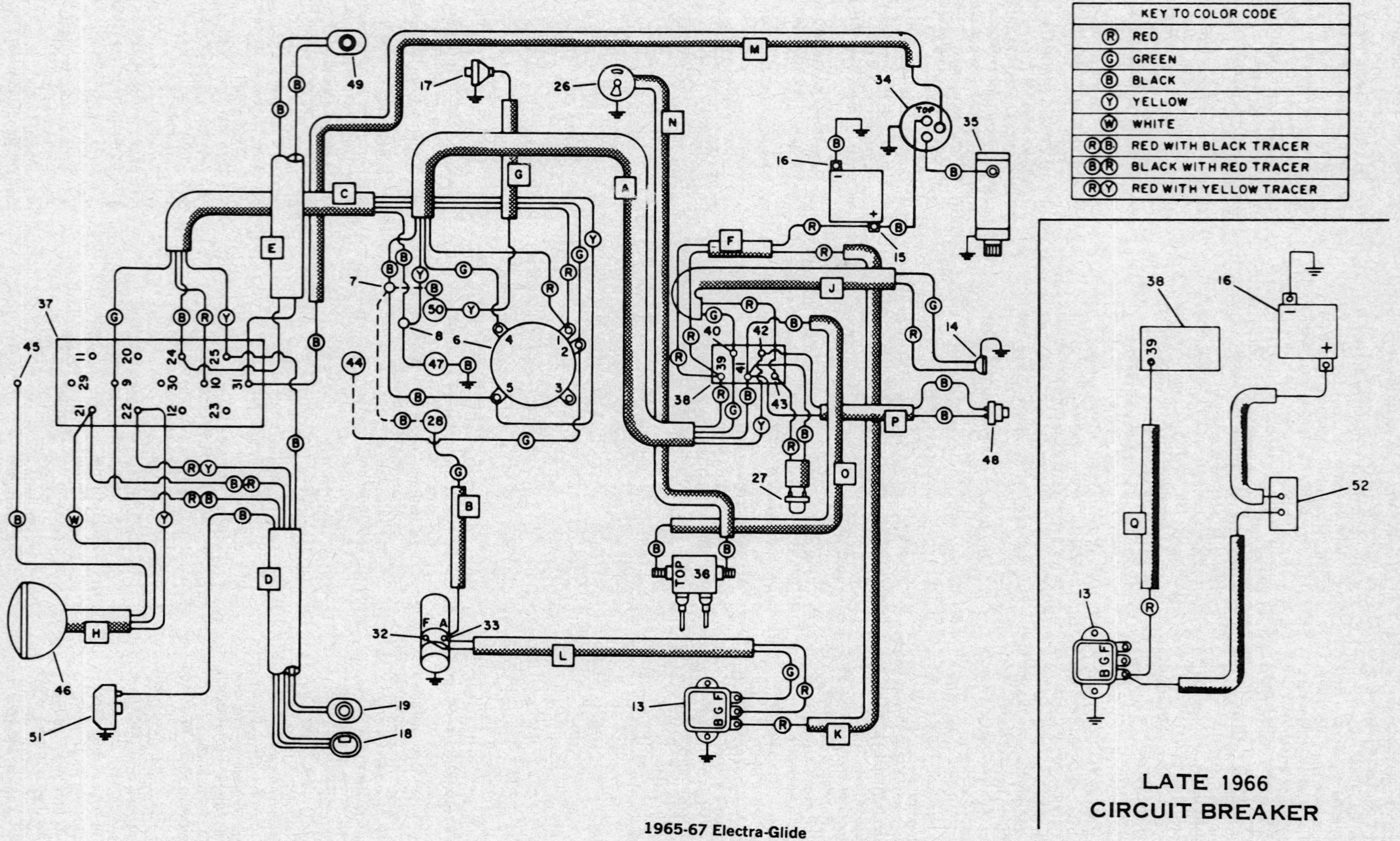

1965-67 Electra-Glide

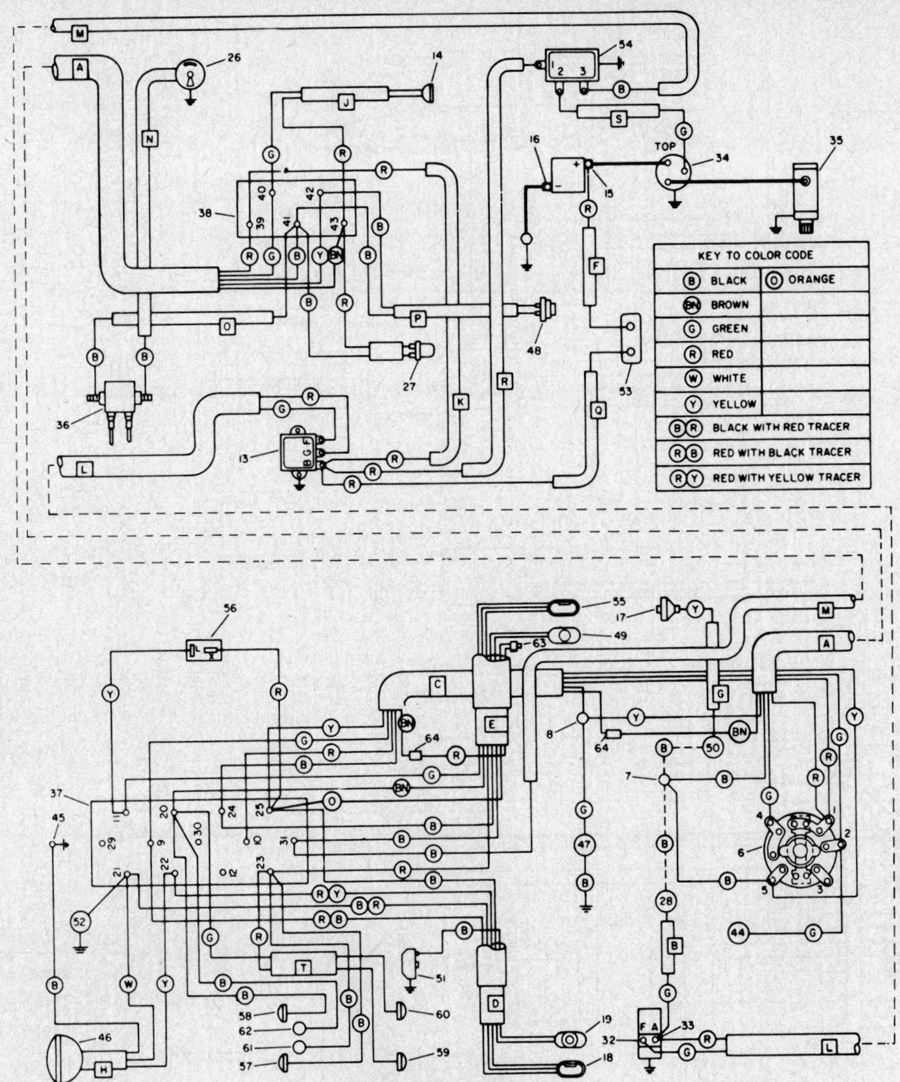

1968-69 Electra-Glide

A. Conduit (four wire)—Red, green, black and yellow
B. Conduit (one wire)—Green
C. Conduit (four wire)—Red, green, yellow and black
D. Left handlebar (loose wires)—Red with black tracer, black with red tracer, red with yellow tracer, 2 black wires
E. Right handlebar (loose wires)—Red, green, brown, 2 black wires
F. Conduit (one wire)—Red
G. Conduit (one wire)—Yellow
H. Conduit (three wire)—Black, white and yellow
J. Conduit (two wire)—Red and green
K. Conduit (one wire)—Red
L. Conduit (two wire)—Green and red
M. Conduit (one wire)—Black
N. Conduit (one wire)—Black
O. Conduit (one wire)—Black
P. Conduit (two wire)—2 Black wires
Q. Conduit (one wire)—Red
R. Conduit (one wire)—Red
S. Conduit (one wire)—Green
T. Conduit (two wire)—Red and green

1. Switch terminal—Switch supply
2. Switch terminal—Headlamp
3. Switch terminal—Not used with standard wiring
4. Switch terminal—Tail lamp
5. Switch terminal—Ignition coil
6. Ignition—Light switch—See terminals 1 through 5
7. Junction terminal
8. Junction terminal
9. Terminal
10. Terminal
11. Terminal
12. Terminal—Not used with standard wiring
13. Regulator
14. Tail and stop lamp
15. Battery positive terminal
16. Battery negative terminal
17. Oil pressure signal switch
19. Horn switch
20. Terminal—Not used with standard wiring
21. Terminal
22. Terminal
23. Terminal
24. Terminal
25. Terminal
26. Ignition circuit breaker
27. Stop lamp switch
28. Generator signal light
29. Terminal—Not used with standard wiring
30. Terminal—Not used with standard wiring
31. Terminal
32. Generator "F" terminal
33. Generator "A" terminal
34. Starter solenoid
35. Starter motor
36. Ignition coil
37. Terminal plate
38. Terminal box—See terminals 39 through 43
39. Terminal
40. Terminal
41. Terminal
42. Terminal
43. Terminal
44. Speedometer light
45. Terminal plate top mounting screw (ground)
46. Headlamp
47. Neutral indicator light
48. Neutral switch
49. Starter button
50. Oil signal light
51. Horn
52. High beam indicator lamp
53. Overload circuit breaker
54. Starter relay
55. Direction signal switch
56. Direction signal flasher
57. Left front direction lamp
58. Right front direction lamp
59. Left rear direction lamp
60. Right rear direction lamp
61. Left direction signal pilot lamp
62. Right direction signal pilot lamp
63. Stop lamp front switch
64. Connector

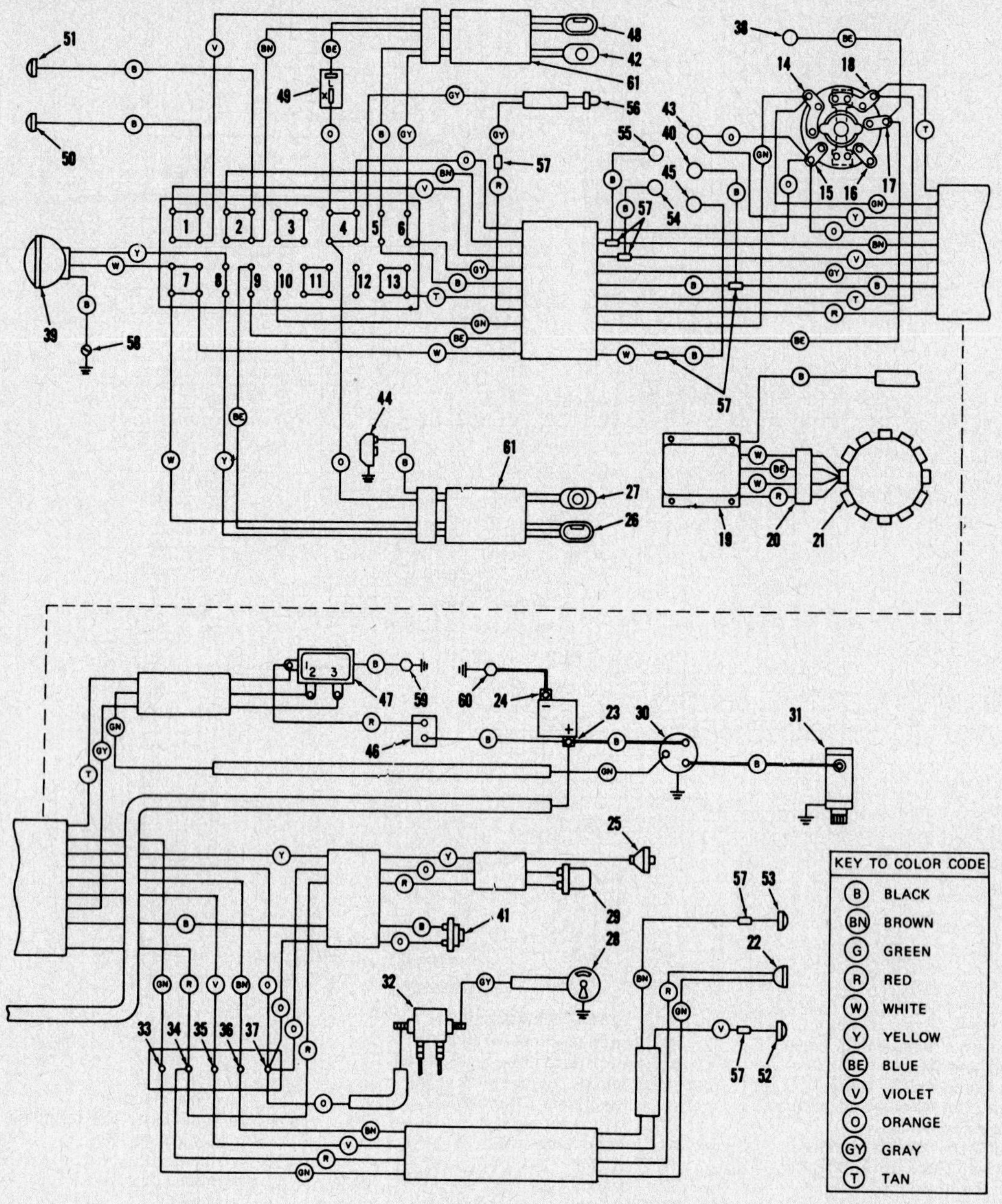

KEY TO COLOR CODE
B BLACK
BN BROWN
G GREEN
R RED
W WHITE
Y YELLOW
BE BLUE
V VIOLET
O ORANGE
GY GRAY
T TAN

1970 Electra-Glide

1. to 13. Front terminal board terminals
14. Switch tail lamp terminal
15. Switch ignition terminal
16. Switch terminal (not used with standard wiring)
17. Switch headlamp terminal
18. Switch supply terminal
19. Regulator-rectifier module
20. Alternator to module connector plug
21. Alternator stator
22. Tail and stop lamp
23. Battery positive terminal
24. Battery negative terminal
25. Oil pressure signal switch
26. Handlebar headlamp switch
27. Horn switch
28. Ignition circuit breaker
29. Stop lamp switch—rear
30. Starter solenoid
31. Starter motor
32. Ignition coil
33. Rear terminal board terminal—top
34. Rear terminal board terminal
35. Rear terminal board terminal
37. Rear terminal board terminal—bottom
38. Speedometer light
39. Headlamp
40. Neutral indicator light
41. Neutral switch
42. Starter button
43. Oil signal light
44. Horn
45. High beam indicator lamp
46. Overload circuit breaker
47. Starter relay
48. Direction signal switch
49. Direction signal flasher
50. Left front direction lamp
51. Right front direction lamp
52. Left rear direction lamp
53. Right rear direction lamp
54. Left direction signal pilot lamp
55. Right direction signal pilot lamp
56. Stop lamp switch—front
57. Connector
58. Terminal board mounting screw
59. Transmission stud
60. Frame lug bolt
61. Handlebar

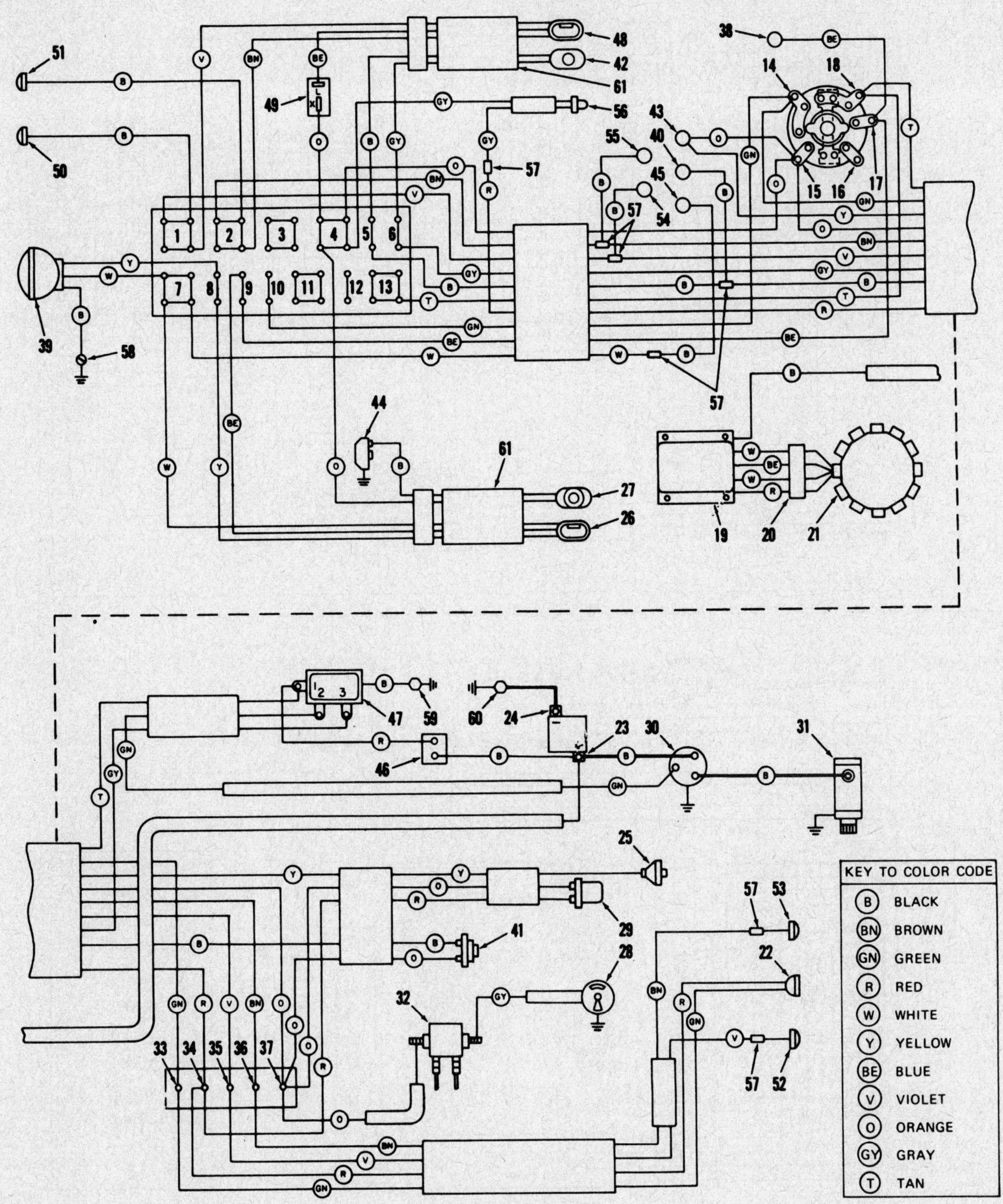

1971 Electra-Glide

1. to 13. Front terminal board terminals
14. Switch tail lamp terminal
15. Switch ignition terminal
16. Switch terminal (not used with standard wiring)
17. Switch headlamp terminal
18. Switch supply terminal
19. Regulator-rectifier module
20. Alternator to module connector plug
21. Alternator stator
22. Tail and stop lamp
23. Battery positive terminal
24. Battery negative terminal
25. Oil pressure signal switch
26. Handlebar headlamp switch
27. Horn switch
28. Ignition circuit breaker
29. Stop lamp switch—rear
30. Starter solenoid
31. Starter motor
32. Ignition coil
33. Rear terminal board terminal—top
34. Rear terminal board terminal
35. Rear terminal board terminal
37. Rear terminal board terminal—bottom
38. Speedometer light
39. Headlamp
40. Neutral indicator light
41. Neutral switch
42. Starter button
43. Oil signal light
44. Horn
45. High beam indicator lamp
46. Overload circuit breaker
47. Starter relay
48. Direction signal switch
49. Direction signal flasher
50. Left front direction lamp
51. Right front direction lamp
52. Left rear direction lamp
53. Right rear direction lamp
54. Left direction signal pilot lamp
55. Right direction signal pilot lamp
56. Stop lamp switch—front
57. Connector
58. Terminal board mounting screw
59. Transmission stud
60. Frame lug bolt
61. Handlebar

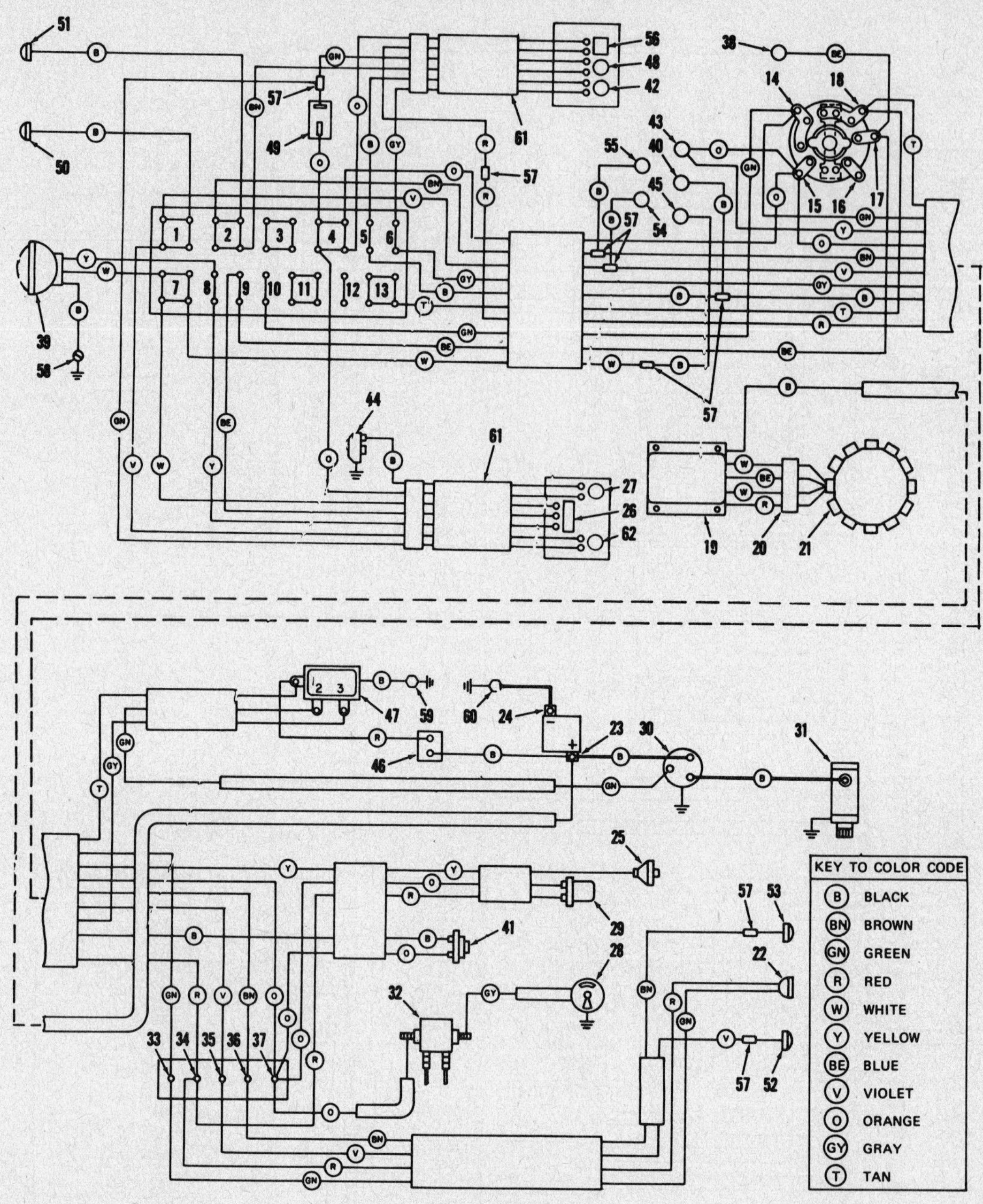

1972 Electra-Glide

1. to 13. Front terminal board terminals
14. Switch tail lamp terminal
15. Switch ignition terminal
16. Switch terminal (not used with standard wiring)
17. Switch headlamp terminal
18. Switch supply terminal
19. Regulator-rectifier module
20. Alternator to module connector plug
21. Alternator stator
22. Tail and stop lamp
23. Battery positive terminal
24. Battery negative terminal
25. Oil pressure signal switch
26. Handlebar headlamp switch
27. Horn switch
28. Ignition circuit breaker
29. Stop lamp switch—rear
30. Starter solenoid
31. Starter motor
32. Ignition coil
33. Rear terminal board terminal—top
34. Rear terminal board terminal
35. Rear terminal board terminal
37. Rear terminal board terminal—bottom
38. Speedometer light
39. Headlamp
40. Neutral indicator light
41. Neutral switch
42. Starter button
43. Oil signal light
44. Horn
45. High beam indicator lamp
46. Overload circuit breaker
47. Starter relay
48. Direction signal switch
49. Direction signal flasher
50. Left front direction lamp
51. Right front direction lamp
52. Left rear direction lamp
53. Right rear direction lamp
54. Left direction signal pilot lamp
55. Right direction signal pilot lamp
56. Stop lamp switch—front
57. Connector
58. Terminal board mounting screw
59. Transmission stud
60. Frame lug bolt
61. Handlebar
62. Left direction signal switch

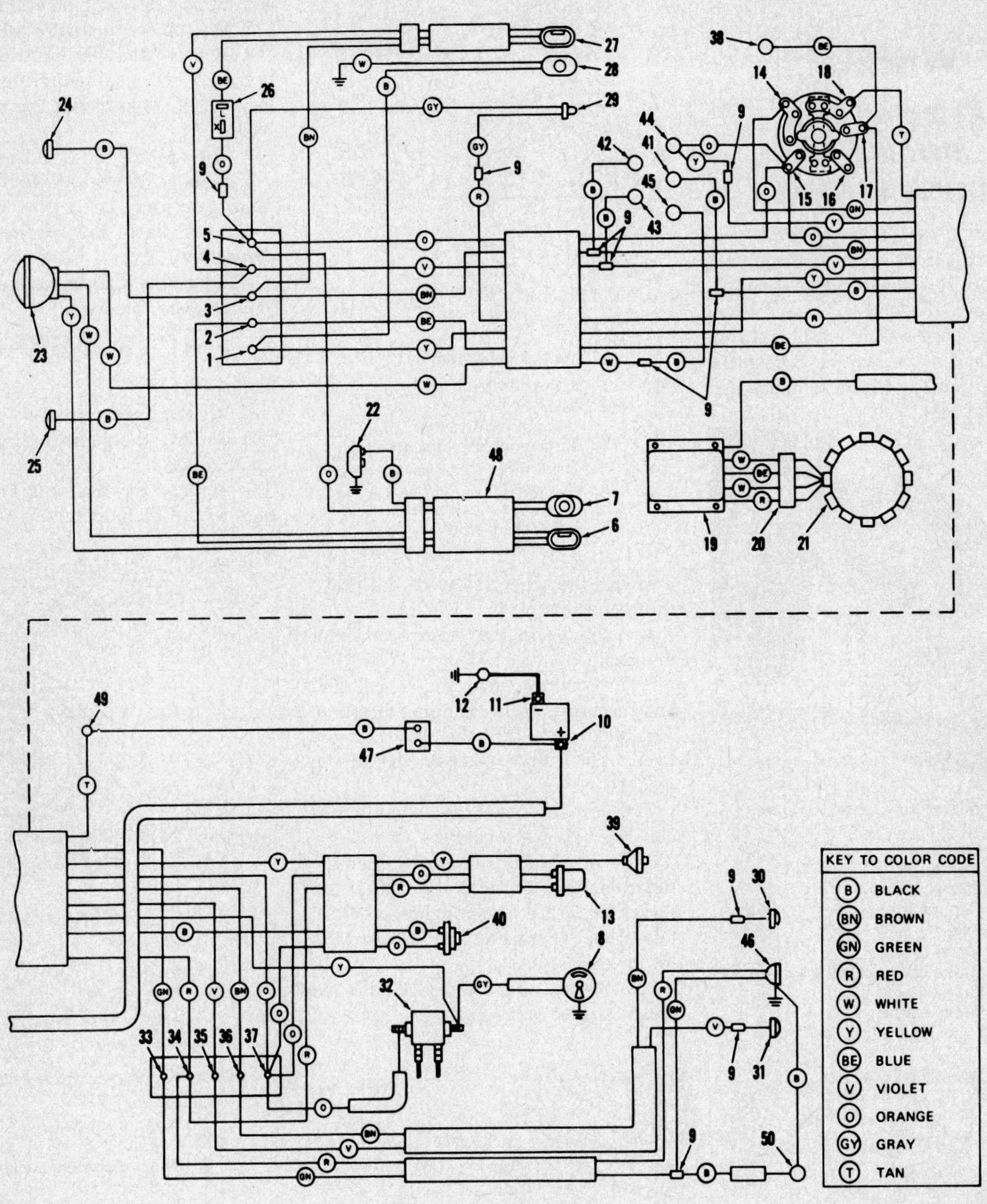

1971 and later Super-Glide

1. to 5. Fork terminal board terminals
6. Headlamp dimmer switch
7. Horn switch
8. Ignition circuit breaker
9. Wire connector
10. Battery positive terminal
11. Battery negative terminal
12. Frame lug bolt
13. Stop lamp switch—rear
14. Switch tail lamp terminal
15. Switch ignition terminal
16. Switch terminal (not used with standard wiring)
17. Switch headlamp terminal
18. Switch supply terminal
19. Regulator—rectifier module
20. Alternator to module connector plug
21. Alternator stator
22. Horn
23. Headlamp
24. Right front direction lamp
25. Left front direction lamp
26. Direction signal flasher
27. Direction signal switch
28. Ignition cutout button
29. Stop lamp switch—front
30. Right rear direction signal lamp
31. Left rear direction signal lamp
32. Ignition coil
33. Rear terminal board terminal—top
34. Rear terminal board terminal
35. Rear terminal board terminal
36. Rear terminal board terminal
37. Rear terminal board terminal—bottom
38. Speedometer light
39. Oil pressure signal switch
40. Neutral switch
41. Neutral indicator light
42. Right direction signal pilot lamp
43. Left direction signal pilot lamp
44. Oil signal lamp
45. High beam indicator lamp
46. Tail and stop lamp
47. Overload circuit breaker
48. Left handlebar
49. Junction terminal
50. License lamp

CHASSIS

WHEELS

Removal and Installation

FRONT WHEEL

Servi-Car and Glide Models

1. Raise the front wheel off the ground and support the machine in this position.
2. Remove the cotter pin (or clevis pin), axle nut, flat washer, bushings (if applicable), and socket screws. Loosen the slider cap nuts (or pinch bolts) and remove the axle.

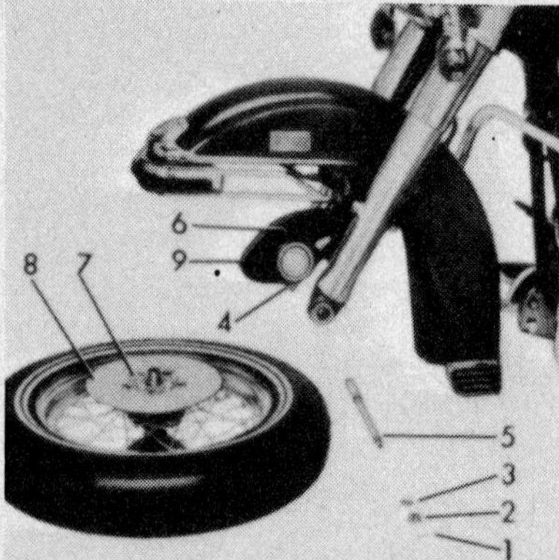

1972 and later front wheel assembly

1. Cotter pin
2. Axle nut
3. Flat washer
4. Cap nuts
5. Axle
6. Bleed fitting
7. Brake disc mounting screws
8. Brake disc
9. Brake caliper

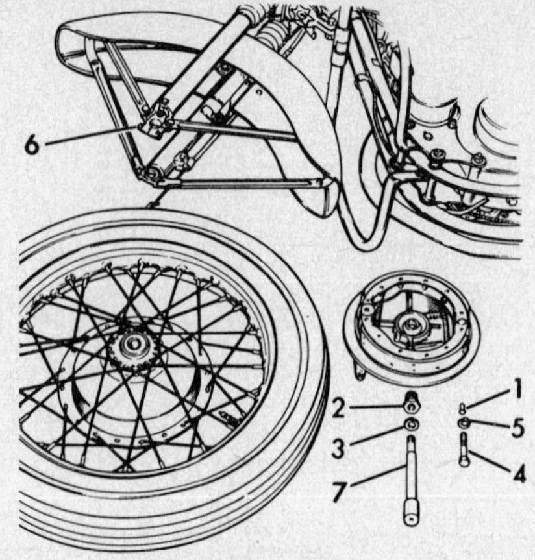

Front wheel assembly

1. Brake clevis pin
2. Axle nut
3. Axle nut lock washer
4. Brake anchor and centering bolt
5. Lock washer
6. Front axle pinch bolt
7. Front wheel axle

3. Lift the wheel clear of the brake drum and remove it.
4. Assemble in the reverse order of disassembly.
5. Thoroughly clean the wheel hub and the brake drum clamping faces.
6. Make sure that the disc slips between the caliper pads on disc brake models.
7. Secure the socket screws with a suitably sized allen wrench.
8. Secure the axle nut evenly, then the slider cap nuts (or pinch bolts), after the socket screws have been tightened, to attain proper alignment. Install a new cotter (or clevis pin).
9. Adjust the brake as described in the "Maintenance" section.

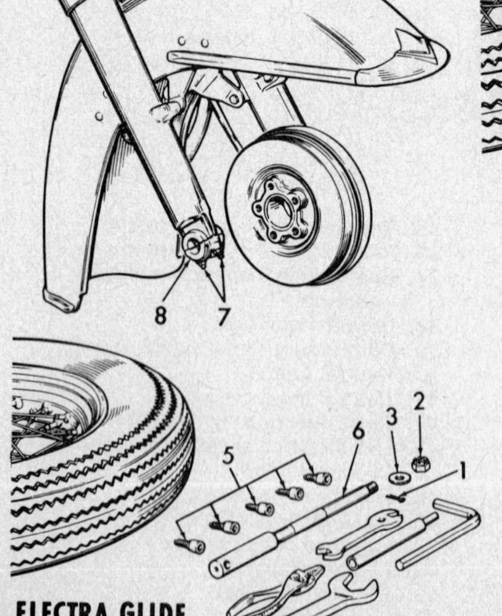

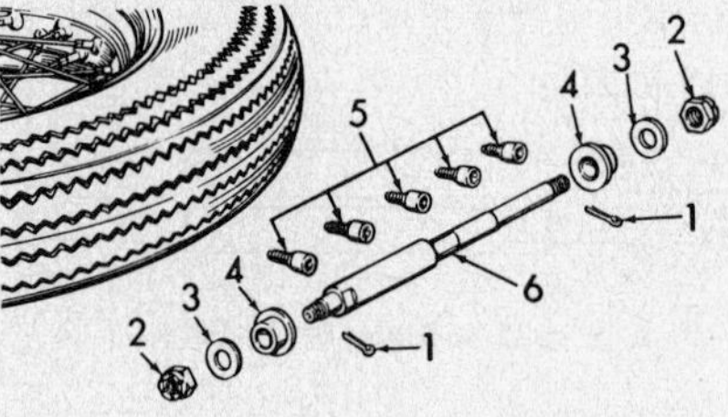

SERVI-CAR

1. Cotter pin
2. Axle nut
3. Flat washer

* Not used on Duo-Glide

*4. Bushing
5. Wheel mounting socket screws
6. Axle
7. Slider cap nuts
8. Slider cap

Front wheel assembly

Sportster and Super Glide

1. Raise the front wheel off the ground and support the machine in this position.
2. Disconnect the brake cable.
3. Remove the axle nut, lockwasher, brake anchor, shoe centering bolt, and lockwasher, then loosen the axle pinch bolt.
4. Tap the axle loose and remove it.
5. Remove the wheel and brake assembly.
6. Assemble in the reverse order of disassembly.
7. Adjust the brake as described in the "Maintenance" section.

REAR WHEEL

Servi-Car

1. Pry the hubcap free.
2. Remove the wheel lug nuts with a suitable tool.
3. Replace the lug nuts finger-tight, then secure them evenly in a cross pattern.
4. Install the hub cap.

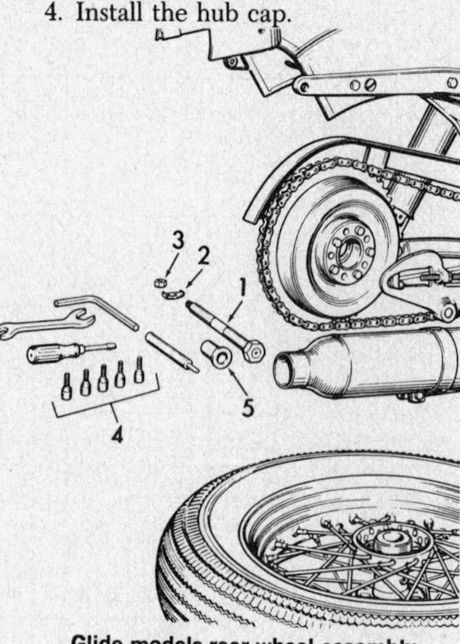

Glide models rear wheel assembly

1. Axle
2. Axle nut lockwasher
3. Axle nut
4. Wheel mounting socket screws
5. Spacer

Glide Models

1. Raise the rear wheel off the ground and support the machine in this position.
2. Remove the fender support screws and raise the fender flap (if applicable).
3. Remove the rear wheel mounting screws with a suitably sized allen wrench.
4. Remove the axle nut, lockwasher, axle, and axle spacer.

NOTE: *Remove the wheel while actuating the rear brake. Brake Pedal Locking Tool (H-D part no. 45875–58) may be used but is not necessary.*

5. Assemble in the reverse order of disassembly.
6. Drum and hub clamping faces must be thoroughly cleaned.

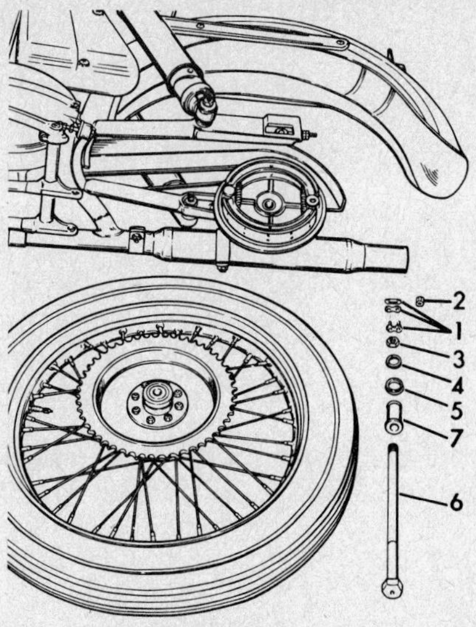

Sportster rear wheel assembly

1. Chain connecting link
2. Rear brake road adjusting nut
3. Axle nut
4. Axle nut lockwasher
5. Axle centering collar, right side
6. Rear axle
7. Axle spacer, left side

7. Secure the wheel mounting screws tightly so that the wheel cannot work free.

8. Secure the axle nut.

Sportster

1. Raise the rear wheel off the ground and support the machine in this position.

2. Remove the drive chain master link and free the chain from the rear sprocket.

3. Remove the brake rod adjusting nut, axle nut, lockwasher, and centering collar, and then loosen the axle by tapping it on the axle nut side.

4. Remove the axle and axle spacer.

5. Pull the wheel to the rear end of the frame and lift it up and out to remove.

6. Assemble in the reverse order of disassembly.

7. Adjust the brake as described in the "Maintenance" section.

SIDE CAR WHEEL

1. Raise the wheel off the ground and support the machine in this position.

2. Loosen the fender front bracket and step lug, and the fender inner brace clip bracket nut.

3. Remove the axle nut, lockwasher, and brace.

4. Tilt the fender forward, taking care to leave slack in the taillight wire.

5. Remove the extension nut, axle nut, washer, and wheel and drum assembly.

6. The wheel can be detached from the drum, if desired, by removing the wheel mounting screws with a suitably sized allen wrench.

7. Assemble in the reverse order of disassembly.

8. Take care to secure the socket screws tightly so that the wheel cannot work free.

WHEEL HUB

Servi-Car and Glide Models (Front and Rear Wheels)

ROLLER BEARING WHEEL HUBS (1966 and earlier)

Disassembly

1. Remove the wheels as described in "Wheel Removal and Installation."

2. Remove the thrust bearing cover screws, lockwashers, outer cover, cork grease retainer, bearing housing, housing gasket, bearing adjusting shims, outer thrust washer, bearing sleeve, and inner thrust washer.

3. Remove the bearing assembly and separate for reassembly.

4. Remove the roller retainer thrust washer.

5. Invert the hub and remove the outer roller retainer-spring lockring, retaining washer, hub inner sleeve, cork grease retainer, inner spring lockring, and roller bearing washer.

6. Remove the rollers, retainer, and thrust washer, and separate them for reassembly.

Inspection and Repair

1. Clean all parts other than the cork grease retainers, if they are to be reused, in a suitable solvent and blow them dry.

2. Inspect all parts for wear and replace if necessary.

3. Eliminate excessive bearing sideplay by adding 0.002 in. adjusting shims until 0.005–0.007 in. clearance is obtained between the thrust bearing sleeve and the thrust bearing outer cover. This measurement must be taken without the cork retainer present.

NOTE: *Bearing assemblies must be replaced as sets.*

4. Fit bearings to eliminate radial play by installing oversize bearing rollers until a clearnace of 0.001–0.005 in. is obtained. Rollers are available in 0.0002 in. gradations from 0.001 in. undersize to 0.001 oversize.

5. Replace the snap-rings and cork retainers.

Assembly

1. Assemble in the reverse order of disassembly.

2. Install a washer under the thrust bearing housing grease fitting.

3. Lightly grease the rollers, races, and thrust washers, and inject 1 oz of grease into the hub when it is assembled. Do not overlubricate the hub, since excess grease may get in the brakes.

4. Check bearings for slight play and free-motion.

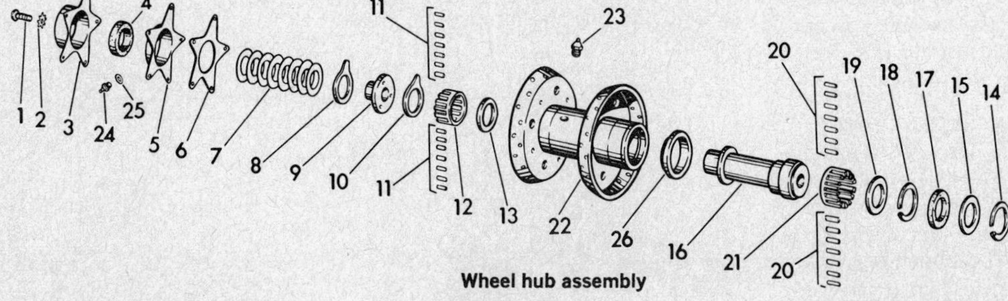

Wheel hub assembly

1. Thrust bearing cover screw (5)
2. Thrust bearing cover screw lockwasher (5)
3. Thrust bearing outer cover
4. Cork grease retainer
5. Thrust bearing housing
6. Thrust bearing housing gasket
7. Thrust bearing adjusting shim (varies) (each 0.002 in. thick)
8. Thrust washer (2) (see item 10)
9. Thrust bearing sleeve
10. Thrust washer (see item 8)
11. Bearing roller (12)
12. Roller retainer
13. Roller retainer thrust washer
14. Roller bearing spring lock ring (2) (see item 18)
15. Retaining washer
16. Hub inner sleeve
17. Cork grease retainer
18. Roller bearing spring lock ring (see item 14)
19. Roller bearing washer
20. Bearing roller (14)
21. Roller retainer
22. Hub shell
23. Grease fitting (2)
24. Grease fitting (see item 23)
25. Plain washer
26. Roller retainer thrust collar

Figure following name of part indicates quantity necessary for one complete assembly.

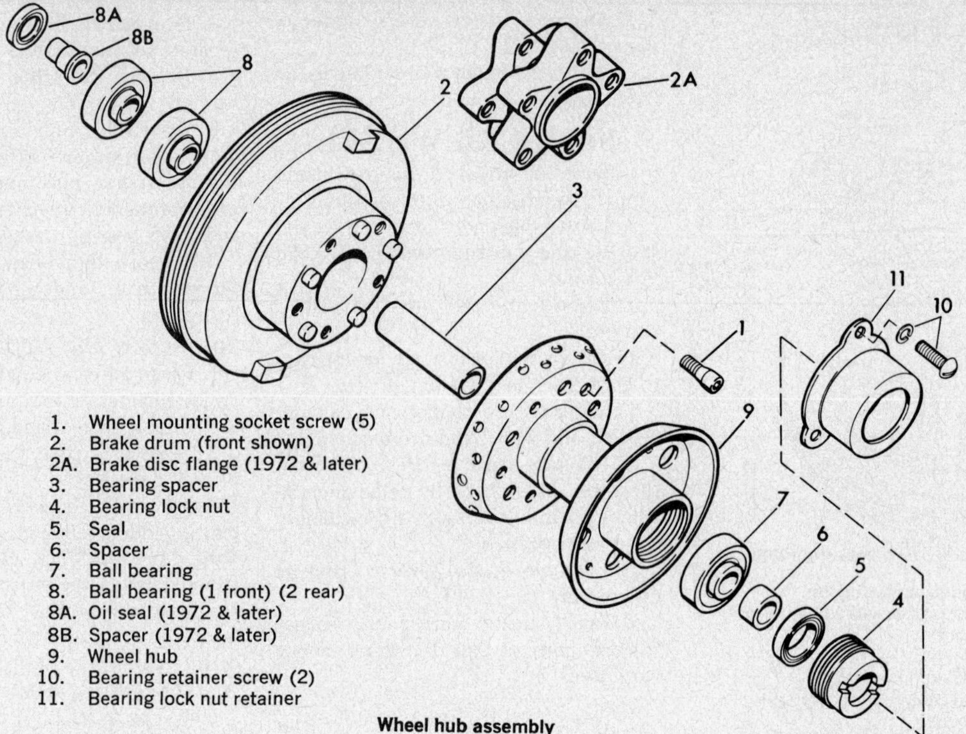

1. Wheel mounting socket screw (5)
2. Brake drum (front shown)
2A. Brake disc flange (1972 & later)
3. Bearing spacer
4. Bearing lock nut
5. Seal
6. Spacer
7. Ball bearing
8. Ball bearing (1 front) (2 rear)
8A. Oil seal (1972 & later)
8B. Spacer (1972 & later)
9. Wheel hub
10. Bearing retainer screw (2)
11. Bearing lock nut retainer

Wheel hub assembly

BALL BEARING WHEEL HUBS (1967 and later)

Disassembly

1. Remove the wheels as described in "Wheel Removal and Installation."

2. Remove the wheel mounting socket screws with a suitably sized allen wrench.

3. Remove the brake drum (or brake disc flange) from the hub.

4. Remove the bearing spacer and press the drum bearing, or bearings, free from the hub side with a suitably sized drift.

5. Remove the retainer screws and retainer (late 1970 and later).

6. Remove the left-hand threaded bearing locknut with special tool (H-D part no. 94630–67) or a suitable substitute, and remove the seal and spacer.

7. Press the hub bearing free with a suitable drift from the drum side.

Inspection and Replacement

1. Check bearing for wear, rough motion, and excessive looseness of the inner and outer races and replace as necessary.

2. Inspect all of the parts for wear or damage, and replace as necessary.

3. Replace the seal if it is worn, cracked, or damaged, taking special note of the condition of the lip.

Assembly

1. Assemble in the reverse order of disassembly.

2. Pack both sides of the bearings and fill the remaining area in the hub and on the inside bearing of the drum with grease.

3. The drum and hub clamping faces must be completely clean so the wheel cannot work free.

Sportster (1963 and Earlier) Front Wheel Hub

DISASSEMBLY

1. Remove the wheel as described in the wheels section "Removal and Installation."

2. Remove the bearing locknut from the hub. It will be necessary to break the stakings.

3. Drift the ball bearing free from the opposite side and remove the bearing washer and spacer.

4. Drift the other bearing free from the opposite side and remove the grease retainer.

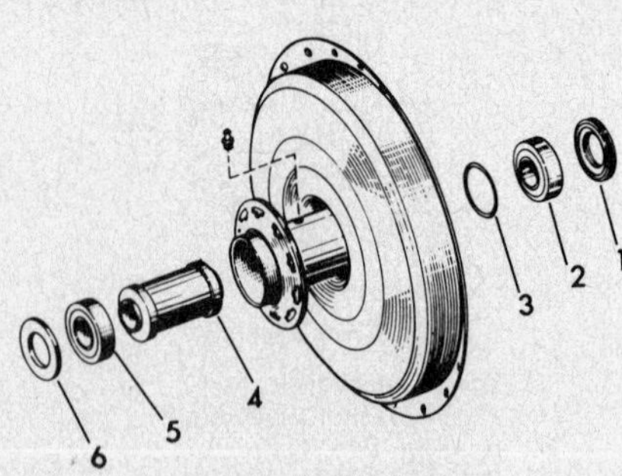

Wheel hub assembly

1. Bearing lock nut
2. Ball bearing
3. Bearing washer
4. Bearing spacer
5. Ball bearing
6. Grease retainer

Sportster (1964 and Later) and Super Glide Front Wheel Hub

DISASSEMBLY

1. Remove the wheel as described in the wheels section "Removal and Installation."

2. Pry the grease retainer free with a pointed instrument.

3. Remove the retaining ring with snap-ring pliers.

4. Gently tap the grease retainer side ball bearing into its seat in the hub. This will cause the spacer to push the other bearing out slightly. Slide the spacer back to the seated bearing.

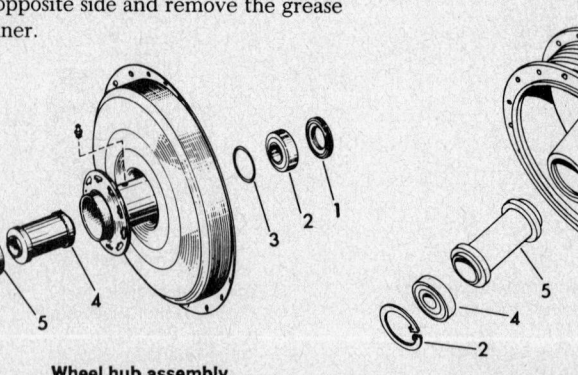

Wheel hub assembly

1. Grease retainer
2. Retaining ring
3. Ball bearing
4. Ball bearing (brake side)
5. Bearing spacer

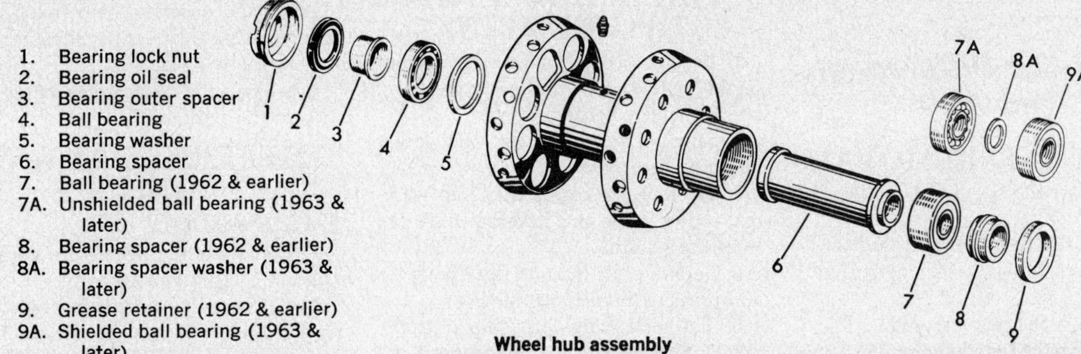

Wheel hub assembly

5. Insert an appropriate sized drift through the seated bearing and drift the opposite bearing out.

6. Remove the spacer and drift the seated bearing out from the opposite end.

Sportster Rear Wheel Hub

DISASSEMBLY

1. Remove the wheel as described in the "Removal and Installation" section.
2. Remove the bearing locknut with the special tool (H-D part no. 94630–67) or a suitable substitute. It will be necessary to break the stakings.
3. Drift the bearing oil seal and the outer spacer free from the opposite side of the hub with a suitable drift.
4. Drift the ball bearing and washer free in the above manner.
5. Remove the bearing spacer.
6. Drift the ball bearing, spacer (or spacer washer), and grease retainer as in the above manner.

REAR WHEEL HUBS (all above models) INSPECTION AND REPLACEMENT

1. Clean all parts in a suitable solvent and blow them dry.
2. Inspect all parts for wear and replace as necessary.
3. Replace any bearings which are worn, damaged, scorched, or have excessive radial play or rough motion.
4. Inspect the spoke flanges for damage or a bent condition and replace if necessary.
5. Clean and pack all ball bearings.

Sportster (1963 and Earlier) Front Wheel Hub

ASSEMBLY

1. Insert the bearing washer, open-end bearing, and locknut in the hub and stake the locknut in two new places.
2. Insert the bearing spacer.
3. Press the closed-end bearing (facing out) until it is seated on the bearing spacer; secure it with a grease retainer.

Sportster (1964 and Later) and Super Glide Front Wheel Hub

ASSEMBLY

1. Press the retaining ring side bearing (shielded side out) against its seat in the hub.
2. Secure the retaining ring with snapring pliers.
3. Insert the bearing spacer, press the bearing against its seat in the hub, and secure the grease retainer.

Sportster Rear Wheel Hub

ASSEMBLY

1. Press the bearing oil seal into the locknut and the outer spacer into the oil seal.
2. Secure the bearing washer, bearing, and assembled locknut to the hub. Stake the locknut in two new places.
3. Insert the bearing spacer in the hub.
4. Press the ball bearing (or unshielded bearing) until it is seated against the bearing spacer.
5. Insert the bearing spacer (or bearing spacer washer) and the grease retainer (or shielded ball bearing).

DRIVE TRAIN

Drive Chain

REMOVAL AND INSTALLATION

1. Loosen the axle housing frame clamps.
2. Loosen the axle adjusting screw locknuts and shift the axle forward about ½ in.
3. Jack up the right wheel and spin it until either side of the master link is visible through the chainguard slot.
4. Loosely connect the chain links on either side of the master link with mechanic's wire to prevent the chain from running off the sprockets.
5. Remove the master link with Chain Tool (from tool kit—H-D part no. 95020–38), Shop Tool (H-D part no. 95021–29) or pry the spring clip from the link with a screwdriver.
6. Attach a new chain to the present chain, or an old chain if chain is to be cleaned, with the master link.
7. Rotate the wheel forward while feeding one chain off the sprockets and the other one on.
8. Attach the loose end of the replacement to the chainguard with a piece of mechanic's wire.
9. Remove the replaced chain and connect the ends of the replacing chain. If a new chain is being mounted, secure it with a new master link, or at least use a new spring clip. If it is only a temporary replacement, connect it with mechanic's wire but do not attempt to run the machine this way.
10. Secure the spring clip with Press Tool (H-D part no. 95020–66) or pry on with a screwcriver.
11. If a second chain is not available, remove the chainguard and feed the chain off from the sprockets by rotating the rear wheel. Replace the chain by putting one end over the rear sprocket. With the transmission in First gear, crank the engine until the chain goes over mainshaft sprocket and secure it with the master link.
12. Adjust the chain as described in "Drive Chain Adjustment."

DETERMINING CHAIN WEAR

1. Lay the chain out on a flat surface.
2. Push the links together, a couple at a time, until all slack has been removed. Measure the overall length.
3. Pull on both ends until the chain is extended to its greatest possible length. Measure the chain again. If the overall length is greater by more than one inch, the chain is excessively worn and must be replaced.
4. This procedure can be used to measure the length of continuous-type primary chains also. Lay the chain on its side

to do this and replace if the difference is greater than ⅜ in.

Servi-Car Differential and Axle

REAR END REMOVAL

1. Remove the Servi-Car box assembly.
2. Block the wheels free from floor.
3. Remove the outer chainguard and cover.
4. Remove the inner chainguard.
5. Remove the speedometer drive unit from the differential.
6. Remove the master cylinder brake line.
7. Remove the stoplight switch wires.
8. Remove the rear muffler clamp.
9. Loosen the frame clamp bolt nuts and slide the rear axle free from the frame.

AXLE HOUSING DISASSEMBLY

1. Remove the hydraulic brake line assembly, wheels, and brake (or brake rod on mechanical brake models).
2. Disconnect the front and lower housing truss rods.
3. Remove the clamp nuts and washers, and drift the axle housing studs free from the housing.
4. Separate the left and right housings and remove them from the axle.
5. The following procedures apply only if the axle bearings, oil seals, or bearing race require service:
    a. Remove the end-bearing spring rings with snap-ring pliers.
    b. Slip the thrust washers, oil seals, roller thrust bushings, roller bearing retainers, bearing rollers, axle bearing race, and bearing cup lockwashers from the axles.
    c. Remove the bearing housing lock screw and unscrew the Timken bearing housing and bearing cup outer race from the left axle.
    d. Press the bearing cup outer race from the right axle.

DIFFERENTIAL AND AXLE

DISASSEMBLY

1. Remove the spring-wire lockring holes in the differential bolts.
2. Remove the differential bolt nuts, washers, lock plates, differential bolts, and drive sprocket.
3. Separate the axle and differential halves, and slip the gear housing from the axle.
4. Strike the wheel end of the axle surface until the sprocket will move down the splines.
5. Remove the axle lockring halves and the differential axle gear.

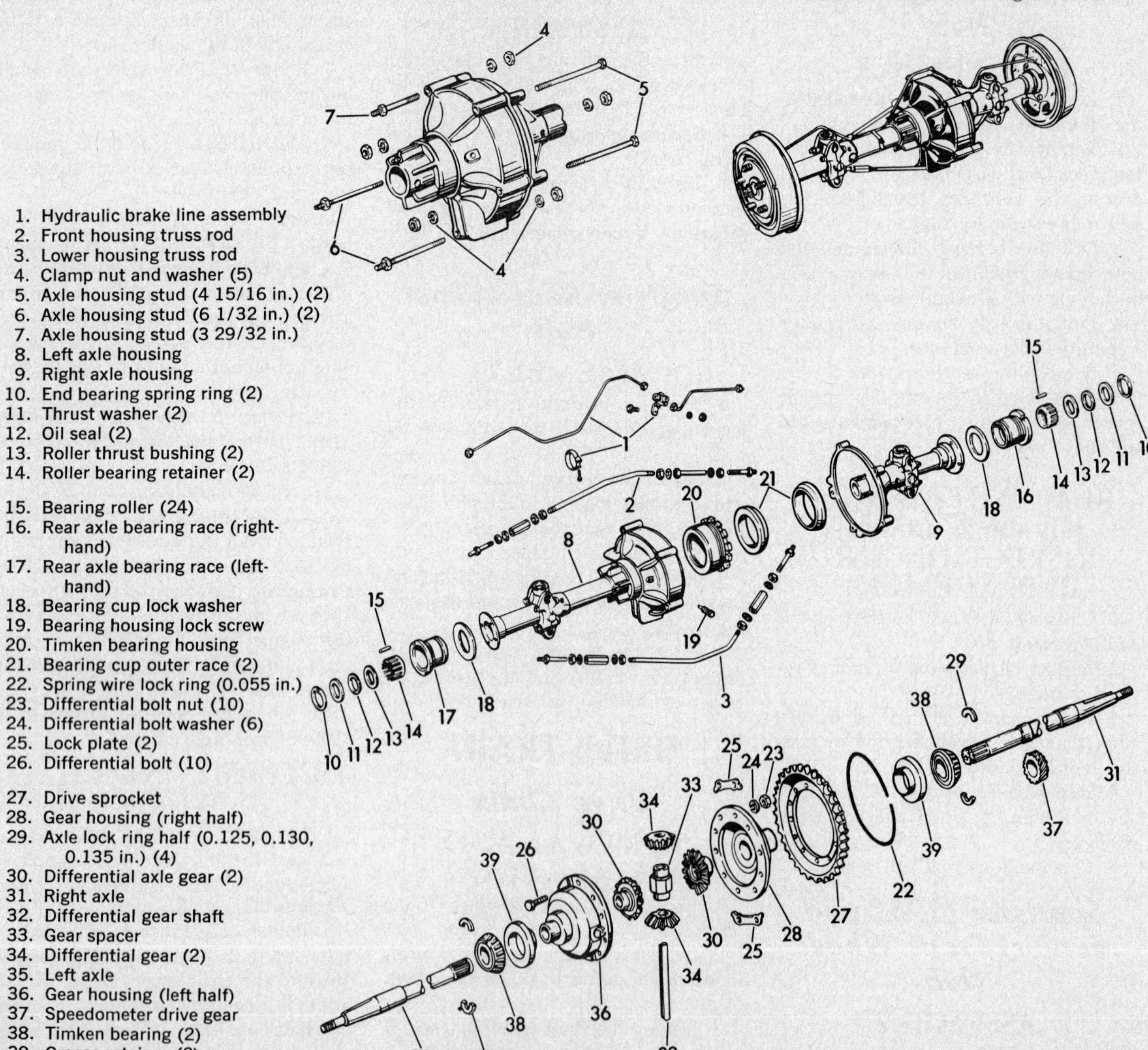

Figure following name of part indicates quantity necessary for one complete assembly.

Servi-Car differential and axle assembly

6. Drive the differential gear shaft out of its case and remove the gear spacer and differential.

7. Disassemble the left axle housing assembly in the same manner as was used for the right.

8. Press the Timken bearings and grease retainers from the differential housing only if replacement is necessary.

9. If the speedometer drive-gear is to be replaced, first measure the distance from the gear face to the end of the axle. Press the new gear in exactly the same position.

INSPECTION AND REPAIR

1. Clean all of the parts in a suitable solvent and blow them dry.

2. Inspect the bearing rollers, races, and gear teeth for a pitted, grooved, gouged, or otherwise worn condition and replace them if necessary. Oversize bearing rollers may be selected to obtain a 0.0015–0.0020 in. free-fit. Bearings are available in 0.0002 in. gradations from 0.-0002–0.0010 in.

3. Axles must be true to within 0.005 in. total runout. Your dealer can true them or advise when to replace them.

4. Axle housings must be true to within 0.010 in. total runout. Your dealer can repair housings that are not badly damaged.

5. Replace any grease retainers and oil seals which leak.

ASSEMBLY

1. Assemble in the reverse order of disassembly.

2. Temporarily secure the housing halves and insert the axles.

3. Correct axle end-play to within 0.-003–0.005 in. by installing thicker or thinner axle lockrings. Rings are available in 0.125, 0.130, and 0.135 in. thicknesses. Each axle must have matching rings but different thicknesses may be used on different axles.

4. Install all of the housing bolts with lock plates over the ends of the differential gear nut and secure the washers and nuts.

5. Run the spring-wire lockring through the holes in the housing bolts and bend it over at the ends. Start the ring in at the grease fittings. Secure the lock plate ears against the nuts.

AXLE HOUSING ASSEMBLY

1. Assemble in the reverse order of disassembly.

2. Pack the axle end bearings, tapered roller bearings, and speedometer drive housing with grease.

3. Fill the assembled gear housing with about 4 oz of grease.

4. Turn the Timken bearing housing into the case until it seats and then back it off 1½–2 notches until the housing lock.

5. Adjust the Timken bearing through the slot in the axle housing after the housing halves are assembled.

6. Turn the Timken bearing housing into the case until it seats and then back it off 1½–2 notches until the housing lock screw seats in the housing adjusting notch.

7. Secure the 6 1/32 and 3 29/32 in. axle stud bolts from the left side of the housing and secure the 4 15/16 in. bolts from the right.

8. Loosen the low-end truss rod fittings and tighten the high-end fittings until the truss rod bearing surfaces are parallel. Equally tighten both ends until the rod seats in the housing notch. Rods should be seated firmly but not tightly.

9. Assemble the brake line, drums, and wheels, and install the axle and box.

Rear Wheel Sprocket Replacement (all models)

1. Remove the wheel as described in the "Replacement and Installation" section for the wheels.

2. Remove the brake drum from the wheel as described in the wheel hub section.

3. On Servi-car models the differential and axle assemblies will have to be taken down. The sprocket is affixed to the right half of the gear housing by the bolts which hold the housing halves together. When the housing is removed the sprocket too may be removed.

4. Free the sprocket from the drum by chiseling off the heads of all rivets and dowel pins from the brake shell side and then by punching them out.

5. If the rivet holes are not worn or elongated and if the drum is still in good condition, proceed as follows:

   a. Using a new sprocket as a template (guide), drill a new rivet hole from the brake shell side between the original dowel and the rivet holes. Use a 5/32 in. drill for 1958 to early 1961 Servi-Car and Glide models, and a no. 10 drill (0.1935 in. diameter) for the 3/16 in. rivets used on early 1961 and later models. Sportster models require a 9/16 in. hole.

   b. Drill another hole opposite the first one and secure both with rivets but do not head them.

   c. Drill the remaining holes and remove the sprocket.

   d. Smooth the drum surface around the river holes.

6. Using the sprocket as a template, drill new 3/16 in. dowel holes and smooth off any burrs which may have resulted.

7. Place the drum on the center support flange of Riveting Jig (H-D part no. 95600–33B) and carefully align the sprocket on the drum. An appropriate riveting device may be substituted. Riveting Set (H-D part no. 95612–42) or Rivet Punch (H-D part no. 95613–42) may be purchased independently of the jig. If substitute rivets are used, make sure that they will provide a strong enough bond. Consult your dealer if you are in doubt.

8. Insert the dowel pins, then the rivets, from the brake shell side in the following manner:

   a. Using a hollow driver, drive the sprocket and hub flange together by seating the dowel pins and rivets.

   b. Work in opposite pairs to ensure an even seat between the sprocket and hub.

   c. Flare the dowel pin and rivet ends with a punch until the heads extend 3/64 in. above the sprocket surface for 5/32 in. rivets. Rivet heads that are 3/16 in. long must extend 3/32 in. above the sprocket surface. Use a concave-end punch for the dowel pins and the smaller rivets, and a flat-end punch for the larger diameter rivets.

BRAKES

Front Brake Cable Removal and Installation

1. Remove the wheel and the outer dust cover on Servi-Car and Glide models (older models are more like the Sportster and need not have the wheel removed).

2. Remove the clevis clamp nut and clamp.

3. Free the cable from the clevis and pull it free from the upper end of the cable housing (coil).

4. Slide a new cable in from the top of the cover, applying a light coat of grease as it goes in.

5. When installing the side slot cable ferrule in the brake lever, position the slot toward the inside, or down, on the earlier type, with the end slot.

6. Turn the adjusting sleeve clockwise to its stop.

7. Pull the cable from the lower end to remove all slack.

8. With the actuating lever in its lowest position, loop the cable around the clevis and secure it with a clevis clamp and clamp nut.

9. Replace the wheel and dust cover if applicable.

10. Adjust the brake cable.

Front Brake

DISASSEMBLY

Sportster and Super Glide

1. Remove the wheel, with the brake drum, from the fork.

2. Remove the operating shaft nut and lever.

3. Remove, as a unit, the brake shoes, springs, operating shaft, washer, and pivot stud, by tapping with a soft mallet on the operating shaft.

4. Remove the shoes and springs from the pivot stud and operating shaft.

Servi-Car and Glide Models

1. Remove the wheel, with the brake drum, from the fork.

2. Remove the dust cover.

3. Remove the shoes and springs by lifting them out and away from the sidecover.

4. Remove the cotter pin, washer, cam lever, lever bushing, set screw, and cam lever stud.

5. Follow the numerical order as depicted in the accompanying illustration.

INSPECTION AND REPLACEMENT (all models)

1. Examine the brake shoes, lining, drum, cam pivot, and the cam for excessive wear, glazing, and imbedded particles.

2. Exposed rivets on linings will gouge the drum and must be replaced. Oil-soaked, hard, cracked, or glazed linings must be replaced. Slightly worn linings can be dressed with medium grade sandpaper.

3. Replace the linings with rivets or replace them with ready-lined shoes. Always set the rivets from one end to the other to ensure a smooth, tight fit. Bevel the end of each brake lining.

4. Lightly lubricate the pivot stud (one squirt from a standard grease gun on Sportster grease fittings).

5. Rough up the drum braking surface with emery paper.

ASSEMBLY

1. Assemble in the reverse order of disassembly.

2. Assemble the brake shoes on the operating camshaft and pivot the stud with the top return spring in place in its groove nearest the brake side plate.

3. Assemble the shoes to the side plate, taking care to register the flat side of the pivot stud correctly in the flat side of the plate.

4. Secure the lower spring in place using a screwdriver as a lever or pilers.

5. Secure the operating nut and lever to the camshaft (Sportster models).

6. Mount the wheel and brake assemblies, adjust the cable, and center the shoes

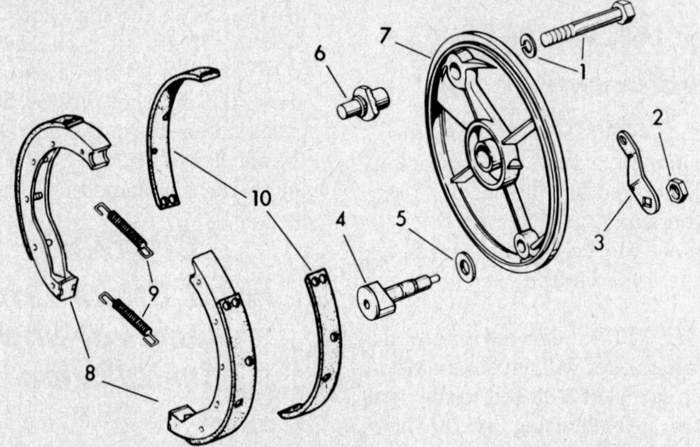

Front brake assembly—Sportster and Superglide models

1. Pivot stud screw and washer
2. Operating shaft nut
3. Operating lever
4. Operating shaft
5. Operating shaft washer
6. Shoe pivot stud
7. Brake side plate
8. Brake shoe and lining (2)
9. Brake shoe spring (2)
10. Brake lining (2)

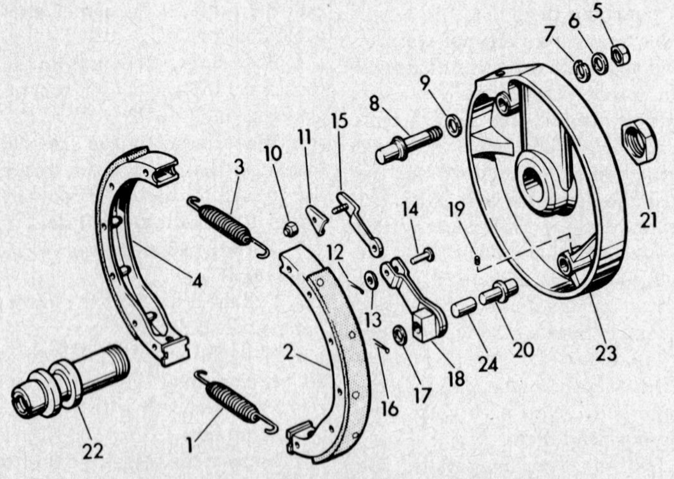

Front brake assembly—Servi-Car and Glide models

1. Brake shoe spring (2)
2. Brake shoe and lining (2)
3. Brake shoe spring (see item 1)
4. Brake shoe and lining (see item 2)
5. Brake shoe pivot stud nut
6. Pivot stud flat washer
7. Pivot stud lock washer
8. Pivot stud
9. Pivot stud washer
10. Clevis clamp nut
11. Cable clevis clamp
12. Cotter pin
13. Flat washer
14. Cam lever clevis pin
15. Cable clevis
16. Cotter pin
17. Cam lever washer
18. Cam lever
19. Set screw
20. Cam lever stud
21. Axle sleeve nut
22. Front axle sleeve
23. Brake side cover
24. Cam lever bushing

Figure following name of part indicates quantity necessary for one complete assembly.

Hydraulic Disc Brake

CALIPER DISASSEMBLY, INSPECTION, AND REPAIR

WARNING: *Hydraulic brake fluid will damage plastic, paint, and chrome surfaces.*

1. Free the hydraulic line from the hose clamp.

2. Remove the caliper bolts, washers, and outer caliper half.

3. Remove the mounting pin and inner caliper half.

4. Remove the brake pads and pad mounting pins.

5. Inspect the brake pad friction material for excessive wear, damage, or a loose fit, and replace as a set if friction material is less than 1/16 in. thick.

6. Inspect the friction material backing plates for damage or a warped condition and replace them if they are not completely flat.

7. Check the piston retraction with a dial indicator or spin the front wheel and check it for drag. The piston should retract 0.020–0.025 in. When the hand lever is released.

8. Replace the piston if fluid leaks through the seal or if the piston does not retract. Replace in the following manner:

a. Pump the hand lever until the piston moves to the end of its travel.

b. Disconnect the hydraulic line or drain the fluid into a clean glass container if the fluid is to be reused.

c. Slide the piston boot away from its groove in the piston and pull the piston free.

d. Remove the retaining ring with snap-ring pliers and slide out the backing plate, wave spring, adjusting ring, and O-ring.

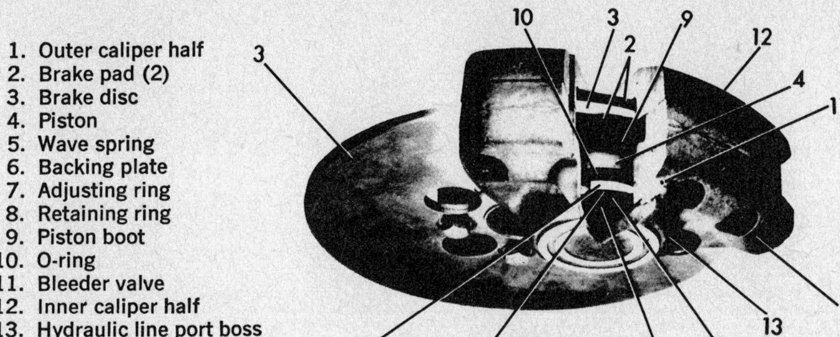

Front disc brake

9. Remove the bleeder valve.

10. Clean all of the metal parts in a suitable solvent and blow them dry.

11. Replace any worn or damaged parts.

12. Replace the outer caliper half if the cylinder bore is scored or damaged.

13. Inspect the brake disc for scoring or warping and replace it if necessary. If the disc is less than 3/16 in. thick, it must be replaced as described in "Brake Disc Removal and Installation."

14. Replace the bushings in the forks slider if they are worn or damaged.

15. Replace the O-ring, adjusting ring, and retaining ring.

CALIPER REASSEMBLY

1. Assemble in reverse order of disassembly.

2. Immerse the piston, retaining ring, backing plate, wave spring, adjusting ring, piston boot, and O-ring in hydraulic fluid, and assemble in bore.

3. Assemble the piston boot in the caliper bore.

4. Press the piston into the assembled bore until it firmly seats, taking care to avoid scoring the bore.

5. Assemble the bleeder valve on the caliper.

6. Assemble the brake pads and calipers to the fork.

7. Apply a graphite compound to the caliper bolts and torque them to 35 ft lbs.

8. Assemble the hydraulic line, hose clamp, screw, and lockwasher.

9. With the bike standing straight up, fill the reservoir with hydraulic brake fluid to the gasket level.

10. Coat the fittings with a hydraulic sealant if leaks are present (Locktite is recommended by the factory).

11. Bleed the system as described in "Bleeding Hydraulic System" until any spongy feeling disappears.

BRAKE DISC REMOVAL AND INSTALLATION

1. Remove the wheel as described in the "Removal and Installation" section for the front wheel.

2. Remove the disc securing bolts and lockwashers.

3. Replace the disc if it is worn to 0.188 in., or less, or it it is warped more than 1/32 in.

4. Replace the brake disc flange if it is damaged.

5. Reassemble using new lockwashers and torque to 35 ft lbs.

6. Assemble the wheel on motorcycle.

MASTER CYLINDER DISASSEMBLY, INSPECTION, AND REPAIR

1. Remove the cover securing screws, cover, and gasket.

2. Disconnect the hydraulic line at the caliper and drain it into a clean glass container if the fluid is to be reused.

3. Disconnect the stoplight wires and remove the handlebar switch assembly.

4. Remove the pivot pin, retaining ring, and pin.

5. Remove the lever, pin, plunger, spring, washers, dust wiper, and retaining ring.

6. Pull the piston, O-ring, piston cup, spring cup, and spring until they are free of the master cylinder.

7. Replace the piston cup and O-ring if they are worn, soft, or swollen.

8. Replace the cylinder walls if they are scratched or grooved.

9. Replace the gasket if it is leaky.

10. Blow the master cylinder vent hole clear.

MASTER CYLINDER ASSEMBLY

1. Assemble in the reverse order of disassembly.

2. Use all components of the repair kit if such a kit is to be used.

3. Immerse all internal parts in hydraulic fluid before assembly.

4. Lightly grease the pivot pin and plunger pin before reassembly.

5. Check to see that the relief port in the master cylinder is open when the lever is released.

1. Hose clamp, screw, and lockwasher
2. Bolt (4)
3. Washer (4)
4. Outer caliper half
5. Mounting pin
6. Inner caliper half
7. Brake pad mounting pins (2)
8. Brake pads (2)
9. Brake piston
10. Hydraulic line
11. Piston boot
12. Retaining ring
13. Backing plate
14. Wave spring
15. Adjusting ring
16. O-ring
17. Bleeder valve
18. Bushing
19. Bushing
20. Bolt and lockwasher (6)
21. Brake disc
22. Brake disc flange

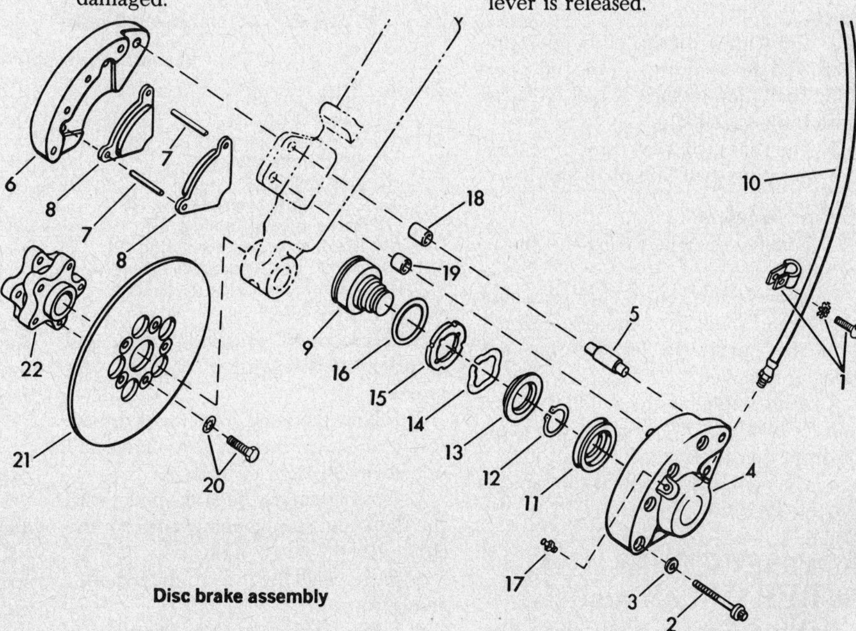

Disc brake assembly

6. Fill the reservoir to the gasket level with brake fluid.

7. Bleed the system as described in "Bleeding Hydraulic Brake System."

8. Install the gasket with the flat side down and secure the cover.

Rear Brake

DISASSEMBLY

Servi-Car

1. Remove the wheel from the brake shell.

2. Remove the cotter pin, axle nut, and axle shaft spacers.

3. Remove the brake shell with a stud or a claw wheel puller.

4. Remove the retangular axle key from its slot.

5. Remove the shoes by removing the upper return spring and lower retainer spring from the hold-down leaf springs.

NOTE: *Do not remove additional parts unless the cylinder or backing plate need repair.*

6. Disconnect the hydraulic brake fluid line.

7. Remove the cylinder mounting screws, washers, cylinders, and bleeders.

8. Pry the cylinder boots free and remove the pistons, cups, and springs.

9. Remove the back plate self-locking nuts, bolts, shims, and back plate. Note the number and placement of these shims for reassembly.

Sportster

1. Remove the wheel from the motorcycle.

2. Free the brake rod from the operating lever by removing the brake rod adjusting nut.

3. Remove the shaft nut and its lockwasher, operating lever, pivot stud nut and its lockwasher, and the locating block.

4. Tap with a soft mallet on operating shaft, and shoes, springs, pivot stud, operating shaft, and washer will all fall away from brake side-plate.

5. The shoes will now come free from the operating shaft and pivot stud.

Glide Models

1. Remove the wheel from the motorcycle.

2. Remove the return spring, anchor spring, and shoes from the side cover.

3. The hold-down leaf springs may now be removed.

4. After removing the cylinder screws and lockwashers, the cylinder will come off from the side-cover.

5. Cylinder disassembly is the same as for the Servi-Car.

INSPECTION AND REPAIR (all models)

1. Consult "Front Brake Inspection and Replacement" for the Sportster and all other models with mechanical rear brakes.

2. Follow the same steps for hydraulic rear brakes but inspect the cylinder and side-cover for signs of leakage.

3. Do not operate the brake pedal with the shoes and springs removed from the back plate.

4. Remove all burrs from the cylinder and piston.

5. If the cylinder is faulty, install a repair kit. Dip the parts in brake fluid and use all of the parts provided. Never use gasoline on any hydraulic parts.

ASSEMBLY

Sportster

1. Assemble in the reverse order of disassembly.

2. Using one spring, mount the shoes on the operating shaft and pivot stud, taking care to seat the spring in its groove on the back plate.

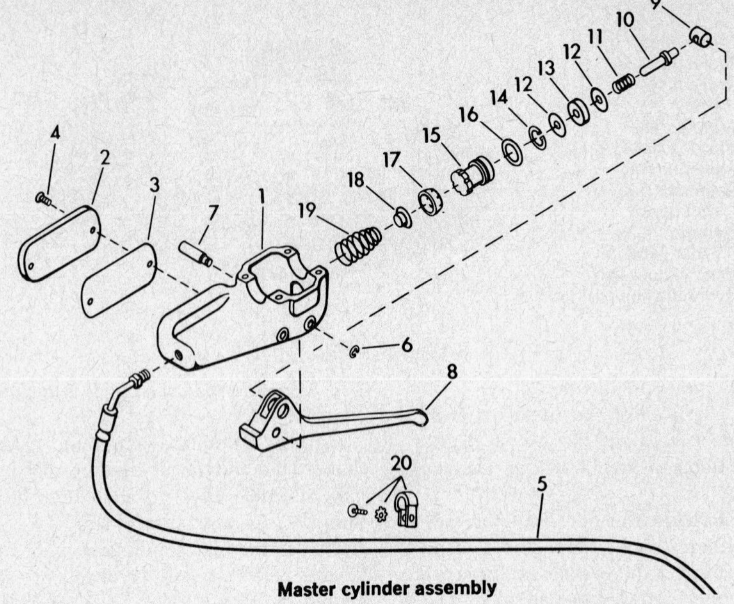

Master cylinder assembly

1. Master cylinder
2. Master cylinder cover
3. Gasket
4. Screw (2)
5. Hydraulic line
6. Retaining ring
7. Pivot pin
8. Brake lever
9. Pin
10. Plunger
11. Spring
12. Washer
13. Dust wiper
14. Retaining ring
15. Piston
16. O-ring
17. Piston cup
18. Spring cup
19. Spring
20. Hose clamp, screw and lock-washer

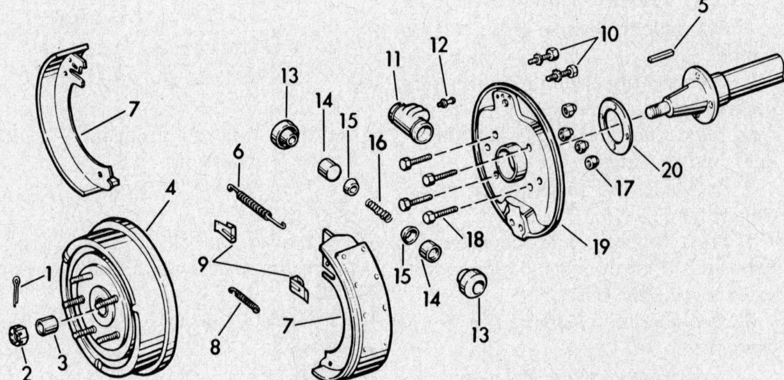

Rear brake assembly—Servi-Car

1. Cotter pin (2)
2. Axle nut (2)
3. Axle shaft spacer (2)
4. Rear brake shell (2)
5. Axle key (2)
6. Brake shoe return spring (2)
7. Brake shoe with lining (4)
8. Brake shoe retainer spring (2)
9. Brake shoe hold down spring (4)
10. Cylinder mounting screw and washer
11. Wheel cylinder (2)
12. Cylinder bleeder nipple (2)
13. Cylinder boot (4)
14. Cylinder piston (4)
15. Cylinder cup (4)
16. Spring (2)
17. Self-locking nut (8)
18. Back plate mounting bolts
19. Brake back plate
20. Brake side plate shim (2 to 8)

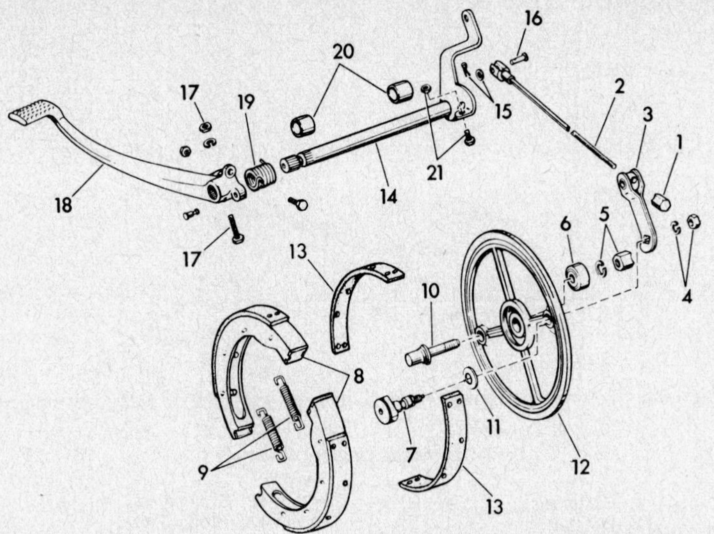

1. Brake rod adjusting nut
2. Brake rod
3. Brake operating lever
4. Operating shaft nut and lock washer
5. Pivot stud nut and lock washer
6. Locating block
7. Operating shaft
8. Shoe and lining (2)
9. Shoe spring (2)
10. Pivot stud
11. Operating shaft washer
12. Brake side plate
13. Brake lining (2)
14. Cross shaft
15. Rod clevis cotter pin and washer
16. Rod clevis pin
17. Foot lever bolt and nut
18. Foot lever
19. Lever torsion spring
20. Frame brake shaft tube bushing (2)
21. Cross shaft adjusting screw and nut

Rear brake and cross shaft assembly

3. Assemble the operating shaft and washer on the side-plate.

4. Mount the locating block, pivot stud nut and lockwasher, operating lever, and the shaft nut and lockwasher on the shaft.

5. Secure the shoes with a second spring. Use a screwdriver as a lever, or pliers, to install it.

6. Place the brake rod through the lever ferrule and secure it with an adjusting nut.

7. Assemble the brake and wheel on the motorcycle.

8. Adjust the adjusting rod and center the shoes.

Hydraulic Brake Models

1. Assemble in the reverse order of disassembly.

2. Lightly grease the hold-down leaf springs, and the area on the side plate where the shoes seat during operation.

3. Connect the shoes with the lower return spring, place the assembly on the back plate, and secure it with the upper spring, using a screwdriver as a lever or else with pliers.

4. Place the short hook in the elongated hole on the front shoe (when applicable).

5. On 1963 and later Glide models, the shoes are of different widths and the narrow shoe must be on the rear of the back plate.

6. Assemble the wheel on the motorcycle.

7. Adjust the linkage and center the shoes.

Rear Brake Cross-Shaft Mechanical Brake Models

DISASSEMBLY

NOTE: *Consult Sportster Rear Wheel Brake Disassembly for Cross Shaft Assembly Illustration.*

1. Disconnect but do not remove the rear chain.

2. Remove the rear cylinder exhaust pipe and muffler.

3. Remove the brake rod, clevis pin, cotter pin, washer, and clevis pin from the lever arm.

4. Back off the pinch bolt until the foot pedal lever and return spring can be slipped from the shaft.

5. Remove the shaft from the right side of the machine.

INSPECTION AND REPAIR

1. Inspect the shaft and the lever pedal splines, and replace them if they are damaged or worn. Excessive wear will cause the lever to slip on the shaft reducing braking accuracy.

2. Assemble the clevis pin in the rod clevis and check for wear. Replace the pin if it is worn; always replace the cotter pin.

3. Check to see if excessive clearance has developed between the bushings and shaft; replace the bushings if necessary.

4. Bushings can be drifted out from the frame by threading in a ¾–16 in. tap from the outside of each bushing.

5. Press in new bushings, install the shaft, and check to see that the shaft rotates freely.

6. Ream the bushing to the correct size of high spots developed during drifting.

ASSEMBLY

1. Replace bushings if they have been removed.

2. Insert the shaft in the frame tube.

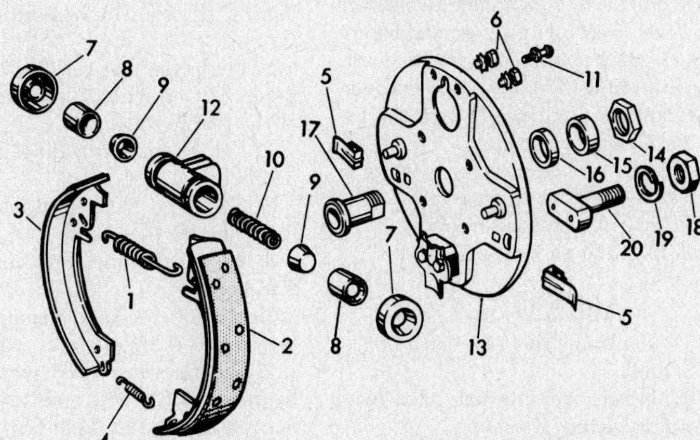

1. Shoe return spring
2. Front brake shoe
3. Rear brake shoe
4. Brake shoe spring
5. Hold-down spring (2)
6. Cylinder screw and lock washer (2 each)
7. Boot (2)
8. Piston (2)
9. Cup (2)
10. Spring
11. Bleeder nipple
12. Wheel cylinder
13. Brake side cover
14. Nut
15. Spacer
16. Collar
17. Brake sleeve
18. Nut
19. Lockwasher
20. Anchor stud

Rear brake assembly—Glide

3. Assemble the shaft arm, if it has been removed, and secure it to the brake rod clevis with the pin, washer, and cotter pin.

4. Mount and adjust the chain on the rear sprocket, and assemble the tail pipe and muffler.

5. Set the cross-shaft adjusting screw so that, when it is stopped against the frame, the cross-shaft arm is slightly behind the center of the rear fork pivot bolt. The arm must never be closer than 1½ in. tc the inner recess of the transmission sprocket cover.

6. Assemble the brake pedal on the shaft so it lies slightly beneath the foot rest. Adjust the cross-shaft adjusting screw until the pedal is correctly positioned. Always adjust it so the arm moves away from the transmission cover.

7. Secure the cross-shaft bolt locknut.

8. Check the brake pedal adustment.

Master Cylinder

DISASSEMBLY

1. Drain the master cylinder of all brake fluid.

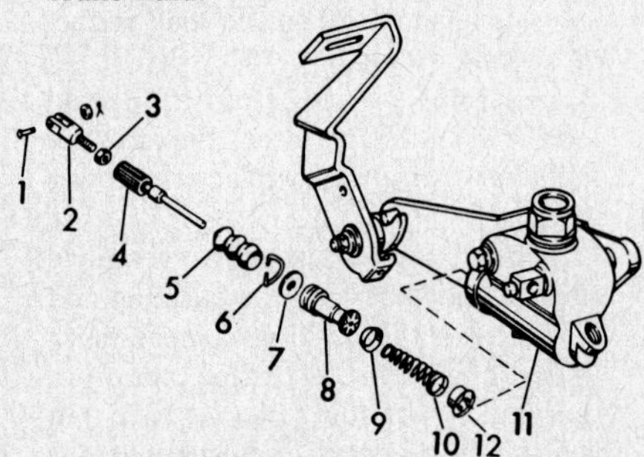

Glide models master cylinder assembly

1. Rod clevis pin with washer and cotter pin
2. Lever clevis
3. Master cylinder plunger lock nut
4. Master cylinder plunger
5. Cylinder boot
6. Stop wire
7. Stop washer
8. Piston assembly
9. Piston cup
10. Piston return spring
11. Master cylinder
12. Valve

2. It is not necessary to remove the master cylinder from the frame to replace the piston assembly.

3. Remove the cotter pin, washer, and clevis pin to free the linkage lever.

4. Disconnect the brake line, remove the mounting bolts, lockwashers and securing bolts, and remove the cylinder from the frame.

5. Loosen the brake adjusting locknut and remove the cylinder clevis and nut.

6. Remove the cylinder pushrod and rubber boot.

7. Remove the stop wire by prying it out with a screwdriver.

8. Slide out the piston and stop washer.

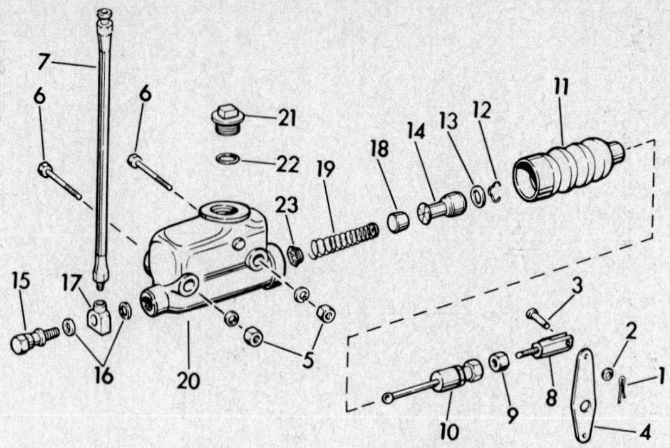

Servi-Car master cylinder assembly

1. Cotter pin
2. Washer
3. Clevis pin
4. Bracket lever
5. Cylinder mounting nut and washer (2)
6. Cylinder mounting bolt (2)
7. Rear brake hose
8. Master cylinder clevis
9. Brake adjusting lock nut
10. Cylinder push rod
11. Boot
12. Stop wire
13. Stop washer
14. Piston
15. Cylinder bolt
16. Bolt gasket (2)
17. Cylinder fitting
18. Cup
19. Spring assembly
20. Master cylinder shell
21. Filler plug
22. Filler plug gasket
23. Valve

9. Remove the cylinder bolt, gaskets, and cylinder fitting.

10. Remove the cup, spring assembly, and valve by gently pressing them out with a small rod.

11. Remove the filler plug and gasket.

INSPECTION AND REPAIR

1. Clean all of the cylinder parts in brake fluid only.

2. Clear, if necessary, the intake and by-pass ports with a wire run through the filler opening.

3. Replace the cup for wear and replace it if it is grooved by the edge of the by-pass port.

4. If the cup was grooved, smooth the by-pass port edges with a burring tool or with a thin, round file.

5. Hone the master cylinder walls until they are free of pits, scratches, or grooves. After honing, check with a hole gauge to see if the bore has been overenlarged. Use a burring tool on the by-pass port after the honing.

6. Inspect rubber parts for swelling or softness and replace as necessary.

7. If any of piston assembly is worn, install all of the parts in a repair kit.

ASSEMBLY

1. Assemble in the reverse order of disassembly.

2. Lubricate all internal parts with brake fluid before assembly.

3. Make all connections firm and check for leaks.

4. Bleed the brake system.

5. Adjust the brake linkage.

Bleeding Hydraulic Brake System

1. The brake must be bled anytime a line or cylinder is opened to remove all air.

2. Place a length of plastic tubing of appropriate size over the bleeder nipple and run the tube into a container with about one inch of brake fluid already in it so bubbles will be visible and so no air can get back in the system. Be sure there is no room for leakage around the nipple because brake fluid removes paint.

3. On Servi-Cars, bleed the left wheel first.

4. Open the bleeder nipple by rotating it counterclockwise about ½ turn.

5. Keep the master cylinder full of fluid at all times to keep air out of the system.

6. Pump the foot pedal or hand lever repeatedly until no air bubbles come out of the plastic tube.

7. Fill the master cylinder to its original leve.

8. Close the bleeder nipple first and then remove the plastic tube.

9. Repeat the operation on the Servi-Car right wheel.

10. If bubbles keep coming, replace the master cylinder check valve.

11. Do not reuse brake fluid since it is hydrascopic (attracts moisture) and will become moisture-ridden from sitting in the draining container. This will cause spongy brake action.

FRONT FORK

Fork Slider and Tube Removal

(ALL MODELS EXCEPT SPORTSTER AND SUPER GLIDE)

1. Remove the front wheel as described in the wheels' "Removal and Installation" section.
2. Remove the brake cable clip from the front fender.
3. Remove the axle sleeve nut, pivot stud nut, and brake side-cover and shoe assembly along with the axle sleeve, from the forks.
4. Remove the front fender.
5. Loosen but do not remove the front fork bracket clamping studs.
6. Remove the upper bracket bolts, oil seals, and fork slider and slider tube assemblies from the bottom of the slider covers.

Preliminary Disassembly

1. Remove the headlight cowlings and headlamp.
2. Disconnect all headlight and handlebar wires at the terminal.
3. Disconnect the throttle and spark cables at the carburetor and the contact breaker.
4. Remove the handlebars.

Disassembly

NON-ADJUSTABLE GLIDE MODELS

1. Remove the fork stem nut, nut lock (if applicable), upper bracket bolts, oil seal, upper bracket cover (if applicable), and handlebar and fork bracket.
2. Using Lock Nut Wrench (H-D part no. 96219–50) or a suitable substitute, remove the head bearing nut, lift the upper bearing free, and pull the fork free from the bottom of the steering head.
3. Loosen, but do not remove, the fork bracket clamping studs and slip the fork bracket and slider cover assembly free of the fork tubes.
4. Remove the slider tube plugs, drain the oil, and remove the fork springs.
5. Remove the damper valve stud locknut and free the slider tube from the slider.
6. Remove the slider tube snap-ring with snap-ring pliers. Remove the damper tube lower bushing, damper tube bushing gasket, and damper valve stud gasket. Discard and replace all parts other than the tube assembly.

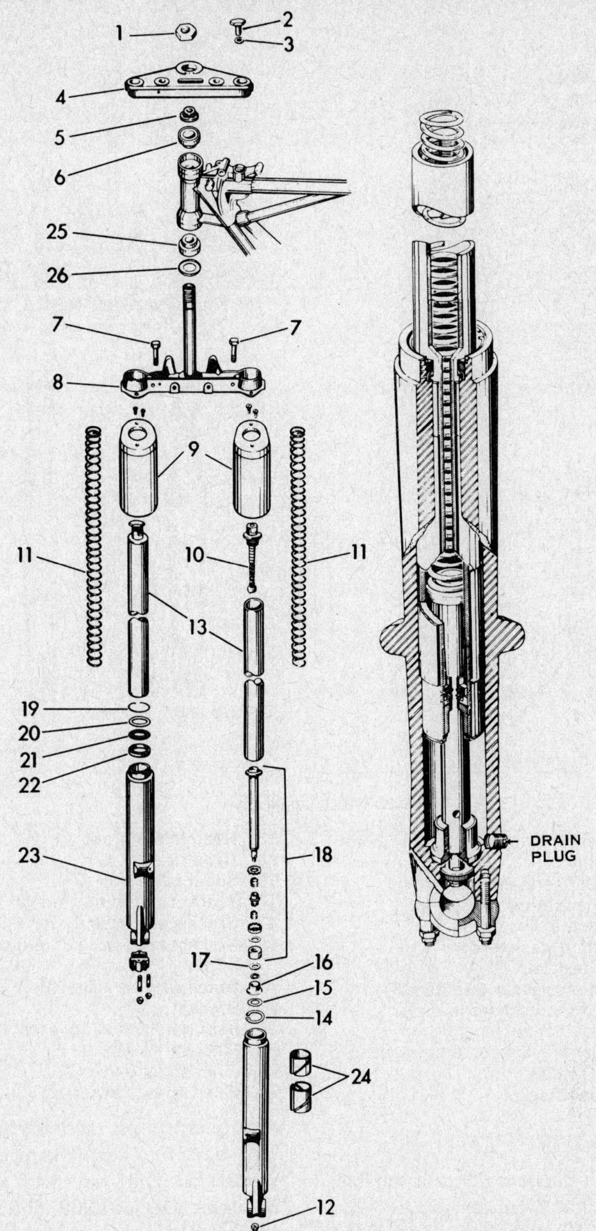

Non-adjustable Hydra-Glide fork assembly

1. Fork stem nut
2. Fork upper bracket bolt and valve (2)
3. Tube plug oil seal (2)
4. Handlebar and fork bracket
5. Head bearing nut
6. Head bearing (2)
7. Fork bracket clamping stud (2)
8. Fork bracket with stem
9. Fork slider cover (2)
10. Slider tube plug (2)
11. Fork spring (2)
12. Damper valve stud lock nut (2)
13. Fork slider tube (2)
14. Slider tube snap ring
15. Damper tube bushing gasket (2)
16. Damper tube lower bushing (2)
17. Damper valve stud gasket (2)
18. Damper tube valve (2)
19. Spring ring (2)
20. Spring ring washer (2)
21. Upper oil seal felt washer (2)
22. Upper oil seal (2)
23. Slider (2)
24. Slider upper and lower bushing (2 each)
25. Head bearing (see item 7)
26. Lower head bearing guard

ADJUSTABLE GLIDE MODELS AND SERVI-CAR

1. Remove the steering damper adjusting screw, spring cover, spider spring, upper pressure disc, friction washer, anchor plate, friction washer, and lower pressure disc by prying all parts loose when necessary.
2. Remove the fork stem nut, upper bracket bolts and washers, bracket cover and bracket.
3. Using Lock Nut Wrench (H-D part no. 96219–50) or a suitable substitute, remove the head bearing nut, lift the upper head bearing free, and pull the fork free from the bottom of the steering head.
4. Remove the slider tube plugs.
5. Loosen but do not remove the bracket clamping studs.
6. Continue as described for Non-Adjustable Glide Models.

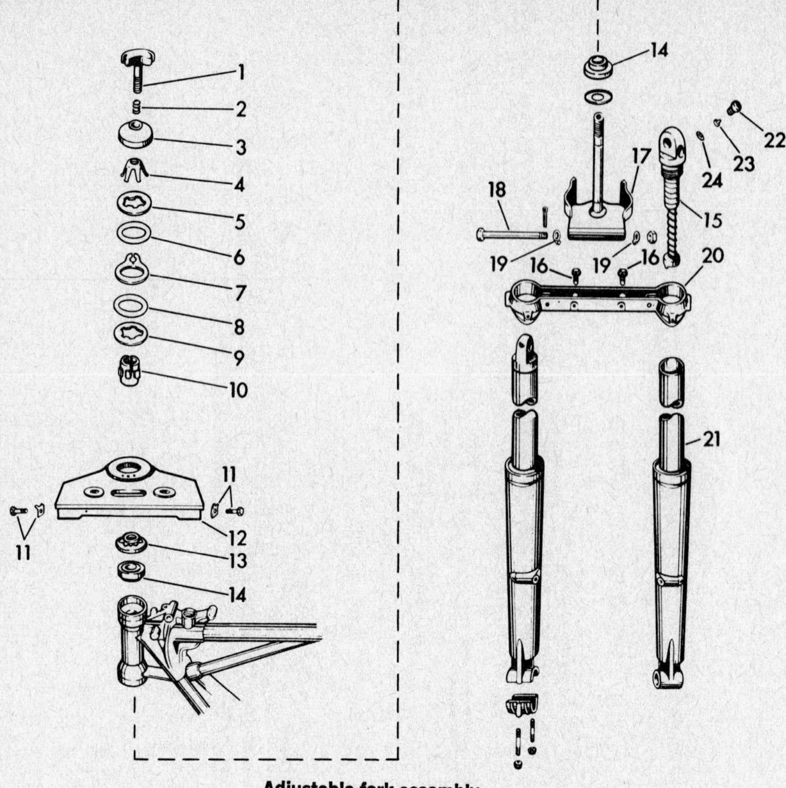

Adjustable fork assembly

1. Steering damper adjusting screw
2. Spring
3. Spider spring cover
4. Spider spring
5. Pressure disc (2)
6. Friction washer (2)
7. Anchor plate
8. Friction washer (see item 6)
9. Pressure disc (see item 5)
10. Fork stem nut
11. Upper bracket bolt and washer (2 each)
12. Upper bracket
13. Head bearing nut
14. Head bearing (2)
15. Slider tube plug (2)
16. Bracket clamping stud (2)
17. Bracket with stem
18. Bracket bolt with nut and cotter pin
19. Bracket bolt washer (2)
20. Bracket
21. Fork tube and slider assembly (2)
22. Filler screw (2)
23. Filler screw valve (2)
24. Filler screw washer (2)

Inspection and Repair

1. Clean all of the parts in a suitable solvent and blow them dry.

2. Inspect the slider tubes and slider for scratches, grooves, wear, and damage, and replace if necessary. Remove minor faults with a fine oil stone or emery paper.

3. Inspect the valve tube assembly components for pitting, rust, wear, and damage, and replace if necessary.

4. Inspect the slider tube plugs for loose cups or damaged springs and replace if necessary. Oil slots in the cups must be arranged on alternate sides.

5. Inspect the steering head bearings and races for pitting, rough motion, wear, or damage, and replace in sets whenever necessary.

6. Bearing races can be drifted free with a suitable drift after the head cups are removed. Replace by pressing new races into the head cup and then pressing both into the head frame.

7. The following distinction is made in steering head bearing assemblies:

a. Bearings on models earlier than 1960 have 16 rollers. The races on 1959 models are ⅜ in. high with an outside diameter (OD) of 1.969. The 1959 type head cup must be used with this bearing race.

b. Bearings on models later than 1959 have 19 rollers. The races on 1960 models are 27/64 in. high with an OD of 1.980 in. The 1960 type head cup must be used with this bearing race.

8. Remove both fork slider bushings, if worn, pitted, or damaged, by installing Fork Slider Bushing Puller (H-D part no. 96255–50) or a suitable substitute. Oil the tool's threads and washer to ease removal. The bushing may be split with a chisel to remove it if care is taken not to damage the slider.

9. Install the new fork slider bushings with Fork Slider Bushing Driver and Guide (H-D part no. 96285–50) or a suitable drift, or else use a piece of pipe with the slide secured in a copper or wood-jawed vise. If the proper bushing driver is not available, mark the tube where the bushings were originally as an aid in replacing them correctly. Lubricate the bushing and the tube to aid installation. The lower bushing should seat at a position where the second groove of the driver is aligned with the top of the guide. The upper bushing should be 1/16 in. below the oil seal counterbore.

10. Ream the bushing with Fork Slider Bushing Reamer and Pilots (H-D part no. 96300–50) or a suitable substitute. Using the long pilot as a guide in the lower bushing, ream the upper bushing by slowly placing the reamer in position while rotating it clockwise. Always continue to rotate the reamer while withdrawing it.

11. Ream the lower bushing with the small pilot as a guide in the same manner as for the upper bushing. Take care not to mar the upper bushing while passing the reamer through it. Pilots can be made from suitably sized lengths of pipe.

12. Fork tubes can be pressed straight, if they are only slightly bent, but should be turned professionally. Consult your dealer for a qualified shop that does this sort of work. Turning is inexpensive and more accurate then pressing. This also applies to sliders, fork stem, and brackets. Your dealer is your best bet.

NON-ADJUSTABLE FRONT FORK ASSEMBLY

1. Install a new upper oil seal and felt washer in a thoroughly cleaned slider. The oil seal may be seated gently in its counterbore with a mallet and Driver (H-D part no. 96250–50) or a suitable substitute.

2. Install a new spring ring washer and a new spring ring with its gap over the slider top water drain hole.

3. Assemble the damper valve, new upper gasket, lower bushing, and a new lower gasket.

4. Secure a length of 1 in. steel rod vertically in a vise with 13½ in. above the jaws.

5. Place the inverted slider tube over the steel rod and drop the damper valve assembly in upside down.

6. Secure the slider snap-ring in the slider tube notch and check the clearance between the ring and the lower bushing. Insert shims if they are necessary to bring clearance to a maximum of 0.004 in.

7. Slide the slider over the lubricated slider tube and secure the damper valve stud locknut. Check slider motion for binding or drag. Llosen the locknut and rotate the slider 180 degrees before securing it to eliminate binding.

8. Install the assembled fork bracket and slider covers over the slider tubes so 5/16 in. of tube extends above the top of the bracket and tighten the bracket clamping studs.

9. Fill each tube with Harley-Davidson Fork Oil (oil may be experimented with freely as long as specified quantities are conformed to) or hydraulic fluid, then install the fork springs and secure the slider tube plugs.

10. Secure the lower head bearing guard and a well-packed head bearing on the stem. Install the stem into the steering head.

11. Install a well-packed upper head bearing and secure the head bearing nut until there is slight bearing draw when the head is turned. Back off the nut until the motion is smooth.

12. Install and secure the fork bracket, bracket cover, and slider tube plugs.

13. Loosen the bracket clamping studs and rotate the slider tubes until the tube plug flat sides are to the sides of the forks.

14. Secure the fork stem nut, bracket clamping studs, tube plug oil seals, upper bracket bolts, and handlebar.

15. Complete assembly in the reverse order of disassembly.

Adjustable Front Fork Assembly

1. Consult "Non-Adjustable Front Fork Assembly."

2. Place the slider tubes in the fork bracket with tubes 5 1/16 in. above the top of the bracket. The slider tube plug flat surfaces must point toward the filler screw.

Adjusting Adjustable Front Fork For Side-Car Use

1. Remove the bracket bolt nut and lockwashers.

2. Loosen the upper bracket bolts.

3. Pull the fork tubes forward until movement is detected.

4. Replace the bracket bolt washers with the pin seated in the bracket boss slot and secure the bracket bolt and nut.

5. To resume solo riding, push the fork tubes back and asjust the washer pins until they point backward.

SPORTSTER AND SUPER GLIDE MODELS

Breather Valve Replacement

1. Remove the headlight housing if it interferes with removing the fork tube cap.

2. Remove the cap and secure it in a wood or copper-jawed vise.

3. Remove the breather valve by breaking the stakings.

4. Apply a suitable sealer when reassembling and stake in the breather valve in three new positions.

Fork Boot Replacement

1. Pull the boot free from the upper retainer.

2. Free the fork slider assembly as described in "Fork Slider and Tubes Removal."

3. Remove the fork vent and plain screws and loosen, but do not remove, the retainer, gasket, and retaining disc.

4. Pry the lower retainer lip to remove it from the slider and then remove the boot.

5. Assemble in the reverse order of disassembly.

6. Replace the fork slider bushings first if this is to be done at this time.

7. Secure the upper retainers by sliding them up to the slider counterbore then by inserting the pilot end of the Oil Seal Driver (H-D part no. 96310–55) through the retainer and into the upper slider bushings. Gently tap the retainer until it is seated. A suitable sized piece of pipe can be used as a drift if the factory tool is not available.

Fork Disassembly

1. Remove the front wheel and brake assembly as described in the "Removal and Installation" for the wheels.

2. Remove the front fender, headlight cowling, and fork tube caps.

3. Loosen, but do not remove, the fork pinch bolts and free the fork boot from the upper retainer.

4. Slide the fork leg assemblies free from the bottom.

5. Remove the piston rod (or spring) retainer with Wrench (H-D part no. 94694–52) or a suitable substitute. Models earlier than 1968 require compressing the fork spring, securing the top of the shock absorber with vise grips, and then removing the piston rod retainer.

6. Remove the fork spring and drain plug, and allow the hydraulic fluid or fork oil to drain into a suitable container. Keep hydraulic fluid away from painted surfaces since it can cause corrosive damage.

7. Invert the assembly and remove the tube end bolt and washer by securing the slot in the top of the shock sbsorber tube with a screwdriver and then turning the end bolt. The shocks will come free on 1967 and earlier models.

8. Free the slider front fork tube and shock absorber assembly.

9. Remove the piston stop bushing with Wrench (H-D part no. 94691–52) or a suitable substitute and remove from shock absorber tube. Remove the piston rod nut to dismantle the piston rod assembly.

10. Remo-e the shock absorber retaining ring with snap-ring pliers and slide the lower valve body, washer, upper body, spring (1971 and later), tube, piston, retaining ring, and piston on 1968 and later models.

11. Remove the headlight assembly and disconnect the speedometer cable at the speedometer head.

12. Remove the stem sleeve end nut and loosen, but do not remove, the upper bracket pinch bolt.

13. Remove the handlebar and upper fork bracket assembly and lay it aside. It is not necessary to disconnect the cables or wires as long as they do not bend sharply.

14. Remove the upper bracket spacer, stem sleeve, stem and bracket assembly,

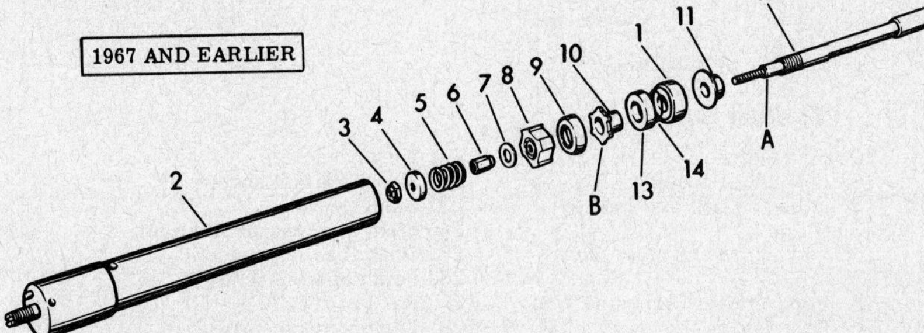

1. Piston stop bushing
2. Shock absorber tube
3. Piston rod nut
4. Recoil valve spring retainer
5. Valve spring
6. Piston spacer
7. Recoil valve washer
8. Piston
9. Piston valve
10. Piston rod stop nut
11. Piston rod guide
12. Piston rod
13. Piston stop collar
14. Piston stop spring

THRU 1970

1971 & LATER

1. Retaining ring
2. Valve body, lower
3. Valve washer
4. Valve body, upper
4A. Spring
5. Piston retaining ring
6. Piston
7. Shock absorber tube
8. Fork tube

A and B fork shock absorber

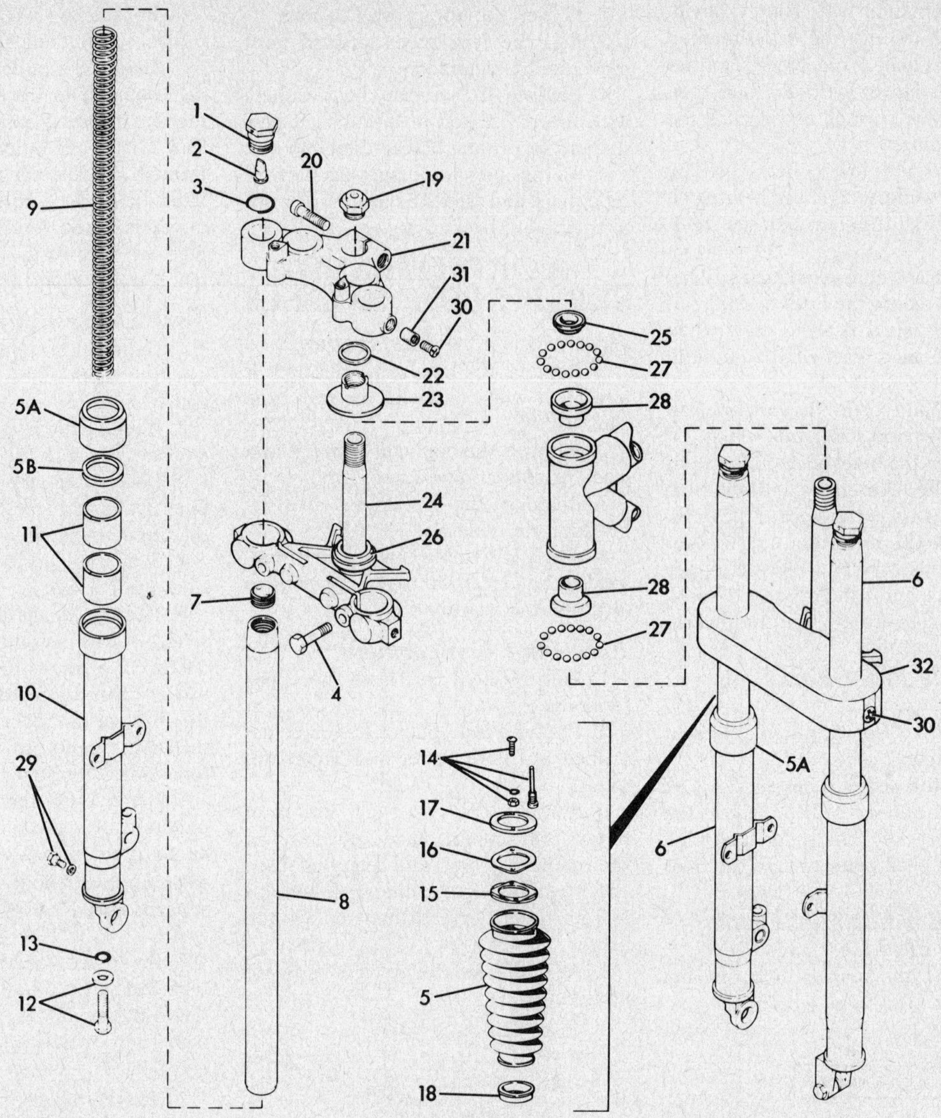

Sportster fork assembly

1. Tube cap
2. Tube breather valve
3. Tube cap seal
4. Pinch bolt
5. Fork boot (1970)
5A. Fork boot (1971)
5B. Seal (1971)
6. Fork side
7. Spring retainer
8. Fork tube and shock absorber assembly
9. Fork spring
10. Fork slider
11. Fork slider bushing (2)
12. Tube end bolt and washer
13. O-ring
14. Vent screw and plain screw (1970)
15. Boot retainer (upper) (1970)
16. Boot gasket (1970)
17. Boot retaining disc (1970)
18. Boot retainer (lower) (1970)
19. Stem sleeve end nut
20. Upper bracket pinch bolt
21. Upper bracket
22. Upper bracket spacer
23. Stem sleeve
24. Stem and bracket assembly
25. Upper bearing cone
26. Lower bearing cone
27. Ball bearings (28)
28. Steering head cups (2)
29. Drain plug and washer
30. Cover screw (2)
31. Insert
32. Cover

upper and lower bearing cones and bearings (and separate for reassembly), and head cups (if necessary). Head cups are easily removed by drifting from the opposite end with a suitable drift.

Inspection and Repair

1. Consult the previous section.

Assembly

1. Assemble 1967 and earlier models in the following manner:

a. Assemble the piston rod guide, piston collar, spring, bushing, and stop nut on the piston rod, with the stop nut face (b) 0.550 in. from the collar (a). Stake around the center of the nut in four new places.

b. Assemble the piston valve, piston, recoil valve washer, piston spacer, valve spring, valve spring retainer, and piston rod nut onto the piston rod.

c. Secure the piston stop bushing in the shock absorber tube with Wrench H-D part no. 94691-52) or a suitable substitute, until the top of the bushing is flush with the end of the tube. Stake the bushing by punching through the hole in the upper end of the tube.

2. Assemble 1968 and later models in the reverse order of disassembly using new gaskets and snap-rings.

3. Assemble 1967 and earlier model forks in the following manner:

a. Insert the rod end of the shock absorber in the fork tube.

b. Place a new shock absorber gasket on the end screw and dowel pin.

c. Assemble the slider on the fork tube so the tube end screw registers in the slider.

d. Secure the tube end nut and washer.

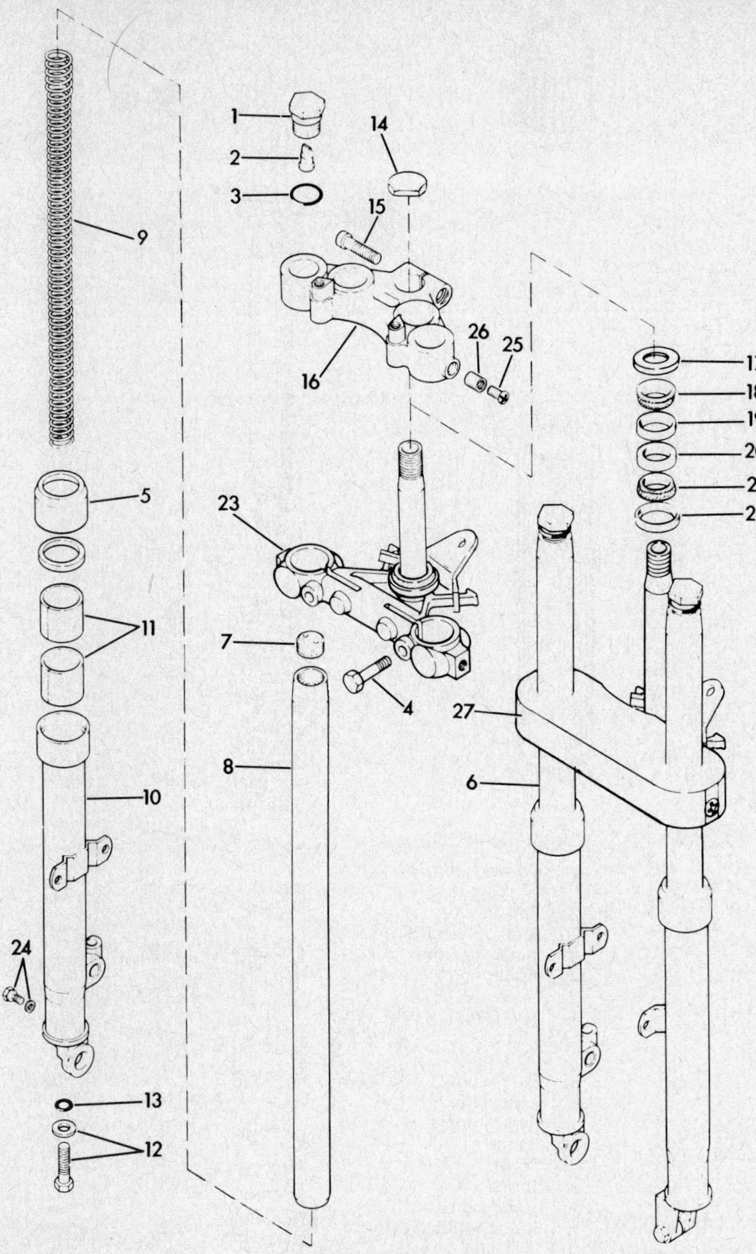

Super-Glide fork assembly

1. Tube cap
2. Tube breather valve
3. Tube cap seal
4. Pinch bolt
5. Fork boot
6. Fork side
7. Spring retainer
8. Fork tube and shock absorber assembly
9. Fork spring
10. Fork slider
11. Fork slider bushing (2)
12. Tube end bolt and washer
13. O-ring
14. Fork stem nut
15. Upper bracket pinch bolt
16. Upper bracket
17. Upper bearing shield
18. Upper bearing cone
19. Upper bearing cup
20. Lower bearing cup
21. Lower bearing cone
22. Lower bearing shield
23. Lower bracket & stem
24. Drain screw & washer
25. Cover screw
26. Cover screw insert
27. Cover

e. Pour 4½ oz of fork oil or hydraulic fluid over the top of the shock absorber rod and into the tube.

f. Insert the fork spring.

g. Screw a 5/16 x 24 thread rod (i.e., brake rod) into the end of the shock absorber rod, compress the spring, and grip the flat portions of the rod with vise grips. Remove the threaded rod.

h. Secure the piston rod retainer and remove the grips.

i. Stake the retainer threads through the hole at the top of the absorber rod.

j. Secure the retainer in the fork tube using Wrench (H-D part no. 94694–52), or a suitable substitute, until the top of the retainer is 9/16 in. below the top of the fork tube.

4. Assemble 1968 and later models in the following manner:

a. Insert the fork tube and shock absorber assembly into the slider.

b. Hold the slotted top of the shock absorber rod with a screwdriver and secure a new O-ring and the tube end bolt and washer.

c. Insert a spring retainer ¾ in. below the surface of the fork tube top using Wrench (H-D part no. 94694–52) or a suitable substitute.

5. Secure the steering head cups, ball bearings, and bearing cones. Bearing cones must be heavily greased.

6. Install the fork stem and bracket assembly and secure it with a stem sleeve until bearing motion is smooth and free and all excessive play has been taken up.

7. Install the upper bracket spacer, handlebar assembly, and upper fork bracket.

8. Install both assembled fork slides into the mounting brackets and secure the tube caps and then the pinch bolts.

9. Count and secure the fork bolts.

10. Check fork motion for smoothness and adjust the sleeve if necessary. All sideways shake should be removed.

11. Secure the upper bracket pinch bolt and nut, and stem the sleeve end.

SWING ARM

Disassembly

1. Remove the rear wheel as described in the "Removal and Installation" section for the wheels.

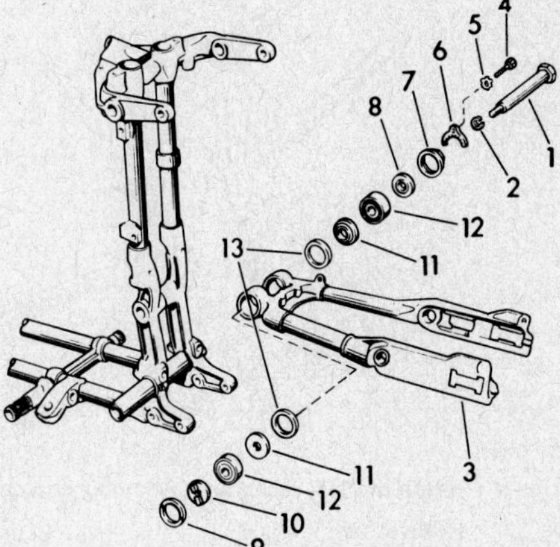

Sportster swing arm assembly

1. Pivot bolt
2. Bearing lock washer
3. Rear fork
4. Bearing screw
5. Shakeproof washer
6. Lockwasher
7. Bearing lock nut—right
8. Outer spacer
9. Bearing lock nut—left
10. Pivot bolt nut
11. Bearing inner spacer (2)
12. Bearing (2)
13. Bearing shield (2)

2. Remove the rear brake assembly and linkage as described in the brake section.

3. Remove the rear shock absorbers as described in "Rear Shock Absorbers."

4. Remove the exhaust pipe and muffler (if necessary).

5. Remove the pivot bolt and rear fork assembly.

6. Remove the bearing screw, washer, lockwasher, right locknut, and outer spacer. Use a punch to remove the left bearing locknut and pivot bolt nut Sportster models.

7. Press the bearing inner spacer, bearing, and bearing shield from each side of the fork Sportster models.

8. Press the bearing spacer, seal, and bearing from each side of the fork (Glide models).

Inspection and Repair

1. Clean all parts in a suitable solvent and blow them dry.

2. Inspect all parts for wear, pitting, rough bearing motion, or damage, and replace as necessary.

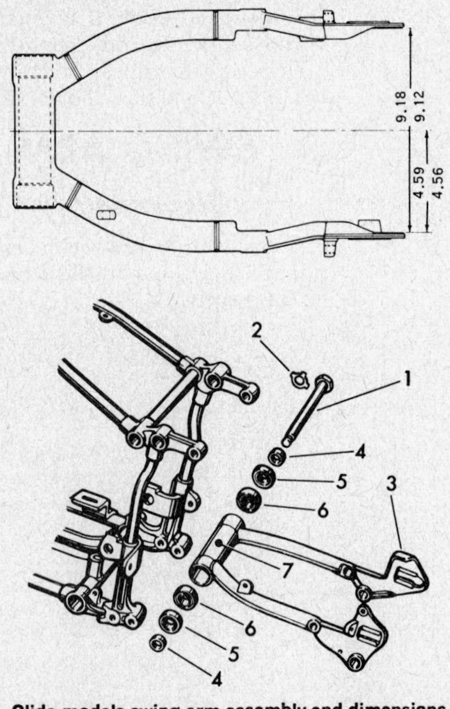

Glide models swing arm assembly and dimensions

1. Pivot bolt
2. Pivot bolt lock washer
3. Rear fork
4. Pivot bearing spacer (2)
5. Bearing seal
6. Bearing
7. Grease fitting

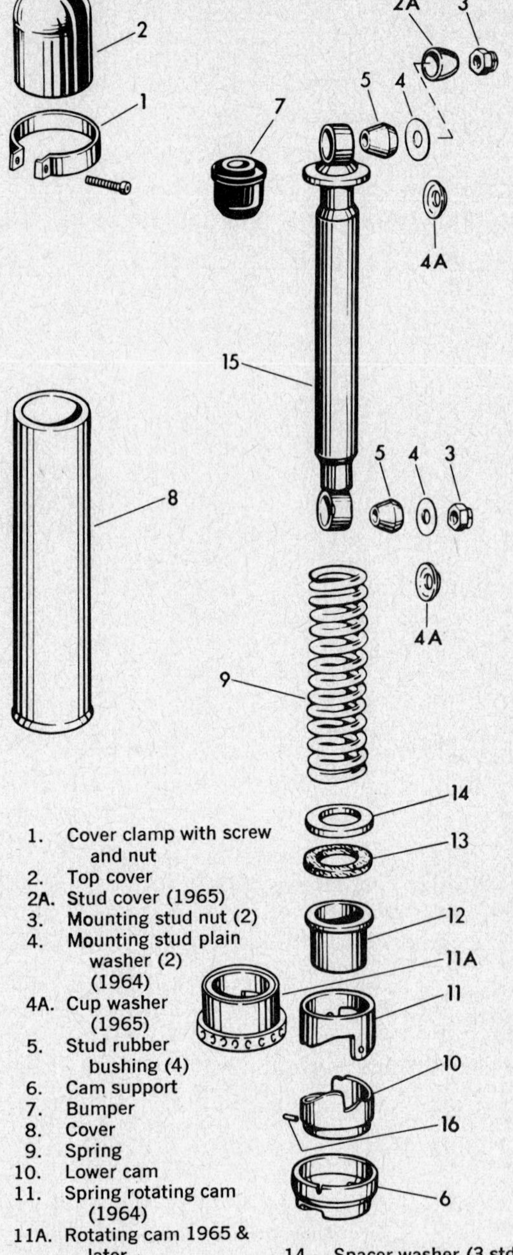

1. Cover clamp with screw and nut
2. Top cover
2A. Stud cover (1965)
3. Mounting stud nut (2)
4. Mounting stud plain washer (2) (1964)
4A. Cup washer (1965)
5. Stud rubber bushing (4)
6. Cam support
7. Bumper
8. Cover
9. Spring
10. Lower cam
11. Spring rotating cam (1964)
11A. Rotating cam 1965 & later
12. Cam sleeve
13. Seal washer
14. Spacer washer (3 std.)
15. Shock absorber
16. Roll pin

1966 and earlier shock absorber

3. Measure the swing arm for correct dimensions as shown and take it to your dealer if alignment or straightening is necessary.

Assembly

1. Assemble in the reverse order of disassembly.

2. Grease the bearings thoroughly. This must be done every 10,000 miles on Sportsters or it must be greased through the fitting every 2,000 miles on Glide models (1962 and later).

3. Press the bearing shield into the fork from the outside until it is flush with the inside. Insert the bearing with the wide side of the race facing out. Assemble and secure the right bearing locknut and then back it off one full turn. Assemble the pivot bolt nut, then secure the left locknut and stake it in three new places Sportster models.

4. Apply grease to the bearing seals in the groove between the sealing lips and secure the seals and spacers Glide models.

5. Preload the bearings in the following manner:

a. Assemble the pivot bolt.

b. Weigh the extreme rear end of the fork in a horizontal position, with a spring scale, and note the reading.

c. Tighten the pivot bolt (sportster) or the right locknut (Glide models) until bearing drag is increased by one or two pounds above the original reading.

6. Complete reassembly in the reverse order of disassembly.

REAR SHOCK ABSORBERS

Harley-Davidson shock absorbers have three riding positions which are regulated by an adjusting cam. The lowest position, which is off the cam, is for the average (150 lbs) solo rider. The first cam position is for heavy solo riders, and the second cam position is for tandem riding. These various riding positions are selected using the Spanner Wrench (H-D part no. 94700–52B) to rotate the cam. Shocks are interchangeable from one side to the other, however both must be adjusted on the same position to provide proper balance.

Disassembly is aided by the use of Rear Shock Absorber Tool (H-D part no. 97010–52A) but any means of compressing the spring for long enough to remove the split key (1967 and later models) will work. This can be done by hand if one person compresses while the other removes the keys.

Disassembly

1966 AND EARLIER MODELS

1. Remove the cover clamp, top cover mounting stud nuts, stud cover, washer, and rubber bushing.
2. Remove the shock from the mounting studs.
3. Compress the spring until the lower mounting eye can be rotated 90° then remove the shock from the tool (if used).
4. Remove the cam support.
5. Strike the lower mounting eye sharply to free the bumper from the cover flange.
6. Remove the cover and disassemble the lower cam, rotating cam, cam sleeve, dirt seal, and spacer washers.
7. Remove the bumper by extending the absorber piston shaft and the springing bumper.

1967 AND LATER MODELS

1. Remove the mounting stud nuts, upper stud cover, and cup washers.
2. Remove the shock absorber from the mounting studs.
3. Press the stud rubber bushings from the mounting eyes.
4. Remove the retaining ring.
5. Compress the spring until the split key can be removed.
6. Remove the compression tool (if used) and disassemble the remaining items.

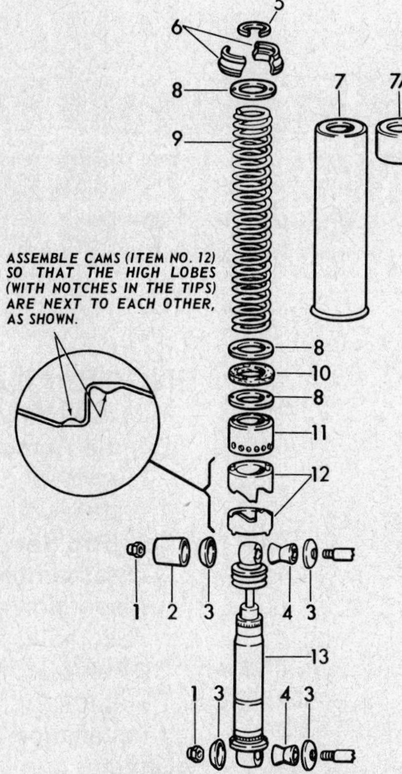

1967 and later shock absorber

1. Mounting stud nut (2)
2. Stud cover
3. Cup washer (4)
4. Stud rubber bushing (2)
5. Retaining ring
6. Split key
7. Cover (long)
7A. Cover (short)
8. Washer (3)
9. Spring
10. Seal washer
11. Adjusting cup
12. Cam (2)
13. Shock absorber unit

Inspection and Repair

1. Clean and inspect all parts for wear or damage and replace as necessary.
2. If possible, compare the old springs with new ones to determine wear.
3. Replace absorbers if they are leaking or if the piston does not compress a little more easily than it extends.

Assembly

1966 AND EARLIER MODELS

1. Lightly grease the cam sleeve and cam surface of the adjusting cam.
2. Secure the roller pin in the lower cam and place it on the cam support with the pin and pin slot aligned. Slot "A" is for the left side assembly and slot "B" is for the right side (1964 and earlier).
3. Extend the piston rod and assemble the bumper.
4. Assemble the spring in the cover, then the shock in the spring, and strike the upper mounting eye to secure the bumper in the cover flange.
5. Slip the spacer and seal washers into the cover and complete assembly in the reverse order of disassembly.
6. Compress the spring and rotate the lower mounting eye 90° to secure it in the cam support notch.
7. Mount units with letters "A" and "B" so they are facing to the rear (1964 and earlier).

1967 AND LATER MODELS

1. Lightly grease the cam surfaces.
2. Assemble in the reverse order of disassembly taking care to align the cam faces.
3. Compress the springs and insert the keys and retaining ring (if applicable).

HONDA TWO-STROKE SINGLES

INDEX

MODEL IDENTIFICATION

MT-125

MT-250

SERIAL NUMBER LOCATION

Each model comes with matching serial numbers stamped on the left-side of the steering head, and on the top of the crankcase at the right rear of the cylinder.

TUNE-UP AND MAINTENANCE

TUNE-UP OPERATIONS

Contact Breaker Points

SERVICE

If the points are heavily pitted, replace the points and condenser. These can be obtained as a unit already mounted on a base plate, or as separate components which can be mounted in place of the worn units. Disconnect the electrical leads, unscrew the components from the base plate or remove the base plate assembly (depending on which method you have chosen for replacement), and mount the new parts. If single components are to be used, be sure to insulate the points properly with insulating washers which must be used in their original positions. When the new parts are mounted, reconnect the electrical leads.

Place a drop or two of gasoline or other non-oily solvent on a piece of paper and pull it through the points to remove any dirt or preservative coating on the contact surfaces. Put a small daub of distributor cam lubricator or another high-melting-point grease on the contact breaker cam.

The rotor is behind the left-side cover
1. Wire harness connector
2. Left crankcase cover
3. Generator rotor cover

REPLACEMENT

1. Remove the left-side plastic cover, disconnect the generator lead connector, then remove the left-side crankcase cover.

NOTE: *Remove the generator rotor cover if you plan to time the bike with the crankcase cover installed.*

2. Engage the transmission in First gear, secure the the drive sprocket with the drive sprocket holder (Tool No. 07922-35700000) or a suitable substitute, and remove the rotor mounting nut.

Securing the drive sprocket
1. AC generator rotor
2. Drive sprocket fixing bolts
3. Drive sprocket holder

NOTE: *The drive sprocket mounting bolts should be positioned as illustrated when the sprocket holder is in use.*

3. Lightly oil the threads of the rotor puller (Tool No. 07933-3580000), then screw the puller in to remove the rotor from the crankshaft.

4. Remove the bolt and nut which secure the points to the points lead, taking care to note the correct sequence for replacement, then remove the screw which secures the points to the stator plate. Put a daub of high-melting-point grease on the points follower cam.

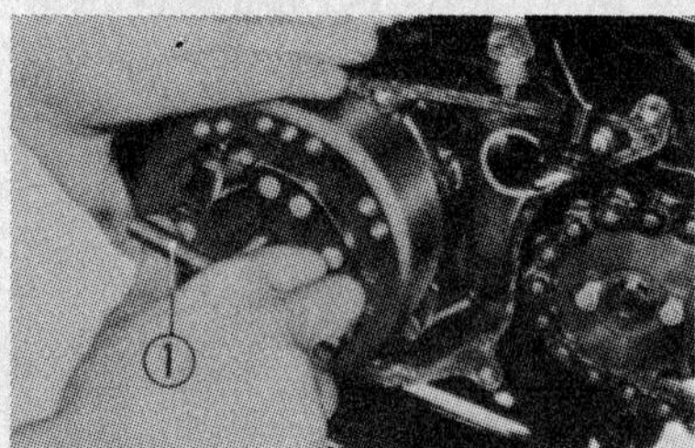

Using a puller (1) to remove the rotor

CAUTION: *Avoid overtightening the points lead nut and bolt as this may damage the fiber washer.*

5. When reinstalling the rotor make sure that the key and keyway are lined up. Avoid pounding the rotor onto the shaft as this may interfere with the magnetic properties of the rotor and play havoc with the crankshaft main bearings.

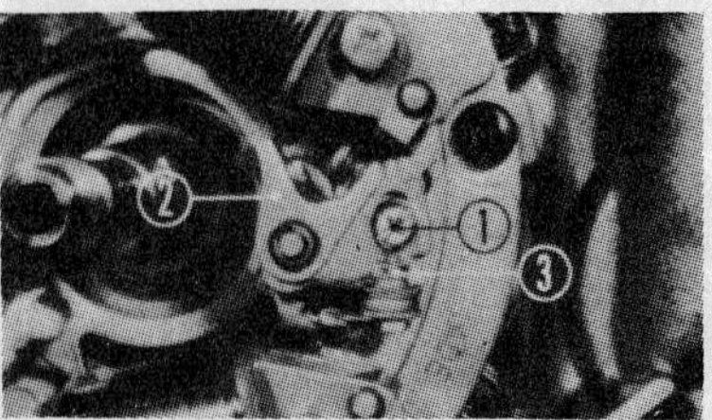

The points (2) are mounted by the screw (1), and connected by the nut and bolt (3)

GENERAL SPECIFICATIONS

	MT-125	MT-250
DIMENSIONS		
Overall length	80.7 in. (2,050 mm)	85.0 in. (2,160 mm)
Overall width	32.7 in. (830 mm)	35.0 in. (890 mm)
Overall height	43.3 in. (1,100 mm)	44.5 in. (1,130 mm)
Wheelbase	53.9 in. (1,370 mm)	56.7 in. (1,440 mm)
Ground clearance	9.3 in. (235 mm)	9.8 in. (250 mm)
Dry weight	207 lbs (94 kg)	260 lbs (118 kg)
FRAME		
Type	Semi-double cradle	Semi-double cradle
Front suspension	Telescopic fork	Telescopic fork
Rear suspension	Swing arm	Swing arm
Front tire size, pressure	2.75-21, 21 psi (1.5 kg/cm^2)	3.00-21, 21 psi (1.5 kg/cm^2)
Rear tire size, pressure	3.50-18, 21 psi (1.5 kg/cm^2)	4.00-18, 21 psi (1.5 kg/cm^2)
Front brake	Internal expanding shoes	Internal expanding shoes
Rear brake	Internal expanding shoes	Internal expanding shoes
Fuel capacity	6.5 lit. (1.7 U.S. gal., 1.4 Imp. gal.)	8.5 lit. (2.2 U.S. gal.)
Fuel reserve capacity	1.5 lit. (0.4 U.S. gal., 0.3 Imp. gal.)	1.5 lit. (0.4 U.S. gal.)
Caster angle	59.5°	59.5°
Trail length	5.5 in. (140 mm)	(5.6 in.) 143 mm
ENGINE		
Type	Air-cooled, 2-stroke	Air-cooled, 2-stroke
Cylinder arrangement	Single-cylinder 15° inclind from vertical	Single-cylinder 15° inclinded from vertical
Bore and stroke	2.205 x 1.969 in. (56.0 x 50.0 mm)	2.756 x 2.535 in. (70.0 x 64.4 mm)
Displacement	7.5 cu. in. (123 cc)	15.1 cu. in. (248 cc)
Compression ratio	7.0 : 1	9.0 : 1
Transmission oil capacity	1.1 U.S. qt/1.0 lt.	1.4 U.S. qt/1.3 lt.
Oil tank capacity	1.6 U.S. qt/1.5 lt.	1.4 U.S. qt/1.3 lt.
Lubrication system	Forced and wet sump	Forced and wet sump
Port timing		
Intake: Open	75° BTDC	80° BTDC
Close	75° ATDC	80° ATDC
Exhaust: Open	85° BBDC	87° BBDC
Close	85° ABDC	87° ABDC
Scavenge: Open	57.5° BBDC	60° BBDC
Close	57.5° ABDC	60° ABDC
Idle speed	1400 rpm	1500 rpm
DRIVE TRAIN		
Clutch	Wet, multi-plates	Wet, multi-plates
Transmission	5-speed constant mesh	5-speed constant mesh
Primary reduction	4.400	3.300
Gear ratio I	2.357	2.235
Gear ratio II	1.611	1.571
Gear ratio III	1.238	1.160
Gear ratio IV	1.000	0.896
Gear ratio V	0.808	0.718
Final reduction	2.933	2.933
Gearshift pattern	Left foot operated return system	Left foot operated return system
ELECTRICAL		
Ignition	Flywheel magneto	Flywheel magneto
Starting system	Kickstarter	Kickstarter
Generator	A.C. generator	A.C. generator
Spark plug	NGK B8ES	NGK B8ES
Spark plug gap	0.024-0.028 in. (0.6-0.7 mm)	0.024-0.028 in. (0.6-0.7 mm)
Ignition timing	20° BTDC	20° BTDC

6. When installing new points you should also install a new condenser. The condenser is located under the gas tank on the ignition coil mounting plate.

NOTE: *Consult the "AC Generator" Section for additional information.*

Ignition Timing

1. Remove the generator cover.
2. Rotate the engine counterclockwise with a suitable wrench while watching the points. They should begin to open at the moment the "F" mark on the rotor passes the index mark on the crankcase. If they don't begin to open at this point, loosen the points mounting screw and use a screwdriver at the adjusting point to make them begin to open, then secure the screw.

NOTE: *The moment the points begin to open can be determined with a timing light, or by allowing the points to close on a piece of cellophane. Tug gently on the cellophane while rotating the engine, and see if it is released when the timing marks come into conjunction.*

3. Connect a timing light to the bike in either of the following manners:
   a. If the light has its own self-contained power source, it should be connected to ground and to the black/white stator lead wire which you'll have to disconnect.
   b. If the light has no power source it should be connected to the black/-white lead, to ground, and to the positive (+) battery terminal. The light must be of the same wattage as the headlight.
4. Rotate the engine counterclockwise until the "F" mark (1) lines up with the index (2) mark. At this point (20° BTDC), the light should flicker.
5. If the light did not react, loosen the adjusting screw and pry at the points with a screwdriver at the adjustment point until the light reacts correctly. Secure the adjusting screw and recheck the timing.
6. Check the point gap with a feeler gauge when the points are fully open. Optimal gap is 0.012-0.016 in. (0.3-0.4 mm), but it may vary as much as 0.008-0.024 in. (0.2-0.6 mm). If the gap is not within the serviceable limits, the points should be replaced and the engine retimed.
7. Run a clean piece of paper through the points to clean them, taking care not to leave a piece of paper between the points, and check the timing with a strobe light if possible after the engine has reached its normal operating temperature.

NOTE: *If the strobe timing indicates a variation from the static timing, disassemble and inspect the advance mechanism as described in the "Electrical System" Section.*

Carburetor Adjustment

1. Run the engine until its normal operating temperature is reached, then adjust the idle speed screw until the engine idles at 1500 rpm. The screw is rotated clockwise to increase idle speed, and counterclockwise, to decrease it.

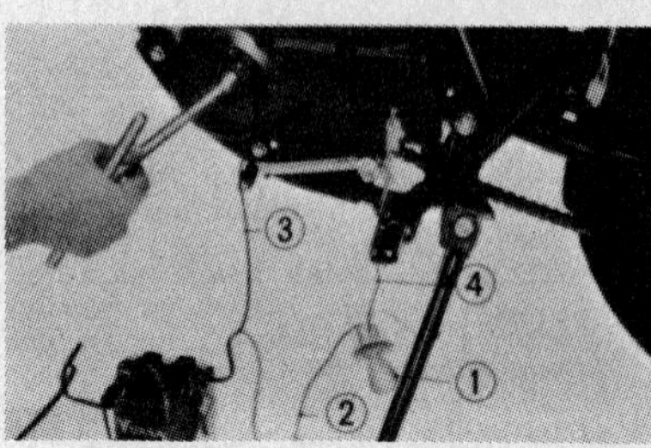

Test light attached to the engine

1. Lamp
2. Connect to positive terminal of battery
3. Ground
4. Connect to black/white lead

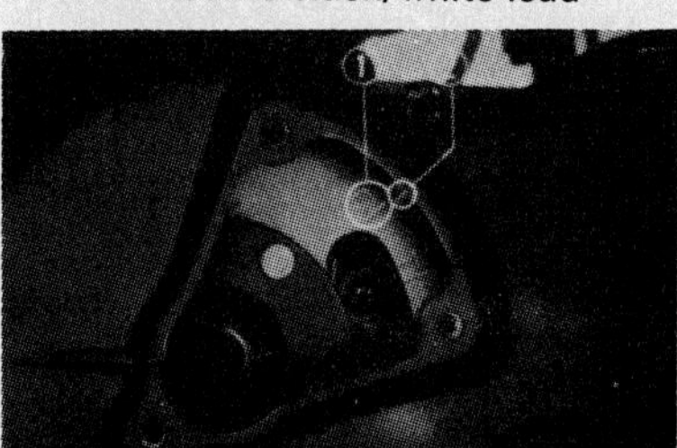

Timing marks in alignment

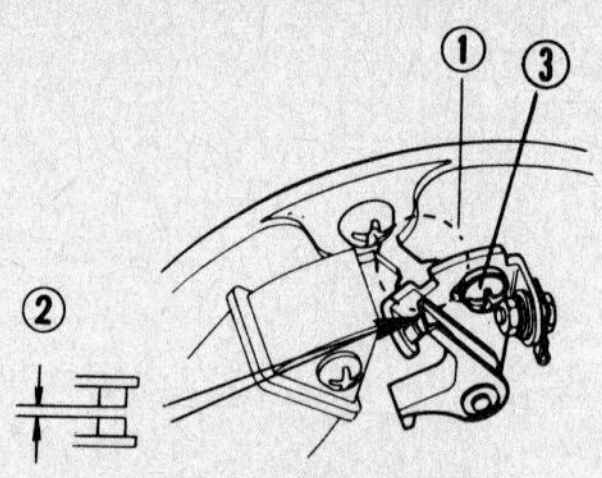

Points pry position

1. Adjustment point
2. Contact breaker point gap
3. Point base locking screw

Testing timing with a strobe (1) light

NOTE: *If the engine does not react to an adjustment of one full turn, remove the screw and inspect it for wear or blockage of the passage which it regulates.*

2. Turn the air screw clockwise until the engine begins to miss or run roughly,

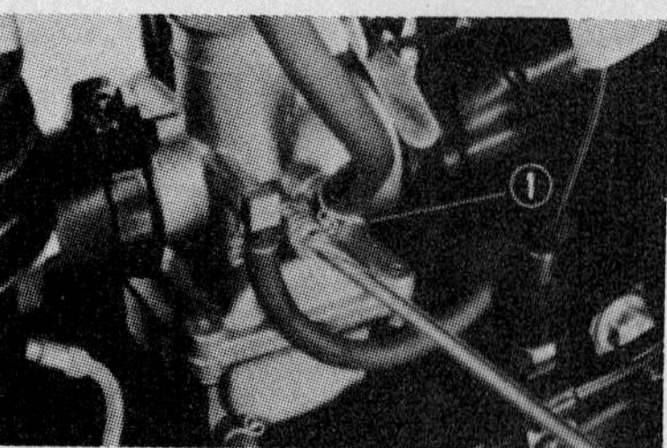

Adjusting the idle speed (1)

Adjusting the air screw (1)

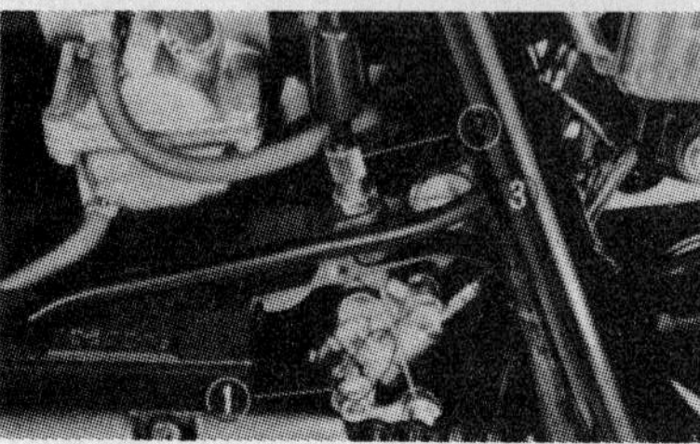

Lining up the adjustment mark (125 shown)

1. Marks on control lever and oil pump
2. Adjusting screw
3. Locknut

then rotate it in the opposite direction until the engine again reacts poorly. The optimal adjustment is exactly between these two points, generally where the idle speed is the smoothest. Readjust the idle speed screw if necessary.

NOTE: *Carburetor adjustments to compensate for a poorly timed engine, or for an engine with insufficient compression, ain't gonna make it.*

Compression Test

1. Run the engine until its normal operating temperature has been reached, then remove the spark plug.
2. Install the compression tester.

NOTE: *If an automotive type tester with a rubber tip is to be used, coat the tip with oil to insure a good seal.*

3. Hold the throttle open all the way and kick the engine through about six times, then remove and read the gauge. The compression should be about 120 psi. If the compression is more than 15 psi less than the specified pressure, the top end should be taken down and inspected to determine the reason.

MAINTENANCE ITEMS

NOTE: *The service intervals given in*

the following Sections are more applicable for street riding than for competition, dirt riding, or use in dusty conditions. Use these only as a guideline and service the machine according to its needs.

TUNE-UP SPECIFICATIONS

MT-125/250

Ignition timing	20° BTDC
Point gap	
optimal gap	0.012-0.016 in. (0.3-0.4 mm)
service limit	0.008-0.024 in. (0.2-0.6 mm)
Spark plug	
standard type	NGK B8ES
gap	0.024-0.028 in. (0.6-0.7 mm)
Carburetor	
idle speed	1500 rpm
air screw adjustment	1-1½ turns off seat
Cranking compression	120 psi

Engine

OIL PUMP (3,000 Mi/6 Mo)

Cable Adjustment

1. Remove the oil pump case cover.
2. Check that the throttle is in the fully closed position, then turn the cable adjusting screw until the control lever and lower cover (250), or lever and pump (125), index marks line up.
3. Snap open the throttle several times to make sure that the adjustment doesn't change, then secure the adjusting screw locknut.

Air Bleeding

1. Remove the left-side crankcase and oil pump covers.
2. Remove the oil check screw, then hold the throttle open and kick the engine through until no more air bubbles are seen coming out of the bleeder hole, then secure the oil check screw.

NOTE: *The throttle should not be allowed to return to the off position before the oil check screw is installed, as this may cause air to be drawn back into the system.*

3. Install and secure the crankcase and oil pump covers, and top off the oil tank supply.

THROTTLE CABLE ADJUSTMENT (3,000 Mi/6 Mo)

1. Adjust the oil pump cable as directed in the "Oil Pump Cable Adjustment" Section, above.

Oil check screw (1)

2. There should be free-play equal to about 5-10° of full-throttle grip rotation. Adjust the cable by loosening the locknut and rotating the adjusting screw clockwise (B) to increase free-play, or counterclockwise (A) to decrease it, then secure the locknut.

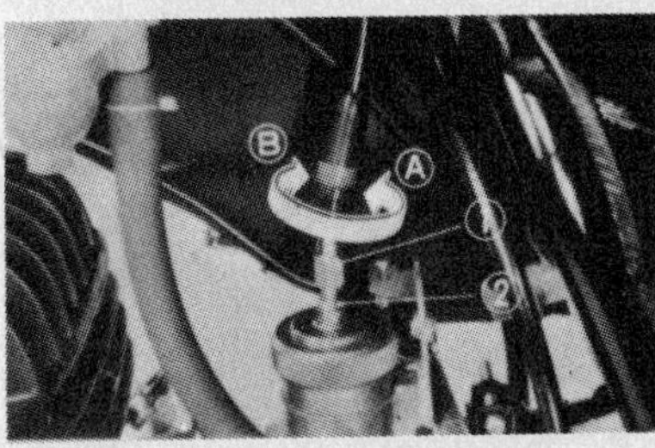

Adjusting the throttle cable
1. Adjusting screw 2. Locknut

3. Snap open the throttle several times and recheck the amount of play. Binding or rough throttle motion should be remedied by rerouting or replacing the cable, or by replacing the throttle slide if scored or damaged.

AIR FILTER (3,000 Mi/6 Mo)

1. Open the seat, remove the tool tray and air cleaner case lid wing nut and lid, then remove and separate the filter element and holder. The element may be reused unless torn.
2. Clean the element thoroughly in clean gasoline and allow to dry. Soak the element in clean gear oil (SAE 80-90) until fully saturated, then wring out thoroughly.

Remove the wing nut (1) to remove the cover (2), element holder (3), and element (4)

3. Install the element and holder so that the word "FRONT" is facing front as shown.

NOTE: *Excessive oil smoking may occur for several minutes following this operation.*

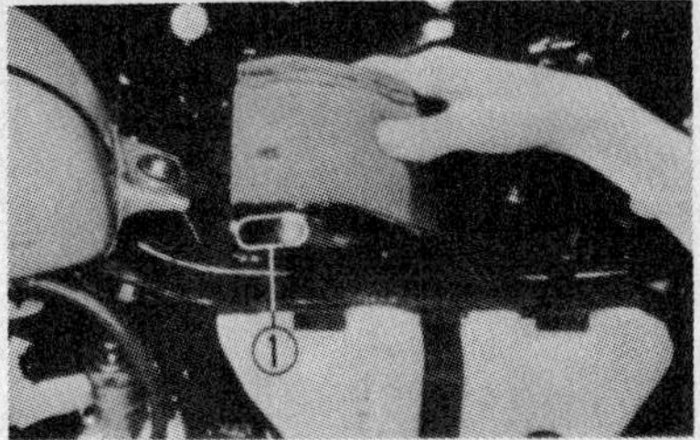

Install the element with the "FRONT" (1) marking forward

FUEL FILTER (3,000 Mi/6 Mo)

1. Turn the petcock to the "S" position, then remove the sediment cup and filter screen. Be prepared to catch the gas in the cup in a rag.
2. Clean the filter and cup in clean gasoline, then reassemble.

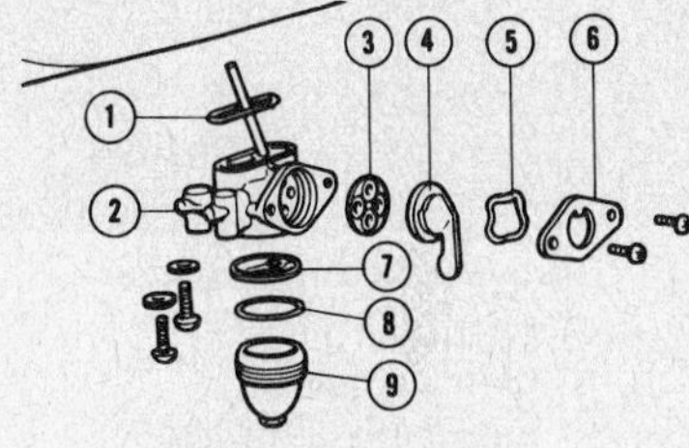

Petcock assembly
1. 23 mm O-ring
2. Fuel valve body
3. Fuel valve gasket
4. Fuel valve lever
5. Fuel valve lever spring
6. Fuel valve lever setting plate
7. Fuel valve strainer screen
8. O-ring
9. Fuel strainer cup

NOTE: *If the rubber O-ring has allowed leakage, or if it appears damaged, replace it. If a replacement is not available, use the old O-ring, and coat the joint between the cup and petcock with liquid steel. The liquid steel will break away the next time the cup is removed.*

CLUTCH ADJUSTMENT (3,000 Mi/6 Mo)

1. Loosen the clutch cable adjuster locknut, rotate the adjusting screw until the lever and crankcase index marks are aligned, then secure the locknut.

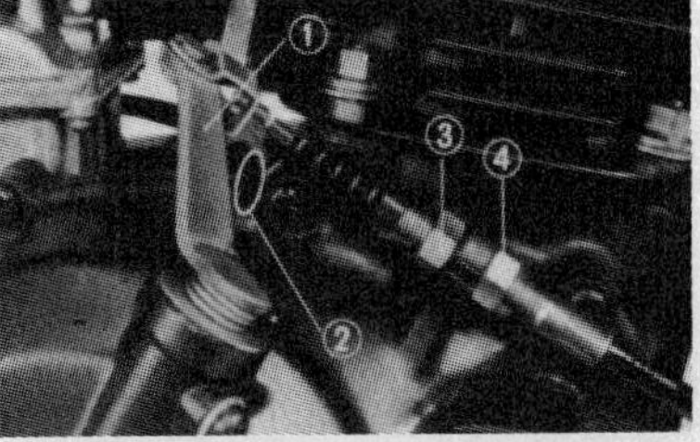

Cable adjusting positions
1. Clutch lifter lever
2. Index mark
3. Locknut
4. Clutch cable lower adjuster

2. Remove the clutch adjuster cap from the right-side crankcase cover.

3. Loosen the adjuster locknut using either the special tool (Tool No. 07908-3570000) or a suitable substitute, and gently rotate the adjusting screw clockwise until it reaches its seat, then back it off ½ turn and secure the locknut.

4. There should be 0.4-0.8 in. (10-20 mm) of free-play at the clutch hand lever. If necessary, remove the dust cover from the clutch lever at the handlebar, and loosen the adjusting screw locknut. Rotate the adjuster clockwise (A) to increase the free-play, and counterclockwise (B) to decrease it, then secure the locknut and replace the dust cover.

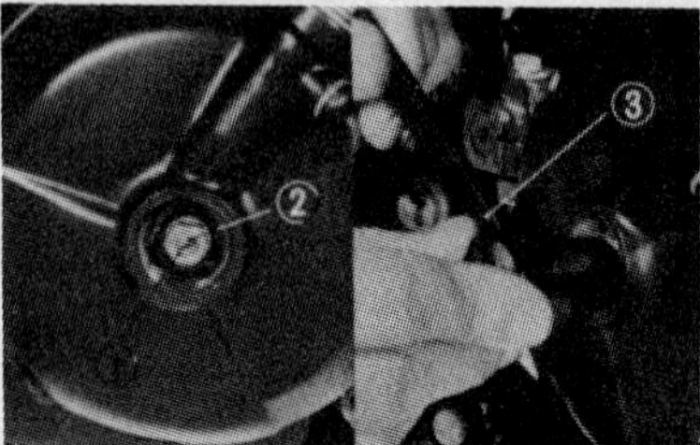

Throwout bearing adjuster

1. Locknut
2. Clutch adjuster
3. Clutch adjusting wrench

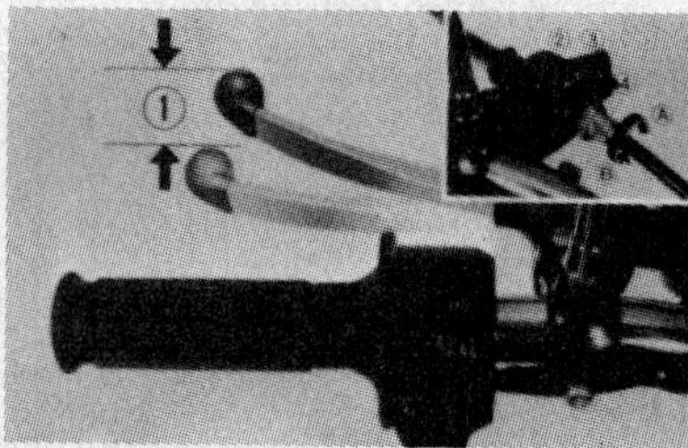

Clutch hand lever adjustment

1. Clutch lever free-play
2. Dust cover
3. Locknut
4. Clutch lever adjuster

TRANSMISSION OIL (6,000 Mi/12 Mo)

Oil Level Check

1. Run the engine until its normal operating temperature is reached, then remove the oil check bolt while holding the bike fully upright, and note whether or not oil flows out of the check bolt hole. Replace the bolt.

2. Add oil as necessary through the filler hole. Check the level on the dipstick. The oil should be up to the upper level mark. If you add too much, allow the excess to run out the oil check bolt hole.

Oil check bolt (1) location

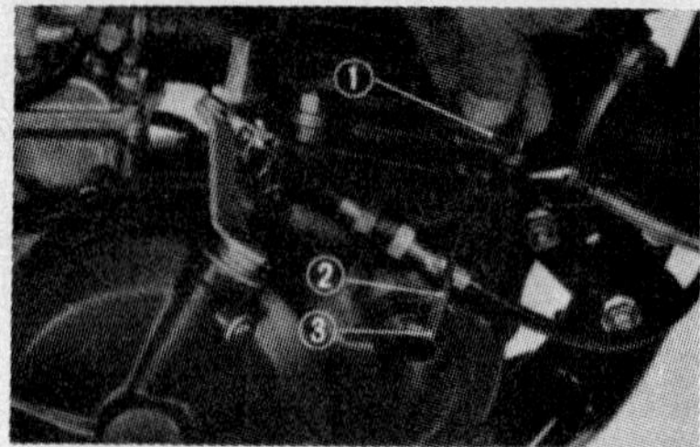

Checking oil level on the dipstick

1. Oil filler cap
2. Upper level mark
3. Lower level mark

NOTE: *Do not screw in the dipstick when taking a level reading as this may yield misleading results.*

Oil Change

1. Run the engine until its normal operating temperature is reached, then remove the oil drain bolt and allow the oil to drain into a suitable receptacle. To insure complete drainage, tilt the machine to the left, and kick the motor through several times with the key in the off position.

2. Install the drain bolt and fill the engine with fresh oil. Consult the "Maintenance Data" chart at the end of this Section for the necessary capacities.

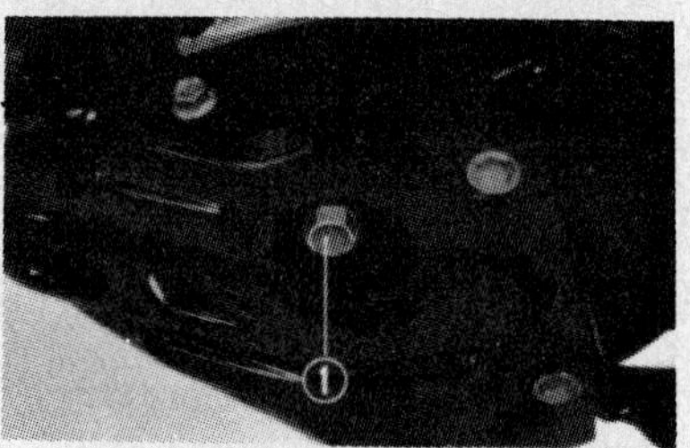

Transmission drain bolt (1)

OIL TANK FILTER (6,000 Mi/12 Mo)

1. Remove the oil tank securing strap and the tank filler cap, then invert the tank and allow it to drain into a suitable receptacle.

2. Disconnect the filter screen cap and remove the filter. Clean the screen thoroughly in a suitable solvent, then blow it dry.

3. Assembly is in the reverse order of disassembly. Make sure that the oil line is secured by the spring clip. It may be necessary to purge the system of any air as directed in the "Oil Pump Air Bleeding" Section. Be sure to refill the tank with fresh oil.

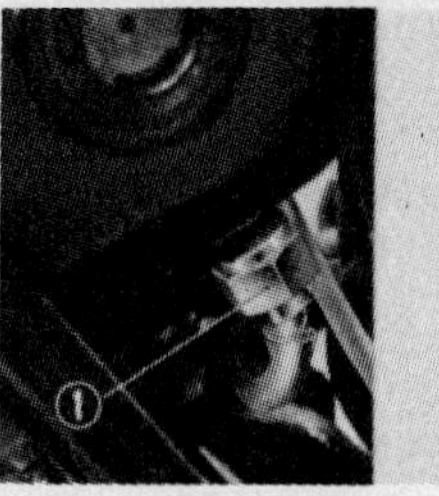

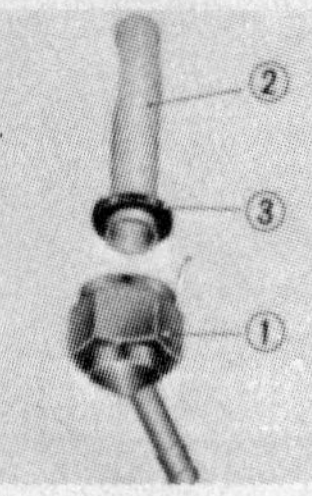

Oil tank filter assembly

1. Joint nut
2. Oil filter screen
3. Gasket

DECARBONIZATION (6,000 Mi/12 Mo)

Periodically disassemble the top end and decarbonize the cylinder head, piston crown, exhaust port, and the muffler.

The head can be dipped in a tank of solvent to loosen the deposits, and then scraped clean with a blunt instrument, such as a butter knife, and the other components can just be scraped clean. Be careful only to remove the deposits and none of the alloy. The cylinder end of the muffler should be done, and the muffler lid should be removed and cleaned.

If the piston rings are to be replaced at this time, clean out the ring lands with the edge of a broken ring. Take care not to allow any carbon flakes to fall into the crankcase.

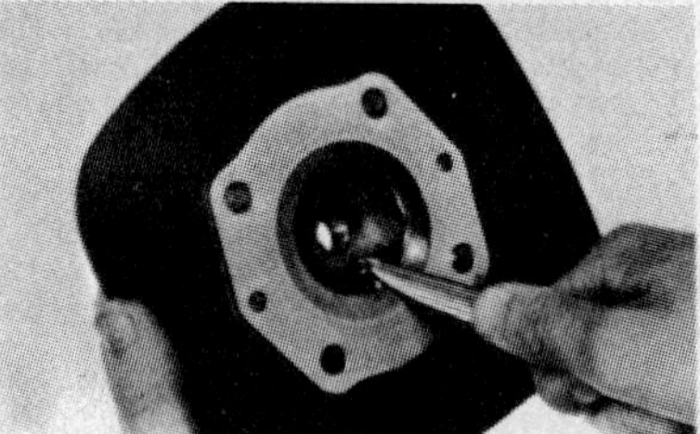

Decarbonizing the cylinder head

Frame

CHAIN

Maintenance (Weekly)

The drive chain should be cleaned and lubricated, or at least lubricated, as often as possible. If the machine is used primarily on the street, the chain should be lubricated at least once a week, or more often as necessary, especially if the machine is used in the dirt. Engine oil can be used, however it is not as effective as a penetrating chain spray.

When lubricating the chain, inspect it for kinking, binding, wear, and adjustment. The chain should not be able to be pulled more than ¼ in. off the middle of the rear sprocket when properly adjusted, and must be replaced if worn to this point.

Adjustment (3,000 Mi/6 Mo)

Check drive chain tension while sitting on the seat. There should be about ¾ in. of slack as illustrated. Adjust the chain in the following manner:

1. Remove the rear axle nut cotter pin, and loosen the axle nut.

2. Loosen the adjusting bolt locknuts, and rotate the bolts in to increase chain

tension, or out to decrease it. Turn both bolts an equal amount, and make sure that the index marks on both sides agree.

3. Secure the rear axle nut and install the cotter pin (use a new pin if the old one is worn), then tighten up the adjusting bolts and locknuts. Recheck the adjustment.

4. Loosen the chain guide roller locking bolt, then position the roller so it is about 0.4 in. (10 mm) from the chain (MT-250).

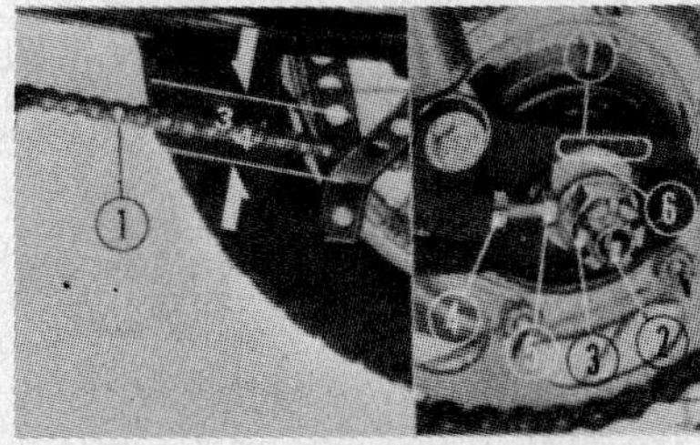

Chain adjusting points and slack

1. Drive chain
2. Cotter pin
3. Rear axle nut
4. Locknut
5. Adjusting bolt
6. Index mark
7. Reference marks

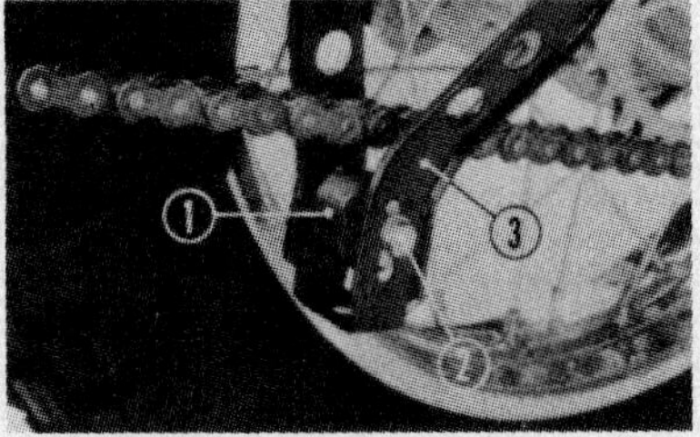

Chain roller adjusting points

1. Chain guide roller
2. Locking bolt
3. Chain protector

BRAKES

NOTE: *The brakes should be taken down and inspected once every 12 months or 6,000 miles.*

Front Brake Adjustment

The front brake lever free-play, as measured at the tip of the lever, should be 0.8-1.2 in. (20-30 mm). Free-play is the distance the lever moves before braking begins.

Adjustment is done in two parts as follows:

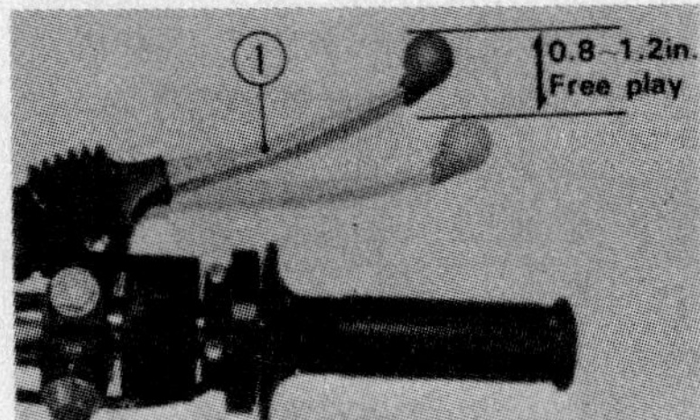

Checking brake lever free-play (1)

1. Large adjustments are made at the front hub. Loosen the locknut and rotate the adjusting screw clockwise (A) to decrease free-play, and counterclockwise (B) to increase it.

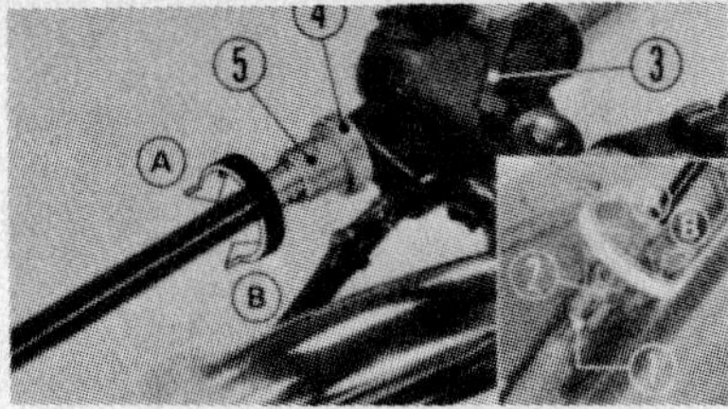

Cable adjusting points

1. Locknut
2. Adjusting nut
3. Dust cover
4. Upper locknut
5. Front brake cable adjuster

2. Minor adjustments can be made at the hand lever by loosening the locknut and rotating the adjusting screw clockwise (B) to increase free-play, and counterclockwise (A) to decrease it.

3. If the above two procedures fail to provide the necessary results, remove the pinch-bolt at the brake drum lever, pry the clamp open with a screwdriver and remove the lever, and rotate the lever one tooth (in relation to the punch mark) when replacing it.

CAUTION: *Do not rotate the lever more than one tooth.*

4. If the above procedure fails to yield the desired results, disassemble the brake and inspect the shoes for wear.

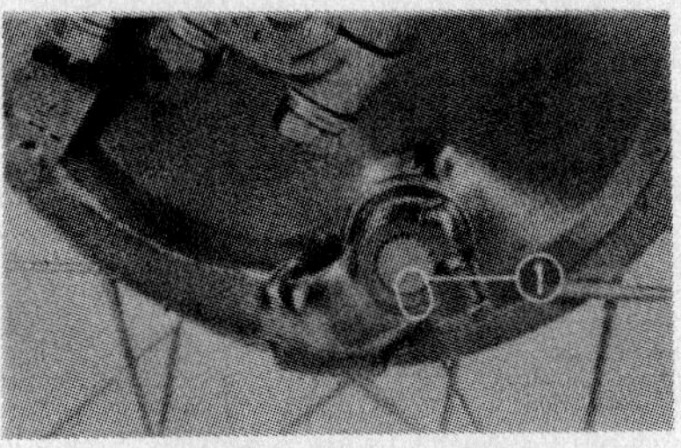

Lever punch marks (1)

Rear Brake

PEDAL HEIGHT ADJUSTMENT

1. Loosen the locknut and rotate the adjusting bolt in either direction until the pedal is at the position preferred by the rider. Rotating the bolt clockwise (A) will decrease the height, and rotating it counterclockwise (B) will increase it.

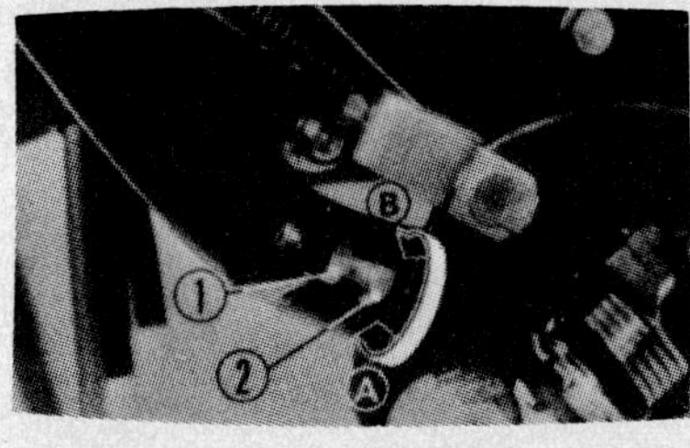

Pedal height is adjusted by loosening the locknut (1) and rotating the adjuster (2)

NOTE: *Braking efficiency is not affected by this adjustment.*

2. Secure the locknut and adjust rear brake pedal free-play.

PEDAL FREE-PLAY ADJUSTMENT

The rear brake should have 0.8-1.2 in. (20-30 mm) of free-play as measured at the tip of the brake pedal. Free-play is the distance the pedal moves before braking begins.

Adjust the free-play by rotating the adjusting nut clockwise (A) to decrease free play, or counterclockwise (B) to increase it.

NOTE: *Pressing the brake lever forward before rotating the adjusting nut will keep the nut lips from wearing out.*

Pedal (1) free-play (2)

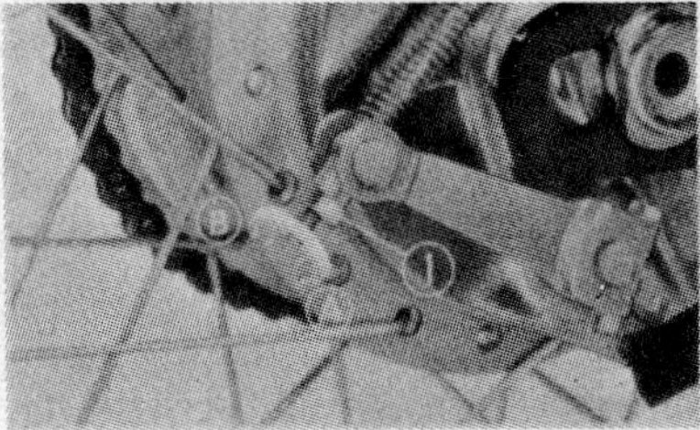

Brake adjusting bolt (1)

FRONT SUSPENSION AND STEERING (6,000 Mi/12 Mo)

Steering Head Bearings

Check for play in the bearings by grabbing the bottom of the forks and trying to move them back and forth in line with the motorcycle. Play can be removed by loosening the steering head main nut and then rotating the fork top thread clockwise. Retighten the main nut and recheck the forks for play. If after the adjustment the forks are still loose, or if their motion is rough when turned from stop to stop, the steering stem must be taken down and the bearings inspected. Consult the "Chassis" Section for additional information.

Fork Oil

Remove the small drain plug at the bottom of each fork leg, and pump the forks until all the oil has been expelled. Remove the top filler plugs, replace the drain plugs, and fill each fork leg with the proper amount and grade of oil (consult the specifications at the end of this Section).

After the oil has been poured into the forks, work them up and down several times to expel any air in the hydraulic passages before replacing the filler caps.

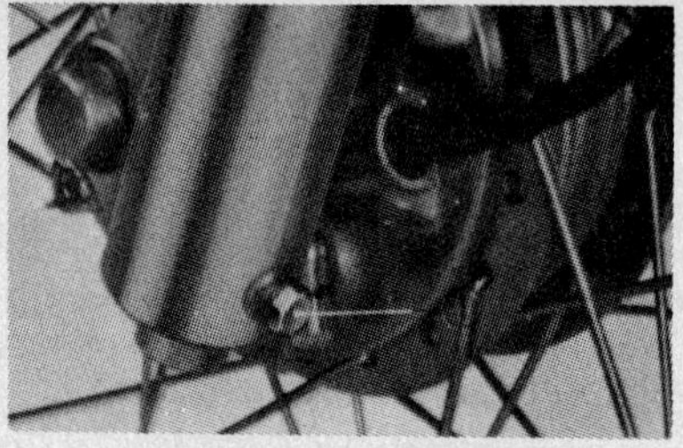
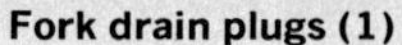
Fork drain plugs (1)

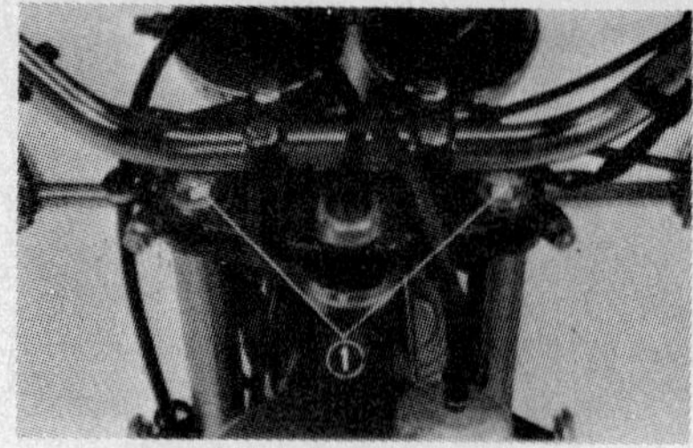
Fork filler plugs (1)

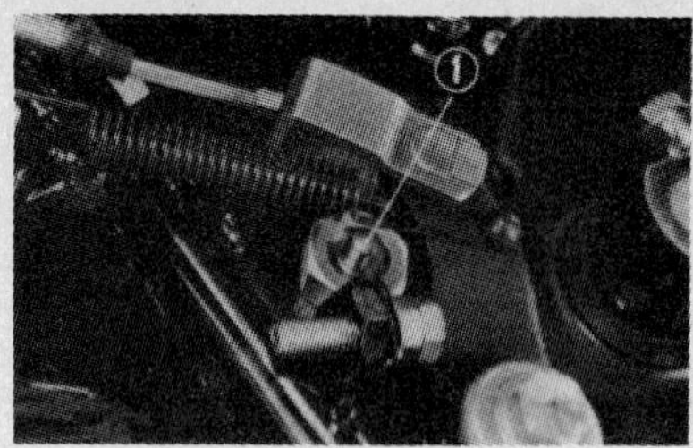
Swing arm grease fitting (1)

PERIODIC MAINTENANCE SCHEDULE

This maintenance schedule is based upon average riding conditions. Machines subjected to severe use, or ridden in unusually dusty areas, require more frequent servicing.

	Regular Service Period Perform at every indicated month or mileage interval, whichever occurs first	
Month	6	12
Mile	3,000	6,000
Km	5,000	10,000
Transmission oil—Change		●
Spark plug—Clean and adjust gap or replace as necessary	●	
Contact point and ignition timing—Clean, check, and adjust or replace as necessary	●	
Polyurethane foam air filter element—Clean and oil (Service more frequently if operated in dusty area)	●	
Carburetor—Check, and adjust as necessary	●	
Oil pump operation—Check	●	
Cylinder head, cylinder, piston, piston rings and muffler—Decarbonize		●
Throttle operation—Inspect cable, check, and adjust free-play	●	
Oil tank filter—Clean		●
Fuel filter screen—Clean	●	
Clutch—Check operation, and adjust as necessary	●	
Drive chain—Check, lubricate, and adjust as necessary	●	
Brake shoes—Inspect, and replace if worn		●
Brake control linkage—Check linkage, and adjust free-play as necessary		●
Wheel rims and spokes—Check. Tighten spokes and true wheels, as necessary	●	
Tires—Inspect		●
Front fork oil—Drain and refill		●
Rear fork bushing—Grease. Check for excessive looseness	●	
Steering head bearings—Adjust		●
Battery—Check electrolyte level, and add water as necessary	●	
All nuts, bolts, and other fasteners—Check security and tighten as necessary	●	

SWING ARM BUSHINGS (6,000 Mi/12 Mo)

The swing arm bushings should be checked for wear at regular intervals by checking for swing arm side-play. The bushings should be thoroughly greased at this time.

ENGINE AND TRANSMISSION

ENGINE REMOVAL AND INSTALLATION

NOTE: *For work on the cylinder head, cylinder and piston, clutch, oil pump, AC generator, kick starter, and external shifter mechanism, it is not necessary to remove the engine from the frame. If the engine is to be removed for bottom end or transmission work, it is best to drain the transmission oil at this time.*

Exhaust pipe removal

1. Muffler
2. Exhaust pipe spring
3. Muffler mounting nut

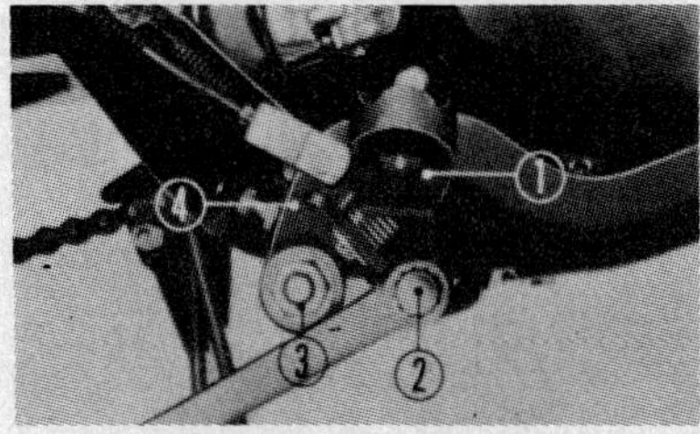

Removing the right footpeg

1. Right footpeg
2. 8 mm bolt
3. 10 mm nut
4. Brake pedal

Removal

1. Disconnect the two exhaust pipe springs and remove the two muffler mounting nuts, then pull the muffler forward and off the cylinder.

2. Remove the right-side foot peg and brake pedal. Then open the seat, turn the petcock to "OFF" disconnect the fuel line, and remove the tank.

3. Disconnect the 3 rubber carburetor lines at the engine, remove the tach cable mounting screw and disconnect the cable, remove the inlet one-way bolt and the two inlet pipe mounting bolts, then separate the pipe from the cylinder.

MAINTENANCE DATA

	MT-125	MT-250
Engine oil tank	1.6 U.S. qt	1.4 U.S. qt
Transmission oil①	1.1 U.S. qt	1.0 U.S. qt
Fork oil②	145-150 cc	145-150 cc
Tire pressure:		
Front	21 psi	21 psi
Rear	21 psi	21 psi

① Use a high detergent SAE 10W-30 or 10W-40 for use in all temperatures, or use SAE 30 for temperatures above 59°F, SAE 20 for temperatures of 32°-59°F, or SAE 10 for temperatures below 32°F.

② Use 165 cc of oil when refilling a completely dry assembly.

Tank mounting bolts (1) and fuel line (2)

4. Remove the six engine mounting bolt nuts, but do not remove the bolts.

5. Loosen the rear wheel and slide it forward in the swing arm until the chain can be removed from the rear sprocket and then the front sprocket, or remove the master link retaining clip and link to remove the chain.

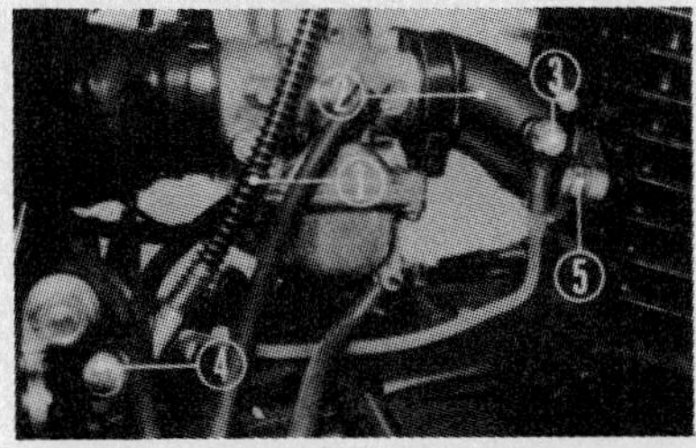

Cable and fuel line connecting points

1. Tachometer cable
2. Inlet pipe
3. Inlet one-way bolt
4. Tach cable mounting screw
5. Inlet pipe mounting bolts

6. Remove the left-side crankcase cover, then disconnect the wiring harness connector.

7. Plug the oil tank to prevent spillage, remove the oil pump cover, and disconnect the oil pipe from the tank.

8. Disconnect the oil pump and clutch cables and the high-tension spark plug lead.

9. Remove the engine mounting bolts and hanger plates, then lift the engine out of the frame. Plug up the carburetor and engine ports to prevent the entry of dust and dirt, and wrap the oil pump pipe assembly to prevent contamination.

Engine mounting bolt nuts (1 and 2)

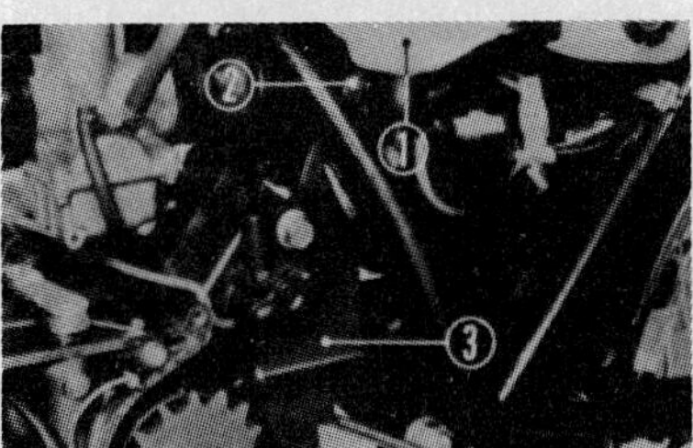

Oil tank (1), pipe (2), and cover (3)

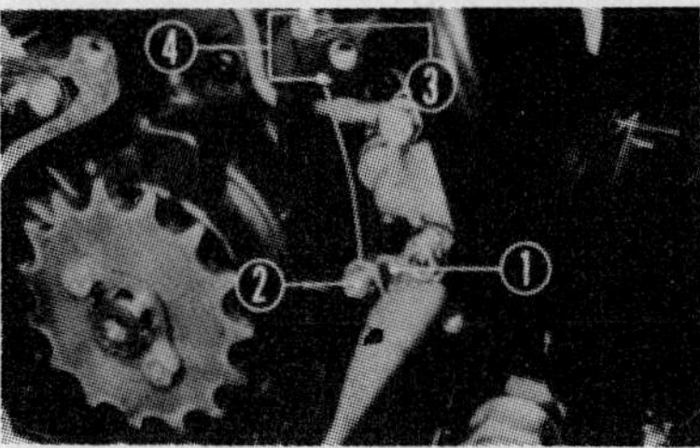

Disconnecting the oil pump cable

1. Lever
2. Cable pin
3. Locknut
4. Adjusting bolt

Disconnecting the clutch cable

1. Clutch cable
2. Stay
3. Clutch lever
4. Clutch lever spring

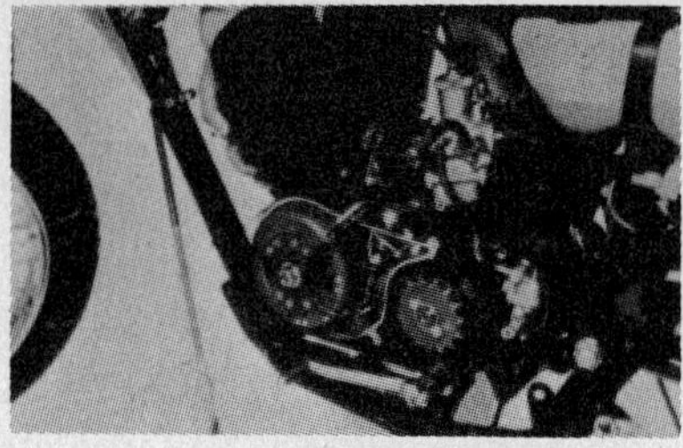

Engine ready for removal

Installation

1. Installation is basically in the reverse order of removal.

2. Install the engine hanger plates as shown, securing the skid plate to the front lower side of the hanger plate.

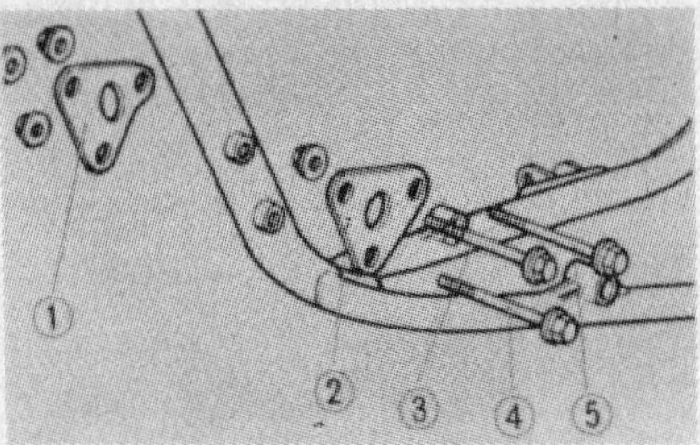

Engine hanger plates

1. Right engine hanger plate
2. Left engine hanger plafe
3. 8 x 59 mm bolt
4. 8 x 63 mm bolt
5. 8 x 68 mm bolt

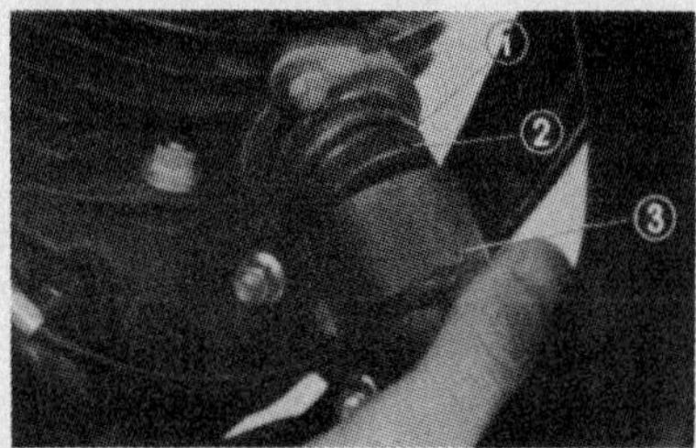

Installing the muffler (3) and gasket (2) with the ring gap (2) up

3. When installing the exhaust pipe, loosely secure the muffler mounting nuts, install the mounting springs, tighten the mounting nuts, and hook the spring ends to lock them into place. The exhaust ring gap must be up, and a new exhaust pipe joint gasket should be used if it has been removed.

4. Take care when installing the rear brake pedal that the pedal shaft seal is not damaged.

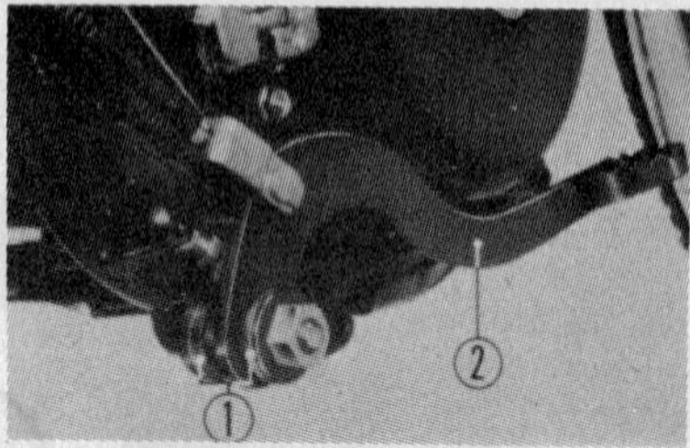

Do not damage the seal (1) when mounting the lever (2)

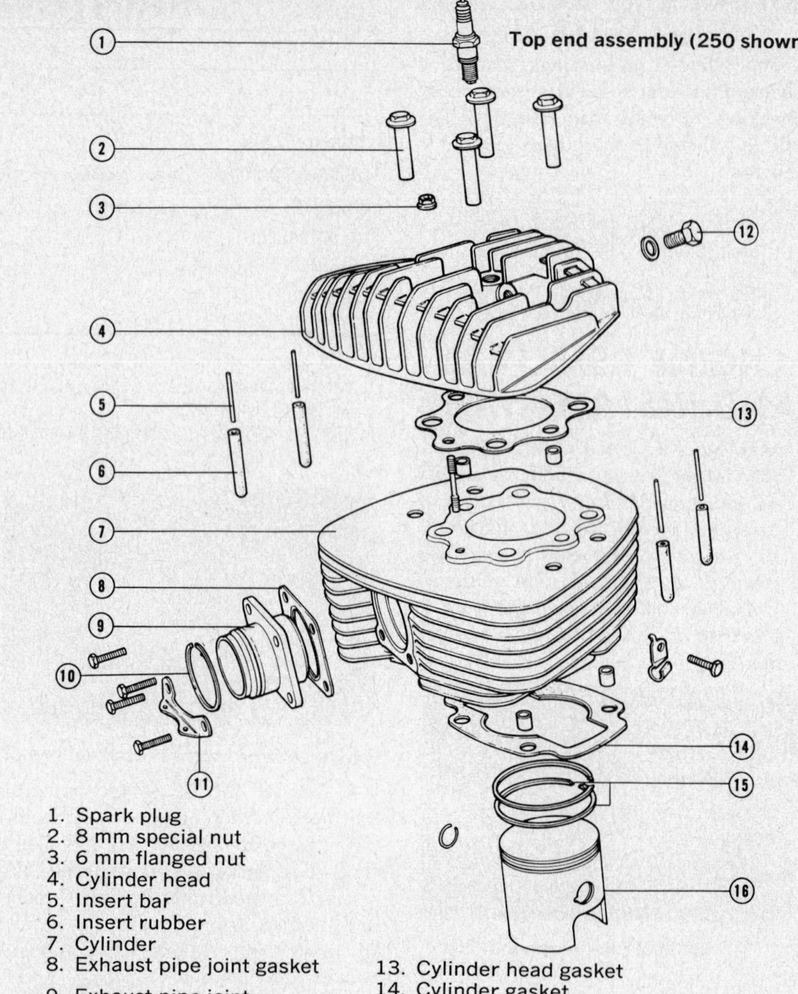

Top end assembly (250 shown)

1. Spark plug
2. 8 mm special nut
3. 6 mm flanged nut
4. Cylinder head
5. Insert bar
6. Insert rubber
7. Cylinder
8. Exhaust pipe joint gasket
9. Exhaust pipe joint
10. Exhaust ring
11. Exhaust pipe spring stay
12. 14 mm sealing bolt
13. Cylinder head gasket
14. Cylinder gasket
15. Piston ring
16. Piston

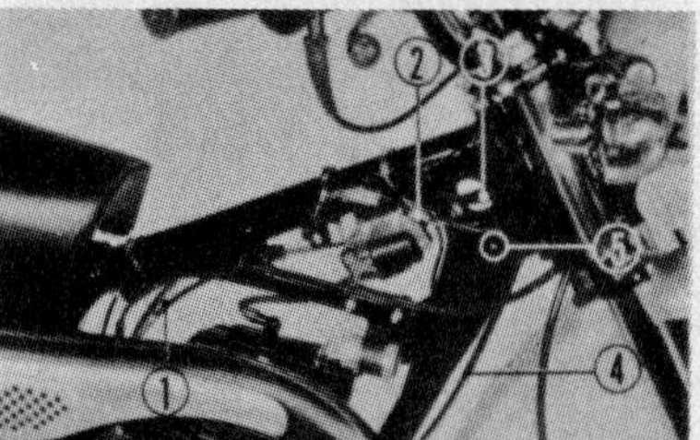

Route the cables as shown when installing the tank

1. Tachometer cable
2. Front stop switch lead
3. Ignition switch lead
4. Clutch cable
5. Tank location

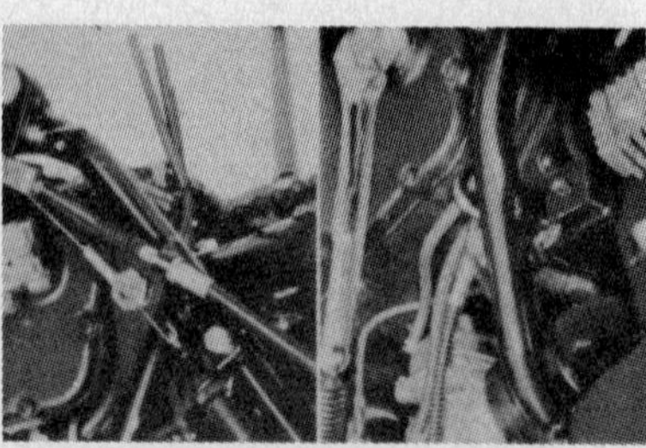

Route the pipes and tubes as shown

5. When installing the gas tank be sure that the cables are routed as shown. Use clips on the fuel line.

6. Route the pipes and tubes as illustrated.

7. Install the drive chain. If the chain has been disconnected, use a new master link spring clip, and install it so that the closed end of the clip is facing the direction of normal rotation, then adjust the chain.

Spring clip (1) properly installed

8. Perform all the tune-up and engine-oriented maintenance operations. Be certain that there is sufficient oil in the transmission and oil tank. The engine should be run for about 7 minutes under

less than half-throttle as a break-in precaution before any hard riding is done.

TOP END SERVICE

Disassembly

1. Open the seat and remove the tank, then remove the muffler as described in the "Engine Removal and Installation" Section.

NOTE: *Before going any further it is imperative that the engine be cleaned thoroughly.*

2. Remove the inlet pipe one-way bolt and the inlet pipe mounting bolts.

3. Disconnect the spark plug lead and remove the cylinder head mounting nuts. Tap the head lightly with a soft mallet to remove the head and gasket.

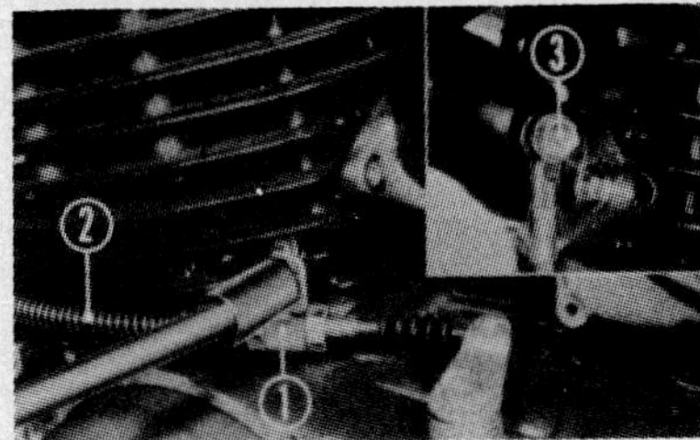

Remove all this stuff

1. Clutch cable clamp stay
2. Clutch cable
3. One-way bolt

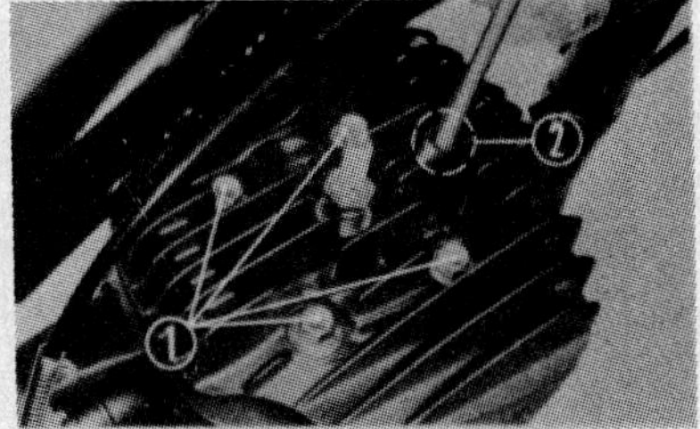

Remove the 8 mm nuts (1). The 250 also has a 6 mm flanged nut (2).

Only the 125 has cylinder base nuts

1. Cylinder
2. Inlet pipe one-way bolt
3. 8 mm nuts
4. Bolt

4. Remove the clutch cable clamp stay, then lift the cylinder barrel off its studs, after removing the 8 mm base mounting nuts (125 only), taking care not to damage the piston assembly. As the barrel is lifted off, clean rags should be stuffed around the connecting rod to prevent foreign matter from falling into the crankcase. Remove the cylinder base gasket.

5. Remove the piston pin circlips with needlenose pliers or a suitable pointed instrument, push out the pin, and remove the piston. When removing the piston rings, the end of the ring opposite the gap should be lifted off the piston first. The small end bearing need not be removed.

6. If the cylinder is to be replaced, remove the exhaust pipe joint, the insert bars, and the insert rubbers.

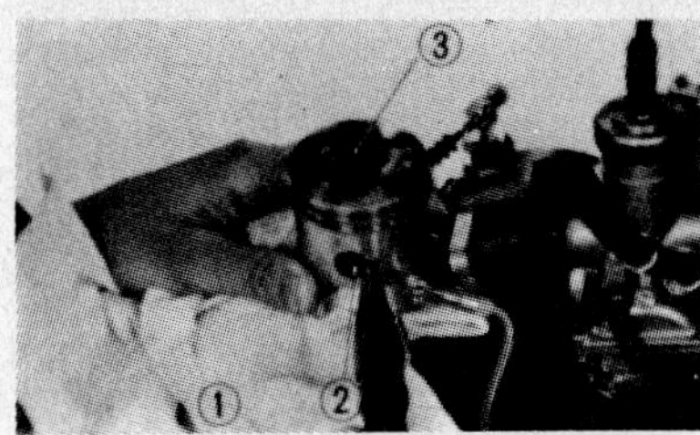

Removing the piston pin circlip

1. Rag
2. Piston pin clip
3. Piston

Inspection and Repair

1. Thoroughly decarbonize the piston, cylinder, and cylinder head assemblies, taking care not to gouge the metal. The ring lands can be cleaned with a piece of broken ring.

2. Inspect the piston, cylinder, and head for signs of wear or damage, and repair or replace them as necessary. If the cylinder is worn or scored, it can be bored out to the first oversize only 0.025 in. (0.65 mm). The cylinder should be honed at least to break the glaze and to help the rings seat properly. Check the piston ring dowels for excessive wear, and replace the piston as necessary.

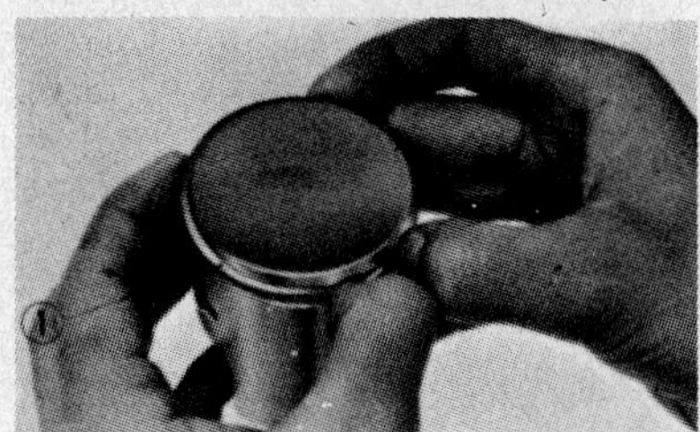

Piston ring (1) removal

3. Measure the inside diameter of the cylinder at the 4 locations shown in the illustration in both directions. Consider the maximum figure to be the measured value.

4. Measure the piston outside diameter at a point 0.2 in. (5.0 mm) above the bottom of the skirt. The difference between this and the measurement taken in the previous step is the piston-to-cylinder clearance.

5. Measure the piston ring end-gap with the ring about ¼ in. down in the bore, and file them flat, as necessary, to meet specifications.

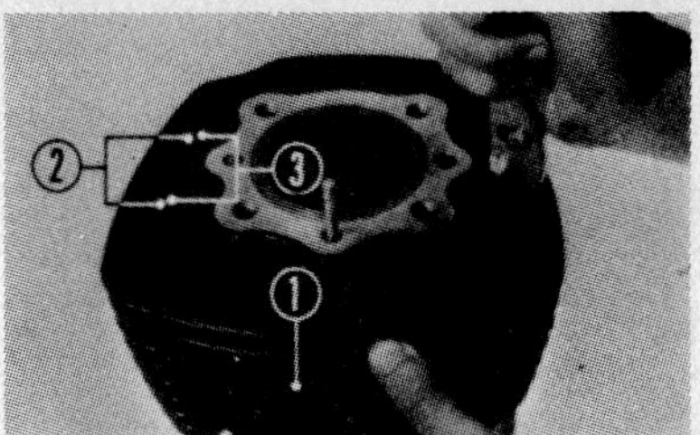

Removing an insert bar

1. Exhaust pipe joint
2. Insert bar
3. Insert rubber

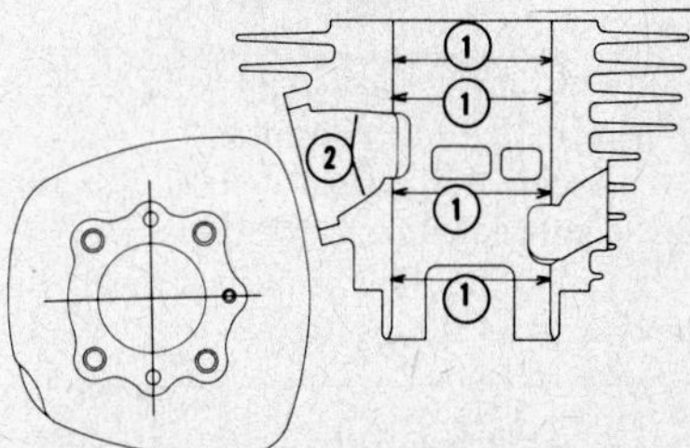

Positions for measuring the cylinder (1). (2) indicates where carbon deposits build up.

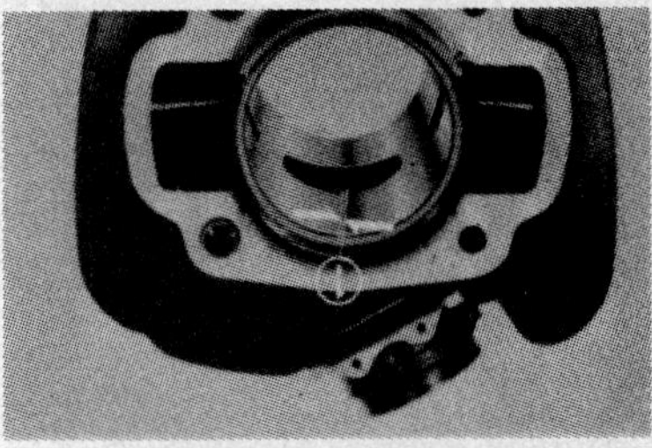

Ring end-gap (1)

6. Measure the piston ring side-clearance in relation to the piston, and replace the piston if the clearance exceeds the specified limits.

7. Inspect the connecting rod small end bearing for a worn or loose condition, and replace it, if necessary, according to the information given in the following chart:

NOTE: *All 125 models are "with notch (A)".*

8. Check the piston pin hole for wear and excessive clearance between the pin and piston, and replace them as necessary.

Piston Pin Dia. Connecting Rod Small End ID	*A (With Notch)*	*B (Without Notch)*
I (One notch)	Red	—
II (Two notches)	Blue	Red
III (Three notches)	White	Blue

NOTE: *All 125 models are "with notch (A)."*

Assembly

1. Assembly is basically in the reverse order of disassembly. Use new gaskets, circlips, and rings if they have been removed from the piston.

2. When installing the rings make sure

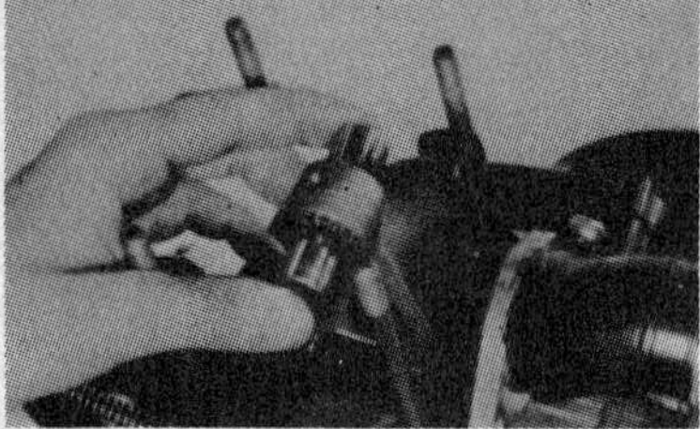

Checking the small end bearing for excessive play

that the keystone ring is in the top groove, and that the ring markings face up.

3. Lubricate the small end needle bearing when installing it.

4. Install the piston so that the ring dowels are facing the inlet port.

5. Lubricate the piston rings and cylinder when installing them.

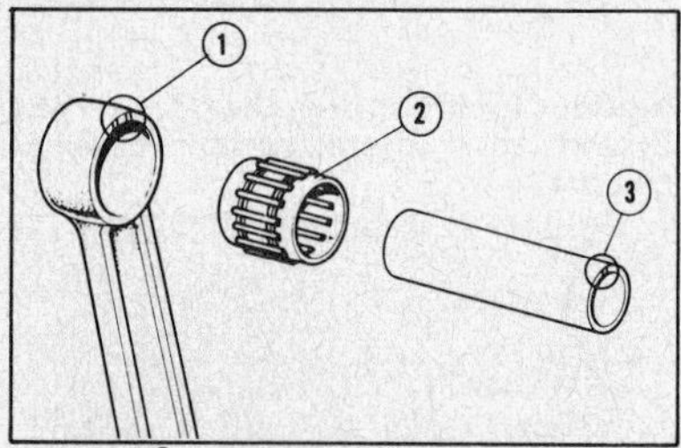

The notches tell the story

1. Connecting rod small end notch
2. Small end bearing
3. Crank pin notch

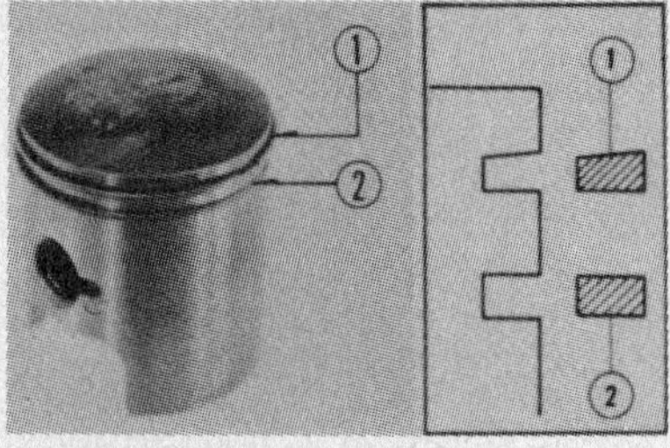

Make sure that the keystone ring (1) is in the top groove, and the oil ring (2) is in the bottom

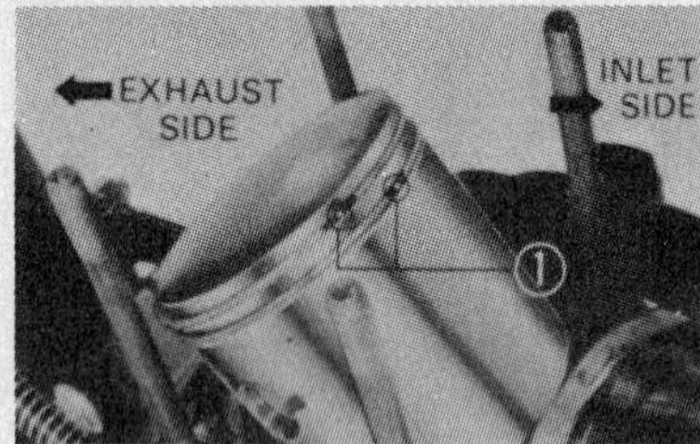

Install the piston with the ring dowels toward the inlet port

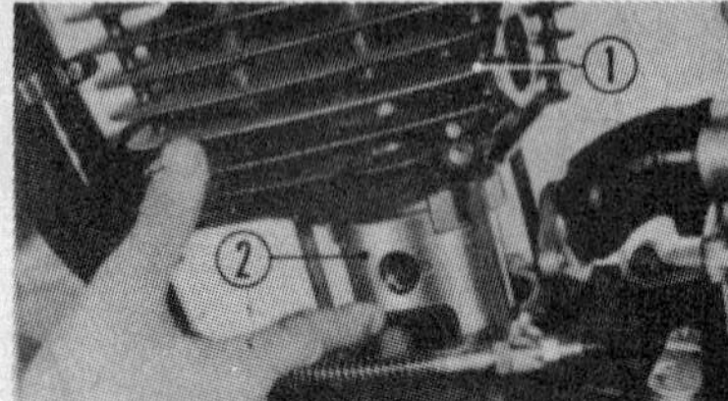

Installing the cylinder (1) over the piston (2)

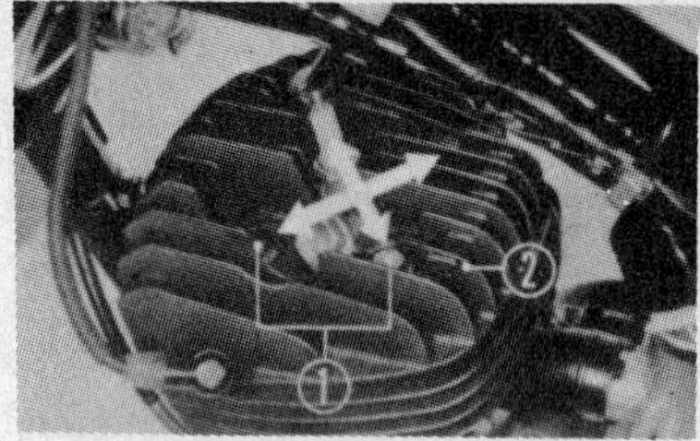

Head nut tightening sequence (250 shown)

1. Head nuts 2. Head

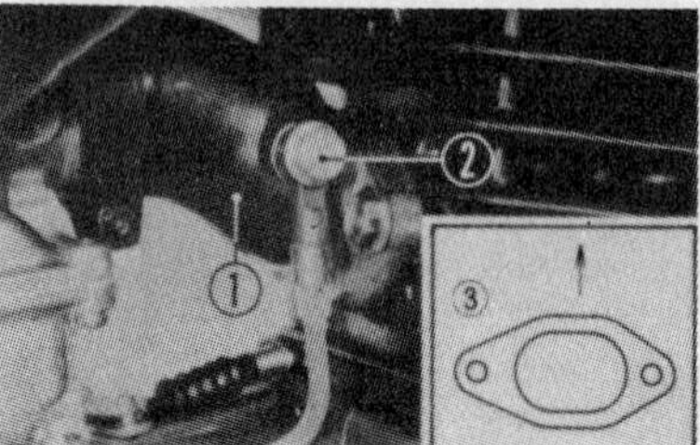

Inlet pipe installed

1. Inlet pipe
2. Inlet pipe one-way bolt
3. Inlet pipe gasket orientation

6. Secure the head nuts, and base nuts (125 only), evenly in the crossed pattern shown in the accompanying illustration. Consult the "Torque Specifications" Chart at the end of this Section for the proper values.

OIL PUMP

Removal

NOTE: *The pump should never be removed unless necessary. It cannot be rebuilt, and therefore must be replaced if defective.*

1. Remove the drive chain, left crankcase cover, and the oil pump case cover.

2. Remove the left-side plastic cover, and disconnect the oil pump at the oil tank. Plug the pump opening to prevent leakage.

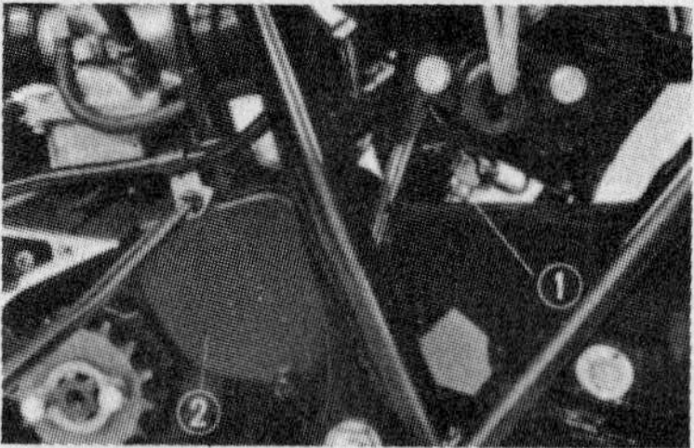

Oil pump cover (2) and tube (1)

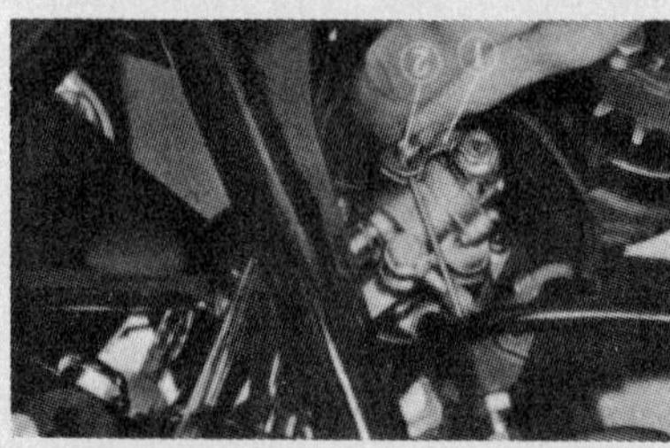

Raise the lever (1) before pulling the pin (2)

3. Raise the pump control lever, remove the control cable pin, and disconnect the cable.

4. Remove the one-way bolt and the two mounting screws, then pull the pump off and out.

Installation

1. Installation is in the reverse order of removal.

2. Slip one end of the oil pipe into the inlet grommet hole, and pull it toward the tank.

3. Fit the pump drive gearshaft into the slotted opening in the crankcase, and push it in by hand until it is in contact with the crankcase gasket, then secure the two parts.

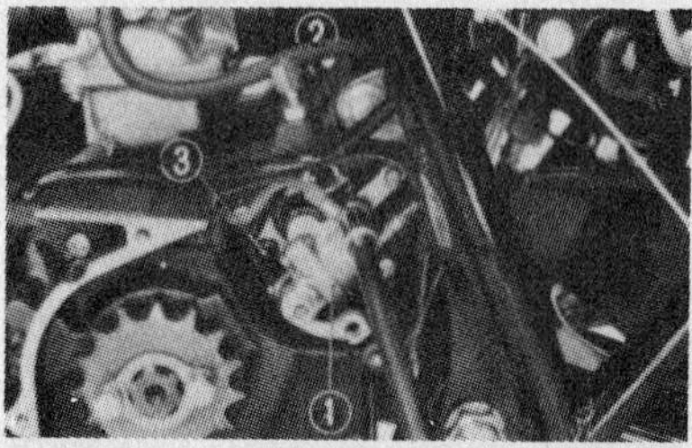

Remove the one-way bolt (2) and the mounting screws (3) before pulling off the pump (1)

Lining up the crankcase opening (1) and the drive gearshaft (2)

4. Use the one-way bolt to secure the outlet hose, the secure the pump control cable in the control lever.

5. Insert the oil pipe into the tank completely, and secure it with the clip, then bleed and adjust the pump as described in the "Tune-Up and Maintenance" Section.

CLUTCH

Disassembly

125

1. Remove the brake pivot shaft, brake pedal, kickstarter bolt, kickstarter lever, and the clutch adjusting cap, then loosen the locknut and clutch adjusting screw.

2. Loosen the cable adjusting screw locknut and screw, then disconnect the cable at the right crankcase cover.

3. Remove the lifter shaft spring from the right crankcase cover, then remove the 6 mm special bolt while keeping the lever pulled up about ½ of its total length.

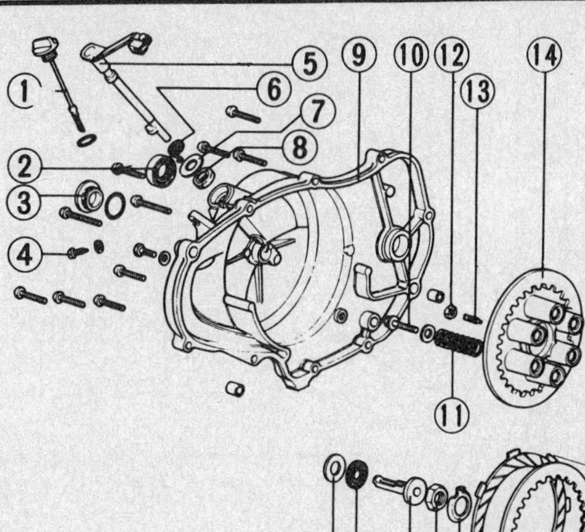

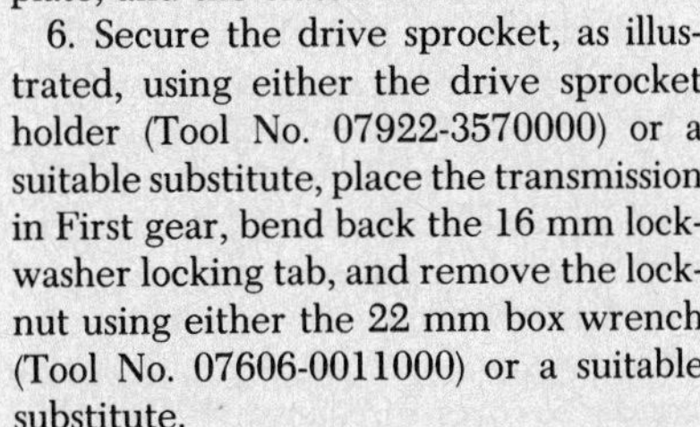

Clutch assembly (125)

1. Oil level gauge
2. 16 x 28 x 7 oil seal
3. Clutch adjusting cap
4. 6 mm special bolt
5. Clutch lever
6. Lifter shaft spring
7. 26 mm special washer
8. 11 x 17 x 4 oil seal
9. Right crankcase cover
10. 6 mm flanged bolt
11. Clutch spring
12. 6 mm nut
13. Clutch adjusting screw
14. Clutch pressure plate
15. 12.5 mm thrust washer
16. 1612 thrust needle bearing
17. Lifter rod
18. 16 mm locknut
19. 16 mm lockwasher
20. Clutch friction disc
21. Clutch plate
22. Clutch center
23. 20 mm splined washer
24. Clutch hub
25. 20 mm thrust washer

Removing the case cover
1. Lifter shaft spring
2. Clutch lever
3. Right crankcase cover

Removing the pressure plate bolts
1. 6 mm flanged bolt
2. Clutch pressure plate
3. Clutch lifter rod

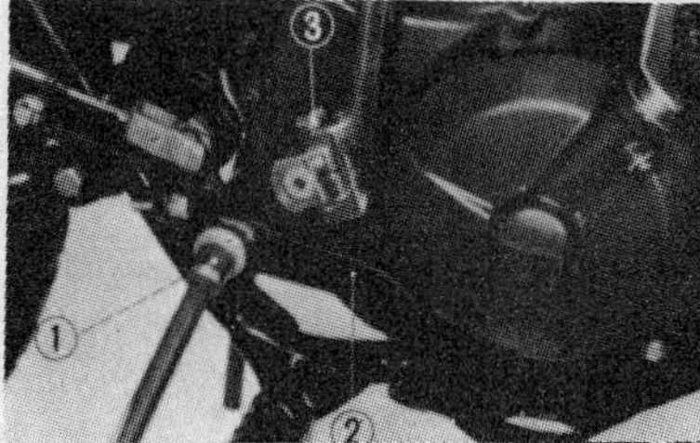

Removing the brake pedal assembly
1. Brake pivot shaft
2. Brake pedal
3. Kickstarter bolt

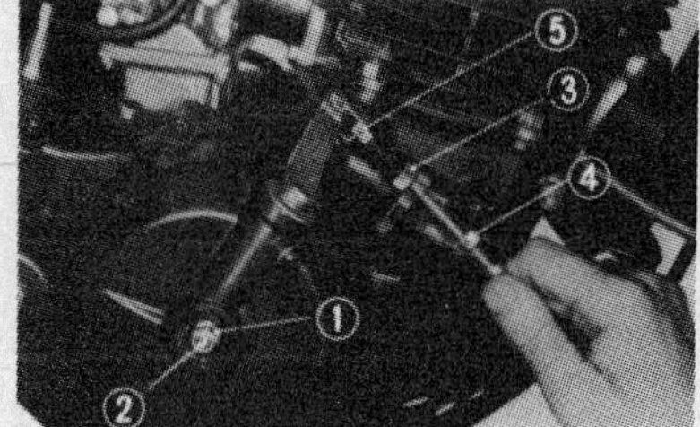

Disconnecting the clutch cable
1. Locknut
2. Clutch adjusting screw
3. Locknut
4. Adjusting nut
5. Cable end

4. Remove the ten 6 mm cover mounting screws, then remove the right cover.

5. Remove the pressure plate bolts evenly to avoid deforming the plate, then remove the clutch springs, the pressure plate, and the clutch lifter rod.

6. Secure the drive sprocket, as illustrated, using either the drive sprocket holder (Tool No. 07922-3570000) or a suitable substitute, place the transmission in First gear, bend back the 16 mm lockwasher locking tab, and remove the locknut using either the 22 mm box wrench (Tool No. 07606-0011000) or a suitable substitute.

7. Remove the clutch center and the discs and plates, then remove the 20 mm splined washer and the clutch hub.

250

1. Either drain the transmission oil or tilt the bike over to the left to prevent it from dripping out.

2. Remove the right-side foot peg, the brake pedal, the kick starter pedal, and the right crankcase cover screws and cover.

NOTE: *Be prepared to catch the oil in the cover. The skid plate will probably become oil soaked, and should be cleaned.*

3. Remove the clutch pressure plate retaining bolts, clutch springs, pressure plate, and pressure plate center piece. The adjusting screw locknut and screw now can be removed from the pressure plate.

Drive sprocket holder (1) installed

Removing the clutch locknut
1. 16 mm locknut
2. 16 mm lockwasher
3. 22 mm box wrench

Removing the washer (1) and center (2) from the hub (3)

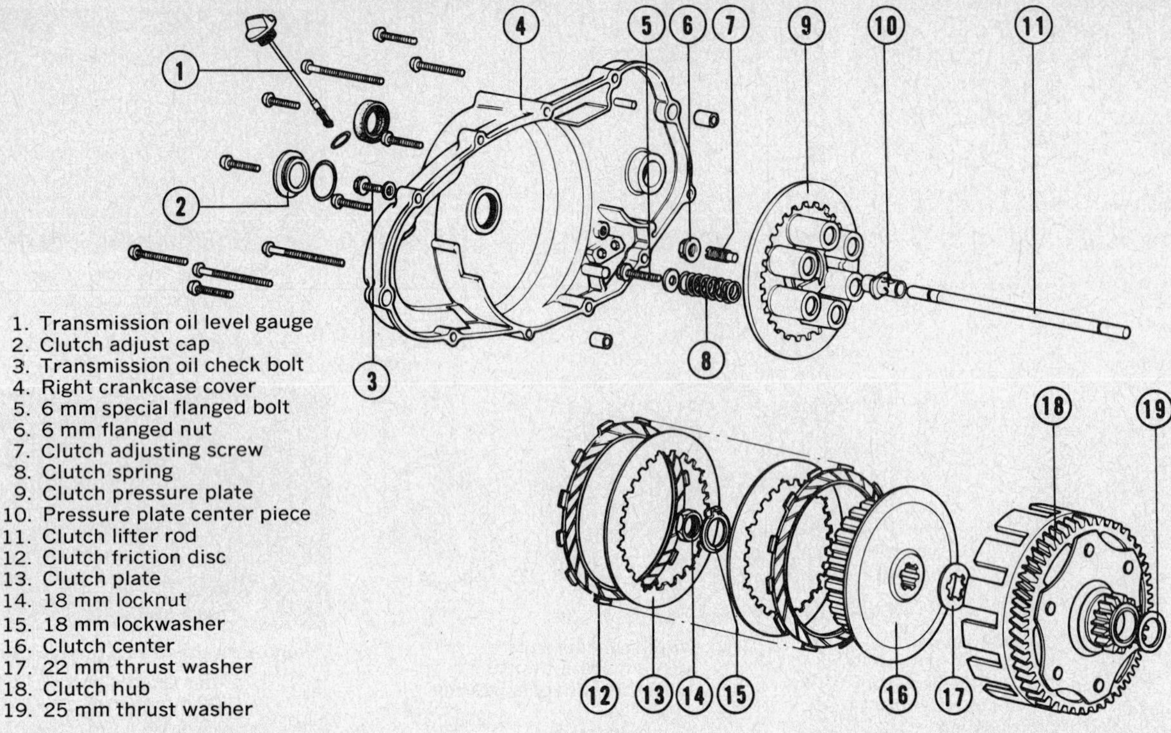

Clutch assembly (250)

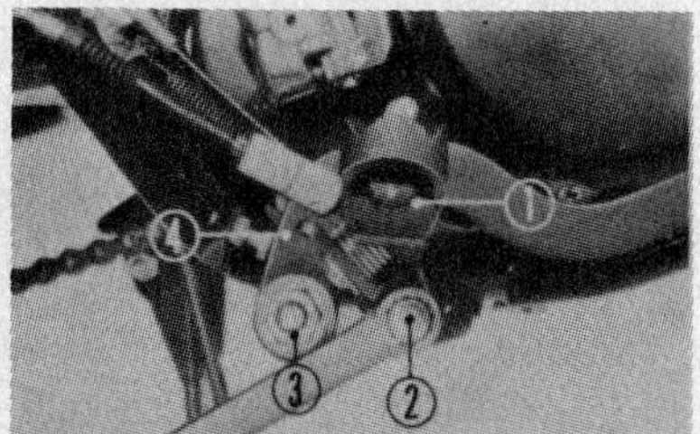

Removing the footpeg

1. Right footpeg
2. 8 mm bolt
3. 10 mm nut
4. Brake pedal

Crankcase cover (1), starter lever (2), and skid plate (3)

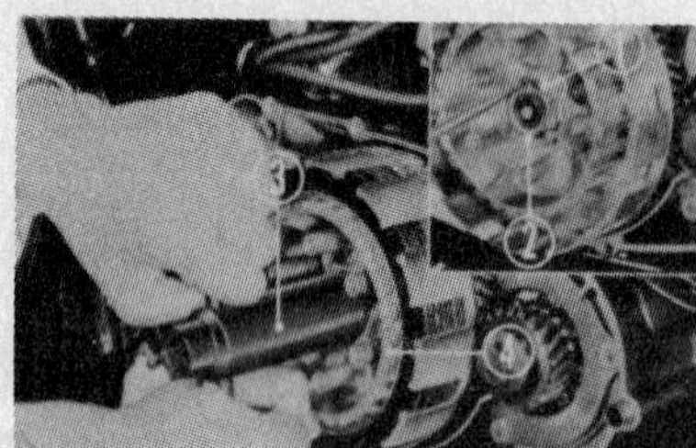

Removing the clutch locknut

1. 18 mm lockwasher
2. 18 mm locknut
3. Locknut wrench
4. Clutch center

4. Remove the clutch friction plates and discs, and bend back the lockwasher locking tab.

5. Place the transmission in First gear, and secure the clutch center with the drive sprocket holder (Tool No. 07922-3570000), or a suitable substitute, then remove the clutch center mounting nut using either the locknut wrench (Tool No. 07907-035000) or a suitable substitute, and remove the clutch center.

6. Remove the 22 mm thrust washer and the clutch hub. The pushrod can be withdrawn from the mainshaft.

7. Remove the clutch actuating lever, as necessary, by removing the left-side crankcase cover, disconnecting the cable, removing the 5 mm special bolt, lever, lever spring, oil seal, and needle bearing.

Inspection and Repair

125 AND 250

1. Clean all parts, other than the friction discs, in a suitable solvent, and blow them dry.

2. Inspect and measure the thickness of the friction discs for a worn, oil impregnated, warped, or damaged condition, and replace them, as a set, as necessary.

3. Inspect the clutch discs for a worn, warped, scored, or damaged condition, and replace them as necessary.

4. Measure the free length of and inspect the clutch springs for a worn, collapsed, or damaged condition, and replace them as a set as necessary.

5. Inspect the remaining parts for wear or damage, and replace them as necessary.

Removing the center (1) and thrust washer (3) from the hub (2)

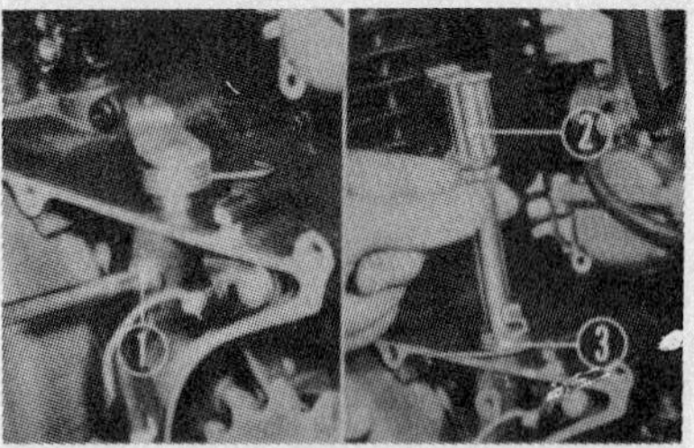

Removing the bolt (1), lever (2), and spring (3)

Assembly

125 AND 250

1. Assembly is basically in the reverse order of disassembly. Use new gaskets and lockwashers.

2. Position the thrust washer on the mainshaft, then install the clutch hub so that it is in mesh with the primary drive gear and the starter idle gear.

3. Install and secure the clutch center, making sure that the splined thrust washer is in place, and that the lockwasher locking tab is seated in the attaching hole in the clutch hub. Secure the

Install the thrust washer (2) and then the hub (1)

Installing the lockwasher (1) so that the lug seats in the hole (2) in the center

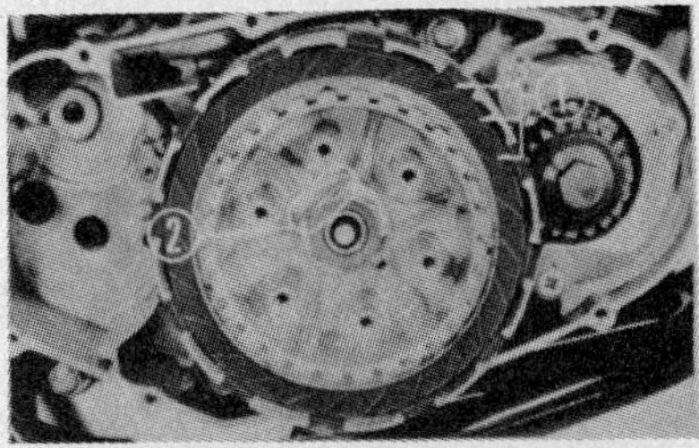
The oil grooves (1) should be positioned this way, and the lockwasher (2) should be secured as shown

locknut by bending the side of the lockwasher opposite the locking tab up against a flat side of the nut.

4. Install a friction disc, then a clutch plate, then a disc, and so on, making sure that the oil grooves on the discs are positioned as shown in the accompanying illustration.

5. Install the pressure plate center piece into its groove in the pressure plate, then install and tighten the adjusting screw and locknut on the plate.

6. Install the clutch pushrod with the spherical end toward the pressure plate (the other end is flat), then install the plate, springs, washers, and mounting bolts. Secure the mounting bolts evenly in a crossed pattern, torquing them to the value given in the "Torque Specifications" chart at the end of this section.

7. When installing the clutch lever (125), hold it at half its length in the position shown in the illustration so that the lever lug will fit the lifter groove.

KICK STARTER, OIL PUMP DRIVESHAFT, AND TACHOMETER GEAR

Disassembly

1. Remove the right-side crankcase cover as described in the "Clutch" section.

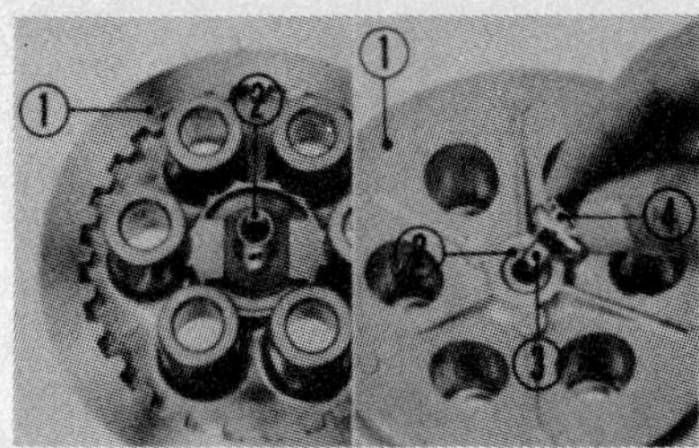
Install the center piece (2) in the pressure plate (1), then install the adjusting screw (3) and locknut (4) in the center piece

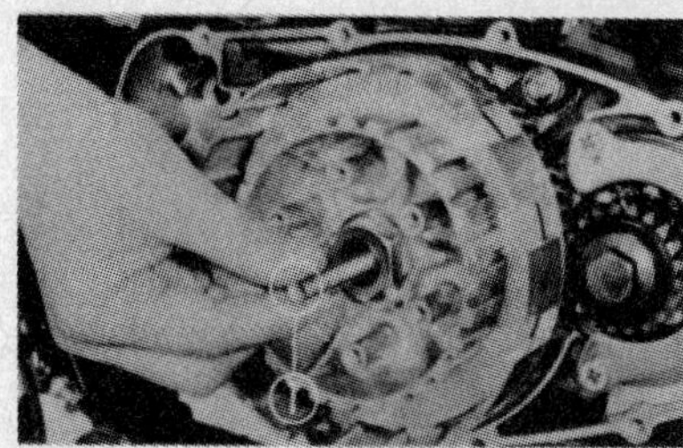
Installing the lifter rod (1) with the spherical end out

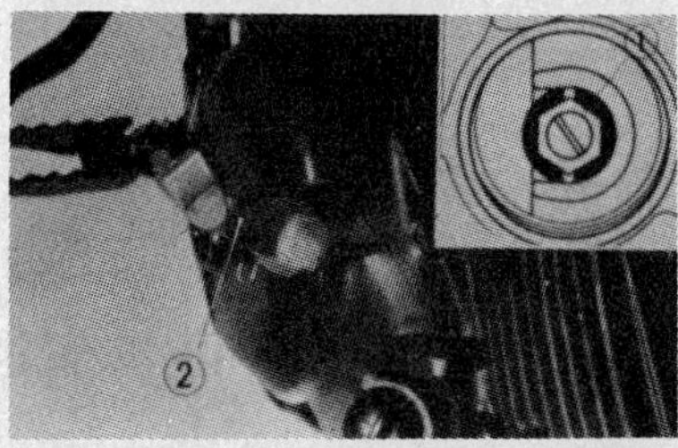
The lever lug (2) should fit the lifter rod (1) groove

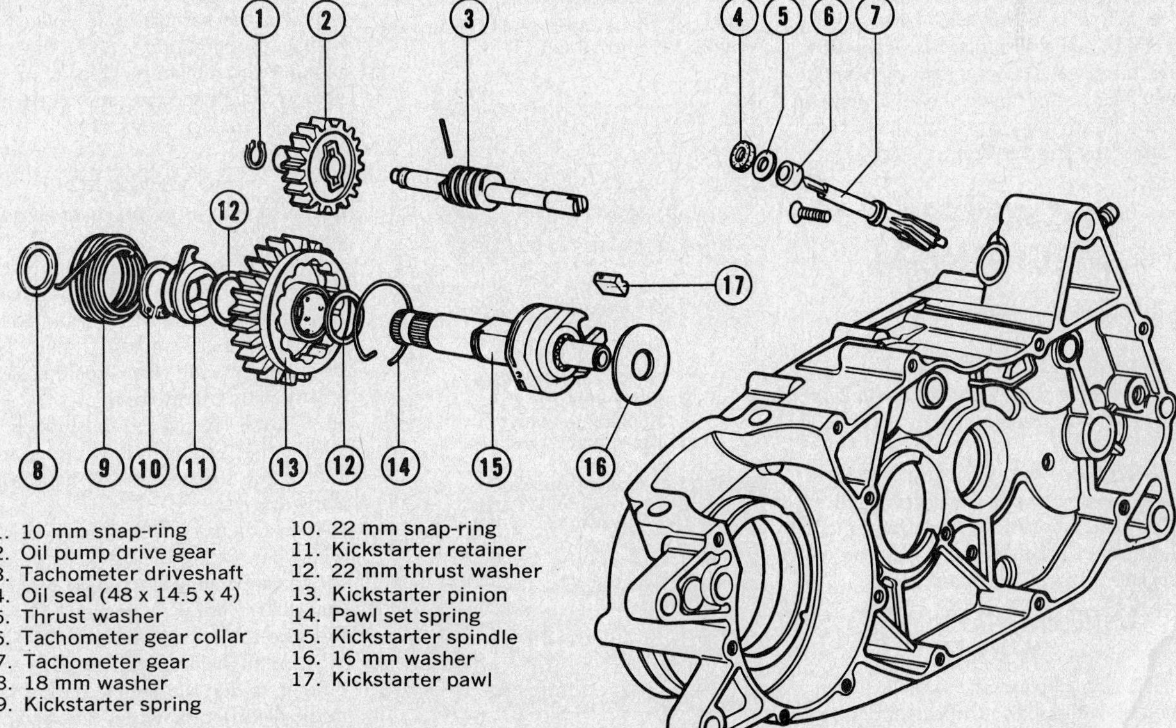
1. 10 mm snap-ring
2. Oil pump drive gear
3. Tachometer driveshaft
4. Oil seal (48 x 14.5 x 4)
5. Thrust washer
6. Tachometer gear collar
7. Tachometer gear
8. 18 mm washer
9. Kickstarter spring
10. 22 mm snap-ring
11. Kickstarter retainer
12. 22 mm thrust washer
13. Kickstarter pinion
14. Pawl set spring
15. Kickstarter spindle
16. 16 mm washer
17. Kickstarter pawl

Kickstarter, oil pump driveshaft, and tach gear assemblies (250)

2. Remove the kickstarter spring and starter assembly, then remove the tachometer driveshaft and oil pump drive gear. Removing the 10 mm snap-ring will permit separation of the drive gear from the driveshaft.

3. Remove the 22 mm external snap-ring from the kickstarter, then remove the spring retainer and starter pinion.

4. Remove the kickstarter pawl set ring, then remove the pawl and starter spindle.

5. Disconnect the tachometer cable, then remove the tachometer drive gear from the crankcase by pressing it out from the bottom.

Inspection and Repair

1. Clean all parts in a suitable solvent, then blow them dry. Inspect all parts for wear or damage, and replace as necessary.

2. Inspect the pawl and pawl stopper for wear or damage, as this may cause the pedal to slip.

Assembly

1. Assembly is basically in the reverse order of disassembly.

2. When installing the tachometer drive gear, push the assembled gear, collar, thrust washer, and oil seal into place using the tachometer cable end as a guide.

3. Install the kickstarter assembly in the order shown in the exploded illustration. Be certain that the stopper is correctly positioned, and avoid expanding the stopper more than necessary.

4. When installing the starter spring retainer, make sure that it faces up when the starter pawl bears against the stopper bolt. The starter pinion should be able to rotate lightly only when the pawl bears against the stopper bolt.

SHIFTER MECHANISM

125

DISASSEMBLY

1. Remove the right-side crankcase cover, clutch assembly, shift lever, and shift spindle.

2. Remove the shift drum stopper plate, neutral stopper, and drum shifter, taking care not to drop the pawl plunger, then remove the drum stopper arm collar, and drum stopper arm.

INSPECTION AND REPAIR

1. Clean all parts in a suitable solvent, then blow them dry. Inspect all parts for signs of wear or damage, and replace them as necessary.

Removing the spring (1) from the starter assembly (2)

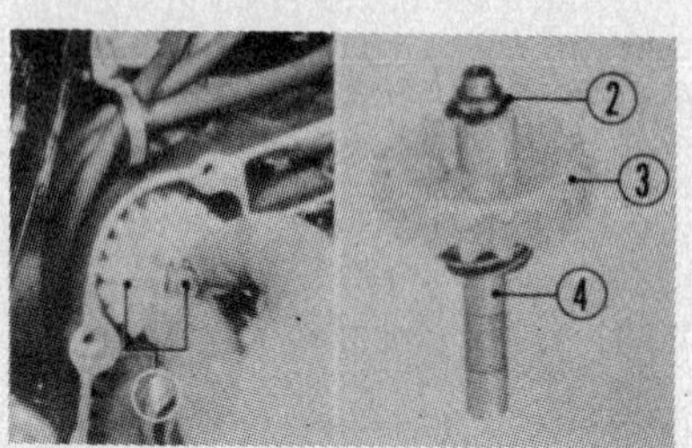

Removing the tach driveshaft and pump drive gear

1. Tachometer driveshaft and oil pump drive gear
2. 10 mm external snap-ring
3. Oil pump drive gear
4. Tachometer driveshaft

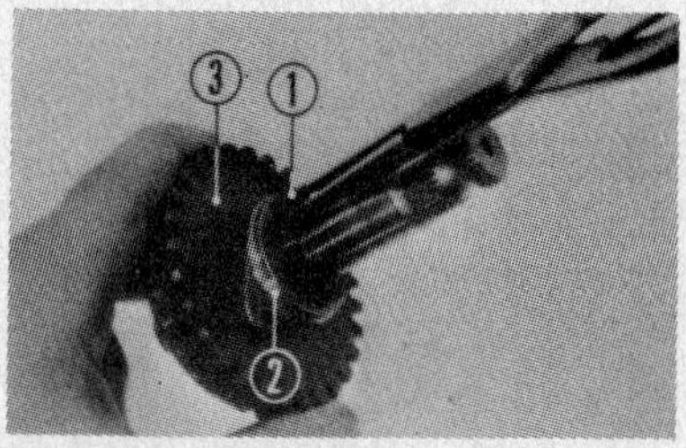

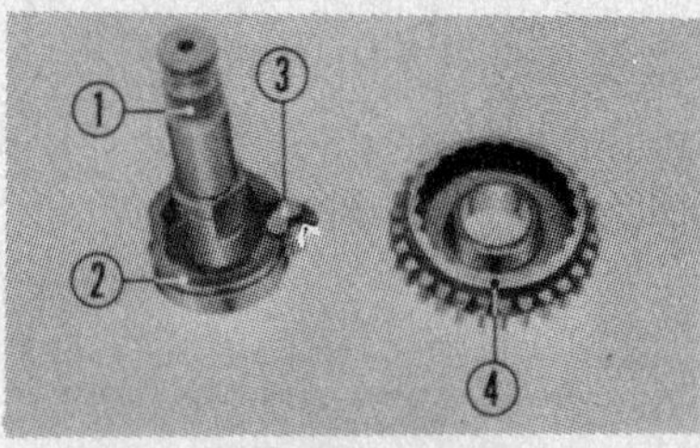

Removing the snap-ring (1) from the retainer (2) and pinion (3)

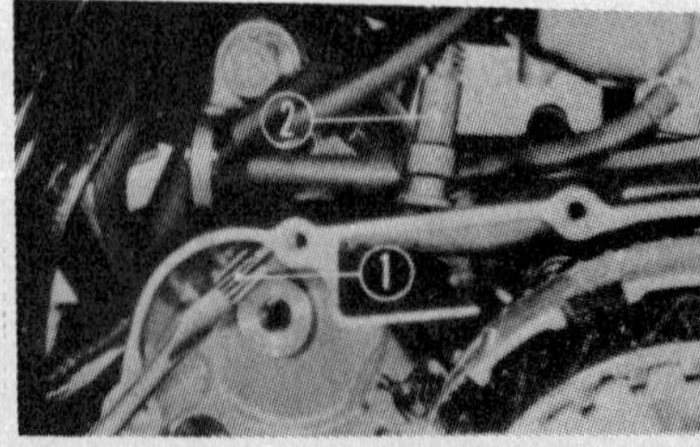

Spindle assembly

1. Kickstarter spindle
2. Pawl set spring
3. Kickstarter pawl
4. Kickstarter pinion

Removing the drive gear (1) and cable (2)

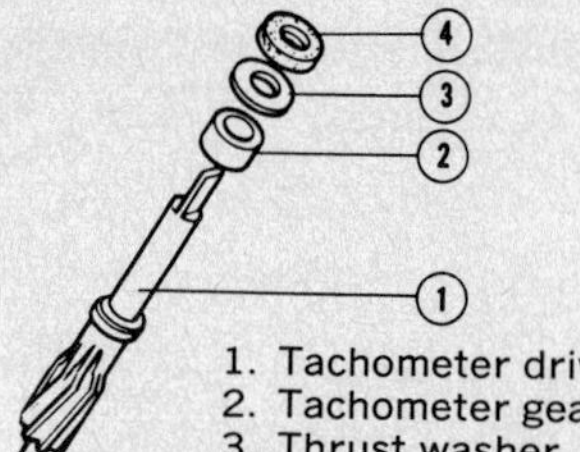

1. Tachometer drive gear
2. Tachometer gear collar
3. Thrust washer
4. Oil seal

Tach drive gear assembly

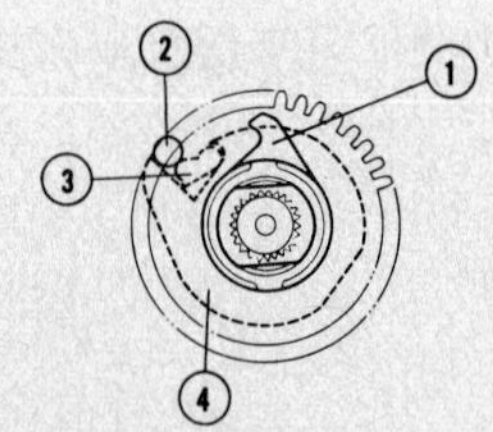

Starter spring retainer properly installed

1. Kickstarter spring retainer
2. Stopper bolt
3. Starter pawl
4. Kickstarter spindle

Removing the gearshift spindle

2. Inspect the shift spindle for wear or damage, the springs for a collapsed or damaged condition, and the pawl plunger and ratchet pawl for wear, damage, or rough motion, and replace any damaged parts as necessary.

ASSEMBLY

1. Assembly is in the reverse order of disassembly.

2. Install the shift drum stopper spring to the drum stopper arm, then install the drum stopper arm, washer, and collar so that the longer threaded part points down. Secure the collar while holding it steady with a screwdriver.

3. Install the neutral stopper arm spring, then assemble the stopper arm to the drum stopper arm collar with a screwdriver.

4. Install the ratchet pawl with the wider part facing the inside as shown in the accompanying illustration. Make sure that the ratchet pawl operates correctly, then assemble it to the drum.

5. Install the drum shifter, after assembling it, so that the punch mark is facing in the direction shown in the accompanying illustration.

6. Assemble the drum plate to the

Removing the stopper plate (1), neutral stopper (2), and drum shifter (3)

Removing the stopper arm collar

1. Return spring pin
2. Drum stopper arm collar
3. Drum stopper arm

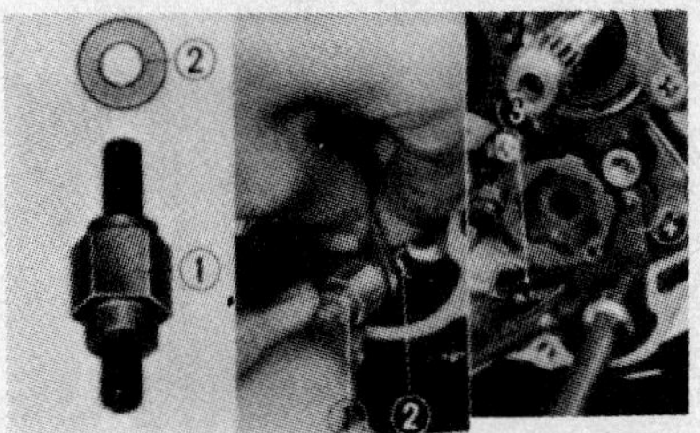

Installing the collar

1. Drum stopper arm collar
2. Drum stopper arm washer
3. Drum stopper arm spring
4. Drum stopper arm

Installing the stopper arm (1) and spring (2)

Install the pawl with the wider part facing in

1. Drum shifter
2. Pawl plunger spring
3. Pawl plunger
4. Ratchet pawl

drum stopper arm collar, then insert the plate pawl between the drum and drum shifter, and secure the plate with the 6 mm screw and nut. Stake the screw to secure it.

7. Assemble the shifter return spring and shifter spindle as shown in the accompanying illustration.

8. Mesh the shift arm gear and the drum shifter gear by aligning them as shown in the accompanying illustration.

250

DISASSEMBLY

1. Remove the clutch hub as described in the "Clutch" Section, then remove the shift lever.

2. Remove the gearshift arm from the shift drum, and pull out the shift spindle, then remove the drum stopper and neutral stopper arms.

INSPECTION AND REPAIR

1. Clean all parts in a suitable solvent, then blow them dry. Inspect all parts for signs of wear or damage, and replace them as necessary.

2. Check all the springs for a weak or damaged condition, and replace them as necessary.

3. Make sure that the shift return spring is secure.

ASSEMBLY

1. Assembly is in the reverse order of disassembly. Install the drum stopper arm and neutral stopper as shown in the accompanying illustration.

2. After the assembly has been installed operate it by hand to check for smooth action. If the operation is stiff, or if it won't work, either the bolts have been over torqued, or the collar and washer are not correctly positioned.

AC GENERATOR

Removal

1. Remove the left-side plastic cover, and disconnect the wire harness connector.

2. Remove the generator rotor cover and the left-side crankcase cover.

3. Place the transmission in First gear, rotate the engine until the two sprocket mounting bolts are positioned as illustrated in the accompanying illustration. Secure the drive sprocket using either the drive sprocket holder, as illustrated, (Tool No. 07933-0010000 for the 125, or 07922-3570000 for the 250), or a suitable substitute, then remove the 12 mm rotor mounting nut.

4. Remove the rotor from the shaft using either the special rotor puller (Tool No. 07933-3580000), or a suitable puller.

NOTE: *The rotor can be kept from rotating by using a "Y" shaped tool which fits in the two slots in the rotor face. Such a tool is also available from Yamaha dealers.*

Lining up the punch mark (1)

Installing the drum plate (1), shifter (2), and collar (3)

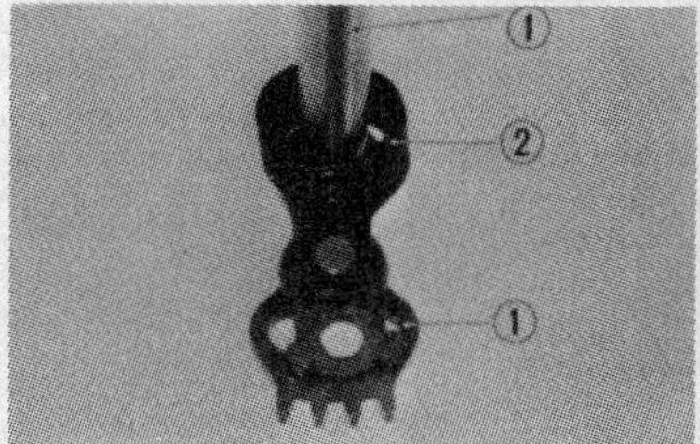

Installing the spindle (1) and spring (2)

Meshing the shift arm and drum shifter gears

1. Gearshift arm
2. Drum shifter
3. Drum plate
4. Neutral stopper arm
5. Stopper pin

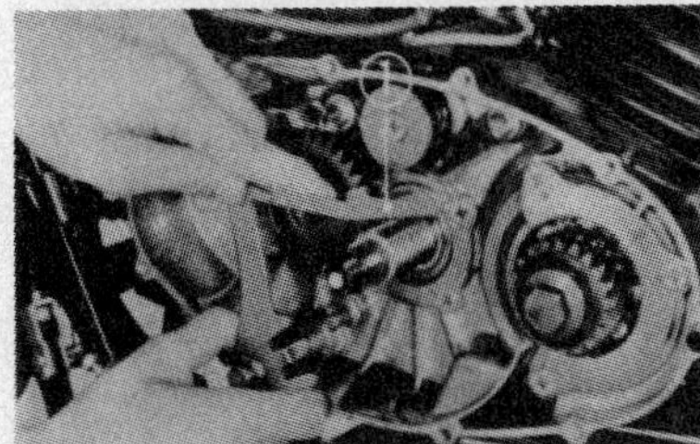

Removing the gearshift spindle (1)

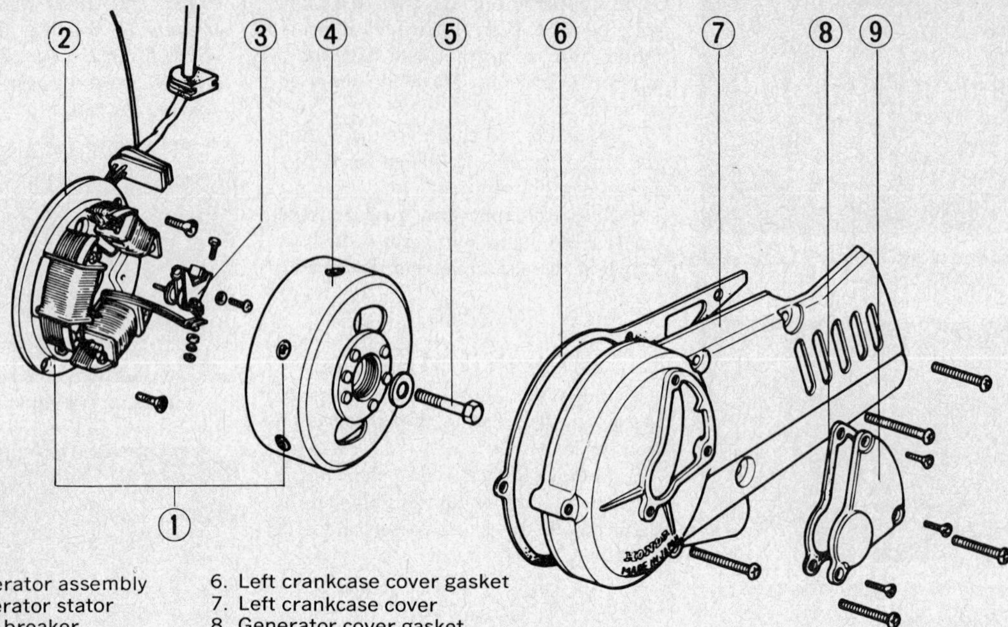

1. AC generator assembly
2. AC generator stator
3. Contact breaker
4. AC generator rotor
5. 8 mm tightening bolt
6. Left crankcase cover gasket
7. Left crankcase cover
8. Generator cover gasket
9. Generator cover

AC generator assembly

Removing the neutral (1) and drum (2) stopper arms

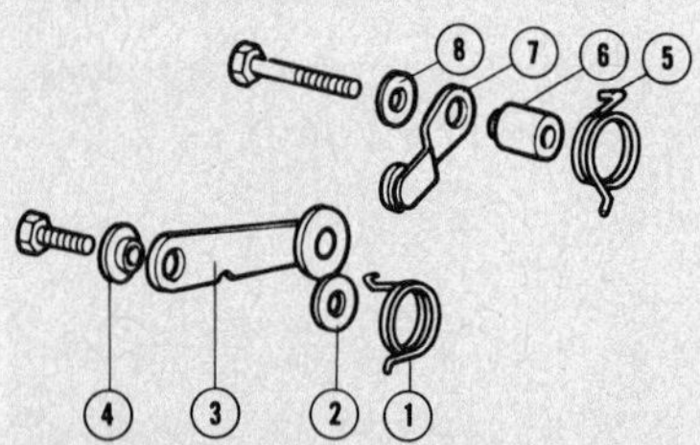

Drum and neutral stopper arm assemblies

1. Drum stopper arm spring
2. Drum stopper washer
3. Drum stopper arm
4. Drum stopper collar
5. Neutral stopper arm spring
6. Neutral stopper collar
7. Neutral stopper arm
8. Washer

Neutral (1) and drum (2) stopper arm assemblies installed

CAUTION: *Do not attempt to secure the rotor by using a screwdriver held against one of the coils through the windows, and do not attempt to pry the rotor from the shaft. Either of these approaches may result in damage to the rotor or stator.*

5. Disconnect the lead from the neutral switch, straighten out the generator clamper, then remove the screws which mount the stator to the crankcase. The points can now be removed from the stator plate.

Inspection and Repair

1. Wipe the assemblies clean if oil or dirt covered, and replace any components which are worn or damaged.

Crankcase cover (1) and electrical connector (2)

Removing the rotor (2) mounting nut with the aid of the factory tool (1)

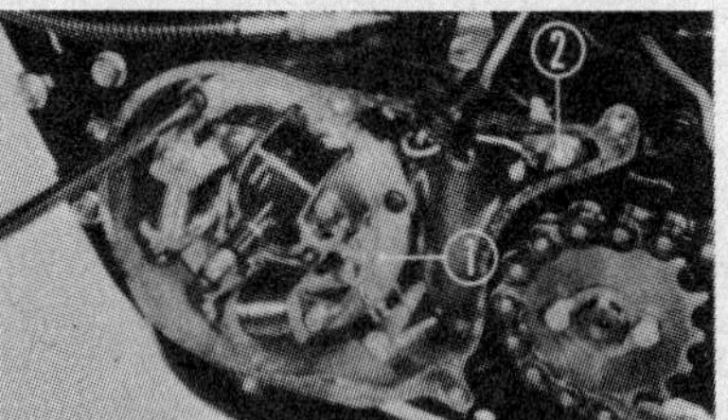

Unscrew the stator plate (1) and disconnect the neutral switch (2)

Generator clamper (1) position

2. Inspect the stator cord for a frayed or damaged condition, and replace it as necessary.

3. Consult the "Electrical System" Section for additional information.

Installation

1. Make sure that no hardware has stuck on the rotor magnets before installing it, and be sure that the key and keyway line up before placing the rotor on the shaft.

2. Draw the rotor down onto the shaft with the mounting nut. Do not attempt to drive the rotor onto the shaft by force.

3. Make sure that the rotor rotates freely and does not rub on the stator before buttoning up the side case.

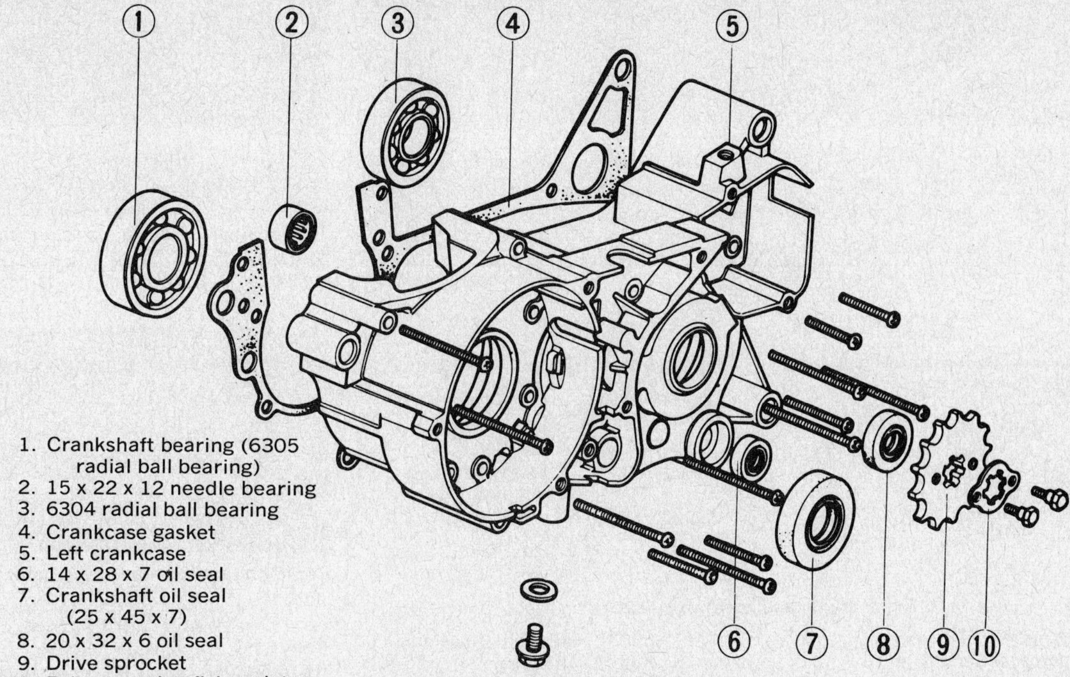

Left crankcase assembly (125)

SEPARATING THE CRANKCASES

NOTE: *In addition to describing how the crankcases are disassembled, this section also deals with the removal, repair, and installation of the crankshaft, internal shifter, and transmission assemblies.*

Disassembly

1. Run the engine, if possible, until its normal operating temperature is reached, then drain the transmission oil.
2. Remove the engine from the frame as described in the "Engine Removal and Installation" Section.
3. Disassemble the cylinder head, cylinder, and piston assemblies as described in the "Top End Service" Section.
4. Remove the AC generator as described in the previous Section, then remove the drive sprocket.
5. Remove the oil pump assembly as described in the "Oil Pump" Section.
6. Remove the right-side crankcase cover, then remove the clutch, oil guide plate, primary gear, kick starter spindle, shifter spindle, shift drum stopper, and

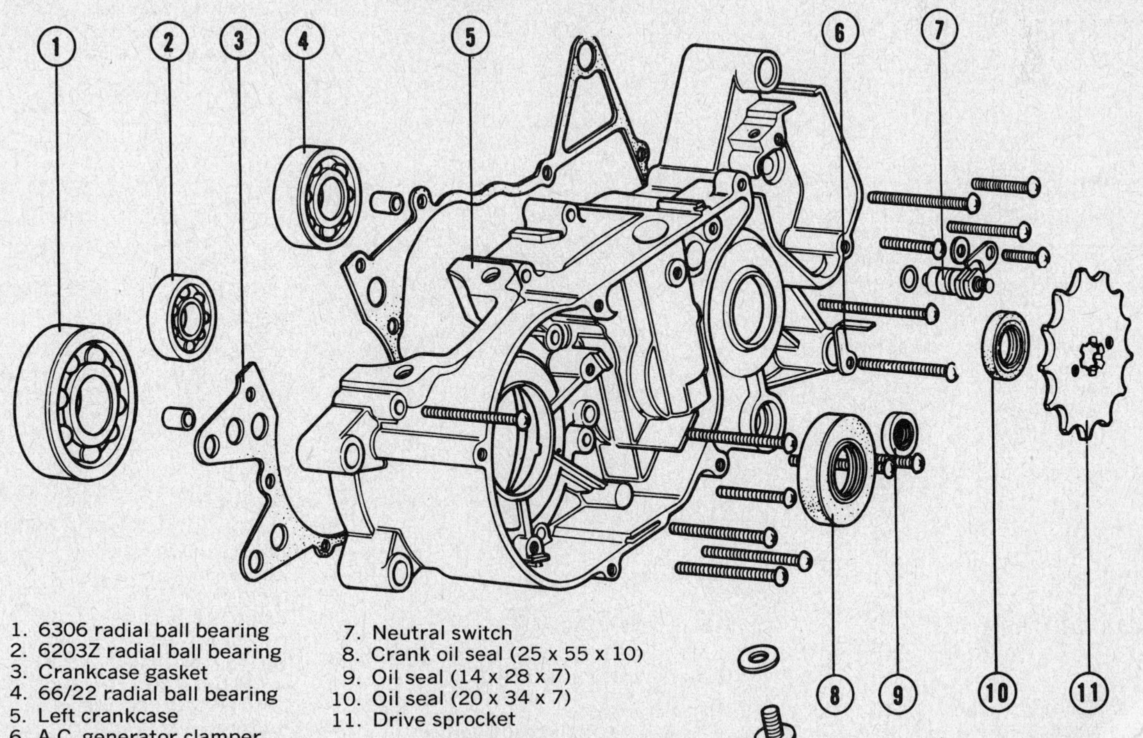

Left crankcase assembly (250)

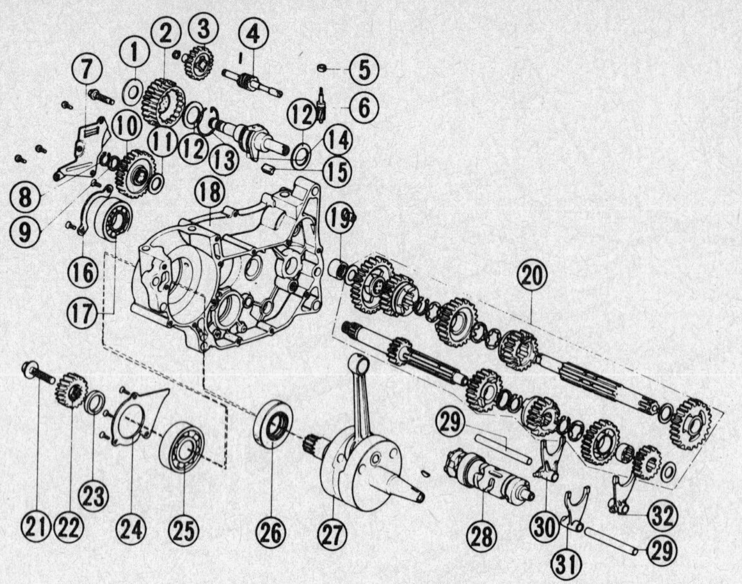

Right crankcase assembly (125)

1. 17 mm thrust washer
2. Starter pinion
3. Oil pump drive gear
4. Oil pump driveshaft
5. 4.8 x 14.5 x 4 oil seal
6. Tachometer gear
7. Oil guide plate
8. 15 mm set ring
9. 16 mm thrust washer
10. Starter idle gear
11. 16.5 mm thrust washer
12. 22 mm thrust washer
13. Starter pawl spring
14. Starter shaft
15. Starter pawl
16. Bearing set plate B
17. 6304Z radial ball bearing
18. Right crankcase
19. 1612 needle bearing
20. Transmission gears
21. 8 mm special bolt
22. Primary drive gear
23. Primary drive gear collar
24. Bearing set plate A
25. 6322 ball bearing
26. 28 x 56 x 9 oil seal
27. Crankshaft
28. Gearshift drum
29. Gearshift fork shaft
30. Right gearshift fork
31. Center gearshift fork
32. Left gearshift fork

Removing the drive sprocket (250)

1. Drive sprocket fixing plate
2. Drive sprocket
3. Oil pump

Removing the primary drive gear (125)

1. 8 mm special bolt
2. Primary drive gear
3. Drive gear holder

Removing the starter idle gear snap-ring (250 shown)

1. 17 mm snap-ring
2. 17 mm thrust washer
3. Starter idle gear
4. Bearing stopper plate
5. Bearing set plate

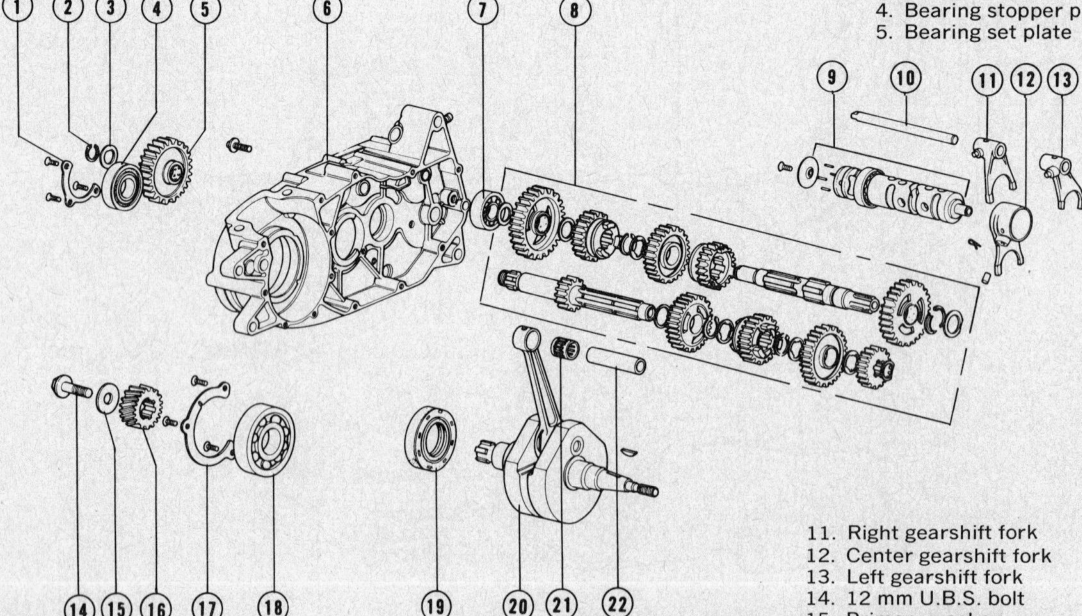

Right crankcase assembly (250)

1. Bearing stopper plate
2. 17 mm snap-ring
3. 17 mm thrust washer
4. 6205Z radial ball bearing
5. Starter idle gear
6. Right crankcase
7. 17 x 42 x 12 radial ball bearing
8. Transmission gears
9. Gearshift drum
10. Gearshift for shaft
11. Right gearshift fork
12. Center gearshift fork
13. Left gearshift fork
14. 12 mm U.B.S. bolt
15. Primary washer
16. Primary drive gear
17. Bearing set plate
18. 6306 radial ball bearing
19. 38 x 64 x 13 crank oil seal
20. Crankshaft
21. Connecting rod small end bearing
22. Piston pin

Removing the oil guide plate (125)

1. Oil guide plate
2. Plate mounting screws

Removing the starter pinion thrust washer (125)

1. Snap-ring
2. Starter idle gear
3. Starter pinion
4. Thrust washer

Fourteen (1) crankcase securing screws (125)

Thirteen (1) crankcase securing screws (250)

neutral stopper as described in the appropriate preceding Sections.

NOTE: *On the 125, the primary drive gear is removed by securing it with the drive gear holder (Tool No. 07924-3600000), which is mounted using the right crankcase cover mounting screws, and then removing the 8 mm bolt.*

7. Remove the snap-ring which secures the starter idle gear, then remove the gear.

8. Remove the bearing set plate and bearing stopper plate (250), then remove the starter pinion thrust washer and pinion (125).

9. Remove the crankcase securing screws, then mount the two studs of the crankcase puller (Tool No. 07937-360000 for the 125, or 07937-3580000 for the 250) into the two 8 mm holes in the left crankcase. Screw the puller in while tapping on the countershaft, and along the crankcase mating surface, with a soft-faced mallet until the case halves separate.

CAUTION: *Do not beat on the rotor shaft with a hammer, and do not attempt to pry the case halves apart as this may damage the mating surface.*

10. Remove the oil seals and ball bearings.

Separating the case halves

1. Crankcase puller
2. Left crankcase
3. Right crankcase

11. Remove the clutch actuating lever mounting bolt, lever, lever spring, oil seal, and needle bearing.

12. Remove the neutral switch plate and the neutral switch.

13. Remove the shift fork shafts and the left-side shift fork, then remove the transmission, gearshift drum, and the remaining two shift forks as a complete assembly.

14. Remove the crankshaft from the case by giving the end of the shaft which protrudes through the bearing a sharp rap with a soft-faced mallet.

15. Remove the tachometer drive gear, the kickstarter stopper pin, the shift return spring, and the ball bearings.

NOTE: *The crankshaft bearing cannot be removed until the oil seal has been disposed of.*

Inspection

1. Clean all parts in a suitable solvent, then blow them dry. Gaskets, O-rings, oil seals, snap-rings, circlips, lockwashers with locking tabs which must be bent, and keys should be replaced.

2. Check the bearings for a loose fit in their housings, excessive play, wear, damage, or rough motion, and replace them as necessary.

3. Inspect the crankcases and their mating surfaces for cracks, damage, or irregularities, and repair or replace them as necessary.

4. Check the connecting rod big end for axial and radial play, and replace the crankshaft assembly if play is excessive, or if the crankcase is damaged in any way.

Removing the shift fork shaft (1) and the left fork (2)

Removing the transmission components

1. Countershaft
2. Mainshaft
3. Gearshift drum
4. Center gearshift fork
5. Right gearshift fork

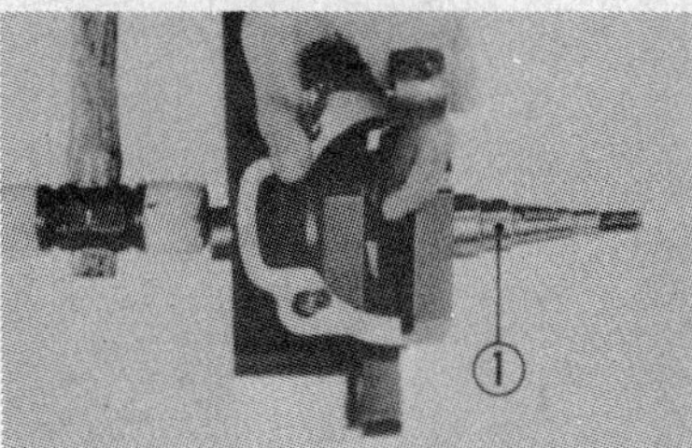

Removing the crankshaft (1)

Bearing installation with the factory driver

1. Left crankcase
2. Bearing attachment
3. Driver handle

5. Inspect the transmission assembly for worn, chipped, pitted, or otherwise damaged gears, and replace them, preferably in sets, as necessary.

6. Measure the shift drum outside diameter, the shift forks inside diameter, the shift fork guide shaft outside diameter, and the shift fork finger thickness, and replace any components which are worn past their serviceable limits, or are damaged in any way.

Assembly

1. Assembly is basically in the reverse order of disassembly. Make sure that all

components are completely clean, and use plenty of lubricant when installing the assemblies.

2. Install the ball bearings using, if possible, the ball bearing driver attachment (Tool No. 07946-360000 for the 125, or 07946-3570000 for the 250). If necessary, the bearings can be driven in with a suitable drift, or by using a wood block and hammer.

NOTE: *The countershaft bearing on the 125 is installed with Tool No. 07946-9370100.*

CAUTION: *When driving bearings in, go from the inside of the case out, and always place the case on a suitable block, preferably made of iron, to avoid damage to the crankcase.*

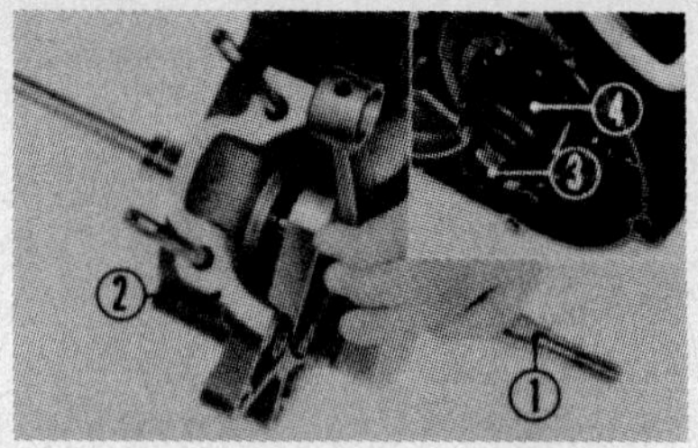

Installing the crankshaft in the right case

1. Crankshaft
2. Right crankcase
3. 12 mm UBS bolt
4. Primary drive gear

3. Grease the lips of the oil seals when installing them. If you nick or distort a seal lip during installation, the seal should be replaced.

4. Install the crankshaft in the right-side crankcase. The primary drive gear can be used to draw the crankshaft into the case by tightening up the 12 mm bolt.

5. Install the shift drum and center fork as shown in the accompanying illustration.

6. Assemble the transmission components as shown in the accompanying illustrations.

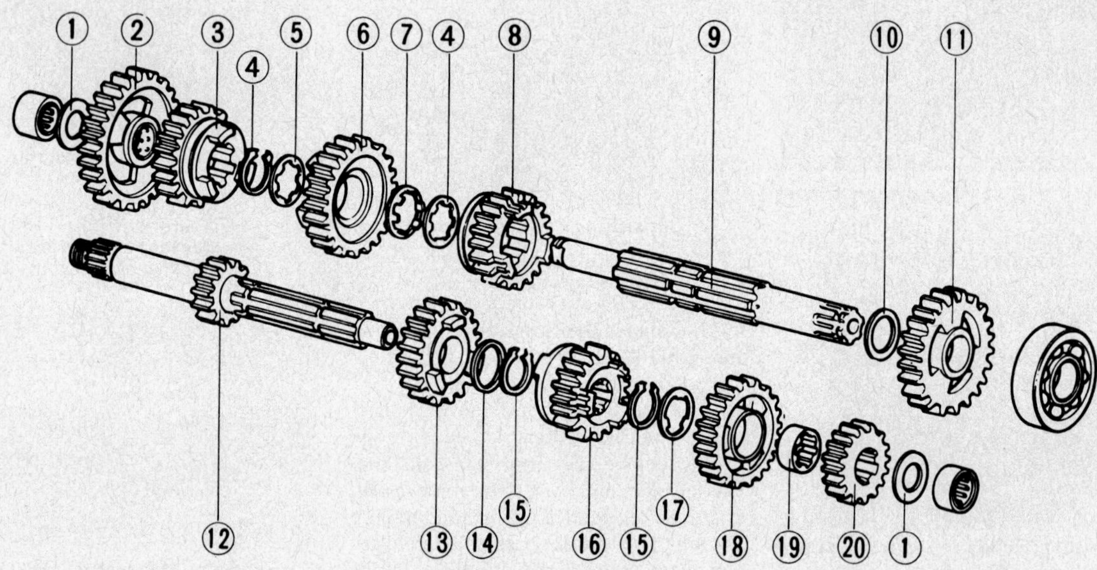

Transmission assembly (125)

1. 16.5 mm thrust washers
2. Countershaft Low gear
3. Countershaft Fourth gear
4. C-3 set ring
5. C-3 splined washer
6. Countershaft Third gear
7. Lockwasher
8. Countershaft Fifth gear
9. Countershaft
10. 30 mm thrust washer
11. Countershaft Second gear
12. Mainshaft
13. Mainshaft Fourth gear
14. 20 mm thrust washer
15. 20 mm set ring
16. Mainshaft Third gear
17. 20 mm splined washer
18. Mainshaft Fifth gear
19. M-5 gear splined washer
20. Mainshaft Second gear

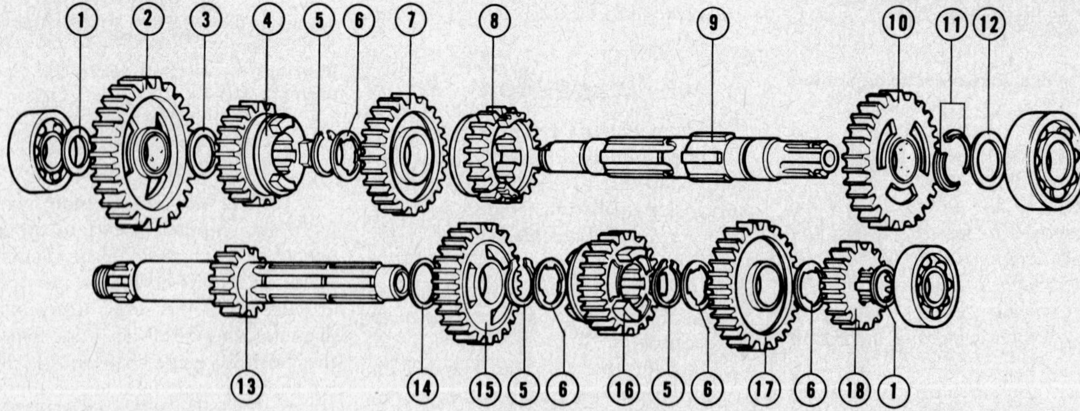

Transmission assembly (250)

1. 17.2 mm thrust washer
2. Countershaft Low gear
3. 18.6 mm thrust washer
4. Countershaft 4th gear
5. 22 mm snap-ring
6. 22 mm spline washer
7. Countershaft 3rd gear
8. Countershaft 5th gear
9. Countershaft
10. Countershaft 2nd gear
11. Countershaft cotters
12. 23 mm thrust washer
13. Mainshaft
14. 22 mm thrust washer
15. Mainshaft 4th gear
16. Mainshaft 3rd gear
17. Mainshaft 5th gear
18. Mainshaft 2nd gear

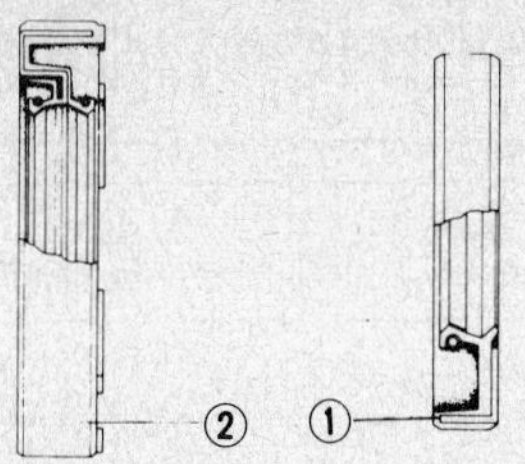
1. Left crankcase oil seal
2. Right crankcase oil seal

Left (1) and right (2) crankcase oil seals

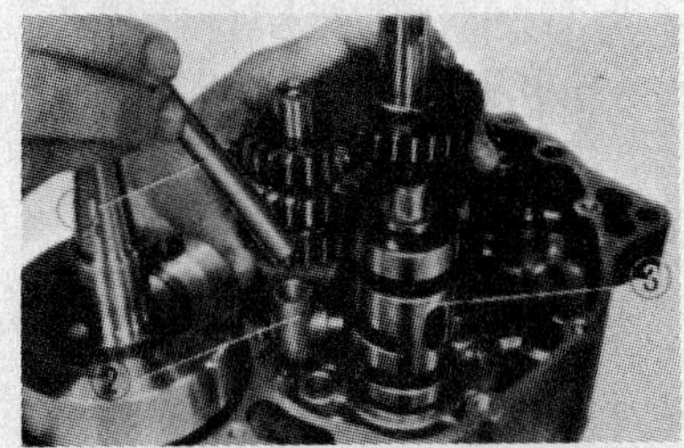

Gearshift shaft (1), center shift fork (2), and shift drum (3) installed

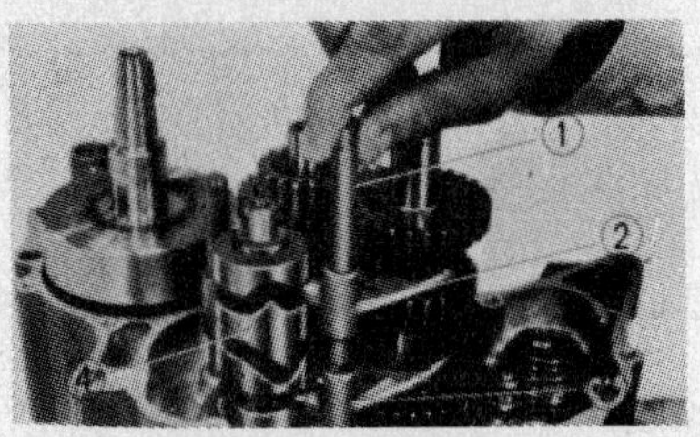

Installing the shift forks
1. Gearshift shaft
2. Left gearshift fork
3. Right gearshift fork
4. Gearshift drum

7. Install the right shift fork (the forks are marked "R" and "L") to the countershaft 4th gear, and the left fork to the countershaft 5th gear, making sure that the fork fingers and gear teeth are properly meshed.

NOTE: *The identifying marks should face toward the left.*

8. Install the center shift fork to the mainshaft 3rd gear, then install the transmission and shift drum assemblies into the right-side crankcase at the same time.

9. Make sure that the mainshaft 25 mm thrust washer and the countershaft 23 mm thrust washer and cotters are properly positioned, then install the left-side crankcase while taking care not to damage the mainshaft bearing oil seal.

NOTE: *Grease the countershaft cotters to keep them in place during installation.*

10. Assemble the case halves using the crankcase assembly tool (Tool No. 07965-3610000), or a suitable substitute. Work slowly.

11. Secure the 14 crankcase screws in a criss-cross pattern to their specified torque, then rotate the crankshaft to check for smooth motion.

ENGINE SPECIFICATIONS

Item	Assembly Standard in. (mm)	Service Limit in. (mm)
MT-125		
Cylinder bore	2.2047-2.2051 (56.00-56.01)	2.2087 (56.1)
Piston OD	2.2024-2.2031 (55.94-55.96)	2.1988 (55.85)
Piston pin hole diameter	0.5513-0.5515 (14.002-14.008)	0.5531 (14.05)
Piston pin OD	0.5509-0.5512 (13.994-14.000)	0.5504 (13.98)
Piston ring groove side-clearane top	0.0012-0.0030 (0.030-0.075)	0.0035 (0.09)
Piston ring groove side-clearance 2nd	0.0010-0.0022 (0.025-0.055)	0.0028 (0.07)
Piston ring end-gap	0.0059-0.0138 (0.15-0.35)	0.0197 (0.50)
Connecting rod big end axial clearance	0.0059-0.0236 (0.15-0.60)	0.0276 (0.70)
Connecting rod big end radial clearance	0.0003-0.0008 (0.008-0.020)	0.0012 (0.03)
Clutch friction disc thickness	0.1031-0.1094 (2.62-2.78)	0.0945 (2.40)
Clutch plate face run-out	0.0059 (0.15)	0.0098 (0.25)
Clutch spring free length	1.3780 (35.0)	1.3583 (34.5)
Clutch spring tension	24.3/14.74 kg (0.9567/32.5 lbs)	—
Transmission gear backlash	—	0.0787 (0.2)
Shift fork guide shaft OD	0.3926-0.3932 (9.972-9.987)	0.3906 (9.92)
Gearshift fork ID	0.3937-0.3944 (10.000-10.018)	0.3957 (10.05)
Shift fork finger thickness	0.1929-0.1941 (4.90-4.93)	0.1772 (4.5)
MT-250		
Cylinder bore	2.7559-2.7563 (70.0-70.01)	2.7598 (70.1)
Piston OD	2.7531-2.7539 (69.93-69.95)	2.7480 (69.8)
Piston pin hole diameter	0.7087-0.7090 (18.002-18.008)	0.7126 (18.1)
Piston pin OD	0.7083-0.7087 (17.992-18.000)	0.7079 (17.98)
Piston ring side-clearance top	0.0018-0.0030 (0.045-0.075)	0.0035 (0.09)
Piston ring side-clearance 2nd	0.0010-0.0022 (0.025-0.055)	0.0028 (0.07)
Piston ring end-gap top	0.0079-0.0157 (0.2-0.4)	0.0197 (0.5)
Piston ring end-gap 2nd	0.0079-0.0157 (0.2-0.4)	0.0197 (0.5)
Connecting rod small end ID	0.8660-0.8665 (21.997-22.009)	—
Connecting rod big end axial clearance	0.0079-0.0157 (0.2-0.4)	0.0236 (0.6)
Connecting rod big end radial clearance	0.0004-0.0009 (0.010-0.022)	0.0012 (0.03)
Clutch friction disc thickness	0.1031-0.1094 (2.62-2.78)	0.0945 (2.4)
Clutch plate face run-out	0.0059 (0.15)	0.0098 (0.25)
Clutch spring free length	1.6220 (41.2)	1.5748 (40.0)
Clutch spring tension	22.5/21 kg (0.8858/46 lbs)	20.5/21 kg (0.8071/46 lbs)
Transmission gear backlash	—	0.0079 (0.2)
Gearshift fork drum OD	1.3366-1.3376 (33.95-33.975)	1.3346 (33.9)
Center gearshift fork ID	1.3386-1.3396 (34.00-34.025)	1.3417 (34.08)
Shift fork guide shaft OD	0.4715-0.4722 (11.976-11.994)	0.4693 (11.92)
R/H & L/H gearshift fork ID	0.4724-0.4731 (12.00-12.018)	0.4744 (12.05)
Shift fork finger thickness	0.1941-0.1969 (4.93-5.0)	0.1811 (4.6)

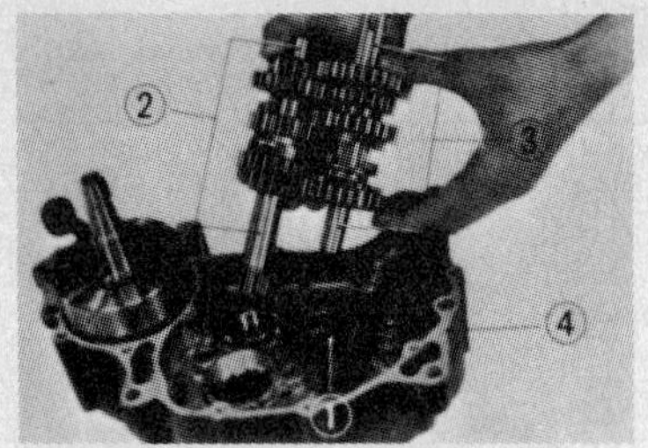

Fitting the transmission assemblies into the case

1. 16.5 mm thrust washer
2. Mainshaft gears
3. Countershaft gears
4. Right crankcase

Installing the mainshaft (1) and countershaft (2) thrust washers

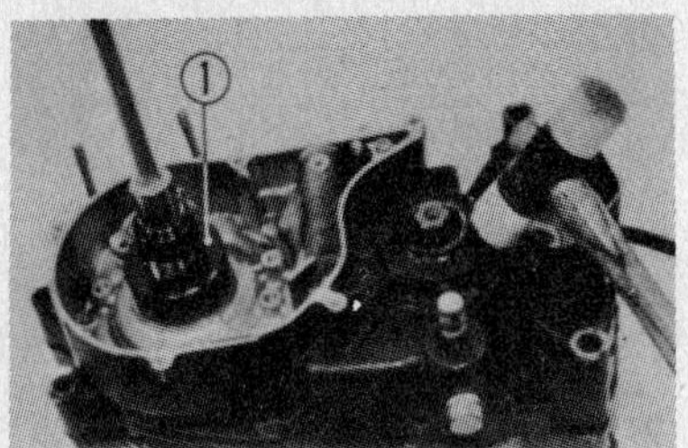

Assembling the cases with the factory tool (1)

Checking for smooth motion

Bearing set plates (1 and 2) and mounting screws (3)

12. Install and secure the bearing set plate and stopper plate screws, then flare out the plate.

13. Install the oil pump as described in the "Oil Pump" Section.

ENGINE TORQUE SPECIFICATIONS

Tightening Point	Thread Dia. (mm)	Torque in. (mm)
MT-125		
Drive sprocket	6	5.8-8.7 (0.8-1.2)
Clutch center	14	27.5-32.5 (3.8-4.5)
Clutch pressure plate	6	5.1-7.2 (0.7-1.0)
A.C. generator rotor	8	13.0-16.6 (1.8-2.3)
Cylinder head special nut	8	14.5-16.6 (2.0-2.3)
Primary drive gear	8	25.3-28.9 (3.5-4.0)
Carburetor insulator band	6	5.8-9.0 (0.8-1.25)
Cylinder	8	14.5-16.6 (2.0-2.3)
Crankcase cover	6	5.1-7.2 (0.7-1.0)
MT-250		
Drive sprocket	6	5.8-8.7 (0.8-1.2)
Drum stopper	6	5.8-8.7 (0.8-1.2)
Neutral stopper	6	5.8-8.7 (0.8-1.2)
Exhaust pipe muffler	6	5.8-8.7 (0.8-1.2)
Clutch center	18	28.9-32.5 (4.0-4.5)
Clutch pressure plate	6	5.8-8.7 (0.8-1.2)
AC generator rotor	12	32.5-36.2 (4.5-5.0)
Cylinder head flanged nut	6	7.2-9.4 (1.0-1.3)
Cylinder head special nut	8	14.5-18.1 (2.0-2.5)
Primary drive gear	12	36.2-43.4 (5.0-6.0)
Spark plug	14	10.8-14.5 (1.5-2.0)
Carburetor insulator band	5	3.6-5.1 (0.5-0.7)
5 mm special bolt	5	2.2-2.9 (0.3-0.4)

14. Install the primary drive gear, but do not secure it, install the clutch assembly as described in the "Clutch" Section, then secure the drive gear using the drive sprocket holder and a suitable wrench.

15. Complete the assembly and installation in the reverse order of disassembly. Be certain to fill the oil tank and transmission with fresh oil, perform all the necessary tune-up and maintenance operations, and run the engine mildly, and below half-throttle, for at least ten minutes before putting a heavy load on the engine. The transmission oil should be changed again in 500 miles.

FUEL SYSTEMS

CARBURETOR

Removal and Disassembly

1. Clean the carburetor and surrounding area thoroughly, place the petcock lever in the "OFF" position, and disconnect the gas line at the carburetor.

2. Remove the intake pipe mounting bolts, remove the connecting tube hose clamp, and separate the carburetor and inlet pipe from the engine.

NOTE: *Clean rags should be used to prevent dirt from getting into the cylinder and air cleaner.*

3. Unscrew the carburetor top and withdraw the throttle valve (slide) from the carburetor bore.

NOTE: *If the slide assembly is not to be disassembled, place it in a plastic bag to keep it clean, and place it, still attached to the cable, out of the way.*

4. Remove the insulator band and disconnect ưe inlet pipe from the carburetor.

5. Remove the needle clip and plate, remove the needle, compress the spring, disconnect the cable from the slide, remove the rubber cap, and disconnect the cable from the carburetor top.

Disconnecting the gas line (2). Petcock (1) is "OFF".

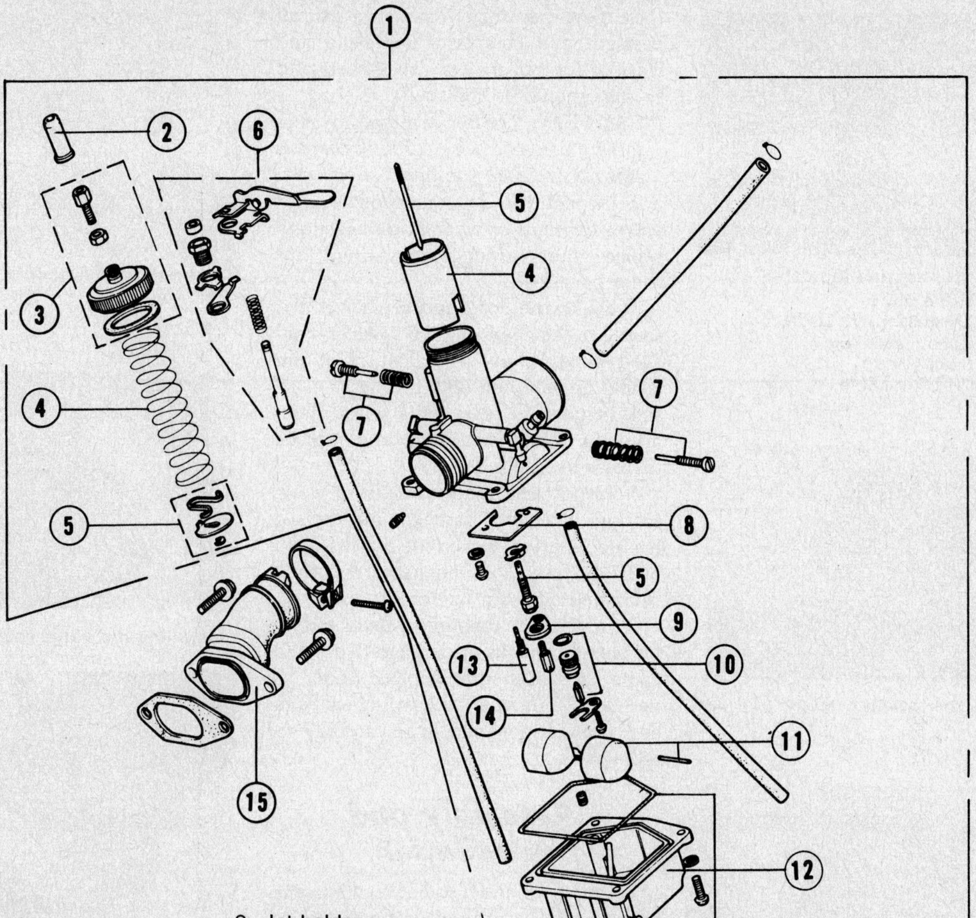

1. Carburetor assy.
2. Rubber cap
3. Top set
4. Throttle valve set
5. Jet needle set
6. Starter valve set
7. Screw set
8. Baffle plate
9. Jet holder
10. Float valve set
11. Float set
12. Float chamber set
13. Slow jet
14. Main jet
15. Inlet pipe

Carburetor assembly

Carburetor mounting points

1. Inlet pipe tightening boi.
2. Carburetor top
3. Connecting tube band

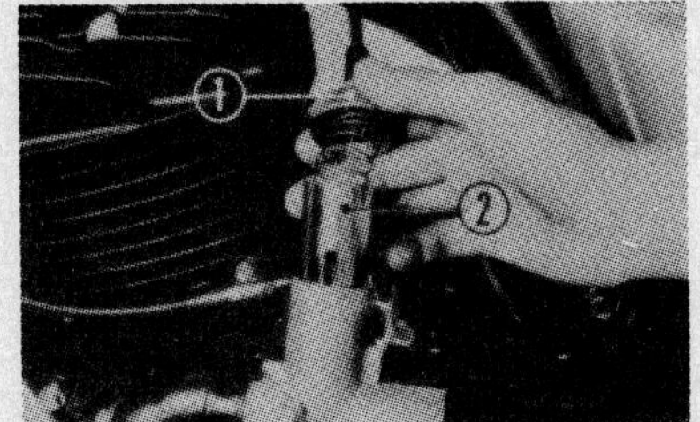

Unscrew the top (1) and withdraw the slide (2)

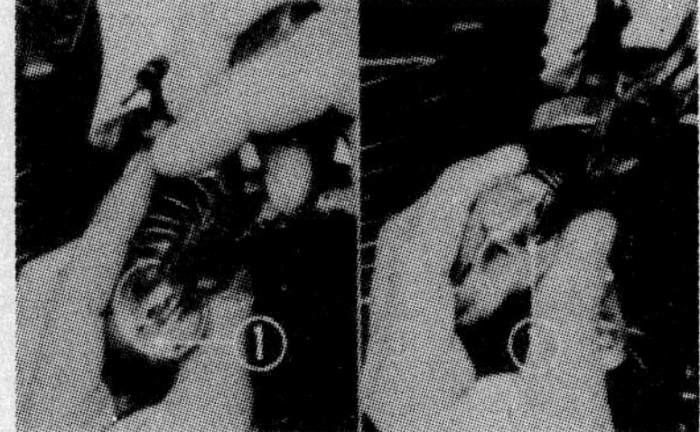

Removing the needle clip plate (1)

6. Remove the starter valve by bending back the lockwasher locking tab and removing the locknut, then pull the starter lever from the starter valve, and the starter valve from the carburetor.

7. Remove the carburetor sealing bolt (drain bolt) from the bottom of the float chamber cover. Be prepared to catch the gas in a suitable receptacle.

8. Remove the 4 screws which secure the float chamber to the carburetor body.

NOTE: *If you are just trying to remove the main jet, this can be done through the drain bolt opening without removing the float chamber.*

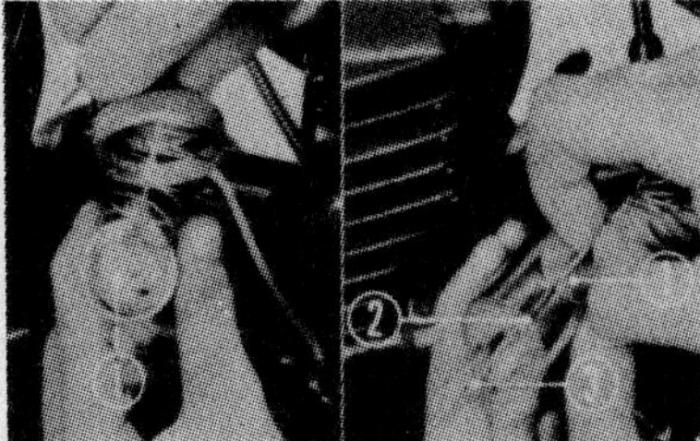

Removing the cable (2) from the valve plate (1). Note that the needle (3) remains in the valve.

9. Remove the float pin and float, then remove the screw which secures the valve seat set plate, and remove the plate and seat.

CAUTION: *The valve may come out with the float, so be careful not to lose it.*

10. Remove the main jet, jet holder, needle jet, and the needle jet plate.

Inspection and Repair

1. Clean all parts in a suitable solvent,

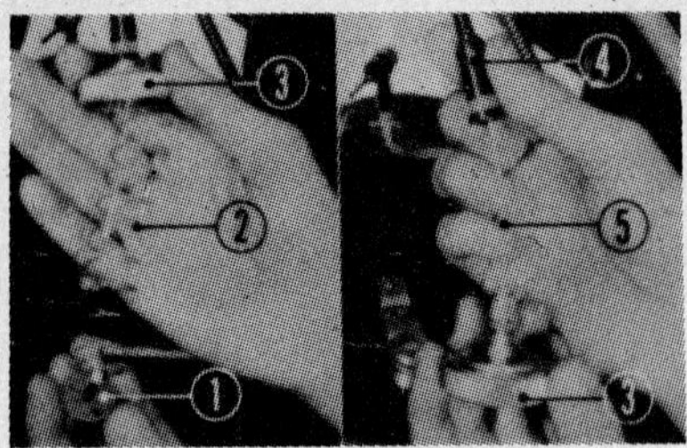

Disconnecting the cable
1. Valve plate
2. Throttle valve spring
3. Carburetor top
4. Rubber cap
5. Throttle cable

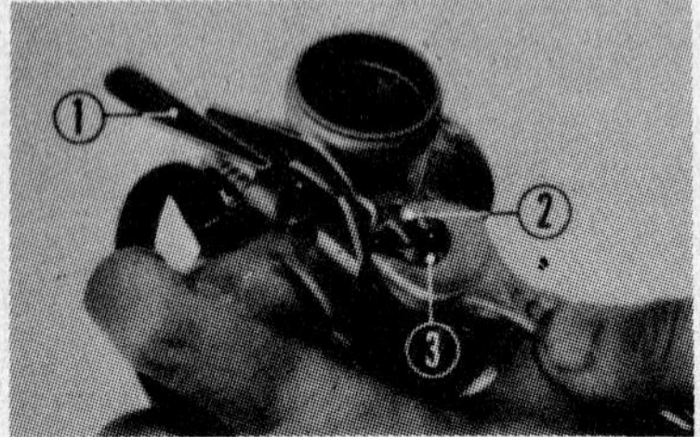

Removing the starter lever (1) and valve (2)

Remove the sealing bolt (1)

Float chamber body (1), main jet (2), and chamber mounting screws (3)

Withdrawing the float pin
1. Float pin
2. Float
3. Valve seat set plate
4. Valve seat

then blow them dry. Make sure that all passages and chambers are clean and clear of foreign matter. All gaskets and O-rings should be replaced.

CAUTION: *Do not attempt to clear jets by poking a wire through them as this may scratch the bore.*

2. Inspect the jets, jet needle, and valves for signs of wear or damage, and replace them as necessary. Blunt tips cause poor seals.

3. Shake the float, and replace it if it sounds fuel-logged, or if it is worn or damaged in any way. The float pivot pin should be replaced with the float.

4. Inspect all seats for a worn, damaged, or pitted condition, and replace them as necessary.

5. Inspect the slide for signs of wear, scoring, pitting, or damage, and replace it as necessary. A worn slide may hang up or fail to fully close. Slight burrs can be smoothed out with fine emery cloth.

6. Inspect the carburetor body and inlet pipe for cracks or damage that could cause air leaks, and replace them as necessary. The inlet pipe will crack from age, and therefore should be carefully inspected.

Assembly and Installation

1. Assembly and installation are in the reverse order of removal and disassembly. If a rebuild kit is available, use all the parts that come in it rather than only those which you know to be worn or damaged. Keep the parts clean during the assembly procedure.

2. Install the valve seat set plate as shown in the accompanying illustration. Make sure that you don't install it upside down.

3. Adjust the float height in the following manner:

a. Hold the carburetor so that the main bore is in a vertical position. The float arm tang should close the float valve without compressing the spring-loaded plunger in the end of the valve.

b. Measure float height with a float level gauge. The distance between the carburetor body and the opposite edge of the float should be 0.94 in. (24 mm) for the 125, and 0.79 in. (20 mm) for the 250, just as the float valve closes.

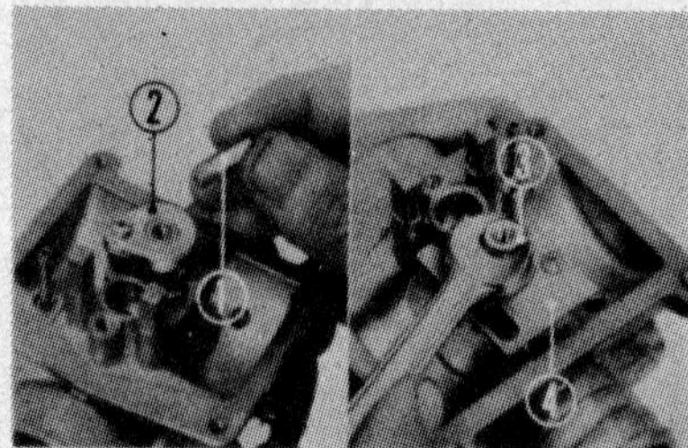

Removing the jets
1. Main jet
2. Jet holder
3. Jet needle
4. Baffle plate

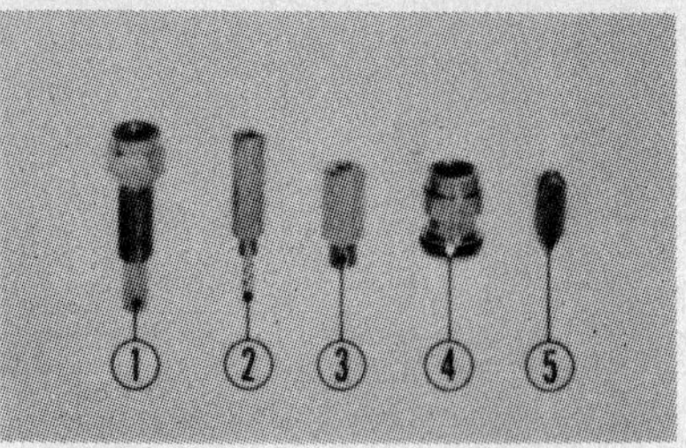

These parts must be in perfect condition
1. Jet needle
2. Slow jet
3. Main jet
4. Valve seat
5. Float valve

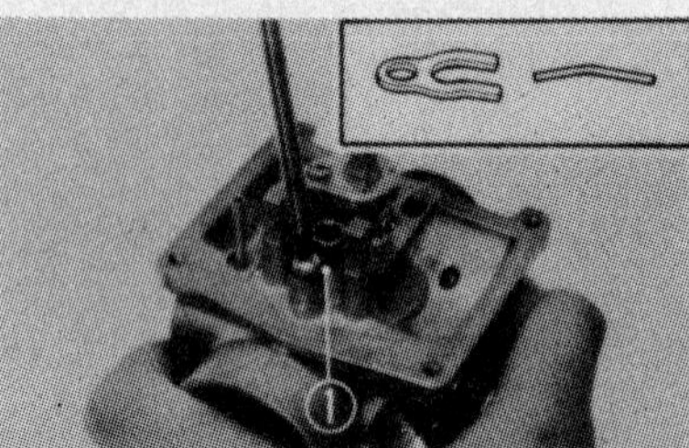

Installing the valve seat set plate (1)

Measuring float (1) height adjustment using the factory tool (2)

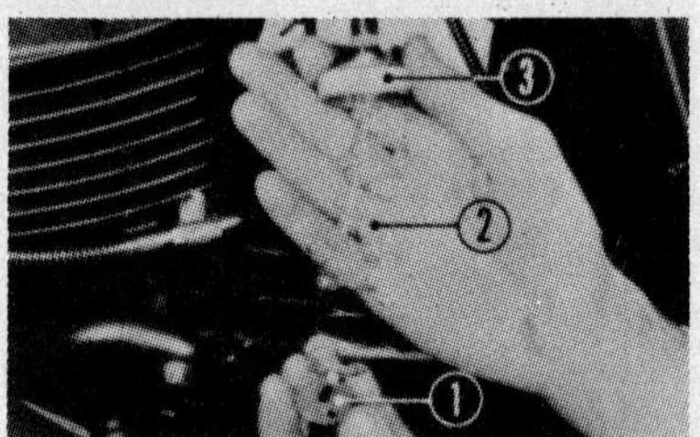

Seat the spring (2) in the carburetor top (3), and run the cable through the spring to the valve plate (1)

c. Adjust the float height, as necessary, by carefully bending the float arm tang toward or away from the valve until the specified height is achieved. Be sure to bend the tang straight.

4. When installing the jet needle in its clip in the slide, use the middle groove to obtain the stock setting. Raising the needle richens the mixture, and lowering it leans it out.

5. Assemble the slide components in the order shown in the accompanying illustration.

6. Install the starter valve lever, secure the nut, and bend up the lockwasher locking tab against a flat of the nut. Make sure that the starter lever operates smoothly.

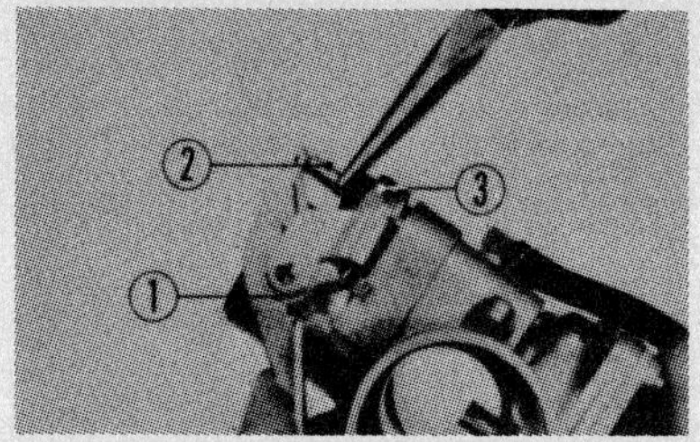

Installing the starter lever (1) and valve (2)

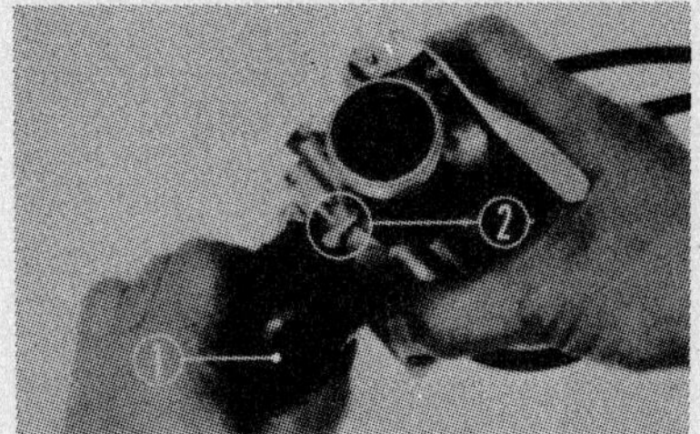

Fitting the inlet pipe (1) to the carburetor body boss (2)

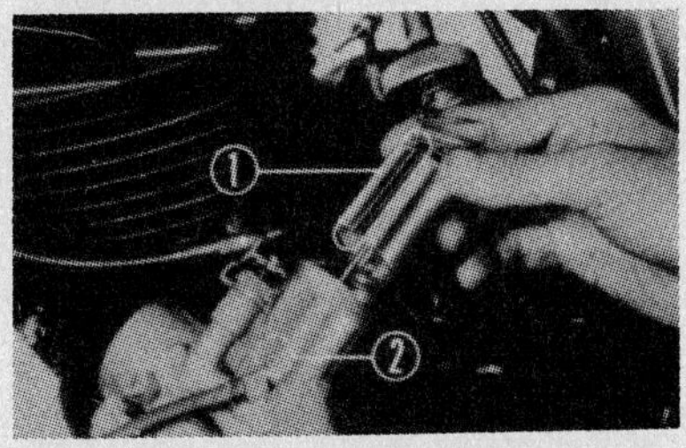

The groove (1) in the valve must mesh with the lug (2) in the bore

7. When installing the inlet pipe to the carburetor body, make sure that the pipe recess meshes with the carb body lug.

8. Install the carb on the air cleaner side first.

9. When installing the slide assembly, make sure not to foul the tip of the jet needle, and make sure that the groove cut in the side of the slide meshes with the lug on the inside of the carb body.

10. Rout the carburetor tubing as shown in the accompanying illustration.

11. Run the engine until its normal operating temperature is reached, then adjust the mixture and idle speed.

CARBURETOR SPECIFICATIONS

Model	MT-125	MT-250
Main jet (standard)①	98	122
Slow jet (standard)	50	60
Air jet (standard)	200	200
Air screw opening	1-1½	1-1½
Idle speed (rpm)	1500	1500
Float height	0.94 in. (24 mm)	0.79 in. (20 mm)
Jet needle position	middle groove	middle groove

① All over- and undersize jets are available in 5 cc increments.

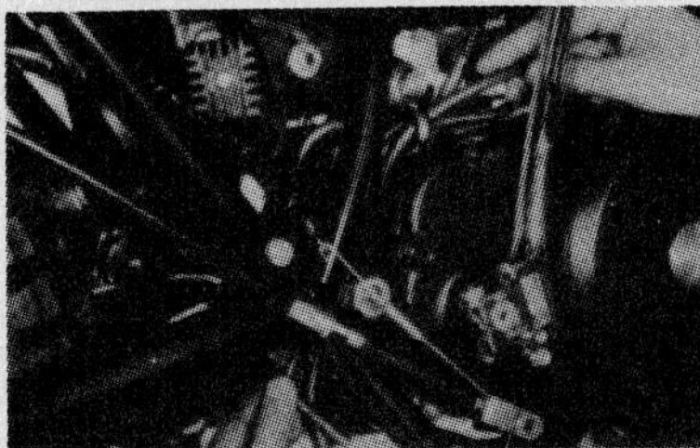
Route the hoses as shown

ELECTRICAL SYSTEMS

CHARGING SYSTEM

AC Generator Output Test

NOTE: *In order to obtain accurate results from this test, the battery must be fully charged. Charge the battery, as necessary, until the specific gravity of the electrolyte is 1.260-1.280 at 20°C (68°F).*

1. Connect the ammeter negative lead (−) to the battery positive terminal (+), and the wire harness to the ammeter positive lead.

2. Connect the leads of a voltmeter to the positive and negative battery terminals.

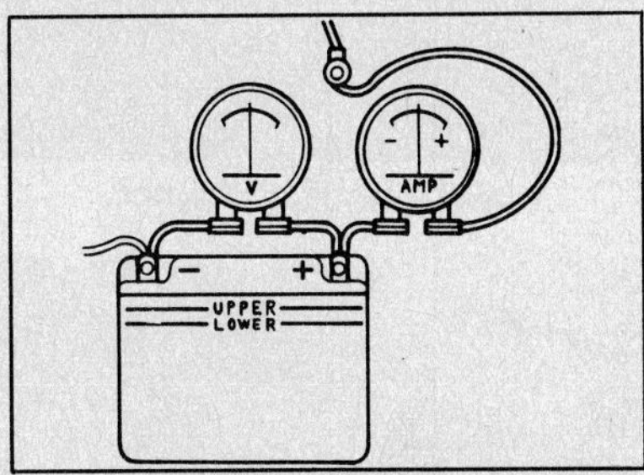

Output test circuit

3. Start the engine and simulate "NIGHTTIME RIDING" and "DAYTIME RIDING" by turning the lights on and off. Check the ammeter and voltmeter readings at each of the engine speeds given in the "Charging Characteristic Chart". If the two values are very different, check the generator in the manner described in the next section.

NOTE: *The output of the generator may vary slightly due to atmospheric conditions.*

AC Generator Stator Test

The stator cannot be repaired, however it can be tested for continuity and resistance using a meter. Excessive resistance, or a lack of continuity, indicates the need for replacement. Check for continuity between:

1. Black/white wire and stator
2. White/yellow wire and stator
3. Pink and yellow wires

	Beginning of Charging		5000 rpm		7500 rpm	
Engine rpm	MT-125	MT-250	MT-125	MT-250	MT-125	MT-250
DAYTIME RIDING						
Charging current	700 rpm max.	1000 rpm max.	2.8A min.	1.5A min.	4.0A max.	4.0A max.
Battery voltage	7.2V	6.3V	8.8V	8.0V	8.9V	8.9V
NIGHTTIME RIDING						
Charging current	2000 rpm max.	1500 rpm max.	0.8A min.	1.2A min.	1.3A min.	1.5A min.
Battery voltage	7.1V	6.3V	8.4V	7.5V	8.6V	8.3V

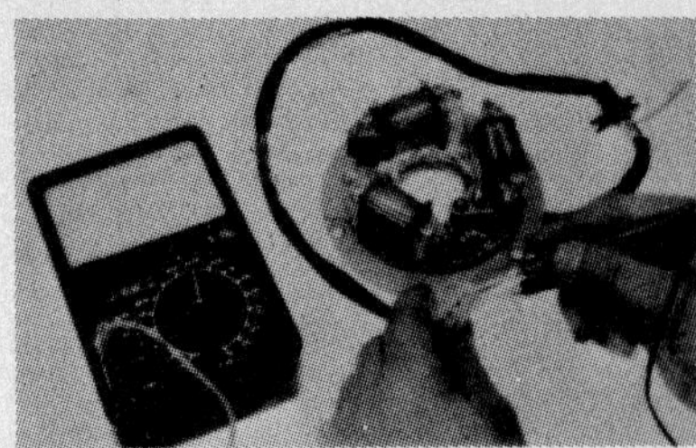
Testing the stator

Silicon rectifier mounted

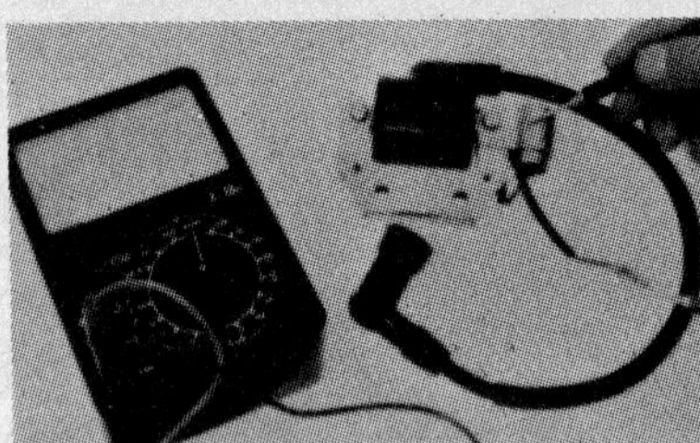
Testing the rectifier

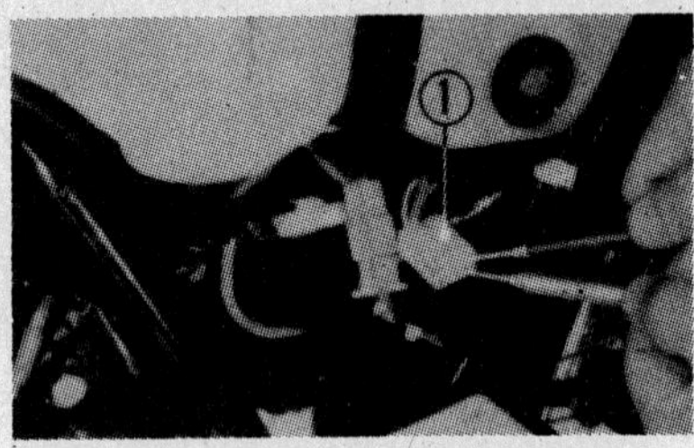

Testing the condenser

Silicon Rectifier Test

The silicon rectifier cannot be repaired, however the diodes can be checked for continuity in each direction. An ohmmeter, set for the K Ω range, should be used. Continuity, or no continuity in both directions indicates a need for replacement.

CAUTION: *Beware of high-voltage input to the rectifier as this may damage the diodes. Make sure that the battery is connected correctly, as reverse polarization may result in damage to the wiring harness or the rectifier. Disconnect the rectifier coupler before recharging the battery from an outside source.*

IGNITION SYSTEM

Ignition Coil Continuity Test

1. Test the primary winding using a tester set in the Ω range. There should be continuity between the attaching stay and the black/white lead.

2. Test the secondary winding with the tester in the Ω range. There should be continuity between the attaching stay and the high-tension lead.

Condenser Test

The condenser is tested with a multitester. If the capacity or resistance is too small, or if the condenser is short circuited, it must be replaced. The condenser capacity is 0.25 mf and its insulation resistance is 10M Ω (at 1,000 megger).

SWITCHES

The switches can be tested for continuity, as indicated by the following charts, and must be replaced if defective.

Main Switch

Terminal	IG	HO	BAT	E
Lead color	Black/white	Black	Red	Green
OFF	○	—	—	○ (ground)
ON		○	○	

Turn Signal Switch

Terminal	IG + terminal	R	L
Lead color	Gray	Light blue	Orange
R	○	○	
(N)			
L	○	—	○

Dimmer Switch

Terminal	IG + terminal	HB	LB
Lead color	Blue/white	Blue	White
H	○	○	
(N)	○	○	○
L	○	—	○

Ignition Switch

Terminal	IG	E
Lead color	Black/white	Green
OFF	○	○ (ground)
RUN	○	○ (ground)
OFF	○	○ (ground)

Headlight Switch

Terminal	C_1	HL	TL	HO
Lead color	White/ yellow	Brown/ white	Black/ white	Black
OFF				
(headlight symbol)	○	○	○	○

WIRING DIAGRAM

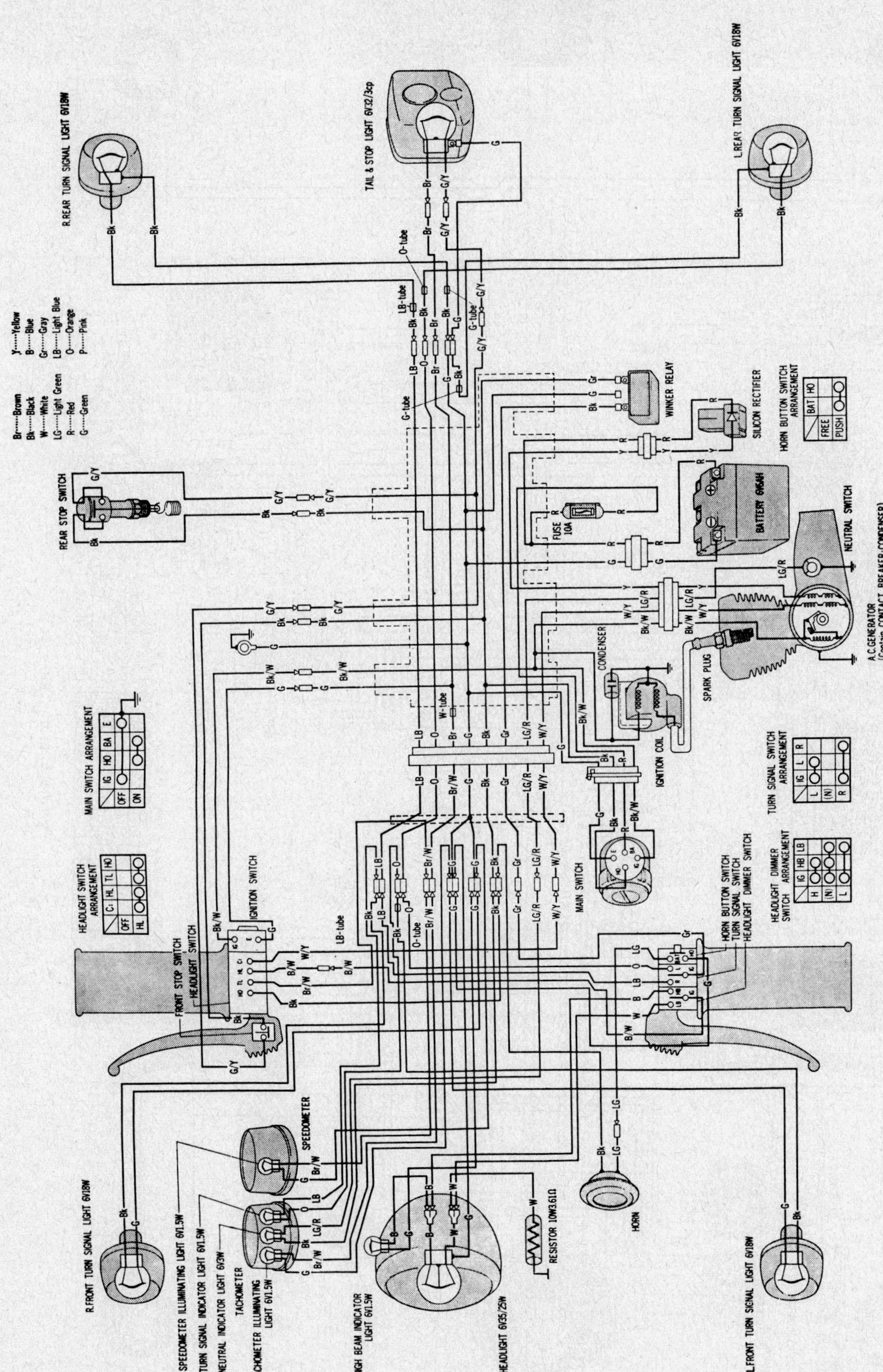

Wiring diagram (125)

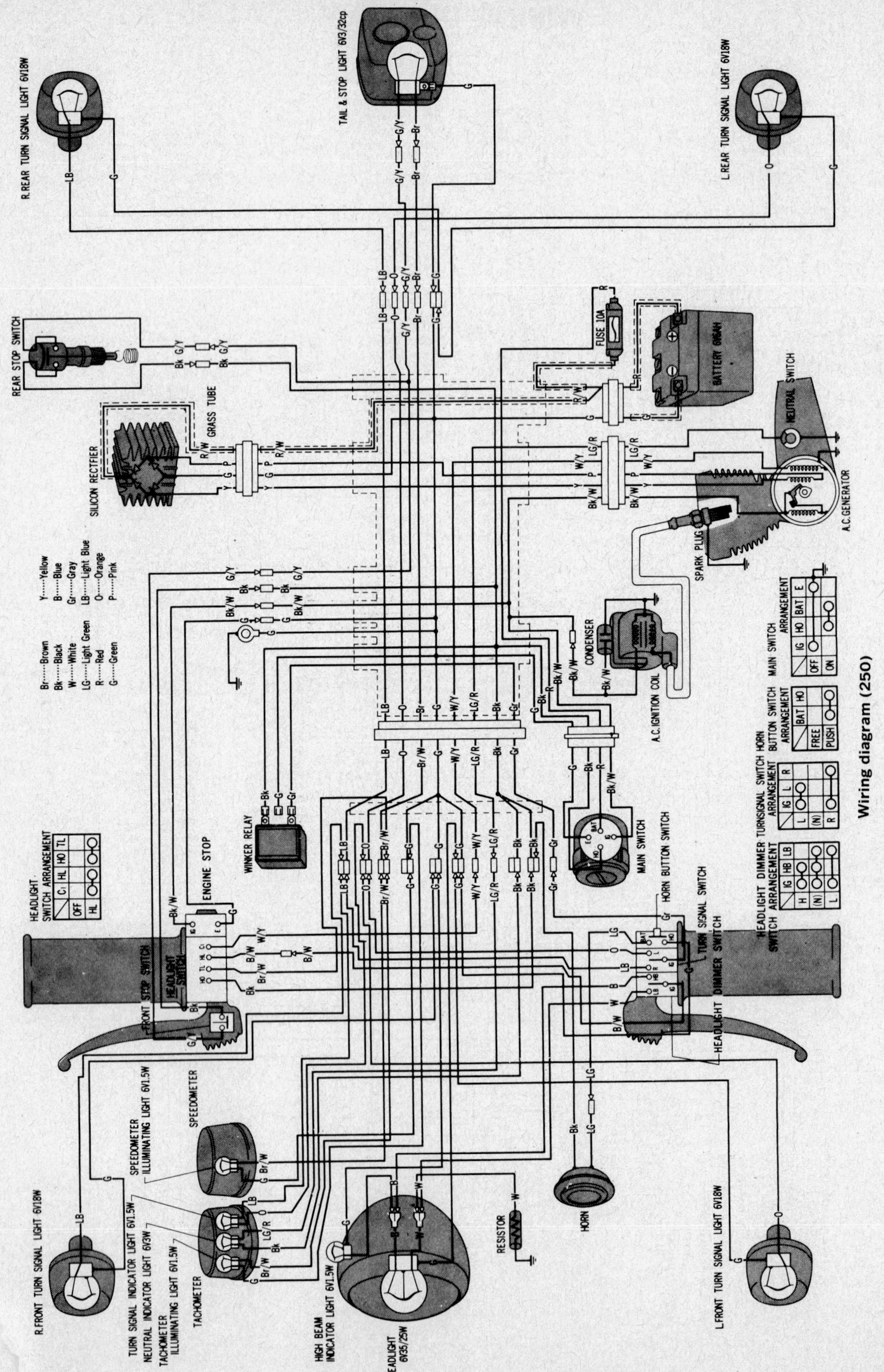

Wiring diagram (250)

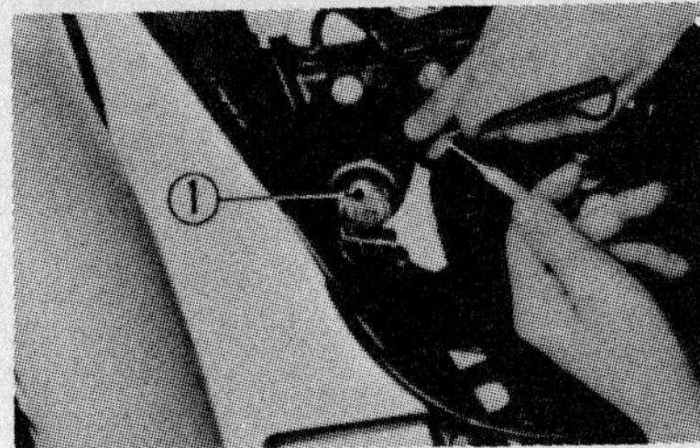
Testing the main ignition switch

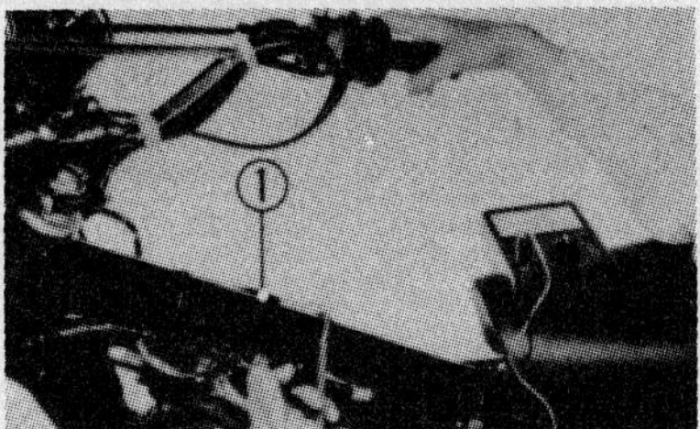
Testing the neutral switch (1)

Neutral Switch

Check continuity between the switch, and the crankcase when the transmission is in Neutral.

Front and Rear Stop Switch

Check for continuity between the green/yellow and black leads when the brake is applied.

Horn

Check for continuity between the black and the yellowish-green leads for the horn which are in the headlight shell.

Horn Button

Disconnect the turn signal/dimmer switch leads in the headlight shell (yellowish-green and green). There should be continuity when the horn button is depressed.

CHASSIS

WHEELS, HUBS, AND BRAKES

Front Wheel

REMOVAL AND INSTALLATION

MT-125

1. Block up the motorcycle so that the front wheel is off the ground, then disconnect the brake cable and the speedometer cable from the hub.
2. Remove the axle nut cotter pin, then remove the axle nut, pull out the axle, and remove the wheel. Remove the brake backing plate.

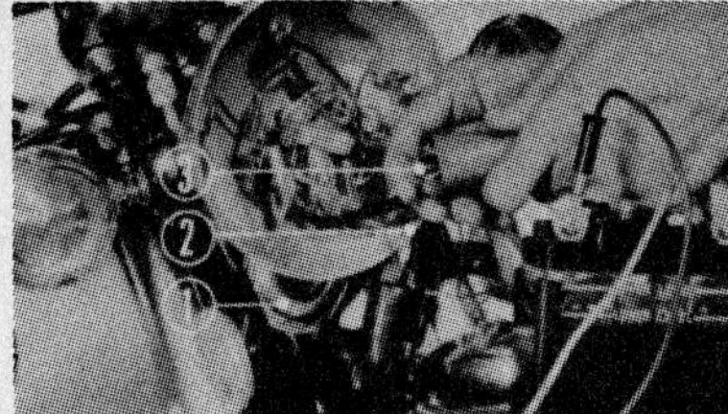
Testing the front brake light switch

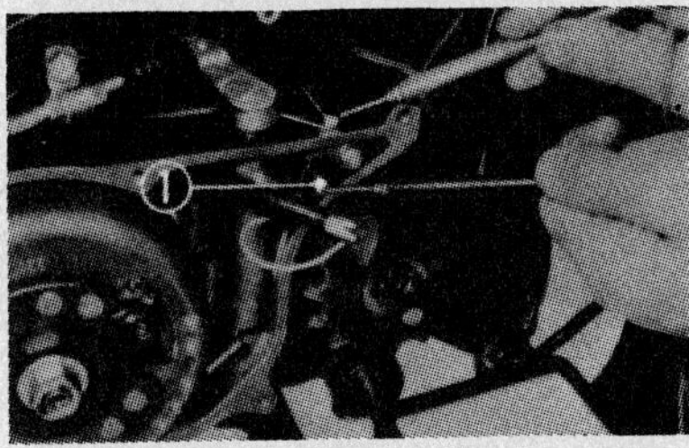
Testing the horn leads

1. Horn
2. Black cord
3. Yellowish-green cord

3. Installation is in the reverse order of removal. Use a new cotter pin.

MT-250

1. Disconnect the brake cable at the brake backing plate, then disconnect the speedometer cable.
2. Remove the 8 axle cap mounting nuts and the caps, then block up the motorcycle so that the front wheel is off the ground, and remove the wheel.
3. When installing the wheel, make sure that the axle caps are installed with the "F" mark toward the front, and secure the nuts in the order shown in the accompanying illustration. There should be no clearance between the cap and the slider at the front.
4. Position the speedometer gearbox in the manner shown in the accompanying illustration, then connect and secure the cable.

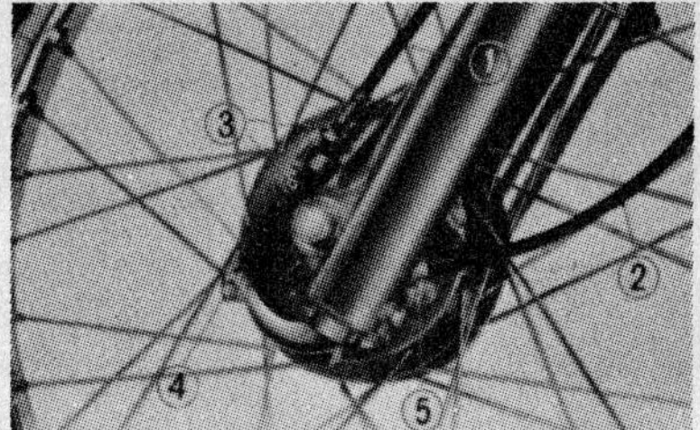
Cable mounting points (125)

1. Front brake cable
2. Speedometer cable
3. Locknut and adjusting nut
4. Cotter pin
5. Screw

DISASSEMBLY

125 and 250

1. Remove the wheel, place the wheel

Remove the cotterpin (1) and axle nut (2), then drive out the axle (3)

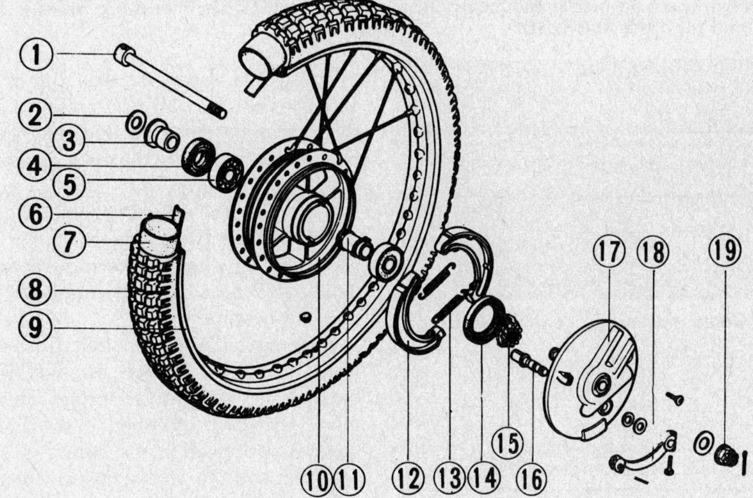
Front wheel assembly (125)

1. Front wheel axle
2. 12 mm plain washer
3. Front wheel side collar
4. 21 x 37 x 7 oil seal
5. 6301 radial ball bearing
6. Tire flap
7. Front wheel tube
8. Front wheel tire
9. Front wheel rim
10. Front wheel hub
11. Front axle distance collar
12. Front brake shoe
13. Brake shoe spring
14. 47 x 60 x 7 oil seal
15. Speedometer gear
16. Brake cam
17. Front brake panel
18. Front brake arm
19. Front wheel axle nut

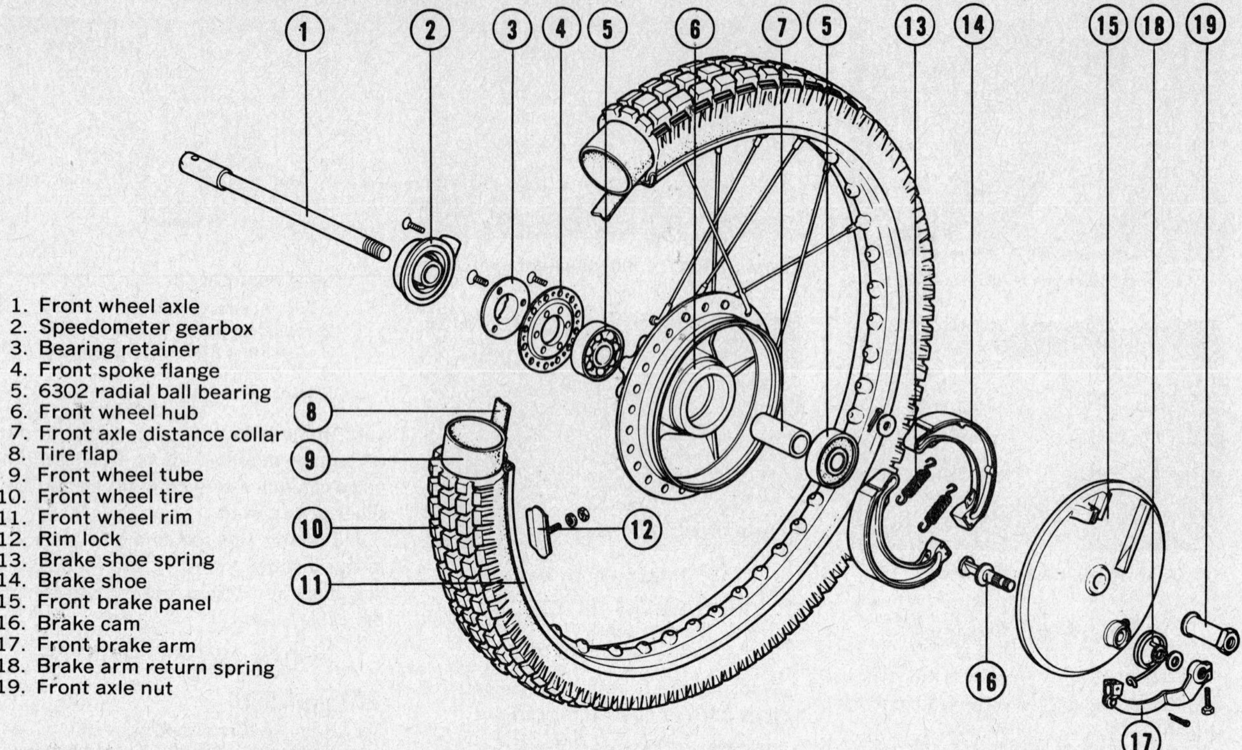

Front wheel assembly (250)

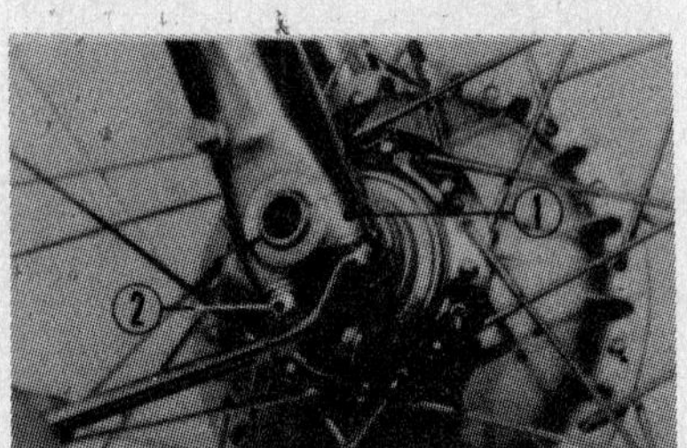

Remove the axle holder mounting nuts (2) and then the holder (1)

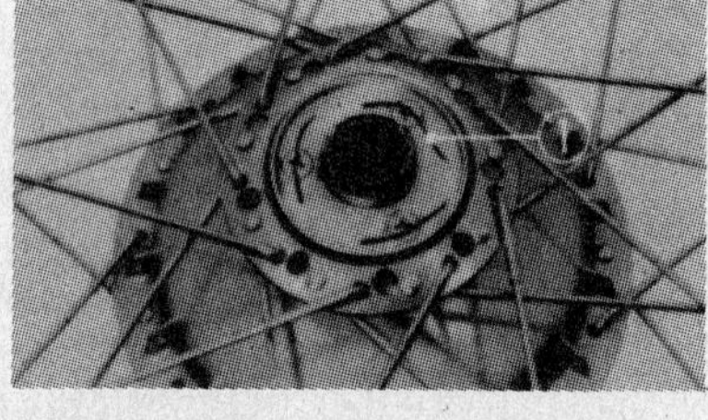
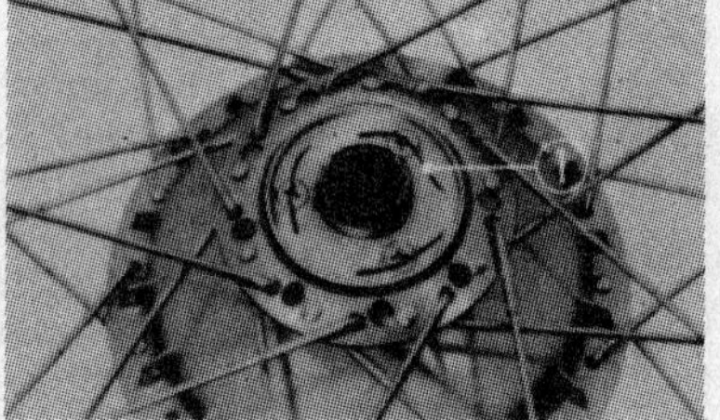

Bearing retainer mounting screws (1) (250)

Install the gearbox (1) and cable (2) as shown

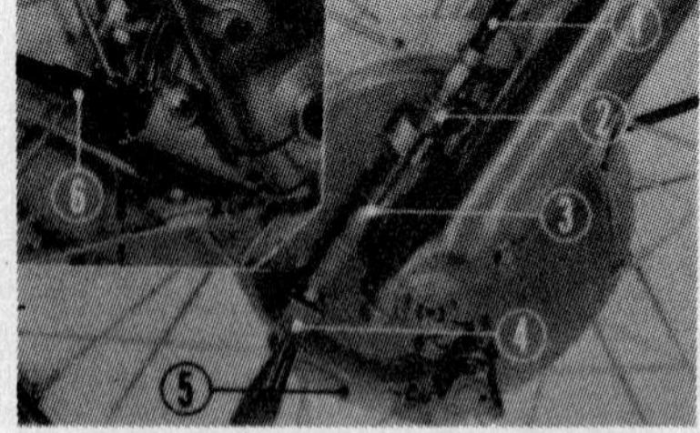

Cable mounting positions (250)

1. Front brake cable
2. Adjusting nut
3. Locknut
4. Cotter pin
5. Front brake arm
6. Speedometer cable

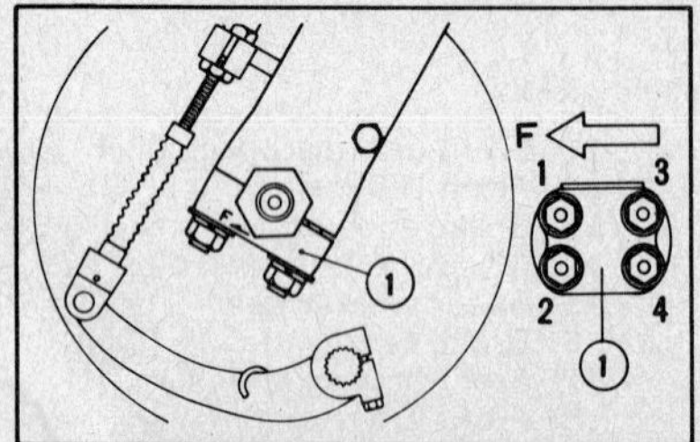

Axle holder (1) bolt tightening sequence

assembly in a vise by the axle nut, or secure the axle nut with a suitable wrench, then break the nut free, and remove it, by rotating the axle in the manner shown (250).

2. Remove the axle, speedometer gear box, and brake backing plate.

3. Remove the 3 bearing retainer mounting screws (250), then remove the two ball bearings.

4. Remove the 6 mm bolt from the front brake panel, then remove front brake lever and return spring. This is more easily accomplished if the brake panel is positioned in the hub.

5. Remove the anchor pin cotter pin and washer, then expand the shoes by hand and remove them and the brake shoe springs from the panel in one movement.

INSPECTION AND REPAIR

125 and 250

1. Check the front axle for excessive run-out, and replace it as necessary.

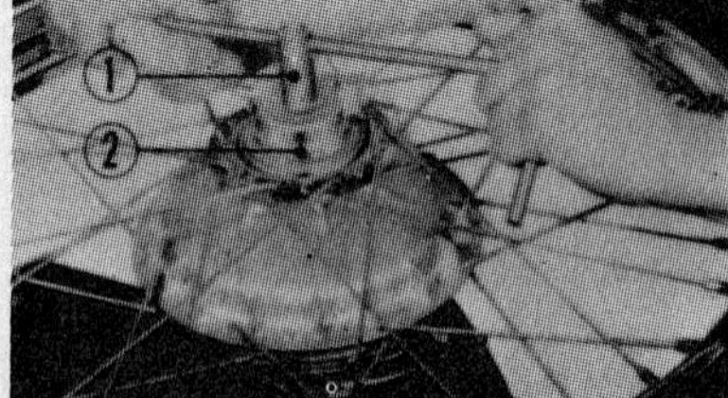

Break the axle (1) from the speedometer gear box side (2)

2. Check the bearings for wear, damage, or rough or loose action, and replace them, preferably as a set, as necessary.

3. Check the rim for excessive run-out and true it as necessary, then inspect the spokes for looseness or damage, and replace or tighten any which require attention.

4. Inspect the brake shoes for wear, damage, or oil impregnation, and replace them, preferably as a set, as necessary.

5. Inspect the brake shoe return springs for a worn, collapsed, or damaged condition, and replace them as necessary.

6. Inspect the brake panel assembly,

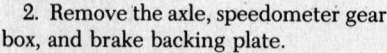

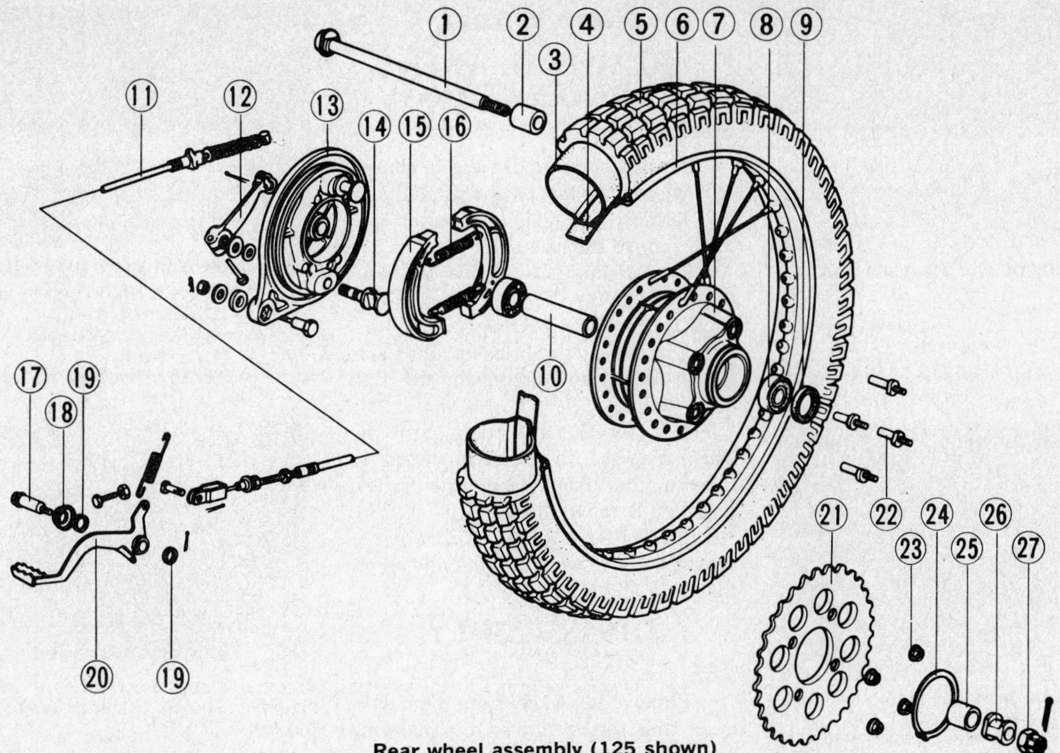

Rear wheel assembly (125 shown)

1. Rear wheel axle
2. Rear wheel side collar
3. Rear wheel tube
4. Rear tire flap
5. Rear wheel tire
6. Rear wheel rim
7. Rear wheel hub
8. 6302 ball bearing
9. 28 x 42 x 7 oil seal
10. Rear axle distance collar
11. Rear brake cable
12. Rear brake arm
13. Rear brake panel
14. Rear brake cam
15. Rear brake shoe
16. Rear brake shoe spring
17. Brake pivot shaft
18. Brake pivot washer
19. Brake pedal dust seal
20. Brake pedal
21. Final driven sprocket
22. Driven sprocket fixing bolt
23. 8 mm flanged nut
24. 58 mm snap-ring
25. Rear wheel side collar
26. Rear axle collar
27. Rear axle nut (14 mm)

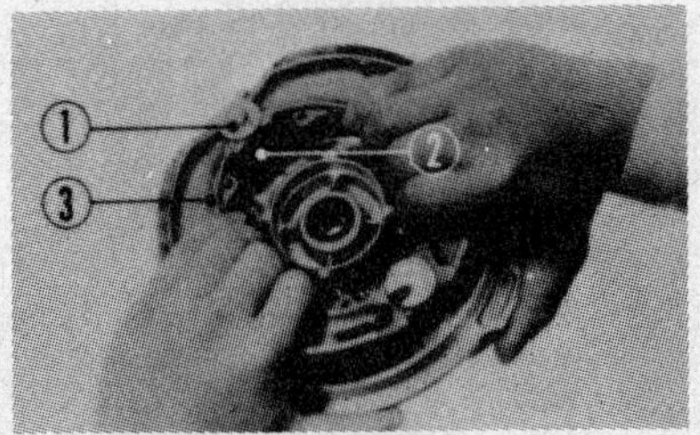

After removing the cotter pin (1), the springs (2) and shoes (3) can be spread and removed

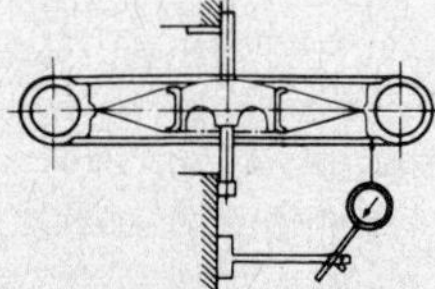

Checking rim run-out

Installing the bearing (1) using the factory driver (3) and driver handle (2)

and the bearing retainer, for wear or damage, and replace parts as necessary.

ASSEMBLY

125 and 250

1. Assembly is basically in the reverse order of disassembly. Use new seals and cotter pins. Sand the glaze off the brake shoes if they are to be reused, and rough up and clean out the hub so that the shoes will seat properly.

2. Pack the bearings with fresh bearing grease, and fill in the area between the bearings with grease also, then drive the bearings in until seated on the distance collar. The factory bearing driver (Tool No. 07946-3330100 for the 125 or 07945-3330100 for the 250) may be used, or the bearings can be driven in using a socket as a drift. The sealed side of the bearing should be facing out. Make sure that the collar isn't tilted.

3. Lightly grease the brake cam and anchor pin before installing the shoes.

4. Grease the bearing dust seal before installing it.

5. Align the punch marks on the brake lever arm and the brake cam.

6. Install the brake backing plate and the speedometer drive box before installing the axle (250). Grease the drive box before installing it.

NOTE: *The 125 has speedometer gear lugs which must mesh with two grooves cut in the hub.*

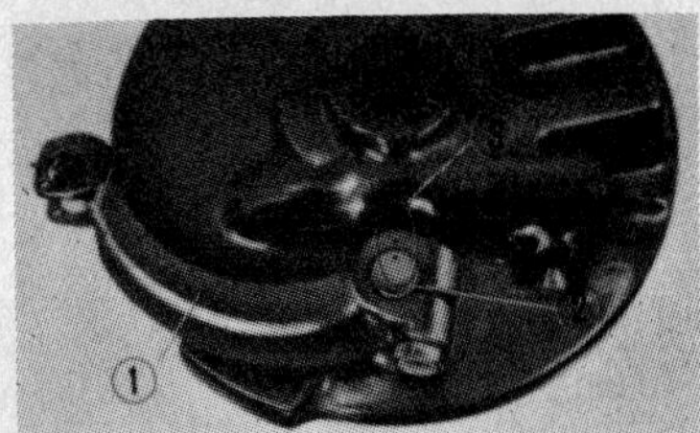

The brake arm (1) and brake cam (2) punch marks (3) lined up

The speedometer gear lugs (1) must mesh with the wheel hub grooves (2)

Backing off the adjusting bolt

1. Locknut
2. Adjusting bolt
3. Cotter pin
4. Axle nut

Rear brake assembly

1. Rear brake stopper arm
2. Rear brake arm
3. Rear brake cable
4. Brake panel

Removing the rear axle (1)

Remove the snap-ring (1) and 8 mm nuts (2)

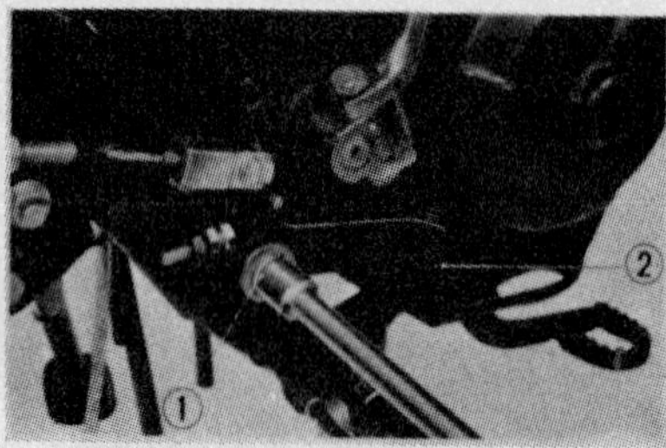

Removing the brake pivot shaft (1) and pedal (2)

Rear Wheel

REMOVAL AND INSTALLATION

125 and 250

1. Place a stand under the engine to raise the rear wheel off the ground.
2. Remove the axle nut cotter pin, then remove the axle nut.
3. Loosen the right- and left-side chain adjuster locknuts, then turn the adjusting bolts in to loosen the chain.
4. Disconnect the brake stopper arm at the hub, then disconnect the rear brake cable.
5. Pull out the axle, then push the wheel forward in the swing arm to remove the chain from the driven sprocket. Remove the wheel.
6. Installation is in the reverse order of removal. Use new cotter pins, and adjust the chain and brake.

DISASSEMBLY

125

1. Remove the wheel from the motorcycle, then remove the 58 mm snap-ring and the 8 mm nuts which secure the driven sprocket, and remove the sprocket.
2. Remove the brake panel, and disassemble it in the same manner given in the "Front Wheel" Section.
3. Drive out the bearings, and remove the distance collar.
4. Remove the brake pivot shaft and brake pedal from the frame, then remove the pedal spring and brake stop light switch spring.
5. Remove the cotter pin which secures the pedal to the cable, then loosen the locknuts and adjusting nuts to disconnect the cable from the frame.

250

1. Remove the wheel from the motorcycle, then remove the 65 mm snap-ring, driven sprocket, driven flange, and the damper rubbers.
2. Remove the brake panel, and disassemble it in the manner given in the "Front Wheel" Section.
3. Remove the rear wheel bearing retainer with the bearing retainer wrench (Tool No. 07910-3290000), then remove the bearings.

INSPECTION AND REPAIR

125 and 250

1. Consult the "Front Wheel Inspection and Repair" Section.
2. Check the drive chain for a kinked, worn, pitted, or otherwise damaged condition, and replace it as necessary. The master link and spring clip must be a snug fit.

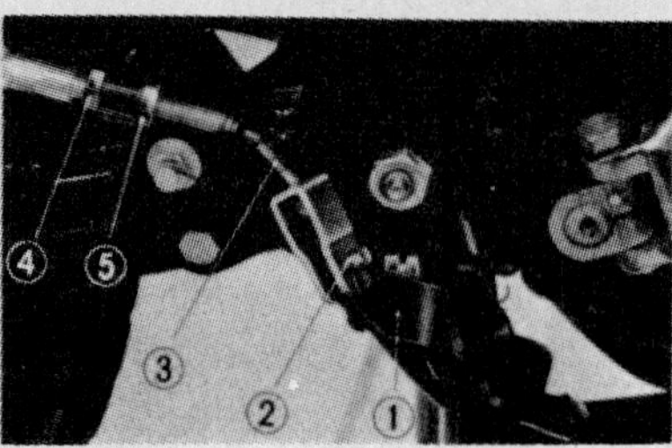

Cable and pedal assembly

1. Rear brake pedal
2. Cotter pin
3. Rear brake cable
4. Locknut
5. Adjusting nut

Using a wood block (1) to drive the driven sprocket (3) and flange (2) off the hub

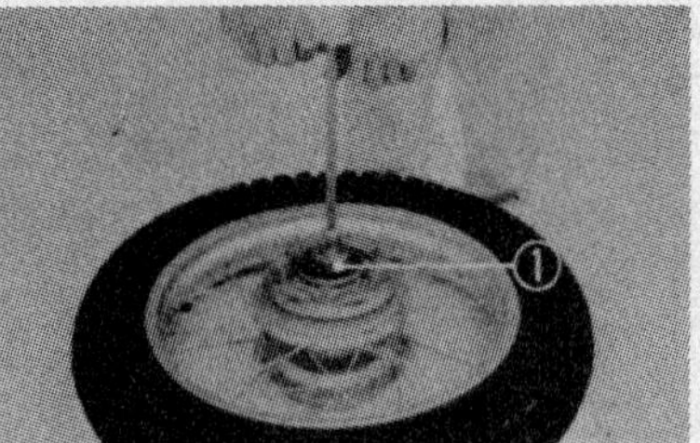

Removing the bearing retainer (1)

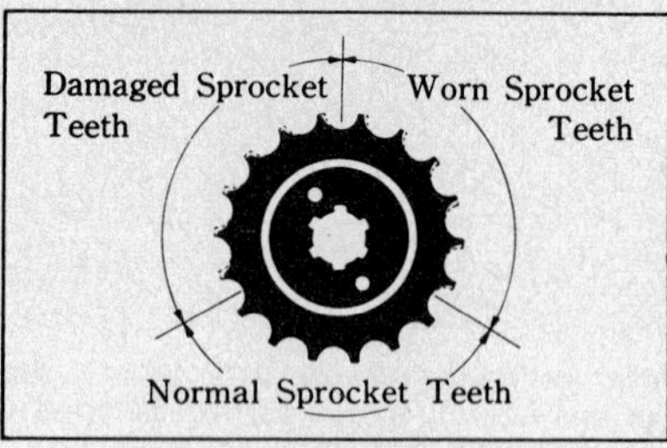

Sprocket wear patterns

3. Inspect the driven sprocket for wear or damage, and replace it as necessary. If the driven sprocket is worn it would be wise to also replace the drive sprocket.
4. Inspect the hub dampers for a damaged or cracked condition, and replace them, as a complete set, as necessary.

NOTE: *Replacing the flange after installing new dampers can be quite a problem, but the job will go more easily if the rubbers are lubricated with oil or dishwashing liquid.*

ASSEMBLY

125

1. Assembly is in the reverse order of

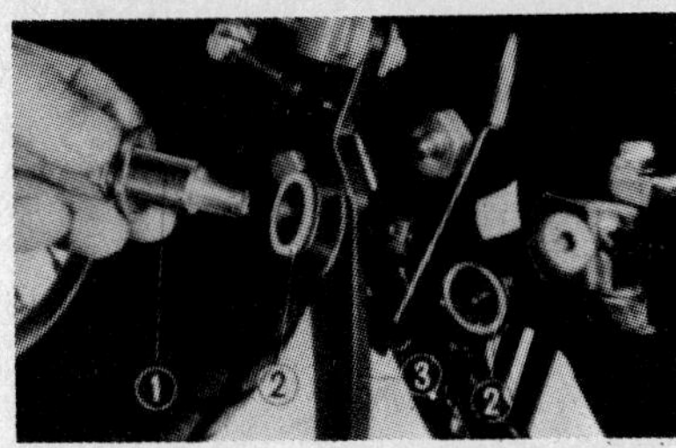

Do not damage the dust seals (2) in the frame or pedal (3) when installing the brake pivot shaft

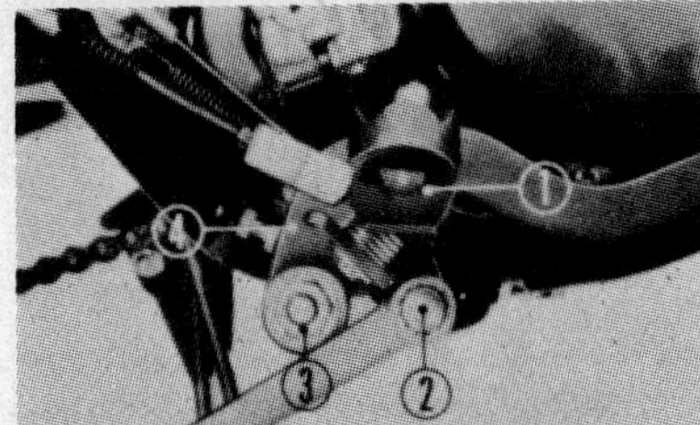

Right foot peg and brake pedal assemblies installed

1. Right footpeg
2. 8 mm bolt
3. 10 mm nut
4. Rear brake pedal

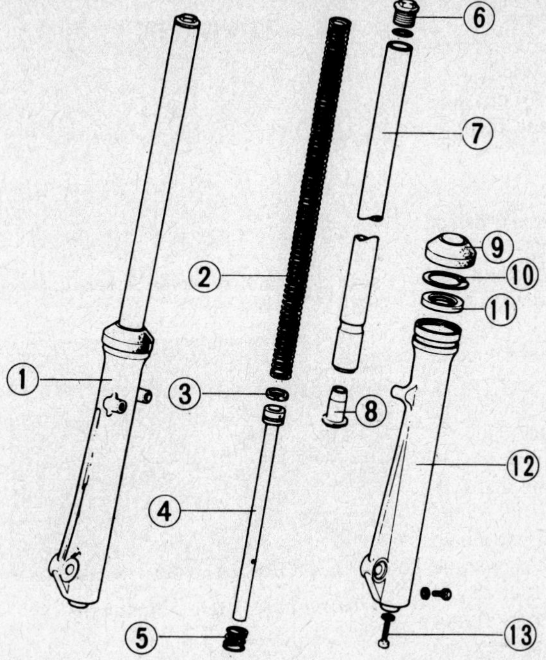

1. Front fork assembly
2. Front shock absorber spring
3. Piston ring
4. Bottom pipe
5. Front shock absorber rebound spring
6. Front fork bolt
7. Front fork pipe
8. Oil lock piece
9. Front fork dust seal
10. 45 mm internal snap-ring
11. 31 x 43 x 12.5 oil seal
12. Front fork bottom case
13. 8 mm socket bolt

Front fork assembly (125 shown)

disassembly. Use new seals, snap-rings (if at all distorted), and cotter pins.

2. Sand the glaze off the brake shoes, and rough up the drum with sandpaper.

3. Pack the bearings with bearing grease, and fill the area between the bearings with grease.

4. Drive in the bearings using either the factory driver (Tool No. 07946-9370100) or a suitable drift. Make sure that the distance collar is not tilted.

5. Mount the driven sprocket to the hub using the 58 mm snap-ring and the 4 8 mm nuts.

6. Grease the brake pedal sliding surface and the brake pivot and cam before installing the shoes and springs, and also oil the lips of the seals.

7. Adjust the chain, brake pedal height, brake light switch and the brakes themselves when the assembly is complete.

250

1. Assembly is in the reverse order of disassembly. Consult the "125" Section, and note the following:

2. Install the 6204 bearing with Tool No. 07946-3290000, and the 6302 bearing with Tool No. 07945-3330100. The left-side bearing should be installed first, and the distance collar should be inserted from the right.

3. Stake the bearing retainer to secure it.

4. Secure the driven flange to the hub using the 66 mm washer and 65 mm snap-ring.

5. When installing the sprocket 8 mm flanged nuts, lubricate the nuts with oil, and secure them in a crossed pattern.

NOTE: *When installing new stud bolts, coat the threads with locking sealant.*

SUSPENSION

Front Forks

125 AND 250

Disassembly

1. Loosen the fork filler bolts, then remove the front wheel as described in the "Front Wheel" Section.

2. Loosen the pinch-bolts, spread the clamps with a screwdriver, and pull out the forks from the bottom.

3. Remove the fork filler bolts and pour out the fork oil into a suitable container. The fork springs will probably slide out during this operation, but if they don't, pull them out.

4. Secure the fork sliders in a wood-jawed vise, or wrap them to protect them and use a metal-jawed vise, then remove the allen bolt from the bottom pipe using either the factory tool (Tool No. 07917-3230000) or a suitable allen wrench. The bottom pipe can now be removed, along with the rebound spring, from the slider.

5. Slide up the dust seal and remove the snap-ring and oil seal from the slider.

NOTE: *Use a pointed instrument to remove the oil seal, but be careful not to gouge the slider.*

6. Pull the fork tube from the slider with a sharp jerk.

Inspection and Repair

1. Clean all parts in a suitable solvent, then blow dry. Make sure that all oil orifices are clear.

2. Inspect the fork piston rings for a worn, pitted, or damaged condition, and replace them as necessary.

Remove the filler caps (1), loosen the pinch-bolts (2), and pull out the fork (3)

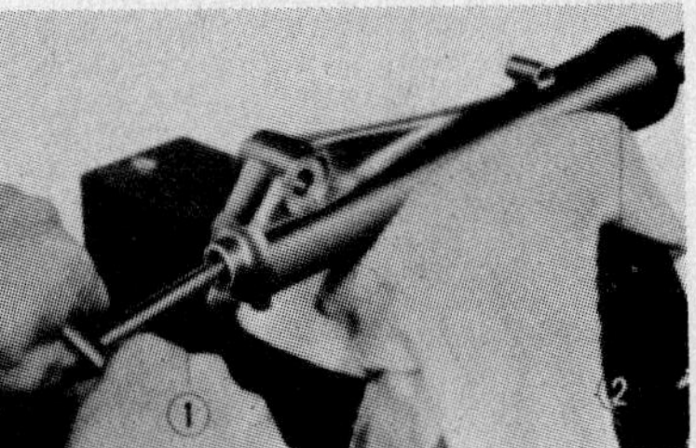

Using an allen wrench (1) to remove the allen bolt from inside the slider (2)

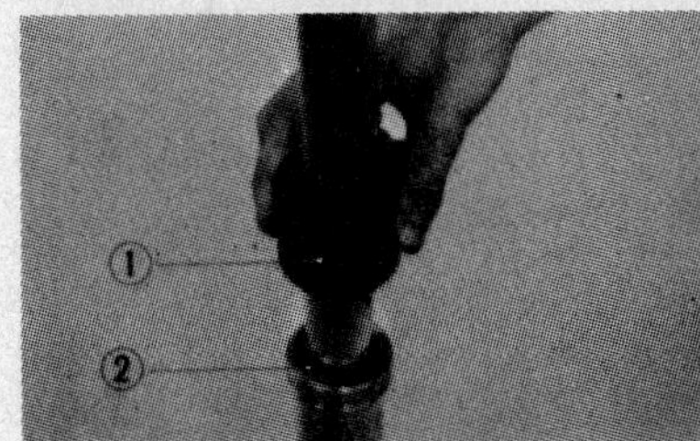

Slide up the dust seal (2) and remove the snap-ring (1)

3. Measure the spring free lengths, inspect them for wear, pitting, or a collapsed condition, and replace them as necessary.

4. Inspect the tubes and sliders for wear, scoring, damage, or pitting, and re-

place them as necessary. Deep scoring may cause oil leaks. Rust and burrs may be removed with fine emery cloth.

5. Inspect the dust covers for cracking or other damage, and replace them as necessary.

Assembly

1. Assembly is in the reverse order of disassembly. Use new oil seals.

2. When securing the fork pipes to the slider, coat the threads of the allen bolts with a locking sealant.

3. The seals can be installed in one of the two following manners:

a. If you have access to the factory oil seal driver (Tool No. 07947-3550000 for the 125, or 07947-3290000 for the 250), lubricate the lips of the seal with ATF (unless you are going to fill the forks with oil, in which case you should lubricate the seals with the same type of oil which you are going to use), and carefully slip the seal onto the lower half of the tube. Slip the tube into the slider, and use the driver to press the seal into its boss in the top of the slider. Be sure that it seats evenly.

b. If you don't have a factory driver, lubricate the seal lips with the same type of oil with which you are going to fill the forks, and drive the seal into the slider with a suitable socket. A piece of flat wood can also be used as a drift.

CAUTION: *Any damage to the seal lips will result in leakage.*

4. Install the snap-ring and dust cover, fill the fork legs with ATF or oil, and install each leg in the triple clamp, making sure that they come up to the same height. Fork height can be adjusted 3 ways.

NOTE: *Add 10 cc more fluid whenever the forks have been disassembled to compensate for the residual oil that*

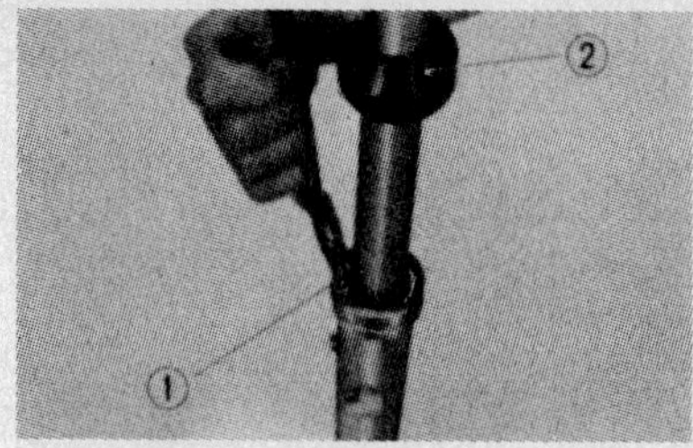

Using the factory seal driver (1) to install the seal (1)

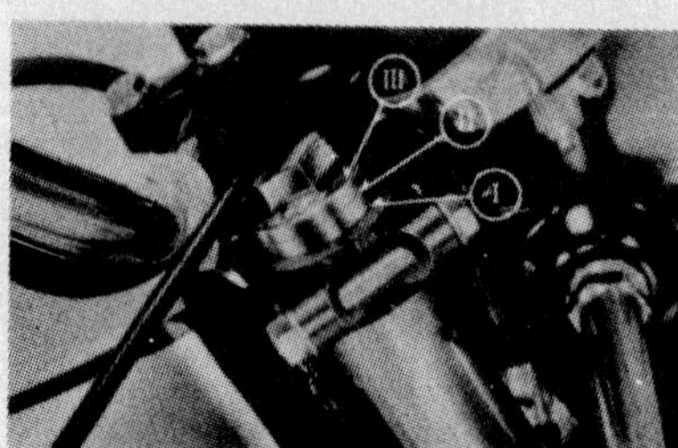

Three fork height adjustments

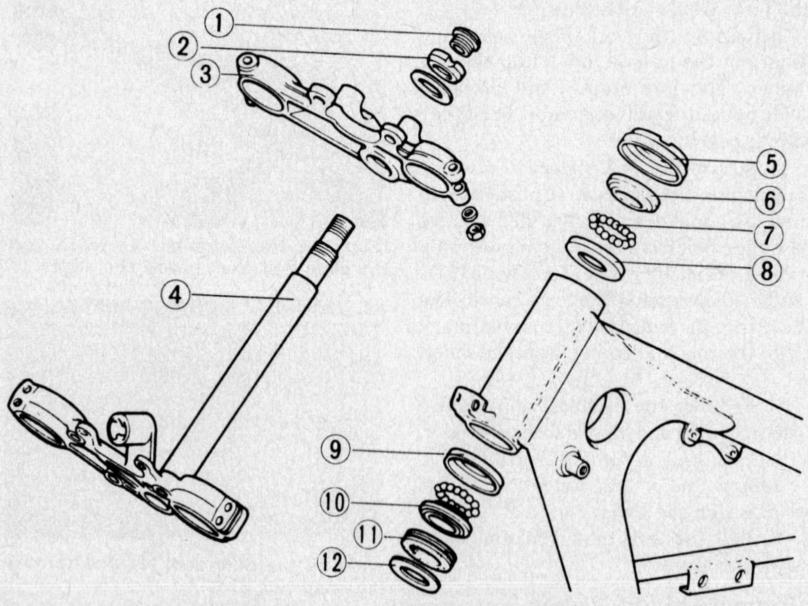

Steering stem assembly (125 shown)

1. Steering stem cap
2. Steering stem nut
3. Fork top bridge
4. Steering stem
5. Steering head top thread
6. Steering head top cone race
7. #6 steel ball
8. Steering top ball race
9. Steering bottom ball race
10. Steering bottom cone race
11. Steering head dust seal
12. Dust seal washer

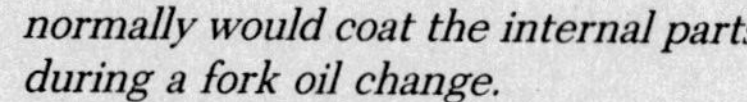

normally would coat the internal parts during a fork oil change.

5. Secure the pinch-bolts and the filler bolts, then check the fork for smooth and proper operation.

Steering Stem

125 AND 250

Disassembly

1. Remove the front wheel, front forks, gas tank, instruments, and handlebars.

Removing the steering stem nut with the factory wrench (1)

Remove the fork bridge (1) after removing the pinch-bolts (2)

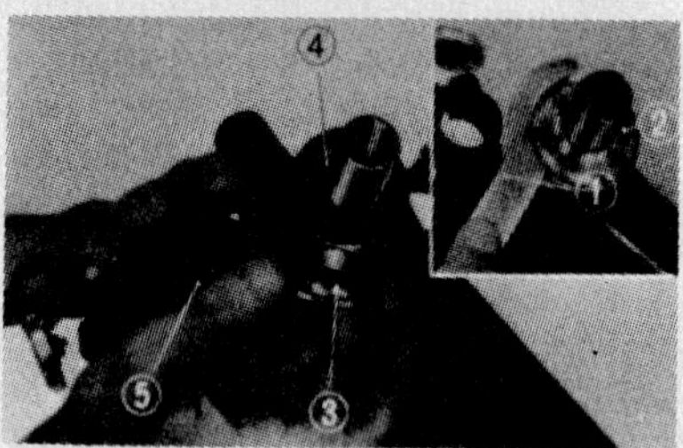

Use a pin wrench (1) to remove the top thread (2), then remove the top cone race (3) and balls (4), and pull the stem (5) out from the bottom

2. Remove the steering stem cap, and then the nut on the 125, using either the stem nut wrench (Tool No. 07915-0300000), or a suitable substitute. On the 250, remove the steering stem nut with a suitable wrench.

3. Remove the top fork bridge.

4. Remove the steering head top thread using a suitable pin wrench, then pull the steering stem out from the bottom.

CAUTION: *When you pull out the stem all the bearings are going to come out also, so be prepared. If you lose one bearing you must replace them all.*

5. Drift out the bearing races using a suitable drift in the manner shown in the accompanying illustration.

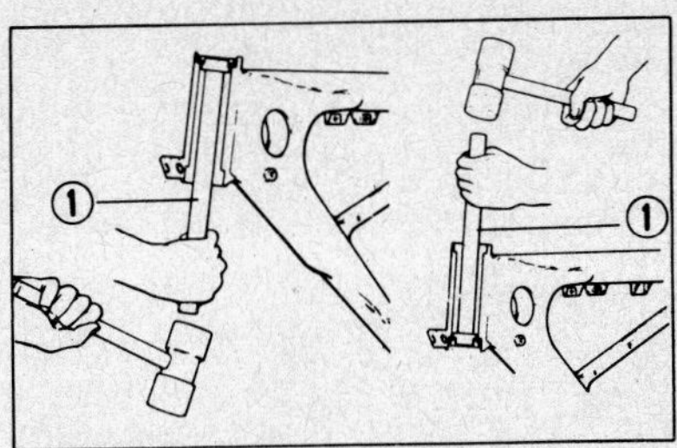

Drifting out the races with the factory drift (1)

Balls (1) installed in top race (2). Note stopper (2) position.

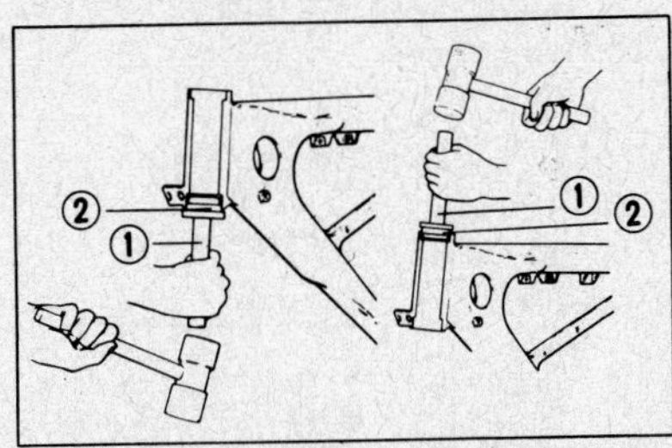

Driving in new races using the factory driver (2) and driver handle (1)

NOTE: *Do not remove races which aren't to be replaced.*

Inspection and Repair

1. Clean all parts thoroughly in a suitable solvent, then blow them dry.
2. Inspect the bearing balls for signs of wear, pitting, or damage, and replace them, as a complete set, as necessary.
3. Inspect the steering stem for signs of wear or damage, and replace it as necessary. Straightening out a bent stem is not recommended.
4. Inspect the bearing races for signs of wear, pitting, or damage, and replace them, as a set, as necessary.

   NOTE: *Replacing balls and not races, or vice versa, is a false economy, since worn balls will quickly wear out new races, and worn races will wear out new balls.*
5. Inspect the steering stem dust seal for a worn or damaged condition, and replace it as necessary.
6. Inspect the triple clamp stopper for signs of wear or damage, and repair it as necessary. The stopper cannot be removed and replaced without a torch.

Assembly

1. Assembly is basically in the reverse order of disassembly. New seals should be used.

FRAME SPECIFICATIONS

	Standard in. (mm)	Serviceable Limit in. (mm)
MT-125		
Front fork bottom pipe OD	1.2175-1.2185 (30.925-30.950)	1.2165 (30.9)
Front fork bottom case ID	1.2205-1.2220 (31.00-31.039)	1.2276 (31.180)
Front wheel axle run-out	0.0004 (0.01)	0.0079 (0.2)
6301 ball bearing axial run-out	0.0008 (0.02)	0.0016 (0.04)
6301 ball bearing radial run-out	0.0006 (0.015)	0.0012 (0.03)
Front and rear wheel rim face run-out	0.0197 (0.5)	0.0787 (2.0)
Front and rear brake drum ID	4.3307-4.3386 (110.0-110.2)	4.3701 (111.0)
Front and rear brake shoe thickness	0.1476 (3.75)	0.0984 (2.50)
Rear wheel axle run-out	0.0004 (0.01)	0.0079 (0.20)
Rear fork pivot bushing ID	0.7098-0.7111 (18.030-18.063)	0.7165 (18.20)
Rear fork center collar OD	0.7074-0.7063 (17.968-17.941)	0.7039 (17.88)
6302 ball bearing axial run-out	0.0008 (0.02)	0.0016 (0.04)
6302 ball bearing radial run-out	0.0006 (0.015)	0.0012 (0.03)
MT-250		
Drive chain length	39.3780 (1000.2)	38.5827 (980)
Front shock absorber spring B free length	19.6535 (499.2)	19.2913 (490)
Rear shock absorber spring A free length	9.9094 (251.7)	9.6850 (246)
Front fork bottom pipe OD	1.3681-1.3780 (34.75-35.00)	1.3661 (34.70)
Front fork bottom case ID	1.3780-1.3795 (35.00-35.039)	1.3850 (35.18)
Front wheel axle bend	0.0004 (0.01)	0.0080 (0.2)
6302 ball bearings axial run-out	0.0028 (0.07)	0.0039 (0.1)
6302 ball bearings radial run-out	0.0012 (0.03)	0.0020 (0.05)
Front wheel rims face run-out	0.0197 (0.5)	0.0787 (2.0)
Front brake drum ID	6.2992-6.3110 (160.0-160.3)	6.3386 (161.0)
Front brake shoe thickness	0.1772 (4.5)	0.0984 (2.5)
Rear wheel rims face run-out	0.0197 (0.5)	0.0787 (2.0)
Rear wheel axle bend	0.0004 (0.01)	0.008 (0.2)
6204 & 6304 ball bearings axial run-out	0.0028 (0.07)	0.0039 (0.1)
6204 & 6304 ball bearings radial run-out	0.0012 (0.03)	0.0020 (0.05)
Rear fork pivot bushing ID	0.8504-0.8524 (21.60-21.65)	0.8583 (21.8)
Rear fork center collar OD	0.8455-0.8449 (21.475-21.46)	0.8425 (21.4)
Rear brake drum ID	5.5118-5.5236 (140.0-140.3)	5.5512 (141.0)
Rear brake shoe thickness	0.1772 (4.5)	0.0984 (2.5)

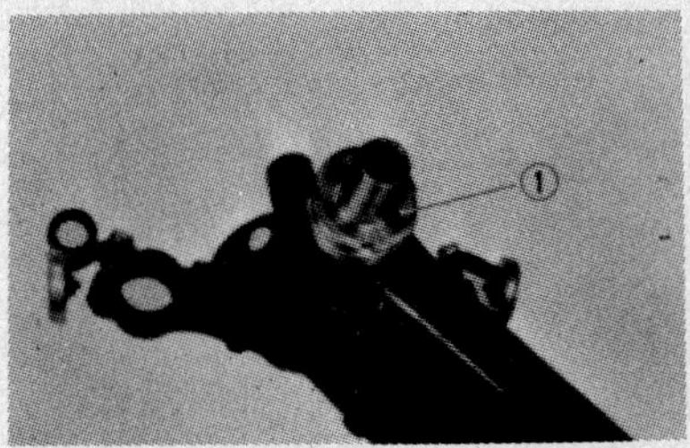

Using the top thread (1) to fully seat the bearing races

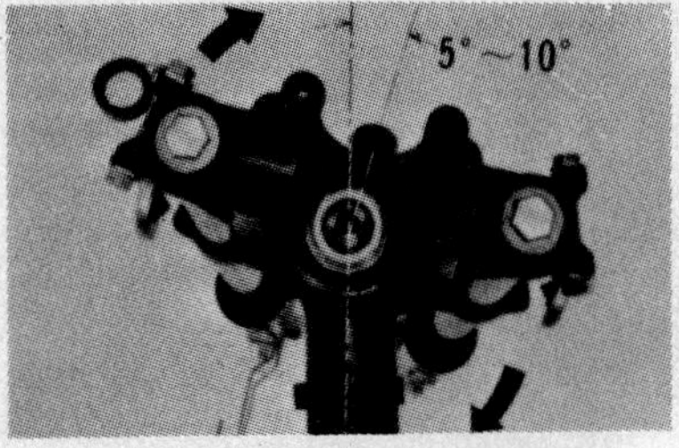

Removing the chain guard (1)

2. Drive new races into the steering head using a suitable drift. Make sure that the races seat evenly. The steering stem race can be installed by slipping it over the stem, positioning the stem between the jaws or a vise, and using the vise to hold the race steady while driving the stem through it from the bottom. Make sure that the washer and seal are in place before installing the race.

3. Liberally grease the races with fresh bearing grease, then arrange the balls in the grease. There should be 18 balls in each race.

4. Slip the stem into place and fully tighten down the top thread to assure that the races are properly seated, then back off the adjustment until the stem can be easily, and smoothly, rotated in either direction.

5. Install the forks in the triple clamp, then see if the forks will fall, for at least 5-10°, to either side of their own volition. The forks should move smoothly without any rough spots or binding. If the forks do not move smoothly, check for any of the following:

a. Improperly adjusted top thread.
b. Bent steering stem.
c. Worn balls or races, or the wrong number of balls.

6. Route the cables as shown in the accompanying illustration, check that everything is tight, fill the forks with oil, and road test the machine.

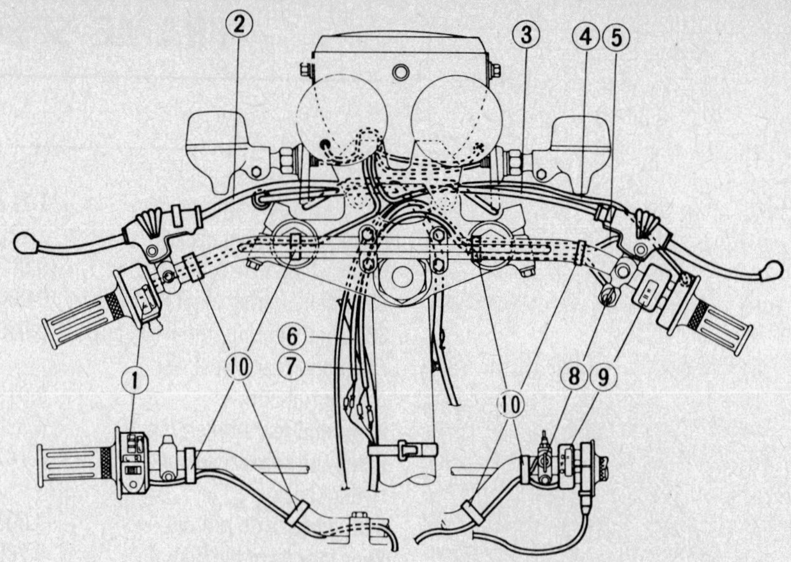

Wire the handlebars like this

1. Turn signal/dimmer switch
2. Clutch cable
3. Front brake cable
4. Throttle cable
5. Front stop switch
6. Front stop switch lead
7. Ignition switch lead
8. Ignition switch
9. Headlight switch
10. Wire bands

Swing Arm

125 AND 250

Disassembly

1. Remove the rear wheel as directed in the "Rear Wheel Removal and Installation" Section.

2. Remove the bolts which secure the rear shock units to the frame and swing arm, then remove the shocks.

3. Remove the chain case and guide.

4. Remove the swing arm pivot bolt locknut, then pull out the pivot bolt and remove the swing arm.

5. Drift out the pivot thrust bushings and spacer using a suitable drift.

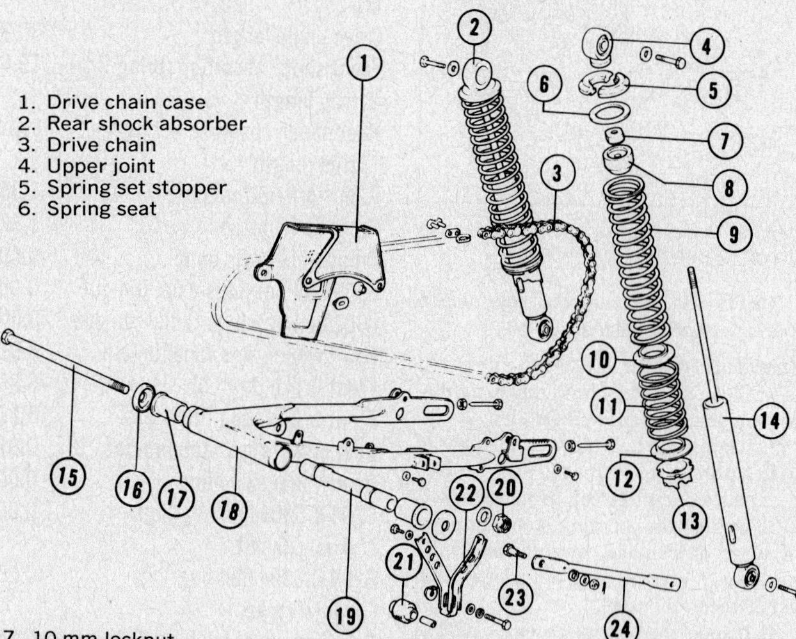

1. Drive chain case
2. Rear shock absorber
3. Drive chain
4. Upper joint
5. Spring set stopper
6. Spring seat
7. 10 mm locknut
8. Stopper rubber
9. Rear suspension spring B
10. Spring joint
11. Rear suspension spring A
12. Under spring seat
13. Spring adjuster
14. Rear damper
15. Rear fork pivot bolt
16. Dust seal cup
17. Rear fork bushing
18. Rear fork
19. Rear fork center collar
20. 14 mm self locknut
21. Tensioner roller
22. Drive chain guide
23. Stopper arm bolt
24. Stopper arm

Swing arm and rear shock assembly (250 shown)

Inspection and Repair

1. Clean all parts thoroughly in a suitable solvent, then blow them dry.

2. Inspect the swing arm for cracks, fatigue marks, misalignment of the arms or axle holes, and repair or replace it as necessary.

NOTE: *Repairs are not recommended unless a suitable jig is available.*

3. Measure the bushing-to-center collar clearance, and replace the bushings as necessary.

4. Check the grease fitting for blockage, and clean or replace it as necessary.

Assembly

1. Assembly is basically in the reverse

The forks should freely fall this far to either side

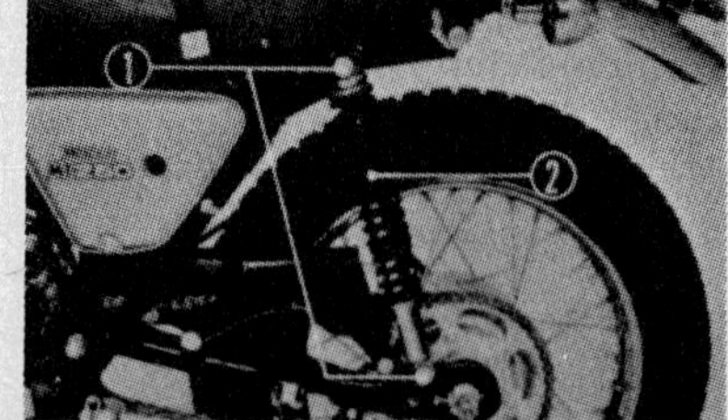

Remove the shock mounting nuts (1), then pull the shock (2) off its mounting studs

FRAME TORQUE SPECIFICATIONS

Tightening Point	Thread Dia. (mm)	Torque ft lb (kg-m)
MT-125		
Steering stem nut	22	43.4-65.1 (6.0-9.0)
Front fork top bridge	8	13.0-18.1 (1.8-2.5)
Handlebar holder	8	13.0-18.1 (1.8-2.5)
Front fork bottom bridge	8	13.0-18.1 (1.8-2.5)
Spoke (front)	—	1.1-2.2 (0.15-0.30)
Spoke (rear)	—	1.4-2.5 (0.2-0.35)
Rear fork pivot bolt	12	39.8-47.0 (5.5-6.5)
Front wheel axle nut	12	39.8-47.0 (5.5-6.5)
Engine hanger bolt	8	20.3-23.9 (2.8-3.3)
Rear axle nut	14	43.4-57.9 (6.0-8.0)
Driven sprocket	8	16.6-20.3 (2.3-2.8)
Brake arm	6	5.8-8.7 (0.8-1.2)
Rear brake torque link	8	13.0-18.1 (1.8-2.5)
Rear shock absorber	10	21.7-28.9 (3.0-4.0)
Change pedal	6	5.8-8.7 (0.8-1.2)
Kickstarter pedal	8	13.0-18.1 (1.8-2.5)
Rear brake pedal pivot nut	10	21.7-28.9 (3.0-4.0)
MT-250		
Steering stem nut	23	57.9-86.8 (8.0-12.0)
Front fork top bridge	8	13.0-18.1 (1.8-2.5)
Handlebar holder	8	13.0-18.1 (1.8-2.5)
Front fork bottom bridge	8	13.0-18.1 (1.8-2.5)
Spoke	—	1.4-2.5 (0.2-0.35)
Rear fork pivot bolt	14	43.4-50.6 (6.0-7.0)
Front wheel axle nut	12	43.4-57.9 (6.0-8.0)
Front axle holder	8	13.0-18.1 (1.8-2.5)
Front engine hanger bolt	8	16.6-20.3 (2.3-2.8)
Rear engine hanger bolt	10	21.7-28.9 (3.0-4.0)
Rear axle nut	14	43.4-57.9 (6.0-8.0)
Driven sprocket	8	16.6-20.3 (2.3-2.8)
Brake arm	6	5.8-8.0 (0.8-1.1)
Rear brake torque link	8	9.4-13.0 (1.3-1.8)
Rear shock absorber	10	21.7-28.9 (3.0-4.0)
R/H foot rest	10	21.7-28.9 (3.0-4.0)
Change pedal	6	5.8-8.7 (0.8-1.2)
Rear brake pedal pivot nut	10	21.7-28.9 (3.0-4.0)
Kickstarter pedal	8	13.0-18.1 (1.8-2.5)
Handle lever bracket	6	2.2-2.9 (0.3-0.4)

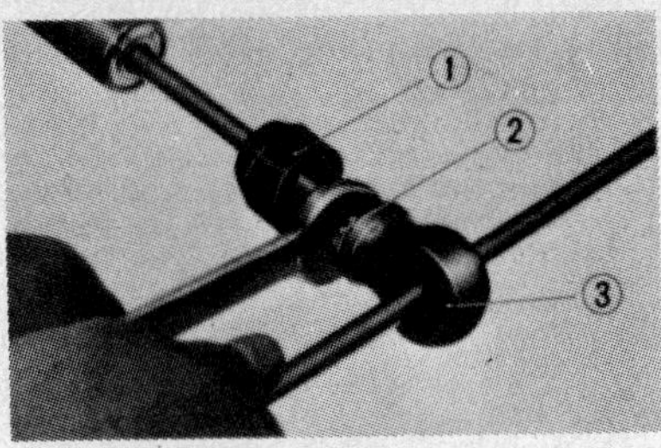

Disassembling the shock

1. Stopper rubber
2. Locknut
3. Mounting eye

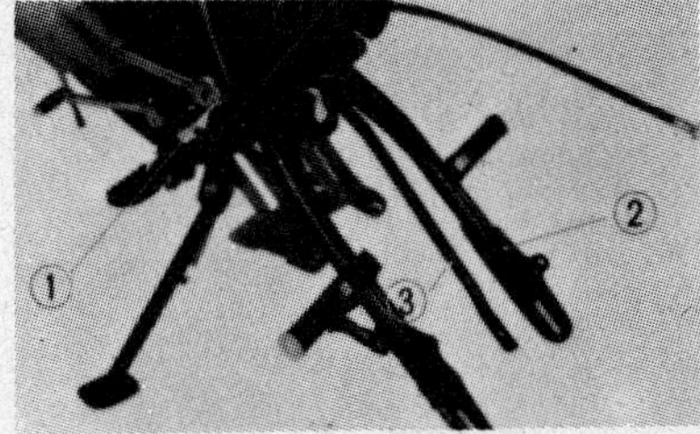

Removing the fork (2) pivot bolt (1). Note the brake stay (3) position.

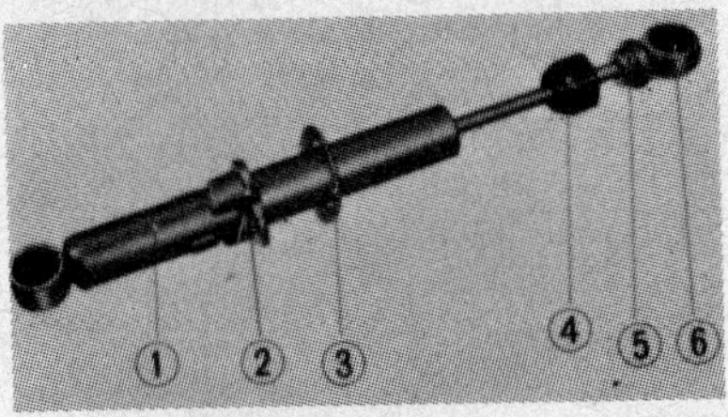

Shock assembly

1. Rear damper
2. Spring adjuster
3. Rear shock absorber spring seat
4. Stopper rubber
5. 9 mm locknut
6. Mounting eye

order of disassembly. Use new dust seals.

2. Thoroughly pack the inside and outside of the fork center collar with bearing grease, and the inside of the bushings, then install them in the swing arm.

3. Install the dust seal cups, then position the swing arm in the frame, grease the pivot bolt, and mount and secure the swing arm. Check the motion of the swing arm for binding, and make sure that there is no side-to-side play.

Rear Shock Absorbers

DISASSEMBLY

1. Remove the rear shocks, place the bottom of the shock on the floor, press down on the spring until the collars are free to be removed, then have someone pull the collars out. Remove the spring.

2. Place a screwdriver in the upper mounting eye to keep it from turning, then remove the locknut. The shock can now be fully disassembled.

INSPECTION AND REPAIR

1. Push in the shock piston and then pull it back out. It should take about twice as long to pull it out as to push it in. If the two take an equal amount of time, the shock is shot and should be replaced.

2. Inspect the rubber stopper for cracks or damage, and replace it as necessary.

3. Inspect the shock for a bent piston rod, and replace the unit if the piston is bent.

NOTE: *When replacing the shock units, it is best to replace them as a set. You definitely don't want unequal suspension in the back end. Also make sure that both shocks are adjusted equally for spring preload and dampening (on shocks which have adjustable dampening).*

4. Measure the shock spring free length, and replace them, as a set, as necessary if worn or damaged. The shock springs shouldn't tilt more than a few degrees.

ASSEMBLY

1. Assembly is in the reverse order of disassembly. Make sure that the collars seat properly.

HONDA FOUR-STROKE SINGLES INDEX

MODEL IDENTIFICATION

The C50 and C50M models were introduced in 1963 and became immediate favorites among the small displacement set. Both models are virtually alike except that the M model came equipped with an electric starter. In 1964 a more powerful version was introduced, the C90. In 1965, the C65 and C65M models were added to the line and in 1969, a C70 model made its debut, soon to be followed in 1970 by a C70M. All of these models use the same basic frame but come with varying engines.

Pictured here is the S65, the sportier version of the 65cc line which was introduced in 1965 to replace the 50cc models which came out in 1963. These S models retained the leading link front end used on the C models, but came with a more traditional multiple plate clutch instead of the centrifugal clutch used in the step-through frames.

In 1964, the S90 was introduced to complement the S50. The 90cc version, in addition to having a hotter engine, featured a telescopic front end.

The CL70 shown here, which first appeared in 1969, is an updated version of the S65. Although the backbone frame design was retained, the smoother lines of the tank and fenders along with the telescopic front end made the CL a much sportier machine than its predecessor.

Here is the original CL90 scrambler, introduced in 1966. The differences between this bike and the S model are the shape of the tank, pipe, and fenders, and a higher gear ratio than on the street model. This machine marked Honda's entrance into the field of dual purpose machines.

In 1969 this SL90 Motosport model was introduced. It's still powered by the same 90cc engine as the rest of the 90cc line, but this one has geniune high fenders, a slightly higher pipe, and a pair of knobbies. In 1971 it was joined by the SL70 which is basically the same machine.

The CT90 shown here was the first real dirt bike Honda offered. It was first introduced in 1966 and then joined by the almost identical CT70 in 1969.

In 1968, Honda introduced the CB, CL, and SL100 models which featured an all new 100cc engine with a five speed gearbox, their first single to be mounted vertically in the frame. In 1971 a CB125S, CD125S, and SL125 were added to the line. They are very similar to the 100cc models and use an engine which is merely a bored out 100. Shown here is the CB100.

Here is the CL100 version of the 100cc line. It's intended to be an off-road bike, but like most of the Japanese dual-purpose machines it's more at home on the blacktop.

Pictured here is the SL125, a true scrambler.

Here is the XL250, Honda's revolutionary four valve single. This is the bike that surprised everyone with its remarkable performance in the 1972 Baja.

GENERAL SPECIFICATIONS

	C50	C50M	S50
DIMENSIONS			
Overall length (in.)	70.67	70.67	69.45
Overall width (in.)	25.19	25.19	24.21
Overall height (in.)	38.4	38.4	35.95
Ground clearance (in.)	5.12	5.12	4.92
Wheelbase (in.)	46.65	46.65	45.28
Net weight (lbs)	152.0	166.6	168.0

GENERAL SPECIFICATIONS

	C50	C50M	S50
ENGINE			
Type		ohc, air-cooled, four-stroke	
Bore and stroke (mm)	39 x 41.4	39 x 41.4	39 x 41.4
Compression ratio	8.8 : 1	8.8 : 1	8.8 : 1
Displacement (cc)	49	49	49
Valve train		chain-driven, overhead-cam	
Lubrication system		pressure and splash, wet sump	
Horsepower @ rpm	4.8 @ 10,000	4.8 @ 10,000	5.2 @ 10,000
Torque (ft lbs @ rpm)	2.7 @ 8,200	2.7 @ 8,200	4.75 @ 8,200
Carburetion (Keihin)		piston valve type, manual choke	
DRIVE TRAIN			
Clutch type	automatic, wet, multiple-disc, centrifugal type		wet, multiple-disc type
Transmission		constant meshed-gear type	
Power reduction (primary)	gear / 3.722	gear / 3.722	gear / 3.300
Power reduction (secondary)		chain and sprocket	
	3.000	3.000	3.154
Gear ratio (total)	N.A.	N.A.	12.2
1st	3.364	3.364	3.000
2nd	1.722	1.722	1.765
3rd	1.190	1.190	1.300
4th	——	——	1.043
5th	——	——	——
ELECTRICAL SYSTEM			
Ignition		battery and coil, high-voltage electrical spark	
Starting system	kick	kick and electric	kick
Charging system		flywheel magneto	
Battery (volts/amp hr)	6/2	6/11	6/2
Fuse (amps)	10	10	10

	C65	C65M	S65
DIMENSIONS			
Overall length (in.)	70.67	70.67	69.13
Overall width (in.)	25.19	25.19	24.02
Overall height (in.)	38.4	38.4	35.83
Ground clearance (in.)	5.12	5.12	4.92
Wheelbase (in.)	46.65	46.65	45.28
Net weight (lbs)	161	174	170
ENGINE			
Type		ohc, air-cooled, four-stroke	
Bore and stroke (mm)	44 x 41.4	44 x 41.4	44 x 41.4
Compression ratio	8.8 : 1	8.8 : 1	8.8 : 1
Displacement (cc)	63	63	63
Valve train		chain-driven, overhead-cam	
Lubrication system		pressure and splash, wet sump	
Horsepower @ rpm	5.5/9,000	5.5/9,000	6.22/10,000
Torque (ft lbs @ rpm)	3.32/7,000	3.32/7,000	3.47/8,500
Carburetion (Keihin/mm)		piston valve type, manual choke	

GENERAL SPECIFICATIONS (con't.)

	C65	C65M	S65
DRIVE TRAIN			
Clutch type	automatic, wet, multiple-disc, centrifugal type		wet, multiple-disc type
Transmission		constant meshed-gear type	
Power reduction (primary)		gear/3.300	
Power reduction (secondary)		chain and sprocket	
	3.154	3.154	3.308
Gear ratio (total)	12.4	12.4	11.4
1st	3.364	3.364	3.000
2nd	1.722	1.722	1.765
3rd	1.190	1.190	1.300
4th	—	—	1.043
5th	—	—	—
ELECTRICAL SYSTEM			
Ignition		battery and coil, high-voltage electrical spark	
Starting system	kick	kick and electric	kick
Charging system		flywheel magneto	
Battery (volts/amp hr)	6/2	6/11	6/2
Fuse (amps)	10	10	10

	CL70	C70	C70M
DIMENSIONS			
Overall length (in.)	70.1	70.7	70.7
Overall width (in.)	29.7	25.2	25.2
Overall height (in.)	39.2	38.4	38.4
Ground clearance (in.)	5.1	5.1	5.1
Wheelbase (in.)	46.5	46.7	46.7
Net weight (lbs)	174.2	165.0	174.2
ENGINE			
Type		ohc, air-cooled, four-stroke	
Bore and stroke (mm)	47 x 41.4	47 x 41.4	47 x 41.4
Compression ratio	8.8	8.8	8.8
Displacement (cc)	72	72	72
Valve train		chain-driven, overhead-cam	
Lubrication system		pressure and splash, wet sump	
Horsepower @ rpm	6.5/9,500	6.2/9,000	6.2/9,000
Torque (ft lbs @ rpm)	3.83/8,000	3.83/7,000	3.83/7,000
Carburetion (Keihin/mm)		piston valve type, manual choke	
DRIVE TRAIN			
Clutch type	wet, multiple-disc type	automatic, wet, multiple-disc, centrifugal type	
Transmission		constant meshed-gear type	
Power reduction (primary)	gear/3.722	gear/3.722	gear/3.722
Power reduction (secondary)		chain and sprocket	
	3.615	2.786	2.786
1st	2.692	3.364	3.364
2nd	1.824	1.722	1.722
3rd	1.300	1.190	1.190
4th	0.958	—	—
5th	—	—	—

GENERAL SPECIFICATIONS (con't.)

	CL70	C70	C70M
ELECTRICAL SYSTEM			
Ignition	battery and coil, high-voltage electrical spark		
Starting system	kick	kick	kick and electric
Charging system	flywheel magneto	flywheel magneto	AC generator
Battery (volts/amp hrs)	6/5.5	6/4	6/11
Fuse (amps)	10	10	10

	CD90	C90	CT90	CT90 (from F. no. 000001A)
DIMENSIONS				
Overall length (in.)	70.72	72.10	70.92	73.6
Overall width (in.)	25.22	25.22	25.61	26.8
Overall height (in.)	37.63	39.20	38.61	41.0
Ground clearance (in.)	5.12	5.12	5.40	6.9
Wheelbase (in.)	45.39	46.89	46.81	47.9
Net weight (lbs)	——	187.00	179.30	200.00
ENGINE				
Type	ohc, air-cooled, four-stroke			
Bore and stroke (mm)	50 x 45.6	50 x 45.6	50 x 45.6	50 x 45.6
Compression ratio	8.2 : 1	8.2 : 1	8.2 : 1	8.2 : 1
Displacement (cc)	89.6	89.6	89.6	89.6
Valve train	chain-driven, overhead-cam			
Lubrication system	pressure and splash, wet sump			
Horsepower @ rpm	7.5	7.5	7.0	7.0
Carburetion (Keihin/mm)	piston valve type, manual choke			
DRIVE TRAIN				
Clutch type	wet, multiple-disc type	automatic, wet, multiple-disc type		
Transmission	constant meshed-gear type			
Power reduction (primary)	gear/3.722	gear/3.722	gear/3.722	gear/3.722
Power reduction (secondary)	chain and sprocket			
	3.000	2.857	3.000	3.000
1st	2.540	2.538	2.538	(4.738)*
2nd	1.610	1.555	1.611	(3.008)*
3rd	1.190	1.000	1.190	(2.222)*
4th	0.96	——	0.958	(1.789)*
5th	——	——	——	——
Sub transmission total ratio			1.000	(1.867)
ELECTRICAL SYSTEM				
Ignition	battery and coil, high-voltage electrical spark			
Starting system	kick	kick	kick	kick
Charging system	AC generator			
Battery (volts/amp hrs)	6/6	6/6	6/5.5	6/5.5
Fuse (amps)	10	10	10	10

* The figures in parentheses indicate a sub-transmission ratio

GENERAL SPECIFICATIONS (con't.)

	CL90, CL90L	S90	SL90
DIMENSIONS			
Overall length (in.)	72.1	74.47	73.6
Overall width (in.)	31.9	26.5	31.5
Overall height (in.)	41.3	38.61	43.3
Ground clearance (in.)	6.3	5.71	9.8
Wheelbase (in.)	47.2	47.08	48.8
Net weight (lbs)	202.9	190.73	216.1
ENGINE			
Type		ohc, air-cooled, four-stroke	
Bore and stroke (mm)	50 x 45.6	50 x 45.6	50 x 45.6
Compression ratio	8.2	8.2	8.2
Displacement (cc)	89.6	89.6	89.6
Valve train		chain-driven, overhead-cam	
Lubrication system		pressure and splash, wet sump	
Horsepower @ rpm	①	8.0 @ 9,500	8.0 @ 9,500
Torque (ft lbs @ rpm)	②	4.70 @ 8,000	4.77 @ 8,000
Carburetion (Keihin)		piston valve type, manual choke	
DRIVE TRAIN			
Clutch type		wet, multiple-disc type	
Transmission		constant meshed-gear type	
Power reduction (primary)	gear/3.72	gear/3.72	gear/3.72
Power reduction (secondary)		chain and sprocket	
	3.21	3.21	3.28
1st	2.54	2.54	2.54
2nd	1.61	1.53	1.61
3rd	1.19	1.09	1.19
4th	0.96	0.88	0.96
5th	—	—	—
ELECTRICAL SYSTEM			
Ignition		battery and coil, high-voltage electrical spark	
Starting system	kick	kick	kick
Charging system		AC generator	
Battery (volts/amp hrs)	6/6	6/6	6/5.5
Fuse (amps)	10	10	10

① CL90: 8.0/9,500
CL90L: 4.9/8,000

② CL90: 4.7 @ 8,000
CL90L: 14.24 @ 3,500

	CB100	CL100	SL100
DIMENSIONS			
Overall length (in.)	74.2	71.6	75.4
Overall width (in.)	29.5	32.5	31.9
Overall height (in.)	40.0	40.5	42.9
Ground clearance (in.)	N.A.	N.A.	N.A.
Wheelbase (in.)	47.4	47.8	49.4
Net weight (lbs)	191.8	191.8	211.7
ENGINE			
Type		ohc, air-cooled, four-stroke	
Bore and stroke (mm)	50.5 x 49.5	50.5 x 49.5	50.5 x 49.5

GENERAL SPECIFICATIONS (con't.)

	CB100	CL100	SL100
Compression ratio	9.5 : 1	9.5 : 1	9.5 : 1
Displacement (cc)	99	99	99
Valve train		chain-driven, overhead-cam	
Lubrication system		pressure and splash, wet sump	
Horsepower @ rpm		11.5 @ 11,000	
Carburetion (Keihin)		piston valve type, manual choke	
DRIVE TRAIN			
Clutch type		wet, multiple-disc type	
Transmission		constant meshed-gear type	
Power reduction (primary)		gear/4.055	
Power reduction (secondary)		chain and sprocket	
	2.857	3.071	3.142
1st	2.500	2.500	2.500
2nd	1.722	1.722	1.722
3rd	1.333	1.333	1.333
4th	1.083	1.083	1.083
5th	0.923	0.923	0.923
ELECTRICAL SYSTEM			
Ignition		battery and coil, high-voltage electrical spark	
Starting system	kick	kick	kick
Charging system		AC generator	
Battery (volts/amp hrs)	6/6	6/6	6/6
Fuse (amps)	15	15	15

	CB125S	CD125S	SL125	XL250
DIMENSIONS				
Overall length (in.)	74.8	74.8	78.5	83.5
Overall width (in.)	29.5	29.5	31.9	33.1
Overall height (in.)	40.0	39.4	44.3	44.3
Ground clearance (in.)	N.A.	N.A.	N.A.	7.5
Wheelbase (in.)	47.4	47.2	50.2	54.53
Net weight (lbs)	220.0	196.2	209.5	277.7
ENGINE				
Type		ohc, air-cooled, four-stroke		
Bore and stroke (mm)	56 x 49.5	56 x 49.5	56 x 49.5	74 x 57.8
Compression ratio	9.5 : 1	9.5 : 1	9.5 : 1	9.1 : 1
Displacement (cc)	122	122	122	248
Valve train		chain-driven, overhead-cam		
Lubrication system		pressure and splash, wet sump		
Horsepower @ rpm	12.0 @ 9,000	12.0 @ 9,000	12.0 @ 9,000	20.0 @ 8,000
Carburetion (Keihin)		piston valve type, manual choke		
DRIVE TRAIN				
Clutch type		wet, multiple-disc type		
Transmission		constant meshed-gear type		
Power reduction (primary)	gear/4.055	gear/4.055	gear /4.055	gear/3.125
Power reduction (secondary)		chain and sprocket		
	3.267	2.800	3.267	3.200
1st	2.500	2.769	2.769	2.352
2nd	1.722	1.722	1.722	1.666
3rd	1.333	1.272	1.272	1.280
4th	1.083	1.000	1.000	1.000
5th	0.923	——	0.815	0.806

GENERAL SPECIFICATIONS (con't.)

	CB125S	CD125S	SL125	XL250
ELECTRICAL SYSTEM				
Ignition	battery and coil, high-voltage electrical spark			
Starting system	kick	kick	kick	kick
Charging system	AC generator			
Battery (volts/amp hrs)	6/6	6/6	6/6	6/6
Fuse (amps)	10	10	15	15

TUNE-UP AND MAINTENANCE

TUNE-UP OPERATIONS

Valve Clearance ADJUSTMENT

1. Remove the left crankcase cover and the tappet caps. It will be necessary to remove the seat and tank on all 100 and 125 cc models, and also on the XL-250. The cam chain should also be adjusted at this time.

2. Rotate the engine until the flywheel "T" timing mark is in alignment with the timing mark scribed on the crankcase. The proper direction of rotation is indicated by an arrow scribed on the rotor.

3. Check the tappet clearance with a suitable feeler gauge. If there is no clearance at the tappet, the engine is on the exhaust stroke and it will be necessary to rotate it 360° to bring it to the top of the compression stroke.

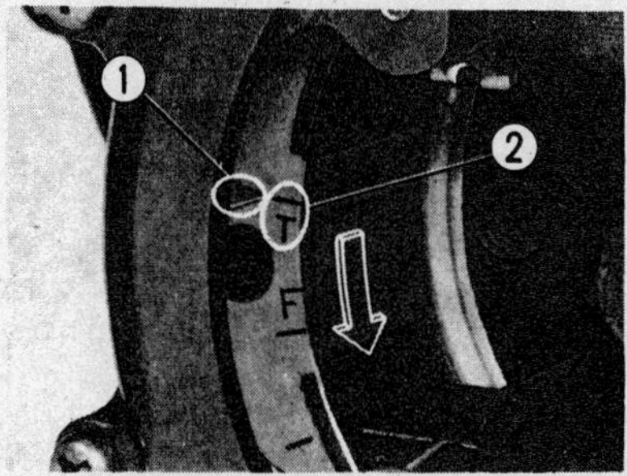

XL-250 timing marks

1. Index mark 2. "T" mark

4. To adjust the tappets, loosen the locknut and turn in the adjusting screw to decrease the clearance and out to increase clearance. The correct clearance for the intake and exhaust valves is 0.05 mm (0.002 in.) for all models other than the XL-250. Adjust both intake valves on the XL-250 to 0.05 mm (0.002 in.) and both exhaust valves to 0.08 mm (0.003 in.)

Aligning the "T" timing mark (50, 65, and 70cc models)

Aligning the "T" timing mark (90, 100, and 125cc models)

Adjusting the tappet clearance (shown is a 50cc engine)

Cam Chain Adjustment 100 AND 125 CC MODELS

1. Remove the tappet covers and rotate the engine until the piston is on the compression stroke and both valves are closed (play at the rocker arms). If there is no clearance at the tappets, rotate the engine 360° to bring the engine from the exhaust stroke to the compression stroke.

2. Loosen the cam chain adjuster locknut and loosen the adjuster screw a few

Cam chain adjuster

1. Adjuster locknut 2. Adjusting screw

turns to free the tensioner. Turn the screw clockwise until there is a noticeable tension on the screw and secure the locknut while holding the screw steady. Be careful not to place too much tension on the chain.

3. Replace the tappet covers.

XL-250

1. Rotate the engine in its normal operating direction until the piston is at TDC on the compression stroke.

2. Remove the tensioner set bolt cap and set nut. Slightly rotate the timing sprocket in a counter clockwise direction to place tension on the chain guide, then loosen the tensioner set bolt.

3. Secure the set bolt and nut and replace the set bolt cap.

Contact Breaker Points SERVICE AND ADJUSTMENT

If the points are heavily pitted, replace the points and condenser. These can be obtained as a unit already mounted on a base plate, or as separate components which can be mounted in place of the worn units. Disconnect the electrical leads, unscrew the components from the base plate or remove the base plate assembly (depending on which method you have chosen for replacement), and mount the new parts. If single components are to be used, be sure to insulate the points properly with insulating washers which must be used in their original

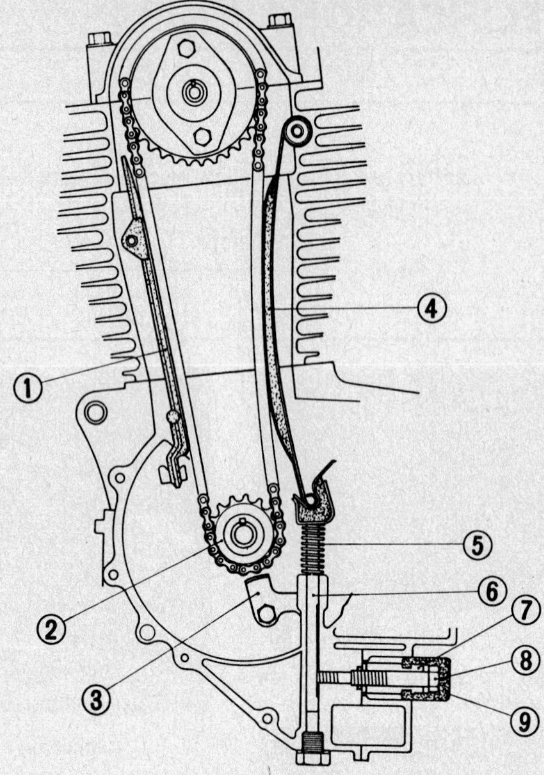

Cam chain guide

1. Cam chain guide
2. Timing sprocket
3. Cam chain set plate
4. Cam chain tensioner
5. Tensioner spring
6. Tensioner set bar
7. Tensioner set nut
8. Tensioner set bolt
9. Tensioner set bolt cap

positions. When the new parts are mounted, reconnect the electrical leads.

Place a drop or two of gasoline or other non-oily solvent on a piece of paper and pull it through the points to remove any dirt or preservative coating on the contact surfaces. Put a small daub of distributor cam lubricator or another high-melting-point grease on the contact breaker cam.

BREAKER POINT GAP ADJUSTMENT

The breaker point arrangement on all of the single-cylinder engines is basically the same, except that on the 50 and 65 cc models the points are located inside the rotor rather than being separate assemblies as on the larger models.

1. Rotate the engine until the points are open as far as they will go.

2. Check the point gap with a 0.3–0.4 mm (0.012–0.016 in.) feeler gauge. If the gap is incorrect, adjust it by loosening the breaker arm retaining screws so there is just a slight drag created by the pressure of the screws. (If the screws are loosened too much, the points will spring shut instead of holding an adjustment.) Pry the points to open or close them by prying with a screwdriver at the adjusting position. Secure the retaining screws when you are satisfied with the adjustment and then check it again to make sure tightening the screws hasn't altered the gap.

Breaker point adjustment

1. Rubbing block 2. Breaker cam

Ignition Timing

STATIC TIMING

50, 55, and 70 cc Models

1. Remove the left crankcase cover. Remove the spark plug and ground it against the cylinder head while it is still attached to the high-tension lead and turn on the ignition switch. The engine can be rotated easily (on hand clutch models) by placing the machine on its center stand, shifting the transmission into high gear, and rotating the rear wheel in its normal direction.

2. Rotate the engine until the spark plug fires and then stop immediately. Observe where the "F" mark on the rotor is. If the "F" mark is aligned with the crankcase timing mark, the engine is correctly timed. If plug fired before the "F" mark reached the crankcase timing mark, the timing is advanced and must be corrected by loosening the breaker lockscrew and shifting the breaker base to the left. If the timing is retarded it must be corrected by shifting the base to the right. Try to move the base a comparable distance between where the "F" mark was when the plug fired and the crankcase timing mark.

3. Secure the breaker lockscrew and recheck the timing. If the timing seems correct, replace the spark plug and the left crankcase cover.

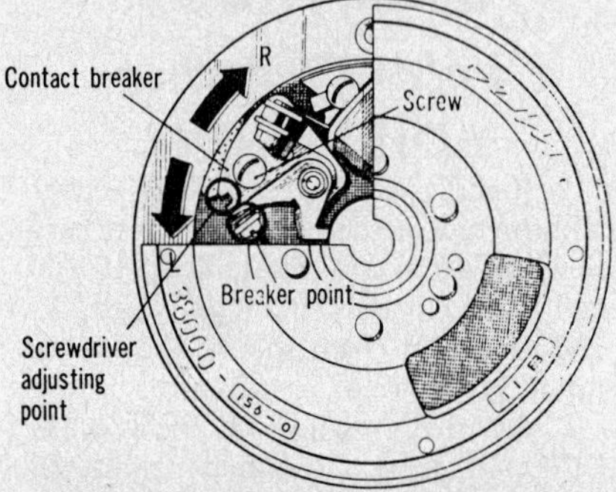

Adjusting the ignition timing (shown is a 100cc engine)

Aligning the "F" mark

90, 100, 125, and 250 cc Models

1. Remove the covers from the points and the left crankcase, attach one test light lead to the contact breaker arm spring and the other lead to ground (i.e., the cylinder cooling fins), and turn on the ignition switch (if applicable to the type of light in use). The engine (on all hand clutch models) can be easily rotated by placing the machine on the center stand, shifting the transmission into high gear, and rotating the rear wheel in its normal direction.

2. Rotate the engine until the test light goes out (for the type of test light that uses the machine's power source) and observe the location of the "F" mark and the crankcase timing mark. The two marks should be aligned if the timing is correct.

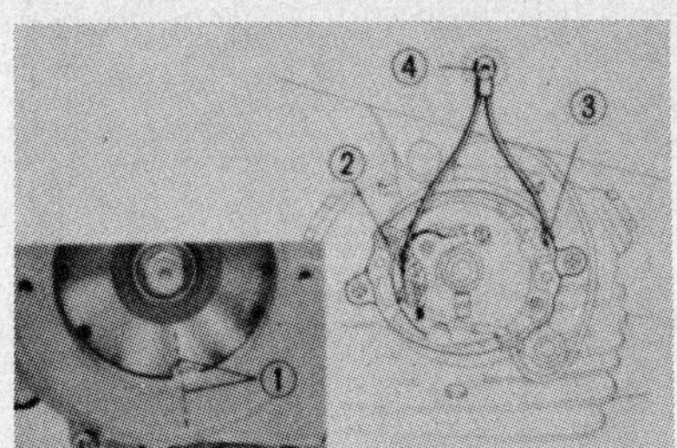

Adjusting the ignition timing and aligning the "F" mark

1. "F" aligning mark
2. Breaker arm spring
3. Ground
4. Test light

3. If the light goes off before the timing marks are aligned, the timing is advanced and can be remedied by loosening the breaker base securing screws and shifting the base clockwise to retard it. If the timing light stays on after the marks are aligned, the timing is retarded and the breaker base must be shifted counterclockwise to advance it.

4. Secure the breaker base and recheck the timing before installing the points and left crankcase covers.

Adjusting the breaker base plate

1. Base plate mounting screws
2. Base plate

DYNAMIC TIMING

50, 65, and 70 cc Models

1. Remove the left crankcase cover and connect the strobe light as directed by the manufacturer of the light.

2. With the engine running at its normal operating temperature at approximately 2500–3000 rpm, train the strobe light at the crankcase timing mark. If the

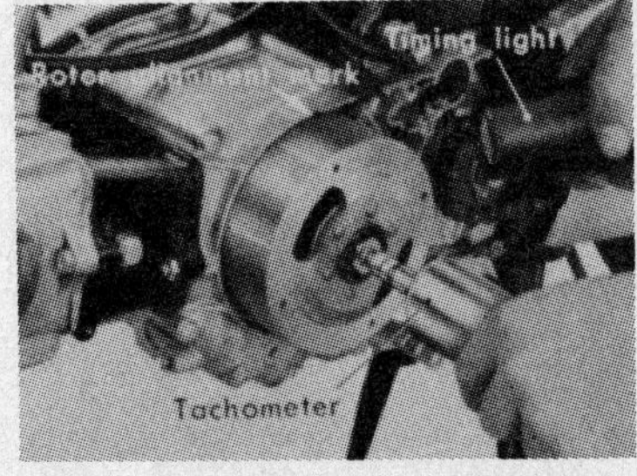

Strobe timing

timing is correct, the timing mark will appear to be between the two parallel lines on the rotor to the left of the "F" timing mark.

3. If the crankcase timing mark doesn't line up correctly, turn off the engine and shift the breaker base to the right to advance the timing and to the left to retard it. Start the motor and check for a proper adjustment again.

90, 100, 125, and 250 cc Models

1. Remove the points and left crankcase covers, and attach the strobe light according to the manufacturer's instructions.

2. With the engine running at its normal operating temperature at approximately 2500–3000 rpm, observe the timing marks on the rotor.

3. If the timing mark falls between the

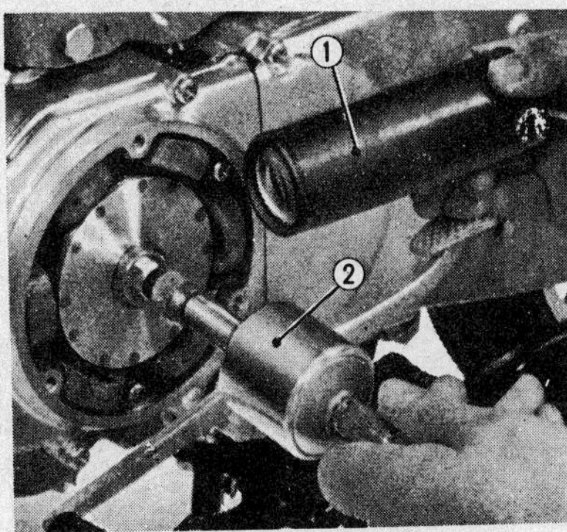

Strobe timing

1. Timing light
2. Tachometer

two parallel lines to the right of the "F" mark, the timing is correct. If the timing is retarded, shift the breaker base counterclockwise; clockwise if the timing is advanced. This can be done with the engine running.

4. Secure the breaker base while watching the timing marks then mount and secure the points and left crankcase covers.

Carburetor Adjustments

1. Run the engine until the normal operating temperature is reached, then set the idle speed as desired. A normal idle speed for models with a traditional clutch set up is about 1200–1350 rpm; a normal speed for models with an automatic clutch is about 1400–1600 rpm. Idle speed is increased by turning the throttle stop screw in; decreased by turning the stop screw out.

2. Adjust the mixture by turning the air screw slowly in until the engine runs irregularly, then back it out until it begins to run irregularly again. The correct adjustment is at that point where the engine runs its smoothest and fastest, and that point is somewhere in the middle. The "Tune-Up Specifications" chart indicates the factory setting which may be used but, due to variations in the manufacturing, this may not always be the most accurate method. The chart indicates the number of turns off its seat the air screw should be turned. Take care not to bevel the seat of the adjuster by applying pressure on it.

3. Readjust the throttle stop screw if the adjustment has changed. Avoid using an idle speed very much slower than that recommended by the factory as this may cause hard starting and poor low-speed operation.

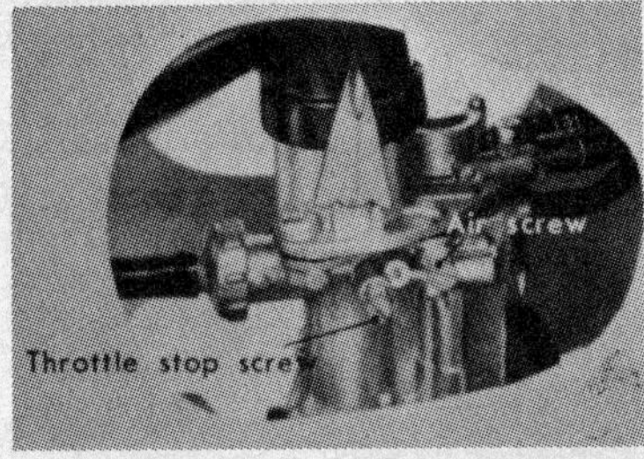

Adjusting the carburetor (50-70cc C series models)

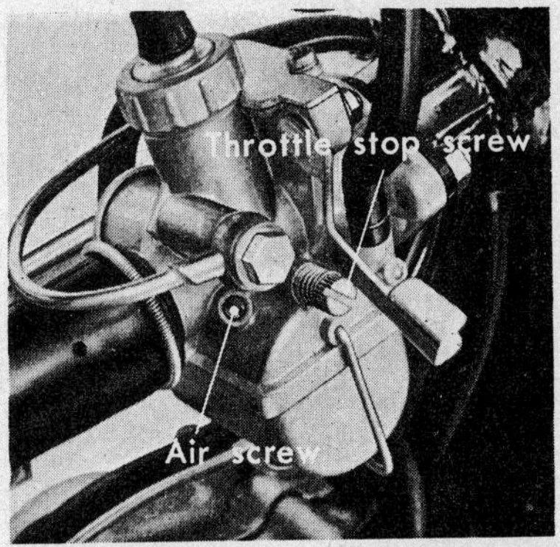

Adjusting the carburetor (50-70cc S series models)

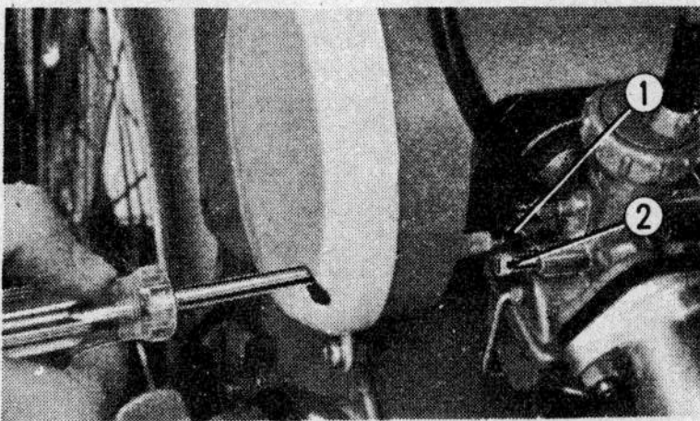

Adjusting the carburetor (90cc models)

1. Throttle stopscrew
2. Air screw

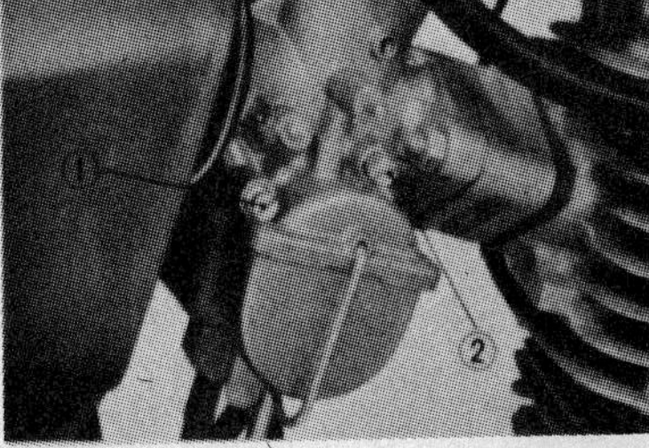

Adjusting the carburetor (100 and 125cc models)

1. Air screw
2. Throttle stopscrew

TUNE-UP SPECIFICATIONS

	C50, C50M, S50, C65, C65M, S65, CL70, C70, C70M, SL70	S90	CL90, CL90L	SL90
VALVE CLEARANCE (cold)				
Intake (in./mm)	0.002/0.05	0.002/0.05	0.002/0.05	0.002/0.05
Exhaust (in./mm)	0.002/0.05	0.002/0.05	0.002/0.05	0.002/0.05
CRANKING COMPRESSION				
Pressure range (psi)	115-170	115-170	115-170	115-170
IGNITION				
Spark plugs:				
Standard make*	NGK	NGK	NGK	NGK
Type	C-7HS	D-6HS	D-6HS	D-8HS
Gap (in./mm)	0.024-0.028/0.6-0.7	0.024-0.028/0.6-0.7	0.024-0.028/0.6-0.7	0.024-0.028/0.6-0.7
Point gap (in./mm)	0.012-0.016/0.3-0.4	0.012-0.016/0.3-0.4	0.012-0.016/0.3-0.4	0.012-0.016-0.3-0.4
CARBURETION				
Idle speed (rpm)	1,000-1,200	1,250-1,350	1,250-1,350	1,250-1,350
Air screw opening	$1\frac{1}{8} \pm \frac{1}{4}$	$1\frac{1}{4} \pm \frac{1}{8}$	$1\frac{3}{8} \pm \frac{1}{8}$	$1\frac{1}{4} \pm \frac{1}{8}$

* Other reputable makes are also acceptable. Be sure to select plugs of the correct heat range, and diameter. Most spark plug application charts also have conversion tables and a heat range chart, enabling you to select the spark plug that best suits your needs. Following the specifications charts is a NGK heat range chart that will enable you to choose a plug to fit the conditions.

	CD90	C90	CT90	CT90 (from F. no. 000001A)
VALVE CLEARANCE (cold)				
Intake (in./mm)	0.002/0.05	0.002/0.05	0.002/0.05	0.002/0.05
Exhaust (in./mm)	0.002/0.05	0.002/0.05	0.002/0.05	0.002/0.05
CRANKING COMPRESSION				
Pressure range (psi)	115-170	115-170	115-170	115-170
IGNITION				
Spark plugs:				
Standard make*	NGK	NGK	NGK	NGK
Type	D-6HS	D-6HS	D-8HS	D-8HS
Gap (in./mm)	0.024-0.028/0.6-0.7	0.024-0.028/0.6-0.7	0.024-0.028/0.6-0.7	0.024-0.028/0.6-0.7
Point gap (in./mm)	0.012-0.016/0.3-0.4	0.012-0.016/0.3-0.4	0.012-0.016/0.3-0.4	0.012-0.016/0.3-0.4
CARBURETION				
Idle speed (rpm)	1,250-1,350	1,250-1,350	1,400-1,060	1,400-1,060
Air screw opening	$1\frac{1}{4} \pm \frac{1}{8}$	$1 \pm \frac{1}{8}$	$1\frac{3}{8} \pm \frac{1}{8}$	$1\frac{1}{8} \pm \frac{1}{8}$

TUNE-UP SPECIFICATIONS (con't.)

	CB100, CL100, SL100, CB125S, CD125S, SL125	XL250
VALVE CLEARANCE (cold)		
Intake (in./mm)	0.002/0.05	0.002/0.05
Exhaust (in./mm)	0.002/0.05	0.003/0.08
CRANKING COMPRESSION		
Pressure range (psi)	115-170	115-170
IGNITION		
Spark plugs:		
Standard make*	NGK	NGK
Type	D-8ES	D-8ESL
Gap (in./mm)	0.025-0.028/0.6-0.7	0.025-0.028/0.6-0.7
Point gap (in./mm)	0.012-0.016/0.3-0.4	0.012-0.016/0.3-0.4
CARBURETION		
Idle speed (rpm)	1,200-1,300	1,200-1,300
Air screw opening	$1\frac{1}{2} \pm \frac{1}{8}$	$1\frac{1}{2} \pm \frac{1}{8}$

* Other reputable makes are also acceptable. Be sure to select plugs of the correct heat range, and diameter. Most spark plug application charts also have conversion tables and a heat range chart, enabling you to select the spark plug that best suits your needs. Following the specifications charts is a NGK heat range chart that will enable you to choose a plug to fit the conditions.

Adjusting the carburetor (XL-250)

1. Idle speed screw 2. Air screw

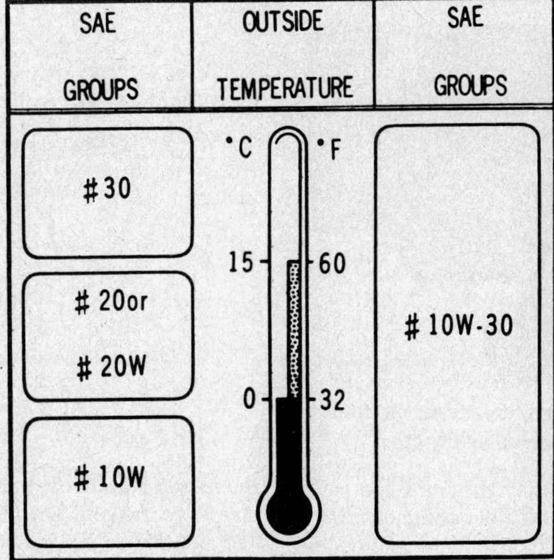

Specified grades of oil

MAINTENANCE ITEMS

Engine

OIL CHANGES (1,000 mi/60 days summer, 30 days winter)

Change the oil after the engine has been run long enough to reach operating temperature. This ensures that the oil is fluid enough to drain completely and that impurities suspended in the circulating oil will be removed. Honda recommends that SAE 10W-40 or 10W-50 oil of SD (previously MS) service rating be used. For even better protection, you can use the new SE-rated oils, which are able to withstand more heat than SD-rated oil before breaking down. If a single-viscosity oil is to be used, it must be a high-detergent (heavy-duty) oil of SD service rating. For temperatures above 60° F, use SAE 30W-30 oil; between 32 and 60° F, use SAE 20W-20; and below 32° F, use SAE 10W-10 oil. Do not use vegetable-based or non-detergent oil.

Remove the drain plug from the crankcase sump and remove the filler cap to assist draining. When most of the oil has drained, kick the engine over a few times to remove any oil remaining in the delivery system. Replace the drain plug and refill the engine with the correct grade and amount of oil. Start the engine and let it idle for a minute or so to circulate the oil. Turn the engine off and check the oil level with the filler dipstick. To obtain a true reading on the dipstick, three precautions must be observed:

1. Allow the oil a few seconds to drain down into the crankcase.
2. Place the machine on its center stand, on a level surface.
3. Do not screw the dipstick/filler cap into the case when checking the oil level or a false (high) reading will be obtained. Add oil if necessary to bring the level to the upper mark on the dipstick.

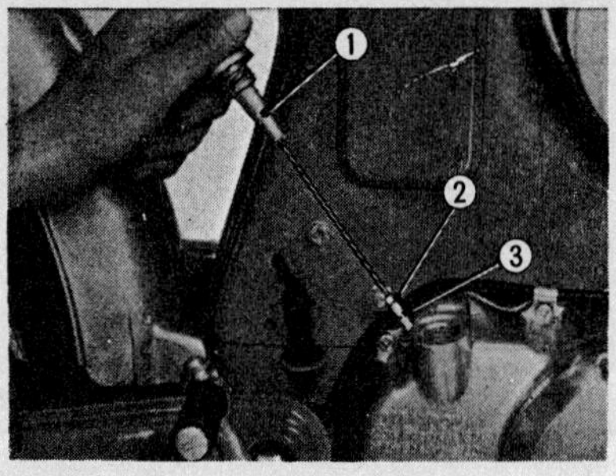

Oil level dipstick

1. Dipstick
2. High level mark
3. Low level mark

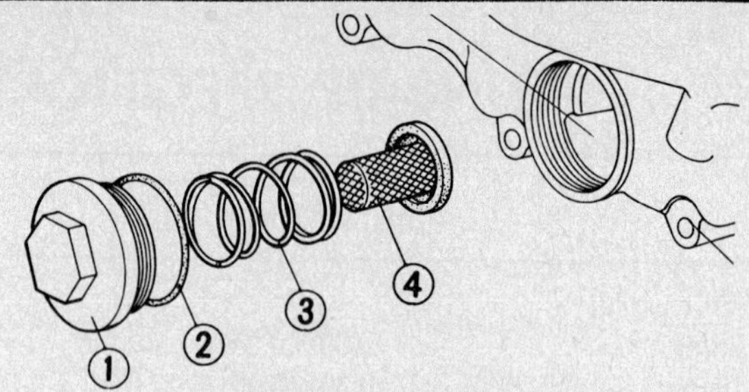

Oil filter assembly (XL-250)

1. Oil filter screen cap
2. O-ring
3. Spring
4. Oil filter screen

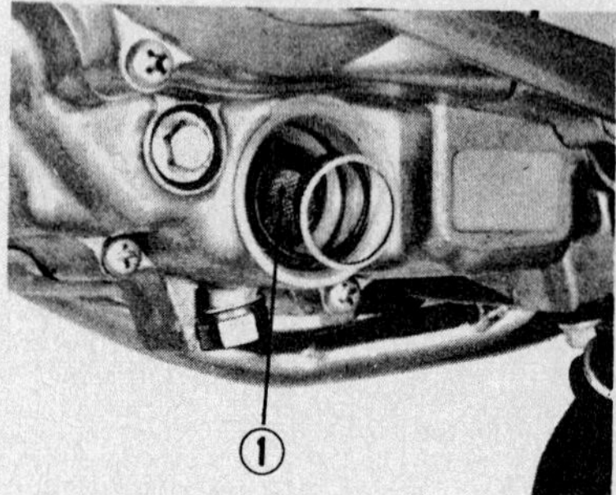

Oil pump screen (100, 125, and 250cc models)

1. Oil pump screen assembly

Crankcase drain plug

1. Drain plug

OIL FILTER (3,000 mi)

A centrifugal oil filter is used on all models other than the 90 cc bikes, and all of the engines have an oil screen filter which must be cleaned periodically. The filters need not be cleaned at every oil change, but they should be attended to about twice a year, or about every sixth oil change on machines that are used daily and accumulate high mileage. Bikes used in the dirt should be serviced more often, and the oil filter should be cleaned more frequently.

1. Clean the oil filter in conjunction with an oil change. Drain the oil, but do not reinstall the drain plug yet.

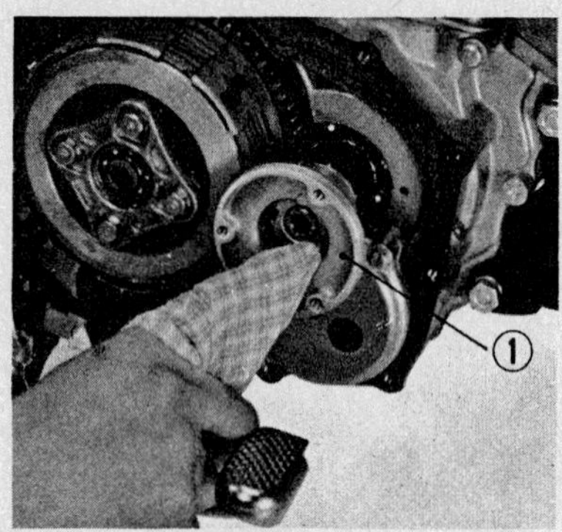

Cleaning the centrifugal oil filter

1. Centrifugal oil filter

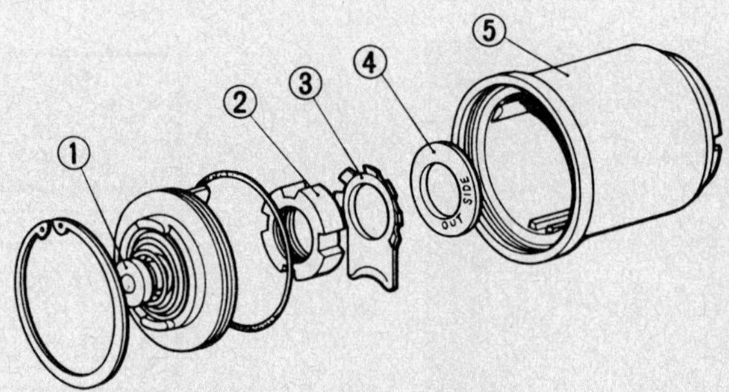

Centrifugal oil filter assembly (100, 125, and 250cc models)

1. Oil passage
2. Lock nut
3. Lock washer
4. Washer
5. Oil filter rotor

2. Remove the right crankcase cover on all models and pull out the oil screen. On 100 and 125 cc models, remove the right crankcase cover to get at the centrifugal oil filter, and the left-side filter cap to get at the pump screen. On the XL-250 the filter is located behind the countershaft sprocket which must be removed prior to filter servicing.

3. Clean centrifugal oil filters by wiping all dirt and grit from the surface with a clean rag. Remove the centrifugal oil filter cap (100, 125, and 250 cc models) and wipe out the inside of the filter with a clean rag.

4. Pull out the oil filter screen and clean it thoroughly with gasoline, blow it dry with compressed air, and replace it. The screen must be installed with the narrow portion toward the inside, and so the screen fin is to the bottom (all 50, 65, and 90 cc models). The filter on the 100, 125 and 250 cc models fits in vertically.

5. Install the drain cap and the filter covers, then replenish the oil supply.

OIL PRESSURE CHECK

XL-250

1. Remove the 10mm cap nut from the cylinder head cover, then start the engine. The engine should not be hot.

2. Watch for oil flow while keeping track of how long the engine has been running. If oil begins to flow within 12 seconds at 1000 rpm (with an oil temperature of 68°F or 20°C), the oil pump is delivering sufficient pressure. Note that the time lag may be increased under cold conditions when the oil will be thicker, but this does not indicate a malfunction.

3. Secure the cap nut to the specified torque of 21.7–26.0 ft lbs (3.0–3.6 kg/m).

NOTE: *Inadequate oil pressure is probably due to blockage of the oil lines rather than an oil pump malfunction. Consult the "Lubrication System" chapter for additional information.*

Removing the air filter element (shown is the S50 model)

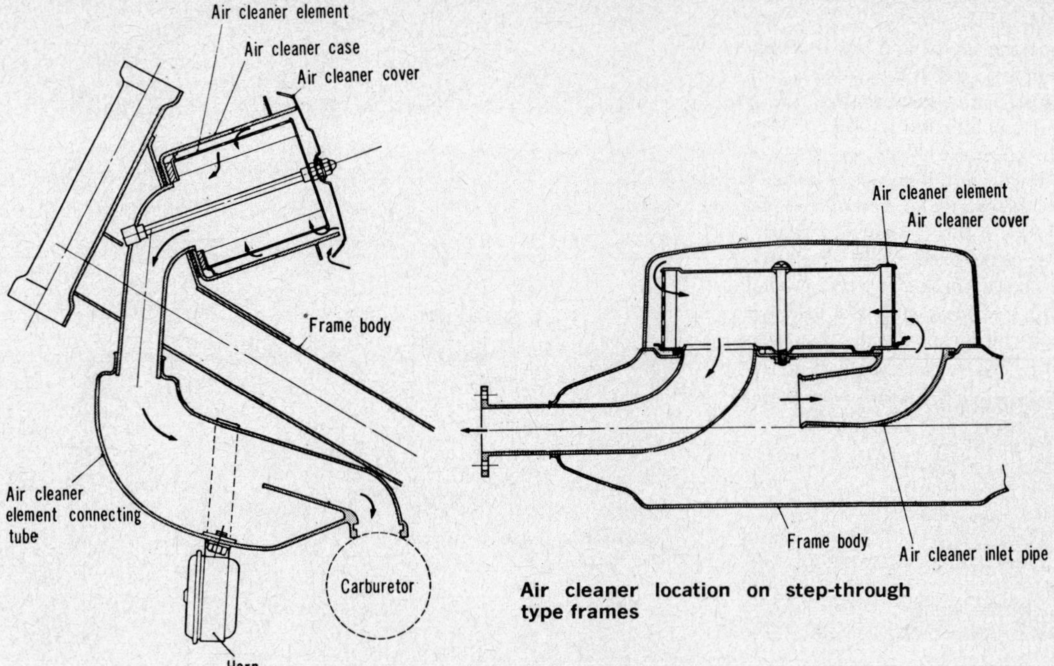

Air cleaner location on step-through type frames

AIR FILTER (3,000 mi/6 mo)

On most models, the filter element is located under a right-side panel, but on step-through machines, it is located on the frame tube. Clean paper elements with compressed air (directed from the inside out) or by tapping the element lightly and brushing away the dirt with a stiff brush. Replace the element if it is torn or wet with oil or water. Clean rubber foam filter elements in solvent and wet the elements with a light-grade oil. Wring out any excess oil before reinstallation. Foam elements must be replaced if torn.

Cleaning the element

CLUTCH ADJUSTMENT (3,000 mi/6 mo)

S50, S65, CL70, and SL70 Models

1. Adjust the clutch cable at the lever by loosening the cable adjuster locknut and rotating the cable adjuster until there is about 0.4–0.8 in. of free-play at the lever, then secure the locknut.

2. Check the operation of the clutch

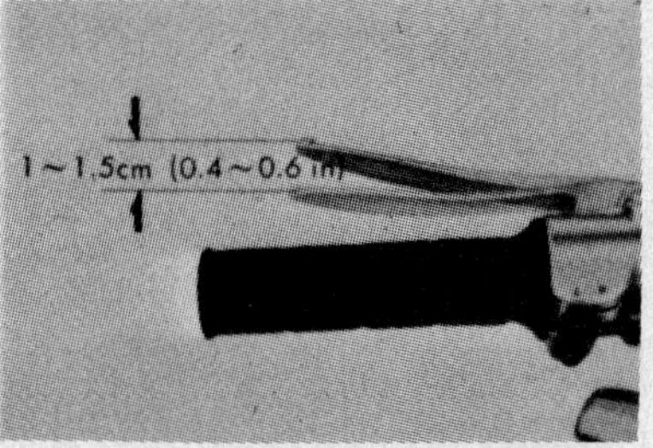

Clutch lever free-play

with the motor running. The gears should engage quietly and smoothly, and the bike should not tend to creep while in first gear with the clutch engaged. Go on to the next step if the clutch drags or slips.

3. If you can't arrive at a suitable adjustment, remove the clutch cover, loosen the adjusting screw locknut, and rotate the adjusting screw to the right until you feel tension on it, then rotate the screw ⅛–¼ turn to the left. This should be the correct adjustment give or take ⅛ of a turn. Secure the locknut while holding the adjusting screw and check the adjustment with the motor running. It may be necessary to readjust the cable at this time.

Adjusting the clutch

C50, C50M, C65, C65M, C70, C70M, C90, and CT90 Models

1. Loosen the clutch adjusting screw locknut located on the right-side crankcase, then rotate the screw to the left until there is tension on it. Rotate the adjusting screw about ⅛ of a turn to the right and secure the locknut while holding the screw steady.

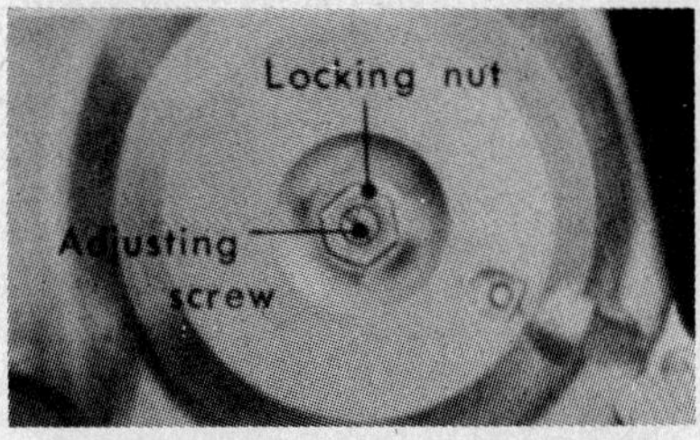

Adjusting the clutch

2. Check the adjustment by starting the motor and placing the transmission in first gear. The adjustment determines how fast the clutch will engage when the throttle is opened. If the bike starts to creep before the throttle is opened, the adjustment will have to be done again and the screw will have to be turned about ⅛ turn to the right. If it takes too long for the clutch to engage when the throttle is opened, the adjusting screw will have to be turned slightly to the left. If the initial adjustment is not correct, you will have to make small adjustments until you arrive at a suitable adjustment.

S90, CL90, CL90L, and CD90 Models

1. Adjust the clutch cable until there is about 0.4–0.6 in. of free-play at the lever by loosening the knurled locknut at the

lever and rotating the upper adjuster of the clutch cable.

2. Start the motor and put the transmission in first gear. If the clutch is properly adjusted, the gear change will be quiet and smooth, and the bike will not creep or stall. If the clutch performs well, secure the locknut. If you were unable to arrive at the proper amount of free-play, check to see if there is another adjuster near the bottom of the cable. This can be used to take up excessive slack, or allow for more free-play, and is adjusted by loosening the locknut and rotating the adjuster.

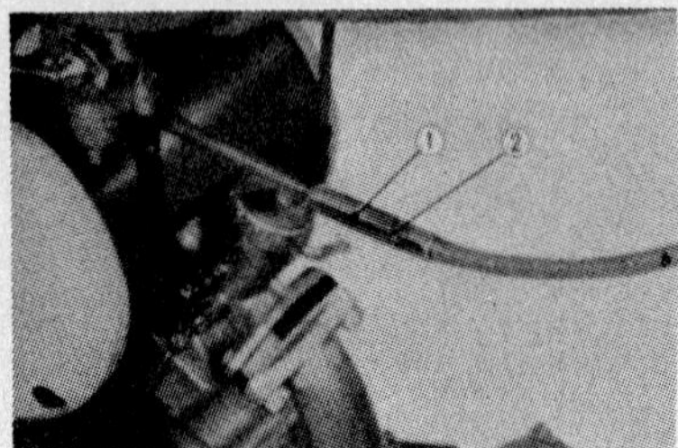

Adjusting clutch cable

1. Clutch cable Adjuster
2. Adjuster locknut

All 100 and 125 cc Models

1. Loosen the locknut at the clutch lever and rotate the cable adjuster until there is excessive play at the lever, then loosen the locknut located near the kickstart lever. Rotate the adjuster screw counterclockwise until a slight resistance is felt, then rotate the screw clockwise about ⅛–¼ of a turn and secure the locknut.

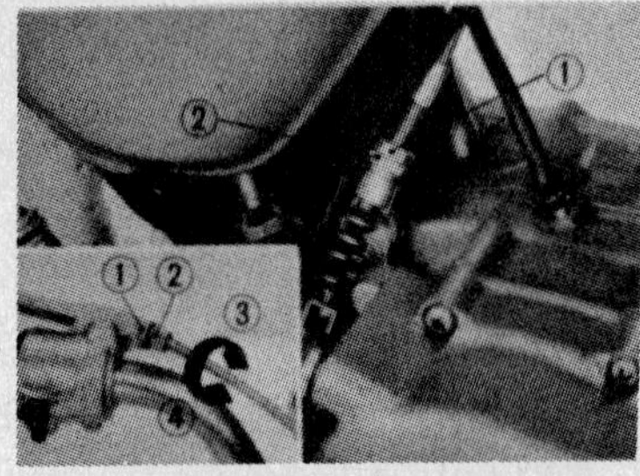

Adjusting clutch cable

1. Adjuster locknut
2. Cable adjuster
3. To increase play
4. To decrease play

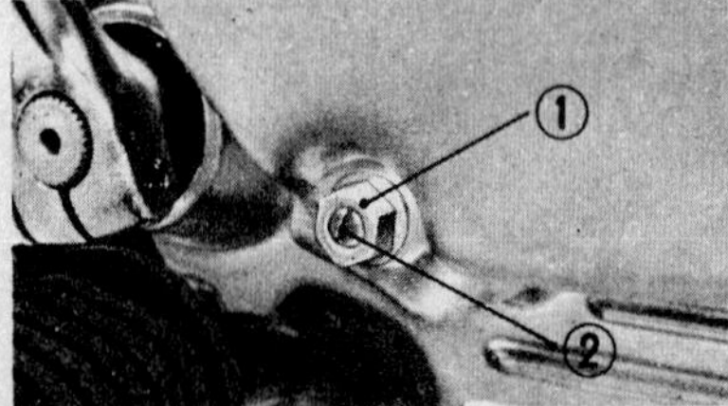

Adjusting the clutch push rod

1. Locknut
2. Adjusting screw

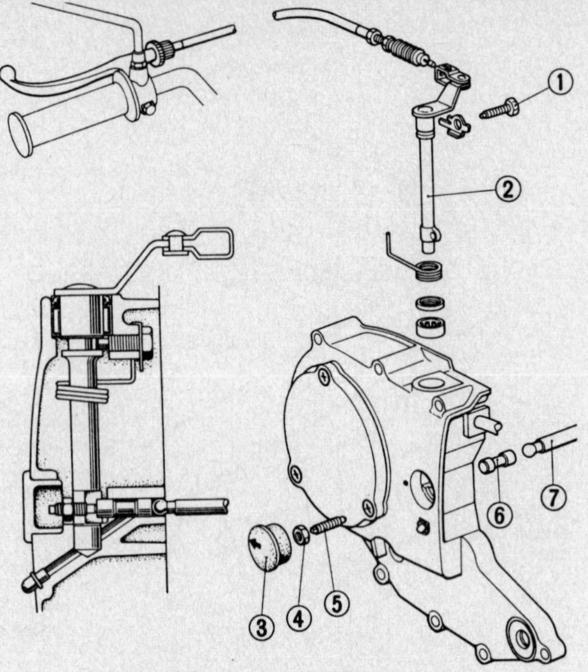

XL-250 clutch adjustment point

1. 6 mm lock bolt
2. Clutch release lever
3. Clutch adjuster cap
4. Lock nut
5. Adjusting screw
6. Clutch push rod end piece
7. Clutch push rod

2. Rotate the cable adjuster until there is about 0.4–0.8 in. of free-play still left at the lever, then secure the cable adjuster locknut.

3. Start the engine and place the transmission in first gear. If the clutch is adjusted correctly, the engagement will be quiet and smooth. If the bike tends to stall, creep, or if the clutch slips, start over and change the adjustment about ⅛ turn. Minor adjustments can be made entirely at the clutch lever if doing so doesn't make the cable too loose or tight.

XL-250

1. Remove the clutch adjusting cap and loosen the locknut.

2. Gently rotate the adjusting screw into its seat, then back it out ½ turn.

3. Secure the locknut while holding the adjusting screw steady, then install the adjusting cap so the arrow on the cap is aligned with the punch mark on the crankcase cover. Take up excess cable slack at the handlebar adjuster.

Fuel System (3,000 mi/6 mo)

The fuel filter, located in the fuel tap, should be removed and cleaned at the prescribed intervals or whenever fuel feed problems are encountered. Simply turn the fuel tap to "stop" and unscrew the cup to gain access to the filter. Fuel flow at both the "on" and "reserve" positions can be checked at this time. If the

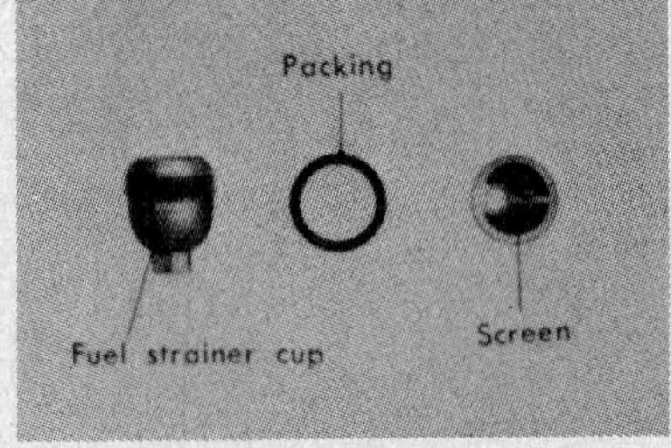

Fuel strainer

tap allows any gasoline to pass while in the "stop" position, the tap should be repaired or replaced, as gasoline may leak into the crankcase and dilute the oil.

Clean the filter screen and reinstall the cup and filter on the fuel tap. Use a new O-ring if necessary. Do not overtighten the cup. Examine the fuel lines for leakage and for restriction caused by kinks or sharp bends. Check to see that the vent hole in the tank filler cap is not plugged to preclude the possibility of fuel starvation.

Front Suspension and Steering (6,000 mi/12 mo)

STEERING HEAD BEARINGS

Check for play in the bearings by grabbing the bottom of the forks and trying to move them back and forth in line with the motorcycle. Play can be removed by tightening the steering head main nut.

Tighten the main nut no more than necessary to remove play, and then recheck the forks' motion. If the steering movement remains unsatisfactory, the bearings should be replaced.

FORK OIL

Remove the small drain plug at the bottom of each fork leg and work the suspension until all the oil has been expelled. Remove the top filler plugs, replace the drain plugs, and fill the fork leg with the proper amount and grade of oil. (Consult the specifications at the end of this section).

After the oil has been poured into the forks, work them up and down to expell any air in the hydraulic passages before replacing the filler caps.

Fork leg filler caps (shown is the CB100)

1. Filler caps

Fork leg drain plugs (shown is the CB100)

1. Drain plug

Brakes

Brake lining wear on drum brakes can be determined by observing the angle formed by the brake operating lever and rod (at the drum) while the brake is applied. When the lever and rod move past perpendicular as the brake is applied, the brake shoes should be replaced.

The brakes on all of the models are adjusted by rotating the adjusting nut at the hub (for front brakes), or at the brake rod (for rear brakes). Rotating the adjuster clockwise will decrease the amount of free-play at the brake lever or pedal, and rotating it counterclockwise will increase the amount of free-play. Make sure the cutaway portion of the adjusting nut is seated against the lever or a false adjustment will result. Minor adjustments can be made at the handlever on the 100 and 125 cc models by loosening the knurled locknut and rotating the adjuster until a satisfactory adjustment is obtained. Free-play should be about ¾–1¼ in. at both brakes but this is mostly a matter of personal preference. Check the adjustment by raising the wheel and rotating it. If you can hear the brakes dragging or if the wheel does not spin freely, back off on the adjuster until there is sufficient clearance between the brake shoes and the drum.

Unless the shoes are worn past their serviceable limit (consult the "Brakes" section for procedures and specifications), the brake actuating lever itself can be adjusted so that what remains of the shoes can be used. Remove the lever by removing the pinch bolt and prying the lever open. When it is spread sufficiently, it will be able to be slipped off the shaft. Rotate the lever a few degrees to the rear for rear brakes and to the front for front brakes, slip it back on the shaft, and secure it with the pinch bolt. The brakes can now be adjusted according to the information given in the previous paragraph. Never do this without taking down the brake and inspecting the shoes, as you may be placing the hub in jeopardy; if the shoes are too thin they may wear down to the rivets quickly, and rivets score brake drums almost immediately.

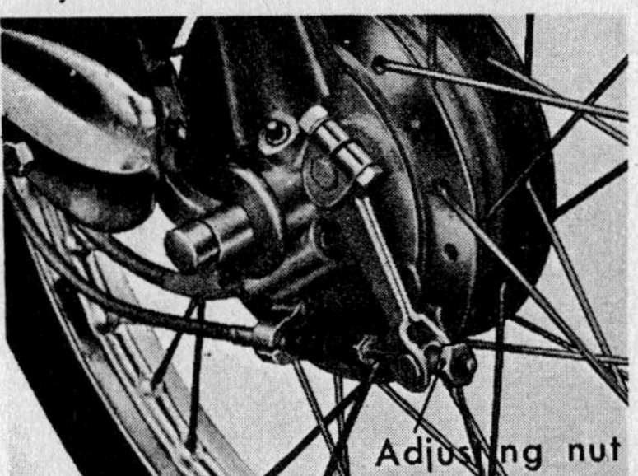

Front brake adjuster

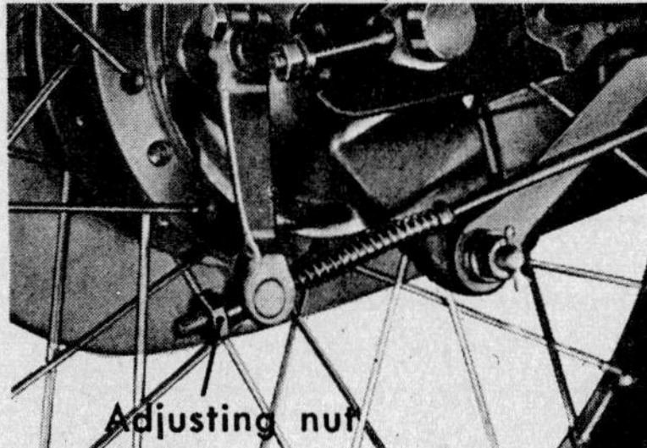

Rear brake adjuster

Rear brake pedal free-play

Final Drive

CHAIN ADJUSTMENT AND LUBRICATION

To check the chain adjustment, place the bike on the center stand and move the chain up and down at the midpoint of either run. On models with a fully enclosed chain, remove the inspection hole cap and check the adjustment through the hole. If the total movement exceeds 1.5 in., the chain is too loose and must be adjusted. The procedure is as follows:

1. Loosen the rear axle nut until it can easily be turned by hand.
2. Rotate the adjuster nuts evenly until the play is reduced to within ½–¾ in. for all models except the XL-250 which is adjusted for ¾ in. of chain slack. Turning the adjusters an unequal amount will adversely affect wheel alignment, so make sure the adjusters are both aligned with the same punch marks on the swing arm.

3. Secure the axle nut firmly and recheck the alignment and chain adjustment.

NOTE: *A dry chain should be lubricated before adjustment so that the links will not bind and restrict chain movement, making it seem tighter than it really is. If tension varies alternately between too loose and too tight as the chain is rotated, remove it and inspect for excessive wear after it has been thoroughly cleaned and lubricated. If the rear suspension has been modified it is a good idea to adjust the chain with someone sitting on the rear portion of the seat so the swing arm is in its riding position.*

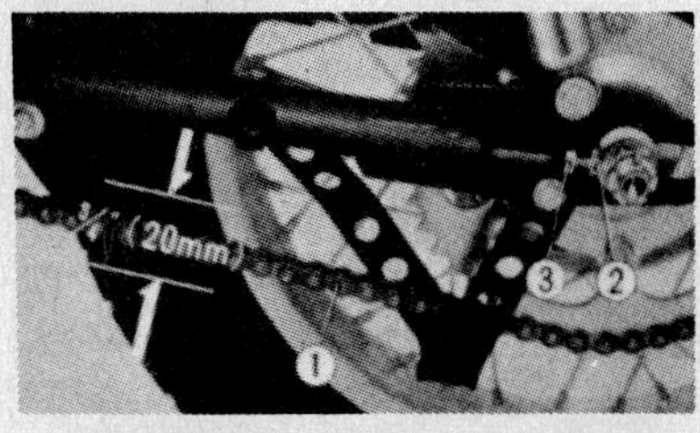

Adjusting the drive chain (XL250)

1. Drive chain
2. Adjusting bolt
3. Locknut

PERIODIC MAINTENANCE CHART

Service Required		Months or Miles, whichever occurs first				
		First	Second	Third	Thereafter Repeat Every	
	Month	——	6	12	6	12
	km	300	5,000	10,000	5,000	10,000
	Mile	200	3,000	6,000	3,000	6,000
Engine Oil—change		X	Every 1,000 Miles (1,600 km)			
Oil Filter—clean		X		X		X
Spark Plug—clean and adjust or replace			X	X	X	
Contact Breaker Points—check or service			X	X	X	
Ignition Timing—check or adjust		X	X	X	X	
Valve Tappet Clearance—check or adjust		X	X	X	X	
Cam Chain—adjust		X	X	X	X	
Air-Cleaner—clean			X			X
Throttle Operation—check			X	X	X	
Carburetor—check or adjust			X	X	X	
Fuel Valve Strainer—clean			X	X	X	
Fuel Tank and Fuel Lines—check			X	X	X	
Clutch—check or adjust		X	X	X	X	
Drive Chain and Sprockets—adjust and lubricate or replace		X	X	X	X	
Front and Rear Brake—adjust		X	X	X	X	
Front and Rear Brake Shoes—check or replace				X		X
Front and Rear Brake Links—check			X	X	X	
Wheel Rims and Spokes—check		X	X	X	X	
Tires—check or replace			X	X	X	
Front Fork Oil—check and			X			X
change				X		X
Steering Head Bearings—check or adjust				X		X
Steering Handle Lock—check for operation				X		X
Side Stand Spring—check			X	X	X	
Battery Electrolyte Level—check and replenish if necessary		X	X	X	X	
Lights, Horn, Speedometer and Tachometer—check for operation or adjust			X	X	X	

MAINTENANCE DATA

Model	C50	C50M	S50	C65	C65M	S65
CAPACITIES						
Engine Oil (pt)	1.7	1.7	1.7	1.7	1.7	1.7
Fork Oil (cc)	——	——	——	——	——	——
Gas Tank (pt)	6.3	6.3	11.6	9.5	9.5	13.7
Fuel Reserve Tank (pt)	N.A.	N.A.	N.A.	N.A.	N.A.	N.A.
TIRES						
Front Tire Size	2.25 x 17	2.25 x 17	2.25 x 17	2.25 x 17	2.25 x 17	2.25 x 17
Front Tire Pressure (psi)	24.2	24.2	24.2	24.2	24.2	24.2
Rear Tire Size	2.25 x 17	2.25 x 17	2.25 x 17	2.25 x 17	2.25 x 17	2.25 x 17
Rear Tire Pressure (psi)	30.0	30.0	30.0	30.0	30.0	30.0

MAINTENANCE DATA

Model	CL70	C70	C70M	SL70	S90	CL90, CL90L
CAPACITIES						
Engine Oil (pt)	1.5	1.5	1.5	1.5	1.9	1.9
Fork Oil (cc)	100-105	—	—	130-140	170-175	170-175
Gas Tank (pt)	12.8	9.6	9.6	N.A.	14.80	15.9
Fuel Reserve Tank (pt)	N.A.	N.A.	N.A.	N.A.	N.A.	N.A.
TIRES						
Front Tire Size	2.50 x 17	2.25 x 17	2.25 x 17	N.A.	2.50 x 18	2.50 x 18
Front Tire Pressure (psi)	25.6	24.2	24.2	N.A.	22.0	22.0
Rear Tire Size	2.50 x 17	2.50 x 17	2.50 x 17	N.A.	2.50 x 18	2.75 x 18
Rear Tire Pressure (psi)	28.5	30.0	30.0	N.A.	28.0	29.5

Model	SL90	CD90	C90	CT90	CT90 (from F. no. 000001A)	CB100
CAPACITIES						
Engine Oil (pt)	1.9	1.9	1.9	1.9	1.9	2.1
Fork Oil (cc)	170-175	—	—	—	130-140	130-140
Gas Tank (pt)	17.6	15.0	11.6	13.7	12.8	16.0
Fuel Reserve Tank (pt)	4.2	N.A.	N.A.	N.A.	N.A.	2.5
TIRES						
Front Tire Size	2.75 x 19	2.50 x 17	2.50 x 17	2.50 x 17	2.75 x 17	2.50 x 18
Front Tire Pressure (psi)	25.6	25.6	25.6	25.6	26.0	22.0
Rear Tire Size	3.25 x 17	2.50 x 17	2.50 x 17	2.75 x 17	2.75 x 17	2.75 x 18
Rear Tire Pressure (psi)	28.5	28.5	28.5	29.5	29.5	26.5

Model	CL100	SL100	CB125S	CD125S	SL125	XL250
CAPACITIES						
Engine Oil (pt)	2.1	2.1	2.0	2.0	2.0	4.0
Fork Oil (cc)	130-140	180-190	130-140	130-140	180-190	145-160
Gas Tank (pt)	16.0	16.0	16.0	16.0	14.4	16.2
Fuel Reserve Tank (pt)	2.5	2.5	2.6	2.6	3.2	N.A.
TIRES						
Front Tire Size	2.50 x 18	2.75 x 19	2.75 x 18	2.50 x 18	2.75 x 21	2.75 x 21
Front Tire Pressure (psi)	22.0	25.6	23.6	22.0	26.4	24.0
Rear Tire Size	3.00 x 18	3.25 x 17	3.00 x 17	2.75 x 18	3.25 x 18	4.00 x 18
Rear Tire Pressure (psi)	28.0	28.5	27.0	26.5	28.0	28.0

ENGINE AND TRANSMISSION

ENGINE SERVICE

Removal and Installation

On most models it is not necessary to remove the engine from the frame to work on the top end, carburetor, clutch, or oil pump. If it should become necessary to work on the bottom end, it is best to remove the engine intact and then disassemble it.

ALL 50, 65, AND 70 CC MODELS EXCEPT FOR THE CL70 AND SL70

1. Remove the air cleaner assembly (all models except S50 and S65), and drain the engine oil.
2. Remove the fairing (if applicable).
3. Remove the muffler and exhaust pipe.
4. Remove the footpeg assembly.
5. Remove the tool box.
6. Remove the oil lines (S50 and S65 models).
7. Remove the carburetor from the cylinder head on all "C" models and also remove the intake pipe from all "S" models. Pinch the fuel line with a hose clamp or block the line to prevent gasoline leakage onto the engine of the "C" models.

Disconnecting the oil lines

8. Disconnect the clutch cable at the lever and then at the engine (all "S" models).

9. Remove the kick-starter and gearshifter levers.

10. Remove the left-side crankcase cover and disconnect the electrical leads.

11. Rotate the rear wheel until the master link is positioned as shown, and remove the master link. Connect the ends of the chain with a length of mechanic's wire as an aid in reassembly.

Disconnecting the drive chain

12. Disconnect the high-tension lead from the spark plug and place the lead out of the way.

13. Remove the high-tension lead clip from the right-side crankcase cover.

14. Remove the brake pedal and stoplight switch return springs.

15. Remove the nuts from the engine mounting bolts and draw out the bolts while taking care not to allow the engine to fall onto the floor. Remove the engine.

Engine mounting bolt positions

16. Installation is in the reverse order of removal. Note the following:

a. Installation can be made easier by temporarily securing the engine by inserting a screwdriver in the mounting holes while inserting the mounting bolts.

b. The brake pedal spring and the stoplight switch are mounted together.

c. Make sure the master link is in excellent condition, and mount it so the closed end is in the direction of normal wheel rotation.

Temporarily mounting the engine

CL70 AND SL70 MODELS

1. Run the engine until its normal operating temperature is reached, then drain all the engine oil.

2. Remove the shifter lever, the footpeg assembly, the left-side crankcase cover, and disconnect the drive chain as described in the previous section.

3. Remove the exhaust system.

4. Disconnect the carburetor intake manifold at the cylinder head.

5. Disconnect the clutch cable at the release lever.

6. Remove the spark plug and move the high-tension lead out of the way.

7. Remove the battery cover and disconnect the three wires at the wiring harness. (The leads should be white, yellow, and pink.)

8. Disconnect the brake pedal return spring at the pedal.

9. Remove the engine mounting nuts and bolts, then remove the engine, taking care not to let it fall out of the frame.

10. Installation is in the reverse order of removal. Take care to have the closed portion of the master link facing in the direction of normal chain rotation.

S90, CL90, CL90L, AND CD90 MODELS

1. Run the engine until the normal operating temperature is reached and then drain the oil.

2. Remove the footpeg assembly, the muffler, and the left-side crankcase cover. Remove the chain as described in the previous section,

3. Disconnect the clutch cable at the release lever.

Disconnecting the clutch cable

1. Clutch cable
2. Clutch actuating lever

4. Disconnect the carburetor intake manifold at the cylinder head and place the assembly out of the way.

5. Disconnect the spark plug high-tension lead and place it out of the way.

6. Disconnect the brake pedal return spring.

7. Remove the engine mounting nuts and bolts, and lift the engine out of the frame.

8. Installation is in the reverse order of removal. Note the following:

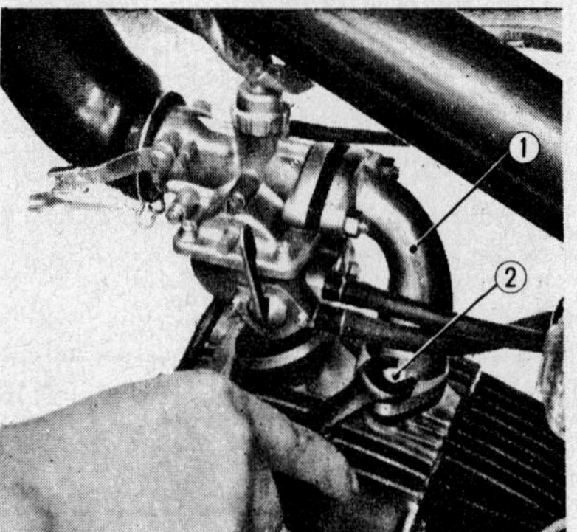

Disconnecting the intake manifold

1. Intake manifold
2. Flange mounting bolt

a. Block up the engine under the frame.

b. Route the wiring harness up to the battery box and suspend the engine from the frame by inserting a screwdriver into a frame and engine mounting point.

c. Insert the engine mounting bolts from the left side, then secure and torque the mounting nuts.

d. Connect the brake pedal return spring to the lower mounting bolt.

e. Connect all the wiring harness leads.

f. Connect the battery leads to the battery terminals, push the wires up into the top of the battery box, install the battery, taking care not to pinch any of the wires, and route the battery overflow tube down through the bottom of the battery box.

g. Connect the clutch cable to the release lever.

h. Install the intake manifold onto the carburetor and mount the assembly to the cylinder head, taking care to correctly position the O-ring between the manifold and the cylinder head.

i. Attach the high-tension lead to the spark plug. The lead should be secured by the clip under the right-side intake manifold mounting bolt.

j. Install the muffler assembly.

k. Connect the drive chain, taking care to have the closed portion of the master link facing the direction of chain rotation. The master link must be in excellent condition.

l. Install the chaincase, the rear crankcase cover, and the footpeg assembly.

C90 AND CT90 MODELS

1. Remove the fairing or mudguard (as applicable), and drain the oil.
2. Remove the footpeg assembly.
3. Remove the chaincase rear cover and disconnect the master link after wiring the chain halves together.
4. Remove the muffler and exhaust pipe.
5. Disconnect the intake manifold at the cylinder head.
6. Disconnect the electrical leads at the connectors.
7. Remove the high-tension lead from the spark plug and place it out of the way.
8. Disconnect the brake pedal return spring.
9. Remove the engine mounting bolts and remove the engine from the frame, taking care not to drop it.
10. Consult step no. eight of the previous section for installation procedures.

SL90 MODELS

1. Run the engine until its normal operating temperature is reached, drain the oil, and then remove the muffler and exhaust pipe.
2. Remove the left crankcase rear cover and disconnect the drive chain master link. Wire the two chain halves together.
3. Disconnect the clutch cable at the release lever.
4. Disconnect the high-tension lead from the spark plug and place it out of the way.
5. Remove the intake manifold at the cylinder head.
6. Remove the kick-starter and gearshifter levers.
7. Disconnect the electrical leads at the connectors.
8. Remove the engine mounting nuts and bolts and remove the engine from the frame.
9. Consult step no. 8 of the "S90, CL90, CL90L, and CD90 Models" section for installation procedures.

100 AND 125 CC MODELS

1. Run the engine until its normal operating temperature is reached, then drain the oil.
2. Remove the exhaust pipe and muffler.
3. Remove the footpeg assembly.
4. Disconnect the clutch cable at the release lever. It will probably be necessary to loosen the adjuster at the handlever to provide the necessary slack in the cable.
5. Disconnect the carburetor at the intake manifold.
6. Remove the gearshifter lever.
7. Remove the left-side, rear crankcase cover, then disconnect the drive chain and wire the halves together.

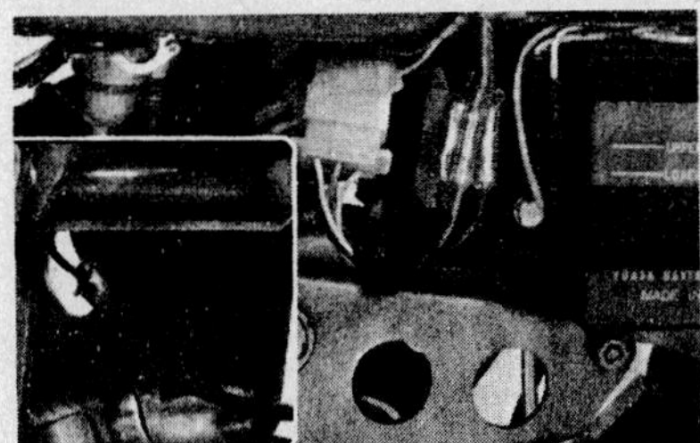

Disconnecting the electrical leads

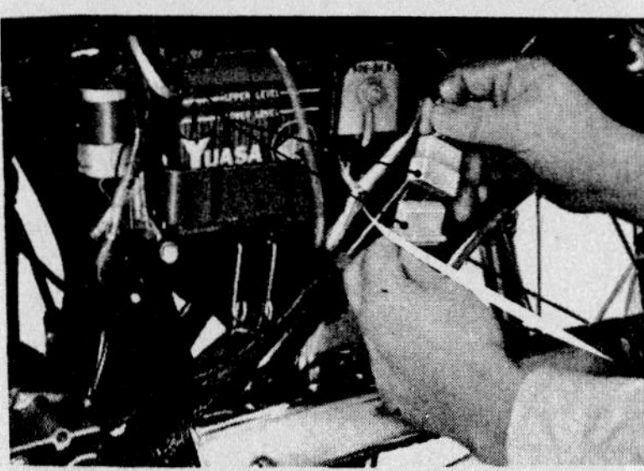

Disconnecting the electrical couplers

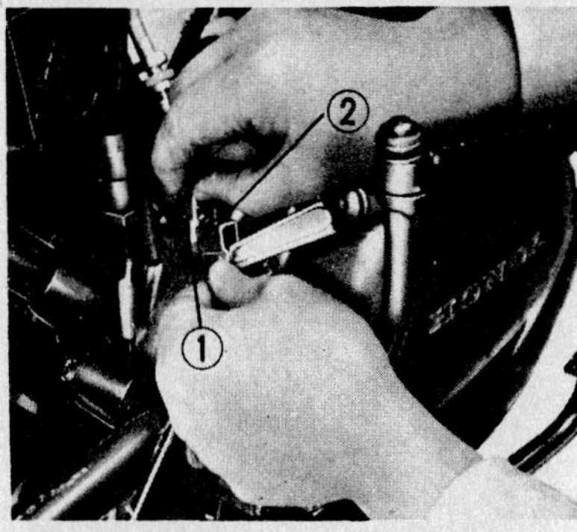

Disconnecting the clutch cable
1. Clutch cable
2. Clutch actuating lever

8. Disconnect the coupler from the wiring harness.
9. Remove the engine support nuts and bolts, then remove the engine from the frame.
10. Install the engine in the reverse order of removal. Note the following:

a. Hang the engine on the frame by inserting a screwdriver through the frame and engine mounting points.

b. Temporarily install the exhaust system before performing the final torquing.

c. Make certain that the closed portion of the master link is facing in the direction of chain rotation, and that the link is in excellent condition.

XL250

Follow the steps indicated in the following illustration.

Engine mounting bolt positions

Engine mounting bolt positions

TOP-END SERVICE

Cylinder Head

50, 65, AND 70 CC MODELS

Removal and Disassembly

1. Run the engine until normal operating temperature is reached, then drain the oil.
2. Remove the left-side crankcase cover, and remove the right- and left-side cylinder head covers.
3. Remove the flywheel using either the Honda puller (tool no. 07016–00102) or a suitable substitute, then remove the stator.
4. Rotate the engine until the key of the left crankshaft is pointing toward the cylinder head, and so the "O" mark on the cam sprocket is at its topmost position.
5. Remove the AC generator rotor and stator from C70M models, then remove the circlip securing the starter motor

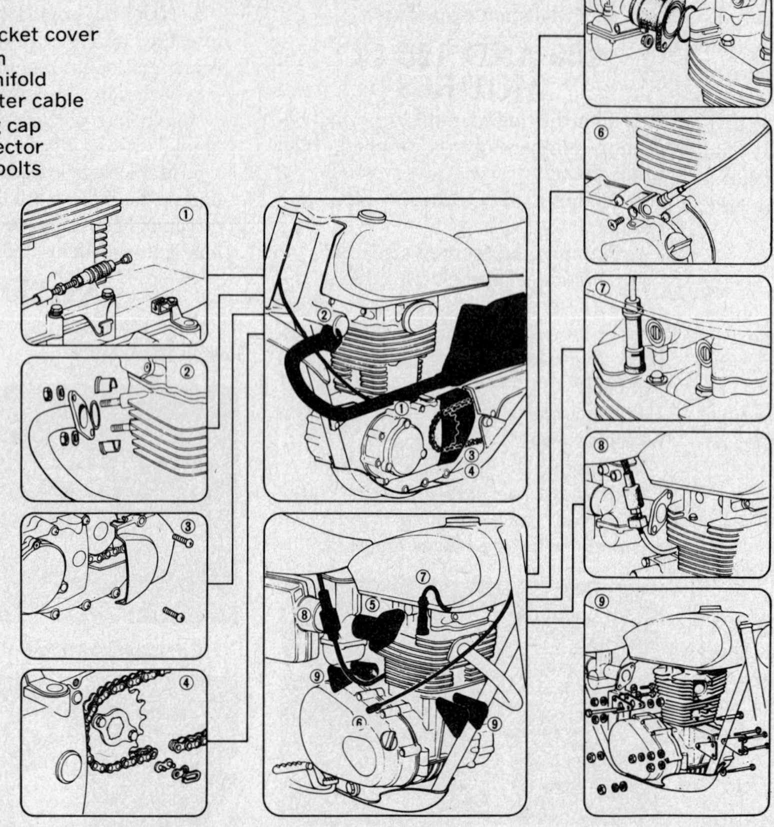

Engine removal and installation (XL250)

sprocket, and remove the starter chain, starter motor sprocket, and the starting sprocket.

6. Remove the three bolts which secure the cam sprocket to the cam, and remove the sprocket.

7. Remove the nuts securing the cylinder head to the cylinder, and remove the cylinder head. Tap the head gently with a hammer and wood block if it is reluctant to come off.

8. Remove the cam chain guide roller pin, then remove the roller.

9. Remove the rocker arms and the cam from the cylinder head. Use a 6 mm bolt for pulling out the rocker arm pin.

10. Using either the Honda valve spring compressor (tool no. 07031-20001) or a suitable substitute, compress

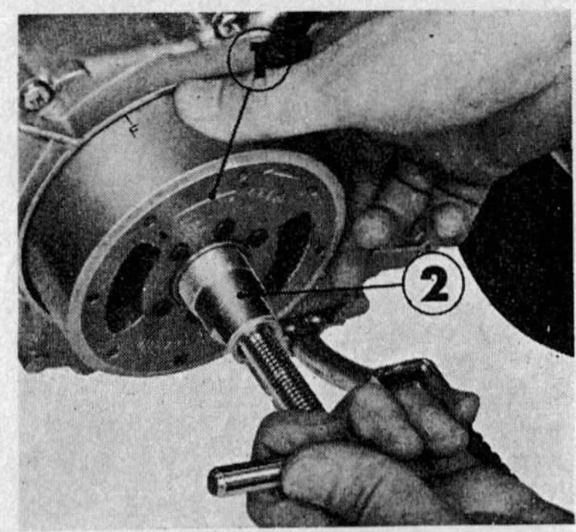
Removing the flywheel
1. Flywheel generator
2. Flywheel puller

1. Cam sprocket
2. Sprocket mounting bolts

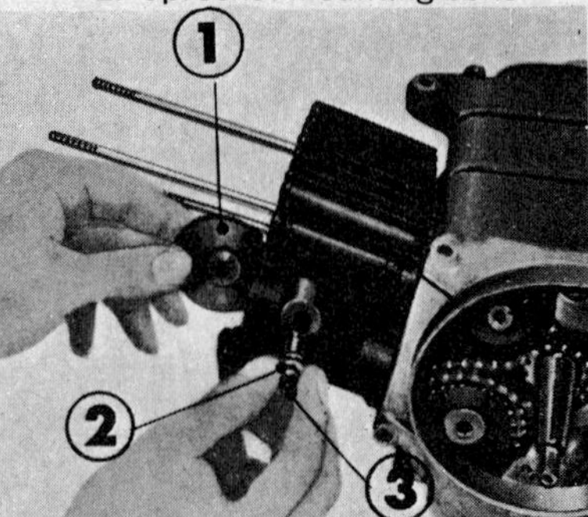
Removing the cam chain roller assembly
1. Cam chain roller guide
2. Sealing washer (8 mm)
3. Roller pin

Cylinder head covers

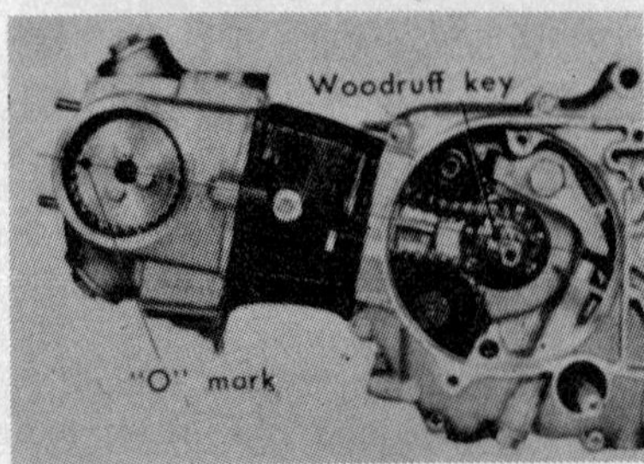

Removing the cam sprocket

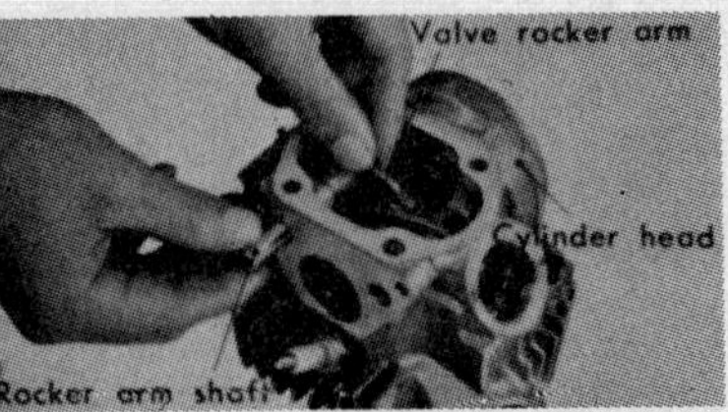

Disassembling the rocker arms →

the valve springs until the keepers can be removed, then remove the valve assemblies. Keep the assemblies separate for reassembly in their original positions.

Inspection and Repair

1. Clean all parts in a suitable solvent and blow them dry. Carbon deposits on the piston and head can be softened with a decarbonizing solvent and scraped off with a blunt instrument such as a butter-knife. Do not use a caustic soda solution to clean aluminum parts. Periodically, as you work, wipe the surface clean with a clean rag soaked in clean gasoline. If this is done with the cylinder still in place, you can catch the carbon flakes by pressing a line of grease around the piston on top of the rings. Rotating the piston will leave the grease ring with the carbon trapped in it on the cylinder, and it can then be wiped out. The cylinder head assemblies should be disassembled before being decarbonized.

2. Inspect the cylinder head for warpage on the gasket surface by laying a straightedge across the head and measuring the distance between the straightedge and the gasket surface with feeler gauges. If the clearance exceeds 0.002 in. (0.05 mm), the head must be repaired or replaced. Repair the head in the following manner:

a. Place a sheet of fine grit emery paper on a flat surface and move the head around in a figure-eight motion while applying mild pressure. It is better to work slowly with mild pressure than quickly with heavy pressure. Don't remove any more metal than is necessary.

b. An alternative method is to use a piece of glass and a fine valve grinding compound instead of the emery paper.

c. Check the results with Prussian blue or red lead. To do this, lay out some very fine sandpaper on a flat surface. Coat the gasket surface of the head with the dye and allow it to dry. Move the head very gently over the sandpaper just long enough to remove the dye, then look at the gasket surface. If the head is flat all of the dye will have been removed. If there is still dye on the head, repeat the entire process.

3. Inspect the valve seat for a contact surface in excess of 0.080 in. (2.0 mm) and cut the seat if necessary until the seat width measures 0.040–0.051 in. (1.0–1.3 mm). For the valve seat contact area, 30° and 60° cutters are used; a 45° cutter is used for the valve contact area. Valve faces and stems may be reground if necessary, but replacement is advised. Valves with a stellite face must be replaced as they cannot be ground. Always lap in a new valve.

4. If the seat has just been cut, or if lapping is desired, lap the valves in at this

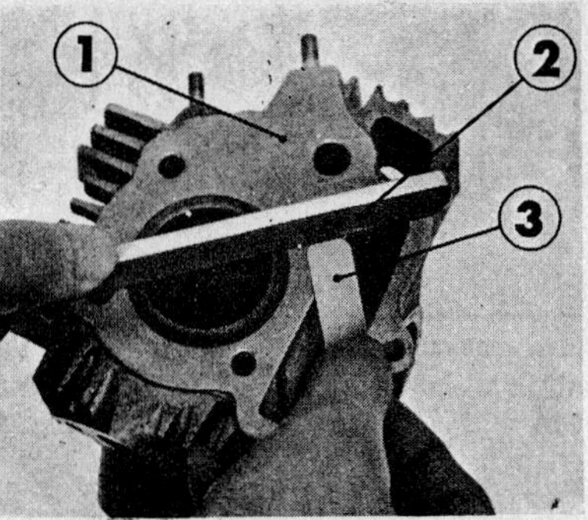

Checking the cylinder head for warpage
1. Cylinder head
2. Straightedge
3. Feeler gauge

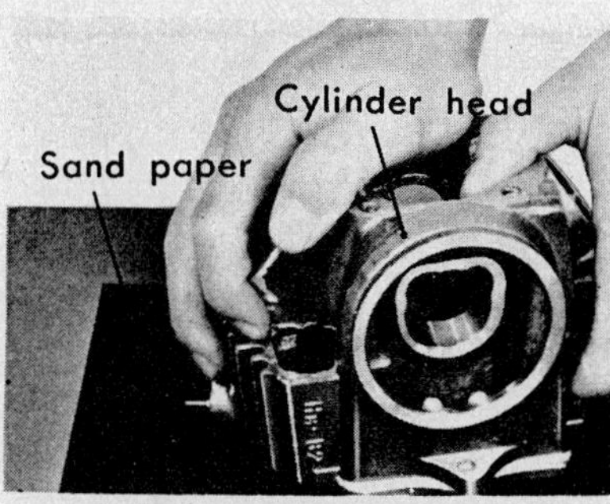

Truing the gasket surface

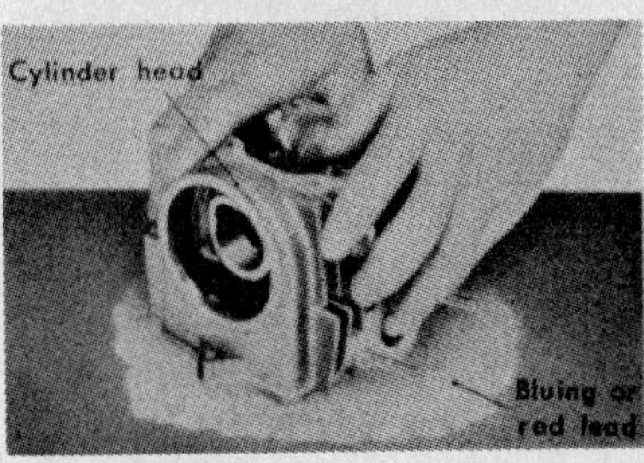

Checking the results with dye

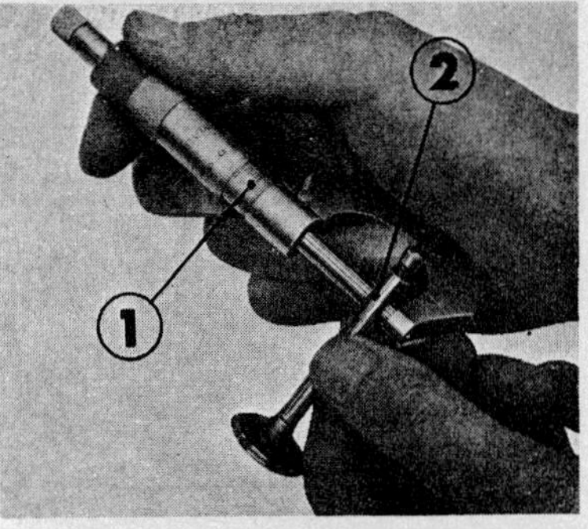

Measuring the valve stem
1. Micrometer 2. Valve

Drifting out the valve guide
1. Valve guide drift

Measuring the clearance between the valve stem and guide
1. Dial indicator

time in the following manner:

a. Lightly oil the valve stem and insert it in the guide.

b. Apply a light coat of lapping compound to the seat. It is best to apply a few evenly spaced daubs rather than a random application.

c. Slip a gas line over the valve stem and rotate it back and forth in your hands while applying mild pressure against the seat by pulling on the gas line.

d. Clean the seat area when smooth and assemble the valve. Pour some gas into the spring-side of the head and allow the head to sit. If there is no leakage through the seat, the lapping has been successful.

5. Measure the clearance between the valve stem and guide with a dial indicator, then measure the diameter of the valve with a micrometer. Measure the valve in several places and replace it if

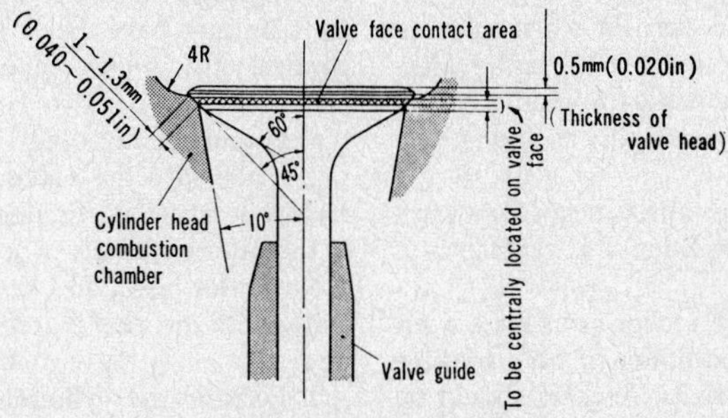

Valve seat contact area

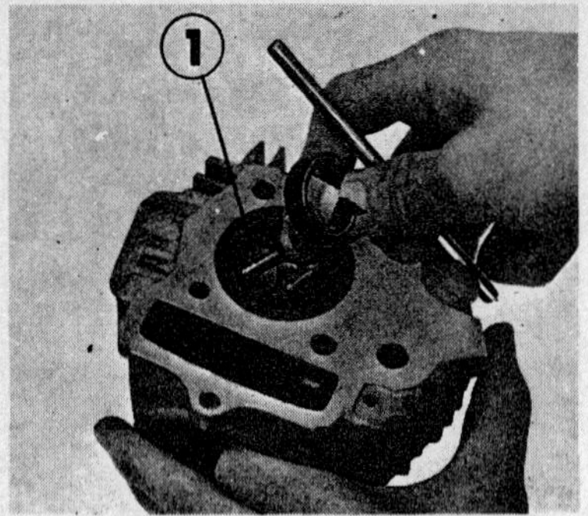

Reaming the valve guide
1. Valve guide reamer

worn or unevenly worn. Replace the guide if worn or damaged in the following manner:

a. Remove the guide from the head with either the Honda valve guide remover (tool no. 07047–04001) or a suitable drift. If drifting, heat the head in an oven to about 200° F to loosen the guide.

b. Install a new guide that is one size over the previous one, then ream it to size with either the Honda reamer (tool no. 07008–24001) or a suitable substitute. Take care not to deform the guide, and oil the reamer lightly when it encounters interference. Remove metal chips as soon as they occur, and always continue to rotate the reamer when removing or installing it.

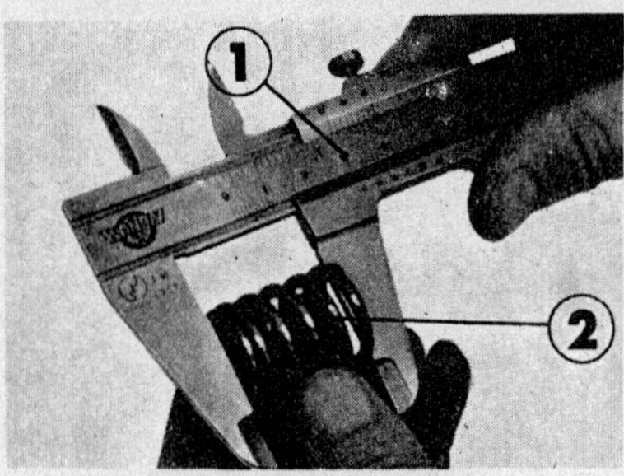

Measuring the valve springs
1. Vernier caliper
2. Valve spring

6. Inspect the valve springs for a worn, collapsed, or damaged condition, and replace them if necessary. If a spring is noticeably shorter than a new one, or if it is shorter than the serviceable limits listed in the specifications charts at the end of this chapter, replace the spring set.

7. Inspect the cam for worn spots or damage and replace it as necessary. Measuring the cam with a micrometer will indicate if it is worn past its serviceable limit.

8. Inspect the cam sprocket for a worn or damaged condition and replace it as necessary.

9. Inspect the rocker arms for a worn or damaged condition, or for excessive play on their shafts. Rockers should be replaced on the valve and shaft from which they came.

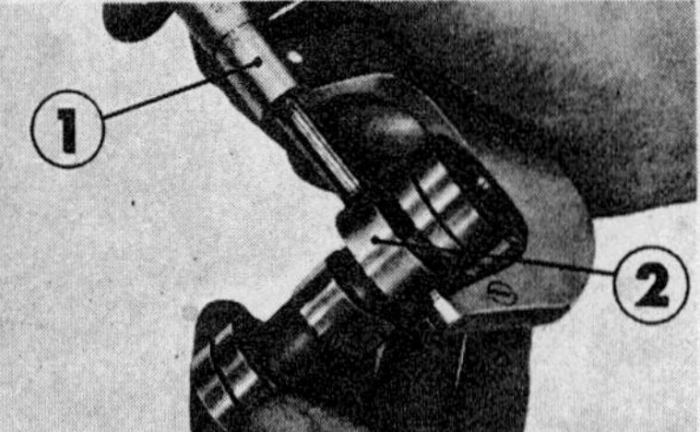

Measuring the camshaft
1. Micrometer
2. Camshaft

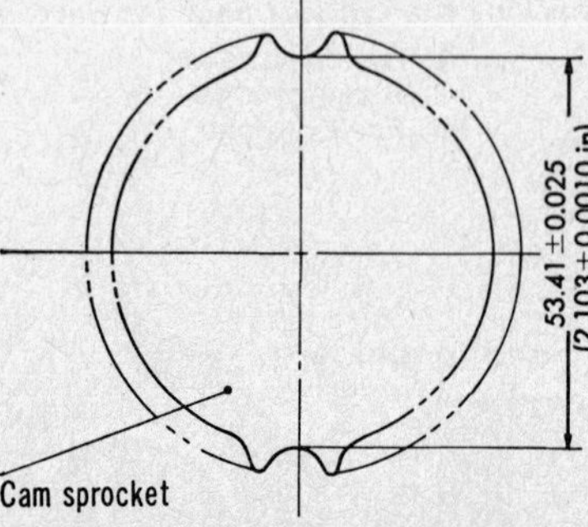

Cam sprocket teeth base contour

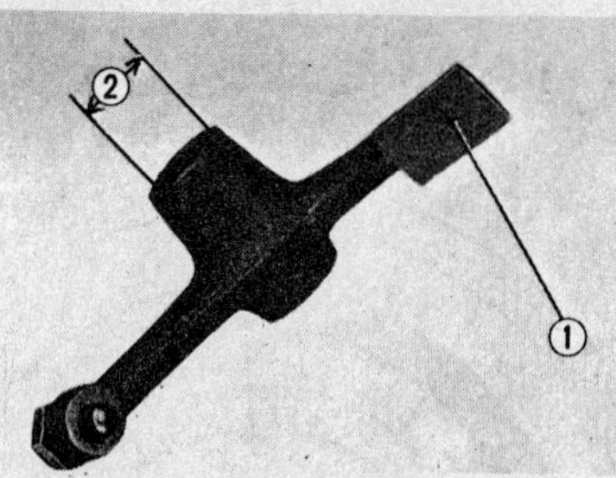

Rocker arm
1. Cam contact area
2. Shaft bore

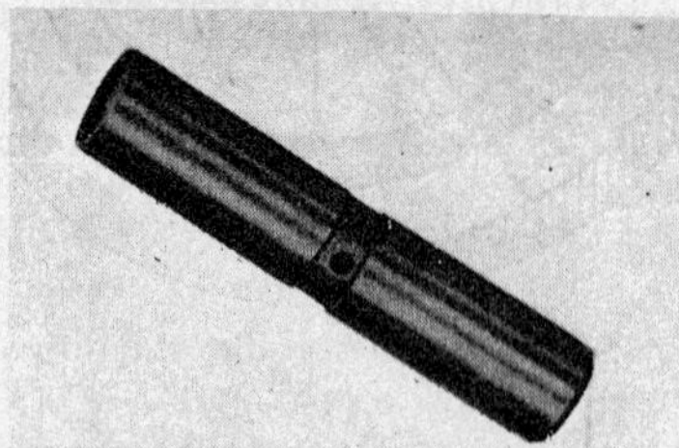

Rocker arm shaft

Assembly

1. Assembly is in the reverse order of disassembly. Make sure you use new inlet seals if they have been disturbed—regardless of how they appear. Use a new head gasket and valve keepers also, as these parts will fail easily if reused.

2. Make sure the valve timing is correct by rotating the engine until the key of the left crankshaft is pointing toward the cylinder head, and so the "O" mark on the cam sprocket is at its topmost position.

3. Position the cylinder head nuts as illustrated and torque them down in the order shown at 6.5–9.0 ft lbs.

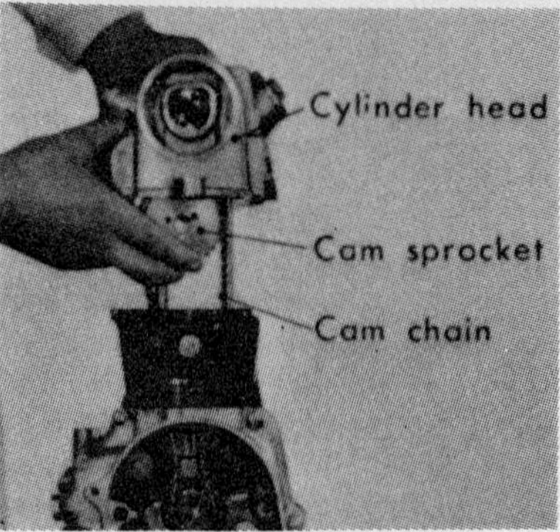

Installing the cylinder head

Cylinder head torquing sequence

Cylinder and Piston Assembly

Disassembly

1. Remove the cylinder head as described in the cylinder head "Removal and Disassembly" section.

2. Remove the cam chain guide roller pin and roller.

3. Remove the cylinder mounting bolts and lift the cylinder off the piston. This is best done with the piston at top dead center (TDC), and, as soon as there is enough room between the cylinder and the crankcase, an oil-soaked, clean rag should be inserted and wrapped around the connecting rod. This is to keep dirt and possible broken ring parts from falling into the crankcase.

4. Remove the piston pin circlip, then push the piston pin out from the opposite side with a suitable instrument. If the pin

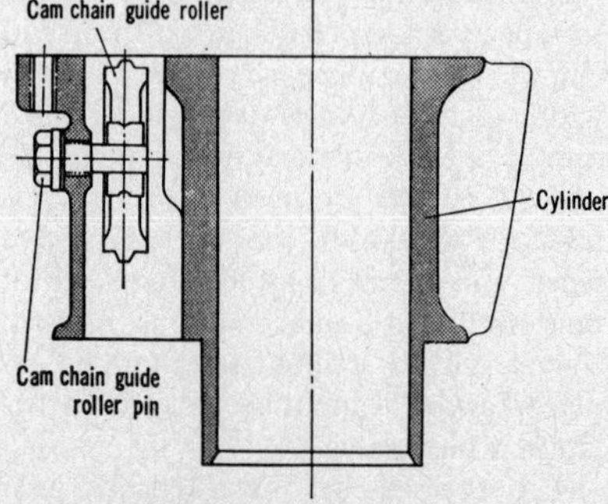

Cylinder cross section

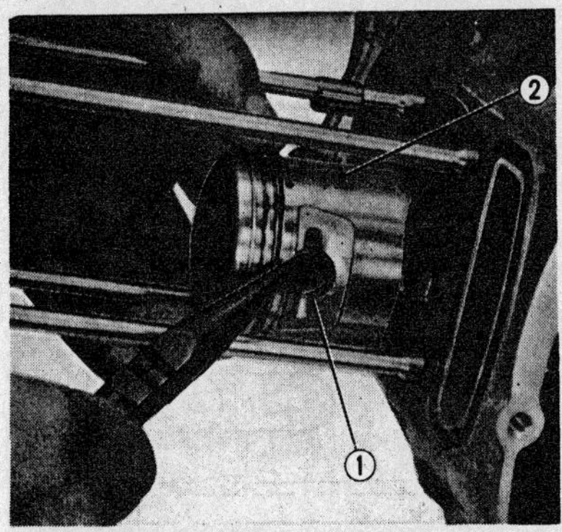

Removing the piston pin circlip
1. Piston pin circlip
2. Piston

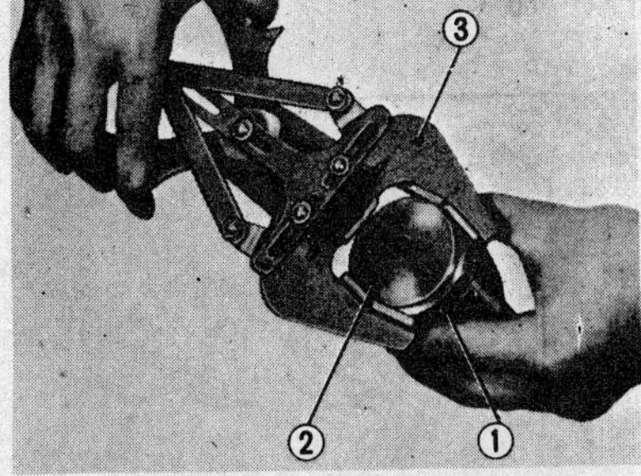

Removing the piston rings
1. Piston ring
2. Piston
3. Ring removing tool

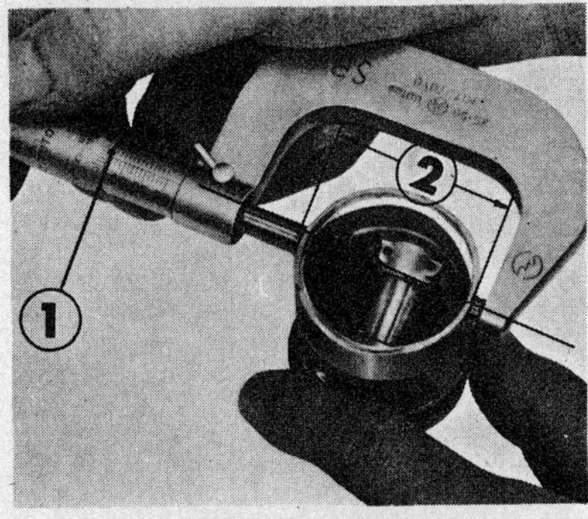

Measuring the piston
1. Micrometer
2. Piston diameter

won't come free, remove the remaining circlip and drift the pin out while securely holding the connecting rod and piston steady. The piston crown may be heated with hot towels or an iron to aid in the pin removal.

5. Remove the piston from the connecting rod, and remove the piston rings if so desired by using a ring expander or by hand, taking care not to score the piston.

Inspection and Repair

1. Consult the decarbonization section in the cylinder head "Inspection and Repair" section.

2. Inspect the piston pin for a worn, scored, pitted, or otherwise damaged condition, and replace it as necessary. Oversize pins may be used if there is excessive clearance in the piston, but replacing the piston and pin is the better method

3. Inspect the piston for a scored, burned, or damaged condition and replace as necessary. Measure the piston with a micrometer at a right angle to the piston pin, and near the bottom of the piston skirt. The piston must be replaced if worn beyond the limit listed in the specifications chart.

4. Inspect the condition of the cylinder walls for a scored condition. The cylinder may be bored out or reamed to a serviceable condition if this will not make the cylinder walls too thin. Measure the cylinder bore at several places and replace the cylinder if worn beyond its serviceable limit.

5. Measure the piston ring end-gap to determine the necessary size of ring. Do this with a feeler gauge at the bottom of the cylinder. Oversize rings are available for standard and oversize pistons.

Measuring the cylinder bore

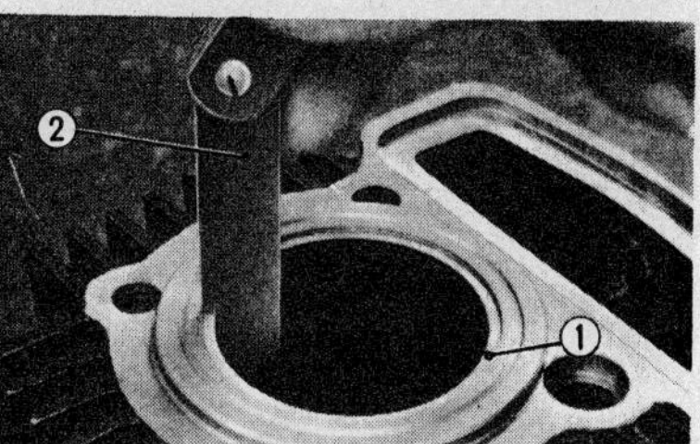

Measuring ring end gap
1. Piston ring
2. Feeler gauge

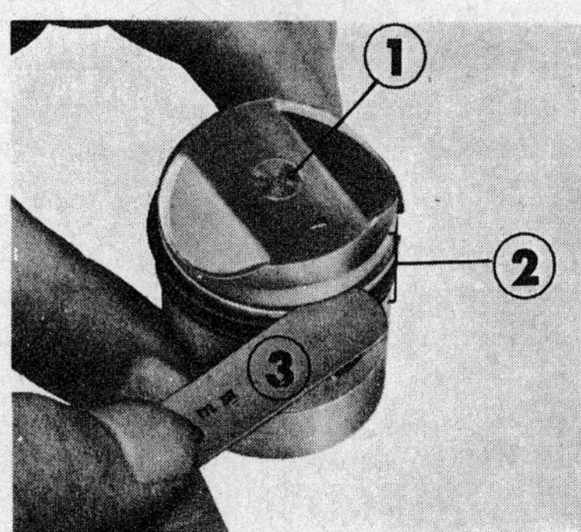

Measuring ring side clearance
1. Piston
2. Piston rings
3. Feeler gauge

6. Measure the ring side clearance with a feeler gauge, using the appropriately sized ring. The piston will have to be replaced if there is too much clearance in the ring grooves.

7. If there is excessive side-play, or up-and-down play on the connecting rod, the lower end bearing may be in need of replacement. Consult the crankcase "Disassembly" section.

Assembly

1. Assembly is basically in the reverse order of disassembly. Use new circlips and gaskets, make sure that all the components are perfectly clean, and lubricate each part with clean engine oil before assembling them.

2. Mount the rings on the piston with a ring expander if possible. The rings should be mounted with the ring mark up. Stagger the ring gaps every 120°, and check to make sure they can rotate freely by rolling them externally in the ring groove.

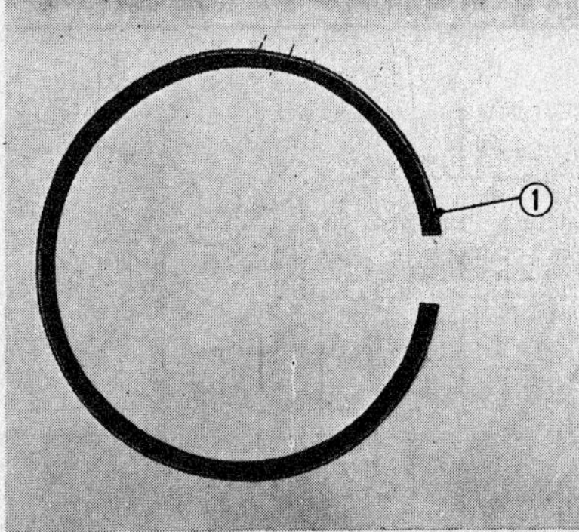

Ring mark
1. Ring mark

Checking piston ring contact
1. Piston ring
2. Ring grooves

3. Install the new cylinder gasket at this time.

4. Install the piston on the connecting rod so the arrow on the piston crown is pointing down. Install one circlip, position the piston on the connecting rod, slip in the piston pin, and install the remaining circlip. Lightly oil the piston pin with clean engine oil, and heat the piston crown if necessary.

The position for mounting the piston

5. Compress the rings with a hose clamp, or hold them closed by hand while slipping the cylinder down over the piston. Liberally coat the cylinder walls with clean engine oil before installing it.

6. Secure the cylinder mounting bolts evenly to avoid damaging the gasket.

Cylinder Head

90 CC MODELS

Removal and Disassembly

1. Run the machine until normal operating temperature is reached, then drain the oil.

2. Remove the point cover and the left-side crankcase cover. Be prepared to catch some oil as the crankcase cover is removed.

3. Remove the stator assembly, then pull the rotor, using either the Honda rotor puller (tool no. 07011–20001) or a suitable substitute.

4. Remove the rocker arm side-cover.

5. Disconnect the contact breaker lead wire, remove the breaker base assembly, remove the hex bolt and the 3 × 5.2 dowel pin, then remove the breaker advance mechanism. Remove the point base which is mounted with three screws.

Removing the stator assembly
1. Stator assembly

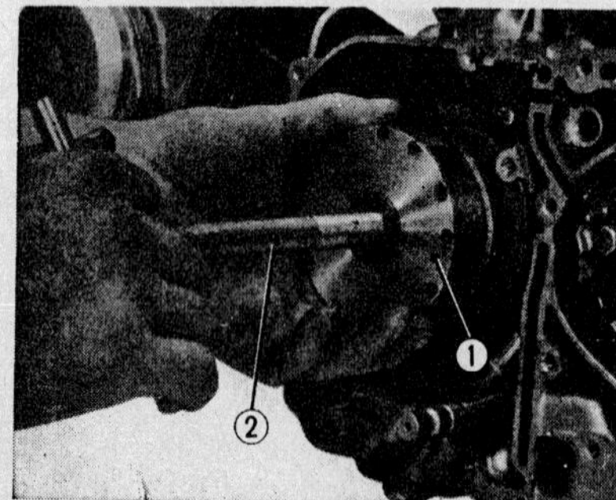

Removing the rotor
1. Rotor
2. Rotor puller

6. Rotate the engine until the left crankcase woodruff key is aligned with the camshaft dowel pin hole, then remove the cam sprocket. The camshaft is now free to be removed along with the rocker arms. This must be done with the head still secure. Keep the rockers separate so they can be assembled as they were removed.

7. Remove the cylinder head cover and the head assembly. If the head is reluctant to separate, tap it gently with a wood block and hammer.

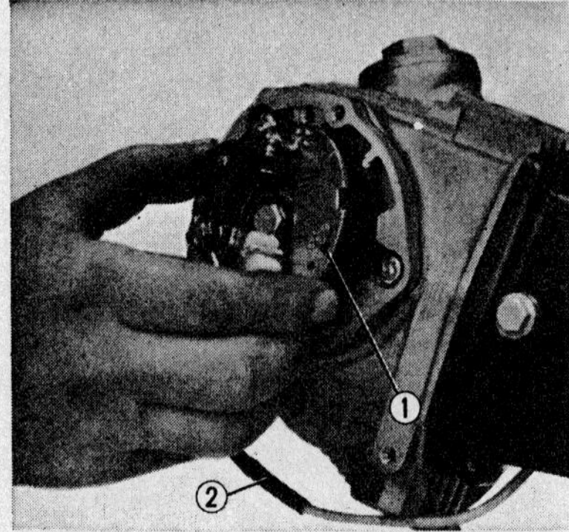

Removing the contact breaker assembly
1. Breaker assembly
2. Lead wire

Removing the point base
1. Point base

8. Disassemble the valves by compressing them with a valve spring compressor until the keepers can be removed. The keepers can be easily handled with a screwdriver with a daub of grease on its tip. Keep the assemblies separate for reassembly in their original locations.

Inspection and Repair

1. Consult the "50, 65, and 70 cc models" cylinder head "Inspection and Repair" section.

2. A good valve seat for these engines is 0.028–0.048 in (0.7–1.2 mm), and the serviceable limit is 0.08 in (2.0 mm).

Assembly

1. Apply engine oil to the valve stems, rocker arm shafts, and cam before assembling them.

2. Assemble the valve assemblies using new keepers, install the rocker assemblies in the cylinder head, and install the rocker arm cover.

3. Position the cylinder head gaskets and slip the head into place, taking care to keep the chain free so it can be drawn up into the head.

Cylinder head torquing sequence

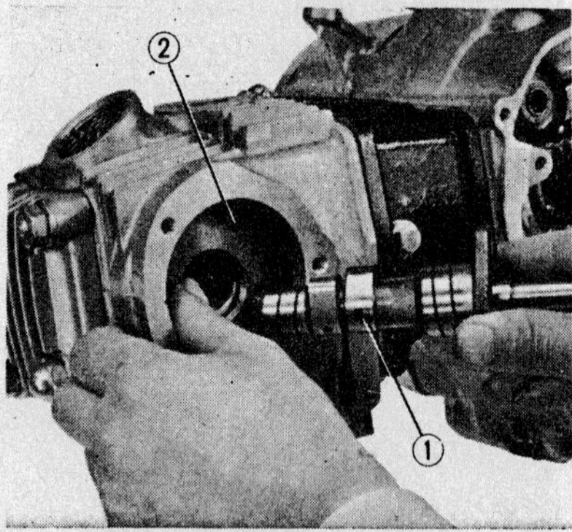

Installing the camshaft
1. Camshaft
2. Cam sprocket

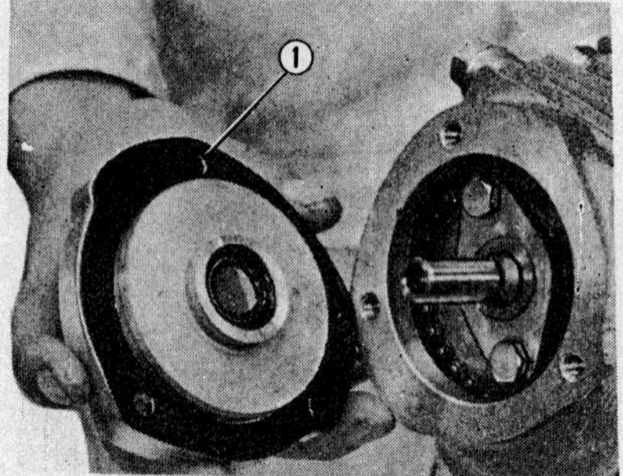

Installing the point base
1. Point base

4. Torque the head to 14.5–18.1 ft lbs in the order shown in the illustration.

5. Rotate the engine so the woodruff key on the crankshaft cam sprocket is aligned as previously illustrated, then align the "O" mark on the sprocket and secure the sprocket. The chain must be placed on the sprocket before it is installed.

6. Slip the camshaft into position so the pin hole is toward the head cover. The valve and piston should be in the TDC position on the compression stroke (no clearance at the tappets).

7. Mount the point base on the camshaft extension using an oil seal guide such as the Honda guide (tool no. 07057–03301) or a suitable substitute. If this operation is performed without some sort of guide, the oil seal will probably leak.

8. Insert the 3 × 5.2 guide pin in its hole and mount the spark advancer unit.

9. Install the contact breaker assembly and connect the leads.

10. Mount the rotor and stator assemblies onto the crankshaft.

11. Tune the engine, replenish the oil supply, and complete the assembly process.

Cylinder and Piston Assembly

Disassembly

1. Consult the 50, 65, and 70 cc models "Cylinder and Piston" assembly and disassembly section.

2. The cam chain and cylinder should be removed together once the chain is free of the timing sprocket.

Inspection and Repair

1. Consult the 50, 65, and 70 cc models "Inspection and Repair" section.

Assembly

1. Consult the 50, 65, and 70 cc models "Assembly" section. The only difference in the procedures is that the piston is marked with "in" on its crown. Make sure the marking is toward the top of the engine.

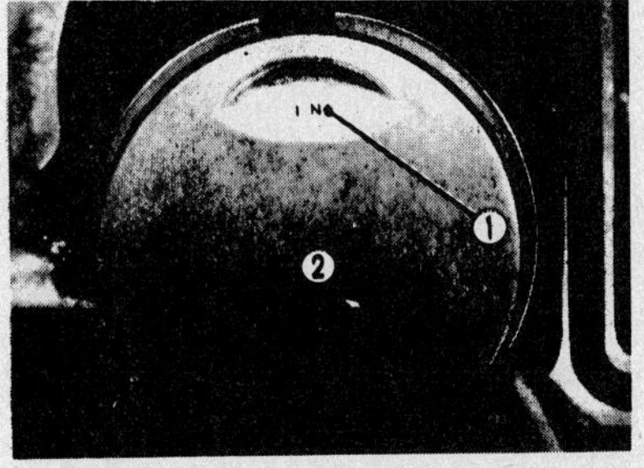

Mounting the piston in the correct position
1. "IN" mark
2. Piston

Cylinder Head

100 AND 125 CC MODELS

Removal and Disassembly

1. Run the machine until its normal operating temperature is reached, then drain the oil. Remove the engine from the frame as directed in the engine "Removal and Installation" section.

2. Remove the points and dynamo covers, then remove the contact breaker baseplate.

3. Remove the hex nut securing the advance mechanism, then remove the advance unit.

4. Remove the point base, thereby revealing the cam sprocket.

5. Rotate the engine until the piston is at TDC, then remove the cam sprocket. Lift the chain over the sprocket in the direction of the cam itself. It is a good idea to attach a thin piece of mechanic's wire to the chain so that if it falls into the crankcase, you can pull it up. Do not loosen the cylinder head bolts until this has been accomplished.

Point base mounting positions
1. 5 mm screws
2. 6 mm bolt
3. 6 mm screws

Aligning the cam sprocket for disassembly
1. Cam chain
2. 6 mm bolts
3. Cam sprocket
4. "T" aligning mark
5. Camshaft

6. Remove the four cylinder head cap nuts, align the cam lobes to the cutout on the cylinder head, and slip the camshaft from the head. It should not require undue pressure to remove the cam.

7. Remove the tensioner stopper bolt and position the tensioner so the head can be removed. Lift off the head. If necessary, gently tap on the head with a hammer and wood block to free it.

8. Remove the rocker arms and shaft, keeping them separate so that they may be replaced in their original positions, then compress the valve springs with a suitable compressor or the Honda compressor (tool no. 07031–10701), until the keepers can be removed, and separate the assemblies for reassembly in their original positions.

Inspection and Repair

1. Consult the 50, 65, and 70 cc models

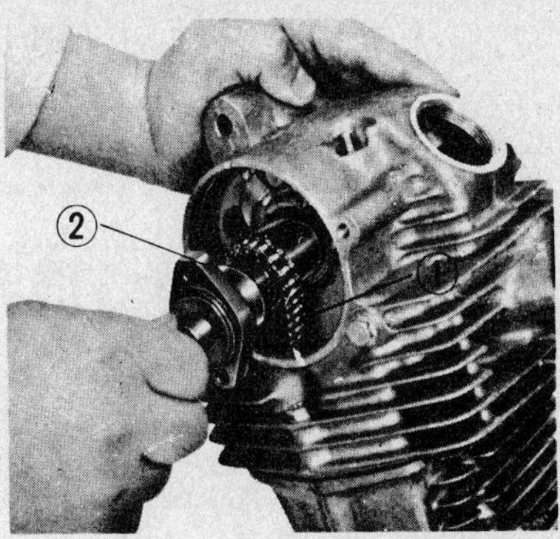

Removing the camshaft
1. Cam chain
2. Camshaft

Positioning the cam chain guide for cylinder removal
1. Screwdriver
2. Cam chain guide

cylinder head "Inspection and Repair" section.

Assembly

1. Install the cam chain guide if it has been removed, then position the O-ring and dowel pins on the head.

2. Assemble the valves using new keepers. The keepers are easy to handle if you place a daub of grease on the tip of a screwdriver. Lubricate all the parts as you install them.

3. Install the rockers in the head, taking care to position them in their original locations if they have not been replaced. Lubricate all parts as you install them, using clean engine oil.

4. Position the cam sprocket on the cam chain, and install the assembly in the head by using the cam chain tensioner to support them. Use a new head gasket between the head and cylinder.

5. Slip the head into place on its studs, and torque the head cap nuts to 5.8–8.7 ft lbs (tighten the cap nuts down finger-tight and then torque them in diagonal pairs) while supporting the cam sprocket and chain with a screwdriver. You should still have a wire on the chain to guard against dropping it into the crankcase.

6. Remove the cam chain from the sprocket and install the camshaft. Make

1. Dowel pins
2. Cam chain tensioner
3. Cam chain guide

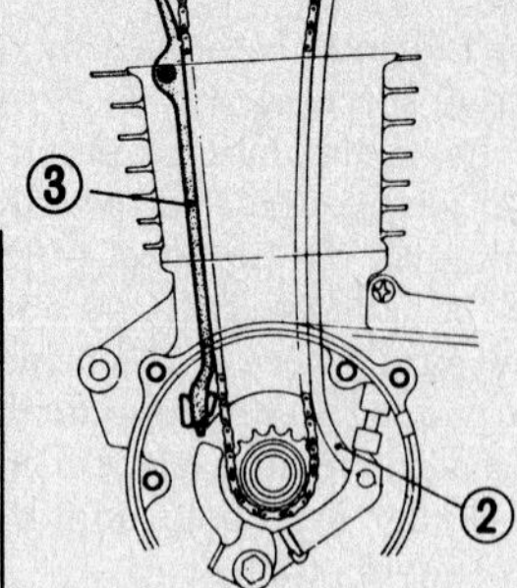

Installing the chain guide, O-rings, and dowel pins

Installing the cam sprocket
1. "T" mark
2. Mounting holes
3. Cam sprocket

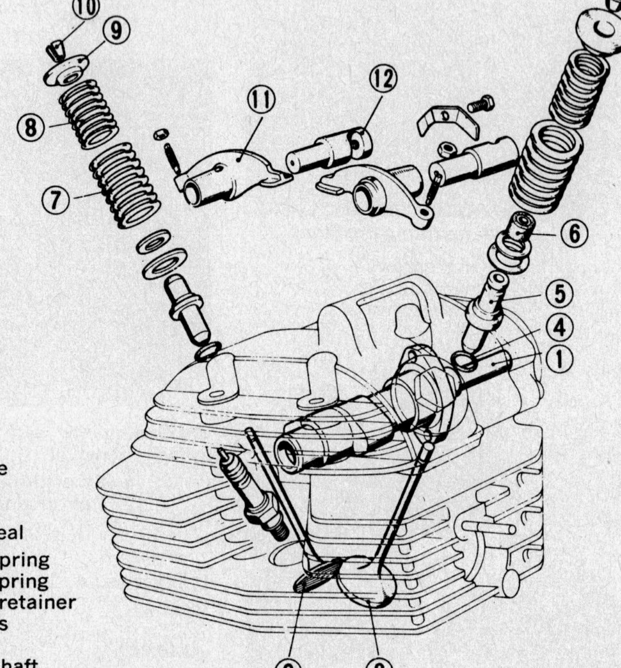

1. Camshaft
2. Inlet valve
3. Exhaust valve
4. O-ring
5. Valve guide
6. Valve stem seal
7. Valve outer spring
8. Valve inner spring
9. Valve spring retainer
10. Valve keepers
11. Rocker arm
12. Rocker arm shaft

Valve mechanism assembly

Installing the automatic advance mechanism
1. Pin
2. Pin hole

Installing the cylinder head
1. Cam chain
2. Screwdriver
3. 8 mm cap nuts

sure the cam lobe is aligned with the cutout on the cylinder head before inserting it. Rotate the cam one full revolution to bring it to a TDC position. This is assured by the cam sprocket mounting holes which won't be properly positioned unless perpendicular to the crankshaft.

7. Check the valve timing by aligning the "T" mark on the crankshaft with the timing mark scribed on the crankcase. Place enough tension on the cam chain to make it taut, then install and secure the cam sprocket with its mounting holes perpendicular to the crankshaft.

8. Use an oil seal guide when replacing the breaker point base assembly or the seal will probably leak.

Installing the camshaft
1. Camshaft
2. Cam lobe

9. Complete the assembly in the reverse order of disassembly, then tune the engine and replenish the oil supply.

Cylinder and Piston Assembly

Disassembly

1. Consult the 50, 65, and 70 cc models "Cylinder and Piston" assembly and disassembly section.
2. Keep a wire on the chain when you lift the cylinder over the piston.

Inspection and Repair

1. Consult the 50, 65, and 70 cc models "Inspection and Repair" section.
2. The "in" mark on the piston crown should be toward the rear.

Assembly

1. Consult the 50, 65, and 70 cc models "Assembly" section.
2. Make sure you install the two dowel pins in the mounting base.

Cylinder Head

XL-250

Removal and Disassembly

1. Remove the contact points base plate and spark advance unit.
2. Remove the tappet adjusting covers and the two 6mm bolts.
3. Remove the 6mm dowel pins and the rocker arm shaft plugs.
4. Remove the cam sprocket mounting bolts and lift the cam sprocket and

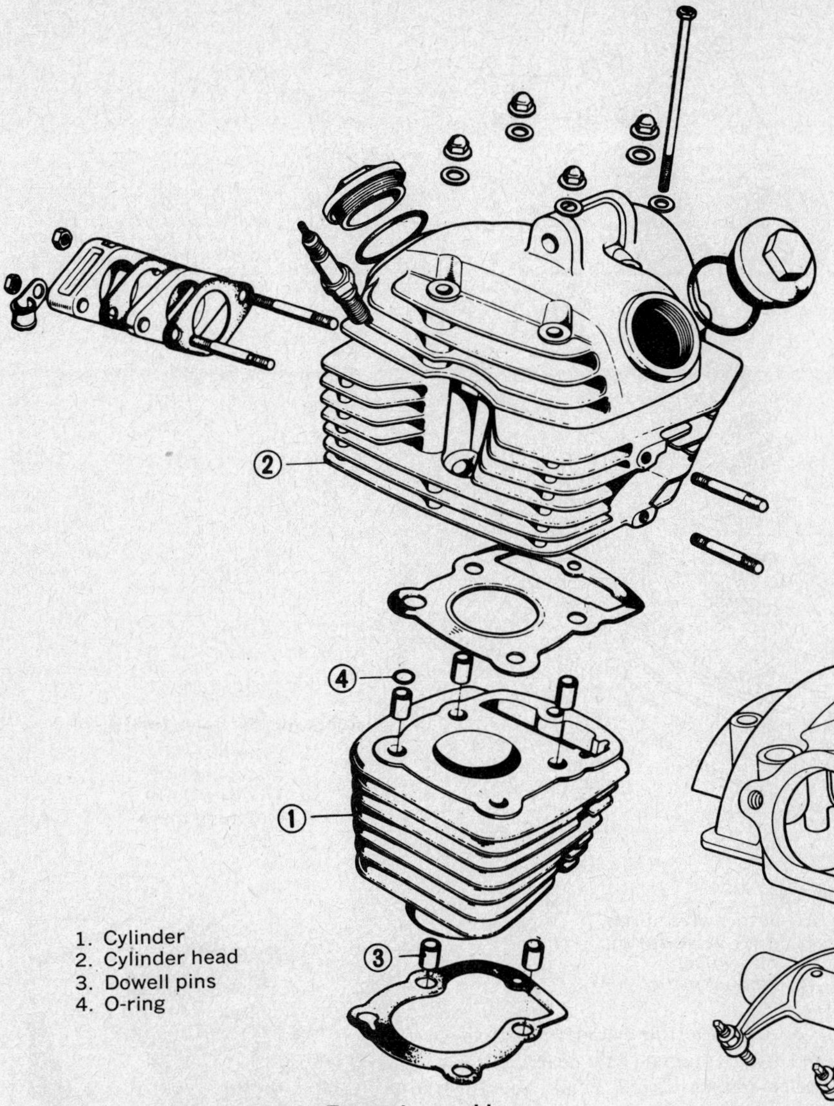

1. Cylinder
2. Cylinder head
3. Dowell pins
4. O-ring

Top end assembly

Contact point base plate

1. Contact point base plate
2. 6 mm bolts

chain off the cam. Take care to avoid dropping the bolts into the crankcase by stuffing the area around the sprocket with a clean cloth.

5. Place the cam chain on the right side of the sprocket and wire the sprocket and chain to something to keep them from falling into the crankcase as the cam is withdrawn, then carefully withdraw the cam.

6. Remove the cam chain tensioner bolt, the 10mm nut from under the sealing cap, and the four nuts which secure the head, then remove the cylinder head and gasket, tapping gently with a soft mallet if necessary.

7. Remove the valves by compressing the valve springs with either the Honda valve spring compressor (tool no. 07031–32901) or a suitable substitute, and then removing the keepers and springs. Keep the assemblies separate for reassembly in their original positions.

Inspection and Repair

1. Consult the "Cylinder Head Inspection and Repair" section, under "50, 65, and 70cc Models", and incorporate the following information.

2. The valve seats should be refaced by using 60°, 120°, and 90° cutters in that order. The proper seat contact width is 0.028–0.039 in. (0.7–1.0 mm).

Cam chain and sprocket assembly

1. Sealing cap
2. Cam chain
3. Cam sprocket
4. Tensioner bolt

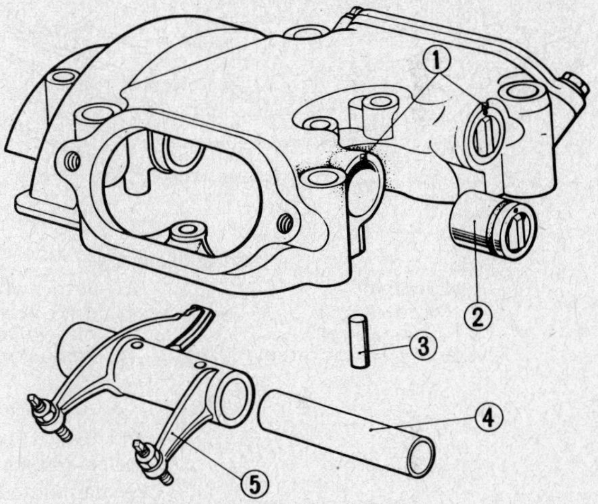

3. When replacing a valve guide always use an oversize OD guide along with a new 10 × 1.6 mm O-ring. The Honda valve guide remover (tool no. 07046–32901) and valve guide driver (tool no. 07047–32901), or suitable substitutes, may be used.

4. Ream newly installed valve guides with either the Honda reamer (tool no. 07008–32301) or a suitable substitute.

Rocker cover assembly

1. Matching marks
2. Rocker arm shaft plug
3. Dowel pin
4. Rocker arm shaft
5. Rocker arm

Assembly

1. Assembly is basically the reverse of disassembly. Use new inlet seals, valve keepers and a new head gasket, and coat all parts liberally with oil during the assembly procedures.

2. Slip the valves into their guides, place the valve springs and gaskets on the valves, compress the valves, and install the new keepers.

NOTE: *The narrower pitch of the valve springs must be on the valve head side of the valve.*

3. Install the cylinder head gasket on the cylinder taking care to align it perfectly. A light coat of gasket sealer may be used at your discretion.

4. Make sure that the oil holes in the camshaft bearing and oil sump are not blocked and clear them if necessary.

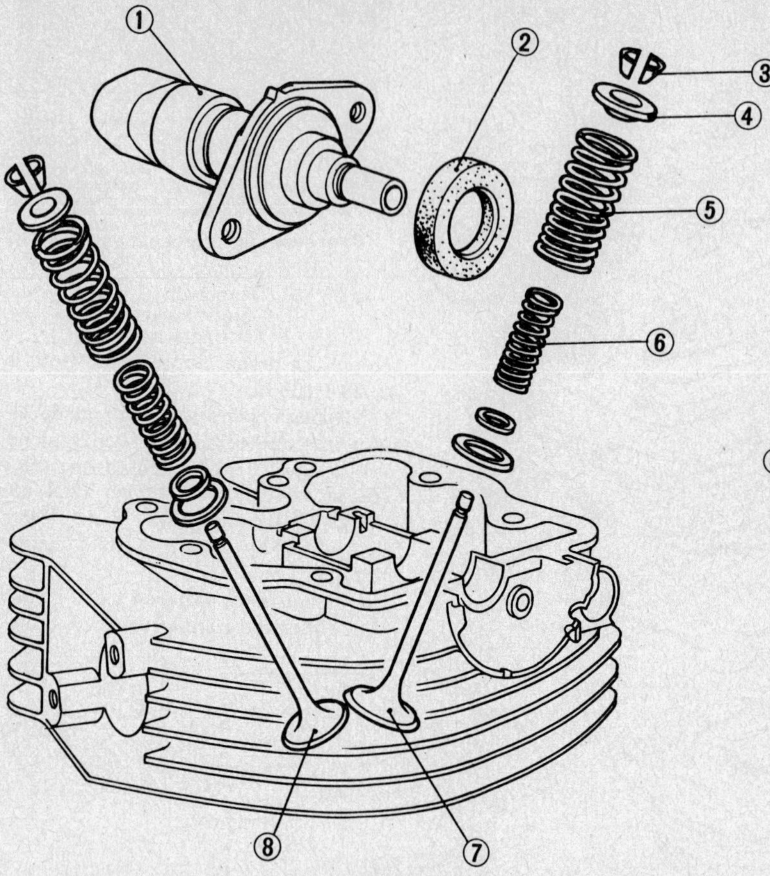

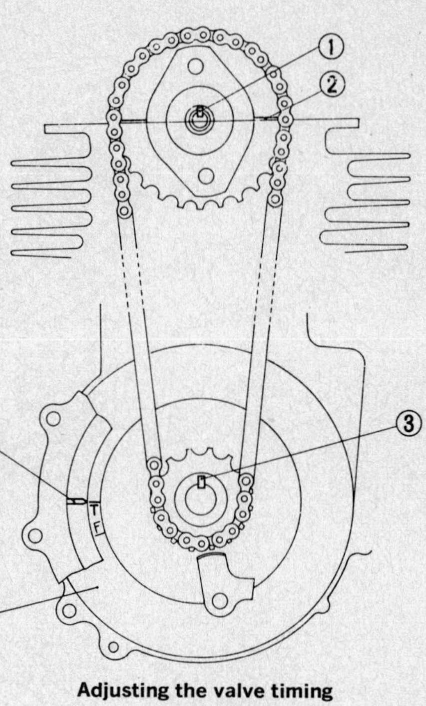

Adjusting the valve timing
1. Dowell pin
2. Matching line
3. Woodruff key
4. Matching mark
5. Flywheel

Valve assembly
1. Camshaft
2. Oil seal
3. Valve keeper
4. Valve spring retainer
5. Outer valve spring
6. Inner valve spring
7. Inlet valve
8. Exhaust valve

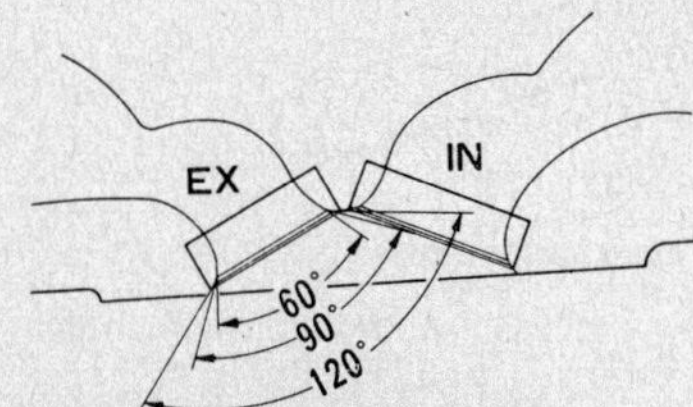

Valve seat angle

Cylinder head ready for installation
1. Oil holes 2. Rubber inserts

5. Make sure all of the rubber inserts on the head are in place. These are provided to prevent resonance.

6. Install the head and torque it down evenly to specifications.

7. Install the cam, cam sprocket, and cam chain.

8. Assemble the cylinder head cover and install it using a light coat of suitable sealer (Super Three Bond No. 10 is recommended by the factory). Wipe away any excess sealer which might have entered the head.

9. Make sure the camshaft dowel pin and the spark advancer dowel pin hole are engaged.

Piston and Cylinder Assembly

Disassembly

1. Remove the cylinder head as described in the "Cylinder Head Removal and Disassembly" section. Keep a safety wire on the cam chain to prevent it from falling into the crankcase.

2. After cleaning the area around the cylinder, remove the cylinder securing bolts and remove the cylinder, tapping gently with a soft mallet if necessary. Cover the crankcase with a clean cloth as soon as there is sufficient clearance to do so.

3. Remove the piston circlips and gently press the piston pin out with a suitable instrument. Heat the piston if necessary to remove the pin, then remove the piston.

Removing the cylinder
1. Rubber inserts

4. Remove the rings taking care not to scratch the piston.

Inspection and Repair

1. Consult the "50, 65, and 70cc Inspection and Repair" section.

Assembly

1. Assembly is basically the reverse order of disassembly.

2. Install the piston rings with their stamped mark facing up and install the piston so the mark "IN" faces the inlet valves.

3. Make sure that the rubber inserts have not been lost or damaged and replace them if necessary.

4. Retighten the 8mm stud bolts to a specified torque of 14.5–18.1 ft lb (2–2.5 kg/m).

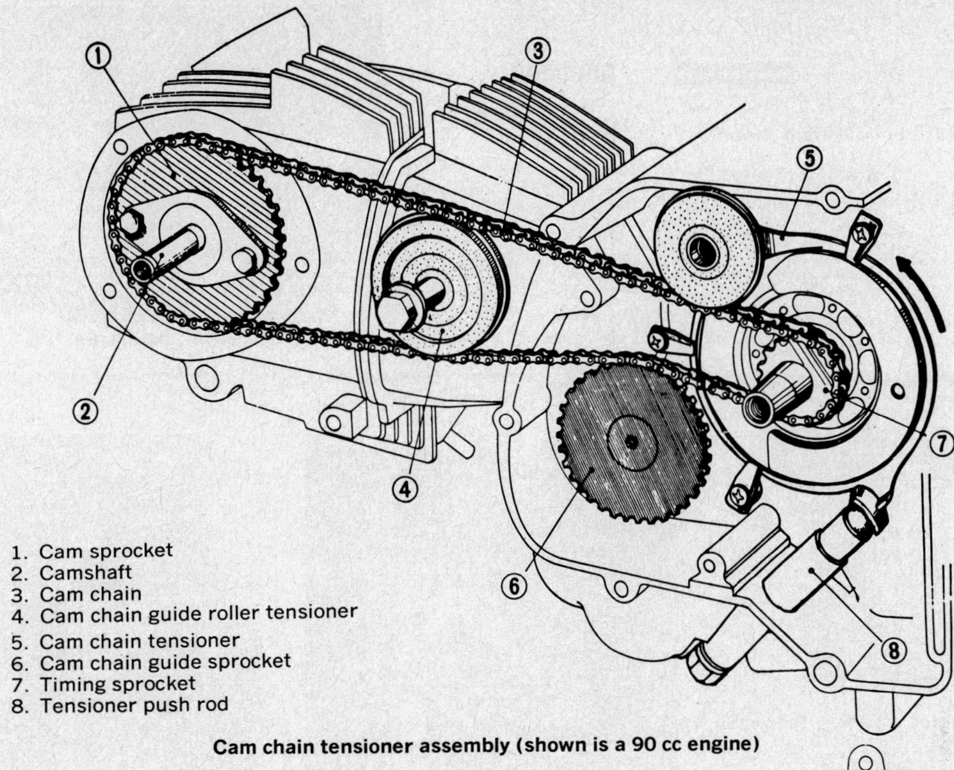

Cam chain tensioner assembly (shown is a 90 cc engine)

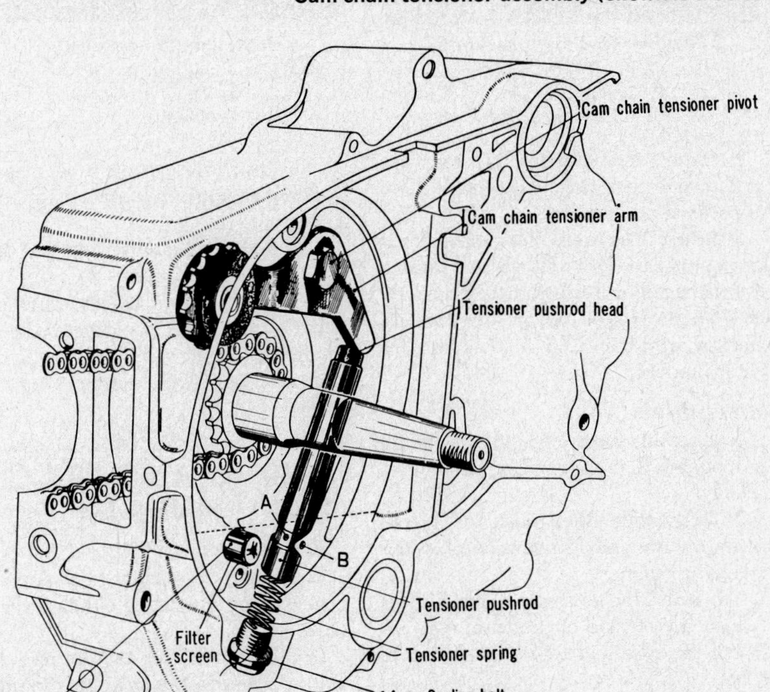

Tensioner mechanism (shown is a 50 cc engine)

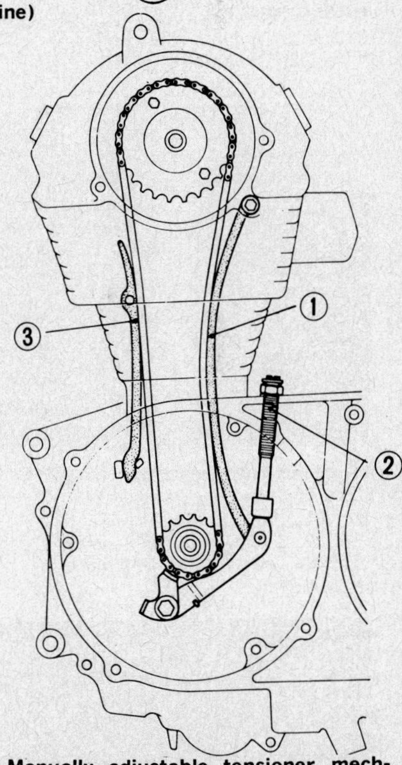

Manually adjustable tensioner mechanism (shown is a 100 cc engine)

1. Tensioner
2. Adjusting bolt
3. Tensioner guide

BOTTOM-END SERVICE

Cam Chain Tensioner

Disassembly

1. Remove the left-side crankcase cover, then remove the rotor and stator assemblies (all models).

2. Remove the camshaft, then remove the cam chain from the timing and guide sprockets. Remove the tensioner from the tensioner setting plate (90 cc models).

3. Remove the sealing plug from the crankcase, and remove the tensioner assembly (50, 65, and 70 cc models).

4. Remove the tensioner pivot bolt, then disassemble the cam chain tensioner and tensioner arm. Remove the push rod assembly, then pull out the tensioner adjusting bolt (100, 125, and 250cc models).

Inspection and Repair

1. Clean all parts in a suitable solvent and blow them dry, taking care to blow clear all of the oil passages.

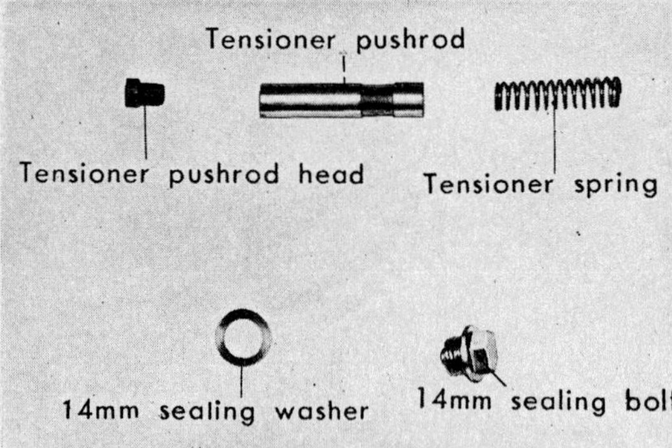

Tensioner components from a 50 cc engine

Tensioner installation

1. Spring
2. Screwdriver

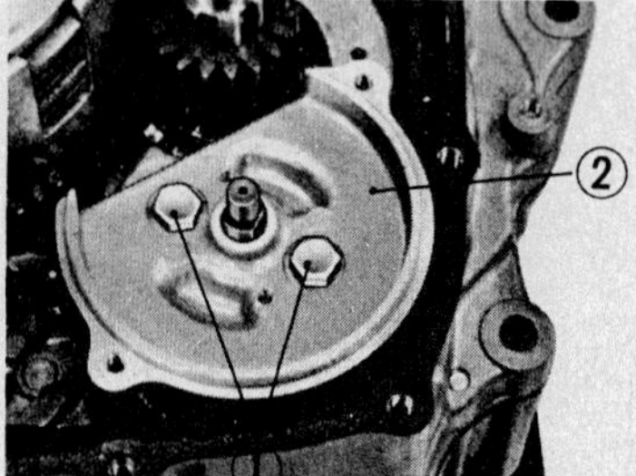

Removing the rotor assembly (shown is a 100 cc engine)

1. Dynamo rotor puller
2. Dynamo rotor

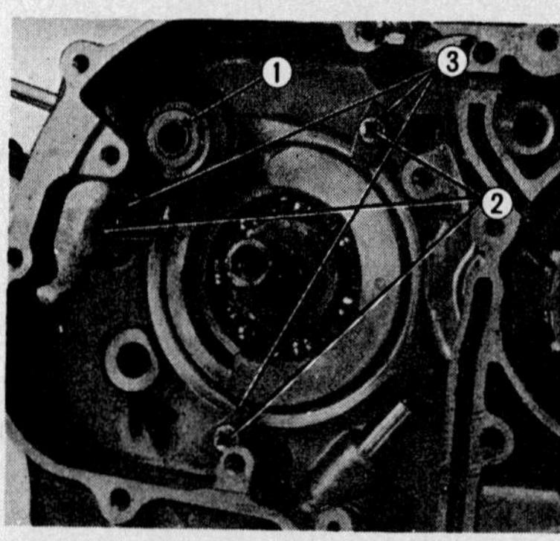

Removing the tensioner (shown is a 90 cc engine)

1. Cam chain tensioner
2. 5 mm cross point screw
3. Tensioner setting plate

Removing the tensioner push rod

1. Sealing plug
2. Spring
3. Push rod

Tensioner and pivot assembly

1. Pivot bolt
2. Tensioner arm
3. Adjusting bolt

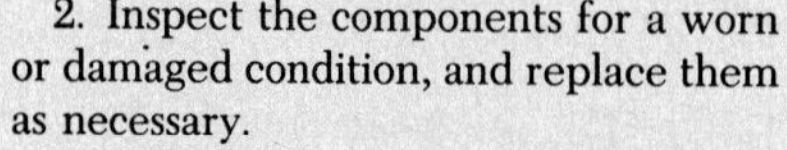

2. Inspect the components for a worn or damaged condition, and replace them as necessary.

3. Inspect the tensioner spring for a worn or collapsed condition, and replace it if damaged or if it is shorter than 2.89 in. (73.5 mm) for 50, 65, or 70 cc models, and if shorter than 2.65 in. (67.4 mm) for 90 cc models.

Assembly

1. Assembly for the 50, 65, 70, and 90 cc models is in the reverse order of disassembly.

2. Reassemble the tensioner mechanism on 100 and 125 cc models in the following manner:

a. Insert the tensioner adjusting bolt from the outside of the case, then install the case and tensioner arm rubber.

b. Mount the tensioner on the tensioner arm pin, connect the spring to the arm, and install the tensioner arm adjusting bolt.

c. Install the rotor assembly, and torque it to 19.0–23.0 ft lbs.

d. Mount the AC generator by installing the cord grommet, mounting the generator, and then aligning the screw mounting holes. Secure the O-ring.

e. Install the left crankcase cover.

3. Assemble the tensioner mechanism on the XL-250 in the following manner:

Installing the generator

1. Stator
2. Cord grommet
3. O-ring

a. Install the cam chain set plate so it doesn't come into contact with the cam chain.

b. Set the tensioner set bar in its fully lowered position.

c. Install the cam chain tensioner on the tensioner set bar concave head.

d. Adjust the cam chain as described in the "Tune-Up" section.

Clutch

50, 65, AND 70 CC MODELS

Disassembly

1. Remove the right-side crankcase cover, then remove the clutch lever and outer cover.

2. Bend back the tab on the lockwasher, remove the locknut, and lift out the clutch assembly. Removing these parts is made simpler by the use of the Honda clutch outer holder (tool no. 07024–03501) and the locknut wrench (tool no. 07086–00102), but substitutes may be used without too much trouble.

3. Disassemble the clutch assembly using either the Honda clutch assembly tool (tool no. 07038–01101) or a suitable substitute.

Inspection and Repair

1. Clean all parts other than the clutch friction plates in a suitable solvent and blow them dry.

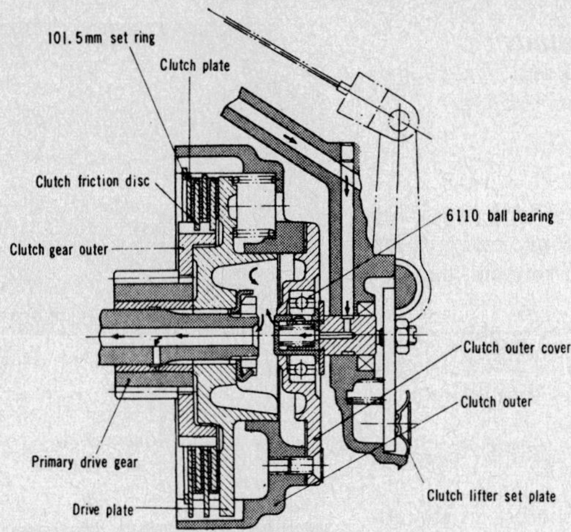

Hand-operated clutch diagram

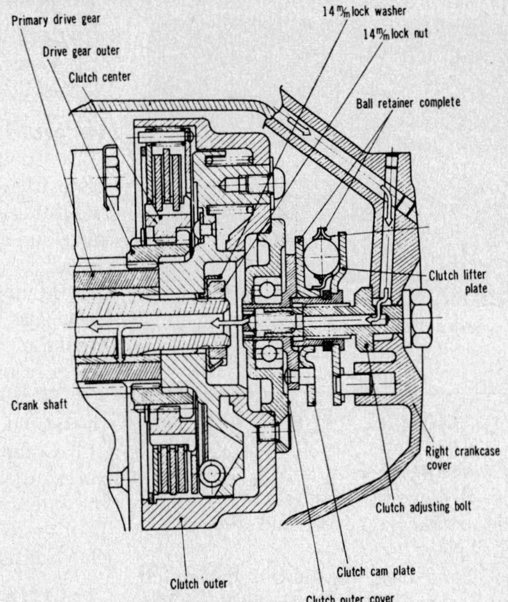

Centrifugal clutch diagram

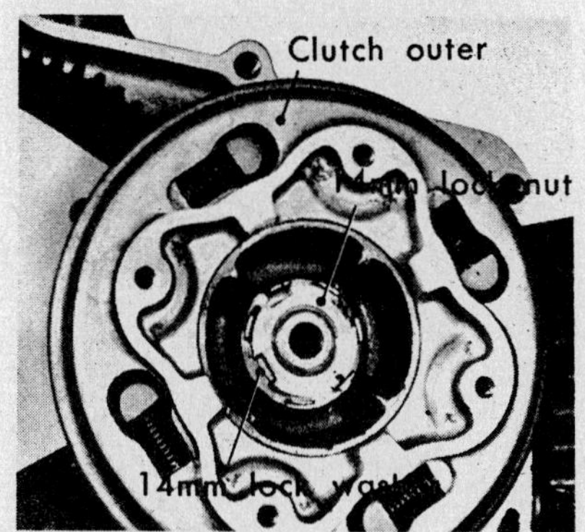

The tabs of the lockwasher seated against the flats of the locknut

2. Inspect the clutch plates and discs for a worn, damaged, scored, or burned condition, and replace them as necessary.

3. Inspect the clutch springs for a worn, damaged, or collapsed condition, and replace them as necessary. The springs may be measured with a vernier caliper or compared to new ones. The springs must be replaced if collapsed beyond their serviceable limit, and must be replaced as a full set.

4. Inspect the clutch center guide and the primary drive gear for a worn or damaged condition and replace them if necessary.

5. Measure the clearance between the clutch outer and the drive plate or clutch plate in the direction of normal rotation, If the clearance exceeds 0.012–0.02 in. (0.3–0.5 mm), the worn parts must be replaced.

Assembly

1. Assembly is in the reverse order of disassembly.

2. Make sure the tab of the lockwasher is seated flat against the side of the locknut.

Removing the clutch assembly

Clutch lever, cover, and ball retainer assemblies

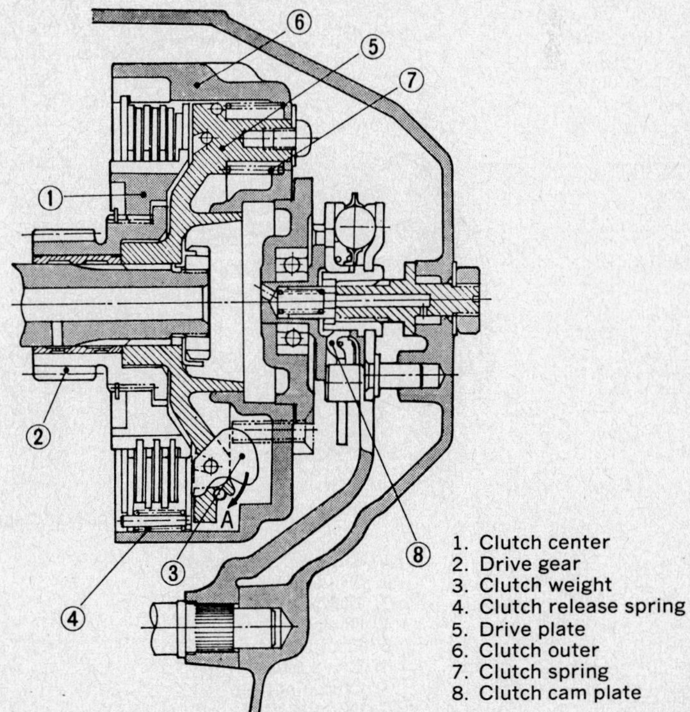

1. Clutch center
2. Drive gear
3. Clutch weight
4. Clutch release spring
5. Drive plate
6. Clutch outer
7. Clutch spring
8. Clutch cam plate

Hand-operated type clutch components

Removing the clutch outer cover
1. Clutch outer cover
2. Clutch outer

90 CC MODELS

Disassembly

1. Remove the clutch cover, the right-side crankcase cover, and the clutch outer cover.

2. Bend back the tab on the clutch lockwasher and remove the locknut. The clutch is now free to be removed as a complete assembly. The job is made simpler by using the Honda clutch outer holder (tool no. 07024–01101), but substitutes may be used without too much trouble.

3. Disassemble the clutch using the Honda clutch tool (tool no. 07038–03001) or a suitable substitute. Avoid pressing on the drive plate and damper spring retainer if the Honda tool is to be used, or the drive plate won't be able to be compressed.

Inspection and Repair

1. Consult the 50, 65, and 70 cc models "Inspection and Repair" section.

Assembly

1. Assemble the clutch spring, drive plate, friction discs, and clutch plates into the clutch outer, then compress the drive plate and install the set ring and damper spring

2. Mount the clutch assembly, clutch drive gear, and the center guide onto the crankshaft and torque the locknut to 54–64 ft lbs.

3. Secure the lockwasher by bending the tab up.

4. Complete the assembly in the reverse order of disassembly by installing the outer cover, crankcase cover, and then the clutch cover together with the clutch lifter and oil guide.

100 AND 125 CC MODELS

Disassembly

1. Remove the right-side crankcase cover, then remove the oil filter rotor as described in the "Lubrication" chapter.

2. Remove the four bolts which secure the clutch lifter plate and remove the plate

3. Remove the set ring and slip out the clutch center and the clutch discs and plates, then remove the spline washer and the clutch outer assembly.

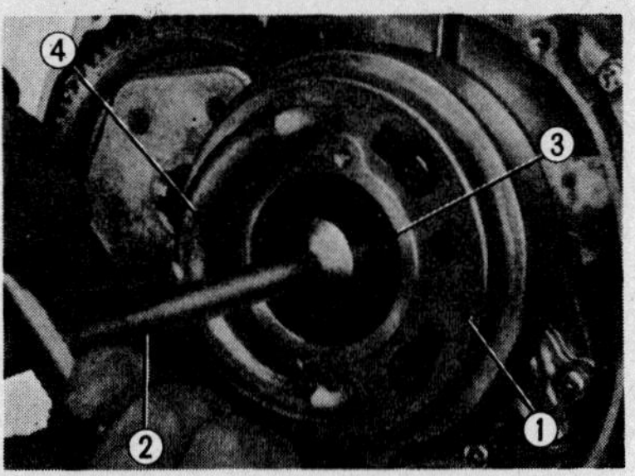

Removing the clutch assembly
1. Clutch outer
2. 16 mm locknut "T" spanner
3. 16 mm locknut
4. Clutch outer holder

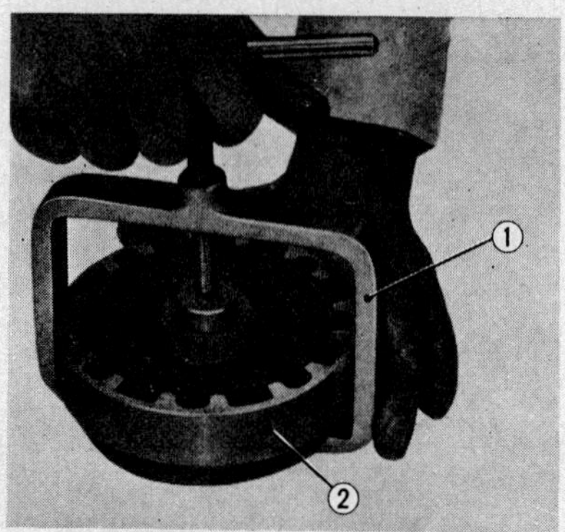

Disassembling the clutch
1. Clutch disassembling and assembling tool
2. Clutch assembly

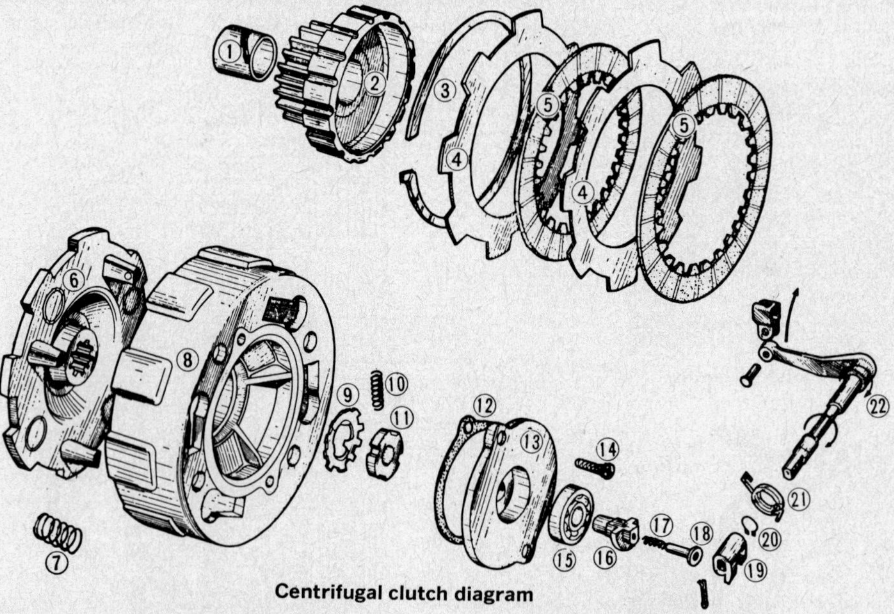

Centrifugal clutch diagram

1. Clutch center guide
2. Drive gear
3. 102.5 mm set ring
4. Clutch plate
5. Friction disc
6. Drive plate
7. Clutch spring
8. Clutch outer
9. 16 mm lockwasher
10. Clutch damper spring
11. 16 mm locknut
12. Clutch outer cover gasket
13. Clutch outer cover
14. 5 mm cross-screw
15. 6000 ball bearing
16. Clutch lifter
17. Oil through spring
18. Oil through
19. Clutch lifter arm
20. 10 mm snap-ring
21. Clutch lever spring
22. Clutch lever

Secure the locknut by bending up the tabs of the lockwasher

1. Lockwasher

Installing the clutch assembly

1. Clutch center
2. Clutch friction discs
3. Splines

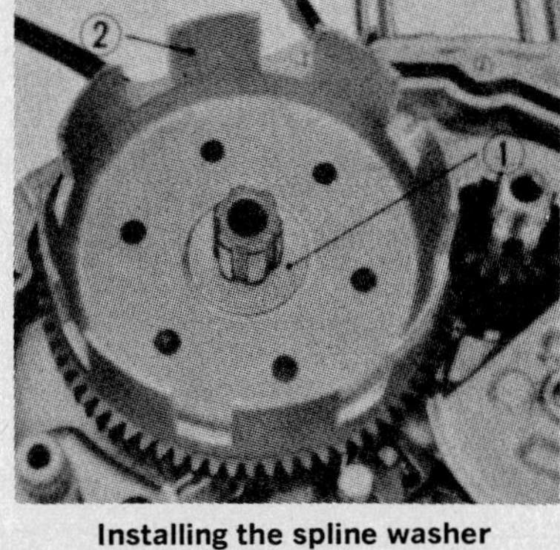

Installing the spline washer

1. 20 mm spline washer
2. Clutch outer assembly

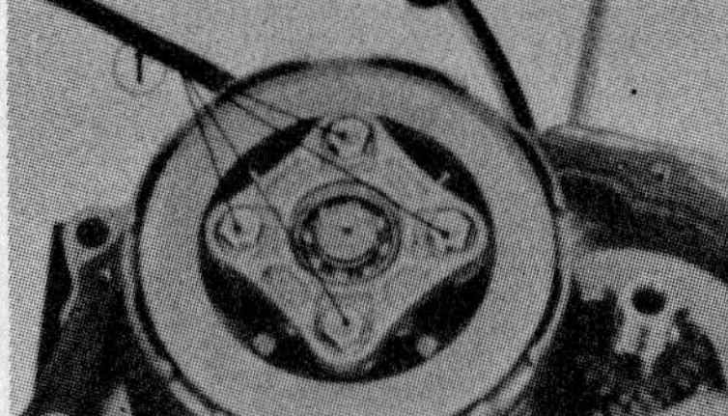

Clutch lifter plate securing bolts

1. 6 mm bolts

Installing the clutch lifter guide pin

1. Clutch lifter guide pin

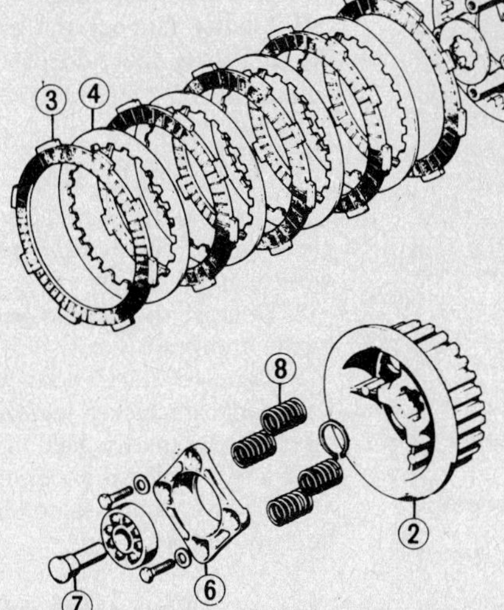

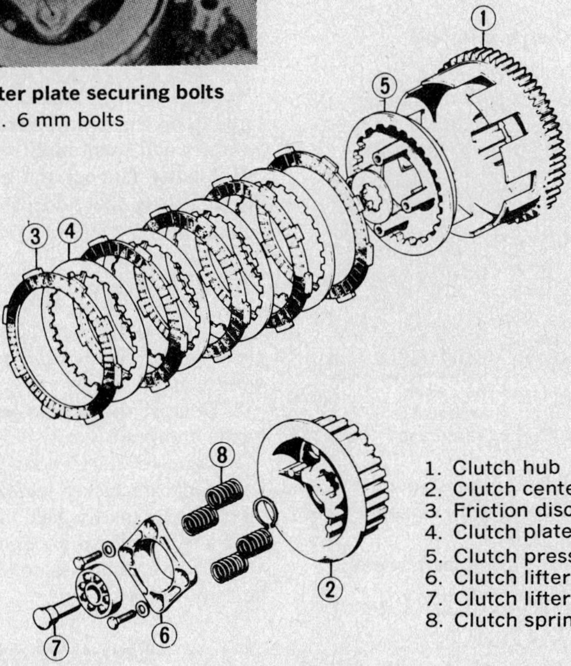

1. Clutch hub
2. Clutch center
3. Friction disc
4. Clutch plate
5. Clutch pressure plate
6. Clutch lifter plate
7. Clutch lifter guide pin
8. Clutch spring

Clutch Assembly

Inspection and Repair

1. Consult the 50, 65, and 70 cc models "Inspection and Repair" section.

Assembly

1. Insert the outer assembly and pressure plate, then slip the splined washer into place.
2. Assemble the clutch discs and plates on the clutch center, then position the center on the mainshaft while rotating each plate and disc into position in their splined passageways.
3. Position the set ring, then assemble and secure the springs and lifter plate. The bolts should be tightened down evenly, then torqued diagonally to 5.8–8.7 ft lbs. Make sure you install the clutch lifter guide pin.
4. Complete the assembly in the reverse order of disassembly.

Removing the clutch outer assembly

1. Snap-ring pliers
2. 20 mm set ring
3. Clutch center

XL-250

Disassembly

1. Run the engine until its normal operating temperature is reached, then drain the oil as directed in the "Maintenance" section.
2. Remove the tachometer cable, the kick starter pedal, the right side foot rest, and the right side crankcase cover.
3. Remove the four 6mm bolts, springs, and washers which secure the pressure plate, then remove the pressure plate and friction discs.
4. Remove the centrifugal oil filter, the 25mm clutch center circlip, the clutch center, and the clutch outer. The clutch pushrod may be withdrawn from the mainshaft at this time.

Inspection and Repair

1. Consult the 50, 65, and 70 cc models "Inspection and Repair" section.

Assembly

1. Assembly is the reverse of disassembly.
2. Install the clutch outer on the mainshaft, then check it for excessive backlash. The outer will have to be replaced if the backlash is greater than the serviceable limit of (0.00079–0.00354 in. (0.02–0.09 mm).
3. After the 25mm circlip is installed, make sure that the clutch hub rotates smoothly.

Splitting the Crankcases

50, 65, AND 70 CC MODELS

1. Remove the engine from the frame, clean it off thoroughly, and place it on the work bench.

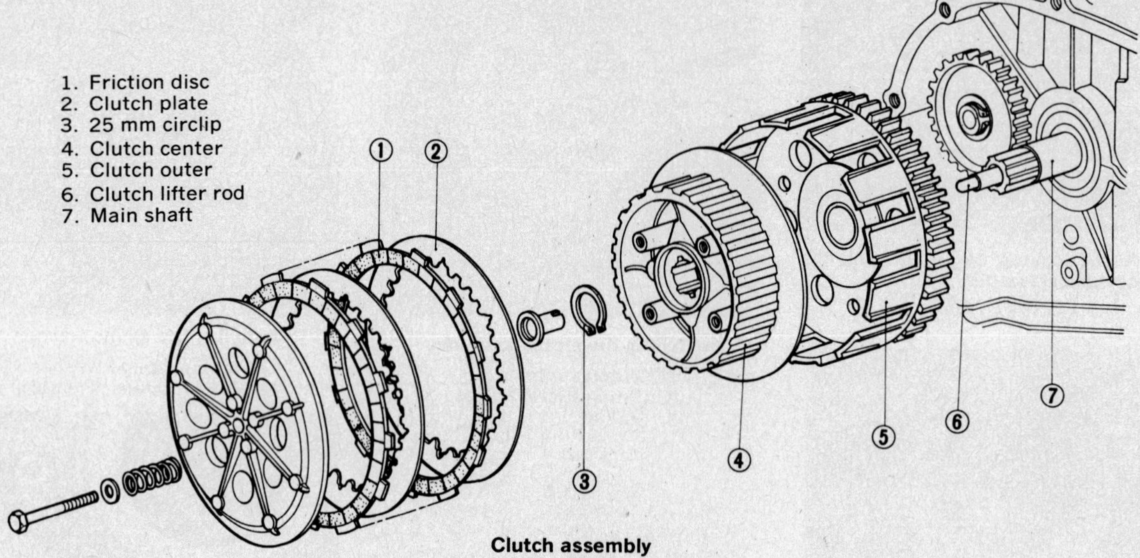

Clutch assembly

2. Remove the cylinder head, the cylinder, and the piston assemblies.
3. Remove the clutch assembly.
4. Remove the primary driven gear and the kick-starter spring.
5. Remove the oil pump assembly.
6. Remove the gearshift stopper and shifter plate.
7. Remove the left-side crankcase cover, flywheel, stator, and cam chain assembly.
8. Remove the rubber plug and gearshift drum stopper bolt.
9. Remove the final drive sprocket.
10. Separate the right crankcase from the left by tapping on the cases with a hammer and wooden block.
11. Remove the crankshaft assembly.

90 CC MODELS

1. Remove the engine from the frame, clean it thoroughly, and place it on the work bench.
2. Remove the clutch and gearshift spindle assemblies.
3. Remove the left crankcase cover.
4. Remove the cylinder head, cylinder, and piston assemblies.
5. Remove the 6 × 16 hex bolt and

Splitting the cases
1. Left crankcase
2. Right crankcase

separate the left crankcase from the right side by tapping on it with a hammer and wood block.

6. Remove the crankshaft assembly.

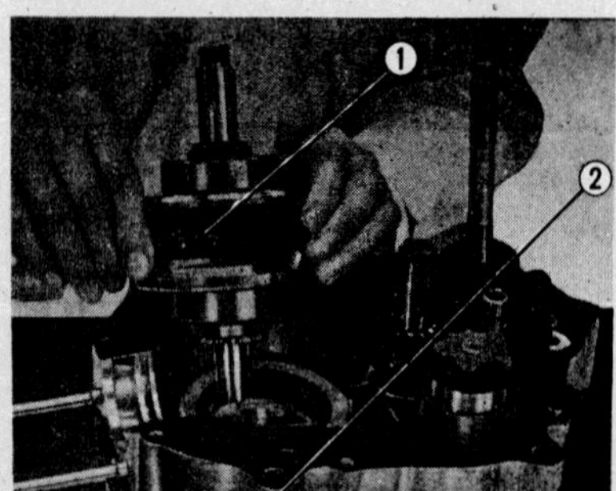

Removing the crankshaft assembly
1. Crankshaft
2. Left crankcase

100 AND 125 CC MODELS

1. Remove the engine from the frame, clean it thoroughly, and place it on the work bench.
2. Remove the cylinder head, cylinder, and piston assemblies.
3. Remove the right-side crankcase cover, the oil filter, and the oil pump.
4. Remove the clutch, shifter, and AC generator assemblies.
5. Remove the drive sprocket, the 11 left-side crankcase securing bolts, and the right-side crankcase securing screw.
6. Separate the crankcase halves by tapping on them with a soft mallet or a hammer and wood block.
7. Gently tap out the crankshaft by tapping on its right side to loosen it, while supporting the crankcase, and then carefully pulling it free.

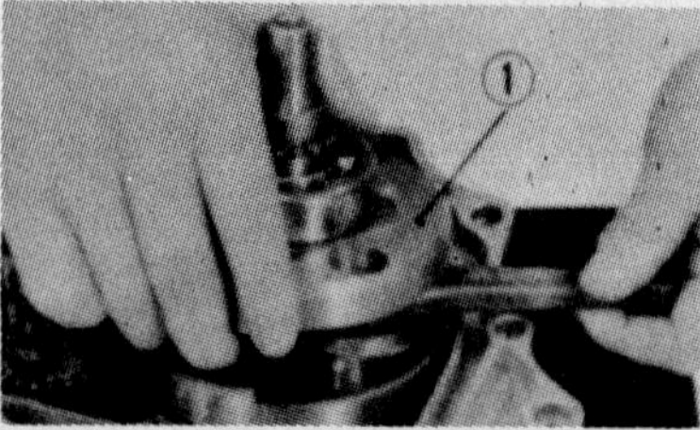

Removing the crankshaft assembly
1. Crankshaft assembly

XL-250

1. Remove the engine from the frame, clean it thoroughly, and place it on a work bench.
2. Remove the top end assembly down to the crankcase.
3. Remove the 15 bolts which secure the crankcase halves together, then lift off the top crankcase half, tapping gently with a soft mallet if necessary.
4. The remaining assemblies may now be removed with ease.

Crankshaft (ALL MODELS)

Inspection and Repair

Honda recommends the replacement of the cranksahft assembly whenever any of its components fail, wear beyond their serviceable limit, or appear ready to fail. Perform the following tests and replace the assembly if your results indicate that the components are past their serviceable limit.

1. Support the crankshaft on a pair of V-blocks, or so it can be rotated smoothly and evenly, then measure the crankshaft run-out with a dial indicator.
2. Support the crankshaft on centers or so the bearings can be moved without disturbing the crankshaft itself. Measure the play in the bearing with a dial indicator or with feeler gauges. Measure the play at various positions on the bearings. Make sure you measure both the axial and vertical play.

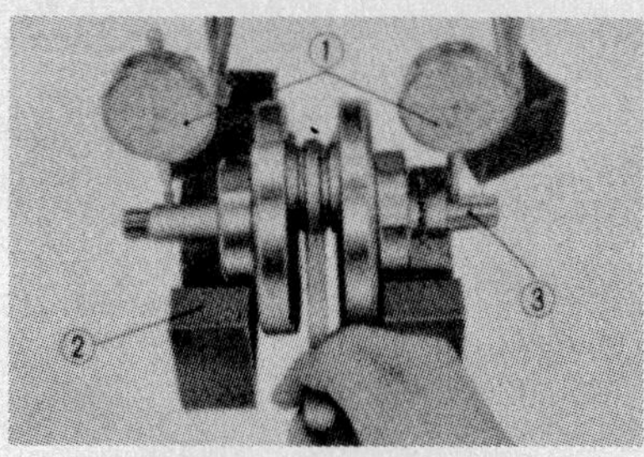

Measuring crankshaft runout
1. Dial indicators
2. "V" block
3. Crankshaft

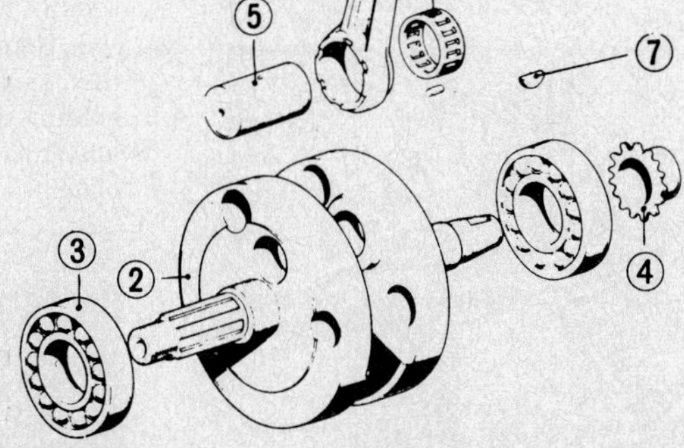

1. Connecting rod
2. Crankshaft
3. Main bearing
4. Timing sprocket
5. Crankpin
6. Connecting rod bearing retainer
7. Woodruff key

Crankshaft assembly (shown is a 100 cc engine)

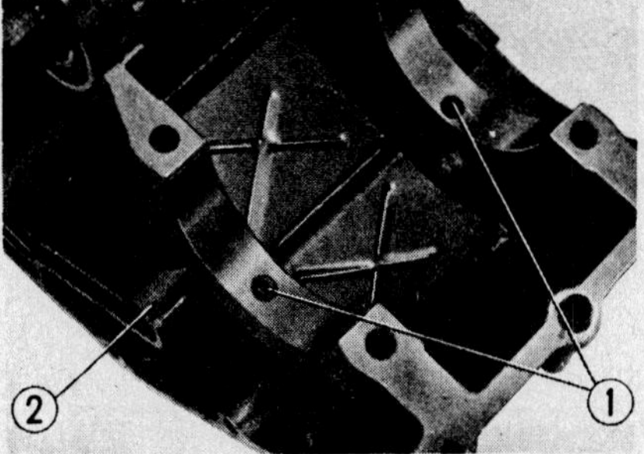

The bearings must seat in these dowel holes
1. Bearing pins
2. Lower crankcase

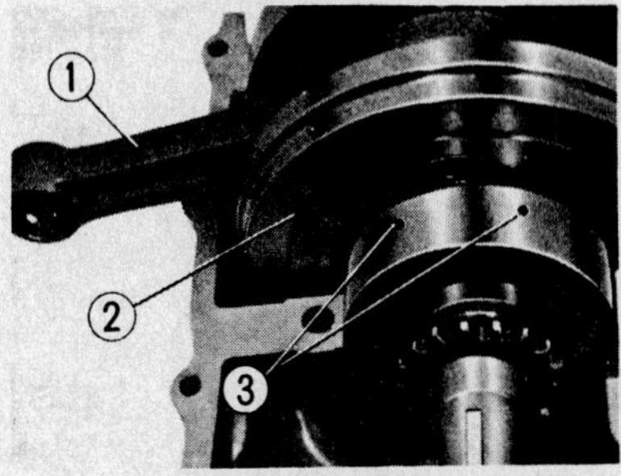

Installing the crankshaft assembly
1. Connecting rod
2. Crankshaft
3. Oil holes

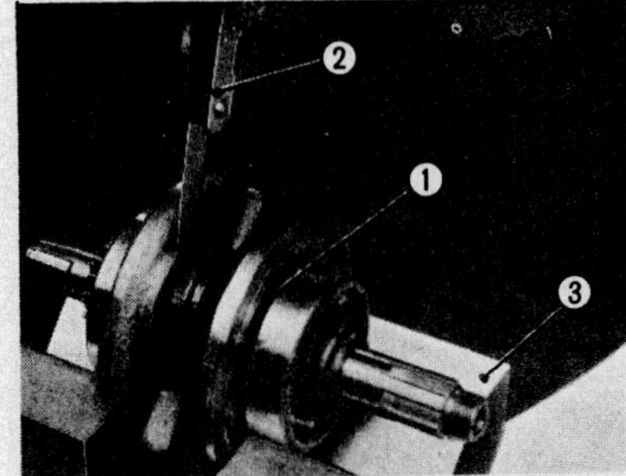

Measuring axial clearance
1. Crankshaft
2. Feeler gauge
3. "V" block

Measuring connecting rod radial-play
1. Dial indicator
2. Connecting rod

Installing the right crankcase (shown is a 50 cc engine)

Measuring connecting rod side-play
1. Crankshaft
2. Connecting rod
3. Feeler guage

3. Measure the connecting rod side- and radial play. Use a feeler gauge for measuring the side-play, and a dial indicator for measuring the radial play.

4. Measure the dimensions of the connecting rod small-end for wear or damage. If it is worn past the point at which the clearance can be taken up by oversize piston pins, the crankshaft will have to be replaced.

5. Inspect the condition of the timing sprocket for cracked, chipped, or worn teeth, and replace it if necessary. If the rest of the crankshaft is in good condition, it may be worth your while to purchase a new sprocket and take the assembly to a machine shop. The sprocket can be pressed off and replaced with an arbor press. Use a new woodruff key if you do this.

6. Before installing the crankshaft assembly in the crankcase, make sure it's perfectly clean, especially the bearing oil passages, and coat it liberally with engine oil. The bearing housing dowel pins and dowel holes must come into alignment.

Crankcase Assembly (ALL MODELS)

1. Assembly is basically the reverse order of disassembly. Make sure you use new gaskets wherever applicable, and install the dowel pins in their correct location when putting the cases together. A light coat of gasket sealer may be used at your own discretion on all models other than the XL-250 on which it definitely should be used.

2. Assemble the crankshaft into the left crankcase on the 90 cc and smaller models, and into the right crankcase on the 100 and 125 cc models. Make sure the crankshaft bearing pins seat in their holes in the lower case on the XL-250.

3. Install the cam chain guide sprocket at this time on 90 cc models. Set the tensioner bar all the way down on the XL-250

4. Assemble the cylinder, cylinder head, gearshift, and clutch assemblies in that order.

Crankcase Breather (XL-250)

When installing the crankcase breather unit make sure the rubber seal

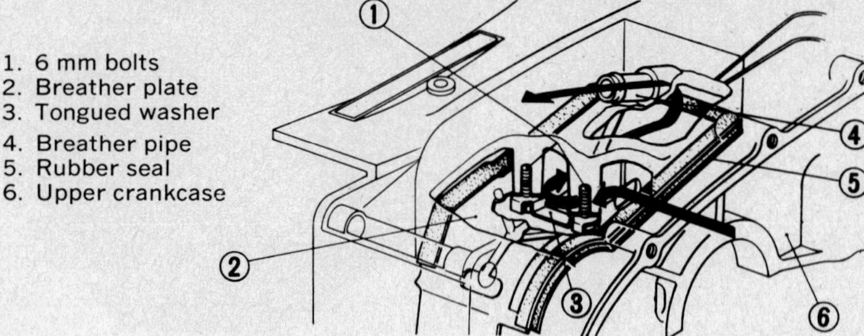

Crankcase breather

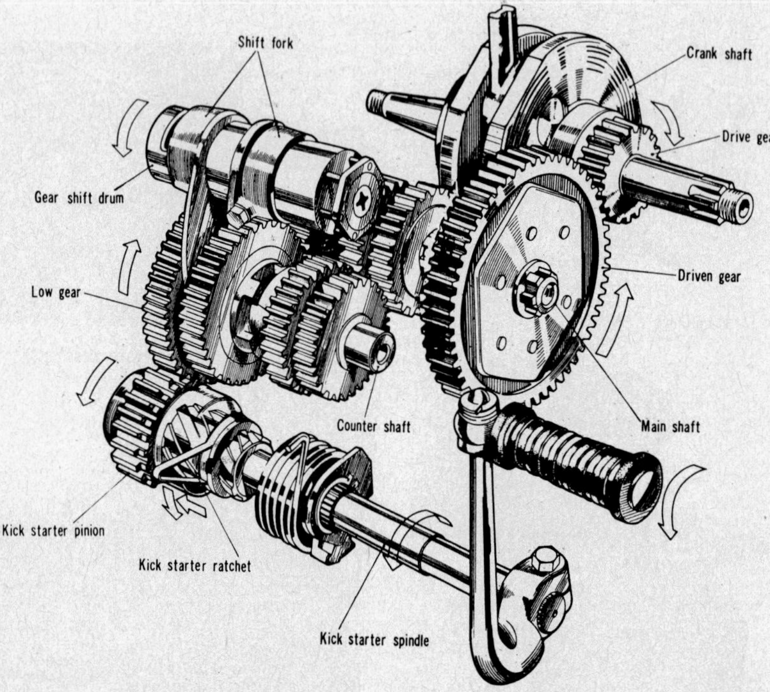

Shifter and kick-starter mechanisms

and the upper crankcase half seal completely. If the breather plate is not adequately sealed, oil leaks through the breather tube may result. When installing the 6mm bolts make sure they are secure by bending the locking tab of the lockwasher against a flat portion of the bolt head. Failure to do this may result in a bolt falling into the transmission gears.

Shifter Mechanism

50, 65, AND 70 CC MODELS

Disassembly

1. Complete the procedures listed in the "Splitting the Crankcases" section.
2. The gearshift drum and fork assembly can be removed along with the transmission assembly after the kick-starter spindle is disengaged.

Inspection and Repair

1. Clean all parts in a suitable solvent and blow them dry.
2. Inspect the components for obvious wear or damage and replace them as necessary.
3. Measure the thickness of the ends of the shifter fork to determine if they have been worn past their serviceable limits.
4. Measure the inside diameter of the shifter fork with an inside micrometer to determine if it has worn past its serviceable limit.
5. Measure the outside diameter of the shifter drum, and replace it if worn past its serviceable limit.

Assembly

1. Assembly is basically in the reverse order of disassembly. Make sure all components are perfectly clean, and lubricate them with clean engine oil before installation.
2. Assemble the shifter forks to the drum and position the assembly on the countershaft in the manner shown in the accompanying illustration. Make sure the guide pin and guide pin clip are in good condition, and that they are installed securely.
3. Apply a daub of a strong screw and bolt sealer to the stopper plate mounting screw.
4. Make sure the transmission engages smoothly and positively in all gears before you complete the assembly.

90 CC MODELS

Disassembly

1. Remove the clutch assembly as described in the "Clutch" section.
2. Remove the 20 mm circlip which secures the primary driven gear, and remove the gear.
3. Remove the shifter drum stopper, then pull the shifter spindle free while holding the shifter arm down so that it is not engaging the shifter drum stopper plate.

Removing the primary driven gear retaining ring
1. Primary driven gear
2. 20 mm circlip

Removing the shifter spindle
1. Shifter arm

4. If you wish to work on the shifter drum and forks, the crankcases will have to be split as described in the "Splitting the Crankcases" section.
5. Remove the kick-starter spindle, then remove the mainshaft, countershaft, and shifter drum assemblies from the left crankcase.
6. Disassemble the shifter forks from the shifter drum by removing the gearshifter guide pin clip and pin, then slide the forks from the drum.

Inspection and Repair

1. Consult the 50, 65, and 70 cc models "Inspection and Repair" section.
2. In addition to the other measurements, measure the shifter drum groove

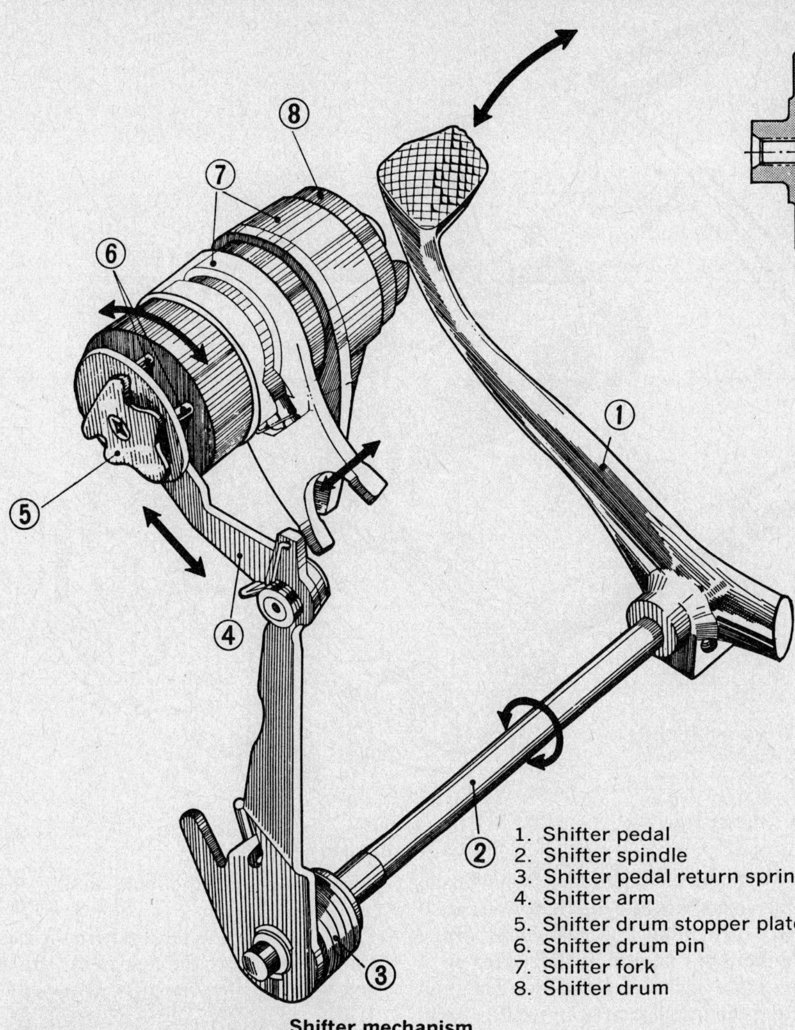

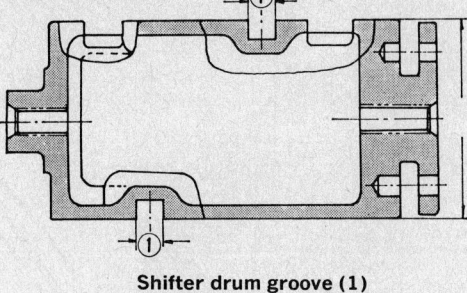

1. Shifter pedal
2. Shifter spindle
3. Shifter pedal return spring
4. Shifter arm
5. Shifter drum stopper plate
6. Shifter drum pin
7. Shifter fork
8. Shifter drum

Shifter mechanism

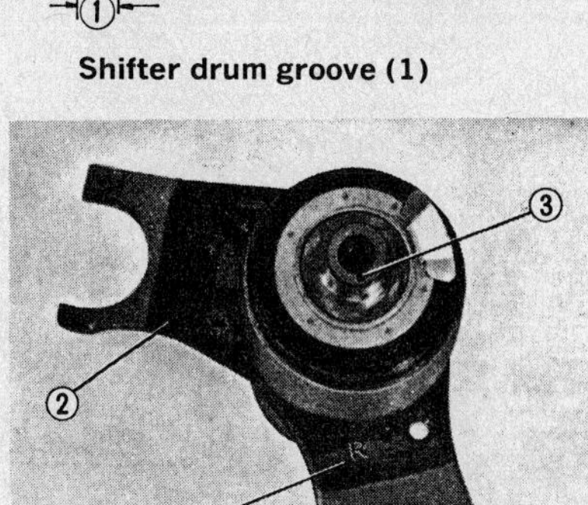

Shifter drum groove (1)

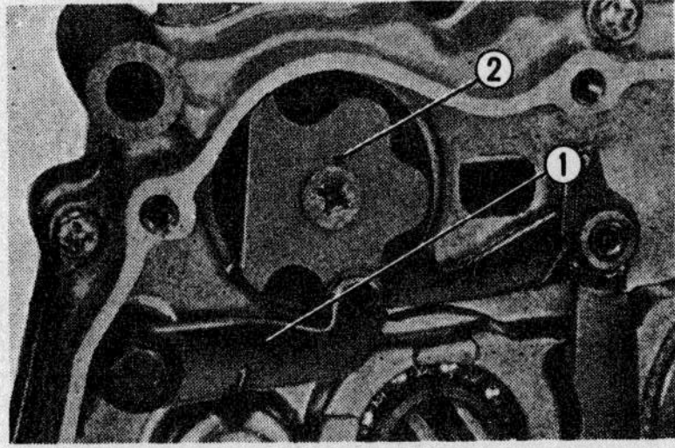

Location of the "R" mark on the right-side shifter fork

1. "R" mark
2. Shifter fork
3. Shifter drum

Assembly the shifter drum stopper

1. Shifter drum stopper
2. Shifter drum stopper plate

Removing the shifter forks

1. Shifter guide pin clip
2. Shifter fork

with feeler gauges or a small inside micrometer, and replace the drum if the grooves are worn past their serviceable limits.

Assembly

1. Slip the shifter forks onto the shifter drum and secure them with the guide pins and clips. Use new pins and clips if the old ones don't look perfect. Make sure that the forks are in their correct position. There is a "R" mark on the right-side fork. Check the operation of the forks for smoothness.

2. Install the transmission assemblies in the left crankcase half and check the action of the forks and gears for smooth and positive action.

3. Install the kick-starter spindle, then assemble the crankcase halves.

4. Complete the assembly in the reverse order of disassembly. Carefully check the operation of all the components as you install them. Make sure the return springs snap the components back into position, and carefully check the operation of the shifter arm on the drum stopper plate.

100 AND 125 CC Models

Disassembly

1. Remove the right-side crankcase cover, then remove the oil filter rotor and clutch assemblies.

2. Remove the circlip with a set of snap-ring pliers, and remove the gearshift plate and spring.

3. Remove the shifter drum stopper and shifter cam.

4. Remove the shifter pedal, then pull the shifter spindle out.

5. If you wish to work on the shifter forks or drum, the crankcases will have to be split as described in the "Splitting the Crankcases" section.

Removing the circlip

1. Snap-ring pliers
2. Circlip

6. Remove the kick-starter spindle, then lift out the mainshaft, countershaft, and shifter drum all at the same time.

7. Remove the shifter fork guide shaft to remove the shifter forks.

Inspection and Repair

1. Consult the 90 cc models "Inspection and Repair" section.

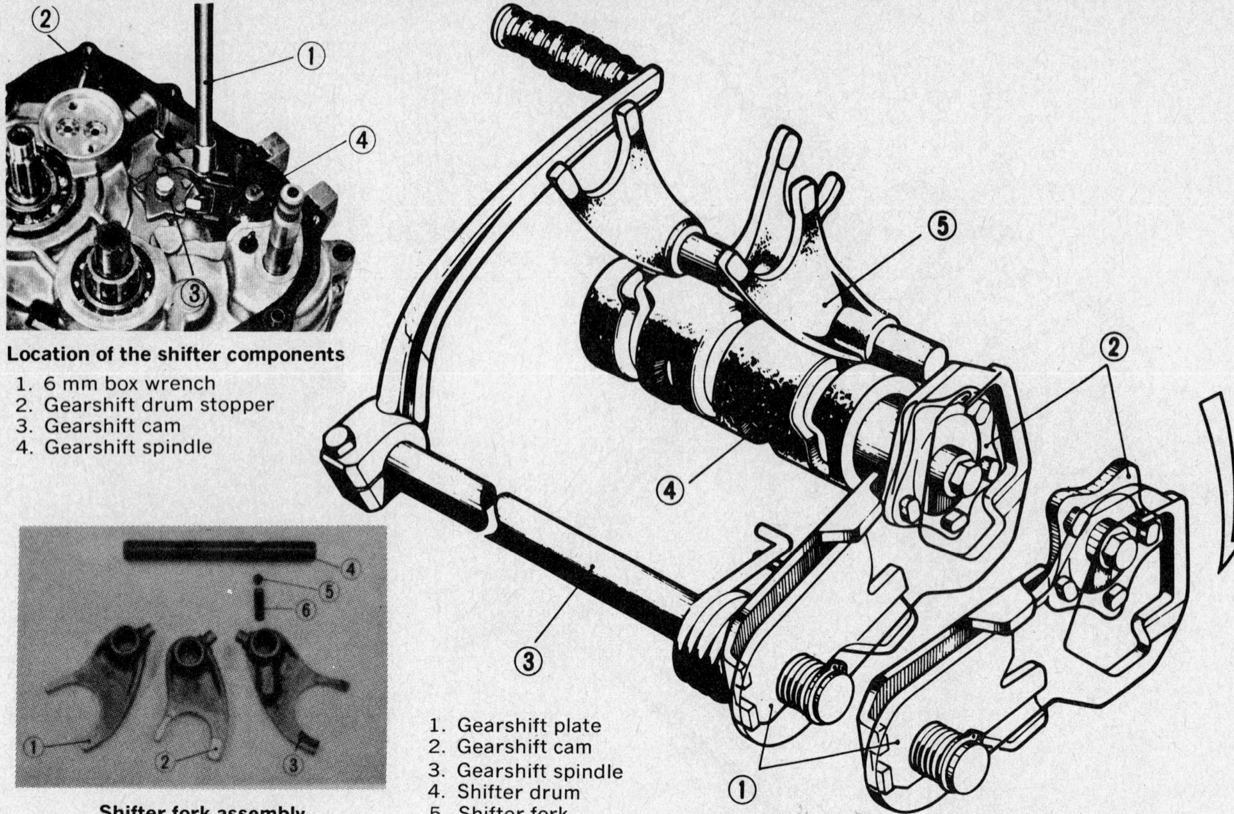

Location of the shifter components

1. 6 mm box wrench
2. Gearshift drum stopper
3. Gearshift cam
4. Gearshift spindle

Shifter fork assembly

1. Right-side shifter fork
2. Center shifter fork
3. Left-side shifter fork
4. Shifter fork guide shaft
5. 4 x 10 roller
6. Spring

Shifter mechanism

1. Gearshift plate
2. Gearshift cam
3. Gearshift spindle
4. Shifter drum
5. Shifter fork

Assembly

1. Slip the left-side gearshifter fork onto the guide shaft. Use a thin screwdriver or some other suitable instrument to install the spring and 4 × 10 rollers on the guide shaft.

2. Assemble the kick-starter (if necessary) spindle into the right-side crankcase. Secure the spring by inserting one end into the hole in the case, and then hook the other end of the spring onto the case boss.

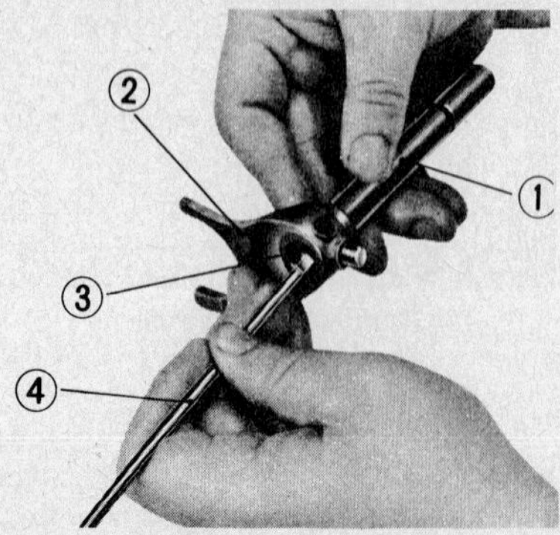

Installing the spring and rollers on the guide shaft

1. Shifter fork guide shaft
2. Left-side shifter fork
3. 4 x 10 roller
4. Screwdriver

3. Mount the countershaft and mainshaft assemblies into the right-side crankcase, then install the gearshifter drum, Position the neutral switch rotor so it faces the cylinder assembly. This will make the installation of the shifter forks much easier.

4. Position the right-side shifter fork on the countershaft high gear, then raise the gear until the cam guide pin can be assembled into the guide groove on the drum, and install the center shifter fork in the same manner. Work from the countershaft end.

5. Position the left-side gearshifter fork, align the holes in the three forks, then insert the shaft from the top.

6. Install the gearshift assembly, then mount the left-side crankcase. Make sure the kick-starter spindle shaft is perfectly perpendicular to the hole in the left crankcase.

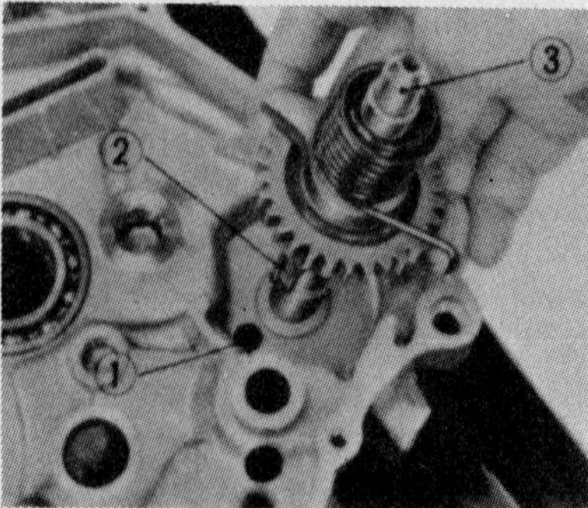

Installing the kick starter spindle

1. Hole
2. Spring
3. Kick starter spindle

7. Assemble the shifter cam so the cam pin is inserted into the hole in the drum.

Proper direction for installing the shifter drum

1. Shifter drum
2. Mainshaft
3. Countershaft

Installing the right side shifter fork

1. Right side shifter fork

Aligning the cam pin
1. Cam pin
2. Pin hole

Positioning the center shifter fork
1. Center shifter fork

Positioning the left side shifter fork
1. Shifter fork guide shaft
2. Left side shifter fork

8. Assemble the gearshifter assembly, making sure that the end of the return spring is hooked onto the crankcase boss.
9. Install the shifter drum stopper and the gearshifter plate, then mount the spring and secure the assembly with the circlip.
10. Complete the assembly in the reverse order of disassembly.

XL-250

Disassembly

1. Remove the engine and separate the crankcase halves as described in the "Splitting the Crankcases" section.
2. Remove the transmission mainshaft and countershaft.
3. Remove the right and left side shifter forks by pulling the shift fork guide shaft out to the right.
4. Remove the bearing set plate and shifter drum.
5. Disassemble the shifter linkage only if necessary.

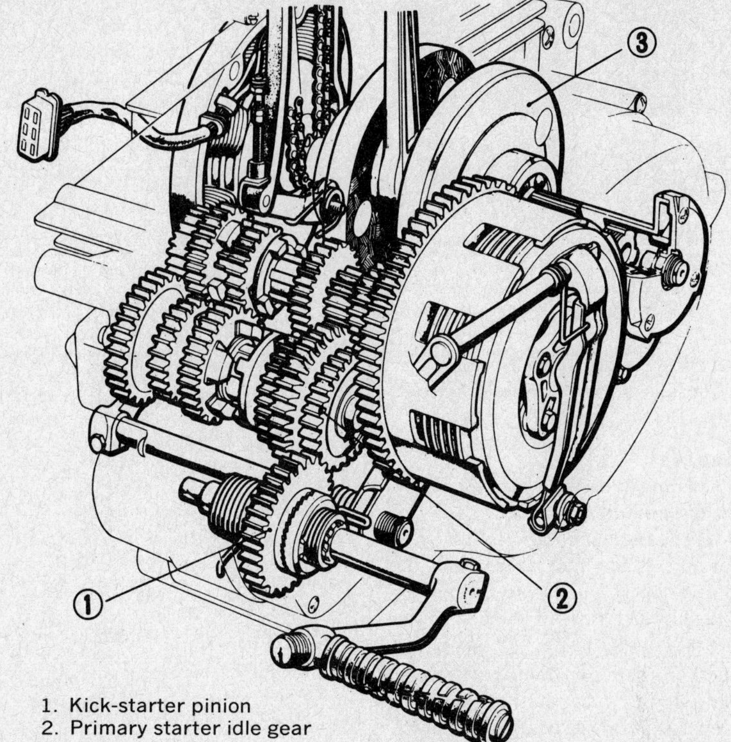

1. Kick-starter pinion
2. Primary starter idle gear

Kick-starter and transmission assemblies (shown is a 100 cc engine)

Installing the spindle
1. Boss
2. Return spring

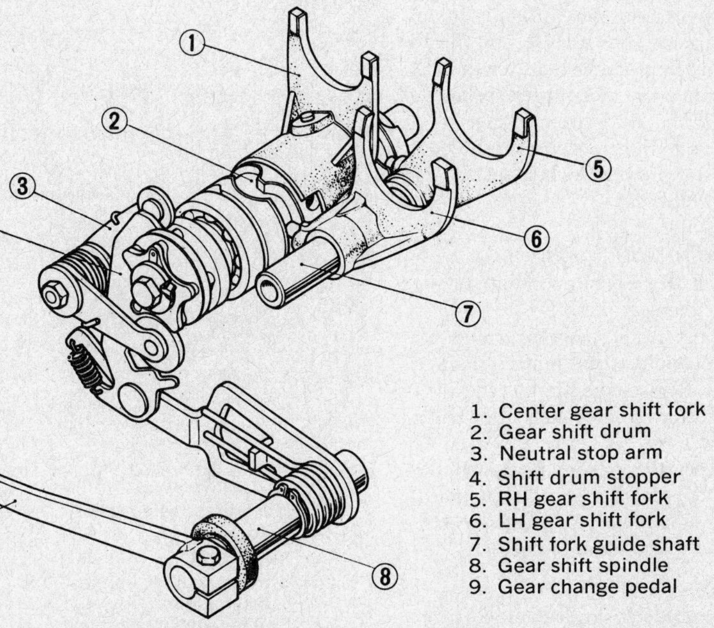

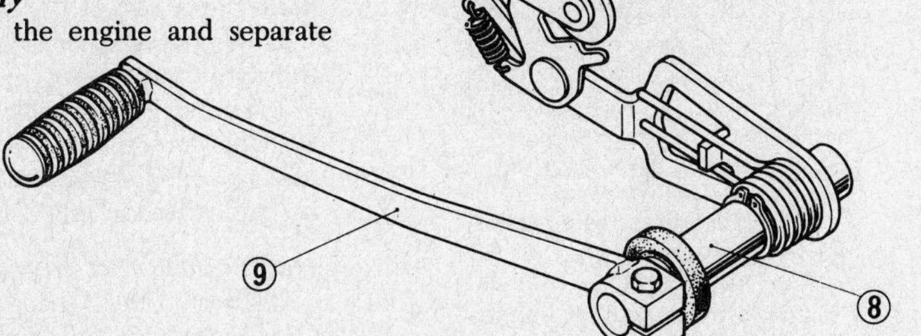

1. Center gear shift fork
2. Gear shift drum
3. Neutral stop arm
4. Shift drum stopper
5. RH gear shift fork
6. LH gear shift fork
7. Shift fork guide shaft
8. Gear shift spindle
9. Gear change pedal

Positioning the shifter forks

Shifter assembly
1. Guide pin
2. Bearing clip
3. L-gear shift fork
4. R-gear shift fork

Inspection and Repair

1. Consult the 90cc models "Inspection and Repair" section.

Assembly

1. Assembly is basically the reverse order of disassembly.
2. When installing the center gear shifter fork guide pin, do so with the guide pin clip groove facing upward.
3. Install the right and left side shifter forks. The forks have "R" and "L" stamped on them for identification.
4. Install the gear shift spindle and shift lever, taking care to align the punch mark on the spindle with the mark on the pedal.
5. Before securing the crankcase halves place them together and check the operation of the shifter mechanism in each gear.

Kick-Starter Mechanism

(ALL MODELS EXCEPT XL-250)

Disassembly

1. Remove the clutch, flywheel and stator assemblies, the primary driven gear, the gearshifter spindle, and the 16 mm circlip from the kick-starter spindle.
2, Remove the kick-starter spring retainer and the kick-starter spring.
3. Separate the crankcases and lift out the kick-starter spindle which seats in the left-side crankcase.

Inspection and Repair

1. Clean all parts in a suitable solvent and blow them dry.
2. Inspect all the parts for a worn or damaged condition and replace them as necessary. Replace the spring if the lever does not return immediately after being depressed.
3. Inspect the ratchet pawl and the kick-starter pinion teeth for a worn, chipped, or otherwise damaged condition, and replace them as necessary.

Assembly

1. Assembly is basically the reverse order of disassembly.

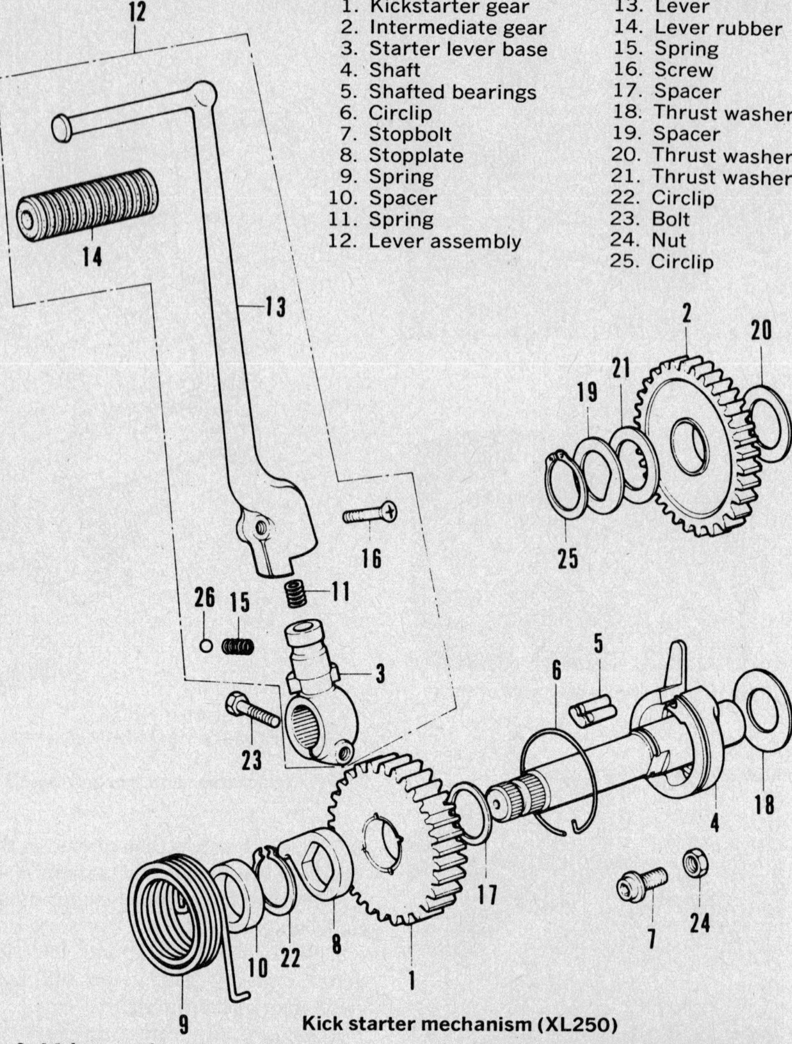

1. Kickstarter gear
2. Intermediate gear
3. Starter lever base
4. Shaft
5. Shafted bearings
6. Circlip
7. Stopbolt
8. Stopplate
9. Spring
10. Spacer
11. Spring
12. Lever assembly
13. Lever
14. Lever rubber
15. Spring
16. Screw
17. Spacer
18. Thrust washer
19. Spacer
20. Thrust washer
21. Thrust washer
22. Circlip
23. Bolt
24. Nut
25. Circlip

Kick starter mechanism (XL250)

2. Make sure the spring will return the kick-starter lever properly before you complete the assembly procedures.
3. Use new circlips and gaskets wherever applicable.

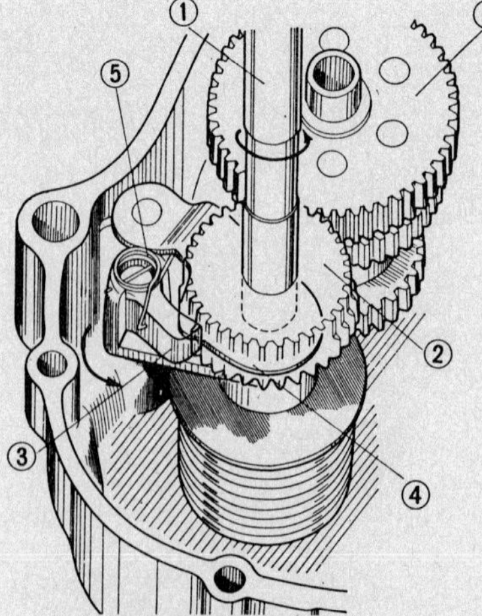

Kick starter assembly
1. Starter spindle
2. Starter pinion
3. Starter ratchet flange
4. Starter guide
5. Starter pawl spring
6. Countershaft low gear

Removing the kick-starter (shown is a 50 cc engine)

XL-250

Disassembly

1. Run the engine until its normal operating temperature is reached, then drain the oil.
2. Remove the kickstarter lever and the right crankcase cover.
3. The kickstarter mechanism is now available for removal. If more working area is needed, remove the clutch assembly as directed in the "Clutch" section.

Inspection and Repair

1. Consult the "Inspection and Repair" section for "All Models".
2. Make sure the stopper bolt is firmly secured.

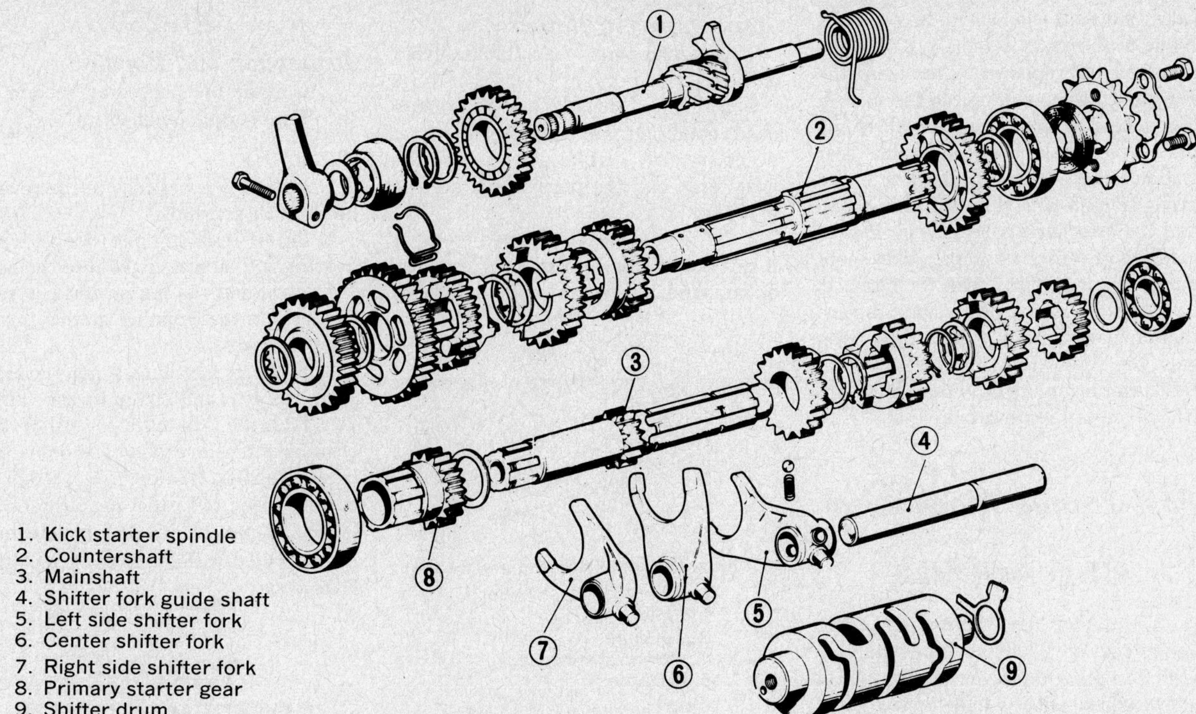

1. Kick starter spindle
2. Countershaft
3. Mainshaft
4. Shifter fork guide shaft
5. Left side shifter fork
6. Center shifter fork
7. Right side shifter fork
8. Primary starter gear
9. Shifter drum

Transmission assembly (shown is the gearbox from a 100cc engine)

Assembly

1. Assembly is the reverse order of disassembly.

2. Install the spring retainer so it faces upward and so the starter pole comes in contact with the stopper bolt.

3. Check the motion of the starter pole. The starter gear should rotate lightly while in contact with the stopper bolt, but not while in its other position if the starter pole is in good condition.

4. Make sure the 17mm thrust washer has been installed before completing the assembly.

TRANSMISSION

The transmissions used on the single-cylinder Hondas can usually be rebuilt unless the shaft is damaged. There is often one gear which is an integral part of the shaft, and of course the splines are a part of the shaft, so if either of these items, or the shaft itself, is damaged or

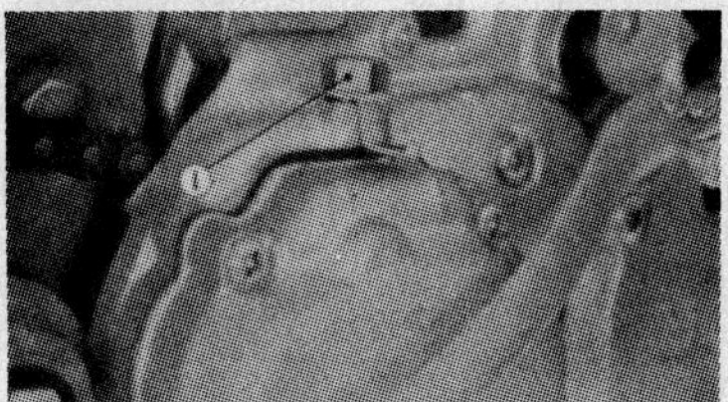

High/Low-speed selector
1. Speed selector

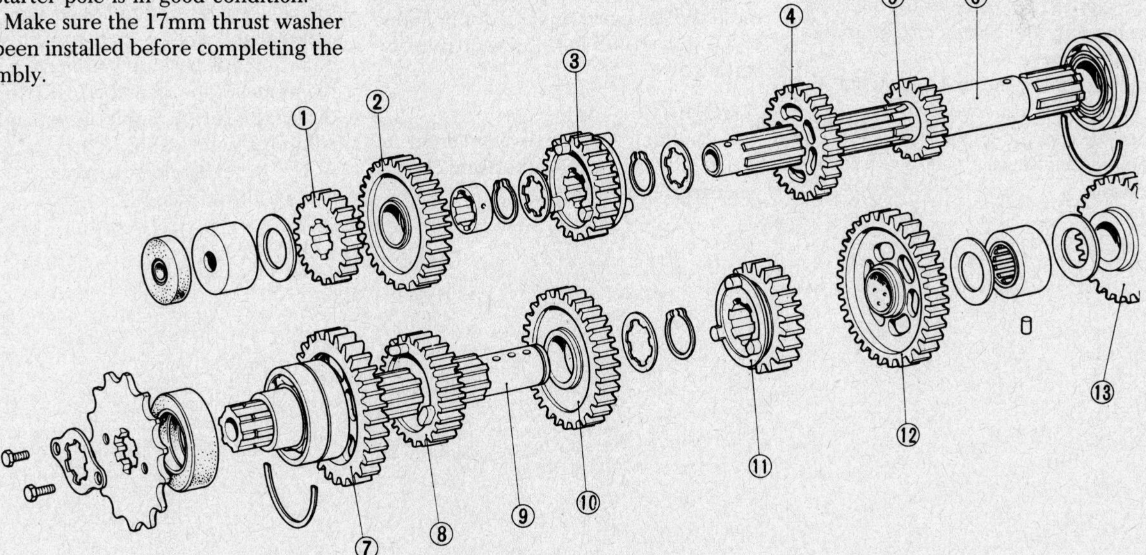

Transmission assembly

1. Main shaft second gear (21 T)
2. Main shaft top gear (31 T)
3. Main shaft third gear (25 T)
4. Main shaft fourth gear (23 T)
5. Main shaft low gear (17 T)
6. Main shaft
7. Countershaft second gear (35 T)
8. Countershaft top gear (25 T)
9. Countershaft
10. Countershaft third gear (32 T)
11. Countershaft fourth gear (28 T)
12. Countershaft low gear (40 T)
13. Idle gear (36 T)

worn, the shaft will have to be replaced. If one of the gears is damaged, it can be removed and replaced by removing the snap-rings which secure it to the shaft. It is a good practice to replace all of the parts which make up an individual gear system, since when one goes it either takes the rest with it or is an indication that the associated parts haven't long to go. This means that if the bike keeps jumping out of third gear, for instance, you should examine and maybe replace the idler gear, the dog gear, the driven gear, the shifter fork, and possibly even the shifter drum. Always use new circlips whenever you remove one.

Posi-Torque Mechanism

CT90 MODELS

CT90 models from frame no. 122551 and engine no. 000001A come equipped with the posi-torque mechanism which allows you to select a high- or low-speed range of gearing by a simple manual adjustment.

Disassembly

1. Remove the posi-torque cover which is located on the left-side crankcase. It may be necessary to remove the gearshifter lever depending on how it has been mounted.
2. Remove the posi-torque low gear and the counter gear assembly along with the countershaft assembly.
3. Remove the posi-torque high gear by removing the 20 mm circlip and the splined washer.
4. To remove the drive sprocket, the left-side crankcase cover will have to be removed, and the chain will have to be removed or at least unhooked from the sprocket.

Inspection and Repair

1. Clean all parts in a suitable solvent and blow them dry.
2. Inspect all parts for a worn or damaged condition and replace them as necessary. Pay careful attention to the gear teeth and the dogs which are the first parts to go.
3. If any gears have chipped teeth, or if any of the dogs or dog holes are worn or damaged, the gears should be replaced along with any gears with which they mesh. When a gear dog is worn in excess of 2.5 mm (0.098 in.), the gear must be replaced.

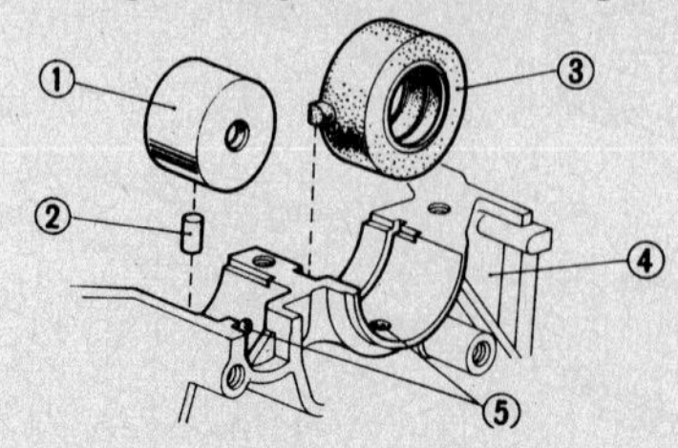

Installing the roller bearing and oil seal

1. Needle roller bearing
2. Dowel pin
3. Oil seal
4. Lower crankcase
5. Oil holes

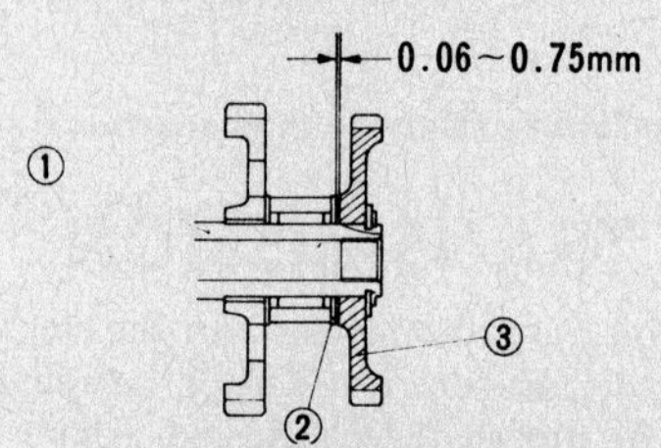

Correct gear to washer side clearance

1. Counter shaft
2. Thrust washer
3. Idle gear

Assembly

1. Assembly is the reverse order of disassembly. Use new gaskets and circlips wherever applicable.

XL-250

Inspection and Repair

1. Consult the preceding section for the "Posi-Torque Mechanism".

Assembly

1. Assembly is basically in the reverse order of disassembly.
2. When installing the needle roller bearing and oil seal, make sure the bearing dowel and the lug on the seal seats properly in their mating grooves in the lower crankcase.
3. If, upon installing a new countershaft idle gear and 20mm thrust washer, you find the idle gear-to-washer side clearance to be in excess of 0.76mm (0.03 in.), add a 20 × 0.7mm (0.79 × 0.028 in.) thrust washer to correct the clearance to 0.06–0.75 mm (0.002–0.03 in.). In most cases a thrust washer of 1.0mm (0.039 in.) is necessary.

TORQUE SPECIFICATIONS

In 1967, Honda started using ISO nuts and bolts instead of the JIS hardware they had been using up to that time. The main difference is in the number of threads per millimeter, and the two can be differentiated by the small figure-eight on the heads of the ISO bolts. ISO hardware will stand up to greater torque values than the JIS type, so know what kind you are torquing before you start. Incidentally, the two types are not interchangeable, so if you start to turn something in and it seems like it's going to fit and then all of a sudden it doens't want to turn anymore, don't force it because you may be using the wrong type and this will strip the threads for sure. Consult the appendix for additional information.

As a general rule you may use the following torque values:

50, 65, 70, AND 90 cc MODELS

Bolts and Nuts	Tightening Torque ft lbs (kg-cm)	Bolts and Nuts	Tightening Torque ft lbs (kg-cm)
R and L Crankcase	5.8- 8.0 (80-110)	Shift drum stopper plate	6.5- 9.4 (90-130)
Cam chain guide roller pin	5.1- 9.4 (70-130)	Shift drum stopper	7.2-11.6 (100-160)
Cylinder head stud nut	6.5- 8.7 (90-120)	Clutch nut	27.5-32.5 (380-450)
Cylinder side bolt	5.8- 8.0 (80-110)	R Crankcase cover	5.8- 8.7 (80-120)
Cylinder head side bolt	7.2-10.8 (100-150)	Stater	5.8- 8.7 (80-120)
Cam sprocket	3.6- 6.5 (50- 90)	Fly wheel	23.9-27.5 (330-380)
Cylinder head R side cover	5.1- 6.5 (70- 90)	Rotor	15.9-21.7 (220-300)
Cylinder head L side cover	5.8- 8.7 (80-120)	Drive sprocket	6.5-10.8 (90-150)
Tappet adjustment	5.1- 7.2 (70-100)	L Crankcase cover	5.8- 8.0 (80-110)
Cam chain tensioner push rod	10.8-18.1 (150-250)	Drain cock bolt	18.1-25.3 (250-350)
Oil pump	5.8- 8.7 (80-120)	Spark plug	8.0-10.8 (110-150)
Shift drum side bolt	6.5-10.8 (90-150)	Carburetor	6.5-10.1 (90-140)

100 AND 125 cc MODELS

Engine		Frame	
Item	Torque values kg-m (ft-lb)	Item	Torque values kg-m (ft-lb)
Cylinder head	1.8- 2.0 (11.5-14.5)	Gearshift drum cam bolt	0.8- 1.2 (5.6- 8.7)
Spark advance	0.8- 1.2 (5.8- 8.7)	Front axle nut	4.0- 5.0 (29.0-36.0)
Cam sprocket	0.8- 1.2 (5.8- 8.7)	Rear axle nut	4.0- 5.0 (29.0-36.0)
Cylinder mount bolt, 6 mm	1.2- 1.8 (8.7-13.0)	Rear fork pivot bolt	3.0- 4.0 (21.7-29.0)
Left crankcase cover	0.8- 1.2 (5.8- 8.7)	Engine mounting bolt	2.0- 2.5 (14.5-18.8)
AC rotor	2.6- 3.2 (18.8-23.2)	Handle mounting bolt	0.9- 1.1 (6.50-7.95)
AC generator mounting screw	0.8- 1.2 (5.8- 8.7)	Steering stem nut	6.0- 8.0 (43.3-57.8)
Cam chain tensioner arm	0.8- 1.2 (5.8- 8.7)	Front cushion mounting bolt	4.0- 5.0 (29.0-36.0)
Right crankcase cover screw	0.8- 1.2 (5.8- 8.7)	Rear cushion mounting nut	3.0- 4.0 (21.7-29.0)
Oil filter cover screw	0.8- 0.4 (2.2- 2.9)	Torque link mounting bolt	2.0- 2.5 (14.5-18.0)
Oil filter (locknut, 16 mm)	4.0- 5.0 (29.0-36.0)	Top bridge locknut	4.0- 4.8 (29.0-34.7)
Oil pump gear cover bolt	0.4- 0.6 (2.9- 4.4)	Final driven sprocket	2.0- 2.5 (14.5-18.0)
Clutch mounting bolt	0.8- 1.2 (5.6- 8.7)	Seat mounting bolt	2.0- 2.5 (14.5-18.0)
Gearshift drum stopper bolt	0.8- 1.2 (5.6- 8.7)		

XL-250

		Tightening point	Torque kg-m (lb-ft)	Bolts mm
1.	Frame	Steering stem nut	8.0-12.0 (57.84-86.76)	23
		Front fork top bridge	1.8-2.3 (13.014-16.629)	8
		Handle holder	1.8-2.3 (13.014-16.629)	8
		Front fork bottom bridge	1.8-2.3 (13.014-16.629)	8
		Spoke	0.2-0.45 (1.446-3.2535)	
		Rear fork pivot bolt	5.5-7.0 (39.765-50.610)	14
		Front wheel axle shaft nut	5.5-6.5 (39.765-46.995)	12
		Front axle holder	1.8-2.3 (13.014-16.629)	8
		Engine hanger bolt	3.0-4.0 (21.69-28.92)	10
		Rear axle	8.0-10.0 (57.84-72.30)	18
		Driven sprocket	1.8-2.3 (13.014-16.629)	8
		Brake arm	0.8-1.1 (5.784-7.953)	6
		Front brake torque link	1.8-2.3 (13.014-16.629)	8
		Rear brake torque link	1.8-2.3 (13.014-16.629)	8
		Rear cushion, upper/lower	3.0-4.0 (21.69-28.92)	10
		Step bar	1.8-2.3 (13.014-16.629)	8
			3.0-4.0 (21.69-28.92)	10
		Change pedal	0.8-1.2 (5.784-8.676)	6
		Kick arm	1.8-2.3 (13.014-16.629)	8
		Seat band	0.8-1.2 (5.784-8.676)	6
2.	Engine	Crankcase cover	0.7-1.1 (5.061-7.953)	6
		Cylinder head	3.0-3.6 (21.690-26.028)	10
		Carburetor insulator	0.8-1.2 (5.784-8.676)	6
		Cam sprocket	1.8-2.2 (13.014-15.906)	7
		Flywheel	6.0-7.0 (43.380-50.610)	12
		Oil filter rotor	4.5-5.5 (32.535-39.765)	16
		Tappet adjusting nut	0.7-1.1 (5.061-7.953)	5
		Upper crankcase	2.4-3.0 (17.352-21.690)	10
		Lower crankcase	2.4-3.0 (17.352-21.690)	10
		Cylinder 8 mm stud bolt	2.0-2.5 (14.460-18.075)	8

Parts other than those specified above should be tightened in accordance with following specifications.

Bolts	Torque kg-m (lb-ft)
6 mm (0.24 in.) machine screw	0.7-1.0 (5.061-7.230)
6 mm (0.24 in.) hex. bolt	0.8-1.2 (5.784-8.676)
8 mm (0.31 in.) hex. bolt	1.8-2.5 (13.014-18.075)
10 mm (0.39 in.) hex. bolt	3.0-4.0 (21.690-28.920)
6 mm (0.24 in.) flange bolt	1.0-1.4 (7.230-10.122)
8 mm (0.31 in.) flange bolt	2.3-3.0 (17.352-21.690)
10 mm (0.39 in.) flange bolt	3.0-4.0 (21.690-28.920)

ENGINE, CLUTCH, AND TRANSMISSION SPECIFICATIONS

C50, C50M, S50

	Standard	Serviceable Limit
CYLINDER HEAD		
Valve guides:		
outside diameter (in./mm)	0.394/10.0	—
interference fit (in./mm)	0.002-0.006/0.40-0.065	—
inside diameter (in./mm)	0.217/5.5	0.199/5.53
Intake valve:		
valve seat (in./mm)	0.040-0.051/1-1.3	0.080/2.0
total length (in./mm)	2.600/66.0	2.530/65.6
stem diameter (in./mm)	0.217/5.5	0.214/5.44
head thickness (in./mm)	0.020/0.5	0.008/0.2
stem-to-guide clearance (in./mm)	0.0004-0.0012/0.010-0.030	0.0023/0.06
Exhaust valve:		
valve seat (in./mm)	0.040-0.051/1-1.3	—
total length (in./mm)	2.573/65.3	2.557/64.9
stem diameter (in./mm)	0.217/5.5	0.213/5.4
head thickness (in./mm)	0.026/0.7	0.016/0.4
stem-to-guide clearance (in./mm)	0.0012-0.0020/0.030-0.050	0.0032/0.08
Outer valve spring:		
free-length (in./mm)	1.110/28.1	1.060/26.9
compressed pressure (lbs/in.)	16.0 ± 1.2/0.980	14.0/0.980
(kg/mm)	7.2 ± 55/24.9	6.4/24.9
tilt	1°30′	2°
Inner valve spring:		
free-length (in./mm)	0.990/25.1	0.940/23.9
compressed pressure (lbs/in.)	18.0 ± 0.88/0.690	15.8/0.690
(kg/mm)	8.2 ± 4/17.5	7.2/17.5
tilt	1°30′	2°
Camshaft:		
left-end diameter (in./mm)	1.140-1.110/29.00-28.927	1.135/28.8
right-end diameter (in./mm)	1.140-1.110/29.00-28.927	1.135/28.8
shaft run-out (in./mm)	N.A.	0.0020/0.05
cam height (in./mm)	0.200/5.076	0.190/4.9
left-end bearing diameter (in./mm)	1.140/29.00	1.145/29.06
right-end bearing diameter (in./mm)	1.140/29.00	1.145/29.06
cam sprocket root diameter (in./mm)	2.104 ± 0.001/53.41 ± 0.025	2.09/53.00
Rocker arm:		
wear slipper (in./mm)	N.A.	N.A.
shaft bore (in./mm)	N.A.	N.A.
Rocker arm shaft:		
shaft diameter (in./mm)	N.A.	N.A.
shaft clearance (in./mm)	N.A.	N.A.
CYLINDER AND PISTON ASSEMBLY		
Cylinder:		
cylinder taper (in./mm)	N.A.	N.A.
cylinder bore (in./mm)	1.54/39.0	1.74/44.1
surface roughness (micron)	1.5	

ENGINE, CLUTCH, AND TRANSMISSION SPECIFICATIONS (con't.)

C50, C50M, S50

	Standard Value	Serviceable Limit
CYLINDER AND PISTON ASSEMBLY		
Piston:		
piston diameter (in./mm)	1.5346-1.5354/38.98-39.00	1.73/33.88
ring side clearance (in./mm)	0.0006-0.00177/0.015-0.045	0.0047/0.12
oil ring side clearance (in./mm)	0.0004-0.0017/0.005-0.12	0.005/0.12
piston-to-piston pin clearance (in./mm)	0.00008-0.00055/0.002-0.014	0.0020/0.05
Piston rings:		
ring thickness (in./mm)	0.079 ± 0.04/2.0 ± 0.1	0.07/1.8
oil ring thickness (in./mm)	0.071 ± 0.0004/1.8 ± 0.1	0.063/1.6
ring end gap (in./mm)	0.004-0.0118/0.1-0.3	0.0197/0.5
oil ring end gap (in./mm)	0.12/0.30	0.020/0.50
CAM CHAIN TENSIONER		
Tensioner spring:		
spring free-length (in./mm)	3.04/77.2	2.89/73.5
spring tension (in./lbs)	0.874/0.99 ± 0.08	0.87/0.79
(mm/kg)	22.2/0.45 ± 0.04	22.2/0.36
roller diameter	0.391-35.3	1.359/34.5
CLUTCH		
Friction disc and clutch plate:		
thickness of disc (in./mm)	0.138/3.5	0.122/3.1
thickness of plate (in./mm)	0.063 ± 0.0020/1.6 ± 0.05	0.059/1.5
warpage of plate (in./mm)	N.A.	0.006/0.15
backlash of plate (in./mm)	N.A.	N.A.
backlash of disc (in./mm)	N.A.	N.A.
Clutch center guide:		
inside diameter (in./mm)	0.670/17.00	0.674/17.1
outside diameter (in./mm)	0.827/21.00	0.787/19.98
length (in./mm)	0.812/20.6	0.8/20.4
run-out (in./mm)	0.0012/0.03	0.006/0.15
crankshaft to guide clearance (in./mm)	N.A.	N.A.
Primary drive gear:		
inside diameter (in./mm)	0.830/21.00	0.833/21.15
chordal distance across three teeth (in./mm)	0.551/14.001	0.540/13.7
Clutch spring:		
free-length (in./mm)	①	②
spring tension (lb/in.)	③	④
(kg/mm)		
CRANKSHAFT		
Crankshaft:		
run-out at the bearings (in./mm)	0.0006/0.015	0.0020/0.05
axial clearance (in./mm)	0.0002-0.001/0.004-0.036	0.004/0.1
clearance normal to axis (in./mm)	0.0004-0.001/0.010-0.025	0.002/0.05
sprocket root diameter (in./mm)	0.994 ± 0.001/25.24 ± 0.025	0.991/25.19
right-side spline play (in./mm)	0.0004-0.0020/0.010-0.040	0.0032/0.08
maximum shaft run-out (in./mm)	0.002 TIR/0.05 TIR	0.008/0.2
Crankpin:		
outside diameter (in./mm)	0.91/23.1	0.908/23.045
interference fit (in./mm)	0.0020-0.0034/0.052-0.087	——

ENGINE, CLUTCH, AND TRANSMISSION SPECIFICATIONS (con't.)

C50, C50M, S50

	Standard Value	Serviceable Limit
CRANKSHAFT		
Connecting rod:		
small-end-to-piston pin clearance (in./mm)	0.001-0.002/0.016-0.043	0.0032/0.08
small-end deflection (in./mm)	0.060/1.5	0.120/3.0
large-end end-play (in./mm)	0.004-0.014/0.10/0.35	0.024/0.6
bearing clearance (in./mm)	0-0.0005/0-0.012	0.002/0.05
small-end bore (in./mm)	0.512/13.00	0.52/13.1

	Model	Value
①	S65	0.756/19.2
	S50	0.744/18.9
	C50, C50M, C65, C65M	0.772/19.6
	CL70, SL70	0.787/20.0
	C70, C70M	0.843/21.4
②	S65	0.717/18.2
	S50	0.717/18.2
	C50, C50M, C65, C65M	0.720/18.2
	CL70, SL70	0.748/19.0
	C70, C70M	0.830/20.4

	Model	(lb/in.)	(kg/mm)
③	S65		
	S50	29.0 ± 1.75/0.504	13.2 ± 0.8/12.8
	C50, C50M,	29.0 ± 1.75/0.504	13.2 ± 0.8/12.8
	C65, C65M	12.8 ± 0.66/0.532	5.85 ± 0.3/13.5
	CL70, SL70	17.4-19.6/0.504	7.9-8.9/12.8
	C70, C70M	13.3-14.7/0.532	6.05-6.65/13.5
④	S65	14.3/0.504	6.5/12.8
	S50	14.3/0.504	6.5/12.8
	C50, C50M, C65, C65M	11.0/0.532	5.0/13.5
	CL70, SL70	16.3/0.504	7.4/12.8
	C70, C70M	11.8/0.532	5.35/13.5

C65, C65M, S65

	Standard Value	Serviceable Limit
CYLINDER HEAD		
Valve guides:		
outside diameter (in./mm)	0.394/10.0	——
interference fit (in./mm)	0.002-0.006/0.040-0.065	——
inside diameter (in./mm)	0.217/5.5	0.199/5.53
Intake valve:		
valve seat (in./mm)	0.040-0.051/1-1.3	0.080/2.0
total length (in./mm)	2.540/64.5	2.580/64.1
stem diameter (in./mm)	0.217/5.5	0.214/5.44
head thickness (in./mm)	0.020/0.5	0.008/0.2
stem-to-guide clearance (in./mm)	0.0004-0.0012/0.010-0.030	0.0023/0.06
Exhaust valve:		
valve seat (in./mm)	0.040-0.051/1-1.3	——
total length (in./mm)	2.483/63.9	2.502/63.5
stem diameter (in./mm)	0.217/5.5	0.213/5.4
head thickness (in./mm)	0.026/0.7	0.016/0.4
stem-to-guide clearance (in./mm)	0.0012-0.0020/0.030-0.050	0.0032/0.08
Outer valve spring:		
free-length (in./mm)	1.080/27.4	1.030/26.2
compressed pressure (lbs/in.)	16.0 ± 1.2/0.980	14.0/0.98
(kg/mm)	7.2 ± 0.55/24.9	6.4/24.9
tilt	1°30′	2°
Inner valve spring:		
free-length (in./mm)	0.990/25.1	0.940/23.9
compressed pressure (lbs/in.)	18.0 ± 0.88/0.690	15.8/0.690
(kg/mm)	8.2 ± 0.4/17.5	7.2/17.5
tilt	1°30′	2°

ENGINE, CLUTCH, AND TRANSMISSION SPECIFICATIONS (con't.)

C65, C65M, S65

	Standard Value	Serviceable Limit
CYLINDER HEAD		
Camshaft:		
left-end diameter (in./mm)	1.140-1.110/29.00-28.927	1.135/28.8
right-end diameter (in./mm)	1.140-1.110/29.00-28.927	1.135/28.8
shaft run-out (in./mm)	N.A.	0.0020/0.05
cam height (in./mm)	0.200/5.076	0.190/4.9
left-end bearing diameter (in./mm)	1.140/29.00	1.145/29.06
right-end bearing diameter (in./mm)	1.140/29.00	1.145/29.06
cam sprocket root diameter (in./mm)	2.10 ± 0.001/53.41 ± 0.025	2.09/53.00
Rocker arm:		
wear slipper (in./mm)	N.A.	N.A.
shaft bore (in./mm)	N.A.	N.A.
Rocker arm shaft:		
shaft diameter (in./mm)	N.A.	N.A.
shaft clearance (in./mm)	N.A.	N.A.
CYLINDER AND PISTON ASSEMBLY		
Cylinder:		
cylinder taper (in./mm)	N.A.	N.A.
cylinder bore (in./mm)	1.750/44.0	N.A.
surface roughness (micron)	1.5	——
Piston:		
piston diameter (in./mm)	1.734/43.5	1.708/42.25
ring side clearance (in./mm)	0.0006-0.00177/0.015-0.045	0.0047/0.12
oil ring side clearance (in./mm)	0.0004-0.0017/0.010-0.045	0.005/0.12
piston-to-piston pin clearance (in./mm)	0.00008-0.00055/0.002-0.014	0.0020/0.05
Piston rings:		
ring thickness (in./mm)	0.079 ± 0.04/2.0 ± 0.1	0.07/1.8
oil ring thickness (in./mm)	0.099 ± 0.004/2 ± 0.1	0.071/1.8
ring end gap (in./mm)	0.0059-0.0138/0.15-0.35	0.0197/0.5
oil ring end gap (in./mm)	0.004-0.014/0.1-0.35	0.020/0.50
CAM CHAIN TENSIONER		
Tensioner spring:		
spring free-length (in./mm)	3.04/77.2	2.89/73.5
spring tension (in./lbs)	0.87/0.99 ± 0.08	0.87/0.79
(mm/kg)	22.2/0.45 ± 0.04	22.2/0.36
roller diameter	0.391/35.3	1.359/34.5
CLUTCH		
Friction disc and clutch plate:		
thickness of disc (in./mm)	0.138/3.5	0.122/3.1
thickness of plate (in./mm)	0.063 ± 0.0020/1.6 ± 0.05	0.59/1.5
warpage of plate (in./mm)	N.A.	0.006/0.15
backlash of plate (in./mm)	N.A.	N.A.
backlash of disc (in./mm)	N.A.	N.A.
Clutch center guide:		
inside diameter (in./mm)	0.670/17.00	0.674/17.1
outside diameter (in./mm)	0.827/21.00	0.787/19.98
length (in./mm)	0.812/21.06	0.8/20.4
run-out (in./mm)	0.0012/0.03	0.006/0.15
crankshaft to guide clearance (in./mm)	N.A.	N.A.

C65, C65M, S65

	Standard Value	Serviceable Limit
CLUTCH		
Primary drive gear:		
inside diameter (in./mm)	0.830/21.00	0.833/21.15
chordal distance across three teeth (in./mm)	0.541/13.723	0.540/13.7
Clutch spring:		
free-length (in./mm)	①	②
spring tension (lb/in.)	③	④
(kg/mm)		
CRANKSHAFT		
Crankshaft:		
run-out at the bearings (in./mm)	0.0006/0.015	0.0020/0.05
axial clearance (in./mm)	0.0002-0.001/0.004-0.036	0.004/0.1
clearance normal to axis (in./mm)	0.0004-0.001/0.010-0.025	0.002/0.05
sprocket root diameter (in./mm)	0.994 ± 0.001/25.24 ± 0.025	0.991/25.19
right-side spline play (in./mm)	0.0004-0.0020/0.010-0.040	0.0032/0.08
maximum shaft run-out (in./mm)	0.002 TIR/0.05 TIR	0.008/0.2
Crankpin:		
outside diameter (in./mm)	0.91/23.1	0.908/23.045
interference fit (in./mm)	0.0020-0.0034/0.052-0.087	——
Connecting rod:		
small-end-to-piston pin clearance (in./mm)	0.001-0.002/0.016-0.043	0.0032/0.08
small-end deflection (in./mm)	0.060/1.5	0.120/3.0
large-end end-play (in./mm)	0.004-0.014/0.10/0.35	0.024/0.6
bearing clearance (in./mm)	0-0.005/0.012	0.002/0.05
small-end bore (in./mm)	0.512/13.00	0.52/13.1

①	S65	0.756/19.2
	S50	0.744/18.9
	C50, C50M, C65, C65M	0.772/19.6
	CL70, SL70	0.787/20.0
	C70, C70M	0.843/21.4
②	S65	0.717/18.2
	S50	0.717/18.2
	C50, C50M, C65, C65M	0.720/18.2
	CL70, SL70	0.748/19.0
	C70, C70M	0.830/20.4

		(lb/in.)	(kg/mm)
③	S65		
	S50	29.0 ± 1.75/0.504	13.2 ± 0.8/12.8
	C50, C50M,	29.0 ± 1.75/0.504	13.2 ± 0.8/12.8
	C65, C65M	12.8 ± 0.66/0.532	5.85 ± 0.3/13.5
	CL70, SL70	17.4-19.6/0.504	7.9-8.9/12.8
	C70, C70M	13.3-14.7/0.532	6.05-6.65/13.5
④	S65	14.3/0.504	6.5/12.8
	S50	14.3/0.504	6.5/12.8
	C50, C50M,		
	C65, C65M	11.0/0.532	5.0/13.5
	CL70, SL70	16.3/0.504	7.4/12.8
	C70, C70M	11.8/0.532	5.35/13.5

CL70, C70, C70M, SL70

	Standard Value	Serviceable Limit
CYLINDER HEAD		
Valve guides:		
outside diameter (in./mm)	N.A.	——
interference fit (in./mm)	N.A.	——
inside diameter (in./mm)	0.2156-0.2159/5.475-5.485	N.A.
Intake valve:		
valve seat (in./mm)	0.040-0.051/1.0-1.3	0.080/2.0
total length (in./mm)	2.600/66.0	2.530/65.6
stem diameter (in./mm)	0.2148-0.2187/5.455-5.465	0.2126/5.40
head thickness (in./mm)	0.020/0.5	0.008/0.2
stem-to-guide clearance (in./mm)	0.004-0.0012/0.01-0.03	0.0032/0.08
Exhaust valve:		
valve seat (in./mm)	0.040-0.051/1.0-1.3	0.080/2.0
total length (in./mm)	2.573/65.3	2.577/64.9
stem diameter (in./mm)	0.2070-0.2109/5.435-5.445	0.2048/5.38
head thickness (in./mm)	0.020/0.5	0.008/0.2
stem-to-guide clearance (in./mm)	0.0012-0.002/0.03-0.05	0.004/0.10
Outer valve spring:		
free-length (in./mm)	1.106/28.1	1.059/26.9
compressed pressure (lbs/in.)	14.66-17.09/0.980	10.14/0.980
(kg/mm)	6.65-7.75/24.9	4.6/24.9
tilt	N.A.	N.A.
Inner valve spring:		
free-length (in./mm)	①	②
compressed pressure (lbs/in.)		
(kg/mm)	③	④
tilt	N.A.	N.A.
Camshaft:		
left-end diameter (in./mm)	N.A.	N.A.
right-end diameter (in./mm)	N.A.	N.A.
shaft run-out (in./mm)	N.A.	N.A.
cam height (in./mm)	1.0266/26.076	1.012/25.8
left-end bearing diameter (in./mm)	N.A.	N.A.
right-end bearing diameter (in./mm)	N.A.	N.A.
cam sprocket root diameter (in./mm)	N.A.	N.A.
Rocker arm:		
wear slipper (in./mm)	N.A.	N.A.
shaft bore (in./mm)	N.A.	N.A.
Rocker arm shaft:		
shaft diameter (in./mm)	N.A.	N.A.
shaft clearance (in./mm)	N.A.	N.A.

① CL70, SL70
1.004/25.5
C70, C70M
0.988/25.1

② CL70, SL70
0.957/24.3
C70, C70M
0.941/23.9

③ CL70, SL70
7.87-8.55/0.894
3.55-3.85/22.7
C70, C70M
5.37-6.03/0.894
2.45-2.75/22.7

④ CL70, SL70
6.84/0.894
3.1/22.7
C70, C70M
4.41/0.894
2.0/22.7

CL70, C70, C70M, SL70

	Standard Value	Serviceable Limit
CYLINDER AND PISTON ASSEMBLY		
Cylinder:		
cylinder taper (in./mm)	N.A.	N.A.
cylinder bore (in./mm)	⑤	⑥
surface roughness (micron)	1.5	——
Piston:		
piston diameter (in./mm)	1.8492-1.8500/46.98-47.00	1.847/46.9
ring side clearance (in./mm)	0.0006-0.0018/0.015-0.045	0.0047/0.12
oil ring side clearance (in/mm)	0.0004-0.0018/0.010-0.045	0.0047/0.12
piston-to-piston pin clearance (in./mm)	N.A.	N.A.
Piston rings:		
ring thickness (in./mm)	N.A.	N.A.
oil ring thickness (in./mm)	N.A.	N.A.
ring end gap (in./mm)	0.0059-0.0138/0.15-0.35	0.0197/0.5
oil ring end gap (in./mm)	0.0059-0.01575/0.15-0.40	0.0197/0.5
CAM CHAIN TENSIONER		
Tensioner spring:		
spring free-length (in./mm)	3.04/77.2	2.89/73.5
spring tension (in./lbs)	0.874/0.99 ± 0.08	0.87/0.79
(mm/kg)	22.2/0.45 ± 0.04	22.2/0.36
roller diameter	0.391/35.3	1.359/34.5
CLUTCH		
Friction disc and clutch plate:		
thickness of disc (in./mm)	0.138/3.5	0.122/3.1
thickness of plate (in./mm)	0.063 ± 0.0020/1.6 ± 0.05	0.059/1.5
warpage of plate (in./mm)	N.A.	0.006/0.15
backlash of plate (in./mm)	N.A.	N.A.
backlash of disc (in./mm)	N.A.	N.A.
Clutch center guide:		
inside diameter (in./mm)	0.670/17.00	0.674/17.1
outside diameter (in./mm)	0.827/21.00	0.787/19.98
length (in./mm)	0.812/20.6	0.8/20.4
run-out (in./mm)	0.0012/0.03	0.006/0.15
crankshaft to guide clearance (in./mm)	N.A.	N.A.
Primary drive gear:		
inside diameter (in./mm)	N.A.	N.A.
chordal distance across three teeth (in./mm)	N.A.	N.A.

⑤ CL70, SL70
1.8510-1.8514/47.015-47.025
C70, C70M
1.8506-1.8510/47.005-47.015

⑥ CL70, SL70
1.854/47.1
C70, C70M
1.854/47.1

CL70, C70, C70M, SL70

	Standard Value	Serviceable Limit
CLUTCH		
Clutch spring:		
free-length (in./mm)	①	②
spring tension (lb/in.) (kg/mm)	③	④
CRANKSHAFT		
Crankshaft:		
run-out at the bearings (in./mm)	0.0006/0.015	0.0020/0.05
axial clearance (in./mm)	0.0002-0.001/0.004-0.036	0.004/0.1
clearance normal to axis (in./mm)	0.0004-0.001/0.010-0.025	0.002/0.05
sprocket root diameter (in./mm)	0.994 ± 0.001/25.24 ± 0.025	0.991/25.19
right-side spline play (in./mm)	0.0004-0.0020/0.010-0.040	0.0032/0.08
maximum shaft run-out (in./mm)	0.002 TIR/0.05 TIR	0.008/0.2
Crankpin:		
outside diameter (in./mm)	0.91/23.1	0.908/23.045
interference fit (in./mm)	0.0020-0.0034/0.052-0.087	——
Connecting rod:		
small-end-to-piston pin clearance (in./mm)	0.001-0.002/0.016-0.043	0.032/0.08
small-end deflection (in./mm)	0.060/1.5	0.120/3.0
large-end end-play (in./mm)	0.004-0.014/0.10-0.35	0.024/0.6
bearing clearance (in./mm)	0-0.0005/0-0.012	0.002/0.05
small-end bore (in./mm)	0.512/13.00	0.52/13.1

	Model	Value
①	S65	0.756/19.2
	S50	0.744/18.9
	C50, C50M, C65, C65M	0.772/19.6
	CL70, SL70	0.787/20.0
	C70, C70M	0.843/21.4
②	S65	0.717/18.2
	S50	0.717/18.2
	C50, C50M, C65, C65M	0.720/18.2
	CL70, SL70	0.748/19.0
	C70, C70M	0.830/20.4

	Model	(lb/in.)	(kg/mm)
③	S65	29.0 ± 1.75/0.504	13.2 ± 0.8/12.8
	S50	29.0 ± 1.75/0.504	13.2 ± 0.8/12.8
	C50, C50M, C65, C65M	12.8 ± 0.66/0.532	5.85 ± 0.3/13.5
	CL70, SL70	17.4-19.6/0.504	7.9-8.9/12.8
	C70, C70M	13.3-14.7/0.532	6.05-6.65/13.5
④	S65	14.3/0.504	6.5/12.8
	S50	14.3/0.504	6.5/12.8
	C50, C50M, C65, C65M	11.0/0.532	5.0/13.5
	CL70, SL70	16.3/0.504	7.4/12.8
	C70, C70M	11.8/0.532	5.35/13.5

S90, SL90, CI90, CL90L, CD90, C90, CT90

	Standard Value	Serviceable Limit
CYLINDER HEAD		
Valve guides:		
outside diameter (in./mm)	0.396-0.3966/10.055-0.1065	——
interference fit (in./mm)	0.002-0.003/0.640-0.065	——
inside diameter (in./mm)	0.215-0.216/5.475-5.485	0.217/5.525
Intake valve:		
valve seat (in./mm)	0.028-0.048/0.7-1.2	0.08/2.0
total length (in./mm)	2.648-2.153/67.2-67.4	2.632/66.8
stem diameter (in./mm)	0.2149-0.2153/5.455-5.465	0.2141/5.435
head thickness (in./mm)	0.024-0.032/0.6-0.8	0.012/0.3
stem-to-guide clearance (in./mm)	0.0004-0.0012/0.01-0.03	0.0028/0.08

S90, SL90, CL90, CL90L, CD90, C90, CT90

	Standard Value	Serviceable Limit
CYLINDER HEAD		
Exhaust valve:		
valve seat (in./mm)	0.028-0.048/0.7-1.2	0.08/2.0
total length (in./mm)	2.593-2.600/65.8-66.0	2.577/65.4
stem diameter (in./mm)	0.214-0.215/5.455-5.465	0.214/5.435
head thickness (in./mm)	0.024-0.032/0.6-0.8	0.012/0.3
stem-to-guide clearance (in./mm)	0.0012-0.0020/0.03-0.05	0.0032/0.1
Outer valve spring:		
free-length (in./mm)	1.253/31.8	1.207/30.6
compressed pressure (lbs/in.)	17.38-19.58/1.095	N.A.
(kg/mm)	7.9-8.9/27.8	N.A.
tilt	N.A.	1.5°
Inner valve spring:		
free-length (in./mm)	1.044/26.5	1.005/25.5
compressed pressure (lbs/in.)	20.90-23.10/1.73	N.A.
(kg/mm)	9.5-10.5/18.4	N.A.
tilt	N.A.	1.5°
Camshaft:		
left-end diameter (in./mm)	1.0208-1.025/25.917-25.930	0.9913/25.180
right-end diameter (in./mm)	0.7060-0.6730/17.927-17.938	0.7147/17.900
shaft run-out (in./mm)	0.0004/0.01	0.0020/0.05
cam height (in./mm)	0.9792-0.98396/24.90-24.98	0.9684/24.6
left-end bearing diameter (in./mm)	1.0236-1.0244/26.00-26.020	1.0256/26.05
right-end bearing diameter (in./mm)	0.7086-0.7093/18000-18018	0.7106/18.05
cam sprocket root diameter (in./mm)	2.103-2.105/53.435-53.385	2.09/53.00
Rocker arm:		
wear slipper (in./mm)	N.A.	6.0012/0.3
shaft bore (in./mm)	0.3937-0.3943/10.00-10.015	0.40-10.1
Rocker arm shaft:		
shaft diameter (in./mm)	0.3926-0.3933/9.972-9.987	0.3934/9.920
shaft clearance (in./mm)	0.0005-0.0017/0.013-0.043	0.0031/0.08
CYLINDER AND PISTON ASSEMBLY		
Cylinder:		
cylinder taper (in./mm)	0.004/0.01	0.002/0.05
cylinder bore (in./mm)	1.9685-1.9688/50.00-50.01	1.9739/50.10
surface roughness (micron)	1.5	——
Piston:		
piston diameter (in./mm)	1.9673-1.9681/49.97-49.99	N.A.
ring side clearance (in./mm)	0.0004-0.018/0.01-0.1	0.004/0.1
oil ring side clearance (in./mm)	N.A.	N.A.
piston-to-piston pin clearance (in./mm)	N.A.	N.A.
Piston rings:		
ring thickness (in./mm)	0.0808-0.0812/1.175-1.190	0.0445/1.13
oil ring thickness (in./mm)	0.9743-0.9802/2.475-2.490	0.0953/2.43
ring end gap (in./mm)	0.006-0.014/0.15-0.35	0.02/0.5
oil ring end gap (in./mm)	0.0059-0.157/0.15-0.40	0.020/0.5
CAM CHAIN TENSIONER		
Tensioner spring:		
spring free-length (in./mm)	2.772/70.4	2.654/67.4
spring tension (in./oz)	1.931/2.275-2.285	1.931/1.400
(mm/g)	49.00/65.00-81.00	49.00/40.00
roller diameter	N.A.	N.A.

S90, SL90, CL90, CL90L, CD90, C90, CT90

	Standard Value	Serviceable Limit
CLUTCH		
Friction disc and clutch plate:		
thickness of disc (in./mm)	0.1102-0.1141/2.8-2.9	0.0944/2.4
thickness of plate (in./mm)	0.0760-0.0815/1.93-2.07	0.073/1.85
warpage of plate (in./mm)	0.0079/0.2	0.0196/0.5
backlash of plate (in./mm)	0.008/0.2	0.036/0.7
backlash of disc (in./mm)	0.008/0.2	0.0196/0.7
Clutch center guide:		
inside diameter (in./mm)	N.A.	N.A.
outside diameter (in./mm)	N.A.	N.A.
length (in./mm)	N.A.	N.A.
run-out (in./mm)	N.A.	N.A.
crankshaft to guide clearance (in./mm)	0.0002-0.0019/0.005-0.047	0.060/0.15
Primary drive gear:		
inside diameter (in./mm)	0.945-0.946/24.00-24.02	0.951/24.15
chordal distance across three teeth (in./mm)	0.5496-0.5504/13.96-13.98	0.5484/13.93
Clutch spring:		
free-length (in./mm)	①	1.0236/26.0
spring tension (lb/in.) (kg/mm)	②	N.A.
CRANKSHAFT		
Crankshaft:		
run-out at the bearings (in./mm)	0.0006/0.015	0.004/0.1
axial clearance (in./mm)	0.004-0.019/0.10-0.35	0.032/0.8
clearance normal to axis (in./mm)	0-0.004/0-0.01	0.002/0.05
sprocket root diameter (in./mm)	N.A.	N.A.
right-side spline play (in./mm)	N.A.	N.A.
maximum shaft run-out (in./mm)	N.A.	N.A.
Crankpin:		
outside diameter (in./mm)	N.A.	N.A.
interference fit (in./mm)	N.A.	N.A.
Connecting rod:		
small-end-to-piston clearance (in./mm)	N.A.	N.A.
small-end deflection (in./mm)	N.A.	N.A.
large-end end-play (in./mm)	N.A.	N.A.
bearing clearance (in./mm)	N.A.	N.A.
small-end bore (in./mm)	0.5517-0.5523/14.012-14.028	0.5531/14.05

① S90, SL90, CL90, CL90L, CD90	1.0551/26.8	
C90, CT90	1.0630/27.0	
	(lb/in.)	**(kg/mm)**
② S90, SL90, CL90, CL90L, CD90	44.453-48.863/0.6890	20.16-22.16/17.5
C90, CT90	22.0-22.9/0.591	10.0-10.4/15.0

CB100, CL100, SL100, CB125S, CD125S, SL125

	Standard Value	Serviceable Limit
CYLINDER HEAD		
Valve guides:		
outside diameter (in./mm)	N.A.	——
interference fit (in./mm)	N.A.	——
inside diameter (in./mm)	N.A.	N.A.
Intake valve:		
valve seat (in./mm)	0.028/0.7	0.059/1.5
total length (in./mm)	N.A.	N.A.
stem diameter (in./mm)	0.214-0.215/5.450-5.565	0.2130/5.420
head thickness (in./mm)	N.A.	N.A.
stem-to-guide clearance (in./mm)	N.A.	N.A.
Exhaust valve:		
valve seat (in./mm)	0.028-0.7	0.059/1.5
total length (in./mm)	N.A.	N.A.
stem diameter (in./mm)	0.214-0.215/5.430-5.445	0.2126/5.400
head thickness (in./mm)	N.A.	N.A.
stem-to-guide clearance (in./mm)	N.A.	N.A.
Outer valve spring:		
free-length (in./mm)	①	②
compressed pressure (lbs/in.) (kg/mm)	N.A.	N.A.
tilt	N.A.	N.A.
Inner valve spring:		
free-length (in./mm)	③	④
compressed pressure (lbs/in.) (kg/mm)	N.A.	N.A.
tilt	N.A.	N.A.
Camshaft:		
left-end diameter (in./mm)	N.A.	N.A.
right-end diameter (in./mm)	N.A.	N.A.
shaft run-out (in./mm)	N.A.	N.A.
cam height (in./mm)	N.A.	N.A.
left-end bearing diameter (in./mm)	N.A.	N.A.
right-end bearing diameter (in./mm)	N.A.	N.A.
cam sprocket root diameter (in./mm)	N.A.	N.A.
Rocker arm:		
wear slipper (in./mm)	N.A.	N.A.
shaft bore (in./mm)	N.A.	N.A.
Rocker arm shaft		
shaft diameter (in/mm)	N.A.	N.A.
shaft clearance (in./mm)	N.A.	N.A.
CYLINDER AND PISTON ASSEMBLY		
Cylinder:		
cylinder taper (in./mm)	N.A.	N.A.
cylinder bore (in./mm)	⑤	⑥
surface roughness (micron)	1.5	——

CB100, CL100, SL100, CB125S, CD125S, SL125

	Standard Value	Serviceable Limit
CYLINDER AND PISTON ASSEMBLY		
Piston:		
piston diameter (in./mm)	⑦	⑧
ring side clearance (in./mm)	0.0008-0.0011/0.025-0.030	0.0275/0.7
oil ring side clearance (in./mm)	N.A.	N.A.
piston-to-cylinder clearance (in./mm)	0.0004-0.0020/0.01-0.05	N.A.
Piston rings:		
ring thickness (in./mm)	N.A.	N.A.
oil ring thickness (in./mm)	N.A.	N.A.
ring end gap (in./mm)	0.0059-0.0138/0.15-0.35	0.0197/0.5
oil ring end gap (in./mm)	0.0059-0.0158/0.15-0.04	0.0197/0.5
CAM CHAIN TENSIONER		
Tensioner spring:		
spring free-length (in./mm)	N.A.	N.A.
spring tension (in. oz)	N.A.	N.A.
(mm/g)	N.A.	N.A.
roller diameter	N.A.	N.A.
CLUTCH		
Friction disc and clutch plate:		
thickness of disc (in./mm)	0.114/2.9	0.102/26.00
thickness of plate (in./mm)	N.A.	N.A.
warpage of plate (in./mm)	N.A.	N.A.
backlash of plate (in./mm)	N.A.	N.A.
backlash of disc (in./mm)	N.A.	N.A.
Clutch center guide:		
inside diameter (in./mm)	N.A.	N.A.
outside diameter (in./mm)	N.A.	N.A.
length (in./mm)	N.A.	N.A.
run-out (in./mm)	N.A.	N.A.
crankshaft to guide clearance (in./mm)	N.A.	N.A.
Primary drive gear:		
inside diameter (in./mm)	N.A.	N.A.
chordal distance across three teeth (in./mm)	N.A.	N.A.
Clutch spring:		
free-length (in./mm)	N.A.	N.A.
spring tension (lb/in.)	N.A.	N.A.
CRANKSHAFT		
Crankshaft:		
run-out at the bearings (in./mm)	0.001/0.03	0.004/0.1
axial clearance (in./mm)	N.A.	N.A.
clearance normal to axis (in./mm)	N.A.	N.A.
sprocket root diameter (in./mm)	N.A.	N.A.
right-side spline play (in./mm)	N.A.	N.A.
maximum shaft run-out (in./mm)	N.A.	N.A.
Crankpin:		
outside diameter (in./mm)	N.A.	N.A.
interference fit (in./mm)	N.A.	N.A.

CB100, CL100, SL100, CB125S, CD125S, SL125

	Standard Value	Serviceable Limit
CRANKSHAFT		
Connecting rod:		
small-end-to-piston pin clearance (in./mm)	N.A.	N.A.
small-end deflection (in./mm)	N.A.	N.A.
large-end end-play (in./mm)	0.004-0.014/0.10-0.35	0.0032/0.8
bearing clearance (in./mm)	0-0.0004/0-0.01	0.0020/0.05
small-end bore (in./mm)	N.A.	N.A.

① CB100, CL100, SL100 1.591/40.4
CB125S, CD125S, SL125 1.610/40.9
② CB100, CL100, SL100 1.535/39.0
CB125S, CD125S, SL125 1.555/39.5
③ CB100, CL100, SL100 1.406/35.7
CB125S, CD125S, SL125 1.318/33.5
④ CB100, CL100, SL100 1.358/34.5
CB125S, CD125S, SL125 1.259/32.0
⑤ CB100, CL100, SL100 1.9881-1.9885/50.50-50.51
CB125S, CD125S, SL125 2.2047-2.2051/56.00-56.01
⑥ CB100, CL100, SL100 1.992/50.6
CB125S, CD125S, SL125 2.2086/56.1
⑦ CB100, CL100, SL100 1.987-1.988/50.47-50.49
CB125S, CD125S, SL125 2.2035-2.2043/55.97-53.99
⑧ CB100, CL100, SL100 1.980/50.3
CB125S, CD125S, SL125 2.1968/55.80

XL250

	Standard Value	Serviceable Limit
Rocker arm-to-shaft clearance (mm/in.)	0.016-0.052/0.0006-0.0020	0.090/0.0035
Camshaft journal OD (mm/in.) (right hand)	21.939-21.960/0.8637-0.8646	21.92/0.8630
(left hand)	23.939-23.960/0.9425-0.9433	23.92/0.9417
Cam height (mm/in.) (intake)	6.260/0.2465*	6.142/0.2418
(exhaust)	6.150/0.2421)*	6.025/0.2372
Valve stem OD (mm/in.) (intake)	5.480-5.490/0.2157-0.2161	5.465/0.2151
(exhaust)	5.460-5.470/0.2149-0.2154	5.445/0.2144
Valve stem-to-guide clearance (mm/in.) (intake)	0.010-0.030/0.00039-0.00118	0.06/0.00236
(exhaust)	0.030-0.050/0.00118-0.00197	0.07/0.00276
Valve spring free length (mm/in.) (inner)	36.5/1.43	36.0/1.41
(outer)	40.7/1.60	39.7/1.56
Valve spring tension (kg/mm (lb/in.)) (inner)	14.5/22 (6.6/0.87)	13.48-15.52/22 (6.1-7.0/0.87)
(outer)	34/26.4 (15.42/1.04)	31.62-36.38/26.4 (14.3-16.5/1.04)
Cylinder bore diameter (mm/in.)	73.99-74.01/2.913-2.914	74.11/2.918
Piston OD (mm/in.)	73.97-73.99/2.912-2.913)	73.88/2.909
Piston pin hole diameter (mm/in.)	19.002-19.008/0.7481-0.7483	19.08/0.7512
Piston pin OD (mm/in.)	18.994-19/0.7478-0.7480)	18.96/0.7465
Piston ring-to-groove clearance (mm/in.) (top)	0.03-0.06/0.0012-0.0024	0.18/0.007
(second)	0.015-0.045/0.0006-0.0018	0.165/0.006
(oil)	0.03-0.045/0.0012-0.0018	0.17/0.007
Piston ring gap (mm/in.) (top)	0.15-0.35/0.0059-0.0138	0.75/0.029
(second)	0.20-0.40/0.0079-0.0157	0.80/0.031
(oil)	0.20-0.40/0.0079-0.0157	0.80/0.031

(con't.)

XL250

	Standard Value	Serviceable Limit
Connecting rod small end ID (mm/in.)	19.020-19.041/0.7488-0.7496	19.07/0.751
Connecting rod big end radial clearance (mm/in.)	——	0.05/0.00197
Connecting rod big end axial clearance (mm/in.)	0.12-0.38/0.00472-0.01496	0.60/0.02362
Radial clearance of right hand and left hand crankshaft bearing (mm/in.)	——	0.05/0.00197
Oil pump delivery flow (l (usgal)/rpm	4.2 (1.11)/5,000 80°C (176°F)	3.4 (0.90)/5,000 80°C (176°F)
Axial clearance of oil pump inner and outer rotors (mm/in.)	0.02-0.08/0.00079-0.00315	0.1/0.004
Clutch friction disc thickness (mm/in.)	2.7/0.106	2.3/0.091
Clutch plate face runout (mm/in.)	0.15/0.006	0.30/0.012
Clutch spring free length (mm/in.)	35.5/1.40	34.2/1.35
Clutch spring tension (kg/mm (lb/in.))	23.8/23 (10.8/0.91)	21.8/23 (9.89/0.91)
Transmission gear backlash (mm/in.)	——	0.2/0.0079
Gear shift fork drum OD (mm/in.)	35.950-35.975/1.4153-1.4163	35.9/1.4133
Center gear shift fork ID (mm/in.)	36.0-36.025/1.4173-1.4183	36.075/1.4203
Shift fork guide shaft OD (mm/in.)	12.968-12.984/0.5106-0.5112	12.9/0.5079)
Right hand and left hand gear shift fork ID (mm/in.)	13.0-13.018/0.5118-0.5125	13.05/0.5138
Shift fork thickness	4.93-5/0.1941-0.1969	4.6/0.1811

* Base Circle 30 (1.1811 in.)

VALVE TIMING

S50, S65, CL70, SL70		S90, CL90, SL90	
Valve timing		Valve timing	
inlet valve opens	5° BTDC	inlet valve opens	5° BTDC
inlet valve closes	30° ABDC	inlet valve closes	35° ABDC
exhaust valve opens	40° BBDC	exhaust valve opens	25° BBDC
exhaust valve closes	5° ATDC	exhaust valve closes	5° ATDC

C50, C50M, C65, C65M		CL90L, CD90, C90, CT90	
Valve timing		Valve timing	
inlet valve opens	0° BTDC	inlet valve opens	5° BTDC
inlet valve closes	20° ABDC	inlet valve closes	20° ABDC
exhaust valve opens	25° BBDC	exhaust valve opens	25° BBDC
exhaust valve closes	5° BTDC	exhaust valve closes	5° ATDC

C70, C70M		CB100, CL100, SL100, CB125S, CD125S, SL125, XL250	
Valve timing		Valve timing	
inlet valve opens	5° BTDC	inlet valve opens	N.A.
inlet valve closes	20° ATDC	inlet valve closes	N.A.
exhaust valve opens	25° BBDC	exhaust valve opens	N.A.
exhaust valve closes	5° BTDC	exhaust valve closes	N.A.

BTDC—before top dead center
ABDC—after bottom dead center
BBDC—before bottom dead center
ATDC—after top dead center

LUBRICATION SYSTEMS

OIL PUMP

50, 65, 70, AND 90 CC MODELS

Disassembly

1. Remove the right-side crankcase cover and clutch assemblies.
2. Remove the oil pump assembly by removing the 6 mm bolts and the hex bolt which secure it to the crankcase.
3. The pump may be further disassembled or replaced as a unit.

Inspection And Repair

1. Clean all components other than the gaskets in a suitable solvent and blow them dry. Replace any obviously damaged parts, and use new gaskets when reassembling the assembly.
2. Rotate the pump driveshaft by hand, check it for smooth motion, and replace it as necessary.
3. Measure the clearance between the outer rotor and the pump body using feeler gauges, and replace the necessary parts if worn beyond their serviceable limits.
4. Measure the rotor-to-rotor clearance using feeler gauges, and replace them as necessary

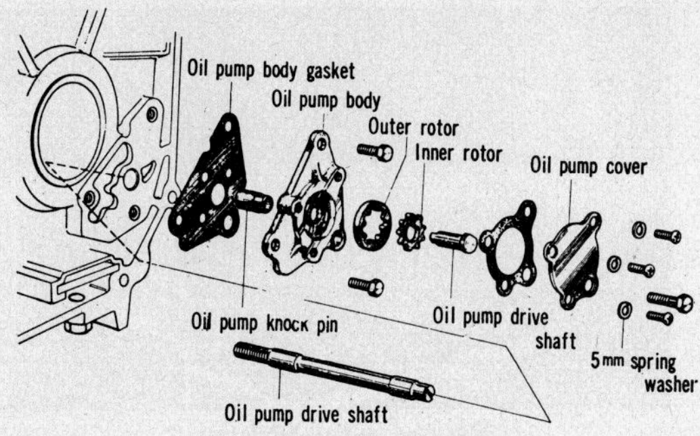

Oil pump assembly

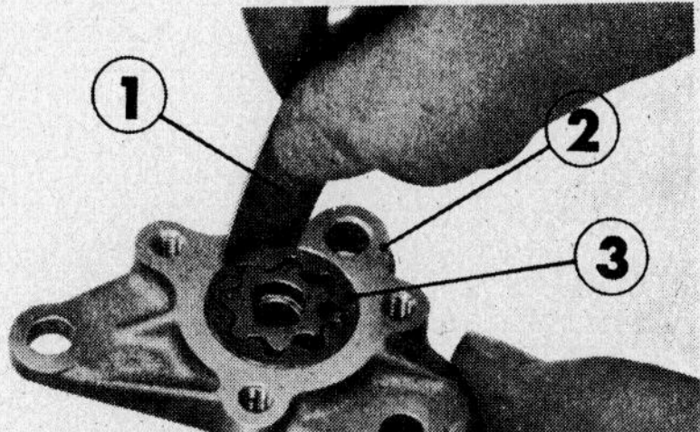
Measuring rotor-to-pump body clearance
1. Feeler gauge
2. Pump body
3. Outer rotor

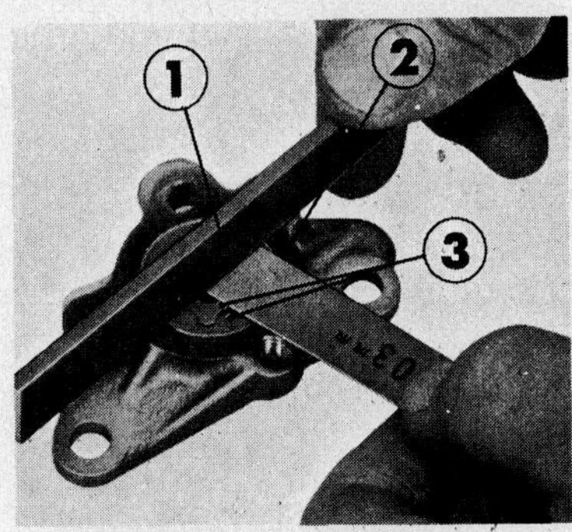
Measuring rotor end-play
1. Straightedge
2. Pump body
3. Rotor

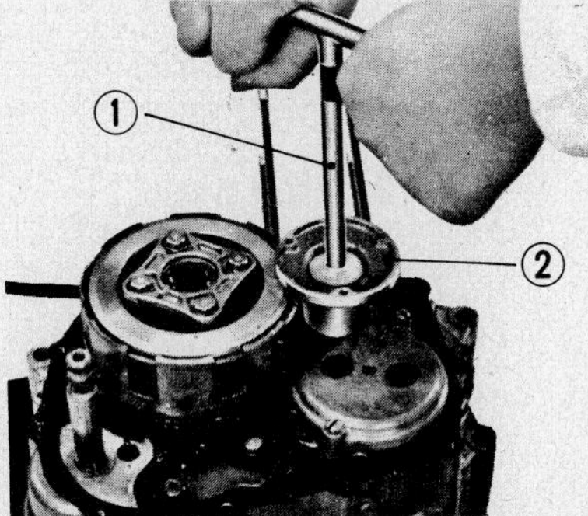
Removing the oil filter rotor
1. 16 mm wrench
2. Oil filter rotor

5. Measure the end-play of the rotor by placing a straightedge over the pump body, and measuring the clearance between the top of the rotor and the straightedge with feeler gauges. Replace the rotor if necessary.

6. On gear and rotor type pumps, check for gear backlash. If the backlash is excessive, the gears should be replaced as a pair. Excessive play will cause the pump operation to be noisy. Backlash, unless extreme, will probably not affect the pumping pressure.

Assembly

1. Assembly is basically the reverse order of disassembly.

2. Place the inner rotor and outer rotor together, then install the assembly in the right crankcase. Use new gaskets whenever applicable.

100 AND 125 CC MODELS

Disassembly

1. Remove the right side crankcase and oil filter rotor covers, then remove the 6 mm locknut and remove the oil filter rotor.

2. Remove the oil pump gear cover.

3. Remove the tachometer pinion gear on the CB and SL 125 cc models.

4. Remove the oil pump drive gear, then remove the pump assembly.

5. Remove the oil pump shaft, then remove the outer rotor.

Removing the oil pump drive gear
1. Oil pump drive gear
2. Shaft

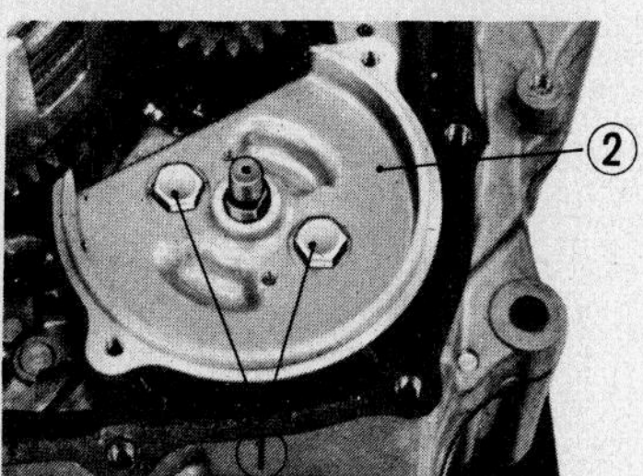
Removing the oil pump body
1. 6 mm bolts
2. Oil pump body

Inspection And Repair

1. Clean all parts other than gaskets in a suitable solvent and blow them dry.

2. Inspect all parts for obvious damage and replace them as necessary. The two rotors must be replaced as a pair.

3. The general practice, if the pump is not putting out, is to replace either the entire assembly, or try to replace individual parts. Since there are no available specifications for these models, it is best to replace the assembly.

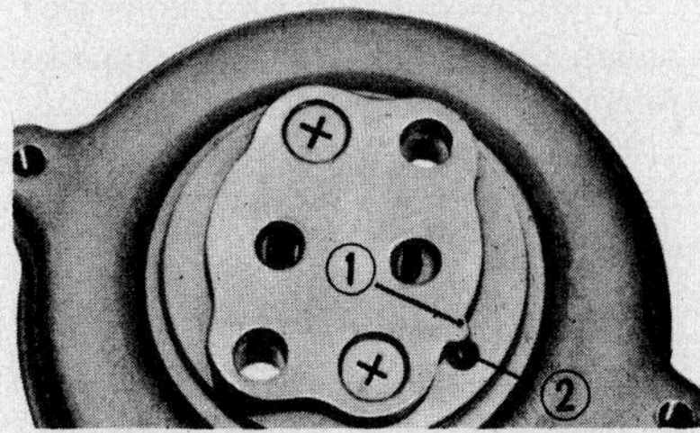
Aligning the cover on the plate
1. Cover mark
2. Plate mark

Installing the O-rings
1. O-ring

Installing the pump shaft
1. Pump shaft

Assembly

1. Assembly is basically in the reverse order of disassembly.

2. Install the pump with the concave portion of the pump on the convex portion of the oil pump plate.

3. Install the pump body, taking care to replace the two O-rings.

4. Bring the oil pump shaft into alignment with the cutout of the inner rotor gear, then assemble the unit.

5. Install the tachometer pinion gear on CB and SL 125 cc models.

6. Assemble the oil pump drive gears,

then mount and secure the pump gear cover.

7. Mount the oil filter rotor and torque the locknut to 29–36 ft lbs. Make sure you use the lockwasher.

8. Install the remaining covers.

XL-250

Disassembly

1. Remove the kickstart lever, right side crankcase cover, clutch assembly, and kickstarter spindle mechanism.
2. Remove the two 6mm bolts which secure the oil pump to the crankcase, remove the oil pump assembly.
3. Remove the two 6mm screws which hold the pump assembly together, and disassemble the pump.

Inspection And Repair

1. Consult the "Inspection and Repair" section for the 50, 65, 70, and 90cc models.

Assembly

1. Assembly is the reverse order of disassembly.
2. Do not forget to install the O-rings and packing.

Removing the oil pump
1. 6 mm bolts
2. 6 mm screws

1. Oil pump body
2. Outer rotor
3. Inner rotor
4. Oil pump drive gear

Oil pump assembly

OIL PUMP SPECIFICATIONS

90 cc and Under, Trochoid Type Pump	Standard Value	Serviceable Limit
Clearance between rotor and housing	0.004-0.006 in. (0.10-0.15 mm)	Replace if over 0.0079 in. (0.20 mm)
Clearance between rotor and top of housing	0.008-0.027 in. (0.02-0.07 mm)	Replace if over 0.0047 in. (0.12 mm)
Clearance between rotors	0.008-0.028 in. (0.02-0.07 mm)	Replace if over 0.0047 in. (0.12 mm)
Rotor backlash	0.006 in. (0.15 mm)	Replace if over 0.008 in. (0.2 mm)
Gear Type Pump		
Clearance between gear and housing	0.0020-0.0035 in. (0.05-0.09 mm)	Replace if over 0.0059 in. (0.15 mm)
Gear backlash	0.0037-0.0014 in. (0.0940-0.188 mm)	Replace if over 0.0118 in. (0.30 mm)
XL250 Axial clearance between rotors	0.00079-0.00315 in. (0.02-0.08 mm)	0.004 in. (0.1 mm)
Oil Pump Pressure		
50, 65, and 70 cc models	N.A.	
90 cc models (trochoid type)	1400 cc (85.43 cu in.)/min @ 8000 rpm	
(gear type)	1200 cc (73.22 cu. in.)/min @ 4000 rpm	
100 and 125 cc models	2.41/min @ 10,000 rpm	
XL250	4.2 l (1.11 gal)/min @ 5000 rpm @ 80°C (176°F)	

FUEL SYSTEMS

CARBURETOR OVERHAUL

Service

When working on any of these carburetors, keep in mind that the components are machined to exacting specifications and must not be treated roughly. It is possible to purchase a rebuilding kit for any of these units, and it is suggested that you use all the parts which come in the kit. Clean all the parts in a suitable solvent such as gasoline, and blow them dry, if possible, with compressed air.

Look for blunted adjusters which indicate that the screws have been forced into their seats, and may have even done damage to them. A situation like this could call for replacing the carburetor body. Carefully examine all passages as they can become blocked partially and cause erratic performance. Check for burrs or score marks on the slide, jet, or jet needle which could cause the carb to hang-up. Inspect the float for a gas-logged condition which would make replacement necessary.

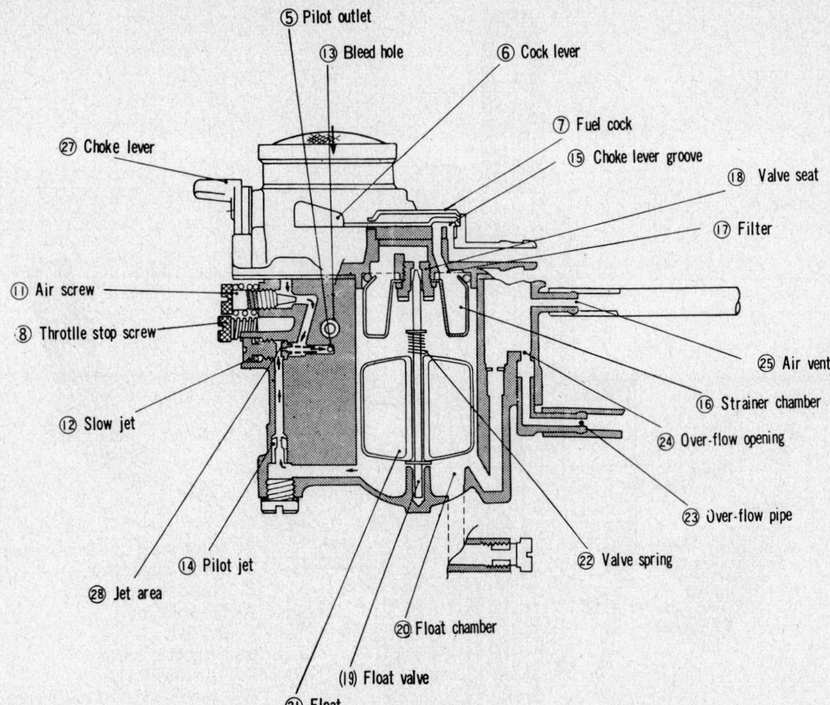

Carburetor used on the C series 50, 65, and 70cc engines

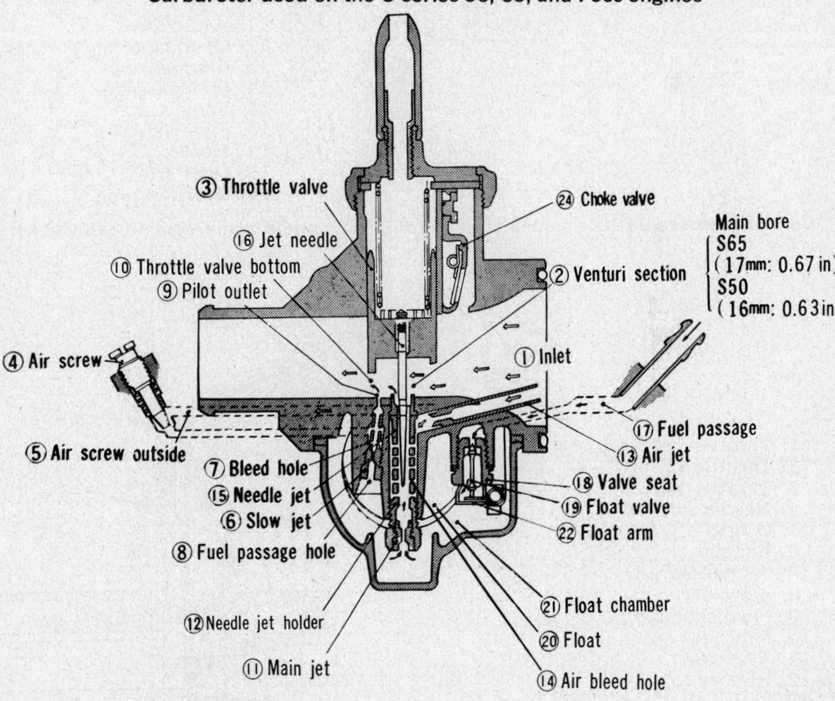

Carburetor used on the S series 50, 65, and 70cc engines

ALL MODELS EXCEPT THE XL-250

Removal And Installation

1. Turn off the fuel tap and disconnect the fuel line.
2. Unscrew the carburetor cap, carefully withdraw the slide, and place the assembly out of the way.
3. Loosen and slide back the air cleaner connecting clamp at the carburetor.
4. Unbolt and remove the carburetor from the manifold. The following points should be noted during installation:

1. Tighten the mounting bolts that secure the carburetor to the manifold evenly to avoid crushing the manifold spacer gasket.
2. When installing the slide in the carburetor, take special care not to damage the needle when dropping it into the jet tube. Make sure the needle starts into the tube, and check to make sure that the tab in the slide bore engages the slot in the slide. Lightly coating the slide with clean engine oil is a good idea as it will help lubricate the slide in the bore.
3. Tighten down the carburetor cap firmly, then check the operation of the throttle linkage. If it binds check the cable for kinks, then check the slide to make sure it is in correctly and that it will slide down the bore of its own weight. The slide may be lightly sanded with fine sandpaper if it is burred or has a high spot.
4. Reset the adjustments after the carburetor is mounted, then run a plug check to make sure your mixture is correct.

Disassembly

1. Disconnect the carburetor slide from the throttle cable by compressing the spring and feeding the inner cable into the slide so that the cable end can be disengaged from the retaining slot. The needle and clip will have to be removed.
2. Release the float bowl by swiveling back the retaining clip.
3. Tap out the float pin from the float tang using a small diameter rod or drift. Remove the float and lift the float valve needle out of the valve seat. Unscrew the valve seat from the carburetor body.
4. Using a small screwdriver, remove the main jet, low-speed jet, throttle stop-screw, and the air screw.
5. Unscrew the main jet tube using a suitably sized wrench.

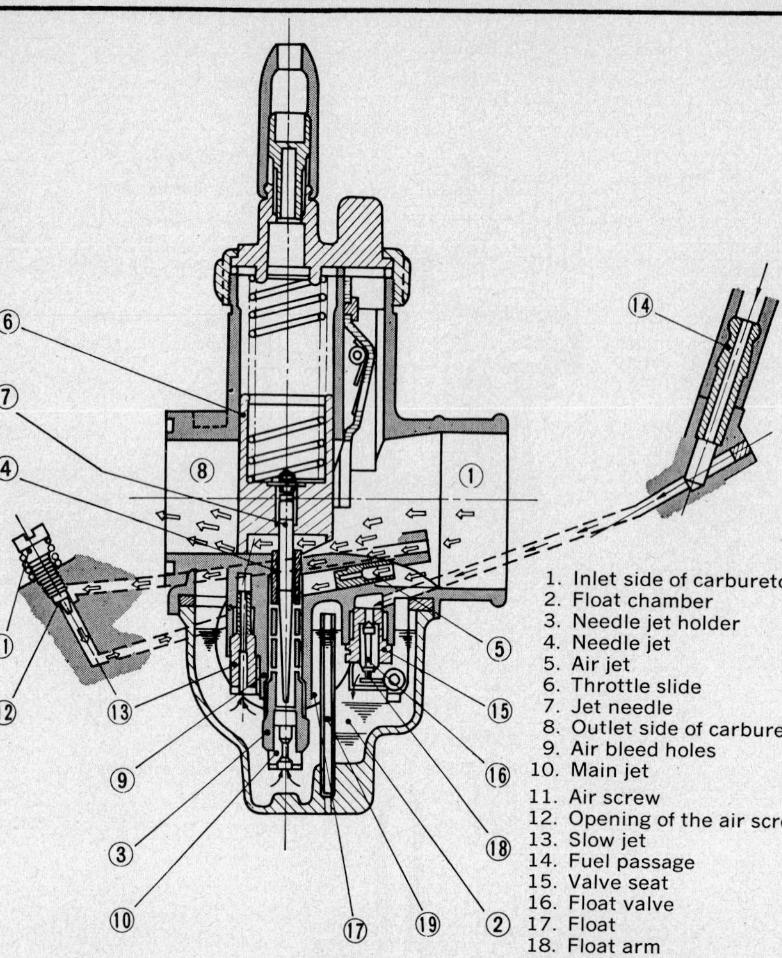

1. Inlet side of carburetor
2. Float chamber
3. Needle jet holder
4. Needle jet
5. Air jet
6. Throttle slide
7. Jet needle
8. Outlet side of carburetor
9. Air bleed holes
10. Main jet
11. Air screw
12. Opening of the air screw
13. Slow jet
14. Fuel passage
15. Valve seat
16. Float valve
17. Float
18. Float arm
19. Overflow pipe

Carburetor used on 90cc models (except for CT90 models from frame no. 000001A)

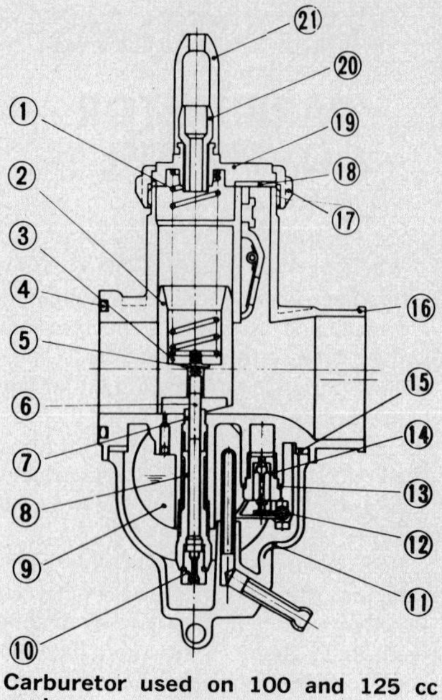

Carburetor used on 100 and 125 cc engines

1. Return spring
2. Throttle slide
3. Needle clip plate
4. O-ring
5. Bar clip
6. Jet needle
7. Needle jet
8. Needle jet holder
9. Float
10. Main jet
11. Float chamber body
12. Arm pin
13. Valve seat
14. Slow jet
15. Float chamber washer
16. Body
17. Cap
18. Top washer
19. Top
20. Cable Adjuster
21. Rubber cap

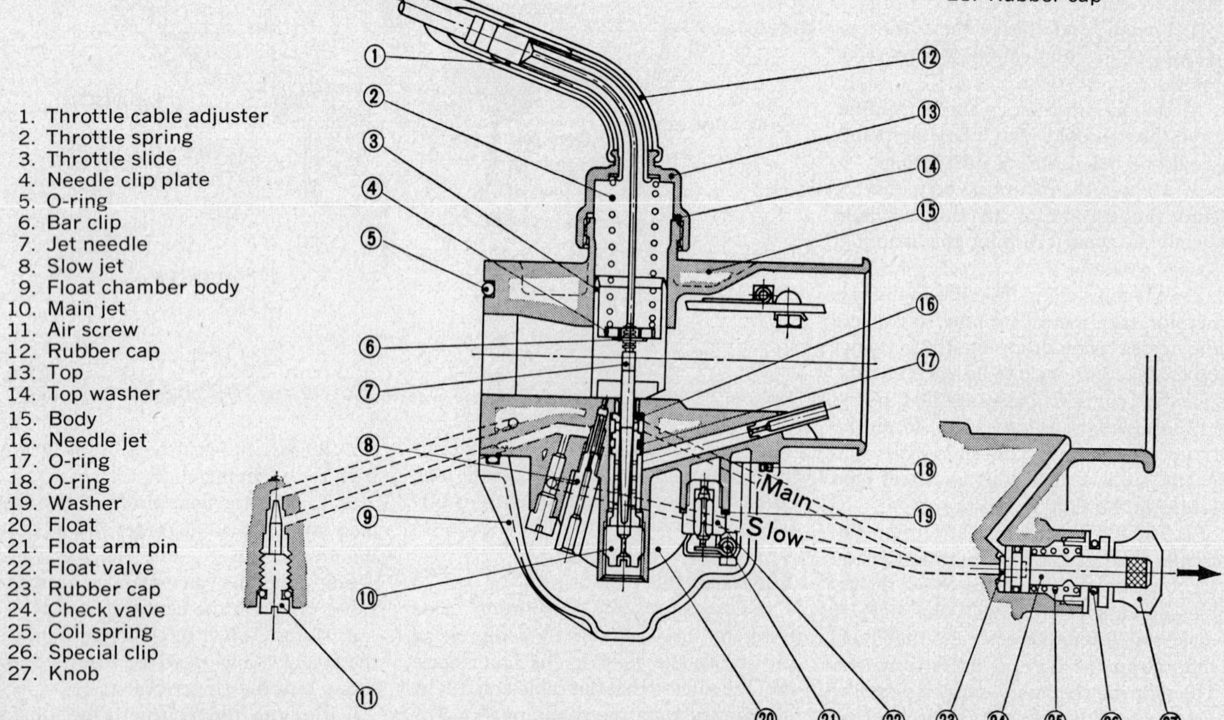

1. Throttle cable adjuster
2. Throttle spring
3. Throttle slide
4. Needle clip plate
5. O-ring
6. Bar clip
7. Jet needle
8. Slow jet
9. Float chamber body
10. Main jet
11. Air screw
12. Rubber cap
13. Top
14. Top washer
15. Body
16. Needle jet
17. O-ring
18. O-ring
19. Washer
20. Float
21. Float arm pin
22. Float valve
23. Rubber cap
24. Check valve
25. Coil spring
26. Special clip
27. Knob

Carburetor used on CT90 models from frame no. 000001A

Adjusting the float level
1. Float level gauge

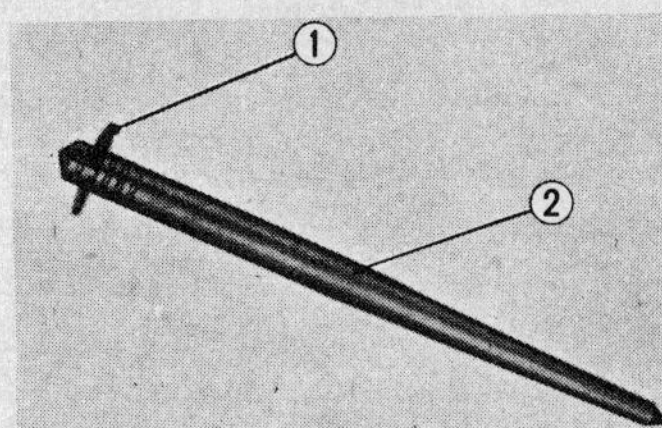

Jet needle and needle clip
1. Needle clip
2. Jet needle

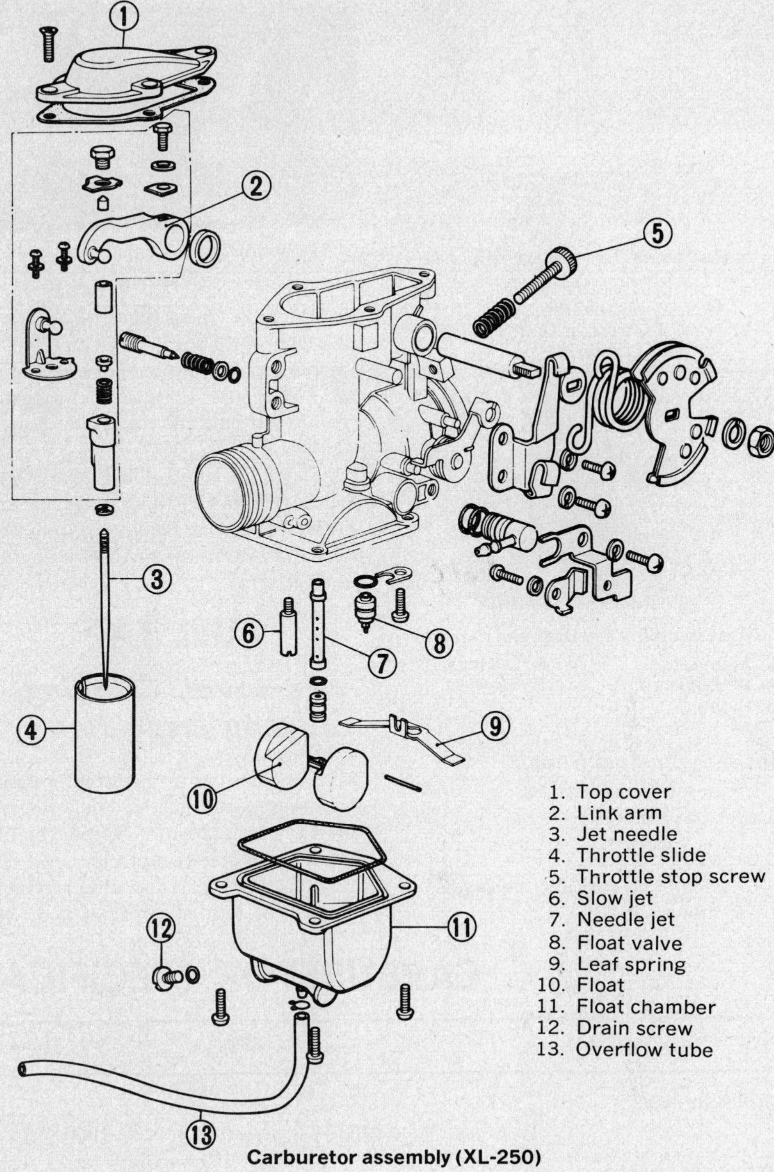

1. Top cover
2. Link arm
3. Jet needle
4. Throttle slide
5. Throttle stop screw
6. Slow jet
7. Needle jet
8. Float valve
9. Leaf spring
10. Float
11. Float chamber
12. Drain screw
13. Overflow tube

Carburetor assembly (XL-250)

Inspection And Repair

1. Clean all parts, other than the gaskets, in a suitable solvent and blow them dry. If you use an acid type carburetor cleaner, do not clean the float or any other rubber or plastic parts in it as they will be damaged by it.
2. Make sure that the surface of the throttle slide is clean and smooth. Light scoring can be smoothed with fine every cloth.
3. Examine the jet needle for wear as indicated by bright spots or an uneven taper. If wear is noticeable, replace both the needle and the needle jet tube.
4. Examine the float needle for wear. If replacement is necessary, replace the needle and seat as a unit.
5. Inspect the carburetor body for cracks, and replace it as necessary.

Assembly

1. Assembly is basically in the reverse order of disassembly. Use new gaskets and O-rings.
2. The float level must be checked and adjusted if necessary. The float should be positioned so that when the float arm just touches the tip of the float needle, the distance from the top of the float to the float bowl mating surface on the carburetor is as close as possible to the specification given at the end of the chapter for the carburetor.
3. Do not overtighten the jets when installing them in the carburetor body.
4. Make sure that the jet needle is installed in the same position as when removed. Changing the needle position in the slide will affect the mid-throttle range operation.
5. After installing the carburetor, check for smooth operation of the choke.

Removing the throttle shaft
1. 13 mm nut
2. Tongued washer
3. Link arm

XL-250

Removal And Installation

1. Turn off the fuel tap and disconnect the fuel line.
2. Remove the screws and carburetor cap.
3. Straighten out the two lockwashers and remove the bolts, remove the 13mm nut located at the side of the throttle shaft, then remove the throttle shaft itself.
4. Remove the two 3mm screws which secure the valve plate, then rotate the plate until the lug is sufficiently cleared for removal of the plate and slide assemblies.
5. Complete the removal and installation procedures as directed in the section for "All Models Except the XL-250".

Disassembly

1. Complete the first four steps in the above section which deal with removing the throttle slide and then remove the jet needle from the slide.
2. Remove the float chamber securing screws and chamber.
3. Remove the leaf spring and main jet, then carefully remove the slow jet using an appropriate screwdriver.
4. Remove the clip plate and the valve seat.

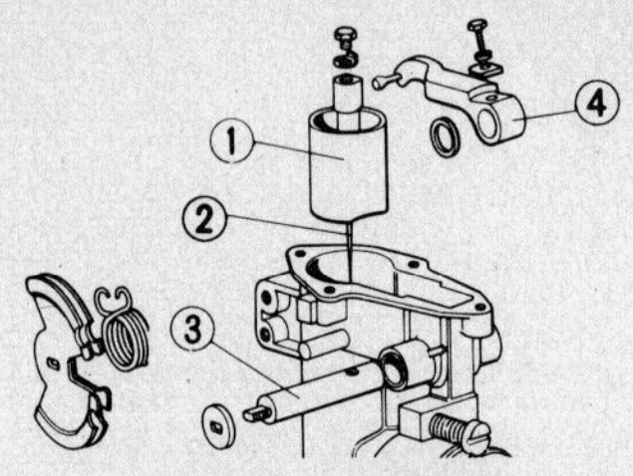

Removing the throttle slide

1. Throttle valve
2. Jet needle
3. Throttle shaft
4. Link arm

Disassembling the float mechanism

1. Main jet
2. Float arm pin
3. Float
4. Leaf spring
5. Slow jet

Inspection And Repair

1. Consult the section for "All Models Except the XL-250".

Assembly

1. Assembly is basically the reverse of disassembly.

Removing the valve seat

1. Valve seat

2. When installing the throttle slide in the carburetor body, do so with the cutaway portion facing the choke assembly.

3. Make sure there is no excessive clearance around the carburetor top and the throttle shaft.

4. Using the Honda Float Level Gauge (tool no. 07144–99998) or a suitable substitute, set the float height at 24mm (0.94 in.). Adjustments are made by bending the float arm.

FUEL TAP

Removal, Cleaning, And Inspection

1. Turn the tap to the "stop" position and disconnect the fuel lines. Be prepared to catch the run-off from the fuel lines in a suitable receptacle.

2. Raise the seat and either remove the tank or raise the rear of it up and support it (if applicable). On step-through type frames, the fuel tap is located at the carburetor and can be reached without removing anything.

3. Drain the strainer cup by removing the drain plug at the bottom of the cup, or just unscrew the cup and hold it in such a way as not to allow the fuel to drip on everything.

4. Remove the O-ring and fuel strainer from the cup.

5. Remove the two mounting screws and remove the fuel tap.

6. Remove the two screws from the lever retaining plate and remove the plate, O-ring, and gasket.

7. Clean all the components in a suitable solvent and blow them dry. Inspect all the parts for wear, cracks, or any other damage which could contribute to a fuel leak.

8. Assemble the tap in the reverse order of disassembly using all new gaskets and O-rings.

9. Install the tap on the tank and check for proper fuel flow by turning on the tap and allowing the gas to run out into a suitable receptacle. Make sure you don't have the reserve and normal supply lines reversed.

10. Lower the tank (if applicable), install the fuel lines, and check the system for leaks. If the system doesn't work, check to make sure that the gas cap vent hole is not plugged.

CARBURETOR SPECIFICATIONS

	C65	C65M	C50
Carburetor type	1000-112 (1000-113)	1000-115	1000-110 (1000-145)
Setting specifications			
Setting mark	65H (Y65H)	65MB	C50C
Throttle bore	13ϕ (0.512 in.)	13ϕ	13ϕ
Venturi bore	14ϕ (0.551)	14ϕ	13ϕ
Main jet	no. 72	no. 72	no. 70
Air jet	no. 150	no. 150	no. 150
Main air bleed: AB 1	0.4ϕ × 2 (0.0157 in.)	0.5ϕ × 2	0.4ϕ × 2
1.5	0.4ϕ × 2	0.4ϕ × 2	——
2	0.4ϕ × 2	0.4ϕ × 2	0.4ϕ × 2
3	0.4ϕ × 2	0.4ϕ × 2	0.4ϕ × 2
4	0.4ϕ × 2	0.4ϕ × 2	0.4ϕ × 2
5	0.4ϕ × 2	0.4ϕ × 2	——
6	0.4ϕ × 2	0.4ϕ × 2	0.4ϕ × 2
Needle jet	3.0 × 2.8 mm (0.118 × 0.110 in.) 3ϕ × 2.8 recess	3ϕ × 2.8	3ϕ × 2.5
Jet needle	13243 3 stage	13243 3 stage	13239 3 stage

CARBURETOR SPECIFICATIONS (con't.)

	C65	C65M	C50
Carburetor type	1000-112 (1000-113)	1000-115	1000-110 (1000-145)
Cutaway (throttle valve)	no. 2.0 [1.2 × 0.15] (0.047 × 0.006 in.) 2.0 (1.2ϕ × 0.15)	no. 2.0 (1.2 × 0.15)	no. 2.0 (1.2ϕ × 0.15)
Air screw	1¼ ~ ⅛	1¼ ~ ⅛	1¼ ± ⅛
Slow jet	no. 35	no. 35	no. 35
Slow air bleed: 1	0.8 mm (0.315 in.) × 2 0.8ϕ × 2	0.9ϕ × 2	0.8ϕ × 2
2	0.8 mm (0.315 in.) × 2 0.8ϕ × 2	0.8ϕ × 2	0.8ϕ × 2
3	0.8 mm (0.315 in.) × 2 0.8ϕ × 2	0.9ϕ × 2	0.8ϕ × 2
4	0.8 mm (0.315 in.) × 2 0.8ϕ × 2	0.8ϕ × 2	0.8ϕ × 2
Valve seat	1.2 mm (0.0473 in.) 1.2ϕ	1.2ϕ	1.2ϕ
Pilot jet	no. 35	no. 35	no. 35
Pilot outlet	0.9 mm (0.0354 in.) P = 5.0	0.9ϕ P = 5.0	0.9ϕ P = 5.0
Fuel level (actual fuel height)	17.5 mm (0.689 in.) 17.5	17.5	15.5

	C50M	S65	S50
Carburetor type	1000-111	PW16FA6 (CF130) PW16FA10 (CYFF130)	PW16FA11
Setting specifications Setting mark	50MB	17-B	K
Throttle bore	13ϕ	16 mm (0.630 in.)	16 mm (0.630 in.)
Venturi bore	13ϕ	17 mm (0.670 in.) equiv	16 mm (0.630 in.) equiv
Main jet	no. 72	no. 85	no. 78
Air jet	no. 150	no. 150	no. 120
Main air bleed: AB 1	0.5ϕ × 2	0.5 mm (0.0197 in.) × 4	0.9 mm (0.0354 in.) × 4
1.5	0.4ϕ × 2	——	——
2	0.4ϕ × 2	0.9 mm (0.0354 in.) × 2	0.6 mm (0.0236 in.) × 2
3	0.4ϕ × 2	——	0.6 mm (0.0236 in.) × 2
4	0.4ϕ × 2	0.5 mm (0.0197 in.) × 2	0.6 mm (0.0236 in.) × 2
5	——	0.5 mm (0.0197 in.) × 2	0.6 mm (0.0236 in.) × 2
6	0.4ϕ × 2	——	——
Needle jet	3ϕ × 2.5	2.6 mm (0.1023 in.) [3.4 (0.134 in.) recess]	2.6 mm (0.1023 in.) [3.4 (0.134 in.) recess]
Jet needle	13239 3 stage	16305 3 stage	16232 3 stage
Cutaway (throttle valve)	no. 2.0 (1.2 × 0.15)	no. 1.5 [1.2 × 0.3] (0.047 × 0.012 in.)	no 1.5 [1.2 × 0.3] (0.047 × 0.012 in.)

(con't.)	C50M	S65	S50
Carburetor type	1000-111	PW16FA6 (CF130) PW16FA10 (CYFF130)	PW16FA11
Air screw	$1^1/_4 \pm {}^1/_8$	$1^1/_2 \sim {}^1/_8$	$1^1/_2 \sim {}^1/_8$
Slow jet	no. 35	no. 38	no 35
Slow air bleed: 1	0.9φ × 2	0.7 mm (0.0276 in.) × 2	0.8 mm (0.0315 in.) × 2
2	0.8φ × 2	0.7 mm (0.0276 in.) × 2	0.8 mm (0.0315 in.) × 2
3	0.9φ × 2	0.7 mm (0.0276 in.) × 2	0.7 mm (0.0276 in.) × 2
4	0.8φ × 2	0.7 mm (0.0276 in.) × 2	0.7 mm (0.0276 in.) × 2
Valve seat	1.2φ	1.0 mm (0.0394 in.)	1.0 mm (0.0394 in.)
Pilot jet	no. 35	——	——
Pilot outlet	0.9φ P = 5.0	1.0 mm (0.0394 in.) P = 5.5	1.0 mm (0.0394 in.) P = 5.5
Fuel level (actual fuel height)	15.5	19.5 mm (0.768 in.) Height of float	19.5 mm (0.768 in.) Height of float

	CL70	C70	C70M
Carburetor type	——	DP 13 N 14 AI	DP 13N 14 AI
Setting specifications Setting mark	AL 70 B	C 70 C	C 70 MA
Main jet	no. 72	no. 75	no. 75
Air jet	no. 90	no. 150	no. 150
Main air bleed: AB 1	0.6 mm (0.024 in.) × 4	0.4 mm (0.016 in.) × 2	0.4 mm (0.016 in.) × 2
1.5	——	0.4 mm (0.016 in.) × 2	0.4 mm (0.016 in.) × 2
2	0.6 mm (0.024 in.) × 2	0.4 mm (0.016 in.) × 2	0.4 mm (0.016 in.) × 2
3	——	0.4 mm (0.016 in.) × 2	0.4 mm (0.016 in.) × 2
4	0.7 mm (0.028 in.) × 2	0.4 mm (0.016 in.) × 2	0.4 mm (0.016 in.) × 2
5	0.7 mm (0.028 in.) × 2	0.4 mm (0.016 in.) × 2	0.4 mm (0.016 in.) × 2
6	——	0.4 mm (0.016 in.) × 2	0.4 mm (0.016 in.) × 2
Needle jet	2.6 mm (0.102) × 3.7R	2.1 mm (0.083) × 3.0R	2.1 mm (0.083 in.) × 3.0R
Jet needle	2°30″ 2 steps 2.535 mm (0.0998 in.)	2°30″ 2.5 steps 2.04 mm (0.0803 in.)	3°00″ 3 steps 2.05 mm (0.0807 in.)
Cutaway	no. 2.5 width 1.2 mm (0.047 in.) depth 0.2 mm (0.008 in.)	no. 2.5 width 1.2 mm (0.047 in.) depth 0.2 mm (0.008 in.)	no. 2.5
Air screw	$1^1/_8 \pm {}^1/_8$	$1^1/_2 \pm {}^1/_8$	$1^1/_8 \pm {}^1/_8$
Slow jet	no. 38	no. 35	no. 35
Slow air bleed: 1	0.9 mm (0.0354 in.) × 2	0.8 mm (0.031 in.) × 2	0.8 mm (0.031 in.) × 2
2	0.9 mm (0.0354 in.) × 2	0.8 mm (0.031 in.) × 2	0.8 mm (0.031 in.) × 2
3	0.9 mm (0.0354 in.) × 2	0.8 mm (0.031 in.) × 2	0.8 mm (0.031 in.) × 2
4	0.9 mm (0.0354 in.) × 2	0.8 mm (0.031 in.) × 2	0.8 mm (0.031 in.) × 2
Pilot jet	——	no. 35	no. 35
Valve seat	1.0 mm (0.039 in.)	1.2 mm (0.047 in.)	1.2 mm (0.047 in.) × 2
By-pass	0.9 mm (0.035 in.) P = 5.4 mm (0.213 in.)	0.92 mm (0.036 in.) P = 50 mm (0.197 in.)	0.92 mm (0.036 in.) P = 50 mm (0.197 in.)
Main bore	15 mm (0.591 in.)	14 mm (0.551 in.)	14 mm (0.551 in.)
Fuel level	7.0 mm (0.276 in.)	13.5 mm (0.531 in.)	15.5 mm (0.610 in.)

	CB100, CL100, SL100	CB125S, SL125S	XL250
Main jet	no. 110	no. 105	no. 120
Air jet	no. 100	no. 100	no. 100
Needle jet	2.6ϕ × 3.8ϕ length 10	2.6ϕ × 3.8ϕ length 10	N.A.
Needle jet holder	5.0ϕ	5.0ϕ	N.A.
Jet needle	2°30″ × 3 step 2.495ϕ	2°30″ × 5 step 2.495ϕ	N.A.
Air screw	$1\frac{1}{2} \pm \frac{1}{8}$	$1\frac{1}{2} \pm \frac{1}{8}$	$1\frac{1}{4} \pm \frac{3}{8}$
Throttle valve	no. 2.5 cutaway width 1.2 depth 0.2	no. 2.5 cutaway width 1.8 depth 0.2	N.A.
Slow jet	no. 38	no. 38	no. 45
Slow air bleed: 1	0.8 × 2	0.9ϕ × 2 × 4	
2	0.8 × 2		
3	0.8 × 2		
Fuel level	24 mm (0.9449 in.)	24 mm (0.9449 in.)	24 mm (0.9449 in.)

	S90	CL90, CL90L	CD90
Carburetor type	1000-133-00	1000-152-00	1000-131-00
Setting specifications			
Main jet	no. 85	no. 85	no. 90
Air jet	no. 150	no. 150	no. 150
Main air bleed: AB 0	—	—	—
1	0.7 × 4	0.7 × 2	0.7 X 2
2	0.6 × 2	0.7 × 2	0.7 X 2
3	0.6 × 2	0.7 × 2	0.7 X 2
4	0.6 × 2	0.7 × 2	0.7 X 2
5	0.6 × 2	0.7 × 4	0.7 X 2
Needle jet	2.60 × 3.7	2.60 × 3.7	2.60 × 3.5
Jet needle	18241 2 stage	18241 2 stage	183011 3 stage
Cutaway (throttle valve)	no. 25 width: 1.2, depth: 0.3 cutout provided	no. 2.5 width: 1.2, depth: 0.3 cutout provided	no. 2.5 cutout not provided
Slow jet	no. 38	no. 35	no. 40
Air screw	$1\frac{1}{4} \pm \frac{1}{8}$	$1\frac{3}{8} \pm \frac{1}{8}$	$1\frac{1}{4} \pm \frac{1}{8}$
Slow air bleed: 1	0.9 × 2	0.9 × 2	0.9 × 2
2	0.9 × 2	0.9 × 2	0.9 × 2
3	0.9 × 2	0.9 × 2	0.9 × 2
4	—	0.9 × 2	0.9 × 2
Valve seat	1.5	1.5	1.5
By-pass	1 2	1 1.0 2	1 2
Pilot outlet	1 1.0 pitch 7.0	1 pitch 7.0	1 1.1 pitch 6.3
Pilot air jet	—	—	—
P.W.J.	—	—	—
P.W.A.J.	—	—	—
Fuel level	16.5	19.5	19.5
Setting mark	S 90 C	L 90 A	B

	C90	CT90	CT90 (from F. no. 000001A)
Setting specifications			
Carburetor type	1000-109-00	1000-108-00	1000-108-00
Main jet	no. 75	no. 72	no. 80
Air jet	no. 120	no. 120	no. 120
Main air bleed: AB 0	—	—	—
1	0.5 × 2	0.4 × 2	1.3 × 2
2	—	0.4 × 2	0.6 × 4
3	0.4 × 2	0.4 × 2	0.4 × 2
4	0.4 × 2	0.4 × 2	—
5	0.4 × 2	0.4 × 2	0.4 × 2
Needle jet	2.60 × 3.7	2.60 × 3.5	2.60 × 3.4
Jet needle	16332 2 stage	16332 3 stage	3 stage
Cutaway (throttle valve)	no. 2.0 width: 1.2, depth: 0.3 cutout provided	no. 2.0 width: 1.4, depth: 0.3	no. 2.5 width: 1.2, depth: 0.2
Slow jet	no. 40	no. 40	no. 38
Air screw	1.0 ± 1/8	1 3/8 ± 1/8	1 1/8 ± 1/8
Slow air bleed: 1	0.8 × 2	0.9 × 2	0.8 × 2
2	0.8 × 2	0.9 × 2	0.8 × 2
3	0.8 × 2	0.9 × 2	0.8 × 2
4	—	0.9 × 2	—
Valve seat	1.2	1.2	1.5
By-pass	1 2	1 2	—
Pilot outlet	1 1.2 pitch 5.1	2 1.0 pitch 5.1	1 0.9 pitch 5.5
Pilot air jet	no. 60	—	—
P.W.J.	—	—	—
P.W.A.J.	—	—	—
Fuel level	19.5	19.5	27 (adjustment height 23.5)
Setting mark	D	B	T 90 KA

ELECTRICAL SYSTEMS

CHARGING SYSTEM

Honda uses two types of electricl system on the models covered in this guide. The simpler method of generating power, and that which is used on all of the 50, 65, and 70 cc models, is the magneto system which uses AC current produced by a permanently magnetized flywheel, an ignition coil, and a lighting coil. The flywheel is secured to the end of the crankshaft and the coils are mounted in a fixed position within the flywheel circumference. The lighting coil is also con-

Flywheel generator

nected to a selenium rectifier which converts the AC current to DC for charging the battery. Of the models equipped with this system, only the C50M, C65M, and the C70M come equipped with electric starting.

The other system which is used on all of the other models is an alternator sys-

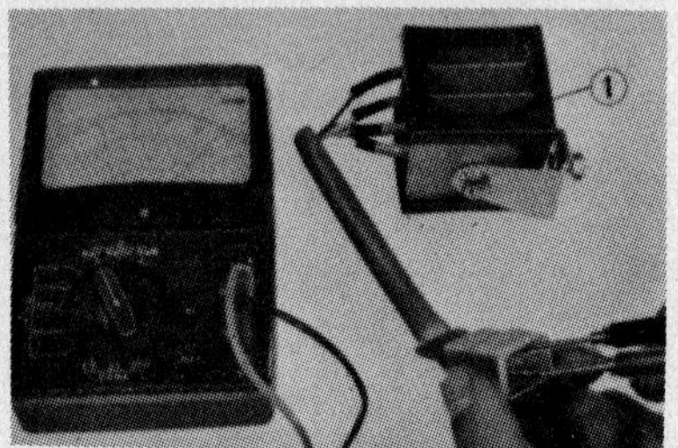
Testing the rectifier
1. Selenium rectifier

tem which produces AC current through a rotor and stator assembly. It operates in basically the same way as the magneto system, but in this case the permanent magnet (rotor) revolves within the fixed coils (stator). The current passes from the stator to a selenium rectifier where it is converted into DC and is used for ignition and lighting.

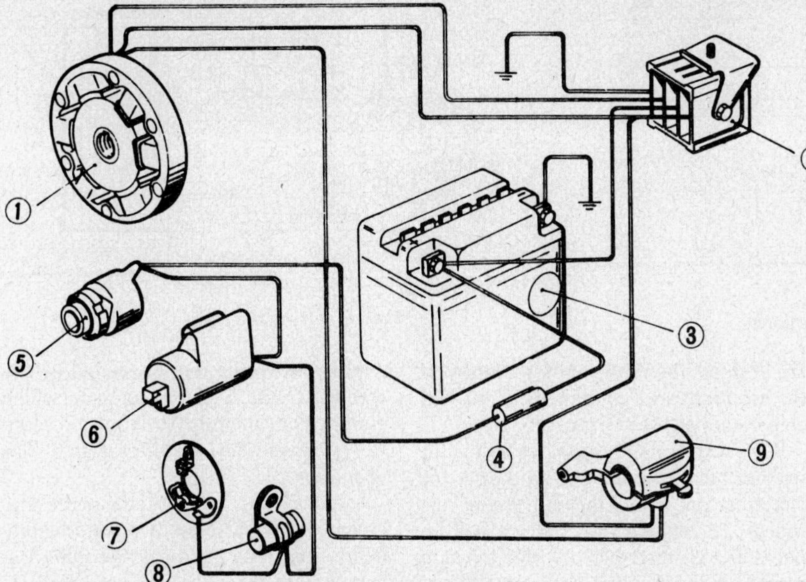

Alternator generating system

1. Alternator
2. Selenium rectifier
3. Battery
4. Fuse
5. Combination switch
6. Ignition coil
7. Breaker points
8. Condenser
9. Lighting switch

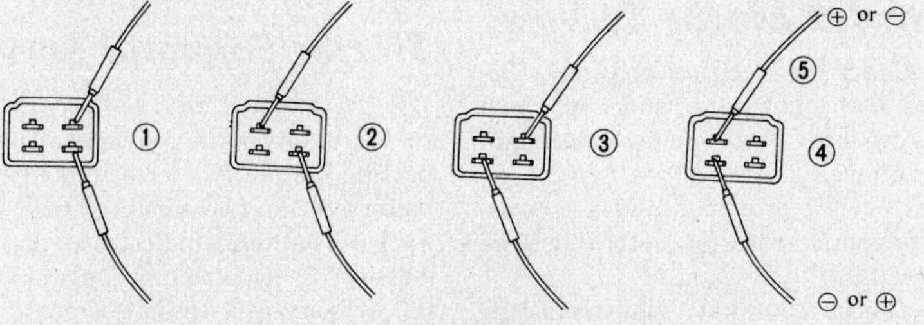

Test positions

1. Green and pink leads
2. Pink and red/white leads
3. Green and yellow leads
4. Red/white and yellow leads
5. Tester leads

COMPONENT TESTING

Rectifier Testing

If alternator output is satisfactory but the battery discharges as the engine is running, it is quite possible that the rectifier is not functioning properly (assuming that the battery is in good condition and is capable of taking on a charge). Before removing and testing the rectifier, make sure that it is mounted solidly on the frame. The rectifier is grounded through its mounting and will not operate without a good ground. Never loosen or tighten the nut that holds the rectifier unit together, as this will adversely affect the operation of the rectifier.

To test the rectifier, first pull apart the plastic connector, unscrew the mounting nut, and remove the rectifier unit. There are four diodes inside the rectifier, which, if functioning properly, will allow electricity to pass in only one direction. To check the diodes you can use either a multimeter or a test light and the motorcycle battery. If the test light and battery are to be used, simply run a length of wire off one battery terminal and connect one of the test light leads to the other terminal. The two free wire ends will be used to check electrical continuity of the diodes.

Connect the positive lead to the yellow wire and the negative lead to the red-white wire, as shown in test one of the accompanying table. Reverse the leads so that the negative lead is connected to the red/white wire. The test light should light (or the gauge needle should respond) in one direction only. Repeat in the same manner for test steps two, three, and four in the table. Continuity in both directions (when reversing the leads) indicates a defective diode, in which case the rectifier unit must be replaced.

Testing the stator coil
1. Stator coil

RECTIFIER TEST TABLE

Connection			Resistance Value
Test Leads		Rectifier Terminal	
1. +	−	Yellow	Satisfactory if between 5-40Ω
−	+	Red/White	
2. +	−	Pink	
−	+	Red/White	
3. +	−	Green	
−	+	Yellow	
4. +	−	Green	
−	+	Pink	

The diodes are quite susceptible to failure from excessive heat and electrical overload. Observe the following precautions to avoid rectifier failure.

1. Do not reverse battery polarity when installing or reconnecting the battery. The electrical system is negative ground.
2. Do not use high-voltage test equipment to test the rectifier diodes.
3. Do not run the engine with the rectifier disconnected.
4. Do not charge the battery without first disconnecting, and isolating one of the battery cables.

Alternator Service

Uncouple the alternator leads at the connector block and check continuity between the three stator coil leads (yellow, pink, and white) using a multimeter or a test light and battery. Connect one of the test leads to the pink wire and the other to first the yellow and then the the white wire. If there is continuity in both cases, the stator coil is satisfactory. Standard stator coil resistance is 1.1 ohms (pink to yellow wire) and 0.55 ohms (pink to white wire). The stator coil assembly can be taken off after the left side cover is removed.

Regulator Testing

1. Connect the regulator in circuit as indicated in the accompanying illustration. The voltage may be altered by manipulating the slide resister.

2.If, when the voltage is low the pointer on the ammeter swings, the regulator is defective and must be replaced.

3. If, when the voltage is between

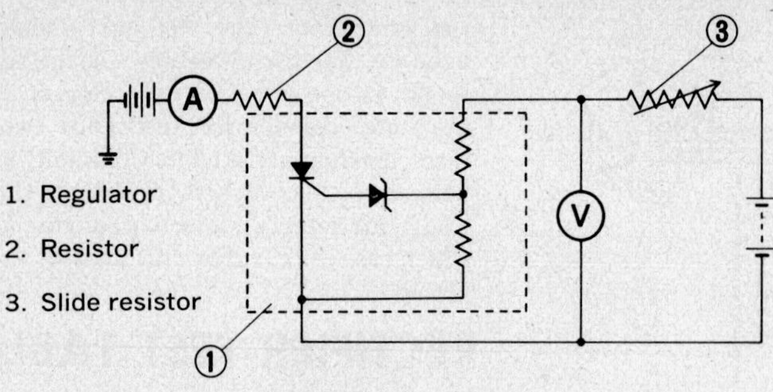

Regulator test connections

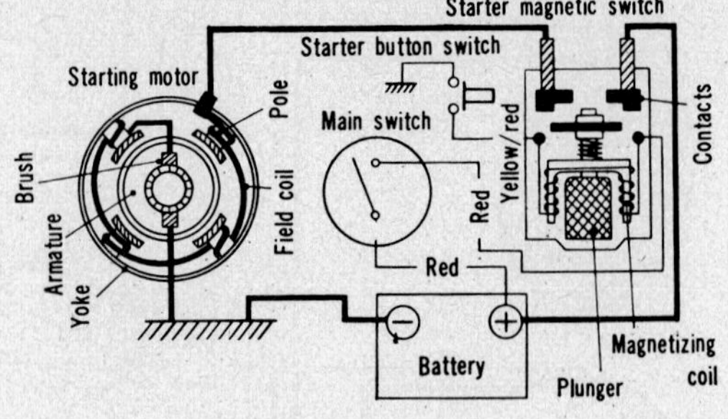

Starter wiring diagram

7–8V the ammeter pointer swings, the regulator is good.

4. If when the voltage is increased normally the ammeter pointer swings, the regulator must be replaced.

STARTING SYSTEM

Testing

1. If the starter will not operate, switch on the headlight and observe its intensity. If it is dim when the starter is not being operated, check the battery connections and recharge the battery. If the headlight doesn't light, check the fuse, and the battery connections, and check the electrical continuity of the wire between the ignition switch and the battery.

If the headlight is bright, press the starter button mementarily and watch the light. If it remains bright, touch a screwdriver blade between the two starter solenoid terminals. If the starter operates, connect a test light between the small yellow/red wire on the solenoid and ground. If the test light comes on as the button is pushed, the solenoid is faulty. If it does not light, look for defective wiring between the starter button and the ignition switch, or simply a burned out starter button switch. If the starter does not operate and the headlight dims as the main solenoid terminals are bridged, the starter motor if faulty. If the headlight does not dim, look for a bad connection at the starter.

If the starter motor operates freely but will not turn the engine over, the starter clutch is not operating (a rare occurrence). To remove the clutch it will be necessary to first take off the left-side crankcase cover and remove the alternator rotor. If the overrunning clutch is defective and the starter keeps spinning after the engine starts, it must be repaired immediately to prevent serious damage to the starter assembly.

Starter Motor Service

1. Check for electrical continuity between the commutator and and armature core using a multimeter or test light and battery. If continuity exists, the armature coil is grounded and the armature or complete starter motor should be replaced.

2. Check continuity between the brush wired to the stator (field) coil and the starter motor cable terminal. Lack of continuity indicates that an open circuit exists in the stator coil and the starter motor unit should be replaced.

3. Examine the carbon brushes for damage to the contact surfaces and measure their length. Replace the burshes as a set if they are damaged in any way or if they measure less than 0.3 in. (7.5mm).

4. Brush spring tension should be determined with a small pull-scale which your dealer can probably supply. Replace the springs if they exert less than 0.8 lbs of tension.

5. Polish the commutator with fine emery cloth and blow it off thoroughly before installing it. Check the following components for excessive wear and damage: clutch spring and rollers; bearings; bushings; oil seal; reduction gears; and the sprockets. Replace all parts as necessary if worn or damaged. When reassembling the starter clutch, apply a thin coat of silicone grease to the rollers.

Starter Solenoid Service

If the solenoid does not work, check the continuity of the primary coil by connecting the multimeter or test light and battery to the two small solenoid leads. Lack of continuity indicates an open circuit and the solenoid must be replaced. If the primary coil winding is continuous, disassemble the solenoid and clean the contact points with emery paper or a small file. The points, after long use, have a tendency to become pitted or burned due to the large current passing across them. Be sure to disconnect the battery before disconnecting the cables from the solenoid when it is to be removed. Replace the solenoid if cleaning the points fails to repair it.

ELECTRICAL SPECIFICATIONS

	C50	C50M	S50	C65
Headlight	6V-15W/15W	6V-25W/25W	6V-15W/15W	6V-15W/15W
Tail/stoplight	6V-3W/6V-10W red	6V-3W/6V-10W red	6V-2W/6V-6W red	6V-3W/6V-10W red
Turn signal light	6V-8WX2 amber	6V-8WX2 amber	6V-8WX2 amber	6V-8WX2 amber
Meter light	N.A.	N.A.	N.A.	N.A.
Neutral indicator light	N.A.	N.A.	N.A.	N.A.
Turn signal indicator light	N.A.	N.A.	N.A.	N.A.
High-beam indicator light	N.A.	N.A.	N.A.	N.A.

ELECTRICAL SPECIFICATIONS (con't.)

	C65M	S65	CL70	C70
Headlight	6V-25W/25W	9V-15W/15W	6V-15W/15W	6V-15W/15W
Tail/stoplight	6V-3W/6V-10W red	6V-2W/6V-6W red	6V-5.3W/17W	6V-3W/10W
Turn signal light	6V-8WX2 amber	6V-8WX2 amber	6V-18W	6V-8W
Meter	N.A.	N.A.	N.A.	N.A.
Neutral indicator light	N.A.	N.A.	——	6V-5W
Turn signal indicator light	N.A.	N.A.	N.A.	N.A.
High-beam indicator light	N.A.	N.A.	N.A.	N.A.
Oil lamp light	——	——	——	6V-3W

	C70M	S90	SL90	CL90, CL90L
Headlight	6V-15W/25W	6V-25W/25W	6V-25W/25W	6V-25W/25W
Tail/stoplight	6V-3W/10W	6V-2W/6V-6W	6V-17W/6V-5.3W	6V-5W/6V-17W
Turn signal light	6V-8W	6V-8W	N.A.	6V-18W
Meter light	N.A.	N.A.	N.A.	N.A.
Neutral indicator light	6V-5W	N.A.	N.A.	N.A.
Turn signal indicator light	N.A.	N.A.	N.A.	N.A.
High-beam indicator light	N.A.	N.A.	N.A.	N.A.
Oil lamp light	6V-3W	——	——	——

	CD90	C90	CT90	CB100 CL100
Headlight	6V-25W/25W	6V-25W/25W	6V-25W/25W	6V-35W/25W
Tail/stoplight	6V-5W/6V-10W	6V-3W/6V-10W	①	6V-5.3W/17W
Turn signal light	6V-10W	6V-8W	②	6V-18W
Meter light	N.A.	N.A.	N.A.	6V-1.5W
Neutral indicator light	N.A.	N.A.	N.A.	6V-1.5W
Turn signal indicator light	N.A.	N.A.	N.A.	6V-1.5W
High-beam indicator light	N.A.	N.A.	N.A.	6V-1.5W

① CT90 — 6V-5W/6V-18W
CT90 (after F. no. 000001A) — 6V-5W/6V-17W
② CT90 — none
CT90 (after F. no. 000001A) — 6V-18W (option)

	SL100	CB125S CD125S	SL125	L250
Headlight	6V-35W/25W	6V-25W/25W	6V-25W/35W	6V25W/35W
Tail/stoplight	6V-5.3W/17W	6V-3W/10W	6V-5.3W/17W	6V-32/3CP
Turn signal light	——	6V-8W	——	——
Meter light	6V-1.5W	6V-1.5W	6V-1.5W	6V-1.5W
Neutral indicator light	6V-1.5W	6V-1.5W	6V-1.5W	6V-1.5W
Turn signal indicator light	——	6V-1.5W	——	——
High-beam indicator light	6V-1.5W	6V-1.5W	6V-1.5W	6V-1.5W

WIRING DIAGRAMS

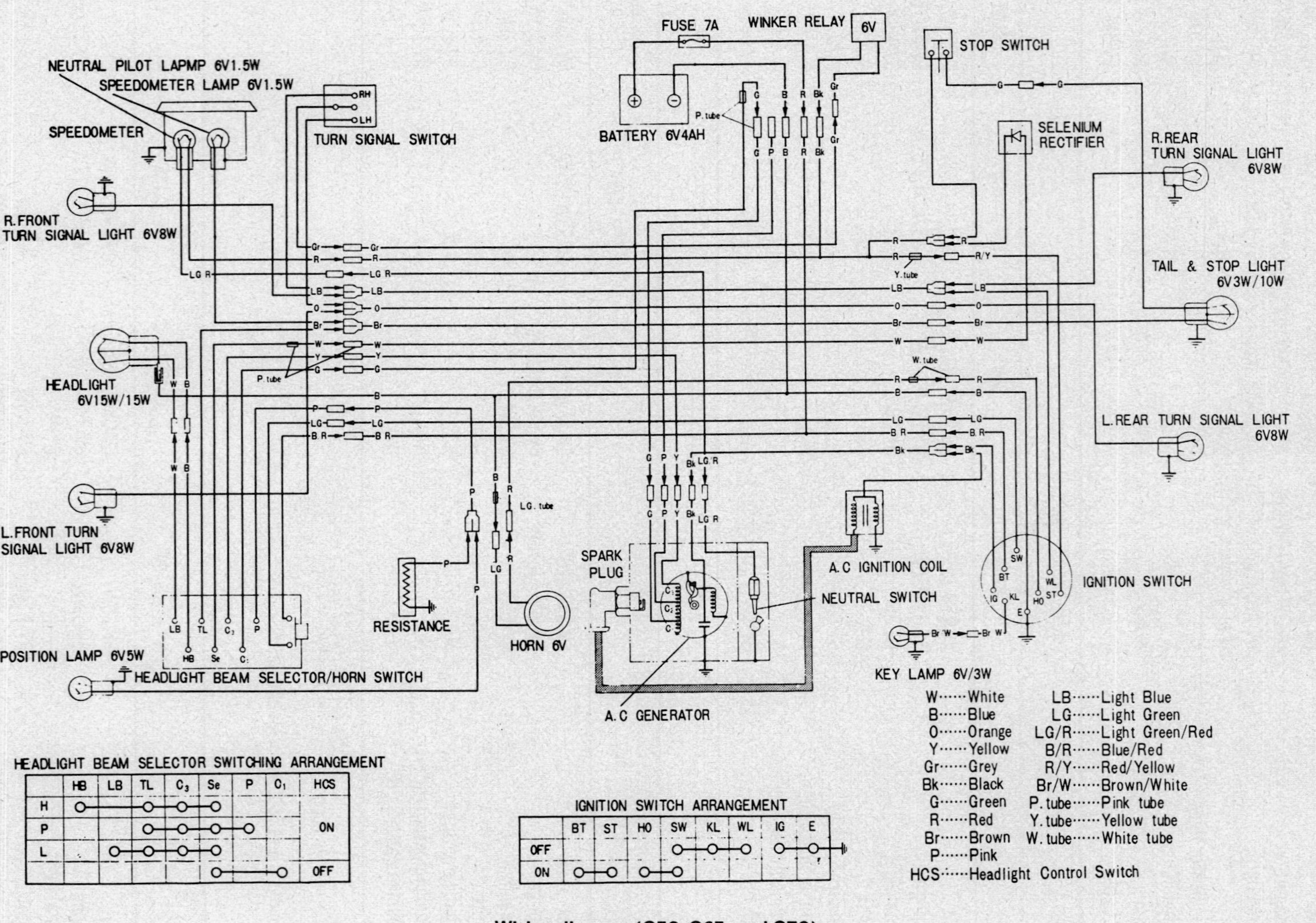

Wiring diagram (C50, C65, and C70)

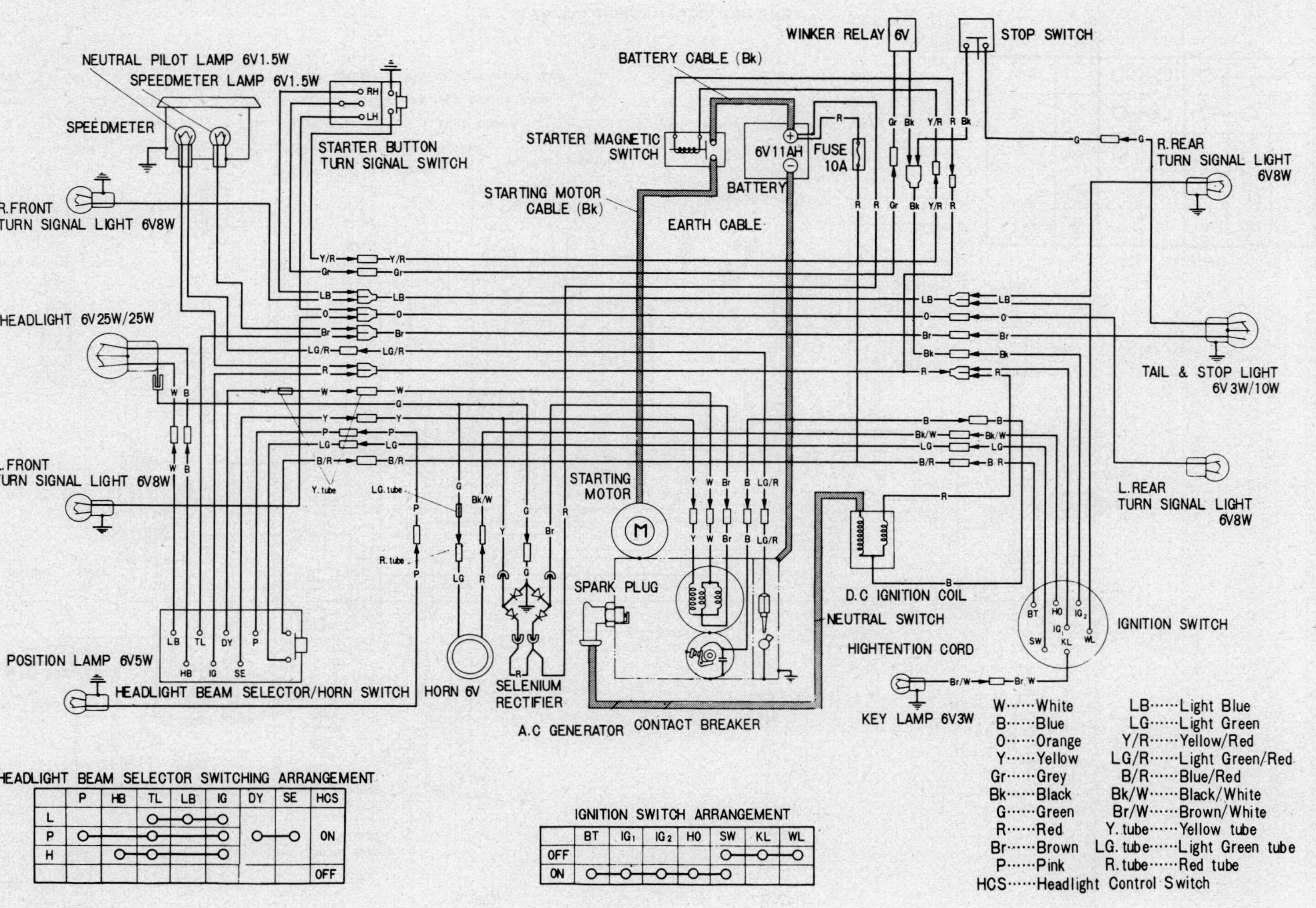

HEADLIGHT BEAM SELECTOR SWITCHING ARRANGEMENT

	P	HB	TL	LB	IG	DY	SE	HCS
L			○	○	○			
P	○		○	○	○	○	○	ON
H		○	○	○	○			
								OFF

IGNITION SWITCH ARRANGEMENT

	BT	IG₁	IG₂	HO	SW	KL	WL
OFF					○	○	○
ON	○	○	○	○	○		

Wiring diagram (C50M, C65M, and C70M)

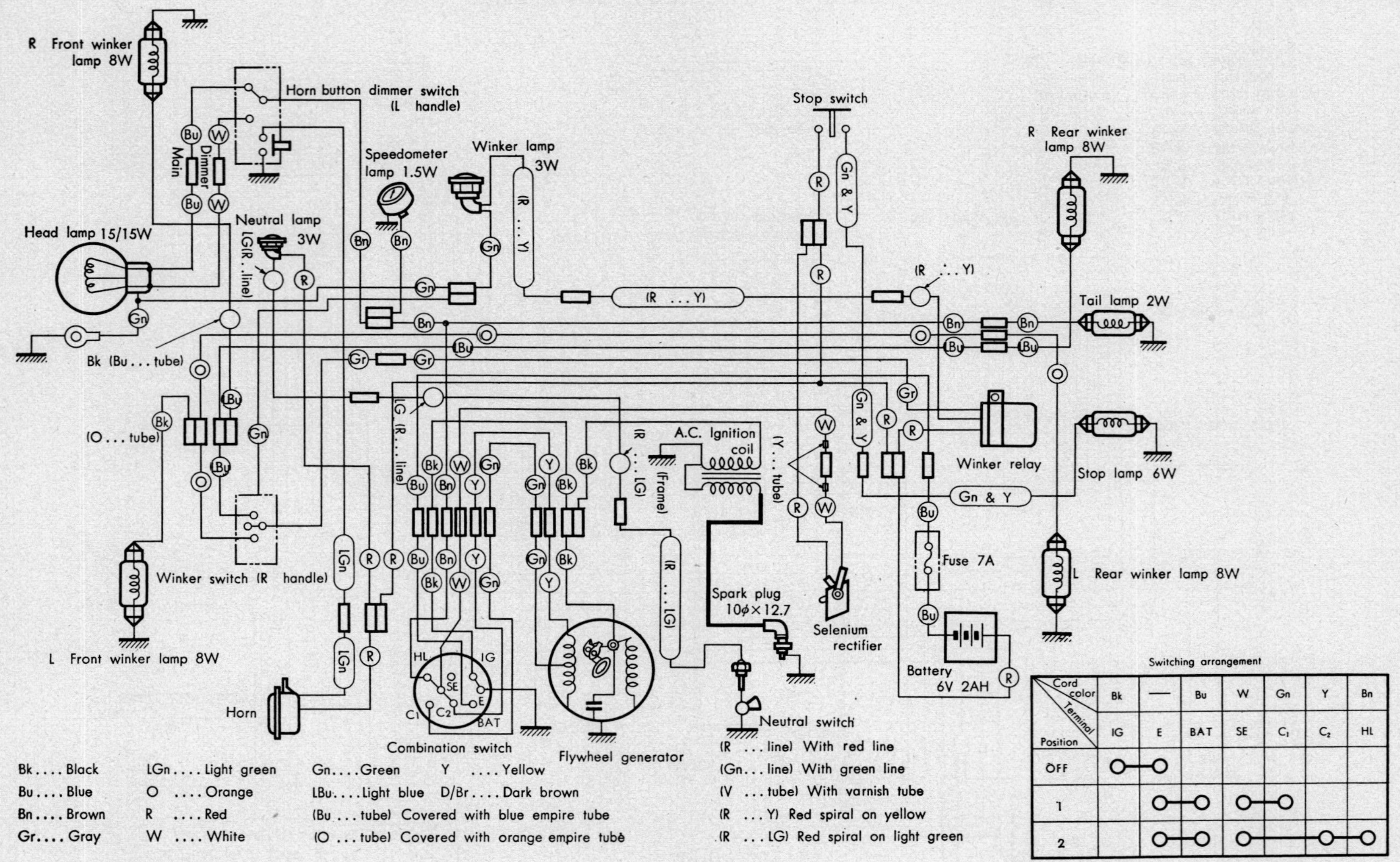

Cord color / Terminal / Position	Bk	—	Bu	W	Gn	Y	Bn
	IG	E	BAT	SE	C_1	C_2	HL
OFF	o—	—o					
1		o—	—o	o—	—o		
2		o—	—o	o—	—	—o—	—o

Wiring diagram (S50, and S65)

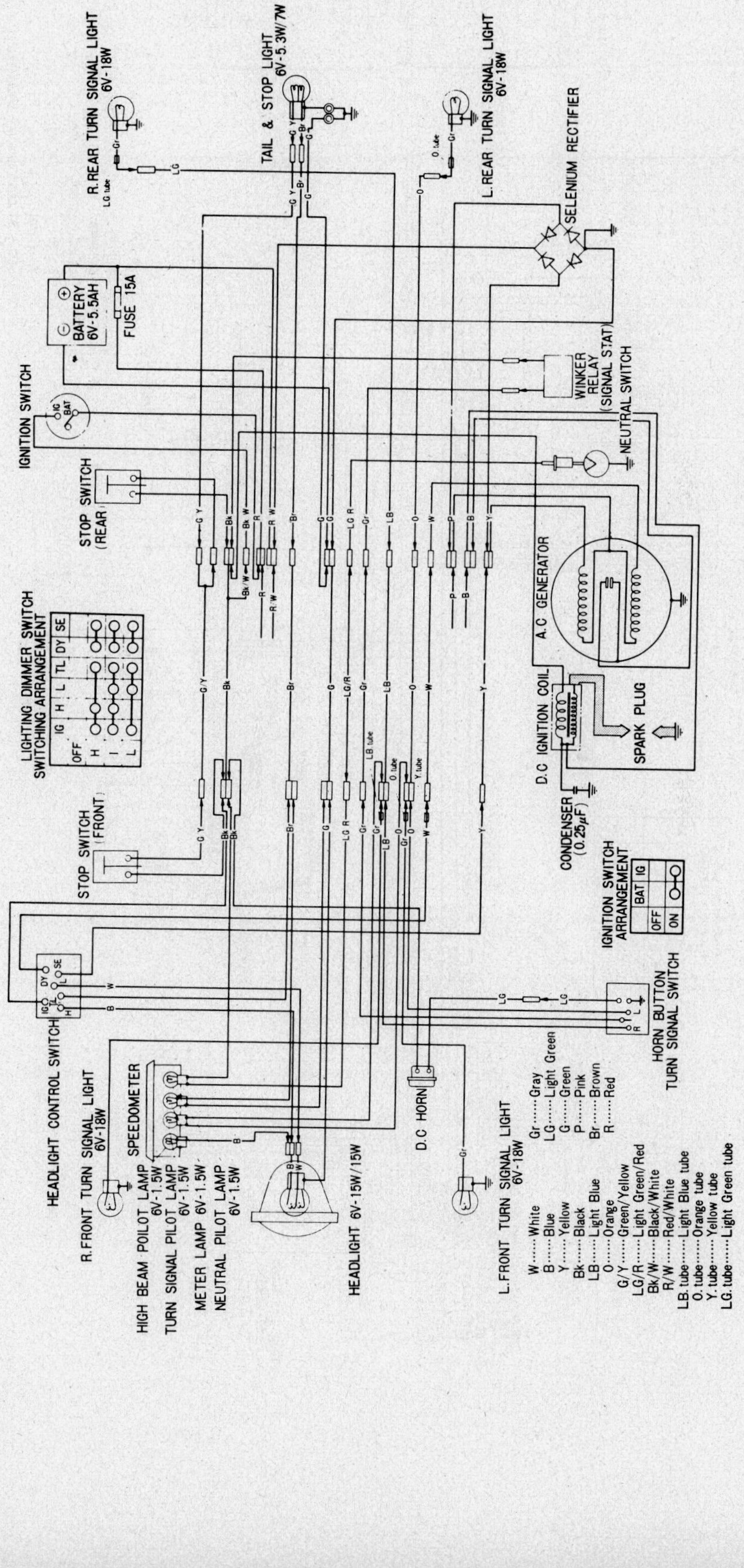

Wiring diagram (CL70)

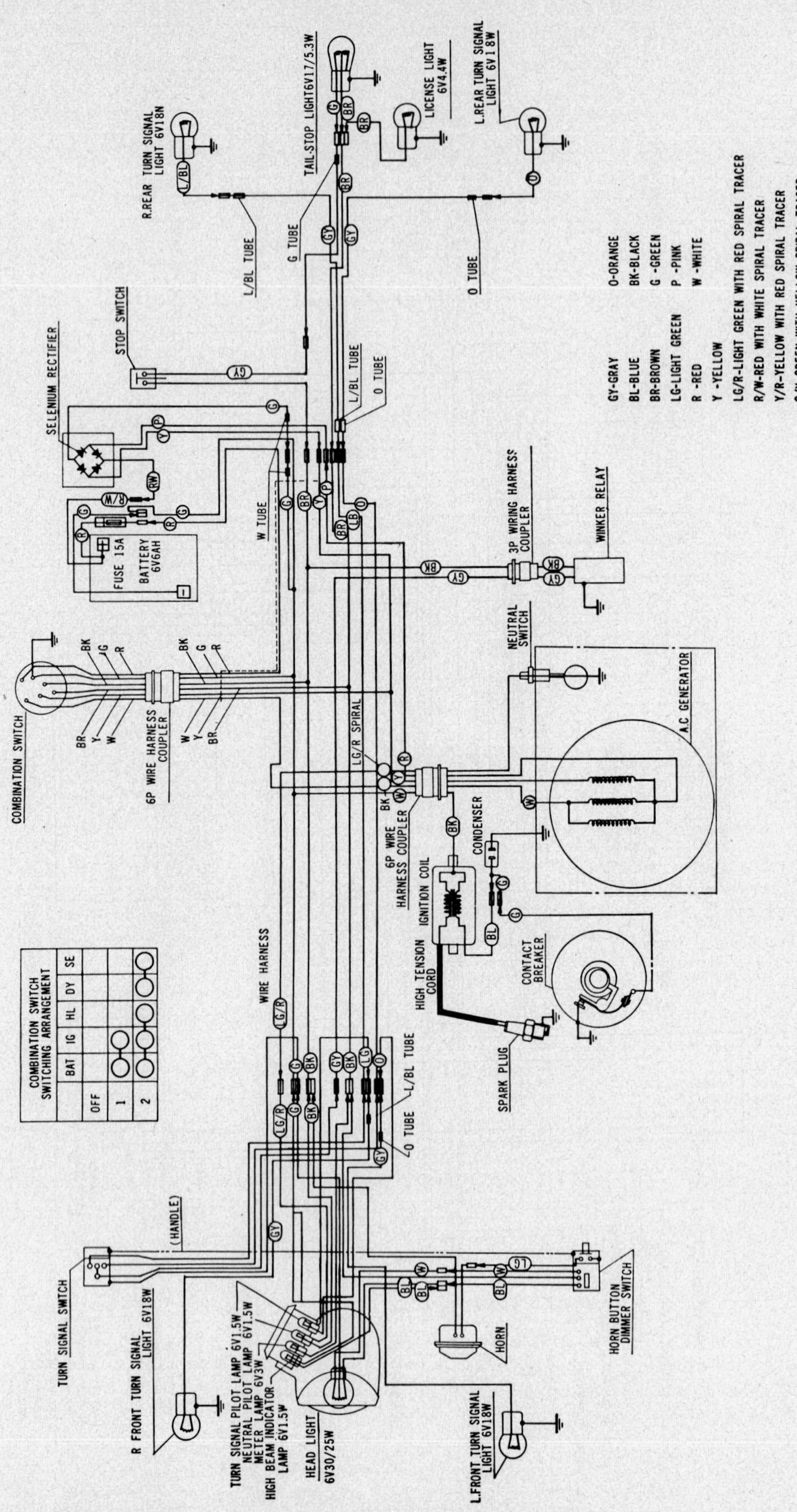
TAIL-STOP LIGHT 6V17/5.3W
R.REAR TURN SIGNAL LIGHT 6V18W
LICENSE LIGHT 6V4.4W
L.REAR TURN SIGNAL LIGHT 6V18W
L/BL TUBE
G TUBE
O TUBE
STOP SWITCH
SELENIUM RECTIFIER
FUSE 15A
BATTERY 6V6AH
W TUBE
3P WIRING HARNESS COUPLER
WINKER RELAY
COMBINATION SWITCH
6P WIRE HARNESS COUPLER
NEUTRAL SWITCH
A.C GENERATOR
LG/R SPIRAL
6P WIRE HARNESS COUPLER
CONDENSER
IGNITION COIL
HIGH TENSION CORD
CONTACT BREAKER
SPARK PLUG
WIRE HARNESS
COMBINATION SWITCH SWITCHING ARRANGEMENT
BAT IG HL DY SE
OFF
1
2
(HANDLE)
TURN SIGNAL SWITCH
R FRONT TURN SIGNAL LIGHT 6V18W
TURN SIGNAL PILOT LAMP 6V1.5W
NEUTRAL PILOT LAMP 6V1.5W
METER LAMP 6V3W
HIGH BEAM INDICATOR LAMP 6V1.5W
HEAD LIGHT 6V30/25W
HORN
HORN BUTTON DIMMER SWITCH
L.FRONT TURN SIGNAL LIGHT 6V18W
GY-GRAY
BL-BLUE
BR-BROWN
LG-LIGHT GREEN
R -RED
Y -YELLOW
O-ORANGE
BK-BLACK
G -GREEN
P -PINK
W -WHITE
LG/R-LIGHT GREEN WITH RED SPIRAL TRACER
R/W-RED WITH WHITE SPIRAL TRACER
Y/R-YELLOW WITH RED SPIRAL TRACER
G/Y-GREEN WITH YELLOW SPIRAL TRACER

Wiring diagram (S90)

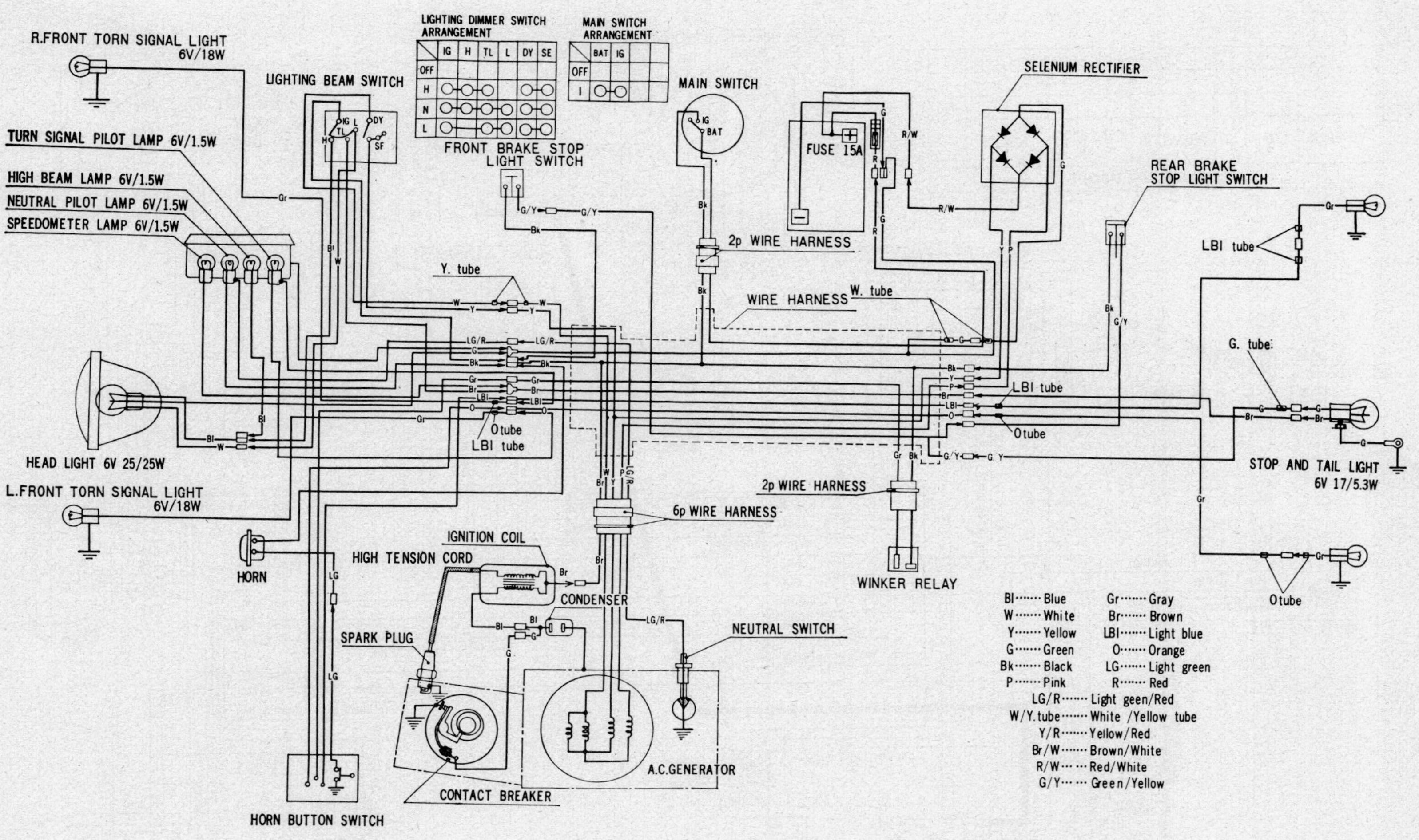
R.FRONT TORN SIGNAL LIGHT 6V/18W
LIGHTING DIMMER SWITCH ARRANGEMENT
MAIN SWITCH ARRANGEMENT
LIGHTING BEAM SWITCH
MAIN SWITCH
SELENIUM RECTIFIER
TURN SIGNAL PILOT LAMP 6V/1.5W
HIGH BEAM LAMP 6V/1.5W
NEUTRAL PILOT LAMP 6V/1.5W
SPEEDOMETER LAMP 6V/1.5W
FRONT BRAKE STOP LIGHT SWITCH
FUSE 15A
REAR BRAKE STOP LIGHT SWITCH
2p WIRE HARNESS
LBI tube
Y. tube
WIRE HARNESS
W. tube
G. tube
LBI tube
O tube
O tube
LBI tube
HEAD LIGHT 6V 25/25W
STOP AND TAIL LIGHT 6V 17/5.3W
L.FRONT TORN SIGNAL LIGHT 6V/18W
2p WIRE HARNESS
6p WIRE HARNESS
IGNITION COIL
HIGH TENSION CORD
HORN
WINKER RELAY
O tube
CONDENSER
NEUTRAL SWITCH
SPARK PLUG
A.C.GENERATOR
CONTACT BREAKER
HORN BUTTON SWITCH
Bl······Blue
W······White
Y······Yellow
G······Green
Bk······Black
P······Pink
Gr······Gray
Br······Brown
LBl······Light blue
O······Orange
LG······Light green
R······Red
LG/R······Light geen/Red
W/Y.tube······White /Yellow tube
Y/R······Yellow/Red
Br/W······Brown/White
R/W······Red/White
G/Y······Green/Yellow

Wiring diagram (CL90 and CL90L)

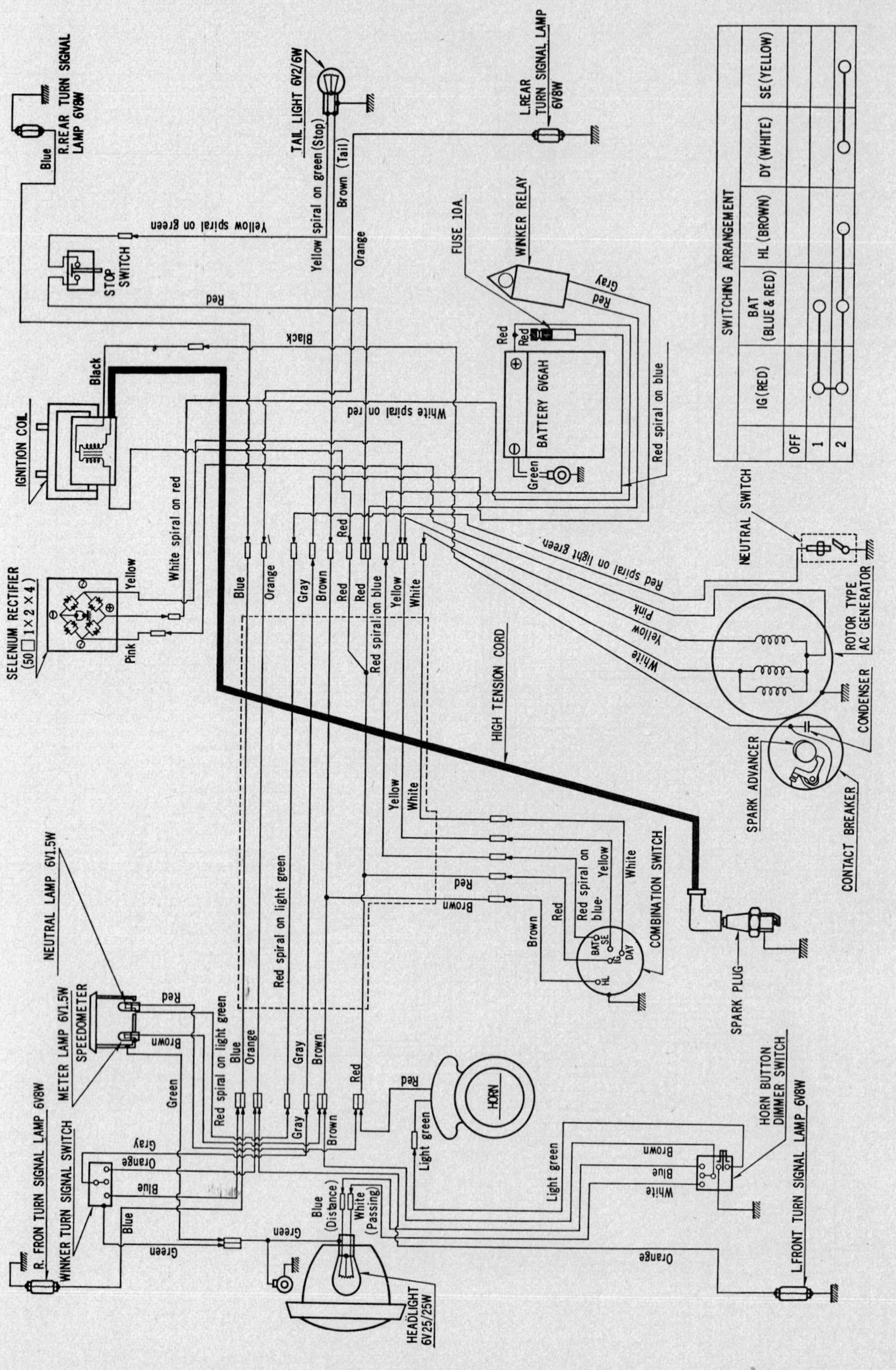

Wiring diagram (CD90)

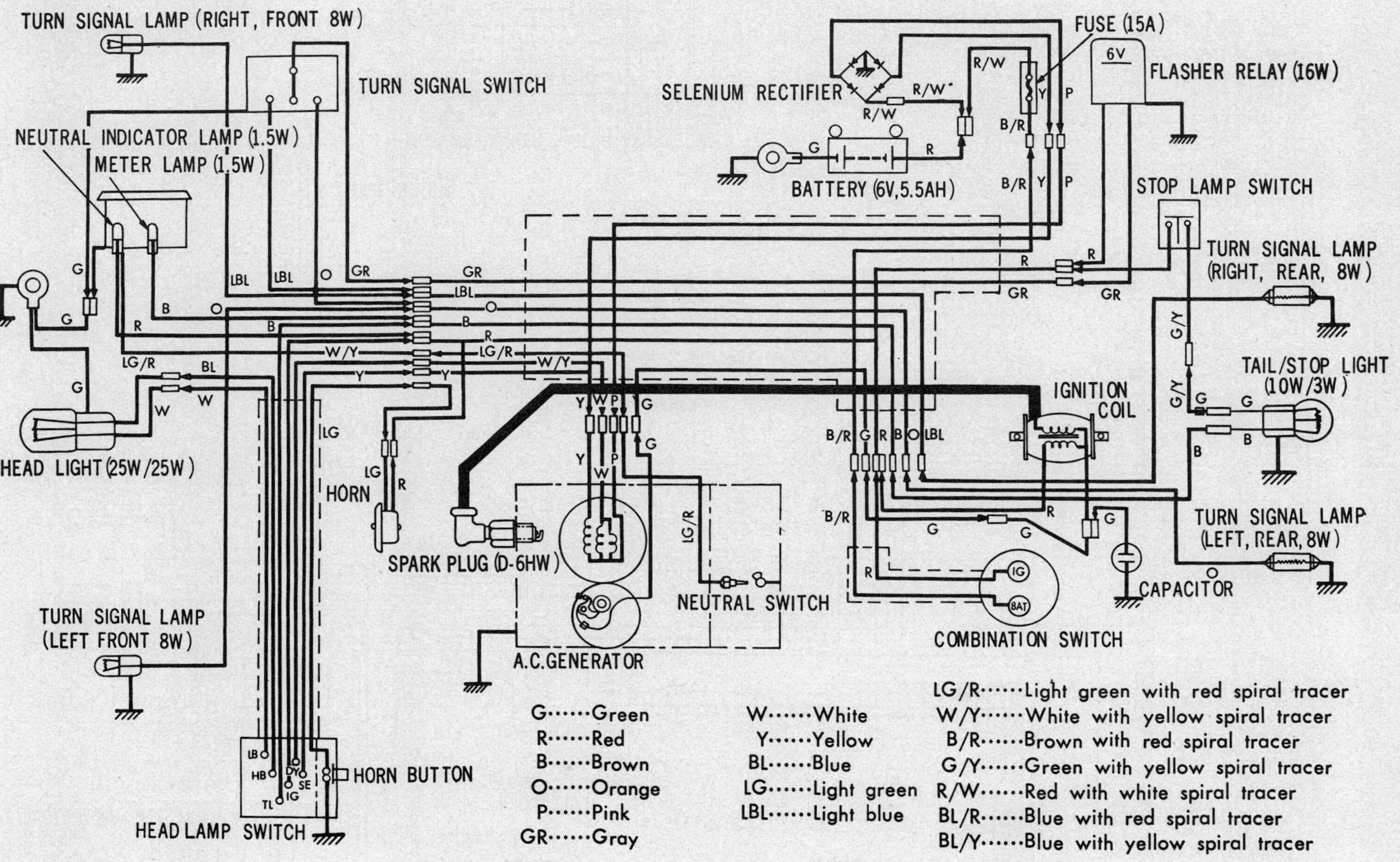
TURN SIGNAL LAMP (RIGHT, FRONT 8W)
TURN SIGNAL SWITCH
NEUTRAL INDICATOR LAMP (1.5W)
METER LAMP (1.5W)
HEAD LIGHT (25W/25W)
HORN
TURN SIGNAL LAMP (LEFT FRONT 8W)
HEAD LAMP SWITCH
HORN BUTTON
SPARK PLUG (D-6HW)
A.C.GENERATOR
NEUTRAL SWITCH
SELENIUM RECTIFIER
BATTERY (6V,5.5AH)
FUSE (15A)
FLASHER RELAY (16W)
STOP LAMP SWITCH
TURN SIGNAL LAMP (RIGHT, REAR, 8W)
TAIL/STOP LIGHT (10W/3W)
IGNITION COIL
TURN SIGNAL LAMP (LEFT, REAR, 8W)
CAPACITOR
COMBINATION SWITCH
G......Green
R......Red
B......Brown
O......Orange
P......Pink
GR......Gray
W......White
Y......Yellow
BL......Blue
LG......Light green
LBL......Light blue
LG/R......Light green with red spiral tracer
W/Y......White with yellow spiral tracer
B/R......Brown with red spiral tracer
G/Y......Green with yellow spiral tracer
R/W......Red with white spiral tracer
BL/R......Blue with red spiral tracer
BL/Y......Blue with yellow spiral tracer

Wiring diagram (C90)

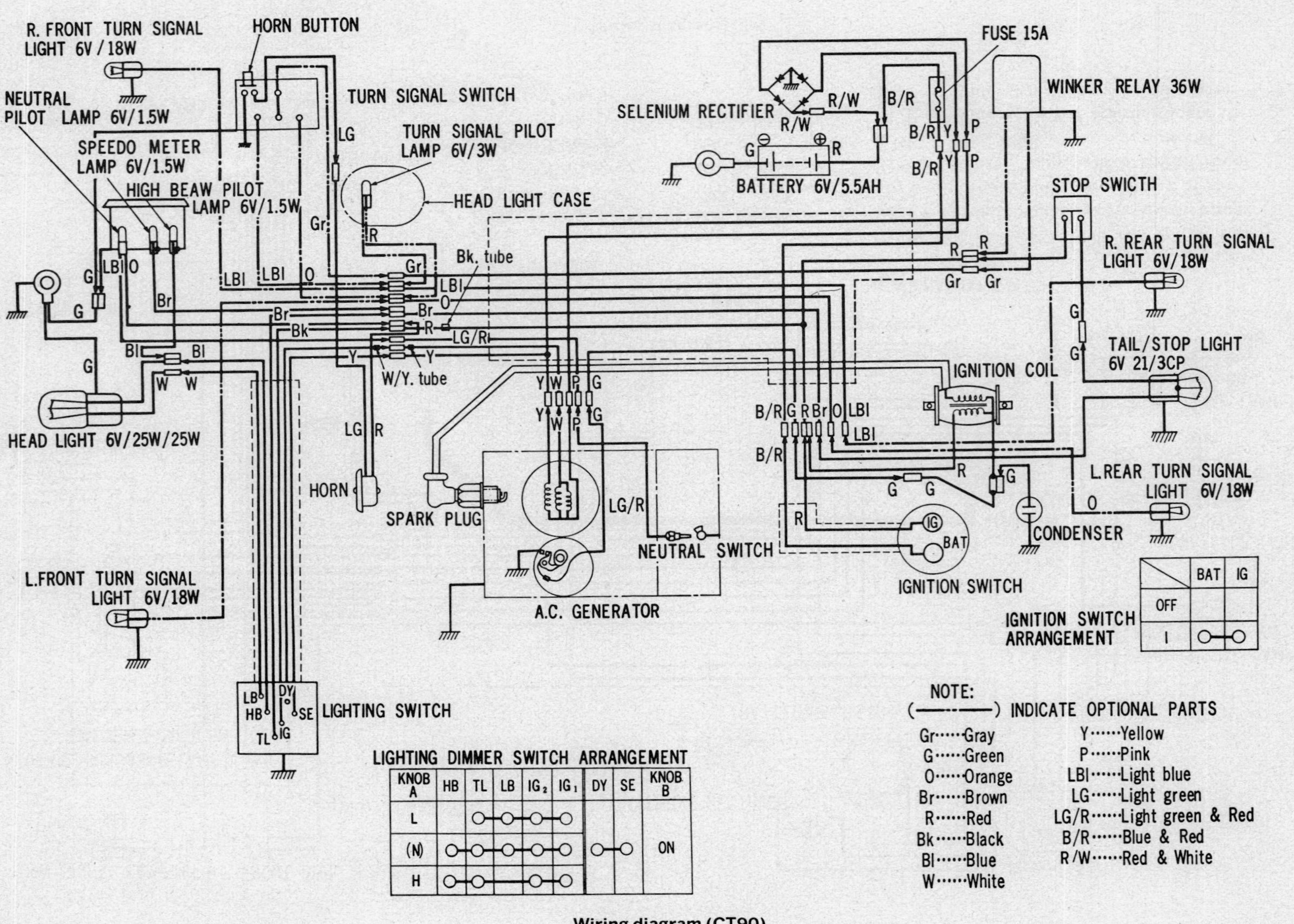
R. FRONT TURN SIGNAL LIGHT 6V / 18W
HORN BUTTON
TURN SIGNAL SWITCH
NEUTRAL PILOT LAMP 6V/1.5W
SPEEDO METER LAMP 6V/1.5W
HIGH BEAW PILOT LAMP 6V/1.5W
TURN SIGNAL PILOT LAMP 6V/3W
HEAD LIGHT CASE
Bk. tube
W/Y. tube
HEAD LIGHT 6V/25W/25W
HORN
SPARK PLUG
L.FRONT TURN SIGNAL LIGHT 6V/18W
A.C. GENERATOR
NEUTRAL SWITCH
SELENIUM RECTIFIER
BATTERY 6V/5.5AH
FUSE 15A
WINKER RELAY 36W
STOP SWICTH
R. REAR TURN SIGNAL LIGHT 6V/18W
TAIL/STOP LIGHT 6V 21/3CP
IGNITION COIL
L.REAR TURN SIGNAL LIGHT 6V/18W
CONDENSER
IGNITION SWITCH
IGNITION SWITCH ARRANGEMENT
BAT
IG
OFF
I
LIGHTING SWITCH
LIGHTING DIMMER SWITCH ARRANGEMENT
KNOB A
HB
TL
LB
IG2
IG1
DY
SE
KNOB B
L
(N)
H
ON
NOTE:
(-------) INDICATE OPTIONAL PARTS
Gr……Gray
G……Green
O……Orange
Br……Brown
R……Red
Bk……Black
Bl……Blue
W……White
Y……Yellow
P……Pink
LBl……Light blue
LG……Light green
LG/R……Light green & Red
B/R……Blue & Red
R/W……Red & White

Wiring diagram (CT90)

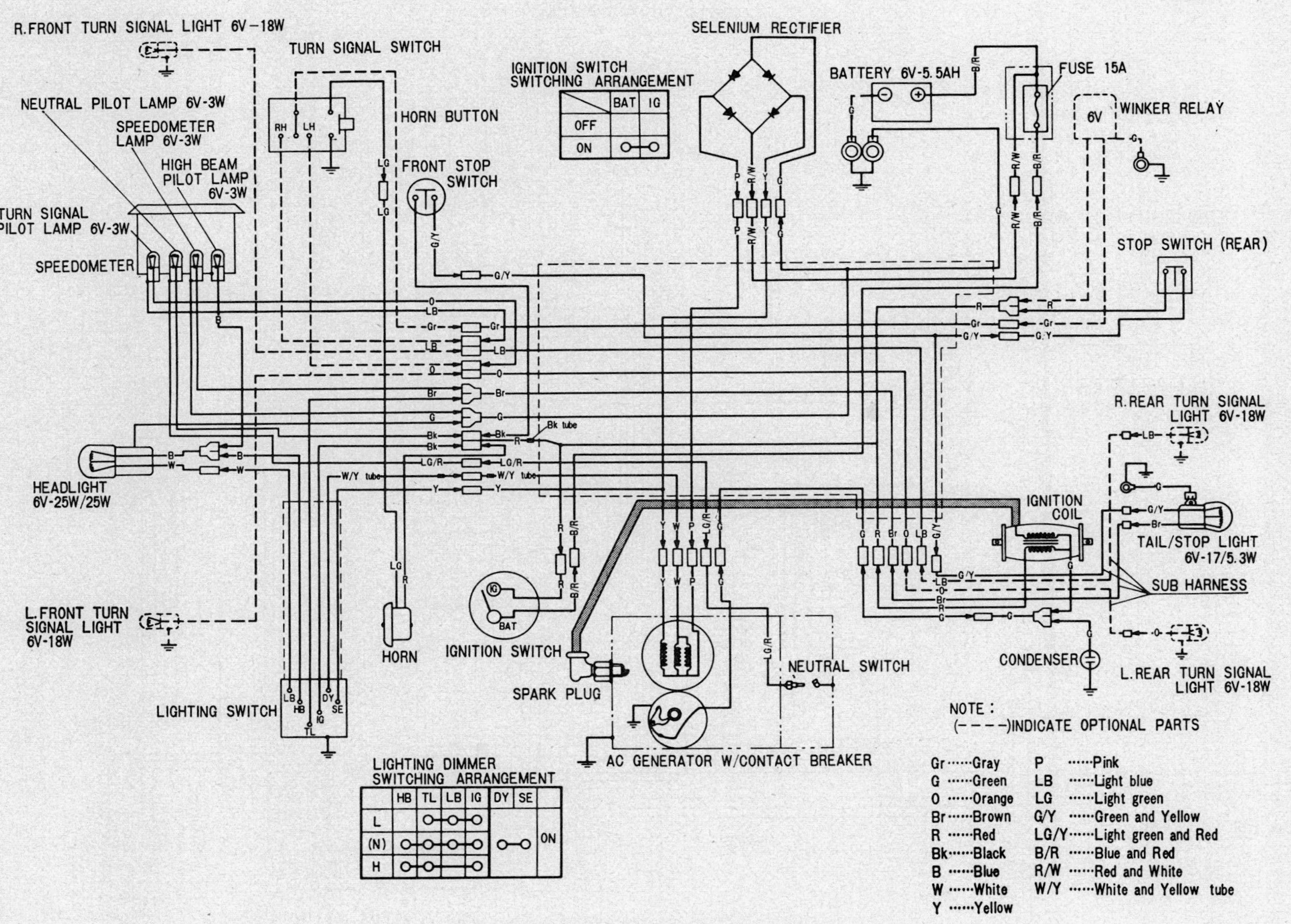

Wiring diagram (CT90 from frame no. 000001A)

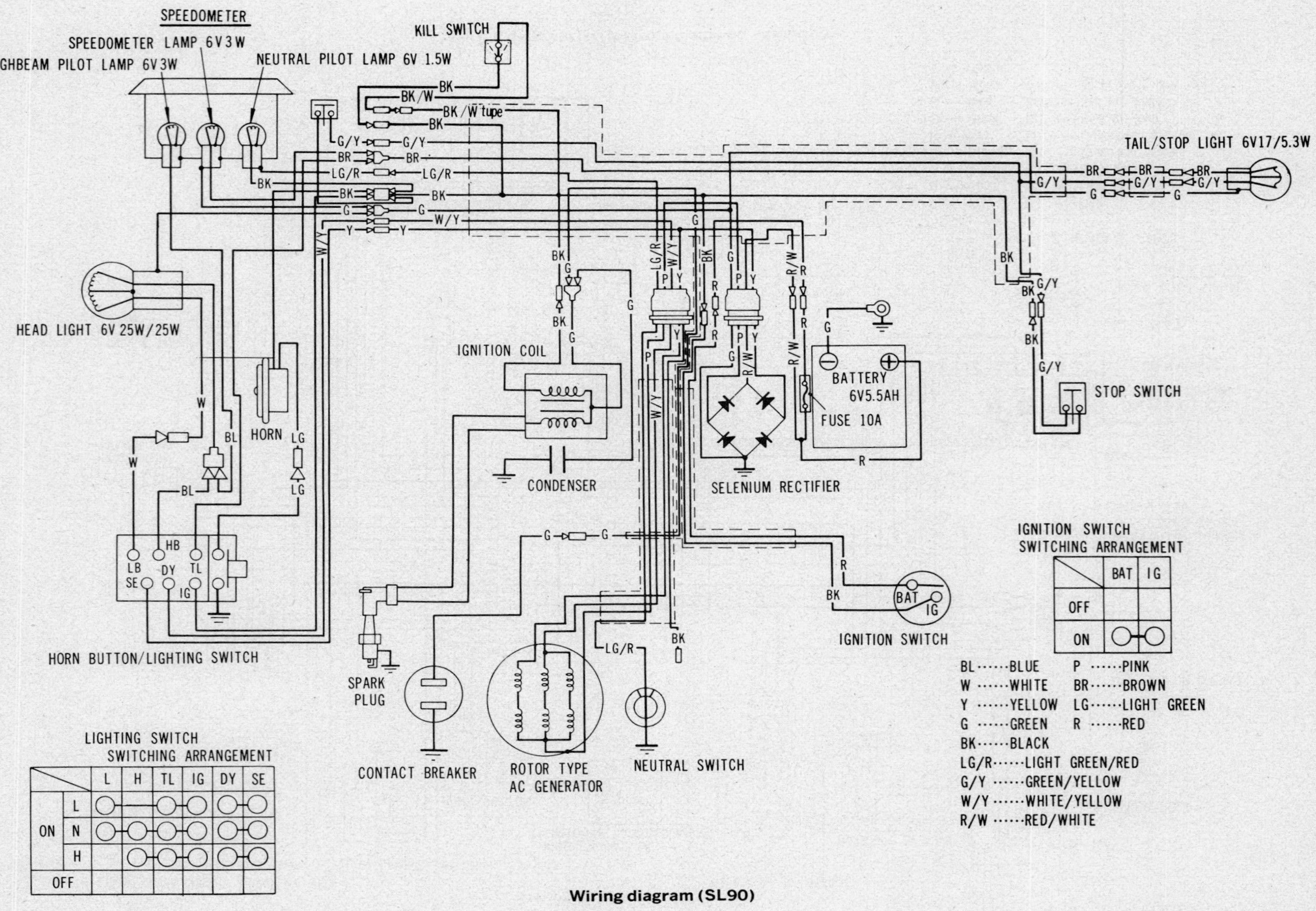
SPEEDOMETER
SPEEDOMETER LAMP 6V3W
HIGHBEAM PILOT LAMP 6V3W
NEUTRAL PILOT LAMP 6V 1.5W
KILL SWITCH
BK/W tupe
TAIL/STOP LIGHT 6V17/5.3W
HEAD LIGHT 6V 25W/25W
HORN
IGNITION COIL
CONDENSER
BATTERY
6V5.5AH
FUSE 10A
SELENIUM RECTIFIER
STOP SWITCH
HORN BUTTON/LIGHTING SWITCH
SPARK
PLUG
CONTACT BREAKER
ROTOR TYPE
AC GENERATOR
NEUTRAL SWITCH
IGNITION SWITCH
IGNITION SWITCH
SWITCHING ARRANGEMENT
BAT IG
OFF
ON
LIGHTING SWITCH
SWITCHING ARRANGEMENT
L H TL IG DY SE
ON L
N
H
OFF
BL......BLUE
W......WHITE
Y......YELLOW
G......GREEN
BK......BLACK
LG/R......LIGHT GREEN/RED
G/Y......GREEN/YELLOW
W/Y......WHITE/YELLOW
R/W......RED/WHITE
P......PINK
BR......BROWN
LG......LIGHT GREEN
R......RED

Wiring diagram (SL90)

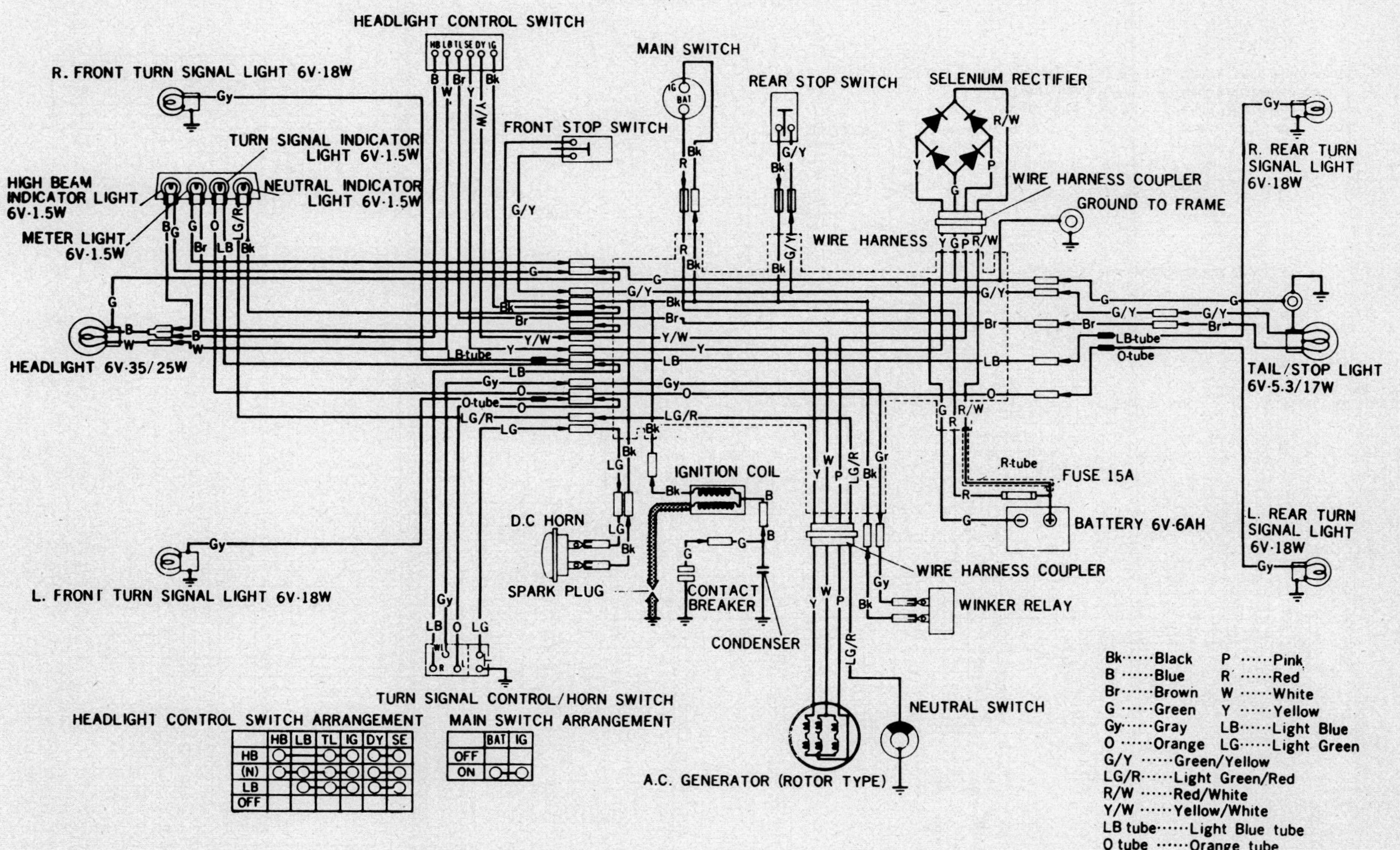
HEADLIGHT CONTROL SWITCH
MAIN SWITCH
REAR STOP SWITCH
SELENIUM RECTIFIER
R. FRONT TURN SIGNAL LIGHT 6V-18W
FRONT STOP SWITCH
TURN SIGNAL INDICATOR LIGHT 6V-1.5W
HIGH BEAM INDICATOR LIGHT 6V-1.5W
NEUTRAL INDICATOR LIGHT 6V-1.5W
METER LIGHT 6V-1.5W
R. REAR TURN SIGNAL LIGHT 6V-18W
WIRE HARNESS COUPLER
GROUND TO FRAME
WIRE HARNESS
HEADLIGHT 6V-35/25W
TAIL/STOP LIGHT 6V-5.3/17W
IGNITION COIL
FUSE 15A
D.C HORN
BATTERY 6V-6AH
L. REAR TURN SIGNAL LIGHT 6V-18W
L. FRONT TURN SIGNAL LIGHT 6V-18W
SPARK PLUG
CONTACT BREAKER
WIRE HARNESS COUPLER
WINKER RELAY
CONDENSER
TURN SIGNAL CONTROL/HORN SWITCH
HEADLIGHT CONTROL SWITCH ARRANGEMENT
MAIN SWITCH ARRANGEMENT
NEUTRAL SWITCH
A.C. GENERATOR (ROTOR TYPE)
Bk.....Black
B.....Blue
Br.....Brown
G.....Green
Gy.....Gray
O.....Orange
P.....Pink
R.....Red
W.....White
Y.....Yellow
LB.....Light Blue
LG.....Light Green
G/Y.....Green/Yellow
LG/R.....Light Green/Red
R/W.....Red/White
Y/W.....Yellow/White
LB tube.....Light Blue tube
O tube.....Orange tube

Wiring diagram (CB100)

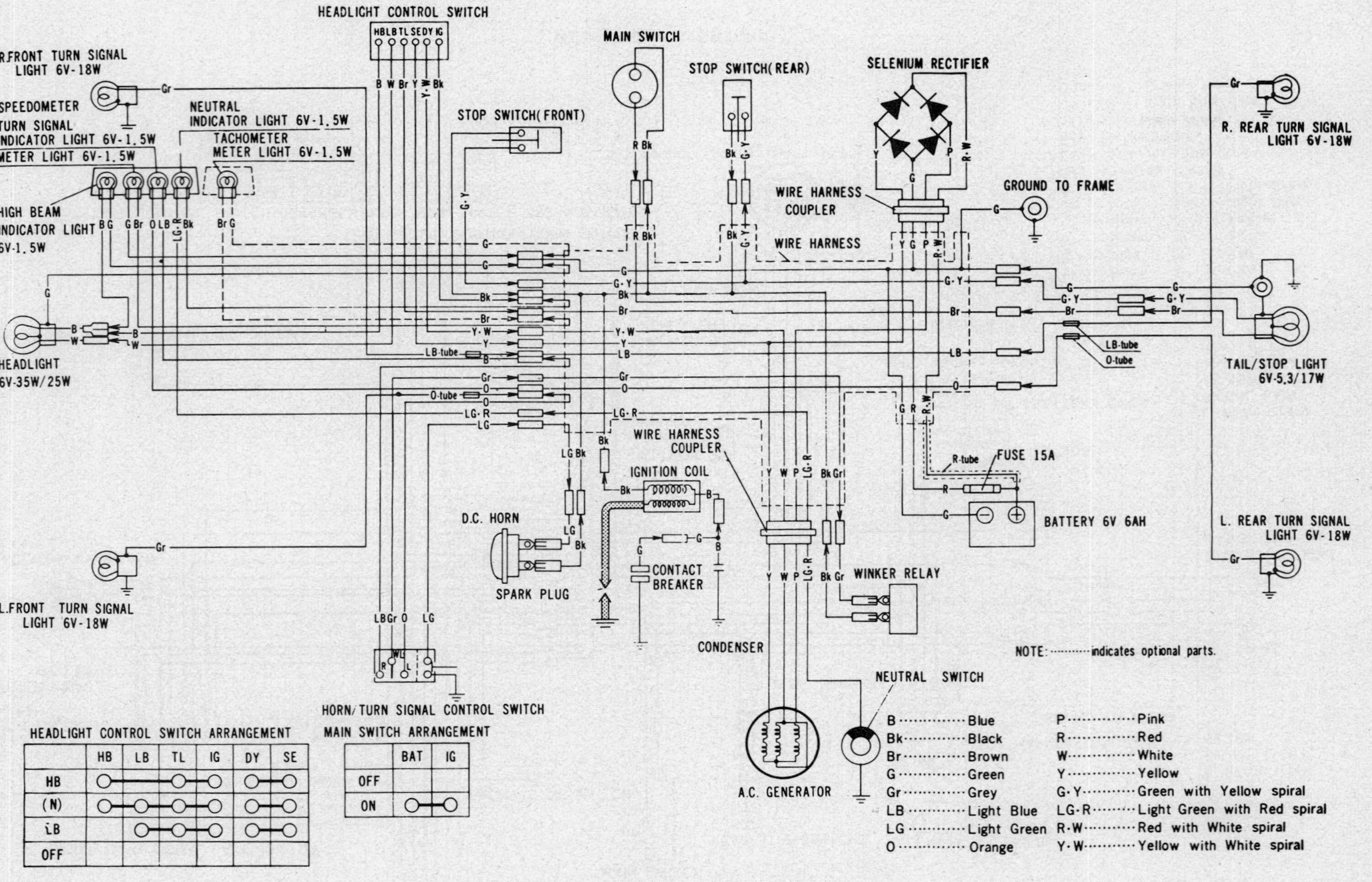

HEADLIGHT CONTROL SWITCH ARRANGEMENT

	HB	LB	TL	IG	DY	SE
HB	○——		——○	——○	○—	—○
(N)	○—	—○—	—○—	—○	○—	—○
LB		○—	—○—	—○	○—	—○
OFF						

MAIN SWITCH ARRANGEMENT

	BAT	IG
OFF		
ON	○—	—○

B .... Blue	P .... Pink
Bk .... Black	R .... Red
Br .... Brown	W .... White
G .... Green	Y .... Yellow
Gr .... Grey	G·Y .... Green with Yellow spiral
LB .... Light Blue	LG·R .... Light Green with Red spiral
LG .... Light Green	R·W .... Red with White spiral
O .... Orange	Y·W .... Yellow with White spiral

Wiring diagram (CL100)

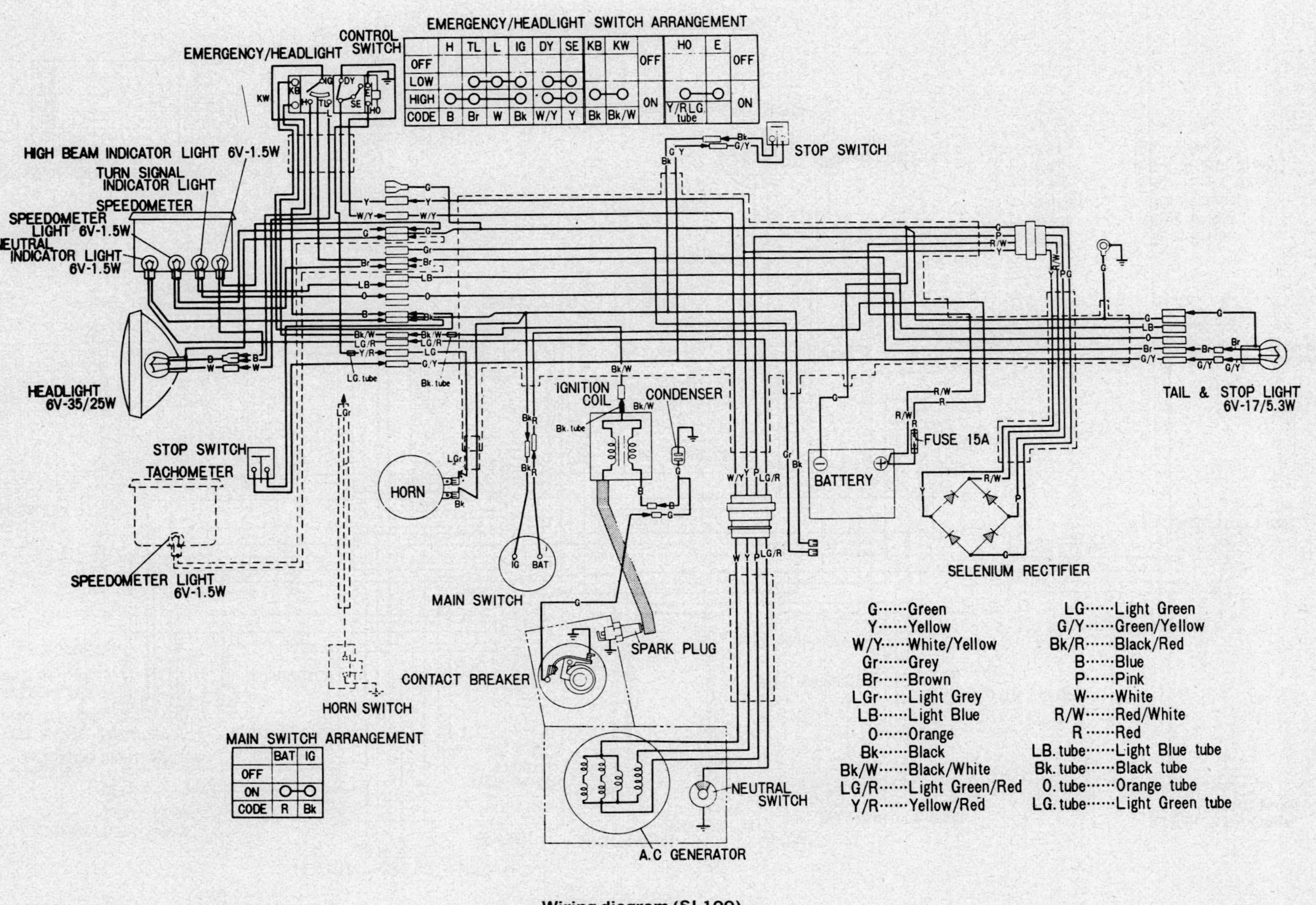
EMERGENCY/HEADLIGHT SWITCH ARRANGEMENT
CONTROL SWITCH
EMERGENCY/HEADLIGHT
HIGH BEAM INDICATOR LIGHT 6V-1.5W
TURN SIGNAL INDICATOR LIGHT
SPEEDOMETER
SPEEDOMETER LIGHT 6V-1.5W
NEUTRAL INDICATOR LIGHT 6V-1.5W
HEADLIGHT 6V-35/25W
STOP SWITCH
TACHOMETER
SPEEDOMETER LIGHT 6V-1.5W
HORN
IGNITION COIL
CONDENSER
MAIN SWITCH
SPARK PLUG
CONTACT BREAKER
HORN SWITCH
MAIN SWITCH ARRANGEMENT
A.C GENERATOR
NEUTRAL SWITCH
BATTERY
FUSE 15A
SELENIUM RECTIFIER
STOP SWITCH
TAIL & STOP LIGHT 6V-17/5.3W
G······Green
Y······Yellow
W/Y······White/Yellow
Gr······Grey
Br······Brown
LGr······Light Grey
LB······Light Blue
O······Orange
Bk······Black
Bk/W······Black/White
LG/R······Light Green/Red
Y/R······Yellow/Red
LG······Light Green
G/Y······Green/Yellow
Bk/R······Black/Red
B······Blue
P······Pink
W······White
R/W······Red/White
R······Red
LB. tube······Light Blue tube
Bk. tube······Black tube
O. tube······Orange tube
LG. tube······Light Green tube

Wiring diagram (SL100)

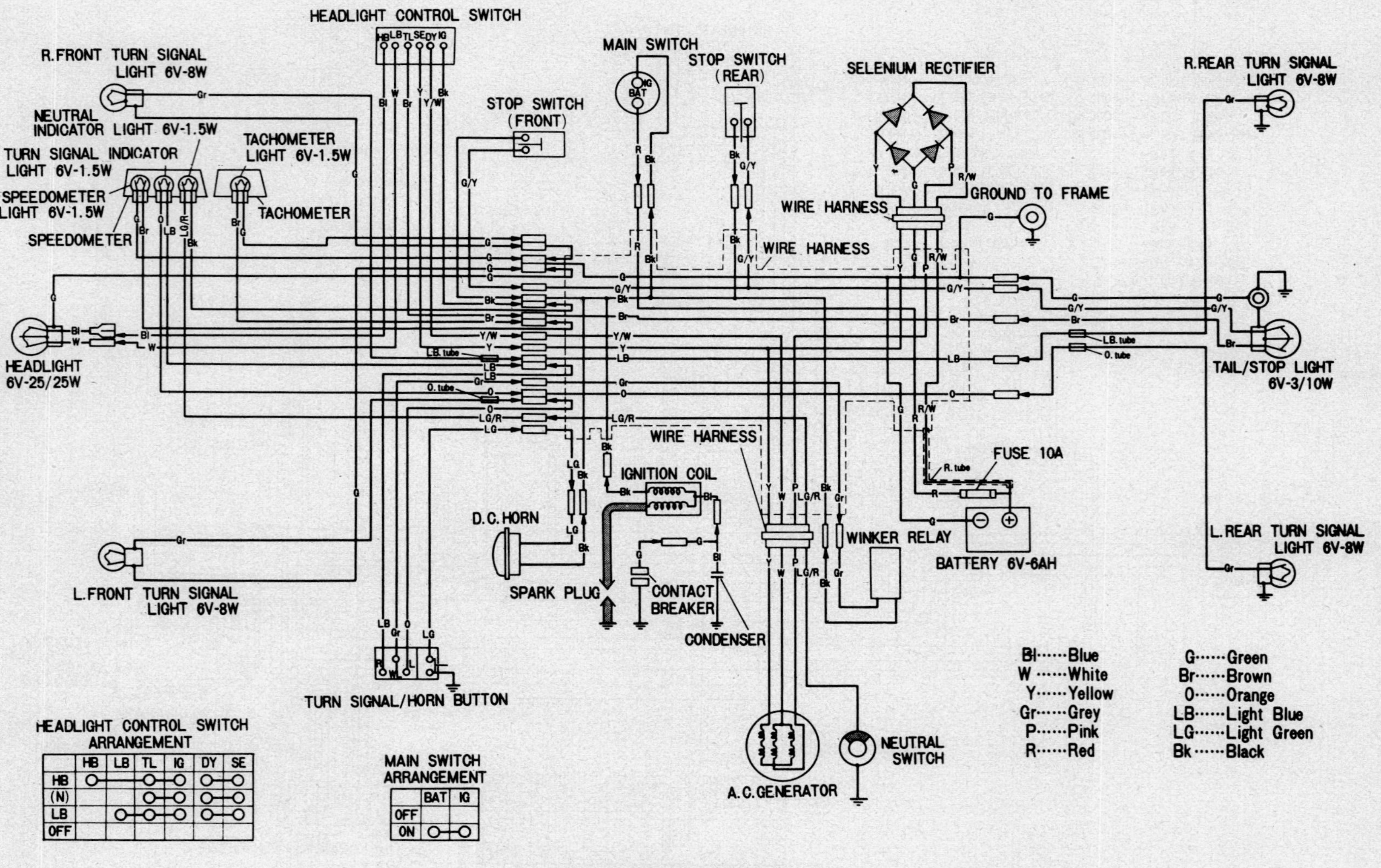
R.REAR TURN SIGNAL LIGHT 6V-8W
TAIL/STOP LIGHT 6V-3/10W
L.REAR TURN SIGNAL LIGHT 6V-8W
GROUND TO FRAME
FUSE 10A
BATTERY 6V-6AH
SELENIUM RECTIFIER
WIRE HARNESS
WIRE HARNESS
WIRE HARNESS
WIRE HARNESS
WINKER RELAY
NEUTRAL SWITCH
A.C.GENERATOR
STOP SWITCH (REAR)
MAIN SWITCH
IGNITION COIL
CONDENSER
CONTACT BREAKER
SPARK PLUG
STOP SWITCH (FRONT)
D.C.HORN
HEADLIGHT CONTROL SWITCH
TURN SIGNAL/HORN BUTTON
MAIN SWITCH ARRANGEMENT
TACHOMETER LIGHT 6V-1.5W
TACHOMETER
R.FRONT TURN SIGNAL LIGHT 6V-8W
NEUTRAL INDICATOR LIGHT 6V-1.5W
TURN SIGNAL INDICATOR LIGHT 6V-1.5W
SPEEDOMETER LIGHT 6V-1.5W
SPEEDOMETER
HEADLIGHT 6V-25/25W
L.FRONT TURN SIGNAL LIGHT 6V-8W
HEADLIGHT CONTROL SWITCH ARRANGEMENT
Bl.....Blue
W.....White
Y.....Yellow
Gr.....Grey
P.....Pink
R.....Red
G.....Green
Br.....Brown
O.....Orange
LB.....Light Blue
LG.....Light Green
Bk.....Black

Wiring diagram (CB125S)

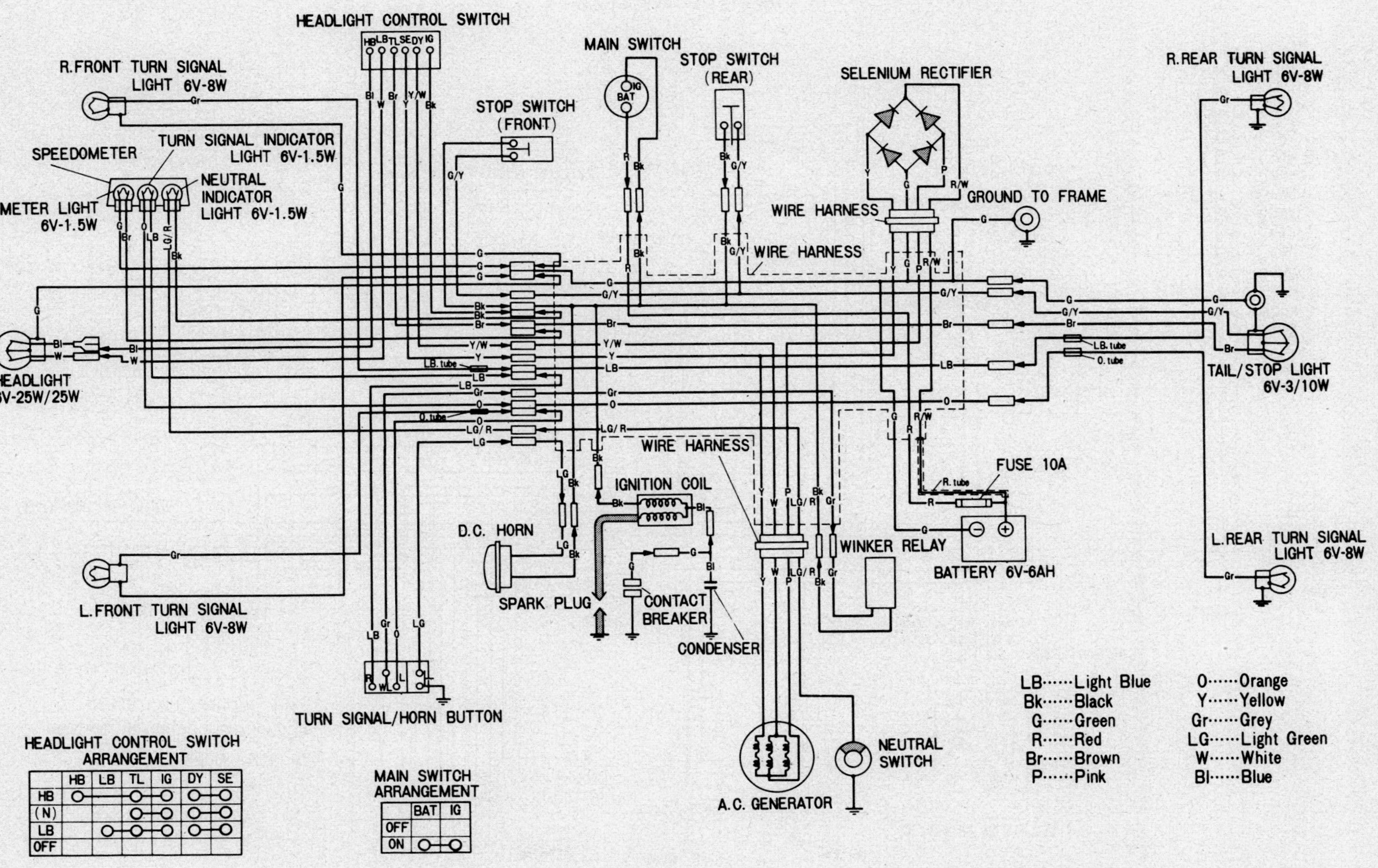

Wiring diagram (CD125S)

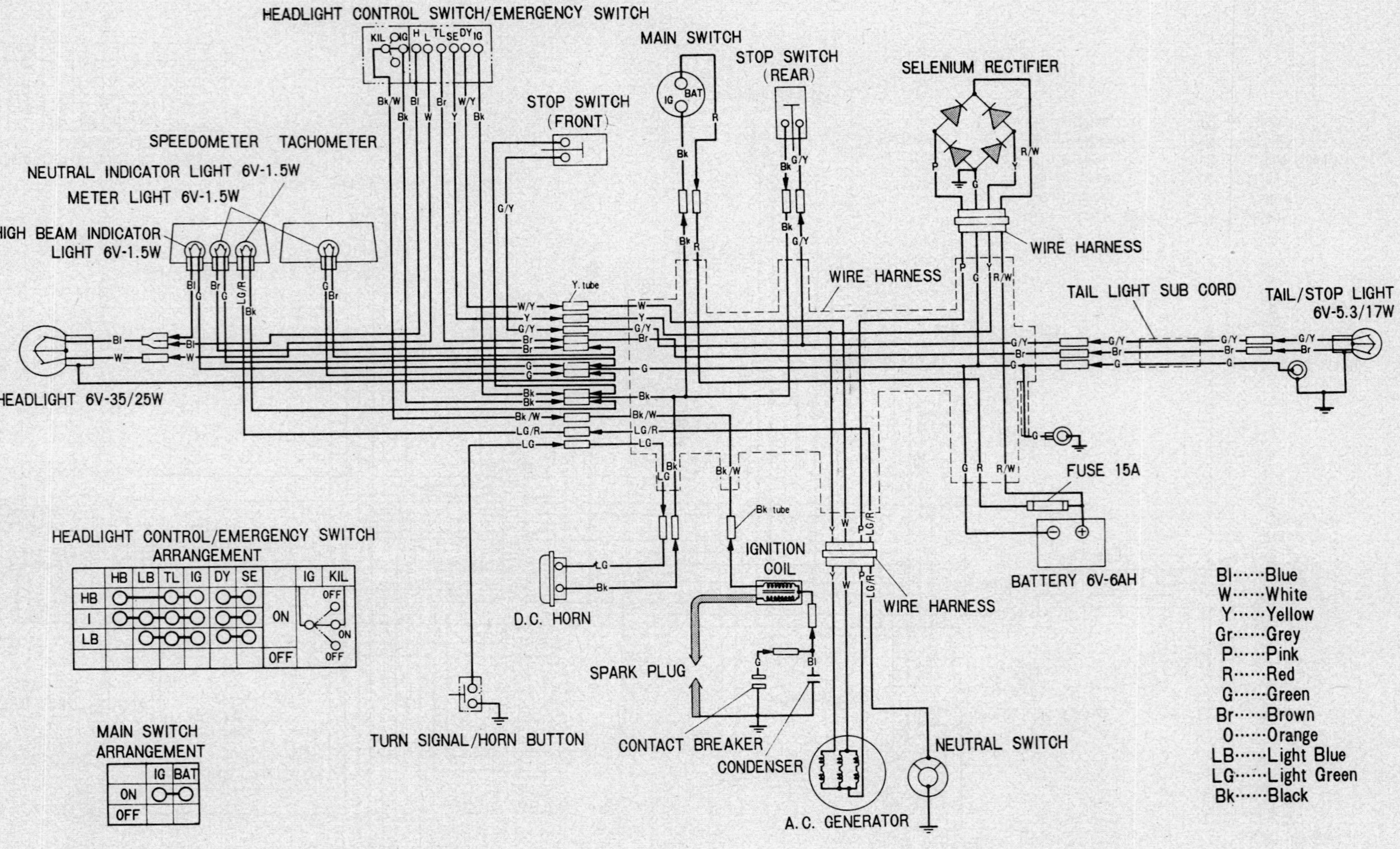
HEADLIGHT CONTROL SWITCH/EMERGENCY SWITCH
MAIN SWITCH
STOP SWITCH
(REAR)
SELENIUM RECTIFIER
STOP SWITCH
(FRONT)
SPEEDOMETER TACHOMETER
NEUTRAL INDICATOR LIGHT 6V-1.5W
METER LIGHT 6V-1.5W
HIGH BEAM INDICATOR
LIGHT 6V-1.5W
WIRE HARNESS
WIRE HARNESS
TAIL LIGHT SUB CORD
TAIL/STOP LIGHT
6V-5.3/17W
HEADLIGHT 6V-35/25W
FUSE 15A
HEADLIGHT CONTROL/EMERGENCY SWITCH
ARRANGEMENT
IGNITION
COIL
D.C. HORN
WIRE HARNESS
BATTERY 6V-6AH
SPARK PLUG
MAIN SWITCH
ARRANGEMENT
TURN SIGNAL/HORN BUTTON
CONTACT BREAKER
CONDENSER
NEUTRAL SWITCH
A. C. GENERATOR
Bl······Blue
W······White
Y······Yellow
Gr······Grey
P······Pink
R······Red
G······Green
Br······Brown
O······Orange
LB······Light Blue
LG······Light Green
Bk······Black

Wiring diagram (SL125)

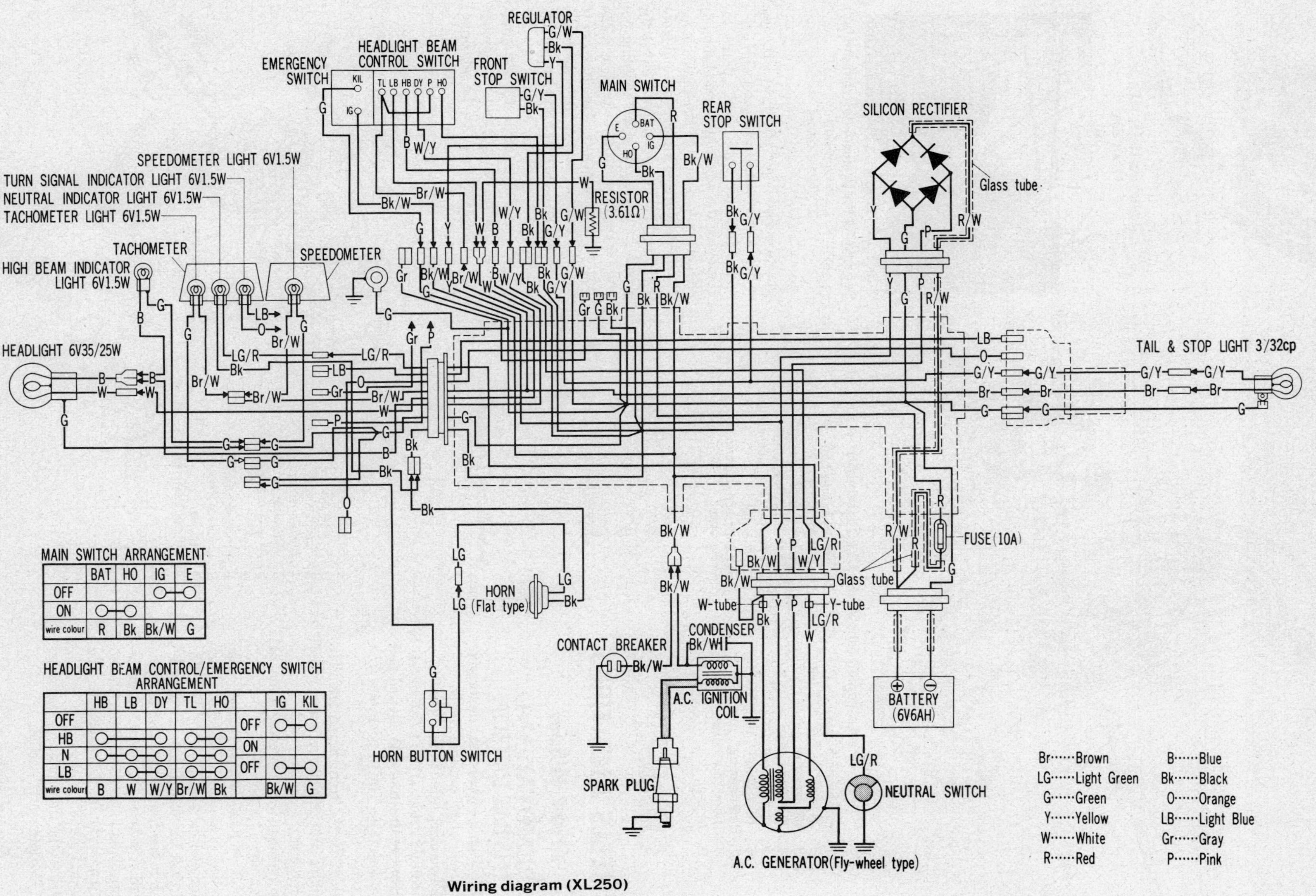

MAIN SWITCH ARRANGEMENT

	BAT	HO	IG	E
OFF			○	○
ON	○	○		
wire colour	R	Bk	Bk/W	G

HEADLIGHT BEAM CONTROL/EMERGENCY SWITCH ARRANGEMENT

	HB	LB	DY	TL	HO		IG	KIL
OFF						OFF	○	○
HB	○		○	○	○	ON		
N	○	○	○	○	○			
LB		○	○	○	○	OFF	○	○
wire colour	B	W	W/Y	Br/W	Bk		Bk/W	G

Wiring diagram (XL250)

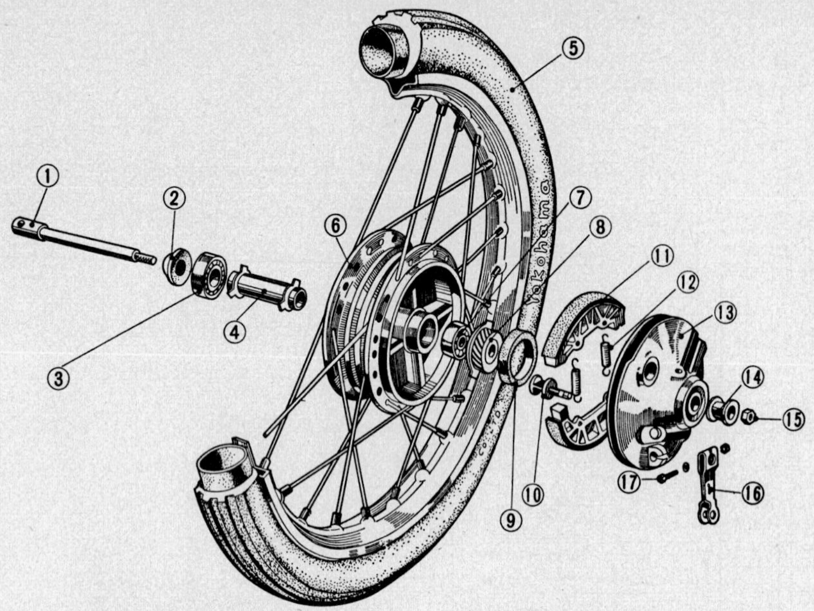

Front wheel assembly (shown is a CL90 assembly)

1. Front wheel axle
2. Oil seal
3. Ball bearing
4. Distance collar
5. Front wheel tire
6. Front wheel hub
7. Ball bearing
8. Speedometer gear
9. Oil seal
10. Front brake cam
11. Brake shoe
12. Brake shoe spring
13. Front brake panel
14. Front wheel side collar
15. Axle nut
16. Front brake arm
17. Hex bolt

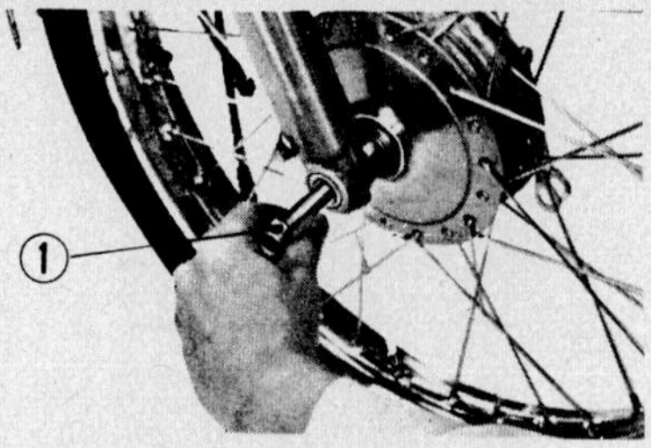

Removing the front axle
1. Front axle

Separating the brake panel from the hub
1. Wheel hub
2. Brake panel

CHASSIS

WHEELS AND TIRES

Front Wheel

REMOVAL AND INSTALLATION

1. Block up the front of the motorcycle so the front wheel can spin freely.
2. Disconnect the front brake and speedometer cables at the front wheel.
3. Remove the front axle nut and pull out the front axle. The wheel is now free to be removed.
4. Remove the front brake assembly by pulling free the front brake panel from the hub.
5. Installation is in the reverse order of disassembly.
6. Make sure the wheel is installed in such a way as to make installation of the speedometer cable easy.
7. Install the axle holder so the "F" mark is to the front and secure the nuts in rotation in the order depicted in the accompanying illustration. There should be no gap at the front between the axle holder and the fork slider.
8. Adjust the front brake as described in the "Maintenance" section.

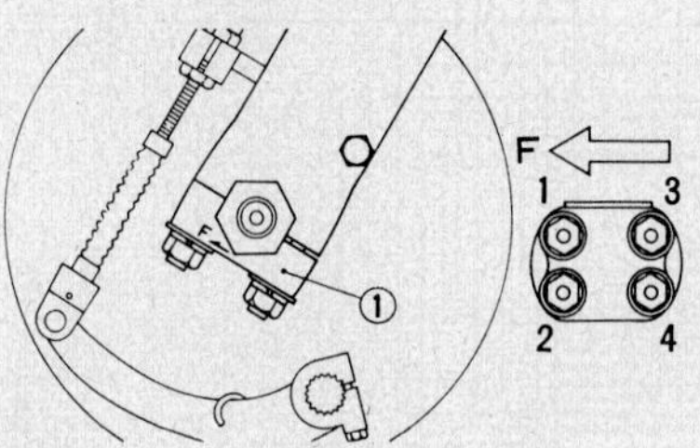

Securing the axle holder
1. Axle holder

Rear Wheel

1. Place the motorcycle on its center stand, or find some way to block the rear wheel up so that it can spin freely.
2. Disconnect the rear brake by removing the adjusting nut and slipping the brake rod out of the brake lever. Press down on the brake pedal and block the pedal's movement, then release the pedal. In this manner the adjusting nut will be kept free from damage as it can turn without resistance. Take care not to lose the cylinder which fits in the brake lever. Remove the rear brake torque link nut and disconnect the link.
3. Remove the muffler if it will interfere in pulling the axle out. Remember that the axle comes out on the side opposite the end on which the axle nut is fitted.

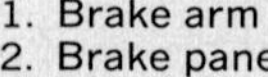

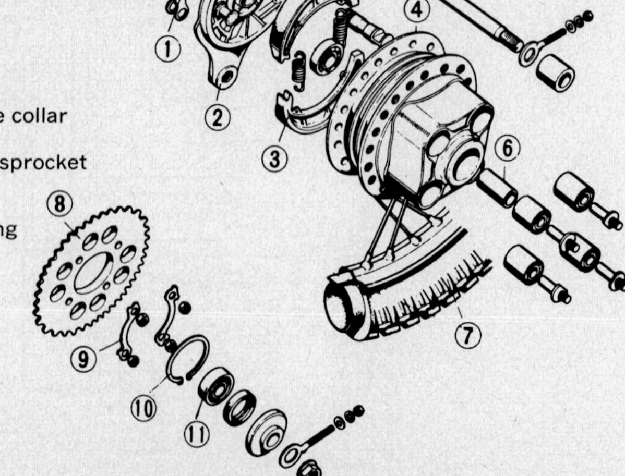

1. Brake arm
2. Brake panel
3. Brake shoe
4. Wheel hub
5. Wheel axle
6. Axle distance collar
7. Tire
8. Final driven sprocket
9. Lockwasher
10. Circlip
11. Wheel bearing

Rear wheel assembly (shown is CL90 assembly)

Removing the rear wheel

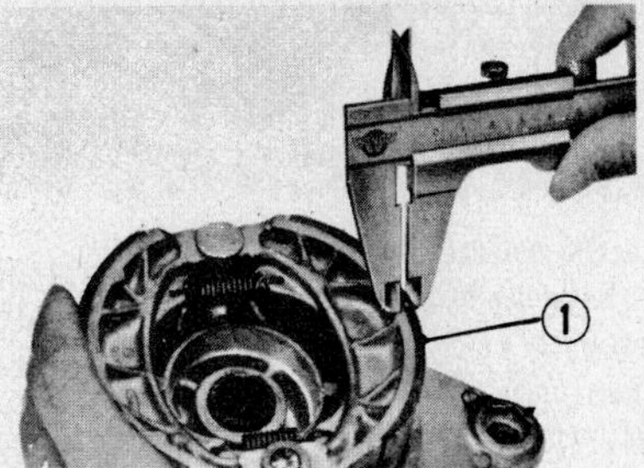
Measuring brake linings
1. Brake lining

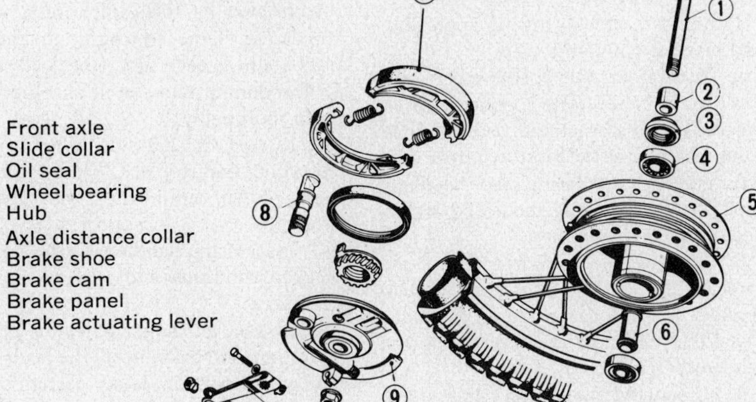

Front brake and hub assembly (shown is a CB100 assembly)

4. Loosen the chain adjusters and push the wheel as far forward as possible, then lift the chain off a few sprocket teeth, and rotate it until the chain comes off. If this fails you, you can still disconnect the master link.

5. Remove the axle nut and pull the axle out. The rear wheel is now free for removal, and the rear brake panel may be removed.

6. Installation is in the reverse order of disassembly. The closed end of the master link spring clip should be in the direction of normal rotation.

BRAKES

Shoe Replacement

(ALL MODELS)

1. Remove the wheel from the motorcycle as described in the "Wheels and Tires" section.

2. Remove the brake panel from the hub assemlby.

3. Measure the drum inside diameter with a vernier caliper and replace it, if out of true or if worn past its serviceable limit.

4. Remove the shoes by spreading them away from the panel and lifting them off.

5. Inspect the springs for a worn or damaged condition and replace them as necessary.

Measuring the hub inside diameter

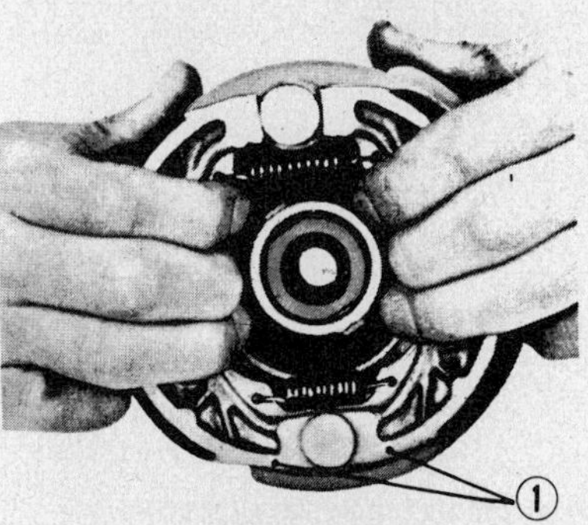
Removing the brake shoes
1. Brake shoes

6. Measure the brake linings and replace them if worn past their serviceable limit.

7. Install the brakes on the panel by attaching them together with the return springs, and pressing them into position on the panel.

8. Mount the drum and check to see if the entire surface of the shoe is contacting the drum. If both ends touch the drum, file down one end of the shoe until it only touches at one end.

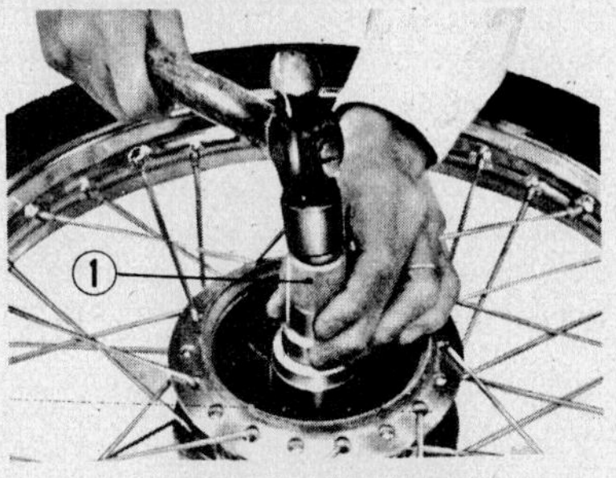
Installing wheel bearings
1. Bearing driver

9. If the brake squeals, you can either wait until it wears in or you can file down the shoe slightly as illustrated. Avoid removing too much of the shoe or the braking performance will be negatively affected.

10. Complete the assembly process in the reverse order of disassembly.

WHEEL BEARINGS

If the balls or races appear worn, pitted, or otherwise damaged, the bearing should be replaced. If the bearing's action when spinning on the axle is not smooth, the bearings should be repacked. If, after rechecking the bearing's motion, it still isn't smooth, the bearing should be replaced. Always replace bearings as sets.

Bearings are removed and replaced by drifting them out with a suitable drift (the rear sprocket will have to be removed to get at the rear wheel bearings). Make sure the spacer and bearing seals are well seated. This is also a good time to check the axle for a warped or bent condition. Spin the axle and check the run-out with a dial indicator, and replace it if the run-out exceeds 0.020 in. (0.5 mm). Always pack the bearings in fresh grease, and always replace the oil seal. Never spin an insufficently lubricated bearing as it may be damaged. You will find that lubricating the bearing with engine oil will make installation easier. Make sure you install the bearing distance collar when applicable.

SPROCKET REMOVAL AND INSTALLATION

To get at the countershaft sprocket the cover will have to be removed and the chain loosened or disconnected. The sprocket can can be unbolted after the locktabs (if applicable) are bent back. The final drive sprocket can be removed from the rear wheel hub only after the wheel has been removed. The disassembly procedure is quite straightforward and should present no problem. Consult the accompanying illustrations if you have any trouble remembering how to put it all back together once the sprockets have been exchanged. Use new locktabs whenever possible as these become fatigued quickly from repeated bending.

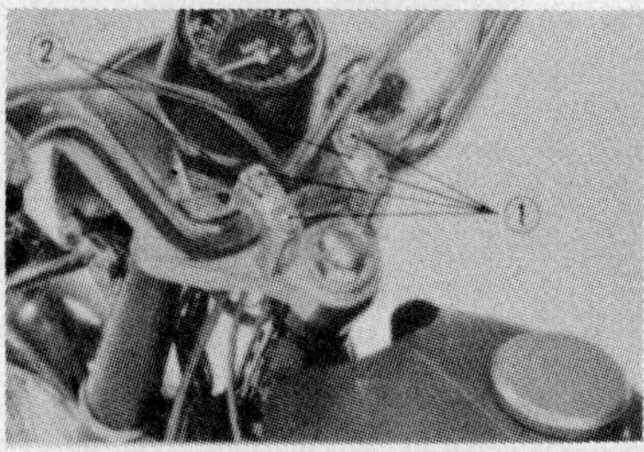

Removing the handlebar
1. 6 mm mounting bolts
2. Handlebar upper holders

On the CT90 models with frame numbers prior to CT 90-122550, both the final drive sprockets are mounted to the driven flange, and may be replaced independently of one another.

At this time it is advisable that you examine the rear hub dampers, bearings, and brakes since the rear wheel assembly will have to be taken down.

FRONT SUSPENSION

Handlebars

REMOVAL

1. Remove the fairing (if applicable) and place it out of the way.
2. Disconnect the speedometer and front brake cables. The speedometer cable can be disconnected at either the front wheel or at the point where it joins the speedometer inside the headlight shell. The brake cable should be disconnected at the handlever.
3. Unscrew the carburetor cap and carefully pull out the side assembly. Disconnect the throttle cable at the slide. The cable can now be disconnected at the handlebar.
4. Disconnect the clutch cable at the clutch lever. It may be necessary to adjust the cable to provide more slack.
5. Remove the headlight unit and disconnect the leads from the switches. The wires from the switch assemblies do not run through the handlebars on the XL-250 model, so merely separate the assembly halves and place them out of the way. It is not necessary to disconnect the electrical leads.
6. Disconnect and remove the handlebar assembly by removing the mounting hardware. On models with the pressed steel type of handlebar, the mounting points are on the bottom of the handlebar; on the steel tube type, the mounting bolts are at the center of the bars and are plainly visible.

Inspection And Repair

1. Inspect all the cables for a worn, kinked, or damaged condition and replace them as necessary. Check all cables for freedom of movement and lubricate them thoroughly.
2. Inspect the handlevers for smooth operation and replace, grease, or file them down until they do operate smoothly.
3. Inspect the handlebar for a bent or cracked condition and replace them as necessary.
4. Inspect all the switches for proper operation, and examine all the leads for a damaged condition. If any portion of the switch is damaged, it should be replaced. These units are designed with replacement rather than repair in mind. If it becomes necessary to replace a switch, you'll find it easiest if you lubricate the leads sleeve, tape the lead ends together, and pull the leads through the bars with a piece of mechanic's wire.

Installation

1. Position the handlebar lower holder, rubber bushings for the handlebars, the turn signals (if applicable), the handlebars, and the handlebar upper holder (if applicable). Temporarily secure the bars to make the rest of the procedures easier.
2. Lubricate the handlebar with fresh grease where the throttle grip rides. Connect the cables in the reverse order of removal. It helps to have as much play as possible when connecting the cables. The clutch and brake cables can be attached to the levers and then the levers can be installed. Adjust all cables as described in chapter two.
3. Connect all of the electrical leads inside the headlight shell, then install the light and make sure everything works correctly. The leads are color-coded to make connecting them simpler. In instances where there is a different colored plastic sheath over the female connector, or a different colored band near the male connector, the color of the sheath or band stands for a tracer color. On the XL-250 model, the wires will not have to be drawn through the handlebar and the leads will not have to be connected in the headlight shell unless for some reason

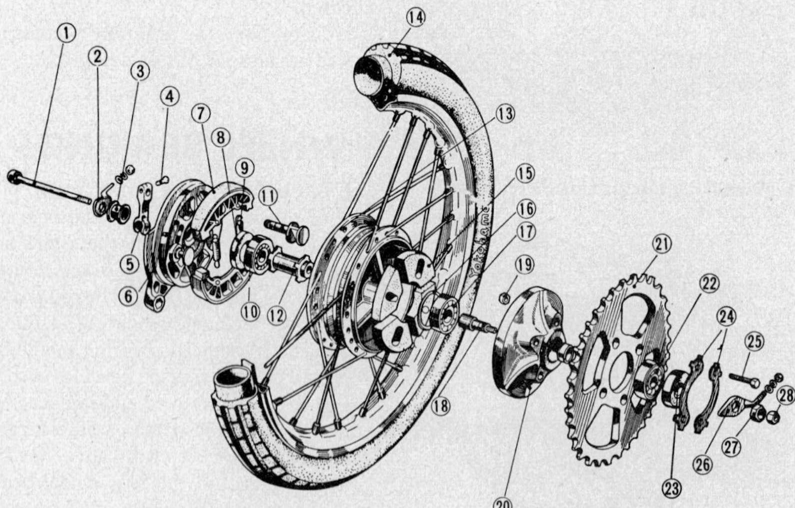

Drive sprocket and rear wheel assembly (shown is a CL90)

1. Rear wheel axle
2. Right drive chain adjuster
3. Rear brake panel side collar
4. Hex bolt
5. Rear brake arm
6. Rear brake panel
7. Brake shoe
8. Oil seal
9. Brake shoe spring
10. Ball bearing
11. Rear brake cam
12. Rear axle distance collar
13. Rear wheel hub
14. Rear wheel tire
15. Rear wheel damper
16. O-ring
17. Ball bearing
18. Rear axle sleeve
19. Thin nut
20. Final driven flange
21. Final driven sprocket
22. Ball bearing
23. Oil seal
24. Tongued washer
25. Driven sprocket setting bolt
26. Left drive chain adjuster
27. Rear axle sleeve nut
28. Axle nut

they have been disturbed. Make sure the wires are attached to the handlebar in such a way as to keep them out of the way.

4. Secure the handlebars. On the steel tube type models the serrated portion of the bars should be centered between the two holders and the punch mark should be at the junction of the two holder halves. Tighten down the securing bolts evenly.

Steering Stem

The front suspension units are attached to the frame at the steering stem. The forks ride on ball bearings which are located in cone-shaped races at the top and bottom of the steering stem itself. It is not necessary to disassemble the front suspension components to work on the stem, and if you can raise the front of the motorcycle enough, it is not even necessary to remove the front wheel (although this is the accepted practice).

Disassembly

LEADING LINK TYPE FORKS

1. Block up the mororcycle so the front wheel can be removed, then remove the front wheel.

2. Remove the handlebar assembly as described in the "Handlebars" section. It is not necessary to disconnect all of the cables, and you may wish to disconnect only those which will interfere with the removal of the forks.

3. Remove the headlight rim, lens, and case. The case is secured by two bolts and a screw on the inside.

4. Remove the steering stem head nut and the two, 8 mm bolts, then remove the fork top bridge.

5. Remove the steering head top thread using a suitable, 36 mm hook spanner or a suitable substitute.

6. Pull out the fork from the bottom of the steering head. Keep a pan ready to catch the steering head bearings as they will probably fall out of the bottom race.

TELESCOPIC TYPE FORKS

1. Remove the handlebar assembly as described in the "Handlebars" section.

2. Remove the two fork bolts and the steering stem nut, then remove the fork top bridge.

3. Remove the headlight rim, lens, and shell assemblies, then remove the left

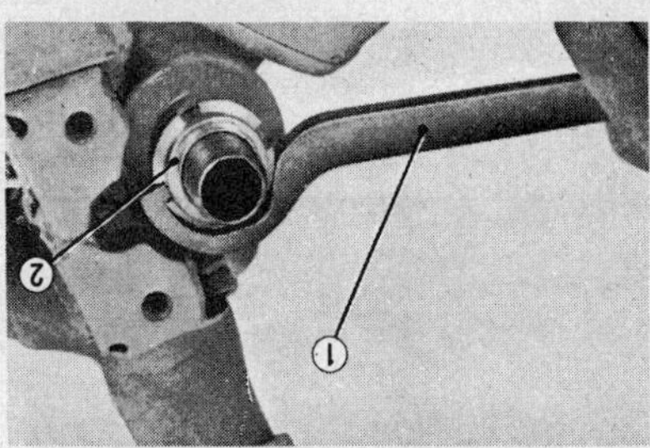

Removing the steering head top thread

1. 36 mm hook spanner
2. Steering head top thread

and right front fork cover if applicable.

4. Block up the motorcycle and remove the front wheel assembly, then remove the front fender. Remove the horn assembly between the two fork legs (if applicable).

5. Loosen the front cushion mounting bolts from the lower triple clamp, then drop out the front fork assembly.

6. Remove the steering head top thread using a suitable, 36 mm hook spanner or a suitable substitute, then pull the stem out through the bottom of the head. Keep a pan ready to catch the steering head bearings as they will probably fall out from the bottom race.

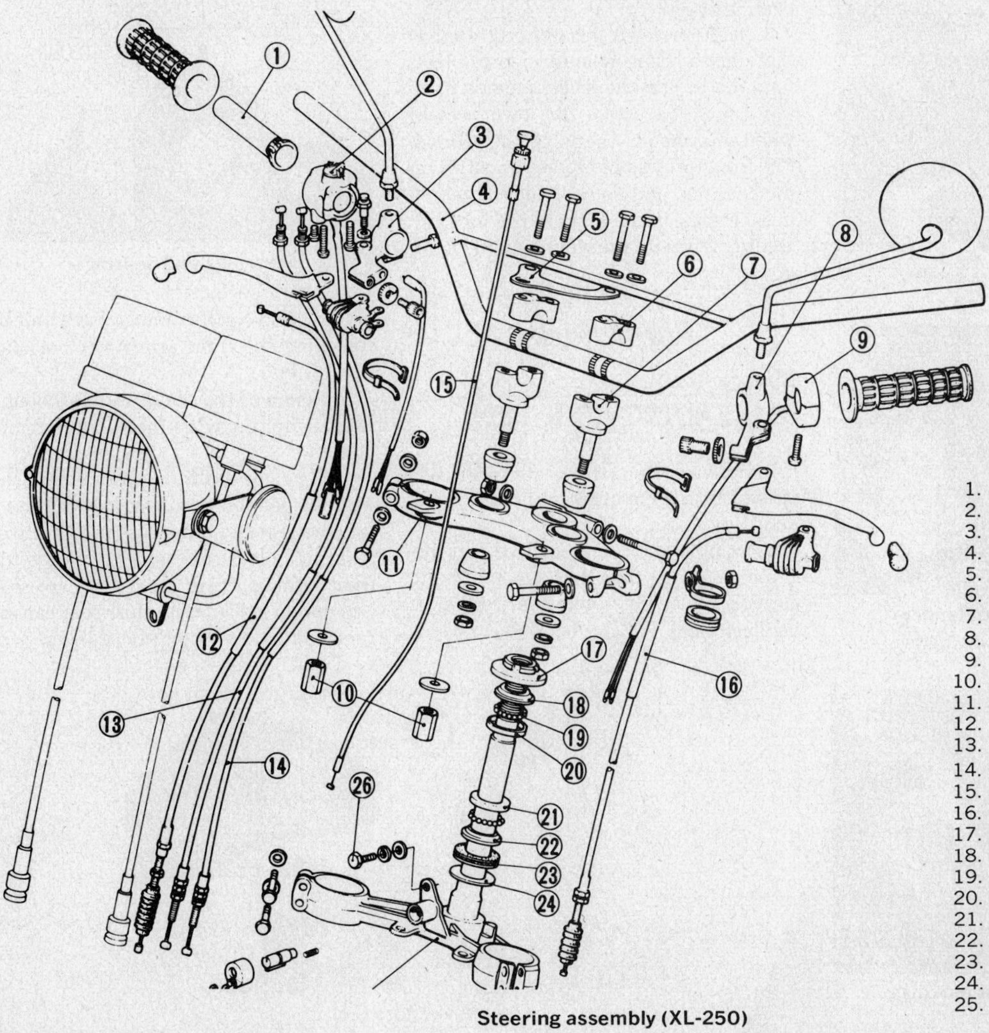

1. Throttle grip pipe
2. Switch housing
3. Handle lever bracket
4. Steering handle pipe
5. Cable holder
6. Handle holder (upper)
7. Handle holder (lower)
8. Handle lever bracket
9. Horn switch
10. Nut
11. Fork top bridge
12. Front brake cable
13. Throttle cable A
14. Throttle cable B
15. Choke cable
16. Clutch cable
17. Fork top thread
18. Top corn race
19. Steel balls
20. Top ball race
21. Bottom ball race
22. Bottom corn race
23. Dust seal
24. Dust seal washer
25. Steering stem

Steering assembly (XL-250)

Removing the front fork
1. Front fork

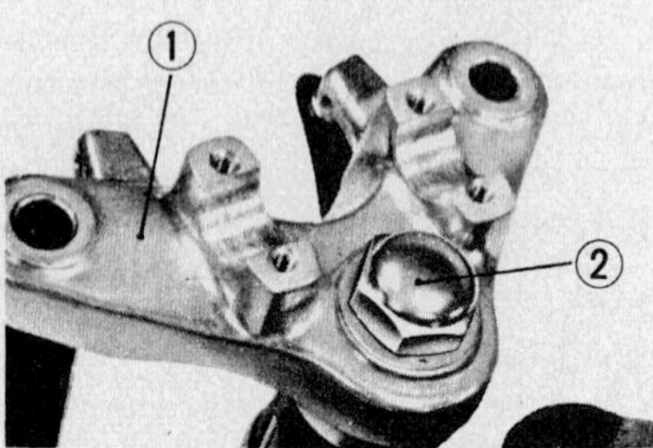
Removing the fork top bridge
1. Fork top bridge
2. Steering stem nut

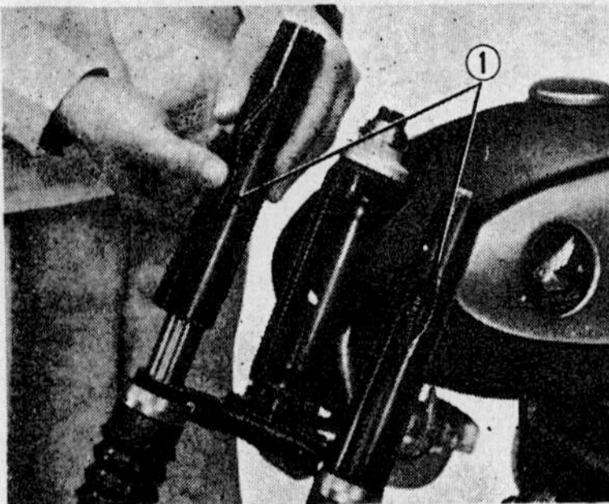
Removing the fork covers
1. Fork ears

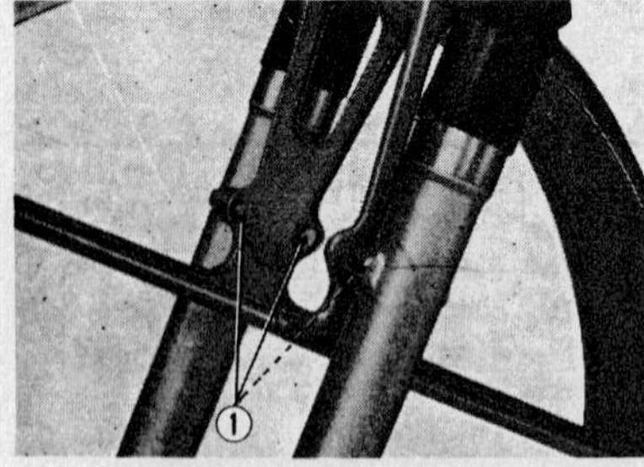
Removing the front fender
1. Fender mounting bolts

Removing the front fork legs
1. Fork legs

Inspection And Repair (All Models)

1. Clean all steering head components in a suitable solvent and blow them dry.

2. Inspect the bearings for a worn, damaged, or pitted condition, and replace them as necessary. Bearings must be replaced as complete sets.

3. Inspect the steering stem for a worn, warped, or otherwise damaged condition and replace it as necessary. In some cases the stem may be repaired. Consult your dealer for additional information.

4. Inspect the steering head top and bottom cone races for wear, score marks, deep scratches, or any other damage, and replace them as necessary by drifting them out from their opposite sides using a suitable drift. The new cone races are then drifted into position.

Assembly

1. Assembly is basically the reverse order of disassembly.

2. Install the steering stem bearings in the races after applying fresh grease to the races. There should be no more than 1–2 mm (0.040–0.080 in.) of clearance left between the bearings after they all have been installed.

3. Tighten down the steering stem so that only a slight amount of pressure is required to start the wheel moving in either direction under its own weight when the wheel is raised off the ground. The front forks should rotate smoothly on the bearings, and there should be no noticeable play in the forks in the fore and aft direction with the wheel raised off the ground.

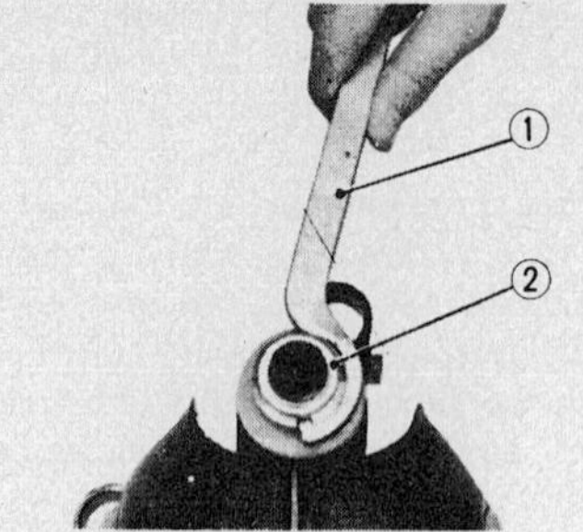
Removing the steering head top thread
1. 36 mm hook spanner
2. Steering headtop thread

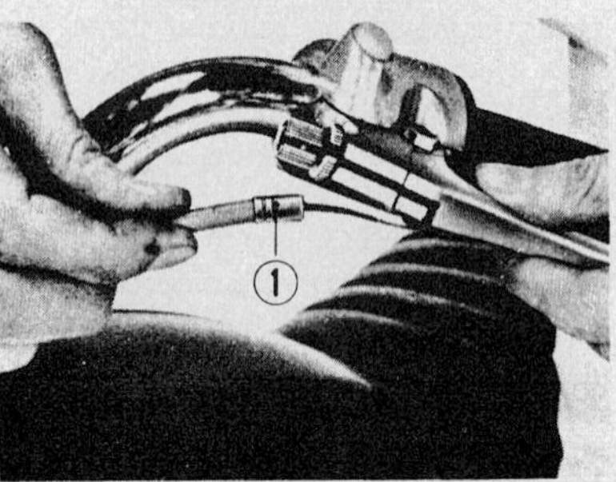
Removing the steering stem
1. Steering stem

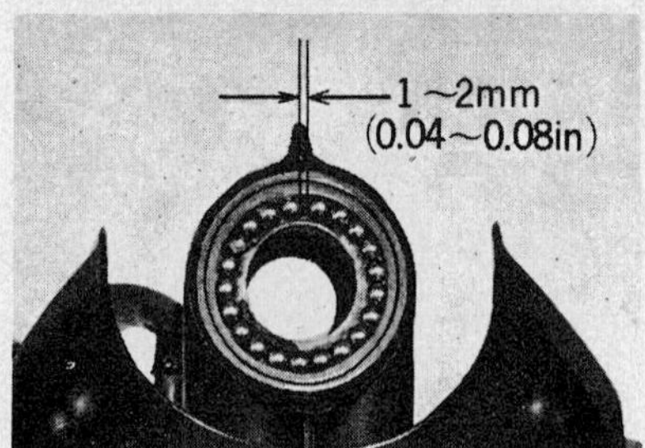

Steering head bearings

Front Forks

Disassembly

LEADING LINK TYPE FORKS

1. Remove the front wheel as described in the "Wheels and Tires" section.

2. Remove the 6 mm lockpin and the 7 mm locknut, then remove the front cushion joint washer and joint rubber A (as illustrated). The front cushion and suspension arm can be removed as a unit by removing the front arm pivot bolt and the hex bolt.

3. Remove the front arm rebound stopper by removing the 8 mm hex nut and bolt.

4. Separate the front cushion and the front suspension arm by removing the 8 mm hex nut and the front cushion lower securing bolt. Take care not to loose the front cushion lower dust seal cap, seal, and spacer collar. The dust seal can be removed by unlocking the staking.

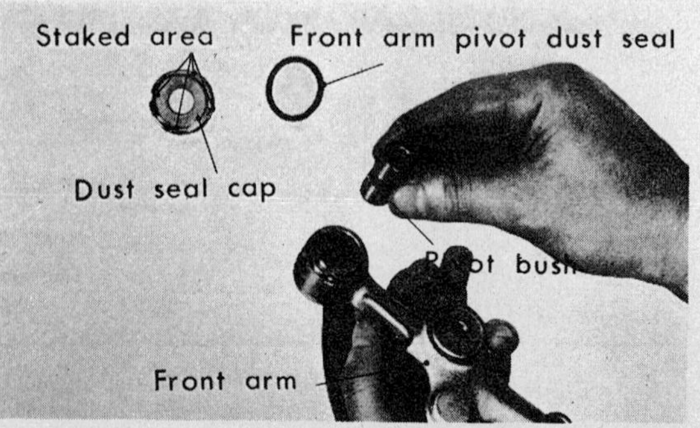

Pivot dust seal

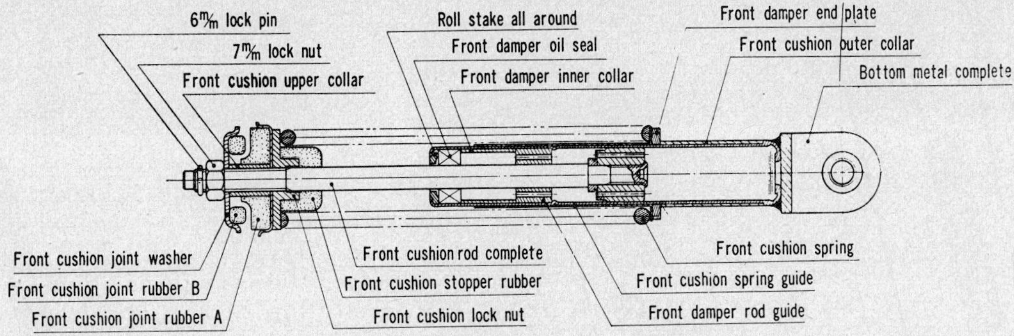

Front cushion sectional diagram

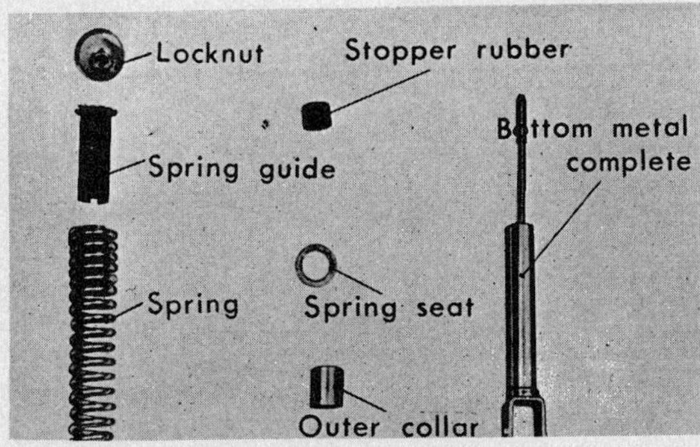

Cushion components

5. The suspension unit is now ready to be dismantled. The lower portion of the cushion is a sealed unit which cannot be rebuilt, and which must be replaced if weak or damaged. Disassemble the cushion by removing the locknut and spring. The spring guide, seat, stopper rubber, and outer collar are now free to be removed.

Inspection And Repair

1. Clean all parts in a suitable solvent and blow them dry. The dust seals should be replaced as a matter of course.

2. Inspect the damper unit for oil leaks, warpage, or inefficient damping characteristics, and replace it as necessary.

3. Inspect the suspension and fork components for a worn or damaged condition and replace them as necessary. If the fork legs are bent slightly they can usually be straightened. Consult your local dealer for additional information.

4. Measure the free-length of the spring and replace it if collapsed, worn, or damaged.

Assembly

1. Assembly is basically the reverse order of disassembly.

2. Lubricate the suspension arm with grease and apply engine oil to the dust seal.

3. Lubricate the assembly when the assembly process is complete, by applying grease through the grease fitting using an automotive type grease gun.

ALL MODELS EXCEPT XL-250

Disassembly

TELESCOPIC TYPE FORKS

1. Remove the handlebars, headlight assembly, and the fork top bridge. The fork ears are now free to be removed.

2. Raise the motorcycle so the front wheel can be removed, then remove the wheel and fender assemblies. The fender is secured by four hex bolts located on the fork legs.

3. Remove the fork pinch bolts from the lower triple clamp and pull the fork assemblies down and out of the clamp.

4. Allow the forks to drain into a suitable receptacle. The forks can be drained by merely inverting them.

5. Remove the fork book or spring cover and the associated cover mounting apparatus, then remove the spring and spring guide.

6. Remove the circlip using a set of snap-ring pliers, then remove the fork piston, stop-ring, and oil and dust seal assemblies from the fork legs. The fork tube can be separated from the fork by securing the fork leg to something and pulling sharply on the tube.

7. Make sure you keep the assemblies separate so they can be reassembled with their original fork legs.

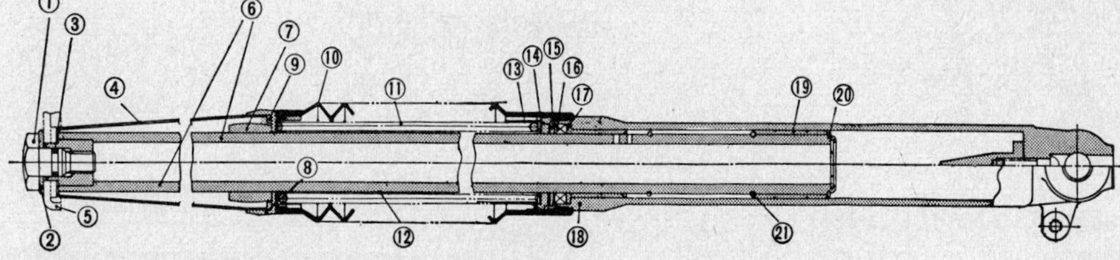

Front fork diagram (90 cc models except for the SL90)

1. Front fork filler bolt
2. Washer
3. O-ring
4. Front fork ear
5. Fork top bridge plate
6. Front fork leg
7. Fork bottom bridge
8. Fork cover lower seat
9. Fork cover lower seat packing
10. Front fork boot
11. Spring
12. Spring guide
13. Lower spring guide
14. Spring lower seat
15. Circlip
16. Front fork oil seal
17. Front fork leg guide
18. Front fork slider
19. Front fork piston
20. Front fork piston snap ring
21. Piston stopper ring

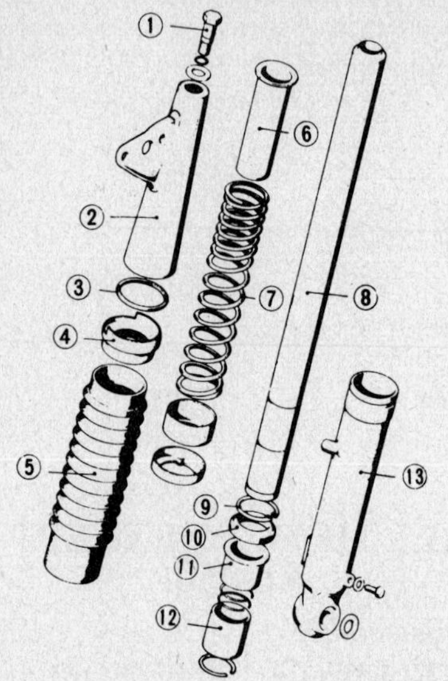

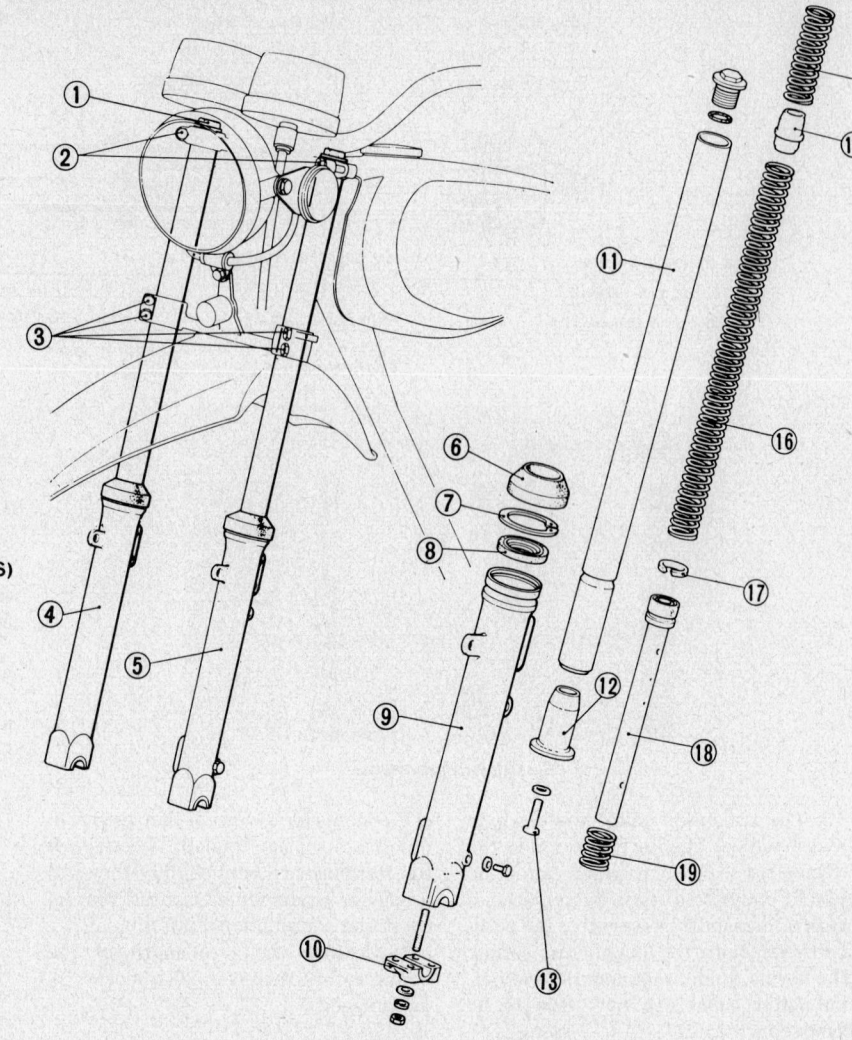

Front fork assembly (CB100 and CB125S)

1. Fork filler bolt
2. Fork ear
3. Fork ear lower seat bushing
4. Fork ear lower seat
5. Fork boot (CB models)/fork cover (CL and CD models)
6. Fork spring guide
7. Fork spring
8. Fork leg
9. Circlip
10. Fork oil seal
11. Fork leg guide
12. Fork piston
13. Fork slider

Front fork assembly

1. Front fork bolt
2. 8 mm bolt
3. 8 mm bolt
4. Right fork slider
5. Left fork slider
6. Dust seal
7. Circlip
8. Oil seal
9. Fork slider
10. Front axle holder
11. Fork tube
12. Oil lock piece
13. 8 mm socket bolt
14. Upper spring
15. Spring joint piece
16. Lower spring
17. Piston ring
18. Damper tube
19. Fork rebound spring

Front fork assembly (CL100 and CD125S)

1. Fork filler bolt
2. Fork ear
3. Fork ear lower seat bushing
4. Fork ear lower seat
5. Fork boot (CB models)/Fork cover (CL and CD models)
6. Fork spring guide
7. Fork spring
8. Fork leg
9. Circlip
10. Fork oil seal
11. Fork leg guide
12. Fork piston
13. Fork slider

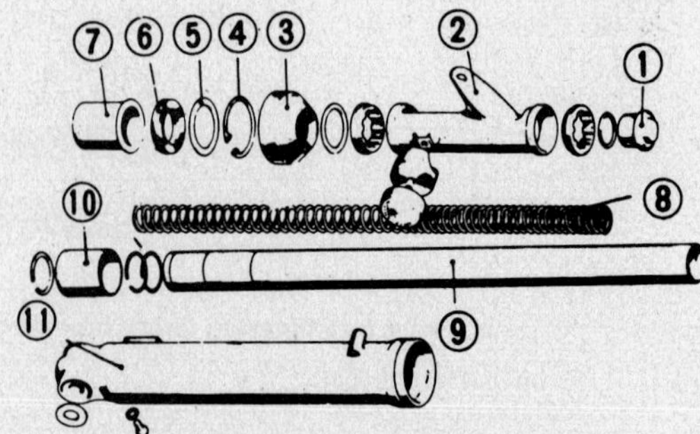

Front fork assembly (SL models)

1. Fork filler bolt
2. Fork ear
3. Fork dust seal
4. Circlip
5. Backup ring
6. Oil seal
7. Fork leg guide
8. Fork spring
9. Fork leg
10. Fork piston
11. Fork slider

1. Fork filler bolt
2. Pinch bolt

Disassembling the forks

Removing the circlip
1. Circlip

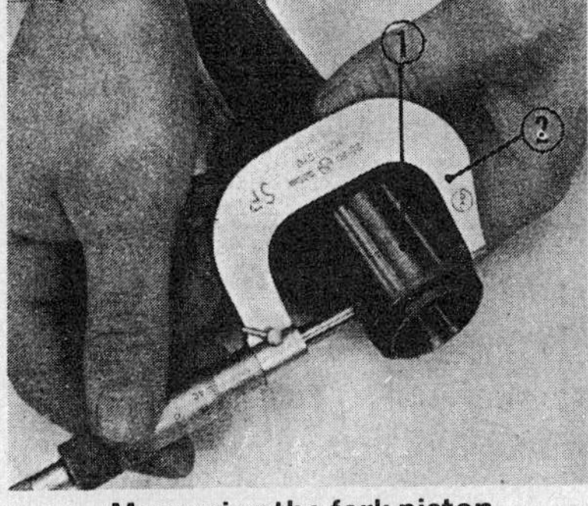

Measuring the fork piston
1. Fork piston
2. Micrometer

XL-250

1. Remove the front wheel and fender assemblies, then drain the fork oil after removing the filler caps and drain plugs from each fork.

2. Remove the 8 mm Allen head screw from the bottom of each slider, then remove the slider by pulling sharply down on it.

3. Loosen the 8mm pinch bolts located at the top and bottom triple clamps.

4. Remove the fork springs and bottom pipes from the top of each tube, then remove the tubes from the triple clamps. This will be difficult if the pinch bolts have not been sufficiently loosened.

5. Complete the disassembly by removing the dust seal, circlip, and oil seal from each of the fork sliders, taking care not to damage the slider lip while prying free the seals.

Inspection And Repair

1. Clean all parts other than the oil seals in a suitable solvent, and blow them dry. The oil seals must be handled gently if you intend to reuse them, but if possible they should be replaced whenever they are removed.

2. Inspect all the components for an obvious worn or damaged condition and replace them as necessary.

3. Insepct the front spring for a worn, collapsed, or damaged condition and replace it if necessary. The spring should be replaced if shorter than the specified free-length, or if tilted at a greater than acceptable angle.

4. Inspect the fork piston for wear or damage and replace it if worn past its serviceable limit. The piston should be measured with a micrometer.

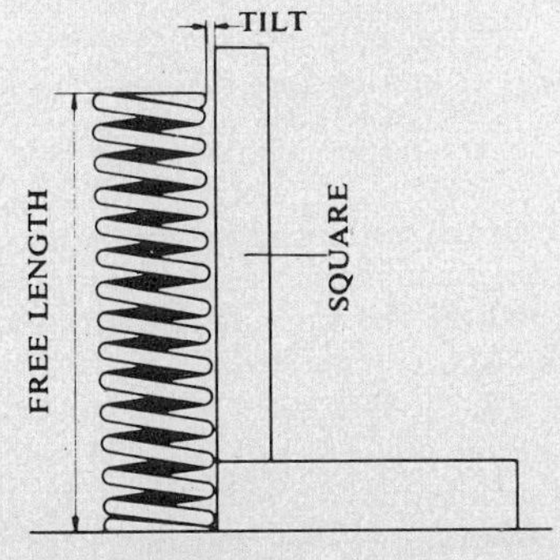

Spring inspection

5. Carefully inspect the circlips and oil and dust seals if you plan to reuse them.

ALL MODELS EXCEPT XL-250

Assembly

1. Assembly is basically the reverse order of disassembly.

2. Apply petroleum-resistant grease, or a suitable substitute, between the main and dust lips of the front oil seal, then install the seal into the bottom of the fork leg. An oil seal driving guide (tool no. 07054–07401) is available to prevent damage to the seal while driving it into the fork leg.

3. Install the circlips into their respective grooves, making sure they are correctly seated in the groove.

4. On internal spring type forks, install the spring into the fork leg so the smaller pitch of the spring is at the bottom of the fork leg. On the exposed type forks, and on the SL 100 and 125, install the spring with the larger pitch to the bottom of the fork leg.

5. Install each fork leg through the triple clamps so the top of the tube is flush with the top of the fork bridge. Remember to install the rubber boot or dust cover, and position the fork ears before running the fork tubes through the clamps. A fork leg puller is available to assist in the operation but is not essential.

6. Slip the axle into position to align the forks, then secure the pinch bolts at the lower triple clamp. The pinch bolts must be secure when the filler bolts are installed. The filler caps can be used to draw the fork tubes into position.

7. When the forks are completely installed and assembled, fill each fork tube with the recommended amount of fork oil, then make all necessary adjustments to the controls.

8. Check the operation of the forks by applying the front brake severely, without locking it, while exerting very little pressure on the handlebars. If everything else is in alignment, the forks should dip down evenly and the bike shouldn't tend to swerve to either side.

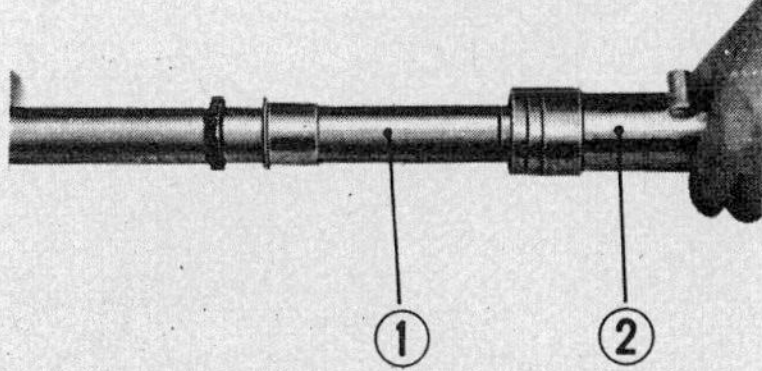

Assembling the fork leg into the slider
1. Fork leg
2. Fork slider

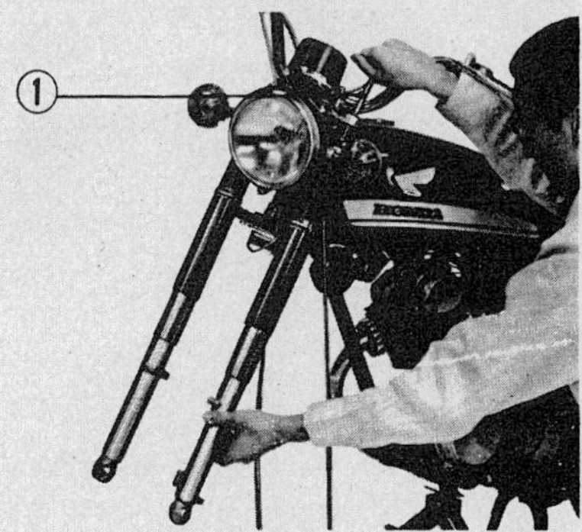

Installing the forks
1. Fork puller

Aligning the forks

XL-250

1. Clean all parts thoroughly with a suitable solvent, then coat them all with assembling oil before installing them. The lips of the oil seals should be lubricated with ATF (automatic transmission fluid) or petroleum jelly as an aid in installation.

2. Position the seal on the slider, insert the fork tube as a guide for the Honda seal driver tool (Tool no. 07054–32901), then seat the seal in the slider. If the tool is not available, a suitable drift such as a socket whose diameter is slightly smaller than the slider, can be used. If the fork tube has been used as a guide, remove it now.

3. Assemble the circlip and dust seal to each fork slider.

4. Slip the fork tube into the fork slider, then insert the rebound spring, bottom pipe, cushion spring (B), joint piece, and cushion spring (A) into the fork tube.

5. Position a washer on the Allen screw which is to be inserted in the bottom of the slider, coat the threads with a suitable thread locking compound, then install and secure the screw.

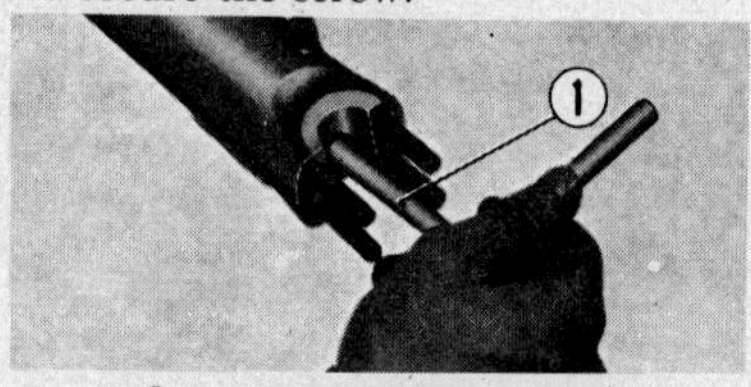

Securing the Allen screw
1. Hollow set wrench

Removing the rear shock absorber
1. Cap nuts
2. Shock absorber

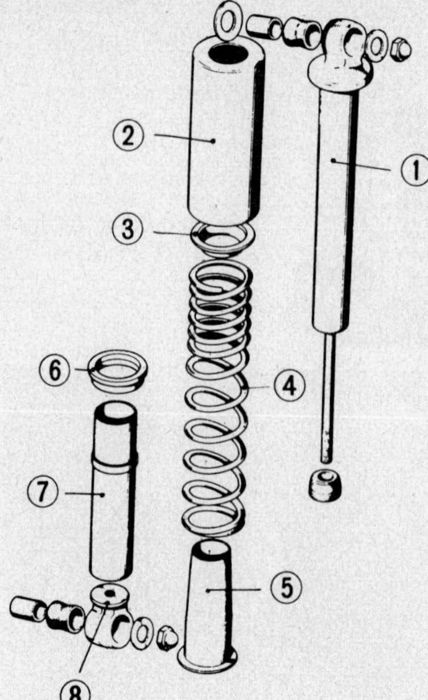

Covered spring type rear shock assembly (shown is a CB100 unit)
1. Shock Absorber unit
2. Upper case
3. Upper seat
4. Spring
5. Spring guide
6. Spring seat
7. Lower seat
8. Bottom mounting eye

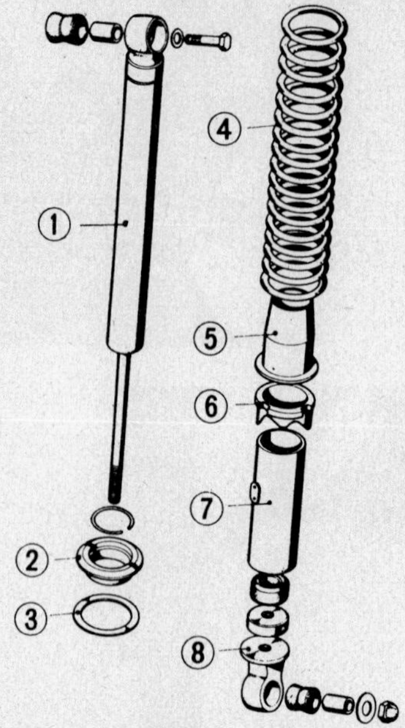

External spring type rear shock assembly (shown is a SL100 unit)
1. Shock absorber unit
2. Spring seat stopper
3. Spring upper seat
4. Spring
5. Spring guide
6. Spring adjuster
7. End case
8. Bottom mounting eye

6. Install the fork assembly into the triple clamp, then secure it when properly aligned for the type of riding the machine is to be used for.

7. Fill the fork tubes with the appropriate amount of fork fluid or ATF, which is the lubricant recommended by the manufacturer. When the the lubricant recommended by the manufacturer. When the of fluid rather than the 145cc (4.9 oz) which they take when the fluid is just changed.

REAR SUSPENSION

Rear Shock Absorbers

To check the effectiveness of the shock absorber, compress and extend it by hand (after the spring has been removed of course). More resistance should be encountered on the extension stroke than on the compression stoke if the shock is operating correctly. Replace the unit if leaking or if the damping is unsatisfactory.

Disassemble the shock after removing it from the two mounting studs by setting

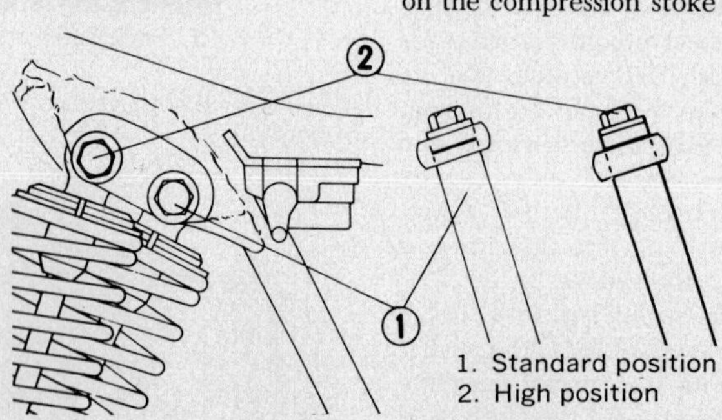

1. Standard position
2. High position

Suspension positions

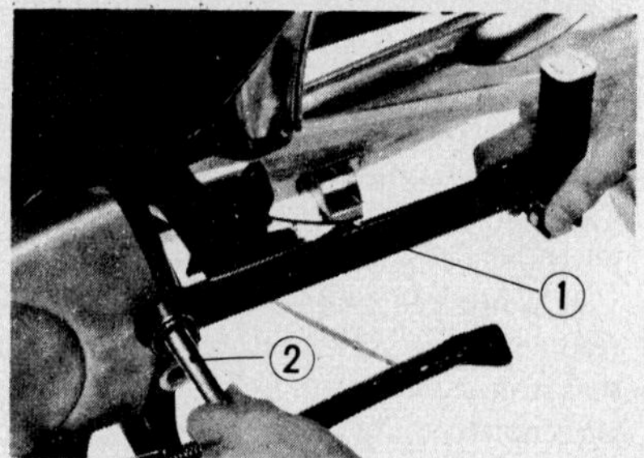

Removing the swing arm assembly (shown is a CB100)
1. Swing arm
2. Pivot bolt

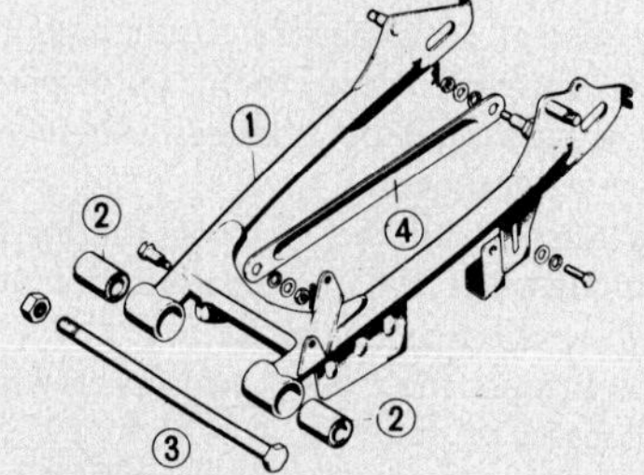

Swing arm assembly (shown is the fork from a CB100)
1. Swing arm
2. Pivot rubber bushing
3. Pivot bolt
4. Rear brake anchor

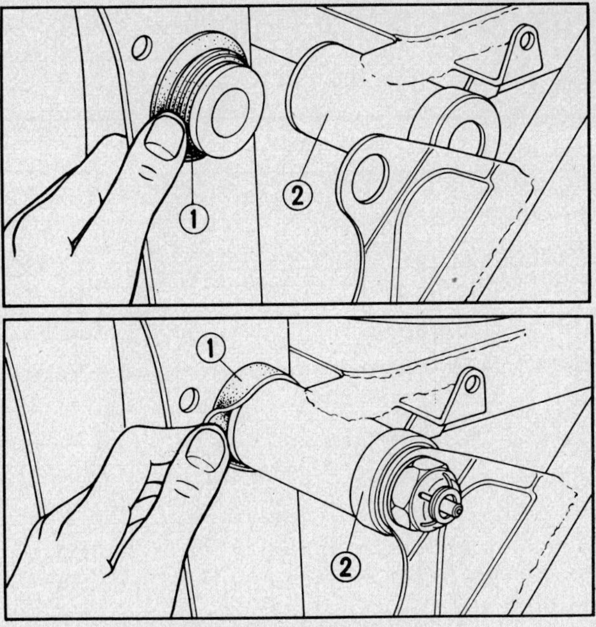

Installing the dust seal
1. Dust seal 2. Rear fork

it on the softest adjustment, then compressing the spring by hand until the locking nut can be removed. The shock can usually be compressed by one person, but it is a good idea to have someone there to remove the locking nut. Replace any worn or broken parts, and replace the spring if collapsed or if shorter than the specified length. When reassembling the shock, always install the spring so the smaller pitch of the coil is down as positioned on the bike.

Rear Swing Arm

Disassembly

1. Place the motorcycle on its centerstand and remove the rear wheel and drive chain. If the machine has a chaincase, that too must be removed.
2. Remove the lower mounting bolts from the shock absorbers and detach the units from the swing arm.
3. Remove the fork pivot bolt nut and pull the pivot bolt out. The swing arm is now free to be removed.

Inspection And Repair

1. Clean all parts in a suitable solvent and blow them dry.
2. Replace all the bushings and the chaincase (if applicable) gasket. The bushings may be reused but as long as you've got it all apart you may as well replace them. If you decide to retain the bushings, use them only if they are in perfect condition, and exhibit no signs of wear, cracking, or age.
3. Inspect the fork pivot bolt for a scored, warped, or otherwise damaged condition, and replace it as necessary. Rolling the bolt on a perfectly flat surface will indicate whether or not it is out of true.

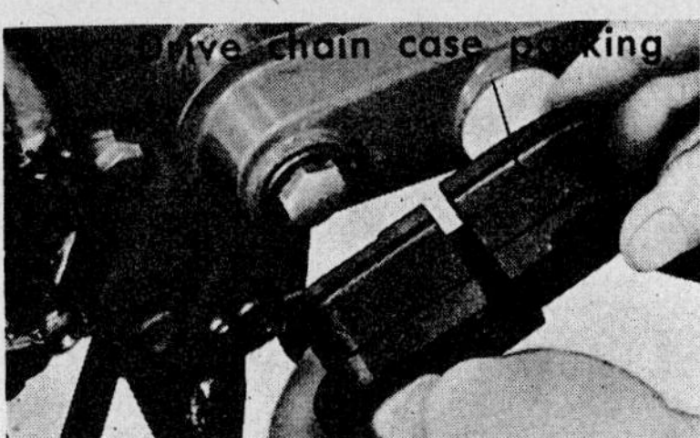

Installing the chaincase packing

4. Inspect the swing arm for cracks, bends, signs of fatigue, warping, or damage, and replace it as necessary. If the fork is slightly bent, it can be repaired.

Assembly

1. Assembly is basically the reverse order of disassembly.
2. Thoroughly grease the rubber bushings before installing them in the fork, and grease the pivot bolt before installing it in the frame. On the XL-250 the fork center collar must be greased before assembly.
3. Make sure the chaincase packing (if applicable) is correctly seated before you install the case.
4. On the XL-250 install the dust seal so the lip seats smoothly as illustrated.

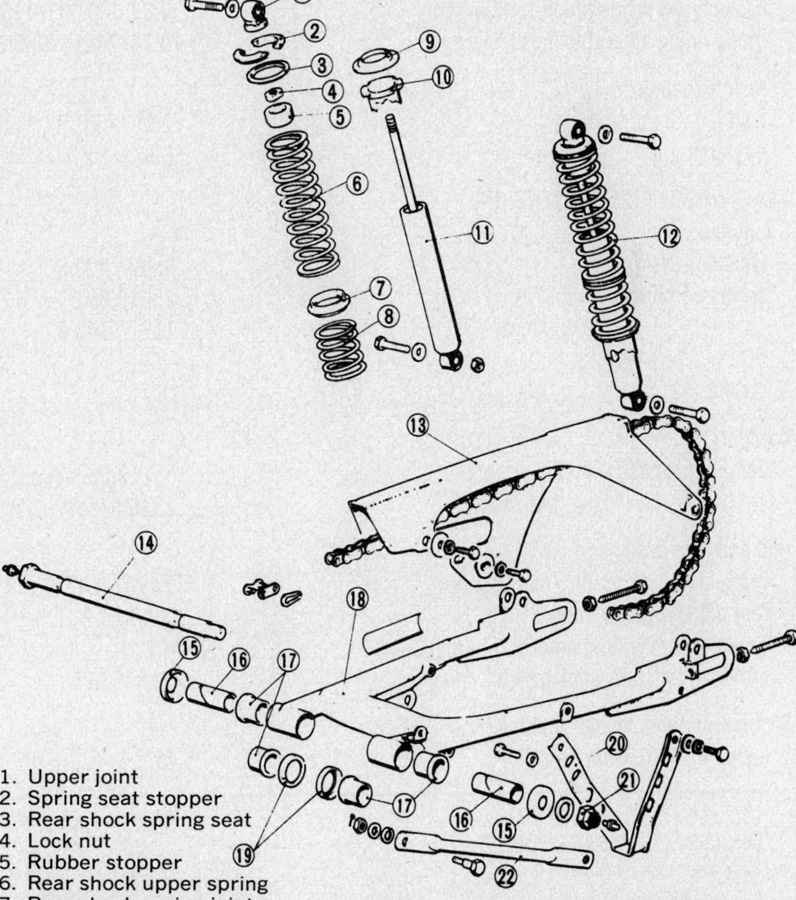

1. Upper joint
2. Spring seat stopper
3. Rear shock spring seat
4. Lock nut
5. Rubber stopper
6. Rear shock upper spring
7. Rear shock spring joint
8. Rear shock lower spring
9. Lower spring seat
10. Spring adjuster
11. Rear damper
12. Rear shock absorber assembled

Rear suspension assembly (XL-250)

13. Drive chain case
14. Rear fork pivot bolt
15. Dust seal rubber
16. Rear fork center collar
17. Fork pivot bushing
18. Rear fork
19. Dust seal cap
20. Chain guide
21. Self lock nut
22. Rear brake anchor

CHASSIS SPECIFICATIONS

C50, C50M, S50, C65, C65M, S65

	Standard Value	Serviceable Limit
FRONT WHEEL AND SUSPENSION		
Cushion spring:		
free-length (in./mm)	5.14/130.7	4.72/120.0
spring compression (lbs/in.)	220.0/3.63	198/3.35
(kg/mm)	100.0/92.1	90.0/92.1
tilt	1°30′	4°
Damper:		
damping capacity (lbs/in./sec)	66-77/19.68/sec	——
(kg/mm/sec)	30-35/0.5/sec	——
Fork piston and bottom case:		
piston diameter (in./mm)	N.A.	N.A.
case inside diameter (in./mm)	N.A.	N.A.
stroke (in./mm)	N.A.	N.A.
damping capacity	N.A.	N.A.
Hub and axle assembly:		
front axle diameter (in./mm)	0.400/10.0	N.A.
front axle bend (in./mm)	0.008/0.2	0.02/0.5
brake drum inside diameter (in./mm)	4.33 ± 0.008/110.0 ± 0.2	4.33/100.0
brake lining shoe thickness (in./mm)	0.1417-0.1476/3.6-3.75	0.984/2.5
Steering geometry:		
trail length (in./mm)	2.95/75.0	——
caster angle	63°	——
REAR WHEEL AND SUSPENSION		
Cushion spring:		
free-length (in./mm)	9.260/209.8	7.874/200.0
spring compression (lbs/in.)	256/5.512	234/5.512
(kg/mm)	116.5/140.0	106/140.0
tilt	——	——
stroke	①	——
Damper:		
damping capacity (lbs/in./sec)	55/19.68/sec	——
(kg/mm/sec)	25/0.5/sec	——
Hub and axle assembly:		
rear axle diameter (in./mm)	0.4707-0.4720	——
rear axle bend (in./mm)	0.008/0.2	0.020/0.5
brake drum inside diameter (in./mm)	N.A.	——
brake lining shoe thickness (in./mm)	0.1378/3.5	0.0590/1.5
Swing arm pivot rubber bushing:		
inside diameter (in./mm)	②	——

① C50, C50M 2.465/62.6
C65, C65M 2.658/67.5
S50, S65 2.492/63.6

② C50, C50M, C65, C65M O.D. 0.9055/23.0
S50 O.D. 0.9842/25.0
S65 I.D. 0.4764/12.1

CHASSIS SPECIFICATIONS (con't.)

C70, C70M

	Standard Value	Serviceable Limit
FRONT WHEEL AND SUSPENSION		
Cushion spring:		
free-length (in./mm)	5.146/130.7	4.803/122.0
spring compression (lbs/in.)	264.3/3.386	—
(kg/mm)	120/86	—
tilt	1°30′	4°
Damper:		
damping capacity (lbs/in./sec)	—	—
(kg/mm/sec)	—	—
Fork piston and bottom case:		
piston diameter (in./mm)	N.A.	N.A.
case inside diameter (in./mm)	N.A.	N.A.
stroke (in./mm)	N.A.	N.A.
damping capacity	N.A.	N.A.
Hub and axle assembly:		
front axle diameter (in./mm)	0.3923-0.3932/9.965-9.987	0.392/9.96
front axle bend (in./mm)	0.0020/0.05	0.008/0.2
brake drum inside diameter (in./mm)	4.323-4.339/109.8-110.2	4.448/113.0
brake lining shoe thickness (in./mm)	0.1417-0.1476/3.6-3.75	0.984/2.5
Steering geometery:		
trail length (in./mm)	2.95	—
caster angle	63°	—
REAR WHEEL AND SUSPENSION		
Cushion spring:		
free-length (in./mm)	8.661/220.0	8.268/210.0
spring compression (lbs/in.)	187.4/5.512	—
(kg/mm)	85/140	—
tilt	1°30′	4°
Damper:		
damping capacity (lbs/in./sec)	—	—
(kg/mm/sec)	—	—
Hub and axle assembly:		
rear axle diameter (in./mm)	0.4704-0.4718/11.957-11.984	0.4705/11.95
rear axle bend (in./mm)	0.0020/0.05	0.008/0.2
brake drum inside diameter (in./mm)	4.323-4.339/109.8-110.2	4.448/113
brake lining shoe thickness (in./mm)	0.1417-1.1476/3.6-3.75	0.984/2.5
Swing arm pivot rubber bushing:		
inside diameter (in./mm)	0.398-0.406/10.1-10.3	0.411/10.45

CHASSIS SPECIFICATIONS (con't.)

CL70

	Standard Value	Serviceable Limit
FRONT WHEEL AND SUSPENSION		
Cushion spring:		
free-length (in./mm)	5.146/130.7	4.803/122.0
spring compression (lbs/in.)	264.6/3.386	——
(kg/mm)	120/86	——
tilt	1°30′	4°
Damper:		
damping capacity (lbs/in./sec)	N.A.	N.A.
(kg/mm/sec)	N.A.	N.A.
Fork piston and bottom case:		
piston diameter (in./mm)	1.1389-1.1402/28.93-28.96	1.1375/28.917
case inside diameter (in./mm)	1.1417-1.1430/29.0-29.033	1.1488/29.18
stroke (in./mm)	3.44/87.5	N.A.
damping capacity	——	——
Hubh and axle assembly:		
front axle diameter (in./mm)	0.3923-0.3932/9.965-9.987	0.392/9.96
front axle bend (in./mm)	0.0020/0.05	0.008/0.2
brake drum inside diameter (in./mm)	4.323-4.339/109.8-110.2	4.448/113.0
brake lining shoe thickness (in./mm)	0.1417-0.1476/3.6-3.75	0.984/2.5
Steering geometry:		
trail length (in./mm)	2.76/70.0	——
caster angle	64°	——
REAR WHEEL AND SUSPENSION		
Cushion spring:		
free-length (in./mm)	8.224/208.9	7.874/200
spring compression (lbs/in.)	257.1/5.472	——
(kg/mm)	116.5/139.1	——
tilt	1°30′	4°
Damper:		
damping capacity (lbs/in./sec)	——	——
(kg/mm/sec)	——	——
Hub and axle assembly:		
rear axle diameter (in./mm)	0.4704-0.4718/11.957-11.984	0.4705/11.9
rear axle bend (in./mm)	0.0020/0.05	0.008/0.2
brake drum inside diameter (in./mm)	4.323-4.339/109.8-110.2	4.448/113
brake lining shoe thickness (in./mm)	01417-1.1476/3.6-3.75	0.984/2.5
Swing arm pivot rubber bushing:		
inside diameter (in./mm)	0.476-0.484/11.957-11.984	0.490/12.45

C90, CD90, CT90 (from F. no. 000001A)

	Standard Value	Serviceable Limit
FRONT WHEEL AND SUSPENSION		
Cushion spring:		
free-length (in./mm)	①	②
spring compression (lbs/in.)	③	——
(kg/mm)	④	——
tilt	1°	1°
Damper:		
damping capacity (lbs/in./sec)	22.1/20.0/sec	——
(kg/mm/sec)	10.0/0.5/sec	——
Fork piston and bottom case:		
piston diameter (in./mm)	N.A.	N.A.
case inside diameter (in./mm)	N.A.	N.A.
stroke (in./mm)	N.A.	N.A.
damping capacity	N.A.	N.A.
Hub and axle assembly:		
front axle diameter (in./mm)	0.394-0.396/9.995-10.050	N.A.
front axle bend (in./mm)	0.008/0.2	N.A.
brake drum outside diameter (in./mm)	4.2992-4.3110/109.2-109.5	4.2323/107.5
brake lining shoe thickness (in./mm)	0.1575/4.0	0.1181/3.0
Steering geometry:		
trail length (in./mm)	2.955/75.0	——
caster angle	⑤	——

① C90 5.2520/133.4
CD90 5.886/149.5
CT90 8.0/203.0
② C90 4.73/120.0
CD90 5.32/135.0
CT90 7.3/185.0
③ C90 104.738-115.763/4.433
CD90 167.58/4.606
CT90 51.7-58.3/4.71
④ C90 47.5-52.5/112.6
CD90 76.0/117.0
CT90 23.5-26.5/119.6
⑤ C90 63°
CD90 63.5°
CT90 63.5°

C90

	Standard Value	Serviceable Limit
REAR WHEEL AND SUSPENSION		
Cushion spring:		
free-length (in./mm)	8.313/212.0	7.48/190.0
spring-compression (lbs/in.)	264.0/5.57	——
(kg/mm)	120.0/141.5	——
tilt	1.5°	2°
Damper:		
damping capacity (lbs/in./sec)	55-68/20/sec	——
(kg/mm/sec)	25-31/0.5/sec	——
stroke (in./mm)	2.46/62.4	——
Hub and axle assembly:		
rear axle diameter (in./mm)	0.472-0.515/11.984-12.957	——
rear axle bend (in./mm)	0.00/0.2	0.020/0.5
brake drum inside diameter (in./mm)	——	——
brake lining shoe thickness (in./mm)	0.5575/4.0	0.1181/3.0
Swing arm pivot rubber bushing:		
inside diameter (in./mm)	——	——

CHASSIS SPECIFICATIONS (con't.)

CD90

	Standard Value	Serviceable Limit
REAR WHEEL AND SUSPENSION		
Cushion spring:		
free-length (in./mm)	8.313/211.0	7.48/190.0
spring compression (lbs/in.)	220.0/5.532	—
(kg/mm)	100.0/140.4	—
tilt	1.5°	2°
Damper:		
damping capacity (lbs/in./sec)	61.6-81.4/19.7/sec	—
(kg/mm/sec)	28-37/0.5/sec	—
stroke (in./mm)	2.41/61.2	—
Hub and axle assembly:		
rear axle diameter (in./mm)	0.472-0.515/11.984-12.957	—
rear axle bend (in./mm)	0.00/0.2	0.020/0.5
brake drum inside diameter (in./mm)	—	—
brake lining shoe thickness (in./mm)	0.5575/4.0	0.1181/3.0
Swing arm pivot rubber bushing:		
inside diameter (in./mm)	—	—

CT90

	Standard Value	Serviceable Limit
REAR WHEEL AND SUSPENSION		
Cushion spring:		
free-length (in./mm)	8.776/222.9	8.16/207.0
spring compression (lbs/in.)	3.473/5.6181	—
(kg/mm)	157.5/142.7	—
tilt	1.5°	2°
Damper:		
damping capacity (lbs/in./sec)	88-110/20/sec	—
(kg/mm/sec)	40-50/0.5/sec	—
stroke (in./mm)	①	—
Hub and axle assembly:		
rear axle diameter (in./mm)	0.472-0.515/11.984-12.957	—
rear axle bend (in./mm)	0.00/0.2	0.020/0.5
brake drum inside diameter (in./mm)	—	—
brake lining shoe thickness (in./mm)	0.5575/4.0	0.1181/3.0
Swing arm pivot rubber bushing:		
inside diameter (in./mm)	—	—

① CT90 2.49/62.4
CT90 (after F. no. 000001A) 3.05/77.5

SL90

	Standard Value	Serviceable Limit
FRONT WHEEL AND SUSPENSION		
Cushion spring:		
free-length (in./mm)	—	—
spring compression (lbs/in.)	—	—
(kg/mm)	—	—
tilt	—	—
Damper:		
damping capacity (lbs/in./sec)	N.A.	N.A.
(kg/mm/sec)	N.A.	N.A.
Fork piston and bottom case:		
piston diameter (in./mm)	1.395-1.396/35.425-35.45	1.39/35.3
case inside diameter (in./mm)	1.399-1.400/35.53-35.57	1.405/35.7
stroke (in./mm)	—	—
damping capacity (lbs/in./sec)	—	—
(kg/in./sec)	—	—
Hub and axle assembly:		
front axle diameter (in./mm)	—	—
front axle bend (in./mm)	—	—
brake drum inside diameter (in./mm)	—	—
brake lining shoe thickness (in./mm)	—	—
Steering geometry:		
trail length (in./mm)	3.66/93.0	—
caster angle	61.5°	—
REAR WHEEL AND SUSPENSION		
Cushion spring:		
free-length (in./mm)	8.492/21.5	7.874/20.0
spring compression (lbs/in.)	—	—
(kg/mm)	—	—
tilt	—	—
Damper:		
damping capacity (lbs/in./sec)	—	—
(kg/mm/sec)	—	—
Hub and axle assembly:		
rear axle diameter (in./mm)	0.472-0.515/11.984-12.957	—
rear axle bend (in./mm)	0.00/0.2	0.020/0.5
brake drum inside diameter (in./mm)	4.32-4.34/109.8-110.2	4.41/112.0
brake lining shoe thickness (in./mm)	0.5575/4.0	0.1181/3.0
Swing arm pivot rubber bushing:		
inside diameter (in./mm)	0.472-0.480/12.0-12.2	—

CHASSIS SPECIFICATIONS (con't.)

S90, CL90, CL90L

	Standard Value	Serviceable Limit
FRONT WHEEL AND SUSPENSION		
Cushion spring:		
free-length (in./mm)	7.789/197.7	7.013/178.0
spring compression (lbs/in.)	22.44/6.686	——
(kg/mm)	10.2/16.97	——
tilt	1°	1°
Damper:		
damping capacity (lbs/in./sec)	N.A.	N.A.
(kg/mm/sec)	N.A.	N.A.
Fork piston and bottom case:		
piston diameter (in./mm)	1.219-1.220/30.950-30.975	——
case inside diameter (in./mm)	1.22-1.223/31.0-31.039	——
stroke (in./mm)	——	——
damping capacity (lbs/in./sec)	22.1/20.0/sec	——
(kg/mm/sec)	10.0/0.5/sec	——
Hub and axle assembly:		
front axle diameter (in./mm)	0.394-0.396/9.995-10.050	——
front axle bend (in./mm)	0.008/0.2	——
brake drum outside diameter (in./mm)	4.2992-4.3110/109.2-109.5	4.2323/107.5
brake lining shoe thickness (in./mm)	0.1575/4.0	0.1181/3.0
Steering geometry:		
trail length (in./mm)	①	——
caster angle	②	——

① S90 2.955/75.0
CL90, CL90L 2.87/73.0

② S90 65°
CL90, CL90L 64°

S90

	Standard Value	Serviceable Limit
REAR WHEEL AND SUSPENSION		
Cushion spring:		
free-length (in./mm)	6.761/171.6	6.139/155.8
spring compression (lbs/in.)	257.4/3.983	——
(kg/mm)	117.0/101.1	——
tilt	1.5°	2°
Damper:		
damping capacity (lbs/in./sec)	55.125-77.175/19.68/sec	——
(kg/mm/sec)	25-35/0.5/sec	——
stroke (in./mm)	2.41/61.1	——
Hub and axle assembly:		
rear axle diameter (in./mm)	0.472-0.515/11.984-12.957	——
rear axle bend (in./mm)	0.00/0.2	0.020/0.5
brake drum inside diameter (in./mm)	——	——
brake lining shoe thickness (in./mm)	0.5575/4.0	0.1181/3.0
Swing arm pivot rubber bushing:		
inside diameter (in./mm)	0.472-0.480/12.0-12.2	

CL90, CL90L

	Standard Value	Serviceable Limit
REAR WHEEL AND SUSPENSION		
Cushion spring:		
free-length (in./mm)	6.7874/172.4	6.139/155.8
spring compression (lbs/in.)	2.280-2.571/4.6457	N.A.
(kg/mm)	103.4-116.6/118.0	N.A.
tilt	1.5°	2°
Damper:		
damping capacity (lbs/in./sec)	55.125-77.175/19.68/sec	N.A.
(kg/mm/sec)	25-35/0.5/sec	N.A.
stroke (in./mm)	2.11/53.6	N.A.
Hub and axle assembly:		
rear axle diameter (in./mm)	0.472-0.515/11.984-12.957	N.A.
rear axle bend (in./mm)	0.00/0.2	0.020/0.5
brake drum inside diameter (in./mm)	N.A.	N.A.
brake lining shoe thickness (in./mm)	0.5575/4.0	0.1181/3.0
Swing arm pivot rubber bushing:		
inside diameter (in./mm)	0.472-0.480/12.0-12.2	N.A.

CB100, CL100, SL100, CB125S, CD125S, SL125

	Standard Value	Serviceable Limit
FRONT WHEEL AND SUSPENSION		
Cushion spring free-length: (in./mm)		
CB100/CL100	7.2440/184.0	6.2992/160.0
SL100	19.0629/484.2	18.1102/460.0
CB125S/CD125S	8.0905/205.5	7.0866/180.0
SL125	18.9881/482.3	18.1102/460.0
XL250	18.94/481.1	18.50/470.0
Front fork piston outside diameter: (in./mm)		
CB100/CL100/CB125S/CD125S	1.2174-1.2194/30.936-30.975	1.2165/30.9
SL100/SL125	1.3946-1.3956/35.425-35.450	1.2937/35.4
XL250	0.9744-0.9843/24.75-25.0	0.9724/24.70
Stroke: (in./mm)		
CB100/CL100	4.2716/108.5	N.A.
SL100	6.2992/160.0	N.A.
CB125S/CD125S	4.5000/114.3	N.A.
SL125	5.5118/142.0	N.A.
XL250	N.A.	N.A.

CB100, CL100, SL100, CB125S, CD125S, SL125 (con't.)

	Standard Value	Serviceable Limit
Brake drum inside diameter: (in./mm)		
CB100/CL100/CB125S/CD125S	4.3229-4.3385/109.8-110.2	4.409/112.0
SL100/SL125	4.3307-4.3425/110.0-110.3	4.409/112.0
XL250	6.2992-6.3110/160.0-160.3	6.339/161.0
Brake Lining shoe thickness: (in./mm)		
All Models except XL250	0.1535-0.1614/3.9-4.1	0.0787/2.0
XL250	0.197/5.0	0.098/2.5
Trail length: (in./mm)		
CB100	2.95/75.0	—
CL100	3.07/78.0	—
SL100	3.70/95.0	—
CB125S/CD125S/SL125	3.15/80.0	—
XL250	N.A.	—
Caster angle:		
CB100	64°	—
CL100	63°40′	—
SL100	61°30′	—
CB125S/CD125S	63°45′	—
SL125	60°	—
XL250	N.A.	—
REAR WHEEL AND SUSPENSION		
Cushion spring free-length: (in./mm)		
CB100/CL100/CB125S/CD125S	7.1200/180.9	6.2992/160.0
SL100/SL125	7.4803/190.0	6.6929/170.0
XL250	9.31/236.4	9.06/230.0
Clearance between rear fork pivot bushing and bolt: (in./mm)		
All Models	0.0031-0.0118/0.1-0.3	0.0196/0.5
Brake drum inside diameter: (in./mm)		
CB100/CL100/CB125S/CD125S	4.3229-4.3385/109.8-110.2	4.409/112.0
SL100/SL125	4.3307-4.3425/110.0-110.3	4.409/112.0
XL250	5.5118-5.5236/140.0-140.3	5.5512/141.0
Brake Lining shoe thickness: (in./mm)		
All Models except XL250	0.1535-0.1614/3.9-4.1	0.0787/2.0
XL250	0.177/4.5	0.098/2.5

INDEX

HONDA TWINS

MODEL IDENTIFICATION

The CD 125 pictured here was introduced in 1967 along with a CB and CL model which featured the same engine mounted in different chassis. The CB model looks like a Superhawk and the CL model has upswept scrambler pipes.

The latest version of the CB 175 pictured here represents the culmination of the 175cc line which Honda introduced in 1967 to replace the 160cc line. The engine is essentially a bored out version of the 125cc models.

Pictured here is the CL 175 which is the street-scrambler version of the 175cc line. There is also a CD 175 which is very similar in appearance to the CD 125 shown above and an SL 175 which was introduced three years later than the CB and CL models.

The CB 350 is the staple of the Japanese motorcycle industry. First introduced in 1968, the sturdy 350 soon proved to be near bullet proof. Older models had a squarish sort of two-toned tank and no vents in the side covers.

Here is the CL 350, the street-scrambler version of the 350cc line. These street-scramblers have upswept pipes but are essentially street bikes as they aren't as ruggedly built as the SL models.

In 1966 Honda introduced the CB 450 which came equipped with a four-speed transmission and an ugly hump-back tank. In 1968 they redesigned the bike a little, changed the tank and side covers (like the one shown here), and added a fifth cog to the gearbox.

In 1968, Honda added the CL 450 to its line. For its first two years, this bike looked very much like the CB models of that era except it had high, scrambler type pipes. In 1970, the CL was redesigned to its present form which is pictured here.

In 1970 the CB 450 went through some further changes: the tank was redesigned once again and a disc brake was mounted up front. The model pictured here is a 1972, but is very similar in appearance to the '70 and '71 models.

The SL 350 shown here came out in 1970 as the vanguard of Honda's entry into the dirt bike market. The SL models have that dirt bike look but that street bike feel. There is also an SL 175 model which looks very much like this one.

GENERAL SPECIFICATIONS

	CB 125 (from serial no. 4,000,001)	CL 125 (from serial no. 4,000,001)
ENGINE		
Displacement (cc)	124	124
Bore and stroke (mm)	44 x 41	44 x 41
Compression ratio	9.4 : 1	9.4 : 1
Carburetion (Keihin)	(2) 18 mm	(2) 18 mm
Horsepower @ rpm	14.8 @ 10,000	13.8 @ 10,000
Torque (ft lb) @ rpm	7.59 @ 8,500	7.66 @ 8,500
Weight (lb)	77.2	68.4
DRIVE TRAIN		
Clutch type	wet, multi-plate	wet, multi-plate
Gear ratios:		
1st	2.692	2.615
2nd	1.667	1.611
3rd	1.286	1.190
Gear ratios:		
4th	1.043	0.880
5th	0.880	——
Primary reduction	3.875	3.875
Final reduction	3.133	3.133
CHASSIS		
Weight (lb)	262	254
Wheelbase (in.)	50.4	50.4
Tire size (in.):		
front	2.50 x 18	2.75 x 18
rear	2.75 x 18	3.00 x 18
Overall length (in.)	77.9	76.0
Overall width (in.)	29.3	31.9
Overall height (in.)	40.9	40.6
Ground clearance (in.)	5.5	6.1
ELECTRICAL SYSTEM		
Ignition	battery and coil	battery and coil
Starting system	electric and kick	electric and kick
Charging system:		
battery (volts/amp hrs)	6/12	6/6
alternator	rotor type	rotor type
regulator	——	——

This section is intended to serve as a guide for the maintenance, tune-up and repair of the following Honda models:

CB 125 (from serial #4,000,001)
CL 125 (from serial #34,000,001)
CD 125 (from serial #2,000,001)
CB 175 (from serial #4,000,001)
CL 175 (from serial #4,000,001)
CD 175 (from serial #2,000,001)
SL 175 (1970 thru 1972)
CB 350 (1968 thru 1972)
CB 350 G (1973)
CL 350 (1968 thru 1972)
SL (1970)
SL 350K1 and K2 (1971 and 1972)
CB 450 (1966 thru 1969)
CL 450 (1968 and 1969)
CB 450K4 and K5 (1970 thru 1972)
CL 450K4 and K5 (1970 thru 1972)

TUNE-UP AND MAINTENANCE

TUNE-UP OPERATIONS

Valve Clearance

125 AND 175—ALL MODELS

1. Remove the circular alternator cover on the left side of the engine.
2. Unscrew the four adjuster access caps on the cylinder head.
3. Remove the spark plugs.
4. Turn the crankshaft in the normal direction of rotation until the "T" mark on the alternator rotor lines up with the timing index mark.

The timing index mark (1) and the "T" mark (2) must be aligned.

5. Both pistons will be at top dead center (TDC) of the stroke, however, one piston will be on the compression stroke and the other will be on the exhaust stroke. To determine which piston is on compression, check to see which pair of valves (intake and exhaust) are fully closed, in which case there will be clearance at both rocker arms. The valves for the piston that is on compression are correctly positioned for adjustment.
6. Check the clearance between the rocker arm and valve stem for the two valves using the appropriate feeler gauge. Correct clearance is 0.002 in. (0.05 mm) for both valves.
7. If adjustment is necessary, loosen the adjuster screw locknut and turn the

	SS 125 (from serial no. 2,000,001)	CB 175 (from serial no. 4,000,001)
ENGINE		
Displacement (cc)	124	174
Bore and stroke (mm)	44 x 41	52 x 41
Compression ratio	9.4 : 1	9.0 : 1
Carburetion (Keihin)	——	(2) 20 mm
Horsepower @ rpm	12.5 @ 10,000	19.8 @ 10,000
Torque (ft lb) @ rpm	6.8 @ 8,500	10.8 @ 8,500
Weight (lb)	75.0	88.2
DRIVE TRAIN		
Clutch type	wet, multi-plate	wet, multi-plate
Gear ratios:		
1st	2.615	2.769
2nd	1.611	1.882
3rd	1.190	1.450
4th	0.880	1.173
5th	——	1.000
Primary reduction	3.875	3.700
Final reduction	3.071	2.375
CHASSIS		
Weight (lb)	265	280
Wheelbase (in.)	50.4	50.4
Tire size (in.):		
front	3.00 x 17	2.75 x 18
rear	3.00 x 17	3.00 x 18
Overall length (in.)	78.0	78.4
Overall width (in.)	29.5	29.3
Overall height (in.)	40.2	40.9
Ground clearance (in.)	5.5	6.6
ELECTRICAL SYSTEM		
Ignition	battery and coil	battery and coil
Starting system	electric and kick	electric and kick
Charging system:		
Battery (volts/amp hrs)	6/12	12/9
alternator	rotor type	rotor type
regulator	——	——

	CL 175 (from serial no. 4,000,001)	CD 175 (from serial no. 2,000,001)
ENGINE		
Displacement (cc)	174	174
Bore and stroke (mm)	52 x 41	52 x 41
Compression ratio	9.0 x 1	9.0 x 1
Carburetion (Keihin)	(2) 22 mm	
Horsepower @ rpm	19.8 @ 10,000	16.8 @ 9,500
Torque (ft lb) @ rpm	10.8 @ 8,500	9.4 @ 7,000
Weight (lb)	82.7	87.1

screw in the required direction until the feeler gauge fits with some resistance. Tighten the locknut while holding the adjuster from turning, and recheck clearance.

8. When both valves are correctly adjusted, rotate the crankshaft through one complete turn (360°) and align the "T" mark with the index mark again. The other piston is now on compression and its two valves are correctly positioned for adjustment. Repeat steps 6 and 7.

A feeler gauge (1) is used to check valve clearance, as shown. Adjustment is made by loosening the locknut (2) and turning the adjuster screw (3).

350—ALL MODELS

1. Remove the alternator rotor cover on the left side of the engine.
2. Remove the ignition points cover and the small matching cover on the right side.
3. Remove the four valve access caps on the cylinder head.
4. Remove the spark plugs.
5. Rotate the crankshaft in the normal direction of rotation while observing the left intake (rear) valve spring and rocker arm. When the valve spring is fully compressed and then starts to return, turn the crankshaft slowly in the same direction until the "LT" mark on the alternator rotor and the timing index mark are aligned. At this point, the left piston is at top dead center (TDC) of its compression stroke and both the intake and exhaust valves on that side should be fully closed (clearance at both rocker arms).
6. Check the clearance between the rocker arm and valve stem on the two left-side valves using the appropriate feeler gauges. Correct clearance is 0.002 in (0.05 mm) for the intake valve, and

To adjust the valves on the left cylinder, the timing index mark must be aligned with the "LT" mark on the alternator rotor (2) and the left piston must be on its compression stroke (clearance at both valves).

(con't.)	CL 175 (from serial no. 4,000,001)	CD 175 (from serial no. 2,000,001)
DRIVE TRAIN		
Clutch type	wet, multi-plate	wet, multi-plate
Gear ratios:		
1st	2.769	2.769
2nd	1.882	1.778
3rd	1.450	1.318
4th	1.173	1.040
5th	1.000	—
Primary reduction	3.700	3.700
Final reduction	2.470	2.294
CHASSIS		
Weight (lb)	274	271
Wheelbase (in.)	50.8	50.4
Tire size (in.):		
front	3.00 x 19	3.00 x 17
rear	3.00 x 18	3.00 x 17
Overall length (in.)	78.3	78.0
Overall width (in.)	32.3	29.5
Overall height (in.)	42.5	40.2
Ground clearance (in.)	7.8	6.1
ELECTRICAL SYSTEM		
Ignition	battery and coil	battery and coil
Starting system	electric and kick	electric and kick
Charging system:		
battery (volts/amp hrs)	12/9	6/12
alternator	rotor type	rotor type
regulator	—	—

	SL 175 (1970-72)	CB 350/CB 350G (1968-72)
ENGINE		
Displacement (cc)	174	325
Bore and stroke (mm)	52 x 41	65 x 50.6
Compression ratio	9.0 : 1	9.5 : 1
Carburetion (Keihin)	—	(2) 28 mm CV
Horsepower @ rpm	20 @ 10,000	36 @ 10,500
Torque (ft lb) @ rpm	—	18.5 @ 9,500
Weight (lb)	—	115.5
DRIVE TRAIN		
Clutch type	wet, multi-plate	wet, multi-plate
Gear ratios:		
1st	2.769	2.353
2nd	1.882	1.636
3rd	1.450	1.269
4th	1.173	1.036
5th	1.000	0.900
Primary reduction	3.700	3.714
Final reduction	2.687	2.250
CHASSIS		
Weight (lb)	262.4	370.0
Wheelbase (in.)	51.6	52.0

0.004 in. (0.1 mm) for the exhaust valve.

7. Adjustment is made by rotating the eccentric rocker arm shafts. If adjustment is necessary, loosen the appropriate adjuster locknut located next to the ignition points base plate, and turn the adjuster in the required direction until the feeler gauge fits with some resistance. Tighten the locknut while holding the adjuster from turning, and recheck clearance.

NOTE: *The small index mark on the end of each adjuster must be pointed outwards (away from the center of the cylinder head) for the valve rocker arms to operate properly. If the mark is pointing inward, rotate the adjuster about ½ turn so that the mark points outward and reset the valve clearance.*

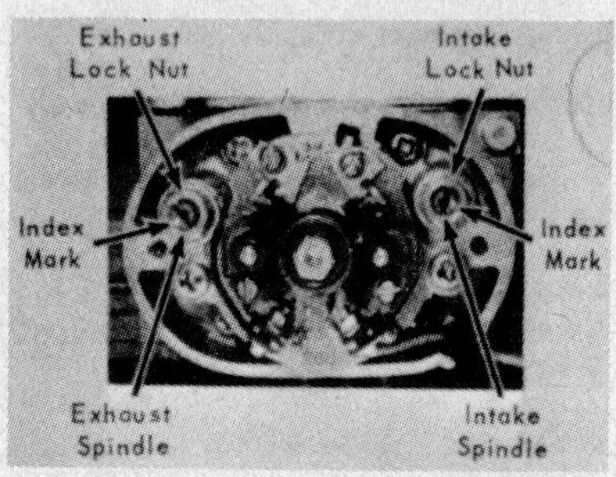

The left-side valve adjuster screws are located under the ignition points cover.

Check valve clearance using a feeler gauge (1). If adjustment is necessary, loosen the locknut (3) and turn the adjusting screw (2) in the required direction.

8. When both left-side valves are correctly adjusted, rotate the crankshaft 180° (½ turn) in the normal direction of rotation to align the "T" mark on the alternator rotor with the timing index mark. The right-side piston is now on compression and its two valves are correctly positioned for adjustment. Repeat steps 6 and 7 for the right-side valves. The adjusters are located under the small chrome cover on the right side.

450—ALL MODELS

1. Remove the fuel tank.
2. Unbolt and remove the front and rear cylinder head covers.
3. Remove the ignition points cover and the alternator rotor cover.
4. Remove the spark plugs.
5. Rotate the crankshaft slowly in the normal direction of rotation and observe the left-side cam followers. When the fol-

(con't.)	SL 175 (1970-72)	CB 350/CB 350G (1968-72)
CHASSIS		
Tire size (in.):		
front	3.00 x 19	3.00 x 18
rear	3.50 x 17	3.50 x 18
Overall length (in.)	78.5	79.2
Overall width (in.)	30.7	30.5
Overall height (in.)	42.9	42.3
Ground clearance (in.)	——	5.9
ELECTRICAL SYSTEM		
Ignition	battery and coil	battery and coil
Starting system	kick	electric and kick
Charging system:		
battery (volts/amps hrs)	12/5	12/12
alternator	rotor type	rotor type
regulator	non-adjustable silicon type	non-adjustable silicon type

	CL 350 (1968-72)	SL 350 (1970)
ENGINE		
Displacement (cc)	325	325
Bore and stroke (mm)	64 x 50.6	64 x 50.6
Compression ratio	9.5 : 1	9.5 : 1
Carburetion (Keihin)	(2) 28 mm CV	(2) 28 mm CV
Horsepower @ rpm	33 @ 9,500	33 @ 9,500
Torque (ft lb) @ rpm	19.5 @ 8,000	19.5 @ 8,000
Weight (lb)	115.5	115.5
DRIVE TRAIN		
Clutch type	wet, multi-plate	wet, multi-plate
Gear ratios:		
1st	2.353	2.353
2nd	1.636	1.636
3rd	1.269	1.269
4th	1.036	1.036
5th	0.900	0.900
Primary reduction	3.714	3.714
Final reduction	2.375	2.500
CHASSIS		
Weight (lb)	366	364
Wheelbase (in.)	52.0	52.8
Tire size (in.):		
front	3.00 x 19	3.25 x 19
rear	3.50 x 18	4.00 x 18
Overall length (in.)	79.5	79.5
Overall width (in.)	32.7	33.3
Overall height (in.)	42.9	46.5
Ground clearance (in.)	7.1	8.3
ELECTRICAL SYSTEM		
Ignition	battery and coil	battery and coil
Starting system	electric and kick	electric and kick
Charging system:		
battery (volts/amp hrs)	12/12	12/12
alternator	rotor type	rotor type
regulator	non-adjustable silicon type	non-adjustable silicon type

lowers have travelled downward fully and start to rise, turn the crankshaft slowly until the "LT" mark on the alternator rotor and the timing index mark are aligned. At this point, the left piston is at top dead center (TDC) of its compression stroke and both the intake and exhaust valves on that side should be fully closed (clearance between the camshaft and cam followers).

6. Check the clearance between the camshaft and cam follower on the two left-side valves using the appropriate feeler gauge. Correct clearance is 0.002 in. for both valves.

7. Adjustment is made by rotating the eccentric cam follower shafts. If adjustment is necessary, loosen the appropriate adjuster locknut and turn the adjuster in the required direction until the feeler gauge fits with some resistance. Tighten the locknut while holding the adjuster from turning, and recheck clearance. (The left-side exhaust valve adjuster is located next to the ignition points base plate.)

NOTE: *The small index mark on the end of each adjuster must be pointed outward (away from the center of the cylinder head) for the cam followers to operate properly. If the mark is pointing inward, rotate the adjuster about ½ turn so that the mark points outward and reset the valve clearance.*

8. When both left-side valves are correctly adjusted, rotate the crankshaft 180° (½ turn) in the normal direction of rotation to align the "T" mark on the alternator rotor with the timing index mark. (On early models with a four speed transmission, rotate the crankshaft one

To adjust the right-side valves, the timing index mark (1) must be aligned with the "T" mark (2) and the right piston must be on its compression stroke (clearance at both valves).

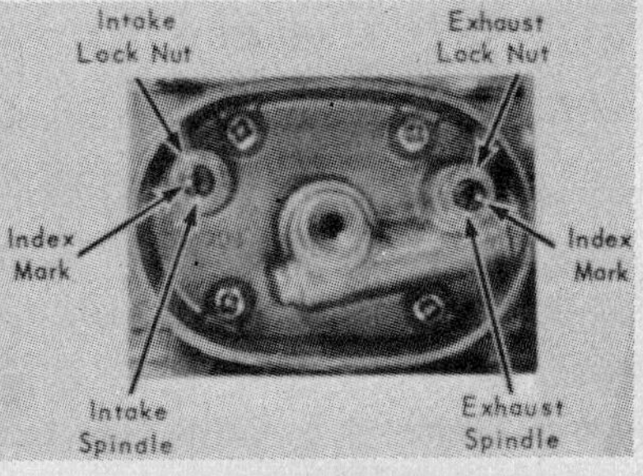

The right-side valve adjusters are located under the small chrome cover on the cylinder head.

	SL 350K1 and K2 (1971-72)	CB 450 (1966-67)
ENGINE		
Displacement (cc)	325	44
Bore and stroke (mm)	64 x 50.6	70 x 57.8
Compression ratio	9.5 : 1	8.5 : 1
Carburetion (Keihin)	(2) 24 mm	(2) 36 mm CV
Horsepower @ rpm	25 @ 8,000	43 @ 8,500
Torque (ft lb) @ rpm	18.1 @ 8,000	27.6 @ 7,250
Weight (lb)	103.5	146.6
DRIVE TRAIN		
Clutch type	wet, multi-plate	wet, multi-plate
Gear ratios:		
1st	2.353	2.411
2nd	1.636	1.400
3rd	1.280	1.034
4th	1.036	0.903
5th	0.900	——
Primary reduction	3.714	3.304
Final reduction	2.500	2.333
CHASSIS		
Weight (lb)	306.5	412
Wheelbase (in.)	54.7	53.2
Tire size (in.):		
front	3.25 x 19	3.25 x 18
rear	4.00 x 18	3.50 x 18
Overall length (in.)	83.07	82.0
Overall width (in.)	33.07	30.2
Overall heigth (in.)	45.08	53.2
Ground clearance (in.)	8.3	5.4
ELECTRICAL SYSTEM		
Ignition	battery and coil	battery and coil
Starting system	kick only	electric and kick
Charging system:		
battery (volts/amps hrs)	12/5.5	12/12
alternator	rotor type	rotor type
regulator	non-adjustable silicon type	non-adjustable silicon type

	CB 450 (1968-69)	CL 450 (1968-69)
ENGINE		
Displacement (cc)	444	444
Bore and stroke (mm)	70 x 57.8	70 x 57.8
Compression ratio	9.0 : 1	9.0 : 1
Carburetion (Keihin)	(2) 36 mm CV	(2) 36 mm CV
Horsepower @ rpm	45 @ 9,000	43 @ 8,000
Torque (ft lb) @ rpm	28 @ 7,500	29 @ 7,000
Weight (lb)	137.8	137.8

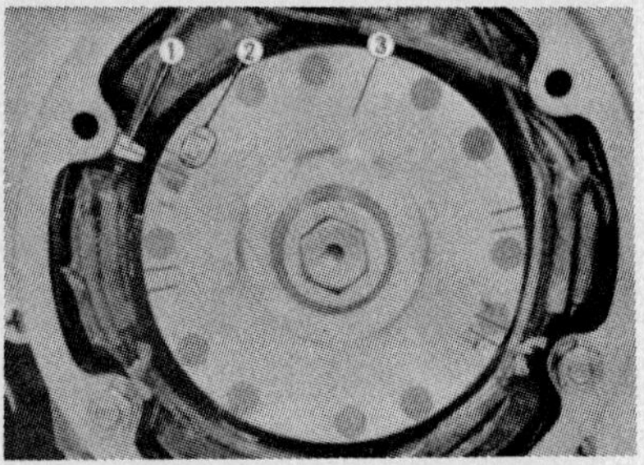

To adjust the valves on the left cylinder, the timing index mark (1) must be aligned with the "LT" mark on the alternator rotor (2) and the left piston must be on its compression stroke (clearance at both valves).

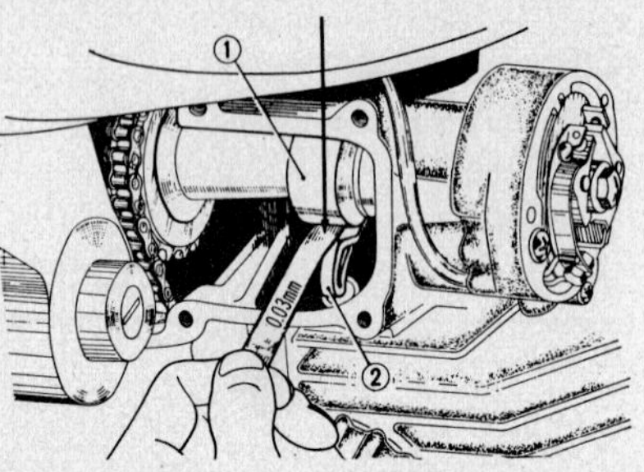

Valve clearance is measured between the camshaft lobe (1) and the cam follower (2).

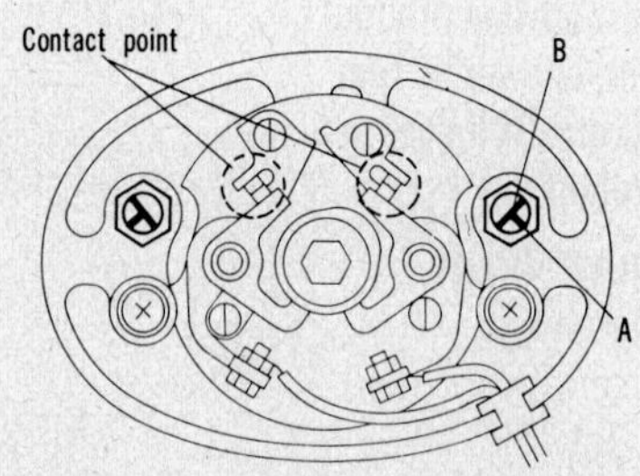

The index marks (A) on the adjusting screws (B) must be pointing away from the center on the cylinder head.

full turn.) The right-side piston is now on compression and its two valves are correctly positioned for adjustment. Repeat steps 6 and 7 for the right-side valves.

Cam Chain Adjustment

125 AND 175—ALL MODELS

1. Remove the alternator rotor cover.
2. Remove the left-side intake valve access cap.
3. Turn the alternator rotor clockwise (the opposite direction of normal rotation) until the left intake valve opens fully (spring compressed) and begins to close.
4. Turn the alternator rotor counterclockwise until the left intake valve barely moves.
5. Loosen the cam chain adjuster locknut and back the adjuster bolt out a few turns to free the tensioner. The tensioner will automatically take up the chain slack. Retighten the adjuster bolt and locknut.

(con't.)	CB 450 (1968-69)	CL 450 (1968-69)
DRIVE TRAIN		
Clutch type	wet, multi-plate	wet, multi-plate
Gear ratios:		
1st	2.412	2.412
2nd	1.636	1.636
3rd	1.269	1.269
4th	1.000	1.000
5th	0.844	0.844
Primary reduction	3.304	3.304
Final reduction	2.333	2.333
CHASSIS		
Weight (lb)	412	401
Wheelbase (in.)	54.0	54.0
Tire size (in.):		
front	3.25 x 18	3.25 x 19
rear	3.50 x 18	3.50 x 18
Overall length (in.)	83.0	84.5
Overall width (in.)	30.5	32.5
Overall height (in.)	43.0	43.5
Ground clearance (in.)	5.5	6.0
ELECTRICAL SYSTEM		
Ignition	battery and coil	battery and coil
Starting system	electric and kick	electric and kick
Charging system:		
battery (volts/amp hrs)	12/12	12/12
alternator	rotor type	rotor type
regulator	non-adjustable silicon type	non-adjustable silicon type

	CB 450K4 and K5 (1970-72)*	CL 450K4 and K5 (1970-72)
ENGINE		
Displacement (cc)	444	444
Bore and stroke (mm)	70 x 57.8	70 x 57.8
Compression ratio	9.0 : 1	9.0 : 1
Carburetion (Keihin)	(2) 36 mm CV	(2) 36 mm CV
Horsepower @ rpm	45 @ 9,000	43 @ 8,000
Torque (ft lb) @ rpm	28 @ 7,500	29 @ 7,000
Weight (lb)	137.8	137.8
DRIVE TRAIN		
Clutch type	wet, multi-plate	wet, multi-plate
Gear ratios:		
1st	2.412	2.412
2nd	1.636	1.636
3rd	1.269	1.269
4th	1.000	1.000
5th	0.844	0.844
Primary reduction	3.304	3.304
Final reduction	2.333	2.333

Cam chain tensioner locknut (1) and the adjuster bolt (2).

350—ALL MODELS

1. Remove the alternator cover.
2. Remove the two left cylinder valve access caps.
3. Turn the alternator rotor slowly in the normal direction of rotation until the "LT" mark lines up with the timing index mark. The left piston is now at TDC.
4. Check to see if the left-side tappets are free. If they are, the left piston is on the compression stroke. If not, rotate the engine 360° (one full turn) in the normal direction of rotation and realign the marks. The left piston should be at TDC of its compression stroke.

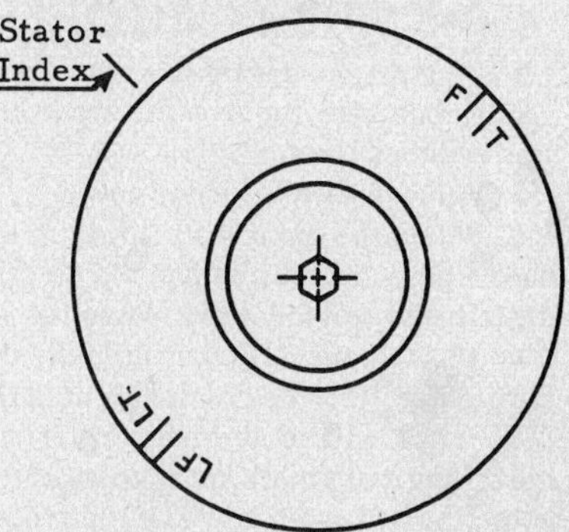

The engine is properly set up for cam chain adjustment when the left piston is 90° past TDC of its compression stroke.

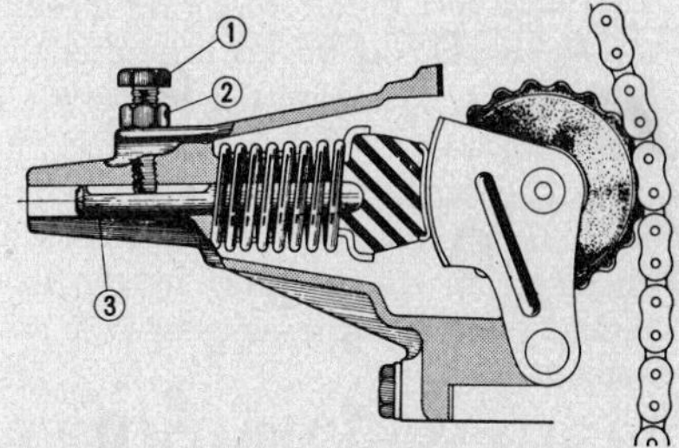

Cross-section of the tensioner assembly, located at the rear of the cylinder barrel. Shown is the adjuster bolt (1), locknut (2), and the tensioner guide rod (3).

5. Now, turn the alternator rotor counterclockwise about 90° (¼ turn after the "LT" mark). The engine is properly set up for adjustment of the cam chain at this point. Loosen the locknut and the adjuster bolt, and the cam chain slack will be taken up automatically by the tensioner. Retighten the adjuster bolt and locknut.

(con't.) Model	CB 450K4 and K5 (1970-72)*	CL 450K4 and K5 (1970-72)
CHASSIS		
Weight (lb)	430	414.5
Wheelbase (in.)	54.3	54.0
Tire size (in.):		
front	3.25 x 19	3.25 x 19
rear	3.50 x 18	3.50 x 18
Overall length (in.)	82.7	82.0
Overall width (in.)	30.5	32.7
Overall height (in.)	42.3	42.9
Ground clearance (in.)	5.7	7.1
ELECTRICAL SYSTEM		
Ignition	battery and coil	battery and coil
Starting system	electric and kick	electric and kick
Charging system:		
battery (volts/amp hrs)	12/12	12/12
alternator	rotor type	rotor type
regulator	non-adjustable silicon type	non-adjustable silicon type

* Disc brake models

450–5-SPEED MODELS

1. Remove the gas tank.
2. Unbolt and remove the front and rear cylinder head covers.
3. Remove the alternator cover.
4. Rotate the crankshaft slowly in the normal direction of rotation and observe the left-side cam followers. When the followers have traveled downward fully and start to rise, turn the crankshaft until the "LT" mark on the alternator rotor and the timing index mark are aligned. At this point, the left piston is at TDC of its compression stroke and both the intake and exhaust valves on that side should be fully closed (clearance between the camshaft and cam followers).
5. Now, turn the alternator rotor counterclockwise about 90° (¼ turn after the "LT" mark). The engine is properly set up for adjustment of the cam chain at this point. Loosen the locknut and the adjuster bolt, and the cam chain slack will be taken up automatically by the tensioner. Retighten the adjuster bolt and locknut.

450–4 SPEED MODELS

Follow steps 1, 2, 3, and 4 in the preceding section on five-speed models, omitting step 5. The crankshaft is correctly positioned for cam chain adjustment when the left piston is at TDC of its compression stroke.

ALTERNATE PROCEDURES—350 AND 450

If you can't obtain satisfactory cam chain adjustment using the previously described methods, try adjusting the tensioner in the following manner:

Loosen the locknut and adjuster bolt. Insert a thin instrument such as a stiff piece of wire or a small screwdriver into the tail section of the tensioner and seat it gently against the end of the tensioner rod inside. (On early 450s, the tensioner rod protrudes from the tail section.) Now, turn the engine over slowly; you can feel the rod move back and forth as the cam chain slack varies. Do this several times and take note of the point at which the rod is farthest in (closest to the engine). Continue turning the engine over slowly until you succeed in stopping it at this point. *Do not use pressure to force the tensioner rod in.* When this is accomplished, the cam chain slack is on the tensioner side of the engine and the tensioner has automatically moved in to take up slack. Tighten the adjuster bolt and locknut to lock the tensioner in this position.

This method has been used for many years and is quite effective if carried out carefully. If you do not use pressure to force the rod in, there is no danger of the cam chain being overtight.

Ignition Points and Ignition Timing

IGNITION POINTS SERVICE—ALL MODELS

Inspection, Cleaning, and Replacement

Examine the contact points for pitting, misalignment, and excessive wear of the rubbing block that rides on the breaker cam. If the points are in good condition except for a slight amount of pitting, they may be cleaned up using an ignition points file. Allow the points to spring shut on the file and move the file back and forth without exerting any extra pressure against the points surface. Remove dirt and grit from between the points by pulling a thick piece of paper, such as a business card, through the points two or three times.

If the points are heavily pitted, replace the points and condenser(s). The components can be unscrewed and removed from the base plate after the electrical leads have been disconnected. Make sure that any insulating washers are replaced in their original positions when reconnecting the wires. Place a drop or two of gasoline or other non-oily solvent on a piece of paper and pull it through the points to remove any dirt or preservative coating on the contact surfaces. Put a *small* dab of distributor cam lubricant or other high-melting-point grease on the contact breaker cam. This will prevent the points rubbing block from wearing excessively and reducing point gap.

125 AND 175

Adjustment

Adjust the point gap by loosening the securing screws and swivelling the stationary contact point toward or away from the moving contact as required. The breaker cam must be positioned where it will give maximum point opening. The gap should be set at 0.012–0.016 in. The gap is not particularly critical, as long as it is within the specified range.

The contact breaker arm (1) and the breaker points (2). The point gap can be adjusted by loosening the two set screws (arrows) and repositioning the stationary contact.

350 AND 450

Adjustment

Point gap should be adjusted to 0.012–0.016 in. Adjust one set at a time by loosening the securing screws and swivelling the stationary contact point toward or away from the moving contact as required. The cam must be positioned where it will give maximum opening for the set of points being adjusted. The point gap is not particularly critical as

Loosen the securing screws (1) for one point set at a time and adjust the points gap (2) by repositioning the stationary contact.

long as it is within the specified range. However, you should try to adjust each set of points so that their gaps are as close to identical as possible.

Ignition Timing

125 AND 175

Static Timing Procedure

1. Connect one of the test light leads to the small bolt that fastens the electrical supply wire to the point set. Ground the other test light lead on the engine.

2. Switch the ignition on and turn the engine in the normal direction of rotation until the "F" mark on the alternator rotor is aligned with the timing index mark.

3. The test light should light at the same instant the marks are aligned. If not, loosen the points base plate securing screws and rotate the base plate in the required direction until the light just comes on as the timing marks are aligned. Retighten the securing screws. Both cylinders are now correctly timed.

350 AND 450

Static Timing Procedure

1. Make sure that the point gaps are as close to identical as possible.

2. Connect one of the test light leads to the small bolt that fastens the electrical supply wire to the left (L) point set. Ground the other test light lead on the engine.

3. Switch the ignition on and turn the engine in the normal direction of rotation until the "LF" mark on the alternator rotor aligns with the timing index mark.

4. The test light should light at the same instant the marks are aligned. If not, loosen the points base plate securing screws and rotate the base plate in the required direction until the light just comes on as the timing marks are aligned. Retighten the securing screws. The left cylinder is now correctly timed.

5. If the point gaps are the same, the right cylinder should also be correctly timed at this point. To check this, transfer the test light lead to the right (R) point set. Turn the alternator rotor counterclockwise 180° (½ turn) until the "F" mark aligns with the timing index mark. If adjustment is necessary, loosen the securing screws on the right point set and alter the point gap until the light comes on as the marks are aligned. Retighten the screws and double-check the timing on both cylinders. Make sure that point gap is still within 0.012–0.016 in.

Connect the test light lead to the terminal shown (arrow). The timing can be altered by rotating the base plate after the securing screws (3) have been loosened.

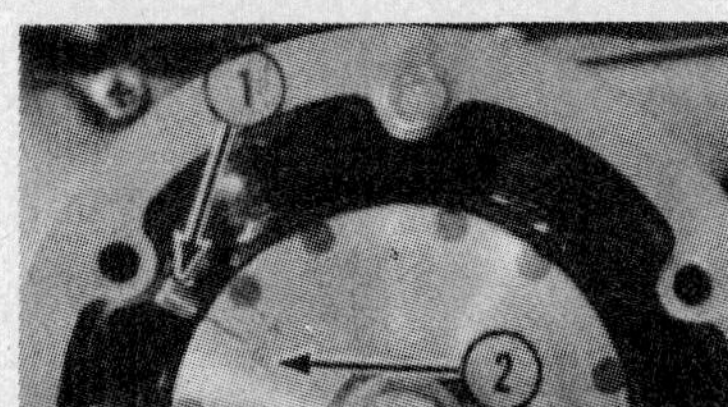

Timing index mark (1) and the "F" mark on the alternator rotor (2).

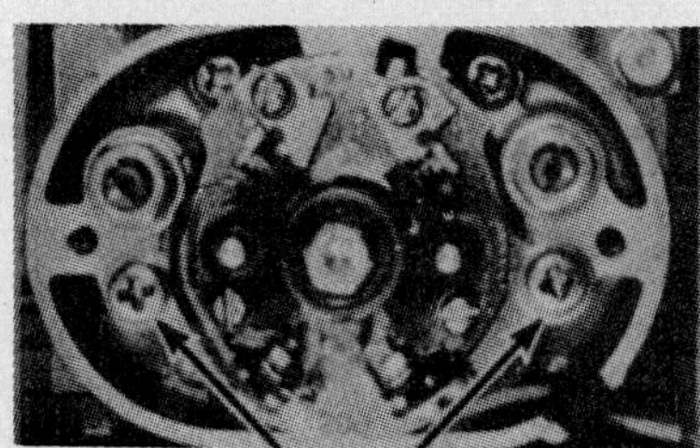

The timing can be adjusted after the base plate securing screws have been loosened.

The timing index mark (1) and the "LF" (left cylinder firing) mark on the alternator rotor.

The timing index mark (1) and the "F" (right cylinder firing) mark.

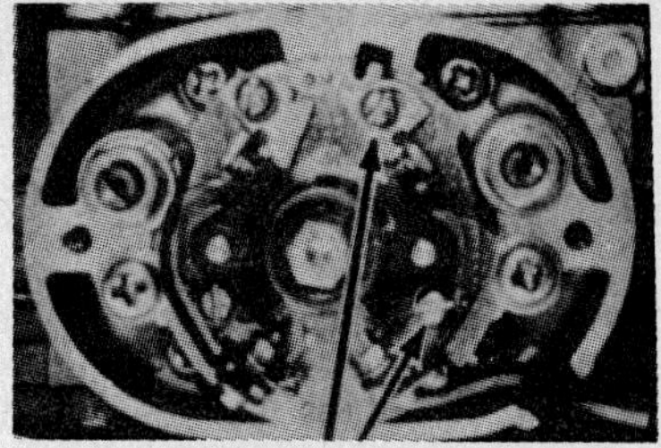

Right cylinder point set securing screws.

125 AND 175

Dynamic Timing Procedure

1. Connect the strobe light as per manufacturer's instructions, picking up the impulses from either cylinder.

2. Start the engine and adjust the idle, if necessary, to the recommended speed. (Refer to the specifications at the end of the chapter.)

3. Aim the light at the timing marks. At idle speed the "F" mark should be aligned with the timing index mark. If not, loosen the points base plate securing screws and rotate the base plate in the required direction until the marks are aligned. Retighten the screws.

4. To check the timing at full ignition advance, increase the engine speed to approximately 2,000 rpm (175) or 4,000 rpm (125) and hold it steady. The timing index mark should be between the two marks on the alternator rotor that are about 35° to the left of the "F" and "T" marks. If it is, both cylinders are correctly timed and the ignition advance unit is functioning properly.

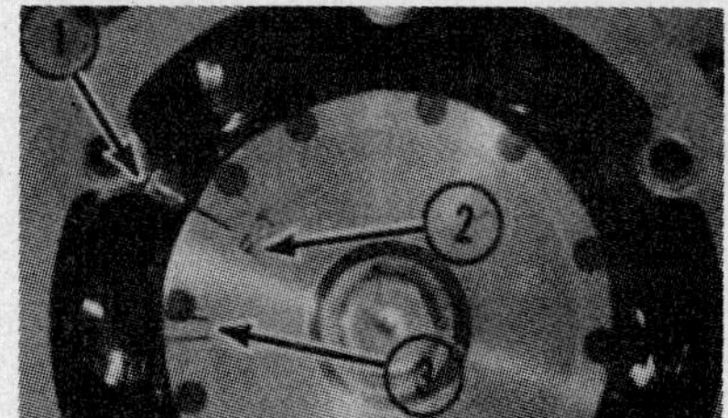

Timing index mark (1), "F" (firing) mark used for static timing (2), and the full advance marks (3) used for dynamic timing.

5. If it is not, or if the timing is unsteady even though the engine speed is held constant, the fault probably lies with either the ignition points or the advance unit springs (assuming that the timing is correct at idle speed). To examine the advance unit, first scribe a line on the contact breaker plate and cylinder head to facilitate correct reassembly, then take out the two screws and remove the breaker plate assembly. The advance unit can be removed, if necessary, after the mounting bolt is unscrewed. Look for weak or broken springs, and stiff governor weight pivots. When installing the advance unit, make sure that the camshaft oil seal is in good condition, and that

the pin in the camshaft is properly located in the groove in the advance unit.

350 AND 450

Dynamic Timing Procedure

1. Make sure that the point gaps are as close to identical as possible.

2. Connect the strobe light as per manufacturer's instructions, picking up the impulses from the left cylinder.

3. Start the engine and adjust the idle, if necessary, to the recommended speed. (Refer to the specifications at the end of the chapter.)

4. Aim the light at the timing marks. At idle speed the "LF" mark should be aligned with the timing index mark. If not, loosen the points base plate securing screws and rotate the base plate in the required direction until the marks are aligned. Retighten the screws.

5. To check the timing at full ignition advance, increase the engine speed to approximately 3,500 rpm and hold it steady. The timing index mark should be between the two advance marks on the alternator rotor. If it is, the left cylinder is correctly timed. If it is not, or if the timing is unsteady even though the engine speed is held constant, the fault probably lies with the ignition points or the advance unit springs (see step 7).

The timing index mark (1), "LF" (left cylinder firing) mark used for static timing (2), and the full advance marks (3) used for dynamic timing.

6. To time the right cylinder, shut the engine off, transfer the strobe light lead to the right cylinder, and restart the engine. If the "F" mark and timing index mark are not aligned at normal idling speed, loosen the screws securing the right point set and alter the point gap until the marks align. Check the timing at full ignition advance in the same manner as for the left cylinder in step 5, above. Make sure that point gap is still within 0.012–0.016 in.

7. If the timing is unsteady as the advance unit comes into operation, scribe a line on the contact breaker plate and cylinder head and remove the breaker plate assembly. The advance unit can be removed, if necessary, after the retaining bolt is unscrewed. Look for weak or broken springs, and stiff governor weight pivots. When reinstalling the advance unit, make sure that the pin in the camshaft is properly located in the groove at the back of the unit.

The timing index mark (1) and the right cylinder firing mark (2), and the full advance marks (3).

Carburetor Adjustments

CB/CL 350, SL 350 (1979 ONLY), AND CB/CL 450

Twin Carburetor Synchronization

Place your hand under the carburetors and note the movement of the throttle levers as the throttle is opened. If adjustment is required, loosen the locknut and turn the cable adjuster in the required direction until both throttle slides open at the same time.

Left carburetor throttle cable adjuster (1) and locknut (2) (shown is a 350cc model).

CB/CL 125 AND 175, SL 350K1 AND K2

Twin Carburetor Synchronization

To synchronize the throttle slides on these models it will be necessary, first, to remove the air filter(s) or air filter tubes so that the slides are accessible. Place a finger into each of the carburetor bores so that you are lightly touching the slides and slowly open the throttle grip a small amount. Both slides should start to rise at the same time. If they do not, raise the rubber boot on top of either carburetor and loosen the adjuster locknut. Turn the adjuster in the required direction until the slides are synchronized. If both slides are rising and falling at the same time a single click (rather than two separate clicks) should be heard as the throttle grip is released and the slides hit bottom.

ALL MODELS

Idle Adjustment

1. Back off the throttle cable adjuster at the handlebar to provide about ¼ in. of slack in the cable.

2. Start the engine and adjust the idle (after it has warmed up) to the recommended speed with the throttle stop screw(s). Refer to the specifications at the end of the chapter.

3. Turn the air screw(s) slowly in or out to obtain the highest idle speed consistent with smoothness. Standard air screw opening is approximately one turn from full open, and it should not be necessary to exceed ¼ turn in either direction from this setting.

Throttle stop screw (1) and air screw (2) (all models except CB/CL 350, CB/CL 450, and SS 125).

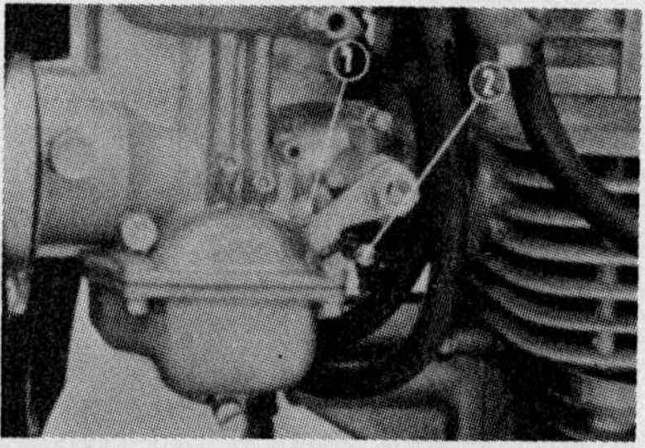

Throttle stop screw (1) and air screw (2) (CB/CL 350 and SS 125).

Air screw (1) and throttle stop screw (2) (all 450cc models).

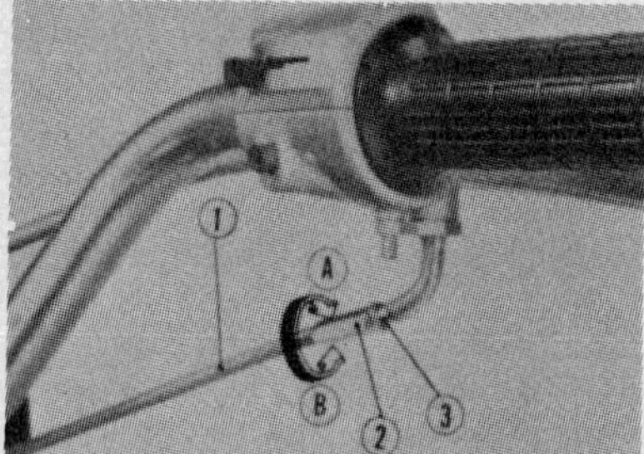

Throttle cable (1), cable adjuster (2), and adjuster locknut (3). Turning the adjuster in direction (A) decreases cable play and turning in direction (B) increases play.

4. Check for even firing of the cylinders by feeling the exhaust pressure with your hand. Reset the throttle stop screws again, if necessary, to obtain the correct idle speed.

NOTE: *If the carburetors are unresponsive to large changes in air screw openings, investigate the following possible causes: clogged air passage, worn air screw, float level too high, or loose low speed jet. If the air screw adjustment requires less than ½ turn opening, look for: clogged low speed jet or jet passage, float level too low, or worn air screw seat.*

5. Adjust the throttle cable play to the desired amount at the adjuster near the throttle grip. Swing the handlebars to full lock in both directions to make sure that the throttle cable is not binding and pulling the carburetors open.

TUNE-UP SPECIFICATIONS

	125	175	350	450
VALVE CLEARANCE (cold)				
Intake: (in./mm)	0.002/0.05	0.002/0.05	0.002/0.05	0.002/0.05
Exhaust: (in./mm)	0.002/0.05	0.002/0.05	0.004/0.1	0.002/0.05
COMPRESSION				
Pressure (psi)	140 (115-170)	140 (115-170)	170 (145-200)	185 (160-210)
Maximum Variation (psi)*	15	15	15	15
IGNITION				
Spark Plugs:				
standard make**	NGK	NGK	NGK	NGK
type	D8HS	D8HS	B8ES or B9E	B8ES or B9E
gap (in.)	0.025-0.028	0.025-0.028	0.025-0.028	0.025-0.028
Point Gap (in.)	0.012-0.016	0.012-0.016	0.012-0.016	0.012-0.016
CARBURETION				
Idle Speed (rpm)	①	①	1,000-1,300	1,000-1,200
Air Screw Opening	1⅛ ± ¼	1⅛ ± ¼	②	1.0 ± ¼

* Between cylinders.
** Other reputable makes are also acceptable. Be sure to select plugs of the correct heat range, reach and diameter. Most spark plug application charts also have conversion tables and a heat range chart, enabling you to select the spark plug that fits your needs exactly.
① Single carburetor models—1,000; twin carburetor models 1,200
② CB/CL 350 and 1970 SL 350—¾ ± ⅛; SL 350K1 and K2—1 ± ¼

MAINTENANCE

Engine

OIL CHANGES (1,000 MI/60 DAYS SUMMER, 30 DAYS WINTER)

Change the oil after the engine has been run long enough to be up to operating temperature. This ensures that the oil is fluid enough to drain completely and that impurities suspended in the oil while it is circulating will be removed. Honda recommends that SAE 10W-40 or 10W-50 oil of SD (previously MS) service rating be used. For even better protection, you can use the new SE rated oils, which are able to withstand more heat than SD rated oil before breaking down. If a single-viscosity oil is to be used, it must be a high detergent (heavy duty) oil of SD service rating. For temperatures above 60°F, use SAE 30W-30 oil; between 32 and 60°F, use SAE 20W-20; and below 32°F, use SAE 10W-10 oil. Do not use a vegetable-based or non-detergent oil.

Remove the drainplug from the crankcase sump and remove the filler cap to assist draining. When most of the oil has drained, kick the engine over a few times to remove any oil remaining in the delivery system. Replace the drainplug and refill the engine with the correct grade and amount of oil. Start the engine and let it idle for a minute or so to circulate the oil. Shut the engine off and check the oil level with the filler dipstick. To obtain a true reading on the dipstick, three precautions must be observed:

1. Allow the oil a few seconds to drain down into the crankcase.
2. Place the machine on its center stand, on a level surface.
3. Do not screw the dipstick/filler cap into the case when checking the oil level or a false (high) reading will be obtained. Add oil, if necessary, to bring the level to the upper mark on the dipstick.

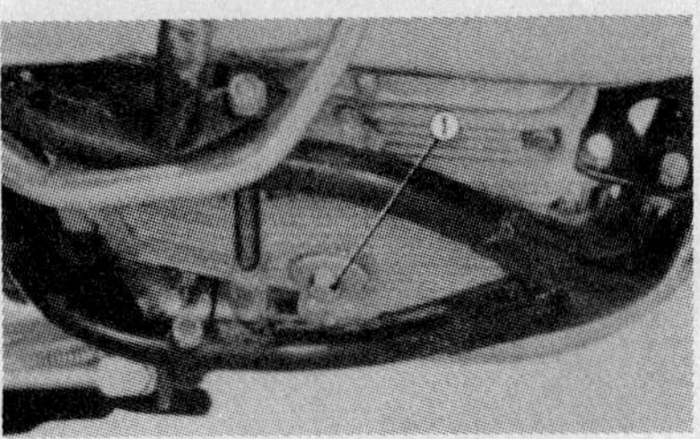

Crankcase drain plug (1).

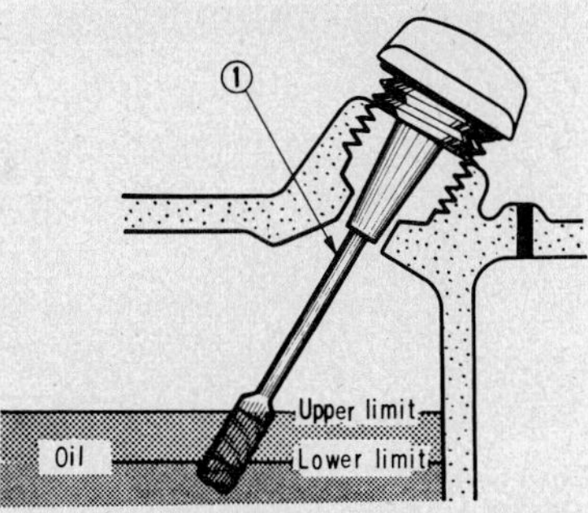

When checking the oil level do not screw the dipstick (1) into the crankcase.

OIL FILTER (3,000 MI)

1. Clean the oil filter in conjunction with an oil change. Drain the oil and do not reinstall the drain plug at this time.
2. Take out the three screws and remove the small circular cover plate at the right side of the engine towards the front.
3. Remove the circlip and gently pull the rotor cap out of the oil filter rotor.

NOTE: *On early 450s the rotor cap is held in place with an aluminum bolt rather than a circlip. When removing and installing the bolt, take great care not to apply sudden or excessive torque to it, as it can be broken off very easily.*

4. Clean the inside of the filter rotor with solvent or gasoline and allow the cleaning agent to drain completely before replacing the oil drain plug. Clean the rotor cap and cover plate, and dry thoroughly.
5. Install the rotor cap with the vanes located in the grooves on the inside of the rotor, and secure with the circlip. Before

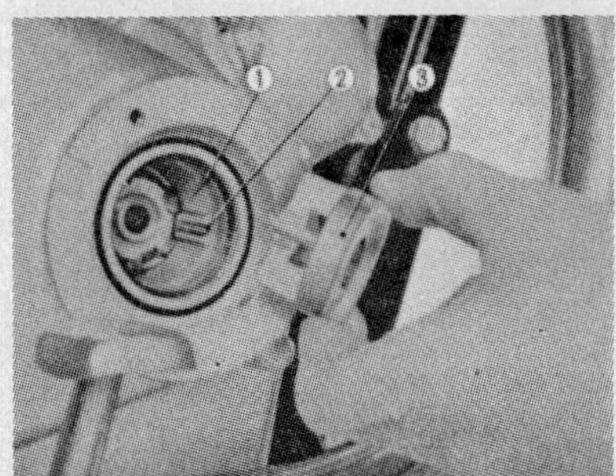

Removing the oil filter rotor cap, showing the rotor (1), rotor cap alignment groove (2), and rotor cap (3).

Checking the operation of the oil guide (1). Some models do not have an oil guide.

With the rotor cap (1) in place, install the cover plate (2) so that its oil holes (3) align with the holes in the crankcase cover.

installing the cover plate, check that the oil guide in the center of the plate (if applicable) is free to operate smoothly and that the gasket or O-rings are in good condition. Install the cover plate so that the matching holes in the plate and crankcase cover are aligned. Install the drainplug and refill the engine with oil.

AIR FILTER (3,000 MI/6 MO)

On all models, the filter elements are located within the side panels. On machines with paper elements, clean, using compressed air (directed from the inside out) or by tapping the elements lightly and brushing away the dirt. Replace the elements if they are torn or wet with oil or water. On machines with rubber foam type filter elements, clean in solvent and wet the elements with oil. Wring out any excess oil before reinstalling. Replace the elements if torn.

CLUTCH ADJUSTMENT (3,000 MI / 6 MO)

The clutch release mechanism should be adjusted at the prescribed intervals, or whenever the clutch begins to drag or slip and satisfactory operation cannot be obtained by adjusting free-play at the lever. At the time of adjustment, lubricate the grease fitting, using only one or two strokes of the grease gun.

1. Screw the cable adjuster at the clutch lever all the way into the lever (increasing lever free-play).

2. Back off the locknut and turn the cable adjuster at the engine case into the case (increasing cable free-play to maximum).

3. Loosen the clutch adjuster locknut or bolt, and turn the adjuster clockwise (125, 175, and 450) or counterclockwise (350) until resistance is felt. Then turn the adjuster in the opposite direction about ⅛–¼ in. (½ turn on the 350) and retighten the locknut or bolt.

NOTE: *On the 350, if a loud click is heard and the cable goes slack (or if the cable goes slack for no apparent reason while riding), turn the lower cable adjuster into the engine case a few more turns and reset the adjuster screw.*

4. Turn the cable adjuster at the engine case out until there is about 1–2 in. freeplay at the end of the clutch lever.

5. Remaining adjustment is made at the lever. Free-play at the end of the lever should be 0.4–0.8 in.

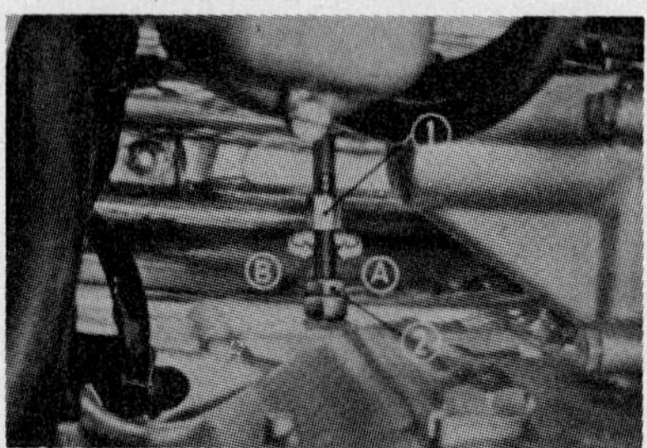

Bottom cable adjuster bolt (1) and locknut (2).

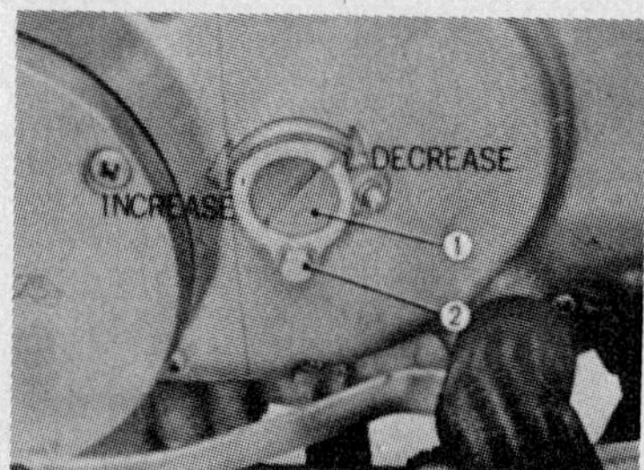

Clutch adjuster (1) and lockbolt (2) (all models except 350).

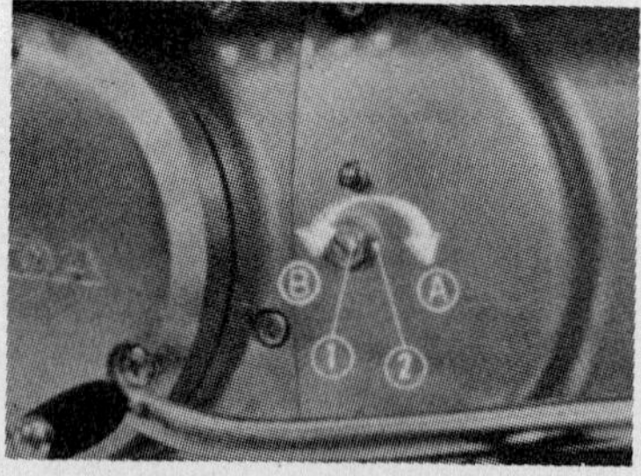

Clutch adjuster (1) and locknut (2) (350cc models).

FUEL FILTER (3,000 MI/6 MO)

The fuel filter, located in the fuel tap, should be removed and cleaned at the prescribed intervals or whenever fuel feed problems are suspected. Simply turn the fuel tap to "Stop" and unscrew the cup to gain access to the filter. Fuel flow at both the "on" and "reverse" positions can be checked at this time.

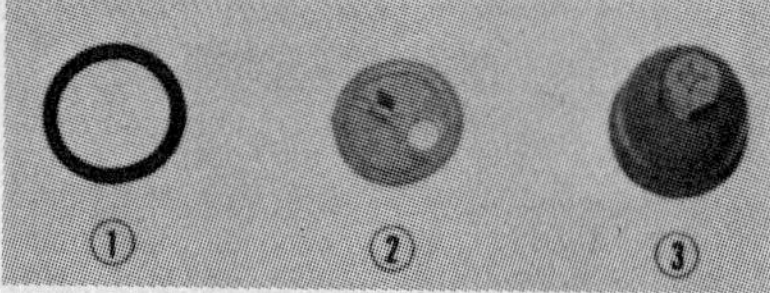

Fuel tap O-ring (1), filter (2), and cup (3).

CAUTION: *Do not start the engine until all spilled gasoline has evaporated or has been wiped off the engine. Use a can or jar to catch gasoline when checking flow.*

If the tap allows any gasoline to pass while in the "stop" position, the tap should be repaired or replaced, as gasoline may leak into the crankcase and dilute the oil.

Clean the filter screen and reinstall the cup and filter on the fuel tap. Use a new O-ring, if necessary. Do not overtighten the cup. Examine the fuel lines for leakage and for restriction caused by kinks or sharp bends. Check to see that the vent hole in the tank filler cap is not plugged, to preclude the possibility of fuel starvation.

Front Suspension and Steering (6,000 mi/12 mo)

STEERING HEAD BEARINGS

To check the bearings, place the bike on its center stand and swing the forks slowly through full steering travel. Movement should be smooth, light, and free from any binding. Check for play in the bearings by grabbing the bottom of the forks and trying to move them back and forth in line with the motorcycle. Play can be removed by tightening the steering head main nut. *Tighten no more than necessary to remove play.* If steering movement remains unsatisfactory the bearings should be replaced.

NOTE: *On machines equipped with a friction type steering damper, back the damper knob completely out when checking the steering. If the damper is operating unevenly or is binding, unbolt the damper components at the bottom of the steering stem and check the spring and plate for wear and damage.*

FORK OIL

Remove the small drain plug at the bottom of each fork leg and work the suspension until all the oil has been expelled. Replace the drain plugs. Remove the top filler plugs and fill each fork leg with the proper amount and grade of oil (see the specifications at the end of the chapter). After the oil has been poured into the forks, work them up and down slowly a few times to expel any air in the hydraulic passages before replacing the filler caps.

Rear Suspension (3,000 mi/6 mo)

Lubricate the swing arm pivot grease fitting(s) using a high-pressure grease gun. Wipe off any excess grease. There should be absolutely no side-play and the swing arm must not be bent or weakened from cracked welds, or else handling (especially at high speeds) will become erratic. Check that the bushings at the shock absorber mounting eyes are in good condition by attempting to move the swing arm up and down by hand and watching for play. Refer to the "Chassis" section.

Brakes

Brake lining wear on drum brakes can be determined by observing the angle formed by the brake operating lever and rod (at the brake drum) while the brake is applied. When the lever and rod move past perpendicular as the brake is applied, the brake shoes should be replaced.

Disc brake pad wear on the 450 can be determined by checking the clearance between the front of the caliper and the brake disc using a feeler gauge. Replace both pads when clearance is less that 0.08 in. (2.0 mm). (On 1972 and later 450s, the K5, and the CB 350 G replace both pads when either one has worn to the wear indicator groove.) Brake squeal can usually be eliminated by careful attention to pad alignment. Refer to the "Chassis" section.

DISC BRAKE ADJUSTMENT

The disc brake is self-adjusting and is not provided with a means for manual adjustment to compensate for wear. If the brake lever feels spongy or lever travel is excessive, bleed the hydraulic system. Use only brake fluid conforming to SAE specification J1703. Refer to the "Chassis" section.

DOUBLE LEADING SHOE FRONT BRAKE ADJUSTMENT

Adjustment can normally be made at the handlebar lever. Turn the adjuster until there is about 0.5–1.0 in. free-play at the lever. When adjustment at the lever is used up, further adjustment can be made at the bottom cable adjuster on the brake plate, after the locknut has been loosened. If both ends of the brake shoes are not contacting the drum at the same time (as evidenced by decreased braking efficiency and a spongy feel at the lever),

Swing arm pivot grease fitting.

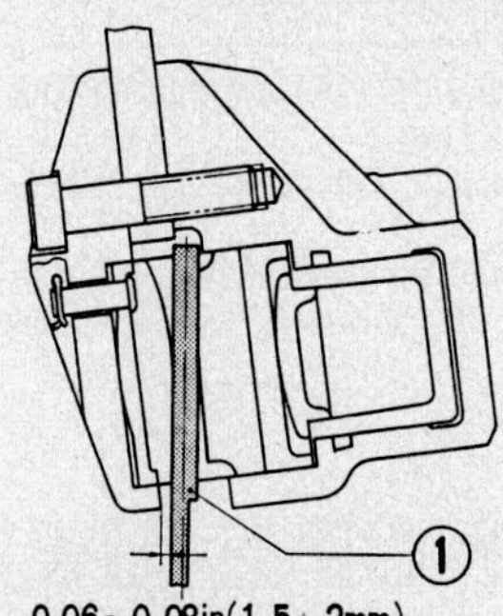

Replace disc pads on the 450K4 when clearance between the disc (1) and caliper is less than 0.08 in.

loosen the locknut on the rod connecting the two brake arms and disconnect the rod from one of the brake arms. Turn the rod in the required direction to lengthen or shorten it to where both ends of the brake shoes are contacting the drum at the same time as the brake is applied. Retighten the locknut after the rod is connected at its correct length.

NOTE: *On the 450, it is not necessary to disconnect the rod. Since the rod is threaded on both ends, it can be rotated to change its working length once the locknuts are loosened. Note that one of the locknuts has a left-hand thread.*

REAR BRAKE ADJUSTMENT

The brake should be adjusted so that there is approximately 1.0 in. (25 mm) free-play at the end of the pedal. Adjustment is made by turning the eccentric nut at the end of the operating rod. Make sure that the nut is seated properly on the lever and readjust the brake light switch if necessary.

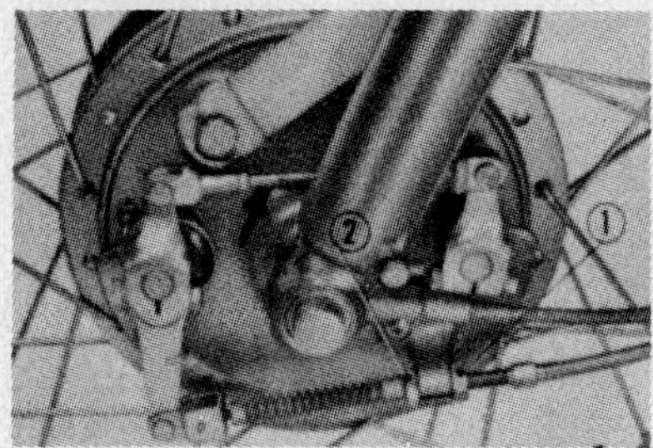

Bottom brake cable adjuster locknuts (1 and 2) and the brake arm connecting rod (arrow).

Rear brake arm (1) and brake adjusting nut (2).

Final Drive

CHAIN ADJUSTMENT AND LUBRICATION

To check chain adjustment, place the bike on the center stand and move the chain up and down at the midpoint of either run. If total movement exceeds 1.5 in., the chain is too loose and must be adjusted. The procedure is as follows:

1. Remove the rear axle nut cotter pin (if applicable), and loosen the nut until it can be turned by hand.
2. Loosen the locknuts on the two chain adjuster bolts at the swing arm ends.

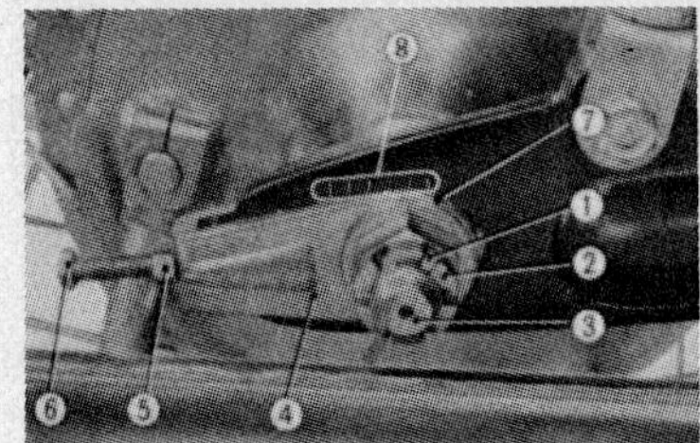

Chain adjuster components.

1. Cotter pin
2. Axle nut
3. Rear wheel axle
4. Chain adjuster
5. Locknut
6. Adjusting bolt
7. Index mark
8. Reference scale

3. To tighten the chain, turn the adjuster bolts in equally until total chain slack is within ½–¾ in. Turning the adjusters an unequal amount will affect wheel alignment. Scales are provided on both sides of the swing arm to facilitate adjustment. Make sure that they are both in the same position.
4. Tighten the adjuster bolt locknuts until they are just snug, while holding the bolts to keep them from turning. Do not overtighten.
5. Tighten the axle nut firmly and recheck chain movement. Do not forget to reinstall the cotter pin.

NOTE: *A dry chain should be lubricated before adjustment so that the links will not bind and restrict chain movement, making it seem tighter than it really is. If tension varies alternately between too loose and too tight as the chain is rotated, remove it and inspect for excessive wear after it has been cleaned.*

PERIODIC MAINTENANCE CHART

EVERY 1,000 MILES
60 DAYS (SUMMER),
30 DAYS WINTER):
Engine—
1. Change oil.
EVERY 3,000 MILES/6 MONTHS:
Engine—
1. Clean centrifugal oil filter.
2. Service air filter element.
Clutch—
1. Perform full clutch adjustment.
Battery—
1. Check electrolyte level and state of charge.
Fuel System—
1. Clean fuel filter.
2. Check fuel flow.
3. Examine fuel lines and filler cap.
Rear Suspension—
1. Lubricate swing arm pivot.

Wheels, Tires, and Brakes—
1. Check tightness of spokes.
2. Check wheel runout.
3. Examine tires for wear and damage.
4. Check brake wear.
Frame—
1. Check tightness of nuts and bolts.
Final Drive—
1. Service chain.
2. Check sprockets for wear and damage.
EVERY 6,000 MILES/12 MONTHS:
Front Suspension and Steering—
1. Check movement of steering head bearings.
2. Change oil in fork legs.
EVERY 12,000 MILES/24 MONTHS:
Fuel System—
1. Examine carburetor rubber caps.
Brakes—
1. Examine the brake hoses and cylinders (CB 450K4 and K5).

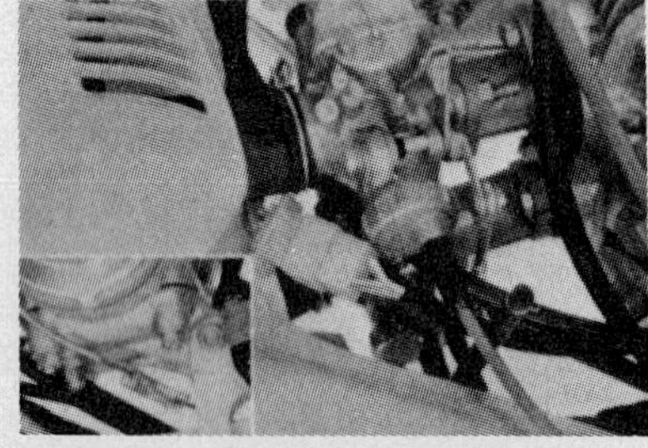
Disconnecting the electrical leads.

RECOMMENDED OILS

	125	175	350	450
Engine Oil	10W-40 or 20W-50, service rating SE (formerly MS)			
capacity (pt)	2.5	3.2	4.2	6.0
Fork Oil capacity oz/cc)	10W-30 4.9/140	10W-30 ①	10W-30 ②	10W-30 ③

① CB and CD 175—4.9/140; CL and SL 175—5.4/160
② CB and CL 350—6.75/200; SL 350—6.5/185
③ CB 450 through 1969, and CL 450—9.25/290; CB 450K4—7.2/225; CB 450K5—5.4/160

ENGINE AND TRANSMISSION

Engine Removal and Installation

125 AND 175 MODELS

1. Remove the footpeg, kick-start pedal, and shift lever. Drain the engine oil.
2. Remove the entire exhaust system from each side as a unit.
3. Disconnect the wires from the spark plugs and tuck them up out of the way.
4. Remove the small cover from the right side of the cylinder head and disconnect the tachometer cable from the tachometer drive.
5. Remove the seat.
6. Turn off the fuel tap and disconnect the fuel lines from the carburetors.
7. Uncouple the electrical leads at the connectors. Refer to the accompanying illustration.
8. Loosen the air filter tube clamps.
9. Unscrew the carburetor caps and withdraw the slides. Tie them out of the way. (Simply disconnect the cable from the carburetor on the CD 125.)
10. Remove the left-side rear crankcase cover. Separate the drive chain at the master link and disconnect the clutch cable from the release lever.
11. Disconnect the starter motor cable from the starter solenoid (if applicable).
12. Take out the nine engine mounting bolts and remove the engine from the right side.

Installation is a reversal of the removal procedure. Note the following points:

1. Do not forget to connect the battery ground cable when installing the engine mounting bolts.

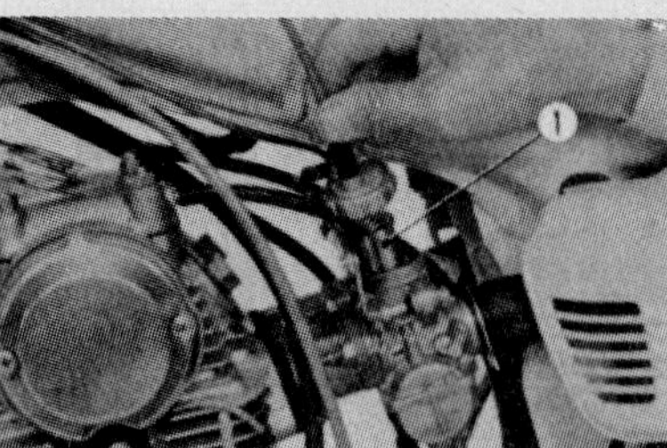
Removing the carburetor slides.

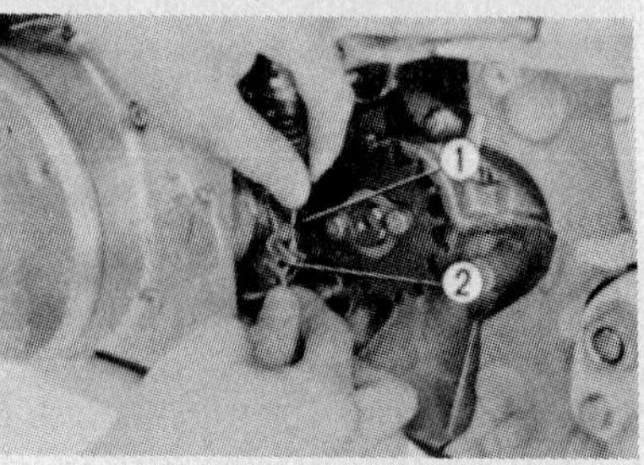
Disconnecting the clutch cable from the release lever.

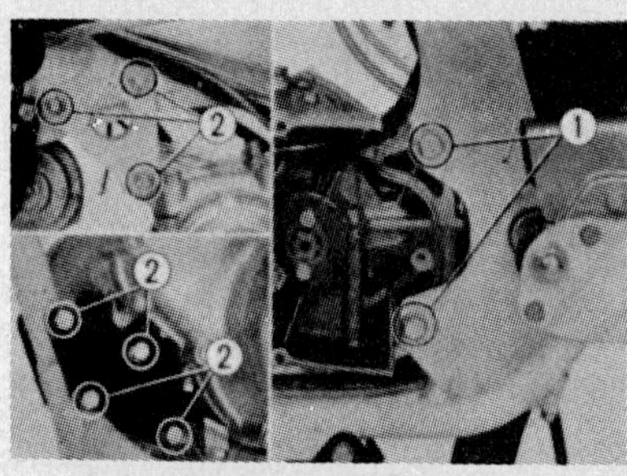
Engine mounting bolts.

2. The chain master link clip should be installed so that the closed end faces the direction of forward rotation.
3. Make sure that the steel ball has been installed in the clutch release lever before reinstalling the crankcase cover.
4. Do not forget to refill the engine with oil.

Top End Overhaul

CYLINDER HEAD REMOVAL

1. Remove the engine from the frame.
2. Unscrew the cylinder head nuts and then the head nut (175 only). Remove the cam cover.
3. Rotate the crankshaft until the cam chain master link is accessible, then dis-

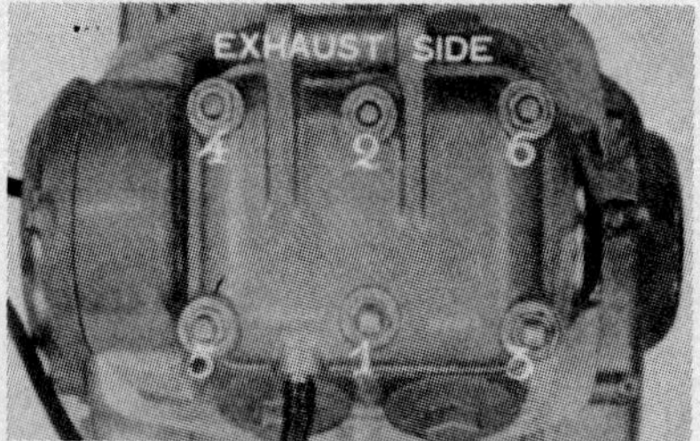

Cylinder head nuts (125cc models).

Cylinder head nuts and bolt (1) (175cc models).

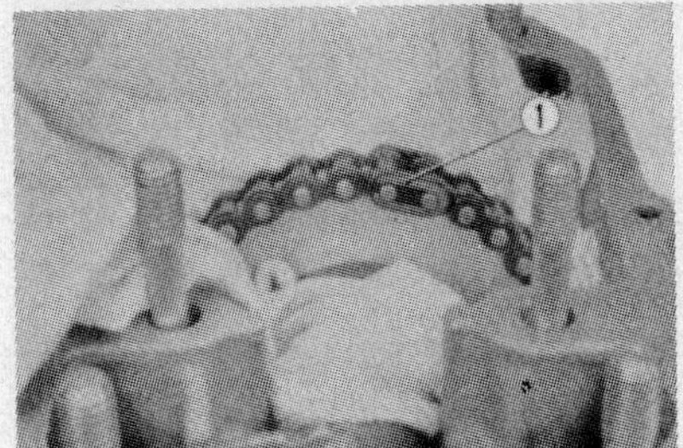
Cam chain master link clip (1).

connect the cam chain. Attach a length of wire to each end of the chain so that it will not fall into the crankcase.

4. Lift the head carefully off of the cylinder barrel.

CYLINDER BARREL AND PISTON REMOVAL

1. Unscrew the cylinder retaining bolt(s) and carefully lift the cylinder off of the crankcase. Take care to prevent the pistons from being damaged on the studs as the cylinder is withdrawn over them.

The cylinder can be removed after the retaining bolt (1) has been unscrewed.

2. Remove the wrist pin circlips from the pistons.

CAUTION: *Do not allow the circlips to fall into the crankcase. To avoid having to split the cases to retrieve a clip, cover the crankcase opening with a cloth.*

3. Remove the wrist pins from the pistons. Mark the pistons, inside the skirt, so that they can be reinstalled in their original positions.

COMPONENT INSPECTION AND SERVICE

Camshaft

The camshaft can be removed, if necessary, after the following components have been removed: left and right head side covers, ignition points breaker plate assembly, ignition advance unit (located under the breaker plate), and the valve adjuster access caps. Rotate the camshaft until the rocker arms are resting on the heel of the cam, and remove the rocker arm shafts and rocker arms. (On the 125 it will be necessary to remove the rocker shaft end plate.) Lift the camshaft out of the cylinder head. Using a micrometer, measure the camshaft end diameters, cam height, and cam base circle diameter. Compare your results with the specifications at the end of the chapter. Replace the camshaft if the measurements are outside the serviceable limit, or if the cam lobes are scored or worn.

Valve Rocker Assembly

Measure the diameter of the rocker arm bores and rocker arm shafts and compare with the specifications. Check that the rocker arm pads that contact the camshaft lobes are not excessively worn. Check the cam chain for stretch and replace it if necessary.

Cylinder Head and Valves

Compress the springs (Honda spring compressor no. 07031-21601) and remove the collars, retainers, springs, and valves. Check the following measurements against the specifications at the end of the chapter: valve length, stem diameter, head thickness, valve face concentricity, and valve spring free length. Replace valves as necessary. When replacing worn valves it is wise also, to replace the valve guides, which can be driven out of the head with a suitably sized drift. Since the guides are an interference fit, oversize guides should be used.

If the valve seat is burnt, worn, or damaged in any way, it should be recut. Valve seat angle is 45°. Seat width should not be greater than 0.08 in. (2 mm). Nominal seat width is 0.04 in. (0.1 mm).

NOTE: *Do not attempt to reface the valves or refinish the valve stem ends, as these surfaces have a thin stellite facing that will be destroyed if cut.*

Carefully scrape carbon deposits from the combustion chambers and thoroughly clean the cylinder head. Before the valves are installed, whether they are the original ones or new, they should be lapped into their seats so that a perfect seal will be obtained.

Check for warpage of the head mating surface with a straightedge and feeler gauge. Cap or mill the head if clearance between the head and straightedge exceeds 0.002 in. (0.05 mm).

Cylinder Bore and Pistons

Measure the cylinder bore diameter at

Take off the cover (1) and remove the points breaker plate assembly (2).

Hold the camshaft from turning with a block of wood (1) and unscrew the ignition advance unit securing bolt (2).

Take out the screws and remove the side covers (1).

Remove the rocker arm shaft end plate (125cc models only).

1. Rocker shaft end plate
2. Plate retaining bolt
3. Rocker arm shafts

Slide the rocker shafts out (2) and remove the rocker arms (1).

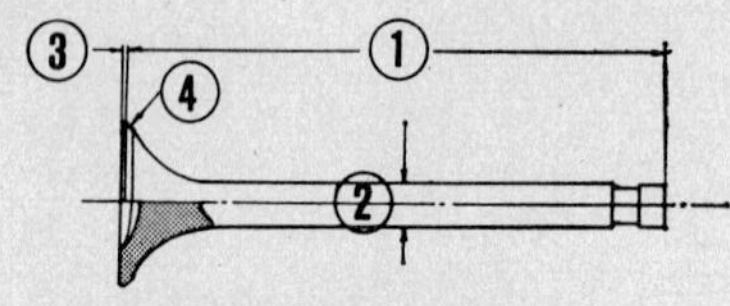

Valve measurements.
1. Length
2. Stem diameter
3. Head thickness
4. Valve face concentricity (out of round)

the top, center, and bottom in both the fore-and-aft and side-to-side directions. Reboring will be necessary if any of the measurements exceeds 1.736 in (125) or 2.051 in. (175), or if the cylinder bore is tapered or out of round more than 0.002 in. (0.05 mm). See the specifications at the end of the chapter for piston oversizes. The bores should be honed if they have been rebored or if new rings are to be used.

Measure the diameter of the piston skirt, perpendicular to the wrist pin. Pistons should be replaced when calculated clearance between the piston and cylinder is greater than 0.004 in. (0.1 mm).

If the original pistons are to be reused, remove the rings and clean the grooves using a piece of one of the old rings. Remove the carbon deposit from the piston tops. Roll the new rings around the grooves before installing them to ensure that there is sufficient clearance. The

Using a dial indicator (1) to measure cylinder bore wear (2).

rings should roll smoothly without binding. Install the rings on the pistons using a ring expander to avoid breaking them. Make sure that the mark on the rings (if any) is facing up.

PISTON AND CYLINDER BARREL INSTALLATION

1. Install the pistons on the connecting rods in their original positions. Be sure to use new wrist pin circlips.
2. Stagger the rings so that the gaps are 120° apart and not in line with or perpendicular to the piston boss axis.
3. Install the cylinder base gasket and two dowel pins.
4. Install piston bases or blocks of wood cut to suitable size under the pistons to hold them in position.
5. Compress the rings (after oiling them liberally) and carefully install the cylinder barrel over them. Take care not to damage the rings.
6. Before seating the cylinder fully, raise the cam chain through the center and hold the ends from dropping back down. Install the cylinder retaining bolt(s).

Cylinder dowel pins (1).

CYLINDER HEAD INSTALLATION

1. Install the head gasket, dowel pins, and O-rings on the cylinder.
2. Loosen the adjuster locknut and bolt, push the cam chain tensioner as far as it will go into the head, and lock it there with the adjuster bolt.
3. Assemble the valves, rocker arms, and camshaft into the head in reverse order of disassembly.
4. Fit the head carefully onto the cylinder.
5. To properly set the valve timing, first turn the crankshaft until the "T" mark on the alternator rotor is aligned with the timing index mark on the alternator stator. Then rotate the camshaft until the "O" mark on the face of the

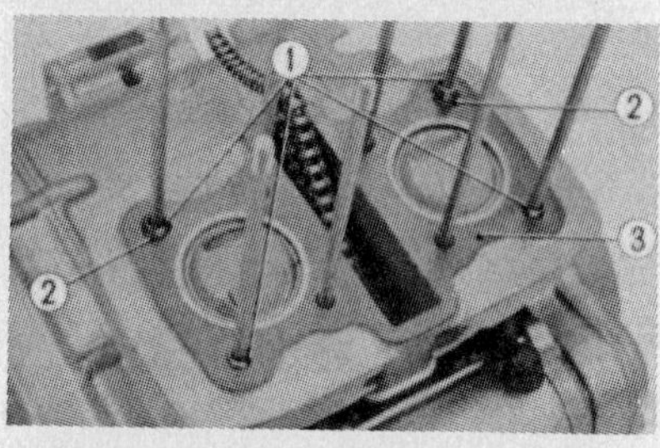

Install the dowel pins (1), O-rings (2), and head gasket (3).

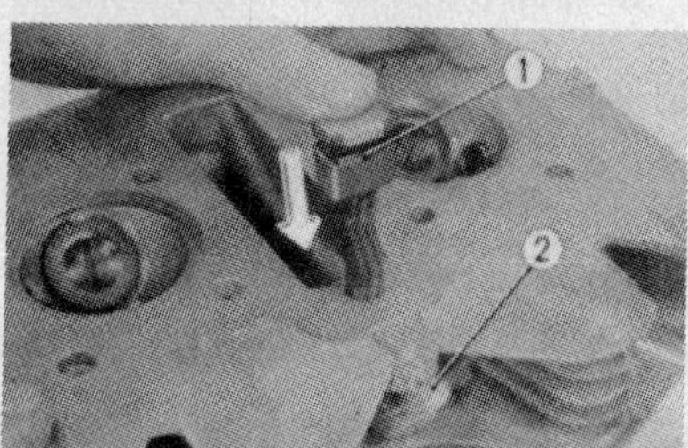

Loosen the adjuster bolt (2) and push the cam chain tensioner (1) into the head.

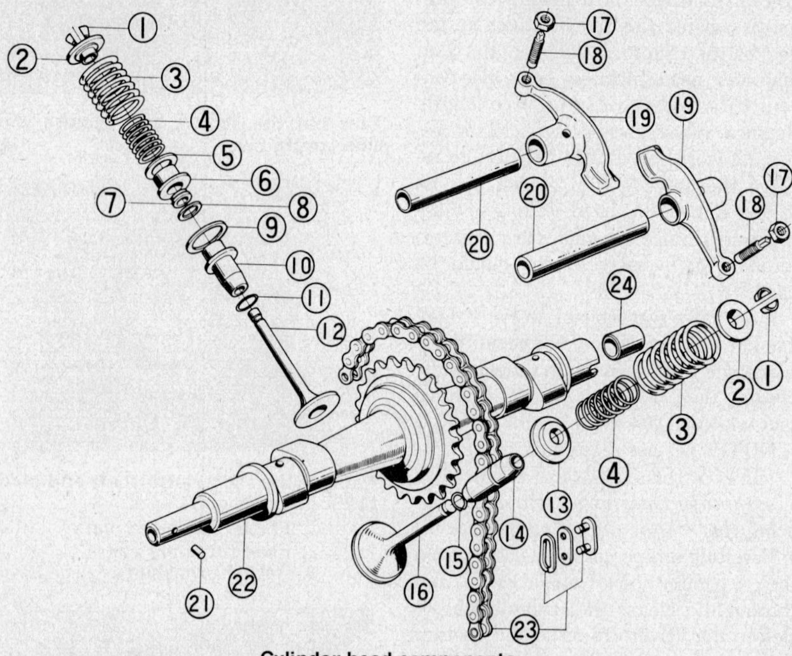

Cylinder head components.

1. Valve collar
2. Valve retainer
3. Outer valve spring
4. Inner valve spring
5. Inner seal
6. Valve stem seal cap
7. Valve stem seal
8. Stem seal rubber cushion
9. Valve spring seat B
10. Exhaust valve guide
11. O-ring
12. Exhaust valve
13. Valve spring seat
14. Intake valve guide
15. Valve guide clip
16. Intake valve
17. Valve tappet adjusting locknut
18. Valve tappet adjuster
19. Rocker arm
20. Rocker arm shaft
21. Knock pin
22. Camshaft
23. Camchain
24. Dowel pin

sprocket is at the top, and install the cam chain. The master link clip must be installed with the closed end facing the direction chain rotation.

6. Install the cylinder head nuts and tighten them gradually, in the sequence shown, to 12–15 ft lb.

7. Reinstall the engine and perform a complete tune-up, paying special attention to valve and cam chain adjustments. Refer to chapter 3. The valves and cam chain should be checked again after approximately 500 miles have been covered. Don't forget to refill the engine with oil.

Connect the cam chain when the "O" mark (1) on the cam sprocket is at the top, with the "T" mark on the alternator rotor, and the timing index mark aligned.

Crankcases

SPLITTING THE CRANKCASES

1. Remove the engine from the frame and remove the cylinder head, barrel, and pistons as described in the preceding section on top end overhaul.

NOTE: *If desired, the cases can be split without disassembling the top end.*

2. Take out the screws and remove the left-side crankcase cover.

3. Unscrew the alternator rotor retaining bolt and remove the rotor using Honda tool no. 07011-21601 or a suitably sized bolt.

4. Take out the three screws and remove the starter clutch. Remove the master link and take off the starter chain. Remove the set plate and pull the starter sprocket off of the crankshaft.

5. Remove the kickstart lever, take out the ten retaining screws, and remove the right-side crankcase cover.

6. Unscrew the four clutch pressure plate retaining bolts and withdraw the clutch discs and plates.

7. Remove the oil filter rotor locknut and then the filter retaining nut, and pull the rotor off of the crankshaft.

8. Take out the 20 mm circlip and remove the clutch center.

9. Unscrew the oil pump mounting nuts and remove the oil pump assembly and clutch outer housing as an assembly.

CAUTION: *Take care not to damage the crankshaft when removing the clutch housing.*

10. Remove the gearshift spindle and kickstart return spring.

11. Remove the crankcase securing bolts and nuts and separate the crankcase halves with a rubber hammer. Do not neglect to remove the bolt under the oil drainplug.

Using a threaded puller (1) to remove the rotor (2).

Starter chain (1).

Pressure plate retaining bolts (1) and clutch assembly (2).

Oil filter rotor (1) and oil pump assembly (2).

Circlip (1) and clutch center (3).

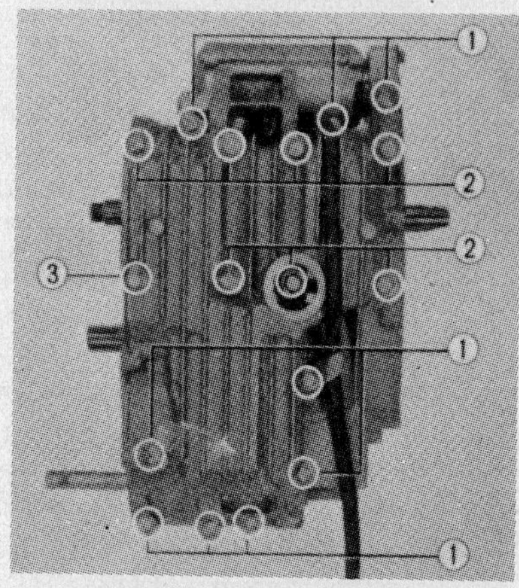

Crankcase securing bolts—6 mm (1) and 8 mm (2) (175cc models).

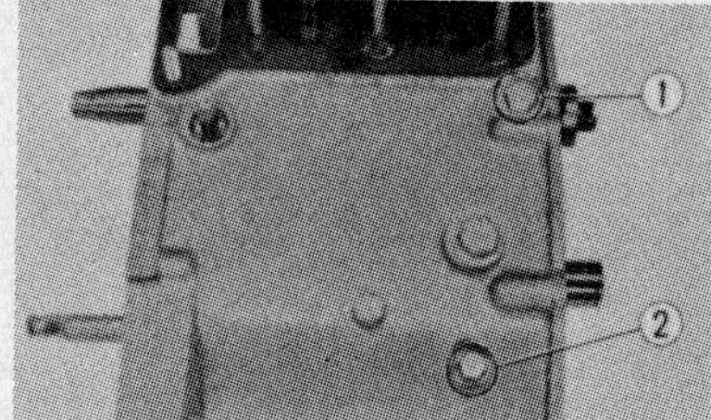

Top crankcase mounting bolts (1 and 2) (125cc models).

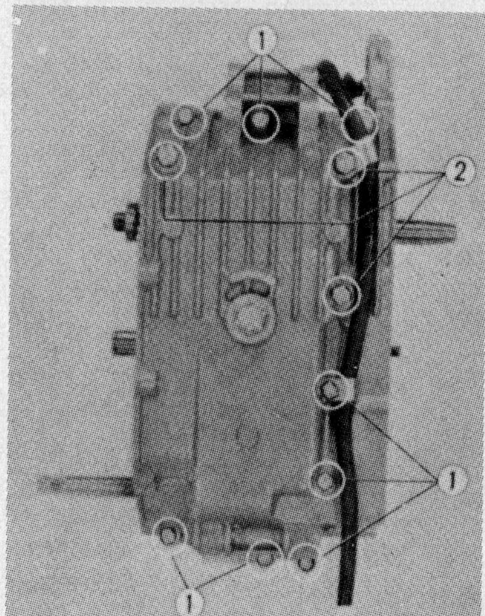

Bottom crankcase securing bolts—6 mm (1) and 8 mm (2) (125cc models).

ASSEMBLING THE CRANKCASES

Assembly is a reversal of the disassembly procedures. Observe the following points:

1. Clean the crankcase mating surfaces carefully and inspect them for scratches, signs of leaks, and other damage. Use a sealing compound on the surfaces to prevent oil leaks.

2. Don't forget to reinstall the two dowel pins in the upper crankcase if they were removed.

Crankshaft and Connecting Rods

DISASSEMBLY

The crankshaft is a built-up unit with one-piece connecting rods and main bearings. It cannot be disassembled and repaired by normal means. Check for excessive wear as described below, and if any of the measurements are beyond the serviceable limits the crankshaft assembly should be replaced.

INSPECTION

Support the outer main bearings in V-blocks, as shown, and measure crankshaft runout 1.3 in. (30 mm) in from each end of the crankshaft with a dial indicator. (Runout equals one-half the dial indicator reading.) Maximum acceptable runout is 0.0032 in. (0.08 mm).

Support the ends of the crankshaft with V-blocks (or any other means that will hold it securely) and check the radial and axial clearance of the main bearings. Maximum acceptable axial clearance is 0.004 in. (0.1 mm), and maximum radial clearance is 0.002 in. (0.05 mm).

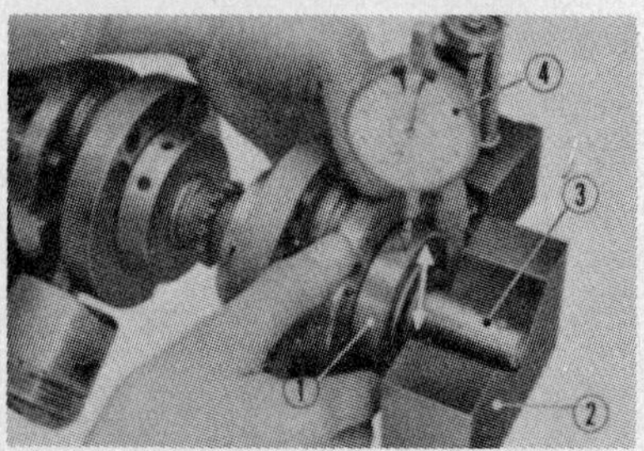

Checking the radial clearance of the main bearing (1) with a dial indicator (4).

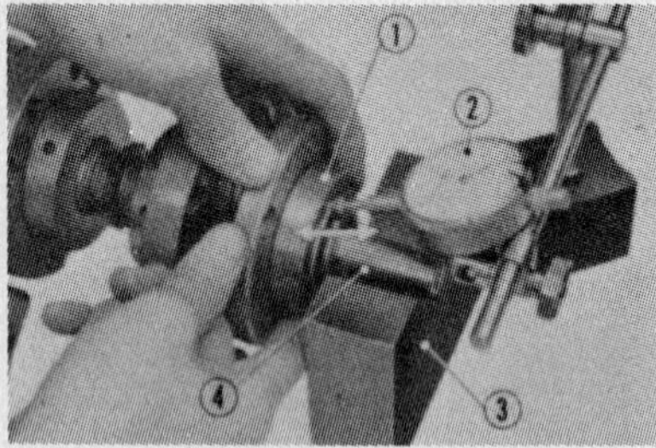

Checking axial clearance of the main bearing (1) with a dial indicator (2).

Measure the amount of side to side movement of the connecting rod at the small end, as shown in the accompanying illustration. Maximum permissible deflection (indicative of worn rod bearings) is 0.118 in. (3.0 mm).

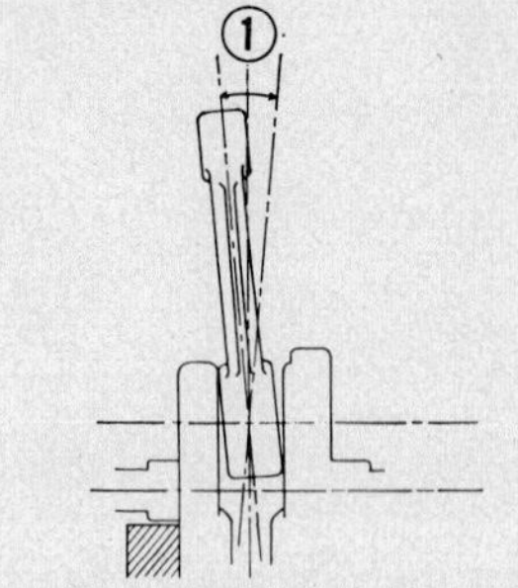

Checking the connecting rod bearings by measuring small end movement (1).

ASSEMBLY

When installing the crankshaft into the crankcase, make sure that the dowel pins in the bearing seats of the upper crankcase are installed, and that the dowels fit into the locating holes in the main bearings. This can be made simpler by aligning the lines scribed into the outside of the bearing races with the crankcase mating surface.

Dowel pins (1), upper crankcase (2).

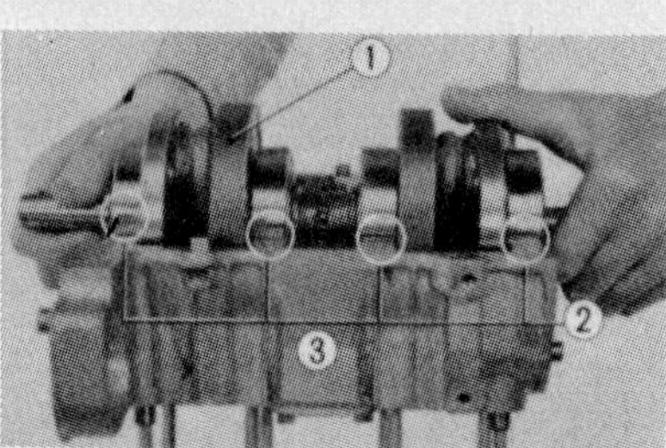

Crankshaft (1), bearing scribe lines (2), and upper crankcase (3).

Clutch Service

DISASSEMBLY

1. Remove the kickstart lever, take out the ten retaining screws, and remove the right-side crankcase cover. Refer to the preceding section on splitting the crankcases.
2. Unscrew the four clutch pressure plate bolts and withdraw the clutch discs and plates.
3. If you wish to remove the clutch housing and hub assembly, first remove the oil filter retaining nut, and pull the filter rotor off the crankshaft.
4. Take out the 20 mm circlip and remove the clutch center.
5. Unscrew the oil pump mounting nuts and remove the oil pump assembly and clutch outer housing as an assembly.

CAUTION: *Take care not to damage the crankshaft when removing the clutch housing.*

INSPECTION

Measure the thickness of the clutch discs and plates with a vernier caliper or micrometer. Replace the discs if they measure less than 0.0984 in. (2.5 mm), and the plates if they measure less than 0.114 in. (2.9 mm). Warpage of the plates and discs should be checked by placing them on a flat surface such as a surface plate or a plate of glass, and measuring any gaps with a feeler gauge. Maximum allowable warpage for the discs and plates is 0.02 in. (0.5 mm). Measure the free length of the clutch springs and replace them if less than 1.20 in. (30.3 mm).

Examine the primary drive gears at this time for chipping, pitting, and excessive wear; replace if necessary. Before reinstalling the plates and discs, make sure that the tabs and slots in the clutch center are in good condition.

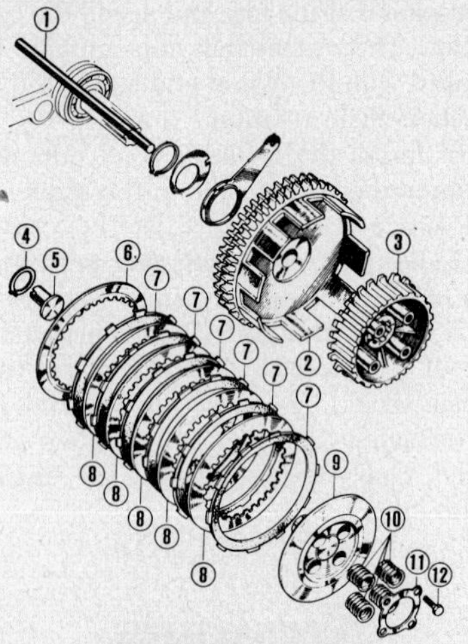

Clutch components.

1. Clutch rod
2. Clutch outer complete
3. Clutch center
4. 20 mm set ring
5. Clutch lifter joint piece
6. Clutch plate B
7. Clutch friction disc
8. Clutch plate
9. Clutch pressure plate
10. Clutch spring
11. Clutch spring retaining plate
12. 6 x 20 hex bolt

ASSEMBLY

Assembly is a reversal of the disassembly procedures. Install the discs and plates alternately, beginning with a disc. Take care to torque the pressure plate bolts evenly. Perform a complete clutch adjustment after assembly. Refer to the "Chassis" section.

Transmission Service

DISASSEMBLY

1. Remove the engine from the frame and follow disassembly steps 2–11 under "Splitting the Crankcases."
2. Lift out the transmission mainshaft and countershaft assemblies.
3. Disassemble the gears from the shafts, taking care to lay them out in order of assembly.

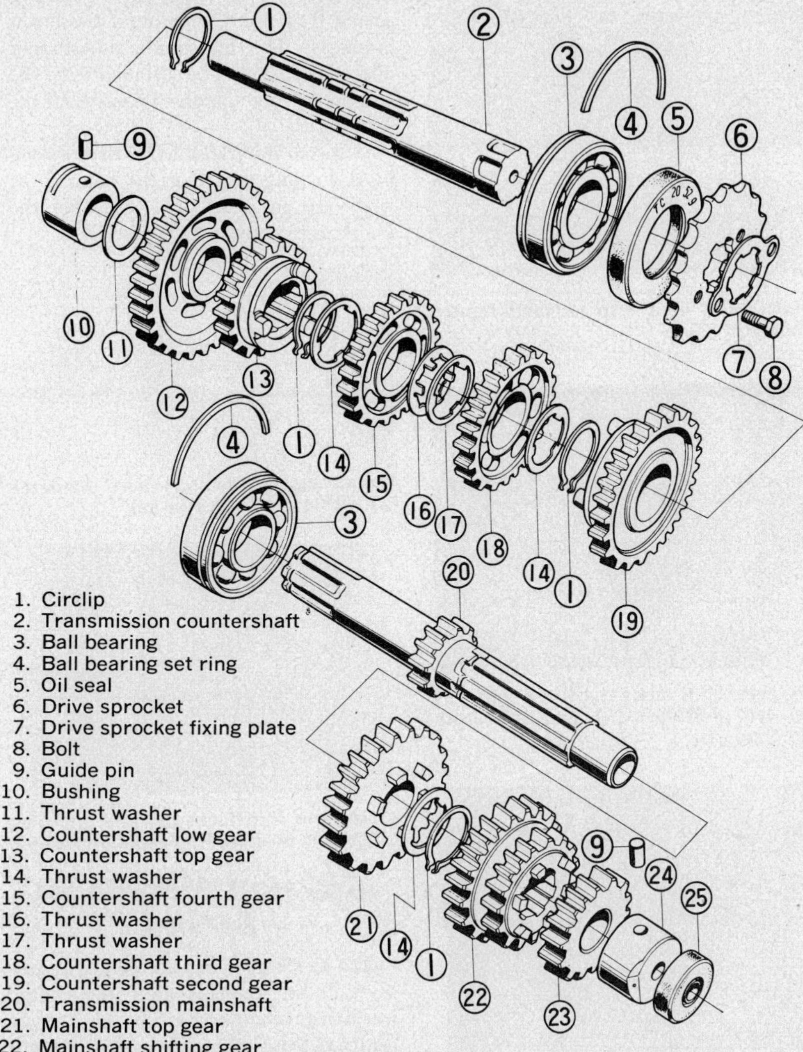

1. Circlip
2. Transmission countershaft
3. Ball bearing
4. Ball bearing set ring
5. Oil seal
6. Drive sprocket
7. Drive sprocket fixing plate
8. Bolt
9. Guide pin
10. Bushing
11. Thrust washer
12. Countershaft low gear
13. Countershaft top gear
14. Thrust washer
15. Countershaft fourth gear
16. Thrust washer
17. Thrust washer
18. Countershaft third gear
19. Countershaft second gear
20. Transmission mainshaft
21. Mainshaft top gear
22. Mainshaft shifting gear
23. Mainshaft second gear
24. Bushing
25. Oil seal

Five-speed transmission components.

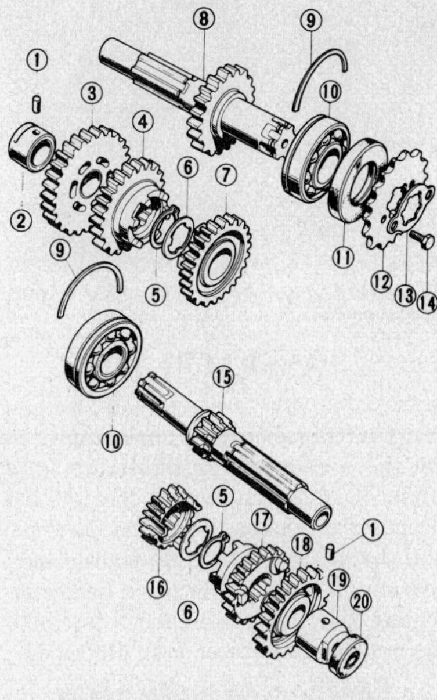

Four-speed transmission components.

1. Knock pin
2. Bushing
3. Countershaft low gear
4. Countershaft second gear
5. Circlip
6. Thrust washer
7. Countershaft third gear
8. Transmission countershaft
9. Bearing set ring
10. Ball bearing
11. Oil seal
12. Drive sprocket
13. Drive sprocket plate
14. Bolt
15. Transmission mainshaft
16. Mainshaft second gear
17. Mainshaft third gear
18. Mainshaft top gear
19. Bushing
20. Oil seal

INSPECTION

1. Examine the dogs on the respective gears and if damaged or excessively worn, the gears should be replaced. Check to make sure that the gears are free to slide smoothly on the shafts.

2. Check the backlash of the mating gears, with the shaft assemblies in the case, using a dial indicator. Replace gears that are outside the limits given in the table.

1st, 2nd, 3rd gears

Standard Value	Serviceable Limit
0.0017 ~ 0.0052 in. (0.044 ~ 0.133 mm)	Replace if over 0.008 in. (0.2 mm)

4th and 5th gears

Standard Value	Serviceable Limit
0.0016 ~ 0.005 in. (0.042 ~ 0.126 mm)	Replace if over 0.008 in. (0.2 mm)

3. Check the gear teeth for pitting, wear, and damage. Gears must be replaced in sets.

4. Compute the gear-to-shaft clearance of the gears in the accompanying table by measuring first the shaft diameter and then the gear bore diameter, and subtracting the former from the latter. (M4 means mainshaft fourth gear, etc.)

4-SPEED TRANSMISSION

M2, C3

Standard Value	Serviceable Limit
0.001 ~ 0.002 in. (0.029 ~ 0.053 mm)	Replace if over 0.0047 in. (0.1 mm)

C1, M4

Standard Value	Serviceable Limit
0.0006 ~ 0.0018 in. (0.016 ~ 0.045 mm)	Replace if over 0.0047 in. (0.1 mm)

5-SPEED TRANSMISSIONS

M4

Standard Value	Serviceable Limit
0.0008 ~ 0.0024 in. (0.02 ~ 0.062 mm)	Replace if over 0.004 in. (0.1 mm)

M5, C1

Standard Value	Serviceable Limit
0.0006 ~ 0.0018 in. (0.016 ~ 0.045 mm)	Replace if over 0.004 in. (0.1 mm)

C2, C3

Standard Value	Serviceable Limit
0.0016 ~ 0.003 in. (0.04 ~ 0.082 mm)	Replace if over 0.0047 in. (0.12 mm)

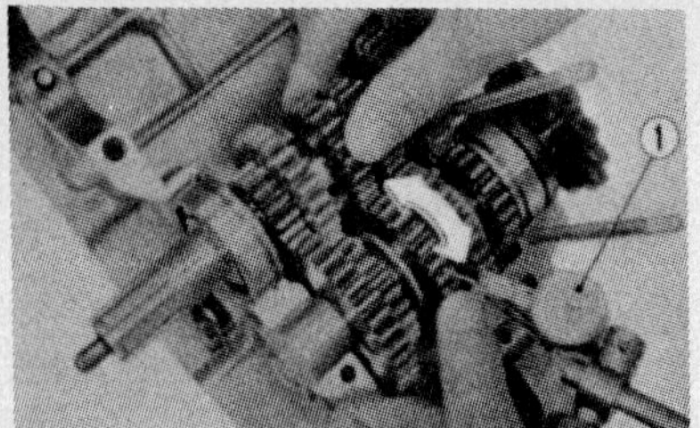
Measuring gear backlash with a dial indicator (1).

ASSEMBLY

Assemble the transmission components in reverse order of disassembly, using the accompanying illustration as a guide. It is very important that the old circlips are not reused on the transmission shafts. Check that the transmission bearing set rings are in place before installing the shaft assemblies. Assemble the crankcases as previously described.

Shifter Mechanism

DISASSEMBLY

1. Follow disassembly steps 1 and 2 under the preceding section on transmission service.
2. Remove the neutral indicator switch limit arm and then remove the switch from the top of the crankcase.
3. Pull out the shift drum guide pin clips and guide pins.
4. Unscrew the 6 mm bolt and remove the shift drum limit arm and limit arm plate. Withdraw the shift drum.
5. The shift spindle and return spring can be removed after the circlip has been removed from the end of the spindle.

INSPECTION

1. Check that the shift spindle and arm are not bent or twisted.
2. Examine the shift fork fingers for damage and excessive wear. The forks must be in good condition for the transmission to shift properly. Replace the forks if the fingers measure less than 0.-200 in., or if the fork bore inside diameter is greater than 1.342 in.
3. Check that the shift drum tracks and shift fork guide pins are not excessively worn.
4. Check the springs for breakage and adequate tension.

ASSEMBLY

1. Install the shift drum from the right side of the upper crankcase and assemble the shift forks onto the drum as shown.
2. Install the shift fork guide pins and pin clips.
3. Assemble the neutral switch into the shift drum.
4. Install the shift drum limit arm and plate.
5. Install the shift return spring in the lower crankcase.
6. Install the shift spindle and return spring from the right side of the lower crankcase. The shift spindle side stopper and oil seal should be installed from the left end of the spindle. Then install the set ring.
7. Install the transmission shaft assemblies, making sure that the bearing set rings are in place, and assemble the crankcases as previously described.

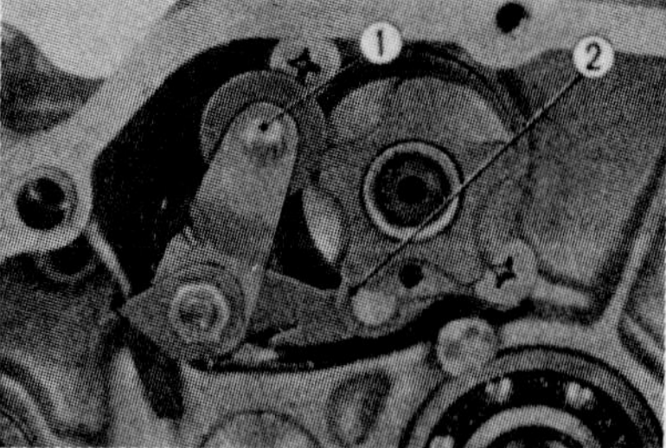
Shift drum limit arm (1) and neutral limit arm (2).

The right shift fork (1), center shift fork (2), left shift fork (3), and the guide pin clips (4).

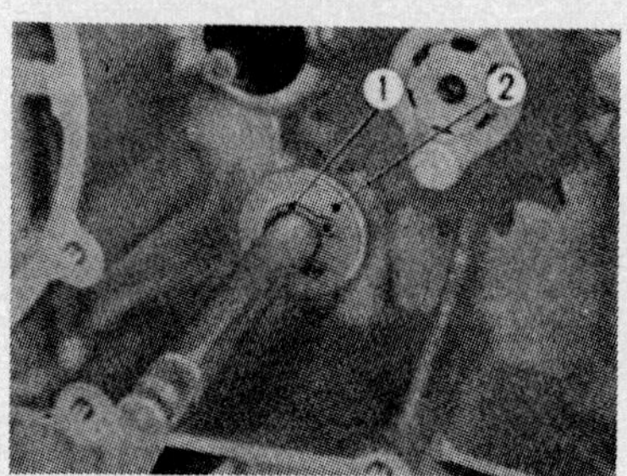
Shift drum spindle circlip (1) and washer (2).

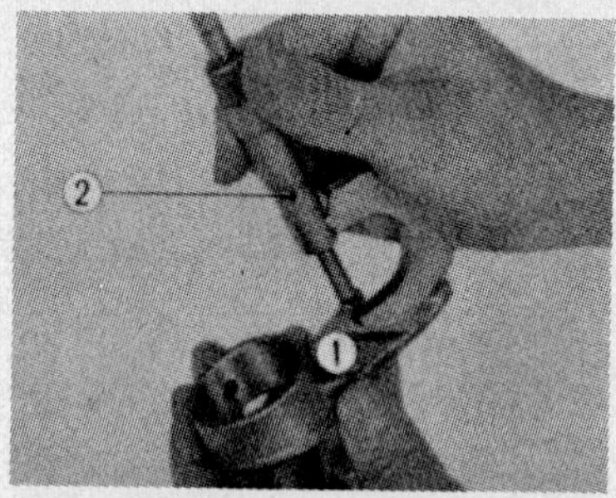
Measuring the thickness of the shift fork fingers (1) with a micrometer (2).

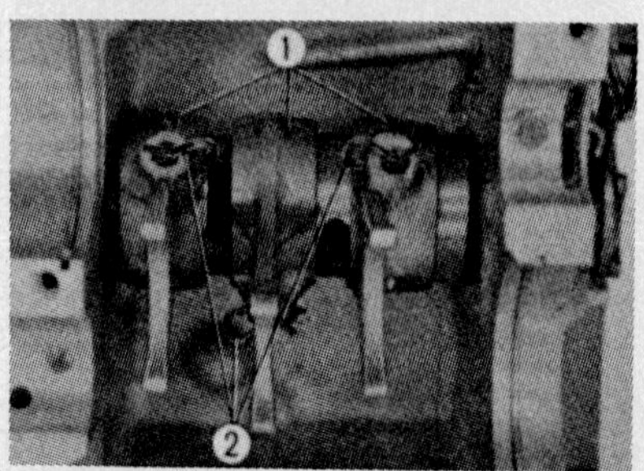
Install the shift forks (1) and pin clips (2) in this position (five-speed models).

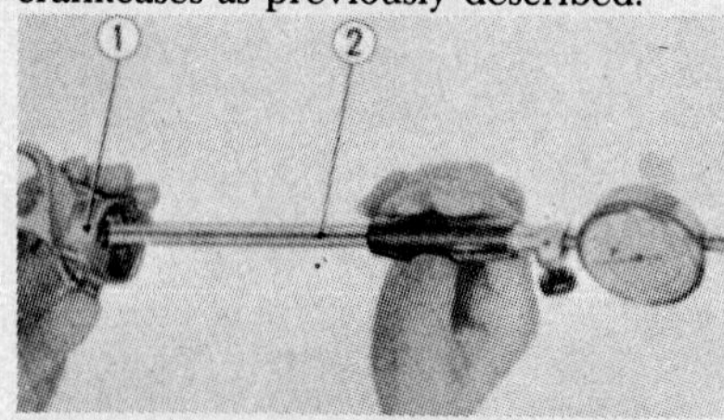
Measuring the shift fork bore diameter (1) with a dial indicator (2).

Install the shift forks (2) and pin clips (1) in this position (four-speed models).

Kickstart Mechanism Service

The kickstart shaft and ratchet assembly can be removed after the shifter mechanism components have been disassembled from the crankcase. A slipping ratchet assembly (normally the only cause for kick-start failure) must be replaced.

Removing the kick-start assembly, showing the locating pin (1).

Engine Removal and Installation

350

1. Drain the engine oil.
2. Turn the fuel tap off, disconnect the fuel lines, and remove the gas tank.
3. Remove the entire exhaust system, as a unit, from each side.
4. Remove the footpeg and shift lever, and take off the left-side rear crankcase cover.
5. Separate the drive chain at the master link and disconnect the clutch cable from the release lever.

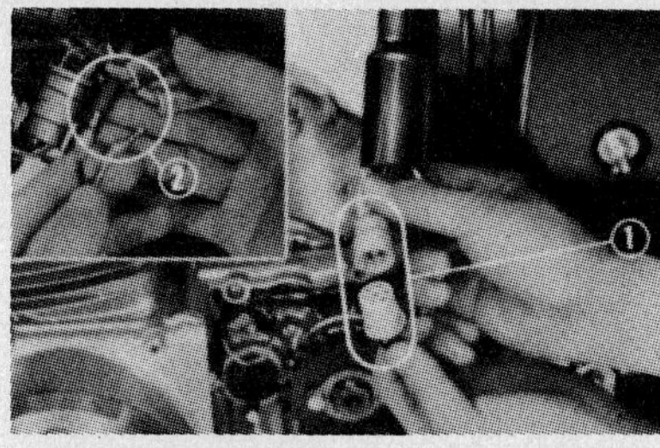

The electrical lead connector (1) and contact breaker connectors.

6. Back the rear brake adjuster nut off so that the brake pedal drops down and out of the way.

7. Disconnect the throttle cables from the throttle sides at the carburetors.

NOTE: *On the SL 350K1 and K2, unscrew the carburetor tops and lift out the slides. Tie them out of the way.*

8. Disconnect the electrical leads at the connectors. Refer to the accompanying illustration.

9. Disconnect the wires from the spark plugs and tuck them up out of the way.

10. Disconnect the starter motor cable from the starter solenoid (if applicable).

11. Disconnect the tachometer cable from the tachometer drive at the engine.

12. Unscrew the engine mounting bolts and remove the engine from the right side.

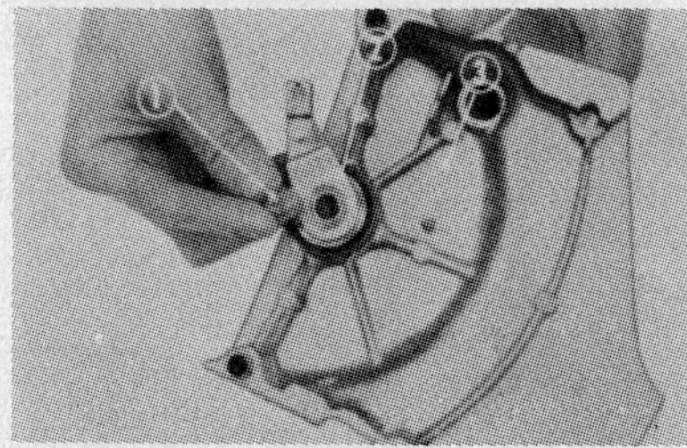

Steel ball (1), clutch release lever (2), and crankcase cover (3).

Installation is a reversal of the removal procedure. The following points should be noted:

1. Do not neglect to reconnect the battery ground cable when installing the engine mounting bolts.

2. The chain master link clip should be installed so that the closed end faces the direction of forward rotation.

3. Make sure that the steel ball has been installed in the clutch release lever before reinstalling the crankcase cover. And replace engine oil.

Top End Overhaul

CYLINDER HEAD REMOVAL

1. Unscrew the eight cap nuts and lift off the cam cover.

2. Remove the alternator cover and ignition points cover.

3. Take out the screws and remove the points breaker plate assembly. Unscrew

Points breaker plate assembly (1) and the ignition advance unit (2).

Rocker arm shaft end nuts (1), rocker arm shafts (2), cylinder head side cover (3), and rocker arms (4).

the bolt from the center of the breaker cam and remove the ignition advance unit.

4. Remove the rocker arm shaft end nuts (valve adjuster locknuts) and then take out the screws and remove the cylinder head side covers. Remove the rocker arm shafts.

5. Unbolt and remove the cam chain tensioner assembly from the rear of the cylinder barrel.

6. Rotate the crankshaft until one of the cam chain sprocket retaining bolts is accessible, and unscrew the bolt. Then rotate the crankshaft one full turn and remove the remaining bolt.

NOTE: *Special bolts are used for this application and are marked on their heads with the number "9". Do not use any substitute bolts.*

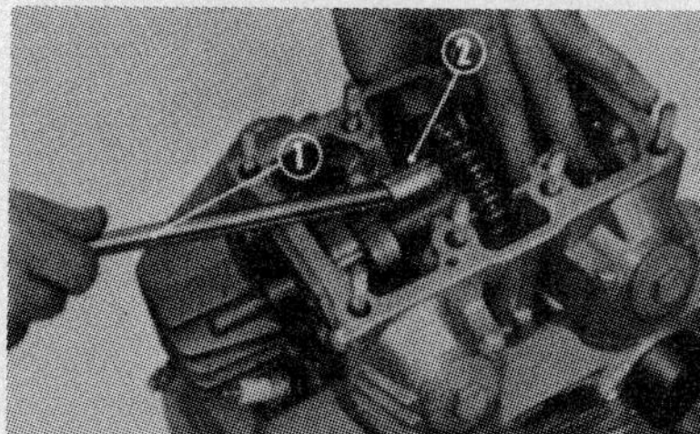

Unscrewing the cam sprocket bolt (2).

Cam case mounting screws (1) and the cam case (2).

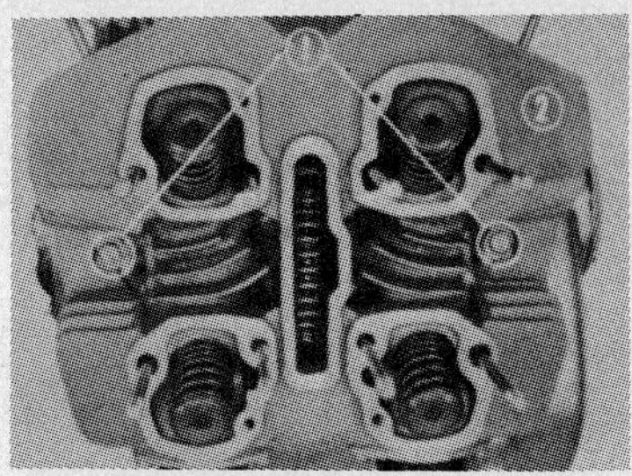

Cylinder head bolts (1) and the cylinder head (2).

7. Withdraw the camshaft through the cam chain sprocket, from the right side of the engine.

8. Take out the four screws and remove the cam case.

9. Remove the spark plugs and unscrew the two head bolts.

10. Lift the cylinder head off of the cylinder.

CYLINDER BARREL AND PISTON REMOVAL

1. Carefully lift the cylinder off of the crankcase. Take care to prevent the pistons from being damaged on the studs as they cylinder is withdrawn over them.

2. Remove the wrist pin circlips from the pistons.

CAUTION: *Do not allow the circlips to fall into the crankcase. To avoid having to split the cases to retrieve a clip, cover the crankcase opening with a cloth.*

3. Push the wrist pins out of the pistons. Mark the pistons, inside the skirt, so that they can be reinstalled in their original positions.

COMPONENT INSPECTION AND SERVICE

Camshaft

Carefully examine the cam lobes for excessive wear and scoring. Temporarily reinstall the camshaft back into the cylinder head and measure the side clearance with a dial indicator. If side clearance exceeds 0.04 in. (0.2 mm), obtain a special 0.2 mm shim available from Honda dealers for use with the camshaft, and install it during reassembly.

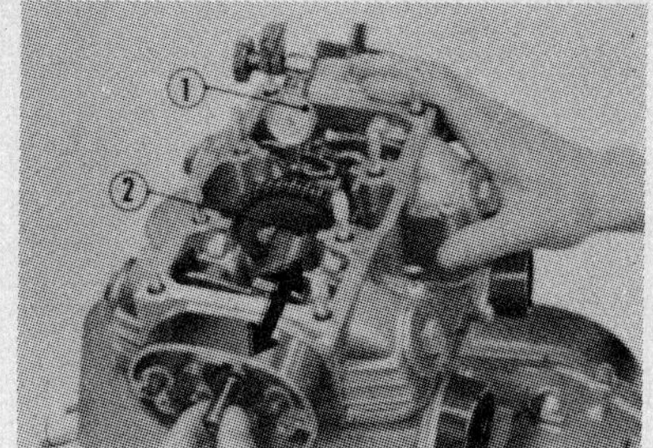

Using a dial indicator (1) to measure the side-clearance of the camshaft (2).

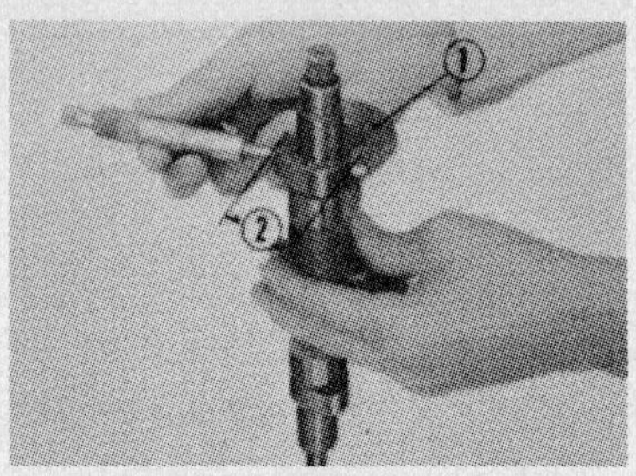
Using a micrometer (1) to measure cam height (2).

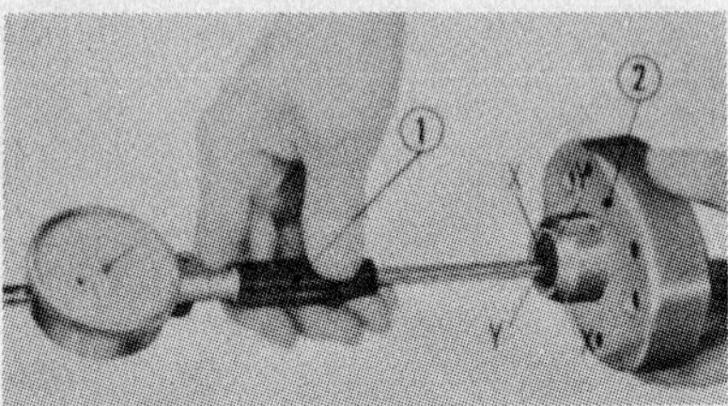
Using a dial indicator (1) to measure the inside diameter of the cylinder head side-cover.

Measure the height of the cam lobes and replace the camshaft if the dimension of either the intake or exhaust lobes is less than 1.444 in. (36.68 mm). The diameter of the left and right bearing surfaces of the camshaft should not measure less than 0.863 in. (20.050 mm). The inside diameter of the left and right cylinder head covers, measured in both the "X" and "Y" directions as shown, should not exceed 0.868 in. (21.920 mm). Replace if necessary. Minor defects on the cams can be finished off with a fine oilstone.

Valve Rocker Assembly

Measure the diameter of the rocker arm shafts. Replace the shafts if less than 0.508 in (12.9 mm). Check the fit of the rocker arms on their shafts, and make sure that the rocker arm pads (cam contact surface) are not excessively worn.

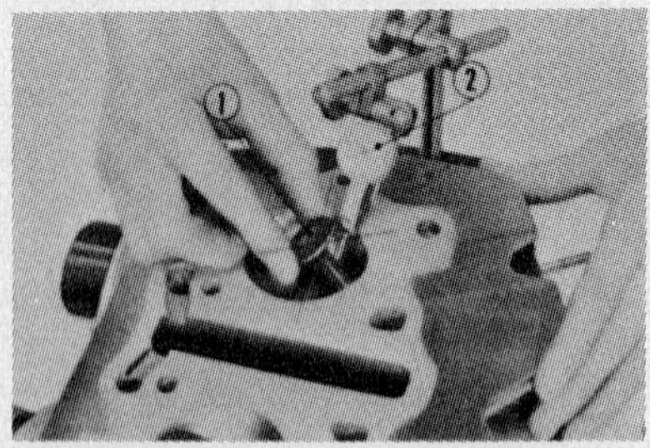
Checking valve guide clearance with a dial indicator (2).

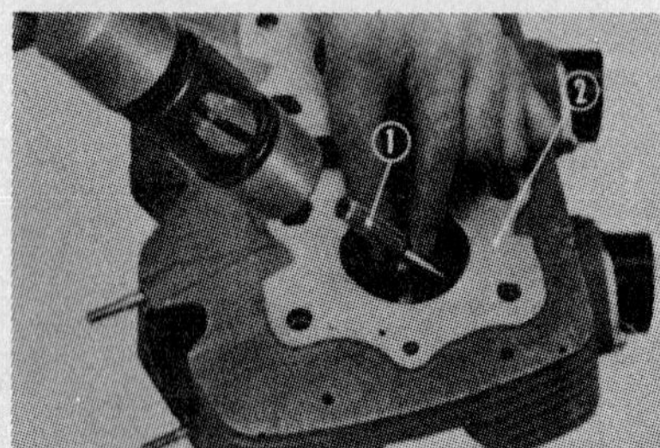
Using a drift (1) to drive a valve guide out of the head (2).

Cylinder Head and Valves

Compress the springs (Honda spring compressor no. 07031-25001) and remove the collars, retainers, springs, and valves. To check valve stem and guide wear, insert the valve into the guide and measure clearance in both the "X" and "Y" directions, as shown, with a dial indicator. If clearance is greater than 0.003 in. (0.08 mm) (intake valves), or 0.004 in. (0.09 mm) (exhaust valves), the valve and guide should be replaced as a set. The replacement guide should be one that is oversize, for a proper fit. Guides can be driven out and installed using Honda service tool no. 07046-25901 or a suitably sized drift. Take care to install the guide straight. The guides should be reamed with tool no. 07008-28601 after installation. Use the reamer carefully, with sufficient lubrication, and recheck valve clearance when completed.

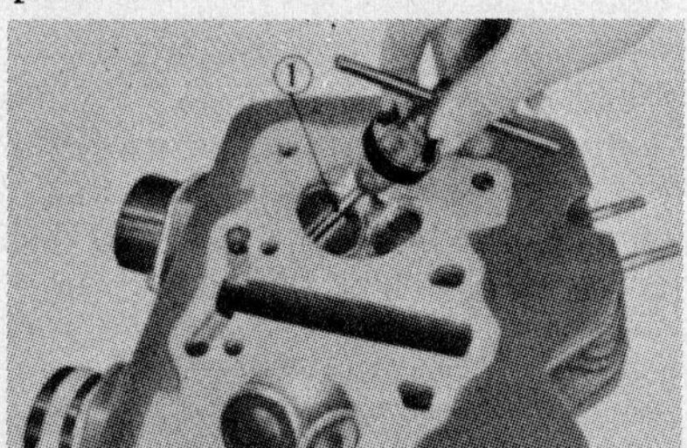
Valve guide reamer (1).

Valve lapping tool (1).

The valve stem diameter should be measured at the top, center, and bottom using a micrometer. Minimum intake valve stem diameter is 0.274 in. (6.955 mm), and minimum exhaust diameter is 0.273 in. (6.935 mm). Maximum valve contact face width is 0.08 in. (2.0 mm). Do not attempt to reface the valves or refinish the valve stem ends, as these surfaces have a thin stellite facing that will be destroyed if cut. If the valve seat is burnt, worn, or damaged in any way it should be recut. Valve seat angle 45°. Seat width should be within 0.04–0.05 in. (1–1.3 mm).

Carefully scrape carbon deposits from the combustion chambers and thoroughly clean the cylinder head. Before the valves are installed, whether they are the original ones or new, they should be lapped into their seats so that a perfect seal will be obtained.

It is a good idea at this time to replace the valve springs. However, if the height of the original springs is not less than 1.547 in. (39.3 mm) (inner springs) or 1.882 in. (47.8 mm) (outer springs), they can be reused if desired.

NOTE: *Be sure to install the springs with the smaller pitch coils toward the head.*

The valve springs (1) should be installed with the smaller pitch (2) toward the head.

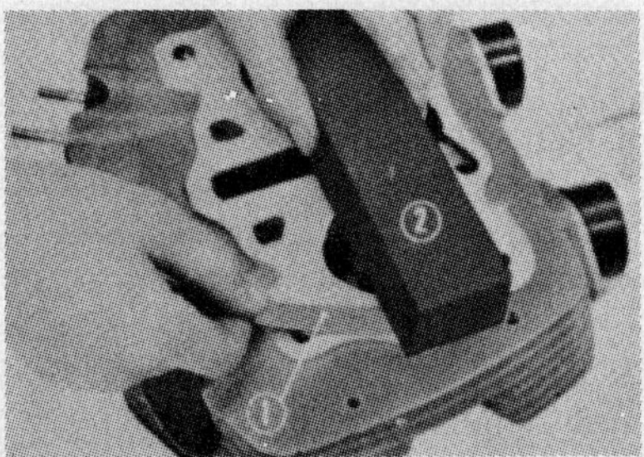
Using a feeler gauge (1) and straightedge (2) to measure cylinder head warpage.

Place a straightedge on the cylinder head surface and measure the clearance with a feeler gauge at several points to determine head warpage or distortion. If the clearance at any point exceeds 0.002 in. (0.05 mm), the head surface should be milled or lapped flat. Lapping can be accomplished using a large, flat oilstone on the head surface with a figure eight motion. It may be helpful to first coat the surface with machinist's blue so that you can observe the removal of high spots.

Make sure that the head is clean and free from grit and install the valves as removed. Lubricate the valve stems before inserting them into the guides.

Cylinder Bore and Pistons

Measure the cylinder bore diameter at the top, center, and bottom of the cylinders in both the fore-and-aft and side-to-side directions. If any measurement exceeds 2.524 in. (64.1 mm), or if bore taper or ovality is greater than 0.002 in. (0.05 mm), the cylinders should be rebored. See the specifications at the end of the chapter for piston oversizes. The cylinders should be honed after boring or whenever new rings are to be used.

Measure the diameter of the piston

skirt, perpendicular to the wrist pin. Pistons should be replaced when less than 2.515 in. (63.9 mm), or if they are scored or damaged in any way. The piston wrist pin hole should be measured at both ends and 90° apart, and the diameter should be no greater than 0.594 in. (15.08 mm). The wrist pin should be a hand press-fit in the piston and connecting rod.

If the original pistons are to be reused, remove the rings and clean the grooves using a piece of one of the old rings. Remove the carbon deposit from the tops of the pistons. Roll the new rings around the grooves before installing them to ensure that there is sufficient clearance. The rings should roll smoothly wihtout binding. Install the rings on the pistons using a ring expander, if possible, to avoid breaking them. Make sure that the mark on the rings is facing up when installed.

PISTON AND CYLINDER BARREL INSTALLATION

1. Install the pistons on the connecting rods in their original positions. Be sure to use new wrist pin circlips.
2. Stagger the rings so that the gaps are 120° apart and not in line with or perpendicular to the piston boss axis.
3. Install the cylinder base gasket and two dowel pins, and check to make sure that the O-ring and cam chain guide are installed on the cylinder skirt.
4. Fit piston bases, or blocks of wood cut to suitable size, under the pistons to hold them in position. Compress the rings (after oiling them liberally) and carefully install the cylinder barrel over them. Take care not to damage the rings.
5. Before seating the cylinder fully, raise the cam chain through the center and stick a screwdriver through the chain to keep it from dropping back down.

CYLINDER HEAD INSTALLATION

1. Install the head gasket onto the cylinder.
2. Check to make sure that the two dowel pins are in position.
3. Mount the cylinder head on the cylinder while pulling the cam chain through the center of the head.
4. To properly set the valve timing, first align the "LT" mark on the alternator rotor with the timing index mark on the stator. The left piston will then be at TDC. Fit the cam sprocket into the chain so that the cutout (flat spot with the "L" mark) is at the top, and fit the camshaft through the sprocket and into position. Bolt the sprocket onto the camshaft.

NOTE: *The two sprocket retaining bolts are different, and their positions must not be reversed. Refer to the accompanying illustration.*

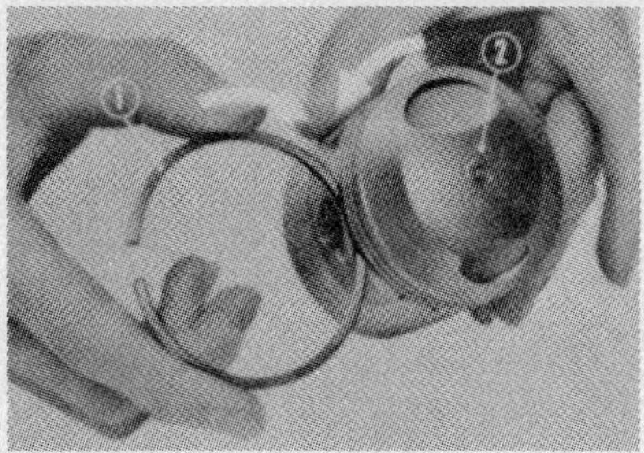

Roll the rings (1) around the piston grooves to check for sufficient clearance.

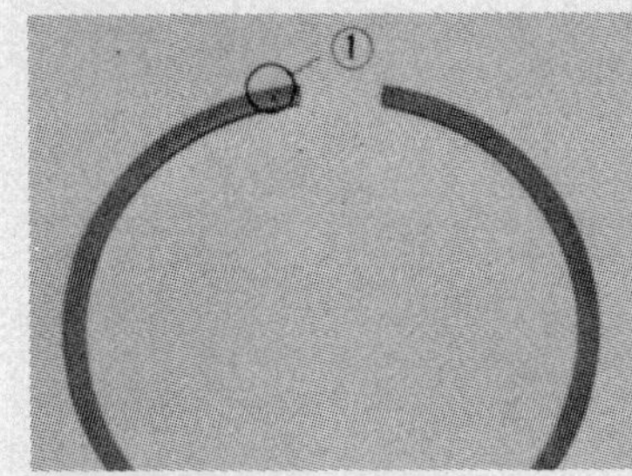

The mark on the rings (1) should face up when installed.

The "L" mark (1) on the cam sprocket (2) should be at the top.

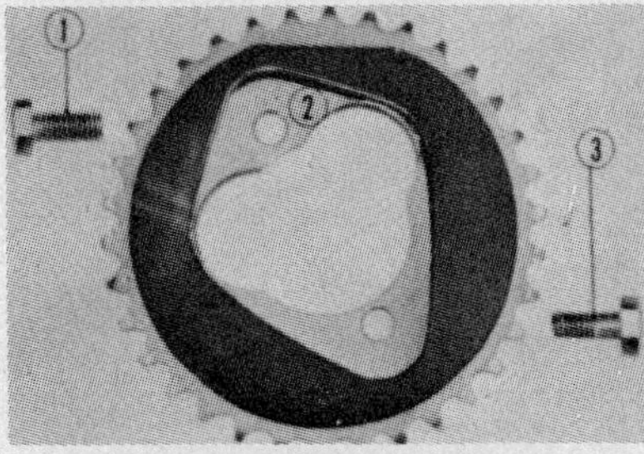

The cam sprocket mounting bolts (1 and 3) and the cam sprocket (2).

Camshaft (1), cam sprocket (2), and pin (3).

5. Install the rocker arms and rocker arm shafts.
6. Install the side-covers.
7. Install the ignition advance unit (taking care to locate it correctly on the camshaft with the dowel pin) and the breaker plate assembly.

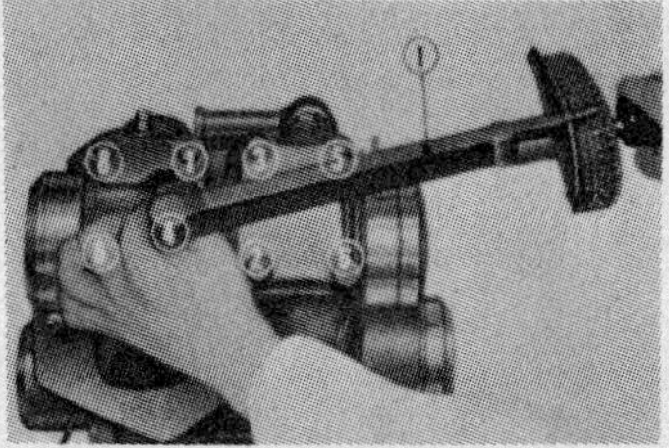

Cylinder head tightening sequence.

8. Install and tighten the two 6 mm nuts near the spark plug holes.
9. Install the cam cover with the head nuts and tighten the nuts evenly, in the sequence shown, to 13–14.5 ft lbs.
10. Install the cam chain tensioner on the cylinder.
11. Reinstall the engine in the frame and perform a complete tune-up, paying special attention to the valve and cam chain adjustments. Refer to chapter three.

Crankcases

SPLITTING THE CRANKCASES

1. Remove the engine from the frame and remove the cylinder head, barrel, and pistons as described in the previous section.

NOTE: *If desired, the cases can be split without disassembling the top end.*

2. Lift the cam chain roller pin and rubber mounts out of the top of the case (between the connecting rods). (When reinstalling, the cutout on the roller pin must be positioned toward the top.)
3. Remove the kick-start lever, take out the mounting screws, and remove the right-side crankcase cover.
4. Take out the circlip and remove the oil filter cap. The cap can be pulled out easily after a 6 mm (10 mm head) bolt is screwed into it.
5. Bend back the locktab and unscrew the 16 mm oil filter rotor retaining nut. Remove the rotor.
6. Unscrew the four clutch pressure plate bolts and remove the clutch springs, plates, and discs.
7. Take out the 25 mm circlip and remove the clutch center hub.
8. Bend back the locktab and unscrew the oil pump mounting bolts.
9. Withdraw the clutch housing and oil pump as a unit, taking care not to damage the end of the crankshaft as the housing is pulled off. (It may be necessary to remove the oil filter cap and rotor for additional clearance.)
10. Remove the gearshift spindle.
11. Disconnect the lead from the neutral indicator switch.
12. Take out the screws and remove the left crankcase cover.

Cam chain roller bracket (1), chain roller (2), and roller pin (3).

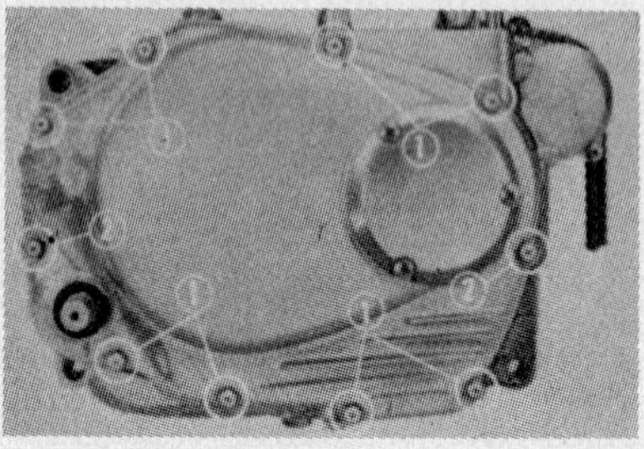

Right-side crankcase cover mounting screws (1 and 2).

Circlip (1), oil filter cap (2), circlip pliers (3), and a 6 mm bolt (4) used to pull off the cap.

Clutch housing (1) and oil pump (2).

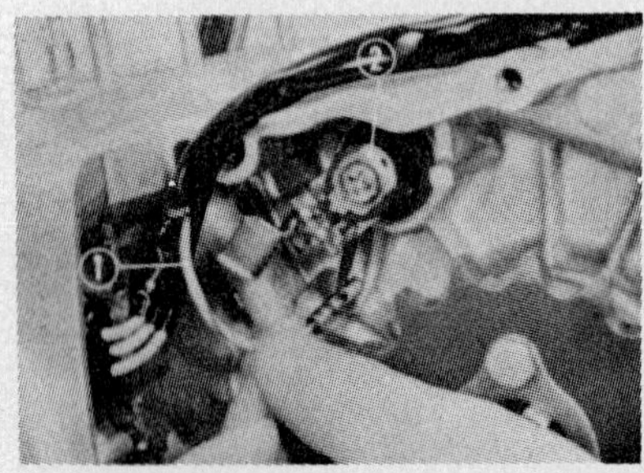

Neutral switch connection (1) and neutral switch (2).

13. Unscrew the retaining bolt and pull off the alternator rotor using Honda service tool no. 07011–21601 or a suitably sized bolt.

14. Remove the starter clutch sprocket set plate and take off the clutch sprocket and starter motor sprocket as a unit (except SL).

15. Unscrew the two crankcase securing bolts on the upper side and the twelve bolts on the lower crankcase. Lift the lower crankcase half away. If necessary, tap the crankcases with a rubber mallet to break the joint seal.

ASSEMBLING THE CRANKCASES

Assembly is a reversal of the disassembly procedures. Observe the following points:

1. Clean the crankcase mating surfaces carefully and inspect them for scratches, signs of leaks, and other damage. Use a sealing compound on the surfaces to prevent oil leaks.

2. Make sure that the kick-starter is properly engaged in the lower crankcase.

3. Handle the starter and alternator cables with care so that the clamps won't be damaged.

4. Tighten the alternator rotor bolt to 16–17.5 ft lbs.

Crankshaft and Connecting Rods

DISASSEMBLY

The crankshaft is a built-up unit with one-piece connecting rods and main bearings. It cannot be disassembled and repaired by normal means. Check for excessive wear as described below. If any of the measurements are beyond the serviceable limits the crankshaft assembly should be replaced.

The crankshaft can be lifted out of the case after the main bearing caps have been unbolted and removed.

INSPECTION

Support the center main bearings in a V-block and measure the amount of runout at the end of the crankshaft and the counterweight with a dial indicator. Maximum allowable runout is 0.006 in. (0.15 mm), at the shaft end, and 0.012 in. (0.3 mm) at the counterweight.

NOTE: *Runout equals one-half the dial indicator reading.*

Support the crankshaft securely at two points and measure the radial (up-and-down) clearance of the main and connecting rod bearings with a dial indicator. Bearing clearance must not exceed 0.002 in. (0.05 mm).

Check the side clearance of the rod bearings with a feeler gauge, as shown. Side clearance should not exceed 0.023 in. (0.60 mm).

Left crankcase cover (1).

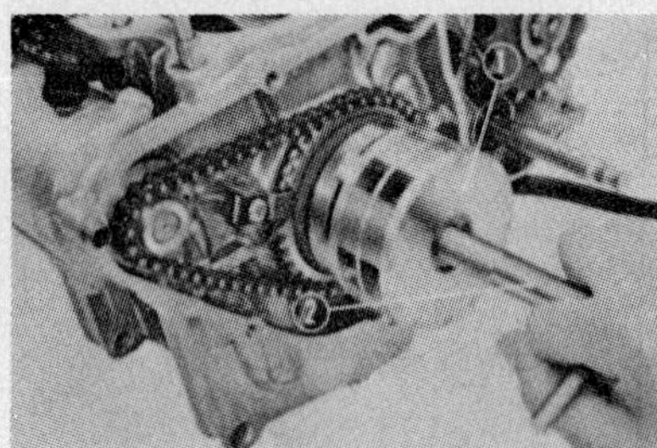

Alternator rotor (1) and rotor puller (2).

Starter motor sprocket (1), starter clutch sprocket (2), and starter chain (3).

Upper crankcase securing bolts (1).

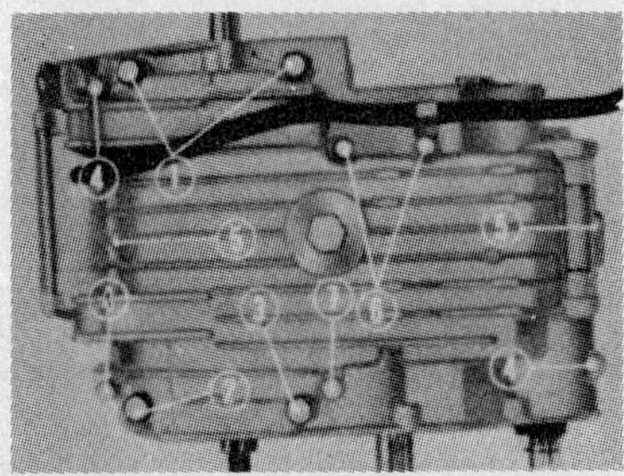

Lower crankcase tightening sequence. Note that the different numbered bolts have different lengths.

Checking main bearing radial clearance with a dial indicator (1).

Checking the connecting rod bearing side clearance with a feeler gauge (1).

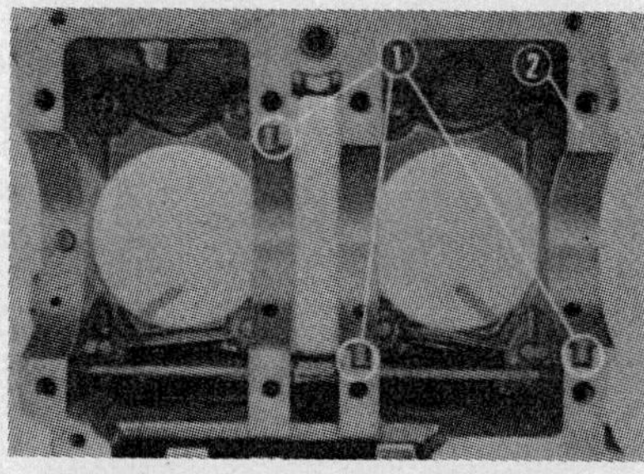

Dowel pin grooves (1) in the upper crankcase (2).

Measure the inside diameter of the connecting rod wrist pin bores with an inside micrometer or dial indicator. A measure of over 0.593 in. (15.07 mm) indicates excessive wear.

ASSEMBLY

When installing the crankshaft into the crankcase, make sure that the dowel pin in each crankcase bearing seat is firmly installed, and that the pins fit into the locating holes in the main bearings. Tighten the four center bearing cap bolts gradually and evenly, in a diagonal sequence, to 16–17.5 ft lbs.

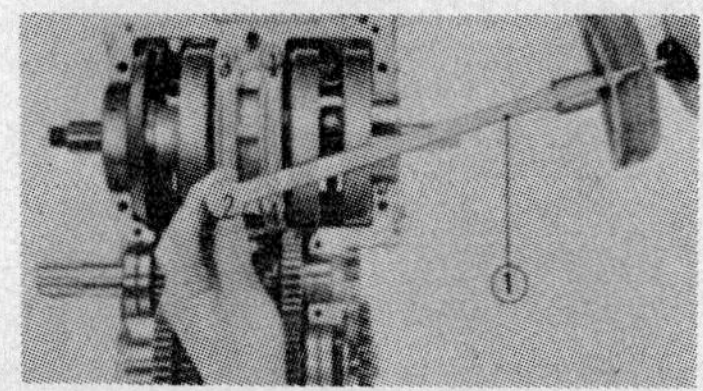

Main bearing cap tightening sequence. Use a torque wrench (1) to tighten the bolts to 16–17.5 ft lbs.

Clutch Service

DISASSEMBLY

1. Remove the kick-start lever, take out the ten retaining screws, and remove the right-side crankcase cover. Refer to the section on splitting the crankcases.

2. Unscrew the four clutch pressure plate bolts and withdraw the clutch discs and plates.

3. If you wish to remove the clutch housing and hub assembly, first take out the 25 mm circlip and withdraw the clutch hub (center). Next, bend back the locktab and unscrew the oil pump mounting bolts. Remove the oil pump and clutch housing as an assembly.

CAUTION: *Take care not to damage the crankshaft when removing the clutch housing. It may be necessary to remove the oil filter cap and rotor to provide additional clearance.*

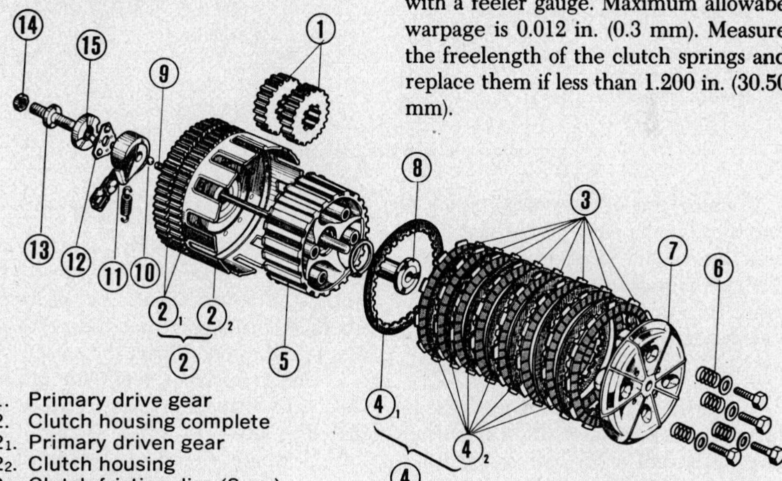

1. Primary drive gear
2. Clutch housing complete
   - 2_1. Primary driven gear
   - 2_2. Clutch housing
3. Clutch friction disc (8 ea.)
4. Clutch plate
   - 4_1. Clutch plate A
   - 4_2. Clutch plate B
5. Clutch center
6. Clutch spring
7. Clutch pressure plate
8. Clutch lifter joint piece
9. Clutch lifter rod
10. No. 10 steel ball
11. Clutch lever
12. Steel ball (clutch ball retainer)
13. Clutch adjuster
14. Clutch adjuster locknut
15. Clutch adjusting cam

Exploded view of the clutch assembly.

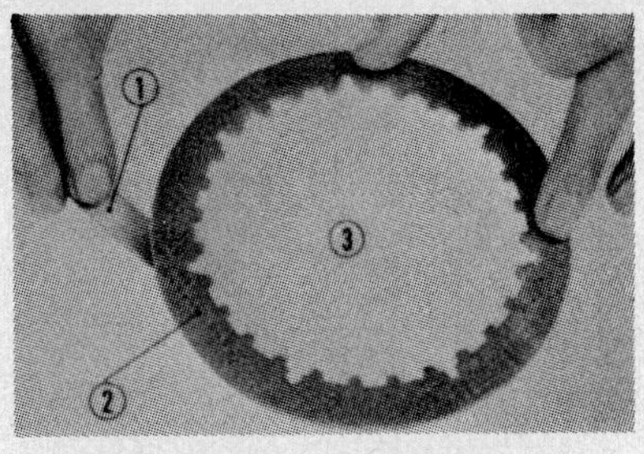

Checking clutch plate warpage. Feeler gauge (1), clutch plate (2), surface plate (3).

INSPECTION

Measure the thickness of the clutch discs with a vernier caliper or micrometer. Replace the discs if they measure less than 0.091 in. (2.3 mm). Warpage of the plates can be checked by placing them on a flat surface such as a surface plate or a plate of glass, and measuring any gaps with a feeler gauge. Maximum allowabe warpage is 0.012 in. (0.3 mm). Measure the freelength of the clutch springs and replace them if less than 1.200 in. (30.50 mm).

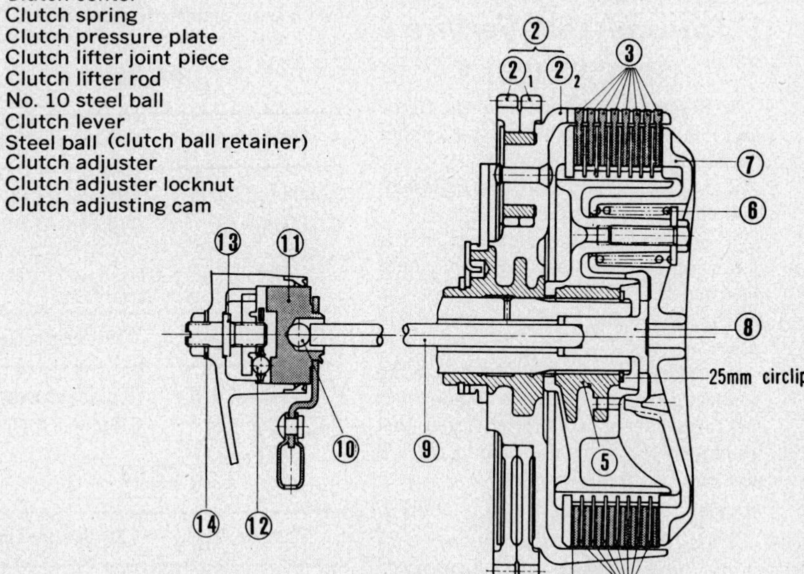

Sectional view of the clutch assembly.

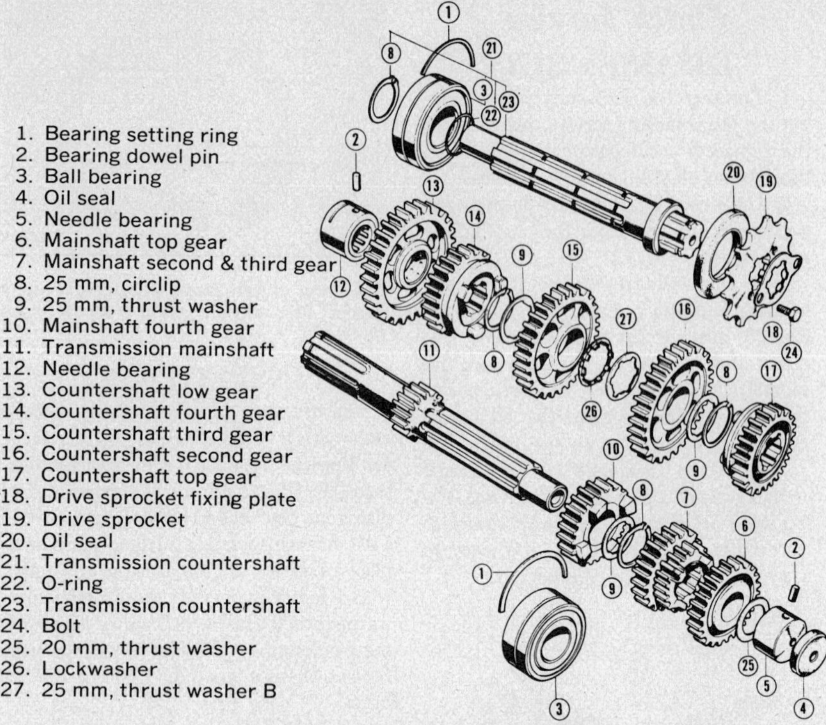

Exploded view of the transmission.

Examine the primary drive gears at this time for chipping, pitting, and excessive wear, and replace if necessary. Before reinstalling the plates and discs, make sure that the tabs and slots in the clutch center are in good condition.

ASSEMBLY

Assembly is a reversal of the disassembly procedure. Install the discs and plates alternately, beginning with a disc. Take care to torque the pressure plate bolts evenly. Perform a complete clutch adjustment after assembly. Refer to chapter two.

Transmission Service

DISASSEMBLY

1. Remove the engine from the frame and follow disassembly steps 3–15 under "Splitting the Crankcases."
2. Lift out the transmission mainshaft and countershaft assemblies.
3. Disassemble the mainshaft in the following order: remove the needle roller bearing, the M5 and M2-M3 gears, the circlip, the thrust washer, and the M4 gear.
4. Disassemble the countershaft in the following order: remove the needle roller bearings, the circlip thrust washer that retains the C3 gear, the C3 and C2 gears, and the C5 circlip and gear.

NOTE: *On later engines (from CB/CL 350E-1042395 and all SL engines) a 25 mm thrust washer and a lockwasher are installed between the C2 and C3 gears. Remove the C3 gear first and then take off the washers.*

INSPECTION

1. Examine the dogs on the respective gears and, if damaged or excessively worn, the gears should be replaced. Check to make sure that the gears are free to slide smoothly on the shafts.
2. Check the gear teeth for pitting, wear, and damage. Gears must be replaced in sets.
3. Compute the gear-to-shaft clearance of the gears in the accompanying table by measuring first the shaft diameter and then the gear bore diameter, and subtracting the former from the latter. (M4 means mainshaft fourth gear, etc.)

M4, M5

Standard Value	Serviceable Limit
0.0008-0.0024 in./ 0.02-0.062 mm	Replace if over 0.004 in./0.10 mm

C1

Standard Value	Serviceable Limit
0.0008-0.0020 in./ 0.02-0.054 mm	Replace if over 0.004 in./0.10 mm

C2, C3

Standard Value	Serviceable Limit
0.0016-0.002 in./ 0.04-0.054 mm	Replace if over 0.004 in./0.10 mm

ASSEMBLY

Assemble the transmission components in reverse order of disassembly, using the accompanying illustration as a guide. Observe the following points:

1. Use only new circlips, and make sure that they are properly seated in their grooves.
2. Make sure that the thrust washers and circlips are installed on the M4, C2, and C3 gears.
3. When installing the bearings on the shafts, be sure to install the bearing with the oil groove on the countershaft, and the bearing without the groove on the mainshaft.
4. Check to make sure that the bearing set rings and dowel pins are in place before installing the shaft assemblies in the crankcase.
5. After the mainshaft and countershaft assemblies are in place, check the backlash of the mating gears with a dial indicator. Maximum allowable backlash is 0.008 in. (0.2 mm) for all gears.
6. Heck to make sure that the left shift fork is fitted to the C4 gear, the right shift fork to the C5 gear, and the center fork to the M2-M3 gear.
7. Assemble the crankcases as previously described.

Checking gear backlash with a dial indicator.

Shifter Mechanism

DISASSEMBLY

1. Follow disassembly steps one and two under the preceding section on transmission service.
2. Remove the neutral indicator switch rotor and the shift drum limit arm.
3. Pull out the shift drum guide pin clips and guide pins.
4. Withdraw the shift drum from the case by gently tapping the case on the neutral switch side.

INSPECTION

1. Examine the shift fork fingers for damage and excessive wear. Measure the thickness of the fingers and replace the fork if less than 0.181 in. (4.6 mm) (right

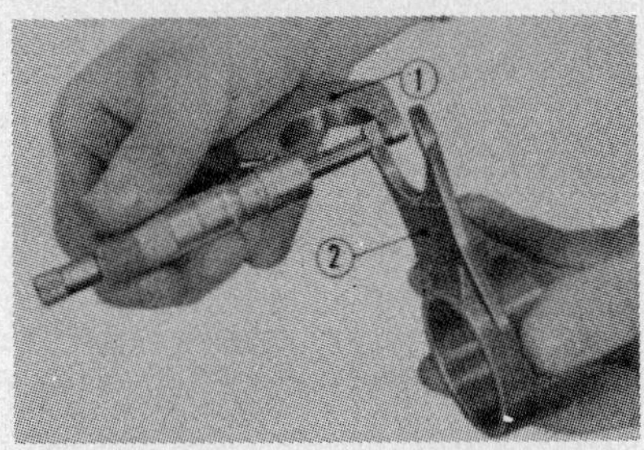

Measuring shift fork fingers with a micrometer (1).

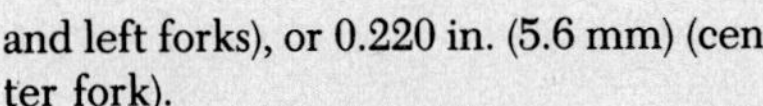

and left forks), or 0.220 in. (5.6 mm) (center fork).

2. Measure the diameter of the shift fork bore. Maximum allowable diameter is 1.577 in. (40.075 mm).

3. Measure the diameter of the shift drum and replace it if over 1.571 in. (39.9 mm).

4. Check to see that the shift drum tracks and shift fork guide pins are not excessively worn.

Measuring the shift fork bore with a dial indicator (1).

ASSEMBLY

1. Install the shift drum and forks into the crankcase and make sure the forks are positioned properly. Refer to the accompanying illustration.

2. Install the shift fork guide pins and clips. Make sure that the clips are securely set.

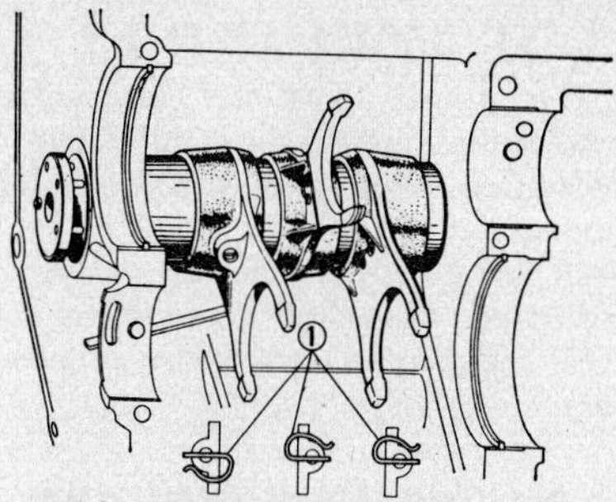

Install the shift forks and guide pin clips (1) in this position.

3. Reassemble the remaining parts in reverse order of disassembly. Check to see that the action of the shifter mechanism is smooth.

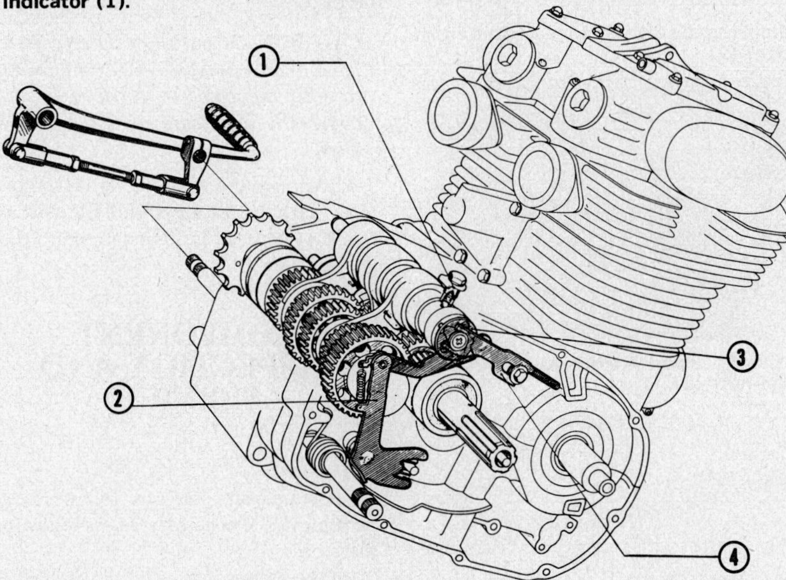

Shifter mechanism. Neutral stopper (1), shift arm (2), drum limit plate (3), and shift drum limit arm (4).

Kick-Start Mechanism Service

CB, CL, AND 1970 SL MODELS

The kick-start shaft and pinion assembly can be removed after the crankcases have been split. If the shaft and pinion are damaged or visibly worn, they should be replaced.

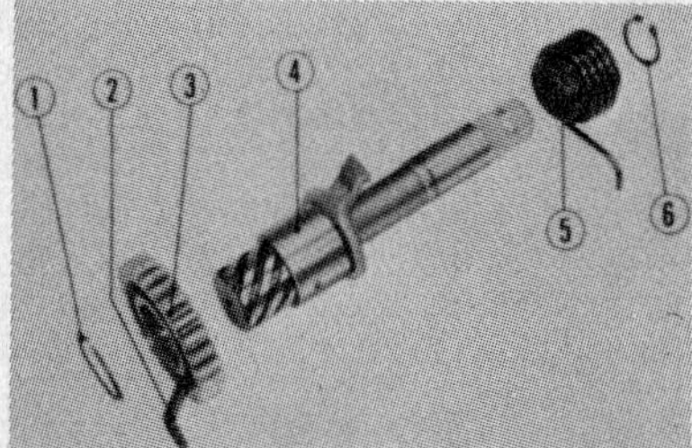

Kick-start components (CB, CL, and 1970 SL 350 models).

1. Circlip
2. Friction spring
3. Kick-start pinion
4. Kick-start spindle
5. Spring
6. Circlip

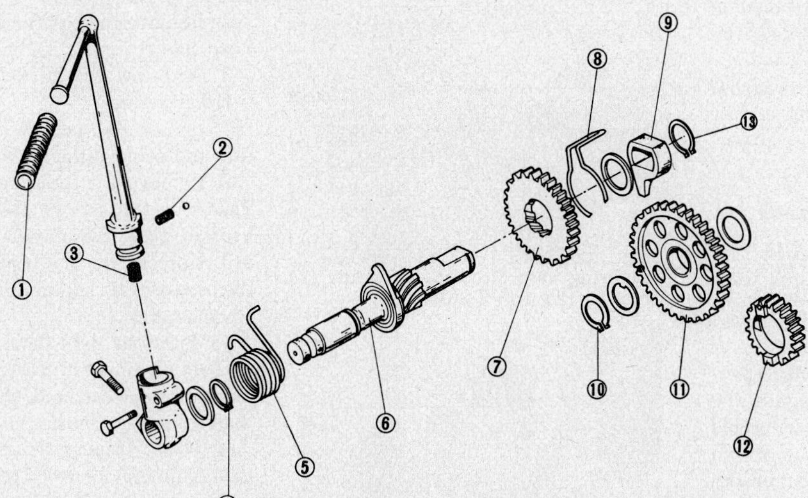

1. Kick-starter rubber
2. Stopper spring
3. Knuckle spring
4. Circlip
5. Kick-starter spring
6. Spindle
7. Pinion
8. Friction spring
9. Spindle stopper
10. Circlip
11. Idle gear
12. Kick-starter gear
13. Circlip

Kick-start components (SL 350K1 and K2 models).

SL 350K1 AND K2

The primary kick-start mechanism used on these models allows the engine to be started in any gear with the clutch disengaged. To remove the kick-start shaft and gears the crankcases must be separated. Check all components for wear and damage, and replace as necessary.

Engine Removal and Installation

450

1. Drain the engine oil.
2. Turn the fuel tap off, disconnect the fuel lines, and remove the gas tank.
3. Disconnect the throttle cables from the throttle linkage at the carburetors.
4. Remove the air filter assemblies, loosen the carburetor-to-intake tube clamps, and remove the carburetors.
5. Remove the entire exhaust system, as a unit, from each side.
6. Remove the footpeg and shift lever, and take off the left-side rear crankcase cover. Separate the chain at the master link and disconnect the clutch cable from the release lever.
7. Uncouple the engine electrical leads at the connectors. Refer to the accompanying illustration.
8. Disconnect the wires from the spark plugs and tuck them up out of the way.
9. Disconnect the starter motor cable from the starter solenoid, and disconnect the tachometer cable from the cylinder head.
10. Unscrew the thirteen engine mounting bolts and remove the engine from the left side.

Installation is a reversal of the removal procedure. Note the following points:

1. Do not forget to connect the battery ground cable when installing the engine mounting bolts.
2. The chain master link clip should be installed so that the closed end faces the direction of forward rotation.
3. Make sure that the steel ball has been installed in the clutch release lever before reinstalling the crankcase cover.

Top End Overhaul

CYLINDER HEAD REMOVAL

1. Remove the front and rear cam covers.
2. Rotate the crankshaft slowly and examine the cam chain links until the master link is located. It can be identified by its brighter color and crimped pin heads (rather than the normal flat heads). The master link should then be removed using Honda tool no. 07050–28303. Observe the following precautions:

Engine mounting bolts (1–4).

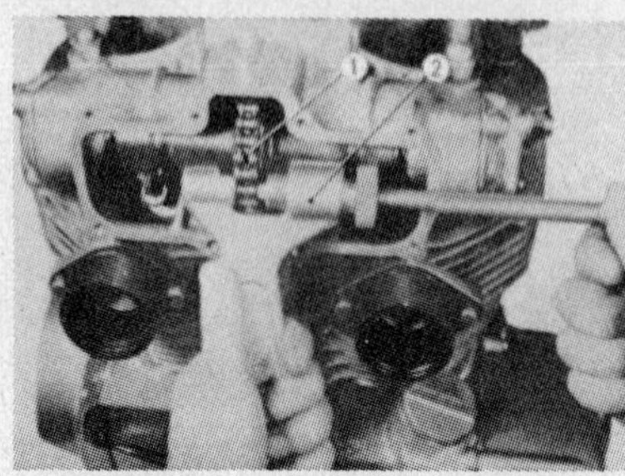

Removing the cam chain (1) with a chain cutter (2).

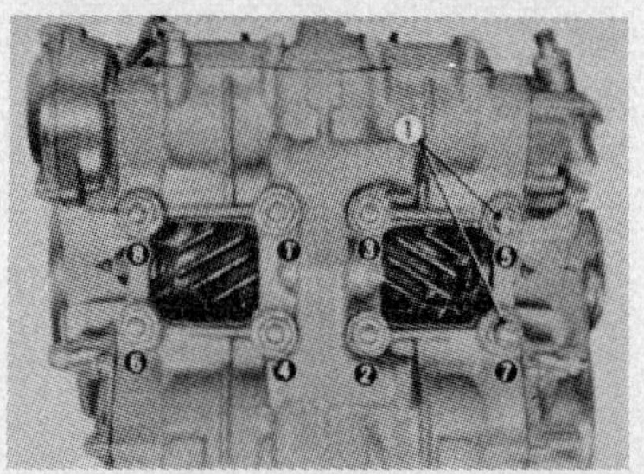

Cylinder head tightening sequence. Cap nuts (1).

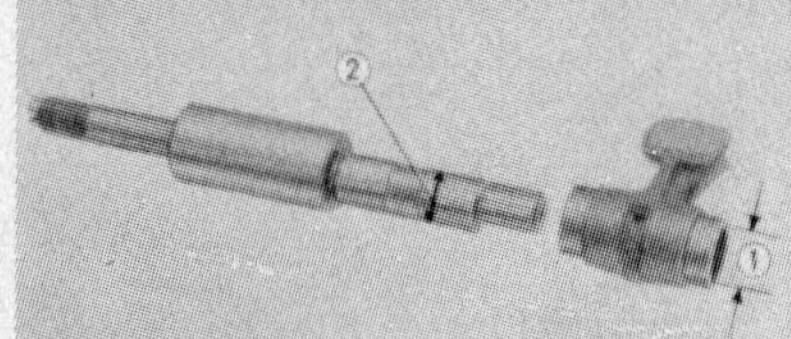

Cam follower bearing diameter (1) and cam follower shaft journal diameter (2).

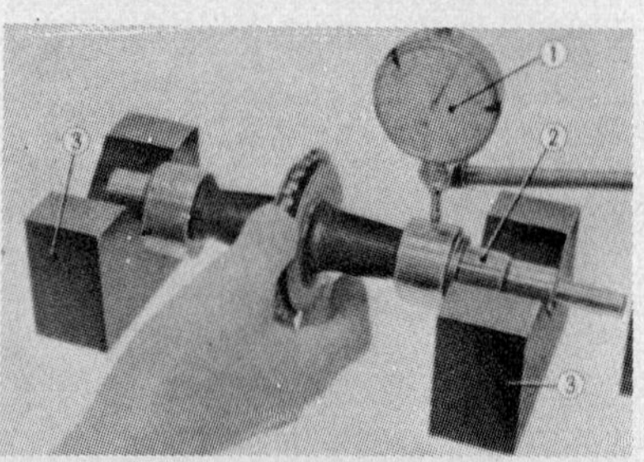

Measuring cam lift. Dial indicator (1), camshaft (2), and V-blocks (3).

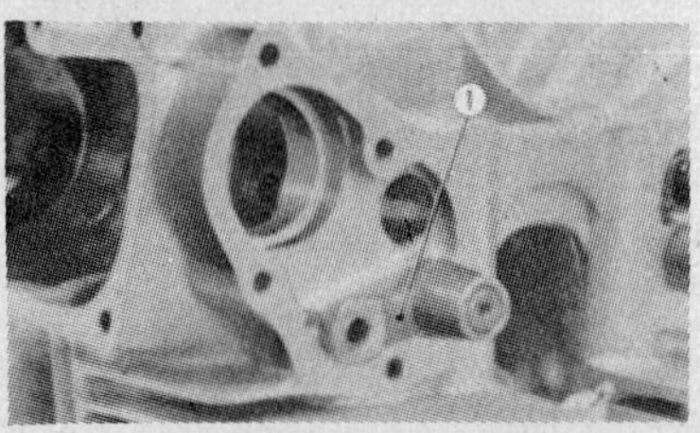

Torsion bar arm (1).

a. Disconnect the chain from the intake side.

b. Take care not to drop the master link into the engine.

c. Attach a length of wire to each end of the cam chain to prevent it from falling into the crankcase.

3. Gradually loosen the eight cylinder head nuts in reverse order of the tightening sequence.
4. Lift the cylinder head off the cylinder barrel.

CYLINDER BARREL AND PISTON REMOVAL

1. Carefully lift the cylinder barrel off the crankcase. Take care to prevent the pistons from being damaged on the studs as the cylinder is withdrawn over them.
2. Remove the wrist pin circlips from the pistons.

CAUTION: *Do not allow the circlips to fall into the crankcase. To avoid having to split the cases to retrieve a clip, cover the crankcase opening with a cloth.*

3. Remove the wrist pins from the pistons. Mark the pistons, inside the skirt, so that they can be reinstalled in their original positions.

COMPONENT INSPECTION AND SERVICE

Camshafts

The camshafts and cam followers can be removed, if necessary, in the following manner:

Intake Side:

1. Remove the cam follower shaft (valve adjuster) locknut from the right and left sides.
2. Remove the right and left cylinder head side covers.
3. Withdraw the intake camshaft.

Exhaust Side:

1. Loosen the locknut from the right side and remove the tachometer drive.
2. Remove the ignition points cover. Take out the screws and remove the breaker plate assembly.
3. Unscrew the bolt from the center of the breaker cam and remove the ignition advance unit.
4. Withdraw the exhaust camshaft.

Carefully inspect the cam lobes for scoring and wear, and check the camshaft dimensions using the accompanying chart. Inspect the cam sprockets (and dampers) for worn teeth and other damage, and replace the camshafts if necessary. Replace the cam followers if they are damaged in any way.

Item	Standard Value	Serviceable Limit
1. Cam follower bearing diameter	0.4016-0.4023 in./10.20-10.218 mm	Replace if over 0.4047 in./10.28 mm
2. Cam follower shaft journal	0.3992-0.4009 in./10.166-10.184 mm	Replace if under 0.3976 in./10.10 mm
3. Camshaft journals, intake and exhaust	0.8648-0.8654 in./21.967-21.980 mm	Replace if under 0.8622 in./21.92 mm
4. Cam lift, intake and exhaust	0.1846-0.1853 in./4.688-4.728 mm	Replace if under 0.1830 in./4.65 mm
5. Breaker point shaft run-out	0.0004 in. max/0.01 mm	Replace if over 0.002 in./0.05 mm

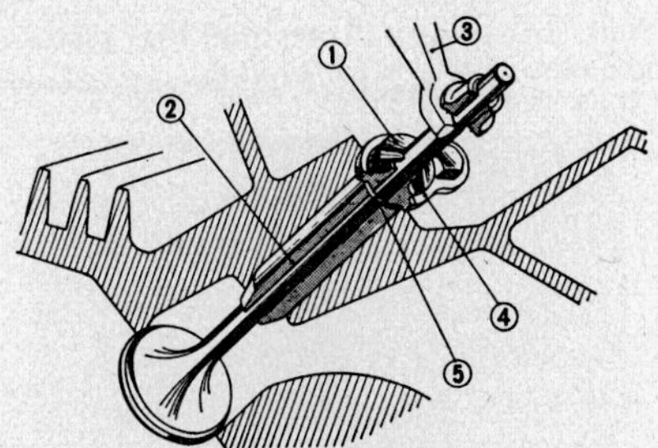

Valve assembly.
1. Valve guide seal cap
2. Valve guide
3. Forked arm
4. Valve guide stop
5. O-ring

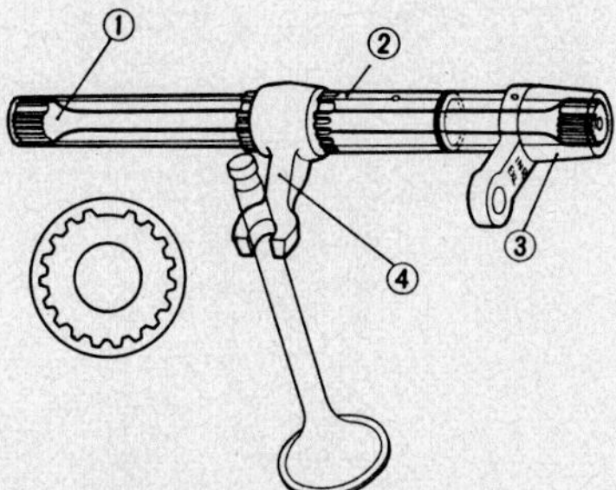

Torsion bar components.
1. Torsion bar
2. Torsion bar housing
3. Torsion bar holder arm
4. Torsion bar forked arm

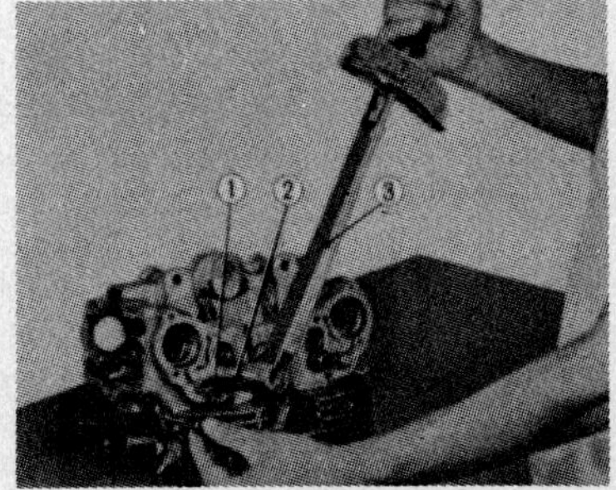
Setting the torsion bar with a torque wrench. Torsion bar arm (1), torque wrench attachment (2), and torque wrench (3).

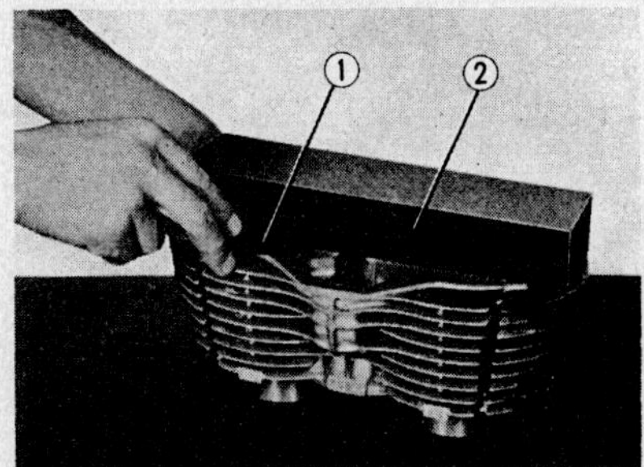

Measuring cylinder head warpage with a feeler gauge (1) and straightedge (2).

Cylinder Head and Valves

To remove the valves and torsion bar valve springs, first hold the torsion bar arm in the direction shown on the end of the bar to relieve the load on the retaining bolt. Then unscrew the bolt, allow the bar to return slowly to the unloaded position, and withdraw it.

CAUTION: *Do not interchange the torsion bar components from side to side or front to rear. Do not scratch or mark the bars in any way. Tag the components for identification upon disassembly.*

To remove the valves, first remove the collars and valve spring retainers. Loosen the bolts and remove the valve guide stopper and guide seal cap. Withdraw the valves.

Replace valves as necessary. When replacing valves due to worn stems, it is wise to also replace the valve guides. The replacement guides should be slightly oversize and new O-rings should be used. Always ream the guides and check valve fit after installation.

If the valve seat is burned, worn, or damaged in any way, it should be recut. Valve seat angle is 45°. Seat width should be within 0.040–0.050 in. (1.0–1.3 mm). Maximum allowable seat width is 0.079 in. (2.0 mm).

NOTE: *Do not attempt to reface the valves or refinish the valve stem ends, as these surfaces have a thin stellite facing that will be destroyed if out.*

The valves can be checked using the accompanying chart as a guide.

Carefully scrape carbon deposits from the combustion chambers and thoroughly clean the cylinder head. Before the valves are installed, whether they are original or new ones, they should be lapped into their seats so that a perfect seal will be obtained.

Place a straightedge on the cylinder head surface and measure the clearance with a feeler gauge at several points to determine head warpage or distortion. If the clearance at any point exceeds 0.002 in. (0.05 mm), the head surface should be milled or lapped flat. Lapping can be accomplished by using a large, flat oilstone on the head surface with a figure eight motion. It may be helpful to first coat the surface with machinist's blue so you can observe the removal of the high spots.

Make sure that the head is clean and free from grit and install the valves as removed. Lubricate the valve stems before inserting them into the guides. Install the valve springs in the following manner:

1. Assemble the torsion bars and their arms.

NOTE: *There are two types of torsion bars; they must not be interchanged. Refer to the accompanying illustration.*

2. Fit the torsion bars into the cylinder head and install the forked arms on the bars from the inside.

Item	Standard Value	Serviceable Limit
1. Valve stem diameter intake	0.2746-0.2751 in./6.974-6.988 mm	Replace if under 0.2740 in./6.96 mm
2. Valve stem diameter, exhaust	0.2743-0.2749 in./6.968-6.982 mm	Replace if under 0.2736 in./6.95 mm
3. Straightness of valve stem	Within 0.0008 in./0.02 mm	Replace if over 0.0008 in./0.02 mm
4. Concentricity of valve face*	0.0012 in./0.03 mm	Replace if over 0.0012 in./0.03 mm
5. Valve guide diameter and exhaust	0.2756-0.2760 in./7.0-7.01 mm	Replace if over 0.2776 in./7.05 mm

* Run-out in this case equals the full dial indicator reading (true indicated reading).

3. Fit the forked arm into the valve stem and check for smooth movement. If the arm is binding, the valve stem may be bent.

4. Check to make sure that the valve guide seal cap is not loose.

5. Finally, the forked arm at the inside end of the torsion bar must be positioned on the splines of the bar so that the bar exerts the correct amount of closing pressure on the valve. To accomplish this, a torque wrench and Honda service tool attachment no. 07039–28302 are absolutely necessary. Fit the torque wrench and attachment onto the end of the bar and turn the bar in the direction of the arrow stamped on its end until the bolt hole in the bar retaining arm aligns with the bolt hole in the head. The wrench should read 3.7–4.6 ft lbs. If it is outside these limits, partially withdraw the torsion bar while holding the forked arm in position on the valve stem, and rotate the bar in the required direction to position the bolt holes in the retaining arm closer or farther apart as necessary. Recheck the torque wrench reading. Install the retaining bolt in the bar arm when the correct torque is reached.

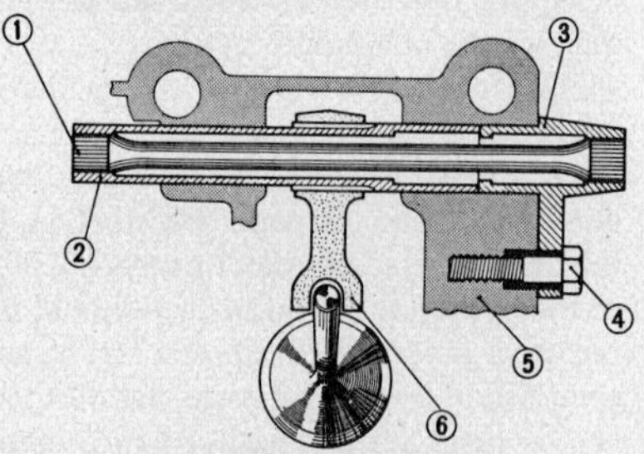

Valve mechanism.

1. Torsion bar splines
2. Torsion bar housing
3. Torsion bar holder arm
4. Holder retaining bolt
5. Cylinder head
6. Torsion bar outer (forked) arm

Cam Chain Guide Rollers

Inspect the rollers for damage and excessive wear. The rollers can be removed after the pins and bracket bolts have been taken out. To install the rollers, assemble rollers A, C, and R in that order. (See the illustration.) Liberally oil them and check for smooth operation after installation.

Cylinder Bore and Pistons

Measure the cylinder bore diameter at the top, center, and bottom of the cylinders in both the fore-and-aft and side-to-side directions. If any measurement exceeds 2.760 in. (70.11 mm), or if bore taper or ovality is greater than 0.002 in. (0.05 mm), the cylinders should be rebored. See the specifications at the end of the chapter for piston oversizes. The cylinders should be honed after boring or whenever new rings are to be used.

Measure the diameter of the piston skirt, perpendicular to the wrist pin. Pistons should be replaced when less than 2.751 in. (69.88 mm), or if they are scored or damaged in any way. The piston wrist pin hole should be measured at both ends and 90° apart, and the diameter should be no greater than 0.6732 in. (17.10 mm). The wrist pin should be a hand press-fit in the piston and connecting rod.

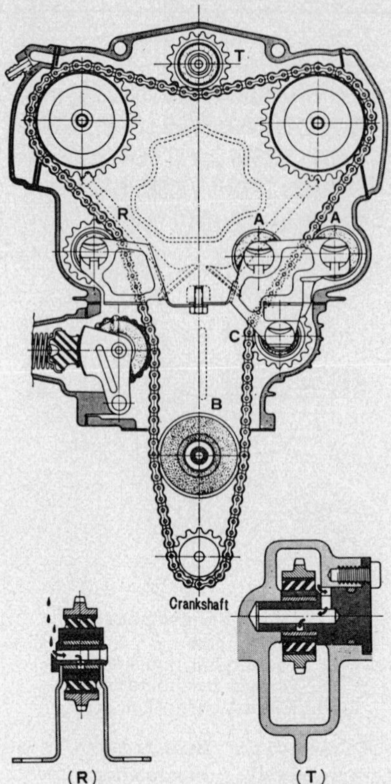

Cam chain guide rollers.

If the original pistons are to be reused, remove the rings and clean the grooves using a piece of one of the old rings. Remove the carbon deposit from the tops of the pistons. Roll the new rings around the grooves before installing them to ensure that there is sufficient clearance. The rings should roll smoothly without binding. Install the rings on the pistons using a ring expander, if possible, to avoid breaking them. Make sure that the mark on the rings is facing up when installed.

PISTON AND CYLINDER BARREL INSTALLATION

1. Install the pistons on the connecting rods in their original positions. Be sure to use new wrist pin circlips.

2. Stagger the rings so that the gaps are 120° apart and not in line with, or perpendicular to, the piston boss axis.

3. Install the O-rings on the base of the cylinder barrel and check to make sure that the dowel pins on the crankcase are in place.

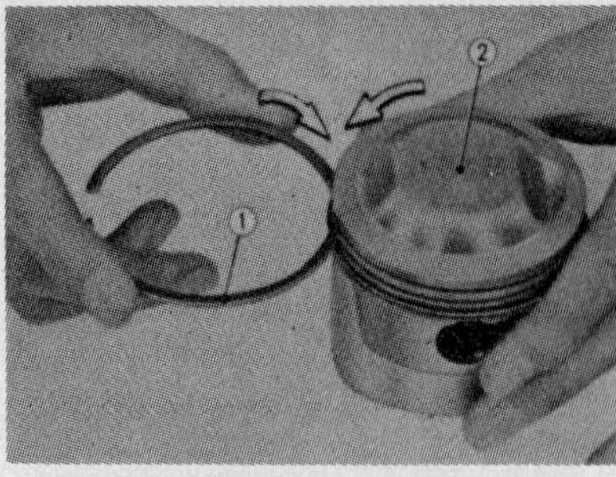

Roll the rings (1) around the piston grooves to check for binding.

After installing the wrist pin circlips (1), shift the cut portion of the clip from the cut portion of the groove.

4. Fit piston bases, or blocks of wood cut to suitable size, under the pistons to hold them in position. compress the rings (after oiling them liberally) and carefully install the cylinder barrel over them. Take care not to damage the rings.

5. Before seating the cylinder fully, raise the cam chain through the center and secure the ends so it won't drop back down.

CYLINDER HEAD INSTALLATION

1. Install the camshafts and cam followers in the following manner:

Intake side:

Assemble the cam followers onto their eccentric shafts. Position the shaft so that it is in approximately the same position as shown in the accompanying illustration.

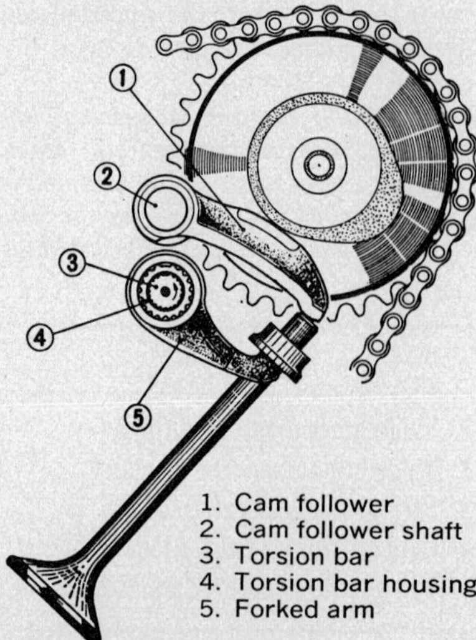

1. Cam follower
2. Cam follower shaft
3. Torsion bar
4. Torsion bar housing
5. Forked arm

Valve mechanism.

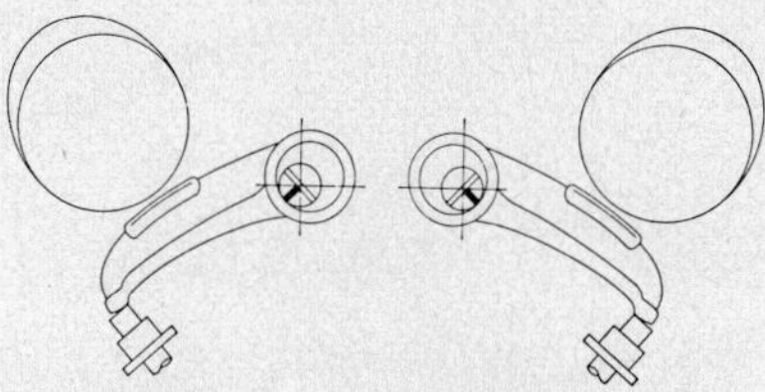

Position the cam follower shafts so that the index mark points away from the center of the cylinder head.

Install the intake camshaft in the head so that the end with the oil line fitting is on the right side. Install the left and right cylinder head side-covers. Check to make sure that the cam rotates freely. Temporarily tighten the cam follower shaft (valve adjuster) locknuts.

Exhaust side:

Assemble the cam followers and shafts into the head, and install the exhaust camshaft. Install the pinion on the tachometer drive. (Don't forget the washer.) Install the tachometer drive, making sure that the pinion is fully seated in the camshaft gear, and then the ignition advance unit and contact breaker plate. Check to make sure that the camshaft rotates freely and temporarily tighten the locknuts.

2. Check the side-clearance of both camshafts. Proper clearance is 0.002–0.014 in. (0.05–0.35 mm). Shims are available for adjusting the side-clearance if this is necessary.

3. Fit the head gasket, stud gaskets, and the three guide pins onto the cylinder.

4. Carefully install the head on the cylinder while pulling the cam chain through the center of the head. Take care not to let the chain drop back down.

Head gasket (1), guide pin (2), and stud gaskets (3).

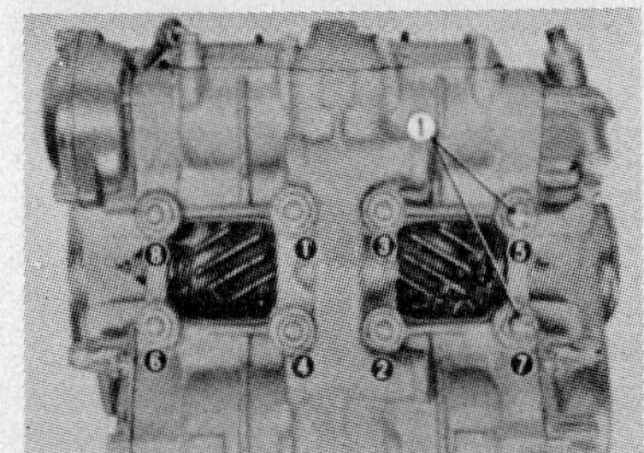

Cylinder head tightening sequence. Cap nuts (1).

Tachometer drive pinion (1), washer (2), and gearbox (3).

5. Install the copper washers on the two right-side studs and the flat washers on the remaining six studs.

NOTE: *The two right-side stud holes are oil passageways, and the copper washers must be correctly installed to prevent leaks. The oil flow to the head can be checked by loosening these two stud nuts.*

6. Install the head nuts and tighten them evenly, in the sequence shown, to 20–22 ft lbs.

7. To properly set the valve timing, align the mark on the right side of each camshaft to the mark on the right-side cam bearings, as shown. Next, align the "LT" mark on the alternator rotor with the timing index mark on the stator.

8. Connect the ends of the cam chain with a new master link. Take care to prevent the master link from dropping into the engine.

NOTE: *The master link cannot be riveted where the chain passes over the sprocket.*

9. To install the cam chain tensioner, first loosen the locknut and adjuster bolt, push the tensioner roller against the inside of the tensioner, and tighten the adjuster bolt to prevent the roller from popping out. Install the tensioner assembly on the cylinder block.

Aligning the valve timing marks. Camshaft (1) and cam bearing (2) marks aligned (circle).

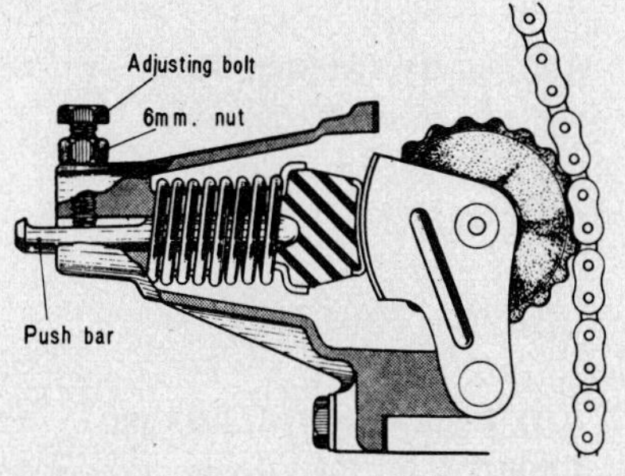

Cross-section of the cam chain tensioner.

10. Reinstall the engine in the frame and perform a complete tune-up, paying special attention to the valve and cam chain adjustments. Refer to chapter three. The valves and cam chain should be checked again after approximately 500 miles have been covered. Don't forget to refill the engine with oil.

Crankcases

SPLITTING THE CRANKCASES

1. Remove the engine from the frame and remove the cylinder head, barrel, and pistons, as described in the previous section.

NOTE: *If desired, the cases can be split without disassembling the top end.*

2. Remove the neutral switch. Take out the screws and remove the left-side crankcase cover.

3. Unscrew the retaining bolt and remove the alternator rotor using a rotor puller or a suitably sized bolt.

Removing the alternator rotor (1) with a puller (2).

Starter motor sprocket (1), set plate (2), and starter clutch sprocket (3).

4. Remove the starter clutch sprocket set plate and withdraw the clutch and starter motor sprockets, together with the chain, as an assembly.

5. Remove the kick-start lever. Take out the screws and remove the right-side crankcase cover.

6. Take out the circlip (or bolt on earlier models) and remove the oil filter cap. Bend back the locktab, unscrew the nut, and remove the oil filter rotor.

7. Unscrew the clutch pressure plate

Clutch assembly (1), oil filter (2), and oil pump (3).

Removing the oil filter rotor (1).

Clutch hub (1), circlip (2), and circlip pliers (3).

bolts and remove the pressure plate, discs, and plates.

8. Take out the 29 mm circlip and remove the clutch hub.

9. Bend back the locktabs and unscrew the oil pump mounting bolts. Remove the oil pump and clutch housing as an assembly.

10. Take out the left circlip and pull out the gearshift spindle. Be careful not to damage the shift drum limit cam plate.

Removing the clutch housing (1) and oil pump (2).

11. Unscrew the four crankcase securing bolts on the upper side and the eleven bolts on the underside. Tap the lower crankcase half with a rubber hammer to break the joint seal and separate the cases.

ASSEMBLING THE CRANKCASES

Assembly is a reversal of the disassembly procedures. Observe the following points:

1. Clean the crankcase mating surfaces carefully and inspect them for scratches, signs of leaks, and other damage. Use a sealing compound on the surfaces to prevent oil leaks. Do not get the sealer on the dowel pin holes.

2. Make sure that the kick-starter is properly engaged in the lower crankcase.

3. Handle the starter and alternator cables with care so that the clamps won't be damaged.

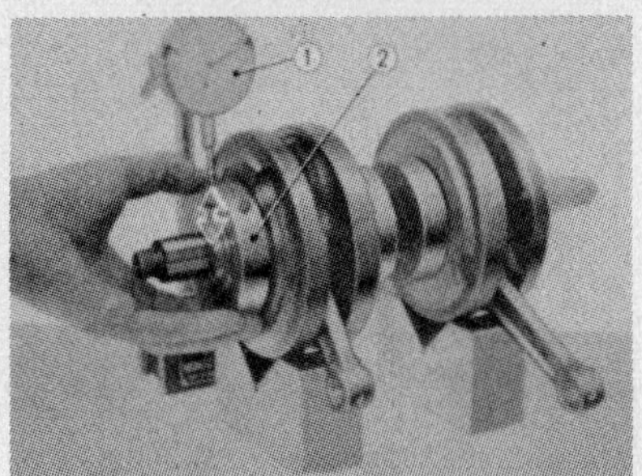

Using a dial indicator (1) to check radial clearance of the main bearing (2).

4. Tighten the crankcase bolts securely, in an even pattern.

Crankshaft and Connecting Rods

DISASSEMBLY

The crankshaft is a built-up unit with one-piece connecting rods and main bearings. It cannot be disassembled and repaired by normal means. Check for excessive wear as described below, and if any of the measurements are beyond the serviceable limits the crankshaft assembly should be replaced.

The crankshaft can be lifted out of the case after the main bearings caps have been unbolted and removed.

INSPECTION

Use the chart below and the illustrations as a guide to checking the crankshaft components.

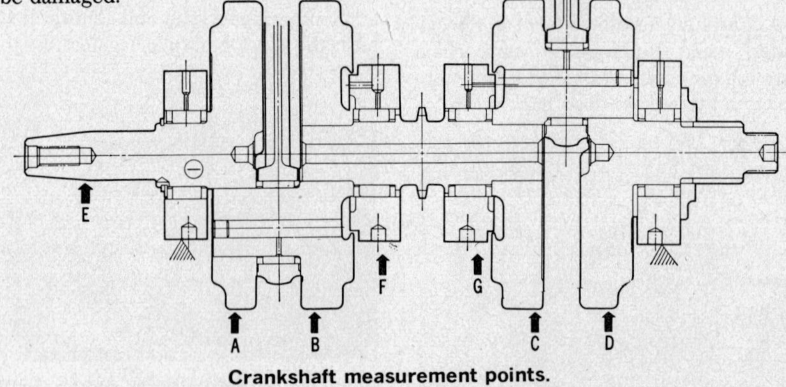

Crankshaft measurement points.

Item	Standard Value	Serviceable Limit
1. Crankshaft run-out*		
A, B, C and D	0.002 in. max/0.05 mm	Replace if over 0.008 in./0.2 mm
E, F and G	0.001 in. max/0.02 mm	Replace if over 0.004 in./0.1 mm
2. Main bearing radial clearance	0.0002-0.0005 in./0.006-0.014 mm	Replace if over 0.001 in./0.03 mm
3. Connecting rod small end	0.6699-0.6706 in./17.016-17.034 mm	Replace if over 0.6721 in./17.07 mm
4. Connecting rod large end radial clearance	0-0.0003 in./0-0.008 mm	Replace if over 0.0020 in./0.05 mm
5. Connecting rod large end side-clearance	0.0028-0.0130 in./0.07-0.33 mm	Replace if over 0.0197 in./0.5 mm
6. Connecting rod large end tilt	0.008-0.04 in./0.2-1.0 mm	Replace if over 0.118 in./3.0 mm

* Run-out equals one-half the dial indicator reading.

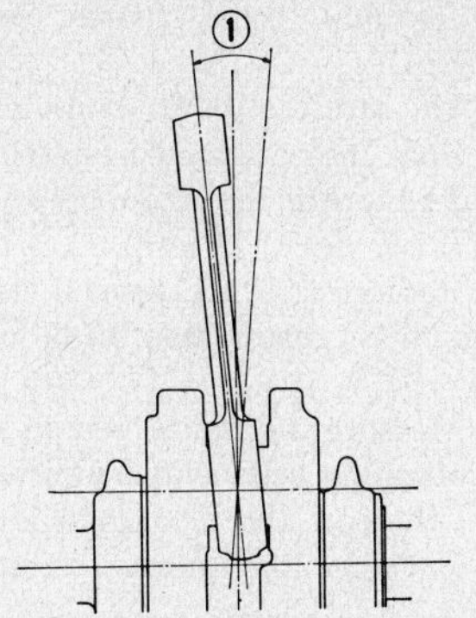

Connecting rod large end tilt measurement (1).

ASSEMBLY

When installing the crankshaft into the crankcase make sure that the dowel pin in each crankcase bearing seat is firmly installed, and that the pins fit into the locating holes in the main bearings. Tighten the four center bearing cap bolts gradually and evenly, in a diagonal sequence, to 12–15 ft lbs.

Main bearing locating pins (1).

Clutch Service

DISASSEMBLY

1. Remove the kick-start lever, take out the retaining screws, and remove the right-side crankcase cover. Refer to the preceding section on splitting the crankcases.
2. Unscrew the clutch pressure plate bolts and withdraw the clutch discs and plates.
3. If you wish to remove the clutch housing and hub assembly, first take out the 29 mm circlip and withdraw the clutch hub (center). Next, bend back the locktab and unscrew the oil pump mounting bolts. Remove the oil pump and clutch housing as an assembly.

Caution: *Take care not to damage the crankshaft when removing the clutch housing. It may be necessary to remove the oil filter cap and rotor to provide additional clearance.*

INSPECTION

Measure the thickness of the clutch discs with a vernier caliper or micrometer. Replace the discs if they measure less than 0.122 in. (3.1 mm). Warpage of the plates can be checked by placing them on a flat surface such as a surface plate or a plate of glass, and measuring any gaps with a feeler gauge. Maximum allowable warpage is 0.014 in. (0.35 mm). Measure the free-length of the clutch springs and replace them if less than 1.55 in. (3.94 mm).

Examine the primary drive gears at this time for chipping, pitting, and excessive wear, and replace if necessary. Check the radial clearance between the clutch hub and the shaft, and replace the hub if the clearance is greater than 0.-0047 in. (0.12 mm). Measure teh backlash of the clutch discs in the clutch housing. Replace the housing or discs as necessary if backlash is greater than 0.032 in. (0.8 mm).

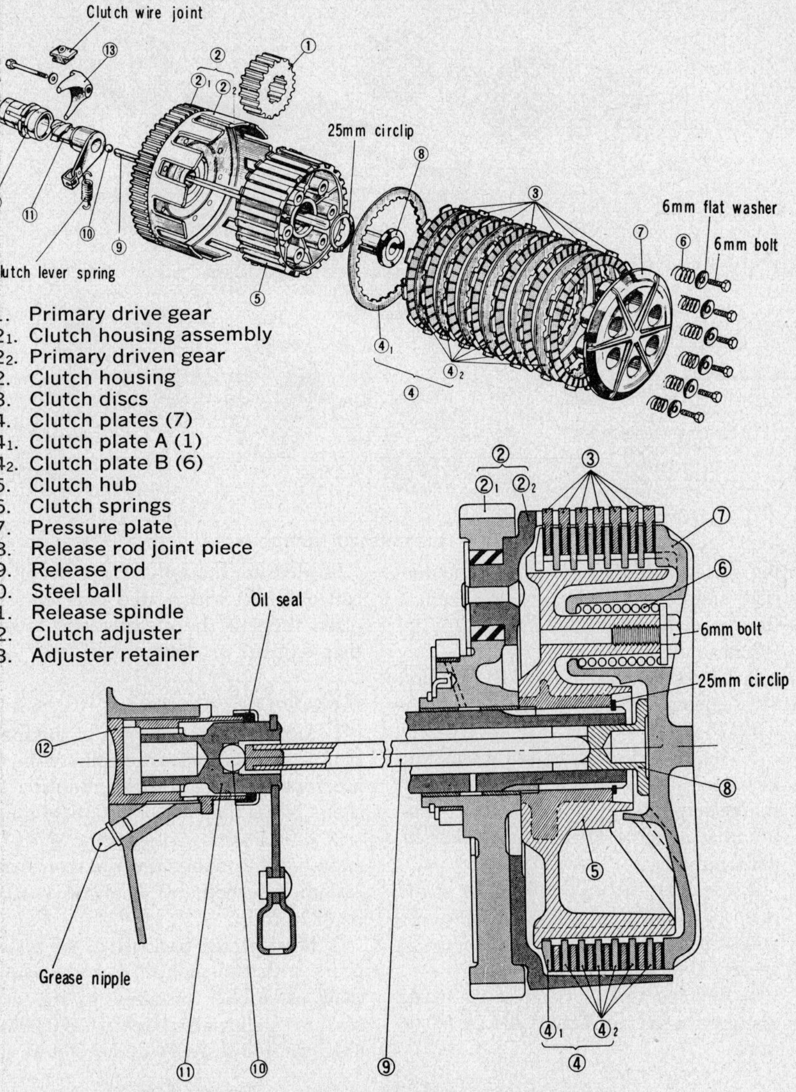

Exploded and sectional views of the clutch assembly.

ASSEMBLY

Assembly is a reversal of the disassembly procedures. Install the discs and plates alternately, beginning with a disc. Take care to torque the pressure plate bolts evenly. Perform a complete clutch adjustment after assembly (refer to chapter two). Observe the following precautions:

1. If the oil pump rod was removed, take care to install it in the correct position. Reversing it will cause pump failure.
2. Use a new oil pump locktab.
3. Before installing the oil pump, make sure that the O-ring is in place. Use a new one if necessary.
4. Take care not to damage the surface of the pressure plate.

Transmission Service

DISASSEMBLY

Remove the engine from the frame and follow disassembly steps 2–11 under "Splitting the Crankcases." Lift out the mainshaft and countershaft assemblies, and refer to the following section for inspection procedures.

INSPECTION

4-Speed

1. Measure the diameter of the bear-

Four-speed transmission components.

ing surfaces at the end of the countershaft and mainshaft. Replace the shafts if the measurement is less than 0.785 in. (19.94 mm).

2. Check the backlash of the C2 and M3 gears on their shafts. Backlash limit is 0.00473 in. (0.12 mm).

3. Measure the backlash of the mating gears with the countershaft and mainshaft assemblies fitted into the case. Maximum acceptable backlash is 0.00826 in. (0.21 mm).

4. Measure the inside diameter of the mainshaft and countershaft bushings, and replace them if the diameter is greater than 0.789 in. (20.06 mm).

5. Replace the C1 gear if its inside diameter is greater than 0.791 in. (20.08 mm).

6. Measure the radial clearance of the ball bearings with a dial indicator. Replace them if the clearance is greater than 0.00197 in. (0.05 mm).

5-Speed

1. Measure the diameter of the mainshaft and countershaft as shown in the accompanying illustration. Replace the shafts if less than 0.785 in. (19.94 mm).

2. Check the backlash of the M2-3, C4, and C5 gears on the splines of their shafts. Maximum acceptable backlash is 0.006 in. (0.15 mm).

3. Measure the backlash of the mating gears with the mainshaft and countershaft assemblies installed in the case. Maximum allowable backlash is 0.006 in. (0.15 mm) (low gear), and 0.008 in. (0.2 mm) (second, third, fourth, and fifth gears).

4. Measure the inside diameter of the mainshaft and countershaft bearings, and replace them if the diameter is greater than 0.789 in (20.05 mm).

5. Replace the C1 gear if its inside diameter is greater than 0.789 in. (20.05 mm).

6. Measure the radial clearance of the ball bearings with a dial indicator. Replace them if the clearance is greater than 0.002 in. (0.05 mm).

ASSEMBLY

Assemble the transmission components in reverse order of disassembly. Observe the following points:

1. Use only new circlips and make sure that they are properly seated in their grooves.

2. Make sure that the thrust washers are installed on the M2 and C3 gears (four-speed) and the M4, C2, and C3 gears (five-speed).

3. When installing the bearings on the shafts, be sure to install the bearing with the oil groove on the countershaft, and the bearing without the groove on the mainshaft.

4. Check that the bearing set rings and dowel pins are in place before installing the shaft assemblies in the crankcase.

5. Assemble the crankcases as previously described.

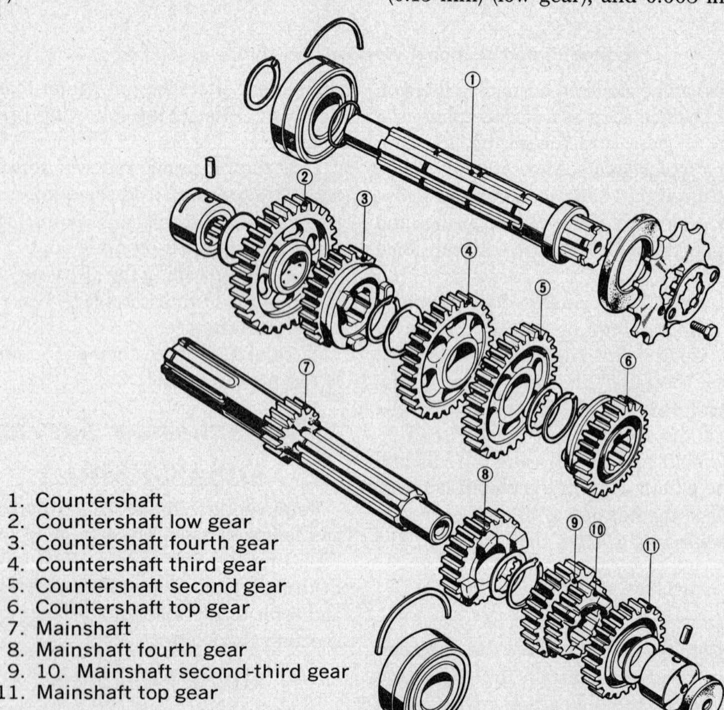

Five-speed transmission components.

Shifter Mechanism

DISASSEMBLY

1. Split the crankcases and lift out the transmission mainshaft and countershaft assemblies as previously described.

2. Remove the shift drum stop (four-speed models). Unscrew the bolt and disassemble the neutral limit arm and shift drum stop (five-speed models).

3. Remove the shift fork guide pin clips and pull out the pins. Withdraw the shift drum from the case by lightly tapping in from the neutral switch side.

INSPECTION

1. Check the shift forks using the chart below as a guide.

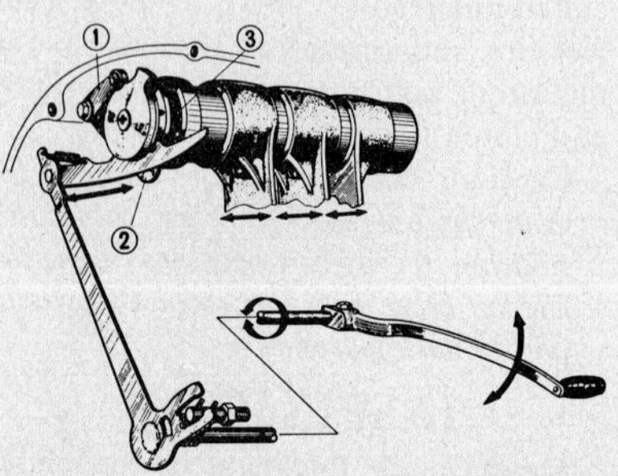

Shifter mechanism. Neutral limit arm (1), shift drum stop (2), and ball bearing (3).

Item	Standard Value	Serviceable Limit
Inside Diameter	1.3385-1.339 in./34.0-34.025 mm	Replace if over 1.3425 in./34.1 mm
End Thickness (left, right)	0.1941-0.1968 in./4.93-5.0 mm	Replace if under 0.181 in./4.6 mm
End Thickness (center)	0.2334-0.236 in./5.93-6.0 mm	Replace if under 0.2205 in./5.6 mm
Bend in fork end (left, right)	Within 0.004 in./0.1 mm	Replace if over 0.031 in./0.8 mm

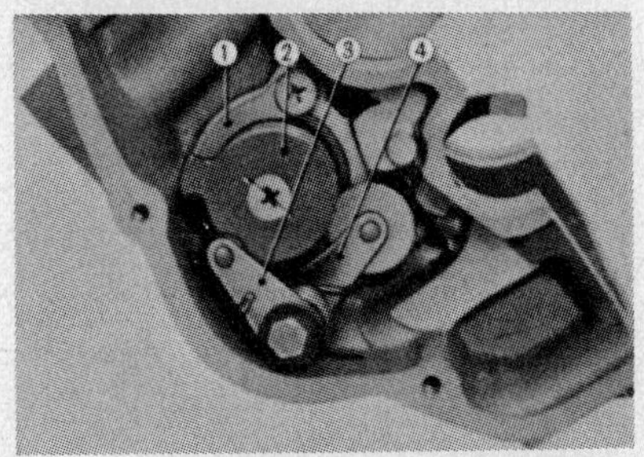

Shifter mechanism installed.
1. Bearing set plate
2. Shift drum
3. Shift drum neutral stop
4. Shift drum stop

2. Measure the width of the tracks in the shift drum. Replace the drum if the width exceeds 0.256 in. (6.5 mm) or if the tracks are damaged.

ASSEMBLY

1. Install the shift drum and forks into the case. Take care not to damage the crankcase oil seal.
2. Install the fork guide pins and pin clips, taking note of the proper clip installation direction.
3. On four-speed models the right shift fork fits around the C2 gear, and the left fork around the M3 gear. On five-speed models the left fork is fitted to gear C4, the right fork on gear C5, and the center fork on the M2–3 gear. Install the transmission shaft assemblies in the case.
4. Reassemble the remaining parts in reverse order of disassembly. Check to make sure that the action of the shifter mechanism is smooth.

Kick-Start Mechanism Service

The kick-start shaft and ratchet assembly can be removed after the crankcases have been split. A damaged shaft and pinion assembly should be replaced. When reassembling, always use a new 8 mm lockwasher.

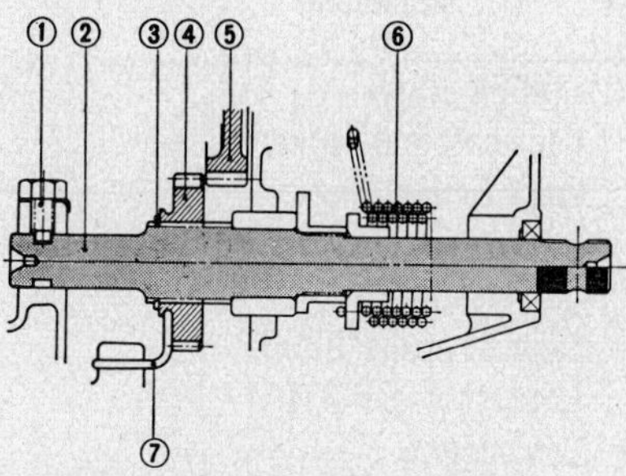

Cross-section of kick-start components.

1. Set bolt
2. Spindle
3. Circlip
4. Pinion
5. Countershaft low gear
6. Spring
7. Friction spring

ENGINE SPECIFICATIONS

	125 in. (mm)	175 in. (mm)	350 in. (mm)	450 in. (mm)
CYLINDER HEAD				
Valves, Guides, and Springs—				
Valve run-out at face:				
maximum	0.001 (0.03)	0.001 (0.03)	0.001 (0.03)	0.001 (0.03)
Valve stem diameter:				
intake (nominal)	0.216 (5.48-5.49)	0.216 (5.48-5.49)	0.275 (6.98-6.99)	0.275 (6.98-6.99)
exhaust (nominal)	0.215 (5.46-5.47)	0.215 (5.46-5.47)	0.274 (6.96-6.97)	0.275 (6.97-6.98)
Valve guide bore:				
nominal	0.217 (5.50-5.51)	0.217 (5.50-5.51)	N.A. (N.A.)	0.276 (7.0-7.01)
maximum	0.219 (5.55)	0.219 (5.55)	N.A. (N.A.)	0.278 (7.05)
Stem-to-guide clearance:				
intake (nominal)	N.A. (N.A.)	N.A. (N.A.)	0.001 (0.01-0.03)	0.001 (0.01-0.03)
(maximum)	0.003 (0.08)	0.003 (0.08)	0.003 (0.08)	0.003 (0.08)
exhaust (nominal)	N.A. (N.A.)	N.A. (N.A.)	0.002 (0.03-0.05)	0.002 (0.03-0.05)
(maximum)	0.004 (0.10)	0.004 (0.10)	0.0035 (0.09)	0.004 (0.10)

(con't.)	125 in. (mm)	175 in. (mm)	350 in. (mm)	450 in. (mm)
CYLINDER HEAD				
Spring free-length:				
inner (nominal)	1.028	1.189	1.567	—
	(26.1)	(30.2)	(39.8)	—
(minimum)	1.008	1.169	1.547	—
	(25.6)	(29.7)	(39.3)	—
outer (nominal)	1.264	1.252	1.929	—
	(32.1)	(31.8)	(49.0)	—
(minimum)	1.221	1.205	1.882	—
	(31.0)	(30.6)	(47.8)	—
CYLINDER HEAD				
Camshaft and Rocker Arms—				
Valve timing: (deg):				
Intake opens (BTDC)	5°	10°	①	10°
Intake closes (ABDC)	30°	40°	①	40°
Exhaust opens (BBDC)	5°	40°	①	40°
Exhaust closes (ATDC)	35°	10°	①	10°
Cam height:				
intake (nominal)	1.031	0.987	1.452	③
	(26.18)	(25.06)	(36.88)	
exhaust (nominal)	1.013	0.979	1.452	③
	(25.74)	(24.87)	(36.88)	
intake (minimum)	1.024	N.A.	1.444	③
	(26.0)	(N.A.)	(36.68)	
exhaust (minimum)	1.008	N.A.	1.444	③
	(25.6)	(N.A.)	(36.68)	
Base circle diameter:				
nominal	0.827	0.827	N.A.	N.A.
	(21.0)	(21.0)	(N.A.)	(N.A.)
minimum	N.A.	N.A.	N.A.	N.A.
	(N.A.)	(N.A.)	(N.A.)	(N.A.)
Side clearance:	N.A.	N.A.	0.008-0.024	0.002-0.014
	(N.A.)	(N.A.)	(0.2-0.6)	(0.05-0.35)
Camshaft end diameter:				
minimum (left)	1.296	0.785	0.862②	0.862
	(32.91)	(19.94)	(21.92)②	(21.92)
minimum (right)	0.785	0.785	0.862②	0.862
	(19.94)	(19.94)	(21.92)②	(21.92)
Rocker arm shaft clearance:				
nominal	0.001	0.001	N.A.	④
	(0.02-0.04)	(0.02-0.04)	(N.A.)	
maximum	0.003	0.003	N.A.	④
	(0.08)	(0.08)	(N.A.)	
Rocker arm shaft diameter:				
nominal	0.393	0.393	0.510	⑤
	(9.98)	(9.98)	(12.950)	
maximum	0.390	0.390	0.508	⑤
	(9.92)	(9.92)	(12.9)	

① Serial numbers prior to CB/CL 350E-1045164—10° BTDC, 35° ATDC, 30° BBDC, 10° ABDC; serial numbers after CB/CL 350E-1045165—5° BTDC, 30° ATDC, 30° BBDC, 5° ABDC; SL 350K1 and K2—TDC, 20° ABDC, 25° BBDC, TDC.
② End cover (cam bearing) inside diameter, maximum—0.868 in. (20.05 mm).
③ Cam lift, intake and exhaust—nominal: 0.185 in. (4.70 mm);
minimum: 0.183 in. (4.65 mm).
④ Cam follower bearing diameter—maximum: 0.405 in. (10.28 mm).
⑤ Cam follower shaft journal diameter—minimum: 0.398 in. (10.10 mm).

(con't.)

	125 in. (mm)	175 in. (mm)	350 in. (mm)	450 in. (mm)
Cylinder Bore—				
nominal	1.732	2.030	2.520	2.756
	(44.0)	(52.00)	(64.01)	(70.0)
maximum	1.736	2.051	2.524	2.760
	(44.1)	(52.1)	(64.1)	(70.11)
Taper and ovality:				
maximum	0.002	0.002	0.002	0.002
	(0.05)	(0.05)	(0.05)	(0.05)
CYLINDERS, PISTONS, AND RINGS				
Pistons—				
Diameter:				
nominal	1.732	2.046	2.519	2.754
	(43.96)	(51.96)	(63.97)	(69.95)
minimum	1.728	①	2.510	2.751
	43.9		(63.9)	(69.88)
Wrist pin hole diameter:				
nominal	0.512	0.551-0.552	0.591	0.669
	(13.00)	(14.00)	(15.00)	(17.00)
maximum	0.513	0.553	0.594	0.673
	(13.05)	(14.05)	(15.08)	(17.1)
Wrist pin diameter:				
nominal	N.A.	N.A.	0.590	0.669
	(N.A.)	(N.A.)	(14.99)	(16.99)
minimum	N.A.	N.A.	0.589	0.667
	(N.A.)	(N.A.)	(14.96)	(16.95)
Available oversizes:	(3) (44.25-44.75)	(4) (52.25-53.00)	(4) (64.25-65.00	(4) (70.25-71.00)
Rings—				
End gap:				
compression (nominal)	0.006-0.014	0.006-0.016	0.008-0.016	0.012-0.03
	(0.15-0.35)	(0.15-0.40)	(0.2-0.4)	(0.3-0.5)
oil control (nominal)	0.006-0.015	0.006-0.016	0.008-0.016	0.008-0.016
	(0.15-0.40)	(0.15-0.40)	(0.2-0.4)	(0.2-0.4)
compression (maximum)	0.032	0.032	0.032	0.032
	(0.8)	(0.8)	(0.8)	(0.08)
oil control (maximum)	0.032	0.032	0.032	0.032
	(0.8)	(0.8)	(0.8)	(0.8)
Side clearance:				
top (nominal)	0.001	0.001-0.002	0.001-0.002	0.002-0.003
	(0.03)	(0.03-0.05)	(0.03-0.05)	(0.04-0.07)
2nd (nominal)	0.001	0.001	0.001	0.001-0.002
	(0.03)	(0.02-0.04)	(0.02-0.04)	(0.02-0.04)
oil (nominal)	0.001	0.001	0.001	0.001
	(0.03)	(0.02-0.04)	(0.02-0.04)	(0.01)
top (maximum)	0.004	0.004	0.007	0.006
	(0.01)	(0.01)	(0.18)	(0.15)
2nd (maximum)	0.004	0.004	0.006	0.006
	(0.01)	(0.01)	(0.17)	(0.15)
oil (maximum)	0.004	0.004	0.006	0.004
	(0.01)	(0.01)	(0.17)	(0.1)

① Piston-to-cylinder clearance, maximum—0.004 in. (0.1 mm).

(con't.)

	125 in. (mm)	175 in. (mm)	350 in. (mm)	450 in. (mm)
CRANKSHAFT AND CONNECTING RODS				
Crankshaft run-out—				
Shaft end:				
nominal	0.001 (0.02)	0.001 (0.02)	0.001 (0.02)	0.001 (0.02)
maximum	0.003 (0.08)	0.003 (0.08)	0.006 (0.15)	0.004 (0.10)
Counterweight:				
nominal	N.A. (N.A.)	N.A. (N.A.)	0.004 (0.10)	0.002 (0.05)
maximum	N.A. (N.A.)	N.A. (N.A.)	0.012 (0.30)	0.008 (0.20)
CRANKSHAFT AND CONNECTING RODS				
Main bearing radial clearance—				
nominal	0.002 (0.05)	0.002 (0.05)	0.001 (0.02)	0.0005 (0.014)
maximum	0.004 (0.1)	0.004 (0.01)	0.002 (0.05)	0.001 (0.03)
Con rod bearing radial clearance—				
nominal	N.A. (N.A.)	N.A. (N.A.)	0.0005 (0.012)	0.0003 (0.008)
maximum	0.004 (0.1)	0.004 (0.01)	0.002 (0.05)	0.002 (0.05)
Con rod side clearance—				
nominal	①	②	0.003-0.0013 (0.07-0.33)	0.003-0.013 (0.07-0.33)
maximum	①	②	0.023 (0.60)	0.020 (0.50)
Wrist pin bushing diameter—				
nominal	N.A. (N.A.)	N.A. (N.A.)	0.592 (15.03)	0.670 (17.03)
maximum	N.A. (N.A.)	N.A. (N.A.)	0.593 (15.07)	0.672 (17.07)

① Main bearing side clearance, nominal—0.002 in. (0.05 mm); maximum—0.004 in. (0.1 mm).
② Main bearing side clearance, nominal—0.001 in. (0.02 mm); maximum—0.002 in. (0.05).

LUBRICATION SYSTEMS

OIL PUMP SERVICE

Removal and Installation

ALL MODELS

To remove the oil pump it is necessary to remove the clutch unit. Refer to chapter four. The oil pump and clutch are unbolted and removed together.

DISASSEMBLY

1. Remove the circlip and separate the pump rod from the clutch housing. The plunger can be removed from the pump rod after the pin is driven out.
2. The pressure relief valve and check valve balls and springs can be removed from the pump after the retaining caps have been unscrewed.

INSPECTION

Examine the plunger bore in the oil pump housing for scoring or other damage. Measure the diameter of the bore and plunger at four points: two points 90° apart at top and bottom. Compare the dimensions obtained with the specifications at the end of the chapter and replace parts as necessary.

Inspect the pressure relief valve balls and ball seats for damage and wear. The complete pump assembly should be replaced if the valve balls show extensive wear.

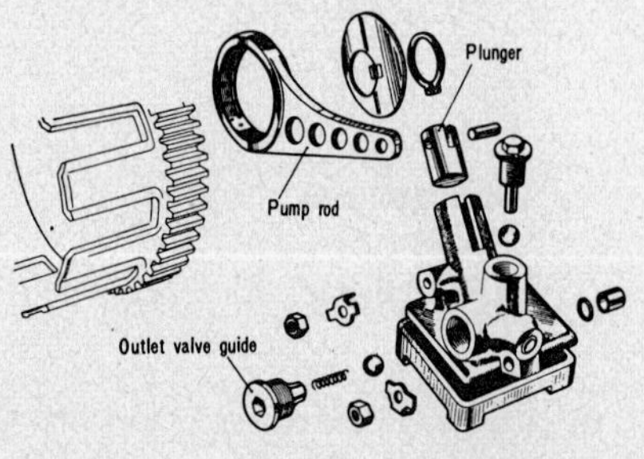

Oil pump (450cc four-speed models).

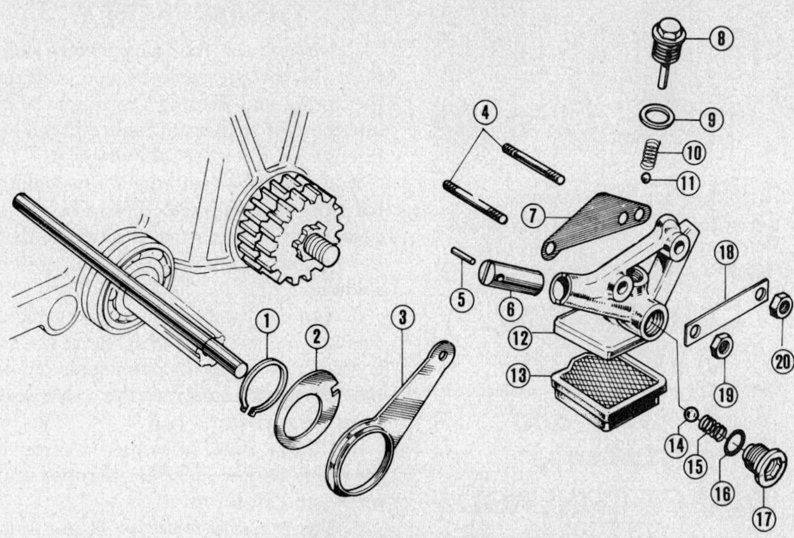

Oil pump (125 and 175cc models).

1. Circlip
2. Pump rod side washer
3. Pump rod
4. Stud
5. Plunger pump pin
6. Plunger
7. Pump body gasket
8. Suction valve bolt
9. Suction valve bolt packing
10. Suction valve spring
11. ⁵⁄₁₆ in. steel ball
12. Oil pump body
13. Pump filter screen
14. ⁵⁄₁₆ in. steel ball
15. Valve spring
16. O-ring
17. Outlet valve guide
18. Pump lockwasher
19. 20. 6 mm hex nut

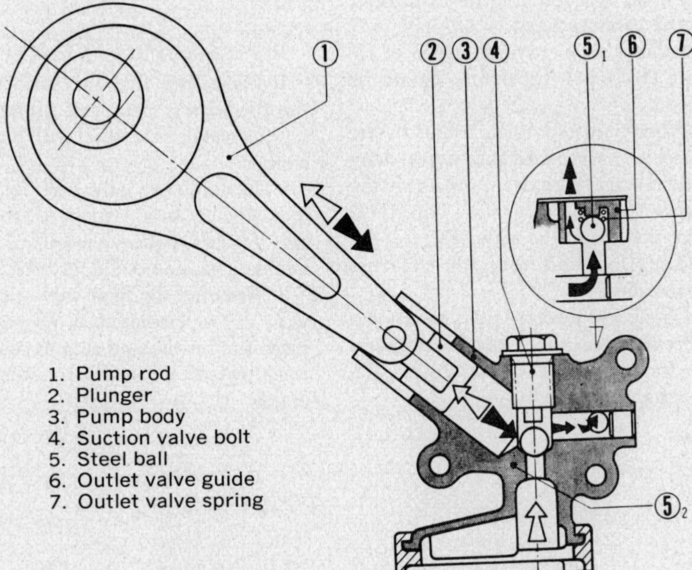

Oil pump (350cc models).

1. Circlip
2. Pump rod side washer
3. Knock pin
4. O-ring
5. Oil pump ball stopper bolt
6. O-ring
7. Steel ball
8. Oil pump ball seat
9. Rubber ring
10. Oil pump ball stopper
11. Rubber seat
12. Oil pump plunger pin
13. Pump plunger
14. Pump rod
15. Oil pump body
16. Filter screen
17. Lockwasher
18. Bolt

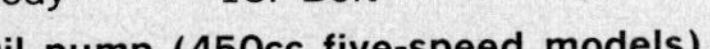

Oil pump (450cc five-speed models).

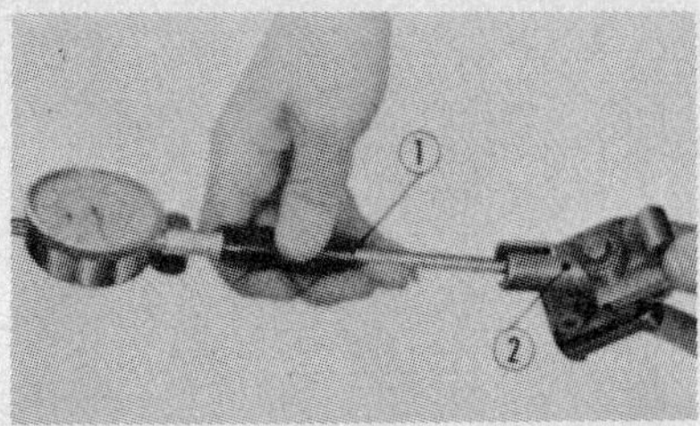

Using a dial indicator (1) to measure the pump body bore (2).

ASSEMBLY

Assemble the oil pump in reverse order of disassembly. Make sure that all components have been cleaned thoroughly and coated with fresh engine oil. Note the following points:

1. Do not overtighten the check valve and pressure relief valve caps.
2. The pump rod retaining circlip is a special type and should not be substituted for with any others.
3. Take care to install the pump rod in the correct position. Reversing it will cause pump failure.
4. Use new O-rings and make sure they are correctly positioned. Refer to the accompanying illustrations.
5. Use a new locktab under the mounting nuts when installing the pump.

125 and 175

	in. (mm)
Plunger-to-housing Calculated clearance:	
nominal	0.001-0.0025 (0.025-0.063)
maximum	0.0067 (0.17)
Oil pump capacity:	
nominal—cc/min @ rpm	3,6000 @ 10,000
minimum—cc/min @ rpm	3,400 @ 10,000

350

Bore diameter:	
nominal	0.630-0.631 (16.000-16.018)
maximum	0.634 (16.10)
Plunger diameter:	
nominal	0.628-0.629 (15.995-15.970)
minimum	0.627 (15.930)

450

Plunger-to-housing Calculated clearance:	
nominal	0.001-0.0025 (0.025-0.063)
maximum	0.0067 (0.017)

Using a micrometer (1) to measure the plunger diameter (2).

FUEL SYSTEMS

FUEL TAP

Removal, Cleaning, and Inspection

ALL MODELS

1. Turn the tap to "stop" and disconnect the lines.
2. Raise the seat, and raise and support the rear of the fuel tank.

Unscrew the cup from the tap, and remove the O-ring and filter strainer.

4. Remove the two mounting screws and the fuel tap.
5. Remove the two screws from the lever retaining plate and remove the plate, O-ring, and gasket.
6. Clean all components in solvent and dry thoroughly. Inspect for wear and cracks.
7. Assemble the tap in reverse order of disassembly, using new gaskets and O-rings.
8. Install the fuel tap on the tank and check for proper fuel flow. (Catch the gasoline in a can or jar.)
9. Lower the tank, install the fuel lines, and check for leaks.

FUEL TANK

Removal and Installation

ALL MODELS

1. Turn the fuel tap to "stop" and disconnect the fuel lines.
2. Raise the seat. On early 125s and 175s it will be necessary to loosen the two seat mounting bolts and remove the seat.
3. Left the rear of the fuel tank out of the rubber mount and withdraw the tank up and toward the rear of the machine, taking care not to snag any cables or wiring on the mounting flanges.

NOTE: *On early 450s the rear of the tank is retained by a bolt and rubber bushings.*

Installation is in reverse order of removal. Be careful not to accidentally strain or reroute any cables when positioning the tank. Make sure that the fuel lines are secured properly at the fuel tap.

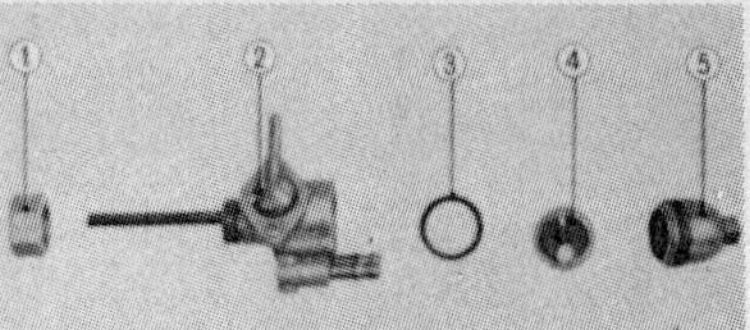

Fuel tap components.

1. Securing nut
2. Fuel top body
3. Gasket
4. Filter screen
5. Cup

CARBURETOR OVERHAUL

Removal and Installation

DIRECT-CONTROL TYPE

1. Turn the fuel tap off and disconnect the fuel line.
2. Unscrew the cap from the top of the carburetor and carefully withdraw the slide.
3. Loosen and slide back the air filter connecting clamp at the carburetor.
4. Disconnect one side of the choke linkage rod (twin carburetors).
5. Unbolt and remove the carburetor from the cylinder head.

Installation is in reverse order of removal. The following points should be noted:

1. When reinstalling the slide in the carburetor, take special care not to damage the needle when dropping it into the jet tube. The tab in the slide bore must engage the slot in the slide. Tighten the cap firmly by hand after the slide has been installed.
2. Check carburetor adjustment and synchronization after installation, and check for smooth throttle operation. Refer to chapter three.

DISASSEMBLY

1. Disconnect the carburetor slide from the throttle cable by compressing the spring and feeding the inner cable into the slide so that the cable end can be disengaged from the retaining slot.
2. Release the float bowl by swivelling back the retaining clip. Try to hold the carburetor in its normal position so that the gasoline in the float bowl will not be spilled.
3. Tap out the float hinge pin using a small diameter rod or drift. Remove the float and lift the float valve needle out of the valve seat. Unscrew the valve seat from the carburetor body.
4. Using a small screwdriver, remove the main jet, low-speed jet, throttle stop screw, and air screw.
5. Unscrew the main jet tube, using the correct size wrench.

CLEANING

Clean all components in solvent or carburetor cleaner and dry thoroughly with compressed air. If an acid type carburetor cleaner is used, do not clean the float or any rubber or plastic parts in it.

INSPECTION

1. Make sure that the surface of the throttle slide is clean and smooth. Light scoring can be smoothed with fine emery cloth.
2. Examine the jet needle for wear as indicated by bright spots or uneven taper. If wear is noticeable replace both the needle and the needle jet tube.
3. Examine the float valve needle for wear. If replacement is necessary, replace the needle and seat as a unit.
4. Inspect the carburetor body for cracks.

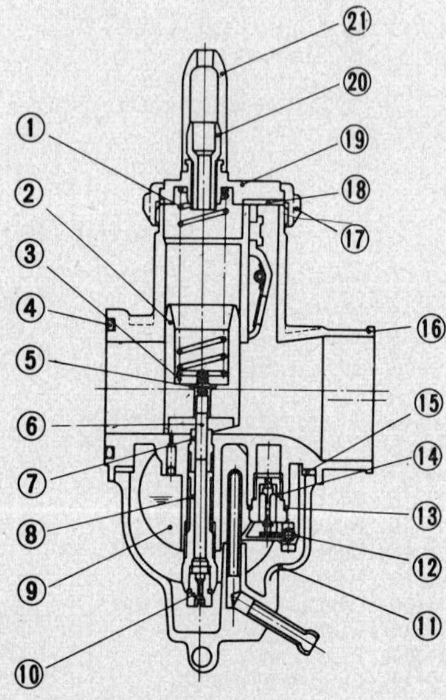

1. Coil spring
2. Throttle slide
3. Needle clip plate
4. O-ring
5. Bar clip
6. Jet needle
7. Needle jet
8. Needle jet holder
9. Float
10. Main jet
11. Float chamber body
12. Arm pin
13. Valve seat
14. Slow jet
15. Float chamber washer
16. Body
17. Cap
18. Top washer
19. Top
20. Cable adjuster
21. Rubber cap

Cross-section of a direct control type carburetor.

CARBURETOR SPECIFICATIONS

	CB 125	CL 125	CD 125	CB 175	CL 175
Type	(2) Keihin	(2) Keihin	(1) Keihin CV	(2) Keihin	(2) Keihin
Bore diameter (mm)	18	18	—	20	22
Main jet (no.)	92	92	—	95	98
Low-speed jet (no.)	35	35	—	35	38
Slide cutaway (no.)	2.0	2.0	—	2.0	3.0
Jet needle	18231 (2 stage)	18234 (2 stage)	—	3°, 2.535 (3 stage)	4°, 2.535 (3 stage)
Air screw openings*	1⅛ ± ¼	1⅛ ± ¼	—	1⅛ ± ¼	1⅛ ± ¼
Air jet (no.)	150	150	—	10	100
Float height (mm)	21	21	—	19.5	28.0

* Number of turns from fully closed.

	CD 175	SL 175	CB/CL 350 †	CB/CL 350 ‡
Type		(2) Keihin	(2) Keihin CV	(2) Keihin CV
Bore diameter (mm)	—	—	28	28
Main jet (no.)	—	—	60/115 (pri/sec)	70/110 (pri/sec)
Low-speed jet (no.)	—	—	38	35
Slide cutaway (no.)	—	—	12°, 1.0	12°, 1.0
Jet needle	—	—	3°30′, 2.595	3°30′, 2.595
Air screw opening*	—	—	¾ ± ⅛	1.0 ± ⅛
Air jet (no.)	—	—	50/50 (pri/sec)	150/50 (pri/sec)
Float height (mm)	—	—	19	21

* Number of turns from fully closed.
† Up to engine number E-1045165.
‡ From engine number E-1045165 to E-1065279.

	CB/CL 350 § SL 350 (1970)	SL 350K1 & K2	CB 450 (4-speed)		CB/CL 450 (5-speed)
Type	(2) Keihin CV	(2) Keihin	(2) Keihin CV		(2) Keihin CV
Bore diameter (mm)	28	24	36		36
Main jet (no.)	70/105 (pri/sec)	120	125		130
Low-speed jet (no.)	35	40	38		38
Slide cutaway (no.)	12°, 1.0	2.5 x 1.8 x 0.2	14°, 1.0		14°, 0.9
Jet needle	3°30′, 2.595	3°, 2.515	2°26′, 2.275		3°, 2.275
Air screw opening*	¾ ± ⅛	1.0 ± ¼	¾ ± ¼	&	1.0 ± ¼
Air jet (no.)	150/50 (pri/sec)	150	50		50
Float height (mm)	26	25	20		20

§ From engine number E-1065279 to present.
* Number of turns from fully closed.

ASSEMBLY

Assemble in reverse order of disassembly. Observe the following points:

1. Use new gaskets and O-rings.
2. The float level must be checked and adjusted if necessary. The float should be positioned so that when the float arm just touches the tip of the float needle, the distance from the top of the float to the float bowl mating surface on the carburetor is as close as possible to the specification given at the end of the chapter for your carburetor.
3. Do not overtighten the jets when installing them in the carburetor body.
4. Make sure that the jet needle is installed in the same position as when removed. Changing the needle position in the slide will affect running at mid-range throttle openings.
5. After installing the carburetor check for smooth operation of the choke. On twin carburetor installations, check to make sure that the clearance between the choke valve and throttle bore is less than 0.02 in. (0.5 mm) and that both chokes operate simultaneously. Adjust with the linkage rod if necessary.

Removal and Installation

CONSTANT VELOCITY TYPE

1. Turn the fuel tap off and disconnect the fuel line.
2. Disconnect the throttle cable from the linkage at the carburetor.

3. Loosen the air filter connecting clamp at the carburetor and loosen or remove the air filter housing so that the carburetor can be moved back slightly.

4. Loosen the carburetor-to-intake tube mounting clamp and remove the carburetor.

Installation is in reverse order of removal. The following points should be noted:

1. Make sure that the carburetor is securely clamped to the intake tube. If necessary, use a new clamp.

2. Check carburetor adjustment and synchronization after installation. (Refer to chapter three.) Check for smooth throttle operation.

DISASSEMBLY, CLEANING, INSPECTION, AND ASSEMBLY

Refer to the preceding section on direct-control type carburetors, as the procedures are nearly identical. In the "disassembly" section, omit step one and substitute the following:

1. Remove the carburetor top and lift out the slide. Take care not to damage the slide diaphragm (350 only).

ELECTRICAL SYSTEMS

ALTERNATOR

Alternator Output Test

125 AND 175

1. Check the state of charge of the battery. (Refer to chapter two.). If necessary, recharge the battery before proceeding with the test.

2. Connect an ammeter between the positive (+) battery terminal and the input (alternator) side of the rectifier. Start the engine and compare the readings obtained with those in the table.

3. If alternator output is insufficient, the fault lies either in the wiring between the alternator and rectifier or in the alternator itself. Check the wiring and refer to the "ALTERNATOR SERVICE" section. If the alternator is producing a sufficient amount of current, it can be assumed that either the rectifier or the wiring between the rectifier and battery is at fault.

NOTE: *Remember that these models do not have a regulator, and running constantly with the lights on or under other heavy electrical load can cause slow battery discharge, which should be considered normal.*

350 AND 450

1. Check the state of charge of the battery. (Refer to chapter two.) If necessary, recharge the battery before proceeding with the test.

2. Connect the positive lead of an ammeter to the yellow alternator lead and ground the negative lead on the engine. Start the engine and run it as a steady 5,000 rpm. The ammeter should read 1.5–2.5 amps (350) or 4.0&5.0 amps (450). Excessive amperage indicates a bad regulator.

3. Next, switch the ammeter lead from the yellow wire to the white alternator wire. Start the engine, turn the headlight on (high beam), and run it at 5,000 rpm. Teh ammeter should read approximately the same as before, 1.5–2.5 amps (350) or 4.0–5.0 amps (450). Battery voltage at 5,000 rpm in either case should be 14.8 volts.

4. If output in steps two and three is sufficient, chances are that the rectifier or wiring between the rectifier and battery is at fault.

5. If alternator output in steps two and three is insufficient, disconnect the yellow wire from the regulator, making sure it does not touch ground, and check the output again at 5,000 rpm with the lights on. If a good reading is obtained, the regulator is at fault (assuming there are no breaks in the wiring). If output is still insufficient, the problem lies in the alternator itself.

Testing the Rectifier–All Models

If alternator output is satisfactory but the battery discharges as the engine is running, it is quite possible that the rectifier is not functioning properly (assuming that the battery is in good condition and capable of taking a charge). Before removing and testing the rectifier, make sure that it is solidly mounted on the frame. Teh rectifier is grounded through its mounting and will not operate without a good ground.

CAUTION: *Do not loosen or tighten the nut that holds the rectifier unit together; this will adversely affect operation of the rectifier.*

ALTERNATOR OUTPUT TABLE, 125 AND 175

Model	Item	Charging Start	Charging Current /3,000 rpm	Charging Current /5,000 rpm	Charging Current /10,000 rpm
CB 175	Daytime	Max 2,400 rpm	—	Min 0.5 A	Max 3.0 A
	Nighttime	Max 2,800 rpm	—	Min 0.5 A	Max 3.0 A
	Battery voltage	12.3 V	—	13 V	16.5 V
CL 175	Daytime	Max 2,400 rpm	—	Min 0.5 A	Max 3.0 A
	Nighttime	Max 2,800 rpm	—	Min 0.5 A	Max 3.0 A
	Battery voltage	13.2 V	—	14 V	16.5 V
CB 125	Daytime	Max 1,300 rpm	Min 2.0 A	Min 2.7 A	Max 4.5 A
	Nighttime	Max 1,900 rpm	Min 1.2 A	Min 2.0 A	Max 4.0 A
	Battery voltage	6.3 V	6.7 V	7 V	8.3 V
CL 125	Daytime	Max 1,300 rpm	—	Min 1.7 A	Max 3.0 A
	Nighttime	Max 2,000 rpm	—	Min 1.7 A	Max 3.5 A
	Battery voltage	6.3 V	—	7 V	8.3 V
CD 175	Daytime	Max 1,300 rpm	Min 3.0 A	Min 4.0 A	Max 6.0 A
	Nighttime	Max 1,800 rpm	Min 1.2 A	Min 2.0 A	Max 4.0 A
	Battery voltage	6.3 V	7 V	7 V	8.3 V
SS 175	Daytime	Max 1,300 rpm	Min 2.0 A	Min 2.5 A	Max 4.5 A
	Nighttime	Max 2,100 rpm	Min 1.2 A	Min 1.5 A	Max 4.0 A
	Battery voltage	6.4 V	6.7 V	7.5 V	8.3 V

To test the rectifier, first pull apart the plastic connector, unscrew the mounting nut, and remove the rectifier unit. Inside the rectifier are four diodes which, if functioning properly, will allow electricity to pass in only one direction. To check the diodes you can use either a multimeter or a test light and the motorcycle battery. If the test light and battery are to be used, simply run a length of wire off one battery terminal and connect one of the test light leads to the other terminal. The two free wire ends will be used to check electrical continuity of the diodes.

Connect the positive lead to the yellow wire and the negative lead to the red/-white wire, as shown in test one of the accompanying table. Then, reverse the leads, so that the negative lead is connected to the yellow wire and the positive lead is connected to the red/white wire. The test light should light (or the gauge needle respond) in one direction only. Repeat in the same manner for test steps two, three, and four in the table. Continuity in both directions (when reversing the leads) indicates a defective diode, in which case the rectifier unit must be replaced.

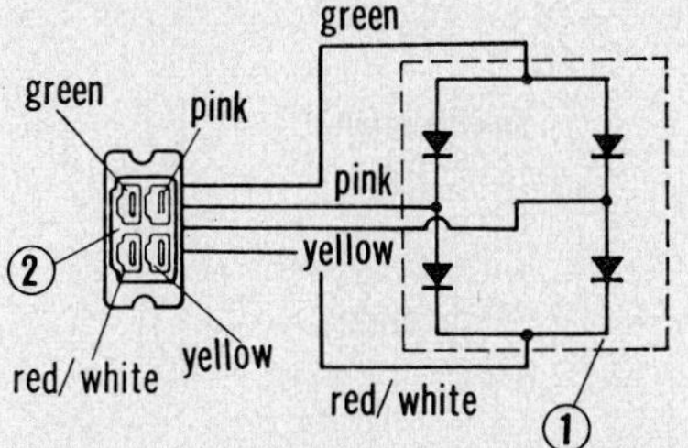

Rectifier wiring diagram. Rectifier pack (1) and connector (2).

Test Leads		Connection Rectifier Terminal	Resistance Value
1. +	−	Yellow	
−	+	Red/white	
2. +	−	Pink	Satisfactory if
−	+	Red/white	between
3. +	−	Green	5—40 Ω
−	+	Yellow	
4. +	−	Green	
−	+	Pink	

The diodes are quite susceptible to failure from excessive heat and electrical overload. Observe the following precautions to avoid rectifier failure.

1. Do not reverse battery polarity when installing or reconnecting the battery. The electrical system is negative ground.
2. Do not use high-voltage test equipment to test the rectifier diodes.
3. Do not run the engine with the rectifier disconnected.
4. Do not charge the battery without first disconnecting one of the battery cables.

Alternator Service

Uncouple the alternator leads at the connector block and check continuity between the three stator coil leads (yellow, pink, and white) using a multimeter or a test light and battery. Connect one of the test leads to the pink wire and the other to first the yellow and then the white wire. If there is continuity in both cases, the stator coil is satisfactory. Standard stator coil resistance is 1.1 ohms (pink-to-yellow wire) and 0.55 ohm (pink-to-white wire). The stator coil assembly can be taken off after the left side cover is removed.

STARTING SYSTEM

Testing

ALL MODELS

If the starter will not operate, switch on the headlight and observe its intensity. If it is dim when the starter is not being operated, check the battery connections and recharge the battery. If the headlight doesn't light, check the fuse, the battery connections, the ignition switch and its connections, and check the electrical continuity of the wire between the ignition switch and the battery.

If the headlight is bright, press the starter button momentarily and watch the light. If it remains bright, touch a screwdriver blade between the two starter solenoid terminals. If the starter operates, connect a test light between the small yellow/red wire on the solenoid and ground. If the test light comes on as the button is pushed, the solenoid is faulty. If it does not light, look for defective wiring between the starter button and solenoid or between the starter button and ignition switch, or simply a burned-out starter button switch. If the starter does not operate and the headlight dims as the main solenoid terminals are bridged, the starter motor is faulty. If the headlight does not dim, look for a bad connection at the starter.

If the starter motor operates freely but will not turn the engine over, the starter clutch is not operating (a rare occurrence). To remove the clutch it will be necessary to first take off the left-side crankcase cover and remove the alternator rotor.

Starter Motor Service

125 AND 175

Removal and Installation

1. Disconnect the electrical cable from the starter motor.
2. Take out the screws and remove the starter motor side cover.
3. Remove the left-side crankcase cover.

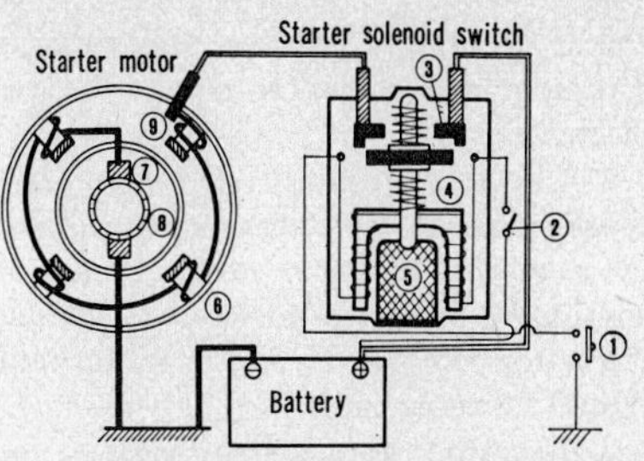

Starting system diagram.

1. Starter button switch
2. Ignition switch
3. Contact unit
4. Coil
5. Plunger
6. Pole
7. Brush
8. Armature
9. Field coil

4. Remove the starter chain and starter motor sprocket.
5. Unscrew the three bolts and remove the starter motor.
6. Installation is a reversal of the removal procedures.

350

Removal and Installation

1. Remove the left-side rear crankcase cover and disconnect the neutral indicator switch lead.
2. Remove the left crankcase cover.
3. Remove the alternator rotor using Honda service tool no. 07011-21601 (which is a long threaded bolt that is screwed into the center of the rotor).
4. Remove the starter clutch sprocket set plate and then remove the starter motor sprocket and clutch sprocket together.
5. Disconnect the electrical cable from the starter.
6. Unscrew the two starter mounting bolts and remove the starter. The brushes can be withdrawn from their holders after the brush lead screws have been taken out.
7. Install the starter in the reverse order of removal.

450

Removal and Installation

1. Disconnect the electrical cable from the starter motor.
2. Take out the two screws and remove the starter side cover.
3. Remove the left-side crankcase cover.
4. Remove the starter chain and starter motor sprocket.
5. Unscrew the three starter mounting bolts and remove the starter.
6. Install the starter in reverse order of removal.

Repair

ALL MODELS

1. Check electrical continuity between the commutator and armature core using a multimeter or test light and battery. If continuity exists, the armature

coil is grounded and the armature or complete starter motor should be replaced.

2. Check continuity between the brush wired to the stator (field) coil and the starter motor cable terminal. Lack of continuity indicates an open circuit in the stator coil and the starter motor unit should be replaced.

3. Examine the carbon brushes for damage to the contact surfaces and measure their length. Replace brushes as a set if they are damaged in any way or if they measure less than 0.3 in. (7.5 mm).

4. Brush spring tension should be determined with a small pull-scale. Replace the springs if they exert less than 0.8 lb (0.4 kg) tension.

5. Polish the commutator with fine emery cloth before installing the starter motor. Check the following components for excessive wear and damage: clutch spring and rollers, bearings, bushings, the oil seal, reduction gears, and sprockets. Replace parts as necessary.

NOTE: *When reassembling the starter clutch, apply a thin coat of silicone grease to the rollers.*

Starter Solenoid Service

The solenoid is an electromagnetic switch that closes and completes the circuit between the starter and battery when activated by the starter button. The solenoid is a necessary addition to the starting circuit because the starter button switch is not capable of handling the amperage load required to operate the starter and because mounting a heavy-duty switch on the handlebar, with the large cable needed to handle the load, is impractical.

If the solenoid does not work, check the continuity of the primary coil by connecting a multimeter or test light and battery to the two small solenoid leads. Lack of continuity indicates an open circuit and the solenoid must be replaced. If the primary coil winding is continuous, disassemble the solenoid and clean the contact points with emery paper or a small file. The points, after long use, have a tendency to become pitted or burned due to the large current passing across them.

NOTE: *Be sure to disconnect the battery before disconnecting the cables from the solenoid when it is to be removed.*

Replace the solenoid if cleaning the points fails to repair it.

STARTER SPECIFICATION TABLES

	125			175		
Item	**Specification**			**Specification**		
Rated voltage	6			12		
Rated output	0.35 kw			0.35 kw		
Intermittent operation	30 seconds			30 seconds		
Reduction ratio	6.44			6.44		

	Without Load	With Load	Lock	Without Load	With Load	Lock
Voltage	5.5	4.2	2.8	11.5	9.4	6.7
Current	Max 40	120	Max 300	Max 28	100	Max 240
Torque	——	Min 0.55 kg/m	Min 1.5 kg/m	——	Min 0.55 kg/m	Min 1.5 kg/m
Rpm	Min 1,900-2,700	Min 400	——	Min 2,000	Min 500	——
Output	——	0.22kw	——	——	Min 0.33 kw	——

	350			450		
Item	**Specification**			**Specification**		
Rated voltage	12			12		
Rated output	0.45 kw			0.5 kw		
Intermittent operation	30 seconds			30 seconds		
Reduction ratio	6.44			6.44		

	Without Load	With Load	Lock	Without Load	With Load	Lock
Voltage	11	9	5	11	9	5
Current	Max 35	120	280	Max 35	120	280
Torque	——	5.06 ft lbs	13.02 ft lbs	——	5.06 ft lbs	13.02 ft lbs
Rpm	Min 1,700	Min 500	——	Min 1,700	Min 500	——
Output	——	N.A.	——	——	N.A.	——

WIRING DIAGRAMS

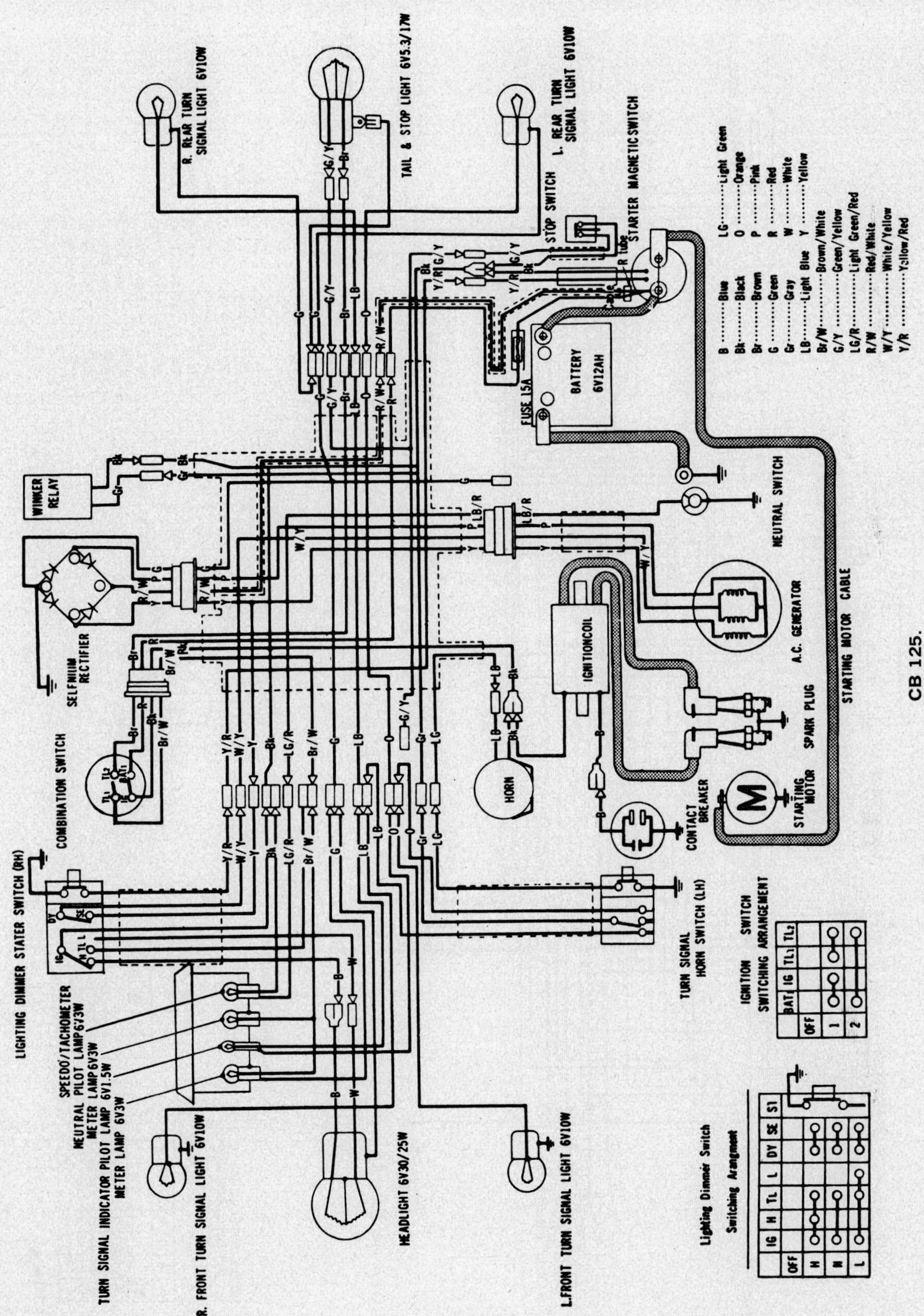

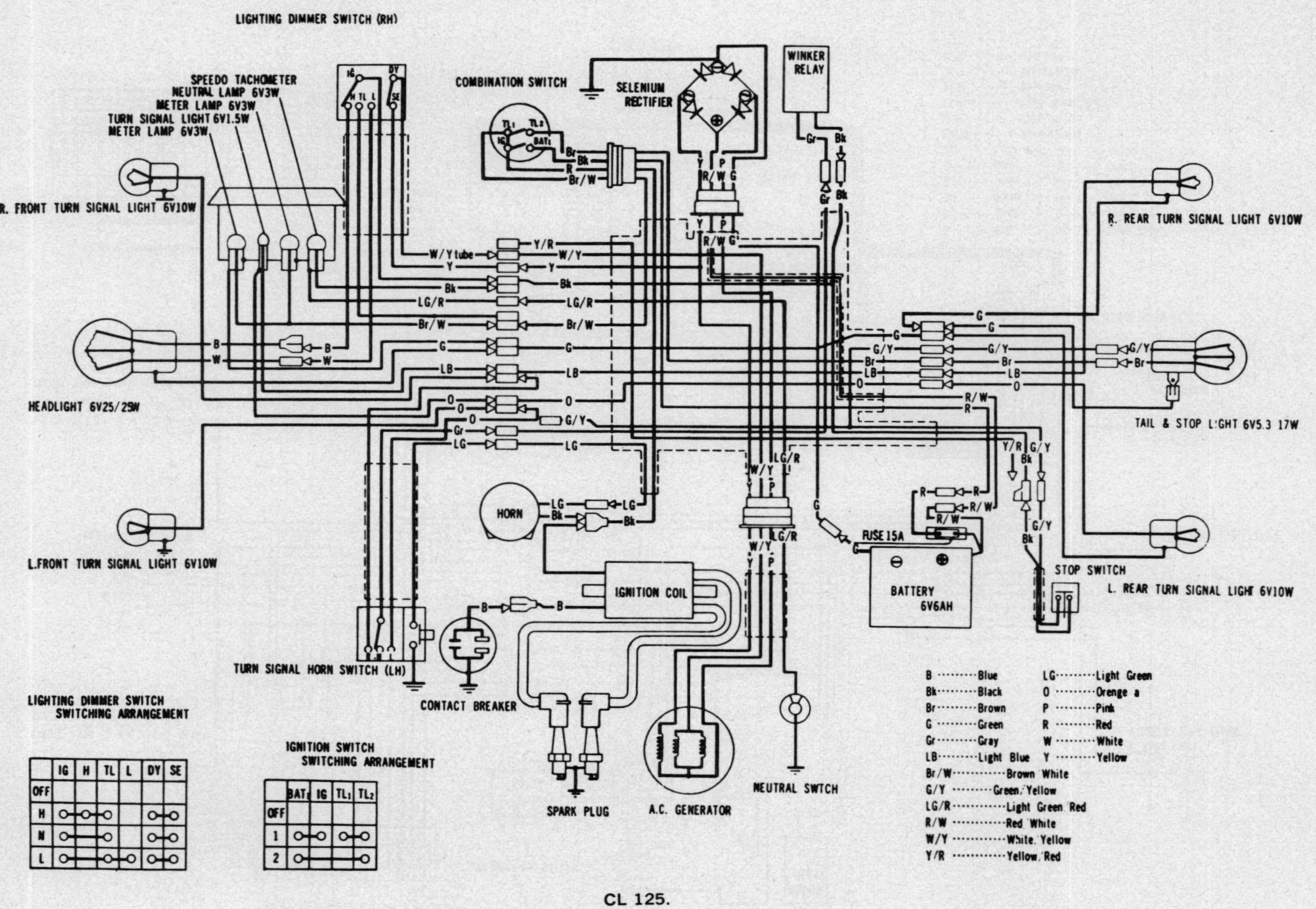
LIGHTING DIMMER SWITCH (RH)
SPEEDO TACHOMETER
NEUTRAL LAMP 6V3W
METER LAMP 6V3W
TURN SIGNAL LIGHT 6V1.5W
METER LAMP 6V3W
COMBINATION SWITCH
SELENIUM RECTIFIER
WINKER RELAY
R. FRONT TURN SIGNAL LIGHT 6V10W
R. REAR TURN SIGNAL LIGHT 6V10W
HEADLIGHT 6V25/25W
TAIL & STOP LIGHT 6V5.3 17W
HORN
FUSE 15A
BATTERY 6V6AH
STOP SWITCH
L.FRONT TURN SIGNAL LIGHT 6V10W
L. REAR TURN SIGNAL LIGHT 6V10W
IGNITION COIL
TURN SIGNAL HORN SWITCH (LH)
CONTACT BREAKER
SPARK PLUG
A.C. GENERATOR
NEUTRAL SWTCH
LIGHTING DIMMER SWITCH SWITCHING ARRANGEMENT
IGNITION SWITCH SWITCHING ARRANGEMENT
B Blue
Bk Black
Br Brown
G Green
Gr Gray
LB Light Blue
Br/W Brown White
G/Y Green Yellow
LG/R Light Green Red
R/W Red White
W/Y White Yellow
Y/R Yellow Red
LG Light Green
O Orange
P Pink
R Red
W White
Y Yellow

CL 125.

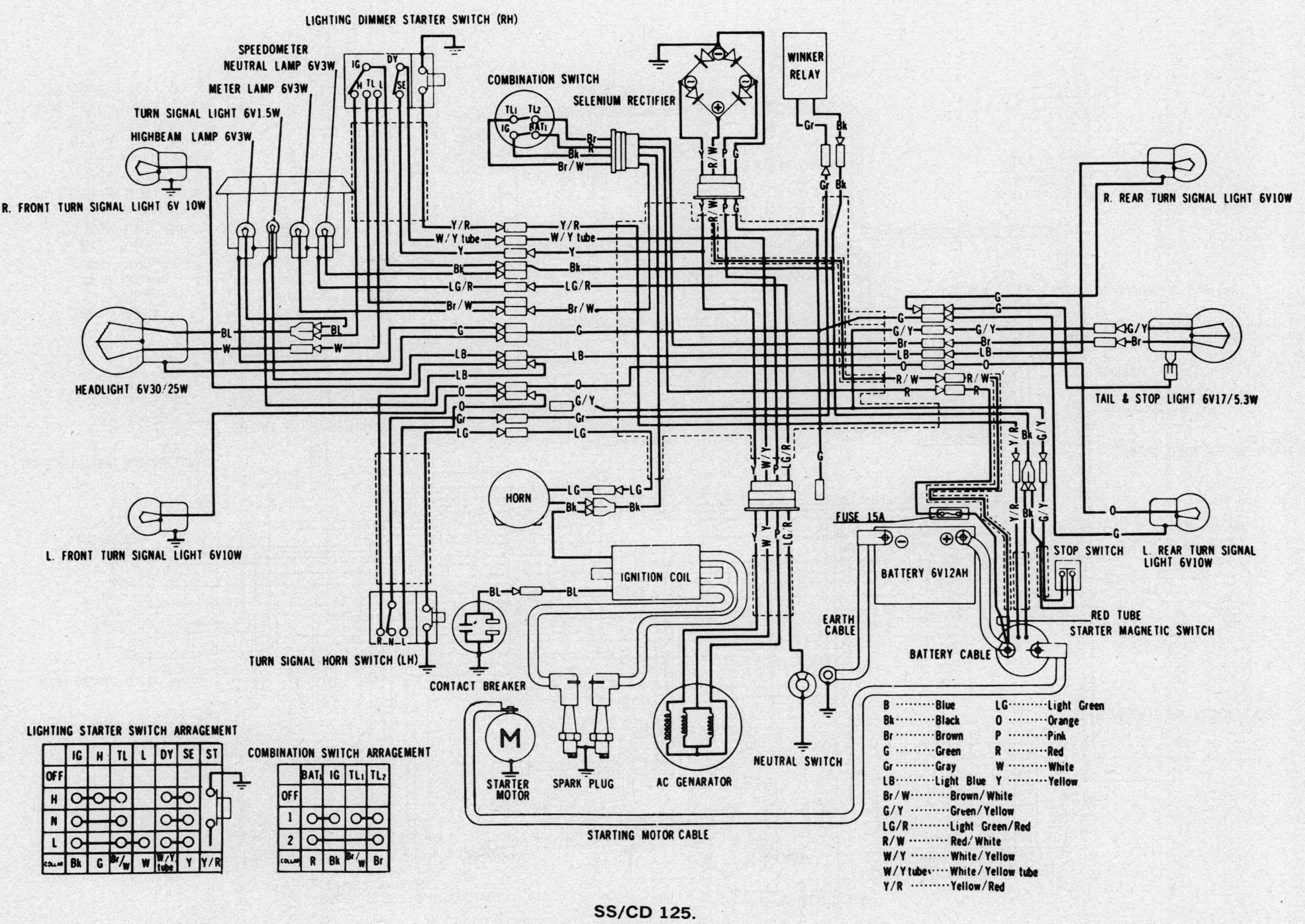
LIGHTING DIMMER STARTER SWITCH (RH)
SPEEDOMETER
NEUTRAL LAMP 6V3W
METER LAMP 6V3W
TURN SIGNAL LIGHT 6V1.5W
HIGHBEAM LAMP 6V3W
R. FRONT TURN SIGNAL LIGHT 6V 10W
COMBINATION SWITCH
SELENIUM RECTIFIER
WINKER RELAY
R. REAR TURN SIGNAL LIGHT 6V10W
HEADLIGHT 6V30/25W
TAIL & STOP LIGHT 6V17/5.3W
HORN
L. FRONT TURN SIGNAL LIGHT 6V10W
FUSE 15A
BATTERY 6V12AH
STOP SWITCH
L. REAR TURN SIGNAL LIGHT 6V10W
IGNITION COIL
EARTH CABLE
RED TUBE
STARTER MAGNETIC SWITCH
BATTERY CABLE
TURN SIGNAL HORN SWITCH (LH)
CONTACT BREAKER
STARTER MOTOR
SPARK PLUG
AC GENARATOR
NEUTRAL SWITCH
STARTING MOTOR CABLE
LIGHTING STARTER SWITCH ARRAGEMENT
COMBINATION SWITCH ARRAGEMENT
B Blue
Bk Black
Br Brown
G Green
Gr Gray
LB Light Blue
Br/W Brown/White
G/Y Green/Yellow
LG/R Light Green/Red
R/W Red/White
W/Y White/Yellow
W/Y tube White/Yellow tube
Y/R Yellow/Red
LG Light Green
O Orange
P Pink
R Red
W White
Y Yellow
SS/CD 125.

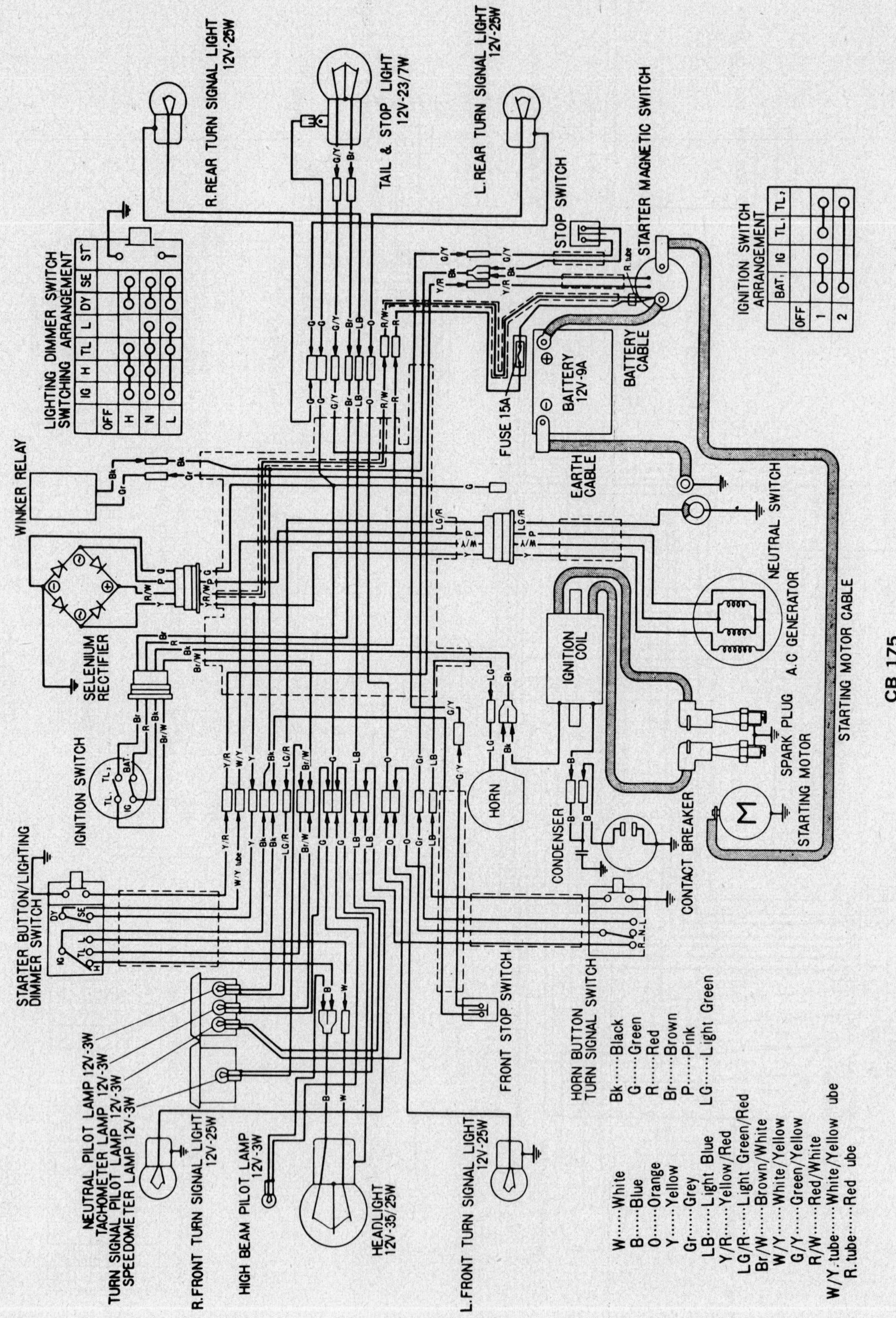
R.REAR TURN SIGNAL LIGHT 12V-25W
TAIL & STOP LIGHT 12V-23/7W
L.REAR TURN SIGNAL LIGHT 12V-25W
STOP SWITCH
STARTER MAGNETIC SWITCH
IGNITION SWITCH ARRANGEMENT
LIGHTING DIMMER SWITCH SWITCHING ARRANGEMENT
WINKER RELAY
FUSE 15A
BATTERY 12V-9A
BATTERY CABLE
EARTH CABLE
NEUTRAL SWITCH
SELENIUM RECTIFIER
IGNITION COIL
A.C GENERATOR
STARTING MOTOR CABLE
SPARK PLUG
STARTING MOTOR
IGNITION SWITCH
HORN
CONDENSER
CONTACT BREAKER
STARTER BUTTON/LIGHTING DIMMER SWITCH
HORN BUTTON TURN SIGNAL SWITCH
FRONT STOP SWITCH
NEUTRAL PILOT LAMP 12V-3W
TACHOMETER LAMP 12V-3W
TURN SIGNAL PILOT LAMP 12V-3W
SPEEDOMETER LAMP 12V-3W
R.FRONT TURN SIGNAL LIGHT 12V-25W
HIGH BEAM PILOT LAMP 12V-3W
HEADLIGHT 12V-35/25W
L.FRONT TURN SIGNAL LIGHT 12V-25W
CB 175.
W......White
B......Blue
O......Orange
Y......Yellow
Gr......Grey
LB......Light Blue
Y/R......Yellow/Red
LG/R......Light Green/Red
Br/W......Brown/White
W/Y......White/Yellow
G/Y......Green/Yellow
R/W......Red/White
W/Y.tube......White/Yellow ube
R.tube......Red ube
Bk......Black
G......Green
R......Red
Br......Brown
P......Pink
LG......Light Green

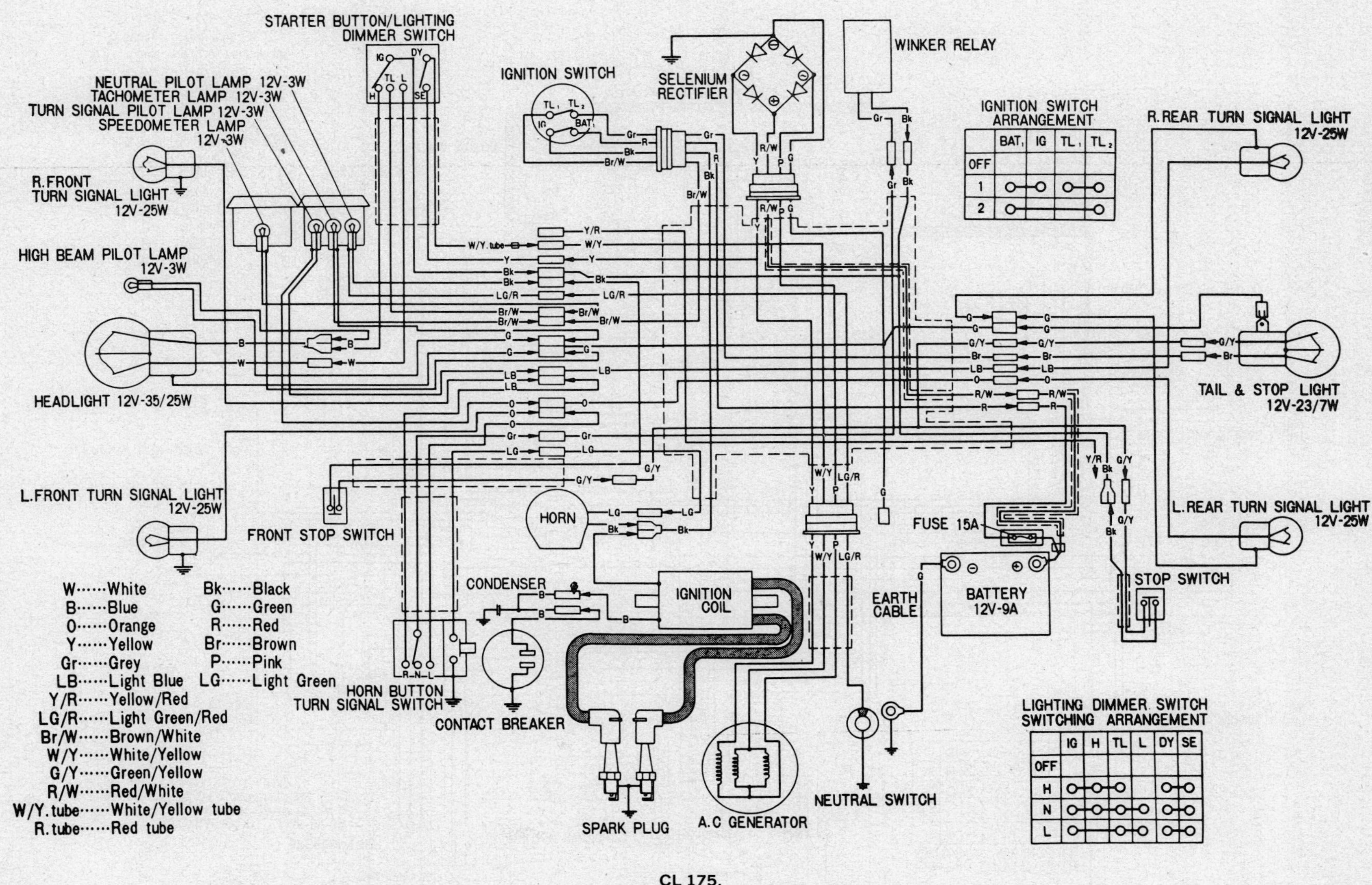
STARTER BUTTON/LIGHTING DIMMER SWITCH
NEUTRAL PILOT LAMP 12V-3W
TACHOMETER LAMP 12V-3W
TURN SIGNAL PILOT LAMP 12V-3W
SPEEDOMETER LAMP 12V-3W
R.FRONT TURN SIGNAL LIGHT 12V-25W
HIGH BEAM PILOT LAMP 12V-3W
HEADLIGHT 12V-35/25W
L.FRONT TURN SIGNAL LIGHT 12V-25W
FRONT STOP SWITCH
IGNITION SWITCH
SELENIUM RECTIFIER
WINKER RELAY
IGNITION SWITCH ARRANGEMENT
R.REAR TURN SIGNAL LIGHT 12V-25W
TAIL & STOP LIGHT 12V-23/7W
L.REAR TURN SIGNAL LIGHT 12V-25W
HORN
FUSE 15A
STOP SWITCH
CONDENSER
IGNITION COIL
EARTH CABLE
BATTERY 12V-9A
HORN BUTTON TURN SIGNAL SWITCH
CONTACT BREAKER
SPARK PLUG
A.C GENERATOR
NEUTRAL SWITCH
LIGHTING DIMMER SWITCH SWITCHING ARRANGEMENT
W······White
B······Blue
O······Orange
Y······Yellow
Gr······Grey
LB······Light Blue
Y/R······Yellow/Red
LG/R······Light Green/Red
Br/W······Brown/White
W/Y······White/Yellow
G/Y······Green/Yellow
R/W······Red/White
W/Y. tube······White/Yellow tube
R. tube······Red tube
Bk······Black
G······Green
R······Red
Br······Brown
P······Pink
LG······Light Green
CL 175.

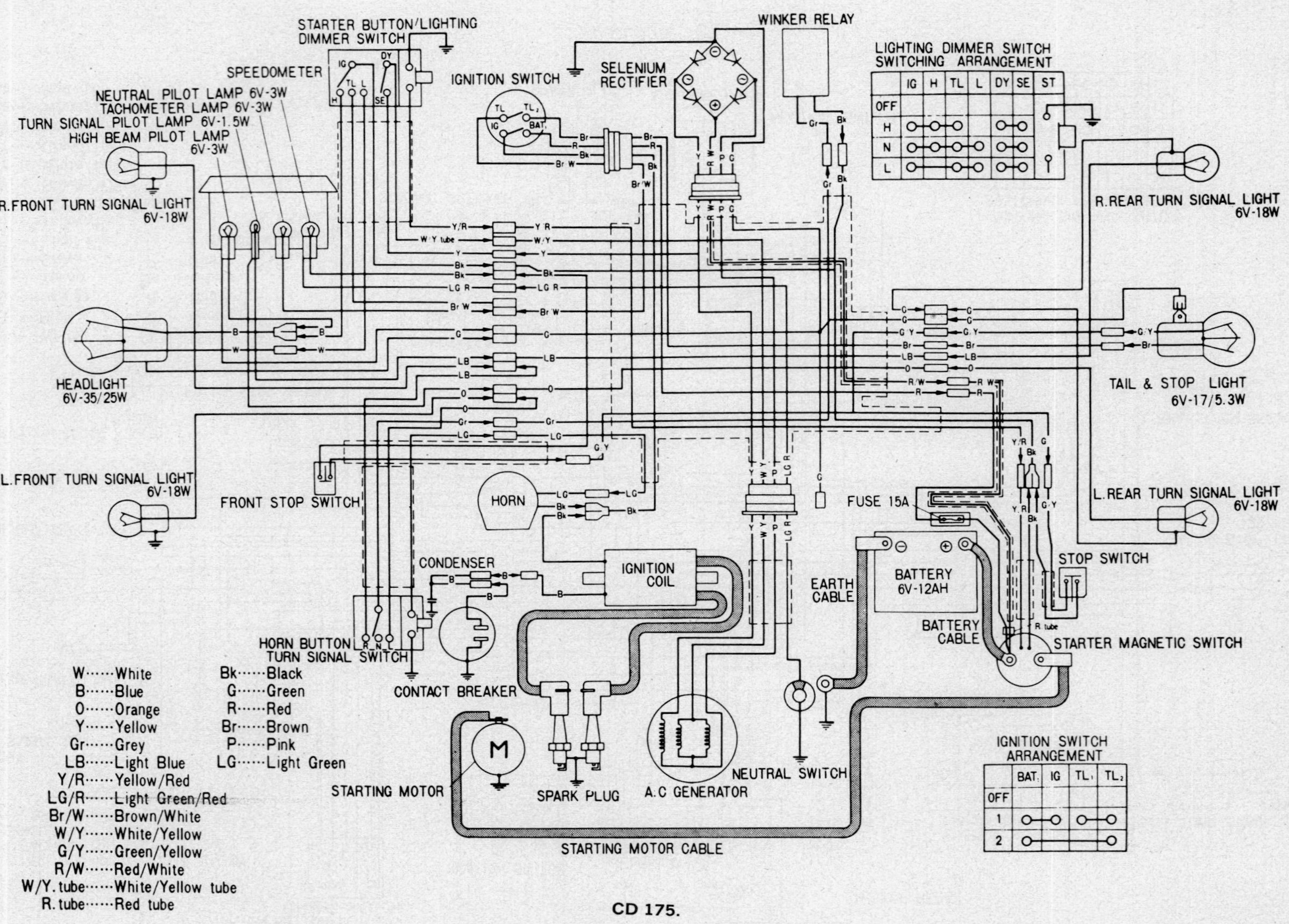
STARTER BUTTON/LIGHTING DIMMER SWITCH
SPEEDOMETER
NEUTRAL PILOT LAMP 6V-3W
TACHOMETER LAMP 6V-3W
TURN SIGNAL PILOT LAMP 6V-1.5W
HIGH BEAM PILOT LAMP 6V-3W
IGNITION SWITCH
SELENIUM RECTIFIER
WINKER RELAY
LIGHTING DIMMER SWITCH SWITCHING ARRANGEMENT
IG H TL L DY SE ST
OFF
H
N
L
R.FRONT TURN SIGNAL LIGHT 6V-18W
R.REAR TURN SIGNAL LIGHT 6V-18W
HEADLIGHT 6V-35/25W
TAIL & STOP LIGHT 6V-17/5.3W
L.FRONT TURN SIGNAL LIGHT 6V-18W
FRONT STOP SWITCH
HORN
FUSE 15A
L.REAR TURN SIGNAL LIGHT 6V-18W
CONDENSER
IGNITION COIL
EARTH CABLE
BATTERY 6V-12AH
STOP SWITCH
BATTERY CABLE
STARTER MAGNETIC SWITCH
HORN BUTTON TURN SIGNAL SWITCH
CONTACT BREAKER
W……White
B……Blue
O……Orange
Y……Yellow
Gr……Grey
LB……Light Blue
Y/R……Yellow/Red
LG/R……Light Green/Red
Br/W……Brown/White
W/Y……White/Yellow
G/Y……Green/Yellow
R/W……Red/White
W/Y. tube……White/Yellow tube
R. tube……Red tube
Bk……Black
G……Green
R……Red
Br……Brown
P……Pink
LG……Light Green
STARTING MOTOR
SPARK PLUG
A.C GENERATOR
NEUTRAL SWITCH
IGNITION SWITCH ARRANGEMENT
BAT. IG TL1 TL2
OFF
1
2
STARTING MOTOR CABLE
CD 175.

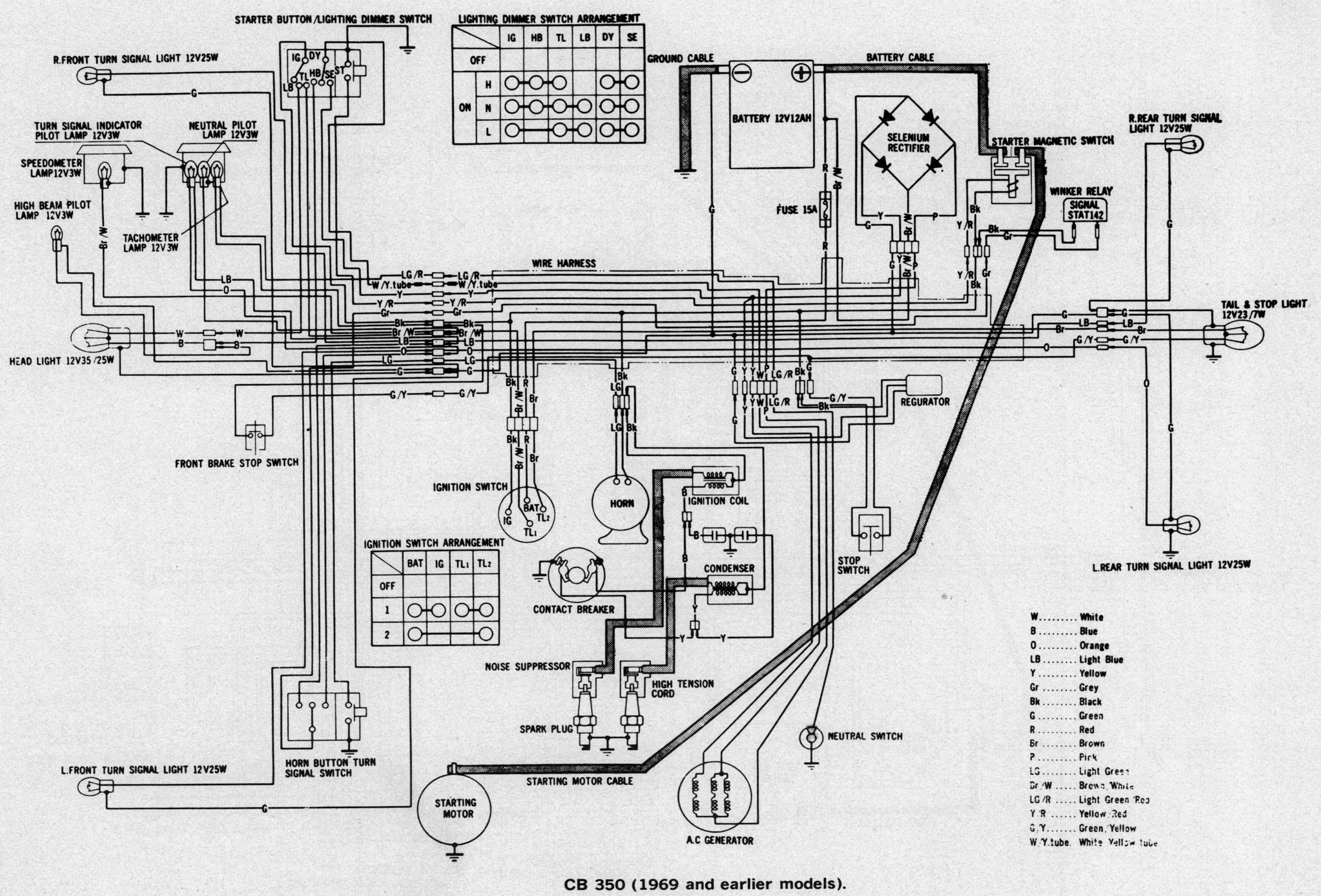
STARTER BUTTON /LIGHTING DIMMER SWITCH
LIGHTING DIMMER SWITCH ARRANGEMENT
R.FRONT TURN SIGNAL LIGHT 12V25W
GROUND CABLE
BATTERY CABLE
BATTERY 12V12AH
SELENIUM RECTIFIER
R.REAR TURN SIGNAL LIGHT 12V25W
STARTER MAGNETIC SWITCH
TURN SIGNAL INDICATOR PILOT LAMP 12V3W
NEUTRAL PILOT LAMP 12V3W
SPEEDOMETER LAMP12V3W
HIGH BEAM PILOT LAMP 12V3W
TACHOMETER LAMP 12V3W
FUSE 15A
WINKER RELAY
SIGNAL STAT142
WIRE HARNESS
TAIL & STOP LIGHT 12V23/7W
HEAD LIGHT 12V35/25W
REGURATOR
FRONT BRAKE STOP SWITCH
IGNITION SWITCH
HORN
IGNITION COIL
IGNITION SWITCH ARRANGEMENT
CONDENSER
CONTACT BREAKER
STOP SWITCH
L.REAR TURN SIGNAL LIGHT 12V25W
NOISE SUPPRESSOR
HIGH TENSION CORD
SPARK PLUG
NEUTRAL SWITCH
L.FRONT TURN SIGNAL LIGHT 12V25W
HORN BUTTON TURN SIGNAL SWITCH
STARTING MOTOR CABLE
STARTING MOTOR
A.C GENERATOR
W.........White
B.........Blue
O.........Orange
LB........Light Blue
Y.........Yellow
Gr........Grey
Bk........Black
G.........Green
R.........Red
Br........Brown
P.........Pink
LG........Light Green
Br/W.....Brown/White
LG/R.....Light Green/Red
Y/R......Yellow/Red
G/Y.......Green/Yellow
W/Y.tube. White Yellow tube

CB 350 (1969 and earlier models).

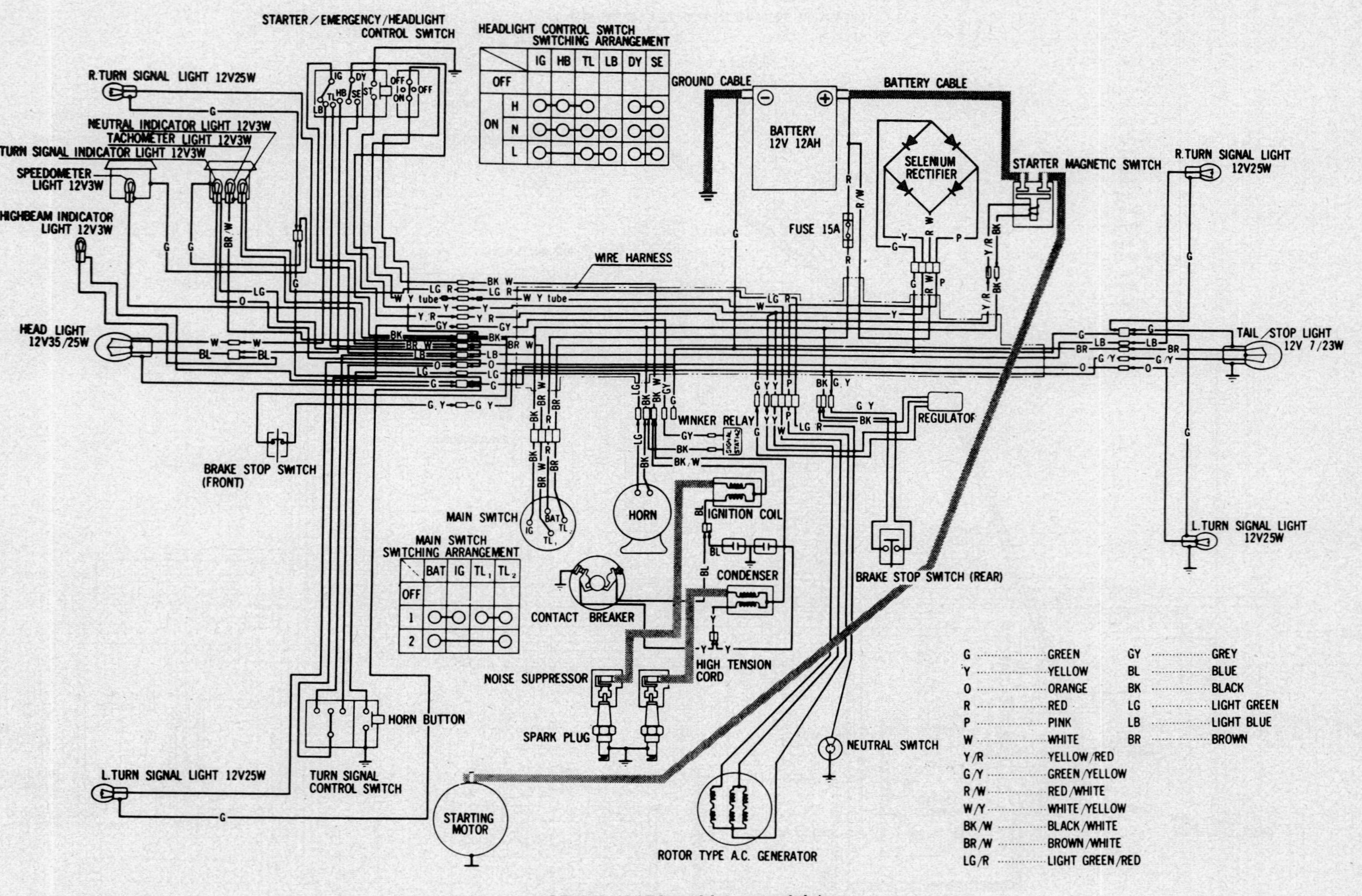
STARTER/EMERGENCY/HEADLIGHT CONTROL SWITCH
HEADLIGHT CONTROL SWITCH SWITCHING ARRANGEMENT
R.TURN SIGNAL LIGHT 12V25W
NEUTRAL INDICATOR LIGHT 12V3W
TACHOMETER LIGHT 12V3W
TURN SIGNAL INDICATOR LIGHT 12V3W
SPEEDOMETER LIGHT 12V3W
HIGHBEAM INDICATOR LIGHT 12V3W
HEAD LIGHT 12V35/25W
GROUND CABLE
BATTERY 12V 12AH
BATTERY CABLE
SELENIUM RECTIFIER
STARTER MAGNETIC SWITCH
FUSE 15A
WIRE HARNESS
R.TURN SIGNAL LIGHT 12V25W
TAIL/STOP LIGHT 12V 7/23W
WINKER RELAY
REGULATOR
BRAKE STOP SWITCH (FRONT)
MAIN SWITCH
HORN
IGNITION COIL
CONDENSER
L.TURN SIGNAL LIGHT 12V25W
BRAKE STOP SWITCH (REAR)
MAIN SWITCH SWITCHING ARRANGEMENT
CONTACT BREAKER
HIGH TENSION CORD
NOISE SUPPRESSOR
SPARK PLUG
HORN BUTTON
NEUTRAL SWITCH
L.TURN SIGNAL LIGHT 12V25W
TURN SIGNAL CONTROL SWITCH
STARTING MOTOR
ROTOR TYPE A.C. GENERATOR
G GREEN
Y YELLOW
O ORANGE
R RED
P PINK
W WHITE
Y/R YELLOW/RED
G/Y GREEN/YELLOW
R/W RED/WHITE
W/Y WHITE/YELLOW
BK/W BLACK/WHITE
BR/W BROWN/WHITE
LG/R LIGHT GREEN/RED
GY GREY
BL BLUE
BK BLACK
LG LIGHT GREEN
LB LIGHT BLUE
BR BROWN

CB 350 (1970 and later models).

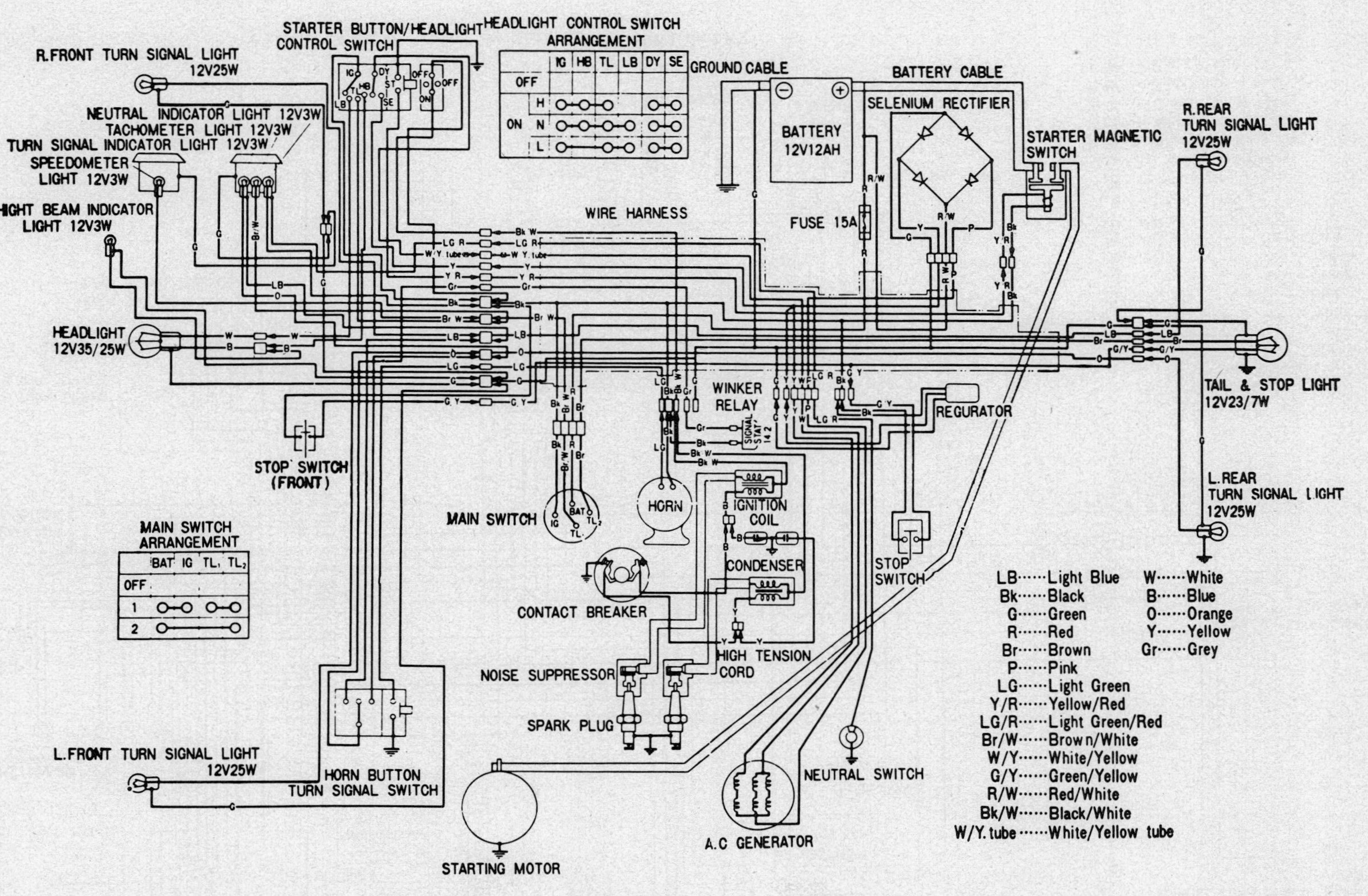
R.FRONT TURN SIGNAL LIGHT 12V25W
STARTER BUTTON/HEADLIGHT CONTROL SWITCH
HEADLIGHT CONTROL SWITCH ARRANGEMENT
GROUND CABLE
BATTERY CABLE
BATTERY 12V12AH
SELENIUM RECTIFIER
STARTER MAGNETIC SWITCH
R.REAR TURN SIGNAL LIGHT 12V25W
NEUTRAL INDICATOR LIGHT 12V3W
TACHOMETER LIGHT 12V3W
TURN SIGNAL INDICATOR LIGHT 12V3W
SPEEDOMETER LIGHT 12V3W
HIGHT BEAM INDICATOR LIGHT 12V3W
WIRE HARNESS
FUSE 15A
HEADLIGHT 12V35/25W
TAIL & STOP LIGHT 12V23/7W
WINKER RELAY
REGURATOR
STOP SWITCH (FRONT)
L.REAR TURN SIGNAL LIGHT 12V25W
MAIN SWITCH
HORN
IGNITION COIL
MAIN SWITCH ARRANGEMENT
CONDENSER
STOP SWITCH
CONTACT BREAKER
HIGH TENSION CORD
NOISE SUPPRESSOR
SPARK PLUG
L.FRONT TURN SIGNAL LIGHT 12V25W
HORN BUTTON TURN SIGNAL SWITCH
NEUTRAL SWITCH
A.C GENERATOR
STARTING MOTOR
LB······Light Blue
Bk······Black
G······Green
R······Red
Br······Brown
P······Pink
LG······Light Green
Y/R······Yellow/Red
LG/R······Light Green/Red
Br/W······Brown/White
W/Y······White/Yellow
G/Y······Green/Yellow
R/W······Red/White
Bk/W······Black/White
W/Y. tube······White/Yellow tube
W······White
B······Blue
O······Orange
Y······Yellow
Gr······Grey

CL 350 (1970 and later models); SL 350 (1970 models).

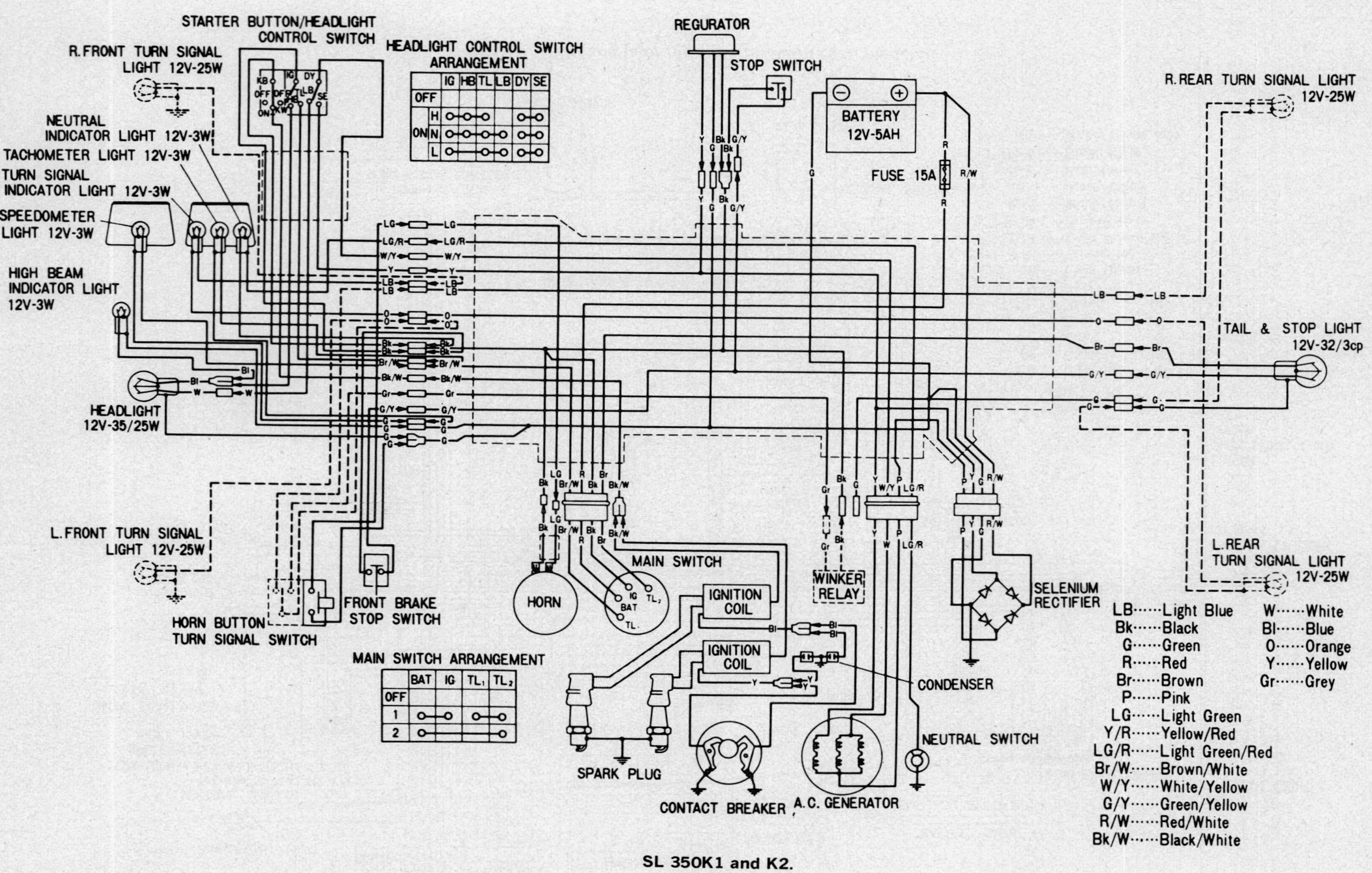
R.REAR TURN SIGNAL LIGHT 12V-25W
TAIL & STOP LIGHT 12V-32/3cp
L.REAR TURN SIGNAL LIGHT 12V-25W
W……White
Bl……Blue
O……Orange
Y……Yellow
Gr……Grey
LB……Light Blue
Bk……Black
G……Green
R……Red
Br……Brown
P……Pink
LG……Light Green
Y/R……Yellow/Red
LG/R……Light Green/Red
Br/W……Brown/White
W/Y……White/Yellow
G/Y……Green/Yellow
R/W……Red/White
Bk/W……Black/White
SELENIUM RECTIFIER
FUSE 15A
BATTERY 12V-5AH
WINKER RELAY
CONDENSER
NEUTRAL SWITCH
A.C. GENERATOR
CONTACT BREAKER
IGNITION COIL
IGNITION COIL
SPARK PLUG
MAIN SWITCH
HORN
REGURATOR
STOP SWITCH
HEADLIGHT CONTROL SWITCH ARRANGEMENT
STARTER BUTTON/HEADLIGHT CONTROL SWITCH
FRONT BRAKE STOP SWITCH
MAIN SWITCH ARRANGEMENT
HORN BUTTON TURN SIGNAL SWITCH
R.FRONT TURN SIGNAL LIGHT 12V-25W
NEUTRAL INDICATOR LIGHT 12V-3W
TACHOMETER LIGHT 12V-3W
TURN SIGNAL INDICATOR LIGHT 12V-3W
SPEEDOMETER LIGHT 12V-3W
HIGH BEAM INDICATOR LIGHT 12V-3W
HEADLIGHT 12V-35/25W
L.FRONT TURN SIGNAL LIGHT 12V-25W

SL 350K1 and K2.

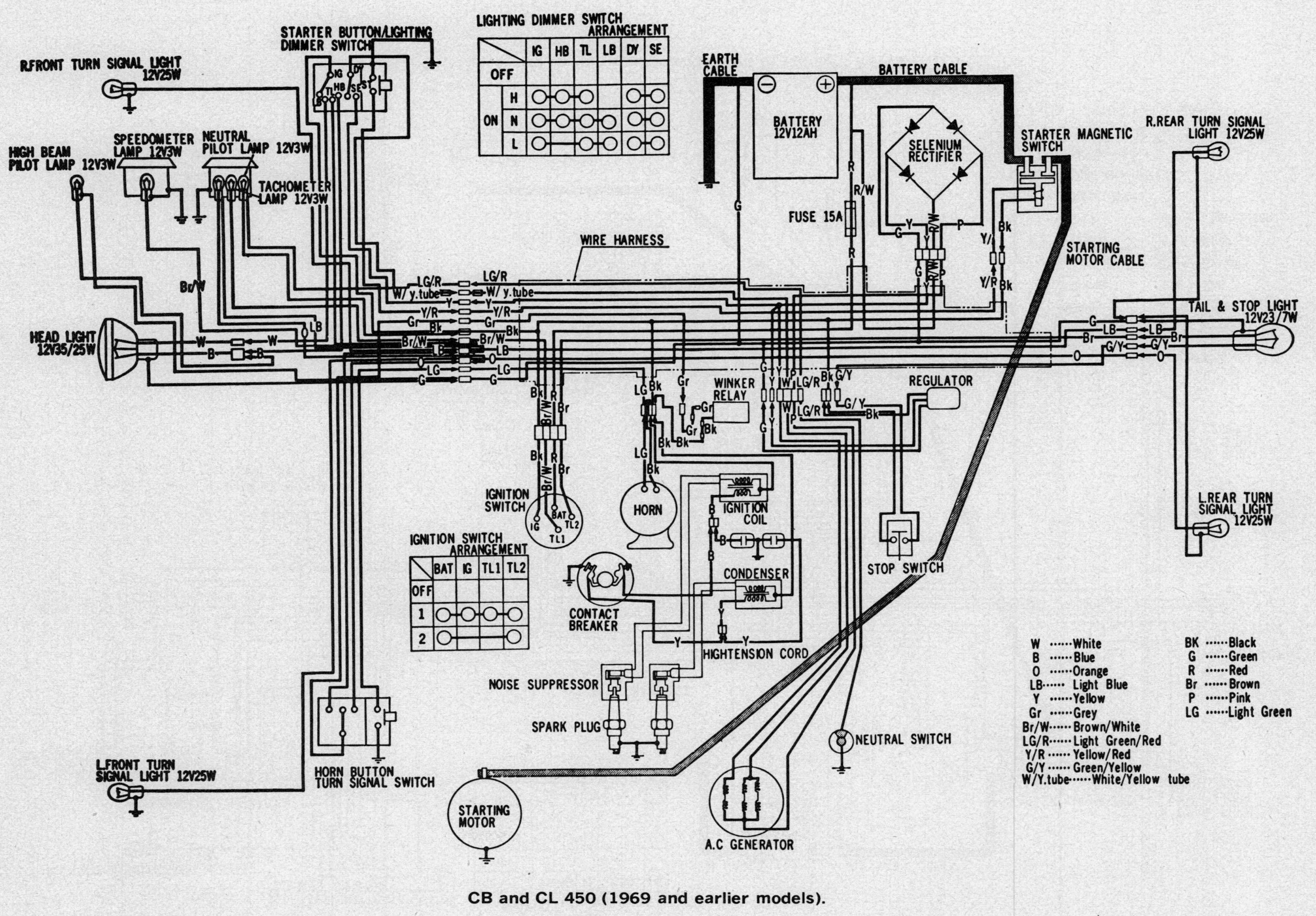

CB and CL 450 (1969 and earlier models).

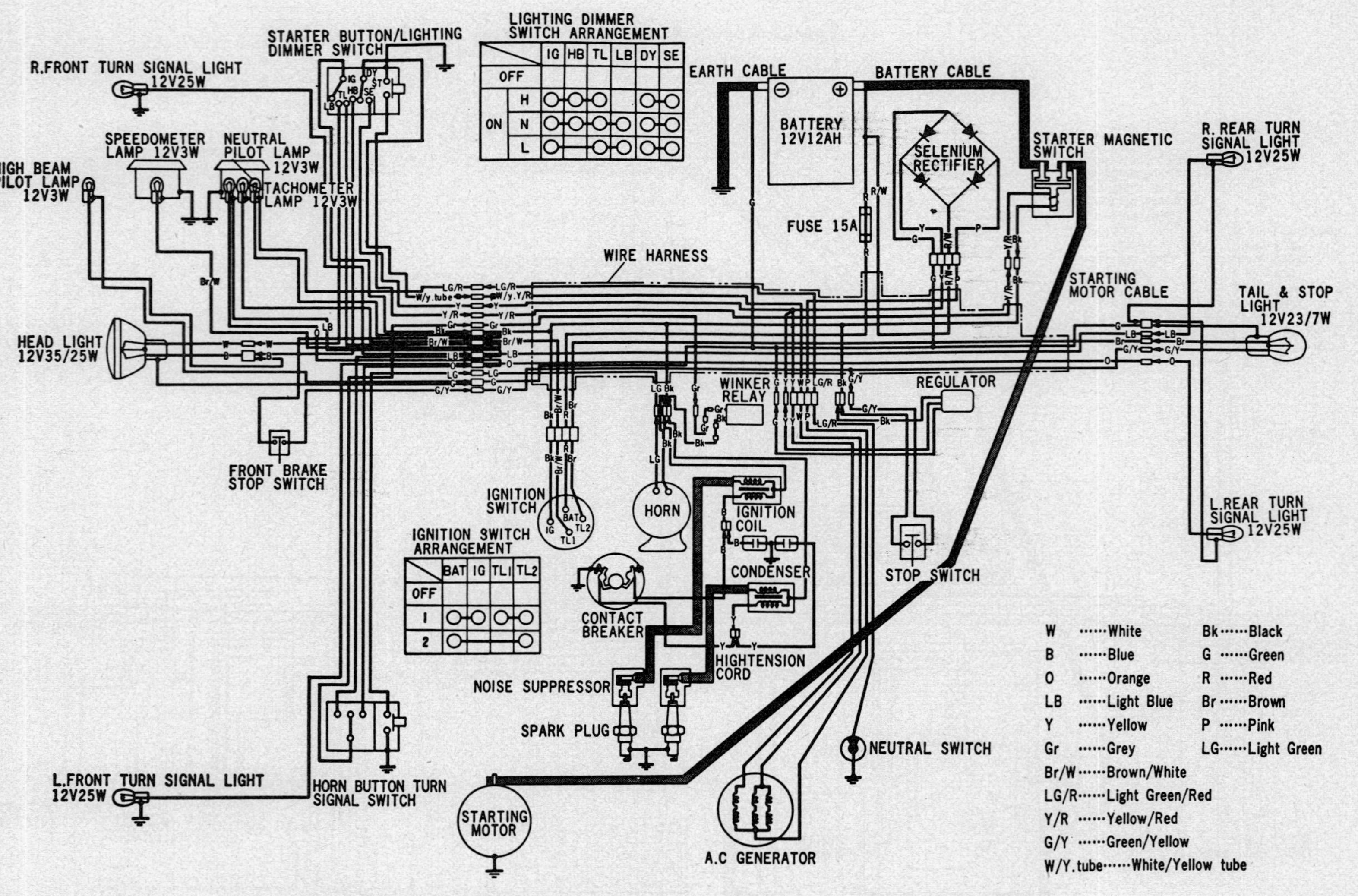

CB and CL 450 (1969 and earlier models with front brake light switch).

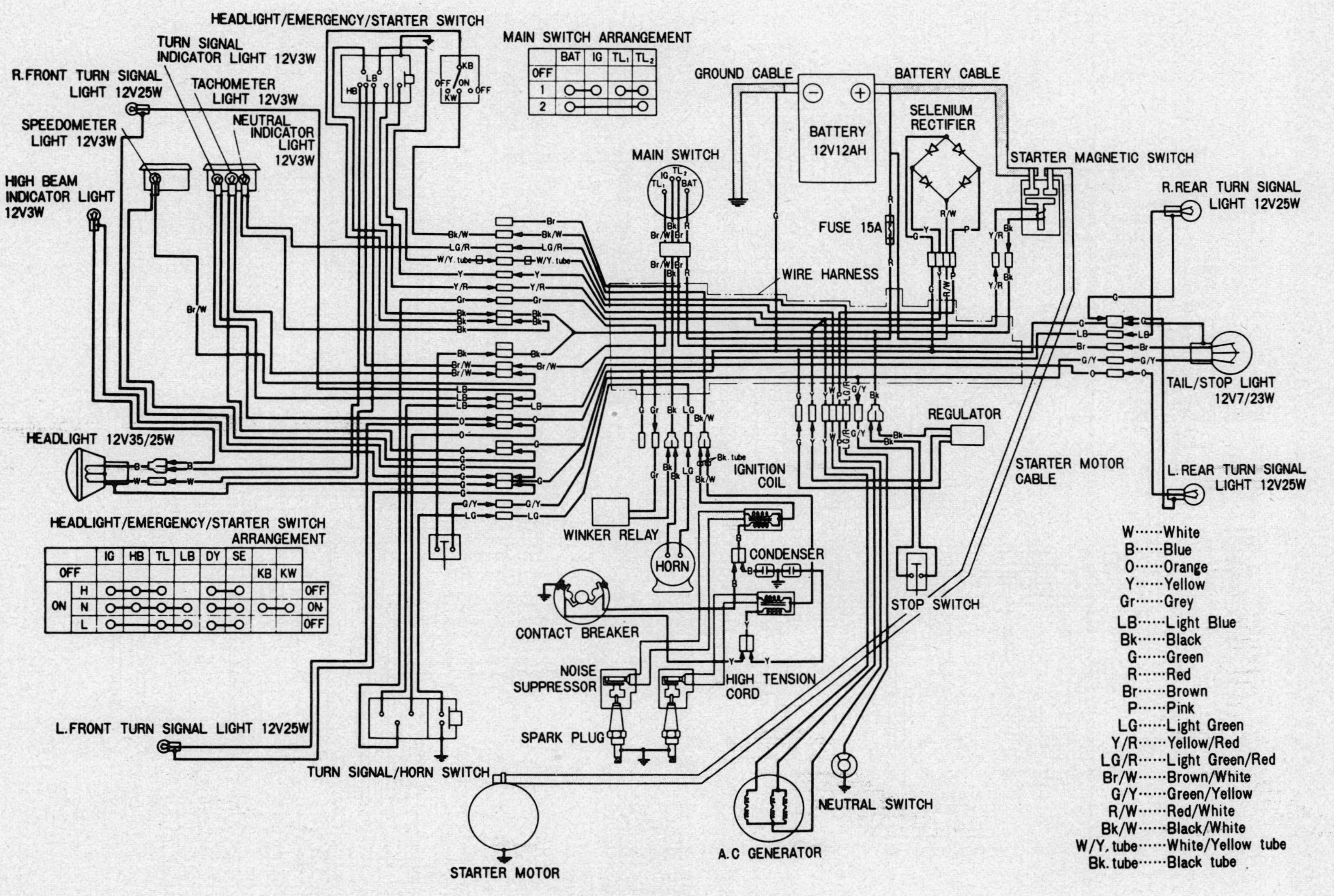
HEADLIGHT/EMERGENCY/STARTER SWITCH
TURN SIGNAL INDICATOR LIGHT 12V3W
R.FRONT TURN SIGNAL LIGHT 12V25W
TACHOMETER LIGHT 12V3W
SPEEDOMETER LIGHT 12V3W
NEUTRAL INDICATOR LIGHT 12V3W
HIGH BEAM INDICATOR LIGHT 12V3W
MAIN SWITCH ARRANGEMENT
GROUND CABLE
BATTERY CABLE
BATTERY 12V12AH
SELENIUM RECTIFIER
STARTER MAGNETIC SWITCH
MAIN SWITCH
R.REAR TURN SIGNAL LIGHT 12V25W
FUSE 15A
WIRE HARNESS
TAIL/STOP LIGHT 12V7/23W
REGULATOR
HEADLIGHT 12V35/25W
IGNITION COIL
STARTER MOTOR CABLE
L.REAR TURN SIGNAL LIGHT 12V25W
HEADLIGHT/EMERGENCY/STARTER SWITCH ARRANGEMENT
WINKER RELAY
HORN
CONDENSER
STOP SWITCH
CONTACT BREAKER
NOISE SUPPRESSOR
HIGH TENSION CORD
L.FRONT TURN SIGNAL LIGHT 12V25W
SPARK PLUG
TURN SIGNAL/HORN SWITCH
NEUTRAL SWITCH
A.C GENERATOR
STARTER MOTOR
W······White
B······Blue
O······Orange
Y······Yellow
Gr······Grey
LB······Light Blue
Bk······Black
G······Green
R······Red
Br······Brown
P······Pink
LG······Light Green
Y/R······Yellow/Red
LG/R······Light Green/Red
Br/W······Brown/White
G/Y······Green/Yellow
R/W······Red/White
Bk/W······Black/White
W/Y. tube······White/Yellow tube
Bk. tube······Black tube

CB 450 (1970 and later models).

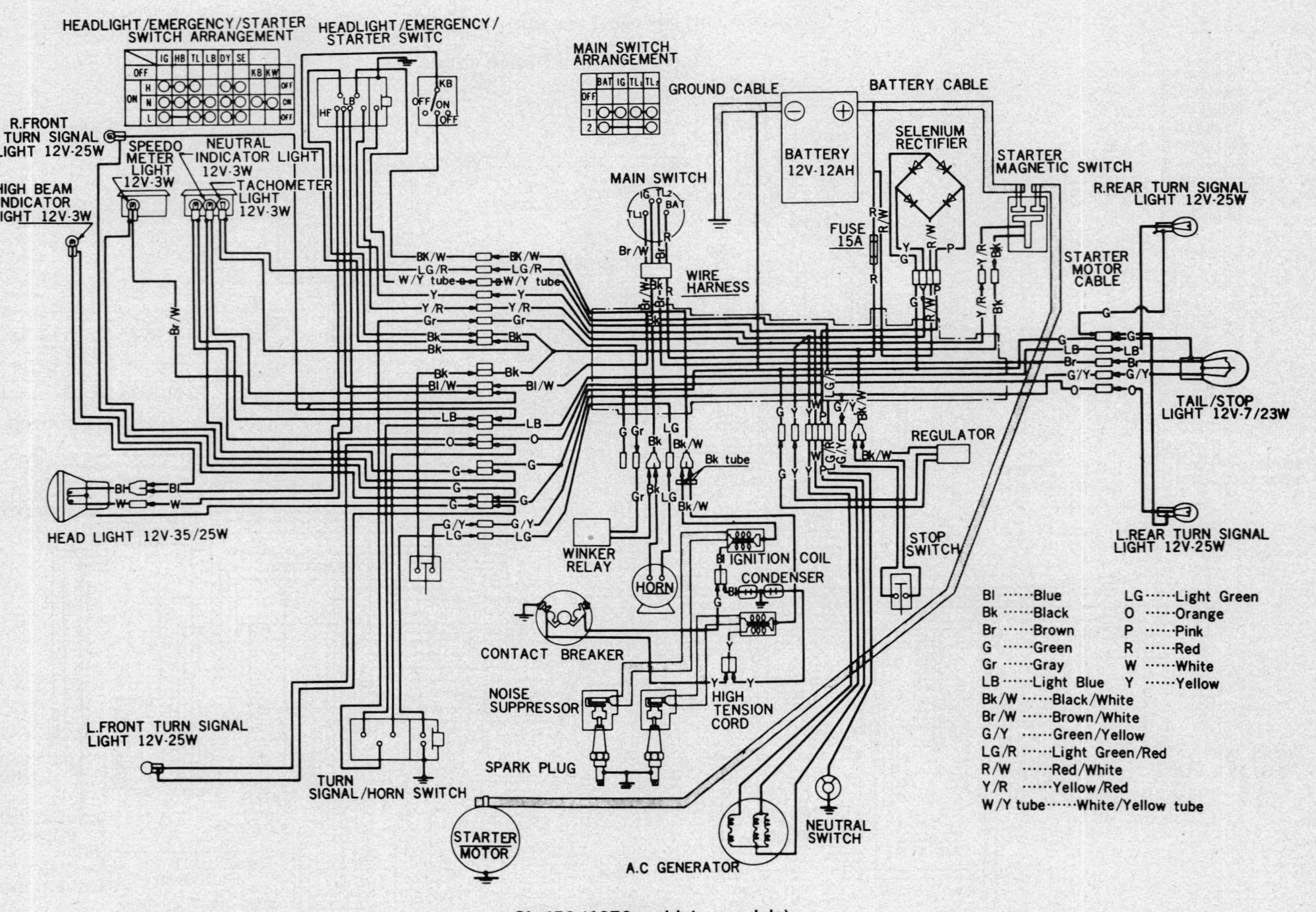
HEADLIGHT/EMERGENCY/STARTER SWITCH ARRANGEMENT
HEADLIGHT/EMERGENCY/STARTER SWITC
MAIN SWITCH ARRANGEMENT
GROUND CABLE
BATTERY CABLE
BATTERY 12V-12AH
SELENIUM RECTIFIER
STARTER MAGNETIC SWITCH
R.REAR TURN SIGNAL LIGHT 12V-25W
R.FRONT TURN SIGNAL LIGHT 12V-25W
SPEEDO METER LIGHT 12V-3W
NEUTRAL INDICATOR LIGHT 12V-3W
TACHOMETER LIGHT 12V-3W
HIGH BEAM INDICATOR LIGHT 12V-3W
MAIN SWITCH
FUSE 15A
STARTER MOTOR CABLE
WIRE HARNESS
TAIL/STOP LIGHT 12V-7/23W
REGULATOR
Bk tube
HEAD LIGHT 12V-35/25W
WINKER RELAY
IGNITION COIL
CONDENSER
STOP SWITCH
L.REAR TURN SIGNAL LIGHT 12V-25W
HORN
CONTACT BREAKER
NOISE SUPPRESSOR
HIGH TENSION CORD
SPARK PLUG
L.FRONT TURN SIGNAL LIGHT 12V-25W
TURN SIGNAL/HORN SWITCH
STARTER MOTOR
A.C GENERATOR
NEUTRAL SWITCH
Bl ......Blue
Bk ......Black
Br ......Brown
G ......Green
Gr ......Gray
LB ......Light Blue
Bk/W ......Black/White
Br/W ......Brown/White
G/Y ......Green/Yellow
LG/R ......Light Green/Red
R/W ......Red/White
Y/R ......Yellow/Red
W/Y tube ......White/Yellow tube
LG ......Light Green
O ......Orange
P ......Pink
R ......Red
W ......White
Y ......Yellow

CL 450 (1970 and later models).

CHASSIS

WHEELS AND TIRES

Front Wheel Removal and Installation

125 AND 175

1. Raise the front wheel off the ground by placing a support under the engine.
2. Disconnect the speedometer cable from the front hub.
3. Disconnect the brake cable and brake torque arm from the brake panel.
4. Unscrew the front axle nut and withdraw the axle. The wheel will drop down as the axle is pulled out.

Installation is a reversal of the removal procedure. Don't forget to readjust the brake after assembly.

350 AND 450

1. Raise the front wheel off the ground by placing a support under the engine.
2. Disconnect the speedometer cable from the front hub.
3. Disconnect the brake cable and the brake torque arm (all except CB 450K4 and K5).
4. Remove the four axle clamp nuts (two on each side) and withdraw the front wheel assembly from the forks.

CAUTION: *On CB 450K4 and K5 models (disc brake), do not operate the front brake while the wheel is removed or the caliper piston will be forced out of the cylinder.*

Installation is in reverse order of removal. The front axle holder clamps are machined so that the forward mating surface is slightly higher than the rear surface, and they must be installed correctly. Place a straightedge on the mating surfaces to determine which end is higher and install the high mating surface forward. Tighten the forward retaining nut first, drawing the forward mating surface of the holder clamp flush against the fork leg mating surface, and then tighten the rear nut.

Wheel Service

ALL MODELS

Check wheel run-out at the rim using a dial indicator. If runout exceeds 0.080 in. (2.0 mm), or if the rim or spokes are damaged, the wheel should be repaired by a shop with the equipment and experience to replace and/or true the wheel properly.

Front Wheel Bearing Service

ALL MODELS EXCEPT CB 450K4 AND K5

Disassembly

1. Remove the front wheel.

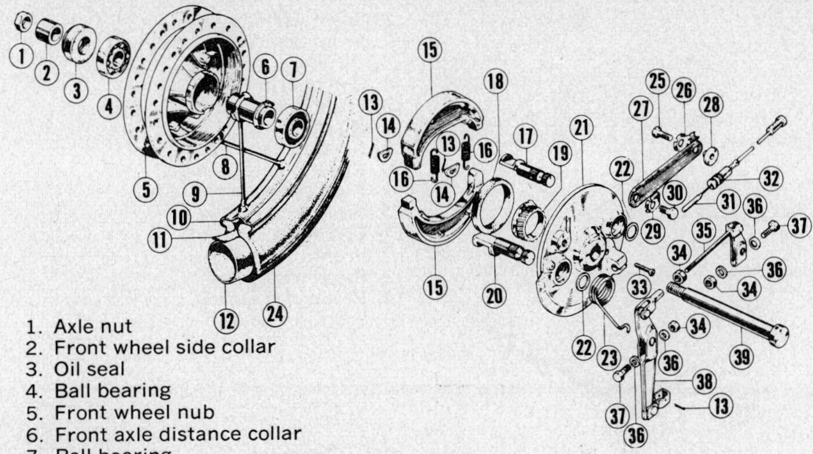

1. Axle nut
2. Front wheel side collar
3. Oil seal
4. Ball bearing
5. Front wheel nub
6. Front axle distance collar
7. Ball bearing
8. Spoke
9. Spoke
10. Front wheel rim
11. Tire flap
12. Front wheel tube
13. Cotter pin
14. Anchor pin washer
15. Front brake shoe
16. Front brake spring
17. Front brake cam
18. Oil seal
19. Speedometer gear
20. Front brake cam
21. Front brake panel
22. Front brake cam dust seal
23. Front brake arm return spring
24. Front wheel tire
25. Bolt
26. Tongued washer
27. Front brake stopper arm
28. Front brake stopper arm collar
29. Tongued washer
30. Front brake stopper arm bolt
31. Speedometer inner cable
32. Speedometer cable
33. 5 x 20 cross screw
34. 6 mm hex nut
35. Front brake arm B
36. 6 mm flat washer
37. 6 x 32 hex bolt
38. Front brake arm
39. Front wheel axle

Front hub components (125 and 175cc models).

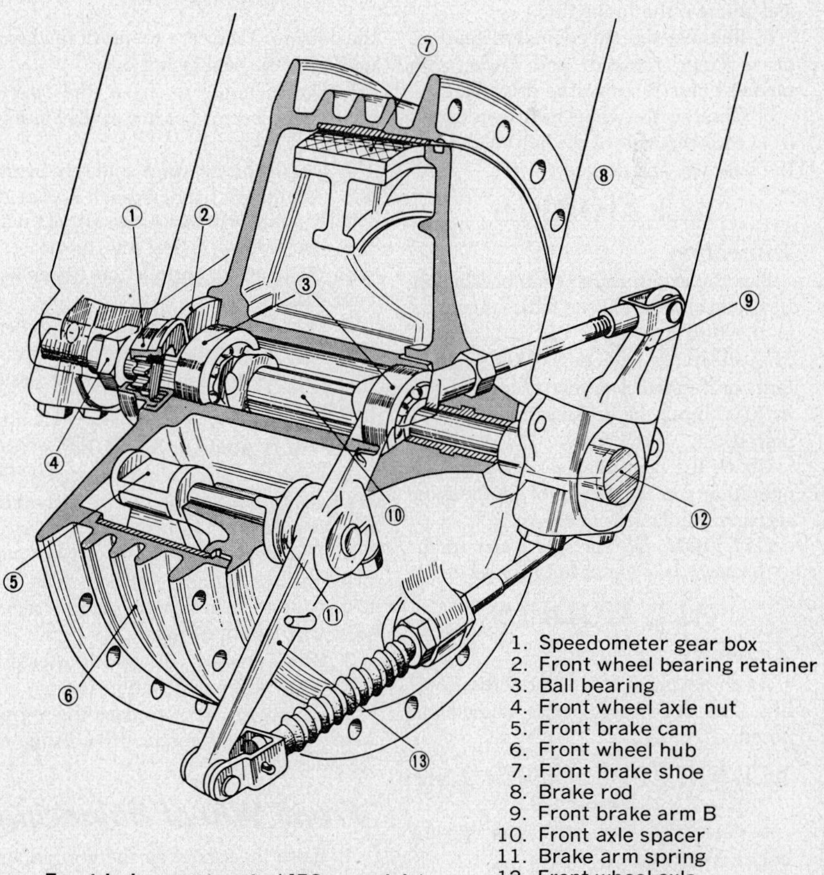

1. Speedometer gear box
2. Front wheel bearing retainer
3. Ball bearing
4. Front wheel axle nut
5. Front brake cam
6. Front wheel hub
7. Front brake shoe
8. Brake rod
9. Front brake arm B
10. Front axle spacer
11. Brake arm spring
12. Front wheel axle
13. Front brake arm

Front hub components (450cc models).

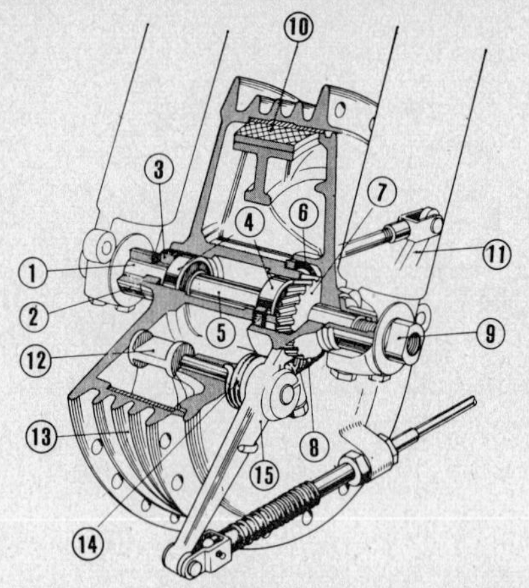

1. Front wheel axle
2. Front wheel side collar
3. Oil seal
4. Ball bearing
5. Front axle spacer
6. Oil seal
7. Speedometer gear
8. Speedometer pinion
9. Front wheel axle sleeve
10. Front brake shoe
11. Front brake cam B
12. Front brake cam
13. Front wheel hub
14. Brake arm spring
15. Front brake arm

Front hub components (350cc models).

1. Bolt
2. Gearbox retainer cover
3. Gearbox retainer
4. Ball bearing
5. Front wheel axle
6. Screw
7. Speedometer gear box
8. Front axle spacer
9. Ball bearing
10. Dust seal
11. Front wheel bearing retainer
12. Front wheel collar
13. Front wheel axle nut
14. Wheel balance weight
15. Front wheel hub
16. Front spoke A
17. Front spoke B
18. Front wheel rim
19. Front tire flap
20. Front wheel tube
21. Front wheel tire

Front hub components (CB 450K4 and K5 models).

2. Remove the front wheel axle nut and pull out the axle (350 and 450). Separate the speedometer gearbox and brake panel from the hub.

3. Remove the spacer and bearing retainer (if applicable), and then remove the two wheel bearings.

CB 450K4 AND K5

Disassembly

1. Remove the front wheel.
2. Unscrew the axle nut and withdraw the axle and axle collar.
3. Take out the screw and remove the speedometer gearbox from the hub.
4. Bend back the locktabs, and unbolt and remove the brake disc.
5. Remove the speedometer gearbox drive flange retainer (and O-ring, K5 models only). Remove the drive flange.
6. Unscrew the wheel bearing retainer from the other side of the hub. Withdraw the bearings and spacer.

ALL MODELS

Inspection

Pass the axle through each bearing, in turn, and check axial and radial clearance of the bearing with a dial indicator. If axial clearance exceeds 0.004 in. (0.1 mm), or if radial clearance exceeds 0.002 in. (0.05 mm), the bearing should be replaced.

Check the bearings for smoothness of operation and for pitting of the bearing surfaces. Replace as necessary.

CAUTION: *Do not spin a dry (unlubricated) bearing at high speed.*

ALL MODELS

Assembly

Assemble in reverse order of disassembly. The following points should be noted:

ALL EXCEPT CB 450K4 AND K5

1. Pack the bearings with grease before installation.
2. The bearings incorporate a seal on the outside. Take care to install the bearings with the seal facing out.
3. Don't forget to insert the spacer before the second bearing is driven into place.
4. Install the bearings squarely in the hub. A suitably sized wrench socket or length of pipe can be used to install them.
5. Use a new oil seal and lubricate it with oil to make installation easier (except 45).
6. To avoid excessive strain on the cable, install the speedometer gearbox so that the cable is in line with the brake cable.

CB 450K4 AND K5

1. Pack the bearings with grease. Do not forget to install the spacer in the hub before installing the bearings.
2. The bearings may be driven into place using Honda service tool no. 07048–30001 or a suitably sized wrench socket or length of pipe.
3. Use a new oil seal and lubricate it with oil to make installation easier.
4. Do not forget to replace the O-ring behind the speedometer drive flange on K5 models.

Front Wheel Balancing

1. Raise the wheel off the ground and rotate it lightly. If the wheel does not rotate freely, back off the brake adjuster (turn the caliper adjuster bolt clockwise, CB 450K4 and K5) until it does.
2. Let the wheel spin until it stops on its own. The heaviest section of the wheel will stop at the lowest point.
3. Attach the weight (available in 5 g, 10 g, 15 g, and 20 g) to the spoke nipple at the highest position where the wheel has stopped. Spin the wheel again and observe where it stops. The idea is to get the proper weight positioned on the wheel so that it does not end up at any particular position when it stops spinning. Different weights may have to be tried at various positions to achieve this. Lock the weight with pliers after you've found the spot.

NOTE: *Solder may be used if weights are not available. Wrap the solder wire around the spoke nipple and secure it with tape.*

Rear Wheel

ALL MODELS WITH REMOVABLE DRIVE CHAIN MASTER LINK

Removal

1. Place the bike on the center stand and remove the drive chain master link.
2. Unscrew the brake adjuster nut and

separate the brake rod from the brake arm.

3. Unscrew the brake torque arm bolt and remove the arm from the brake panel.

4. Remove the cotter pin, unscrew the axle nut, and pull out the axle.

NOTE: *Unless you can compress the suspension enough for the axle to clear, it will be necessary to remove the muffler.*

5. Tilt the wheel slightly and remove it from the swing arm.

ALL MODELS WITH ENDLESS DRIVE CHAIN

Removal

1. Place the bike on the center stand. Unscrew the brake adjuster nut and separate the brake rod from the brake arm.
2. Unscrew the bolt and disconnect the brake torque arm from the brake panel.
3. Loosen the chain adjuster bolt on both sides. Remove the cotter pin and loosen the axle nut.
4. Remove the lockbolts and chain adjuster stop plates. Push the wheel forward and lift the chain off the rear sprocket. Withdraw the wheel rearward from the swing arm.

Installation

Install the wheel in reverse order of removal. Adjust the drive chain, if necessary, and adjust the brake. Use a new cotter pin to lock the axle nut in position.

Service

Refer to the preceding section on the front wheel.

Rear Wheel Bearing Service

ALL MODELS

Disassembly

1. Remove the wheel and withdraw the axle from the hub.
2. Take out the circlip, bend back the locktabs, and unbolt the rear sprocket.
3. Remove the oil seal internal retainer (125 and 175). Unscrew the bearing retainer (350 and 450).
4. Remove the bearings and spacer for the hub.

Inspection

Pass the axle through each bearing, in turn, and measure the axial and diametrical clearance of the bearing with a dial indicator. If axial clearance exceeds 0.004 in. (0.1 mm), or if diametrical clearance exceeds 0.0024 in. (0.06 mm), the bearing should be replaced.

Check the bearings for smoothness of operation and for pitting of the bearing surfaces. Replace as necessary.

1. Rear wheel axle
2. Drive chain adjuster
3. Rear brake panel side collar
4. Nut
5. Drive chain adjusting bolt
6. 6 mm flat washer
7. Rear brake arm
8. Bolt
9. Rear brake panel
10. Rear brake shoe
11. Brake shoe spring
12. Brake cam dust seal
13. Rear brake cam
14. Ball bearing
15. Handle holder setting washer A
16. Cotter pin
17. Rear wheel hub
18. Rear axle spacer
19. Spoke
20. Spoke
21. Rear wheel rim
22. Tire flap
23. Rear wheel tube
24. Rear tire
25. Ball bearing
26. Rear wheel damper bushing
27. Oil seal
28. Rear wheel side collar
29. Final driven sprocket
30. Circlip
31. Axle nut

Rear hub components (125 and 175cc models).

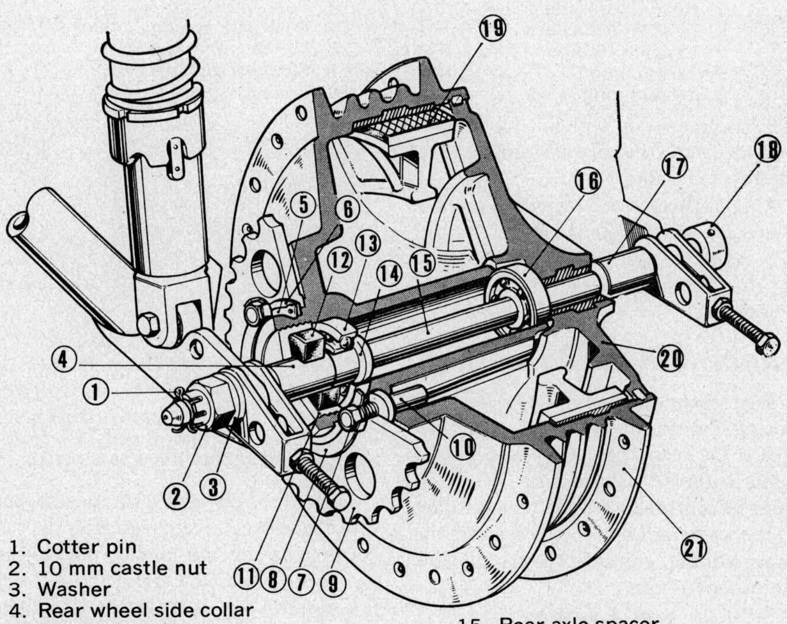

1. Cotter pin
2. 10 mm castle nut
3. Washer
4. Rear wheel side collar
5. External circlip
6. 70 mm washer
7. 10 mm thin nut
8. 10 mm tongued washer
9. Final driven sprocket
10. Driven sprocket fixing bolt
11. Rear wheel bearing retainer
12. Dust seal
13. Ball bearing
14. Rear axle spacer
15. Rear axle spacer
16. Ball bearing
17. Rear wheel collar
18. Rear wheel axle
19. Rear brake shoe
20. Rear wheel brake panel
21. Rear wheel hub

Rear hub components (350cc models).

Check to see if the axle is bent by rolling it on a flat surface. A bent axle should be replaced.

Assembly

Assemble in reverse order of disassembly. Note the following points:

1. Pack the bearings with grease. Do not forget to install the spacer in the hub before installing the second bearing.
2. The bearings may be driven into place using a suitably sized wrench socket or length of pipe.

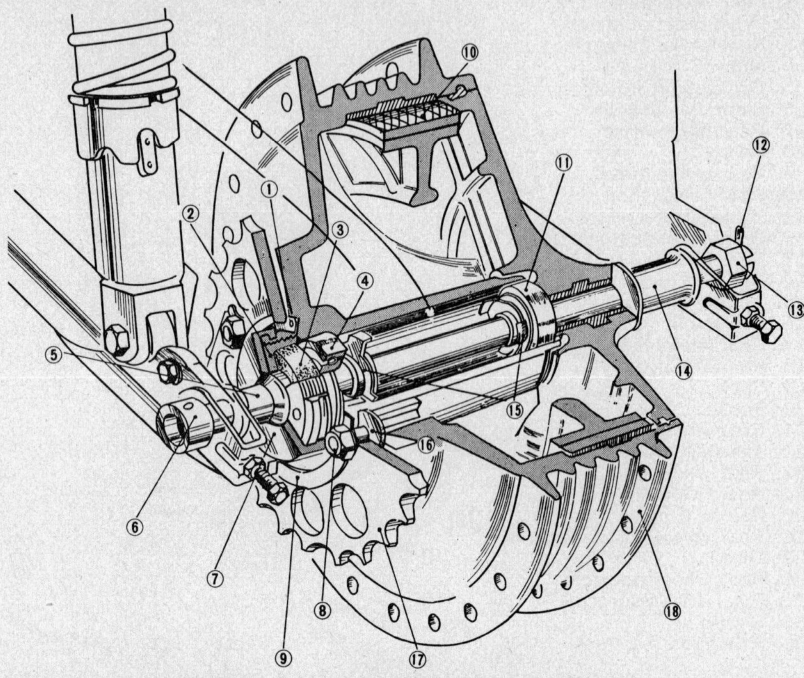

Rear hub components (450cc models).

1. 73.8 mm circlip
2. Rear wheel bearing retainer
3. Dust seal
4. Ball bearing
5. Rear wheel side collar
6. Rear wheel axle
7. Bearing retainer
8. 10 mm nut
9. 10 mm tongue washer
10. Rear brake shoe
11. Ball bearing
12. 4.0 x 10 mm center pin
13. Rear axle nut
14. Rear brake panel collar
15. Rear axle spacing collar
16. Driven sprocket bolt
17. Final driven sprocket
18. Rear wheel hub

3. Use a new oil seal and lubricate it with oil to make installation into the bearing retainer easier.

4. Use thread-lock cement on the bearing retainer (350 and 450).

5. Apply a small quantity of grease to the friction surfaces of the flange and wheel hub.

Rear Wheel Balancing

Refer to the section on front wheel balancing. Procedures are the same, except that if the rear wheel is to be balanced while mounted on the bike, the chain must be removed from the rear sprocket so the wheel will spin freely. Back off the brake adjuster nut if necessary to allow the wheel to spin.

BRAKES

Front Brake Service

DRUM BRAKE

Shoe Replacement

The brake shoes should be replaced when the brake cable and operating lever at the brake panel move over-center or past perpendicular as the brake is applied. The replacement procedure is as follows:

1. Remove the wheel.

2. Remove the axle and separate the brake panel from the brake drum.

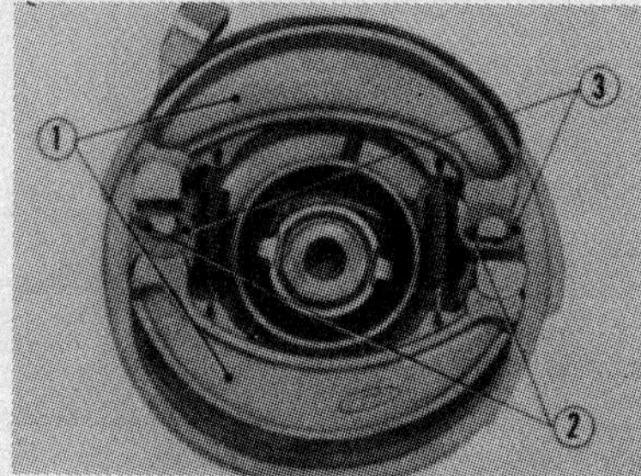

Front brake panel assembly (shown is a 175cc model). Brake shoes (1), cotter pins (2), and anchor pin washers (3).

3. On the 125 and 175 models, the brake shoes can be removed after the two cotter pins and the anchor pin washer have been taken off. On the 350 and 450, first remove the brake levers from the panel and then spread the shoes apart and lift them away.

4. Minimum acceptable lining thickness is 0.080 in. (2.0 mm). Shoes must always be replaced as a set.

5. Examine the brake actuating cams for wear and replace them if they are damaged. Apply a *light* coat of grease to the cams, and then install the shoes and springs as removed. If the brake shoe springs are stretched or damaged, they should be replaced.

6. Wipe the brake drum clean and examine it for damage and wear. Light scoring can be tolerated, but the drum should be replaced if badly scored or worn out of round.

7. Assemble the drum and hub, and reinstall the wheel.

8. Adjust the brake operating lever interconnecting rod on double leading shoe brakes so that both ends of the shoes contact the drum at the same time. Finally, adjust the cable so that there is about ½ in. of free-play at the handlebar lever.

DISC BRAKE

Pad Replacement

To determine pad wear on the CB 450K4, measure the clearance between the front of the caliper and the disc face using a feeler gauge. When clearance is less than 0.08 in. (2.0 mm), the pads should be replaced.

Pads should be replaced on the K5 (1972) model when either one has worn down to the red wear indicator groove.

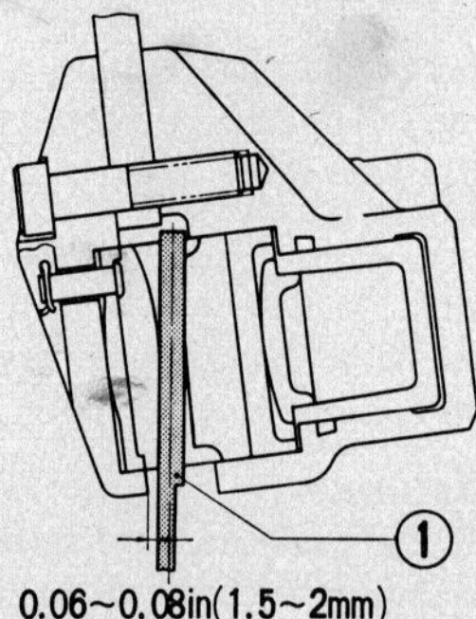

Replace the disc pads on the CB 450K4 when clearance between the disc (1) and the caliper is less than 0.08 in.

1. Remove the front wheel.

2. Using the proper size allen wrench, remove the two bolts from the side of the caliper and remove the right-side caliper half.

3. Remove the pad from the piston side of the caliper. Withdraw the cotter pin and remove the pad from the other caliper half.

4. Before installing the new pads, apply a small amount of silicone grease to the pad sliding surfaces on the caliper, as shown. The grease serves to keep pad operation smooth by repelling dust and wa-

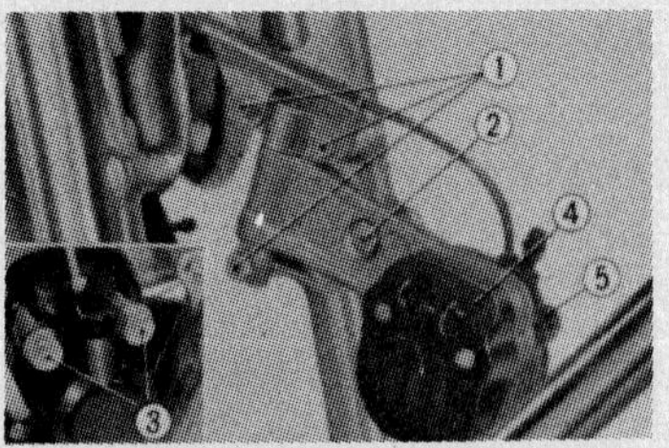

Caliper assembly.

1. Caliper mounting bolts
2. Caliper adjusting bolt
3. Caliper half retaining bolts
4. Right caliper
5. Left caliper

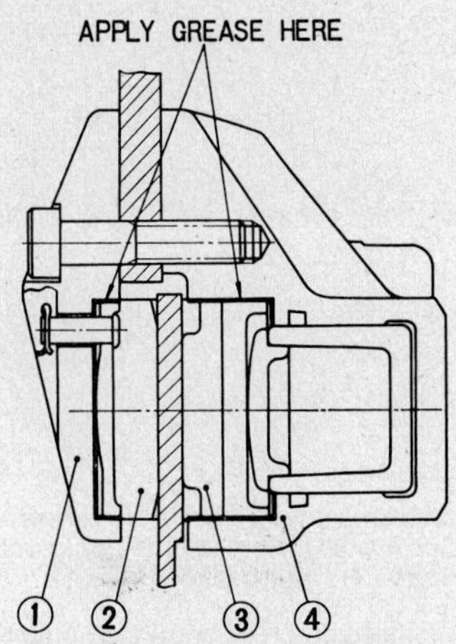

Lubrication points of the caliper.

1. Right caliper half
2. Right brake pad
3. Left brake pad
4. Left caliper half

ter as well as providing lubrication. Use grease sparingly and do not allow it to contact the pad friction material

5. Install the new pads in the caliper halves and bolt the caliper together.

6. Install the front wheel and adjust the brake as explained in the following section. Avoid heavy braking until at least 500 miles have been covered.

Adjustment

1. Loosen the caliper adjuster bolt locknut and turn the bolt until the inside pad (closest to the wheel) lightly contacts the disc.

2. Turn the adjuster bolt in the opposite direction until the front wheel rotates with as little drag as possible (about ¼–½ turn) and tighten the locknut.

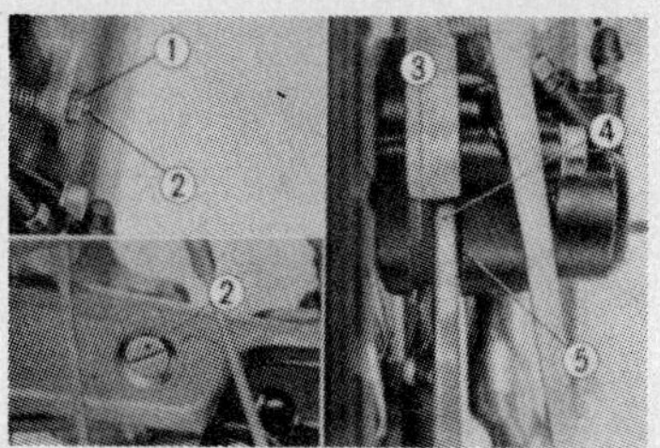

Adjusting points.

1. Nut
2. Caliper adjusting bolt
3. Right pad
4. Brake disc
5. Left pad

About 0.006 in. clearance should exist between the pads and disc.

1. Caliper assembly
2. Brake pads
3. Nut
4. Caliper adjusting bolt

Caliper Service

Leakage of brake fluid from around the caliper piston indicates that the caliper assembly is worn or damaged, and the cause should be investigated immediately. To remove, inspect, and rebuild the caliper assembly:

1. Remove the front wheel.

2. Unscrew the hydraulic line connection at the caliper. Catch the fluid that drains from the line in a suitable container and dispose of it. Do not reuse old brake fluid.

3. Unscrew the three caliper mounting bolts at the left fork leg and remove the caliper.

4. Remove the two bolts and separate the caliper halves.

5. Remove the pad seat from the caliper piston and withdraw the piston.

6. Remove the seal from the cylinder using a plastic or wood instrument to avoid damaging the bore.

7. Examine the cylinder bore and piston surface for scoring and pitting, and replace if damaged. Cylinder bore diameter should not exceed 1.540 in. (38.215 mm), and piston diameter should not be less than 1.500 in. (38.105 mm). Maximum calculated clearance between the piston and cylinder is 0.0045 in. (0.115 mm). Replace parts as necessary. Clean all components and dry with compressed air.

8. Use a new seal in the cylinder bore and lubricate it thoroughly with fresh brake fluid before installing. Make sure it is seated properly in its groove.

9. Lubricate the piston with brake fluid and install it in the cylinder. Be careful not to twist the seal or force it out of the groove. Install the pad seat on the piston.

10. Reinstall the brake pads in the caliper halves. Use new pads if the old ones have been in contact with brake fluid.

11. Bolt the caliper halves together and remount the caliper assembly on the fork leg.

12. Connect the hydraulic line and replace the front wheel. Bleed and adjust the brake (refer to the appropriate headings in this section).

Master Cylinder Service

Brake fluid leakage around the brake lever and excessive lever travel (after bleeding the brake to make sure that there is no air trapped in the hydraulic system) are indications of master cylinder malfunction. The rebuilding procedure is as follows:

NOTE: *Be very careful when filling or emptying the reservoir. Brake fluid can damage paint and plastic, and extreme care should be exercised in handling the stuff. Wipe up any spills immediately.*

1. Place a cloth underneath the connection to absorb any spilled fluid, and disconnect the brake hose from the master cylinder.

2. Unscrew the clamp bolts and remove the master cylinder from the handlebar. Unscrew the reservoir cap and discard the brake fluid.

3. Remove the rubber boot. Remove the circlip and withdraw the washer, piston, seal, spring cap, spring, and check valve.

4. Check the cylinder bore for scoring and pitting, and measure the wear using a dial indicator. Bore diameter should not exceed 0.553 in. (14.055 mm). Replace the master cylinder assembly if damaged or worn.

5. Clean all components in solvent and dry with compressed air.

6. Use a new seal and lubricate it with

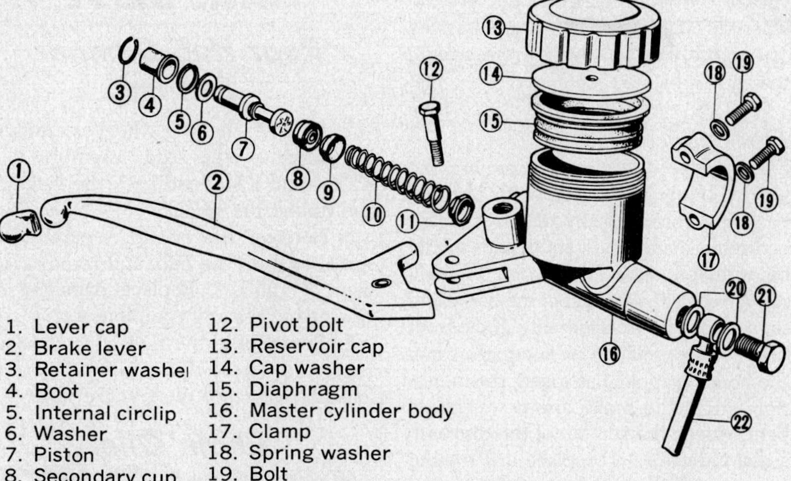

1. Lever cap
2. Brake lever
3. Retainer washer
4. Boot
5. Internal circlip
6. Washer
7. Piston
8. Secondary cup
9. Primary cup
10. Spring
11. Check valve
12. Pivot bolt
13. Reservoir cap
14. Cap washer
15. Diaphragm
16. Master cylinder body
17. Clamp
18. Spring washer
19. Bolt
20. Joint washers
21. Bolt
22. Brake hose

Exploded view of the master cylinder assembly.

fresh brake fluid. Install the components in the bore as removed.

7. Mount the master cylinder on the handlebar and connect the brake hose. Do not forget to install the two washers at the connection. (Use brake fluid conforming to SAE specification J1703).

Bleeding the Hydraulic Brake System

The brake hydraulic system must be bled whenever any part of the system has been disconnected or removed for service. When refilling the master cylinder reservoir, use only brake fluid conforming to SAE specification J1703. Any brand meeting this requirement is acceptable. The brake fluid container of all reputable brands will be plainly marked with the standards the fluid meets or exceeds.

1. Top up the reservoir with brake fluid and replace the cap to keep dirt and moisture out and the fluid in.
2. Attach one end of a small rubber hose to the bleed valve at the caliper and place the other end in a container to catch the fluid.
3. Pump the brake lever rapidly several times until some resistance is felt and, holding the lever against the resistance, open the bleed valve about ½ turn. When the lever bottoms, close the valve (do not overtighten) and then release the lever.
4. Repeat this operation until no more air is released from the hose and the brake lever is firm in operation. Check the fluid level in the reservoir often to make sure it doesn't go dry and draw more air into the system. Do not reuse fluid that has been pumped out of the system. Do not use fluid that has been stored for more than a few weeks after the seal on its container has been opened, as brake fluid will absorb moisture from the air and may corrode the master cylinder and caliper. Be sure to refill the reservoir to the level mark (do not overfill) when through. Avoid overtightening the cap or the fluid will weep from around the cap edge.

Disc Service

The brake disc normally requires no service of any kind. However, if the disc becomes scored for any reason it should be replaced and a new set of pads should be installed. A badly scored disc will reduce the effectiveness of the brake and shorten pad life considerably. If the front brake lever oscillates or fluctuates when the brake is applied at speed, the indication is that the brake disc is warped or bent. Check the run-out of the disc with a dial indicator and replace it if run-out exceeds 0.012 in. (0.3 mm). To replace the disc:

1. Remove the front wheel.
2. Bend back the locktabs, unscrew the six nuts, and remove the disc from the hub.
3. Mount the new disc on the hub and tighten the nuts evenly, using new locktabs to secure them.
4. Examine the brake pads and replace them if they are close to the limit of wear or have worn in an unusual pattern.
5. Install the wheel on the bike and check brake adjustment.

Rear Brake Service

ALL MODELS

Brake Shoe Replacement

The brake shoes should be replaced when the brake operating rod (or cable) and lever move over-center or past perpendicular as the brake is applied. The replacement procedure is as follows:

1. Remove the rear wheel.
2. Unscrew the axle nut and withdraw the axle (CB 450K4 and K5). Separate the brake panel from the hub.
3. Remove the cotter pin and washer from the brake shoe pivots and lift the shoes away from the brake panel. Minimum acceptable lining thickness at any point is 0.080 in. (2.0 mm).
4. Apply a light coat of grease to the brake shoe pivots and the actuating cam. Install the shoes and springs as removed, using new cotter pins. (Use new springs if the original ones are stretched or damaged.)
5. Wipe the brake drum clean with a cloth and examine for scoring and wear. Light scoring can be tolerated, but the drum should be replaced if badly scored or worn out of round.
6. Assemble the drum and hub, and install the wheel. Adjust the brake so that there is about 1.0 in. free-play at the pedal. Avoid heavy braking until at least 500 miles have been covered.

FINAL DRIVE

Rear Hub Damper Service

1. Remove the rear wheel assembly.
2. Remove the axle assembly (CB 450K4 and K5). Bend back the locktabs and unbolt the sprocket.
3. Remove the circlip, separate the sprocket from the hub, and remove the damper rubbers. Replace damaged or worn dampers as a complete set.
4. Reassemble the hub and wheel in reverse order of disassembly. Use new locktabs to secure the sprocket nuts.

Chain Oiler Adjustment—CB 450K4 and K5

1. Remove the countershaft sprocket

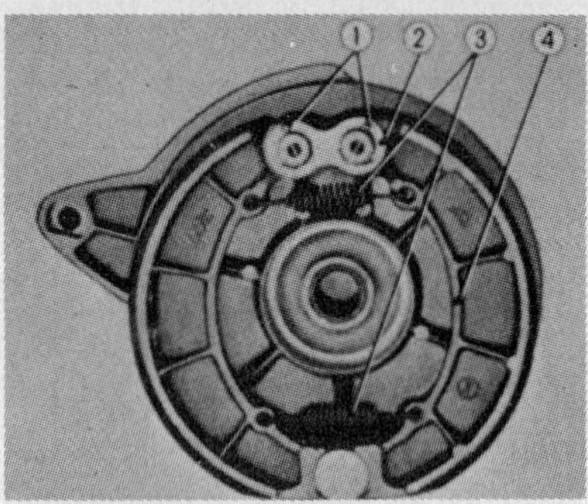

Rear brake panel assembly (shown is a 450cc model). Cotter pins (1), pivot (2), springs (3), and brake shoe (4).

cover (left-side rear crankcase cover) and wipe the sprocket and chain clean.

2. Turn the oiler adjusting screw in until seated (fully closed).
3. Ride the bike a minute or two at about 50–60 mph and then check the oil output to the chain. If additional oiling is desired, back the adjusting screw out about ¼ turn and recheck output. Maximum oiling is achieved when the screw is backed out three full turns from closed.

NOTE: *Since the chain is lubricated with oil from the engine crankcase, the engine oil level should be checked frequently to make sure that it does not run low.*

Chain oiler adjusting screw (1).

FRONT SUSPENSION

Fork Service

125 AND 175–ALL MODELS

Disassembly

1. Remove the front wheel.
2. Unscrew the mounting bolts and remove the fender.
3. Partially loosen the two headlight shell mounting bolts.
4. Unscrew the two top fork bolts and loosen the two lower triple clamp pinchbolts. Pull the fork legs out from the bottom.
5. Raise the fork dust seal (if applicable) and remove the oil seal circlip. Separate the bottom fork leg case from the fork tube and discard the oil in the bottom fork leg.
6. Carefully pry out the oil seal, taking

care not to damage the inside surface of the bottom fork leg.

Inspection

Examine all components for damage and scoring. If the fork assembly was not operating properly, check the spring height and damper component dimensions against the specifications in the accompanying table. Clean all components in solvent and dry thoroughly. Even a small piece of grit can impair damper action. Make sure that the slider tube is not bent by rolling it on a flat surface. Replace if bent.

Assembly

Assemble in reverse order of disassembly. Observe the following points:

1. Lubricate the seal with oil before installation. If the proper oil seal driver is not available, a piece of wood cut to fit the inside of the bottom fork leg will do the job without damaging the inside surface.
2. New fork piston stopper rings and circlips should be used since the old parts may be fatigued and liable to break.
3. Before tightening the lower triple clamp pinch-bolts, insert the axle through the fork legs to make sure that they are level.
4. Fill the forks with the proper amount and grade of oil (refer to chapter two), and install the top fork bolts before fully tightening the triple clamp pinch-bolts.

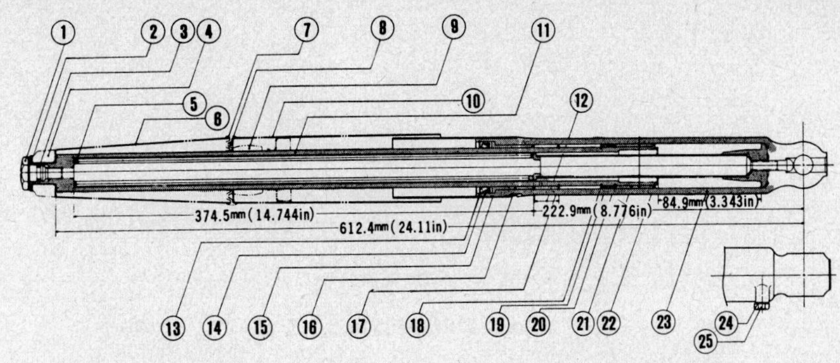

Cross-section of fork leg (CB and SS 125 and CB and CD 175).

1. Front fork bolt
2. Front fork washer
3. O-ring
4. Fork top bridge
5. Front cushion spring
6. Front fork upper cover
7. Front fork rib
8. Front fork rib packing
9. Steering stem
10. Front fork under cover
11. Front fork pipe complete
12. Rebound stroke (19 mm : 0.748 in.)
13. 41 mm internal circlip
14. Front fork oil seal
15. Bottom case cover
16. Front fork pipe guide
17. Fork pipe stopper ring
18. Fork valve stopper ring
19. Front damper valve
20. Piston stopper ring
21. Front fork piston
22. Fork piston snap-ring
23. Front fork bottom case comp.
24. Fork drain cock packing
25. Bolt

CB/XL 350, AND CB/CL 450 (Except K4 and K5)

Refer to the preceding section on the 125 and 175. Procedures are virtually identical. Before the oil seal circlip can be removed on the 350 and 450, the front fork under cover (CB) or fork boot (CL) must be removed.

SL 350

Refer to the preceding section on the 125 and 175. Procedures are virtually identical. Before the fork legs can be withdrawm, both the upper and lower triple clamp pinch-bolts must be loosened. Refer to the accompanying illustrations.

CB 450K4 AND K5

Disassembly

1. Remove the top fork bolts and the piston rod locknuts.
2. Remove the front wheel and fender.
3. Remove the three caliper mounting bolts and the adjuster nut, and lift the caliper assembly away from the fork leg. Do not let the caliper hang by the brake hose; tie it up out of the way with some string or wire.
4. Loosen the upper and lower triple clamp pinch-bolts. Remove the fork legs by pulling gently downward.

FORK SPECIFICATIONS (IN./MM)

	CB/CL/SS 125	CB/175	CL/SL 175	CB/CL 350(G)
Spring free-length:				
nominal	16.331/414.8	16.331/414.8	N.A.	8.27/210
minimum	15.1/384	15.1/384	N.A.	7.72/196
Damper piston:				
minimum diameter	1.395/35.42	1.395/35.42	1.394/35.4	1.472/37.39
maximum taper	0.002/0.04	0.002/0.04	0.002/0.04	N.A.
Lower fork leg case:				
maximum inside diameter	1.406/35.72	1.406/35.72	N.A.	1.484/37.68
maximum taper	0.002/0.04	0.002/0.04	0.002/0.04	N.A.

	SL 350	CB/CL 450 up to 1970	CB 450K4	CB 450K5
Spring free-length:				
nominal	N.A.	8.35/211.9	19.075/484.5	17.78/451.7
minimum	N.A.	8.06/205	18.11/460	16.73/425
Damper piston:				
minimum diameter	1.472/37.39	1.551/39.4	1.551/39.4	N.A.
maximum taper	N.A.	0.002/0.03	0.001/0.02	N.A.
Lower fork leg case:				
maximum inside diameter	1.484/37.68	N.A.	1.559/39.68	N.A.
maximum taper	N.A.	N.A.	0.0012/0.03	N.A.

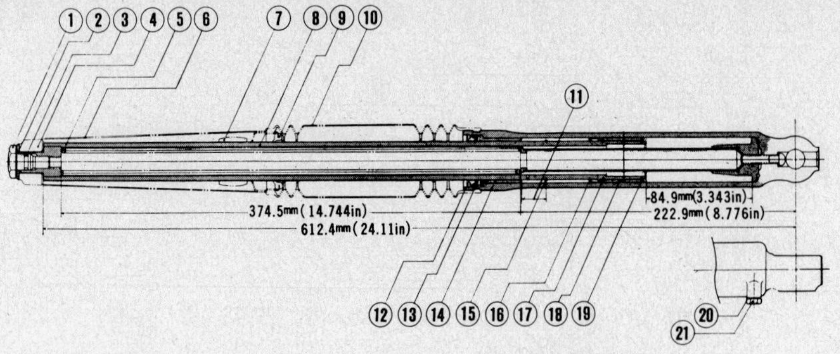

Cross-section of fork leg (CL 125).

1. Front fork bolt
2. Front fork washer
3. O-ring
4. Fork top bridge
5. Front cushion spring
6. Front fork cover
7. Steering stem
8. Front fork pipe comp.
9. Front fork dust seal
10. Front fork boot
11. Rebound stroke (19 mm : 0.748 in.)
12. 41 mm internal circlip
13. Front fork oil seal
14. Front fork pipe guide
15. Fork pipe stopper ring
16. Fork valve stopper ring
17. Piston stopper ring
18. Front fork piston
19. Fork piston snap-ring
20. Fork drain cock packing
21. Bolt

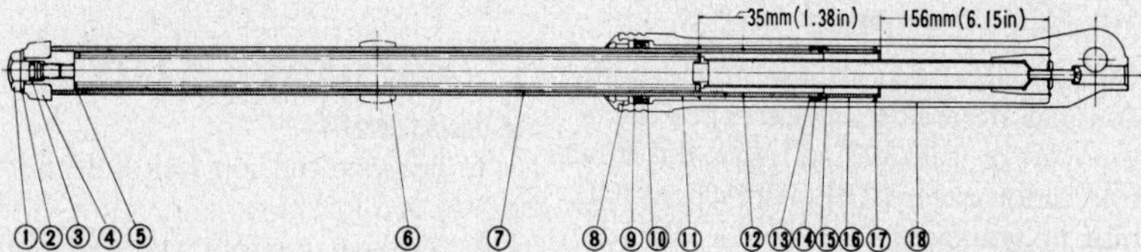

Cross-section of fork leg (CL and SL 175).

1. Front fork bolt
2. 24 mm washer
3. O-ring
4. Front fork top bridge
5. Front cushion spring
6. Front fork bottom bridge
7. Front fork pipe
8. Front fork dust seal
9. 41 mm internal circlip
10. Front fork oil seal
11. Front fork pipe guide
12. Front`piston stopper ring
13. Fork valve stopper ring
14. Front damper valve
15. Fork piston stopper ring
16. Front fork piston
17. Fork piston snap ring
18. Front fork bottom case

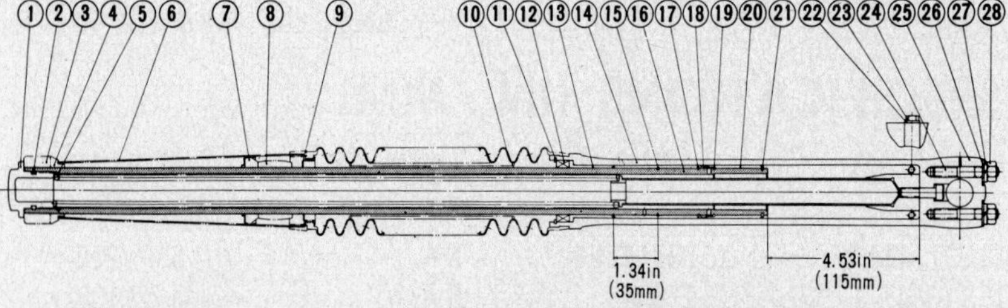

Cross-section of front fork assembly (CB, CL 450K5).

1. Top bolt
2. O-ring
3. Top triple clamp
4. Fork cover upper cushion
5. Spring cushion
6. Fork cover
7. Fork cover lower cushion
8. Steering stem
9. Fork rib
10. Fork boot
11. Circlip
12. Oil seal
13. Guide
14. Bottom case
15. Travel limit ring
16. Slider tube
17. Valve limit ring
18. Damper valve
19. Piston limit ring
20. Damper piston
21. Piston circlip
22. Washer
23. Bolt
24. Bolt
25. Axle clamp
26. Flat washer
27. Spring washer
28. Nut

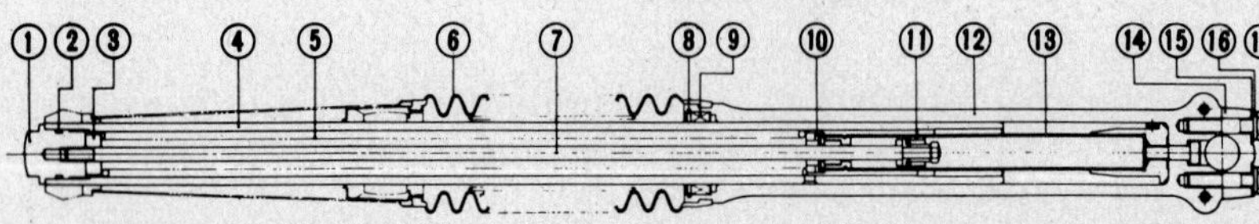

Cross-section of front fork assembly (CB 450 K4).

1. Top bolt
2. O-ring
3. Locknut
4. Slider tube
5. Spring
6. Fork boot
7. Damper rod
8. Circlip
9. Oil seal
10. Holder
11. Collar
12. Bottom case
13. Damper case
14. Axle clamp
15. Flat washer
16. Spring washer
17. Nut

5. Pull the spring out of the slider tube and invert the fork leg assembly over a suitable container to drain the oil.

6. Pull the rubber boot off the leg if it remained attached when the leg was removed. Remove the circlip at the top of the lower fork leg, and separate the lower fork leg and slider tube.

7. Pry the seal out of the fork leg, taking care not to damage the inside surface.

8. The damper assembly can be removed from the lower fork leg after unscrewing the allen bolt that is recessed into the bottom of the leg.

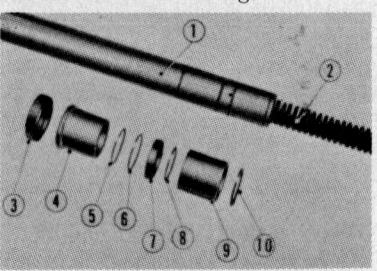

Damper components.

1. Front fork pipe
2. Front cushion spring
3. Front fork oil seal
4. Front fork pipe guide
5. Piston stopper ring
6. Fork valve stopper ring
7. Front damper valve
8. Piston stopper ring
9. Front fork piston
10. Fork piston snap ring

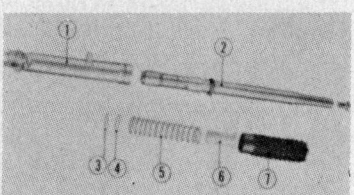

Fork leg components (CB, CL 350, and CB, CL 450).

1. Front fork bottom case
2. Front fork pipe
3. 44 mm internal circlip
4. Spring under seat
5. Front cushion spring
6. Front fork under cover guide
7. Front fork boot

Inspection

Refer to the preceding section on the 125 and 175.

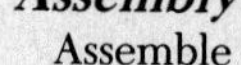

Assembly

Assemble in reverse order of disassembly. Observe the following points:

1. Lubricate the seal with oil before installation. If the proper oil seal driver is not available, a piece of wood cut to fit inside the lower fork leg will do the job without damaging the inside surface.

2. Fill the forks with the proper amount and grade of oil (refer to chapter two), and install the top fork bolts before fully tightening the triple clamp pinch-bolts.

3. Adjust the brake caliper after assembly is complete.

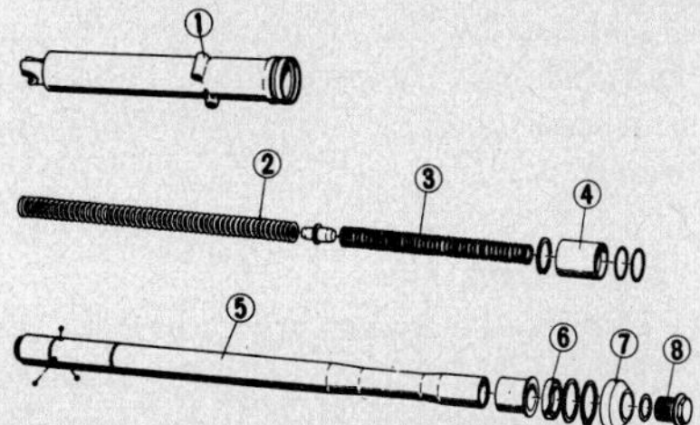

Front fork components (SL 350 K1 and K2).

1. Front fork bottom case
2. Front fork cushion spring (B)
3. Front fork cushion spring (A)
4. Front fork piston
5. Front fork pipe
6. Front fork oil seal
7. Front fork dust seal
8. Front fork bolt

1. Damper lock spring setting bolt
2. Steering damper locking spring
3. Steering head stem nut
4. Steering stem washer
5. Steering head top thread
6. Steering top cone race
7. Steering bottom cone race
8. Steering head dust seal
9. Steering head dust seal washer
10. Steering stem
11. 8 x 32 hex bolt
12. Handle lock spring
13. Handle lock
14. Handle lock case cover
15. 3 mm flat washer
16. 3 x 8 cross screw
17. Steering damper knob
18. Steering damper plate A
19. Steering damper friction disc
20. Friction disc anchor bolt
21. Steering damper plate B
22. Steering damper spring
23. Steering damper nut
24. 6 mm snap-pin

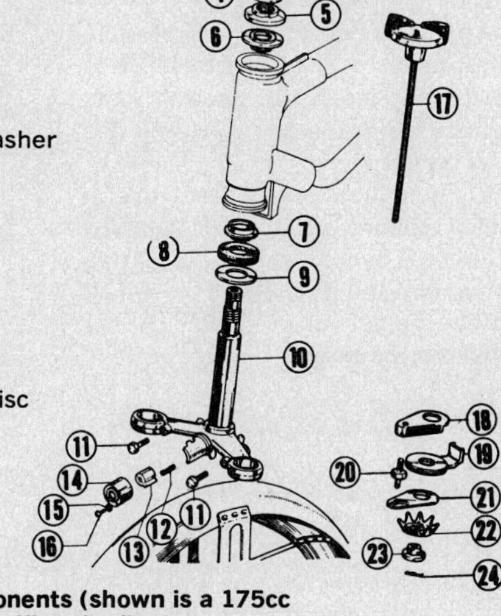

Steering components (shown is a 175cc model which typifies the line).

Steering Head Service

ALL MODELS

The steering head bearings will not require attention unless a steering fault develops. The procedure for checking the bearings can be found in chapter two.

Disassembly

1. Unscrew the master cylinder mounting bolts and remove the master cylinder from the handlebar (CB 450K4 and K5 only).
2. Disconnect the electrical switches, throttle cable, and clutch and brake cable from the handlebar.
3. Remove the headlight unit from the headlight case and disconnect the wiring at the connectors.
4. Unbolt and remove the handlebar.
5. Loosen the instrument mounting clamp and remove the speedometer/tachometer unit from the upper triple clamp. On models equipped with a steering damper, unscrew the nut at the bottom of the damper and remove the disc, plates, and washer.
6. Remove the front fork assembly.
7. Loosen the center (steering stem) triple clamp pinch-bolt and unscrew the large triple clamp cap nut. Remove the upper triple clamp.
8. The steering stem and lower triple clamp can be withdrawn from the bottom of the steering head after the large steering stem retaining nut is unscrewed. Be careful not to lose the steel balls when removing the steering stem.

Inspection

Examine the steel balls and the bearing races for wear, pitting, and damage. Replace both bearing assemblies if they are not in perfect condition. Make sure that the steering stem is not cracked or bent. If the original bearings are to be reused, clean the races and balls in solvent and dry them thoroughly. If the bearings are to be replaced, drive the races out of the steering head with a soft metal drift. Take care not to damage the inside surface.

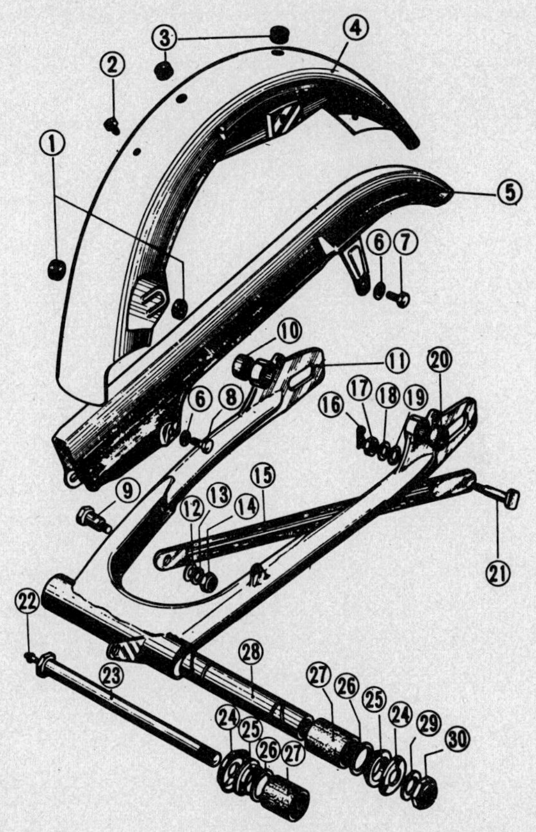

Swing arm components (shown is a 450cc model which typifies the line).

1. Front fuel tank cushion
2. Wire cord grommet
3. Wire cord grommet
4. Rear fender
5. Drive chaincase
6. 6 mm flat washer
7. Bolt
8. Bolt
9. Rear brake stopper arm bolt
10. Rear cushion under rubber bushing
11. Rear fork
12. Spring washer
13. Flat washer
14. Locknut
15. Rear brake stopper arm
16. Lockpin
17. Hex nut
18. Rear fork thrust bushing
19. Spring washer
20. Rear cushion under rubber bushing
21. Rear brake panel stopper bolt
22. Grease nipple
23. Rear fork pivot bolt
24. Rear fork dust-seal cap
25. Rear fork thrust bushing
26. Rear fork felt ring
27. Rear fork pivot bushing
28. Rear fork center collar
29. Rear fork pivot bolt washer
30. Locknut

Assembly

Assemble in reverse order of disassembly. Note the following points:

1. Apply a liberal amount of grease to the bearing races. Place the steel balls in the races and install the steering stem. Take care not to drop the balls as the stem is installed.

2. Tighten the steering stem nut in small increments, checking frequently, until there is no fore-and-aft play at the steering stem and it can move freely and smoothly throughout its travel. Do not overtighten the nut.

REAR SUSPENSION

Shock absorber and Spring Replacement

The shock absorber/spring unit can be removed after the upper and lower mounting bolts are taken out. To remove the spring, first set the spring adjustment cam in the soft position. Then compress the spring slightly by hand and have a helper remove the split retainer at the top.

To check the effectiveness of the shock absorber, compress and extend it by hand. More resistance should be encountered on the extension stroke than the compression stroke if the shock is operating correctly. Replace if leaking or if the damping is unsatisfactory. Make sure that the spring/shock unit is not binding after it has been reassembled.

Swing Arm Pivot Service

Disassembly

1. Remove the mufflers.
2. Remove the rear wheel.
3. Remove the rear shock absorber/-spring units.
4. Take off the left-side rear crankcase cover (125 and 175 only).
5. Unscrew the swing arm pivot nut and withdraw the pivot shaft. The swing arm can now be separated from the frame.

Inspection

Inspect the swing arm carefully for cracks and distortion. Check to make sure that the pivot shaft is not bent by rolling it on a flat surface. Replace it if bent. Examine the pivot tube (collar) and pivot bushings for damage. If calculated clearance between the pivot tube and bushings exceeds 0.008 in. (0.2 mm), the bushings and tube should be replaced. Check also to make sure that the pivot bolt is a snug fit in the pivot tube.

Assembly

Assembly is a reversal of the disassembly procedures. Liberally grease the pivot tube before installing, and lubricate the pivot at the grease fitting after it is assembled.

INDEX
HONDA FOURS

MODEL IDENTIFICATION

The first CB 750 models were introduced in 1969 and remained unchanged through 1970. The pre-K1 models are easily distinguished from the later models by their vented side covers and the old type throttle linkage.

The first CB 500 models came out in 1972. There have been no major mechanical changes since then.

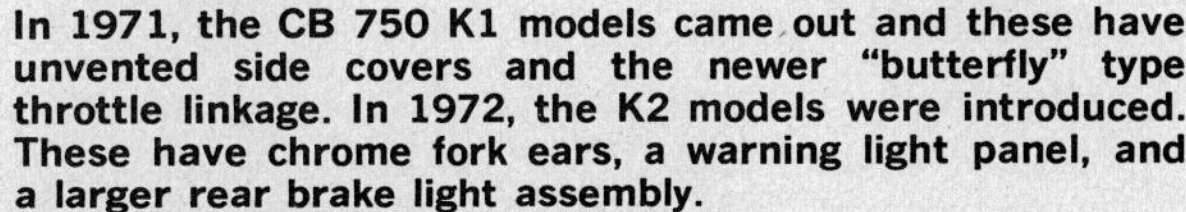

In 1971, the CB 750 K1 models came out and these have unvented side covers and the newer "butterfly" type throttle linkage. In 1972, the K2 models were introduced. These have chrome fork ears, a warning light panel, and a larger rear brake light assembly.

The little brother of the line, the CB 350F, was first introduced in 1972.

TUNE-UP AND MAINTENANCE

GENERAL SPECIFICATIONS

	CB 350F	CB 500	CB 750	CB 750K1—K3
ENGINE				
Type	Four-cylinder, single overhead camshaft, air cooled			
Displacement (cu in./cc)	21.1/347	30.38/498	44.93/736	44.93/736
Bore and Stroke (in./mm)	1.850 x 1.969/ 47.0 x 50.0	2.205 x 1.992/ 56.0 x 50.6	2.401 x 2.480 61 x 63	2.401 x 2.480 61 x 63
Compression Ratio	9.3 : 1	9.0 : 1	9.0 : 1	9.0 : 1
BHP (SAE @ rpm)	32 @ 9,500	50 @ 9,000	67 @ 8,000	67 @ 8,000
Torque (ft lb @ rpm)	19.5 @ 8,000	30.4 @ 7,500	44.12 @ 7,000	44.12 @ 7,000
Carburetion	(4) 21 mm Keihin	(4) 22 mm Keihin	(4) 28 mm Keihin	(4) 28 mm Keihin
Lubrication System Type	wet sump	wet sump	dry sump	dry sump
Weight (lb)	N.A.	152	192	192
DRIVE TRAIN				
Clutch	wet, multi-plate			
Primary Reduction	3.423	2.0	1.708	1.708
Transmission Ratios (overall)				
1st	2.733	2.353	2.500	2.500
2nd	1.850	1.636	1.708	1.708
3rd	1.416	1.269	1.333	1.333
4th	1.148	1.036	1.097	1.097
5th	0.965	0.900	0.939	0.939
Final Reduction	2.235	2.0 (17/34)	2.812 (16/45)	2.667 (18/48)
CHASSIS				
Dry Weight (lb)	373	403.5	480	480
Frame Type	semi-double cradle	Full double cradle, tubular steel		
Wheelbase (in.)	53.3	55.5	57.3	57.3
Tire Size (in.): front	3.00 x 18	3.15 x 19	3.25 x 19	3.25 x 19
rear	3.50 x 18	3.50 x 18	4.00 x 18	4.00 x 18
Overall Length (in.)	81.1	83.0	85.0	85.0
Overall Width (in.)	30.7	32.5	34.8	34.8
Overall Height (in.)	42.9	44.0	45.5	45.5
Ground Clearance (in.)	6.1	6.5	6.3	5.5
ELECTRICAL SYSTEM				
Ignition	Battery and coil			
Starting System	Electric and kick			
Charging System				
battery (volts/amp hrs)	12/12	12/12	12/14	12/14
alternator	Three-phase, excited-field-type with silicon rectifier			
regulator	Dual-contact-type voltage regulator			

Frame serial number location (1)

Engine serial number location (1)

TUNE-UP OPERATIONS

Valve Clearance Adjustment

NOTE: *Valves should be adjusted with the engine cold.*

CB 350 F, CB 500, CB 750, CB 750K1—K3

1. Remove the fuel tank.
2. Unscrew the eight adjuster access caps.
3. Remove the ignition points cover.
4. Remove the spark plugs.
5. Turn the crankshaft in its normal direction or rotation and observe the no. 1 cylinder (far left) intake and exhaust valves. When both valves are fully closed (clearance at both rocker arms), the piston is close to top dead center of its compression stroke. Next, align the timing index mark and the "T" (1.4) mark on the ignition advance rotor, as shown.
6. Measure the clearance between the adjusting screw and the valve stem of the "A" valves in the chart below, using a feeler gauge. Correct clearances for the intake and exhaust valves of both the 500 and 750 are 0.002 in. (0.05 mm) intake, and 0.003 in. (0.08 mm) exhaust. Adjust both the intake and the exhaust valves on the 350 to 0.002 in. (0.05 mm).
7. If the feeler gauge of the proper clearance thickness will not fit between the adjuster screw and valve stem, or if it slides through with little or no resistance, the clearance should be adjusted. To obtain the proper clearance, loosen the adjuster screw locknut and turn the screw until the feeler gauge just fits, and slides with some resistance. Tighten the locknut firmly (but do not overtighten) while holding the screw to keep it from turning. Recheck clearance in case it changed as the locknut was tightened.

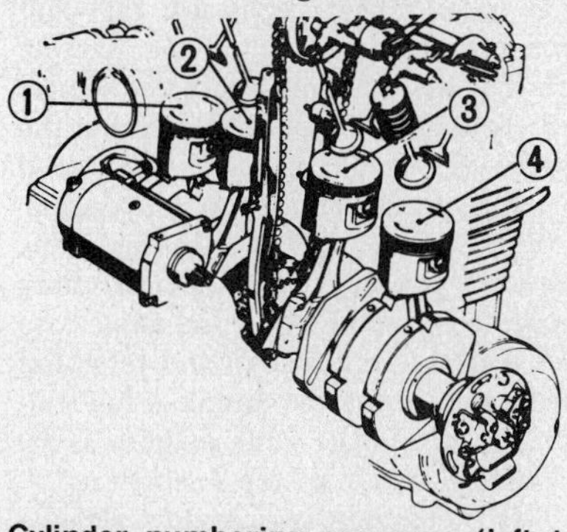

Cylinder numbering sequence (left to right)

8. After all four "A" valves have been checked and adjusted, rotate the crankshaft one turn (360°) in its normal direction of rotation and align the timing index mark and "T" mark exactly as before. This will position no. 4 cylinder on its compression stroke, and the "B" valves in the chart can be checked and adjusted in the same manner as the "A" valves.

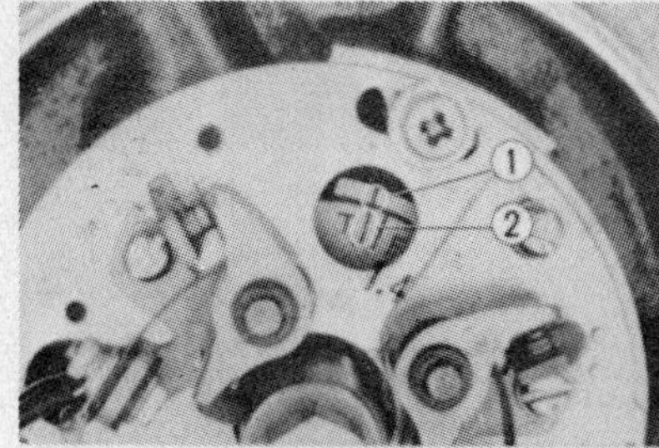

Align the timing index mark (1) with the "T" mark on the ignition advance rotor (2). Make sure that No. 1 cylinder is at TDC on the compression stroke (play at both rockers).

Measure valve clearance with a feeler gauge (3). Loosen the locknut (1) and turn the adjusting screw (2) to alter the clearance.

(Looking down on the engine, from the rider's position.) — Right side

	No. 1 Cyl.	No. 2 Cyl.	No. 3 Cyl.	No. 4 Cyl.
Exhaust Valves	A	A	B	B
Intake Valves	A	B	A	B

Cam Chain Tensioner Adjustment

CB 350 F and CB 500

1. Remove the valve adjuster access caps from no. 1 (left outside) cylinder.
2. Rotate the crankshaft in the normal direction of rotation until both valves are closed (clearance at both rocker arms).
3. Remove the ignition points cover (if you have not already done so) and turn the crankshaft clockwise, slowly, until the spring peg on the ignition advance unit is just to the right of the timing index mark (see illustration). At this point, no. 1 piston is positioned 15° After Top Dead Center and the chain tensioner can now be adjusted.

CAUTION: *Do not rotate the crankshaft counterclockwise (opposite direction of normal rotation) if you have turned it too far and gone past the timing mark. Instead, rotate the crankshaft clockwise through two complete turns so that no. 1 piston will again be on the compression stroke and you can position the spring peg just to the right of the timing mark without having to turn the crankshaft back. Otherwise, the chain slack will not be positioned properly and the tensioner may not be able to take up the full amount of slack.*

4. Finally, loosen the tensioner locknut and the proper chain tension will be obtained automatically. Retighten the locknut and install the valve adjuster access caps.

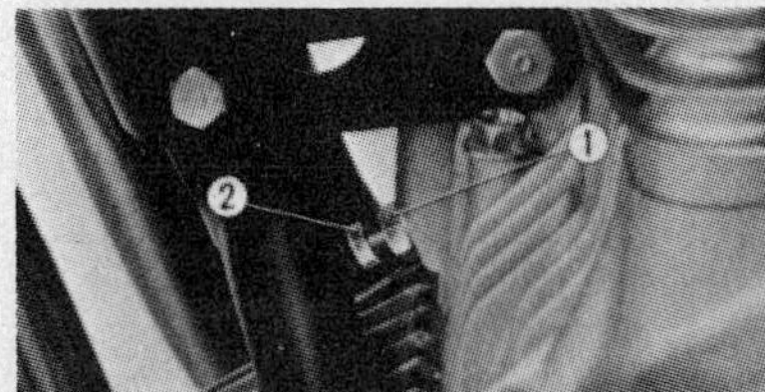

Cam chain adjuster location (CB 350F).
1. Lock nut
2. Adjusting bolt

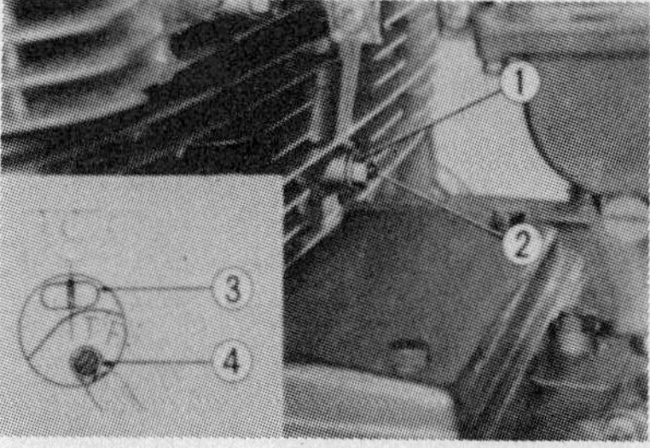

Cam chain tensioner locknut (1) and adjusting screw (2). Chain adjustment is automatically made when the locknut is loosened. Inset shows relationship of of the spring peg (4) to the timing index mark (3) when the crankshaft is correctly positioned for chain adjustment (CB 500 models).

CB 750, CB 750K1—K3

1. Consult Steps 1–3 of the CB 350 F and CB 500 "Cam Chain Tensioner Adjustment" section.
2. Finally, loosen the locknut and back out the adjuster bolt until you can turn it with your fingers. At this point, the adjuster bolt has released pressure on the tensioner rod, which has automatically moved in to take up chain slack. Retighten the adjuster bolt until it is just snug. *Do not overtighten.* Lock it in position with the locknut.

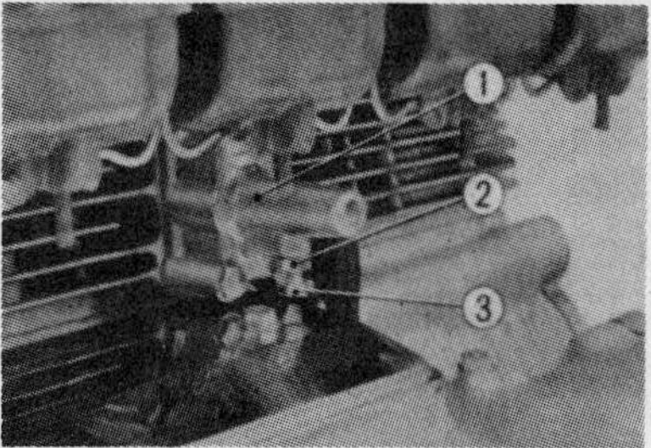

Cam chain tensioner (1) is at the rear of the cylinders. After the crankshaft has been correctly positioned, loosen the locknut (2) and adjuster bolt (3) and the tensioner will automatically take up the slack in the chain (CB 750 models).

NOTE: *If you follow this method you should have no further trouble with the cam chain. However, if it is still excessively noisy, try adjusting the tensioner in the following manner:*

Loosen the locknut and adjuster bolt. Insert a thin instrument such as a stiff piece of wire or a small screwdriver into the tail section of the tensioner and seat it gently against the end of the tensioner rod inside. Now, turn the engine over slowly; you can feel the rod move back and forth as the cam chain slack varies. Do this several times and take note of the point at which the rod is farthest in (closest to the engine). Continue turning the engine over slowly until you succeed in stopping it at this point. *Do not use pressure to force the tensioner rod in.* When this is accomplished, the cam chain slack is on the tensioner side of the engine and the tensioner has automatically moved in to take up the slack. Tighten the adjuster bolt and locknut to lock the tensioner rod in this position.

This method has been used for many years on the overhead cam Honda engines and is quite effective if carried out carefully. If you have not used pressure to force the rod in, there is no danger of the cam chain being overly tight.

Ignition Points and Ignition Timing

Ignition Points Service

CB 350 F, CB 500, CB 750, AND CB 750K1—K3

If the points are heavily pitted, replace both sets of points and condensers. The components can be unscrewed and removed from the base plate after the electrical leads have been disconnected. Make sure that any insulating washers are replaced in their original positions when reconnecting the wires. Place a drop or two of gasoline or other non-oily solvent on a piece of paper and pull it through the points to remove any dirt or preservative coating on the contact surfaces. Put a *small* dab of distributor cam lubricant or other high-melting-point grease on the contact breaker cam. This will prevent the rubbing blocks that run on the cam from wearing excessively and reducing point gap.

Point gap should be adjusted to 0.012–0.016 in. Adjust one set at a time by loosening the locking screw and swivelling the stationary contact point toward or away from the moving contact as required. The cam must be positioned where it will give maximum opening for the set of points being adjusted. The point gap is not particularly critical as long as it is within the specified range; however, you should try to adjust each set of points so that their gaps are as close to identical as possible.

Adjust the gap of each set of points when the high side of the breaker cam is toward them. Arrow shows the direction of cam rotation. Points (1) are adjusted by loosening the locking screw (2) and moving the stationary contact.

Ignition Timing

CB 350 F, CB 500, CB 750, AND CB 750K1—K3

STATIC TIMING PROCEDURE

1. Connect one of the test light leads to the small bolt that fastens the condenser and coil wires to the rear (1.4) point set. (The 1.4 point set fires cylinders 1 and 4.) Ground the other test light lead on the engine.

2. Switch the ignition on and turn the crankshaft clockwise until the "F" (1.4) mark on the ignition advance rotor aligns with the timing index mark. The test light should light at the same instant the marks are aligned. If not, loosen screws "B" and move base "B" in the required direction until the light just comes on as the marks are aligned. (Moving the base clockwise will retard timing, counterclockwise will advance timing.) Cylinders 1 and 4 are now correctly timed. Tighten screws "B" and recheck the setting.

"F" mark for cylinders 1 and 4 (1) aligned with timing index mark (2)

3. To time cylinders 2 and 3, switch the test light lead from the rear (1.4) point set to the front (2.3) point set and turn the crankshaft until the "F" (2.3) mark on the ignition advance rotor aligns with the timing index mark. The test light should light at the instant the marks are aligned, as before. If not, loosen screws "C" and move base "C" in the required direction until the light comes on just as the marks are aligned. Tighten the screws and recheck the setting. Cylinders 2 and 3 are now correctly timed.

Timing adjustment points

1. Screw B
2. Point base plate
3. Base B of the breaker plate
4. Screw C
5. Base C of the breaker plate

DYNAMIC TIMING PROCEDURE

1. Connect the strobe light as per manufacturer's instructions, picking up the impulses from no. 1 (left outside) cylinder.

2. Start the engine and adjust the idle, if necessary, to the recommended speed. (Refer to the specifications at the end of the chapter.)

3. Aim the light at the timing marks. At idle speed, the "F" (1.4) mark should be aligned with the timing index mark. If not, loosen screws "B" and move base "B" in the required direction to align the marks. Retighten the screws.

4. To check the timing at full ignition advance, increase the engine speed to 2,500–3,000 rpm and hold it steady. The timing index mark should be between the two lines scribed into the ignition advance rotor. If it is, the advance unit is functioning properly and cylinders 1 and 4 are correctly timed. If it is not, or if the timing is unsteady even though the engine speed is held constant, the fault probably lies with either the ignition points or advance unit spring (see step 6).

5. To time cylinders 2 and 3, shut the engine off, transfer the strobe light lead to no. 2 cylinder, and restart the engine. If the "F" (2.3) mark and timing index mark are not aligned at normal idling speed, loosen screws "C" and move base "C" until the marks align and retighten the screws. Check the timing at full ignition advance in the same manner as for cylinders 1 and 4 in step 4, above.

6. If the timing is unsteady, remove the contact breaker plate assembly and examine the advance unit. Look for weak or broken springs, or a bent advancer shaft. If either spring is defective, replace both of them. If the advancer shaft is bent (noticeable as the engine is turned over), remove the advance unit and bend the shaft until total runout is less than 0.004 in. (0.1 mm).

When reinstalling the advance unit, make sure that the pin is located in the hole, as shown.

Remove the breaker plate assembly (1) by removing the retaining screws (2), nut (5), and washers (3 and 4)

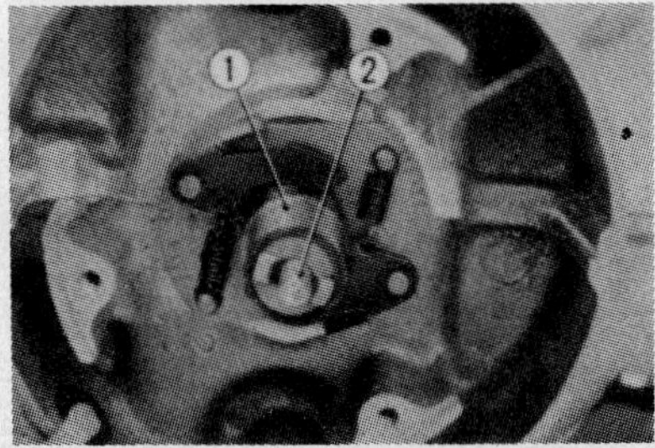

The breaker cam and advancer assembly (1) fit over the advancer shaft

Make sure the advancer dowel fits in its locating hole

1. Locating hole
2. Dowel pin
3. Automatic advance unit

Carburetor Synchronization and Adjustment

CB 350 F AND CB 500

Synchronization

1. Raise the rear of the fuel tank as far as the fuel lines will allow and support the tank in this position. (If the carburetors are not fully accessible, it may be desirable to fit longer fuel lines, temporarily, so that the tank can be raised higher.)

2. Adjust the throttle stop screw so that the throttle lever is 2.205 in. (350) or 1.938 in. (500) from the cable adjuster bracket, as shown.

3. Install the vacuum gauge hoses at the intake manifold tubes.

4. Start the engine, loosen the carburetor adjuster locknuts, and turn the adjuster screws so that all four carburetors are indicating within 3.0 cm Hg of each other, 16–24 cm Hg. Turning the screw clockwise decreases vacuum, and counterclockwise increases vacuum. Try to maintain the correct idle speed during adjustment.

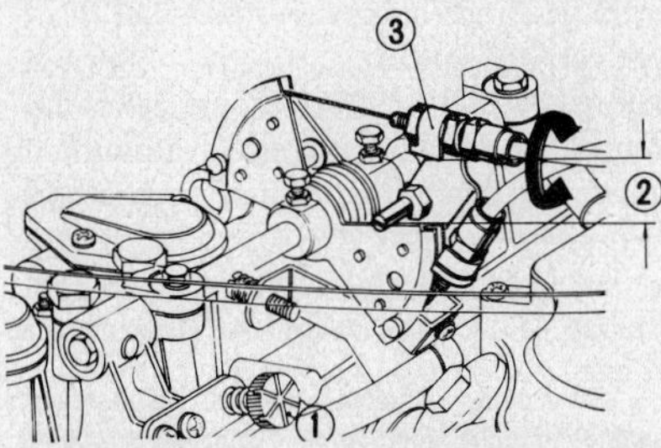

Throttle stop screw adjustment

1. Throttle stop screw
2. $1^{15}/_{16}$–2.0 in.
3. Bracket

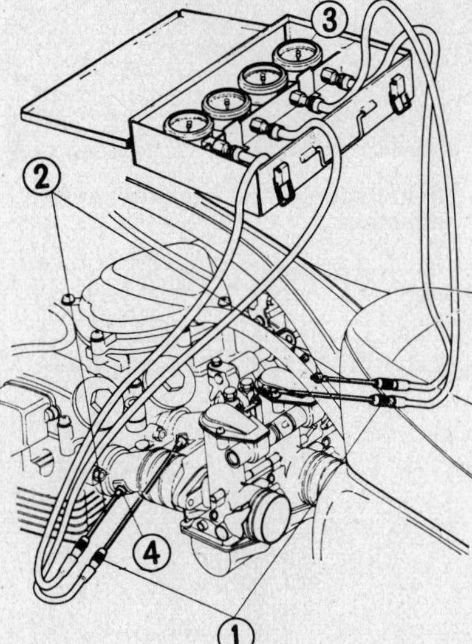

Adjusting manifold vacuum pressure

1. Long adapter
2. Short adapter
3. Vacuum gauge set
4. Vacuum pick-up hole

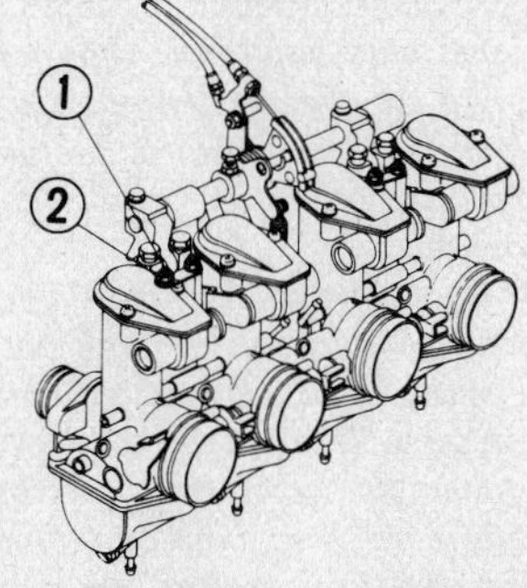

Carburetor adjuster screw (1) and locknut (2)

NOTE: *Provision is made on some vacuum gauges for dampening needle movement if the needle tends to oscillate over a wide range. This will facilitate obtaining accurate vacuum settings.*

5. After the desired settings have been achieved, snap the throttle open several times and recheck vacuum readings after the engine has settled down. Readjust any carburetor(s) that show a lack of uniformity.

CAUTION: *Do not run the engine for more than about five minutes while the motorcycle is stationary. Either ride the bike at moderate speeds for a few minutes to cool it down or place an electric fan in front of the engine to provide a stream of air to keep it cool while running.*

If the vacuum reading is less than 15 cm Hg for any carburetor, check the following: ignition timing, valve clearances, spark plug gap, and compression. Check also for air leaks at the carburetor and intake manifold tube.

Idle Adjustment

1. After all four carburetors have been adjusted to the same vacuum draw, adjust the carburetor air screws to obtain maximum idle speed consistent with smoothness. Standard air screw opening is one turn from the fully closed position and it should not be necessary to deviate from this setting more than ¼ of a turn in either direction to obtain the desired results.

2. Adjust idle speed to 1,200 rpm (350) or 1,000 rpm (500) with the throttle stop screw.

3. Recheck vacuum uniformity and idle smoothness. Remove the vacuum gauge tubes and tighten the intake manifold plugs firmly.

Throttle Cable Adjustment

PLAY ADJUSTMENT

1. Back off the cable adjuster at the handlebar to increase cable play. Leave a small amount of adjustment range available so that final, small adjustments can be made.

Throttle cable adjuster at the handgrip

1. Adjuster 2. Locknut

2. Loosen the cable locknut at the carburetor end and turn the adjuster until there is about ⅛–1/6 in. (3–4 mm) play at the throttle grip. Retighten the locknut.

NOTE: *The throttle lever should hit the eccentric pin when the throttle grip is forced to the fully closed position. If the lever will not hit the pin, replace the return cable.*

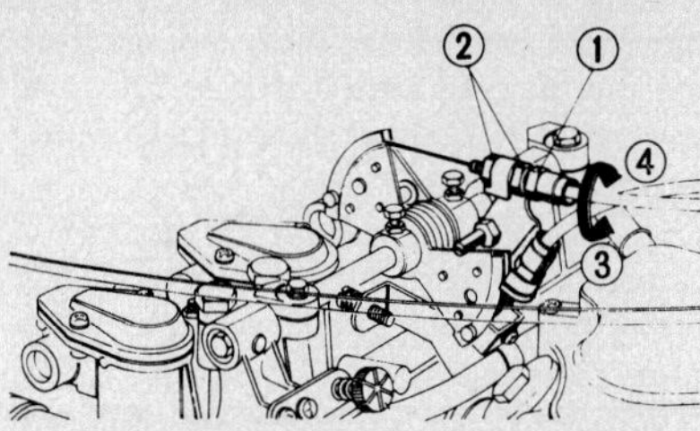

Throttle cable adjuster at the carburetor

1. Adjuster
2. Locknut
3. Decrease play
4. Increase play

3. Make any desired, final cable play adjustment at the handlebar adjuster.

OVERTRAVEL LIMIT ADJUSTMENT

Simply loosen the locknut and turn the eccentric pin, as illustrated, until clearance between the pin and throttle lever is 0.08–0.083 in. (2–2.1 mm) for the 350, or 0.08–0.12 in. (2–3 mm) for the 500.

FULL THROTTLE LIMIT ADJUSTMENT

Adjust the throttle lever stop screw so that the carburetor slides are pulled 0–0.04 in. (0–1.0 mm) above the top of the carburetor bore at full throttle.

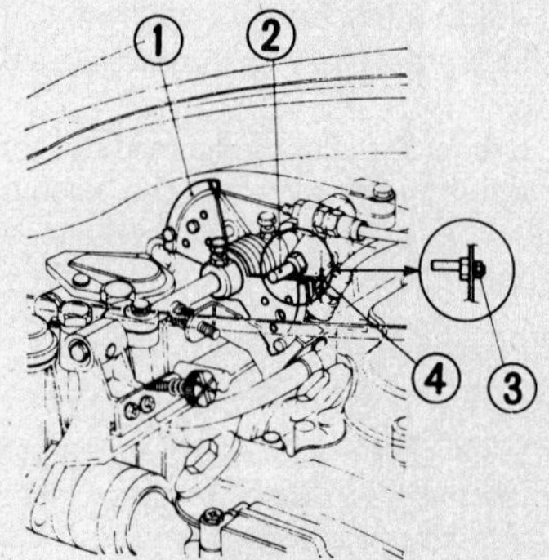

Adjusting overtravel

1. Throttle lever
2. Eccentric pin
3. Locknut
4. 0.08–0.12 in. (2–3 mm)

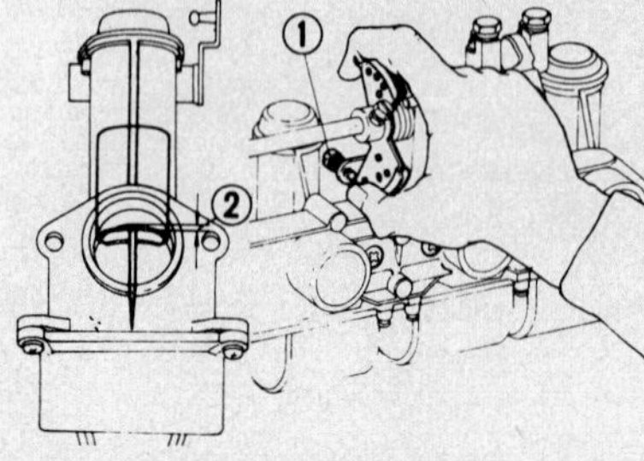

Adjusting full throttle limit

1. Stop screw
2. 0–0.04 in. (0–1.0 mm)

CB 750

Carburetor Synchronization

1. Connect the vacuum gauge hoses at the carburetors. It may be helpful to raise the rear of the fuel tank as described in the preceding section for the CB 500.

2. Start the engine and drop the idle below 1,000 rpm using the throttle stop screws. Next, lift up the rubber boots at the top of the carburetors, loosen the locknuts, and rotate the individual throttle cable adjusters until the engine is idling at 1,000–1,100 rpm and the carburetors are drawing an equal amount of vacuum (within 3 cm Hg of each other). It may be necessary to decrease throttle cable slack with the adjuster at the handlebar to provide sufficient adjustment range.

Installation of the vacuum gauge adapters

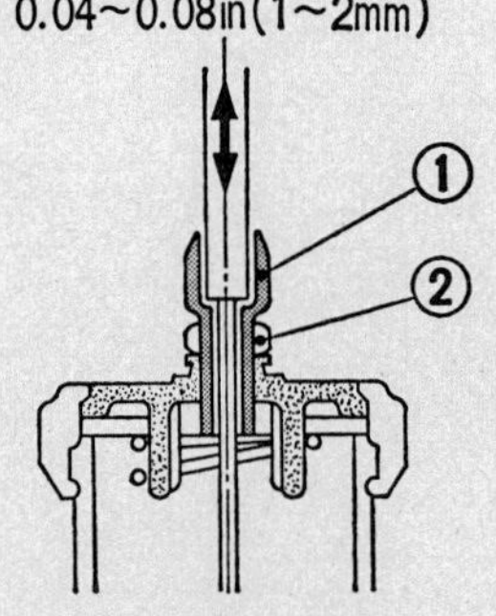

Throttle cable adjuster

1. Cable adjuster
2. Locknut

NOTE: *Some vacuum gauges are equipped with adjustable dampers to eliminate needle oscillation. Do not overdampen the needles. A fluctuation of about one gradation on the scale is acceptable.*

CAUTION: *Do not allow the engine to overheat by idling it for long periods while stationary. A household electric fan can be used to provide a flow of air over the engine when adjustment time exceeds more than about five minutes.*

3. After the carburetors have been synchronized, tighten the locknuts on the adjusters and fit the rubber boots down over the carburetor tops. Proceed to the following section on idle adjustment. If the vacuum reading is less than 15 cm Hg at normal idle speed, investigate the following possibilities: intake air leak, low compression due to insufficient valve clearance or a sticking valve, loose spark plug, or idle speed set too high.

Idle Adjustment

1. Back off the throttle cable adjuster at the handlebar to provide about ¼ in. of slack in the cable.

2. Start the engine and adjust the idle to about 1,000 rpm with the throttle stop screws. The vacuum gauge can be used to obtain equal throttle screw settings.

3. Turn the air screws slowly in or out to obtain the highest idle speed consistent with smoothness. Standard air screw opening is one turn from fully closed, and it should not be necessary to exceed ¼ turn in either direction from this setting. Individual cylinders can be checked for even firing by feeling the exhaust pressure with your hand. Reset the throttle stop screws again, if necessary, to obtain the correct idle speed.

NOTE: *If the carburetors are unresponsive to large changes in air screw openings, investigate the following possible causes: clogged air passage, worn air screw, float level too high, or loose low-speed jet. If air screw adjustment requires less than ½ turn opening, look for: clogged low-speed jet or jet passage, float level too low, or worn air screw seat.*

4. Adjust throttle cable play to the desired amount at the adjuster near the grip. Swing the handlebars to full-lock in both directions to make sure that the throttle cable is not binding and pulling the carburetors open.

Idle adjustment points; air screw (1) and throttle stop screw (2)

CB 750K1—K3

Synchronization

1. Raise the rear of the fuel tank as far as the fuel lines will allow and support the tank in this position. It may be helpful to temporarily fit longer fuel lines so that the tank can be raised higher.

2. Slide the rubber boots on the carburetor tops back on the linkage arms.

3. Connect the vacuum gauge tubes to the carburetors.

4. Start the engine and adjust the idle speed with the throttle stop screw to about 1,000 rpm.

5. Loosen the adjuster nut locknuts and turn the adjuster nuts until all carburetors are indicating uniformly (within 3.0 cm Hg) between 16–24 cm Hg. Turning the adjuster nuts clockwise increases

vacuum, and counterclockwise decreases vacuum. Try not to increase the idle speed while making adjustments.

NOTE: *Some vacuum gauges are equipped with adjustable dampers to eliminate needle oscillation. Do not overdampen the needle. A fluctuation of about one graduation on the scale is acceptable.*

CAUTION: *Do not allow the engine to overheat by idling it for long periods while stationary. A household electric fan can be used to provide a flow of air over the engine to prevent overheating when adjustment time exceeds more than about five minutes.*

6. After adjustment has been made, check to see that at least one thread on each throttle rod protrudes above the locknuts. If not, turn all four adjuster nuts in an equal amount until at least one thread on each throttle rod is exposed, reset the idle speed with the throttle stop screw, and recheck the vacuum readings.

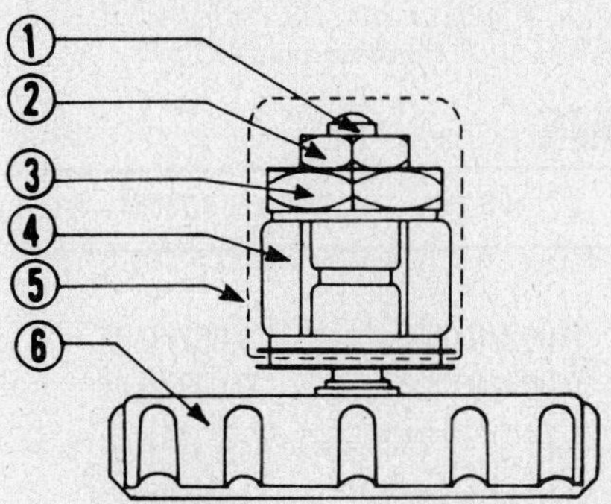

Adjuster components

1. Throttle rod
2. Locknut
3. Adjuster nut
4. Linkage arm
5. Rubber boot
6. Cap

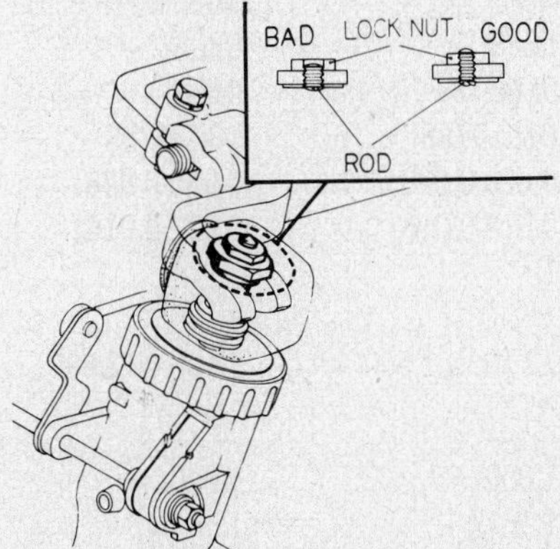

At least one thread of the throttle rod should protrude above the locknut

7. Snap the throttle open several times to verify synchronization before tightening the locknuts.

CAUTION: *When tightening the locknuts, hold the adjuster nut in position with a wrench to prevent the torque from being transferred through the throttle rod and twisting it off. Tighten the locknuts to 11–17 in. lbs, or about 1 ft lb. Do not overtighten.*

8. When refitting the rubber boots, make sure that the bottom rim is fully seated in the groove at the base of the adjuster linkage. It is a good idea at this time to open the throttle wide to expose the throttle rods and lubricate the rods and adjuster linkage with silicone grease. *Do not use a petroleum-base lubricant.* The throttle shaft pivots may be lubricated with motor oil.

Idle Adjustment

Adjust the carburetor air screws so that the maximum vacuum draw is obtained, consistent with engine smoothness. Standard air screw adjustment range is ¾–1¼ turns from the fully closed position. Readjust the throttle stop screw, if necessary, to reduce idle speed to about 1,000 rpm. Recheck vacuum uniformity and idle smoothness. Remove the vacuum gauge tubes and tighten the carburetor plugs firmly.

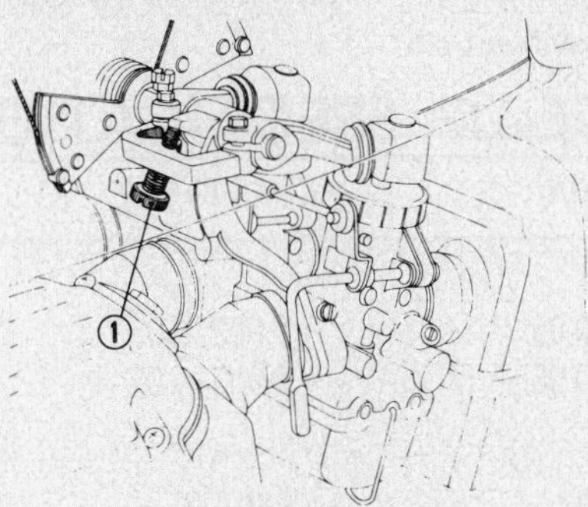

Throttle stop screw (1)

Throttle Cable Adjustment

PLAY ADJUSTMENT

1. Back off the cable adjuster at the handlebar to increase cable play. Leave a small amount of adjustment range available so that final, small adjustments can be made.

2. Loosen the cable locknut at the carburetor end and turn the adjuster until there is about ⅛–1/6 in. (3–4 mm) play at the throttle grip. Retighten the locknut.

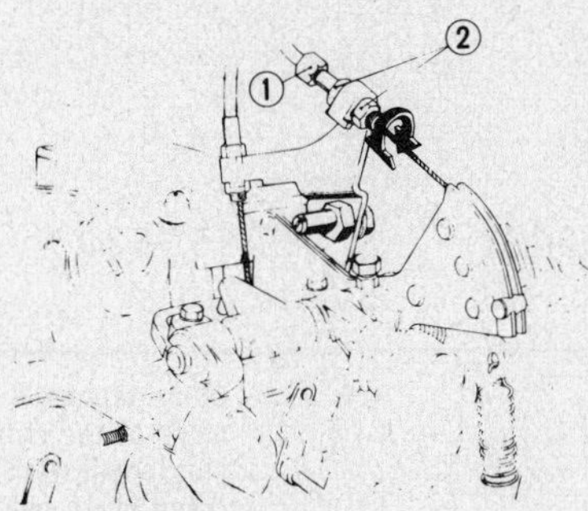

Throttle cable play adjustment

1. Adjuster nut
2. Locknut

NOTE: *The throttle lever should hit the eccentric pin when the throttle grip is forced to the fully closed position. If the lever will not hit the pin, replace the return cable.*

3. Make any desired final cable play adjustment at the handlebar adjuster.

OVERTRAVEL LIMIT ADJUSTMENT

Simply loosen the locknut and turn the eccentric pin, as shown, until clearance between the pin and the throttle lever is 0.08–0.12 in. (2–3 mm).

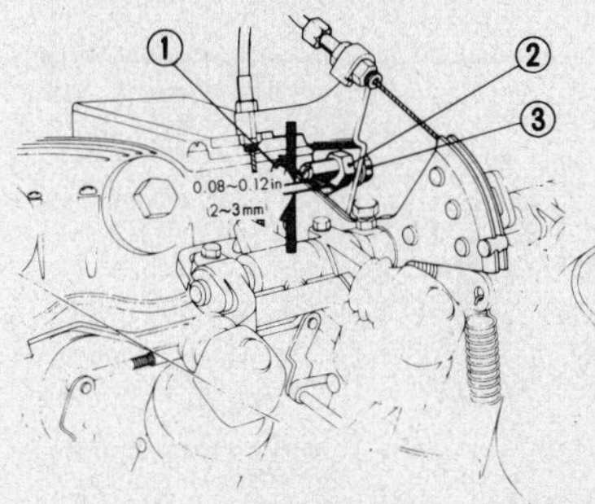

Throttle cable overtravel adjustment

1. Throttle lever
2. Eccentric pin
3. Locknut

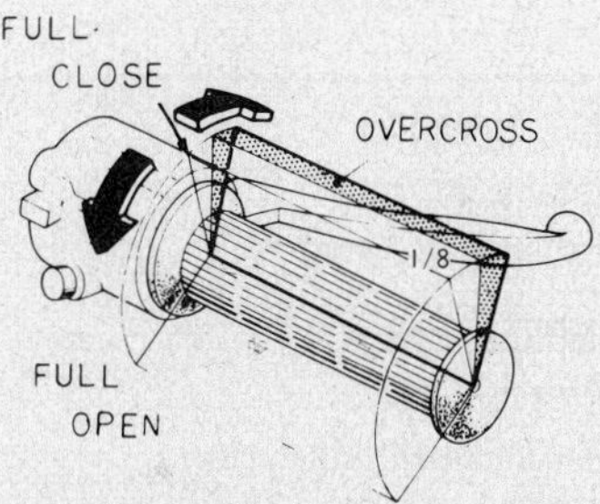

Overtravel comes into play just before the throttle is fully closed

FULL THROTTLE LIMIT ADJUSTMENT

Adjust the throttle lever stop screw so that there is a distance of 1.28–1.29 in. (32.5–33.0 mm) between the carburetor top and the bottom of the adjuster linkage with the throttle fully open, as shown.

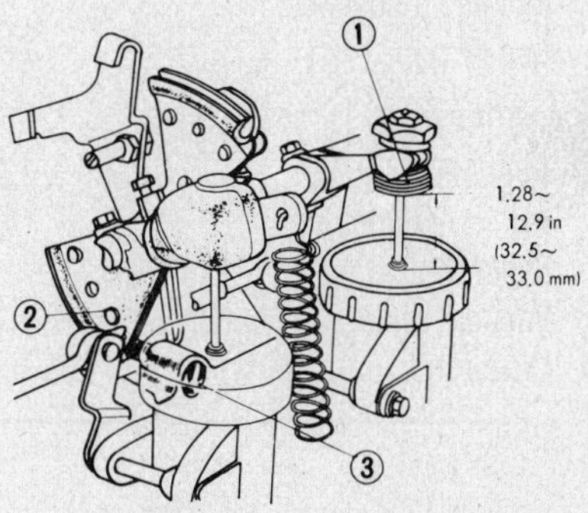

Full throttle limit adjustment

1. Adjuster linkage
2. Throttle lever
3. Full throttle limit screw

THROTTLE ROD AND LINKAGE LUBRICATION

Lubricate the throttle rods and seals, and the linkage pivot points as shown in the illustration. If this does not restore smooth throttle operation, the carburetor tops should be removed, the throttle components thoroughly cleaned and dried, and the throttle rod guides and seals lubricated with silicone grease. *Do not use a petroleum base grease.*

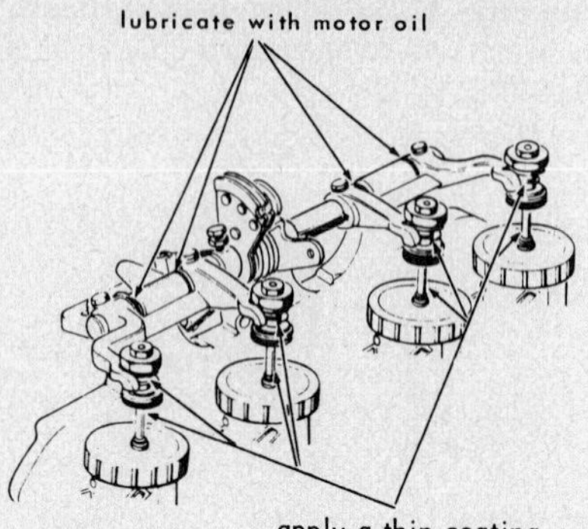
lubricate with motor oil
apply a thin coating of silicone grease

Throttle rod and linkage lubrication points

MAINTENANCE ITEMS

Engine Oil

NOTE: *Oil changes—(1,000 mi/60 days summer, 30 days winter)*

Change the oil after the engine has been run long enough to be up to operating temperature. This ensures that the oil is fluid enough to drain completely and that impurities suspended in the oil while it is circulating will be removed. Honda recommends that SAE 10W–40 or 20W–50 oil of SC (previously MS) service rating be used. Also recommended are the new 10W–50 oils of SE rating, which withstand heat even better than the SD oils. If a single-viscosity oil is to be used, it must be a high detergent, heavy-duty oil of SD service rating. For temperatures above 60 deg F, use SAE 30W–30 oil. Between 32 and 60 deg F, use SAE 20W–20, and below 32 deg F, use SAE 10W–10 oil. Do not use a vegetable-based or non-detergent oil.

CB 350 F AND CB 500

Remove the drain plug from the crankcase sump and remove the filler cap to assist draining. When most of the oil has drained, kick the engine over a few times to remove any oil remaining in the delivery system. Replace the drain plug and add approximately 3.5 qts of oil. Start the engine and let it idle for a few minutes to circulate the oil. Shut the engine off and check oil level with the filler dipstick. To obtain a true reading on the dipstick, three precautions must be observed:

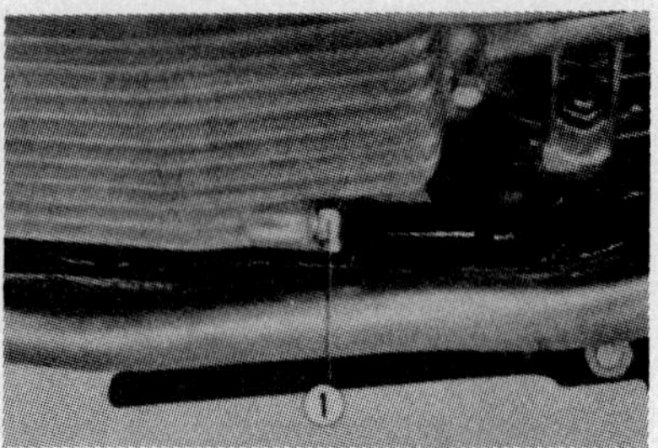
1

Oil drain plug (1)

TUNE-UP SPECIFICATIONS

	CB 350F	CB 500	CB 750	CB 750K1—K3
VALVE CLEARANCE (cold)				
Intake: (in./mm)	0.002/0.05	0.002/0.05	0.002/0.05	0.002/0.05
Exhaust: (in./mm)	0.002/0.05	0.003/0.08	0.003/0.08	0.003/0.08
COMPRESSION				
Pressure, psi	140-170	140-170	140-170	140-170
Maximum Variation, psi	15	15	15	15
IGNITION				
Spark Plugs				
Standard make*	NGK	NGK	NGK	NGK
Type: standard	D8ESL	D7ES	D8ES	D8ES
cold	D10E	D8E, D8ES	D10E	D10E
hot	D8E, D7ES	D7E	D8E, D7ES	D8E, D7ES
Gap, in.	0.025-0.028	0.025-0.028	0.025-0.028	0.025-0.028
Point Gap, in.	0.012-0.016	0.012-0.016	0.012-0.016	0.012-0.016
Static Timing, deg BTDC	5	5	10	10
Maximum Advance,** deg @ rpm	28-31 @ 2,500	28-31 @ 2,500	33-36 @ 2,500	33-36 @ 2,500
CARBURETION				
Idle Speed, rpm	1,200	1,000	1,000	1,000
Air Screw Opening	$7/8 \pm 3/8$	$1 \pm 1/4$	$1 \pm 1/4$	$1 \pm 1/4$
Synchronization				
Vacuum range, (in./cm Hg)	6.2-9.5 (16-24)	6.2-9.5 (16-24)	6.2-9.5 (16-24)	6.2-9.5 (16-24)
Uniformity, (in./cm Hg)	1.2/3.0	1.2/3.0	1.2/3.0	1.2-3.0

* Other reputable makes are also acceptable. Be sure to select plugs of the correct heat range, reach, and diameter. Most spark plug application charts also have conversion tables and a heat range chart, enabling you to select the spark plug that fits your needs exactly. The Fours use 12 mm diameter plugs with a half-inch (12.7 mm) reach.

** Includes initial (static) advance.

1. Allow the oil a few seconds to drain down into the crankcase.

2. Place the machine on its center stand, on a level surface.

3. Do not screw the dipstick/filler cap into the case when checking oil level or a false (high) reading will be obtained.

Add oil, if necessary, to bring the level to the upper mark on the dipstick.

CB 750 AND CB 750K1—K3

Remove the oil tank filler cap and unscrew the oil tank and crankcase drain plugs. When most of the oil has drained, operate the kick-starter several times to chase out any oil remaining. Install the drain plugs and tighten firmly. Pour 3.0 qts of oil into the oil tank and start the engine. After the oil pressure light goes off, run it at 1,000–1,500 rpm for a minute or two. Shut the engine off and check the level. Make sure that the machine is level to obtain an accurate dipstick reading. Add oil, if necessary, to bring the level to the upper mark on the dipstick.

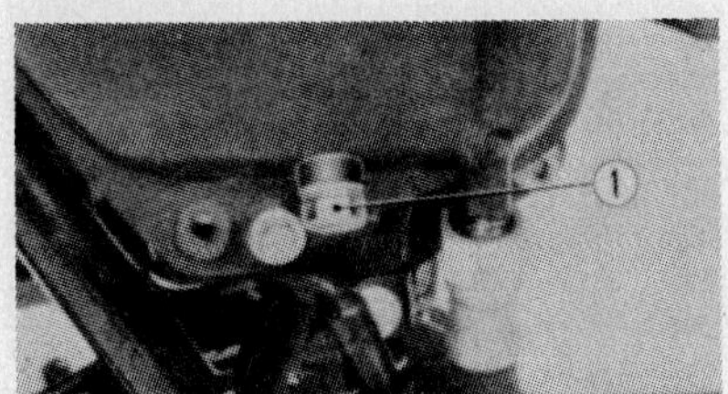

Oil tank drain plug (1)

Crankcase sump drain plug (1)

Oil Filter, Disposable Type (2,000 mi)

CB 350 F, CB 500, CB 750 AND CB 750K1—K3

A disposable cartridge, automotive-type oil filter is used as the main filter on the Honda Fours. It should be replaced initially at the first oil change and thereafter at every second oil change. To replace the cartridge, place a pan underneath the filter and unbolt the housing. Discard the old element and O-ring and clean the housing in solvent. Dry thoroughly. Install the new element and O-ring in the housing and reinstall on the engine. *Do not overtighten the bolt.* Start the engine and check for oil leakage around the filter.

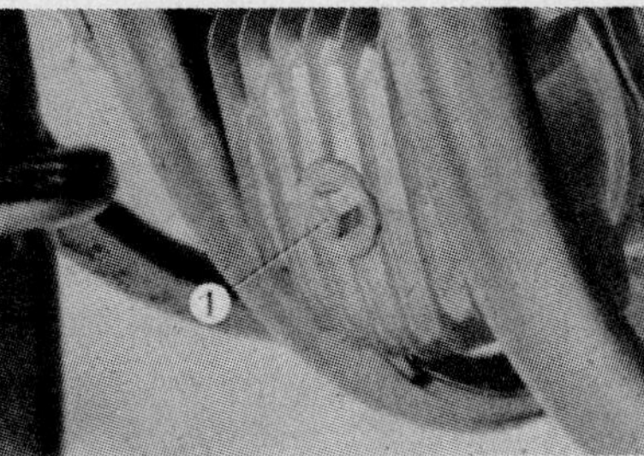

Oil filter mounting bolt (1)

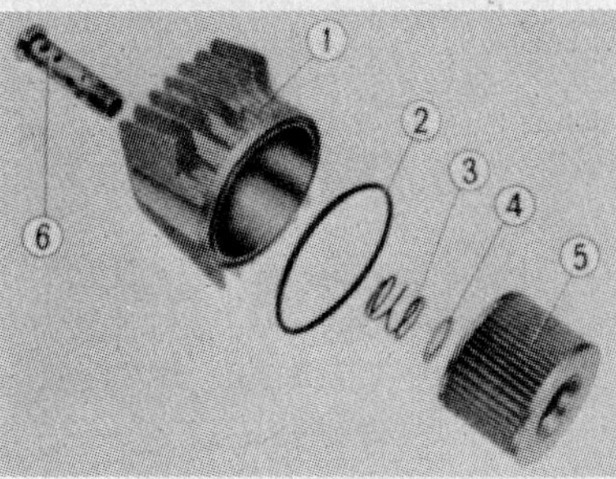

Oil filter components

1. Filter housing
2. O-ring
3. Spring
4. Washer
5. Filter element
6. Filter mounting bolt

Oil Filter, Strainer Type (12,000 mi/24 mo)

CB 350 F, CB 500, CB 750 AND CB 750K1—K3

The oil strainer is located at the oil pump pick-up and may be removed for cleaning after the oil pan is unbolted and lowered. (Do not forget to drain the oil.) Withdraw the strainer from the pump body and clean it in solvent, or replace it with a new one if damaged. Refit the strainer in the oil pump and install the oil pan using a new gasket. After refilling with oil, start the engine and check for oil leaks.

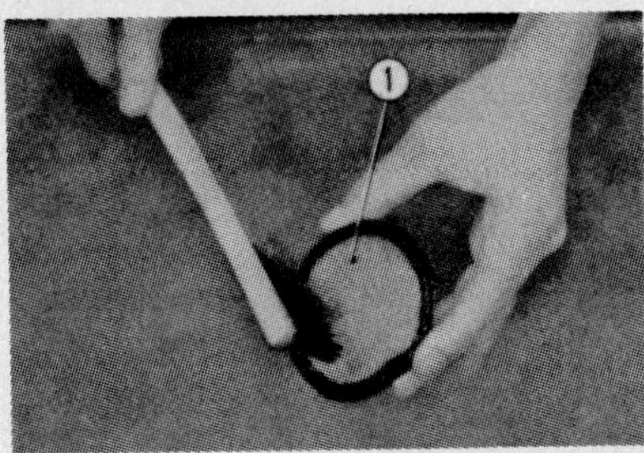

Cleaning the oil strainer (1)

Oil Pressure (6,000 mi/12 mo)

CB 750 AND CB 750K1—K3

A gauge may be connected at the oil gallery access hole at the right side of the engine after the plug has been removed. Honda service tools 07068–30001 (adaptor) and 07065–30001 (pressure gauge) may be used. The gauge should register 50–64 psi when the engine is warm (oil temperature 140–160 deg F) and running at approximately 3,000 rpm. If oil pressure is unsatisfactory, determine and correct the fault (restricted oil passage, clogged filter, pressure relief valve failure, etc.). Refer to the "Lubrication" section.

Checking oil pressure on the 750

Air Filter (3,000 mi/6 mo)

CB 350 F, CB 500, CB 750 AND CB 750K1—K3

To remove the filter on the 350 and 500, simply raise the seat and pull out the spring clip.

The element can then be withdrawn. On the 750, it is necessary to remove the left side-cover and loosen the lower, filter-housing wing bolts to gain access to the element.

Clean the filter element using compressed air (directed from the inside out) or by tapping it lightly and brushing away the dirt. Wipe the inside of the filter housing clean before replacing the element.

The air filter element (1) is secured by a spring clip (2)—CB 500 models

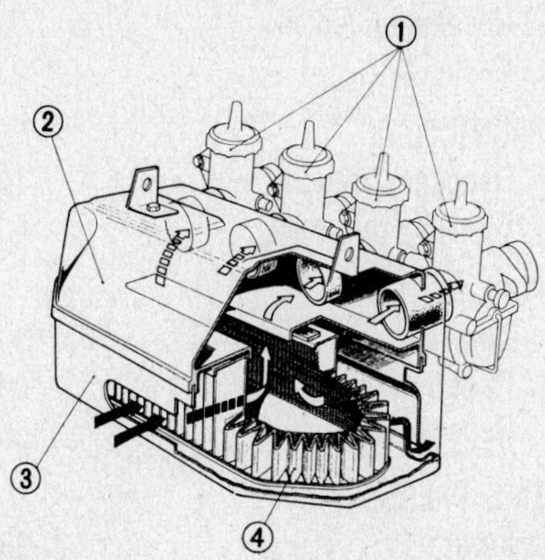

Cutaway of the air filter assembly on the 750

1. Carburetors
2. Upper housing
3. Lower housing
4. Filter element

PERIODIC MAINTENANCE CHART CB 350F, CB 500, CB 750, CB 750K1—K3

EVERY 1,000 MILES/60 days (summer) 30 days (winter)
- Engine
  - 1) Change oil

EVERY 2,000 MILES/4 months (summer) 2 months (winter)
- Engine
  - 1) Replace oil filter

EVERY 3,000 MILES/ 6 months
- Engine
  - 1) Service air filter element
- Clutch
  - 1) Adjust clutch
- Battery
  - 1) Check electrolyte level and state of charge
- Fuel System
  - 1) Clean fuel filter
  - 2) Check fuel flow
  - 3) Examine fuel lines and tank filler cap
- Rear Suspension
  - 1) Lubricate fork pivot
- Wheels, Tires, and Brakes
  - 1) Check spokes
  - 2) Check wheel runout
  - 3) Examine tires for wear and damage
  - 4) Check brake wear
- Frame
  - 1) Examine for cracks and misalignment check tightness of nuts and bolts
- Final Drive
  - 1) Service chain
  - 2) Check sprockets for wear and damage

EVERY 6,000 MILES/12 months
- Engine
  - 1) Check oil pressure (750 only)
- Front Suspension and Steering
  - 1) Check movement of steering head bearings
  - 2) Change oil in front fork legs

EVERY 12,000 MILES/24 months
- Engine
  - 1) Clean oil strainer
- Fuel System
  - 1) Examine carburetor rubber caps
- Brakes
  - 1) Examine brake hose (front) and cable (rear)

Clutch Adjustment (3,000 mi/6 mo)

CB 350 F

1. Align the clutch lever and right crankcase index marks as illustrated, then loosen the clutch adjuster locknut.

2. Rotate the clutch adjuster counterclockwise until resistance is felt, then back it off about ¼ turn and secure the locknut.

3. Check the ball end of the clutch lever for free play. The lever should have 0.4–0.8 in. (10–20 mm) of free movement.

4. Adjust the play if necessary by loosening the locknut at the lower adjuster, and rotating the adjuster clockwise (direction "A") to increase play, and counterclockwise (direction "B") to decrease it. Secure the lower adjuster locknut, and make fine adjustment at the hand lever by loosening the upper adjuster locknut and rotating the adjuster until free play is within the specified limits. Secure the locknut when satisfied with the adjustment.

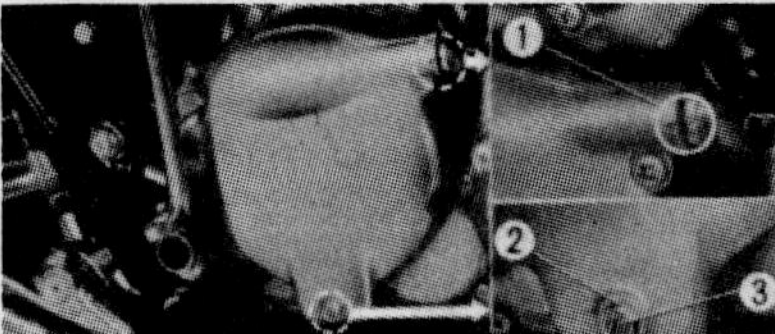

Adjusting the clutch release mechanism (350) 1. Matching mark 2. Lock nut 3. Clutch adjuster

MAINTENANCE DATA

	CB 350F	CB 500	CB 750	CB 750K1—K3
ENGINE OIL				
Recommended oil	10W-40 or 20W-50, service rating SD (previously MS)			
Capacity (qt)	3.7	3.2	3.7②	3.7②
Oil pressure (psi)	N.A.	N.A.	50-64③	50-64③
TRANSMISSION OIL				
Recommended oil	①	①	①	①
Capacity	①	①	①	①
FRONT FORK				
Recommended oil	10W-30	10W-30	10W-30	10W-30
Capacity (oz/cc)	4.2/125	5.4/160	7.0-7.3/220-230	7.0-7.3/220-230
FUEL TANK				
Total capacity (gal)	3.2	3.7	4.5	4.5
Reserve (gal)	0.5	1.6	1.3	1.3
Recommended fuel	premium	premium	premium	premium
TIRE PRESSURE				
Front	26	25	28	28
Rear	28	28	30	30

① Transmission lubricated by engine oil.
② Oil tank capacity at upper mark on dipstick is 2.1 qt. The crankcase sump and oil filter contain the remaining 1.6 qt.
③ With engine warm (oil temperature 140-160 deg F) and running at 3,000 rpm.

Fine adjustments can be made at the cable (350)

1. Lock nut
2. Clutch cable lower adjuster
3. Clutch cable upper adjuster

CB 500

1. Screw the cable adjuster at the clutch lever all the way into the lever (increasing lever free-play).

2. Back off the locknut and turn the cable adjuster at the engine into the housing (increasing cable free-play to maximum).

3. Loosen the clutch adjuster lockbolt and, using a large screwdriver, turn the adjuster clockwise until a slight resistance is felt. At this point, back the adjuster out approximately ⅛ in. and tighten the lockbolt.

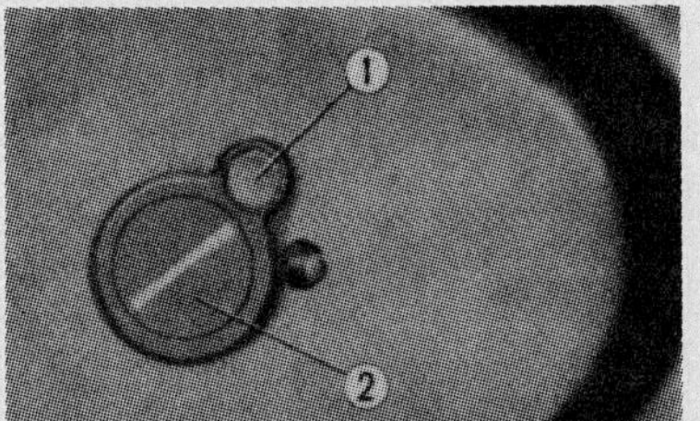

Clutch adjuster locknut (1) and adjuster screw (2). The grease fitting is shown immediately to the right of the adjuster screw.

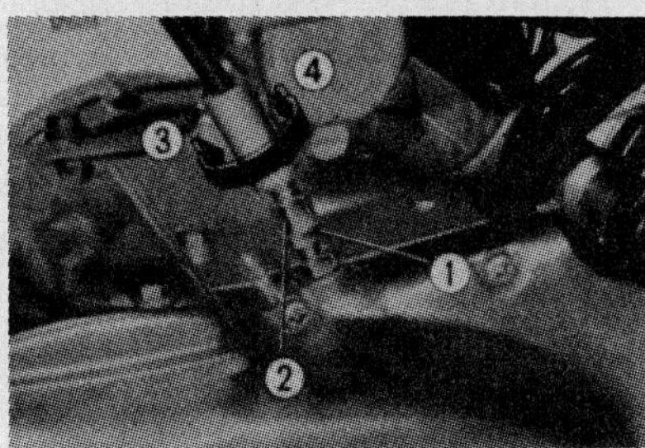

Cable adjuster at the clutch housing

1. Locknut
2. Adjuster
3. Turning clockwise increases play
4. Turning counterclockwise decreases play

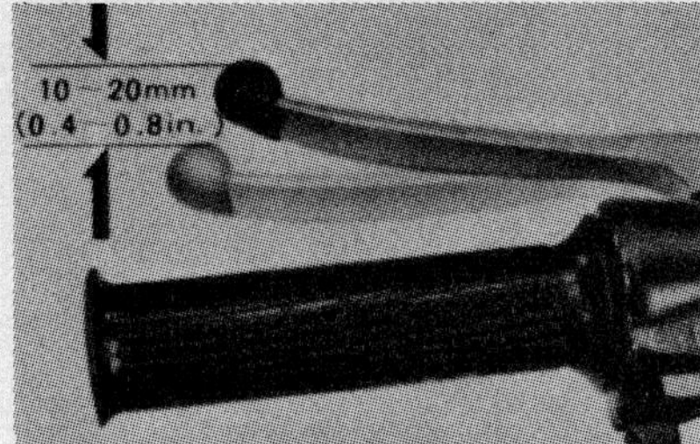

Final free-play at the lever end should be approximately ¾ in.

4. Turn the cable adjuster at the engine out until there is about 2–3 in. free-play at the clutch lever.

5. Remaining adjustment is made at the lever. Free-play at the end of the lever should be 0.4–0.8 in.

6. Lubricate the release mechanism, located at the cable adjuster, by giving it one or two squirts with the grease gun.

CB 750 AND CB 750K1—K3

1. Screw the cable adjuster at the clutch lever all the way into the lever (increasing lever free-play).

2. Back off the locknut and turn the cable adjuster at the engine into the housing (increasing cable free-play to maximum).

3. Remove the clutch housing cover plate and loosen the adjusting screw locknut.

4. Turn the adjusting screw clockwise until a slight resistance is felt, and then counterclockwise ¼–½ turn (90–180 deg). Tighten the locknut while holding the screw in position. Replace the cover plate.

5. Turn the cable adjuster at the engine until there is about 2–3 in. free-play at the end of the clutch lever.

6. Turn the adjuster at the clutch lever until 0.4–1.0 in. free-play remains at the end of the lever.

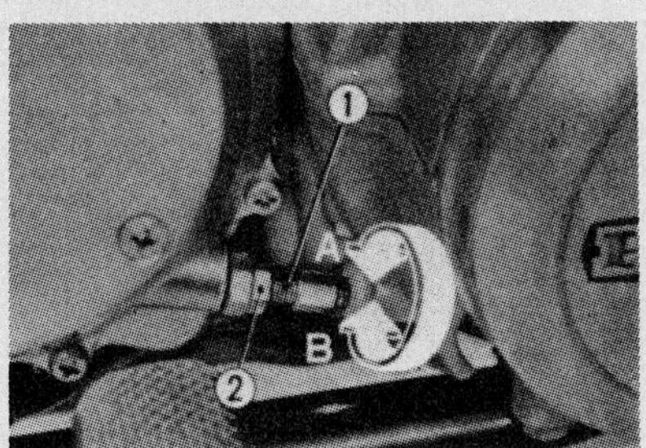

Cable adjuster at the clutch housing

1. Adjuster 2. Locknut

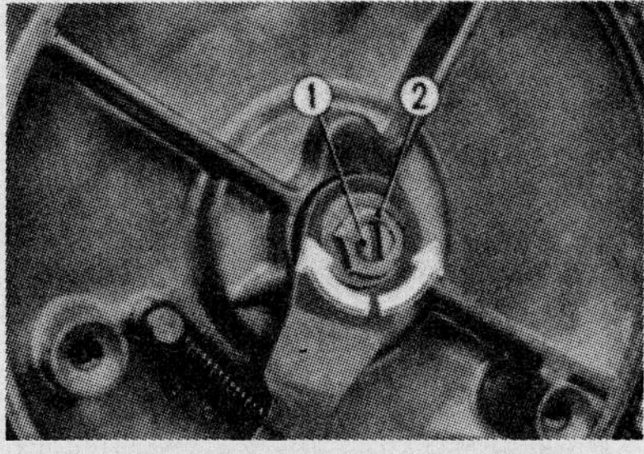

Clutch adjuster screw (1) and locknut (2) located under the cover plate

Fuel System (3,000 mi/6 mo)

CB 350 F, CB 500, CB 750, AND CB 750K1—K3

The fuel filter, located in the fuel tap, should be removed and cleaned at the prescribed intervals or whenever fuel feed problems are suspected. Simply turn the fuel tap to "stop" and unscrew the cup to gain access to the filter. Fuel flow at both the "on" and "reserve" positions can be checked at this time.

CAUTION: *Do not start the engine until any gasoline spilled has evaporated or has been wiped off the engine. Use a can or jar to catch gasoline when checking flow. If the tap allows any gasoline to pass while in the "stop" position, the tap should be repaired or replaced, or gasoline may leak into the crankcase and dilute the oil.*

Clean the filter screen and reinstall the cup and filter on the fuel tap. Use a new O-ring if necessary. Do not overtighten. Examine the fuel lines for leakage and for restriction caused by kinks or sharp bends. Check to see that the vent hole in the tank filler cap is not plugged to preclude the possibility of fuel starvation.

Front Suspension and Steering (6,000 mi/12 mo)

CB 500, CB 750, CB 750K1, AND CB 750K2

Steering Head Bearings

To check the bearings, place the bike on its center stand and swing the forks slowly through full steering travel. Movement should be smooth, light, and free from any binding. Check for play in the bearings by grabbing the bottom of the forks and trying to move them back and forth in line with the motorcycle. Play can be removed by tightening the steering head main nut. *Tighten no more than necessary to eliminate play.* If steering movement remains unsatisfactory the bearings should be replaced. Refer to the "Chassis" section.

Fork Oil

Remove the small drain plug at the bottom of each leg and work the suspension until all the oil has been expelled. Replace the drain plugs. Remove the top filler plugs and fill each leg with 4.-202/125 cc (350), 5.4 oz/160 cc. (500) or 7.0–7.3 oz/220–230cc (750) of SAE 10W-30 engine oil or special fork oil (available from most dealers).

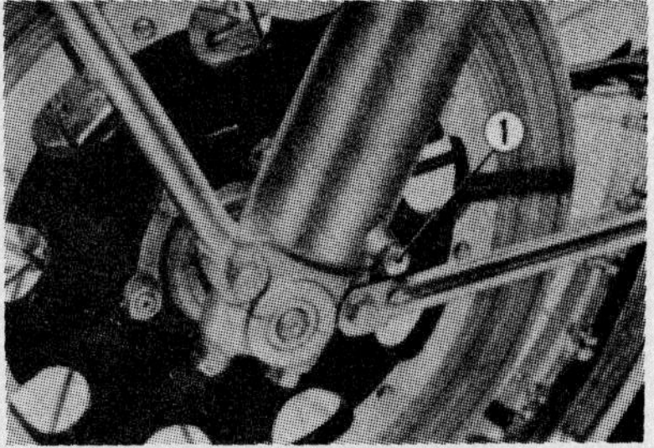

Fork drain plug (1)

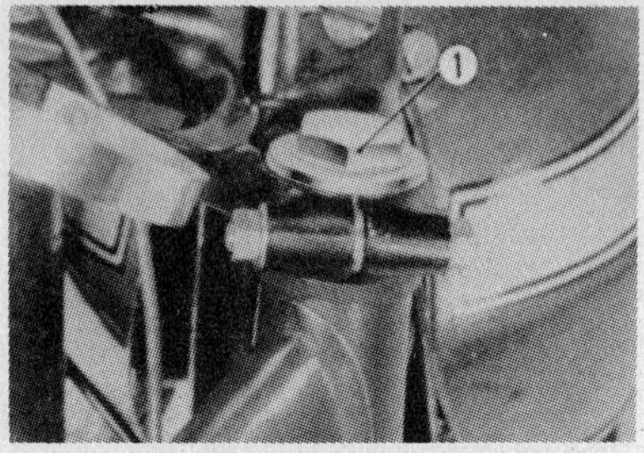

Filler plug (1)

NOTE: *Fork oil is not available in multi-viscosity form and viscosity selection must be made relative to riding and temperature conditions. Generally, SAE 30 is acceptable for summer and SAE 20 is acceptable for winter riding.*

After the oil has been poured into the forks, work them up and down slowly a few times to expel any air in the hydraulic passages before replacing the filler caps.

Rear Suspension (3,000 mi/6 mo)

CB 350 F, CB 500, CB 750, AND CB 750K1—K3

Lubricate the swing arm pivot grease fittings using a high-pressure grease gun. Wipe off any excess grease. There should be absolutely no side-play and the swing arm must not be bent or weakened from cracked welds, or else handling (especially at high speed) will become quite erratic and dangerous.

Fork pivot grease fittings (1). Inset shows right side fitting.

Brakes (3,000 mi/6 mo)

CB 350 F, CB 500, CB 750, AND CB 750K1—K3

Front Brake

Replace both brake pads on the 350, 500, or 750K2—K3when either one has worn to the red wear indicator groove. On the 750 and 750K1 pad wear is measured by checking the clearance between the front of the caliper and the brake disc using a feeler gauge. Replace both pads when clearance is less than 0.08 in./2.0 mm. Brake squeal can usually be eliminated by careful attention to pad alignment. Refer to the chassis section.

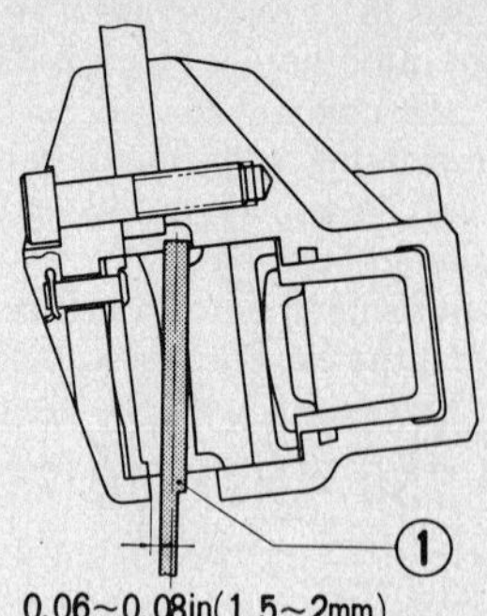

Brake pads on the 750 models must be replaced when the clearance between the disc (1) and caliper is less than 0.08 in.

Examine the hydraulic lines for leaks and damage. Check the operation of the brake and if the lever feels spongy or lever travel is excessive, bleed the hydraulic system. Use only brake fluid conforming to SAE specification J1703. Refer to the "Chassis" chapter.

Rear Brake

Rear brake lining wear can be determined by observing the angle formed by the brake operating lever and rod (at the brake drum) while the brake is applied. When the lever and rod move past perpendicular as the brake is applied, the brake shoes should be replaced. The brake should be adjusted so that there is approximately 1.0 in./25 mm free-play at the end of the pedal. Adjustment is made by turning the eccentric nut at the end of the operating rod. Make sure that the nut is seated properly on the lever and readjust the brake light switch if necessary. Examine the following components: brake pedal, brake operating rod, operating lever, backing plate, and torque link.

Final Drive

CB 350 F, CB 500, CB 750 AND CB 750K1—K3

Chain Adjustment

To check chain adjustment, place the bike on the center stand and move the chain up and down at the midway point on either run. If total movement exceeds 1.5 in., the chain is too loose and must be adjusted. The procedure is as follows:

1. Remove the rear axle nut cotter pin and loosen the nut until it can be turned by hand.
2. Loosen the locknuts on the two chain-adjuster bolts. To tighten the chain, turn the adjuster bolts in equally until total chain slack is within ½–¾ in. Turning the adjusters an unequal amount will affect wheel alignment. Scales are provided on both sides of the swing arm to facilitate adjustment. Make sure that they are both in the same position.
3. Tighten the adjuster bolt locknuts until they are just snug, while holding the bolts to keep them from turning. Do not overtighten.
4. Tighten the axle nut to 58–72 ft lbs and install a new cotter pin. Recheck chain movement.

NOTE: *A dry chain should be lubricated before adjustment so that the links will not bind and restrict chain movement, making it seem tighter than it really is. If tension varies alternately between too loose and too tight as the chain is rotated, remove it and inspect for excessive wear.*

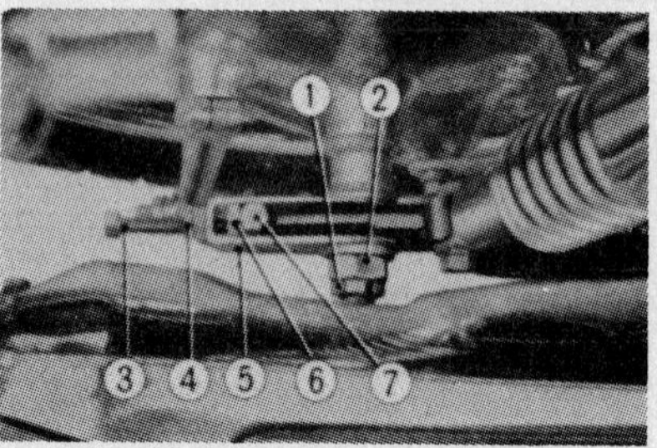

Rear axle nut and right-side chain adjuster assembly—shown is a 750
1. Cotter pin
2. Axle nut
3. Chain adjuster bolt
4. Locknut
5. Adjuster bracket
6. Swing arm end cap
7. End cap retaining bolt

ENGINE AND TRANSMISSION

ENGINE SERVICE

Engine Removal and Installation

NOTE: *The following components can be serviced or replaced without removing the engine from the frame: cylinder head and cylinder head components, cylinder barrel unit, pistons, cam chain tensioner, clutch, gearshift linkage, generator, and starter motor. Refer to the appropriate sections in this chapter for service procedures.*

CB 350 F

The accompanying illustration depicts the appropriate steps to be taken when removing the engine from the frame. Installation is in the reverse order of removal.

CB 500

1. Turn the fuel tap off, disconnect the fuel lines, and remove the tank.
2. Unscrew the drain plug and filter housing bolt, and drain the oil.
3. Unbolt and remove all four exhaust pipes and mufflers.

4. Remove the wires from the spark plugs and disconnect the ground cable at the battery terminal.

5. Remove the 5 mm screw and withdraw the tachometer cable from the tachometer drive at the cylinder head.

6. Raise the seat and remove the air filter element. Unscrew the three bolts and remove the air filter housing.

7. Disconnect the throttle cables from the throttle linkage at the carburetors.

8. Loosen the air filter intake clamp and intake manifold tube clamp at each carburetor. Remove the carburetors as a unit.

9. Disconnect the starter motor cable from the solenoid and the alternator output wire at the connector near the battery.

10. Remove the shift lever. Unbolt and remove the starter motor cover and left crankcase cover. Disconnect the clutch cable from the release mechanism.

Electrical leads to be disconnected

1. Starter cable
2. Solenoid
3. Connector

11. Remove the countershaft sprocket and drive chain. Disconnect the contact breaker point leads (yellow and blue) at the connectors.

12. Remove the engine mounting bolts and plates as illustrated. Raise the rear of the engine slightly and remove it from the right side of the frame.

Installation is in reverse order of removal. The following points should be noted:

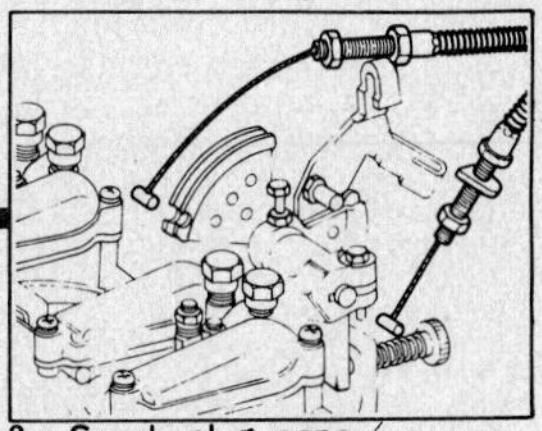

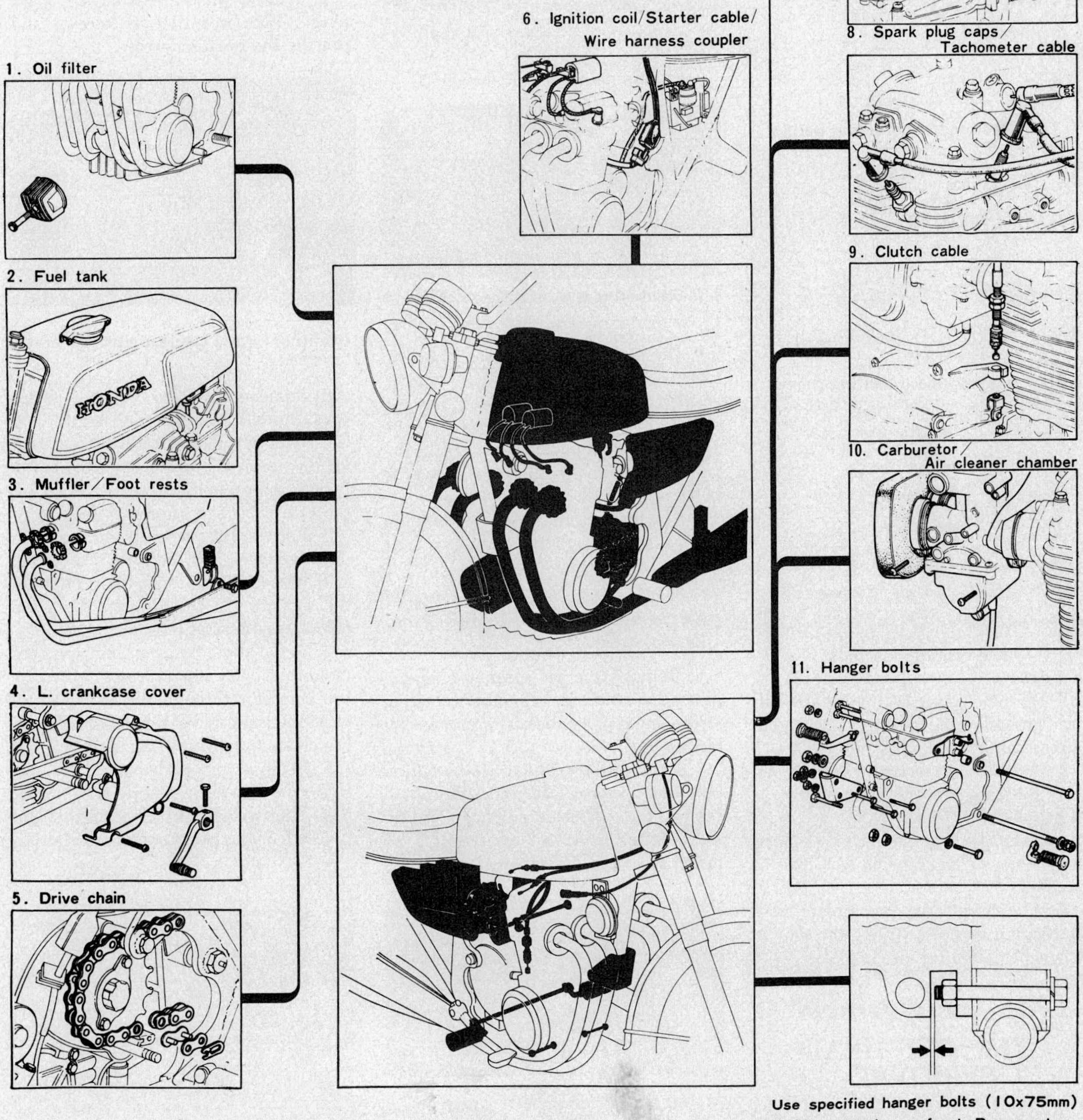

1. Oil filter
2. Fuel tank
3. Muffler/Foot rests
4. L. crankcase cover
5. Drive chain
6. Ignition coil/Starter cable/Wire harness coupler
7. Throttle cable
8. Spark plug caps/Tachometer cable
9. Clutch cable
10. Carburetor/Air cleaner chamber
11. Hanger bolts

Use specified hanger bolts (10x75mm) at lower crankcase front. Be sure to install spring washer

Engine removal sequence (350)

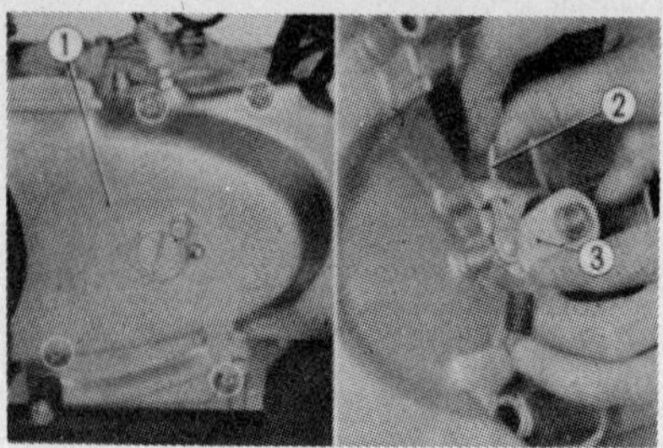

Disconnecting the clutch cable
1. Left crankcase cover
2. Clutch cable
3. Clutch release lever

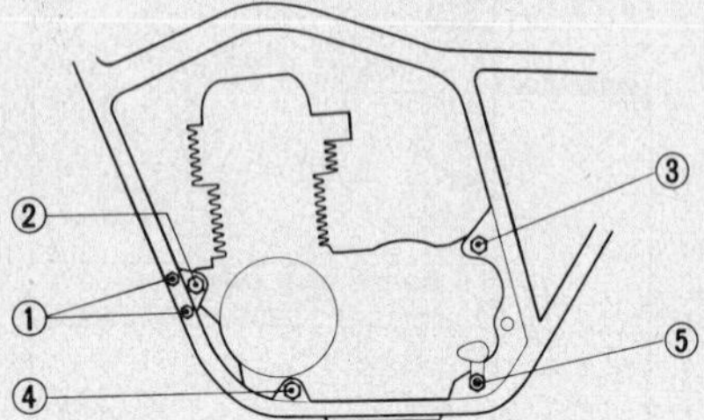

Left-side engine mounting points

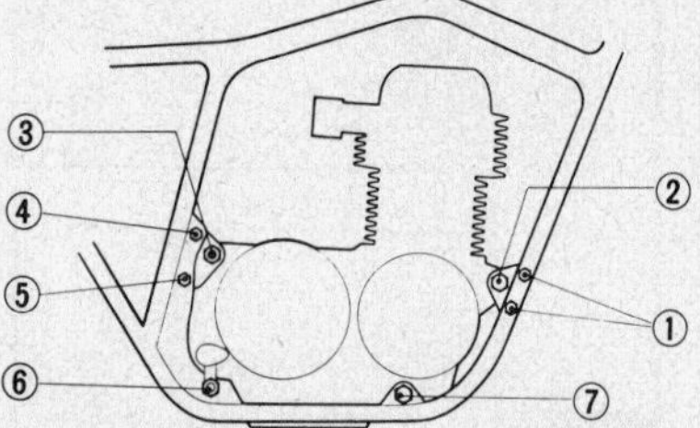

Right-side engine mounting points

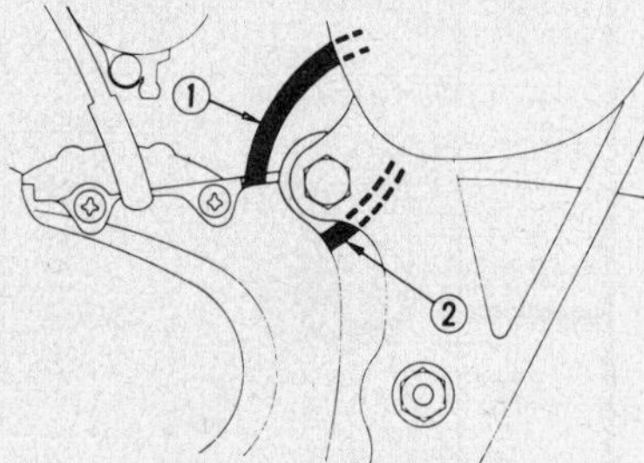

Cable routing positions

1. Do not neglect to connect the battery ground cable to the rear engine mount bolt as the bolt is installed.

2. Route the starter motor and alternator cables behind the frame tube, as shown.

3. Make sure that the muffler connecting clamps are in place on each pair of mufflers.

4. When installation is complete, refill the engine with oil. Adjust the clutch, drive chain, and carburetors.

Top End Overhaul

CYLINDER HEAD REMOVAL

CB 350 F

1. Remove the fuel tank, ignition coils, and breather cover, then disconnect the tachometer cable at the cylinder head.

2. Remove the eight tappet access caps, loosen the rocker arm adjusting screws, and remove the cylinder head cover. Remove the rocker arm shafts from the cover by removing the cap nuts and screwing a 10mm (1.25mm pitch) bolt into the shaft.

3. Remove the exhaust system, spark plugs, and cam chain tensioner holder, then remove the tensioner holder and slipper.

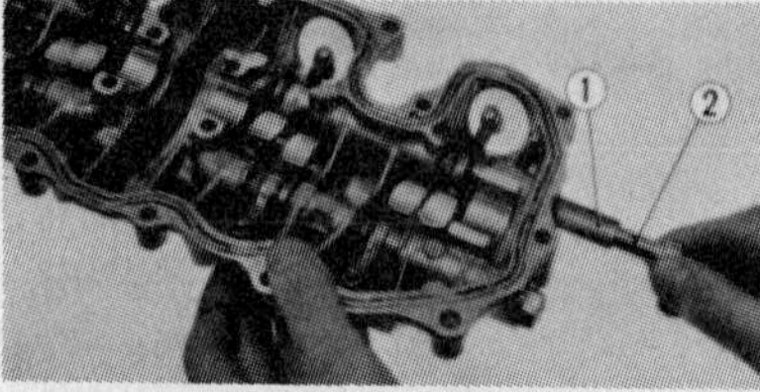

Removing the rocker arm shaft
1. Rocker arm shaft
2. 10 mm (pitch 1.25 mm) bolt

Removing the tensioner holder
1. Tensioner holder 2. 6 x 20 bolts

4. Remove the point cover, then rotate the crankshaft, by means of a suitable wrench on the special nut, until the one of the cam sprocket bolts is vertical to the cylinder head, and remove the bolt. Rotate the crankshaft 180° and remove the remaining sprocket bolt.

5. Lift the cam chain to avoid scratching the camshaft, then slip the camshaft out from the right.

NOTE: *Loop a piece of wire around the chain to prevent it from falling into the crankcase.*

6. Remove the air cleaner element, loosen the air cleaner chamber retaining screw, and remove the carburetor assembly.

7. Remove the cylinder head securing bolts in a crisscross pattern as illustrated, remove the cam chain guide, and lift off the cylinder head, striking it with a soft mallet to loosen it if necessary.

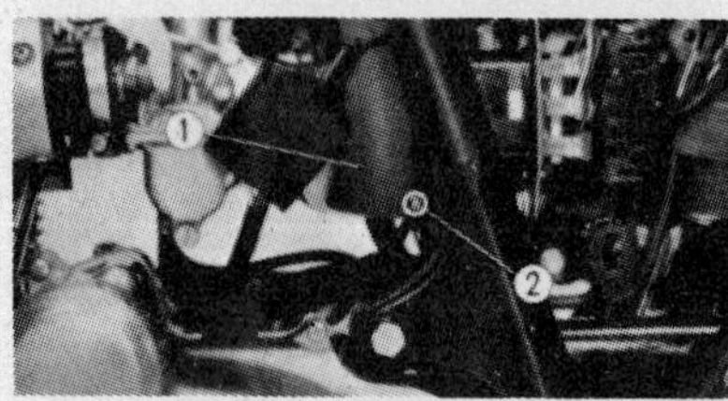

Air cleaner chamber location
1. Air filter chamber
2. Chamber retaining screw

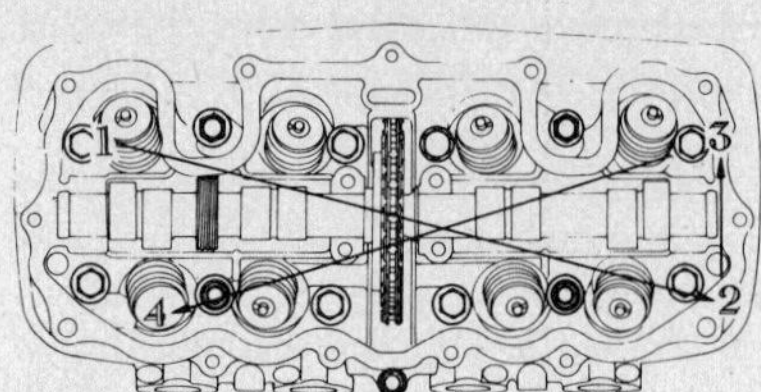

Head bolt removal and installation sequence

CB 500

1. Turn the fuel tap off and disconnect the fuel lines. Remove the fuel tank.

2. Unbolt and remove all four exhaust pipes and mufflers.

3. Disconnect the tachometer cable from the tachometer drive at the cylinder head.

4. Remove the wires from the spark plugs. Take out the six screws and remove the breather cover.

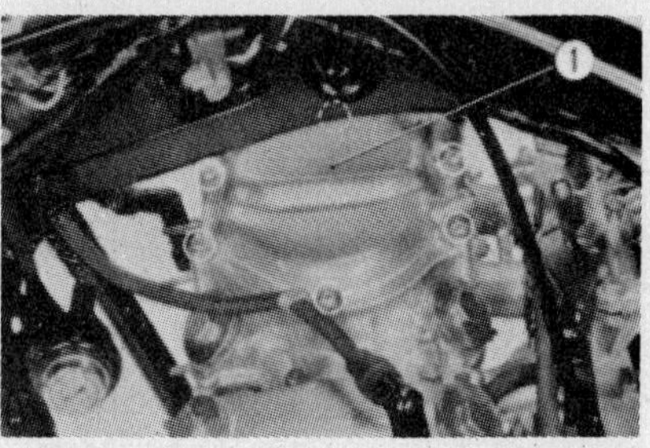

Breather cover (1) and mounting screws (circled)

5. Remove the valve adjuster access caps, the left and right side-covers, and the cover set plate. Gradually and uniformly (to prevent distortion) loosen the twelve screws and six bolts that secure the camshaft cover. Remove the cover.

6. Loosen the locknut on the cam chain adjuster and turn the screw fully clockwise (about ¼ turn), then retighten the locknut. In this position the cam chain is relieved of tension.

7. Remove the two camshaft sprocket mounting bolts and carefully withdraw the camshaft through the sprocket toward the right side of the engine. Lift off the chain and remove the sprocket.

8. Remove the carburetors and unscrew the cam chain tensioner mounting bolt. The twelve cylinder head nuts and two flange bolts can now be removed and

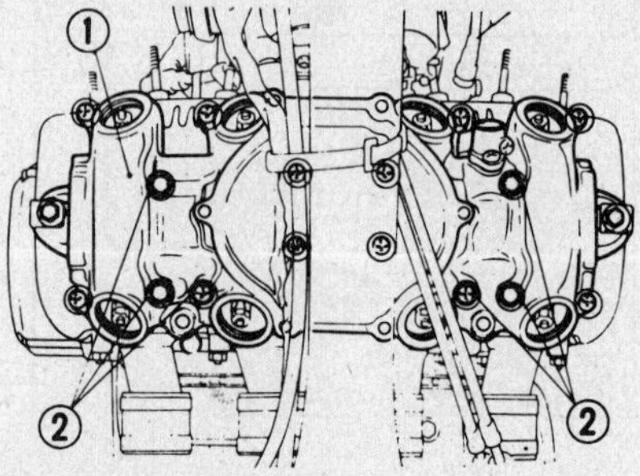

Cam cover
1. Cam cover 2. Copper washers

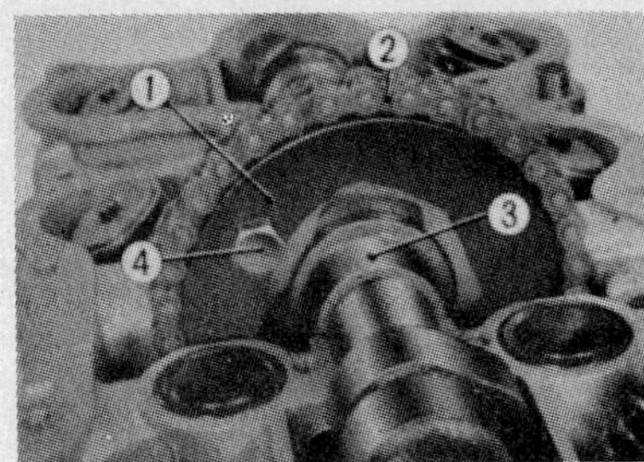

Removing the cam sprocket and shaft

1. Sprocket
2. Cam chain
3. Camshaft
4. Sprocket mounting bolt

Cylinder head (1) and cylinder head nuts (circled). The two flange bolts are circled with a broken line.

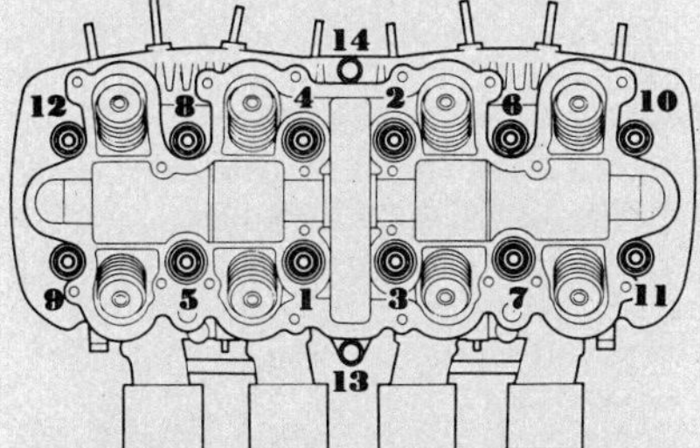

Cylinder head tightening sequence

the cylinder head can be lifted off the engine. It is important that the bolts and nuts are loosened gradually and evenly in reverse order of the tightening sequence.

CYLINDER BARREL AND PISTON REMOVAL

CB 350 F and CB 500

1. After the cylinder head has been removed, raise the cam chain guide slightly, rotate it ¼ turn, and lift it out. Take care not to drop the cam chain.

2. Unscrew the locknut on the cam chain adjuster, raise the cylinder barrel unit about one inch, and lift out the chain tensioner assembly.

NOTE: *If the cylinder cannot be raised easily, tap the sides lightly with a rubber mallet or pry with a screwdriver at the groove in the base of the cylinder to break it loose.*

3. The cylinder can be lifted away after the tensioner is removed. Do not allow the pistons and connecting rods to fall to one side and be damaged by the case or studs as the cylinder is withdrawn.

The cylinder barrel (1) can be broken free by prying carefully at the groove in the base (2)

4. Remove the wrist pin circlips from the pistons.

CAUTION: *Do not allow the circlips to fall into the crankcase. To avoid having to split the cases to retrieve a clip, cover the crankcase openings with a cloth.*

5. Remove the wrist pins from the pistons. You should be able to push them out by hand. If the need arises, the pins can be tapped out using a soft metal drift. Mark the pistons, inside the skirt, so they can be reinstalled in their original bores.

Component Inspection and Service

CAMSHAFT

Examine the camshaft bearing journals, bearing caps, and bearing surfaces in the cylinder head for scoring and excessive wear. If the journals and bearings are not in perfect condition they should be replaced.

Measure cam lobe height and replace the camshaft if any of the intake or exhaust lobes are less than 1.1024 in. (28.0 mm) on the 350, or if on the 500, any intake lobes are less than 1.3720 in. (34.85 mm) or if any exhaust lobes are less than 1.3563 in. (34.45 mm). The cam lobes must not be scored or pitted in any way.

Check camshaft runout, as illustrated, using a dial indicator. Maximum acceptable runout is 0.004 in. (0.1 mm). Do not attempt to straighten a bent camshaft. (Runout equals one-half the dial indicator reading.)

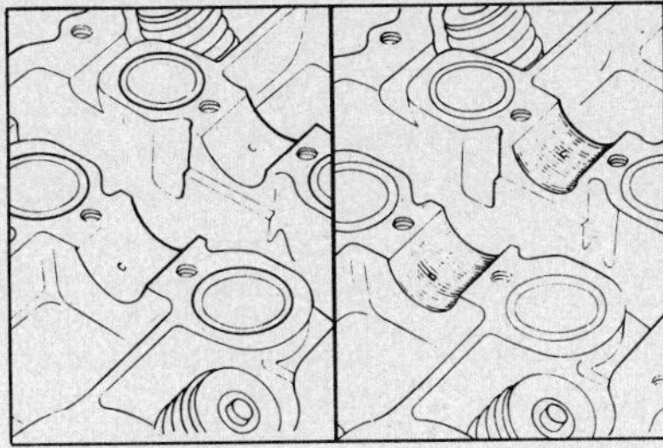

Look for scored or damaged camshaft bearing surfaces, as shown on the right. Surfaces should be smooth and clean, as are those on the left.

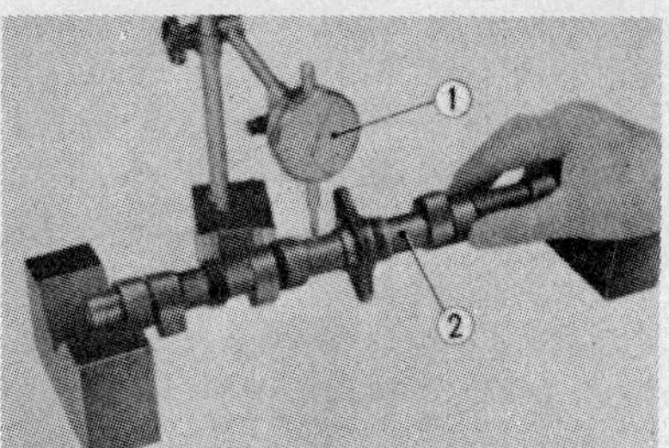

Checking camshaft runout

1. Dial indicator 2. Camshaft

VALVE ROCKER ASSEMBLY

There should be no detectable play of the rocker arms on the rocker arm shaft. To remove the shaft for inspection or replacement, screw a 6 mm bolt into the end of the shaft and pull it out of the camshaft cover.

CYLINDER HEAD AND VALVES

Compress the valve springs and remove the collars, seals, retainers, and valves. Remove the valve guide cap from the guide. To check valve guide and stem wear, insert the valve into the guide and measure clearance in the X and Y directions, as shown, with a dial indicator. If, on the 350, the valve-to-guide clearance in either direction exceeds 0.0118 in. (0.3 mm) for either the intake or exhaust valves, or if on the 500 clearance in either direction exceeds 0.0031 in. (0.080 mm) (intake valves) or 0.0039 in. (0.10 mm) (exhaust valves), the valve and guide should be replaced as a set. If the guides are to be replaced, they can be driven out of, and installed into, the head without the need for heat application. After installation, the guides should be finish-reamed to fit the matching valve stem. Standard inside diameter for both intake and exhaust valve guides is 0.2153–0.-2157 in. (5.475–5.485 mm).

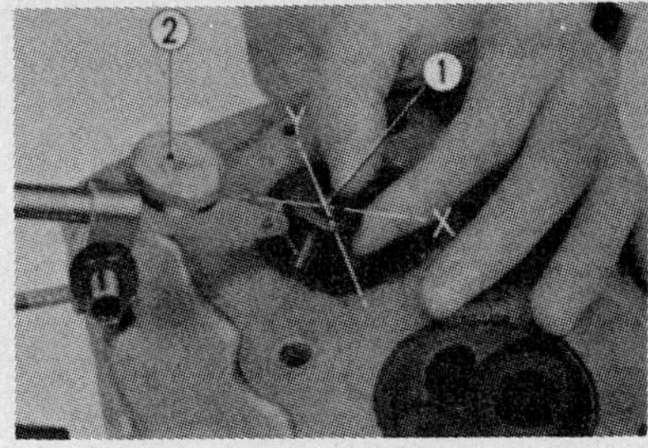

Checking valve stem and guide wear

1. Valve 2. Dial indicator

If the valve seat is burnt, worn, or damaged in any way, it should be recut. Valve seat angle is 45°. Seat width should be within 0.039–0.059 in. (1.0–1.5 mm) on all models except the 350, whose seat width should be within 0.03–0.06 in. (0.7–1.5 mm). If the valve stem is suspected of being bent or the valve face out of round, check the runout with a dial indicator at

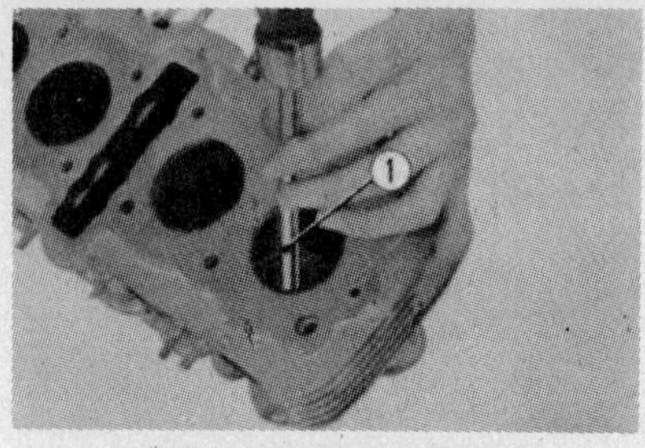

Valve guides can be driven out and installed using a suitably sized drift (1) or Honda tool no. 07031-30011

the valve face. Place the valve in a V-block and slowly rotate the valve while observing the dial indicator. If runout exceeds 0.002 in. (0.05 mm), the valve should be replaced. (Runout is one-half the dial indicator reading.)

NOTE: *Do not attempt to reface the valves or refinish the valve stem ends, as these surfaces have a thin stellite facing that will be destroyed if cut.*

Carefully scrape carbon deposits from the combustion chambers and thoroughly clean the cylinder head. Before the valves are installed, whether they are the original ones or new, they should be lapped into their seats so that a perfect seal will be obtained.

It is a good idea at this time to replace the valve springs as a matter of course. However, if the height of the original springs on the 350 is not less than 1.06 in. (27.0 mm) (inner springs) or 1.28 in. (32.5 mm) (outer springs), or, on the 500, is not less than 1.35 in. (34.5 mm) (inner springs) or 1.53 in. (39 mm) (outer springs), they can be reused if desired.

NOTE: *Modified seals are used from engine number CB 500E-1002378. These new seals, along with the redesigned oil control rings, will cure excessive oil consumption experienced on some early models.*

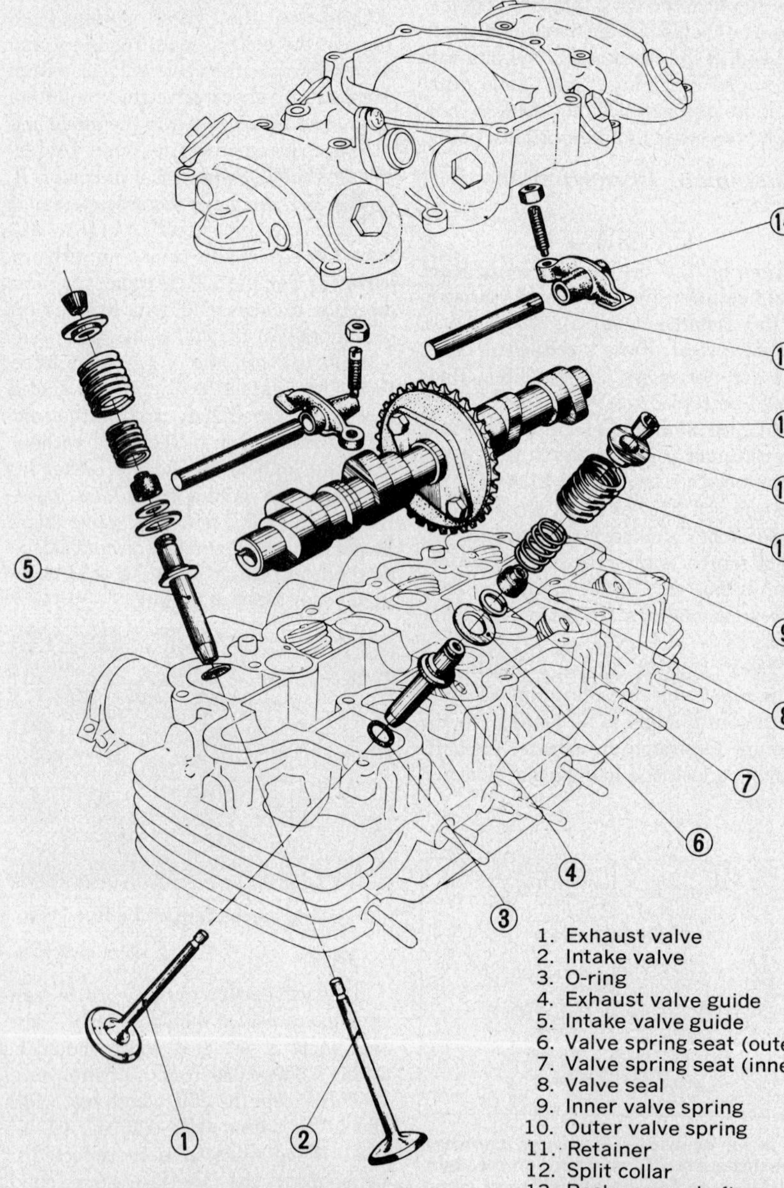

1. Exhaust valve
2. Intake valve
3. O-ring
4. Exhaust valve guide
5. Intake valve guide
6. Valve spring seat (outer)
7. Valve spring seat (inner)
8. Valve seal
9. Inner valve spring
10. Outer valve spring
11. Retainer
12. Split collar
13. Rocker arm shaft
14. Rocker arm

Valve train components

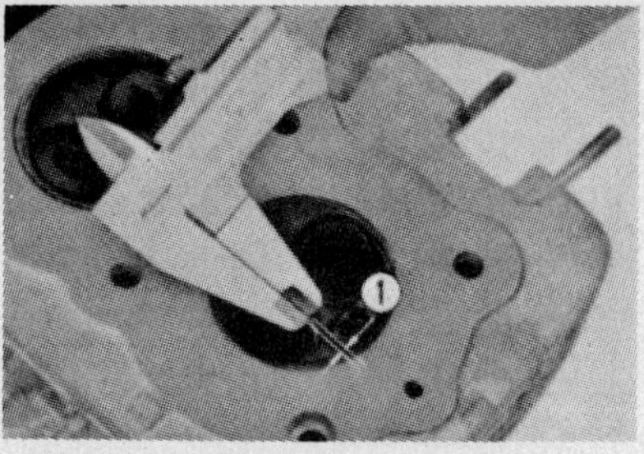

Valve seat width (1) can be measured with a vernier caliper

Place a straightedge on the cylinder head surface and measure the clearance with a feeler gauge at several points to determine head warpage or distortion. If measured clearance at any point exceeds 0.011 in. (0.3 mm), the head surface should be lapped. Spread some lapping compound or a large sheet of no. 400 emery paper on a flat surface such as a glass plate. If emery paper is used, it should be wetted with water or oil. Place the head on the plate and move it lightly and evenly from side to side in a figure-eight pattern. Unless the head is badly warped, this method will usually prove quite satisfactory in preventing head gasket sealing problems. Check the surface with the straightedge again after a smooth, even finish is obtained. Clean the head thoroughly after the lapping operation is complete. Lubricate the valve stems with fresh oil and install the valves as removed, using new seals.

Checking for cylinder head warpage
1. Straightedge 2. Feeler gauge

CYLINDER BORE AND PISTONS

Measure the cylinder bore diameter at the top, center, and bottom in both the X and Y directions as shown. Reboring will be necessary if any of the measurements exceeds the specifications at the end of this section. The cylinders should be honed if new rings are to be used.

Measure the diameter of the piston skirt, perpendicular to the wrist pin. Pistons should be replaced when the diameter is less than the specified limits. Pistons that are scored or damaged in any way should not be reused. The diameter of the wrist pin hole must not exceed the specified limits.

Measure cylinder diameter in both directions with an inside micrometer or dial indicator (1)

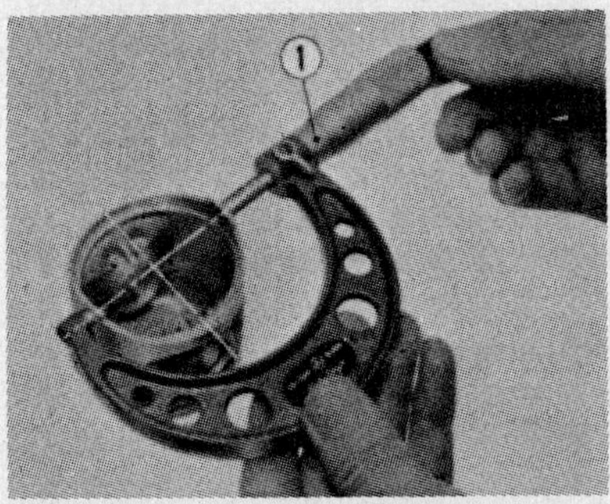
Use a micrometer (1) to measure the piston diameter perpendicular to the wrist pin

If the original pistons are to be reused, remove the rings and clean the grooves using a piece of one of the old rings. Remove the carbon deposit from the piston tops. Roll the new rings around the grooves before installing them to ensure that there is sufficient clearance. The rings should roll smoothly without binding. Install the rings on the pistons using a ring expander to avoid breaking them. Make sure that the mark on the rings is facing up.

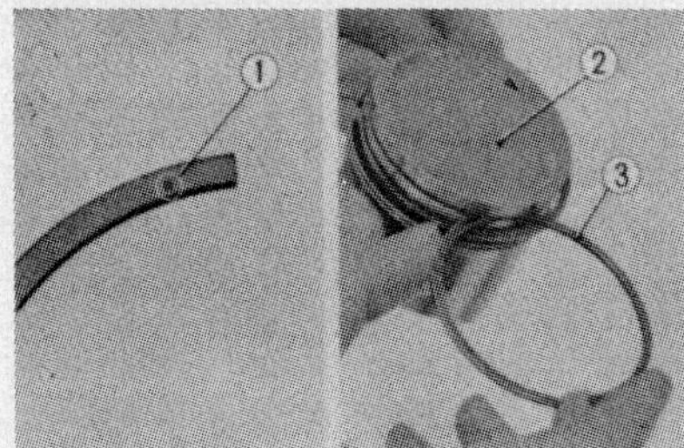
Marks on the rings (1) should face up. Roll the rings (3) around the grooves in the pistons (2) to check for sufficient clearance.

NOTE: *Three-piece oil rings are used from engine number CB 500E-1002378, in an effort to eliminate excessive oil consumption experienced on some earlier models. Old and new-type oil rings are interchangeable.*

PISTON AND CYLINDER BARREL INSTALLATION

Install the pistons on the connecting rods so that the mark on the piston crown points toward the front (exhaust side). Be sure to use new wrist pin circlips. Stagger the rings so that the gaps are 120° apart and not in line with or perpendicular to the piston boss axis. Install the cylinder base gasket, the two dowel pins (orifice valve), and two O-rings on the top of the crankcase.

NOTE: *Blow compressed air through the dowel pin holes to make sure they are not clogged before installing the pins.*

Rotate the engine until no. 2 and 3 pistons are at top dead center and place a piston base (Honda part number 07033-33301 for the 350, or, for the 500, 07033-55102) under the pistons to hold them in position. (A block of wood cut to suitable size works just as well). Compress the rings on no. 2 and 3 pistons (after oiling them liberally) and slide the cylinder down over them. Rotate the engine until no. 1 and 4 pistons contact the base of the cylinder (taking care not to pull no. 2 and 3 pistons out of their bores), compress the rings, and slide the cylinder against the crankcase, raise the cam chain through the center of the cylinder and put a screwdriver through the center of it to keep it from dropping down. Also, with the cylinder about one in. from the crankcase, install the cam chain tensioner in the cylinder. Hold the tensioner down by hand and install the O-ring and washer, and tighten the locknut. Install the cam chain guide into the cylinder as illustrated.

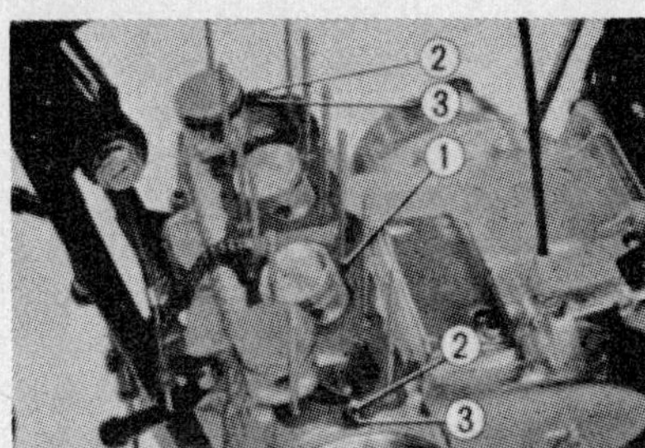
Make sure the dowel pins and O-rings are in position

1. Cylinder gasket
2. Dowel pins
3. O-rings

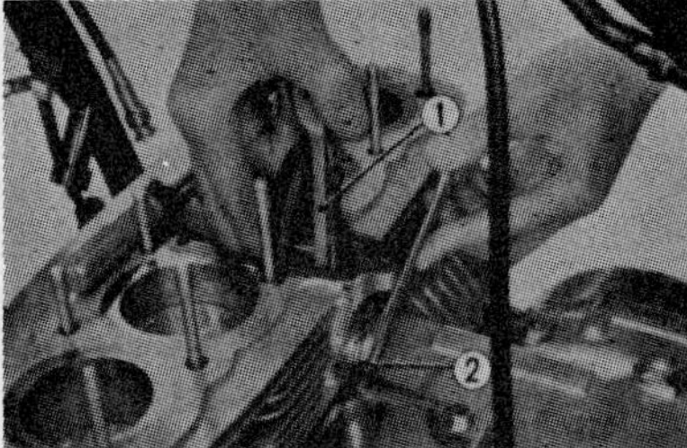
Securing the cam chain tensioner

1. Cam chain tensioner
2. Locknut

NOTE: *If the cylinder studs are to be replaced, a special stud wrench (Honda part number 07779-99902) should be used because the studs are secured with thread-locking compound. When installing new studs, thoroughly clean the stud holes, apply thread-locking compound, and torque the studs to 15-16 ft lbs.*

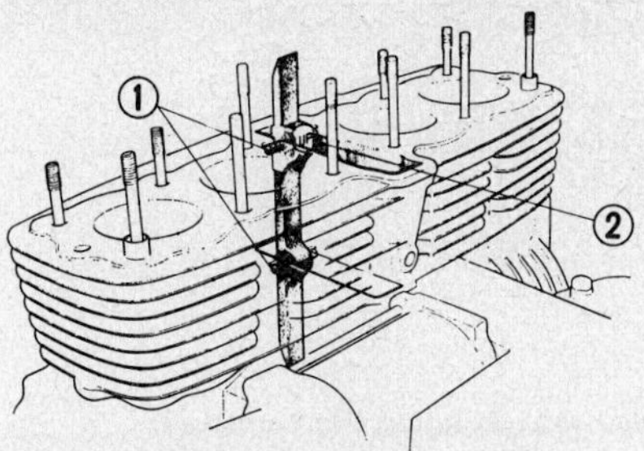
Installing the cam chain guide

1. Guide pins
2. "Up" mark

CYLINDER HEAD INSTALLATION

Install the cylinder head gasket, two dowel pins, and two O-rings on the cylinder. Mount the cylinder head on the cylinder while pulling the cam chain through the center of the head. Hold the chain from dropping down using a screwdriver as before. Tighten the head nuts gradually, in the sequence shown, to a final torque value of 14.5-16.5 ft lbs. After the nuts have been properly torqued, install and tighten the two 6 mm flange bolts (500).

CAUTION: *Take care not to drop any hardware into the crankcase.*

Make sure the dowel pins and O-rings are in position

1. Head gasket
2. Dowel pins
3. O-rings

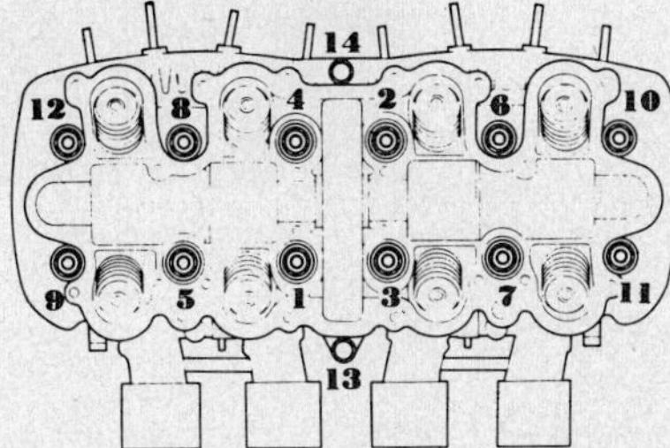

Cylinder head tightening sequence

Hold the cam chain and cam chain sprocket together and install the camshaft through them from the right side of the engine. To set the valve timing properly, remove the ignition points cover and rotate the engine clockwise until the

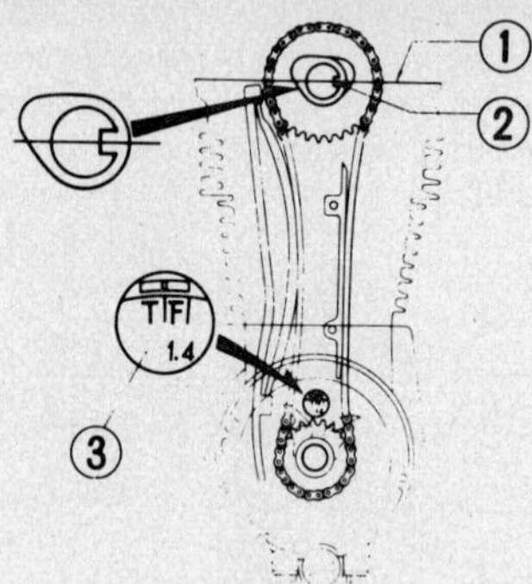

Aligning the camshaft

1. Cylinder head flange surface
2. Cutout notch
3. Ignition advance unit marks

T (1.4) mark on the ignition advance unit aligns with the timing mark. Turn the camshaft until the center of the notch on the right end of the shaft is aligned with the cylinder head flange surface. Place the chain over the sprocket, and bolt the sprocket onto the camshaft.

Install the carburetor assembly on the head. Install the two dowel pins and six rubber seals, as shown. Install the camshaft cover and torque the bolts to 5.-1–8.0 ft lbs for the 350, or, for the 500, 6.0–8.5 ft lbs. (Maximum torque variance between all bolts must not exceed 1.4 ft lbs.) Do not forget the copper washers. Insert a finger into the cam cover to check the contact of the valve adjuster screw on the valve stem end. (See illustration.) Install the small, cam cover, side set-plate with the chrome washer on top and the aluminum washer on the bottom. Install O-rings on the dowel pins of the left and right side covers and mount them on the head. Install the breather cover.

Make sure the dowel pins and rubber seals are in position

1. Dowel pins
2. Rubber seals

NOTE: *Spark plug wire clips should face forward on both sides.*

Install the exhaust system and connect the tachometer cable. Perform a complete engine tune-up, paying special attention to valve and cam chain adjustments. The valves and cam chain should be checked again after approximately 500 miles have been covered. It is also a good idea to change the oil after the tune-up has been completed and again at the 500 mile check.

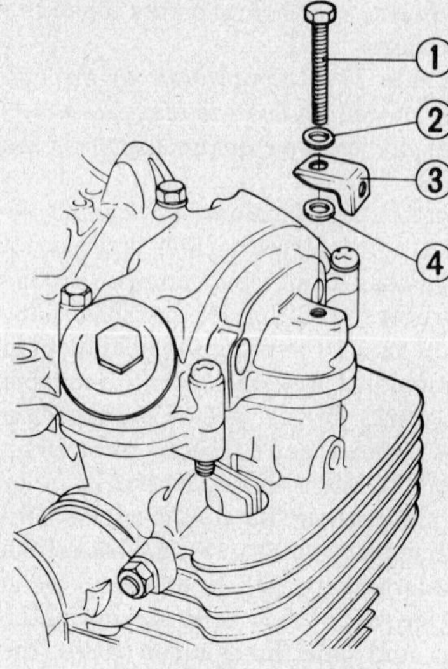

Securing the cam cover

1. Bolt
2. Chrome washer
3. Side cover set plate
4. Aluminum washer

Bottom End Overhaul

DISASSEMBLY

CB 350 F

1. Drain the oil from the sump and oil filter, then remove the engine from the frame as directed in the "Engine Removal and Installation" section.
2. Disassemble the top end as described in the "Top End Overhaul" section.
3. Remove the alternator rotor using a suitable rotor puller (Honda part number 07011–33301).
4. Remove the right crankcase cover and gearshift spindle, then disassemble the positive stopper, gearshift drum stopper, and the neutral stopper arm.
5. Remove the contact breaker and automatic advance mechanism.
6. Invert the engine and remove the oil pan and oil pump assembly.
7. Remove the 12mm bolt from the end of the primary shaft, slide the secondary drive gear off of the primary shaft, then slip the primary shaft out to the right.
8. Remove the internal circlip (52mm), the ball bearing, and the 25 mm collar as illustrated.
9. Evenly loosen the bolts from the lower crankcase, working in a criss-cross

The valve tappet adjusting screw is not properly contacting the valve.

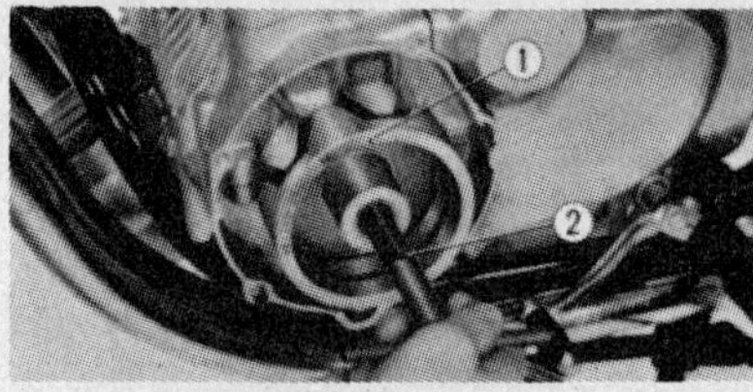

Removing the alternator rotor

1. Alternator rotor
2. Rotor puller

Removing the gearshift spindle (1)

Removing the stoppers

1. Positive stopper
2. Gear shift drum stopper
3. Neutral stopper arm

Primary shaft securing bolt

1. 12 mm bolt
2. Primary shaft lock washer
3. Secondary drive gear

Removing the primary shaft (1)

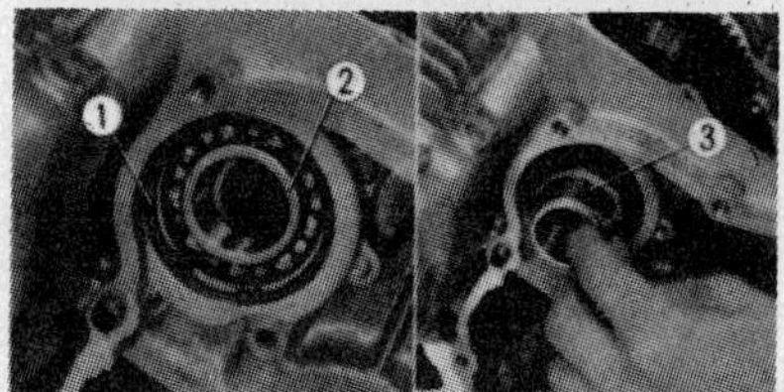
Removing the bearing and collar

1. 52 mm internal circlip
2. Ball bearing
3. Collar

pattern from the inside out, then gently tap the cases with a soft mallet to separate them.

10. Remove the transmission and shifter components if necessary. The gear assemblies should be removed simultaneously.

CB 500

1. Remove the engine from the frame and remove the cylinder head, cylinder barrel, and pistons as described in the preceding section on top end overhaul.
2. Take off the alternator cover and remove the rotor using, if possible, a rotor puller (Honda part number 07011–21601).

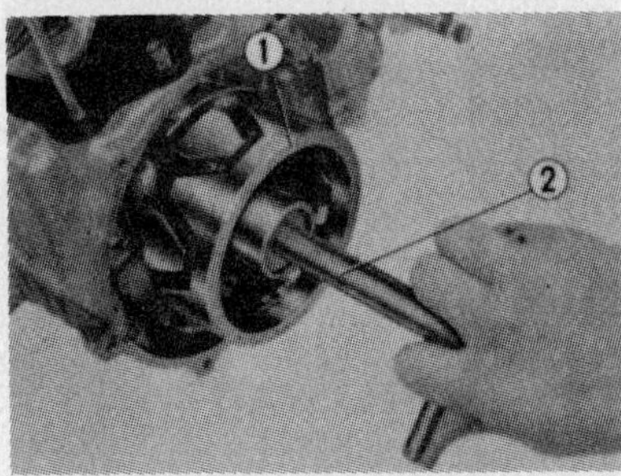
Removing the alternator rotor

1. Alternator rotor
2. Rotor puller

3. Remove the ignition points cover and unscrew the 6 mm bolt at the end of the breaker cam. Remove the hexagonal washer. Take out the three phillips head screws and remove the complete breaker plate assembly.
4. Remove the clutch unit as described under "Clutch Service" in this section.
5. Remove the shift lever. Withdraw the shift linkage from the right side of the engine while holding the shift arm down.
6. Take off the starter cover and remove the starter motor.
7. Place the engine upside down, preferably on a large piece of cardboard. Unscrew the ten bolts, and remove the oil pan and oil pump pick-up.
8. Unscrew the ten 8 mm lower crankcase bolts gradually, in reverse order of the tightening sequence. Remove the thirteen 6 mm bolts from the lower crankcase.
9. Turn the engine over again so that it is resting on the lower crankcase in its normal position and remove the three 8 mm and three 6 mm bolts.
10. Separate the crankcase halves by tapping with a rubber mallet and lifting the upper crankcase away. Lift the transmission mainshaft and countershaft assemblies out of the case. Do not lose the bearing set rings.

Tightening the sequence of the 8 mm lower crankcase bolts

6 mm crankcase bolts (circled)

Upper crankcase mounting bolts

1. 6 mm bolts
2. 8 mm bolts

NOTE: *Be very careful not to mar the mating surfaces of the crankcase halves during handling or when removing old gasket cement.*

11. Unscrew the two bolts and remove the transmission primary shaft bearing set plate. Remove the circlip and pull out the primary shaft using tool number 07009–32301 or a suitable gear puller. Lift out the starter clutch and primary sprocket assembly.

Primary shaft bearing set plate (1)

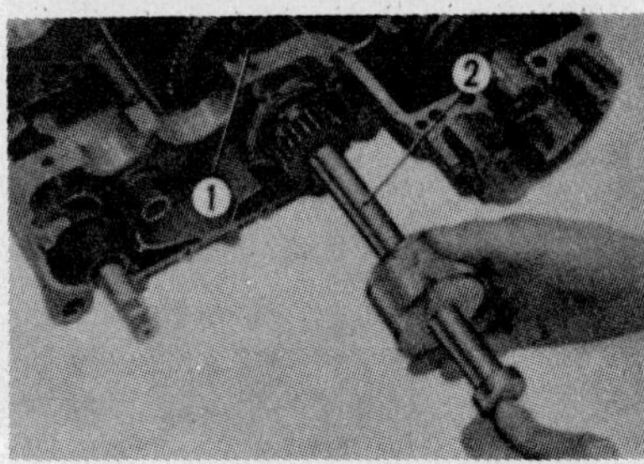
Removing the primary shaft

1. Primary shaft
2. Shaft puller

12. Lift out the crankshaft. Unbolt the connecting rod bearing caps, remove the rods, and slip the cam and primary chains off the crankshaft. Mark or tag the rods so they may be installed in their original positions.

CRANKSHAFT INSPECTION

CB 350 F and CB 500

Check the crankshaft runout by placing the ends of the crankshaft in V-blocks and rotating it while taking a reading with a dial indicator at the center journal. Replace the crankshaft if runout exceeds 0.0019 in. (0.05 mm). (Runout equals one-half the dial indicator reading.)

A dial indicator (1) is used to measure crankshaft runout at the center journal (2)

MAIN BEARINGS

CB 350 F and CB 500

Inspect the bearing journals for scoring and damage. Measure the journal diameter in several places to check for ovality and taper. Maximum acceptable variation of journal diameter is 0.002 in. (0.05 mm).

Journal wear can be checked using a material such as plastigauge. Cut strips of plastigauge to fit across each bearing, install the crankshaft and lower crankcase, and torque the ten 8 mm lower crankcase bolts in the correct sequence to 15 ft lbs. Do not turn the crankshaft, and measure the plastigauge as shown with the scale provided. If clearance exceeds 0.0032 in. (0.08 mm), the bearings should be replaced. Bearings that are damaged in any way should not be reused.

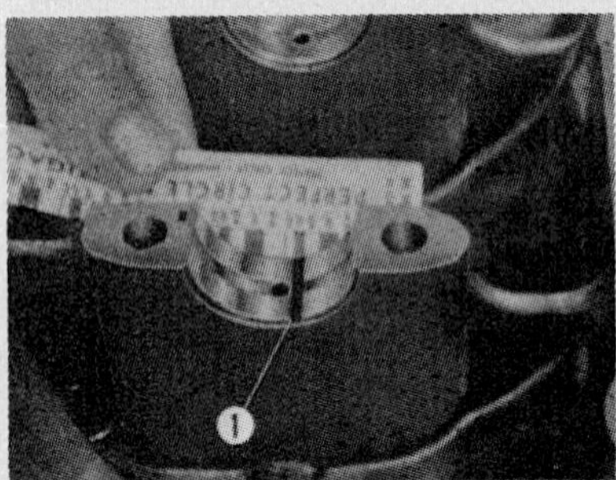

Plastigauge® strip

CODE LETTER SIZE CHART (BEARING SEAT DIAMETER)

Seat Diameter	Code
1.4173-1.4176 in./ 36.000-36.008 mm	A
1.4176-1.4179 in./ 36.008-36.016 mm	B
1.4179-1.4182 in./ 36.016-36.024 mm	C

Main Bearing Selection

If the main bearings are to be replaced, two measurements must be made: inside diameter of the bearing seats and crankshaft journal diameter. To check bearing seat diameter, assemble the upper and lower crankcases with the ten bolts, as described above. Measure the seats with an inside dial indicator in the vertical direction and select from the following code letters according to measurements obtained for each bearing seat.

Next, measure the crankshaft bearing journal diameters with a micrometer and select one of the following two code numbers for each journal.

Use the codes obtained to pick out the proper bearings from the bearing selection chart.

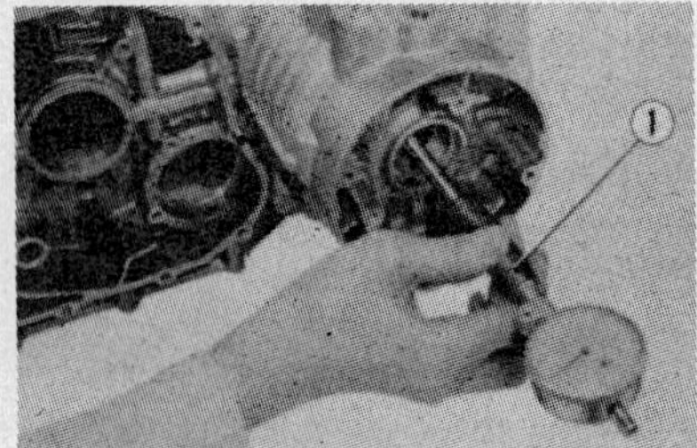

Measuring bearing seat diameter with a dial indicator and adapter (1)

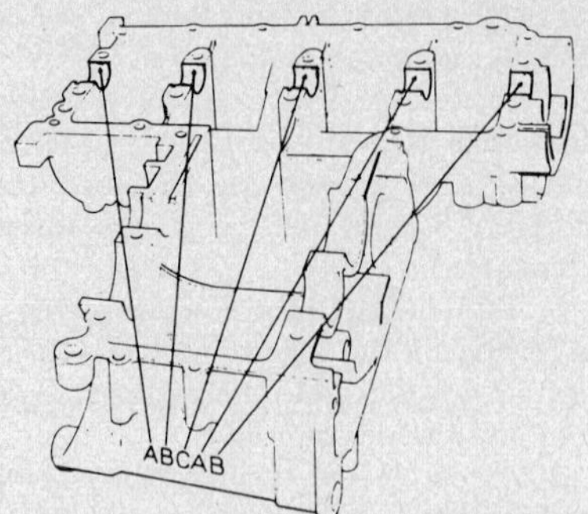

Original (new) bearing seat diameter code. These production codes should not be used or referred to during overhaul.

CODE NUMBER SIZE CHART (JOURNAL DIAMETER)

Journal Diameter	Code
1.2987-1.2992 in./ 32.99-33.00mm	2
1.2983-1.2987 in./ 32.98-32.99 mm	2

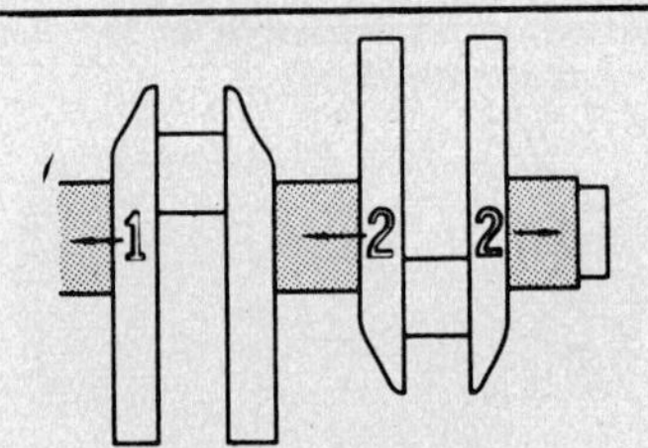

The original crankshaft journal diameter codes, stamped on the weights, should not be referred to during overhaul. Make your own measurements.

BEARING SELECTION CHART

Code Letters	Code Number 1	Code Number 2
A	D yellow	C green
B	C green	B brown
C	B brown	A black

CONNECTING RODS AND BEARINGS

CB 350 F and CB 500

Rod Bearing Selection

Connecting rod bearings need not be replaced unless the bearing shells show signs of wear and/or damage, of if there is excessive clearance between the bearing and crankpin. To check the clearance, cut a strip of plastigauge and place it across the bearing shell, as when checking main bearing clearance. Install the rod bearing cap and torque the nuts to 15 ft lbs. Do not turn the crankshaft or move the connecting rod. Remove the bearing cap and measure the plastigauge with the scale. Maximum acceptable clearance is 0.0032 in. (0.08 mm).

If the rod bearings are to be replaced, measure the diameter of the crankpin and select from the following bearing code letters.

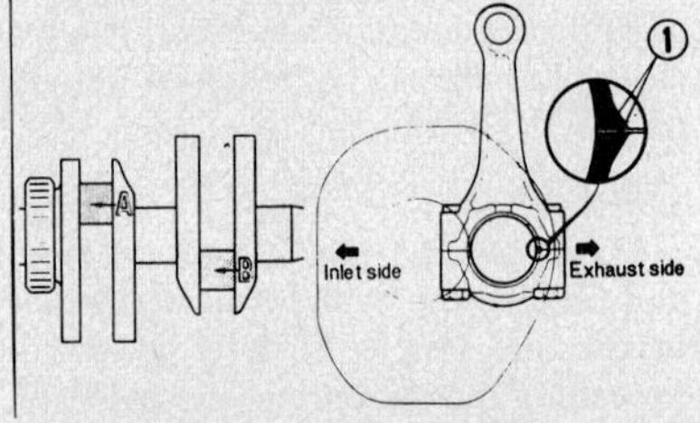

The original crankpin diameter codes are stamped on the weights adjacent to the crankpins. The crankpin diameters should be remeasured before bearings are selected.

CODE LETTER SIZE CHART (CRANKPIN DIAMETER)

Crankpin Diameter	Code
1.3775-1.3780 in./ 34.99-35.00 mm	A
1.3771-1.3775 in./ 34.98-34.99 mm	B

CRANKSHAFT JOURNAL O.D.
Unit: mm (in.)

Crankcase Bearing I.D.	31.99-32.00 (1.2594-1.2598)	31.98-31.99 (1.2590-1.2594)	31.97-31.98 (1.2586-1.2590)
35.00-35.008 (1.3780-1.3783)	D (yellow)	C (green)	B (brown)
35.008-35.016 (1.3783-1.3786)	C (green)	B (brown)	A (black)
35.016-35.024 (1.3786-1.3789)	B (brown)	A (black)	AA (blue)

Crankcase bearing chart

CRANKSHAFT PIN O.D.
Unit: mm (in.)

Connecting Rod Code No.	31.99-32.00 (1.594-1.2598)	31.98-31.99 (1.2590-1.2594)	31.97-31.98 (1.2586-1.2590)
1	E (red)	D (yellow)	C (green)
2	D (yellow)	C (green)	B (brown)
3	C (green)	B (brown)	A (black)

Connecting rod code chart

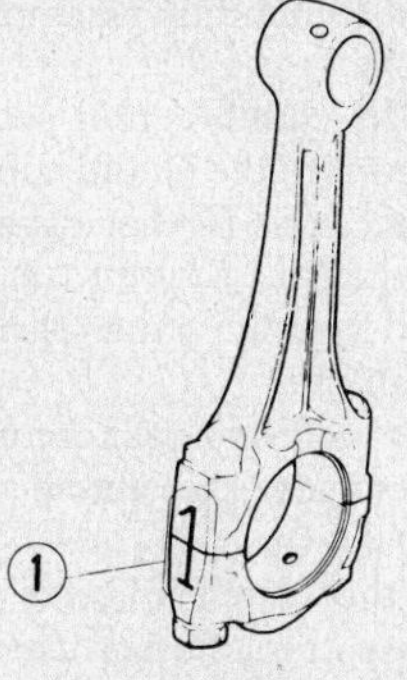

Code	Weight (gr.)
A	281~285
B	286~290
C	291~295
D	296~300
E	301~305
F	306~310
G	311~315

The rod weight code letter (1)

Connecting rod code numbers (1) refer to the bearing seat diameter, which need not be remeasured

BEARING SELECTION CHART

Code Number	Code Letter A	B
1	D yellow	C green
2	C green	B brown
3	B brown	A black

Now, using the code letter obtained above and the code *number* stamped on the connecting rod, select the proper bearings from this chart.

Connecting Rod Replacement

Connecting rod side clearance for the 350 must not exceed 0.0059 in. (0.15 mm), and for the 500, must not exceed 0.0138 in. (0.08 mm), and the wrist pin bushing inside diameter for the 350 must not exceed 0.5158 in. (13.10 mm), and for the 500, must not exceed 0.5930 in. (15.07 mm). If either measurement is beyond the limit, replace the rod. A replacement connecting rod of the same weight as the original should be selected. Rod weight can be determined by the code *letter* stamped on the big end of the rod. When replacing all four rods, ensure that weight variation between them does not exceed five grams.

NOTE: *Rod weight includes the bearing cap and bolts but does not include the bearing shells.*

ASSEMBLY

CB 350 F

1. Assembly is basically in the reverse order of disassembly. Make sure all components are thoroughly clean, and coat all bearing surfaces with a suitable lubricant. New gaskets, oil seals, and O-rings should be used.

2. When installing the cam chain tensioner push bar, do so with the mark facing upward. Depress the bar by hand and lock it in place with the adjusting bolt and lock nut.

3. Install the primary chain guide with its recessed mark facing the transmission.

4. Apply a uniformly thin coat of a suitable liquid gasket compound to the crankcase mating surfaces, taking care not to foul any bearing surfaces.

5. Check that all dowel pins are properly installed before fitting the case halves together.

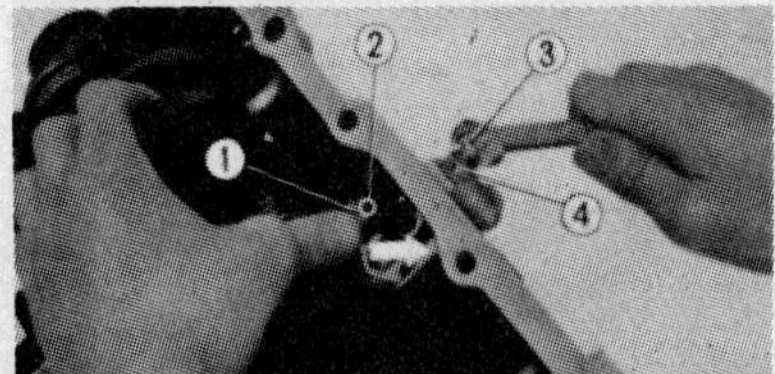

Installing the tensioner push-bar

1. Push bar
2. Mark
3. Tensioner adjusting bolt
4. Lock nut

Primary chain guard installation

1. Primary chain guide
2. Recessed mark

Tightening sequence

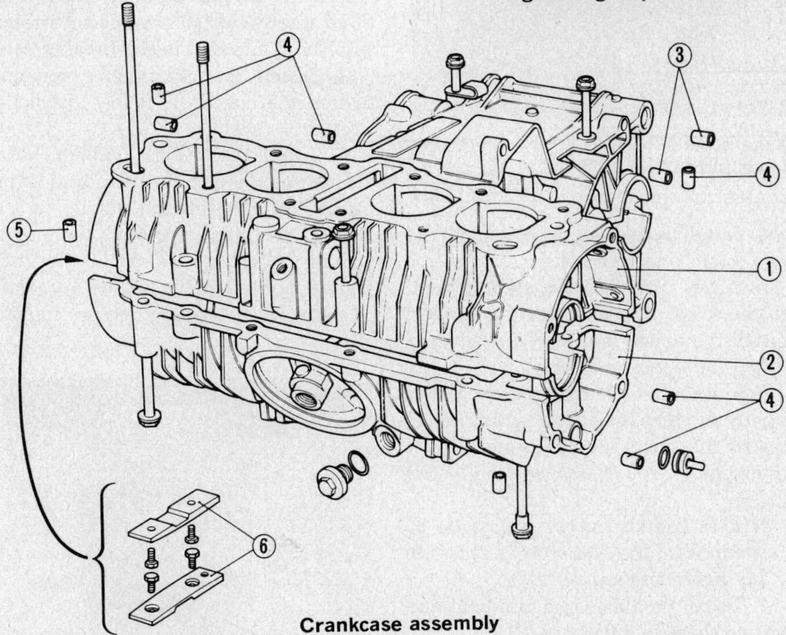

Crankcase assembly

1. Upper crankcase
2. Lower crankcase
3. Dowel pins (two), 8 x 10
4. Dowel pins (six), 8 x 14
5. Dowel pins (two), 10 x 14
6. Primary chain guides (two)

6. Secure the ten bolts on the crankcase in the order shown, torquing them to 16.6–18.1 ft/lbs (2.3–2.5 kg/m).

CB 500

1. Position the main bearing shells in the crankcase halves and coat them with engine oil.

2. Install the primary and cam chains on the crankshaft and install the connecting rods, in their original positions, tightening the nuts to 15 ft lbs. Place the crankshaft assembly in the upper crankcase.

Connecting rod cap (1)

3. Install the primary chain around the starter clutch and, holding the starter gear and clutch in position, drive the primary shaft in from right to left. Be careful not to damage the needle bearings in the starter gear hub and do not forget to install the circlip. Install the mainshaft and countershaft gear assemblies, taking care to position the bearing set rings and dowel pins correctly.

Make sure the bearing set rings and dowel pins are in position

1. Bearing set rings 2. Dowel pins

4. Install the bearing set plate with the two 6 mm retaining bolts.

5. Apply a *thin* coat of gasket cement to the lower crankcase mating surface, install the dowel pins (if removed), and install the upper crankcase.

6. Hold the crankcases together tightly and turn the engine upside down. Install the ten 8 mm bolts and torque them, in the sequence shown, to 17–18 ft lbs.

NOTE: *Position the two bolts with "9" stamped on the bolt head as shown in the tightening sequence.*

7. Install the thirteen 6 mm bolts and torque them to 8 ft lbs.

8. Turn the engine over again so it is resting on the bottom crankcase and install the three 6 mm and three 8 mm

Tightening sequence of the 8 mm lower crankcase bolts

6 mm crankcase bolts (circled)

bolts. Position the two 8 mm bolts marked "8" on the bolt head as indicated in the illustration.

9. Install the oil pump pick-up and mount the oil pan with the ten 6 mm bolts.

10. Install the starter motor.

11. Install the shift linkage, as removed, and install the shift lever.

12. Mount the clutch assembly in accordance with procedures given in the section on clutch service.

13. Place the ignition advance dowel pin in the hole in the crankshaft and mount the oil pan with the ten 6 mm three screws. Install the special washer with the 6 mm bolt in the breaker cam.

14. Install the alternator rotor and tighten the bolt to 30 ft lbs. Install the alternator cover.

15. Install the pistons, cylinder, head, etc., as described under "Top End Overhaul," and reinstall the engine in the frame. Do not forget to refill the engine with oil. Turn the kill switch to the "off" position and crank the engine over until oil pressure is developed before starting it.

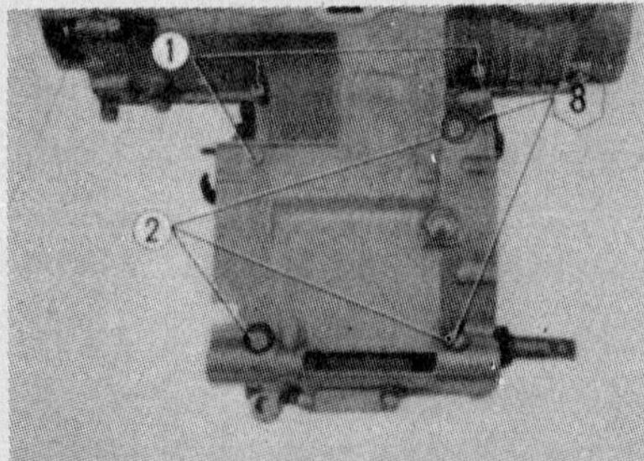

Upper crankcase mounting bolts

1. 6 mm bolts 2. 8 mm bolts

Clutch Service

DISASSEMBLY

CB 350 F and CB 500

1. Drain the engine oil.

2. Remove the kick-start lever and right-side footrest.

3. Take out the screws and pull off the right-side rear crankcase (clutch) cover.

4. Unscrew the four pressure-plate mounting bolts and remove the plate and four springs. Remove the release piston.

5. Remove the large circlip and shims (if any). Pull the clutch hub assembly off the mainshaft.

6. Remove the clutch center section, discs, and plates from the clutch housing. On the 350 this can be further disassembled by removing the 12 mm set ring.

If it is desired to remove the release or adjuster mechanisms:

7. Remove the left side, rear crankcase cover and disconnect the clutch cable from the release lever.

8. Unscrew the clutch adjuster lockbolt and remove the adjuster from the left crankcase cover. Pull the release rod out of the crankcase.

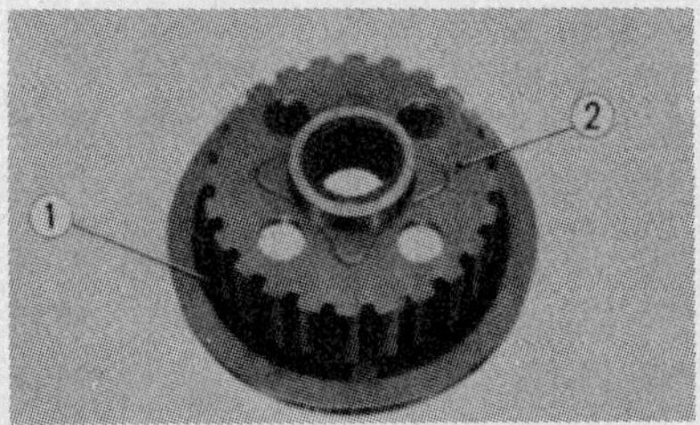

Clutch center assembly (350)

1. 92 mm special set ring
2. Clutch center

Removing the circlip

1. Circlip
2. Clutch assembly

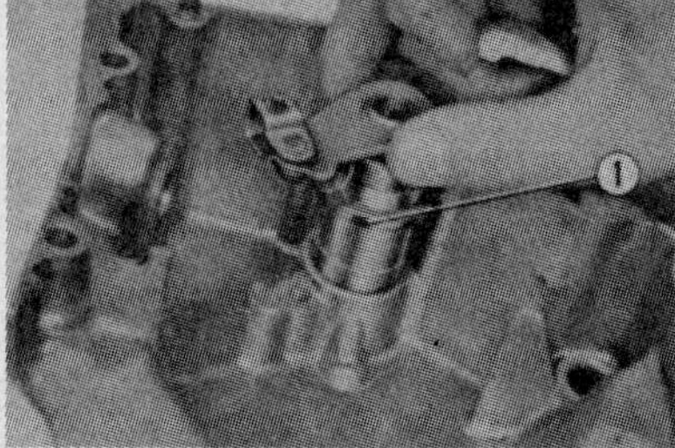

Removing the clutch

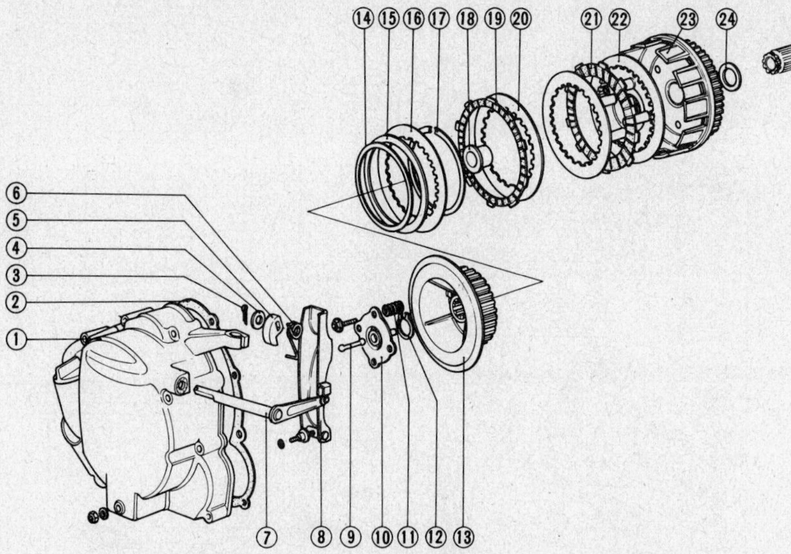

Clutch assembly (350) adjuster (1)

1. Crankcase cover, R
2. Cover packing
3. Cotter pin, 20 x 15
4. Washer, 10 mm
5. Clutch lifter cam
6. Clutch lever return spring
7. Clutch lever
8. Clutch adjusting lever
9. Clutch lifter rod
10. Clutch lifter plate
11. Clutch springs (four)
12. Snap ring, 25 mm
13. Clutch center
14. Disc spring seat
15. Clutch disc spring
16. Clutch plate B
17. Special set ring, 92 mm
18. Collar, 25 mm
19. Clutch friction disc
20. Clutch plates (six)
21. Clutch friction disc (six)
22. Clutch pressure plate
23. Clutch outer
24. Thrust washer, 25 mm

INSPECTION

CB 350 F and CB 500

1. Measure the thickness of the friction discs and replace if less than 0.01 in. (2.3 mm) for the 350, or 0.11 in. (3 mm) for the 500.

2. Place the clutch plates on a flat surface and check for excessive warpage with a feeler gauge. Replace if warpage is greater than 0.008 in. (0.2 mm) for the 350, or 0.011 in. (0.3 mm) for the 500.

3. Measure the free-length of the clutch springs. Replace the springs if they measure less than 1.339 in. (34.0 mm) for the 350, or 1.20 in. (30.5 mm) for the 500.

4. Make sure that the clutch housing rivets, as shown, are tight. If not, the clutch housing should be replaced.

5. On the 350, check the clutch center to clutch plate "B" clearance as illustrated, and replace the plate if worn beyond its serviceable limit of 0.004–0.020 in. (0.1–0.5 mm).

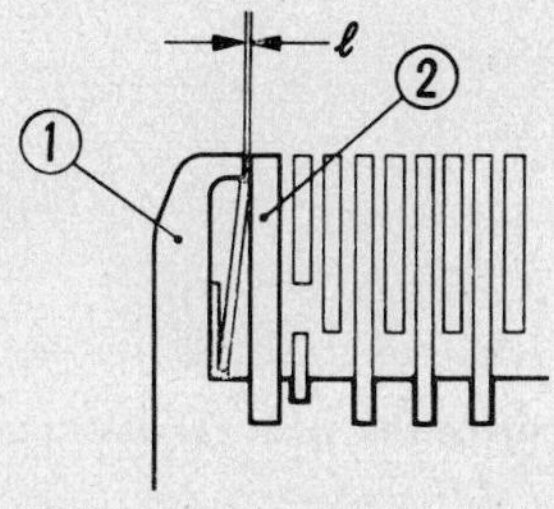

Checking center-to-plate clearance

1. Clutch center
2. Clutch plate B

ASSEMBLY

1. Install the release rod into the crankcase so that the round end is toward the right side.

2. Apply grease to the clutch release, assemble it into the adjuster, and install it in the left crankcase cover. Tighten the lockbolt and connect the clutch cable to the release lever.

3. Install the steel ball into the clutch release and mount the left crankcase cover on the engine.

4. Coat the friction discs with fresh engine oil and assemble the discs and plates onto the center section. Install the center section in the clutch housing.

NOTE: *Beginning with engine number CB 500E-1018728, modified clutch discs and plates have been used. Earlier engines suffering from clutch slip may be modified with these parts, as they are interchangeable.*

5. Install the clutch assembly on the mainshaft and lock it in place with the circlip. Check end-play of the clutch assembly with a dial indicator, and if end-play exceeds 0.004 in. (0.1 mm), a shim should be installed behind the circlip. Shims are available in thicknesses of 0.1, 0.3, and 0.5 mm.

6. Slip the release piston into the main-

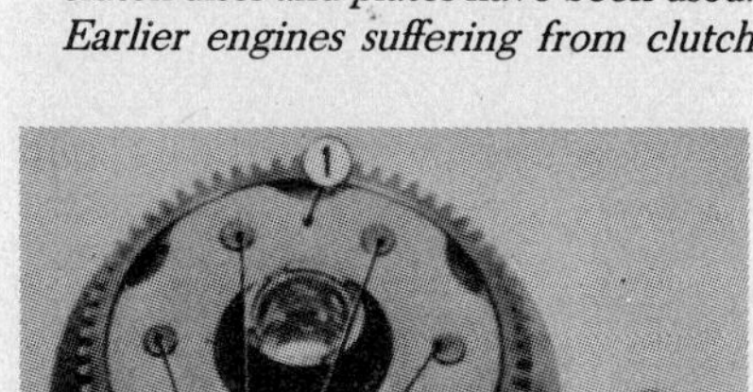

The rivets in the housing must be tight

1. Driven gear
2. Clutch housing
3. Rivets

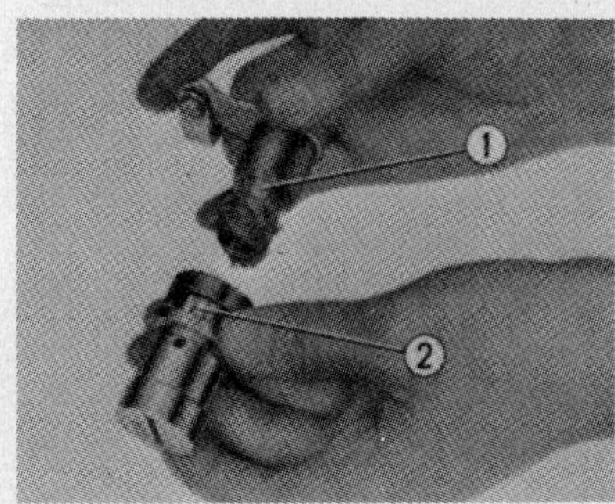

Grease the release mechanism before installing it in the adjuster

1. Clutch release 2. Adjuster

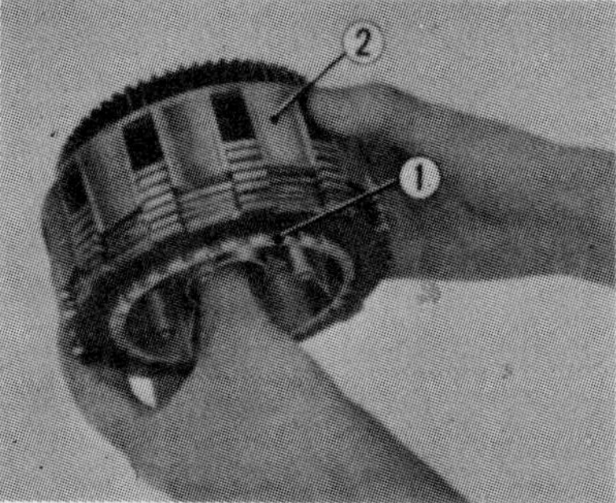

Assembling the clutch housing in the clutch center

1. Clutch center 2. Clutch housing

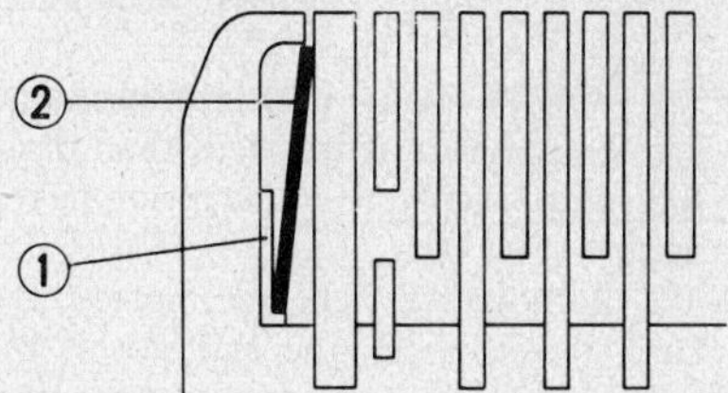

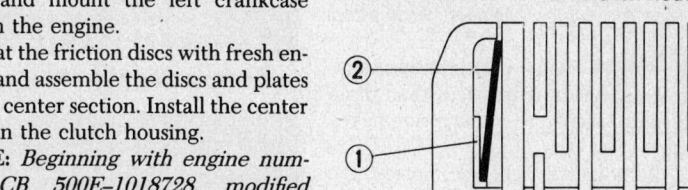

Spring seat and spring properly installed (350)

1. Disc spring seat
2. Clutch disc spring

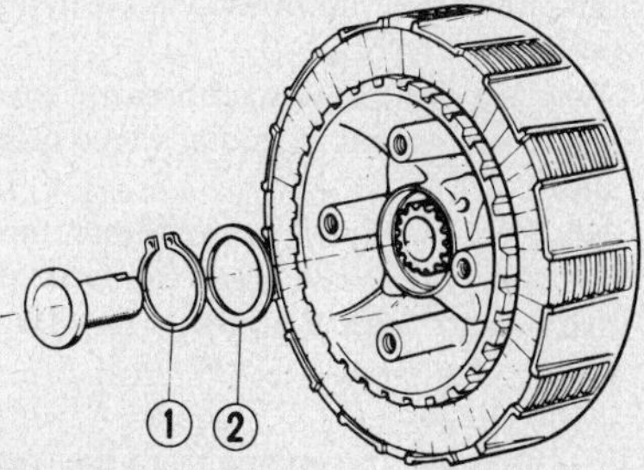

Shims are used to correct excessive end play

1. Circlip 2. Shim

Don't forget the 25 mm thrust washer (350)
1. 25 mm thrust washer

shaft and install the pressure plate, with springs, on the clutch housing.

7. Install the crankcase (clutch) cover using a new gasket.

8. Refill the engine with oil, and adjust the clutch.

Installing the release piston (1)

Shifter Mechanism Service

DISASSEMBLY

CB 350 F

NOTE: *For convenience sake, Honda breaks the shifter mechanism down into two sub-groups. Group "A" components can be serviced with the engine still mounted in the frame, Group "B" components can only be serviced once the engine has been dismantled.*

(Group A)

1. Run the engine until normal operating temperature is reached, then drain the sump. Place the transmission in the neutral position.

2. Remove the right-side footrest, the kick starter pedal, the shift lever, the right-side crankcase cover, and the gear shift spindle.

3. Remove the positive stopper, the gear shift drum stopper, and the neutral stopper arm. The accompanying illustration shows the transmission in the neutral position.

4. Remove the contact breaker cover, base plate assembly, and advance mechanism.

5. Remove the oil pump, then remove the secondary drive gear from the primary shaft after removing the 12mm bolt.

(Group B)

1. Remove the engine from the frame as directed in the "Engine Removal and Installation" section, then perform all of the steps listed in the preceding section.

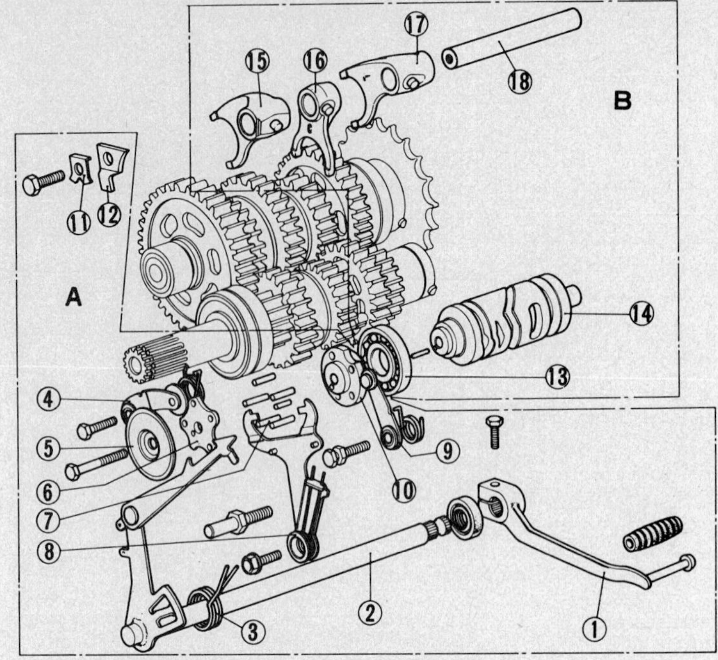

Shifter assembly (350)

Group A
On-vehicle servicing

1. Gear change pedal
2. Gear shift spindle
3. Return spring
4. Gear shift drum stopper
5. Gear shift side plate
6. Drum stopper plate
7. Rollers (six)
8. Positive stopper
9. Neutral stopper arm

Group B
On-work stand servicing

10. Gear shift drum center
11. Lock washer, 8 mm
12. Guide shaft set place
13. 16004 ball bearing
14. Gear shift drum
15. Gear shift fork, R (right)
16. Gear shift fork, C (center)
17. Gear shift fork, L (left)
18. Shift fork guide shaft

Removing the gearshift spindle (1)

Stopper assemblies installed
1. Positive stopper
2. Shift drum stopper
3. Neutral stopper arm

2. Pull the primary shaft out through the right side of the case.

3. Remove the internal circlip, ball bearing, and collar as illustrated.

4. Evenly remove the crankcase securing bolts, then tap on the case halves with a soft mallet, and remove the lower crankcase.

5. Remove the transmission mainshaft and countershaft at the same time.

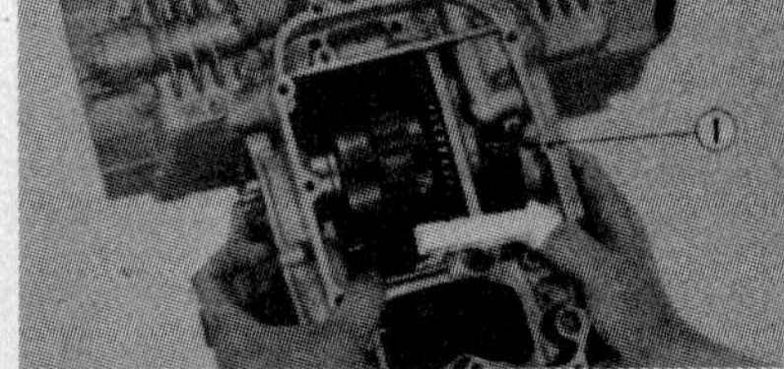

Removing the primary shaft (1)

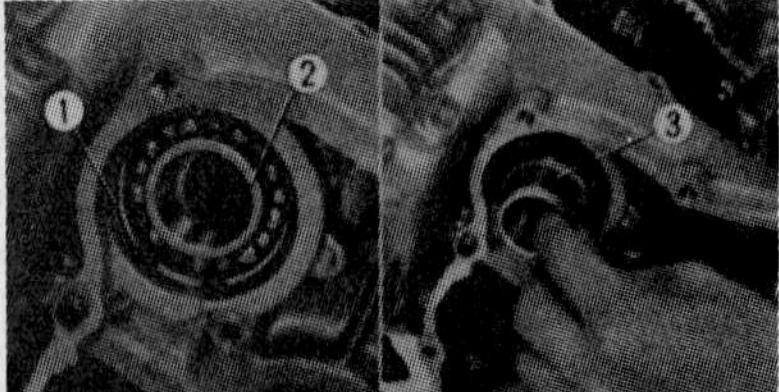

Circlip (1), bearing (2), and collar (3)

Removing the main (1) and counter (2) shafts

6. Remove the gear shift set plate, then remove the shift fork guide shaft and gear shift drum.

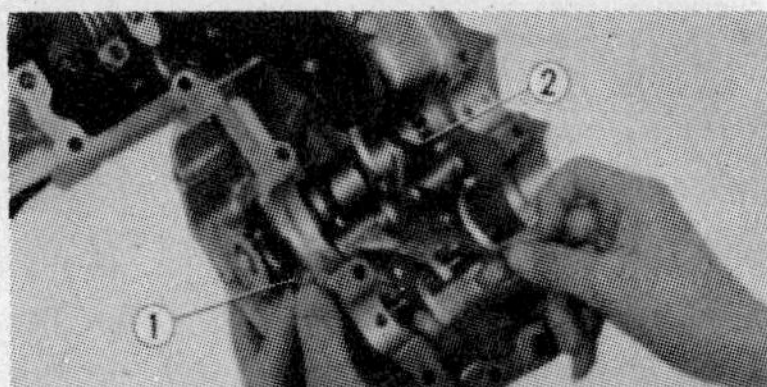

Removing the guide shaft (1) and drum (2)

Removing the shift arm (1)

Shifter assembly installed

1. Shift drum limit bolt
2. Shift drum limit arm
3. Cam plate retaining screw
4. Cam plate

CB 500

1. Remove the engine.

2. Remove the clutch assembly as described in the previous section.

3. Remove the shift lever. Depress the gearshift arm and withdraw the linkage from the right side.

4. Unscrew the shift-drum limit bolt and remove the limit arm. Take out the camplate retaining screw and remove the camplate.

5. Take out the three 8 mm, and three 6 mm bolts on top of the rear section of the upper crankcase. Turn the engine upside down and remove the thirteen, 6 mm bolts and ten, 8 mm bolts that hold the crankcases together. Loosen the 8 mm bolts in reverse order of the tightening sequence. Tap the lower crankcase with a rubber mallet to break the seal and lift it off the engine.

6. Remove the neutral switch from the shift drum.

7. Unscrew the shift-drum guide screw from the upper crankcase and remove the spring, spring cap, and ball.

8. Lift the transmission mainshaft and countershaft assemblies out of the crankcase, taking care not to lose the bearing set rings. Remove the shift fork guide pin clips and pins, and pull the shift drum out of the crankcase.

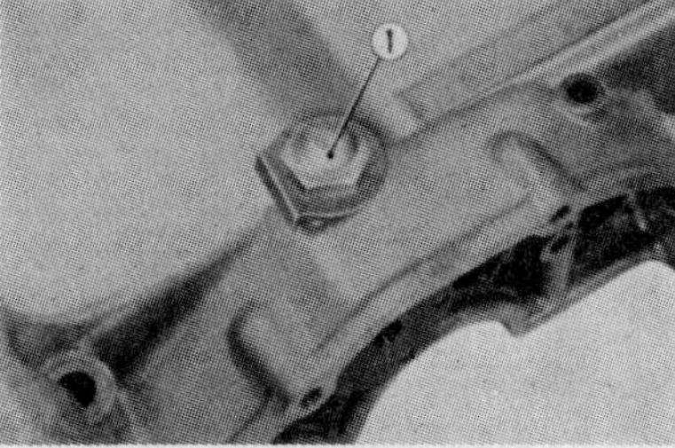

Take care not to lose the spring, spring cap, and ball which are located beneath the guide screw (1)

The guide pin and clip must be removed in order to remove the shift drum

1. Guide pin clip
2. Guide pin
3. Shift drum

INSPECTION

CB 350 F and CB 500

1. Clean all components thoroughly in a suitable solvent, then blow dry.

2. Inspect the shift fork fingers for signs of wear or damage, measure the width of each fork finger, and the inside diameter of each fork, and replace any components worn past their serviceable limits.

3. Inspect the shift fork guide shaft for signs of wear or damage, measure the outside diameter of the shaft, and replace it if worn past its serviceable limit.

4. Inspect the shift drum for signs of wear (as indicated by bright spots along the drum grooves) or damage, measure the outside diameter of the drum, and replace it as necessary.

5. Measure the gear shift fork guide-to-gear shift drum groove clearance, and replace the components if worn past their serviceable limits.

ASSEMBLY

CB 350 F

1. Install the shift drum and gears in the neutral position.

2. Install the guide set plate, securing it by bending the lock washer locking tab against the flat of the bolt.

3. Install the shift forks in their respective positions. Note that the forks are marked "R", "C", and "L" for identification.

4. Make sure that the shift drum stopper, neutral stopper, and positive stopper are in their proper positions, and that they work properly.

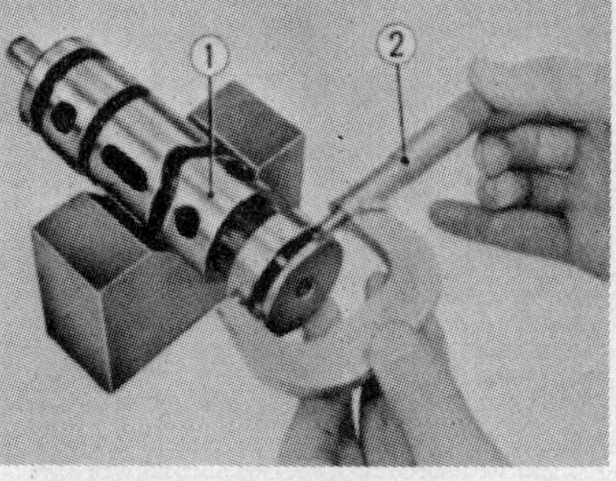

Measuring the shift drum for wear

1. Shift drum 2. Micrometer

Shiftforks (1) properly installed

Stoppers properly installed

1. Guide set plate
2. Lock washer
3. 8 mm bolt

5. Rotate the spindle to check for proper operation.

6. Install the transmission components as directed in the "Transmission" section.

7. Assemble the case halves together as directed in the "Bottom End Overhaul" section.

CB 500

NOTE: *Modified shift-drum limit assemblies (making neutral selection easier) are used from engine number CB 500E–1018728. Old and new parts are interchangeable. The new parts are available, along with the clutch plates mentioned in the clutch service section, in kit form, from Honda dealers so that earlier models can be updated.*

1. Place the shift forks in the crankcase as shown and install the shift drum.

2. Insert the guide pins into the forks and secure them with the clips. Be sure the clips are installed in the proper direction. Refer to the accompanying illustration.

3. Align the counterbored section of the shift drum with the guide screw hole and install the steel ball, spring cap, and spring. Install the O-ring and locktab, and tighten the guide screw. Lock the guide screw in position with the locktab.

Installing the shift drum and forks

1. Shift forks 2. Shift drum

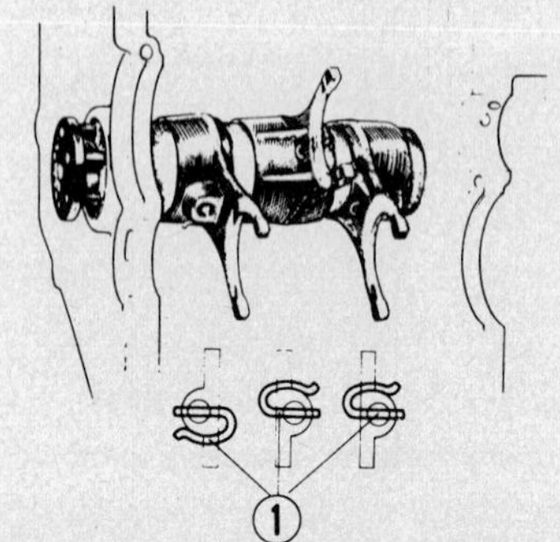

Be sure to install the guide pin clips (1) as shown

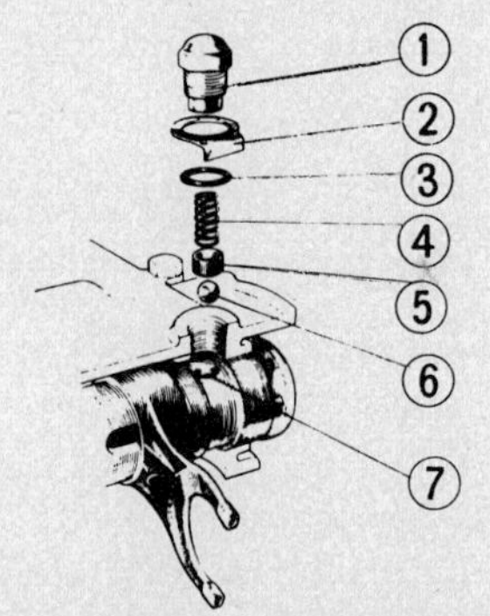

Shift drum guide screw assembly

1. Guide screw
2. Lockwasher
3. O-ring
4. Spring
5. Spring cap
6. Steel ball
7. Counterbored section

4. Align the neutral switch with the groove in the shift drum and lock in place with the 6 mm screw.

5. Replace the transmission mainshaft and countershaft assemblies in the upper crankcase, taking care to locate the bearing settings and dowel pins properly, and apply a thin coat of gasket cement to the crankcase mating surface. Carefully join the crankcase halves and install the ten, 8 mm bolts. Tighten the bolts, in the correct sequence, to 17–18 ft lbs. Install and tighten the thirteen, 6 mm bolts to 8 ft lbs. (Refer to "Bottom End Overhaul".)

NOTE: *Position the two, 8 mm bolts with "9" stamped on the bolt head as shown in the tightening sequence.*

6. Turn the engine up so it is resting on the lower crankcase and install the three, 8 mm and three, 6 mm bolts through the upper crankcase. Position the two, 8 mm bolts marked "8" on the bolt head as indicated in the illustration.

7. Install the camplate on the shift drum, making sure that the pin in the drum and hole in the camplate are aligned. Coat the threads of the retaining screw with the thread-locking compound before installing.

8. Place the spring on the end of the shift drum limit arm and install the end of the spring into the crankcase groove. Install and tighten the limit bolt, and make sure that the arm operates smoothly. If there is excessive vertical movement, the arm should be replaced.

9. Install the shift linkage and shift arm, and make sure the arm operates smoothly in both directions. Install the shift lever.

10. Fit the clutch on the engine and reinstall the engine in the frame. Do not forget to refill the engine with oil.

Transmission, Primary Drive, and Kick-Starter Service

DISASSEMBLY

CB 350 F

1. Follow all the steps listed in the "Shifter Mechanism Service" section.

2. Remove the primary driven sprocket and the starter driven gear, then remove the driven sprocket hub from the primary driven sprocket, and remove the hub rubber dampers.

3. Disassemble the transmission shafts assemblies as necessary, keeping the components separate for assembly in their original positions.

Upper crankcase mounting bolts

1. 6 mm bolts 2. 8 mm bolts

Installing the cam plate (2). Make sure the locating pin (1) is properly seated.

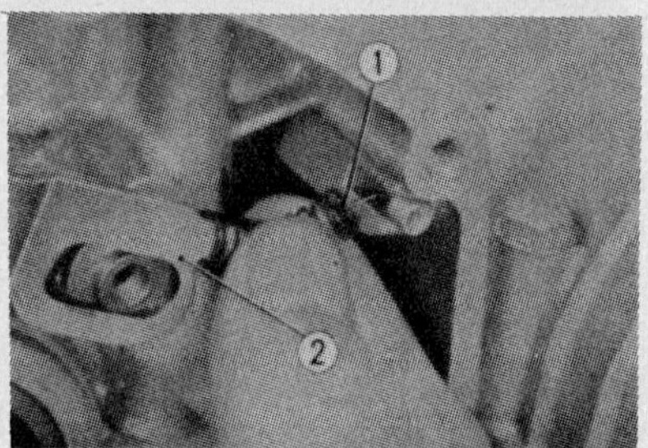

Installing the limit arm spring

1. Spring
2. Shift drum limit arm

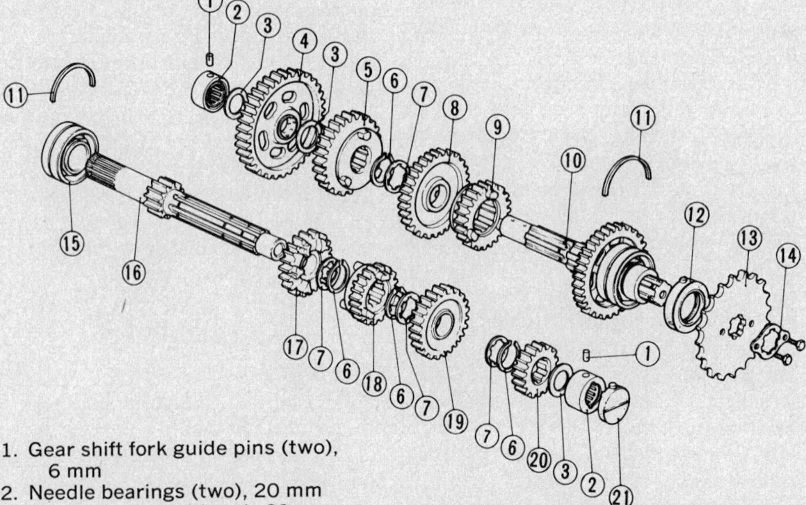

Transmission assembly (350)

1. Gear shift fork guide pins (two), 6 mm
2. Needle bearings (two), 20 mm
3. Thrust washers (three), 20 mm
4. Countershaft low hear, 41 T
5. Countershaft fourth gear, 31 T
6. Circlips (four), 25 mm
7. Thrust washers (four)
8. Countershaft third gear, 34 T
9. Countershaft top gear, 28 T
10. Countershaft, 37 T
11. Bearing set rings (two), 52 mm
12. Oil seal
13. Drive sprocket, 17 T
14. Drive sprocket fixing plate
15. Ball bearing, 5205 HS
16. Main shaft
17. Main shaft fourth gear, 27 T
18. Main shaft third gear, 24 T
19. Main shaft top gear, 29 T
20. Main shaft second gear, 20 T
21. Oil seal

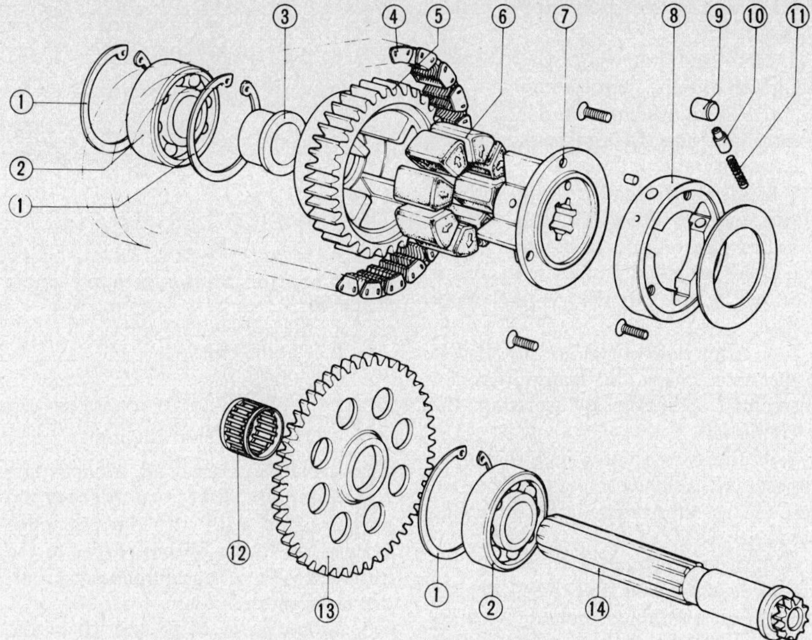

Primary drive assembly (350)

1. Internal circlips (three), 52 mm
2. Ball bearings (two), 6205
3. Collar, 25 x 21.8
4. Primary drive chain
5. Primary driven sprocket
6. Rubber dampers (eight)
7. Driven sprocket hub
8. Clutch outer
9. Rollers (three), 10.2 x 9.5
10. Caps (three)
11. Springs (three)
12. Needle bearing
13. Starter driven gear
14. Primary shaft

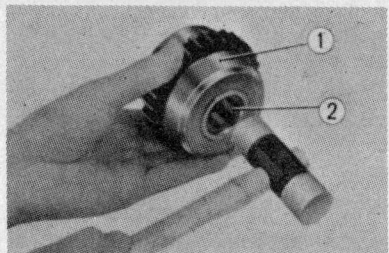

Removing the primary driven sprocket (1) and starter driven gear

Removing the driven sprocket hub (2) from the driven sprocket (1)

CB 500

1. Follow steps 1, 2, and 5 in the preceding section on shifter mechanism disassembly.

2. Lift the transmission mainshaft and countershaft assemblies out of the crankcase. Do not lose the bearing set rings.

3. To remove the kick-start gear and shaft, first remove the 18 mm circlip and return spring from the end of the shaft. Remove the 12 mm circlip from the end of the shaft inside the case and withdraw the shaft from the lower crankcase.

4. To remove the primary shaft, unscrew the two bolts and remove the primary shaft bearing set plate. Remove the 20 mm circlip at the end of the shaft and pull out the primary shaft using tool number 07009-32301 or a suitable gear puller. Lift out the starter clutch and primary sprocket assembly.

5. Pull the large primary shaft bearing off the shaft. The primary sprocket and starter clutch can be removed and separated after the primary sprocket circlip has been removed.

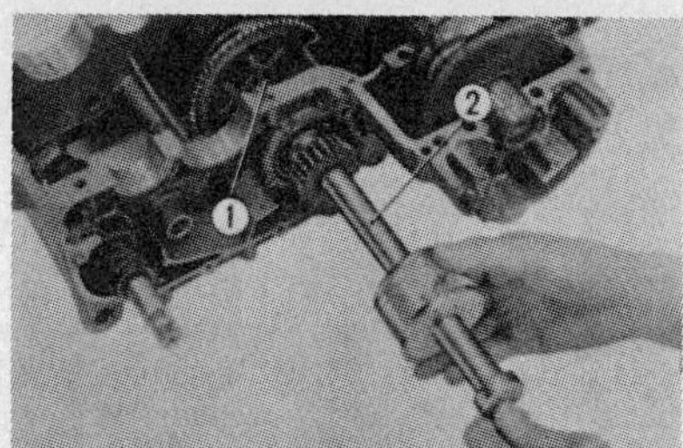

Removing the primary shaft

1. Primary shaft 2. Shaft puller

INSPECTION

CB 350 F and CB 500

1. Set the mainshaft and countershaft gear assemblies into the crankcase and measure backlash. Maximum acceptable backlash is 0.008 in. (0.2 mm) for all gearsets. Replace gears (mating pairs) on both shafts that exceed the limits. Inspect the dogs and replace any gears with damaged or excessively worn dogs. Check the ball bearings for excessive play and make sure the gears slide smoothly on the shaft splines.

2. Examine the damper rubbers in the primary sprocket and replace them if they do not appear to be in perfect condition.

3. If it is necessary to replace the starter clutch needle bearing assembly or to replace other components, the housing can be removed after the three phillips head screws have been taken out.

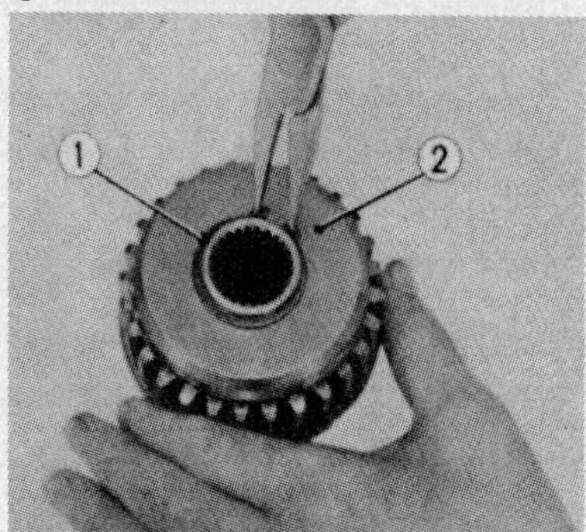

Removing the primary sprocket circlip

1. Circlip 2. Primary sprocket

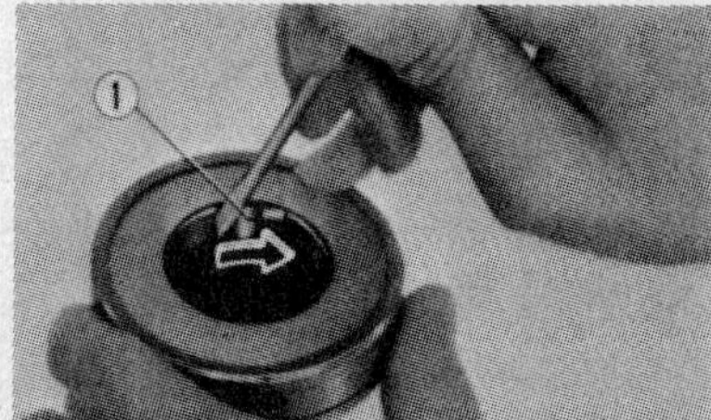

Testing the starting clutch rollers (1)

Installing the starter spring

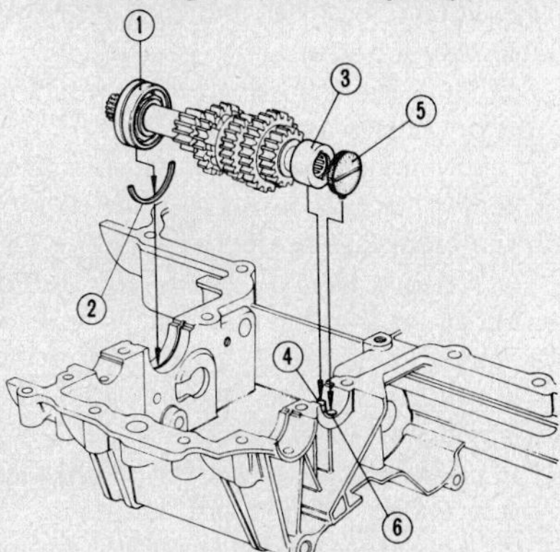

Mainshaft installation

1. 5205 HS ball bearing
2. 52 mm bearing set ring
3. 20 mm needle bearing
4. 6 mm guide pin
5. Oil seal
6. Pin hole

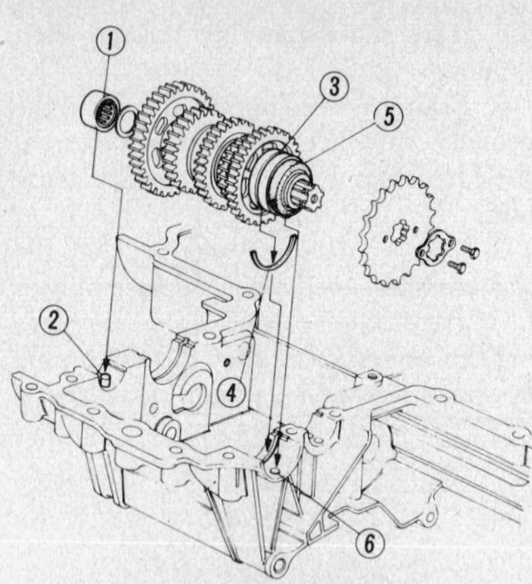

Countershaft installation

1. 20 mm needle bearing
2. 6 mm guide pin
3. 5205 ball bearing
4. 50 mm bearing set ring
5. Oil seal
6. Pin hole

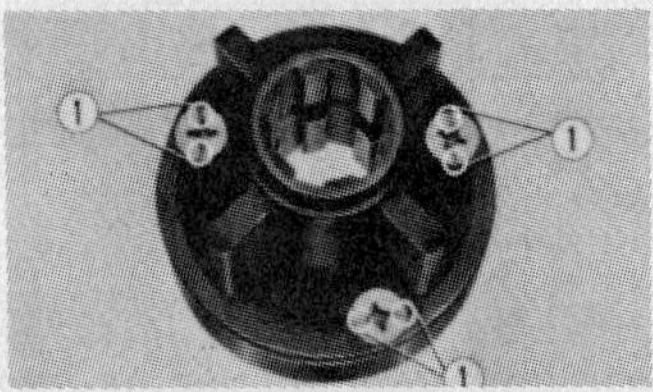

Stake (1) the retaining screws to prevent loosening

Primary shaft (1) and collar (2) installed

ASSEMBLY

CB 350 F

1. Assembly is in the reverse order of disassembly. New circlips and seals should be used, and all components should be liberally coated with a suitable assembly lubricant.

2. Note the following when installing the kickstarter assembly;

a. The hair pin section of the starter pinion friction spring is inserted into the crankcase stopper groove.

b. Hook the "A" end of the starter spring as shown, then install the kick starter assembly. The "B" end of the spring should be hooked onto the crankcase rib as illustrated.

c. Make sure the starter pinion gear is properly meshed with low gear.

3. Note the following when assembling the main shaft assembly;

a. Install the ball bearing with the bearing set ring installed in its groove.

b. Install the needle bearing so its guide pin fits in the guide pin hole.

c. Install the oil seal so its dowel fits into the pin hole in the upper crankcase half.

4. Note the following when assembling the counter shaft assembly;

a. When installing the needle bearing, make sure the crankcase guide pin is seated in its pin hole.

b. Install the ball bearing with its ring groove fitted onto the ring installed in the upper case half.

c. Install the oil seal so its pin is seated in the pin hole in the upper case.

d. After both shafts are installed in the case, check the transmission for smooth operation by rotating the crankshaft.

5. If the clutch outer body has been disassembled, stake each of the three flat screws, as illustrated, after screwing them in.

6. Insert the primary shaft through the right side of the case after the case halves have been assembled, but not secured, then install the collar.

7. The primary shaft ball bearing will have to be driven into place with a suitable drift, and then secured with the 25mm internal circlip.

Installing the bearing (1) retaining circlip (2)

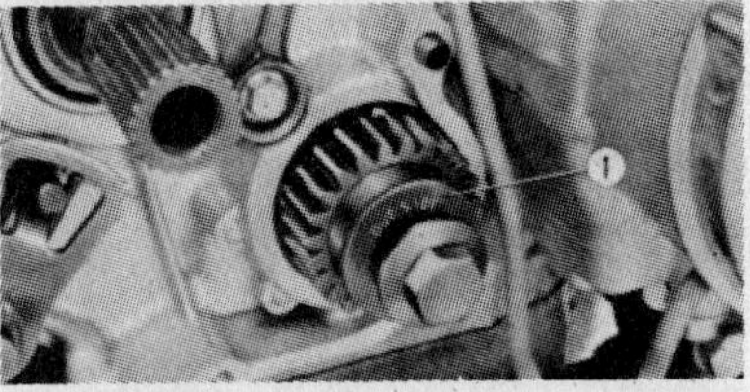

Lockwasher (1) properly installed

8. Secure the case halves as directed in the "Bottom End Overhaul" section.

9. Install the primary shaft lock washer so the word "OUTSIDE" faces outward.

CB 500

1. Assemble the starter clutch housing and clutch hub, coating the threads of the three screws with thread-locking compound. Stake the screws with a punch, as illustrated, to prevent loosening.

2. Assemble the primary shaft components onto the shaft in reverse order of removal. Refer to the accompanying illustration.

3. Assemble the kick-starter components onto the shaft and install in the crankcase. Refer to the exploded view of the components for order of assembly.

4. If the mainshaft and countershaft gears have been removed, *do not reuse the old circlips.* Take care to install the new circlips with the smooth edge against the thrust washer. Refer to the exploded view of the components for order of assembly.

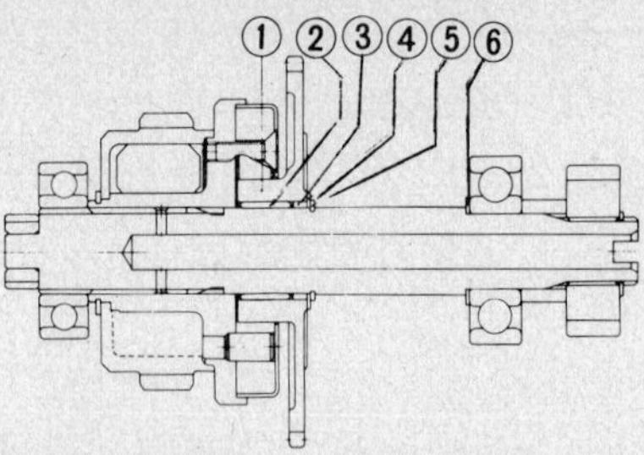

Cross section of the primary shaft assembly

1. Starter clutch gear
2. Needle bearing
3. Spacer
4. Thrust washer
5. Circlip
6. Thrust washer (22 mm)

5. Follow steps 5, 6, and 10 in the preceding section on shifter mechanism assembly.

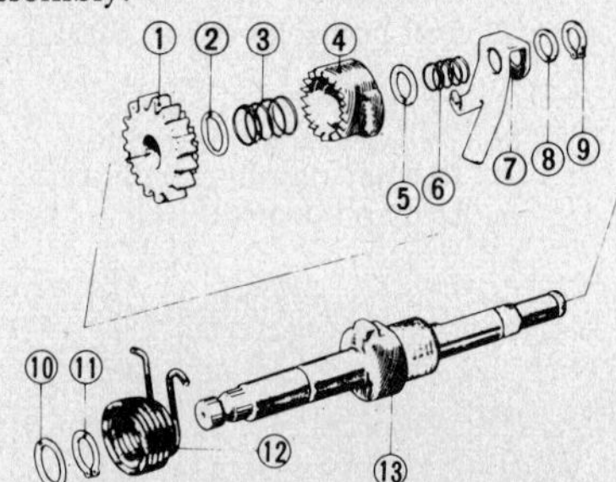

Exploded view of kick-starter components

1. Kick-start gear
2. Thrust washer
3. Starter gear spring
4. Ratchet
5. Thrust washer
6. Ratchet spring
7. Ratchet guide plate
8. Thrust washer
9. Circlip
10. Flat washer
11. Circlip
12. Return spring
13. Kickstart shaft

ENGINE SERVICE

Engine Removal and Installation

CB 750 AND CB 750K1—K3

NOTE: *The following components can be serviced or replaced without removing the engine from the frame: clutch, alternator, cam chain tensioner, and gearshift linkage.*

1. Turn the fuel tap off, disconnect the fuel lines, and remove the tank.

2. Drain the oil from the crankcase and oil tank, and remove the oil filter.

3. Remove the exhaust system on both sides.

1. Bearing set ring
2. Circlip
3. Ball bearing
4. O-ring
5. Countershaft
6. Oil seal
7. Countershaft sprocket
8. Sprocket mounting plate
9. Shift fork pin
10. Needle bearing
11. Countershaft first gear, 40 T
12. Countershaft fourth gear, 29 T
13. Thrust washer
14. Countershaft third gear, 33 T
15. Lockwasher
16. Thrust washer
17. Countershaft second gear, 36 T
18. Countershaft fifth gear, 27 T
19. Bearing set ring
20. Ball bearing
21. Mainshaft
22. Mainshaft fourth gear, 28 T
23. Mainshaft second and third gears, 22 & 26 T
24. Mainshaft fifth gear, 30 T
25. Thrust washer
26. Needle bearing
27. Oil seal

Exploded view of transmission mainshaft and countershaft components (CB 500)

Disconnecting the clutch cable

1. Clutch lever
2. Clutch cable
3. Clutch case

The oil lines (1) are bolted to the engine

4. Disconnect the tachometer cable from the cylinder head and remove the wires from the spark plugs.

5. Unscrew the carburetor caps and withdraw the slides (750) or disconnect the throttle cables from the carburetor linkage (750K1 and K2).

6. Remove the air filter housing, disconnect the carburetors from the intake tubes, and remove the carburetors as an assembly.

7. Remove the kick-start lever and the clutch housing cover. Disconnect the clutch cable from the clutch lever.

8. Disconnect the brake-light switch spring and remove the brake pedal and footpeg.

9. Unbolt the two oil lines from the engine and remove the oil tank. Disconnect the oil tank breather line from the upper crankcase.

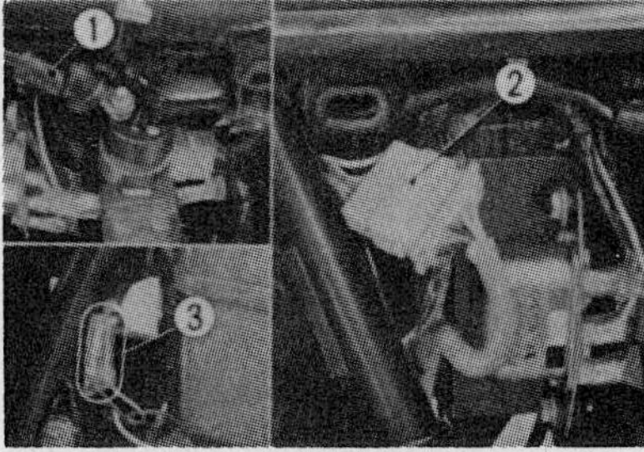

Disconnecting the electrical leads

1. Starter cable
2. Alternator connector
3. Brake light switch connector

10. Remove the shift lever and take off the countershaft sprocket (rear crankcase) cover. Loosen the rear axle nut and drivechain adjusters so that the wheel can be moved forward and the chain can be lifted off the countershaft sprocket.

11. Disconnect the positive battery cable, then disconnect the starter motor cable at the solenoid, the alternator lead at the connector near the battery, and the brake light switch lead at the upper, right-side, rear motor mount.

12. Remove the engine mount bolts, as illustrated. Raise the rear of the engine and lift it out from the right side of the frame.

Installation is in reverse order of removal. The following points should be noted:

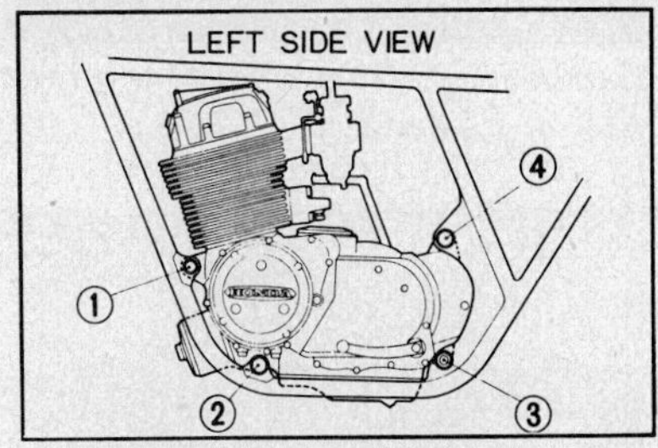

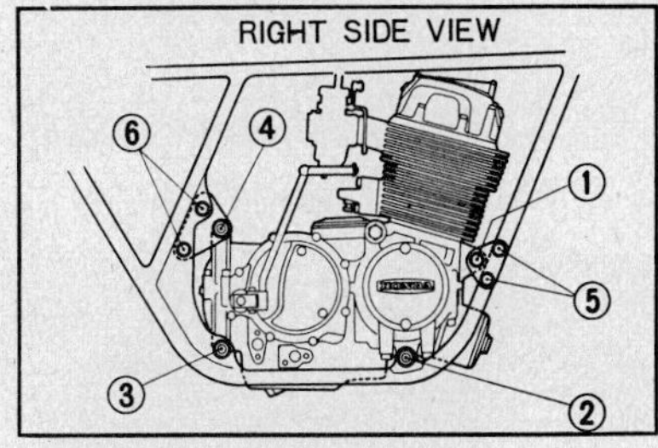

Engine mounting points

1. Be sure to connect the battery ground strap to the upper, rear engine-mount bolt as the bolt is installed.

2. Take care to connect the scavenge and delivery oil lines in their original positions.

3. Make sure that the muffler connecting clamps are in place on each pair of mufflers.

4. When installation is complete, refill the engine with oil. Adjust the clutch, drive chain, and carburetors.

Top End Overhaul

CYLINDER HEAD REMOVAL

1. Remove the engine from the frame.

2. Take out the three, 6 mm screws and remove the breather cover.

3. Remove the remainder of the screws and lift off the camshaft cover.

4. Turn the crankshaft to align the valve timing marks at the right end of the camshaft with the cam bearing joint, as illustrated. Unbolt and remove the cam bearing caps.

5. Unscrew the three bolts and remove the cam chain tensioner from the rear of the cylinder.

6. Remove the two, cam-chain sprocket mounting bolts and loosen the valve-adjusting screws. Remove the four rocker arm shaft retaining bolts and drive out the shafts using a suitable drift. Be careful not to damage the shaft holders.

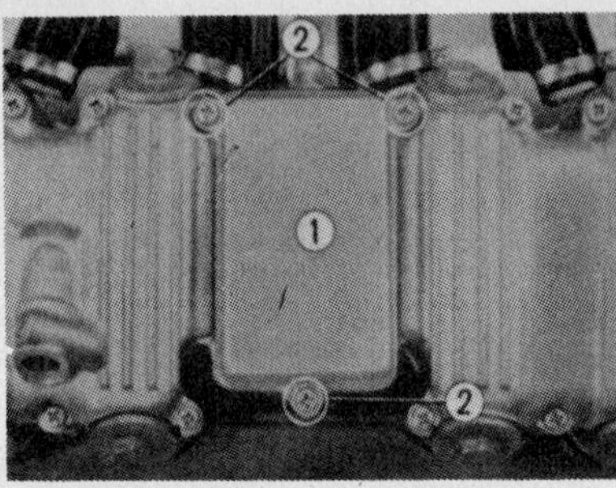

Breather cover (1) and retaining screws (2)

1. Camshaft
2. Valve timing index lines

Aligning the camshaft marks

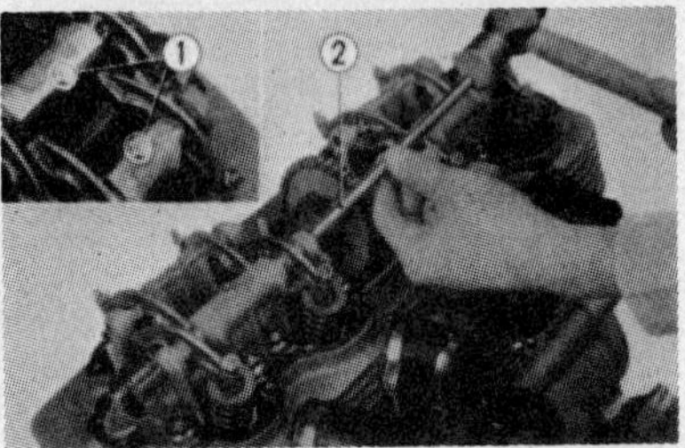

Removing the rocker arm shafts

1. Rocker shaft retaining bolts
2. Using a drift to tap the shafts out

CYLINDER BARREL AND PISTON REMOVAL

1. Carefully lift the cylinder unit away from the crankcase. If it can't be raised easily, tap the sides *lightly* with a rubber mallet to break the seal.

2. Remove the two, cam-chain tensioner rubber mounts from the crankcase and lift out the tensioner roller assembly. The guide roller can be removed from the tensioner by pushing the roller pin.

3. Remove the cam chain guide pin from the bottom of the cylinder and withdraw the guide assembly.

4. Remove the wrist pin circlips from the pistons.

CAUTION: *Do not allow the circlips to fall into the crankcase. To avoid having to split the cases to retrieve a clip, cover the crankcase openings with a cloth.*

5. Remove the wrist pins from the pistons and mark the pistons, inside the skirt, so they can be replaced in their original bores.

COMPONENT INSPECTION AND SERVICE

Camshaft

To check camshaft bearing wear, install the camshaft holder on the cylinder head and install the bearing caps on the holder. Check the marks on the holder and caps to ensure that the caps are installed in their original positions. Torque the cap nuts and bolts to 8 ft lbs. Measure the inside diameter of one of the bearings with an inside micrometer in both the horizontal and verticle directions and then calculate the average value. Next, measure the diameter of the corresponding camshaft journal and compute the bearing clearance. Repeat this operation for the remaining camshaft bearings. Replace the holder and caps as a set if clearance of any bearing exceeds 0.0083 in. (0.21 mm).

NOTE: *Bearing clearance may also be measured using a material such as plastigauge.*

Examine the camshaft lobes for scoring and wear. If the lobes are visibly imperfect, the camshaft should be replaced. Measure the cam height as illustrated. Minimum acceptable measurements are:

Intake cam—1.411 in. (35.86 mm);

Exhaust cam—1.392 in. (35.36 mm).

In addition, the base circle diameter of each cam should not be less than 1.099 in. (27.93 mm). The base circle measurement is taken in a plane perpendicular to the cam height measurement, through the camshaft centerline. Replace the camshaft if any of the above measurements are not within the limits.

Cylinder head tightening sequence. Arrows point to the five small head bolts.

7. Lift the chain off the cam sprocket and withdraw the camshaft from the left side. Unbolt and remove the camshaft holder from the head.

8. Gradually loosen the sixteen cylinder head nuts, in reverse order of the tightening sequence. Remove the five bolts and lift the cylinder head assembly off the engine.

Cam chain tensioner rubber mounts

1. Rubber mounts
2. Tensioner

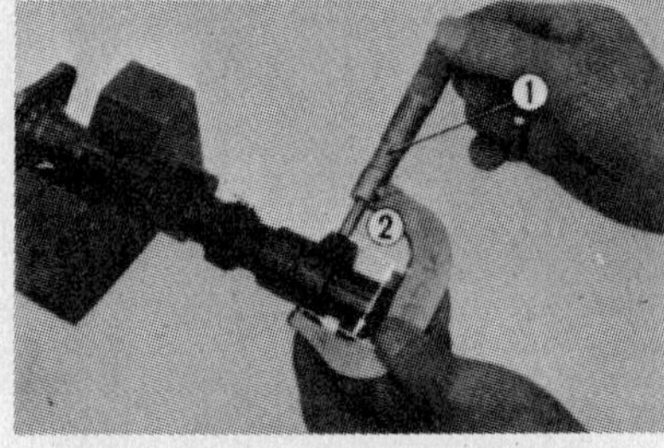

Checking camshaft measurements

1. Micrometer
2. Cam lobe height

Check camshaft runout using a dial indicator, as illustrated, while rotating the camshaft. To obtain an accurate reading, the ends of the camshaft should be supported in machined V-blocks. Camshaft runout must not exceed 0.004 in. (0.1 mm). (Runout equals one-half the dial indicator reading.)

Checking camshaft runout

1. Dial indicator
2. Camshaft

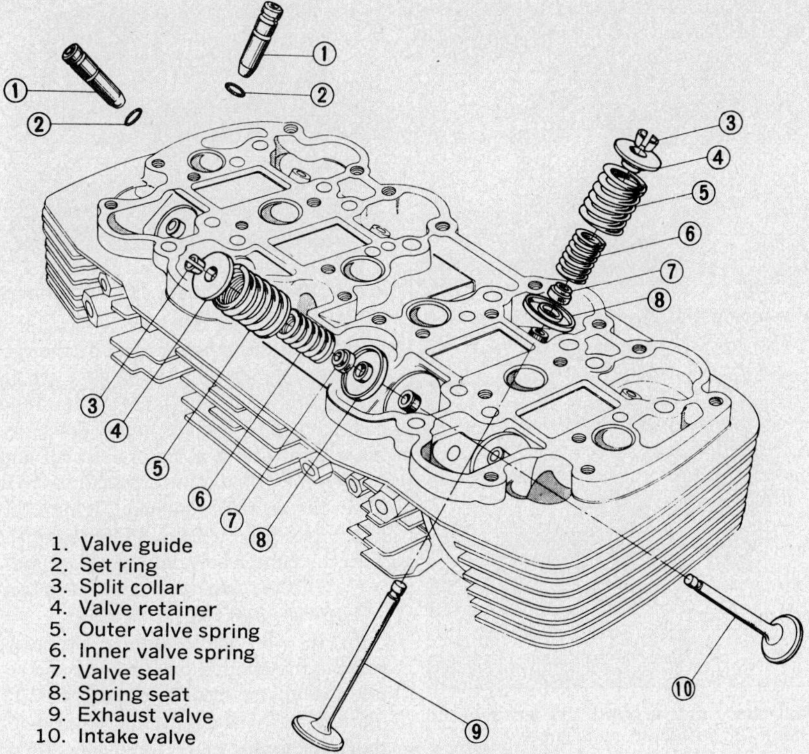

1. Valve guide
2. Set ring
3. Split collar
4. Valve retainer
5. Outer valve spring
6. Inner valve spring
7. Valve seal
8. Spring seat
9. Exhaust valve
10. Intake valve

Valve assembly—exploded view

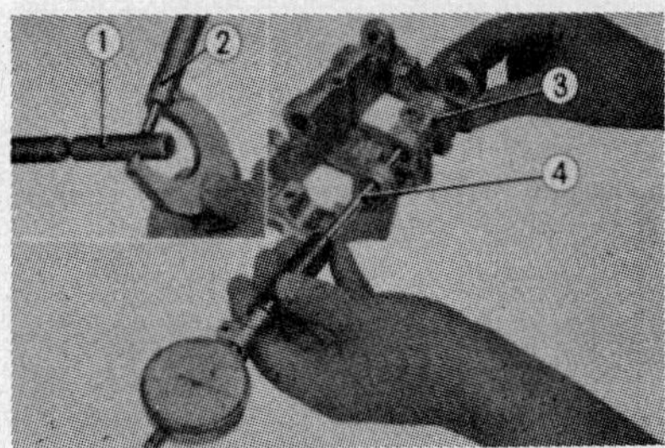

Checking rocker shaft dimensions

1. Rocker shaft
2. Micrometer
3. Measuring rocker shaft bore in cam holder
4. Dial indicator

Valve Rocker Assembly

Measure the inside diameter of the rocker arm supports and measure the diameter of the rocker arm shafts in the area of bearing contact. If calculated clearance exceeds 0.0044 in. (0.11 mm), replace parts as necessary to reduce clearance to within the limit. Check the fit of the rocker arms on the shafts and replace the arms and/or shafts if play is excessive.

Cylinder Head and Valves

Compress the valve springs and remove the collars, retainers, springs, seals, and spring seats. To check valve stem and guide wear, insert the valve into the guide and measure clearance in both the X and Y directions, as shown, with a dial indicator. If clearance is greater than 0.003 in. (0.08 mm) (intake valves) or 0.004 in. (0.1 mm) (exhaust valves), the valve and guide should be replaced as a set. The replacement guide should be one that is oversize, for a proper fit. Guides can be driven out and installed using Honda tool 07046–30001 or a suitably sized drift. New guides should be reamed to 0.2598–0.2602 in. (6.60–6.61 mm) after installation, using a valve guide reamer (Honda part number 07008–30001).

If the valve seat is burnt, worn, or damaged in any way, it should be recut. Valve seat angle is 45°. Seat width should be within 0.039–0.051 in. (1.0–1.3 mm). If either the valve stem is suspected of being bent or the valve face out of round, check the runout with a dial indicator at the valve face. Place the valve in a V-block and slowly rotate the valve while observing the dial indicator. If runout exceeds 0.002 in. (0.05 mm), the valve should be replaced. (Runout equals one-half the dial indicator reading.) Measure the width of the valve face, and replace any valve that has a face contact width greater than 0.079 in. (2.0 mm).

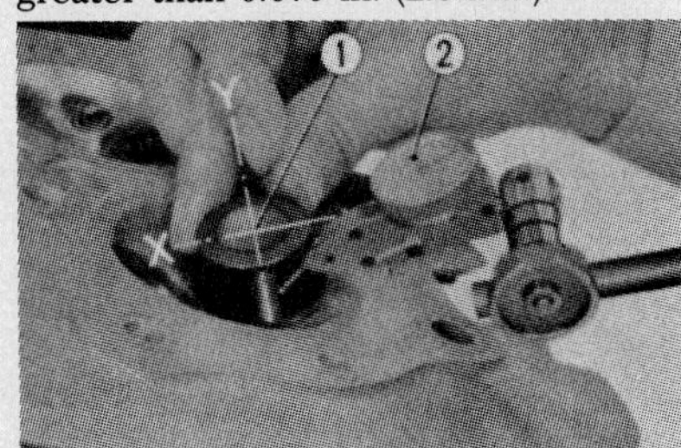

Checking valve guide and stem wear

1. Valve
2. Dial indicator

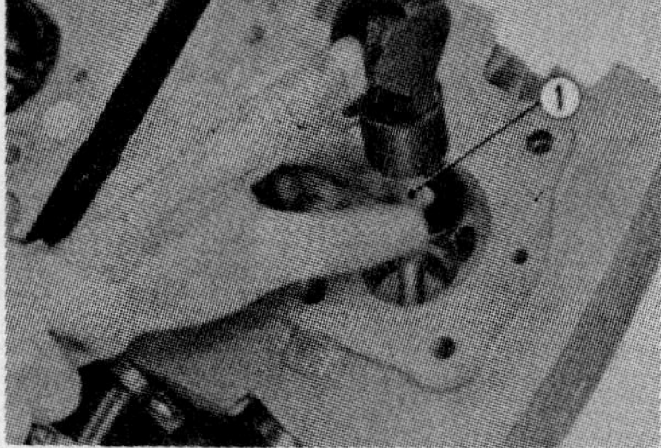

Using a drift (1) to remove a valve guide

NOTE: *Do not attempt to reface the valves or refinish the valve stem ends, as these surfaces have a thin stellite facing that will be destroyed if cut.*

Carefully scrape carbon deposits from the combustion chambers and thoroughly clean the cylinder head. Before the valves are installed, whether they are the original ones or new, they should be lapped into their seats so that a perfect seal will be obtained.

It is a good idea at this time to replace the valve springs as a matter of course. However, if the height of the original springs is not less than 1.4567 in. (37.0 mm) (inner springs) or 1.5748 in. (40.0 mm) (outer springs), they can be reused if desired.

Place a straightedge on the cylinder head surface and measure the clearance with a feeler gauge at several points to determine head warpage or distortion. If clearance at any point exceeds 0.009 in. (0.25 mm), the head should be milled flat or replaced. Ideally, head warp should be no greater than 0.002 in. (0.05 mm).

Make sure that the head is clean and free from grit, and install the valves as removed. Lubricate the valve stems

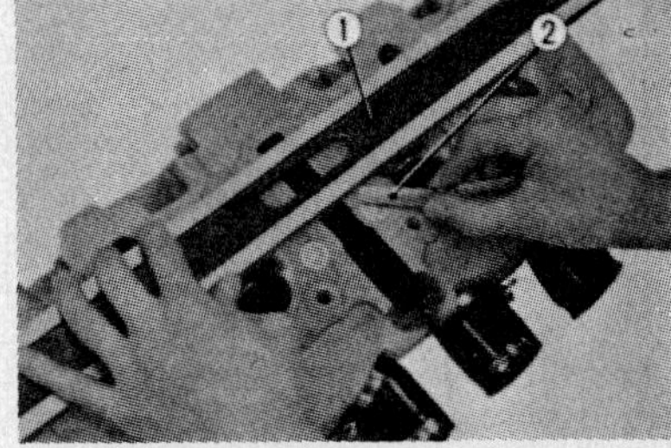

Checking for cylinder head warpage with a straightedge (1) and a feeler gauge (2)

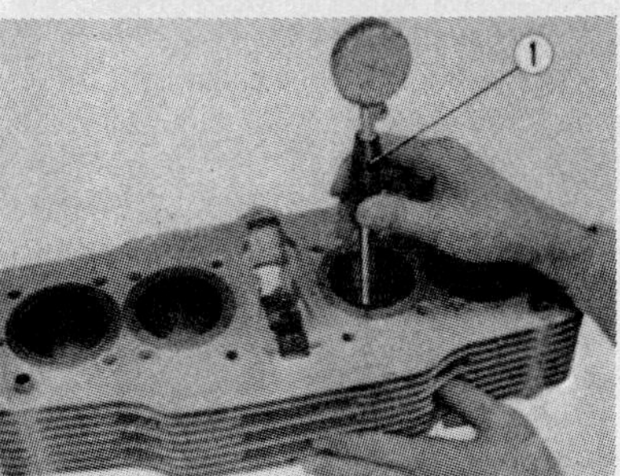

A dial indicator with inside micrometer adapter (1) used to measure bore diameter

before inserting them into the guides, and use new seals.

Cylinder Bore and Pistons

Measure the cylinder bore diameter at the top, center, and bottom of the cylinders in both the fore-and-aft and side-to-side directions. If any measurement exceeds 2.406 in. (61.1 mm), or if bore taper or ovality is greater than 0.002 in. (0.05 mm), the cylinders should be rebored. See the specifications at the end of the chapter for piston oversizes. The cylinders should be honed when new rings are to be used.

Measure the diameter of the piston skirt, perpendicular to the wrist pin. Pistons should be replaced when the diameter is less than 2.3957 in. (60.85 mm). Pistons that are scored or damaged in any way should not be reused. The diameter of the wrist pin hole should measure no less than 0.5937 in. (15.08 mm).

If the original pistons are to be reused, remove the rings and clean the grooves using a piece of one of the old rings. Remove the carbon deposit from the tops of the pistons. Roll the new rings around the grooves before installing them to ensure that there is sufficient clearance. The rings should roll smoothly without binding. Install the rings on the pistons using a ring expander to avoid breaking them. Make sure that the mark on the rings is facing up.

PISTON AND CYLINDER BARREL INSTALLATION

Install the pistons on the connecting rods so that the mark on the piston crown points toward the front (exhaust side). Be sure to use new wrist pin circlips. Stagger the rings so that the gaps are 120° apart. Route the cam chain through the chain tensioner roller, mount the roller assembly on the upper crankcase, and install the rubber mounts. Make sure the chain guide is positioned correctly in the cylinder. Install the cylinder base gasket, two dowel pins, and two O-rings on top of the crankcase.

Rotate the engine until no. 2 and 3 pistons are at top dead center and place a piston base (Honda part number 07033-30001) under the pistons to hold them in position. (A block of wood cut to suitable size works just as well.) Compress the rings on no. 2 and 3 pistons (after oiling them liberally) and slide the cylinder barrel down over them. Rotate the engine until no. 1 and 4 pistons contact the base of the cylinder (taking care not to pull no. 2 and 3 pistons out of their bores), compress the rings, and slide the cylinder over the pistons. Before seating the cylinder against the crankcase, raise the cam chain through the center of the cylinder

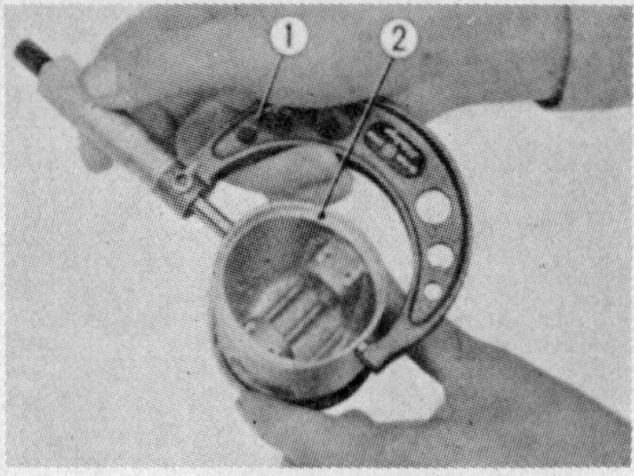

Measuring the diameter of the piston skirt
1. Micrometer
2. Piston skirt

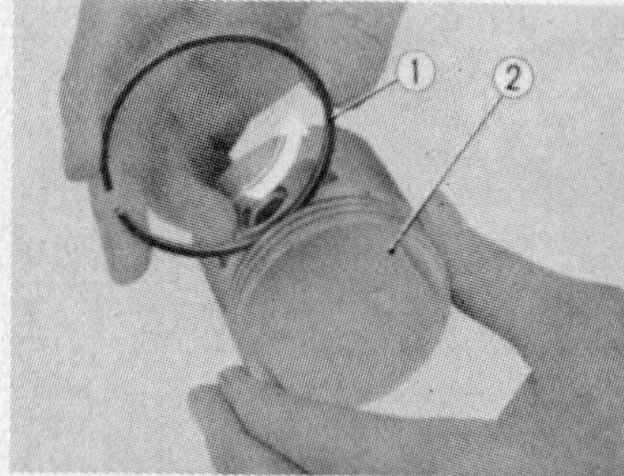

Roll the rings around the grooves to check for sufficient clearance

Tensioner roller rubber mounts (1)

and put a screwdriver through the center of it to keep it from dropping down.

CYLINDER HEAD INSTALLATION

Install the cylinder head gasket, two dowel pins, and two O-rings on the cylin-

Make sure the O-rings (1) and dowel pins (2) are in position

der. Mount the cylinder head on the cylinder while pulling the cam chain through the center of the head. Hold the chain to keep it from dropping down, using a screwdriver as before. Install and tighten the cylinder head nuts to 14–15 ft lbs in the proper sequence. Tighten the five, 6 mm head bolts to 8 ft lbs, starting with the center bolts and working out.

CAUTION: *Take care not to drop any hardware into the crankcase.*

To set the valve timing properly, remove the ignition points cover and rotate the engine clockwise until the "T" mark (for no. 1 and 4 pistons) aligns with the index timing mark (top dead center). Bolt the camshaft holder onto the head, hold the cam chain and sprocket together, and install the camshaft through them from the right side of the engine. Rotate the camshaft until the marks at the end of the shaft are aligned with the bearing cap joint, as illustrated. The groove must be toward the top.

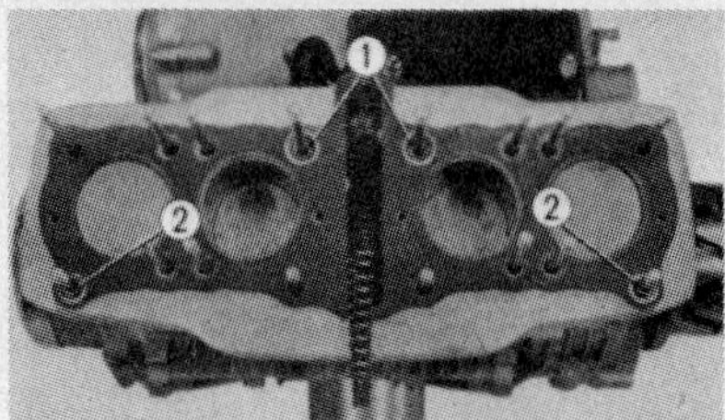

Make sure the O-rings (1) and dowel pins (2) are in position

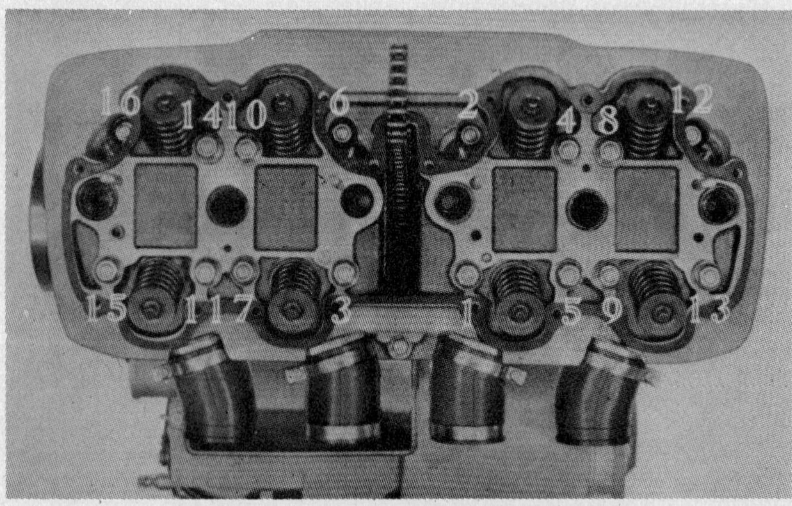

Cylinder head nut tightening sequence. Arrows point to the five small head bolts.

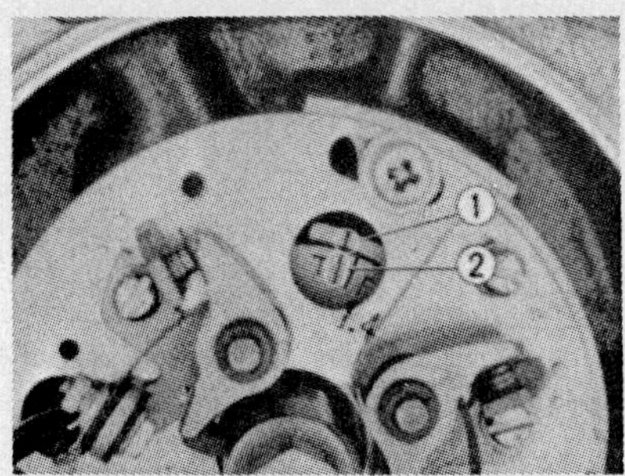

Aligning the index mark (1) and the "T" (2) mark

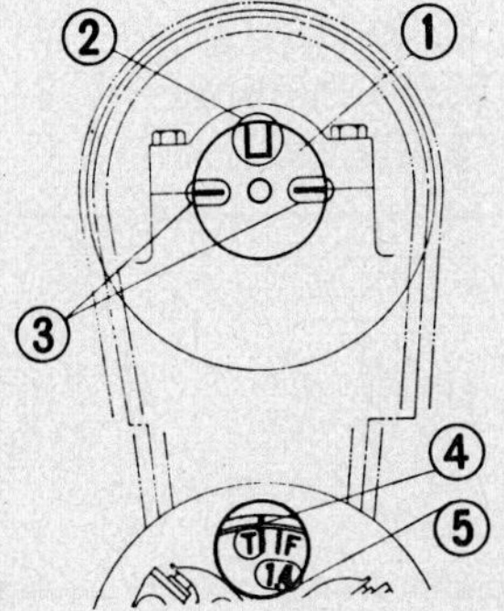

Aligning the camshaft timing marks

1. Camshaft
2. Groove
3. Index lines
4. T mark
5. 1.4 mark

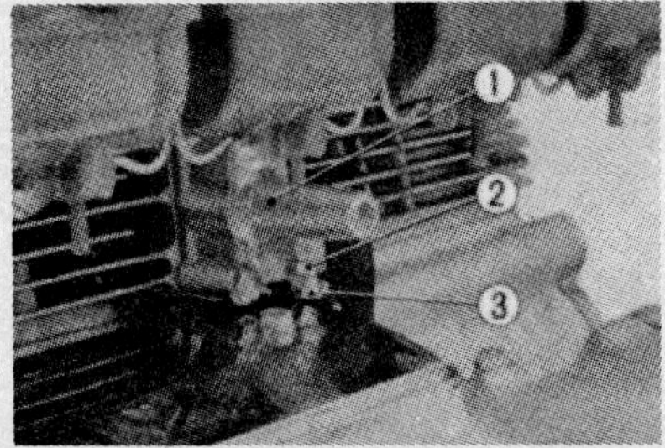

Cam chain tensioner (1) is at the rear of the cylinders. After the crankshaft has been correctly positioned, simply loosen the locknut (2) and the adjuster bolt (3). Chain tension is automatically adjusted when the adjuster bolt is loosened.

Place the cam chain over the sprocket, bolt the sprocket onto the camshaft, and install the bearing caps. Make sure that the caps are replaced in their original positions (note the matching marks on cap and holder), and tighten the cap nuts and bolts to 7–9 ft lbs.

Install the rocker arms and rocker arm shafts, tightening the shaft retaining bolts to 6–8 ft lbs. Make sure that the rocker arms are installed in their original positions. Loosen the cam-chain tensioner locknut and adjuster bolt, and install the tensioner on the rear of the cylinder.

Adjust the valve clearance in accordance with procedures in chapter 3, and install the camshaft cover.

NOTE: *Before the cover is installed, take out the tachometer drive-gear limit bolt, coat the threads with thread-lock compound, and tighten the bolt firmly to prevent the possibility of it loosening from heat and vibration.*

Fit the breather cover and install the engine in the frame. Perform a complete tune-up. Do not neglect to adjust the cam chain tension and refill the engine with oil.

Bottom End Overhaul

DISASSEMBLY

1. Remove the engine from the frame, and remove the cylinder head, cylinder, pistons, and cam chain tensioner as described in preceding sections.
2. Take off the left-side crankcase covers and remove the alternator rotor using, if possible, a rotor puller (Honda part number 07011–30001).
3. Remove the starter motor reduction gear and starter clutch gear.
4. Remove the shift linkage arm, shift-drum side plate, and shift-arm limit plate.
5. Take off the ignition points cover, unscrew the nut at the end of the breaker cam, and remove the special washer. Remove the three screws and withdraw the complete breaker plate assembly. Remove the ignition advance unit and advance shaft.
6. Remove the clutch unit. Refer to the clutch service section in this chapter.
7. Remove the transmission countershaft bearing retainer.
8. Take out the upper crankcase mounting bolts, turn the engine upside down, and remove the lower crankcase mounting bolts. Tap the crankcases with a rubber mallet and lift the lower crankcase away.

NOTE: *The starter motor cover must be removed to gain access to one of the upper bolts.*

Starter clutch gear (1) and starter motor reduction gear (2)

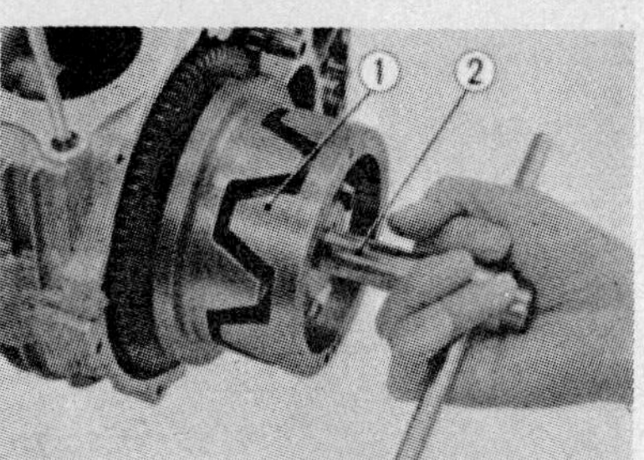

Removing the alternator rotor

1. Alternator rotor
2. Rotor puller

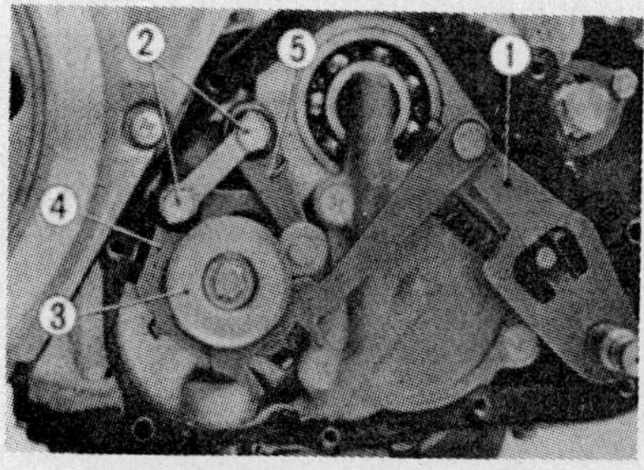

Installed shifter mechanism

1. Shift arm
2. 6 mm bolts
3. Shift drum side plate
4. Shift arm stopper
5. Shift drum stopper

Transmission bearing retainer (1)

Upper crankcase mounting bolts

1. 6 mm bolts
2. 10 mm bolt
3. 8 mm bolts

9. Raise the transmission mainshaft and lift the primary chain off the sprocket. Put the mainshaft assembly aside.
10. Lift out the crankshaft. Unscrew the connecting rod bearing cap nuts and remove the rods from the crankshaft. Mark or tag the rods so they may be installed in their original positions.

CRANKSHAFT INSPECTION

Check crankshaft runout by placing

2
1
2
2
4 3

Lower crankcase mounting bolts
1. 8 mm bolts
2. 6 mm bolts
3. 10 mm nut
4. 8 mm nut

the ends of the crankshaft in V-blocks and rotating it while taking a reading with a dial indicator at the center journal. If runout exceeds 0.002 in. (0.05 mm), the crankshaft should be replaced. (Runout equals one-half the dial indicator reading.)

MAIN BEARINGS

Journal wear can be checked using a material such as plastigauge. Cut strips of plastigauge to fit across each bearing, install the crankshaft and lower crankcase, and torque the 8 mm lower crankcase bolts in the correct sequence to 15 ft lbs. Do not turn the crankshaft. Unbolt the case, lift out the crankshaft, and measure the plastigauge with the scale provided. If clearance exceeds 0.0032 in. (0.08 mm), the bearings should be replaced. Do not reuse bearings that are damaged in any way.

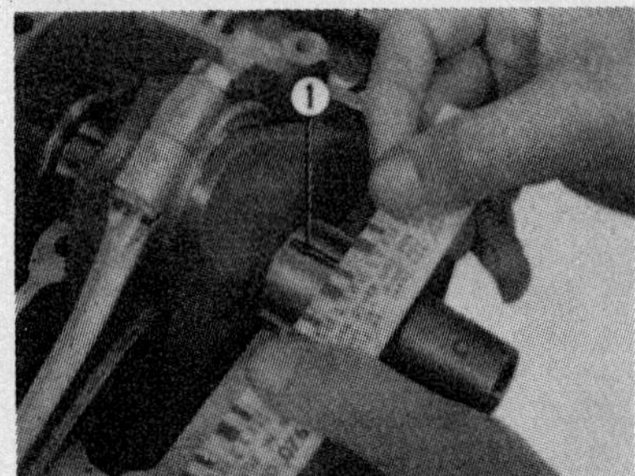
1

Measuring a Plastigauge® strip (1) to determine main bearing clearance

Inspect the journals for scoring and damage. Measure the journal diameter in several places to check for ovality and taper. Maximum acceptable variation of journal diameter is 0.002 in. (0.05 mm).

NOTE: *When the bearing halves are installed in the crankcases, the tops of the bearings should protrude 0.0027–.0039 in. (0.068–.098 mm) above the crankcase flanges.*

Main Bearing Selection

In most cases, the original bearing inserts can be replaced with new bearings of the same size. Size identification is made by the color code on the end surface of each bearing. Simply replace each main bearing insert with one of the same color.

It may be desirable, however, to measure the diameter of the crankshaft journals so that journal wear (if any) can be taken into account when selecting bearing size. In this case, it will be necessary to convert journal sizes into code letters so that the appropriate bearings can be selected. After the diameter of each journal has been measured, refer to the following chart for journal size codes.

JOURNAL DIAMETER CODE CHART

Journal Diameter	Code
36.000-35.995 mm	A
35.995-35.990 mm	B
35.990-35.985 mm	C

NOTE: *The original (new) crankshaft journal size codes, which you may want to refer to, can be found stamped on the side of the crankshaft weight adjacent to the primary drive sprocket. (See the illustration.) However, on very early engines (up to engine number CB 750E–1015587), Japanese symbols were used instead of letters for journal size coding. Disregard these symbols and rely on your own journal diameter measurements.*

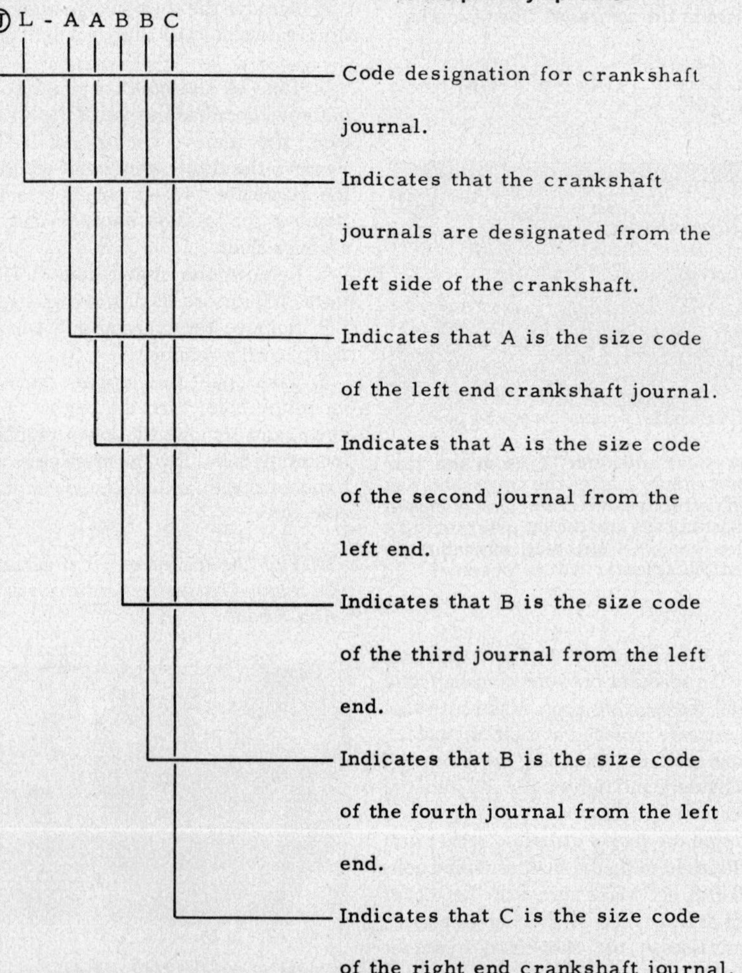
Ⓙ L - A A B B C
Code designation for crankshaft journal.
Indicates that the crankshaft journals are designated from the left side of the crankshaft.
Indicates that A is the size code of the left end crankshaft journal.
Indicates that A is the size code of the second journal from the left end.
Indicates that B is the size code of the third journal from the left end.
Indicates that B is the size code of the fourth journal from the left end.
Indicates that C is the size code of the right end crankshaft journal.

Description of a typical journal diameter code

After the journal size codes have been determined, locate the main-bearing seat diameter code which is stamped on the lower crankcase as shown in the accompanying illustration. For reference purposes, the code letters convert as follows:

BEARING SEAT DIAMETER CODE CHART

Seat Diameter	Code
39.000-39.008 mm	A
39.008-39.016 mm	B
39.016-39.024 mm	C

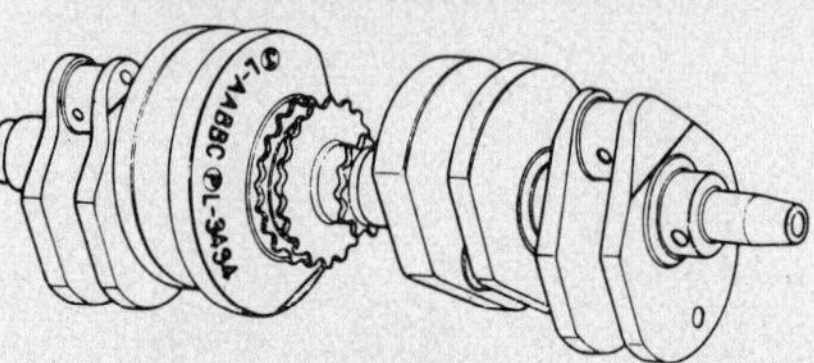

The original crankshaft journal diameter code is stamped on the weight adjacent to the primary sprocket

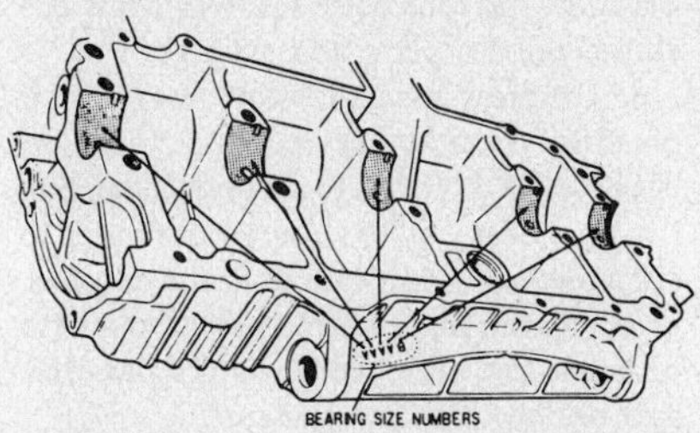
BEARING SIZE NUMBERS

Bearing seat diameter production (original) code

BEARING SELECTION CHART

Seat Code	Journal Code A	B	C
A	yellow	yellow	green
B	green	green	brown
C	brown	brown	black

Finally, using the journal and seat diameter code letters you have arrived at for each bearing, select the proper bearing color codes.

CONNECTING RODS AND BEARINGS

Rod Bearing Selection

Connecting rod bearings need not be replaced unless the bearing shells show signs of wear and/or damage, or unless there is excessive clearance between the bearing and crankpin. To check the clearance, cut a strip of plastigauge and place it across the bearing shell, as when checking main bearing clearance. Install the rod bearing cap and tighten the nuts to 14.5 ft lbs. Do not turn the crankshaft or move the connecting rod. Remove the cap and measure the plastigauge with the scale. Maximum acceptable clearance is 0.0032 in. (0.08 mm).

CRANKPIN DIAMETER CODE CHART

Crankpin Diameter	Code
36.000-35.995 mm	3
35.995-35.990 mm	4
35.990-35.985 mm	5

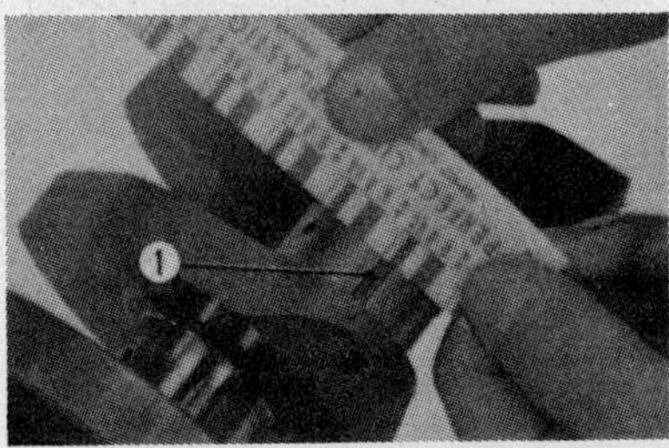
1

Measuring a Plastigauge® strip (1) on the crankpin to determine rod bearing oil clearance

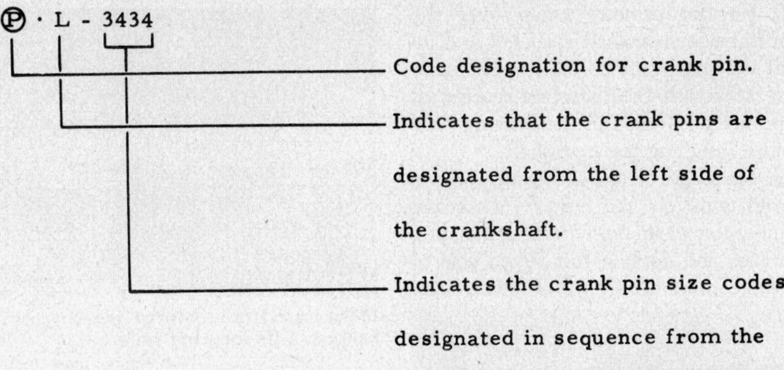
Ⓟ · L - 3434
Code designation for crank pin.
Indicates that the crank pins are designated from the left side of the crankshaft.
Indicates the crank pin size codes designated in sequence from the left side of the crankshaft.

The original crankpin diameter codes are stamped on the crankshaft next to the journal codes

In most cases, the original bearings can be replaced with new bearings of the same size. Size identification is made by the color code on the end surface of each bearing. Simply replace each rod bearing with one of the same color.

It may be desirable, however, to measure the diameter of the crankpins so that wear can be taken into account when selecting bearing size. In this case it will be necessary to convert crankpin sizes into code numbers so that the appropriate bearings can be selected, in the same manner as main bearing selection. After the diameter of each crankpin has been measured, refer to the following chart for crankpin size codes.

After the crankpin size codes have been determined, locate the rod bearing seat diameter code, stamped on the side of the connecting rod big end.

CAUTION: *The connecting rod must be held with the small end down, as shown, when reading the code number. Otherwise, the rod* weight *code (stamped on the bearing cap) could become confused with the* seat diameter *code.*

Bearing Seat Diameter Code Chart

Seat Diameter	*Code*
39.000–39.008 mm	1
39.008–39.016 mm	2
39.016–39.024 mm	3

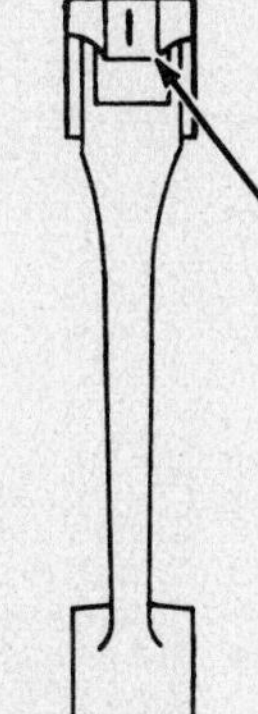

The bearing seat diameter code number (arrow) is stamped on the big end of the rod.

For reference purposes, the seat diameter code numbers convert as follows:

Finally, using the crankpin and seat diameter code numbers you have arrived at for each bearing, select the proper bearing color codes.

BEARING SELECTION CHART

Seat Code	Crankpin Code 3	4	5
1	yellow	yellow	green
2	green	green	brown
3	brown	brown	black

CONNECTING ROD REPLACEMENT

If a connecting rod is to be replaced, a replacement of the same weight code as the original should be selected. Rod weight can be determined by the code letter stamped on the rod bearing cap. When replacing all four rods, ensure that the weight codes are the same. Rod weight includes the bearing cap and bolts, but does not include the bearing shells.

NOTE: *Prior to engine number CB 750E–1017739, Japanese symbols were used for the rod weight code. The connecting rods used in engines produced after this engine number use letter codes and the machined surfaces on either side of the big end are slightly redesigned. The old and new type rods are interchangeable; however, when replacing an old-type rod with a new-type, always select one having a weight code of A, regardless of the symbol that appears on the old rod.*

ASSEMBLY

1. Fit the cam and primary drive chains onto the crankshaft and install the connecting rods in their original positions, as marked. Tighten the rod bolts to 15 ft lbs. Lubricate the bearings and install the crankshaft in the upper crankcase.

2. Fit the primary chain over the transmission mainshaft sprocket and install the mainshaft in the upper crankcase. Make sure the mainshaft bearing set rings are positioned in the bearing seats before installing the mainshaft.

3. Install the oil collar, O-ring, and two dowel pins on the upper crankcase. Thoroughly clean both crankcase mating surfaces and apply a thin, even coat of gasket cement to only one of the surfaces.

Make sure the oil collar (1), O-ring (1), and dowel pins (2) are correctly positioned

4. Carefully fit the lower crankcase half on the upper one. Install and tighten the ten, 8 mm lower crankcase mounting bolts to 17–18 ft lbs. Next, install the 6 mm mounting bolts and tighten to 8 ft lbs.

Tightening sequence for the 8 mm crankcase bolts. The 6 mm bolts are circled.

5. Turn the engine over so that it is resting on the lower crankcase in its normal position and then install the upper crankcase mounting bolts. Refit the starter motor cover and install the transmission countershaft bearing retainer.

6. Install the clutch assembly, shift linkage arm and limit plate, and shift-drum side plate.

7. Install the ignition advance shaft and mount the advance unit on the shaft. The pin at the back of the advance unit must fit into the crankshaft pin hole. Install the contact breaker plate assembly with the three screws, fit the special washer on the end of the cam, and install the nut.

8. Install the starter motor reduction gear and starter clutch gear.

9. Fit the alternator rotor on the end of the crankshaft and tighten the rotor retaining nut to 70 ft lbs.

Make sure the advancer locating pin is seated in its locating hole

1. Locating hole
2. Dowel pin
3. Ignition advancer shaft

NOTE: *Make sure that the crankshaft and rotor mating surfaces are perfectly smooth. If the rotor has a tendency to slip on the shaft, even after the nut has been properly torqued, apply a thin layer of valve lapping compound to the crankshaft taper and reinstall the rotor. This will cure slipping problems.*

10. Reassemble the top end components as described in the top end overhaul section. Install the engine in the frame. Do not forget to refill the engine with oil. Turn the kill switch to the "off" position and crank the engine over until oil pressure is developed before starting it.

Clutch Service

DISASSEMBLY

1. Remove the clutch cover plate and disconnect the clutch cable from the release lever.

2. Take out the mounting screws and remove the clutch (rear crankcase) cover. Unscrew the four bolts and withdraw the clutch release plate and springs.

3. Unscrew the clutch locknut using, if possible, Honda service tool number 07086–30001. If the tool is not available, the next best way to remove the nut is to cut a piece of steel plate to fit the notches, gripping the plate with a pair of pliers to unscrew the nut. Avoid using a hammer and punch to loosen the nut.

4. After the nut has been removed, the clutch center section can be withdrawn.

Disconnecting the clutch cable

1. Release lever
2. Clutch cable
3. Clutch cover

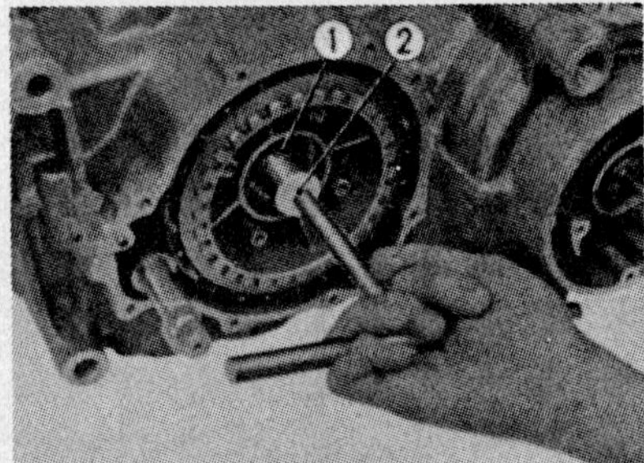

Removing the clutch locknut

1. Clutch locknut
2. Locknut removing socket

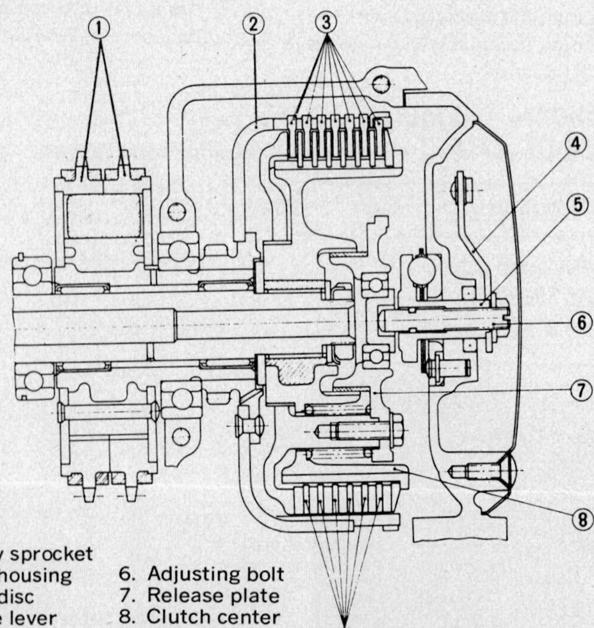

1. Primary sprocket
2. Clutch housing
3. Clutch disc
4. Release lever
5. Release shaft
6. Adjusting bolt
7. Release plate
8. Clutch center
9. Clutch plate

Schematic diagram of the clutch assembly

Clutch release plate (1)

Then remove the outside (smaller diameter) clutch disc and the outer ring; now the remaining discs and plates can be removed.

5. Remove the washer and pressure plate, and pull the clutch housing off the transmission mainshaft.

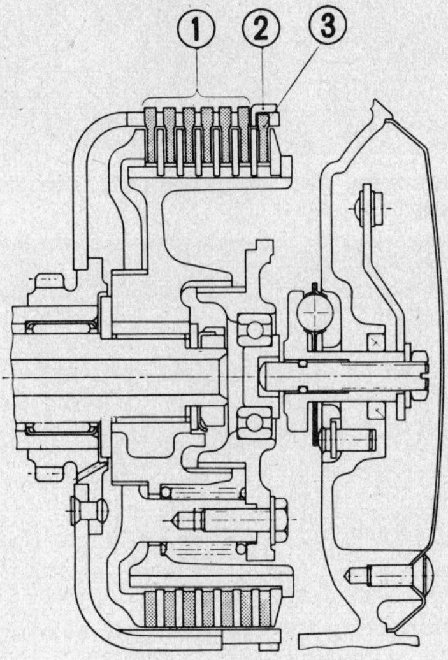

Clutch disc placement

1. Clutch discs
2. Outer ring
3. Outer disc (smaller diameter)

INSPECTION

1. Measure the thickness of the friction discs and replace if less than 0.122 in. (3.1 mm).

2. Place the clutch plate on a flat surface and check for excessive warpage with a feeler gauge. Replace the plates *and discs* if warpage is greater than 0.012 in. (0.3 mm).

3. Measure the free-length of the clutch springs and replace if less than 1.2 in. (30.5 mm), or if they are not all of the same length.

ASSEMBLY

1. Install the clutch housing and spline washer on the mainshaft.

2. Place the pressure plate inside the housing and install the clutch discs and plates, alternately (beginning with a disc), until all but the outside (smaller diameter) disc is in place. Fit the outer ring and then install the outside disc.

3. Install the clutch center section, spring washer (tab toward the front),

Installing the clutch housing on the mainshaft

1. Clutch housing
2. Spline washer
3. Pressure plate

lockwasher, and locknut in that order. Tighten the locknut to 33–36 ft lbs.

4. Install the clutch springs and the release plate using the four mounting bolts.

5. Install the crankcase (clutch) cover and connect the clutch cable to the release lever. Adjust the clutch.

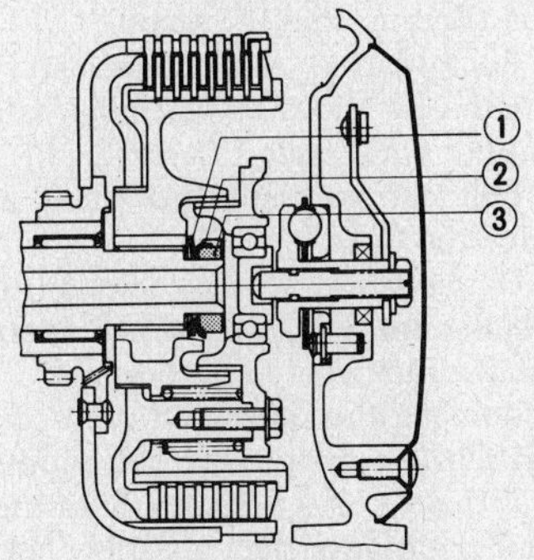

Locking components placement

1. Spring washer
2. Lockwasher
3. Locknut

Primary Drive and Kick-Starter Mechanism Service

PRIMARY DRIVE CHAIN INSPECTION

An automatic primary chain tensioner is incorporated to reduce chain vibration, wear, and noise. However, it is possible for the chain to stretch beyond the range

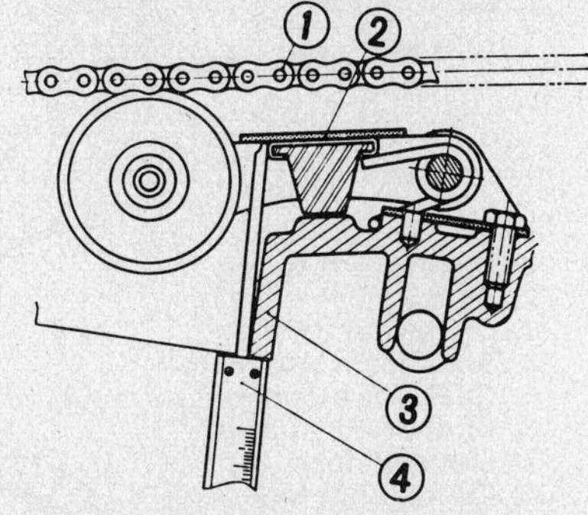

Primary tensioner assembly

1. Primary chain
2. Chain tensioner
3. Lower crankcase
4. Vernier caliper

of the tensioner, resulting in excessive primary drive noise. Chain wear can be checked without disassembling the engine. Proceed as follows:

1. Drain the oil from the crankcase.

2. Unscrew the ten oil pan mounting bolts and drop the pan.

3. Measure the distance between the chain tensioner bracket and the oil-pan mounting flange with a vernier caliper, as shown. The chain should be replaced if the measurement exceeds 2.756 in. (70 mm).

4. Examine the tensioner roller and replace it if damaged or noticeably worn.

Primary chain tensioner (1) installed in crankcase

DISASSEMBLY

Disassembly of the primary drive or kick-start mechanism entails splitting the crankcases. The crankcases can be separated *without* disassembling the top end components, however. Remove the engine and follow disassembly steps 2–9 under "Bottom End Overhaul."

Primary Drive

To remove the drive chain, simply lift the crankshaft out of the case and slip the chain off. If necessary, the mainshaft chain sprocket can be removed from the shaft and replaced. However, if the crankshaft sprocket is worn or damaged, the crankshaft itself must be replaced.

Kick-Start Mechanism

To disassemble the kick-start mechanism, first remove the kick-start shaft retaining pin and withdraw the shaft. Remove the gear assembly and return spring. Finally, take off the ratchet spring and remove the kick-start pawl.

Check to make sure that the gear turns smoothly in one direction and locks in the other. The kick-start shaft diameter should not measure less than 0.7847 in. (19.930 mm), and the inside diameter of the gear (shaft bore) should not exceed 0.7904 in. (20.075 mm). Replace parts as necessary.

Install the gear, kick-start flange, and return spring together in the lower crankcase. Hook the end of the spring on the case and force the flange down with a screwdriver to hook it on the pin. Install the kick-start shaft and shaft retaining pin.

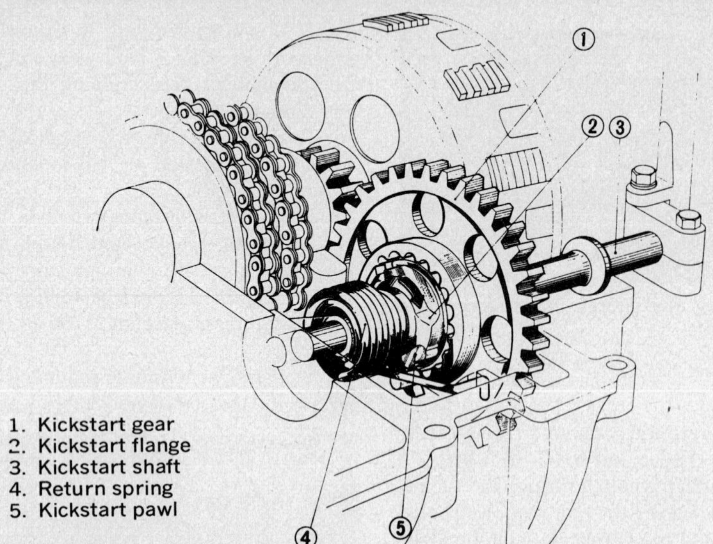

Kickstarter assembly

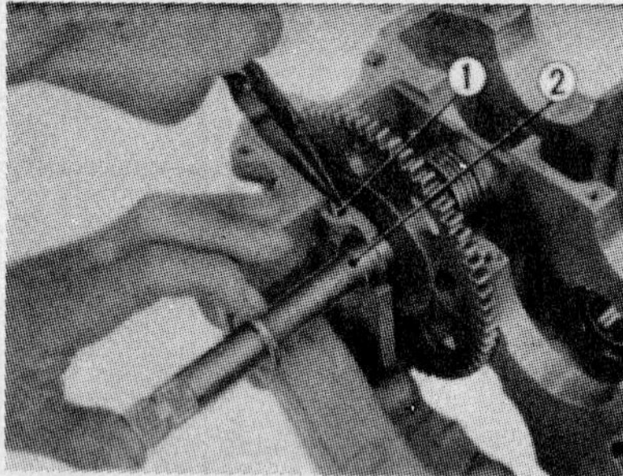

Removing the kickstart shaft retaining pin (1) to free the shaft (2)

Seating the kickstart return spring (2) on the kickstart flange (1)

ASSEMBLY

Reassemble the engine in accordance with the assembly procedures given in the bottom end overhaul section, omitting steps 1 and 10. Install the engine in the frame and refill the engine with oil. Before starting the engine, crank it over on the starter (with the kill switch off) until oil pressure is developed.

Transmission and Shifter Mechanism Service

DISASSEMBLY

1. It will not be necessary to disassemble the top end components in order to work on the transmission. It is necessary, however, to split the cases. Remove the engine and follow disassembly steps 3–9 under "Bottom End Overhaul."

2. Remove the final driveshaft oil guide and lift the shaft assembly out of the upper crankcase.

3. Pull out the shift fork shaft and remove the forks.

4. Unscrew the neutral detent (stopper) bolt, remove the detent, and remove the shift drum from the crankcase.

5. Remove the outer (left-side) countershaft ball bearing, slide the countershaft fifth gear off the shaft as illustrated, and lift the countershaft assembly out of the lower crankcase.

6. The inner (right-side) countershaft bearing can now be removed if it is to be replaced. Drive the bearing out or pull it out using a slide-hammer type puller, Honda part number 07048–30025.

INSPECTION

1. Set the mainshaft and countershaft gear assemblies into the lower crankcase and measure gear backlash. Maximum acceptable backlash is 0.008 in. (0.20 mm) for all five gearsets. Replace gears (mating pairs) on both shafts that exceed the limits.

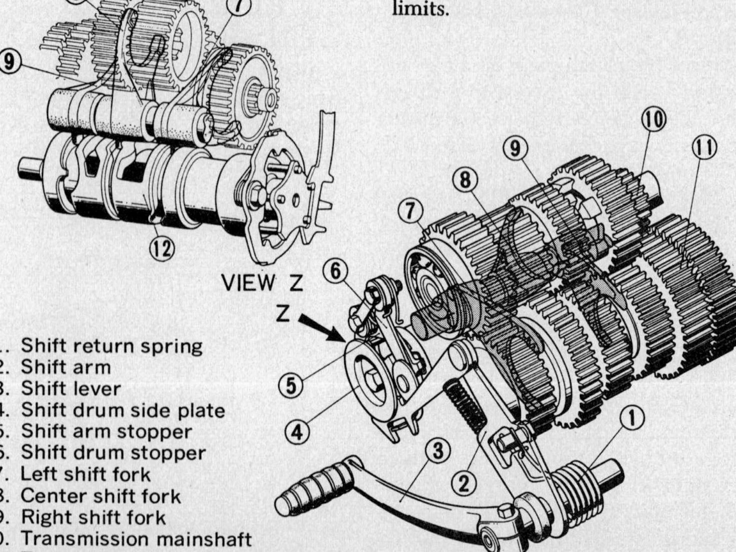

Shifter mechanism assembly

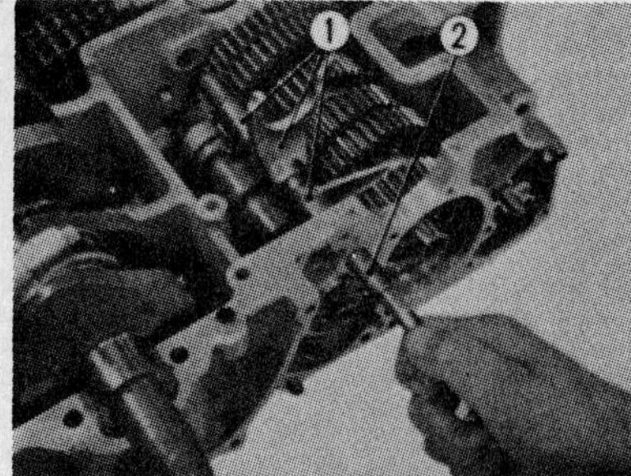

Removing the shift fork shaft (2) and forks (1)

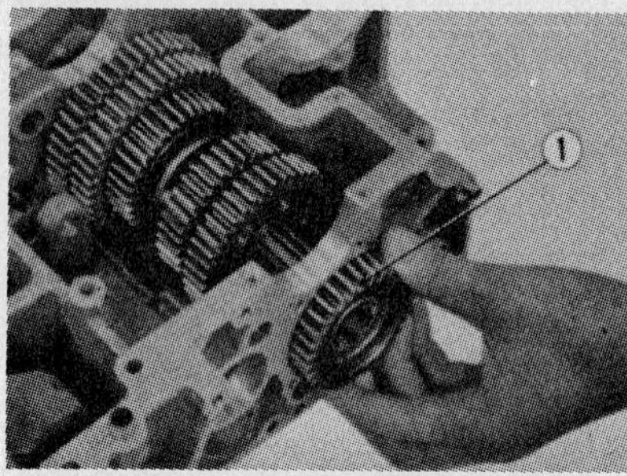

Removing the countershaft fifth (c5) gear (1)

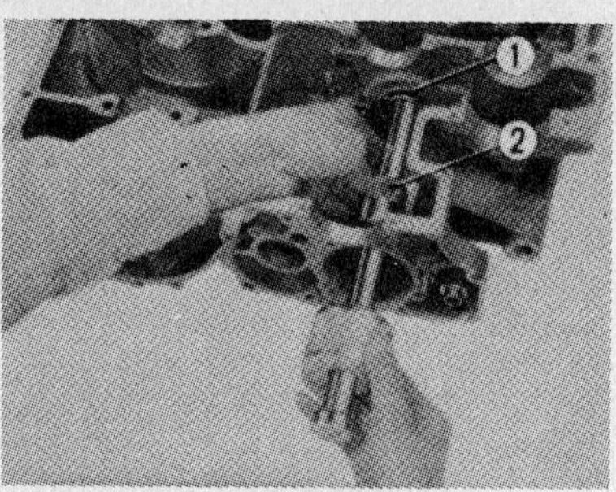

Removing the countershaft bearing

1. Countershaft bearing
2. Bearing puller

2. Examine the dogs on the respective gears and if damaged or excessively worn, the gears should be replaced. Check to make sure that the gears are free to slide smoothly on the shafts.

3. Compute the gear-to-shaft (or bushing) clearance of gears C_1, C_2, C_3, M_4, and M_5 by measuring shaft (or bushing) diameter and gear inside (bore) diameter. Replace the shaft, gear, or bushing if clearance exceeds 0.0072 in. (0.182 mm).

4. Measure the thickness of the shift fork fingers. Replace the fork if the fingers are worn to less than 0.240 in. (6.1 mm), or if the diameter of the dog (cam track roller) is worn to less than 0.260 in. (6.6 mm). Check the inside diameter of the forks (shaftbearing), which should be no greater than 0.5134 in. (13.04 mm). Correspondingly, the fork shaft diameter must not be worn to less than 0.5079 in. (12.9 mm).

5. Examine the shift drum cam tracks for damage and wear, and measure the diameter of the drum, as illustrated. Replace the drum if the diameter has worn to less than 0.5154 in. (11.95 mm) (right side) or 1.4142 in. (35.92 mm) (left side), or if the cam tracks do not appear to be in perfect condition.

ASSEMBLY

NOTE: *Press fit ball bearings must be heated before installation on their shafts.*

1. Assemble the mainshaft and countershaft components onto their shafts. *Do not reuse the old circlips.* Take care to install the new circlips with the smooth edge against the thrust washer. Refer to the exploded view of the components for order of assembly.

2. Install the right-side countershaft bearing in the crankcase (if removed) and fit the countershaft assembly into place. Install the countershaft fifth gear and left-side bearing on the end of the countershaft.

3. Install the shift drum and neutral detent. Neutral position on the shift drum is at the depression on the drum.

4. Install the shift forks as shown, with the forks marked "R" and "L" fitted to the grooves in the countershaft fourth and fifth (C4 and C5) gears, respectively. The fork marked "C" is fitted to the mainshaft second and third-gear unit. The rollers (dogs) at the back of the shift forks should be located in the shift drum cam tracks. Install the fork shaft into the case and through the forks.

5. Place the bearing set ring in the bearing seat and install the final driveshaft assembly in the upper crankcase. Install the final driveshaft oil guide.

6. Mount the primary chain on the mainshaft sprocket and lower the mainshaft assembly into place. Do not forget to position the bearing set rings in the bearing seats before installing the mainshaft. Make sure all gears are in neutral before assembling the cases.

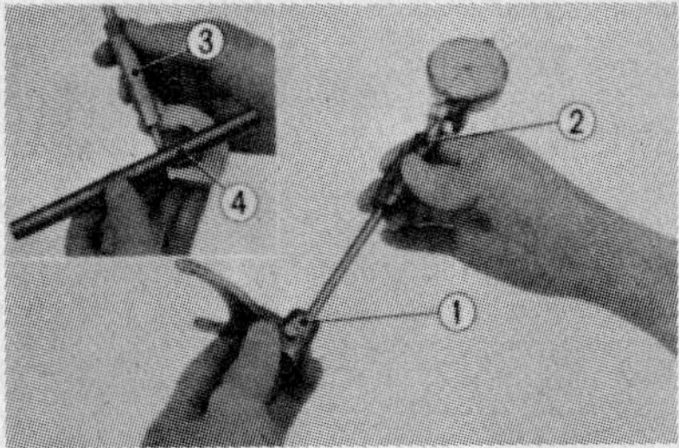

Checking clearances of the shift forks and shaft

1. Shift fork
2. Dial indicator
3. Micrometer
4. Shift fork shaft

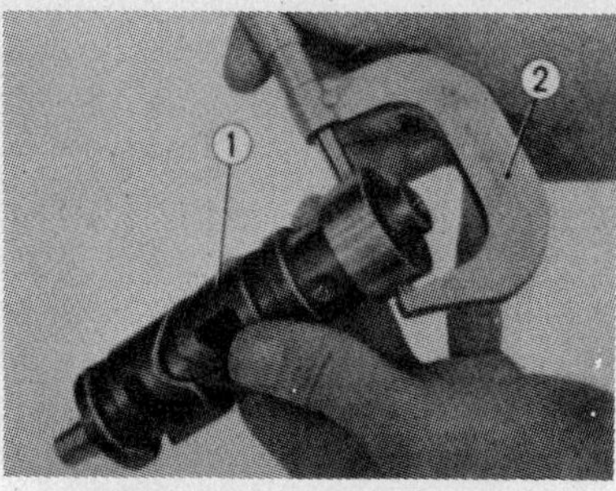

Measuring the shifter drum

7. Follow assembly steps 3–8 under "Bottom End Overhaul," and install the engine in the frame. Refill the engine with oil and crank the engine over (with the kill switch off) until oil pressure is developed before allowing it to start.

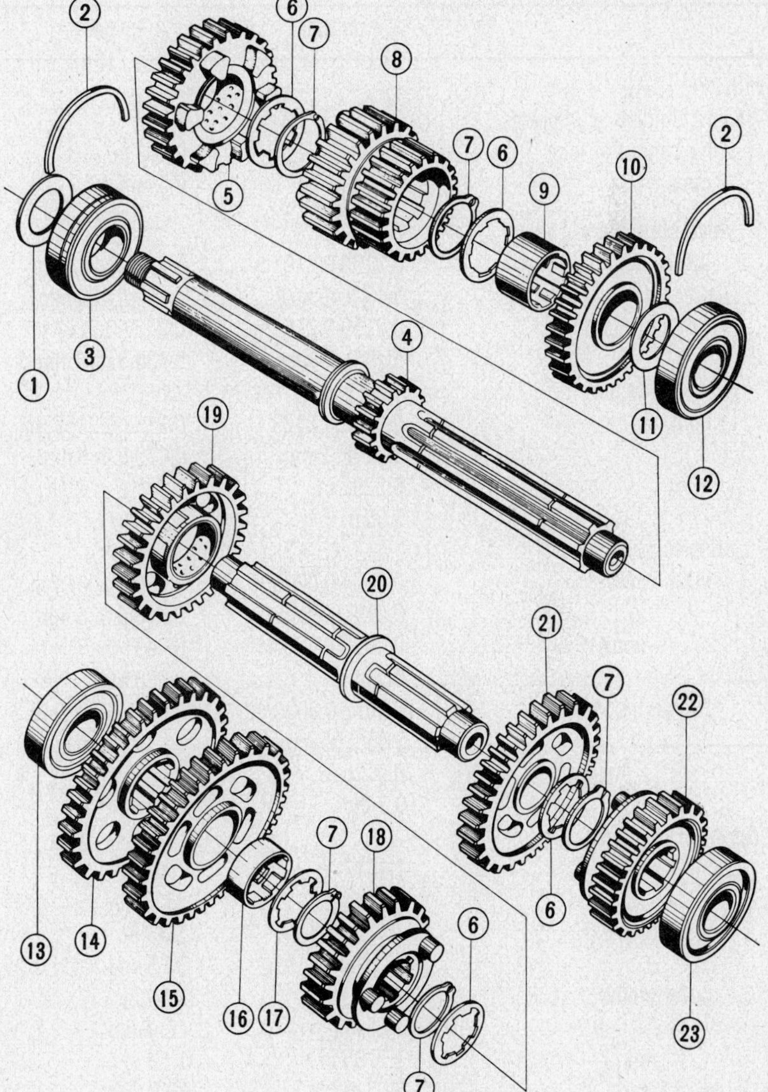

Exploded view of the transmission components

1. Thrust washer
2. Bearing set ring
3. Ball bearing
4. Mainshaft
5. M4 gear (37 T)
6. Thrust washer
7. Circlip
8. M2 and M3 gear (24 & 27 T)
9. Bushing
10. M5 gear (33 T)
11. Thrust washer
12. Ball bearing
13. Ball bearing
14. Final drive gear
15. C1 gear (47 T)
16. Bushing
17. Thrust washer
18. C4 gear (34 T)
19. C3 gear (36 T)
20. Countershaft
21. C2 gear (41 T)
22. C5 gear (31 T)
23. Ball bearing

Correct positioning of the shift forks (1)

Final drive shaft assembly (2) and oil guide (1) installed
1. Shift drum 2. Micrometer

ENGINE SPECIFICATIONS

	CB 350F	CB 500	CB 750	CB 750K1—K3
CYLINDER HEAD				
Valves, Guides, and Springs				
valve runout at face max.	0.002 in. 0.5 mm	0.002 in. 0.5 mm	0.002 in. 0.05 mm	0.002 in. 0.05 mm
valve stem diam.				
intake (nom.)	0.2158-0.2161 in. 5.48-5.49 mm	0.2145-0.2150 in. 5.450-5.465 mm	N.A.	N.A.
exhaust (nom.)	0.2150-0.2161 in. 5.46-5.47 mm	0.2137-0.2142 in. 5.430-5.445 mm	N.A.	N.A.
Valve guide bore				
nom.	0.2162-0.2173 5.49-5.52 mm	0.2153-0.2157 in. 5.475-5.485 mm	0.2598-0.2602 in. 6.60-6.61 mm	0.2598-0.2602 in. 6.60-6.61 mm
max.	0.2292 in. 5.55 m	N.A.	0.2614 in. 6.64 mm	0.2614 in. 6.64 mm
stem-to-guide clear.				
intake (nom.)	0.0004-0.0012 in. 0.01-0.03 mm	0.0004-0.0014 in. 0.010-0.035 mm	0.004-0.0012 in. 0.010-0.030 mm	0.0004-0.0012 in. 0.010-0.030 mm
(max.)	0.0018 in. 0.3 mm	0.0031 in. 0.080 mm	0.0031 in. 0.080 mm	0.0031 in. 0.080 mm
Exhaust (nom.)	0.0012-0.0020 in. 0.03-0.05 mm	0.0011-0.0019 in. 0.030-0.050 mm	0.0016-0.0024 in. 0.040-0.060 mm	0.0016-0.0024 in. 0.040-0.060 mm
(max.)	0.0118 in. 0.3 mm	0.0039 in. 0.10 mm	0.0039 in. 0.10 mm	0.0039 in. 0.10 mm
Spring free-length				
inner (nom.)	1.1417 in. 29.0 mm	1.40 in. 35.7 mm	1.50 in. 38.1 mm	1.50 in. 38.1 mm
(min.)	1.0630 in. 27.0 mm	1.35 in. 34.5 mm	1.4567 in. 37.0 mm	1.4567 in. 37.0 mm
outer (nom.)	1.3583 in. 34.5 mm	1.59 in. 40.4 mm	1.622 in. 41.2 mm	1.622 in. 41.2 mm
(min.)	1.2795 in. 32.5 mm	1.53 in. 39.0 m	1.5748 in. 40.0 mm	1.5748 in. 40.0 mm
Camshaft & Rocker Arms				
Valve timing (deg.)				
intake opens (BTDC)	5	N.A.	5	5
intake closes (ATDC)	35	N.A.	30	30

(con't.)	CB 350F	CB 500	CB 750	CB 750K1—K3
Exhaust opens (BTDC)	35	N.A.	35	35
Exhaust closes (ATDC)	5	N.A.	5	5
Cam height				
intake (nom.)	1.1096-1.1112 in. 28.185-28.225 mm	1.3742-1.3768 in. 34.93-34.97 mm	①	①
Exhaust (nom.)	1.1096-1.1111 in. 28.184-28.224 mm	1.3595-1.3610 in. 34.53-34.57 mm	②	②
intake (min.)	1.1024 in. 28.0 mm	1.3720 in. 34.85 mm	1.411 in. 35.86 mm	1.411 in. 35.86 mm
exhaust (min.)	1.1024 in. 28.0 mm	1.3563 in. 34.45 m	1.392 in. 35.36 mm	1.392 in. 35.36 mm
Base circle diam.				
nom.	N.A.	N.A.	1.1016-1.1030 in. 27.98-28.02 mm	1.1016-1.1030 in. 27.98-28.02 mm
min.	N.A.	N.A.	1.0996 in. 27.93 mm	1.0996 in. 27.93 mm
Runout max.	0.004 in. 0.1 mm	0.004 in. 0.1 mm	0.004 in. 0.1 mm	0.004 in. 0.1 mm
Cam bearing diam.				
nom.	N.A.	N.A.	0.8669-0.8678 in. 22.02-22.041 mm	0.8669-0.8678 in. 22.02-22.041 mm
max.	N.A.	N.A.	0.8701 mm 22.0 mm	0.8701 in. 22.0 mm
Rocker arm bearing diam.				
nom.	N.A.	N.A.	0.4724-0.4731 in. 12.00-12.018 mm	0.4724-0.4731 in. 12.00-12.018 mm
max.	N.A.	N.A.	0.4744 in. 12.05 mm	0.4744 in. 12.05 mm
Rocker arm shaft diam.				
nom.	N.A.	N.A.	0.4711-0.4718 in. 11.966-11.984 mm	0.4711-0.4718 in. 11.966-11.984 mm
min.	N.A.	N.A.	0.4701 in. 11.94 mm	0.4701 in. 11.94 mm
Rocker arm-to-rocker shaft clear.				
nom.	0.0020-0.0006 in. 0.016-0.052 mm	N.A.	N.A.	N.A.
min.	0.0039 in. 0.1 mm	N.A.	N.A.	N.A.
CYLINDERS, PISTONS, AND RINGS				
Cylinder Bore				
nom.	1.8504-1.8508 in. 47.00-47.01 mm	2.204-2.205 in. 56.00-56.01 mm	2.402-2.4024 in. 61.01-61.02 mm	2.402-2.4024 in. 61.01-61.02 mm
max.	1.8543 in. 47.1 mm	2.208 in. 56.1 mm	2.4055 in. 61.1 mm	2.4055 in. 61.1 mm
Taper and ovality max.	N.A.	N.A.	0.002 in. 0.05 mm	0.002 in. 0.05 mm
Pistons diameter				
nom.	1.8492-1.8500 in. 46.97-46.99 mm	2.204-2.203 in. 55.99-55.97 mm	2.4002-2.4009 in. 60.965-60.985 mm	2.4002-2.4009 in. 60.965-60.985 mm
min.	1.8445 in. 46.85 mm	2.198 in. 55.85 mm	2.3957 in. 60.85 mm	2.3957 in. 60.85 mm

(con't.)	CB 350F	CB 500	CB 750	CB 750K1—K3
Wrist pin hole diam.				
nom.	0.5119-0.5121 in. 13.002-13.008 mm	0.5906-0.5909 in. 15.002-15.008 mm	0.5906-0.5909 in. 15.002-15.008 mm	0.5906-0.5909 in. 15.002-15.008 mm
max.	0.5138 in. 13.05 mm	0.5937 in. 15.08 mm	0.5937 in. 15.08 mm	0.5937 in. 15.08 mm
Wrist pin diam.				
nom.	0.5116-0.5118 in. 12.994-13.00 mm	N.A.	0.5903-0.5906 in. 14.994-15.000 mm	0.5903-0.5906 in. 14.994-15.000 mm
min.	0.5079 in. 12.9 mm	N.A.	0.589 in. 14.96 mm	0.589 in. 14.96 mm
Available oversizes	0.25, 0.50, 0.75, and 1.00 mm			
Rings				
End gap				
compression (nom.)	0.0039-0.0118 in. 0.1-0.3 mm	0.005-0.013 in. 0.15-0.35 mm	0.0079-0.016 in. 0.2-0.4 mm	0.0079-0.016 in. 0.2-0.4 mm
oil control (nom.)	0.0039-0.0118 in. 0.1-0.3 mm	0.005-0.13 in. 0.15-0.35 mm	0.0004-0.0012 in. 0.1-0.3 mm	0.0004-0.0012 in. 0.1-0.3 mm
compression (max.)	0.0276 in. 0.7 mm	0.0276 in. 0.7 mm	0.0276 in. 0.7 mm	0.0276 in. 0.7 mm
oil control (max.)	0.0276 in. 0.7 mm	0.0276 in. 0.7 mm	0.0276 in. 0.7 mm	0.0276 in. 0.7 mm
Side clearance				
top (nom.)	0.0012-0.0022 in. 0.03-0.055 mm	0.0015-0.0029 in. 0.040-0.075 mm	0.0015-0.0028 in. 0.040-0.070 mm	0.0015-0.0028 in. 0.040-0.070 mm
2nd (nom.)	0.0006-0.0018 in. 0.015-0.045 mm	0.0010-0.0023 in. 0.025-0.060 mm	0.0010-0.0022 in. 0.025-0.055 mm	0.0010-0.022 in. 0.025-0.055 mm
oil (nom.)	0.0006 in. 0.015 mm	0.0007-0.0022 in. 0.020-0.055 mm	0.0004-0.0012 in. 0.010-0.040 mm	0.0004-0.0012 in. 0.010-0.040 mm
top (max.)	0.0059 in. 0.15 mm	0.007 in. 0.18 mm	0.007 in. 0.18 mm	0.007 in. 0.18 mm
2nd (max.)	0.0059 in. 0.15 mm	0.006 in. 0.15 mm	0.0065 in. 0.165 mm	0.0065 in. 0.165 mm
oil (max.)	0.0059 in. 0.015 mm	0.006 in. 0.15 mm	0.0045 in. 0.114 mm	0.0045 in. 0.114 mm
CRANKSHAFT AND CONNECTING RODS				
Crankshaft journals diam.				
nom.	1.2594-1.2598 in. 31.99-32.00 mm	1.2987-1.2992 in. 32.99-33.00 mm	1.4169-1.4173 in. 35.99-36.00 mm	1.4169-1.4173 in. 35.99-36.00 mm
min.	1.2586 in. 31.97 mm	1.2969 in. 32.94 mm	1.415 in. 35.94 mm	1.415 in. 35.94 mm
Taper and ovality				
max.	0.002 in. 0.05 mm	0.002 in. 0.05 mm	0.002 in. 0.05 mm	0.002 in. 0.05 mm
Oil clearance				
nom.	0.0008-0.0018 in. 0.020-0.046 mm	0.008-0.0018 in. 0.020-0.046 mm	0.0008-0.0018 in. 0.020-0.046 mm	0.008-0.0018 in. 0.020-0.046 mm
max.	0.0032 in. 0.08 mm	0.0032 in. 0.08 mm	0.0032 in. 0.08 mm	0.0032 in. 0.08 mm
Crankpins diam.*				
nom.	1.2594-1.2598 in. 31.99-32.00 mm	1.3775-1.3780 in. 34.99-35.00 mm	1.4169-1.4173 in. 35.99-36.00 mm	1.4169-1.4173 in. 35.99-36.00 mm
min.	1.2586 in. 31.97 mm	1.3757 in. 34.94 mm	1.415 in. 35.94 mm	1.415 in. 35.94 mm

(con't.)	CB 350F	CB 500	CB 750	CB 750K1—K3
Oil clear.				
nom.	0.0008-0.0018 in. 0.020-0.046 mm	0.0008-0.0018 in. 0.020-0.046 mm	0.0008-0.0018 in. 0.020-0.046 mm	0.0008-0.0018 in. 0.020-0.046 mm
max.	0.0032 in. 0.08 mm	0.0032 in. 0.08 mm	0.0032 in. 0.08 mm	0.0032 in. 0.08 mm
Connecting rods				
Wrist pin bushing diam.				
nom.	0.5123-0.5131 in. 13.012-13.033 mm	0.5912-0.5919 in. 15.016-15.034 mm	0.5912-0.5919 in. 15.016-15.034 mm	0.5912-0.5919 in. 15.016-15.034 mm
max.	0.5158 in. 13.10 mm	0.5933 in. 15.07 mm	0.5933 in. 15.07 mm	0.5933 in. 15.07 mm
Side clear.				
nom.	0.0008-0.0028 in. 0.02-0.07 mm	0.0047-0.0106 in. 0.12-0.27 mm	N.A.	N.A.
max.	0.0059 in. 0.15 mm	0.0138 in. 0.35 mm	N.A.	N.A.
Weight		③	③	③

N.A. Not Available.
* Main and connecting rod bearings are select-fitted to the crankshaft and bearing seats. See text.
① Valve lift—0.3142-0.3158 in./7.98-8.02 mm
② Valve lift—0.2945-0.2961 in./7.48-7.52 mm
③ Connecting rods are grouped and coded according to weight. Individual engines use rods of the same weight group. See text.
NOTE: When measuring the runout of any engine components, runout equals one-half the observed dial indicator reading.

CLUTCH AND TRANSMISSION SPECIFICATIONS

	CB 350F	CB 500	CB 750	CB 750K1—K3
CLUTCH				
Disc Thickness				
nom.	0.1032-0.1095 in. 2.62-2.78 mm	0.13 in. 3.30 mm	0.1347-0.1409 mm 3.42-3.58 mm	0.1347-0.1409 mm 3.42-3.58 mm
min.	0.0906 in. 2.3 mm	0.12 in. 3.0 mm	0.122 in. 3.1 mm	0.112 in. 3.1 mm
Plate Warpage				
max.	0.012 in. 0.03 mm	0.012 in. 0.03 mm	0.012 in. 0.03 mm	0.012 in. 0.03 mm
Springs				
Free-length				
nom.	1.3976 in. 35.5 mm	1.25 in. 31.9 mm	1.2575 in. 31.94 mm	1.2575 in. 31.94 mm
min.	1.3386 in. 34.0 mm	1.201 in. 30.5 mm	1.201 in. 30.5 mm	1.201 in. 30.5 mm
Strength				
nom., lb @ in.	42.557-45.643 @ 0.9842	228-238 @ 0.90	215-227 @ 0.98	215-227 @ 0.98
min., lb @ in.	N.A.	N.A.	199 @ 0.98	199 @ 0.98

(con't.)	CB 350F	CB 500	CB 750	CB 750K1—K3
TRANSMISSION				
Shift Drum				
outside diam.				
nom.	N.A.	1.5738-1.5728 in. 39.975-39.950 mm	N.A.	N.A.
min.	N.A.	1.5709 in. 39.9 mm	①	①
Shift Forks				
inside diam.				
nom.	0.5118-0.5125 in. 13.000-13.018 mm	1.5748-1.5757 in. 40.000-40.025 mm	N.A.	N.A.
max.	0.5098 in. 12.95 mm	1.5797 in. 40.075 mm	N.A.	N.A.

① 0.5154 in./11.95 mm (right side), 1.4142 in./35.92 mm (left side).

N.A. Not Available.

	CB 350F	CB 500	CB 750	CB 750K1—K3
Bearing inside diam.				
max.	N.A.	N.A.	0.5134 in. 13.04 mm	0.5134 in. 13.04 mm
Finger width				
center (nom.)	0.2335-0.2362 in. 5.93-6.00 mm	0.233-0.236 in. 5.93-6.00 mm	N.A.	N.A.
right & left (nom.)	0.2335-0.2362 in. 5.93-6.00 mm	0.194-0.197 in. 4.93-5.00 mm	N.A.	N.A.
center (min.)	0.2165 in. 5.5 mm	0.220 in. 5.60 mm	0.240 in. 6.10 mm	0.240 in. 6.10 mm
right & left (min.)	0.2165 in. 5.5 mm	0.181 in. 4.60 mm	0.240 in. 6.10 mm	0.240 in. 6.10 mm
Gear Backlash				
1st: nom.	②	0.0017-0.0052 in. 0.044-0.133 mm	0.0017-0.0055 in. 0.044-0.140 mm	0.0017-0.0055 in. 0.044-0.140 mm
max.		0.008 in. 0.20 mm	0.008 in. 0.20 mm	0.008 in. 0.20 mm
2nd & 3rd: nom.	③	0.0017-0.0052 in. 0.044-0.133 mm	0.0018-0.0055 in. 0.046-0.140 mm	0.0018-0.0055 in. 0.046-0.140 mm
max.		0.008 in. 0.20 mm	0.008 in. 0.20 mm	0.008 in. 0.20 mm
4th & 5th: nom.	0.0018-0.0056 in. 0.046-0.142 mm	0.0018-0.0055 in. 0.046-0.140 mm	0.0018-0.0055 in. 0.046-0.140 mm	0.0018-0.0055 in. 0.046-0.140 mm
max.	0.0079 in. 0.2 mm	0.008 in. 0.20 mm	0.008 in. 0.20 mm	0.008 in. 0.20 mm

② 1st and 2nd: nom. 0.0017-0.0053 in.
0.044-0.134 mm
max. 0.0079 in.
0.2 mm

③ 3rd: nom. 0.0018-0.0056 in.
0.046-0.142 mm
max. 0.0079 in.
0.2 mm

TORQUE SPECIFICATIONS

	CB 350F	CB 500	CB 750, CB 750K1—K3
Camshaft bearing cap nuts	N.A.	N.A.	7-9
Camshaft cover	1	1	6-8
Camshaft sprocket bolts	11.6-14.5	12-14	12-14
Clutch locknut	N.A.	N.A.	33-36
Connecting rod cap nuts	15	15	15
Crankcase bolts (6 mm)	5.1-8.0	8	8
Crankcase bolts (8 mm)	17-18	17-18	17-18

	CB 350F	CB 500	CB 750, CB 750K1—K3
Crankcase drain plug	26-29	26-29	26-29
Cylinder head bolts (6 mm)	14.5	N.A.	8
Cylinder head nuts	14.5	14.5-16.5	14-15
Cylinder studs	15-15	15-15	N.A.
Oil filter housing bolt	20-24	20-24	20-24
Oil pressure switch	11-14	11-14	11-14
Rocker arm shaft bolts	N.A.	N.A.	6-8
Spark plugs	9-12	9-12	9-12

— Not Applicable
N.A. Not Available

LUBRICATION SYSTEMS

LUBRICATION SYSTEM REPAIR

CB 350 F and CB 500

OIL PUMP REMOVAL AND INSTALLATION

The oil pump can be removed without removing the engine from the frame. The procedure is as follows:

1. Drain the engine oil.
2. Remove the starter motor cover 500.
3. Remove the shift lever and left footrest.
4. Remove the left crankcase cover. A hammer-driven impact wrench will aid in removing the screws without damaging the heads.
5. Disconnect the wire from the pressure switch, located on top of the pump.
6. Remove the pump mounting bolts and withdraw the pump.

Installation is in reverse order of removal. The following points should be observed:

1. Use new gaskets and O-rings.
2. Do not forget to refill the engine with oil.

OIL PUMP SERVICE

Disassembly

1. Remove the cap and withdraw the relief valve and spring.
2. Remove the three screws and the side cover, exposing the rotors. Withdraw the rotors and mark them as shown (if not already marked).
3. Remove the drive pin and withdraw the drive-gear shaft.
4. Unscrew the pressure switch from the pump body.

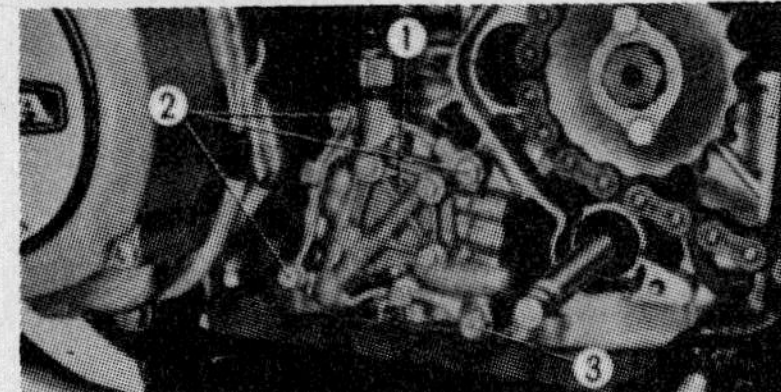

Oil pump mounting bolts (350)

1. Oil pump 3. 8 mm bolts
2. 6 mm bolts

The pump screen (1) should be cleaned at this time (350)

O-ring locations (350

1. O-ring, 15 x 2.5 3. O-ring, 9.9 x 1.5
2. O-ring, 63 x 2.5

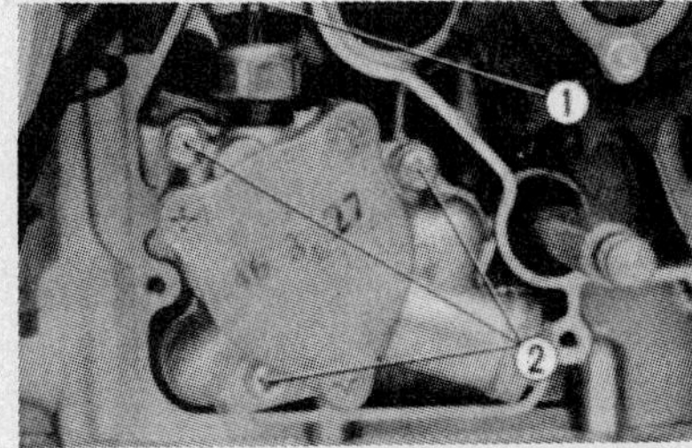

Oil pump installed (500)

1. Oil pressure switch lead
2. Oil pump mounting screws

Inspection

1. Measure the clearance between the inner and outer rotors, as illustrated. Replace both rotors if clearance exceeds 0.12 in. (.30 mm) (350) or 0.013 in. (0.35 mm) (500).
2. Measure the clearance between the outer rotor and housing. If clearance exceeds 0.013 in. (0.35 mm), the complete pump should be replaced.

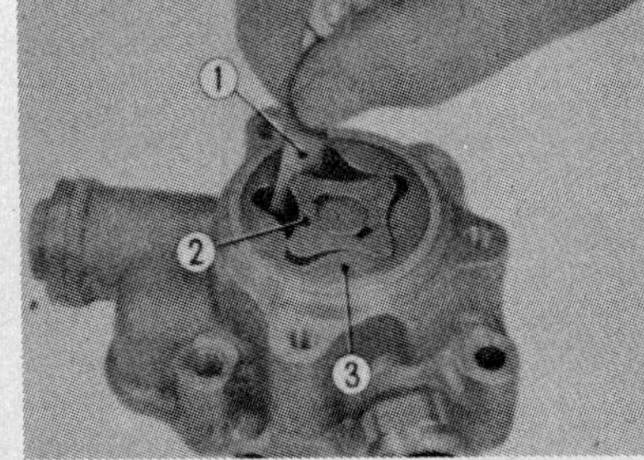

Checking rotor-to-rotor clearance (500)

1. Feeler gauge 3. Outer rotor
2. Inner rotor

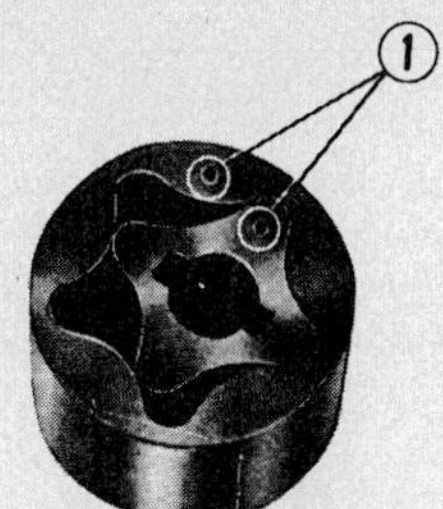

Rotor marks (1) allow the rotors to be assembled in their original positions (500)

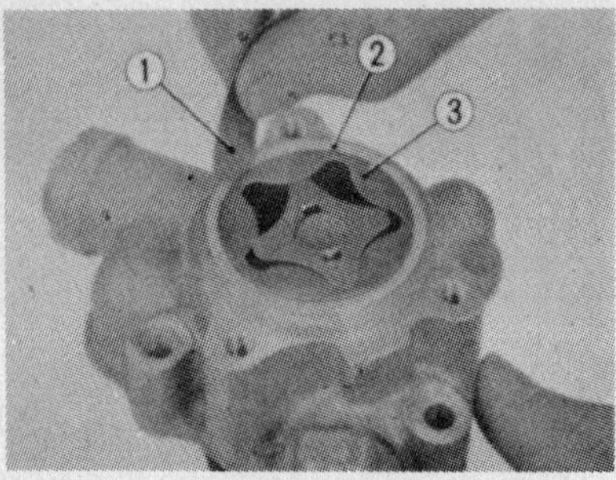

Checking rotor-to-housing clearance (500)
1. Feeler gauge
2. Pump body
3. Outer rotor

Oil pump mounting points
1. Oil pump
2. Oil pump mounting bolts

The shaft dowel pin (2) must be removed in order to remove the rotor shaft (1)

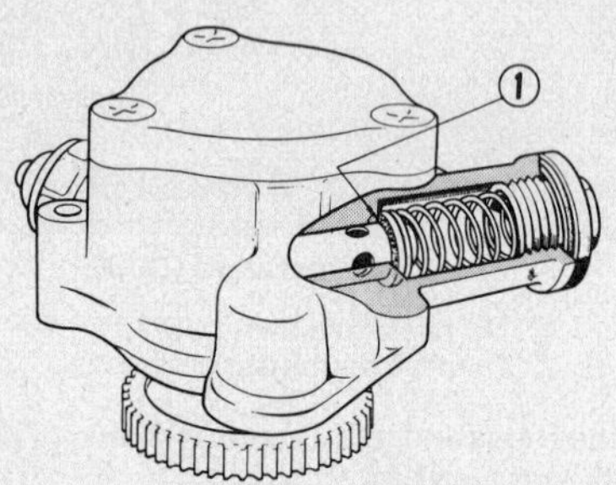

Check for foreign objects which may become lodged between the relief valve and seat (1) (500)

Make sure the collars and O-rings are correctly positioned (500)
1. Collar 2. O-ring 3. O-ring

3. Examine all components for damage and stress cracks.

4. Examine the relief valve for wear and replace if necessary. It is a good idea to replace the spring at this time to be sure of maintaining proper oil pressure.

Assembly

Assemble in reverse order of disassembly. Observe the following points:

1. Do not reuse old O-rings.

2. Lubricate all moving parts with oil before installing.

3. Be sure the drive pin is securely installed in the shaft.

4. When installing the rotors, make sure that the mark in the side of each faces in the same direction. The rotors may be installed with the marks facing either toward or away from the side cover.

5. Use extreme care when installing the pressure-relief valve cap. *Overtightening will cause the cap to fracture.* Tighten to 7.5–10 ft lbs.

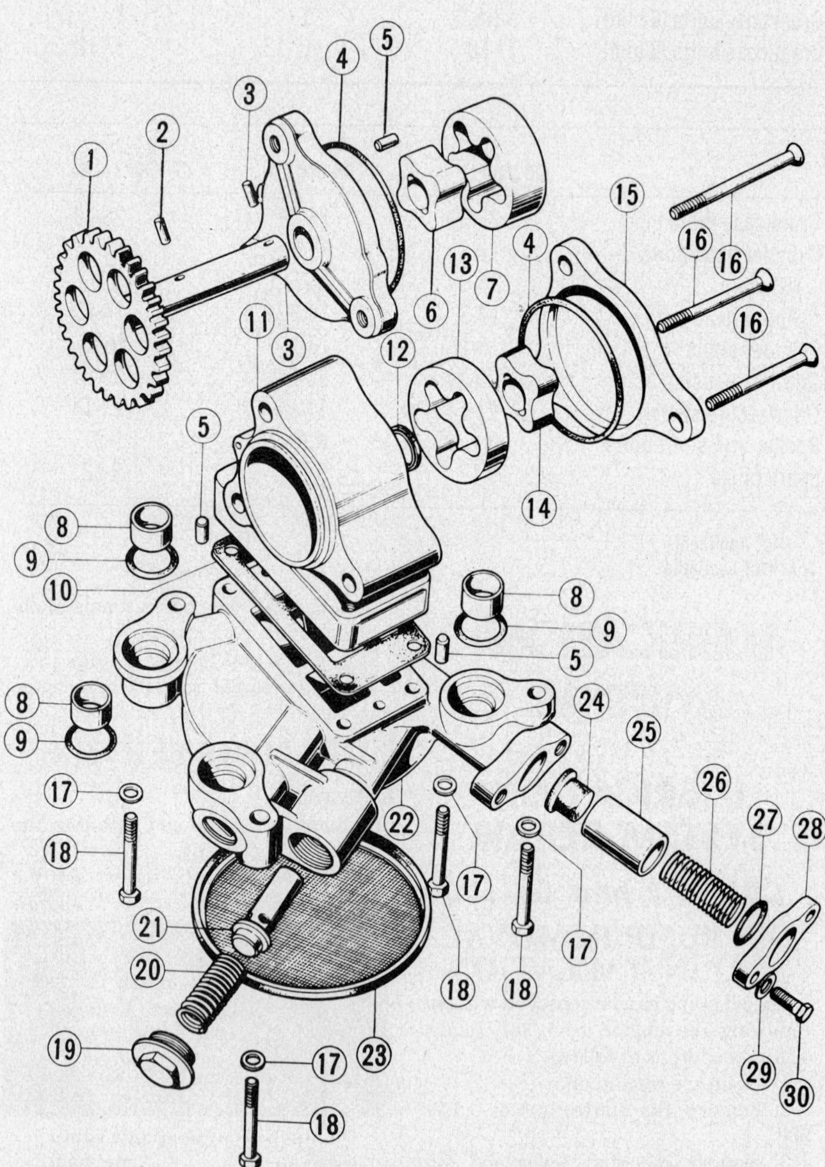

Expoded view of the oil pump

1. Drive gear
2. Pin
3. Right cover
4. O-ring
5. Dowel pin
6. Inner rotor B
7. Outer rotor B
8. O-ring collar
9. O-ring
10. Gasket
11. Pump housing
12. Oil seal
13. Outer rotor A
14. Inner rotor A
15. Left cover
16. Screw
17. Flat washer
18. Bolt
19. Relief valve cap
20. Relief valve spring
21. Relief valve
22. Pump base
23. Filter screen
24. Check valve seal
25. Check valve
26. Check valve spring
27. O-ring
28. Check valve cap
29. Flat washer
30. Bolt

CB 750 and CB 750K1 —K3

OIL PUMP REMOVAL AND INSTALLATION

The oil pump can be removed without removing the engine from the frame. The procedure is as follows:

1. Unbolt and remove the oil filter housing.
2. Drain and remove the crankcase sump (oil pan).
3. Remove the three oil-pump mounting bolts and withdraw the pump.

Installation is in reverse order of removal. Observe the following points:

1. Use new gaskets and O-rings.
2. Do not forget to install the three oil guide pins and O-rings when installing the pump.
3. Refill the engine with oil.

OIL PUMP SERVICE

Disassembly

1. Remove the three side-cover mounting bolts from the oil pump.
2. Remove the left cover (opposite the oil pump drive-gear) and remove the inner and outer delivery rotors (A).
3. Remove the dowel pin from the drive-gear shaft and withdraw the shaft.

4. Remove the inner and outer scavenge rotors (B).
5. Remove the metal oil strainer from the bottom of the pump. Remove the four bolts at the pump base and separate the rotor housing from the pump body.

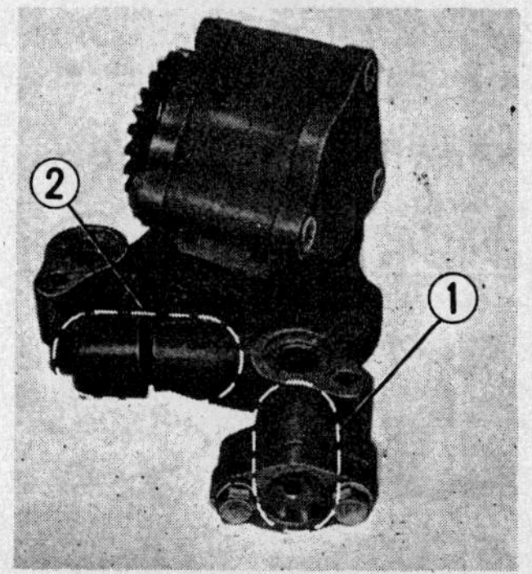

Check (1) and relief (2) valve positions

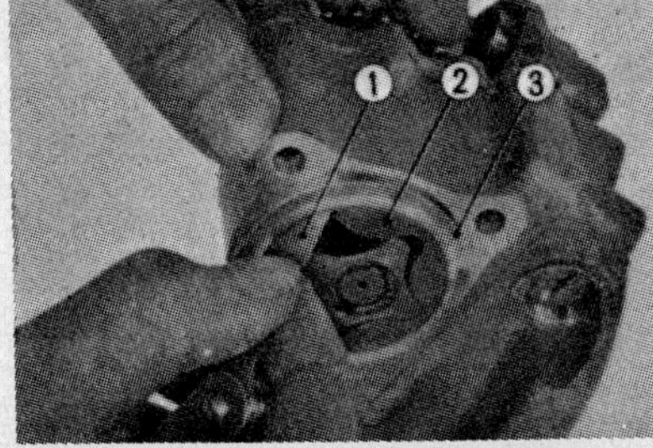

Checking rotor-to-housing clearance

1. Feeler gauge
2. Outer rotor
3. Pump housing

6. Remove the check valve cap bolts and remove the cap. Withdraw the check valve and spring.
7. Unscrew the oil-pressure relief-valve cap and withdraw the valve and spring.

Component Inspection

1. Clean the oil strainer in solvent and replace it if damaged in any way.
2. Examine the side covers, rotor housing, and pump body for damage and stress cracks.
3. Assemble each outer rotor, in turn, into the housing and measure the clearance between the rotor and housing. Clearance should not exceed 0.0138 in. (0.35 mm).
4. Install each inner rotor, in turn, into its matching outer rotor and measure clearance between the inner rotor tips and the outer rotor, as illustrated. Clearance should not exceed 0.0138 in. (0.35 mm).

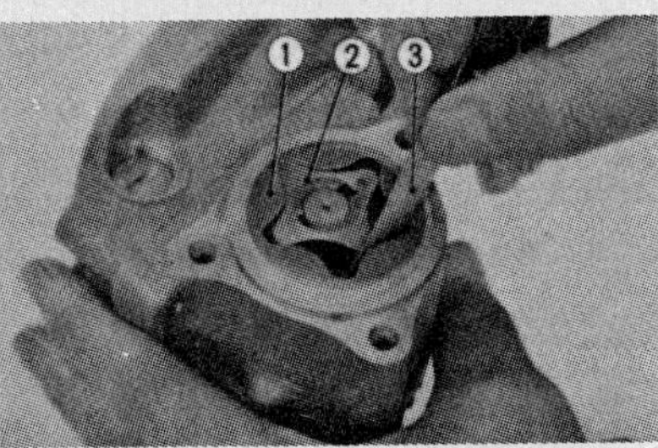

Checking rotor-to-rotor clearance

1. Outer rotor
2. Inner rotor
3. Feeler gauge

5. If the clearance limit is exceeded in steps 2 or 3 above, the housing and rotors should be measured for wear and should be replaced as necessary. Rotors should be replaced in sets (inner and outer) only.
6. Measure the diameter of the check valve and check-valve cylinder bore. Measurements should be within the limits given in "Oil Pump Specifications," and the calculated clearance between the valve and bore should not exceed 0.0067 in. (0.17 mm). Replace the valve and/or oil pump body if worn beyond specification.
7. Check the oil pressure relief valve and bore in the same manner as above (step 6). Calculated clearance should not exceed 0.0039 in. (0.10 mm).
8. Check rotor end-play by measuring the thickness of each outer rotor, in turn, and subtracting this from the measured depth of the corresponding rotor housing. Calculated end-play at either side of the pump should not exceed 0.0047 in. (0.12 mm). Replace the rotor housing or rotors as necessary (refer to "Oil Pump Specifications").

Assembly

Assembly is in reverse order of disassembly. The following points should be noted:

1. Do not reuse old O-rings.
2. Lubricate all moving parts with fresh oil before installing.
3. Be sure that the drive pins are securely installed in the drive-gear shaft.
4. After the pump is assembled turn the drive-gear by hand to make sure that the pump operates smoothly.
5. Before installing the pump in the crankcase, immerse it in oil and turn the drive-gear until the pump is filled.

OIL PUMP SPECIFICATIONS CB 500

	Nominal	Limit
Inner and outer rotor clearance		
in.	N.A.	0.013
mm	N.A.	0.350
Outer rotor to housing clearance		
in.	N.A.	0.013
mm	N.A.	0.350

OIL PUMP SPECIFICATIONS CB 750, CB 750K1—K3

	Nominal	Limit
Rotor housing diam.		
in.	1.600-1.602	1.6083
mm	40.65-40.68	40.85
Rotor housing depth—delivery side		
in.	0.7095-0.7102	0.7114
mm	18.02-18.04	18.07
scavenge side		
in.	0.4732-0.4740	0.4744
mm	12.02-12.04	12.07
Rotor diam.		
in.	1.589-1.600	1.5945
mm	40.53-40.56	40.50
Rotor thickness delivery side		
in.	0.7079-0.7087	0.7067
mm	17.98-18.00	17.95
scavenge side		
in.	0.4717-0.4724	0.4705
mm	11.98-12.00	11.95
Check valve diam.		
in.	0.7059-0.7067	0.7051
mm.	17.93-17.95	17.91

OIL PUMP SPECIFICATIONS CB 750, CB 750K1—K3

(con't.)	Nominal	Limit
Check valve cylinder bore		
in.	0.7087-0.7097	0.7117
mm	18.00-18.027	18.077
Relief valve diam.		
in.	0.4707-0.4718	0.4697
mm	11.957-11.984	11.93
Relief valve cylinder bore		
in.	0.4714-0.4724	0.4736
mm	11.973-12.000	12.03
Inner and outer rotor clearance		
in.	N.A.	0.0138
mm	N.A.	0.350
Outer rotor-to-housing clearance		
in.	N.A.	0.1083
mm	N.A.	0.350

OIL PUMP SPECIFICATIONS CB 350F

Outer rotor to pump body clearance	
Main pump	
nom.	0.0024-0.0047 in. 0.06-0.12 mm
limit	0.0138 in. 0.35 mm
Auxiliary pump	
nom.	0.0059-0.0079 in. 0.15-0.20 mm
limit	0.0138 in. 0.35 mm
Rotor to rotor clearance	
Main pump	
nom.	0.0059 in. 0.15 mm
limit	0.0118 in. 0.3 mm
Auxiliary pump	
nom.	0.0059 in. 0.15 mm

FUEL SYSTEMS

FUEL TAP

Removal, Cleaning, and Inspection

CB 350 F, CB 500, CB 750 AND CB 750K1—K3

1. Turn the tap to "stop" and disconnect the lines.
2. Raise the seat, and raise and support the rear of the fuel tank.
3. Unscrew the cup from the tap, and remove the O-ring and strainer.
4. Remove the two mounting screws and the fuel tap.
5. Remove the two screws from the lever retaining plate and remove the plate, O-Ring, and gasket.
6. Clean all components in solvent and dry thoroughly. Inspect for wear and cracks.

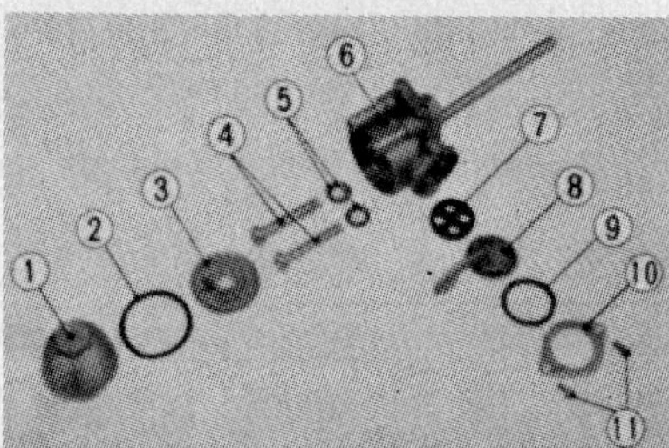

Exploded view of a fuel tap

1. Cup
2. O-ring
3. Filter screen
4. Mounting screws
5. Washers
6. Fuel tap body
7. Gasket
8. Lever
9. Spring
10. Plate
11. Screws

7. Assemble the tap in reverse order of disassembly, using new gaskets and O-rings.
8. Install the fuel tap on the tank and check for proper fuel flow. (Catch the gasoline in a can or jar.)
9. Lower the tank, install the fuel lines, and check for leaks.

CARBURETOR

Overhaul

CB 350 F AND CB 500

Removal and Installation

1. Remove the fuel tank.
2. Raise the seat and remove the air filter element. Unbolt and remove the air filter housing.
3. Disconnect the throttle cables from the carburetor linkage.
4. Loosen the air filter intake clamp at each carburetor.
5. Loosen the carburetor-to-intake tube clamps and withdraw the carburetors toward the rear.

Installation is in reverse order of removal. The following points should be noted:

1. Make sure that the carburetors are securely clamped to the intake tubes. Use new clamps if necessary.
2. Check carburetor adjustment and synchronization after installation as described in the "Tune-Up" section.

Disassembly

1. Remove the throttle return spring. Be careful not to damage the spring hook.
2. Unscrew the nuts and remove the dust plate, as illustrated.

1. Adjuster screw locknuts
2. Dust plate
3. Cap nuts

Removing the adjuster holders

1. Linkage arm 2. Adjuster holders

3. Remove the adjuster holders from the linkage arms.
4. Unbolt and separate the carburetors from the mounting plate.
5. Separate the carburetors. Do not misplace the connecting tubes.

NOTE: *Disassembly procedure from this point on is given for one carburetor, but applies to all four. Keep each carburetor and its components separate from the others; do not interchange parts between carburetors.*

6. Remove the two screws and lift off the carburetor cap.
7. Position the throttle slide to full-open and bend back the two locktabs.
8. Remove the bolt from the shaft end and remove the linkage arm in direction "A" using a screwdriver.
9. Loosen the bolt on the throttle slide about one-half turn and pry the linkage arm loose as shown.
10. Remove the two screws and rotate the slide plate one-quarter turn in either direction to align the tap on the plate with the groove in the shaft. Remove the plate.

Locktabs (1)

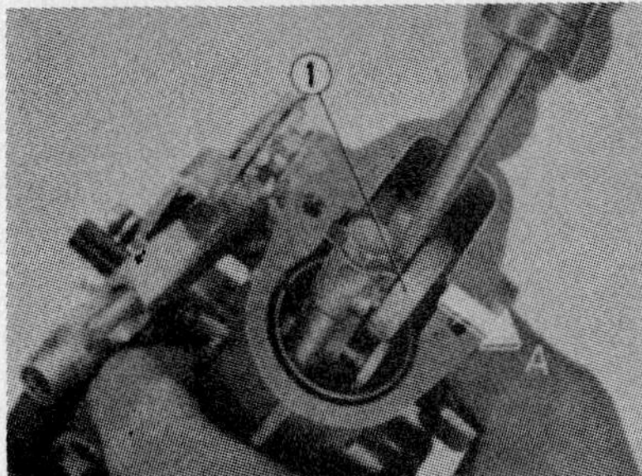
Linkage arm (1)

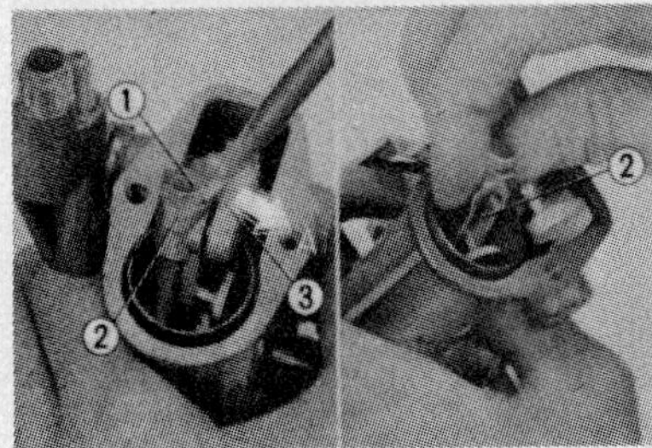
Removing the linkage arm

1. 6 mm bolt
2. Throttle shaft
3. Arm

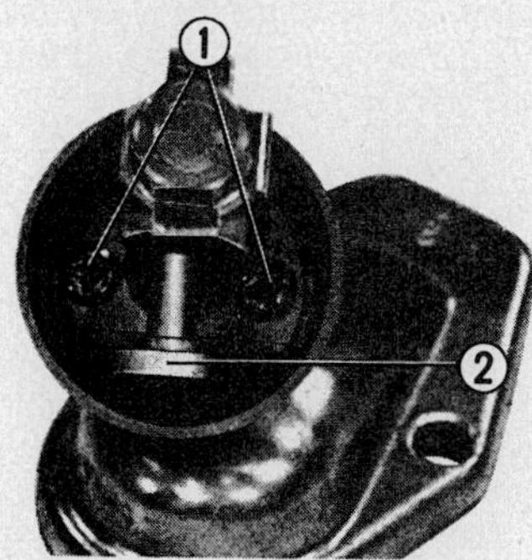
Removing the side plate

1. Screws
2. Valve plate

11. Remove the jet needle from the throttle slide.

12. Remove the float bowl.

13. Remove the leaf spring and unscrew the main jet.

14. Pull out the float hinge pin and remove the float.

15. Remove the screw and clip plate, and withdraw the float needle and seat.

16. Remove the main jet tube, low-speed jet, and air screw.

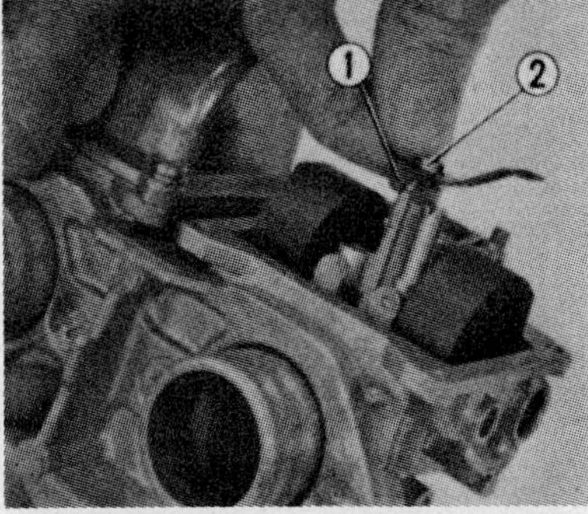
Removing the leaf spring (1), and main jet (2)

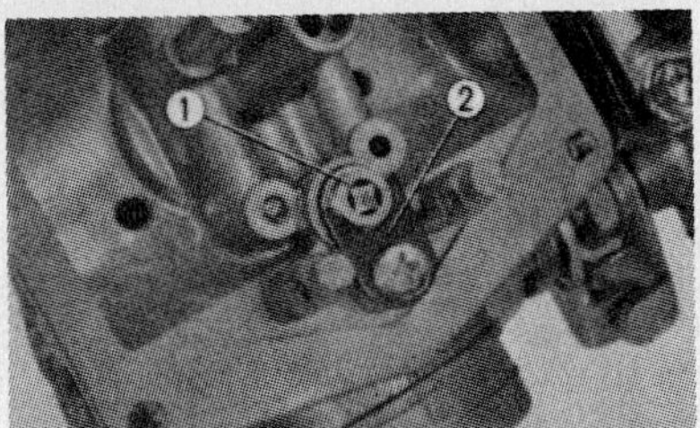
The clip plate (2) must be removed in order to remove the needle and seat (1)

Cleaning

Clean all components in solvent or carburetor cleaner and dry thoroughly with compressed air. If an acid-type carburetor cleaner is used, do not clean the float or any rubber parts in it.

Inspection

1. Make sure that the surface of the throttle slide is clean and smooth. Examine the jet needle for wear as indicated by bright spots or uneven taper. If wear is noticeable, replace both the needle and the main jet tube.

2. Examine the float valve needle for wear. If replacement is necessary, replace the needle and seat as a unit.

3. Check the carburetor body for cracks.

Assembly

Assembly is in reverse order of disassembly. The following points should be noted:

1. Use new gaskets and O-rings.

2. The float should be positioned so that when the float arm just touches the tip of the float needle, the distance from the top of the floats to the float bowl mating surface on the carburetor 0.82 in. (21 mm) on the 350, or 0.89 in. (22 mm) on the 500. Bend the float arm in the desired direction if adjustment is necessary. Make sure that *both* floats are positioned correctly.

NOTE: *A special float level gauge (part number 07144-99998) is available from Honda dealers.*

3. Do not overtighten the jets when installing them in the carburetor body.

4. Make sure that the jet needle is installed in the same position as when it was removed. Changing needle position in the slide will affect running at mid-range throttle openings.

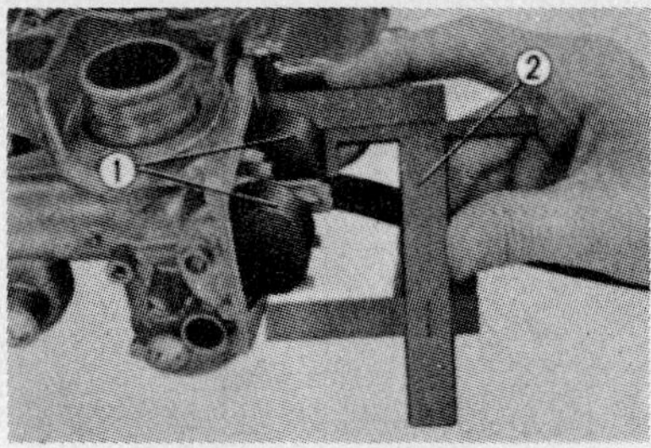
Adjusting the float level

1. Float 2. Level gauge

5. To install the adjuster holder (if removed), first insert the spring and spring seat. Open the throttle slide about half-way and install the holder onto the shaft while holding the spring seat down with a thin screwdriver.

6. Install the locktabs as shown.

7. Do not forget the spring under the cap nut on the adjuster holders.

8. Install the special washers and dust plate as shown.

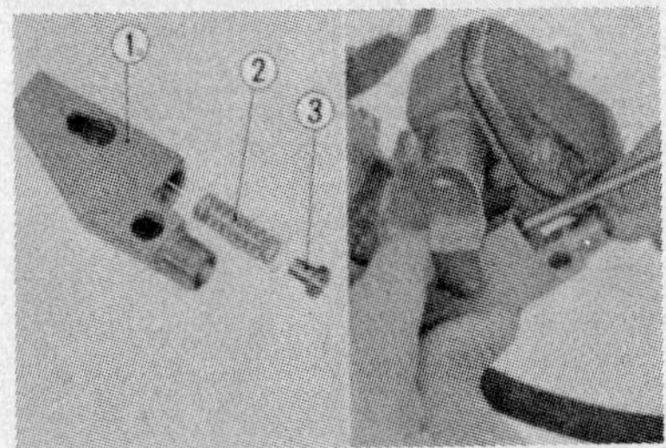
Installing the adjuster holder

1. Adjuster holder
2. Spring
3. Spring seat

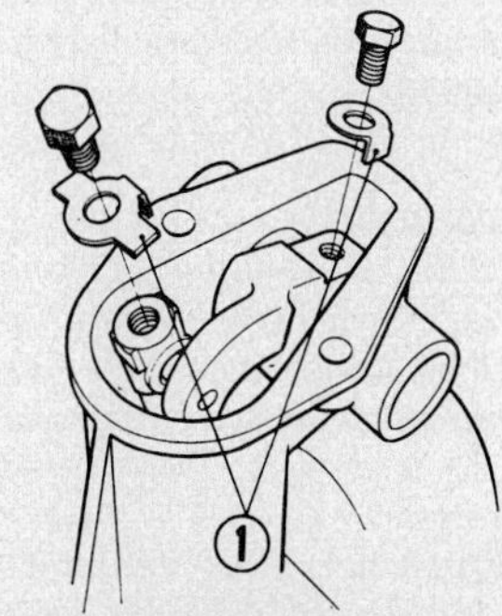
Locktabs (1)

Installing the cap nut (2) over the adjuster spring (1)

Special washers and dust plate locations

1. Special washers
2. Dust plate
3. Washers
4. Nuts

CB 750

Removal and Installation

1. Remove the fuel tank.

2. Unscrew the cap from the top of each carburetor and carefully withdraw the slides.

3. Loosen the air filter connecting clamp at each carburetor and loosen or remove the air filter housing so that the carburetors can be moved back at least one inch.

4. Loosen the carburetor-to-intake tube mounting clamps and remove the carburetors as a unit.

Installation is in reverse order of removal. The following points should be noted:

1. Make sure that the carburetors are securely clamped to the intake tubes. If necessary, replace the clamps.

2. When reinstalling the slides in the carburetors, take special care not to damage the needles when dropping them into the jet tubes. The tab in the slide bore must engage the slot in the slide. Tighten the caps firmly by hand after the slides have been installed.

3. Check carburetor adjustment and synchronization after installation. Check for smooth throttle operation as described in the "Tune-Up" section.

Disassembly

NOTE: *Disassembly procedure is given for one carburetor but applies to all four. Keep each carburetor and its components separate from the others; do not interchange parts between carburetors.*

1. Disconnect the carburetor slide from the throttle cable by compressing the spring and feeding the inner cable into the slide so that the cable end can be disengaged from the retaining slot.

2. Disconnect the choke linkage and remove the screws holding the carburetors to the mounting plate. Remove all four carburetors and separate them. Do not misplace the connecting tubes.

3. Release the float bowl by swivelling back the retaining clip. Try to hold the carburetor in its normal position so that the gasoline in the float bowl will not be spilled.

4. Tap out the float hinge pin using a small diameter rod or drift. Remove the float and lift the float valve needle out of the valve seat. Unscrew the valve seat from the carburetor body.

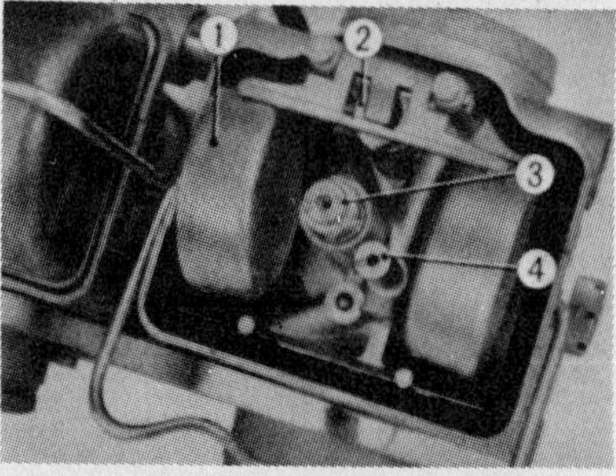

Float and jet locations

1. Float
2. Float needle and seat assembly.
3. Main jet
4. Low speed jet

5. Using a small screwdriver, remove the main jet, low-speed jet, throttle stop screw, and air screw.

6. Unscrew the main jet tube, using the correct size wrench.

Cleaning

Clean all components in solvent or carburetor cleaner and dry thoroughly with compressed air. If an acid-type carburetor cleaner is used, do not clean the float or any rubber parts in it.

Inspection

1. Make sure that the surface of the throttle slide is clean and smooth. Examine the jet needle for wear as indicated by bright spots or uneven taper. If wear is noticeable replace both the needle and the main jet tube.

2. Examine the float valve needle for wear. If replacement is necessary, replace the needle and seat as a unit.

3. Inspect the carburetor body for cracks.

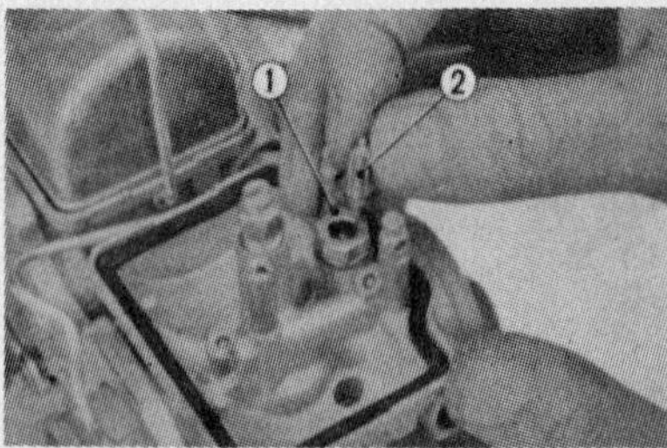

Installing the needle (2) into the needle seat (1)

Assembly

Assembly is in the reverse order of disassembly. Observe the following points:

1. Use new gaskets and O-rings.

2. The float should be positioned so that when the float arm just touches the tip of the float needle, the distance from the top of the float to the float bowl mating surface on the carburetor is 1.02 in. (26 mm). Bend the float arm in the desired direction if adjustment is necessary.

NOTE: *A special float level gauge (part number 07144-99998) is available from Honda dealers.*

3. Do not overtighten the jets when installing them in the carburetor body.

4. Make sure that the jet needle is installed in the same position as when

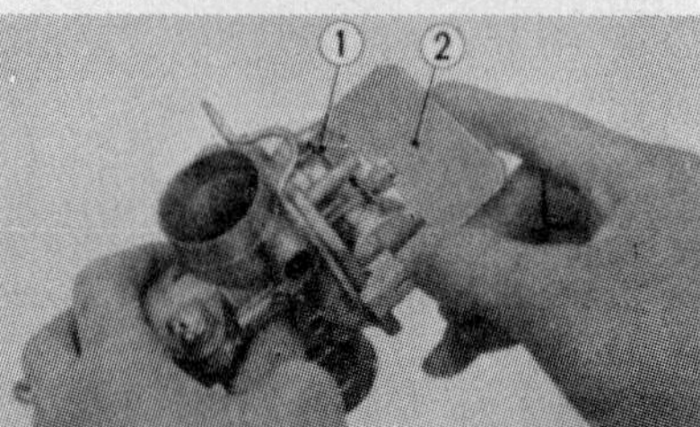

Adjusting the float level

1. Float
2. Level gauge

removed. Changing needle position in the slide will affect running at mid-range throttle openings.

5. Check for smooth operation of the chokes after the linkage has been connected. If a clearance greater than 0.02 in. (0.5 mm) exists between the choke valve and throttle bore with the choke fully closed, the adjusting rod should be lengthened or shortened as required.

NOTE: *The carburetors on the CB 750 (pre-K1 models) were modified during the production run, and all early models without the modifications are entitled to have this update performed by the dealer, regardless of whether or not the machine is out of warranty or was purchased used. An examination of the caps will reveal whether or not the carburetors incorporate the modifications. The original caps are 0.45 in. (11.5 mm) high and the modified caps are 0.57 in. (14.5 mm) high.*

CB 750K1—K3

The 750K1 and K2 uses basically the same carburetors as those used on earlier models. The major change is in the throttle linkage arrangement, with separate throttle cables being used to positively open and close the throttle slides via a single linkage operating all four carburetors. This eliminates the need for a spring in each carburetor to return the slides when the throttle is closed.

Except for removal and installation, all service procedures are the same as for the CB 750. Refer to the preceding section.

NOTE: *The throttle rod guides and seals should be lubricated with silicone grease during assembly. Do not use a petroleum base grease, as it will disintegrate the seals.*

Removal and Installation

1. Remove the fuel tank.

2. Disconnect the throttle cables from the carburetor linkage.

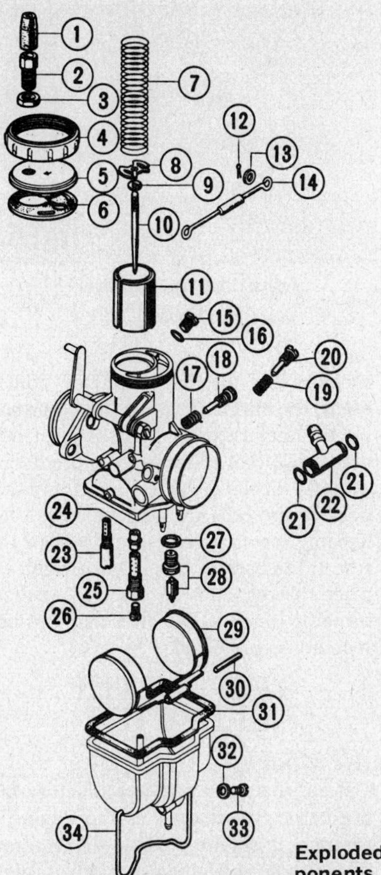

1. Rubber cap
2. Cable adjuster
3. Locknut
4. Cap
5. Top
6. Rubber gasket
7. Slide return spring
8. Needle retaining clip
9. C-clip
10. Jet needle
11. Slide
12. Cotter pin
13. Flat washer
14. Choke linkage rod
15. Plug
16. Flat washer
17. Air screw spring
18. Air screw
19. Throttle stop screw spring
20. Throttle stop screw
21. O-ring
22. T-connector
23. Low speed jet
24. Main jet tube
25. Main jet holder
26. Main jet
27. Flat washer
28. Needle and seat assembly
29. Float
30. Float hinge pin
31. Float bowl gasket
32. Flat washer
33. Drain plug
34. Float bowl clip

Exploded view of the carburetor components

Adjust the choke linkage
1. Choke lever
2. Choke valve
3. Clearance between choke valve and throttle bore

Carburetor mounting locations
1. Carburetor
2. Mounting plate
3. Retaining screws

3. Loosen the air filter connecting clamp at each carburetor and loosen or remove the air at least one inch.

4. Loosen the carburetor-to-intake tube mounting clamps and remove the carburetors as a unit.

5. After removing the carburetors from the mounting plate, it will be necessary to loosen the throttle shaft pinch-bolts and disconnect the choke linkage in order to separate them.

Installation is in reverse order of removal. Make sure that the carburetors are securely clamped to the intake tubes. Check carburetor adjustment and synchronization after installation.

ELECTRICAL SYSTEMS

CHARGING SYSTEM

CB 350 F, CB 500, CB 750, CB 750K1—K3

ALTERNATOR OUTPUT TEST

1. Check the state of the battery. If battery voltage is less than 12 volts, or if specific gravity of the electrolyte is less than 1.26, recharge the battery before proceeding with the test.

2. The test is performed using an ammeter and a voltmeter. Connect the ammeter as follows: Disconnect the positive (+) battery cable and connect it to the positive side of the ammeter. Connect the negative (−) side of the ammeter to the positive battery terminal. Connect the voltmeter as follows: connect the positive side of the ammeter to the positive battery cable, and ground the negative voltmeter lead on the engine.

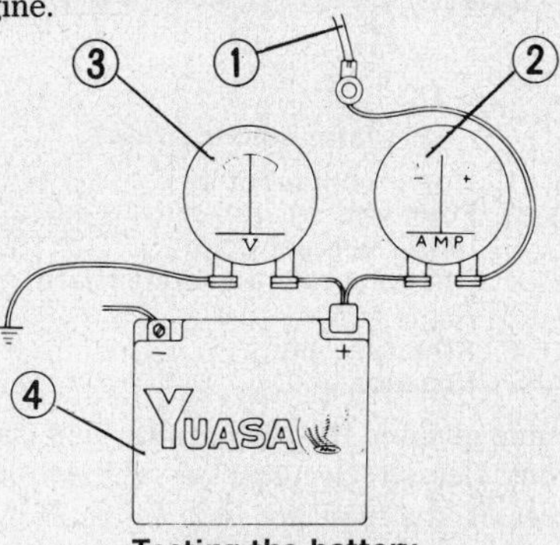

Testing the battery
1. Red/white lead
2. Ammeter
3. Voltmeter
4. Battery

3. Start the engine and check the amperage and voltage output of the alternator under both day riding (lights off) and night riding (lights on) conditions. If the readings obtained are noticeably greater or smaller than those in the accompanying table, adjust the regulator. Slight variation is acceptable due to the effect of the state of charge of the battery upon alternator output. If alternator output is satisfactory but the battery has discharged during use, refer to the section on testing the rectifier.

REGULATOR ADJUSTMENT

CB 350 F

NOTE: *Perform the following tests with a fully charged battery.*

1. Connect a DC voltmeter from the regulator ignition terminal (1) to ground, then disconnect the white lead from the field terminal (F), and connect an ammeter between the lead and the terminal.

2. Take a field current reading with the engine idling, and compare it with the Mode 1 limits given in the accompanying chart. If the value found exceeds the value given, either the regulator or alternator field coil is defective.

MODE	FIELD CURRENT	VOLTAGE
I (idle)	2.4 - 2.6 A	to 13.2 V
II	1.2 - 1.3 A	13.5 - 14.5 V
III	0 - 1.2 A	14.0 - 15.0 V

3. Slowly increase the engine speed until the ammeter needle deflects to read half the Mode 1 value, and compare the reading at the moment of deflection with the Mode 11 value given in the accompaning chart.

4. Increase the engine speed to at least 4,000 rpm, and note the maximum voltage reading. The field current and voltage should agree with the Mode 111

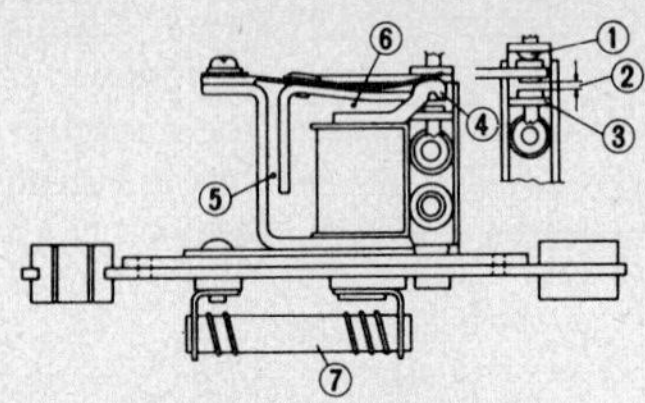

Regulator construction

1. Upper contact point
2. Point gap
3. Lower contact point
4. Charging rate adjustment arm
5. Angle gap
6. Armature gap
7. Resistor

value given in the chart. If the field current doesn't decrease as voltage increases, the regulator is defective. If the field current and voltage values do not agree with those given in the chart, the regulator should be adjusted. If the voltage is in excess of 15.0V, the system is overcharging.

5. Armature and angle gap are adjusted simultaneously by loosening the point base screw, and raising or lowering the point assembly until a gap of 0.02–0.04 in. (0.6–1.0 mm) is attained.

6. Adjust the point gap by bending the lower point bracket until a gap of 0.012 in. (0.3 mm) is attained.

Checking point gap with a feeler gauge

7. Correct the voltage readings by bending the adjusting arm up to increase the charging rate, or down to decrease it.

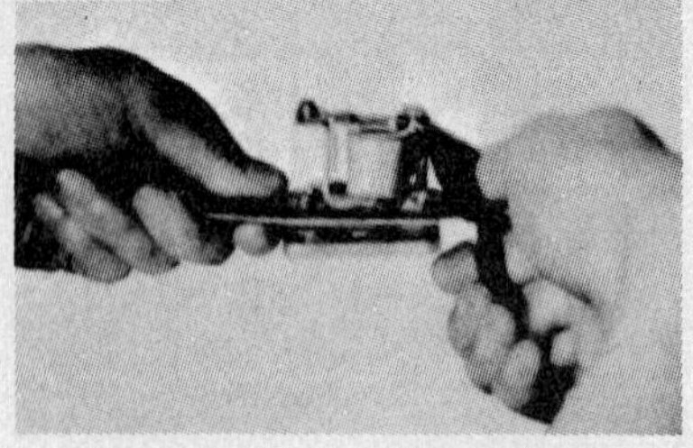

Adjusting the charging rate

CB 500, CB 750, and CB 750K1—K3

1. Disconnect the three wires at the regulator, marking them so they can be replaced on the same terminals. Take out the two mounting bolts and remove the regulator unit.

2. Remove the two screws and take off the regulator cover.

3. Examine the condition of both sets of contact points. If dirty or pitted, they may be cleaned up with fine emery paper.

4. Measure the core gap with a feeler gauge. If the gap does not measure within 0.024–0.040 in. (0.6–1.0 mm), loosen the core gap adjusting screw and move the point body up or down as required.

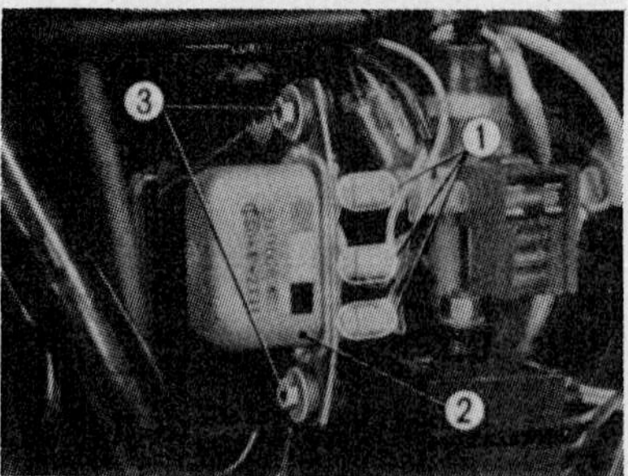

The regulator is located under the side cover—shown is a 750

1. Connectors
2. Regulator
3. Mounting bolts

Regulator adjusting points

A. Core gap
B. Point gap
1. Core gap adjusting screw
2. Point gap adjusting screw
3. Moveable contact

5. Measure the gap of the upper point set in the same manner. The points should be gapped at 0.008 in. (0.2 mm) on the 500, and 0.012–0.016 in. (0.3–0.4 mm) on the 750. To adjust the gap, loosen the adjusting screw and move the lower contact up or down as required.

6. Temporarily install the regulator with one of the mounting bolts, leaving the cover off. Connect the three wires.

7. Loosen the voltage adjusting screw locknut. If the alternator output test showed insufficient output, turn the voltage adjusting screw clockwise about one-quarter turn. If the test showed output to be excessive, turn the screw counterclockwise about one-quarter turn. Tighten the locknut and rerun the alternator output test. Readjust the screw as necessary to obtain satisfactory alternator output.

8. If alternator output is unstable or excessive after the regulator has been adjusted properly, chances are that the regulator is faulty. If alternator output is insufficient and cannot be brought up to specification through regulator adjustment, the alternator itself should be suspected. Before proceeding any further, make sure that the battery is producing at least 12 volts at the terminals, and that none of the cells are dead or have a noticeably lower specific gravity than the rest. If the battery checks out alright, replace the regulator or check into the alternator (refer to the alternator service section), as indicated.

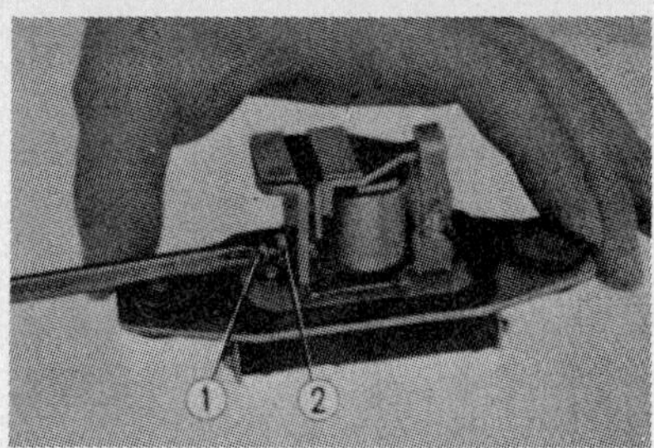

Adjusting the regulator

1. Voltage adjusting screw
2. Locknut

TESTING THE RECTIFIER

All Models

If alternator output is satisfactory but the battery discharges as the engine is running, it is quite possible that the rectifier is not functioning properly. (This is assuming, of course, that the battery is not old and tired or has one or more bad cells.) Before removing and testing the rectifier, make sure that it is solidly mounted on the frame. The rectifier is grounded through its mounting and will not operate without a good ground.

CAUTION: *Do not loosen or tighten the nut that holds the rectifier unit together, as this will adversely affect operation of the rectifier.*

To test the rectifier, first pull apart the plastic connector, unscrew the mounting nut, and remove the rectifier unit. Inside the rectifier are six diodes which, if functioning properly, will allow electricity to pass in only one direction. To check the diodes, you can use either a multi-meter or a test light and the motorcycle battery. If the test light and battery are to be used, simply run a length of wire off of one of

Rectifier installed

1. Rectifier
2. Mounting nut
3. Connector block

the battery terminals and connect one of the test light leads to the other terminal. The two free wire ends will be used to check electrical continuity of the diodes.

Connect one of the leads to pin number 4 in the connector block and touch the other lead to pins 1, 2, and 3, in turn. Now, reverse the leads and repeat the procedure. The test light should light (or the gauge needle respond) in one direction only. If all is well so far, connect one of the leads to pin 5 and touch the other to pins 1, 2, and 3 again. Reverse the leads, as before, and repeat. Continuity in both directions (when reversing the leads) indicates a defective diode, in which case the rectifier unit must be replaced.

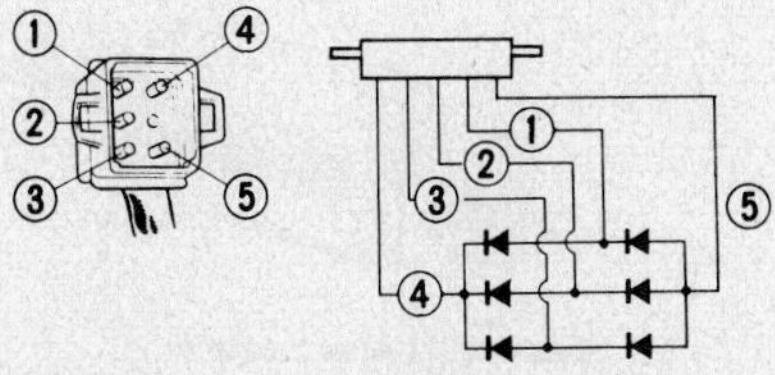

Schematic diagram of rectifier showing connector pin arrangement

1. Yellow
2. Yellow
3. Yellow
4. Yellow/white
5. Green

The diodes are quite susceptible to failure from excessive heat and electrical overload. Observe the following precautions to avoid rectifier failure:

1. Do not reverse battery polarity. The electrical system is negative ground.
2. Do not use high-voltage test equipment to test the rectifier diodes.
3. Do not run the engine at high rpm with the rectifier "P" terminal disconnected, or else the high voltage that is produced will damage the rectifier.
4. Do not quick-charge the battery (high-output charging equipment) without first disconnecting one of the battery cables.

ALTERNATOR SERVICE

Remove the alternator cover and the components will be accessible for testing.

Field Coil Test

CB 350 F AND CB 500

Check continuity between the two

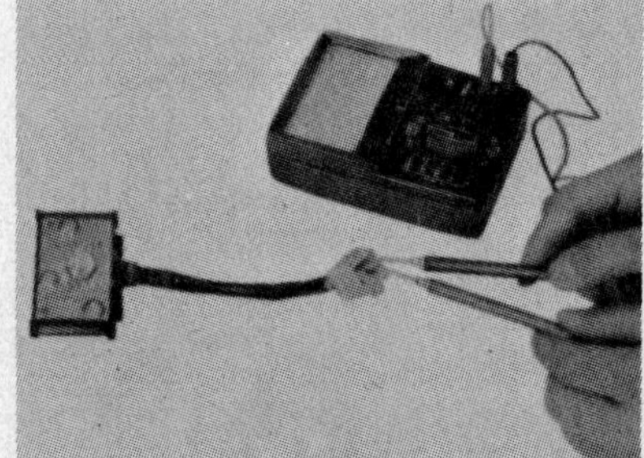

Checking the diodes with a multi-tester

field coil leads (white and green) using a multi-tester or a test light and the battery. If there is continuity, the field coil is satisfactory. Standard field coil resistance is 4.9 ohms, ± 10 percent. The field coil can be removed from the cover by simply taking out the three mounting screws under the plate on the outside of the cover.

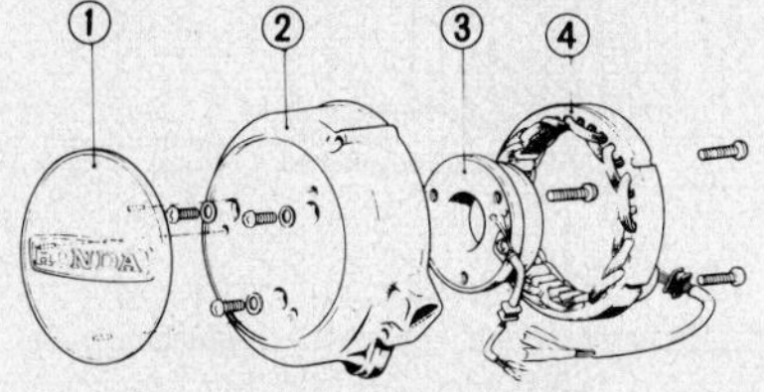

Alternator assembly

1. Side cover
2. Alternator cover
3. Field coil
4. Stator coil

CB 750 AND CB 750K1—K3

Check continuity between the field coil leads and the core, using a multi-tester or test light and battery. If there is continuity between the leads and core, the coil is grounded. If there is no continuity between the two leads, the coil has an open circuit. In either case, the field coil is defective and must be replaced. Standard field coil resistance is 7.2 ohms. The coil can be removed from the cover by taking out the mounting screws.

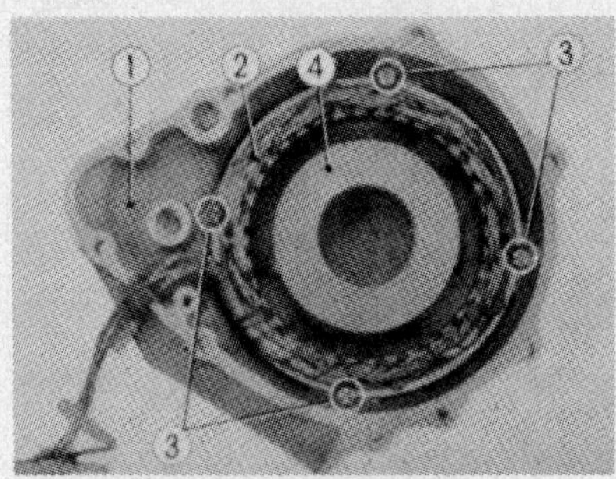

Alternator installed in the cover

1. Alternator cover
2. Stator coil.
3. Mounting screws
4. Field coil

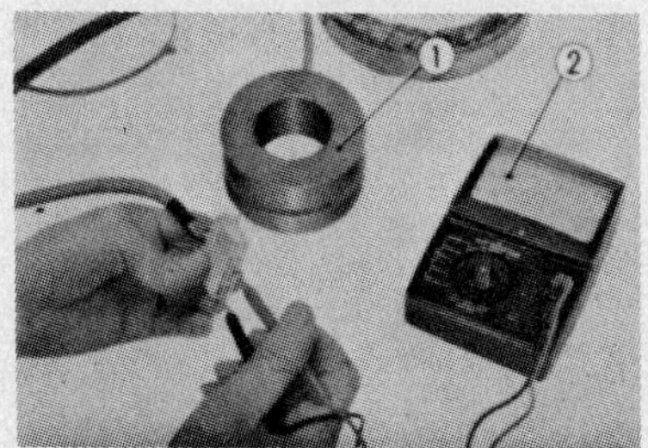

Testing the rectifier

1. Field coil
2. Tester

Stator Coil Test

CB 350 F AND CB 500

Check for continuity between the three stator coil leads (yellow) in the same manner as the field coil test. If there is continuity, the stator coil is satisfactory. Standard stator resistance is 0.61–0.69 ohm for the 350, or 0.32–0.38 ohm for the 500. To remove the stator from the cover, simply take out the three mounting screws.

CB 750 AND CB 750K1—K3

Check for continuity between the three stator coil leads in the same manner as in the field coil test. If there is continuity, the stator coil is satisfactory; if not, it must be replaced. Standard coil resistance is 0.2 ohm. The stator coil can be removed after the three mounting screws in the coverplate have been taken out.

Alternator cover (1) with field coil mounting screws (2)

Rotor

CB 350 F, CB 500, CB 750 AND CB 750K1—K3

The alternator rotor need not be removed at this time. If it must be taken off, pull it off the crankshaft after the retaining nut has been removed, using Honda tool no. 07011-33301 (350), 07011-21601 (500), or 07011-30001 (750) to avoid damage to the rotor or crankshaft taper. When reinstalling the rotor, tighten the retaining nut to 29 ft lbs (350), 30 ft lbs (500), or 70 ft lbs (750).

NOTE: *On some 750s, the rotor has a tendency to slip on the crankshaft taper as the engine is running, decreasing alternator output and causing the battery to discharge. To prevent this, the crankshaft and rotor tapers must be absolutely clean and smooth before installing the rotor and the retaining nut must be tightened to specification. If the slipping persists, apply a thin layer of valve lapping compound to the crankshaft taper and install the rotor over it. This will lock the rotor firmly on the crankshaft after the retaining nut is tightened.*

STARTING SYSTEM

CB 350 F, CB 500, CB 750, And CB 750K1—K3

The starting system consists of the starter motor and clutch, the solenoid, and the handlebar-mounted starter switch. When the button is pressed, the electrical circuit to the solenoid is closed and the solenoid is activated, sending the battery current directly to the starter

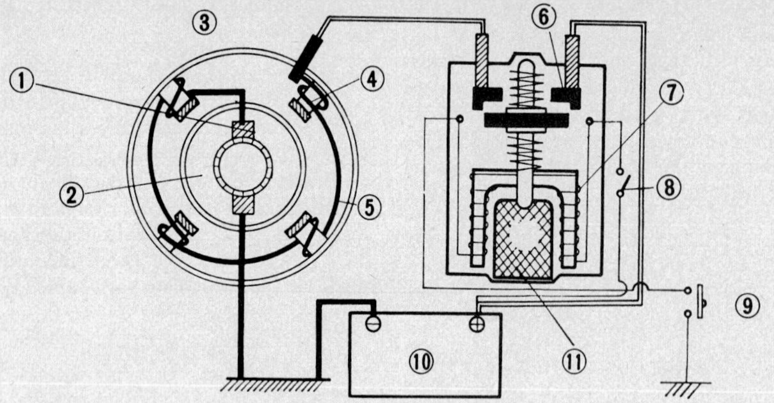

Starting system diagram

1. Brush
2. Armature
3. Starter motor
4. Pole
5. Field coil
6. Solenoid switch
7. Solenoid electromagnet
8. Ignition switch
9. Starter button
10. Battery
11. Solenoid plunger

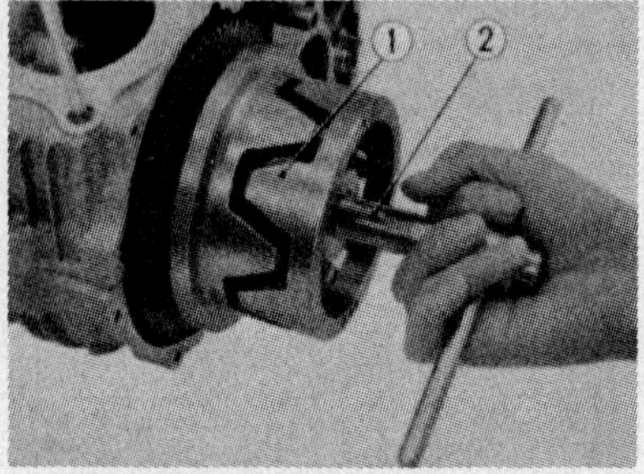

Pulling the alternator off of the crankshaft—shown is a 750

1. Rotor 2. Puller

motor. The starting system is quite reliable and it is unlikely that you will experience any major problems.

TESTING

If the starter will not operate, switch on the headlight and observe its intensity. If it is dim when the starter is not being operated, check the battery connections and recharge the battery. If the headlight doesn't light, check the fuse, the battery connections, the ignition switch and its connections, and check the continuity of the wire between the ignition switch and the battery.

If the headlight is bright, press the starter button momentarily and watch the light. If it remains bright, touch a screwdriver blade between the two starter solenoid terminals. If the starter operates, connect a test light between the small yellow/red wire on the solenoid and ground. If the test light comes on as the button is pushed, the solenoid is faulty. If it does not light, look for defective wiring between the starter button and solenoid or between the starter button and ignition switch, or simply a burned out starter button switch. If the starter does not operate and the headlight dims as the main solenoid terminals are bridged, the starter motor is faulty. If the headlight does not dim, look for a bad connection at the starter.

If the starter motor operates freely but will not turn the engine over, the starter clutch is not functioning (a rare occurrence). To remove the starter clutch from the 350 and 500, it is necessary to remove the engine and split the cases. Refer to the section on transmission and primary drive service for removal and installation procedures. To remove the starter clutch on the 750, it is necessary only to remove the alternator cover and pull off the rotor to gain access to the clutch. Refer to the previous section on alternator service in this chapter.

STARTER MOTOR SERVICE

Removal and Installation

1. Disconnect the cable from the positive battery terminal.
2. Disconnect the starter motor cable from the solenoid.
3. Remove the starter motor cover and the left-side crankcase cover.
4. Unscrew the two starter motor mounting bolts and lift the starter out.

Starter motor location—shown is a 500

1. Starter 2. Mounting bolts

5. Installation is in reverse order of removal.

Repair

1. Take out the two screws and remove the starter side cover.
2. Check electrical continuity between the commutator and armature core, as shown, using a multi-tester to test

Starter motor location—shown is a 750

1. Starter 2. Mounting bolts

light and battery. If continuity exists, the armature coil is grounded and the armature or complete starter motor unit should be replaced.

3. Check continuity between the brush that is wired to the stator coil and

Testing the armature

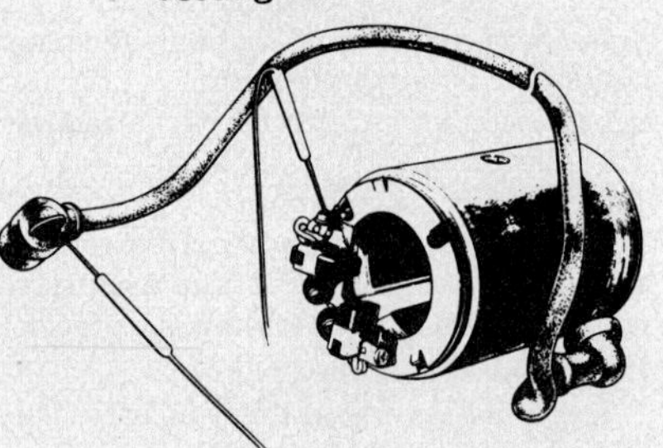

Testing the stator coil

the starter motor cable. Lack of continuity indicates an open circuit in the stator coil and the starter motor unit should be replaced.

4. Examine the carbon brushes for damage to the contact surfaces and measure their length. Replace the brushes as a set if either one measures less than 0.22 in. (5.5 mm), or if they are damaged in any way.

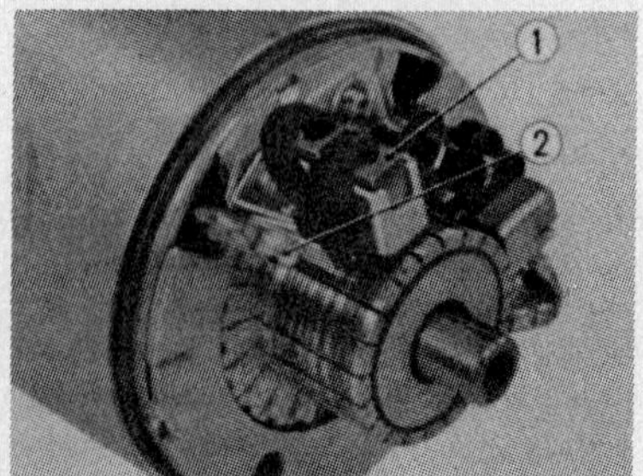

Brush location

1. Brush
2. Brush mounting screw

5. Brush spring tension should be measured with a small pull-scale. Replace the springs if they have weakened to less than 0.8 lb (0.4 kg) tension.
6. Polish the commutator with fine emery paper before reinstalling the starter motor.

STARTER SOLENOID SERVICE

If the solenoid does not work, check the continuity of the primary coil by connecting a multi-tester or test light and battery to the two small solenoid leads, as shown. Lack of continuity indicates an open circuit, and the solenoid must be replaced. If the primary coil winding is continuous, disassemble the solenoid and clean the contact points with emery paper or a small file. The points, after long use, have a tendency to become pitted or burned due to the large current passing across them.

NOTE: *Be sure to disconnect the battery before disconnecting the cables from the solenoid when it is to be removed.*

Replace the solenoid if cleaning the points fails to repair it.

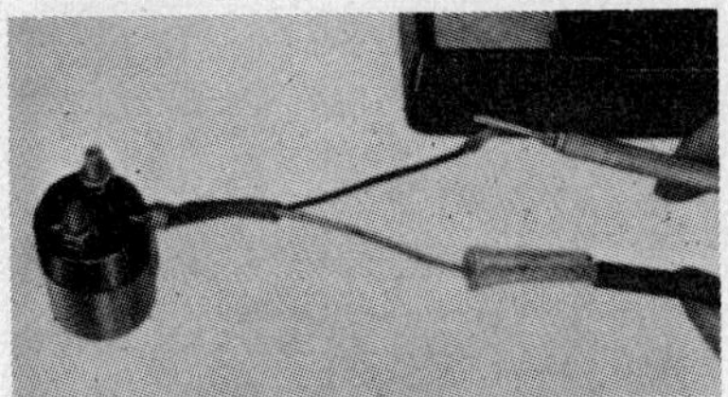

Solenoid primary coil continuity test

ELECTRICAL EQUIPMENT

CB 350 F, CB 500, CB 750 and CB 750K1—K3

TURN SIGNAL FLASHER

If none of the turn signals will flash, chances are that the turn signal flasher has failed. A Signal-Stat 142 flasher is used on the Fours and is located near the battery. Replacements are available at most auto supply stores.

NOTE: *The flasher must be properly grounded to operate properly.*

SWITCHES

Testing and Replacement Procedures

The operation of any switch can be checked using a multi-tester or test light to determine the electrical continuity of the switch in its different positions. Follow the procedures given below for testing the individual switches. If, during any test, you find that electricity is available at the switch but the switch won't work, make sure it is not simply a bad ground that is sabotaging it before you rush out to buy a replacement. Removal and installation procedures are given after the testing information, as it is not necessary to remove the switches in order to check them.

Ignition (Main) Switch

Pull the ignition switch connector apart and check continuity of the switch in its three positions using the accompanying chart as a guide. If any part of the test shows the switch to be faulty, the switch should be replaced.

The switch can be removed after the retaining nut has been unscrewed.

NOTE: *You may want to relocate the switch to a more convenient position. Many dealers carry brackets that allow you to mount the switch between the instruments, where it is much more accessible.*

Front and Rear Brake Light Switches

The front brake light switch is located between the fork legs just under the headlight. To check its operation, connect the two test leads to the switch terminals, leaving the switch wires connected, and operate the front brake lever. If the tester does not show continuity as the brake is applied (ignition on), check to see if there is electricity at the switch power supply lead (black wire). If there is, replace the brake light switch. If there is not, check the continuity of the black wire between its connections at the brake light switch and ignition switch to determine if there is a loose connector, a short circuit, or a break in the wire.

The front brake light switch can be removed by pulling off the wires and unscrewing it. It may be necessary to bleed the brake after installation.

The rear switch may be tested in the same manner as the front switch. Make sure that it is not simply improperly adjusted and that the spring is strong enough to actuate it. Adjustment can be made by turning the large nut on the switch.

Horn Button and Horn

If the horn is not working, check to see if it is receiving electricity by connecting the tester between the light green wire at the horn and a good ground (such as the engine crankcase). Turn on the ignition and press the horn button. If the tester responds, the horn is faulty or is not properly grounded. If the tester does not respond, connect the tester lead to the light green wire in the headlight shell and press the horn button again (ignition on). If there is still no electricity available, replace the horn button. If there is electricity at the headlight shell but not at the horn, check the green wire for loose connections or a short circuit between the headlight and horn.

NOTE: *Horn loudness can be increased by turning the adjusting screw in (clockwise). The horn button and turn signal switch are in the same switch case, which can be removed after the screws in the bottom half of the case are taken out.*

Turn Signal Switch

To check operation of the turn signal switch, pull apart the connectors for the orange, gray, and blue wires in the headlight shell. Check continuity of the switch in its three positions with a multi-tester or test light and battery, using the accompanying chart as a guide. (Be sure to connect the tester to the three wire ends leading to the switch, not the turn signal bulbs.) If any part of the test shows the switch to be faulty, it should be replaced.

To remove the switch, take out the screws at the bottom of the switch case and separate the upper and lower halves of the switch.

Lighting Switch

To check operation of the lighting switch, pull apart the connectors for the black, blue, brown/white, and white leads in the headlight shell. Check continuity of the switch in its different positions, using the accompanying chart as a guide. (Be sure to connect the tester to the three wire ends leading to the switch, not the lights. The brown/white wire is for the highbeam indicator light.) If any part of the test shows the switch to be faulty, it should be replaced. The switch can be removed after the screws in the bottom half of the case have been taken out.

Ignition Kill Switch

Check operation of the kill switch by pulling apart the connectors for the black and black/white wires in the headlight shell, and testing for continuity of the switch in both the "on" and "off" positions. Electrical continuity in either of the "off" positions, or *lack* of continuity in the "on" position, indicates a bad switch. (Be sure to connect the tester to the wire ends leading to the switch, and not to the ignition coil and ground.)

The switch can be removed after the screws in the bottom half of the case have been taken out.

Starter Button

Check operation of the starter button by connecting the tester between the yellow/red wire in the headlight shell and ground. Lack of continuity with the button depressed indicates a bad switch.

The switch can be removed after the screws in the bottom half of the case have been taken out.

Oil Pressure Switch

When oil pressure drops below approximately 4.3 psi on the 350, or 7 psi on any of the other fours, the oil pressure switch closes, completing the ground circuit of the oil pressure warning light which will then light up. There is no power supplied to the oil pressure switch and it must be tested using equipment with its own power source such as a multi meter or test light and battery. Connect the meter leads to the oil pressure switch lead and to ground. If the tester does not respond, the switch has not closed and is defective. (The engine must not be running or else oil pressure will be too high to allow the switch to close.)

The oil pressure switch is located on top of the crankcase (just behind the cylinders) on the 750, and on top of the oil pump on the 350 and 500. To remove, simply unscrew the switch unit after the lead has been disconnected.

Neutral Indicator Switch

In the same manner as the oil switch closes and completes the ground circuit to the neutral indicator light when the transmission is placed in neutral, at which time the light should commence to smile at you from its nest in the instrument cluster. If it refuses to do this and you suspect that an evil spirit has taken over the switch, connect a tester with its own power supply to the switch lead and to ground. Lack of continuity (with the transmission in neutral) means that the switch has definitely turned against you and it should be dispatched with all due haste.

The switch is located at the underside of the engine on the 750, and on the left side of the upper crankcase on the 350 and 500.

ELECTRICAL SPECIFICATIONS

	CB 350F	CB 500	CB 750	CB 750K1—K3
CHARGING SYSTEM				
Alternator				
type		Three phase, excited field, automotive type		
battery voltage			12	
output (watts)			150	
polarity		negative ground		
stator coil resistance (ohms)	0.61-0.69	0.35	0.2	0.2
field coil resistance (ohms)	4.6-5.0	4.9	7.2	7.2
weight (lbs)	N.A.	6.6	11.0	11.0
Regulator				
type		Dual contact type voltage regulator		
point gap (in./mm)			0.024-0.040/ 0.6-1.0	
Rectifier				
type		6 silicon diodes, full-wave rectification		
STARTING SYSTEM				
Starter Motor				
rated voltage			12	
rated output (kw)			0.6	
rated operation		30 seconds continuous		
carbon brush length				
nominal (in./mm)			0.47-0.51 12-12	
minimum (in./mm)			0.22/5.5	
brush spring tension minimum (lbs/kg)			0.8/0.4	
mica undercut minimum (in./mm)			0.012/0.3	
load test: volts			8.5	
amps			120	
rpm (min.)			3,200	
no-load test: volts			11	
amps (max.)			35	
rpm			11,000-20,000	
max. draw (amps)			280	
Solenoid				
operating voltage			7.5	

(con't.)

ELECTRICAL SPECIFICATIONS

	CB 350F	CB 500	CB 750	CB 750K1—K3
ELECTRICAL EQUIPMENT (12 volt rated)				
Battery				
capacity, amp hrs	12/12	12/12	14/14	14/14
Light Bulbs (wattage)				
headlight (SAE 6012)			40w/50w	
tail/brake			7w/25w	
turn signals			25w	
warning lights			3w	

WIRING DIAGRAMS

		BAT	IG	TL1	TL2
Color of cords		Red	Black	Brown/white	Brown
Key position	OFF				
	1	○—	—○	○—	—○
	2	○—	—	—	—○

Emergency switch		
Cord color	Black	Black/white
ON	○—	—○
OFF		

Cord color		IG Black	HB Blue	TL Brown/white	LB White
ON	H	○—	—○—	—○	
	P	○—	—	—○	
	L	○—	—	—○—	—○
OFF					

Knob	Blue cord	Gray cord	Orange cord
R	○—	—○	
OFF (center)			
L		○—	—○

Starter switch		
Cord color		Yellow/red
ON	○—	—○
OFF		

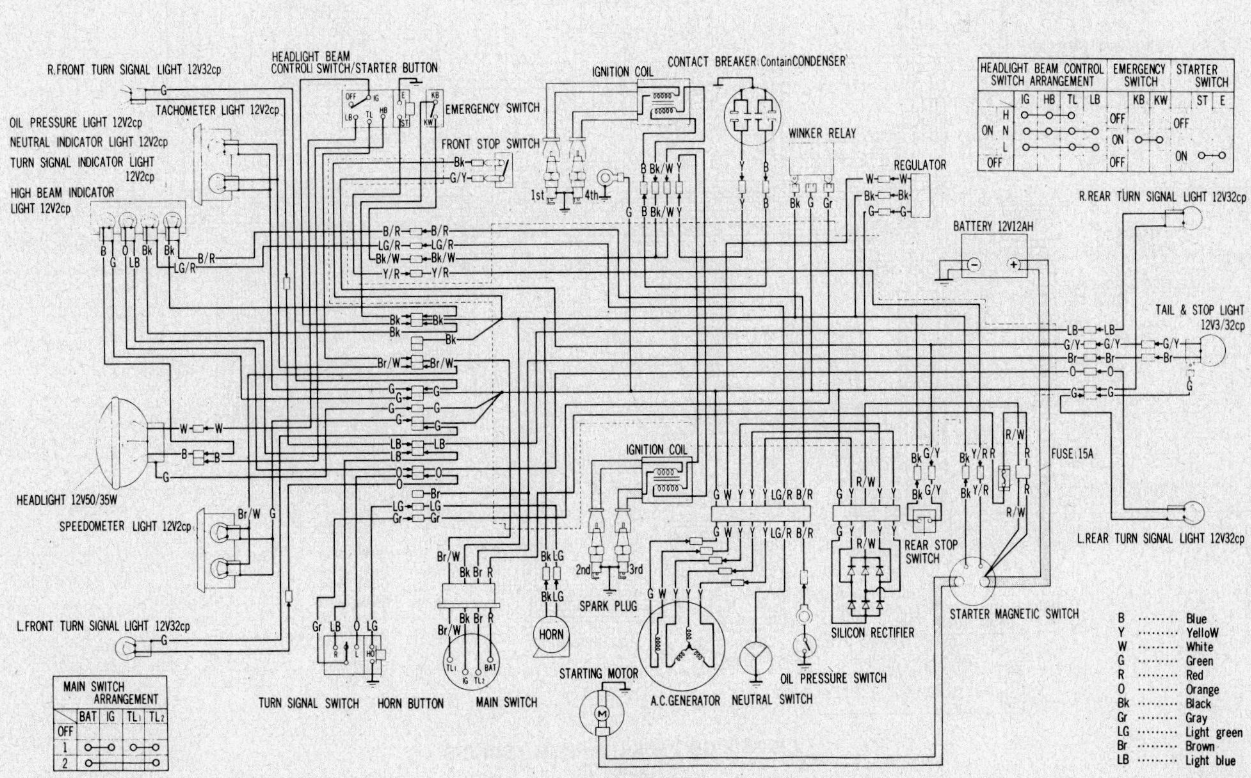

CB 350F

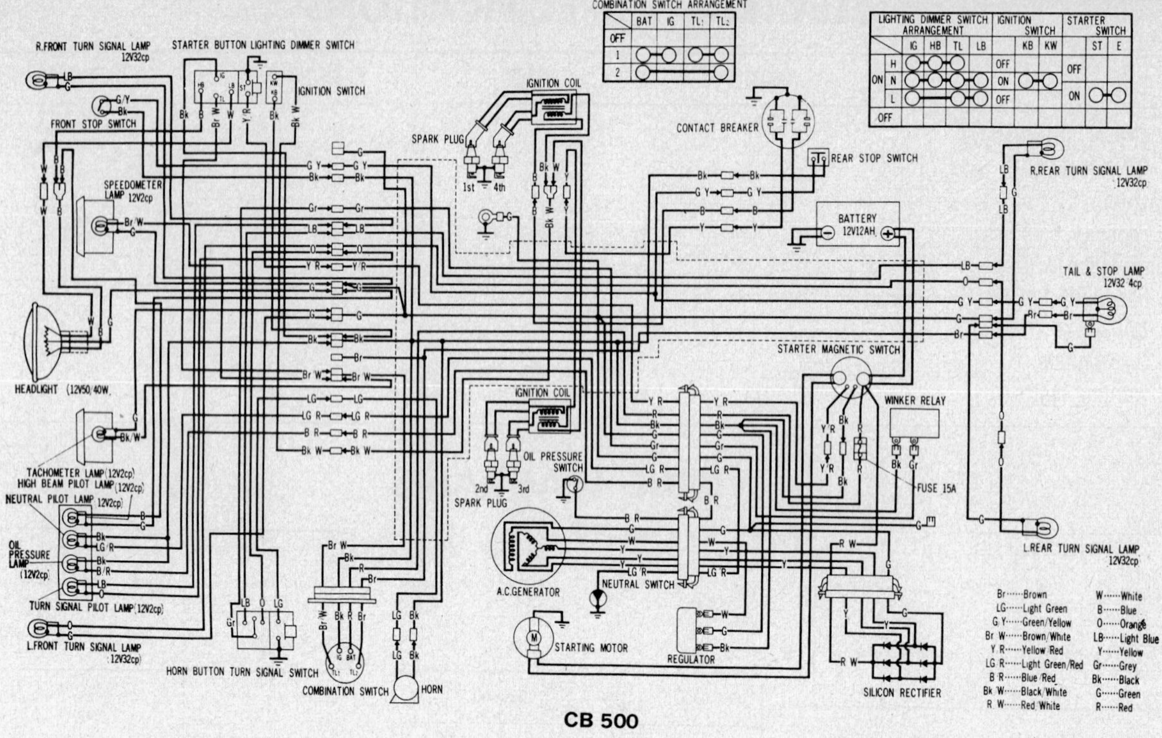

CB 500

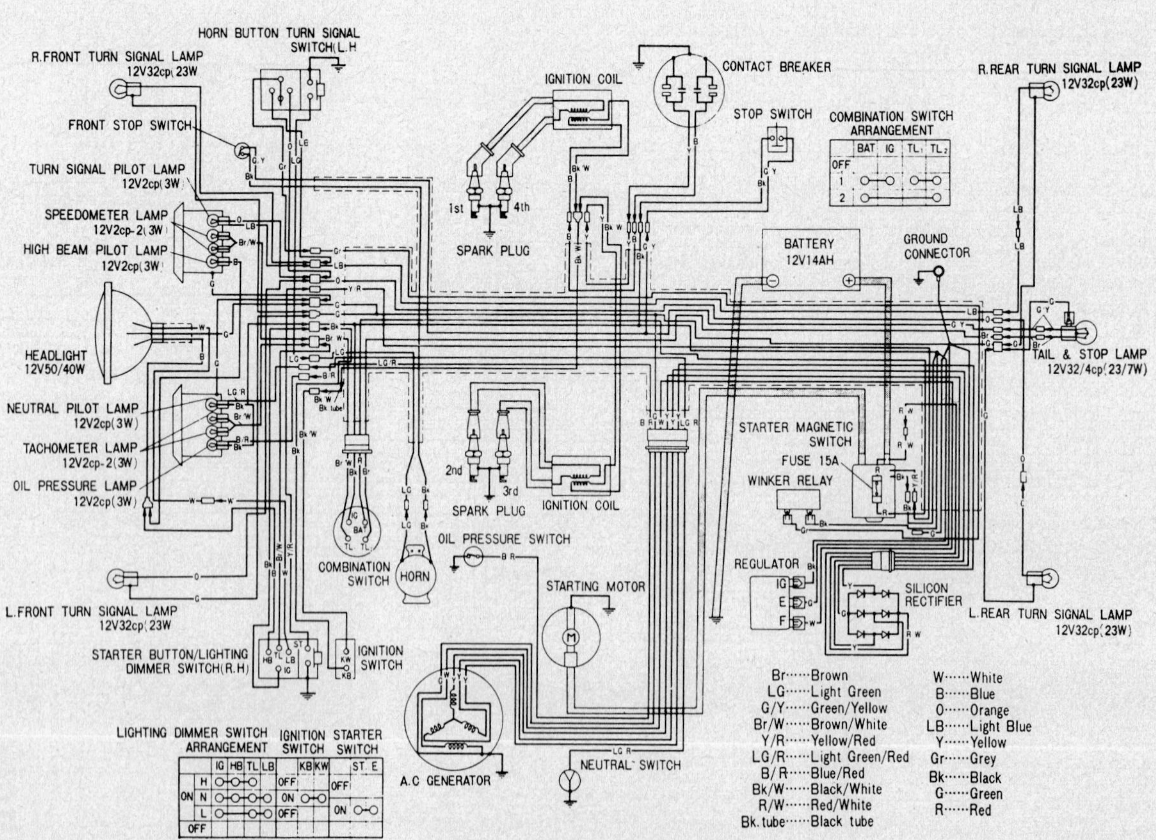

CB 750, CB 750K1, and CB 750K2-3

CHASSIS

WHEELS AND TIRES

CB 350 F, CB 500, CB 750 and CB 750K1—K3

FRONT WHEEL REMOVAL AND INSTALLATION

1. Raise the front wheel off the ground by placing a support under the engine.
2. Disconnect the speedometer cable from the front hub.
3. Remove the four axle clamp nuts (two on each side) and withdraw the front wheel assembly from the forks.

CAUTION: *Do not operate the front brake while the wheel is removed or the caliper piston will be forced out of the cylinder.*

Installation is in reverse order of removal. The front axle holder clamps are machined so that the forward mating surface is slightly higher than the rear mating surface and they must be installed correctly. Place a straightedge on the mating surfaces to determine which end is higher, and *install the high mating surface forward.* Tighten the forward retaining nut first, drawing the forward mating surface of the holder clamp flush against the fork leg mating surface and then tighten the rear nut.

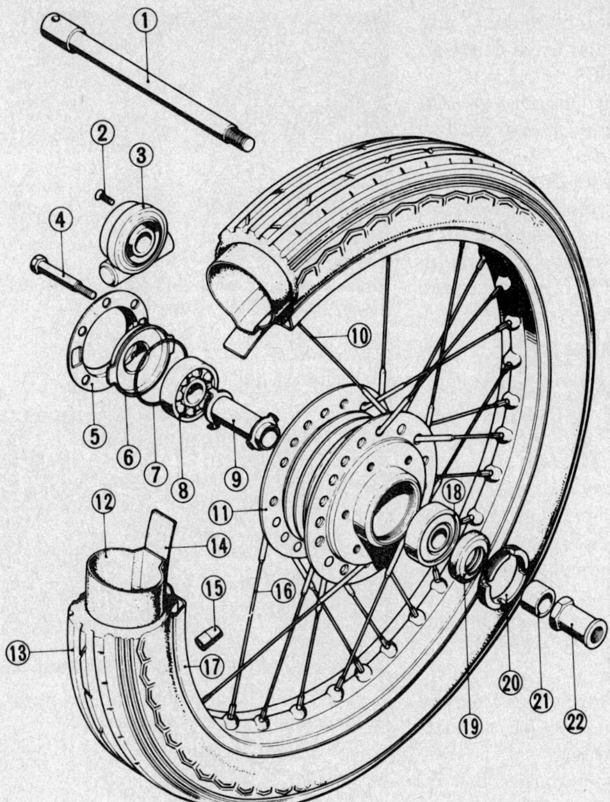

1. Axle shaft
2. Screw
3. Speedometer gearbox
4. Bolt
5. Speedometer drive flange retainer
6. Speedometer drive flange
7. O-ring (500 only)
8. Wheel bearing
9. Spacer
10. Spoke
11. Hub
12. Tire tube
13. Tire
14. Tube protector
15. Wheel balance weight
16. Spoke
17. Wheel rim
18. Wheel bearing
19. Oil seal
20. Wheel bearing retainer
21. Spacer
22. Axle nut

Exploded view of the front wheel and hub

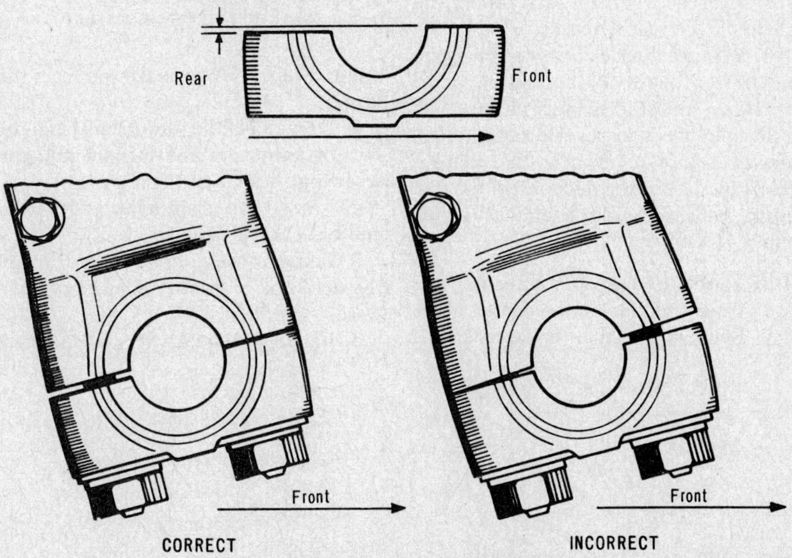

Rear
Front

Front
CORRECT
Front
INCORRECT

Installation of front axle clamps

FRONT WHEEL BEARING SERVICE

Disassembly

1. Remove the front wheel.
2. Unscrew the axle nut and withdraw the axle and axle collar.
3. Remove the screw and remove the speedometer gearbox from the hub.
4. Bend back the locktabs, and unbolt and remove the brake disc.
5. Remove the speedometer gearbox drive flange retainer (and O-ring, CB 350 F and CB 500 only). Remove the drive flange.
6. Unscrew the wheel bearing retainer from the other side of the hub. Withdraw the bearings and spacer.

Inspection

Pass the axle through each bearing, in turn, and check axial and diametrical runout of the bearing with a dial indicator. If axial runout exceeds 0.004 in. (0.1 mm), or if diametrical runout exceeds 0.-002 in. (0.05 mm), the bearing should be replaced.

Check the bearings for smoothness of operation and for pitting of the bearing surfaces. Replace as necessary.

Assembly

Assemble in reverse order of disassembly. The following points should be noted:

1. Pack the bearings with wheel bearing grease. Do not forget to install the spacer in the hub before installing the bearings.
2. The bearings may be driven into place using Honda service tool 07048-30001 or a suitably sized wrench socket or length of pipe.
3. Use a new oil seal and lubricate it with oil to make installation into the bearing retainer easier.

Using a dial indicator to check a wheel bearing for axial runout. Inset shows a diametrical runout check.

4. Do not forget to replace the O-ring behind the speedometer drive flange on CB 350 F and CB 500.

NOTE: *The front hub on the CB 750K1—K3 is narrower than that on the CB 750. In addition, the speedometer drive flange and flange retainer, and the brake disc mounting bolts are changed to fit the narrower hub. It is important that the correct disc mounting bolts are used (if replaced) or the disc will not be securely mounted.*

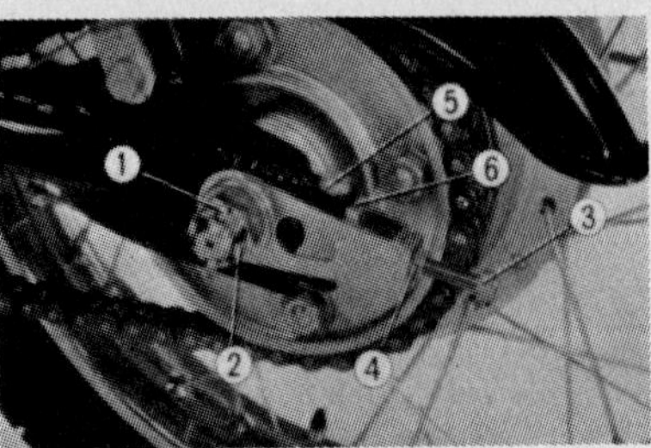

Rear axle nut and left-side chain adjuster assembly—shown is a 500

1. Cotter pin
2. Axle nut
3. Adjuster bolt
4. Locknut
5. Lockbolt
6. Adjuster stopper

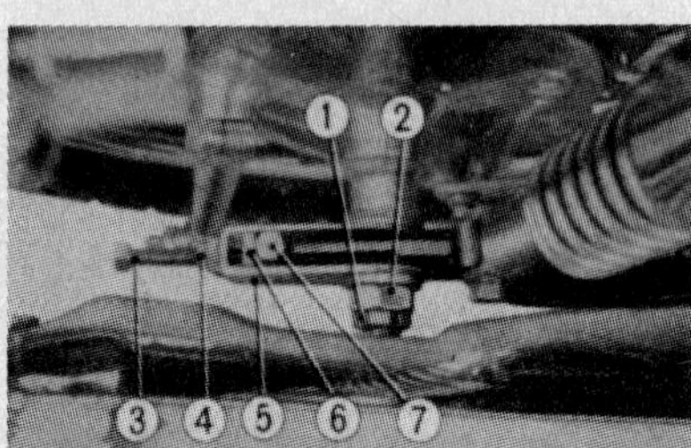
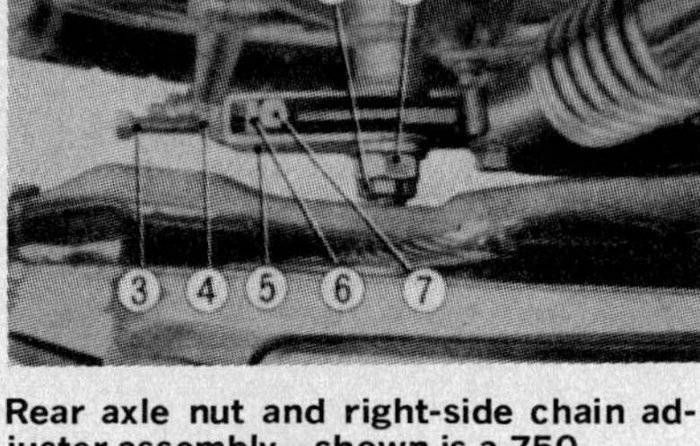

Rear axle nut and right-side chain adjuster assembly—shown is a 750

1. Cotter pin
2. Axle nut
3. Chain adjuster bolt
4. Locknut
5. Adjuster bracket
6. Swing arm end cap
7. End cap retaining bolt

REAR WHEEL REMOVAL AND INSTALLATION

CB 350 F and CB 500

1. Place the bike on the center stand and remove the mufflers. (On some machines there may be enough clearance to remove the wheel without removing the mufflers. Try it.)

2. Remove the rear brake adjuster nut and separate the brake rod from the lever.

3. Disconnect the torque link from the hub by removing the lockpin and unscrewing the nut and bolt.

4. Loosen the chain adjuster bolt on both sides. Remove the cotter pin and loosen the axle nut.

5. Push the wheel forward and lift the chain off the rear sprocket.

6. Remove the lock bolts and chain adjuster stop plates. Withdraw the wheel rearward from the swing arm.

Installation is in reverse order of removal. Adjust the chain so that there is ½–¾ in. slack at the midpoint of the run. Brake pedal free-play should be 1 in. (25 mm).

CB 750 and CB 750K1—K3

1. Place the bike on the center stand.

2. Remove the rear brake adjusting nut and separate the brake rod from the lever.

3. Disconnect the torque link from the hub by removing the lockpin and unscrewing the nut and bolt.

4. Loosen the chain adjuster locknuts and back the bolts out.

5. Remove the cotter pin and loosen the axle nut. Turn the adjusters downward.

6. Remove the lockbolts and chain adjuster stop plates. Push the wheel forward and lift the chain off the rear sprocket. Withdraw the wheel rearward from the swing arm.

Installation is in reverse order of removal. Adjust the chain so that there is ½–¾ in. slack at the midpoint of the run. Brake pedal free-play should be 1 in. (25 mm).

REAR WHEEL BEARING SERVICE

Disassembly

1. Remove the wheel.
2. Remove the axle from the hub.
3. Bend back the locktabs and unbolt the sprocket.
4. Unscrew the bearing retainer and drive the bearings out of the hub.

NOTE: *The bearing retainer on the CB 350 F and CB 500 has a left-hand thread.*

Inspection

Pass the axle through each bearing, in turn, and check axial and diametrical runout of the bearing with a dial indicator as for the front wheel bearings. If axial runout exceeds 0.004 in. (0.1 mm), or if diametrical runout exceeds 0.0024 in. (0.06 mm), the bearing should be replaced.

Check the bearings for smoothness of operation and for pitting of the bearing surfaces. Replace as necessary.

Check the runout of the axle shaft. If beyond 0.009 in. (0.2 mm), replace it.

Assembly

Assemble in reverse order of disassembly. The following points should be noted:

1. Pack the bearings with wheel bearing grease. Do not forget to install the spacer in the hub before installing the bearings.

2. The bearings may be driven into place using Honda service tool 07048–30001 or a suitably sized wrench socket or length of pipe.

3. Use a new oil seal and lubricate it with oil to make installation into the bearing retainer easier.

4. Use thread-lock cement on the bearing retainer.

5. Apply a small quantity of grease to the friction surfaces of the flange and wheel hub.

BRAKES

CB 350 F, CB 500, CB 750 and CB 750K1—K3

FRONT BRAKE SERVICE

Pad Replacement

To determine pad wear on the 750 and

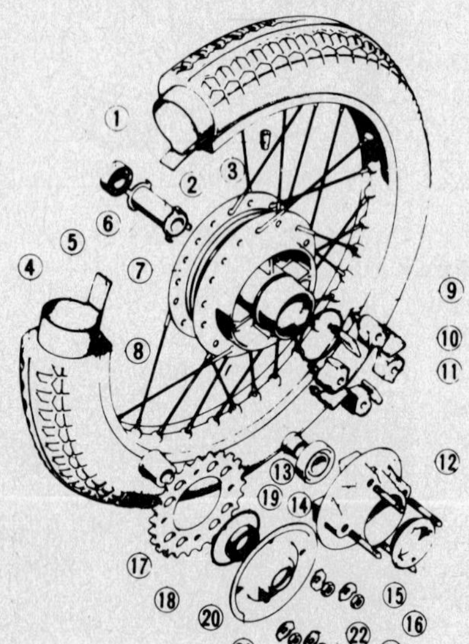

1. Wheel bearing
2. Spacer
3. Wheel balance weight
4. Tire
5. Tube
6. Tube protector
7. Wheel hub
8. Wheel rim
9. O-ring
10. Rear hub damper rubber
11. Rear hub damper rubber
12. Hub flange
13. Spacer
14. Wheel bearing
15. Bearing retainer
16. Sprocket mounting stud
17. Spacer
18. Sprocket
19. Oil seal
20. O-ring
21. Sprocket side plate
22. Tab washer
23. Nut

Exploded view of the rear wheel and hub

750K1 measure the clearance between the front of the caliper and the disc face by using a feeler gauge. When clearance is less than 0.08 in. (2.0 mm), the pads should be replaced.

Pads should be replaced on the 350, 500, and 750K2-K3when either one has worn down to the red wear indicator groove.

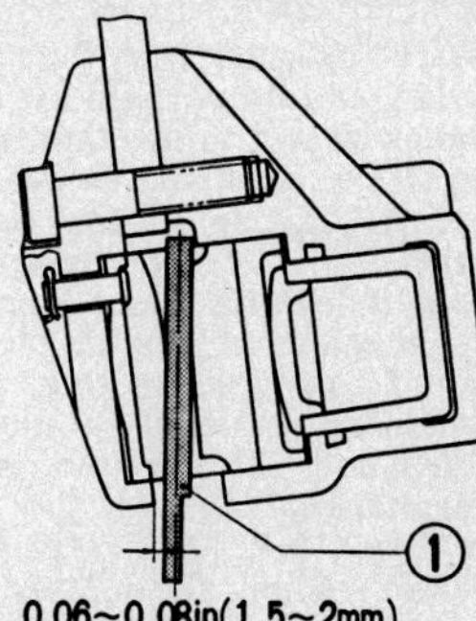

Replace disc pads on the 750 when clearance between the disc (1) and caliper is less than 0.08 in.

1. Remove the front wheel.
2. Using the proper size allen wrench, remove the two bolts from the side of the caliper and remove the right-side caliper half.
3. Remove the pad from the piston side of the caliper. Withdraw the cotter pin and remove the pad from the other caliper half.
4. Before installing the new pads, apply a small amount of silicone grease to the pad sliding surfaces on the caliper as shown. The grease serves to keep pad operation smooth by repelling dust and water as well as providing lubrication. Use grease sparingly and do not allow it to contact the pad friction material.
5. Install the new pads in the caliper halves and bolt the caliper together.
6. Install the front wheel and adjust the brake as explained in the following section. Avoid heavy braking until at least 500 miles have been covered.

Adjustment

1. Loosen the caliper adjuster bolt locknut and turn the bolt until the inside pad (closest to the wheel) lightly contacts the disc.
2. Turn the adjuster bolt in the opposite direction until the front wheel rotates with as little drag as possible (about ¼–½ turn) and tighten the locknut.
3. On the CB 750, provisions is made for adjustment of brake lever free-play at the lever. Loosen the locknut and turn the adjuster screw until ¼–½ in. free-play is obtained at the end of the lever. Retighten the locknut to 13–17 ft lbs. The lever is not adjustable on the CB 350 F, CB 500, and CB 750K1—K3.

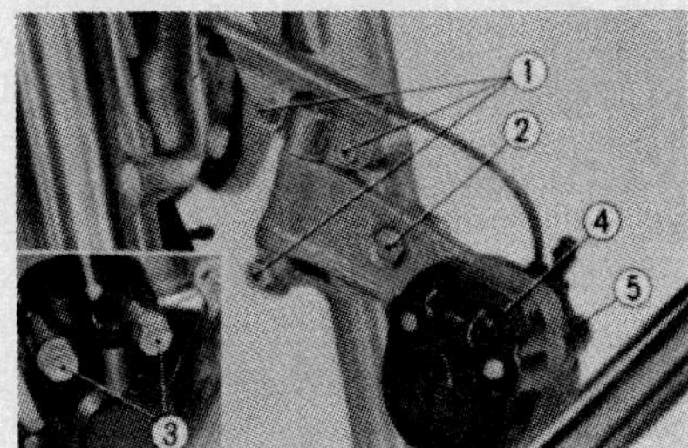

Caliper mounting positions

1. Caliper mounting bolts
2. Caliper adjusting bolt
3. Caliper half retaining bolts
4. Right caliper
5. Left caliper

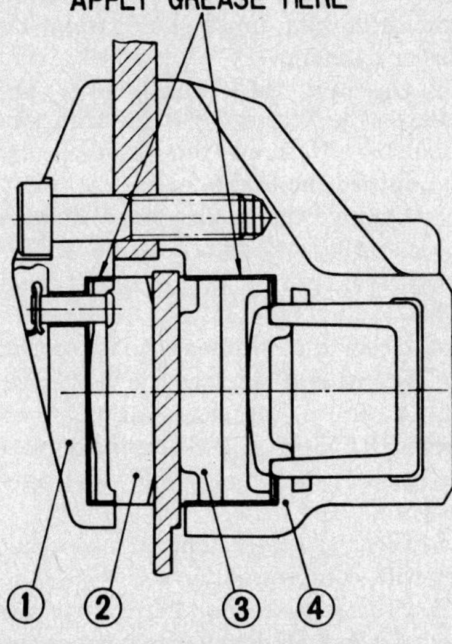

Lubrication points

1. Right caliper half
2. Right brake pad
3. Left brake pad
4. Left caliper half

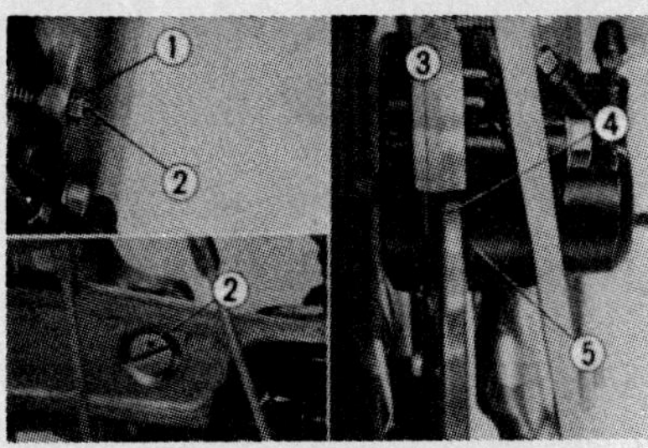

Caliper adjusting points

1. Nut
2. Caliper adjusting bolt
3. Right pad
4. Brake disc
5. Left pad

Caliper Service

Leakage of brake fluid from around the caliper piston indicates that the caliper assembly is worn or damaged and the cause should be investigated immediately. To remove, inspect, and rebuild the caliper assembly:

1. Remove the front wheel.
2. Unscrew the hydraulic line connection at the caliper and catch the fluid that drains from the line in a suitable container and dispose of it. (Do not reuse old brake fluid.)
3. Unscrew the three caliper mounting bolts at the left fork leg and remove the caliper.

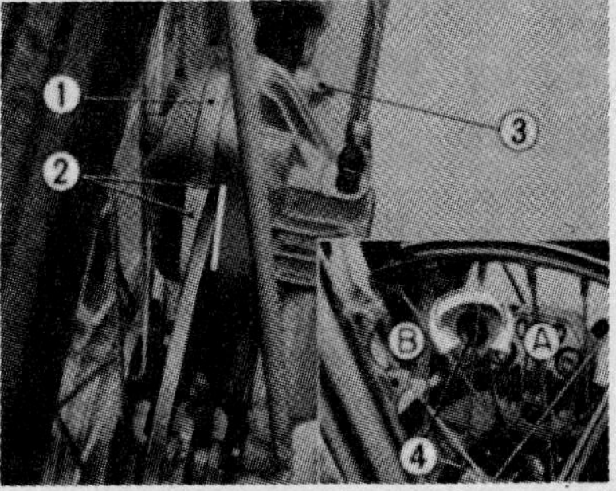

About 0.006 in. (0.15 mm) clearance should exist between the pads and disc

1. Caliper assembly
2. Brake pads
3. Nut
4. Caliper adjusting bolt

4. Remove the two bolts and separate the caliper halves.
5. Remove the pad seat from the caliper piston and withdraw the piston.
6. Remove the seal from the cylinder using a plastic or wood instrument to avoid damaging the bore.
7. Examine the cylinder bore and piston surface for scoring and pitting, and replace if damaged. Cylinder bore diameter should not exceed 1.540 in. (38.215 mm) and piston diameter should not be less than 1.500 in (38.105 mm). Maximum calculated clearance between the piston and cylinder is 0.0045 in. (0.115 mm). Replace parts as necessary. Clean all components and dry with compressed air.
8. Use a new seal in the cylinder bore and lubricate it thoroughly with fresh brake fluid before installing. Make sure it is seated properly in its groove.
9. Lubricate the piston with brake

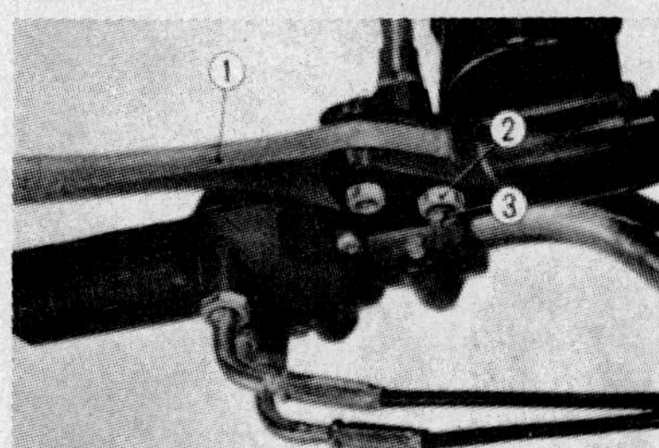

If the locknut has a tendency to loosen, coat the threads with locking compound, install a locktab, and tighten the nut to 13-17 ft lbs

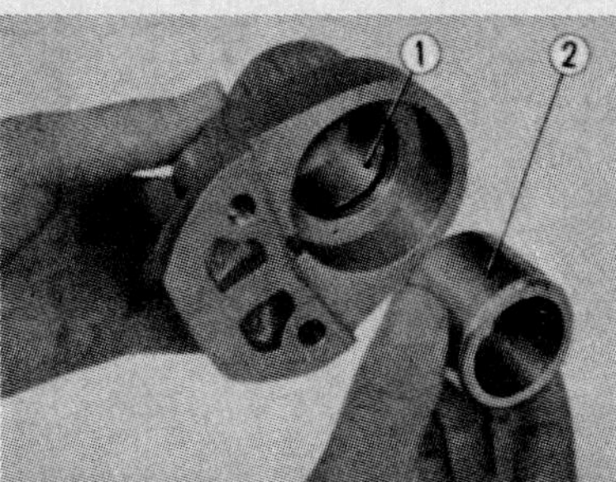

The left caliper half (1) and the piston (2). The piston seal is visible in the caliper bore—shown is a 750

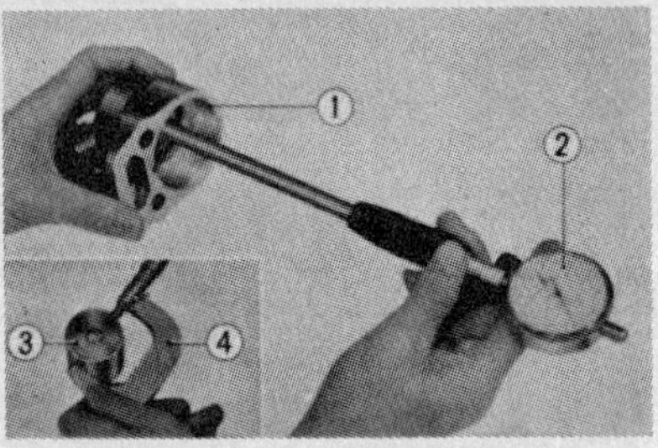

Measuring caliper bore and piston diameter

1. Left caliper half
2. Dial indicator
3. Caliper piston
4. Micrometer

fluid and install it in the cylinder. Be careful not to twist the seal or force it out of the groove. Install the pad seat on the piston.

10. Reinstall the brake pads in the caliper halves. Use new pads if the old ones have been in contact with brake fluid.

11. Bolt the caliper halves together and remount the caliper assembly on the fork leg.

12. Connect the hydraulic line and replace the front wheel.

13. Bleed and adjust the brake. Refer to the appropriate headings in this section.

Master Cylinder Service

Brake fluid leakage around the brake lever and excessive lever travel (after bleeding the brake to make sure that there is no air trapped in the hydraulic system) are indications of master cylinder malfunction. The rebuilding procedure is as follows.

NOTE: *Be very careful, when removing and replacing the master cylinder, of filling the reservoir. Brake fluid can damage paint and plastic, and extreme care should be exercised in handling the stuff. Wipe up any spills immediately.*

1. Place a cloth underneath the connection to absorb any spilled fluid and disconnect the brake hose from the master cylinder.

2. Unscrew the clamp bolts and remove the master cylinder from the handlebar. Unscrew the reservoir cap and discard the brake fluid.

3. Remove the rubber boot. Remove the snap-ring and withdraw the washer, piston, seal, spring cap, spring, and check valve.

4. Check the cylinder bore for scoring and pitting, and measure the wear using a dial indicator. Bore diameter should not exceed 0.553 in. (14.055 mm). Replace the master cylinder assembly if damaged or worn.

5. Clean all components in solvent and dry with compressed air.

6. Use a new seal and lubricate it with fresh brake fluid. Install the components in the bore as removed.

7. Mount the master cylinder on the handlebar and connect the brake hose. Do not forget to install the two washers at the connection.

8. Fill the reservoir to the level mark with brake fluid and bleed the brake. (Use brake fluid conforming to SAE J1703 specification.)

Bleeding the Hydraulic Brake System

The purpose of bleeding the brake is to expel any air trapped in the hydraulic system. Air, since it is compressible, will cause the brake lever to feel spongy and will decrease braking effectiveness. If the brake lever begins to feel spongy for no apparent reason, it is likely that there is a fault in the hydraulic system. It would be wise to determine and remedy the fault rather than merely bleed the brake and hope the problem will disappear.

The brake hydraulic system must be bled whenever any part of the system has been disconnected or removed for service. When refilling the master cylinder reservoir, use only brake fluid conforming to SAE specification J1703. Any brand meeting this requirement is acceptable. The brake fluid container of all reputable brands will be plainly marked with the standards the fluid meets or exceeds.

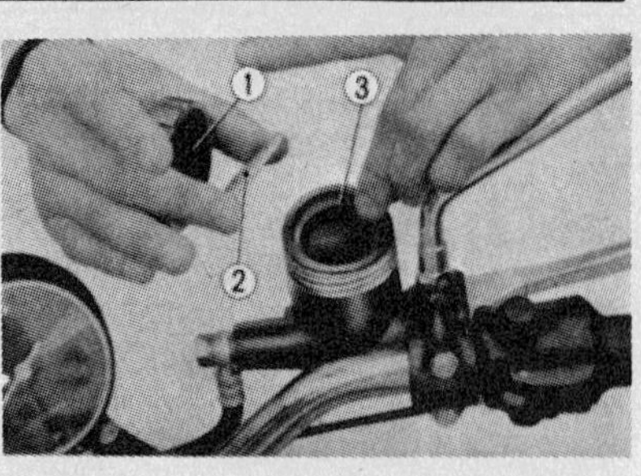

The master cylinder reservoir cap (1), washer (2), and diaphragm (3) must be installed as shown to prevent leaks. Do not overfill the reservoir or overtighten the cap. If the cap is too tight, the diaphragm will become distorted and cause slight leaking around the edge. The diaphragm and washer have been redesigned to eliminate this, and the new parts are installed on most 500s and 750K1 and K2s. Old and new parts are interchangeable.

1. Top up the reservoir with brake fluid and replace the cap to keep dirt and moisture out and the fluid in.

2. Attach one end of a small rubber hose to the bleed valve at the caliper and place the other end in a container to catch the fluid.

3. Pump the brake lever rapidly several times until some resistance is felt and, holding the lever against the resistance, open the bleed valve about one-half turn. When the lever bottoms, close the valve (do not over-tighten) and then release the lever.

4. Repeat this operation until no more air is released out of the hose and the brake lever is firm in operation. Check the fluid level in the reservoir often to make sure it doesn't go dry and draw more air into the system. Do not reuse fluid that has been pumped out of the system. Do not use fluid that has been stored for more than a few weeks after the seal on its container has been opened, as brake fluid will absorb moisture from the air and may corrode the master cylinder and caliper. Be sure to refill the reservoir to the level mark (do not overfill) when through. Avoid over-tightening the cap or fluid will weep around the cap edge.

Disc Service

The brake disc normally requires no service of any kind. However, if the disc becomes scored for any reason, it should be replaced and a new set of pads should be installed. A badly scored disc will reduce the effectiveness of the brake and shorten pad life considerably. If the front brake lever oscillates or fluctuates when

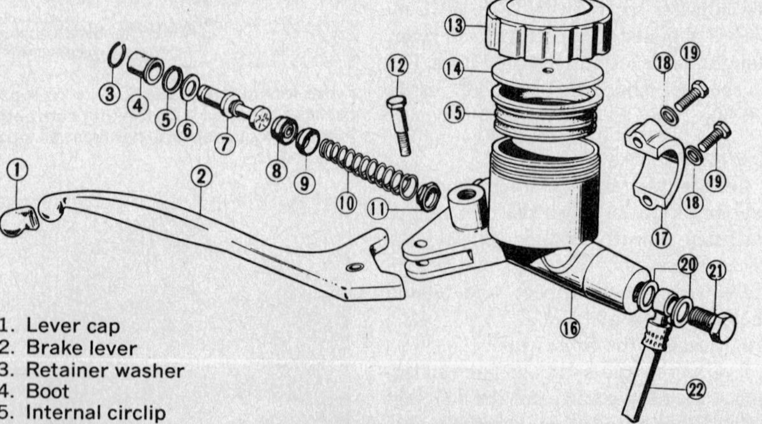

Exploded view of the master cylinder components

1. Lever cap
2. Brake lever
3. Retainer washer
4. Boot
5. Internal circlip
6. Washer
7. Piston
8. Secondary cup
9. Primary cup
10. Spring
11. Check valve
12. Pivot bolt
13. Reservoir cap
14. Cap washer
15. Diaphragm
16. Master cylinder body
17. Clamp
18. Spring washer
19. Bolt
20. Joint washers
21. Bolt
22. Brake hose

the brake is applied at speed, the indication is that the brake disc is warped or bent. Check the runout of the disc with a dial indicator and replace it if runout exceeds 0.012 in. (0.3 mm). To replace the disc:

1. Remove the front wheel.
2. Bend back the locktabs, unscrew the six nuts, and remove the disc from the hub.
3. Mount the new disc on the hub and tighten the nuts evenly, using new locktabs to secure the nuts.
4. Examine the brake pads and replace them if they are close to the limit of wear or have worn in an unusual pattern.
5. Install the wheel on the bike and check brake adjustment.

REAR BRAKE SERVICE

Brake Shoe Replacement

The brake shoes should be replaced when the brake operating rod and lever move over-center or past perpendicular as the brake is applied. The replacement procedure is as follows:

1. Remove the rear wheel.
2. Unscrew the axle nut and withdraw the axle. Separate the backing plate from the brake drum.

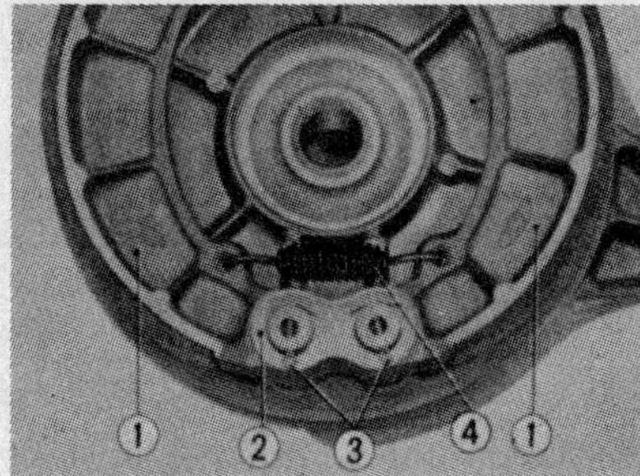

Brake shoes mounted on the backing plate

1. Brake shoes
2. Pivot washer
3. Cotter pins
4. Brake shoe spring

3. Remove the cotter pin and washer from each brake shoe pivot and lift the shoes away from the backing plate. Minimum acceptable lining thickness at any point is 0.080 in. (2.0 mm) for all models except the 350, which requires a minimum of 0.1 in. (2.5 mm).
4. Apply a *light* coat of grease to the brake shoe pivots and the actuating cam. Install the shoes and springs as removed, using new cotter pins.
5. Wipe the brake drum clean with a cloth and examine for damage and wear. Light scoring can be tolerated, but the drum should be replaced if badly scored or worn beyond the limit.
6. Assemble the drum and hub with the axle and install the wheel.
7. Adjust the brake so that there is about 1.0 in. (25 mm) free-play at the pedal. Avoid heavy braking until at least 500 miles have been covered.

FINAL DRIVE

CB 350 F, CB 500, CB 750 and CB 750K1—K3

SPROCKET REMOVAL AND INSTALLATION

To gain access to the countershaft sprocket, it is only necessary to remove the left-side rear crankcase cover. Removal of the rear wheel sprocket requires that the rear wheel assembly be removed from the bike. The sprocket can be unbolted after the locktabs are bent back from the nuts. Be sure to use new locktabs upon reassembly.

REAR HUB DAMPER SERVICE

1. Remove the rear wheel assembly and withdraw the axle.
2. Bend back the locktabs and unbolt the sprocket.

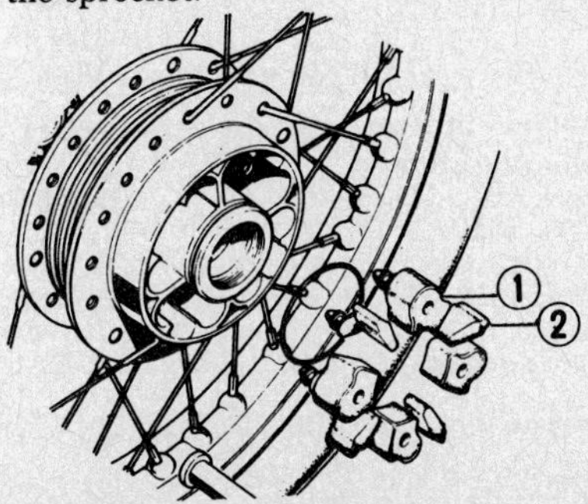

New type damper rubbers (1 and 2)

3. Separate the driving flange from the hub and withdraw the damper rubbers. The damper rubbers used in the CB 750 may be replaced with the modified K1 type. The CB 500 is equipped as standard with the K1-type damper rubbers.

Replace damaged or worn damper rubbers as a complete set. Assemble in reverse order of disassembly. Use new locktabs to secure the sprocket nuts.

CHAIN OILER ADJUSTMENT

The early type chain oiler (through engine number CB 750E–1026143) can be adjusted as follows:

1. Remove the countershaft sprocket cover (left-side rear crankcase cover) and wipe the sprocket and chain clean.
2. Remove the shaft plug, lockwasher, and shim washer.
3. To reduce oil flow from the oiler, use a thinner shim washer. To increase oil flow, use a thicker shim washer. Change shim thickness in approximately one-half mm increments to avoid overdoing it.
4. Install the shim washer, lockwasher, and plug. Ride the bike at about 60 mph for a minute or two and examine the amount of oil metered by the oiler. Readjust if necessary.

Drive chain oiler adjusting screw

NOTE: *If you are not able to regulate the chain oiler to your satisfaction, a replacement oiler of the later type K1—K3 design is available from Honda dealers to fit the CB 750. The CB 350 and CB 500 is not equipped with a chain oiler.*

To adjust the K1—K3-Type chain oiler:

1. Remove the countershaft sprocket cover (left-side rear crankcase cover) and wipe the sprocket and chain clean.
2. Turn the oiler adjusting screw in until seated (fully closed).
3. Ride the bike for a minute or two at about 60 mph and then check the oil output to the chain. If additional oiling is desired, back the adjusting screw out about one-fourth turn and recheck output. Maximum oiling is achieved when the screw is backed out three full turns from closed.

FRONT SUSPENSION

CB 350 F, CB 500, CB 750 and CB 750K1—K3

FORK SEAL REPLACEMENT AND DAMPER COMPONENT INSPECTION

Fork Disassembly

1. Remove the top fork bolts and the piston rod locknuts.
2. Remove the front wheel and fender.
3. Remove the three caliper mounting bolts and the adjuster nut, and lift the caliper assembly away from the fork leg. Do not let the caliper hang by the brake hose; tie it up out of the way with some string or wire.
4. Loosen the fork leg pinch bolts at

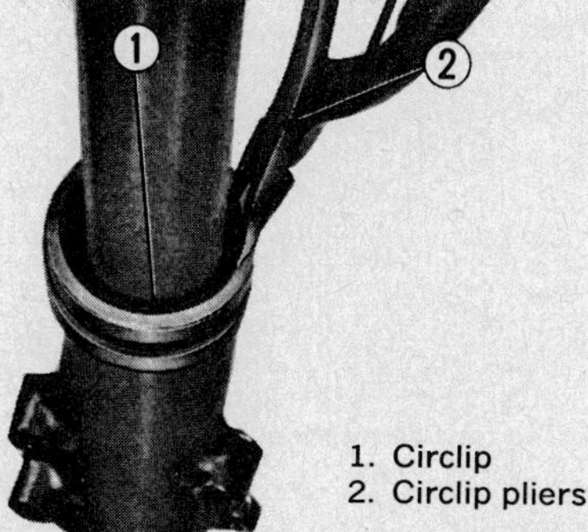

1. Circlip
2. Circlip pliers

Removing the fork seal circlip

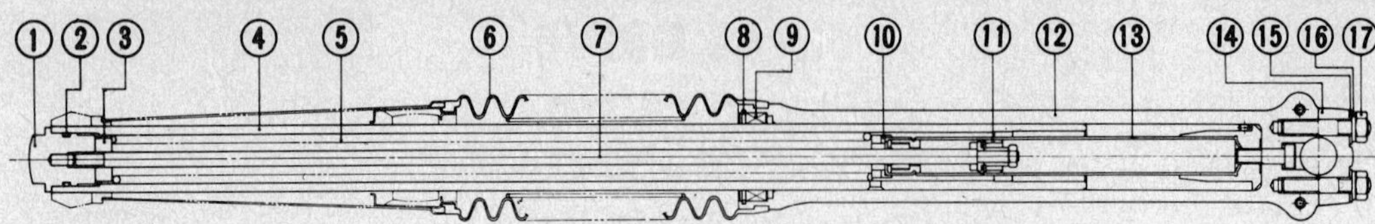

Cross-section of front fork assembly (500cc models)

1. Top bolt
2. O-ring
3. Locknut
4. Slider tube
5. Spring
6. Fork boot
7. Damper rod
8. Circlip
9. Oil seal
10. Holder
11. Collar
12. Bottom case
13. Damper case
14. Axle clamp
15. Flat washer
16. Spring washer
17. Nut

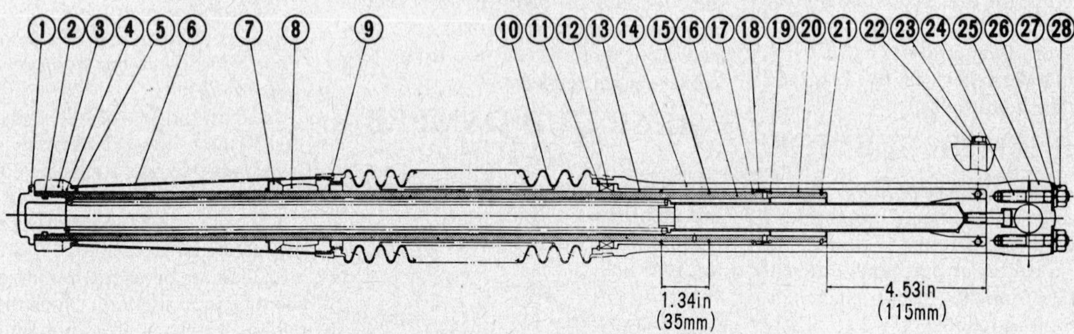

Cross-section of front fork assembly (750cc models)

1. Top bolt
2. O-ring
3. Top triple clamp
4. Fork cover upper cushion
5. Spring cushion
6. Fork cover
7. Fork cover lower cushion
8. Steering stem
9. Fork rib
10. Fork boot
11. Circlip
12. Oil seal
13. Guide
14. Bottom case
15. Travel limit ring
16. Slider tube
17. Valve limit ring
18. Damper valve
19. Piston limit ring
20. Damper piston
21. Piston circlip
22. Washer
23. Bolt
24. Bolt
25. Axle clamp
26. Flat washer
27. Spring washer
28. Nut

the top and bottom triple clamps. Remove each fork leg assembly by pulling gently downward.

NOTE: *From this point on, disassembly and inspection refers to one fork leg but applies to both.*

5. Pull the spring out of the slider tube and invert the fork leg assembly over a suitable container to drain the oil.

6. Pull the rubber boot off the leg if it remained attached when the leg was removed. Remove the circlip at the top of the lower fork leg, and separate the slider tube and lower fork leg.

7. Pry the seal out of the lower fork leg using a screwdriver, taking care not to damage the inside surface.

8. The damper assembly can be removed from the lower fork leg after unscrewing the allen bolt that is recessed into the bottom of the leg.

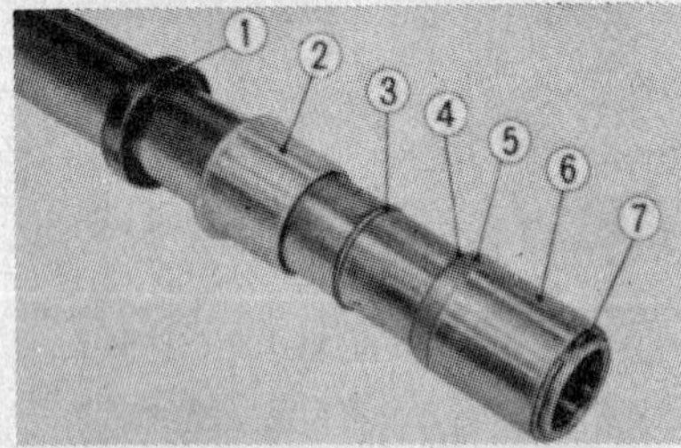

Damper components (750cc models)

1. Oil seal
2. Guide
3. Travel limit ring
4. Valve limit ring
5. Damper valve
6. Damper piston
7. Circlip

Fork components (500cc models)

1. Top bolt
2. Locknut
3. Spring seat
4. Circlip
5. Oil seal
6. Bottom case
7. Bolt
8. Damper unit
9. Spring
10. Slider tube
11. Removing the allen bolt

Inspection

Examine all components for damage and scoring. If the fork assembly was not operating properly, check the spring height and damper component dimensions against the specifications at the end of the chapter. Clean all components in solvent and dry thoroughly. Even a small piece of grit can impair damper action. Make sure that the slider tube is not bent by rolling it on a flat surface. Replace if bent.

Assembly

Assemble in reverse order of disassembly. Observe the following points:

1. Lubricate the seal with oil before installing it. If the proper oil seal driver is not available, a piece of wood cut to fit inside the lower fork leg will do the job without damaging the inside surface.

NOTE: *The oil seals and circlips used on the CB 750K1—K3 are slightly larger than those used on earlier models. Parts are not interchangeable.*

2. Fill the forks with the proper amount and grade of oil, and install the top fork bolts before fully tightening the triple clamp pinch bolts.

3. Adjust the brake caliper after assembly is complete.

STEERING HEAD

CB 350 F, CB 500, CB 750 and CB 750K1—K3

DISASSEMBLY

1. Unscrew the master cylinder mounting bolts and remove the master cylinder unit from the handlebar.

2. Disconnect the electrical switches, the throttle cable, and the clutch cable from the handlebar.

3. Remove the headlight assembly from the headlight case and disconnect the wiring at the connectors.

4. Unbolt and remove the handlebar assembly.

5. Loosen the instrument mounting clamp and remove the speedometer/ta-

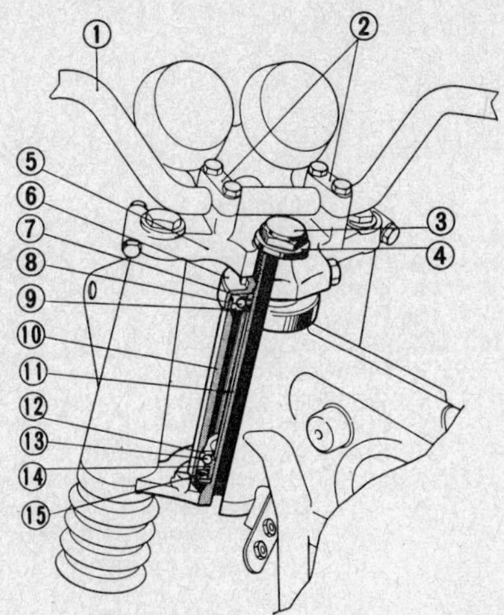

Steering components

chometer unit from the upper triple clamp.

6. Follow steps 1 through 4 in the preceding section to remove the front fork assembly.

7. Loosen the center triple-clamp pinch bolt and remove the large steering stem nut. Lift off the upper triple clamp.

Securing bolt locations

1. Top triple clamp
2. Top fork bolts
3. Stem nut
4. Pinch bolts

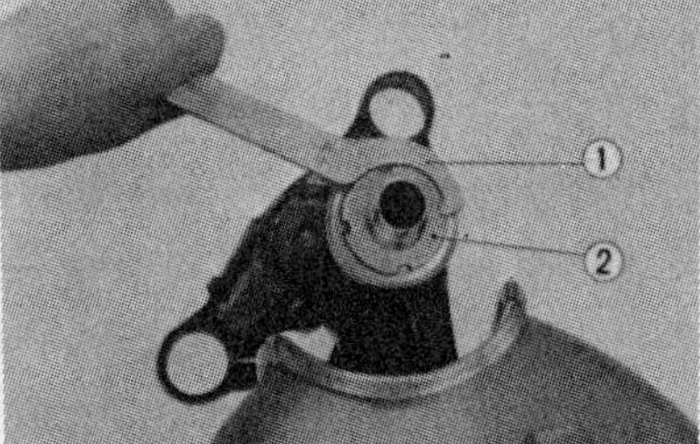

Removing the flat stem nut

1. Pin wrench
2. Flat stem nut

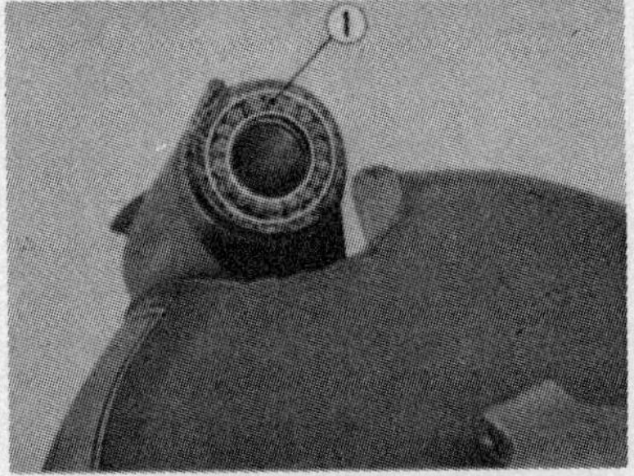

Top ball bearing assembly (1)

8. The steering stem and lower triple clamp can be withdrawn from the bottom after the large flat steering stem nut is removed. A special pin wrench, Honda part number 07072–20001, is available to facilitate removal of the nut. Be careful not to lose the steel balls when removing the steering stem.

INSPECTION

Examine the steel balls and the bearing races for wearing, pitting, and damage. Replace both bearing assemblies if they are not in perfect condition. Make sure that the steering stem is not cracked or bent. If the original bearings are to be reused, clean the balls and races in solvent and dry thoroughly. If the bearings are to be replaced, drive the races out of the steering head using a soft metal drift. Take care not to damage the inside surface.

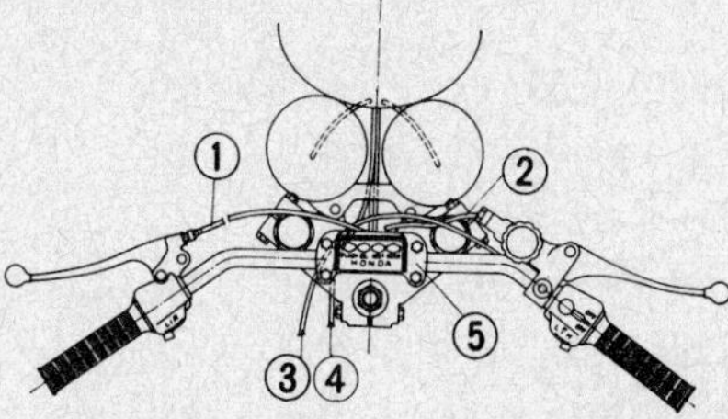

1. Clutch cable
2. Front brake hose
3. Throttle cable
4. Wire harness
5. Top triple clamp

ASSEMBLY

Assemble in reverse order of disassembly. Note the following points:

1. Apply a liberal amount of grease to the bearing races. Place eighteen steel balls in the upper race and nineteen in the lower race. Take care not to drop the balls as the steering stem is installed.

2. Tighten the flat steering stem nut *in small increments,* checking frequently, until there is no fore and aft play at the steering stem and it can move freely and smoothly throughout its travel. *Do not overtighten the flat stem nut.*

3. Route the control cables and electrical wires as shown in the accompanying illustration. Check clutch and throttle cable play when assembly is complete.

REAR SUSPENSION

CB 350 F, CB 500, CB 750 and CB 750K1—K3

SHOCK ABSORBER AND SPRING REPLACEMENT

Check the free-length of the spring against the correct dimension given at the end of the chapter. Place the spring on its end on a flat surface and check the amount of tilt from vertical. Replace the spring if the free-length is off or if tilt exceeds 2.5 degrees. Make sure that the spring/shock unit is not binding after it has been reassembled.

CAUTION: *The De Carbon type shock units which are supplied by the factory are not repairable and attempted disassembly may be potentially dangerous. If the units leak or do not provide satisfactory service they must be replaced.*

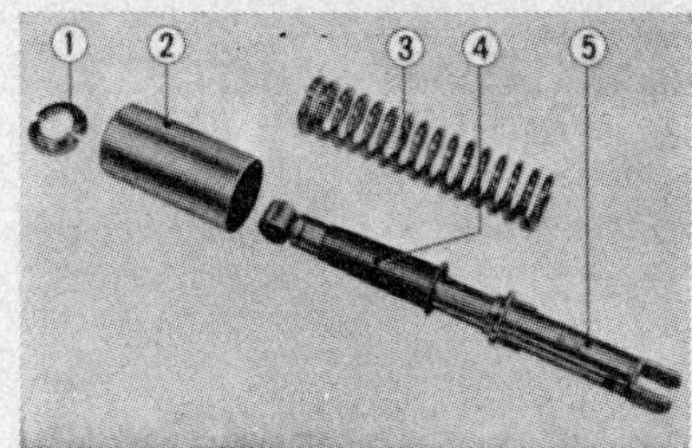

Rear shock assembly

1. Split retainer
2. Upper cover
3. Spring
4. Spring guide
5. Shock absorber unit

SWING ARM AND SWING ARM PIVOT SERVICE

Disassembly

1. Remove the mufflers.
2. Remove the rear wheel.
3. Remove the rear shock absorber/-spring units.
4. Remove the swing arm pivot nut and withdraw the pivot shaft. The swing arm can now be separated from the frame.

Inspection

Check the swing arm carefully for cracks and distortion. It is very important that the swing arm is aligned properly and in perfect condition. It is also very important that the pivot tube and pivot bushings are in perfect condition. The inner diameter of the pivot bushings must not exceed 0.858 in. (21.8 mm), and the outside diameter of the pivot tube must not be less than 0.8425 in. (21.4 mm). Replace parts as required.

Assembly

Installation is in reverse order of removal. Observe the following points:

1. Liberally grease the pivot tube before installing.
2. Refer to the illustration for pivot component installation details.
3. Lubricate the swing arm pivot at the grease fittings after it is assembled, and make sure that no more than 0.02 in. (0.5 mm) of free-play exists at the pivot.

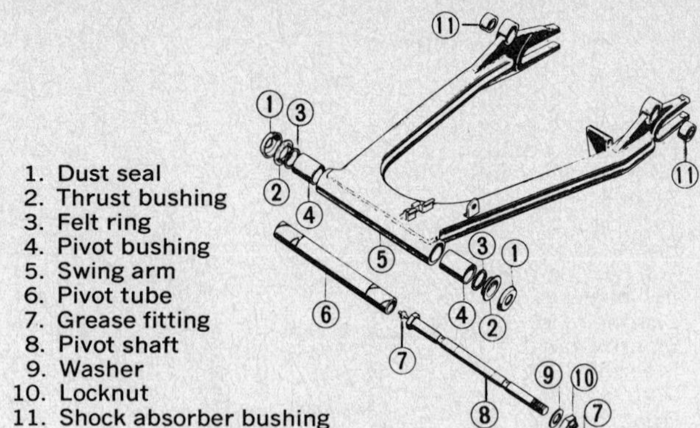

Exploded view of swing arm components—shown is a 750

CHASSIS SPECIFICATIONS

	CB 350F	CB 500	CB 750	CB 750K1—K3
WHEELS				
Rim Runout				
nom. (in./mm)	0.0197/0.5	0.02/0.5	0.02/0.5	0.02/0.5
max.	0.079/2.0	0.08/2.0	0.08/2.0	0.08/2.0
WHEEL BEARINGS				
Front				
axial runout				
max. (in./mm)	0.0039/0.1	0.004/0.1	0.004/0.1	0.004/0.1
diametrical				
runout max.				
(in./mm)				
Rear	0.0020/0.05	0.002/0.05	0.002/0.5	0.002/0.05
axial runout				
max. (in./mm)				
diametrical	0.0039/0.1	0.004/0.1	0.004/0.1	0.004/0.1
runout max.				
(in./mm)	0.0020/0.05	0.0024/0.06	0.0024/0.06	0.0024/0.06
BRAKES				
Front Brake				
Disc thickness				
nom. (in./mm)	0.275/7.0	N.A.	0.275/7.0	0.275/7.0
min. (in./mm)	0.217/5.5	N.A.	0.217/5.5	0.217/5.5
Disc runout				
nom. (in./mm)	0.0118/0.3	N.A.	0.004/0.1	0.004/0.1
max. (in./mm)	0.0118/0.3	0.012/0.3	0.012/0.3	0.012/0.3
Master cylinder				
bore diameter				
maximum				
(in./mm)	0.553/14.055	0.553/14.055	0.553/14.055	0.553/14.055
piston diam.				
minimum				
(in. mm)	0.549/13.940	0.549/13.940	0.549/13.940	0.549/13.940
Caliper				
bore diameter				
maximum				
(in./mm)	1.504/38.215	1.504/38.215	1.504/38.215	1.504/38.215

	CB 350F	CB 500	CB 750	CB 750K1—K3
piston diam. minimum (in./mm)	1.500/38.105	1.500/38.105	1.500/38.105	1.500/38.105
Pad to disc clear. (in./mm)	0.006/0.15	0.006/0.15	0.006/0.15	0.006/0.15
Rear Brake				
Drum diameter max. (in/mm)	6.3386/161.0	7.125/181.0	7.205/183.0	7.205/183.0
Lining thickness min. (in./mm)	0.0984/2.5	0.080/2.0	0.080/2.0	0.080/2.0
Pedal free travel (in./mm)	1.0/2.5	1.0/25	1.0/25	1.0/25
FRONT SUSPENSION				
Suspension Travel (in./mm)	4.5/114.6	4.8/121	5.6/143	5.6/143
Spring				
free-length min. (in./mm)	16.378/416	16.73/425	18.11/460	18.11/460
installation load (approx, lbs)	58.212	N.A.	71	71
tilt max. (deg)	2.5	2.5	2.5	2.5
Damper Piston				
diameter min. (in./mm)	1.2944/32.875	N.A.	1.5512/39.4	1.5512/39.4
taper and ovality max. (in./mm)	N.A.	N.A.	0.0006/0.015	0.0006/0.015
Lower Fork Leg Case				
inner diameter max. (in./mm)	13.063/33.18	N.A.	1.5591/39.68	1.5591/39.68
taper and ovality max. (in./mm)	N.A.	N.A.	0.0012/0.03	0.0012/0.03
STEERING				
Rake (deg)	26.60	26	27	27
Trail (in./mm)	3.3/85	4.1/105	3.74/95	3.74/95
REAR SUSPENSION				
Suspension Travel (in./mm)	3.6/91.0	3.1/78.5	3.3/85	3.3/85
Swing Arm Length (in.)	N.A.	17.75	17.75	17.75
Spring				
free-length min. (in./mm)	7.480/190	8.070/205	8.504/216	8.504/216
installation load (approx, lbs)	N.A.	N.A.	67	67
tilt max. (deg)	2.5	2.5	2.5	2.5
inner diam. (in./mm)	N.A.	N.A.	1.415/36.0	1.710/40.0
Swing Arm Pivot				
bushing inner diam. max. (in./mm)	0.8543/21.70	0.858/21.8	0.858/21.8	0.858/21.8
pivot tube outer diam. min. (in./mm)	0.8406/21.35	0.8425/21.4	0.8425/21.4	0.8425/21.4

INDEX KAWASAKI TWO-STROKES

MODEL IDENTIFICATION

G3SS—90 cc street model, single cylinder, rotary valve induction, Super Lube lubrication, magneto ignition, 5-speed.
GA1, GA2—identical to G3SS in most respects; GA1 has 4-speed transmission.

G3TR, G4TR—99 cc trail models, single cylinder, rotary valve induction, Super Lube lubrication, magneto ignition, 5-speed, high pipe, raised front fender, knobby tires.

A1—247cc twin, rotary valve induction, Super Lube lubrication, 12 volt electrics, dual carbs.
A7—same as A1, but 338cc; displacement increased by boring cylinder.

B1L-A—124cc road bike, early Japanese styling, pressed steel frame, fully enclosed drive chain, electric starter, 4-speed transmission, 12 volt electrical system.

A1SS, A7SS—247cc and 338cc respectively, the SS models are high-pipe versions of the A1 and A7; identical in other respects.

F-Series—all basically similar in appearance, engine specifications vary, displacement from 124cc to 346cc, single cylinder, upswept pipe, off-road trim.

S2, H1, H2—Kawasaki's line of triples displace 346cc, 498cc and 748cc respectively; H1 and H2 have front disc brake, S2 has twin leading shoe; the S2 also has Super Lube system, while the H1 and H2 are equipped with Injecto Lube; all three have Piston Port induction, 12 volt electrics; S2 has three 24mm carbs; H1 has 28mm, and H2 comes with three 30mm.

GENERAL SPECIFICATIONS

GA1-A, GA2-A, G3SS-A, G3TR-A, G4TR, B1L-A

	GA1—A	GA2—A	G3SS—A	G3TR—A	G4TR	B1L—A
DIMENSIONS						
Net Weight (lbs)	174	174	183	183	185	257
Overall Length (in.)	71.3	71.3	72.1	72.1	76.7	77.4
Overall Width (in.)	29.1	29.1	33.0	33.0	33.0	31.1
Overall Height (in.)	40.2	40.2	40.7	40.7	41.8	40.4
Wheelbase (in.)	45.3	45.3	45.3	45.3	50.0	49.2
Ground Clearance (in.)	5.9	5.9	6.7	6.3	9.41	5.3
Tire Size: front	2.50 x 18	2.50 x 18	2.75 x 18	2.75 x 18	3.00 x 18	3.00 x 16
rear	2.50 x 18	2.50 x 18	2.75 x 18	2.75 x 18	3.00 x 18	3.00 x 16
ENGINE						
Displacement (cc)	89	89	89	99	99	124
Bore x Stroke (mm)	47 x 51.8	47 x 51.8	47 x 51.8	49.5 x 51.8	49.5 x 51.8	55 x 52.5
Compression Ratio (:1)	7.0	7.0	7.0	7.0	7.0	6.4
Horsepower @ RPM	NA	NA	NA	NA	NA	12 @ 6500
Torque @ RPM	NA	NA	NA	NA	NA	9.75 @ 5000
Induction (RV, PP)*	RV	RV	RV	RV	RV	RV
Lubrication (SL, IL)**	SL	SL	SL	SL	SL	SL
Carburetion Mikuni)	VM19SC	VM19SC	VM19SC	VM19SC	VM19SC	VM22SC
TRANSMISSION						
Clutch Type	All Models—Wet, Multi-plate					
Primary Reduction	3.52	3.52	3.52	3.52	3.52	3.24
Secondary Reduction	2.79	2.57	2.64	3.00	2.80	2.80
Overall Reduction	9.82	8.68	8.92	10.14	9.46	8.16
Gearbox Ratios: 1st	2.92	2.92	2.92	2.92	2.92	2.67
2nd	1.71	1.72	1.77	1.77	1.77	1.62
3rd	1.24	1.30	1.30	1.30	1.30	1.20
4th	1.00	1.09	1.09	1.09	1.09	0.90
5th	—	0.96	0.96	0.96	0.96	—
ELECTRICS						
Generator Type	Magneto	Magneto	Magneto	Magneto	Magneto	Starter/ Generator
System Voltage	6V	6V	6V	6V	6V	12V
CHASSIS						
Frame Type	Tubular, Dbl.-cradle	Tubular, Dbl.-cradle	Tubular, Dbl.-cradle	Tubular, Dbl.-cradle	Tubular, Dbl.-cradle	Pressed Steel
Steering Angle (deg)	45	45	45	45	45	43
Caster (deg)	64	64	64	64	62.5	63
Trail (in.)	3.1	3.1	3.5	3.5	3.94	3.6
PERFORMANCE						
Turning Radius (in.)	70.9	70.9	70.9	70.9	79.0	74.8
Climbing Ability (deg)	29	27	27	33	①	30
Braking Distance (ft/mph)	21.3/22	21.3/22	21.3/22	21.3/22	21.3/22	16.4/22
Top Speed (mph)	62	68	70	66	66	68
Fuel Consumption (mpg)	176	176	176	165	153	153

* RV—Rotary Valve; PP—Piston Port
** SL—Super Lube; IL—Injecto Lube
NA—Not Available
① 29°—high range; 40°—low range

GENERAL SPECIFICATIONS

F6, F7, F8, F5, A1, A1SS

	F6	F7	F8	F5	A1	A1SS
DIMENSIONS						
Net Weight (lbs)	231	233	270	265	318.5	323.3
Overall Length (in.)	78.5	80.5	82.0	82.0	78.3	78.3
Overall Width (in.)	33.5	33.5	82.0	32.3	31.9	32.6
Overall Height (in.)	38.5	43.0	43.5	40.0	43.1	42.5
Wheelbase (in.)	51.5	52.0	55.0	55.0	51.2	51.0
Ground Clearance (in.)	9.5	9.84	8.3	9.0	6.5	6.7
Tire Size: front	3.00 x 18	3.00 x 19	3.25 x 19	3.00 x 21	3.00 x 18	3.00 x 18
rear	3.25 x 18	3.50 x 18	4.00 x 18	4.00 x 18	3.25 x 18	3.50 x 18
ENGINE						
Displacement (cc)	124	174	246.8	346	247	247
Bore x Stroke (mm)	52 x 58.8	61.5 x 58.8	68 x 68	80.5 x 68	53 x 56	53 x 56
Compression Ratio (:1)	7.2	7.1	6.8	6.8	7.0	7.0
Horsepower @ RPM	15 @ 7500	20 @ 7500	23.5 @ 6800	33 @ 6500	31 @ 8000	31 @ 8000
Torque @ RPM	10.8 @ 7000	14.3 @ 7000	19.1 @ 6000	28 @ 5500	21.1 @ 7500	21.1 @ 7500
Induction (RV, PP)*,	RV	RV	RV	RV	RV	RV
Lubrication (SL, IL)**	SL	SL	IL	IL	SL	SL
Carburetion (Mikuni)	VM24SC	VM26SC	VM30SC	VM32SC	VM22SC (2)	VM22SC (2)
TRANSMISSION						
Clutch	All Models—Wet, Multi-plate					
Primary Reduction	3.13	3.13	3.04	3.04	3.40	3.40
Secondary Reduction	3.93	3.57	3.21	3.22	2.46	2.60
Overall Reduction	8.84	8.04	9.28	7.00	6.52	6.89
Gearbox Ratios: 1st	2.67	2.67	2.45	2.45	2.50	2.50
2nd	1.75	1.75	1.71	1.71	1.53	1.53
3rd	1.20	1.20	1.17	1.17	1.13	1.13
4th	0.91	0.91	0.96	0.90	0.92	0.92
5th	0.72	0.72	0.71	0.71	0.78	0.78
ELECTRICS						
Generator Type	Magneto	Magneto	Magneto	Magneto	Magneto	Magneto
System Voltage	6V	6V	6V	6V	12V	12V
CHASSIS						
Frame Type	Tubular, Dbl.-cradle	Tubular, Dbl.-cradle	Tubular, Dbl.-cradle	Tubular, Dbl.-cradle	Tubular, Dbl.-cradle	Tubular, Dbl.-cradle
Steering Angle (deg)	48	48	45	45	40	40
Caster (deg)	62	61	60.5	60	63	63
Trail (in.)	4.9	4.37	4.65	5.12	3.4	3.4
PERFORMANCE						
Turning Radius (in.)	79.0	74.8	90.0	88.0	86.6	86.6
Climbing Ability (deg)	34	36	36	40	38	39
Braking Distance (ft/mph)	19.5/22	33.0/31	49.0/31	39/31	39/31	39/31
Top Speed (mph)	72	78	80	84	103	103
Fuel Consumption (mpg)	141	118	94	90	80	80

* RV—Rotary Valve; PP—Piston Port
** SL—Super Lube; IL—Injecto Lube

GENERAL SPECIFICATIONS

A7, A7SS, S2, H1, H2

	A7	A7SS	S2	H1	H2
DIMENSIONS					
Net Weight (lbs)	327.7	329.0	329.6	382.0	423.4
Overall Length (in.)	79.0	78.7	79.1	82.5	81.9
Overall Width (in.)	31.9	31.9	31.5	33.1	33.5
Overall Height (in.)	43.5	43.5	43.1	42.5	45.1
Wheelbase (in.)	51.0	51.0	52.4	55.1	55.5
Ground Clearance (in.)	6.7	6.7	6.3	5.3	6.9
Tire Size: front	3.25 x 18	3.25 x 18	3.00 x 18	3.25 x 19	3.25 x 19
rear	3.50 x 18	3.50 x 18	3.50 x 18	4.00 x 18	4.00 x 19
ENGINE					
Displacement (cc)	338	338	346.2	498	748
Bore x Stroke (mm)	62 x 56	62 x 56	53 x 52.3	60 x 58.8	71 x 63
Compression Ratio (:1)	7.0	7.0	7.3	6.8	7.0
Horsepower @ RPM	42 @ 8000	42 @ 8000	45 @ 8000	60 @ 7500	74 @ 6800
Torque @ RPM	28.9 @ 7000	28.9 @ 7000	30.7 @ 7000	42.3 @ 7000	57.1 @ 6500
Induction (RV, PP)*	RV	RV	PP	PP	PP
Lubrication (SL, IL)**	IL	IL	SEL	IL	IL
Carburetion (Mikuni)	VM28SC (2)	VM28SC (2)	VM24SC (3)	VM28SC (3)	VM30SC (3)
TRANSMISSION					
Clutch Type	All Models—Wet, Multi-plate				
Primary Reduction	3.40	3.40	2.22	2.41	1.88
Secondary Reduction	2.40	2.40	3.07	②	3.13
Overall Reduction	6.36	6.36	6.56	③	4.76
Gearbox Ratios: 1st	2.50	2.50	2.86	2.20	2.17
2nd	1.53	1.53	1.79	1.40	1.47
3rd	1.113	1.13	1.35	1.09	1.11
4th	0.92	0.92	1.12	0.92	0.92
5th	0.78	0.78	0.96	0.81	0.81
ELECTRICS					
Generator Type	Magneto	Magneto	Alternator	Alternator	Alternator
System Voltage	12V	12V	12V	12V	12V
CHASSIS					
Frame Type	Tubular, Dbl.-cradle	Tubular, Dbl.-cradle	Tubular, Dbl.-cradle	Tubular, Dbl.-cradle	Tubular, Dbl.-cradle
Steering Angle (deg)	40	40	42	42	39
Caster (deg)	63	63	62	61	62
Trail (in.)	3.6	3.6	4.3	4.3	4.3
PERFORMANCE					
Turning Radius (in.)	86.6	86.6	82.5	90.5	94.5
Climbing Ability (deg)	40	40	40	40	40
Braking Distance (ft/mph)	39/31	39/31	39.4/31	34.5/31	39.4/31
Top Speed (mph)	110	109	111	118	126
Fuel Consumption (mpg)	80	80	75	78	45

* RV—Rotary Valve; PP—Piston Port
** SL—Super Lube; IL—Injecto Lube
② Early Models—2.81; late models—3.00
③ Early models—5.46; late models—5.84

TUNE-UP AND MAINTENANCE

TUNE-UP OPERATIONS

Contact Breaker Points and Ignition Timing

G SERIES, F6, AND F8

These models are equipped with a flywheel magneto in which contact breaker adjustment and ignition timing are accomplished in one operation.

1. Remove the ignition access cover, then separate the points and check their condition.

2. Clean up a set of used points by running a point file or piece of fine sandpaper between them. Remove any deposits and smooth out pitted surfaces, then apply laquer thinner or point cleaner.

NOTE: *Apply thinner or point cleaner to a new set of points as well, since many of them are coated with a protective film.*

3. Snap the points shut on a white business card (or piece of heavy paper) to remove the filings and cleaning fluid. Repeat this step until the points leave a clean imprint.

4. Rotate the engine by putting it in gear and turning the rear wheel. Observe the points as they open and close. If they do not meet squarely, replace the set.

NOTE: *Use the accompanying illustration for reference when performing the remaining steps.*

5. Rotate the engine until the mark "A" on the flywheel is aligned with the mark "C" on the crankcase.

6. Loosen lockscrew "E" just enough to enable you to move the breaker plate.

7. Adjust the position of the points so that they are just opening. This is accomplished by prying the breaker plate between points "F" and "G" with a screwdriver blade.

Flywheel magneto (G Series, F6, and F8)

Magneto (flywheel removed)

8. Tighten lockscrew "E," making certain that the breaker plate does not move when the screw is tightened.

9. Check the adjustment by rotating the engine and observing the points. They should just begin to open when the flywheel and crankcase marks fall into alignment.

10. When the timing is correctly adjusted, the maximum gap between the points should be between 0.012 and 0.-016 in.

NOTE: *The F8 is equipped with slotted magneto mounting holes to provide a means of adjustment. The crankcase and magneto base mark must be aligned before adjustment can be performed.*

11. Lubricate the breaker cam felt with a high-melting-point grease.

B1L—A

This model is equipped with a combination starter/DC generator, in which the contact breaker point gap and ignition timing are set separately.

1. Inspect and clean the breaker points as previously described for the flywheel magneto models.

2. Rotate the engine until the points are at their widest gap.

NOTE: *Use the accompanying illustration for reference when performing the following steps.*

3. Loosen lockscrews "A" just enough so that the position of the breaker plate can be shifted.

4. Shift the position of the plate so that the gap between the points is between 0.012 and 0.016 in. (0.3–0.4 mm).

5. Tighten lockscrews "A," making certain that the plate does not shift position when the screws are tightened.

6. Align the timing pointer "C" with the mark "D" on the breaker cam.

7. Loosen both breaker plate adjusting screws "E" and shift the plate up or down until the points just begin to open. Tighten the adjusting screws "E," making certain that the plate does not move when the screws are tightened.

NOTE: *This position can best be determined by connecting a timing light between the point set and ground.*

8. Recheck the adjustment by rotating the engine and observing the points. They should just be opening as the marks "C" and "D" align.

Starter/generator (B1L-A)

IGNITION TIMING

G Series, F6 and F8

Model	Standard ignition timing	Piston Position Before TDC 17° in. (mm)	18° in. (mm)	19° in. (mm)	20° in. (mm)	21° in. (mm)	22° in. (mm)	23° in. (mm)	24° in. (mm)	25° in. (mm)
G Series	20°	0.055	0.061	0.068	0.077	0.083	0.091	0.099	0.110	—
		(1.40)	(1.56)	(1.72)	(1.96)	(2.11)	(2.32)	(2.51)	(2.78)	—
G31M-4	23°	0.055	0.061	0.068	0.077	0.083	0.091	0.099	0.110	—
		(1.40)	(1.56)	(1.72)	(1.96)	(2.11)	(2.32)	(2.51)	(2.78)	—
F6	23°	0.064	0.071	0.080	0.088	0.097	0.106	0.116	0.125	0.136
		(1.62)	(1.81)	(2.02)	(3.23)	(2.46)	(2.69)	(2.94)	(3.19)	(3.46)
F8	20°	0.074	0.083	0.092	0.102	0.112	0.123	0.134	0.145	0.158
		(1.88)	(2.10)	(2.34)	(2.59)	(2.85)	(3.12)	(3.41)	(3.70)	(4.01)
F81M	19°	0.074	0.083	0.092	0.102	0.112	0.123	0.134	0.145	0.158
		(1.88)	(3.10)	(2.34)	(2.59)	(2.85)	(3.12)	(3.41)	(3.70)	(4.01)

9. Lightly lubricate the breaker cam felt with a high-melting-point grease.

F5 AND F7

These models are equipped with capacitor discharge ignition, which does not use contact breaker points. Instead, it has a signal generator which does not emit a pulse unless the engine is running. Therefore, ignition timing cannot be set statically as is the case with flywheel magneto and DC generator systems. It can only be observed with a stroboscopic timing light.

NOTE: *Since this system does not employ contact breaker points, it is not subject to their wear. As a result, once initial timing has been set (as it is at the factory) it very rarely requires adjustment.*

1. Remove the magneto cover, then connect a strobe light according to manufacturer's instructions.

2. Start and run the engine at 4000 rpm.

3. Aim the strobe light beam at the marks on the flywheel and crankcase.

4. If the marks are in alignment at 4000 rpm, no adjustment is necessary. If they are not aligned, stop the engine, insert a screwdriver blade through the hole in the magneto (see illustration), and loosen screws "B," "C," and "D."

5. Shift the position of the magneto base by prying it with a screwdriver inserted into notch "A." To retard the timing, turn the base counterclockwise; to advance the timing turn it clockwise.

6. Tighten magneto base lockscrews "B," "C," and "D."

CID magneto (F5 and F7)

7. Start the engine up again and run it at 4000 rpm. Recheck the mark alignment with the strobe light beam. Readjust again if necessary.

8. Lightly lubricate the breaker cam felt with a high-melting-point grease.

A SERIES (CONVENTIONAL IGNITION)

1. Clean and inspect the breaker points as previously described for the flywheel magneto models.

NOTE: *Use the accompanying illustration for reference when performing the following adjustments.*

2. Turn the alternator rotor shaft with an appropriate open end wrench on nut "F" until the left contact breaker points are fully opened.

3. Loosen lockscrews "D" and "E."

4. Set the left contact breaker point gap to between 0.012 and 0.016 in. by turning adjusting screw "B." Turning the screw clockwise decreases the gap; turning it counterclockwise increases the gap.

5. Tighten lockscrews "D" and "E," making certain that the points do not shift position when the screws are tightened.

6. Adjust the right point set gap in the same manner. Turning the right contact breaker adjusting screw clockwise increases gap; turning it counterclockwise decreases gap.

7. Align ignition timing pointer "K" with the red painted mark "O" on the plate "P." When these marks are aligned, the crankshaft is located 23° before top dead center.

8. Loosen base plate screws "L" and "M" on plate "N."

9. Shift the position of the base plate until the left points are just about to open by prying it with a screwdriver between the projections on the rear cover "D" and the projection of the base plate "E."

10. Tighten base plate lockscrews "L" and "M," making certain that the plate does not move when the screws are tightened.

11. Set the timing at the right points in the same manner. Align ignition timing pointer "K" with mark "Q" to locate the crankshaft at 23° before top dead center.

12. After the right contact breaker timing has been set, check the left set again to make sure that its position has not shifted.

13. Apply a small amount of high-melting-point grease to breaker cam felt "R."

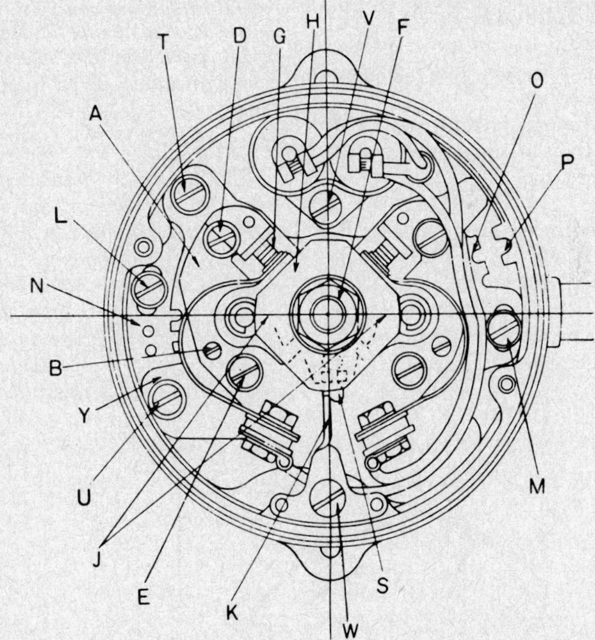

Alternator (A Series with conventional ignition)

IGNITION TIMING

B1L-A

Model	Standard timing	Piston Position Before TDC								
		17° in. (mm)	18° in. (mm)	19° in. (mm)	20° in. (mm)	21° in. (mm)	22° in. (mm)	23° in. (mm)	24° in. (mm)	25° in. (mm)
B1L-A	20°	0.055 (1.40)	0.062 (1.57)	0.069 (1.75)	0.076 (1.93)	0.084 (2.13)	0.088 (2.33)	0.100 (2.55)	0.110 (2.77)	— —

S SERIES (CONVENTIONAL IGNITION)

Ignition timing for the three-cylinder 350 is accomplished the same way as described for the H1 with conventional ignition. However, piston position should be 23° BTDC (0.1024 in.; 2.60 mm) rather than 25°. The timing pointer and marks are also slightly different. See the accompanying illustration for reference.

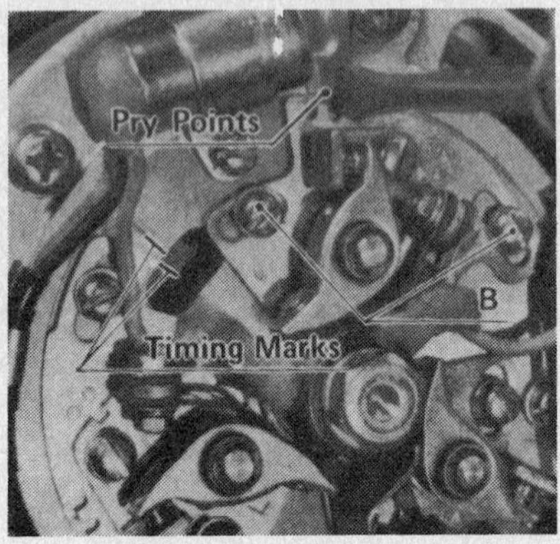

S2 timing marks and point base plate screws

H1

(CONVENTIONAL IGNITION)

1. Clean and inspect the points as previously described.
2. Turn the crankshaft until each set of points are at their maximum gap (one at a time). Check the gap with a feeler gauge.
3. If the clearance is not within specifications, loosen screw A (see accompanying illustration) and pry the points until the gap is correct. Tighten screw A.
4. Remove the spark plug from the left cylinder and install a dial gauge in its place.
5. Position the crankshaft so that the left piston is set at 25° (0.1362 in.; 3.46 mm) before top dead center.
6. Loosen the stator base plate securing screws A (see accompanying illustration).
7. Connect a timing light or ohmmeter to ground and left cylinder point wire B.
8. Using a screwdriver blade for leverage, pry the stator base plates so that the left cylinder points are just opening (as indicated by the timing light or ohmmeter).
9. Tighten stator base plate screws A.
10. Line up pointer E with the circled L mark on the rotor by moving the pointer. *Do not turn the rotor.*
11. After the marks are aligned, *then* turn the rotor to align the circled R mark with the pointer E.
12. Connect an ohmmeter or timing light to point set F and ground.
13. Loosen screws G and adjust the timing for this cylinder in the same manner as described above.
14. Turn the rotor until circled mark C aligns with pointer E, then set the timing for the center cylinder point set J as previously described.
15. Lightly lubricate the breaker cam felt with a high melting point grease.

NOTE: *Reference marks C, H, and K in the accompanying illustration are prying points for the left, right, and center cylinder points sets, respectively.*

(CD Ignition)

NOTE: *It is rarely necessary to adjust the ignition timing on this system. If you are in doubt that the timing is correct, it is best to connect a strobe timing light to each cylinder (see F5 and F7 section) and check the alignment of the rotor and crankcase timing marks at 4000 rpm. If an adjustment is needed, proceed as described below.*

1. Loosen pick-up lockscrews "1" and "2" (see illustration).
2. Adjust the gap between the top of the pick-up and the projection of the signal generator rotor to 0.4–0.6 mm.
3. Tighten lockscrews "1" and "2."
4. Insert a dial guage into a spark plug hole and set the piston position at 3.45 mm (25°) before top dead center.
5. Loosen lockscrews "3," "4," and "5" of the pick-up and adjust them so that the mark of the signal generator aligns with that of the pick-up.
6. Bend the pointer "6" so that it too aligns with the corresponding mark on the signal generator.

H2 (CD IGNITION)

NOTE: *It is rarely necessary to adjust the timing on the capacitive discharge ignition system. If you are in doubt as to the accuracy of the timing, however, you can check and reset it by following the procedure given below.*

1. Remove the two securing screws and the left case cover.
2. Using a feeler gauge, measure the gap between the signal generator pickup coil of each cylinder and the magnet projection on the rotor. The correct gap is 0.020–0.031 in. (0.5–0.8 mm).
3. If the gap is incorrect, loosen the two coil mounting screws and move the coil by hand until the gap is correct.

Rotor and pickup coil gap (H2)

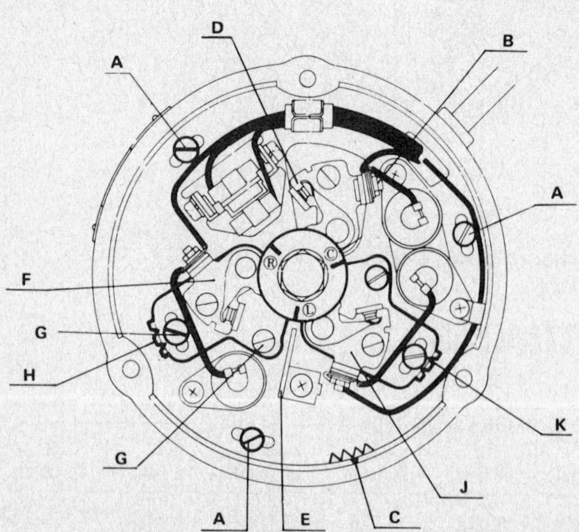

Ignition breaker points arrangement (H1 w/out CDI)

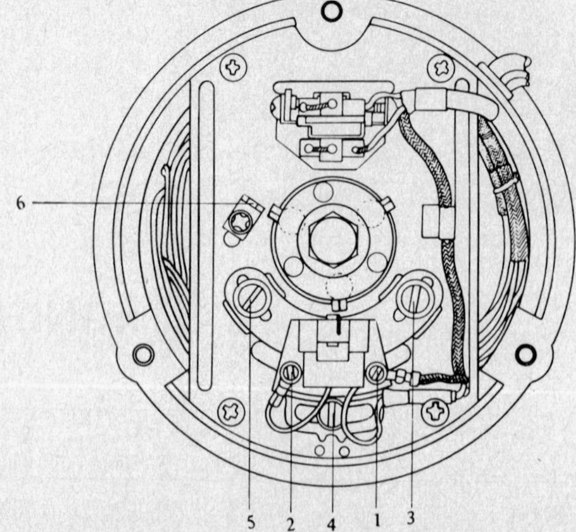

Alternator (H Series with CD ignition)

4. Remove the spark plug and install a dial guage in the left cylinder. Position the piston at 0.1231 in. (3.13 mm) before top dead center.

5. Bend the pointer on the magneto stator so that it aligns perfectly with the mark L on the rotor.

6. Turn the rotor slightly so that the pointer is aligned with the S mark.

7. Examine the trailing edge of the rotor magnet to make certain it coincides with the mark on top of the left cylinder signal generator coil housing. If it does not, loosen the coil base plate screws and shift the plate until it does. Retighten the securing screws.

8. Repeat the previous steps for the right and center cylinders, aligning the right and center S marks with the pointer.

Bending the pointer to align with circled mark L

9. Reinstall the spark plugs and attach a strobe light to the left cylinder.

10. After having started and warmed up the engine, increase engine speed to 4000 rpm and aim the strobe light beam at the pointer; the pointer and L mark should be in line. If not, readjust the left cylinder timing.

Checking ignition timing with a strobe light (H2)

11. Repeat step 10 for the other cylinders to make certain that the R and C marks also align with the pointer.

TUNE-UP SPECIFICATIONS

Model	Breaker Point Gap (mm)	Ignition Timing BTDC (deg/mm)	Spark Plug (NGK)	Spark Plug Gap (mm)	Spark Plug Tightening Torque (ft lbs)	Carburetor Air Screw (no. turns)	Carburetor Idle Speed (rpm)
GA1—A	0.3-0.4	20/1.96	B7HZ	0.6-0.7	18	1½	1300-1500
GA2—A	0.3-0.4	20/1.96	B7HZ	0.6-0.7	18	1½	1300-1500
G3SS—A	0.3-0.4	20/1.96	B8HC	0.6-0.7	18	1½	1300-1500
G3TR—A	0.3-0.4	20/1.96	B8HC	0.6-0.7	18	1¾	1300-1500
G4TR	0.3-0.4	20/1.96	B7HZ	0.6-0.7	18	1¾	1300-1500
B1L—A	0.3-0.4	20/1.93	B6H	0.6-0.7	18	1½	900-1100
F6	0.3-0.4	23/2.94	B9HC	0.6-0.7	18	1¾	1300-1500
F7	—	23/2.94	①	—	18	1¾	1000-1300
F8	0.3-0.4	20/2.59	B8HC	0.6-0.7	18	1¾	1000-1300
F5	—	23/3.41	①	—	18	1¼	1000-1300
A1 (Con)	0.3-0.4	23/N.A.	B9HC	0.6-0.7	18	1½	1500-1800
A1 (CDI)	②	25/3.28	①	—	18	1½	1500-1800
A1SS (Con)	0.3-0.4	23/N.A.	B9HC	0.6-0.7	18	1½	1500-1800
A1SS (CDI)	②	25/3.28	①	—	18	1½	1500-1800
A7 (Con)	0.3-0.4	23/N.A.	B9HC	0.6-0.7	18	1½	1500-1800
A7 (CDI)	②	25/3.28	①	—	18	1½	1500-1800

TUNE-UP SPECIFICATIONS

Model	Breaker Point Gap (mm)	Ignition Timing BTDC (deg/mm)	Spark Plug (NGK)	Spark Plug Gap (mm)	Spark Plug Tightening Torque (ft lbs)	Carburetor Air Screw (no. turns)	Carburetor Idle Speed (rpm)
A7SS (Con)	0.3-0.4	23/N.A.	B9HC	0.6-0.7	18	1½	1500-1800
A7SS (CDI)	②	25/3.28	①	—	18	1½	1500-1800
S2	0.3-0.4	23/2.60	B9HC	0.6-0.7	18	1½	1300-1500
H1 (Con)	0.3-0.4	25/3.46	B9HC	0.6-0.7	18	1½	1500-1800
H1 (CDI)	②	25/3.45	①	—	18	1¼	1500-1800
H2	③	④/3.13	B9HS-10	0.5	18	1½	1400-1600

① Champion L—19V or NGK BUHX
② Set the gap between the signal generator projection and signal pickup to 0.4-0.6 mm
③ Set the gap between the coil pickups and the rotor projection to 0.5-0.8 mm
④ 23° @ 4000 rpm

Carburetor Adjustment

IDLE SPEED AND MIXTURE

1. Turn the idle mixture (air) screw(s) IN until it seats lightly.

2. Back out the idle mixture (air) screw(s) the recommended number of turns.

3. Start and warm up the engine; then, with the throttle grip completely closed, turn the idle speed (throttle stop) screw(s) in or out until the engine idles at the specified rpm.

NOTE: *On multis, you can check idle speed synchronization by holding one hand behind each muffler and noting the exhaust pulse frequency. Reset the idle speed screws until the cylinders are firing alternately and at the same rate. If one cylinder is backfiring or its pulses are erratic, stop the engine; turn all idle speed screws IN until lightly seated, then turn them back OUT equally a couple of turns (enough to prevent stalling). Start the engine and turn one cylinder's idle speed screw IN, then OUT, and note any increase or decrease in engine speed. At the position where ½–1 turn does not cause a variation in rpm, the cylinders should be firing smoothly and at the same rate. The idle rpm may be higher than specified, but by equally backing out the idle mixture screws, you can lower it to normal.*

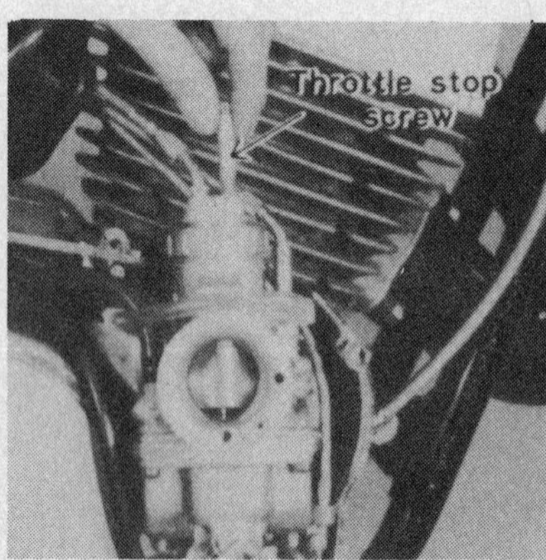

Adjusting idle speed (G Series, B1L-A, and F Series)

Adjusting idle mixture (H1)

Adjusting idle speed (H1)

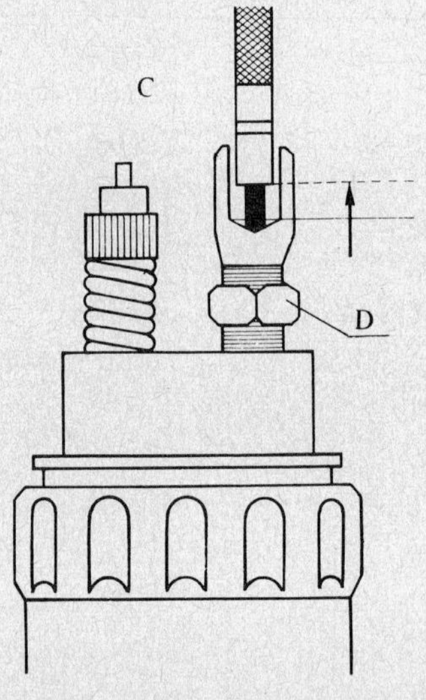

Turn cable adjuster "C", then tighten locknut "D" to raise or lower the throttle slides

MULTI-CARBURETOR SYNCHRONIZATION

1. Make certain that the carburetor bodies are level and parallel to each other (H1) by viewing the float bowl joining gaskets from the side and rear.

2. If the bodies are misaligned, loosen the carburetor mounts. Reposition the bodies correctly and tighten the mounting clamp screws, then check the starter jet cables to make certain that some freeplay exists and that all jets will close fully.

3. Remove the carburetor/air cleaner elbow(s).

4. Twist the throttle grip fully open to lift up the slides.

5. Position a mirror behind the carburetors (H1) or reach into both carburetor bores (A series) with your fingers and have a helper hold the throttle.

6. Slowly close the throttle grip and watch or feel the slides as they are being lowered; they should enter their carburetor bores simultaneously.

7. If the slide positions are unequal, raise or lower one to match the other by turning the cable end adjuster at the top of the carburetor.

STARTER AND THROTTLE CABLE ADJUSTMENT

On most models, a cable runs from the twist grip to a junction block and, from the junction block, one or more cables are routed to the carburetor(s). One end of each cable is fitted with an adjustment nut, located at the twist grip cable guide and the carburetor top(s).

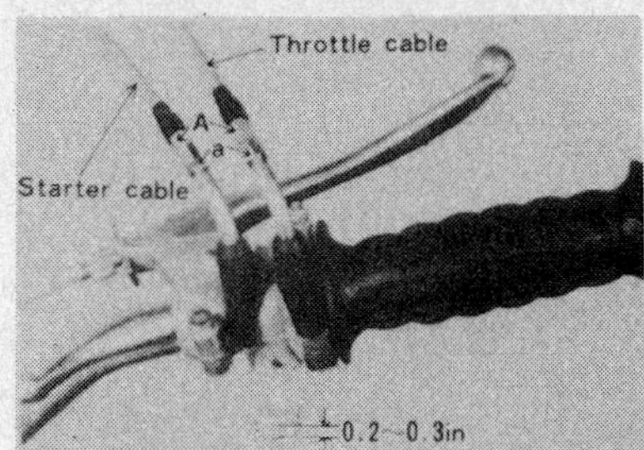

Starter and throttle cable adjustment points at the handlebar (G Series, B1L-A, and F Series)

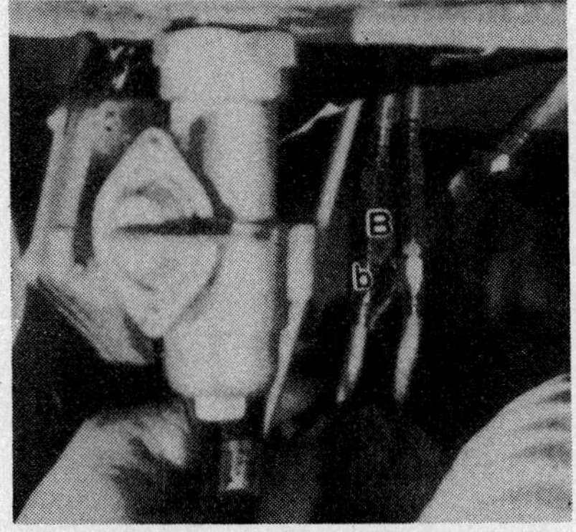

Single cylinder engine starter and throttle cables can also be adjusted at their midway point. Play of the bottom cable sleeves must be zero

After setting the specified free-play at each cable separately, start and warm up the engine, then turn the handlebars from side to side and note any change in idle rpm. If a variation occurs, one of the cables is either adjusted incorrectly (not enough free-play) or is binding somewhere along its routing.

Throttle Cable Free-Play

AT THROTTLE GRIP

G Series and F Series—5–6 mm

A Series, S Series and H Series—2–3 mm

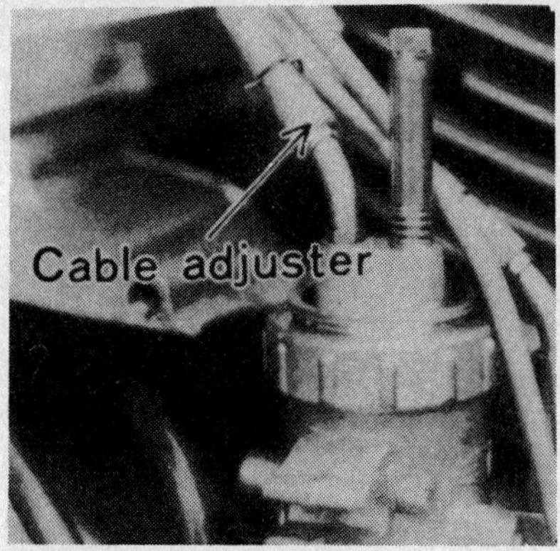

Throttle cable adjustment at the carburetor top (G Series, B1L-A, and F Series)

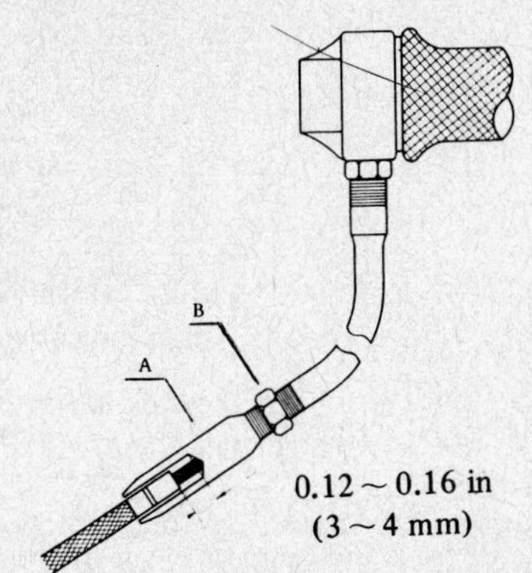

Starter cable adjustment at the handlebar (H1)

Starter cable adjustment at the carburetor (H1)

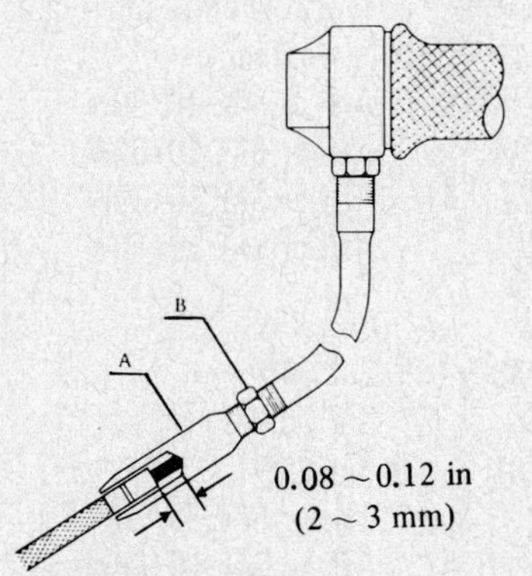

Throttle cable adjustment at the twist grip (H1)

Throttle cable adjustment at the carburetor (H1)

AT CARBURETOR

G Series and F Series—Zero

A Series, S Series and H Series—Zero

Starter Cable Free-Play

AT LEVER

G Series and F Series—5–6 mm

A Series, S Series and H Series—3–4 mm

AT CARBURETOR

G Series and F Series—Zero

A Series, S Series and H Series—Zero

Oil Pump Adjustment

Before making this critical adjustment, it is imperative that the carburetor(s) and carburetor cables be set correctly.

G SERIES B1L—A AND F SERIES

1. Remove the oil pump access cover.

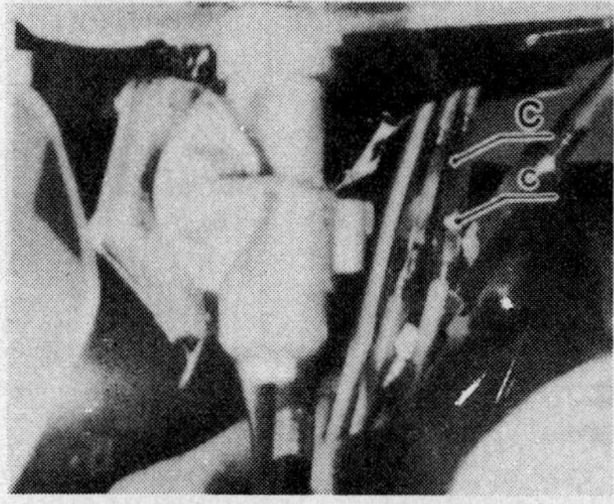

Oil pump cable adjustment (G Series, B1L-A, and F Series)

Oil pump control lever alignment marks (G Series, B1L-A, and F Series)

NOTE: *Use the accompanying illustrations for reference when performing the following steps.*

2. Loosen oil pump cable locknut "c" and turn adjuster "C" until the mark on the oil pump lever and lever stop align.
3. Retighten the cable locknut "c."

A SERIES, S SERIES AND H SERIES

1. Remove the right side engine cover.
2. Remove the ignition distributor cap.

NOTE: *Use the accompanying illustration for reference when performing the following procedure.*

3. Loosen locknut "F" or "H" and turn the cable adjuster "E" or "G" IN to give the cable some free-play.
4. Align the marks on the control lever and lever stop, then adjust the cable to have zero free-play by turning adjuster "E" or "G."
5. Tighten locknut "F" or "H."

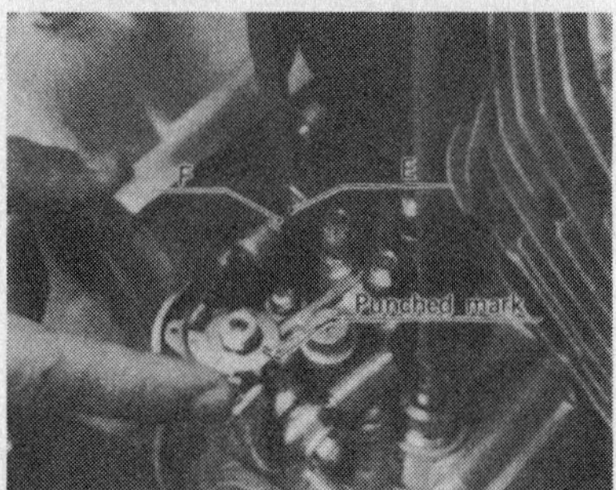

Oil pump cable adjustment and control lever alignment marks (H1)

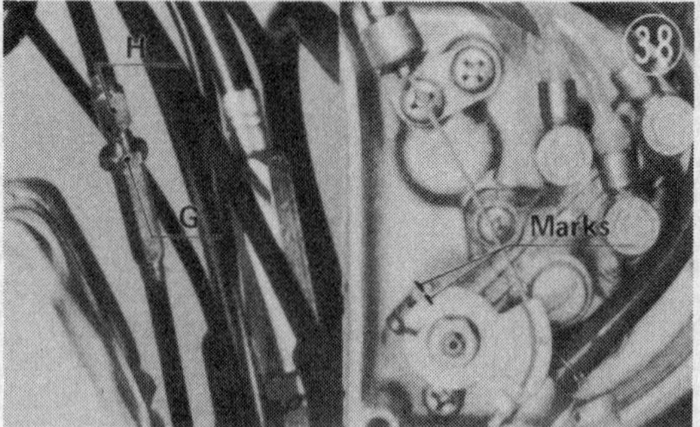

Oil pump cable arrangement (S2)

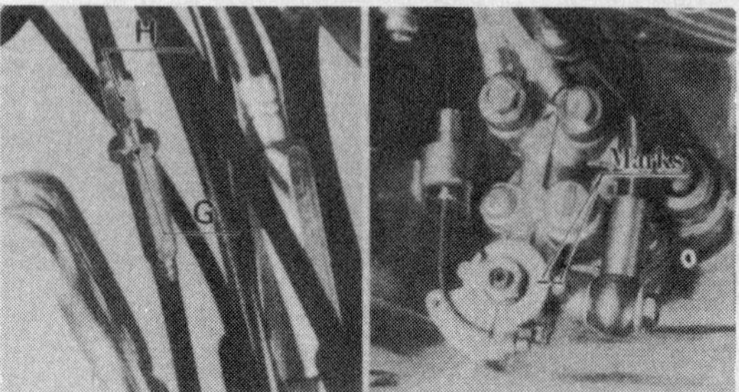

Oil pump cable arrangement (H2)

MAINTENANCE ITEMS

Oil Changes and Lubrication

Engine

These are all good to 18° F or less. Colder than this, use a multiviscosity oil SAE 10/30W.

American	Permalube SAE 30W
Atlantic	Atlantic Aviation SAE 30W
Castrol	Heavy Duty SAE 30W
Gulf	Gulfpride SAE 30W
Humble	ESSO, ENCO, Humble SAE 30W
Kendall	Dual Action, Super Duty SAE 30W
Mobil	Mobil A SAE 30W
Phillips	Sixty-Six SAE 30W
Pure	Super Duty Purelube SAE 30W
Richfield	Richlube Premium SAE 30W
Shell	Shell X—100 SAE 30W
Texaco	Havoline SAE 30W

Gearbox

Front Fork

1. Remove the drain screw at the bottom of each fork leg.
2. Drain the oil, then pump the fork up and down a few times to make sure the tubes are clear.
3. Reinstall the drain screws and remove the cap at the top of each fork leg.

GA1—A	SAE 30W or 10/30W in cold weather
GA2—A	SAE 30W or 10/30W in cold weather
G3SS—A	SAE 30W or 10/30W in cold weather
G3TR—A	SAE 30W or 10/30W in cold weather
G4TR	ATF or SAE 30W
B1L—A	SAE 30W or 10/30W in cold weather
F6	ATF or SAE 10/30W
F7	ATF or SAE 10/30W
F8	ATF or SAE 10/30W
F5	ATF or SAE 10/30W
A1	SAE 30W
A1SS	SAE 30W
A7	SAE 30W
A7SS	SAE 30W
S2	ATF or SAE 10/30W
H1	ATF or SAE 10/30W
H2	ATF or SAE 10/30W

4. Add the proper amount of the appropriate oil to the inner tubes, then work the fork up and down a few times to expel any air present in the fork.
5. Reinstall the fork caps.

Kawasaki recommends that the following oil mixtures be used:

Model	Mixture (SAE 30W: Spindle Oil 60W)
GA1—A	8:2
GA2—A	8:2
G3SS—A	8:2
G3TR—A	8:2
G4TR	6:4
B1L—A	8:2
F6	6:4
F7	6:4
F8	6:4
F5	6:4
A1	8:2
A1SS	8:2
A7	8:2
A7SS	8:2
H1	6:4

On the newer H1, H2 and S2 models, Kawasaki recommends the use of SAE 10W motor oil.

Decarbonization

1. Remove the cylinder head, cylinder, exhaust pipe, and muffler baffle. (See "Engine and Transmission.")

2. Scrape carbon deposits off the cylinder head and piston top, and out of the exhaust port, ring grooves (if rings are to be replaced), and exhaust pipe.

3. Place the muffler baffle in a vise and burn the carbon deposits with a torch.

4. Lightly tap the baffle against a wooden block or bench to remove the deposits.

Starter/DC Generator Brushes (B1L—A)

Begin regular inspections after 4000 miles. Dust from the generator brushes tends to collect on the mica undercut, so, if necessary, polish up the commutator surface with emery cloth and remove any accumulated dust with a knife or screwdriver blade.

Drum Brakes

INSPECTION

Remove any surface glaze with emery cloth or fine sandpaper and replace the linings if they are worn down near the rivets or show signs of oil penetration.

ADJUSTMENT

The front brake is adjusted by turning the adjusting nut on the brake cam actuating lever. Actuation should occur after about 1 in. of lever free-play is taken up. The cable incorporates a stoplight switch which is not adjustable because it does not require adjustment. Minor adjustment can also be performed at the handlebar lever. This adjuster has a slot which should be facing downward to keep water from entering the cable sleeve.

The rear brake is also adjusted at the cam actuating lever. Pedal free-play should be approximately 1 in. The rear brake also incorporates a stoplight switch, but this unit is mounted in an adjustable bracket. Position the switch so that the stoplight comes on just before the brake shoes make contact with the drum. The rear brake must be adjusted whenever the final drive chain is removed and/or adjusted.

Disc Brake

Brake fluid should be changed every 6000 miles or at least once a year.

To change the fluid and bleed the system:

1. Attach a hose to the bleeder valve and insert the other end into a container.

2. Open the bleeder valve and pump the handlever until all the fluid has drained into the can. Make sure no fluid remains.

3. Fill the reservoir with fresh fluid, then pump the handlever until all air in the brake line is expelled and only pure fluid is in the hose.

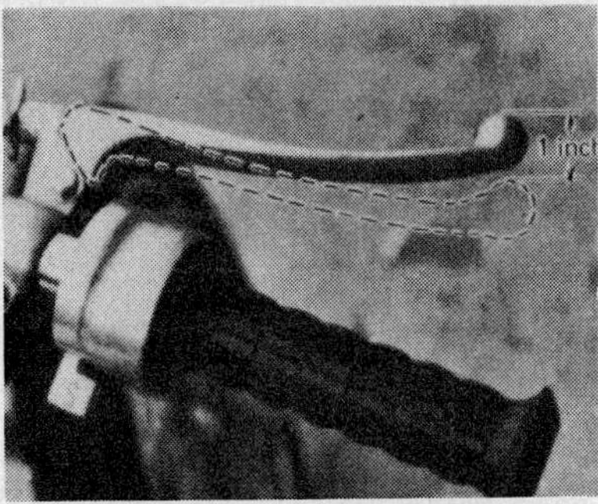

Front brake adjustment

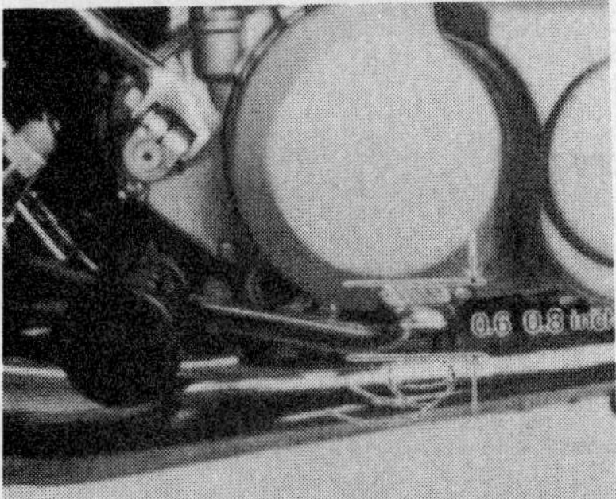

Rear brake adjustment

Front stoplight switch

NOTE: *During the above operation, add brake fluid as necessary so that the level in the reservoir remains high.*

4. After having just squeezed the handlever, close the bleeder valve, then disconnect the hose.

5. Operate the handlever several times to make certain it has a stiff, hard feel.

Arrangement for bleeding hydraulic disc brake

Use only a brake fluid specified for disc brake use, as the boiling point of many hydraulic fluids is unsatisfactorily low.

Disc pad replacement and caliper service is covered in the Chassis section. No brake adjustment is provided for, although lever freeplay can be set by way of an adjustment bolt at the handlebar.

Clutch

G SERIES AND F SERIES

1. Remove the clutch pushrod cap on the left case cover (F5, F8), magneto cover (F6, F7), or carburetor cover (G Series).

2. Loosen locknut "a," then back out adjustment screw "A" three complete turns.

3. Loosen locknut "b" and turn the clutch cable adjuster "B" until the release lever angle is 90°.

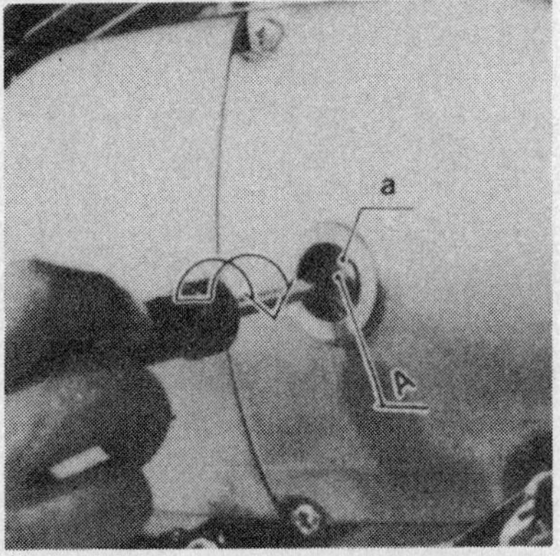

Clutch pushrod adjustment (F5 and F8)

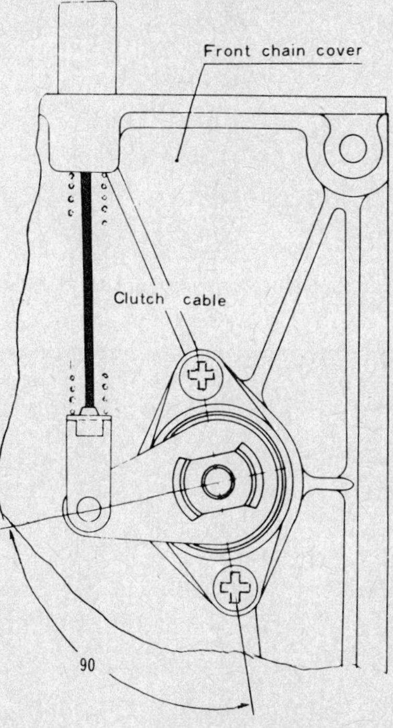

Release lever angle should be 90°

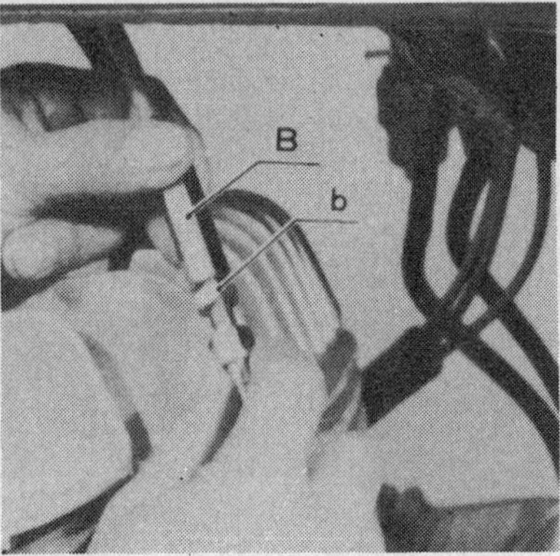

Clutch cable adjustment (G and F Series)

Clutch pushrod adjustment (F6 and F7)

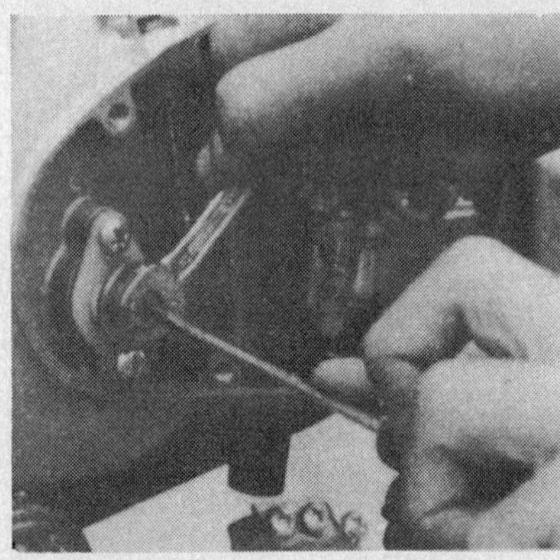

Clutch pushrod adjustment (G Series)

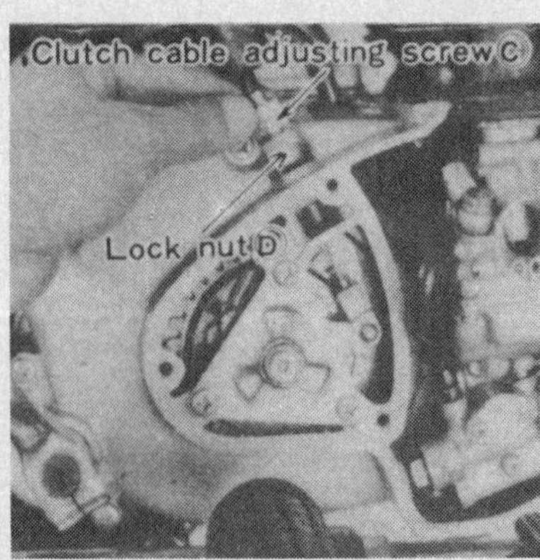

Clutch cable adjustment (B1L-A)

4. Turn adjustment screw "A" clockwise until lightly seated, then hold it in that position and tighten locknut "a." Make certain that there is no movement of screw "A" when the locknut is tightened, otherwise there will be clutch slippage.

5. Tighten locknut "b," taking care not to disturb the position of adjusting screw "B."

6. Make final adjustment at the handlever to suit the individual rider. Freeplay should be approximately ½ to ¾ in.

B1L—A

1. Remove the carburetor cover from the right side of the engine.

2. Loosen locknut "D" and cable adjusting screw "C."

3. At the handlever, loosen locknut "B," then turn adjusting screw "A" until the clutch cable is completely slack.

4. Loosen clutch pushrod adjusting screw locknut "F," then tighten adjusting screw "E" until it seats lightly. Back out screw "E" ¼–½ turn, then hold it in this position and lighten locknut "F."

5. Turn cable adjusting screw "C" as necessary to obtain ½–¾ in. free-play, then tighten locknut "D" at the top of the right engine case.

A SERIES

The A Series clutch is adjusted in the same manner as the B1L—A.

S AND H SERIES

1. Remove the countershaft sprocket cover and loosen locknut "B." Back out adjusting screw "A" three or four turns until the lever is free.

2. At the handlever, loosen locknut "D" and adjust the lever to the free-play shown in the accompanying illustration by turning adjuster "C."

3. Loosen the cable adjuster locknut "F" and turn adjuster "E" until the clutch actuating lever angle is 100°.

4. Back near the countershaft sprocket, turn adjusting screw "A" IN until you begin to feel resistance. Hold it in this position, then tighten locknut "B."

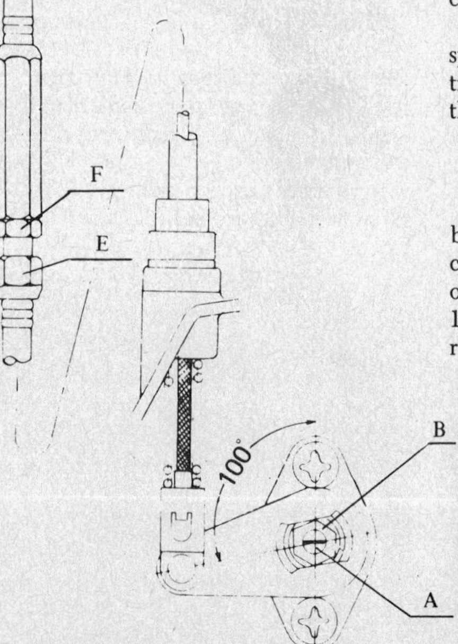

Clutch cable adjustment and release lever angle (H1)

Clutch pushrod adjustment (B1L-A)

Clutch pushrod adjustment (H Series)

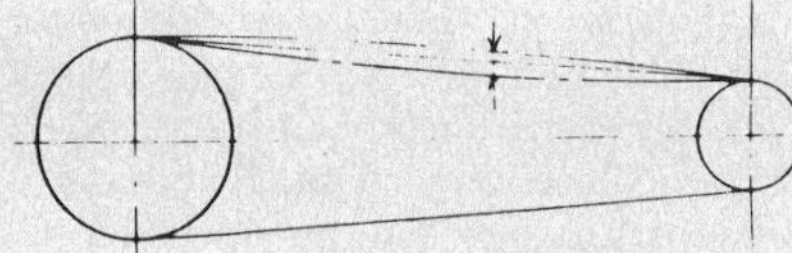

Drive chain freeplay

Final Drive Chain

To check chain adjustment, put the bike up on its center stand and move the chain up and down at the midway point of either run. If total movement exceeds 1 in., the chain is too loose and must be readjusted.

Drive chain adjustment

SPECIFICATIONS OF SPROCKETS AND DRIVE CHAIN

Model	Number of teeth of the sprocket		Gear ratio	Chain	
	Engine	Rear	(Secondary)	Type	Links
GA1—A	14	39	2.79	EK428	104
GA2—A	14	36	2.57	EK428	102
G3SS—A	14	37	2.64	EK428	104
G3TR—A	14	42	3.00	EK428	106
G4TR	15	42	2.80	EK428	110
G31M—A	14	50	3.57	EK428SH	114
B1L—A	15	42	2.80	EK428	112
F6	14	55	3.93	EK428SH	118
F7	14	50	3.57	EK428SH	114
F8, F81M	14	45	3.21	EK525SH	96
F5	14	41	2.93	EK525SH	94
A1	15	37	2.46	EK525SH	92
A1SS	15	39	2.60	EK525SH	92
A7	15	36	2.40	EK530SH	90
A7SS	15	36	2.40	EK530SH	90
H1	15	45	3.00	DID50HT	102
	16	45	2.81	DID50HT	102

1. Remove the rear axle nut cotter pin and loosen the nut(s) until it can be turned by hand.

2. Loosen the locknuts on the two chain adjuster bolts.

3. Loosen or tighten the adjuster bolts *an equal amount* until the prescribed free-play is achieved. Scales are stamped on the adjuster bolts and swing arm to provide correct alignment.

4. Tighten adjuster bolt locknuts while holding the adjustment steady. Pull the locknuts up snug, but do not overtighten them.

5. Tighten the axle nut(s) to the specified torque and install a new cotter pin.

Periodic Maintenance

Weekly (In Hot Weather)
Check battery fluid level

Monthly (In Normal Weather)
Check battery fluid level

Bi-Monthly
Charge battery if stored

Every 200 Miles
Lubricate drive chain

Every 2000 Miles
Change gearbox oil
Lubricate grease fittings
Lubricate cables
Soak drive chain in solvent
Adjust brakes
Adjust clutch
Tighten nuts and bolts
Wash Filtron-type air cleaner
Clean fuel petcock strainer
Perform complete tune-up

Every 3000 Miles
Replace paper-type air cleaner

Every 4000 Miles
Change front fork oil
Decarbonize engine
Check brake linings
Clean carburetors

Every 10,000 Miles
Repack steering head bearings
Repack wheel bearings

MAINTENANCE DATA

Model	Fuel Tank Capacity (gal)	Oil tank Capacity (qt)	Gearbox Capacity (qt)	Front Fork Capacity Each Leg cc (qt)	Tire Pressure (psi) Front	Tire Pressure (psi) Rear	Chain Adjustment mm (in.)
GA1—A	1.73	1.3	0.74	130 (0.135)	23	28	25 (25/32)
GA2—A	2.26	1.3	0.74	130 (0.135)	23	28	25 (25/32)
G3SS—A	2.26	1.3	0.74	130 (0.135)	23	28	25 (25/32)
G3TR—A	2.26	1.3	0.74	130 (0.135)	23	28	25 (25/32)
G4TR	2.5	1.3	0.74	170 (0.18)	23	28	25 (25/32)
B1L—A	2.24	1.9	0.95	175 (0.185)	23	28	25 (25/32)
F6	2.4	1.6	0.74	170 (0.18)	23	28	25 (25/32)
F7	2.4	1.6	0.74	115 (0.12)	23	28	25 (25/32)
F8	3.3	1.7	1.27	175 (0.185)	24	31	25 (25/32)
F5	3.3	1.7	1.27	175 (0.185)	24	31	25 (25/32)
A1	3.5	2.4	1.27	200 (0.22)	23.8	31.2	25 (25/32)
A1SS	3.5	2.4	1.27	200 (0.22)	23.8	31.2	25 (25/32)
A7	3.5	2.4	1.27	200 (0.22)	23.8	31.2	25 (25/32)
A7SS	3.5	2.4	1.27	200 (0.22)	23.8	31.2	25 (25/32)
S2	3.7	1.6	1.16	210 (0.22)	24	31	25 (25/32)
H1	4.0	2.5	1.70	230 (0.25)	25.5	31.2	25 (25/32)
H2	4.5	2.1	1.5	160 (0.15)	26	31	25 (25/32)

ENGINE AND TRANSMISSION

ENGINE SERVICE

G SERIES, F SERIES, and B1L—A

Engine Removal and Installation

1. Disconnect the retaining springs (if so equipped) and remove the exhaust header pipe or ring nut.
2. Remove the muffler securing bolts and/or nuts, then lift off the header pipe and muffler as an assembly.
3. On all but the GA models, remove the air cleaner assembly.
4. Remove the carburetor cover from the right side of the engine, then slide the rubber cap up out of the way over the carburetor cables.
5. Turn the fuel petcock off, then disconnect the fuel delivery line from the carburetor.

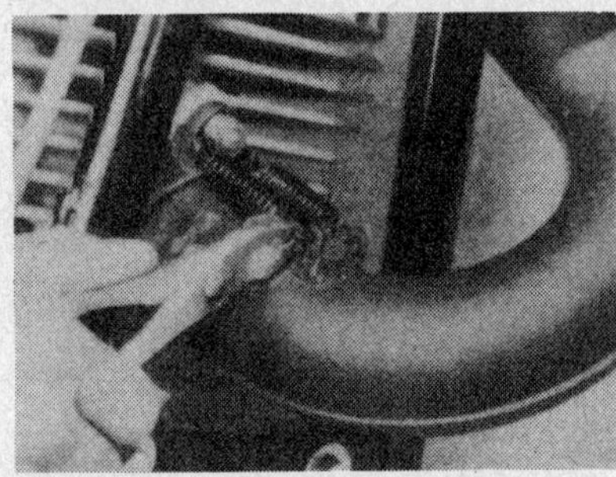

Removing the exhaust header pipe (F Series)

6. Remove the carburetor securing screw (if so equipped) from the front of the crankcase, then lift the carburetor out of the case cavity and tie it aside. The carburetor starter and throttle cables can remain connected unless the carburetor is to be serviced. If it does require service, unscrew the carburetor cap and pull out the throttle slide. The cable can then be disconnected and pulled through. To disconnect the starter cable, unscrew the cable guide and pull out the plunger.
7. Remove the oil pump cover (G Series).
8. Disconnect the oil pump cable from the pump control lever, then disconnect and plug the oil tank delivery line.
9. On the F Series, disconnect and pull out the tachometer cable.
10. On the B1L—A and F Series, remove the gearshift pedal, then remove the securing screws and lift off the front chaincase cover. The clutch release mechanism and cover should be tied aside unless they require service.
11. On the G Series, back off the clutch adjustment, then disconnect the cable

Front chaincase removed (B1L-A and F Series)

Removing the cylinder

from the release mechanism and draw it through the case cover.

12. On the G Series, remove the gearshift pedal and the left engine cover.
13. Remove the drive-chain master link, then withdraw the chain.
14. Disconnect the magneto or starter/generator wiring connectors near the battery.
15. Disconnect the spark plug cap.
16. Drain the gearbox oil and reinstall the plug.
17. Remove the engine mounting bolts, then lift the engine out of the frame.

Installation is a reversal of the removal procedure.

Cylinder Head

The cylinder head is made of aluminum alloy, for heat dissipation qualities. On the F Series, a hole is tapped opposite the spark plug so that a decompression valve can be installed.

REMOVAL

1. Remove the four securing nuts in an "X" pattern, a little at a time, to prevent distortion.
2. Lift off the head and gasket. If necessary, tap the bottom of the cooling fins with a rubber mallet to free the head.

INSTALLATION

1. Install a new gasket.
2. Install the head and securing nuts, then tighten the nuts a little at a time in an "X" pattern to prevent distortion. Final tightening torque is 18 ft lbs.

Cylinder

The cylinder of the G Series, B1L—A and F6 are made of cast iron, whereas the F5, F7, and F8 cylinder is made of aluminum alloy with a bonded cast-iron liner.

REMOVAL

1. With the cylinder head removed, lift the cylinder up over the studs. If necessary, tap the bottom of the exhaust port with a mallet to break it free.
2. Remove the cylinder base gasket.

NOTE: *As the cylinder is being raised, stuff some clean, lint-free rags into the case opening to prevent anything from dropping down into the bottom end. Also support the piston as it falls free from the cylinder.*

INSPECTION

Remove carbon deposits from the exhaust and transfer ports. Examine the cylinder walls for scoring, seizure spots, or hairline cracks. Measure the bore diameter as described in "Piston and Cylinder Fit" to determine whether boring and/or honing is necessary. If it is not necessary, clean up the cylinder walls with no. 400 emery cloth, in a 45° crosshatch pattern.

INSTALLATION

1. Install a new cylinder base gasket.
2. Lubricate the piston and rings with oil, then slide the cylinder over the studs.
3. Insert the top of the piston into the cylinder bore, then, while compressing one ring at a time with your fingers, lower the cylinder.
4. Remove the rags in the case opening, then let the cylinder slide fully down.

PORT DIMENSIONS (G SERIES, BIL-A, AND F SERIES)

Model	A in. (mm)	B in. (mm)	C in. (mm)	D in. (mm)	E in. (mm)
GA1—A G3SS—A GA2—A	1.248 (31.7)	1.661 (42.2)	1.260 (32.0)	0.886 (22.5)	0.472 (12.0)
G3TR—A	1.292 (32.8)	1.705 (43.3)	1.260 (32.0)	0.886 (22.5)	0.472 (12.0)
G4TR	1.315 (33.4)	1.728 (43.9)	1.260 (32.0)	0.886 (22.5)	0.472 (12.0)
G31M—A	1.126 (28.6)	1.626 (41.3)	1.339 (34.0)	1.055 (26.8)	0.516 (13.1)
B1L—A	1.366 (34.7)	1.693 (43.0)	1.496 (38.0)	0.886 (22.0)	0.472-0.571 (12.0)
F6	1.382 (35.1)	1. 98 (48.2)	1.378 (35.0)	1.028 (26.1)	0.5 0 (12.7)
F7	1.496 (38.0)	1.945 (49.4)	1.614 (41.0)	0.921 (23.4)	0.512 (13.0)
F8	1.693 (43.0)	2.177 (55.3)	1.752 (44.5)	1.087 (27.6)	0.571 (14.5)
F81M	1.598 (40.6)	2.177 (55.3)	1.752 (44.5)	1.181 (30.0)	0.571 (14.5)
F5	1.732 (44.0)	2.224 (56.5)	2.008 (51.0)	1.063 (27.0)	0.563 (14.3)

PORT TIMING (G SERIES, BIL-A, AND F SERIES)

	Intake open	Intake close	Exhaust open	Exhaust close	Scavenging open	Scavenging close
GA1—A GA2—A G3SS—A G3TR—A	120°	50°	84° 30′	84° 30′	57° 30′	57° 30′
G4TR	120°	55°	84° 30′	57° 30′	57° 30′	57° 30′
G31M—A	140°	70°	93°	93°	62°	62°
B1L—A	110°	45°	80°	80°	59°	59°
F6	115°	55°	87°	87°	57° 30′	57° 30′
F7	115°	55°	82°	82°	55°	55°
F8	110°	50°	83°	83°	59°	59°
F81M	130°	65°	87° 40′	87° 40′	59°	59°
F5	110°	50°	82°	82°	57°	57°

Piston, Piston Pin, and Piston Rings

REMOVAL AND DISASSEMBLY

1. Make certain that the crankcase opening is protected with rags, then remove the piston pin circlips with a pair of needle-nose pliers.
2. Press the pin out of the piston with the tool shown in the accompanying illustration or a suitable substitute.
3. Remove the piston rings, one at a time, over the top of the piston.

NOTE: *It may be necessary to initially spread the ends of the expander rings (if so equipped) with a screwdriver blade.*

INSPECTION

Remove carbon deposits from the piston crown and ring grooves.

Examine the piston for seizure spots, crown damage, or hairline cracks. If the seizure spots are minor, they can be smoothed out with no. 400 emery cloth. However, it is recommended to replace the piston to be on the safe side.

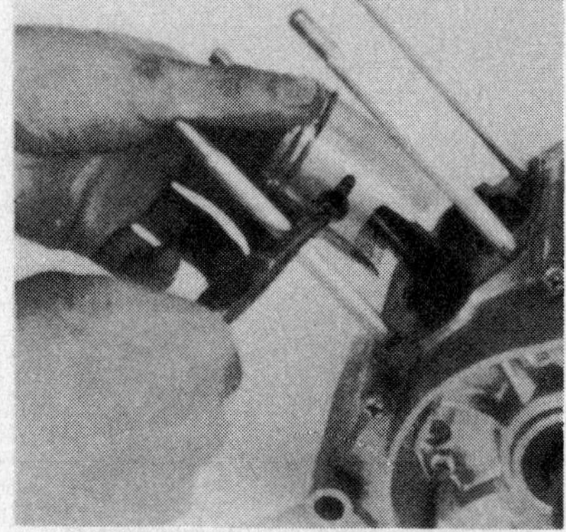

Removing the piston pin circlips

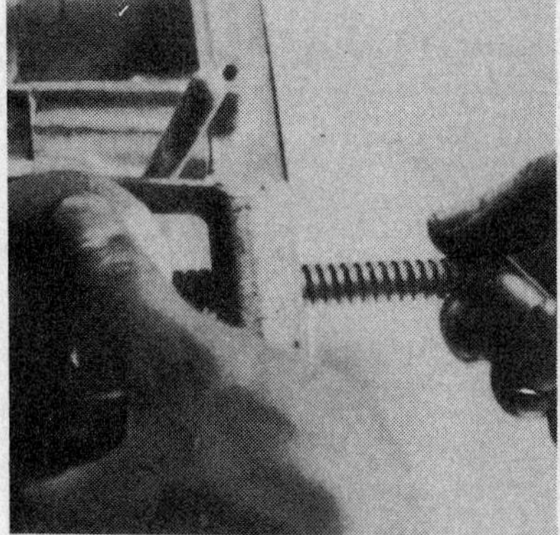

Removing the piston pin

Examine the piston pin for step wear in the center. Insert it into the connecting rod bearing and check for radial play; there should be an absolute maximum of 0.05 mm (0.002 in.). This can be checked with a dial indicator. If radial play is excessive, replace both the piston pin and connecting rod small end bearing.

The rings can be checked in the following manner:

1. Insert each ring, one at a time, into

RING END GAP (G SERIES, BIL-A, AND F SERIES)

	G Series in. (mm)	G31M-A in. (mm)	B1L-A in. (mm)	F6 in. (mm)	F7, FB, F81M in. (mm)	F5 in. (mm)
Free Gaps	0.0059 ~ 0.0137 (0.15 ~ 0.35)	0.0137 ~ 0.0216 (0.35 ~ 0.55)	0.0059 ~ 0.0137 (0.15 ~ 0.35)	0.0059 ~ 0.0173 (0.15 ~ 0.35)	0.0078 ~ 0.0157 (0.20 ~ 0.40)	0.0098 ~ 0.0177 (0.25 ~ 0.45)

the cylinder bore and push it 0.2 in. (5 mm) from the bottom of the barrel.

2. Measure the end-gap of the ring with a feeler gauge and compare your measurement with the specified gap given in the accompanying chart. If beyond the wear limit, the ring must be replaced.

3. Insert an edge of each ring, one at a time, into its respective groove. Measure the clearance between the ring and the top or bottom of the groove with a feeler gauge. If the clearance exceeds 0.05 mm, the ring must be replaced.

ASSEMBLY AND INSTALLATION

1. Install the piston rings.
2. Position the ring end-gaps at the ring groove locating (knock) pins.
3. Position the piston over the connecting rod with the arrow stamped in the crown pointing forward (toward the exhaust port).

NOTE: *It is very important that the piston be correctly positioned, as the piston pin is slightly offset to counteract uneven combustion thrust.*

4. First lubricate, then press the piston pin through the piston and connecting rod small end bearing, using the same tool that was illustrated during removal.
5. Install new piston pin circlips.

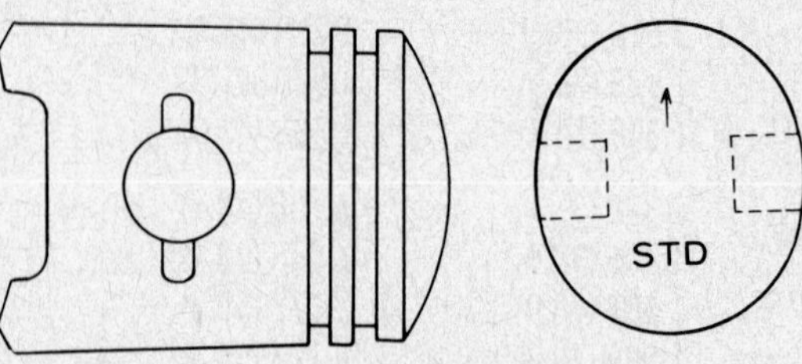

Piston markings

PISTON AND CYLINDER FIT

When the cylinder and piston are removed, it is a good idea to measure cylinder and piston wear, even if it is not your intention to replace them.

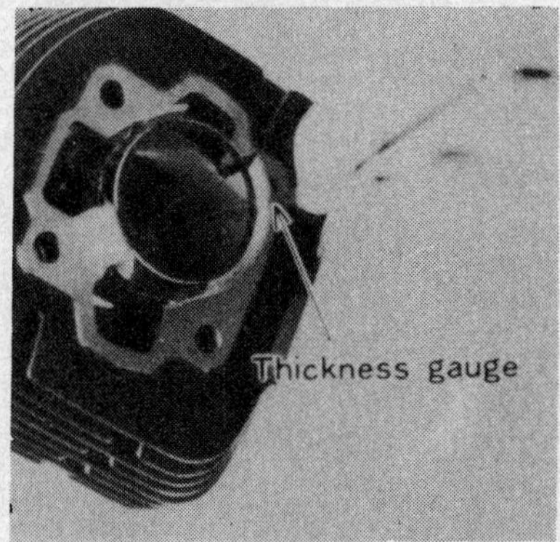

Measuring ring end-gap

CYLINDER MEASUREMENT

Measure cylinder bore diameter at the points indicated in the accompanying illustration. At each level, make two measurements perpendicular to each other. If wear exceeds 0.006 in. (0.15 mm) at any given point, or if the difference in inside diameter between any two points exceeds 0.002 in. (0.05 mm), the cylinder must be bored.

PISTON MEASUREMENT

Measure piston diameter with a micrometer positioned perpendicular to the piston pin 0.2 in. (5.0 mm) from the bottom of the skirt. Standard diameters are given in the accompanying chart. If the cylinder is to be bored, the piston must be replaced.

NOTE: *Pistons are available in two oversizes: 0.50 mm and 1.00 mm.*

CYLINDER DIMENSIONS (G SERIES BIL-A, AND F SERIES)

Models	Standard Dimension in. (mm)	A in. (mm)	B in. (mm)	C in. (mm)	D in. (mm)
GA2—A GA1—A G3SS—A	1.850 (47.0)	0.4 (10)	1.0 (25)	2.0 (50)	1.0 (25)
G3TR—A	1.949 (49.5)	0.4 (10)	1.0 (25)	2.0 (50)	1.0 (25)
G4TR	1.949 (49.5)	0.4 (10)	1.0 (25)	2.0 (50)	1.0 (25)
G31M—A	1.949 (49.5)	0.4 (10)	1.0 (25)	2.0 (50)	1.0 (25)
B1L—A	2.165 (55.0)	0.4 (10)	1.2 (30)	2.0 (50)	1.0 (25)
F6	2.047 (52.0)	0.4 (10)	1.2 (30)	2.4 (60)	1.0 (25)
F7	2.421 (61.5)	0.4 (10)	1.2 (30)	2.4 (60)	1.0 (25)
F8	2.677 (68.0)	0.4 (10)	1.4 (35)	3.8 (70)	1.0 (25)
F81M	2.677 (68.0)	0.4 (10)	1.4 (35)	2.8 (70)	1.0 (25)
F5	3.169 (80.5)	0.4 (10)	1.6 (40)	2.8 (70)	1.0 (25)

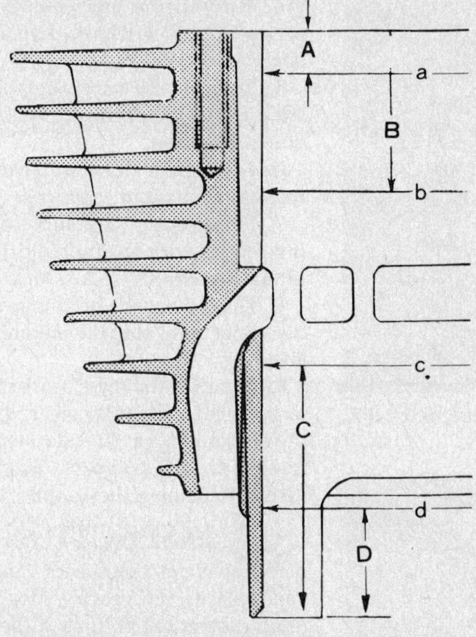

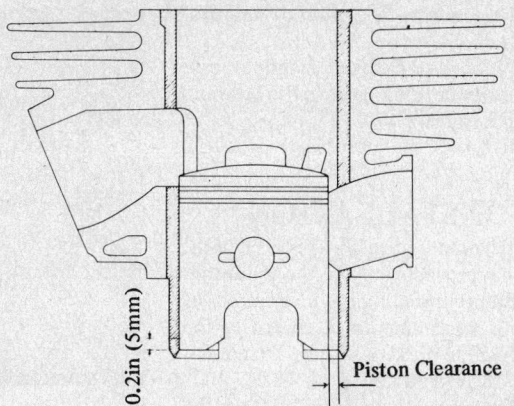

Cylinder dimensions

Piston to cylinder wall clearance

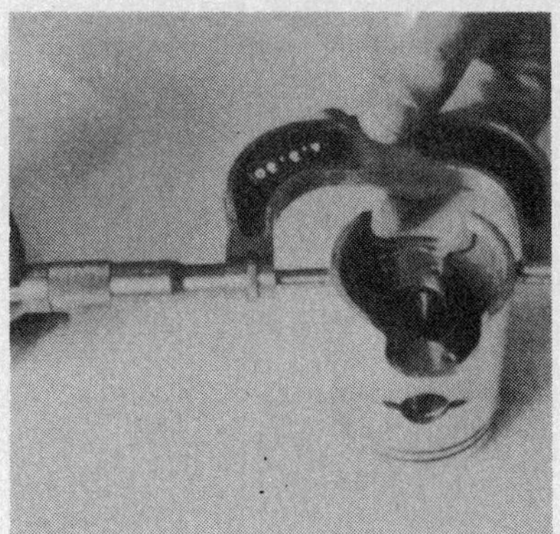

Measuring the piston diameter

Piston Clearance (G Series, BIL-A, and F Series)

Models	Piston Clearance in. (mm)
GA1—A GA2—A G3SS—A	0.0026 (0.067)
G3TR—A G4TR	0.0018 (0.046)
G31M—A	0.0025 ~ 0.0033 (0.066 ~ 0.086)
B1L—A	0.0020 (0.051)
F6	0.0032 (0.083)
F7	0.0025 (0.064)
F8	0.0021 ~ 0.0023 (0.055 ~ 0.060)
F81M	0.0030 (0.077)
F5	0.0039 (0.100)

Left Case Cover

The left case cover contains the flywheel magneto (or starter/generator) and countershaft sprocket. G Series and B1L—A models use a one-piece cover, whereas the F Series models are equipped with a magneto cover and a front chaincase cover.

REMOVAL (G SERIES AND B1L—A)

1. Completely remove the gearshift pedal pinch bolt, then spread the clamp open slightly and pull the pedal off the shaft.
2. Remove the cover securing screws with an impact driver or screwdriver.
3. Pull the cover off the engine and lay it aside.

INSTALLATION (G SERIES AND B1L—A)

1. Replace the gearshift shaft oil seal if there has been any seepage in that area, then install the cover and securing screws.
2. Tighten the securing screws snugly with an impact driver.
3. Slide the gearshift pedal over the shaft in a comfortable position for the rider, then secure it with the pinch bolt.

REMOVAL (F SERIES)

1. On F6 and F7 models, remove the contact breaker cover securing screws and cover.
2. Remove the chaincase cover securing screws with an impact driver, then lift the cover off the engine.
3. Remove the case cover securing screws with an impact driver, then lift the cover off the engine.
4. Tie the chaincase cover (with clutch cable attached) out of the way.

INSTALLATION (F SERIES)

Installation is a reversal of the removal procedure. Tighten all cover securing screws snugly with an impact driver.

Flywheel Magneto or Starter/Generator (G Series, B1L—A, and F6)

REMOVAL

1. Remove the flywheel center bolt, then remove the flywheel with an extractor, (See illustration.)

Removing the flywheel magneto (G Series, B1L-A, and F6)

Removing the magneto base bolts

2. Disconnect the neutral indicator switch wire.

3. Remove the three magneto base securing bolts, then remove the base and wiring harness.

4. Remove the crankshaft woodruff key.

INSTALLATION

Installation is basically a reversal of the removal procedure. Note the following:

1. Before installing the magneto base, apply a small amount of grease to the crankshaft to prevent seizure. Do not forget the woodruff key.

2. Make sure that marks "A" and "B" on the magneto base and crankcase align. (See accompanying illustration.)

3. Tighten the magneto base securing bolts to 36.0 ft lbs, if possible.

Flywheel Magneto (F7, F8, and F5)

REMOVAL

1. Remove the flywheel securing nut. **NOTE:** *Insert a screwdriver blade through the flywheel and magneto base hole to keep the flywheel from turning as the nut is removed.*

2. Remove the flywheel, using an extractor as shown in the accompanying illustration.

INSTALLATION

Installation is a reversal of the removal procedure. Note the following:

1. Before installing the magneto base, apply a small amount of grease to the crankshaft to prevent magneto base seizure. Do not forget the woodruff key.

2. Make sure that marks "A" and "B" on the magneto base and crankcase align. (See illustration.)

3. Tighten the magneto base securing screws to 7.2 ft. lbs. (if possible).

Countershaft Sprocket

REMOVAL

1. Bend back the tab on the sprocket securing nut lockwasher.

2. Hold the sprocket secure in any way you can devise, then remove the securing nut and lockwasher.

3. Remove the sprocket.

INSPECTION

Examine the sprocket teeth for wear. A hooked condition indicates that the sprocket, and possibly the drive chain and rear wheel sprocket, should be replaced.

INSTALLATION

Installation is a reversal of the removal procedure. Make sure that the securing nut lockwasher is correctly positioned with the tang engaging the sprocket and remember to bend up one side of the washer against the nut.

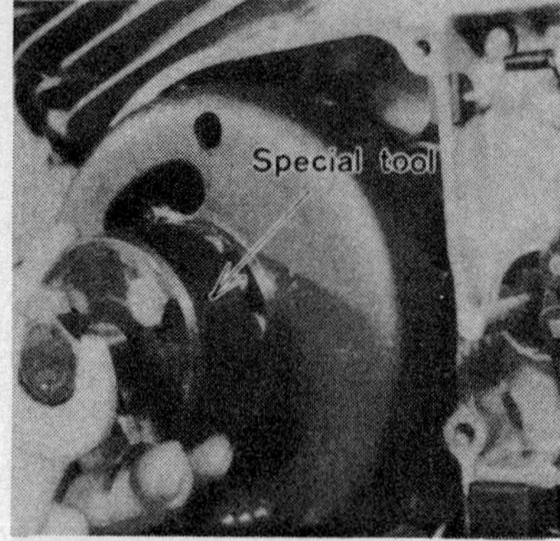

Removing the flywheel magneto (F7, F8, and F5)

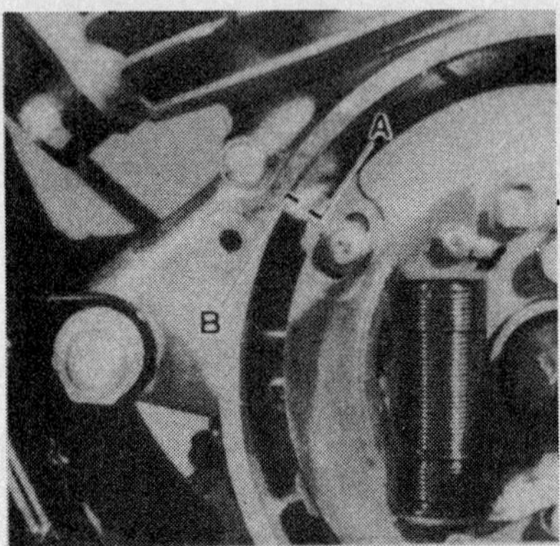

Magneto base plate and crankcase alignment marks (F7, F8, and F5)

Removing the countershaft sprocket (note special tool used)

Right Case Cover (G Series and B1L—A)

REMOVAL

1. Completely remove the kick-starter pedal pinch bolt, then spread the clamp slightly and withdraw the pedal.

2. Remove the carburetor cover securing screws with an impact driver, then lift off the cover.

3. Remove the carburetor securing screw at the front of the crankcase (if so equipped).

4. Turn off the fuel petcock and disconnect the fuel delivery line at the carburetor.

5. Remove the carburetor and tie it aside with cables connected unless it requires servicing.

6. Disconnect the clutch cable at the release mechanism.

7. Remove the oil pump cover securing screws with an impact driver, then lift off the cover.

8. Disconnect the oil pump cable and disconnect and plug the oil tank delivery line.

9. Remove the case cover securing screws with an impact driver, then lift off the oil pump cover. It is not necessary to remove the oil pump or clutch release mechanism unless they require servicing.

INSPECTION

Examine the kick-starter shaft oil seal and replace it if necessary. Also check the drain tube at the bottom of the cover to make certain there are no obstructions.

INSTALLATION

Installation is a reversal of the removal procedure. Note the following:

1. Use a new case cover gasket on reassembly.

2. Make sure that the rotary-valve and check valve O-rings seat properly.

3. Make sure that the clutch holder assembly is correctly positioned.

4. Make sure that the oil pump drive gears mesh properly when the cover is installed.

Right Case Cover (F Series)

REMOVAL, INSPECTION, AND INSTALLATION

The procedure for these models is the same as that for the G Series and B1L—A, with the exception that the clutch release mechanism is located on the other side of the engine.

Primary Drive (G Series, F6, and F7)

REMOVAL

1. Bend back the tab on the primary drive gear securing nut lockwasher.

2. Keep the primary drive gear from turning by installing the clutch holding tool (see accompanying illustration) or stuffing a rag between the primary and clutch gear teeth, then remove the securing nut and lockwasher.

3. Remove the crankshaft woodruff key.

INSPECTION

Examine the gear teeth for burrs, nicks, or any other signs of damage. Re-

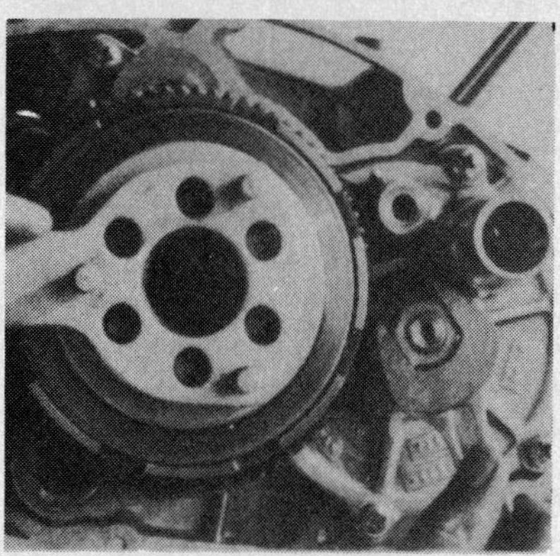

Primary drive gear securing nut removal (G Series, F6 and F7)

place it if necessary. Excessive wear or any of the above will cause the primary drive to whine while riding and make grinding noises at idle speeds.

INSTALLATION

Installation is a reversal of the removal procedure. Note the following:

1. Torque the primary gear securing nut to 36 ft lbs.
2. Make sure to bend one side of the lockwasher against the securing nut.

Primary Drive (B1L—A, F5, and F8)

REMOVAL

1. Bend back the oil pump pinion securing nut lockwasher tab, then install the clutch holding tool or stuff a rag between the primary and clutch gear teeth.
2. Remove the oil pump pinion securing nut and lockwasher, then slide off the primary and oil pump pinion gear set.
3. Remove the crankshaft woodruff key.

INSPECTION

See the preceding section for G Series, F6, and F7 primary gear inspection.

INSTALLATION

Installation is a reversal of the removal procedure. Note the following:

1. Torque the oil pump pinion securing nut to 36 ft lbs.
2. Make sure to bend one side of the securing nut lockwasher against the nut.
3. On F5 and F8 models, center-punch the lockwasher into the small hole in the oil pump pinion.

Clutch Release Mechanism (G Series)

Refer to the following section for the F Series Clutch Release Mechanism. The only difference on the G Series is that the mechanism is located on the opposite side of the engine and, as a result, the two pushrods used on the F Series are not needed.

Installing the clutch release mechanism (F Series)

Clutch Release Mechanism (B1L—A)

The accompanying illustration shows the construction of the release mechanism. Remove the mechanism by taking out the three mounting screws and withdrawing the assembly. Check the balls for pitting, scoring, or excessive wear. Replace as necessary. Install the mechanism by reversing the removal instructions.

Clutch Release Mechanism (F Series)

REMOVAL

1. Remove the left case cover as previously described.
2. Remove the two clutch release mechanism housing securing screws.
3. Remove the housing from the case cover and pull the short pushrod out through the oil seal.

INSPECTION

Inspect the inner and outer release for excessive wear, scoring, or any other signs of damage. Replace as necessary.

INSTALLATION

Installation is a reversal of the removal procedure. When assembling the inner and outer release, set the lever angle at approximately 90° so that the correct clutch adjustment can be achieved.

Clutch

REMOVAL (G SERIES AND B1L—A)

1. On G Series models, remove the clutch retaining circlip.
2. On the B1L—A, remove the clutch securing nut. This can be accomplished by installing the clutch holding tool or by stuffing a rag between the primary and clutch gear teeth to keep the clutch from turning as the nut is removed.
3. Pull the clutch assembly off the shaft, then remove the shock absorber (G Series).
4. Remove the six retaining bolts, then disassemble and inspect the clutch components as described in a following section.

REMOVAL (F SERIES)

1. Unscrew the five retaining bolts, then pull out the clutch springs and spring guides.
2. Remove the pressure plate, friction plates, steel plates, and steel rings.
3. Pull out the pressure plate pusher.
4. Hold the clutch housing secure with

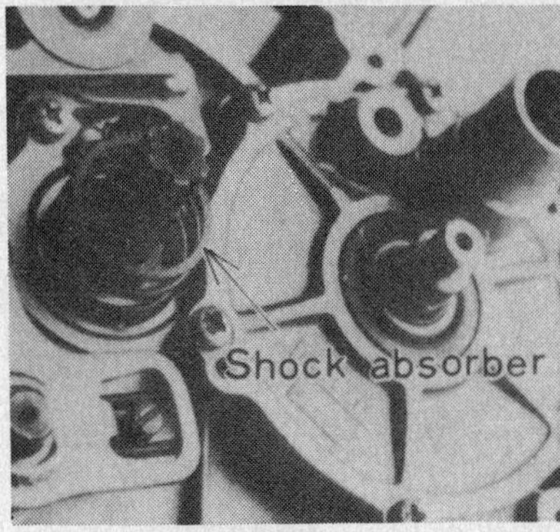

Clutch shock absorber (G Series)

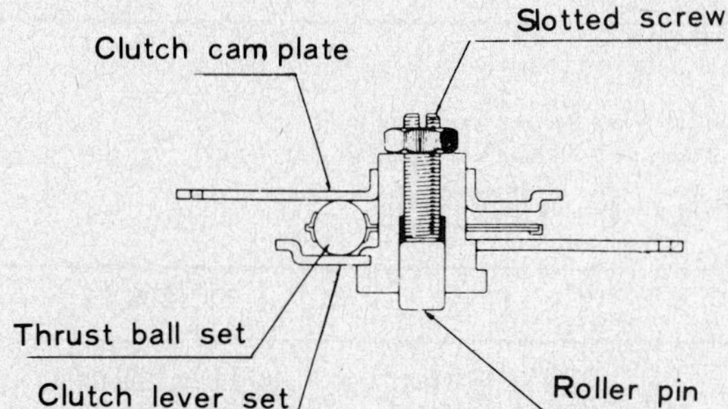

Cross section of clutch release mechanism (B1L-A)

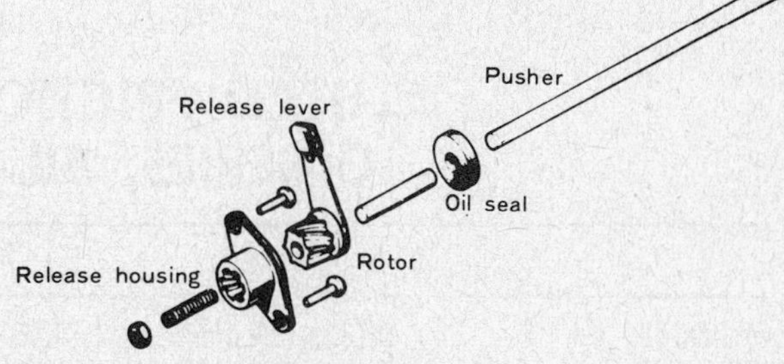

Clutch release mechanism (G and F Series)

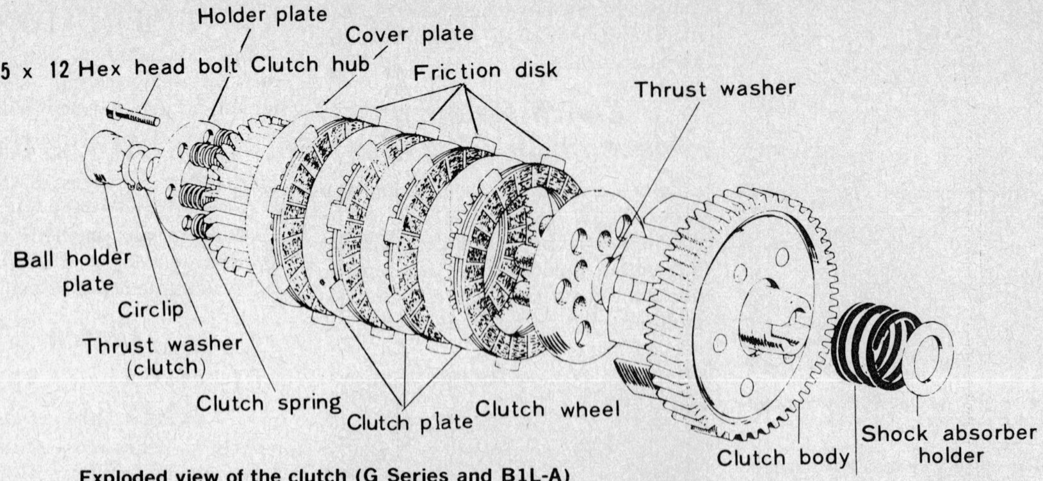

Exploded view of the clutch (G Series and B1L-A)

the special tool illustrated or by stuffing a rag between the primary and clutch gear teeth.

5. Remove the hub securing nut and thrust washer, then slide off the clutch hub and housing.

6. Remove the clutch bushing and thrust washer from the shaft.

INSPECTION (ALL MODELS)

1. Measure clutch spring free-length. Replace them all if any is shorter than the specified wear limit.

2. Measure the thickness of the friction discs at several points and compare your measurements with the specifications. Replace any discs that are unevenly worn or beyond the specified wear limit.

3. Using a feeler gauge, measure the gap between the friction disc tabs and the clutch housing. (See accompanying illustration.) If the gap is greater than 0.-0016–0.012 in. (0.04–0.3 mm), the disc should be replaced.

Removing the clutch retaining bolts (F Series)

4; Examine the gear teeth on the clutch housing for burrs, nicks, or any other signs of damage. If any of the above cannot be cleaned up with an oilstone, or if normal wear is excessive, replace the housing.

5. Insert the clutch bushing into the housing and check radial free-play. If play is noticeable, the bushing should be replaced.

INSTALLATION (ALL MODELS)

Installation is a reversal of the removal procedures. Note that there are three thrust washers in each type of clutch.

Rotary Valve (All Models)

As mentioned previously, the rotary valve is mounted directly to the end of

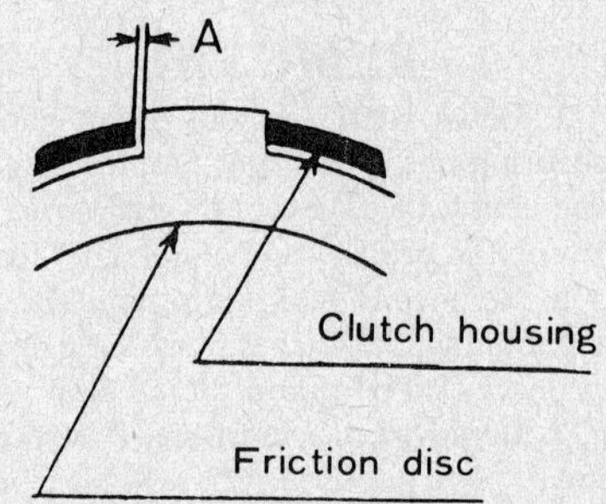

Friction disc pad clearance

CLUTCH SPRING FREELENGTH (G SERIES, BIL-A, AND F SERIES)

	G Series	B1L-A	F6, F7	F8	F81M, F5
Free length	0.85 in. (21.6 mm)	108 in. (27.5 mm)	1.36 in. (34.5 mm)	1.32 in. (33.6 mm)	1.42 in. (36.0 mm)
Repair limit	Over 0.08 in. (2.0 mm)	Over 0.1 in. (2.5 mm)	Over 0.14 in. (3.5 mm)	Over 0.14 in. (3.6 mm)	Over 0.14 in. (3.5 mm)

CLUTCH FRICTION DISC THICKNESS (G SERIES, BIL-A, AND F SERIES)

	G Series	B1L-A, F6	F7	F8, F81M, F5
Standard	0.13 in. (3.2 mm)	0.16 in. (4.0 mm)	0.12 in. (3.0 mm)	0.11 in. (2.8 mm)
Repair limit	0.01 in. (0.3 mm)	0.015 in. (0.4 mm)	0.01 in. (0.3 mm)	0.01 in. (0.3 mm)

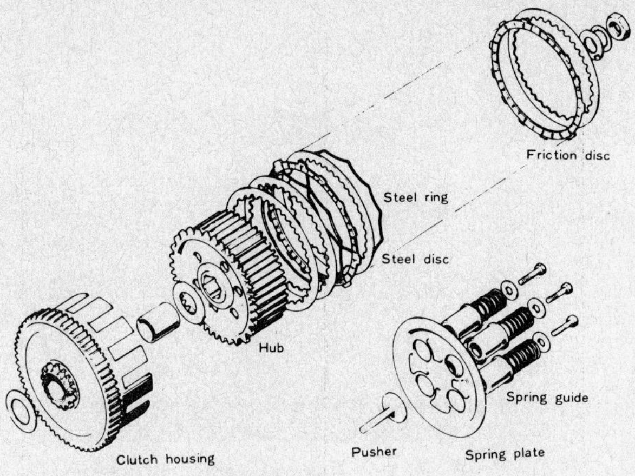

Exploded view of the clutch (F Series)

the crankshaft and rotates within a sealed disc cover. On all models but the F8 and F5, the disc is made from phenol resin. The F8 and F5 models are equipped with a steel disc.

REMOVAL

1. Remove the six valve cover securing screws in the reverse order of the tightening sequence shown.
2. Remove the valve cover.
3. Slide the valve disc off the end of the crankshaft.
4. Remove the spacer and O-ring from the crankshaft.
5. Remove the locating dowel pin.

INSPECTION

1. Examine the valve cover oil seals for signs of leakage or lip damage. Replace as necessary.

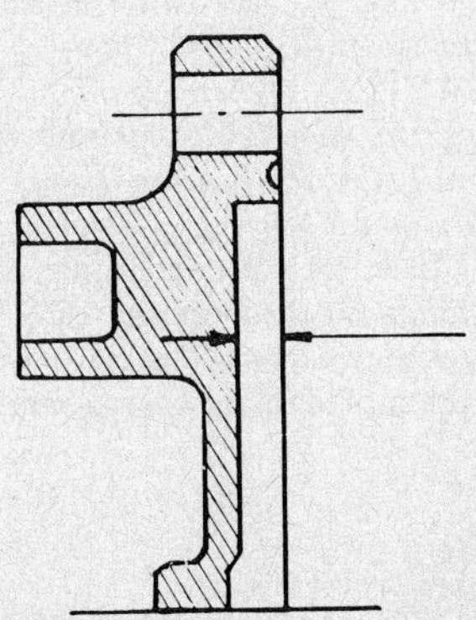

Valve cover depth

2. Examine the valve cover for any deep scratches, excessive wear, or distortion. Also measure the depth of the cover and replace it if it is beyond the specified wear limit.
3. Inspect the valve disc for scratches, distortion, or any other signs of damage. Also measure valve disc thickness and replace it if beyond the specified wear limit.

Valve Cover Thickness

Models	Standard in. (mm)	Repair limit in. (mm)
G Series	0.12 (3.1)	0.11 (2.8)
G31M—A	0.12 (3.1)	or less
B1L—A	0.16 (4.0)	0.14 (3.6) or less
F6, F7	0.12 (3.1)	0.11 (2.8) or less
F8, F81M, F5	0.02 (0.4)	0.01 (0.36) or less

Valve Disc Thickness

Models	Standard in. (mm)	Repair limit in. (mm)
G Series	0.13 (3.4)	Over 0.16 (4.0)
G31M—A	0.14 (3.5)	Over 0.16 (4.0)
B1L—A	0.16 (4.0)	Over 0.16 (4.0)
F6, F7	0.14 (3.45)	Over 0.16 (4.0)
F8, F81M, F5	0.03 (0.7)	Over 0.01 (0.2)

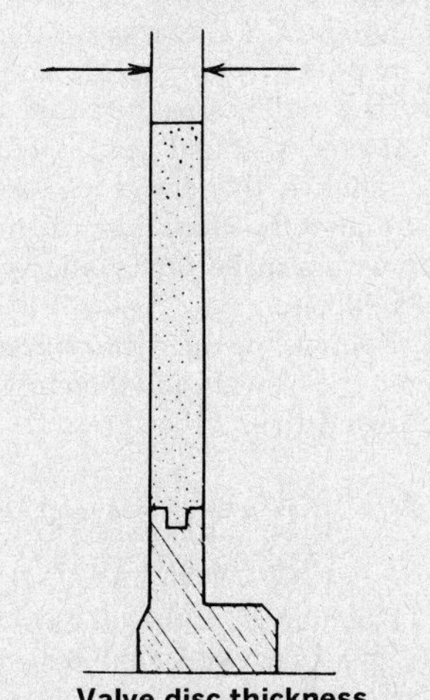

Valve disc thickness

Checking clutch bushing free-play

INSTALLATION

Installation is a reversal of the removal procedure. Note the following:

1. Apply 30W oil to both sides of the valve disc before installation.
2. Install new O-rings.
3. On F6 and F7 models, make sure you align the valve disc mark with the locating dowel pin. (See accompanying illustration.)
4. Tighten the valve cover securing screws, a little at a time, in the order shown.

Shifter Mechanism (All Models)

REMOVAL

1. Disengage the set lever from the change (shift) drum.

Rotary-valve alignment mark (F6 and F7)

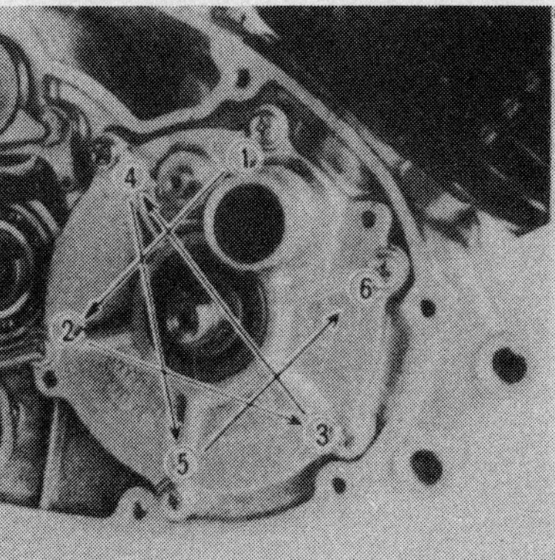

Valve cover tightening sequence

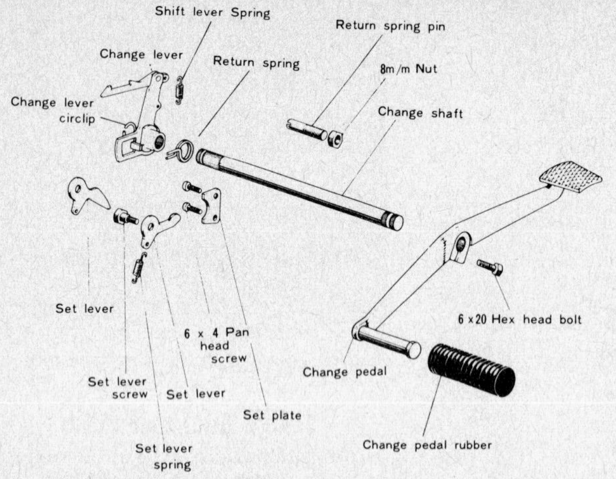

Shifter mechanism construction

Removing the neutral indicator switch

Removing the shifter change lever

2. Draw out the change lever and shaft as an assembly.

3. Remove the change lever circlip, then remove the set lever by removing the attaching pan head screws.

INSPECTION

1. Check the return spring and shift lever spring for fatigue and general condition. Replace if necessary.

2. Examine the change lever and set lever for wear and any other signs of damage. Replace as necessary.

INSTALLATION

Installation is a reversal of the removal procedure. Note the following:

1. On F Series models, adjust the shift lever position as necessary by rotating the return spring pin.

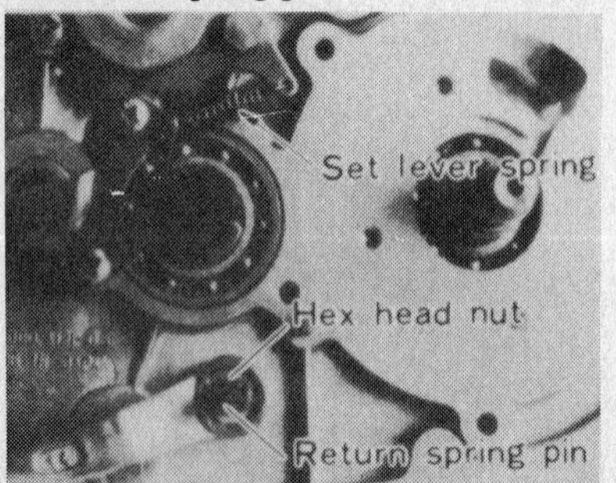

Adjusting shift lever position (F Series)

2. Make sure that each spring is correctly installed.

Crankcase (All Models)

The crankcase is split vertically into two aluminum alloy halves and joined with Kawasaki Bond. No gasket is used. Two dowel pins are provided to locate the crankcase halves.

DISASSEMBLY

1. Remove the transmission neutral indicator switch body and set plate.

2. On F5 and F8 models, remove the circlips on the ends of the Fourth and Fifth gear shift rods.

3. Remove the crankcase halves securing screws.

4. Split the cases by tapping each half alternately with a mallet or plastic hammer. Leave the transmission and all shafts in the right case.

5. Tap the end of the transmission drive shaft lightly with a mallet, then remove the change drum and transmission as a complete assembly.

6. On the G Series and B1L—A, remove the kick-starter spring and holder from the right case half, then remove the kick-starter gear and shaft together.

7. On the F Series, remove the retaining snap-ring, return spring and holder from the right case, then pull out the kick-starter shaft and gear together.

8. Remove the dowel pin from the right end of the crankshaft, then tap the shaft with a mallet and remove it from the right case.

9. Remove the main bearing retainers, pry out the oil seals, and then remove the bearings with an arbor press.

CRANKCASE INSPECTION

1. Examine all of the oil passages and blow them out with compressed air to make sure that there are no obstructions.

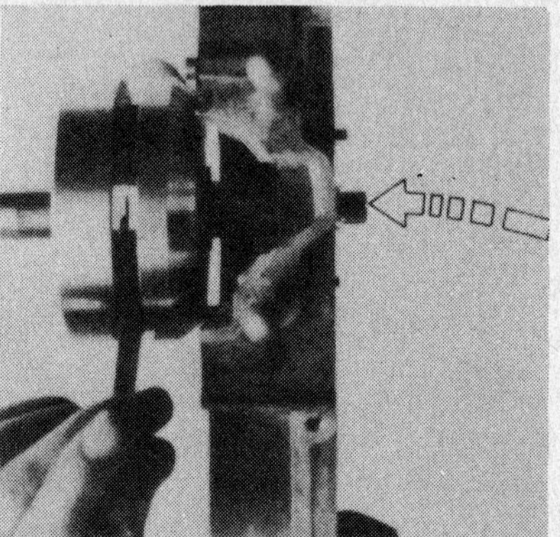

Removing the crankshaft. Arrow indicates dowel pin

2. Make sure that the breather hole is free from obstruction.

3. Inspect the main and transmission shaft bearings for pitting, rust, and general condition. Also check radial clearance and replace any bearing that exceeds 0.002 in. (0.05 mm)

CAUTION: *When cleaning the bearings in solvent, do not spin the races until after the bearing has been blown dry and lubricated with oil.*

4. Examine the transmission shaft bushings (in the opposite case half) for excessive wear and replace if necessary. An arbor press is necessary for this operation.

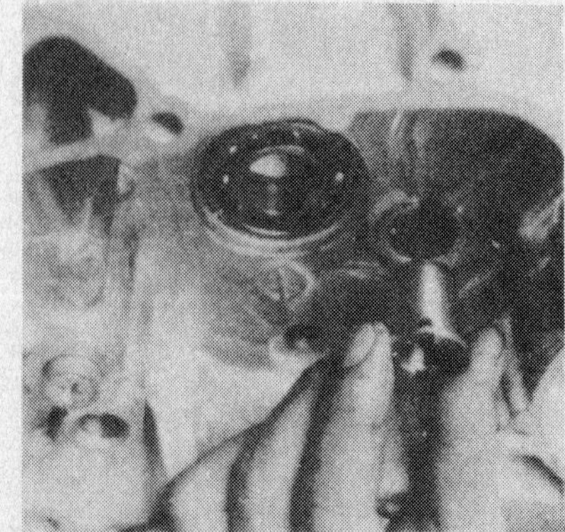

Transmission driveshaft bushing

LEFT CASE SPECIFICATIONS (G SERIES, BIL-A, AND F SERIES)

Models	Crankshaft Ball bearing	Crankshaft Oil Seal	Output Shaft Ball bearing	Output Shaft Oil Seal	Drive Shaft Needle bearing	Drive Shaft Oil Seal	Shift Shaft Oil Seal
G Series	#6204	TB20407	#6004	SC25376	Bushing	—	SB12205
G4TR	#6204	TB20407	#6005	SC32435.5	Bushing	—	SB12205
B1L—A	#6305	TB25407	#6204	SC25476	Bushing	—	VB12185
F6, F7	#6205	TB25407	#6204N	SC30426	7E-HKS162412-1	TB7246	SB12205
F8, F81M, F5	#6305	TB25407	#6205	TB30407	7E-HMK2015	TCY 8 27 55 65	SB12205

CRANKSHAFT INSPECTION

The crankshaft is of the two-piece type, consisting of the left and right crankshafts, crank pin, large end connecting rod needle bearing, side thrust washers, and the connecting rod.

Unless you are experienced in crankshaft repair, it is recommended that you deliver the whole unit to a qualified specialist. You can, however, check the connecting rod large-end, needle bearing, radial play with a dial gauge and the side clearance with a feeler gauge. Specifications are given in the accompanying charts.

RIGHT CASE SPECIFICATIONS (G SERIES, BIL-A, AND F SERIES)

Models	Crankshaft Ball bearing	Crankshaft Oil Seal (Valve cover)	Output Shaft Needle bearing	Drive Shaft Ball bearing
G Series	#6204	TB25407	Bushing	#6005
B1L—A	#6305	TB32457	#6203	#6204
F6, F7	#6305	TB32457	7E-HKS162412-1	#6204N
F8, F81M, F5	SC0626	TB35488	7E-HMK2015	#6205

ASSEMBLY

NOTE: *Before beginning this procedure, thoroughly lubricate all parts.*

1. Install new main bearings and transmission shaft bearings with an arbor press.
2. Install all new oil seals.
3. Insert the crankshaft in the right case.
4. Insert the kick-starter shaft and gear.
5. Install the transmission as an assembly.
6. Apply Kawasaki Bond to the crankcase halves, then reassemble the remaining parts in the reverse order of disassembly.

NOTE: *On the G Series, do not forget the ball and shim at the tip of the transmission driveshaft.*

Transmission Service

The transmissions used in Kawasaki single-cylinder engines are all quite conventional and all operate in basically the same manner. There are three units used: one type in the G Series (five-speed, return change); one in the B1L—A (four-speed, return change); and one in the F Series (five-speed, return change).

LARGE END RADIAL PLAY (G SERIES, BIL-A, AND F SERIES)

	G Series	G4TR	B1L-A	F6, F7	F8, F81M, F5
Big end radial	0.001 in. (0.027 mm)	0.0006 in. (0.017 mm)	0.0007 in. (0.020 mm)	0.0009 in. (0.024 mm)	0.0019 in. (0.050 mm)
Repair limit	0.0023 in. (0.060 mm)	0.0019 in. (0.050 mm)	0.0021 in. (0.055 mm)	0.0023 in. (0.060 mm)	0.0035 in. (0.090 mm)

LARGE END SIDE PLAY (G SERIES, BIL-A, AND F SERIES)

	G Series	G4TR	B1L-A	F6, F7	F8, F81M, F5
Big end side clearance	0.016 in. (0.40 mm)	0.011 in. (0.28 mm)	0.011 in. (0.28 mm)	0.015 in. (0.38 mm)	0.017 in. (0.43 mm)
Repair limit	0.024 in. (0.60 mm)	0.018 in. (0.45 mm)	0.018 in. (0.45 mm)	0.024 in. (0.60 mm)	0.024 in. (0.60 mm)

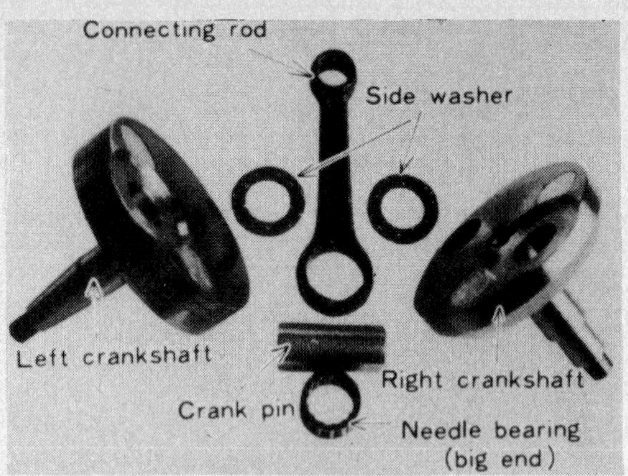

Crankshaft construction

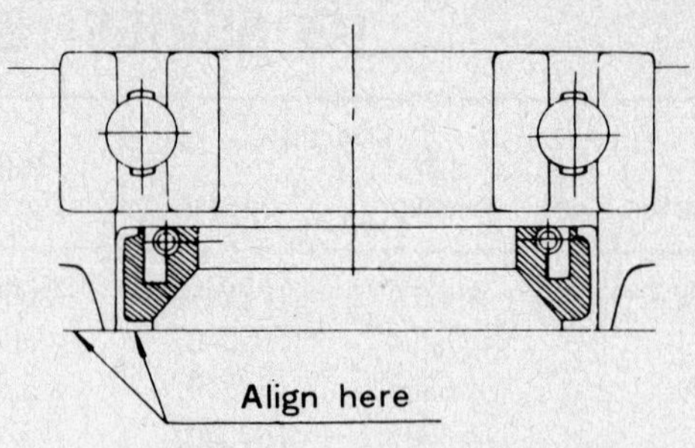

Main bearing oil seal installation

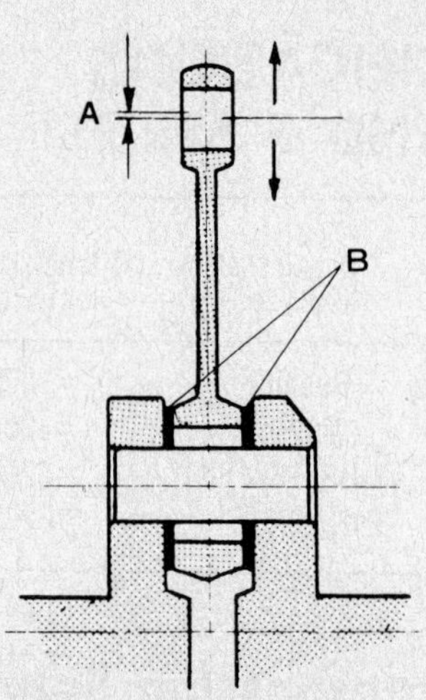

A-large end radial play; B-large end side play

DISASSEMBLY

1. Remove the shift fork cotter pins and shift fork pins.
2. Remove the shift fork from the change drum.

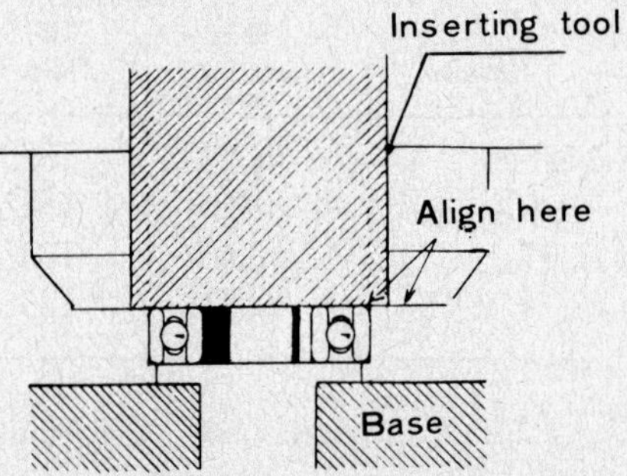

Main bearing installation

NOTE: *On F8 and F5 models, the shift forks are mounted on the shift rods and are easily removed when the fork pin is removed.*

3. Remove the retaining circlip on each gear, then disassemble the gears and thrust washers.

INSPECTION

1. Measure the clearance between the shift forks and the side of the groove in their respective gears. Also check the general condition of the forks and replace them if they are excessively worn.

2. Examine the gears for burrs, pitting, broken teeth, etc. Replace as necessary.
3. Examine the transmission shafts for excessive wear and general condition.

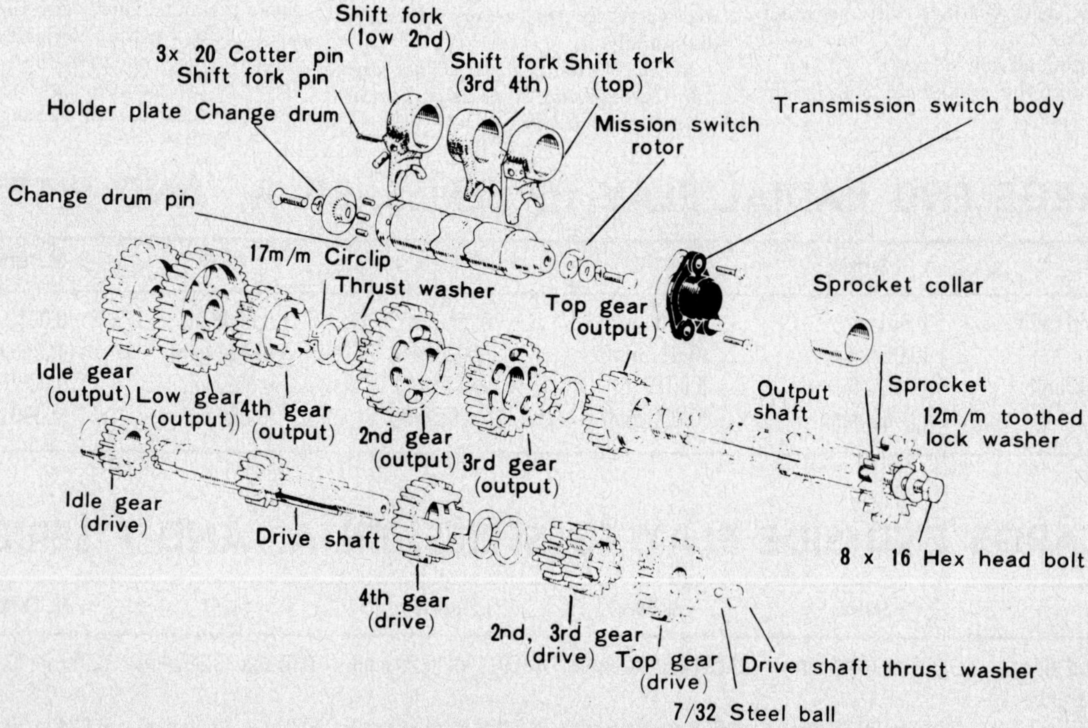

Exploded view of the transmission (GAI-A, G3SS-A, G4TR, and G31M-A)

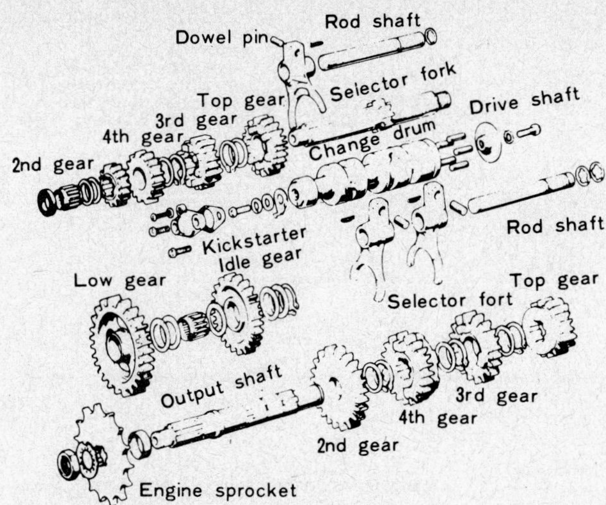

Exploded view of the transmission (F Series)

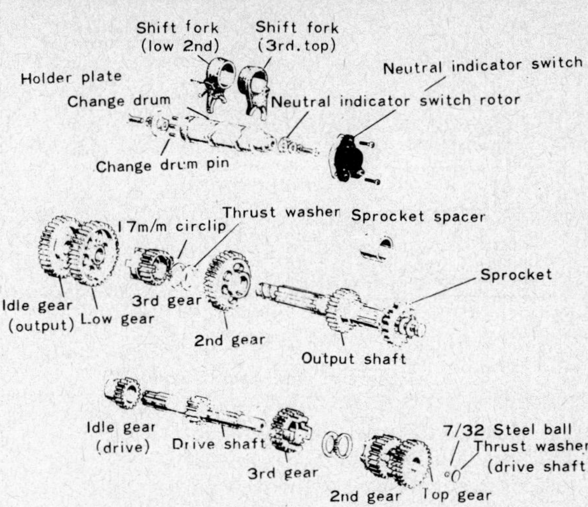

Exploded view of the transmission (B1L-A)

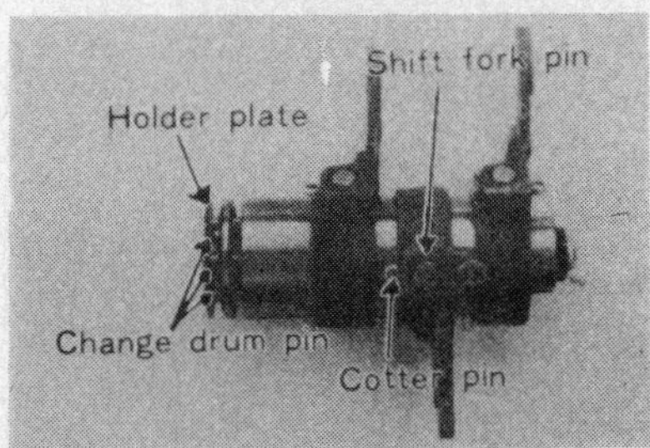

Gear change drum assembly

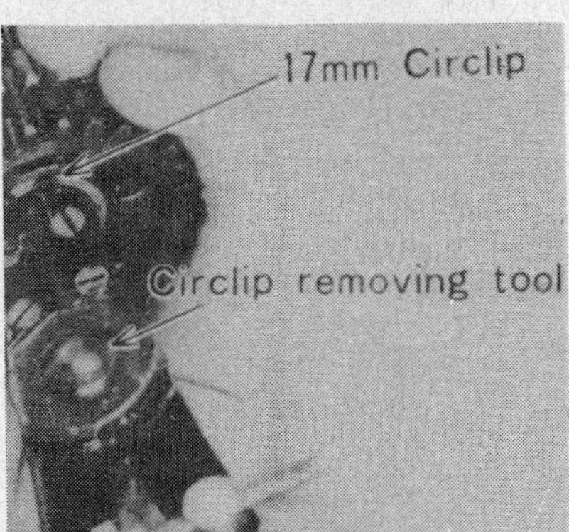

Removing the gear retaining circlips

ASSEMBLY

Assembly is a reversal of the disassembly procedure. Note the following:

1. Engage the shift forks on their respective gears and install the gear assemblies, forks, and change drum as an assembly.
2. On G Series models, make certain that the kick-starter gear and the two idler gears are properly engaged.
3. Apply grease to the output shaft bearing balls to hold them in place.

Kickstarter

DISASSEMBLY (G SERIES AND B1L—A)

1. Remove the gear from the kick-starter shaft.

Measuring fork and gear groove clearance

2. Separate the gear, shaft, pawl push pin, pawl, and spring.
3. Remove the kick-starter stopper from the left case.

DISASSEMBLY (F6 AND F7)

1. Remove the spring guide and spring.
2. Remove the two retaining circlips.
3. Separate all parts.

Clearance Between Shift Fork and Gear Slot (G Series, BIL-A, and F Series)

Model	Standard	Repair limit
All Models	0.1 ~ 0.25 mm	0.6 mm

DISASSEMBLY (F8 AND F5)

1. Remove the kick-starter gear snap-ring, then separate the gear from the shaft.
2. Leaving the kick-starter shaft in the case, remove the ratchet, spring holder plate, and spring from the shaft.

INSPECTION—(G SERIES AND B1L—A)

1; Examine the gear teeth and the inner surface in which the pawl engages the gear. If excessively worn or deformed, replace the gear.

2. Inspect the kick-starter pawl tip for wear.

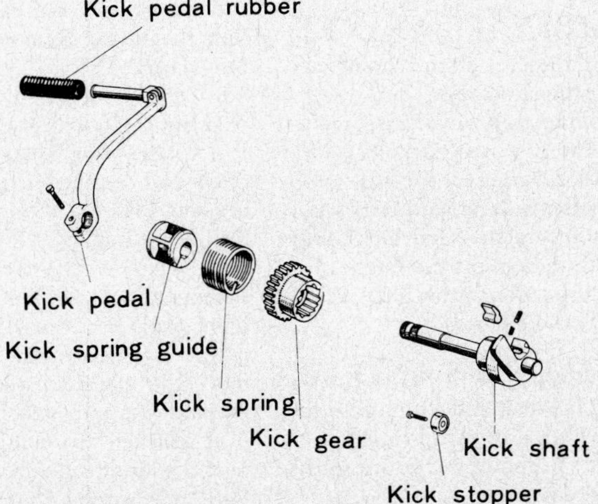

Exploded view of the kickstarter (G Series and B1L-A)

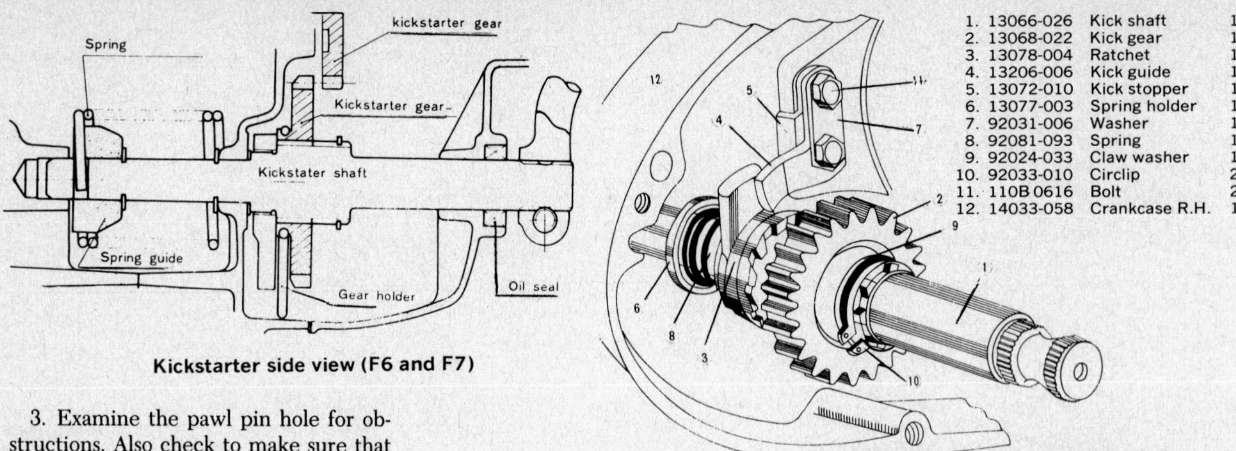

Kickstarter side view (F6 and F7)

Kickstarter construction (F8 and F5)

3. Examine the pawl pin hole for obstructions. Also check to make sure that there is free movement of the pawl pin and spring.

INSPECTION (F6 AND F7)

1. Inspect the kick-starter gear guide and splines for excessive play. Also roll the shaft on a flat surface to be sure that it is not bent.
2. Examine the gear teeth for general condition.

INSPECTION (F8 AND F5)

1. Make sure the ratchet slides along the kick-starter guide freely.
2. Roll the kick-starter shaft on a flat surface to make sure that it is not bent.

ASSEMBLY (G SERIES AND B1L—A)

1. Install the kick-starter stopper in the left case.
2. Install the pawl spring and then the pawl push pin in the hole in the shaft.
3. Install the pawl, then while holding it down, install the kick-starter gear.
4. Insert the assembly in the right case.
5. Insert one end of the kick-starter spring in the case hole, then twist the spring about 120° and insert the other end in the kick-starter shaft.
6. Install the kick-starter shaft holder.

ASSEMBLY (F6 AND F7)

1. Install the kick-starter guide and stopper on the crankcase.
2. Install the shaft in the case and secure with the two snap-rings. Install the spring holder, spring, and collar as described for the G Series and B1L—A
3. Align the ratchet and kick-starter shaft marks, then insert the ratchet.
4. Install the kick-starter gear and secure it with the circlips.

ASSEMBLY (F8 AND F5)

1. Insert the shaft in the right case and secure it with the two snap-rings.
2. Insert one end of the return spring in the right case.
3. Twist the spring 120° and insert the other end in the kick-starter shaft.
4. Install the spring guide.
5. Install the kick-starter gear with holder and secure with the circlip.

ENGINE SERVICE

A AND H SERIES

Engine Removal and Installation

1. Turn on the fuel tap, disconnect the fuel lines at the carburetors, and unbolt and remove the gas tank (H series only).
2. Remove the exhaust header pipe retaining rings, unscrew the muffler mounting bolts, and remove the entire exhaust system.
3. Take off the left side cover and remove the air filter housing and element.
4. Remove the shift lever and the right and left side carburetor covers (A Series only).
5. Unbolt and remove the carburetors. Tie them out of the way with the cables attached.
6. Take out the securing screws and slide the oil pump cover up on the tachometer cable (H Series only).
7. Disconnect the tachometer cable from the engine. Remove the distributor cap (H1 only).
8. Disconnect the oil pump control cable from the pump control lever.
9. Unscrew the banjo bolt from the oil pump and disconnect the oil tank delivery line. Plug the line to prevent the oil tank from draining.
10. Take off the front chain cover. Remove the master link and take off the drive chain. On the H2, which has no master link loosen the rear axle nuts, move the wheel forward, and slip the chain off the sprockets.
11. Slacken the clutch cable, disconnect the inner cable from the clutch release mechanism, then disconnect the outer cable from the engine cover.

Disconnecting the clutch cable (H Series)

12. Disconnect the alternator leads from the main harness at the connectors under the seat.
13. Remove the high-tension wires from the spark plugs.
14. Drain the transmission oil.
15. Take out the engine mounting bolts and remove the engine from the frame.

Installation is basically a reversal of the removal procedure.

Cylinder Heads

The cylinder heads are made of aluminum alloy for heat dissipation qualities and light weight. An individual head is used for each cylinder.

REMOVAL

1. Remove the securing nuts gradually and evenly to prevent distortion of the head.
2. Lift off the head and gasket. If necessary, tap the bottom of the cooling fins with a rubber mallet to free the head.

INSPECTION

Remove the carbon buildup from the head as described in "Maintenance." Examine the spark plug hole threads for signs of stripping or other damage.

INSTALLATION

1. Install a new head gasket.
2. Install the head and securing nuts,

then tighten the nuts gradually and evenly, in an "X" pattern, to prevent distortion. Final tightening torque is 18 ft lbs.

Cylinder

The individual cylinders are made of aluminum alloy, with bonded, cast iron liners.

REMOVAL

1. Remove the cylinder head, then lift the cylinder up over the studs. If necessary, tap the bottom of the exhaust port with a rubber mallet to break the cylinder free. Take care to steady the piston as the cylinder is withdrawn.
2. Cover the crankcase openings with clean rags.
3. Remove the cylinder base gasket.

INSPECTION

Remove the carbon deposits from the exhaust and transfer ports as described in "Maintenance." Examine the cylinder walls for scoring, seizure spots, or hairline cracks. Measure the bore diameter as described in "Piston and Cylinder Fit" to determine if boring and/or honing is necessary. If it is not, clean up the cylinder walls with no. 400 emery cloth, in a 45° crosshatch pattern.

INSTALLATION

1. Install a new cylinder base gasket.
2. Lubricate the piston and rings with oil, then slide the cylinder over the studs.
3. Insert the top of the piston into the cylinder bore, then, while compressing one ring at a time with your fingers, lower the cylinder.
4. Remove the rags in the case opening and seat the cylinder on the gasket.

Piston, Piston Pin, and Piston Rings

REMOVAL AND DISASSEMBLY

1. Make certain that the crankcase opening is protected with rags, then remove the piston pin circlips with a pair of needle-nose pliers.
2. Press the pin out of the piston with the tool shown in the accompanying illustration.
3. Remove the piston rings, one at a time, beginning with the top one, over the top of the piston.

INSPECTION

Remove carbon deposits from the piston crown and ring grooves as described in "Maintenance." Examine the piston for seizure spots, crown damage, and hairline cracks. If the seizure spots are minor, they can be smoothed out with no. 400 emery cloth. However, it is best in these cases to replace the piston.

Removing the piston pin circlip

Removing the piston pin

Examine the piston pin for step wear in the center. Insert it into the connecting rod bearing and check for excessive clearance. Maximum allowable radial play is 0.004 in. (0.10 mm). This can be checked with a dial indicator. Nominal radial play is 0.00012–0.00086 in. (0.003–0.022 mm). If play is excessive, replace both the piston pin and connecting rod small end bearing.

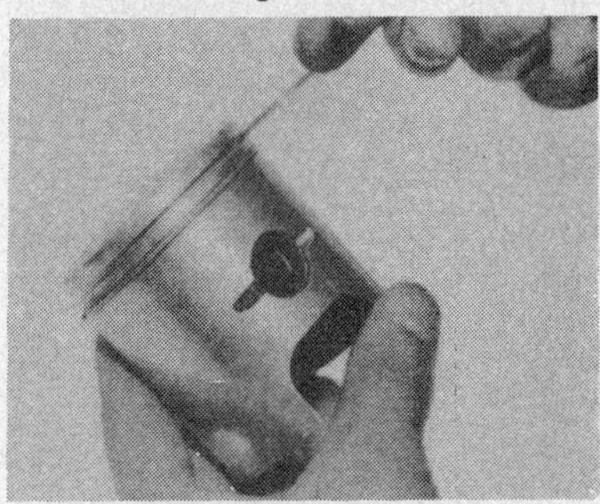
Measuring ring side-clearance

The rings may be reused if they are checked in the following manner:

1. Insert each ring, one at a time, into the cylinder bore and locate it 0.2 in. (5 mm) from the bottom of the barrel.
2. Measure the end-gap of the ring with a feeler gauge. If the measurement is beyond the wear limit shown in the accompanying chart, the ring must be replaced.
3. Insert an edge of each ring, one at a time, into its respective groove. Measure the clearance between ring and the top or bottom of the groove with a feeler gauge. If the clearance exceeds specifications the ring must be replaced.

Small End Radial Play (A Series and H1)

Model	Standard Item	Max. limit
A1, A7, H1	0.00012-0.00086 in. (0.003-0.022 mm)	more than 0.004 in. (0.10 mm)

Ring End Gap (S2 and H2)

Model	Top	2nd
S2	.256 in. 6.5 mm	.256 in. 6.5 mm
H2	.315 in. 8.0 mm	.315 in. 8.0 mm

Ring End Gap (A Series and H1)

Series	Standard Item	Max. limit
A1, A7, H1	0.008-0.012 in. (0.2-0.3 mm)	more than 0.0315 in. (0.8 mm)

PISTON SPECIFICATIONS (S2 AND H2)

Model	Skirt Diam. in. (mm)	Top Groove width x depth in. (mm)	Second Groove width x depth in. (mm)
S2	2.08563 (52.975)	.0591 +.0039 × .0984 ±.0039 +.0031 (1.5 +0.10) × (2.5 ±0.1) +0.08)	.0591 +.0024 × .0984 ±.0039 +.0016 (1.5 +0.06) × (2.5 ±0.1) +0.04)
H2	2.79314 (70.946)	.0591 +.0039 × .1272 ±.0039 +.0031 (1.5 ±0.10) × (3.23 ±0.1) +0.08)	.0591 ±.0024 × .1272 ±.0039 +.0016 (1.5 +0.06) × (3.23 ±0.1) +0.04)

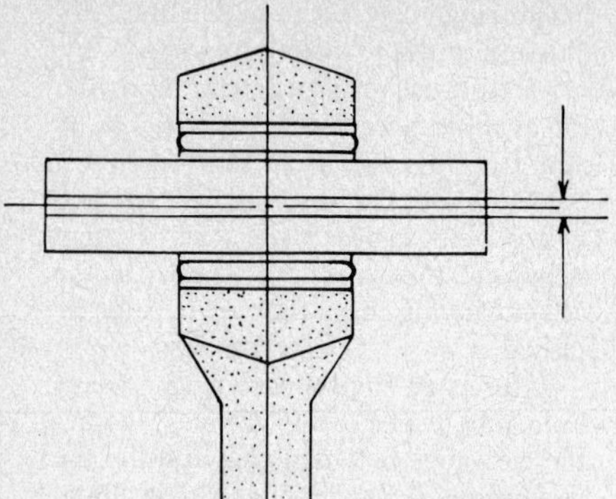

Connecting rod small end clearance

ASSEMBLY AND INSTALLATION

1. Install the piston rings. The rings must be installed with the number and letter facing up.
2. Position the ring end-gaps at the ring groove locating pins (H and S Series only).
3. Position the piston over the connecting rod with the arrow stamped in the crown pointing forward (toward the exhaust port).

NOTE: *It is very important that the piston be correctly located, as the piston pin is slightly offset to counteract uneven combustion thrust.*

4. Install the piston pin using the same tool used for removal. Lubricate it before installation.
5. Install new piston pin circlips.

Piston and Cylinder Fit

When the cylinder and piston are removed, it is a good idea to measure cylinder and piston wear, even if it is not your intention to replace them.

CYLINDER MEASUREMENT

Measure cylinder bore diameter at the points indicated in the accompanying illustration. At each level, make two measurements perpendicular to each other. If wear exceeds 0.006 in. (0.15 mm) at any given point, or if the difference in inside diameter between any two points exceeds 0.002 in. (0.05 mm), the cylinder must be bored and/or honed.

Cylinder Bore Diameter (A and H Series)

Item	Standard	Maximum limit
Inner diam.		
A1	2.09 in. (53.0 mm)	Over
A7	2.44 in. (62.0 mm)	0.006 in.
H1	2.36 in. (60.0 mm)	(0.15 mm)

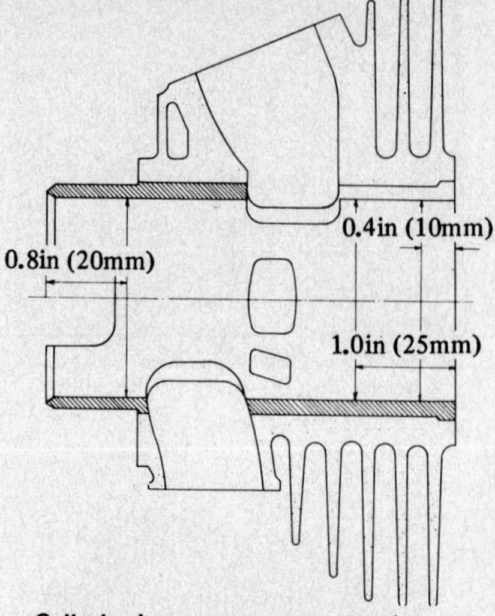

Cylinder bore measurement points

PISTON MEASUREMENT

Measure piston diameter with a micrometer positioned perpendicular to the piston pin 0.2 in. (5.0 mm) from the bottom of the skirt.

NOTE: *Pistons are available in two oversizes: 0.50 mm and 1.00 mm.*

Piston Ring Dimensions (S2 and H2)

Model		A	B
S2	Top	.0591 +.0004- −.0012 in. 1.5 0.01- −0.03 mm	.0906 ±.004 in. 2.3 ±0.1 mm
	2nd	.0591 +.0004- −.0012 in. 1.5 +0.01- −0.03 mm	.0906 ±.004 in. 2.3 ±0.1 mm
H2	Top	.0591 +.0004- −.0012 in. 1.5 +0.01- −0.03 mm	.118 ±.004 in. 3.0 ±0.1 mm
	2nd	.0591 +.0004- −.0012 in. 1.5 +0.01- −0.03 mm	.106 ±.004 in. 2.7 ±0.1 mm

Measuring cylinder bore wear with a dial indicator

Clutch Release Mechanism (S and H Series)

REMOVAL

1. Take off the left-side rear engine cover (front chain cover) and disconnect the clutch cable.

Cylinder Diameter (S2 and H2)

Model	Standard Diameter	Service Limit
S2	2.0866 +.0007 in. −0	2.0925 in.
	53 +.019 mm −0	53.15 mm
H2	2.7953 +.0007 in. −.0	2.8012 in.
	71 +.019 mm −.0	71.15 mm

Piston to Cylinder Wall Clearance (A Series and H1)

Model	Standard
A1	0.0015 in. (0.037 mm)
A7	0.0032 in. (0.081 mm)
H1	0.0022 in. (0.056 mm)

Piston Clearance (S2 and H2)

Model	Standard
S2	0.0012 in. (0.031 mm)
H2	0.0029 in. (0.074 mm)

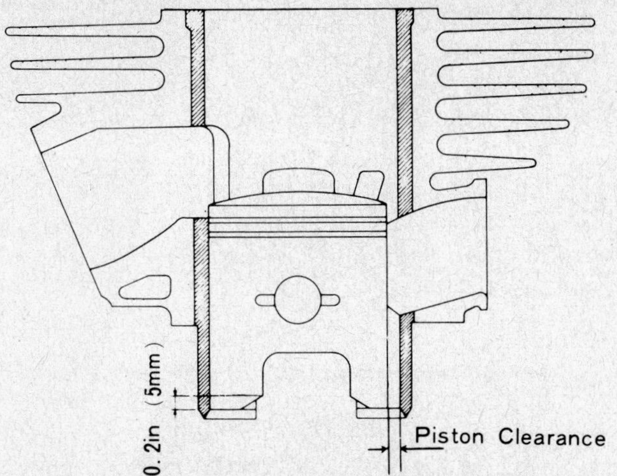

Piston to cylinder wall clearance

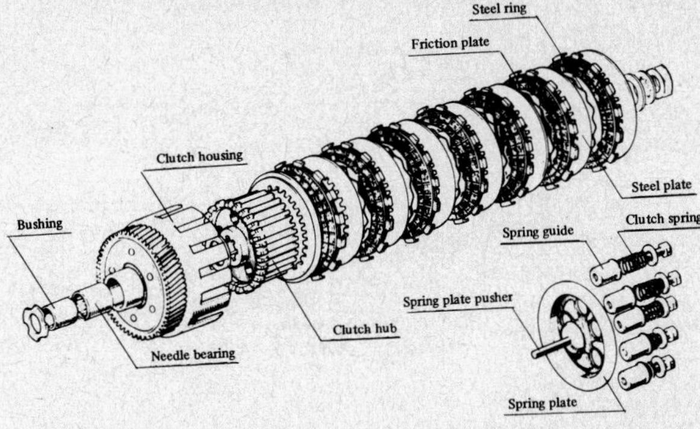

Exploded view of the clutch. The H Series has 7 discs, the A1 has 5, and the A7 has 6. The H Series has 6 plates, the A1 has 4, and the A7 has 5.

Removing the clutch release mechanism (H Series)

2. Take out the screws on the outer release and pull out the assembly. Do not attempt to pry it out

INSPECTION

Insert the inner release into the outer release and check for smooth movement.

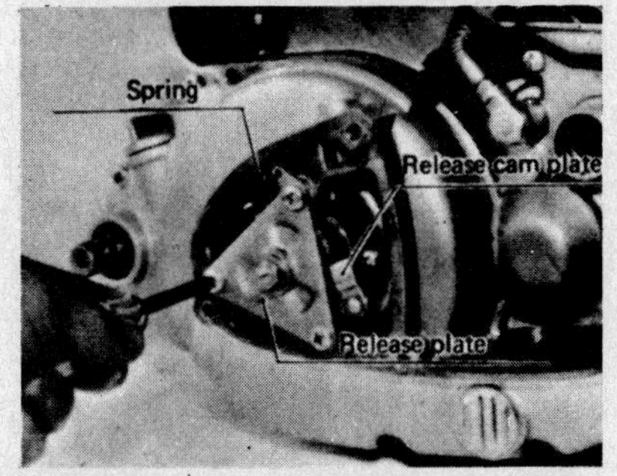

Removing the clutch release mechanism (A Series)

INSTALLATION

1. Install the inner release into the outer release so that the angle of the release arm is the same as it was before removal.
2. Tighten the outer release screws evenly to avoid distortion.
3. Reconnect the clutch cable and adjust the clutch. Install the cover.

Clutch Release Mechanism (A Series)

REMOVAL

1. Take off the right-side carburetor cover and disconnect the clutch cable.
2. Pull off the return spring, take out the three screws, and remove the release assembly.

INSPECTION

Check to make sure that the release mechanism operates freely. Make sure that the cam plate, thrust ball set, and roller pin are not worn excessively or damaged.

ASSEMBLY

1. Install the assembly in its original position and tighten the three retaining screws evenly to avoid distortion. Refit the return spring.
2. Reconnect the clutch cable and adjust the clutch.
3. Install the cover.

Clutch

REMOVAL (S AND H SERIES)

1. If the engine is still in the frame, unscrew the banjo bolt and disconnect the oil tank delivery line. Plug the line to prevent the oil tank from draining. Disconnect the oil delivery lines and mark them for correct replacement. Disconnect the oil pump control cable.
2. Remove the kick-start lever.
3. Take out the securing screws and remove the right-side engine cover. The tachometer and distributor drive gears and the kick-start shaft oil seal are located in the cover and may be removed for inspection or replacement at this time.
4. Remove the clutch springs and bolts.
5. Remove the pressure plate, discs, and plates. Take out the release pushrod.
6. Keep the clutch housing from turning by using the special tool or by stuffing a rag between the primary and clutch gear teeth, and unscrew the housing retaining nut.
7. Remove the clutch hub and housing from the transmission shaft.
8. Pull out the bushing and remove the thrust washer.

REMOVAL (A SERIES)

1. Remove the kick-start lever.
2. Take out the securing screws and

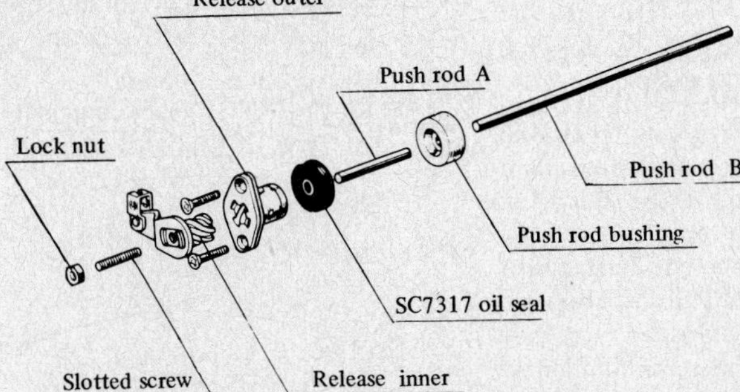

Clutch release mechanism (H Series)

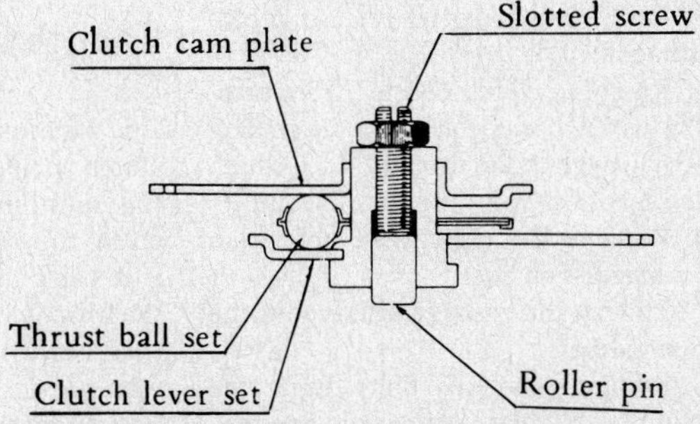

Clutch release mechanism (A Series)

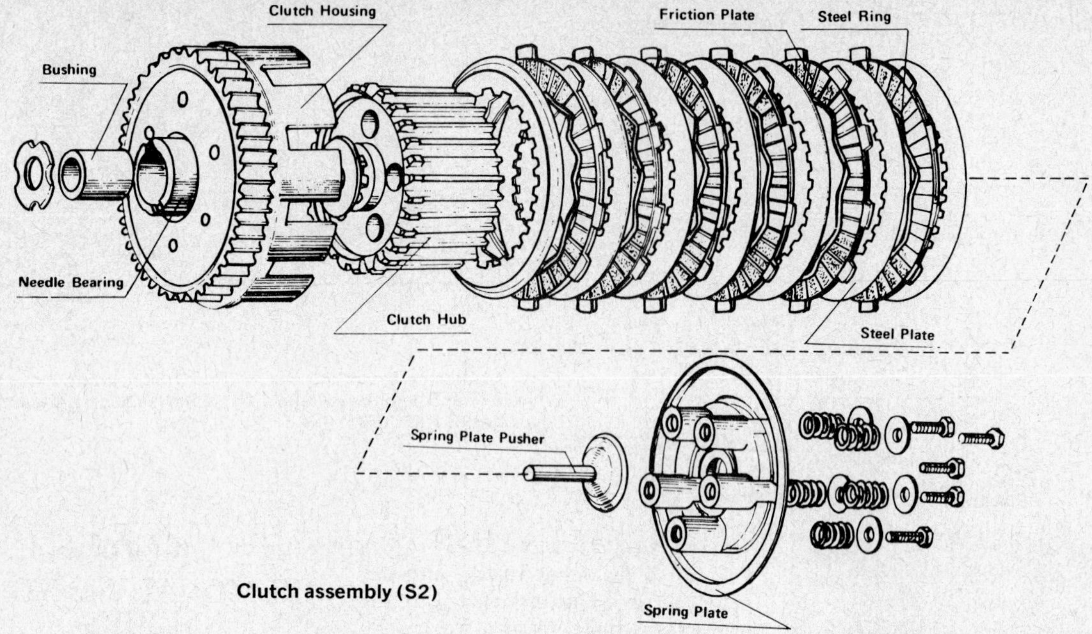

Clutch Housing
Friction Plate
Steel Ring
Bushing
Needle Bearing
Clutch Hub
Steel Plate
Spring Plate Pusher
Spring Plate

Clutch assembly (S2)

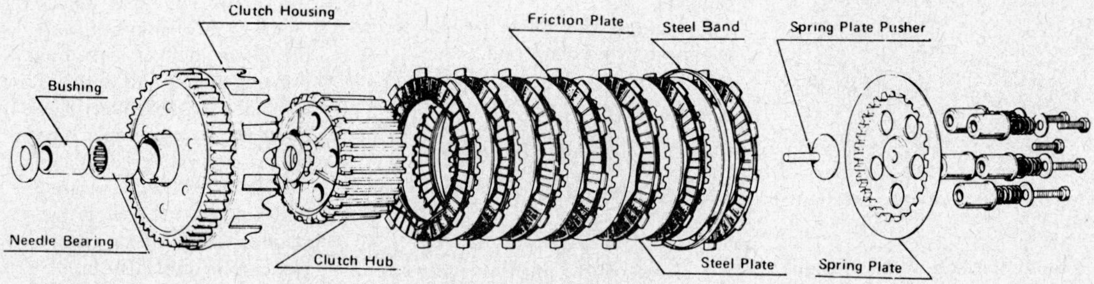

Clutch Housing
Friction Plate
Steel Band
Spring Plate Pusher
Bushing
Needle Bearing
Clutch Hub
Steel Plate
Spring Plate

Clutch assembly (H2)

Removing the clutch housing nuts (H Series)

Removing the clutch assembly nut (A Series)

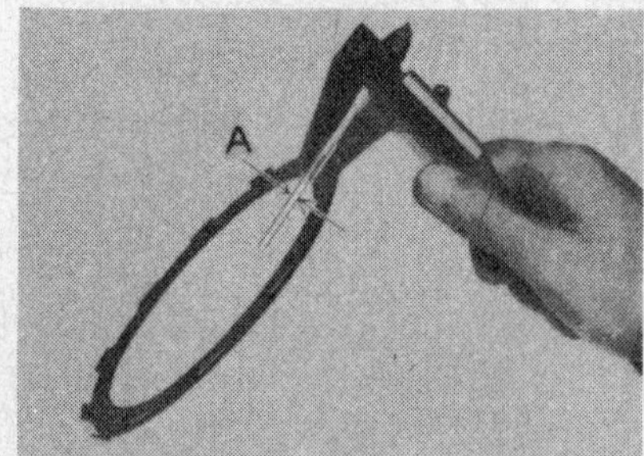

Measuring friction disc thickness

remove the right-side carburetor cover.

3. Disconnect the clutch cable from the release mechanism.

4. Remove the clutch release mechanism.

5. Keep the clutch housing from turning by using the special tool or by stuffing a rag between the primary and clutch gear teeth. Unscrew the housing nut.

6. Remove the clutch assembly from the transmission shaft.

7. Pull out the bushing and remove the thrust washer.

8. Remove the six bolts from the clutch housing and remove the pressure plate, discs, and plates.

NOTE: *Take care not to lose the rubber rings during disassembly of the clutch.*

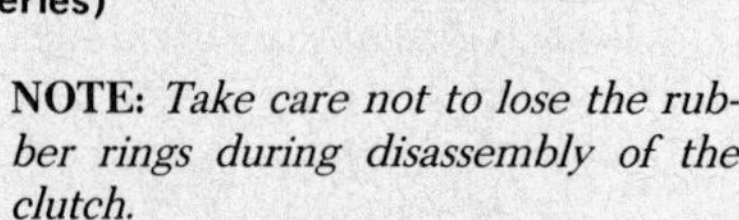

INSPECTION (A, S AND H SERIES)

1. Measure the free-length of the clutch springs. If they measure less than the minimum given in the following chart, they should be replaced.

2. Check for damage and burn-out of the friction material on the discs. Replace the discs if they are damaged or if they measure less than the minimum thickness given in the accompanying chart.

3. Examine the clutch plates for scoring and warpage. Replace them if they do not appear to be in perfect condition.

4. Measure gap B, shown in the accompanying illustration, between the disc

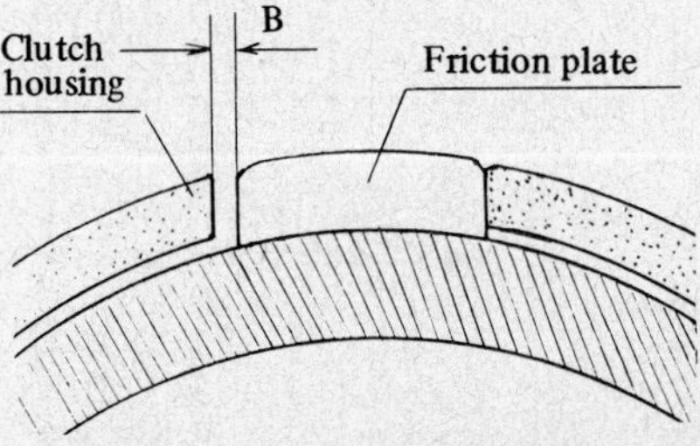

Clutch disc tab and clutch housing gap

Clutch Spring Freelength (A Series and H1)

Model	Standard	Repair Limit
A1	1.18 in. (29.5 mm)	1.10 in. (28.0 mm) or less
A7	1.20 in. (30.0 mm)	1.13 in. (28.5 mm) or less
H1	1.40 in. (36.0 mm)	1.32 in. (34.5 mm) or less

Spring Length (S2 and H2)

Model	Standard	Service Limit
S2	1.130 in. (28.7 mm)	1.051 in. (26.7 mm)
H2	1.26 in. (32 mm)	1.18 in. (30 mm)

Clutch Return Rubber and Steel Rings (A Series and H1)

Model	Part Name	Quantity
A1	Return rubber—short	24
	long	6
A7	Return rubber—short	30
	long	6
H1	Steel ring	7

Friction Plate Thickness (S2 and H2)

Model	Standard	Service Limit
S2	0.118 in. (3.0 mm)	0.106 in. (2.7 mm)
H2	0.110 ±0.004 in. (2.8 ±0.1 mm)	0.098 in. (2.5 mm)

Clutch Disc Thickness (A Series and H1)

Model	"A" Dimension Standard	Repair Limit
A1	0.16 in. (4.0 mm)	0.14 in. (3.65 mm)
A7	0.12 in. (3.1 mm)	0.11 in. (2.85 mm)
H1	0.11 in. (2.8 mm)	0.10 in. (2.50 mm)

Clutch Disc Tab and Housing Gap (A Series and H1)

Model	"B" Dimension Standard
A1, A7, H1	0.002-0.012 in. (0.05-0.3 mm)

Clutch Housing/Plate Clearance (S2 and H2)

Model	Standard
S2	.0020-.0217 in. (0.05-0.55 mm)
H2	.0035-.0157 in. (0.09-0.40 mm)

tabs and clutch housing slots. Replace parts as necessary if the gap is not within the specifications given in the chart.

5. Check the clutch gear teeth for damage and excessive wear. Refinish the teeth with an oilstone or replace the clutch housing if necessary.

6. Check the clearance between the bushing and needle bearing in the clutch housing. If clearance is excessive, replace the bushing and bearing.

ASSEMBLY (A, S AND H SERIES)

Assembly is a reversal of the disassembly procedure. The following points should be noted:

1. On the A Series models, take care to correctly position the long and short return rubbers.
2. When mounting the clutch housing, align the timing marks on the sides of the gears as shown in the illustration (A Series).
3. Tighten the clutch springs evenly.
4. On H Series models, bleed the oil pump after assembly and adjust the pump cable.

Primary Drive

REMOVAL (S AND H SERIES)

1. Remove the right-side engine cover as described in the "Clutch" section and take off the oil pump drive gear.
2. Bend back the locktab, hold the clutch from turning by using the special tool or a prybar, and unscrew the gear retaining nut.
3. Pull off the distributor drive gear and primary gear. Remove the woodruff key from the crankshaft.

REMOVAL (A SERIES)

1. Remove the right-side engine cover.
2. Bend back the locktab, hold the clutch from turning by using the special tool or a prybar, and unscrew the gear retaining nut.
3. Pull the gear off of the crankshaft.

Primary and clutch gear alignment marks (A Series)

Primary gear, oil pump pinion, and distributor pinion (H Series)

Removing the primary gear nut (H Series)

INSPECTION

Examine the gear teeth for damage and excessive wear. Refinish the teeth with an oilstone or replace the gear as necessary.

ASSEMBLY

Assembly is a reversal of the removal procedures. Don't forget to secure the nut with the locktab and, on the H Series models, bleed the oil pump and adjust the pump cable.

Countershaft Sprocket

REMOVAL AND INSTALLATION

1. Remove the front drive chain cover.
2. Bend back the sprocket nut locktab.
3. Put the machine in gear, apply the rear brake, and loosen the sprocket retaining nut.
4. Remove the master link and disconnect the drive chain.

Removing the countershaft sprocket

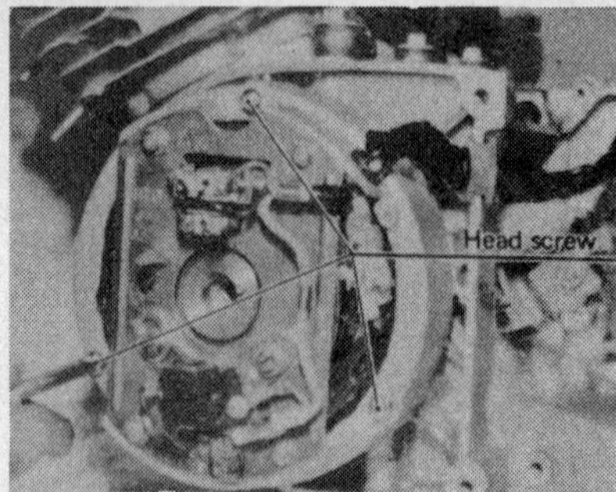

Removing the alternator yoke (H Series)

Removing the signal generator rotor (H Series with CD ignition)

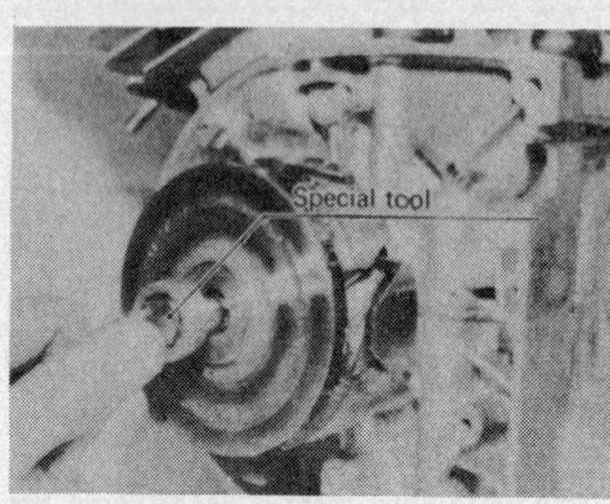

Removing the alternator rotor (H Series)

5. Pull the sprocket off the transmission shaft.

6. Installation is in reverse order of removal. Don't forget to secure the nut with the locktab.

Alternator

REMOVAL (H SERIES)

1. Remove the right-side engine cover as described in the "Clutch" section.

2. Unbolt and remove the timing signal generator rotor.

3. Take out the screws and remove the alternator yoke.

4. Pull off the alternator rotor using an extractor (a special threaded bolt).

5. Remove the woodruff key from the crankshaft.

REMOVAL (A SERIES)

1. Remove the right-side engine cover.

2. Unscrew the bolt and remove the alternator drive gear.

3. Remove the alternator cover from the crankcase and remove the alternator assembly.

INSTALLATION

Installation is in reverse order of removal. Note the following points:

1. Make sure that the timing alignment marks on the clutch gear, primary reduction gear, and alternator drive gear are aligned. Refer to the accompanying illustration. (A Series only.)

2. On the H Series models, install the signal generator rotor after installing the locating (knock) pin on the rotor shaft. Be sure to bleed the oil pump and adjust the control cable after assembly.

Shifter Mechanism

REMOVAL

1. Remove the right-side engine cover

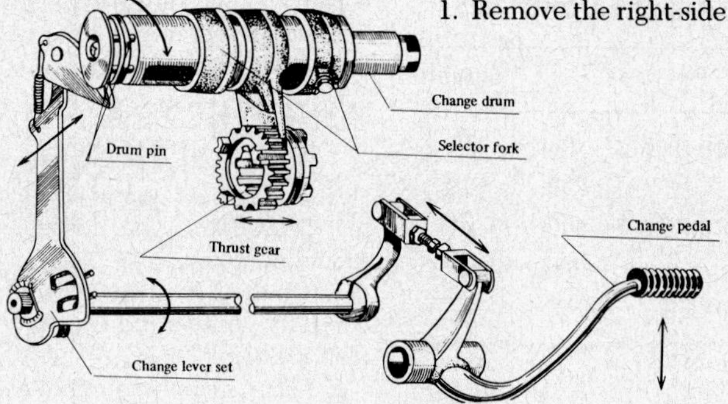

Change lever assembly

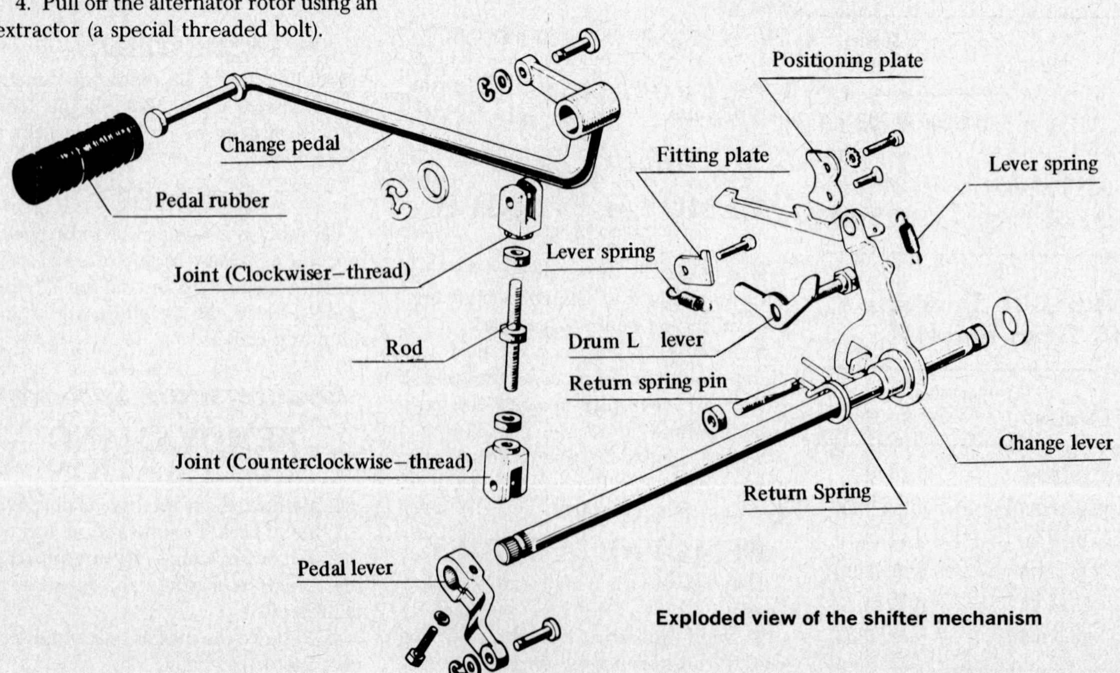

Exploded view of the shifter mechanism

as previously described. The shifter arms, return springs, and pivot shaft will then be accessible.

2. Remove the arm retaining clip from the end of the shaft and remove the arm and return spring assembly.

3. Unscrew the bolt and remove the small set plate and spring.

INSPECTION

1. Examine the springs for cracks and weakness. Replace if necessary.

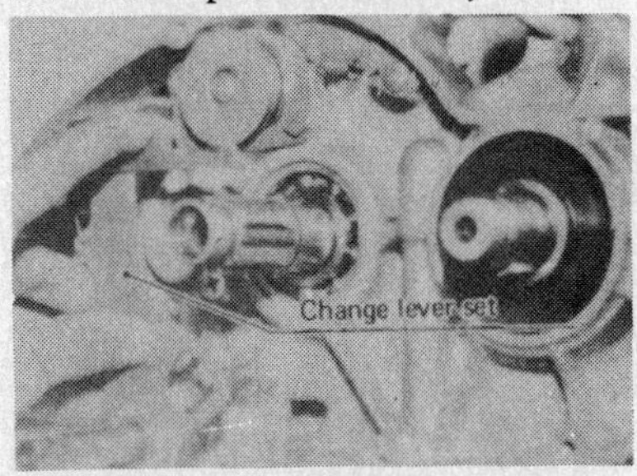

Removing the change lever

2. Check to make sure that the set pin locknut is tight. If it is not, the shifter may not index properly.

ASSEMBLY

Assembly is a reversal of the removal procedure. On S and H Series models, don't forget to bleed the oil pump and adjust the pump control cable after assembly.

Rotary Valve (A Series)

REMOVAL

1. Remove the carburetor covers.

2. Loosen the carburetor clamps, remove the carburetor, and tie the clamps out of the way.

3. Disconnect the lines from the oil pump and mark them to facilitate correct reassembly.

4. Unbolt and remove the oil pump assembly.

5. Take out the screws and remove the left and right-side valve covers. Take off the collars and O-rings and pull the valves off of the crankshaft.

INSPECTION

1. Examine the oil seal in each of the valve covers for wear and damage, and replace them if necessary.

2. Make sure that the oil injection nozzles are not clogged.

3. Examine the inside surface of the valve covers for scoring and wear, and measure the depth of the covers as shown in the illustration. If the measurements exceed 0.16 in. (4.0 mm), replace the covers.

4. Measure the thickness of the valve discs. Replace the valves if they are damaged in any way or are worn beyond 0.12 in. (3.0 mm). Nominal thickness is 0.14 in. (3.5 mm).

Valve Cover Depth (A Series)

Standard	Repair Limit
0.14 in. (3.5 mm)	Over 0.16 in. (4.0 mm)

Valve Disc Thickness (A Series)

Standard	Repair Limit
0.14 in. (3.5 mm)	0.12 in. (3.0 mm) or less

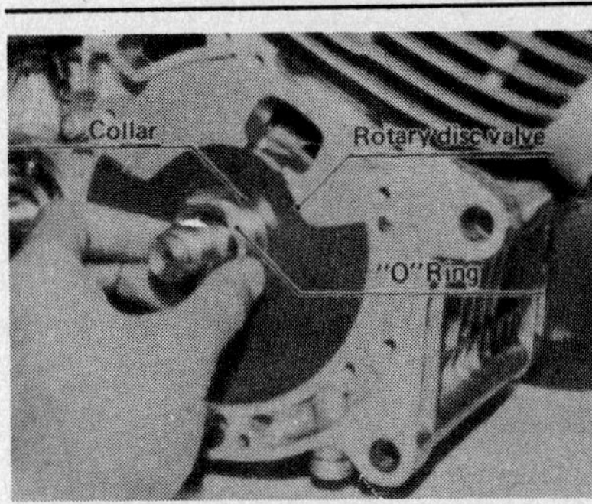

Removing the rotary valve (A Series)

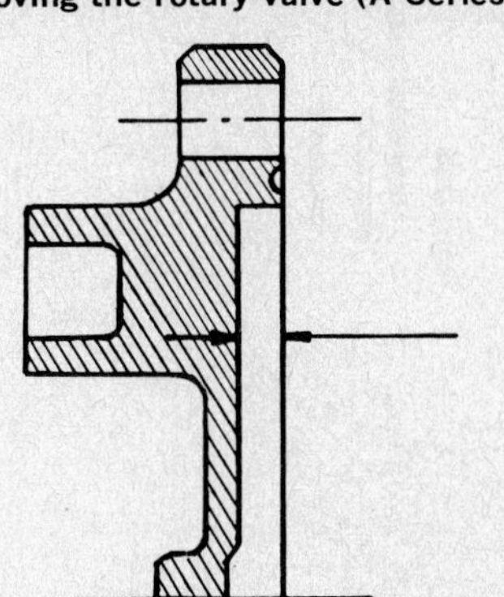

Valve cover depth measurement (A Series)

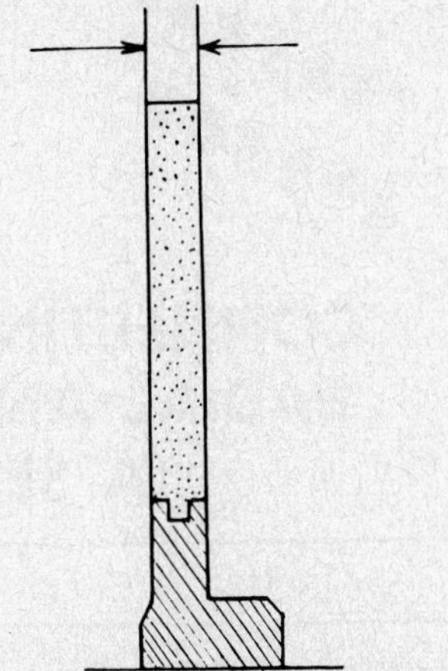

Valve disc thickness (A Series)

INSTALLATION

Installation is a reversal of the removal procedure. Note the following points:

1. Use new O-rings.

2. Soak the valves well in fresh motor oil before installing them.

3. Bleed the oil pump and adjust the pump control cable before running the engine.

Crankcase

In order to split the cases, it will first be necessary to remove the engine from the frame. Then remove the clutch, clutch release mechanism (S and H Series only), alternator yoke (S and H Series only), shifter mechanism, and rotary disc valve covers (A Series only). If the crankshaft is to be removed, it will also be necessary to disassemble the cylinder heads, cylinders, and pistons. The crankcases can then be separated in the following manner:

1. Remove the oil guide from the end of the transmission output shaft.

2. Turn the engine upside down and remove the crankcase securing nuts.

3. Break the crankcase joint seal by tapping both sides of the cases and the shifter shaft boss with a rubber mallet. Lift the lower crankcase away and the crankshaft and transmission assemblies will be accessible.

CRANKSHAFT REMOVAL

Tap both ends of the crankshaft gently with a rubber mallet and lift it out of the crankcase.

CRANKSHAFT DISASSEMBLY

The crankshaft cannot be disassembled. If the bearings, connecting rods, or the crankshaft itself are excessively worn, the entire assembly must be replaced.

CRANKSHAFT RUNOUT

Place the ends of the crankshaft in V-blocks and measure runout at the points shown in the illustration with a dial indicator. Replace the crankshaft if it is not within the specification given in the following chart.

MAIN BEARINGS

Thoroughly clean the bearings and lu-

Removing the oil guide from the transmission output shaft

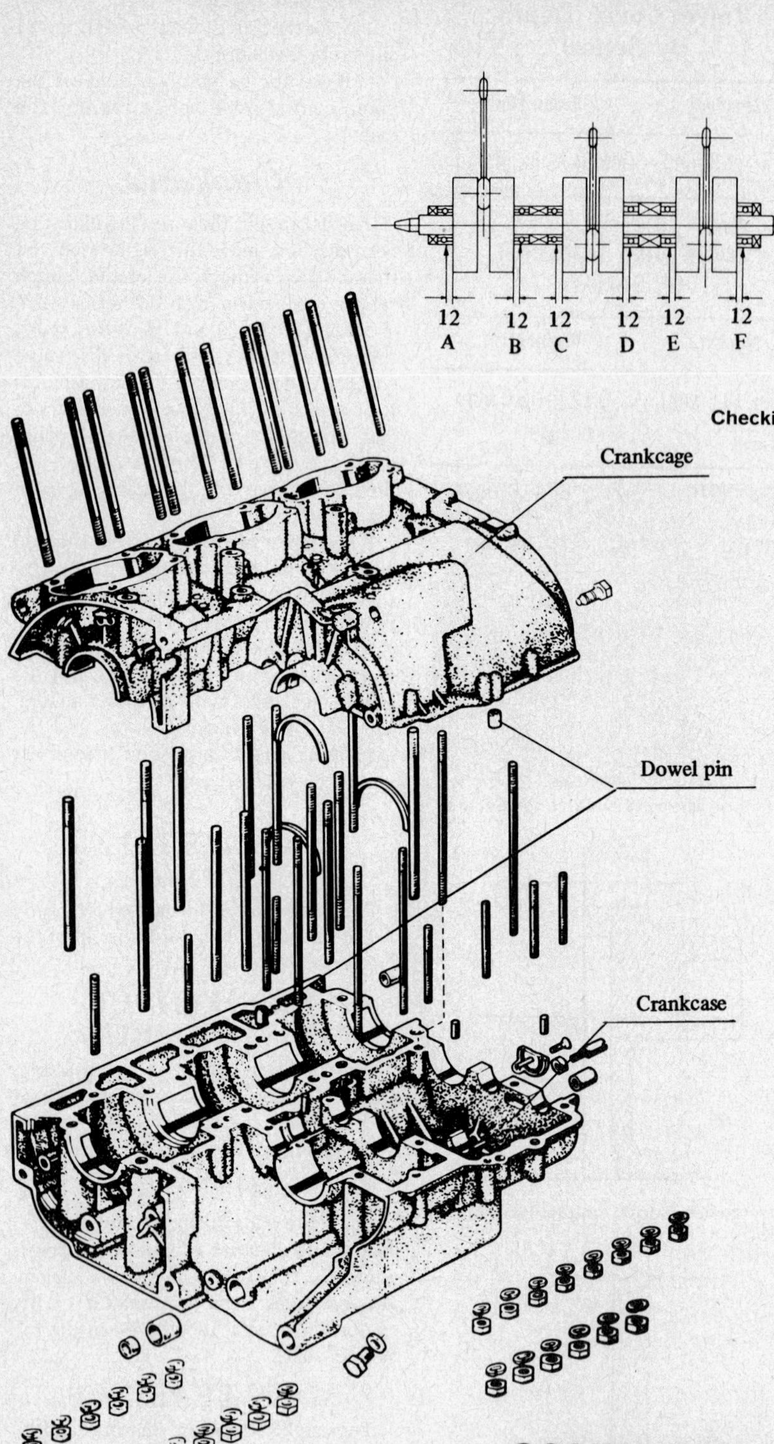

0.47in (12mm) A
0.47in (12mm) B
0.47in (12mm) C
0.47in (12mm) D

Checking crankshaft runout

Crankcase assembly (H Series)

bricate them with a good quality engine oil. Spin the bearings and check for smooth operation and acceptable clearance. *Do not spin the bearings until they have been cleaned and lubricated.*

OIL SEALS

The crankshaft oil seals must be in good condition to maintain fuel transfer compression in the individual crankcase compartments. If the seal lips are damaged or worn, or if there is evidence of leaking (discoloration), the seals should be replaced. Scratches on the surface of the outer seals, caused by pinching when the crankcases are assembled, are not harmful.

CONNECTING ROD BEARINGS

Measure the radial (up and down) and clearance of the rod bearings using a dial indicator, and measure the side clearance with a feeler gauge. Steady the big end of the rod with your hand while checking the radial movement so that side movement of the rod will not affect the reading. The crankshaft assembly should be replaced if the specifications given in the chart are exceeded.

Crankshaft Runout (A and H Series)

Model	Measuring Point	Standard	Maximum Limit
A H	ABCD ABCEF	0.0008 in. (0.02 mm)	0.0024 in. (0.06 mm)

CONNECTING ROD LARGE END RADIAL AND SIDE CLEARANCE (A SERIES AND H1)

Items	Standard	Maximum Limit
Big end radial clearance	0.00016-0.00047 in. (0.004-0.012 mm)	0.002 in. (0.05 mm)
Big end side clearance	0.016-0.020 in. (0.40-0.50 mm)	0.028 in. (0.7 mm)

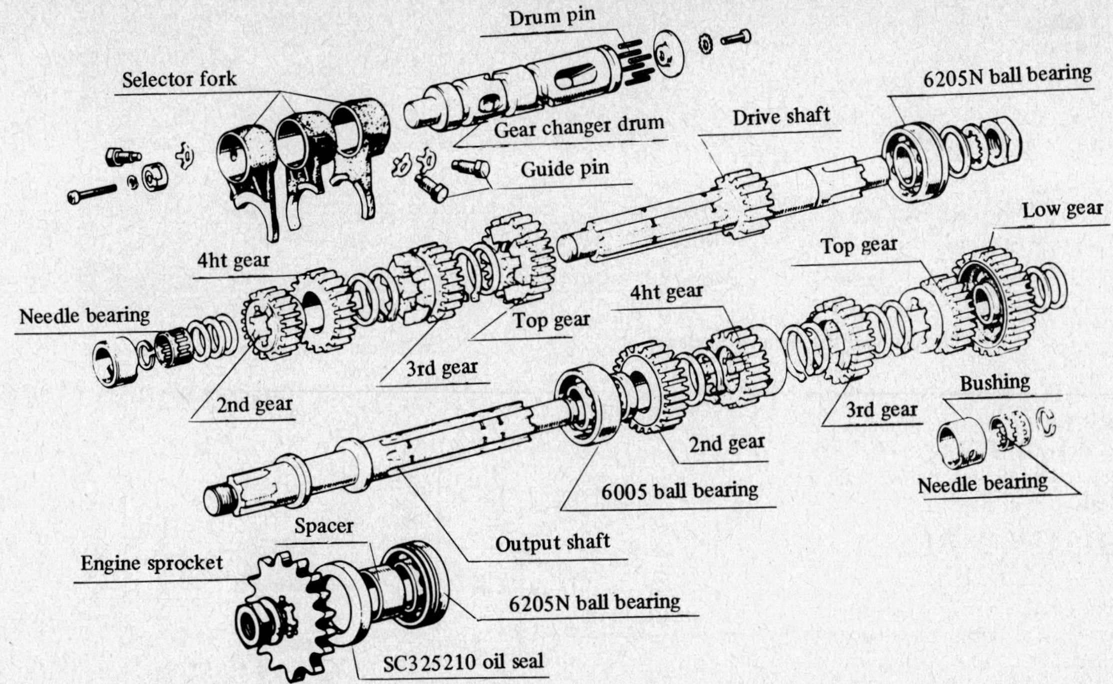

Exploded view of the transmission. The A Series uses plain bearings and the H Series uses needle bearings.

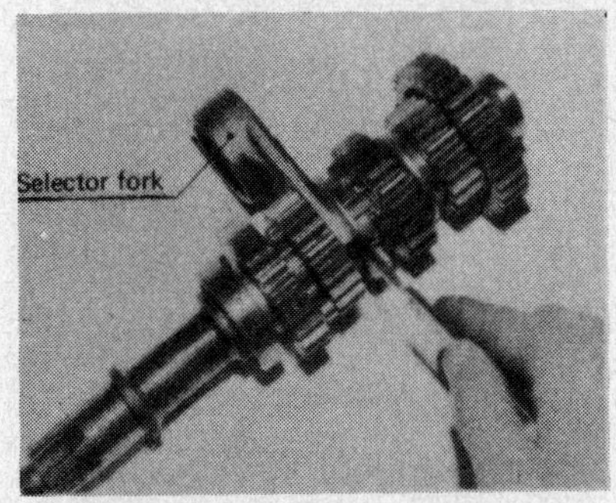

Measuring shift fork and gear groove clearance

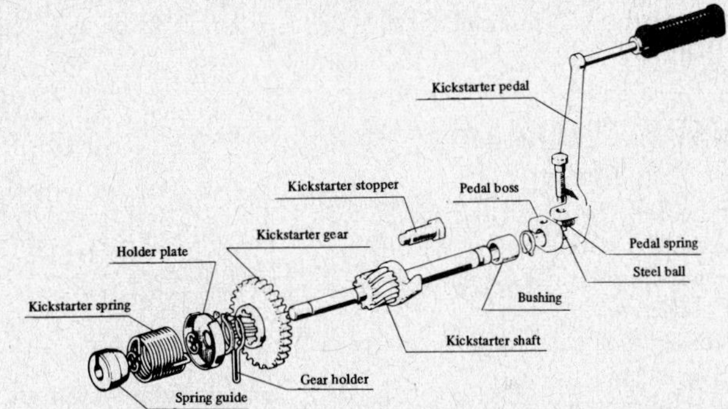

Kickstart mechanism (H Series)

TRANSMISSION SERVICE

DISASSEMBLY

1. Bend back the locktabs and unscrew the shift fork guide pins, then pull the shift fork shaft out of the case.

2. Lift the transmission shafts out of the crankcase.

3. Remove the bearing circlips from the ends of the transmission shafts and remove the bearings. The shafts can then be disassembled.

INSPECTION

1. Examine the gear teeth for damage and excessive wear. Refinish damaged teeth with an oilstone or else replace the gear. If the dogs on the gears are damaged or rounded off, the gears should be replaced.

2. Install the shift forks on the shift grooves in their gears and measure the side clearance with a feeler gauge. Replace the gears or forks if they are damaged or overheated, or if the side clearance is less than the specifications given in the chart below.

ASSEMBLY

Assemble the components in reverse order of disassembly, using the illustrations as a guide. Note the following points:

1. If possible, use new circlips and make sure they are properly seated.

2. Before inserting the shaft through the shift forks, make sure that the bearing set rings (two each) are properly installed.

3. Secure the shift fork guide pins with the locktabs.

Shift Fork and Gear Groove Clearance (A Series and H1)

Standard Limit	Repair Limit
0.0039-0.01 in. (0.1-0.25 mm)	Less than 0.023 in. (0.6 mm)

Kick-Starter Mechanism

DISASSEMBLY (S AND H SERIES)

1. Remove the spring guide and spring.

2. Remove the two circlips and the spring holder plate.

3. Remove the circlips from the kick-starter shaft guide and remove the gear.

INSPECTION (S AND H SERIES)

Examine the kick-starter shaft guide and gear inner ring for excessive clearance. Spin the gear and check for smooth operation.

ASSEMBLY (S AND H SERIES)

Assemble the kick-starter mechanism in the reverse order from disassembly. The following points should be noted:

1. Make sure that the circlips are seated properly.

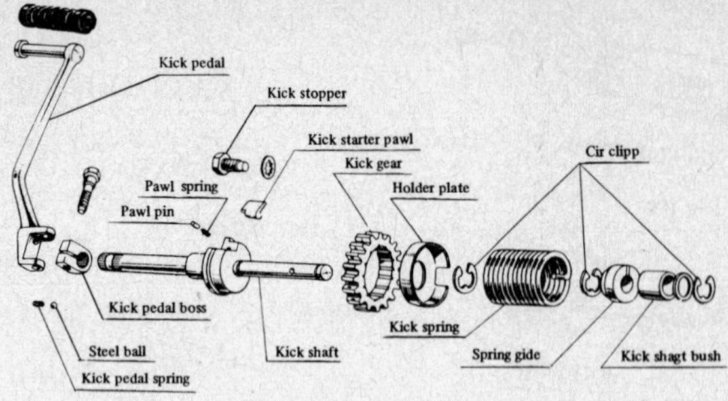

Kickstart mechanism (A Series)

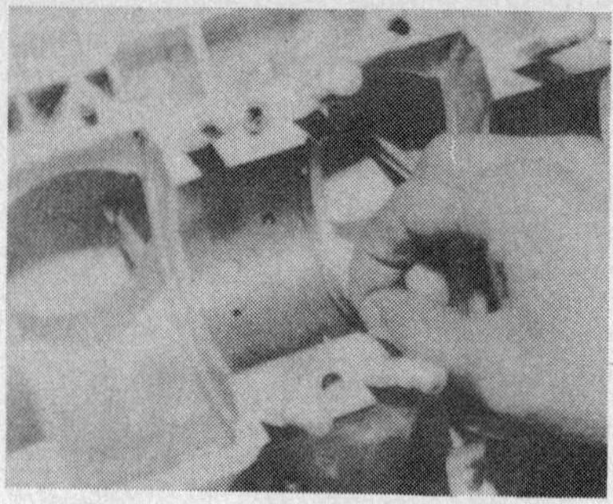

Installing the main bearing set rings

2. After assembling the crankcases, install the kick-stopper with the kick-start lever rotated from its original position about 150°.

DISASSEMBLY (A SERIES)

1. Take off the circlip, then remove the thrust washer, bushing, spring guide, and spring.
2. Remove the circlip and holder plate, then slide the gear off the shaft.
3. Remove the pawl, pin, and spring from the shaft.

INSPECTION (A SERIES)

1. Examine the teeth and the inside machined surface of the kick gear. Replace the gear if it does not appear to be in perfect condition.
2. Replace the kick pawl if the top end is worn or damaged.
3. Install the spring and kick pawl push pin and check to see if they can move freely. Repair or replace as necessary.

ASSEMBLY (A SERIES)

Assemble in the reverse order from disassembly. Make sure that the circlips are seated properly. After the crankcases have been assembled, install the kick-stopper with the kick-start lever rotated about 150° from its original position.

Crankcase Assembly

1. Make sure that the crankshaft main bearing set rings are properly located in the upper crankcase. Seat them with a rubber mallet.
2. Check to make sure that the oil supply and breather holes are not plugged. Clear them, if necessary, with compressed air.
3. Clean the crankcase flanges thoroughly and apply a thin coat of gasket sealer (Kawasaki Bond).
4. Fit the crankshaft, transmission shafts, and kick-start shaft into position, then install the lower crankcase.

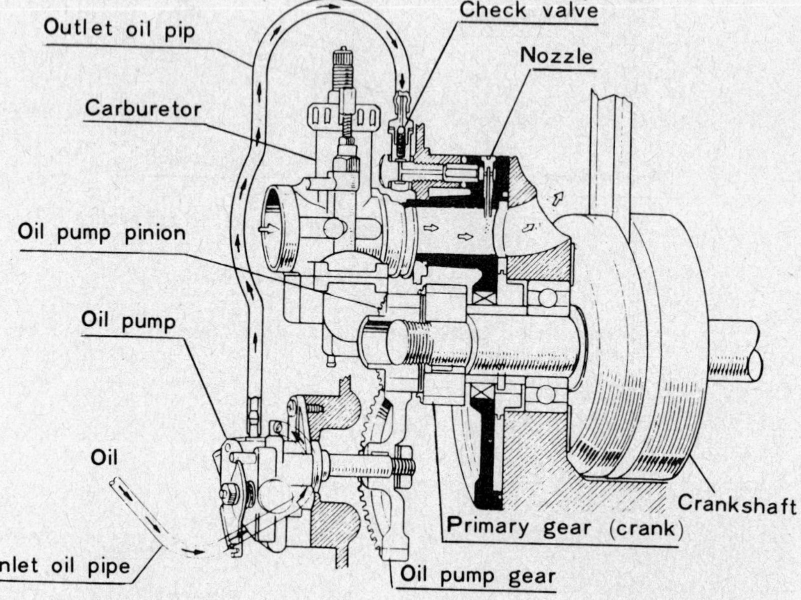

Superlube system (G Series and B1L-A)

5. Install and tighten the crankcase securing nuts. Torque 8 mm nuts to 18 ft lbs; 6 mm nuts to 11 ft lbs. Tighten all nuts in a cross pattern, starting from the center.
6. The remainder of the assembly procedure is a reversal of the disassembly steps. Refer to the appropriate sections in this chapter for assembly details on the remaining engine components.

LUBRICATION SYSTEMS

OIL PUMP

Repair

The factory advises against attempting to disassemble and repair the oil pump. The internal parts are machined to very exacting tolerances and it is highly unlikely that the pump can be reassembled to factory specifications. In addition to this, oil pump failure is *very* seldom due to internal malfunction.

Adjustment

See "Tune-Up" procedures.

Bleeding

The oil pump must be bled of air between the pump and check valve, and between the reservoir and pump whenever the pump is removed, the delivery lines are disconnected, or the reservoir has run dry.

1. Remove the oil pump access cover.
2. Start and run the engine at 2000 rpm while holding the pump control lever in the fully open position.
3. Observe the output delivery line. Any air bubbles in the system should disappear quickly. If they do not, check the tightness of the input and output line banjo bolts.
4. If there are air bubbles in the reservoir oil delivery line, disconnect it at the pump and allow oil to flow through it until the bubbles are gone, then reconnect it and repeat steps 2 and 3. The reservoir delivery line must not be disconnected while the engine is running.

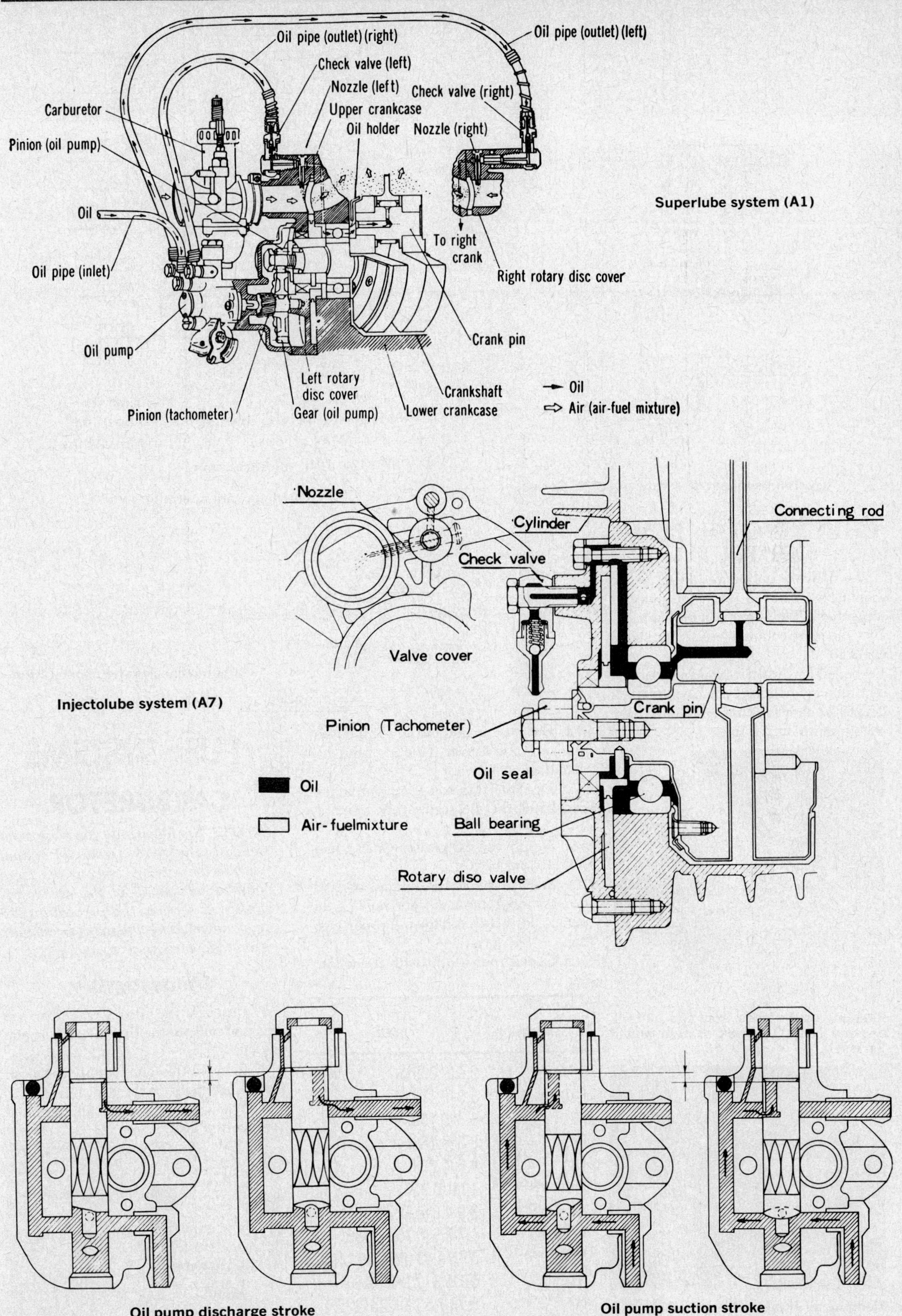

Superlube system (A1)

Injectolube system (A7)

Oil pump discharge stroke

Oil pump suction stroke

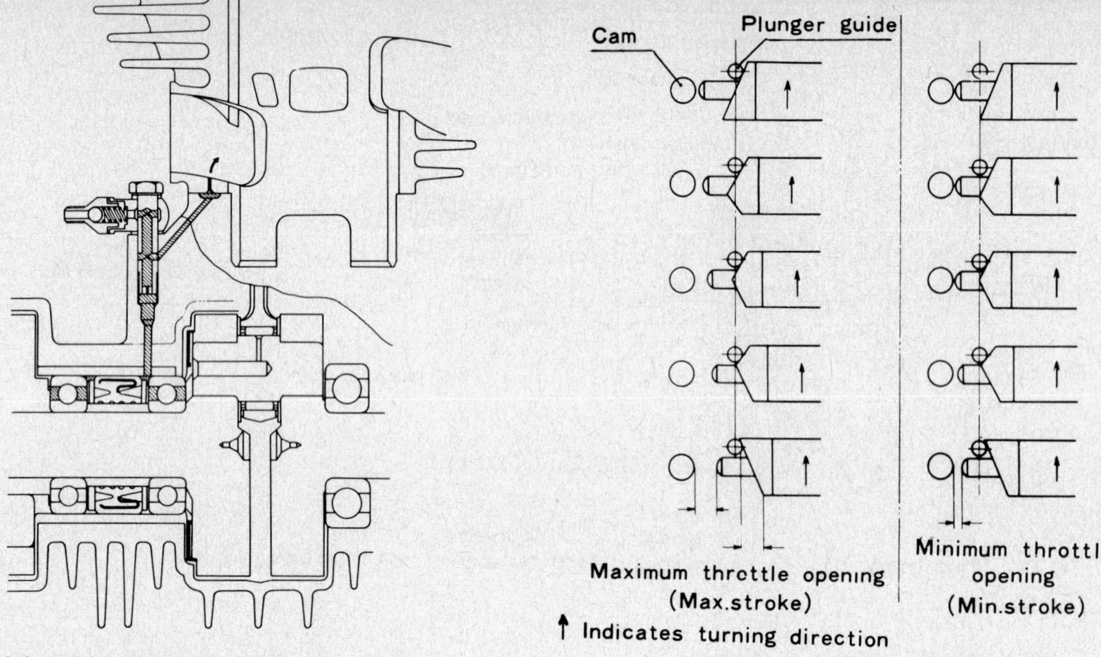

Injectolube oil nozzle arrangement (H Series)

Oil pump cam operation

CHECKING OIL PUMP OUTPUT

The delivery output of the oil pump should be measured when the pump is suspected as the source of a problem and after the more common causes have been checked.

Needed for this operation are: a laboratory tube graduated in cubic centimeters (tenths) or ounces (hundreths), and an extra oil pump output line.

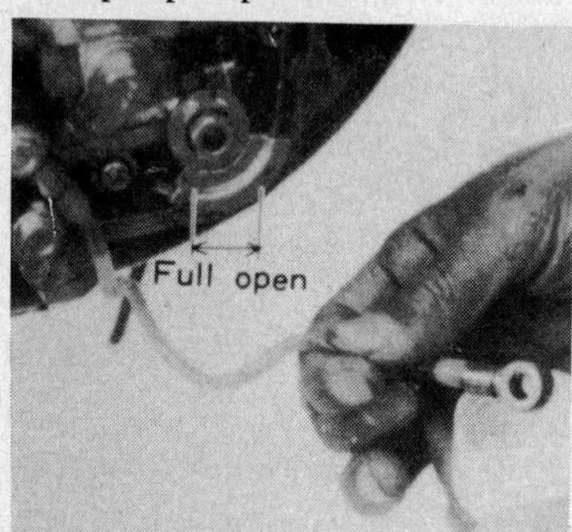

Bleeding air bubbles from the oil tank delivery line (G Series, B1L-A, and F Series)

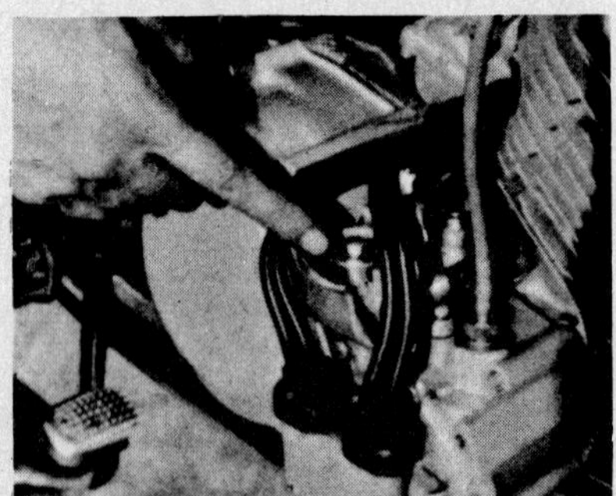

Bleeding air bubbles from the oil pump output line (A and H Series)

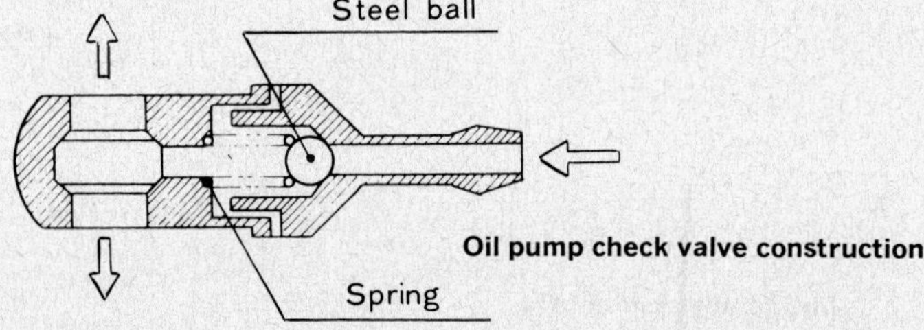

Oil pump check valve construction

1. Cut off one end of the extra output line and slide it over the end of the graduated tube.
2. Disconnect the oil pump output line and install the measuring tube assembly in its place.
3. Supply the carburetors with a fuel/oil mixture of 20:1.
4. Start and run the engine at 2000 rpm for three minutes while holding the pump control lever in the fully open position.
5. Check your results with the following:

Model	Output cc (oz)
G Series	2.8 (0.095)
B1L—A	3.6 (0.112)
F6	4.1 (0.139)
F7	5.5 (0.186)
F8	6.0 (0.203)
F5	10.0 (0.338)
A1, A1SS	3.9-4.6 (0.127-0.155)
A7, A7SS	4.7-5.5 (0.159-0.186)
S2	3.75-4.43 (0.127-0.150)
H1	5.1-5.8 (0.172-0.196)
H2	6.75-7.53 (0.228-0.255)

FUEL SYSTEMS

CARBURETOR

NOTE: *The following procedure is intended to serve as a guide for Mikuni carburetor service. Due to the large number of models of this make currently in service, the procedures are general in nature and may vary slightly from one carburetor to another.*

Disassembly

1. Unscrew the mixing chamber top ring and pull out the throttle slide assembly.
2. Remove the four bottom float bowl screws and take off the float bowl.
3. Take out the float spindle and remove the float.

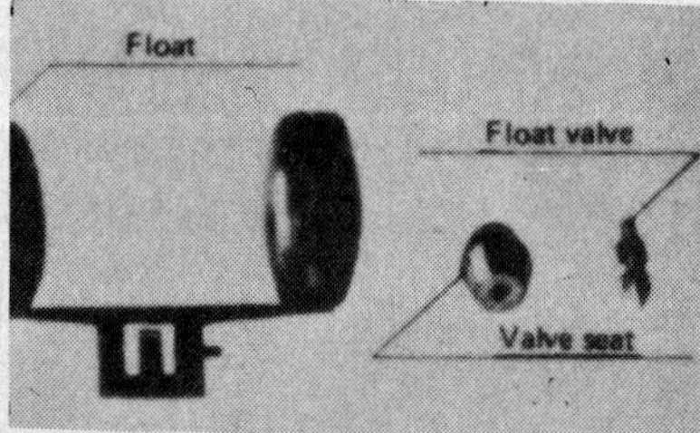

Float assembly

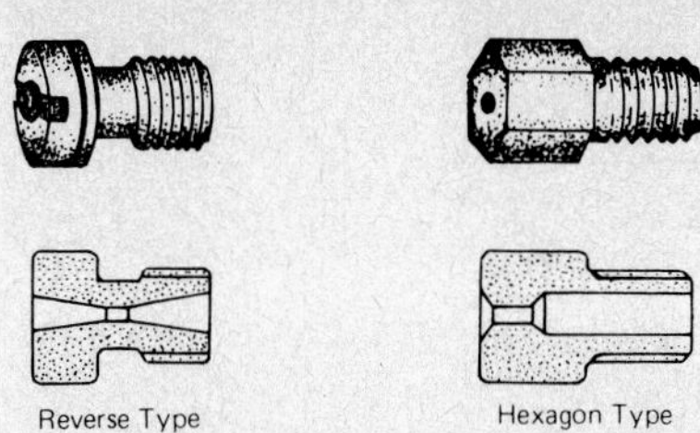

Two types of main jets fitted to Mikuni carburetors

4. Remove the starter plunger mechanism (if fitted).
5. Remove the float needle and unscrew and remove the needle seat.
6. Remove the pilot jet.
7. Remove the main jet.
8. Remove the needle jet.

NOTE: *Mikuni carburetors have two types of needle jets—one screws into position, the other is held in place by a small clip. If the latter, remove the clip and push out the jet from the top of the carburetor.*

9. Remove the pilot air screw and the throttle stop screw.
10. Remove the needle from the throttle slide by first removing the throttle slide rod (if fitted), compressing the return spring against the carburetor cap, and removing the clip which secures the needle.

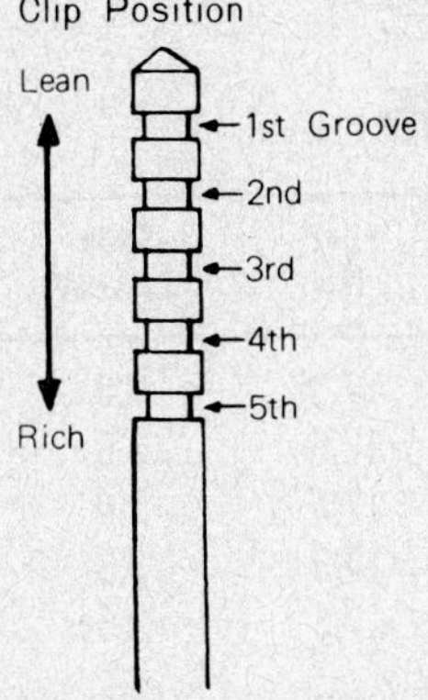

NOTE: *Ascertain the needle clip setting before removing the clip.*

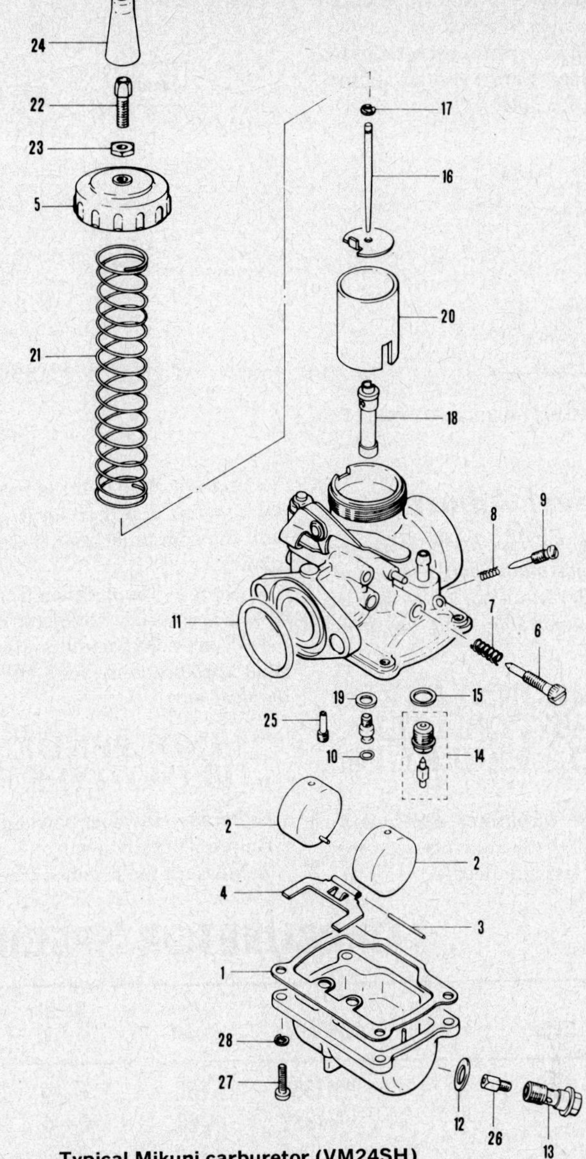

Typical Mikuni carburetor (VM24SH)

Cleaning and Inspection

1. Wash out the carburetor body in a suitable solvent and blow out all air and fuel passages.
2. Check the body for deformation at the mounting flange, minute cracks in the casting, or scoring or wear of the throttle slide bore.
3. The float bowl mating surface should be flat and free from nicks, etc.
4. Shake the float to assure that no gasoline has leaked in. The float cannot be repaired. Replacement is recommended if a leak is discovered.
5. The tip of the float needle must be perfectly clean, smooth, and unworn as must the needle seat. Both items must be cleaned thoroughly to remove any foreign matter. If a good seal of the needle against the seat is not accomplished by cleaning, there may be corrosion in the seat.

Grinding the needle against the seat is not recommended. The components should be replaced.

The ability of the needle to form a good seal with its seat may be checked by reassembling the carburetor except for the float bowl. Fit the seat, needle, and float into position, then connect the fuel line to the carb. Turn on the gas only AFTER the float has been gently lifted until the needle is seated. There should be no noticeable gas leakage.

6. Clean the fuel jets and blow them dry. The air bleed holes in the needle jet and pilot jet must also be clear.
7. Make sure that the needle is free of any nicks. The tapered portion must be smooth.

NOTE: *After many miles, the needle and the needle jet will begin to show signs of wear due to their contact. They must both be replaced if this happens. It is usually noticeable as a rich running condition in the mid-throttle range.*

8. The throttle slide is also subject to some wear after considerable mileage. If the slide is too loose in its bore, it should be replaced. Also inspect the slide for scoring or scratches.
9. The tapered portion of the pilot air screw should be smooth and free of foreign matter.
10. All gaskets, fiber washers, and O-rings should be replaced upon reassembly.

Assembly

Assemble the carburetor in the reverse order of disassembly. Note the following points:

1. The throttle slide must move freely in the bore.

2. The float level should be checked before reassembly (see below).

3. The pilot air screw must be adjusted with the engine warm. Use an approximate setting for now.

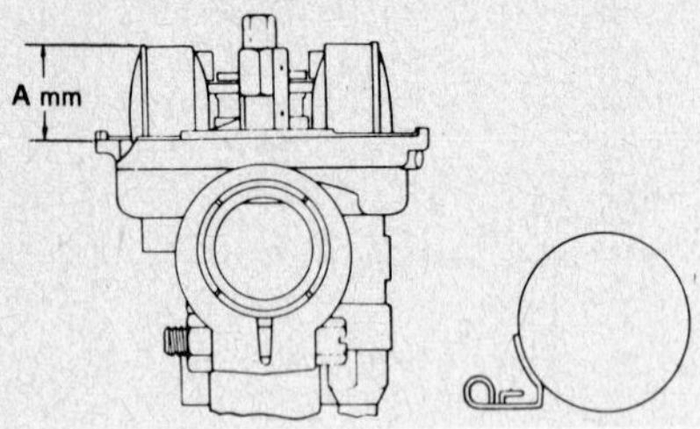

Float level setting (all models except F5)

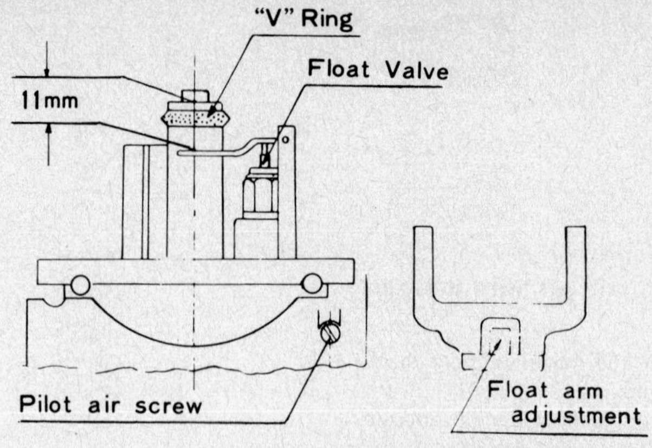

Float level setting (F5)

Float Level Adjustment

NOTE: *Float level is present at the factory. An adjustment should be necessary only after installing a new float or when the adjustable tang has been bent.*

INTERCONNECTED FLOAT-TYPE (ALL MODELS EXCEPT F5)

1. Turn the carburetor upside-down and tilt it until the float pivots up against the fuel inlet passage needle.

2. Make certain that the fuel inlet needle is seated, and then let it spring back until the adjustable tang is lightly touching it.

3. Measure the distance from the float bowl gasket surface to the top of the float.

4. If an adjustment is necessary to meet specifications, bend the tang, *not the float arm.*

INDEPENDENT FLOAT-TYPE (F5)

1. Remove the float bowl and turn the carburetor upside-down.

2. Measure the distance from the needle jet housing surface to each of the float arms.

3. If necessary, bend the adjustable tang to achieve the proper clearance.

FUEL PETCOCK

If you experience any fuel delivery problems, first check the gas tank vent, then the fuel petcock. Any sediment, water, etc., in the gas tank will eventually settle in the petcock filter or bowl. Remove the petcock, disassemble it, wash the filter in solvent, then blow everything dry with compressed air and reinstall it.

CARBURETOR SPECIFICATIONS

Model	Carburetor	Main Jet	Needle Jet	Jet Needle	Pilot Jet	Slide Cutaway	Air Screw (turns out)
GA1—A	VM19SC	160	E—4	512—3	17.5	2.0	1½
GA2—A	VM19SC	160	E—4	512—3	17.5	2.0	1½
G3SS—A	VM19SC	160	E—4	512—3	17.5	2.0	1½
G3TR—A	VM19SC	170	0—2	4L6—3	17.5	2.5	1¾
G4TR	VM19SC	180	E—6	5I1—3	17.5	2.5	1¾
B1L—A	VM22SC	190	0—0	4L6—2	30.0	3.0	1½
F6	VM24SC	125	0—4	4J13—3	25.0	2.5	1¾
F7	VM26SC	105	0—2	4EJ3—3	30.0	2.5	1¾
F8	VM30SC	117.5	0—8	5EL9—2	30.0	2.5	1¾
F5	VM32SC	132.5	0—8	5FL11—2	35.0	2.5	1¼
A1	VM22SC	140	0—6	4J13—3	30.0	2.5	1½
A1SS	VM22SC	140	0—6	4J13—3	30.0	2.5	1½
A7	VM28SC	97.5	0—4	5E14—4	30.0	1.5	1½
A7SS	VM28SC	97.5	0—4	5E14—4	30.0	1.5	1½
S2	VM24SC	85	0—2	4EJ4—3	25.0	2.0	1½
Early H1 (with CDI)	VM28SC	100	0—2	5GL—3	30.0	3.0	1¼
Early H1 (without CDI) (Europe)	VM28SC	90.0	0—2	5EH7—3	30.0	2.5	1½
Late H1 (with KA4 carb)	VM28SC	100	0—4/2	5DJ19—3	30.0	2.5	1¼
Late H1 (with KA5 carb)	VM28SC	95	0—4/8	5DJ19—4	30.0	2.5	1½
H2	VM30SC	105	0—6	5FL14—3	35.0	2.5	1½

Float Level Settings (G Series, BIL-A, and F Series)

Model	Fuel Level A
G Series	1.01 in. (25.7 mm)
G31M	1.04 in. (26.5 mm)
B1L—A	1.01 in. (25.7 mm)
F6, F7, F8, F81M	1.04 in. (26.5 mm)
F5	0.43 in. (11 mm)

Float Level Setting (A Series and H1)

Model	Height of Float
A1	1.06-1.14 in. (27-29 mm)
A7	1.14-1.22 in. (29-31 mm)
H1	1.14-1.22 in. (29-31 mm)

Float Level Setting (S2 and H2)

Model	Float Level Actual Level	Float Level Measurement "A"
S2	1.06 ± .04 in. (27 ± 1 mm)	1.00 ± .04 in. (25.5 ± 1 mm)
H2	Same as H1	(23-24 mm) .90-.94 in.

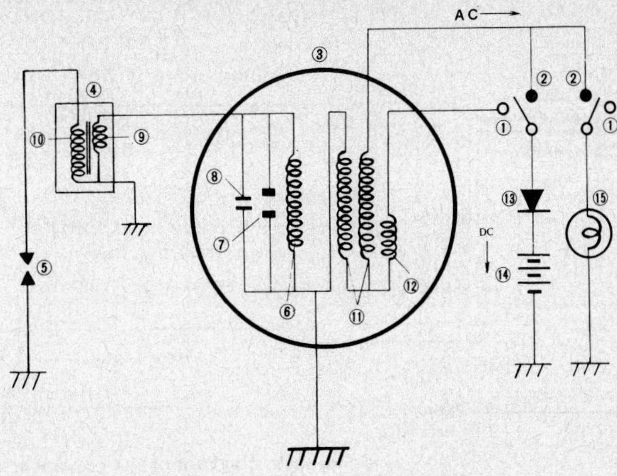

Flywheel magneto wiring diagram

1. Daytime running
2. Nighttime running
3. Flywheel magneto
4. Ignition coil
5. Spark plug
6. Magneto coil
7. Contact breaker
8. Capacitor
9. Ignition primary coil
10. Ignition secondary coil
11. Lighting coil
12. Differential winding coil
13. Rectifier
14. Battery
15. AC lamp load (head lamp and tail lamp)

FLYWHEEL MAGNETO SPECIFICATIONS (G SERIES, BIL-A, AND F SERIES)

Model	Type	Manufacturer	Cut-in rpm Day time	Cut-in rpm Night time	Battery
GA1—A,	FE101	Kokusan	1400	1600	6V 4AH
GA2—A	FE101	Kokusan	1400	1600	6V 4AH
G3SS—A	FE109	Kokusan	s.t.d. 1800	2100	6V 4AH
G3TR—A	FE109	Kokusan	spare 2700	2100	6V 4AH
G4TR	FE109	Kokusan	s.t.d. 1800 spare 2700	2100	6V 2AH
G31M—A	NJ101	Kokusan	—	—	—
F6	F6079BL	Mitsubishi	s.t.d. 2000 spare 3000	3000	6V 4AH
F7	HM-01	Kokusan	s.t.d. 2000 spare 3000	1800	6V 4AH
F8	FP6309	Kokusan	s.t.d. 1600 spare 3000	2000	6V 2AH
F81M	X016	Kokusan	—	—	—
F5	HM-01	Kokusan	1000	1800	6V 2AH

ELECTRICAL SYSTEMS

MAGNETO SYSTEMS

Flywheel Magneto Component Tests (G Series, F6, and F8)

MAGNETO IGNITION COIL

Place a strip of paper between the breaker points to insulate them. Perform the following resistance tests using an ohmeter.

1. Coil Resistance:

a. Measure the resistance between the black lead and ground. The coil is good if the ohmeter reading is approximately 0.5 ohms.

2. Insulation resistance:

a. Disconnect the ground wire from the coil to the magneto base.

b. Measure the insulation resistance between the iron core and the coil. The reading should be over 5.0 megohms.

CONDENSER

1. Capacity:

a. The condenser capacity should be between 0.18–0.25 microfarads.

2. Spark quality:

a. Connect the positive and negative wires of the condenser to a 6 volt DC power source for a few seconds to charge it.

b. Disconnect the power source and touch the two wires together. If a spark is produced, the condenser is good.

3. Insulation resistance:

a. Disconnect the ground wire of the condenser.

b. Measure the insulation resistance between the outer case and the positive terminal. The reading should be above 5.0 megohms.

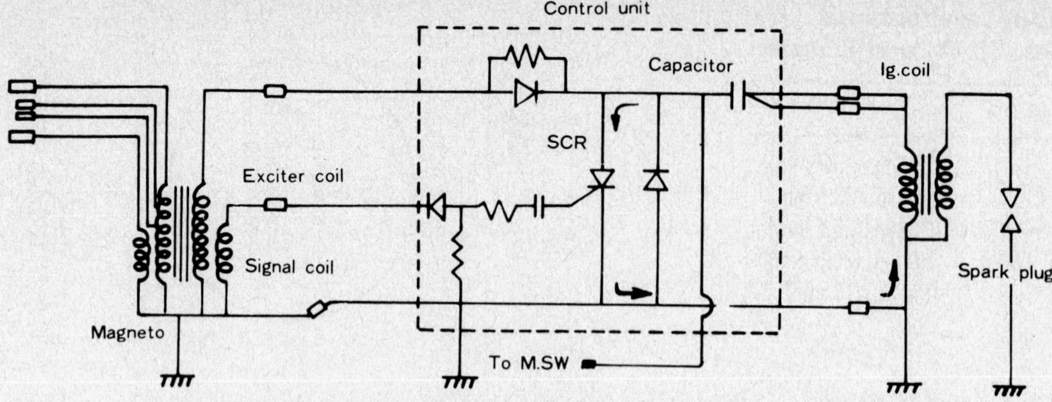

Schematic diagram of the capacitor discharge ignition system

LIGHTING AND CHARGING SPECIFICATIONS (G SERIES AND F SERIES)

Model	Lighting Coil Yellow	Pink	Charging Coil Blue	Yellow/Green
GA1—A, GA2—A	0.41 Ω ± 10%	—	0.36 Ω ± 10%	—
G3SS—A, G3TR—A, G4TR	0.55 Ω ± 10%	0.55 Ω ± 10%	1.20 Ω ± 10%	0.29 Ω ± 10%
F6	0.48 Ω ± 10%	0.48 Ω ± 10%	0.60 Ω ± 10%	0.54 Ω ± 10%
F8	0.30 Ω ± 10%	0.30 Ω ± 10%	0.58 Ω ± 10%	0.57 Ω ± 10%

LIGHTING AND CHARGING COILS

1. Coil resistance:

a. Measure the resistance of each coil with an ohmeter and compare the readings with the specifications in the accompanying chart.

NOTE: *The lighting coil for the GA1—A and GA2—A models also serves as a charging coil when the headlight is turned on.*

2. Insulation resistance:

a. Disconnect the ground wire.

b. Check insulation resistance between the iron core and the coil. The coil is good if the reading is above 0.5 megohms.

CAPACITOR DISCHARGE IGNITION SYSTEM

Operation

With the capacitor discharge ignition system, the primary winding of the ignition coil is supplied with current from the capacitor, in response to a timed signal at the time of ignition. Because the capacitor discharges current to the primary windings instantly, high voltage is induced in the secondary windings of the coil and a very strong spark is produced at the spark plug. Self-induction in the primary winding occurs faster in the CD ignition system and this short-rise time is why a good spark can be produced across even a fouled spark plug.

Contact breaker points are not used with the CD ignition system. Instead, an electronic timing detector and electric switch are used to fire the spark plug at the right moment. The signal coil (timing detector) generates a small voltage at every crankshaft revolution and sends it to the electric switch (silicon-controlled rectifier, or SCR), which triggers the capacitor.

Adjustment

FLYWHEEL MAGNETO

The coils installed in the magneto should be checked with an ohmeter.

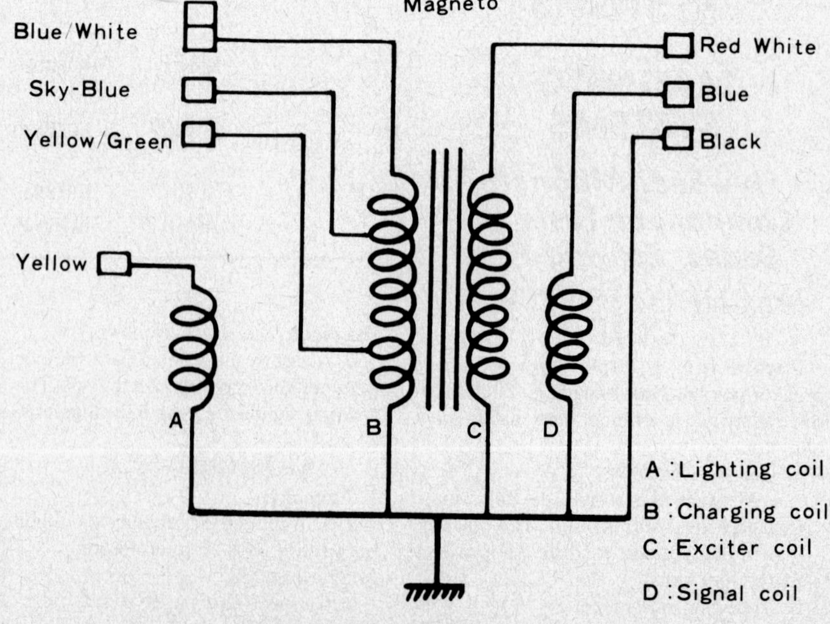

Magneto coils and coil leads

When testing the coils, be sure to disconnect the wires from the control unit, the rectifier, and the main switch. Resistance values are given in the accompanying table.

IGNITION COIL

Check the ignition coil with an ohmeter. Connect the meter to the terminals of each of the windings (primary and secondary), in turn. Resistance values are given in the accompanying table.

CONTROL UNIT

A special tester is necessary for checking the CDI control unit to avoid damage to the components. It is recommended that this operation be left to a Kawasaki dealer.

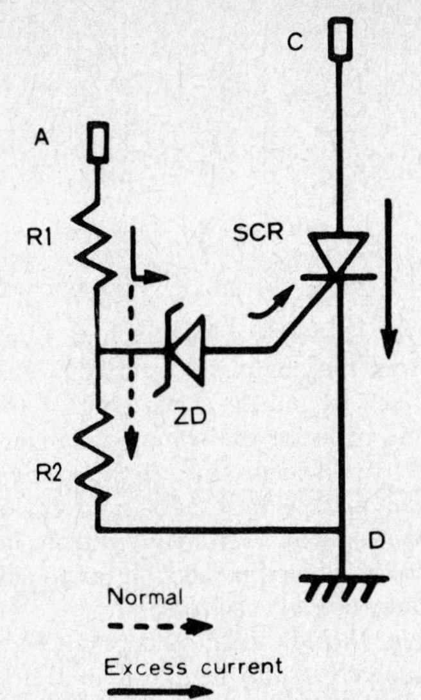

Voltage regulator wiring diagram (F7 and F5)

Voltage Regulator Service (F5)

PRECAUTIONS

1. Do not remove the rubber cap which projects from the regulator body. Do not loosen the nut in the rubber cap, which controls the rate of heat transfer of the rectifier.
2. Be sure to turn off the ignition before disconnecting any wiring.

TESTING

NOTE: *Use the accompanying illustration for reference when performing the following tests.*

Check for electrical continuity between points C and D by using a test light connected in series with a 6 volt battery or a multimeter with its own power source. Check continuity in both directions by reversing the test leads. Check also for continuity between the regulator case and point C. If continuity exists in any case, the regulator should be replaced.

STARTER/DC GENERATOR—B1L—A

Model B1L—A is equipped with a starter/dc generator unit rather than a magneto, as with other models. When the starter/generator acts as a starter, it converts electrical energy into mechanical energy. When it acts as a generator, it converts the mechanical energy of the engine into electrical energy. Its function is dependent upon the type of energy fed into it: electrical or mechanical. The starting/charging circuit, including the starter switch and regulator, is shown in the accompanying illustration.

Removal

1. Remove the shift lever.
2. Remove the engine left cover.
3. Unscrew the contact breaker cam mounting bolt and remove the cam.
4. Take out the screw and remove the yoke assembly.
5. Remove the armature from the end of the crankshaft using an armature puller.

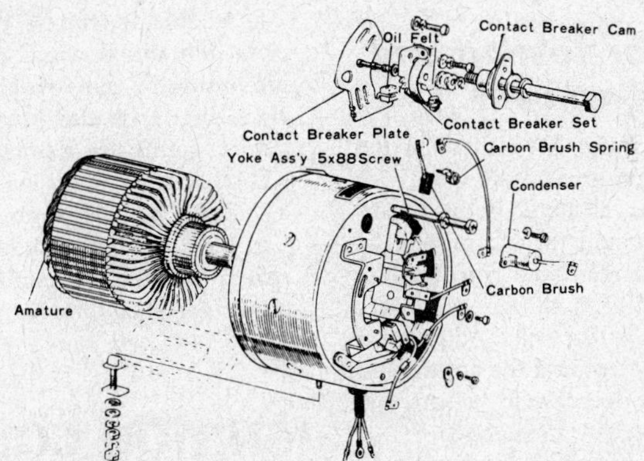

Starter/generator components (B1L-A)

MAGNETO COIL RESISTANCE (F7 AND F5)

Coils	Connection of Tester		Standard Resistance
Exciter Coil	Red/White	Black	220 Ω ± 10%
Signal Coil	Blue	Black	75 Ω ± 10%
Charging Coil	Blue/White	Black	0.23 Ω ± 10%
Lighting Coil	Yellow	Black	0.23 Ω ± 10%

IGNITION COIL RESISTANCE (F7 AND F5)

Coils	Connection of Tester		Standard Resistance
Primary Coil	Green/White	Black	0.21 Ω ± 10%
Secondary Coil	High voltage terminal	Black	1.8 Ω ± 10%

Service

YOKE ASSEMBLY

1. Check for electrical continuity between the positive brush and ground using a test light and battery or multimeter. Continuity indicates a short circuit at the brush holder or terminal D. (The negative brush is not insulated.)
2. Measure field coil resistance by connecting an ohmeter between terminals F and D. The reading should be 5–8 ohms.
3. Check for electrical continuity between terminal F and ground. If continuity exists, or if the reading obtained in step 2 was not within specifications, the yoke assembly should be replaced.
4. Remove and examine the brushes. If either brush is not making full contact or is worn excessively, both should be replaced. Make sure that they are free to slide in their holders.
5. When installing the brushes, make sure that the leads are not unintentionally short-circuited on the holders, springs, or other components.

ARMATURE

1. Check for electrical continuity be-

tween the armature core and the commutator. If continuity exists, the armature should be replaced.

2. Examine the commutator for wear and damage. It can be cleaned up using fine sandpaper or, if the damage is severe, it can be turned down on a lathe. The mica between the commutator segments should be undercut 0.02–0.04 in. with a hacksaw blade.

3. Thoroughly clean the armature before reinstalling it. Make sure that there is no grit between the commutator segments.

Installation

Installation is a reversal of the removal procedure. Note the following points:

1. Do not forget to install the woodruff key.

2. Install the carbon brushes and springs after the yoke assembly has been installed.

Regulator Testing and Adjustment

1. Disconnect the B terminal at the regulator. Do not ground the wire.

2. Connect a voltmeter between terminal B at the regulator and ground.

3. Start the engine and run it at approximately 2,500 rpm. The voltmeter should read 14.7–15.7 volts. Adjustment can be made by bending the adjustment spring up for a decrease in voltage and down for an increase in voltage.

NOTE: *The battery must be disconnected before performing any adjustments on the regulator.*

4. The cutout relay contacts should close at 12.5–13.5 volts. If adjustment is necessary, first clean the points and then bend the spring retainer up or down as required. Bending the retainer down will increase voltage.

Starter/DC Generator Fault Diagnosis

1. Starter does not turn engine over:

a. Check battery terminal connections and state of charge.

b. Switch on the headlight and press the starter button. If the headlight goes dim, it is likely that current is getting to the starter and the starter itself is faulty. If the light does not dim and a click can be heard at the regulator as the button is pressed, then the starter brushes or contact points of the starter switch are at fault. If a click is not heard at the regulator and normal voltage is available at the starter switch, it is probable that the starter switch coil is bad and the switch will have to be replaced.

2. Undercharging, as indicated by the charge light staying on, or overcharging:

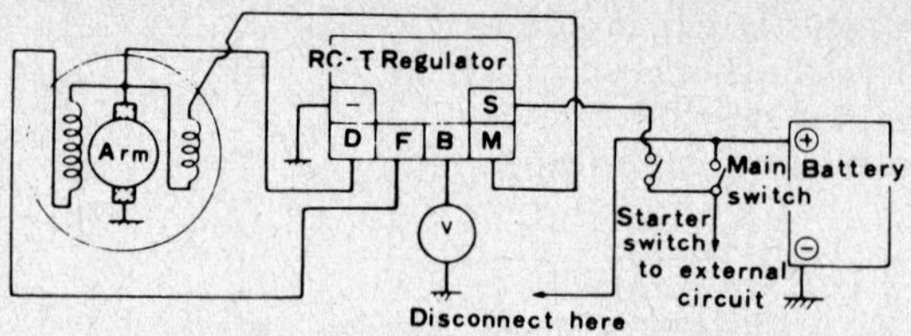

Voltage regulator test connections

a. Disconnect the D and F wires from the engine and start the engine.

b. Ground the F wire on the frame and measure the voltage between the D wire and ground. If the reading is above 13 volts at 2,200 rpm, the voltage regulator is probably at fault. Refer to the preceding section for regulator tests and adjustments.

c. If a low reading is obtained, it is likely that the field coil of the starter/dc generator is broken off or short-circuited.

3. Charge light dimly lit:

a. Regulator cutout points fail to close fully due to break-off of the coil, grounding of the regulator, or short-circuiting. It is also possible that the cutout points are damaged or out of adjustment.

4. Charge light flickers:

a. Most often due to the iminent destruction or short-circuiting of the generator or regulator coil.

IGNITION COIL (ALL MODELS)

The number of windings on the primary and secondary coils varies with the different engine models. If a coil is suspected of being faulty, the most reliable method of checking it on any magneto-equipped model is to check the spark produced at the spark plug. This can be accomplished by removing the plug, reconnecting the cable, and cranking the engine over with the ignition turned on, while grounding the plug body on the engine. A fat, hot spark should be produced.

The ignition coil of the B1L—A model can be checked either with the above method or using an electro-tester.

Rectifier (All Models B1L—A)

BIL—A)

PRECAUTIONS

1. Do not run the motorcycle with the battery removed or disconnected.

2. Do not run the motorcycle without the fuse being installed properly.

TESTING

1. Connect the negative lead from the battery (6 volt) to the blue/white wire on the rectifier.

2. Connect a test light between the positive battery lead and the brown wire on the rectifier.

3. If the bulb lights, the rectifier is defective and must be replaced.

4. Reverse the leads (negative battery lead to brown wire and positive lead to blue/white wire).

5. If the bulb does not light in this case, the rectifier should be replaced.

MULTICYLINDER MODELS (A SERIES, S SERIES AND H SERIES)

Alternator

An alternator is used on all twins, S Series and H1 models to keep the battery charged and to power the electrical components. Very basically, the alternator consists of field coil which rotates inside of—and induces a current in—a stator (armature) coil. The A, S and H1 models, with contact breaker point ignition systems, use a permanent, magnet-type field coil, while the A and H1 Series models with CD ignition use an electro magnetic field coil.

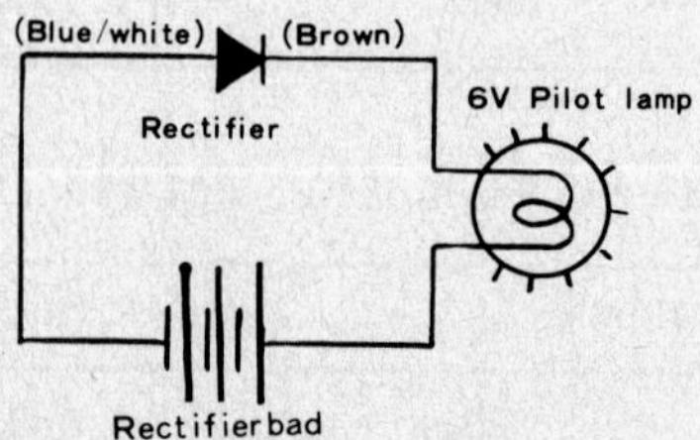

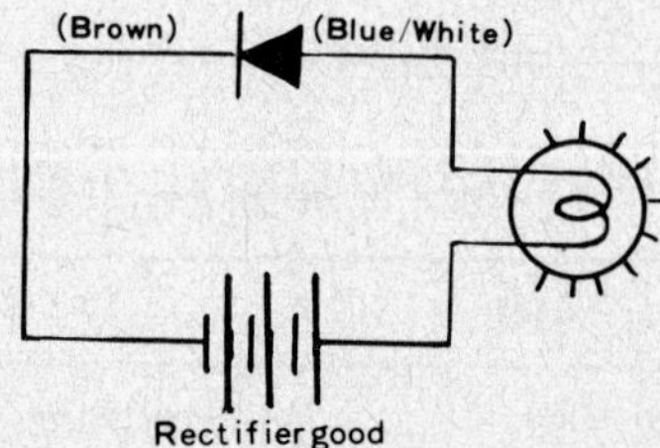

Rectifier test connections

ALTERNATOR SERVICE

1. Field coil:

a. Connect an ohmeter between the slip rings as shown in the accompanying illustration. Resistance should be within 3.5–5.5 ohms. If not, the field coil should be replaced.

Testing the field coil (A Series)

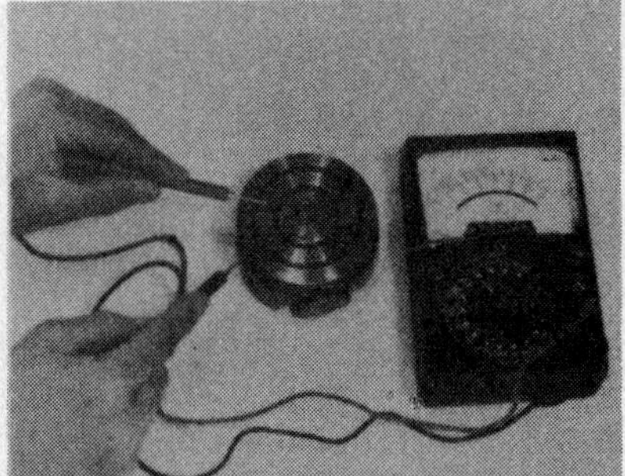

Testing the field coil (H1)

NOTE: *Use low-powered test equipment or else the field coil may be damaged.*

2. Stator (armature):

a. On the A Series with contact breaker ignition, check for electrical continuity between the two yellow wires and one green wire leading out of the alternator, as shown. If there is no continuity, one of the wires is broken or disconnected. Check for continuity between the yellow terminal and the alternator housing. Continuity indicates a short circuit between the stator and housing.

b. On A Series models with CD ignition systems, there is no way to test the stator with simple meters since the silicon diodes are assembled within it.

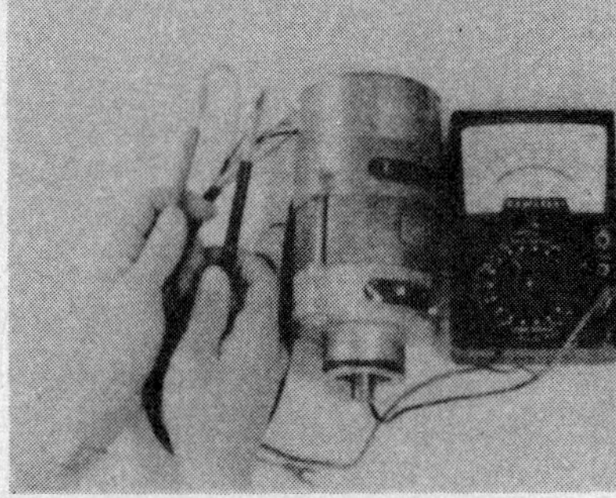

Testing the stator (A Series)

c. On S and H1 Series models, check for electrical continuity by connecting the tester between the three yellow wires (pink, yellow and white for S2) from the alternator, as shown. If there is no continuity, one of the wires is broken or disconnected. Check for continuity between the terminals and alternator housing. Continuity indicates a short circuit between the stator and housing.

Rectifier

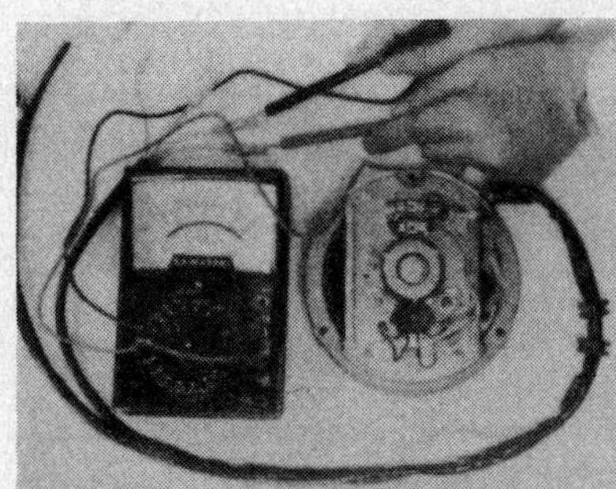

Testing the stator (H1)

RECTIFIER TESTS

A Series with Conventional Ignition

Using a test light and battery or multimeter, check the electrical continuity of the seven wires leading from the rectifier. The current should flow in the directions of red-yellow, and yellow-black. If it flows in the reverse direction, the rectifier is defective and should be replaced.

H1

Using a test light and battery or multimeter, check the electrical continuity of the six wires leading from the rectifier. The current should flow in the directions of red-yellow and yellow-black. (Yellow-black, blue-black, red-black, blue-yellow, and red-yellow on '72 models). If it flows in the reverse direction, the rectifier is defective and should be replaced.

Voltage Regulator SERVICE

A And S Series With Conventional Ignition

A silicon voltage regulator is used on the A and S Series models with contact breaker ignition. This regulator has no moving parts and should never require replacement.

Check for electrical continuity between points 2 and 3 using a test light connected in series with a 12 volt battery, or a multitester with its own power source. Check continuity in both directions by reversing the test leads. Check also for continuity between the regulator case and point 2. If continuity exists in any case, the regulator should be replaced.

H1 with Conventional Ignition

The H1 uses a sealed contact-type voltage regulator rather than the silicon type.

1. Measure the resistance between the battery wire (brown) and ground (black). A good regulator will give a reading of between 53 and 55 ohms. If the reading is less than this, usually coil B is at fault.

2. Connect a voltmeter between ground and the battery lead with the engine running at about 5000 rpm. If output voltage is 14–15 volts, the regulator is good; if less than this, the regulator may be bad, but first check the alternator before discarding the regulator.

A Series and H1 with CD Ignition

1. Internal short-circuit:

a. Check resistance at the four regulator terminals using an ohmeter after disconnecting the wires. The readings obtained should be approximately 29.5 ohms at terminals 1 and 2, 29.5 ohms at terminals 1 and 3, and 54.0 ohms at terminals 1 and 4. If the readings vary greatly from these specifications, the regulator should be replaced.

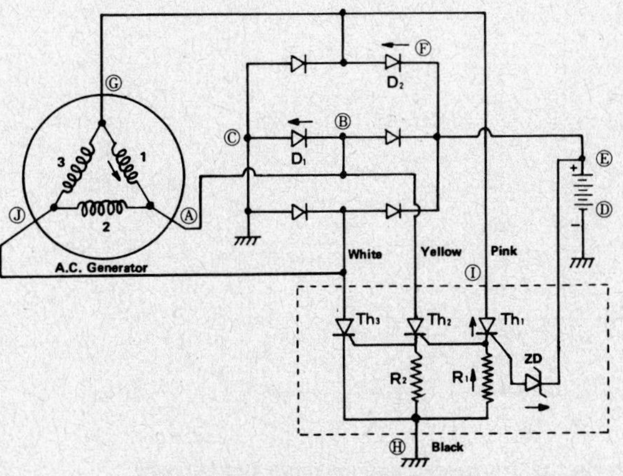

Voltage regulator circuit (S2)

2. Internal contact check:

a. Check battery voltage with a voltmeter, as shown, since engine speed is increased to 5,000 rpm. If the voltmeter indicates 14–15 volts, the voltage regulator is satisfactory.

CAPACITOR DISCHARGE IGNITION

SERVICE

Precautions

1. Do not reverse battery polarity.
2. Do not run the engine with the battery disconnected.
3. Take care to connect any wiring correctly. Improperly connected wiring can damage the CDI components.
4. The battery and ignition coil are matched to the CDI system. When replacement is necessary, use identical parts.
5. Make sure to install any rubber insulators correctly when a component has been removed and reinstalled.
6. The igniters (amplifiers) are sealed with epoxy and cannot be disassembled.

Testing The Igniter Units

Use the following illustration and tables to test ignitor units A and B singly and together.

H2

The H2 model is equipped with an electrical system different from any of the other models.

Whereas conventional CDI takes a low battery voltage and raises it to 370–500 volts with a converter, magneto CDI taps its high voltage directly from a special generator winding and then rectifies it. Another advantage is that magneto CDI can use the signal generator voltage directly, without amplification.

Magneto CDI also differs from conventional magneto ignition in that two primary ignition coils are used: one contains a high number of windings so that high voltage can be tapped at relatively low rpm, the other contains a low number of windings so that, as rpm rises, voltage can be produced quickly enough to fire the plugs properly.

In addition to the above, magneto CDI differs from the CDI used on other

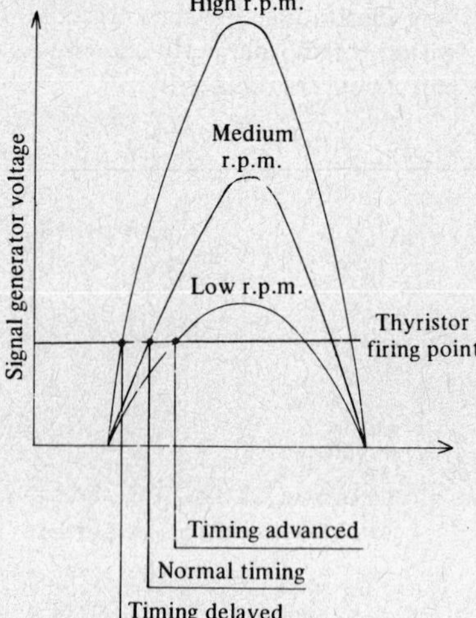

Magneto CDI timing advance curve

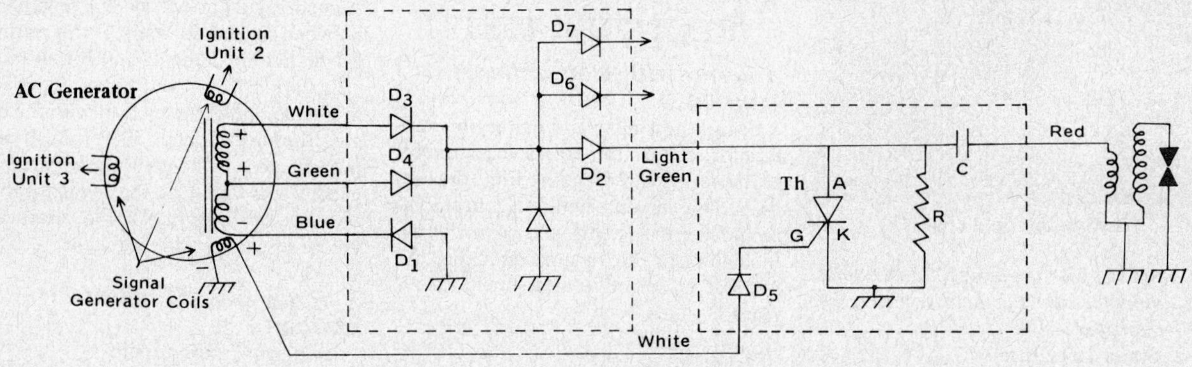

Magneto CDI schematic

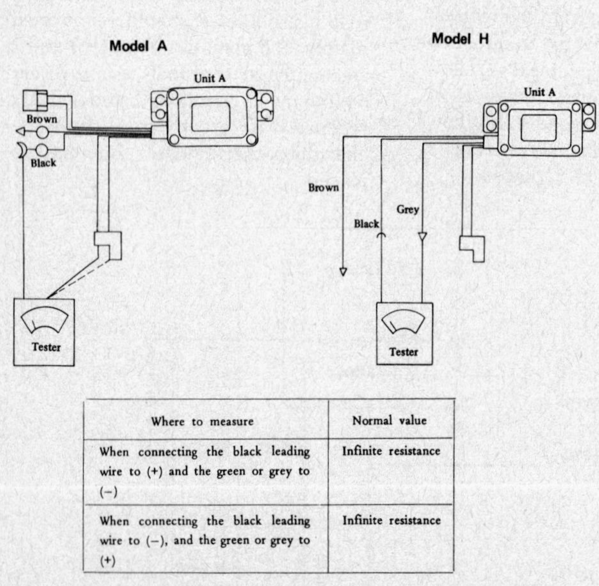

Where to measure	Normal value
When connecting the black leading wire to (+) and the green or grey to (−)	Infinite resistance
When connecting the black leading wire to (−), and the green or grey to (+)	Infinite resistance

Apply 12 volts to the brown lead and measure the current and voltage while grounding the black lead

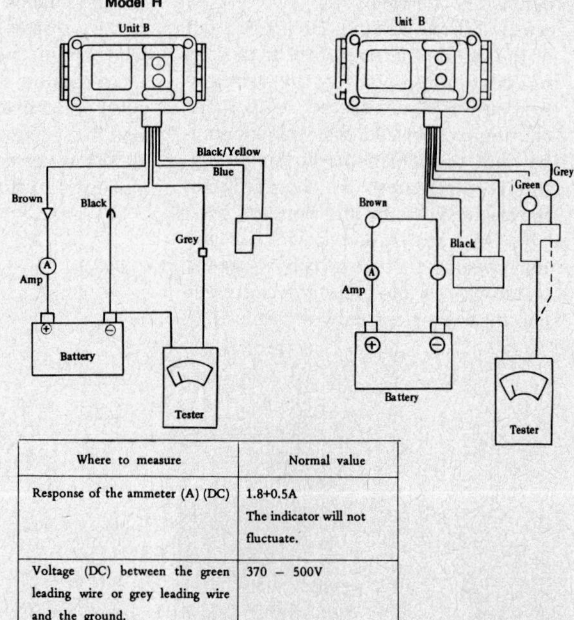

Where to measure	Normal value
Response of the ammeter (A) (DC)	1.8+0.5A The indicator will not fluctuate.
Voltage (DC) between the green leading wire or grey leading wire and the ground.	370 – 500V

Apply 12 volts to units A and B and check current and voltage while grounding the black wire

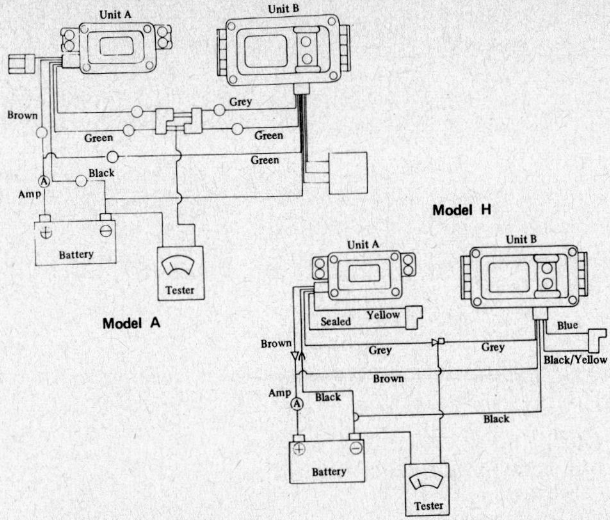

Check the units together, in the same manner as singly, if the earlier test did not show any faults

Kawasaki models in that 3 separate CDI units, one for each cylinder, are used.

Component tests are given in the accompanying illustrations.

NOTE:

1. In the following tests using an ohmmeter, some meters will have to be connected in reverse to obtain the correct readings.

2. "+" and "−" indicate the positive and negative meter leads, respectively.

3. All resistance readings in ohms (Ω) are approximate.

4. If meter readings do not correspond to the values given, the part can be considered defective.

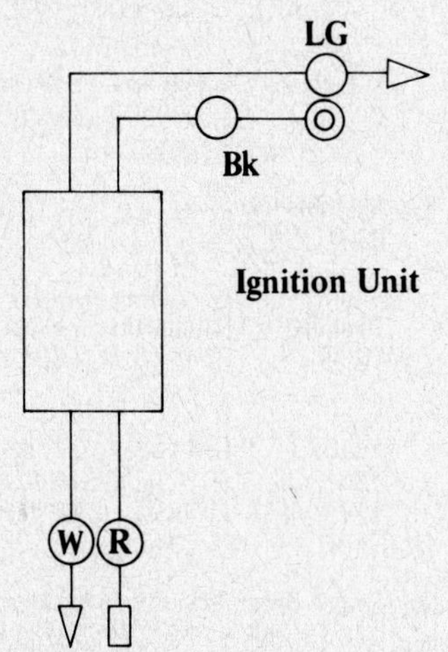

+ to Bk, − to LG	R = infinity (no reading)
− to Bk, + to LG	R = infinity

+ to LG, − to R	For either measurement the meter needle should jump and then return to infinity (no reading).
− to LG, + to R	

Ignition Unit

1. Check resistance between the black and light green wires using the "R×100" range of the ohmmeter.

2. Check resistance between the light green and red wires using the "R×100" range of the ohmmeter.

Ignition Rectifier Unit

1. Measure resistance between the black-white lead and the blue, white and green leads, one at a time, using the "R×10" ohmmeter range.

2. Measure the resistance between the black-white lead and each light-green wire in turn, using the "R×10" ohmmeter range.

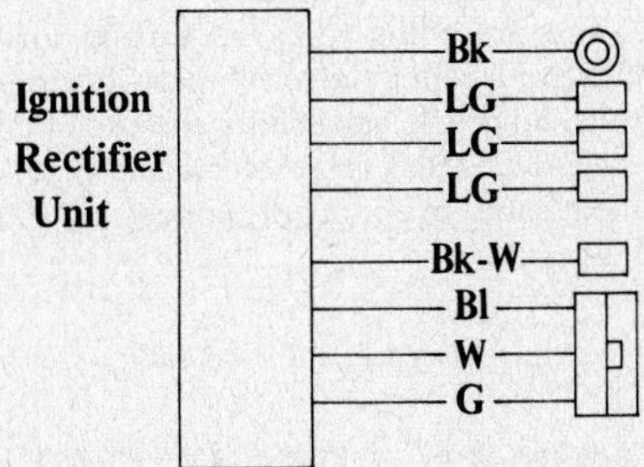

+ to Bk − W,	− to Bl	R = 35 Ω
	− to G	R = 35 Ω
	− to W	R = 90 Ω
− to Bk − W,	+ to Bl	R = infinity,
	+ to G	all three
	+ to W	readings

+ to Bk − W, − to LG	R = infinity (no reading)
− to Bk − W, + to LG	R = 35 Ω

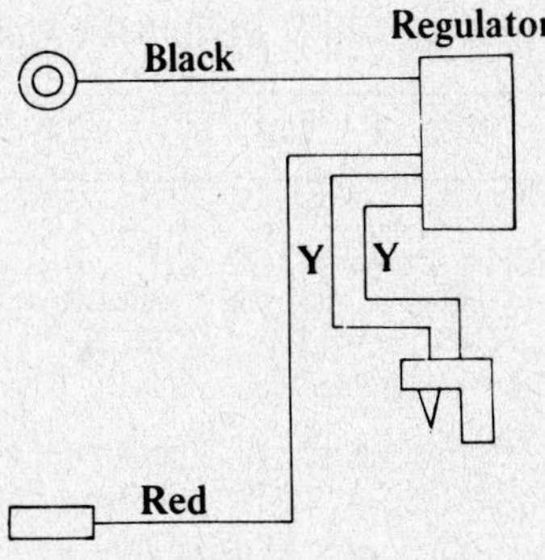

+ to Bk, − to Red	R = 70 Ω
− to Bk, + to Red	R = 1K Ω

+ to Bk, − to Y	R = 25 Ω
− to Bk, + to Y	R = 1K Ω

+ to R, − to Y	One Y lead:	R = 1K Ω
− to R, + to Y	Other Y lead:	R = 4K Ω
		R = 25 Ω

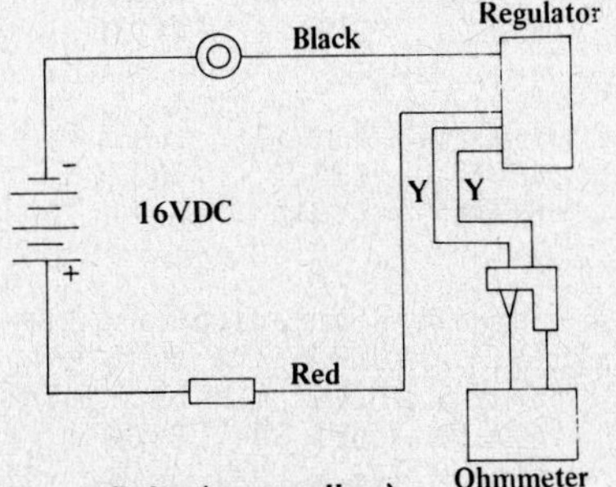

R = infinity (no reading) with test leads reversed R = 500Ω

R = infinity (no reading) with test leads reversed R = 500 Ω

R = infinity (no reading) either direction

Regulator

1. Measure the resistance between the black and red leads using the "R×10" range of the ohmmeter.

2. Measure resistance between the black lead range.

3. Measure resistance between the red lead and each yellow lead using the "R×10" ohmmeter range.

4. Connect the battery voltage indicated (−) to the black lead and (+) to the red lead. Then measure resistance between the two yellow leads.

AC Generator

Generator resistance readings should be taken with the generator at normal temperatures, not when it is excessively hot from running,

1. Resistance between the two yellow leads is 0.4Ω.

2. Resistance between either yellow lead and ground should be infinite (no reading).

3. Resistance between the blue and green leads is 5.0Ω.

4. Resistance between the black lead and each white lead is 200Ω; (Signal generator test)

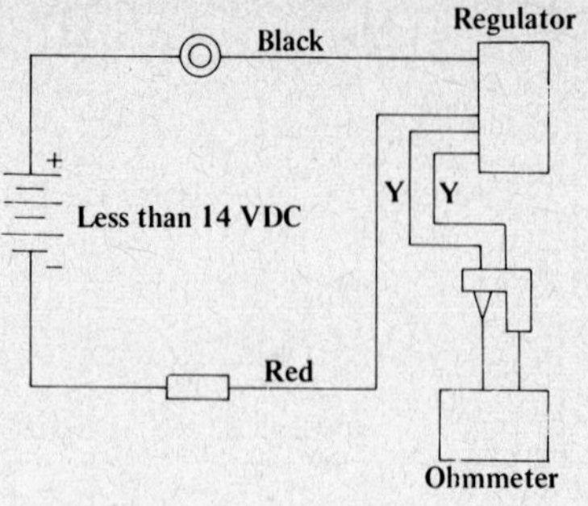

R = infinity (no reading) either direction

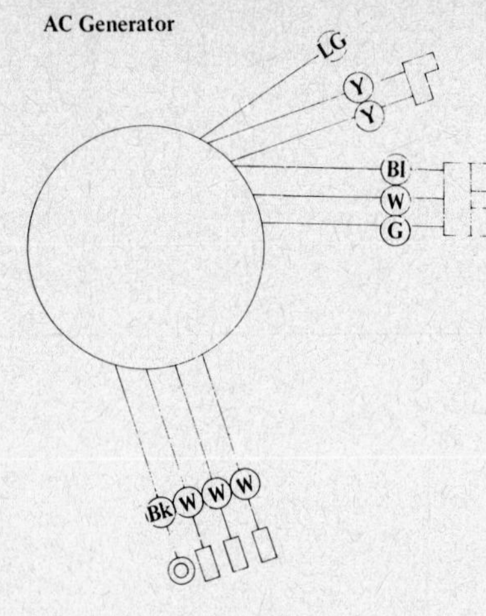

Ignition Coil

1. Resistance between the white lead and the core is 0.8Ω.

2. If an inductance tester is available, inductance between the white lead and the core is 2.5 mh, and between the plug wire and core it is 14h.

The preceding tests are usually sufficient to locate a defective part. Further tests, however, necessitate the use of an oscilloscope and other electronic equipment and are not explained in this manual.

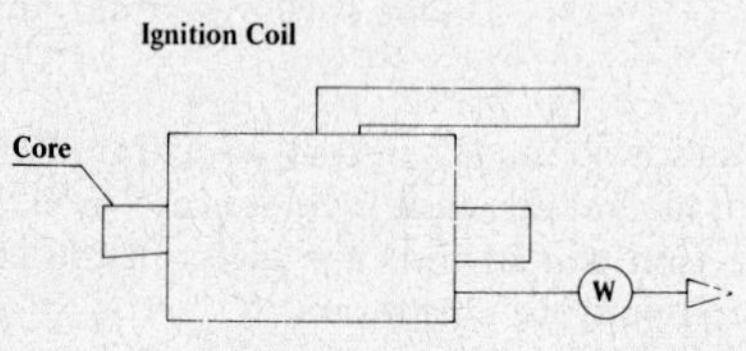

ELECTRICAL SPECIFICATIONS

GA1-A, GA2-A, G3SS-A, G3TR-A, G4TR, G31M-A, B1L-A, F6, F7

	GA1—A	GA2—A	G3SS—A	G3TR—A	G4TR	G31M—A	B1L—A	F6	F7
GENERATOR or MAGNETO									
Made by	Kokusan	Kokusan	Kokusan	Kokusan	Kokusan	Kokusan	Mitsubishi	Mitsubishi	Kokusan
Type	FE101	FE101	FE109	FE109	FE109	NJ 101	CE-TIR	F-6079BL	HM-01
REGULATOR									
Made by	—	—	—	—	—	—	Mitsubishi	—	—
Type	—	—	—	—	—	—	RC-T	—	—
IGNITION COIL									
Made by	Kokusan	Kokusan	Kokusan	Kokusan	Kokusan	Kokusan	Diamond	Mitsubishi	Kokusan
Type	ST94	ST94	ST98	ST98	ST 98	ST 98	TU-25	HD-D	SU 101
BATTERY									
Made by	Furukawa	Furukawa	Furukawa	Furukawa	Furukawa	—	Yuasa	Furukawa	Furukawa
Type	6N4-2A-3	6N4-2A-3	6N4-2A-3	6N4-2A-5	6N2-2A-5	—	12N12-3B	6N4-2A-5	6N4-2A-5
Capacity	6V 4AH	6V 4AH	6V 4AH	6V 4AH	6V 2AH	—	12V 12AH	6V 4AH	6V 4AH
LAMP BULBS									
Head Lamp Type	Semi-Sealed	Semi-Sealed	Sealed Beam	Sealed Beam	Sealed Beam	—	Sealed Beam	Sealed Beam	Sealed Beam
Head Lamp Bulb	67 25/25W	6V 25/25W	6V 25/25W	6V 25/25W	6V 25/25W	—	12V 35/35W	6V 25/25W	6V 35/35W
Brake/Tail Lamp Bulb	67 17/5. 3W	6V 17/5. 3W	6V 17/5. 3W	6V 17/5. 3W	6V 17/5. 3W	—	12V 20/5W	67 17/5. 3W	6V 17/5. 3W
Speedometer Lamp Bulb	6V 1. 5W	6V 1. 5W	6V 1. 5W	6V 1. 5W	6V 3W	—	12V 3W	6V 3W	6V 3W
Neutral Indicator Lamp Bulb	6V 1. 5W	6V 1. 5W	6V 1. 5W	6V 1. 5W	6V 3W	—	12V 1. 5W	6V 3W	6V 3W
Tachometer Indicator Lamp Bulb	—	—	—	—	—	—	—	6V 3W	6V 3W
Top Indicator Lamp Bulb	—	—	—	—	—	—	12V 1. 5W	—	—
Charge Indicator Lamp Bulb	—	—	—	—	—	—	12 1. 5W	—	—
High-Beam Indicator Bulb	—	—	6V 1. 5W	6V 1. 5W	6V 1. 5W	—	—	6V 1. 5W	6V 1. 5W
Turn Signal Lamp Bulb	6V 8W	6V 8W	6V 8W	6V 8W	6V 8W	—	12V 8V	6V 8W	6V 8W

F8, F81M, F5, A1 Conventional, A1 CDI, A1SS Conventional, A1SS CDI, A1R Conventional, A1R CDI

	F8	F81M	F5	A1 Convent.	A1 CDI	A1SS Convent.	A1SS CDI	A1R Convent.	A1R CDI
GENERATOR or MAGNETO									
Made by	Kokusan	Kokusan	Kokusan	Kokusan	Mitsubishi	Kokusan	Mitsubishi	Kokusan	—
Type	FP 6309	X 016	HM-01	EN10	AW2010A	EN10	AW2010A	EN04	—
REGULATOR									
Made by	—	—	Kokusan	Kokusan	Mitsubishi	Kokusan	Mitsubishi	—	—
Type	—	—	ZR910(SVR)	ZR 905	RL2128T	ZR 905	RL2128T	—	—
IGNITION COIL									
Made by	Kokusan	Kokusan	Kokusan	Diamond	Diamond	Diamond	Diamond	Kokusan	—
Type	IG 3125	IG 3125	SU 101	TU-25M-7	TU-51-1	TU-25M-7	TU-51-1	ST-70	—
BATTERY									
Made by	Furukawa	—	Furukawa	12N 6-4 A	12V 6AH	12N 6-4 A	12V 6AH	—	—
Type	6N2-2A-5	—	6N2-2A-5						
Capacity	6V 2AH	—	6V 2AH						
LAMP BULBS									
Head Lamp Type	Sealed Beam	—	Sealed Beam	Semi-Sealed		Semi-Sealed		—	
Head Lamp Bulb	6V 35/35W	—	6V 35/35W	12V, 35/25W		12V, 35/25W		—	
Brake/Tail Lamp Bulb	6V 17/5. 3W	—	6V 17/5. 3W	12V, 8/25W		12V, 8/25W		—	
Speedometer Lamp Bulb	6V 3W	—	6V 3W	(4/32 cp)		(4/32 cp)		—	
Neutral Indicator Lamp Bulb	6V 3W	—	6V 3W	12V, 3W		12V, 3W		—	
Tachometer Indicator Lamp Bulb	6V 3W	—	6V 3W	12V, 3W		12V, 3W		—	
Top Indicator Lamp Bulb	—	—	—	12V, 3W		12V, 3W		—	
Charge Indicator Lamp Bulb	—	—	—	—		—		—	
High-Beam Indicator Bulb	6V 1. 5W	—	6V 1. 5W	12V, 1.5W		12V, 1.5W		—	
Turn Signal Lamp Bulb	6V 8W	—	6V 8W	12V, 8W		12V, 8W		—	

A7 Conventional, A7 CDI, A7SS Conventional, A7SS CDI, A7R Conventional, A7R CDI, S2, H1 Conventional, H1 CDI, H2

	A7 Convent.	A7 CDI	A7SS Convent.	A7SS CDI	A7R Convent.	A7R CDI	S2	H1 Convent.	H1 CDI	H2
GENERATOR										
Made by	Kokusan	Mitsubishi	Kokusan	Mitsubishi	Kokusan	—	Kokusan	Mitsubishi	Mitsubishi	Mitsubishi
Type	EN8	AW2010A	EN8	RL2128T	EN04	—	AR2101	AZ-2010M	AZ-2010A	F-6061DL
REGULATOR										
Made by	Kokusan	Mitsubishi	Kokusan	Mitsubishi	—	—	Kokusan	Mitsubishi	Mitsubishi	Mitsubishi
Type	ZR 905	RL2128T	ZR 905	AM2010A	—	—	RS-2114	RL-2128T	RL-T	X006T30171
IGNITION COIL										
Made by	Diamond	Diamond	Diamond	Diamond	Kokusan	—	Diamond	Diamond	Diamond	Mitsubishi
Type	TU-25M-7	TU-51-1	TU-25M-7	TU-51-1	ST-70	—	TU-29M-14	TU-25	TU-51-2	F006T00171
BATTERY										
Made by							Furukawa			Furukawa
Type	12N 6-4 A	12V 6AH	12N 6-4 A	12V 6AH	—	—	12N5.5-4A	12N 9-4B	12V 9AH	12N5.5-4A
Capacity							12V, 6AH			12V 6AH
LAMP BULBS										
Head Lamp Type	Semi-Sealed		Semi-Sealed		Semi-Sealed		Sealed Beam	Semi-Sealed		Sealed Beam
Head Lamp Bulb	12V, 35/25W		12V 35/25W		—		12V, 35/25W	12V 35/25W		12V, 35/25W
Brake/Tail Lamp Bulb	12V, 8/25W (4/32 cp)		12V, 8/25W (4/32 cp)		—		12V, 8/23W	12V, 8/25W (4/32 cp)		12V, 8/23W

ELECTRICAL SPECIFICATIONS

A7 Conventional, A7 CDI, A7SS Conventional, A7SS CDI, A7R Conventional, A7R CDI, S2, H1 Conventional, H1 CDI, H2

	A7 Convent.	A7 CDI	A7SS Convent.	A7SS CDI	A7R Convent.	A7R CDI	S2	H1 Convent.	H1 CDI	H2
Speedometer Lamp Bulb	12V, 3W		12V, 3W		—		12V, 3WX2	12V, 3W		12V, 3WX2
Neutral Indicator Lamp Bulb	12V, 3W		12V, 3W		—		12V, 3W	12V, 3W		12V, 3W
Tachometer Indicator Lamp Bulb	12V, 3W		12V, 3W		—		12V, 3WX2	12V, 3W		12V, 3WX2
Charge Indicator Lamp Bulb	—		—		—		—	12V, 3W		—
High-Beam Indicator Bulb	—		12V, 1.5W		—		12V, 1.5W	12V, 1.5W		12V, 15W
Turn Signal Lamp Bulb	12V, 8W		12V, 8W		—		12V, 23WX4	12V, 8W		12V, 23WX4

WIRING DIAGRAMS

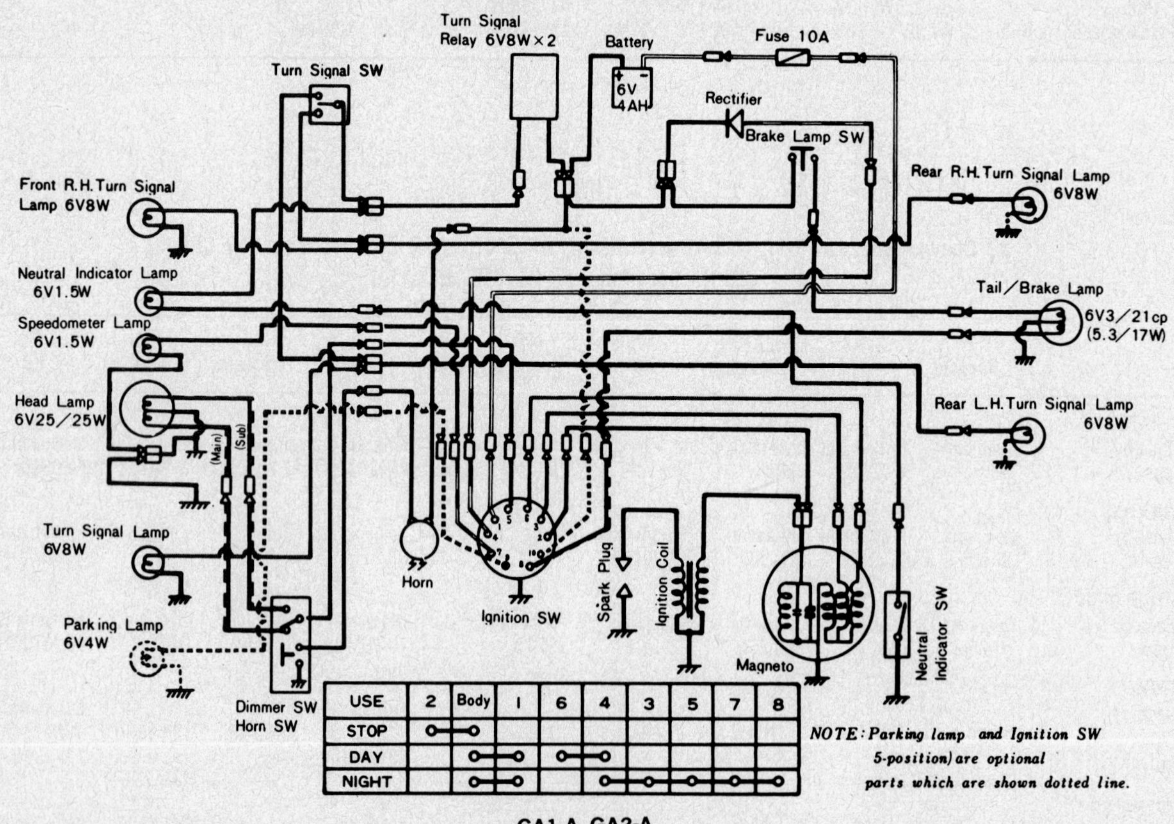

GA1-A, GA2-A

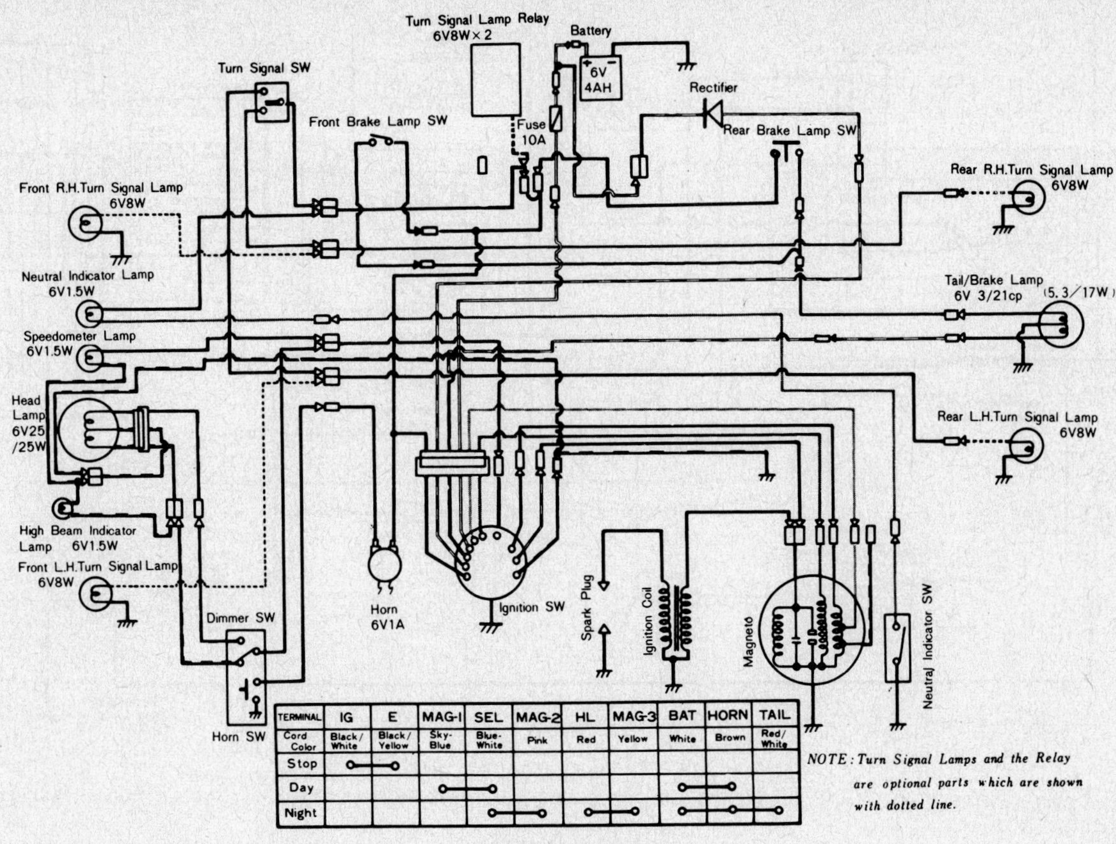

TERMINAL	IG	E	MAG-1	SEL	MAG-2	HL	MAG-3	BAT	HORN	TAIL
Cord Color	Black/White	Black/Yellow	Sky-Blue	Blue-White	Pink	Red	Yellow	White	Brown	Red/White
Stop	o	o								
Day			o	o				o	o	
Night				o	o	o	o	o	o	o

NOTE: Turn Signal Lamps and the Relay are optional parts which are shown with dotted line.

G3TR-A, G3SS-A

Battery
6V
2AH
Rectifier
Front Brake Lamp SW
Rear Brake Lamp SW
Fuse
10A
Neutral Indicator Lamp
6V3W
Speedometer Lamp
6V3W
Tail/Brake Lamp
6V 3/21cp
(5.3/17W)
High Beam Indicator Lamp
6V1.5W
Head Lamp
6V25/25W
Spark Plug
Ignition Coil
Horn
6V1A
Ignition SW
Dimmer SW
Magneto
Neutral Indicator SW
Horn SW

TERMINAL	IG	E (ground)	MAG-1	SEL	MAG2	HL	MAG3	BAT	HORN	TAIL
Cord Color	Black	Black/Yellow	Sky-Blue	Blue/White	Pink	Red	Yellow	White	Brown	Red/White
Stop	o	o								
Day			o	o				o	o	
Night				o	o	o	o	o	o	o

G4TR

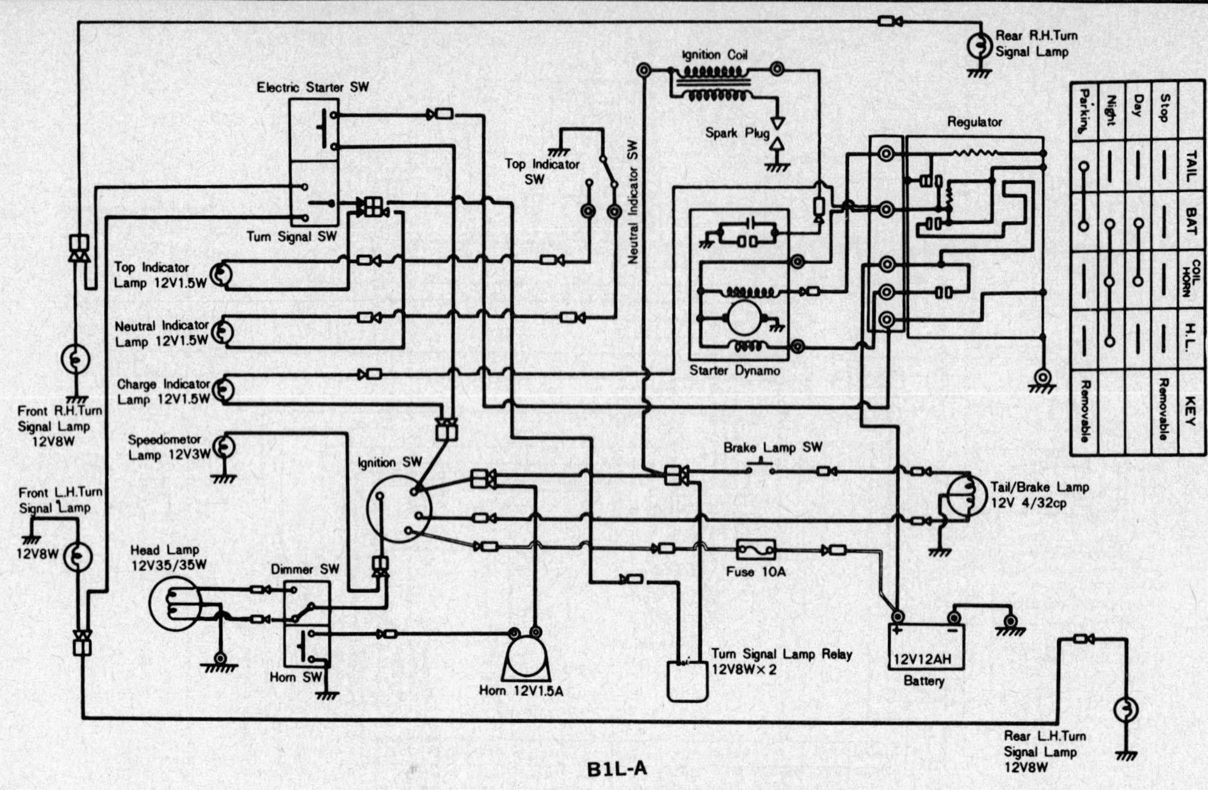

B1L-A

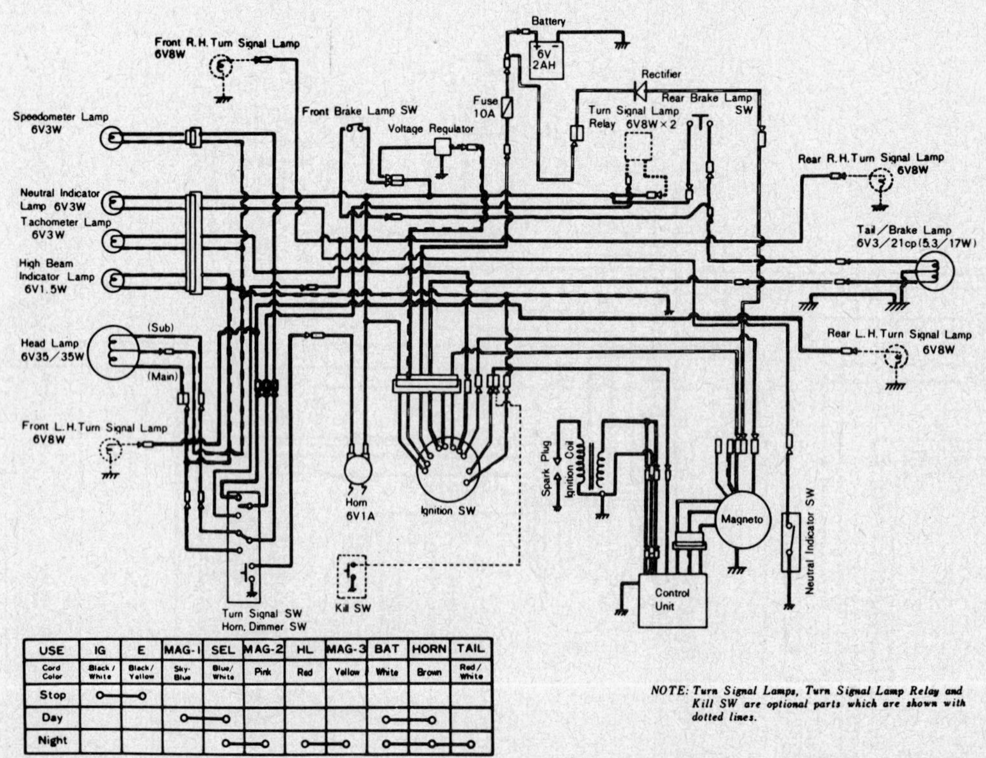

USE	IG	E	MAG-1	SEL	MAG-2	HL	MAG-3	BAT	HORN	TAIL
Cord Color	Black/White	Black/Yellow	Sky-Blue	Blue/White	Pink	Red	Yellow	White	Brown	Red/White
Stop	o—	—o								
Day			o—	—o				o—	—o	
Night				o—	—o	o—	—o	o—	—o—	—o

NOTE: Turn Signal Lamps, Turn Signal Lamp Relay and Kill SW are optional parts which are shown with dotted lines.

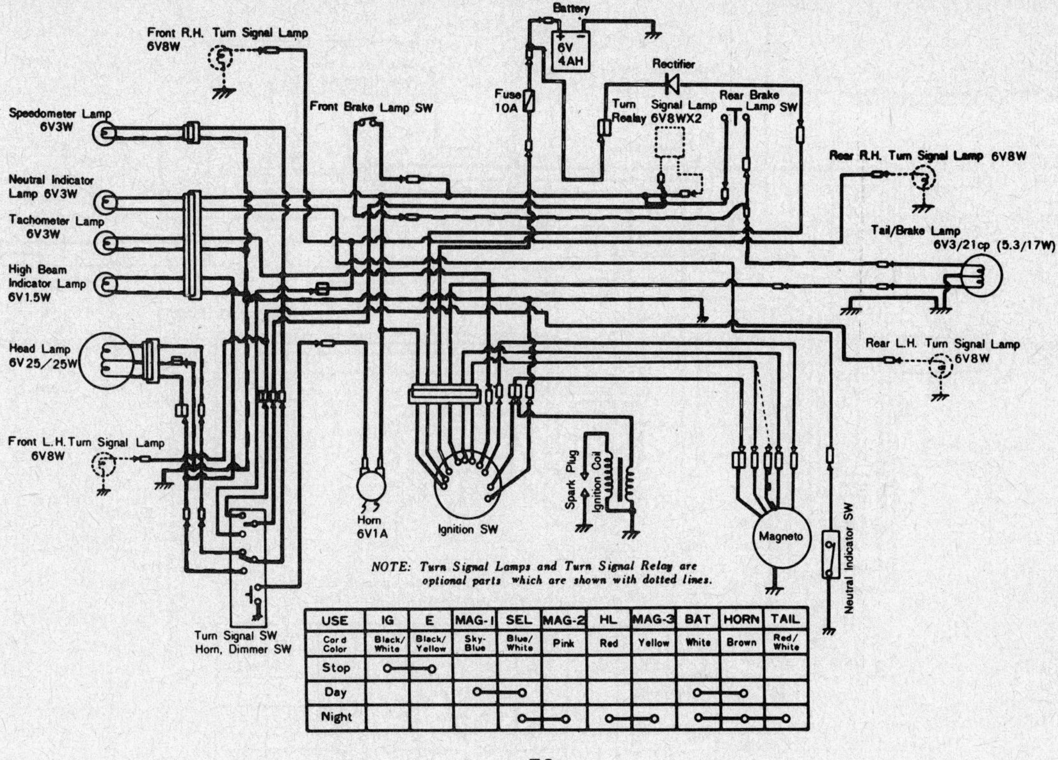

USE	IG	E	MAG-I	SEL	MAG-2	HL	MAG-3	BAT	HORN	TAIL
Cord Color	Black/White	Black/Yellow	Sky-Blue	Blue/White	Pink	Red	Yellow	White	Brown	Red/White
Stop	○	○								
Day			○	○				○	○	
Night				○	○	○	○	○	○	○

F6

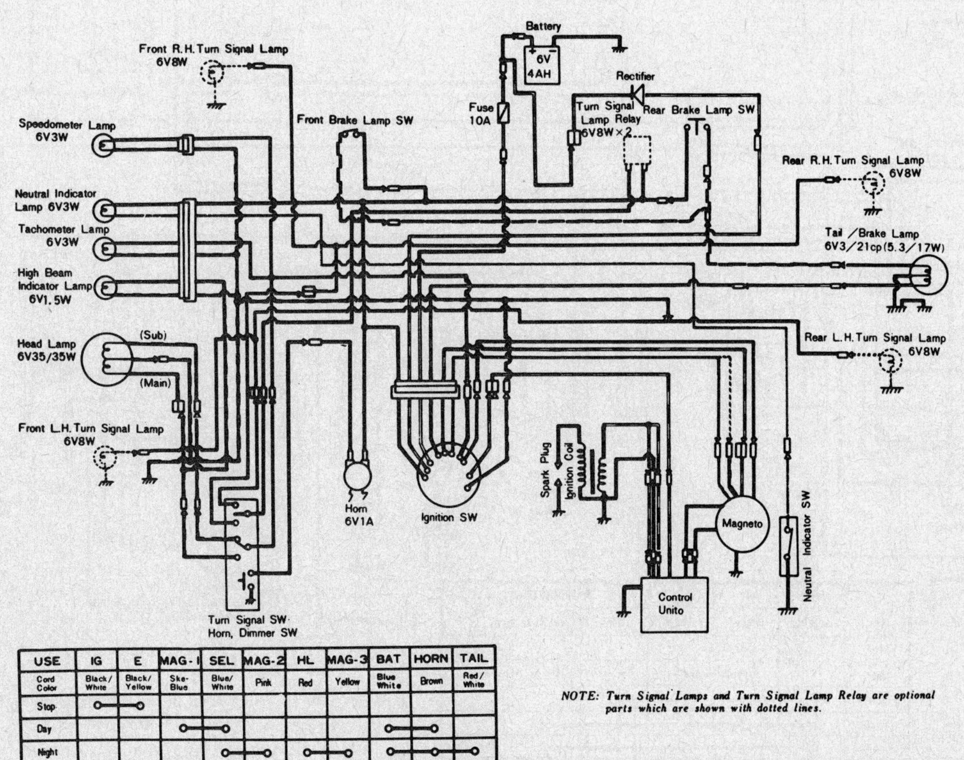

USE	IG	E	MAG-I	SEL	MAG-2	HL	MAG-3	BAT	HORN	TAIL
Cord Color	Black/White	Black/Yellow	Ske-Blue	Blue/White	Pink	Red	Yellow	Blue White	Brown	Red/White
Stop	○	○								
Day			○	○				○	○	
Night				○	○	○	○	○	○	

F7

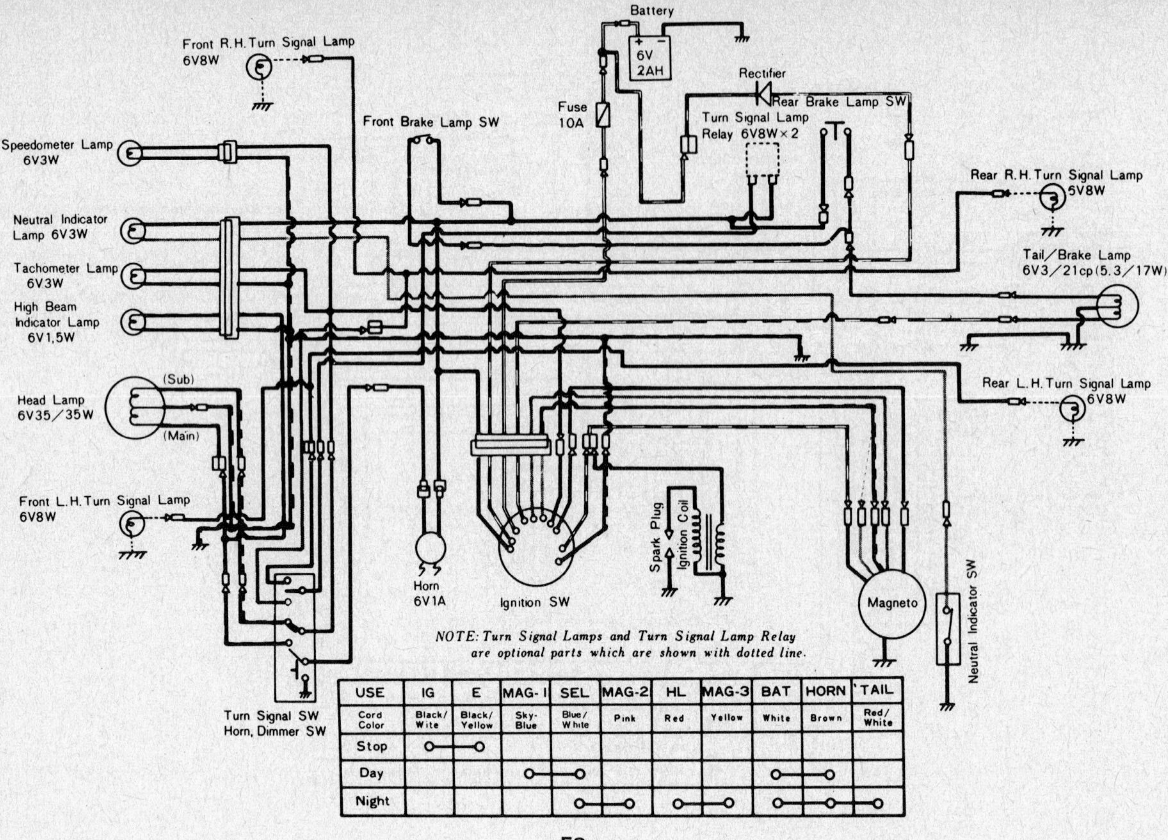

USE	IG	E	MAG-1	SEL	MAG-2	HL	MAG-3	BAT	HORN	TAIL
Cord Color	Black/White	Black/Yellow	Sky-Blue	Blue/White	Pink	Red	Yellow	White	Brown	Red/White
Stop	O	O								
Day			O	O				O	O	
Night				O	O	O	O	O	O	O

F8

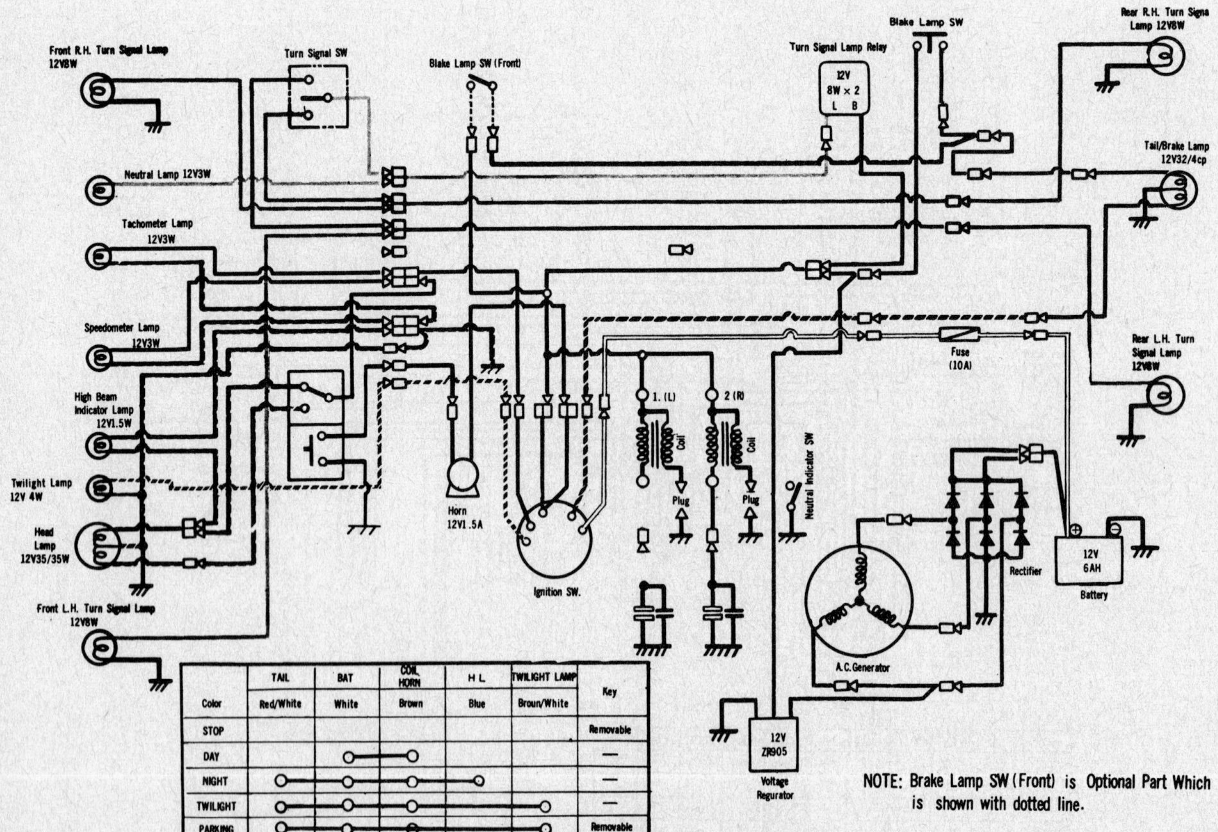

	TAIL	BAT	COIL, HORN	HL	TWILIGHT LAMP	Key
Color	Red/White	White	Brown	Blue	Broun/White	
STOP						Removable
DAY		O	O			—
NIGHT	O	O	O	O		—
TWILIGHT	O	O	O		O	—
PARKING	O	O	O		O	Removable

A Series with contact breaker ignition

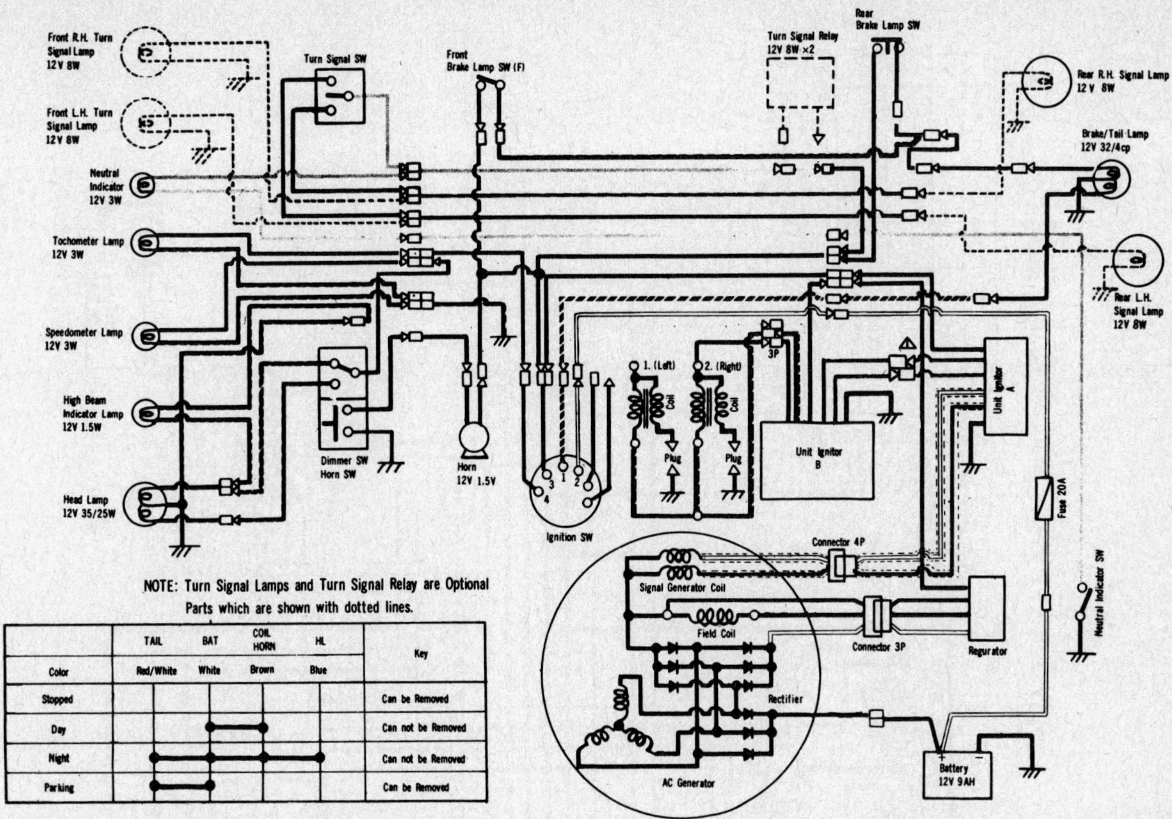

	TAIL	BAT	COIL HORN	HL	Key
Color	Red/White	White	Brown	Blue	
Stopped					Can be Removed
Day		●	●		Can not be Removed
Night	●	●	●	●	Can not be Removed
Parking	●	●			Can be Removed

A Series with CDI

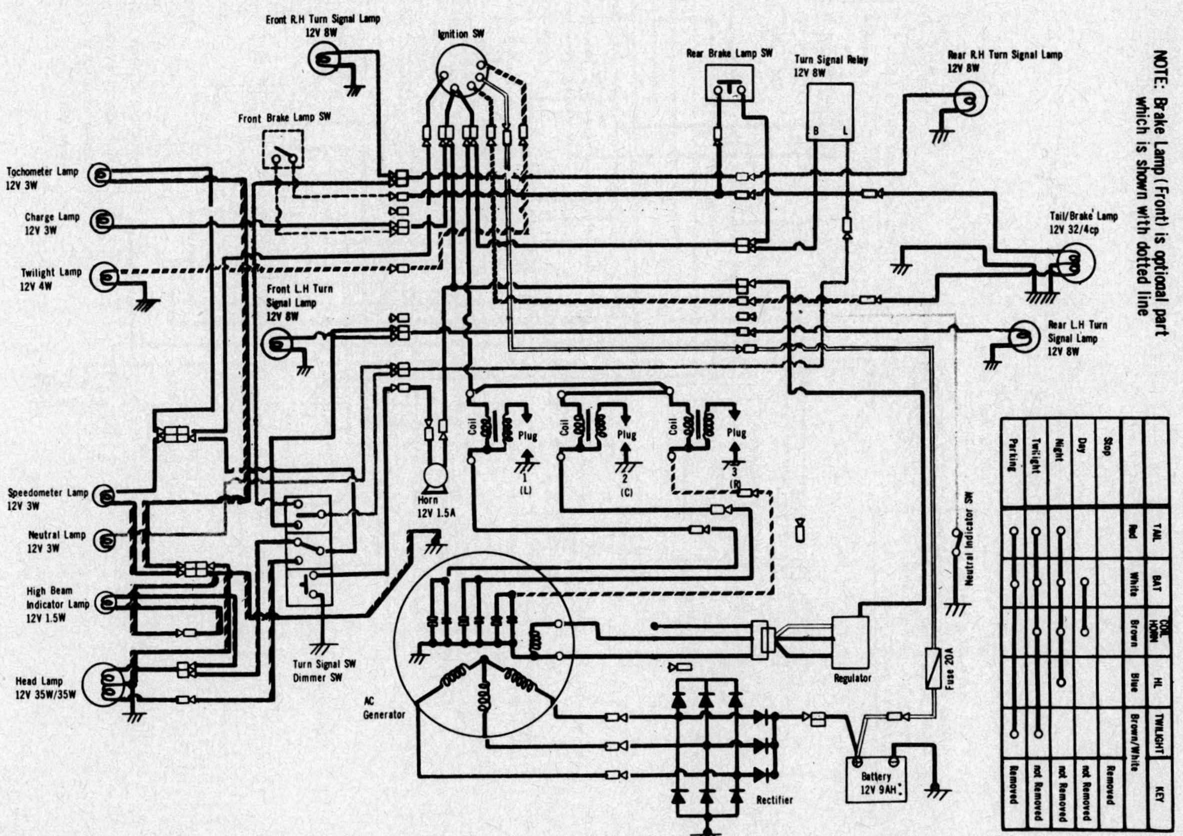

	TAIL	BAT	COIL HORN	HL	TWILIGHT	KEY
	Red	White	Brown	Blue	Brown/White	
Stop						Removed
Day		●	●			not Removed
Night	●	●	●	●		not Removed
Twilight	●	●	●		●	not Removed
Parking	●	●			●	Removed

H Series with contact breaker ignition

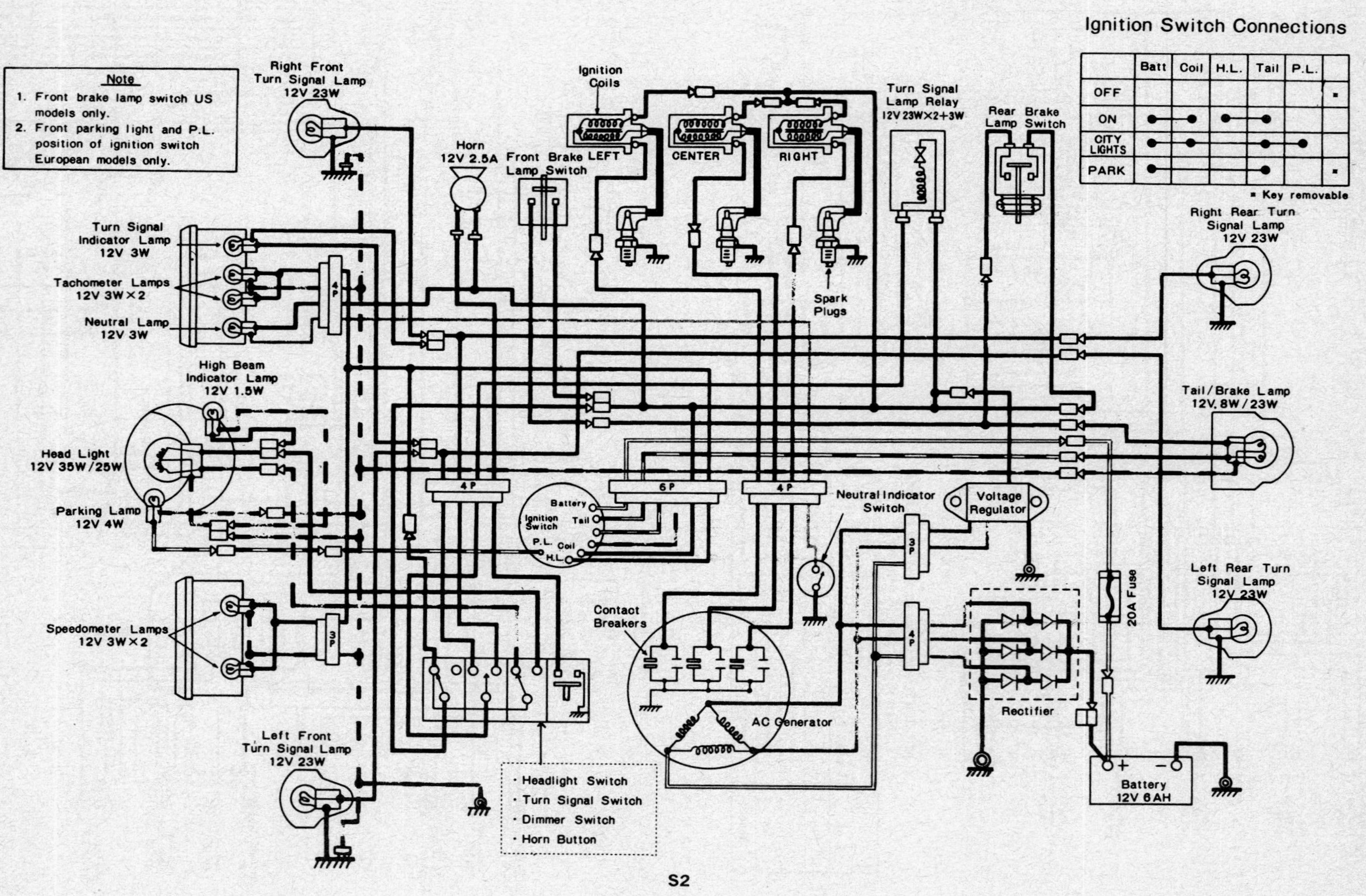
Note
1. Front brake lamp switch US models only.
2. Front parking light and P.L. position of ignition switch European models only.
Right Front Turn Signal Lamp 12V 23W
Horn 12V 2.5A
Front Brake Lamp Switch
Ignition Coils
LEFT
CENTER
RIGHT
Turn Signal Lamp Relay 12V 23W×2+3W
Rear Brake Lamp Switch
Ignition Switch Connections
Batt
Coil
H.L.
Tail
P.L.
OFF
ON
CITY LIGHTS
PARK
■ Key removable
Right Rear Turn Signal Lamp 12V 23W
Turn Signal Indicator Lamp 12V 3W
Tachometer Lamps 12V 3W×2
Neutral Lamp 12V 3W
Spark Plugs
High Beam Indicator Lamp 12V 1.5W
Tail/Brake Lamp 12V 8W/23W
Head Light 12V 35W/25W
4P
6P
3P
Battery
Ignition Switch
Tail
P.L.
Coil
H.L.
Neutral Indicator Switch
Voltage Regulator
Parking Lamp 12V 4W
Left Rear Turn Signal Lamp 12V 23W
20A Fuse
Speedometer Lamps 12V 3W×2
Contact Breakers
Rectifier
AC Generator
Left Front Turn Signal Lamp 12V 23W
Battery 12V 6AH
· Headlight Switch
· Turn Signal Switch
· Dimmer Switch
· Horn Button
S2

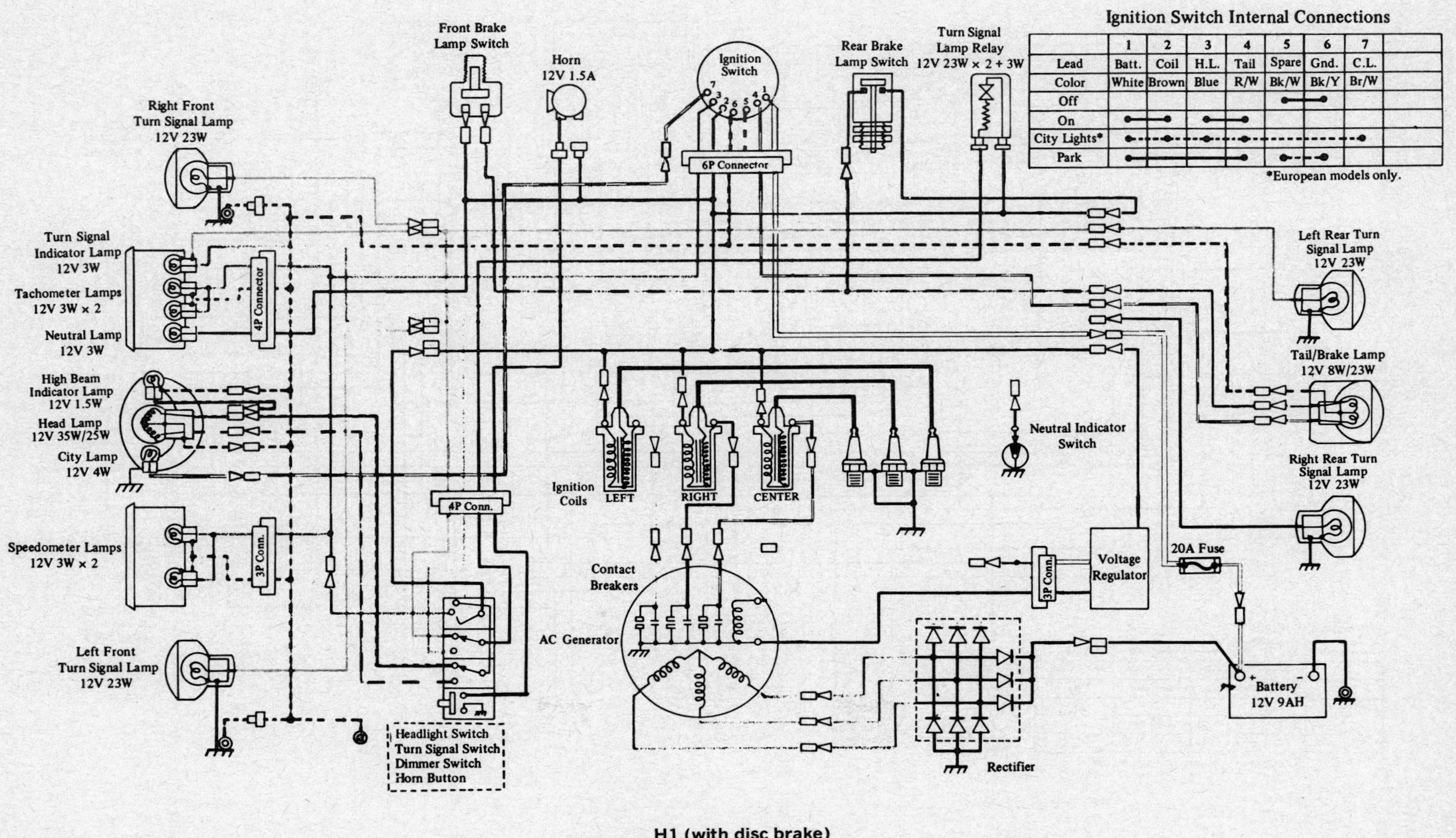

	1	2	3	4	5	6	7
Lead	Batt.	Coil	H.L.	Tail	Spare	Gnd.	C.L.
Color	White	Brown	Blue	R/W	Bk/W	Bk/Y	Br/W
Off					●—	—●	
On	●—	—●	●—	—●			
City Lights*	●- - -	- - -●- - -	- - -●- - -	- - -●- - -	- - -	- - -	- - -●
Park	●—	—●—	—●—	—●	●- - -	- - -●	

*European models only.

H1 (with disc brake)

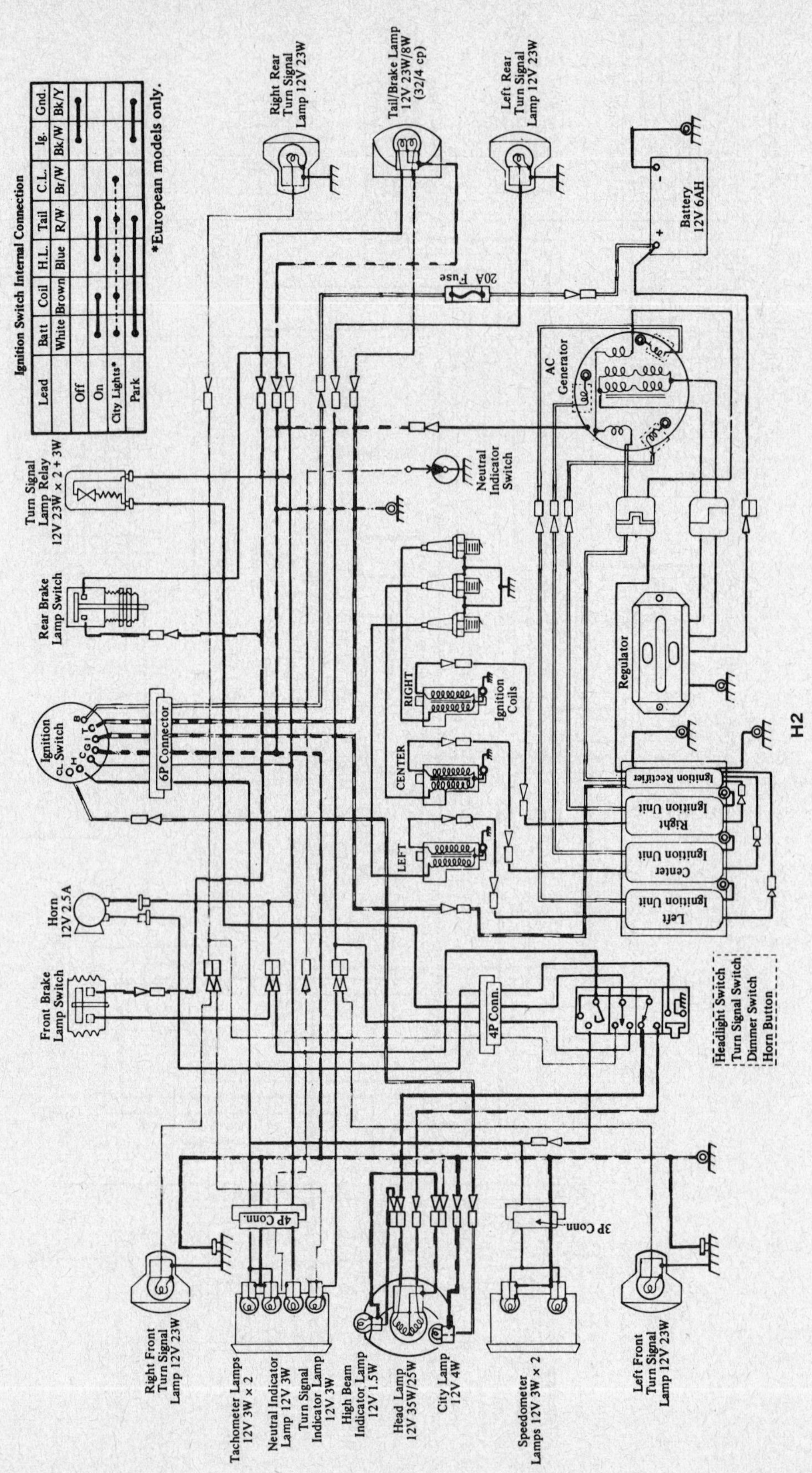
Ignition Switch Internal Connection
Lead
Batt White
Coil Brown
H.L. Blue
Tail R/W
C.L. Br/W
Ig. Bk/W
Gnd. Bk/Y
Off
On
City Lights*
Park
*European models only.
Right Rear Turn Signal Lamp 12V 23W
Tail/Brake Lamp 12V 23W/8W (32/4 cp)
Left Rear Turn Signal Lamp 12V 23W
Battery 12V 6AH
20A Fuse
AC Generator
Turn Signal Lamp Relay 12V 23W × 2 + 3W
Neutral Indicator Switch
Rear Brake Lamp Switch
Ignition Coils
RIGHT
CENTER
LEFT
Regulator
Ignition Switch
6P Connector
Ignition Rectifier
Right Ignition Unit
Center Ignition Unit
Left Ignition Unit
H2
Horn 12V 2.5A
Front Brake Lamp Switch
4P Conn.
Headlight Switch
Turn Signal Switch
Dimmer Switch
Horn Button
3P Conn.
Right Front Turn Signal Lamp 12V 23W
Tachometer Lamps 12V 3W × 2
Neutral Indicator Lamp 12V 3W
Turn Signal Indicator Lamp 12V 3W
High Beam Indicator Lamp 12V 1.5W
Head Lamp 12V 35W/25W
City Lamp 12V 4W
Speedometer Lamps 12V 3W × 2
Left Front Turn Signal Lamp 12V 23W

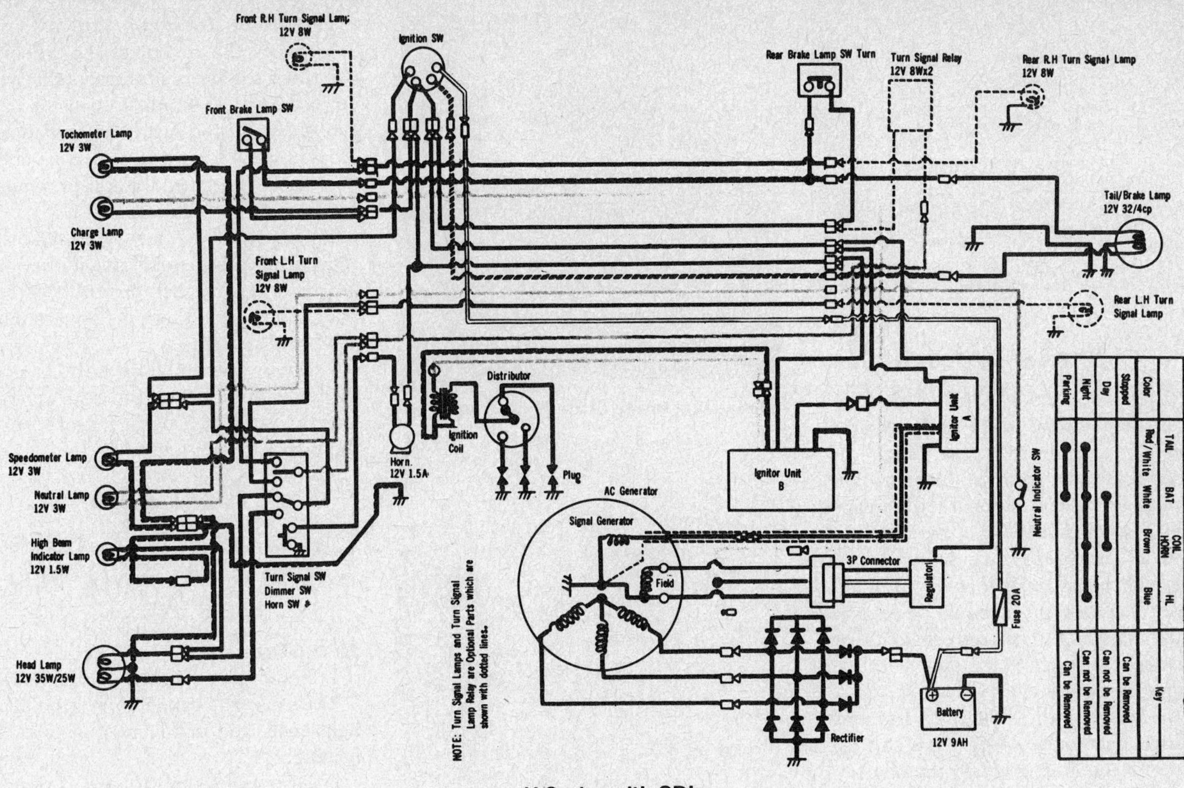

H Series with CDI

CHASSIS

SINGLE-CYLINDER MODELS

Wheel Removal

FRONT

1. Loosen the brake adjusting nut and remove the brake cable.
2. Loosen the speedometer cable nuts and remove the cable.
3. Place a stand under the engine and loosen the axle shaft nut. Do not remove the nut because it is caulked in the axle shaft.
4. Pull out the shaft and remove the wheel. On the F5 and F8, the torque arm is separated from the front fork. Remove this arm when taking off the front wheel.

REAR

1. Remove the brake adjusting nut and remove the brake cable from the lever.
2. Disconnect the torque link.
3. Take out the screws and remove the chainguard. Remove the master link clip and separate and remove the chain.

NOTE: *It is not necessary to remove the chainguard on the GA and B1L models.*

4. Pull the axle shaft out of the hub after loosening the nut. Do not remove the nut.
5. Take out the spacer and remove the rear wheel assembly.

Wheel Installation

Installation is a reversal of the removal procedure. Note the following points:

1. The brake lever should be installed so that the cable and lever are at right angles when the brake is applied.
2. Apply a small amount of grease to the brake lever and cam bushings in the brake panel before reassembly.
3. Install the master link clip on the chain so that its closed end faces in the direction of forward rotation.
4. Adjust the brake and stop light switch, if necessary, after installation.

Standard Drum Inside Diameters (G Series, BIL-A, and F Series)

Model	Standard Value	Repair Limit
G Series	4.33 in. (110 mm)	4.36 in. (110.75 mm)
G31M—A F6, F7	5.12 in. (130 mm)	5.15 in. (130.75 mm)
B1L—A, F8 F81M, F5	5.91 in. (150 mm)	5.94 in. (150.75 mm)

Lining Thicknesses (G Series, BIL-A, and F Series)

Model	Standard Value	Repair Limit
G Series F6, F7	0.138 in. (3.5 mm)	0.079 in. (2 mm)
B1L—A, F8 F81M, F5	0.197 in. (5 mm)	0.118 in. (3 mm)

Free Length of Brake Shoe Spring (G Series, BIL-A, and F Series)

Model	Standard Value	Repair Limit
G Series F6, F7	1.23 in. (31.2 mm)	1.34 in. (34.0 mm)
B1L—A	1.87 in. (47.5 mm)	1.97 in. (50.0 mm)
F8, F81M F5	1.89 in. (48.0 mm)	2.01 in. (51.0 mm)

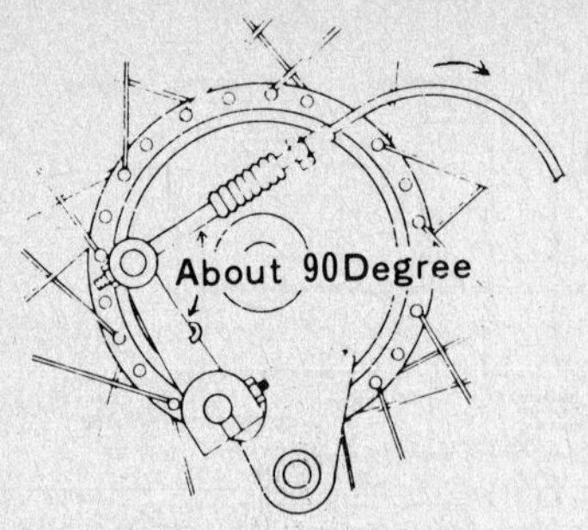

Brake Service

1. Remove the wheel.
2. Remove the brake shoes by prying them away from the brake panel.
3. Measure the inside diameter of the brake drum and compare the reading with the specifications in the chart.
4. If the brake shoe lining is worn beyond the limit shown, or if it is cracked or broken, the shoes should be replaced.
5. If the lining is glazed or making uneven contact, correct the fault with sandpaper or emery cloth.
6. Measure the length of the brake spring and replace it if it has stretched beyond the limit given in the chart.
7. Clearance between the brake cam shaft and the brake panel bushing should not exceed 0.02 in. (0.5 mm). If it does, replace parts as necessary.

Gaps Between the Brake Camshaft and the Bushing (G Series, BIL-A, and F Series)

Model	Standard Value	Repair Limit
All	0.0008 ~ 0.0028 in. (0.02 ~ 0.07 mm)	0.02 in. (0.5 mm)

Measuring brake drum inside diameter

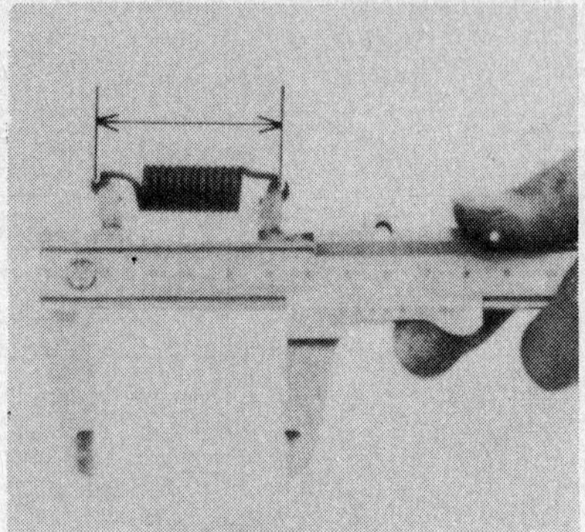
Measuring brake spring free length

Wheel Bearing Service

1. Remove the wheel(s).
2. Drive the oil seal and outer bearing out of the hub from the inner side of the brake drum.
3. Insert the drift from the outside of the brake drum and drive out the inner bearing. Remove the bearing uniformly to avoid damaging the hub.
4. Measure the runout of the axle shaft and repair or replace it if it is bent more than 0.016 in. (0.4 mm).
5. Check the runout of the wheel at the rim also. Maximum acceptable runout is 0.12 in. (3.0 mm).
6. Examine the bearings for damage. Measure axial and radial clearance of the bearings and replace them if the specification limit is exceeded.
7. Use a new oil seal if possible and replace the oil seal metal ring if it is worn.
8. Examine the damper rubbers (rear hub) and replace them if they are damaged or distorted.
9. When reassembling the hub, press or drive the bearings and seal squarely into the housing. Do not forget to pack the bearings with grease.

Front Fork

GA1—A, GA2—A, G3SS—A, G3TR—A, AND B1L—A

Removal

1. Remove the front wheel and fender.
2. Unsnap the connectors in the headlight shell, and unbolt and remove the headlight.
3. Disconnect the cables and remove the speedometer and tachometer.
4. Loosen the lower triple clamp pinch bolts and remove the top filler bolts.
5. Withdraw the forks downward from the clamps.

Disassembly

1. Remove the dust seal, spring, dust boots, and spring guide. Drain the oil from the fork legs.
2. Place the fork leg in a vise, that is protected with strips of rubber, and clamp the jaws on the outer tube nut.

NOTE: *Do not use excessive pressure or the tube will be distorted.*

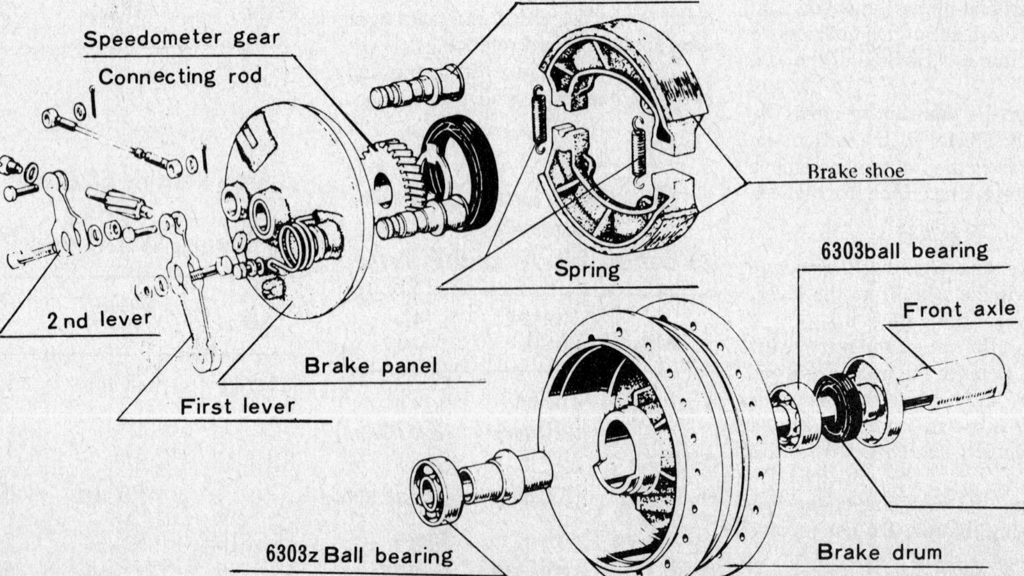

Front hub components

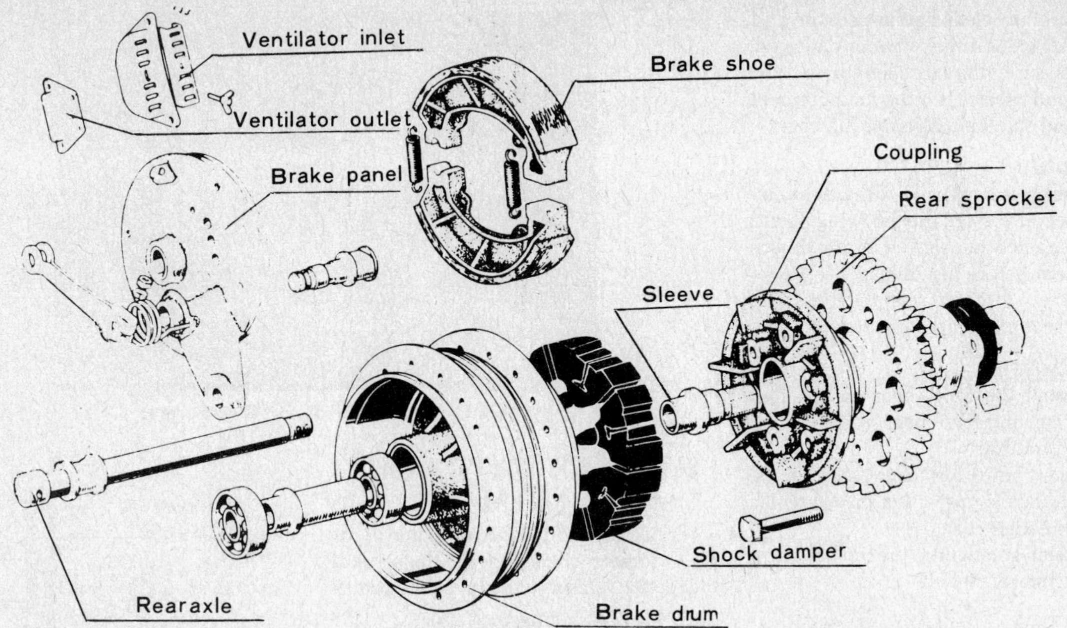

Rear hub components

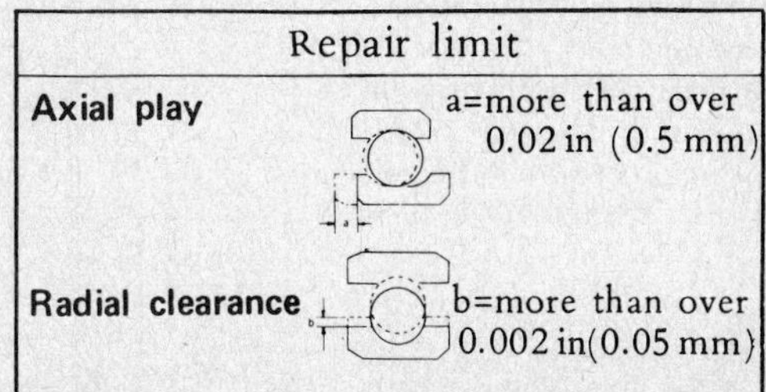

Repair limit	
Axial play	a=more than over 0.02 in (0.5 mm)
Radial clearance	b=more than over 0.002 in(0.05 mm)

Wheel bearings (G Series, B1L-A, and F Series)

Lower triple clamp pinch bolt

Protect the fork leg with rubber

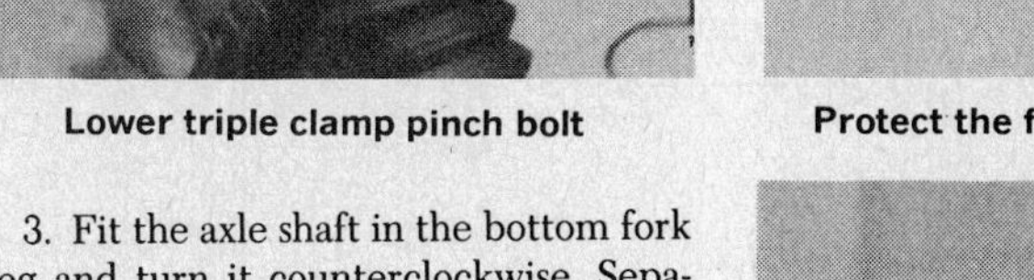

3. Fit the axle shaft in the bottom fork leg and turn it counterclockwise. Separate the inner tube and bottom fork leg.

Inspection

1. Insert the inner tube into the bottom fork leg and install the slide. Check to make sure that the inner tube slides smoothly, with a minimum of play. If clearance is excessive, replace the tube.
2. Examine the inner tube for wear and scratches, which can ruin the oil seal. Repair or replace as necessary. Make sure that the tube is not bent.

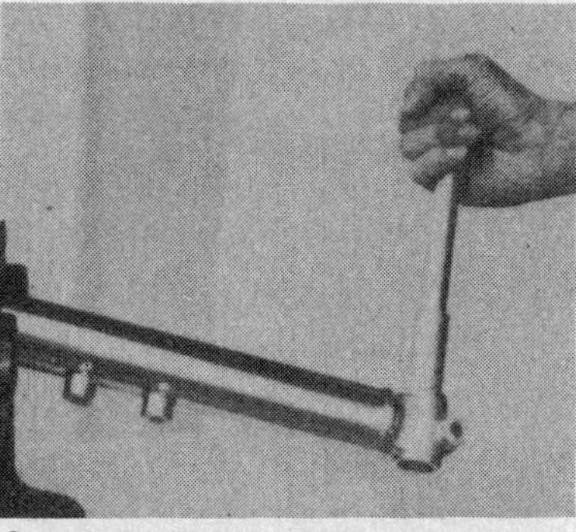

Separating the fork tube and lower leg

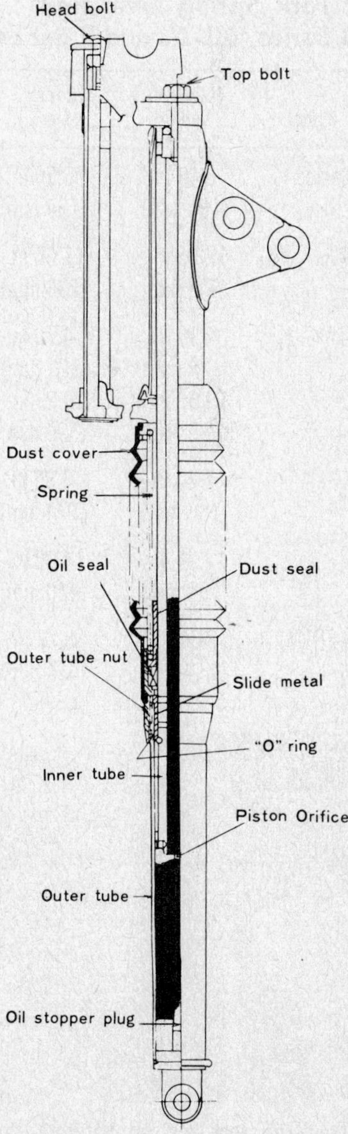

Cross section of the fork leg

3. Carefully clean and inspect the dust seal. Replace it if it is worn or damaged.

4. Measure the free-length of the spring and replace it if the measurement is beyond the limit given in the chart.

Assembly

Assembly is a reversal of the disassembly procedure. Note the following points:

1. Use a new oil seal and O-ring. Lubricate them before installation.
2. Do not forget to refill the forks with the correct grade and amount of oil.

Installation

1. Install the fork cover gasket, fork cover ring, and fork cover to the bottom clamp assembly.
2. Insert the fork and pull it up through the clamps with a special tool (a long, threaded rod).
3. Install and tighten the top bolt, then tighten the pinch-bolt.

Fork Spring Freelength (G Series, BIL-A, and F Series)

Model	Standard Value	Repair Limit
G Series	6.46 in. (164 mm)	6.06 in. (154 mm)
G4TR	12.05 in. (306 mm)	11.65 in. (296 mm)
G31M—A,	4.96 in. (126 mm)	4.76 in. (121 mm)
F7	13.63 in. (346 mm)	13.23 in. (336 mm)
B1L—A	7.24 in. (184 mm)	6.85 in. (174 mm)
F6	12.29 in. (490 mm)	18.90 in. (480 mm)
F8, F81M, F5	18.66 in. (474 mm)	18.27 in. (464 mm)

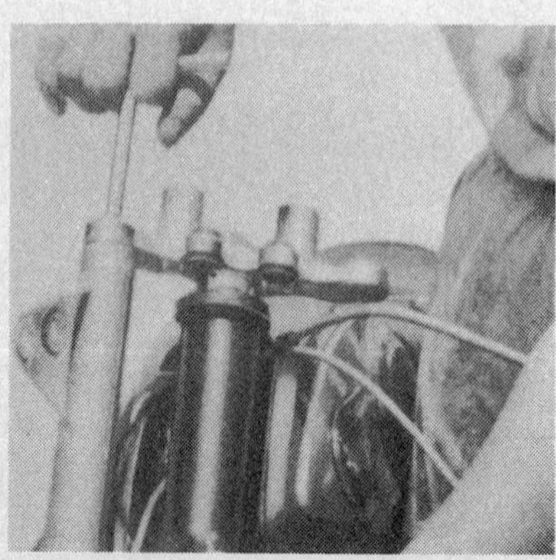

Pulling the fork leg up through the clamps (using the special tool)

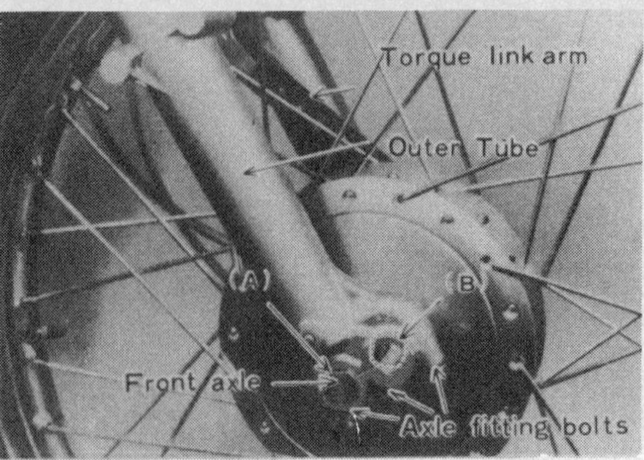

Front axle positions A and B (F Series)

F SERIES, G4TR, AND G31M

Service procedures are the same as for the G Series models. Refer to the preceding section. Observe the following procedure when installing the forks:

1. Place the headlight brackets and insulating rubber between the upper and lower triple clamps, insert the forks, and tighten the mounting bolts.
2. The three lines on the inner tube should be symmetrically adjusted according to the adjusting procedure in the following section.

Front axle positions A and C (F Series)

FORK ADJUSTMENT—F5, F7, F8, AND G31M—A

Front Axle Position

A is the standard position.

Position B increases caster and reduces trail, resulting in faster steering and less stable operation at high speeds. This position is suitable for relatively low-speed operation where light, quick steering is an asset.

Position C is the most desirable setting for high-speed riding, where slow steering and stability are necessary.

In any case, do not forget to install the torque line and remember to make sure that the link bolts are secured.

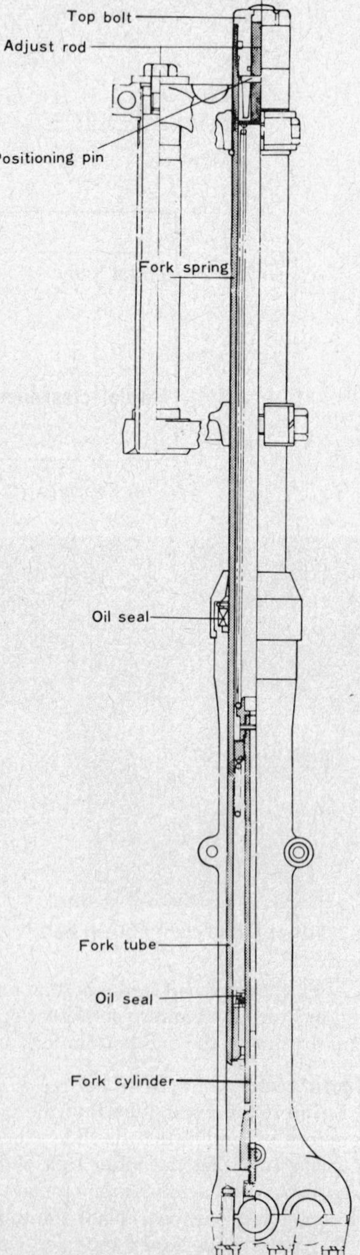

Cross section of the Ceriani-type fork leg

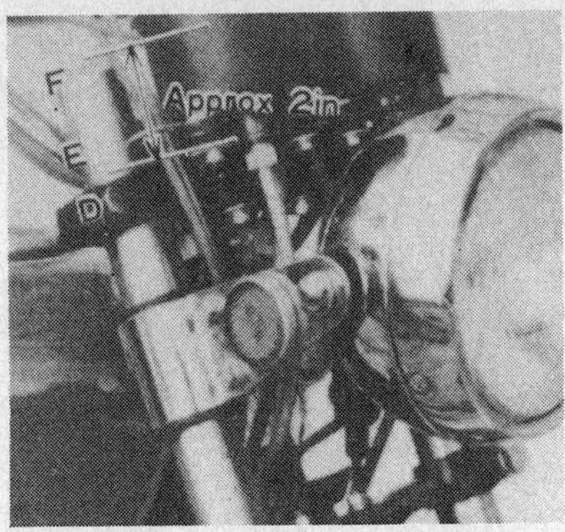

Steering stem positions (F Series)

Steering Stem Position (F6 Also)

D is the standard position. E and F decrease caster and increase trail, resulting in greater stability at high speeds, and heavier steering. To adjust, loosen the four, triple clamp pinch-bolts, move both forks to the desired setting, and retighten the bolts.

Fork Spring Length

A is the standard setting for the fork springs. B and C positions progressively decrease the length of the spring, increasing the initial spring load and thus increasing spring strength. To adjust, simply remove the rubber cap and turn the adjuster rod to the desired position. Make sure that both springs are adjusted to the same position.

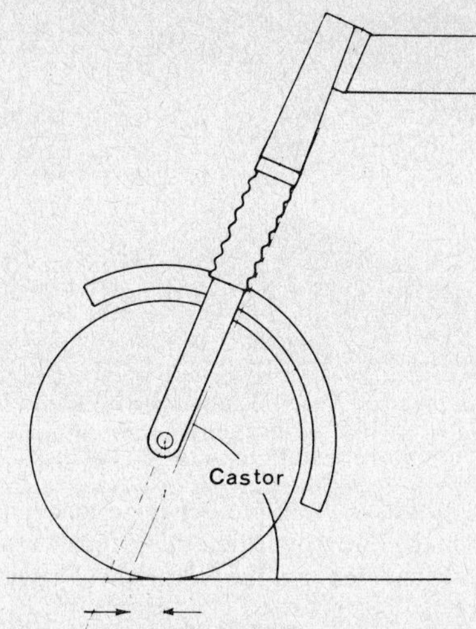

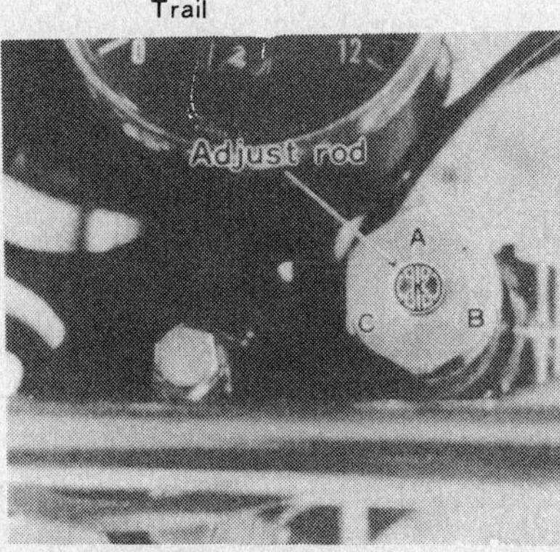

Spring tension adjustment

STEERING GEOMETRY

(F5)

Axle Shaft		Steering Stem Position D		E		F	
A	Castor Trail	60°	5.16 in.	59°	5.46 in.	58°	5.76 in.
B	Castor Trail	60° 23′	4.06 in.	59° 54′	4.36 in.	58° 26′	4.66 in.
C	Castor Trail	50° 40′	6.26 in.	58° 07′	6.56 in.	57° 34′	6.86 in.

(F6)

	Steering Stem Position D		E		F	
Castor Trail	62°	3.86 in.	61°	4.09 in.	60°	4.33 in.

(F7)

Axle Shaft		Steering Stem Position D		E		F	
A	Castor Trail	61°	4.37 in.	60°	4.61 in.	59°	4.88 in.
B	Castor Trail	61° 37′	2.91 in.	60° 41′	3.14 in.	59° 46′	3.88 in.
C	Castor Trail	60° 23′	5.85 in.	59° 26′	6.12 in.	58° 30′	6.39 in.

Steering Stem

DISASSEMBLY

1. Remove the handlebar, handlebar bracket, and the front fork assembly.
2. Loosen the stem nut with a pin wrench and withdraw the stem downwards, taking care not to lose the bearing balls.
3. Drive the upper and lower bearing races out of the stem housing using a suitable drift, as shown. Take care not to damage the housing.
4. Pry the lower race off from the stem using a chisel or screwdriver.

INSPECTION

1. Check the steering stem and clamp assembly, and replace it if the stem is damaged or bent.
2. Carefully examine the bearing balls and races for wear and damage. If any defects are found, replace both complete bearing assemblies.

ASSEMBLY

1. Press or drive the bearing races into the housing, taking care to install them squarely.
2. Grease the bearing balls, fit them into the races, and install the steering stem. Partially tighten the stem nut. On the G Series, twenty-three balls are used at each bearing; on the F Series there are nineteen at each bearing, and on the B1L—A, there are eighteen at each bearing.

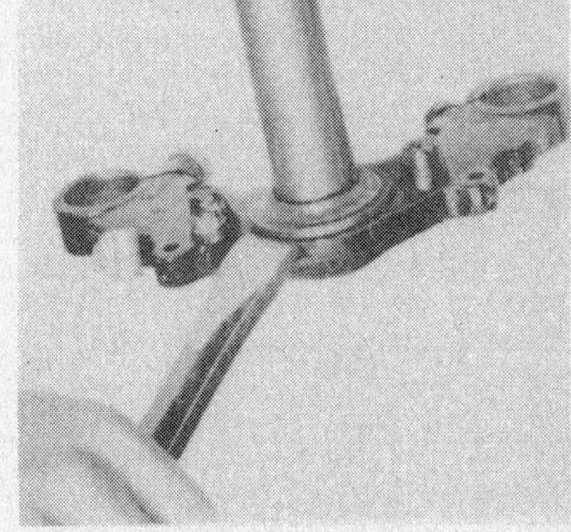
Removing the lower race from the steering stem

3. Install the front forks, and tighten the steering stem nut slowly, until steering play is eliminated.

Rear Shock Absorbers

ADJUSTMENT

The spring tension on the shock absorbers of the G4TR, B1L—A, and F Series models is adjustable. Rotate the adjustment cam at the bottom of the spring to the desired setting. Make sure that both springs are set equally.

INSPECTION

If the shock absorbers are leaking or if

damping action is weak or inconsistent, the shock unit should be replaced. They are not rebuildable.

CAUTION: *The shock absorbers on the GA1—A, GA2—A, G3SS, and G3TR—A models contain nitrogen gas under extreme pressure. Under no circumstances should you attempt to disassemble these units.*

REMOVAL AND INSTALLATION

Simply unscrew the upper and lower mounting bolts and pull the shock/spring unit away from the mounting points. To remove the spring, have a helper compress the spring slightly and remove the retaining collar at the top of the spring. Installation is in reverse order of removal.

Swing Arm

DISASSEMBLY

1. Remove the rear wheel.
2. Unscrew the nut at the end of the swing arm pivot shaft and withdraw the shaft.
3. Remove the swing arm from the frame.

INSPECTION

1. Carefully inspect the pivot sleeves for wear and damage. If there is excessive clearance between the sleeves and bushings, replace all of the related parts.
2. Measure the pivot shaft for bending with a dial indicator. If the shaft is bent beyond 0.02 in. (0.5 mm), it should be replaced. Ideally, there should be no greater than 0.004 in. (0.1 mm) bend in the shaft.
3. Examine the swing arm for distortion and cracked welds. Replace it if it does not appear to be in perfect condition.
4. Check the sprocket for distortion by placing it on a flat surface and measuring any gaps between the surface and sprocket with a feeler gauge.

ASSEMBLY

Assembly is a reversal of the disassembly procedures. Lubricate all pivot shaft components before installation.

MULTICYLINDER MODELS

Wheel Removal

FRONT

1. Unscrew the bolt and disconnect the speedometer cable from the front hub.
2. Disconnect the front brake cable at the brake.

The spring adjustment cam, showing the different positions (F Series shown)

3. Place a stand under the engine and remove the front axle nut. Withdraw the axle and remove the front wheel assembly.

REAR

1. Disconnect the brake cable from the brake arm at the hub.
2. Disconnect the torque link at the mounting ear on the rear hub.
3. Remove the master link clip and separate and remove the chain.
4. Unscrew the rear axle nut and loosen the chain adjuster bolts. Withdraw the axle and remove the rear wheel assembly.

Wheel Installation

Installation is a reversal of the removal procedure. Note the following points:

1. The brake lever (or arm) should be installed so that the cable and lever are at right angles when the brake is applied.
2. Apply a small amount of grease to the brake lever and cam bushings in the brake panel before reassembly.
3. Install the master link clip on the chain so that its closed end faces in the direction of forward rotation.
4. Adjust the brake and stop light switch, if necessary, after installation.

Drum Brake Service

1. Remove the wheel.
2. Remove both brake shoes by lifting them away from the panel at the same time.
3. Measure the inside diameter of the brake drum and compare the reading with the specifications in the chart.
4. If the brake shoe lining is worn beyond the limit shown, or if it is cracked or broken, the shoes should be replaced.
5. If the lining is glazed or making uneven contact, correct the fault with sandpaper or emery cloth.

Gap Between the Swing Arm Sleeve and the Bushing (F Series)

Standard Value	Repair Limit
0.005 ~ 0.008 in. (0.128 ~ 0.199 mm)	0.014 in. (0.35 mm)

FRONT WHEEL

Model	Bearing		Oil Seal	
	Drum	Panel	Drum	Panel
S2	6302	6302Z	WTC25 42 8	WOC55 68 7
H1*, H2	6203	6203	BJN25406	BJN54656

* Disc brake models

REAR WHEEL

Model	Bearing			Oil Seal
	Drum	Coupling	Panel	Coupling
S2	6205	6205	6205Z	WTC35 52 7
H1	6303Z	6305	6205Z	AJN40 62 7
H2	6304Z	6206	6304	AJN40 62 7

Front axle torque value
Model A series 44-58 ft lb (6-8 kg.m)
Model H series 65-93 ft lb (9-13 kg.m)

Rear axle torque value
A and H series 65-93 ft lb (9-13 kg.m)

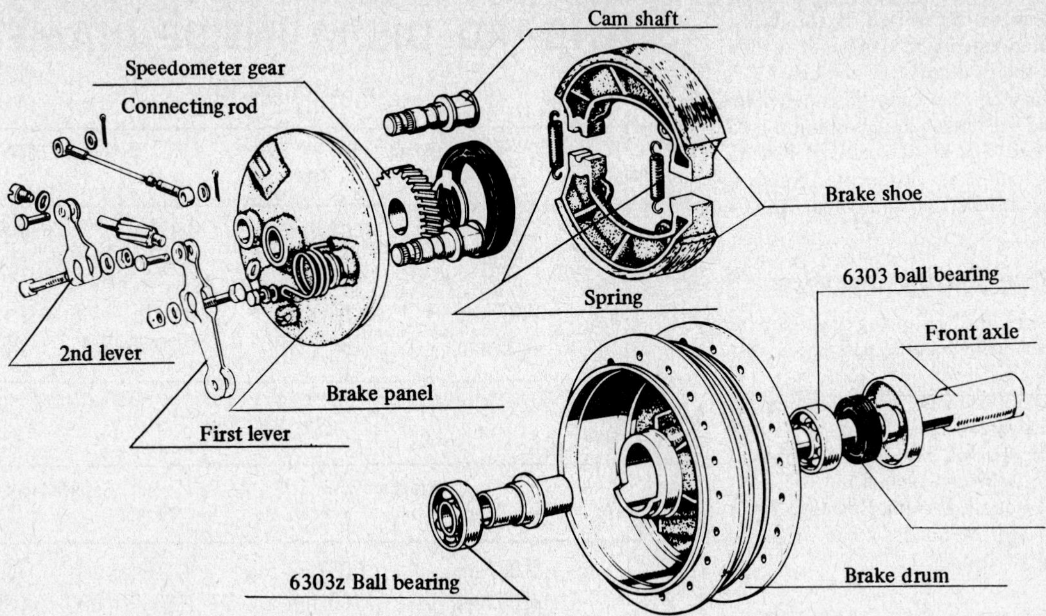

Front hub components

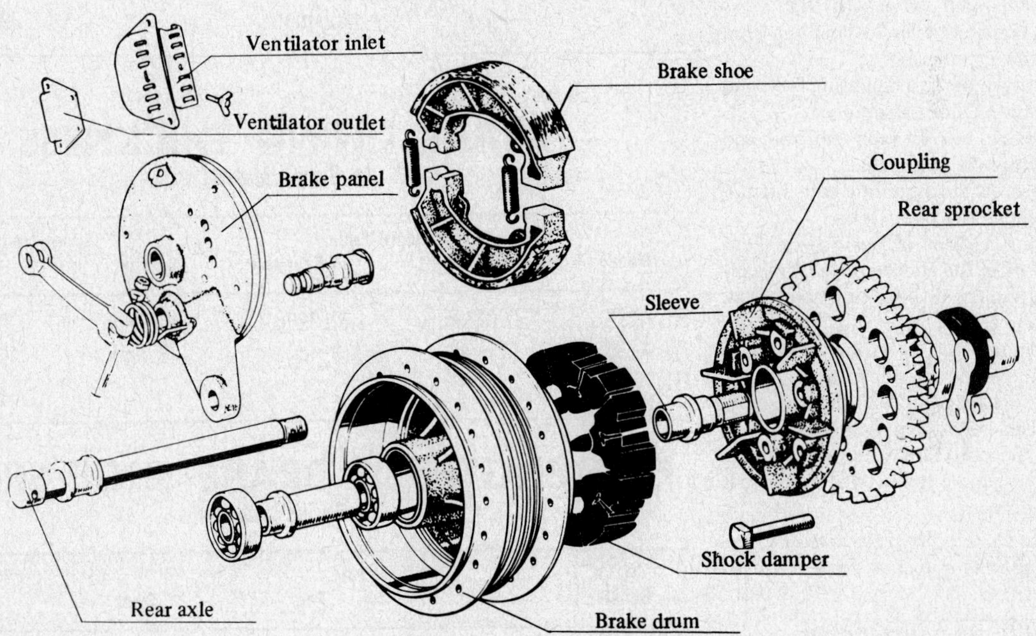

Rear hub components

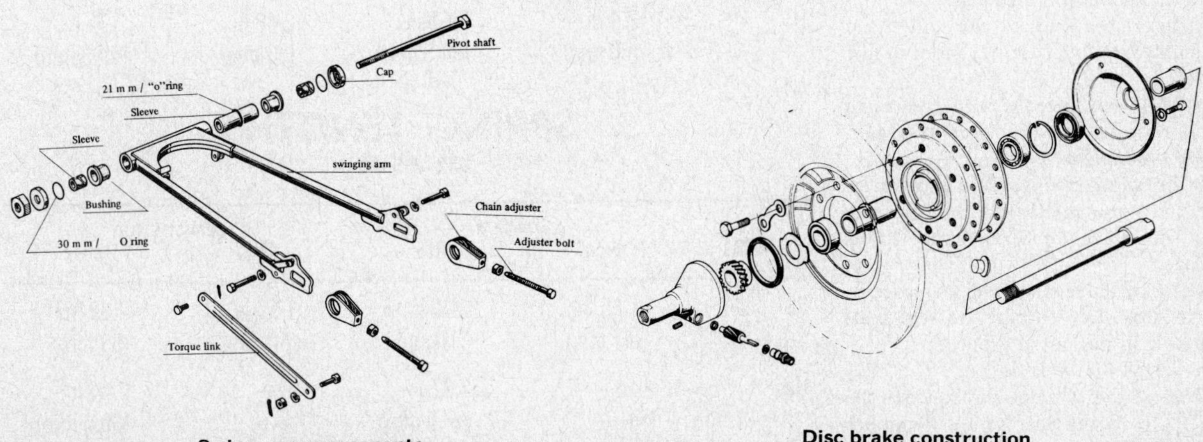

Swing arm components

Disc brake construction

6. Measure the length of the brake spring and replace it if it has stretched beyond the limit given in the chart.

7. Clearance between the brake cam shaft and the brake panel bushing should not exceed 0.02 in. (0.5 mm). If it does, replace parts as necessary. Nominal clearance is 0.0008–0.0028 in. (0.02–0.07 mm).

Disc Brake Service

Observe the following precautions when performing any repairs on the disc brake:

1. Do not use gasoline or any mineral based solvent to clean brake parts. Use only glycol-based brake fluid, ethyl alcohol, or isopropyl alcohol.

2. Do not allow rubber parts to be in contact with cleaning alcohol for more than thirty seconds.

MASTER CYLINDER

Removal And Disassembly

1. Disconnect the brake fluid line from the master cylinder.

2. Remove the two mounting bolts and the master cylinder assembly.

3. Remove the reservoir cap, seal, and plate. Drain the brake fluid.

4. Unscrew the mounting bolt and nut, then remove the brake lever.

5. Using a piece of heavy wire bent into a hook at the end, remove the securing ring and the dust seal. Be careful not to damage the seal.

6. Remove the securing snap-ring, then remove the stopper plate, piston assembly, primary cup, spring assembly, and check valve. Leave the secondary cup on the piston unless replacement is necessary. Do not remove the spring seat from the spring.

NOTE: *Do not clamp the master cylinder tightly in a vise, as distortion may result.*

Assembly And Installation

1. Thoroughly lubricate the piston assembly, primary cup, and check valve with brake fluid prior to assembly.

2. Insert the primary cup and piston assembly into the master cylinder in that order.

NOTE: *Make sure the primary cup and check valve do not turn sideways during installation.*

3. Install the stopper, then fit the snap-ring in its groove. Replace the snap-ring if it does not rotate smoothly in its groove.

4. Install the dust seal and seal stopper. Make absolutely certain the seal seats properly in the piston groove.

5. Install the brake lever.

6. Hold the cylinder and squeeze the lever to make certain it operates smoothly. Put a finger over the hose con-

STANDARD DRUM INSIDE DIAMETERS

(A Series and H1)

Model	Standard Value Front	Standard Value Rear	Service Limit Front	Service Limit Rear
A1, A1SS A7, A7SS	— —	7.08 in. (180 mm)	7.12 in. (180.75 mm)	7.12 in. (180.75 mm)
H1	7.87 in. (200 mm)	7.08 in. (180 mm)	7.90 in. (200.75 mm)	7.12 in. (180.75 mm)

(S2, H2)

Model	Standard Front	Standard Rear	Service Limit Front	Service Limit Rear
S2	7.087 in. (180 mm)	7.087 in. (180 mm)	7.116 in. (180.75 mm)	7.116 in. (180.75 mm)
H2	— —	7.874 in. (200 mm)	— —	7.904 in. (200.75 mm)

BRAKE LINING THICKNESS

(A Series and H1)

Model	Standard Value Front	Standard Value Rear	Service Limit Front	Service Limit Rear
A1, A1SS A7, A7SS H1	0.192 in. (5 mm)	0.192 in. (5 mm)	0118 in. (3 mm)	0.118 in. (3 mm)

FREELENGTH OF BRAKE SHOE SPRING

(A Series and H1)

Model	Standard Value Front	Standard Value Rear	Service Limit Front	Service Limit Rear
A1, A1SS A7, A7SS	1.8 in. (46 mm)	2.2 in. (56 mm)	1.92 in. (49 mm)	2.32 in. (59 mm)
H1	2.4 in. (60 mm)	2.62 in. (66.5 mm)	2.48 in. (63 mm)	2.74 in. (69.5 mm)

SPRING LENGTH

(S2 and H2)

Model	Standard Front	Standard Rear	Service Limit Front	Service Limit Rear
S2	1.85 in. (47 mm)	2.20 in. (56 mm)	1.97 in. (50 mm)	2.32 in. (59 mm)
H2	— —	2.62 in. (66.5 mm)	— —	2.74 in. (69.5 mm)

nection: you should be able to detect suction when the lever is released.

7. Fill the reservoir with brake fluid and install the cap.

8. Squeeze and release the lever several times until the fluid is pumped out the hose connection. Do not squeeze the lever to the limit of its travel or damage to the secondary cup may result.

9. Squeeze the lever, cover the hose connection with a finger, then release the lever: it should return to its original position quickly and smoothly.

10. Mount the assembly on the handlebar, and tighten the top mounting bolts first.

11. Adjust the brake lever to have less than 3/16 in. freeplay.

12. Connect the brake hose, fill the reservoir, and bleed the system.

Master Cylinder

Measurement	Standard	Service Limit
Cyl. inside diam.	.5512-.5529 in. (14.000-14.043 mm)	.5543 in. (14.080 mm)
Piston outside diam.	.5495-.5506 in. (13.957-13.984 mm)	.5496 in. (13.960 mm)
Prim., sec. cup diam.	.577-.596 in. (14.65-15.15 mm)	.571 in. (14.50 mm)
Spring length (free)	2.01 in. (51 mm)	1.89 in. (48 mm)

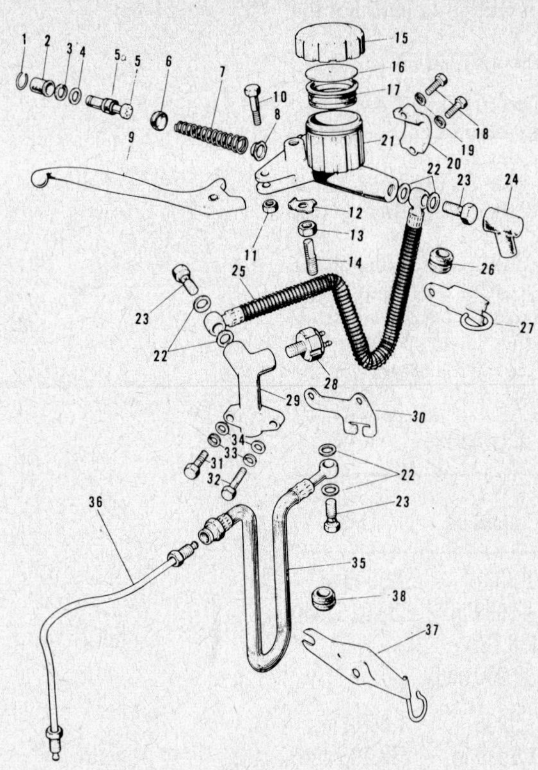

Master cylinder construction

1. Stopper, dust seal
2. Dust seal
3. Circlip
4. Stopper, piston
5. Piston assembly
5.a Secondary cup
6. Primary cup
7. Spring assembly
8. Check valve assembly
9. Brake lever
10. Bolt
11. Nut
12. Lock washer
13. Nut
14. Bolt
15. Cap
16. Plat
17. Cap seal
18. Bolt
19. Washer
20. Master cylinder mounting
21. Master cylinder body
22. Washer
23. Banjo bolt
24. Dust cover
25. Hose
26. Grommet
27. Bracket
28. Pressure switch
29. 3-way fitting
30. Guide
31. Bolt
32. Bolt
33. Lock washer
34. Washer
35. Hose
36. Pipe
37. Bracket
38. Grommet

DISC BRAKE ASSEMBLY TORQUE SETTINGS

Part	Location	Torque ft-lb	kg-M
Banjo bolt	master cylinder/hose	18.1-23.9	2.5-3.3
Banjo bolt	3-way fitting/hose (top)	18.1-23.9	2.5-3.3
Banjo bolt	3-way fitting/hose (bottom)	18.1-23.9	2.5-3.3
Pressure switch	3-way fitting	10.8-14.5	1.5-2.0
Pipe fitting	both ends of pipe	12.3-13.0	1.7-1.8
Bolt	caliper/front fork	18.1-23.9	2.5-3.3
Bolt	3-way fitting mounting	3.6-4.3	0.5-0.6
Nut	brake lever mounting	3.6-5.1	0.5-0.7
Nut	brake lever adjuster	5.8-8.7	0.8-1.2
Shaft, allen head	caliper assembly	21.7-26.0	3.0-3.6

CALIPER

Removal And Disassembly

1. Disconnect the brake fluid line at the caliper and plug it so that no more fluid escapes.

2; Loosen the two allen head shafts and remove the mounting bolts and caliper assembly.

3. Remove the brake pads.

4. Unscrew the two allen head shafts and divide the caliper halves.

NOTE: *Remove the allen head shafts by loosening them a little at a time to prevent damage to seals and O-rings.*

5. Pull the caliper mounting off the shafts evenly, taking care not to damage the seals and O-rings.

6. Remove the band and dust seal from the piston. Blow compressed air into the

caliper hose connection to push out the piston.

7. Remove the cylinder oil seal.

Assembly And Installation

1. Thoroughly clean all parts, observing the precautions given earlier.
2. Lubricate the oil seal and piston with brake fluid, then install them in that order.
3. Install the dust seal and band on the piston, making certain they keep dry.
4. Install the two O-rings on each shaft, then apply a thin layer of PBC (Poly Butul-Cuprysil) to the shafts between the O-rings.

Caliper

	Standard	Service Limit
Cylinder inside diam.	1.5031-1.5039 in. (38.180-38.200 mm)	1.5045 in. (38.215 mm)
Piston outside diam.	1.5006-1.5019 in. (38.115-38.148 mm)	1.5002 in. (38.195 mm)

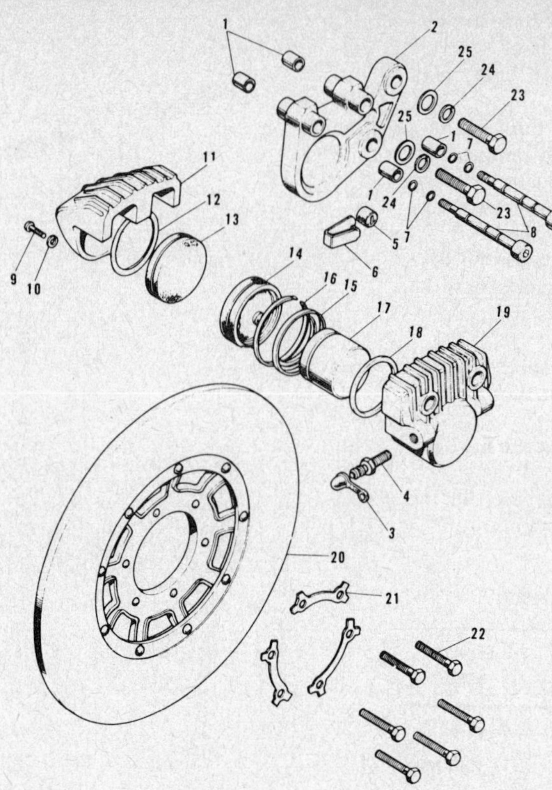

1. Dust seal
2. Caliper mounting
3. Bleeder valve cap
4. Bleeder valve
5. Bushing
6. Stopper
7. O ring
8. Shaft
9. Screw
10. Lock washer
11. Caliper B
12. Ring
13. Pad B
14. Pad A
15. Dust seal
16. Band
17. Piston
18. Ring
19. Caliper A
20. Disc
21. Lock washer
22. Bolt
23. Bolt
24. Lock washer
25. Washer

Caliper construction

5. Insert the two shafts into caliper half A, position the first two dust seals on the caliper mounting, and slide the mounting onto the shafts. Make sure the seals seat.
6. Install the second set of dust seals, then join the two caliper halves.

Disc

Measurement	Standard	Service Limit
Thickness	0.276 in. (7 mm)	0.217 in. (5.5 mm)
Runout	less than 0.004 in. (less than 0.1 mm)	0.012 in. (0.3 mm)

7. Move the caliper mounting back and forth to make certain it operates smoothly.
8. Install the brake pads.
9. Install the caliper on the fork leg, connect the brake fluid line, and bleed the system.

PAD REPLACEMENT

1. Remove the front wheel.
2. Remove the securing screw and pad B.
3. Squeeze the brake lever and remove pad A.
4. Open the bleeder valve slightly to relieve pressure, then push the piston in all the way and close the valve.
5. Install pad A, making certain that the groove is properly aligned with the positioning pin.
6. Install pad B, apply a small dab of locktite to the securing screw, then tighten the screw.
7. Install the front wheel and, if the lever is soft or spongy, bleed the system.

Wheel Bearing Service

Refer to the preceding section on single-cylinder models. Procedures are identical. On the H1, make sure that the rear brake ventilator is clean and free of grit.

Front Fork

REMOVAL

1. Remove the front wheel and fender.
2. Loosen the lower triple clamp pinch bolts and remove the top filler bolts.
3. Withdraw the fork legs individually from the clamps.

Loosening the lower triple clamp pinch bolts

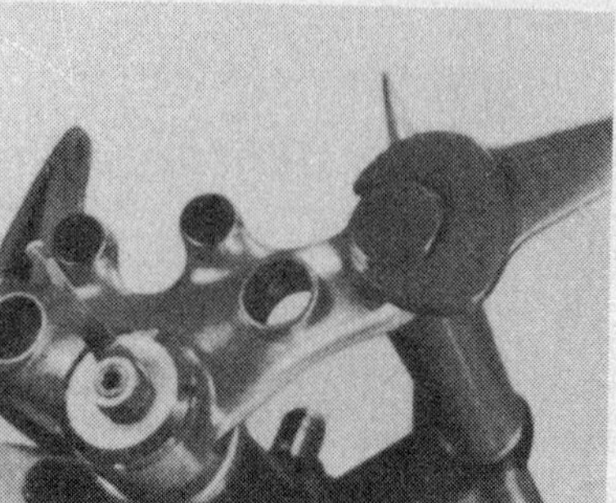

Removing the top filler bolts (the handlebar and steering damper do not have to be removed to take off the forks)

DISASSEMBLY

1. Drain the oil from the fork legs.
2. Place the fork leg in a vice that is protected with strips of rubber and clamp the jaws on the outer tube nut.

NOTE: *Do not use excessive pressure or else the tube will be distorted.*

3. Fit the front axle in the bottom fork leg and unscrew the bottom fork leg from the inner tube.

INSPECTION

1. Insert the inner tube into the bottom fork leg and install the guide. Check to make sure that the inner tube slides smoothly, with a minimum of play. If clearance is excessive, replace the tube;

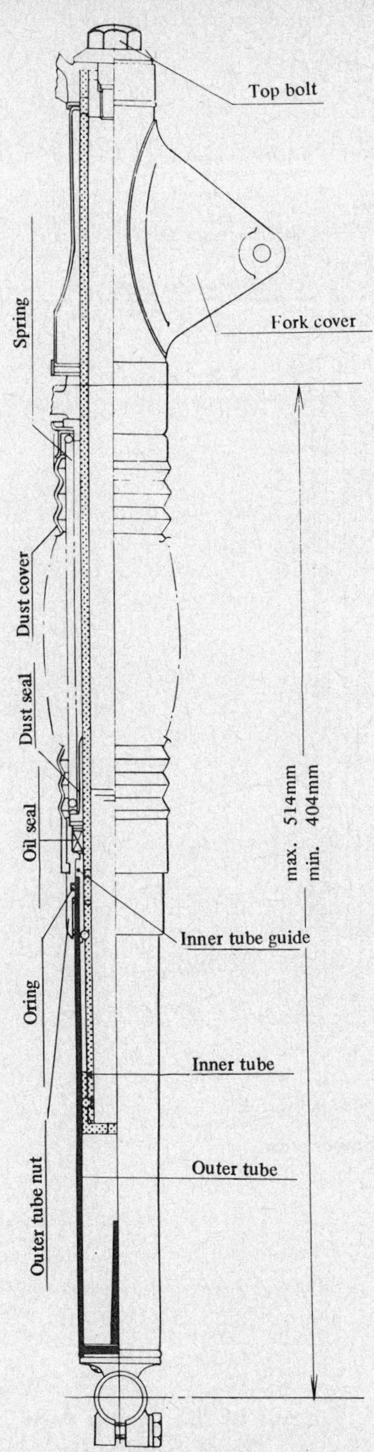

Cross section of the fork leg (A Series)

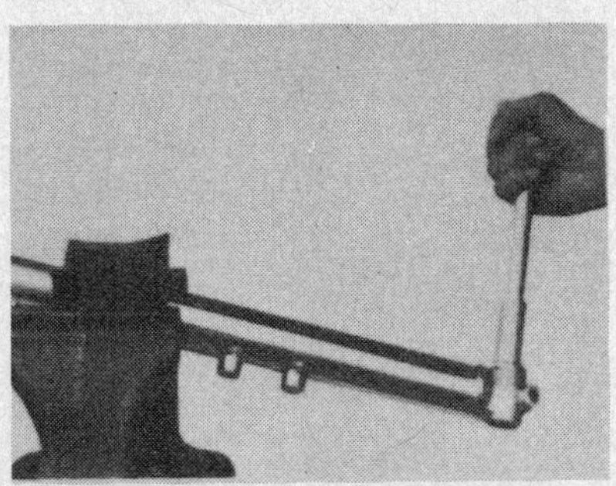

Removing the bottom fork leg

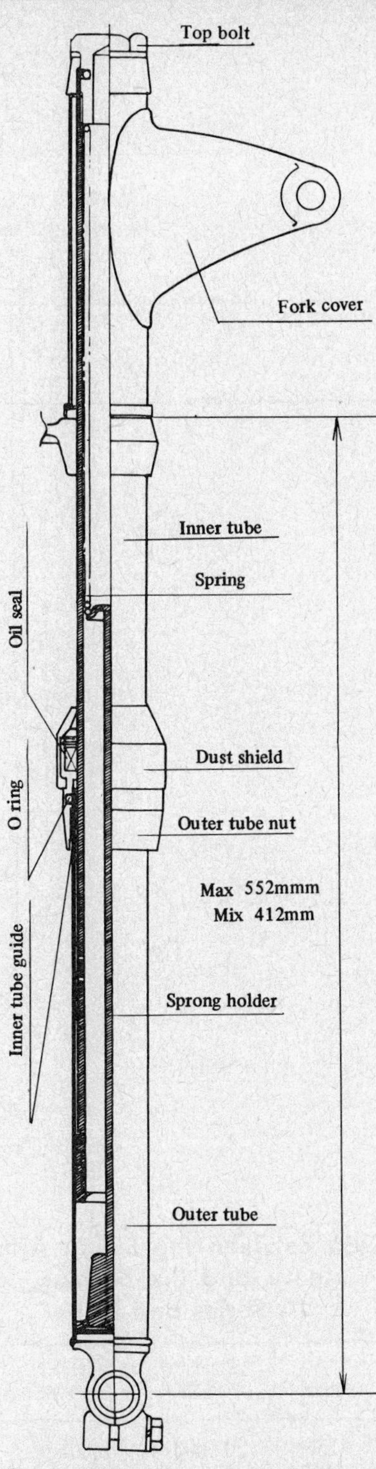

Cross section of the Ceriani-type fork leg (H Series)

2. Examine the inner tube for wear and scratches; these can ruin the oil seal. Repair or replace parts as necessary. Make sure that the tube is not bent.

3. Carefully clean and inspect the dust seal. Replace it if it is worn or damaged

4. Measure the free-length of the spring and replace it if the measurement is beyond the limit given in the chart.

ASSEMBLY

Assembly is a reversal of the disassembly procedure. Note the following points:

1. Use a new oil seal and O-ring. Lubricate them before installation.

2. Do not forget to refill the forks with the correct grade and amount of oi.

INSTALLATION

A Series Models

1. Insert the fork from the lower part of the clamps and pull it into position with a special tool (a long, threaded rod).

2. Secure the fork in position with the top filler bolts and then tighten the pinch bolts.

Fork Spring Freelength (A Series and H1)

Model	Standard Value	Service Limit
A1, A1SS, A7, A7SS	8.0 in. (202.5 mm)	7.56 in. (192 mm)
H1	13.58 in. (345 mm)	13.18 in. (335 mm)

Spring Length (S2 and H2)

Model	Standard	Service Limit
H2	13.58 in. (345 mm)	13.19 in. (335 mm)
S2	14.21 in. (361 mm)	13.78 in. (350 mm)

H Series Models

1. Insert the fork leg through the triple clamps, pushing up until the end of the inner tube reaches the step portion in the steering head.

2. Install the top filler bolt and then tighten the pinch bolt. Install the other leg in the same manner.

Steering Stem

DISASSEMBLY

1. Remove the front fork assembly (optional) and handlebar.

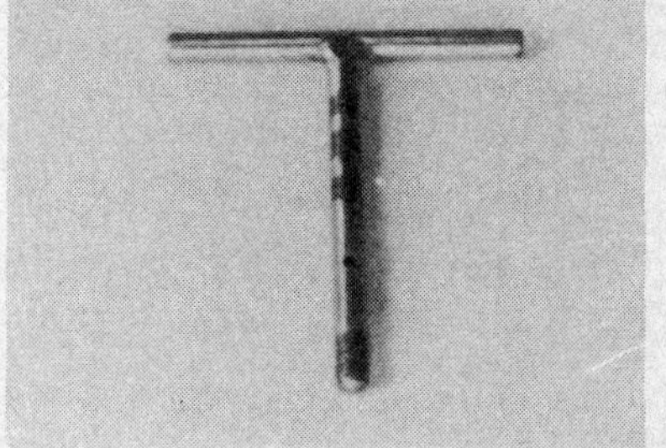

Fork installation tool (A Series)

2. Unsnap the connectors in the headlight shell, and unbolt and remove the headlight assembly.

3. Disconnect the cables and remove the speedometer and tachometer.

4. Remove the cotter pin from the lower end of the steering damper rod, loosen the damper knob, and remove the damper assembly.

5. Unscrew the steering stem nut with a pin wrench and remove the steering stem.

6. Drive the upper and lower bearing races out of the stem housing, using a suitable drift, as shown.

7. Pry the lower race off of the stem using a chisel or screwdriver.

INSPECTION

1. Check the steering stem and clamp assembly and replace it if the stem is damaged or bent.

2. Carefully examine the bearing balls and races for wear and damage. If any defects are found, replace both complete bearing assemblies.

ASSEMBLY

1. Press or drive the bearing races into the housing, taking care to install them squarely.

2. Grease the bearing balls, fit them into the races, and install the steering stem. There are 19 steel balls in each bearing. Partially tighten the stem nut.

3. Install the front forks (if removed) and tighten the steering stem nut slowly until steering play is eliminated.

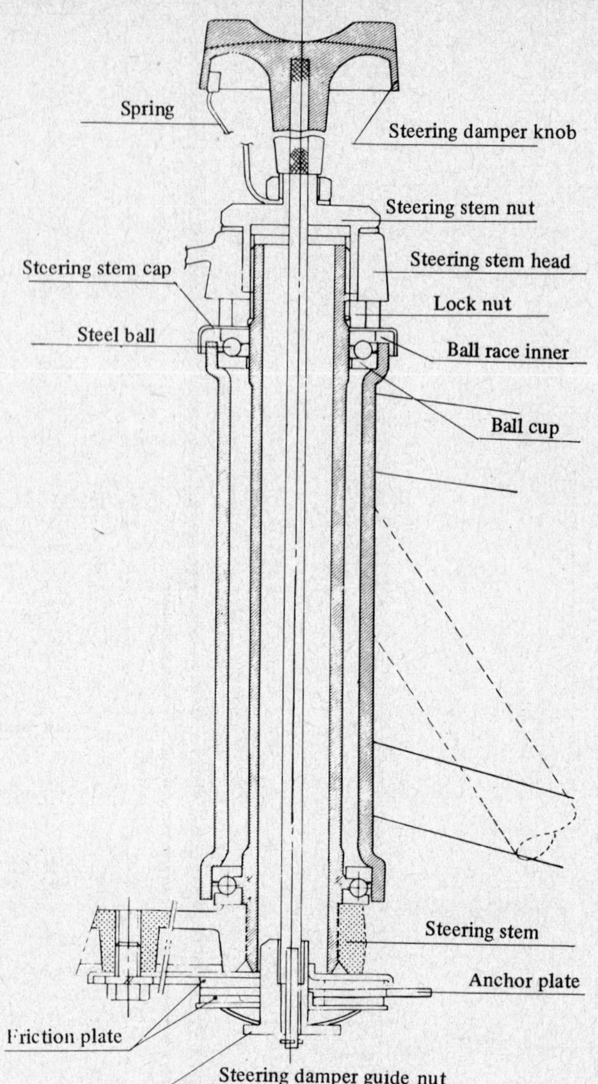

Steering stem components

Rear Shock Absorbers

Refer to the preceding section on single-cylinder models. Procedures are identical. All A and H Series models have adjustable spring tension.

Swing Arm

Refer to the preceding section on single-cylinder models. Procedures are identical. The charts below give the necessary specifications for the A and H Series swing arm.

Runout of the Rear Wheel Sprocket (A Series and H1)

Model	Standard Value	Service Limit
A1, A1SS, A7, A7SS, H1	0.12 in. (Under 0.3 mm)	0.2 in. (0.5 mm)

Gap Between the Swing Arm Sleeve and the Bushing (A Series and H1)

Model	Standard Value	Service Limit
A1, A1SS A7, A7SS	0.0003-0.002 in. (0.007-0.05 mm)	0.008 in. (0.2 mm)
H1	0.005-0.007 in. (0.13-0.19 mm)	0.014 in. (0.35 mm)

Runout of the Swing Arm Pivot Shaft (A Series and H1)

Model	Standard Value	Service Limit
A1, A1SS, A7, A7SS, H1	Under 0.004 in. (0.1 mm)	0.02 in. (0.5 mm)

INDEX

KAWASAKI 900

MODEL IDENTIFICATION

Each machine comes from the manufacturer with a serial number stamped on the right side of the crankcase, and on the left side of the steering head lug. When ordering certain parts from your dealer, it may be necessary to present him with this information.

Frame number location

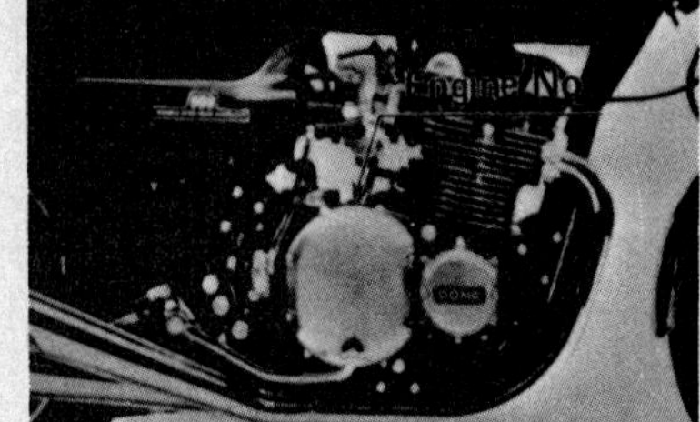

Engine number location

GENERAL SPECIFICATIONS

DIMENSIONS	
Overall length	
U.S.	86.8 in. (2,205 mm)
European	88.5 in. (2,250 mm)
Overall width	
U.S.	31.5 in. (800 mm)
European	32.3 in. (820 mm)
Overall height	
U.S.	45.3 in. (1,150 mm)
European	46.3 in. (1,175 mm)
Wheelbase	58.7 in. (1,490 mm)
Road clearance	6.3 in. (160 mm)
Dry weight	506 lb. (230 kg)
Fuel tank capacity	4.7 U.S. gal. (18 ltr.)
Oil tank capacity	0.95 U.S. qt. (0.9 ltr.)
PERFORMANCE	
SS 1/4 mile	12.0 sec.
Climbing ability	30°
Fuel consumption	40 mil./gal. @ 70 mph (17 km/2 @ 113 kph)
Braking distance	36 ft. @ 31 mph (11 M @ 50 kph)
Minimum turning radius	98.5 in. (2,500 mm)
ENGINE	
Type	DOHC 4 cylinder, transverse inline 4 stroke, air-cooled
Bore and stroke	2.6 x 2.6 in. (66 x 66 mm)
Displacement	55.1 cu. in. (903 cc)
Compression ratio	8.5 : 1
Maximum horsepower	82 HP @ 8,500 rpm
Maximum torque	54.3 ft lb @ 7,000 rpm (7.5 kg-M @ 7,000 rpm)
Valve timing:	
Inlet	
Open	30° BTDC
Close	70° ABDC
Exhaust	
Open	70° BBDC
Close	30° ATDC
Carburetor	VM 28SC
Lubrication system	Forced lubrication

TRANSMISSION	
Type	5-speed, constant-mesh, return-shift
Clutch	Wet, multi-disc.
Gear ratio:	
1st	3.17 (38/12)
2nd	2.19 (35/16)
3rd	1.67 (35/21)
4th	1.38 (29/21)
5th	1.22 (28/23)
Primary reduction ratio	1.73 (97/56)
Final reduction ratio	2.33 (35/15)
Overall drive ratio	4.92 (5th)
ELECTRICAL EQUIPMENT	
Generator	Kokusan AR3701
Regulator	Kokusan RS21
Ignition coil	Kokusan IG3303, IG3304
Battery	Yuasa 12N 14-3A 12V 14AH
Starter	Kokusan SM-226-K
Head lamp type	
U.S.	Sealed beam
European	Semi-sealed
FRAME	
Type	Tubular, double-cradle
Steering angle	41° to either side
Caster	64°
Trail	3.54 in. (90 mm)
Tire size	
Front	3.25-19 4PR
Rear	4.00-18 4PR
Suspension	
Front	Telescopic fork
Rear	Swing arm
Suspension stroke	
Front	5.51 in. (140 mm)
Rear	3.15 in. (80 mm)
Front fork oil capacity (each fork)	5.7 oz. (U.S.) (169 cc)
Front fork oil type	SAE 10W, non-detergent
Brakes	
Front	Disc brake

GENERAL SPECIFICATIONS (con't.)

ENGINE		FRAME	
Engine oil	SE class SAE 10W-40	Rear	Internal expansion, leading-trailing
Engine oil capacity:		Rear brake drum inside dia.	7.9 x 1.4 in. (200 x 35 mm)
Less filter	3.5 U.S. qt. (3.3 ltr.)	Disc diameter	11.65 in. (296 mm)
Total incl. filter	4.2 U.S. qt. (4.0 ltr.)		
Starting system	Electric & kick		
Ignition system	Battery & coil		
Firing order	1-2-4-3		
Ignition timing	From 5° BTDC @ 1,500 rpm to 40° BTDC @ 3,000 rpm		
Spark plugs	NGK B-8ES		

MAINTENANCE ITEMS

Engine

OIL CHANGES (1,000 Mi/60 Days Summer, 30 Days Winter)

Change the oil after the engine has been run long enough to be up to operating temperature. This ensures that the oil is fluid enough to drain completely, and that impurities suspended in the oil while it is circulating will be removed. Kawasaki recommends that SAE 10W-40 or 20W-50 oil of SD (previously MS) service rating be used. Also recommended are the new 10W-50 oils of SE rating, which withstand heat even better than the SD oils. If a single-viscosity oil is to be used, it must be a high detergent, heavy-duty oil of SD service rating. For temperatures above 60 deg F, use SAE 30W-30 oil. Between 32 and 60 deg F, use SAE 20W-20, and below 32 deg F, use SAE 10W-10 oil. Do not use a vegetable-based or non-detergent oil.

Drain the oil from the engine and oil filter in the following manner;

1. Run the engine until normal operating temperature is reached, and place the motorcycle on its center stand.

Engine and oil filter drain plug and filter mounting bolt locations

2. Remove the engine and oil filter drain plugs, and allow the oil to drain into a suitable receptacle.

3. Remove the oil filter, if it is to be replaced, at this time by removing the

Removing the oil filter assembly

filter mounting bolt, and dropping out the filter.

4. Rotate the engine several times, with the key off, to assure complete drainage.

5. Wipe off any metal filings which may be stuck to the magnetic drain plug, and install the plug. Install the filter assembly or filter drain plug only, as the case may be.

6. Torque the drain plug to 29 ft lbs (4.0 kg/m), the filter mounting bolt to 18 ft lbs (7.5 kg/m), and the filter drain plug to 16 ft lbs (2.2 kg/m).

7. Fill the engine with 4.2 qts (4.0 l) of SE or SD class SAE 10W-40, 10W-50, or 20W-50 motor oil. The oil level should be

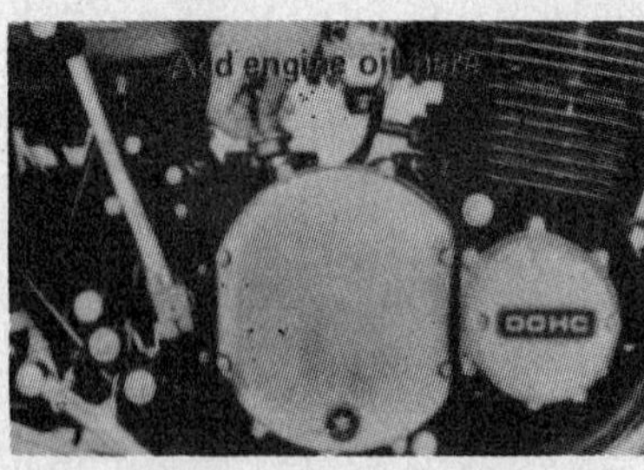

Engine oil filler location

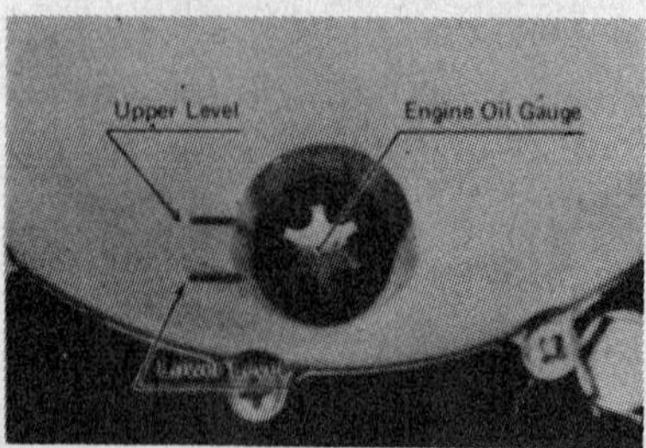

Oil level view window

between the two lines at the level window located on the right side crankcase clutch cover.

OIL FILTER, DISPOSABLE TYPE (2,000 Mi)

An automotive type, disposable filter cartridge is used as the main filter on the Z1, and it should be changed every 2,000 miles, or every second oil change. In addition to this, the filter should be changed after the first 500 and 1,000 miles on a new or rebuilt engine.

When installing a new filter, make sure that the spring and both O-rings are in

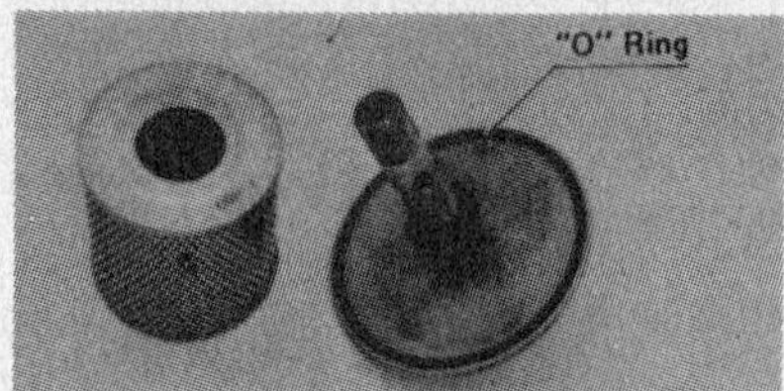

Oil filter O-ring

good condition, and replace them as necessary. The filter mounting assembly should be cleaned with clean gasoline, and blown dry, before the new filter is installed.

After securing the bolt to 18 ft lbs (2.5 kg/m), replenish the oil supply, and run the engine to check for any possible oil leaks.

Oil pump oil filter location

OIL FILTER, STRAINER TYPE (12,000 Mi/12 Mo)

The oil strainer is located at the oil pump pickup, and may be removed for cleaning after the oil pan is unbolted and lowered as described in the "Lubrication System" Section. The strainer is secured to the pump body by 3 screws.

Clean the strainer in solvent, or replace it with a new one if it is damaged, then install the strainer and oil pan using a new pan gasket. After refilling the engine with oil, start the engine and check for oil leaks.

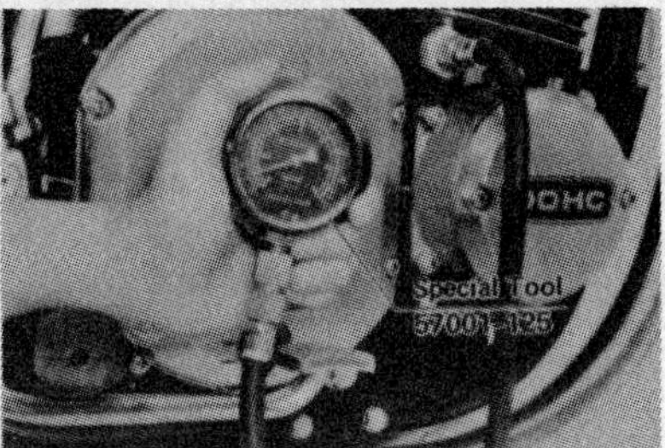

Checking oil pressure

OIL PRESSURE (6,000 Mi/12 Mo)

The engine oil pressure should be checked once a year, or whenever an oil pressure problem is suspected. Either the factory gauge (Part No. 57001-125), or a suitable substitute, can be connected at the oil gallery access hole at the right side of the engine after the plug has been removed. The gauge should read 2.8 lbs/in.^{2} (0.2 kg/cm^2) with the engine running at 3,000 rpm, and the engine oil temperature approximately 140°F (60°C). If the reading proves unsatisfactory, determine and correct the fault (restricted oil passage, clogged filter, pressure relief valve failure, etc.). Consult the "Lubrication System" Chapter for additional information.

NOTE: *Apply Loctite® to the plug threads before installing it in the gallery access hole.*

POINTS REQUIRING USE OF LOCTITE®

(Number required follows item)

Tension stud, 12
Dynamo rotor-to-crankshaft, 1
Dynamo rotor-to-starter clutch, 3
Dynamo stator installation, 3
Oil pump gear (crankshaft), 1
Positioning bolt, 1
Oil passage plugs, 1
Carburetor installation screw, 8
Return spring pin, 1
Oil pump housing mounting screw, 6
Crankcase (crankshaft back both end), 2
R.H. engine cover, 3
Crankcase (left-side between drive/output shaft), 1
Starter mounting bolt, 2
Clutch release mounting screw, 2
Drive chain oil pump screw, 2
Camshaft sprocket mounting bolt, 3
Oil pump mounting bolt, 3

Chain Oiler

The Z1 is equipped with a drive chain oiler, which, in conjunction with hand lubrication using a chain lubricant, is intended to keep chain wear to a minimum. The tank for the oiler is located under the seat, and has a dipstick and a filler cap. The tank should be kept filled with 30W or 40W oil.

Chain oiler tank location

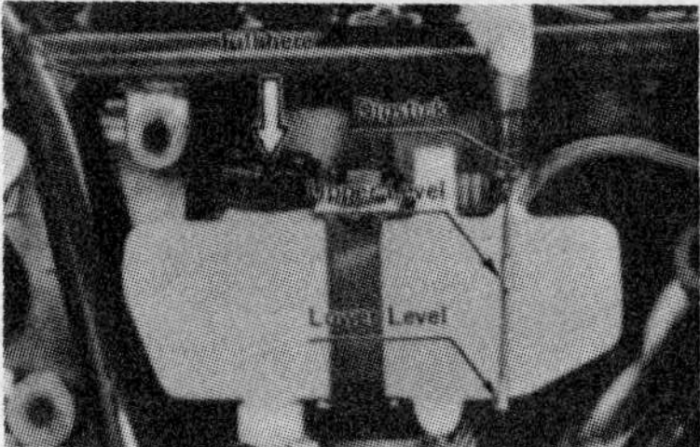

Keep the tank filled with 30 or 40W

The pump can be adjusted for oil flow. "0" supplies the least oil, and "5" is for maximum output. The chain should be kept wet, but not dripping.

Pump cover location

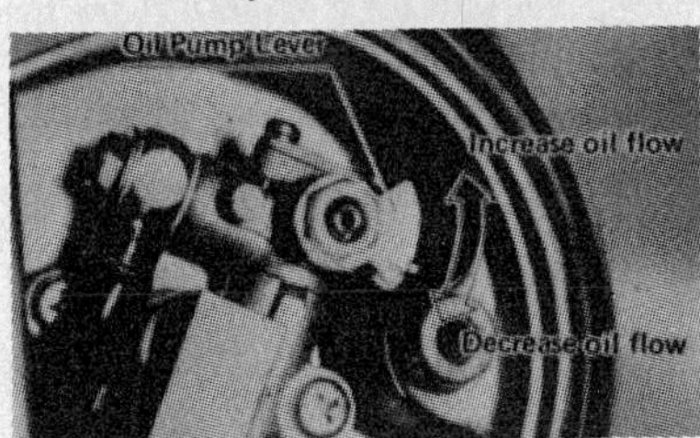

Pump output adjuster

Do not rely on the oiler to provide all the necessary chain lubrication these machines require. Every 200 miles, or more often if used in wet or dusty conditions, the chain should be hand lubricated with graphite, a commerical spray, or 90W oil.

Air Filter

(2,000 Mi/6 Mo)

To remove the filter element, open the seat, take the screen off the air cleaner,

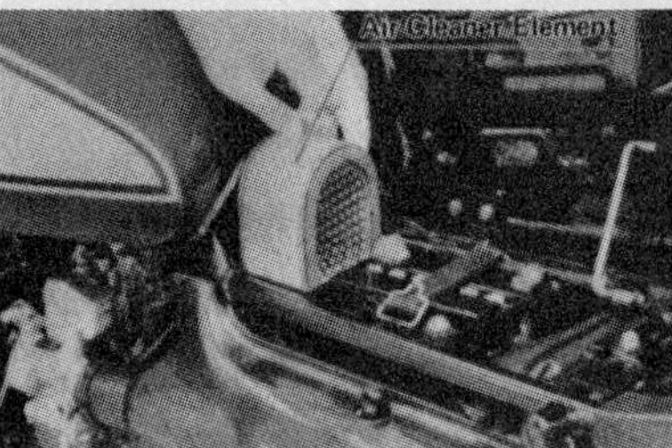

Removing the air filter element

and pull the element out.

Clean the element with gasoline or some other volatile solvent, then blow it dry from the inside out with compressed air. Do not use any cleaner which will not evaporate completely.

Inspect the element and sponge gaskets for signs of wear or damage, and replace the element if either are damaged. The gaskets can be glued on if they've come loose and are still in good condition. Be careful that when installing the element not to crimp the gaskets.

The average useful life span of one of these elements is approximately 8,000 miles or 12 months, or sooner if it has been cleaned 3 or 4 times due to use in dusty conditions.

Fuel System

(2,000 Mi/6 Mo)

The fuel filter, located in the fuel tap, and the fuel lines, should be removed and cleaned at the prescribed intervals, or whenever fuel delivery problems are suspected. Simply turn the fuel tap to the stop ("S") position, and unscrew the cup to gain access to the filter. Fuel flow at both the on and reserve positions can be checked at this time.

The sediment cup must be removed to gain access to the filter

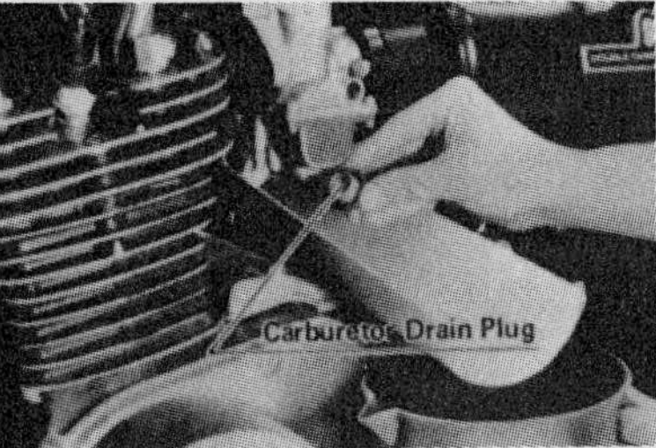

Make sure that the O-ring is in good condition

If there is any indication of water in the gas, turn the tap to the reserve position, and allow the fuel to flow out into a suitable container until only pure gas comes out. Remove the drain plugs from the bottom of each carburetor, and drain the float bowls also.

CAUTION: *Do not start the engine until any spilled gasoline has completely evaporated, or has been wiped up. If the tap allows any gas to pass while in the stop position, the tap should be repaired or replaced, or gas may leak into the crankcase and dilute the oil. Consult the "Fuel System" Chapter for additional information.*

Clean the filter screen and cup, and reinstall them on the tap using a new O-ring, if necessary. Inspect the fuel lines for cracks or damage, and replace them as necessary. Straighten out any kinks or sharp bends in the lines, and make sure that the filler cap vent is not plugged, as this can interfere with normal fuel delivery.

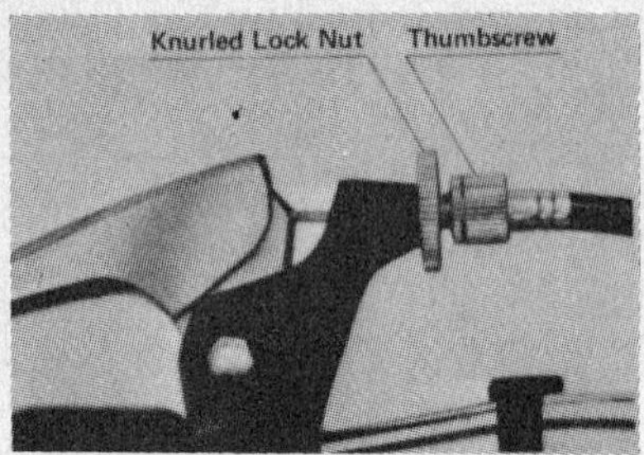

Clutch Adjustment

(2,000 Mi/6 Mo)

1. Loosen the knurled locknut at the hand lever, turn the thumbscrew in to its seat to provide maximum cable play, then secure the locknut.

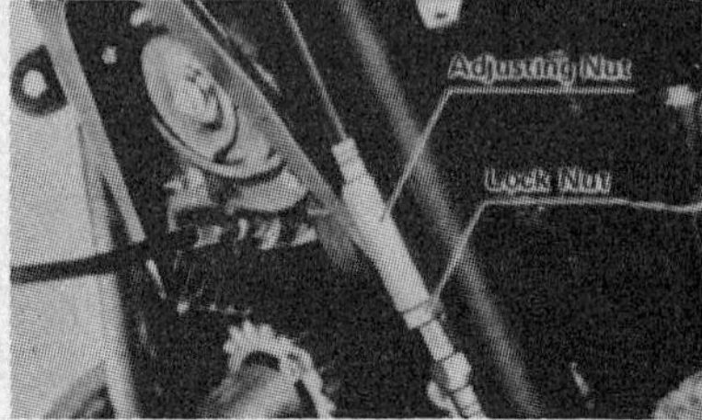

Cable adjusting points

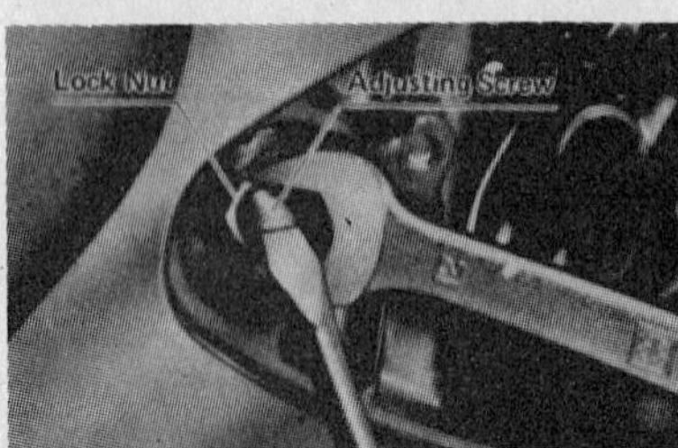

2. Loosen the locknut at the center of the cable, and screw in the adjuster to provide maximum cable play.

3. Remove the chain oil pump cover to gain access to the pushrod adjusting screw.

5. Gently turn in the adjusting screw to the point where it suddenly becomes hard to turn, then back it out ½ turn from that point, and secure the locknut while holding the screw steady with a screwdriver.

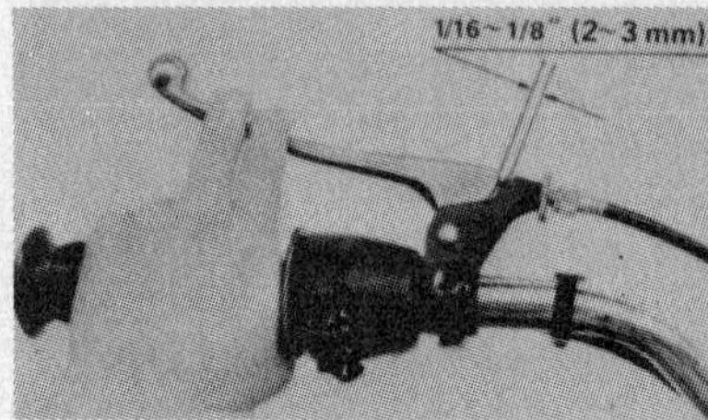

6. Making sure that the cable sleeve ends do not catch on the edge of the cable seat, take up the cable play at the cable center until there is from 1/16-⅛ in. (2-3 mm) play at the hand lever, then secure the cable center adjuster locknut.

7. Make fine adjustments at the hand lever, if necessary, until the cable play is within its specified limits, then secure the thumbscrew locknut, and replace the oil pump cover.

Throttle Cables

The Z1 has a butterfly-tye throttle linkage which is controlled by two cables; one for opening the throttle, and one for closing it down all the way. Rotating the throttle in the opposite direction from open, serves to lower the idle speed for a smoother shift into first gear.

The cables are adjusted to compensate for stretching, and to provide satisfactory throttle action. If the cables are adjusted too loosely, the engine will not respond immediately when the throttle grip is rotated; if the cables are too tight, the throttle will be too sensitive to minute changes in the throttle grip position, and in extreme cases, may cause the idle speed to vary as the handlebars are turned.

Adjust the cables by loosening the locknut on the opening cable, and adjusting out any slack before securing the locknut again. Loosen the locknut on the closing cable, and adjust it so there is about 1/16 in. (2 mm) of play in the throttle grip, then secure the locknut. The adjustment may be varied according to personal preference and riding style, however too tight an adjustment may cause the cables to stretch prematurely. Consult the "Tune-Up" Section for additional information.

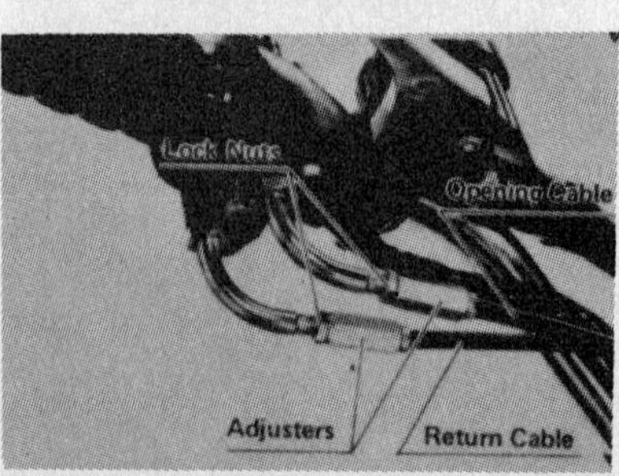

Always adjust the opening cable first

Chassis

STEERING HEAD (4,000 Mi/12 Mo)

Check the bearings by placing the bike on its center stand, and swinging the forks slowly through their full steering travel from stop-to-stop. Movement should be smooth, light, and free from any binding or rough spots, and the forks should be free to fall to either side of their own volition.

Any noticeable play means it's adjustment time

Check for play in the bearings by grabbing the bottom of the forks and trying to move them back and forth in line with the motorcycle. There should be no noticeable play.

Adjust the bearings in the following manner:

1. Loosen the steering stem head bolt, and the clamp bolt shown in the accompanying illustration.

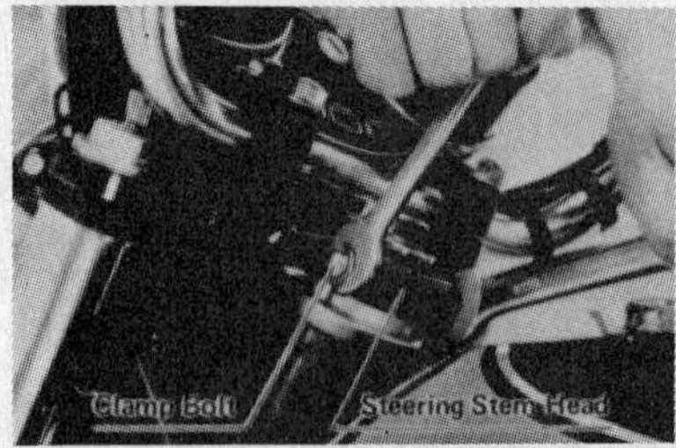

These operation should really be done with the tank removed

Make the adjustment slightly snug if the bearings and race have just been replaced

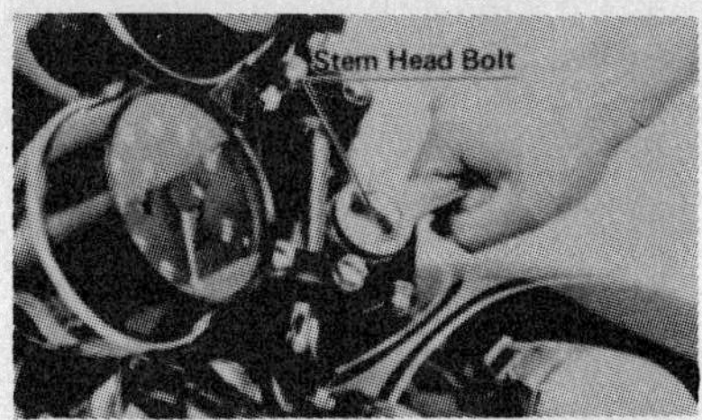

There are 4 clamp bolts to be attended to

2. Use a suitable hook spanner to turn the steering stem locknut down to tighten the steering, or up to loosen it.

3. Secure the head bolt and clamp, then loosen the two lower clamp bolts to let them reseat themselves, and re-tighten the bolts evenly. The upper clamp bolts should be torqued to 12-13 ft lbs (1.6-1.8 kg/m), and the two lower clamp bolts should be torqued to 40-43 ft lbs (5.4-6.0 kg/m).

FORK OIL (6,000 Mi/12 Mo)

Remove the drain screws from both fork sliders, then pump the forks several times while both wheels are on the ground to expel the old oil. Replace the drain screws, remove the top bolt from each fork tube, pour in the specified amount of oil, and replace the top bolts.

NOTE: *Draining the forks after the machine has been run hard will make the oil flow more readily.*

Drain plug location

Remove the top bolt after the oil has been drained

Kawasaki recommends using SAE-10W non-detergent oil, but heavier weights may be used to tune the suspension to your particular needs. Many aftermarket fork oils are available in various weights, or you could try ATF (automatic transmission fluid) if you like a really tight ride.

Make sure that you add the same amount of oil to each leg. A plastic baby bottle works well for measuring and pouring the oil. The oil level can be measured in either of the following manners:

1. Simply measure off and add 5.7 oz (169 cc) to each leg. If the fork has just been disassembled and cleaned, add 10 cc more to compensate for the oil that normally would be coating the parts.

2. Add oil until the level of the oil is 17 15/16 in. (455 mm) below the top of the tube. This is a particularly good way to check the fluid level if leaks are suspected, or if you simply wish to bring the level up to standard.

CAUTION: *Overfilling the forks will result in ruptured oil seals.*

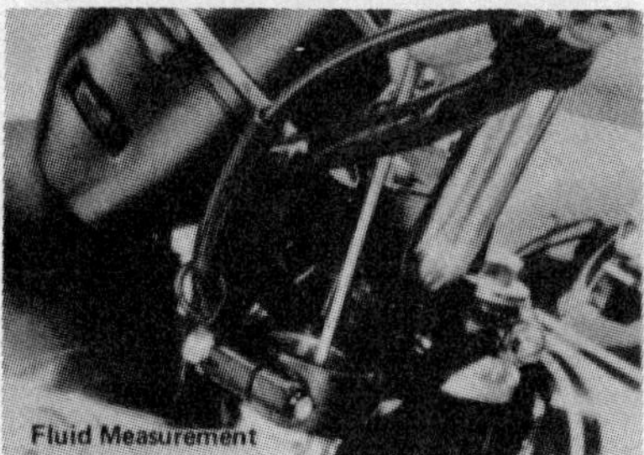

Measuring the height of the oil

REAR SUSPENSION (2,000 Mi/6 Mo)

Lubricate the swing arm pivot grease fitting using a high-pressure grease gun if possible, or a hand gun, using regular cup grease. Force the grease into the fitting until it comes out at both sides of the swing arm, and wipe off any excess. If the grease doesn't come out, first check the fitting for blockage or damage, and if that doesn't do it, disassemble the swing arm and thoroughly clean out the old grease.

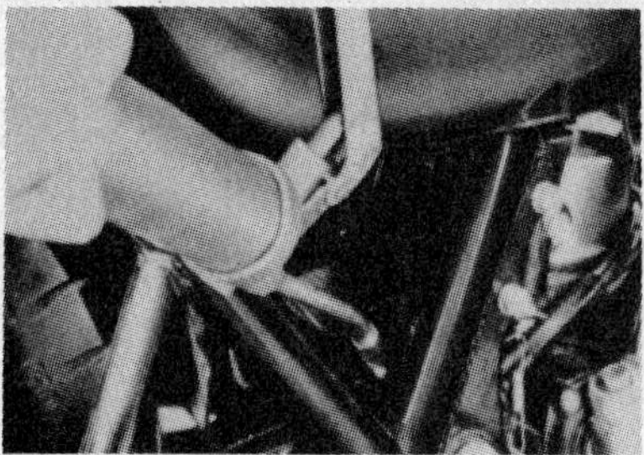

Swing arm lubrication

Inspect the swing arm at this time for signs of cracked welds, fatigue marks, or a bent or otherwise damaged condition. There should be absolutely no side-play in the bushings. Consult the "Chassis" Section for additional information.

Brakes

FRONT DISC BRAKE (2,000 Mi/6 Mo)

The front disc brake is atuomatically adjusted when in use, and therefore the condition of the brake pads should be checked periodically for wear. When either pad is worn down to the red line, the pads should be replaced.

The brake lever is adjustable, however, the need for adjustment, other than to reduce vibration of the lever, indicates excessive wear of some of the brake components.

Adjust the lever by loosening the locknut, and turning the adjusting bolt a fraction of a turn so that the lever has less than 3/16 in. (5 mm) of play. Hold the adjusting bolt steady while securing the locknut, and make sure that there is still play in the lever after the locknut is tightened.

The brake fluid should be drained and refilled, along with a careful check of each component in the system once each year, or every 6,000 miles. Leaks or a spongy feel at the lever should be corrected immediately. Consult the "Chassis" Section for additional information.

REAR BRAKE (2,000 Mi/6 Mo)

Brake adjustment to compensate for wear actually consists of 3 separate adjustments: brake pedal position, cam lever angle, and brake pedal travel.

Adjust the brake in the following manner:

1. Check the position of the brake pedal in relation to the right front foot rest. It should be about 1/16 in. (2 mm) lower than the foot rest, and can be adjusted by loosening the adjusting bolt locknut, and rotating the bolt until the desired adjustment is attained. Be sure to secure the locknut, once a suitable adjustment is arrived at.

2. Lightly depress the brake pedal by

hand and note the angle formed between the actuating lever and the brake rod. If the angle is not within 80-90°, remove the lever and reposition it to correct the angle.

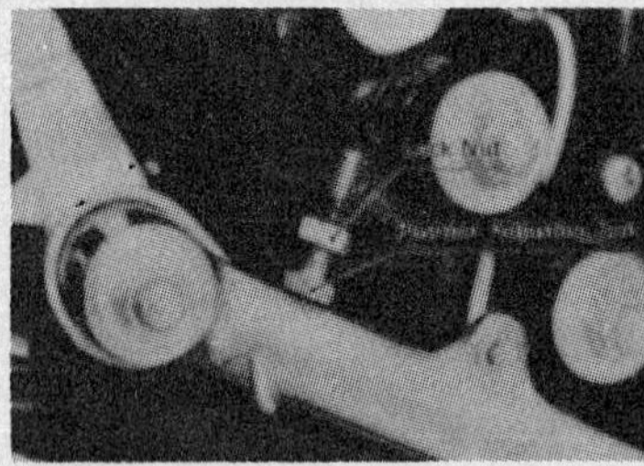

CAUTION: *The brake linings must be checked for wear before the lever is repositioned to avoid damage to the drum caused by worn linings.*

3. Make the fine adjustment by screwing in the brake rod adjusting nut until the brake pedal travel is within ¾-1¼ in. (20-30 mm) from the rest position to the fully applied position when the pedal is lightly depressed by hand.

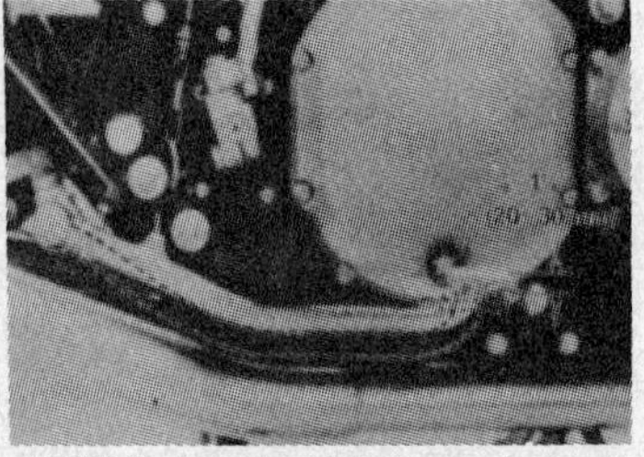

4. With the machine on the center stand, spin the rear wheel to check for dragging, and either readjust the brakes, or disassemble and repair the assembly to adjust for this.

NOTE: *An adjustment made with the machine on its center stand may not be the same once the machine is resting on both wheels.*

BRAKE LAMP SWITCH

The front brake lamp switch is hydraulically operated, and therefore needs no adjustment. The rear brake lamp switch is mechanical, and requires periodic adjustment to compensate for stretching of its spring, damage to the brake pedal, or to suit your preference for when the lamp comes on.

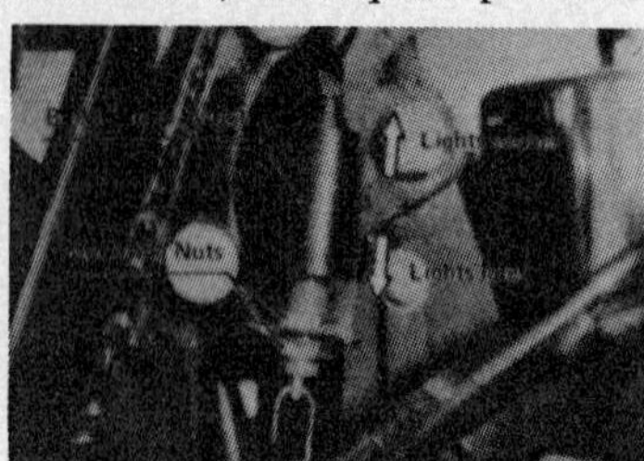

Adjust the switch by loosening the two mounting nuts, and moving the switch up or down so that the brake lamp will light after ½-¾ in. (15-20 mm) of pedal movement. Secure the locknuts when a suitable adjustment has been attained.

CAUTION: *Do not rotate the switch body itself while performing the adjustment, as this may damage the wiring.*

Final Drive

DRIVE CHAIN (2,000 Mi/6 Mo)

NOTE: *A dry chain should be lubricated before adjustment so that the links will not bind and restrict chain movement, making it seem tighter than it really is. If tension varies alternately between too loose and too tight as the chain is rotated, remove it and inspect for excessive wear.*

Chain slack, as measured at the center of the bottom run with the machine on its center stand, should be within 1-1½ in. (25-40 mm). Otherwise, the chain must be adjusted as follows:

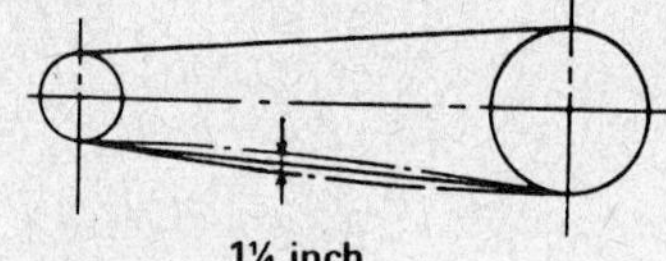

1¼ inch
(30~35 mm)

Adjustment must be checked with both wheels on the ground on the seat

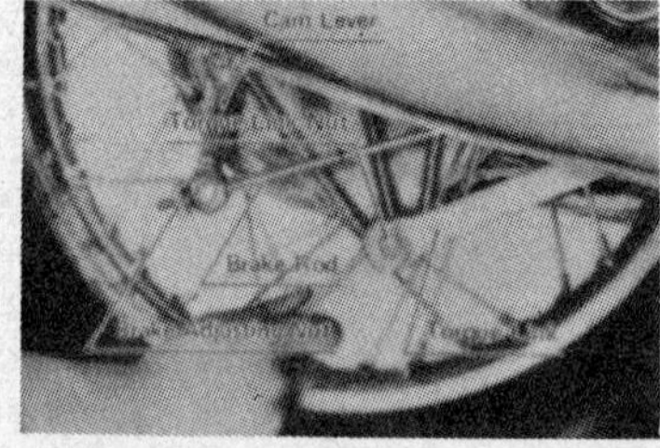

1. Place the machine on its center stand, then loosen the brake torque link nut, the axle nut (after removing the cotter pin), and the chain adjuster locknuts.

2. If the chain seems too tight, kick the wheel forward to loosen it. The tips of the adjusters must be firmly seated in their seats in the adjusting block at all times during adjustment.

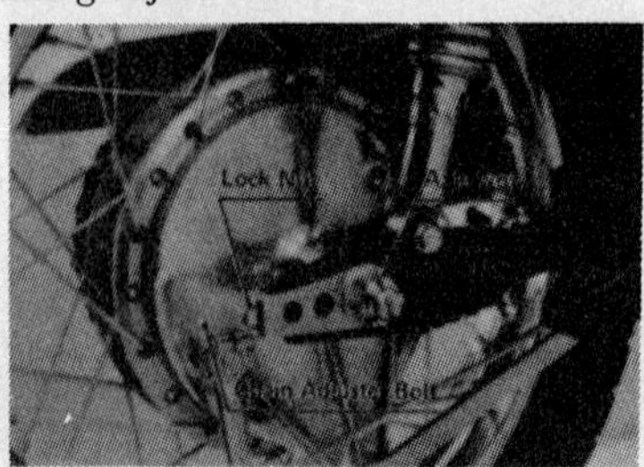

3. Turn the adjusters in evenly until the chain has the correct amount of slack, then secure the locknuts. The chain adjuster marks on both sides must be even or the rear wheel will be out of alignment.

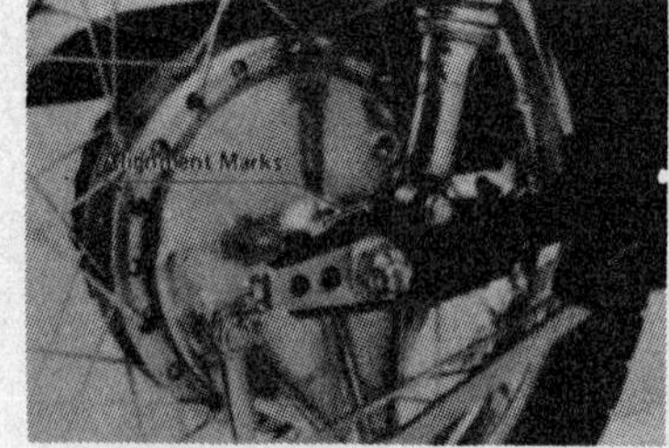

4. Torque the axle nut to 95-115 ft lbs (13-16 kg/m), install a new cotter pin, and recheck the adjustment.

5. Torque the brake torque link nut to 22-25 ft lbs (3-3.5 kg/m).

6. Check the rear brake and brake lamp adjustments.

Wheels

(3,000 Mi/6 Mo)

Tighten any loose spokes until they are approximately as taut as the neighboring spokes. If any spokes are broken, or if a large number are loose, the wheel should be removed for complete servicing.

Check the run-out of the wheel rim with a dial indicator or a fixed stylus if the

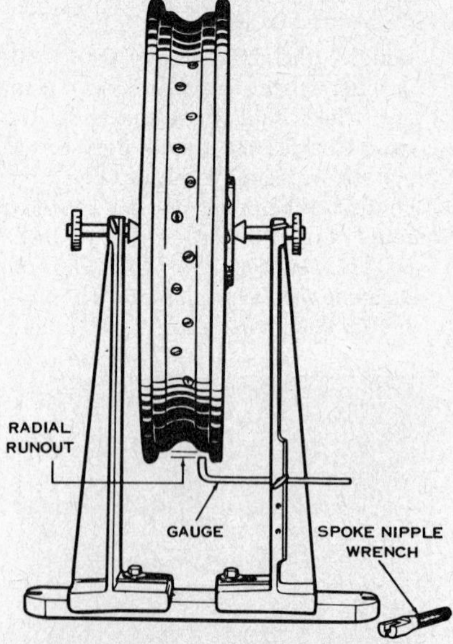

Checking rim run-out with a fixed stylus

Checking rim run-out with a dial indicator

tire is wearing unevenly, or if a wobble is apparent. If run-out exceeds 0.04-0.012 in. (1.0-3.0 mm) the wheel will have to be trued, and if the wheel consistantly stops at any particular position when spun, it will have to be balanced. Consult the "Chassis" Section for additional information.

Check the wheel bearings for side-play, and the axles for a bent condition, and replace any damaged components as described in the "Chassis" Section.

Tires

(3,000 Mi/6 Mo)

Examine the tires for casing damage (splits, bubbles, etc.) and for objects lodged in the tread. Replace any tire whose tread depth is below the specifications given below:

Standard	*Service Limit*	
	Normal Speed	*Over 80 mph*
FRONT		
0.157 in. (4.0 mm)	0.04 in. (1 mm)	0.04 in. (1 mm)
REAR		
0.276 in. (7.0 mm)	0.08 in. (2 mm)	0.12 in. (3 mm)

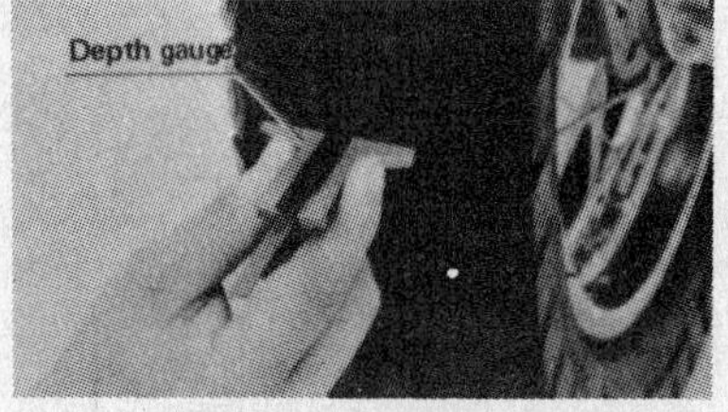

Checking for tire wear

The maximum recommended load, in addition to vehicle weight, is 330 lbs (150 kg), and this should not be exceeded as a safety precaution.

The following chart gives the recommended tire pressures and sizes. Wider profile tires may be used at the same pressures, and all tires should be overinflated by 3-6 psi for better heat dissipation when used for high-speed touring.

Tire Pressure Table

Brand/ Type	*Size*	*Air Pressure*	
		One Rider	*Two Riders*
FRONT Dunlop F6	3.25-19 4PR	26 psi (1.8 kg/ cm²)	26 psi (1.8 kg/ cm²)
REAR Dunlop K87	4.00-18 4PR	31 psi (2.2 kg/ cm²)	36 psi (2.5 kg/ cm²)

Routine Lubrication

When giving the bike a thorough going over, or when necessary, lubricate the components shown in the accompanying illustrations.

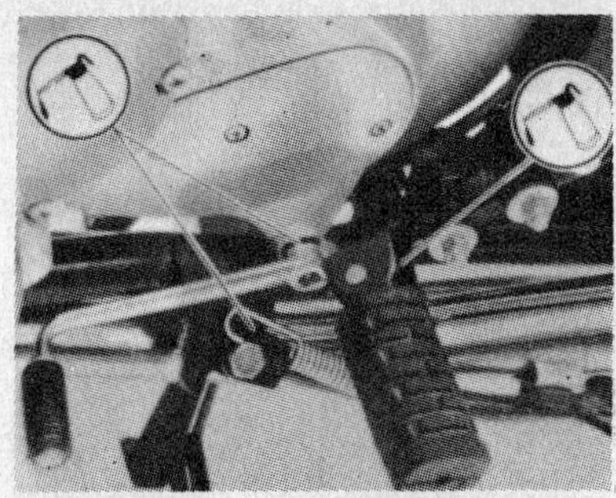

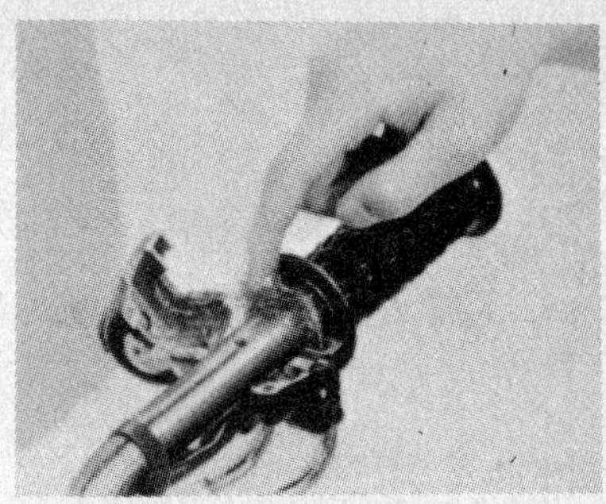

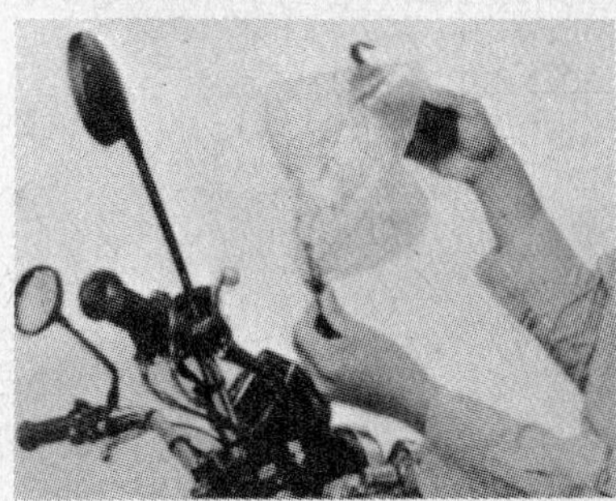

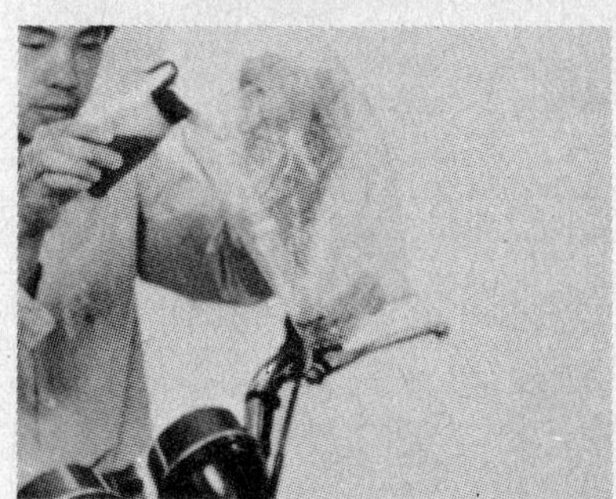

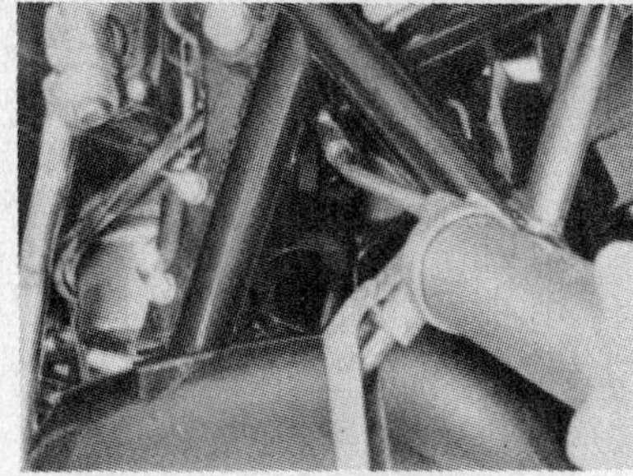

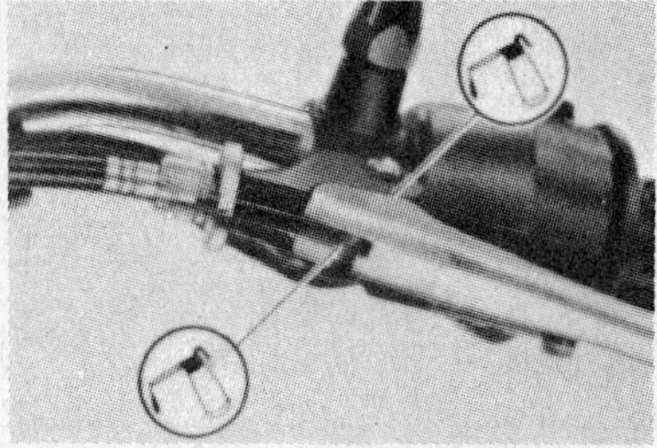

TUNE-UP AND MAINTENANCE

TUNE-UP OPERATIONS

Valve Clearance

NOTE: *Before you start, read the following as it may save you a lot of unnecessary aggravation:*

An oil film can form between the adjusting shim and the top of the valve which can cause misleading measurements. You may find that the clearance isn't what you expected it to be after the correct shim is installed, and this film is the reason. To avoid this, do the following:

1. Measure the clearance as directed in the "Adjustment" Section.
2. Remove and measure the shim to determine what you need (i.e., if the clearance is 0.006 in., a 0.002 in. shim will result in a clearance of 0.004 in.).
3. Kick the engine through a couple dozen times with the spark plugs out and the ignition switch "Off" to remove the film, then measure the clearance again.

CAUTION: *Never rotate the engine with any of the adjusting shims removed as this may damage the cam and tappet.*

NOTE: *The type of valve tappets used in all models up to engine number Z1E-08979 have caused shim fracturing problems on some machines. If your machine is equipped with this type of tappet, consult the "Engine Disassembly; Camshafts" Section for additional information.*

PERIODIC MAINTENANCE CHART

	Frequency			
Operation	After initial 500 miles (800 km)	After initial 2,000 miles (3,000 km)	Every subsequent 2,000 miles (3,000 km)	Every 4,000 miles (6,000 km)
Lubricate drive chain	Every 200 miles (300 km)			
Adjust cam chain	Every 1,000 miles (1,500 km)			
Check, tighten spokes	●	●	●	
Adjust drive chain	●	●	●	
Adjust brakes	●	●	●	
Adjust clutch	●	●	●	
Tighten nuts and bolts	●	●	●	
Change engine oil	●	●	●	
Replace oil filter element	●	●		●
Clean air cleaner element		●	●	
Lubricate motorcycle		●	●	
Clean, set spark plugs		●	●	
Adjust points, check timing		●	●	
Check tire wear		●	●	
Check chain wear			●	
Check brake shoes and drum			●	
Clean fuel lines			●	
Check valve lifter clearance				●
Check steering play				●
Change brake fluid	Every 1 year or 6,000 miles (10,000 km)			
Change front fork oil				
Re-grease wheel bearings	Every 12,000 miles (20,000 km)			

Removing the valve cover

ADJUSTMENT

1. Open the seat all the way and remove the fuel tank, then remove the valve cover and cover gasket.
2. Rotate the engine so that the cam lobe (the highest portion of the cam) for the valve to be checked is pointing directly away from the valve lifter.
3. Measure the clearance between the cam and the valve shim using a thickness gauge. The clearance should be within 0.002-0.004 in. (0.05-0.10 mm) for both the intake and exhaust valves. If the feeler gauge of the proper clearance will not fit between the cam and the shim, or if it slides through with little or no resistance, the clearance should be adjusted. It should be noted that some of the valves may not require adjustment. Clearance is correct if the next size thinner gauge fits easily and if the next size thicker will not fit, or fits with great resistance.

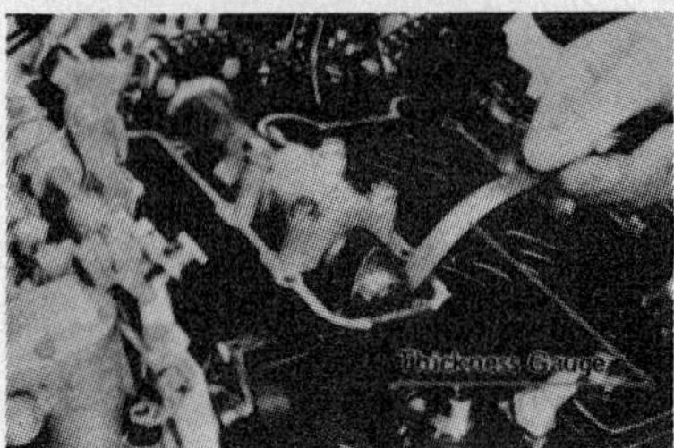

Be sure the gauge is between the shim and the cam lobe

4. If the clearance is in need of adjustment, use either of the following methods for removing the valve shim:

   a. Rotate the engine so that the cam lobe presses the lifter down, install the special tool (Part No. 57001-109) as illustrated, then rotate the engine so

MAINTENANCE DATA

ENGINE AND TRANSMISSION OIL	
Recommended oil	SAE 10W-40, 10W-50, or 20W-50. Service Rating SE or SD
Capacity	4.2 qt.
Oil pressure	2.8 psi at 3,000 rpm (Oil temperature 140°F, 60°C)
FRONT FORK	
Recommended oil	10W, 10W-30
Capacity	5.7 oz (169 cc)
FUEL TANK	
Total capacity	4.7 U.S. gal. (18 l.)
Reserve tank capacity	4.2 qt. (4 l.)
Recommended fuel	Regular
CHAIN OILER TANK	
Recommended oil	30W or 40W
Capacity	0.95 U.S. qt. (0.9 l.)
TIRE PRESSURE*	
Front	
one rider	26 psi
two riders	26 psi
Rear	
one rider	31 psi
two riders	36 psi

* Add from 3-6 psi to each tire for high-speed riding

that the cam lobe points directly away from the tappet and remove the shim.

NOTE: *The tappet is notched so that the shim can be grasped.*

b. Unbolt the camshafts to remove and replace the shims.

Using the special tool to remove the shim

CAUTION: *If the camshafts are unbolted, the valve timing will probably be altered. Consult the "Camshaft Timing" Section for additional information before securing the camshafts.*

5. If the valve clearance was less than 0.002 in., use a thinner shim; if the clearance was greater than 0.004 in., use a thicker shim. Shims are available in 0.05 mm increments from 2.00 mm to 3.20 mm. Consult the accompanying Valve Adjustment Chart.

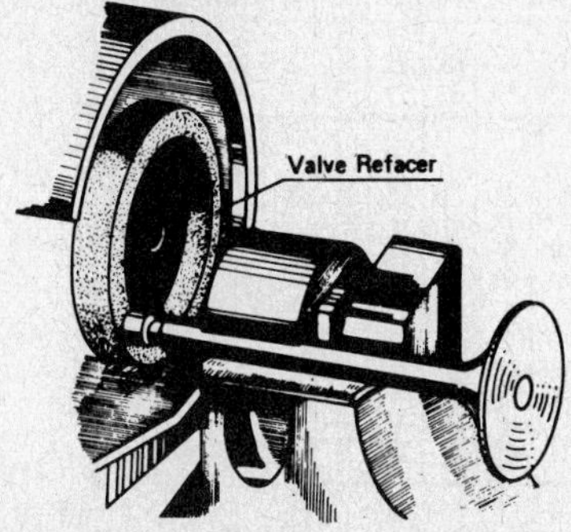

CAUTION: If the valve stem is ground down, be sure to leave at least .16 inch (4.1 mm) of stem end above the wide groove portion.

Grinding the valve stem

6. If the valve seat is worn to the point where the smallest shim will not provide the correct clearance, check for excessive wear or burning of the valve and seat. Bring the clearance within the specified limits by removing the valve and grinding down the top of the stem slightly while holding the valve in a V-block to keep it at right angles to the side of the grinder. There must be at least 0.16 in. (4.1 mm) of stem above the valve spring collar groove.

Camshaft Chain

ADJUSTMENT

1. Loosen the adjuster locknut and bolt.

2. Rotate the engine slowly a couple times to allow the spring loaded tensioner to take up the slack evenly, then secure first the bolt, and then its locknut.

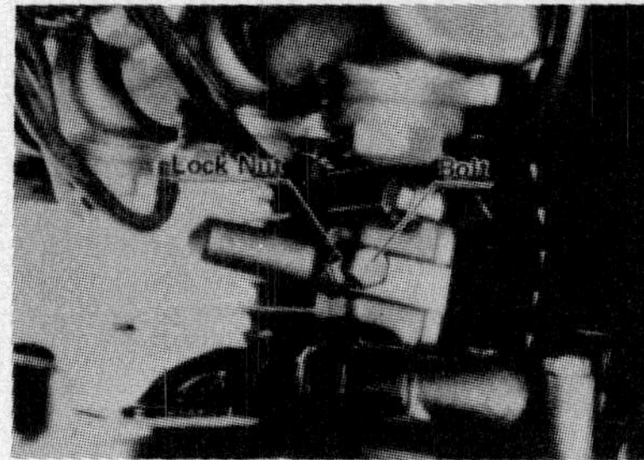

Cam chain adjuster

Contact Breaker Points

SERVICE

If the points are heavily pitted, replace them and the condensers together. Disconnect the electrical leads, taking care to note where everything goes; unscrew the points and condensers from their base plate, and mount the new parts. An alternative method is to install a new plate, points, and condensers assembly which comes ready to mount. If you take it all apart yourself, be careful not to crush the fiber washers during reassembly, and this may cause electrical leaks which can short out the points.

Place a drop or two of some non-oily solvent on a piece of paper and pull it through the points to remove any dirt or preservative coating from the contact surfaces. Put a small daub of distributor cam lubricator, oil, or another high-melting point grease on the contact breaker cam (oil should be placed directly on the felt pad but use it sparingly to avoid contaminating the contact surfaces). This will prevent the points' rubbing block and cam from wearing excessively, thereby reducing the points' gap.

BREAKER POINT GAP ADJUSTMENT

1. Rotate the crankshaft until the points set to be adjusted is at its widest opening (the highest point of the cam lobe). Check the gap using a suitable thickness gauge. If the gap is not within the specified limits of 0.012-0.016 in. (0.-3-0.4 mm), loosen the screws and use a

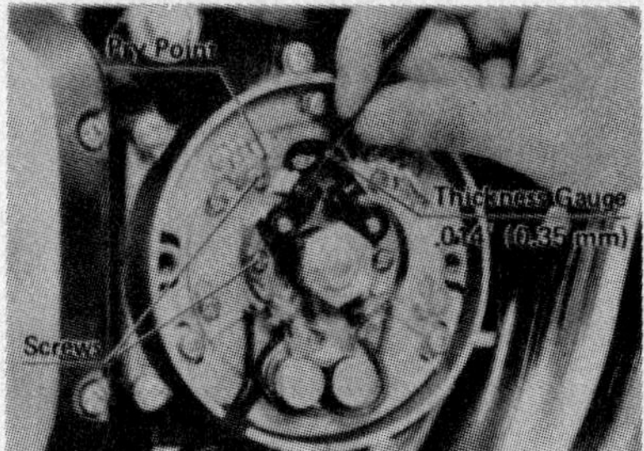

Adjusting the point gap

screwdriver at the pry point to increase or decrease the gap as necessary. The optimal setting is 0.014 in. (0.35 mm), and the thickness gauge should move between the points with some slight resistance; the next larger and smaller sizes should be obviously too thin and too thick respectively. Recheck the adjustment

Kawasaki Z1 Valve Adjustment Chart

PART NUMBER PREFIX 12037-

PRESENT SHIM SIZE

VALVE CLEARANCE

	P/N SUFFIX	-001	-002	-003	-004	-005	-006	-007	-008	-009	-010	-011	-012	-013	-014	-015	-016	-017	-018	-019	-020	-021	-022	-023	-024	-025
	INCHES	.079	.081	.083	.085	.087	.089	.091	.093	.094	.096	.098	.100	.102	.104	.106	.108	.110	.112	.114	.116	.118	.120	.122	.124	.126
	MILLIMETERS	2.00	2.05	2.10	2.15	2.20	2.25	2.30	2.35	2.40	2.45	2.50	2.55	2.60	2.65	2.70	2.75	2.80	2.85	2.90	2.95	3.00	3.05	3.10	3.15	3.20
INCHES	MILLIMETERS																									
.000-.001	0.00-0.04		2.00	2.05	2.10	2.15	2.20	2.25	2.30	2.35	2.40	2.45	2.50	2.55	2.60	2.65	2.70	2.75	2.80	2.85	2.90	2.95	3.00	3.05	3.10	3.15
.002-.004	0.05-0.10	SPECIFIED CLEARANCE/ NO CHANGE REQUIRED																								
.005-.007	0.11-0.19	2.10	2.15	2.20	2.25	2.30	2.35	2.40	2.45	2.50	2.55	2.60	2.65	2.70	2.75	2.80	2.85	2.90	2.95	3.00	3.05	3.10	3.15	3.20		
.008-.009	0.20-0.24	2.15	2.20	2.25	2.30	2.35	2.40	2.45	2.50	2.55	2.60	2.65	2.70	2.75	2.80	2.85	2.90	2.95	3.00	3.05	3.10	3.15	3.20			
.010-.011	0.25-0.29	2.20	2.25	2.30	2.35	2.40	2.45	2.50	2.55	2.60	2.65	2.70	2.75	2.80	2.85	2.90	2.95	3.00	3.05	3.10	3.15	3.20				
.012-.013	0.30-0.34	2.25	2.30	2.35	2.40	2.45	2.50	2.55	2.60	2.65	2.70	2.75	2.80	2.85	2.90	2.95	3.00	3.05	3.10	3.15	3.20					
.014-.015	0.35-0.39	2.30	2.35	2.40	2.45	2.50	2.55	2.60	2.65	2.70	2.75	2.80	2.85	2.90	2.95	3.00	3.05	3.10	3.15	3.20						
.016-.017	0.40-0.44	2.35	2.40	2.45	2.50	2.55	2.60	2.65	2.70	2.75	2.80	2.85	2.90	2.95	3.00	3.05	3.10	3.15	3.20							
.018-.019	0.45-0.49	2.40	2.45	2.50	2.55	2.60	2.65	2.70	2.75	2.80	2.85	2.90	2.95	3.00	3.05	3.10	3.15	3.20								
.020-.021	0.50-0.54	2.45	2.50	2.55	2.60	2.65	2.70		2.80	2.85	2.90	2.95	3.00	3.05	3.10	3.15	3.20									
.022-.023	0.55-0.59	2.50	2.55	2.60	2.65	2.70	2.75	2.80	2.85	2.90	2.95	3.00	3.05	3.10	3.15	3.20										
.024-.025	0.60-0.64	2.55	2.60	2.65	2.70	2.75	2.80	2.85	2.90	2.95	3.00	3.05	3.10	3.15	3.20											
.026-.027	0.65-0.69	2.60	2.65	2.70	2.75	2.80	2.85	2.90	2.95	3.00	3.05	3.10	3.15	3.20												
.028-.029	0.70-0.74	2.65	2.70	2.75	2.80	2.85	2.90	2.95	3.00	3.05	3.10	3.15	3.20													
.030-.031	0.75-0.79	2.70	2.75	2.80	2.85	2.90	2.95	3.00	3.05	3.10	3.15	3.20														
.032-.033	0.80-0.84	2.75	2.80	2.85	2.90	2.95	3.00	3.05	3.10	3.15	3.20															
.034-.035	0.85-0.89	2.80	2.85	2.90	2.95	3.00	3.05	3.10	3.15	3.20																
.036-.037	0.90-0.94	2.85	2.90	2.95	3.00	3.05	3.10	3.15	3.20																	
.038-.039	0.95-0.99	2.90	2.95	3.00	3.05	3.10	3.15	3.20																		
.040-.041	1.00-1.04	2.95	3.00	3.05	3.10	3.15	3.20																			
.042-.043	1.05-1.09	3.00	3.05	3.10	3.15	3.20																				
.044-.045	1.10-1.14	3.05	3.10	3.15	3.20																					
.046-.047	1.15-1.19	3.10	3.15	3.20																						
.048-.049	1.20-1.24	3.15	3.20																							
.050-.051	1.25-1.29	3.20																								

INSTALL THIS SHIM

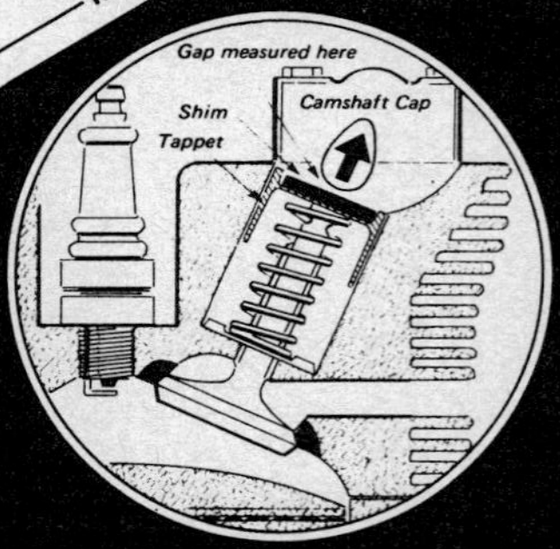

1. To use the chart, locate the measured gap on the vertical column on the left. Find the thickness of the old shim in the top horizontal column and look down that column to find the required new shim.

2. If the valve clearance is greater than 0.10mm (.004"), use a thicker shim to correct to the specified clearance.

3. If the valve clearance is less than 0.05mm (.002"), select a thinner shim. NOTE: If there is no clearance between the shim and the cam, select a shim which is several sizes smaller and then remeasure the gap.

4. Do not put shim stock under the shim. This may cause the shim to pop out at high rpm.

5. NOTE: Check the valve clearance with the cam lobe pointing directly away from the valve, as pictured. Checking the clearance at any other cam position may result in improper valve clearance.

after securing the screws, and run a business card through the points to remove any dirt from the thickness gauge.

2. Rotate the engine until the other points set is at its widest position, and adjust them in the same manner.

Ignition Timing

STATIC TIMING

1. Clean and adjust the points as described in the "Contact Breaker Points" Section.

2. Rotate the engine until the "F" mark on the timing advancer for the set of points to be adjusted is slightly to the left of the timing mark located just above the advancer.

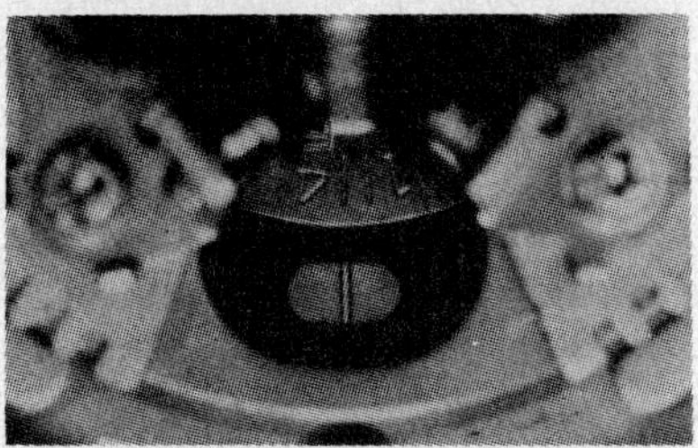

Aligning the timing mark

3. Connect a timing light or ohmmeter to the appropriate set of points with one lead on either the leaf spring on the points wire mounting bolt, and the other on a ground (i.e., an engine cooling fin, the frame, etc.). Turn on the ignition switch, if an ohmmeter or timing light without a power source is used.

4. Rotate the engine until the "F" mark is aligned with the timing mark. The light should flicker as the two come together. If it does, the timing is correct and you should now do the other set of points; if not, go on to the next step.

Adjusting the points adjusting plate

5. Loosen the adjusting plate mounting screws, and use a screwdriver at the pry points to position the points so that they just begin to open as the timing marks come into alignment. Always rotate the engine back past the point of alignment by a few degrees before trying again. If the adjusting plate will not travel far enough to arrive at a suitable adjustment, loosen the 3 mounting plate screws and rotate the plate to provide more room for adjustment. Secure the screws and recheck the timing before going on to the other set of points.

Mounting plate mounting screws

DYNAMIC TIMING

1. Clean and adjust the points as described in the "Contact Breaker Points" section.

2. Run the engine until its normal operating temperature is reached, and adjust the idle, if necessary, to within 800-1,000 rpm as described in the "Carburetor Synchronization and Adjustment" Section.

Dynamic timing with a strobe light

3. Connect the strobe light according to the manufacturer's instructions, so that the impulses from cylinders 1 and 4 are monitored. Aim the light at the timing marks. The "F" 1.4 mark should be aligned with the timing index mark. If it isn't, loosen the mounting screws, and use a screwdriver at the pry points until the marks do line up.

4. Repeat the above steps on the "F" 2.3 mark.

5. Advance the engine speed to about 2,900-3,100 rpm and check both sets of points. If the timing if off, the advance mechanism is probably at fault.

NOTE: *The idle speed can be regulated by either the throttle stop screw or the throttle grip tensioner.*

6. If the timing is unsteady, remove the contact breaker plate assembly and examine the advance unit. Look for weak or broken springs, or a bent advancer shaft. If either spring is defective, replace both of them. If the advancer shaft is bent (noticeable as the engine is turned over), remove the advancer unit and bend the shaft until total run-out is less than 0.004 in. (0.1 mm), or replace the assembly. When reinstalling the advance unit, make sure that the pin is located in the hole. Consult the "Electrical System" Section for additional information.

Turning in the adjusting screw will keep the throttle where you want it

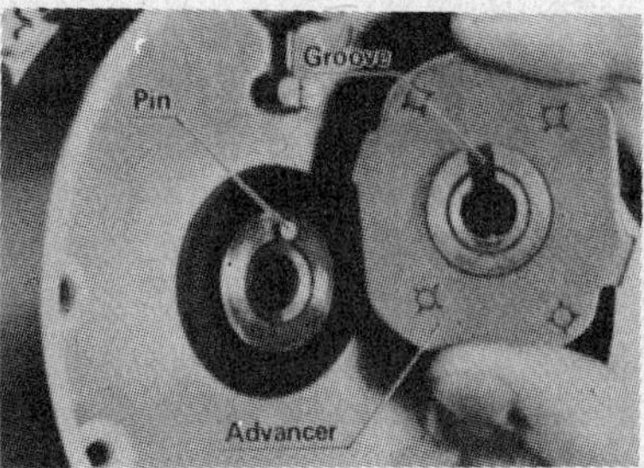

Installing the advance mechanism

Carburetor Synchronization and Adjustment

PRELIMINARY ADJUSTMENT

Perform the following operations as a prelude to the actual adjustment anytime the carbs are rebuilt or replaced, or if the engine idles especially rough.

1. Remove the carburetors as described in the "Fuel System" Chapter.

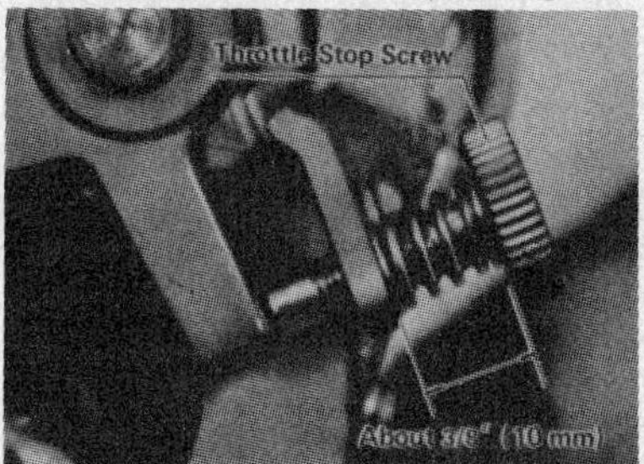

Throttle stop screw adjustment

2. Turn the throttle stop screw in or out until there is about ⅜ in. (10 mm) between the bracket and the underside of the screw head.

3. Loosen the closed-throttle stopper locknut, and rotate the eccentric stopper screw until there is about 1/16 in. (1.5-2.0 mm) clearance between the stopper and the top of the pulley.

4. Locate the notch cut into the throttle valve, then loosen the locknut and rotate the adjusting screw until there is about 0.024-0.028 in. (0.6-0.7 mm) clearance between the notch and the bottom of the carburetor bore, and secure the locknut.

NOTE: *This is a very delicate operation which must be performed on each of the carbs, so that the adjustment is as close as possible for all 4.*

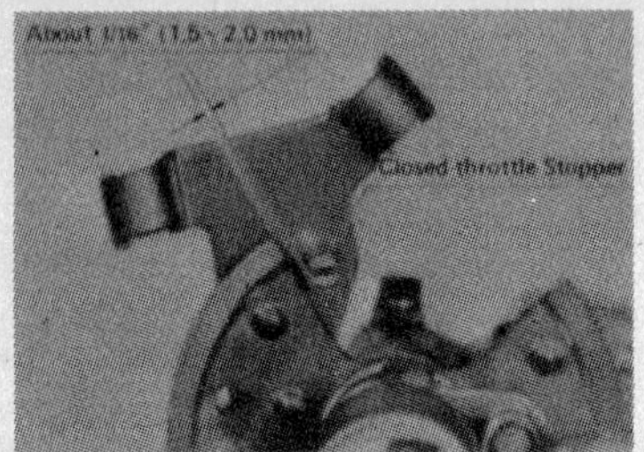

Closed-throttle stopper adjuster

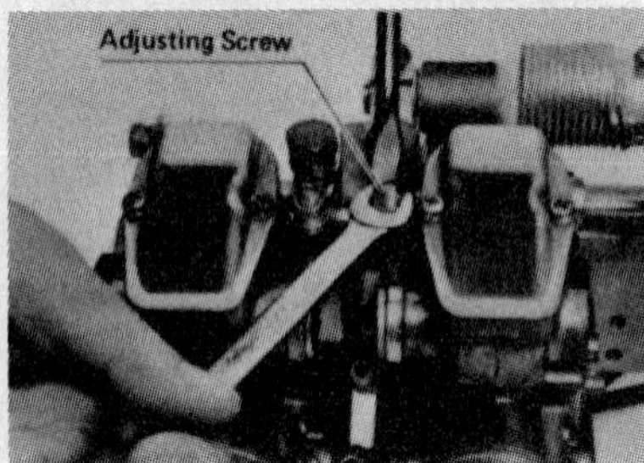

Throttle valve adjusting screw and locknut

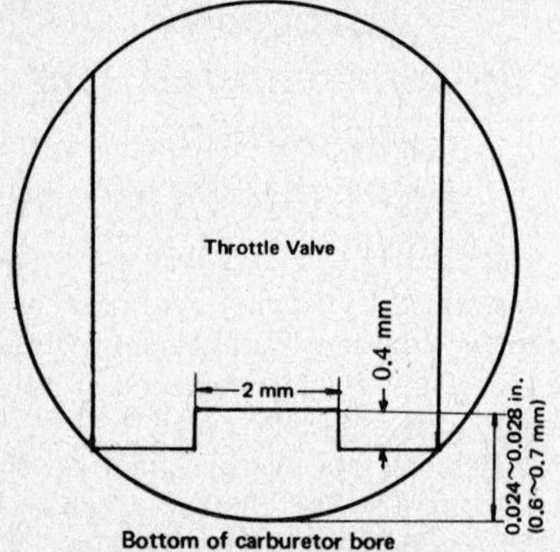

Throttle valve clearance

5. Open the throttle by rotating the pulley until the bottom edge of the lowest of the 4 throttle valves is even with the top of the carburetor bore, then rotate the open-throttle stopper screw so that the pulley is stopped at that point.

Adjusting the opened-throttle stopper

6. Gently turn each of the carburetor pilot air screws in to their seats, then back them all out 1½ turns to provide an equal arbitrary adjustment.

7. Mount the carburetor bank onto the engine, and adjust the throttle cables as described in the "Maintenance" Section.

ADJUSTMENT

1. Run the engine for at least 5 minutes until normal operating temperature is reached, then adjust the engine idle speed using the throttle stop screw until the idle speed is about 800-1,000 rpm according to the tachometer.

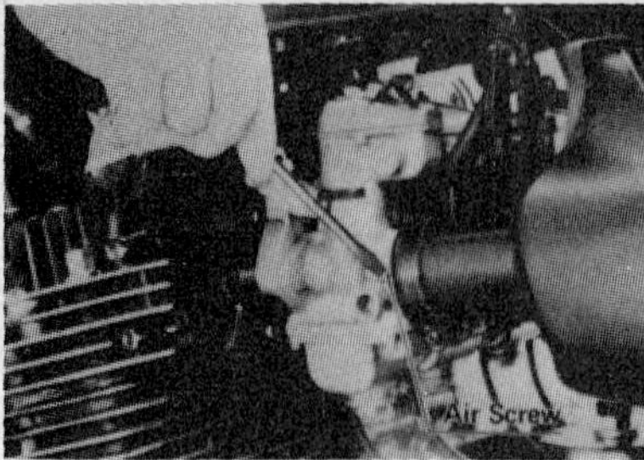

Adjusting the pilot mixture

2. Adjust the pilot air screw on each carburetor to that position where the highest idle speed is reached. If the idle speed exceeds the limits given in the previous step, lower the idle speed to within the limits using the idle stop screw.

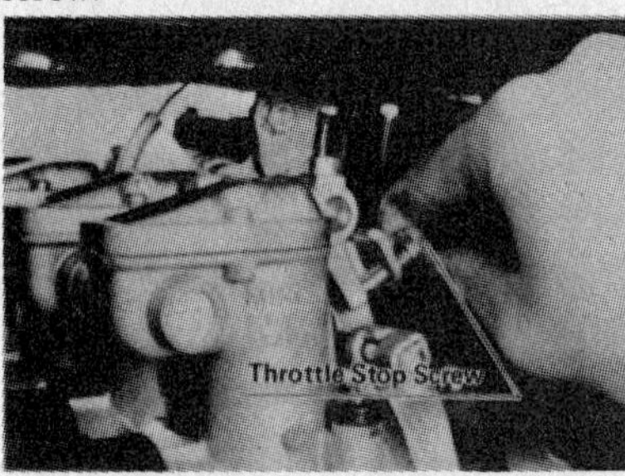

Adjusting the throttle stop screw

NOTE: *If any air screw can be turned in to within ½ turn from its seat without any appreciable rise in idle speed, there is probably something wrong inside that carb.*

3. Turn in each air screw evenly some small arbitrary number of turns (i.e., ¼-½ turn), then readjust the idle speed to within the specified limits.

4. Adjust the manifold vacuum of each carburetor using one of the following methods, depending on the equipment available. The machine should be standing in a good airflow to keep the engine operating temperature down.

Without Vacuum Gauges

1. Pay careful attention to the exhaust noise, and place your hands behind the mufflers to feel the exhaust pressure.

2. Compensate for any variations in exhaust noise or pressure by making adjustments to the throttle valve adjusting screws for the carburetor(s) in question. Use either the special tool (Part No. 57001-120), or suitable substitutes to loosen the locknut and rotate the adjusting screws. Backing the screw(s) out will increase pressure, and turning it in will decrease it. Try to keep the idle speed as low as possible while maintaining a balanced pressure for all 4 carbs. Be sure to secure each locknut while holding the adjusting screw steady with a screwdriver.

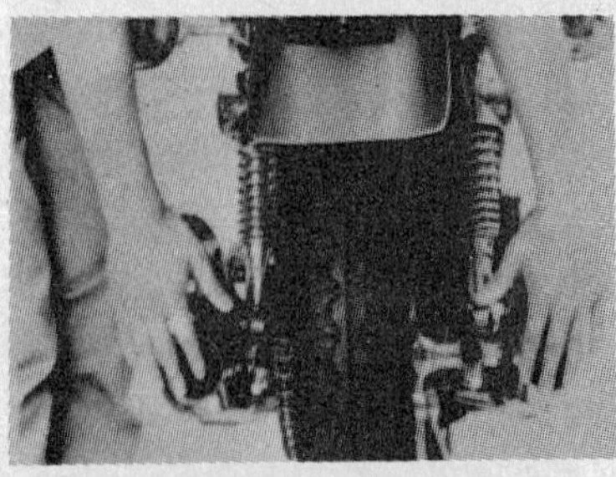

Feeling for even exhaust pulses

Adjusting the throttle valves using the special tool

CAUTION: *If the special tool is not available, you can use a screwdriver and a box-end wrench, but be careful not to bend or place excessive pressure on any of the adjusting screws while loosening or securing the locknuts as this may cause damage to the carburetor. It will be helpful when doing this if the gas tank is removed or raised. An empty 16 oz beer can will probably help by raising both the tank and your spirits.*

NOTE: *Adjusting the vacuum on one carb will cause changes in the pressure on all of the others, so be prepared to compensate for this.*

3. Readjust the air screws on any carburetors which have been readjusted, then readjust the idle speed to within 800-1,000 rpm by adjusting the throttle stop screw.

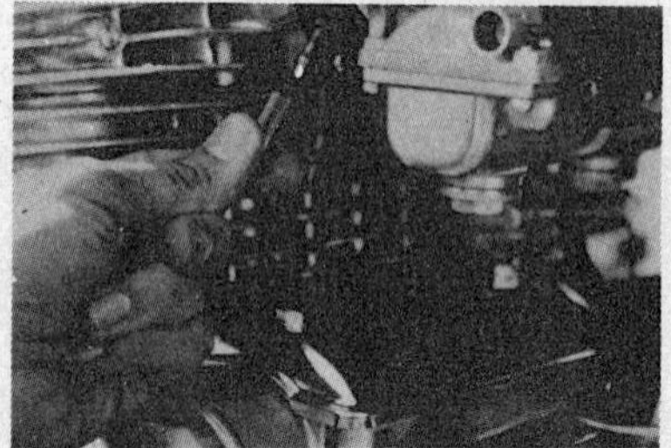

Vacuum gauge fitting (shown is a later model; earlier models were pressed into the head)

Vacuum gauge installation

With Vacuum Gauges

1. Remove the rubber caps from the vacuum fittings on the cylinder head (Engine Nos. up to Z1E-01000) or carb holders (Engine Nos. from Z1E-02174), and attach the vacuum gauges.

2. With the engine running at idle speed, close down the the vacuum gauge intake valve until the gauge needle flutters less than 2 cm Hg (0.8 in. Hg).

3. The normal manifold vacuum gauge reading is 20-23 cm Hg (8-9 in. Hg) for each cylinder. If any gauge reads less than 15 cm Hg (6 in. Hg), recheck the air screw adjustment, and make sure that the carb holder hose clamps and spark plugs are secure.

4. Balance the carbs by readjusting the throttle valve adjusting screws as described in Step 2 of the "Without Vacuum Gauges" Section. All of the carbs should be adjusted to within 2 cm Hg (0.8 in. Hg) of each other. Read the Caution after Step 2.

The intake valve reduces needle fluctuation

5. Open the throttle and allow it to snap shut several times while watching to see if the vacuum gauge readings remain the same. Readjust any carburetor whose reading has changed.

6. Remove the vacuum gauges, replace the rubber covers, readjust the pilot air screws on any carbs which have been adjusted, and adjust the idle speed to about 800-1,000 rpm.

ENGINE AND TRANSMISSION

NOTE: *The following components can be serviced or replaced* **without** *removing the engine from the frame: cylinder head components, cylinder barrel assembly, pistons, cam chain tensioner, clutch, gearshift linkage, generator and starter motor. Refer to the appropriate sections in this Chapter for service procedures.*

ENGINE REMOVAL AND INSTALLATION

Removal

1. Remove the engine and oil filter drain plugs, and allow the engine to drain thoroughly.

2. Remove the plastic side covers, open and unhook the seat, turn the fuel tap to the "S" position, disconnect the fuel lines, disengage the gas tank tang from the rubber retaining band, and pull the tank off from the back.

3. Disconnect the black and green ignition coil leads at the coils, then disconnect the spark plug leads at the plugs.

4. Unscrew the tachometer cable at the cylinder head, and place it out of the way.

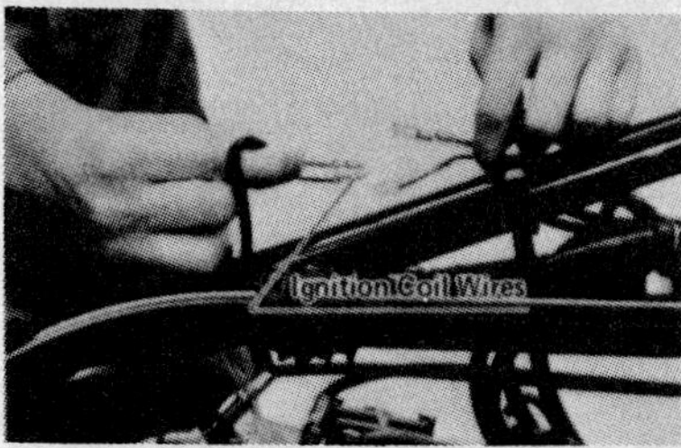

Disconnecting the coil leads

5. Disconnect the blue connector at the electrical panel, then disconnect the starter wire at the starter relay terminal.

6. Remove the right footrest, then unbolt the battery ground wire (−) from the engine.

7. Loosen the 8 clamps which secure the carburetor assembly, then pull the assembly off to the rear. The throttle cables can now be disconnected at the pulley with greater ease.

8. Remove the screen from the top of the air cleaner, slide back the clamp on the oil breather hose, disconnect the

TUNE-UP SPECIFICATIONS

VALVE CLEARANCE	
Intake/exhaust (cold)	0.002-0.004 in. (0.05-0.10 mm)
COMPRESSION	
Standard	121 psi (8.5 kg/cm^2)
Service limit	84 psi (6 kg/cm^2)
Maximum variation	14 psi (1 kg/cm^2)
IGNITION	
Spark plugs	
standard make	NGK
standard type	B-8ES
one step colder	B-9ES
one step hotter	B-7ES
gap	0.028-0.031 in. (0.7-0.8 mm)
reach	3/4 in. (19 mm)
thread diameter	9/16 in. (14 mm)
Point gap	0.012-0.016 in. (0.3-0.4 mm)
Ignition timing	From 5° BTDC @ 1500 rpm to 40° BTDC @ 3000 rpm
CARBURETION	
Idle speed	800-1000 rpm
Air screw opening	1 1/2 turns off seat
Synchronization	
vacuum range	20-23 cm Hg (8-9 in. Hg)
maximum variation	2 cm Hg (0.8 in. Hg)

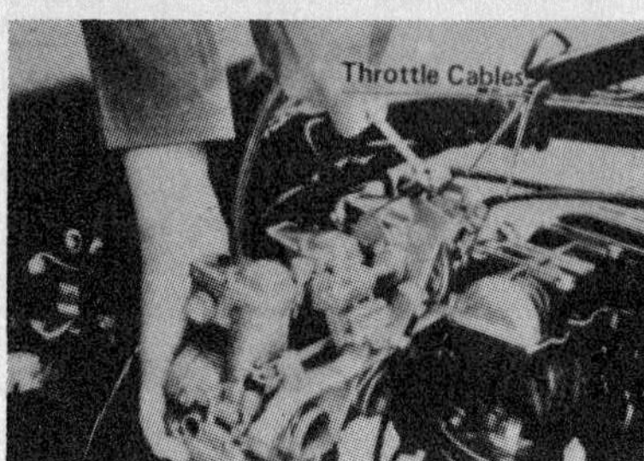

Removing the carburetor assembly

hose, and remove the air cleaner assembly.

9. Remove the nuts which secure the exhaust pipe collars, free the collars from the cylinder head studs, and remove the split keepers.

Removing the air cleaner assembly

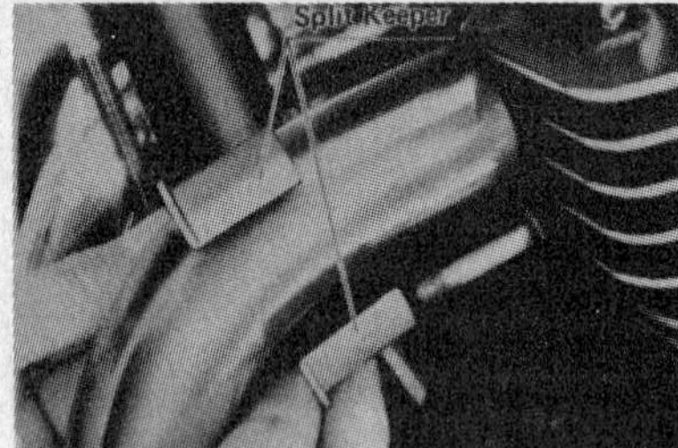

Removing the keepers

NOTE: *Keep the keepers separate for installation in their original locations.*

10. Remove the exhaust system rear mounting bolts, then push the two mufflers on either side forward to remove them. If you wish to contend with each pipe individually, disconnect the muffler connecting hose clamp from each pair.

11. Remove the left front foot rest, shift lever, and starter cover and gasket.

12. Remove the chain oiler pump cover, disconnect the inlet hose from the pump, and plug it with a screw as shown in the illustration.

13. Remove the chain cover, pull the cotter pin out of the clutch release lever, disengage the clutch cable, remove the engine sprocket guard, and remove the clutch pushrod from the driveshaft.

14. Bend back the lockwasher locking tab, secure the sprocket with either the special tool (Part No. 57001-118), or a suitable substitute, and remove the sprocket nut and sprocket.

15. Remove the brake lamp switch and spring, back off the brake rod adjusting nut until maximum pedal play is reached, then loosen the brake pedal position adjusting bolt locknut, and back out the bolt so that the pedal is held down, out of the way.

16. Jack or lever the engine up to take the weight off the mounting bolts, then remove the nuts from the 3 long engine mounting bolts.

17. Remove the short engine mounting bolt from the lower center mounting on each side, the right rear engine mounting bracket bolts, the center and right side front mounting brackets, and the 3 long bolts.

Securing the intake hose

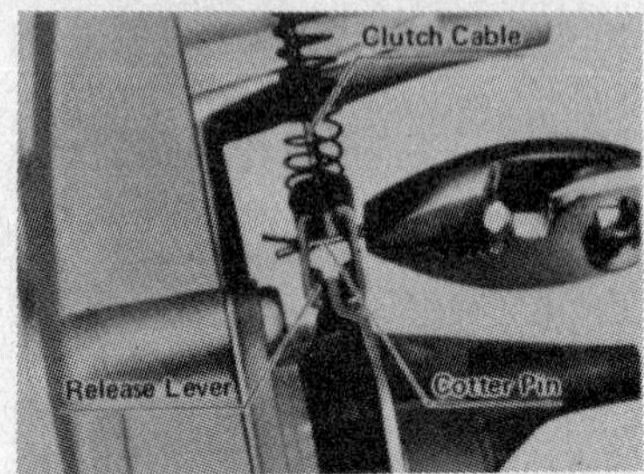

Disconnecting the clutch cable

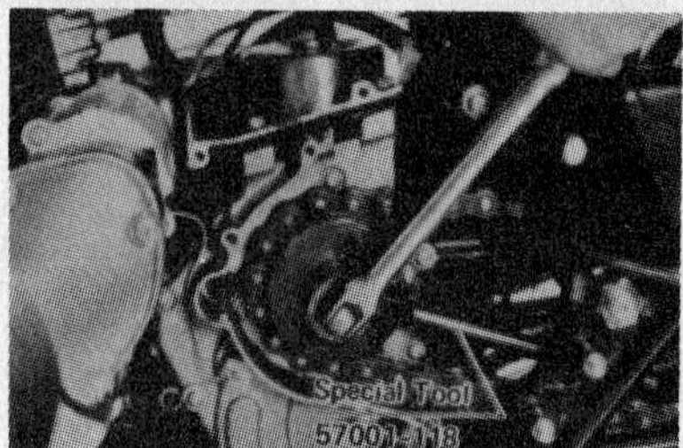

Removing the sprocket nut

Keeping the pedal out of the way

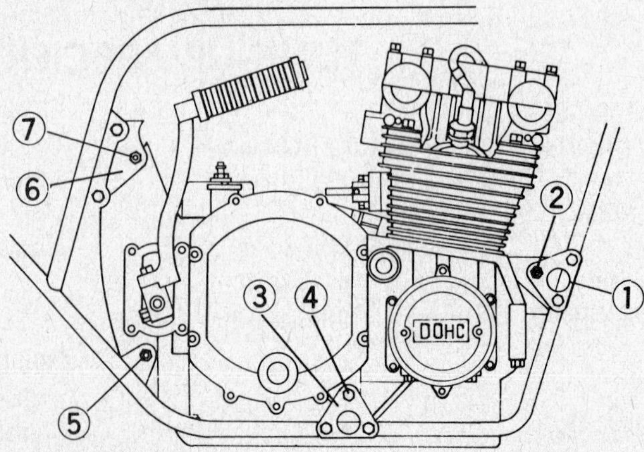

1. Front bracket
2. Front bolt
3. Lower center bracket
4. Lower center bolt
5. Rear lower bolt
6. Rear upper bracket
7. Rear upper bolt

Engine mounting bolt locations

18. With the engine held level, slowly lift it up about 1 in., then move it to the right slightly until the rear of the engine slips over the lower right rear mounting.

19. Raise the front of the engine a little so that it will clear the frame, then drop down the left side, and pull the engine out diagonally and upwards to the right.

The brackets must clear before the engine can come free

Arghhh!

Installation

1. Mount, but do not secure, the 3 engine mounting brackets before inserting the engine bolts. Insert the engine bolts, secure the bracket mounting bolts, and then tighten the engine mounting bolts. The 3 long bolts are inserted from the left side of the machine. Two spacers go on the rear upper bolt; a long one on the left side of the engine, and a short one on the right side. Secure the bracket bolts to 14.-5-16.5 ft lbs (2.0-2.3 kg/m), the 3 long (12 mm) bolts to 47-50 ft lbs (6.5-7.0 kg/m), and the two shorter bolts (10 mm) to 26-29 ft lbs (3.5-4.0 kg/m).
2. Install the engine sprocket with the chain already on it, and secure the sprocket nut to 87-108 ft lbs (12-15 kg/m). A new lockwasher should be used, and the chain adjustment can be loosened if the sprocket and chain will not go on the shaft.
3. An oil seal guide (Part. No. 57001-130), or a suitable substitute, should be used when installing the chain cover in order to avoid damaging the rubber seal. The pin in the output shaft must be aligned with the groove in the chain oil pump shaft before the cover will go on.
4. Install the carburetor assembly, taking care that the clamps are secured well enough to prevent any air leaks.
5. Install the inside mufflers first, and then the outside ones. The collar can be

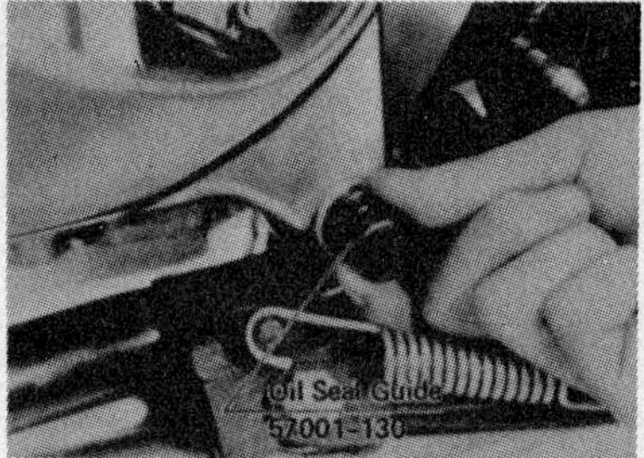

Using the guide to protect the cover oil seal

Lining up the pin and groove

used to hold the split keeper while installing the pipe. Secure the muffler connecting hose clamp to prevent any exhaust leaks, then secure the rear mounting bolts and the bolts at the cylinder head, in that order.

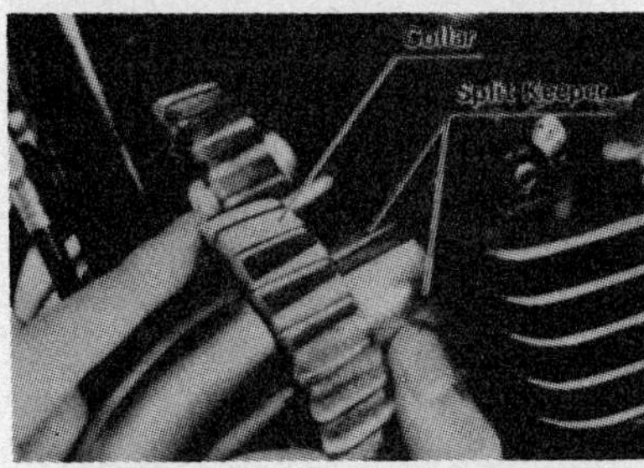

Installing the split keepers and collar

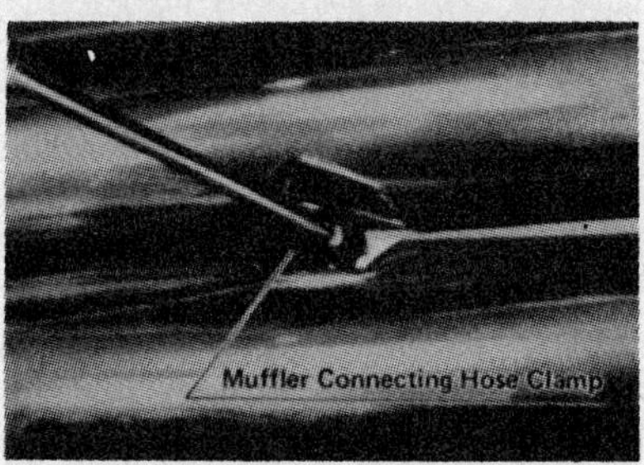

Securing the hose clamp

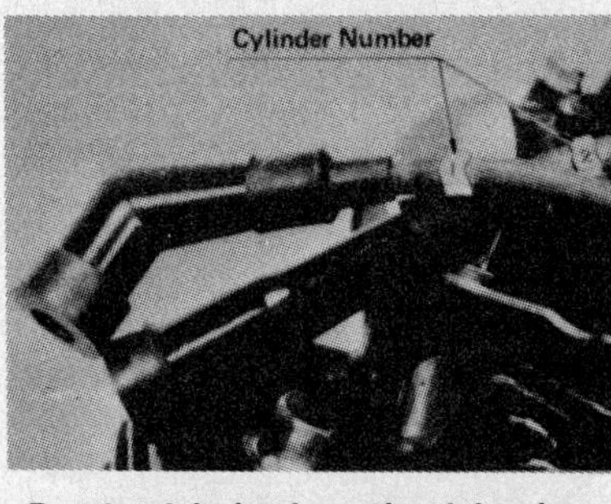

Put the right leads on the right plugs

6. Connect the spark plug wires to the plugs. The wires are numbered in accordance with their respective cylinders counting from left to right.
7. Replenish the oil supply with a little over 4 quarts of high quality (SE or SD) oil, and kick the engine through several times to circulate the oil before firing it up.
8. Give the machine a thorough going over, and make all the necessary adjustments.

ENGINE DISASSEMBLY

Camshafts

REMOVAL

1. Remove the gas tank, disconnect the spark plug wires, and remove the valve cover and gasket.
2. Remove the chain guide sprocket, then unbolt the camshafts caps and separate the split bushing halves for installation in their original positions unless they are to be replaced. Remove the camshafts.
3. Unscrew the tachometer cable, and remove the tach pinion to avoid any possible damage to the camshaft worm during the installation procedure.

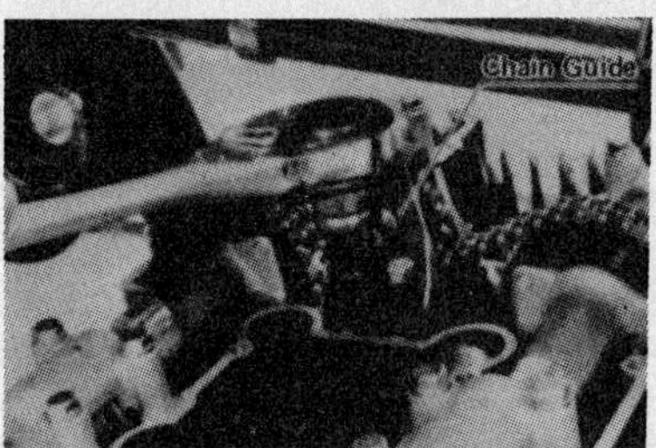

Removing the cam chain guide

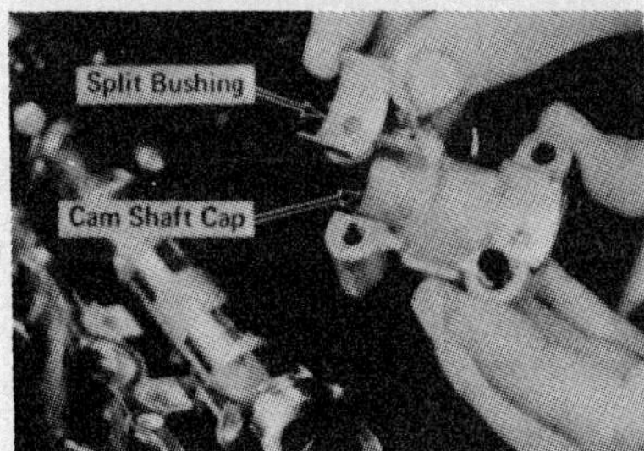

Removing the bushings and caps

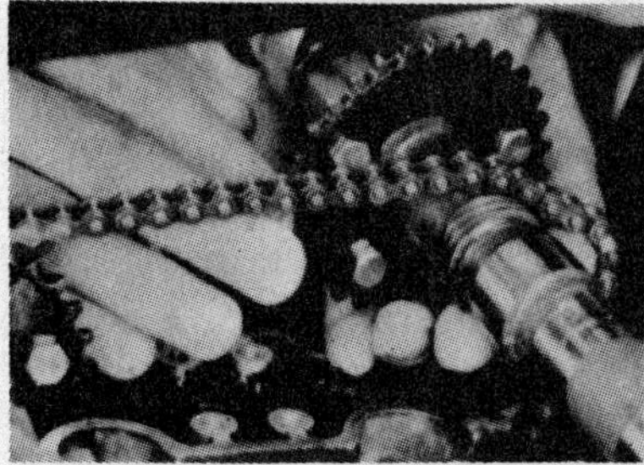
Removing the exhaust camshaft

INSPECTION AND REPAIR

1. Clean all parts in a suitable solvent, then blow them dry.

2. Inspect the camshafts for signs of wear, scored lobes, or damage, and replace them as necessary, based on the following information.

a. Measure the height of each cam lobe with a micrometer, and replace the cam as necessary if the lobes are worn past their serviceable limits as given below:

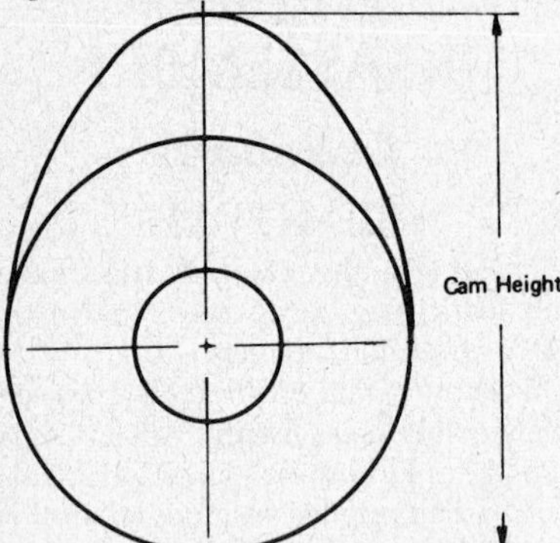

Make the measurement along here

Camshaft Lobe Limits Table

Standard	*Service Limit*
INTAKE	
1.4276-1.4307 in. (36.26-36.34 mm)	1.4236 in. (36.16 mm)
EXHAUST	
1.4079-1.4110 in. (35.76-35.84 mm)	1.4039 in. (35.66 mm)

b. Measure the diameter of each of the camshaft bearing surfaces with a micrometer, and replace the camshaft as necessary if either bearing surface is worn past its serviceable limit as given below:

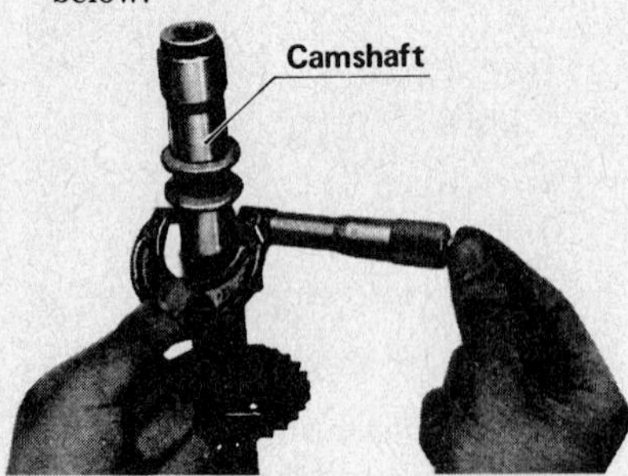

Measuring the bearing surfaces

Camshaft Bearing Chart

Standard	*Limit*
0.9633-0.9638 in. (24.467-24.480 mm)	0.9614 in. (24.420 mm)

3. Remove the cam chain sprocket from the camshafts, keeping them separate for replacement in their original locations, and place the shafts on V-blocks so that they ride on the bushing surfaces, or in a lathe. Rotate the shafts and use a dial indicator to check run-out along the sprocket mounting surface. Replace any cam whose run-out exceeds the service limit given below:

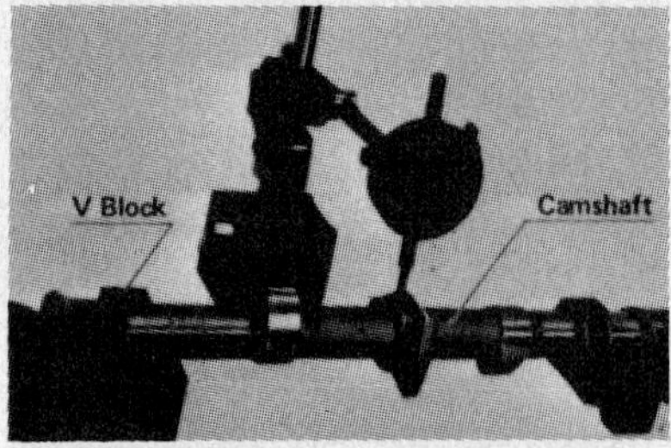

Checking camshaft run-out

Camshaft Runout Chart

Standard	*Limit*
under 0.0008 in. (under 0.02 mm)	0.004 in. (0.10 mm)

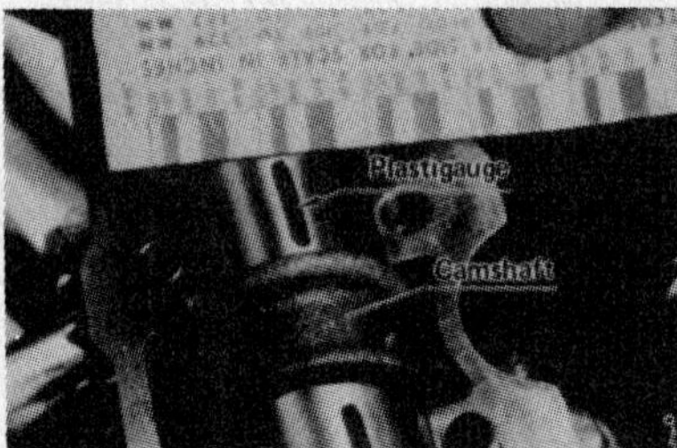

Checking bearing wear with plastigage

4. Inspect the camshaft bushings for signs of wear, scoring, or damage, and replace them as a set per camshaft if worn past their serviceable limit of 0.0063 in. (0.16 mm). The standard clearance between the bushings and the camshafts is 0.008-0.0025 in. (0.020-0.064 mm). Measure the clearance in the following manner:

a. Remove the camshafts and cut sections of Plastigage® to the width of the bushing, and place a strip on the lower half of each bushing, parallel to the camshaft, and so that the plastigage will be between the bushing and the shaft.

b. Fit the cam chain over the sprocket so that the cam is held stationary, and fit and secure the caps and bolts as directed in the "Camshaft Installation" Section.

c. Remove the camshaft and use a micrometer to measure the plastigage in order to determine the camshaft-/bushing clearance. Excessive clearance in any of the 4 bushings for each of the camshafts will necessitate replacing all 4 bushings for that cam.

5. The cam chain is of the endless variety and should not be removed unless replacement is necessary. In most cases excessive chain noise can be traced to wear of the guide rollers, in which case they should be replaced. Consult the "Crankshaft" Section for cam chain replacement information if this becomes necessary.

6. Inspect the cam sprockets for signs of wear or damaged teeth, and replace them as necessary. If one sprocket is damaged, the chances are good that the other is also in need of replacement, and the chain has probably also been affected. It's best, for that reason, to replace the sprockets and chain as a complete system.

NOTE: *On models with engine numbers before Z1E-04654, there have been instances of severe engine damage caused by the sprocket mounting bolts loosening and backing out. A new shouldered bolt (Part No. 92003-41) is available, and should be used to replace the original bolts. Use Liquid Lock-Super (Part No. K41012-014) or a suitable thread locking compound, and torque the bolts to 7 ft lbs (1.0 kg/m).*

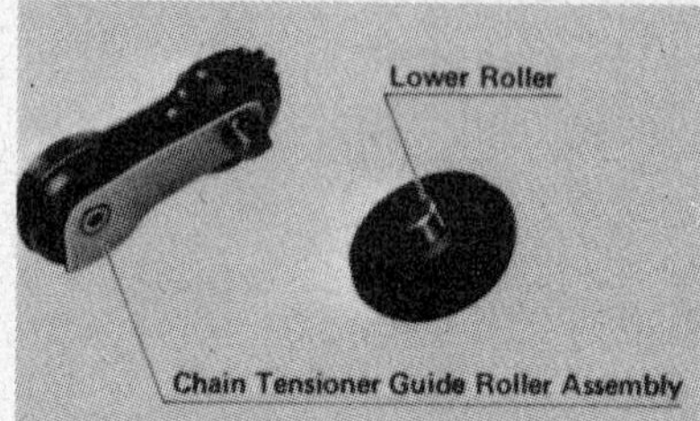

Check these for wear

A sprocket secured with a new type bolt

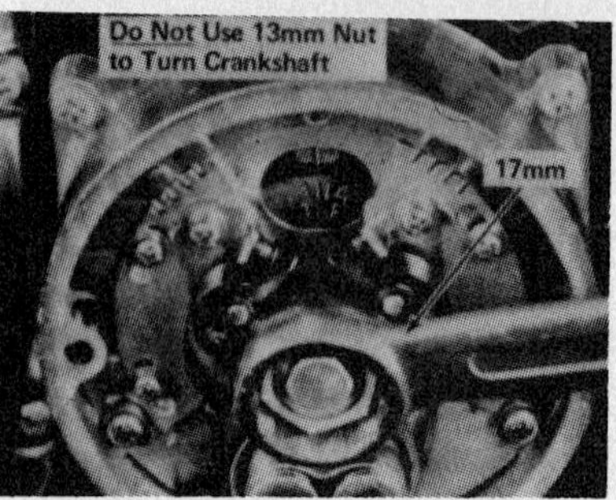

Rotate the engine forward

INSTALLATION AND CAMSHAFT TIMING

1. Installation is basically in the reverse order of removal. Use new gaskets whenever possible.

2. Remove the breaker point cover, then rotate the crankshaft, using a

Lining up the sprocket mark

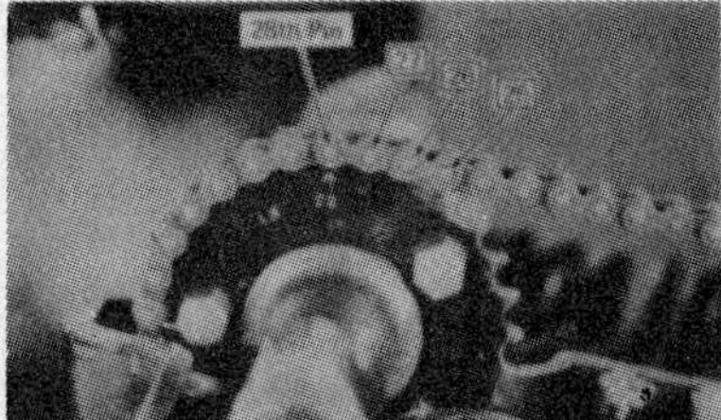

Lining up the 28th pin and mark

Start counting here

Put the right caps in the right places

Torque it down in a crossed pattern

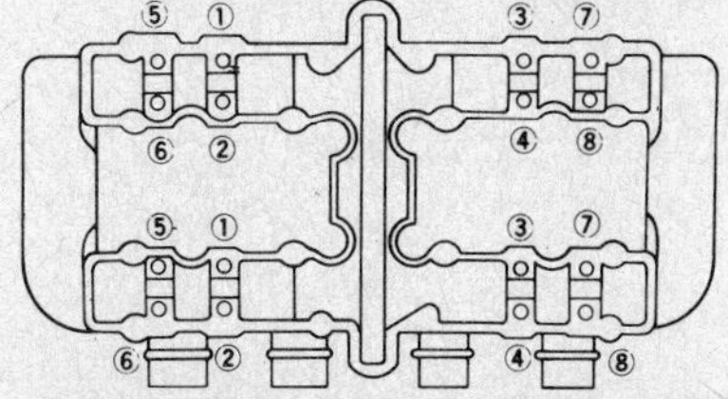

Bolt tightening pattern

wrench on the large crankshaft nut while holding the cam chain up so that it doesn't get caught and so that the slack between the crankshaft and the exhaust cam sprocket is taken up, until the "T" mark for cylinders 1 and 4 is aligned with the timing mark. This brings the number 1 and 4 pistons into the TDC (top dead center) position.

3. Slip the exhaust camshaft through the cam chain, and position it so that the mark on the sprocket is aligned with the cylinder head surface, then pull the chain taut and fit it onto the exhaust camshaft sprocket.

CAUTION: *The chain must be properly seated on the crankshaft and chain guide or the timing will not be accurate.*

4. Starting with the next chain link pin above the one which coincides with the exhaust sprocket mark, count to the 28th, then slip the intake camshaft through the chain so the 28th pin and the "28" mark on the intake camshaft sprocket are aligned as illustrated.

NOTE: *Do not begin counting at the exhaust sprocket mark; start at the next pin* **above** *that point.*

5. Position all the split bushing halves in their original locations unless they've been replaced.

6. Position the camshaft caps so that the arrow points toward the exhaust side, and so that the number on the cap matches the number on the head.

7. Seat the camshaft by partially tightening the left-side cap bolts, then fully torque all of the bolts to 105 in. lbs (1.2 kg/m) in the order shown in the accompanying illustration.

CAUTION: *If you are bench assembling the head without the cam chain installed, great care must be taken not to bend any valves by securing the bearing caps with the cams improperly positioned. Be sure that the cam lobes do not depress both valves of any one cylinder at the same time, and place styrofoam under the head to prevent bending the valves on the bench surface. Do not tighten both camshafts into place at the same time, and do not secure the caps until the valve timing is set (Step nos. 2-4) with the cam chain in position.*

8. Liberally oil the cam assembly, then install the chain guide sprocket assembly, and adjust the cam chain tension as described in the "Tune-Up" Chapter.

9. Rotate the crankshaft two or 3 complete revolutions until number 1 and 4 pistons are at TDC ("T" mark aligned with timing mark), then check that the marks on the exhaust and intake camshaft sprockets are properly aligned, as illustrated, indicating that the cam timing is correct.

Both lobes pointing down . . .

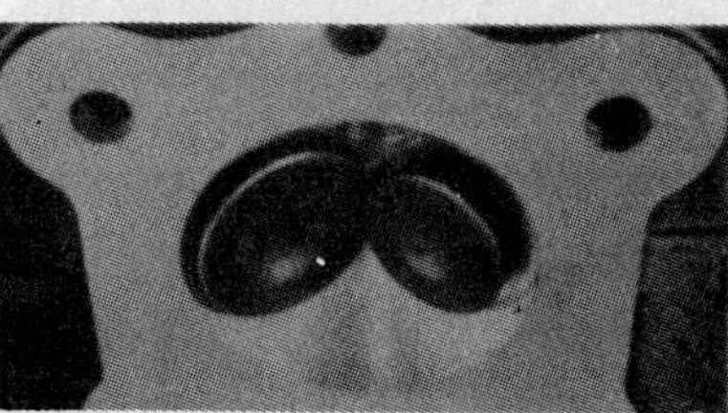
. . . will cause the valves to hit . . .

. . . and this is the result

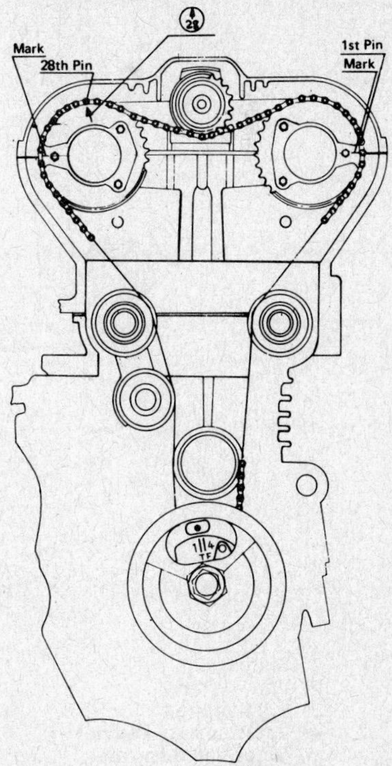

How it all lines up

CAUTION: *Do not attempt to rotate the engine by using a wrench on the camshaft sprocket mounting bolts; use the large nut on the crankshaft instead.*

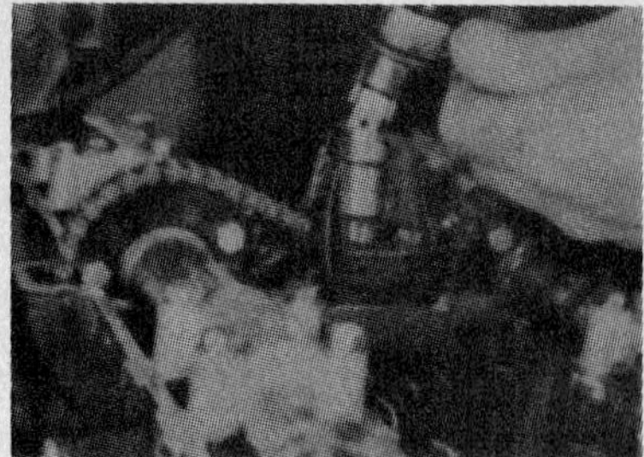

Securing the chain guide

Installing the tachometer pinion

If any unusual resistance is felt when rotating the engine, stop immediately and make sure that the timing is correct or valve damage may occur.

10. Install the tachometer pinion and cable, then mount and secure the valve cover and cover gasket to 70 in. lbs (0.8 kg/m) torque.

11. Adjust the valve clearances as described in the "Tune-Up" Section.

Cylinder Head

The cylinder head is made of aluminium alloy into which the valve guides are pressed, and the valve seats are cast. The valve seats must be cut to their specified angles to assure efficient sealing, and to prevent the valve from overheating by promoting heat dissipation.

Normal wear to the valve lifter and cam surfaces can be adjusted for up to 0.04 in. (1.0 mm). Once this limit has been exceeded through seat wear or grinding, the valve stem end can be ground down to increase clearance. The head will have to be replaced if the adjustment limit is exceeded again.

REMOVAL AND DISASSEMBLY

1. Fully open the seat, and remove the tank.

2. Remove the exhaust system as described in Steps 9 and 10 of the "Engine Removal" Section.

3. Remove the carburetor assembly after loosening the 8 hose clamps which secure it.

4. Remove the camshafts as described in the "Camshafts Removal" Section.

5. Disconnect the spark plug wires from the plugs, and remove the plugs.

Removing the head bolts

6. Remove the bolt from either end of the head, and the 12 cylinder head nuts using either the special tool (Part No. 57001-111) or any suitable socket wrench.

7. Remove all of the valve tappets and shims, keeping them separate for installation in their original locations.

8. Remove the cylinder head and head gasket. Tap the head with a soft mallet to break it free from its seat if necessary.

9. Compress the valve springs, using either the special tool (Part No. 57001-107) or a suitable substitute, until the split keepers can be removed, then remove the valve, springs, and spring retainer, keeping them separate for installation in their original locations.

NOTE: *All of the valves do not necessarily have to be removed, however this is the recommended practice.*

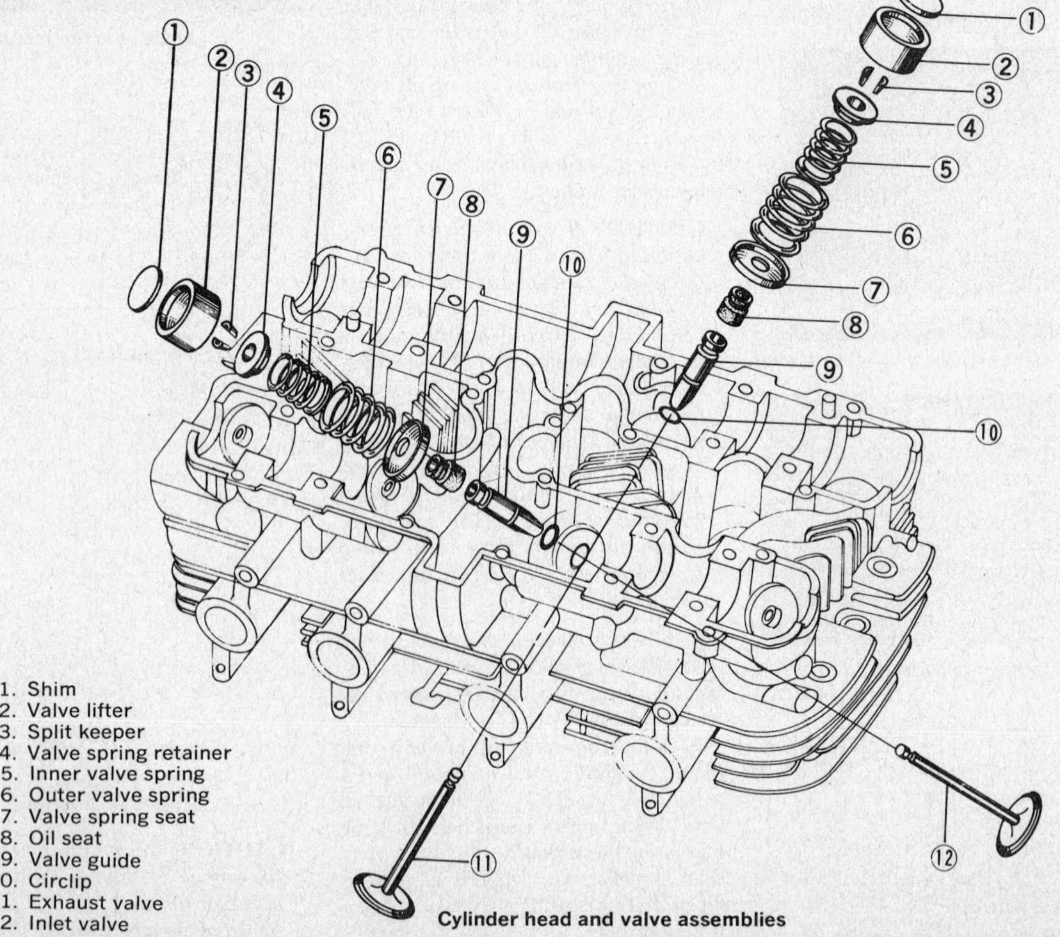

Cylinder head and valve assemblies

Disassembling the valves

Drifting out a valve guide

One complete valve and tappet assembly

10. Remove the oil seal from the valve guide, then heat the area around the guide with a torch to about 250°-300°F (120°-150°C), and drift the guide out from the bottom at the head using either the special drift (Part No. 57001-108) or a suitable substitute.

NOTE: *Do not remove any guide which doesn't have to be replaced. Any guide oil seal which is damaged or removed should be replaced. Consult Step 4 of the following section for additional information.*

INSPECTION AND REPAIR

1. Clean all parts other than seals and gaskets in a suitable solvent, then blow them dry. Carbon deposits on the piston and head assemblies can be softened with a decarbonizing solvent, and scraped off with a blunt instrument such as a butter-knife. Do not use a caustic soda solution to clean aluminum parts such as the head and pistons, however it may be used on the valves. Avoid gouging the piston crown or removing any metal. It is not necessary to restore the components to a like-new condition. Periodically, as you work, wipe the surface clean with a clean rag soaked in clean gasoline. If this is done with the cylinder still in place, you can catch the carbon flakes by pressing a line of grease around the piston on top of the rings. Rotating the piston will leave the grease ring with the carbon trapped in it on the cylinder, and it can then be wiped out. The cylinder head assembly should be disassembled before being decarbonized.

2. Inspect the cylinder head for warpage on the gasket surface by laying a straightedge across the head and measuring the distance between the straightedge and the gasket surface with feeler

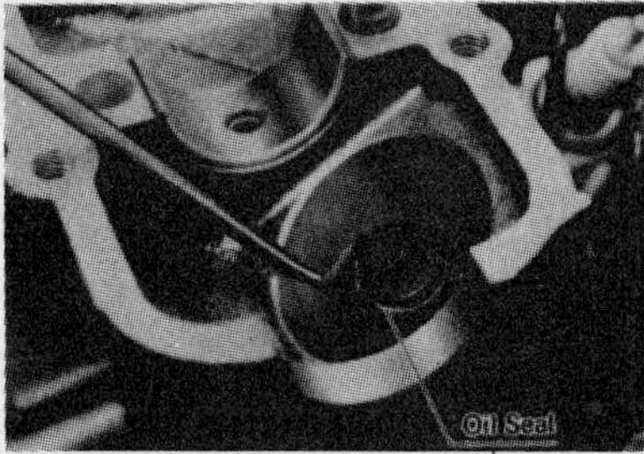

Removing the oil seal

gauges. The standard warpage is under 0.002 in. (0.05 mm), and the serviceable limit is 0.10 in. (0.25 mm). If the warpage exceeds this limit, the head must be replaced. It is possible to straighten a warped head using one of the following procedures;

a. Place a sheet of fine grit emery paper on a flat surface and move the head around in a figure-eight motion while applying mild pressure. It is better to work slowly with mild pressure than quickly with heavy pressure. Don't remove any more metal than is necessary.

b. An alternative method is to use a piece of glass and a fine valve grinding compound instead of the emery paper.

c. Check the results with Prussian blue dye or red lead. To do this, lay out some very fine sandpaper on a flat surface. Coat the gasket surface on the

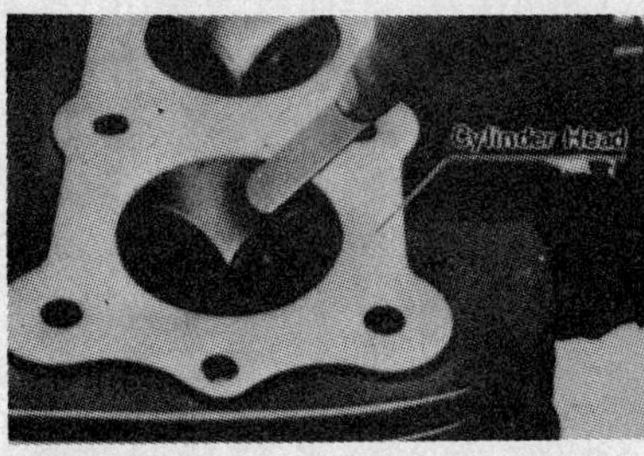

Decarbonizing an assembled head assembly

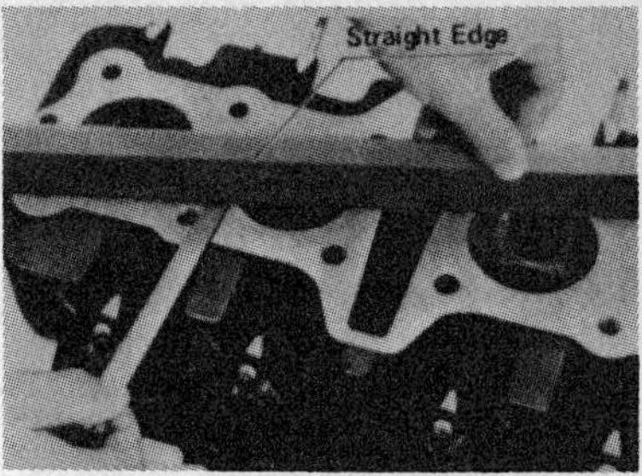

Checking the head for warpage

head with the dye and allow it to dry. Move the head very gently over the sandpaper just long enough to remove the dye, then look at the gasket surface. If the head is flat, all of the dye will have been removed. If there is still dye on the head, repeat the entire process, replace the head, or consult your local dealer.

3. Inspect the valves for a worn, bent, burned or damaged condition, and replace them as necessary. Perform the following operations on each valve:

a. Measure the valve head thickness using vernier calipers, and replace the valve if the head is thinner than the service limit given below:

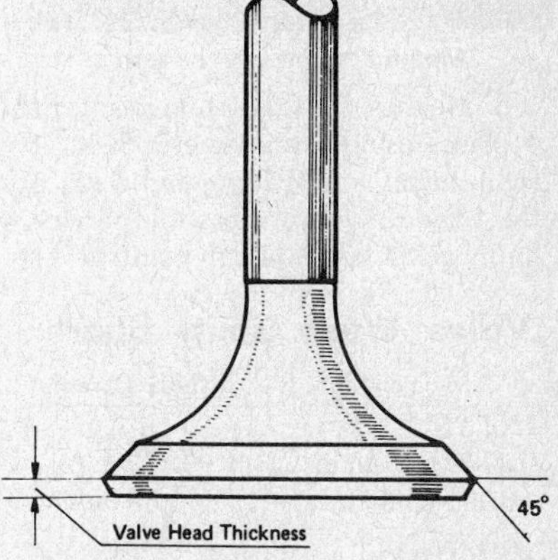

Measure valve head thickness here

Valve Head Thickness Chart

Standard	*Limit*
0.034-0.045 in. (0.85-1.15 mm)	0.020 in. (0.5 mm)

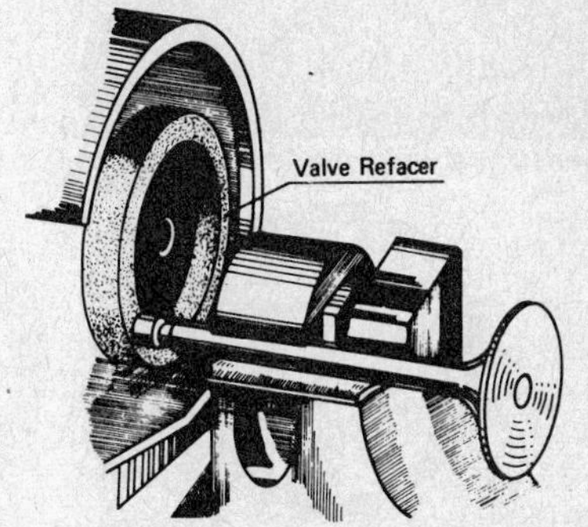

Refacing the valve stem

b. Carefully inspect the seating surface of the valve and the condition of the stem, and repair the valve if possible using a valve refacer. The valve seating surface angle is 45°.

c. Place the valve in a pair of V-blocks, and check its run-out with a dial indicator. The valve must be replaced if its run-out exceeds the service limit of 0.002 in. (0.05 mm).

Measuring valve run-out

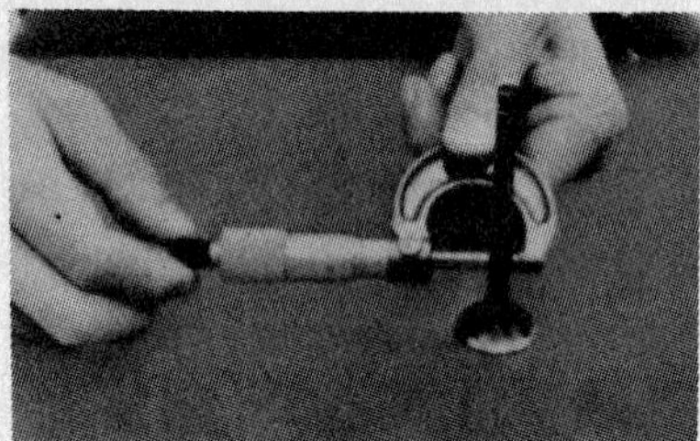
Measuring the valve stem

d. Measure the valve stem in at least 4 places using a micrometer held at right angles to the stem, and replace the valve if it is worn past the service limits given below at any point:

Valve Wear Limits Chart

Standard	*Service Limit*
INTAKE	
0.2742-0.2748 in.	0.270 in.
(6.965-6.980 mm)	(6.86 mm)
EXHAUST	
0.2738-0.2744 in.	0.270 in.
(6.955-6.970 mm)	(6.85 mm)

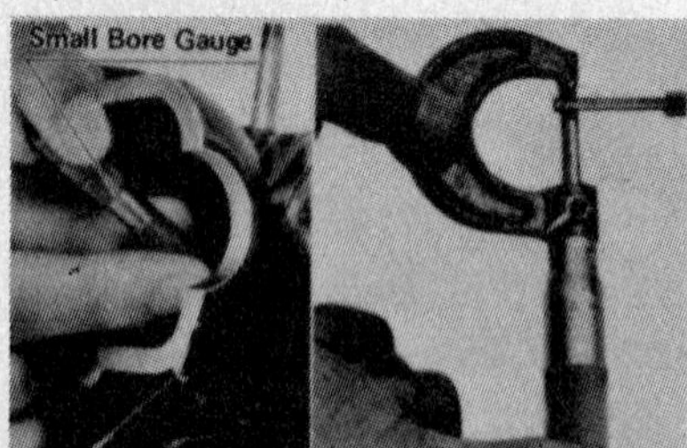

Measuring valve guide inside diameter

4. Measure the bore of each valve guide in at least 4 places, using a small bore gauge and a micrometer, and replace the guide if any of the measurements exceed the service limits given below:

Valve Bore Chart

Standard	*Limit*
0.2756-0.2762 in.	0.280 in.
(7.000-7.015 mm)	(7.10 mm)

If a bore gauge and micrometer are not available, insert a new valve into the guide, set a dial indicator against the stem, and move the stem back and forth to measure valve/valve guide clearance, then do it again while moving the stem in a direction at right angles to the first measurement. The guide will have to be replaced if the valve/valve guide clearance exceeds the service limits given below:

Valve Clearance Chart

Standard	*Service Limit*
INTAKE	
0.0008-0.0002 in.	0.004 in.
(0.02-0.05 mm)	(0.10 mm)
EXHAUST	
0.0012-0.0024 in.	0.004 in.
(0.03-0.06 mm)	(0.10 mm)

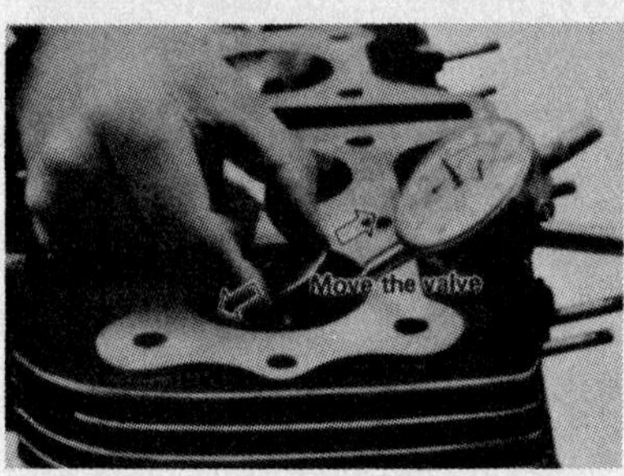

Measuring valve/valve guide clearance

5. Inspect the valve seat for signs of wear, scoring, burning, or damage, then measure the width of the seat. The seat must be smooth and undamaged, and must measure 0.04-0.06 in. (1.0-1.5 mm). 30°, 45°, and two 60° cutters are available for valve seat repairs. Proceed in the following manner;

NOTE: *The following procedure will be of value only if the valve and seat are in good condition.*

a. Remove the valve and apply machinist's dye to the valve seat, then use a lapper to lap the valve lightly into place. The dye pattern on the valve will give an indication of the condition of the seat. Compare it with the illustration.

b. Carefully cut the seating surface with the 45° cutter, taking care to remove only as much metal as is necessary to provide a good surface.

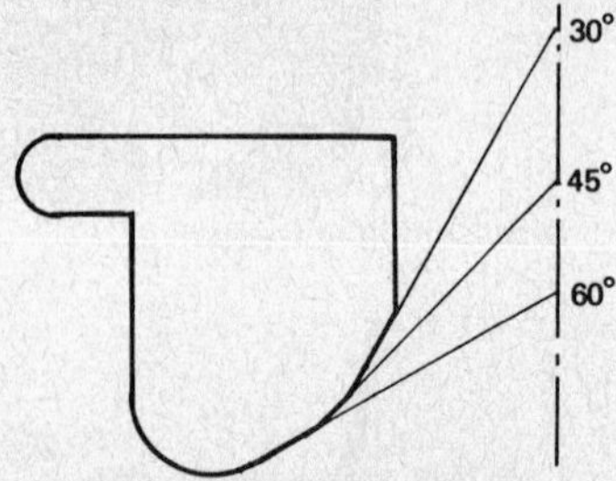

Valve seat dimensions

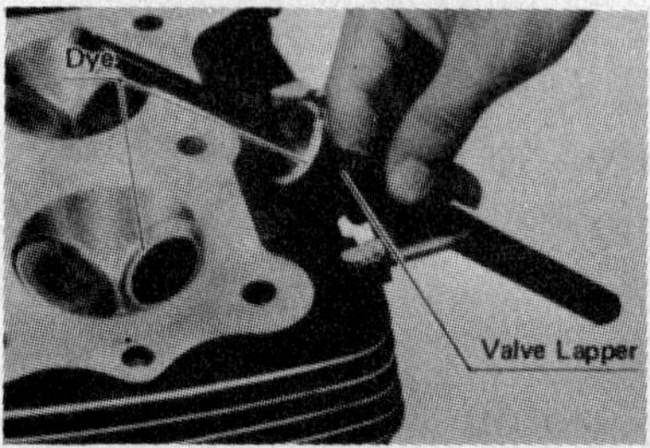

Checking valve/valve seat contact

Cutting a valve seat

c. Carefully cut the area inside the seating surface with the 30° cutter, then cut the area outside the seating surface with the 60° cutter. If done properly, the seating surface should be within the specified limits all the way around.

6. If the seat has just been cut, or if the seat looks alright and you just wish to ensure a good seal between the seat and valve, lap the valves in at this time in the following manner:

a. Lightly oil the valve stem and insert it into the guide.

GOOD

TOO WIDE

TOO NARROW

UNEVEN

Valve/valve seat contact patterns

Lapping in a valve

b. Apply a light coat of lapping compound to the seat. It is best to apply a few evenly spaced daubs rather than a random application, and its a good idea to start off with coarse compound and finish with fine compound.

c. Slip a gas line, or a valve lapper, over the stem and rotate it back and forth in your hands while applying mild pressure against the seat by pulling on the gas line. Stop and clean the seat periodically to check on your progress.

d. Clean the seat area when smooth, and assemble the valve. Pour some gas into the spring side of the head and allow the head to sit. If there is no leakage through the seat after 15 minutes, the lapping has been successful.

7. Inspect the valve springs for a pitted, collapsed, or damaged condition, and replace them as necessary. Perform the following checks also:

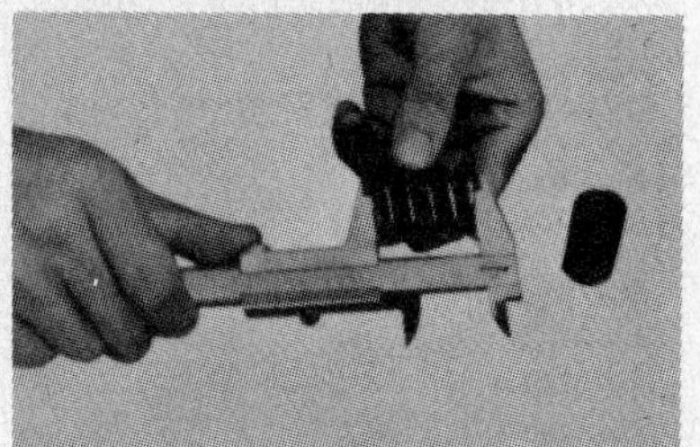
Checking valve spring free length

a. Measure the valve spring free lengths using vernier calipers, and replace the springs as a complete set if any are shorter than the serviceable limits given below:

Valve Spring Chart

Standard	*Limit*
INNER	
1.42 in.	1.38 in.
(36.0 mm)	(35.0 mm)
OUTER	
1.55 in.	1.50 in.
(39.3 mm)	(38.0 mm)

b. Stand each spring up on a flat surface, and set a perpendicular reference point next to them. If any spring is tilted more than 0.075 in. (1.9 mm) replace it.

NOTE: *Valve springs should always be replaced as a complete set to assure efficient operation.*

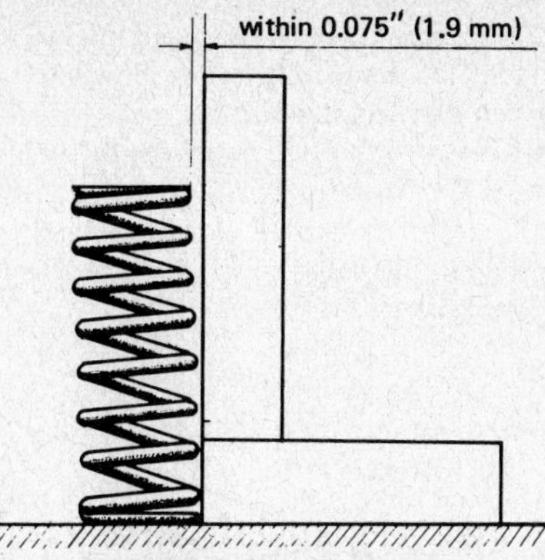

Measuring valve spring tilt

The old style tappets should be replaced

8. Inspect the valve tappets and adjusting shims for signs of wear or damage and replace them as necessary.

NOTE: *The type of valve tappets used in all models up to engine number Z1E-08979 have caused shim fracturing problems on some machines. A new redesigned tappet (Part No. 12032-005) is available as a replacement for the old type (Part No. 12032-004). It is recommended that all old style tappets be replaced. The new type of tappet, recognizable by the lack of a navel in the tappet/shim mating area, can be used in conjunction with the shim already in use, however, this is not recommended as the old shim may have begun to fracture.*

ASSEMBLY AND INSTALLATION

1. Assembly is basically in the reverse order of disassembly and installation is in the reverse order of removal. Use new gaskets, valve guide seals, O-rings, and valve split keepers.

2. Install the circlip in its groove in the valve guide, and liberally oil the guide. Heat the area around the guide hole with a torch to about 250°-300°F (120°-150°C), and drive the guide in from the top of the head using either the special tool (Part No. 57001-108) or a suitable drift, until the circlip reaches its seat.

3. Use a 7 mm reamer to ream the guides. This must be done even if the old guides are used. Always rotate the reamer to the right, and keep rotating it as it's withdrawn.

4. Lap the valve into its seat as directed in the preceding "Inspection and Repair" Section.

Drifting in a valve guide

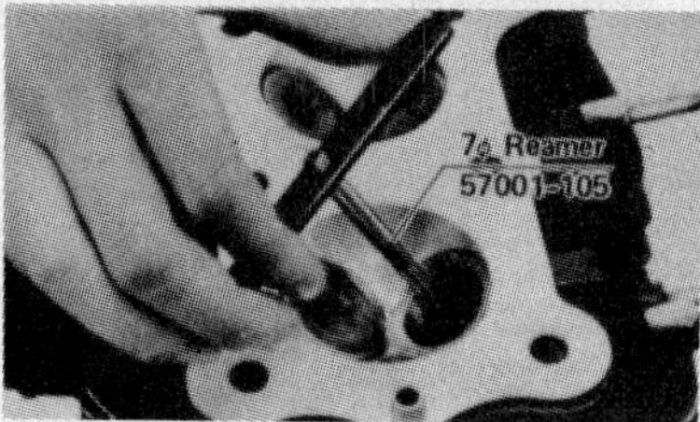

Reaming out a valve guide

5. Install the tappets and shims to their original locations.

6. Use a new head gasket to prevent compression leakage, and install the gasket so the side with the wider folded-over metal edges is facing up.

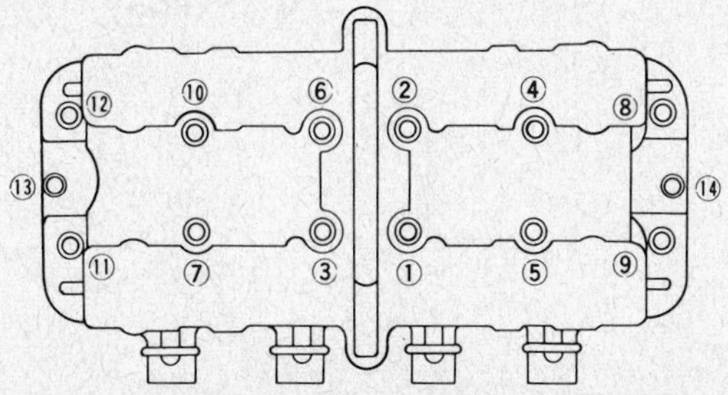

Cylinder head bolt tightening pattern

Installing a new head gasket

7. Secure the cylinder head nuts to 25 ft lbs (3.5 kg/m) in the order shown in the accompanying illustration.

8. Secure the two end bolts to 105 in. lbs (1.2 kg/m).

9. Adjust the valve clearances before installing the valve cover, and use a new cover gasket.

Cylinder and Piston

REMOVAL AND DISASSEMBLY

1. Remove the cylinder head as described in the previous Section, then remove the cam chain tensioner assembly and guide sprocket.

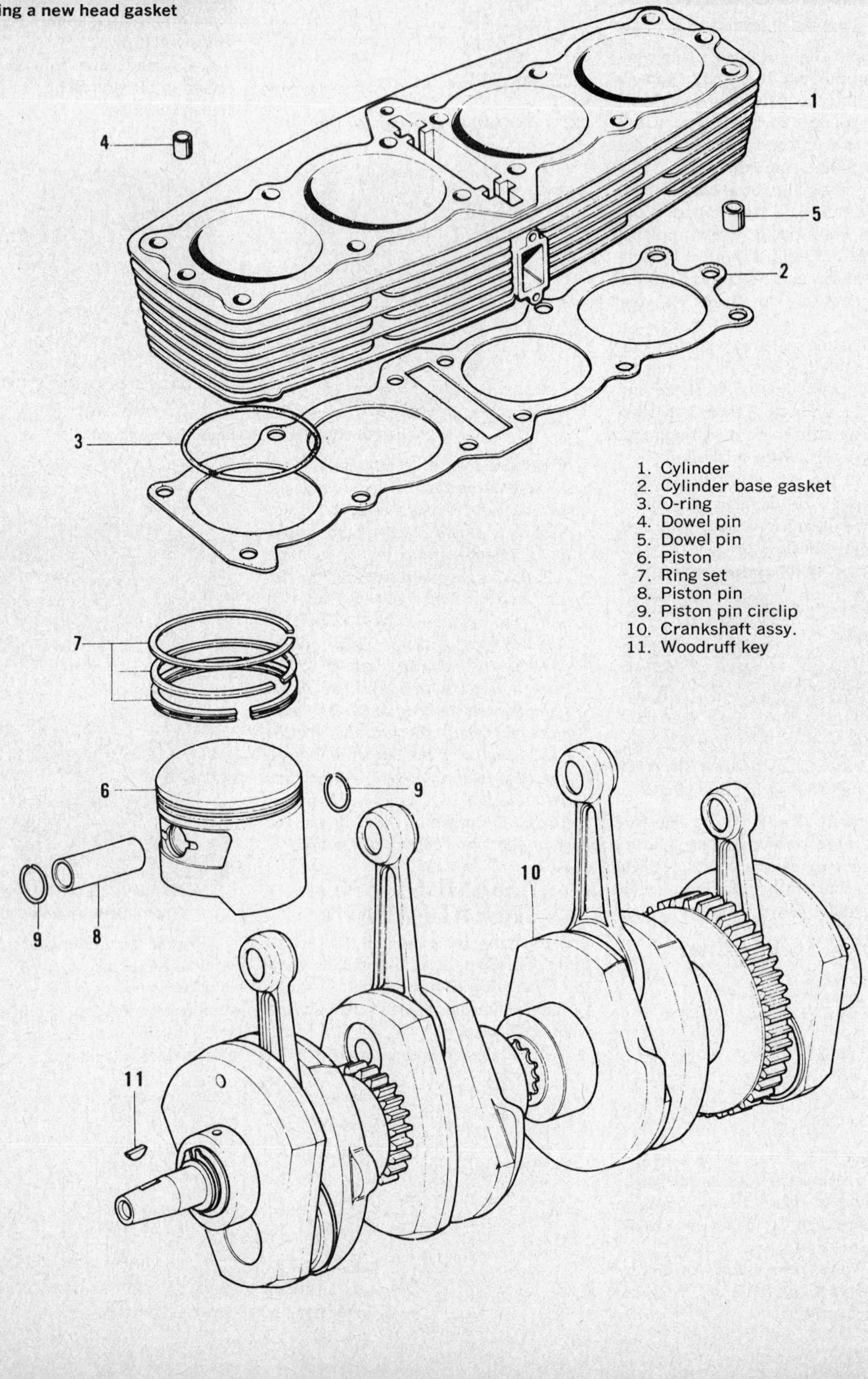

1. Cylinder
2. Cylinder base gasket
3. O-ring
4. Dowel pin
5. Dowel pin
6. Piston
7. Ring set
8. Piston pin
9. Piston pin circlip
10. Crankshaft assy.
11. Woodruff key

Removing the tensioner and guide sprocket assemblies

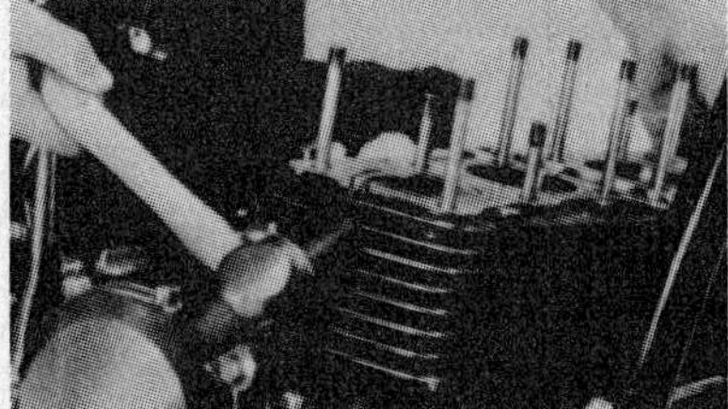
Make sure that it's a soft mallet

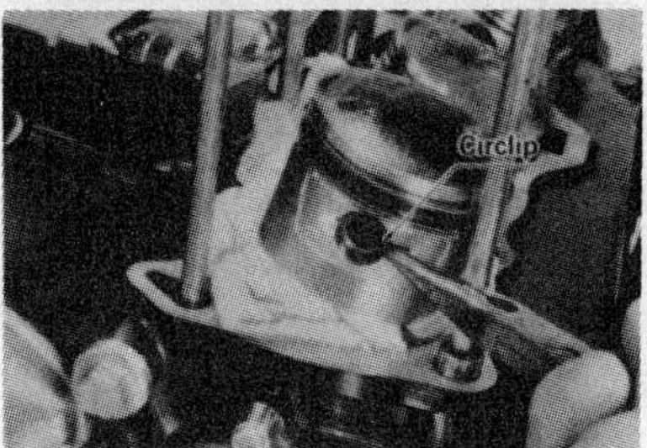

Removing the piston pin circlip

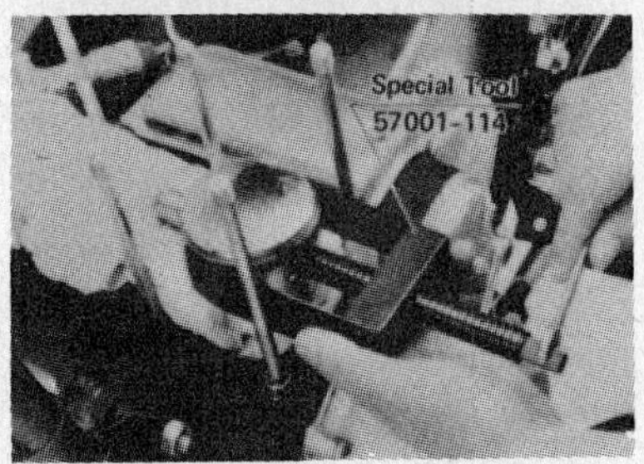

Removing the piston pin

2. Loosen the cylinder block by gently tapping up on alternate ends with a soft mallet, then lift the cylinder and gasket off the crankcase studs.

CAUTION: *As you lift the cylinder block, stuff clean rags in the crankcase openings to prevent foreign matter, such as broken rings, from falling into the crankcase, and to prevent possible piston damage caused by pistons striking the crankcase studs.*

3. Remove the piston pin circlips with a sharp pointed instrument, then remove the piston pin with the special tool (Part No. 57001-114) or a suitable substitute. The pins can be removed also by heating the piston crown with a torch, and driving the pin out while carefully supporting the connecting rod to prevent damage to it or the big end bearings. Keep the pins with their pistons, and mark the pistons for replacement in their original positions.

4. Remove the piston rings using either the special tool (Part No. 57001-115), a suitable substitute, or by hand, taking care not to damage the piston. When removing rings by hand, spread the ring ends with your thumbs, and push up on the opposite side of the ring to remove it.

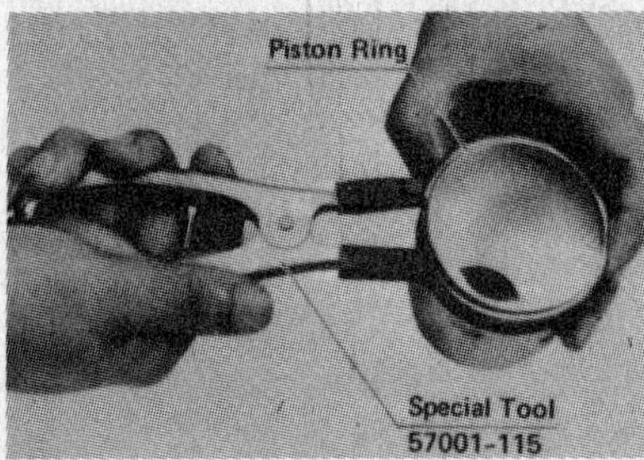

Removing the rings with the special tool

Removing the rings by hand

NOTE: *Do not remove the rings unless you are planning to replace them, as rings shouldn't be reused once they've been removed.*

INSPECTION AND REPAIR

1. Clean all parts other than gaskets, O-rings, and seals, in a suitable solvent, then blow them dry taking care to blow clear all oil passages. Decarbonize all components as described in the preceding "Inspection and Repair" Section. Piston ring grooves can be cleaned with a broken piece of piston ring.

Decarbonizing the piston crown

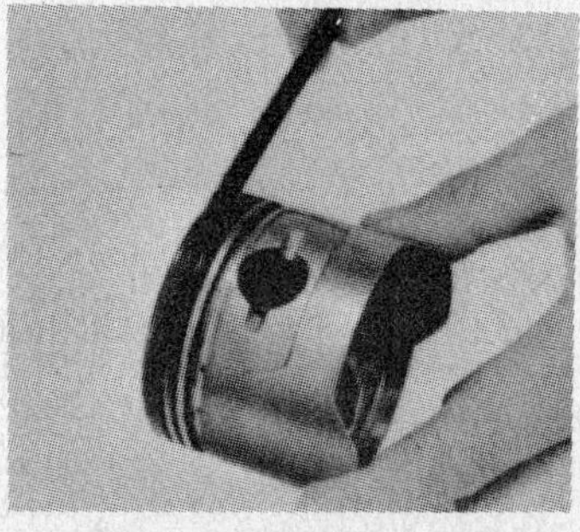
Decarbonizing the piston ring grooves

2. Inspect the cylinder block for damage to the cooling fins or either of the gasket mating surfaces, or for badly scored cylinder walls, and replace the assembly as necessary. Use a cylinder gauge to check the cylinder wall dimensions of each cylinder in the three areas shown, and take two measurements, at 90° from one another, at each location. If any of the measurements exceeds the service limits given below, or if there is a difference of more than 0.002 in. (0.005 mm) between any two measurements, all the cylinders will have to be bored and honed.

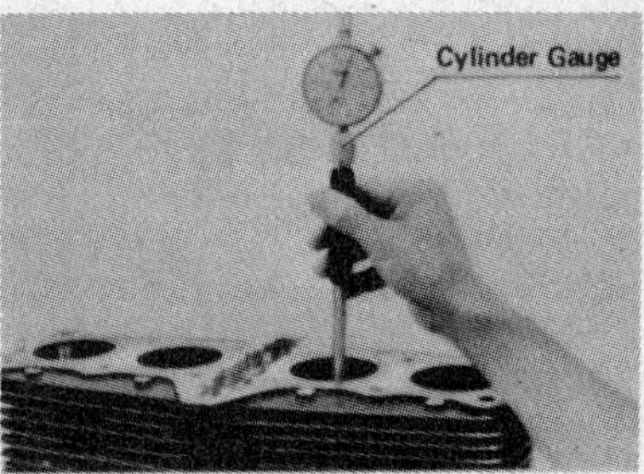

Measuring the cylinder bore

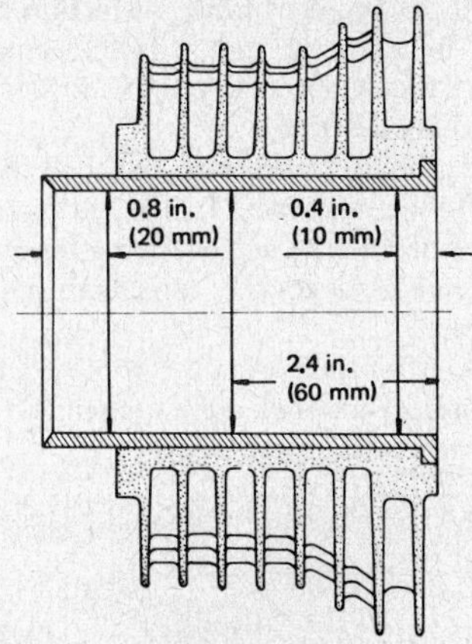

Cylinder dimensions

Piston Wall Dimensions Chart

Standard	*Service Limit*
2.5984-2.5992 in. (66.000-66.019 mm)	2.602 in. (66.10 mm)

3. Measure the piston diameter at a point about 0.2 in. (5 mm) up from the bottom of the piston skirt and at right angles from the piston pin holes. Replace the piston if the diameter is under the service limits given below:

Piston Diameter Chart

Standard	*Service Limit*
2.5956-2.5965 in. (65.93-65.95 mm)	2.590 in. (65.80 mm)

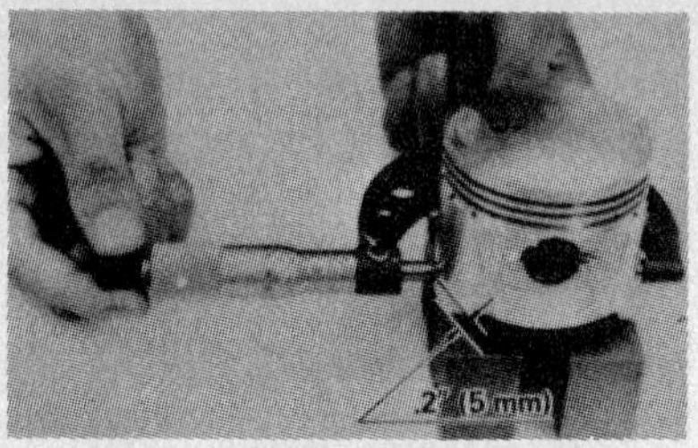

Measuring the piston

4. Subtract the piston diameter from the cylinder measurement to arrive at the piston/cylinder clearance. The clearance must be returned to standard whenever the cylinder is replaced or bored, however, if only the piston is replaced, clearance may exceed the limit, but must not be less than the minimum clearance of 0.0025-0.003 in. (0.060-0.079 mm).

5. When boring and honing the cylinders, adhere to the following rules:

a. The inside diameter of any cylinder must not vary by more than 0.0004 in. (0.01 mm) at any point along its bore.

b. Replacement pistons are available in 0.020 in. (0.5 mm) and 0.04 in. (1.0 mm) oversizes. If boring in excess of 1 mm over standard is ever necessary, the cylinder block must be replaced since replacement sleeves are not made available by the factory.

c. To avoid cylinder distortion due to unbalanced metal temperatures, bore the cylinders in either the 2-4-1-3 or 3-1-4-2 order.

d. Allow the metal to cool completely after boring before taking any measurements, as the diameter may change due to the temperature increase.

e. After the boring is completed, the piston/cylinder clearance should be returned to standard.

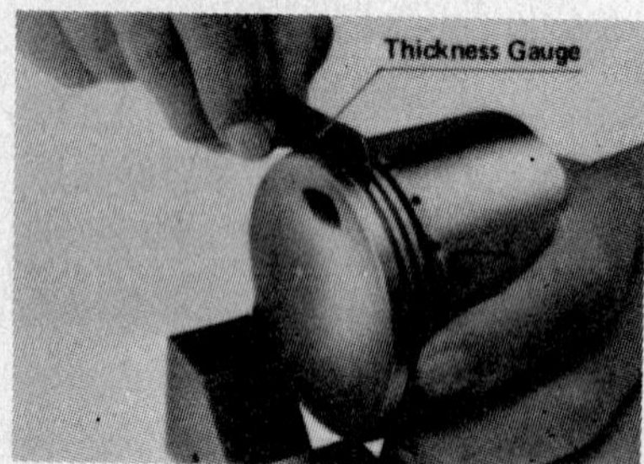

Measuring the piston ring grooves

6. In the event of piston seizure in the bore, the cylinder should be honed, or at least smoothed out with #400 emery cloth, and the piston should be treated likewise. Make sure that the rings are still free if they aren't to be replaced. If the damage is heavy, the cylinder will have to be bored and the piston replaced. Try and determine why the piston seized before running the engine again. Look for air leaks, improper mixture adjustments, improper timing, or insufficient piston/cylinder clearance.

7. Inspect the piston rings and ring grooves for signs of wear or damage. The rings should be replaced if their condition is even slightly questionable, and the piston must be replaced if the ring grooves are unevenly worn or damaged. Make the following measurements;

a. Measure the width of the ring grooves using a thickness gauge, and replace the piston if the grooves exceed the service limits given below:

Ring Groove Thickness Table

Standard	*Service Limit*
Top groove	
0.059-0.060 in. (1.50-1.52 mm)	0.063 in. (1.60 mm)
Second groove	
0.059-0.060 in. (1.50-1.52 mm)	0.063 in. (1.60 mm)
Bottom groove	
0.098-0.099 in. (2.50-2.52 mm)	0.102 in. (2.60 mm)

b. Measure the thickness of the piston rings using a micrometer, and replace the rings if worn thinner than the service limits given below:

Piston Ring Thickness

Standard	*Service Limit*
Top ring	
0.0567-0.0573 in. (1.440-1.455 mm)	0.0535 in. (1.36 mm)
Second ring	
0.0579-0.0587 in. (1.470-1.490 mm)	0.055 in. (1.40 mm)
Oil ring	
0.0973-0.0980 in. (2.470-2.490 mm)	0.0945 in. (2.40 mm)

c. Measure the clearance between the ring grooves and rings using a thickness gauge at various points around the piston, and replace the necessary components if the clearance exceeds the service limits given below:

Ring Clearance

Standard	*Service Limit*
0.0018-0.0031 in. (0.045-0.080 mm)	0.007 in. (0.18 mm)
Second ring oil ring	
0.0004-0.0020 in. (0.010-0.050 mm)	0.006 in. (0.15 mm)

d. Measure ring end gap by placing the ring in a new cylinder, and using a thickness gauge to determine wear. If a new cylinder is not available, make the measurement at the bottom of the least worn cylinder where wear is minimal. If the gap is less than the limits given below, the ring ends can be filed as long as care is taken to file them flat, and if all burrs are removed. If the gap is worn greater than the service limits, the ring must be replaced.

Measuring the piston ring end gap

Ring Gap

Standard	*Service Limit*
0.008-0.016 in. (0.2-0.4 mm)	0.028 in. (0.7 mm)

e. Determine ring tension by measuring the ring gap while the ring is free. If the gap is less than the service limits given below, the ring is weak and should be replaced.

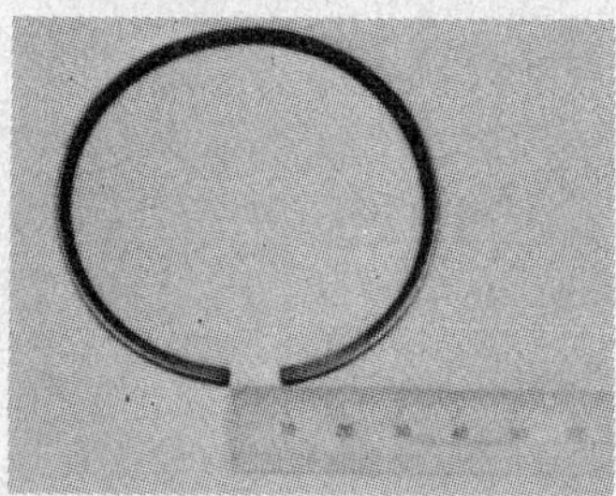
Determining ring tension

Ring Tension

Standard	*Service Limit*
Top ring	
0.354 in. (9 mm)	0.236 in. (6 mm)
Second ring	
0.354 in. (9 mm)	0.236 in. (6 mm)
Oil ring	
0.315 in. (8 mm)	0.197 in. (5 mm)

8. Measure the diameter of the piston pin using a micrometer, then measure the inside diameter of the piston pin hole in the piston, and the diameter of the connecting rod small end bearing. Replace the necessary components if the pin diameter is too small, or if the pin hole or bearing diameter is too large as indicated by the service limits given below:

Piston Pin

Standard	*Service Limit*
Piston pin	
0.6691-0.6693 in. (16.994-17.000 mm)	0.6677 in. (16.96 mm)
Piston pin hole	
0.6694-0.6701 in. (17.0035-17.0115 mm)	0.6724 in. (17.08 mm)
Small end I.D.	
0.6694-0.6698 in. (17.003-17.014 mm)	0.6713 in. (17.05 mm)

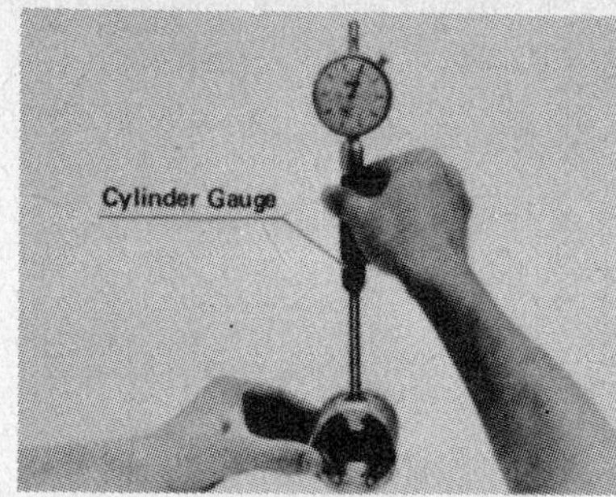

Measuring the piston pin hole

NOTE: *When a new piston or pin is used, check that the piston-to-pin clearance is within the limits of 0.0026-0.00057 in. (0.0066-0.0145 mm), and that the pin-to-small end bearing clearance is within the limits of 0.00012-0.-00079 in. (0.003-0.020 mm), and replace any necessary parts.*

ASSEMBLY AND INSTALLATION

1. Assembly is basically in the reverse order of disassembly, and installation is in the reverse order of removal. Use new gaskets, seals, O-rings, and piston pin circlips.

Be sure that the pistons are installed correctly

2. Liberally lubricate the piston pins before installing them, and install the pistons so that the arrow marked on the piston crown points forward.

CAUTION: *Do not attempt to drive in a pin without firmly supporting the connecting rod to prevent possible damage to the rod and big end bearing. Heat the piston crown with a torch or heated rags as an aid in installation.*

3. Always use new piston pin circlips, taking care to position the clip so that its open end is not aligned with either groove in the piston.

4. Install the piston rings with their lettered ("N") side up. Be careful not to mix the first and second rings. The outer edge of the top ring is chamfered, and the lower outer edge of the second ring is notched as illustrated.

NOTE: *The green coating on the top and bottom rings is to prevent scuffing, and is not intended to be permanent.*

5. Place the two alignment pins into the forward tension stud hole on either side of the crankcase. **Do not put the pins into the rear holes.**

6. Rotate the top and bottom rings so that their end gaps are facing forward, and the center ring so that its gap faces the rear, then thoroughly lubricate the pistons and rings with fresh engine oil

7. Lift up the cam chain so that it doesn't get caught, then rotate the crankshaft until all of the pistons are at about the same height, and install the positioning rods (Part No. 57001-112) to hold them level. Wooden slats can be used effectively in place of the special tool.

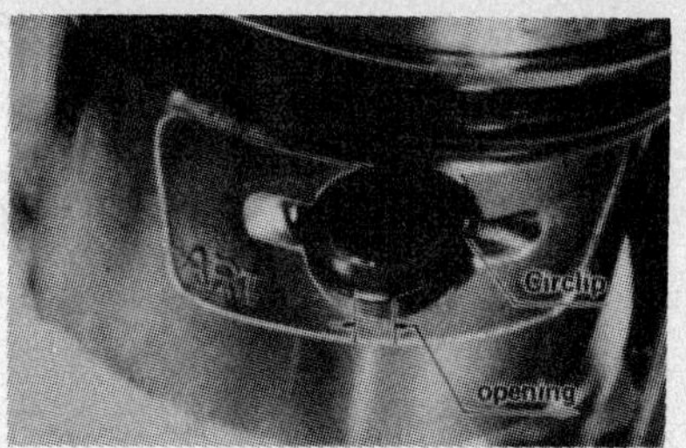

This will prevent the clip from coming free

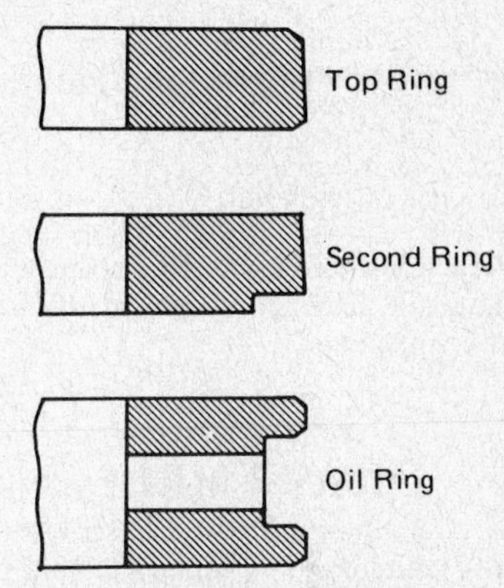

The rings must go on the correct lands

8. Compress the piston rings using either the special positioning rod, ring compressors, or suitable hose clamps, lubricate the cylinder walls thoroughly with fresh engine oil, and start the cylinder block down on the pistons. The ring compressors will have to be lowered and then removed as the rings enter the cylinder. Remove the positioning rod after the rings are in the bore.

9. After the engine is fully assembled, tuned, and lubricated, crank it through

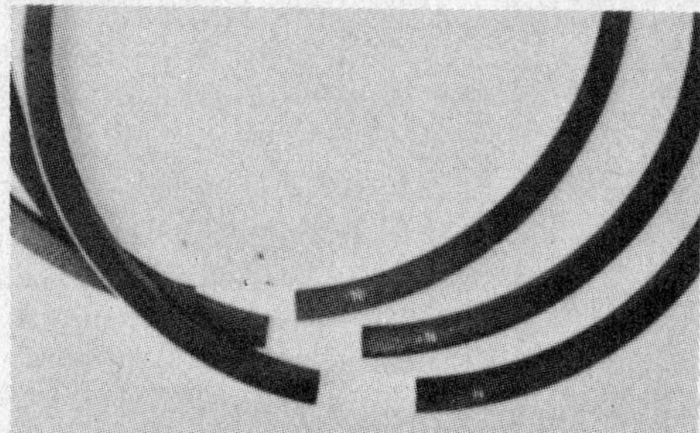
Install the rings with the "N" up

Alignment pin installation

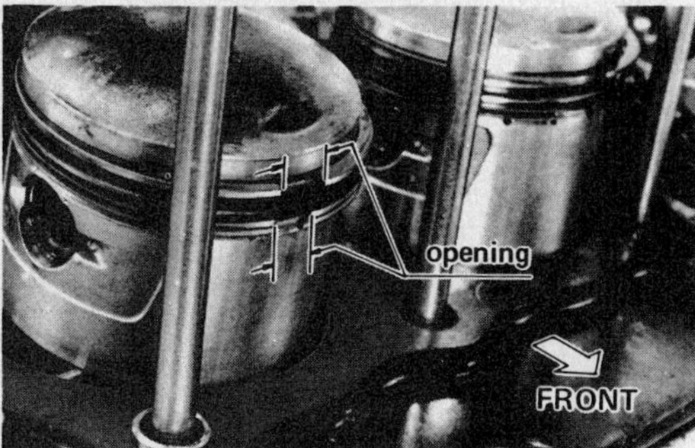

Aligning the ring gaps for maximum compression

Lining up the pistons with the special tool

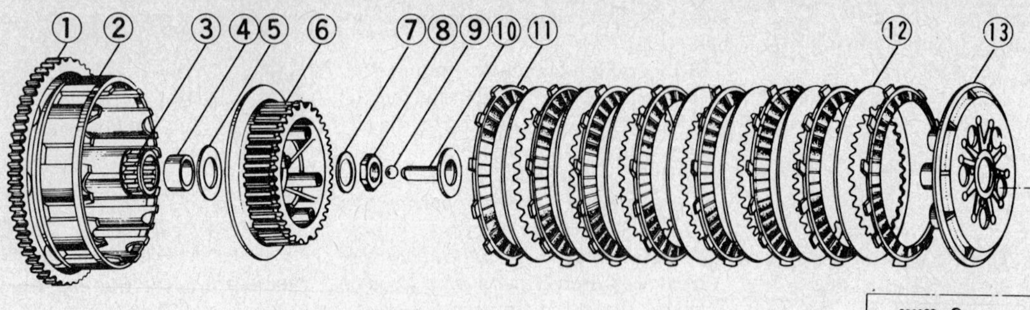

1. Reduction drive gear
2. Clutch housing
3. Needle bearing
4. Bushing
5. Washer
6. Clutch hub
7. Washer
8. Nut
9. Steel ball
10. Pusher
11. Friction plate
12. Steel plate
13. Pressure plate
14. Clutch spring
15. Washer
16. Bolt

Clutch assembly

several times before actually starting it to ensure adequate lubrication of the top end components.

Clutch

DISASSEMBLY

1. Drain the engine oil as described in the "Maintenance" Chapter. The oil in the oil filter, and the filter assembly, can be left as is.

2. Remove the clutch cover and cover gasket, then remove the pressure plate bolts, clutch springs, and the pressure plate.

3. Remove the clutch pushrod, and tilt the motorcycle so the steel ball (release bearing) will fall out.

Removing the pressure plate bolts

Removing the release bearing

NOTE: *The clutch assembly need not be further disassembled unless the clutch hub or housing is damaged.*

4. Remove the clutch plates by either tilting the bike or by lifting them out with a hooked piece of wire, then keep the clutch hub from turning by using either the special tool (Part No. 57001-119) or a

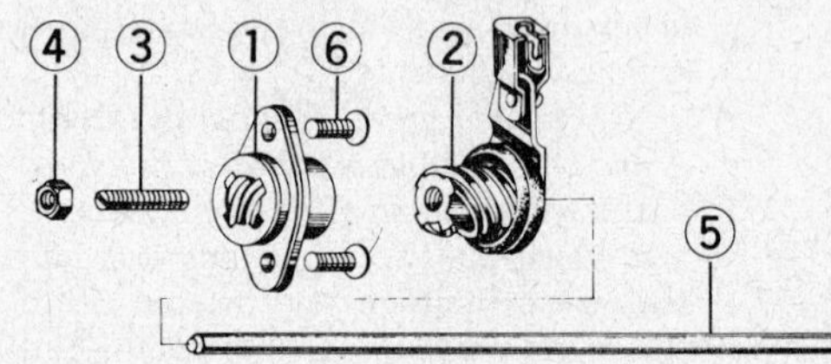

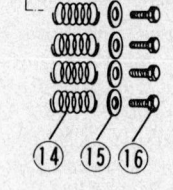

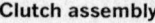

1. Outer release gear
2. Inner release gear
3. Adjusting screw
4. Locknut
5. Pushrod
6. Screw

Clutch release mechanism assembly

suitable substitute, and remove the hub mounting nut.

5. Remove the outer washer, the hub, and the inner washer. Clutch housing removal will necessitate complete engine disassembly with the engine removed from the frame as described in the "Splitting the Crankcases" Section.

6. Remove the chain cover as described in the "Final Drive" Section of the "Chassis" Section, then remove the clutch release inner gear by twisting it out, and the outer gear.

Removing the hub mounting nut

INSPECTION AND REPAIR

1. Clean all parts other than the cover gasket and the friction plates in a suitable solvent, then blow them dry.

2. Inspect the clutch plates and discs for a worn, damaged, scored, or burned condition, and replace them as necessary. A good indication of whether or not a friction disc is worn past its usable limits is if it holds the imprint of a thumb nail pressed against it, or the disc may be measured with a vernier caliper. Friction discs should be replaced as a complete set if any are damaged or worn past the serviceable limits given below:

Friction Disc Wear Table

Standard	*Service Limit*
0.146-0.154 in. (3.7-3.9 mm)	0.134 in. (3.4 mm)

3. Measure the clearance between the friction disc tangs and the fingers of the clutch housing using a thickness gauge. Excessive clearance will result in noisy operation. If you replace the discs check the clearance again, and if it still exceeds the service limit given below, replace the housing.

Disc Clearance Chart

Standard	*Service Limit*
(0.002-0.012 in) (0.04-0.30 mm)	0.020 in. (0.5 mm)

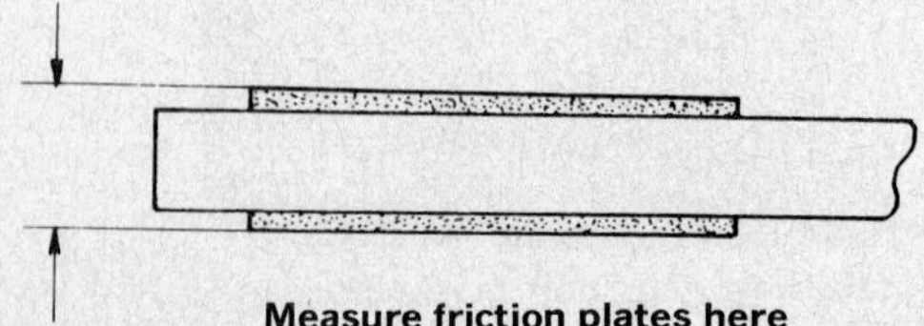

Measure friction plates here

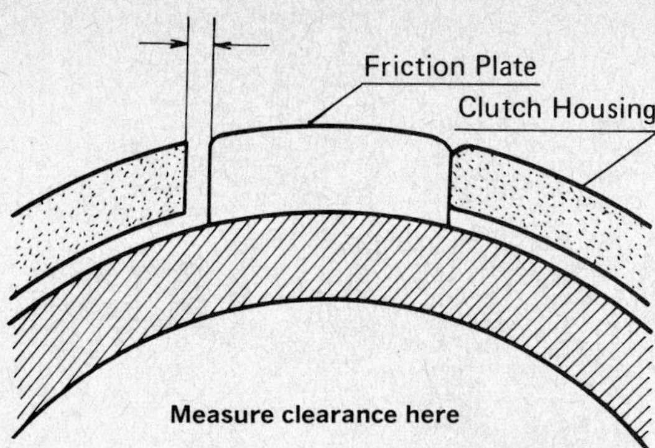

4. Place the clutch plates on a flat surface, and use a thickness gauge to measure warpage. Replace any plate if it is warped more than the limits given below:

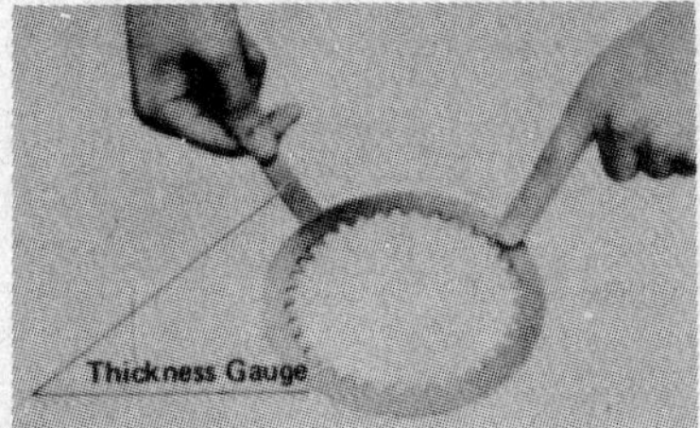

Checking for a warped plate

Clutch Plate Wear Chart

Standard	*Service Limit*
Friction plate	
under 0.006 in.	0.012 in.
(under 0.15 mm)	(0.30 mm)
Steel plate	
under 0.008 in.	0.016 in.
(under 0.20 mm)	(0.40 mm)

5. Inspect the clutch springs for a worn, pitted, or collapsed condition, and replace the entire set if any are worn past the following free length limits:

Clutch Spring Wear Chart

Standard	*Service Limit*
1.33 in.	1.27 in.
(33.8 mm)	(32.3 mm)

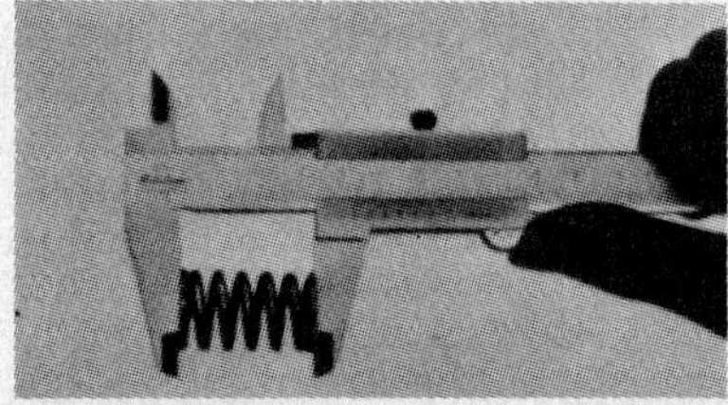

Measuring clutch spring free length

6. Inspect the clutch hub and housing for signs of wear or damage, and replace them as necessary. Light damage to any gear teeth can be repaired with an oilstone, but severly damaged teeth, fingers, or hub splines will necessitate replacing the housing and/or hub.

7. Inspect the clutch pushrod, release bearing, and worm teeth of the release

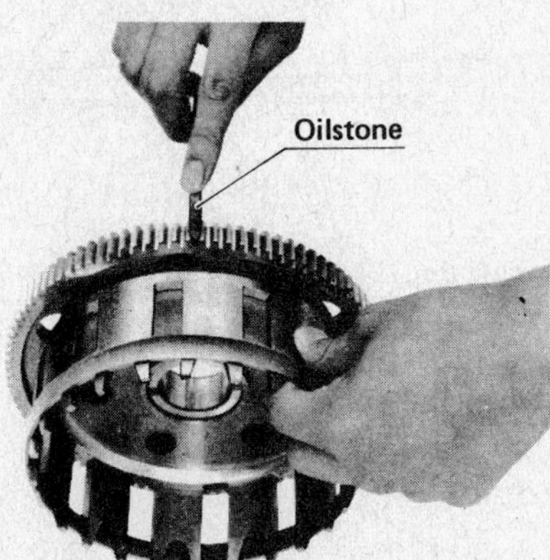

The hub teeth can be gone over with an oilstone

gears for signs of wear, pitting, or damage, and replace them as necessary. The release gears must be replaced as a set.

8. Inspect the pressure plate for signs of wear, fatigue, cracks, or severe warpage, and replace it as necessary.

ASSEMBLY

1. Assembly is basically in the reverse order of disassembly. Use new cover gaskets wherever applicable.

2. Keep the clutch hub from rotating as in the disassembly procedure, and secure the hub nut to 87-108 ft lbs (12-15 kg/m). Remember that the correct order is washer-hub-washer-hub nut.

3. Install the friction and steel plates, starting with a friction disc and then alternating them.

4. Install the release bearing and pushrod in the driveshaft, then install the pressure plate, springs, washers, and mounting bolts, securing them in a crossed pattern.

5. Liberally lubricate the two release

The release lever should be positioned like this

gears with cup grease before installing them. The release lever should be positioned as illustrated.

6. Secure the outer gear mounting after applying Loctite® (which is recommended by the factory), or a suitable thread sealer, to the threads.

7. Refill the engine with 3.5 qts (3.3 l) of a suitable engine oil.

External Shift Mechanism

REMOVAL

1. Remove the chain cover and drive sprocket as described in the "Final Drive" Section of the "Chassis" Chapter.

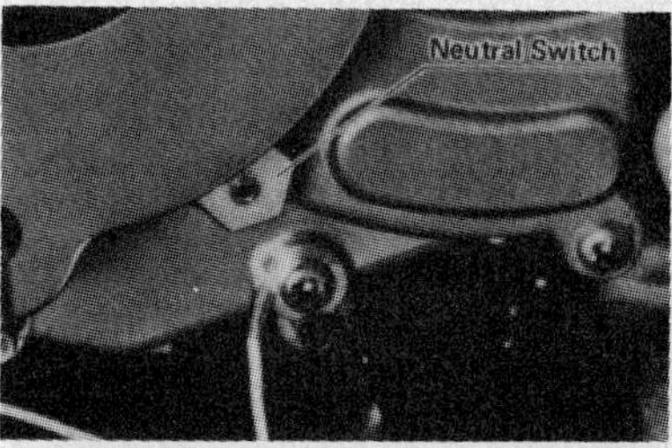

Disconnecting the neutral switch lead

2. Disconnect the neutral switch lead.

3. Remove the transmission cover, cover gasket, sprocket distance collar, and O-ring. A bearing puller may be used if the collar proves difficult to remove.

4. Remove the shift lever assembly and detent lever mounting bolt, then unhook the spring and remove the lever.

INSPECTION AND REPAIR

1. Clean all parts other than gaskets and O-rings in a suitable solvent, then blow them dry.

2. Inspect the shift lever spring, shift pawls, pawl spring, and detent arm spring for signs of wear or damage, and replace them as necessary.

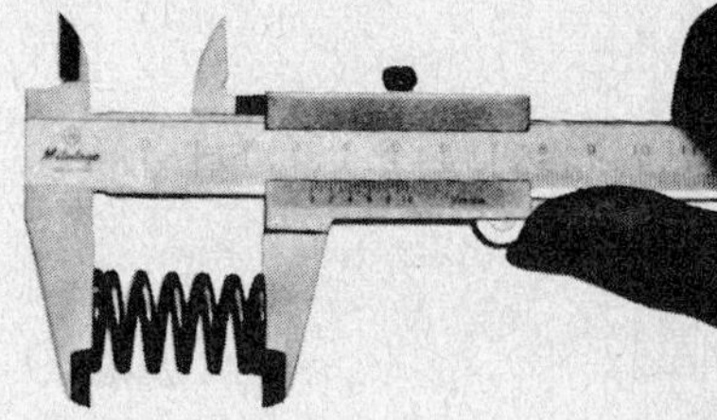

Measuring the return spring free length

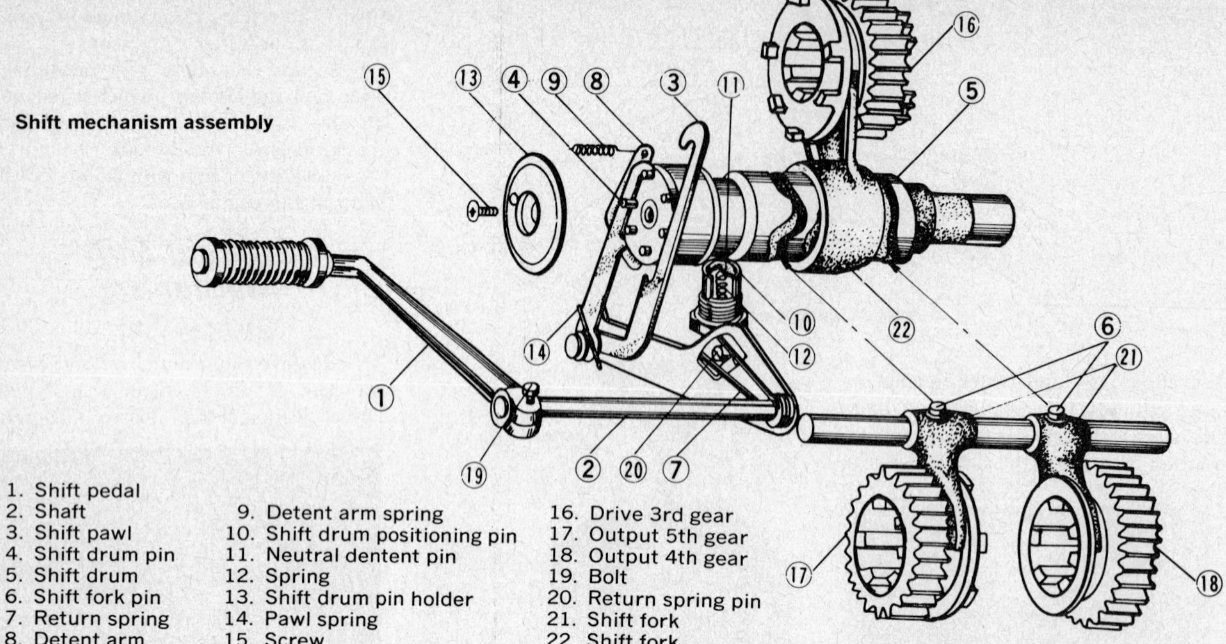

3. Measure the free length of the detent arm spring using vernier calipers, and replace it if it is longer than the service limits given below;

Detent Arm Length Chart

Standard	*Service Limit*
0.917 in. (23.3 mm)	0.984 in. (25 mm)

INSTALLATION

1. Check the return spring pin for a tight fit, and remove it and coat the threads with Loctite before installing it if it was loose.

2. Make sure that the longest shift drum pin is in the position illustrated, if the pins were removed. Failure to properly position the long pin will keep the Neutral light from operating correctly.

3. Install the detent lever taking care to position it so that it rides on the shoulder of its mounting bolt, and so that it doesn't get caught between the bolt and crankcase.

4. Install a new O-ring behind the sprocket to prevent oil leakage.

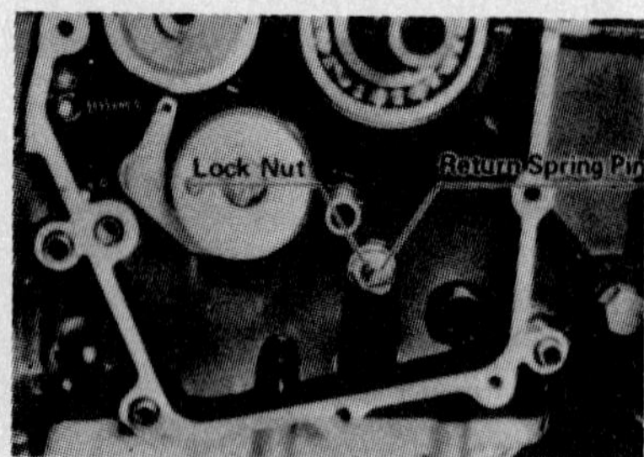

Make sure that the return spring pin is secure

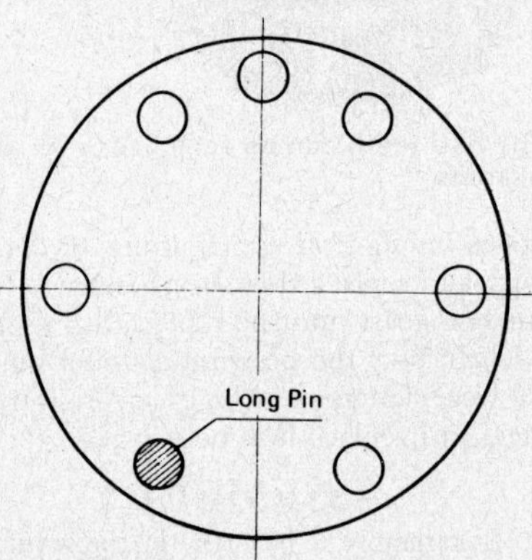

Correct positioning of the long pin is essential

Long pin installed

The detent lever must be able to move freely

Always use a new O-ring to be sure

Protecting the seal will pay off

5. Use an oil seal guide (Part No. 57001-130) or a suitable substitute while installing the transmission cover so that the shift shaft seal isn't damaged.

6. Install the sprocket collar after the transmission cover is installed to avoid damaging the output shaft oil seal.

7. Grease the pushrod before installing it.

Splitting the Crankcases

DISASSEMBLY

1. Remove the engine from the frame as described in the "Engine Removal and Installation" Section.

2. Remove the kickstarter pedal, spring cover, and cover gasket, then pull

out the spring guide and unhook and remove the spring.

3. Remove the clutch hub as described in the "Clutch" Section only if the clutch housing or ball bearing is to be removed from the driveshaft.

Removing the kick starter spring

4. Remove the contact breaker cover, breaker plate assembly, and advance mechanism as described in the "Electrical System" Section then remove the right-side engine cover.

5. Disconnect the leads from the Neutral light switch and the oil pressure switch.

6. Remove the dynamo wires from the clamps, then remove the dynamo cover and cover gasket.

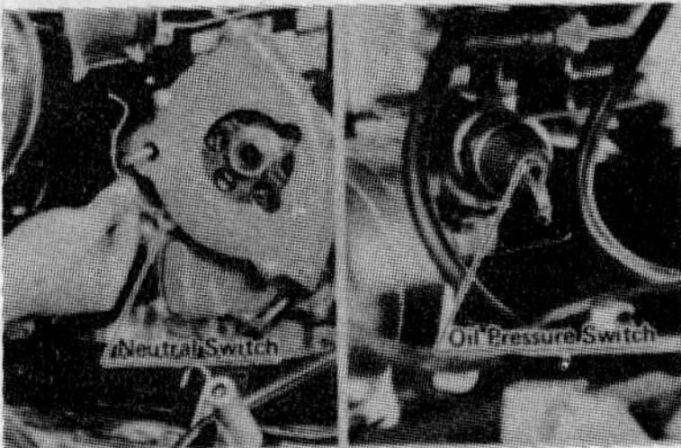

Disconnecting the switch leads

7. Remove the transmission cover and cover gasket, then remove the sprocket distance collar and O-ring. A bearing puller may be used to remove the collar if necessary.

8. Remove the shift lever assembly.

9. Remove the starter assembly as described in the "Electrical System" Chapter.

10. Remove the 5 crankcase bolts from the top side of the crankcase. The two cable clamps will also come free, and these should be replaced in their original positions.

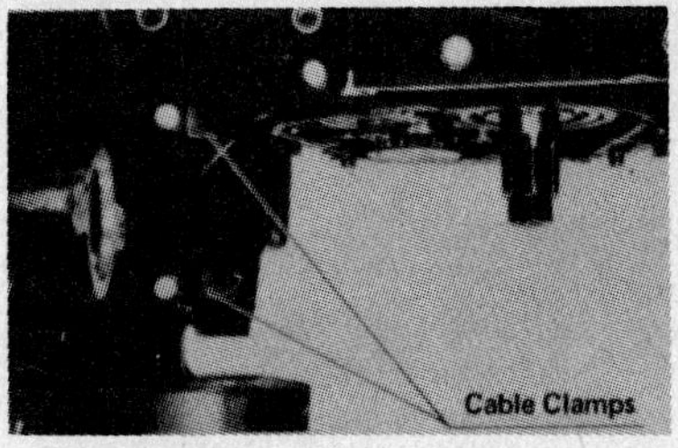

Cable clamp locations

11. Invert the engine and remove the oil filter, oil pan, and pan gasket, then remove the oil pump as described in the "Lubrication System" Section.

12. Remove the 17 6 mm crankcase bolts (two of which have cable clamps under them and both should be replaced in their original positions), and the 8 8 mm bolts.

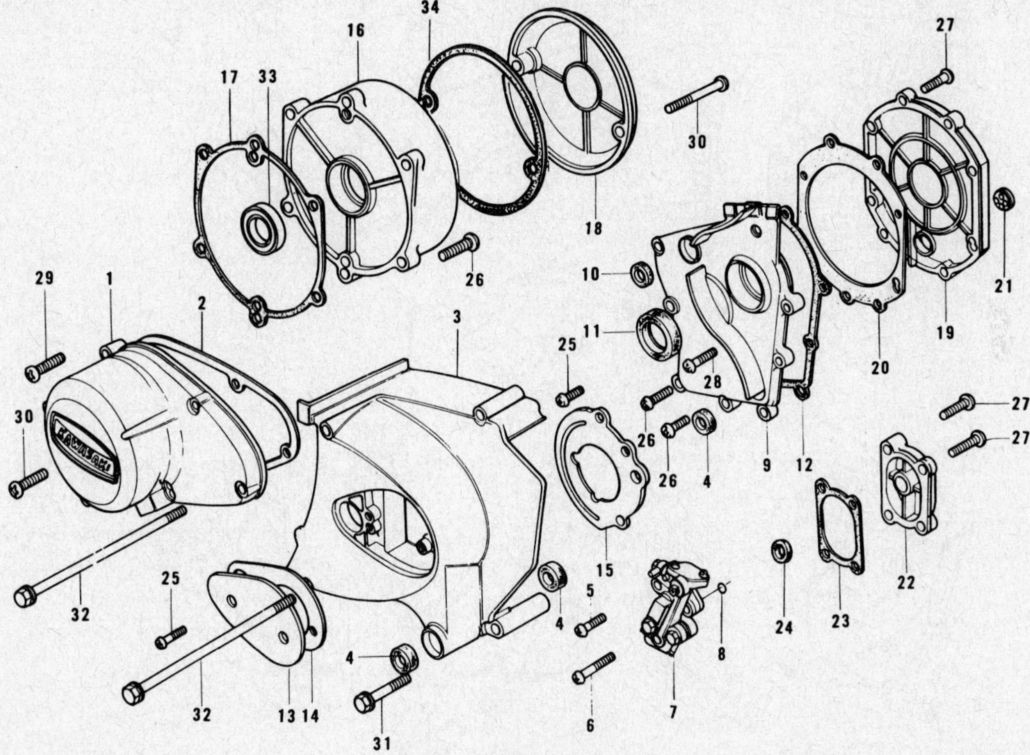

Engine cover assemblies

1. L.H. engine cover
2. L.H. engine cover gasket
3. Front chain cover
4. Oil seal
5. Pan head screw
6. Pan head screw
7. Oil pump assy
8. Oil pump O-ring
9. Transmission cover
10. Oil seal
11. Oil seal
12. Transmission cover gasket
13. Oil pump cover
14. Oil pump cover gasket
15. Engine sprocket cover
16. R.H. engine cover
17. R.H. engine cover gasket
18. Contact breaker cap
19. Clutch cover
20. Clutch cover gasket
21. Oil level gauge
22. Kickshaft cover
23. Kickshaft cover gasket
24. Oil seal
25. Pan head screw
26. Pan head screw
27. Pan head screw
28. Pan head screw
29. Pan head screw
30. Pan head screw
31. Hex head bolt
32. Hex head bolt
33. Oil seal
34. Contact breaker cap gasket

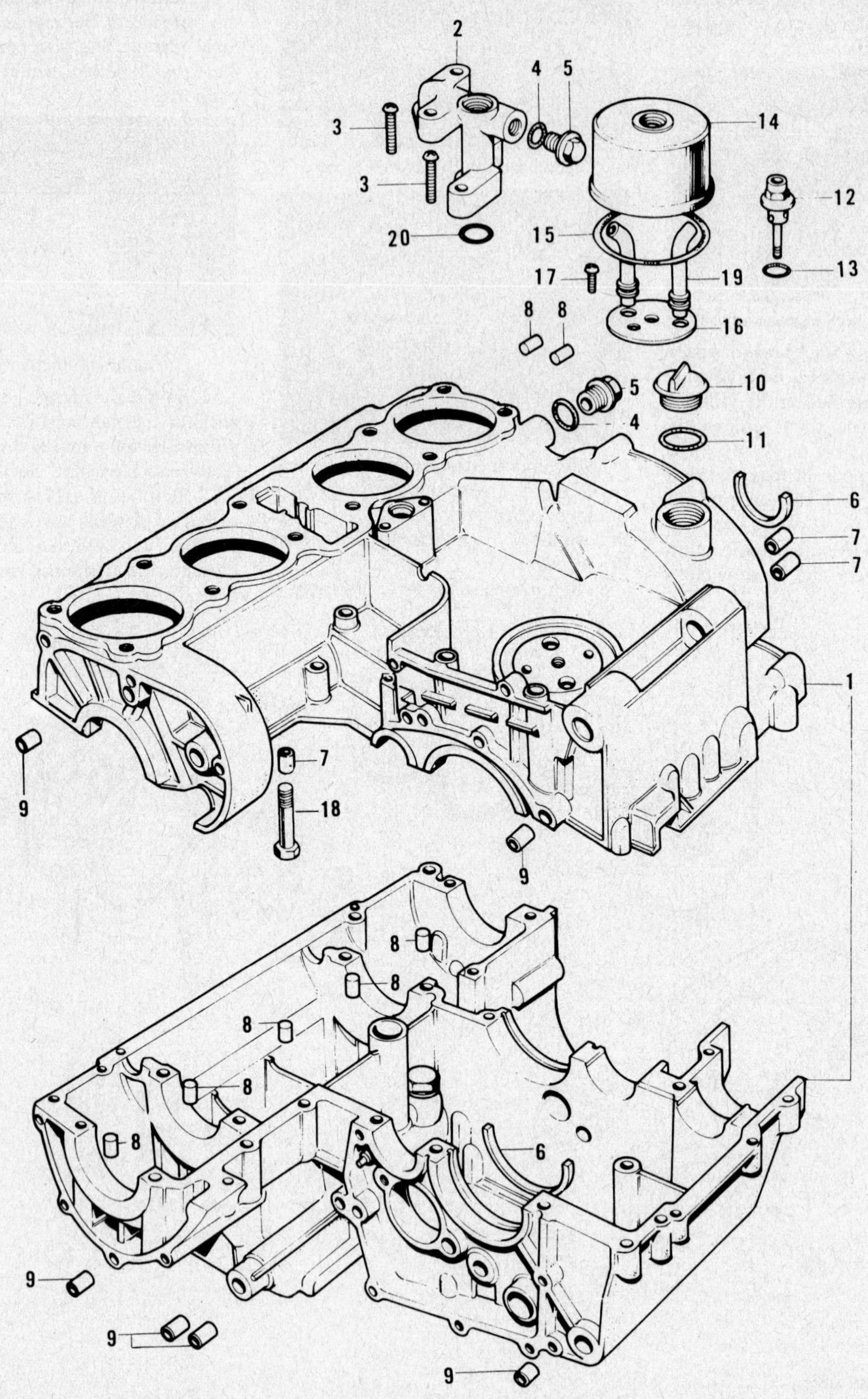

Crankcase assembly

1. Crank case set
2. Pipe
3. Pan head screw
4. O-ring
5. Plug
6. Bearing set ring
7. Dowel pin
8. Dowel pin
9. Dowel pin
10. Oil filler plug
11. O-ring
12. Breather bolt
13. O-ring
14. Breather body
15. Breather body O-ring
16. Breather plate
17. Pan head screw
18. Hex head bolt
19. Tube
20. O-ring

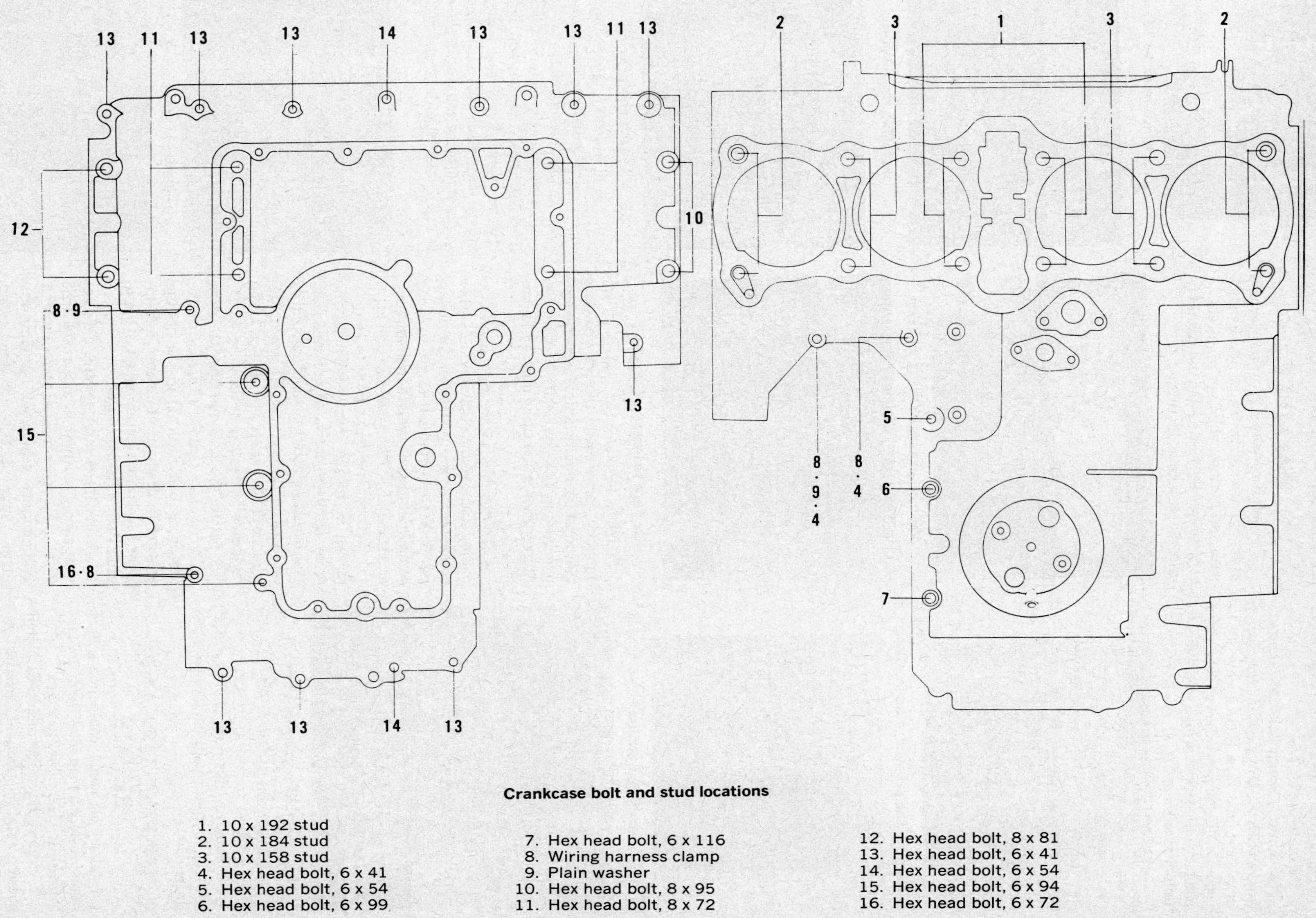

Crankcase bolt and stud locations

1. 10 x 192 stud
2. 10 x 184 stud
3. 10 x 158 stud
4. Hex head bolt, 6 x 41
5. Hex head bolt, 6 x 54
6. Hex head bolt, 6 x 99
7. Hex head bolt, 6 x 116
8. Wiring harness clamp
9. Plain washer
10. Hex head bolt, 8 x 95
11. Hex head bolt, 8 x 72
12. Hex head bolt, 8 x 81
13. Hex head bolt, 6 x 41
14. Hex head bolt, 6 x 54
15. Hex head bolt, 6 x 94
16. Hex head bolt, 6 x 72

CAUTION: *Do not accidentally remove the 4 bolts which hold down the crankshaft.*

13. Screw 3 8 mm bolts into the jack bolt positions provided in the lower crankcase, and turn them in evenly to separate the crankcase halves. The cases can be gently tapped with a soft mallet to help loosen them.

Remove the crankcase bolts evenly

Jack bolt positions

The assemblies ready for removal

CAUTION: *Do not attempt to pry the cases apart.*

14. Remove the driveshaft, clutch housing, output shaft, and kickstarter shaft.

INSPECTION AND REPAIR

1. Clean all metal components in a suitable solvent, then blow them dry taking care to clear all oil passages.

2. Inspect the crankcases, studs, clutch housing, and component systems for signs of wear or damage, and either repair or replace them as necessary. Further disassembly procedures for the kick starter driveshaft, output shaft, shift drum, crankshaft, and cam chain follow the following "Assembly" Section.

ASSEMBLY

1. Assembly is basically in the reverse order of disassembly. Use all new gaskets, seals and O-rings wherever applicable.

2. Install the O-ring for the main engine oil passage as illustrated.

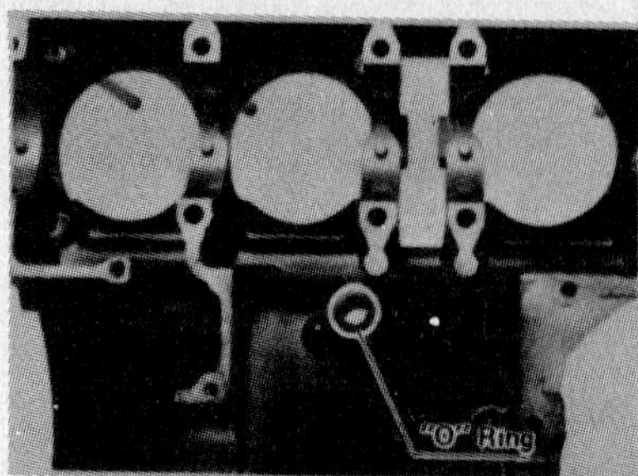

Main oil passage O-ring location

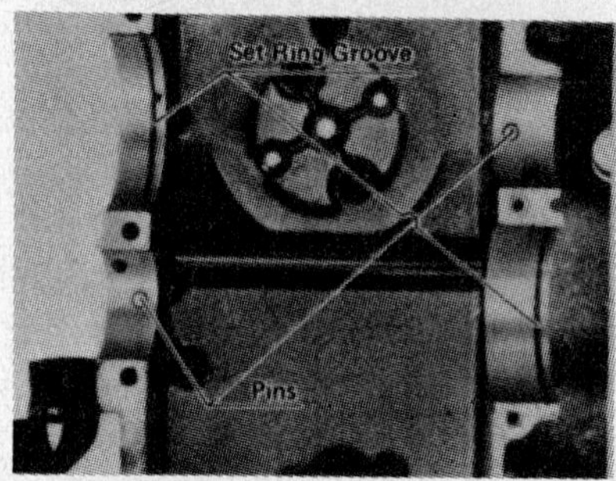

Be sure to install all the pins

3. When installing the output, drive, and kick starter shafts, the crankcase set pins must go into the holes in the respective bushings on the shafts, and the set ring for each ball bearing must be fit into its groove.

4. Thoroughly clean the crankcase mating surfaces, and apply a liquid gasket compound to the surface of the lower case half. Be careful not to use so much compound that it runs down into the crankcase after the halves are joined.

5. Secure the 8 8 mm bolts to 18 ft lbs (2.5 kg/m) torque, evenly following the order numbers on the lower case half. The threads of bolts 6 and 8 should be coated with Loctite, and #1 sealer (the hardening type) should be applied to the underside of the bolt heads.

6. Secure the 22 6 mm bolts to 70 in. lbs (0.8 kg/m). Coat the threads of the remaining bolt depicted in the accompanying illustration with Loctite, and apply #1 sealer (the hardening type) to the underside of the bolt head.

7. Install the O-ring depicted in the accompanying illustration, and check that the oil pump gear meshes correctly with the crankshaft gear when installing the pump. Apply Loctite to the pump mounting bolts, and secure them to 70 in. lbs (0.8 kg/m) torque.

8. To aid in installing the starter, lightly oil the O-ring.

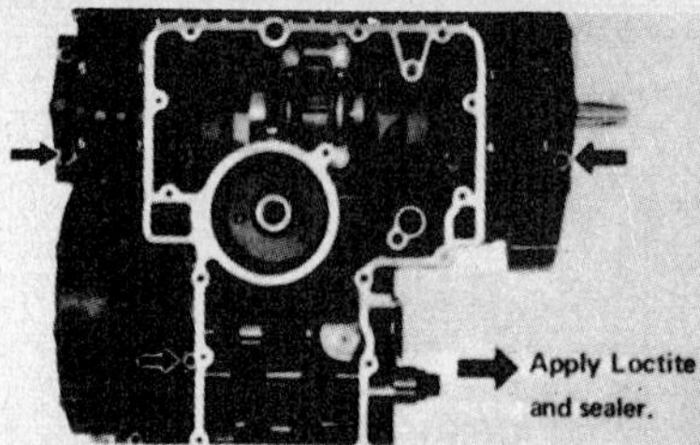

Bolts which must be sealed

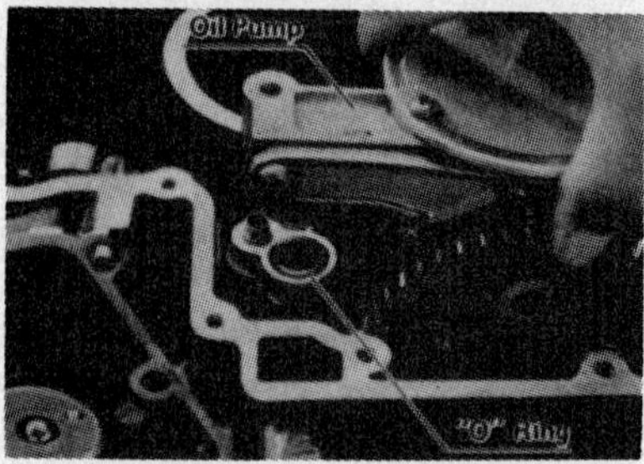

Installing the oil pump

Output shaft O-ring

9. Install the O-ring on the output shaft before installing the transmission cover to prevent oil leaks.

10. Use either the factory oil seal guide (Part No. 57001-130), or a suitable substitute, to protect the oil seal while installing the transmission cover, and install the sprocket distance collar after the cover is in place, otherwise the seal will be damaged.

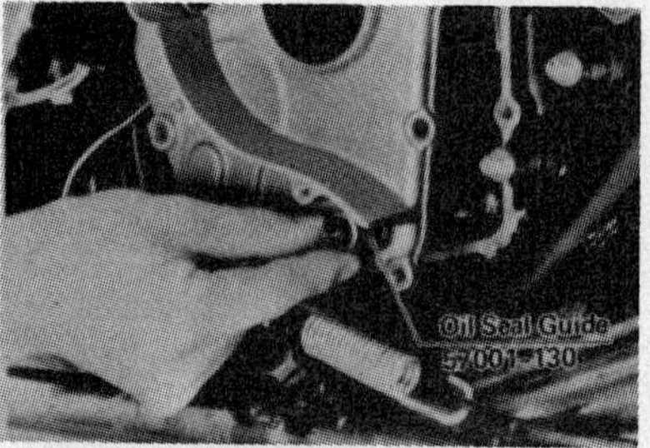

Installing the transmission cover

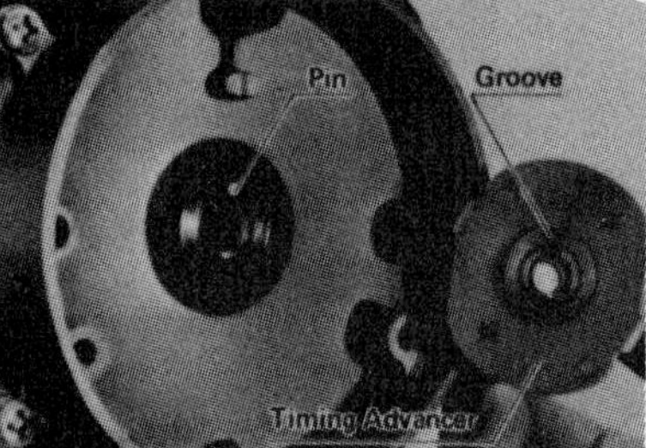

Installing the advance mechanism

11. Apply Loctite to the 3 upper right engine cover mounting screws.

12. Align the pin and groove when installing the advance mechanism.

13. Rotate the kickstarter shaft all the way to the right before hooking the spring into the hole in the shaft.

14. Mount and secure the kick starter cover using either the factory oil seal guide (Part No. 57001-131) or a suitable substitute, to protect the oil seal.

The kickstarter must be preloaded before the spring is installed

Installing the kick starter cover

Kick Starter

DISASSEMBLY

1. Remove the engine from the frame, and separate the crankcases as described previously.

2. Remove the circlip (1), cap (2), coil spring (3), ratchet (4), circlips (1), washer (5), kick gear (6), washer (7), and bushing (8) from the kick shaft (10).

INSPECTION AND REPAIR

1. Clean all parts in a suitable solvent, then blow them dry.

2. If the kick starter made a ratcheting noise while the engine was running, check the pedal return spring and the kick gear bushing and shaft for wear. Wear on these parts, and damage to the kick gear teeth are the most common kick starter problems. If any of these parts appear worn, pitted, collapsed (in the case of the spring), or damaged, they should be replaced. The ratcheting gears should be replaced as a set if either is damaged, as indicated by slipping of the kick starter pedal.

3. Measure the inside diameter of the kick gear, and replace it if it is worn past its service limit given below:

Kick Gear Table

Standard	*Service Limit*
0.8653-0.8661 in. (21.979-22.000 mm)	0.8681 in. (22.05 mm)

4. Measure the outside diameter of the kick start shaft, and replace it if it is worn past its service limit given below:

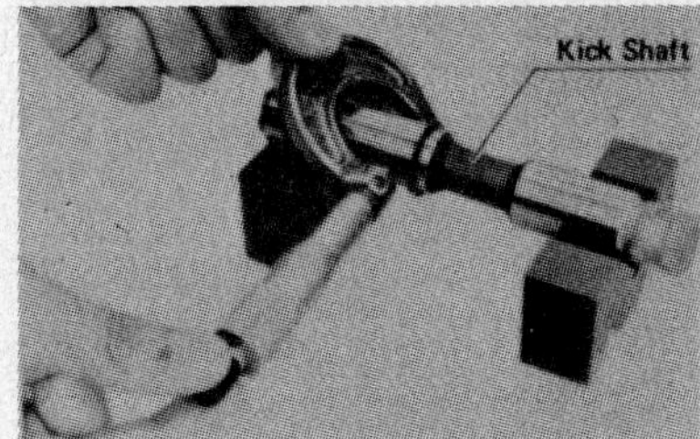

Measuring the diameter of the shaft

Kick Shaft Table

Standard	*Service Limit*
0.8637-0.8646 in. (21.939-21.960 mm)	0.8626 in. (21.91 mm)

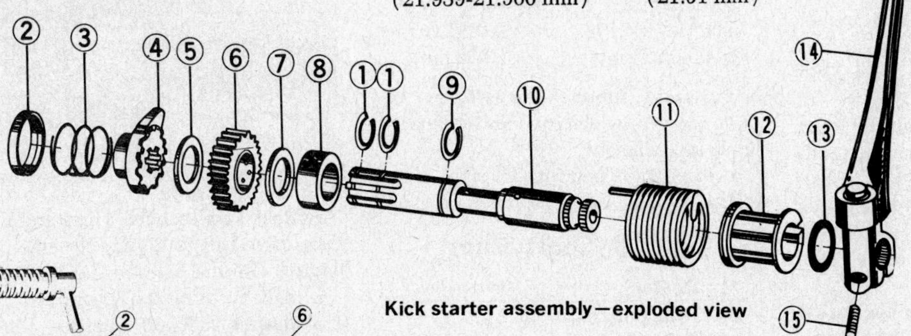
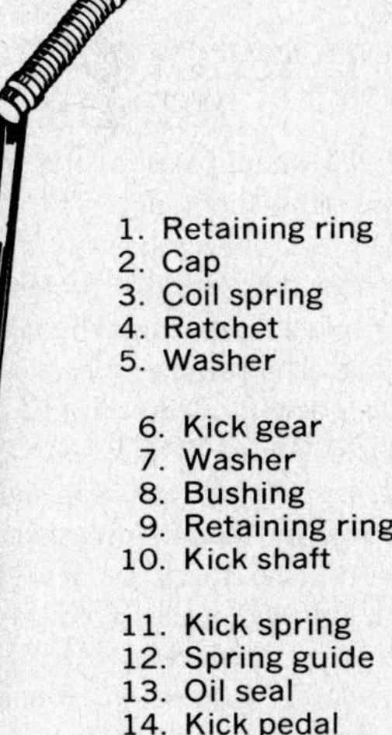

Kick starter assembly—exploded view

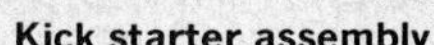

Kick starter assembly

1. Kick shaft
2. Kick pedal
3. Ratchet gear
4. Spring
5. Kick spring
6. Stopper
7. Spring guide
8. Kick gear

ASSEMBLY

1. Assembly is basically in the reverse order of disassembly. The oil seal (13) should be replaced.

2. When the ratchet is assembled to the kick shaft, align the mark on the ratchet with the mark on the shaft.

These marks must be alignment

Transmission

DISASSEMBLY

1. Remove the engine from the frame, and separate the crankcases as described previously. Before removing the gear clusters from the crankcase, the gears should be checked for backlash. Consult the "Inspection and Repair" Section for additional information.

2. Remove the bushing (1), circlip (2), shim (3), needle bearing (4), washers (5 and 6), Second gear (7), Fifth gear (8), Fifth gear bushing (9), and the toothed washer (10).

3. Remove the retaining ring (11), Third gear (12), the next retaining ring (11), the toothed washer (10), and Fourth gear (13), then pull the bearing (14) with a suitable bearing puller.

4. Remove the bushing (15), retaining ring (2), shim (3), needle bearing (4), washers (5 and 6), First gear (16), and shim (17).

5. Rotate the shaft while removing the fourth gear (29) so that the 3 balls (30) will move, then pull the bearing (18) from the shaft using a suitable bearing puller, and remove the washer (19), Second gear (20), the Second gear bushing (21), and the toothed washer (22) from the shaft.

6. Remove the circlip (23), Fifth gear (24), the next circlip (23), the toothed washer (22), Third gear (25), and the washer (26).

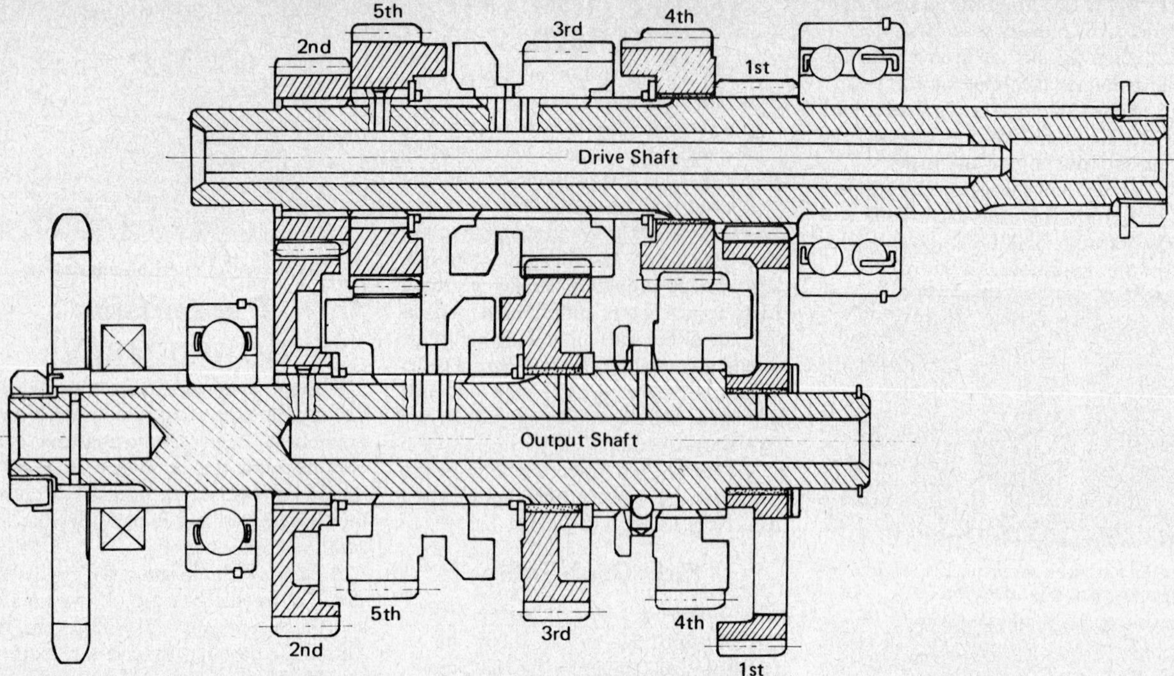

Transmission assembly cross-section

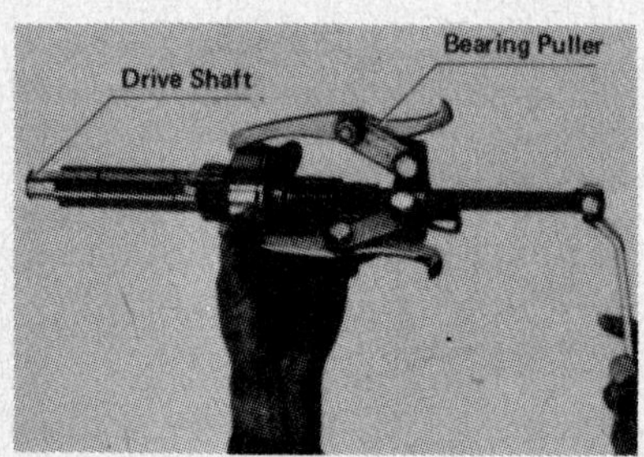

Pulling the bearing from the driveshaft

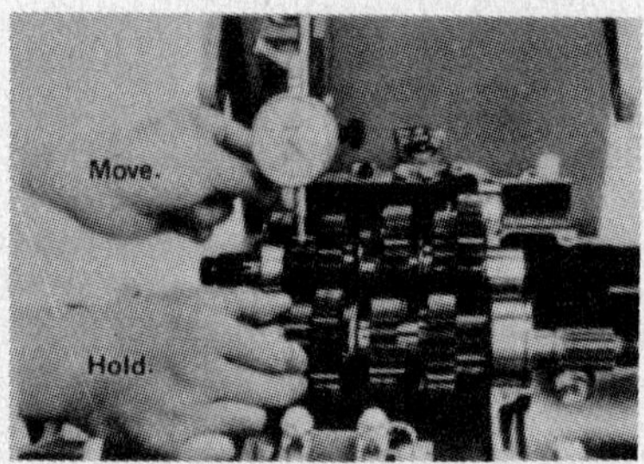

Measuring gear backlash

INSPECTION AND REPAIR

1. Clean all parts in a suitable solvent, then blow them dry. The oil seal (35) which has already been removed during the initial disassembly procedure, should be replaced. Bearings should be washed with clean gasoline, blown dry, and lubricated with clean oil. DO NOT SPIN UNLUBRICATED BEARINGS.

2. Inspect all parts for signs of wear, damage, pitting, or chipped gear teeth, and replace them as necessary. Gears with chipped or damaged teeth, dogs, or dog holes should be replaced as gear systems rather than as individuals since they act upon one another.

3. Check for excessive gear backlash in all 5 gears by holding one gear steady while rotating the gear it meshes with back and forth. A dial indicator set against the gear which is moved will provide the necessary information. The difference between the highest and lowest reading is the backlash. In cases where the backlash exceeds the limits given below, replace both gears:

Backlash Limits

Standard	*Service Limit*
1st gear	
0.0008-0.0075 in.	0.0098 in.
(0.02-0.19 mm)	(0.25 mm)
2nd-5th gears	
0.0024-0.0091 in.	0.0118 in.
(0.06-0.23 mm)	(0.30 mm)

4. Measure the inside diameter of each gear, then measure the outside diameter of the shafts, subtract the two, and replace any gear which exceeds the service limits given below:

Gear & Shaft Chart

Standard	*Service Limit*
Drive 4th, output 3rd	
0.0008-0.0024 in.	0.0064 in.
(0.020-0.062 mm)	(0.162 mm)
Drive 5th	
0.0063-0.0096 in.	0.0136 in.
(0.160-0.245 mm)	(0.345 mm)
Output 1st	
0.0011-0.0024 in.	0.0063 in.
(0.027-0.061 mm)	(0.161 mm)
Output 2nd	
0.0118-0.0182 in.	0.0222 in.
(0.300-0.463 mm)	(0.563 mm)

5. Inspect the bearings for signs of external damage, and spin them (ONLY WHEN LUBRICATED) to check for rough motion or noisy operation, and replace them as necessary.

6. Inspect all the assorted hardware, and replace any circlips which are twisted, or any washers which are worn or scored.

ASSEMBLY

1. Assembly is basically in the reverse order of disassembly. Use plenty of fresh motor oil as an assembly lubricant.

2. Press on the ball bearings so that the set ring groove is toward the end of the shaft.

The set ring groove should be toward the end of the shaft

3. Make sure that the Third and Fifth gear driveshaft bushing oil holes are aligned with the holes in the shaft.

4. Make sure that the Second and Fifth gear (output shaft) oil holes are aligned with the holes in the shaft.

5. Do not grease the Fourth gear steel balls (30) during assembly, as the balls must be able to move freely.

Shift Mechanism

DISASSEMBLY

NOTE: *Consult the "External Shift Mechanism" Section for an operational description and illustration.*

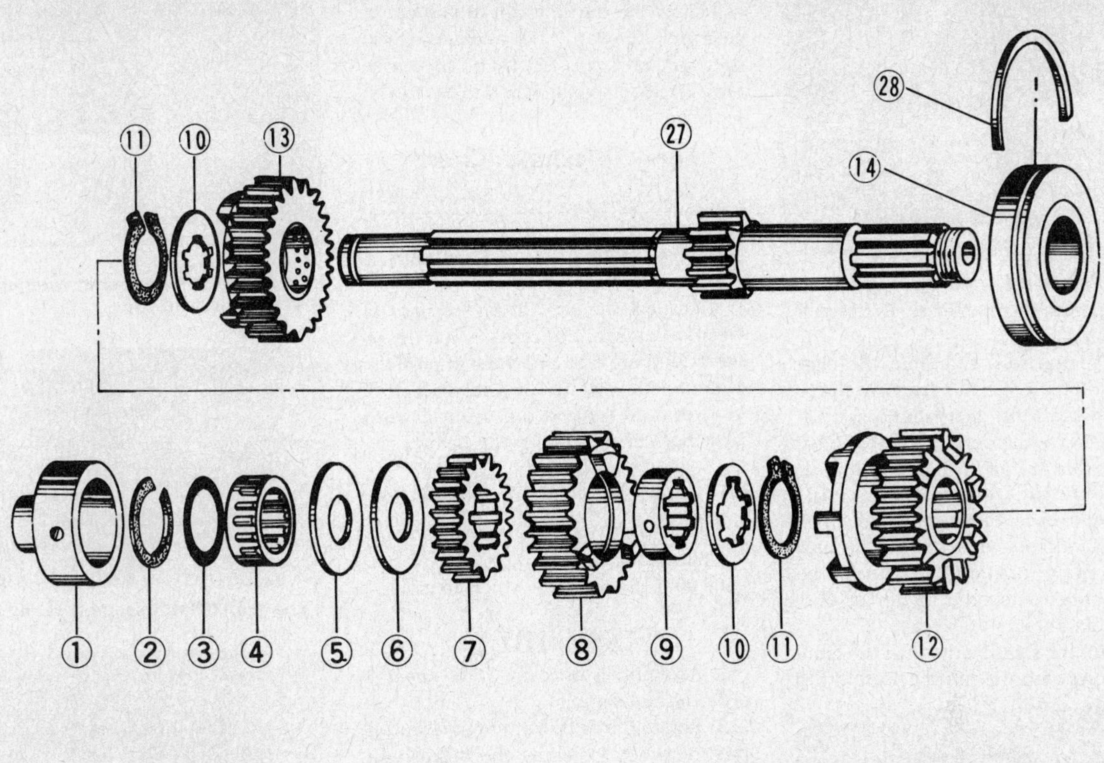

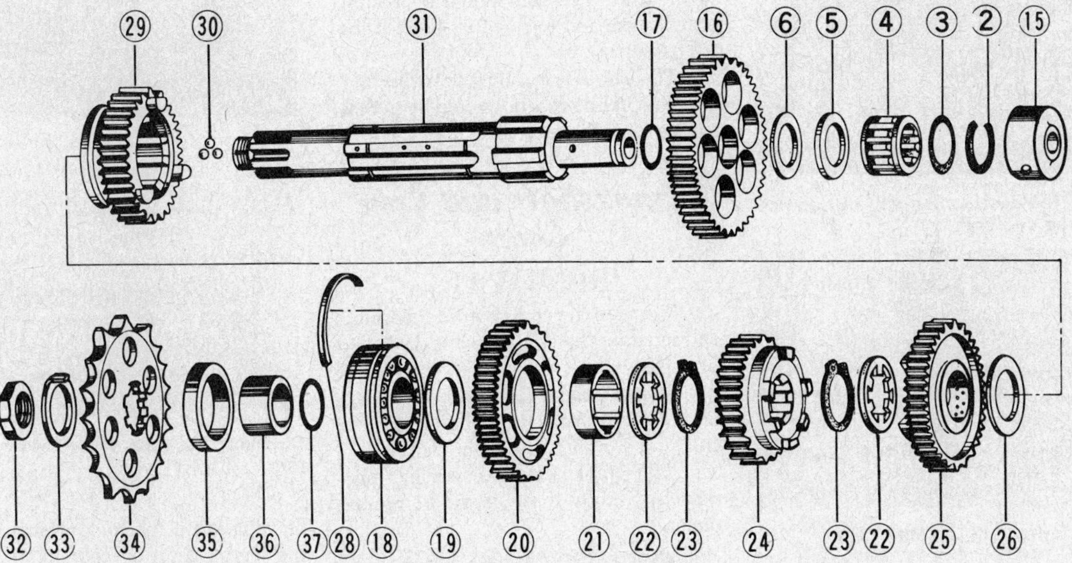

Transmission assembly—exploded view

1. Bushing
2. Retaining ring
3. Shim
4. Needle bearing
5. Washer
6. Washer
7. 2nd gear (D)
8. 5th gear (D)
9. 5th gear bushing
10. Toothed washer
11. Retaining ring
12. 3rd gear (D)
13. 4th gear (D)
14. Bearing
15. Bushing
16. 1st gear (O)
17. Shim
18. Bearing
19. Washer
20. 2nd gear (O)
21. 2nd gear bushing
22. Toothed washer
23. Retaining ring
24. 5th gear (O)
25. 3rd gear (O)
26. Washer
27. Main shaft
28. Set ring
29. 4th gear (O)
30. Steel balls
31. Counter shaft
32. Nut
33. Lockwasher
34. Engine sprocket
35. Oil seal
36. Engine sprocket collar
37. O-ring

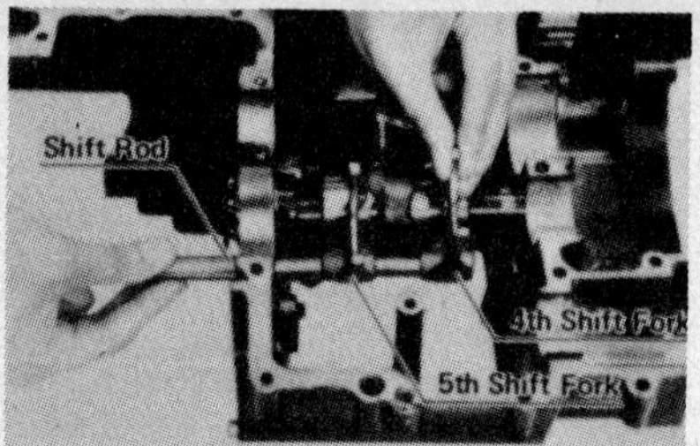

Removing the shift rod and forks

1. Remove the engine from the frame, and separate the crankcases as described previously.
2. Tap the shift rod from the clutch end and pull it out, then remove the two (Fourth and Fifth gear) shift forks.
3. Remove the detent arm, bend back the locking tab of the lockwasher, and remove the shift fork pin.
4. Bend back the locking tab of the lockwasher, then unscrew and remove the drum positioning bolt. The cap bolt need not be removed from the top of the positioning bolt.
5. Pull the shift drum out of the crankcase along with the Third gear shift fork.

Remove the positioning bolt, but do not loosen the cap bolt

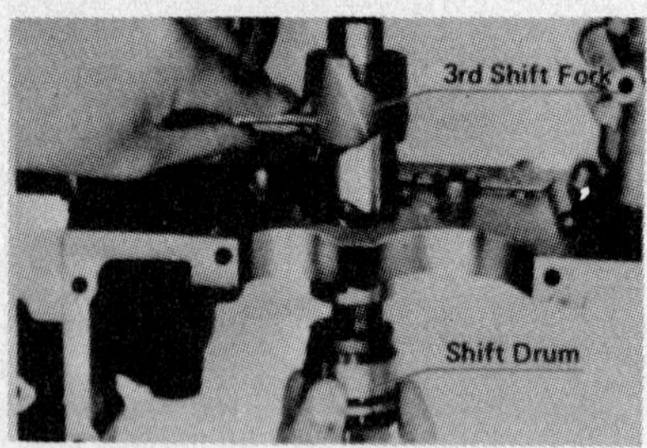

Removing the shift drum

INSPECTION AND REPAIR

1. Clean all parts in a suitable solvent, then blow them dry.
2. Inspect the shift forks for a worn, pitted, bent, or damaged condition, and replace them as necessary. A bent fork will allow the transmission to pop out of gear under power. If the thickness of the shift fork prongs is less than the service limit listed below, the fork will have to be replaced.

Measuring the shifter forks

Fork Thickness Chart

Standard	*Service Limit*
0.228-0.236 in. (5.80-6.00 mm)	0.224 in. (5.70 mm)

3. Inspect the shift drum for signs of wear or damage, and replace it as necessary. Compare it to a new one if possible. Measure the width of the shift fork grooves, and replace the drum if worn past the service limits given below:

Groove Width Chart

Standard	*Service Limit*
0.238-0.242 in. (6.05 6.15 mm)	0.246 in. (6.25 mm)

ASSEMBLY

1. Assembly is basically in the reverse order of disassembly.
2. Rotate the shift drum to the Neutral position when installing the drum positioning bolt. The bolt should be coated with Loctite and torqued to 44-57 ft lbs (6.0-8.0 kg/m).
3. The Third gear shift fork is different from the other two, and should be so that it faces the Neutral switch.

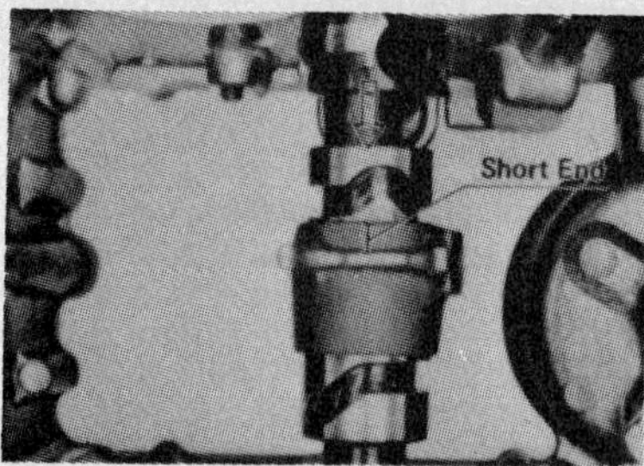

Install the third gear shift fork with the short end as shown

Crankshaft and Cam Chain

REMOVAL

1. Remove the engine from the frame, and separate the crankcases as described previously.
2. Remove the crankshaft bearing cap, lift the crankshaft out of the upper case half, and slip the cam chain from it.
3. The crankshaft end bearings may now be removed by using a suitable puller.

The crankshaft assembly ready to go

INSPECTION AND REPAIR

1. Clean the assembly in a suitable solvent, then blow it dry, taking care to clear any oil passages. Lubricate the assembly with fresh motor oil before attempting to spin the bearings.
2. Remove the bearing from each end of the crank, and place it in a V-block. Place a suitable arbor into the connecting rod small end, and measure the difference in height over a 100 mm (4 in.) length, using a dial indicator, to determine the amount which a connecting rod is bent. The standard for this is under 0.002 in./100 mm (under 0.05 mm/100 mm), and the crankshaft assembly should be replaced if the measurement is over the service limit of 0.008 in. (0.20 mm).

Checking the rods for a bent condition

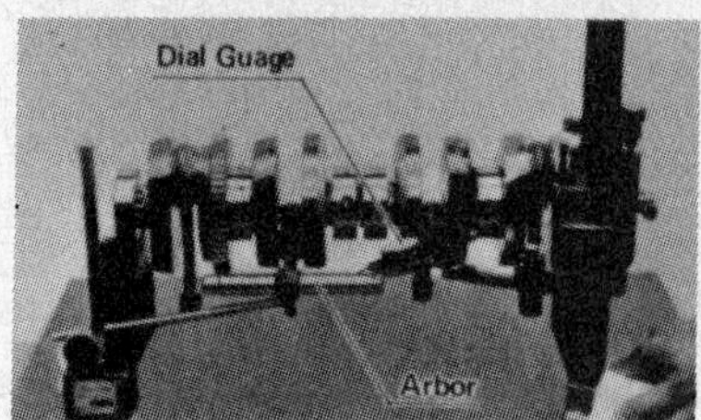

Checking the rods for a twisted condition

3. Use the method described above to determine whether or not a rod is twisted by checking the amount in which the arbor varies from parallel over a 100 mm length of arbor. The standard for this is the same as for bending.
4. Check for big end radial clearance by setting the crank, with the end bearings removed, in V-blocks with a dial indicator set against the connecting rod to be checked. Push the rod against the gauge, and then pull it away. The difference between the two readings is the radial clearance. If the clearance for any of the rods exceeds the service limit listed below, the crankshaft will have to be replaced.

Measuring bearing radial clearance

Radial Clearance Chart

Standard	Service Limit
0.0006-0.0012 in. (0.016-0.030 mm)	0.0031 in. (0.08 mm)

5. Measure the connecting rod side clearance using a thickness gauge as shown in the illustration. If the clearance on any of the connecting rods exceeds the service limits given below, the crankshaft will have to be replaced.

Measuring bearing side clearance

Connecting Rod Chart

Standard	Service Limit
0.012-0.016 in. (0.3-0.4 mm)	0.024 in. (0.6 mm)

6. With the end bearings removed and the crankshaft in that old V-block setup once again, rotate the crank slowly with a dial indicator set against each of the bearings in order. The difference between the highest and lowest reading is the run-out. The crankshaft must be replaced if the runout exceeds the service limit given below:

Measuring crankshaft run-out

Crankshaft Runout Chart

Standard	Service Limit
under 0.0012 in. (under 0.03 mm)	0.004 in. (0.10 mm)

7. Clean the bearings with clean gasoline, blow them dry, then lubricate them with fresh motor oil. DO NOT SPIN UNLUBRICATED BEARINGS. Spin the bearings by hand and check for smooth motion and quiet operation. If the bearings are noisy or rough they must be replaced. Only the end bearings can be replaced without a major crankshaft rebuild.

NOTE: *The crankshaft can be completely rebuilt by the factory if necessary. Consult your local dealer for additional information.*

8. Inspect the bearing cap for signs of wear or damage. Since it is machined along with the crankcase, it must be replaced in conjunction with the crankcase if it is damaged.

INSTALLATION

1. Installation is in the reverse order of removal.
2. Align each pin in the upper crankcase with the pin hole in each bearing before slipping the crankshaft into place.

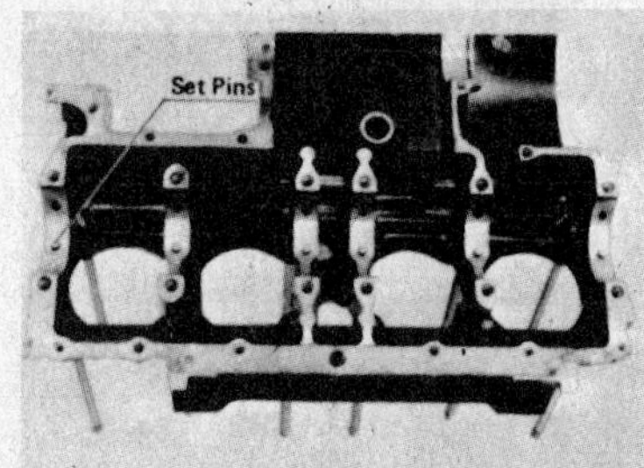

Set pins installed

Bearing cap installed

3. The crankshaft bearing cap is bored along with the crankcase, so that it must be installed with the arrow pointing toward the front of the engine. Secure the bolts with 18 ft lbs (2.5 kg/m) torque in the numbered sequence.

LUBRICATION SYSTEMS

ENGINE LUBRICATION

NOTE: *Excessive oil consumption, as indicated by heavy smoking at the exhaust pipes, possibly accompanied by poor performance and spark plug fouling, has been a problem with with some Z1s. This is caused by either excessive oil buildup in the plenum chamber, or by oil getting past the rings.*

First check the plenum chamber and air cleaner for oil buildup, and if this is the case, check the passage from the air-/oil separator in the plenum chamber to the lower half of the crankcase. Blockage here will prevent oil from flowing back into the crankcase, resulting in oil buildup in the aforementioned areas.

If this is not the problem, the rings may be worn or incorrectly assembled. Do a compression check, and if the results are poor, take down the top end and check for wear, damage, or incorrect assembly as described in the "Engine and Transmission" Section.

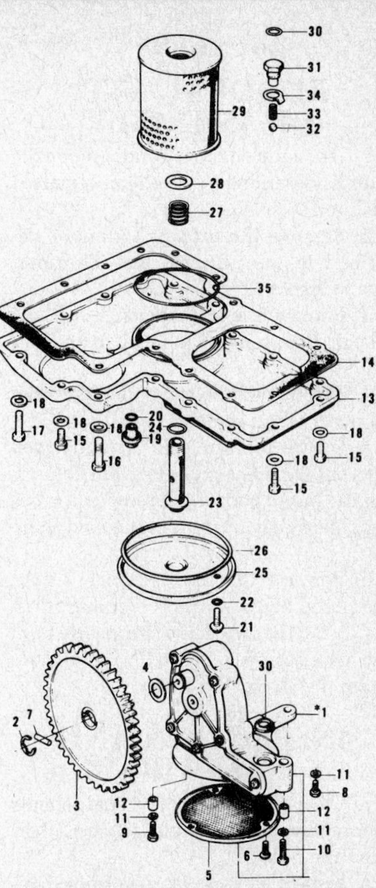
Lubrication system assembly

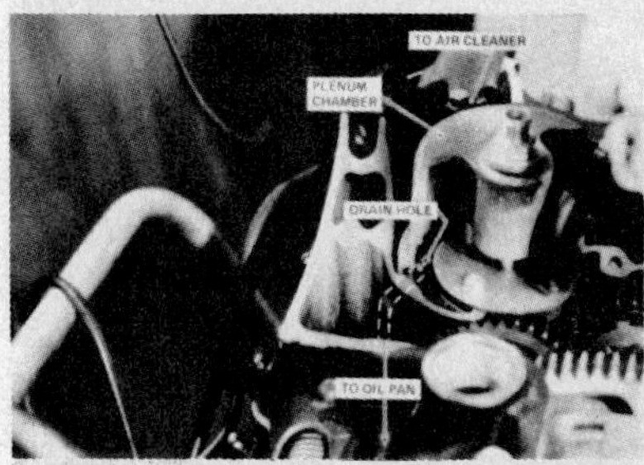

Engine cutaway showing problem area

Oil Pump

REMOVAL AND DISASSEMBLY

1. Drain the engine oil and remove the filter as described in the "Maintenance" Chapter.
2. Remove the exhaust system as described in the "Engine and Transmission" Chapter.
3. Remove the bolts which secure the oil pan, then remove the oil pan and gasket.
4. Remove the bolts which secure the oil pump, then remove the oil pump.
5. Secure the pump in a wood-jawed vise, or take precautions to avoid deforming the pump body, then remove the circlip, main gear, alignment pin, and shim.

6. Remove the screws which secure the pump housing halves together, then gently tap the two shafts alternately until the halves can be separated without damaging the shafts.

INSPECTION AND REPAIR

1. Clean the pump components thoroughly in a suitable solvent, then blow them dry.
2. Inspect all parts for a worn or damaged condition, and replace them as necessary. All gaskets and O-rings should be replaced as a matter of course.

Engine with oil pan removed

Removing the circlip and main gear

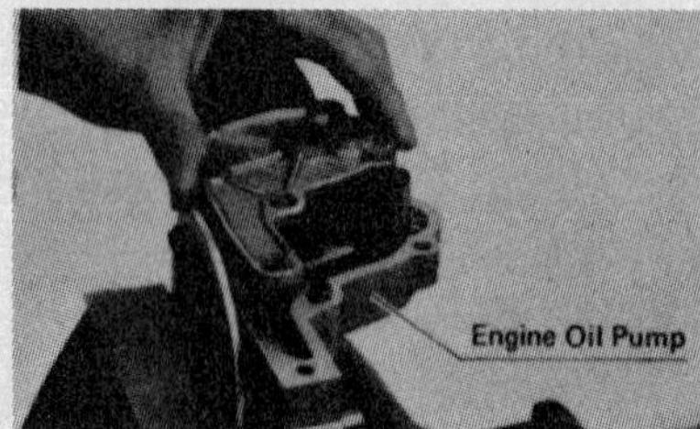

Separating the pump body halves

Checking gear/pump body clearance

3. Assemble the two internal gears in one side of the pump body, and check the clearance between each gear and the pump body with feeler gauges. The standard clearance is 0.0001-0.0014 in. (0.-003-0.036 mm), and the pump must be replaced if it is worn past its serviceable limit of 0.004 in (0.10 mm).
4. Inspect the strainer screen for a damaged, worn, or permanently clogged condition, and replace it as necessary.

ASSEMBLY AND INSTALLATION

1. Assembly is in the reverse order of disassembly, and installation is in the reverse order of removal.
2. Make sure that the gasket surface of both pump body halves is in perfect condition, and is absolutely clean, and always use a new gasket during assembly.
3. Use Loctite or a suitable thread sealing compound, on all of the assembling screws and mounting bolts, and torque the mounting bolts to 70 in. lbs (0.8 kg/m).
4. Make sure that the pump and crankshaft gears mesh properly.
5. Make sure that the sump pan gasket surfaces are perfectly clean, use a new pan gasket, and tighten the pan securing bolts in a crossed sequence to avoid deforming the gasket.

Oil Pressure Switch

For information on oil pressure switch repair and trouble shooting, consult the "Electrical System" Section.

Drive Chain Oil Pump

PUMP REMOVAL AND DISASSEMBLY

1. Remove the oil pump cover, slide back the hose clamp, and disconnect the hose.

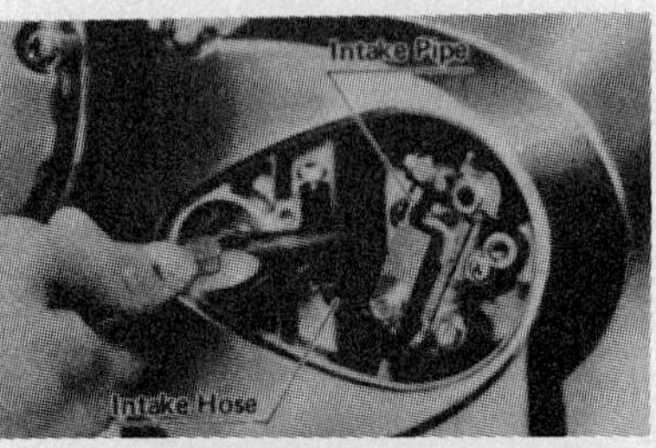

Pliers can be used to stop flow until a screw is inserted

NOTE: *Insert a cover screw into the hose, as illustrated, to prevent oil leakage.*

2. Remove the two pump mounting screws, and the pump.
3. Wrap cloth around the pump shaft

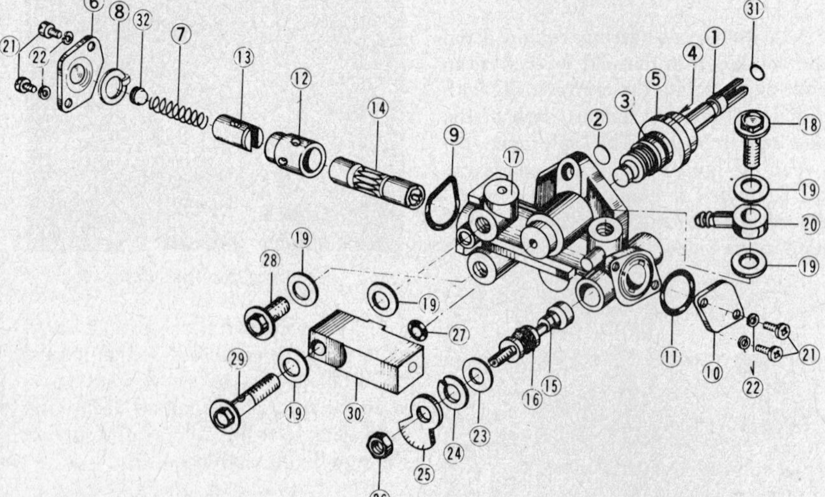

Pump assembly

1. Pump shaft
2. Spacer
3. O-ring
4. Oil seal
5. Bushing
6. Cap
7. Plunger spring
8. Plunger guide stopper
9. O-ring
10. Cap
11. O-ring
12. Plunger guide
13. Plunger
14. Plunger
15. Control cam
16. V-ring
17. Oil pump body
18. Banjo bolt
19. Washer
20. Banjo
21. Bolt
22. Lockwasher
23. Washer
24. Lockwasher
25. Control lever
26. Nut
27. O-ring
28. Bleeder bolt
29. Bolt
30. Check valve
31. O-ring
32. Spring seat

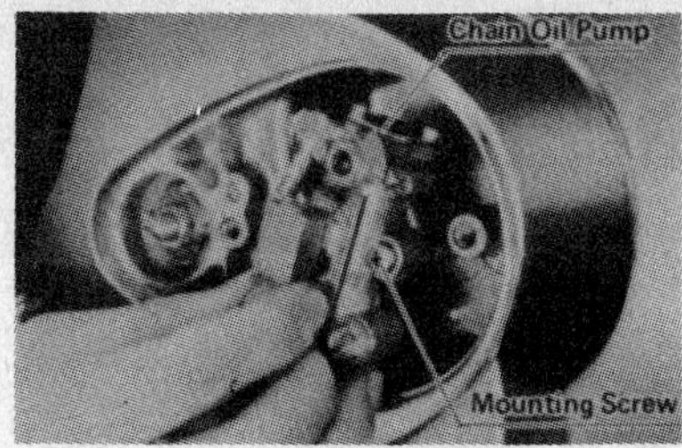

Removing the pump

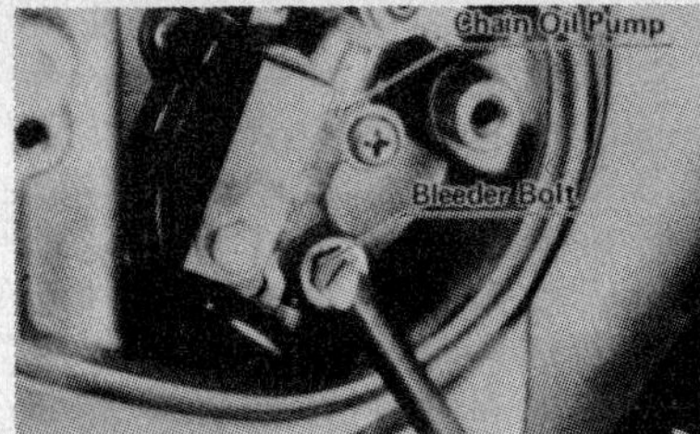

Bleeding the pump

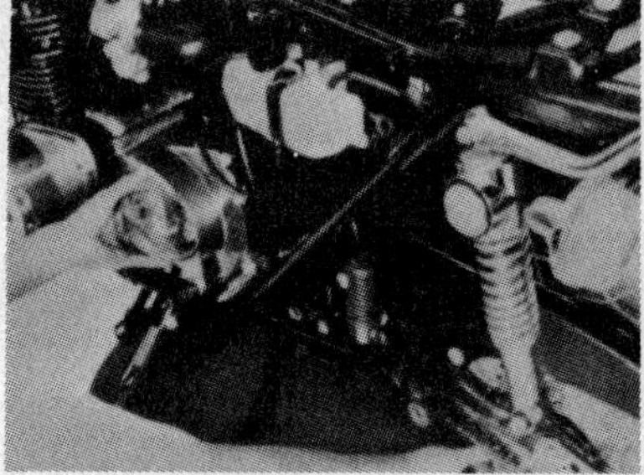
Lining up the pin and groove

(1) to protect it, then pull it out with pliers. A spacer (2) should come out with the shaft.

4. Remove the shaft bushing (5), then remove the O-ring (3) and oil seal (4).

5. Remove the cap screws and top cap (6), then remove the plunger spring (7), plunger guide stopper (8), and O-ring (9).

6. Remove the cap screws and bottom cap (10), then remove the O-ring (11).

7. Gently press on the bottom of the plunger (14) with a thin rod to remove the top plunger (13), guide (12), and bottom plunger (14) from the pump body (17).

8. Remove the control cam (15) and V-ring (16).

9. Remove the banjo bolt (18) and banjo assembly, and the check valve securing bolt (29) and check valve housing (30).

INSPECTION AND REPAIR

1. Clean all but the rubber parts in a suitable solvent, then blow all but the check valve assembly dry.

CAUTION: *The pressure exerted by compressed air may damage the check valve.*

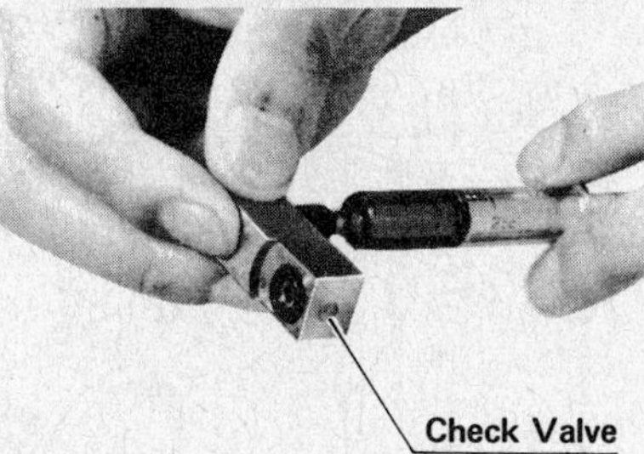

Testing the check valve

2. Inspect all parts for a worn or damaged condition, the O-rings and the check valve are the only parts which are expected to wear, and consequently are the only available replacement components available. If other parts are worn or damaged, the entire pump assembly should be replaced.

3. Check that the check valve will pass oil in only one direction, and that it isn't clogged. The valve can be easily cleaned with gasoline or solvent in a syringe.

4. Whenever the pump is disassembled, or if the pump oil tank runs dry while the pump is in operation, air will enter the pump, which must then be bled. Do this by removing the bleeder bolt (28) until oil starts to run from the hole, then secure the bolt.

ASSEMBLY AND INSTALLATION

1. Assembly and installation are in the reverse order of removal and disassembly.

2. Lubricate the oil seal with clean oil before pressing it into position.

3. Lubricate the O and V-rings, plungers, and plunger guide before assembly.

4. Rotate the rear wheel until the pin in the output shaft is brought into alignment with the groove in the oil pump shaft. This is essential for correct installation as otherwise the pump will not seat correctly.

5. Apply Loctite, or some other suitable thread sealer, to the pump mounting screws before installing them.

6. Bleed the pump as directed in Step 4 of preceding Section before securing the pump cover.

7. Check the oil level in the chain oiler pump tank.

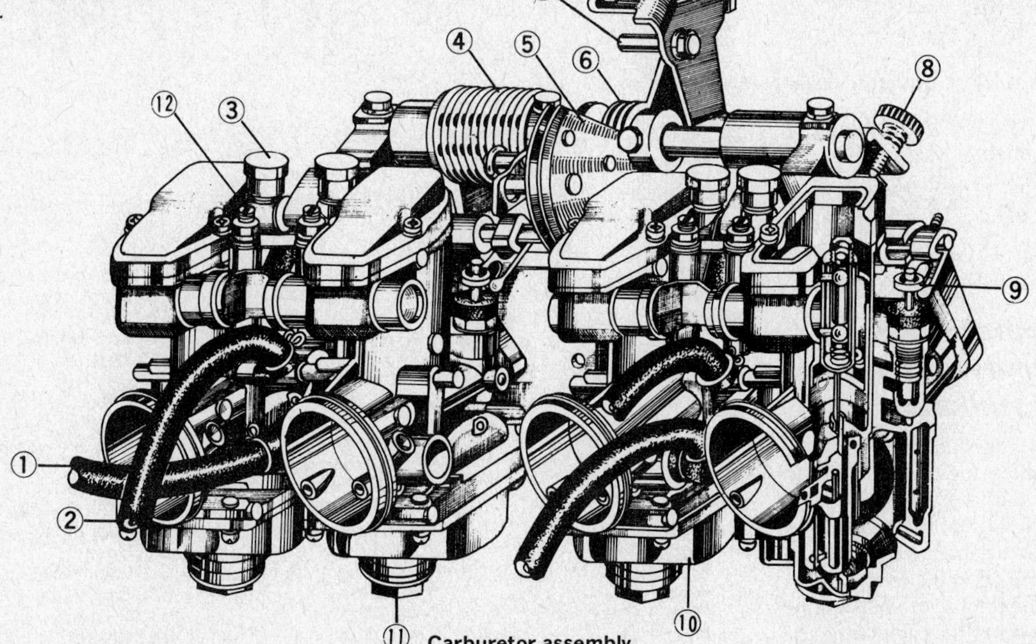

Carburetor assembly

1. Fuel pipe
2. Air vent pipe
3. Guide screw
4. Return spring
5. Pulley
6. Crossover spring
7. Full closed stopper
8. Throttle stop screw
9. Starter plunger
10. Float bowl
11. Drain plug
12. Throttle adjuster

FUEL SYSTEMS

CARBURETOR OVERHAUL

When working on a carburetor, cleanliness and a deftness of touch are the factors which ultimately determine the success or failure of the operation. All parts must be thoroughly cleaned with a carburetor cleaner, and then should be blown dry with compressed air. If a rebuild kit is being used, install all of the parts which came with it rather than only those which obviously must be used, as the installation of only selected components is a false economy.

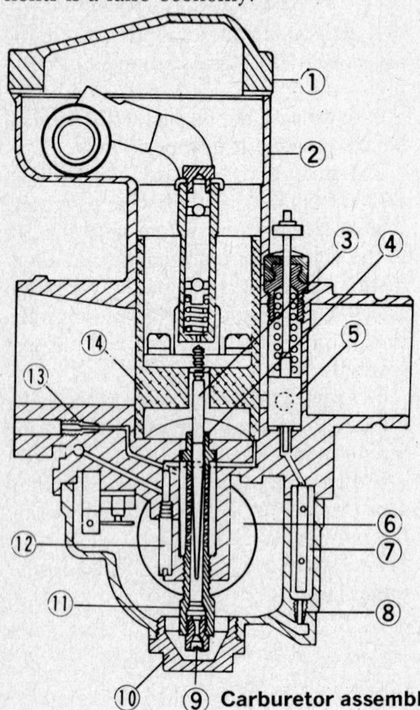

Carburetor assembly cross-section

1. Top cover
2. Mixing chamber
3. Jet needle
4. Needle jet
5. Starter plunger
6. Float
7. Starter pipe
8. Starter jet
9. Main jet
10. Drain plug
11. Air bleed pipe
12. Pilot jet
13. Air jet
14. Throttle valve

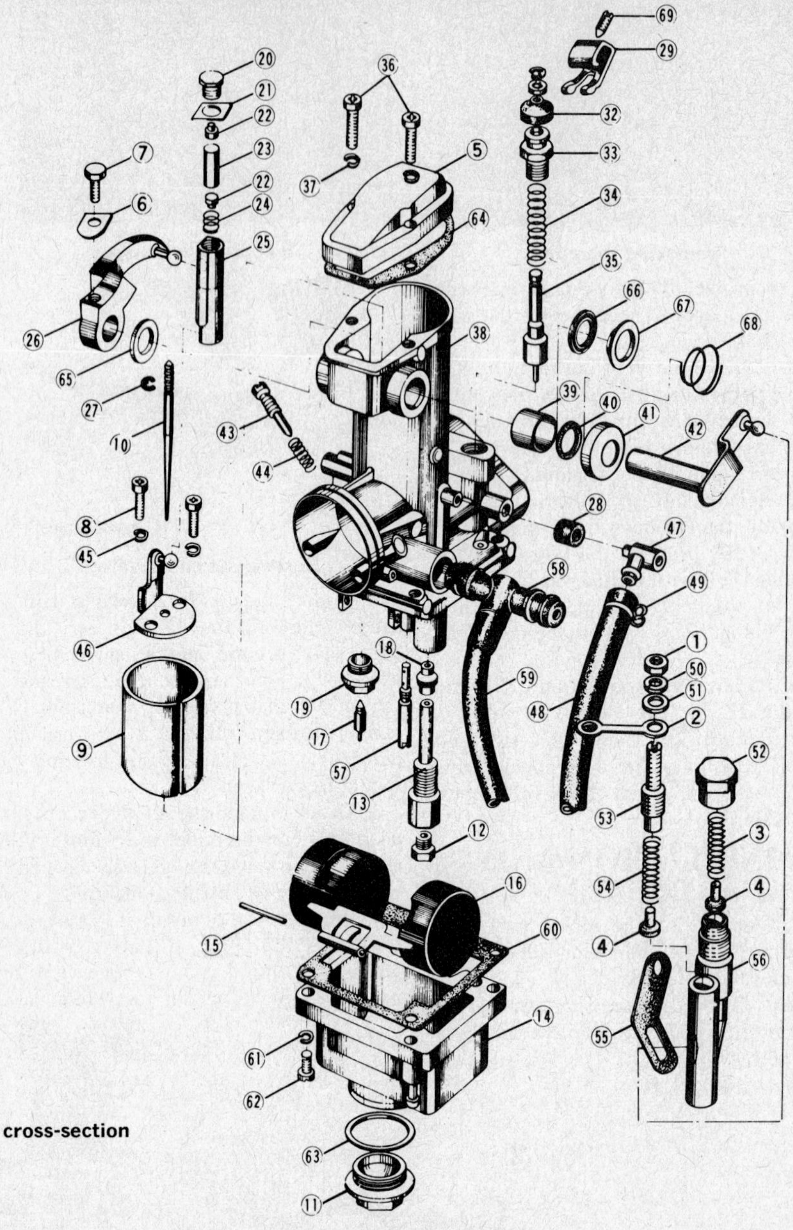

Carburetor assembly

1. Throttle stop screw locknut
2. Double washer link
3. Spring
4. Spring seat
5. Top cover
6. Lockwasher
7. Bolt
8. Screw
9. Throttle valve
10. Jet needle
11. Drain plug
12. Main jet
13. Air bleed pipe
14. Float bowl
15. Pin
16. Float
17. Float valve needle
18. Needle jet
19. Valve seat
20. Guide screw
21. Lockwasher
22. Spring seat
23. Pin
24. Spring
25. Connector
26. Lever assembly
27. Circlip
28. Hose
29. Lever
30. Circlip
31. Ring
32. Cap
33. Guide screw
34. Spring
35. Plunger assembly
36. Bolt
37. Lockwasher
38. Mixing chamber
39. Hose
40. Washer
41. Cup
42. Lever assembly
43. Air screw
44. Spring
45. Lockwasher
46. Bracket assembly
47. Air vent pipe fitting
48. Air vent pipe
49. Clamp
50. Lockwasher
51. Washer
52. Cap nut
53. Throttle stop screw
54. Spring
55. Rubber washer
56. Connector
57. Pilot jet
58. Fuel pipe fitting
59. Fuel pipe
60. Gasket
61. Lockwasher
62. Bolt
63. O-ring
64. Gasket
65. Spacer
66. Oil seal
67. Collar
68. Spring
69. Screw

Carburetor Bank Removal and Installation

1. Disconnect the fuel lines at the gas tank, then remove the tank.

2. Loosen the 4 intake manifold clamps at the front, and the 4 air cleaner hose clamps at the back, then pull the carburetor bank off to the rear.

3. Loosen the throttle cable mounting nuts, and disconnect the cables from the pulley.

4. Installation is in the reverse order of removal. Note the following:

a. All clamps must be secure enough

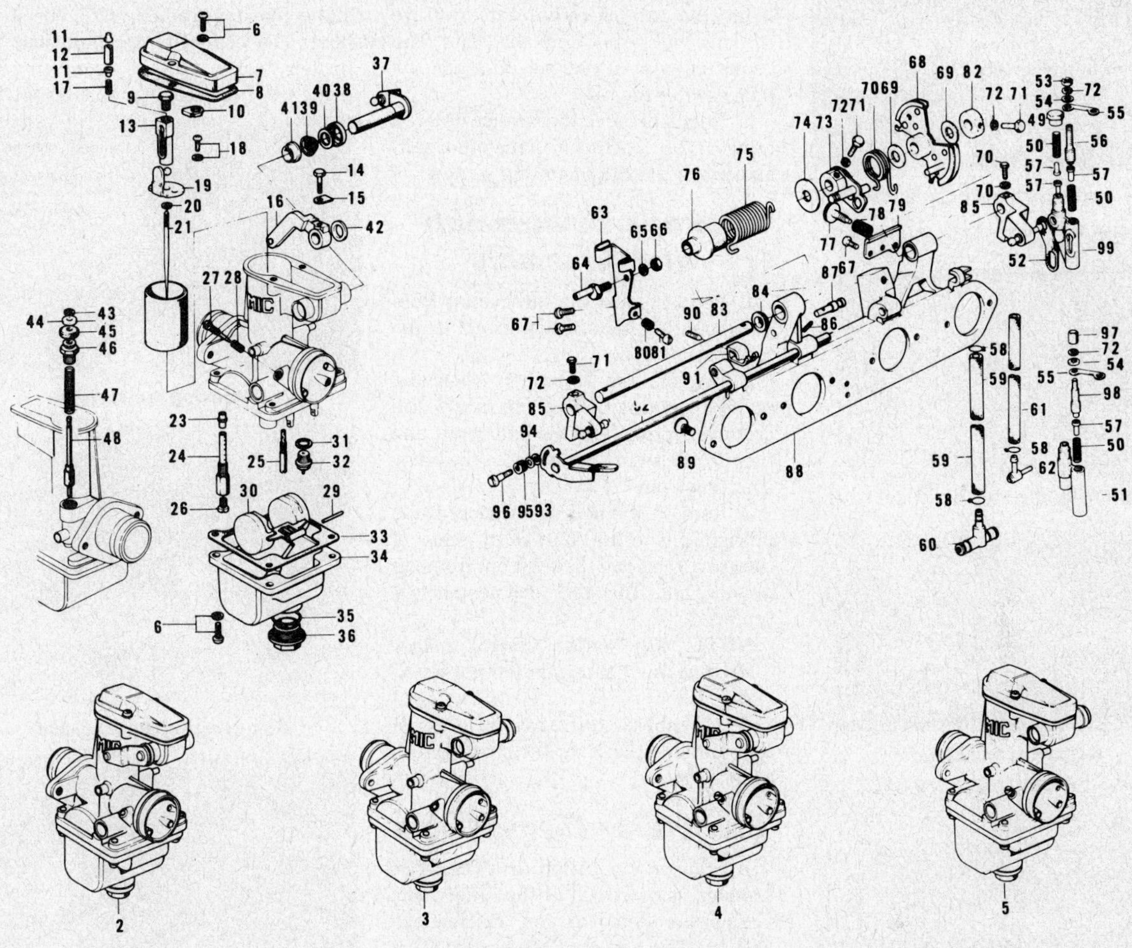

Carburetor and linkage assemblies

1. Carburetor assy
2. Carburetor, A
3. Carburetor, B
4. Carburetor, C
5. Carburetor, D
6. Float chamber fitting screw
7. Mixing chamber top
8. Mixing chamber top gasket
9. Bolt, A
10. Lockwasher, A
11. Spring seat
12. Throttle shaft holder
13. Throttle valve shaft
14. Bolt, B
15. Lockwasher, B
16. Lever, A
17. Spring, A
18. Pan head screw
19. Throttle valve plate
20. Jet needle clip
21. Jet needle
22. Throttle valve
23. Needle jet
24. Needle jet holder
25. Pilot jet
26. Main jet
27. Pilot air adjusting screw
28. Pilot air adjusting spring
29. Float pin
30. Float
31. Float valve seat washer
32. Float valve assy
33. Float chamber gasket
34. Float chamber body
35. Main jet cover O-ring
36. Main jet cover
37. Lever, B
38. Collar, A
39. Spring, B
40. Plain washer
41. Collar, B
42. Plain washer
43. Circlip
44. Plain washer
45. Plain washer
46. Starter plunger cap
47. Starter plunger spring
48. Starter plunger
49. Bolt, C
50. Spring, C
51. Holder
52. Dust plate
53. Nut
54. Plain washer
55. Lockwasher, C
56. Throttle stop adjuster
57. Spring seat
58. Fuel pipe clamp
59. Fuel pipe
60. Fuel pipe joint
61. Over flow pipe
62. Over flow pipe joint
63. Control cable guide
64. Screw stopper pin
65. Spring washer
66. Nut
67. Pan head screw
68. Control cable wheel
69. Plain washer
70. Spring, D
71. Hex head bolt
72. Spring washer
73. Lever, A
74. Plain washer
75. Spring, E
76. Collar, D
77. Throttle stop screw
78. Throttle stop screw spring
79. Throttle stop plate
80. Throttle adjuster spring
81. Throttle lever adjuster
82. Collar, E
83. Shaft
84. Collar, F
85. Lever, B
86. Cotter pin
87. Spring hook pin
88. Carburetor holder
89. Countersunk head screw
90. Slotted screw
91. Starter plunger lever
92. Starter plunger shaft
93. Plain washer
94. Plain washer
95. Spring, F
96. Starter lever screw
97. Lock nut
98. Throttle stop adjuster
99. Holder

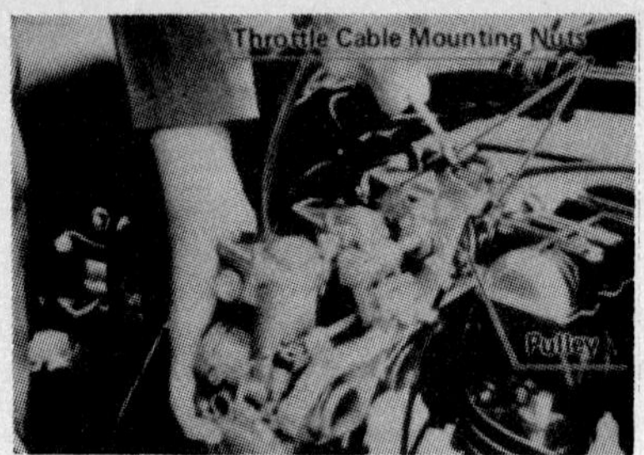

Removing the carburetor bank assembly

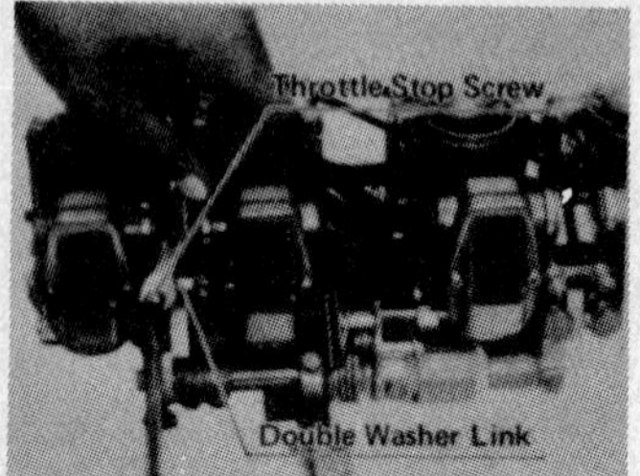

Removing the stop screw locknut

Removing the cap nut

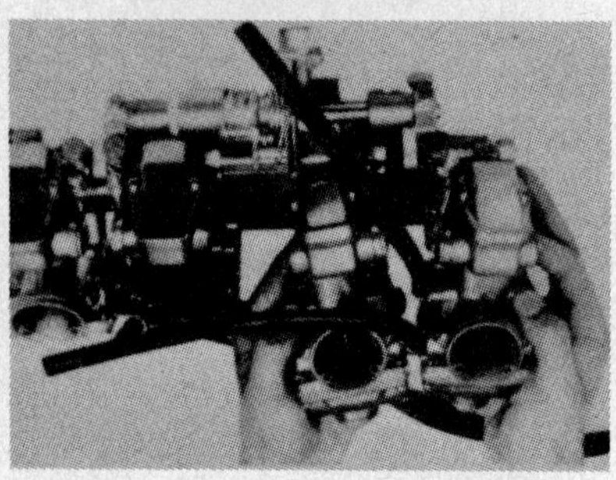
Removing a pair of carbs

to prevent air leaks, especially at the intake manifold.

b. Adjust the throttle cables as described in the "Tune-Up" Chapter.

Individual Carburetor Removal and Installation

1. Remove the carburetor bank as described in the previous Section.

2. Remove the throttle stop screw locknut (1) from both the carburetor to be removed and its companion, then remove the double washer link (2).

3. Remove the throttle stop screw (53), stop screw spring (54), and the spring seat (4).

4. Remove the cap nut (52) from the linkage of the carburetor which is to be removed, then remove the spring (3) and seat (4).

CAUTION: *Upon removal of the cap nut the spring may pop out. Be prepared to catch it.*

5. Remove the 4 mounting screws and swing the pair of carburetors you are working with away from the plate. The object of your attentions may now be pulled off to the side.

6. Installation is in the reverse order of removal. Use Loctite, or some other suitable sealer, on the mounting screws.

Linkage Disassembly and Assembly

1. Remove all of the carburetors from the mounting plate as described in the previous Section.

2. Remove the crossover lever and pulley mounting bolts, then unhook the crossover spring from the pulley pin, and the throttle return spring from the crossover lever pin.

3. Remove the bolt which secures the linkage arm to the shaft from either of the arms, then pull the shaft out from the opposite end. The other arm need not be removed.

NOTE: *The starter (choke) linkage need not be removed unless it is defective.*

4. Assembly is in the reverse order of disassembly. Lubricate the shafts at this time.

Carburetor Disassembly

1. Remove the carburetor to be disassembled as described in the "Individual Carburetor Removal and Installation" Section. The fuel may be drained from the float bowl by removing the drain plug (11) and washer (63).

NOTE: *Consult the "Individual Carburetor Removal and Installation" Section for a labled exploded view illustration.*

2. Remove the top cover mounting screws (36) and washers (37), then remove the cover (5) and cover gasket (64).

3. Bend flat the lockwasher tab (6), then remove the bolt (7). The lever assembly (42) can now be removed along with its associated components. The connector assembly (56) can now be further disassembled if so desired.

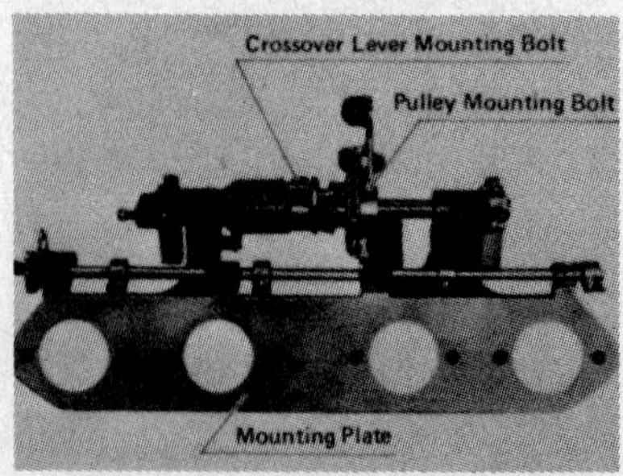

Mounting plate assembled

4. Remove the two screws (8) which secure the bracket assembly (46) to the throttle valve (9), and lift the bracket, complete with the lever assembly (26) and connector assembly (25), out of the bore. The connector assembly may be further broken down by removing the guide screw (20) and components (21-24).

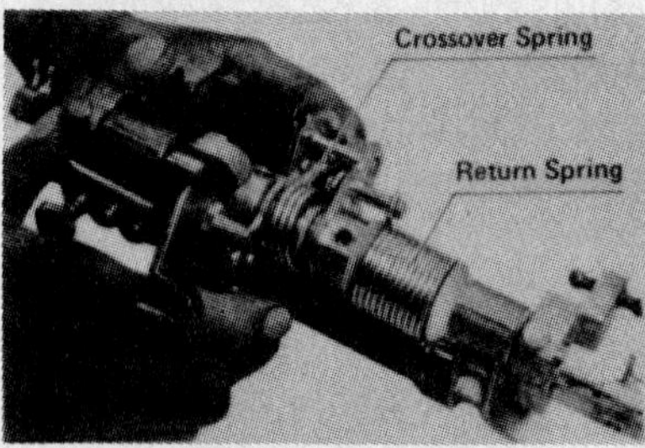

Removing the springs

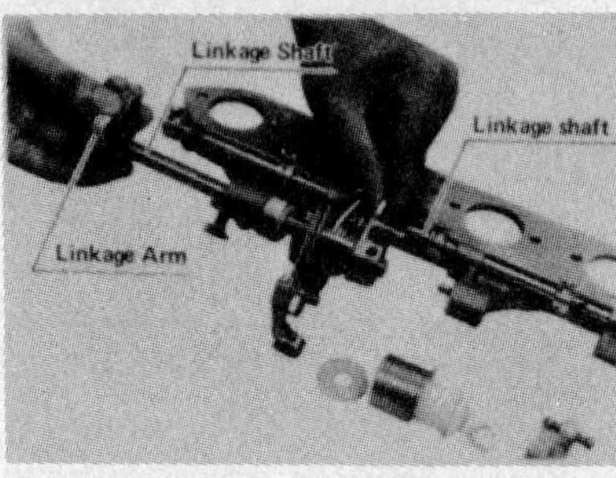

Removing the linkage shaft

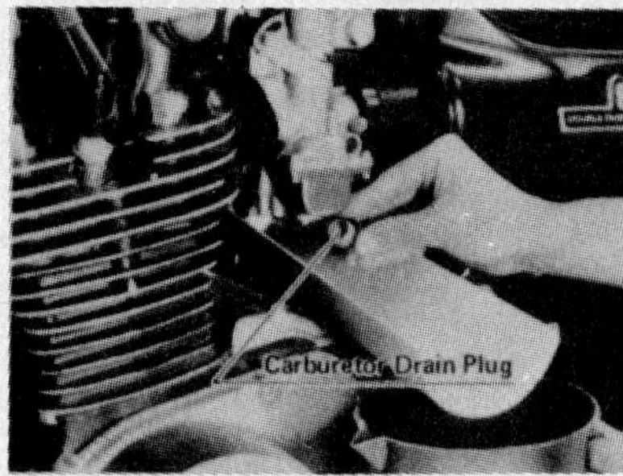

Draining the float bowls

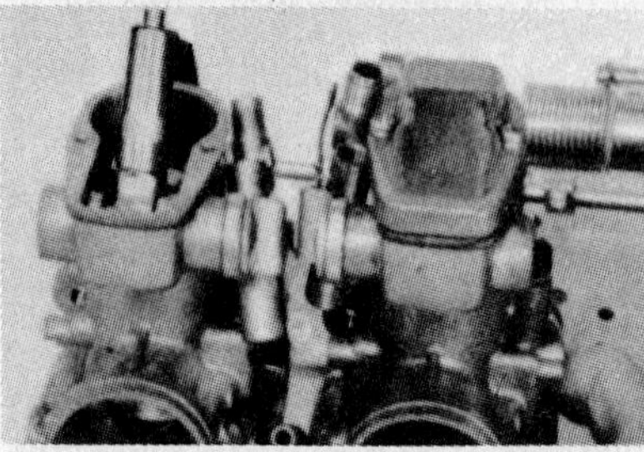
Removing the lever assembly mounting bolt

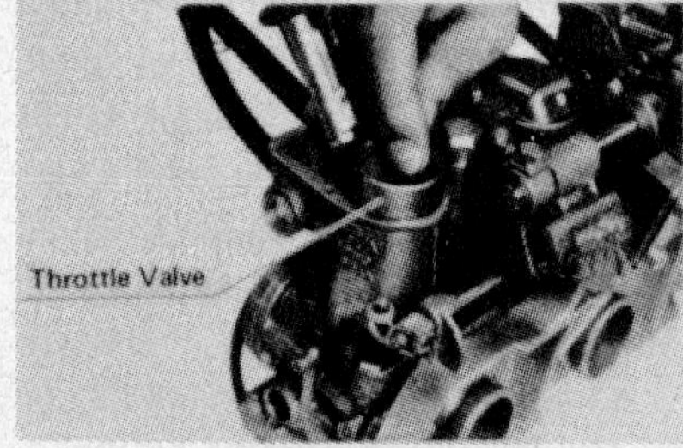

Removing the throttle valve

5. Remove the throttle valve (9) and needle (10) from the bore, taking care not to damage the needle.

6. Remove the plunger assembly (35) after removing the lever (29), cap (32), and the guide screw (33).

7. Remove the float bowl securing screws (62), the float bowl (14), the bowl gasket (60), the float (16), float pivot (15), and the float valve needle (17).

8. Remove the main jet (12) and air bleed pipe (13), then invert the carburetor and gently press out the needle jet (18) with a wooden rod or some other suitable instrument.

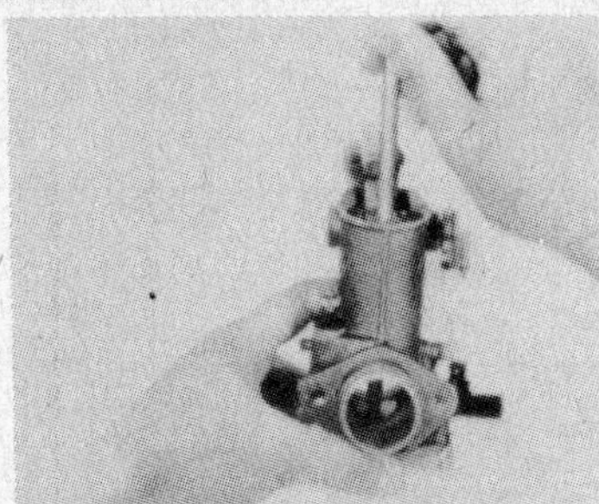

Removing the needle jet

9. Remove the valve seat (19), the pilot jet (57), the pilot air screw (43), and spring (44), and any other remaining items such as the fuel lines and their hardware.

Inspection and Repair

1. Clean all metal components in a suitable solvent, then blow them dry with compressed air taking care to clear all passages.

CAUTION: *Do not attempt to clear clogged jets or cast passages by poking with a wire, as this may cause scoring of the surfaces.*

2. Inspect all parts for signs of wear or damage and replace them as necessary.

3. Carefully inspect the condition of the jet needle, the needle seat, the pilot air screw, the float needle, and the float needle seat for any signs of wear indicated by bright spots or an uneven taper. These parts must be perfectly smooth, and if excessive clearance exists between the needles and their seats they must be replaced as sets.

4. Inspect the float and its pivot pin for rough motion, wear, damage, or a saturated float condition, and replace them as necessary.

5. Inspect the throttle valve and carburetor bore for signs of wear or scoring. The valve may be lightly sanded if necessary, but if the bore is scored, or if the carburetor body is in any way damaged, it must be replaced.

NOTE: *The throttle valve should be able to slide down the bore to its seat of its own weight. If it will not do this even when lightly oiled, it will not function correctly.*

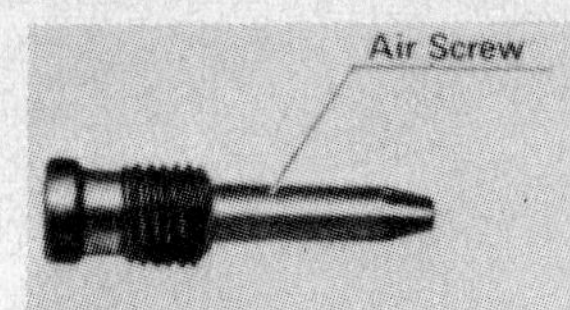

Check the pilot air screw for a blunted tip

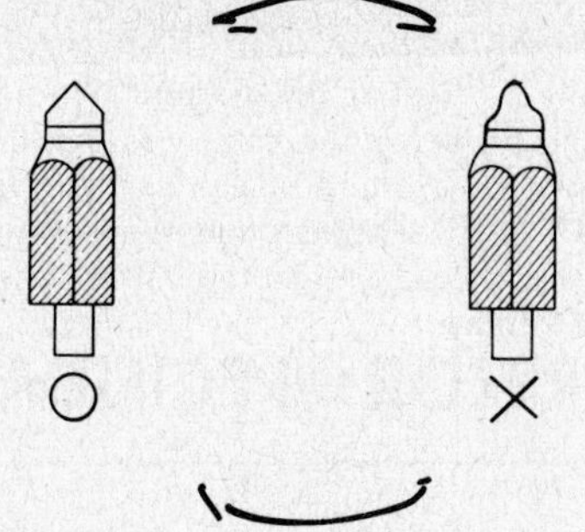

A good (left) and bad (right) float needle

Assembly

1. Assembly is in the reverse order of disassembly. Use all new gaskets and O-rings.

2. Do not overtighten the jets when installing them in the carburetor body.

3. Make certain that the jet needle is installed in the same position as when it was removed. The clip should be in the third groove from the top.

4. Adjust the height of the float as described in the following Section if necessary, and adjust the carburetor as described in the "Tune-Up" Chapter.

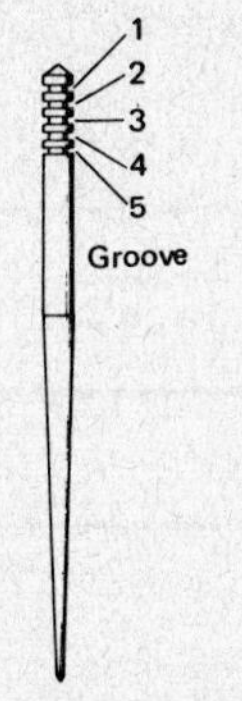

Jet needle clip positions

Float Height Adjustment

1. Turn the fuel tap to the "Off" position, remove the overflow vent tube (which will interfere with the knurled knob), and remove the float bowl drain plug. Be prepared to catch the fuel which will run out.

2. Install the fuel level measuring device (Part No. 57001-122) in place of the drain plug.

NOTE: *The original fuel level gauge hose (Part No. 99990-020) was incorrectly calibrated, and has been subsequently replaced with the part number*

Special tool installed

given in the above Step. This new hose is provided free of charge by the factory.

3. Hold the plastic tube against the carburetor body and turn the fuel tap to the "On" position. The gas level in the hose should come up to 0.10-0.18 in. (2.5-4.5 mm) below the edge of the carburetor body.

4. If the fuel level is incorrect, the float must be adjusted in the following manner:

Checking the fuel level

a. Drain the fuel from the float bowl, then remove the bowl. Be prepared to catch the float, float pivot pin, and float needle.

b. Bend the tang on the float slightly to adjust the float height. Bending the tang up will lower the fuel level, and bending it down will raise it.

NOTE: *When checking the fuel level of the inside two carburetors, the outside carb base may be used as a reference point for the gauge.*

Bending the tang adjusts the float height

FUEL TAP

1. Turn the tap to the "Off" position, and disconnect the fuel lines.

2. Remove the tank, or raise and support the back of it.

3. Unscrew the sediment cup and remove the O-ring and strainer.

4. Remove the screw which secures the valve and lever, and remove those parts.

5. The tap may be removed from the tank by loosening the nut which secures it to the tank.

NOTE: *Removing the fuel tap body from the gas tank is not recommended unless replacement is necessary.*

6. When assembling the tap a suitable gas-resistant sealer should be used if new O-rings are not available. Leaks at the sediment bowl can be stopped with epoxy or some other sealer if necessary.

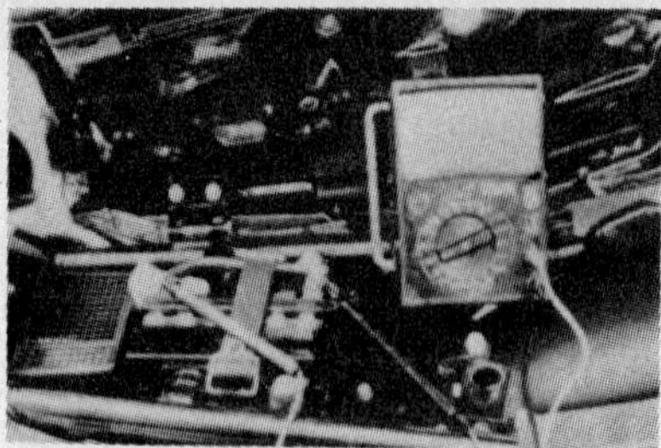

Testing the dynamo

connect it across the battery so that the negative (−) tester lead goes to the negative battery terminal, and the positive (+) tester lead goes to the battery positive terminal.

5. Disconnect the wire which runs from the fuse to the starter relay, and connect the positive (+) tester lead to the white wire on the fuse side, and the nega-

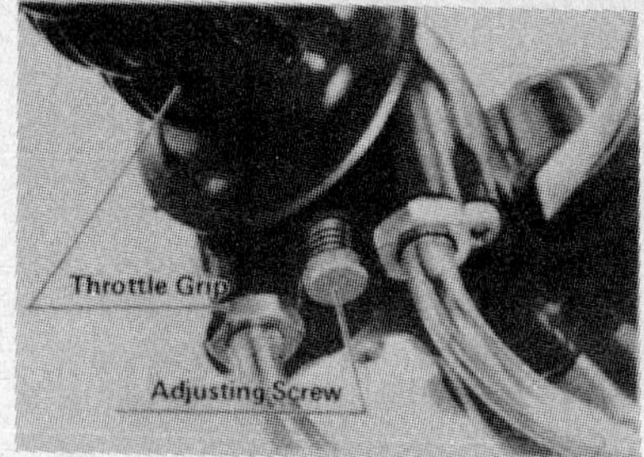

The throttle grip tensioner

CARBURETOR SPECIFICATIONS

Type	Main Jet	Air Jet	Needle Jet	Jet Needle	Pilot Jet	Throttle Valve Cutaway	Air Screw	Fuel Level
VM28SC	112.5	1.0	P-8	5J9-3*	20	2.5	1½ turns out	32 ± 1 mm (1.26 ± .04 in.)

* The 9 of 5J9-3 shows lot no., and may vary. The 3 is the groove no. for the C ring, counting from the top.

ELECTRICAL SYSTEMS

CHARGING SYSTEM

Dynamo

DYNAMO OUTPUT TEST

Before checking the dynamo, make sure that the battery, rectifier, and regulator are all good, and be sure that the battery is fully charged. Dynamo failure can be traced to either a short, an open circuit (burned-out wire), or a loss of rotor magnetism.

Test the dynamo in the following manner:

3. Start the engine and run it at 4000 rpm, taking note of the meter reading. A reading of 15-20 VDC is normal, and a lower reading indicates a defective dynamo.

NOTE: *For convenience sake, the throttle grip adjusting screw can be used to keep the engine turning at 4,000 rpm. Hold the throttle open until*

tive (−) tester lead to the white wire on the relay side. This puts the tester in series with the rectifier and battery so that battery charging current can be measured.

CAUTION: *Do not use the electric starter if the tester is connected in series directly at the battery terminal instead of as directed in the preceding*

Dynamo test connections

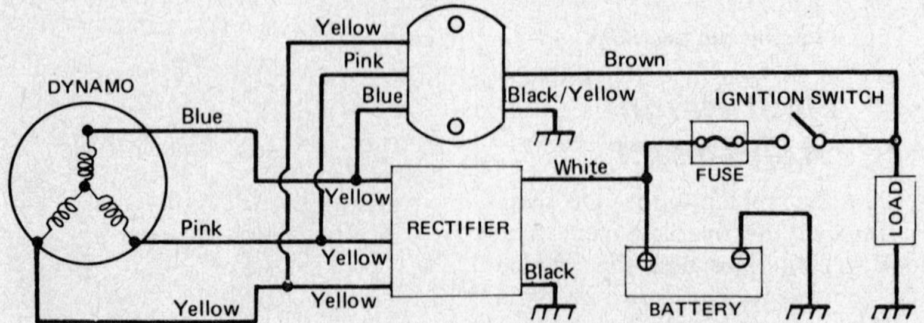

Dynamo circuit

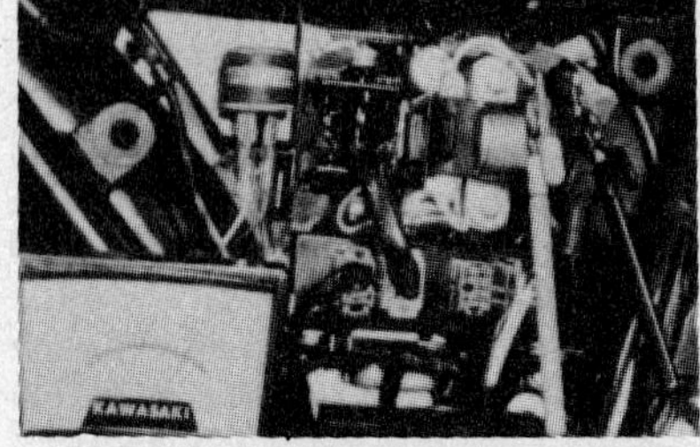

Measuring battery charging current

1. Remove the right-side plastic cover, and disconnect the green regulator lead from the connector panel. Be sure that all accessories are turned off.

2. Rotate the hand tester switch to the 30 VDC (from 0-30 volts of DC) scale, and

the tach reads correctly, then turn in the adjusting screw.

4. Turn off the engine and disconnect the tester leads from the battery, then set the tester to the 12 amp DC range, and switch the tester leads to the appropriate meter sockets.

Step, or the reverse starting current will damage the meter.

6. Start the engine and run it at 4000 rpm, taking note of the meter reading. A reading of 9.5 amps or more is normal, and a lower reading indicates a defective dynamo.

7. Determine whether the problem is in the windings or the rotor in the following manner:

a. Disconnect the blue plug from the connector panel, and use the R x 1 scale on the tester to determine the resistance between each pair of wires going to the plug: blue/pink, blue/yellow, and pink/yellow.

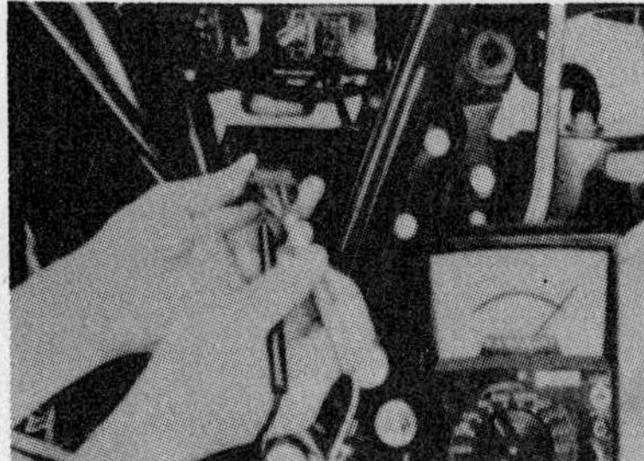

Testing the connector panel plug

b. The resistance between any two of the wires should be 0.45-0.6 ohms; less indicates shorted coils, and a higher resistance or none at all indicates open coils. If the coils are defective, the stator must be replaced.

c. Measure the resistance between each dynamo wire and ground (the chassis, engine, etc.) using the highest resistance scale on the tester.

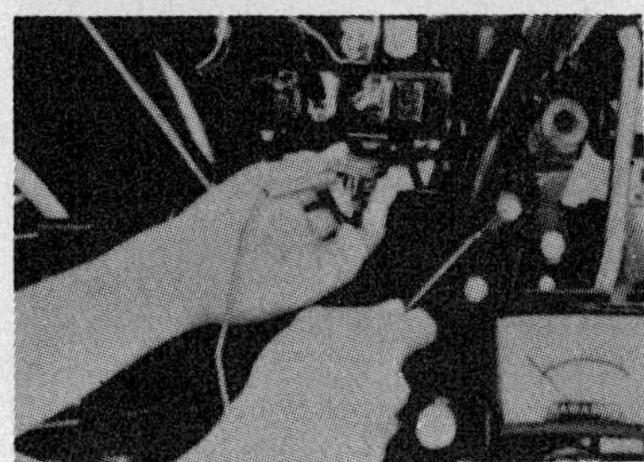

Measuring resistance between the leads and ground

d. No reading (∞) is normal, and any reading indicates a short which means the stator must be replaced.

e. If the coils have normal resistance, but voltage and current checks indicate that the dynamo is defective, the rotor magnets are probably bad, and the rotor will have to be replaced.

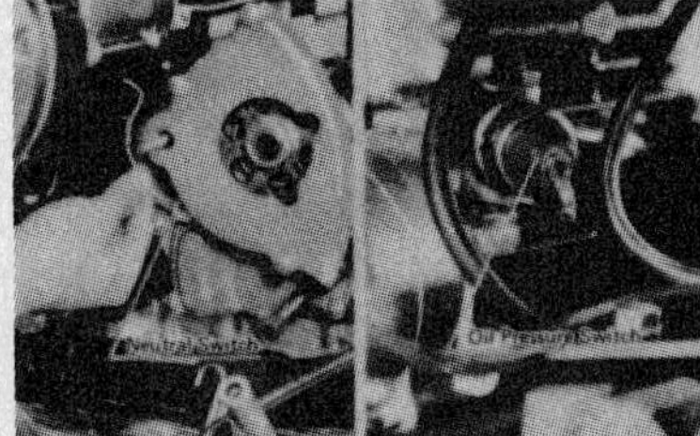

Disconnecting the switches

DYNAMO REMOVAL AND INSTALLATION

1. Remove the chain cover as described in the "Engine Removal and Installation" Section.

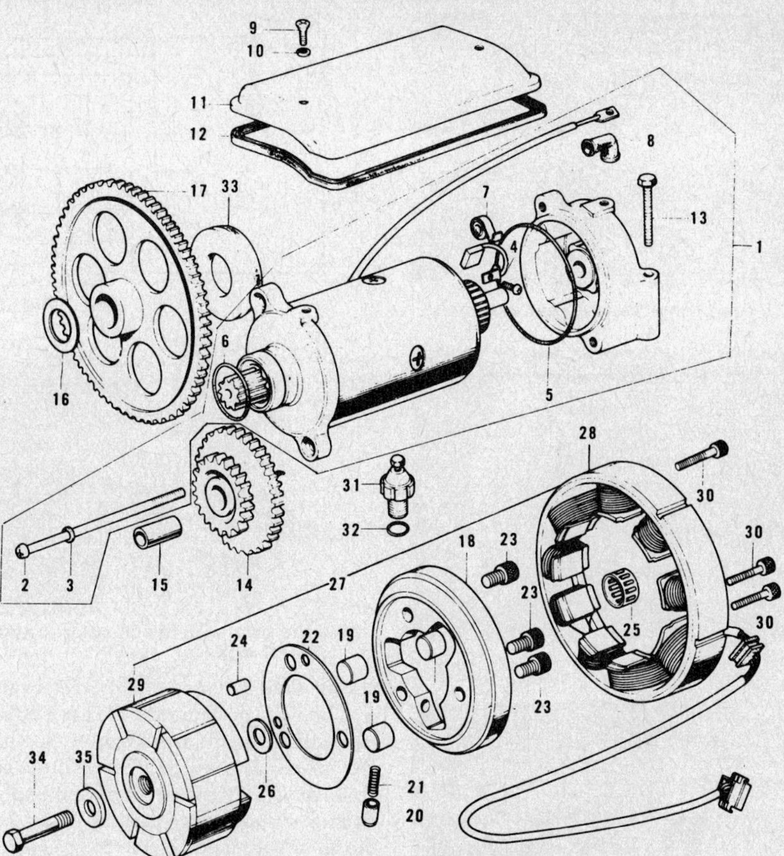

Dynamo and starter assemblies

1. Starting motor assy
2. Pan head screw
3. Spring washer
4. Carbon brush
5. O-ring
6. O-ring
7. Carbon brush spring
8. Starting motor terminal cap
9. Hex head bolt
10. Plain washer
11. Starting motor cover
12. Starting motor cover gasket
13. Hex head bolt
14. Starting motor gear
15. Piston pin
16. Thrust washer
17. Starting clutch gear
18. Starting clutch
19. Roller
20. Plug
21. Spring
22. Clutch starting plate
23. Bolt
24. Dowel pin
25. Needle bearing
26. Plain washer
    Plain washer
27. Dynamo assy
28. Stator assy
29. Rotor
30. Allen bolt
31. Oil pressure switch assy.
32. Oil pressure switch O-ring
33. Damper rubber
34. Hex head bolt
35. Plain washer

2. Remove the right-side plastic cover, and disconnect the blue dynamo wire, and the wires from the oil pressure and Neutral indicator switches, then release the wires from the cable clamps.

3. Remove the left-side engine cover, and remove the allen bolts which secure the stator to the cover.

NOTE: *If only the rotor is to be removed, it is not necessary to disconnect the wiring or remove the stator.*

4. Remove the starter idle gear.

5. Keep the rotor from turning by holding it with either the special tool (Part No. 57001-117) or a suitable substitute, and remove the rotor mounting bolt.

6. Hold the rotor still as described above, and use either the special tool (Part No. 57001-116) or a suitable substitute to remove the rotor/starter clutch assembly.

CAUTION: *Hammering the rotor will demagnetize the magnets, leaving the rotor useless.*

7. Remove the woodruff key, thin shim, starter clutch gear, needle bearing,

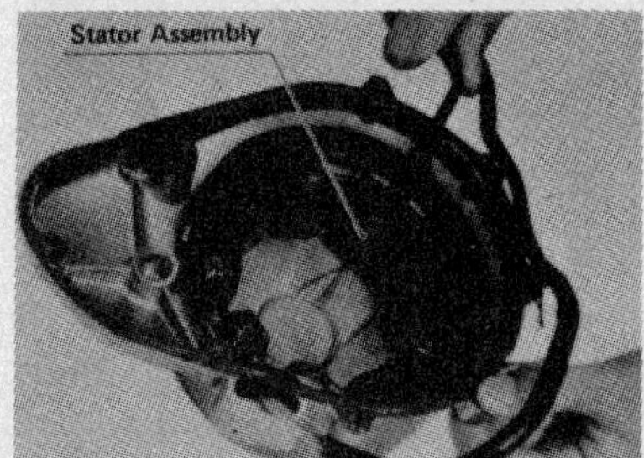

The stator assembly is secured to the engine cover

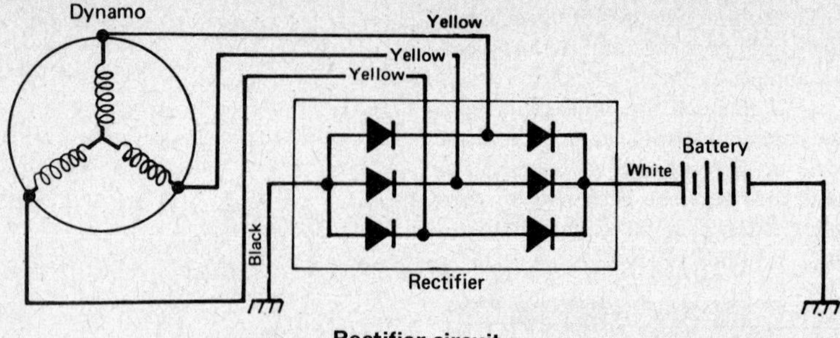

Rectifier circuit

Removing the idle gear assembly

Removing the rotor mounting bolt

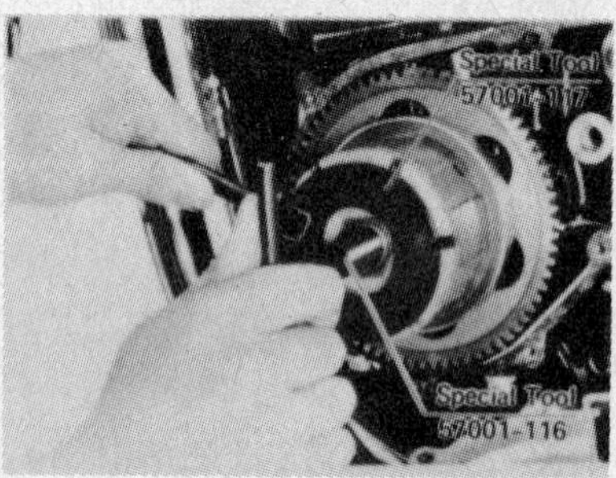

Removing the rotor and starter clutch assembly

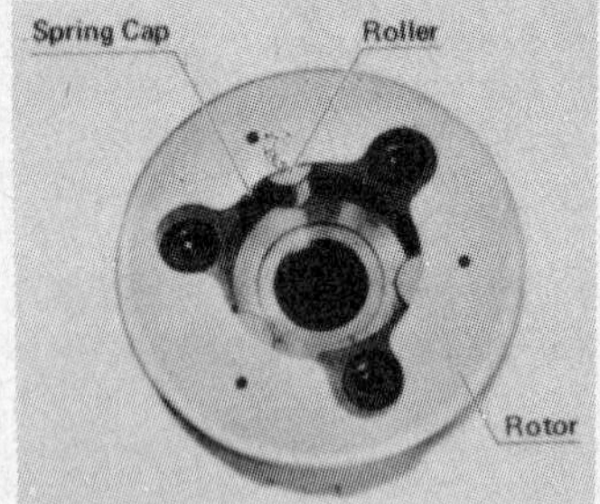

Starter clutch assembly

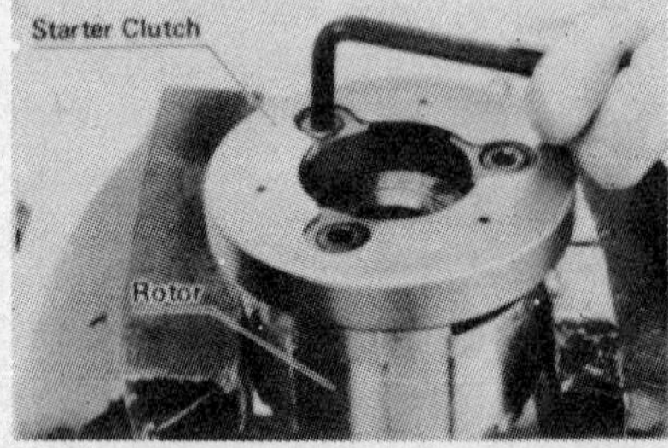

Disassembling the starter clutch

gear damper, and thick shim, in that order, from the crankshaft, then remove the rollers, springs, and spring caps from the starter clutch.

8. Secure the rotor in a wood-jawed vise, or wrap it to protect it if a metal vise is to be used, and remove the allen bolts to separate the rotor and starter clutch.

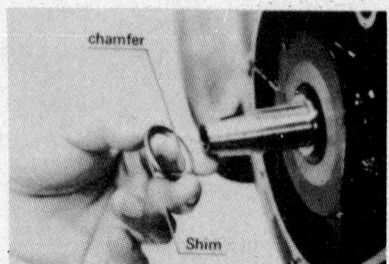

Install the shim with the chamfered side in

9. Installation is in the reverse order of removal. Use a new cover gasket, apply Loctite or some other suitable sealer, to the allen bolts, and be sure to use an oil seal guide when installing the chain cover.

10. Place the thick shim onto the crankshaft with its chamfered side facing it before installing the starter clutch.

11. Spin the clutch gear so that the rollers will move enough to allow it to go on when installing the starter clutch.

12. Apply Loctite, or another suitable sealer, to the rotor mounting bolt threads before installing it, and torque the bolt to 18 ft lbs (2.5 kg/m).

Rectifier

A six-diode (two for each of the dynamo's 3 output phases) rectifier is used to convert the AC current produced by the dynamo into the DC current needed to run the battery charging, ignition, lighting, and horn circuits.

Diodes can only conduct current from negative to positive, and therefore they convert AC to DC. If the rectifier, or any of the diodes, goes bad it will conduct in both directions, or not at all, leading to a discharged battery.

RECTIFIER RESISTANCE TEST

1. Disconnect the white rectifier plug from the connector panel, and the white lead going to the battery.

2. With the tester set on the R x 10, or the R x 100 range, check the resistance between the white rectifier lead and each of the yellow leads, the yellow leads and the white lead, the black lead and each yellow lead, and each yellow and black lead. This means a total of 12 measurements.

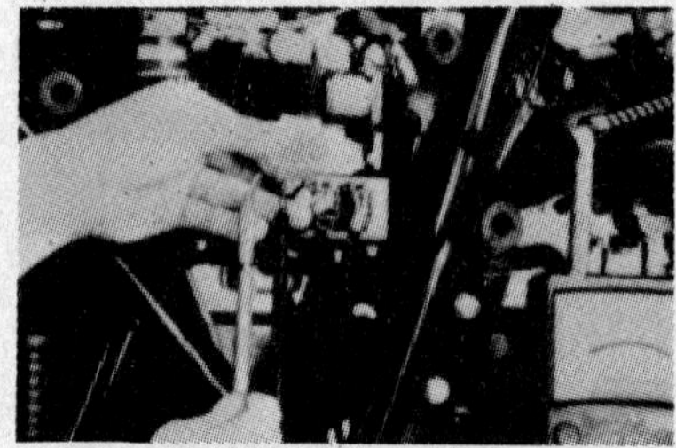

Testing the rectifier

3. The resistance should be low in one direction, and about ten times as great in the other. If the readings are high or low in either direction for any pair of wires, the rectifier is defective and must be replaced.

NOTE: *The lower reading should be within 1/3 scale of zero ohms regardless of the type of tester used.*

CAUTION: *When removing or installing a rectifier, do not loosen or tighten the nut which holds the rectifier assembly together as this will damage the unit.*

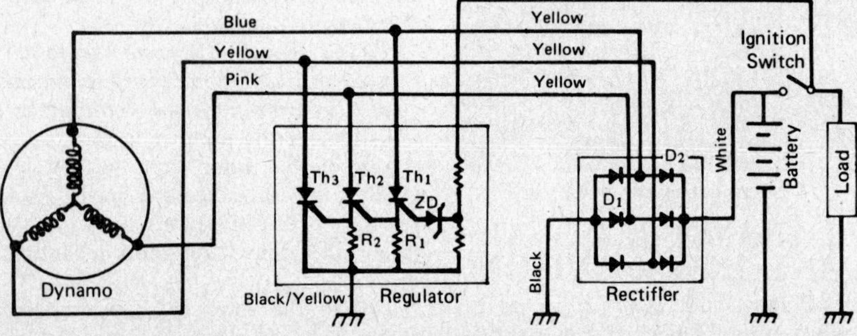

Rectifier and regulator circuit

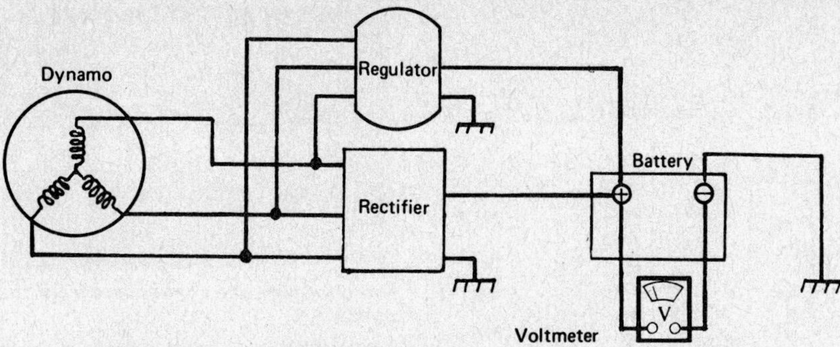

Testing with the regulator in circuit

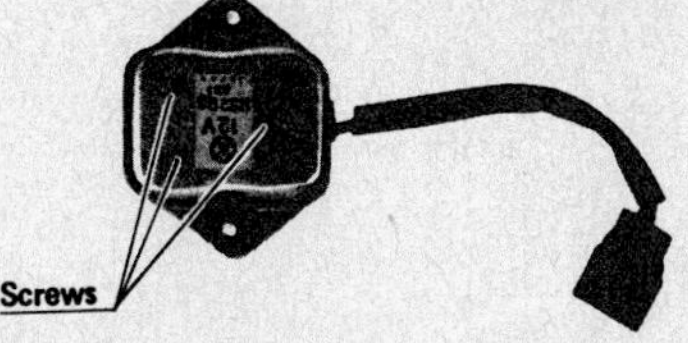

Do not remove these screws

Regulator

REGULATOR OPERATIONAL TEST

In Circuit

NOTE: *Make sure that the battery is in good condition, and is well charged before beginning the test.*

1. Set the tester to the 30 VDC range, and connect it across the battery (tester negative lead to battery negative terminal, and tester positive lead to battery positive terminal).

2. Run the engine, with all lights and accessories turned off, at 4000 rpm while checking the meter. If the meter reads between 15-16 volts, the regulator is functioning normally; if it reads over 16 volts the regulator is either improperly connected or defective; and if the reading is less than 15 volts either the dynamo, rectifier, or regulator needs to be replaced. Go on to the next Step if the reading was low.

3. Turn off the engine, but leave the tester connected as is. Disconnect the green regulator plug from the connection panel under the right-side plastic cover. Run the engine at 4000 rpm and check the meter reading. If the reading is within 15-20 volts the regulator is defective; if the reading is less, then either the dynamo or rectifier is defective.

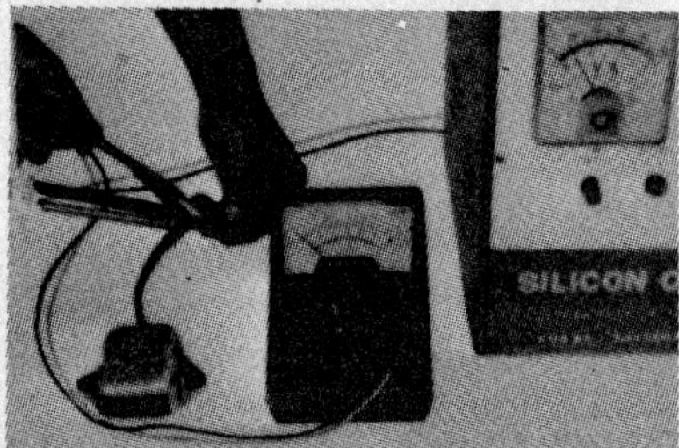
Testing the regulator out of circuit

4. Before replacing the regulator, make sure that all the connections are clean and snug, as poor connections could cause misleading test results.

Out of Circuit

CAUTION: *When removing the regulator do not loosen or remove the screws in the regulator body. The screws aid in heat dissipation, and the unit will overheat if they are not properly installed.*

1. Set the meter on the R × 10 or R × 100 scale. There should be 1,000-1,100 ohms resistance between the black and brown leads, and no reading (∞) between any other two leads, or between the black or brown and any other lead. Any other results indicate that the regulator is defective.

2. For this test a 14 VDC and a 16-17 VDC power source must be available. If the sources used cannot provide sufficient power, the tests will be inaccurate, and if more than 18 volts are passed through the regulator it may be damaged. Proceed as follows:

CAUTION: *If the voltage source and regulator are connected backwards for even a moment, the regulator will be damaged.*

a. Connect the regulator to the 14 VDC source as shown in the accompanying illustration.

b. Set the meter to either the R × 10 or the R × 100 range, and check that there is no reading (∞) between the black lead and the pink, yellow, or blue lead. If the meter gives any reading for any wire, the regulator is defective.

CAUTION: *When performing the next test, be sure that the black and brown leads never touch the meter leads at the same time or the meter will be damaged.*

c. Connect the regulator to the 16-17 VDC source in the same manner as in Step "a", and set the meter on the R x 1 scale. This should result in a very low reading when the meter is connected one at a time between the black lead and the blue, pink, or yellow leads. If there is no reading between any or all of the leads, or if any one reading is higher than the other two, the regulator is defective and must be replaced.

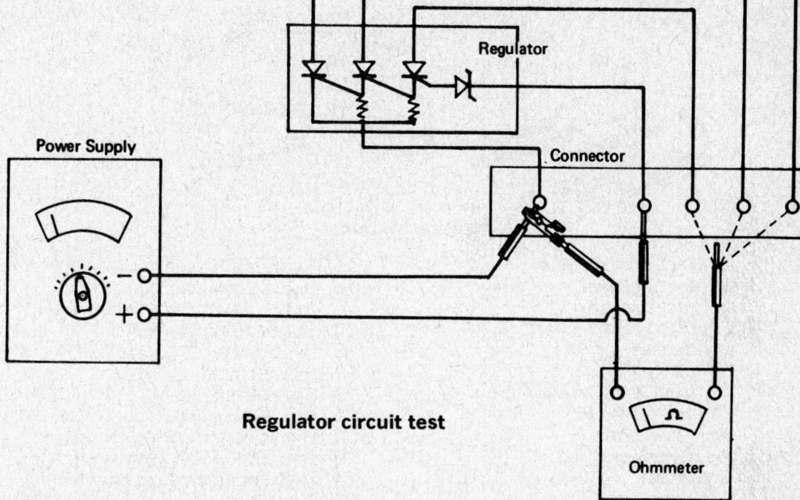

Regulator circuit test

IGNITION SYSTEM

Component Removal and Installation

CONTACT BREAKER POINTS

1. Remove the breaker point cover and cover gasket, then remove the two mounting screws for each set of points, and remove the points.

NOTE: *You may remove the mounting plate with the points and condensers in place, and then install a new plate with the points and condensers already mounted on it. Consult the "Automatic Advance Mechanism" Section for further information.*

2. Loosen the nut at the leaf spring, and disconnect the condensers if they are to be reused. It is best to replace the points and condensers at the same time.

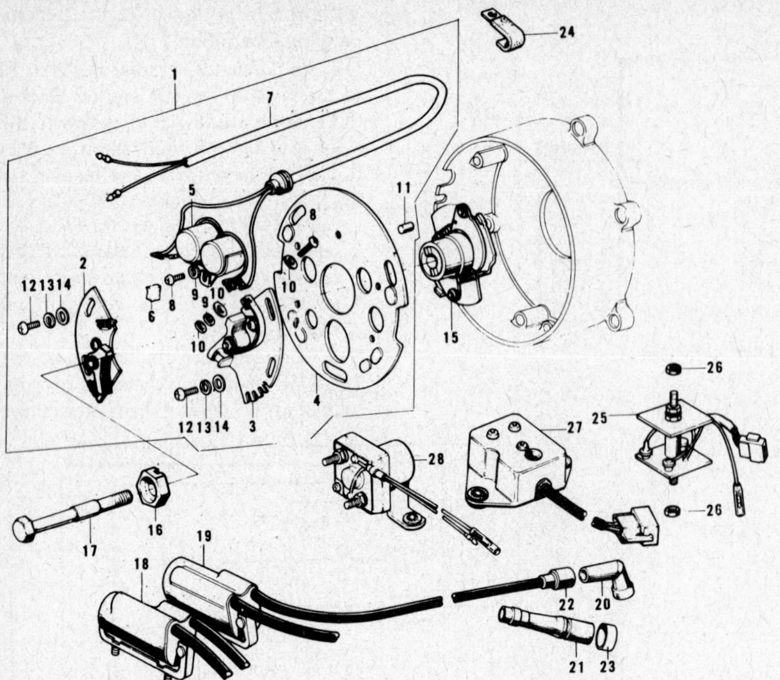

Ignition system

1. Contact breaker assy
2. Contact breaker
3. Contact breaker
4. Contact breaker plate
5. Condenser
6. Oil felt
7. Contract breaker wiring harness
8. Pan head screw
9. Spring washer
10. Plain washer
11. Dowel pin
12. Pan head screw
13. Spring washer
14. Plain washer
15. Spark advancer assy
16. Spark advancer washer
    Spark advancer washer
17. Spark advancer bolt
18. Ignition coil
19. Ignition coil
20. Spark plug cap
21. Spark plug cap
22. High tension cord grommet
23. Spark plug cap grommet
24. High tension coard clamp
25. Rectifier
26. Nut
27. Voltage regulator
28. Magnetic switch assy.

3. When installing the points make sure that the wire connectors are positioned on the outer part of the insulating washer. Do not overtighten the nuts as this may damage the washers causing electrical leakage.

CONDENSERS

1. The condensers are secured to the mounting plate by a single mounting screw. If they are being removed in conjunction with the points, follow Step 1 in the previous section, then remove the condensers mounting screw and disconnect the lead wires.

2. If the condensers alone are to be removed, remove the mounting screw and loosen the nuts at the leaf spring to free the wires. Consult Step 3 in the previous Section.

Testing Condensers

Condensers are generally not tested for poor operation since they are so inexpensive to replace. Arcing across the points when they are open, badly pitted or burned points, or damaged leads indicate the need for condenser replacement.

Removing the point mounting screws

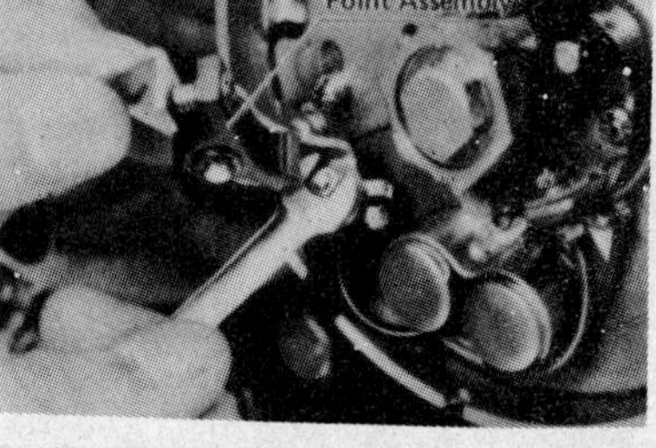

Disconnecting the condensers from the points

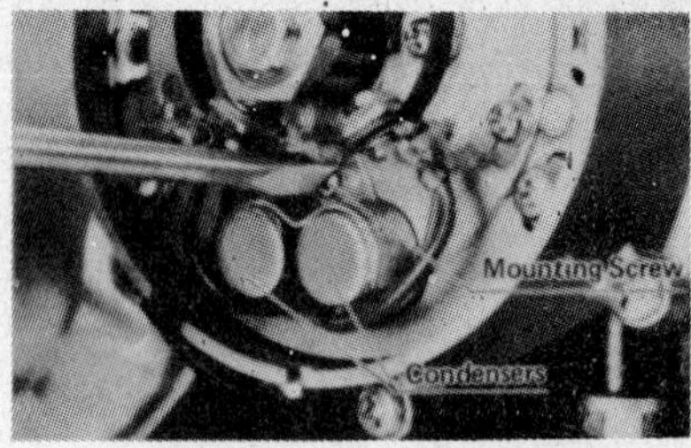

Removing the condensers

The condensers can be tested by replacing them and checking for improved performance, or by testing them with a capacitor tester as illustrated. The condenser specifications are 0.25 ± 0.03 Mfd.,1,000 VDC.

AUTOMATIC ADVANCE MECHANISM

1. Remove the points cover and cover gasket.

2. Hold the crankshaft rotation nut steady with one wrench, then remove the bolt from the end of the shaft with another.

Removing the plate mounting screws

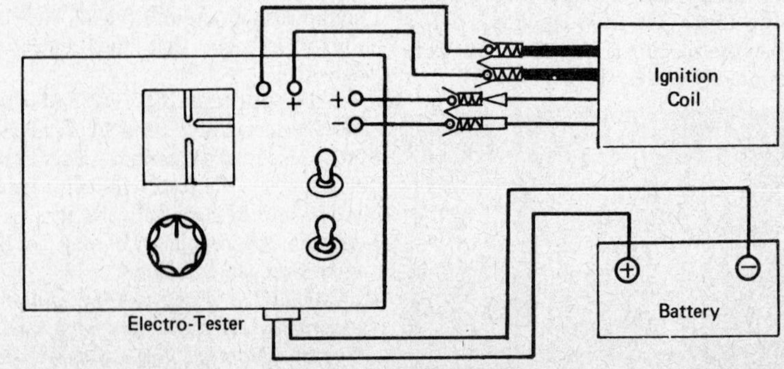

Condenser test circuit

Removing the shaft nut

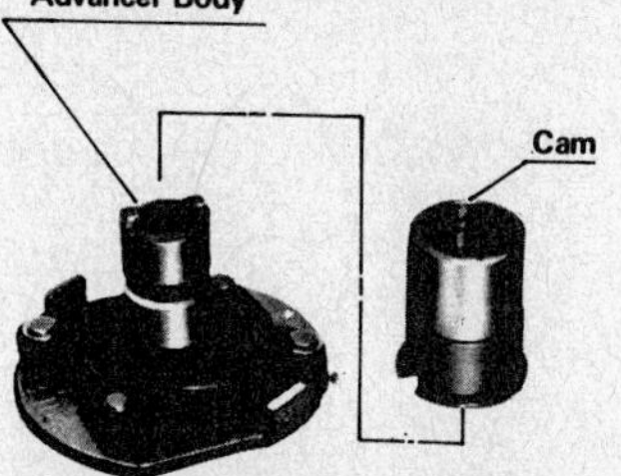

The cam slips right off the advancer body

Line up these marks when assembling the unit

3. Remove the 3 mounting plate mounting screws to remove the plate, and remove the advance mechanism.

4. Disassemble the unit, replace any damaged parts (or the whole unit), assemble it so that the marks line up, and grease the shaft before installing the breaker cam.

5. When installing the mechanism be sure that the pin on the crankshaft fits into the groove in the back of the advancer, and that the crankshaft rotation nut is properly seated.

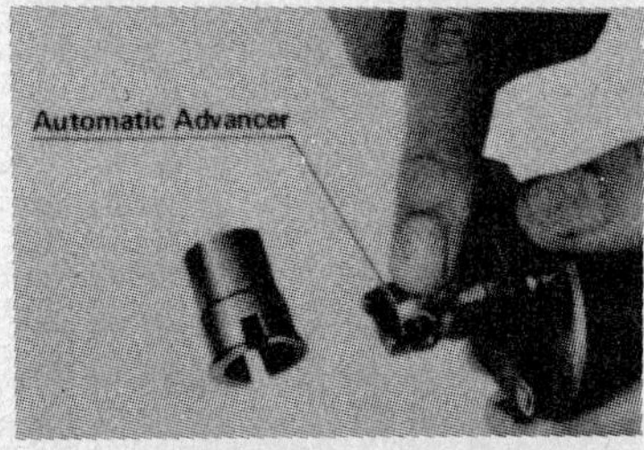

Greasing the shaft

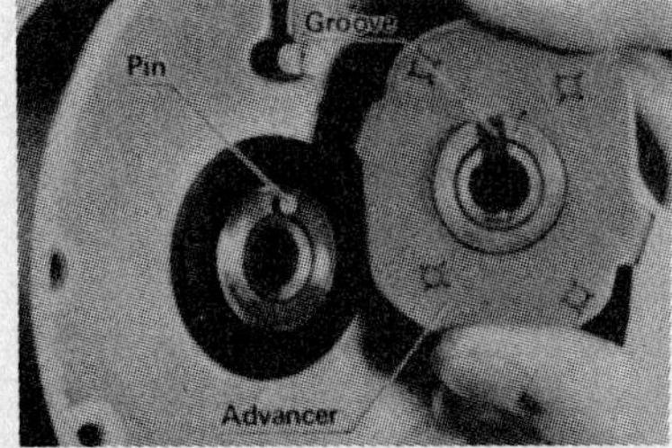

Lining up the groove and pin

IGNITION COILS

1. Remove the fuel tank.

2. Disconnect the black or green wire (as the case may be), and the brown wire, remove the spark plug leads from the plugs, and unbolt and remove the coil(s).

NOTE: *The high tension leads cannot be removed from the coil.*

3. When installing coils match the color coded black and green wires. The brown goes with the yellow/red lead from the battery. Each plug lead is numbered for the appropriate cylinder.

Testing Coils

Coils can be tested by replacing them and seeing if performance is enhanced, by testing them with an electro-tester, or by checking for a shorted or open condition using an ohmmeter.

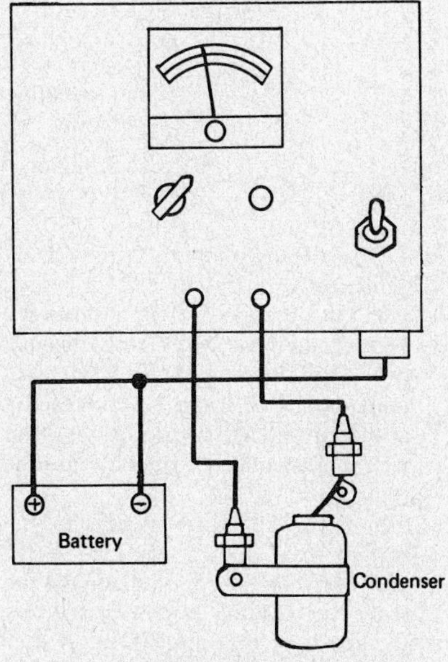

Coil test circuit

Hook up the coil to the electro-tester as indicated in the accompanying illustration. Replace the coil if it won't produce a spark at least 7 mm (0.28 in.) long.

Test the coil using an ohmmeter in the following manner:

1. Check the primary winding resistance between the red/yellow lead and the green or black lead. If the results are not between 3.2-3.8 Ω the coil must be replaced.

2. Check the secondary winding resistance between the two spark plug high tension wires. If the result is not about 30K Ω the coil must be replaced.

3. Set the ohmmeter on its highest scale and check the resistance between the brown wire and the plug wires or the coil core. If the reading is not infinity (∞), the coil must be replaced.

NOTE: *The test with an ohmmeter is not 100% accurate as it doesn't test for high voltage shorts (insulation breakdown).*

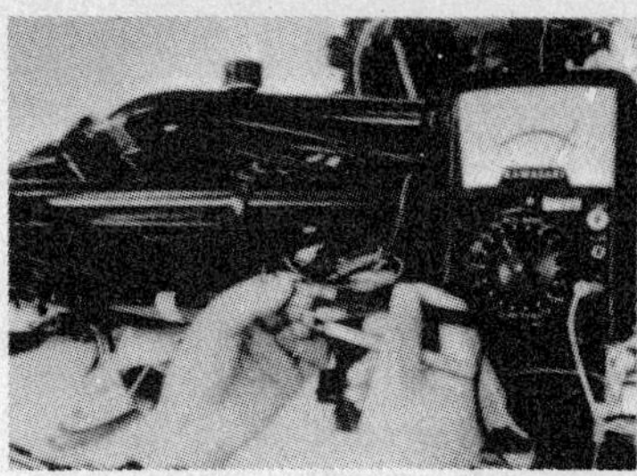

Testing the primary windings

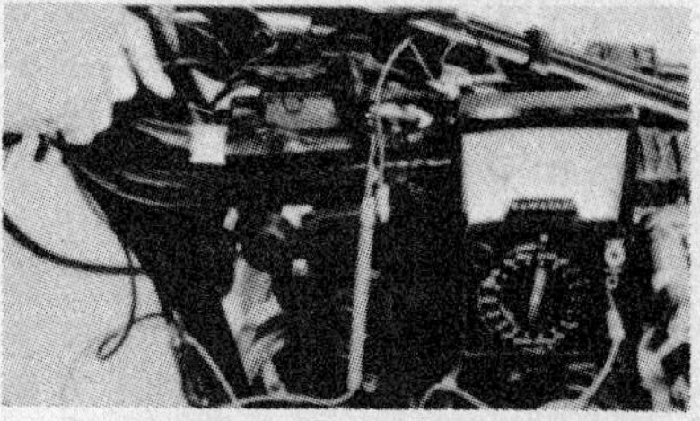

Testing the secondary windings

Starter System

CAUTION: *Do not keep the starter button depressed if the starter motor doesn't respond as this may burn out the starter windings. Do not continue to operate the starter for more than 30 seconds if the engine doesn't start, and let it cool off for about 2 minutes if you do not operate it for long.*

REMOVAL AND DISASSEMBLY

1. Remove the fuel tank, carburetors, starter cover and cover gasket, and the chain cover.

2. Remove the right-side plastic cover, unscrew the starter wire from the starter relay terminal, and free the wire from the cable clamp.

3. Remove the two starter mounting bolts, and remove the starter.

4. Remove the two mounting screws (1), and remove the end cover (2).

5. Disconnect the brush assembly (3) from the field coil lead, then remove the brush plates (4) and remove the brushes.

6. Remove the remaining end cover (5), and remove the yoke assembly (6) and armature (7).

7. Remove the starter clutch as described in the "Dynamo Removal and Installation" Section.

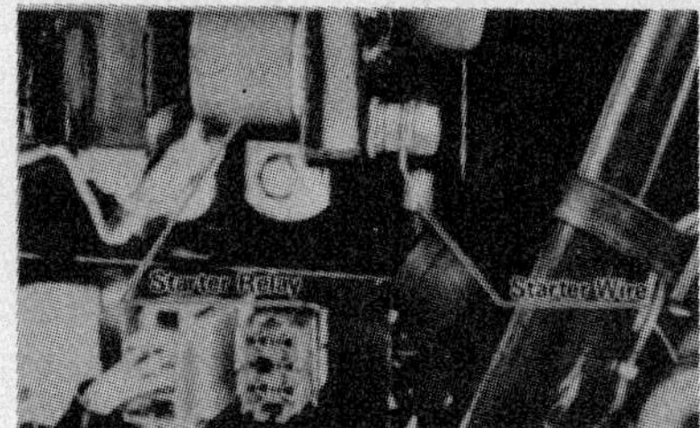

Disconnecting the starter leads

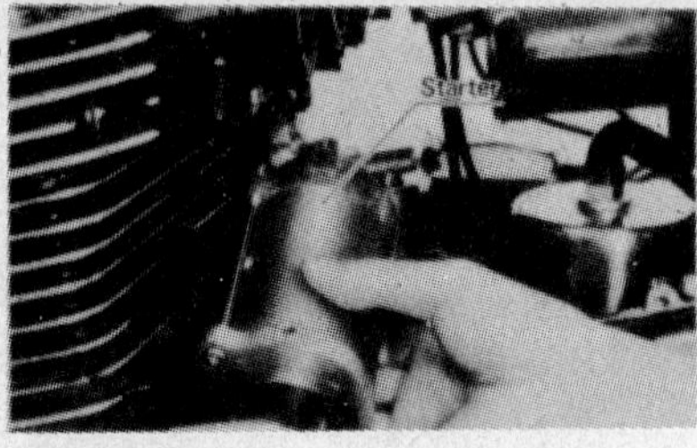

Removing the starter motor

INSPECTION AND REPAIR

1. Inspect the carbon brushes for excessive wear or damage, and replace them if worn past the standard of ½ in. (12-13 mm) by ¼ in. (7 mm) or more. Always replace the brushes as a pair.

2. Inspect the brush springs for a worn, damaged, or collapsed condition and replace them as necessary. The spring tension should be 20-24 oz (560-680 g) as measured with a spring gauge, but the spring may be considered serviceable if it will snap the brush firmly into place.

3. Inspect the commutator for a worn, scored, or otherwise damaged condition, and turn it down or clean it up with fine emery paper if necessary. If brush dust is caught in the commutator grooves it must be cleaned out thoroughly, and the mica should be cut square as illustrated.

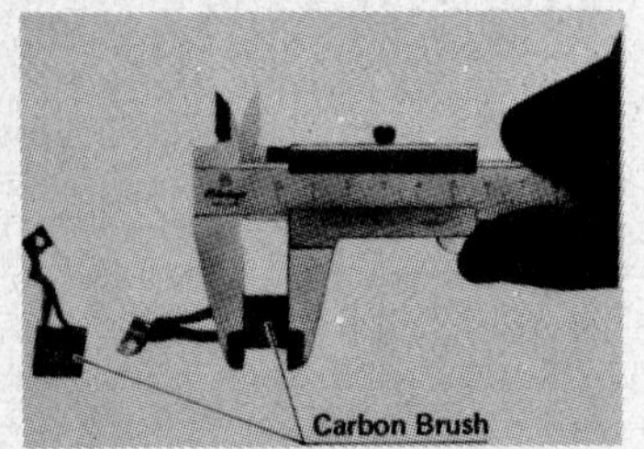

Measuring a carbon brush

Smoothing out the commutator

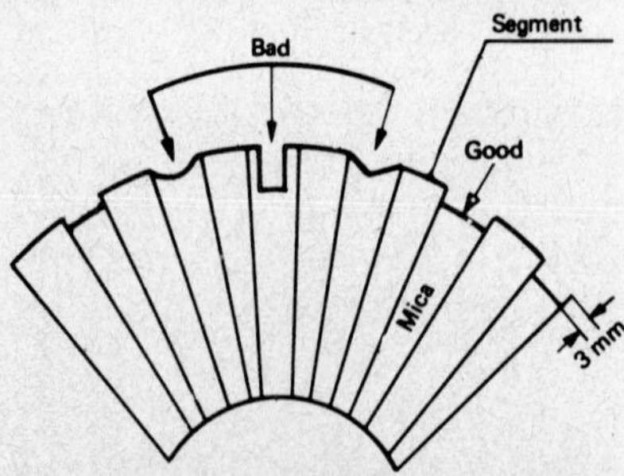

The commutator grooves should look like the "good" one

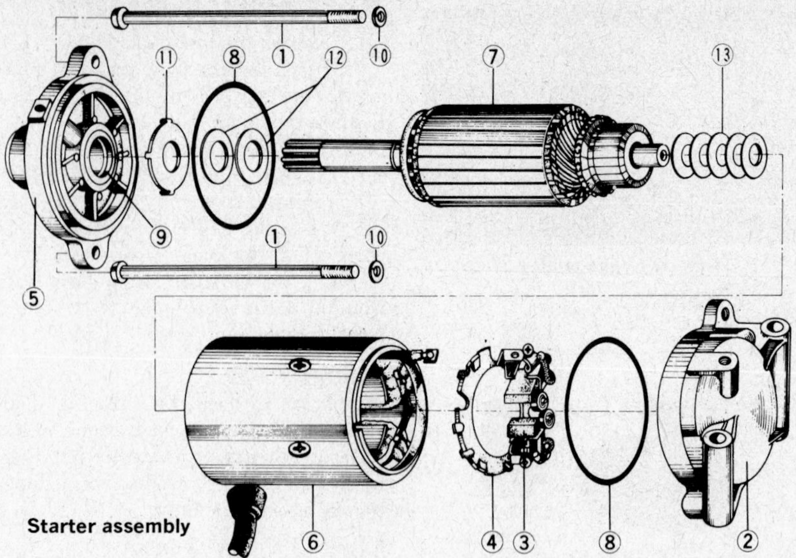

Starter assembly

1. Mounting screw
2. End cover
3. Brush assembly
4. Brush plate
5. End cover
6. Yoke assembly
7. Armature
8. O-ring
9. Oil seal
10. Lockwasher
11. Lockwasher
12. Shim
13. Shim

4. Test the commutator in the following manner:

a. Turn the meter switch to the R x 1 scale, and measure the resistance between each two segments of the commutator. High resistance, or no reading at all between any two, indicates that a wire is open and the armature must be replaced.

b. Turn the meter switch to the highest scale, and measure the resistance between the commutator and the shaft. Any reading at all indicates that the armature is grounded.

c. If the above checks do not reveal a problem, and after checking the other starter circuit components no fault is discovered, the nature of the problem may be such that it cannot be isolated with a meter. Therefore if after thoroughly checking the system the starter still fails to turn over, or only operates feebly, replace the armature.

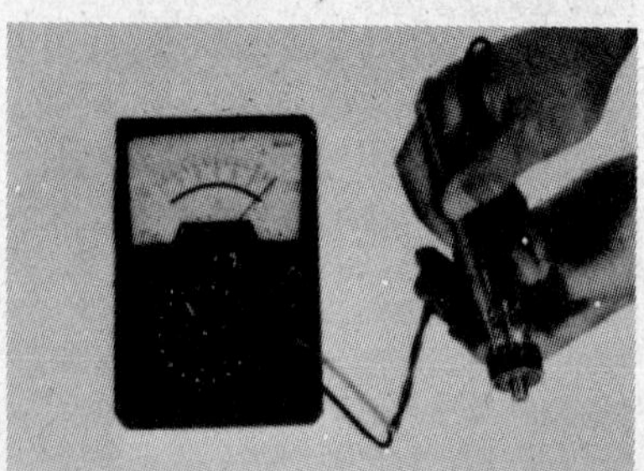
Testing resistance between segments

5. Test the field coils in the following manner:

a. Turn the meter switch to the R x 1 scale, and measure the resistance between the carbon brush on the positive side, and the starter lead. If the reading is not close to zero ohms, or if there is no reading, the field coils are open and the yoke assembly must be replaced.

b. Turn the meter switch to the highest scale, and measure the resistance between the positive side brush and the yoke (housing). Any reading indicates that the coils are shorted to round, and the yoke must be replaced.

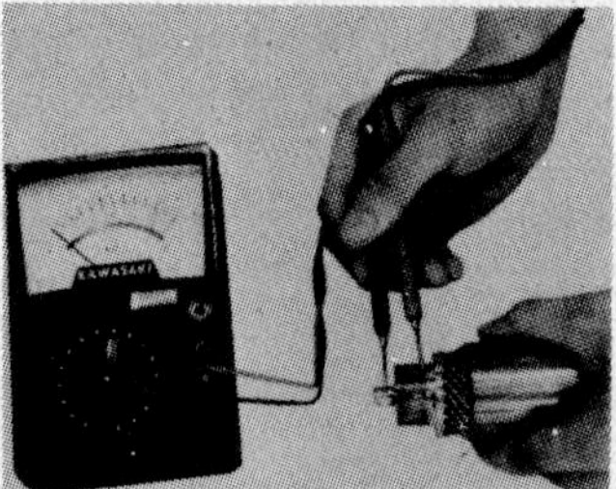

Testing resistance between the commutator and shaft

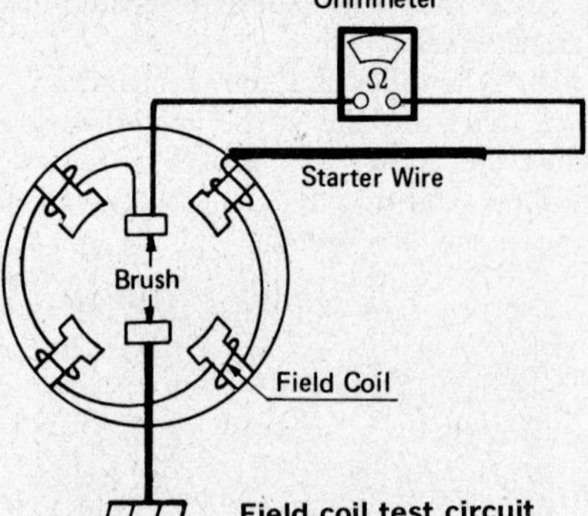

Field coil test circuit

6. Test the starter relay in the following manner:

Testing the resistance between the positive brush and the yoke

a. Disconnect the starter wires from the relay, and connect a meter set on the R x 1 scale, across the relay terminals.

b. Press the starter button and see if the meter reads zero ohms. If the relay clicks once and the meter reads zero, the relay is good. If it clicks, but the meter does not read zero, the relay is defective and must be replaced. If the relay doesn't click at all, disconnect the black and yellow/black wires and measure the resistance across them. If the reading is not close to zero, the relay is defective.

c. If the reading is zero, the relay may be good, but there may be no current getting to it. Turn the tester switch to the 30 VDC scale and connect the negative (–) meter lead to the yellow/black relay lead, and the positive (+) tester lead to the black wire. When the starter button is pushed, the meter should read battery voltage. If it doesn't the problem is in the wiring. If the meter reads battery voltage, but the relay doesn't click, the relay is defective.

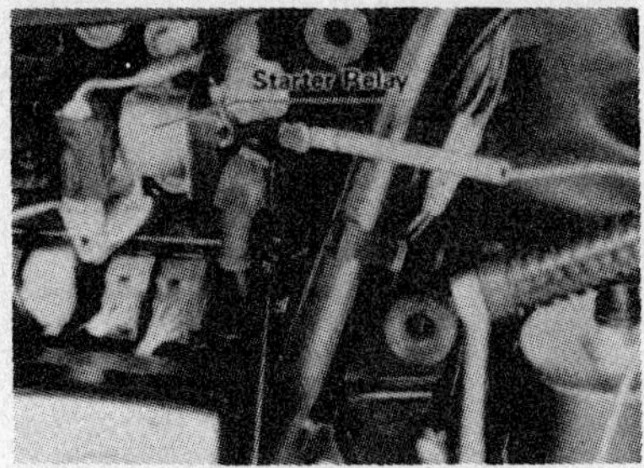

Testing the relay

7. If the starter works, but doesn't disengage after the engine starts, the starter clutch rollers or gear may be damaged or worn. Such damage could also prevent the starter from engaging properly, or could cause noisy operation while the engine is running.

Test the clutch by rotating the clutch gear by hand. It should not be able to turn in the direction of the arrow, but should turn freely in the opposite direction. If the clutch does not operate correctly, or if it operates noisily, disassemble and inspect all components for wear or damage, and replace those whose condition is even marginal.

NOTE: *Damage to either the starter clutch gear, the idle gear, or the starter gear may cause damage to the other gears. Inspect them all carefully if any are damaged or excessively worn.*

The clutch should not be able to rotate in the direction of the arrow

ASSEMBLY AND INSTALLATION

1. Assembly is in the reverse order of disassembly, and installation is in the reverse order of removal.
2. Carefully clean off any dust from the shaft as this may result in premature wear, and dampen the shaft felts with fresh oil.

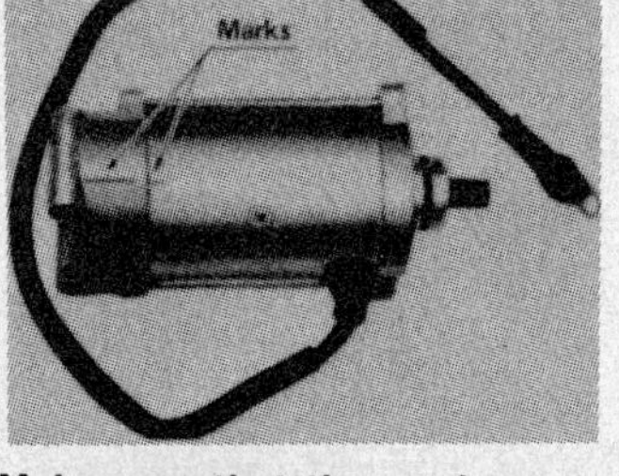

Make sure that the marks are aligned on both ends

3. Take care not to damage the O-rings and oil seals when installing the end covers, and align the marks on the covers and housing.
4. Lubricate the O-rings with a small amout of fresh oil before slipping the starter into place.
5. Apply Loctite, or another suitable sealer, to the starter mounting bolts before installing them.

ELECTRICAL EQUIPMENT

Switches

The switches used on the Z1 are not repairable, and must be replaced if defective. The switches can be disassembled and cleaned, but no replacement parts are available.

Use a meter to determine whether the connectors given in the following chart are good. The meter should read zero ohms for any of these connections.

Intermittent loss of spark to either pair of cylinders may be caused by a shorted kill switch. The best way to test for this situation is to eliminate (by-pass) the switch from the circuit, and see whether or not you continue to drop cylinders.

IGNITION SWITCH

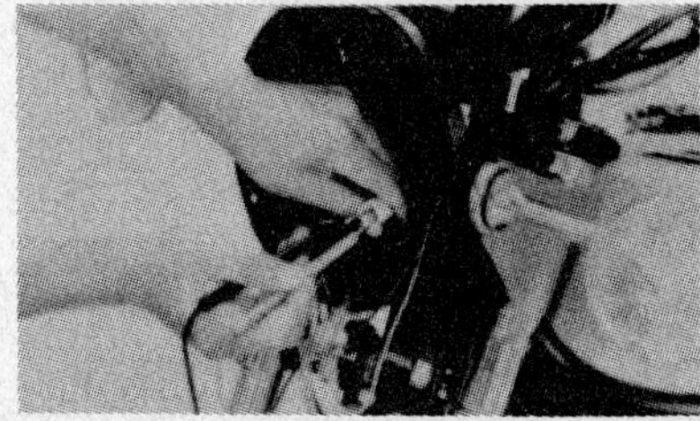

Testing the ignition switch

LEAD	Batt	Ig	Tail 1	Tail 2
Off				
On	•	•	•	•
Park	•			•
COLOR	White	Brown	Blue	Red

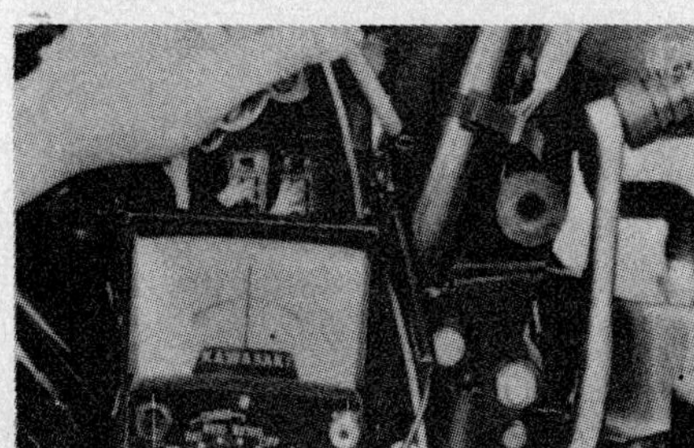

Checking for voltage to the relay

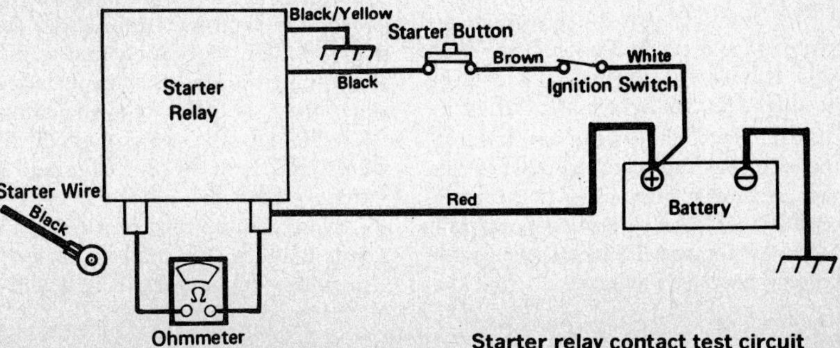

Starter relay contact test circuit

KILL SWITCH

On	●	●
Off		
Color	Brown	R/Y

DIMMER SWITCH

High	●	●		
Low		●	●	
Pass	●			●
COLOR	R/Bk	Blue	R/Y	Brown

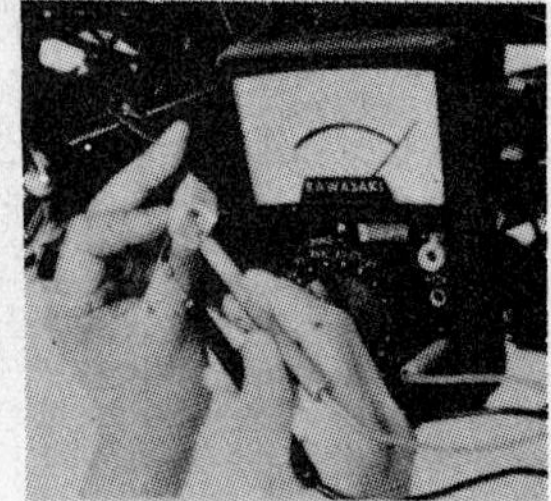

Testing the dimmer switch

HEADLIGHT SWITCH

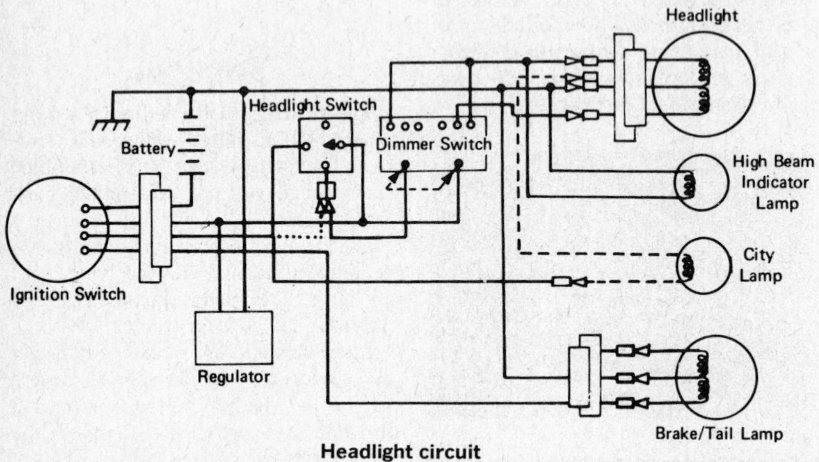

Headlight circuit

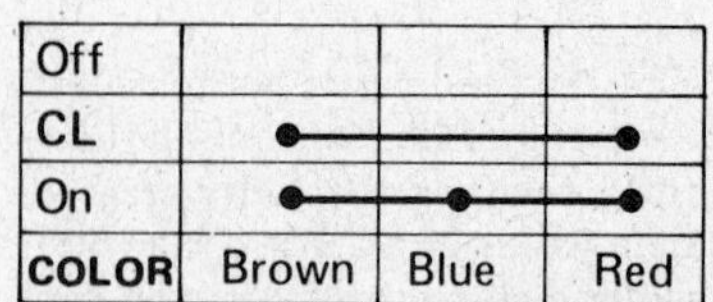

Off			
CL	●		●
On	●	●	●
COLOR	Brown	Blue	Red

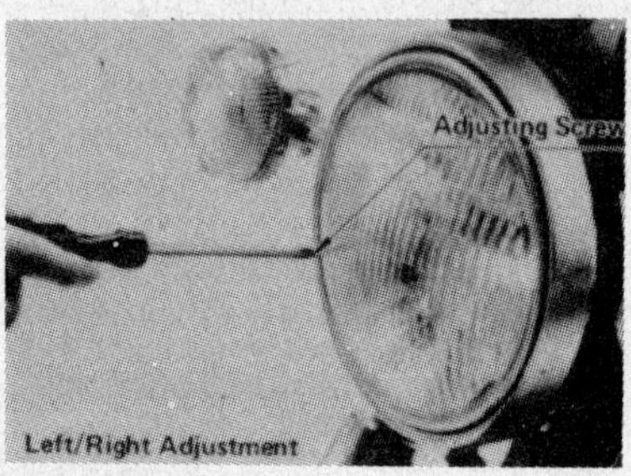

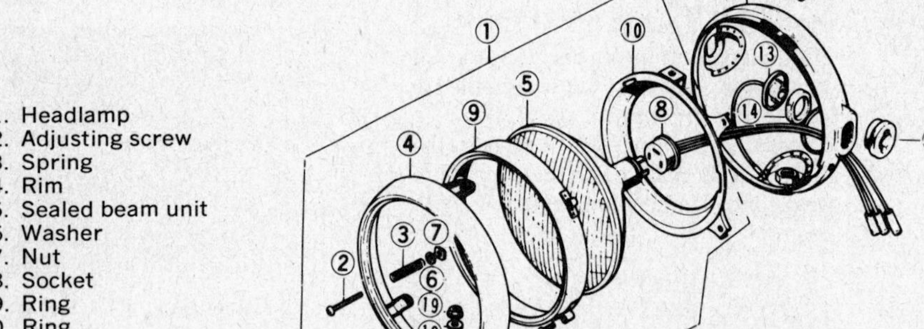

1. Headlamp
2. Adjusting screw
3. Spring
4. Rim
5. Sealed beam unit
6. Washer
7. Nut
8. Socket
9. Ring
10. Ring
11. Body
12. Screw
13. Collar
14. Damper rubber
15. Damper rubber
16. Plug
17. Screw
18. Washer
19. Nut
20. Screw

Headlight assembly

Headlight

The headlight switch connections are given in the previous Section. If the headlight fails on the European model, the headlight or city light bulbs can be replaced. Headlight failure on the U.S. model means replacing the sealed beam unit. A similar automotive unit may be used as a temporary measure, however it will not withstand vibration as well as the unit supplied by Kawasaki.

BEAM ADJUSTMENT

1. Adjust the horizontal (left to right) aim of the light by turning the small screw in the front of the rim.
2. Adjust the vertical (up and down) aim of the light in the following manner:
   a. Remove the two screws which secure the light in the housing, and remove the light.
   b. Loosen the turn signal mounting nuts, hold the light in place, loosen the mounting bolt under the light, and adjust the aim of the unit.
   c. Secure the bolt under the headlight, and tighten the turn signal nuts before reinstalling the unit.

Brake Lights

The brake light is activated by either the front or rear brake light switch. The front switch is activated by hydraulic pressure, and is set to come on when 45-70 psi of pressure is exerted on it. The front switch is neither adjustable nor repairable.

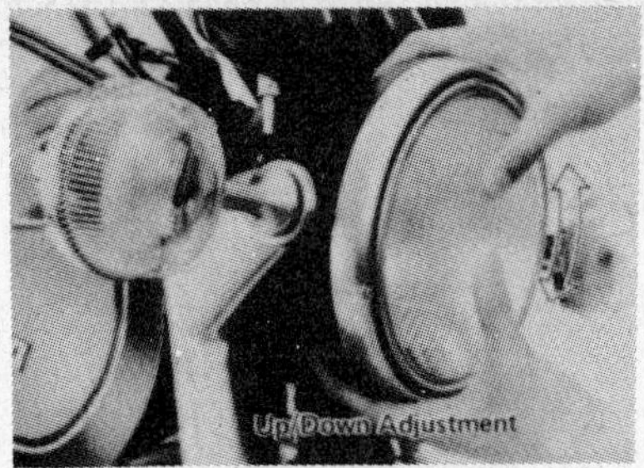

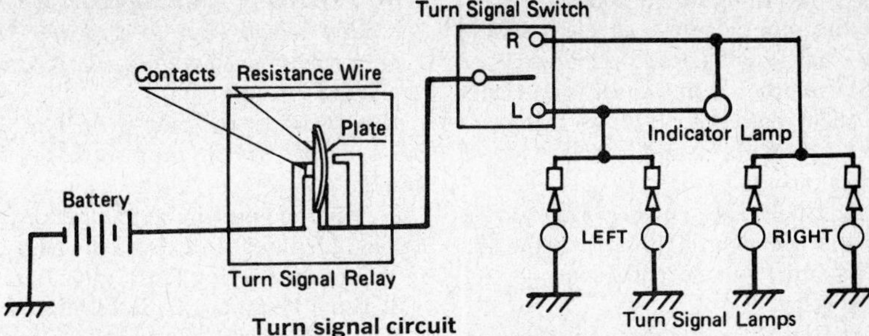

Turn signal circuit

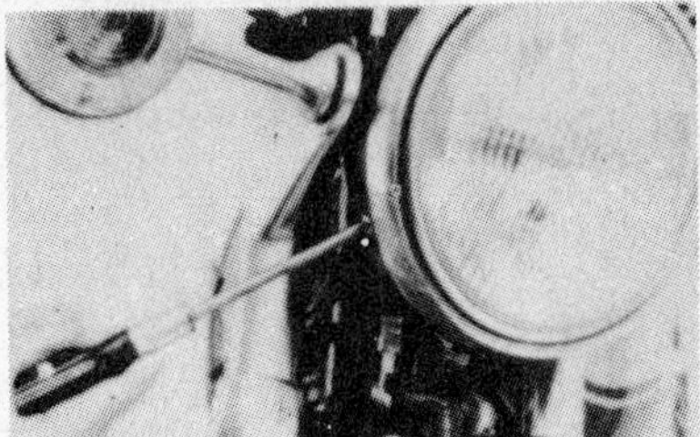
Removing the headlight unit

Mounting bolt location

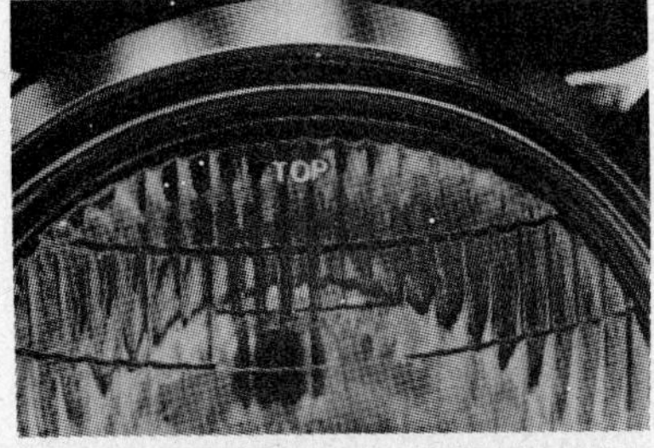

When installing the unit, the word "TOP" should be at the top

Testing the front brake light switch

The rear switch is of the plunger type, and is adjusted in the manner described in the "Maintenance" Chapter.

Check the switches with a meter connected across the terminals. The meter should read zero ohms when the switch is activated, and the switch must be replaced if it doesn't.

Note the following when installing a new front switch:

1. Clean up any spilled brake fluid immediately.
2. Apply Loctite, or another suitable sealer, to the switch threads, taking care not to get any in the switch itself.
3. Bleed the brake lines as directed in the "Chassis" Chapter after the new switch is installed.

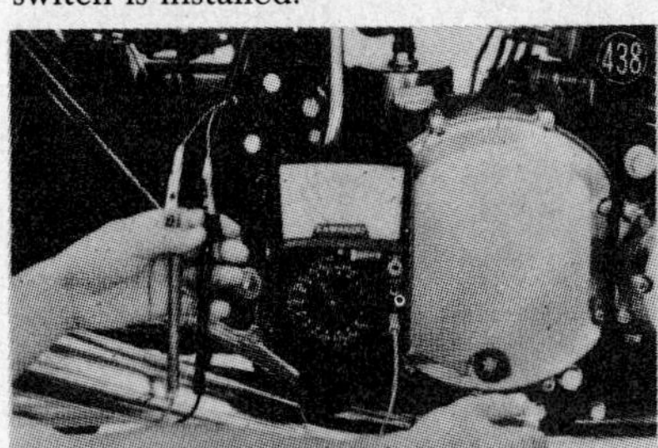
Testing the rear brake light switch

Turn Signals

The turn signals are a complete circuit, and a loose connection, bad wiring, or a burned out bulb will incapacitate the entire system. Usually, if the trouble is common to both the left and right turn signals, the problem is in the relay, although it may be in the switch, wiring, or due to a poorly charged battery. If the problem is isolated in either the right or left sides, the problem is not in the relay, but may be in the switch, wiring, or bulbs.

Troubleshoot the system in the following manner:

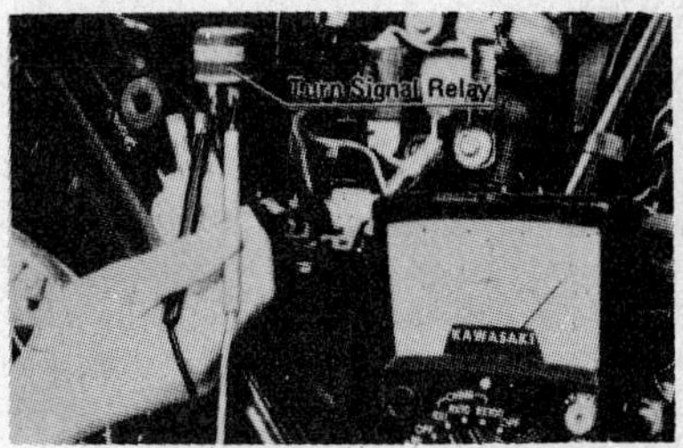

Testing the turn signal relay

1. If neither the right or left signals come on, check the following:
   a. Check the state of battery charge.
   b. Disconnect the relay and use a meter to check for continuity through the relay terminals. If the reading is not close to zero ohms (i.e., no reading or one of several ohms), replace the relay.
   c. If the relay is good, turn the meter switch to the 30 VDC scale, and connect the positive (+) meter lead to the brown wire which goes to the relay, and the negative (−)tester lead to the orange wire. Turn on the ignition, and flip the turn signal switch from right to left. If the meter registers battery voltage but the lamps don't work, recheck the wiring and bulbs. If the meter doesn't register battery voltage, either

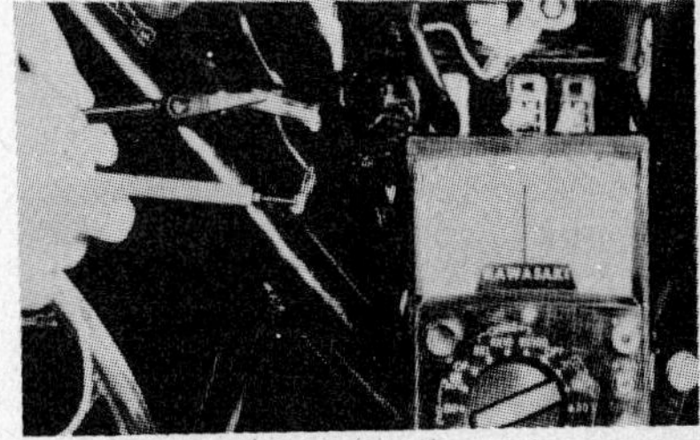

Testing the relay leads

the switch or wiring is bad.

2. If both the right or left signals come on and stay on, on blink too slowly, check the following:
   a. Check the state of battery charge.
   b. Check all of the wiring connections.
   c. Check that the bulbs, both the flasher and the indicator, are of the correct wattage.
   d. Replace the relay if the above Steps check out.

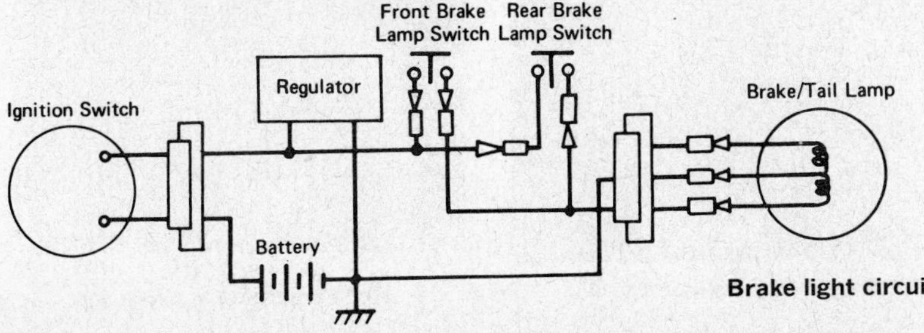

Brake light circuit

3. If one lamp on one side comes on, but the other doesn't, check the lamp that's out for a bad bulb or bad wiring.

4. If neither lamp on one side comes on, check both bulbs and the switch.

5. If the flashing rate is too fast, check the following:

a. Check for an overcharged battery if this occurs on both sides. If the battery and dynamo check out, replace the relay.

b. If this only occurs on one side, check that the wattage of the bulbs is correct.

Instruments

Both instruments are sealed units which cannot be repaired except for bulb replacement. Replace the bulbs by disconnecting the instrument from its cable and mount (it is not necessary to disconnect the wiring in the headlight shell), and pull out the plug connector for the offending bulb. Make sure that you replace the bulb with one of the correct wattage.

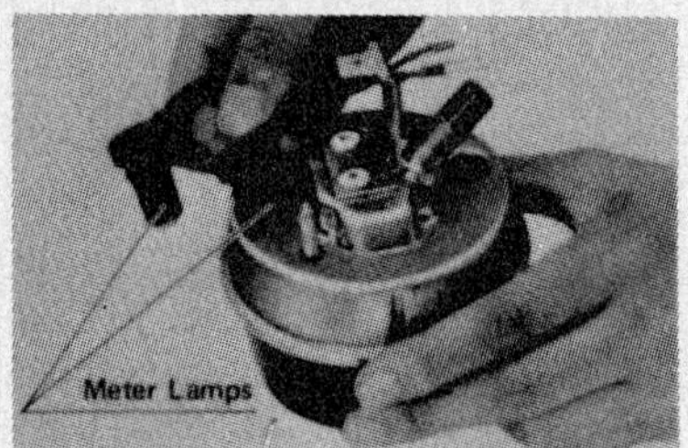

Replacing instrument bulbs

Oil Pressure Switch

SWITCH REPAIR

If the oil pressure lamp comes on and stays on when the oil is hot and the motorcycle is being rapidly accelerated, the problem is probably in the switch. This can often be temporarily remedied by revving the engine up past 6000 rpm.

CAUTION: *If the switch comes on the engine oil flow is cut off. Stop the machine immediately if a quick high rev doesn't turn the light back off or engine damage may result.*

Correct this problem by relieving oil pressure at the switch in the following manner:

NOTE: *This is a warranty covered operation which your local dealer will perform for you if your warranty hasn't expired.*

1. Disconnect the blue wire from the oil pressure switch, and remove the switch.

2. Mark and punch the plunger disc at a point 2.5 mm (0.1 in.) from the edge, as in the accompanying illustration.

3. Use a 1/16 in. (1.5 mm) drill to drill a hole at this point. Do not use a larger drill, and try to be as precise as possible.

4. Reinstall the switch, after applying Loctite, or another suitable sealer, to the threads and connect the blue wire.

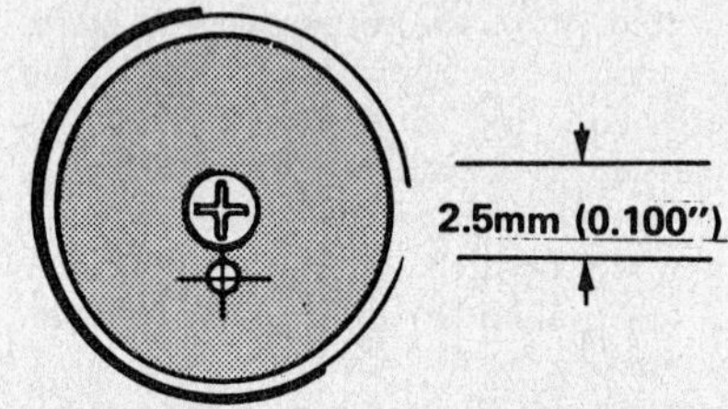

Drill here

SWITCH TESTING

The switch should turn on the indicator light when the key is on but the engine is not running. If the light doesn't come on, disconnect the lead from the switch and use an ohmmeter to check for continuity between the switch body and the switch terminal. A dead short indicates that the problem is either in the wiring or bulb. If the reading is not zero ohms, the switch is defective and must be replaced.

If the lamp stays on and you've already followed the instructions in the preceding Section, disconnect the lead from the switch, and connect an ohmmeter between the switch terminal and ground. With the engine off the meter should read zero ohms, and with the engine running the meter should indicate an open (∞) condition. If the meter still indicates a short when the engine is running, shut it down and run a pressure test as directed in the "Lubrication System" Chapter. The switch is probably defective.

NOTE: *Always coat the switch threads with Loctite, or another suitable sealer, when installing it.*

Horn

Most horn troubles, unless caused by maladjustment, can be traced to the contacts. The contacts wear and must be periodically adjusted. If adjusting the contacts doesn't correct the problem, the contacts are probably dirty or pitted.

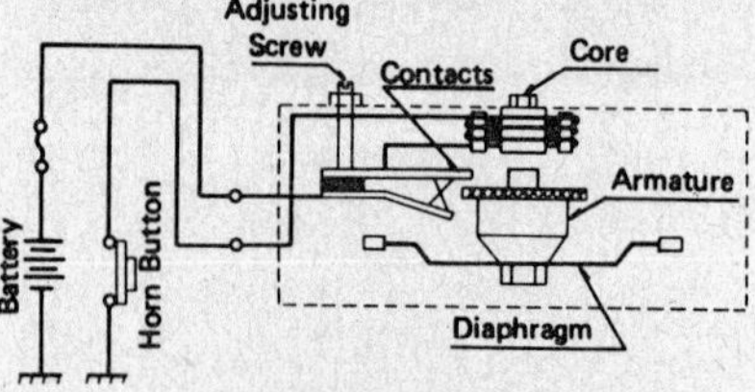

Horn diagram

ADJUSTMENT

1. Remove the fuel tank, then disconnect the black horn wire, and connect a meter into the circuit so that the positive (+) tester lead goes to the black wire on the horn side, and the negative (−) tester lead goes to the remaining black wire.

2. Turn on the ignition, and depress the horn button while turning in the adjusting nut until the horn sounds its best. Keep the horn current between 1.8 and 2.5 amps.

CAUTION: *Do not turn the adjusting nut in too far as this may damage the spring inside the horn, and increase the horn current to a point where the horn coil may be burned out.*

3. If the horn doesn't sound right, first make sure that no cables or other components are touching it, and if this doesn't help, clean the contacts as described in the following Section.

NOTE: *Disassembling the horn during the warranty period will invalidate the horn warranty.*

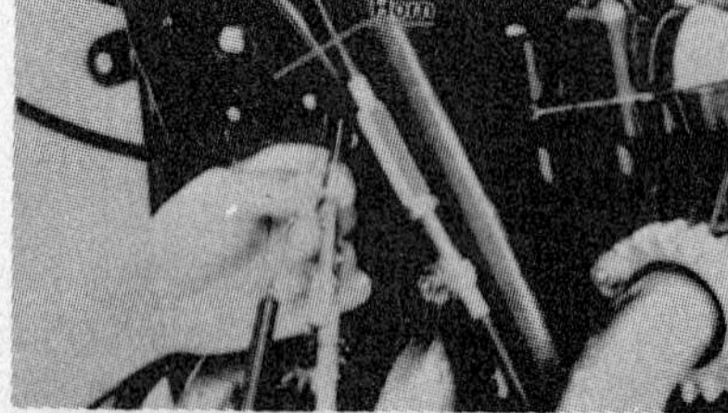

Testing the horn

Oil pressure switch location

Testing the oil pressure switch

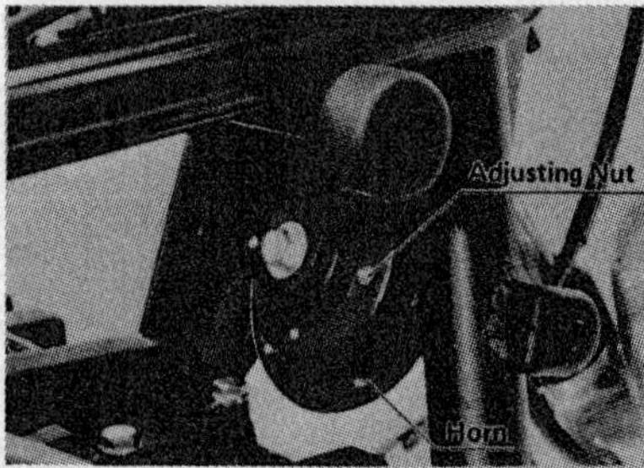

Horn adjusting nut location

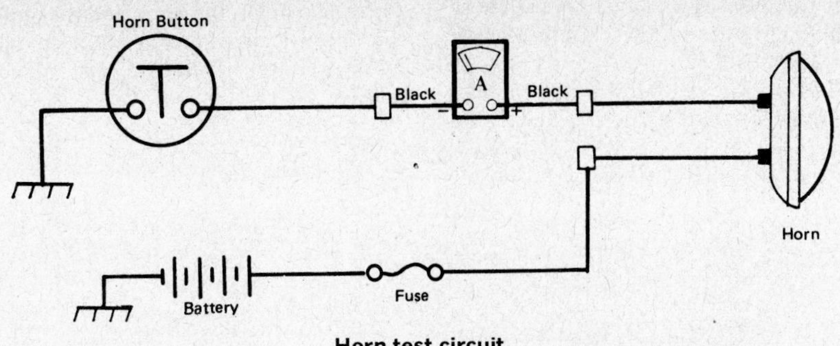

Horn test circuit

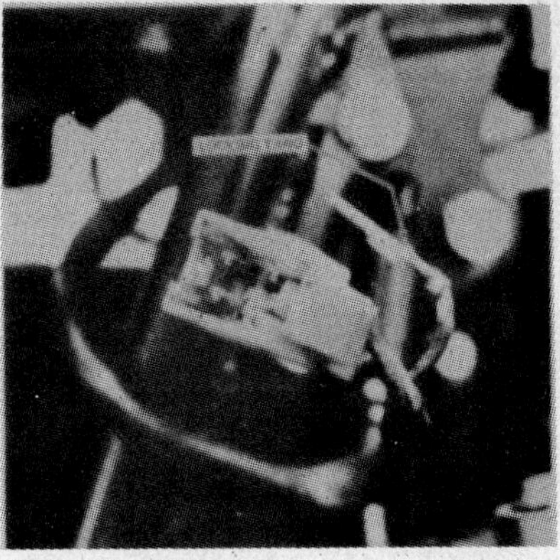

Make sure that the locking tangs are firmly seated

REPAIR

CAUTION: *Do not loosen the core or armature mounting as this will necessitate fine adjustments not given here.*

1. Check horn continuity with a meter connected to the black and brown leads. If the reading is close to zero ohms, the horn should be adjusted.
2. If the reading is several ohms, if there is no reading, or if adjustment will not correct the problem, remove the screws around the perimeter of the horn to disassemble it.
3. Clean the contacts with fine sandpaper or emery cloth until you get a reading of zero ohms resistance across the contacts.
4. If there is still high resistance, or if there is still no reading, the coil is burned out and the horn must be replaced.
5. Inspect the horn assembly for signs of water damage, and replace the gasket with a homemade one if it appears to be water damaged.

Cleaning the contacts

ELECTRICAL TROUBLESHOOTING

If you've got an electrical problem that you can't trace, especially if it is an intermittent one, chances are that it's due to poor contact of the male and female connectors in the electrical panel. This may be due to the failure of one of the connectors to seat properly in the plastic plug jack, so when the panel is plugged together one of the pins or receptors backs out causing a poor contact. Vibration can also figure in this, causing a poor connection while the machine is running, but checking out okay when sitting dormant.

Alleviate this sort of problem by tugging at each wire until a loose one is discovered, then push it back in until you feel the small locking tang reach its seat. Pull on the offending wire a few times again to make sure that it's now properly seated.

The following will help you locate a connector-based problem more easily:

Blue Plug: The blue plug contains 3 leads from the dynamo, one lead from the Neutral light, and one from the oil pressure warning light. A poor connection here could mean the battery would not charge, leading to a dead battery, or failure of one of the warning lights to illuminate.

Green Plug: The green plug goes to the voltage regulator. A poor connection

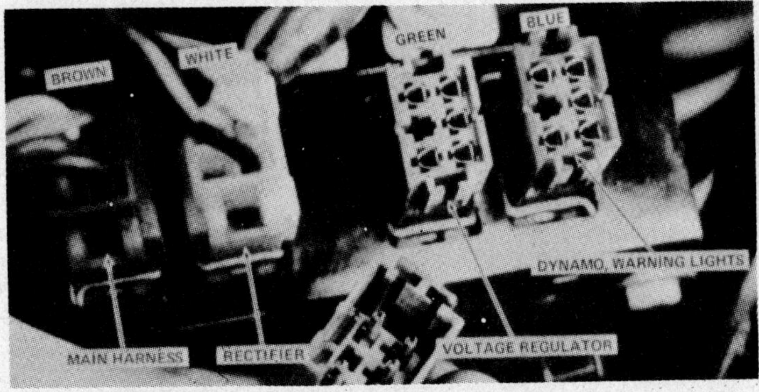

Electrical panel location

ELECTRICAL SPECIFICATIONS

Generator	Kokusan AR3701	Tail/Brake lamp	12V 4/32 cp 8/23W
Regulator	Kokusan RS21	Speedometer lamp	12V 3.4W x 2
Ignition coil	Kokusan IG3303, IG3304	Tachometer lamp	12V 3.4W x 2
Battery	Yuasa 12N 14-3A	Neutral indicator lamp	12V 3.4W
	12V 14AH	High beam indicator lamp	12V 3.4W
Starter	Kokusan SM-226-K	Turn signal lamps	12V 23W x 4
Headlamp type		Turn signal indicator lamp	12V 3.4W
U.S.	Sealed beam	Oil pressure indicator lamp	12V 3.4W
European	Semi-sealed	City lamp	12V 4W
Headlamp	12V 50W/35W	Horn	12V 2.5A max.

here could overcharge the battery, possibly causing it to boil over. Usually, the first indication of a problem is burning out of the headlamp or other lamps.

White Plug: The white plug leads to the rectifier. A bad connection here could fail to charge the battery, leading to a dead battery.

Brown Plug: The brown plug supplies the main electrical harness, including the starter, the lights, the horn, and the ignition. Poor connection could mean no lights, no horn, no electric start, or no ignition.

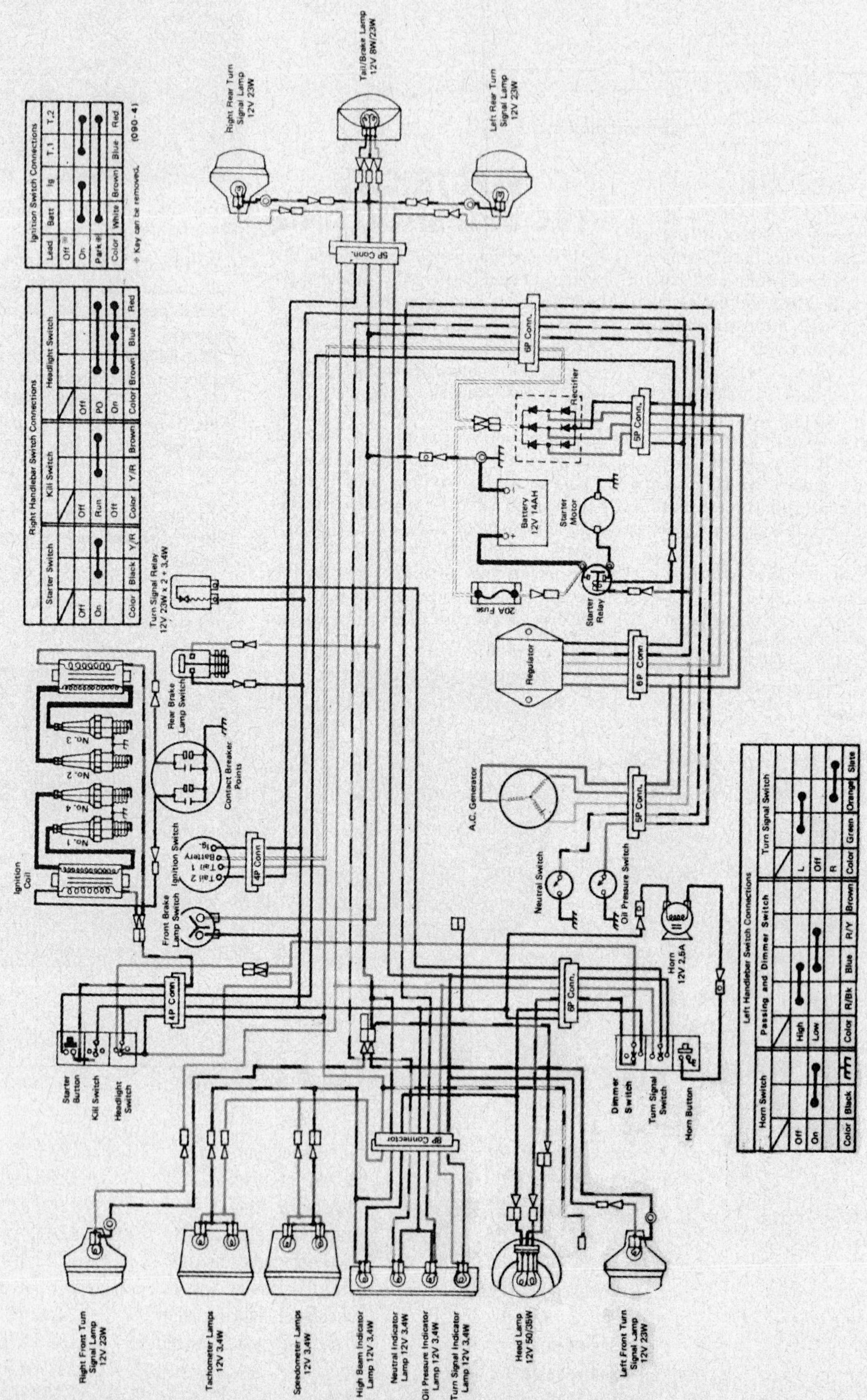

Wiring diagram for U.S. models

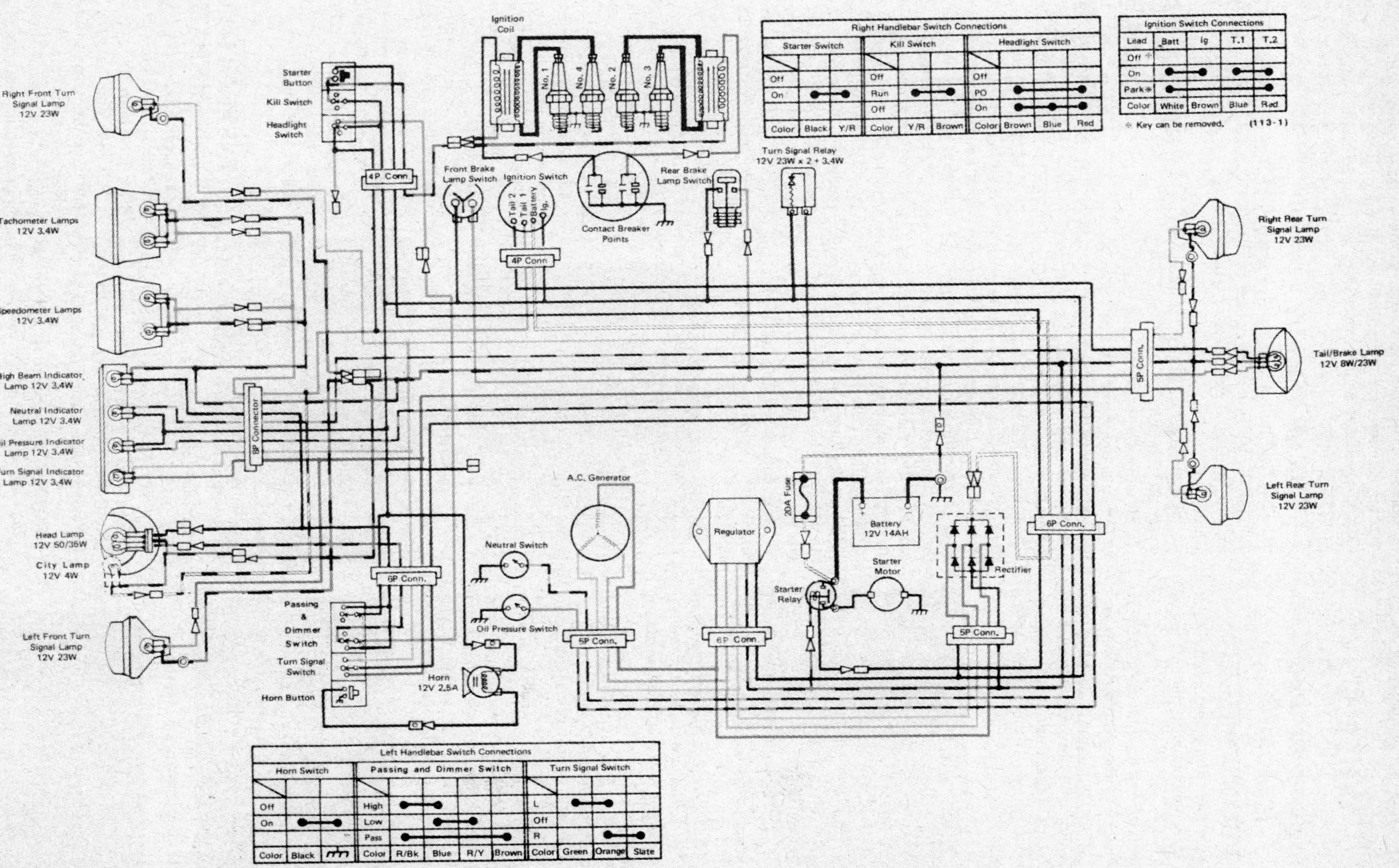

Wiring diagram for European models

CHASSIS

WHEELS

Removal and Installation

FRONT WHEEL

1. Disconnect the speedometer cable at the front wheel, using pliers if necessary.
2. Block up the motorcycle so that the front wheel is off the ground, or use a jack placed under the engine to raise the bike.
3. Remove the nuts which secure the axle clamps, then remove the clamps. The front wheel is now free to be removed.

Disconnecting the speedometer cable

CAUTION: *Do not operate the front brake while the front wheel is removed or the caliper piston will be forced out of the cylinder.*

4. Installation is in the reverse order of removal. Note the following:

a. The axle clamp has a front and rear end, and must be installed so that the gap at the rear is even.

b. Secure the front clamp nut first, and then the rear, to a specified torque of 13-14.5 ft lbs (1.8-2.0 kg/m). Check for an even gap at the rear.

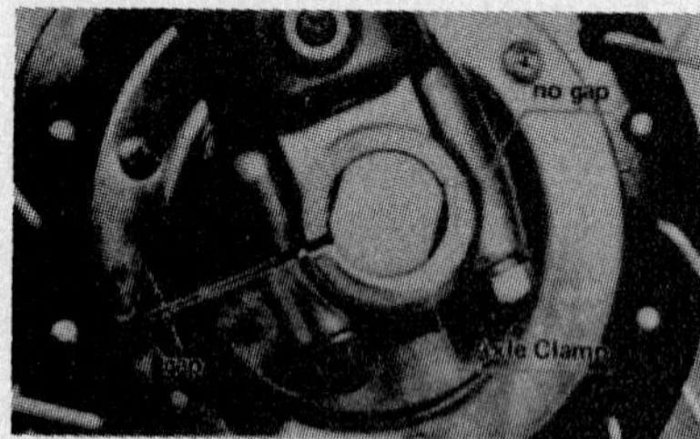

Axle clamp correctly installed

Axle clamp incorrectly installed

c. Rotate the front wheel while installing the speedometer cable until the speedometer drive shaft will seat in the grooved end of the cable, then secure the cable.

REAR WHEEL

1. Place the motorcycle on its center stand, or block up the rear wheel of the machine so that it isn't resting on the ground.
2. Remove the axle nut cotter pin, and loosen the axle nut.
3. Remove the brake torque link cotter pin, nut, and washer at the brake hub, then disconnect the torque link.
4. Remove the brake adjuster nut from the brake rod.
5. Remove the bolts which secure the chain adjuster stoppers, pull back on the rear wheel to take up any slack in the chain, rotate the adjusters down out of the way, and remove the stoppers.
6. Push the rear wheel forward until the chain can be slipped off the sprocket to the left, then pull the wheel back and off the frame. It may be necessary to shift the wheel to the right to get it past the rear fender.
7. Installation is basically in the reverse order of removal. Note the following:

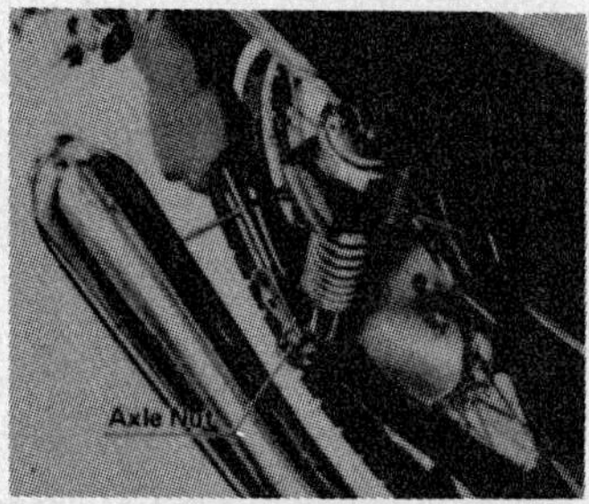

Loosening the axle nut

Chain adjuster stopper location

a. Start the chain onto the sprocket before slipping the wheel assembly onto the frame or it will get stuck on the nuts which secure the sprocket.

NOTE: *If this operation proves too difficult, loosen the left-side muffler mounting, and remove the chain guard to gain greater access.*

b. Adjust the chain, as described in the "Maintenance" section, before securing the axle and torque link nuts.

c. Secure the torque link nut to 22-25 ft lbs (3-3.5 kg/m) and install a new cotter pin.

d. Center the brakes by spinning the rear wheel and sharply applying the brake, then secure the axle nut without releasing the brake. Secure the axle nut to 95-115 ft lbs (13-16 kg/m), and install a new cotter pin. Adjust the brakes as described in the "Maintenance" Section.

WHEEL HUBS AND BRAKES

Front Hub

DISASSEMBLY

1. Remove the wheel as described in the "Wheels Removal and Installation" Section. Refer to the accompanying illustration and the Note, below.
2. Hold the gearbox (9) stationary, and unscrew the axle (17). The speedometer pinion (16) and bushing (14) are secured by the bushing set pin (13), and may be removed if necessary. The speedometer gears (12 and 10), and the oil seal (11) may be removed at this time.

CAUTION: *If the axle is held stationary and the gearbox is rotated, the speedometer drive gear will be damaged.*

3. Remove the collar (18) caps (8), and wheel cap (6). If you wish to remove the disc, remove the six bolts which secure it.
4. Use a suitable drift to knock the left-side bearing (4) free from its seat. Approach it from the right, and apply pressure only to the inner race.
5. Remove the distance collar (5) and oil seal (2).
6. Remove the retaining ring (3) from the left-side of the wheel, and tap evenly around the inner race of the right-side bearing until it comes out.
7. Consult the "Front Disc Brake" Section for additional information on the front disc brake master cylinder and caliper assemblies.

INSPECTION AND REPAIR

1. Clean all parts, except the bearings and seals, thoroughly in a suitable solution, then blow them dry.
2. Clean the bearings with gasoline and blow them dry. Lubricate them with clean oil, then spin them to check for wear or damage. If the bearing doesn't spin smoothly and quietly it must be replaced. If the bearings are good, they must be rewashed with gasoline, blown dry, and repacked with a suitable high quality bearing grease. Spin the bearing a few times to circulate the grease evenly.

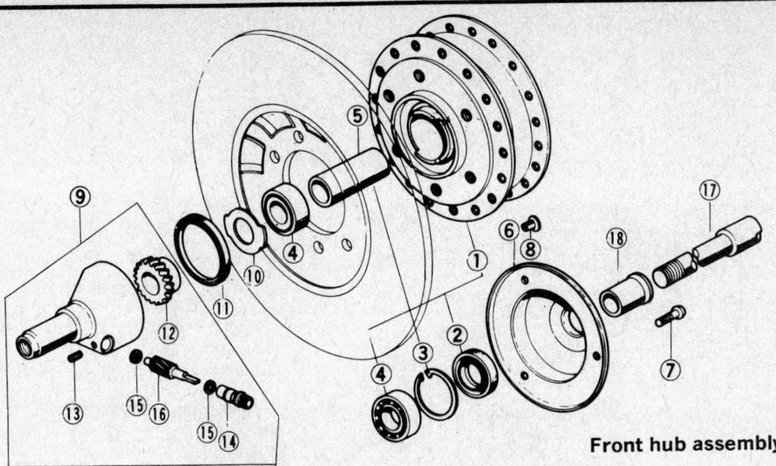

Front hub assembly

1. Drum assembly
2. Oil seal
3. Circlip
4. Bearing
5. Distance collar
6. Wheel cap
7. Screw
8. Cap
9. Gearbox
10. Speedometer gear
11. Oil seal
12. Speedometer gear
13. Pin
14. Bushing
15. Washer
16. Speedometer pinion
17. Axle
18. Collar

CAUTION: *Never spin dry bearings under any circumstances.*

3. Check all parts for a worn or damaged condition, and replace them as necessary. Oil seals must be replaced if even only slightly damaged or cracked, and should be replaced as a matter of course.

4. Consult the "Front Disc Brake—Disc" Section for additional information concerning the disc.

ASSEMBLY

1. Assembly is basically in the reverse order of disassembly.

2. Replace the oil seals with new ones, and install the bearings using either the special bearing driver holder and bearing driver (Part No. 57001-139 and 57001-140) or a suitable substitute.

3. Align the speedometer drive, as illustrated, during installation.

4. Remember to hold the gearbox stationary and screw in the axle to avoid damaging the speedometer gear drive.

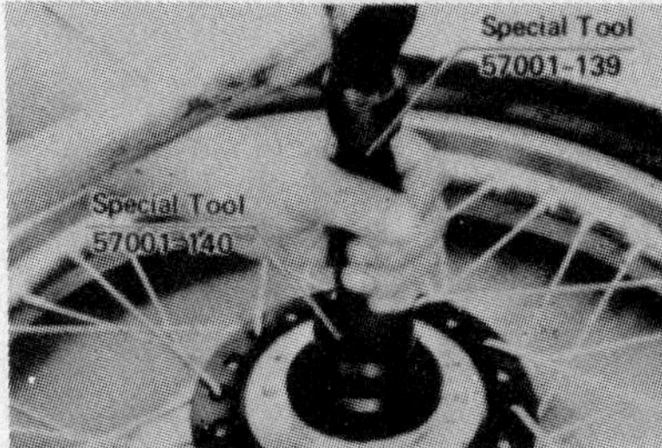

Installing a wheel bearing

Front Disc Brake

CAUTION: *Read and observe the following before beginning any work on the disc brake assemblies:*

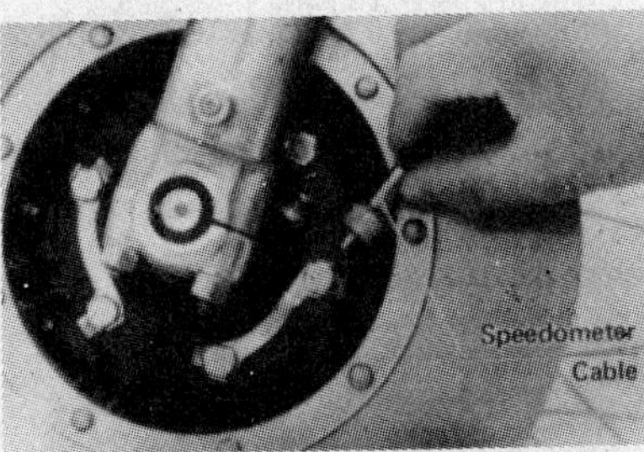

1. Never re-use old brake fluid.

2. Do not use fluid from a container that has been left unsealed, or that has been open a long time.

3. Do not mix two types of fluid for use in the brakes. This lowers the brake fluid boiling point and could cause the brake to be ineffective. It may also cause the rubber brake parts to deteriorate. Recommended fluids are shown below.

NOTE: *The type of fluid originally used in the disc brake is not available in most areas, but it should be necessary to add very little fluid before the first brake fluid change. After changing the fluid, use only that one type thereafter.*

Atlas Extra Heavy Duty
Shell Super Heavy Duty
Texaco Super Heavy Duty
Wagner Lockheed Heavy Duty
Girling Amber

The correct fluid will come in a can labeled SAE J-1703 or D.O.T.3. Do not use fluid that does not have one of these markings.

4. Don't leave the reservoir cap off for any length of time as moisture may be absorbed into the fluid.

5. Don't change the fluid in the rain, or when a strong wind is blowing.

6. Use only disc brake fluid, isopropyl alcohol or ethyl alcohol for cleaning brake parts, but do not allow rubber parts to remain in contact with the alcohol for more than 30 seconds.

7. Brake fluid will damage painted surfaces; any spilled fluid should be wiped off immediately.

8. Do not use gasoline, motor oil, or any other mineral oils near disc brake parts, these oils cause deterioration of rubber brake parts. If oil spills on any brake parts it is very difficult to wash off and will eventually reach and break down the rubber.

9. If any of the brake line fittings or the bleeder valve is loosened at any time the air must be bled from the brake.

10. Prescribed torque values for tightening disc brake parts mountings are as follows:

Brake Torque Value Chart

Items	*Value (in. lbs)*	*Value (kg/m)*
Brake lever	45-60	0.5-0.7
Brake lever adjuster	70-100	0.8-1.2
Master cylinder clamp	55-75	0.63-0.88
Fitting (banjo) bolts	19-23*	2.5-3.3
Brake pipe nipple	150-155	1.7-1.8
3-way fitting mounting	45-50	0.5-0.6
Pressure switch	135-170	1.5-2.0
Caliper shafts	22-26*	3.0-3.6
Caliper mounting	19-23*	2.5-3.3
Bleeder valve	70-85	0.8-1.0
Disc mounting bolts	140-190	1.6-2.2

* *These dimensions are in ft lbs*

BRAKE PADS

Replacement

1. Read the cautionary notes at the beginning of the "Front Disc Brake" Section.

2. Remove the front wheel as described in the "Wheels Removal and Installation" Section.

3. Remove the mounting screw which secures pad B (see the illustration), and remove the pad.

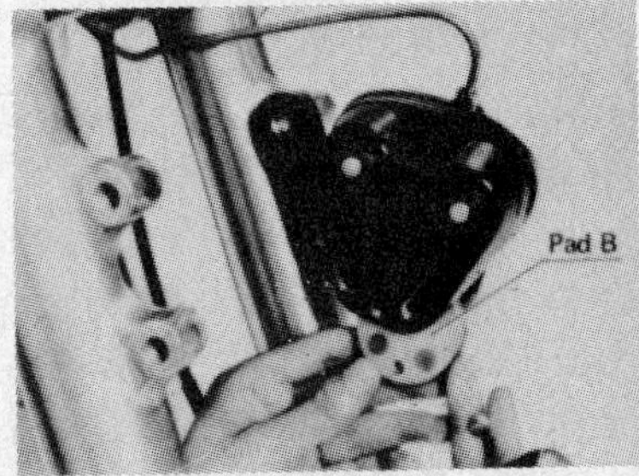

Removing pad B

4. Pump the brake lever several times until the piston forces pad A out, and remove the pad.

5. Loosen the bleeder valve slightly, press the piston in by hand as far as it will go, then close the valve.

CAUTION: *Some brake fluid will leak out of the bleeder during this operation. Be prepared to catch it with a rag.*

6. Align the groove in pad A with the ridge in the caliper, then insert the pad.

7. Install pad B in the caliper, and use either Loctite or some other suitable thread sealer on the mounting screw.

8. Replenish the brake fluid supply in the master cylinder reservoir.

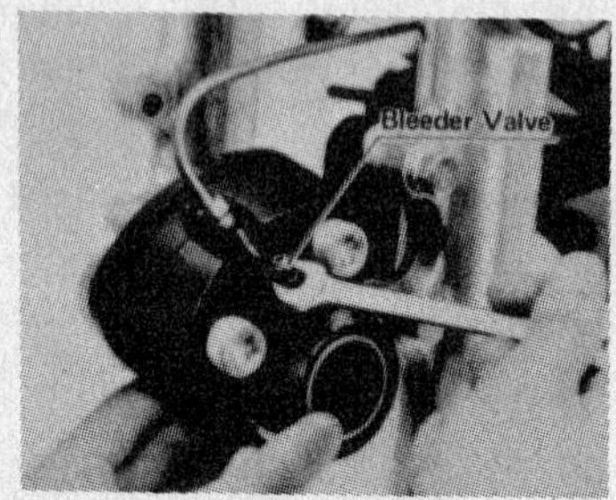

Opening the bleeder valve reduces the pressure in the caliper slightly

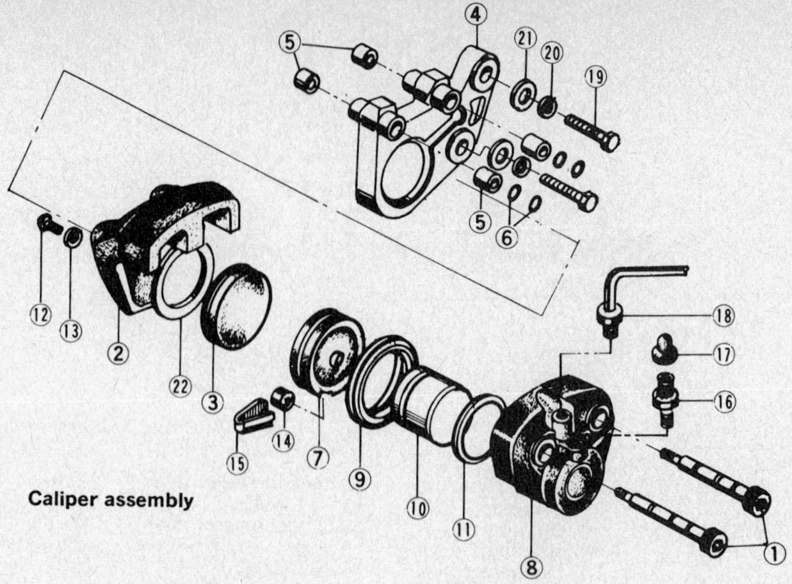

Caliper assembly

1. Allen head shaft
2. Caliper B
3. Pad B
4. Caliper holder
5. Boots
6. O-ring
7. Pad A
8. Caliper A
9. Piston dust seal
10. Piston
11. Seal
12. Screw
13. Lock washer
14. Bushing
15. Stopper
16. Bleeder valve
17. Bleeder valve cap
18. Nipple
19. Mounting bolt
20. Lock washer
21. Washer
22. Ring

CALIPER

Removal and Disassembly

1. Read the cautionary notes at the beginning of the "Front Disc Brake" Section.

2. Remove the front wheel as described in the "Wheels Removal and Installation" Section.

3. Unscrew the brake pipe nipple and disconnect the pipe.

CAUTION: *Disconnecting the brake pipe will result in brake fluid leakage. Have a rag handy to catch the fluid, and use the rubber bleeder valve cap to block off fluid flow at the pipe.*

4. If the caliper is to be disassembled, loosen the allen head shafts at this time.

Loosening the brake pipe nipple

Removing the caliper

5. Remove the mounting bolts, then remove the caliper.

6. Unscrew the allen head shafts (1) evenly, alternating between the two a little at a time, then remove caliper B (2). Pad B (3) may be removed at this time by removing its securing screw (12).

7. Remove the bolts which secure the caliper holder (4), taking care not to damage the boots (5) or O-rings (6), then remove pad A (7).

8. Remove the two shafts (1) from caliper A (8), then remove the piston dust seal (9) and pull the piston (10) straight out without twisting it. The piston may also be blown out with compressed air through the brake line outlet, if it is reluctant to leave its seat.

9. Remove the seal (11), taking care not to damage the cylinder wall. A special tool (Part No. 56019-111) is available for this job, however a suitable substitute may be used.

10. All remaining parts such as the bleeder valve (16) and nipple (18) may be removed at this time if so desired.

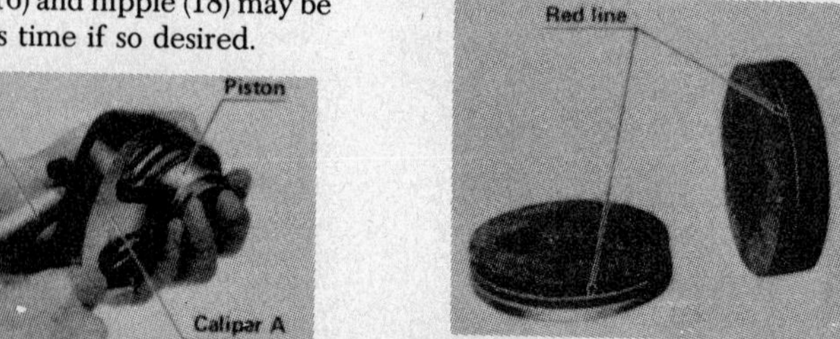

Blowing out the piston

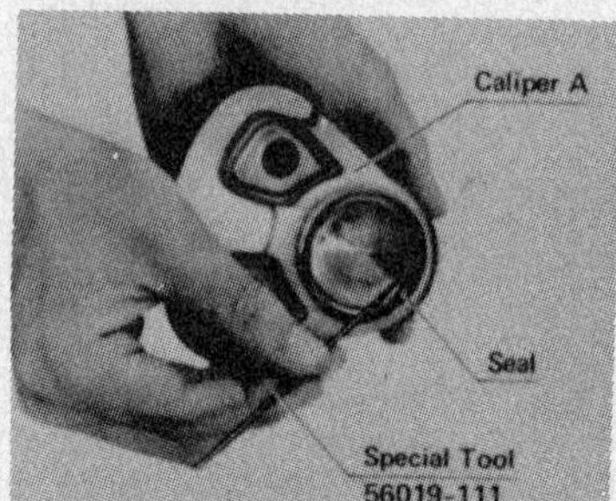

Removing the seal

Inspection and Repair

1. Clean all parts other than brake pads and oil seals in a suitable solvent, then blow them dry, taking care to pass air through all of the passages.

2. Inspect all parts for a worn or damaged condition, and replace them as necessary.

3. Inspect the brake pads for damage or excessive wear and replace them as necessary. If the surface of either pad is

Replace the pads before worn to the red line

worn to the red warning line, the pads should be replaced, preferably as a pair. Grease or oil on the pads can be removed with triclorethylene or gasoline. If the pads are oil impregnated, they should be replaced.

4. Inspect the oil seals for a worn, damaged, or cracked condition and replace them as necessary. If the seal around the piston, which serves to maintain the proper pad/disc clearance, is bad, one pad will wear more rapidly than the other, and the constant friction caused by the dragging pad will cause a sharp increase in brake and brake fluid temperature which might result in damage to the various assemblies. Replace the seal if any of the following conditions exist:

a. Oil leakage around pad A.

b. The brake overheats under normal conditions.

c. Pad A and pad B wear unevenly.

d. The seal is stuck to the piston.

e. If the seal has been reused once already.

5. Check the oil and dust seals, and the O-rings, for signs of wear, damage, or cracking, and replace them as necessary.

6. Inspect the caliper and piston for damage or wear past the following specifications, and replace them as necessary:

Piston Wear Chart

Standard	*Service Limit*
Cylinder, inside diameter	
1.5031-1.5039 in. (38.180-38.200 mm)	1.5045 in. (38.215 mm)
Piston, outside diameter	
1.5006-1.5019 in. (38.180-38.200 mm)	1.5002 in. (38.105 mm)

7. If there is a mushy feeling at the hand lever when the brake is applied, it may be due to excessive clearance between the caliper halves. This is not a problem concerning braking efficiency, and has only to do with the feeling at the hand lever. Check on this in the following manner:

a. Assemble the caliper as described in the "Assembly and Installation" Section. Be sure that the caliper shafts are torqued to 22-26 ft lbs.

b. Check the clearance between the caliper halves using a 0.012 in. (0.30 mm) feeler gauge. If the clearance is greater than this, the caliper must be replaced.

NOTE: *This is a quality control, warranty covered problem which exists on some machines from the beginning of production to serial number Z1E-01498, and from Z1E-04860 to Z1E-05322. The caliper part number is 43041-004.*

Checking clearance between the caliper halves

Assembly and Installation

1. Assembly is basically in the reverse order of disassembly. Use new O-rings and oil seals whenever possible, and use the torque specifications given at the beginning of the "Front Disc Brake" Section.

2. Clean all of the caliper components with either brake fluid or alcohol, then coat them all liberally with fresh brake fluid.

3. Bleed the system thoroughly, after it is installed, as described in the "Bleeding the Brake System" Section.

DISC

Removal and Installation

1. Remove the front wheel as described in the "Wheels Removal and Installation" Section.

2. Bend down the lockwasher (1) locking tabs, and remove the disc mounting bolts (2) to free the disc (3) for removal.

3. When installing the disc, use new lockwashers whenever possible. Torque the mounting bolts to 140-190 ft lbs (1.-6-2.2 kg/m), then bend the locking tab against the flat of the bolt.

Inspection and Repair

1. Clean any oil off the surface of the disc using either trichlorethylene or gasoline.

2. Inspect the disc for deep score marks or wear, and measure the disc with a micrometer at its most worn part. The disc can be cut safely up to 0.050 in. to remove score marks, but if the scoring, or wear, runs deeper than the disc's serviceable thickness of 0.217 in. (5.5 mm), the disc must be replaced. Standard thickness for the disc is 0.276 in. (7.0 mm).

3. Check the disc for a warped condition. Warping causes both the disc and pads to wear down quickly, and also results in overheating and poor braking efficiency. Check for warpage in one of the following ways:

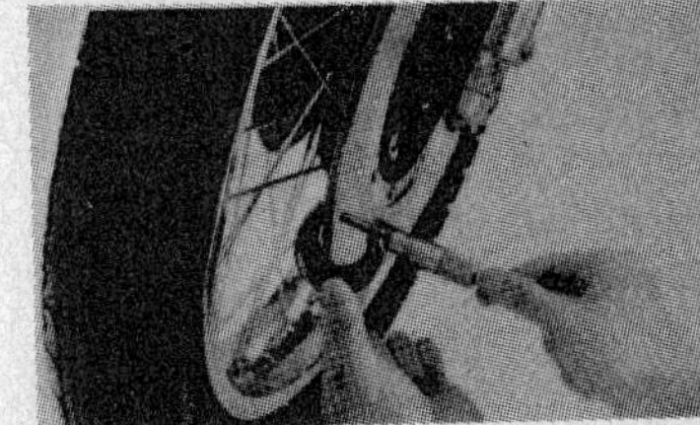

Checking the disc for wear

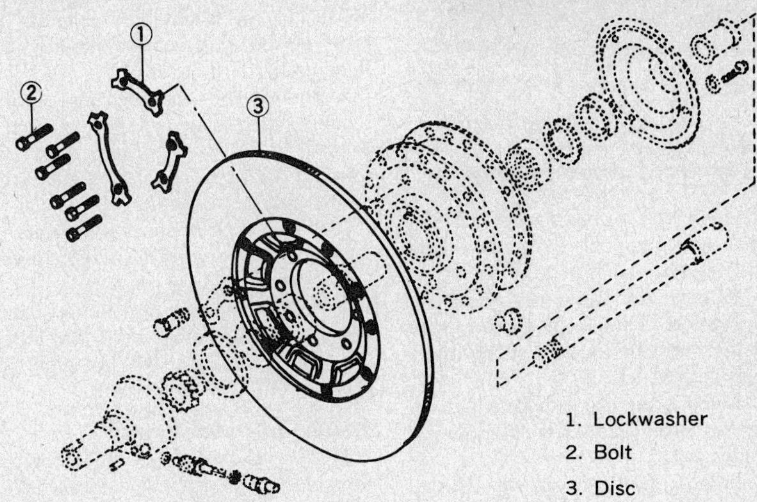

Disc assembly

Checking the disc for a warped condition

a. Place the disc on a perfectly flat surface, and use a feeler gauge under the rim to check for clearance which would indicate warpage.

b. With the completely assembled wheel still on the bike, check the runout with a dial indicator as illustrated.

c. If the disc is warped less than 0.-004 in. (0.1 mm) it needn't be replaced, but if it is warped in excess of 0.012 in. (0.3 mm), it must be replaced.

MASTER CYLINDER

Removal and Disassembly

1. Read the cautionary notes at the beginning of the "Front Disc Brake" Section.

.2 Remove the right-side rear view mirror.

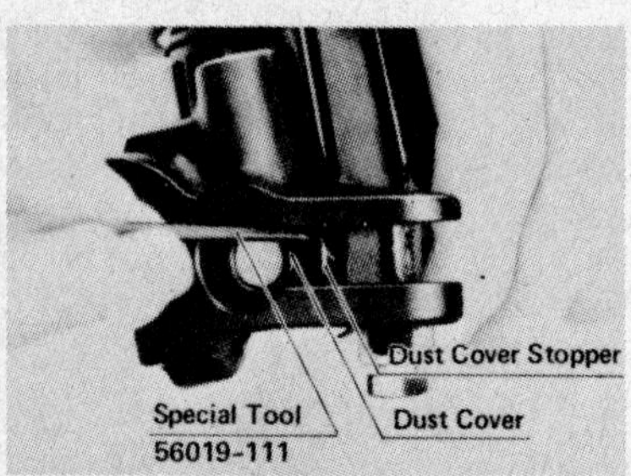

Removing the dust cover stopper

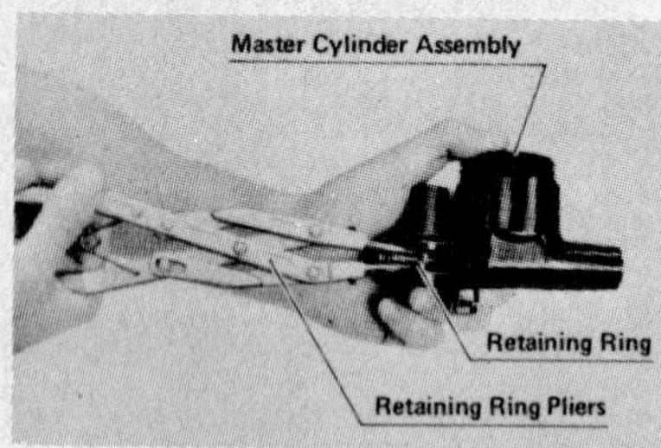

Removing the retaining ring

3. Open the bleeder valve on the caliper, and pump all of the brake fluid out of the system.

4. Remove the banjo bolt which secures the brake line to the master cylinder, then remove the rest of the brake line as desired.

5. Remove the clamp bolts which secure the master cylinder, and remove the cylinder.

6. Remove the reservoir cap (1), diaphragm plate (2), and diaphragm (3), then empty out any residual brake fluid.

7. Remove the brake lever (4), then use either the special tool (Part No. 56019-111) or a suitable substitute to remove the dust cover stopper (5). Remove the dust cover (6).

8. Remove the retaining ring (7) using retaining ring pliers, then remove the stopper (8), piston (9), primary cup (10), spring (11), and check valve (12) from the master cylinder body (22).

CAUTION: *Do not attempt to remove the secondary cup (13) from the piston as this will damage the cup.*

9. Any remaining components such as the pressure switch (29), the 3-way fitting (30), the brake lines (35) and pipe (31) may be removed at this time.

Inspection and Repair

1. Clean all parts in a suitable solvent, then blow them dry. Use compressed air to blow out all passages. A clogged relief port will result in the pads dragging on the disc.

2. Inspect the master cylinder bore for signs of wear, rust, pitting, or damage, and replace it as necessary. The master cylinder and piston must also be replaced if worn past their serviceable limit.

3. Inspect the primary and secondary cups for signs of wear, damage, rotting, or swelling, and replace them as necessary. Leaking at the brake lever is an indication of bad cups. The piston must also be replaced if the secondary cup is damaged, however, it's best to replace the cups as a set.

4. Inspect the spring for signs of wear or damage, and replace it as necessary.

5. Replace the rubber dust cover if it is damaged or aged.

6. Inspect the fittings, hoses, and pipes for signs of wear, cracking, rust, or other damage, and replace them as necessary.

7. The necessary specifications for determining the serviceability of the master cylinder components are as follows:

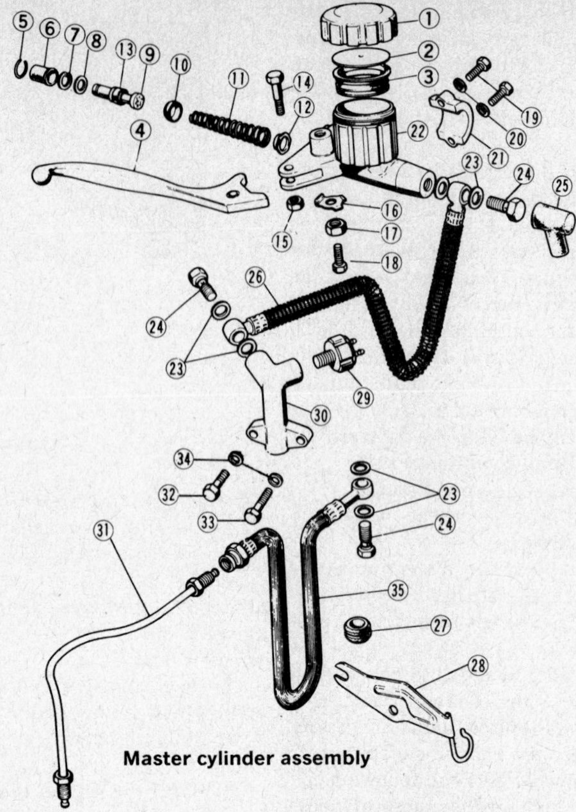

Master cylinder assembly

1. Cap
2. Plate
3. Cap seal
4. Brake lever
5. Dust seal stopper
6. Dust seal
7. Circlip
8. Piston stopper
9. Piston assembly
10. Primary cup
11. Spring assembly
12. Check valve assembly
13. Secondary cup
14. Bolt
15. Nut
16. Lockwasher
17. Nut
18. Bolt
19. Bolt
20. Washer
21. Master cylinder mounting
22. Master cylinder body
23. Washer
24. Banjo bolt
25. Dust cover
26. Hose
27. Grommet
28. Bracket
29. Pressure switch
30. 3-way fitting
31. Pipe
32. Bolt
33. Bolt
34. Washer
35. Hose

Master Cylinder Specifications

Measurement	Standard		Service Limit	
	Single Disc	Dual Disc	Single	Dual
Cylinder inside diameter	0.5512-0.5529 in. (14.000-14.043 mm)	0.6248-0.6265 in. (15.870-15.913 mm)	0.5543 in. (14.080 mm)	0.6280 in. (15.950 mm)
Piston outside diameter	0.5495-0.5506 in. (13.957-13.984 mm)	0.6231-0.6242 in. (15.827-15.854 mm)	0.5472 in. (13.900 mm)	0.6209 in. (15.770 mm)
Primary, secondary cup diameter	0.5768-0.5965 in. (14.650-15.150 mm)	0.6476-0.6673 in. (16.450-16.950 mm)	0.5709 in. (14.500 mm)	0.6417 in. (16.300 mm)
Spring length (free)	2.008 in. (51.0 mm)	1.709 in. (43.4 mm)	1.890 in. (48.0 mm)	1.504 in. (40.? mm)

Assembly and Installation

1. Assembly is basically in the reverse order of disassembly. Make sure that all internal parts are perfectly clean, and liberally coat them all with clean brake fluid before installing.
2. Make sure that the primary cup and the check valve are not installed backwards, and make sure that they aren't distorted or turned sideways after insertion.
3. Use either the factory tool (Part No. 56019-110) or a suitable substitute to install a new retaining ring in its groove in the cylinder wall. The same tool can be used to install the boot and boot stopper.

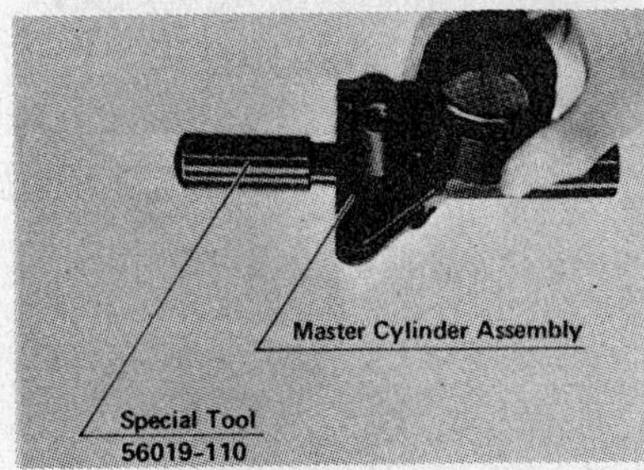

Installing the retaining ring

Installing the master cylinder

4. Install the master cylinder so that the small projection is toward the throttle grip. Secure the lower clamp bolts first, then secure the upper bolts. The bolts should be torqued to 55-75 in. lbs (0.63-0.88 kg/m).
5. Fill the master cylinder with brake fluid and bleed the system as described in the "Bleeding the Brake System" Section. Do not overtighten the master cylinder cap.

BLEEDING THE BRAKE SYSTEM

A mushy feeling at the brake hand lever can often be traced to air in the brake system. Brake fluid is not easily compressed, so that when the lever is operated, almost all of the force applied to the lever is transmitted to the brake caliper. Air, on the other hand is easily compressed, so that any air in the system quickly compresses before the fluid does. This means that some of the lever travel is used in compressing the air without actually applying force to the caliper, resulting in inefficient braking.

The brake system should be bled whenever the action at the hand lever feels soft or spongy, whenever brake fluid is changed, or whenever a brake line fitting has been loosened or disconnected. Bleed the brake system in the following manner:

NOTE: *Read the cautionary notes at the beginning of the "Front Disc Brake" Section.*

1. Remove the reservoir cap and check that there is plenty of fluid in the reservoir. The fluid level must be checked several times during the bleeding operation, and replenished as necessary. If the fluid in the reservoir runs completely out at any time during the bleeding operation, air will enter the system, and the procedure will have to be begun again.
2. Slowly pump the brake lever until no air bubbles can be seen rising up through the fluid from the holes at the bottom of the reservoir. When no more bubbles appear, the master cylinder end of the brake system has been purged of all air.
3. Replace the reservoir cap, and run a clear plastic hose from the caliper bleeder valve into a container. Pump the brake lever until it becomes hard, then, while holding the lever squeezed, quickly open (turn counterclockwise) and close the bleeder valve. Repeat the operation until no more air can be seen coming out into the plastic hose. During this process repeatedly check the fluid level in the reservoir, and replenish it as necessary.

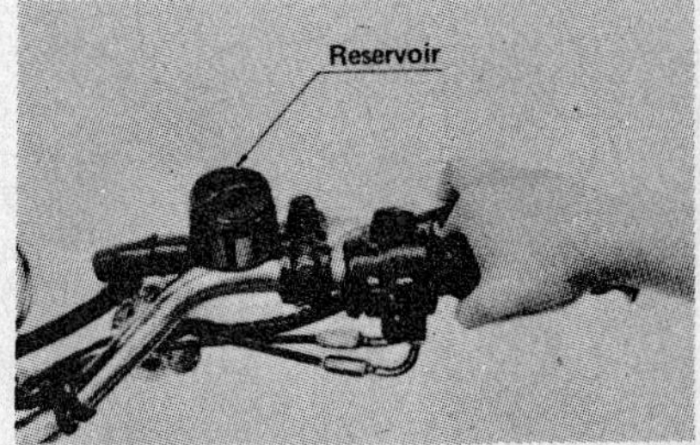

Pumping the brakes

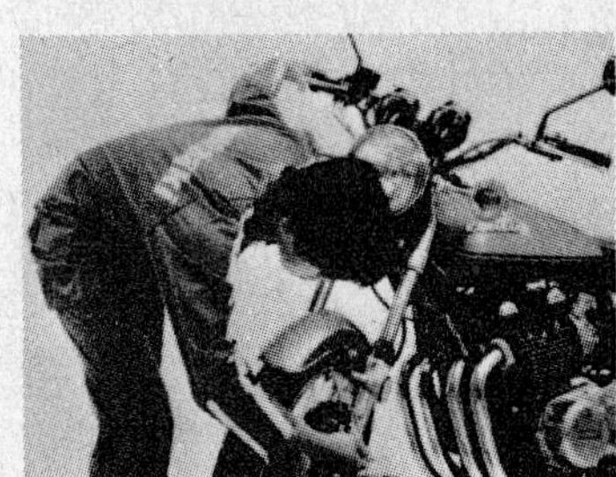

Bleeding the brakes

4. If a double disc has been fitted, repeat the above Step on the other side.
5. When the system has been bled, replace the rubber cap on the bleeder valve(s), and check the fluid level in the reservoir once more. The handlebars must be turned so that the reservoir is level, and the fluid must come up to the level line scribed inside the reservoir.

Fill the reservoir to the level line

NOTE: *If twin brakes are used and it becomes difficult to get a firm feeling at the lever, bleed the brake closest to the master cylinder first. Stretching the brake hoses while pumping up the system will help eliminate air bubbles trapped in the system.*

Rear Hub

DISASSEMBLY

1. Remove the rear wheel as described in the "Wheels Removal and Installation" Section. Refer to the accompanying illustration.
2. Remove the axle nut (25), washer (27), and distance collar (24), then remove the axle (23) by withdrawing it through the left side.
3. Remove the panel assembly (1) from the hub (10), then disassemble the panel assembly in the following manner:
   a. Remove the two cotter pins (9) and double washer (8) which secure the brake shoes.
   b. Use a punch to mark the original position of the brake cam lever (2) and the brake cam (5), then remove the pinch bolt (3) and lever.
   NOTE: *Lever removal can be made easy by using a screwdriver to pry at the pinch bolt slot while pulling the lever off the cam.*
   c. Remove the dust seal (4), then remove the brake shoes (6) and cam (5) by prying the shoes up evenly and removing them along with the cam.
   d. Remove the brake return springs (7) from the shoes.
4. Separate the coupling assembly (15) from the hub (10), then disassemble it in the following manner:
   a. Remove the shock damper rubbers (12), distance collar (16), axle sleeve collar (20), and oil seal (19).
   b. Tap evenly around the bearing (18) inner race from the inside of the coupling assembly (15) with a suitable drift until the bearing comes out.
5. Tap evenly around the inner race of the panel side bearing (14) from the sprocket side until it comes out, remove the distance collar (13), then tap evenly around the inner race of the coupling assembly side bearing (11) from the panel side until it comes out.
6. The rear sprocket (28) can be removed by bending up the lockwasher locking tabs, and removing the mounting nuts and bolts.
   NOTE: *If just the sprocket is to be removed it is not necessary to disassemble the hub. Remove the left-side mufflers, the sprocket mounting bolts, the rear wheel, and then the sprocket.*

INSPECTION AND REPAIR

1. Clean all parts, other than the brake shoes, seals, and rubber dampers in a suitable solvent, then blow them dry.
2. Inspect the brake drum for a warped, scored, or damaged condition, and replace it as necessary. Measurements should be taken in no less than two different places. If the drum is scored or worn out of round it can be turned down as long as turning it doesn't exceed the specified limits which are as follows:

Brake Drum Diameter Chart

Standard	*Service Limit*
7.874-7.881 in. (200.000-200.185 mm)	7.904 in. (200.75 mm)

Measuring the rear hub

3. Inspect the brake shoes for excessive or uneven wear, or for oil or grease impregnation, and replace them as necessary. Surface glazing or high spots can be removed by sanding. The shoes should be measured in several spots, and they must be replaced if worn anywhere past their serviceable limits which are as follows:

Brake Shoe Wear Chart

Standard	*Service Limit*
0.1909-0.2146 in. (4.85-5.45 mm)	0.118 in. (3.00 mm)

Measuring brake shoe lining thickness

4. Inspect the brake return springs for a worn, pitted, collapsed, or otherwise damaged condition, and replace them as

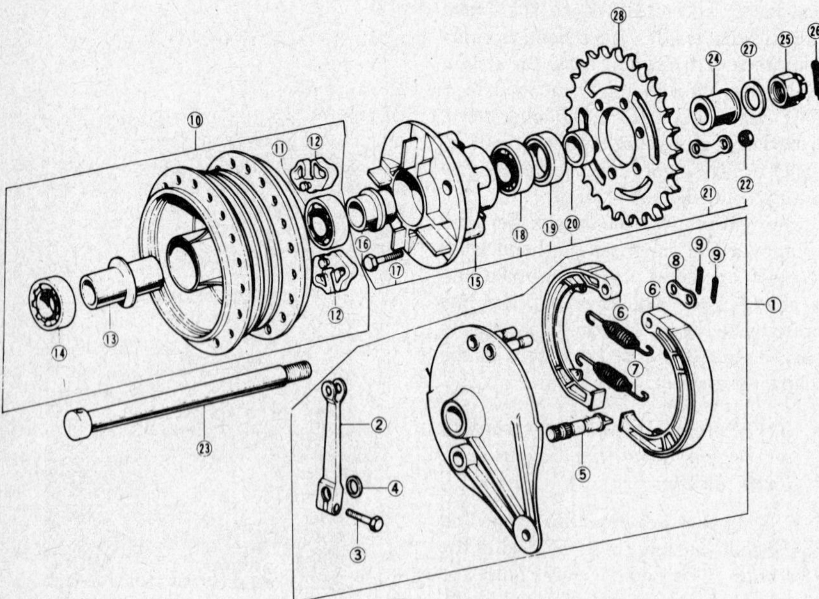

Rear hub assembly

1. Panel assembly
2. Brake cam lever
3. Bolt
4. Dust seal
5. Brake cam
6. Brake shoe
7. Spring
8. Double washer
9. Cotter pin
10. Drum assembly
11. Bearing
12. Shock damper rubber
13. Spacer
14. Bearing
15. Coupling
16. Distance collar
17. Bolt
18. Bearing
19. Oil seal
20. Sleeve collar
21. Washer
22. Nut
23. Axle
24. Distance collar
25. Nut
26. Cotter pin
27. Washer
28. Rear sprocket

necessary. The brake spring free length specifications are as follows:

5. Inspect the brake camshaft and backing plate for signs of wear or damage, and replace them individually or as a pair as necessary. These measurements are critical if efficient braking is to be maintained, and therefore should be done with micrometers as illustrated. The service limits for these items are as follows:

Brake Springs Length Chart

Standard	*Service Limit*
2.62 in. (66.5 mm)	2.72 in. (69.0 mm)

Measuring brake spring free length

6. Measure the rear axle run-out in the manner indicated, and replace it if run-out exceeds 0.008 in. (0.2 mm).

7. Inspect the rubber dampers for signs of cracking, damage, or rotting, and replace them as necessary.

8. Consult the "Maintenance" Chapter for additional information concerning the rear sprocket.

Brake Camshaft/Backing Plate Specs.

Standard	*Service Limit*
Camshaft	
0.6676-0.6687 in. (16.957-16.984 mm)	0.6626 in. (16.83 mm)
Shaft hole	
0.6693-0.6704 in. (17.000-17.027 mm)	0.6764 in. (17.18 mm)

Measuring the brake camshaft

Measuring rear axle run-out

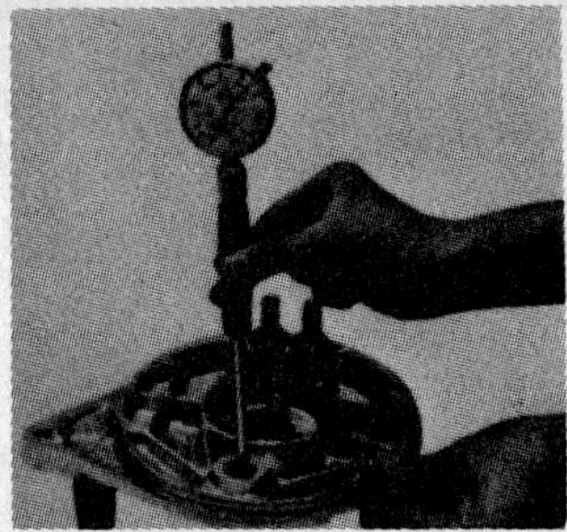

Measuring the inside diameter of the camshaft hole

Lubricating the dampers will make hub assembly easier

ASSEMBLY

1. Assembly is in the reverse order of disassembly. Use new oil seals, locking tabs, and cotter pins whenever possible.

NOTE: *The small cotter pins which secure the brake shoes to the backing plate are sometimes difficult to locate. In a case like this, mechanic's wire will work as a substitute. Loop it through the holes in the pivots at least twice.*

2. Use either the special factory tools (Part Nos. 57001-139 and 57001-140), or a suitable substitute, when installing the bearings and oil seals.

3. When installing the rear sprocket, torque the mounting nuts to 23-30 ft lbs (3.1-4.2 kg/m), and bend the locking tab up against a flat of the nut.

4. Lubricate the brake pivots, brake shoe anchor pins, brake return spring ends, and the brake camshaft surface and groove with grease. Be sure that the camshaft groove is filled, but take care not to overlubricate, as this may result in grease on the brake shoes and drum.

5. Install the rear wheel on the machine as described in the "Wheels Removal and Installation" Section, then adjust the rear brake and chain as described in the "Maintenance" Section.

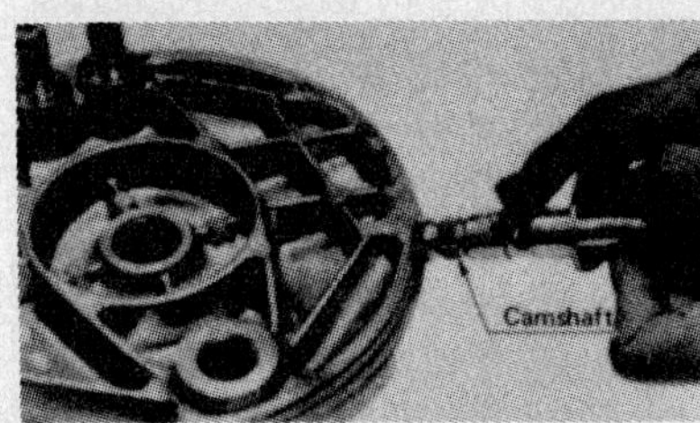

Lubricating the camshaft

FINAL DRIVE

Drive Chain

REMOVAL

NOTE: *The drive chain may be cut or broken with a chain breaker if it is going to be discarded and replaced with a master link type chain. Otherwise, the chain must never be cut.*

1. Remove the chain cover in the following manner:

a. Remove the chain oil pump cover screws and cover.

b. Slide back the hose clamp and disconnect the inlet hose from the pump. One of the cover screws can be used to plug the hose to prevent oil leakage.

c. Remove the left footrest and shift pedal. The clamp bolt must be completely removed before the shifter can be removed.

d. Remove the starter cover and cover gasket.

e. Remove the chain cover mounting bolts, then remove the cover.

f. Remove the cotter pin from the clutch release lever, and disconnect the clutch cable.

2. Loosen the cylinder exhaust flange bolts and the muffler mounting bolts for the two left-hand mufflers, and either remove or swing the pipes up out of the way.

3. Remove the lower mounting bolt from the left-side rear shock absorber.

4. Loosen the chain adjusters and back off the adjusting nuts so that the chain is as loose as possible.

5. Remove the rear axle cotter pin, loosen the axle nut, and push the rear wheel forward in the swing arm.

6. Remove the engine sprocket in the following manner:

a. Remove the clutch pushrod and sprocket guard.

b. Send back the lockwasher locking tab.

c. Secure the sprocket so that it won't turn by using a special tool (Part No. 57001-118), a suitable substitute, or by engaging the transmission in Low gear, then remove the sprocket and disengage the chain.

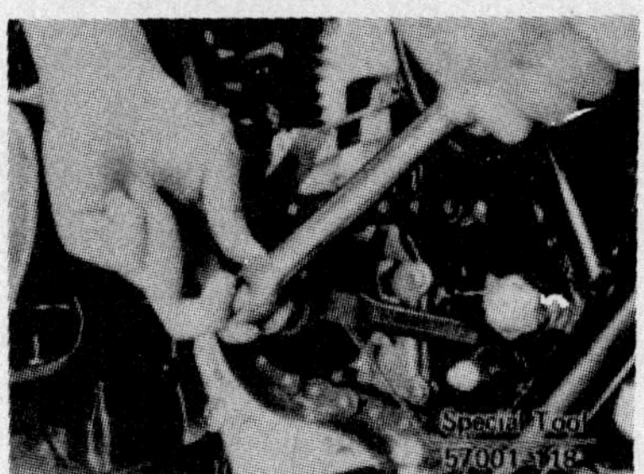

Removing the engine sprocket

7. Disconnect the rear brake torque link at the rear hub, remove the brake rod adjusting nut and disconnect the rod from the lever by rotating the brake backing plate, and remove the two pinch bolts and stoppers at the swing arm chain adjusters.

NOTE: *Remove the spring and link pin from the brake lever and put them back on the rod to avoid losing them.*

8. Push the left shock absorber out of the swing arm, loop the chain over the swing arm, and slide the rear wheel out of the swing arm.

9. Remove the nut from the swing arm pivot shaft, and withdraw the shaft. Tilt the swing arm until the pivot section clears the frame, then drop the chain through the gap.

INSPECTION

1. Check the drive chain for signs of wear, cracks on the rollers, bushings, or roller links, or for kinking or binding, and replace it if any of these conditions exist. Thoroughly lubricating the chain may help free kinked or bound links.

2. Replace the chain if it is worn more that 2% of its original length. This can be determined by either measuring the chain in the following manner:

a. Stretch the chain taut by using the

Stretching the chain with a weight

chain adjusters, or by hanging a 20 lb (10 kg) weight on the bottom run of the chain.

b. Remove the chain guard and measure the length of 20 links along a straight line from the center of the first pin to the center of the twenty-first pin.

Measuring the chain

c. If the length of the chain exceeds the standard length of 15.0 in. (381 mm) by more than 5/16 in. (8 mm), the chain must be replaced.

3. Inspect both the drive (engine) and

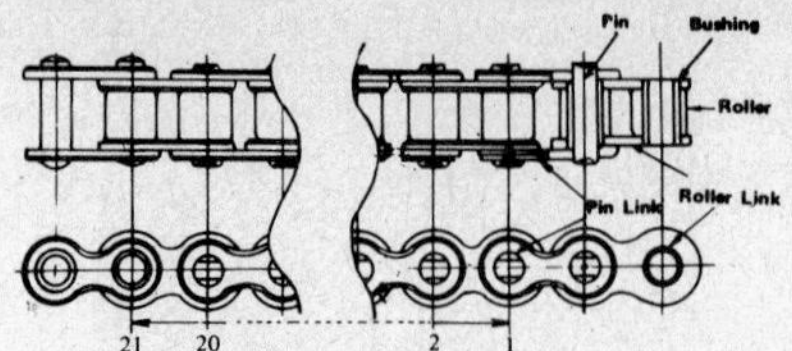

Measure along here

driven sprockets for signs of wear, damage, or a warped condition, and replace them as necessary if worn past the service limits given below:

Measuring rear sprocket diameter

Engine Sprocket Diameter Chart

Standard	*Service Limit*
3.376-3.384 in. (85.76-85.96 mm)	3.346 in. (85.0 mm)

Rear Sprocket Diameter and Run-out Chart

Standard	*Service Limit*
Diameter	
8.560 in. (217.4 mm)	8.484 in. (215.5 mm)
Runout	
under 0.012 in. (under 0.3 mm)	0.020 in. (0.5 mm)

INSTALLATION

1. Installation is basically in the reverse order of removal.

2. Make sure that the chain adjustment is loose enough to allow the engine sprocket and chain to fit properly, then readjust it afterwards.

3. Make sure that the lockwasher tab seats in the hole in the sprocket, and bend up one side of the washer after securing the sprocket nut.

4. Secure the sprocket nut to 87-108 ft lbs (12-15 kg/m).

Disassembling the fork tube and slider

5. Use an oil seal guide (Part No. 57001-130) to prevent damage to the seal while installing the chain cover.

6. Rotate the rear wheel until the pin inside the output shaft and the groove in the chain oil pump shaft are in alignment before installing the cover.

SUSPENSION

Front Forks

FORK TUBES

Removal and Disassembly

1. Remove the front wheel as described in the "Wheels Removal and Installation" Section.

2. Remove the front fender mounting bolts and fender.

3. Remove the brake caliper and place it out of the way.

NOTE: *The caliper need not be disconnected from the brake line pipe, however the assembly should be tied to or rested on something to avoid bending the pipe.*

4. Remove the bolt (2) from the top of the tube if the fork is to be disassembled once it's removed. If only the slider is to be removed, it may be done now by removing the allen bolt (30) from the bottom.

NOTE: *If you've removed or loosened the top bolt (2), the cylinder assembly (19) will rotate and you wont't be able to remove the allen bolt without the assistance of the special factory tool (Part No. 57001-142).*

5. If you wish to remove the entire fork leg, remove the top bolt (2) and the clamp bolts (6 and 16), and pull the assembly down and out. If you use screwdrivers to spread the clamps on the stem head (4) and stem (15) assemblies the legs will come out more easily.

6. Invert the assembly and dump out the spring (18) and fork oil. If the allen bolt (30) has been removed, the inner tube assembly (19) will also come out.

7. Remove the circlip (36) from the inner tube using snap-ring pliers, and remove the cylinder assembly (20) from the tube.

8. Remove the dust seal (21) from the outer tube (25), then remove the circlip (22) and oil seal (24) using a sharp hook.

Clamp bolt locations

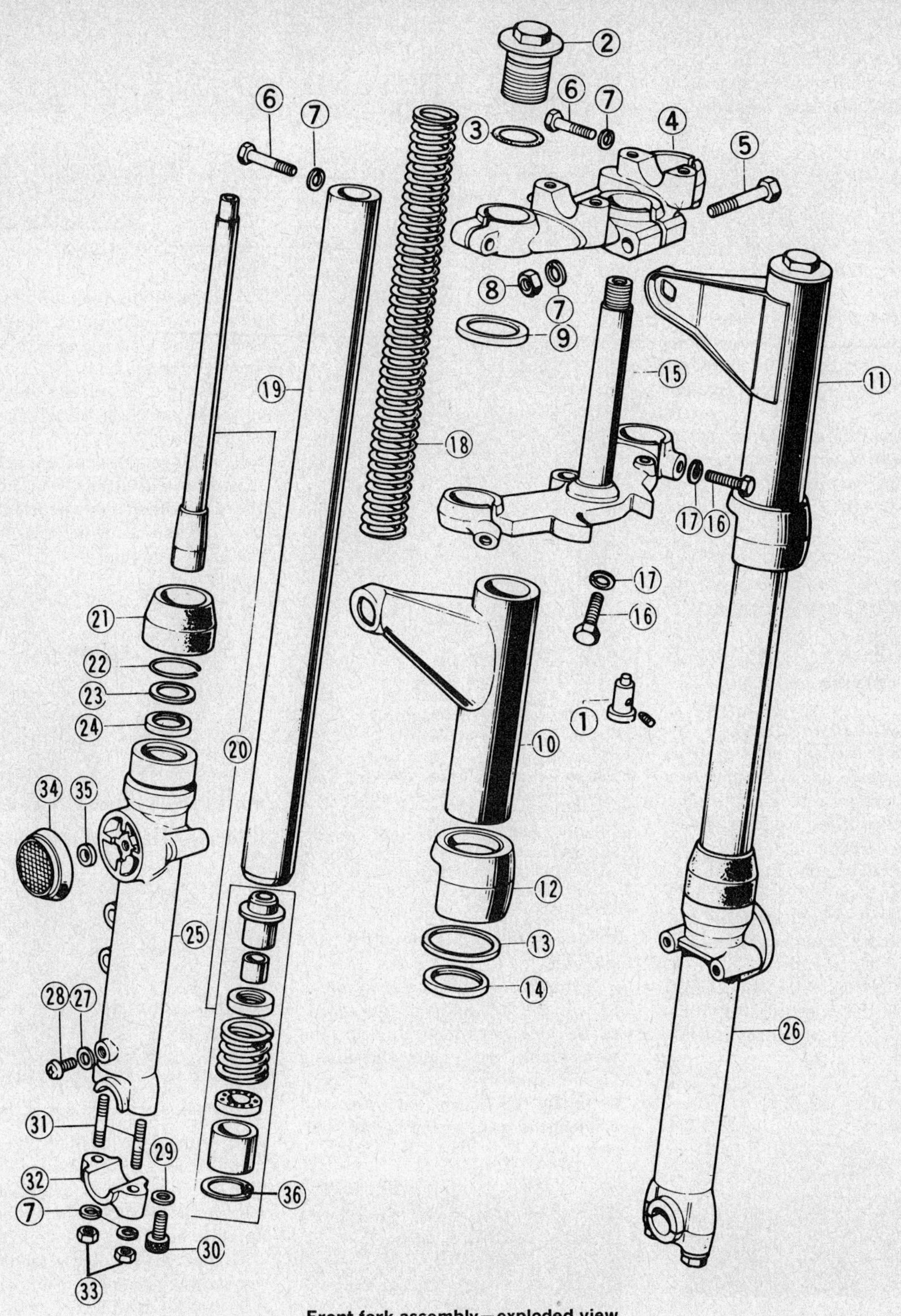

Front fork assembly—exploded view

1. Lock assy
2. Top bolt
3. O-ring
4. Stem head
5. Clamp bolt
6. Clamp bolt
7. Lockwasher
8. Nut
9. Washer
10. Headlight stay
11. Headlight stay
12. Stay guide
13. Washer
14. Gasket
15. Steering stem
16. Bolt
17. Lockwasher
18. Spring
19. Inner tube
20. Cylinder
21. Dust seal
22. Circlip
23. Washer
24. Oil seal
25. Outer tube
26. Outer tube
27. Gasket
28. Drain plug
29. Gasket
30. Allen bolt
31. Stud
32. Axle
33. Nut
34. Reflector
35. Rubber washer
36. Circlip

NOTE: *Once the oil seal has been disturbed it must be replaced.*

Inspection and Repair

1. Clean all of the components in a suitable solvent, then blow them dry.
2. Inspect all parts for signs of wear, scoring, stripped threads, warpage, or other damage and replace them as necessary.
3. Inspect the inner tube for a bent condition by rolling it across a flat surface, and have it straightened out if it isn't too severely bent.
4. Inspect the spring for a collapsed or damaged condition, and measure it to check its free length. If the spring is shorter than 19 1/16 in. (485 mm) it must be replaced.

NOTE: *If one spring is shorter than its serviceable limit, and the other is only marginally above the limit, it's a good idea to replace them both at this time.*

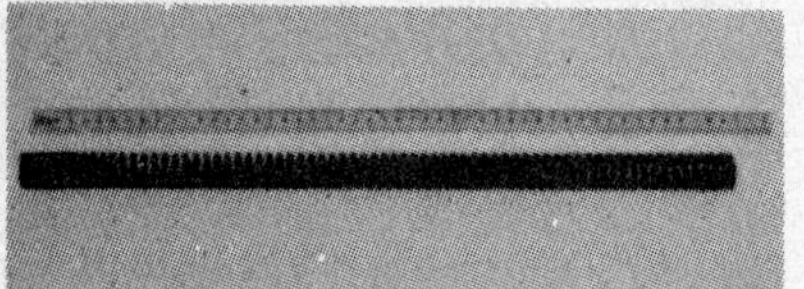

Measuring spring free length

Assembly and Installation

1. Assembly is basically in the reverse order of disassembly, and installation is in the reverse order of removal. Use new seals and circlips if the old ones are of questionable condition.
2. When installing new oil seals, use either the specail tool (Part No. 57001-141) or a suitably sized socket to drift the seal cleanly in to its seat. Lubricating the seal will make installation easier.
3. Before tightening the top clamp, make sure that the flange surface of the bolt in the top of the tube is level with the top of the steering stem.

Installing the oil seal

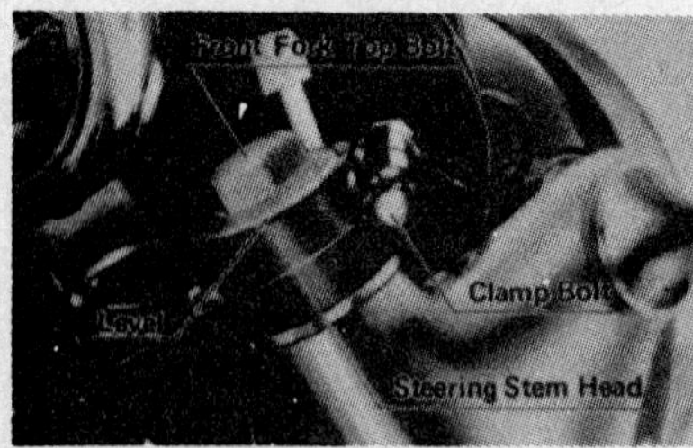

Lining up the tube in the triple clamp

4. Secure the upper clamp bolt to 140-155 in. lbs (1.6-1.8 kg/m), and the lower clamp bolt to 40-43 ft lbs (5.4-6.0 kg/m).

STEERING STEM AND BEARINGS

Removal

1. Remove the front wheel as described in the "Wheels Removal and Installation" Section.

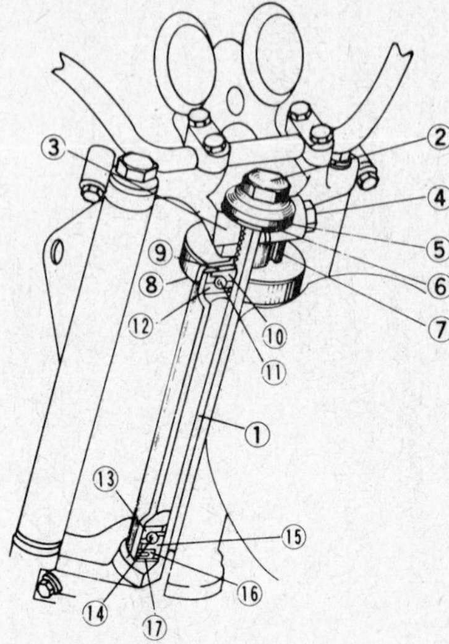

Steering stem assembly

1. Steering stem	10. Inner race
2. Stem head bolt	11. Bearing ball
3. Stem head	12. Outer race
4. Stem head clamp	13. Outer race
5. Washer bolt	14. Bearing ball
6. Spring washer	15. Inner race
7. Stem locknut	16. Oil seal
8. Steering cap	17. Washer
9. Washer	

2. Remove the fender mounting bolts and fender.
3. Remove the bolt from the bottom of the headlight shell and the two screws from the sides which serve to secure the beam assembly, and remove and unplug the beam assembly.
4. Unplug the turn signal wires, and disconnect the main wiring harness connectors.

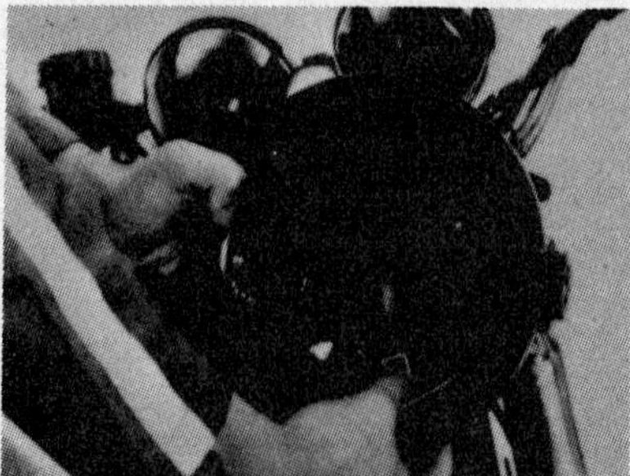

Removing the headlight shell

5. Remove the turn signals and headlight shell after removing the mounting hardware.
6. Disconnect the tachometer cable at the cylinder head.

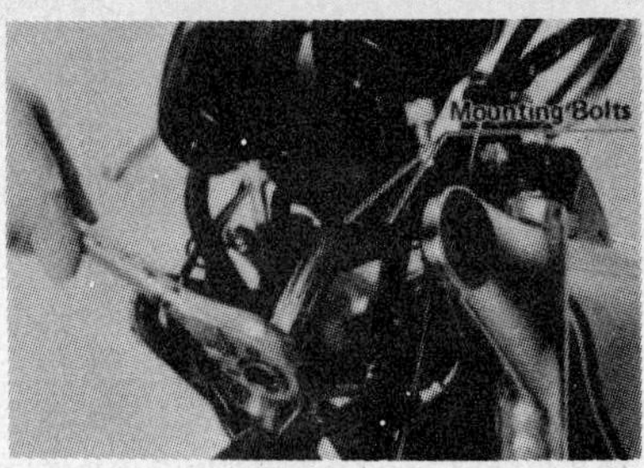

Removing the instrument cluster mounting bolts

7. Remove the mounting bolts which secure the instrument and ignition switch cluster, and remove the assembly. Remove the gas tank.
8. Remove the mirrors (if applicable), then disconnect the front brake pressure switch wires.
9. Remove the mounting bolts for the master cylinder, the 3-way fitting, and the caliper, then remove the entire brake system while taking care not to damage the brake line pipe.

Removing the front brake assembly

Handlebars placed out of the way

10. Unbolt the handlebars and allow them to rest on the tubes as illustrated, then loosen the 3 stem head clamp bolts, remove the stem head bolt, and remove the stem head.
11. Rest the handlebars on the frame, remove the two lower clamp bolts, the fork ears (headlight stay), and the fork tubes.

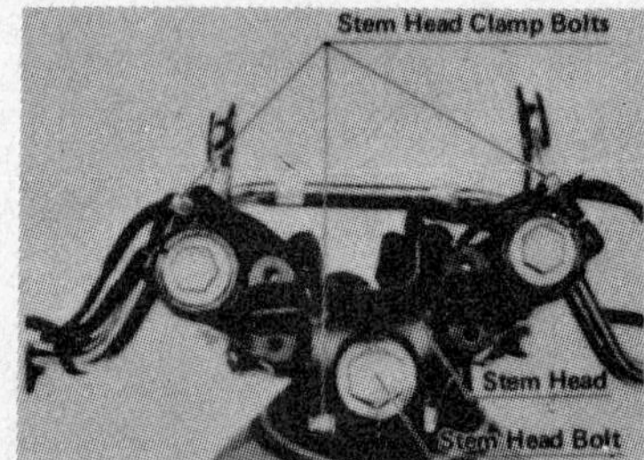

Clamp bolt locations

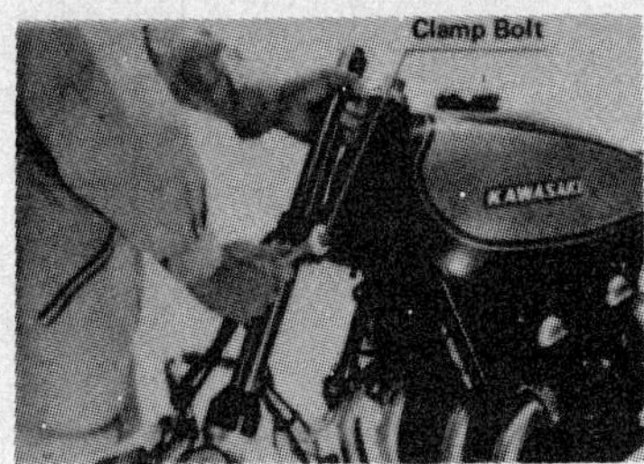

Removing the lower clamp bolts

12. Remove the steering stem locknut using a suitable hook spanner, and drop the stem out from the bottom. Remove the stem cap, upper inner race, and the bearings.

CAUTION: *When withdrawing the stem, be prepared to catch the lower race bearings in a suitable receptacle. Always keep the two bearing groups separate for installation in their original locations.*

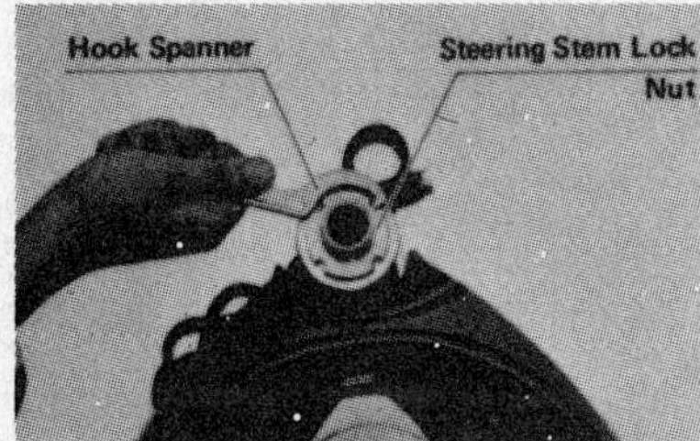

Removing the stem locknut

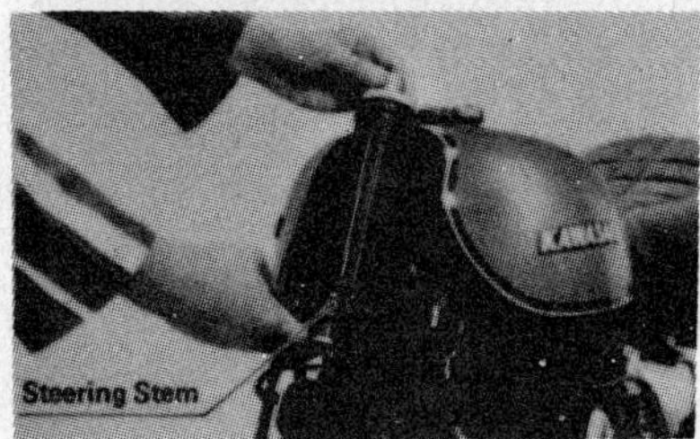

Removing the steering stem

13. Remove the bearing races, only if they must be replaced, by drifting them out with a suitable soft face drift. Drive the lower race out from the top, and the upper race out from the bottom. Tap evenly around the circumference of the race while removing the races.

14. Pull off the lower race which is pressed onto the steering stem by using either the special tool (Part No. 57001-135) or a suitable substitute. Try not to damage the grease seal under the race, or stretch it and pull it off over the race.

Inspection and Repair

1. Clean all parts, other than gaskets and seals, in a suitable solvent, and blow them dry.
2. Inspect all parts for signs of wear, stripped threads, or damage, and replace them as necessary.
3. Visually inspect the stem for a tilted condition and replace it if not perpendicular to the clamp.

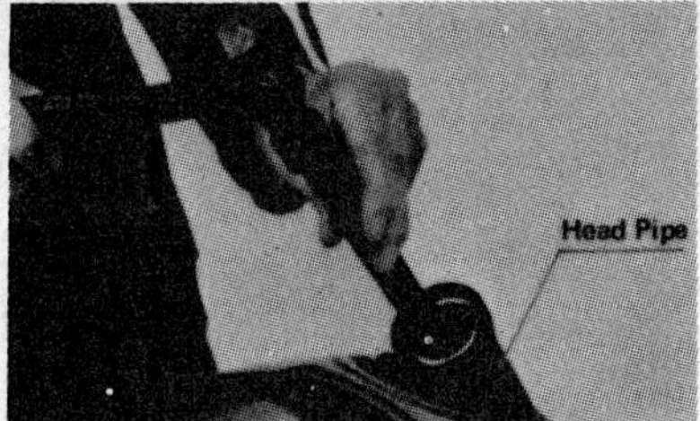

Drifting out the lower race

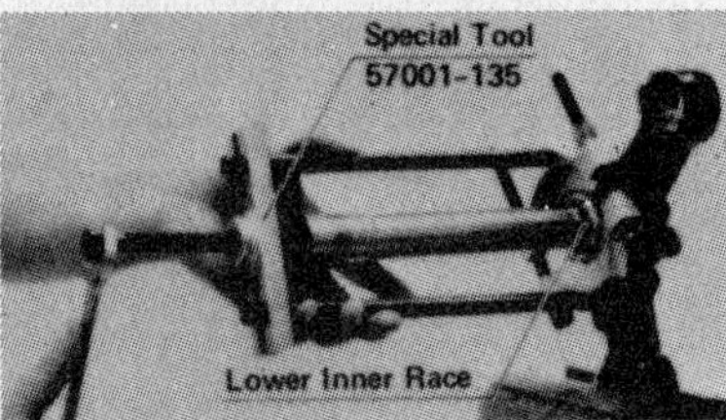

Pulling off the stem lower race

4. Inspect the bearings and races for signs of wear, scoring, or damage, and replace them as complete sets as necessary. Bright spots on the inner portion of the race indicate advanced wear, and will result in jerky steering.

Installation

1. Installation is basically in the reverse order of removal.
2. Liberally oil the outer races and drive them into the head pipe using either the special tools (Part Nos. 57001-139 and 57001-138) or suitable substitute such as a soft-faced drift. Be sure that they seat evenly in the pipe.
3. Oil the lower inner race and drive it onto the stem using either the special tool (Part No. 57001-137) or a suitable substitute. The race can be driven on using the clamping edges of a vise if necessary, but this is hard on the bottom of the clamp.

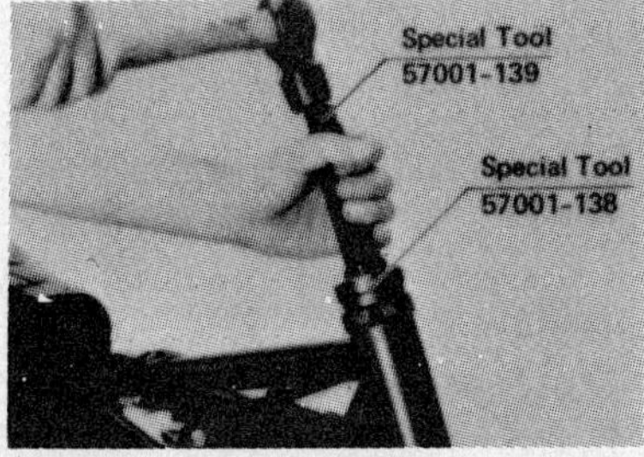

Installing the races using the special tools

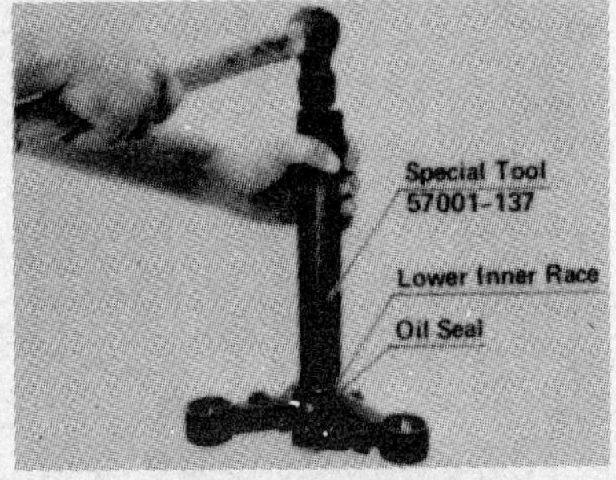

Driving on the lower inner race

NOTE: *If the special tools are being used, install a new seal before driving on the race. If you are going to drive it on using the edges of a vise, it's best to drive on the race and then stretch the seal on over the race.*

4. Liberally grease the bearing races, and stick the bearing in the grease. The upper race takes 19 bearings, and the lower race takes 20. Placing the lower bearings on the stem race will make installation easier.

Upper bearings in position

5. Insert the stem into the frame head, then install the upper inner race, cap and locknut.
6. Use a suitable hook spanner to tighten the locknut until the stem moves smoothly and freely to either side, but no play exists in the bearings.
7. Position the fork ears and guides between the two halves of the stem assembly, then slide the fork tubes up through them so that they protrude about 1¼ in. (30 mm) at the top. Snugging up the lower clamp bolt will hold the tubes in position.

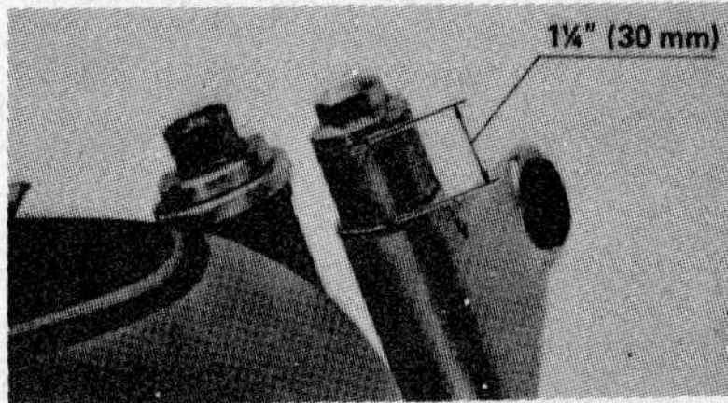

Fork tubes properly positioned

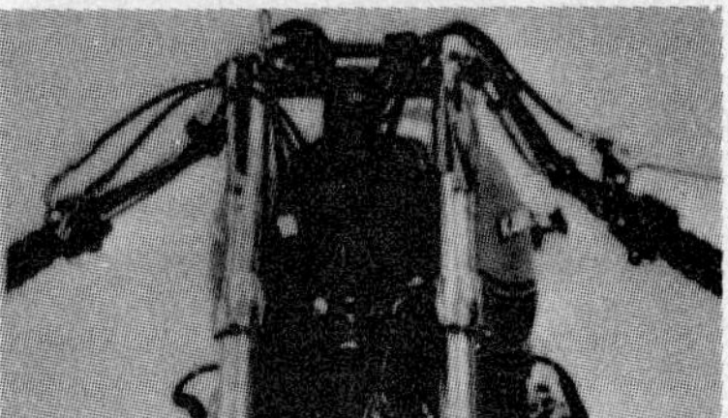
Handlebars out of the way

8. Position the handlebar assembly as illustrated, making sure that all the wires and cables are correctly routed.
9. Install the stem head, and secure the stem head bolt and the rear clamp bolt.
10. Loosen the lower clamp bolt, position the fork tube so that the flange surface of the fork top bolt is flush with the upper surface of the steering stem head,

then secure the upper and lower clamp bolts. The 3 upper clamp bolts should be secured to 140-155 in. lbs (1.6-1.8 kg/m), and the two lower clamp bolts should be torqued to 40-43 ft lbs (5.4-6.0 kg/m).

NOTE: *Secure the lower clamp bolts first, then the upper bolts.*

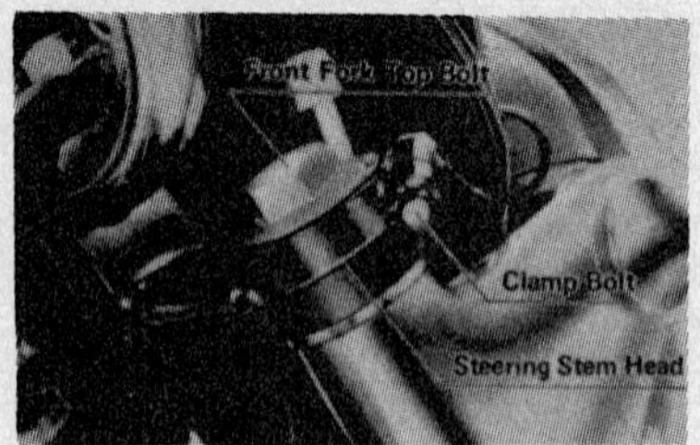

Fork tubes ready to be secured

11. Mount and bleed the disc brake assembly as described in the "Front Disc Brake" Section.

12. Mount and secure the ignition switch and instrument cluster, then mount, but do not secure, the headlight shell and turn signals.

13. Start, but do not tighten, the bolt which goes in the bottom of the headlight. Adjust the vertical height of the shell, then secure the shell, the bottom bolt, and the turn signals.

14. Connect the wiring harness connectors, then connect and install the headlight lamp unit.

NOTE: *The left turn signal lead goes to the green wire, and the right lead goes to the gray wire.*

15. Mount and secure the front fender, the brake hose clamp, and the front wheel.

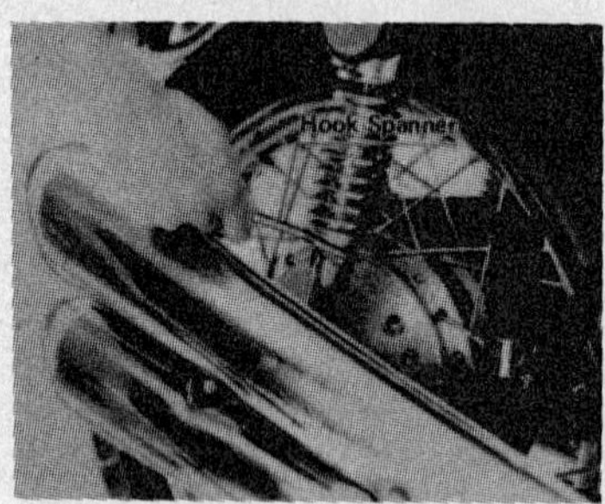

Adjusting the rear shocks

Rear Shock Absorbers

REMOVAL, DISASSEMBLY, AND INSTALLATION

1. Remove the mounting nut from the upper end, and the bolt from the lower end of each shock. If there is not sufficient clearance for the removal of the bottom mounting bolt, it will be necessary to loosen or remove the mufflers on the side in question.

2. Remove the mounting bolts for the chrome bar, and remove the bar, then pull the shock free of the mounting stud.

3. Disassemble the shock by compressing it until the upper keepers are free to be removed, the remove the keepers, cover, and spring. The upper mounting eye can now be unscrewed and removed if it or the rubber stopper is to be replaced.

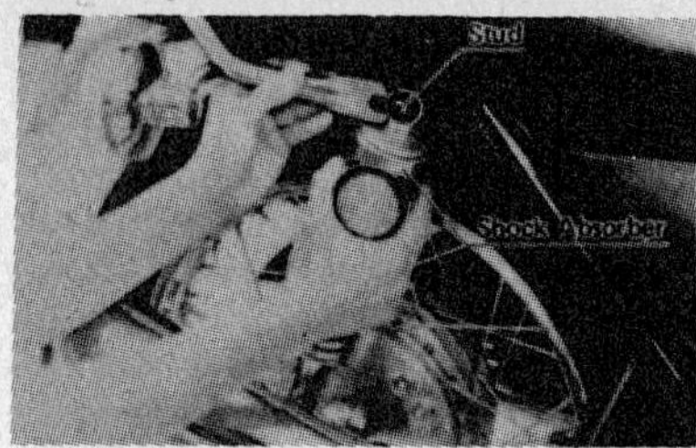

Removing the rear shocks

NOTE: *The shock can be compressed in a vise or by pressing it against the*

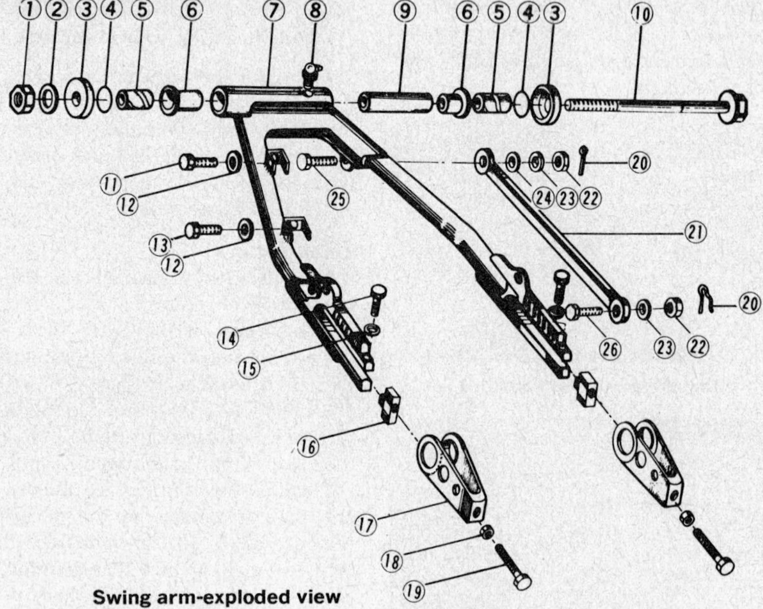

Swing arm-exploded view

1. Self-locking nut
2. Washer
3. Cap
4. O-ring
5. Sleeve
6. Bushing
7. Swing arm
8. Grease nipple
9. Distance collar
10. Pivot shaft
11. Chain guard mounting bolt 1
12. Washer
13. Chain guard mounting bolt 2
14. Chain adjuster stopper mounting bolt
15. Washer
16. Chain adjuster stopper mounting
17. Chain adjuster
18. Locknut
19. Adjuster bolt
20. Cotter pin
21. Torque link
22. Nut
23. Lockwasher
24. Washer
25. Bolt
26. Bolt

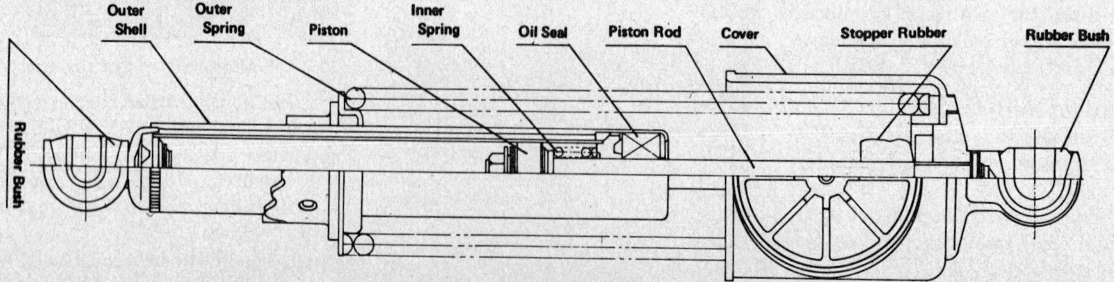

Rear shock absorber cross-section

floor while someone else removes the keepers.

4. Assembly and installation are in the reverse order of removal and disassembly. If you want to look racy, it's not necessary to replace the cover.

INSPECTION

1. Once the shock is disassembled, check its dampening action by pushing in the piston rod, and then pulling it back out. The rod should slip smoothly in until seated, and should take more effort to pull it back out than to push it in. Both shocks should react to this test in the same manner.

2. Replace the shocks, preferably as a set, if one or both fails the above test, if the seals leak, or if the rod is bent.

Swing Arm

REMOVAL AND DISASSEMBLY

1. Remove the rear wheel as described in the "Wheels Removal and Installation" Section.

2. Remove the rear shock absorber lower mounting bolts, then unscrew the swing arm pivot shaft nut, withdraw the shaft, and remove the swing arm.

3. Pull the sleeve (5) out of each end of the swing arm.

4. Position the distance collar (9) so that it seats against either bushing (6), or at least so it's off center, then, using a suitable bar as a drift, gently drift out the opposite side bushing. Invert the swing arm and remove the remaining bushing.

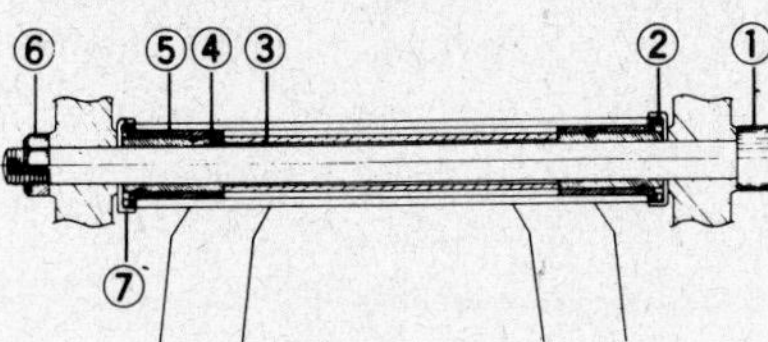

Swing arm cross-section

1. Pivot shaft
2. O-ring
3. Collar
4. Sleeve
5. Bushing
6. Self locknut
7. Cap

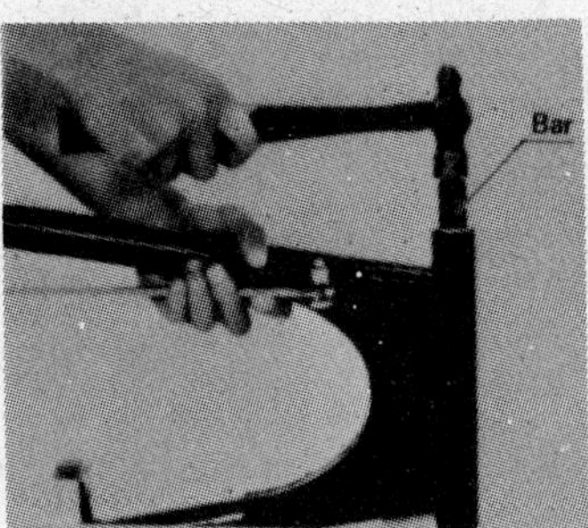

Drifting out a bushing

INSPECTION AND REPAIR

1. Clean all parts in a suitable solvent, then blow them dry.

2. Inspect the swing arm for stress signs, cracks, bends, or other damage, and have it repaired or replace it as necessary.

NOTE: *Any necessary welding should be done by a professional to assure rigidity and correct alignment.*

3. Inspect the sleeves for signs of wear or damage, and replace them as a set if either is in need of replacement. The standard outside diameter of a sleeve is 0.8653-0.8661 in. (21.979-22.171 mm), and the sleeve must be replaced if worn past its serviceable limit of 0.864 in. (21.95 mm).

4. Inspect the bushings for signs of wear or damage, and replace them as a set if either is in need of replacement. The standard inside diameter of a bushing is 0.8712-0.8729 in. (22.128-22.171 mm), and the bushing must be replaced if worn past its serviceable limit of 0.881 in. (22.37 mm).

5. Inspect the pivot shaft for signs of wear, scoring, excessive run-out, or other damage, and replace it as necessary. Check the run-out with a dial indicator and a pair of V-blocks as illustrated. If the run-out exceeds the standard allowance of under 0.004 in. (under 0.1 mm), the shaft must be straightened or replaced.

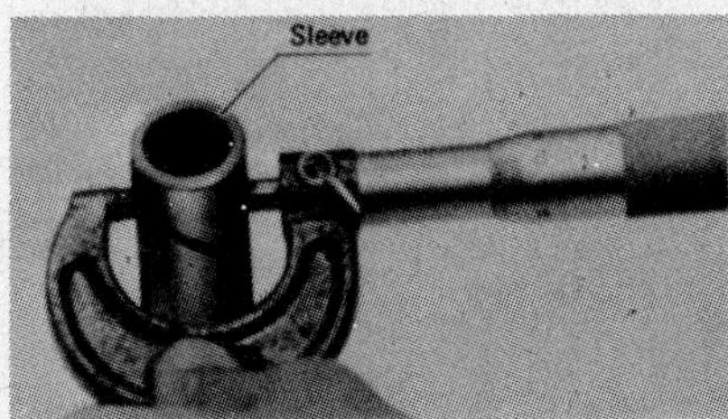

Measuring a sleeve for wear

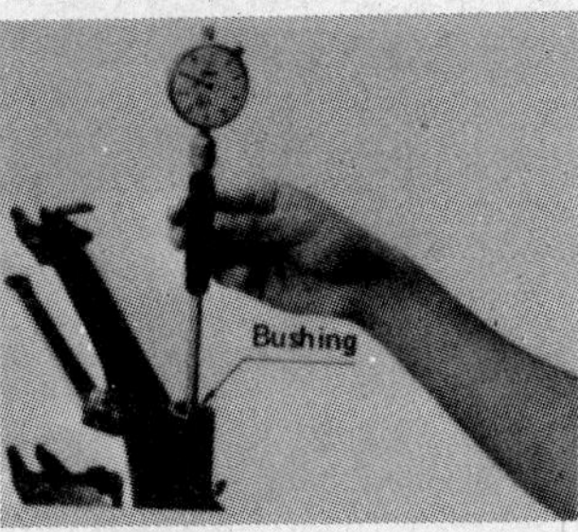

Measuring a bushing

Checking a pivot shaft run-out

ASSEMBLY AND INSTALLATION

1. Assembly is in the reverse order of disassembly, and installation is in the reverse order of removal. New O-rings and bushings should be used whenever possible, and the bushings should be oiled before being installed.

2. Thoroughly grease the swing arm by applying grease through the grease nipple until it runs out either end of the swing arm, then wipe off the excess.

3. Secure the pivot shaft to 87-108 ft lbs (12-15 kg/m).

MUFFLERS

The mufflers do not require any periodic maintenance, however if the gaskets leak or if the rubber connecting hose becomes hard and cracks, these parts should be replaced. Mufflers which are badly rusted or damaged should also be replaced in order to maintain efficient, and quiet, exhaust emission. Also, holes or leaks in the exhaust system may result in annoying popping sounds while the engine is backing down.

On models before engine number Z1E1100, the baffle tube fitted in the end of each muffler was secured by a rivet. In many cases, the rivet broke off causing the baffle to loosen up or fall out. On models with engine numbers from Z1E1100-Z1E2101, this condition was corrected by inserting a 3 mm screw through the rivet, and then securing it with a nut. On mod-

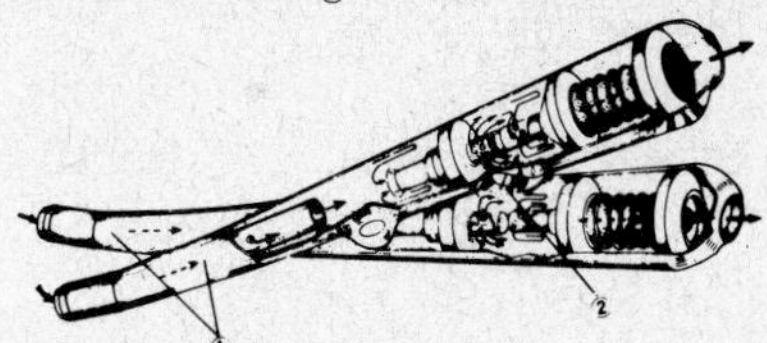

Muffler cross-section

1. Muffler 2. Connecting hose

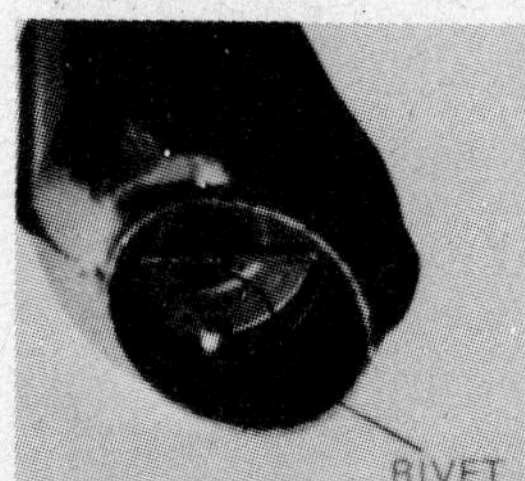

Rivet location

Drilling out the rivet

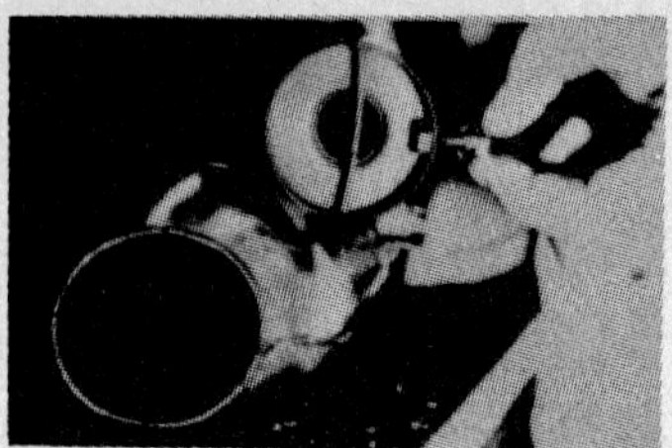

Installing a new baffle

els with engine numbers from Z1E2102-on, the rivet and screw have been replaced by a 6 mm bolt, secured by a 6 mm nut, which has been welded to the inside of the baffle tube.

Replacement baffles with a nut welded on are available, and should be installed as follows:

1. Remove the muffler from the machine, and drill out the rivet using either a 15/64 or a ¼ in. drill bit, then remove the old baffle.

2. Insert a new baffle (Part No. 18033-058), and secure it with a 6 mm hex bolt and lockwasher.

TORQUE SPECIFICATIONS

	English	Metric
Banjo bolt	19-23 ft lbs	2.5-3.3 kg/m
Bleeder valve	70-85 in. lbs	0.8-1.0 kg/m
Brake lever adjuster locknut	70-100 in. lbs	0.8-1.2 kg/m
Brake lever mounting nut	45-60 in. lbs	0.5-0.7 kg/m
Brake pipe nipple	150-155 in. lbs	1.7-1.8 kg/m
Caliper connecting shaft	22-26 ft lbs	3.0-3.6 kg/m
Caliper-to-front fork bolts	19-23 ft lbs	2.5-3.3 kg/m
Camshaft cap bolts	105 in. lbs	1.2 kg/m
Clutch hub nut	87-180 ft lbs	12-15 kg/m
Crankcase nuts (6φ)	70 in. lbs	0.8 kg/m
Crankcase nuts (8φ)	18 ft lbs	2.5 kg/m
Crankshaft cap bolts	18 ft lbs	2.5 kg/m
Cylinder head bolts	105 in. lbs	1.2 kg/m
Cylinder head cap nuts	25 ft lbs	3.5 kg/m
Cylinder head cover bolts	70 in. lbs	0.8 kg/m
Disc mounting bolts	140-190 in. lbs	1.6-2.2 kg/m
Drum positioning bolt	44-57 ft lbs	6.0-8.0 kg/m
Dynamo rotor-to-crankshaft	18 ft lbs	2.5 kg/m
Engine bolt (10φ)	26-29 ft lbs	3.5-4.0 kg/m
Engine bolt (12φ)	47-50 ft lbs	6.5-7.0 kg/m
Engine bracket (8φ)	14.5-16.5 ft lbs	2.0-2.3 kg/m
Engine oil pump bolts	70 in. lbs	0.8 kg/m
Engine sprocket nut	87-108 ft lbs	12-15 kg/m
Front axle clamp bolts	13.0-14.5 ft lbs	1.8-2.0 kg/m
Front brake lamp switch	135-170 in. lbs	1.5-2.0 kg/m
Front fork pinch-bolt (8φ)	12-13 ft lbs	1.6-1.8 kg/m
Front fork pinch-bolt (12φ)	40-43 ft lbs	5.4-6.0 kg/m
Handlebar mounting bolts	18 ft lbs	2.5 kg/m
Master cylinder clamp bolts	55-75 in. lbs	0.63-0.88 kg/m
Pivot shaft nut	87-108 ft lbs	12-15 kg/m
Rear axle nut	95-115 ft lbs	13-16 kg/m
Rear shock absorber bolt (lower)	22-25 ft lbs	3.0-3.5 kg/m
Rear shock absorber bolt (upper)	44-47 ft lbs	6.0-6.5 kg/m
Rear sprocket bolts	23-30 ft lbs	3.1-4.2 kg/m
Spoke	22-26 in. lbs	0.25-0.30 kg/m
3-way fitting bolts	45-50 in. lbs	0.5-0.6 kg/m
Torque link nut	22-25 ft lbs	3.0-3.5 kg/m

INDEX

MONTESA

MODEL IDENTIFICATION

The Cota 25 is a 50 cc trials mount for the young rider. It features all of the same handling characteristics as its two big brothers

The Cota 123 is a 125 cc trials machine

The Cota 247 is a 250 cc trials machine that stands at the top of the Montesa trials line

The Cappra 125MX is a 125 cc motocross machine

The Cappra 250MX is a 250 cc motocross machine and can be differentiated from the 125MX by its different seat and exhaust configurations

The Cappra 250VR; 250 cc Vehkonen Replica

The King Scorpion 250 cc enduro bike which features "Automix", an automatic oil mixing device

MODEL LISTING

Impala Sport
Impala
Commando 175
Kenya
Cota 25
250 Trail
Texas
Impala-Cross 175
Impala-Cross 250
Enduro 175
Sport 250
Cappra 250 MX
Cota 247
LaCross 250
Scorpion 250
Sport 250
Cota 123
Cappra 250 MX
King Scorpion 250
Cappra 360 GP
Cappra 250 Five
Cappra 360 GP
Cappra 360 DS
Cappra 250 GP

TUNE-UP AND MAINTENANCE

TUNE-UP OPERATIONS

Ignition Timing

BREAKER POINT IGNITION

1. Disconnect the spark plug lead and remove the plug.

2. Remove the right side crankcase cover.

3. Disconnect the wire from the No. 1 terminal at the ignition coil and connect one lead of a continuity tester (with built-in battery) to the wire that was disconnected. Ground the other test lead on the crankcase.

4. Install a dial gauge into the spark plug hole. Rotate the flywheel until the piston is at Top Dead Center.

NOTE: *If a dial gauge is not available, a thin rod or a pencil may be used to locate the piston at TDC. Scribe a line on the marker you use, which is even with the top of the plug threads, to indicate TDC and another line the proper distance above the first for the firing point. Refer to the accompanying chart for the proper distance before TDC for individual engines.*

5. Rotate the flywheel backward, after establishing TDC, until the continuity light shows that the points have just opened. The dial gauge or market should indicate close to the following values of piston distance before TDC.

IGNITION TIMING

Model	in.	mm
Texas	0.118	3.00
Impala, Impala Sport	0.118	3.00
Commando 175	0.118	3.00
Kenya	0.118	3.00
250 Trial	0.118	3.00
Impala Cross 175	0.138	3.50
Impala Cross (250)	0.216	5.50
Enduro	0.138	3.50
Sport 250	0.157	4.00
Cota 257		
To Serial No. 21M2999	0.157	4.00
Cota 247		
From Serial No. 21M3000	0.098	2.50
LaCross	0.236	6.00
Scorpion 250	0.157	4.00
Cappra 250	0.151	4.00
Cappra 250 GP	0.152	4.00
Cappra 250 Five	0.157	4.00
Cappra 250 MX	0.118	3.00
Cappra 360 GP/DS	0.157	4.00
Cappra 125 MX		
To Serial No. 18M0052	0.157	4.00
Cota 123	0.118	3.00
Cota 25	0.098	2.50

6. If the ignition timing is off by a small amount, it is possible to correct it by altering the point gap. The gap should be between 0.35–0.45 mm.

7. If the timing cannot be brought within specifications in this way, the flywheel must be removed. The flywheel nut has a left-hand thread. The magneto stator plate can then be turned after loosening the mounting screws.

8. Reinstall the flywheel and check the timing.

ELECTRONIC IGNITION

1. Install a dial gauge or a marker (see above) in the spark plug hole. Turn the engine until the piston is at TDC.

2. Rotate the engine backward until the piston is at the correct timing position. The is 0.118 in. (3.0 mm) BTDC for all models.

3. Insert a thin phillips head screwdriver blade through the small timing hole provided in the flywheel (at about 8 o'clock) and into the hole in the stator plate. If the holes are aligned, the timing is correct.

4. If the holes are not aligned, slowly turn the flywheel until they do, noting the distance the flywheel was turned.

5. Take off the flywheel (the nut has a left-hand thread), loosen the stator plate screws slightly, and turn the stator plate the same amount it was necessary to turn the flywheel for the holes to align, but in the opposite direction.

6. Install the flywheel loosely and recheck the timing.

Carburetor Adjustment

Montesa models use the same types of carburetors as Bultaco. For tune-up adjustments, refer to the "Bultaco, Tune-Up and Maintenance" section.

Carburetor disassembly and repair procedures are found in the Bultaco "Fuel Systems" section.

Spark Plugs

Refer to the accompanying chart for the proper plug for individual models.

Plug gap for all models is 0.016–0.020 in. (0.4–0.5 mm).

MAINTENANCE ITEMS

Lubrication

ENGINE OIL

The transmission and the clutch are lubricated by separate oil supplies in all models except the Cota 123.

Oil should be changed every 1500 miles (street bikes), or more often depending on how the machine is used.

All models use SAE 90 gear oil in the transmission and SAE 20 in the clutch. Capacities are as follows:

FRONT FORKS

For all models except the Cota 123, the capacity of each fork leg is 175 cc (6.5 oz). For the Cota 123 the proper quantity is 150 cc (5 oz) each leg.

Drain the oil by removing drain plug at the bottom of each leg. Pump the slider up and down to expel all the oil.

Refill after removing the fork cap nut for each leg. It may be necessary to remove the handlebars depending on the type fitted.

Service Checks And Adjustments

CLUTCH CABLE

Adjustment is made at the handlebar. The clutch lever should move about 0.08 in. before engagement begins.

BRAKES

The rear brake is adjusted by means of a butterfly nut on the brake rod.

Front brakes are adjusted at the handlebar. Adjustment can be made to suit individual preference. Brakes must not drag when the lever or pedal is released.

RECOMMENDED SPARK PLUGS

Model	NGK	Bosch	Champion
Impala Sport	B7H	W 260 T1	L5
Impala	B6H	W 225 T1	L86
Commando 175	B6H	W 225 T1	L86
Kenya	B6H	W 225 T1	L86
Cota 25	B6H	W 225 T1	L86
250 Trial	B6H	W 225 T1	L86
Texas	B6H	W 225 T1	L86
Impala-Cross 175	N.A.	N.A.	N.A.
Impala-Cross 250	N.A.	N.A.	N.A.
Enduro 175	B7H	W 260 T1	L5
Sport 250	B7H	W 260 T1	L5
Cappra 250 MX	B8EN	W 310 T16	L57R
Cota 247	B4L	W 145 T1	L10
LaCross 250	B8EN	W 310 T16	L58R
Scorpion 250	B7H	W 260 T17	L5
Sport 250	B7H	W 260 T1	L5
Cota 123	B6H	W 225 T2	N4
Cappra 250 MX	B8EN	W 310 T16	L57R
King Scorpion 250	B7H	W 260 T17	L5
Cappra 360 GP/DS	B8EN	W 310 T16	N58R
Cappra 250 Five	B8EN	W 310 T16	N58R
Cappra 250 GP	B8EN	W 310 T16	L58R

Removing the crankcase drain plug

Model	Transmiss. (oz)	Clutch (oz)
Cota 247	10	6.75
250 Trial	13.5	11.75
Cappra 250, King Scorpion, Cappra 125, and 360 GP/DS	11	10
Cota 123	20	20
All Others	13.5	10

Removing the fork leg drain plug

Adjusting the rear brake

DRIVE CHAIN

1. Loosen the rear axle nut.
2. Loosen the brake anchor nut on the brake drum. Also, back the brake adjuster nut off a few turns.
3. Turn the chain adjuster cam discs on the axle back equal amounts.
4. Check chain free-play at the middle of the top run of the chain. The machine should be off the stand and with a rider in position on it. Chain freeplay should be no more than 1 in. total up and down play.
5. Tighten the axle nut, brake anchor nut, and readjust the rear brake.

Adjusting the drive chain—increasing slack

ENGINE AND TRANSMISSION

ENGINE REMOVAL AND INSTALLATION

1. Remove the drain plugs and allow the oil to drain from the gearbox and the primary case.
2. Turn the fuel valve off and disconnect the fuel line from the carburetor.
3. Disconnect the exhaust pipe from the cylinder flange.
4. Remove the air filter (or disconnect the rubber tube) from the carburetor.
5. Disconnect the clutch and throttle cables from the engine.
6. Disconnect the high tension cable and remove the spark plug.
7. Remove the kickstart and shift levers.
8. Take out the screws and remove the right-side crankcase cover (left side on the Cota 123).
9. Remove the master link and take off the drive chain.
10. Disconnect the wires from the magneto.
11. Unscrew the engine mounting bolts and lift the engine out of the frame.
12. To install the engine, reverse the preceding operations. The master link clip should always be installed so that its closed end faces in the direction of forward chain rotation.

TOP END SERVICE

Cylinder head

REMOVAL AND INSTALLATION

1. Unscrew the head nuts gradually and evenly, in a criss-cross pattern, and

remove the bolts (if applicable). Tap the head with a rubber mallet to break the seal and lift it off the cylinder.

2. Installation is in the reverse order of removal. Torque the head nuts to the following specification: 250 Trial, Cota 247, King Scorpion, Cappra 250 (all), and Cota 123—25 ft lbs. All other models—15 ft lbs. No torque specification is given for the head bolts.

Cylinder Service

REMOVAL AND INSPECTION

1. Unscrew the cylinder securing bolts (if applicable). Otherwise, simply lift the cylinder off the crankcase. Take care not to let the piston or connecting rod fall against the case flange.

2. Measure the cylinder bore at several points, from top to bottom, using an inside micrometer or other suitable instrument. Maximum cylinder diameter should not exceed the standard measurement by more than 0.006 in (0.15 mm). Cylinder ovality must not exceed 0.002 in. (0.05 mm). If necessary, the cylinder can be bored and honed, or a new liner installed. Pistons are available in 0.25mm and 0.50mm oversizes.

STANDARD CYLINDER DIAMETER

Model	in.	mm
Impala Sport	2.3988	60.93
Impala	2.3988	60.93
Commando 175	2.3988	60.93
Kenya	2.3988	60.93
250 Trial	2.8563	72.55
Impala Cross 175	2.3988	60.93
Texas	2.3988	60.93
Impala Cross 250	2.8541	72.49
Enduro	2.3988	60.93
Sport 250	2.8563	72.55
Cota 247	2.8563	72.55
La Cross	2.8568	72.56
Scorpion 250	2.8563	72.55
Cappra 250	2.8568	72.56
King Scorpion	2.8563	72.55
Cappra 360 GP/DS	3.0724	78.04
Cappra 125 MX	2.0276	51.50
Cota 123	2.1263	54.01
Cota 25	—	—

CYLINDER LINER REPLACEMENT

Heat the cylinder to 1100° F. to remove the liner and then hold the new liner in position using a press (75 psi) while the cylinder cools.

PISTON TO CYLINDER CLEARANCE

Model	in.	mm
Impala Sport	0.0012	0.030
Impala	0.0012	0.030
Commando 175	0.0012	0.030
Kenya	0.0012	0.030
250 Trial	0.0033	0.085
Impala Cross 175	0.0012	0.030
Impala Cross 250	0.0010	0.025
Enduro	0.0012	0.030
Sport 250	0.0033	0.085
Cota 247	0.0033	0.085
La Cross	0.0039	0.099
Scorpion 250	0.0033	0.085
Cappra 250	0.0039	0.099
King Scorpion	0.0014	0.035
Cappra 360	0.0033	0.085
Cappra 125 MX	0.0019	0.048
Cota 123	0.0017	0.045
Texas	0.0012	0.030
Cota 25	—	—

CYLINDER INSTALLATION

1.Check to see that the small pin in each ring groove is between the ends of the rings.

2. Install a new cylinder base gasket.

3. Oil the piston and cylinder bore and slide the cylinder down over the piston. Carefully compress each ring so that it slips easily into the bore (or use a ring compressor).

4. Seat the cylinder on the crankcase and install and torque the securing bolts to 15 ft lbs (18 ft lbs on the King Scorpion).

Piston Service

REMOVAL

1. Stuff a towel into the crankcase flange to prevent any foreign material from entering.

2. Remove the wrist pin snap-rings with needle nose pliers.

3. Heat the crown of the piston with an electric iron or with rags soaked in hot water, then push the wrist pin out using a drift that is slightly smaller in diameter than the pin. On bikes with uncaged needle bearings, take care not to loose the needles. Inspect the wrist pin and bearing needles for wear and excessive clearance; replace if necessary.

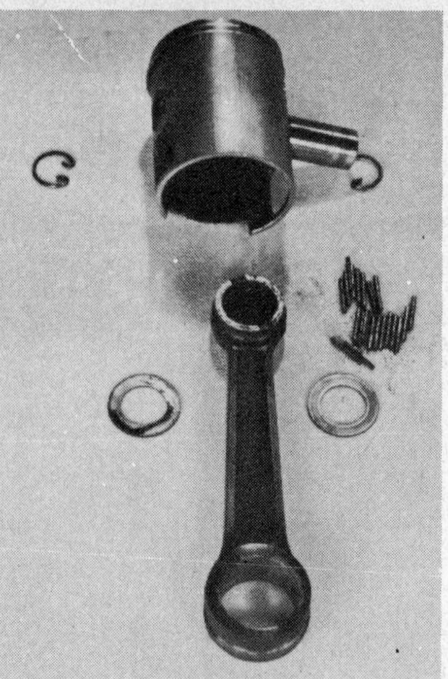

Piston and connecting rod assembly

Piston Rings

REMOVAL AND INSPECTION

1. Carefully remove the rings using a ring spreader or by spreading the ends gently with your thumbs.

2. Clean the ring grooves with a scraper or with a broken piece of a ring.

3. Place each ring, in turn, into the cylinder and push it to the middle with the piston. Measure the end-gap. Eng-gap tolerance for all except 360cc models is 0.-078–0.0137 in. (0.20–0.35mm). On 360cc models, the specification is 0.0118–0.0177 in. (0.30–0.45 mm).

4. "Roll" the rings completely around their grooves to check for any binding. Measure the clearance between the top of the ring and the groove at several places; this measurement should not exceed 0.0067 in (0.07mm).

5. When installing the rings, take care to align the notch in the ring ends with the small pin in the ring groove. If one of the rings is chrome plated, it is installed in the top groove. Do not spread the rings any more than necessary when installing them.

INSTALLATION

1. Installation is basically a reversal of the removal procedure. The piston crown is usually marked "ESCAPE" with an arrow pointing toward one side. This arrow must be made to point toward the exhaust port. If the piston is not marked, the longer skirt should be positioned toward the front of the engine.

2. On models with uncaged needle bearings at the connecting rod small end, a special tool is used, as shown, to arrange the needles for reassembly. Some stiff grease is used to hold them in place.

3. Use new wrist pin circlips upon reassembly.

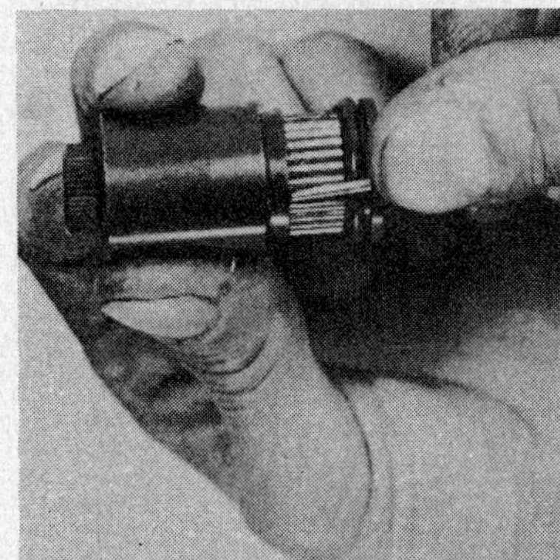

Fitting needle bearing into special tool

Fitting needle bearings into connecting rod

LOWER END AND TRANSMISSION SERVICE

Engine Sprocket

REMOVAL

1. Remove the right side engine cover.
2. Bend the locktab away from the sprocket nut.
3. Use the special tool, or wrap a length of chain around the sprocket, and clamp the ends in a vise. Unscrew the nut. It has a LEFT-HAND thread.
4. Pull the sprocket off of its shaft with a gear puller. Remove the woodruff key from the shaft.

Magneto

REMOVAL AND INSTALLATION

1. Remove the right side engine cover.
2. Hold the flywheel in position and unscrew the securing nut (LEFT-HAND thread). Note that the lock washer also has a special left-hand bias.
3. Install a flywheel puller and pull the flywheel off of the shaft. Mark the position of the magneto plate with one or more scribed lines to facilitate reassembly. Remove the three screws and take off the magneto plate.
4. Installation is the reversal of the removal procedures. Torque the flywheel nut to 72 ft lbs. Check and, if necessary, adjust the ignition timing.

Removing the magneto flywheel

Magneto flywheel with removal tool in position

Auxiliary Flywheel

REMOVAL AND INSTALLATION

On models equipped with an auxiliary flywheel on the left side of the engine:

1. Remove the left side engine case.
2. Remove the lockwire from the flywheel securing nut.
3. Unscrew and remove the flywheel nut.
4. Pull the flywheel off of the crankshaft with a flywheel puller. Remove the woodruff key from the shaft.
5. Install the flywheel in the reverse order of removal. When installing new lockwire, position it so that it will tend to tighten the nut, rather than loosen it.

Clutch Service

REMOVAL

1. Remove the left side engine cover.
2. Pull the pronged release mechanism plate out of the clutch hub.
3. Bend back the locktab and unscrew the clutch hub nut. (Note that the shoulder of the nut faces inward.)
4. Withdraw the clutch plates from the hub.
5. Pull off the bushing and remove the clutch hub from the shaft.
6. Remove the spacer(s) from the shaft. The thicker of the two spacers (if applicable) should be closer to the engine.

Right side crankcase disassembled

Left side crankcase components

Clutch hub

Clutch plate assembly and hub

CLUTCH HUB INSPECTION

Check the hub teeth for wear and damage. Minor damage can be repaired with an oilstone. If the teeth are in bad shape, replace the hub.

Check the operation of the center bearing. If it does not operate smoothly and noiselessly, it should be replaced. If necessary, remove the snap-ring and press out the bearing.

If the small brass piece in the release mechanism shows signs of wear, replace it. When reassembling, install it so that the chamfer faces the release lever.

Clutch hub bearing components

CLUTCH DISC REPLACEMENT

1. Mount the clutch disc assembly on a press, so that the disc tabs are securely located.
2. Apply pressure to the spring plate until it is compressed enough so that the pins can be removed. Release the press slowly.
3. Remove the spring plate, discs, and springs.
4. Install the new discs in the same manner and tighten the retaining nut to 15 ft lbs.

NOTE: *Do not change the order of the clutch plates. They are prearranged at the factory.*

CLUTCH ADJUSTMENT

Rotate the clutch adjustment nut to provide about half an inch of free-play at the end of the clutch lever. Retighten the locknut after adjustment.

Primary Drive Gear

REMOVAL

1. Unscrew and remove the gear securing nut.
2. Pull the gear off of the shaft using a suitable gear puller. *Do not attempt to pry or heat the gear in order to remove it.*
2. If, on your machine, the gear is integral with the auxiliary flywheel, use the tapped holes in the flywheel to mount a puller.

Fitting the crankshaft (primary) gear

INSPECTION

If the gear is badly damaged or worn, replace it. Minor defects can be repaired with an oilstone.

INSTALLATION

When installing the gear, take particular care to clean the crankshaft and gear tapers. Wipe them with a non-oily solvent before assembly. Tighten the securing nut to 72 ft lbs.

Shifter Mechanism

MODELS WITH THE MECHANISM LOCATED UNDER THE LEFT CRANKCASE COVER

NOTE: *If inspection or repair of the shifter mechanism is not required, the mechanism may be removed, complete with its shaft, after the crankcases have been separated.*

Disassembly

1. Unscrew and remove the shifter detent plunger.
2. Bend back the locking tabs and remove the two bolts on the shifter mechanism.
3. Remove the shifter return spring and plates.
4. Remove the two shifter pawls. Take care when removing the pawls; they are positioned with springs.
5. Take off the sector gear. Remove the securing nut, then the adjusting cam.
6. Remove the stop plate after marking it so that it can reinstalled in the same position.

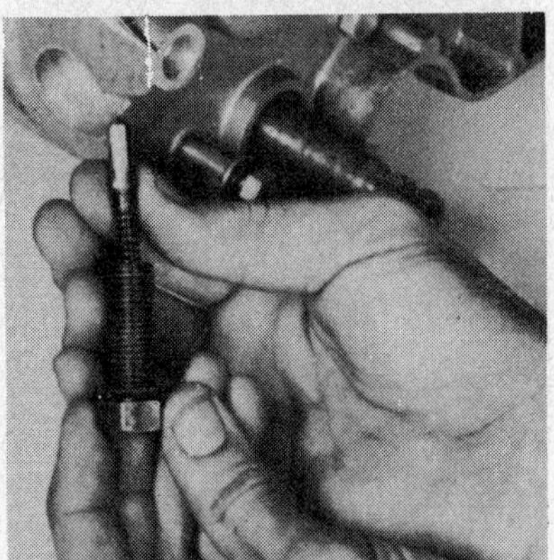

Removing the detent plunger

Inspection

Replace any parts which show excessive wear. Examine the gear teeth and the detents on the stop plate; these items are more subject to damage.

Assembly

Assembly is the reverse of the disassembly procedure. Note the following points:

1. The transmission should be in Neutral during reassembly.
2. The diagonal slot in the end of the selector shaft (into which the pawls are installed) is closer to the TOP bolt hole.
3. Align the slash mark located on the third tooth from the right of the sector gear with the punch mark on the shift drum gear as shown in the illustration.

4. Screw in one of the two shifter assembly bolts, then move the shift lever to align the other bolt with its hole.

Adjustment

1. Loosen the locknut and set the adjustment cam on its center position. Retighten the nut.

2. Select each gear with the shift lever. If any gear won't engage properly, select First gear and then rotate the transmission input shaft a small amount. Continue to turn the shaft and check gear operation until all gears engage properly.

3. Loosen the locknut again and turn the adjusting cam so that when the plunger bottoms in each detent, the pawl engages its stop. Tighten the locknut.

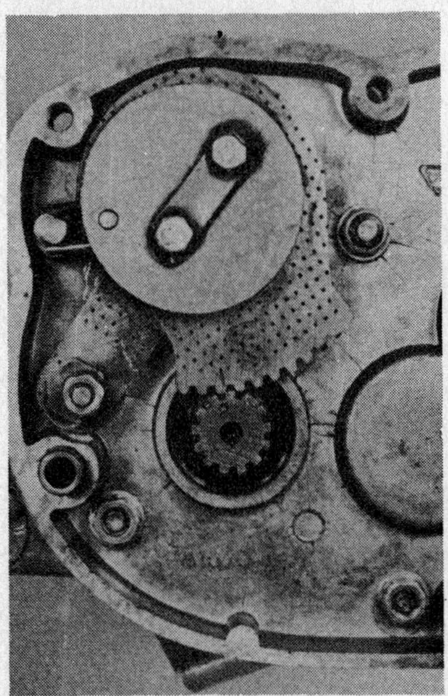

Gear selector mechanism

MODELS WITH THE SHIFTER MECHANISM LOCATED UNDER THE RIGHT CRANKCASE COVER

Disassembly

1. Unscrew the shift detent screw at the left, top of the crankcases, and remove the detent ball with a magnetic screwdirver or suitable substitute.

2. Remove the retainer and take off the small shift cam gear.

3. Remove the snap-ring and washer from the end of the selector shaft and remove the shaft.

4. Take off the shift pawl cover, (three screws) taking care not to lose the pawls.

Inspection

Check the tips of the pawls for wear. Examine the gears for damage and wear. Check the rack guide bushing for wear. Replace parts as necessary.

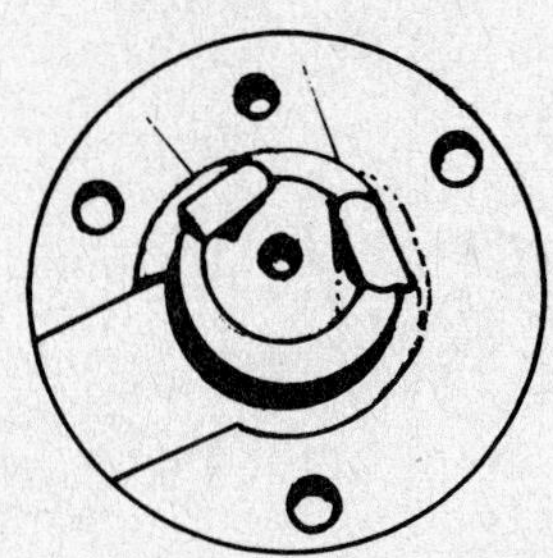

Gear selector pawls positioned for installation

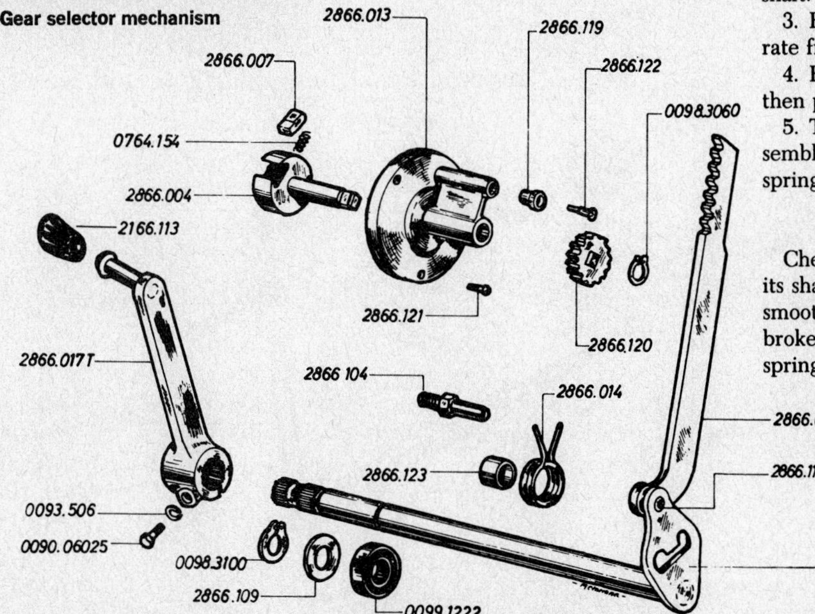

Gear shift mechanism components

Gear shift mechanism correctly positioned

Assembly

Assemble the shifter mechanism in reverse order of disassembly, noting the following points:

1. The transmission must be in Neutral during assembly.

2. Position the square shaft midway between its stops.

3. Install the small gear on its shaft so that its mark aligns with the mark on the rack.

Kickstart Mechanism

On some models, the kickstart mechanism is housed in the crankcase. This type of kickstarter is covered in the "Transmission Section". The other type of kickstart mechanism is accessible upon removal of the right side crankcase cover. Service procedures for this type are as follows.

DISASSEMBLY

1. Unhook the return spring from its anchor and pull out the kick gear assembly.

2. Remove the clutch gear from its shaft.

3. Remove the spacer, keeping it separate from the other one.

4. Remove the snap-ring and washer, then pull the idler gear from its shaft.

5. The kick gear assembly can be disassembled by removing the thrust washer, spring guide, and snap-ring.

INSPECTION

Check the splines in the kick gear and its shaft. The gear must be able to slide smoothly. Examine the gears for worn or broken teeth. Make sure that the return spring is healthy and in one piece.

ASSEMBLY

Assemble the kickstart mechanism in the reverse order of disassembly.

Splitting The Crankcases

1. Perform the following operations, as previously described:
   a. Remove the crankcase covers.
   b. Disassemble the clutch.
   c. Remove the magneto flywheel.
   d. Remove the engine sprockets.
   e. Remove the cylinder head and cylinder.
   f. Remove the piston, if desired.
2. Remove the crankshaft oil seal housings on either side of the crankshaft. Watch for any shims behind the seals and note their location.

Removing the crankshaft oil seal housing

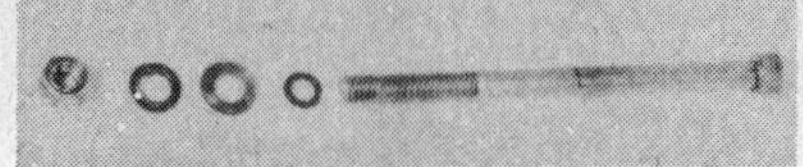

Crankcase bolt and components

3. Unscrew and remove the crankcase securing bolts and nuts. Note that one of the bolts has a flat washer under the bolt and nut heads. This bolt and washer must be replaced in their original positions. Do not take out the nut above and to the left of the kickstarter shaft. On models with the shifter mechanism located under the right crankcases cover, the kickstarter spring anchor serves as a crankcase bolt.

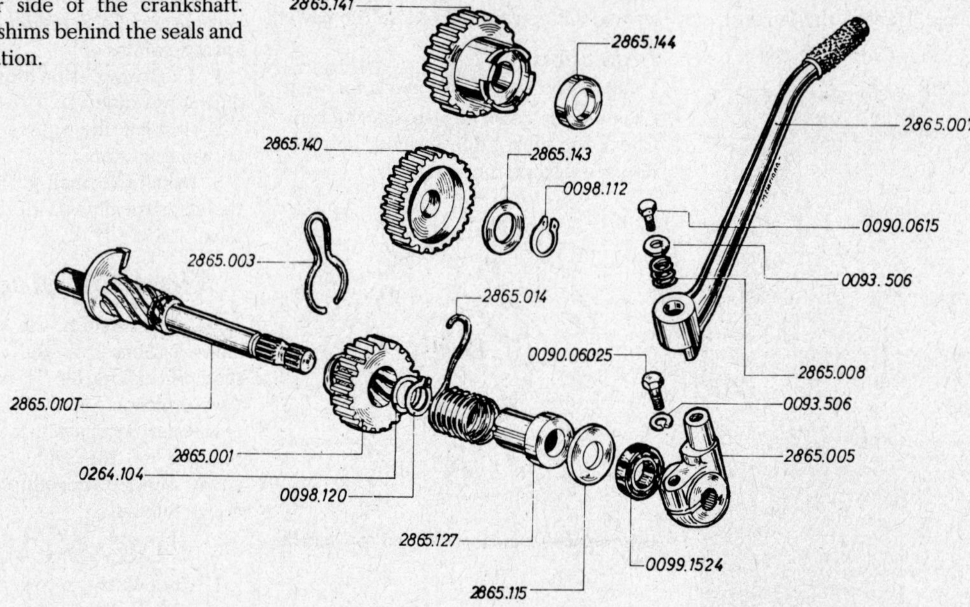

Kickstart components (Cota 123)

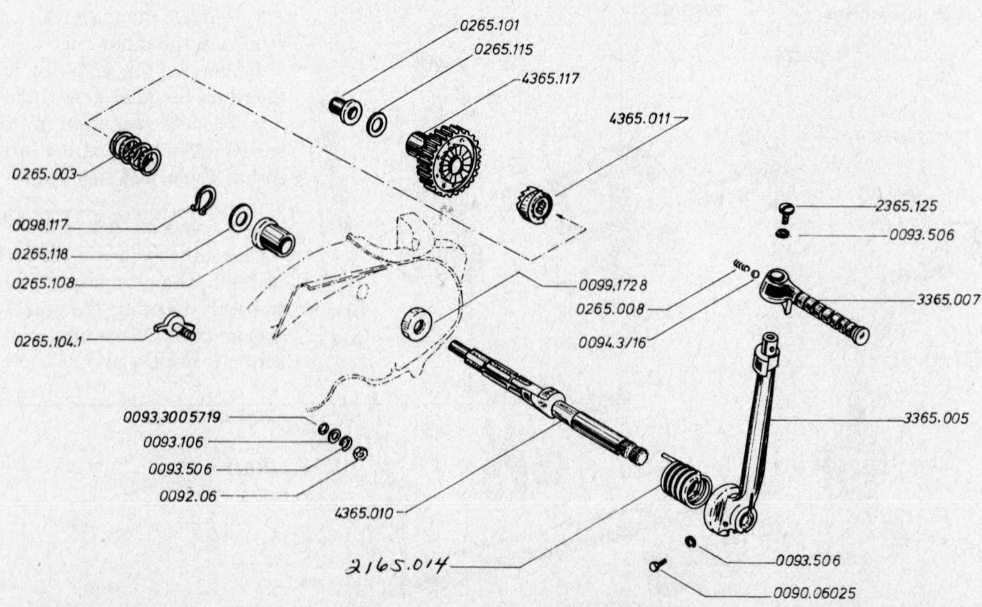

Kickstart components (Cappra 250-VR)

4. If there are any scratches or nicks on the gear shift selector shaft, smooth them with emery cloth before separating the cases.

5. Place the engine on the bench and carefully heat the area around the left side bearing.

6. Lift the engine, holding the left side of the engine up, and tap on the crankshaft and transmission shaft ends with a soft-faced mallet until the cases separate.

Gear cluster shims

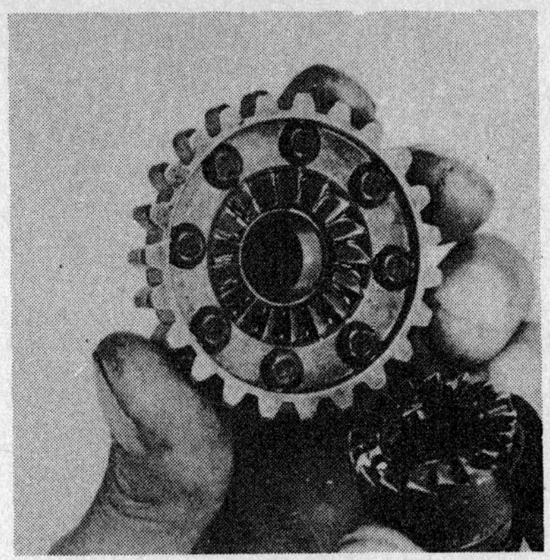
Kickstart ratchet

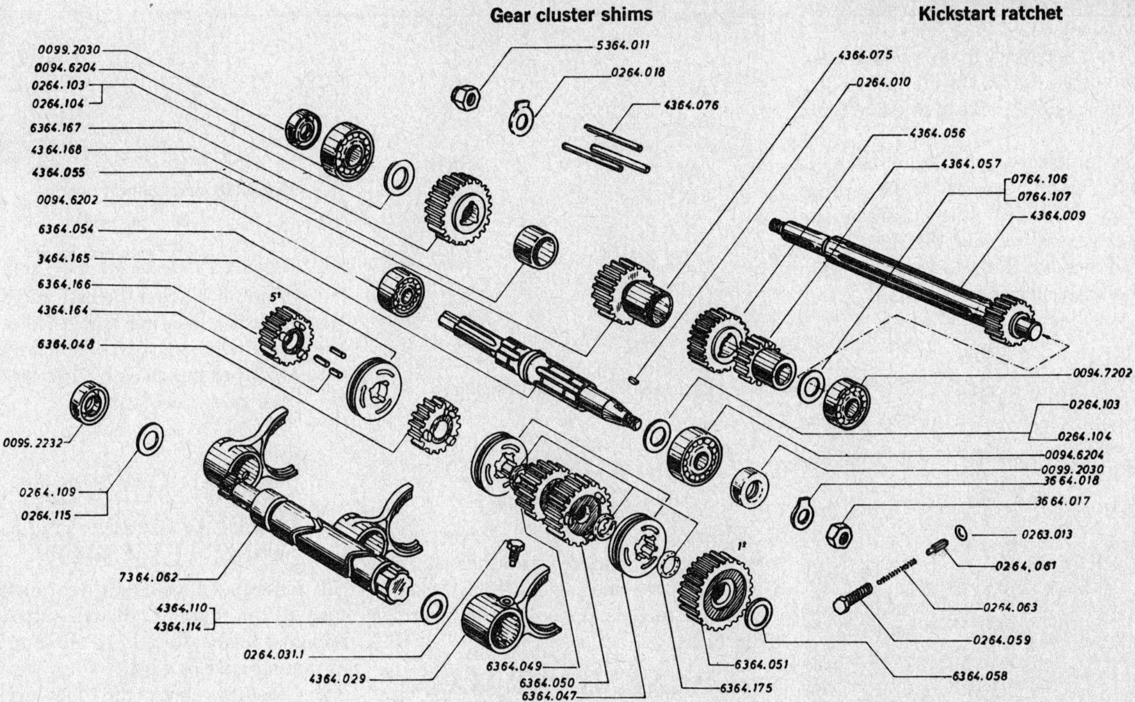

Transmission components (Cappra 250-VR)

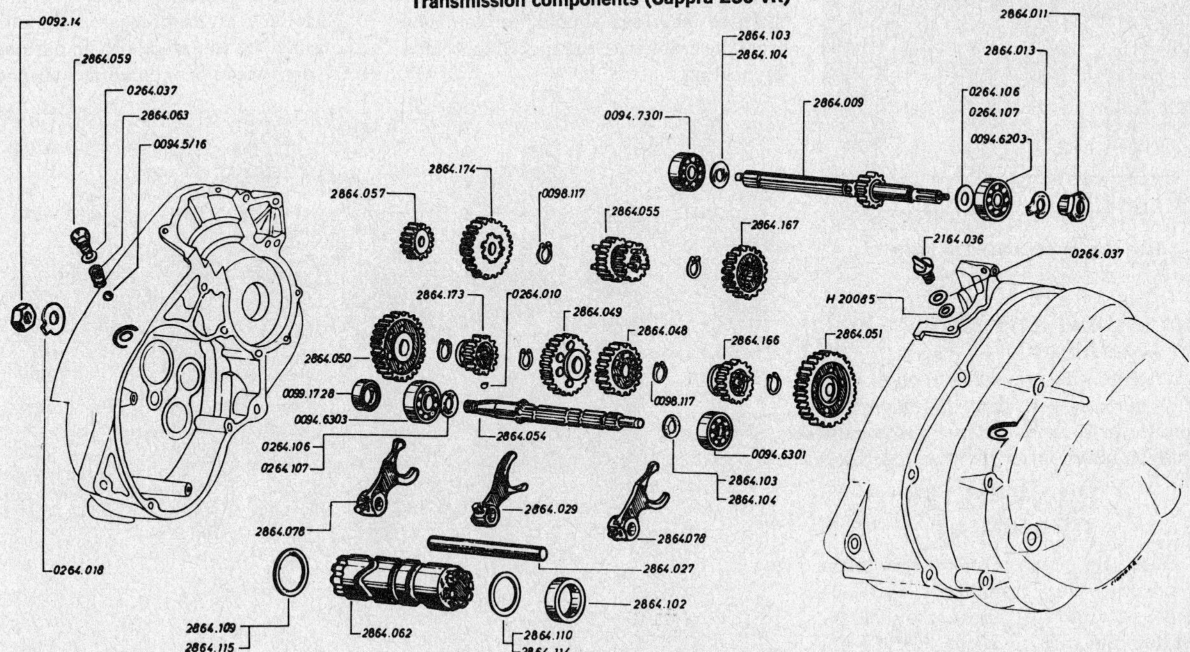

Transmission components (Cota 123)

TRANSMISSION REMOVAL

Sliding Gears On Mainshaft

After the cases have been separated, procede as follows:

1. Remove the kickstart gear, ratchet and spring.
2. Unscrew the detent plunger from the case.
3. Lift out the mainshaft while tapping lightly on the countershaft with a soft-faced mallet. Take out the countershaft, along with the shift drum and forks.
4. Remove and tag the shims on the shafts and disassemble the gears on the countershaft.
5. If it is necessary to remove the bearings or bushings from the crankcase, heat it to about 325° F. and then drive them out.
6. To remove the gears from the mainshaft, it may be necessary to use a press.
7. Cut the safety wire, unscrew the guide pegs, and remove the shift forks.
8. To remove the selector shaft, take out the snap-ring and its washer.

Gear cluster positioned as installed

Models that have Sliding Gears on the Mainshaft

Refer to the preceding section. The only difference is that the mainshaft, countershaft, and shifter mechanism must be lifted out of the case together.

CRANKSHAFT REMOVAL

After the transmission has been removed, the crankshaft may be removed from the crankcase half by heating the case to about 325° F. and driving out the crankshaft and bearing. Note the location of any shim washers on the crankshaft

The crankshaft is pressed together and must be disassembled and reassembled in the same way. Any play in the connecting rod big end bearing will require this operation.

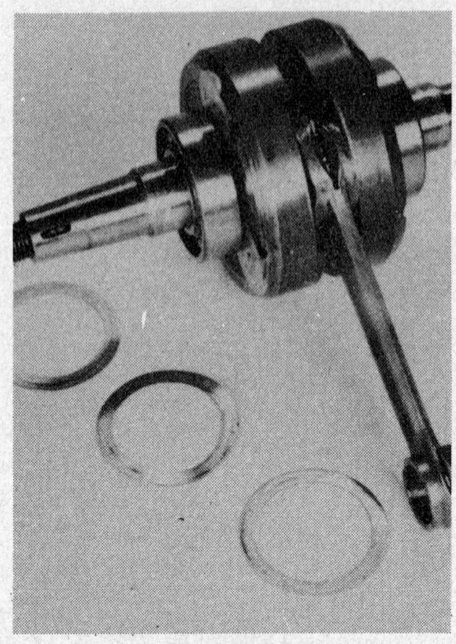

Crankshaft assembly with shims

ASSEMBLY AND ALIGNMENT

Refer to the "Bultaco" section (four-speed models) under "Crankshaft Assembly," Steps 4 and 6. Note that some Montesa models use caged connecting rod bearings.

CRANKSHAFT MAIN BEARINGS

These bearings should be removed from the crank with the special tool aided by heating.

Installing a crankshaft bearing

INSTALLATION

As on removal, heat the case and drive the crankshaft bearing home. Note that the side of the crankshaft which is slotted for a woodruff key must be inserted into the drive side crankcase.

TRANSMISSION INSPECTION AND INSTALLATION

1. Examine all gears for wear or damage. If the gear teeth are pitted or broken, replace the gear in question and its mating gear as a set.
2. Carefully check the dogs on the gears. If they are badly worn or broken, replace the gear. Light wear or chipping can usually be repaired with an oilstone. If the dogs are in poor condition, chances

Left and right crankcases stripped except for transmission bearings

are that the slots in the engaging gears are also damaged.

3. Make sure that the shift forks do not bind. There should not be excessive wear on the shift fork sides. Clearance between each shift fork and the groove in its gears should not be greater than about 0.20 in.

Right side crankshaft bearing installed

4. To install new bearings or bushings in the crankcases, heat the cases to 325° F. Drive the bearings in quickly.

5. It is necessary to check and adjust the end-play if any of the transmission shaft components or bearings have been replaced. The procedure is as follows:

a. Refer to the accompanying illustration. Measure the dimensions of H, Hs, and Hp on the right side crankcase.

H= height from the crankcase surface to the bottom of the shift drum.

Hs = height from the crankcase surface to the top of the inner race of the countershaft bearing.

Hp = height from the crankcase surface to the top of the inner race of the mainshaft bearing.

b. Refer to the next illustration; measure the dimension of h, hs, and hp on the left side crankcase.

h = height from the crankcase surface to the surface of the shift drum

hs = height from the crankcase surface to the top of the inner race of the countershaft bearing.

hp = height from the crankcase surface to the top of the inner race of the mainshaft bearing.

c. Add the measurements obtained as shown below, also adding the thickness of the center crankcase gasket (S).

h + H + S = A

hs + Hs + S = B

hp + Hp + S = C

d. Measure the length of the shift drum (the result to be referred to as dimension (a). Assemble the gears onto the countershaft and measure the distance between the outer sides of the two end gears (to be referred to as dimension (b). Finally, assemble the gears onto the mainshaft and, as for the countershaft, measure the distance between the outer sides of the two end gears (dimension (c).

e. To determine the end-play of the shafts, perform the following computations:

a) A-a = shift drum end-play (xa)

b) B-b = countershaft end-play (xb)

c) C-c = mainshaft end-play (xc)

f. Since you now know the end-play of each shaft without any shims in place, it will be easy to determine the correct number of shims to use. The correct end-play for all of the shafts is 0.1–0.2 mm. Proper shim thickness (Z) can be determined in this manner:

Xa, Xb, or Xc − 0.15 mm = Z

The mainshaft shims should be installed on the left side of the shaft.

The countershaft shims should be installed on the right side of the shaft.

6. Install the mainshaft, countershaft, and shift drum (with forks in place) in the right side crankcase, and operate the drum. Distribute the shims on each side of the shift drum so that there is equal distance between each sliding gear and its engaging gears.

Crankcase Assembly

1. With the transmission gear clusters and the crankshaft in place in the right side crankcase, install a new crankcase gasket, held in place by a small amount of gasket compound if necessary.

2. Gently heat the left side crankshaft bearing and fit the crankcase halves together.

3. Check immediately for free rotation of the crankshaft in the assembled cases, as it is quite possible for the flywheel to hit the cases if bearing alignment is not correct. The connecting rod small end should be exactly centered on the crankcase mating surface.

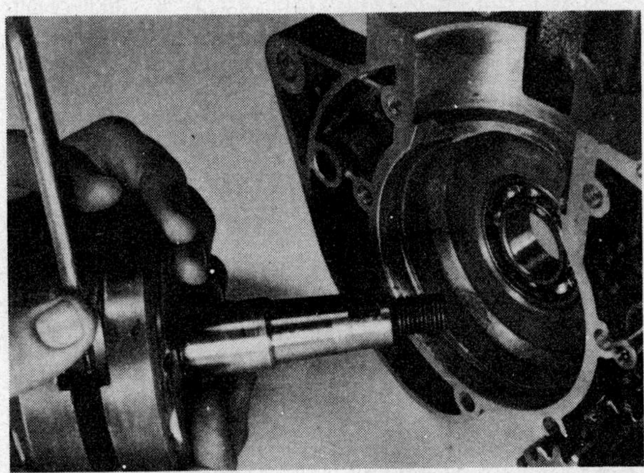

Installing the crankshaft

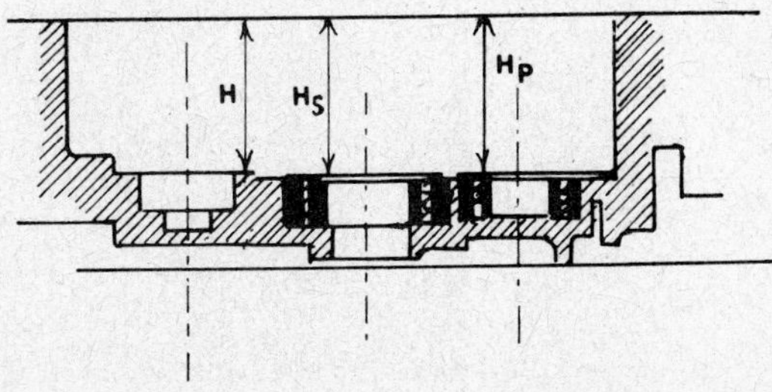

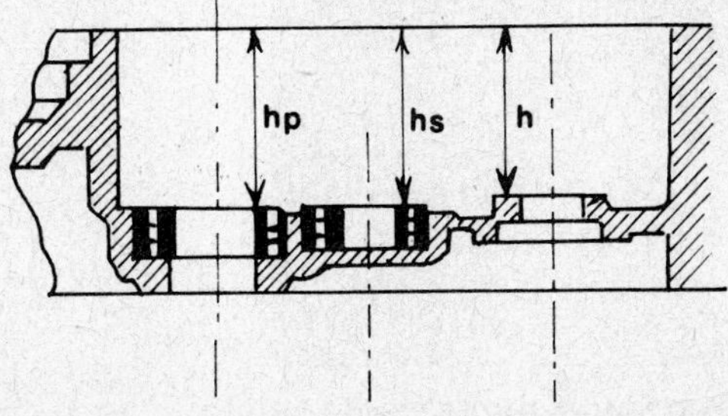

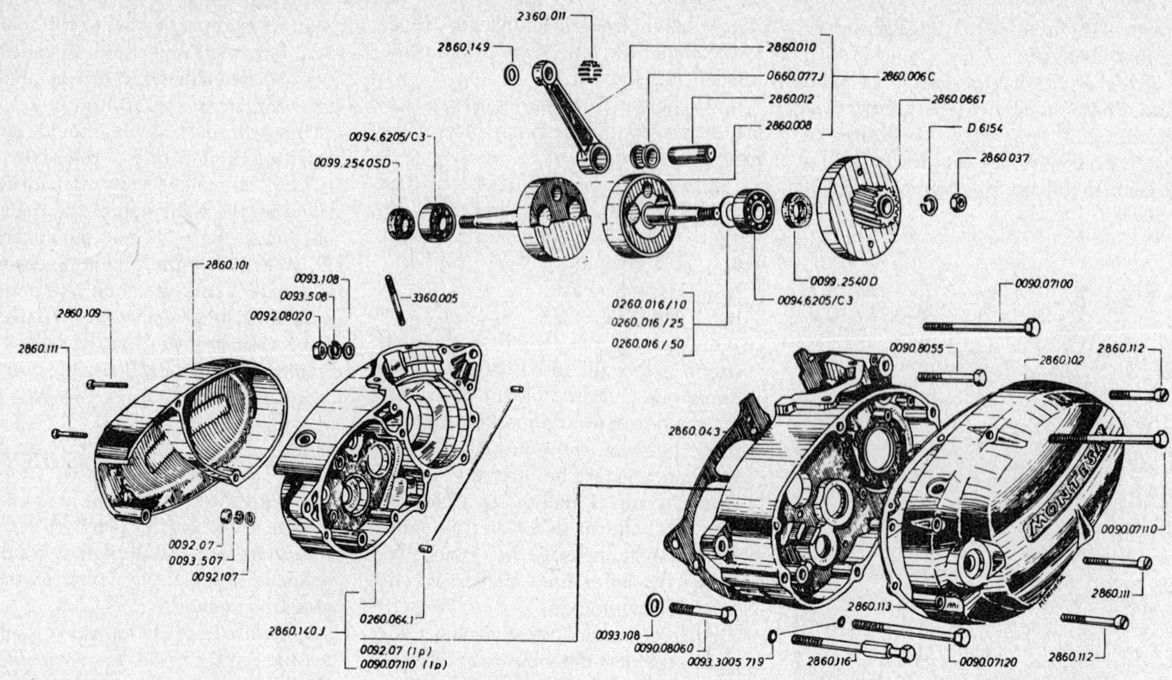

Crankshaft components (Cota 123)

Fitting the crankcase gasket

Heating the crankshaft bearing prior to fitting the crankshaft

4. Refit the crankcase bolts, washers, and nuts in the correct order. Fit the crankcase oil seal assemblies. New seals should be used. These are pressed into the seal housings as shown.

FUEL SYSTEMS

For disassemby and repair procedures, refer to the "Bultaco" section "Fuel Systems." Montesa uses the same makes and types of carburetors.

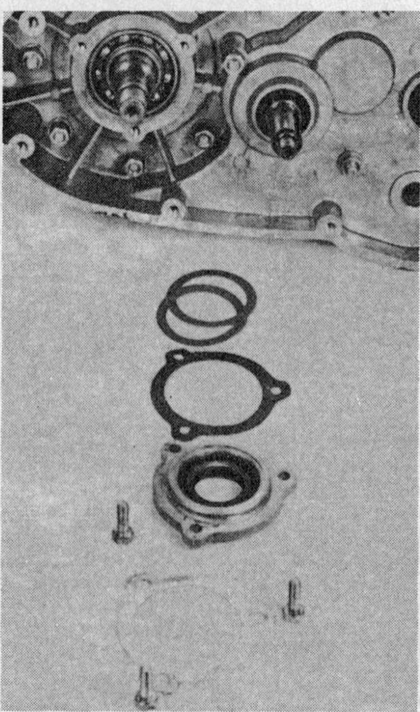

Crankshaft oil seal housing components

ELECTRICAL SYSTEMS

Montesa uses both an electronic ignition system and a conventional magneto ignition system.

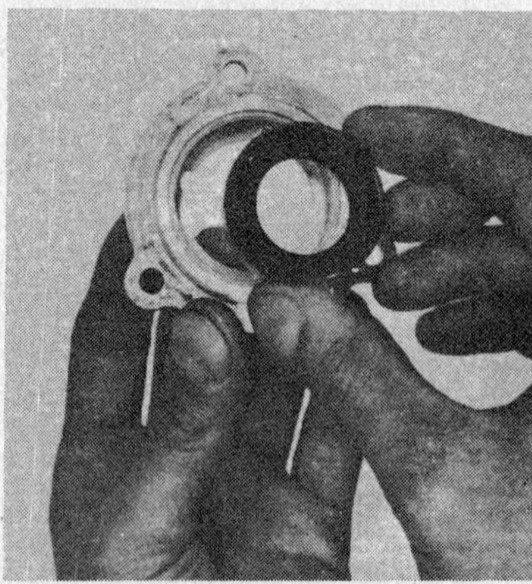

Crankshaft oil seal and housing

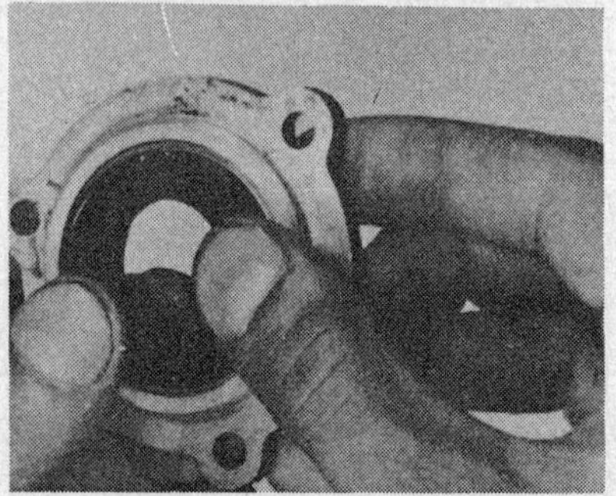

Fitting the oil seal to the housing

COMPONENT TESTS

Tests can be made with an ohmeter or a multimeter

Magneto Ignition Models

IGNITION COIL

1. Measure the resistance between the primary terminals of the coil. The meter should read about 1 ohm.
2. Measure the resistance between one of the primary terminals and the center (high tension) terminal, where the spark plug cable plugs in. The meter should read 5,000–11,000 ohms.
3. Measure resistance between the coil housing and any terminal. For an accurate reading, the paint should be scraped off the housing where the test lead is connected. If the meter does not read infinity, the insulation resistance has broken down.
4. If any of the above tests is not within specification, the coil should be replaced.

CONDENSER

Connect the body of the condenser to the negative terminal of a 12 volt battery and connect the condenser wire to the positive battery terminal. After allowing the condenser to charge for a few seconds, disconnect the battery and touch the condenser wire to the condenser body. If it sparks, the condenser is probably OK. If there is any doubt, replace it.

MAGNETO COILS

1. Remove the flywheel and make sure that the coils are not being rubbed by the flywheel.
2. Disconnect the wires to the magneto. Place a piece of paper between the breaker points. Measure the resistance between each magneto wire and ground. You should obtain the following results:
   a) Light equipped models—black wire, 0.6 ohms pink wire, 0.6 ohms green wire, 0.3 ohms yellow wire, 0.3 ohms
   b) Racing models—resistance of all coils should be about 0.5 ohms.

Electronic Ignition Models

COIL

1. Connect the negative ohmeter lead to ground and connect the positive lead to the blue and black wires, in turn. The meter should read 200–800 ohms. Reverse the ohmeter leads and retest. You should get an infinite reading in this case.
2. Connect the ohmeter between the blue and black wires. It should read 10 ohms.
3. Connect the ohmeter between the spark plug cable and the coil mounting bracket. The meter should read about 10,000 ohms.
4. Connect the ohmeter between the coil mounting bracket and the blue terminal. As the connection is made, the meter needle should jump down the scale, then move to infinity. Repeat this test, using the black terminal.
5. If any of the above tests are failed, the coil should be replaced.

RECTIFIER

1. Using a continutiy light with a self-contained battery, connect the leads to the rectifier one way, then reverse the leads. The continuity light should light when connected one way, and *not* light when connected the other way. If it lights both ways, or not at all, replace the rectifier.

CHASSIS

FRONT FORKS

All Models

DISASSEMBLY

1. Disconnect the front brake cable at the brake drum.
2. Disconnect the brake anchor on the fork slider.

Removing the brake anchor bolt

3. Remove the axle nut, and pull out the axle while supporting the front wheel. Remove the wheel and brake drum. Remove the front fender.

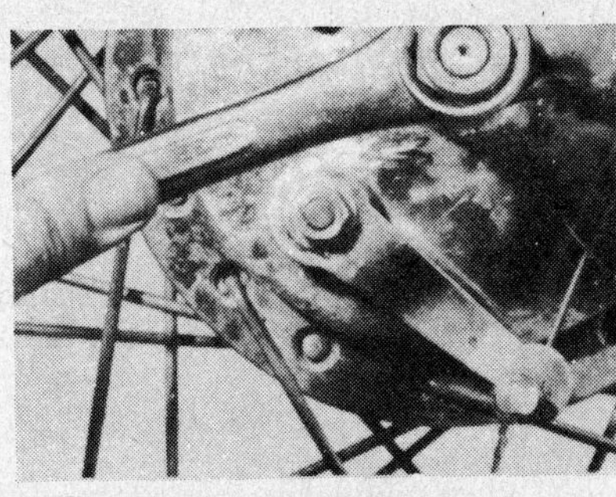

Removing the axle nut

4. Drain the oil from each of the fork legs. Early models may have the drain plug located directly above the axle. Other models are equipped with a drain plug at the rear of the fork slider. Pump each slider up and down several times to assure that all the oil is expelled.
5. Remove the allen bolt from the bottom of each slider.
6. Lift up the dust seal at the top of each slider, and remove the circlip there.
7. Pull the slider off of the fork leg. A rubber bush and a plain steel washer are located at the very bottom of the damper. Usually the washer will remain in the slider when it is removed.

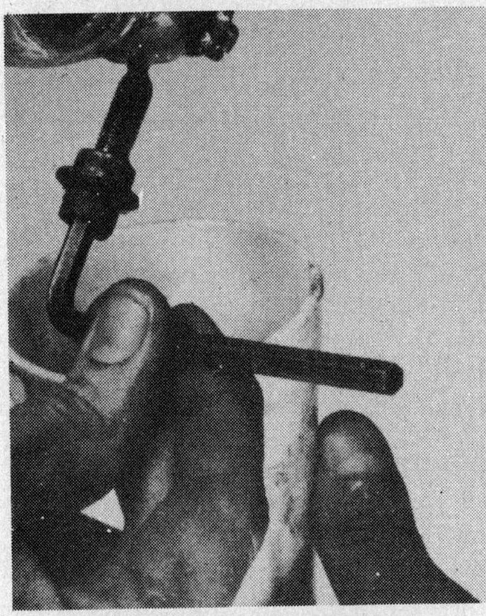

Removing the fork slider allen bolt

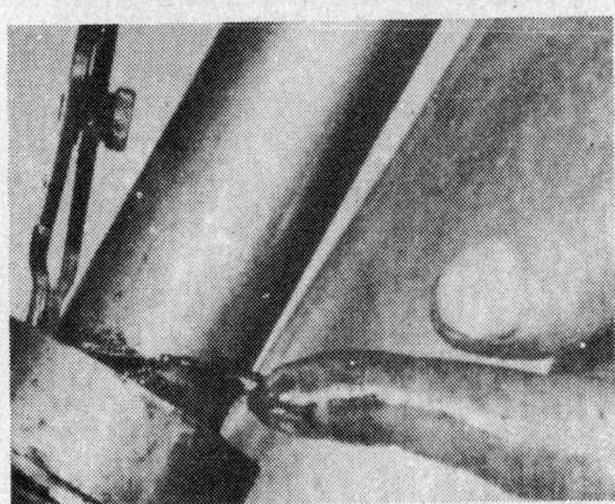

Removing the slider circlip

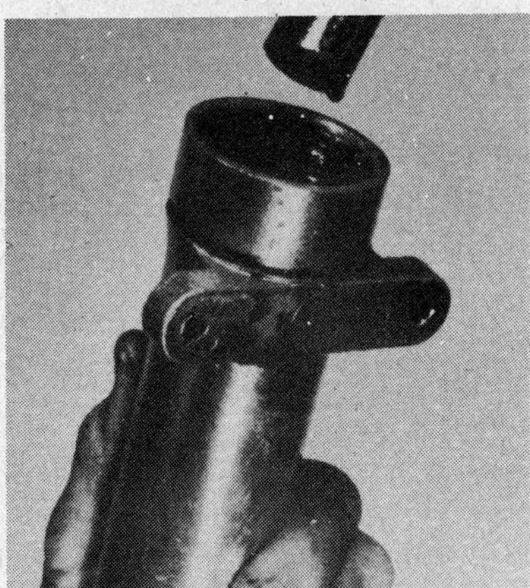

Removing the fork slider

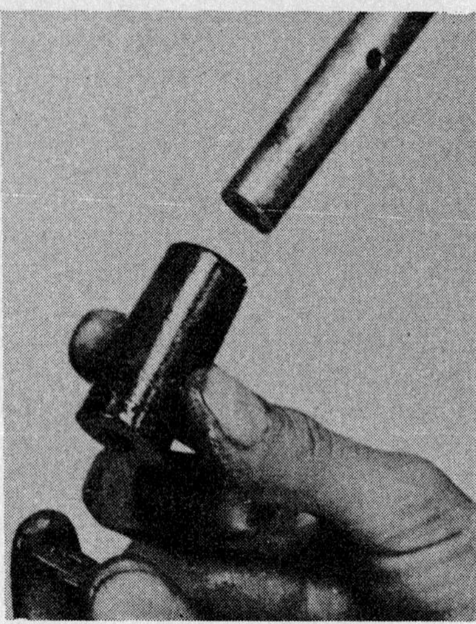

Damper tube rubber bush and washer

8. Remove the fork cap nut. It may be necessary to remove the handlebars to enable the nut to be removed.

9. A check valve is fitted in the fork cap nut. If the valve sticks, oil will be forced out around the top of the cap nut. If this happens, take out the screw from the top of the cap nut, remove the small spring beneath the screw with the aid of a magnetic philips screwdriver, and remove the ball. Clean the assembly, then lightly reseat the ball in the cap nut with a hammer and drift. Reinstall the spring and plug.

10. Remove the large spring from the fork tube.

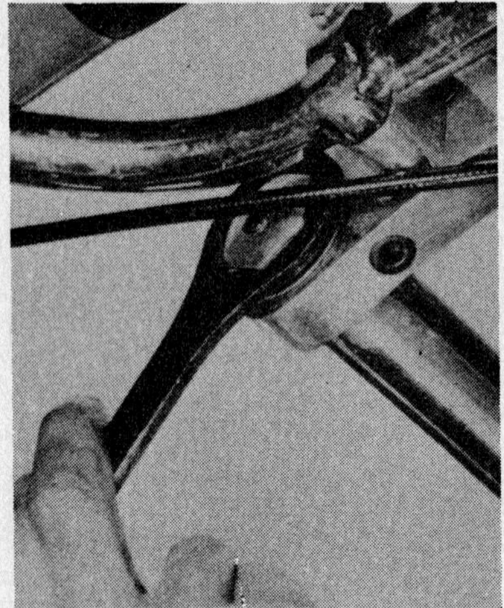

Removing the fork cap nut

11. The damper assembly may be removed by first removing the circlip at the bottom of the fork tube.

12. If it is necessary to remove the fork tube itself, loosen the upper and lower triple clamp nuts; replace the fork cap nut, screwing it in several turns, and strike it sharply with a mallet to break the fork tube free from the triple clamps.

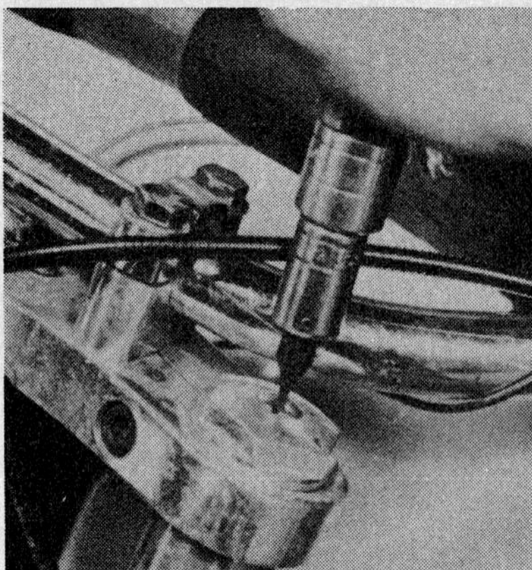

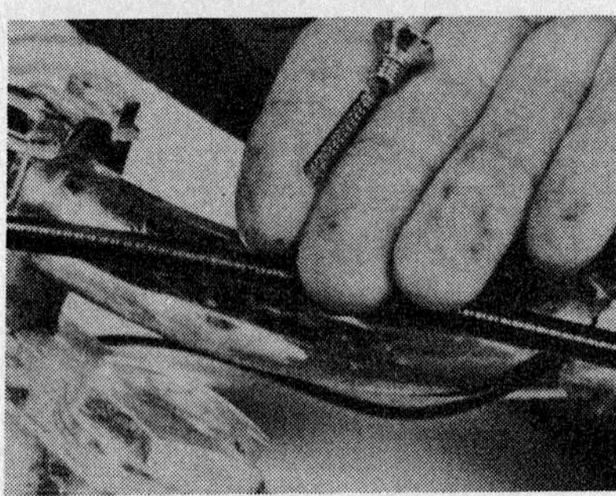

Check valve screw and spring

INSPECTION

1. Check all rubber seals, O-rings, etc. for torn or damaged condition.

2. The holes in the damper must be free of foreign matter.

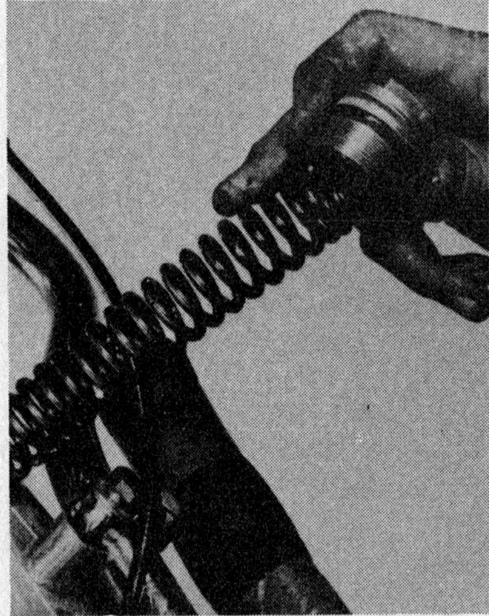

Removing the fork spring

3. Fork tubes must be perfectly straight.

4. Fork slider oil seals are replaced after prying the old seal out with a suitable instrument.

ASSEMBLY

1. When reinstalling the fork tube in the triple clamp, it is important that the tube be driven home until the top of the tube is perfectly flush with the top surface of the upper triple clamp.

2. The remainder of the assembly procedure is the reverse of disassembly.

3. Be sure that the rubber bush is positioned at the bottom of the damper, and

Loosening the lower triple clamp nut

that the plain steel washer is at the bottom of the fork slider before refitting the slider.

4. Refill each fork leg with the correct amount and grade of oil. Fork leg capacity for the Cota 123 is 150cc (5 oz.) for each leg. For all other models, the correct amount is 175cc (6.5 oz.).

STEERING ASSEMBLY

Montesa steering assembly is similar to that of the Ossa machines. Refer to the Ossa chassis section.

Removing the fork tube from the triple clamp

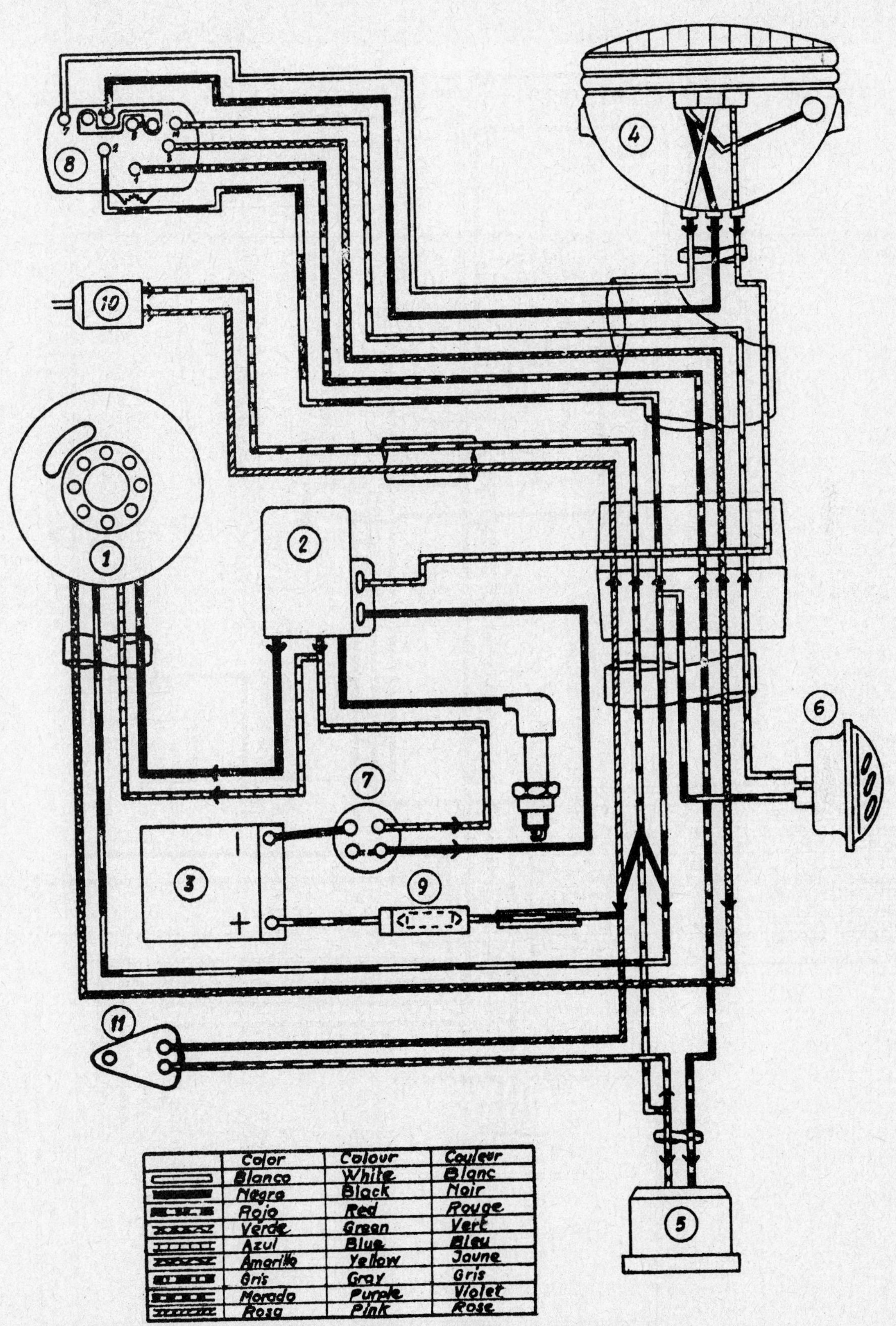

	Color	Colour	Couleur
	Blanco	White	Blanc
	Negro	Black	Noir
	Rojo	Red	Rouge
	Verde	Green	Vert
	Azul	Blue	Bleu
	Amarillo	Yellow	Jaune
	Gris	Gray	Gris
	Morado	Purple	Violet
	Rosa	Pink	Rose

King Scorpion

WIRING DIAGRAMS

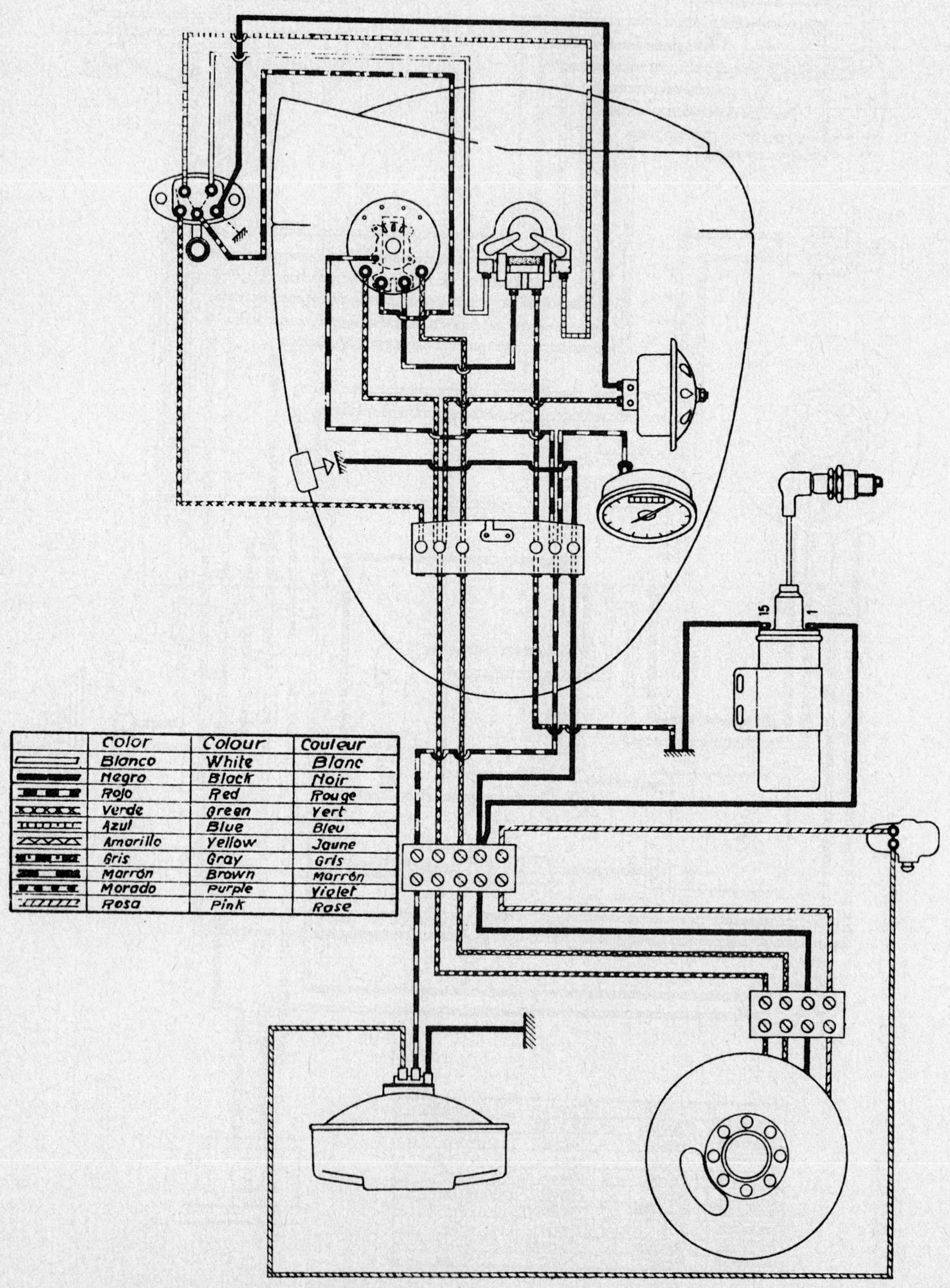

Impala Sport

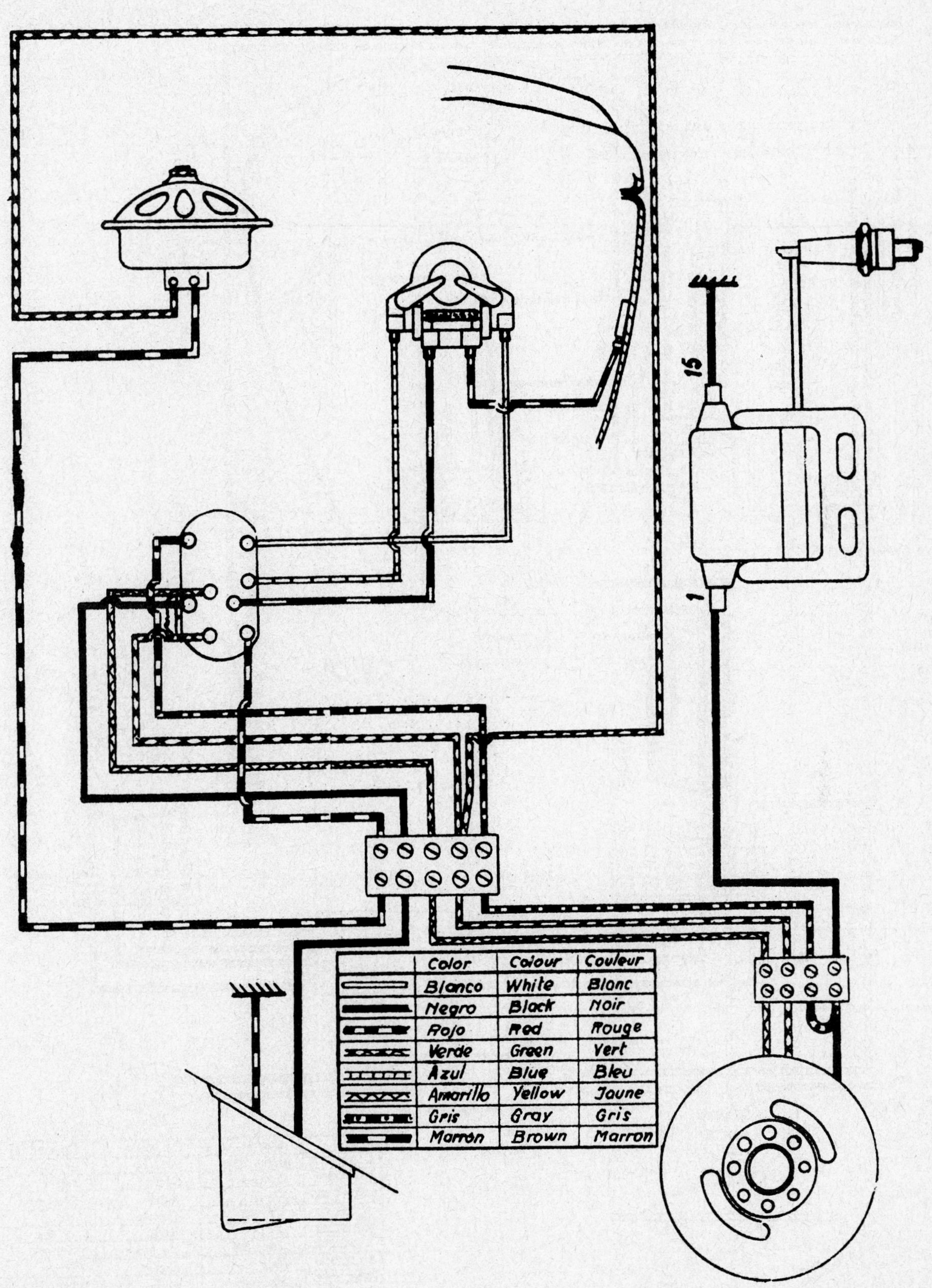

	Color	Colour	Couleur
	Blanco	White	Blanc
	Negro	Black	Noir
	Rojo	Red	Rouge
	Verde	Green	Vert
	Azul	Blue	Bleu
	Amarillo	Yellow	Jaune
	Gris	Gray	Gris
	Marrón	Brown	Marron

Commando 175

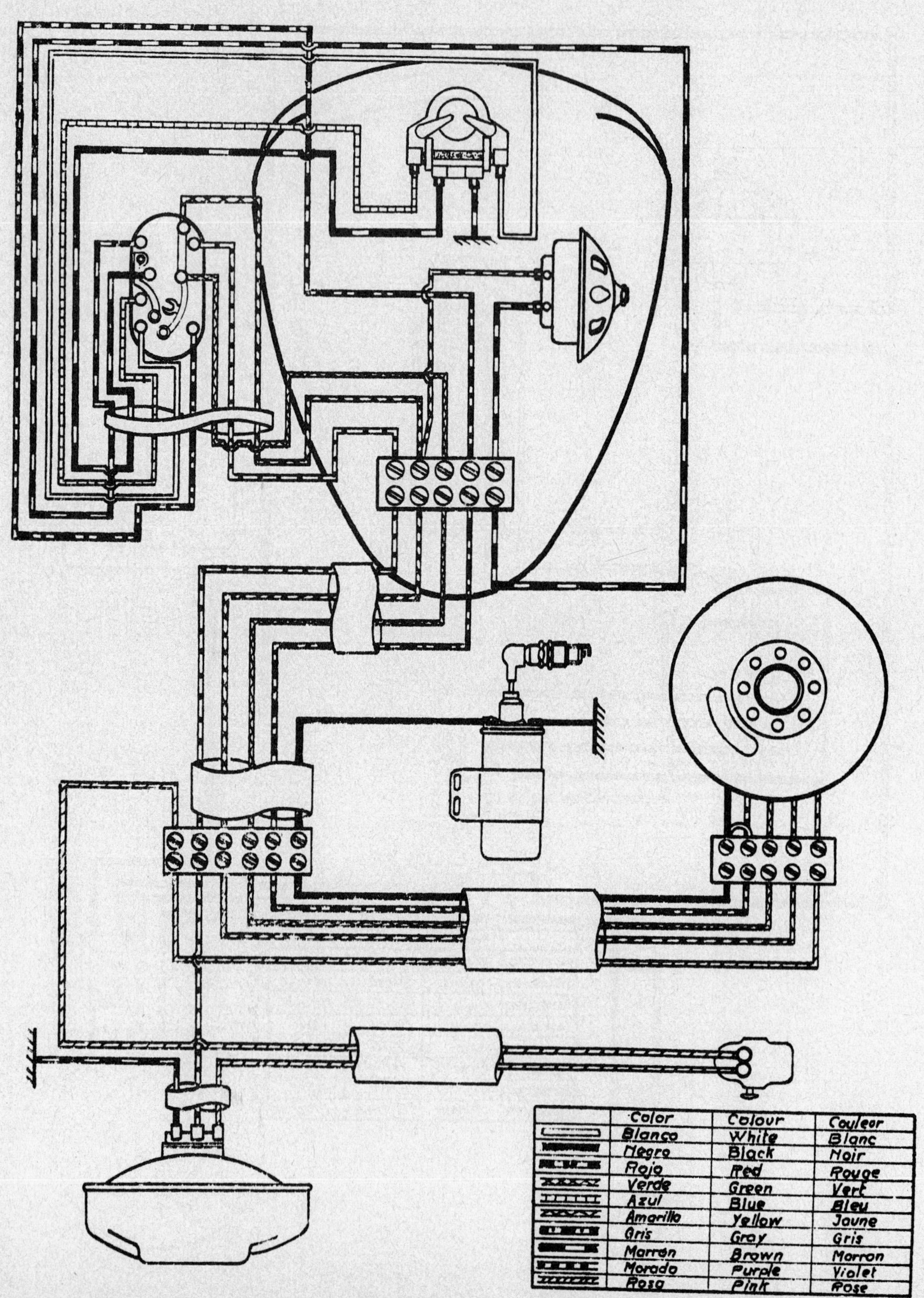
Color | Colour | Couleor
Blanco | White | Blanc
Negro | Black | Noir
Rojo | Red | Rouge
Verde | Green | Vert
Azul | Blue | Bleu
Amarillo | Yellow | Jaune
Gris | Gray | Gris
Marrón | Brown | Marron
Morado | Purple | Violet
Rosa | Pink | Rose

Kenya

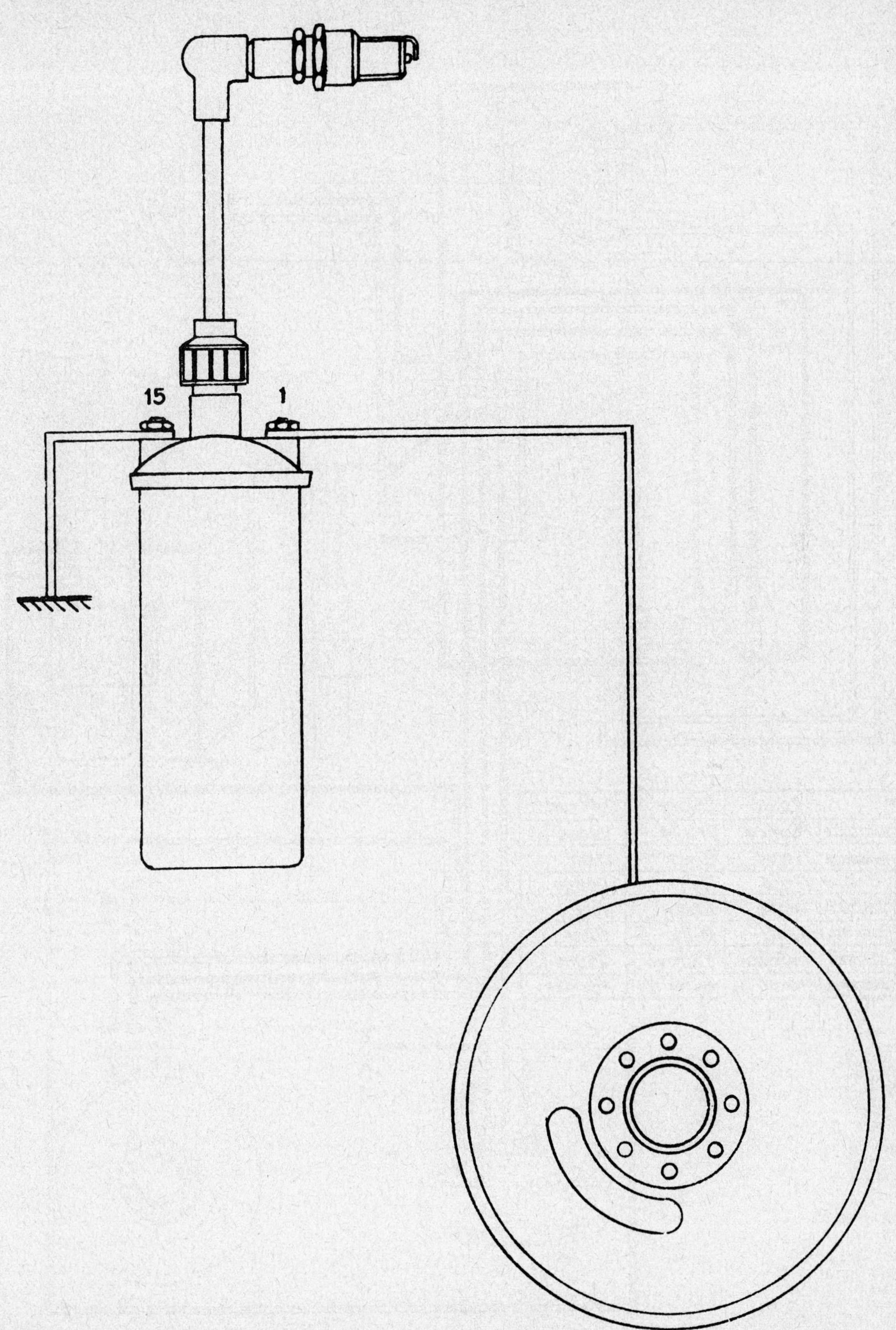

Cappra 250-GP

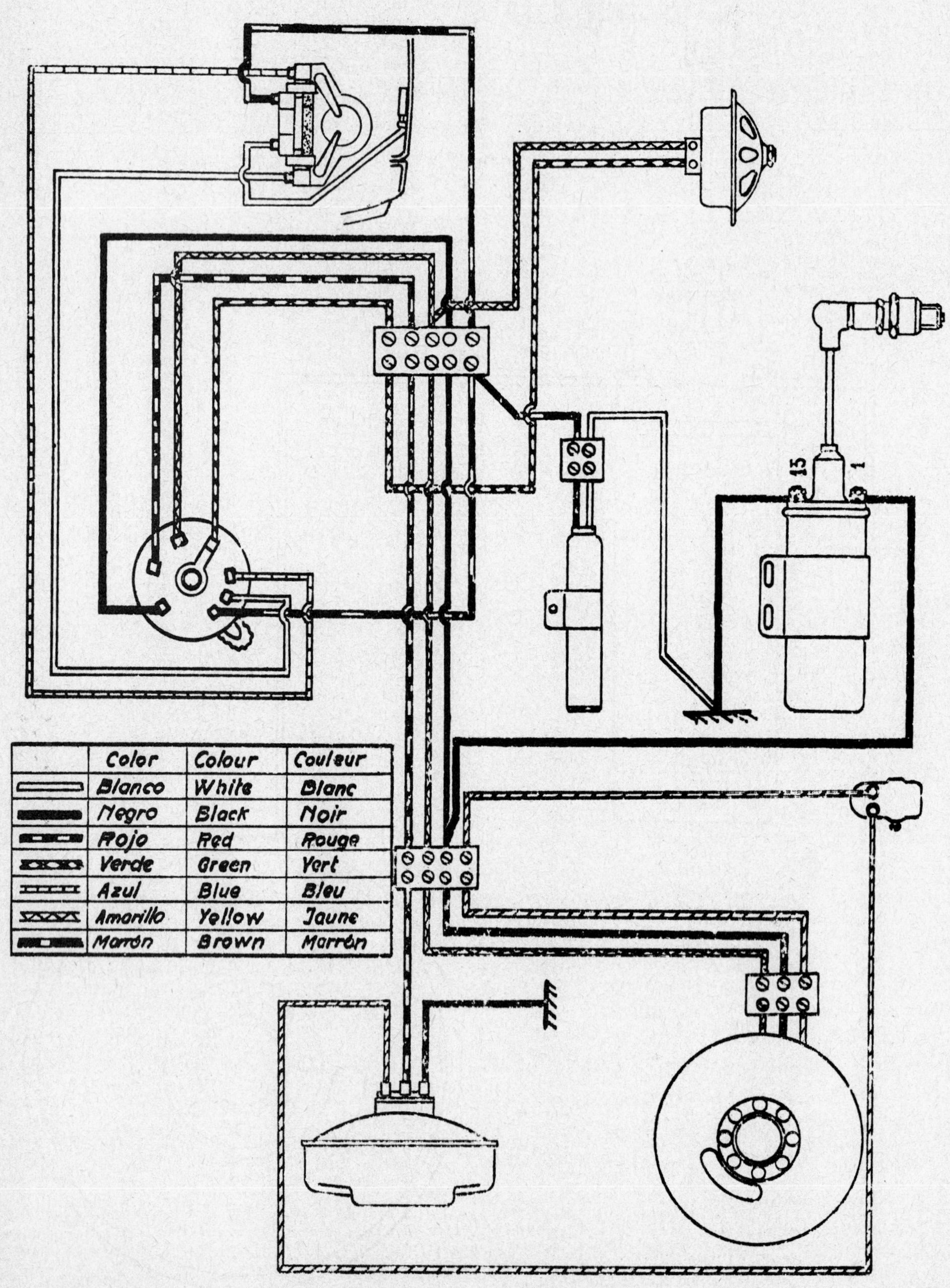
15
1
Color Colour Couleur
Blanco White Blanc
Negro Black Noir
Rojo Red Rouge
Verde Green Vert
Azul Blue Bleu
Amarillo Yellow Jaune
Marrón Brown Marrón

Enduro

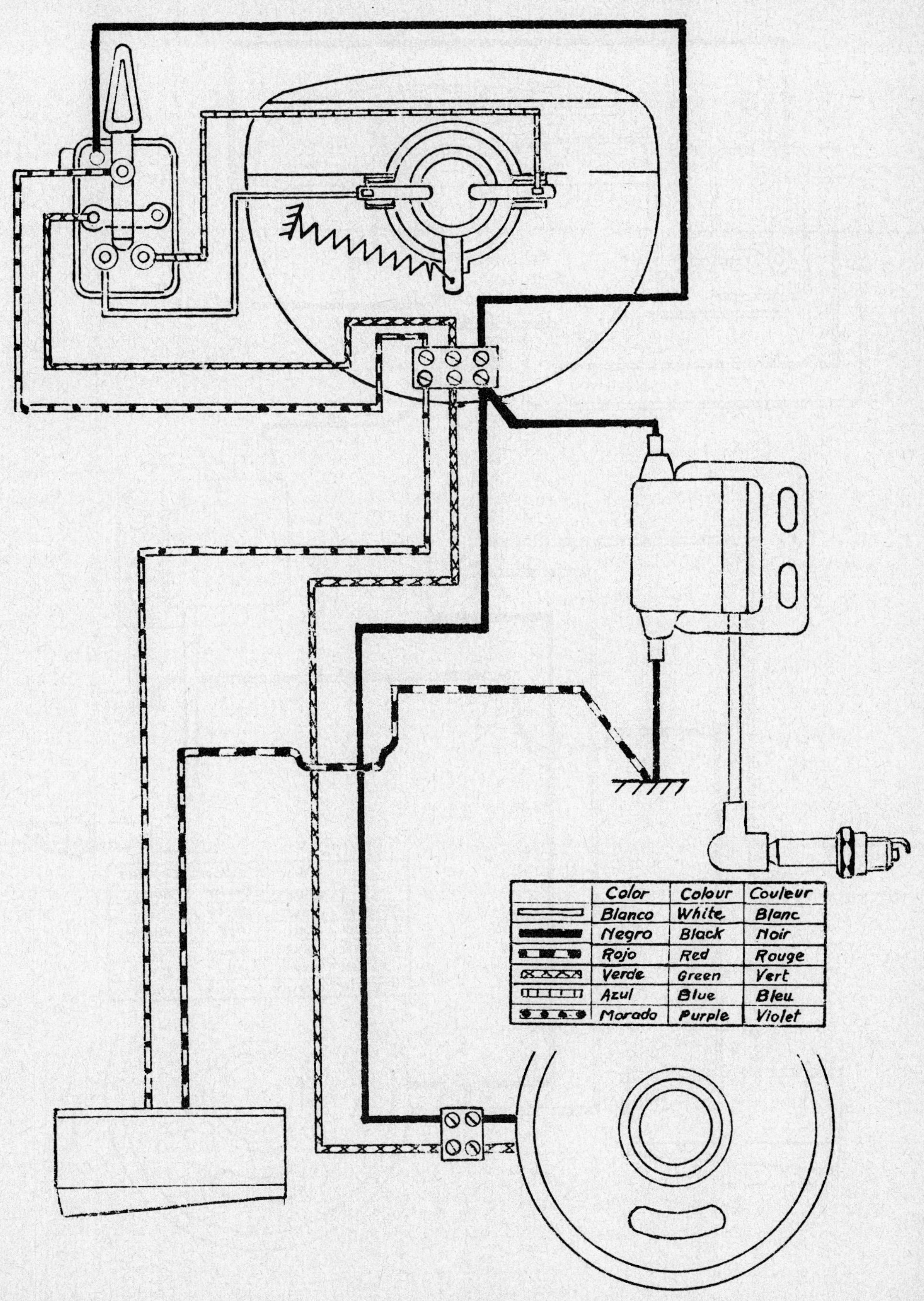
Color
Colour
Couleur
Blanco
White
Blanc
Negro
Black
Noir
Rojo
Red
Rouge
Verde
Green
Vert
Azul
Blue
Bleu
Morado
Purple
Violet

Cota 247

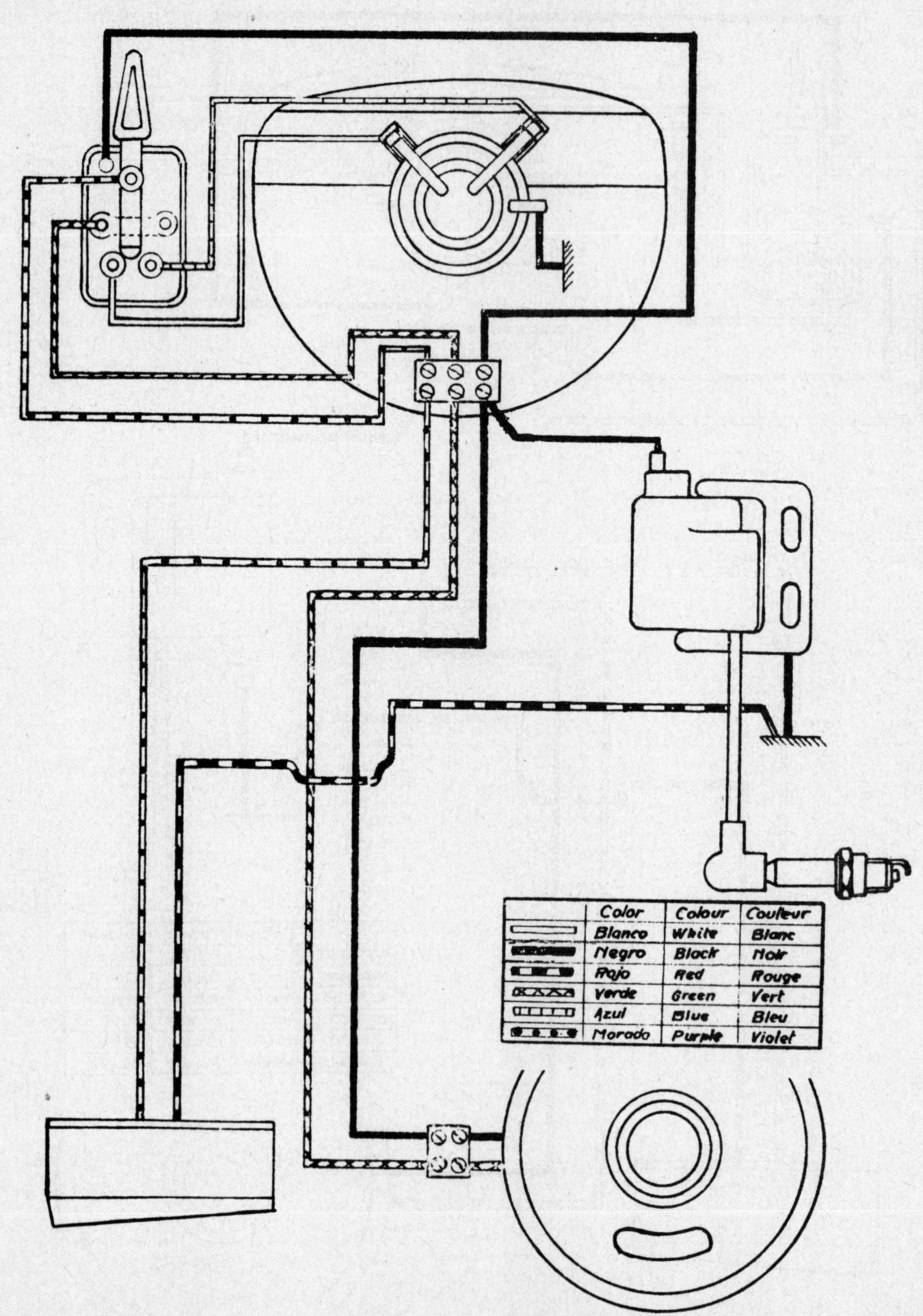
Color | Colour | Couleur
Blanco | White | Blanc
Negro | Black | Noir
Rojo | Red | Rouge
Verde | Green | Vert
Azul | Blue | Bleu
Morado | Purple | Violet

Cota 247

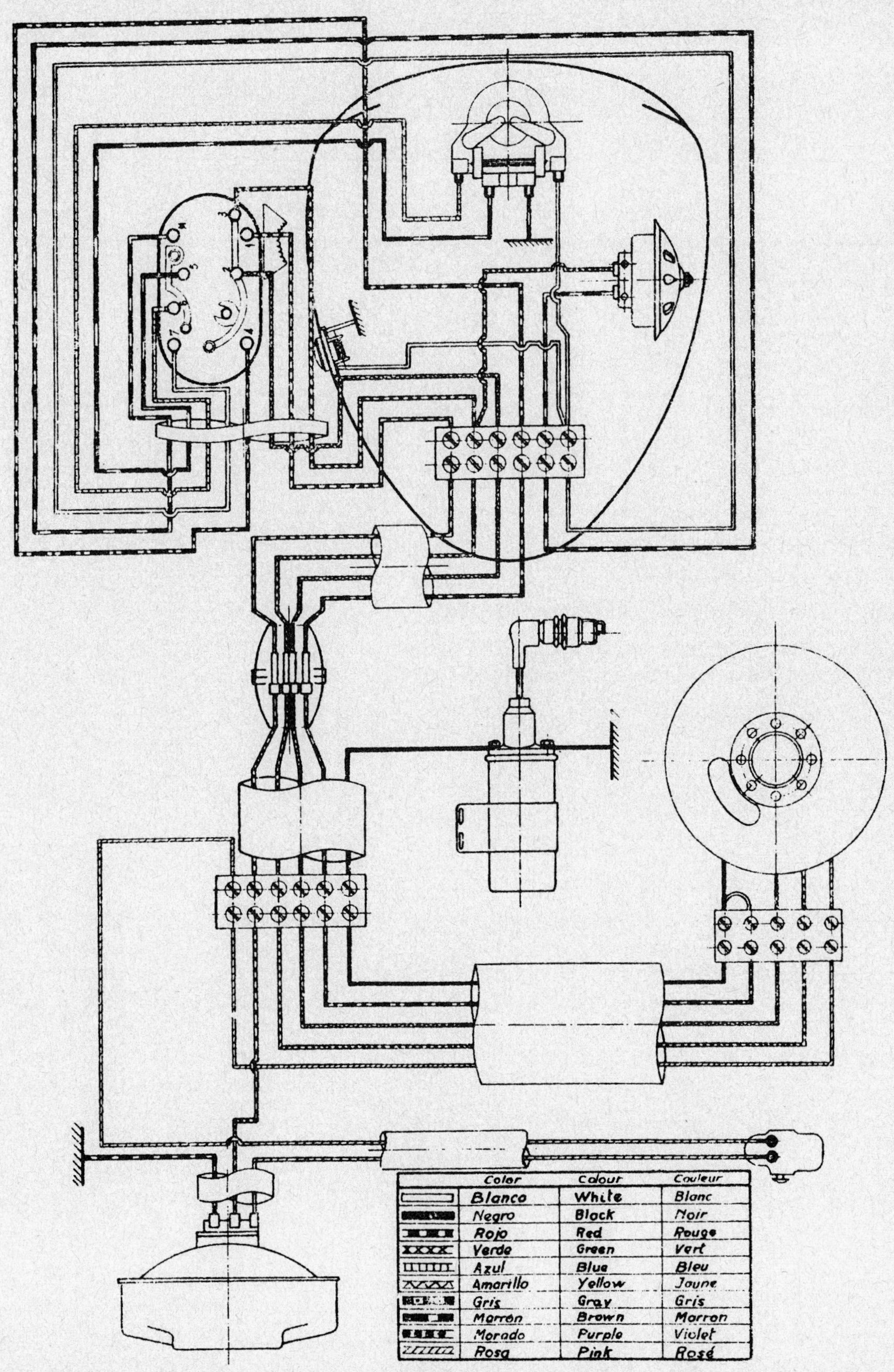
Color
Colour
Couleur
Blanco
White
Blanc
Negro
Black
Noir
Rojo
Red
Rouge
Verde
Green
Vert
Azul
Blue
Bleu
Amarillo
Yellow
Jaune
Gris
Gray
Gris
Marrón
Brown
Marron
Morado
Purple
Violet
Rosa
Pink
Rosé

Scorpion 250

INDEX
MOTO GUZZI

MODEL IDENTIFICATION

The V7, a 700cc former police bike, was the first tourer offered in this country. It produces 50 horsepower at 6000 rpm and is noted for its ability to plod along in traffic without balking.

In 1969, the bore was increased from 80 to 83mm, and the V7 became known as the 750 Ambassador. The redesigned instruments and covers don't do much for performance, but the new clutch throwout bearing makes life easier.

1972 marked the advent of the 850 Eldorado which has 64.5 horses, an all new five-speed transmission, turn signals, a self-returning choke, increased webbing in the crankcases for additional strength, new shift and clutch linkage, a stronger rear hub assembly and a larger oil capacity.

The 750 Sport is a racy version of the Ambassador which comes with clip-ons, a racing tank and seat combination, alloy rims, higher compression, a four leading shoe front brake, and numerous other modifications aimed at reducing weight, cleaning up the lines of the touring bikes, and making this Guzzi a real cafe contender.

MODEL IDENTIFICATION

Each machine comes from the factory with a serial number stamped on the frame down tube and on the left hand crankcase cover. When ordering parts from your dealer mention these numbers to avoid winding up with parts for the wrong model year.

CONTROLS AND ACCESSORIES

Conversion kits are available to mount the gear shift lever on the left side and the rear brake lever on the right side.

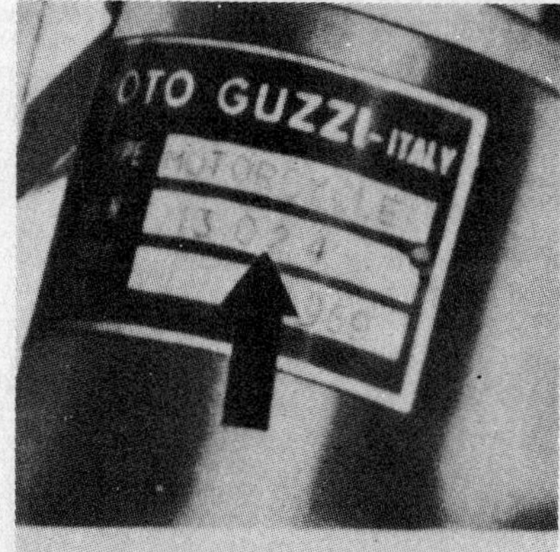

Serial number locations

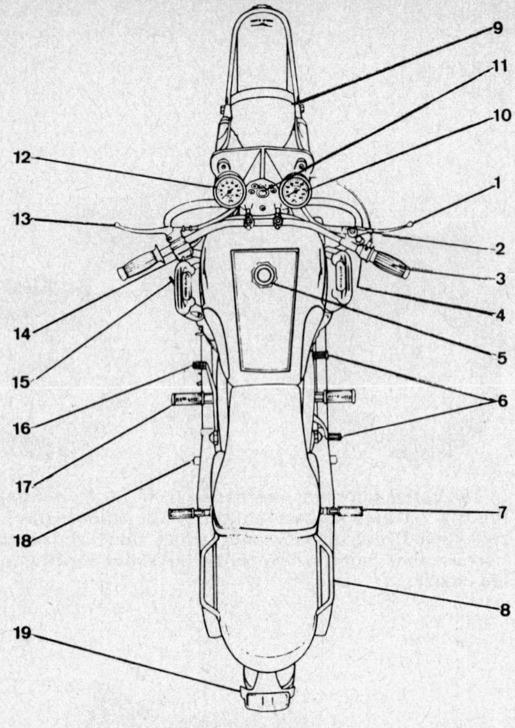

Control layouts

1. Front brake lever
2. Air control lever
3. Throttle control grip
4. Starter button
5. Filler cap
6. Gearshift lever
7. Pillion footrest
8. Pillion handgrip
9. Headlight
10. Speedometer
11. Ignition key
12. Rev-counter
13. Clutch lever
14. Light switch and horn button
15. Side stand
16. Rear brake pedal
17. Footrests
18. Center stand
19. Tail light

GENERAL SPECIFICATIONS

	V700	V750	V850
DIMENSIONS			
Wheelbase (in.)	56.9	57.8	58.8
Length (in.)	87.5	88.3	88.3
Width (in.)	31.2	32.6	31.3
Height (in.)	41.2	42.1	32.5
Min. ground clear. (in.)	5.9	5.9	5.9
Curb weight (lbs)	536	502	548
CAPACITIES			
Fuel tank (gals)	5.28	5.84	5.84
Reserve tank (gals)	1.0	1.0	1.0
Sump (qts)	3.25	3.25	3.25
Transmission (pts)	1.75	1.75	1.75
Drive box (oz)	4.0	4.0	11.4
Fork legs (oz)	5.4	5.4	5.4

	V700	V750	V850
ENGINE			
Type	Four-stroke; push-rod operated overhead valves		
Number of cylinders	2	2	2
Cylinder disposition	"V" 90°		
Bore x stroke (mm)	80 x 70	83 x 70	83 x 78
Displacement (cc)	703.717	757.486	844.050
Compression ratio (:1)	9	9	9.2
Maximum rpm	6000	6500	6500
Horsepower at max. rpm (SAE)	50	60	64
Carb. (Del Orto)			
right	S.S.I.	VHB 29 CD	VHB 29 CD
left	S.S.I.	VHB 29 CS	VHB 29 CS
Lubrication	Pressure; gear driven off crankshaft		
TRANSMISSION			
Clutch type	Flywheel mounted, dry, twin		
Gearbox type	driven plates constant meshed gears bolted to crankcase		
Engine/gearbox ratio (1:)	1.375	1.375	1.235
Internal gear ratios (1:)			
First gear	2.230	2.230	2.000
Second gear	1.333	1.333	1.388
Third gear	0.954	0.954	1.047
Fourth gear	0.750	0.750	0.869
Fifth gear	—	—	0.750
Secondary drive type	Constant speed homokinetic double joint cardan shaft		
Overall gear ratios (1:)			
First gear	14.180	13.413	11.424
Second gear	8.473	8.015	7.929
Third gear	6.063	5.735	5.980
Fourth gear	4.768	4.510	4.964
Fifth gear	—	—	4.284
PERFORMANCES			
Max. speed per gear (solo) (mph)			
First gear	41.0	38.5	42.2
Second gear	59.6	64.6	61.2
Third gear	74.5	89.2	81.9
Fourth gear	106.0	115.0	102.1
Fifth gear	—	—	120.1
Climbing ability per gear (solo) (%)			
First gear	60	60	87
Second gear	34	40	47
Third gear	23	20	28
Fourth gear	14	8	17
Fifth gear	—	—	9

TUNE-UP AND MAINTENANCE

TUNE-UP OPERATIONS

Valve Tappet Adjustment (1800 mi.)

1. Rotate the engine until the piston is at TDC (top dead center) of the compression stroke (clearance at both tappets).

2. Remove the rocker box covers and check the clearances with appropriate size feeler gauges. The inlet valves should be set at 0.15 mm (0.0059 in.), and the exhaust valves should be set at 0.25 mm (0.0098 in.).

Adjusting the valves

3. If the tappets were not properly adjusted, do so using the wrench supplied in the tool kit or a suitable substitute. Loosen the locknut (A) and screw in the adjusting screw (B) to reduce the clearance and out to enlarge it. Upon arriving at a correct adjustment secure the nut while holding the adjusting screw stationary. Recheck the adjustment as securing the nut may have altered it.

4. Repeat the above procedures on the remaining cylinder.

5. When securing the rocker box cover securing screws, do so evenly in a crossed pattern to avoid deforming the gasket.

NOTE: *Ideally, the gasket should be replaced each time it is removed.*

Breaker Point Gap Adjustment (1800 mi.)

1. Remove the distributor cap and rotor, then rotate the engine until the points are open as far as they will go. This is the point where the rubbing block is on the highest point of the breaker cam.

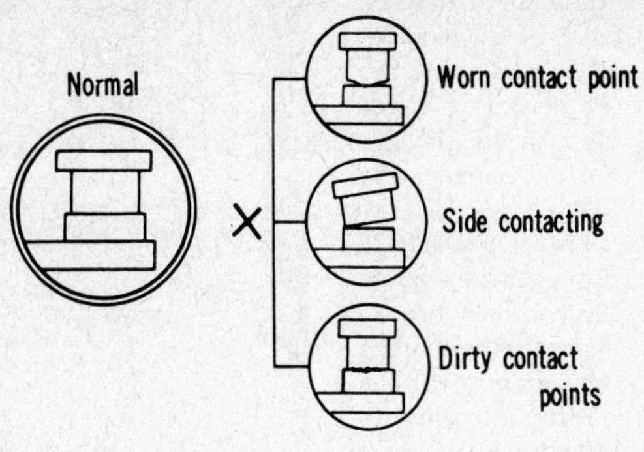

Breaker point contact conditions

2. Check the point gap (A) with a 0.-42–0.48 mm (0.16–0.18 in.) feeler gauge. If the gap is incorrect, adjust it by loosening the adjusting screw (B) slightly so the points can be moved but will not spring shut. Pry the points to open or close the gap by prying with a screwdriver at the adjusting position. Secure the retaining screw when you are satisfied with the adjustment, then check it again to make sure the adjustment hasn't been altered by the securing of the screw.

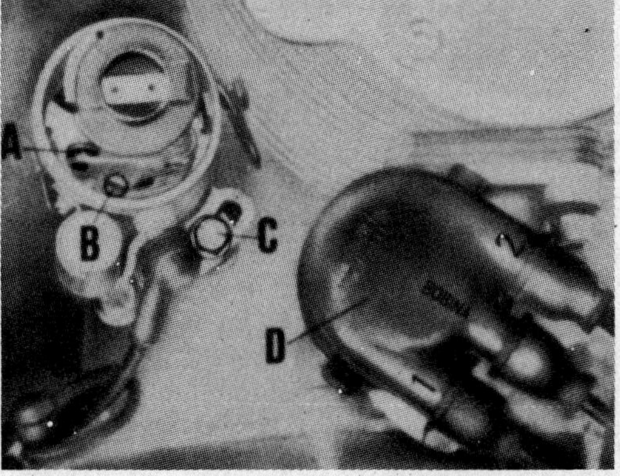

Adjusting the point gap

Ignition Timing

STATIC TIMING

1. Remove the spark plugs, distributor cap (D) and rotor, and the generator belt cover. Rotate the engine where necessary by rotating the generator belt pulley.

2. Make sure that the contact points are correctly gapped at 0.42–0.48 mm (0.-016–0.018 in.) as described in the "Breaker Point Gap Adjustment" section.

3. Rotate the engine until the No. 2 cylinder (the one on the left hand side) is at TDC on its compression stroke (clearance at both tappets). The arrow (D) on the timing cover should be in alignment with the slot (E) on the generator belt pulley. If you go past the slot, rotate the engine around again rather than turning it backward. If you find that the mark and slot don't line up when the piston is at TDC, and you're sure you're on the compression stroke, then the valve timing may be off a few degrees. Consult the "Valve Timing" section of the "Engine and Transmission" chapter for additional information.

4. Position the distributor rotor so the metal contact will skim the metal contact piece in the distributor cap pertaining to No. 2 cylinder. This can be approximated by positioning the cap and making sure

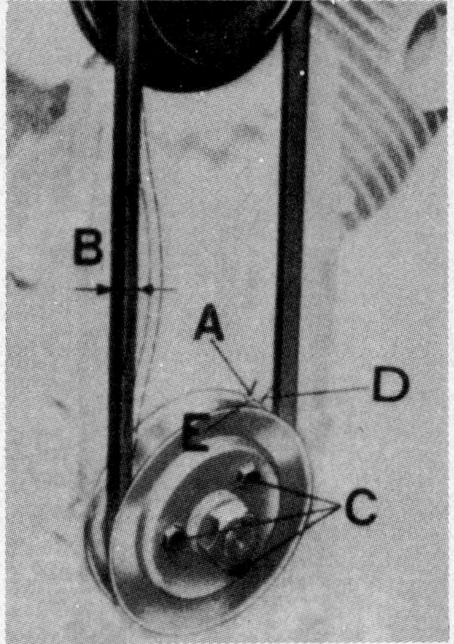

Static timing marks

that the rotor contact piece is directed toward the "2" on the cap. It may be necessary to loosen the bolt which secures the distributor (C), and rotate the distributor body a few degrees. Consult the "Breaker Point Gap Ajustment" section for an illustration of the securing bolt.

5. Connect one lead of the test light to the contact breaker spring or the hot line to the points, and the other lead to ground. Rotate the generator belt pulley until the pulley slot (E) is aligned with the left hand mark (A) on the timing cover. This mark is in a position 10° advanced of the TDC arrow.

6. At this point the contact points should just begin to open and the timing light should come on. If the timing is not dead on, loosen the distributor adjusting bolt (C) and rotate the distributor body to the right or left as necessary. Secure the distributor when a correct timing is achieved and recheck the results with the light.

7. Secure the distributor cap to the distributor and the cables to the plugs and coil. The plug lead labeled "2" must be attached to the plug in No. 2 cylinder. The lead labeled "Bobina" goes to the coil. Replace the generator belt cover.

DYNAMIC TIMING

There are three possible degrees of advanced timing which may be used when timing any of the engines covered in this guide. The marks in the accompanying illustration indicate:

A. the timing reference arrow stamped on the timing chest

B. the TDC mark for the No. 2 cylinder

C. this mark is 10° fixed advanced of TDC

D. this mark is 28° automatically advanced of TDC

E. this mark is the fully advanced position (38°) of TDC.

Dynamic timing marks

This mark is a total of both the fixed and advanced positions.

By checking the timing at all of these three positions you can determine if the advance mechanism works through its three phases. Proceed with the timing in the following manner:

1. Remove the generator belt pulley cover, then run the machine until its normal operating temperature is reached.

2. Connect a strobe light as directed by its manufacturer. There should be one lead to the No. 2 cylinder spark plug, one to a battery positive (+) terminal and one to the battery negative (−) terminal.

3. Start the engine and aim the light at the timing cover arrow (A). Make sure to check that the "C, D, and E" pulley marks align with the arrow at the following engine speeds:

a. Mark "C" at 1200 ± 100 rpm
b. Mark "D" at 2200 ± 100 rpm
c. Mark "E" at 3600 ± 100 rpm

4. If the strobe shows that the timing is advanced or retarded, adjust it by loosening the distributor adjusting bolt and rotating the distributor body slightly until the pulley mark corresponding to the selected engine rpm is in alignment with the timing chest arrow when the arrow is under the beam of the strobe light. The adjustment to the distributor can be made with the engine running.

5. If the strobe indicates a fault with the advance mechanism consult the "Electrical System" section for additional information.

Carburetor Adjustment

All adjustments to the carburetors should be made after the valves have been set according to specification and after the engine has reached its normal operating temperature.

Make sure the choke is in the closed position (C) before making any adjustments. The other position (A) is for cold weather starting.

V700

1. Turn in the idle adjusting screws of both carburetors until they reach their seat, then back them out 1 ½ turns to make sure they're even.

2. Start the engine and run it until its normal operating temperature is reached.

3. Synchronize the carburetors by adjusting the throttle cables in such a way that both throttle slides open simultaneously. This can be done by placing your fingers in the carburetor throat and feeling for when both slides lift up and seat at the same time. Verify, or adjust in this manner, the adjustment by feeling for an even exhaust pulse when the bike is running at about ¼ throttle. The adjustment is made with the throttle cable adjusters which are located where the cables meet the carburetor cap. Secure the locknut to prevent engine vibration from altering the adjustment.

4. Adjust the idle speed as desired by acting on the throttle slide adjusters (B) which are located on the carburetor caps. Both cylinders should be running at the

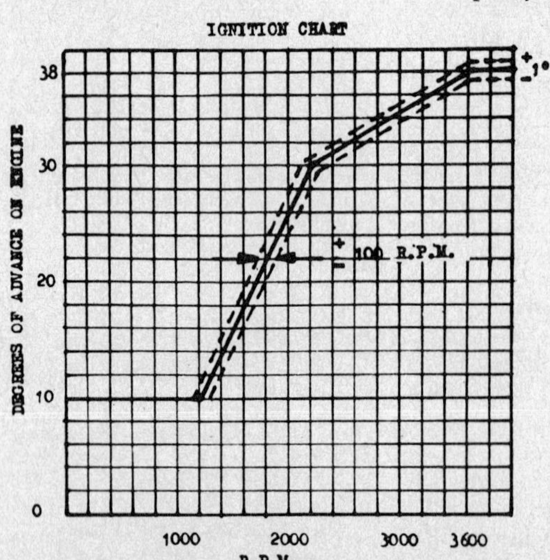

Advance curve for V700 and V750 models

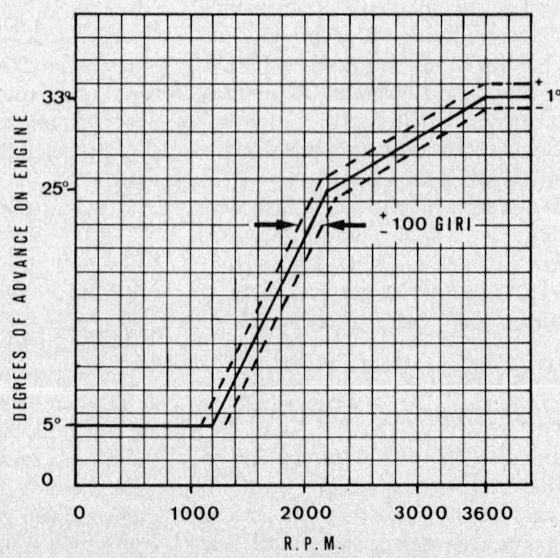

Advance curve for V850 models

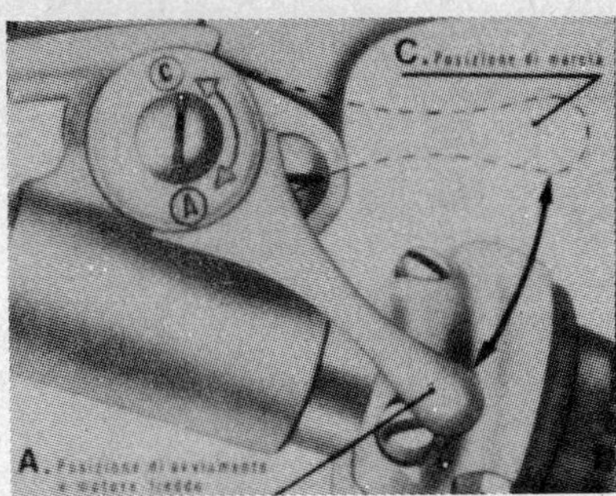

Choke positions

Adjustment points on the V700 carburetor

same speed as evidenced by an even exhaust pulse.

5. Adjust the idle mixture screws (A) to obtain the smoothest idle mixture. It may be necessary to readjust the idle speed (B) to keep the engine running. Turn the idle mixture screw in until the engine rpm begins to drop off, then turn it out until it begins to drop off again. The ideal mixture is somewhere in the middle at that point where the smoothest and strongest idle is. Readjust the idle speeds as necessary.

6. If it was necessary to close the idle mixture screws (A) all the way, the pilot jets are probably too small and larger ones should be fitted. If it was necessary to turn the idle screws out more than 1 ½ turns, the pilot jets are probably too large and smaller ones should be fitted. Change jets one size at a time until the desired results are attained.

7. Recheck the throttle slide synchronization and make sure the locknuts on the slide and idle speed adjusters have been secured.

V750 AND V850

1. Check the adjustment of the choke mechanism. It should have about 4 mm (0.016 in.) of free play when in the fully closed position to ensure that engine vibration can't cause the choke to open.

2. Remove the air filter box and inlet sleeves, then check the throttle slide synchronization by touching the slides with your fingers while operating the throttle. If both slides don't open simultaneously, adjust them by means of the cable adjusters (A).

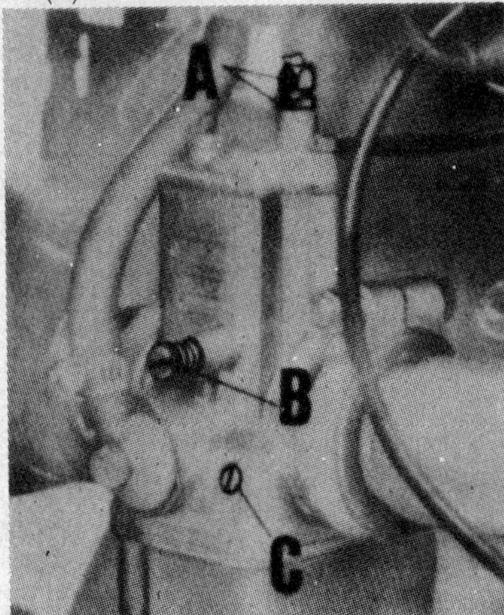

Adjustment points on the V750 and V850 carburetor

3. Adjust the idle speed by rotating the idle speed adjusting screw (C) in to reduce the idle speed and out to increase it. The optimal setting under normal conditions is about 1 ½ turns off its seat for the left hand carb and 1 ¾–2 turns for the right hand unit. Consult Step 4 of the previous section for additional information. The idle speed should be about 1000–1200 rpm.

4. Disconnect the right hand cylinder plug lead with the engine turned off, then start the engine and count the number of pulses before it stalls. If the engine did not fire four or five times, adjust the idling screw (B) and repeat the process until it does so. Reconnect the plug lead and perform the same operation on the opposite cylinder.

CARBURETOR MIXTURE ADJUSTMENT

Adjust the carburetors as directed in the "Carburetor Adjustment" section. In most cases, adjustments at the needles can compensate for mixture deficiencies, but the jets may be exchanged if necessary.

If, upon opening the throttle, the engine is sluggish about picking up speed and shows a tendency to backfire, decelerate, or refuse to run at peak rpm, and if opening the choke makes things a little better, the mixture is too lean due to a restrictive main jet. Going one or two sizes larger will probably improve the performance. Raising the jet needle a notch may also help as this will also enrich the mixture.

If, upon opening the throttle, the exhaust note becomes duller and the engine emits black smoke, and if opening the choke up somewhat accentuates the condition, the mixture is too rich and a smaller main jet is called for. Lowering the jet needle may also help as this will lean out the mixture.

If a change of more than one size is required, change step-by-step. New needle adjustments will probably be necessary, but this can only be determined by trial and error.

TUNE-UP SPECIFICATIONS (All Models)

Ignition Timing	
Breaker point gap	0.42-0.48 mm (0.016-0.018 in.)
Ignition timing (fully advanced)	38°
Spark Plugs	
Type	Marelli CW 25 LVT Bosch W2 75 T2
Gap setting	0.6 mm (0.23 in.)
Tappet Adjustment	
Clearance (cold)	
Intake	015 mm (0.0059 in.)
Exhaust	0.25 mm (0.0098 in.)
Carburetor Adjustment	
Consult "Carburetor Adjustment" section	

MAINTENANCE ITEMS

Oil Changes and Lubrication

ENGINE OIL

The engine oil level should be checked using the dipstick (A) at least every 300 miles without fail and the oil should be changed every 1,800 miles under normal conditions, or more often if used in dusty or extremely cold climates. The oil level should be above the minimum mark on the dipstick, but below the top mark as measured with the engine at its normal operating temperature. Turn down the filler cap one turn when taking a reading to get accurate results.

Drain the oil with the engine at its normal operating temperature by removing

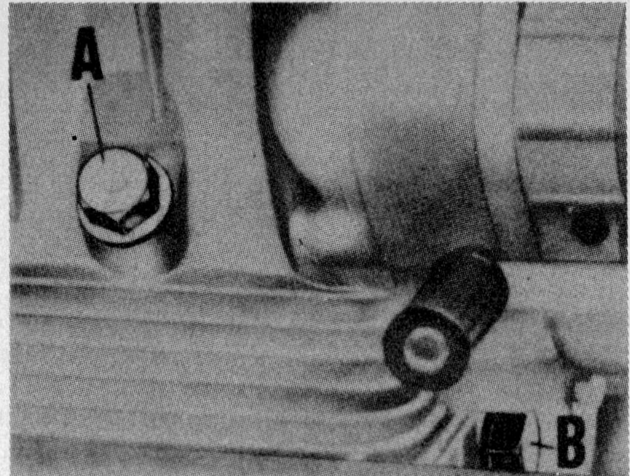

Engine oil filler and drain plugs

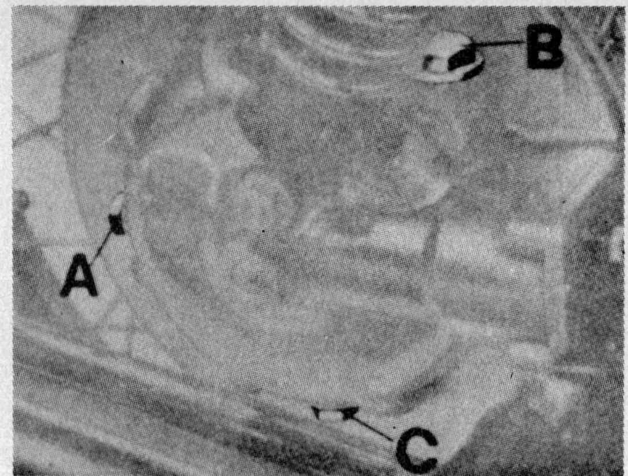

Drive box level, filler, and drain plugs (V700 and V750)

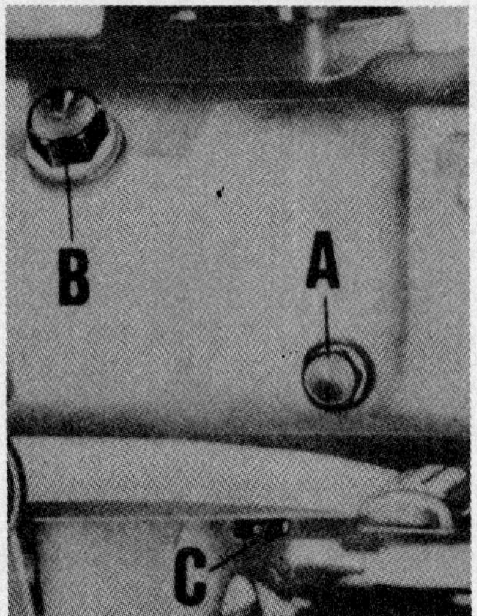

Transmission oil level, filler, and drain plugs

first the filler plug (A), and then the drain plug (B), and allow the oil to drain into a suitable receptacle. Remember to replace the drain plug before refilling.

TRANSMISSION OIL

The oil level of the transmission should be checked every 1,800 miles, or more often if the transmission leaks. Check the level with the engine at its normal operating temperature by removing the level plug (A); the oil should come right up to the lower lip of the level plug hole. If it looks like the transmission needs oil and it's getting close to replacement time, replace it now, but if the level is down due to leakage, add fresh oil until it begins to run out the level hole.

The transmission oil should be changed every 6,000 miles or at least once annually. With the engine at its normal operating temperature remove the filler plug (B), level-plug (A),and drain plug (C) and allow the oil to drain into a suitable receptacle. Secure the drain plug and add fresh oil through the filler plug until it begins to run out through the level plug, then secure the remaining two plugs.

REAR WHEEL DRIVE OIL

The rear wheel drive oil should be checked every 1,800 miles and changed every 6,000 miles (or annually) as in the case of the transmission oil. Follow all of the above procedures given in the above section.

NOTE: *On the Sport and V850 models, there is no drain plug. Instead, the bottom cover is removed to drain the oil.*

FRONT FORK OIL

The oil in the forks should be changed every 12,000 miles, annually, or whenever necessary.

Drain the oil after riding the machine so the oil is flowing freely in the forks. Draining is accomplished by removing the drain plugs and washers (A) from the bottom of each fork leg and then removing the filler caps from the top of each leg. Pumping the forks several times will

Drive box level and filler plugs, and drain cover (V850)

Front fork drain and filler plugs

ensure that all the oil has drained. To refill the forks, install the drain plugs, renewing the washers if necessary, and add the necessary amount of lubricant. If the forks have been taken apart and cleaned you should add an additional 10cc to make up for the oil that normally would be coating the internal parts.

STEERING HEAD BEARINGS

The steering head bearings should be removed and repacked with fresh bearing grease every 12,000 miles or whenever necessary.

WHEEL BEARINGS

The wheel bearings should be removed and repacked with fresh bearing grease every 12,000 miles or whenever necessary.

SWING ARM BEARINGS

The swing arm bearings do not require periodic maintenance, however it is a good idea to inspect and thoroughly repack them any time work on the swing arm assembly becomes necessary.

OIL BREATHER UNIT

Whenever you place the machine in storage for an extended period of time the possibility of undesireable deposits forming on the breather diaphragm is present. This may cause the diaphragm to stick resulting in oil leakage. Before returning the machine to active duty it is advisable to remove and inspect the unit in the following manner:

1. Remove the breather unit securing bolt.
2. Remove the breather by backing it out to the left.
3. Soak the unit in a suitable solvent, then blow it dry.
4. Check the action of the pressure relief valve by moving it with a suitable rod inserted into the central tube of the breather. Free the rod, if necessary, then clean the unit thoroughly in solvent, blow it dry, and install it on the machine.

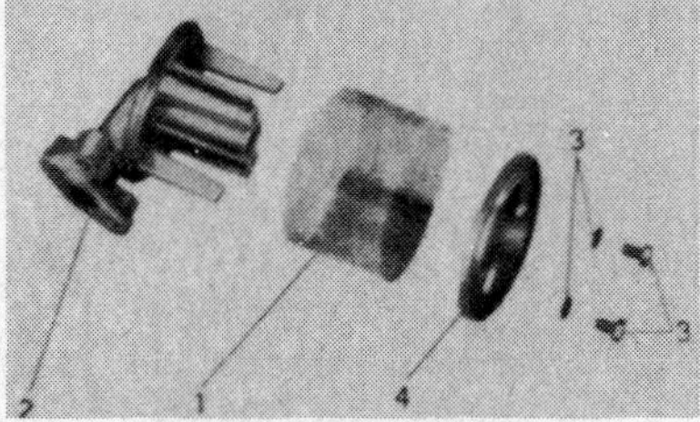

Oil filter assembly
1. Wire mesh
2. Filter body
3. Filter cover mounting bolts
4. Filter cover

OIL FILTER

An oil filter is fitted to all of the models covered in this guide, but is not a regular maintenance item. However, if for any reason you suspect that there may be foreign objects in the oil supply, the filter should be removed, thoroughly cleaned, and then remounted in conjunction with a flushing of the crankcase. The filter is mounted above the oil pump which is located in the right hand lower corner of the crankcase immediately behind the oil pump gear. Access to the filter is most easily gained by removing the sump pan, but can also be reached by removing the oil pump assembly.

Routine Checks and Adjustments

GENERATOR BELT

Over a period of time the generator belt will become loose and the need for adjustment will arise to prevent slipping and the subsequent loss of generating efficiency. Normal belt slack (A) is about 1 cm per 10 kgs (0.39 in./21 lbs). Avoid overtightening the belt as this may cause premature wear to the belt and generator bearings.

Adjust the generator belt in the following manner:

Adjusting the generator belt tension

1. Remove the three bolts (B) which secure the outer half-pulley to the pulley hub, then remove the half-pulley.
2. Add or remove spacing collars as necessary. Removing spacers will increase belt tension and installing spacers will decrease it. Spacers should be removed or installed one at a time and, if more than one spacer is removed, the extras should be placed at the front and rear of the pulley so as not to throw the pulleys out of alignment.
3. Replace the outer half-pulley and secure the three mounting bolts. Recheck the adjustment and repeat the operation until a satisfactory adjustment is attained.

GENERATOR

Every 6000 miles, or whenever necessary, the generator commutator should be cleaned with a clean cloth slightly moistened with clean gasoline.

If carbon or copper dust has settled in the mica insulators, it should be blown clean with compressed air.

At this time inspect the brushes and replace them if chipped, excessively worn, or if they look like they won't last another 6000 miles. Make sure you use authorized replacement parts, and be sure the brushes make perfect contact with the commutator.

REGULATOR

The regulator is sealed to keep you from tampering with it if you don't know what you're doing. If the unit is malfunctioning it should be replaced or returned to your dealer for repair.

STARTER MOTOR

Every 12,000 miles, or whenever necessary, the starter motor commutator should be cleaned with a clean cloth moistened with clean gasoline.

Carbon or copper dust between the rotor segments should be blown away with compressed air. At this time the brushes should be inspected and replaced if worn, damaged, or if they look like they won't make it for another 12,000 miles. They must be in perfect contact with the commutator to avoid damage to it.

CLUTCH LEVER

Check the clutch adjustment periodically or whenever clutch engagement or gear-shifting problems are experienced. Free play at the lever should be about ⅛ in. (4 mm) and can be adjusted by loosening the thumb screw (B) at the lever and screwing the adjuster (A) in or out as necessary until a correct adjustment is achieved. Secure the thumb screw before riding the machine or the adjustment may be lost.

If the clutch has been slipping, the adjuster should be backed out; if the clutch has been dragging, as evidenced by loud gear engagements or creeping at stop lights, the adjuster should be turned in. If adjustment at the hand lever does not prove sufficient, additional adjustment may be made at the release lever by loosening the locknut (D) and adjusting the cable adjuster (C) as necessary. Make sure that the clutch releases completely to avoid accelerated wear to the clutch mechanism and make sure that adjustments at the release lever do not adversely affect the adjustment at the hand lever which may have to be done again.

Adjusting the clutch cable

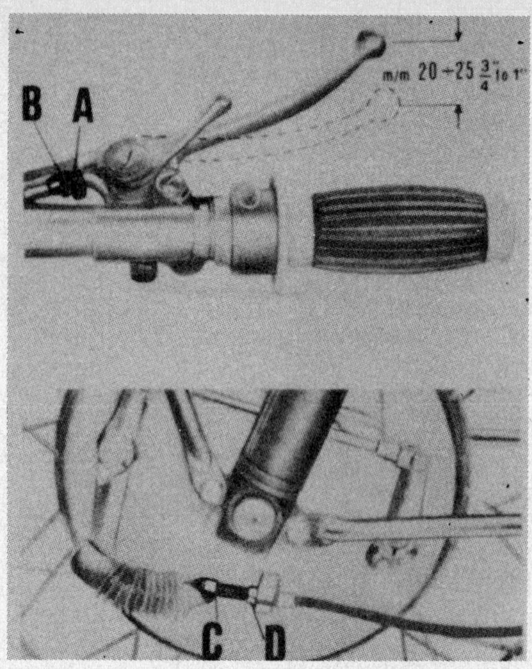

Front brake adjustment

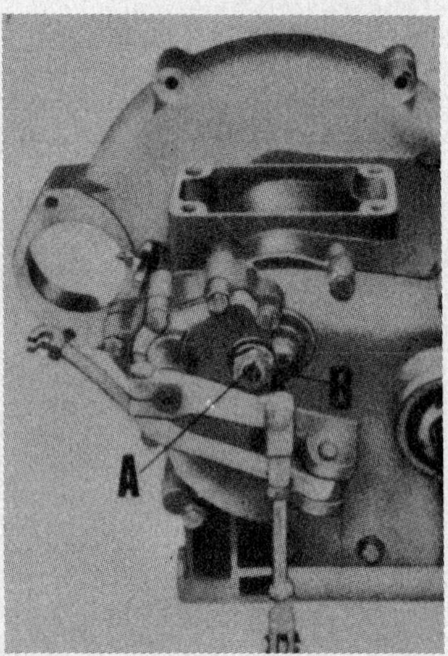

Gearbox adjustment (V700 and V750)

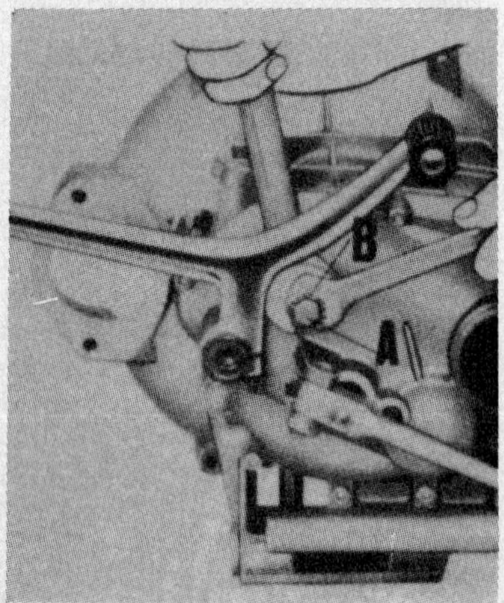

Gearbox adjustment (V850)

SHIFTER MECHANISM

If noisy gear shifts cannot be alleviated by adjusting the clutch, try adjusting the shifter mechanism. Loosen the locknut (B), then rotate the adjusting screw (A), on V700 and V750 models, or the eccentric nut (B) on the V850 model, in and out until a position is reached where the gears will shift smoothly both up and down throughout the range, and where Neutral can be readily found.

When the best adjustment is found, the locknut should be secured while the adjusting screw or eccentric nut is held steady by means of a screwdriver.

Brakes

FRONT BRAKE ADJUSTMENT

There should be about ¾–1 in. (20–25 mm) of free play at the hand lever when the brake is properly adjusted. This is the distance the tip of the lever can move before the brake shoes contact the drum.

Adjust the brake by loosening the thumbscrew (A) and rotating the adjuster (B) until the proper adjustment is arrived at, at which time the thumbscrew should once again be secured. If you are unable to attain the desired results at the hand lever, further adjustments can be made by loosening the locknut (D) and adjusting the adjuster (C) located on the brake backing plate.

REAR BRAKE ADJUSTMENT

There should be about ¾–1 in. (20–25 mm) of free play at the tip of the brake pedal (B) before the brake shoes begin to contact the brake drum. All adjustments to the rear brake are made at the thumb screw (A) located on the end of the brake rod. Usually, the linings are completely worn by the time the adjuster reaches the end of the threaded portion of the brake rod.

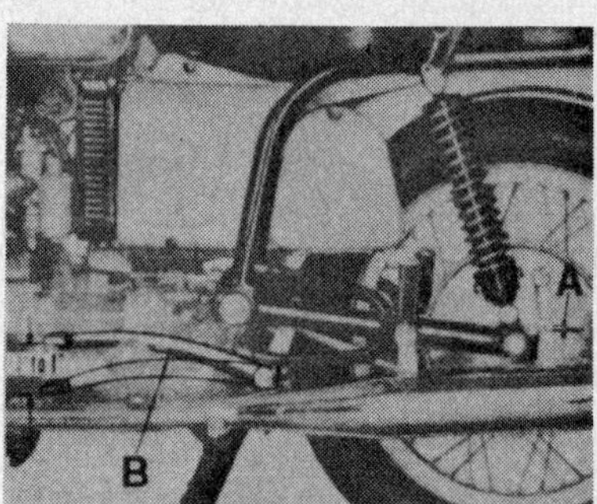

Rear brake adjustment

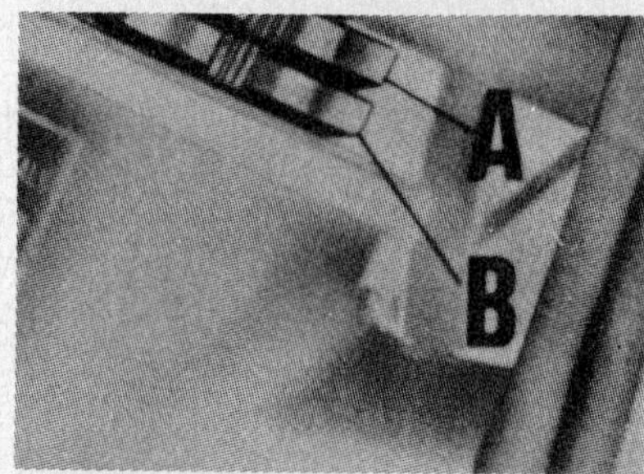

Steering head bearing adjustment

STEERING HEAD

Excessively loose steering may be remedied provided it is not due to wear of the steering head bearings. Loosen the locknut (A) and adjust the lockring (B), using a suitable wrench, to a position where the steering is smooth and free but not loose. The forks should fall to either side, rather than only one side each time they are released, and there should not be an appreciable amount of play when the forks are grasped at the bottom and pulled back and forth.

When the play is as desired, secure the locknut while keeping a firm hold on the lockring so the adjustment is not lost. If the steering is adjusted too loose or too tight it will result in rapid wear of the bearings and their races.

REAR SHOCK ABSORBERS

The rear shocks require no periodic adjustment, but various circumstances may warrant adjusting the load level to a more suitable position.

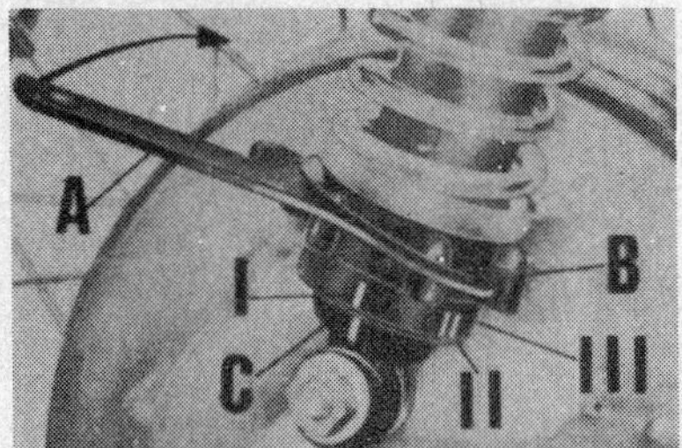

Shock absorber adjustments

The shocks come with three possible adjustments designed to meet all load requirements. The first position is for normal conditions, the second position is for carrying additional equipment or a passenger, and the third position is for two-up riding with additional equipment.

The shocks are adjusted by means of the special wrench (A) which comes with each machine. Using the wrench to turn the adjusting cam (B) counterclockwise will move the shock from position "1" to position "2" and so on. The shock is properly adjusted when the mark for the desired setting is aligned with the fixed mark (C). Make sure both shocks are always kept on the same setting.

AIR CLEANER

The air filter element used on these machines is a dry paper type and can be found in the air filter box which is secured to the frame. The element can be cleaned with kerosene and blown dry, or the dirt can merely be blown off with compressed air. If the element ever becomes saturated with oil or becomes too dirty to clean, it must be replaced. The air filter should be attended to at least every 9000 miles or whenever necessary as conditions dictate.

PERIODIC MAINTENANCE AND LUBRICATION CHART

Weekly

①1. Check battery electrolyte level
2. Check tire pressure

After 300 miles on a rebuilt motor

3. Drain and replace the crankcase oil
4. Secure all nuts and bolts
5. Check and adjust if necessary

Every 600 miles

6. Check the level of the crankcase oil and replenish if necessary
7. Lubricate the cables

Every 1,800 miles

8. Replace crankcase oil supply
9. Check and adjust tappets if necessary
10. Clean and gap spark plugs
11. Check transmission oil and replenish supply if necessary
12. Check drive box oil supply and replenish if necessary

Every 6,000 miles

13. Clean gas taps, filters, lines, and tank vent
14. Disassemble carburetors and rebuild if necessary, but if she's running good leave her alone
15. Change transmission oil
16. Change drive box oil
17. Check the battery terminals then clean, secure, and vaseline them if necessary
18. Clean generator commutator with a clean cloth slightly moistened with gasoline

Every 12,000 miles

19. Check condition of wheel bearings and replace or repack the assembly as necessary
20. Inspect steering head bearings and replace or repack as necessary.
21. Replace fork oil
22. Clean starter motor commutator with a clean cloth slightly moistened with gasoline

① The numbers indicate reference points on the accompanying illustration

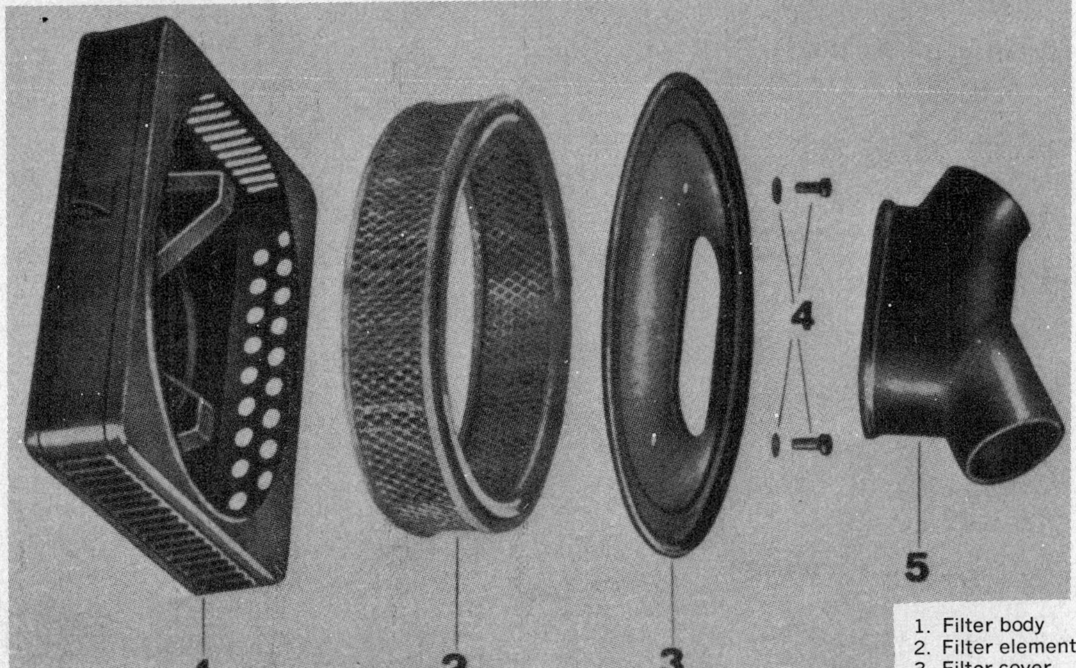

Air cleaner assembly

1. Filter body
2. Filter element
3. Filter cover
4. Cover securing bolts
5. Junction tube

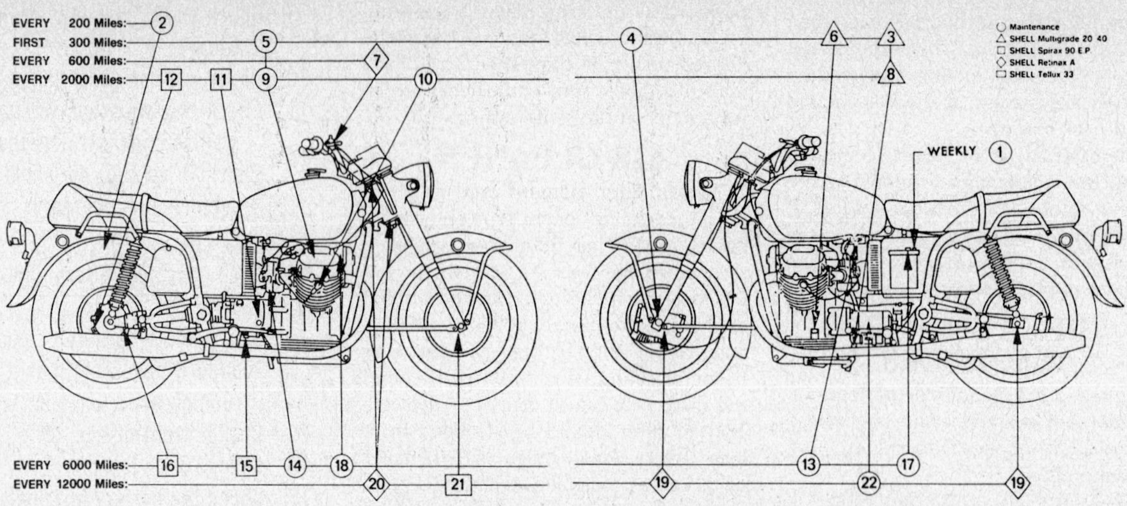

Maintenance and lubrication points

MAINTENANCE DATA

	V700	V750	V850
Engine Oil Capacity (qts)	3.25	3.25	3.25
Transmission Oil Capacity (pts)	1.75	1.75	1.75
Drive Box Oil Capacity (oz)	4.0	4.0	11.4
Fork Oil Capacity (oz)	5.4	5.4	5.4

Tires (all models)
Front (in.) 4.00 x 18 Pressure (psi): 21
Rear (in.) 4.00 x 18 Pressure (psi): Solo 25 Duo 28

ENGINE AND TRANSMISSION

ENGINE REMOVAL AND INSTALLATION

1. Run the engine until its normal operating temperature is reached, then drain the oil.
2. Remove the battery covers from both sides, then disconnect the battery cables.
3. Disconnect the speedometer cable from the transmission housing.
4. Remove the tank, seat, and battery, then remove the battery support plate.
5. Disconnect the throttle and choke cables at the carburetors, or remove the carburetors and position them out of the way as indicated in the accompanying illustration.
6. Disconnect the clutch, starter, and neutral indicator cables from their mounting positions on the engine.
7. Disconnect and remove the ignition coil, distributor cap, spark plug leads, and the distributor rotor.
8. Remove the generator covers, generator belt guard, and the generator unit. It is not entirely necessary to remove the generator; it may be repositioned as in the accompanying illustration to gain sufficient clearance.
9. Remove the exhaust system.
10. Block the engine to keep it from falling out of the frame, then remove the

Removing the engine and transmission from the frame

bolts which secure the engine/transmission assembly to the frame. Remove the engine by slipping it forward, tilting it to the right, and lifting it out of the frame. At this point, the engine should be thoroughly cleaned and degreased before any further disassembling is carried out.

11. Installing the engine is merely a reversal of the removal process. Make sure you replenish the oil supply and readjust the various systems as necessary.

TOP END SERVICE

Cylinder Head

REMOVAL AND DISASSEMBLY

1. Remove the spark plug leads and plugs, then disconnect the cylinder head lubrication pipe.

2. Remove the rocker cover securing screws, rocker covers, and cover gaskets.

Removing the rocker spindles

If the cover is reluctant to leave its seat, tap it gently with a hammer and wood block.

CAUTION: *Do not attempt to pry the cover off or it will probably never be oil tight again.*

3. Remove the rocker spindle bolts and washers, then remove the rocker arm spindles, rocker arms, and the rocker

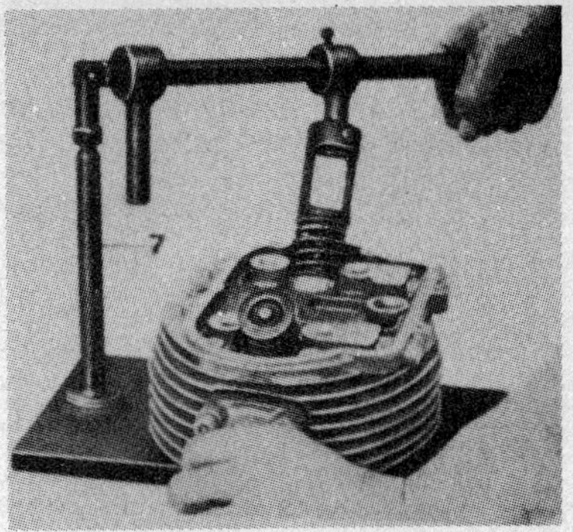

Removing the valves with the special tool

arm springs and washers. The tappet adjusting screw and locknut may be removed from the rockers.

4. Remove the push rods, keeping them separate for installation in their original locations.

5. Remove the rocker arms support by removing the four long and two short bolts which secure the support to the

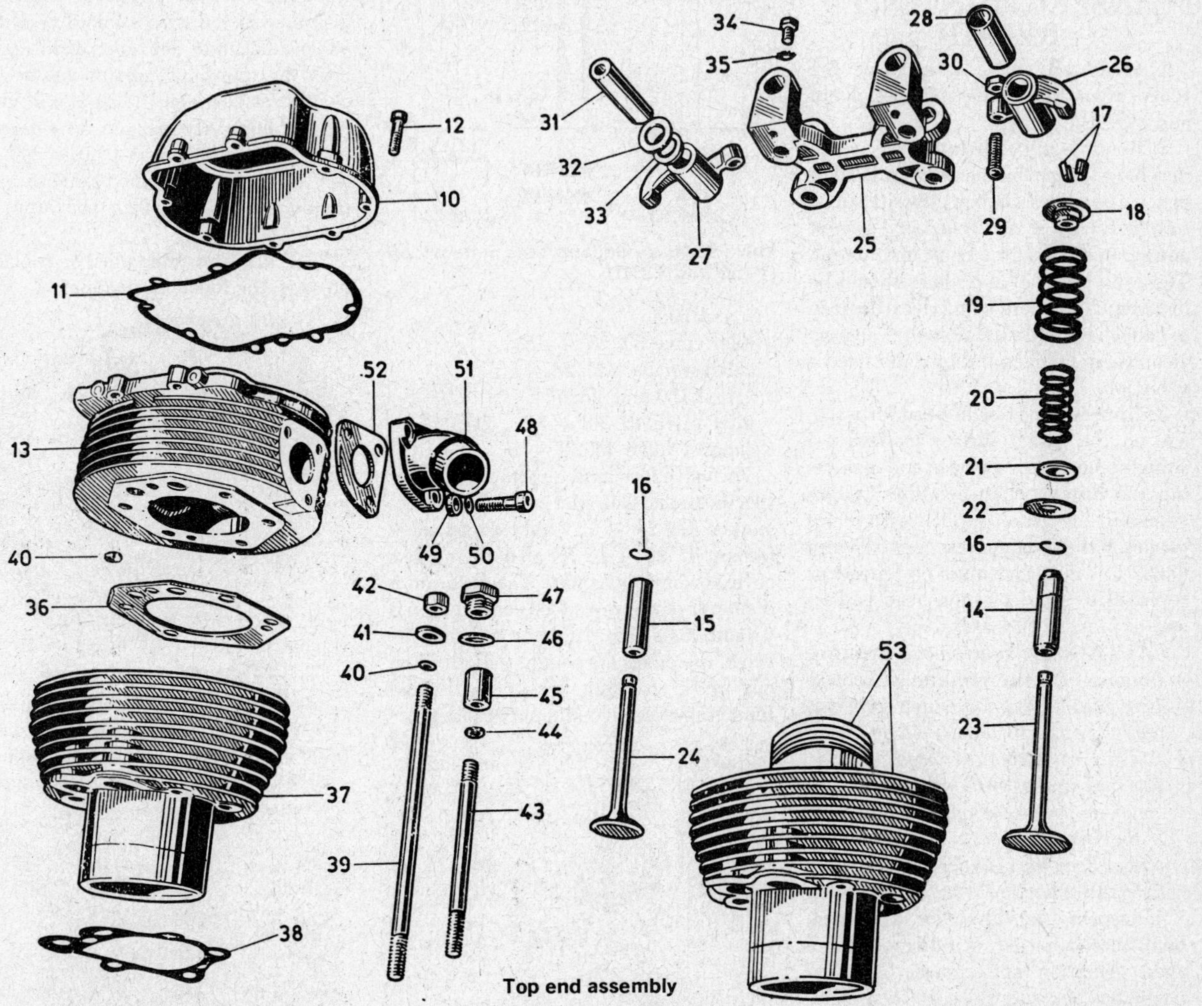

Top end assembly

10. Rocker box cover
11. Rocker box gasket
12. Rocker box cover screw
13. Cylinder head r/h
14. Inlet valve guide
15. Exhaust valve guide
16. Valve guide circlip
17. Valve keepers
18. Valves top collar
19. Outer valves spring
20. Inner valves spring
21. Collar bottom
22. Bottom collar-to-cylinder head washer
23. Inlet valve
24. Exhaust valve
25. Rocker arm support
26. Rocker arm bushings
27. Rocker arm bushings

head, the head to the cylinder, and the cylinder to the crankcase.

NOTE: *If you wish to remove the intake manifold, do so before the cylinder securing studs are removed.*

6. Lift the cylinder head off of the cylinder and remove the head gasket. Tap the side of the head gently with a hammer and wood block to free it if necessary.

7. Remove the valves by compressing the valve springs with either the factory tool (No. 60907200 which is indicated by No. 7 in the accompanying illustration), or a suitable valve spring compressor. With the spring compressed, remove the keepers then remove the compressor and complete the disassembly.

8. The valve guides may be removed by drifting them out with a suitable drift.

NOTE: *Do not remove valve guides unless they must be replaced. Consult the following "Inspection and Repair" section for additional information.*

INSPECTION AND REPAIR

1. Clean all parts, other than the rocker cover gasket, in a suitable solvent and blow them dry.

2. Remove any carbon deposits which may have formed on the cylinder head or piston assemblies. Carbon deposits can be softened with a decarbonizing solvent and scraped off with a blunt instrument. The cylinder head assemblies should be disassembled before being decarbonized so you'll have to disassemble the valves to clean them up even if they don't need a valve job.

3. Inspect the cylinder head for warpage on the gasket surface by laying a straightedge across the head and measuring the distance between the straight edge and the gasket surface with feeler gauges. If the clearance exceeds 0.05 mm (0.002 in.) the head must be lapped or replaced to avoid blowing head gaskets and to prevent oil leaks.

CAUTION: *Do not remove excessive amounts of metal from the gasket surface. If the operation is not done correctly the head will have to be milled and this may result in a raised compression ratio in that cylinder. This must be corrected for in the opposite cylinder. If the lapping process fails to correct leaks, check the cylinder gasket surface for flatness and lap it too, if necessary.*

4. Inspect the valves for a burned, bent, scored, pitted, or otherwise damaged condition and replace them as necessary. Measure the valve stem diameter and replace the valve if not within its serviceable limits of 7.982–7.987 mm (0.3138–0.3142 in.) for the inlet valve, and 7.965–7.980 mm (0.3136–0.3142 in.) for the exhaust valve. These figures apply to all of the models covered in this guide.

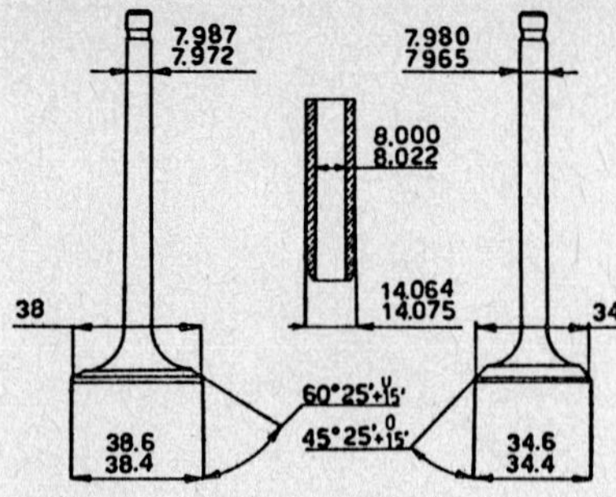

Valve stem guide, and seat dimensions (V700)

5. Inspect the condition of the valve face contact area and the valve seat for a pitted, burned, or otherwise damaged condition. If the valve is burned, worn, or damaged it must be replaced.The valve seat may be cut to restore it to its intended dimensions which are as follows:

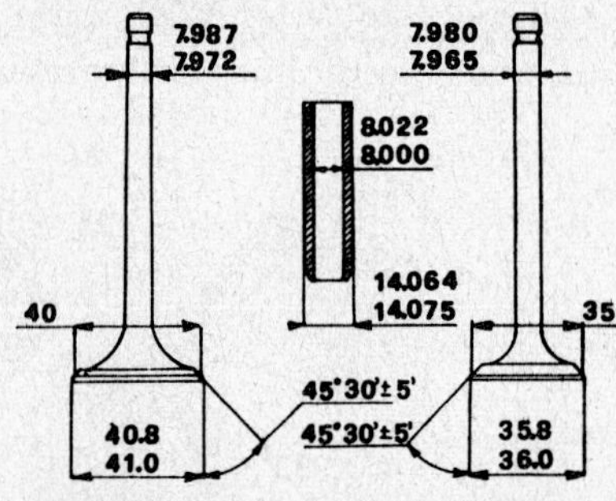

Valve stem, guide, and seat dimensions (V750 and V850)

a. V700:
inlet valve 60° 25' ± 15'
exhaust valve 45° 25' ± 15'
b. V750 and V850:
inlet valve 45° 30' ± 5'
exhaust valve 45° 30' ± 5'

The valve face must also be cut to these specifications. Cut inlet valve faces at an angle of 60° 25' ± 15', and exhaust valve faces at 45° 25' ± 15' for all of the models covered in this guide. The minimum diameter of the valve face contact area is 0.8 mm (0.0315 in.). If, after grinding the valve, the edges are rough, smooth them out on a grinding wheel, but avoid removing excessive amounts of metal.

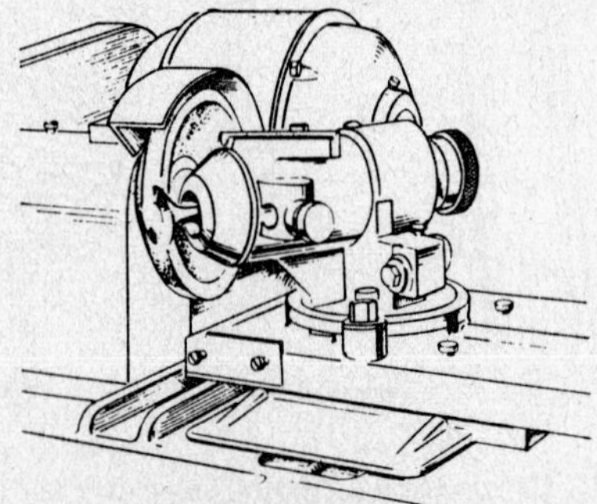

Refacing a valve

NOTE: *Whenever you cut valve seats you change the distance from the seat to the valve keepers and this means that the spring will be too short. If the compressed length of the valve spring is not within its limits of 37–38 mm (1.456–1.496 in.), and you are sure it's not because the spring is worn and slightly collapsed, shim the spring by installing suitable washers between the bottom valve spring collar and the surface of the cylinder head.*

6. If the seat has just been cut, or if the seat looks alright and you just want to ensure a good seal between the seat and valve, lap the valves in at this time.

7. Measure the clearance between the valve stem and guide with a dial indicator, then measure the diameter of the stem with a micrometer in several places along the stem. The valve stem should be of the same diameter all along its length and should be replaced if uneven (consult Step 4 of this section). If the stem is within specifications and the clearance between the stem and guide is excessive, the guide must be replaced. The inside diameter of the guide should be within 8.000–8.022 mm (0.3149–0.3158 in.) for both the inlet and exhaust valves. The clearances between the stem and guide for the inlet valve should be within 0.013–0.050 mm (0.0005–0.0019 in.), and the clearances for the exhaust valve should be within (0.020–0.057 mm (0.0008–0.0022 in.).

8. If the valve guide must be replaced, do so in the following manner:

Drifting out a valve guide

a. Remove the guide by drifting the valve out with a suitable drift. Heating the head to about 200°F. will loosen the guide slightly and facilitate its removal.

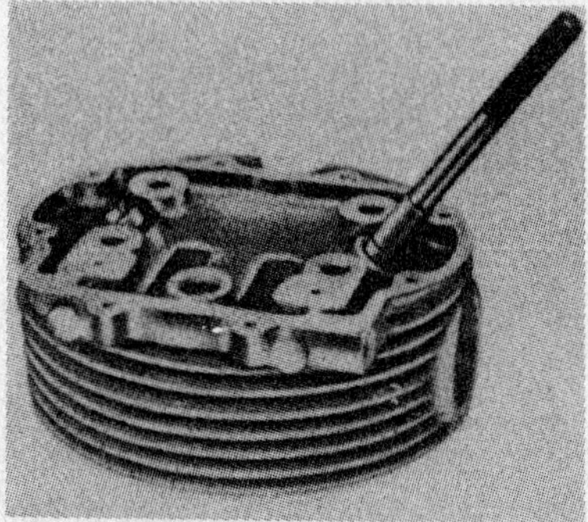

Installing a valve guide

b. Lubricate the new guide and carefully drift it into place. Again, heating the head will make the job easier.

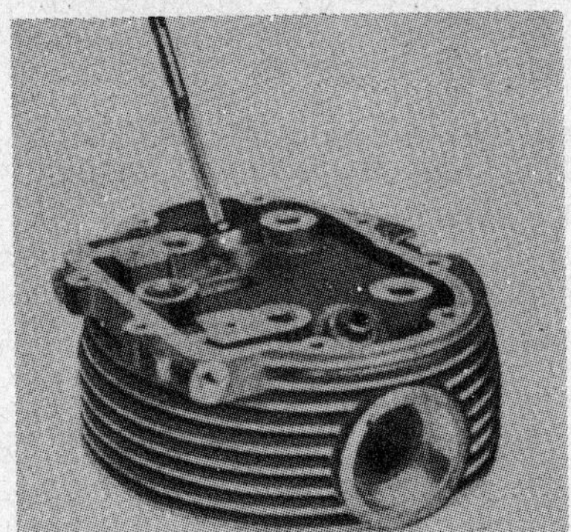

Reaming out a newly installed guide

c. Ream the newly installed guide with a suitably sized reamer to make sure it hasn't collapsed slightly inside. Take care not to deform the guide and oil the reamer slightly when it encounters interference. Remove metal chips as soon as they occur and always continue to rotate the reamer when removing or installing it. The condition of the valve seat should be carefully inspected at this time.

9. Inspect the valve springs for a worn, pitted, collapsed, or otherwise damaged condition and replace them as necessary. The spring tension can be checked on a suitable tester, which you probably won't have access to, so either take the springs to your dealer for testing, visually compare them to new ones, or replace them.

NOTE: *Valve springs should always be replaced in complete sets.*

The correct valve spring tensions are as follows:

V700:

With the valve in its CLOSED position, the spring tension should be 72±2% lbs (33±2% kg) and the spring should compress to 37 mm (1.456 in.).

With the valve in its OPEN position, the spring tension should be 132±2% lbs (60±2% kg) and the spring should compress to 28 mm (1.024 in.).

V750 and V850 (external spring):

With the valve in its CLOSED position, the spring tension should be 65±3% lbs (29.5±3% kg) and the spring should compress to 36 mm (1.417 in.).

With the valve in its OPEN position, the spring tension should be 100±3% lbs (45.5±3% kg) and the spring should compress to 27 mm (1.063 in.).

V750 and V850 (internal spring):

With the valve in its CLOSED position, the spring tension should be 37±3% lbs (16.7±3% kg) and the spring should compress to 31 mm (1.220 in.).

With the valve in its OPEN position, the spring tension should be 60±4% lbs (27.4±4% kg) and the spring should compress to 22 mm (0.866 in.).

10. Inspect the rocker arms and spin-

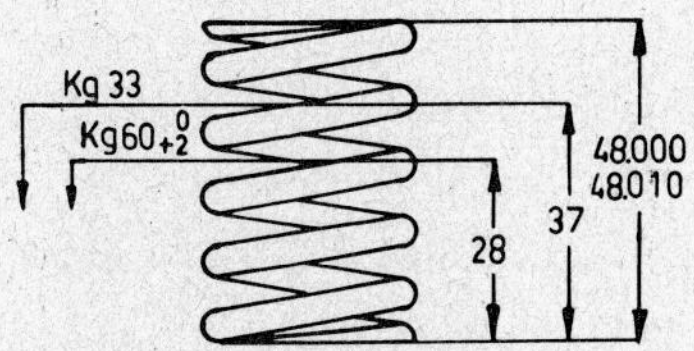

Valve spring dimensions (V700)

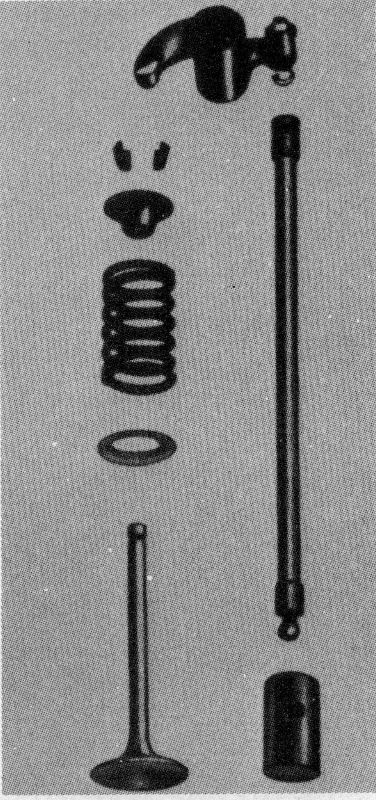

Valve mechanism

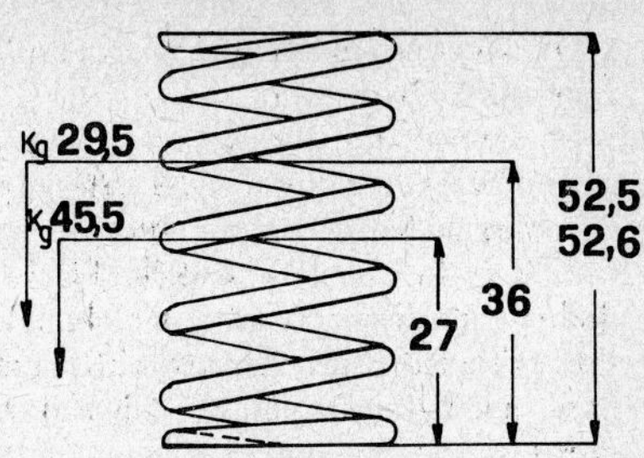

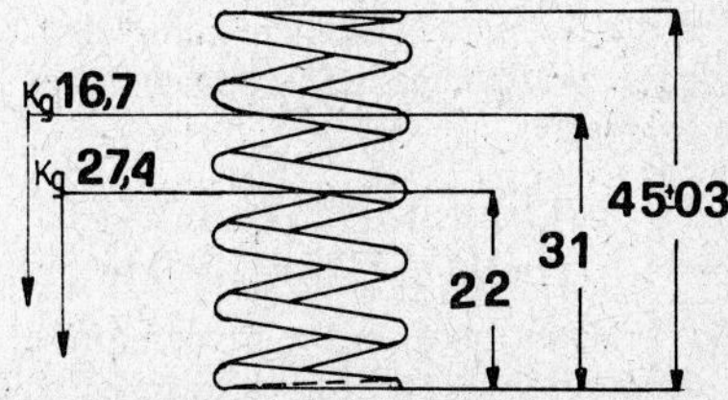

Valve spring dimensions (V750 and V850)

dles for signs of wear, pitting, other damage, or excessive side play between the rockers and their spindles, and replace them as necessary. If the tappet adjusters are damaged, they may be replaced independently of the rockers and bushings are available to replace those in the rockers. The following are useful specifications:

I/D of rocker arm bushing (after pressing-in and machining)
15.032-15.059 mm (0.5918-0.5929 in.)

Diameter of rocker arm spindle
14.983-14.994 mm (0.5899-0.5903 in.)

Fitting clearance
0.038-0.076 mm (0.0015-0.0029 in.)

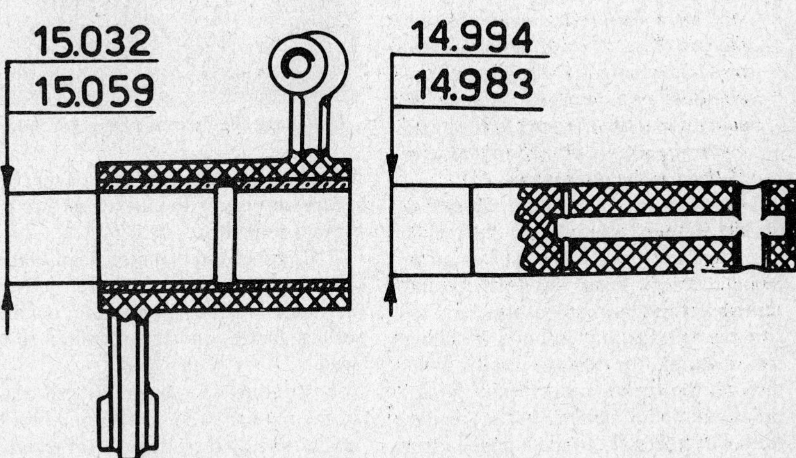

Rocker arm dimensions

CAUTION: *The contact surfaces must be mirror polished.*

11. Inspect the rockers arms support and spindles for signs of wear, scoring, or other damage and replace the necessary components. Check for a smooth operation of the rocker on the spindle and either replace or turn down the damaged parts until they operate smoothly. If there is excessive side play between the rocker and spindle they must be replaced.

12. Inspect the remaining hardware, washers, head gasket, etc. for signs of wear or damage and replace them as necessary.

ASSEMBLY AND INSTALLATION

1. Assembly is in the reverse order of disassembly. New head gaskets and valve keepers should be used for sure and any other gaskets whose condition seems questionable should also be replaced. Lightly lubricate all parts as they are installed.

2. Place a new head gasket between the cylinder and cylinder head, taking care to correctly align all oil hole passages in the cylinder and gasket.

NOTE: *Although it is not recommended specifically by the manufacturer, a light coating of gasket sealer may be used at your own discretion. If you do this, make absolutely sure that none of the oil passages become blocked and that none of the sealer gets in the cylinder.*

3. Position the cylinder head, with the valves already assembled, on the cylinder mounting studs, insert the pushrods in their original locations, then slip the rocker arms support over the studs and into place.

4. Place washers over the studs, then install the nuts and tighten them down finger tight. Secure the nuts progressively in the order shown in the accompanying illustration to a specified torque of 27.48 ft lbs (3.8 kg/m).

CAUTION: *Failure to secure the nuts progressively or tightening them excessively may result in a warped cylinder head or a damaged head gasket. Failure to secure the nuts to their correct torque setting may result in loss of compression or oil leakage.*

5. Position the rocker arm assemblies on the support, then insert the rocker arm spindles through the rocker arms, taking care to keep the washers and springs in their correct locations, and secure the spindles in position by installing and securing the rocker spindle bolts through the rocker support and the appropriate mounting holes in the spindle. It may be necessary to use a punch as an aid in installing the spindles.

6. Position a new rocker cover gasket between the head and the cover, then secure the cover mounting screws in a crossed sequence.

7. Connect the cylinder head lubrication pipe, then mount and secure the inlet manifold reducing bushing, manifold sealing gasket, and the manifold to the head.

8. Complete the assembly procedures in the reverse order of disassembly. The engine should be spun over several times to lubricate the top end before it is started.

Cylinder head bolt torquing sequence

Removing the piston pin

Checking the cylinder bore for wear

Cylinder and Piston Assembly

DISASSEMBLY

1. Remove, but do not disassemble, the cylinder head as described in the cylinder head "Removal and Disassembly" section.

2. Rotate the engine to TDC on the cylinder on which you are working, then carefully lift the cylinder off of the piston, and remove the cylinder base gasket.

NOTE: *As soon as there is sufficient clearance, a clean oil soaked rag should be placed between the cylinder and crankcase to prevent any foreign objects, such as pieces of broken rings, from falling into the crankcase. This rag should be kept in position as long as the crankcase is vulnerable.*

3. Remove the piston pin circlips by prying them out with a pointed instrument, then press out the pin using either the factory tool (No. 26907800, for the V700 and V750, or by No. 13907860 for the V850) which is indicated by No. 17, in the accompanying illustration, or a suitable drift, then remove the piston.

CAUTION: *To avoid deforming the connecting rod, hold it steady while drifting out the pin. Applying heat to the piston crown with an iron or hot towels will make it easier.*

4. Remove the piston rings with a ring expander or by hand. Take care to avoid damaging the piston.

INSPECTION AND REPAIR

1. Clean all parts, other than the gaskets, in a suitable solvent and blow them dry. Make sure the oil passages are clear. Thoroughly decarbonize the piston and cylinder assemblies. The piston ring grooves can be easily decarbonized with a piece of broken piston ring.

2. Inspect all parts for signs of excessive wear or damage and replace them as necessary.

3. Measure the cylinder in at least three places along the piston's path using an inside micrometer after the measurement for each position is taken, rotate the micrometer 180° to make sure you've gotten the most accurate measurement possible. If the cylinder is scored or ovalized in excess of 0.10 mm (0.00394 in.), the liner must be replaced. The sizes of the available liners which may be used are indicated in the accompanying illustrations for each of the models covered in this guide. Various pistons and rings, which must be used in conjunction with the appropriate cylinder class, are available for each of the cylinder diameters listed in the following charts:

V700			V750			V850		
Class A	Class B	Class C	Class A	Class B	Class C	Class A	Class B	Class C
80.000 mm (3.14963 in.)	80.006 mm (3.14987 in.)	80.012 mm (3.15010 in.)	83.000 mm (3.2677 in.)	83.006 mm (3.2679 in.)	83.012 mm (3.2681 in.)	83.000 mm (3.2677 in.)	83.006 mm (3.2679 in.)	83.012 mm (3.2681 in.)
80.006 mm (3.14987 in.)	80.012 mm (3.15010 in.)	80.018 mm (3.15034 in.)	83.006 mm (3.2679 in.)	83.012 mm (3.2681 in.)	83.018 mm (3.2683 in.)	83.006 mm (3.2679 in.)	83.012 mm (3.2681 in.)	83.018 mm (3.2683 in.)

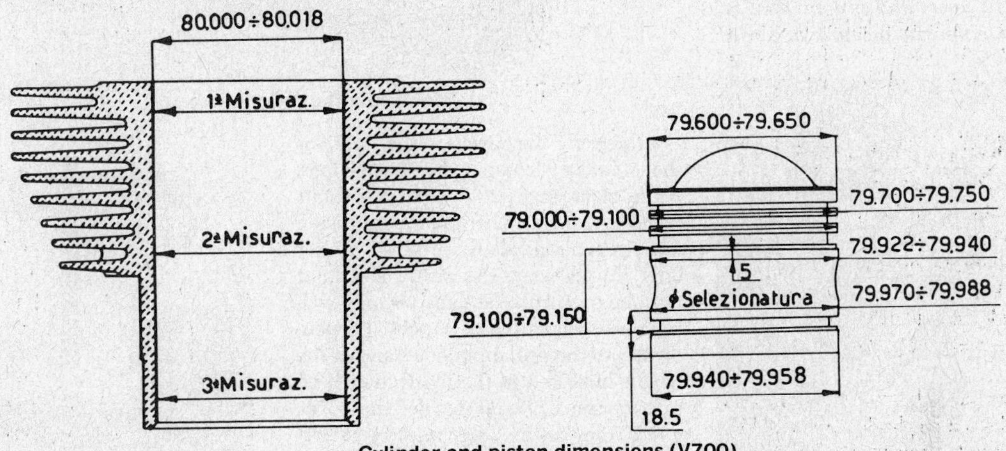

Cylinder and piston dimensions (V700)

Cylinder and piston dimensions (V750)

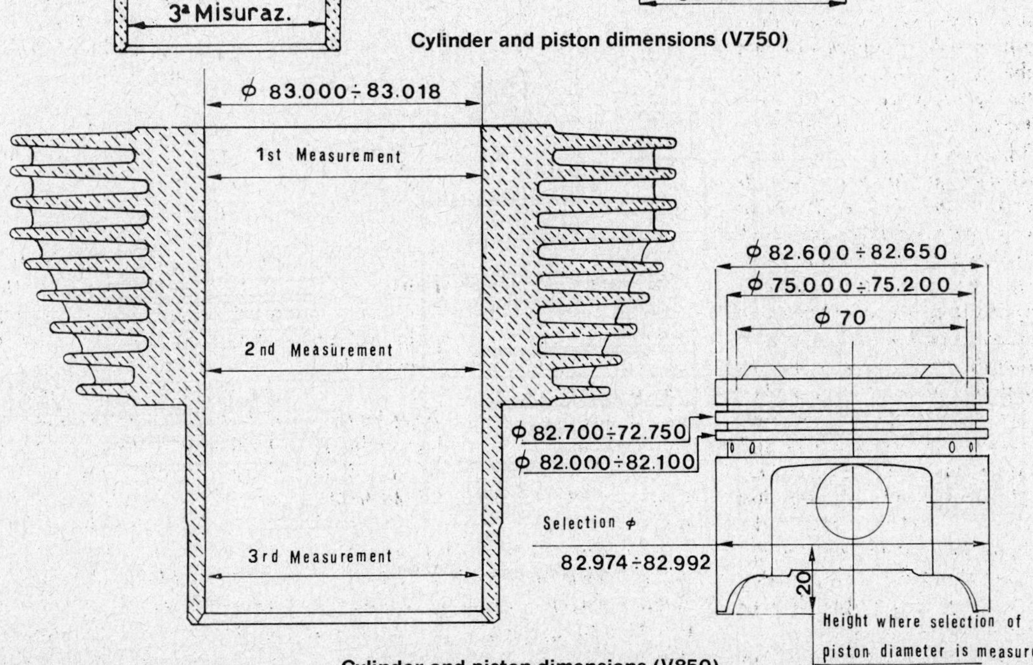

Cylinder and piston dimensions (V850)

The liners can be removed by boiling the cylinder in oil to expand the cylinder away from the liner. Tapping the heated assembly should loosen the liner which should then slip out. The new liner can then be carefully pressed into the cylinder. The piston to be used with the new liner should be selected after the liner is installed.

NOTE: *Although it is not recommended by the factory, Volkswagen replacement liners and pistons may be used as a temporary measure in case of emergency.*

Measuring the piston diameter

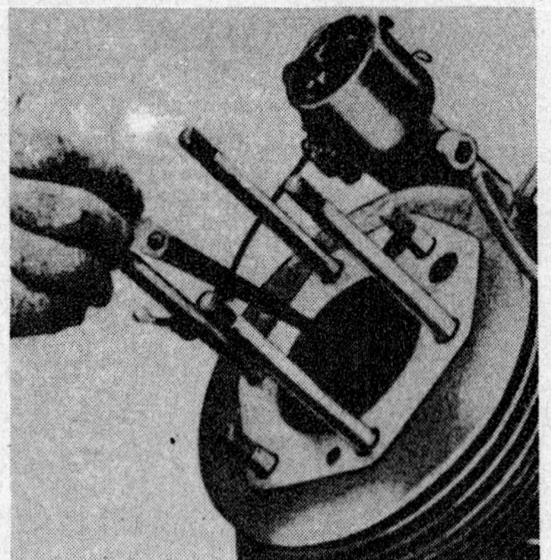

Measuring piston-to-cylinder clearance

4. Measure the pistons in the locations shown in the accompanying illustrations. If the clearances are beyond the limits specified in the illustrations, the piston must be replaced along with the cylinder liner. In all cases, the piston and liner must be compatible and the piston's ovalization as measured at a point perpendicular to the piston pin holes and at the height indicated in the illustration (18.5 mm for the V700, 35 mm for the V750, and 20 mm for the V850) must be at least 0.055–0.065 mm (0.0021–0.0025 in.) less than the selected size. The available pistons are listed in the following charts:

Balancing the pistons

V700

Class A	Class B	Class C
79.952 mm (3.14774 in.)	79.958 mm (3.14798 in.)	79.964 mm (3.14821 in.)
79.958 mm (3.14798 in.)	79.964 mm (3.14821 in.)	79.976 mm (3.14845 in.)

V750

Class A	Class B	Class C
82.958 mm (3.2260 in.)	82.964 mm (3.2262 in.)	82.970 mm (3.2264 in.)
82.964 mm (3.2262 in.)	82.970 mm (3.2264 in.)	82.976 mm (3.2266 in.)

V850

Class A	Class B	Class C
82.968 mm (3.2664 in.)	82.974 mm (3.2666 in.)	82.980 mm (3.2668 in.)
82.974 mm (3.2666 in.)	82.980 mm (3.2668 in.)	82.986 mm (3.2671 in.)

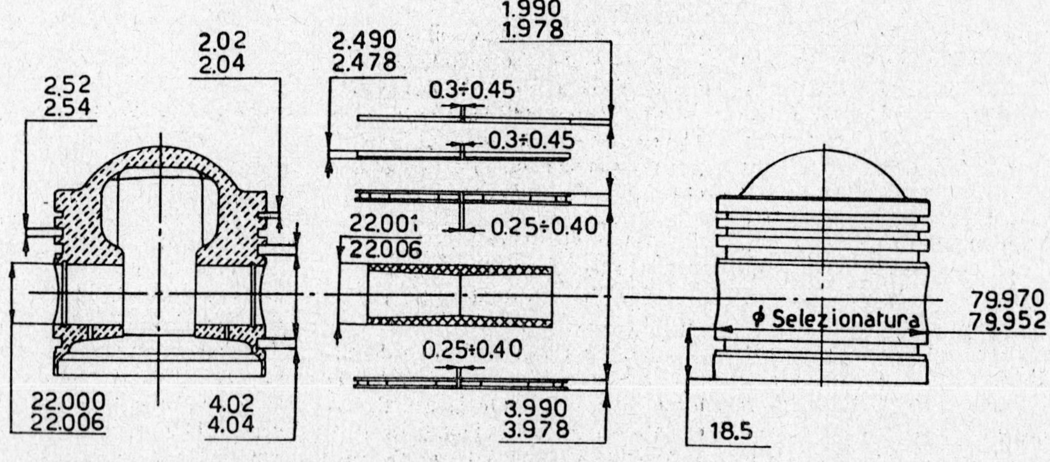

Piston dimensions (V700)

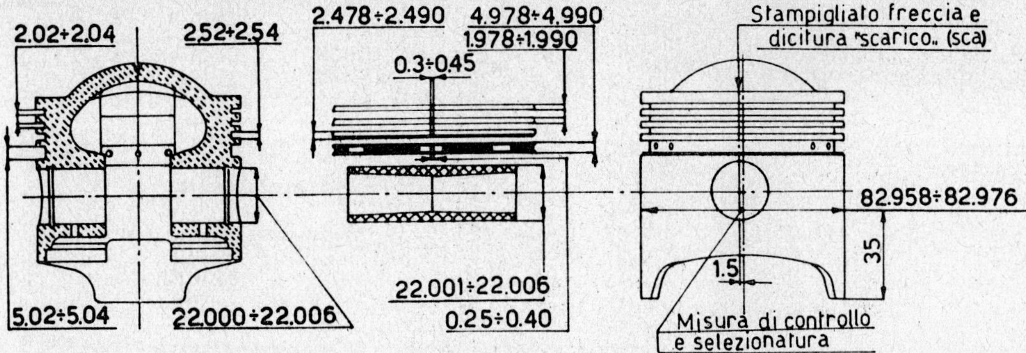

Piston dimensions (V750)

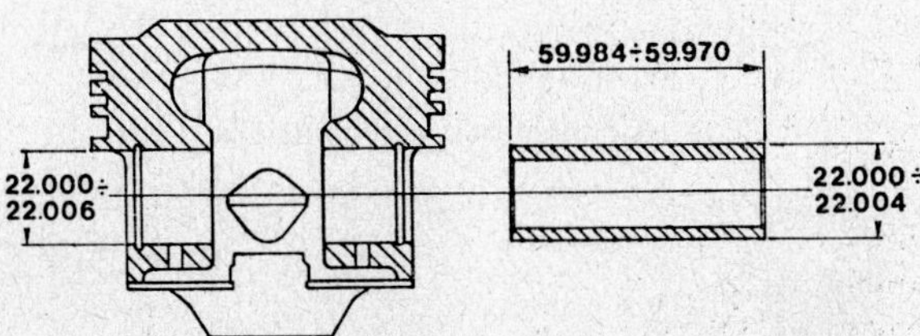

Piston dimensions (V850)

5. Weigh the two pistons which are to be used. If the difference is in excess of 1.5 g, the heavier of the two should be lightly and evenly filed along the bottom edge of its skirt. Remove any burrs which may have been formed by gently sanding with fine emery cloth.

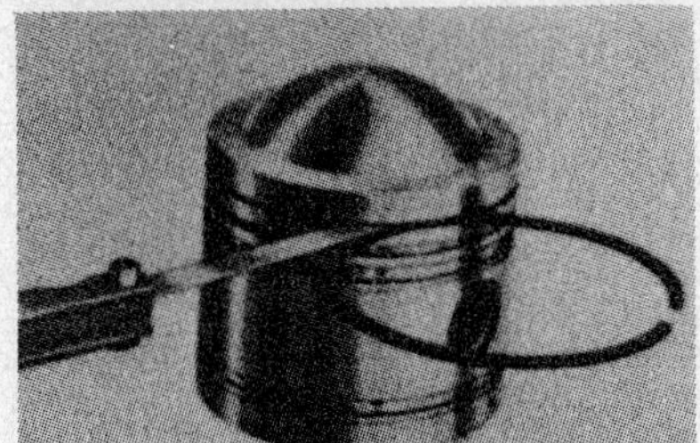

Checking ring-to-piston side clearance

6. Measure the vertical clearance between the new piston rings which are to be fitted and the ring grooves in the piston. If the clearance for any of the grooves exceeds the limits of 0.030–0.062 mm (0.001–0.0024 in.), the piston must be replaced.

7. Measure the end gap on each of the rings to be fitted. The measurement can be made with feeler gauges, when the ring is inserted in the cylinder, just below its lip. The end gap for piston compression rings is 0.30–0.45 mm (0.012–0.018 in,), and the gap for the oil scraper rings is 0.25–0.40 mm (0.010–0.016 in.). Correct the gap if necessary by filing the end of the ring. Make sure you file it evenly and finish it so it's smooth and straight across.

8. Inspect the piston pin for signs of wear, scoring, pitting, or other damage and replace it as necessary. The pin is a press fit and the negative allowance between it and the piston pin hole is 0.001 mm (0.00004 in.) for the V700 and V750, and 0.004 mm (0.00015 in.) for the V850. The correct specifications for the piston pin hole can be found in the illustrations of the pistons found in Step No. 4.

Checking ring end gap

ASSEMBLY AND INSTALLATION

1. Assembly is basically in the reverse order of disassembly.

2. Install the piston rings on the pistons by using a ring expander or do it by hand, taking care not to damage the piston. Make sure they will rotate smoothly around the piston, then stagger their end gaps every 90°.

3. Install the pistons on the connecting rods; use the same tool which you used to remove the piston pin to secure it, then install a new pair of circlips.

NOTE: *As an aid in installation, the piston should be heated and well lubricated and the piston pin holes should be heated to about 140° in a bath of oil. Secure the connecting rod to avoid damaging it or the big end bearing.*

4. Position the cylinder base gasket on the cylinder. The mating surfaces of the cylinder and crankcase must be perfectly clean.

5. Start the cylinder on the mounting studs, then carefully bring it down over the piston, taking care to avoid damaging the piston rings. Thoroughly lubricate the cylinder bore and the piston assembly as an aid in installation. A ring compressor (a suitably sized hose clamp will work also) may be used, but you'll probably find it as easy to use your hands.

NOTE: *The rag should remain over the crankcase until the last moment to prevent any possible pieces of broken ring from falling into the crankcase cavity.*

BOTTOM END SERVICE

Connecting Rods

SMALL END BEARING

Removal and Installation

1. Run the engine until its normal operating temperature is reached, then drain the oil. This job may be done with the engine in or out of the frame, but the oil must be drained.

2. Remove the cylinder head, cylinder, and piston assemblies as directed in the "Top End Service" section.

3. Remove the crankcase sump pan, then unbolt the bottom half of the connecting rod after bending back the locking tab of the lockwashers and remove it and the lower bearing shell.

4. Pull the connecting rod up and out of the crankcase. The big end bearing is a plain bearing in two half shells, so don't forget to remove the top shell if it hasn't fallen out.

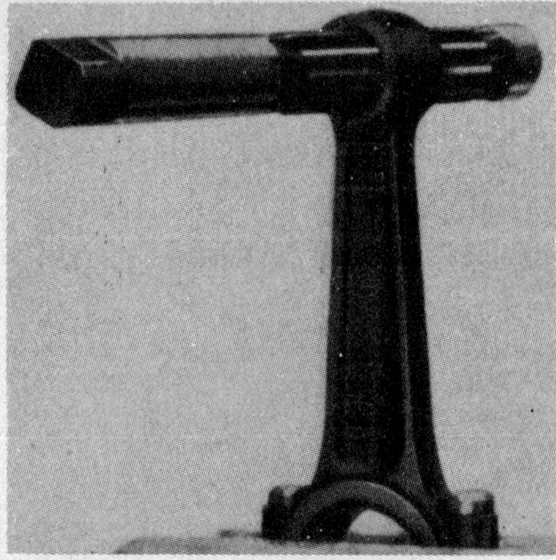

Reaming the small end bearing to size

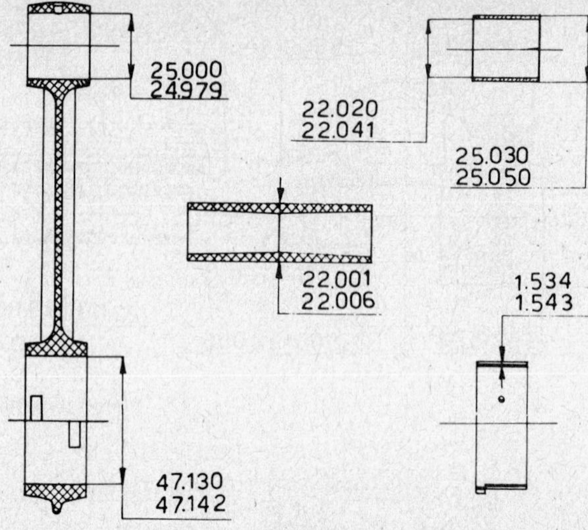

Connecting rod dimensions

NOTE: *Connecting rod assemblies must be kept separate for reassembly in their original positions.*

5. Secure the connecting rod in a wood-jawed vise, then remove the small end bearing by drifting it free with a suitable drift if it appears to be marked, scored, or excessively worn.

6. Replace the bearing by pressing it in, then drill through the oil passage in the connecting rod with a suitable drill. Ream the bearing out with a suitable reamer until you arrive at a perfectly rounded inside diameter of 22.020–22.041 mm (0.8669–0.9678 in.).

7. Reinstall the connecting rod on the crankshaft as directed in the "Connecting Rod Installation" section, then complete the assembly in the reverse order of disassembly. Don't forget to replace the sump pan gasket and refill the sump with oil.

NOTE: *The diameter of the piston pin should be 22.001–22.006 mm (0.8662–0.8663 in.) and the clearance between the pin and the small end bearing should be 0.014–0.040 mm (0.0005–0.0015 in.). Replace the pin at this time if necessary.*

BIG END BEARING

Removal and Installation

1. Run the engine until its normal operating temperature is reached, then drain the sump and remove the sump pan.

2. Remove the nuts and lockwashers which secure the bottom halves of the connecting rod together and then remove the bottom half of the rod and the lower bearing shell.

3. Remove the two bolts which secure the connecting rod halves together, taking care not to scratch the crankshaft journal, then carefully push the connecting rod up until the upper bearing half is free for removal.

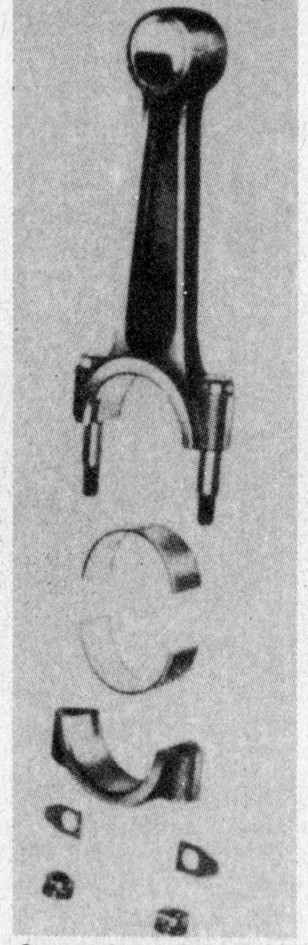

Connecting rod assembly

4. Replace the big end bearing while installing the connecting rod on the crankshaft as described in the "Connecting Rod Installation" section, then complete the reassembly in the reverse order of disassembly. Be sure to replace the sump pan gasket and refill the sump with oil.

CONNECTING ROD INSTALLATION

1. Make sure that the rod is perfectly straight. The axis of the big and small bearing holes must be parallel to each other. If the rod is bent slightly, but

Straightening a connecting rod

shows no signs of fatigue or other damage, it may be bent back as indicated in the accompanying illustration. The rod must not be bent more than 0.03 mm (0.00118 in.) when measured at a point 200 mm (7.874 in.) from the big end bearing hole.

NOTE: *When bending the rod, make sure the jaws of the vise are wood or use some other means of protecting the rod.*

2. Weigh the two connecting rods in their completely assembled form (i.e. including big and small end bearings, nuts, bolts, and lockwashers). The weight of an assembled rod should be 560 ± 10 g (1 lb 3-¾ oz) and the maximum permissible difference is 3 g (46 grains). If the difference is greater, you should get a rod to match one or the other or try to file off some of the material from the heavier one; however, matching is a better idea than filing.

3. Select new big end bearings to fit the crankshaft journal. The following charts list the oversize bearings available to fit an undersize crankshaft. If the crankshaft must be ground to remove

BIG END BEARINGS INSIDE DIAMETER

Original Thickness	Oversize 0.254 mm (.010 in.)	0.508 mm (.020 in.)	0.762 mm (.030 in.)	1.016 mm (.040 in.)
1.534-1.543 mm (0.06039-0.06074 in.)	1.661-1.670 mm (0.06539-0.065748 in.)	1.788-1.797 mm (0.07-0.07074 in.)	1.915-1.924 mm (0.07539-0.07574 in.)	2.042-2.051mm (0.08039-0.08074 in.)

CRANKSHAFT JOURNAL OUTSIDE DIAMETER

Original Diameter	Undersize 0.254 mm (.010 in.)	0.508 mm (.020 in.)	0.762 mm (.030 in.)	1.016 mm (.040 in.)
44.013-44.033 mm (1.7328-1.7336 in.)	43.759-43.779 mm (1.7228-1.7236 in.)	43.505-43.525 mm (1.7128-1.7136 in.)	43.251-43.271 mm (1.7028-1.7036 in.)	42.997-43.017 mm (1.6928-1.6936in.)

score marks or to make the available bearings fit it, remove it as described in the "Crankshaft" section and have your local dealer or a qualified machinist match the rods and bearings to it.

NOTE: *Even if a crankshaft journal is only slightly scored or marked, it must be reground before it is put back into service or a violent failure may occur.*

4. Temporarily secure the connecting rods on the crankshaft journal. The oil passages (A) on the big end must be facing upward for the left hand cylinder's rod and facing downward for the right hand cylinder's rod. When the bottom cap is fitted, it should be done so the numbers marked on the side of the top and bottom halves are aligned.
5. Make sure that the bearing-to-crankshaft journal lateral play is within the specified limits of 0.011–0.061 mm (0.000433–0.0024 in.). This is best measured with a dial indicator and is corrected by installing larger bearings.
6. Make sure that the connecting rod-to-crankshaft journal side clearance is within the specified limits of 0.3–0.5 mm

Balancing the connecting rods

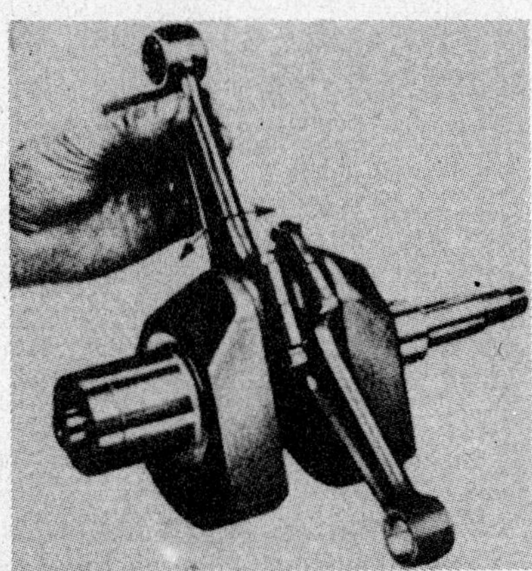

Checking lateral play

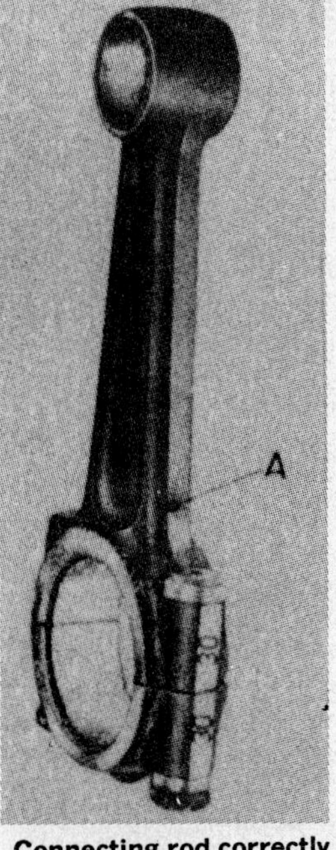

Connecting rod correctly assembled

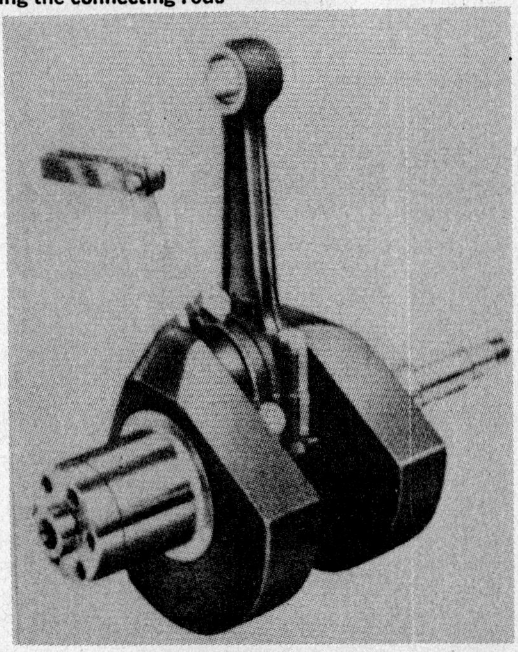

Checking rod-to-journal clearance

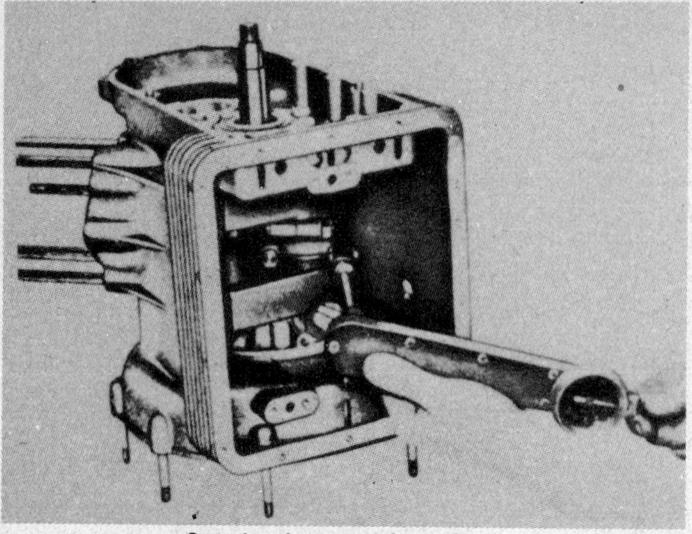
Securing the connecting rods

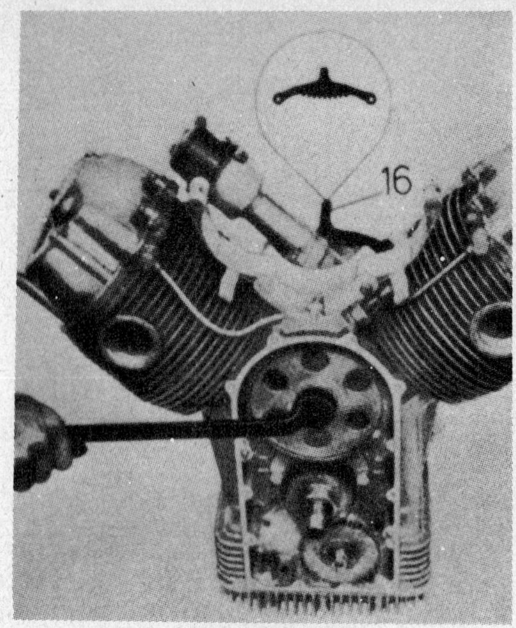

Removing the cam wheel

(0.0118–0.0196 in.). This is best measured with feeler gauges and is usually corrected by grinding the journal down to the next undersize and then compensating by installing the appropriate oversize bearings.

7. When you are satisfied with the way the rods fit on the crankshaft, torque the nuts to 25.31 ft lbs (3.500 kg m) then bend the locking tab up against a flat side of the nut. If you wish, a small amount of thread sealer may be used.

Timing Chest

DISASSEMBLY

1. Remove the engine from the frame as directed in the "Engine Removal and Disassembly" section.

2. Remove the generator belt cover and belt. The belt can be removed by withdrawing the three bolts which secure the outer half of the driving pulley.

3. Secure the clutch assembly with the special tool (No. 12911801) or a suitable substitute, then remove the nut which secures the inner half of the generator driving pulley and remove the pulley half. Then mount either the special tool (No. 12905300 which is indicated by No. 24 in the accompanying illustration), or a suitable substitute, to the pulley hub and remove the crankshaft nut.

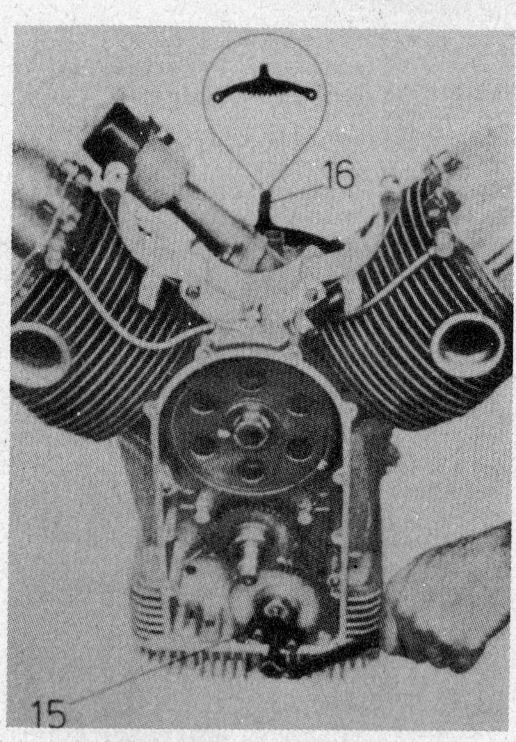

Pulling the oil pump gear

Removing the pulley hub

4. Remove the screws which secure the timing cover to the crankcase, then remove the cover. Tap the cover gently with a wood block and hammer to break its seal, if necessary. Remove the seal ring from the cover if necessary.

5. Remove the cam wheel securing nut, then remove the cam wheel. The clutch should still be secured as directed in Step No. 3 by the special tool (16).

6. Remove the oil pump gear from its tapered shaft with the pump gear puller (No. 32906302 which is indicated by No. 15 in the accompanying illustration) or a suitable substitute. The clutch must be secured by the special tool (16).

7. Remove the crankshaft timing gear from the end of the crankshaft. The gear is a keyed on press fit and must be pulled with a suitable puller.

INSPECTION AND REPAIR

1. Clean all parts other than gaskets and rubber seals in a suitable solvent, then blow them dry.

2. Inspect all parts for signs of wear or damage and replace them as necessary.

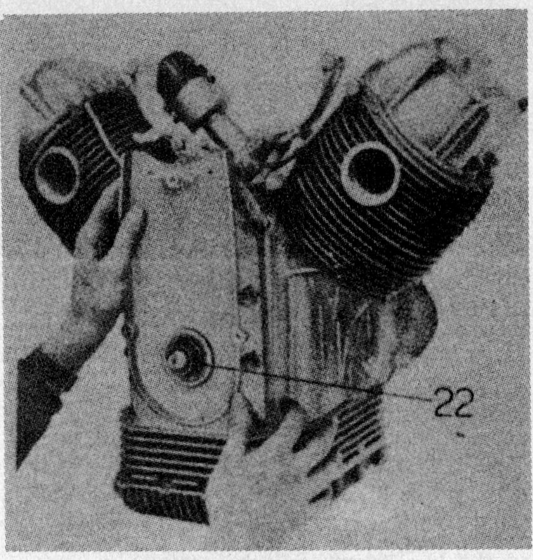

Installing the timing cover

Removing the starter ring gear

The gear teeth must be in good condition and gears which mesh together must be replaced in sets.

3. Woodruff keys, gaskets, and rubber seals should all be replaced as these are short-life items.

4. Inspect the generator belt for signs of wear, cracking, or other damage and replace it at this time if necessary.

ASSEMBLY

1. Assembly is in the reverse order of disassembly.

2. Consult the "Valve Timing" section for instructions on installing the three timing chest gears.

3. When installing the timing cover, some provision must be made to protect the seal ring. This is easily done by using the special tool (No. 12908300 which is indicated by No. 22 in the accompanying illustration).

4. Install and adjust the generator belt as described in the "Maintenance" chapter then tune the engine, if necessary, as directed in the "Tune-Up" section.

5. Install the engine in the frame as described in the "Engine Removal and Installation" section, then replenish the crankcase oil supply.

Clutch

DISASSEMBLY

1. Remove the engine as directed in the "Engine and Transmission" section, or remove the engine mounting hardware, disconnect the transmission, and slide the engine forward as far as it will move in the frame. Removing the engine will make the job go easier.

2. Secure the starter ring gear using either the factory tool (No. 12911801 which is indicated by No. 16 in the accompanying illustration) or a suitable substitute. Remove the bolts which secure the ring gear to the flywheel, then remove the clutch assembly.

NOTE: *The bolts must be removed evenly in a crossed pattern to avoid deforming the pressure plate.*

3. Remove the eight bolts which secure the flywheel, which serves as a clutch hub to the crankshaft, and remove the flywheel. It is not necessary to remove the flywheel unless it is obviously damaged.

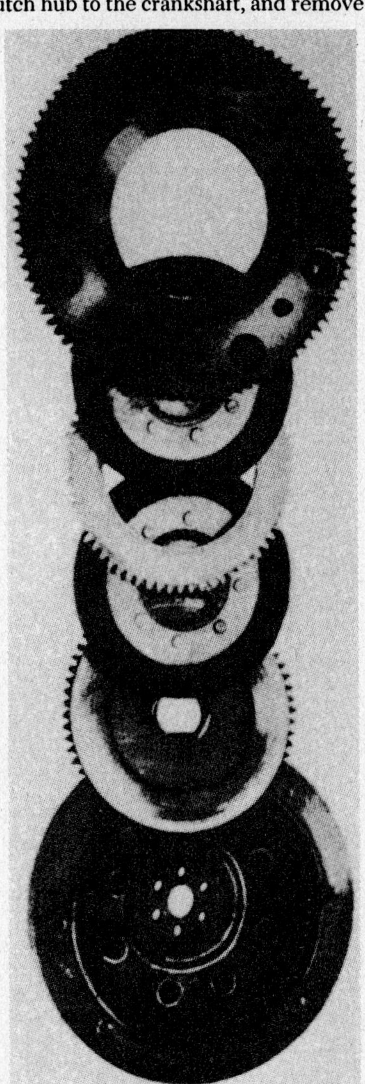
Clutch assembly

4. The release mechanism may be disassembled if so desired.

INSPECTION AND REPAIR

1. Clean all parts other than the friction plates in a suitable solvent, then blow them dry.

2. Inspect the clutch springs for a worn, damaged, or collapsed condition and replace them, as a set, if necessary. The springs should be pressure tested to check their efficiency. If, however, the necessary test equipment is not available, compare them with new springs and replace them if their condition seems doubtful. The following are the necessary test specifications:

V700:

With the spring compressed to 20 mm (0.7874 in.), the load should be 16 ± 10% kg (35.27 ± 10% lbs).

With the spring compressed to 17 mm (0.6692 in.), the load should be 24 ± 10% kg (52.9 ± 10% lbs).

V750 and V850:

With the spring compressed to 20 mm (0.7874 in.), the load should be 21 ± 25% kg (46.3 ± 25% lbs).

With the spring compressed to 17 mm (0.6692 in.), the load should be within 28.-7–29.7 kg (64.6–66.8 lbs).

3. Inspect the pressure plate for signs of wear, cracks, warpage, chipped teeth, or other damage, and replace it as necessary.

4. Inspect the starter ring gear for signs of wear, warpage, cracked or chipped teeth, or other damage and replace it as necessary.

5. Inspect the driven plates for signs of wear, scoring, chipped teeth, grease impregnation, warpage, or other damage, and replace them (as a complete set) if

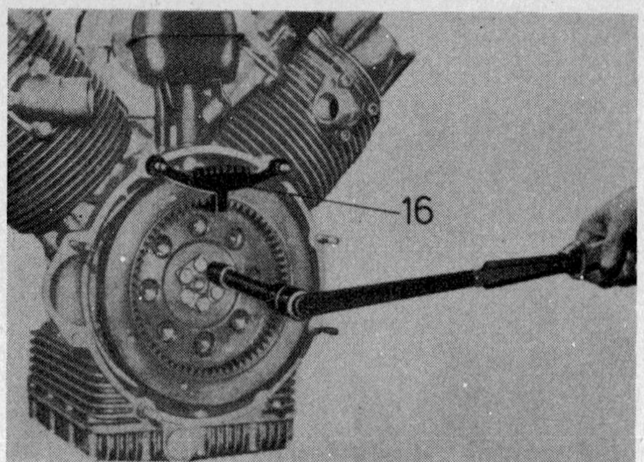

Removing the flywheel from the crankshaft

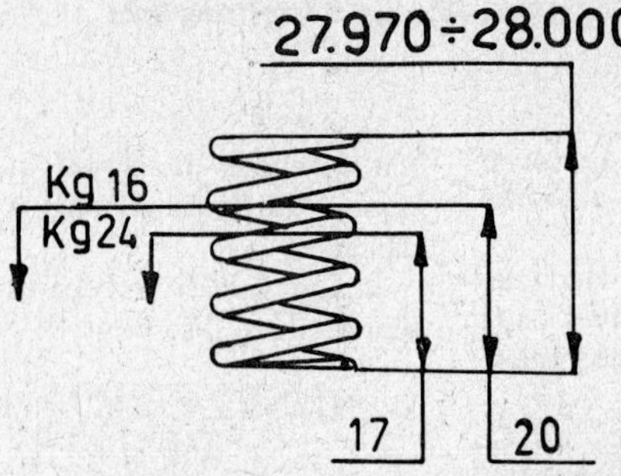

Clutch spring dimensions (V700)

Clutch spring dimensions (V750 and V850)

necessary. Each plate should be 8 mm (0.3149 in.) thick as measured at a point on which there is friction material and the plates must be replaced if worn down to 7.5 mm (0.2953 in.).

6. Inspect the drive plates for signs of wear, scoring, heat damage, chipped teeth, warpage, or other damage and replace them (as a set) if necessary.

7. Inspect the release mechanism and cable for signs of wear or damage and replace the damaged components as necessary. The mechanism should move smoothly and easily throughout its range. Lubricate the assembly with oil or a light grease.

ASSEMBLY

1. Assembly is basically in the reverse order of disassembly.

2. Secure the flywheel to the crankshaft by means of bolts and lockwashers, then torque the bolts down to 25 ft lbs (3.5 kg/m).

3. Insert the clutch springs into their housings in the flywheel, then mount the pressure plate so that the punch-marked tooth on the pressure plate is in alignment with the arrow marked on the flywheel.

NOTE: *There is an arrow on the flywheel which indicates TDC and which serves as a reference mark for assembling the clutch pressure plate.*

4. Mount the clutch dismantling and assembling tool (No. 17906500 which is indicated by No. 21 in the accompanying illustration) on the crankshaft, screwing it down enough so the clutch plates and ring gear can be so positioned that the securing bolts can be screwed down into the flywheel. The flywheel's motion must be blocked by using either the factory tool (No. 12911801 which is indicated by No. 16 in the accompanying illustration) or a suitable substitute. Remove the dismantling and assembling tool.

5. Complete the assembly in the reverse order of disassembly, then adjust the clutch and refill the crankcase sump as necessary.

Throwout Bearing Replacement

1. Drill a 2 × 3 in. hole in the battery shelf to make the bearing more accessible. You'll find this hole also helpful in adjusting the transmission.

NOTE: *This is not absolutely necessary if you aren't into drilling a hole in the bike, but it will make the job considerably easier.*

2. Disconnect the clutch cable and remove the release lever.

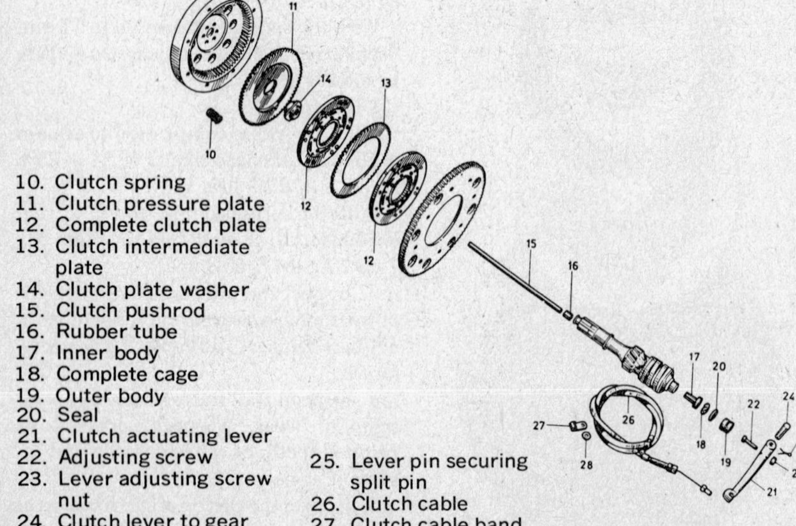

10. Clutch spring
11. Clutch pressure plate
12. Complete clutch plate
13. Clutch intermediate plate
14. Clutch plate washer
15. Clutch pushrod
16. Rubber tube
17. Inner body
18. Complete cage
19. Outer body
20. Seal
21. Clutch actuating lever
22. Adjusting screw
23. Lever adjusting screw nut
24. Clutch lever to gear box pin
25. Lever pin securing split pin
26. Clutch cable
27. Clutch cable band
28. Washer

Clutch assembly

Securing the starter ring gear

3. Remove the bearing components (parts 17–20 in the exploded illustration) using either of the following methods:

a. Apply air pressure to the 17 mm plug located on the left hand front of the transmission, almost under the left hand carburetor. There is a small vent hole in the plug, so applying pressure to it will cause the bearing to pop out of its housing.

NOTE: *Along with the bearing will probably be some oil, so be ready to catch it with a rag.*

b. If you don't have access to an air pressure source, remove the race by drawing it out with a magnet until you can grasp or hook it with something. The damaged bearing parts can be removed with a magnet, too.

Crankshaft and Camshaft

REMOVAL

1. Remove the engine from the frame as directed in the "Engine Removal and Disassembly" section. Then remove the distributor body and gasket by removing the screws and washers which secure the support.

2. Remove the cylinder heads as directed in the "Cylinder Head" section.

3. Disassemble the timing chest as described in the "Timing Chest" section.

4. Disassemble the clutch as directed in the "Clutch" section.

5. Withdraw the cam tappets from their tunnels in the crankcase by lowering a magnet down to them. You may also remove them by removing the cylinders as directed in the "Cylinder and Piston Assembly" section and then plucking the tappets off of their seats.

NOTE: *Keep the tappets separate for installation in their original locations.*

6. Remove the crankcase sump pan, then remove the connecting rods and their big end bearings as directed in the "Big End Bearing" section.

7. Remove the bolts which secure the camshaft mounting flange to the crankcase, then remove the flange and camshaft.

8. Remove the bolts and lockwashers which secure the crankshaft timing side bearing flange to the crankcase, then remove the flange complete with the timing side main bearing. Support the crankshaft while working on the flywheel side bearing.

9. Remove the lockwashers and bolts which secure the flywheel side crankshaft main bearing flange to the crankcase, then pull the flange from the case using either the factory puller (No. 12913600 which is indicated by No. 19 in the accompanying illustration) or a suitable substitute. The factory puller presses on the crankshaft. As you withdraw the flange, be prepared to support the crankshaft, then remove the crankshaft.

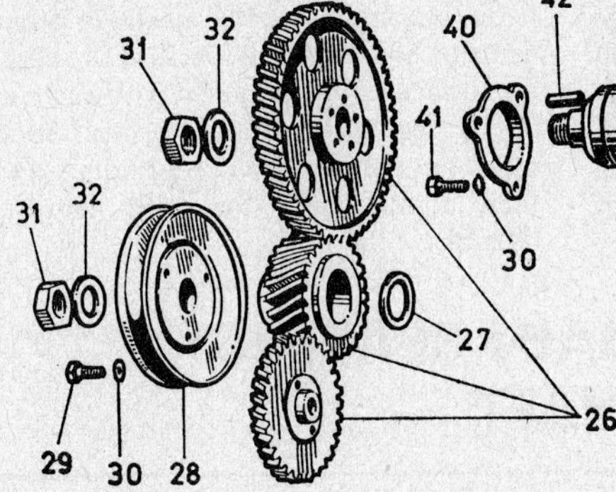

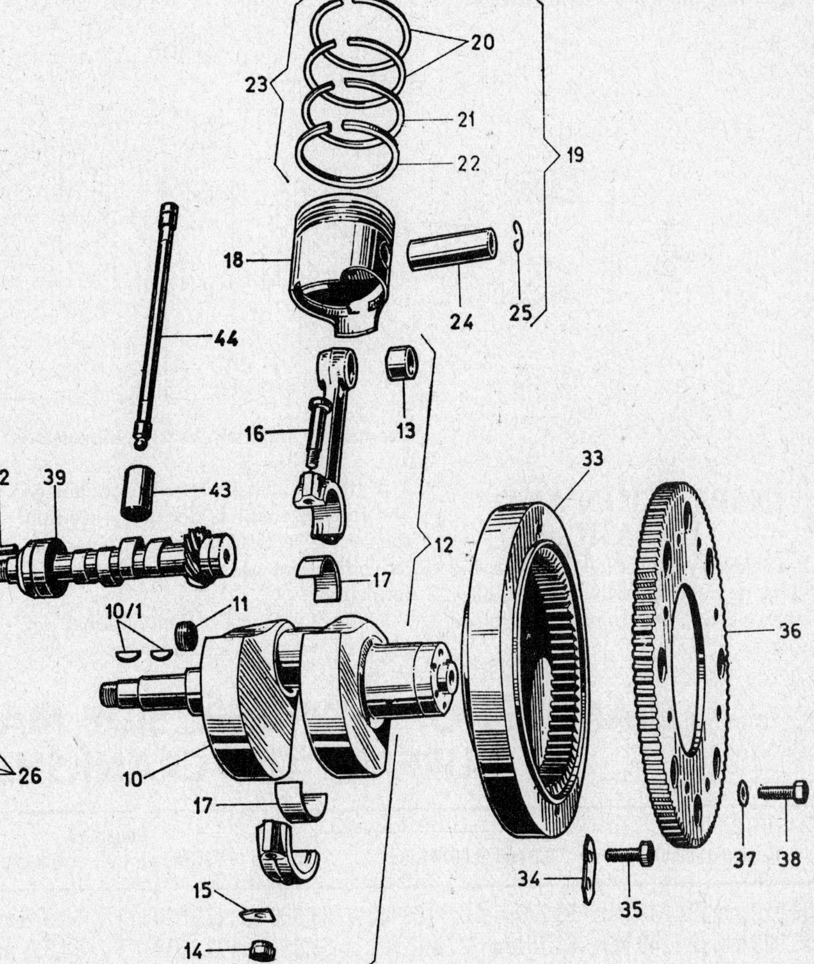

Crankshaft and camshaft assemblies

10. Crankshaft
10-1. Timing gear and pulley key
11. Crankshaft plug
12. Connecting rod c/w bushings, bolts, nuts and lock-plates
13. Small end bush
14. Big end bolts nut
15. Big end bolts lock plate
16. Big end securing bolt
17. Big end, standard size, half bearing
    u/s 0.254 mm (0.01 in.) half bearing
    u/s 0.508 mm (0.02 in.) half bearing
    u/s 0.762 mm (0.03 in.) half bearing
    u/s 1.016 mm (0.04 in.) half bearing
18. Bare piston
19. Piston c/w rings, pin and circlip
20. Top piston ring, compression
21. Center piston ring compression
22. Oil scraper
23. Oil scraper
24. Piston pin
25. Circlip
26. Crankshaft timing and oil pump gears gear set
27. Crankshaft gear seal
28. Generator pulley
29. Pulley assembly securing screw
30. Flange-to-camshaft and pulley assembly screw washer
31. Pulley securing screws nut
32. Pulley securing nut washer
33. Flywheel
34. Flywheel bolts plate
35. Flywheel securing bolt
36. Starter motor ring gear
37. Ring gear-to-flywheel washer
38. Ring gear-to-flywheel bolt
39. Camshaft
40. Camshaft flange
41. Flange-to-camshaft screw
42. Camshaft wheel pin
43. Standard size tappet
    o/s 0.05 mm (0.0019 in.) tappet
    o/s 0.10 mm (0.0039 in.) tappet
44. Complete pushrod

Removing the main bearing flange

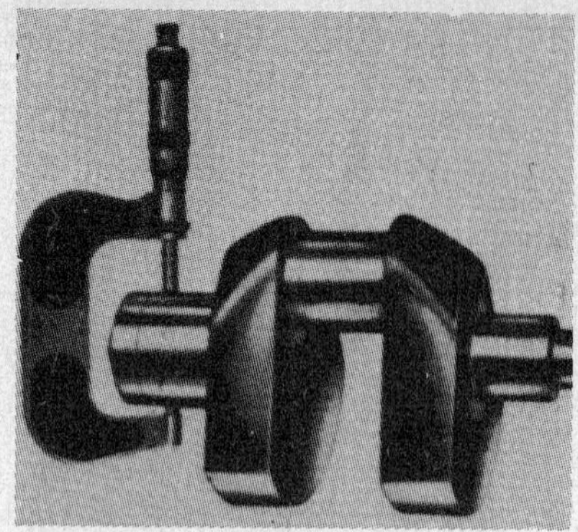
Measuring the flywheel and main bearing journal surface

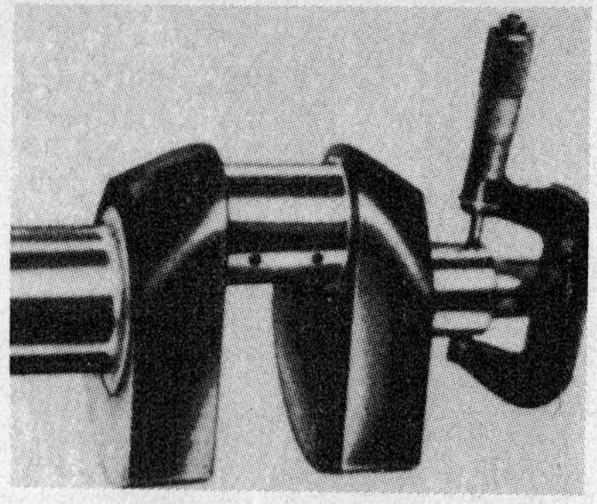
Measuring the timing side main bearing surface

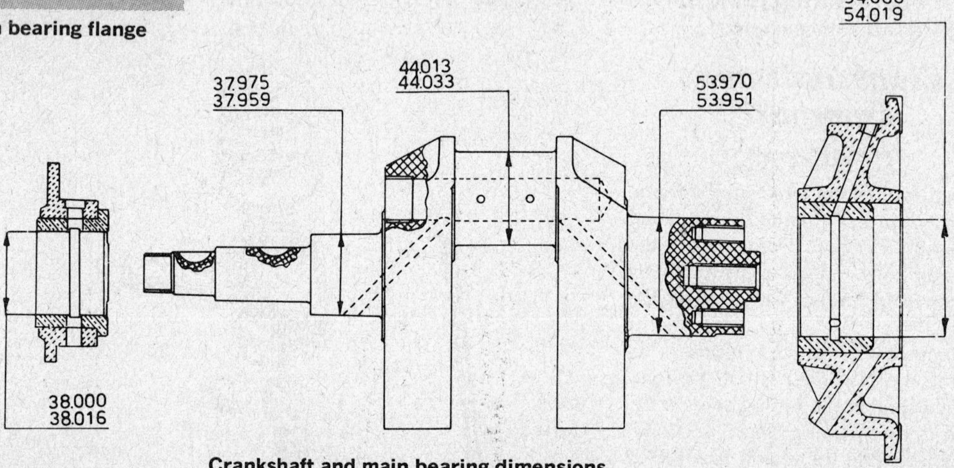

Crankshaft and main bearing dimensions

INSPECTION AND REPAIR

1. Clean all parts, other than seals and gaskets, in a suitable solvent; then blow them dry taking care to blow clear all oil passages.

2. Inspect all parts for wear or damage and replace them as necessary. Consult the various sections dealing with particular component systems for additional information.

3. Carefully inspect the crankshaft for signs of wear, ovalization on bearing paths, scoring or seizing marks, or other damage. Slight seizure marks of the bearing surface can be removed with fine emery paper, but scoring or ovalization must be corrected by regrinding and then compensated for with oversize bearings.

DIAMETER OF FLYWHEEL SIDE MAIN BEARING SURFACE ON CRANKSHAFT

Original Diameter	Undersize 0.2 mm (0.00787 in.)	0.4 mm (0.01574 in.)	0.6 mm (0.02362 in.)	0.8 mm (0.03149 in.)
53.970 mm (2.1248 in.) 53.926 mm (2.1240 in.)	53.770 mm (2.1169 in.) 53.751mm (2.1162 in.)	53.570 mm (2.1090 in.) 53.551 mm (2.1033 in.)	53.370 mm (2.1013 in.) 53.351 mm (2.1004 in.)	53.170 mm (2.093 in.) 53.151 mm (2.0926 in.)

DIAMETER OF TIMING SIDE MAIN BEARING SURFACE ON CRANKSHAFT

Original Diameter	Undersize 0.2 mm (0.00787 in.)	0.4 mm (0.01574 in.)	0.6 mm (0.02362 in.)	0.8 mm (0.03149 in.)
37.975 mm (1.4951 in.) 37.959 mm (1.4944 in.)	37.775 mm (1.4872 in.) 37.759 mm (1.4866 in.)	37.575 mm (1.4793 in.) 37.559 mm (1.4787 in.)	37.375 mm (1.4715 in.) 37.359 mm (1.4707 in.)	37.175 mm (1.4638 in.) 37.159 mm (1.4629 in.)

INSIDE DIAMETER OF FLYWHEEL SIDE MAIN BEARING

Original Diameter	Undersize 0.2 mm (0.00787 in.)	0.4 mm (0.01574 in.)	0.6 mm (0.02362 in.)	0.8 mm (0.03149 in.)
54.000 mm (2.1260 in.)	53.800 mm (2.1171 in.)	53.600 mm (2.1102 in.)	53.400 mm (2.1024 in.)	53.200 mm (2.0945 in.)
54.019 mm (2.1267 in.)	53.819 mm (2.1188 in.)	53.619 mm (2.1109 in.)	53.419 mm (2.1031 in.)	53.219 mm (2.0952 in.)

INSIDE DIAMETER OF TIMING SIDE MAIN BEARING

Original Diameter	Undersize 0.2 mm (0.00787 in.)	0.4 mm (0.01574 in.)	0.6 mm (0.02362 in.)	0.8 mm (0.03149 in.)
38.000 mm (1.4961 in.)	37.800 mm (1.4883 in.)	37.600 mm (1.4803 in.)	37.400 mm (1.4725 in.)	37.200 mm (1.5646 in.)
38.016 mm (1.4967 in.)	37.816 mm (1.4889 in.)	37.616 mm (1.4809 in.)	37.416 mm (1.4731 in.)	37.216 mm (1.5652 in.)

e. Bearing-to-crankshaft clearances:

Crankshaft—timing side main bearing clearance must be within 0.025–0.057 mm (0.00098–0.00224 in.)

Crankshaft—flywheel side main bearing clearance must be within 0.030–0.068 mm (0.00118–0.0027 in.)

Crankpin—big end bearing clearance must be within 0.011–0.061 mm (0.0004–0,0024 in.)

NOTE: *Consult the "Connecting Rod Installation" section for additional information on the available bearings and for fitting instructions.*

f. Check the static balance of the crankshaft by applying a weight of 1.-586±0.015 Kg (3.50 lbs).

g. When regrinding the crankshaft, the shoulder relief radiuses for the crankpin and the flywheel side of the crankshaft must be restored. The shoulders for the crankpin must be 1.5 mm (0.059 in.) and for the flywheel side they must be 3 mm (0.118 in.).

NOTE: *Replacement main bearings come already mounted in their flanges.*

4. Inspect the flywheel and timing side main bearing assemblies for signs of wear, damage, scoring, or ovalization and replace them as necessary.

5. Inspect the seals for signs of wear or damage to their lips and replace them, during the assembly process, as necessary.

6. Inspect the camshaft for signs of wear, pitting, scoring, or other damage, especially on the lobes and bearing journals, and replace it, if necessary. Slight score marks can be removed with fine emery paper. The following specifications will enable you to determine when wear necessitates replacing either the cam or the bearings in which it rides:

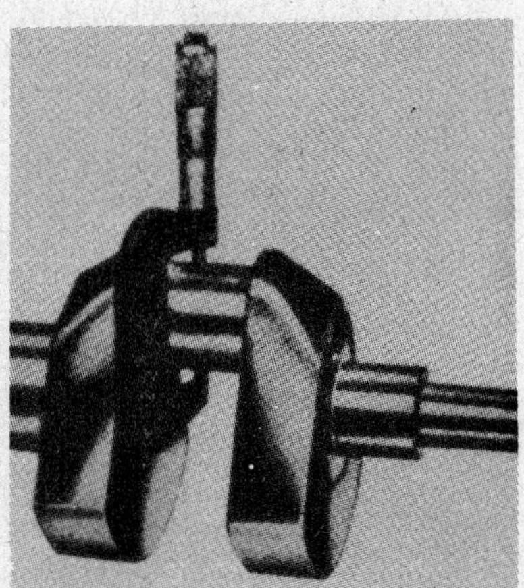

Measuring the crankpin diameter

The flywheel side camshaft bearing is a plain type bearing which is pressed into the crankcase and probably will never have to be replaced. If, however, the bearing becomes worn or damaged it can be replaced by either reaming, cutting, or pulling it out of the crankcase, pressing in a new one and then reaming the new one to size.

CAUTION: *When removing the bushing, especially if you plan to ream or cut it out, take care not to remove or damage any of the crankcase material.*

7. Inspect the tappets for signs of wear, scoring, or other damage, and replace them as necessary; slight score marks can be removed with fine emery paper. The tappet-camshaft contact area must be perfectly smooth or both components will wear out quickly. The tappets must move smoothly in their guides with no hesitation or binding and the guides must not be scored or worn out of shape. Oversize tappets are available, but if the

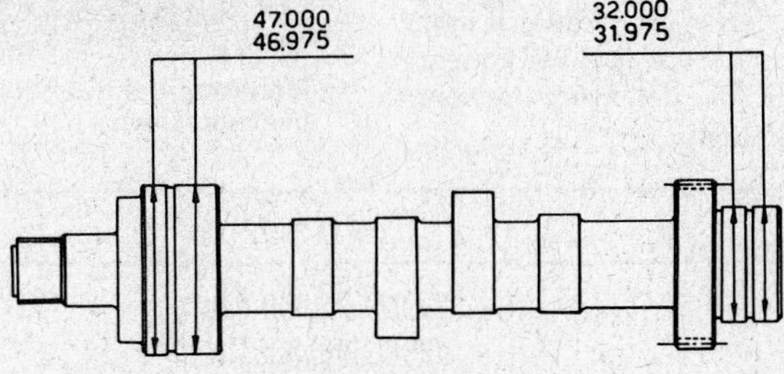

Camshaft dimensions

	Camshaft Journals Diameter	Housing in Crankcase Diameter	Fitting Clearance
Timing side	46.975-47.000 mm (1.8494-1.8504 in.)	47.025-47.064 mm (1.8511-1.8529 in.)	0.025-0.089 mm (0.0009-0.0035 in.)
Flywheel side	31.975-32.000 mm (1.2588-1.2598 in.)	32.025-32.064 mm (1.2607-1.2623 in.)	0.025-0.089 mm (0.0009-0.0035 in.)

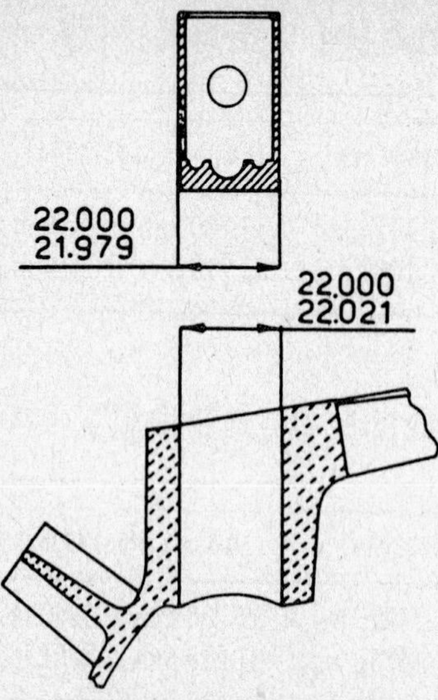

Tappet and guide dimensions

Reaming a tappet guide to size

guide is scored or deformed, you should consult your dealer for additional information, unless you are qualified to ream out the guide. The following are some useful specifications:

	I/D of Guides	O/D of Tappets	Fitting Clearance
Original	22.021-22.000 mm (0.08669-0.8661in.)	22.000-21.979 mm (0.8661-0.9046 in.)	0-0.042 mm (0-0.0016 in.)
Oversize			
0.05 mm (0.0019 in.)	22.071-22.050 mm (0.8688-0.8680 in.)	22.050-22.029 mm (0.8680-0.8672 in.)	0-0.042 mm (0-0.0016 in.)
0.10 mm (0.0039 in.)	22.121-22.100 mm (0.8708-0.8700 in.)	22.100-22.079 mm (0.8700-0.8692 in.)	0-0.042 mm (0-0.0016 in.)

8. Inspect the pushrods for score marks, warpage, wear, or other damage and replace them as necessary.

9. Inspect the crankcase for signs of wear or damage, especially at mating surfaces, and replace it if necessary. The studs themselves are replaceable separately and pressed-in bushings can be pulled or reamed out, pressed-in, and then reamed to size.

ASSEMBLY

1. Assembly is basically in the reverse order of disassembly. Consult the assembly sections pertaining to the various component systems. As a matter of course, all gaskets, seals, keys, and valve keepers should be replaced. All components should be thoroughly oiled during their installation and all parts and mating surfaces should be kept scrupulously clean.

2. Mount and secure the timing side main bearing flange assembly by means of the bolts and lock washers.

3. Install the crankshaft into the timing side flange, then mount and secure by means of the bolts and lock washers, the flywheel side flange so the crankshaft is supported by both main bearings. The lubrication ducts in the flange must be aligned with the passages in the crankcase and the seal in the flange should be protected during installation by using either the special tool (No. 12912000 which is indicated in the accompanying illustration by No. 12) or a suitable substitute.

Mounting the flywheel side main bearing flange

CAUTION: *Failure to protect the seal will probably result in it leaking and this will cause the dry clutch to become oil impregnated causing it to slip and provide generally unsatisfactory performance.*

4. Install the camshaft in its flywheel side bearing, then secure the camshaft support flange to the crankshaft so the camshaft is supported.

5. Install the connecting rods on the crankshaft as described in the "Connecting Rod Installation" section. Remember to bend up the locking tab against a flat on the nut.

6. Install the oil pump, filter, and pipe assemblies, if they have been removed, as directed in the "Lubrication" chapter; then mount and secure the sump pan.

7. Install the piston assemblies as described in the "Cylinder and Piston Assembly" section, install the tappets in their guides, then mount the cylinders.

8. Install the cylinder head assembly as directed in the "Cylinder Head" section, then slip the pushrods into place. Do not secure the rocker box cover as the tappets will have to be adjusted.

9. Mount the flywheel and clutch assemblies on the crankshaft as described in the "Clutch" section.

10. Assemble the timing chest as directed in the "Timing Chest" section and set the valve timing correctly as described in the "Valve Timing" section.

11. Install and adjust the generator belt as described in the "Maintenance" section.

12. Adjust the tappets as directed in the "Tune-Up" chapter, then secure the rocker box covers, tightening the screws in a cross pattern.

13. Install the spark plugs, oil pressure gauge cable, and distributor support assembly. Insert the distributor so its teeth mesh with the gear on the camshaft, then set the points gap and adjust the timing.

14. Install the engine in the frame as directed in the "Engine Removal and Installation" section, then fill the sump with 3 ¼ quarts of fresh oil.

Valve Timing

The inlet valve opens at 24° before top dead center (BTDC) and closes 58° after bottom dead center (ABDC); the exhaust valve opens at 58° before bottom dead center (BBDC) and closes 22° after top dead center (ATDC).

WITH THE ENGINE REMOVED FROM THE FRAME:

1. Adjust the tappets to 0.5 mm (0.-0195 in.), to provide an arbitrary wide

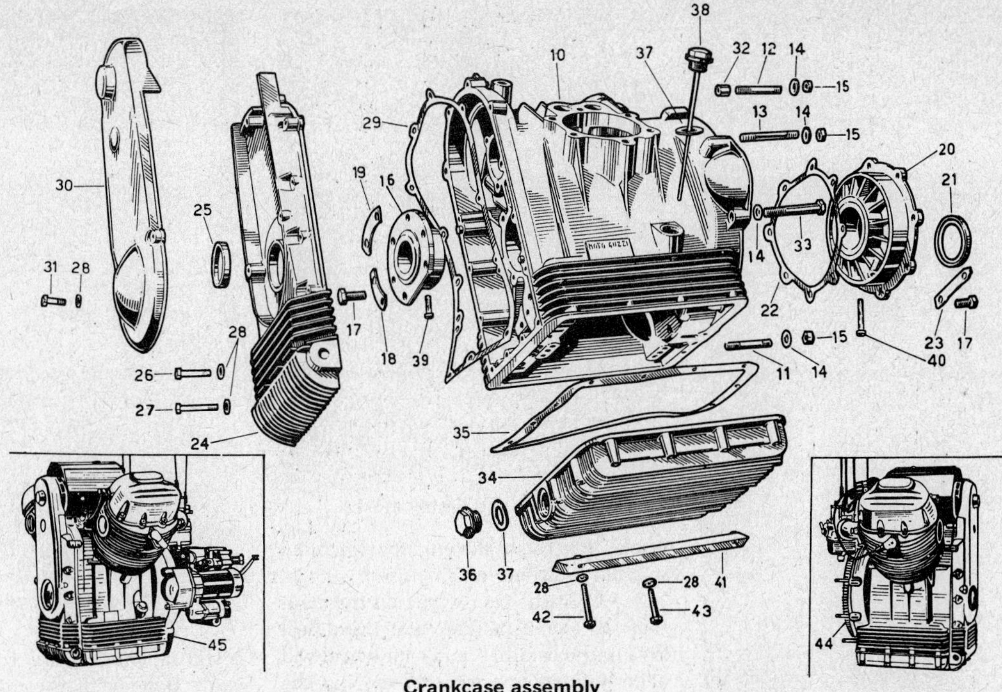

Crankcase assembly

10. Crankcase
11. Gear box fixing bolt
12. Gear box fixing bolt
13. Gear box fixing bolt
14. Gear box and starter motor fixing bolts washer
15. Gear box fixing bolts nut
16. Timing side flange, c/w journal bearing
    Timing side (u/s .0078 in.) flange, c/w journal bearing
    Timing side (u/s .015 in.) flange, c/w journal bearing
    Timing side (u/s .023 in.) flange, c/w journal bearing
    Timing side (u/s .031 in.) flange, c/w journal bearing
17. Flange-to-crankcase and timing cover bolt
18. Flange-to-timing cover nuts lockplate
19. Flange securing nut lockplate
20. Flywheel side flange, c/w main bearing
    Flywheel side (u/s .0078 in.) flange, c/w main bearing
    Flywheel side (u/s .015 in.) flange, c/w main bearing
    Flywheel side (u/s .023 in.) flange, c/w main bearing
    Flywheel side (u/s .031 in.) flange, c/w main bearing
21. Seal on crankshaft, flywheel side
22. Flange, flywheel side, gasket
23. Flywheel side bolt lockplate
24. Timing cover
25. Timing cover seal
26. Short, timing cover screw
27. Long, timing cover screw
28. Timing cover screws, generator belt cover and oil sump washer
29. Timing cover gasket
30. Belt cover
31. Belt cover screw
32. Locating bush
33. Starter motor retaining bolt
34. Oil sump
35. Oil sump gasket
36. Oil drain plug
37. Oil drain and filler plug washer
38. Oil filter plug
39. Main bearing-to-timing side flange pin
40. Main bearing-to-flywheel side flange pin
41. Oil sump guard plate
42. Guard plate securing screw
43. Oil sump screw
44. Engine c/w clutch, without gearshift
45. Engine c/w clutch with gearshift

clearance, either as directed in the "Tune-Up" section, or by following these simpler procedures:

a. Rotate the flywheel until its timing mark is in alignment with the timing mark scribed on the crankcase. If the crankcase mark (A) is no longer there, line the flywheel up with the nub on the crankcase flange.

b. The valves on the left hand cylinder are now closed and are ready to be adjusted.

2. Mount a degree wheel on the flywheel in such a manner that the zero on the degree wheel, the arrow on the flywheel, and the line on the crankcase are all aligned. (See (A) on the accompanying illustration.)

3. Rotate the flywheel 122° (the dis-

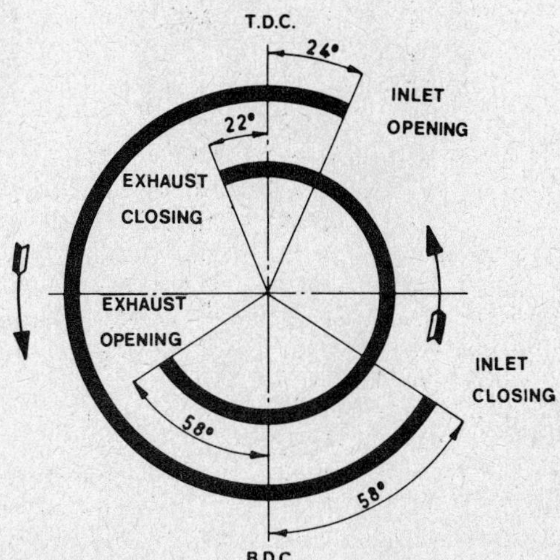

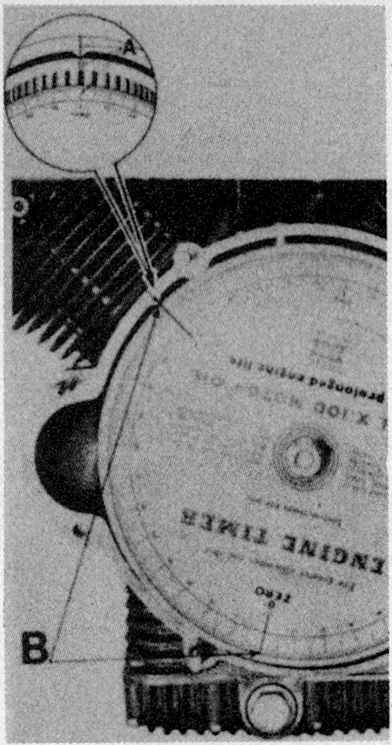

Checking the timing

tance indicated by (B) in the illustration) in the direction of normal engine operation until the exhaust valve of the left-hand cylinder begins to open.

4. At this point, the only timing gear which should be installed is the oil pump gear. Mount the crankshaft timing gear on the crankshaft, then, using a screwdriver, rotate the camshaft counterclockwise until the rocker arm on the exhaust valve of the left hand cylinder begins to touch the valve. A special factory tool (No. 12912900 which is indicated by No. 20 in the accompanying illustration) is

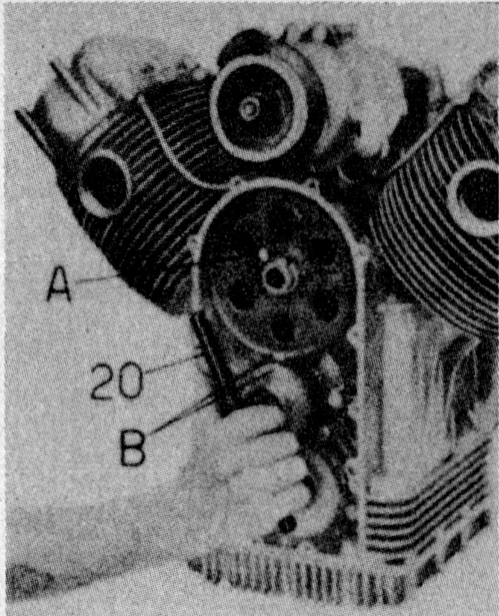

Lining up the timing marks

available to rotate the engine with, but a suitable substitute may be used.

5. Mount the cam wheel on the camshaft in such a manner that the dowel slots in the camshaft and cam wheel will align without necessitating moving the crank or camshaft. A new key should be used.

NOTE: *It is a good idea, when installing new gears, to mark the teeth (B) which are engaged in the cam wheel and the crankshaft timing gear, and the point on the wheel where it is keyed to the shaft (A), with a daub of paint for future reference.*

6. Adjust the tappets to their correct specifications.

WITH THE ENGINE INSTALLED IN THE FRAME

If it ever becomes necessary to replace one of the timing gears while the engine

Mark the engaging gears as shown

is still mounted in the frame, it can be easily done with the special tool (No. 12913800 which is indicated by No. 25 in the accompanying illustration) made available from the factory. If you don't have access to this tool and can't fabricate one to do its job, you'll have to pull the engine from the frame.

1. Remove the gears and wheel as described in the "Timing Chest" section. Even if only one gear appears extensively damaged it is a good practice to replace them all since they all act upon each other at least indirectly.

2. Install the special tool on the cam wheel so the dowel on the tool fits into the wheel's Keyway, which was used to mount the wheel, and which is marked by a daub of paint.

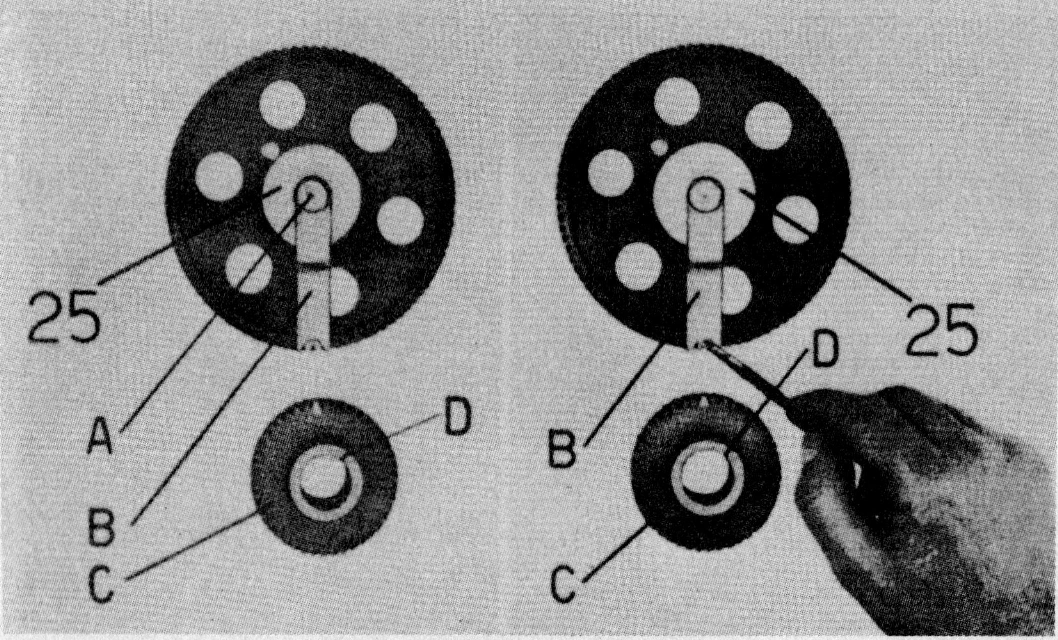

Using the special tool to mark the new gears

3. Loosen the bolt (A) on the tool and rotate the tool arm (B) until the notch on its end spans the two marked teeth, then secure the bolt.

4. Remove the tool from the damaged wheel and install it on the new wheel. Keep repositioning the dowel on the tool, in each of the five keyways of the wheel, until the notch on the end of the arm exactly spans two teeth of the wheel. Mark the keyway, where the tool's dowel is inserted, and the two teeth with a daub of paint for future reference.

5. Determine the position of the new mark on the timing gear, by counting the number of teeth between the mark and the keyway, and then mark the corresponding tooth on the new gear.

6. Install the gears as directed in the "Timing Chest" section.

7. Check the timing by rotating the engine, with the tool described in the "With the Engine removed from the Frame" section, and checking to make sure the painted teeth engage.

REAR WHEEL DRIVE

Transmission

REMOVAL AND DISASSEMBLY

Four-Speed Models

1. Remove the engine from the frame as directed in the "Engine Removal and Installation" section, unbolt the transmission from it (or loosen the motor mounts), slide the engine forward in the frame, and then unbolt the gearbox. In any event, the transmission must be removed from the engine and frame before it is worked on.

2. Drain the transmission oil as directed in the "Maintenance" section.

3. Remove the clutch release lever and the shifter pedal, then disconnect the tachometer cable.

4. Disengage the tab washer by using either the special factory tool (No. 12907100 which is indicated by No. 18 in the accompanying illustration), or a suitable substitute, and then remove the layshaft lock-ring by using either the factory tool (No. 12905400 which is indicated by No. 5 in the accompanying illustration) or a suitable substitute.

Removing the layshaft lock-ring

5. Remove the layshaft spacer and the tachometer drive gear, taking care not to lose the ball.

6. Remove the shifter cover screws, then remove the cover assembly which includes the shaft, sector, return spring, and offset adjusting screw.

7. Remove the gearbox cover mounting screws and cover, then remove the clutch outer body, clutch cage, and clutch pushrod. Tap the cover with a wood block and hammer, if necessary, to loosen it.

8. Remove the clutch inner body circlip, the oil pick-up plate, the drain plug, and the pawl and spring which are housed in the drain plug.

9. Remove the gear control cam plate and the shifter inner body assembly which includes the plungers, pawls, and pawl springs.

10. Remove the shifter drum rod, disengage the shifter forks from the drum grooves, then remove the drum.

11. Remove the shifter fork shaft, then disengage and remove the forks from the layshaft sliding gears.

12. Remove the layshaft assembly and disassemble it in the following order:

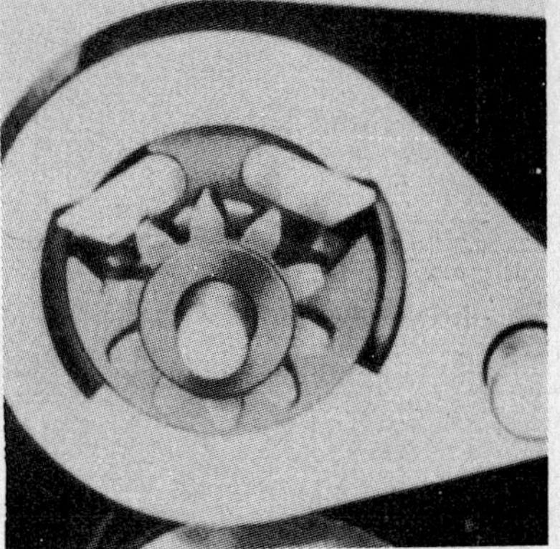
Shifter inner body assembly

a. Adjusting washer
b. First gear
c. Circlip
d. Second gear
e. Fourth gear floating bushing
f. Fourth gear
g. Thrust washer
h. Third gear

13. Remove the mainshaft assembly including the thrust washers and spacers.

14. Remove the clutch shaft complete with the cush drive assembly, then remove the two cush drive plate keepers, the cush drive plate, the cush drive spring, the sliding sleeve, and the clutch shaft-to-mainshaft driving gear. The easiest way to disassemble this assembly is by clamping the shaft on a press or in a wood-jawed vise and using either the special tool (No. 12905900 which is indicated by No. 23 in the accompanying illustration), or a suitable substitute to compress the spring.

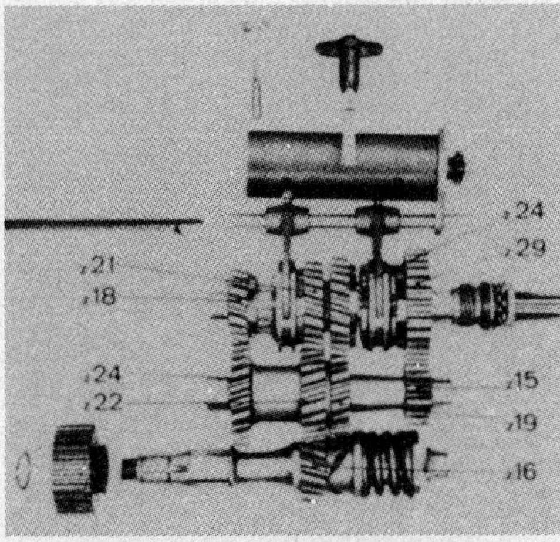

Assembled four-speed transmission

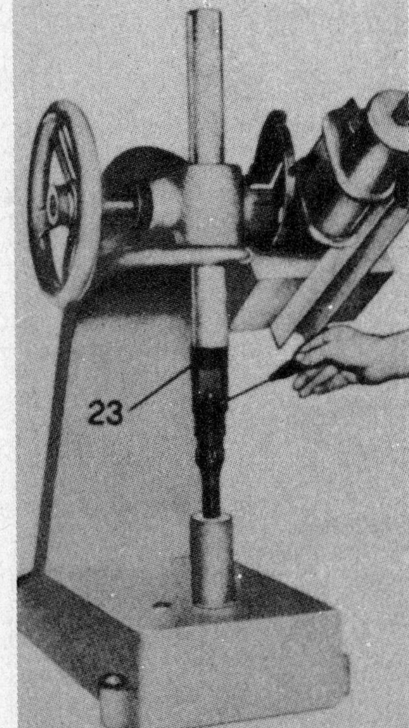

Disassembling the clutch shaft

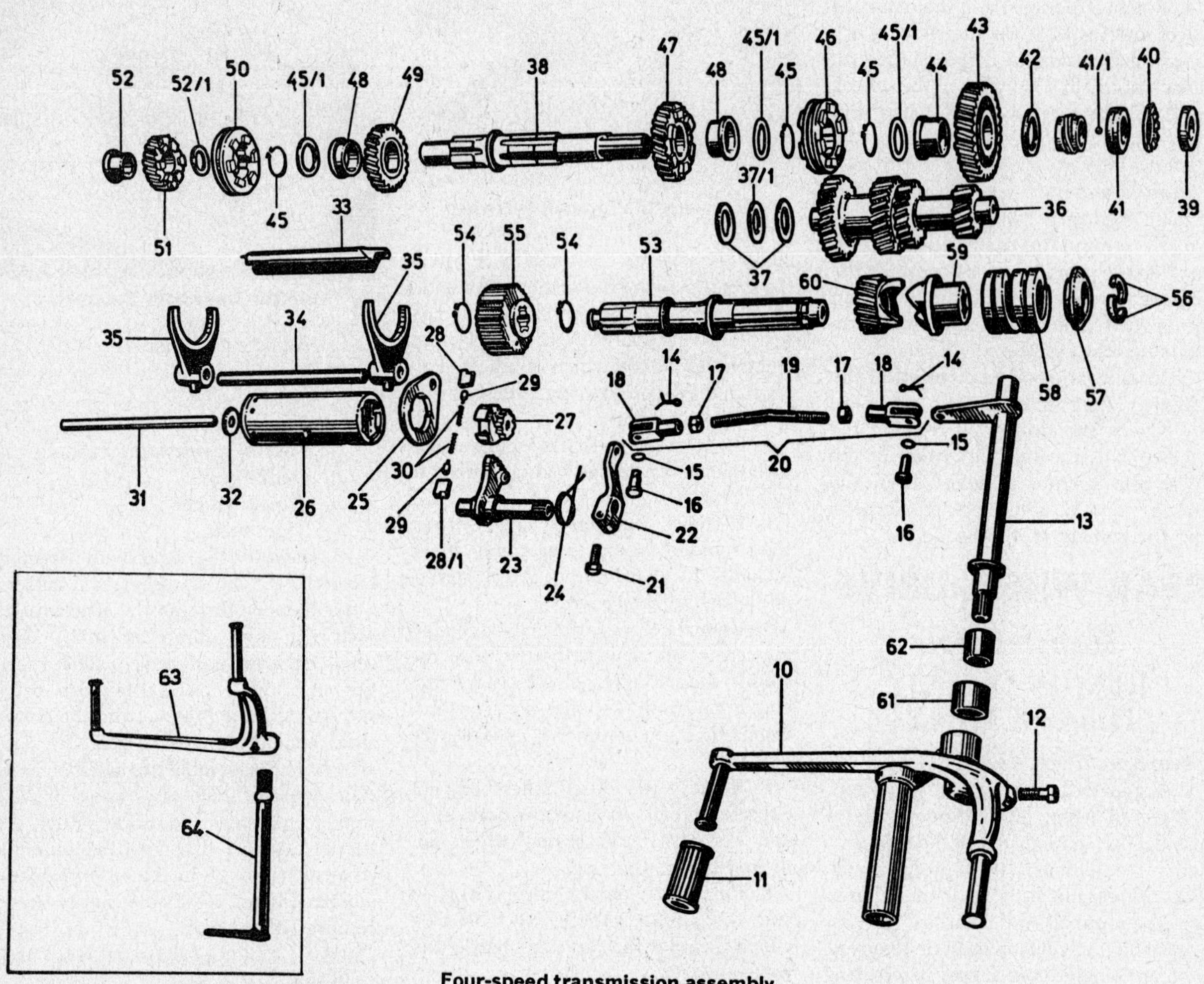

Four-speed transmission assembly

10. Gearshift, rocket type, l/h pedal
11. Gearshift pedal rubber
12. Gearshift pedal screw
13. Operation shaft c/w lever, l/h
14. Gearshift operating rod cotter pin
15. Gearshift rod pins washer
16. Gearshift control rod pin
17. Adjusting on rod nut
18. Gearshift rod fork
19. Gearshift rod
20. Rod c/w forks
21. Lever-to-crankcase screw
22. Gearshift operating lever
23. Shifter guard nut
24. Starter pin return spring
25. Camplate
26. Gear selection drum
27. Inner selector body
28. r/h selector plunger

28/1. l/h selector plunger

29. Selector plunger pawl
30. Plunger spring
31. Selector drum rod

32. Shim, 0.6 mm (0.023 in.)
    Shim, 0.8 mm (0.031 in.)
    Shim, 1 mm (0.039 in.)
    Shim, 1.2 mm (0.047 in.)
33. Oil pick up cup
34. Fork operating shaft
35. Gear selector fork
36. Gear box main shaft
37. Main shaft high gear end thrust washer

37/1. Main shaft seal intermediate

38. Layshaft
39. Layshaft lock ring
40. Safety, lock ring washer
41. Spacer

41/1. Tachometer gear retaining ball

42. Adjusting washer
43. 1st gear c/w bushing gear
44. 1st gear bushing
45. Layshaft circlip

45/1. Thrust, circlip-to-bush washer

46. Sliding, 1st. and 2nd. gear sleeve
47. 2nd. gear, c/w bushing gear
48. 2nd. and 3rd. gear bushing
49. 3rd. gear, c/w bushing gear
50. Sliding, 3rd. and high gear sleeve
51. Top gear
52. Floating, high gear bush

52/1. Bush-to-shaft thrust washer

53. Clutch shaft
54. Clutch inner body circlip
55. Inner clutch body
56. Cush drive plate semi-collar
57. Cush drive plate
58. Cush drive spring
59. Sliding muff
60. Clutch shaft counter gear
61. Guiding operating shaft bush
62. Inner operating shaft bush
63. Gearshift r/h lever
64. R/H lever shaft

NOTE: *Use a screwdriver with a daub of grease on its tip to remove the keepers.*

15. Remove the neutral indicator unit (A).
16. Remove the filler and drain plugs from the housing.
17. Remove the clutch shaft seal from the gearbox and the layshaft seal from the gearbox cover.
18. Remove, only if replacement is deemed necessary, the following bearings in the manner indicated:
    a. Using either the special tool (No. 12913700 which is indicated by No. 8 in the accompanying illustration) or a suitable substitute, remove the layshaft bearing.
    b. Using either the special tool (No. 12913100 which is indicated by No. 9 in the accompanying illustration) or a suitable substitute, remove the mainshaft bearing.
    c. Drift out the clutch shaft bearing with an appropriate drift.
    d. Remove the gearbox cover mainshaft and clutch shaft bearings using either the special puller (No. 12907000 which is indicated by No. 10 in the accompanying illustration) or a suitable substitute.
    3. Drift out the layshaft bearing with an appropriate drift.

NOTE: *Heating the cases to about 150–160° C (300–350°F) will make removing the bearing-considerably easier.*

Five-Speed Models

1. Follow Steps 1–7 in the "Four Speed Models" section. The transmission should be in its Neutral position.

NOTE: *When loosening the layshaft securing nut, use the special tools designed for use on the V850 rather than those listed in the "Four-Speed Models" section. These are Nos. 12907100 and 14905400 which are indicated by Nos. 18 and 26 in the accompanying illustration.*

Neutral indicator

2. Remove the layshaft from its bearing in the cover, taking care not to lose the tachometer gear shim.
3. Remove the shifter fork rod, then remove the high gear shifter fork.

Removing the layshaft bearing

4. Remove the high gear sliding dog gear from the layshaft, then remove the layshaft high gear.
5. Remove the mainshaft high gear along with its roller cage and bushing in the following manner:
    a. Depress the stop pin down into its housing using a suitable pointed instrument, then turn the bushing in either direction and withdraw the gear, complete with roller cage and bushing, to within reaching distance of the shaft hole.
    b. Place your left thumb against the spring-loaded stop pin, to prevent it from springing off into the cosmos, and at the same time withdraw the gear assembly with your right hand.
    c. Remove the stop pin and spring assembly.
6. Remove the breather plug from the top of the transmission housing and remove the spring. The pawl will remain in the housing for removal only after the entire assembly has been taken down.
7. Remove the screws which secure the neutral indicator in the housing, then remove the indicator.
8. Remove the shifter drum and rod, taking careful notice of the way in which the shims are positioned on the drum and the way the drum is positioned in the gear box, so they may be replaced in their original locations, then remove the rod from the drum.
9. Remove the layshaft from the gear-

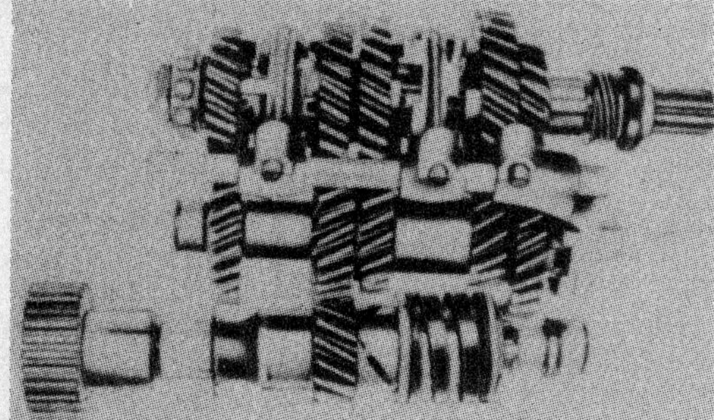
Assembled five-speed transmission

Removing the mainshaft bearing

Removing the mainshaft bearing from the cover

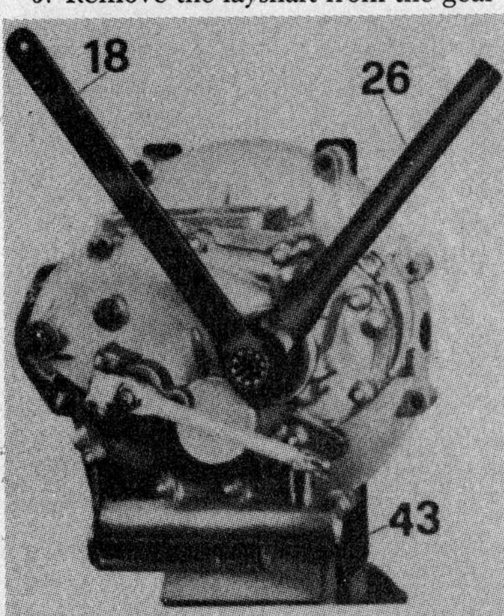

Loosening the layshaft nut

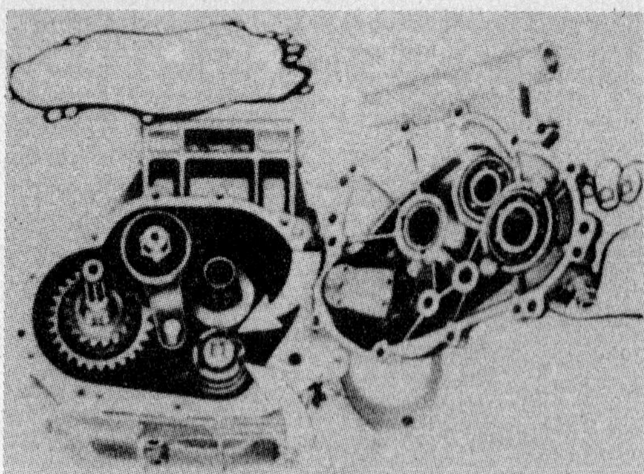

Shifter drum assembly

box, then disassemble it in the following order:

a. Cover side seal ring
b. First gear, roller cage, and bushing
c. First gear sliding dog gear
d. Nut located on the side of fourth gear
e. Roller bearing
f. Adjusting washers
g. Fourth gear, roller cage, and bushing
h. Fourth gear sliding dog gear
i. Fixed sleeve on shaft
j. Shim
k. Third gear, roller cage, and bushing

10. Remove the mainshaft assembly from the gearbox, taking care to note the positions of the shims for reassembly in their original positions. The mainshaft inner bearing race may be removed with either the special puller (No. 14928500 which is indicated by No. 29 in the accompanying illustration) or a suitable substitute.

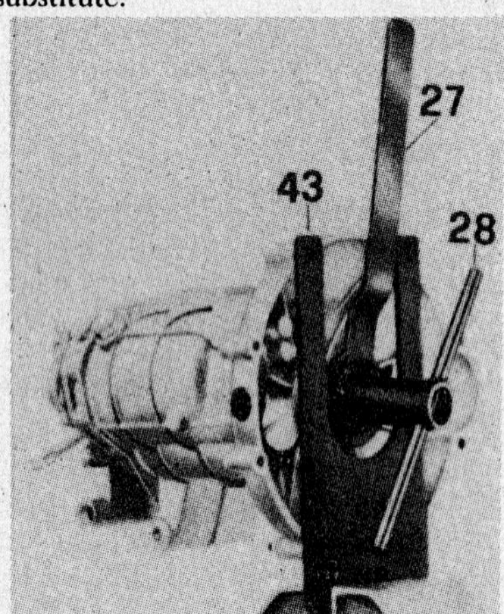

Removing the retaining ring

11. Bend back the locking tabs, then remove the clutch body retaining ring from the clutch side of the clutch shaft using either the special tools (Nos. 14912800 and 14912600 which are indicated by Nos. 27 and 28 in the accompanying illustration) or suitable substitutes.

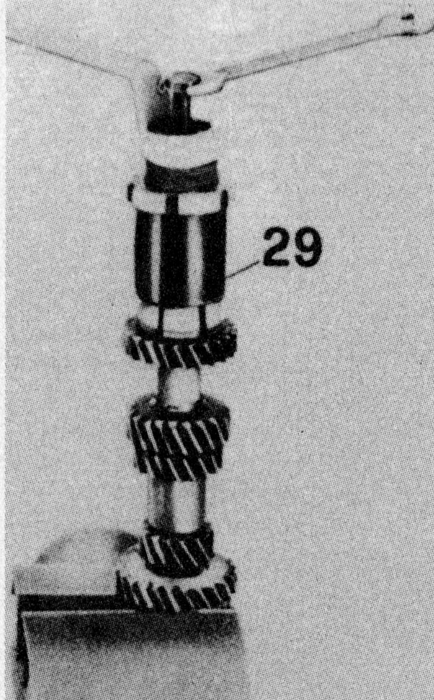

Removing the mainshaft inner bearing race

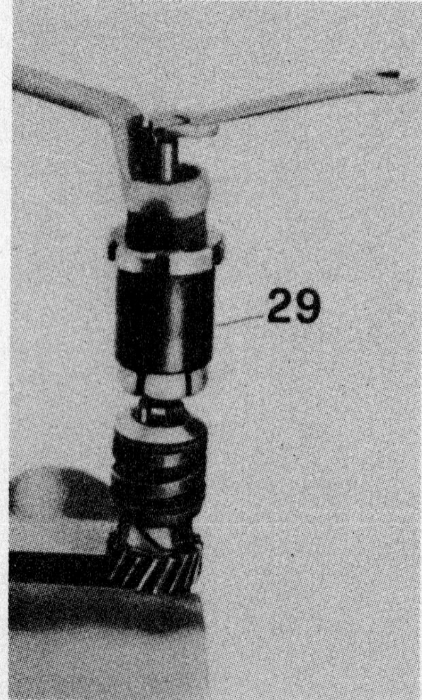

Removing the clutch shaft inner bearing race

NOTE: *The transmission mount (No. 14929600 which is indicated by No. 43 in the accompanying illustration) is a useful item for such work as this, but is in no way necessary for the successful completion of the task.*

12. Remove the clutch fixed body, taking care to note the position of the seals between the body and the bearing and the seals in the shaft groove.

13. Remove the clutch shaft from the bearing taking care not to lose the oil scoop between the shaft and bearing.

NOTE: *Tap the end of the shaft gently with a soft mallet if it is reluctant to leave its seat.*

14. Remove the inner roller bearing race and the spacer nut from the clutch shaft using either the special puller (No. 14928500 which is indicated by No. 29 in the accompanying illustration) or a suitable substitute.

15. Install the clutch shaft in a wood-jawed vise, then use either the special tool (No. 12905900), or a suitable substitute, to compress the spring enough so the keepers can be removed; then remove the tool and slip off the cush plate, spring, sliding sleeve and the intermediate gear.

NOTE: *Use a screwdriver with a daub of grease on its tip to remove the keepers.*

16. Remove the bearings from the gearbox in the following manner, especially if they have been secured with Loctite®.

a. Place the gearbox in an oven and heat it up to 150–160° C (300–350° F).

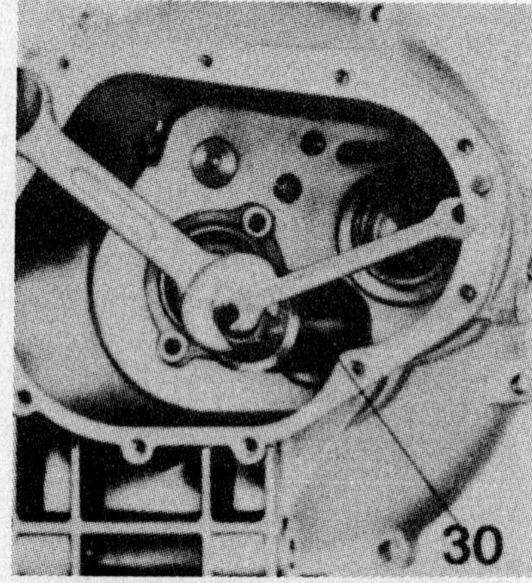

Removing the mainshaft roller bearing

b. Remove the mainshaft roller bearing by using either the special puller (No. 14913100 which is indicated by No. 30 in the accompanying illustration) or a suitable substitute.

c. Remove the mainshaft roller bearing outer race by using either the special puller (No. 14913700 which is indicated by No. 31 in the accompanying illustration) or a suitable substitute.

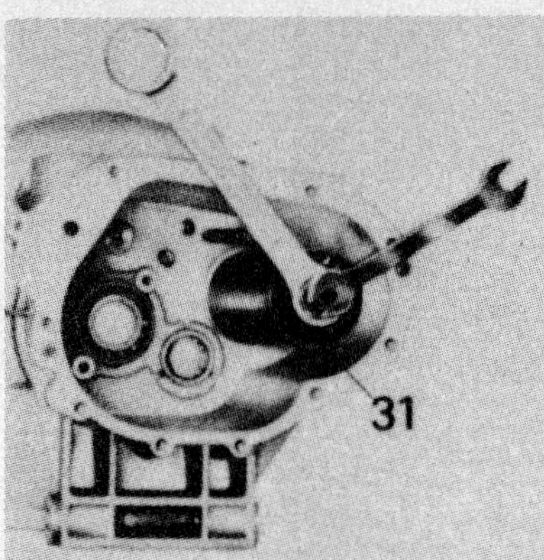

Removing the mainshaft bearing outer race

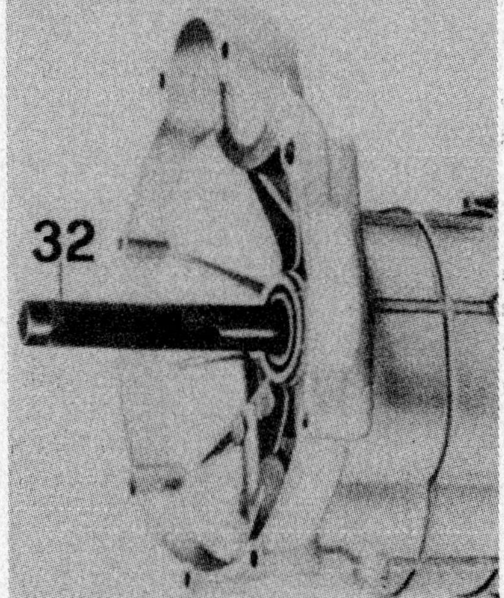

Drifting out the clutch shaft bearing

Removing the mainshaft bearing

Removing the clutch shaft bearing

c. Remove the clutch shaft seal, the lockplate securing bolts, and the lockplate, then drift out the clutch shaft bearing by using either the special drift (No. 14929200 which is indicated by No. 32 in the accompanying illustration) or a suitable substitute.

17. Remove the shifter mechanism from the transmission cover by carefully tapping the assembly free with a soft mallet, then remove the shifter return spring, the spring guide pin, the operating pawls, the pawl return springs, and the shifter adjusting screw and locknut. If the pawls must be removed, do so by removing the pins with the aid of a 3–4 mm (0.11–0.15 in.) tool; the pawl springs will come out with the pins. A 10 mm (0.39) reamer may be used to ream out the pawl housings.

18. Remove the bearings from the gearbox cover in the following manner, especially if they have been secured with Loctite®.

a. Place the cover in an oven and heat it up to 150–160° C (300–350° F).

b. Remove the mainshaft bearing by using either the special puller (No. 14907000 which is indicated in the accompanying illustration by No. 33) or a suitable substitute.

Removing the layshaft bearing

c. Remove the clutch shaft bearing by using either the special puller (No. 14913100 which is indicated by No. 30 in the accompanying illustration) or a suitable substitute.

d. Remove the layshaft seal and the lockplate securing screw, then remove the lockplate.

e. Remove the layshaft bearing by using either the special tool (No. 14929200 which is indicated by No. 32 in the accompanying illustration) or a suitable substitute.

INSPECTION AND REPAIR

All Models

1. Clean all parts, other than gaskets and seals, in a suitable solvent, then blow them dry. Take care to blow clear all oil passages.

2. Inspect the transmission housing and cover for signs of wear, damage, stripped threads of the bosses, or irregularities on mating surfaces, and replace them as necessary.

NOTE: *When purchasing transmission components it is important to provide the serial number so you can be sure of receiving the correct components.*

3. Inspect all gaskets, seals, circlips, washers, and keepers for signs of wear, damage, or distorted or crushed lips and replace them as necessary.

CAUTION: *It is generally considered to be a good practice to replace all of these short-life components any time they are removed. Failure to do this may very well result in serious damage. In all cases, replace the keepers and circlips, as these usually will not perform properly once they have been disturbed.*

4. Inspect the bearings for signs of wear, pitting, scoring, excessive play, or rough motion and replace them as necessary. Do not spin unlubricated bearings and do not attempt to replace individual balls or races as this is a false economy.

5. Inspect the mainshaft and layshaft assemblies for signs of wear, pitting, scoring, seizure marks, chipped or damaged gear teeth, dogs, or splines, and replace them as necessary. The sliding dog gears and the free wheeling idler gears must move freely.

NOTE: *Whenever you have one obviously damaged gear, slight damage has at least probably occured to any gears with which it directly or indirectly engages. For this reason, gears should be replaced as gear systems to insure that there will be no subsequent failure.*

6. Inspect the fifth gear (on five-speed models) bushing retainer and spring for signs of wear, damage, or, in the case of the spring, a collapsed condition and replace them as necessary. The spring should show a load of 1.40 kgs (3.08 lbs) when compressed to a length of 8 mm (0.031 in.).

7. Check the clearances between the layshaft gear bushings and the shaft (V700 and V750 models). The clearances should be as follows:

a. The inside diameter of the first, second, and third gear bushings must be within 27.040–27.061 mm (1.0646–1.0655 in.).

b. The outside diameter of the layshaft bushing support for first, second, and third gears must be within 26.987–27.000 mm (1.0624–1.0630 in.).

c. The bushing-to-layshaft fitting clearance must be within 0.040–0.074 mm (0.0016–0.0028 in.).

d. The inside diameter of the fourth gear floating bushing must be within 20.007–20.028 mm (0.7877–0.7885 in.).

e. The outside diameter of the layshaft floating bushing support for fourth gear must be within 19.987–20.000 mm (0.7868–0.7874 in.).

f. The bushing-to-layshaft fitting clearance must be within 0.007–0.041 mm (0.0003–0.0016 in.).

8. Check the clearances between the layshaft bushings and gears (V700 and V750 models). The clearances should be as follows:

a. The outside diameter of the first, second, and third gear bushings must be within 31.060–31.099 mm (1.2228–1.2243 in.).

b. The inside diameter of the first, second, and third gears must be within 31.000–31.025 mm (1.2205–1.2214 in.).

c. The negative clearance for the gear bushings must be within 0.035–0.099 mm (0.0014–0.0039 in.).

d. The outside diameter of the fourth gear floating bushing must be within 22.960–22.939 mm (0.9309–0.9031 in.).

3. The inside diameter of the fourth gear must be within 23.021–23.000 mm (0.9063–0.9055 in.).

f. The clearance between the fourth gear and its floating bushing must be within 0.040–0.082 mm (0.0016–0.0032 in.).

9. Inspect the clutch shaft assembly for signs of wear or damage and replace the necessary components. The sliding sleeve must be able to slide smoothly and freely and the engaging teeth must be devoid of chips, score marks, or other damage.

10. Inspect the cush plate assembly, making sure that the retainer is not cracked or damaged, the plate grooves are not rough or damaged, and that the drive spring is not collapsed or damaged, and replace any parts as necessary.

11. Inspect the shifter drum assembly for worn or damaged drum grooves, camplate, pawl holes, pawl, pawl spring, shifter inner body teeth, or any other damage, and replace any parts as necessary.

12. Inspect the shifter forks for wear or damage, especially to the nub which rides in the drum grooves, and replace them as necessary.

13. Generally inspect all remaining parts not listed above and replace any which appear to be worn or damaged.

ASSEMBLY

Four-Speed Models

1. Assembly is basically in the reverse order of disassembly. Lubricate all parts, other than those surfaces on which a sealant is used, with clean oil as you put them together and make certain that all parts are perfectly clean.

2. Press all bearings into the cover and case using light applications of green Loctite® (which is the sealant recommended by the factory) at your own discretion. Make absolutely certain that no Loctite® gets into the bearings. When installing the layshaft bearing in the case, make sure you use a bottom plate to protect the fourth gear floating bushing.

CAUTION: *The Loctite® must be allowed to set for at least 12 hours before you continue with the assembly.*

3. Install the clutch shaft seal ring on the gearbox.

4. Install the mainshaft with the two thrust washers and the intermediate washer between the roller bearing and the fourth gear side of the shaft.

5. Place the fourth gear, its floating bush, and the thrust washer on the bearing, then insert the assembled layshaft (except for the first gear) through the thrust washer and gear and into the bearing.

Protect the seal before installing the clutch shaft

6. Install the assembled clutch shaft assembly in the gearbox, using either the special tool (no. 12910700 which is indicated by No. 14 in the accompanying illustration) or a suitable substitute, to protect the seal ring.

NOTE: *Failure to install the shaft correctly will result in damage to the seal ring and eventual oil leakage on the clutch.*

7. Install the shifter forks to the two sliding dog gears, install the shifter drum, then insert the fork ends in the drum grooves.

8. Slip the fork shaft through the forks, then mount the camplate on the shaft.

9. Rotate the shifter drum until the shifter pawl enters the fourth gear position hole and the sliding dog gear engages the second gear.

10. Install the assembled shifter inner body which includes the springs, plungers, and pawls.

11. Slip the first gear and an adjusting washer on the layshaft.

12. Install the oil pick-up plate and the neutral indicator unit in the gearbox, then mount the gearbox cover and a new cover gasket, making sure the indicator doesn't interfere with the mating of the box and cover. A light coating of a gasket sealer may be used at your discretion.

NOTE: *When securing the cover screws, do so evenly in a cross pattern to avoid deforming the cover gasket.*

13. Mount the tachometer driving gear, spacer, and lockwasher on the layshaft; then install the lock ring using either the special tools (Nos. 12907100 and 12905400) or suitable substitutes. Secure the ring by bending the locking tab in the lock ring slot.

14. Assemble the sector quadrant and shifter shaft assembly, the shifter return spring and the offset adjusting screw, along with its washer and locknut, to the shifter cover, then mount the cover assembly using a new gasket and making sure that the quadrant is engaging the shifter inner body. A light coat of a gasket sealer may be used at your discretion.

NOTE: *When securing the cover, tighten the short and long screws evenly in a cross pattern to avoid deforming the cover gasket.*

15. Mount the gear shifter operating lever on the shifter shaft, securing it by means of the two circlips which fit in the clutch shaft grooves.

16. Install the clutch rubber tube, pressure rod, inner body, cage and outer body, and seal ring, then mount the clutch operating lever to the gearbox by means of its pin and cotterpin.

17. Install the drain plug, add 1¾ pts of either Shell Spirax 90 E.P. oil, or a suitable substitute to the gearbox, then install the filler and level plugs.

18. Mount the transmission to the engine, complete the assembly in the reverse order of disassembly, and adjust the transmission as described in the "Transmission Adjustment" section.

Five-Speed Models

1. Assembly is basically in the reverse order of disassembly. Lubricate all parts other than those surfaces on which a sealant is used, with clean oil as you put them together and make sure that all parts are perfectly clean.

2. When installing the bearings, it is recommended that a light coat of green Loctite® be used on the outer races and bearing housings. Be very careful to avoid getting any Loctite® in the bearings and allow them to set for about 12 hours before continuing with the assembly. Install the bearings as follows:

Installing the clutch shaft bearing

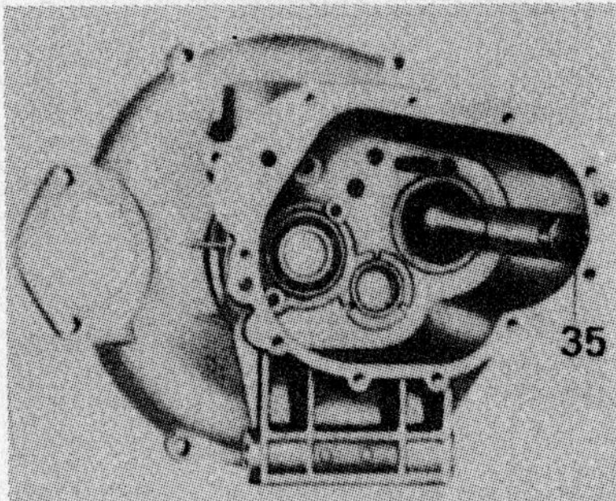

Installing the layshaft bearing outer race

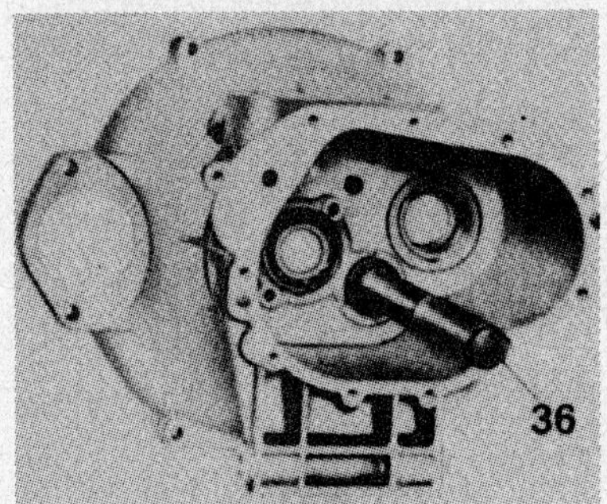

Installing the mainshaft bearing

a. Install the clutch shaft bearing into its gearbox housing using either the special drift (No. 14928900 which is indicated in the accompanying illustration by No. 34) or a suitable substitute.

b. Press the outer layshaft bearing race into its gearbox housing using either the special drift (No. 14929100 which is indicated by No. 35 in the accompanying illustration) or a suitable substitute.

c. Install the mainshaft bearing in its gearbox housing using either the special drift (No. 14928800 which is indicated in the accompanying illustration by No. 36) or a suitable substitute.

d. Press the layshaft bearing in its housing in the gearbox cover using either the special drift (No. 14928900 which is indicated by No. 34 in the accompanying illustration) or a suitable substitute.

e. Install the mainshaft bearing in its cover housing using either the special drift (No. 14929000 which is indicated by No. 37 in the accompanying illustration) or a suitable substitute.

f. Install the clutch shaft bearing in its cover housing using either the special drift (No. 14928800 which is indicated by No. 36 in the accompanying illustration) or a suitable substitute.

3. Install the layshaft bearing retainers in the gearbox cover, making sure that they seat absolutely flush with the outer bearing races. Mill away any projections which may prevent a perfect seal and use a light coat of green Loctite®, taking care not to allow any of it to penetrate the bearing.

NOTE: *Use only the modified type retainers (part No. 14213802) for the best results.*

Installing the mainshaft bearing

4. Install the clutchshaft seal in the gearbox using either the special drift (No. 14929400 which is indicated by No. 38 in the accompanying illustration) or a suitable substitute.

5. Install the layshaft seal in the gearbox cover using either the special drift

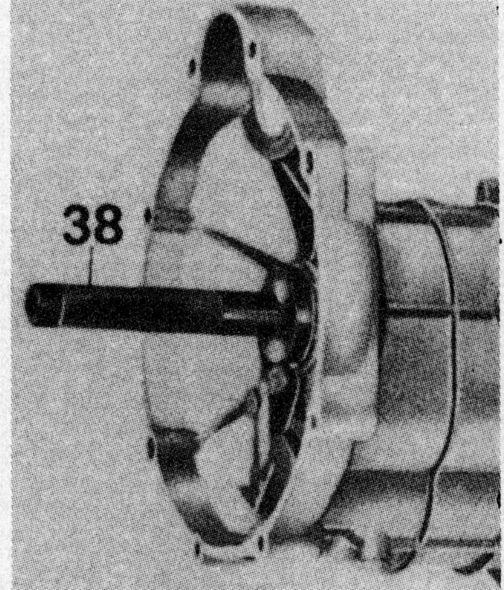

Installing the clutch shaft seal

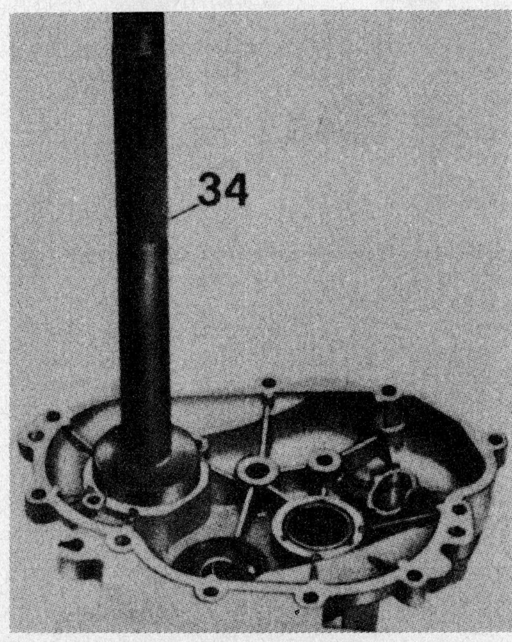

Installing the layshaft bearing

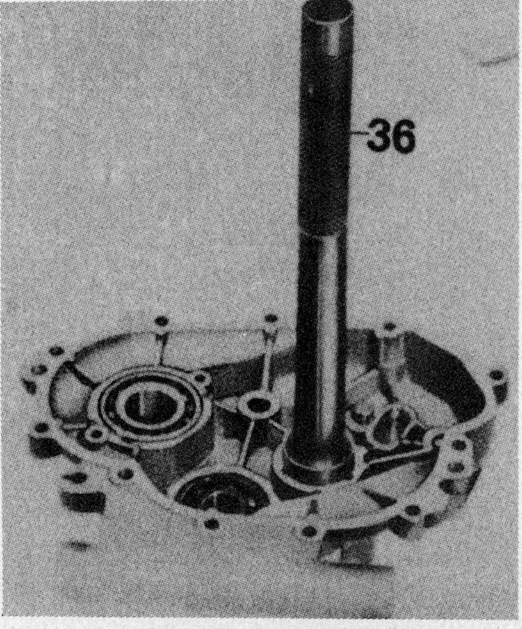

Installing the clutch shaft bearing

Installing the layshaft seal

(No. 14929500 which is indicated by No. 39 in the accompanying illustration) or a suitable substitute.

6. Install the selector shaft seal in its housing in the gearbox cover.

7. Assemble the shifter body by inserting the pawls and springs and securing them to the shifter body with flexible pins; then install the shifter quadrant shaft, gear, and return spring to the shifter body and mount the assembled body to the gearbox cover.

8. Shim up the mainshaft so the distance between the cover bearing and the gearbox bearing is within 167.1–167.2 mm (6.578–6.582 in.). Shims are available in the following sizes: 0.2, 2.1, 2.2, and 2.4 mm (0.078⁸, 0.8274, 0.8668, 0.9456 in.) and may be fitted on the gearbox end of the shaft with bronze spacers between them. The part numbers are given in the accompanying illustration.

9. Press the mainshaft roller bearing inner race onto the shaft using either the special tool (No. 14928600 which is indicated by No. 40 in the accompanying illustration) or a suitable substitute.

10. Assemble the following components on the layshaft gearbox end:

a. Slip the second gear bushing on

Installing the mainshaft bearing inner race

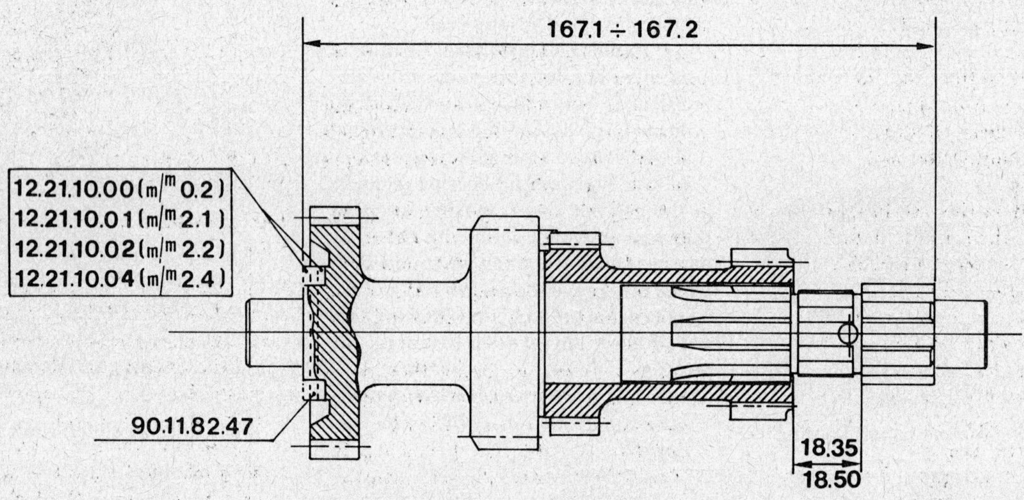

Shimming the mainshaft

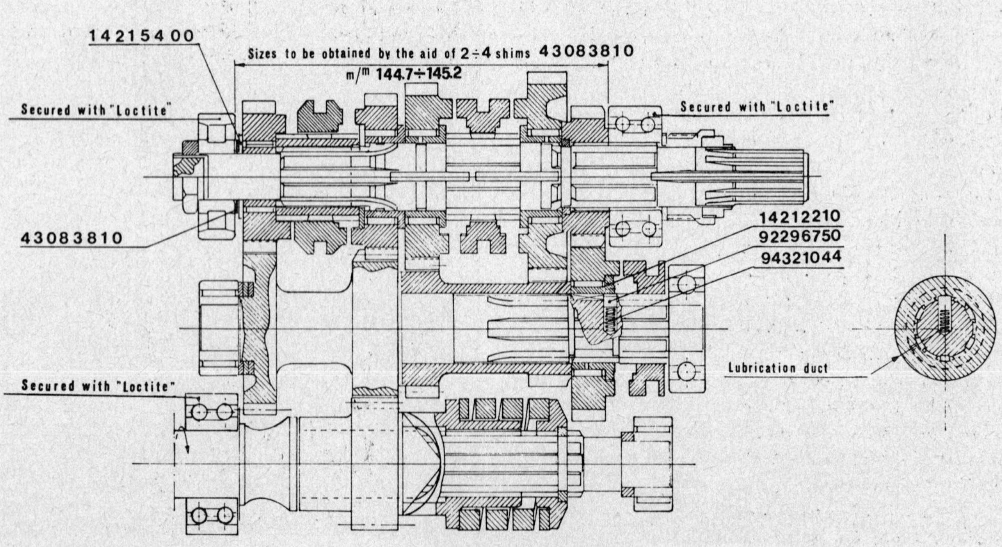

Shimming the layshaft

the shaft so the bushing head faces the transmission cover.

b. Fit the second gear roller cage on the second gear bushing, then mount the second gear on the cage so its engaging dogs are facing the gearbox cover.

c. Slip the third gear bushing on the shaft so its head faces the second gear, assemble the third gear roller cage on the bushing, then install the third gear on the roller cage so its engaging dogs are facing the gearbox.

d. Place a shim on the shaft, install the fixed sleeve on the shaft with its stepped down end facing the third gear, then slip the third and fourth gear sliding sleeve onto the shaft with its stepped down end facing the third gear.

e. Slip the fourth gear bushing on the shaft, install the roller cage on the bushing, then position the fourth gear on the shaft so its engaging dogs face the sliding sleeve.

11. Assemble the following components on the layshaft gearbox cover end:

a. Slip the first and second gear engaging sleeves on the shaft.

b. Position the first gear bushing on the shaft so its head faces second gear, fit the first gear roller cage on the bushing, then install the first gear on the roller cage.

c. Position the seal in its groove in the shaft, then slip the fourth gear on the shaft so its stepped down end is fitted on the seal ring.

12. Shim the layshaft on the fourth gear side until the distance between the shims and the fourth gear is within 144.-7–145.2 mm (5.692–5.715 in.). This can generally be accomplished with between two and four shims.

13. Mount the roller bearing on the fourth gear end of the layshaft, secure the nut on the fourth gear end of the shaft by hammering the nut tang with a chisel along the line of the shaft groove, then mount the assembled layshaft in the transmission housing.

14. Assemble the first, second, third, and fourth gear shifting forks on the layshaft dog gears.

15. Install the splined shifter drum, along with its shaft and a spacer, in the gearbox. Then look through the hole in the ratchet pawl to see if the pawl hole is aligned with one of the six holes in the drum. If the holes are misaligned, replace the spacer with larger or smaller ones until both holes are in perfect accord.

16. Position the knobs of the shifter forks nubs in the drum grooves, using either the special tool (No. 14929300 which is indicated by No. 41 in the accompanying illustration) or a suitable substitute.

17. Temporarily secure the peg, spring, and cap in their gearbox housing.

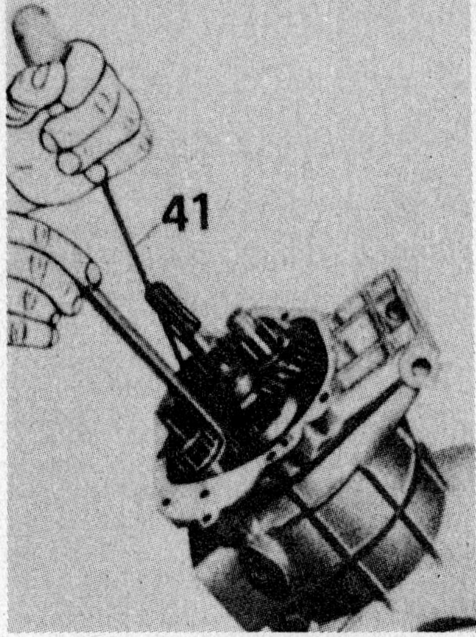

Fitting the shifter forks to the drum

18. Slip the shifter fork retaining rod through the fork eyes.

19. Mount and secure the neutral indicator to the gearbox, making sure that the blade contacts the button on the drum.

20. Assemble the clutch shaft assembly in the following manner:

a. Install the idle gear so its engaging dogs face the gearbox cover, then position the coupling sleeve so its engaging dogs face the idle gear.

b. Slip the cush spring and spring plate on the shaft, then use either the special tool (No. 12905900), or a suitable substitute, to compress the spring enough so two new keepers can be installed.

c. Secure the spacer nut, then install the clutch shaft roller bearing inner race in the cover using either the special tool (No. 14928600 which is indicated by No. 40 in the accompanying illustration) or a suitable substitute.

d. Install, on the gearbox end of the shaft, the oil seal in its groove, and the oil scoop between the shaft and gearbox bearing, then mount the shaft assembly in the gearbox bearing and retaining ring.

21. Assemble the mainshaft assembly in the following manner:

a. Mount the fifth gear roller cage and gear on the bushing, then slip the gear, cage, and bushing assembly on the splined portion of the shaft.

b. Mount the spring in its drilling in the shaft, then position the stop pin on top of the spring.

Installing the clutch shaft bearing inner race

c. Depress the spring with the thumb of your left hand while slipping the fifth gear assembly over it, then rotate the bushing to either the right or left until the stop peg seats into one of the bushing's six splines.

d. Slip the fifth gear engaging sleeve and shifter fork onto the shaft, so the fork eye slips over the fork rod, then engage the fork nub in the drum groove.

22. Assemble the gearbox cover in the following manner:

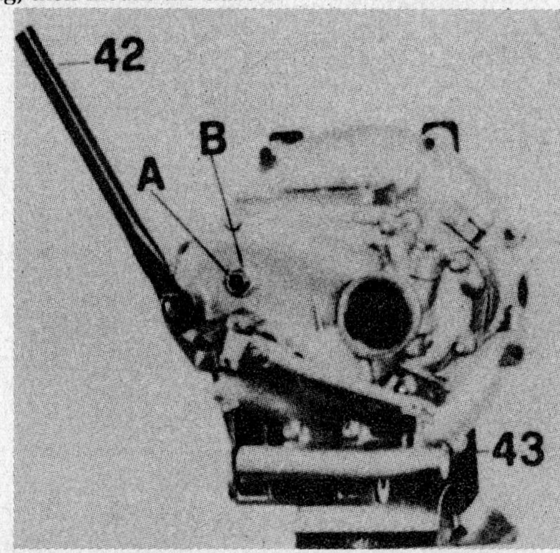

a. Install the retaining washer on the shifter drum along with one or more shims.

b. Shift the drum into the neutral position, place a new cover gasket on the mating surface, mount the cover while tapping it lightly with a soft mallet to properly seat all of the shafts and mating surfaces, then lightly screw in the four cover screws.

NOTE: *A sparing application of a suitable gasket sealer may be used at your own discretion, but make sure none of it gets inside the gearbox.*

c. Slip the shim, tachometer drive gear, and the drive gear stop ball onto the layshaft, then temporarily secure the layshaft securing nut.

d. Mount either the special tool (No. 14928700 which is indicated by No. 42 in the accompanying illustration), or any suitable substitute which you can use to shift the transmission, onto the shifter shaft.

e. Loosen the locknut (B) and rotate the adjusting screw (A) until a suitable adjustment is achieved in which all gears, including neutral, can be easily engaged. If ease of shifting cannot be attained, remove the gearbox cover and add or remove spacer shims from between the gearbox and the shift drum to alleviate shifting problems related to First and Third gears or between the gearbox cover and the drum to alleviate shifting problems related to Second and Fourth gears. 0.6, 0.8, 1.0, and 1.2 mm (0.023, 0.031, 0.039, and 0.047 in.) shims are available.

f. Remount the cover and recheck the gearbox operation. If all of the gears engage smoothly, including Neutral, secure the layshaft nut using either the special tools (Nos. 14905400 and 12907100) or suitable substitutes, then hammer the nut with a chisel at the shaft groove to lock it into place.

g. Secure the cover mounting screws, remove the tool from the shifter shaft, and mount and secure the shift lever on the shifter shaft.

h. Secure the oil breather plug which serves to secure the gearbox spring and stop peg.

23. Mount the bearing inner body seal, inner body, safety washer, and the inner body locking nut on the clutch shaft using either the special tools (Nos. 14912800 and 14912600) or suitable substitutes, then bend one of the locking tabs into one of the locknut grooves.

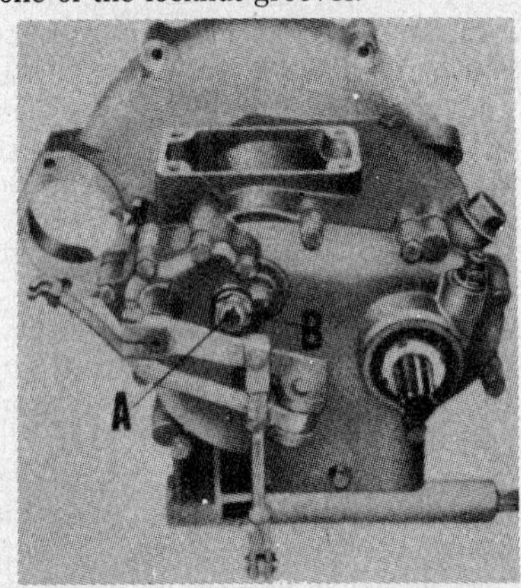

Adjusting the transmission (four-speed models)

24. When installing the clutch unit on the main shaft and gearbox cover, position the small rubber tube in the shaft, mount the inner body, mount the throwout bearing on the inner body, and mount the inner body and seal on the gearbox cover. Then slip the clutch pushrod into the operating shaft at the gearbox end, mount the release mechanism on the cover along with the adjusting screw and locknut and then, using cotters and pins to secure it, install the shifter lever return spring in its housing in the cover.

25. Adjust the gearbox as described in the "Transmission Adjustment" section.

26. Replenish the gearbox oil supply as directed in the "Maintenance" section, then mount the transmission to the engine and frame.

TRANSMISSION ADJUSTMENT

Four-Speed Models

1. Loosen the locknut (B), and turn the

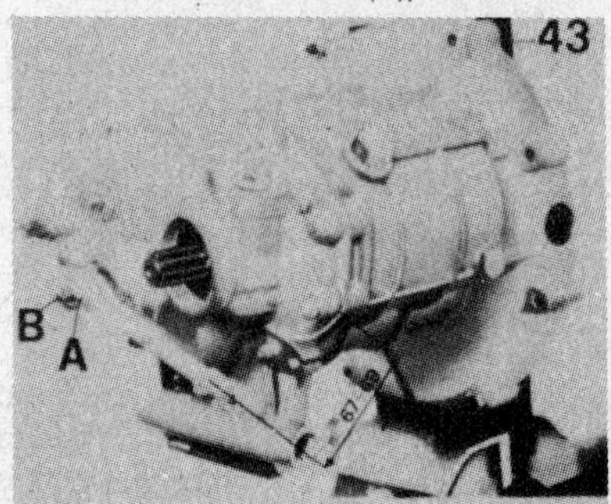

Adjusting the transmission (five-speed models)

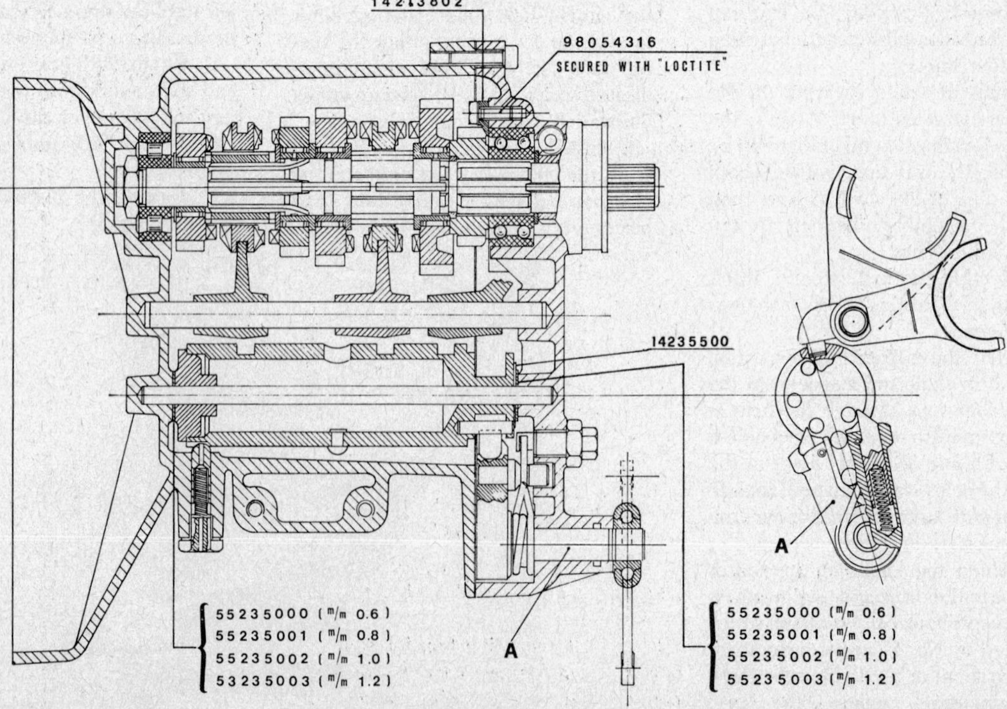

Shimming the gearbox

adjusting screw (A) in or out until a position is located where all gears engage smoothly and quietly.

2. Secure the locknut while holding the adjusting screw steady with a screwdriver.

Five-Speed Models

1. Loosen the locknut (A) and turn the adjusting screw in or out until a distance of 67–69 mm (2.63–2.71 in.) is established between the gearbox cover to the center of the round slot which secures the cable.

2. Secure the locknut while holding the adjusting screw steady with a screwdriver.

Drive Box

DISASSEMBLY (with the engine and transmission mounted in the frame)

1. Remove the drive box drain plug (C) and filler plug (B), and allow the oil to drain.

2. Remove the rear wheel as described in the "Chassis" chapter.

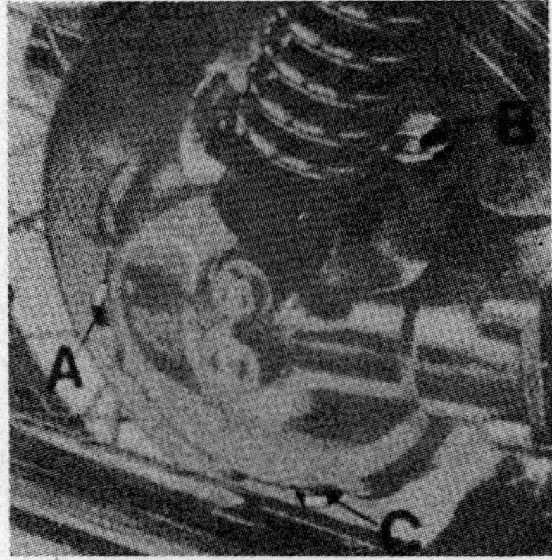

Drive box plug locations

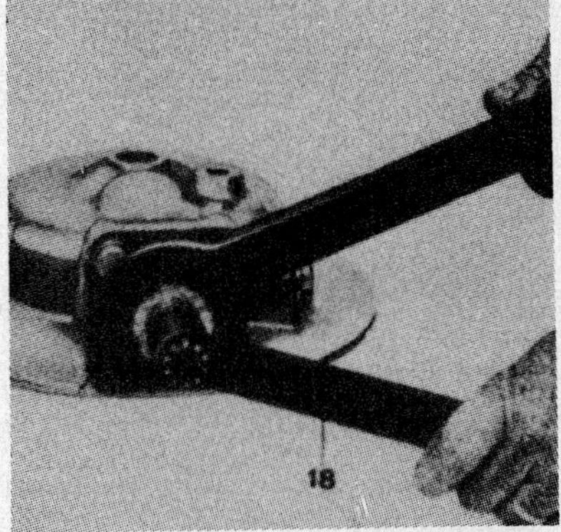

Removing the bevel pinion lock-ring

3. Remove the four nuts or bolts which secure the drive box and remove the box along with the shaft and sleeve.

4. Remove the drive shaft from the sleeve, the two circlips from the shaft, and the sleeve from the bevel pinion.

5. Remove the drive box gasket and oil seal.

6. Bend back the locking tab then, using either the special tool (No. 12907100 which is indicated by No. 18 in the accompanying illustration) or a suitable substitute, remove the lock-ring which secures the bevel pinion.

7. Remove the bearing housing, then further disassemble it by removing the bevel pinion, both bearings, the shims, and the spacer.

8. Remove the housing-to-drive box gasket and seal ring.

9. Bend back the locking tabs, remove the eight bolts which secure the flange to the drive box, then remove the flange. Remove the seal ring and bearing from the flange.

10. Remove the gaskets from between the flange and shim, and from between the shim and drive box.

11. Remove the internally-toothed sleeve and bevel crown from the rear wheel coupling, then remove the bevel crown gear from the sleeve by removing the lockwashers and bolts.

Removing the roller bearing outer race

12. Remove the roller bearing stop screw, plate, bearing cage, and the inner race, then remove the outer race by using either the special puller (No. 12906900 which is indicated by No. 2 in the accompanying illustration) or a suitable substitute.

13. Remove the roller bearing cage retaining ring, drive box oil seal, wheel-to-drive box spacer, and the level plug and gasket.

14. If you wish to remove the universal double joint, gaiters, and bands, you'll have to either remove the engine and transmission assemblies from the frame or remove the swing arm assembly as directed in the "Chassis" section.

INSPECTION AND REPAIR

1. Clean all parts, other than seals and gaskets, with a suitable solvent, then blow them dry.

2. Inspect the drive box for signs of cracks, scoring, or damage of the bearing housing surfaces or drive box mating surfaces, or other damage and replace it as necessary. All gaskets and seals should be replaced as a matter of course.

3. Inspect the drive box flange for cracks, scoring, or damage, especially to the mating surfaces and bearing and seal ring housings, and replace it as necessary. The seal ring should be replaced as a matter of course.

NOTE: *Although the hot set-up is to replace the seal rings, they may be reused in a pinch if completely undamaged.*

4. Inspect the distance shims for signs of wear or damage and replace them as necessary. The shim sizes are 0.10, 0.15, 1.00, 1.20, 1.50 mm (0.0039, 0.0059, 0.0394, 0.0472, 0.0591 in.).

5. Inspect the internally-toothed sleeve for signs of wear or damage to the bearing surface and teeth, and replace it if not perfect.

6. Inspect the bevel gear pinion and crown for signs of wear, scoring, or damage to any of the teeth or splines.

7. Inspect the cage retaining ring for signs of wear or scoring of the contact surface and replace it if not in perfect condition.

8. Inspect the distance pieces for signs of wear or damage and replace them if necessary.

9. Inspect the bearings, cages, housings, spacers, etc. for any signs of wear or damage and replace them as necessary. Bearing action must be perfectly smooth.

CAUTION: *Do not spin bearings when dry.*

10. Inspect all remaining hardware for signs of wear or damage and replace them as necessary. Rubber bands and gaiters must be free of cracks or wear and should retain their original elasticity if they are to be reused.

ASSEMBLY

1. Assembly is in the reverse order of disassembly. Use new gaskets, seals, and lockwashers whenever possible.

2. Replace the oil drain plug, position the rear wheel-to-drive box spacer and press the drive box oil seal into place.

3. Install the bearing cage retaining ring, roller bearing outer race, bearing cage, and inner race, then secure the bearing stop screw and plate.

4. Assemble the bevel crown to the internally toothed sleeve by means of the securing bolts and locking tabs.

5. Press the bearing and seal ring into the drive box flange, position new gaskets on the drive box and box flange, then mount the flange to the box.

NOTE: *Do not secure the locking tabs until after the bevel gear adjustment is performed as directed in the "Bevel Gear Adjustment" section.*

6. Install the front bearing, bearing spacer, distance adjusting shims, and the rear bearing into the bearing housing.

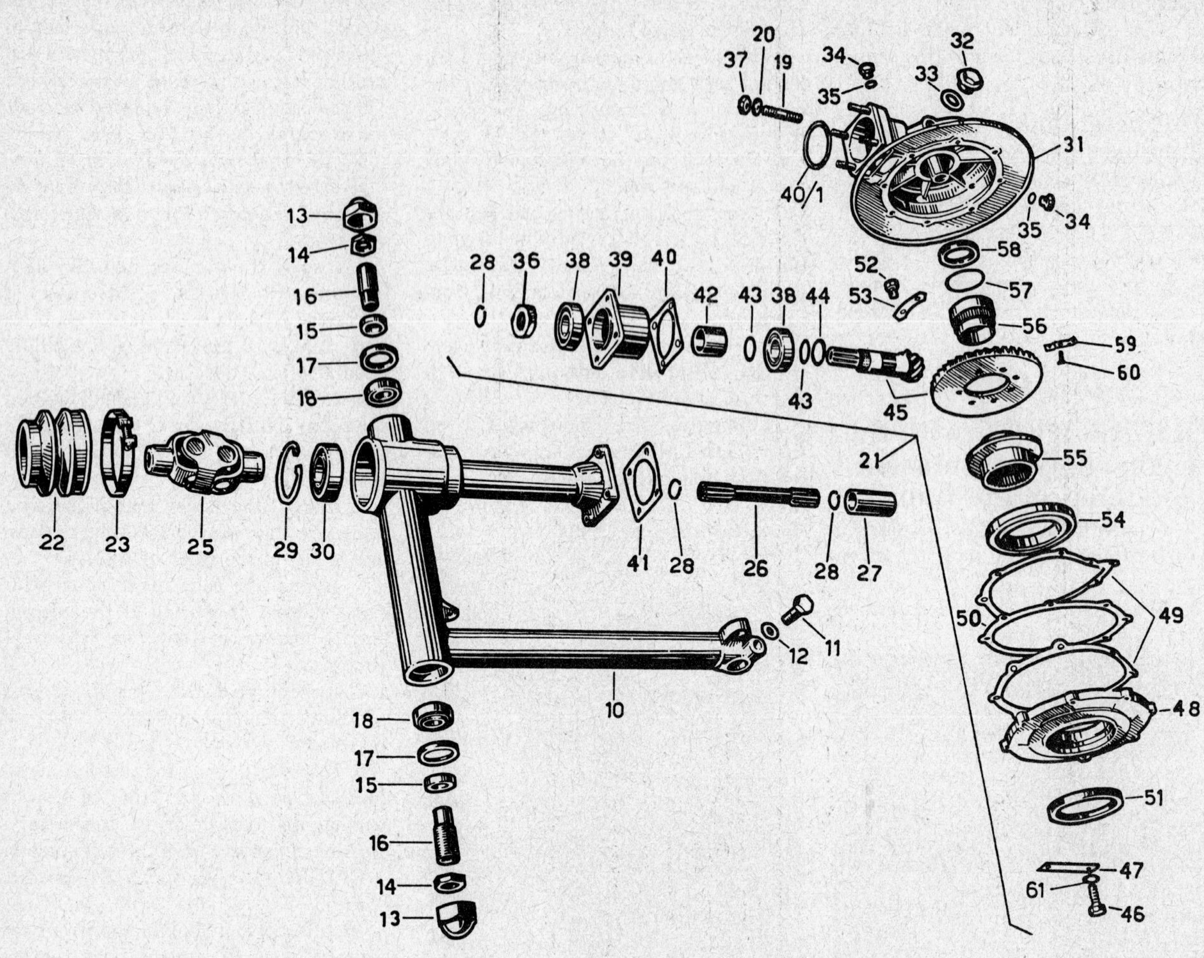

Drive box and rear swing arm assembly

10. Rear fork
11. Rear fork clamp screw
12. Clamp screw washer
13. Rear fork-to-frame cap nut
14. Fork spindle nut
15. Spacer
16. Rear fork support spindle
17. Rear fork spindle seal
18. Taper roller bearing
19. Drive box-to-swing arm bolt
20. Drive box bolts washer
21. Wheel drive complete, rear
22. Rubber gaiter
23. Large gaiter-to-drive box band
24. Small gaiter-to-drive box band
25. Layshaft-to-drive shaft double joint
26. Drive shaft
27. Drive shaft and bevel drive sleeve
28. Drive shaft and bevel gears seal
29. Circlip
30. Ball rear fork bearing
31. Rear drive box
32. Drive box oil filler plug
33. Oil filler plug gasket
34. Oil level and drain plug
35. Oil level and drain plug washer
36. Bevel gear retaining nut
37. Drive box bolts nut
38. Taper roller in housing bearing
39. Housing bearing
40. Drive box-to-bearing housing gasket

40/1. Rear drive box seal
41. Bearing housing-to-rear fork gasket
42. Bearings distance piece
43. Spacer-to-bearing shim
Bevel gears spacer shim
44. Bevel set spacer
Bevel set spacer
Bevel set spacer
45. Bevel gear set
46. Flange
47. Flange fixing bolt lockplate
48. Drive box flange
49. Flange-to-spacer and spacer-to-drive box gasket
50. Shim 0.8 mm (0.031 in.)
Shim 0.9 mm (0.035 in.)
Shim 1.0 mm (0.039 in.)
Shim 1.1 mm (0.043 in.)
Shim 1.2 mm (0.047 in.)
Shim 1.3 mm (0.051 in.)
51. Seal
52. Bevel gear-to-journal bolt
53. Bevel gear bolts-to-journal bearing lockplate
54. Ball bearing
55. Journal bearing
56. Roller bearing
57. Cage retaining ring
58. Seal
59. Bearing stop plate
60. Roller bearing stop plate screw
61. Flange securing screw washer

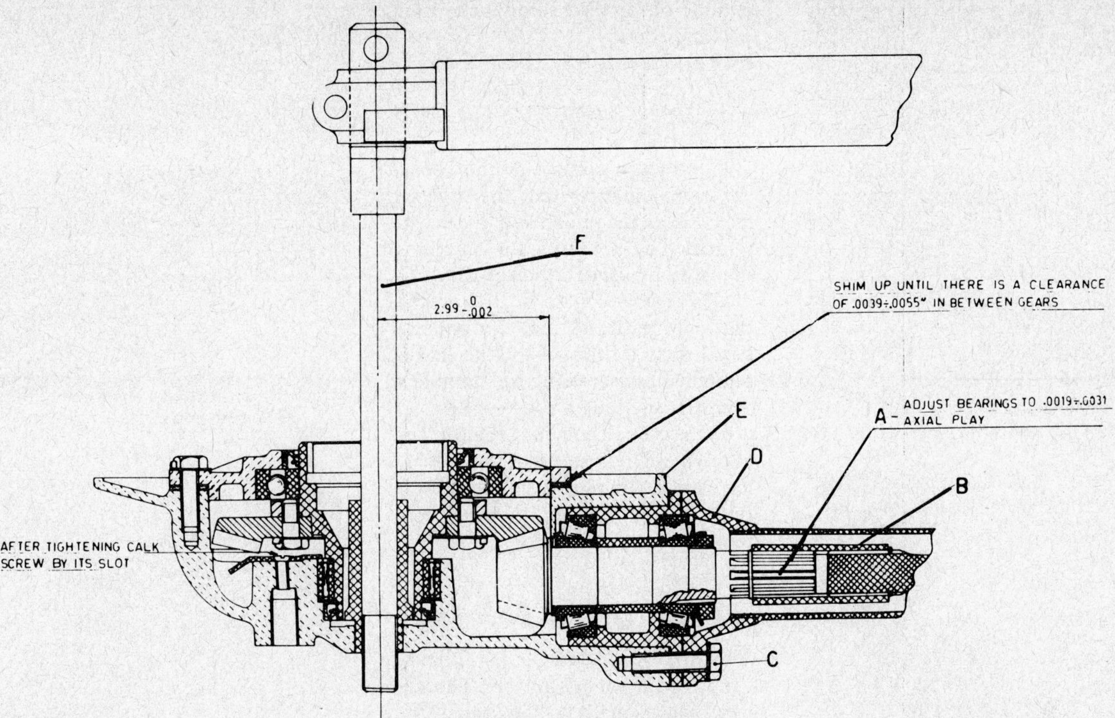
F
2.99 - 0 .002
SHIM UP UNTIL THERE IS A CLEARANCE OF .0039÷.0055" IN BETWEEN GEARS
E
D
ADJUST BEARINGS TO .0019÷.0031 AXIAL PLAY
A
B
AFTER TIGHTENING CALK SCREW BY ITS SLOT
C

Assembling the drive box

7. Mount the spacer shim and adjusting shims onto the bevel pinion and slip the pinion shank into the bearing housing, then secure it with a lock-ring and lockring safety washer using either the special tool (No. 12907100) or a suitable substitute.

NOTE: *After the bevel gear adjustment is carried out, secure the lockring by bending the lockwashers locking tab. Consult the "Bevel Gear Adjustment" section for additional information.*

8. Secure the bearing housing and bevel pinion to the drive box by means of the securing nuts and washers.

NOTE: *This must not be done until the bevel gear adjustment is carried out as directed in the "Bevel Gear Adjustment" section.*

9. Install the ball bearing to the swing arm and secure it with a circlip.

10. Install the double joint in the swing arm bearing and fit the gaiters and bands over the joint. The bands should be used to secure the gaiters on the swing arm side only.

NOTE: *If the engine and transmission have been removed from the frame, the front side of the gaiters must be secured when installed in the engine and transmission assembly.*

11. Position the circlips in their grooves in the drive shaft, then install the shaft into the double joint and bevel drive sleeve.

12. Insert the splined portion of the bevel pinion (A) into the sleeve (B) and secure it without locking the four bolts and lockwashers which secure the drive box (E) to the swing arm (D). Then insert the rear wheel spindle (F) through the left-hand side of the swing arm and into the drive box, then secure the four bolts (C) and remove the spindle (F).

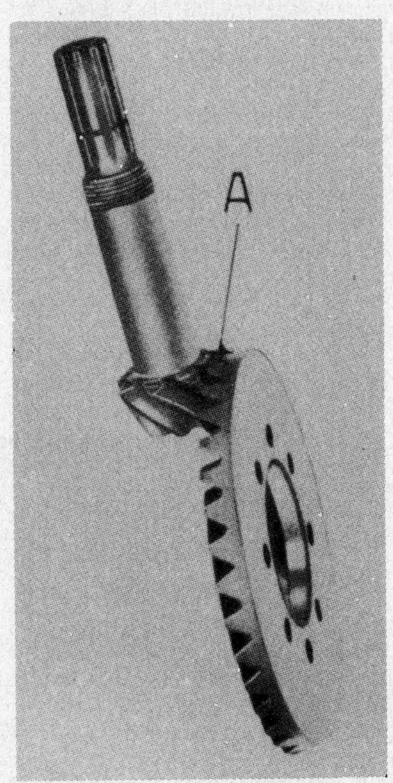
A

Proper gear engagement

13. Replenish the drive box oil supply with 0.4 pts for the V700 and V750, or 0.9 pts for the V850, or a high quality 90 E.P. weight gear oil.

Bevel Gear Adjustment

1. Adjust the pinion-to-crown clearance of the bevel gear set to 0.010–0.15 mm (0.0039–0.0059 in.). Make sure the meshing surfaces (A) of the gears are in proper contact.

2. Check for correct teeth contact in the following manner:

a. Coat the crown teeth with lead oxide, then rotate the pinion while keeping the crown braked so the rotation will take place under load, so contact marks will appear on the coated surface of the crown.

Correct gear engagement

b. Make sure that the contact is correct by comparing it with the accompanying illustration. If the contact marks are incorrect, go onto the next step.

3. If the contact pattern is not correct, consult the following steps and illustrations to arrive at a solution:

Pinion too deep in the crown

Crown too far from pinion

NOTE: *After adding or removing shims, readjust the pinion-to-crown clearance before rechecking the contact pattern.*

a. Excessive contact at the bottom of the tooth flank indicates that the pinion is too deeply inserted in the crown and this may be remedied by reducing the number of adjusting shims, or by using a thinner shim.

NOTE: *Shims are available in the following sizes: 0.10, 0.15, 1.00, 1.20, 1.50 mm (0.0039, 0.0059, 0.0394, 0.472, 0.-591 in.).*

b. Excessive contact at the heel of the tooth indicates that the crown is too far from the pinion and this may be remedied by increasing the number of shims, or by using a thicker shim.

c. Excessive contact at the crest of the tooth indicates that the pinion is too far from the crown and this may be remedied by increasing the number of shims, or by using a thicker shim.

d. Excessive contact at the top land of the tooth indicates that the crown is too close to the pinion and this may be remedied by reducing the number of shims, or by using thinner shims.

Crown too close to pinion

Pinion too far from crown

Final Drive Service

The drive shaft dust boot will have to be replaced about once a year. There is a special replacement boot available that is split for easy installation, but it will not function as satisfactorily as the standard item.

The easiest way to install a new boot is by removing the rear wheel and swing arm, not by sliding the engine forward. Before installing the boot, clean off the drive shaft assembly and swing arm with clean gasoline or some other suitable solvent, and use a sealer on the mating surfaces. Allow the sealer to dry thoroughly before proceding with the assembly, then secure the boot clamps to ensure an oil tight seal.

Drilling a small breather hole in the drive box filler plug will allow excessive pressure to be vented. A No. 50 drill will do the trick and a small rubber boot can be fashioned to prevent dirt or water from getting into the oil supply.

NOTE: *If excessive oil build-up in the drive boot is a problem, try setting the shocks up a step higher, and make sure they aren't worn out.*

ENGINE AND TRANSMISSION SPECIFICATIONS CAMSHAFT AND VALVE TRAIN ASSEMBLIES

V700		V750 and V850	
I/D of camshaft housings in crankcase		I/D of camshaft housings in crankcase	
Timing side	47.025-47.064 mm (1.8511-1.8529 in.)	Timing side	47.025-47.064 mm (1.8511-1.8529 in.)
Flywheel side	32.025-32.064 mm (1.2607-1.2623 in.)	Flywheel side	32.025-32.064 mm (1.2607-1.2623 in.)
Diameter of camshaft journals		Diameter of camshaft journals	
Timing side	49.975-47.000 mm (1.8494-1.8504 in.)	Timing side	46.975-47.000 mm (1.8494-1.8504 in.)
Flywheel side	31.975-32.000 mm (1.2588-1.2598 in.)	Flywheel side	31.975-32.000 mm (1.2588-1.2598 in.)
Diameter of tappet guides	22.021-22.000 mm (0.8669-0.8661 in.)	Diameter of tappet guides	22.021-22.000 mm (0.8669-0.8661 in.)

ENGINE AND TRANSMISSION SPECIFICATIONS CAMSHAFT AND VALVE TRAIN ASSEMBLIES

V700		V750 and V850	
O/D of original tappet	22.000-21.979 mm (0.8661-0.9046 in.)	O/D of original tappet	22.000-21.979 mm (0.8661-0.9046 in.)
Tappet oversize range	0.05-0.10 mm (0.0019-0.0039 in.)	Tappet oversize range	0.05-0.10 mm (0.0019-0.0039 in.)
I/D of rocker arms	15.032-15.059 mm (0.5918-0.5929 in.)	I/D of rocker arms	15.032-15.059 mm (0.5918-0.5929 in.)
Diameter of rocker arms spindles	14.983-14.994 mm (0.5899-0.5903 in.)	Diameter of rocker arms spindles	14.983-14.994 mm (0.5899-0.5903 in.)
I/D of inlet and exhaust valve guide housings	14.000-14.018 mm (0.5512-0.5519 in.)	I/D of inlet and exhaust valve guide housings	14.000-14.018 mm (0.5512-0.5519 in.)
O/D of inlet and exhaust valve guides		O/D of inlet and exhaust valve guides	
Original	14.064-14.075 mm (0.5537-0.5541 in.)	Original	14.064-14.075 mm (0.5537-0.5541 in.)
Spares	14.107-14.118 mm (0.55541-0.55545 in.)	Spares	14.107-14.118 mm (0.55541-0.55545 in.)
I/D of inlet and exhaust valve guides (after pressing-in)	8.000-8.022 mm (0.3149-0.3158 in.)	I/D of inlet and exhaust valve guides (after pressing-in)	8.000-8.022 mm (0.3149-0.3158 in.)
Diameter of inlet valve stem	7.972-7.987 mm (0.3138-0.3144 in.)	Diameter of inlet valve stem	7.972-7.987 mm (0.3138-0.3144 in.)
Diameter of exhaust valve stem	7.965-7.980 mm (0.3136-0.3142 in.)	Diameter of exhaust valve stem	7.965-7.980 mm (0.3136-0.3142 in.)
Diameter of inlet valve head	38.4-38.6 mm (1.5118-1.5197 in.)	Diameter of inlet valve head	40.8-41.0 mm (1.605-1.615 in.)
Diameter of exhaust valve head	34.4-34.6 mm (1.3543-1.3622 in.)	Diameter of exhaust valve head	35.8-36.0 mm (1.409-1.417 in.)

PISTON, CYLINDER, AND CRANKSHAFT ASSEMBLIES

V700		V750 and V850	
Cylinder barrel diameter	80.000-80.018 mm (3.1496-3.1503 in.)	Cylinder barrel diameter	80.000-80.018 mm (3.1496-3.1503 in.)
Piston diameters		Piston diameters	
at piston top	79.600-79.650 mm (3.1338-3.1358 in.)	at piston top	82.600-82.650 mm (3.2520-3.2538 in.)
below top ring	79.700-79.750 mm (3.1378-3.1397 in.)	below top ring	82.700-82.750 mm (3.2558-3.2578 in.)
below 2nd ring	79.000-79.100 mm (3.1102-3.1141 in.)	below 2nd ring	82.000-82.100 mm (3.2283-3.2322 in.)
at recess below oil scrapers	79.100-79.150 mm (3.1149-3.1161 in.)	at recess below oil scrapers	82.100-82.150 mm (3.2322-3.2342 in.)

PISTON, CYLINDER, AND CRANKSHAFT ASSEMBLIES

V700		V750 and V850	
Piston diameters		Piston diameters	
5 mm (0.196 mm) below top oil scraper recess	79.922-79.940 mm (3.1465-3.1472 in.)	5 mm (0.196 in.) below top oil scraper recess	82.928-82.946 mm (3.2648-3.2655 in.)
selection diam. at 18.5 mm (0.728 in.) over piston bottom edge	79.952-79.970 mm (3.1477-3.1484 in.)	selection diam. at 18.5 mm (0.728 in.) over piston bottom edge	82.958-82.976 mm (3.2660-3.2667 in.)
at piston bottom	79.922-79.940 mm (3.1465-3.1472 in.)	at piston bottom	82.928-82.946 mm (3.2648-3.2665 in.)
piston pin housing diameter	22.000-22.006 mm (0.8661-0.8663 in.)	piston pin housing diameter	22.000-22.006 mm (0.8661-0.8663 in.)
Piston pin diameter	22.001-22.006 mm (0.86614-0.86634 in.)	Piston pin diameter	22.001-22.006 mm (0.86614-0.86634 in.)
Main shaft diameter flywheel side	53.970-53.951 mm (2.1248-2.1240 in.)	Main shaft diameter flywheel side	53.970-53.951 mm (2.1248-2.1240 in.)
Main shaft diameter timing side	37.975-37.959 mm (1.4951-1.4944 in.)	timing side	37.975-37.959 mm (1.4951-1.4944 in.)
I/D of main bearings c/w flange		I/D of main bearings c/w flange	
flywheel side	54.000-54.019 mm (2.1260-2.1268 in.)	Flywheel side	54.000-54.019 mm (2.1260-2.1268 in.)
timing side	38.000-38.016 mm (1.4961-1.4967 in.)	Timing side	38.000-38.016 mm (1.4961-1.4967 in.)
Undersize range of main bearings available as spare parts 0.2 mm (0.00787 in.) 0.4 mm (0.01574 in.) 0.6 mm (0.02362 in.) 0.8 mm (0.03149 in.)		Undersize range of main bearings available as spare parts 0.2 mm (0.00787 in.) 0.4 mm (0.01574 in.) 0.6 mm (0.02362 in.) 0.8 mm (0.03149 in.)	
Crankpin diameter	44.013-44.033 mm (1.7328-1.7336 in.)	Crankpin diameter	44.013-44.033 mm (1.7328-1.7336 in.)
Diameter of con-rod big end bearing housing	47.130-47.142 mm (1.9016-1.8559 in.)	Diameter of con-rod big end bearing housing	47.130-47.142 mm (1.9016-1.8559 in.)
Original thickness of con-rod bearings	1.534-1.543 mm (0.06039-0.06070 in.)	Original thickness of con-rod bearings	1.534-1.543 mm (0.06039-0.06070 in.)
Oversize range of big end bearings 0.254 mm (0.010 in.) 0.508 mm (0.020 in.) 0.762 mm (0.030 in.) 1.016 mm (0.040 in.)		Oversize range of big end bearings 0.254 mm (0.010 in.) 0.508 mm (0.020 in.) 0.762 mm (0.030 in.) 1.016 mm (0.040 in.)	
I/D of small end bushing (after pressing in)	22.020-22.041 mm (0.8669-0.8677 in.)	I/D of small end bushing (after pressing in)	22.020-22.041 mm (0.8669-0.8677 in.)

TRANSMISSION

	V700	V750	V850
Gearbox			
Type	four-speed	four-speed	five-speed
Engine-gearbox ratio (1:)	1.375 (16-22)	1.375 (16-22)	1.235 (17-21)
Internal gear ratios (1:)			
First gear	2.230 (13-29)	2.230 (13-29)	2.000 (14-28)
Second gear	1.333 (18-24)	1.333 (18-24)	1.388 (18-25)
Third gear	0.954 (22-21)	0.954 (22-21)	1.047 (21-22)
Fourth gear	0.750 (24-18)	0.750 (24-18)	0.869 (23-20)
Fifth gear	——	——	0.750 (24-18)
Secondary drive			
Type	shaft	shaft	shaft
Bevel layshaft gear			
Rear wheel ratio (1:)	4.625 (8-37)	4.375 (8-35)	4.625 (8-37)
Overall gear ratios (1:)			
First gear	14.180	13.413	11.424
Second gear	8.473	8.015	7.929
Third gear	6.063	5.735	5.980
Fourth gear	4.786	4.510	4.964
Fifth gear	——	——	4.284

LUBRICATION SYSTEMS

OIL PUMP

Oil Pressure Relief Valve

The oil pressure relief valve is designed to be a maintenance free item and must be replaced if it fails to function correctly. The unit is mounted on the oil pipe and works by opening whenever the oil pressure exceeds its prescribed rating.

The prescribed maximum rate of delivery pressure for a 700cc engine is 35.-6–42.7 lbs/sq. in. (2.5–3.0 kgs/sq. cm.); the pressure for 750 and 850cc engines is 54.0–60.0 lbs/sq.in. (3.8–4.2 kgs/sq. cm.). Consult your local dealer for additional information.

Oil Pressure Gauge

The oil pressure gauge (A) is a crankcase mounted, non-repairable item which must be replaced if defective.

Removal and Disassembly

1. Run the engine until its normal operating temperature is reached, then drain the oil.

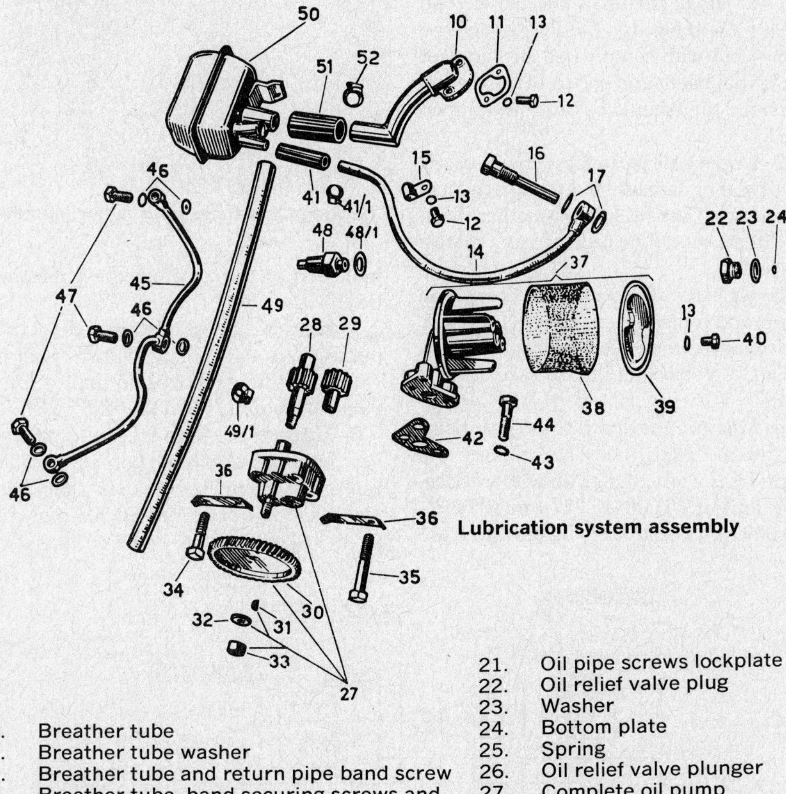

Lubrication system assembly

10. Breather tube
11. Breather tube washer
12. Breather tube and return pipe band screw
13. Breather tube, band securing screws and bottom plate bolt washer
14. Oil return from breather box tube
15. Oil return tube band
16. Return pipe securing hollow bolt
17. Hollow bolt washer
18. Oil pipe
19. Oil pipe washer
20. Oil pipe securing bolt
21. Oil pipe screws lockplate
22. Oil relief valve plug
23. Washer
24. Bottom plate
25. Spring
26. Oil relief valve plunger
27. Complete oil pump
28. Gear driving spindle
29. Driven gear
30. Driving gear
31. Oil pump driving gear key
32. Driving gear nut washer
33. Driving gear nut
34. Oil pump securing screw
35. Oil pump securing screw
36. Pump securing screws lockplate
37. Oil cleaner, complete
38. Oil filter, gauze
39. Bottom plate
40. Plate securing bolt
41. Flexible return pipe line
41/1. Recovery pipe-to-flexible line band
42. Washer
43. Filter screw spring washer
44. Filter securing screw
45. Oil delivery-to-cylinder heads pipe
46. Oil pressure solenoid washer
47. Oil pipes-to-cylinder heads screw
48. Oil pressure solenoid
48/1. Oil pressure solenoid seal
49. Vent tube
49/1. Breather tube band
50. Complete oil breather assembly
51. Flexible center tube
52. Breather tube-to-flexible pipe band

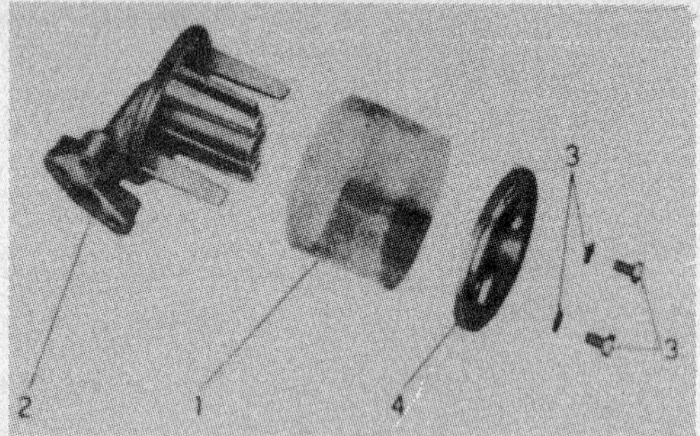

Oil filter assembly
1. Filter element
2. Filter body
3. Cap mounting bolts
4. Filter cap

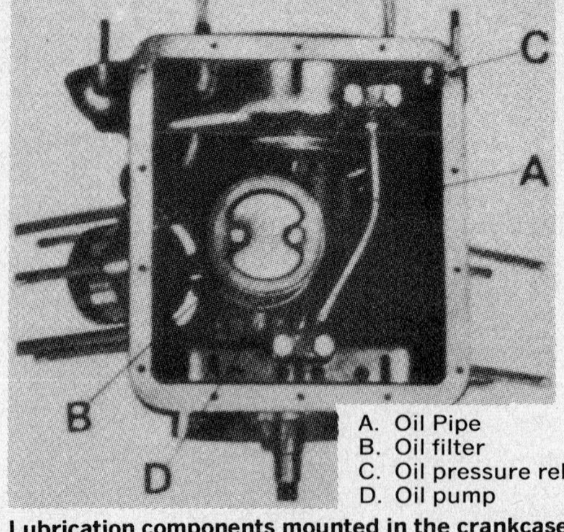

A. Oil Pipe
B. Oil filter
C. Oil pressure relief valve
D. Oil pump

Lubrication components mounted in the crankcase

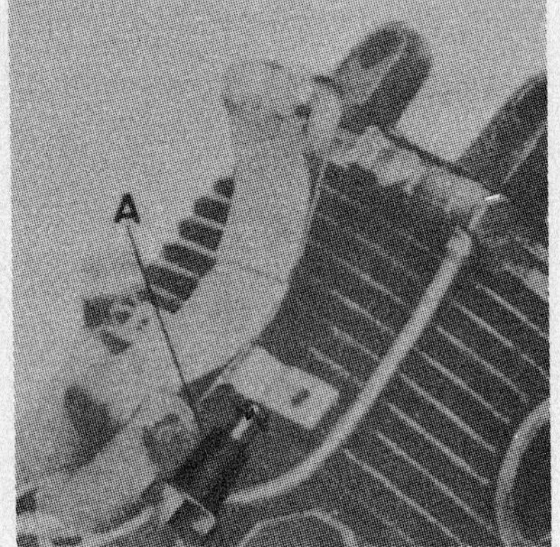

Oil pressure gauge solenoid

2. Remove the generator belt cover and the driven generator pulley. The outer half of the generator pulley can be removed after removing the three securing bolts, spacer washers, and drive belt, and the inner half can be removed after unscrewing the nut which secures it to the crankshaft. A special tool (No. 12911801) is available to secure the clutch while breaking the nut loose, but a suitable substitute may be used.

3. Remove the timing chest cover by removing the bolts which secure it to the crankshaft, then remove the sealing ring from the timing cover.

4. Remove the oil pump gear by breaking loose the nut which secures it to its shaft in the same manner in which the generator belt pulleys were removed. The gear is a press fit on a tapered shaft, and must be pulled off with an oil pump gear puller (No. 32906302) or a suitable substitute.

5. Remove the oil pump mounting screws and pump, then remove the key, the driven gear, and the driving shaft.

6. Remove the oil pump filter retaining screws and filter assembly from the oil pipe located above the pump. The filter can be further broken down by removing the gasket, bottom plate (4), wire gauze, and the filter housing (2). You may wish to approach the filter from below by removing the sump.

7. Remove the oil pipe by bending back the lockwasher locking tabs, then removing the securing bolts and washers. The relief valve assembly can now be removed from the pipe and this assembly can be further broken down into a plunger, spring, bottom plate, and plug.

8. Remove the oil pressure gauge solenoid from the crankcase at this time if it has refused to function as intended.

INSPECTION AND REPAIR

1. Clean all parts in a suitable solvent, then blow them dry. Oil lines should be blown out with compressed air. If gasket sealer has been used on any of the mating surfaces, they should be carefully scraped clean.

2. Inspect all parts for signs of excessive wear or damage, and replace them as necessary. Gaskets, keys, and other short-life items should be replaced as a matter of course.

3. Measure the width of the pump gears and replace them if worn past their serviceable limit. The gears should be 15.983–15.994 mm (0.6293–0.6297 in.) wide.

4. Measure the depth of the gear housing in the pump body and replace the unit if it is worn greater than its serviceable limit of 16.000–16.027 mm (0.6299–0.6309 in.). The areas to be measured are indicated in the accompanying illustration.

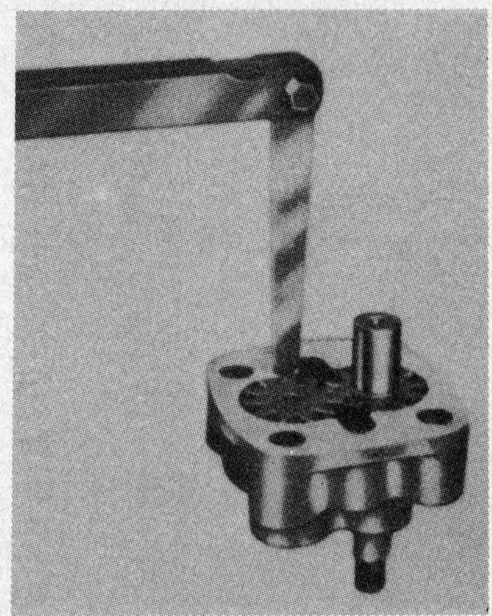

Checking clearances with feeler gauges

5. Measure the outside diameter of the pump gears and replace them as a set if worn past their serviceable limit of 25.-993–25.980 mm (1.0233–1.0227 in.).

6. Measure the inside diameter of the gear housings within the pump body and replace the unit if worn past their serviceable limits of 26.000–26.033 mm (1.-0236–1.0249 in.).

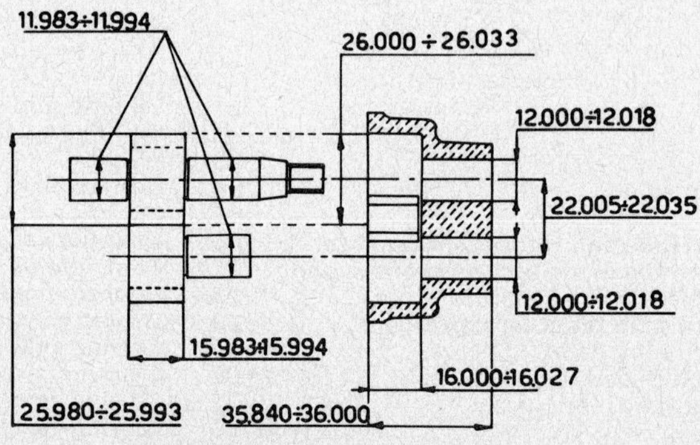

Pump assembly dimensions

7. Check the clearance between the pump gear shafts and the supports upon which they ride in the pump body. The outside diameter of the gear shafts should be within serviceable limits of 11.994–11.983 mm (0.4722–0.4717 in.), and the inside diameter of the supports should measure 12.000–12.018 mm (0.4724–0.4731 in.). The clearance between the supports and the shafts must be within 0.006–0.035 mm (0.00023–0.00137 in.) or the worn components must be replaced.

8. Inspect the wire gauze type oil filter strainer for a clogged or damaged condition and replace it as necessary.

9. If the oil pressure relief valve has not been functioning correctly, replace it at this time. Consult the "Oil Pressure Relief Valve" section for additional information.

10. Replace the oil pressure solenoid if it has failed to function. Before replacing the unit, you should make sure that the problem isn't in the bulb or associated wiring.

ASSEMBLY

1. Assembly is basically in the reverse order of disassembly.

2. Secure the oil pipe, filter, and pump assemblies to the crankcase, then consult the "Engine and Transmission" chapter for information on how to reassemble the timing case and the generator pulley assemblies. Make sure you correctly time the valve gear if the correct timing has been lost. Instructions on adjusting the generator belt tension can be found in the "Maintenance" chapter.

3. Remember to refill the sump with oil before starting the engine.

OIL PUMP SPECIFICATIONS

OIL PUMP (all models)	
Gear width	15.983-15.994 mm 0.6293-0.6297 in.
Depth of housing in pump body	16.000-16.027 mm 0.6299-0.6309 in.
Gear outside diameter	25.993-25.980 mm 1.0233-1.0227in.
Gear housing inside diameter	26.000-26.003 mm 1.0236-1.0249 in.
Gear shaft outside diameter	11.994-11.983 mm 0.4722-0.4717 in.
Shaft support inside diameter	12.000-12.018 mm 0.4724-0.4731 in.
Clearance between shafts and supports	0.006-0.035 mm 0.0023-0.0137 in.

OIL PRESSURE	
Maximum delivered pressure	
V700	35.6-42.7 lbs/sq. in. 2.5-3.0 kgs/sq. cm.
V750	54.0-60.0 lbs/sq. in. 3.8-4.2 kgs/sq. cm.
V850	54.0-60.0 lbs/sq. in. 3.8-4.2 kgs/sq. cm.

FUEL SYSTEMS

DISASSEMBLY AND ASSEMBLY

V700

1. Remove the spring clip (2) from the mixing chamber cap (1) on the top of the carburetor, then remove the chamber cap.

2. Taking care not to foul the needle against the carburetor bore, lift up the mixing chamber cover (3) assembly complete with the throttle slide spring (4), slide (5), tapered needle (6), and venturi block. The cover assembly can be further disassembled, if necessary, by compressing the spring up against the cover, removing the needle clip and needle and disengaging the throttle and choke cables from their respective slides.

3. Remove the air adjusting screw (7) and its spring, then remove the pilot jet (8).

4. Remove the float chamber plug (22) and allow the fuel to drain into a suitable receptacle.

5. Remove the float bowl plug (9), float chamber securing bolt (10), bolt washers (11), float chamber (12), main jet (13), and the jet holder assembly (14) which includes the atomizer and the atomizer nozzle.

6. Disconnect the carburetor from the air cleaner, remove the carburetor body (15) from the intake manifold by loosening the pinch bolt, and remove the choke (16).

7. Remove the float chamber cover and tickler assembly (17), then remove

Pump assembly

the banjo cap (18), banjo (19), fuel filter (20), and the banjo washers (21).

8. Remove the float (23) and float needle (24) assembly from the float chamber.

9. Assembly is in the reverse order of disassembly. Make sure all parts are perfectly clean and avoid overtightening any of the jets or adjusting screws.

V750 and V850

1. Remove the screws (3) which secure the mixing chamber cap (1) to the carburetor body, then lift off the cap and carefully pull the throttle slide (4) out of the carburetor bore taking care not to foul the taper needle (5) on the sides of the bore.

2. Disassemble the cap assembly by compressing the slide spring (2) against the cap, removing the needle clip and needle, and then disengaging the throttle cable from the slide. The cable can now be withdrawn and the cable adjuster can be removed from the top of the cap.

3. Remove the throttle slide stop screw and spring (6) and the pilot air screw and spring (17).

4. Remove the float bowl drain plug (7) and allow the fuel to drain into a suitable recepticle.

5. Remove the float bowl (8) and pilot jet (9).

6. Remove the accelerator pump (10), main jet (11), needle jet (12), and pilot jet (13).

7. Remove the float (14), float pivot pin (15), and the float needle (16).

8. Remove the banjo securing bolt and washer (18), banjo (19), and fuel filter (20).

9. Remove the screw (22) which secures the choke fitting (21), withdraw the choke slide (24), spring (23), and fitting, then disengage the choke cable from the slide.

10. Disconnect the air cleaner from the carburetor, then remove the carburetor body from the intake manifold by loosening the pinch bolt and pulling the body free.

11. Assembly is in the reverse order of disassembly. Make sure all parts are perfectly clean and avoid overtightening any of the jets or adjusting screws.

INSPECTION AND REPAIR

All Models

1. Clean all parts in a suitable solvent, then blow them dry. Pay special attention to the ducts and jet passages which should be blown rather than poked clear.

2. Inspect the throttle slide for score or wear marks or for cracks and replace it as necessary. The slide should be able to easily slide down the carburetor bore under its own weight and without the aid of lubrication. If the slide does not move smoothly it may be lightly sanded with a fine emery cloth to remove burrs, as long as the sanding does not mar the surface of the slide.

3. Inspect the taper needle for signs of wear along the shaft and in the clip grooves. If the needle is worn or blunted or if its fit in the spring clip is loose, the offending component must be replaced.

4. Inspect the jets for signs of wear or damage to their threads and bores, and replace them as necessary.

5. Inspect the float for a fuel clogged or otherwise damaged condition and replace it as necessary. The float needle should be secure in the float on the V700 model.

6. Inspect the float needle and needle seat for wear, damage, or anything which could prevent them from seating together properly.

7. Inspect the adjusting screws for blunt tips or damage to their shafts or threads and replace them as necessary.

8. Inspect the fuel filter for a clogged condition and clean or replace it as necessary.

9. Inspect the float chamber, bowl, and carburetor body for cracks or damage which could cause air or fuel leaks, and

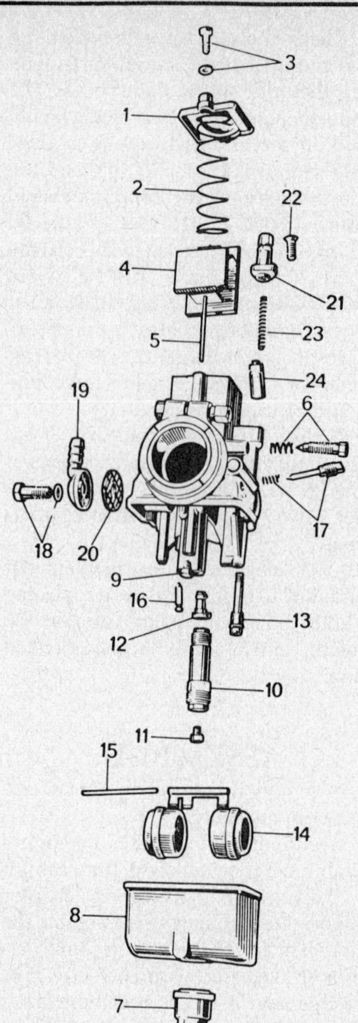

V750 and V850 carburetor assembly

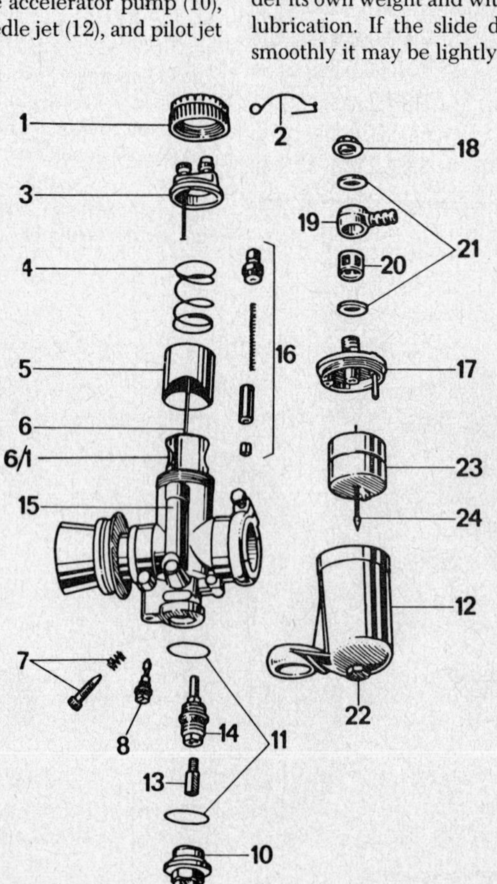

V700 carburetor assembly

look for sediment deposits which could interfere with the proper operation of any of the components. Damaged parts must be replaced, and sediment must be carefully removed with a blunt blade and a deft touch to avoid scoring the surface of the part in question.

CARBURETOR SPECIFICATIONS

Standard Carburetor Settings

	V700	V750 and V850
Model		
Type: (Dell 'Orto)		
Right side	S.S.I.	VHB 29 CD
Left side	S.S.I.	VHB 29 CS
Choke tube diameter	29 mm	29 mm
Throttle slide	80	60
Atomizer	265	265
Main jet	120	145
Pilot jet	55	45
Needle	M14	SV5/SV9
Float	14 gm	NA
Starter atomizer	NA	80
Idling screw (number of turns off seat)		
Right side	1-1½	2-2½/1-1½
Left side	1-1½	1½-2/1¾-2
Needle setting (number of notches from top)	3	2

ELECTRICAL SYSTEMS

CHARGING SYSTEM

Generator

The models covered in this guide come equipped with a Marelli DN 62 Type N generator which, at 2400 rpm, produces 300 watts at 12 volts. The unit is of the open construction type, has two poles, and operates in conjunction with a separate regulator unit. The rotor spins on two permanently lubricated ball bearings which are intended to be maintenance free items. The cover assembly is attached by means of two studs which pass through the unit. There are two terminals D+/51 (A) and DF (B), located on the commutator end of the housing which are used to connect the regulator wiring to the generator. The D+ terminal is connected to the positive brush and the DF terminal is connected to one end of the rotor assembly. When the generator is attached to the regulator, the D+ and DF terminals of both units must be connected.

TROUBLESHOOTING THE GENERATING SYSTEM

The following is the most direct approach to take in locating generating system difficulties:

1. The following items are indicators of a faulty generating system:

a. Failure of the generator light to operate.

b. Repeated or sudden battery discharging.

c. Excessive battery water evaporation indicating an overcharged state.

2. In testing the generating system do not commit the following mistakes which will result in damage to the system:

a. Do not reverse the generator polarity.

b. Do not short or ground any wires unless specifically instructed to do so.

c. Do not operate the engine while the generator output terminal is disconnected.

d. Always connect positive to positive and the negative to negative when connecting a charger or booster to the battery.

e. Keep the generator and regulator units connected.

3. Check for a faulty generator light in the following manner:

a. If the ignition is on and the light remains on, disconnect the generator leads at their terminals. If the light stays on, check for a short between these two leads.

b. If the generator light doesn't go on when the ignition switch is turned on, check for a short between the two leads. If the light still doesn't come on, reverse the two leads. If the light still

Generator terminals

GENERATOR TESTING DATA

Type No.	Rated voltage V	Current A	Direction of rotation	Operating speed Min.*	Operating speed Max.	Regulator unit Type No.	Regulator unit No. of cores
DN 62 N	12	25	CW	2400 RPM	10000 RPM	IR 50 BA	3

* At full power.

GENERATOR WITHOUT REGULATOR

Electrical tests at room temperature of 20°C (68°F)	
Overall resistance of field winding (CD)	4.6 ± 0.2 Ω
Rating of damping resistance (RS)	——
Connection speed with no load (tension 13 V)	1500 RPM
Load rating (tension 13 V, current 23 A)	2300 RPM

TENSION AND INSULATION TESTS

Check dielectric rigidity by feeding for 3 sec. with 50 V, 50 Hz, A.C. Check insulation resistance by feeding with 500 V, D.C.—Resistance value must be over 2 MΩ

MECHANICAL TESTS AND DIMENSIONS

Brush spring load	1000-1100 gms	(2.2-2.4 lbs)
I/D of pole shoes after installation	65.7-66.0 mm	(2.5865-2.5984 in.)
O/D of rotor	64.9-65.0 mm	(2.551-2.559 in.)

NOTE: When carrying out above tests, temporarily disconnect possible groundings.

GENERATOR WITH REGULATOR

Regulator	Connection voltage V	Recovery current A	No-load voltage adjusting V	Loaded adjusting voltage V	Current limiter on A	Load at rated voltage W
IR 50 BA	11.5 ÷ 13	2 ÷ 8	13.8 ÷ 14.4	—	28.5-30.5	300

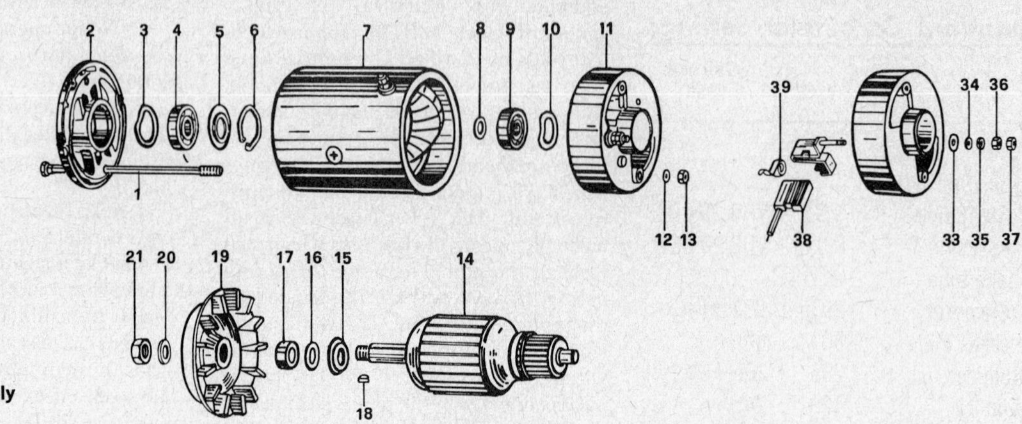

Generator assembly

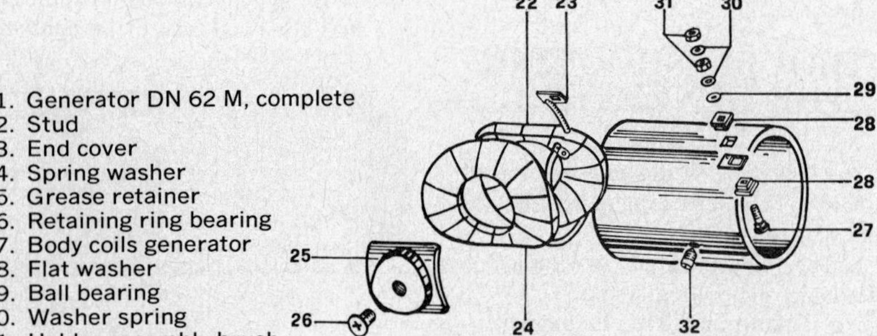

1. Generator DN 62 M, complete
2. Stud
3. End cover
4. Spring washer
5. Grease retainer
6. Retaining ring bearing
7. Body coils generator
8. Flat washer
9. Ball bearing
10. Washer spring
11. Holder assembly brush
12. Washer spring
13. Fixing nut cover
14. Armature
15. Grease retainer
16. Shim, 0.1 mm
    Shim, 0.2 mm
17. Spacer
18. Woodruff key
19. Pulley with fan
20. Washer spring
21. Securing nut pulley
22. Oil with square terminal feed
23. Cable connector grounding
24. Coil with small terminal field
25. Shoe pole
26. Pole shoe screw
27. Terminal screw DF
28. Insulating block
29. Flat washer
30. Washer spring
31. Terminal nut
32. Dowel locating
33. Washer insulating
34. Flat washer
35. Washer spring
36. Terminal securing nut
37. Terminal end nut
38. Brush
39. Spring brush
    IR 50 BA complete regulator
40. Screw for terminals D/61 DF, OF, D/31
41. Washer spring
42. Screw for DF terminal
43. Toothed washer

doesn't come on, check for an open circuit in the following manner:

(A) Connect the two leads of a voltmeter to ground and the DF generator terminal and check for a reading. Go on to the next step if a reading is obtained. No reading indicates an open circuit between the DF terminal and the battery. Correct this, then see if the light goes on when the ignition is turned on.

(B) Either connect or disconnect both generator leads, turn the ignition switch on, and momentarily ground the D+ terminal lead only. If the light does not come on, check for a burned out bulb, blown fuse, faulty bulb socket, or an open condition between the D+ terminal and the ignition switch. Remove the ground from the D+ terminal, if the light comes on and, with both terminals connected, ground the generator.

(C) If the light still hasn't come on, check for open circuits between the wiring harness and the no. 1 terminal, generator brushes, slip rings, and field windings.

(D) If the light came on in the first step and there was a voltmeter reading, replace the regulator.

(E) Consult the next section if the light stays on when the motor is running.

4. Locate the reason for an undercharged battery in the following manner:

a. Make sure the reason the battery keeps going down is not because the accessories have been left on without the engine running.

b. Check the drive belt for proper tension.

c. Check the battery for shorting with a voltmeter or hydrometer indicated by one or more dead cells.

d. Inspect all wiring for loose or poor connections.

e. Connect the leads of a voltmeter from ground to the generator D+ terminals, then the no. 1 terminals, then the no. 2 terminal. No reading indicates an open condition between the battery and the voltmeter connection.

5. Check the generator in the following manner if the problem hasn't yet been discovered:

a. Disconnect the battery ground wire, connect an ammeter so the current will pass through it from the generator D+ terminal to the lead which was connected to the D+ terminal, and reconnect the battery ground wire.

b. Turn on all of the accessories and attach a carbon pile across the battery terminals. Operate the engine until its maximum current output is obtained.

c. If the generator is good, amperage output will be within 10 percent of its rated output. Go back and recheck the previous steps.

d. Ground the generator by inserting a screwdriver through the generator test hole if amperage isn't within 10 percent of its normal rating.

e. Recheck with a carbon pile as described above. If the reading is still not within 10 percent, the regulator must be replaced.

f. Recheck with a carbon pile and overhaul the generator if the reading still isn't within 10 percent of its rated amperage.

6. Locate the reason for an overcharged battery in the following manner:

a. Check the state of battery charge with a voltmeter or hydrometer.

b. Connect the leads of a voltmeter to ground and to the generator DF terminal to check for an open reading (zero). The voltage, in any case, should not exceed 12 volts at 0° F. Discrepancies in measurements taken in cold and hot conditions are to be expected.

7. If the above test proves that the circuit is good and excessive water evaporation still indicates an overcharged battery, separate the generator end frames and check the field windings for a shorted condition in the following manner:

a. Connect the leads of an ohmmeter from the brush lead clip to the end frame and then reverse the connections. The ohmmeter must be set on its lowest range scale.

b. If both readings are zero, check for a grounded brush lead. This is probably caused by a missing or damaged insulating washer or insulating screw sleeve.

c. If, after replacing the insulating elements, both readings are still zero, the regulator is defective and must be replaced.

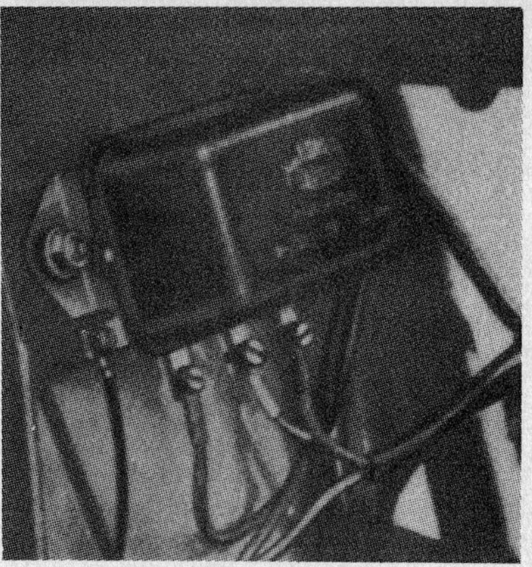

Mounted regulator

Consult the "Troubleshooting" chapter for additional information. If the generator is in need of attention, it should be returned to your dealer or a qualified specialist.

Regulator

All of the models covered in this guide use the Marelli IR 50 BA type regulator which is a three coil unit and is mounted to the frame. The unit is not repairable or adjustable and must be replaced if defective.

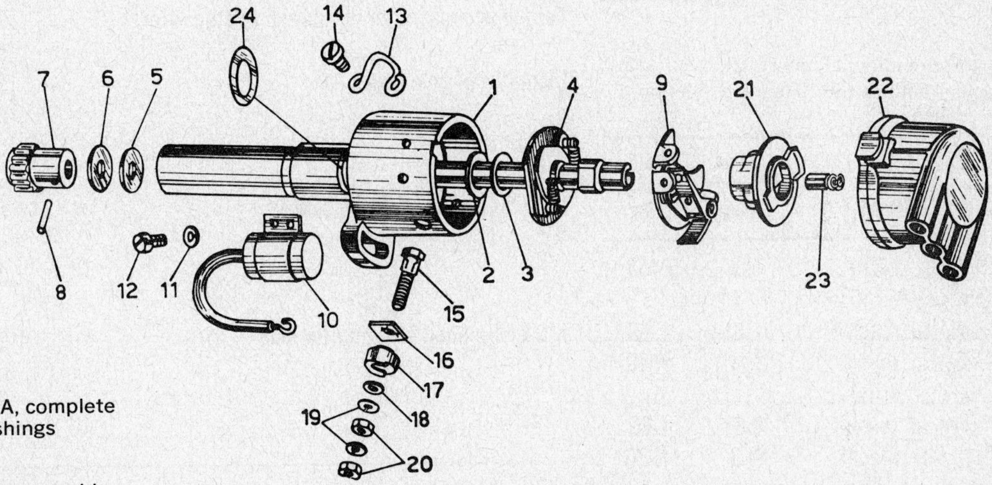

Distributor S 123 A, complete
1. Housings with bushings
2. Bakelite washer
3. Flat washer
4. Automatic advance assembly
5. Spacer
6. Shim, 0.1 mm
   Shim, 0.2 mm
   Shim, 0.5 mm
7. Driving pinion
8. Securing peg pinion
9. Breaker unit, complete contact
10. Condenser CE 29 D
11. Spring washer
12. Condenser fixing screw
13. Securing spring cap
14. Spring fixing screw cap
15. Terminal bolt
16. Insulating plate
17. Insulating block
18. Flat washer
19. Spring washer
20. Terminal nut
21. Distributor rotor
22. Distributor cap
23. Carbon brush
24. Seal

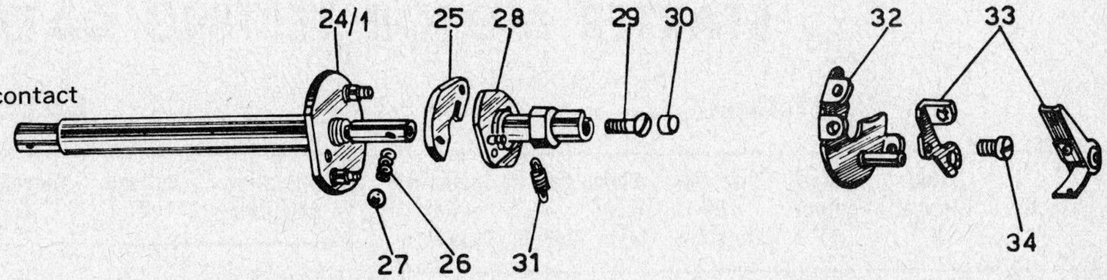

Distributor assembly

24/1. Shaft
25. Advance weight
26. Ball retaining spring
27. Ball
28. Cam
29. Cam retaining screw
30. Cam felt pad
31. Weight spring—8 coils
    Weight spring—9 coils
32. Complete plate with pin
33. Breaker set, contact
34. Point plate fixed screw

MISCELLANEOUS ELECTRICAL COMPONENTS

Automatic Spark Advance

If the advance mechanism is suspected of improper operation, the best way to check it is to static time the engine and then check the timing with a strobe light. Any irregularities should show up immediately. If the cam has become worn the entire unit must be replaced. If the advance springs become damaged or stretched out, they may be replaced. Any other damage to the assembly will result in the need for replacement.

Spark Plugs

Moto Guzzi recommends the use of either Marelli CW 225 LVT or Bosch W 225 T 2 type spark plugs, however any suitable plug manufactured by another company may be used. The following are the Champion plugs which may be used in Moto Guzzis:

For additional information on spark plugs consult the "Tune-Up" section.

Model	Standard Plug	Gold Palladium Plug
850 cc—V-850	N-3	N-3G
750 cc—V-750		
(1/2 in. reach)	L-81	L-6G
(3/4 in. reach)	N-4	N-4G
700 cc—V-700		
(3/4 in. reach)	L-81	L-6G
(1/2 in. reach)	N-3	N-3G

Battery

Voltage	12V
Capacity	32Ah
Length	230 mm (9.0551 in.)
Width	139 mm (5.4724 in.)
Height	180 mm (7.0866 in.)
Weight (wet)	28.6 lbs

Starter Motor

The starter assembly is a long-life unit which, under normal operating conditions, should not require attention. If the starter fails, the unit should be removed and returned to your dealer or a qualified specialist for repairs. The following is some useful testing information and specifications which may be of assistance:

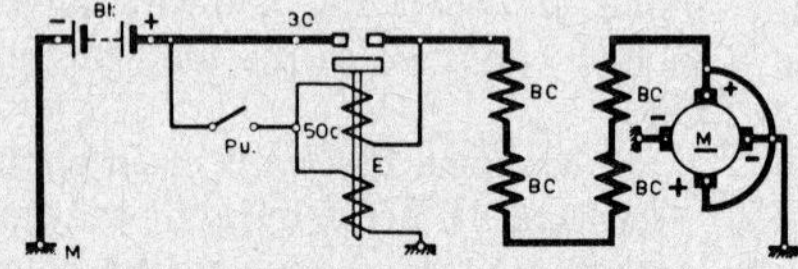

BC. Field coil
Bt. Battery
E. Electromagnet
Pu. Ignition key
M. Ground

Starter wiring diagram

MECHANICAL TESTS AND DIMENSIONS

Torque under no load	0.4-0.5 Kg/cm^2 (2.89-3.61 ft lb)
Torque necessary for disc brake to stop rotor	2.5-4.0 Kg/cm^2 (18-28.9 ft lb)
Diameter of pole shoes	52.6-53.0 mm (2.0708-2.0865 in.)
0/0 of rotor	51.9-52.0 mm (2.0468-2.0472 in.)
I/D of bushing, coupling side	10 + 0.015 mm − 0 (0.3937 + 0.0005 in.) − 0
I/D of bushing, commutator side	10 + 0.015 mm − 0 (0.3937 + 0.0005 in.) − 0

STARTER MOTOR TESTING DATA

Features

Type No.	Rated voltage V	Rated output HP	Direction of rotation	Pinion gear No. of teeth	Pinion gear Module	Solenoid switch Type No.
MT 40 H	12	0.7	CW	8	2.5 D.P.	IE 13 DA

Electrical Tests

Operating condition	Voltage V	Current A	RPM	Torque Kg cm	Torque ft lb
No-Load	11.6	+25	11000-11500	—	—
Full Load	10	+100	3200-3500	0.15	1.08
Short circuit	7	−300	—	0.75	5.42

Solenoid Repair

The solenoid is a non-repairable item which must be replaced if defective. The easiest way to determine whether or not the solenoid is operating, is to listen for the distinctive click it makes when activated. If it doesn't click, it's probably bad and should be replaced.

TEETH CONTACT TEST

There should remain about 1 mm (0.-0394 in.) of coupling lever travel when the tooth faces of the pinion and ring gears come into contact. Therefore, when the switch contacts are completely closed, the coupling spring should have to be compressed one millimeter more before the coils of the spring touch each other. Perform the test by inserting a 1 mm thick feeler between the pinion and ring gears, then push the coupling lever and use a continuity tester to determine if the switch contacts have closed.

Fuses

Fuses must be replaced with 25 A fuses only.

Bulbs

All bulbs used on the models covered in this guide are 12 V. The following list are their wattage ratings:

Headlight	45-45 W*
Taillight (twin filament)	20-5 W
Speedometer (A)	3 W
High beam indicator (B)	3 W
Ammeter (C)	3 W
Neutral indicator (D)	3 W
Oil pressure gauge (E)	3 W

* USA models; European and police models, 45-40w

VOLTAGE AND INSULATION TESTS

Check dielectric rigidity by feeding for 3 secs. with 500 V, 50 Hz, A.C. Check insulation resistance feeding with 100 V, D.C.—Resistance value must be 2 M Ω.
NOTE: When carrying out above tests, temporarily disconnect possible ground connections

SOLENOID SWITCH TEST

Type No.	Absorption A	Coupling voltage V	Release voltage V	Load force Kg	Load force lbs	Total core travel
DE 13 DA	27-53	4	1-6 0.4-2	15	33.06	9.5 mm (0.374 in.)

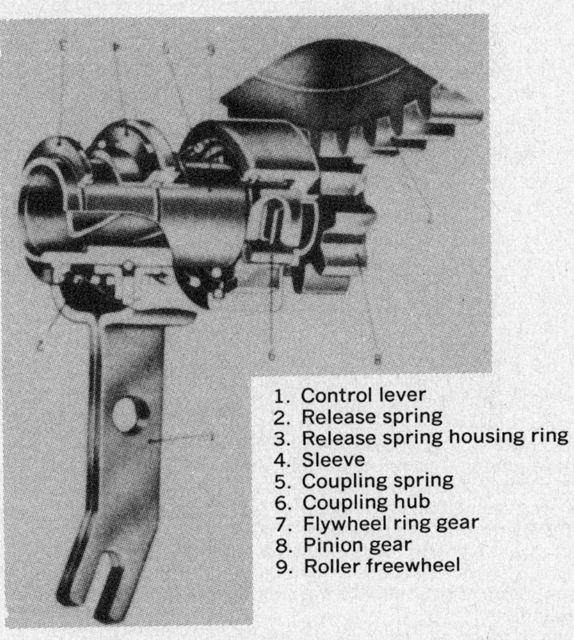

Cutaway view of the engaging mechanism

Wiring Diagrams

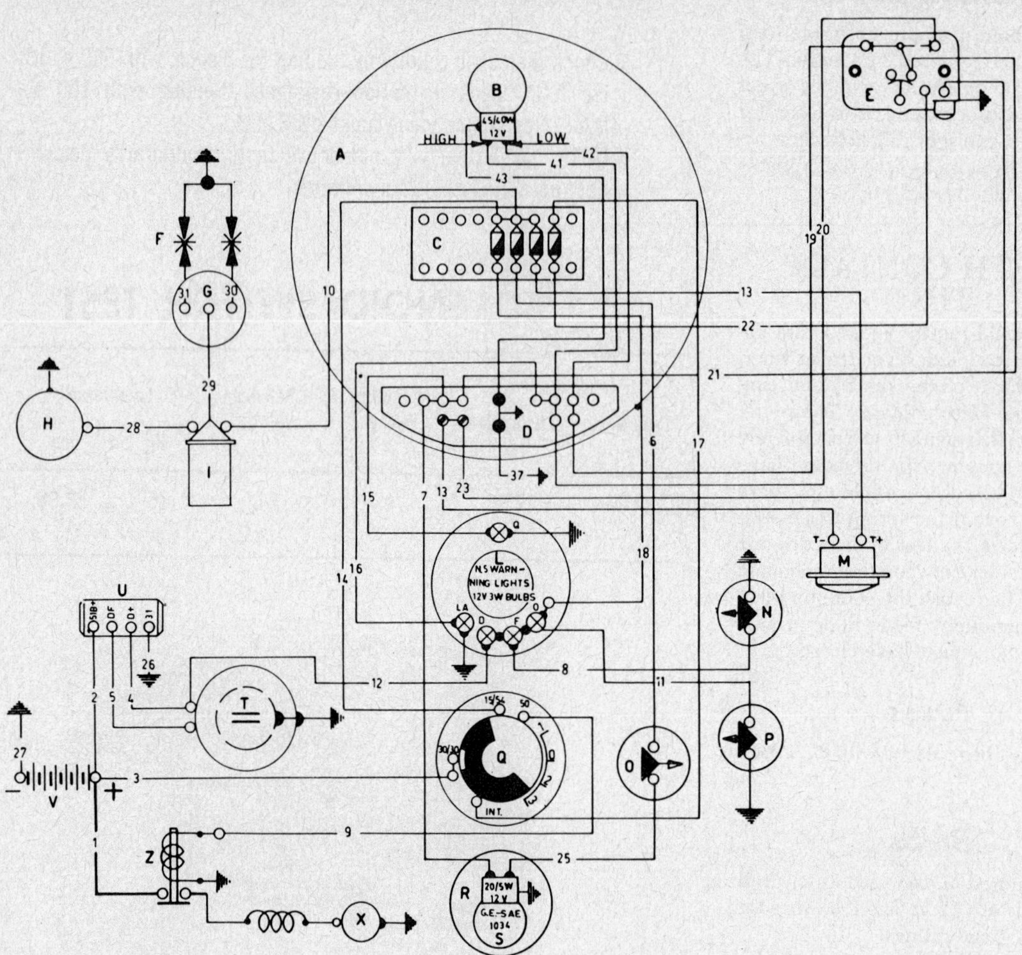

Wiring diagram (V700 USA model)

1. Black: battery V to starter motor relay Z
2. Red: regulator U 51B+ to battery V+
3. Red: battery V to ignition switch Q
4. Grey-red: generator T to regulator U (D+)
5. White: generator T to regulator U (DF)
6. Black: terminal with fuses C to stop cutout O
7. Yellow: distributing block D to tail light bulb R
8. Green: neutral cut-out N to warning light F on speedometer
9. Brown: ignition switch Q (50) to starter relay Z
10. Blue-black: terminal block C to H.T. coil I
11. Grey: oil pressure cut-out P to speedometer L
12. Red: generator T to warning light D on speedometer L
13. Black: distributing block D to horn M (T−)
14. Red: terminal block with fuses C to ignition switch Q
15. White: distributing block D to warning bulb Q in speedometer L
16. Yellow-black: distributing block D to warning light LA on speedometer
17. Brown: terminal block C to ignition switch Q (Int.)
18. White-black: terminal block C to speedometer L
19. Green: distributing block C to light switch E
20. Green-black: distributing block D to light switch E
21. Grey-red: distributing block D to light switch E
22. Brown: terminal block C to light switch E
23. Black: distributing block D to light switch E
25. Black: stop light cut-out O to tail light bulb S
26. Black: regulator U to ground
27. Black: battery V to ground
28. Black: H.T. coil I to contact breaker H
29. Black: H.T. coil I to distributor G
30. Black: distributor G to spark plug F
31. Black: distributor G to spark plug F
37. Black: distributing block D to ground
41. Green-black: distributing block D to high beam filament B
42. Green: distributing block D to low beam filament B
41. Black: headlight bulb B to distributing block D

Ignition Switch Position

0.
1. 30/30 int.
2. 30/20 int. 15/54
3. 30/30 int. 15/54-50

Legend

A. Headlight
B. Main light bulb
C. Terminal block with fuses
D. Distributing block
E. Light switch and horn button
F. Spark plug
G. Distributor
H. Contact breaker
I. H. T. coil
L. Speedometer and warning light bulbs
M. Horn
N. Neutral indicator cut-out
O. Stop light cut-out
P. Oil pressure cut-out
Q. Ignition switch
R. Number plate and tail light
S. Plate illumination and stop light
T. Generator
U. Regulator
V. Battery
Z. Starter motor relay
X. Starter motor

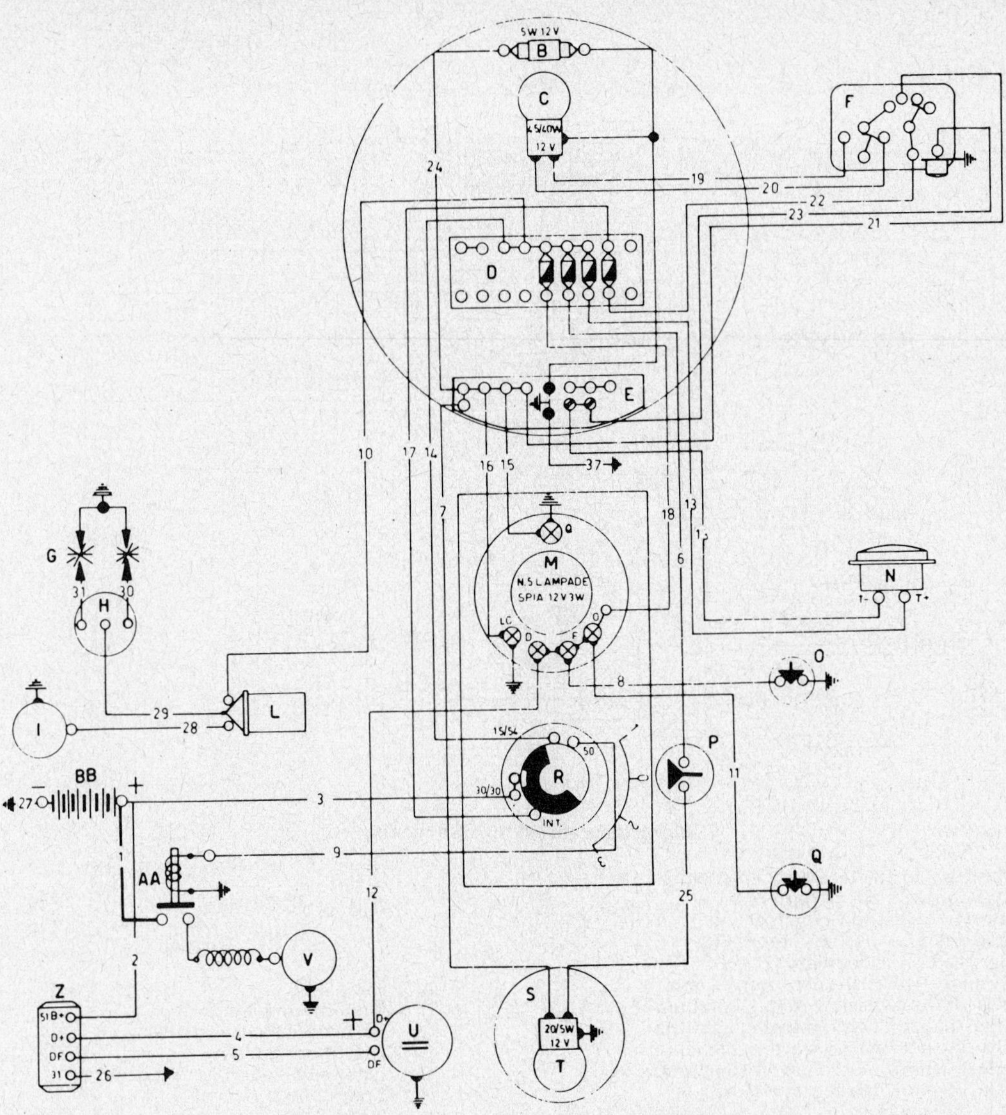

Wiring diagram (V700 European model)

KEY TO CABLE COLORS

1. Black: battery + to start motor
2. Red: battery to regulator 51 B +
3. Red: ignition switch 30/30 to battery +
4. Grey-red: regulator to generator D +
5. White: regulator DF to generator DF
6. Black: terminal with fuses to stop cut-out
7. Yellow: distributing block to tail light bulb
8. Green: instrument board F to neutral indicator cut-out
9. Brown: ignition switch to starter motor
10. Blue-black: terminal block to coil
11. Grey: instrument panel 0 to oil pressure solenoid
12. Red: instrument panel D to generator D +
13. Black: terminal box with fuses to horn
14. Red: ignition switch 15/54 to terminal block
15. White: instrument panel 0 to distributing block
16. Yellow-black: instrument panel LC to distributing block E
17. Brown: ignition switch int. to terminal block with fuses
18. White black: instrument panel D to terminal block with fuses
19. Green: light switch to headlight bulb
20. Green-black: light switch to headlight bulb
21. Grey-red: light switch to distributing block
22. Brown: light switch to terminal with fuses
23. Black: horn button to distributing block
24. Blue: town driving bulb to distributing block
25. Black: stop cut-out to stop bulb
26. Black: regulator to ground
27. Black: battery to ground
28. Black: H.T. coil to contact breaker
29. Black: H.T. coil to distributor
30. Black: distributor to spark plug
31. Black: distributor to spark plug
37. Black: headlight D to ground

IGNITION SWITCH POSITION

0.
1. 30/30 int.
2. 30/30 int. 15/54
3. 30/30 int. 15/54-50

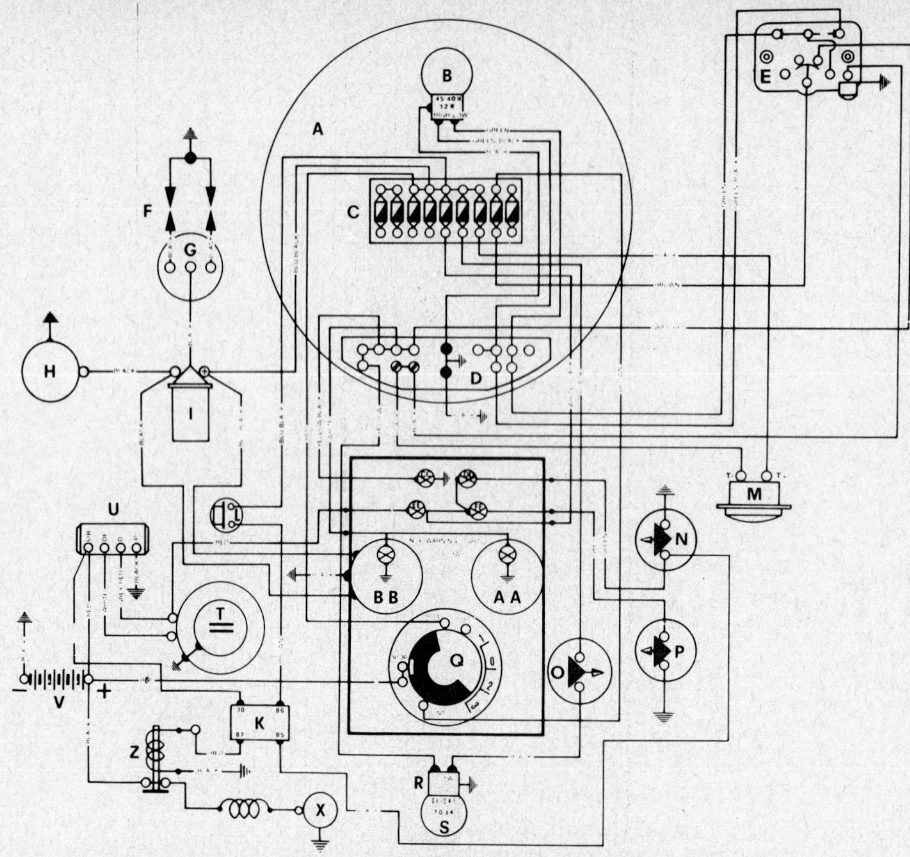

Wiring diagram (V750 USA model)

1. Black: Battery V to starter motor solenoid Z
2. Red: Regulator U 51 B+ to battery V
3. Red: Battery V to ignition switch Q
4. Grey-red: Generator T to regulator U (D+)
5. White: Generator T to regulator U (DF)
6. Black: Terminal with fuses C to stop cutout O
7. Yellow: Distributing block D to tail light bulb R
8. Green: Neutral cutout N to warning light DD
9. Brown: Starter button L to starter solenoid Z

9/1. Blue-black: Terminal block C to starter button

10. Blue-black: Terminal block C to H.T. coil I

10/1. Blue-black: Rev-counter BB (+) to H.T. coil I

11. Grey: Oil pressure cutout P to oil pressure indicator FF
12. Red: Generator T to warning light EE
13. Black: Distributing block D to horn M (T−)
14. Red: Terminal block C to ignition switch Q (15-54)
15. White: Distributing block D to speedometer AA
16. Yellow-black: Distributing block D to warning light CC
17. Brown: Terminal block C to ignition switch Q (Int.)
18. White-black: Terminal block C to warning light EE
19. Green: Distributing block D to light switch E
20. Green-black: Distributing block D to light switch E
21. Grey-red: Distributing block D to light switch E
22. Brown: Terminal block C to light switch E
23. Black: Distributing block D to light switch E
25. Black: Stop light cutout O to tail light bulb S
26. Black: Regulator U to ground
27. Black: Battery V to ground
28. Black: H.T. coil I to contact breaker H
29. Black: H.T. coil I to distributor G

29/A. Black: H.T. coil I to revcounter BB

30. Black: Distributor G to spark plug F
31. Black: Distributor G to spark plug F
37. Black: Headlight B to ground

37/A. Black: Rev-counter BB to ground

37/B. Black: Starter motor solenoid Z to neutral indicator N

41. Green-black: Distributing block D to high beam filament B
42. Green: Distributing block D to low beam filament B
43. Black: Headlight bulb B to ground on distributing block D

Legend

- A. Headlight
- B. Main driving lights
- C. Terminal block with fuses
- D. Distributing block
- E. Light switch and horn button
- F. Spark plugs
- G. Distributor
- H. Contact breaker
- I. H.T. coil
- L. Starter button
- M. Horn
- N. Neutral indicator cutout
- O. Stop light cutout
- P. Oil pressure cutout
- Q. Ignition switch
- R. Number plate and tail light
- S. Plate illumination and stop light
- T. Generator
- U. Regulator
- V. Battery
- Z. Starter motor solenoid
- X. Starter motor
- AA. Speedometer (with illumination bulb)
- BB. Rev counter (with illumination bulb)
- CC. Lights indicator (red)
- DD. Neutral indicator (orange)
- EE. Generator change indicator (red)
- FF. Oil pressure indicator (red)
- K. Relay for starter solenoid

IGNITION SWITCH POSITION

0.
1. 30/30—INT.
2. 30/30—INT. 15/54
3. 30/30—INT. 15/54—50

NOTE: Position—3—does not serve on machines with starter button

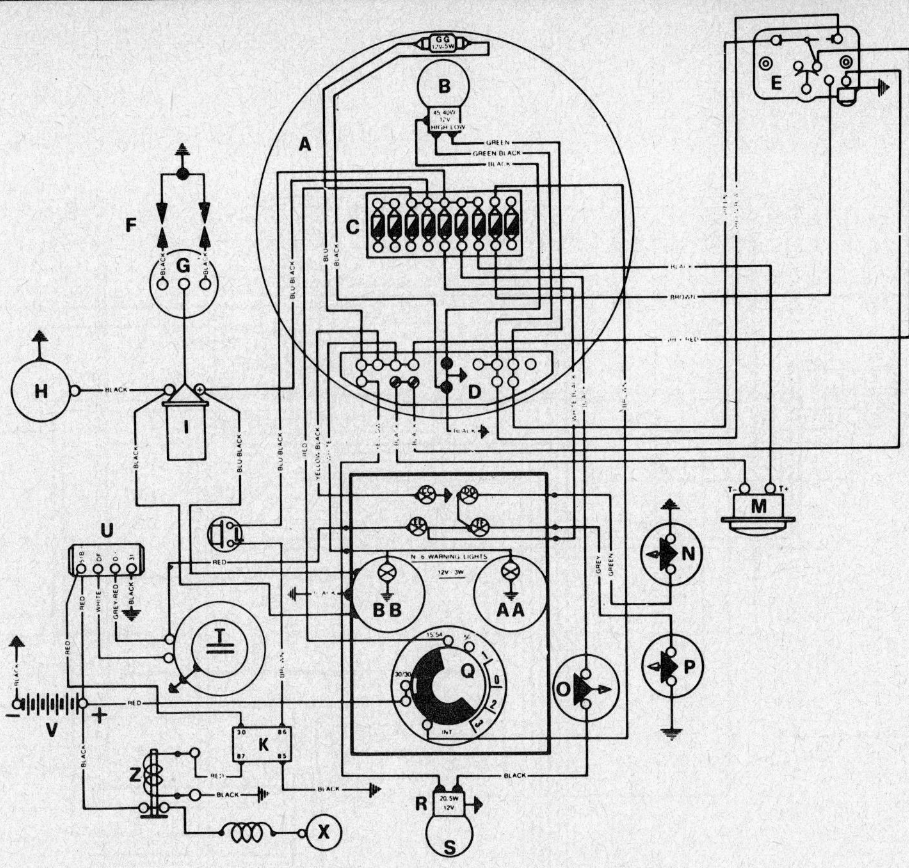

Wiring diagram (V750 European model)

1. Black: Battery (+) to starter motor
2. Red: Battery to regulator 51 B +
3. Red: Ignition switch 30/30 to battery +
4. Grey-red: Regulator to generator D +
5. White: Regulator DF to generator DF
6. Black: Headlight to stop cutout
7. Yellow: Headlight terminal to tail light
8. Green: Warning light F to neutral indicator cutout
9. Brown: Starter button to starter motor solenoid
10. Blue-black: Headlight terminal to H.T. coil
11. Grey: Warning light F to oil pressure cutout
12. Red: Warning light A to generator
13. Black: Distributing block to horn
14. Red: Ignition key 15/54 to headlight terminal
15. White: Speedometer AA to distributing block
16. Yellow-black: Warning light CC to distributing block
17. Brown: Ignition switch INT to headlight terminal
18. White-black: Warning light FF to headlight terminal
19. Green: Light switch to distributing block
20. Green-black: Light switch to distributing block
21. Grey-red: Light switch to distributing block
22. Brown: Light switch to headlight terminal
23. Black: Horn button to distributing block
24. Black: Horn T + to headlight terminal
25. Blue: Parking light to distributing block
26. Black: Stop light cutout to tail bulb
27. Black: Regulator to ground
28. Black: Battery to ground
29. Black: H.T. coil to contact breaker
30. Black: H.T. coil to distributor
31. Black: Distributor to spark plug
32. Black: Distributor to spark plug
33. Black: Headlamp to ground
34. Green: Distributing block to low beam light
35. Green-black: Distributing block to high beam light
36. Black: Headlight bulb to ground
37. Black: Parking light to ground
38. Blue-black: Headlight terminal to button horn
39. Blue-black: H.T. coil + to rev-counter
40. Black: H.T. coil—to rev-counter I

41. Black: Rev-counter BB to ground
42. Black: Starter motor to ground

Legend

- A. Headlight
- B. Main light bulb
- C. Terminal block with fuses
- D. Distributing block
- E. Light switch and horn button
- F. Spark plug
- G. Distributor
- H. Contact breaker
- I. H.T. coil
- L. Starter button
- M. Horn
- N. Neutral indicator cutout
- O. Stop light
- P. Oil pressure cutout
- Q. Ignition switch
- R. Number plate and tail light
- S. Plate illumination
- T. Generator
- U. Regulator
- V. Battery
- Z. Starter motor solenoid
- X. Starter motor
- AA. Speedometer with illumination bulb
- BB. Rev-counter
- CC. Lights indicator (red)
- DD. Neutral indicator (orange)
- EE. Charge indicator (red)
- FF. Oil pressure indicator (red)
- GG. Parking light
- K. Relay for starter solenoid

IGNITION SWITCH POSITION

0.
1. 30/30—INT.
2. 30/30—INT. 15/54
3. 30/30—INT. 15/54—50

NOTE: Position—3—does not serve on machines with starter button

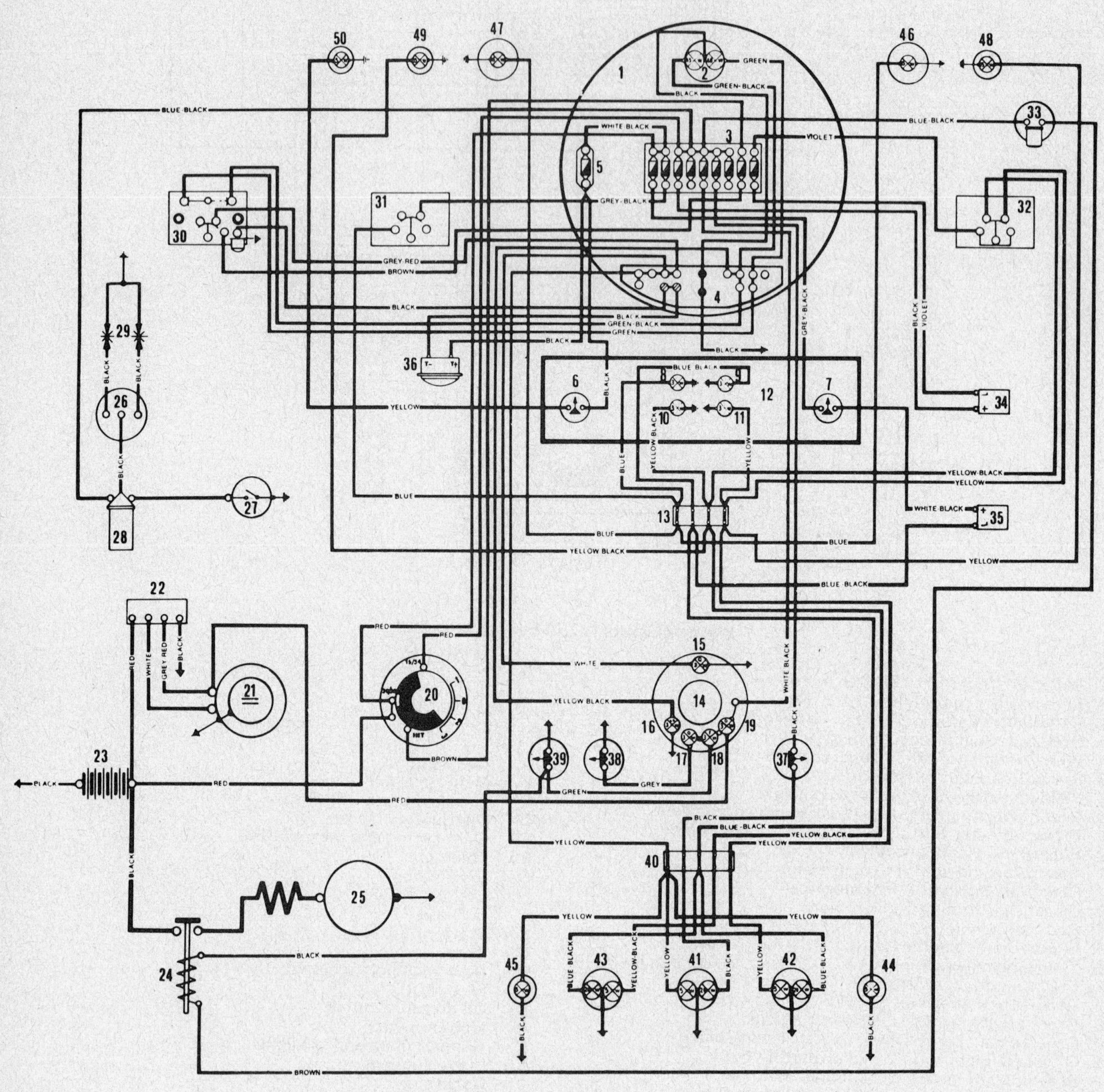

Wiring diagram (V750 Police model)

1. Black: Battery 23 to starter motor relay 24
2. Red: Regulator 22 to battery 23
3. Red: Battery 23 to ignition switch 20
4. Grey-red: Generator 21 to regulator 22
5. White: Generator 21 to regulator 22
6. Black: Terminal with fuses 3 to stop cutout 37
7. Black: H light bulb 2 to distributing block 4
8. Green-black: H light bulb 2 to distributing block 4
9. Green: High beam bulb 2 to distributing block 4
10. Brown: Terminal block with fuses 3 to ignition switch 20
11. Blue-black: Terminal with fuses 3 to start button 33
12. Blue-black: Terminal with fuses 3 to H.T. coil 28
13. Red: Terminal with fuses 3 to ignition switch 15/54
14. White-black: Terminal with fuses 3 to separate fuse 5
15. Red: Terminal with fuses 3 to ignition switch 30/30
16. Grey-black: Terminal with fuses 3 to front side red light switch 31
17. White-black: Terminal with fuses 3 to rear flasher cutout 7
18. Black: Terminal with fuses 3 to turn flasher cutout 34
19. Orange: Terminal with fuses 3 to light switch and horn button 30
20. Violet: Terminal with fuses 3 to turn signal switch 32
21. Violet: Terminal with fuses 3 to flasher cutout 34
22. Black-white: Terminal with fuses 3 to red indicator light 19
23. Grey-red: Distributing block 4 to light switch 30
24. Yellow-black: Distributing block 4 to red warning light for high beam 16
25. White: Distributing block 4 to speedo lamp 15
26. Black: Distributing block 4 to light switch 30
27. Black: Distributing block 4 to horn 36
28. Black: Distributing block 4 to ground
29. Green: Distributing block 4 to light switch 30
30. Green-black: Distributing block 4 to light switch 30
31. Black: Fuse 5 to horn 36
32. Black: Fuse 5 to cutout 36
33. Black-yellow: L/H turn indicator 43 to rear block 40
34. Yellow-black: Distributing block 40 to front block 30
35. Yellow: Supplementary light 50 to cutout 6
36. Blue: Front lateral light switch (red) 31 to front block 13
37. Red: Generator 21 to indicator light 19
38. Black: H.T. coil 28 to contact breaker 27
39. Black: H.T. coil 28 to distributor 26
40. Black: Distributor 26 to plug 29
41. Black: Starter motor relay 24 to starter motor 25
42. Black: Starter motor relay 24 to neutral indicator cutout 39
43. Yellow: H light distributing block 4 to rear distributing 40
44. Brown: Starter relay 24 to start button 33
45. Yellow: L/H rear light 45 to rear block 40
46. Blue-black: Rear amber flasher 43 to rear distributing block 40
47. Yellow: Number plate and stop light 41 to rear block 40
48. Black: Number plate and stop light 41 to rear block 40
49. Yellow: R/H rear flasher 42 to rear block 40
50. Yellow: R/H rear blue light 44 to rear block 40
51. Yellow: R/H rear block 40 to front distributing block 13
52. Blue-black: Rear distributing block 40 to front distributing block 13
53. Green: Neutral indicator cutout 39 to amber indicator 18
54. Blue: Front distributing block 13 to red warning lamp for front red light 8
55. Blue: Front distributing block 13 to R/H front red light 46
56. Blue-black: Front distributing block 13 to amber rearlight cutout 35
57. Yellow: Front distributing block 13 to turn signal 32
58. Yellow: Front distributing block 13 to green warning lamp for R/H flasher 11
59. Yellow-black: Front distributing block 13 to green warning light 18
60. Yellow-black: Front distributing block 13 to turn signal lamp switch 32
61. Black-white: Rear amber cutout 35 to cutout 7
62. Black: Rear block 40 to stop light cutout 37
63. Blue-black: Rear light amber flasher 42 to rear block 40
64. Yellow-black: Front distributing block 13 to amber turn indicator bulb 49
65. Blue-black: Front block 13 to blue warning light 9

LEGEND

1. Headlight
2. High and low beam lamp (45/40W—12V)
3. Terminal block with fuses
4. Distribution block in headlight
5. Fuse for horn and additional light
6. Cutout for additional light
7. Cutout for rear amber flashers
8. Red warning lamp for front red lights (bulb 3W—12V)
9. Blue warning light for amber rear lamps (bulb 3W—12V)
10. Green warning lamp for L/H flasher (bulb 3W—12V)
11. Green warning lamp for R/H flasher (bulb 3W—12V)
12. Instrument panel
13. Front distributing block
14. Mile speedometer
15. Speedometer illumination lamp (3W—12V)
16. Red warning light for high beam (bulb 3W—12V)
17. Red oil pressure indicator (bulb 3W—12V)
18. Amber neutral indicator lamp (bulb 3W—12V)
19. Red indicator light for insufficient battery charge
20. Ignition switch
21. Generator
22. Regulator
23. Battery
24. Starter motor relay
25. Starter motor
26. Distributor
27. Contact breaker
28. H.T. coil
29. Spark plug
30. Light switch and horn button
31. Front side red lights switch
32. Turn signal flashing lamps switch
33. Start button
34. Turn flashers cutout (28W—12V)
35. Amber rear lights cutout (40W—12V)
36. Horn
37. Stop light cutout, rear brake
38. Oil pressure solenoid
39. Neutral indicator cutout
40. Rear distributing block
41. Number plate and stop light (5/20W—12V)
42. R/H rear light amber flasher (bulb 5/20W—12V)
43. R/H rear light amber flasher (bulb 5/20W—12V)
44. R/H rear light, blue (bulb 5W—12V)
45. L/H rear light, blue (bulb 5W—12V)
46. R/H red front light (bulb 15W—12V)
47. L/H red front light (bulb 15W—12V)
48. R/H amber turn indicator (bulb 15W—12V)
49. L/H amber turn indicator (bulb 15W—12V)
50. Additional light for police duties
51. Stop light cutout, front brake

IGNITION SWITCH POSITION

0.
1. 30/30 int.
2. 30/30 int. 15/54
3. Not applicable for systems incorporating starter button.

Wiring diagram (V750 Police model)

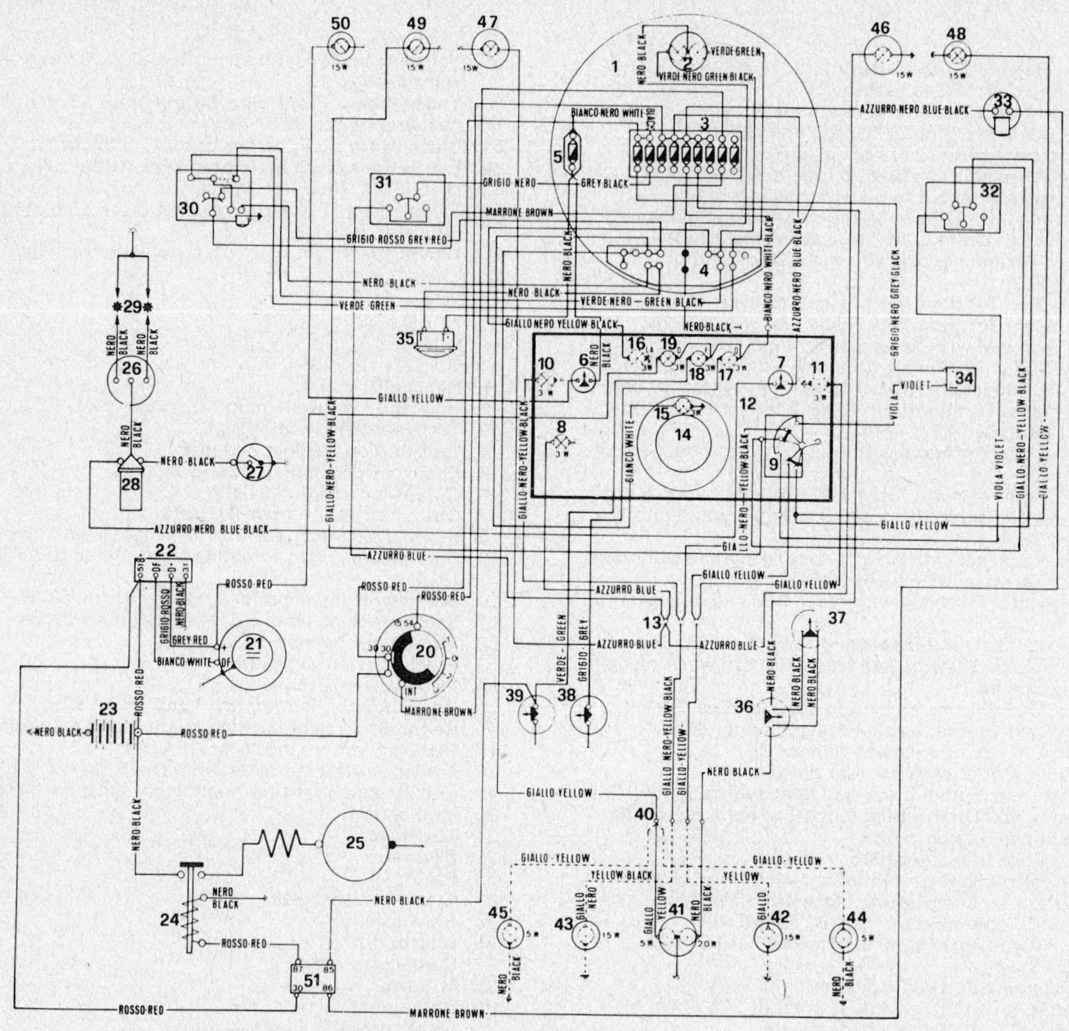

Wiring diagram (V850 Police model)

LEGEND

1. Headlight
2. High and low beam bulb (45/40W—12V)
3. Terminal block with fuses
4. Distributing block in headlight
5. Horn fuse
6. Courtesy light cutout
7. Coil disconnection cutout
8. Red warning light, front red lights on
9. Turn lights and rear flashing lights switch
10. Green warning light, L/H turn light on (3W—12V bulb)
11. Green warning light, R/H turn light on (3W—12V bulb)
12. Instrument panel
13. Shunting connection, front
14. Mile speedometer
15. Bulb, speedo illumination (3W—12V)
16. Red warning light, high light on (3W—12V bulb)
17. Red warning light, oil pressure (3W—12V bulb)
18. Orange warning light, neutral indicator (3W—12V bulb)
19. Red warning light, generator charge (3W—12V)
20. Ignition switch
21. Generator
22. Voltage regulator
23. Battery
24. Starter motor relay
25. Starter motor
26. Distributor
27. Contact breaker
28. Coil
29. Spark plug
30. Light switch and horn button
31. Ground switch for relay
32. Turn lights, front red lights, and radio control switch
33. Starter button
34. Flasher unit for turn lights, and rear lights
35. Horn
36. Rear brake stop cutout
37. Front brake stop cutout
38. Oil pressure hydraulic cutout
39. Neutral indicator cutout
40. Rear shunting connections
41. Plate and stop light (5/21W—12V bulb)
42. Rear orange flashing light (21W—12V bulb), R/H
43. Rear orange flashing light, L/H (21W—12V bulb)
44. Rear R/H blue light (5W—12V bulb)
45. Rear L/H blue light (5W—12V bulb)
46. Front R/H red light (21W—12V bulb)
47. Front L/H red light (21W—12V bulb)
48. Front R/H turn light indicator (orange) (15W—12V bulb)
49. Front L/H orange turn light indicator (15W—12V bulb)
50. Supplementary light
51. Starter motor solenoid relay

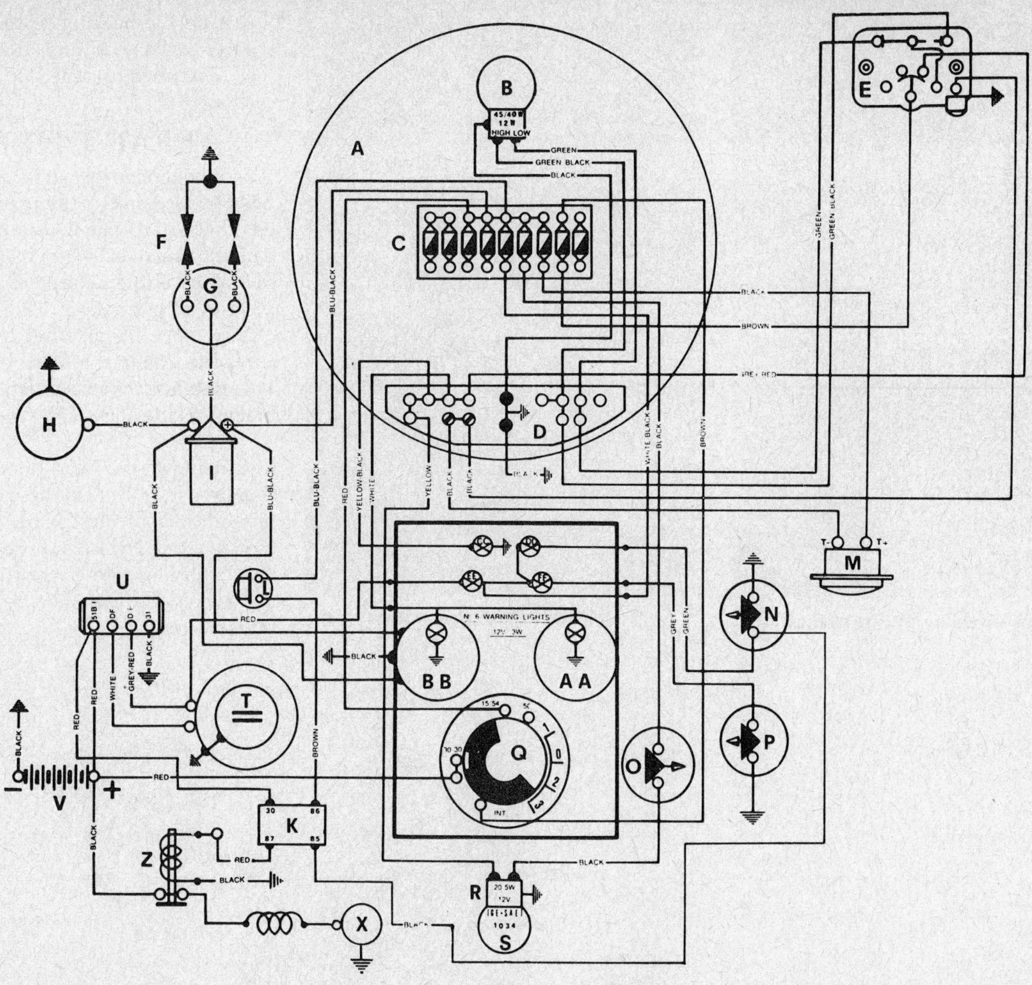

Wiring diagram (V850 Eldorado)

A. Headlight
B. Main driving lights
C. Terminal block with fuses
D. Distributing block
E. Light switch and horn button
F. Spark plugs
G. Distributor
H. Contact breaker
I. H.T. coil
L. Starter button
M. Horn
N. Neutral indicator cutout
O. Stop light cutout
P. Oil pressure cutout
Q. Ignition switch
R. Number plate and tail light
S. Plate illumination and stop light
T. Generator
U. Regulator

V. Battery
Z. Starter motor solenoid
X. Starter motor
AA. Speedometer (with illumination bulb)
BB. Rev-counter (with illumination bulb)
CC. Lights on indicator (red)
DD. Neutral indicator (orange)
EE. Generator charge (red)
FF. Oil pressure indicator (red)
K. Relay for starter solenoid

IGNITION SWITCH POSITION

0.
1. 30/30—INT.
2. 30/30—INT. 15/54
3. 30/30—INT. 15/54—50

NOTE: Position 3 does not serve on machines with starter button.

CHASSIS

WHEELS

Removal and Installation

FRONT WHEEL

1. Block up the machine so the front wheel remains raised off the ground.

2. Disconnect the front brake cable (A) from the brake actuating lever. This can be easily accomplished by applying the brake and stopping the lever from returning to its seat, thus causing an excessive amount of slack in the cable. Remove the cable adjuster (B).

3. Remove the axle nut (C) and both axle pinch bolts (D), then remove the axle taking care not to score it, by gently pressing it out through the left-hand side.

4. Gently push the wheel down far enough to disengage the brake backing plate from its anchoring lug on the left hand slider, then remove the wheel.

5. Installation is done in the following manner:

a. Position the wheel assembly between the sliders, making sure that the brake backing plate is anchored to the lug on the left hand fork slider.

b. Install the axle from the left hand side, working it gently through until it meets its seat.

c. Secure the slider pinch bolts and the axle nut.

d. Screw the cable adjuster into its

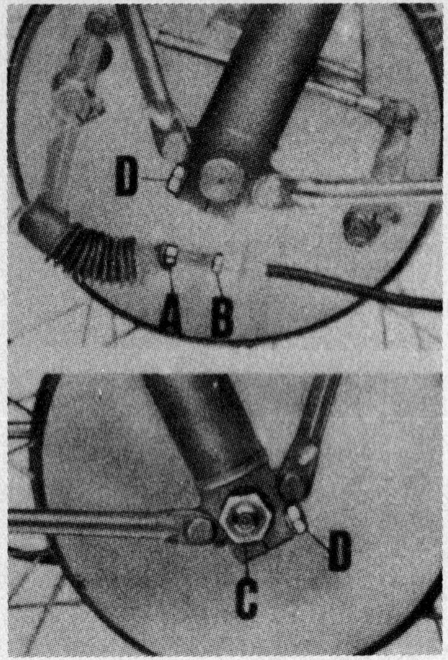

Front wheel mounting points

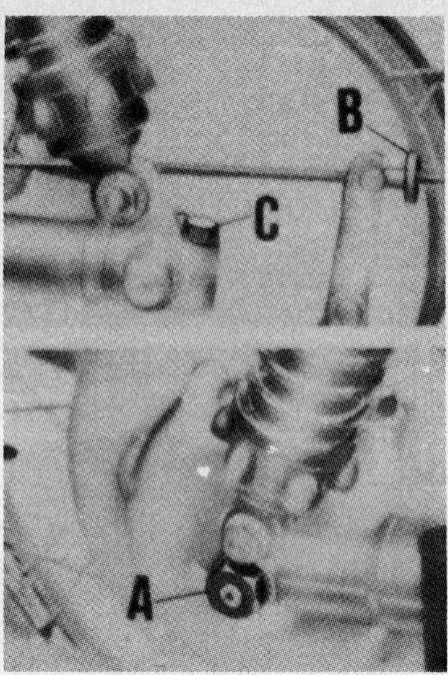

Rear wheel mounting points

seat on the backing plate, secure the cable to the lever, and adjust the brake as described in the "Maintenance" chapter.

REAR WHEEL

1. Wheel removal can be greatly facilitated by blocking up the rear wheel sufficiently so the wheel can be removed without having to lay the bike over on its side. If this is impractical don't hesitate to lay it over, but not yet.
2. Remove the axle nut (A) which secures the axle in the drive box.
3. Remove the nut which secures the brake backing plate to the anchoring lug.

4. Remove the rear brake adjusting thumb screw (B). This is easily accomplished by applying the brake, blocking the actuating lever from returning to its seat by prying with a screwdriver at the pinch bolt (C), and then removing the thumb screw.

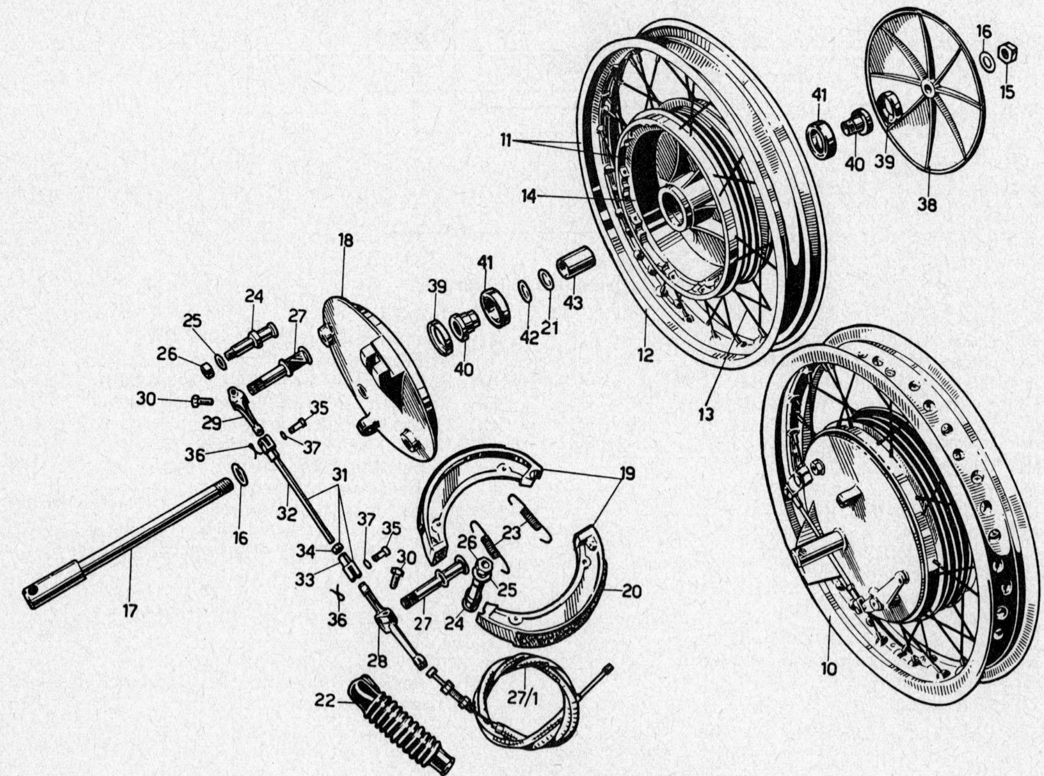
Front hub assembly

10. Complete front wheel
11. Front wheel with bearings
12. Front wheel rim
13. Front wheel, c/w spoke nipples
14. Front wheel, hub
15. Front wheel spindle nut
16. Front wheel spindle washer
17. Front wheel spindle
18. Rear hub cover
19. Brake shoe, c/w linings
20. Brake shoe lining
21. Shim
22. Cable end rubber-protector
23. Front brake shoe spring
24. Brake shoes pin
25. Brake shoe pins washer
26. Brake shoe pins nut
27. Front brake shoes cam
27/1. Front brake cable
28. Cam, double action lever
29. Brake cam lever
30. Lever-to-cams bolt
31. Tie-rod c/w forks for operating levers
32. Tie-rod
33. Tie-rod fork
34. Adjusting tie rod nut
35. Rod-to-operating lever pin
36. Tie-rod-to-control levers split pin
37. Lever pin washer
38. R/H hub cover
39. Hub seal
40. Bearing housing bush
41. Roller bearing
42. Shim
43. Bearings distance piece

5. Remove the pinch bolt (C) which locks the axle to the swing arm and carefully remove the axle while taking care not to score it.

6. Press the wheel to the left enough to disengage it from the internally toothed sleeve in the drive box.

7. If you haven't got the rear wheel blocked up, carefully tilt or lay the machine over to its right-hand side and remove the wheel from the machine.

CAUTION: The gas tank and battery should be removed before laying the machine over.

8. Installation is done in the following manner:

a. With the machine tilted over on its right-hand side, carefully insert the wheel so the central body teeth engage the teeth of the drive box sleeve.

b. Place the brake control rod in the actuating lever, then install the positioning pin and secure the thumb screw.

c. Carefully install the axle from the left-hand side until it reaches its seat.

d. Secure the anchor rod to the backing plate, then secure the axle setting bolt.

e. Secure the axle nut and adjust the brake as described in the "Maintenance" section.

WHEEL HUBS AND BRAKES

Front Wheel

DISASSEMBLY

1. Remove the wheel assembly as described in the previous section.

2. Remove the brake backing plate.

3. Remove the bolts which secure the actuating lever to the cam, then remove the levers and rod from the backing plate.

4. Remove the brake shoes, cams, and brake shoe pins.

5. Remove the seal ring, bearing housing, taper roller bearing, adjusting washers, and distance collar from the left-hand backing plate.

6. Remove the seal ring, bearing housing, and roller bearing from the right hand backing plate.

REAR WHEEL

1. Remove the wheel assembly as described in the "Rear Wheel Removal and Installation" section.

2. Remove the brake backing plate.

3. Remove the bolt and nut which secure the lever to the cam on the shoe pin, then remove the shoes, cam, and shoe pin.

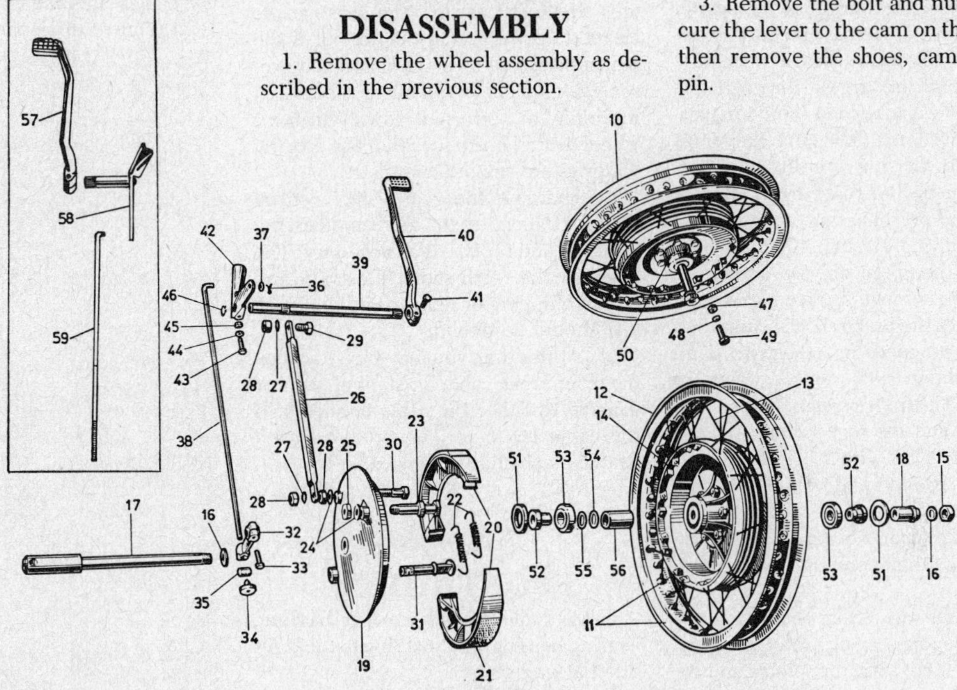

Rear hub assembly

10. Complete rear wheel
11. Rear wheel c/w bearings
12. Rear wheel rim
13. Rear wheel spoke
14. Rear wheel hub
15. Rear wheel spindle nut
16. Rear wheel spindle washer
17. Rear wheel spindle
18. Rear wheel spindle spacer
19. Rear hub cover
20. Rear brake, c/w linings and plates shoe
21. Rear brake shoes lining
22. Rear brake shoes spring
23. Rear brake shoes pin
24. Rear brake shoes washer
25. Shoe pin nut
26. Rear hub cover tie-rod
27. Rear hub cover rod washer
28. Rear hub cover rod nut
29. Tie-rod securing-to-rear fork screw
30. Hub cover securing screw
31. Rear shoes control cam
32. Cam operating lever
33. Lever-to-cam screw
34. Rear brake adjusting rod thumb screw
35. Lever on rear hub cover roller
36. Tie-rod-to-shoe split pin
37. Tie-rod-to-lever washer
38. Rear brake control tie-rod
39. C/W lever spindle
40. Rear brake control lever
41. Rear brake lever-to-spindle screw
42. Rear brake spindle lever
43. Lever to spindle screw
44. Lever securing screw washer
45. Lever securing screw-to-pin nut
46. Pin retaining circlip
47. Central body securing bolt nut
48. Central body bolt washer
49. Central body securing bolt
50. Central body
51. Seal
52. Taper roller bearing housing
53. Taper roller, hub bearing
54. Bearing-spacer washer
55. Washer
56. Hub bearings spacer

FOR MACHINES WITH REAR BRAKE PEDAL ON L/H SIDE:

57. Rear brake lever
58. Spindle c/w lever
59. Rear brake tie-rod

4. Remove the seal ring, bearing housing, taper roller bearing, adjusting washers, and the bearing spacer from the left-hand cover.

5. Remove the seal ring, bearing housing, and taper roller bearing from the right-hand cover.

6. Remove the six central body securing bolts, then separate the body and hub.

Inspection and Repair

BOTH WHEELS

1. Inspect the wheel rims and spokes for damage or an out-of-true condition, and repair or replace them as necessary.

2. Clean all parts in a suitable solvent, except for the brake shoe linings, and blow them dry.

3. Examine the linings and shoes for signs of damage, such as cracks or excessive wear, and replace them as necessary. If the linings are grease impregnated, cracked, or worn beyond their serviceable limit of 2.5 mm (0.984 in.), they must be replaced. Glazing or a slightly greasy surface can be remedied by soaking in gasoline and brushing with a wire brush. When removing glazing, it is not necessary to go deep; go only as deep as is necessary to remove surface glazing.

4. Inspect the brake shoe springs for a collapsed, fatigued, or otherwise damaged condition and replace them as necessary. The front springs, under a load of 46.2 lbs and the rear springs under a load of 132.2 lbs, with a 5% load variation, must extend to 98 mm (3.8583 in.). If measuring devices are not available, compare the springs to a new set and replace them if their condition seems questionable.

5. Examine the brake shoe cams for shiny wear spots, scoring, pitting, or damage to the lobe, stem, or splines and replace them as necessary.

6. Examine the brake shoe pins for scoring or an otherwise damaged condition at both the contact surface and at the threads, and replace them as necessary.

7. Inspect the hub seals for burrs, cracks, stiffness, or damage and replace them as necessary. It's not a bad idea to replace them as a matter of course since you've got them out, but that's up to you.

8. Inspect the roller bearing housings for scoring, wear, or damage, especially to the surface on which the bearing is pressed, and make sure that the contact ends are not damaged. Replace them as necessary.

9. Inspect the roller bearing outer raceway for the inner ring, and the inner raceway for the outer ring, for signs of wear, scoring, pitting or any other damage that might mar the smooth and glossy surface of the races. Balls and rollers must be perfectly smooth all over their surface and their motion within the races must be smooth and free; however DO NOT SPIN DRY BEARINGS. Bearings must be replaced as a complete assembly as repaired bearings will not provide satisfactory operation.

When installing bearings, press only on the ring which is going to be coupled with the housing or shaft, and check to make sure that the bearing will spin freely, with some backlash, after it is installed.

10. Examine the adjusting washers for warpage or damage to their faces and replace them as necessary.

11. Inspect the brake cam actuating levers for damage, especially to the splines, and replace them as necessary.

12. Inspect the brake drums for a smooth surface along the brake swept area. If slightly scored, the area can be cleaned up with emery cloth, but if the scoring is deep, or if the drum is out of round, it should be taken to a qualified machinist to be turned down. On front wheel drums, make sure that the bearing housings are smooth and clean.

13. Examine the rear wheel central body for damage to the teeth and bearing housings and replace it as necessary. The edges of the teeth should be clean and free of chipping or scoring and the housings should be smooth.

14. At this time you may wish to check the front brake cable for signs of wear or damage to either the cable or sheath. If the cable has even one or two frayed strands, it should be replaced.

Assembly

FRONT WHEEL

1. Assemble the taper roller bearing, bearing housing, and seal ring to the right side backing plate.

2. Assemble the bearing distance collar, adjusting washers, taper roller bearing, bearing housing, and seal ring to the left-hand backing plate.

3. Check for excessive end play and alleviate it if necessary by removing one adjusting washer. If the wheel does not rotate freely, it will be necessary to add washers until the desired results are obtained.

4. Mount the brake shoes, cams, shoe pins, levers, and rod to the backing plate and install the assembly. If rod play is excessive, disconnect the rod from the double acting lever, undo the adjusting nut, adjust the fork on the rod enough to just take up the play, then secure the nut and connect the rod fork to the lever by using the pin and cotter pin.

5. Mount the wheel and adjust the front brake. The wheel should spin freely and bearing side play should remain minimal.

REAR WHEEL

1. Secure the central body to the hub using its six mounting nuts, washers, and bolts.

2. Assemble the taper roller bearing, bearing housing, and seal ring to the left side backing plate.

SUSPENSION

Front Forks

DISASSEMBLY

1. Disconnect the clutch and brake cables at the handlebars, remove the clamp screws and caps, and remove the handlebars.

2. Remove the instrument panel mounting screws, disconnect the electrical cables and the speedometer drive, then remove the instrument panel.

Fork drain and filler plugs

3. Remove the speedometer from the instrument panel.

4. Remove the nut and fork filler caps (B) from the top triple clamp plate, then pull the plate using an appropriate wrench and Tool No. 60910500 (labeled "3" in the accompanying illustration) or a suitable substitute puller.

5. Remove the steering stem lock-ring (B) and lock-cap (A) from the top of the steering stem.

6. Remove the pinch bolts which secure the bottom triple clamp to the fork tubes.

7. Either drain the forks now by

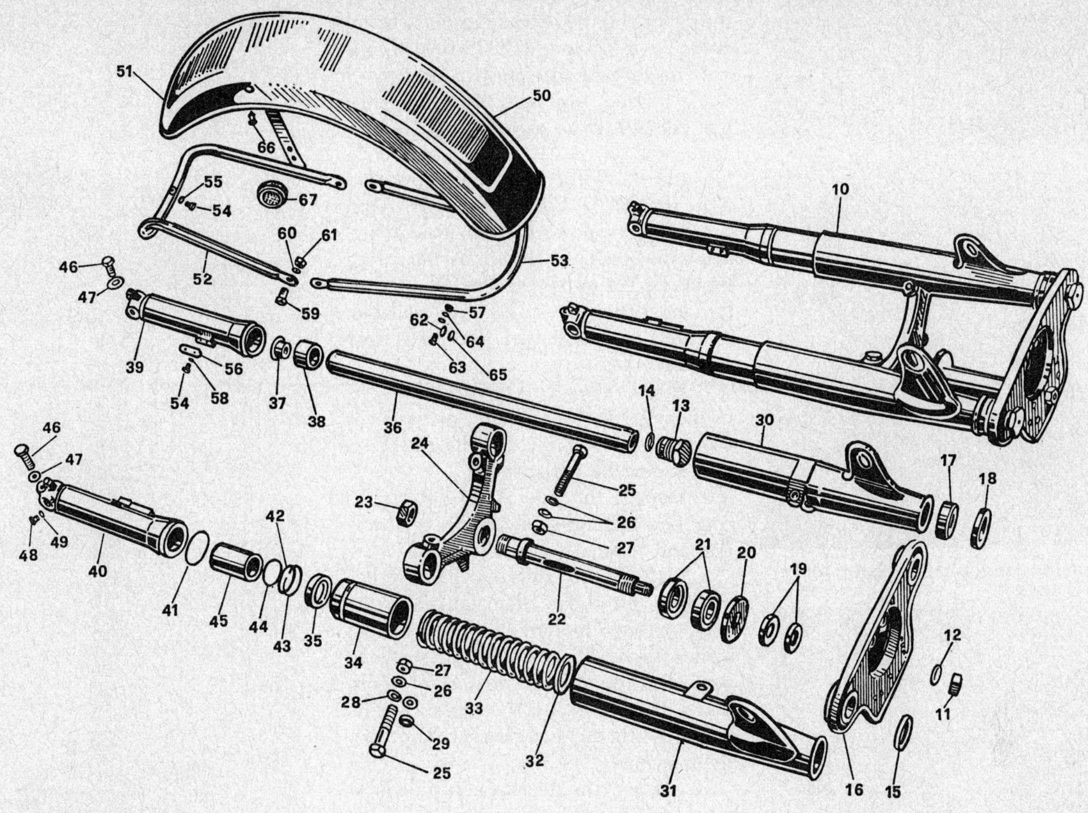

Front end assembly

10. Complete front fork
11. Top linking plate securing nut
12. Top linking plate nut washer
13. Top fork plug
14. Top fork plugs gasket
15. Top fork plugs washer
16. Top linking plate
17. Circlip
18. Headlight bracket cap
19. Bottom yoke lock-ring
20. Steering tube cap
21. Taper roller, steering bearing
22. Bottom yoke steering tube
23. Steering tube-to-bottom yoke nut
24. Bottom yoke
25. Handlebar clamps bolt
26. Clamp bolts-to-bottom yoke washer
27. Clamp bolts-to-bottom yoke nut
28. Front brake cable eyelet
29. Rubber front brake cable guide ring
30. Headlight bracket, r/h
31. Headlight bracket l/h
32. Headlight bracket bottom plate
33. Front fork spring
34. Fork springs housing
35. Seal
36. Fork rod
37. Fork rod bottom for link-retaining lock-ring
38. Bottom fork rod bushing
39. R/H fork cover
40. L/H fork cover
41. Fork cover gasket
42. Adjusting top bush washer 0.1 mm (0.0139 in.)
43. Fork cover circlip
44. Fork cover adjusting 2.0 mm shim (0.078 in.)
    Fork cover adjusting 2.1 mm shim (0.082 in.)
    Fork cover adjusting 2.2 mm shim (0.086 in.)
    Fork cover adjusting 2.3 mm shim (0.090 in.)
    Fork cover adjusting 2.4 mm shim (0.094 in.)
45. Top fork cover bush
46. Handlebar clamp-to-headlight bracket bolt
47. Handlebar clamp-to-headlight bracket bolt washer
48. Oil drain from forks screw
49. Oil drain screw washer
50. Front fender
51. Front fender decal
52. Top front fender stay
53. Bottom front fender stay
54. Stay and center attachment plate screw
55. Stay securing screws washer
56. Center fender securing plate
57. Eyelet securing screw nut
58. Plate securing screws-to-fender washer
59. Front fender-to-fork screw
60. Front fork-to-fender screws washer
61. Front fork-to-fender screws nut
62. Cable guide eyelet
63. Eyelet securing screw
64. Eyelet securing screw spring washer
65. Front brake guiding eyelet rubber ring
66. Front fender plug
67. Front fender amber reflector

removing the drain plugs (A), or pull out the tube and slider assemblies and then invert and drain the oil.

8. Remove the spring housings and springs as an assembly, then remove the headlight bracket bottom plate.

9. Remove the spring housings, then remove the seal ring and rubber ring from the housings.

10. Remove the circlip and adjusting washer, then remove the fork bottom cover and bushing.

11. Remove the bottom slider bushing lock-ring, then extract the bushing.

12. Remove the nut which secures the steering stem from the bottom of the lower triple clamp, then remove the stem.

INSPECTION AND REPAIR

1. Clean all parts in a suitable solvent, then blow them dry.

2. Inspect the fork tubes for signs of warpage, damage, or scoring of the chromed portion which slides inside the bushings. Replace the tube(s) if badly scored or if the threads are stripped or damaged. Using a micrometer or caliper, check the diameter of the tubes at the chromed portion, which must extend 120 mm (4.722 in.), and replace them if worn past their serviceable limit of 34.720–34.695 mm (1.3669–1.3659 in.). Using feeler gauges, check the clearance between the tubes and bushings and replace them if worn past their serviceable limit of 0.040–0.105 mm (0.0015–0.0041 in.) at the top bushing, and 0.020–0.044 mm (0.0007–0.0017 in.) at the bottom bushing.

3. Inspect the top bushings for signs of wear, damage, or scoring which would

Removing the top triple clamp plate

Steering stem lock ring and cap

interfere with the proper operation of the forks, or which could damage the fork tubes, and replace them as necessary. Using inside and outside micrometers, measure the bushings and replace them if worn past their serviceable limits of 34.760–34.800 mm (1.3685–1.370 in.) for the inside diameter, and 40.010–39.971 mm (1.5751–1.5735 in.) for the outside diameter.

4. Inspect the bottom bushings as described above. Their values are 34.700–34.739 mm (1.3661–1.3676 in.) for the inside diameter, and 39.950–39.911 mm (1.5728–1.5712 in.) for the outside diameter.

5. Inspect the fork bottom covers for damage or scoring of their inner surfaces and replace them as necessary. Using an inside micrometer, measure the inside diameter of the cover, then use feeler gauges to measure the clearances between the cover and the top and bottom bushings, and replace the components if worn past their serviceable limits. The inside diameter of the cover should be 40.010–40.050 mm (1.5751–1.5767 in.). The clearance between the cover and the top bushing should be 0–0.079 mm (0–0.10031 in.), and the clearance between the cover and the bottom bushing should be 0.099–0.100 mm (0.0038–0.0039 in.).

6. Inspect the fork springs for signs of wear, fatigue, excessive tilt, or damage and replace them as necessary. A new spring should be 230 ± 15 mm (9.0551 in.), and should be replaced if collapsed more than 3%. With a load of 110 ± 4 lbs, the spring should be 170 mm (6.6929 in.), and with a load of 231 ± 8 lbs, the spring should be 104 mm (4.0945 in.). If a device for measuring load is not available, merely measure the spring free length or compare them to a new set.

7. Inspect the spring housings for wear or damage. If the seal ring or gasket is burred, worn, or has lost its elasticity, they should be replaced.

8. Inspect the filler plug rubber O-rings and seals for wear, cracks, or distortion and replace them as necessary.

9. Inspect the steering head roller bearings for wear, damage, excessive play, or rough motion and replace them as necessary. The bearings must all be perfectly round and devoid of score marks or pitting and the races must be perfectly smooth and glossy. Do not spin the bearings when dry.

10. Inspect the steering adjusting lock-rings for signs of wear or damage, especially to the threads, and replace them as necessary.

11. Inspect the fork neck steering tube and the steering stem for signs of wear, scoring, dings, damage, or anything which could hinder their smooth motion, and replace or repair damaged components as necessary. If there are cracks around the frame neck, they should be immediately attended to by your local dealer or a qualified welder.

ASSEMBLY

1. Install the top and bottom fork cover bushings, then secure them with bushing lock-rings. Use new lock-rings if the old ones are distorted.

2. Install the fork tubes complete with the sliders, then position the adjusting washer in the top portion of the cover and install the circlip in the cover groove.

3. Place the fork cover gasket, cover, and spring housing in position.

4. Carefully press the seal ring into position, then secure the spring housing using Tool No. 12912600 (labeled "11" in the accompanying illustration) or a suitable substitute.

5. Slip the fork spring over the fork tubes and position them in the spring housing; then insert the fork tubes in the bottom triple clamp and headlight bracket using Tool No. 12909500 (labeled "4" in the accompanying illustration), or a suitable substitute, to position them.

6. Install the pinch bolts and secure the headlight bracket, then secure the steering stem to the bottom triple clamp with its nut.

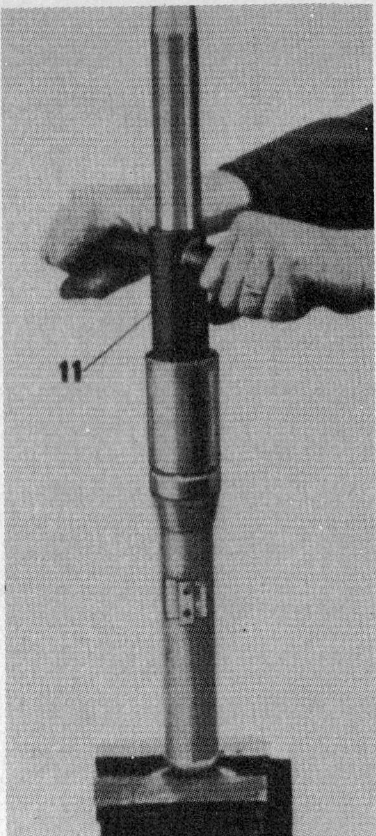

Installing the seal

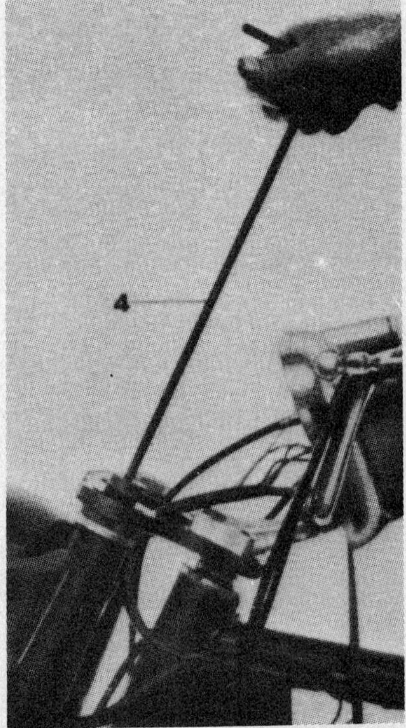

Lining up the fork components with the factory tool

7. Pack the steering head bearings with fresh grease and install them in the frame neck, then slip the steering stem and fork assembly into position so the

stem seats fully inside the neck, and install the steering stem cap.

8. Position the steering stem lock-ring and adjust the steering play as desired. The forks should pivot freely in the fork neck without binding or falling to one side. When the steering is to your satisfaction, fit and secure the lock cap using Tool No. 60910500 or a suitable substitute.

9. Position the rubber rings and caps in the headlight brackets, then position the top triple clamp plate.

10. Install the fork drain plugs and their gaskets, then fill each tube with 5.4 oz (0.160 1) of fork oil. Shell Tellux 33 is the factory recommended lubricant, but substitutes can be made.

11. Position the filler plug seals, washers, and plugs, then fit the top triple clamp plate washer, and the nut which secures the plate, to the steering stem.

12. Mount the handlebar clamps on the top triple clamp plate, install the speedometer drive on the instrument panel, connect the electric cables, and secure the speedometer.

13. Mount the instrument panel on the top triple clamp plate, then install the handlebars and their clamp caps and screws.

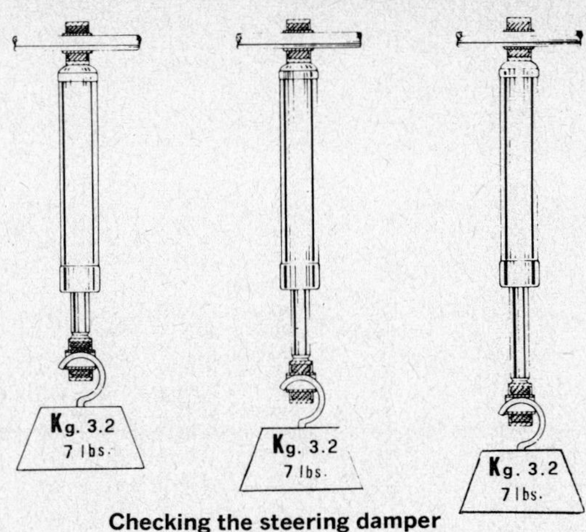

Checking the steering damper

Swing Arm

DISASSEMBLY

1. Remove the rear wheel drive as described in the "Engine and Transmission" chapter.

2. Remove the cap nuts and lock nuts from the fork support spindles, then remove the support spindles.

3. Remove the spacers and sealing rings, then remove the two roller bearings. The bearing outer races can be easily pulled from the swing arm using Tool No. 12904700, (labeled "1" in the accompanying illustration) however a suitable substitute may be used.

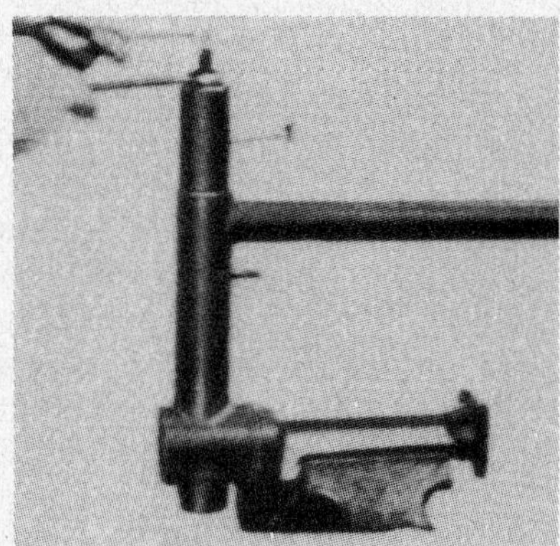
Removing the outer bearing races

INSPECTION AND REPAIR

1. Clean all parts in a suitable solvent, then blow them dry.

2. Inspect the swing arm for signs of fatigue, wear, bends, twist, or cracks, and replace it as necessary. Pay special attention to the condition of the bearing housings and the flange surface which contacts the drive box; these must be smooth and unmarred.

3. Inspect all threaded parts, especially the support spindles, for damage or stripping and replace them as necessary.

4. Inspect the seals for signs of wear, cracks, damage, or loss of elasticity and replace them as necessary. It isn't a bad idea to replace them at this time as a matter of course.

5. Inspect the bearings for wear, damage, excessive play, or rough motion and replace them as necessary. The bearings must all be perfectly round and devoid of score marks or pitting, and the races must be perfectly smooth and glossy. Do not spin the bearings when dry.

Securing the swing arm

ASSEMBLY

1. Carefully press the lubricated bearings into their housings, then press in the two sealing rings.

2. Position the spacers while slipping the swing arm into position in the frame.

3. Insert the support spindles then temporarily secure the assembly with the lock nuts.

4. Tighten the lock nuts evenly using Tool No. 12903000 (labeled "13" in the accompanying illustration), or a suitable substitute, and an appropriate wrench to hold the locknuts. The fork should be able to swing freely when secured.

5. Complete the assembly in the reverse order of disassembly.

Steering Damper (V850)

The steering damper is a non-repairable item which must be replaced, if defective. The damper unit should be periodically checked for efficiency, and should be considered suspect if high speed wobbling develops. Check the damper in the following manner:

1. Hang the damper by it's fixed eyehole as depicted in the accompanying illustration.

2. Attach a weight of 7 lbs to the pushrod eyehole.

3. Pull the rod into various positions and observe whether or not the weight is sufficient to move the rod. If it does move, the dampening ability of the unit is defective and the unit should be replaced. It is particularly important to check the unit with the rod withdrawn halfway out of the damper body.

NORTON INDEX

MODEL IDENTIFICATION

Norton Atlas 750

N15CS: Norton engine and Matchless frame

P-11

Commando Fastback (1968)

Commando Roadster

All Norton models covered in this section feature a 750cc or 828cc vertical twin engine with separate four-speed gearbox. Three different executions (Commando, Atlas, Scramblers) differ in frame design and running equipment, although engine procedures are similar. Engine specifications, however, are different for different models.

On Commando models, the engine is tilted slightly forward and is mounted with Norton's Isolastic System. On other models, the engine is rigidly mounted to the frame, and the cylinders are vertical.

Engine numbers on all models are stamped on the left side of the crankcase just below the cylinder flange.

Frame numbers on the pre-Commando models are found on the left side of the machine, on the lower frame gussets. On the Commando, they are stamped on the left side of the steering head lug. The engine and frame numbers should match.

The transmission has its own serial number stamped on the top of the shell.

GENERAL SPECIFICATIONS

	Commando 850	Commando 750 (Standard)	Commando 750 (Combat)	Atlas	G15CS N15CS	P-11
DIMENSIONS						
Net Weight (lbs)	418-430	390	390	410	N.A.	N.A.
Ground Clearance (in.)	6	6	6	6	N.A.	N.A.
Wheelbase (in.)	57	$56^3/_4$	$56^3/_4$	N.A.	N.A.	N.A.
Overall Length (in.)	88	$87^1/_2$	$87^1/_2$	N.A.	N.A.	N.A.
Overall Width (in.)	26	26	26	26	26	26
Seat Height (in.)	31	31	31	N.A.	N.A.	N.A.
ENGINE						
Displacement (cc)	828	745	745	745	745	745
Bore x Stroke (mm)	77 x 89	73 x 89	73 x 89	73 x 89	73 x 89	73 x 89
Compression Ratio	8.5 : 1	8.9 : 1	10 : 1	7.5 : 1	7.5 : 1	7.5 : 1
Carburetor (Amal)	932	930	932	389 Monobloc or 930	389 Monobloc	930
Ignition	Battery and coil	Battery and coil	Battery and coil	Magneto	Magneto	Battery and coil
TRANSMISSION						
Clutch Type	Diaphragm, multi-plate	Diaphragm multi-plate	Diaphragm, multi-plate	Dry-type, multi-plate	Dry-type, multi-plate	Dry-type, multi-plate
Gear Ratios (:1)						
First	11.20	12.40	12.4	11.6	12.65	12.65
Second	7.45	8.25	8.25	7.70	8.40	8.40
Third	5.30	5.90	5.90	5.52	6.03	6.03
Fourth	4.38	4.84	4.84	4.53	4.96	4.96
CHAINS						
Rear (in.)	$^5/_8$ x $^3/_8$ (99 pitches)	$^5/_8$ x $^3/_8$ (98 pitches)	$^5/_8$ x $^3/_8$ (98 pitches)	$^5/_8$ x $^1/_4$ (97 pitches)	$^5/_8$ x 0.380 (97 pitches)	$^5/_8$ x 0.380 (97 pitches)
Primary (in.)	$^3/_8$ (triple row) (92 pitches)	$^3/_8$ (triple row) (92 pitches)	$^3/_8$ (triple row) (92 pitches)	$^1/_2$ x 0.305 (76 pitches)	$^1/_2$ x 0.305 (76 pitches)	$^1/_2$ x 0.305 (76 pitches)
Camshaft (in.)	$^3/_8$ x 0.225 (38 pitches)	$^3/_8$ x 0.225 (38 pitches)	$^3/_8$ x 0.225 (38 pitches)	$^3/_8$ x 0.225 (38 pitches)	$^3/_8$ x 0.225 (38 pitches)	$^3/_8$ x 0.225 (38 pitches)
Magneto (in.)	——	——	——	$^3/_8$ x $^5/_{32}$ (42 pitches)	$^3/_8$ x $^5/_{32}$ (42 pitches)	——
CHASSIS						
Front Suspension	Rod damper hydraulic forks on all					
Rear Suspension	Swing arm and hydraulic damped shock absorbers on all					
Tire Size						
Front	4.10 x 19	4.10 x 19	4.10 x 19	3.25 x 19	3.25 x 19	3.25 x 19
Rear	4.10 x 19	4.10 x 19	4.10 x 19	4.00 x 18	4.00 x 18	4.00 x 18
ELECTRICAL						
System Voltage	12	12	12	12	12	12
Generator	Alternator on all					

TUNE-UP AND MAINTENANCE

TUNE-UP OPERATIONS

Valve Tappet Adjustment

ALL MODELS

1. Remove the gas tank.
2. Remove the spark plugs, the two exhaust rocker covers, and the intake rocker cover.
3. Kick the engine over with the kick-starter until the left side intake valve is fully open (the rocker arm will be depressed). The right intake valve will be closed at this point. Check the clearance with a feeler gauge. It should be 0.006 in. for all models except Combat-equipped Commandos where it is 0.008 in.

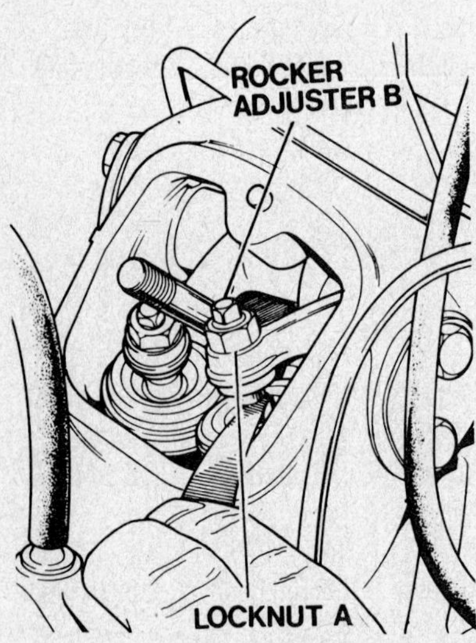

Adjusting valve clearance

4. Adjust, if necessary, by loosening the locknut a few turns and turning down the adjuster until it just touches the feeler gauge blade.
5. Hold the adjuster in position and tighten the locknut. Recheck the clearance.
6. Turn the engine over again until the right intake valve is open, then adjust the left intake valve. Repeat the same procedure for the exhaust valves. Proper exhaust valve clearance is 0.008 in. for all engines except the Combat (0.010 in.).

Contact Breaker Points

MAGNETO IGNITION

The contact breaker points are located beneath the magneto cover on the left side of the machine.

Removal

1. Loosen the kill-button wire knurled nut at the magneto. This is attached to the post in the center of the magneto cover.
2. Unscrew the cover and place it aside.
3. Loosen the central hex-head securing screw until it is clear of its threads, but is still in the center of the contact breaker. It can be used to "break" the points off their tapered shaft by gently levering sideways with the fingers.
4. When the points have been taken off the shaft, remove them completely.

Installation

Installation is the reverse of the removal procedure. Clean the new points with a non-oily solvent to remove the preservative coating. Do not forget to replace the fiber washers on the pivot post. Refer to the illustration for correct position of various parts. Also, apply a drop of oil to the post for lubrication. Note that the points assembly has a key which must fit in its slot. Set the gap upon installation. The ignition timing need not be readjusted.

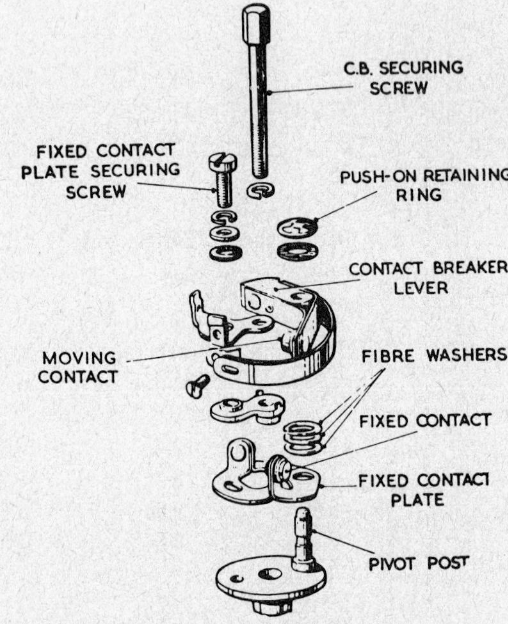

Lucas K2F magneto breaker points

Gap Adjustment

1. Turn the engine over slowly until the points are fully open. The points will be open at two positions on the cam ring. These points can be determined by looking at the cam ring itself. There are two "thick" areas. The points will open when the contact breaker lever heel passes over these points which are about 6 o'clock and 12 o'clock.

Gap adjustment: magneto models

2. Loosen the fixed contact plate securing screw, then use a screwdriver, as shown, to move the fixed contact plate to the correct gap. Check the gap with the appropriate feeler gauge. It should be 0.012–0.015 in.
3. Tighten the fixed contact plate securing screw and recheck the gap.

CAPACITOR IGNITION

Capacitor ignition systems (or battery and coil ignition) are found on 1967 models as well as on Commandos. The earliest machines equipped with this system had the ignition points located in a canister behind the cylinder barrels and attached to the timing case. The first machines utilized dual points with the condensers mounted on the breaker plate. This setup was soon replaced with yet another system: Lucas 6CA dual points, individually mounted on the breaker plate, the

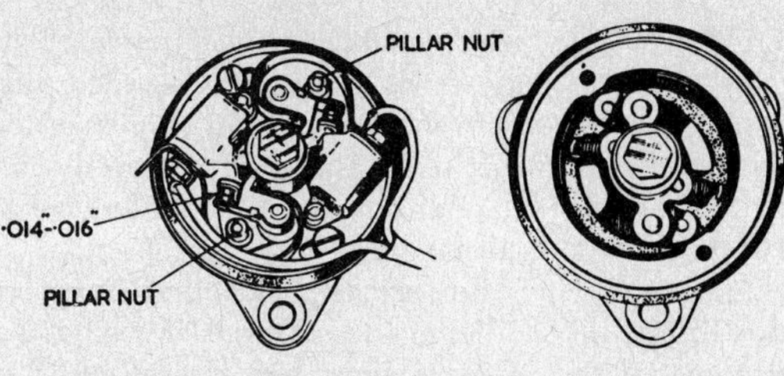

Early battery-and-coil ignition breaker points and advance mechanism

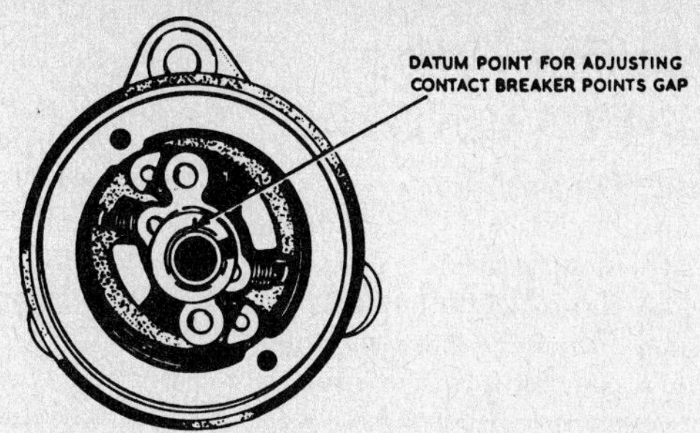

Slash mark on point cam

condensers being remotely positioned. The points on this later system allow each cylinder to be timed separately. This system was used on Commando models also up to engine No. 131257, when the points were relocated to the timing case. Aside from the new location, the points assembly is the same. The procedures for each system are as follows:

Early 1967 Models

REMOVAL

1. Remove the ignition point cover.
2. If desired, the points assembly may be removed as a unit to reveal the automatic timing advance mechanism. Disconnect the two wires from the snap connectors; remove the two screws which secure the breaker plate and remove the plate.
3. If replacement of the points only is desired, remove the two wires from the snap connectors, release the nut which holds the spring of each breaker point to its condensor, being careful of the insulating washers and their positions.
4. Remove the pillar nut which holds each breaker point onto the plate and take away the points.

INSTALLATION

Installation is the reverse of the removal procedure. Be sure that all insulating washers are in their proper positions. Apply a drop of oil to the pivot posts.

NOTE: *When refitting the contact breakers, assure that the wires are connected correctly. The yellow-black wire attached to the top contact breaker goes to the coil mounted on the left rear frame down tube. Also, the high tension lead from this coil goes to the drive side cylinder.*

When refitting the contact breaker cover, be sure that the two insulated strips for each condenser are in position.

GAP ADJUSTMENT

1. Turn the engine over until one of the breaker points is fully open.
2. Loosen the pillar nut which secures the breaker point fixed plate.
3. Use a screw driver to adjust the gap by prying between the fixed plate and the contact breaker housing.
4. Using a feeler gauge, set the gap for each breaker point at 0.014–0.016 in.
5. Tighten the pillar nut and recheck the gap.

Late 1967 Models and Commando to Engine No. 131257

These models utilize the Lucas 6CA points assembly, located behind the cylinders.

REMOVAL

1. Remove the points cover.
2. If desired, the breaker points assembly may be removed as a unit to reveal the automatic timing advance mechanism by removing the two large screws which secure the breaker assembly plate.
3. To remove the points themselves, remove the hexagon nut which secures the wire and the contact breaker spring.
4. Remove the locking screw (D) and take off the breaker.

INSTALLATION

Installation is the reverse of the removal procedure. Refer to the illustration to assure that the insulating washers and insulator sleeve are correctly positioned. Smear the pivot post with a bit of grease before refitting. Clean new points with a solvent to remove the preservative coating.

GAP ADJUSTMENT

1. Turn the engine over until the slash mark on the point cam aligns with the nylon heel of one of the breaker points.
2. Check the gap with the appropriate feeler gauge. It should be 0.014–0.016 in.
3. If adjustment is necessary, loosen the locking screw (D) and turn the eccentric screw (C) until the proper gap is attained.
4. Tighten the locking screw and recheck the gap.

Commando From Engine No. 131258

The points are located beneath the cover on the timing case. This is also a 6CA breaker set and the procedure for removal replacement, and adjustment is exactly the same as described in the preceding section.

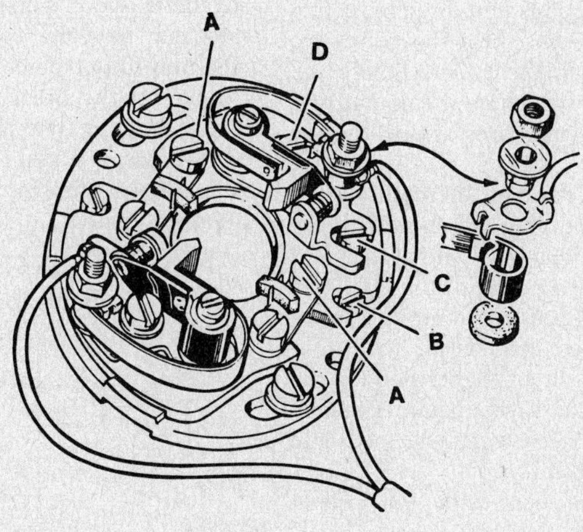

6CA points assembly

Ignition Timing

MAGNETO IGNITION

Adjusting Timing

1. Remove the left and right footpegs and the tachometer drive.
2. Remove the magneto points cover after loosening the kill button wire nut.
3. Place a pan beneath the primary chaincase cover, and remove the cover.
4. Take out all of the screws which secure the timing cover. Place a receptacle for oil beneath the timing cover and pull it off, being careful that the conical oil seal fitted the oil pump nipple is not misplaced.

Oil will dribble out of the drilling in the crankcase. It can be blocked off by inserting one of the cover screws.

5. Remove the spark plugs.
6. Remove the alternator rotor nut and affix a timing disc to the crankshaft.
7. The pistons must be set at top dead center. Kick the engine over slowly until compression is felt in one of the cylinders. Place a thin stick into that spark plug hole and turn the engine over using a wrench on the rotor nut until the piston's highest point has been ascertained. Work the pistons up and down several times until you are sure that you have it right.
8. Attach a stiff wire anywhere that is convenient so that it points to "zero" on the timing disc.
9. Loosen the self-extracting bolt on the timing advance mechanism until the points can be turned freely.
10. Using a small block of wood, or suitable substitute, lock the bob weights of the timing advance mechanism in the "full advance" position.
11. Turn the rotor nut clockwise until the pointer indicates 32° on the timing wheel.
12. Place a very thin piece of paper between the points and, tugging gently at the paper, assure that the points are closed, trapping the paper. Rotate the points with a wrench on the center nut, maintaining gentle pressure on the paper.
13. The very instant the points begin to separate, the plug will fire. With the small wrench, hold the points at the point that the paper slips out of the points.
14. Turn the self-extracting bolt on the timing advance mechanism with your hand until it is finger tight, then tap the bolt head lightly with a hammer so that the advance mechanism will lock onto the tapered shaft.

Tighten the bolt with the proper wrench.

15. Turn the engine over once or twice, then recheck the timing.

NOTE: *The correct amount of timing advance is 32° of crankshaft rotation which is equivalent to 0.343 in. (8.69 mm) of piston travel. It is possible to use this measurement if the head has been removed, but it would be inaccurate if an attempt is made to measure piston travel through the plug holes due to their angle.*

Also, the point of separation for the ignition points cannot be determined with a test light due to the characteristics of the magneto. A special ohmmeter, however, can be used if one is available.

CAPACITOR IGNITION

Early 1967 Models

CHECKING TIMING

1. Remove the left footpeg, and primary chain cover, placing a pan beneath it to catch the oil.
2. Remove the spark plugs and the ignition points cover.
3. Fit a timing disc onto the crankshaft, and place the pistons at top dead center. The left cylinder should be on the firing stroke, as indicated by compression in that cylinder as the piston approaches top dead center.
4. The timing, when fully advanced, is 32°. The advance mechanism is behind the points and it is therefore easier to check the timing in the unadvanced position. This is fine on machines which have not covered a large number of miles. In this case, rotate the crankshaft clockwise a few degrees past 8° as indicated on the timing wheel, then turn it counterclockwise. When the pointer indicates 8°, the points should just be beginning to open. Verify this by using a piece of paper between the points as described in the previous section.

For machines with this system which have covered a large number of miles, the timing should be checked in the full advance position since the advance unit stops may be worn. To lock the advance unit into full advance position, remove the bolt of the breaker cam and use a screwdriver to turn the cam clockwise until it stops. Using this method, the points should start to open at 32° before top dead center.

ADJUSTING TIMING

To set the timing, proceed as outlined above. Loosen the two securing screws which hold the contact breaker plate and move the plate in the needed direction until the points begin to open at the correct time. The plate is moved clockwise to retard the timing, counterclockwise to advance it.

Be sure to check the timing on the other cylinder as well. If there is a difference greater than 1° between the two, position the breaker plate so as to split the difference.

Late 1967 Models and Commando to Engine No. 131257

CHECKING TIMING

1. Remove the primary chain cover after taking off the left side footpeg and the exhaust pipe, if necessary. Catch the oil in a suitable container.
2. Remove the ignition points cover and the spark plugs.
3. Remove the alternator rotor bolt and fit a degree wheel.
4. Place your finger over the right spark plug hole and kick the engine over until compression is felt in the cylinder.
5. Insert a short drinking straw or a swizzle stick into the plug hole and continue turning the engine over with a wrench on the rotor nut until top dead center has been established.
6. Remove the center bolt of the contact breaker cam and find a washer with a hole large enough to fit over the cam post and bear on the cam itself. Refer to the washer illustrated. Replace the bolt and this washer, turn the cam clockwise to the full advance position, and tighten the bolt. This should lock the cam in the advanced position.
7. Using a piece of wire as a pointer, position it anywhere that is convenient so that it indicates "zero" on the timing disc.

If you have placed the right cylinder piston at TDC on the compression stroke, you will be working with the top set of points. The spark plug will fire at exactly the moment when these points begin to open. There are two methods of determining this point. A test light, connected as shown in the accompanying illustration, is probably the best method. One clip is connected to a ground anywhere on the engine, while the other is connected to the point terminal.

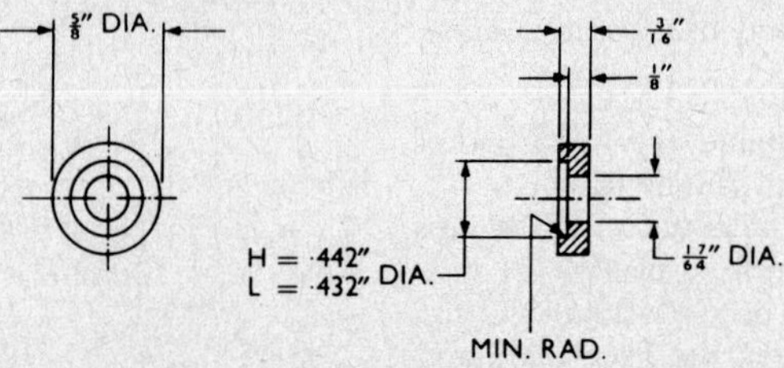

Lock washer for timing advance unit

The instant of points separation can also be found using a very thin piece of paper (cigarette paper is suitable). Placed between the points when they are closed and maintaining a very gently pressure

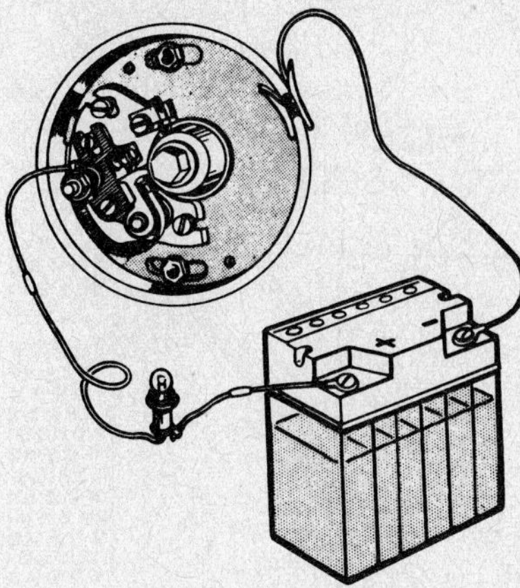

A simple timing light

on the paper as the engine is rotated, the paper will slip out as the points open.

8. Rotate the crankshaft backward by turning the rotor nut clockwise several degrees past the normal timing advance as indicated by the degree wheel. This will be either 32° or 28° depending on the model. Turn the nut to about 40° before TDC to assure that the points are closed.

9. Slowly turn the nut counterclockwise until the timing wheel indicates the correct reading. At this very point the test light bulb should go out, or the paper should slip out of the points.

10. Repeat this procedure for the left cylinder.

ADJUSTING TIMING

If the points do not begin to open at the correct time, refer to the illustration of the 6CA points assembly.

1. Loosen the two securing screws (A) and turn the brass eccentric screw (B) until the points open.

2. If the correct timing cannot be attained in this manner, set the individual contact breaker at about the middle of its adjustment range using screw (B), then tighten the securing screws.

3. Loosen the large screws which hold the contact breaker plate to the housing and rotate the entire plate until the points begin to open.

4. Secure the two screws. Turn the engine over 360° and adjust the other points set as previously described. It should not be necessary to move the entire breaker plate again, only the individual point set.

Commando Models After Engine No. 131257

These machines have the points assembly mounted in the timing case on the right side of the camshaft and are fitted with a timing mark on the rotor and an indicator plate beneath a cap at the front of the primary chain cover. The system may be checked for proper timing either with the engine running or at a standstill.

CHECKING TIMING

1. Remove the points cover and the inspection plug from the primary chaincase.

2. Hook up a strobe light in accordance with the manufacturer's recommendations.

3. Start the engine and run it at 2,000 rpm so that the timing is fully advanced. The mark on the rotor should register with the 28° mark on the indicator plate. (Each line indicates two degrees.)

4. If no strobe light is available, the engine can be checked at rest; Remove the points cover and the inspection cap on the primary chaincase.

5. Remove the spark plugs. Remove the intake valve rocker cover; Rotate the engine until the drive side (left) intake rocker opens and closes. This will place the drive side cylinder on the firing stroke.

6. Remove the center bolt of the contact breaker cam. With a washer which has a hole large enough to clear the cam post and bear on the cam itself, replace the bolt, turn the breaker cam until it is in the full advance position, and then tighten the bolt.

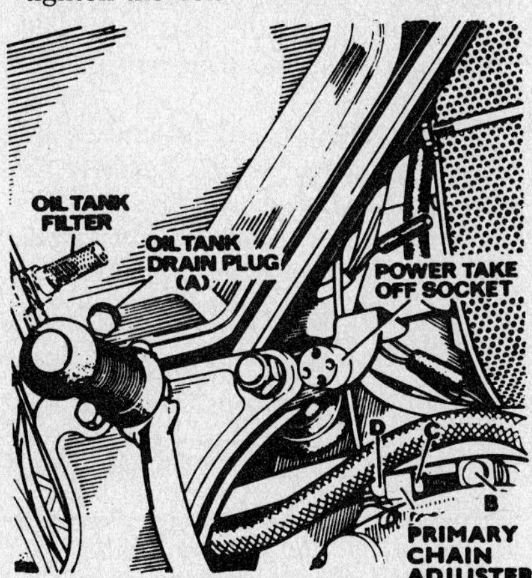

Oil tank drain plug (Commando)

7. Connect a test light to ground and to the spring of the LEFT contact breaker and rotate the engine until the indicator plate on the primary chaincase reads 28°. The test light bulb should blink off at this point as the points separate.

NOTE: *A thin piece of paper can also be used to determine when the points open. For more information on this and the test light construction, see the previous section.*

8. Repeat the procedure to check the timing for the right cylinder.

ADJUSTING TIMING

1. Proceed as above. If the points do not open at the correct time, refer to the illustration of the Lucas 6CA ignition points earlier in this section.

2. Loosen the securing screws (A) and turn the brass eccentric adjusting screw (B) until the points open at the proper time. Tighten the screws.

3. Rotate the engine 360° and repeat the procedure for the other cylinder.

4. Be sure to remove the breaker cam bolt and the oversized washer, replace the standard washer, and tighten the bolt. Make sure that the advance mechanism works freely.

IGNITION TIMING- WHEN TIMING HAS BEEN LOST

1. If, for any reason, the breaker cam assembly has been removed from its shaft (and this applies to all models equipped with the 6CA points system), it is necessary to align it in approximately the correct position before timing can be accomplished.

2. Refering to timing information previously given, locate the drive side (left) cylinder on its compression stroke, and palce the piston at 28° before TDC.

3. Place the breaker cam assembly onto its shaft so that the bobweight pivots of the automatic timing advance mechanism line up with the point assembly cover screw holes (see illustration). The slot on the cam face (not the timing slash mark, but the slot) will be at approximately 9 o'clock.

4. Set the ignition timing as previously described.

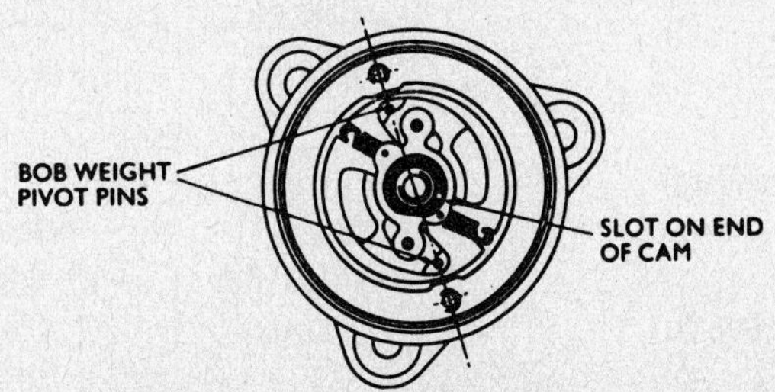

Correct location of timing advance unit

Carburetor Adjustments

IDLE SPEED AND MIXTURE

1. Warm the engine thoroughly.
2. Turn in the throttle stop screws so that the idle speed is slightly higher than normal.
3. Remove one of the spark plug leads. If the engine dies, turn in the throttle stop screw on the cylinder you want to fire until the engine will run on one cylinder.
4. Turn the pilot air screw in or out until the exhaust pulse from the single cylinder is smooth and even.
5. Reconnect the spark plug lead which was removed, disconnect the lead for the cylinder just tuned, and repeat the procedure.
6. Connecting both leads will now raise the idle to a very high level. Back down each throttle stop screw in small, even increments until the desired idle speed is reached.

MULTIPLE CARBURETOR SYNCHRONIZATION

1. Remove the air cleaner assembly.
2. Twist the throttle fully open to lift up the slides.
3. Position a mirror behind the carburetors or reach into the carburetor bores with the thumb and index finger of one hand.
4. Slowly close the throttle and watch, or feel, the slides as they are being lowered; they should enter their respective bores simultaneously.
5. If the slide positions are unequal, raise or lower one to match the other by turning the adjuster at the top of the carburetor.
6. Another check is to place a finger on each carburetor slide when the throttle is fully closed, then move the twist grip very slightly. Both slides should begin to lift at the same time. Adjust as described above if necessary.

THROTTLE CABLE ADJUSTMENT

Adjust the long cable so that there is about 2mm of freeplay before actuation.

Adjust the short cables so that there is as close to zero freeplay as possible. Check carburetor synchronization as previously described.

After setting the freeplay at each cable, start and warm up the engine. Turn the handlebars from side to side and notice any variation in rpm. If a variation occurs, one of the cables is either incorrectly adjusted (not enough freeplay) or is binding somehwere along its routing.

MAINTENANCE ITEMS

Oil Changes and Lubrication

ENGINE OIL

1. Let the engine run until it is warm, then remove the seat (if necessary as on Commando models) and the right side cover (if fitted) to gain access to the tank filler cap and the drain plug, respectively.

2. Drain the warm oil out into a suitable receptacle. On the 1970 Roadster, the filter junction bolt must be removed.

3. Remove the crankcase sump drain plug and allow the sump to drain completely; There should only be a pint or so of oil in the sump.

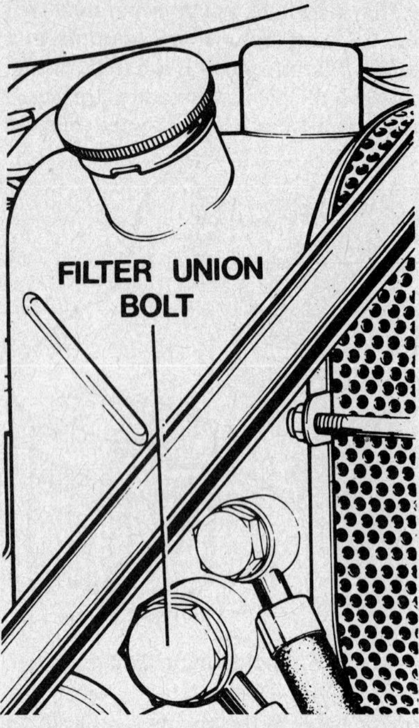

Roadster "S" tank oil filter bolt (1970)

On early 1973 Commando 750 models, only a small drain plug is fitted to the sump. On the 850 Commando, a large plug with filter is fitted along with a smaller magnetic plug. This small plug should be removed and cleaned when the oil is changed.

4. Clean the sump filter by removing the spring clip (this can be done by hand), taking out the washer, and pulling out the filter mesh.
5. Wash the filter thoroughly in a suitable solvent to remove all impurities trapped in it. Also wash out the plug itself checking closely for metal particles.
6. Reassemble the filter in the plug and replace. Tighten the plug firmly.

Commando only:

TUNE-UP SPECIFICATIONS

	Magneto Ignition	Capacitor Ignition (pre-Commando)	Commando (Standard)	Commando (Combat)
Carburetion	Refer to "Fuel System" for standard carburetor settings			
Valve Tappet Clearance (cold)				
Intake (in.)	0.006	0.006	0.006	0.008
Exhaust (in.)	0.008	0.008	0.008	0.010
Ignition				
Spark Plug (standard)				
Champion	N5	N5	N6Y-N7Y	N7Y
Plug Gap (in.)	0.018-0.022	0.023-0.028	0.023-0.028	0.023-0.028
Breaker Point Gap (in.)	0.012-0.015	0.014-0.016	0.014-0.016	0.014-0.016
Ignition Timing (full advance) BTDC	32°	32°	28°	28°

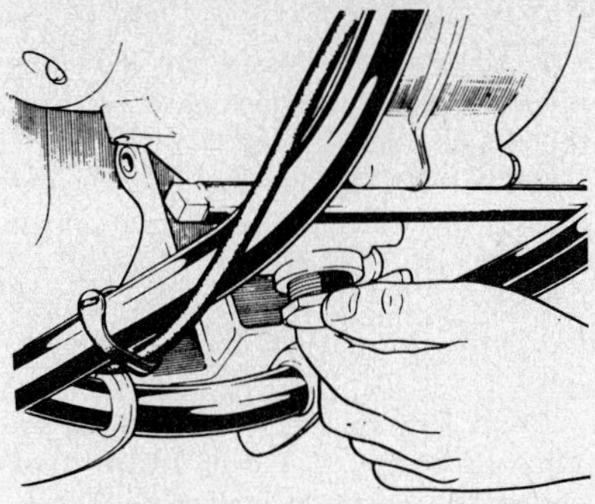

Removing the crankcase sump drain plug

7. Remove the oil feed line at the tank by loosening the securing nut. Remove the filter (held by a circlip) and clean it as for the sump filter. Let the filter dry before refitting it.

On some 1973 Commando 750s, and on the 850 Commando, an automotive-type screw-on cartridge oil filter is fitted to the oil return line, and is located behind the gearbox. This filter should be removed and replaced about every other oil change.

Pre-Commando:

For the other models, the factory did not recommend removing the filter on the oil feed pipe as just described for the Commando for fear of causing a leak at this spot by breaking the seal. Instead, the recommended procedure was to remove the oil tank completely and wash it out with kerosene or another suitable solvent.

a. Take off the metal oil pipe junction at the engine by removing the single fastening bolt.

b. Remove all other hose connections to the oil tank such as the crankcase breather, tank breather, etc.

c. Remove the three or four bolts which hold the oil tank to the frame (depending on the model) and remove the tank.

d. Flush the tank with the solvent several times to assure a complete cleansing job. Let the tank drain and dry thoroughly before refitting.

It is not necessary or recommended to perform this operation at every oil change. It should be done occasionally though, and for certain if the engine has just been rebuilt.

Although this procedure should not be necessary for the Commando under normal conditions, the procedure is as follows:

a. Remove the seat and sidecovers from both sides of the machine.

b. Drain the oil as described above.

c. Take off the chain oiler pipe at the point where it enters the felt cartridge by compressing the spring clip and pulling the pipe away. Also remove the oil tank breather and crankcase breather pipes.

d. Unscrew the front and rear oil tank rubber mountings and remove the tank by lifting it to clear the bottom grommet and taking the bottom of the tank out of the frame first;

e. Reassembly is the reverse of the above procedure.

8. Occasionally check the filter in the oil pressure relief valve. To remove the valve, it may be necessary to take out the rocker oil feed banjo bolt immediately below it.

9. Refill the oil tank with the correct amount and grade of oil. Start the engine and let it run for three minutes; Then shut it off and let it sit for another two minutes. Recheck the oil level and fill it up as necessary.

GEARBOX

1. Remove the clutch lever inspection cap on the outer cover.

2. Remove the drain plug at the bottom rear of the gearbox and allow the oil to drain out. Replace the drain plug and tighten it firmly, but avoid damaging the fiber washer.

3. Using a small funnel or other suitable device, add oil through the inspection cap. Add the oil slowly, as it is quite thick and must drain through a drilling in the outer cover to get to the gear compartment. When you have added the correct amount of oil (Commando: 1.2 pints; other models: 1 pint), let the oil sit for a minute to ensure that the level is equal in both the inner and outer compartments then remove the level plug. Oil level should be even with the plug hole.

4. Replace the level plug and the inspection cap.

The gearbox oil should be changed every 5,000 miles.

PRIMARY CHAINCASE

1. Remove the left-side footpeg.

2. Place a long metal tray or suitable substitute beneath the chaincase, unscrew the central fixing bolt, or the screws around the chaincase cover as on some models, and pull off the chaincase cover just enough to break the joint and let the oil escape.

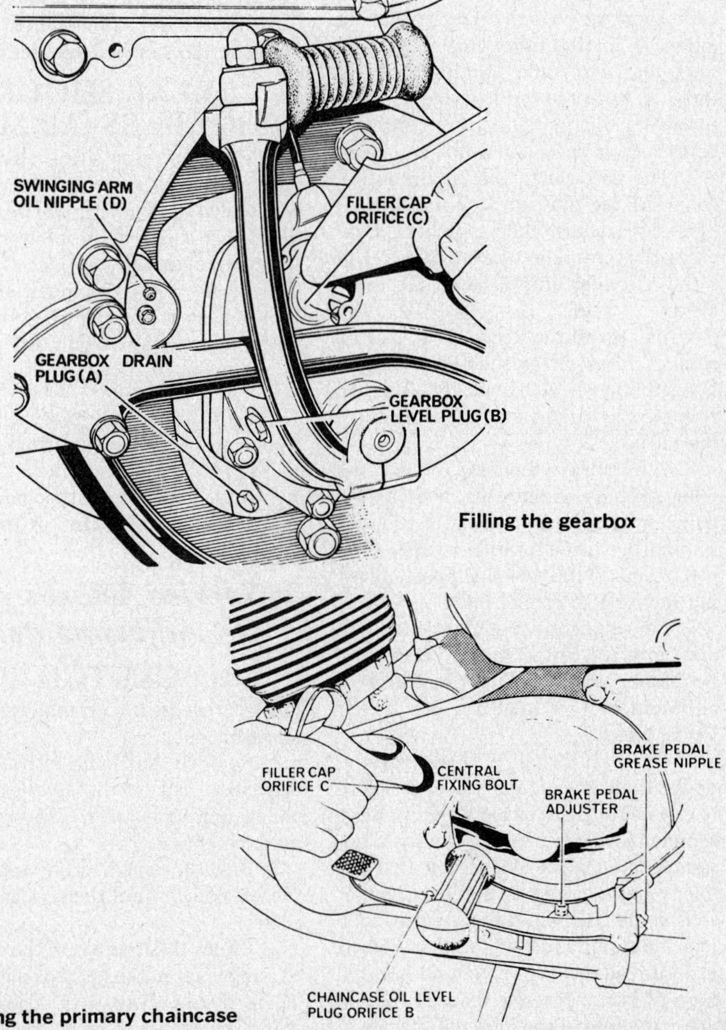

Filling the gearbox

Filling the primary chaincase

3. Let the cover sit for a moment until as much of the oil as possible has drained out, then remove the cover.

4. Wash out the cover with kerosene or another suitable solvent.

5. Replace the cover, remove the chain inspection cap, and add the correct amount and grade of oil with the aid of a small funnel. Check the oil level as before.

Primary chaincase oil should be changed every 3,500 miles. The primary chaincase for the Commando should be filled with 7 oz of oil, while on the other models, the correct amount is 4.5 oz.

Use the same type and grade of oil recommended for the engine in the primary chaincase. The grades, capacities, and changing intervals for all components are given at the end of this section.

FRONT FORKS

The oil should be changed every 5,000 miles (Commando) or 10,000 miles (pre-Commando).

1. Remove the drain screw at the bottom of one fork leg. Work the forks up and down to expel all of the oil.

2. Allow the oil to drain for several minutes. Drain the other fork leg in the same manner. While draining the right fork leg, have the forks turned as far as possible to the right; fork the left fork leg, turn the forks as far as possible to the left.

3. The large filler plug at the top of each fork leg must now be removed. If necessary, remove the handlebars for increased accessibility to the plugs. Unscrew the filler until it clears the triple clamp.

4. Pull up on the front wheel, placing a block of wood or suitable substitute beneath the wheel to hold it up. This will result in the springs and damper rods rising in the fork tubes.

5. Using two wrenches, remove the filler plug by unscrewing it from the damper rod. Hold the damper rod lock nut in place while turning the filler plug.

6. Remove the wheel support, allowing the forks to extend fully.

7. Pour the correct amount of oil into each fork leg. For Commandos this will be 5.5 oz, while the Atlas requires 5 oz, and Scrambler models 6.5 oz due to their longer fork tubes.

7. Give all the oil a chance to run down, then support the wheel as before to expose the damper rod locknuts. Reassemble in the reverse order of the disassembly procedure. Be certain that the filler plugs are screwed onto the damper rods as far as their threads allow, then lock the damper rod nuts against them. A little thread locking compound is useful here to insure that the damper rods do not come free of the filler plugs while in operation.

STEERING HEAD BEARINGS

Late Model Commando

If the machine does not have a large chrome hexagon nut at the top of the steering stem, it is the latest design. The fork bearings are therefore ball journal type, but pre-packed with grease at the factory which lasts for the life of the motorcycle. These bearings need neither lubrication nor adjustment of any kind.

All Other Models

No attention need be paid for at least 20,000 miles. If frequent steering head adjustments have been necessary, chances are the bearings will have to be replaced. If desired, lubricate the bearings by:

1. Removing the front forks and steering head as described in the "chassis" section.

2. Removing the bearings and cupped rings, cleaning, and repacking with an approved brand of grease after checking the bearings for any signs of wear, cracking, or pitting.

3. Adjustment procedures can be found in the "chassis" section.

REAR SHOCK ABSORBERS (All Models)

The Girling rear shock absorbers, as used on Norton Twins, are maintenance-free sealed units and cannot be disassembled. If a shock absorber weeps oil, it must be replaced.

On some early machines, the upper part of the spring might be greased if it grates against the metal dust cover.

WHEEL BEARINGS

The maintenance interval for both front and rear wheel bearings is 10,000 miles, at which time they should be removed, cleaned, inspected, packed with the approved brand of grease.

Service Checks and Adjustments

CLUTCH

The procedure is essentially the same for all models,

1. Remove the clutch activating lever inspection cap on the gearbox and the clutch adjusting screw cap on the primary chaincase.

2. Run the clutch cable adjusters all the way down until there is slack in the cable.

3. Check the freeplay of the clutch activating lever in the gearbox outer cover. There should about ⅛ in. of free movement before the lever engages the clutch.

4. Adjust, if necessary, by loosening the locknut on the adjusting screw. Back the nut off a few turns.

5. Loosen the adjusting screw a few turns until you note the freeplay in the lever.

6. Screw in the adjusting screw until the screw just touches the clutch pushrod.

7. On Commando models, back the adjusting screw off 1/3 of a turn, then tighten the locknut. On all other models, back the screw off 1/2 to 2/3 of a turn, then tighten the locknut.

8. Make sure that the activating lever has the required freeplay. Take up the extra cable slack with the cable adjusters at the gearbox or the handlebar. There should be about ⅛ in. of free movement in the handlebar lever before it engages the clutch for pre-Commando models. On the Commando, the cable play is measured at the gearbox and there should be between 3/16 in. and 1/4 in. free movement between the cable outer casing and the adjuster.

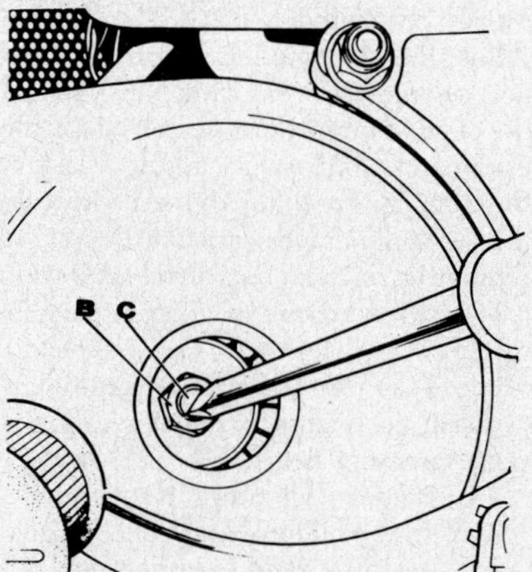

Clutch adjuster locknut (B) and adjusting screw (C)

BRAKE ADJUSTMENT

Commandos are fitted with either a single hydraulic disc brake at the front, or a twin leading shoe drum type, and a single leading shoe at the rear wheel. Drum brakes are cable operated on both wheels.

Other models usually had single leading shoe brakes front and rear, and the rear brake was usually rod-operated.

Commando

FRONT, DRUM TYPE

Two adjusters are provided on the front brake cable: at the handlebar and at the drum itself. Usually, the adjuster at the drum is used. Adjust the brake as needed, by screwing out the adjuster(s). The angle made by the cable and the operating lever should not be greater than 90°.

The link rod for the twin leading shoe brake should be correctly set as it is and does not need adjustment. If the linkage has been disassembled, reset by taking out the top clevis pin and, with the help of an assistant, pull both operating levers until the shoes are in contact with the drum. Then loosen the rod locknut and screw the rod in or out until, with the shoes still in contact with the drum, the clevis pin can be refitted. Retighten the locknut. Readjust the brakes with the cable adjuster.

The pins should be replaced if they seem to be worn.

The front brake is equipped with an air scoop and an outlet, both of which are blocked off. These plates can be removed if desired, but a wire mesh must be fitted to the scoop to protect the linings from debris.

FRONT, DISC TYPE

The disc brake needs no adjustment other than a regular brake fluid check. Remove the master cylinder reservoir cap and take out the bellows seal. The fluid level should be ½ in. from the top of the reservoir. Fill it up with the recommended fluid if necessary. Replace the bellows seal closed end downward and firmly refit the cap.

Bleeding and flushing procedures for the hydraulic disc brake should be necessary only if the system has been disassembled or after very many miles. The information is given in the "chassis" section.

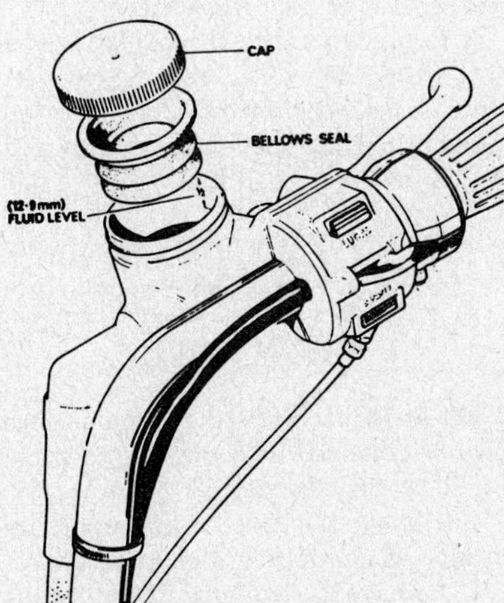

Hydraulic disc brake fluid level

REAR

When the rear brake is fully applied, the lever should not be past the "6 o'clock" position (pointing straight down). After this, new linings will be needed. The brake is adjusted by screwing in the adjuster on the end of the brake cable.

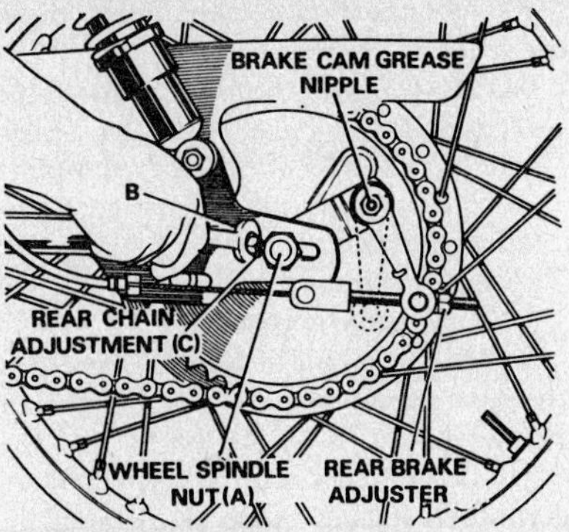

Rear brake lever operating range (Commando)

Pre-Commando Models

FRONT AND REAR

1. There may be one or two adjusters on the front brake cable, depending on the model. Simply screw the adjuster out to adjust the brake as desired. The angle of the brake arm and the cable should not exceed 90°.

2. If the machine is equipped with a pedal stop for the rear brake this should be adjusted to the desired position first. Back off the brake rod nut a few turns if necessary, fill the pedal stop, then adjust the brake.

3. The rear brake, if rod-operated, must be adjusted with the motorcycle off the centerstand and with a rider on the seat, as if in operation. Because the rod will exert pull on the brake arm as the wheel rises, adjusting the brake with the bike on the center stand will cause it to drag in operation.

Cable operated rear brakes are adjusted as described for the Commando rear brake.

In all cases, the wheels should be free to turn with no dragging or rubbing noises coming from the brakes.

If the wheels have been removed, after reinstallation, centralize the brakes in the drum by backing off the axle nut a few turns, holding the brake hard on, and retightening the nut. This applies to both front and rear drum brakes.

PRIMARY DRIVE CHAIN (All Models)

1. Remove the primary chaincase inspection cap and observe the primary chain.

2. Loosen the large nut on the adjustment assembly on top of the gearbox. Also loosen one of the nuts on the lower gearbox mounting stud at the very bottom of the gearbox.

On some Scrambler models, refer to the accompanying illustration. Screw in the adjuster bolt several turns; pull down hard on the rear chain to take up the slack in the primary chain, then turn the adjuster bolt out until the primary chain

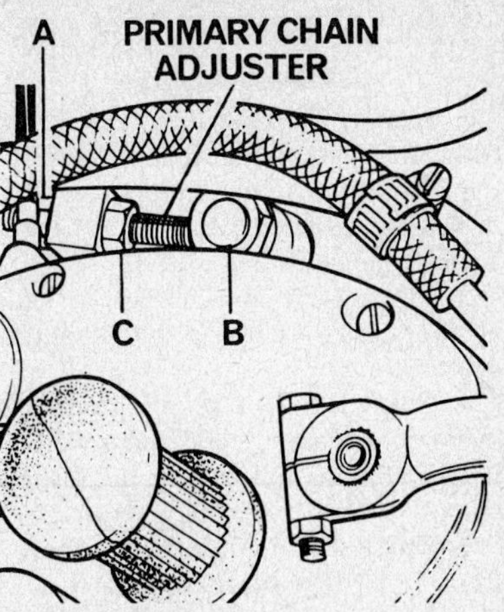

Primary chain adjuster locknuts (A & C) and locking bolt (B)

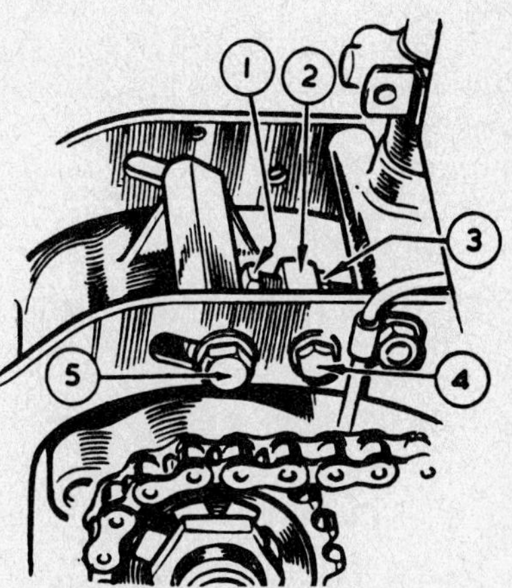

G15CS primary chain adjuster with adjuster bolt (1), lock nut (3), and gearbox lock bolt (5)

tension is correct. Tighten the adjusting bolt lock nut.

.3 Back off the adjuster nut on the right several turns. Then tighten the nut on the left. The gearbox will be drawn to your left to tighten the chain. Tighten this nut until the chain slack is completely gone; then back it off several turns and tighten the right nut until the desired chain slack is attained. For Commandos this will be ⅜ in. of total up and down movement. For other models (those with single-row chains) the correct chain slack is ½–¾ in.

4. Slowly rotate the chain (use the kick-starter) and check the slack at several points. If the chain has a tight spot, the slack must be reset to the correct measurement at this spot.

5. Securely tighten the large adjuster nut and the stud nut. Recheck chain slack. Replace the chaincase cap.

6. The final drive chain adjustment will be altered and must be reset. Perform as described below.

FINAL DRIVE CHAIN (All Models)

1. Loosen the rear axle nuts a few turns, then loosen the adjuster locknuts.

2. Pull down on the bottom run of the drive chain to bring the axle nuts hard up against the adjusters.

3. Screw each adjuster out an equal amount until the chain is a bit looser than you desire.

4. Check the chain slack with the machine off its center stand and a rider on board with his full weight on the machine.

5. Readjust, if necessary, until there is from ¾ in. to 1 in. total up and down chain slack as measured in the middle of the bottom chain run with the machine off the stand and a rider aboard.

6. Retighten the axle nuts and recheck the adjustment. Tighten the adjuster locknuts.

Be sure the rear brake is not dragging. This adjustment will also have changed. Readjust as described.

ENGINE AND TRANSMISSION

ENGINE SERVICE

Commando

REMOVAL

On Commando models, the cylinder head and barrels can be removed with the engine still in the frame. For lower end service, however, it is necessary to remove the engine. The engine must also be removed first to remove the transmission. It is also possible to remove the engine-transmission and primary chaincase as a unit.

1. Remove the seat if necessary (as on Fastback models), by loosening the two coined knobs, lifting the seat to clear the brackets, and pulling backward.

2. Be sure that the fuel petcocks are turned OFF and disconnect the gas lines at the tank. Remove the two bolts at the front of the tank, the rubber strap at the rear, and lift the tank clear of the frame.

3. Drain the oil from the tank and disconnect the oil pipe junction (one bolt) at the engine. Kicking the engine over a few times before removing the junction will minimize the amount of oil which will leak out when the junction is removed. Also, remove the sump drain plug to remove the oil in the crankcase. The engine can be taken out without the gearbox, but if this unit is to be removed, drain it also.

4. Remove the spark plugs.

5. Disconnect the tachometer drive cable at the engine.

NOTE: *On early Commandos with the tachometer drive mechanism mounted on the outside of the timing case, it is preferable to remove the drive mechanism (two screws) rather than just the cable. This component is vulnerable in its position.*

6. Remove the carburetor caps and the slide assemblies. Also, remove the air cleaner.

7. Loosen the clamp bolts which secure each exhaust pipe to its muffler. Loosen the header pipe cross-over tube bolt (if fitted). Using a C-spanner or a suitable replacement, unscrew the two finned nuts which fasten the pipes to the head and remove the exhaust pipes.

NOTE: *The latest Commandos have locking tabs installed to prevent the finned nuts from working loose during operation. These must be taken care of first.*

The washers behind the finned nuts should be replaced when reassembling.

8. Remove the small engine steady side plates on the cylinder head. There are three nuts for each plate. Unbolt the larger engine steady plate at this location. This is secured with three allen screws.

9. Remove the gear shift lever.

10. Remove the battery cover. Disconnect the positive terminal of the battery to obviate the possibility of a short circuit.

11. Disconnect the (two or three) leads from the alternator at the snap connector.

12. Remove the left side footpeg and the rear brake lever.

13. The primary chaincase can be left intact if the engine and transmission are to be removed together. If the engine alone is being removed, refer to "clutch and Primary Drive" later in this section to disassemble the chaincase.

14. Disconnect the crankcase breather tube from the elbow union just above the chaincase, if so equipped.

On late models, the breather is located at the rear of the crankcase. On the 850, it can be found at the top, rear, of the timing case.

If the engine and transmission are to be removed as a unit, remove the oil filter assembly on the engine mounting plates if so equipped (850 and early 1973 750s).

15. Disconnect the ground wire attached to the bottom crankcase stud on the left side.

16. Take off the self-locking nut from the bolt which passes through the front engine mount. Withdraw the bolt from the right side of the frame. Remove the front engine mounting assembly.

17. Remove the three studs which pass through the rear engine mounting plates and the crankcase.

18. The engine can now be removed from the right side of the frame.

19. If removel of the transmission is desired as well, first disconnect the final drive chain masterlink. Remove the right footpeg.

20. Remove the clutch activating lever inspection cover (fastened by two small screws) on the upper right hand side of the transmission gearbox. Detach the clutch cable from the lever and unscrew the cable adjuster.

21. Remove the two gearbox mounting bolts which are directly above and below the gearbox.

22. From the right side of the motorcycle, turn the gearbox a few degrees counterclockwise and remove it from the frame.

INSTALLATION

Installation of the engine and transmission is basically a reversal of the removal procedure.

1. Place the engine in the frame from the right side of the motorcycle.

2. Fit the three studs and nuts which pass through the rear engine mounting and the crankcase.

3. Supporting the engine, place the front engine mounting assembly in position.

4. Insert the front engine mounting bolt and tighten the self-locking nut to the correct torque setting. Tighten the nuts on the three rear engine mounting studs.

5. Continue reassembly in the reverse of the sequence described in "Removal."

6. The washers for the finned exhaust pipe nuts should be replaced.

7. Be sure that the exhaust pipe finned nuts are tightened securely. These nuts are best looked after by safety wire fastened by drilling one lobe of the nut and the top cylinder head fin.

Atlas

REMOVAL

On Atlas machines, the cylinder head may be removed with the engine in the frame, as may the barrels.

To remove the Atlas engine and transmission as a unit, follow this procedure:

1. Remove the gas tank, disconnecting the fuel lines at the carburetors and taking off the mounting nuts.

2. Remove the head steady bracket.

3. Remove the air cleaner and the carburetors.

4. Drain the oil tank and the engine sump. If work is to be performed on the transmission drain it also.

5. Unbolt the oil pipe junction at the crankcase. Kicking the engine over a few times after draining the oil tank and

PERIODIC MAINTENANCE INTERVALS

EVERY 2,500 MILES
- Check timing and adjust contact breaker points
- Clean spark plugs and set gaps
- Change primary chaincase oil and check adjustment
- Check clutch adjustment
- Change engine oil
- Clean crankcase oil filter
- Clean, lubricate, and adjust rear chain
- Grease rear brake pedal pivot
- Grease speedometer drive

EVERY 3,000 MILES
- Lubricate magneto cam ring

EVERY 5,000 MILES
- Change gearbox oil
- Change oil in forks (Commando)
- Check steering head bearing adjustment
- Clean contact breaker points
- Lubricate contact breaker cam and auto advance unit
- Grease brake spindles (one stroke of grease gun)
- Check and adjust valve rocker clearances
- Check and adjust cam chain
- Replace air filter element
- Disassemble and clean both carburetors
- Lubricate swing arm bushes (Commando only)
- Change cartridge oil filter (if fitted)

EVERY 10,000 MILES
- Change oil in front forks (pre-Commando)
- Re-pack wheel bearings with grease
- Check front and rear rubber engine mountings for side play (Commando only)

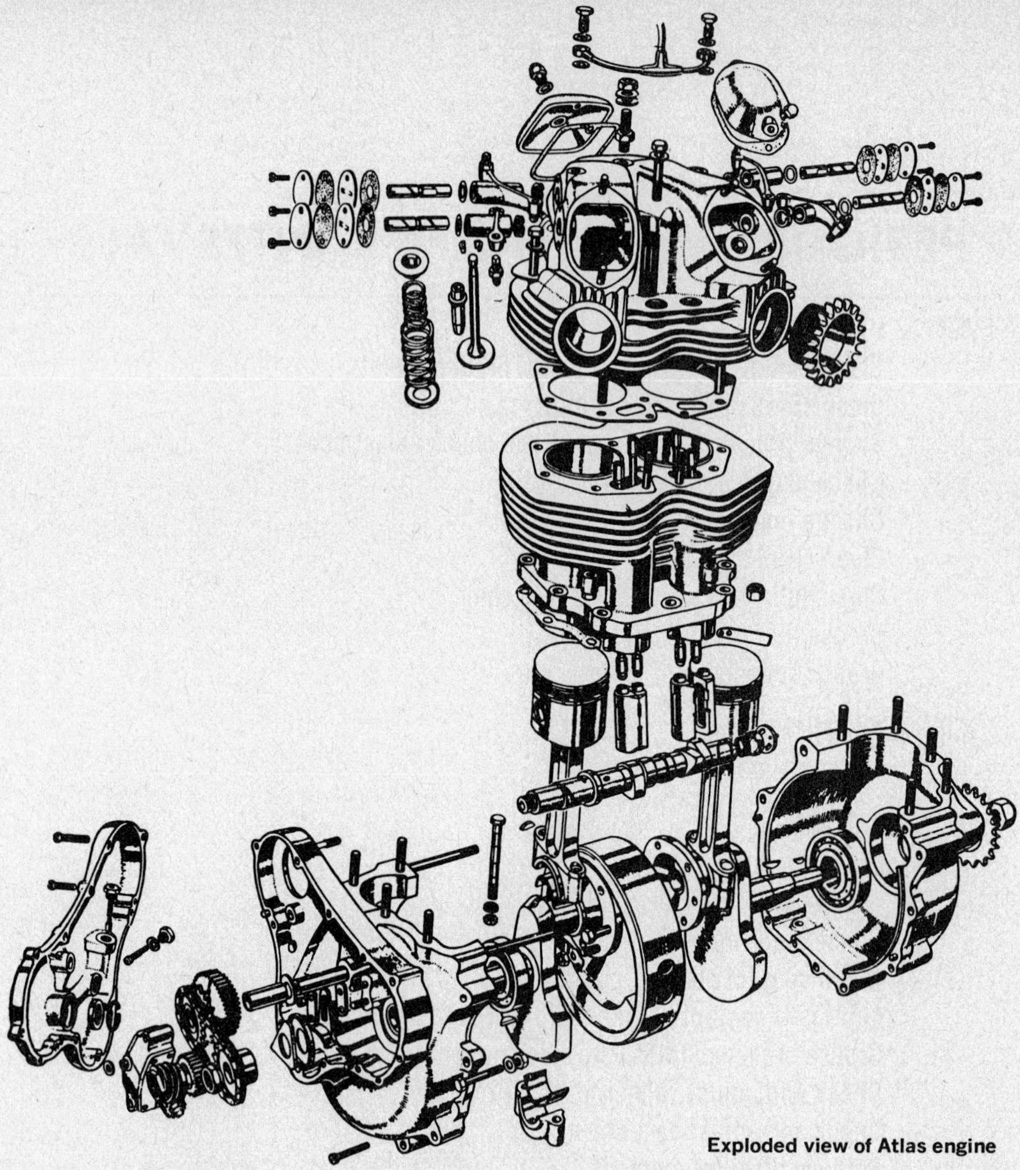

Exploded view of Atlas engine

before removing the junction will minimize the amount of oil which will dribble out.

6. Remove the exhaust pipes and mufflers by removing the muffler bolt and the exhaust pipe finned nut.

7. Disconnect the tachometer drive (two screws) at the engine. It is advisable to remove the drive rather than just the cable to avoid hitting it on something as the engine is removed from the frame.

8. Disconnect the battery leads and remove the battery.

9. Remove the rectifier.

10. Remove the battery box.

11. Disconnect the crankcase and tank breather hoses to the oil tank and remove the tank (4 bolts).

12. Remove the oil tank platform.

13. Remove the clutch activating lever inspection cap at the top right-hand side of the transmission, pry up the lever

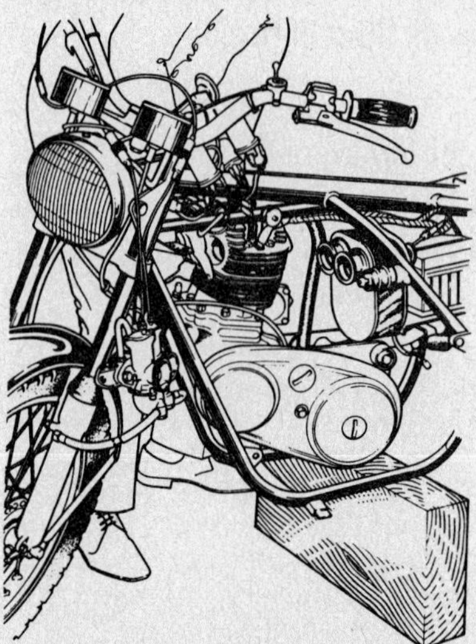

Removing the engine (Commando)

with a suitable screwdriver and remove the clutch cable. Next, remove the adjuster from the case.

14. Remove both footpegs. Place a pan beneath the primary chaincase cover to catch the oil when it is removed. Some of the oil can be drained off by placing the bike on the sidestand and removing the oil level plug in the chaincase cover. Remove the large hexagon nut on the footpeg stud and carefully take off the chrome cover and the rubber washer. Pull off the chaincase cover.

15. Disconnect the three alternator leads at the snap connector.

16. Remove the four nuts and bolts which secure the upper and lower arms of the engine mounting plates (just in front of the swing arm).

17. Remove the center stand spring.

18. Unbolt the two triangular engine mounting plates at the front of the en-

gine. These may be wedged between the frame and the crankcase. Lift the engine slightly to free them if necessary and remove them from the frame.

19. Disconnect the rear chain and take it off of the countershaft sprocket.

20. Remove the engine and transmission from the frame.

If so desired, the engine alone can be removed, leaving the transmission in the frame. In this event, follow Steps 1–7 in the procedure just described, then:

8. Remove the four bolts which secure the oil tank to the engine mounting plates; remove the battery box.

9. Disconnect the crankcase breather hose at the elbow junction.

10. Remove the left side footpeg, place a pan under the primary chaincase cover to catch the oil, and remove the cover after removing the hexagon nut, cover, and rubber washer.

11. Disconnect the alternator leads at the snap connector and carefully pull the wires through the inner chaincase half.

12. Remove the clutch pressure plate by unscrewing the three spring adjustment nuts. These are cylindrical and have two small tabs on the face that bears against the clutch spring to prevent loosening during operation. Removing the nuts will invariably sheer off the tab, making replacement of the nuts advisable. If you must reuse the nuts on the clutch, a knife blade or suitable substitute can be placed between the nut and the spring while removing.

13. Remove the clutch springs and cups.

14. Remove the main clutch nut on the transmission mainshaft and the lock washer. A spark plug socket wrench fits this nut. It is necessary to keep the clutch hub from turning while this nut is removed. Stuffing a rag or similar object between the clutch sprocket and the primary chain is not recommended. Rather, a special tool can be used. This can be fabricated at home. Refer to "Clutch Service" (pre-Commando) in this section.

15. Remove the three nuts and washers which secure the alternator stator to the stator housing. Pull off the stator.

16. Remove the nut which secures the rotor to the crankshaft and remove the rotor and its woodruff key. A small gear puller is sometimes needed to take the rotor off of the shaft.

17. The engine sprocket, primary chain, and clutch hub can be removed together. The clutch hub may require a special puller to remove it from the transmission mainshaft, especially if it has not been removed before. This is a special shop tool which screws into the center of the clutch hub; there is on alternative tool. In addition, the engine sprocket is fitted onto a tapered portion of the crankshaft and will require a puller. A smaller gear puller can be used in place of the factory sprocket extractor. Be sure to remove the engine sprocket woodruff key.

18. Remove the three screws which fix the stator housing to the mounting plate and the three screws fixing the plate to the crankcase.

19. Remove the nut which is found about halfway between the engine sprocket and the clutch which secures the inner chaincase half.

20. The inner chaincase half is also secured by means of a tab by the nut on the bottom transmission stud. Remove this nut and take away the chaincase half.

21. Proceeding to the four bolts which fasten the upper and lower arms of the engine mounting plates (just before the swing arm), remove the lower bolts and loosen the upper two.

22. Remove the two studs, two bolts, and their respective nuts at the front engine plates.

23. Lift the engine slightly to remove the front mounting plates. Remove the two studs which pass through the crankcase and engine mounting plates at the rear of the crankcase.

24. Remove one of the nuts from the stud at the very bottom of the engine which passes through the crankcase and, lifting the engine so that the stud will clear the bottom frame tubes, remove the stud.

25. The engine can now be taken out of the frame,

INSTALLATION

Installation is the reverse of the removal procedure.

Scramblers

REMOVAL

For engine service on Scrambler models, note the following points:

1. The engine and transmission are best removed as a unit.

2. The primary chaincase can be left intact during removal.

Refer to removal procedure for Atlas models for initial steps if additional information is needed.

MAINTENANCE DATA

	Atlas	G15CS, N15CS, P-11	Fastback	Commando 750 and 850 Roadster	SS Hi-Rider	Interstate
Fuel Tank (gal)	3.5	2.5	3.9	2.7, 3.0	2.3	6.0, 7.0
Oil Tank (pts)	4.5	4.5	6.0	6.0	6.0	6.0
Gearbox (pts)	1.0	1.0	1.2	1.2	1.2	1.2
Primary Chaincase (oz)	4.5	4.5	7.0	7.0	7.0	7.0
Front Forks @ (oz)	5.0	6.5	5.5	5.5	5.5	5.5
Tire Pressure (lbs per sq. in.)						
Front	24	24	26	26	26	26
Rear	24	24	26	26	26	26
Chain Slack (in.)						
Primary Drive	1/2-3/4	1/2-3/4	3/8	3/8	3/8	3/8
Rear Drive	3/4-1	3/4-1	3/4-1	3/4-1	3/4-1	3/4-1

RECOMMENDED LUBRICANTS

Commando (All Models)

Brand	Engine and Primary Chain Ambient Temperature Above 32°F	Below 32°F	Gearbox Ambient Temperature Above 32°F	Below 32°F	Front Forks	Hub and Frame Parts	Rear Chain
Mobiloil	S.A.E. 20/50 or straight S.A.E. 30	S.A.E. 10/30 or straight S.A.E. 20	S.A.E. 90EP	S.A.E. 30	Arctic S.A.E. 20	Mobilgrease MP	Mobilgrease MP
Castrol	S.A.E. 20/50 or straight S.A.E. 30	S.A.E. 10/30 or straight S.A.E. 20	S.A.E. 90EP	S.A.E. 30	Castrolite S.A.E. 10W-30	Castrolease LM	Castrolease Graphited
Energol	S.A.E. 20/50 or straight S.A.E. 30	S.A.E. 10/30 or straight S.A.E. 20	S.A.E. 90EP	S.A.E. 30	S.A.E. 20	Energrease C3	Energrease A.O.
Essolube	S.A.E. 20/50 or straight S.A.E. 30	S.A.E. 10/30 or straight S.A.E. 20	S.A.E. 90EP	S.A.E. 30	S.A.E. 20	Esso Multipurpose	Fluid Grease
Shell	S.A.E. 20/50 or straight S.A.E. 30	S.A.E. 10/30 or straight S.A.E. 20	S.A.E. 90EP	S.A.E. 30	X-100 Motoroil 20/20W	Retinax A or C.D.	Retinax A or C.D.
Regent Advanced Havoline	S.A.E. 20/50 or straight S.A.E. 30	S.A.E. 10/30 or straight S.A.E. 20	S.A.E. 90EP	S.A.E. 30			Regent S.A.E. 20

RECOMMENDED LUBRICANTS

Atlas, G15CS, N15CS, P-11

Brand	Engine and Primary Chain Ambient Temperature Above 32°F	Below 32°F	Gearbox Ambient Temperature Above 32°F	Below 32°F	Front Forks	Hub and Frame Parts	Rear Chain
Mobiloil	S.A.E. 20/50 or straight S.A.E. 30	S.A.E. 10/30 or straight S.A.E. 20	S.A.E. 50	S.A.E. 30	Arctic S.A.E. 20	Mobilgrease MP	Mobilgrease MP
Castrol	S.A.E. 20/50 or straight S.A.E. 30	S.A.E. 10/30 or straight S.A.E. 20	S.A.E. 50	S.A.E. 30	Castrolite S.A.E. 10W-30	Castrolease Heavy	Castrolease Graphited
Energol	S.A.E. 20/50 or straight S.A.E. 30	S.A.E. 10/30 or straight S.A.E. 20	S.A.E. 50	S.A.E. 30	S.A.E. 20	Energrease C3	Energrease A.O.
Essolube	S.A.E. 20/50 or straight S.A.E. 30	S.A.E. 10/30 or straight S.A.E. 20	S.A.E. 50	S.A.E. 30	S.A.E. 20		Fluid Grease
Shell	S.A.E. 20/50 or straight S.A.E. 30	S.A.E. 10/30 or straight S.A.E. 20	S.A.E. 50	S.A.E. 30	X-100 Motoroil 20/20W	Retinax A or C.D.	
Regent Advanced Havoline	S.A.E. 20/50 or straight S.A.E. 30	S.A.E. 10/30 or straight S.A.E. 20	S.A.E. 50	S.A.E. 30			

1. Prepare the engine and transmission for removal in the manner outlined for the Atlas, removing the gas tank, exhaust pipes and mufflers, air cleaners, carburetors, oil from tank, and sump.

2. Remove the tachometer drive from the engine, clutch cable at the transmission, oil junction, oil tank, and crankcase breather pipes, and alternator connections.

3. Disconnect the rear drive chain.

4. Remove the metal cover over the transmission.

5. Remove the upper front engine mounting bolts. Loosen, but do not remove, the lower front mounts.

6. Remove the right side footpeg and remove the rod from the left side. There are two spacers involved.

7. Unhook the center stand spring.

8. Remove the left side rear engine mounting bolts.

9. Raise the engine slightly to take the pressure off of the lower front bolts which are still in place and remove the nuts. Take away the engine plates, watching for the spacer.

10. Lever the engine forward and lift it up and out of the right side of the frame.

INSTALLATION

Installation is somewhat simplified by first removing the skid plate.

Before replacing the engine in the frame, be certain that the left side footpeg is in its proper position since it cannot be replaced after the engine is in the frame.

1. Begin by placing the engine in the frame from the right side of the bike, rear end first.

2. Insert a length of steel rod or a suitable screwdriver through the rear engine plates and the frame to align the bolt holes.

3. Lever the front of the engine up to replace the lower small mounting bolt and tighten the nuts firmly.

4. Lower the engine and refit the front and rear engine plate bolts.

5. The remainder of the installation procedure is the reverse of the removal procedure.

TOP END OVERHAUL

Cylinder Head and Cylinder

REMOVAL (All Models)

The cylinder head on all models may be removed with the engine in the frame if desired. On 750s only, if the cylinder head does not require service or inspection, the head and cylinders may be taken off as a unit, after removing the engine from the frame by simply removing the cylinder base bolts. This has the advantage of saving time and effort and not disturbing the cylinder head torque settings. Refer to "Cylinder Removal."

The following procedure gives instructions for removing the head with the engine still in the frame.

1. Remove the gas tank, the seat (if necessary (as on Fastback models), spark plug leads, spark plugs, and exhaust pipes. Refer to initial steps of "Engine Removal" for your models if additional information is needed.

2. Disconnect the rocker oil feed pipe on each side of the head.

CAUTION: *Each junction has two copper washers. A rag placed over the spark plug hole is a good idea when removing the banjo bolts.*

The rocker oil feed pipe must be placed out of the way so that the head can be removed. On models with neoprene lines, this is not a problem. Earlier machines, however, are equipped with a copper pipe to feed the rockers. This pipe is only flexible to a certain degree. It can be bent out of the way, but take care to avoid crimping it anywhere along its length. The alternate method is to also disconnect the pipe banjo at the crankcase and turn the pipe aside.

3. Remove the small engine steady side plates at the cylinder head (there are three nuts for each one) and the larger head steady plate secured by three allen screws (Commando). On other models, remove the head steady bracket.

4. Remove the exhaust rocker covers and the intake rocker cover.

5. Remove the air cleaner, the carburetors, and the manifolds.

6. On magneto models, removing the front spark plug lead is a good idea.

NOTE: On Scrambler models, additional steps must be taken at this point.

a. Remove all of the cylinder head nuts and the bolt on the center of the head. This will leave only the four bolts flanking the spark plug holes.

b. Remove both exhaust rocker spindle retaining plates and remove the spindles. This requires a special tool. Refer to "Cylinder Head Service" later in this section. Be extremely careful of the washer and spring which are found on the spindle.

c. Remove the four remaining cylinder head bolts.

The remainder of the procedure is the same as that for other models.

7. The cylinder head can now be taken off. It is secured to the cylinders by five bolts and five nuts. Loosen the bolts or nuts gradually, and in the order shown.

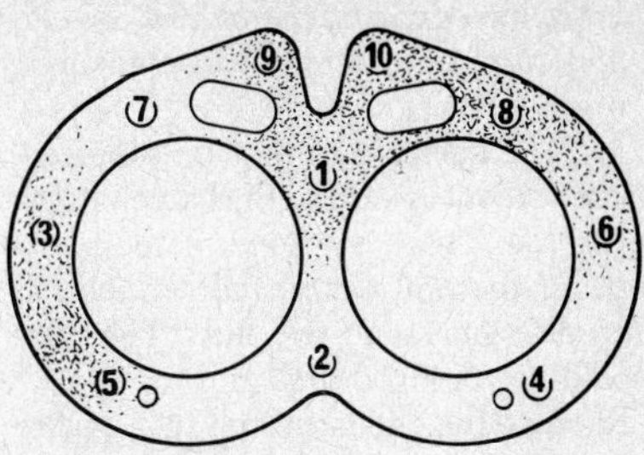

Cylinder head bolt loosening and tightening order

There are two long barrel nuts concealed in the fins.

As the last of the fasteners is loosened, the head should begin to rise off its seat slightly, due to the pressure of the valve springs. If the head is not free after the last of the fasteners has been removed, it is probably due to carbon build-up as on engines with many miles on them or those with an oil burning problem. In this event, place a block of wood against the cylinder fins at the exhaust port (the fins are strongest here) and rap sharply with a hammer.

8. Remember that there are two studs at the front of the cylinder barrels and three shorter ones in the head itself which must clear. The most important consideration at this point, however, is the pushrods.

9. Straddle the bike. Lift the head several inches off its seat. Slipping your fingers between the head and barrels, push the four pushrods up into the head as far as they will go. They should only protrude about two inches from the head.

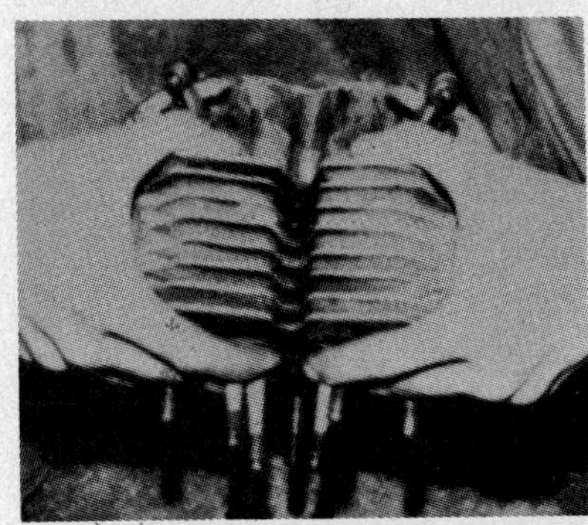

Pushrod position for removing or installing the head with the engine in the frame

10. Pull the head straight up as far as possible and tilt it backward and to one side until two of the pushrods clear their tunnel. Then tilt it to the opposite side so that the other two are clear. After both sets are out of the tunnels, the head can be taken out to one side.

NOTE: *The pushrods are of two lengths. The longer ones activate the intake rockers. These are placed clos-*

est to the center of the barrels. Be certain they are correctly located upon reassembly.

11. The barrels can now be removed. Loosen all nuts securing the barrels to the crankcase. There are nine of them, except on the 850 Commando which has four allen bolts and five nuts. The bolts should be removed first.

Remove the one large and two smaller nuts at the front of the barrels. The others must be loosened as much as possible until they hit the cooling fins. Lift the barrels as much as you can, then loosen the nuts again. Continue until the nuts can be taken off of the studs.

As soon as you have removed the nuts, remove and account for all washers. Be sure that none are left on the barrels, or one can easily fall into the crankcase later.

12. Lift the barrels clear of the crankcase.

INSPECTION

1. Check the cylinder head for warpage.

Place the head on a flat surface, such as a piece of glass, and probe around the mating surface with a feeler gauge. Maximum allowable warpage is 0.002 in.

2. Make sure that the mating surface is smooth and free from any scoring. This must be removed if present.

3. Check the combustion chamber for scoring marks which might have been caused by a piece of valve if the engine was blown. Also inspect for any cracks in the head. This is unlikely unless the macine has been subject to extreme abuse. The most likely spot for a crack to be found is between the spark plug hole and the exhaust port.

4. Make sure that the oil passage drilled behind the right combustion chamber is clear.

ROCKER ARMS

Removal

1. For each rocker arm, remove the rocker spindle retaining plate assembly. This consists of an outer plate, a gasket an inner plate with two tabs to engage the slots of the rocker spindle and assure it maintains its position, and another gasket.

2. The rocker spindle is press-fit on the cylinder head. First note the position of the slots in the spindle end. Removal is made much easier, and there is less chance of scoring the spindle or the head, if the head is heated first. Ideally, the head should be placed in an oven and heated to not more than 100° F. In the case of the Scrambler models, where the factory recommends removing the exhaust rocker spindles prior to removing the head (engine in the frame), a propane

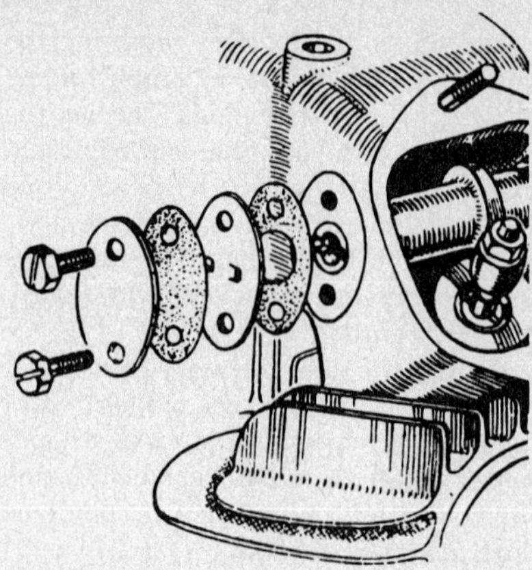

Rocker spindle retaining plate assembly

torch can be used, with caution, to heat the area around the spindle very gently.

The spindle is threaded internally and can be removed with a 5/16 in. bolt (an old head bolt works fine) and a short piece of steel tubing, ½ in. in diameter.

3. Insert the bolt through the steel tube and thread it into the rocker spindle. The spindle will begin to come out of the head.

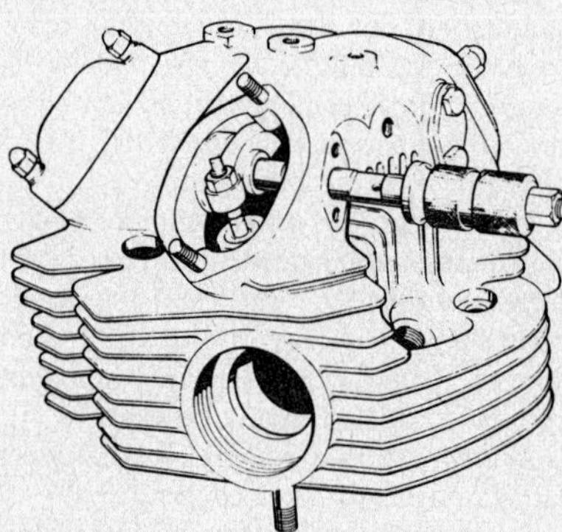

Removing the rocker spindles

4. The rocker arm is flanked by a spring washer, fitted on the side closest to the center of the head, and a plain thrust washer on the opposite side. Be positive that both are accounted for. The thickness of the plain thrust washer should be 0.015 in.

NOTE: *The exhaust rockers can be taken directly out of the head after pulling out the spindle. The intake rockers must be turned upside down and then removed on older models.*

Inspection

1. Check the spindle surface for scuffing or signs of wear. Any roughness or scratches should be removed with a fine grade of emery cloth.

On older models, there are oil grooves machined into the spindles. They must be clear of any obstructions.

On all models, the spindle oil drilling must not be obstructed.

The rocker spindle diameter should be 0.4985 in.–0.4998 in.

2. Check the rocker arm for minute cracks where the arm joins the barrel. Be sure that the ball end of the rocker is spherical. It should also have a bright, mirror finish.

The ball end is press-fit in the rocker arm. To remove it, support the rocker arm on an appropriate surface to prevent damage to it, then drive the ball shaft out with a drift. The rocker arm has a drilled oil passage from the spindle to the ball end to lubricate the ball and pushrod cup. Make sure that this passage is clear. Also, note that the ball shaft's oil hole must line up with the oil drilling in the rocker. To reassemble, press the ball shaft into position as far as possible. A standard bench vise faced with wood will do the job.

3. The inside diameter of the rocker bore should be 0.5003 in.–0.4998 in, Check for excessive play of the rocker on the spindle.

4. Check the valve clearance adjuster. The end of the adjuster which bears on the valve stem should be smooth and slightly spherical to mate well with the stem.

Installation

1. The rocker spindle must be located so that the slots on the outer end are HORIZONTAL; the oil hole on the spindle must face away from the center of the head.

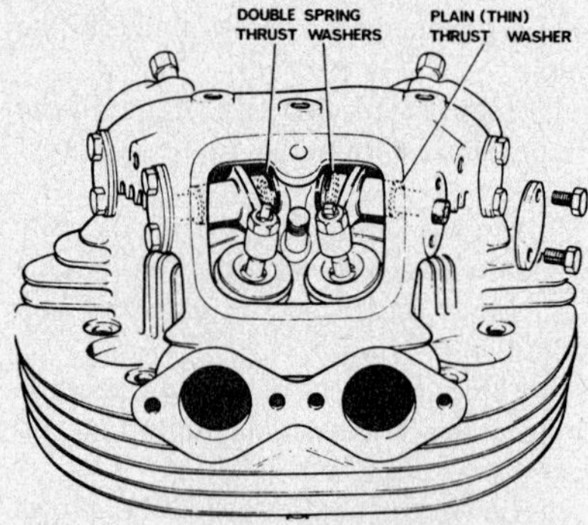

Correct installation of rocker arm spindle spring and plain thrust washers

2. Fit the spring washer, the rocker arm, and the thrust washer in their proper locations. Remember that the spring washer is closest to the center of the cylinder head.

3. Heat the head, as was done on removal, and press in the spindle. Make sure that the spindle slots are horizontal to engage with the tabs on the spindle locating plate. Also, check to make certain that the spindle is just below flush with the gasket face on the cylinder head.

4. Fit the spindle locating plate. The correct order, from the head out, is:

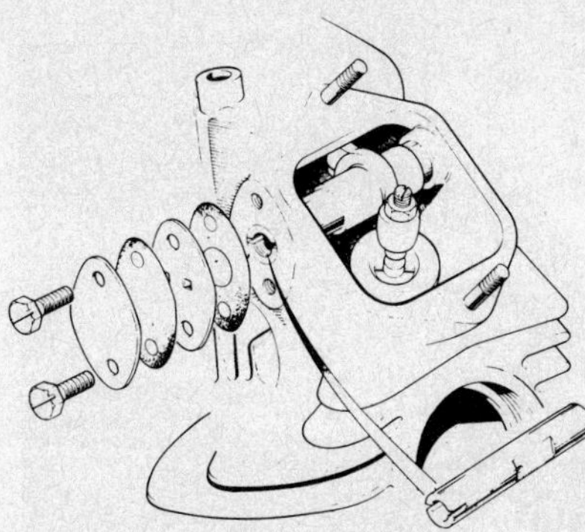

Rocker arm spindle installation: note oil hole location

a. Paper gasket with large center hole
b. Plate with locating tabs
c. Paper gasket
d. Plain oval plate
e. Two fixing bolts

A late modification has been the fitting of copper washers beneath the plate bolts (Part No. 063129). These may be fitted to all previous models.

VALVES AND VALVE SPRINGS

Removal and Inspection

To check the condition of the seats, stand the cylinder head on end and pour some gasoline into the intake ports. Let it stand for a little while in this way, then check to see if any of the gas has leaked through to the combustion chamber. If any is present here, the valves should be lapped into their seats.

Dry off the combustion chamber, if necessary, and repeat the procedure for the exhaust valves.

1. Take out the stud for the intake rocker cover if you are going to remove the intake valves.
2. Using the valve spring compressor, compress the springs far enough to remove the two tapered valve keepers (collets) and release the spring.
3. The valve collar, inner and outer springs, spring seat, and heat insulating washer can be removed.

NOTE: *The valve springs are "rated," that is, they have a smaller coil pitch at one end (like a progressively wound spring). This end should bear against the head upon reassembly.*

4. Remove the oil seals from the intake valves if so equipped.

Remove the valve from its guide. Any sticking or binding upon attempting removal will indicate a very bad condition for the valve stem or the guide.

5. Inspect the valve paying close attention to the condition of the edges of the valve head for pitting, burnt or broken edges, excessive carbon build-up, etc. Deposits should be carefully scraped off with a dull knife, or with a wire wheel, and the valve finished with a fine emery cloth.
6. Check the diameter of the valve stem with a micrometer against the values given in the technical data. A value of less than 0.3095 in. would necessitate replacement of the valve.

Intake valves are larger than the exhaust valves, so telling them apart is no problem. The Commando valves, however, are about 0.07 in. longer than those found on previous models, with a corresponding decrease in the length of the pushrods. The shorter valves can be fitted to the Commando, if necessary, provided that a winkel cap of the proper thickness is installed.

Commando valves cannot be fitted to a pre-Commando engine. The pushrods for Commando and pre-Commando models are in no way interchangable.

7. Check the valve spring free length, for both inner and outer springs, against the figures given in the technical data. If the measured length is less than 0.187 in. from the standard value, the spring must be replaced. Note that valve springs should be replaced as a set.

Lapping

Valve lapping is accomplished in the usual manner. Refer to the BSA "Engine and Transmission" section for information, if necessary.

If lapping has been done several times or if new valve guides are to be installed, it is necessary to machine the valve face and recut the seat.

The seat angle on all models is 45°.

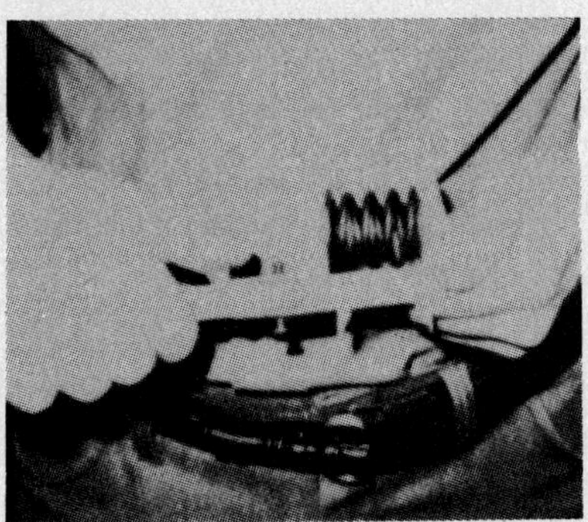

Measuring valve spring free length

Installation

1. Put some clean oil on the valve stem and place the valve in the guide.
2. Refit the valve seal, if so equipped.
3. Replace the heat insulating washer in its seat, then the valve spring seat, the springs (close coils against the head), and the spring collar.
4. Compress the spring and slip the two keepers into place.
5. Check the valve sealing ability as previously described.

VALVE GUIDES

Removal and Inspection

Nortons are equipped with cast iron guides, the newer models being fitted with guides grooved to accept an oil seal on the intake side,

All 750 models have a flange around the guide which rests against the surface of the head when the guide is installed. The 850, however, has a spring clip around the guide which accomplishes the same purpose.

Valve guide to valve stem clearance is 0.002–0.004 in.

1. To remove the guides, strip the head of valves, springs, rocker arms, etc.
2. Heat the head on a hot plate or in an oven. This is essential as the guides are force fit in the head and any attempt to drive them out without heating is sure to result in either a broken guide or a scuffed or enlarged guide bore. Do not heat the head in excess of 200° C.
3. Use a special drift to drive out the guides. The dimensions of this drift are shown in the accompanying illustration.

If the guides are broken, or have a great amount of carbon build-up as in the case of the exhaust guides, some difficulty will be encountered in removing them. If this is the case, use a chisel to break off the lower portion of the guide which protrudes into the port.

This operation should be an emergency recourse undertaken only after the standard procedure has been attempted.

Installation

1. To replace the guides, again heat the head to 200°C. The guide must be accurately inserted in the bore so that the

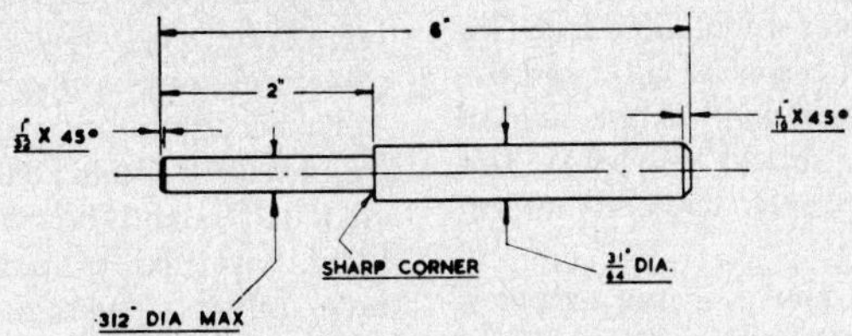

DRIFT FOR REMOVING VALVE GUIDES T 2011

valve can seat properly. To accomplish this, take the valve, which will be used in the port on which you are working, and place it in its normal seated position. The valve stem will be used to locate the valve guide in the head as it is driven in. Use the drift again, this time from the other end, and press home the guide until the flange abuts against the head. Guide bore size on all models is 0.3145–0.3135 in. Use the appropriate ream to check the bore after installation.

2. Accurate refitting of the guide may save you the trouble of recutting the valve seat. The valve should be lapped, however.

3. Refit the spring assembly, and test the valve for sealing ability as previously described.

NOTE: *The newer Commandos have been fitted with oil seals on the intake guides to eliminate the oil burning which was a problem on some motorcycles. The guides are grooved to accept these seals which must* not *be fitted on the exhaust side. These guides are identical in other respects to the previous units, so changing over to a seal-type is possible, if so desired, by simply replacing the old guides with the new units.*

Oversized outside diameter guides are available, if needed, in the following sizes over standard: 0.002 in., 0.005 in., 0.010 in., and 0.015 in.

Cylinder Barrel Service

INSPECTION

1. Check the pushrod length against the specifications given at the end of this section. Check the pushrod ball end and cup for signs of wear. The ball should be smooth and have a mirror-like finish.

2. The steel tappets in the barrels at the front of the cylinder block may be removed for inspection by cutting the safety wire which fastens the two 2BA screws for each pair of tappets and removing the screws. Draw out the tappets and the locating plate. The tappets are machined in pairs, and it is therefore imperative that each pair be kept together, and reinstalled in the same position.

Ensure that the pad at the camshaft end of the tappet is smooth and flat. This is constructed of a special alloy and the seam where it is bonded to the steel of the tappet body should be visible. The pad should, naturally, have a uniform thickness.

As mentioned above, if one tappet is damaged, the pair must be replaced.

The pad may be worked on an oil stone to remove any minor imperfections.

3. Upon reassembly, be sure to refit the tappets with the bevelled edges facing the front of the engine. Oil them before replacing them in the tunnels to assure some primary lubrication. Be sure that the locating plate is correctly installed and that the 2BA screws are securely tightened and fastened with safety wire.

Bevelled edges of cam followers must face forward

4. The cylinder bore should be smooth and without scoring.

When inspecting the bore, it must be checked for both taper and ellipticity.

5. Measure the diameter of the bore with an inside micrometer at the top (about ½ in. below the top of the barrels), middle, and bottom, keeping the micrometer in the same plane. If the readings differ by more than 0.005 in. (0.13 mm), the cylinders should be rebored.

Boring will also be necessary if any of the readings is greater than 2.8758 in. (standard bore), or if the bore is worn more than 0.008 in.

Turn the micrometer 90° and again measure the bore at the three locations. This is the test for ellipticity. The readings in this plane should be the same as the others if the cylinder is circular.

6. A ridge reamer can be used, if needed, to remove the ridge at the top of the cylinder.

7. If reboring is necessary, note that oversized pistons and rings are available in four sizes: 0.010 in., 0.020 in., 0.030 in., and 0.040 in. and the cylinder should be bored with the proper clearance for these pistons. Average clearance between the piston and cylinder wall should be 0.0045 in. Refer to "Pistons, Installation," in the following section.

8. Make sure that the oil passage behind the right cylinder is clear.

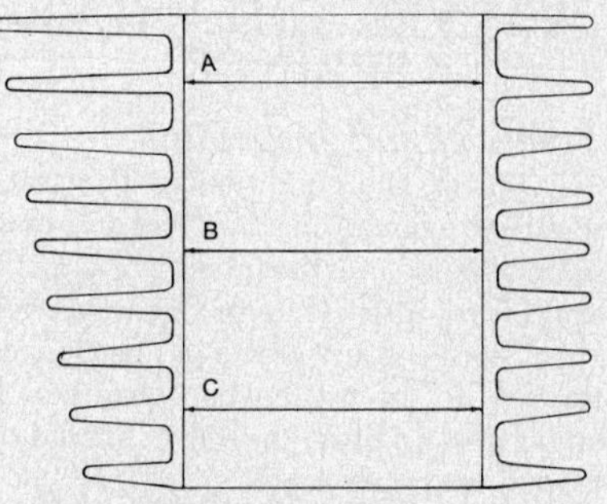

Measure the bore diameter at points A, B, and C

9. Carbon deposits at the top of the bores can be removed with a small steel rule.

Pistons, Rings, and Piston Pin

REMOVAL

1. With needle-nosed pliers, remove the circlips which locate the piston pin.

2. Heat the piston crown gently and evenly with a propane torch. Apply heat only to the crown.

3. Press out the pin using a special piston pin tool, or push out the pin with a suitable drift.

INSPECTION

1. A visual inspection of the pistons and rings in in order. Over the years, various compression ratios have been found on Nortons and, by extension, various types of pistons.

The Atlas and Scrambler models had a 7.4: 1 ratio and the piston for these models has a dished crown. Early Commandos used an 8.9:1 piston which is easily identifiable because of the large vertical slots cut on either side of the piston pin bush.

The pistons used on the Combat Commando are identical to those found on the standard 750 Commando. The increase in compression ratio was attained by milling the cylinder head.

2. Scuff marks at the front and rear of the piston (relative to the engine) is evidence of a seizure. If scuffing is minimal, it is possible to remove it with a very fine emery cloth, although it is best, in any event, to replace the pistons and have the cylinders honed.

NOTE: *In this case, boring might not be necessary. Check the condition of the cylinder walls, noticing any scoring. The bores should be very smooth throughout.*

3. Carbon deposits on the piston crown should be removed. Use the edge of a short steel rule to scrape away the deposits.

4. Inspect the piston wrist pin bushes which should be free of any score marks or obvious signs of wear.

5. The piston rings should be free to rotate in their grooves.

NOTE: *If the rings are tight in the grooves, and there doesn't seem to be an appreciable amount of carbon build-up which would cause this, pay close attention to the piston crown. The Commando pistons are slotted behind the oil ring for a great degree of their circumference. The crown is really only attached to the piston skirt at the wrist pin area. Therefore, a valve hitting a piston can very easily cause the crown to collapse onto the skirt. Check for minute cracks on the edges of the crown.*

6. Brown deposits extending from the piston crown downward past the rings are evidence that the rings are not sealing properly. If they are not binding in the grooves, they are probably worn and should be replaced anyway.

INSTALLATION

1. Before new piston rings are installed, each one should be checked for the proper end gap.

Place the ring in the cylinder bore and insert the piston afterwards, making the ring abut against the piston. This is to make sure that the ring is perpendicular to the cylinder wall.

2. Check the end gap with the aid of a feeler gauge. It should be about 0.013 in. For any value greater than 0.014 in., the ring must be replaced. If the end gap is too small, the ring ends may be filed. Close the ring over a small file so that both ends are filed equally.

On late model Commandos, compression ring gap is acceptable if within 0.010–0.019 in.

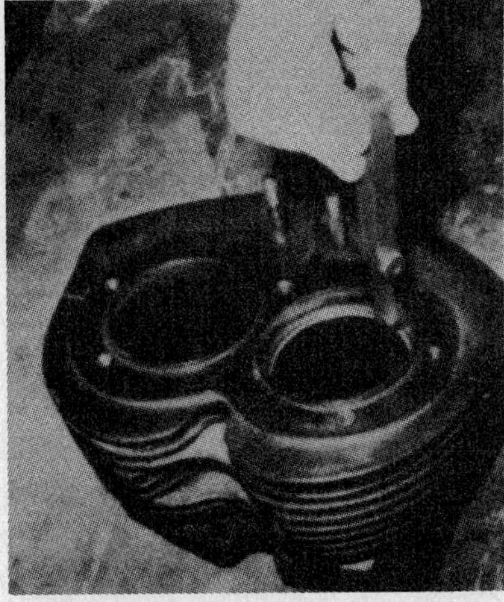

Measuring piston ring end gap with a feeler gauge

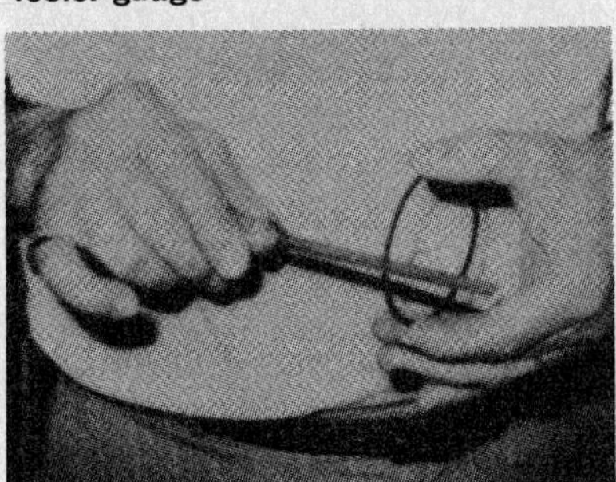

Filing ring ends

On models with the newest type of oil scraper ring (two rails), ring end gap of 0.010–0.040 in. is satisfactory.

3. Nortons have used a variety of oil rings in recent years. The current type has two scraper rails and an expander. Wind the first scraper rail over the piston crown and place it just below, and clear of, the oil ring groove.

4. Fit the corrugated expander ring in the groove. The ends should abut, but must not overlap. The ends are colored, and the color should be visible.

5. Move the first scraper rail up into the groove and position it on the stepped part of the expander ring.

6. Wind the second rail over the piston and place it on the upper stepped portion of the expander.

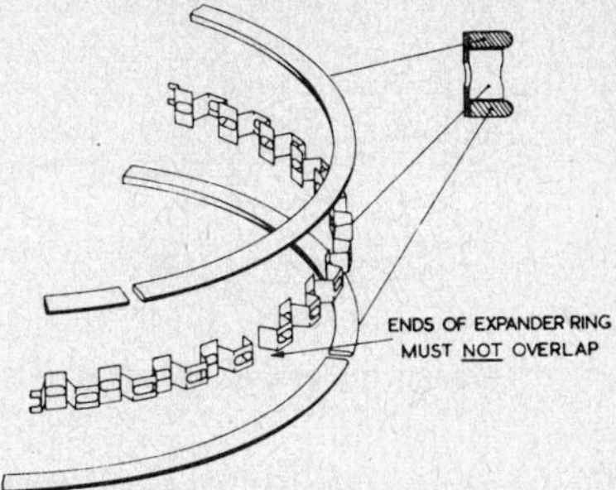

Three-piece oil ring installation

7. The gaps of the two rings should be spaced 180° apart around the piston.

8. Fit the lower compression ring. This ring must be installed with the side up. "Top" is marked on the ring.

NOTE: *If a "stepped type" lower compression ring is fitted, it must be installed as shown in the accompanying illustration.*

9. Fit the upper compression ring. The red coating on this ring must not be removed.

10. Arrange the rings so that the end gaps are not aligned.

11. With the appropriate feeler gauge, check the piston ring side clearance as shown in the illustration. It should be 0.0015–0.0035 in.

12. If replacement of the pistons is necessary, the proper clearance between the piston skirt and the cylinder wall must be observed. Measure the diameter of the piston at the bottom of the skirt, perpendicular to the piston pin. Clearance should be 0.0045 in. on all models.

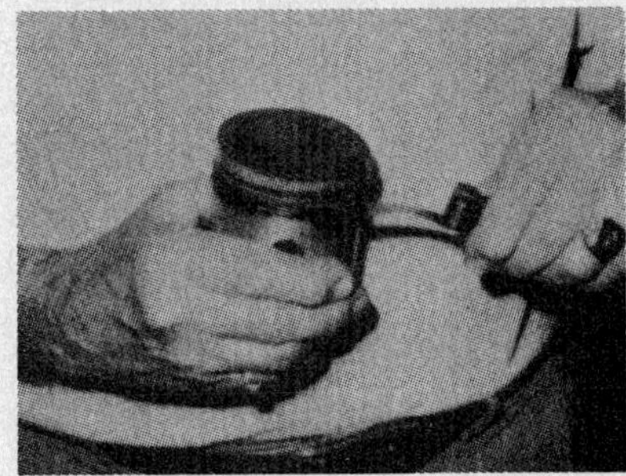

Measuring piston ring side clearance

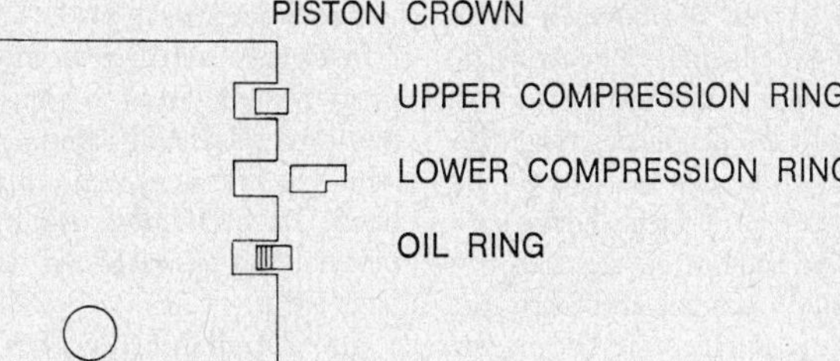

Correct installation of "stepped" compression ring

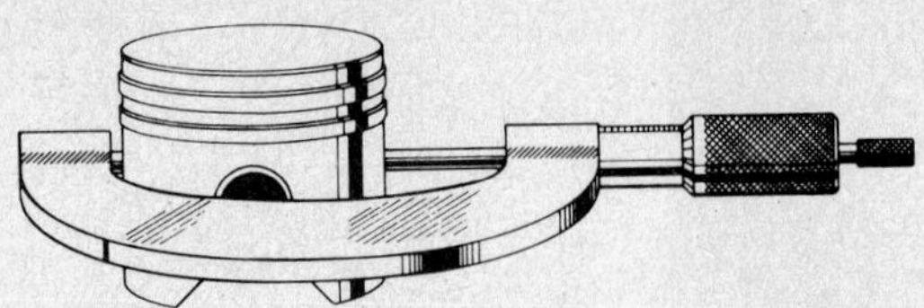

Measuring piston diameter with a micrometer

2 IN.
3⅞ IN.
1⅛ IN.
1⅛ IN.
12 IN.

Piston stand

This may vary somewhat if non-standard pistons are used. In this case, check the manufacturer's recommendation.

NOTE: *Pistons are available in four oversizes in increments of 0.010 in. The oversizes are stamped on the piston crown.*

13. Because of the unsymmetrical arrangement of the ports, the Norton pistons have a definite "left" and "right." In addition, it is possible to put the pistons in "upside down." Remember that the valves are of different sizes and so, therefore, are the valve cut-outs. The exhaust valve cut-out is closer to the edge of the piston and the piston must be positioned accordingly. The pistons will have "left" and "right" stamped on the crown as well.

14. Refit the pistons by replacing one of the circlips, usually the inside one, and making sure that it is seated in its groove. Heat the piston crown as on removal and apply some clean oil to the wrist pin. Press it into the piston until it clears the groove for the outside circlip. Refit the remaining circlip.

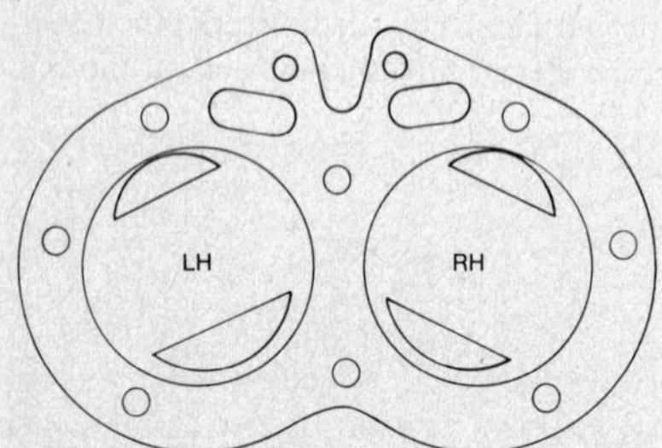

Proper piston installation

Cylinder Head and Cylinders

ASSEMBLY

1. To properly refit the barrels, a device to support the pistons is a great help. A stand can be made, using either steel or wood, refering to the accompanying diagram.

2. Clean any traces of old gasket or gasket material from the bottom mating surface of the cylinder barrels and from the crankcase mating surface. If there are any abrasions, scratches, or score marks on the crankcase mating surface, remove them with an oil stone.

3. Fit a new cylinder base gasket onto the crankcase, making certain that the oil hole in the case (behind the right cylinder) corresponds with that in the gasket.

NOTE: *Commando engines after engine No. 219999 are not fitted with a cylinder base gasket. A plastic gasket compound is used to seal this joint. Since the thickness of the base gasket is normally 0.016–0.020 in. (0.5 mm), deleting the gasket results in an increase in compression ratio as shown below.*

If you desire to retain the original compression ratio, a thicker head gasket must be used. Solid copper head gaskets for the Commando are available in two thicknesses: 0.040 in. (Part No. 064071) and 0.080 in. (Part No. 064072).

4. Support the pistons on the stand and lubricate the rings and skirts with some clean oil.

5. Compress the rings using the piston ring clamps.

6. Slide the barrels down over the pistons, far enough to cover all of the rings, and take out the clamps.

7. Slide the barrels down until you can fit the cylinder base washers and the nuts.

8. Tighten all of the nuts diagonally until the cylinder base is seated against the crankcase, then torque the nuts (again, in a diagonal pattern) until the proper torque setting (20 ft lbs) is attained for each.

Year	Compress. with base gasket	Compress. without base gasket
68-72	8.9 : 1	9.2 : 1
72 (Combat)	9.8 : 1	10.0 : 1
72-73	8.9 : 1	9.2 : 1
72-73	9.3 : 1	9.6 : 1

9. Before refitting the head, select the proper head gasket to be used. Pre-Commando models had a spigot on the barrels which fit into a corresponding joint in the head. These models usually used an asbestos head gasket faced with copper on both sides.

The Commando does not have a spigot, relying solely on the gasket to provide the seal. On early Commandos, this gasket was asbestos. Recent models feature an improved version with steel "eyelets" around the cut-out holes for added strength. This can replace the earlier Commando gasket with no change to the compression ratios. On this gasket, "Top" is marked. Note, however, that the gaskets for the Commando and pre-Commando models are not interchangable.

There are, in addition, gaskets of varying thickness which are described earlier in this section.

10. Place the pistons at top dead center.

11. Place the four pushrods up into the head as far as they will go, as described in "Removal." The longer pushrods are to be positioned closest to the center of the head.

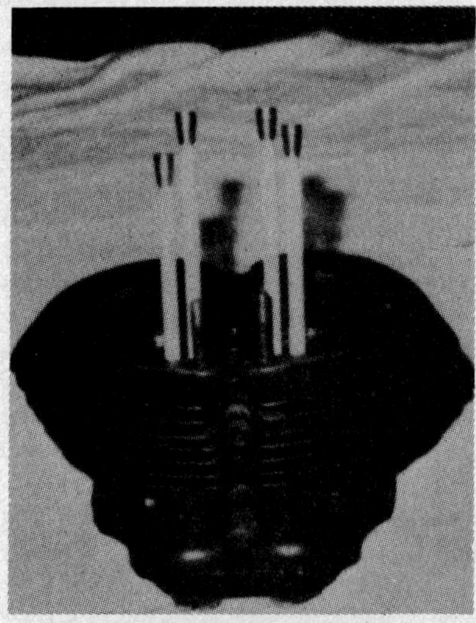

Proper pushrod positions

12. Carefully position the head over the barrels, so that the pushrods will drop directly into the tunnels, and take care that the three studs in the head do not damage the gasket.

14. Let the pushrods drop into their tunnels and make sure that they are properly fit into the tappet cups.

15. Lower the head onto the barrels. The upper end of the pushrods must now be fit with their respective rocker arm ball ends.

CAUTION: *On Scrambler models for which the rocker arm had to be removed before taking the head out of the frame, this rocker arm must now be replaced. This is an operation requiring extreme caution lest the washer or* *spring drop out of reach. It is probably wise to replace the rocker arm now, before bolting down the head.*

16. Support the head about ¼ in. off of the barrels. Those two long cylinder sleeve nuts, which are found beneath the exhaust ports, can be used to support the head in this position.

17. Looking through the exhaust and intake rocker boxes, fit each pushrod with the proper ball end. A short piece of wire with a hook at one end can be used to move the pushrods to accomplish this.

18. When you think you have engaged all of the pushrods, remove the nuts which support the head. Check again. Be absolutely certain all of the pushrods are engaged before proceeding further.

19. Tighten all of the cylinder head bolts and nuts in the order shown. Tightening should be done in increments of 5 ft lbs.

20. Adjust rocker clearances as described in "Tune-Up."

21. The remainder of the assembly procedure is the reverse of that given for disassembly. Before starting, squirt some clean engine oil into the pushrod tunnels, the rocker spindles, and the valve stems.

22. After the engine has been warmed up, allow it to cool and retorque the head bolts and nuts. After the engine is cold, readjust the valves.

CLUTCH AND PRIMARY DRIVE

Commando

DISASSEMBLY

1. Remove the left side footpeg and place a pan beneath the primary chaincase to catch the oil (some can be removed by placing the bike on the sidestand and removing the oil level plug); take off the chaincase fixing bolt and pull of the cover.

2. Disconnect the alternator wires at the snap connectors. Unbolt the stator and pull the wires (carefully) through the inner chaincase half.

3. Remove the sleeve nut and the lock washer which secures the alternator rotor to the carnkshaft. Remove the rotor, using a gear puller if needed, and take out the woodruff key. Use a pair of pliers if it is tight.

4. The triplex chain is endless variety and, therefore, the engine and clutch sprockets and the chain must be removed simultaneously.

CAUTION: *The clutch can only be removed with the aid of a special tool and it is dangerous to attempt to do so without it.*

5. Loosen the clutch adjuster nut and remove the adjuster screw.

6. With the special clutch compressor tool (Part No. 06-0999), screw the center bolt of the tool into the diaphragm spring center. Tighten the nut on the tool's center bolt until the diaphragm spring is free to turn in the clutch sprocket. Stop at this point.

7. Remove the large circlip which retains the diaphragm spring (there is a groove provided to make removal easier) and take away the spring and the tool together.

8. Remove the nut and washer which

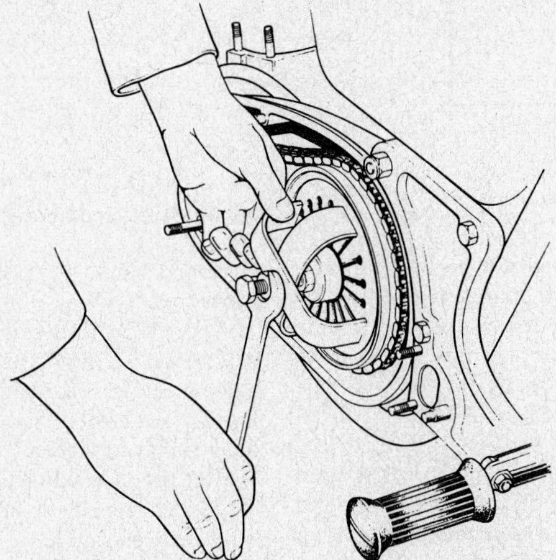

Removing the diaphragm spring with the special tool

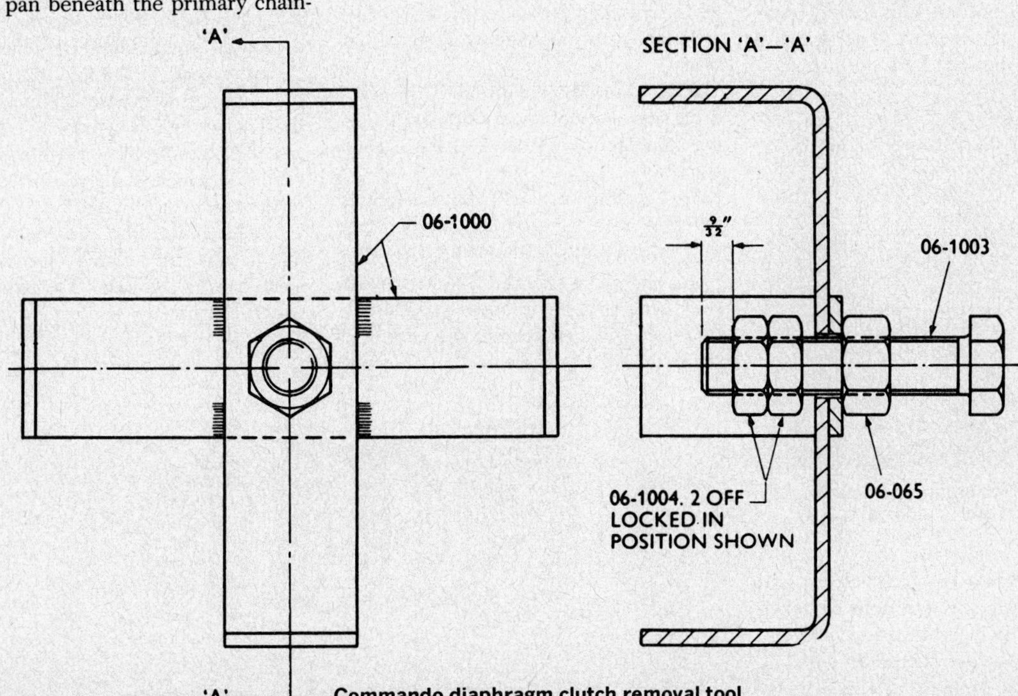

Commando diaphragm clutch removal tool

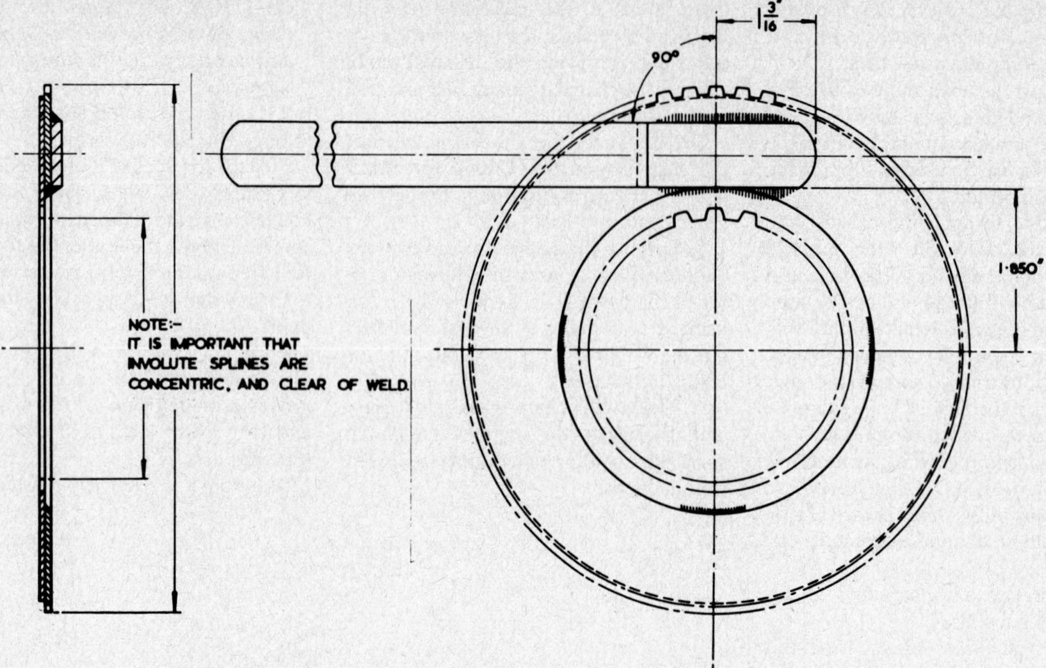

Tool to stop Commando clutch from turning

secures the clutch hub to the transmission mainshaft (a spark plug socket fits this nut); it is necessary to stop the clutch from turning so that this nut can be broken loose. Use the clutch hub tool (Part No. 06-1015) or a suitable substitute.

9. Remove the engine sprocket from its tapered shaft. It is press fit here and must be removed from the taper with a special tool. The procedure here is to attach the extractor to the sprocket and, after tightening the center bolt, rap it once with a hammer. This should break the sprocket off the shaft. If necessary, a small gear puller can be used instead.

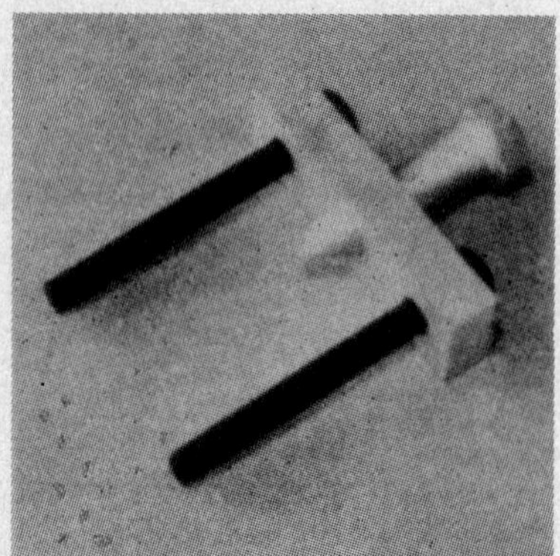

Commando engine sprocket extractor tool

10. The engine sprocket, chain, and clutch hub sprocket can now be taken away. There may be shims behind the clutch hub sprocket. These are used to adjust the true running of the primary chain and should be reassembled in their proper place.

If necessary, a special tool is available which screws into the center of the clutch to aid in removing it from its shaft. It might not be necessary if the clutch has been removed before.

After the assembly has been taken out of the chaincase, remove the engine sprocket woodruff key.

INSPECTION

1. Inspect both sprockets for worn teeth. This is a very strong primary drive assembly, so any damage would be rather rare.

2. Examine the condition of the woodruff keys and notice any signs of tapering or chipping. These must be in good condition.

3. The clutch assembly construction is revealed in the accompanying illustration. The condition of the fiber friction plates should be checked. Extreme wear should not be evident unless foreign matter has become trapped in the assembly.

The 850 Commando has an all-metal clutch assembly, the driven plates being sintered bronze instead of fiber. These should be inspected for scoring and for warpage.

4. Check the plates for warping as shown in the illustration.

5. Although it operates in the primary chaincase which contains oil to lubricate the chain, this clutch is the "dry" type. The friction plates must have dispersal grooves to get rid of any excess oil which accumulates on them. It may be necessary to cut these grooves if the plate does not have them. Four dispersal grooves spaced 90° apart should be sufficient. On the other side of the friction plate, cut four more grooves offset 45° in relation to the first set and also spaced at 90°.

The plates may have a single groove on each side which is elliptical in reference to the center of the plate.

6. The clutch hub runs on a bearing fitted into the clutch sprocket and located with circlips. To remove the clutch bearing:

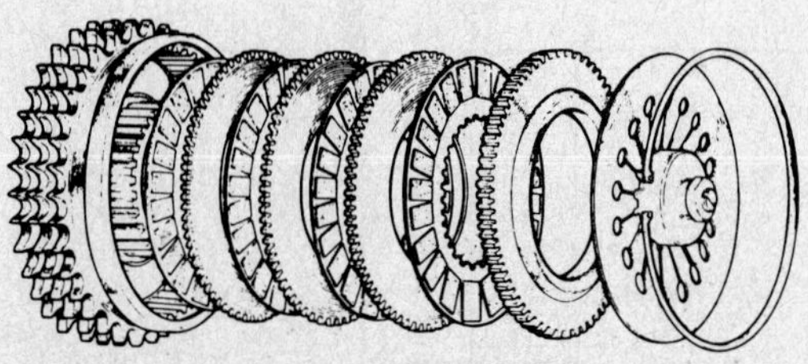

Commando clutch assembly, exploded view

Commando clutch bearing assembly

a. Take out the small circlip which holds the clutch hub with sleeve extension

b. Press out the clutch hub

c. Take out the circlip bearing (the large one)

d. Press out the bearing from the inside of the clutch sprocket

To replace the bearing, apply some grease and reassemble in the reverse of the disassembly procedure.

ASSEMBLY

1. Assembly procedure is essentially the reverse of the preceeding sequence. Be sure that both woodruff keys are in place on the crankshaft. Also, make sure that the chain line is true. Using a straight edge placed over both engine and clutch sprockets, check the chain line and adjust it with shims placed behind the clutch sprocket, if necessary. Tighten the clutch hub nut securely. Use thread locking compound to be safe.

2. Adjust the clutch as described in "Maintenance."

Pre-Commando

DISASSEMBLY

1. Remove the left side footpeg.

2. Place the machine on the sidestand and remove the primary chaincase oil level plug to remove some of the oil therein.

3. Place a pan beneath the chaincase and unscrew the large hex nut which secures the case; remove the washer and the rubber seal; and pull off the chaincase. Some models have the chaincase secured with screws around their circumference; is so, remove these and the cover.

4. Disconnect the alternator leads at the snap connector and carefully pull the wires through the inner chaincase half.

5. Remove the alternator stator.

6. Remove the rotor, using a gear puller if needed, and take the woodruff key out of the crankshaft.

7. Remove the clutch pressure plate by unscrewing the three spring adjustment nuts. Each nut has two small tabs, on the face which bears against the spring, to prevent loosening in operation. It is possible to place a thin knife blade between the spring and the nut to prevent the tabs from being sheared off upon removal. Otherwise, the nuts should be replaced upon reassembly.

8. Remove the clutch springs, cups, and pressure plate.

9. Remove the nut and washer which secure the clutch assembly to the transmission mainshaft.

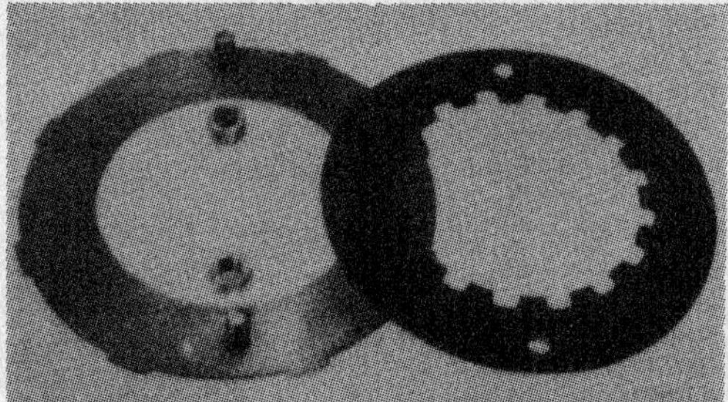

Tool to stop clutch from turning (pre-Commando)

NOTE: *It may be necessary to stop the clutch from turning so that this nut can be removed. You can make a simple, though effective, tool to do this. This consists of a standard clutch plain metal plate and a standard friction plate. As illustrated, both plates are drilled and the metal plate is fitted with two short studs. Bolting the two together takes the place of spring pressure and will make removal of the center nut much easier.*

10. Disconnect the master link of the primary chain and remove the chain.

11. Using the special tool, if necessary, remove the clutch assembly. This tool screws into the center of the clutch and pulls it off the shaft. It may not be necessary to use the tool if the clutch has been removed before.

Clutch hub removal tool (pre-Commando)

12. Using a small gear puller, take the engine sprocket off of the tapered portion of the crankshaft. Remove the woodruff key.

INSPECTION

1. Check the condition of the sprocket teeth; wear should not be noticeable.

2. Inspect the fiber friction plates and the steel plates to see if they are warped. The fiber plates should be in good condition if foreign matter has not become trapped in the clutch mechanism. Replace the plates if they, or any one of them, is scored or the friction material is worn.

3. Plates which have become oil-impregnated through long service should be replaced, although they can be salvaged by dusting them with an oil absorbing material and washing afterward in a solvent.

4. The clutch bearing may be inspected by removing the three nuts at the back of the clutch hub and removing the plate. These nuts are center punched and should be replaced rather than reused. Grease the bearing and replace the plate. Peen the nuts as they were before.

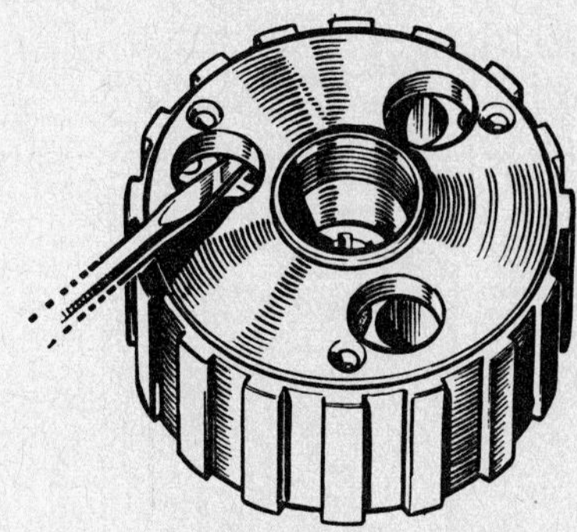

Removing clutch hub cover plate

5. The clutch has rubber shock absorbers in the hub to prevent "snatching" and the damage it might cause. To inspect them, unscrew the three countersunk retaining screws at the front of the clutch hub and pry off the steel plate. The rubber blocks will come out of the hub easily if they are worn. If difficulty is encountered, the thick rubbers can be com-

pressed with the aid of the tool shown in the illustration and the thin rubbers removed.

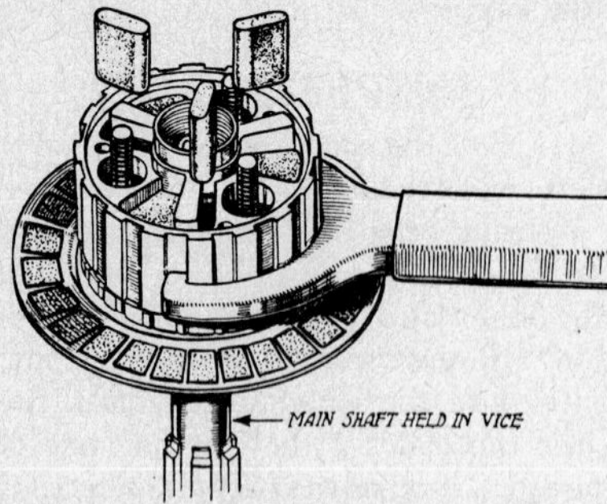

Removal and installation of clutch hub shock absorbers

When reinstalling the rubbers, a soap and water solution will make them slide into place easier. Tighten the three screws very firmly and center punch them for security.

ASSEMBLY

1. Replace the clutch hub on its shaft, refit the woodruff key and engine sprocket, thread the primary chain over the sprockets, and then secure the master link. The closed end of the spring clip should face the direction of chain rotation.

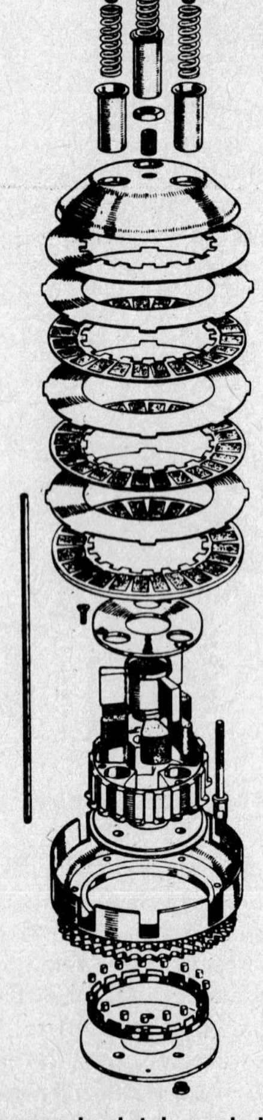

Pre-Commando clutch, exploded view

2. Replace the clutch hub washer and tighten the nut securely. Some thread locking compound is useful here.
3. Assemble the clutch in the following order:
   a. Thick steel plate, step facing inward
   b. Double-sided friction plate
   c. Steel plate
   d. Double-sided friction plate
   e. Steel plate
   f. Double-sided friction plate
   g. Steel plate
   h. Single-sided friction plate, plain side outward
   i. Pressure plate
4. Replace the spring cups and springs; the cups have a tab to fit a slot on the pressure plate.
5. Screw down the adjusting nut with a fork-like tool. These should be flush with the spring cups after assembly.
6. Replace the rotor and tighten the rotor nut very firmly. It is advisable to secure this nut with thread locking compound.
7. Bolt on the alternator, run the leads through the inner chaincase half, and reconnect them.
8. Kick the engine over several times while watching the rotor, to be sure that it does not contact the alternator stator at any point. An even gap all around the rotor is preferred and washers may be placed behind the stator to accomplish this.

A spacer, about 0.010 in. thick, can be placed around the rotor and used as a guide while tightening the stator nuts.

9. Work the handlebar clutch lever several times and notice the operation of the clutch. The pressure plate must remain parallel to the other plates when it disengages. If it does not (you will notice it coming off the assembly at an angle), adjust the clutch springs.
10. Adjust the clutch.
11. The primary chain should be adjusted when the engine-transmission unit is warm because of the expansion of the mountings due to heat. Adjust the chain tension as described in "Tune-Up and Maintenance." Make sure that the chain has no tight spots. If it does, replace it or adjust normally at the tightest spot of the chain. Remember to readjust the rear chain also.

BOTTOM END OVERHAUL

All Models

The Norton crankcase contains the crankshaft itself, the main bearings, and the camshaft. Disassembly, therefore, is quite straightforward and should present no problems.

To check the bearings, or to inspect the crankshaft or connection rods, the cases must be split.

The following procedure applies to all models.

DISASSEMBLY

1. Remove the engine from the frame and remove the cylinder head and barrels as previously outlined. See "Engine Removal."
2. Remove the timing cover. All of the timing and ignition gear in the case must be removed if the timing side bearing is to be inspected or replaced. This equipment can be left intact if the drive side bearing or the camshaft is the reason you are taking the engine apart. Procedures for removing the ignition points, oil pump, timing chain(s), and sprockets are given in a following section.

   NOTE: *If the machine is fitted with a magneto or has the ignition points in a canister behind the barrels, the unit need not be removed, although it is better to do so.*

3. Unbolt all the studs passing through the crankcase halves and the two screws at the bottom of the cases.
4. Take the crankcase up and position it so that the drive side of the crankshaft is pointing straight down.
5. Tap the drive end of the crankshaft on a wooden block until the cases begin to separate. Be careful to split the cases gradually, or the camshaft will fall out if the drive side case comes off too quickly (if the cam sprocket has been removed). If difficulty is encountered, the drive side case half may be heated gently with a propane torch, although care should be taken not to get the flame anywhere near the protruding end of the crankshaft. There is a rubber oil seal here, which, obviously, will suffer from the effects of heat. Heating the case should only be necessary on relatively new engines. Even in this case, the amount of heat needed to split the cases is not great.
6. The cases will separate, leaving the outer bearing race for the drive side bearing in the case; the rollers will remain on the crankshaft.
7. Take out the camshaft, the crankcase breather plate, and the spring from the drive side case half. On newer models, the breather has been relocated to the rear of the crankcase and needs no attention.
8. The timing side main bearing is a ball type on all but the most recent models, which have a roller bearing fitted. In either case, the procedure for removal and installation is essentially the same as for the drive side bearing. The crankshaft will be held in the timing side case half by the bearing. Check the operation of the bearing by noting any lateral play in the crankshaft, or any unusual sounds as the

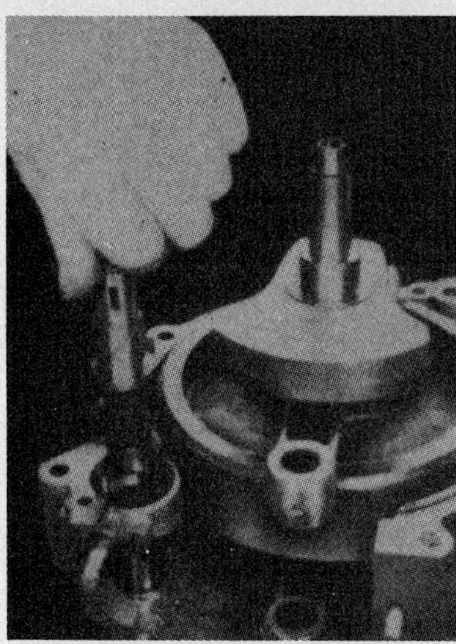

Removing the camshaft

shaft is rotated. This rotation should be smooth and effortless.

9. Heat the case as previously described for the drive side bearing.

10. Holding the case with the drive side of the crankshaft pointing down, have a helper tap on the timing side of the crank with a soft-faced mallet.

NOTE: *It is a good idea to use a sleeve over the crankshaft end to avoid damage to it, the oil pump worm gear threads, or to avoid getting any foreign matter in the oil passage. Also, be sure the intermediate gear shaft does not move.*

11. The timing side ball bearing must be taken off the crankshaft as a single piece. A claw-type puller should be used to get the bearing off of the shaft.

INSPECTION

1. Check the condition of the drive side bearing. The outer race must be free of all scratches and score marks.

Note the condition of the rollers themselves. A single roller may be removed for inspection by grasping it by the end with pliers and jerking quickly upward. Again, check for scoring and signs of wear.

2. Having removed a roller in this manner, the roller path can be examined by looking through the gap left by the removed roller and rotating the cage around the inner race. The race must be free from all imperfections.

3. If necessary, the inner bearing race and the rollers can be removed by two sharp steel wedges which should be placed on either side of the bearing assembly. Use the wedges to lever the bearing away from the crankshaft cheek until there is enough room for a claw-type extractor to be used.

4. The outer race can be taken out of the crankcase in which it is a very tight fit. Of course, if the rollers are replaced, the outer race must be replaced as well. Heat the crankcase half in an oven, being sure not to exceed the recommended temperature of 200°C. and then drop the case (from about a six inch height) onto a wooden bench. This should knock out the bearing race. If you run into trouble, a damp rag stuffed into the race after heating the case should cool the race enough to make removal easy.

5. The timing side ball bearing should also be inspected for wear, pitting of the bearings, rough movement, and true alignment on the shaft.

INSTALLATION

1. The drive side bearing outer race can be refitted after heating the case as described above. The roller assembly must be replaced using an arbor press to fit in onto the crankshaft. Press it on as far as it will go.

2. The timing side bearing (if ball-type), should be raplaced with a "single dot" type which is a close fitting bearing. This is Part No. 17822.

3. If the motorcycle is equipped with one of the newer roller type bearings (as after engine No. 200,004), be sure that the replacement is a Skefco double-lipped outer, single-lipped inner spool type NJ 306. The internal diametrical clearances should be 0.0008–0.0012 in.

Models fitted with the roller bearing on the timing side have an "H" stamped on the timing side crankshaft cheek at the bearing.

The fitting of the roller bearing on the timing side has also resulted in a slight increase in the crank journal diameter.

4. It is imperative in all cases, especially in the case of the timing side roller bearing, to lubricate the bearing after assembly and before running the engine. For the timing side bearing, this lubrication must be done from the outside. Accomplish this by pouring clean engine oil into the intake rocker box. This oil will work its way down into the timing chest and then to the bearing.

Pour a good amount of clean engine oil on the drive side bearing before assembly of the crankcase halves.

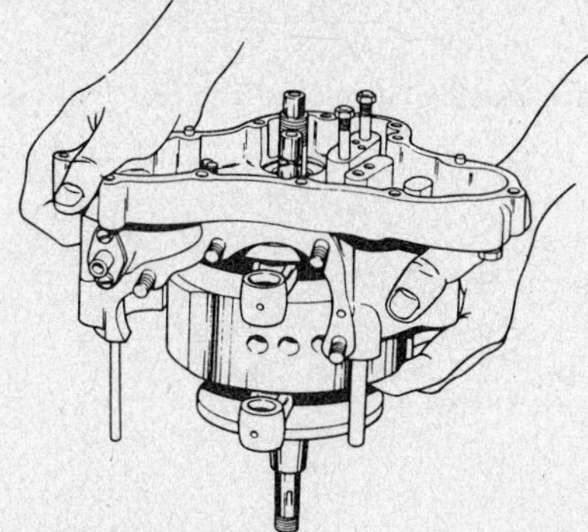

Installing timing side main bearing in crankcase

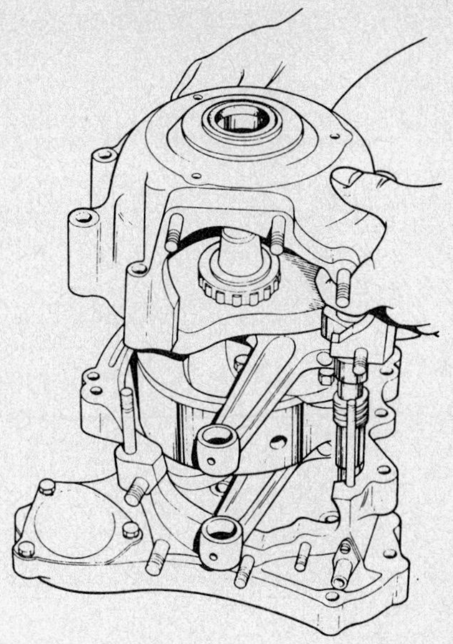

Assembling crankcase halves

5. Heat the timing side crankcase half and press in the bearing, which should already be fitted to the crankshaft. Be sure the bearing is pressed in as far as possible. It should be possible to press the assembly in by hand if the case has been sufficiently heated.

6. Replace the crankcase breather plate and spring and fit the crankcase halves. Some gasket forming compound on the crankcase halve's mating surface is essential, as no gasket is fitted.

Crankcase Oil Seals

1. Both sides of the crankcase are fitted with an oil seal on the crankshaft. For the timing side, the seal is in the timing cover. For inspection or replacement procedures, refer to that section.

2. The drive side seal can be pressed out from the inside of the crankcase. The new seal (Part No. T.2187) is pressed in with the sharp edge facing inward (to the inside of the crankcase).

Connecting Rods and Journals

REMOVAL AND INSPECTION

1. Connecting rods should be checked for vertical play on their journals. There should not be any at all. Some side play is not significant.

2. To remove the connecting rods, remove the two self-locking nuts which hold the rod to the cap and pull the rod away from the journal with a sharp jerk. Keep each rod with its own cap for reassembly. There is a slash mark on each rod and cap unit which indicates the correct position for reassembly. It is essential that each unit be correctly installed (i.e. that the slash marks align).

Crankshaft disassembled

3. The crankshaft journals and the rod big end bearings can now be inspected. The bearing shells in the connecting rod must be absolutely free of scratches or abrasions. A series of parallel grooves running lengthwise along the shells indicate that oil contaminated with metal particles has been circulating. To be safe, the entire lubrication system should be cleaned out to remove the inevitable foreign matter elsewhere in the system. Be sure to flush out the tank and clean the crankshaft sludge trap. It would also be wise to disassemble and carefully inspect the oil pump for damage.

4. Before replacing the bearing shells, check the dimensions of the crank journals. Not even the slightest mar can be tolerated on the journal surface. Minor imperfections must be removed. Use the finest grade of emery cloth available.

A micrometer must be used to check the journals. They must be within 0.001 in. of perfectly circular (measurements obtained by reading the diameter of the journal at two locations, 90° apart) and must be within 0.003 in. of the diameter given at the end of this section.

If either wear or ovality exceeds these figures, the journal must be reground. Never remove material from the connecting rod or cap to take up play.

When grinding the journal, be sure to restore the radius on each as shown in the illustration. The radius is 0.090 in.

5. Undersized big end shells are available in four sizes: 0.010 in., 0.020 in., 0.030 in., and 0.040 in. For the first journal regrind, the journal diameter should therefore be 1.7405–1.7400 in. The size of the replacement shell should be stamped on the end cheek.

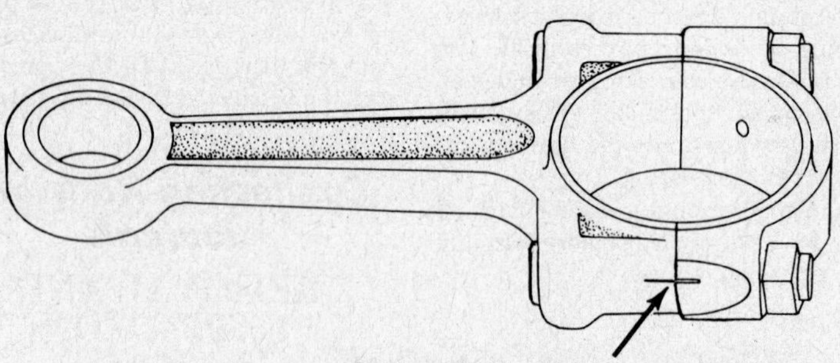

Slash mark identifying con rod and cap

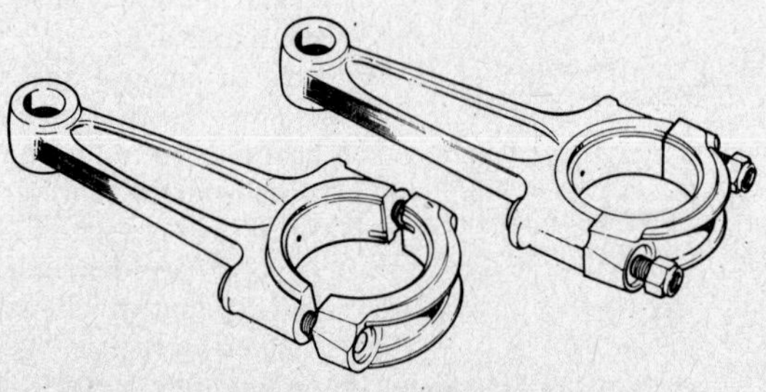

Connecting rod showing bearing shell tab locations

6. The connecting rod body must be free of scratches. Many experts recommend polishing the rods with a fine emery cloth to remove all minor imperfections which may develop into cracks during running.

7. There is no bush at the small end of the connecting rod. The wrist pin rides directly on the rod itself. The small end bore should not exceed 0.6868 in. with the wrist pin in place; check for play.

ASSEMBLY

1. Use the correct undersize bearing shells if the journal has been reground.

2. Be sure that the rod assembly is perfectly clean, especially that the bolt holes and mating surfaces are free of even the minutest particles.

3. Assemble the rods with the small oil hole at the base pointing AWAY FROM the center of the crankshaft.

4. Use the self-locking nuts (Part No. 23253) on the rod bolts and torque them down to 25 ft/lbs. Force some oil through the passages in the crankshaft until some emerges from each side of the rods.

NOTE: *It is advisable to use new rod bolts and nuts when installing the rods.*

Crankshaft

DISASSEMBLY AND INSPECTION

The crankshaft is a three-piece unit consisting of a center flywheel and two end cheeks which have the rod journals. The crank is bolted together, the end cheeks being located with a dowel.

1. The crankshaft cheeks are accidentally interchangable which, of course, will seriously affect the bearings, so avoid the possibility of a mistake on reassembly by marking the position of the cheeks.

2. Straighten the locking tabs and remove the two nuts from the studs, then the four nuts on the bolts. Separate the crankshaft elements.

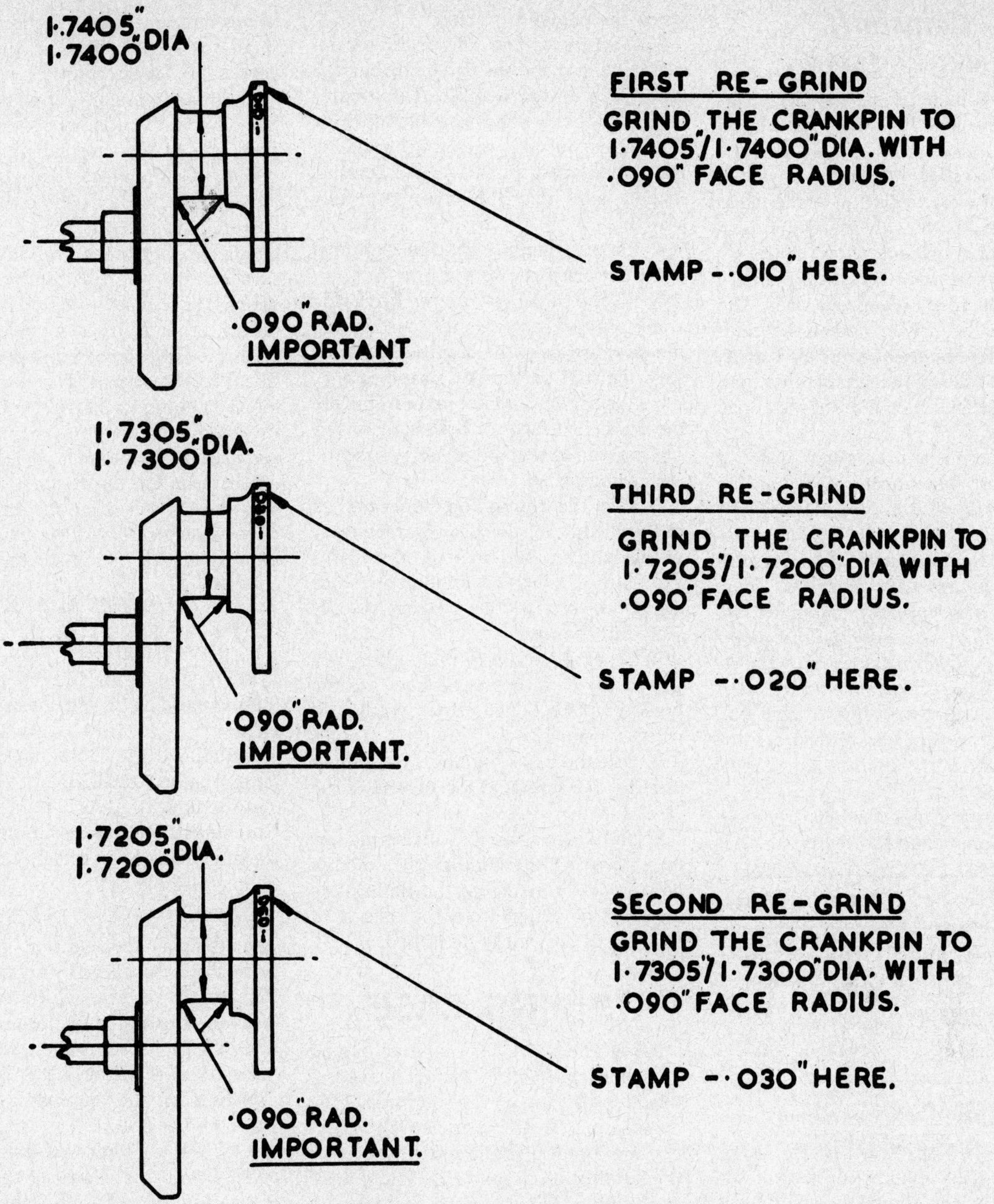

1·7405"
1·7400" DIA
FIRST RE-GRIND
GRIND THE CRANKPIN TO 1·7405"/1·7400" DIA. WITH ·090" FACE RADIUS.
STAMP -·010" HERE.
·090" RAD.
IMPORTANT
1·7305"
1·7300" DIA.
THIRD RE-GRIND
GRIND THE CRANKPIN TO 1·7205"/1·7200" DIA WITH ·090" FACE RADIUS.
STAMP -·020" HERE.
·090" RAD.
IMPORTANT.
1·7205"
1·7200" DIA.
SECOND RE-GRIND
GRIND THE CRANKPIN TO 1·7305"/1·7300" DIA. WITH ·090" FACE RADIUS.
STAMP -·030" HERE.
·090" RAD.
IMPORTANT.

Crankshaft journal regrinding instructions

3. A good mechanic will realize the importance of the mating surfaces of the flywheel and end cheeks and ensure that they are in no way damaged and are completely free of foreign matter. It can easily be seen that this would affect the true running of the crankshaft.

4. Clean out the sludge trap machined into the flywheel.

REASSEMBLY

1. When reassembling the crank, be certain that all of the nuts are very tight. They should be torqued to 35 ft lbs.

2. Tighten the bolts in a diagonal pattern and peen the nuts with a punch afterwards. If the nuts have been peened before, it might be wise to replace thwm with new ones. Do not forget to turn up the locking tabs on the stud nuts.

SMALL NUT ON BOLT
LARGE NUT ON BOLT
STUDS
TAB WASHER

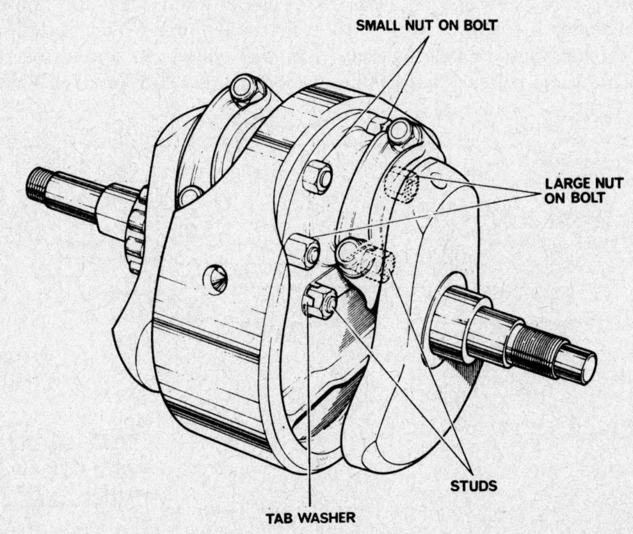

Crankshaft and nuts

Camshaft

INSPECTION

1. Little can be done with the camshaft, as the lobes are calibrated in all their dimensions and should not be touched. You should check for any obvious signs of wear or pitting of the lobes. Replacement is the only solution if damage or wear is evident.

2. Make sure that the cam bushes are smooth and free of imperfections. The bushes can be driven out of the cases after heating, if necessary. If this is done, be sure that the oil hole in the bush lines up with the one in the crankcase upon reassembly.

3. The crankcase breather plate, if fitted, must be smooth and can be worked on an oil stone if necessary.

IMPORTANT: *As of 1972, factory Nortons are equipped with oil grooves machined in the cam bushings. These grooves were formerly machined into the camshaft. It is essential that either the cam or the bushings have the oil grooves or severe damage will result. It does not matter if BOTH cam and bushings are grooved, but either the cam or the bushings must have the oil grooves.*

The following specifications are applicable to Commando camshafts:

	Standard	Combat
Inlet opens BTDC	50°	59°
Inlet closes ABDC	74°	89°
Exh. opens BBDC	82°	88°
Exh. closes ATDC	42°	60°

CRANKCASE ASSEMBLY

1. Check the mating surfaces of the crankcase halves, removing any old gasket compound and rubbing off abrasions with an oil stone.

2. Oil both bearings and bearing races well to insure some primary lubrication when the engine is started.

3. With the timing side bearing (complete) in place and the drive side bearing inner race on the crankshaft (the outer race is in the case), apply heat to the drive side crankcase half, preferably by heating in an oven, then slip it over the bearing, making sure that the bearing is fully seated.

4. Fit the breather plate in its tunnel and then place the spring in.

5. Fit the camshaft into the drive side crankcase making absolutely certain that the driving tabs of the breather plate engage the slots on the end of the cam.

6. Apply gasket compound carefully to the mating surfaces of both case halves. There is no gasket fitted here, so some seal is necessary.

7. Heat the timing side crankcase half in the vicinity of the bearing race (very little heating should be necessary, if any) and slide it over the crankshaft. Once again, make sure the bearing is fully seated in the case.

If the cases refuse to mate after they are about ⅛ in. apart, chances are the breather plate is not properly engaged with the cam.

8. Bolt the cases together, not forgetting the two screws at the bottom of the case.

9. Make sure again that all bearing surfaces have oil. Remember that models with a roller bearing on the timing side must be lubricated from the outside of the case as previously described.

TIMING CASE

All of the valve and ignition timing gear on the Norton 750s and 850s is contained in the case on the right side of the crankcase. The oil pump as well as several important oil seals and junctions for the lubrication system are found here also.

The timing is accomplished by means of a small pinion which is fitted to the end of the crankshaft and drives an intermediate gear and sprocket. This sprocket drives the camshaft by means of a short, single-row chain. The oil pump drive gear is also located on the crankshaft.

Commando engines after No. 131257 have the ignition points operating at the right end of the camshaft. Prior to this model, Commandos had the points located in a canister behind the cylinder barrels. The points were timed by another chain from the intermediate sprocket to the distributor sprocket which was secured to its shaft by a pin.

Most other Nortons, including the Atlas and G15CS, were equipped with the Lucas K2F magneto. This unit, too, was located behind the barrels and it was also driven by chain from the intermediate sprocket. The automatic spark advance mechanism for the magneto was integrated with the magneto sprocket and they were secured to the magneto's tapered shaft with a self-locking bolt.

Timing Cover

REMOVAL

1. Disconnect the tachometer drive if it is mounted on the outside of the timing cover.

2. Remove the ignition points cover (after engine No. 131257)

3. Remove the rocker oil feed pipe banjo at the rear of the timing cover. If the engine has been recently run, a little oil may dribble out.

After engine No. 131257:

4. Remove the ignition point base plate which is secured by two screws, also the wires. It may be helpful to mark the location of base plate before removal, so that it can be reinstalled without the necessity of resetting the timing.

5. Remove the automatic timing advance center bolt.

6. Screw a withdrawal bolt (Part No. 060934) into the center of the advance mechanism to pull it off of the camshaft.

All models:

7. Place a can beneath the cover to catch the oil. Take out the timing cover screws.

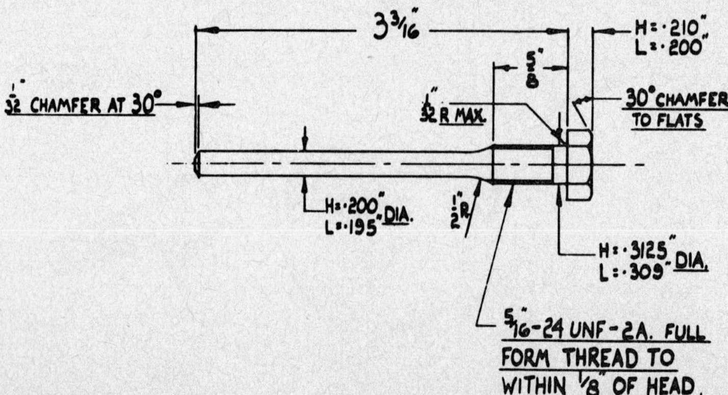

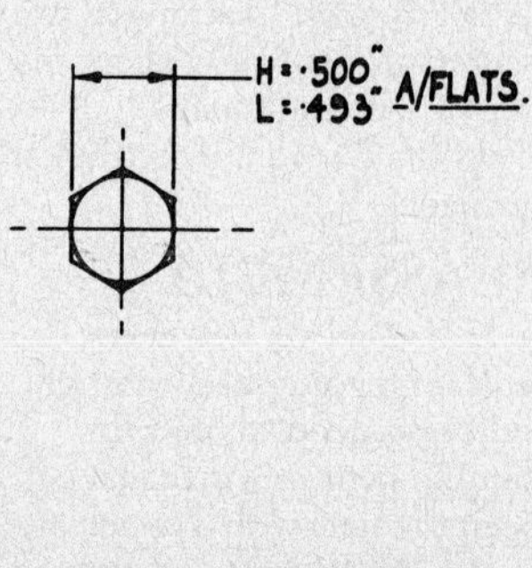

Timing advance mechanism withdrawal bolt

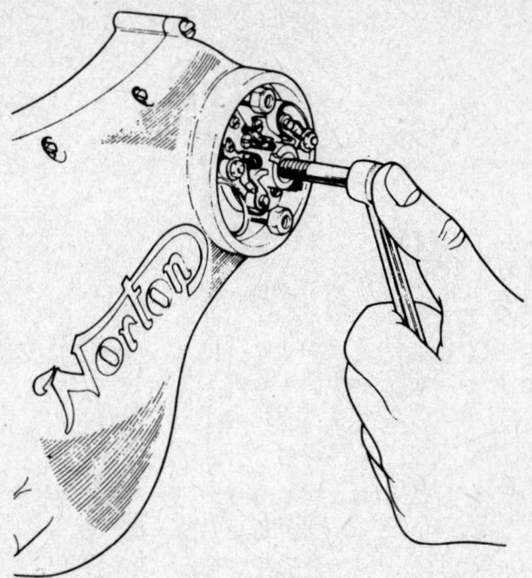
Removing the advance mechanism

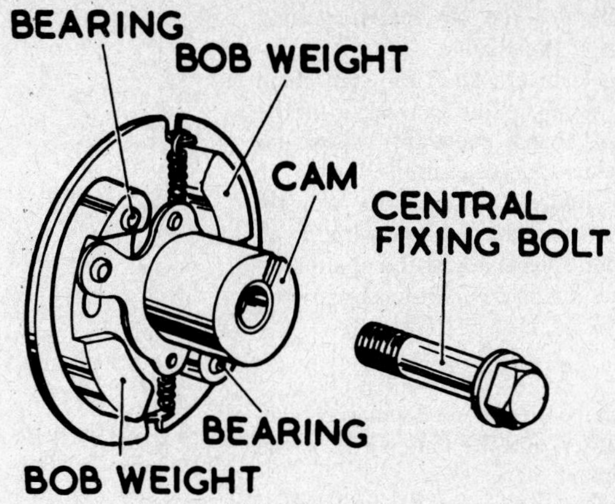

Timing advance mechanism

8. Pull off the timing cover.
9. Oil will dribble out of the drilling in the crankcase at the left (as you look at it) of the timing case. Use one of the cover screws to block off the flow of oil.

Timing Assembly

REMOVAL

If the sprockets and chain are to be removed, mark both with paint before removal.

1. Remove the oil pump. It is secured by two nuts. Make sure that the pump has the conical oil seal fitted on the nipple of the pump body. Sometimes this seal comes away with the timing cover, so check there if it is missing.
2. Remove the oil pump drive gear. This has a LEFT-HAND thread onto the crankshaft.
3. Remove the camshaft chain adjuster. This assembly consists of two plain metal plates of varying thickness and a metal slipper which bears on the cam chain and it is fastened by two nuts. The thin metal plate goes on the engine side of the slipper.

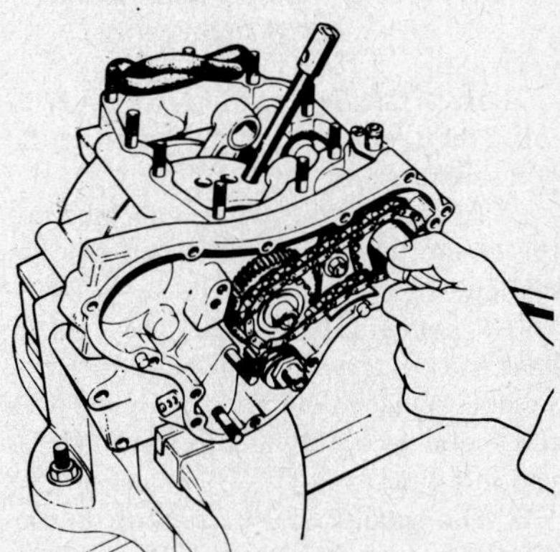
Removing the camshaft sprocket nut

4 Remove the nut which secures the camshaft sprocket. The sprocket can be taken off with a gear puller or with the extractor tool (Part No. EST12). The cam sprocket cannot be removed at this point on models with a separate ignition timing chain. For these models:

5. Loosen the magneto sprocket bolt and make sure that the automatic advance mechanism can be removed from the magneto shaft or, on capacitor ignition models, drive out the pin passing through the distributor sprocket and shaft.

All models:

6. Remove the intermediate sprocket, cam sprocket, and ignition sprocket (if applicable) together. Pinch the chain or chains in the center of their runs to ensure that the sprockets do not change their position on the chain relative to the intermediate sprocket. This will of course affect the timing. Remove the thrust washer behind the intermediate sprocket if fitted. Take the woodruff key off of the camshaft.
7. Remove the small timing pinion from the crankshaft. This necessitates the use of the special extractor (Part No. ET.2003). Remove the pinion key, the triangular washer, and the metal oil seal from the crankshaft.

Timing pinion removal tool

INSPECTION

1. Check all of the sprockets for signs of wear. This would be rare in any case,

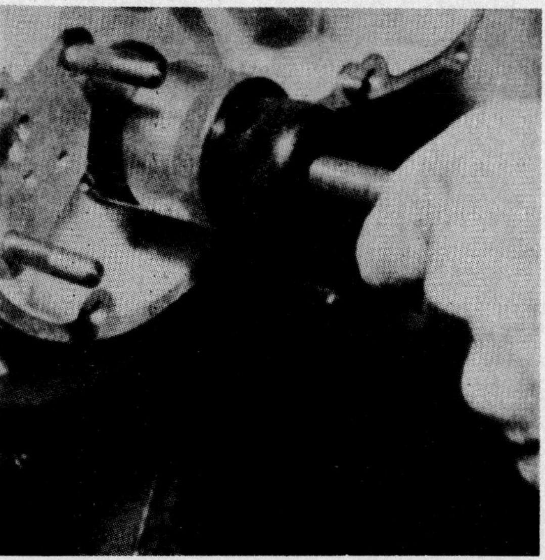
Special tool in use to remove timing pinion

due to the ideal (i.e. oil soaked) running condition of the chains.

2. Check for cracks in the cam chain adjuster slipper. This can occur if the chain had been overtight. Allow for proper play upon reassembly.

3. The magneto or points canister have a small amount of movement on their mountings to adjust the chain tenison. Once this movement has been used up, the chain must be replaced.

ASSEMBLY

1. Replace the metal oil seal, the triangular washer, and the pinion key on the crankshaft.

2. Replace the pinion. Be sure the bevelled edge faces outward. There is a timing "dot" on the outer side of the pinion also.

3. Replace the thrust washer on the intermediate shaft if fitted.

4. Rotate the crankshaft until the small timing dot on the timing pinion is at 12 o'clock.

5. Take the cam timing chaing with the intermediate sprocket and cam sprocket, and the ignition timing chain and sprocket if applicable, and position the intermediate gear so that its timing dot aligns with that on the timing pinion.

Timing pinion correctly meshed with intermediate sprocket

6. Also fit the cam sprocket on the cam. It is keyed.

7. There are timing dots on both the intermediate sprocket and the cam sprocket. When the intermediate sprocket is in the correct position, there should be SIX outer plates of the drive chain between the two dots.

8. Replace the distributor or magneto sprocket. If a magneto is fitted, do not tighten the fixing bolt all the way, as the timing must be reset.

9. Stop the engine from turning by placing the transmission in gear or, if the engine is disassembled, place a steel bar through the connecting rod small ends and the bearing on the top of the crankcase. Tighten the camshaft sprocket nut.

10. Replace the oil pump drive gear on the crankshaft (left-hand thread) and tighten it also. The nut should be very tight. Some thread locking compound here is a good idea.

11. Apply a thin coat of gasket compound on the face of the oil pump unless a gasket is fitted and replace the pump on its studs. Tighten the two nuts evenly and torque both to the proper setting.

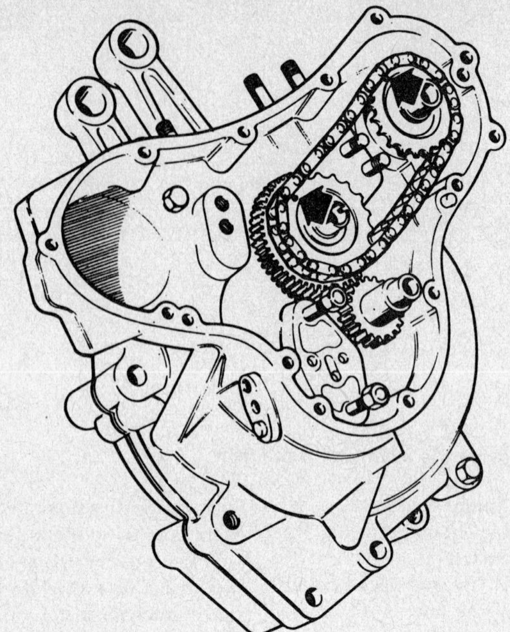

Cam chain correctly timed (six chain plates between the dots on the sprockets

12. Replace the thin metal plate on the cam chain tensioner with the longest portion from the bolt hole downward.

13. Replace the tensioner slipper itself, and finally, the thick plate. Replace, but do not tighten, the two nuts on the tensioner.

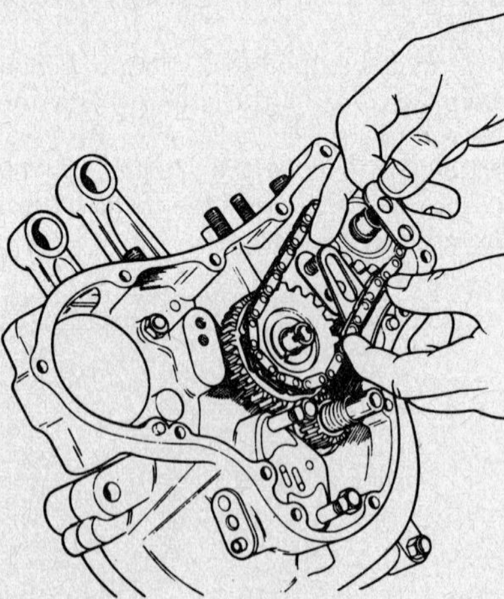

Installing the cam chain tensioner

14. The cam chain tension must now be adjusted. A cut-away timing cover is handy to have for the adjustment of the chain, since it supports the intermediate sprocket spindle and allows a more accurate setting of the chain slack to be made.

The tensioner should be adjusted to bear against the lower chain run until there is 3/16 in. play measured in the middle of the upper chain run.

15. If an ignition chain is fitted, this can be adjusted (also to 3/16 in. play in the middle of the upper run) by loosening the two nuts and one bolt which secure the distributor or magneto, and pivoting the unit until the desired tension is reached. A screwdriver can be used to pry behind the unit, as there is a shoulder provided on the case for this.

CAUTION: *Overtightening of the magneto chain can cause binding of the automatic spark advance mechanism. Therefore, ensure that the chain slack is correct and that the advance mechanism moves freely after the timing is adjusted.*

TIMING COVER OIL SEALS

There are two oil seals in the cover itself. The larger seal is for the end of the crankshaft.

1. To remove the large seal, take out the circlip which secures it and pry the seal out.

1. When replacing the seal, gently heat the cover with a propane torch or suitable replacement and fit the seal with the metal face outward (toward you as you install it).

3. The smaller seal is present on machines after engine No. 131257 and is intended to prevent oil from getting into the points compartment. It fits directly over the camshaft. Pry out the seal with a sharp pointed tool.

4. Warm the cover as before and press the seal into position, metal backing facing you as you install it.

5. The timing cover also has the oil pressure relief valve which is located just above the rocker oil feed pipe junction. The relief valve is spring loaded to operate at a pre-determined pressure and therefore, needs no attention. The valve does have a wire filter screen fitted which might be checked and cleaned if necessary.

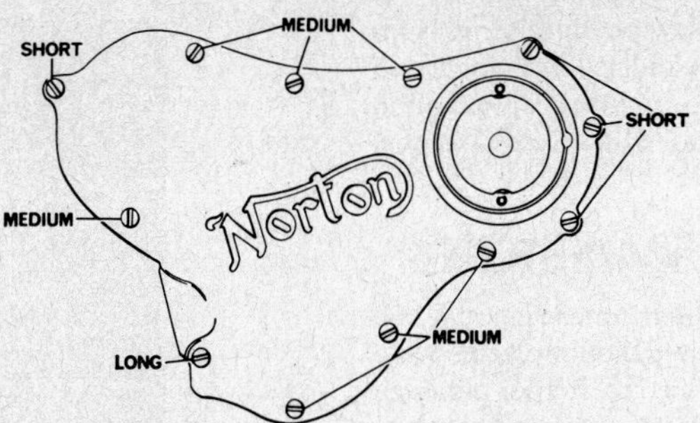

Timing cover screw location

Timing Cover

INSTALLATION

1. Remove all traces of old gasket and gasket compound from the mating surfaces. The timing cover can be worked on an appropriate surface (such as a sheet of emery cloth placed on a piece of glass) to remove any surface irregularities, scratches, etc.

NOTE: *Early model Nortons had a rather thin paper gasket for the timing cover which was effective only if the mating surfaces were in very good condition. The Commando has a thicker gasket which may be used to advantage on earlier models also. The only difference between this and the earlier gasket (aside from the thickness and composition of the material) is an extra hole for the points wires. This is not needed for early models and can be removed.*

2. Models fitted with the ignition points at the camshaft must use a guide bush (Part No. 06-1359) over the cam to prevent damage to the oil seal in the timing cover. The threaded portion of the bush is screwed on to the camshaft by hand, as far as possible. Add a little oil to the outside of the bush to make assembly easier.

3. Check the condition and efficiency of the conical seal on the oil pump. If it is deformed, replace it. It should be able to push the timing cover away from the case about 0.010 in. when fitted. If it does not, replace it, or use shim washers behind the seal.

If a thicker than standard gasket has been fitted, as described above, shim washers may be necessary.

4. Refit the timing cover, screw in the 12 cover screws, and tighten them evenly and in a diagonal pattern.

5. Reconnect the rocker oil feed pipe banjo.

6. Reconnect the tachometer drive cable if applicable.

For Commando models after engine No. 131257:

7. Remove the inspection cap on the primary chaincase to expose the indicator plate.

8. Position the engine so that the timing mark on the rotor registers 28° on the indicator plate (each mark equals two degrees).

9. Insert the timing advance mechanism and position it so that the rivets for the bob weights are in line with the two screw holes for the point cover. The slot (not the slash mark) in the breaker cam should now be about 9 o'clock.

10. Replace the ignition point base as-

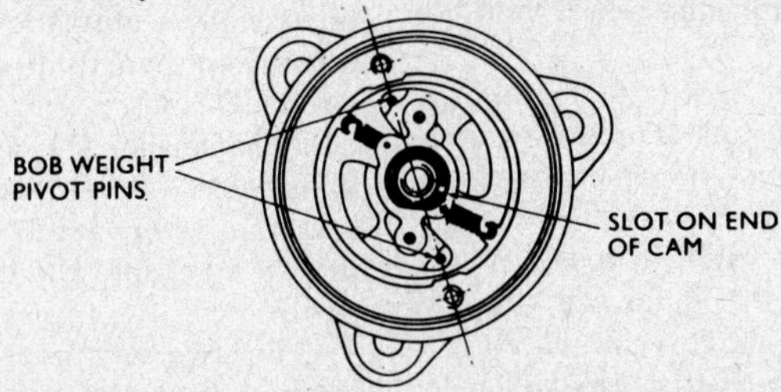

Timing advance mechanism positioned for installation

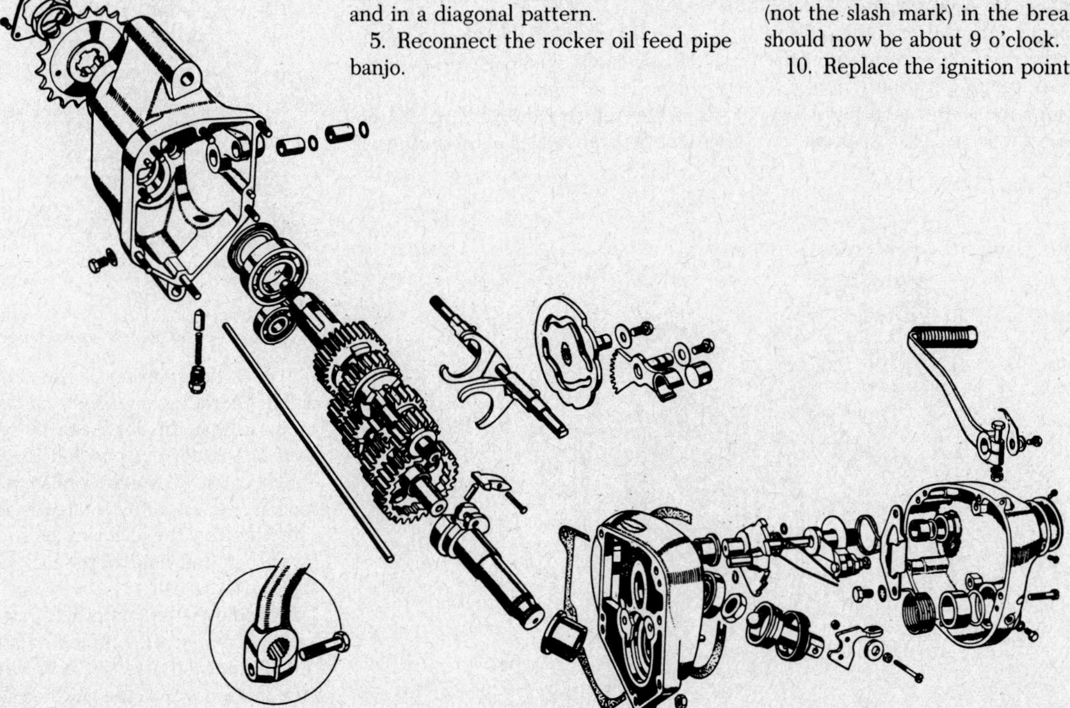
Norton gearbox, exploded view

sembly. The yellow and black lead is for the drive side cylinder (left point set).

11. Adjust the timing as described in the "Tune-Up and Maintenance" section.

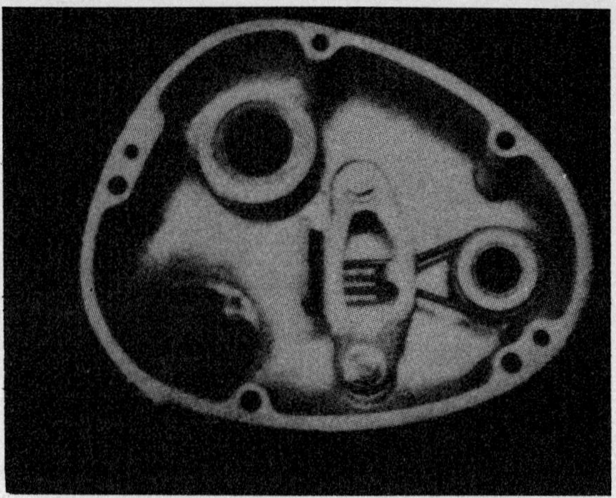

Shifter stop plate and return spring in outer cover

TRANSMISSION

The transmission internals may be removed, inspected, and replaced while the case is still in the frame, although removing the transmission case involves taking out the engine as well. This applies to all models.

To remove the transmission as a unit, refer to the beginning of this section under "Engine Removal."

Transmission Outer Cover

DISASSEMBLY

1. Take off the clutch lever inspection cap on the outer cover and disconnect the clutch cable by prying up the lever and slipping out the nipple. Unscrew the cable adjuster from the case. Drain the transmission oil.
2. Remove the kickstarter crank bolt and remove the crank. It might be necessary to use a claw-type puller to get the crank off the splined shaft.
3. Remove the right footpeg.
4. Remove the bolt for the gearshift lever, but leave the lever in place.
5. Remove the five screws which secure the outer cover.
6. Carefully pull off the cover, using the gearshift lever to assist you.
7. Remove the pawl spring.
8. Disengage the shifter return spring legs from the pawl pin, and withdraw the pawl carrier, tapping it if necessary.
9. Remove the shifter stop plate (two bolts) and remove the return spring.

INSPECTION

1. Check the shifter pawl for unusual wear.
2. The outer cover has two rubber O-rings which act as oil seals. The larger of the two is found on the kickstarter shaft behind a steel bush. The bush may be removed by heating the case and driving it out from the outside after first prying out the O-ring.
3. The smaller O-ring is for the gear shifter shaft. To remove the bush here, heat the cover, gently screw a coarse threaded tap into the bush, and pull it out.
4. Remove any traces of old gasket material from the outer cover mating surface and check the condition of the surface. All abrasions, scratches, etc. should be removed with an oil stone.

REASSEMBLY

1. Reassembly is the reverse of the previous procedure.
2. When refitting the pawl spring, notice that the cranked leg of the spring will be in the lowest position, the straight leg in the higher.
3. Assure that the pawl concave side is facing the gearshift spindle so that it can remesh with the ratchet plate.
4. Put some clean oil on the kickstarter shaft to avoid bruising the O-ring on reassembly.

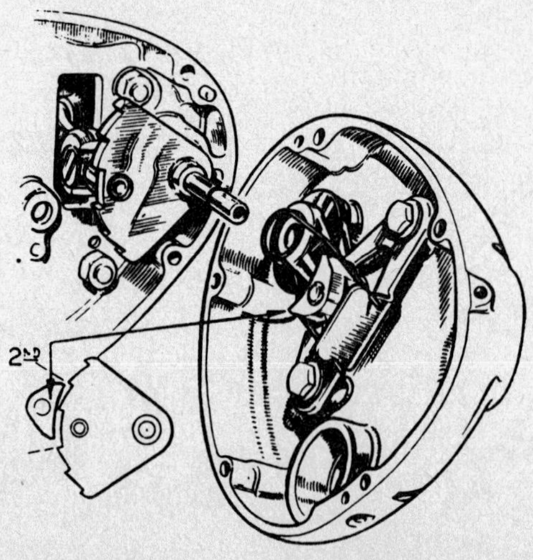

Gearbox outer cover assembly

Inner Cover

DISASSEMBLY

1. Remove the ratchet plate with spindle.
2. Unbolt the clutch operating lever and remove it and its roller from the shaft.

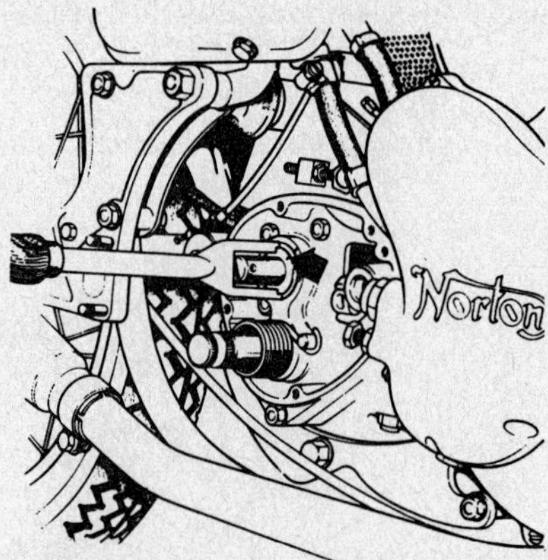

Removing the clutch operating lever

3.Mark the position of the slot in the clutch operating lever shaft on the inner cover so that the shaft can be reassembled in the correct position to give the clutch cable a straight pull. On recent models, the assembly is already marked.

4. Unscrew the lock ring on the clutch lever shaft and remove the lock ring, the shaft and the ball.
5. Remove the mainshaft nut which will be exposed after removing the shaft.
6. Remove the seven nuts which secure inner cover to the gearbox shell and pull off the inner cover, tapping lightly at the front end if necessary.

7. Take the kickstarter return spring out of the hole in the kickstarter shaft.

8. Pull the kickstarter shaft out of its bush from the inside of the cover.

INSPECTION

1. Check the mating surfaces of the inner cover for scratches, abrasions, or knicks. If present, these may be removed with emery cloth. In addition, place the cover on a flat surface, such as a piece of glass, and make sure that it is flat. Warpage of the inner cover is rare, but possible.

2. Check the mainshaft bearing for excessive play, roughness or binding in rotation, or obvious marks of wear. Replace the bearing if necessary by heating the case gently and driving out the bearing.

3. If the kickstarter bush is worn, it can also be removed after heating the case. After the new bush is driven in, it should be reamed to 0.6875–0.6865 in.

4. Check the condition of the kickstarter pawl very carefully. Be sure that the pawl shows no signs of wear or chipping along the edge. The pawl is easily replaced by removing the pin. If this is done, watch for the plunger or spring.

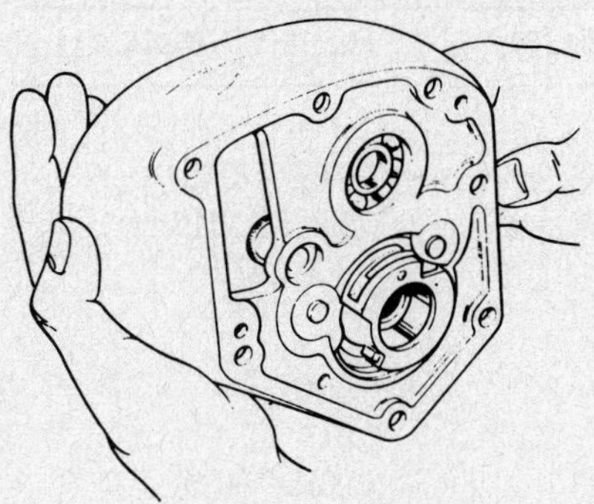

Inner cover removed

5. Examine the kickstarter stop-piece and the pawl cam which are riveted to the inner cover. Check for looseness on the rivets and re-rivet the stop-piece if necessary.

ASSEMBLY

1. Assemble the inner cover in the reverse of the disassembly procedure. Be certain that the clutch operating lever shaft is correctly aligned to give the cable a straight pull.

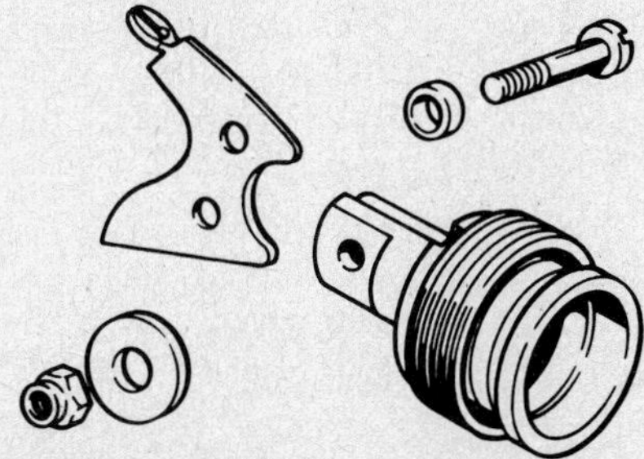

Clutch operating lever disassembled

2. Be sure that the mating surfaces are clean and in good condition. Refit new gaskets.

3. Tighten the inner cover nuts evenly and diagonally until the proper torque is attained.

Gear Cluster

DISASSEMBLY

1. Proceed with the disassembly procedures outlined above. Removing the inner cover will expose the gear assemblies on the two shafts. The upper shaft is the mainshaft and the lower is the countershaft (or layshaft).

2. Remove the low gear pinion on the mainshaft. Note that the boss on this gear faces outward.

3. Unscrew the shifter fork spindle and remove it.

4. Remove the shifter forks.

5. Remove the clutch pushrod from the mainshaft.

6. Remove the mainshaft and the gears on it. The sleeve gear will remain in place.

7. Take out the layshaft and layshaft gears.

8. If disassembly is required past this point, it is necessary to remove the primary chaincase and the clutch, etc. to gain access to the transmission sprocket.

9. Remove the screw which secures the lock plate on the transmission sprocket.

10. Remove the transmission sprocket nut, which has a LEFT-HAND thread, and remove the sprocket from the shaft.

11. Remove the sleeve gear from the bearing.

12. Remove the dome nut at the bottom of the transmission case and take out the plunger and spring.

13. Remove the bolt fixing the quadrant and the bolt which secures the camplate and remove these components.

14. To remove the layshaft bearing, it is necessary to remove the case. Heat it in an oven (do not exceed 200° C.), then tap the case on a wooden bench to knock out the bearing.

15. The mainshaft bearing can be removed after prying out the oil seal and again heating the case, driving out the bearing with a suitable drift.

INSPECTION

1. Check the condition of the mainshaft and layshaft bearings. All gears should rotate with little friction and should be smooth throughout.

2. The bushes for the camplate and quadrant mounting bolts should be checked. Wear would make shifting difficult. The bushes may be removed by heating the case and tapping them out.

3. There are O-ring oil seals on both the camplate and the quadrant. If oil leakage is noticed at the bolts for these components, the seals should be replaced.

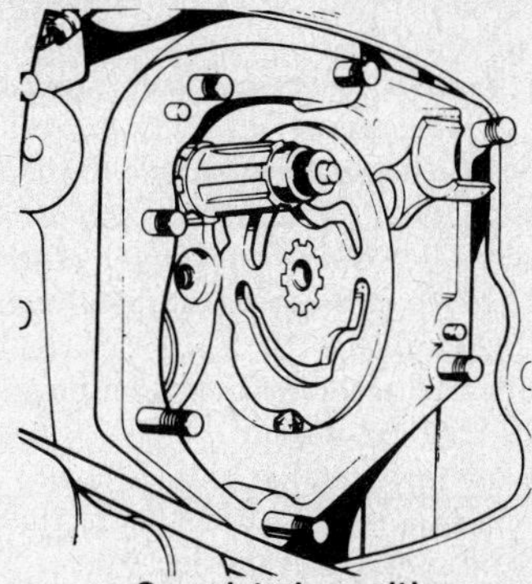

Camplate in position

4. Check all of the transmission gears for wear of the teeth.

A chipped tooth would require a thorough examination, and perhaps replacement, of all of the gears in the case. Also check the bottom of the transmission case for any metallic residue which may have accumulated.

5. Examine the gear bushes. They should be free from any score marks and have a smooth finish.

The bushes are easily removed, but are quite thin and brittle, so caution is advised. Note the location of each bush before removal.

6. Inspect the dogs on each gear for wear, chipping, or cracks.

7. The grooves in the camplate must also be examined; they should show no appreciable wear at all.

8. Check the condition of the shifter forks. Be certain they are not bent or worn and that the shaft bores do not show appreciable wear.

9. Check the condition of the camplate plunger and its spring.

10. Check the inside (ratchet annulus) of the layshaft first gear pinion. The kickstarter pawl bears on this and it is thus subject to some stress. It must not reveal signs of wear, or it must be replaced, at which time it might also be advisable to replace the pawl too.

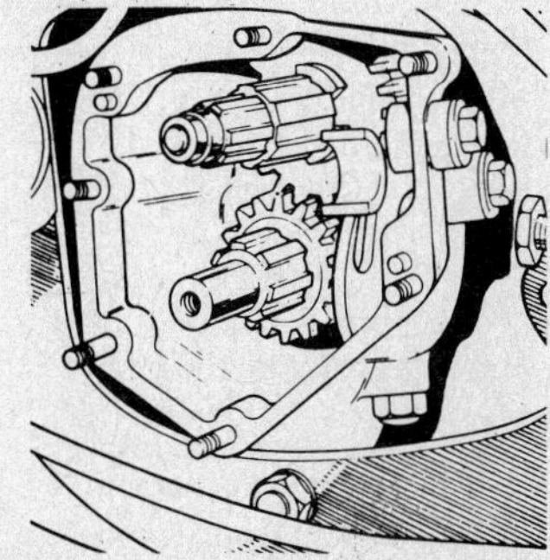

Mainshaft and layshaft in position

11. Check the condition of the splines on the layshaft and mainshaft. Measure the diameters of the shaft ends and compare these figures with the values given in the technical data.

ASSEMBLY

1. Refit the mainshaft and layshaft bearings in the case after heating as on removal.

NOTE: *On refitting, the layshaft should be pressed into its bearing by hand and should be reasonably tight once in place. If the shaft cannot be inserted by hand, use a fine emery cloth to work the end of the shaft until this is possible.*

2. Fit the quadrant first, securing it with its bolt and washer.
3. Raise the quadrant so that the lever arm top radius is in line with the top right hand stud in the transmission case.
4.Insert the camplate, positioning it so that only the first two teeth on the quadrant are visable through the camplate slot.
5. Making sure that the teeth on the camplate and the quadrant are engaged, secure the camplate with its bolt and washer.
6. Replace the camplate plunger, spring, and domed nut.
7. Replace the sleeve gear, making sure that the spacer which bears on the oil seal is in position.
8. Replace the transmission sprocket and secure it with its nut. Remember, the nut has a left-hand thread. Be sure to tighten it firmly. Fit the locking plate and screw.
9. Replace the mainshaft with the third gear pinion on the shaft.
10. Fit the mainshaft second gear pinion on the shaft along with the shifter fork correctly positioned in the slot in the pinion.
11. Engage the stud at the rear of the shifter fork into the slot in the camplate.
12. Replace the first gear pinion on the mainshaft; be sure that the boss on the gear faces outward.
13. Assemble the layshaft gears for fourth, third, and second gears on the layshaft. Also fit the other shifter fork into the slot in the second gear pinion. Insert the layshaft and gears, and engage the shifter fork stud with the slot in the camplate.
14. Line up the bores of the two shifter forks, insert the spindle, and tighten it.
15. Fit the first gear pinion on the layshaft.
16. Fit the inner cover assembly as previously described.
17. Insert the roller into the quadrant radius and confirm the engagement of the ratchet plate stud with the hole in the roller.
18. Reassamble the remainder of the transmission as previously described.
19. Refill the transmission with the correct quantity and grade of oil.

LUBRICATION SYSTEMS

OPERATIONAL DESCRIPTION

The Norton engine employs a dry-sump lubrication system. The oil is contained in a separate tank and is fed to the

ENGINE AND TRANSMISSION SPECIFICATIONS

	Commando 850	Commando 750	Atlas, G15CS, N15CS, P-11
CYLINDER			
Bore Size (in.)	N.A.	2.8750-2.8758 (73.025-73.045 mm)	2.8750-2.8758 (73.025-73.045 mm)
Tappet Bore Size (in.)	1.865-1.875	1.865-1.875	1.865-1.875
PISTONS			
Clearance (in.)	0.0045	0.0045	0.0045
Ring End Gap (in.)	0.013	0.013	0.013
Ring Side Clearance (in.)	0.0015-0.0035	0.0015-0.0035	0.0015-0.0035
Wrist Pin Diameter (in.)	0.6866-0.6868	0.6866-0.6868	0.6866-0.6868
VALVE TRAIN			
Intake Valve			
Head Diameter (in.)	1.500	1.500	1.500
Stem Diameter (in.)	0.309-0.310	0.309-0.310	0.309-0.310
Exhaust Valve			
Head Diameter (in.)	1.312	1.312	1.312
Stem Diameter (in.)	0.309-0.310	0.309-0.310	0.309-0.310
Valve Guides			
Bore (in.)	0.3135-0.3145	0.3135-0.3145	0.3135-0.3145
Valve Springs			
Free Length (inner) (in.)	1.531	1.531	1.531
Free Length (outer) (in.)	1.700	1.700	1.700
Pushrods			
Length (Intake) (in.)	8.130-8.166	8.130-8.166	8.194
Length (Exhaust) (in.)	7.285-7.321	7.285-7.321	7.351
Rocker Arms			
Spindle Bore (in.)	0.4998-0.5003	0.4998-0.5003	0.4998-0.5003
Spindle Diameter (in.)	0.4985-0.4998	0.4985-0.4998	0.4985-0.4998
CONNECTING ROD			
Small End Bore (in.)	0.6873-0.6878	0.6873-0.6878	0.6873-0.6878

ENGINE AND TRANSMISSION SPECIFICATIONS

	Commando 850	Commando 750	Atlas, G15CS, N15CS, P-11
CRANKSHAFT			
Con Rod Journal Diameter (in.)	1.7500-1.7505	1.7500-1.7505	1.7500-1.7505
Bearing Journal (drive) (in.)	1.812-1.815	1.1812-1.1815	1.1812-1.1815
Bearing Journal (timing) (in.)	1.812-.1815	1.1807-1.1812	1.1807-1.1812
Main Bearing (drive) (mm)	30 x 72 x 19 (1 Dot)	30 x 72 x 19 (1 Dot)	30 x 72 x 19 (3 Dot) R330L
Main Bearing (timing) (ball) (mm)	30 x 72 x 19	30 x 72 x 19	30 x 72 x 19 (MJ30)
Main Bearing (timing) (roller) (mm)	30 x 72 x 19	30 x 72 x 19	
CAMSHAFT			
Bearing Diam. (drive side) (in.)	0.8735-0.8740	0.8735-0.8740	0.8735-0.8740
Bearing Diam. (timing side) (in.)	0.8730-0.8735	0.8730-0.8735	0.8730-0.8735
Bush Bore (in.)	0.8745-0.8750	0.8745-0.8750	0.8745-0.8750
PRESSURE RELIEF VALVE SPRING			
Free Length (in.)	1.171	1.171	1.171
O.D. (in.)	0.430-0.435	0.430-0.435	0.430-0.435
INTERMEDIATE PINION			
Shaft Diameter (in.)	0.5610-0.5615	0.5610-0.5615	0.5610-0.5615
Bush Bore	0.5620-0.5627	0.5620-0.5627	0.5620-0.5627

TRANSMISSION—All Models	
Mainshaft Diameter (Clutch side) (in.)	0.8095-0.8105
Mainshaft Diameter (Kickstarter side) (in.)	0.6244-0.6248
Mainshaft Ball Bearing (in.)	$5/8 \times 1\,9/16 \times 7/16$
Layshaft Bearing (mm)	17 x 40 x 12
Layshaft Diameter (Clutch side) (in.)	0.6687-0.6692
Layshaft Diameter (Kickstarter side) (in.)	0.6845-0.6855
Sleeve Gear Bearing (O.D., in place) (in.)	1.2495-1.2500
Sleeve Gear Bush (O.D.) (in.)	0.9055-0.906
Sleeve Gear Bush (reamed in place) (in.)	0.81200-0.81325
Layshaft Bush (Bore diameter) (in.)	0.6865-0.6875
Clutch Bearing (Commando only) (mm)	35 x 62 x 14

TORQUE WRENCH SETTINGS

	ft lbs		ft lbs		ft lbs
Cyl. Head $3/8$ in. nuts and bolts	30	Gearbox inner cover nuts	12	Alternator mounting nuts	10
Cyl. Head $5/16$ in. bolts	20	Cam chain tensioner nuts	15	Crankshaft Nuts	35
Cyl. base nuts	20	Oil pump stud nuts	15	Rotor Nut	80
Connecting rod bolts	25	Oil feed banjo bolts	15	Oil Pressure Relief Valve	25
Rocker shaft cover plate bolts	8.3	Engine mounting nuts	25		

engine as required by gravity feed assisted by the suction of the oil pump. The pump itself is driven off the crankshaft by a worm gear. It is a gear-type unit, consisting of two sets of gears which are located in the pump body and rotate on common shafts, but which are really independent in function. The narrow set of gears feeds the oil to the engine, while the wider ones take the oil which has accumulated in the crankcase and returns it to the tank.

Oil from the tank passes, under pressure, from the feed side of the pump, through the metal nipple visible on the outside of the pump body to a passage in the timing cover. Most of the oil is conveyed through the passage to the timing end of the crankshaft, through which it is forced to lubricate the big end bearings. While passing through the drillings in the crankshaft, the oil also enters the sludge trap machined into the flywheel.

A somewhat smaller amount of oil leaving the feed side of the pump is directed to the rocker oil feed pipe which runs externally from the back of the timing case to the head, where it provides lubrication for the rocker arms and valves. From here it is returned to the timing chest via a passage drilled throught the head, barrels, and crankcase. Oil dripping from the exhaust valve assemblies drains through the pushrod tunnels to the tappets, then to the sump.

The oil accumulating in the timing case lubricates the chains here and its level is determined by a hole on the inside of the case. Any excess flows into the sump.

On early models, it is important to note that oil to the rockers was taken from the return line to the oil tank.

The oil which collects in the bottom of the sump is scavenged by the return side of the oil pump. After passing through a wire mesh filter contained in the sump drain plug, the oil is sucked up to the return side of the oil pump and then forced to the tank.

A pressure relief, or "blow off" valve is located on the timing case cover just above the junction of the rocker feed pipe. When oil pressure reaches 45–55 lbs. per sq. in., the valve is activated and the oil escaping from it is diverted back to the feed side of the oil pump.

The system incorporates three or four filters depending on model, three of which are wire-mesh types. The first is located in the oil tank itself, on the feed line. There is a finer filter in the crankcase sump drain plug already mentioned, and a filter on the end of the pressure relief valve.

The filter in the oil tank is a coarse mesh. This assures that it will not restrict the flow of cold, thick oil when starting.

In addition to these filters, the latest Commando models feature an automotive-type cartridge filter which is mounted behind the gearbox. This is inserted in the oil return line.

Most models also have some provision for oiling the rear chain, usually by overflow from the oil tank itself.

OIL PUMP

Removal and Inspection

When rebuilding a severly damaged engine, the pump should always be inspected.

1. Remove the timing cover, after taking off the tach drive (if necessary), and disconnect the rocker oil feed pipe at the cover.

2. Remove the two nuts which secure the pump body and pull off the pump. Removal should be easy. If not use a wrench on the pump drive gear as shown in the accompanying illustration.

3. Slowly turn the drive shaft and note any roughness or binding in the movement. The drive shaft should turn smoothly.

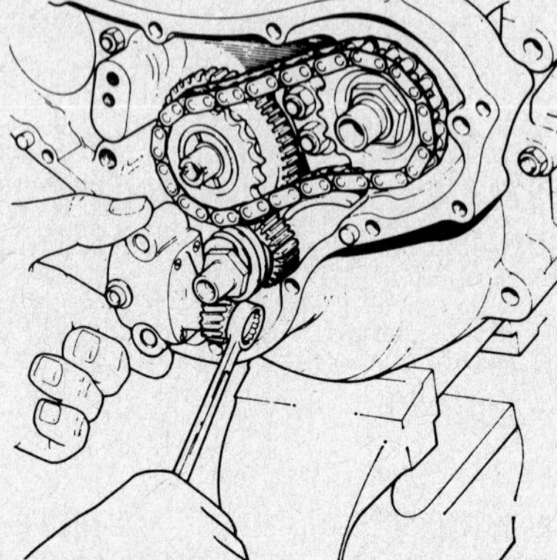

Removing the oil pump

4. Grasp the drive shaft gear firmly and push and pull on it. There should be no end play whatsoever.

5. Check the face of the pump body which mates with the crankcase. Place a straightedge across the stud holes to insure that the body is not warped. It must, of course, be perfectly flat, or air will be introduced into the oil flow. The mating surface may be lapped flat if necessary after dismantling the pump.

6. Check the conical oil seal on the steel nipple. It must be in very good condition and not deformed. If the seal has been subject to too much pressure, the tapered end will be forced into, and perhaps obstruct, the major oil passage in the timing cover.

Disassembly

1. It is not necessary to remove the pump drive gear to get at the internals, but it may be taken off the drive shaft if desired by taking off the nut which secures it to the shaft and pulling off the gear. Take out the woodruff key also.

2. Remove the four screws in the pump body and take off the brass end plate.

3. Remove the iron plate from the pump body.

4. Using a brass drift, if necessary, tap out the drive shaft. The return side (wide) gear is a close fit on the shaft so the drift will probably be needed.

5. Tap out the shaft for the idler gears. Remove it from the feed side of the pump.

6. Remove both sets of gears.

Inspection

1. Foreign matter in the gear teeth or chipped or worn teeth will be very obvious.

2. If the engine oil in the tank runs down to the crankcase sump after the bike has been sitting for a short time, the problem may be due to loose pump body screws. Another reason may be excessive wear of the shaft bores in the pump body. There is no remedy for this latter cause, other than replacement of the pump body.

Reassembly

1. Clean all of the components thoroughly by washing them in a solvent such as kerosene.

2. Reassemble the gears in their proper positions. The small radius on the return (wider) gears must face the inside of the pump body.

3. Replace the idler shaft and the drive shaft.

4. Place the brass and iron end plates in position and insert the screws, but do not tighten them yet.

5. The end plates must be either perfectly flush or slightly below flush with the edge of the pump body surface which

Oil pump disassembled

mates with the crankcase. The reason for this should be obvious. There should be just a minimum of play in the end plates which will allow their correct alignment. This is extremely important.

6. **Tighten the** four screws very securely.

7. **Replace the** drive shaft key, the drive gear, and the fixing nut.

Installation

1. Oil the pump internals well before installing the pump.

2. Apply some gasket compound to the face of the pump, using it sparingly and being very careful not to get it anywhere near the oil passages. No gasket compound should be used if a gasket is used between the pump body and the engine as on the 850. A new gasket, however, should always be used.

3. Replace the pump on the studs, and gradually tighten the two nuts until the proper torque has been reached.

OIL PUMP WORM GEAR

The worm gear has a left-hand thread. All of the Norton Twins manufactured for the past several years have had a worm gear with six "starts." Very early 750 models, however, had a three-start gear. A six-start gear will drive the pump twice as fast, resulting naturally, in twice the amount of oil being pumped into and out of the engine in any given length of time. If your model has the old type of gear, simply replacing it with the six-start variety is a worthwhile modification.

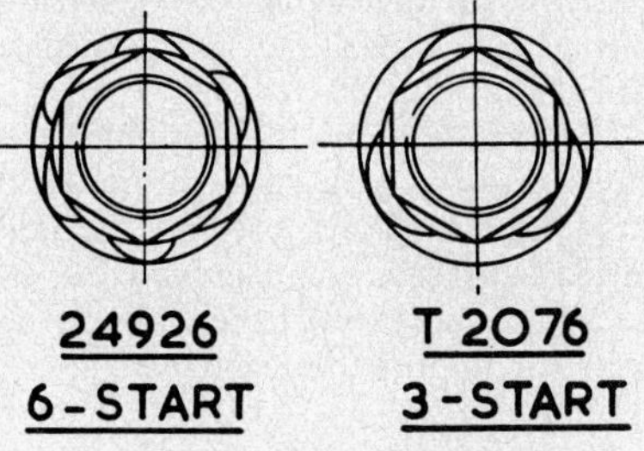

New six-start worm gear and older three-start unit

CRANKCASE BREATHER

Latest Commandos have the crankcase breather fitted to the rear of the crankcase and no attention is needed for this type. All others, however, have the breather fitted to, and timed by, the camshaft. The breather mechanism consists of a slotted plate with driving tabs to engage the end of the camshaft, and a spring.

The rotating plate opens and closes openings in a stationary plate and this accomplishes the timing of the breather.

The rotating breather plate must be flat on the mating side and it may be worked on a stone to make it so if necessary. The driving tabs should also be in good condition.

The crankcase breather is connected to the oil tank via a rubber hose. If the engine has been standing a while, oil will usually seep into the crankcase and, when the bike is started, it will come out of the breather for a few moments until the oil pump has completely scavenged the sump. While the motorcycle is in operation, especially at high speeds, the breather will pass oil mist or even pure oil. This is normal; the amounts, however, should not be excessive, as this is indicative of oil remaining in the sump.

OIL PRESSURE RELIEF VALVE

The oil pressure relief valve is located on the timing case cover just above the junction for the rocker oil feed pipe. The valve has a spring-loaded steel sleeve which is pre-set to open the valve at an oil pressure of 45–55 lbs per square inch (Commando) or 40–50 lbs per square inch (pre-Commando models). Oil passing through the open valve is diverted back to the feed side of the oil pump on Commandos or into the timing case on earlier machines. Although the valve itself does not require attention, it does have a wire mesh filter fitted over one end which is easily cleaned after unscrewing the valve.

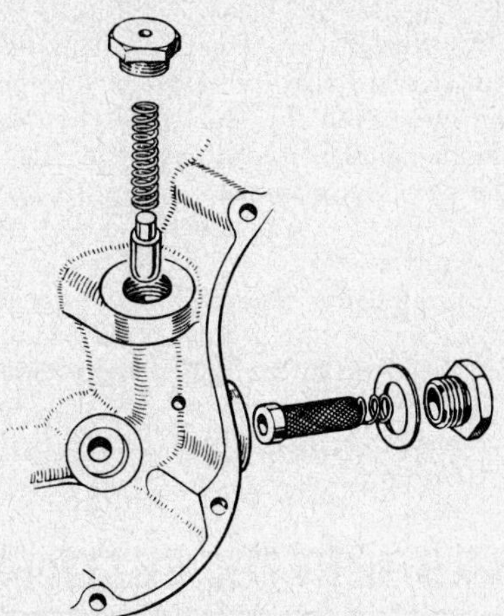

Atlas oil pressure relief valve

OIL LINES

1. All external oil lines should be checked periodically for potential cracks or splits, especially at the joints. If the hoses are secured by screw-type hose clamps, these should not be overtightened or they will crack the rubber.

2. The rocker oil feed pipe is especially important. This unit has been known to crack from vibration. It should therefore be inspected closely, especially if engine work has been done, and the pipe moved about. Arrange the pipe so that it does not touch the barrels or head except at the banjo junctions. Alternately, it can be replaced with a fexible hose as used on the lates Commandos.

NOTE: *After rebuilding an engine, and periodically thereafter, the factory recommends placing a finger over the oil return line in the oil tank for a few seconds while the engine is running. This has the effect of forcing more oil through the rocker oil feed line, clearing it of any possible obstructions. This is to be done for a few seconds ONLY, and is* **only** *for machines with rocker feed taken from the return pipe, and is therefore* **definitely NOT to be performed on the Commando.**

OIL FILTERS

The crankcase sump filter may be removed and cleaned by removing the spring clip at the top, working the cover washer loose very carefully, and pulling out the filter. When refitting, be sure that the spring clip is firmly seated in its groove.

Some 1973 Commando 750s and the Commando 850 are equipped with an automotive-type screw-on filter on the oil return line. This filter is replaced when necessary.

REAR CHAIN OILER

On most models, the rear chain automatically receives lubrication via a run-off from the oil tank breather. This system should not need attention.

CHECKING THE LUBRICATION SYSTEM

Oil Pressure

Oil pressure can be readily checked on Commando models with the use of the proper gauge. This is fitted at the rocker oil feed pipe junction and a reading is taken when the engine is at operating temperature. The reading should be 45–55 lbs per square in. at 3,000 rpm.

This method cannot be used for the other models because the rocker arms are fed from the oil return line. The alternative method is to acquire another timing cover. This is then drilled centered with the large oil seal (see illustration) and the gauge inserted. There should be 40–50 lbs per square in. pressure when checked as above, or a minimum of 5 lbs at idle, with the pressure rising with the rpm.

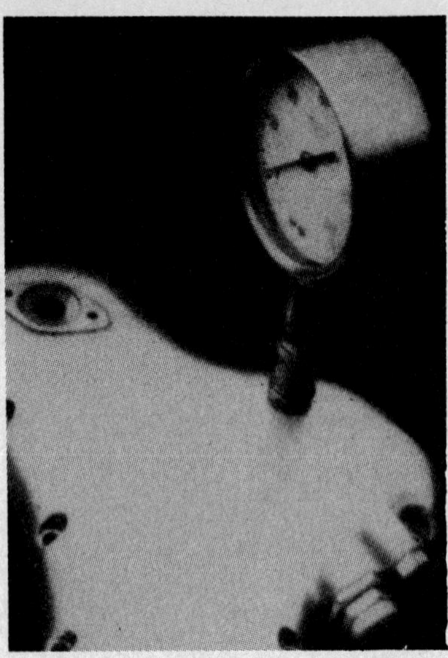
Oil pressure gauge in position (Atlas)

Operational Checks

If you do not have the proper gauge, the lubrication system can be checked over in some manner by doing the following:

1. Run engine for several minutes until the oil is warm, then check the oil level at the tank and top up if necessary.
2. Take a short ride to thoroughly circulate the oil. Stop and remove the crankcase sump drain plug. No more than one or two pints of oil should come out as this is done. Be sure to replace the correct amount of oil.
3. Loosen one of the banjo fittings at the cylinder head and, with the ignition OFF, kick the engine over briskly several times. Oil should seep from the loosened banjo as you do this, proving that it is being fed to the cylinder head rocker assembly.
4. Let the machine sit overnight. Upon starting, observe the flow of oil at the return line inside the oil tank. There should be a steady stream for a few moments and then a sputtering return of oil as the sump is scavenged.
5. Check the condition of the oil seals contained in the timing cover. Removal and installation of these seals is described in the "Engine and Transmission" section.

CAUTION: *Because of a difference in the oil passages, the timing covers found on the Commando are NOT INTERCHANGEABLE with those on earlier machines although they are similar at first sight. Therefore, always be sure that you get the proper timing cover in the event that it must be replaced.*

OIL PUMP PRESSURE RELIEF VALVE SPECIFICATIONS

Oil Pump Body Material	Cast Iron
Type	Double Gear
Ratio, Feed: Return	1:2
Pump Stud Nuts Torque	15 ft lbs
Pressure Relief Valve Spring Free Length	1.171 in.
Spring Outside Diameter	0.430-0.435 in.
Pressure Relief Valve Torque	25 ft lbs

FUEL SYSTEMS

All Nortons are equipped with two Amal carburetors, pre-1967 models being fitted with the Monobloc-type. Machines manufactured after that year have the Concentric model carburetor. Specifications for individual models are given below.

All necessary disassembly and repair procedures for both types of carburetor can be found in the BSA section under "Fuel Systems."

NOTE: *Some models, especially in 1966, were equipped by the factory with main jets ranging up to 420 in size. This is far too rich for most applications, especially if the air cleaner and muffler are left stock. The settings were later revised to those shown above.*

Prior to 1967, Norton 750s were equipped with a Lucas K2F magneto for ignition and an alternator to charge the battery for lighting.

In that year, the magneto was replaced with a "capacitor ignition" system which remains standard today. Not to be confused with the "capacitor discharge ignition" currently found on many two-stroke machines, the Norton uses a standard battery and coil set-up with a large capacitor (Lucas 2MC) wired in parallel with the battery: hence the name. This system allows the machine to be started and run with a low or even dead battery.

CAUTION: *On 1971 and later models, disconnect the green-yellow lead to the warning light assimilator at the alternator snap-connector before performing an electrical test.*

IGNITION SYSTEM

Lucas K2F Magneto

The magneto consists of an armature (with a condenser incorporated) rotating in a magnetic field. The armature is driven by chain from the intermediate sprocket. The centrifugal timing advance mechanism is incorporated in the magneto sprocket and is located in the timing case. The contact breaker points are found on the opposite side of the armature, beneath the magneto cover, and are opened and closed as they rotate inside a cam ring.

The high tension leads contact the magneto slip ring via carbon brushes and these brushes are also used for the "kill button" and the magneto ground, the latter being found beneath the screw on the right side (top) of the magneto.

CARBURETOR SETTINGS

	Commando 850	Commando 750 (Combat Engine)	Commando 750 (Standard)	Atlas (after 1966) P-11	Atlas, G15CS, N15CS
Amal Type	932	932	930	930	389/88 R.H.* 389/87 L.H.
Venturi Size	32 mm	32 mm	30 mm	30 mm	$1^1/_8$ in.
Main Jet	220	220	220	250	320
Needle Jet	0.107	0.106	0.107	0.107	0.106
Needle Position	central notch	top notch	central notch	central notch	lowest notch
Needle Taper					D
Throttle Slide	3	3	3	3	3
Pilot Jet	25	25	25	25	25

* Without float bowl

SERVICE

1. Every 2,000 miles, clean the breaker points and adjust the gap. Check the gap opening at both firing points on the cam ring. If one is greater than the other, it is best to compromise the value.

2. Apply a small drop of oil to the breaker point pivot. Also, use some high temperature grease to lubricate the cam ring.

3. Every 5,000 miles, remove the high tension pick-ups and clean off the carbon brushes. The brushes are mounted on springs and should slide freely in the pick-ups. There must be at least ⅛ in. of the brush protruding from the pick-up for the magneto to work.

Also clean the ground brush after removing its mounting screw.

4. Stuff a clean rag into one of the pick-up holes and kick the engine over a few times to clean off the slip ring. A good deal of oil on the slip ring ring will indicate a defective oil seal which must be replaced.

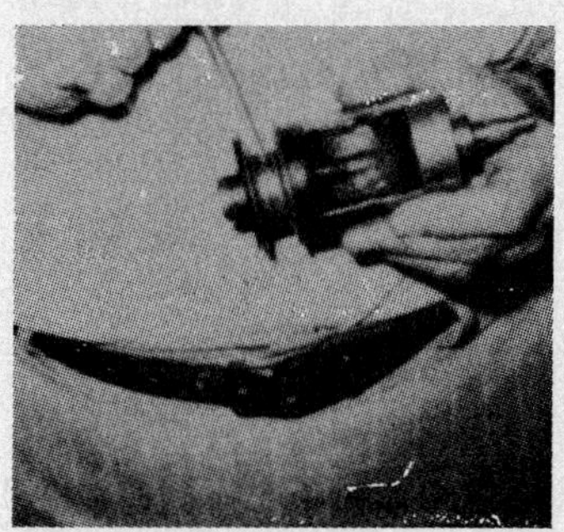

Magneto armature slip ring must be clean

5. Remove the timing cover and check the play (up and down) of the magneto sprocket nut. If there is more than 0.005 in. of play, the magneto should be disassembled and the bearings replaced.

The following procedure is given for either mechanical (i.e. bearing) or electrical faults:

REMOVAL AND DISASSEMBLY

1. Remove the timing cover.
2. Remove the magneto points cover.
3. Remove the pick-ups.
4. Unscrew the magneto sprocket bolt and remove the advance mechanism. Remove the two nuts (on studs) and the nut and bolt which secure the magneto to the timing case.
5. Hold the rocker oil feed pipe aside and pull off the magneto.
6. Remove the two safety screws located just by the pick-up holes.

CAUTION: *These screws must be removed before the armature is taken out.*

7. Remove the points; then remove the cam ring, which is a slip fit in the magneto case and must be pulled straight out (with the fingers only). Be careful of the lubricating wicks.
8. Remove the two end cover screws and take off the cover. Be careful of the thin metal shims which may be fitted behind the cover.
9. Remove the ground brush and pull out the armature, watching the location of the insulator and oil seal on the drive side of the armature.

INSPECTION

1. A simple but relatively effective armature test can be made with a two-volt battery.

Screw out the hexagon screw which secures the points into the armature, then connect one of the battery leads to this screw, the other to an ammeter. Then connect the other lead of the ammeter to the ground of the armature itself. The ammeter reading should be about four amps. This is a test of the primary winding.

2. To test the secondary winding (this is the high tension side of the circuit) set up as above. Obtain a length of high tension wire and clamp one end to ground at the armature, supporting the other end from ⅛ to 3/16 in. from the slip ring contact. Make and break the connection at the hexagon screw several times quickly, and observe the spark produced. The high tension spark must be able to jump at least a ⅛ in. gap.

If no spark is produced, the armature windings or the condenser is defective. Replacement of the complete assembly is the only practical solution.

3. On occasion, a magneto will go intermittent, producing spark on one cylinder, or severe misfiring while running. This is sometimes due to a broken wire within the windings. Unfortunately, this cannot be rectified and the armature should be replaced.

4. The magneto magnets are permanent and should never give trouble. They may, however, be recharged by placing them in the proper magnetic field.

5. Magneto bearing failure is rare. The bearings are adjustable by removing the thin metal shims from behind the end cover until the end play of the shaft is within acceptable limits.

When the last of these shims have been removed, there is still some possibility of adjustment by adding shims behind the inner races on the armature shaft. However, it requires a special tool to remove or replace the inner races.

Excessive bearing play is most often the result of the drive side outer bearing race, which rides on a rather flimsy fiber insulator, becoming loose.

The ball bearings themselves are held on the inner races by a standard cage. They can be easily removed by simply pulling off by hand as the cage is somewhat flexible.

6. The timing advance mechanism should be inspected. Check for worn sprocket teeth. This is usually not a prob-

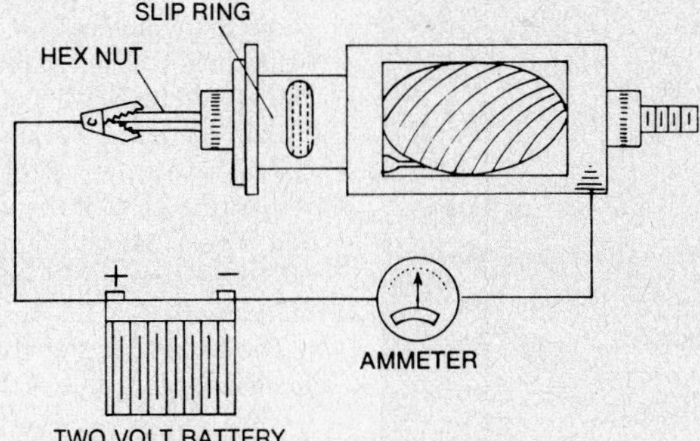

Magneto armature low-tension test

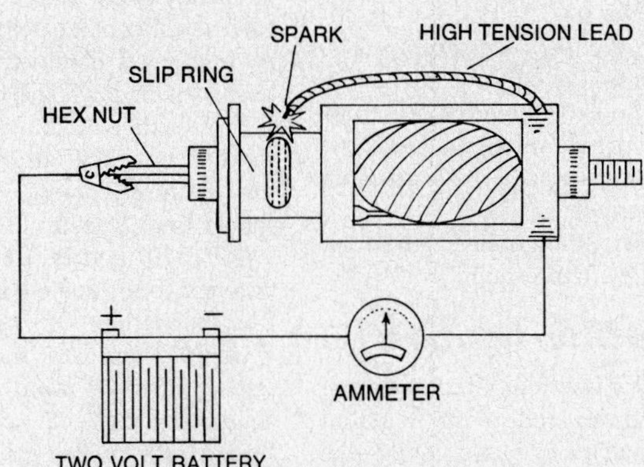

Magneto armature high-tension test

lem. The two springs which control bob-weight movement should have from 12–14 oz of tension at 1/16 in. extension.

If the machine has been idle for some time, bathe the advance mechanism in light penetrating oil to assure free movement of the weights.

If the timing cover has not been removed, the efficiency of the timing advance mechanism can be checked by moving the points into the full advance position. They should return immediately to their normal position when released. If they do not, the advance mechanism is sticking (perhaps the drive chain is too tight) or one or both of the springs may be broken.

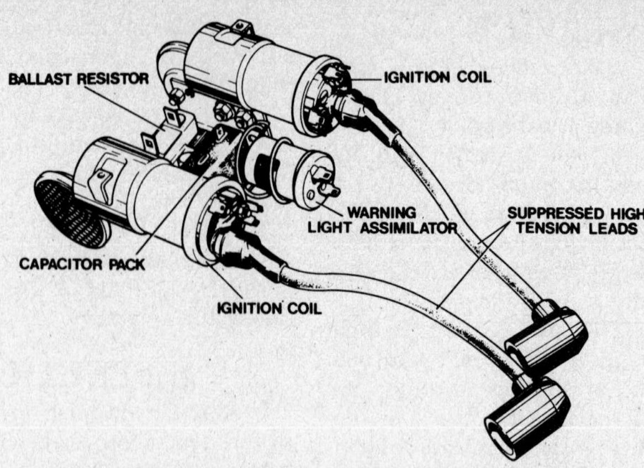

Latest coil assembly: 6 volt coils with ballast resistor

ASSEMBLY

1. Grease the bearings with a good grade of high temperature grease before installation.
2. Replace the fiber insulator and the oil seal.
3. Refit the armature, the ground brush, safety screws, and end cover.
4. Replace the point's cam ring.

NOTE: *As on removal, the cam ring must slide directly in. It must be done by hand. Do not force the ring into place. Note that the ring is notched to align with a small stud in the end cover.*

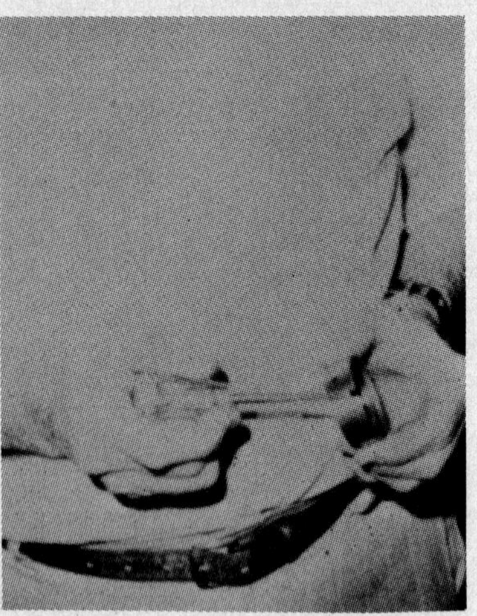

Notch in cam ring must engage stud in magneto body

5. Replace the points assembly. The backing plate is "keyed" and must align with its slot. Replace the hexagon screw.
6. Replace the complete magneto and place the timing advance mechanism on the armature shaft.
7. Reset the ignition timing. Adjust the magneto drive chain tension.

Capacitor Ignition

The capacitor ignition system utilizes a dual-point and dual-coil set-up. As stated earlier, a capacitor is wired in parallel with the battery and should provide spark even if the battery condition is low.

To check each of the components in the event of a lack of spark, follow these procedures:

POINTS ASSEMBLY

The assembly must be cleaned, re-gapped, or replaced at the specified intervals.

IGNITION COILS

1. The ignition coil for each cylinder can be checked by inserting a nail or other suitable conductive object into the spark plug cap and holding this about ⅛ in. away from the cylinder fins while kicking the engine over briskly. A spark should be able to jump the gap.
2. Most models use the Lucas 17M12 coil. The primary winding can be checked by connecting an ohmmeter across the low tension terminals (white and black-white leads or white and black-yellow leads). The reading for the 17M12 coil should be 3.3–3.8 ohms.

Late models are equipped with 17M6 coils. These are 6 volt coils, although the rest of the electrical system remains 12 volt. The 17M6 coils have a ballast resistor wired in series. Resistance for the primary winding is 1.7–1.9 ohms.

The ballast resistor can be tested and should yield a value of 1.8–2.0 ohms.

CONDENSERS

To test the condensers, turn on the ignition and take voltage readings across each set of contact points when open. If no reading is obtained, the condensers have broken down and must be replaced.

If a voltage reading is obtained but there is noticable arcing and pitting of the ignition points, the condensers should be replaced.

On 1970 models, the condensers are fastened to the coil clips and are reached from beneath.

On 1971 and later models, the coil assembly must be removed and then the condenser pack (2 screws and nuts). Remove the rubber cover which will reveal the condensers mounted individually to the base plate.

2MC CAPACITOR

The large Lucas 2MC capacitor is mounted in a coil spring secured to the frame.

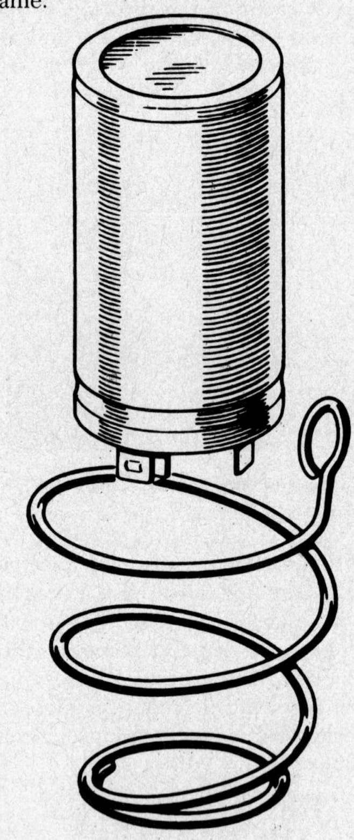

Lucas 2MC capacitor

1. The capacitor should be checked periodically; this can be done by simply disconnecting the battery (tape up the leads to avoid the possibility of a short circuit). The machine should be able to start and run normally. The lights should still work, although they may be dim at low revs, getting brighter as engine speed increases.
2. The capacitor should be mounted as shown with the terminals downward. The single terminal (marked with a red dot) is positive and the double terminal is negative. The terminals are also different sizes, making reversal of the connections almost impossible.

3. The capacitor can also be checked by removing it from the machine and connecting a fully charged 12 volt battery across it, leaving it this way for about five minutes. Then, disconnect the battery and let the capacitor sit for another five minutes. At the end of this time, a DC voltmeter connected across the capacitor terminals should give an instantaneous reading of at least 8 volts.

The capacitor has a limited storage life of approximately 18 months at 68°F. or 9 to 12 months at 86°F. Therefore, it would be wise to check the condition of the capacitor regularly.

CHARGING SYSTEM

IMPORTANT: *All models are equipped with a 12 volt POSITIVE GROUND system.*

The charging system consists of the alternator, rectifier, zener diode, and the battery itself.

The alternator produces alternating current by means of a permanent magnet rotor mounted on the left side of the crankshaft, which rotates within a stationary six-pole laminated iron stator assembly. Two stators have been used and they are easily distinguishable: the RM15 has three leads while the later type, RM21, has two leads.

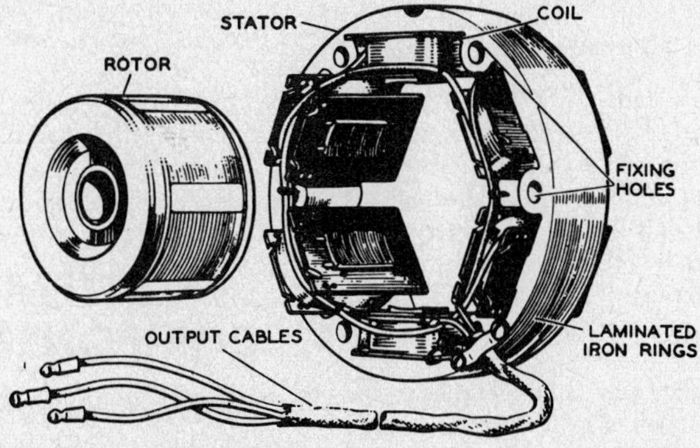

Lucas RM15 Alternator. Cable colors: green-white; green-black; green-yellow

The current produced by the alternator is "rectified" (changed to direct current) by the three-plate rectifier.

This current is used to charge the battery which, in turn, supplies power to the lights, horn, and so on.

The amount of charge which the battery receives is determined by the zener diode. This is essentially a variable resistance ("semi-conductor" is the proper term) which automatically raises or lowers the amount of current flowing into the battery according to its condition and needs.

Although the two types of alternator are similar, charging system troubleshooting procedures are provided for each alternator model.

NOTE: *All Commandos use the RM21 Alternator.*

RM15 System

There are several types of this model alternator fitted. Nos. 540, 210, and 18 are found on magneto equipped machines, and 047 and 534 on coil ignition machines.

IMPORTANT: *For the results of the following tests to be valid, the battery must be in good condition and more than half charged.*

Test the system as whole first by assuring that the battery is receiving the proper charge:

1. Be certain that all electrical connections are clean and tight.
2. Disconnect the 2MC capacitor if fitted.
3. Disconnect the battery negative cable and connect a DC ammeter between the cable and the negative terminal of the battery.
4. Start the engine and run it at 3,000 rpm.
5. Observe the ammeter readings at each of the lighting switch positions.
6. If the readings are higher than those given, the battery may be overcharged. This would most probably be caused by a defective zener diode.

Switch Position	Alternator RM15 Type 540, 210, 18	047, 534
Off	2.75 amps	2.75 amps
Park. Light	2.0	1.5
Headlight	2.0	1.5

7. If the readings are lower than those given, any one of the other components may be at fault. Perform the test again, but disconnect the diode cable. If the readings become higher, the fault is in the diode, which must be replaced.

If the diode cannot be faulted, the alternator should be checked for voltage output. This requires an AC voltmeter (20 volt range) and a 1 ohm resistor capable of carrying 20 amps without overheating.

1. Disconnect the three alternator leads at the snap connector.
2. Connect the resister in parallel with the AC voltmeter and check the voltage output between the alternator leads. The following values are the minimum acceptable for an alternator in good condition, with the engine turning 3,000 rpm.

Voltmeter and Resistor connected between leads	Alternator RM15 Type 540, 210, 18	047, 534
White-Green and Green-Black	4.0 v.	4.0 v.
White-Green and Green-Yellow	6.5	6.5
White-Green and Green-Black*	8.5	9.0
Each lead and ground	0.0	0.0

* With Green-Yellow connected to Green-Black

The following conclusions can be drawn from the test results:

A. If all readings are low, the rotor has become demagnetized.

B. If any individual readings are low, a single coil or coils are short circuited.

C. Zero reading indicates that individual coil or coils are open circuits.

D. Any voltage reading obtained with the voltmeter and resistor connected to any lead and ground indicates coil or coils internally grounded.

NOTE: *Although early RM15 stators could be rewound, later varieties were plastic encapsulated and replacement of the assembly is all that can be done.*

If the alternator tests out okay, the trouble is probably the rectifier. This component is best checked by replacing it with a known workable rectifier. A bench test is given later in this chapter, however.

RM21 System

IMPORTANT: *Before the following tests are carried out, the battery must be in good condition and close to a full state of charge.*

1. Leave the cable connections to the rectifier in place; connect the negative lead of a DC voltmeter (20 volt range) to the center terminal of the rectifier, and the other lead to a ground on the frame or engine. The voltmeter should read battery voltage at this point, if the proper connections are in order.

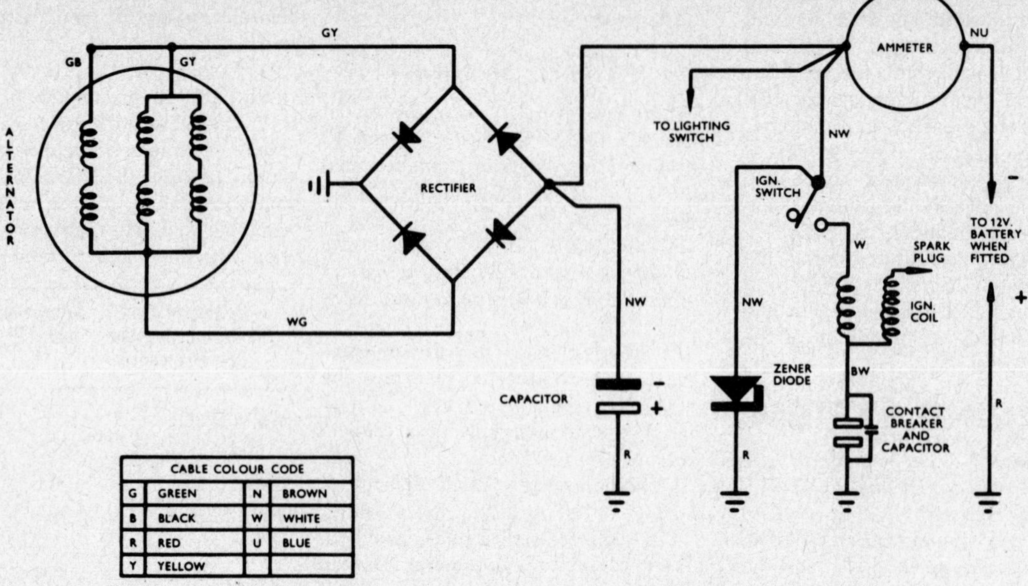

CABLE COLOUR CODE			
G	GREEN	N	BROWN
B	BLACK	W	WHITE
R	RED	U	BLUE
Y	YELLOW		

Simplified diagram of Commando wiring system

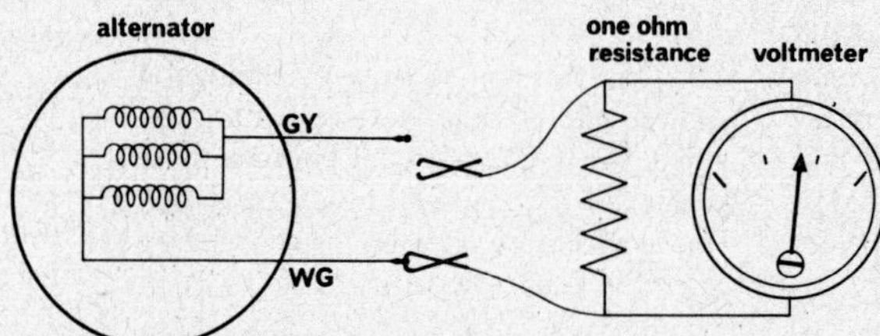

Testing RM21 Alternator voltage output

2. Start the engine and run it at about 3,000 rpm. The voltmeter should register 14.4–16.4 volts.

3. If the voltmeter reading is the proper value, all components are working properly and any trouble with battery charging must be due to the battery itself or to the battery connections.

4. If the voltage reading is higher than the given value, the zener diode is faulty and must be replaced.

5. If the voltage reading is lower than normal, the alternator, rectifier, diode, or 2MC capacitor can be at fault.

6. If the voltage reading is lower than the given value, perform the test again, but disconnect the diode. The voltage reading should read higher than the regulated value of 14.4–16.4 volts. If it does, the diode is faulty. If it does not, the alternator, rectifier, or capacitor may be at fault.

7. Disconnect the 2MC capacitor and repeat the test. If the voltage reading reaches the normal value, the capacitor is faulty and must be replaced. If it does not, the trouble must be in either the alternator or the rectifier.

8. Test the voltage output of the alternator. Disconnect the two leads at the snap connector and connect an AC voltmeter (20 volt range), with a 1 ohm resistor wired in parallel with it, to the two alternator leads.

9. Start the engine and run it up to about 3000 rpm. The voltmeter should give a reading of 9 volts if the alternator is satisfactory. If it does, the rectifier is at fault and must be replaced. If it does not, further checks can be carried out to determine the cause of the alternator failure.

The alternator may fail due either to a short or an open circuit in the stator windings or a demagnetized rotor.

1. Connect a 110 volt AC 15 watt test light circuit between the alternator leads (one at a time) and the stator laminations. If the light goes on there is a short circuit in the windings.

2. It is extremely difficult to carry out a test for an open circuit, so at this point the best thing to do is to fit a replacement rotor and see if this cures the problem. If it does not, the stator is at fault. Since it is plastic encapsulated, no service is possible and the stator must be replaced.

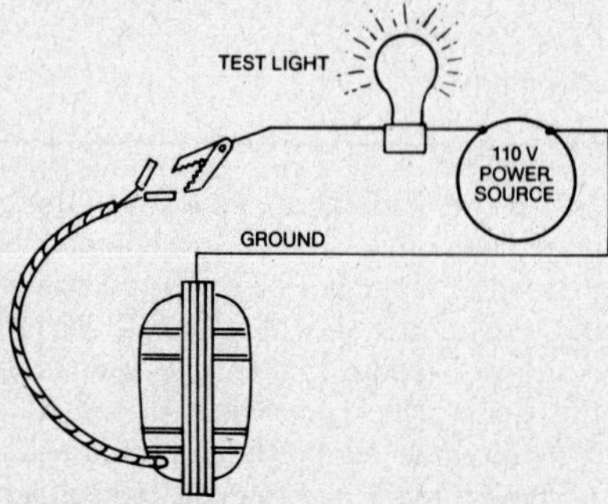

Testing the stator for short circuits

SYSTEM COMPONENTS

Rectifier Bench Test

1. Disconnect and remove the rectifier from the machine. Never put a wrench on any but the rectifier mounting nut. The stud and nut which hold the plates together are set at the factory and disturbing them will affect the rectifier output.

2. Connect the rectifier to a 12V battery and a 1-ohm load resistor.

3. Connect a DC voltmeter in the V_1 position as shown in the accompanying illustration. The meter should read 12 volts.

4. Disconnect the voltmeter and, using the accompanying illustrations for guidance, test each of the diodes with the voltmeter leads. Keep the testing time as short as possible so that the rectifier does not overheat. No reading should be greater than 2.5 volts in Test 1, and no reading should be more than 1.5 volts less than the battery voltage in Test 2 (i.e.,

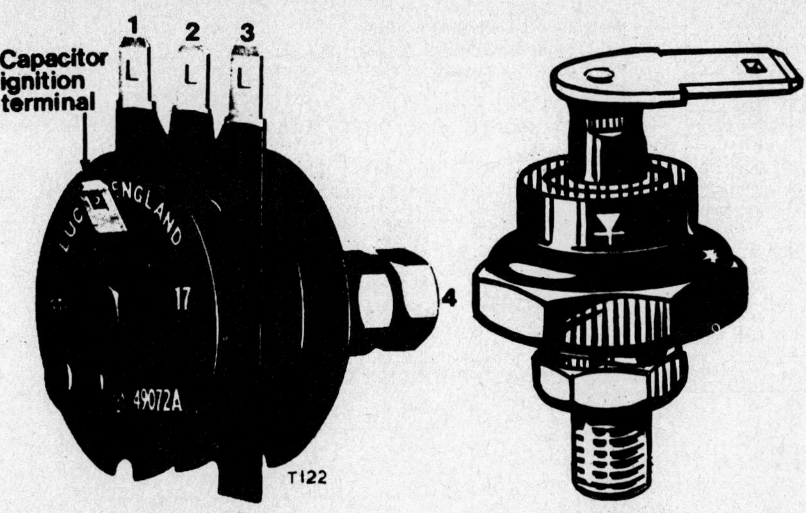

Rectifier

Zener diode

10.5 volts minimum).

5. If the rectifier does not meet specifications, it should be replaced.

Zener Diode

It is important that the diode always be securely mounted to the heat sink and that the heat sink is firmly attached to the frame. Also, the heat sink should be placed in the cooling airstream.

Alternator

The alternator requires no maintenance as such, but the following points should be noted:

1. Clean off the rotor and the stator poles from time to time removing any foreign matter, metal particles, etc.

2. Make sure that the rotor is not worn or scored from contact with the stator poles.

3. There must be no contact between the rotor and the stator poles. Ideally, there should be an even gap between the two all around the rotor. This can be checked with a feeler gauge. Clearance should be about 0.010 in. The position of the stator can be altered by using shim washers behind it placed on the housing studs.

4. Before tightening the stator mounting nuts, place an appropriate spacer around the rotor, then place the stator on its studs. Tighten the nuts with the spacer in place. This will help centralize the stator.

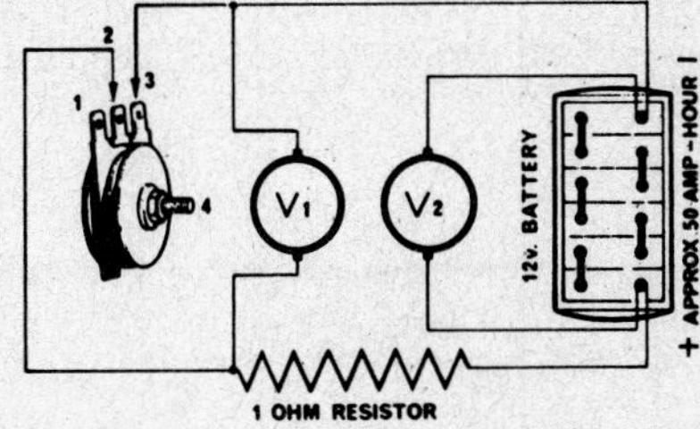

Rectifier bench-test wiring diagram

BULB SPECIFICATIONS

Headlight	12 volt, 50/40 watt Lucas No. 446
Parking light	12 volt, 6 watt; No. 989
Stoplight, tail light	12 volt, 6/21 watt; No. 679
Instrument lights	12 volt, 2.2 watt; L643
Hi-Beam indicator	24 volt, 2 watt; No. 281

WIRING DIAGRAMS

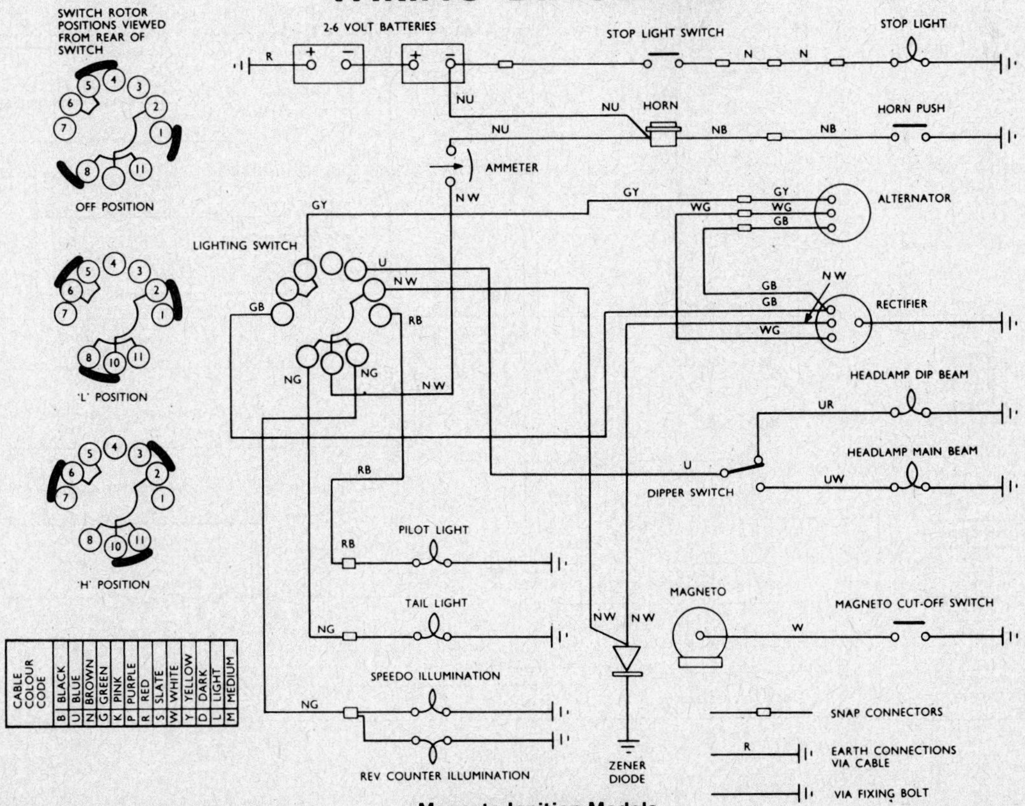

Magneto Ignition Models

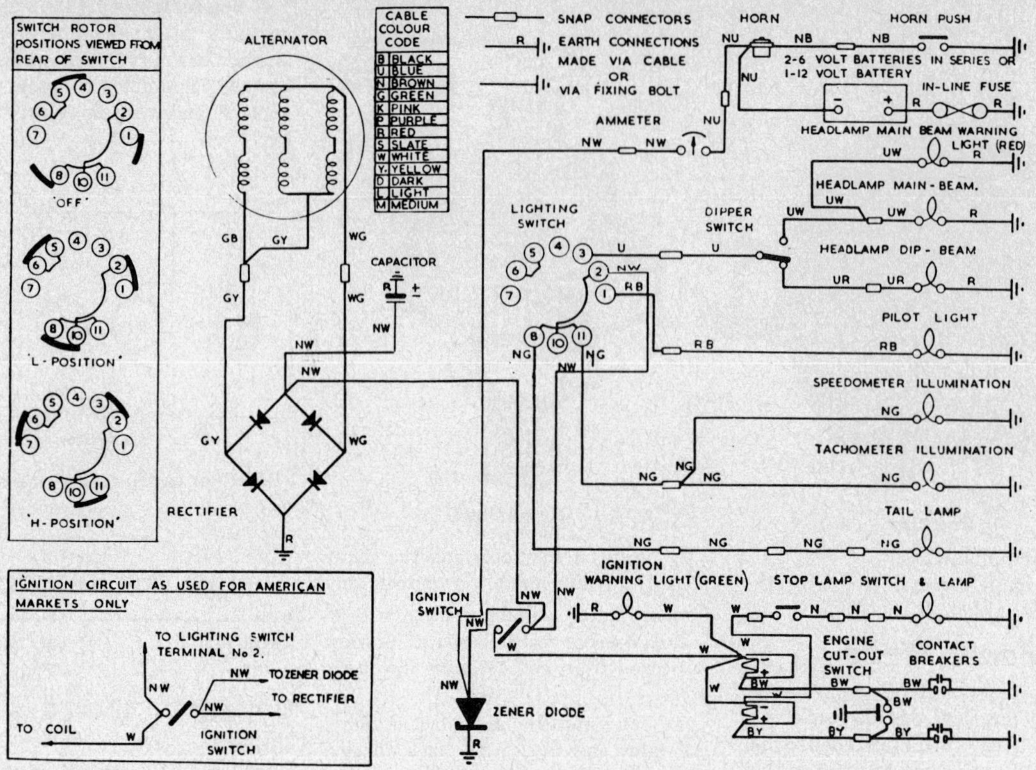

Capacitor Ignition 1967 Models

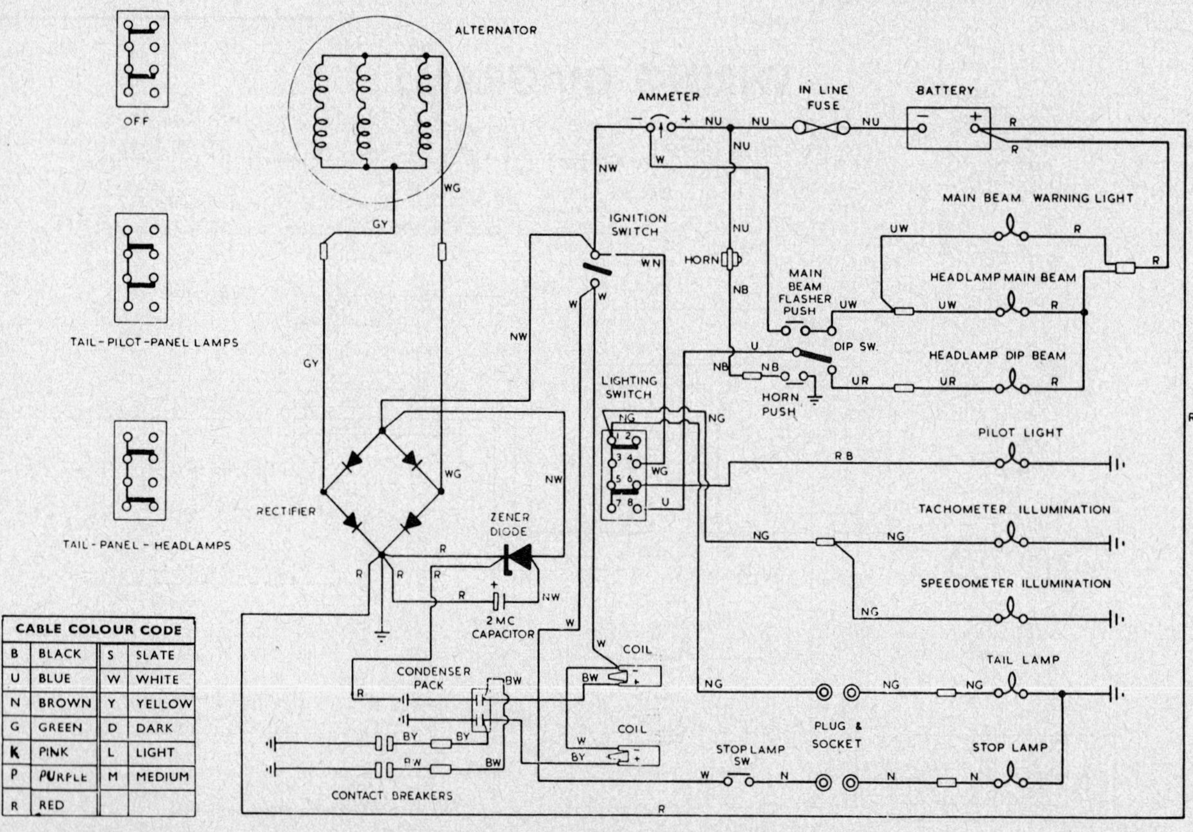

CABLE COLOUR CODE			
B	BLACK	S	SLATE
U	BLUE	W	WHITE
N	BROWN	Y	YELLOW
G	GREEN	D	DARK
K	PINK	L	LIGHT
P	PURPLE	M	MEDIUM
R	RED		

Commando (1968-1970)

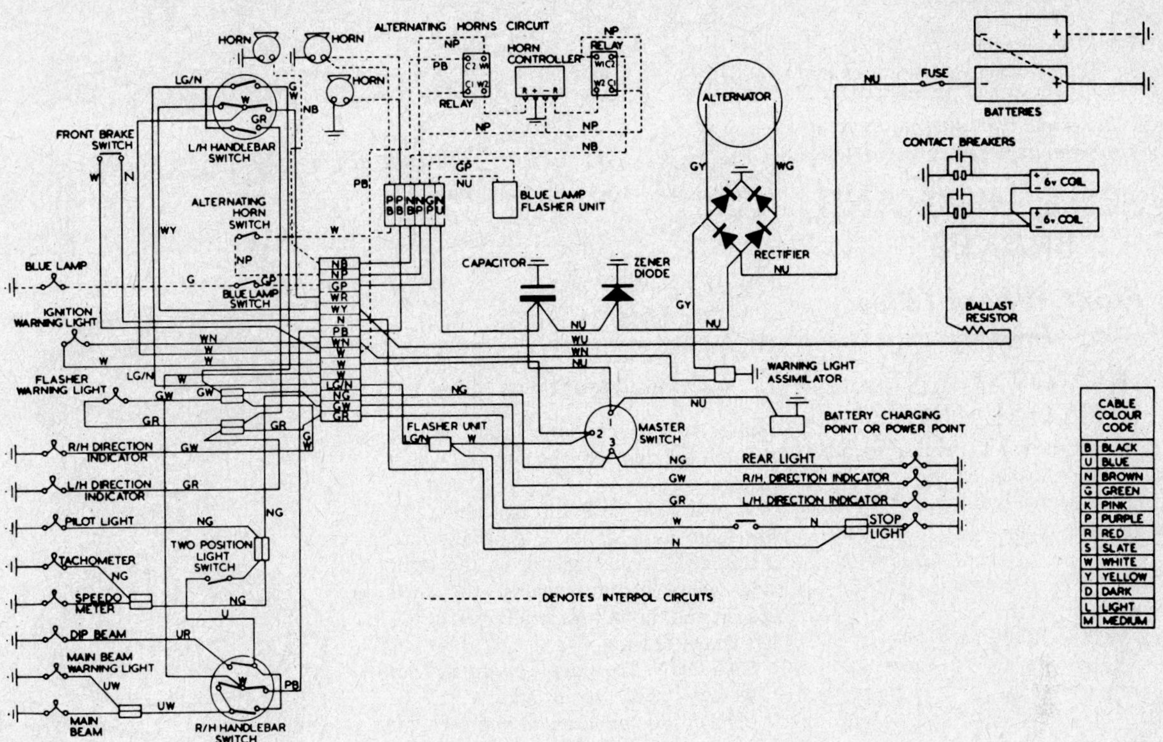

Commando (1971)

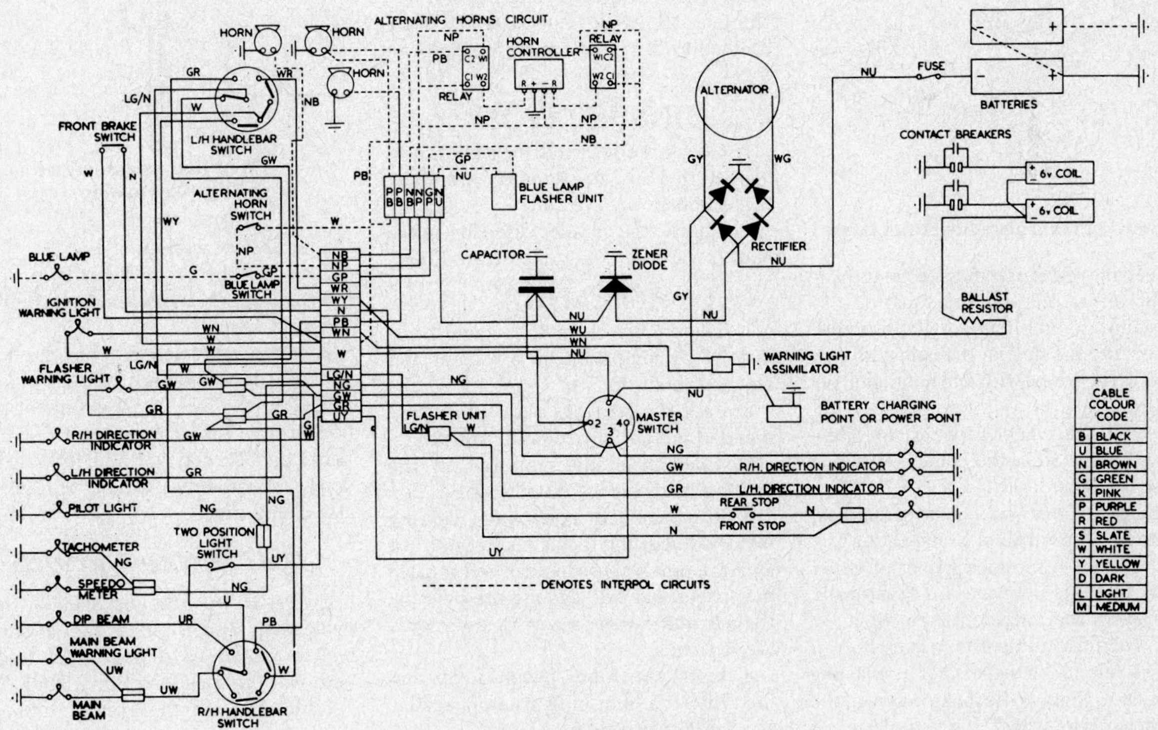

Commando (1972-1973)

CHASSIS

NOTE: *All references to "left" and "right" in the following procedures are taken from the frame of reference of a rider in normal operating position on the machine, unless otherwise noted.*

WHEELS, HUBS AND BRAKES

Front Wheel (Disc Brake)

REMOVAL AND DISASSEMBLY

1. Support the front wheel of the machine about six inches off the ground by placing a wooden box or wire milk basket beneath the engine.

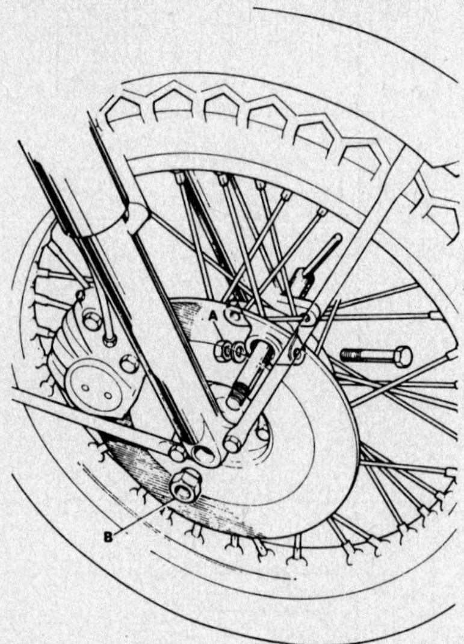

Removing the front wheel (disc brake)

2. Remove the axle nut; loosen the axle clamp nut on the left fork tube.
3. Slip a suitable bar or a philips screwdriver into the hole in the axle and, supporting the wheel with one hand, pull out the axle.
4. Pull the wheel forward, to disengage the disc from the pads, and take it away from the forks.
5. Take off the wheel bearing dust covers to avoid the risk of losing them.
6. Place a ¼ in. thick spacer of either wood or metal between the brake pads, to prevent their accidental ejection.
7. To disassemble the wheel hub, if this is felt to be necessary, use a peg wrench to remove the lock ring from the left side of the wheel. If a peg wrench is not available, the ring can be threaded out by tapping, very carefully, at one of the peg holes with a suitable punch, and unscrewing the ring in this manner.
8. Remove the felt washer. Be very careful with this item unless you have a replacement; remove the spacer, noting that the flat side bears against the wheel bearing.

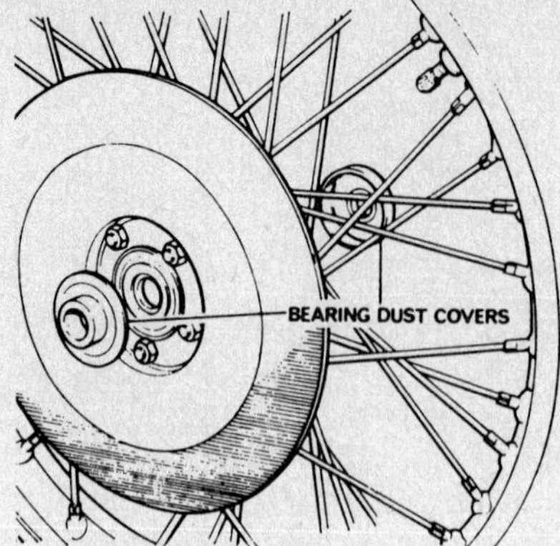

Disc brake bearing dust covers

9. Insert the axle through the right (disc) side of the wheel. A few blows with a soft-faced mallet will drive the right side wheel bearing against the tube spacer, and this in turn will force out the left wheel bearing.

CAUTION: *The wheel bearing will not usually "pop" out. In fact, it will be difficult in many cases to notice that it has moved at all. Therefore, after hitting the end of the axle once or twice, try taking out the bearing with your fingers. Under no circumstances should you use undue force on the axle.*

10. Take out the axle and insert it into the left side of the hub. Use the same method to drive out the right side bearing.

INSPECTION

1. Check the bearings for smoothness of operation and any signs of wear to either the balls or races.
2. Check the brake disc for score marks, warpage, and general condition.

ASSEMBLY

1. Thoroughly clean the wheel bearings by washing them in a solvent and blowing them dry.
2. Pack the bearings with the recommended grease or suitable substitute; clean and check the condition of the bearing lands before installation.
3. Press the left side wheel bearing into the hub using the axle as a drift, just as in the removal procedure, and replace the spacer, flat side against the bearing, the felt washer, and screw in and secure the lock ring.
4. Insert the tube spacer, small end first, into the hub, until it abuts against the bearing already fitted.
5. Fit the right side bearing. Be sure that it is fitted squarely into the hub, then use the axle to drive it home until it abuts against the tube spacer.
6. Fit the thin steel washer (the smaller of the two), the felt washer, and the large steel washer.

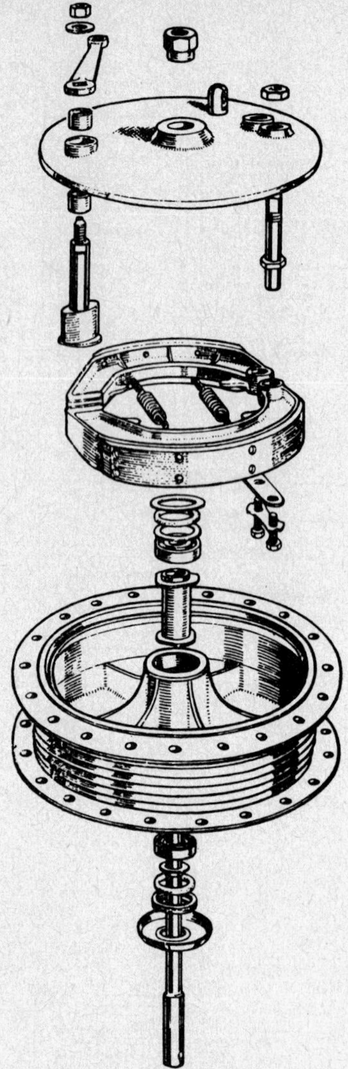

Front hub disassembled (pre-Commando)

7. Secure the large washer by peening it with a punch across the hub. Replace the dust covers.
8. Remove the spacer from the brake pads and reposition the wheel.
9. Refit the axle and tighten the axle bolt firmly. Take the support out from under the bike and work the forks up and down several times. Then, tighten the axle clamp nut.

Disc Brake Service

Every 18 months or 24,000 miles (whichever comes first), the hydraulic system should be drained and refilled with Norton-Lockheed brake fluid.

1. Attach a length of plastic tubing to the bleeder screw of the hydraulic unit (as illustrated), placing the other end in a suitable container, assuring that the end of the tube is immersed in a small amount of new brake fluid.
2. Turn the bleeder screw one-half turn.

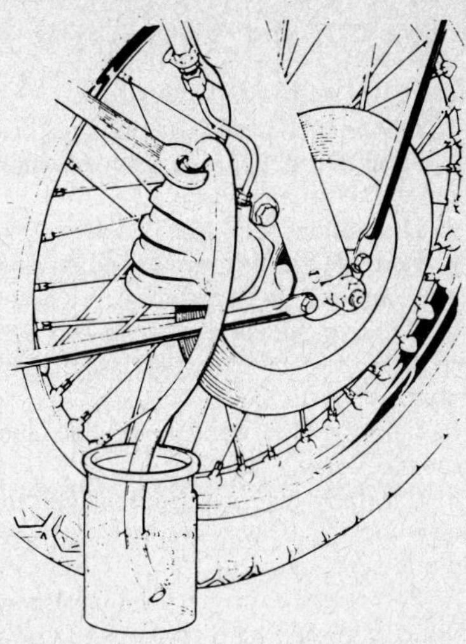

Bleeding hydraulic disc brake system

3. Apply the brake slowly, allowing it to return unassisted. Allow a slight pause between each brake application. Be sure that the master cylinder is kept full by adding the new fluid as needed.

4. When clean fluid, which is completely free of bubbles, emerges from the plastic tube, the flushing operation is complete.

5. Apply the brake lever hard, hold it on, and tighten the bleeder screw.

6. Refill the master cylinder to the correct fluid level (one half inch below the top of the cylinder).

In the event of excessive lever travel or a spongy feel in the front brake, the system must be bled, after first determining the cause of the malfunction.

The bleeding procedure is identical to that for flushing the system as described above, except that it is only necessary to continue the process until the bubbles cease to come out of the plastic tube.

FRICTION PAD REPLACEMENT

1. Remove the front wheel.
2. Rotate the friction pads slightly and remove them from the caliper.
3. The pads should be inspected for uneven or excessive wear or scoring.
4. Clean the pad with the aid of a soft brush. Do not use any solvent or wire brush for removing deposits from the pads.
5. Smear the piston faces and brake pad recesses lightly with disc brake lubricant.
6. Remove the master cylinder cap and bellows seal.
7. Press the pistons back into the caliper, observing the brake fluid level in the master cylinder.
8. Smear the edges of the pad backing plate with disc brake lubricant and press the pads against the pistons.
9. Replace the front wheel and spin the wheel while applying the brake lever several times.
10. Check the master cylinder fluid level.

NOTE: *If new pads are fitted, they must always be fitted in pairs. Also, the correct pad must be obtained depending on whether the machine is equipped with case iron, or newer stainless steel, discs. The latter is identifiable by the part number (063464) stamped on the outer rim. When new pads are fitted, they must be "broken in" for at least fifty miles by avoiding hard application of the brake.*

CALIPER

If the pistons will not move freely in the caliper, this unit should be disassembled and inspected.

Disassembly

1. Loosen, but do not remove, the caliper end plug.
2. Remove the two caliper bolts and washers and swing the caliper clear of the fork leg, watching for the brake hose.
3. Remove the two friction pads from the caliper.
4. Clean the outer ends of the pistons and the caliper body with alcohol.

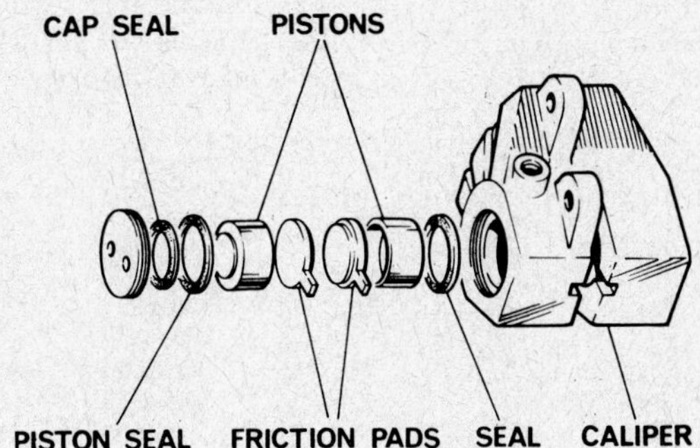

Disc brake caliper assembly

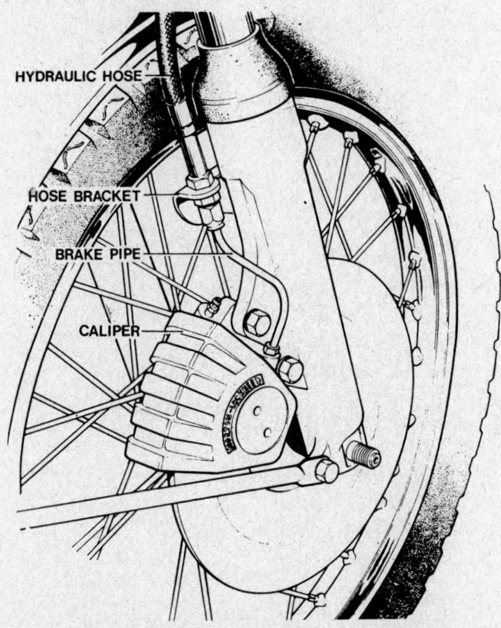

Hydraulic brake system fittings at fork leg

5. Place a can below the caliper to catch the brake fluid. Apply the brake lever, and the inner piston will come out into the pad cavity and the fluid will be released.

IMPORTANT: *If the piston is seized, the entire caliper assembly must be replaced.*

6. Loosen the lower brake pipe junction nut and separate the pipe from the caliper.
7. Remove the caliper end plug which was previously loosened and drain out the remaining fluid.
8. Remove the piston from the caliper.
9. Remove the pressure seal from the outer bore.

CAUTION: *Take extreme care not to damage the seal grooves.*

10. Remove the inner piston through the outer cylinder bore. Then remove the pressure seal from the outer bore.
11. Mark the friction pads for position ("inner" and "outer").

Inspection

1. Clean the pistons, caliper bores, and seal grooves with ethyl alcohol or clean brake fluid.

2. Examine the pistons for corrosion, wear, scoring, or unevenness of the thrust faces. If there are any irregularities present, the pistons must be replaced.

3. Check the caliper bores for corrosion, scratches, abrasion, or damage to the seal grooves.

Assembly

1. Coat new pressure seals with disc brake fluid and insert the first seal into the inner bore with your fingers, making sure that is correctly fitted.

2. Coat the inner piston with the brake fluid and insert it into the inner cylinder bore (closed. end first) after passing it through the outer bore. Let the piston protrude about 5/16 in. from the inner bore.

3. Fit the other pressure seal to the outer bore groove.

4. Insert the other piston into the other bore (open end first) until about 5/16 in. protrudes from the inner mouth of the bore.

5. Replace the end plug. A new O-ring must be fitted.

6. Fit the friction pads and replace the caliper assembly on the fork leg.

7. Torque down the end plug to 26 ft lbs.

8. Examine the fitting of the metal brake fluid pipe for distortion, cracks, or other damage. Fit the pipe into the caliper. Screw down the junction screw until the metal pipe is just lightly seated.

CAUTION: *Tighten the junction nut with a wrench no more than 60°. This is VERY important.*

9. Loosen the bleed nipple one full turn and connect a bleed tube to it as described earlier in this section. Fill the master cylinder with the recommended brake fluid.

10. Work the brake lever until the fluid begins to flow through the bleed tube. Be sure to keep the master cylinder topped up or air will be drawn into the lines. Hold the brake lever on while adding fluid.

11. When fluid without bubbles begins to flow through the bleeder tube, hold the brake lever on and tighten the bleed nipple.

12. Check the brake for sponginess and examine the system for leaks. Recheck the master cylinder fluid level, and fill it up as necessary.

MASTER CYLINDER

Removal and Disassembly

1. Disconnect the brake light switch and lift off the rubber switch cover which exposes the hose junction.

2. Disconnect the hose.

3. Remove the four screws and take off the master cylinder assembly.

4. Remove the reservoir cap and bellows seal. Also remove the brake light switch.

5. Remove the brake lever bolt and the brake lever.

6. Carefully pry out the boot circlip, then remove the boot complete with piston and secondary cup.

7. Remove the primary cup washer, primary cup, spreader, spring, and valve assembly. These parts may be removed by GENTLY tapping the edge of the master cylinder assembly on a wooden block.

Inspection

1. Clean the master cylinder and piston in brake fluid or methyl alcohol. Inspect the cylinder body for wear of the piston bore.

2. Make sure that the two ports in the reservoir chamber are clear.

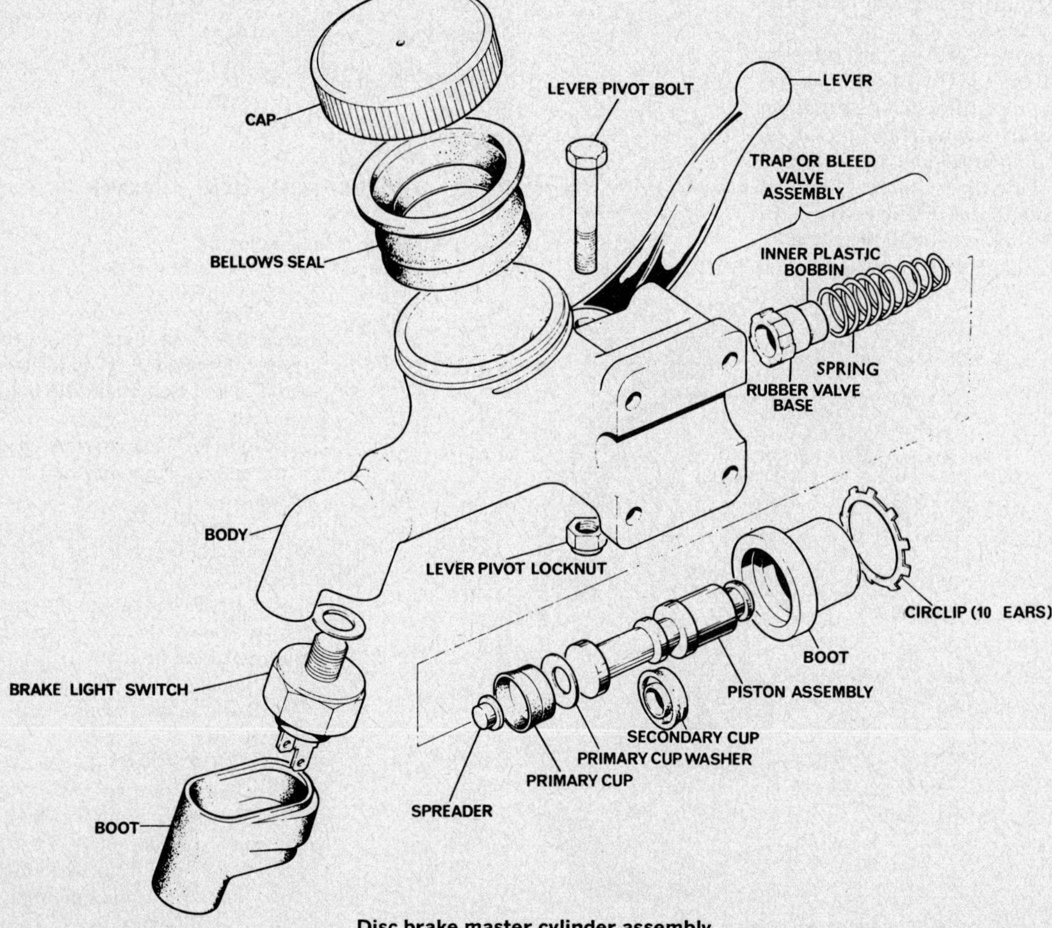

Disc brake master cylinder assembly

3. Inspect the hose junction for cleanliness.

4. Check the body of the master cylinder assembly for any cracks or fractures, especially in the area of the lever bolt.

5. Check for wear of the piston thrust face.

Assembly

1. Clean all parts and lay them out for reassembly, referring to the exploded diagram.

2. New primary and secondary cups MUST be fitted. Soak the new cups in hydraulic brake fluid for fifteen minutes, kneading them occasionally.

3. Take the secondary cup and place its non-lipped side against the ground "crown" diameter of the piston. Work the cup over the crown by hand, down the piston body, over the shoulder, and into its groove.

4. Fit the boot over the piston (open end toward the piston crown) and ensure that the boot upper end is fitted into the piston groove. Oil the piston assembly lightly with brake fluid.

5. Assemble the valve to the spring. Make sure that the inner plastic bobbin is seated in the valve base and that the plastic spreader is pressed securely into the spring.

6. Fit this assembly into the master cylinder, valve end first, holding the master cylinder bore vertical.

7. Place the primary cup into the bore (open end inward), the washer (convex side upward toward the open end of the cylinder bore). Lightly oil the mouth of the cylinder bore.

8. Take the master cylinder assembly in your left hand and insert the piston assembly into the bore.

9. Apply a gentle rotary action to the piston assembly with your right hand, at the same time maintaining pressure downward against the valve spring assembly.

10. Be sure that the lip of the secondary cup enters the bore freely. When the piston has entered the bore, use your left thumb to hold it there and press the lower boot shoulder in.

11. Maintain pressure on the piston and slide the brake lever into position, engaging the thrust pad. Replace the lever bolt.

12. The remainder of the assembly procedure is the reverse of disassembly. Bleed the system as previously described.

Front Wheel (Drum Brake)

Late models are equipped with a twin leading shoe front brake, while earlier ones feature a single leading shoe unit. In either case, the procedures are similar.

REMOVAL AND DISASSEMBLY

1. Place the machine on the center stand.

2. Disconnect the front brake cable from the hub.

3. Remove the axle nut, then loosen the axle clamp nut on the left fork leg.

4. Support the wheel to take the weight off the axle, then insert a bar or a philips screwdriver into the hole on the left side of the axle and pull it out.

5. Watching that the brake anchor clears the slot in the right fork leg, take the wheel out of the forks.

On the P-11, loosen the axle nut, disconnect the brake anchor, remove the axle caps, and remove the wheel.

6. Remove the dust cover on the left side of the wheel. Remove the brake backing plate assembly from the drum.

7. Removal of the wheel bearings is the same as described above for disc brakes (Steps 7–10). It is permissible to heat the hub very gently in the vicinity of the lock ring, if the ring resists removal.

8. Remove the brake shoes from the backing plate by taking out the bolts which secure the fixed end of the shoes (single leading shoe brake), or removing the circlips (twin leading shoe brake).

Commando twin-leading shoe front brake

9. Pull off the brake springs with a vise-grip pliers and lift off the brake shoes.

INSPECTION

1. Inspect the bearing assembly as outlined under "Disc Brake," above.

2. Check the brake linings for excessive wear, dirt embedded in the linings material, scoring, or cracks.

3. Inspect the shoes for general condition, especially the pivots and anchors. Do the same for the brake cam(s).

5. The brake drum should be free of dirt, scoring, and should be as close to circular as possible. It is possible to turn the drum on a lathe to remove imperfections on the brake surface or to restore concentricity.

ASSEMBLY

1. Assembly is the reverse of disassembly. See "Disc Brake" assembly procedure. If new linings are fitted, use a file to bevel the leading and trailing edges.

2. Grease the brake cam spindle(s). Be sure to wipe off any excess.

3. Replace the wheel, slide in the axle, and replace the axle nut, screwing it down a few times by hand.

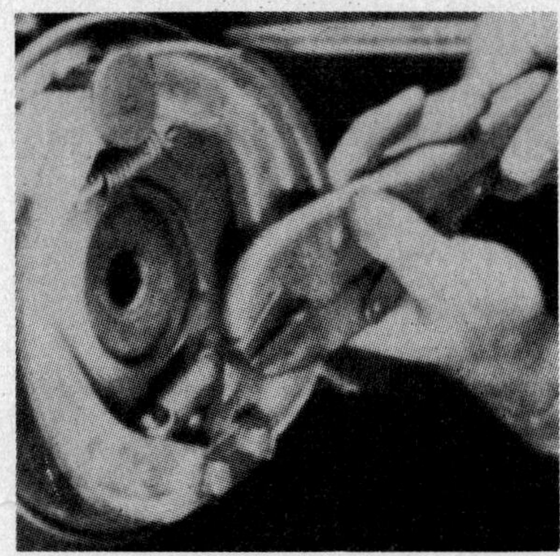

Fitting the brake springs

4. Apply the brake lever on the handlebar firmly and, while maintaining pressure here, secure the axle nut with the appropriate wrench. This will serve to centralize the brakes in the drum.

5. Take the bike off the center stand and work the forks up and down several times. Then tighten the axle clamp nut.

Rear Wheel

REMOVAL

1. It is possible to remove the rear wheel without disturbing the rear brake, drive chain, etc. The wheel is secured to

Removing the rear wheel (pre-1971 models)

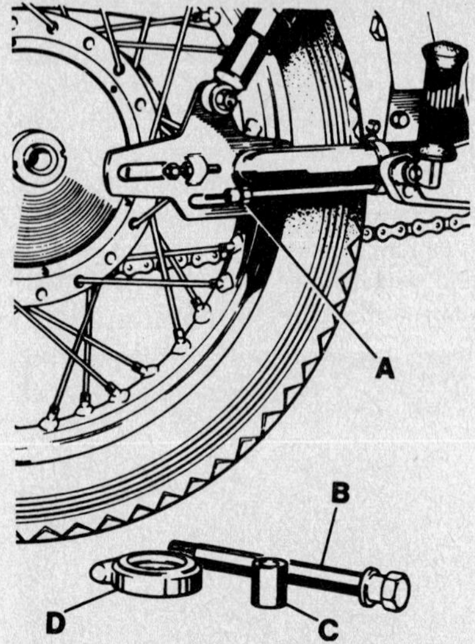

Removing the rear wheel (1971–1973 models). Speedometer cable (A), axle (B), spacer (C), and speedometer drive (D) are shown

the brake drum by three sleeve nuts beneath the rubber caps on the rear hub or, as on more recent models, by three tongues on the brake hub. If your machine has the rubber caps, remove them and remove the sleeve nuts with a suitable socket wrench. On P-11 models, disconnect the brake anchor.

2. Loosen the axle on the right side of the wheel and pull it out.

3. Remove the spacer on the right side of the wheel and remove the speedometer drive. It is not necessary to disconnect the cable, simply place the drive mechanism out of the way.

4. Pull the wheel as far as possible to the right side of the machine, until it is clear of the studs or tongues, then tilt it as necessary to clear the rear fender and pull it out of the machine.

NOTE: *It is permissible to pry between the wheel and the brake drum to free the wheel from the studs or tongues if necessary.*

5. If so desired, the rear brake drum can be removed by removing the chain guard (not necessary on late Commando models with the "chopped" chain guard) and disconnecting the drive chain.

6. Remove the axle nut.

7. Remove the rear brake adjuster nut if the brake is rod-operated, or disconnect the brake cable if it is cable-operated.

8. Take out the brake drum and backing plate, taking care not to loose the large spacer. Remove the brake shoes, if desired, refering to "Front Wheel, Drum Brake," above.

9. If it is desired to remove or lubricate the bearing, remove the lock ring on the right side of the rear hub. This ring has a LEFT-HAND thread. Use a peg wrench or a suitable punch and tap the ring to unscrew it. The hub may be heated gently in the vicinity of the ring if it resists removal.

10. Take out the felt washer, being very careful with this item as it is very fragile; also remove the spacer.

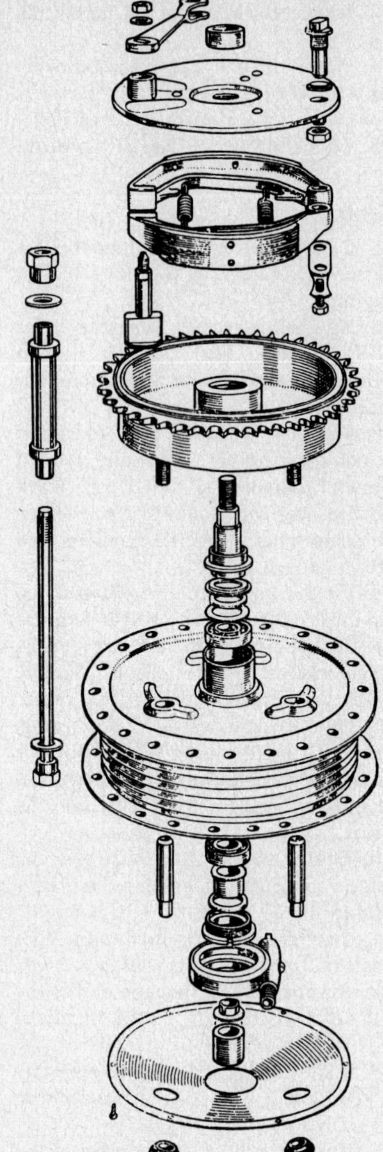

Exploded view of rear hub (Atlas)

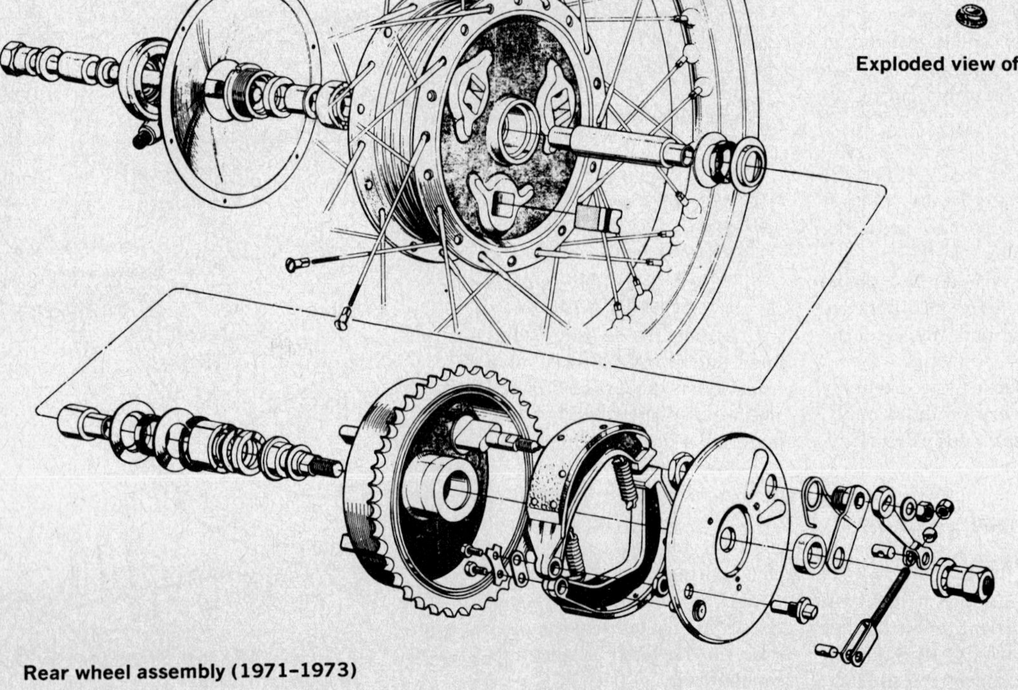

Rear wheel assembly (1971–1973)

11. To the axle, fit the large lock washer with which it is equipped and the large spacer found between the speedometer drive and the swing arm.

12. Insert the axle into the left (brake) side of the wheel and use a soft-faced mallet to strike the axle smartly once or twice. You will feel the brake side bearing give until it bears against a shoulder in the hub. It will have pushed the right side bearing out by an equivalent amount. Stop at this point and withdraw the axle.

13. Obtain a short piece of steel tubing with a diameter just slightly smaller than the inside diameter of the bearing. The front wheel axle is suitable for this purpose. Insert the tubing, or the threaded end of the axle, into the brake side bearing, center it, and tap lightly until the right side bearing is driven out. The axle will bear against the spacer inside the hub, which in turn will serve to drive out the right side bearing.

14. Take out the spacer, if it is still in place, and remove the drift you used. Insert the rear axle (and spacer) into the right side of the wheel. Carefully center it on the brake side bearing and drive this bearing out with a couple of blows on the end of the axle with a soft-faced mallet. The steel cup washer, felt washer, and thin steel washer will come out with the bearing.

INSPECTION

Inspect all bearings and the brake components refering to "Front Wheel, Drum Brake," above. Be especially attentive to grease or oil on the rear brake linings. The linings may have to be replaced if badly impregnated.

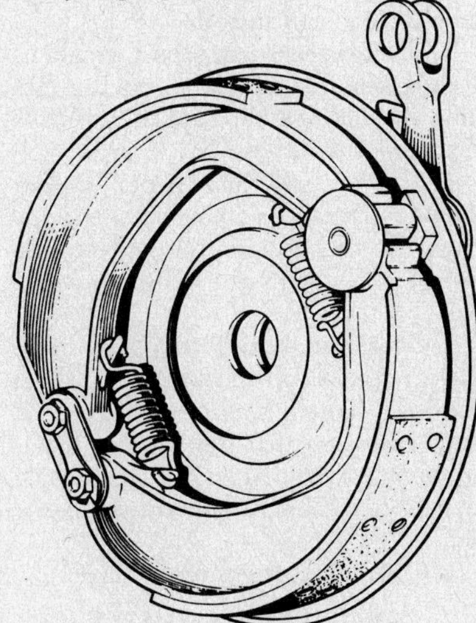

Commando rear brake assembly

1. In 1971, an additional bearing was introduced in the rear brake drum. This bearing should be inspected and lubricated at the same time as the wheel bearings.

2. The three tongues on the brake assembly which drive the wheel must be inspected for security. The tongues are brazed into the brake drum. Note that the brazing material must have run all around the tongue bosses when viewed from inside the drum.

ASSEMBLY

1. Fit the right side (single row) bearing into the threaded side of the hub.

2. Fit the tube spacer from the left side with the long end inserted into the single row bearing.

3. Refit the spacer, the felt washer, and the lock ring on the right-hand side of the hub and tighten the lock ring. Remember, it has a left-hand thread.

4. Replace the brake side bearing and drive it home using the rear axle and spacer as on removal.

5. Fit the thin steel washer, the felt washer, and the cup washer in that order. Peen the cup washer against the hub with a suitable punch.

6. The rest of the assembly is a reverse of the disassembly procedure. Be sure that the speedometer drive is correctly engaged in the slots of the lock ring before tightening the axle.

Also, apply the rear brake pedal hard, then tighten the axle nut (left side), while holding the brake pedal on to centralize the brakes in the drum.

FRONT FORKS

The fork legs can be removed individually, leaving the steering column in place, or the entire assembly can be taken off at once. The first procedure is given below.

Fork Legs

REMOVAL AND DISASSEMBLY

1. Support the front wheel well off the ground. Remove the front wheel, as previously described, and also remove the front fender.

2. Remove the drain plug at the bottom of the fork legs to drain the oil. On disc brake models, remove the hydraulic system completely after placing a ¼ in. spacer between the brake pads.

3. Loosen the filler cap nut at the top of the fork leg until it is clear of the threads in the triple clamp. Then use a thin wrench to loosen the lock nut on the damper rod so that the cap nut can be removed from the rod. It may be necessary to push up on the fork leg to raise the damper rod enough to gain access to the lock nut.

4. Loosen the clamp nut on the lower triple clamp. On models with "Ceriani-type" front forks, loosen the allen bolt.

5. A sharp downward yank on the fork leg should free the upper end from the upper triple clamp. If necessary, the cap nut can be threaded a few turns into place. Then, a sharp blow with a soft-faced mallet should be enough to free the fork leg.

6. Repeat the procedure with the other fork leg.

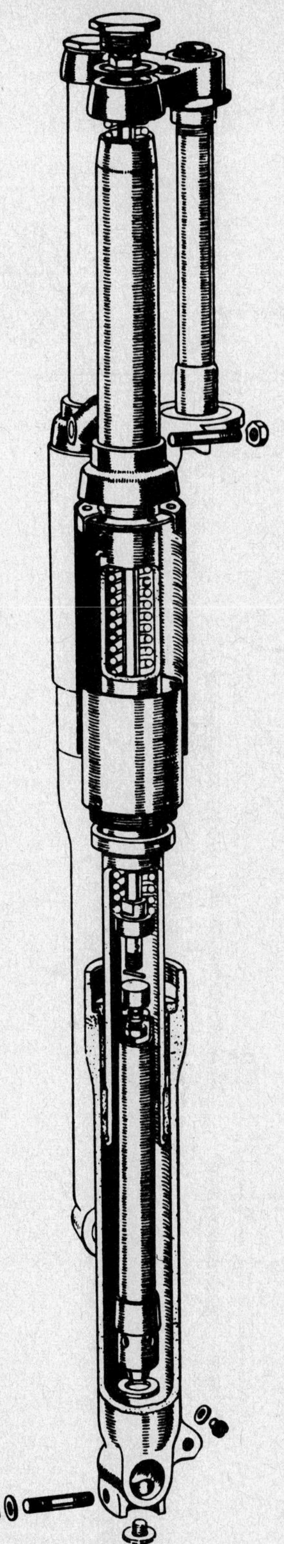

Roadholder forks (Atlas)

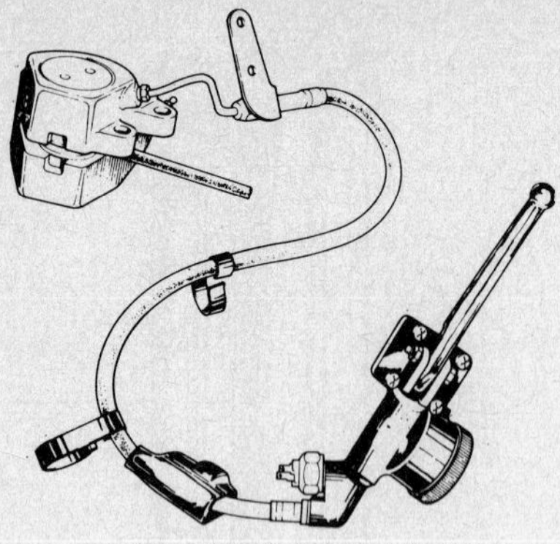

Disc brake system removed without disassembly

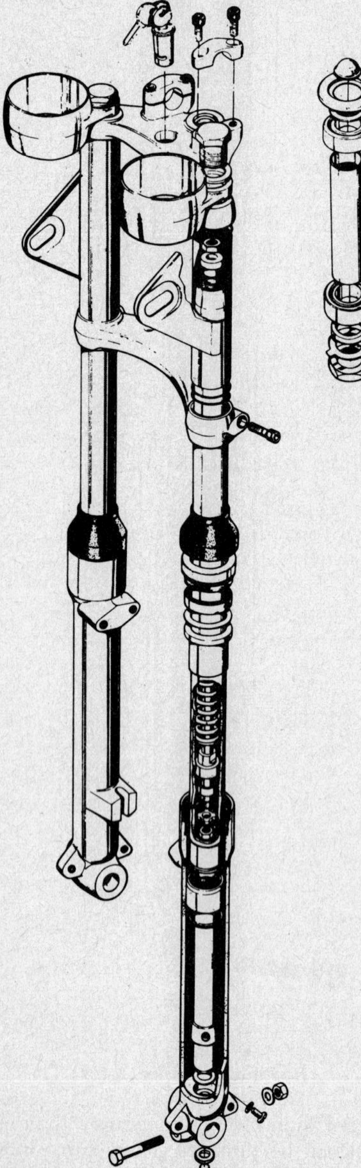

Ceriani-type front forks as fitted to the Commando

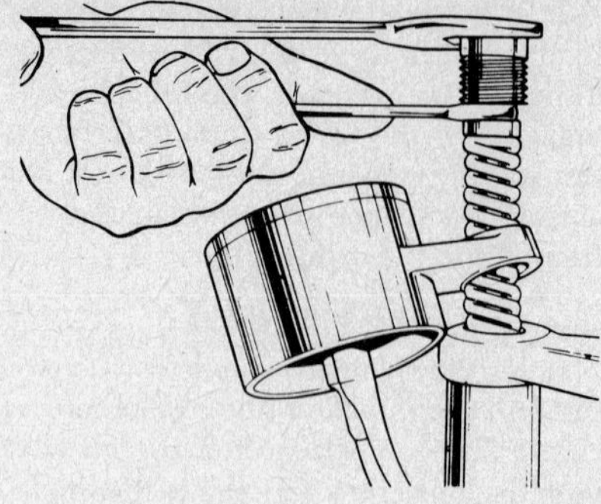

Removing fork cap nut from damper rod

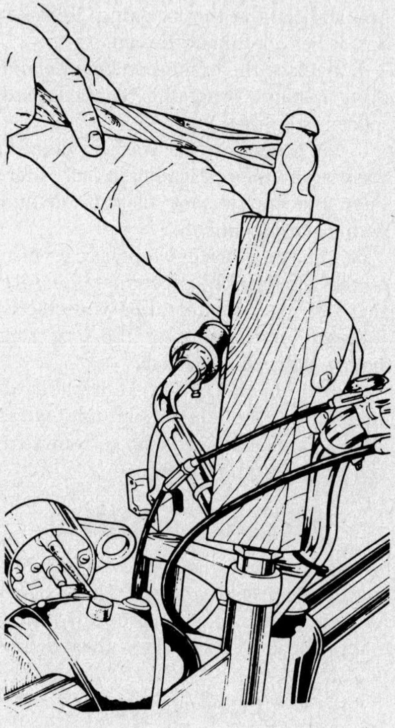

Freeing fork tube from upper triple clamp

7. On Scrambler models, remove the external fork springs.

8. Remove the rubber fork gaiter, if fitted, or the rubber dust cover on Ceriani-type front forks.

9. Remove the bolt and washer at the very bottom of the fork slider (a thin-walled socket is needed to reach this bolt) and take out the spring and damper assembly from the top of the fork tube.

A fiber washer is placed at the bottom of the damper tube and may remain in the fork slider.

10. The alloy fork slider has an extension screwed into it, the length and type of the extension depending on the model of the machine. To remove the slider, the extension must be taken off first. Most models have holes for the appropriate peg wrench on the extension and, if this tool is available, removal is a simple matter. If the peg wrench is not to be had, however, an alternative method is to fasten a heater hose clamp to the extension (at the bottom portion of the long chrome plated extensions, if that is what you have); vise-grip pliers can then be locked on to the screw assembly of the clamp and used to turn the extension.

Unscrew the extension all the way, then take off the slider from the bottom of the fork tube.

11. Remove the extension from the top of the fork tube and also remove the oil seal, paper washer, and flanged bush (bronze), in that order, from the top of the tube as well.

12. The bottom bush (steel) is held in place by a circlip and can be removed after the circlip is taken off.

13. The damper tube can be disassembled on Atlas and Commando models, if desired, by taking off the nut at the top of the rod, the spacer, and the long spring.

14. Insert a suitable rod through the holes in the damper tube to keep it from turning, and unscrew the damper tube cap nut. Removing the nut at the bottom of the rod will allow the slotted washer, cup, and crosspin to be removed.

15. On Scramblers, the damper tube is disassembled by taking off the bottom nut, the brass seat for the damper valve, the damper valve itself, and the crosspin. Remove the circlip and take off the plunger sleeve.

NOTE: *The oil groove is closest to the bottom of the rod when installed.*

INSPECTION

1. Remove any rust from the exterior of the fork tube with emery cloth. This is most likely to form beneath the headlight supports.

2. Make sure that the inside of the fork tube is clean and smooth.

3. The flanged (bronze) bush should be a close but free sliding fit on the fork tube. It must be replaced if excessive clearance is noticed.

4. The oil seal and paper washer should be replaced with new items if possible. The rubber lip of the seal must be free of cracks, signs of age, dirt, or corrosion.

5. Check the damper tube and assure that it is free of corrosion, foreign matter, and has a smooth interior surface.

6. Make sure that the damper rod is not bent as might happen if it has come loose from the fork cap nut during operation.

7. Check the springs for damage.

ASSEMBLY AND INSTALLATION

1. Thoroughly clean all components before assembly. Give all pieces a coat of light oil.

2. Reassemble the damper tube components if this has been taken apart: crosspin, cup, slotted washer. Secure the nut

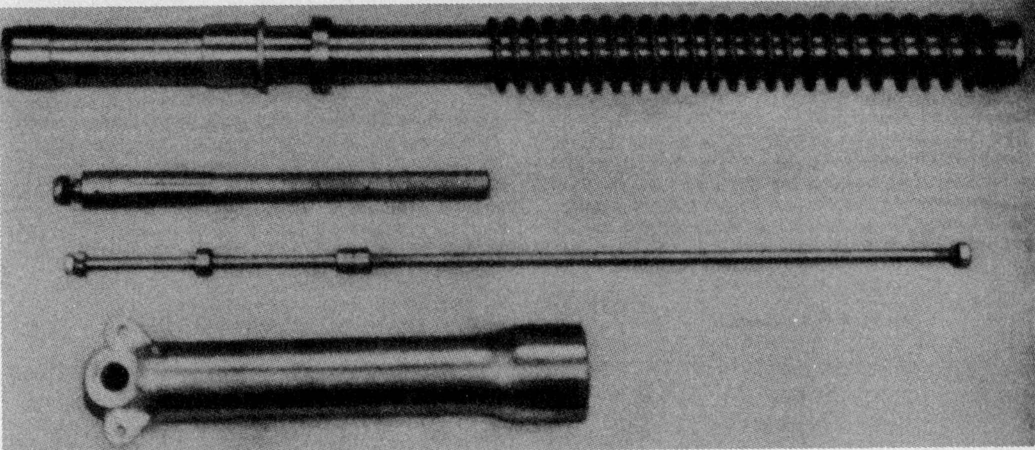

Front fork assembly (G15CS)

at the bottom of the rod, then fit the assembly into the damper tube and secure the damper cap nut.

For Scramblers, the plunger sleeve (oil groove closest to the bottom of the rod), circlip, crosspin, damper valve, valve seat, and rod nut are fitted in that order.

3. Replace the fiber washer on the lower end of the damper tube and insert the tube into the fork slider; secure it there with the bolt and washer at the very bottom of the slider.

4. Fit the bottom (steel) bush and secure it with the circlip. Be sure the circlip is not deformed. Fit a new one if in doubt.

5. From the top of the fork tube, slide on the flanged bush, the paper washer, and the oil seal. Be very careful when sliding the oil seal along the fork tube. It is advisable to apply some oil to the seal lip before refitting. Also, note that the seal is installed with the spring side (open side) facing the flanged bush.

6. Take up the damper rod and fork slider, which have been assembled as directed above, and slip the internal fork spring over the damper rod. Also, fit the spacer and the nut. Be sure that the bevelled side of the nut faces the spring. Screw the nut all the way down to the end of the threads of the damper rod.

7. Take up the slider and damper assembly and insert the spring into the bottom of the fork tube. Carefully bring the fork slider up over the lower and upper bushes.

8. Place the extension into position from the upper end of the fork tube and use it to centralize and press the oil seal into the fork slider. Hand tighten the extension. Final tightening is best left until the axle has been replaced, as this will keep the slider from turning as the extension is turned.

9. Replace the external spring (if fitted) and the fork gaiter or dust cover.

10. Lightly grease the upper portion of the fork tube and position it in the triple clamps. The clamp nut on the lower triple clamp may be gently tightened to hold the fork leg in place, if necessary.

11. Refill the fork leg with the correct grade and quantity of oil.

12. Push up the fork leg to expose the damper rod and replace the cap nut and washer. Tighten the cap nut against the lock nut on the damper rod, then (loosen the clamp nut on the lower triple clamp if this has been tightened) tighten the fork cap nut all the way to pull the fork tube up into its proper position. Retighten the lower triple clamp nut. Replace the brake lines (hydraulic). Torque the caliper bolts to 30 ft lbs.

13. Refit the fender and wheel. Tighten the fork slider extension securely.

STEERING HEAD

The steering head assembly should be removed to lubricate the bearings at the appropriate maintenance interval, or to inspect the condition of the bearings if normal adjustment procedures do not take play out of the front forks.

NOTE: *Latest Commando models have sealed steering head bearings installed and, therefore, the steering head should not be removed except if damage is suspected as after a collision.*

Removal

1. Remove the handlebars, the instrument drive cables, and the light wires.

2. Unbolt the headlight and let it hang from the wiring harness.

3. Remove the fork cap nuts and remove the tach and speedometer.

4. Remove the front wheel and fender as previously described.

5. Remove the steering damper, if fitted.

6. Remove the fork crown nut (this is the large nut at the rear center of the upper triple clamp). Give the upper triple clamp a blow from beneath with a soft-faced mallet and remove it.

7. Support the forks and unscrew the bearing race adjuster nut; this is a sleeve nut. Watch for the 18 ball bearings in the upper race.

8. Lower the forks and remove the assembly from the frame.

9. The bearing cups in the frame are press-fit. They can be drifted out, if necessary, using a short piece of steel tubing. The cups must come out parallel to the housing, so move the tubing around the circumference of the cup while driving it out.

10. The cone on the steering column can be removed with a suitable chisel or a screwdriver.

Inspection

1. There are 36 bearings in the steering head assembly (18 in each ball race). Be sure that all are present.

2. Inspect the bearing race surfaces for cracks, rust, pitting, or signs of wear. The bearing surfaces should be smooth.

3. Make sure that the steering column is parallel with the top ends of the fork tubes.

4. Ball bearings are ¼ in. in size. They must be in good condition and free from any deformation.

Installation and Adjustment

1. Replace the cone on the steering column and the bearing races in the frame. A draw bolt should be used to press home the races, as illustrated. All traces of paint or foreign matter msut be removed to enable the bearings to be repositioned correctly.

2. Place 18 balls in the cone and in the top cup on the frame, holding them in place by embedding them in stiff grease.

3. Replace the dust cover, then thread on the bearing race adjuster nut (sleeve nut). This must be adjusted later. Make it reasonably tight for now.

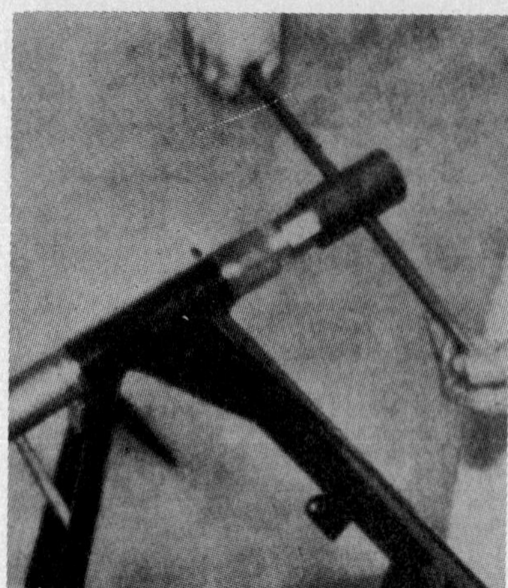

Installing steering head bearing races (Commando)

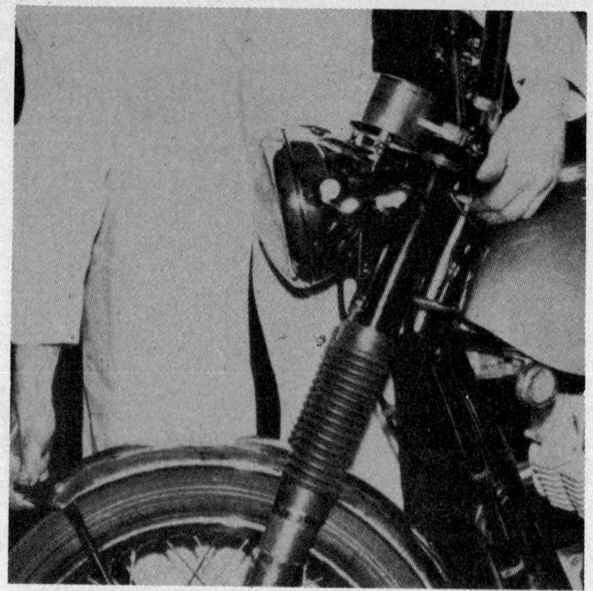

Checking steering head bearings for excessive play

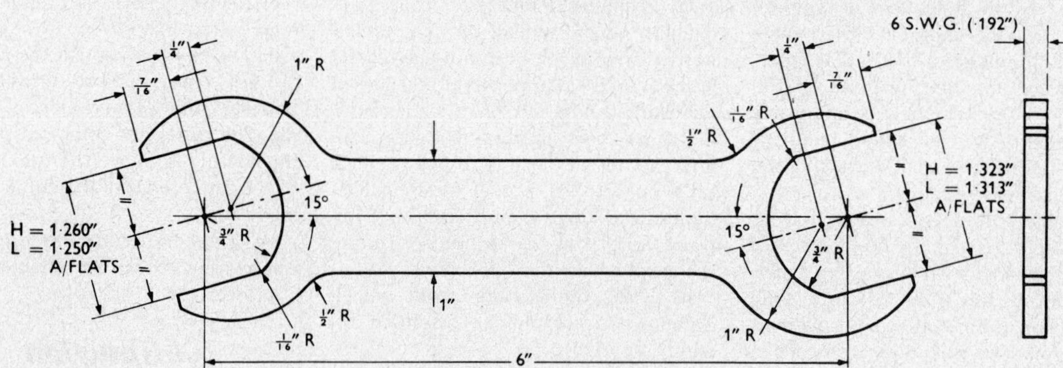

Steering head bearing adjustment wrench

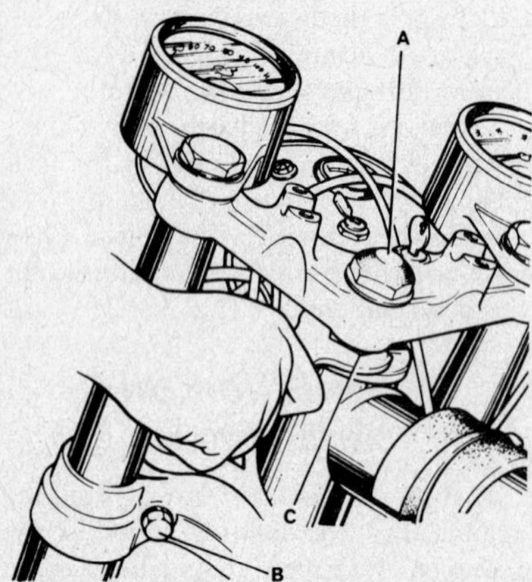

Adjusting steering head bearings (pre-1971 models); lower triple clamp bolt (B) is shown

4. Replace the upper triple clamp and seat it properly. Replace the fork crown nut, but do not tighten it.

5. Replace the front fender and wheel assembly.

6. Check the play in the front forks by grasping the tip of the front fender, pulling forward, and feeling for play with the other hand placed at the junction of the upper triple clamp and the frame.

7. To adjust the bearings, loosen the clamp nuts on the lower triple clamp (be sure the fork crown nut is also loose) and tighten the sleeve nut with the appropriate wrench (see illustration) until all play in the forks is taken up.

8. Retighten the clamp nuts and the crown nut. Recheck the forks for play and also see that they can be rotated from lock to lock with no binding or tight spots.

9. The remainder of the procedure is the reverse of the removal instructions.

REAR SHOCK ABSORBERS

The rear shock absorbers are sealed units and the hydraulic damper cannot be serviced. They are adjustable for load and this change is made with the appropriate "C" wrench.

The springs can be removed by:

1. Removing the shocks (one at a time) from the frame.

2. Compressing the spring sufficiently to take out the two keepers at the top.

3. Removing the dust cover (if fitted), and taking off the spring.

NOTE: *Grating noises while in operation are usually eliminated by greasing the inside of the dust cover before installation.*

SWING ARM

Atlas

REMOVAL

1. Remove the chainguard. Disconnect the final drive chain.

2. Remove the rear wheel and the brake assembly.

3. Remove the bolts which attach the bottom of the shock absorbers to the frame.

4. Remove the nut and washer from one end of the swing arm spindle and take out the spindle from the other side

of the frame.

5. Push the swing arm forward, turn it to one side, and take it out of the frame.

INSPECTION

The swing arm bearings do not need maintenance. If they are defective, play will be noticeable in the swing arm when in the frame.

DISASSEMBLY

The bearings must be pressed out and replaced with an arbor press. There are two bearings, separated by a spacer.

ASSEMBLY AND INSTALLATION

1. Press in the new bearings with the arbor press.
2. Replace the swing arm in the frame.
3. Replace and tighten the shock absorber bottom bolts before tightening the swing arm spindle nut.
4. Tighten the swing arm spindle nut and proceed with assembly in the reverse of the removal sequence.

G15CS, N15CS

These scrambler models incorporate two oilite bearings in a steel sleeve.

REMOVAL

1. Remove the chainguard, disconnect the chain, and unbolt the rear shocks from the swing arm.

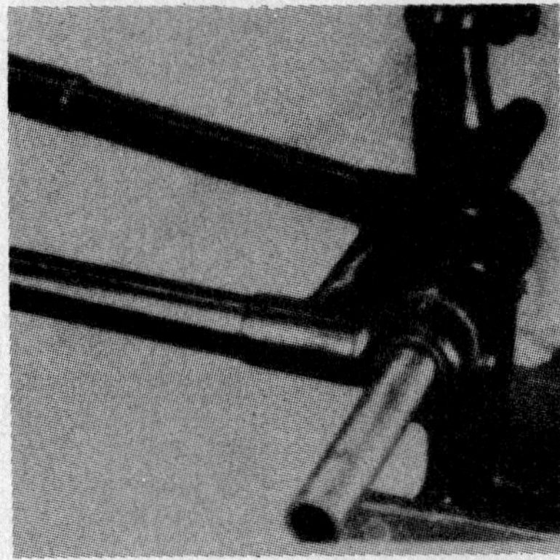

Removing the swing arm bushings (G15CS)

2. Remove the rear wheel and the brake assembly.
3. Take out the cotter pin on the swing arm spindle and press out the steel sleeve. Remove the swing arm. Watch for the two felt washers as the swing arm is removed.

DISASSEMBLY

Each bush must be pressed out in turn with an arbor press. Note that they are flanged.

ASSEMBLY AND INSTALLATION

1. The spindle diameter is 0.990–0.995 in. The bushes are reamed, after installation, to 1.001 in.
2. The steel sleeve is oil filled and this is accomplished by removing the filler screw in the cover plate and injecting a heavy grade of oil until the cavity is filled.
3. The remainder of the procedure is the reverse of removal.

Commando

The swing arm pivots on two flanged bushes which are supported by the swing arm spindle which passes through the rear engine mounting plate.

REMOVAL

1. Remove the threaded rod which secures the end plates for the swing arm bushes.

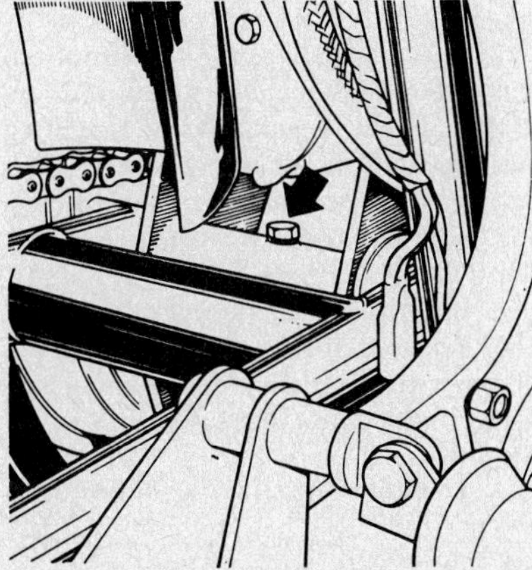

Swing arm spindle lock bolt location (Commando)

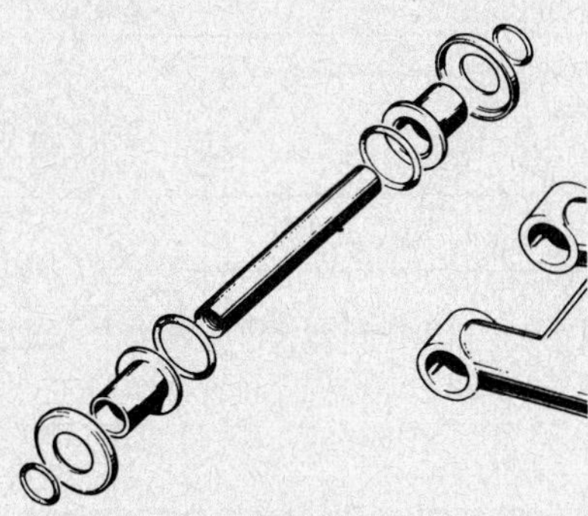

Commando swing arm bushings in order of assembly

2. Remove the lock bolt, in the middle of the rear engine mounting, which secures the swing arm spindle.
3. The spindle is threaded on the right side. It must be removed with a ½ in. bolt. Thread in the bolt and pull out the spindle.
4. Remove the chainguard. Disconnect the drive chain.
5. Remove the rear wheel and the brake assembly.
6. Remove the bottom bolts on the rear shock absorbers.
7. The swing arm can now be removed from the frame.

DISASSEMBLY

1. Remove the large O-rings and dust covers from the swing arm.
2. Take out the small O-rings in the recesses of the bushing housings, then support the ends of the swing arm properly and press out the bushes with an arbor press.

INSPECTION

In the event of a damaged or worn swing arm pivot spindle, oversized units are available. These are 0.005 in. larger in diameter than the stock unit.

The spindle bore clearance should be 0.0005–0.0020 in.

To fit the oversized spindle, the bearings should be bored, in place, to 0.8807–0.8817 in.

ASSEMBLY AND INSTALLATION

1. Place the dust cover over the bush. The recess in the dust cover for the large O-ring should face inward.
2. Press in the bushes. Again, an arbor press is used.
3. Refit the large O-rings in the dust covers and the small O-rings in the recess in the bush housing.
4. The rest of the procedure is the reverse of that for removal.

FRAME

Pre-Commando

The rigid frame Nortons require no maintenance in this area other than routine checks of the frame gussets and steering lug for cracks if vibration is high or handling poor.

In the event of a broken frame tube, it is better to braze the joint than weld it. The broken or fractured tube should first be strengthened by inserting a piece of tubing smaller than the frame tube, spanning the tube for several inches. Depend-

Vibration Range	Probable Cause	Solution
0-3000 rpm	Front Mounting OK, Rear Tight	Remove 0.005 in. shim
3000-5000 rpm	Rear Mounting OK, Front Tight	Remove 0.005 in. shim
0-5000 rpm	Front and Rear Mountings Tight	Remove 0.005 in. shim

CHASSIS SPECIFICATIONS

Wheel Bearings (mm)	
Front, left side	17 x 40 x 12
Front, right side	17 x 40 x 16
Rear, left side	17 x 40 x 12
Rear, right side	17 x 40 x 16
Torque Wrench Settings (ft lbs)	
Engine Mounting Bolts (All)	25
Disc Brake Caliper Bolts	25
Disc Brake	
Pad type: Steel backed, molded and bonded friction material	
Pad friction area diam. (in.)	1.65
Pad thickness (in.)	0.37-0.38
Disc diameter (in.)	10.70
Disc width (in.)	0.250-0.260

ing on the location of the fault, a sleeve over the frame tubes can also be used.

Commando

The engine and transmission are bolted rigidly together by the rear engine mounting plate. The swing arm, instead of being attached to the frame, is bolted to this assembly, although it pivots independently in the normal manner. Now, the entire engine-transmission-swing arm unit is mounted in the frame at three places by means of polymer filled absorption units. These are located at the very top of the cylinder head, at the front of the crankcase, and above and to the rear of the transmission.

The absorption units must be assembled properly if the system is to work as the designers intended.

The front and rear engine mounting units must be checked for side play if vibration occurs.

FRONT MOUNTING

1. For the front engine mounting, be sure that the engine mounting bolt is torqued to the correct value of 25 ft lbs.

2. The total side-play of the front engine mounting should be 0.020–0.025 in. If the side play is reduced, the mounting bush will not function. Side play is adjusted by means of shim washers of varying thickness. These are available in four sizes: 0.005, 0.010, 0.020, and 0.030 in.

3. If the engine plate is moved and then released, the assembly should react through the elasticity of the mounting bush. If it does not, the shim washers are too thick.

4. To fit new shims, remove the nut on the left side of the assembly, drive out the bolt far enough so that the spacer and the cap can be removed for access to the shim washer, and replace this with one which will give the correct side play.

Checking clearance in the front engine mounting

5. Reassemble the mounting, torque down the nut to 25 ft lbs, and recheck the side-play.

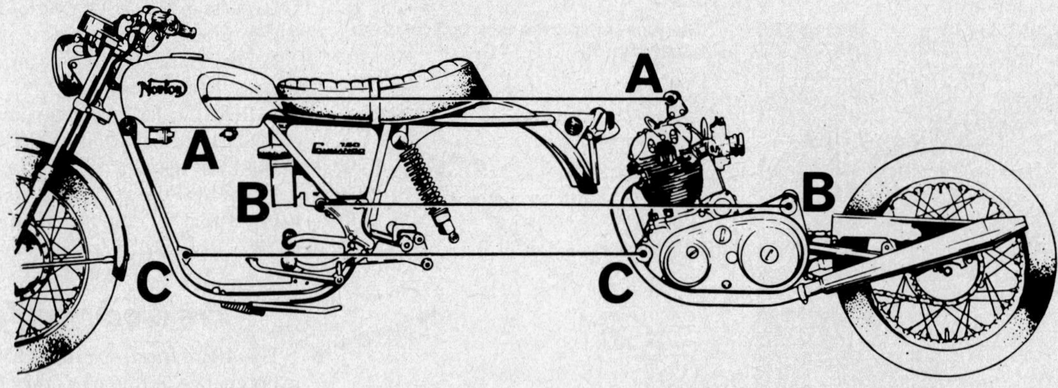

Norton Commandos' "Isolastic" suspension system

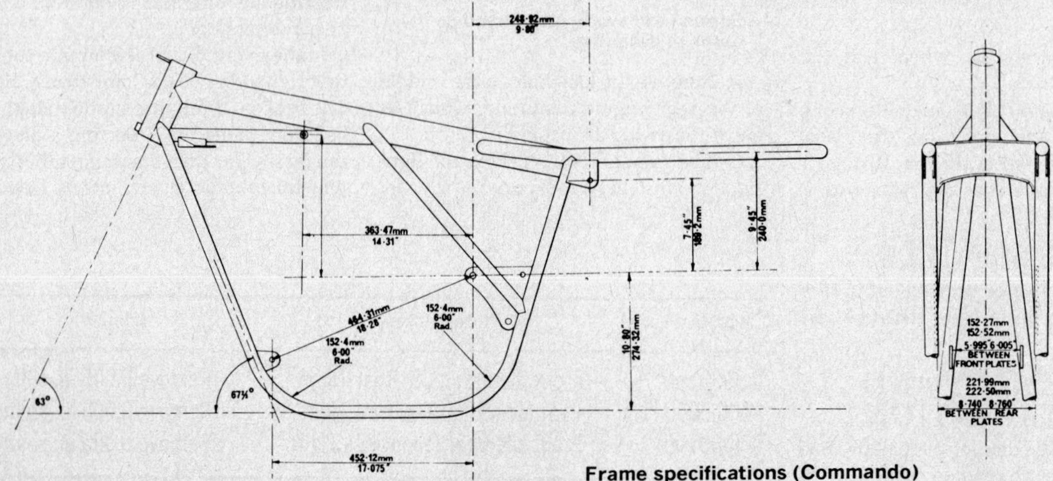

Frame specifications (Commando)

REAR MOUNTING

1. Checking the side-play for the rear mount is the same as for the front. The value is 0.010–0.015 in. It should be checked on the right side of the machine.

2. New shims can be fitted by taking off the nut on the right side and driving out the bolt far enough so that the spacer and cap can be removed.

3. Replace the shim washer with the one selected and refit the cap and spacer.

4. Torque down the nut (25 ft lbs) and recheck side-play.

5. To remove the rear engine mounting, the engine, transmission, oil tank, and the swing arm spindle must be removed. Refer to the appropriate sections for these procedures.

6. The main mounting bush and the rubber spacers are removed with an arbor press. This is also true for the front assembly, although this unit may be taken out of the frame by itself.

NOTE: *If proper side-play cannot be obtained, the engine mounting tube may be partially collapsed and must be replaced.*

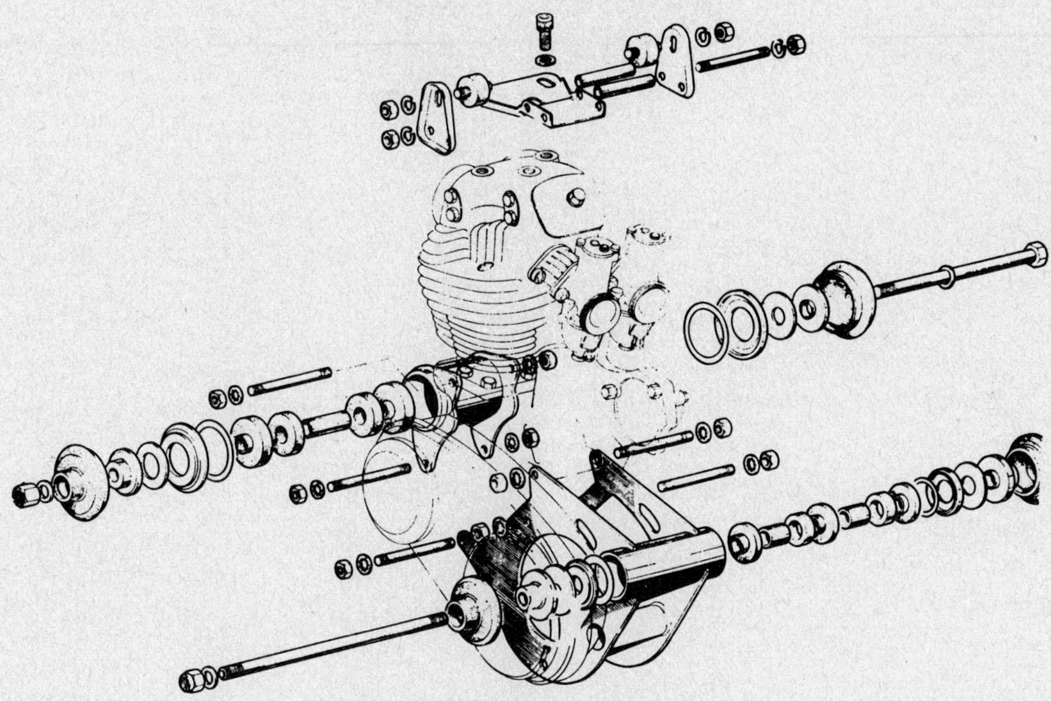

Isolastic suspension system exploded view

INDEX
OSSA

MODEL IDENTIFICATION

The Stilleto model comes in 125, 175, and 250 cc versions, and is intended to be used as a competition machine

The Pioneer is best suited as a scrambles or enduro machine and comes in 175 and 250 cc models

The Plonker is a trials bike with low compression and excellent low speed handling

For around town riding Ossa produces the Wildfire, their only strictly street machine

TUNE-UP AND MAINTENANCE

TUNE-UP OPERATIONS

Ignition Timing

1. Remove the spark plug. Remove the right side engine cover.
2. Turn the magneto flywheel until the small hole in its face is at 11 o'clock. Insert a pin into the hole and work the flywheel back and forth until the pin drops into the hole in the backing plate. This is the position at which the spark plug will fire.
3. Place a dial gauge in the spark plug hole, and zero the gauge.
4. Remove the timing pin from the flywheel and rotate the flywheel clockwise, counting the number of complete revolutions of the gauge needle. Continue rotating the flywheel until the piston is positioned at TDC. Stop at this point, and add to the number of revolutions of the gauge the decimal fraction that the dial gauge now reads.

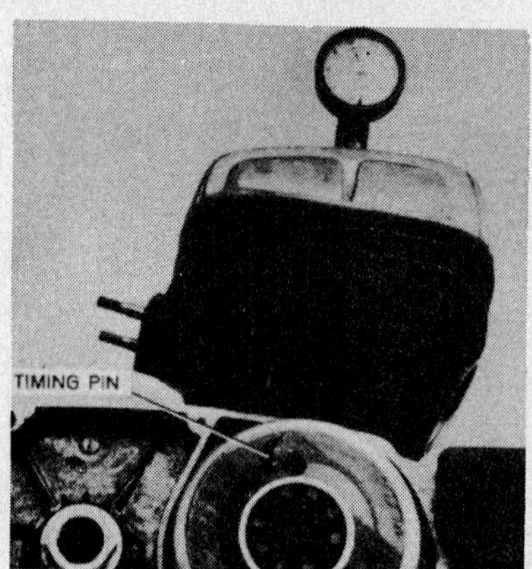

Timing pin and dial gauge installed

The correct timing specification for all models is 3.25–3.50 mm BTDC.

5. If the timing is not within specification, remove the flywheel, and loosen the three magneto backing plate screws just enough to allow the plate to be rotated. If the reading was less than 3.25 mm BTDC, rotate the plate counterclockwise a small amount. If the reading was greater than 3.50 mm BTDC, rotate the plate clockwise. Tighten the screws, install the flywheel and recheck the timing.

Spark Plugs

All models use an NGK B-7ES plug or equivalent: Champion N8Y, N9Y; KLG FE80; Bosch 225T2. Plug gap on all models is 0.020 in.

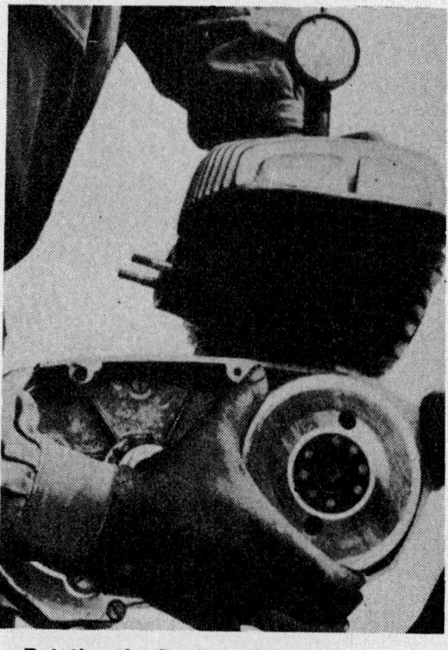

Rotating the flywheel for ignition timing

Carburetor Adjustment

Refer to Bultaco "Tune-up and Maintenance" for carburetor adjustments; disassembly and repair procedures are found under Bultaco "Fuel Systems."

MAINTENANCE ITEMS

Lubrication

TRANSMISSION OIL

Drain the oil when the engine is warm, and refill through the inspection hole in the primary chaincase with 1,000 cc (about 1 qt.) of SAE 90 gear oil.

FRONT FORKS

1. Loosen the two fork clamp bolts on the fork crown.
2. Unscrew and remove the plug at the top of one of the fork tubes.
3. Loosen the drain plug in the same slider leg. The drain plug is located just above the axle mount. Unscrew the plug, but do not remove it, as it also connects the slider leg to the damper in the fork tube.
4. Allow the oil to drain out of the leg, then gently work the forks up and down to expel the rest of the oil
5. Tighten the drain plug and refill the fork tube with 250 cc (Pioneer, Stiletto, and Plonker), or 125 cc (Wildfire), of SAE 20 or 30W oil.
6. Support the front wheel off the ground. Install and tighten the top plug. Tighten the fork tube clamp bolts.
7. Repeat the above procedure for the other fork leg.

Front fork components

Service Checks and Adjustments

DRIVE CHAIN

The drive chain should be adjusted for a maximum of 1 in. total up and down play when measured in the middle of the top chain run.

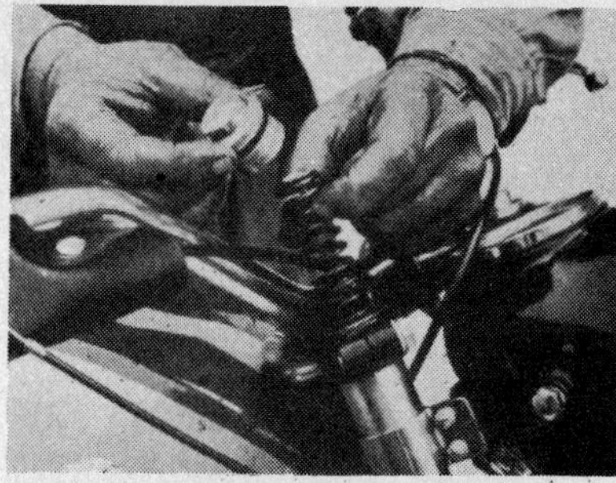

Removing the fork tube filler plug

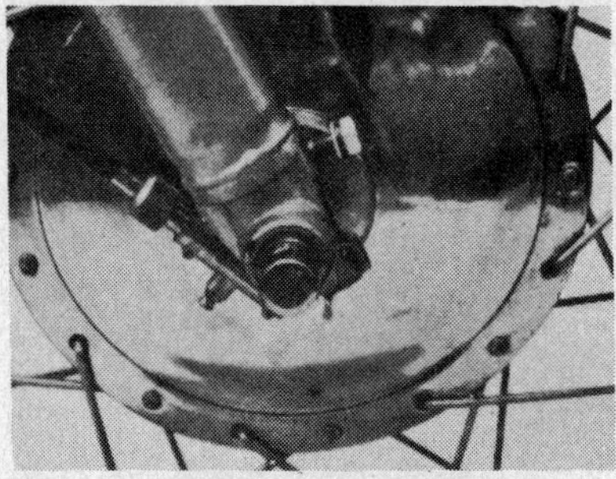

Front fork oil drain plug

CLUTCH CABLE

The cable lever should have a very small amount of free movement before it engages the clutch pushrod.

STEERING HEAD

Refer to the "Chassis" section for steering head service and adjustment.

ENGINE AND TRANSMISSION

ENGINE REMOVAL

1. Before removing the engine, clean the motorcycle thoroughly.
2. Loosen the clamp and remove the air filter from the carburetor.
3. Loosen the two nuts and bolts (or one nut) at the muffler mount.
4. Using a pin wrench, unscrew the exhaust pipe collar from the cylinder head flange.
5. Remove the muffler mount bolts (or nut) and take off the exhaust system.
6. Off-road models: Remove the six rear fender nuts and bolts. Remove the taillight lens (if applicable). Loosen the screw clamping the wire that goes out through the rear of the taillight assembly and remove the wire from the rear fender. Remove the rear fender.
7. Off-road models: Remove the four bolts and two nuts from the saddle mount portion of the gas tank.
8. Wildfire: Remove the spring hanger from the rear of the gas tank using a hook.
9. Remove the gas tank from the frame.
10. Take off the two screws from the plastic side panel on each side, then unscrew the nut and bolt from the panels and remove them.
11. Pioneer: Loosen the terminal screw that mounts the wiring to the taillight assembly in the electrical junction block near the top of the rear downtube.
12. Take out the two screws at the top of the carburetor and remove the top and slide from the body of the carburetor.
13. Loosen the two carburetor mounting nuts so that you can pull the carburetor back enough to be able to remove the nuts, then remove the carburetor.
14. With the Ossa magneto flywheel holding tool, rotate the clutch arm clockwise and remove the cable from the clutch arm.
15. Take out the four screws and remove the magneto case from the engine. Be careful not to lose the clutch cam plunger from the case.
16. Remove the master link from the drive chain and remove the chain.
17. Cut the tape that mounts the electrical wiring to the rear downtube. Remove the wiring from the clamps on the rear tube.
18. Loosen all the terminal screws on the side of the electrical junction block that goes to the engine. Remove the wires from that side of the junction block.
19. Disconnect the two wires from the high tension coil. Unscrew the two bolts and remove the coil from the frame.
20. Remove the nuts from the top and bottom rear engine mount bolts.
21. Remove the nuts from the right and left front engine mount bolts; then tap out the two rear mount bolts using a drift. Remove the two front bolts; lift up the front of the engine so that the bolts come out easily.

Removing the engine from the frame

ENGINE OVERHAUL

Removing The Piston

1. Mount the engine on the bench and remove the sparkplug.
2. Looking down on the cylinder head and viewing the front of the cylinder as being 12 o'clock, loosen the four head nuts ¼ turn each in the following sequence: 10 o'clock, 4 o'clock, 2 o'clock,

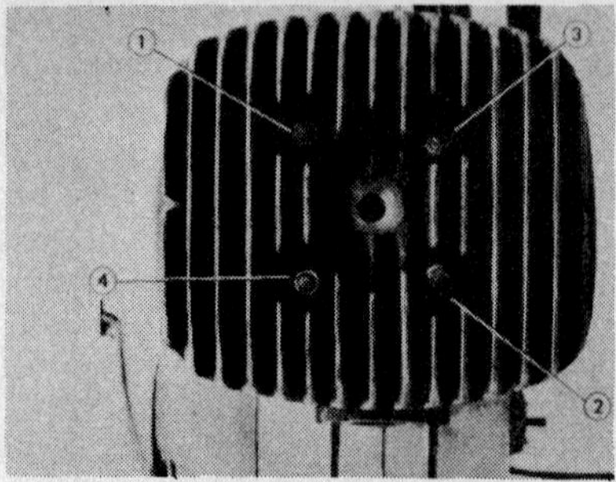

Cylinder head nut loosening and tightening sequence

and 8 o'clock. Loosen the nuts another ¼ turn in the same sequence and then unscrew them completely.

3. Lift off the cylinder head and its gasket.

4. Remove the cylinder, taking care not to tear the cylinder base gasket or to allow the piston and rod to fall against the crankcase flange.

5. Stuff a towel in around the crankcase opening. Using a pair of needle nose pliers, remove the two wrist pin snaprings.

6. Using a soft drift that is slightly smaller than the diameter of the wrist pin, press the pin out while supporting the piston to prevent any side-loading of the connecting rod. If the pin is tight, heat the crown of the piston with an electric iron or with rags soaked in hot water; DO NOT DRIVE THE WRIST PIN OUT.

7. Remove the piston from the rod and remove the needle bearing from the pin guide (or rod).

8. Remove the cylinder base gasket.

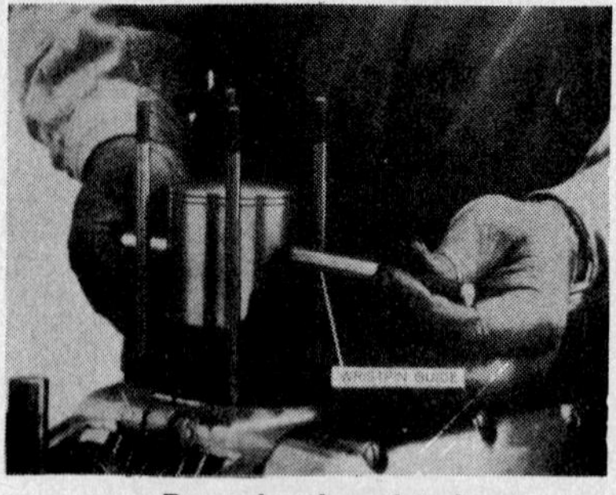
Removing the wrist pin

Disassembling The Magneto Side Engine Case

1. Fit the Ossa flywheel holding tool to the two holes in the flywheel. (You can get by without the tool by inserting a steel bar into each of the two flywheel holes and placing a pry-bar between them to hold the flywheel in position.) Unscrew and remove the flywheel retaining nut.

2. Back out the center bolt of the Ossa flywheel puller. Screw the puller into the flywheel (with the holder still in position). Tighten the puller in the flywheel, then tighten the center bolt of the puller until the flywheel is freed from the end of the crankshaft. Remove the flywheel and is washer.

3. Scribe a line across the edge of the magneto backing plate and one of its mounting bosses (to be used as a reference when reassembling the engine).

4. Take out the three screws and remove the magneto backing plate; fit it to the flywheel to prevent damage to either part.

5. Remove the woodruff key from the end of the crankshaft and place it on the side of the flywheel to prevent losing it.

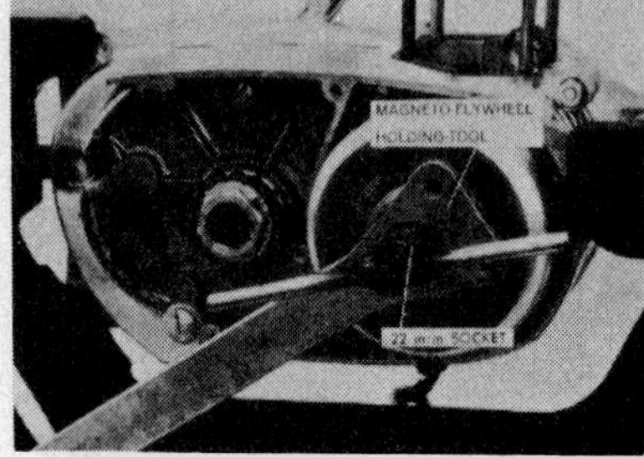

Removing the check valve screw

Disassembling The Primary Side Engine Case

1. Unscrew the bolt completely from the shift lever and remove the shift lever from the selector shaft.

2. Remove the bolt from the kickstart lever and remove the lever from its shaft.

3. Place a pan beneath the engine and remove the drainplug. Tip the engine forward so that most of the gearbox and primary drive lubricant will drain.

4. Unscrew the ten screws that mount the primary case to the crankcase; leave the screws in the case.

5. Remove one of the screws that secures the inspection cover; loosen the other screw and swing the inspection cover aside. Insert a large screwdriver and pry it up against the outer clutch plate to break loose the primary case. If necessary, tap upward on the right edge of the primary case with a rubber mallet to free it. Hold the selector shaft in position in the cases as you remove the primary case.

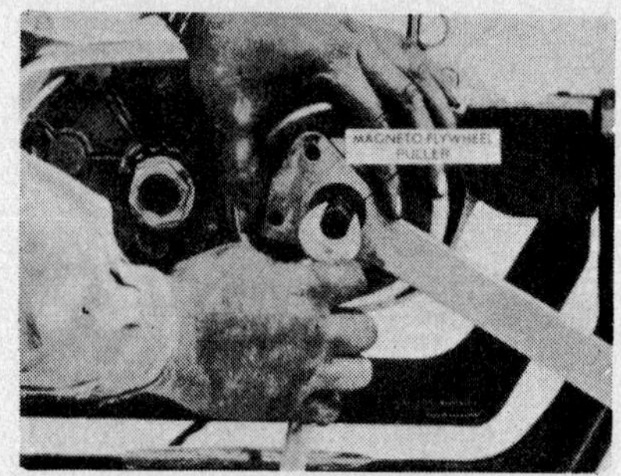

Removing the flywheel

Marking the magneto backing plate for reassembly

6. Remove the case and the case gasket. Take care not to lose the two locating dowels in the case.

7. Remove the spring washer and the flat washer from the selector shaft.

8. Remove the five cotter pins from their studs at the outer clutch plate.

9. Unscrew the clutch spring nuts and remove the springs and spring cups.

10. Withdraw all the clutch plates except the inner one. Loosen the inner plate using two thin screwdrivers and then remove it.

11. Use a clutch holder tool as shown. Brace it against the cush drive hub and unscrew the clutch hub nut.

12. With the holding tool still in position, loosen the allen bolt in the cush drive hub (using a pipe on the allen wrench for additional leverage).

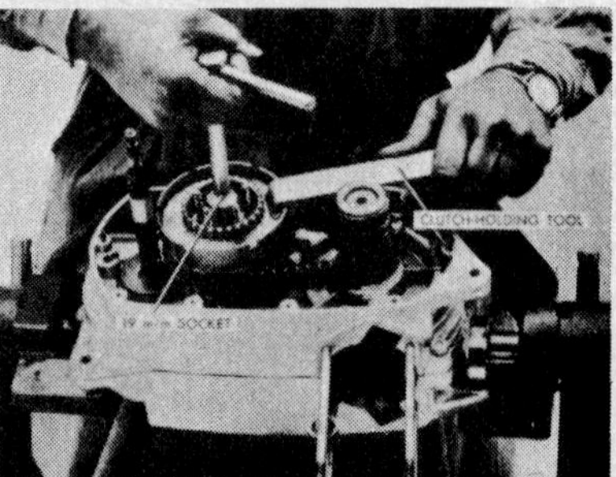

Removing the clutch hub nut

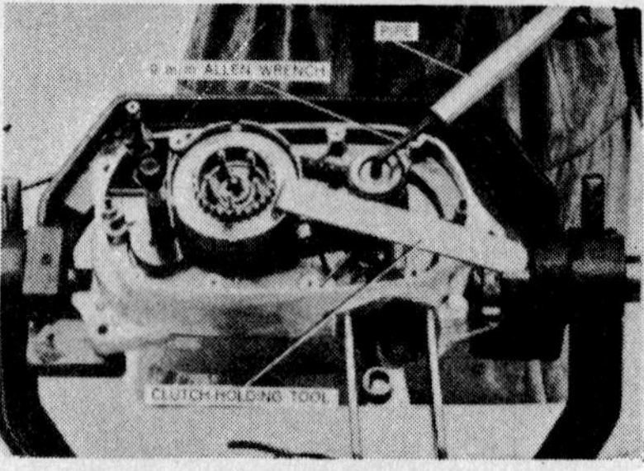

Removing the cush-drive allen nut

13. Remove the clutch nut, then remove the cush drive allen bolt, the flange, spring, and the coupling.

14. Take off the inner clutch hub and remove the hub spacer from the mainshaft.

15. Remove the outer clutch hub, the engine sprocket and the primary chain as an assembly. Remove the bushing and spacer from the mainshaft.

16. To remove the cush drive shaft, which is a press fit on the end of the crankshaft, you will need several Ossa tools. First, screw the cush drive holder into the crankshaft threads, then fit the spanner tool to the cush drive shaft. Install the two collars on the end of the cush drive holder and back out the center bolt in the puller. Mount the puller to the collars on the holder. Hold the spanner and tighten the center bolt of the puller to free the cush drive shaft from the crankshaft.

17. Remove the snap-ring from the kickstart shaft using snap-ring pliers.

18. Disengage the looped end of the kickstart return spring from its mount in the engine case using a large screwdriver. Free the other end of the spring from the kickstart shaft.

19. Remove the spring and large washer from the kickstart shaft.

Splitting The Crankcases

1. Loosen the eleven engine case screws on the right side of the engine ¼ turn each. Remove the screws, working from the middle of the engine outward.

Spanner tool fitted to cush drive shaft

2. Unscrew and remove the engine case nut and bolt at the front of the engine. Do not let the cases fall apart.

3. Loosen the large screw with the nylon washer (the shift drum detent) at the bottom rear of the engine.

4. With the primary side engine case facing up, tap upward on it to separate it from the magneto side case. Lift off the primary side engine case, which will retain the crankshaft assembly. Check the mounting bosses on the primary side case for the mainshaft, layshaft, shift drum and the selector shaft. Look for washers that might have stuck to the bosses in the case. If any washers have stuck to the bosses, remove them and put them on their shafts.

Installing the collars on the end of the cush drive holder

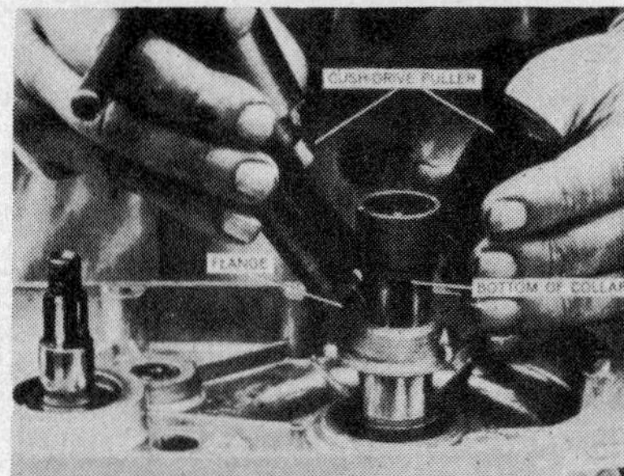

Mounting the puller to the collars on the holder

NOTE: *The washers control the endplay of the different shafts; it is very important not to mix the washers as you disassemble the gearbox.*

5. Lift the washers off the main bearing in the magneto side case and tag them.

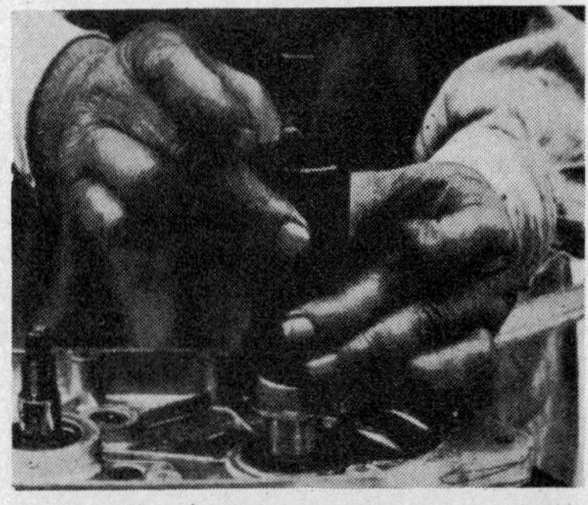

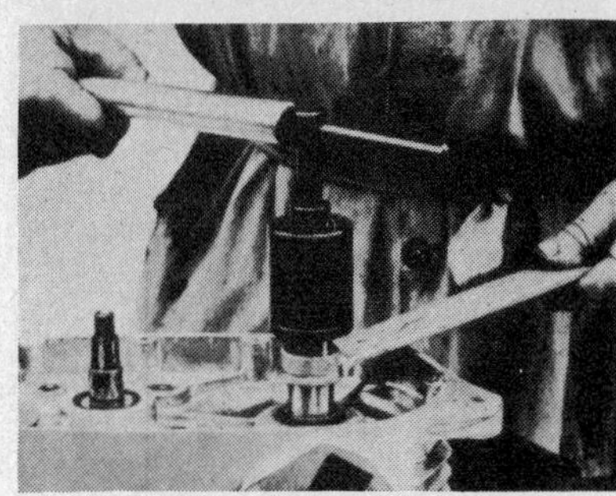
Removing the cush drive shaft

Removing The Transmission Components

1. If the gearbox is not in need of repair, it is not necessary to remove the components. If you are going to remove them, first remove the engine case gasket and discard it.

2. Rotate the kickstart shaft clockwise until the cam on the engaging ratchet is free of the gears and the large screw in the case. Lift out the shaft and its washers.

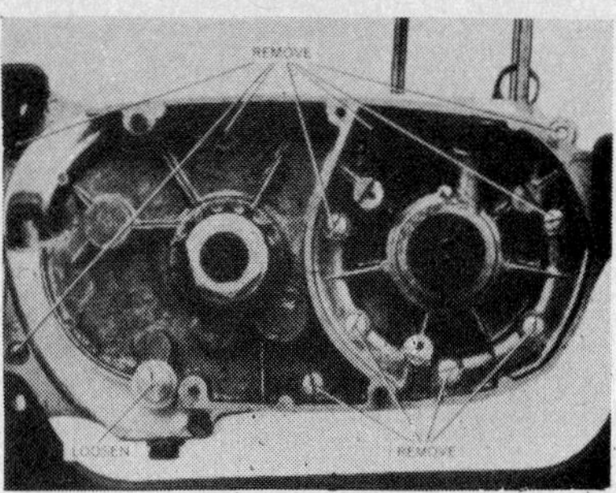

Engine crankcase screws to be removed

3. Lift out the selector shaft with its washers.

4. Pull up the shift fork shaft until the forks can be disengaged from the cam grooves in the shift drum. Lift out the drum with its washers.

5. Remove the large screw with the nylon washer from the outside of the engine case. (This is the detent plunger).

6. Lift out the shift forks on their shaft.

7. Lift out the layshaft along with its washers.

8. Lift the mainshaft, with its bushing and washers, out of the countershaft.

9. Remove the plastic breather tube.

Removing The Countershaft Assembly

1. Lift the two needle bearings out of the countershaft from the inside of the case.

2. Bend back the locktab on the countershaft nut on the outside of the case.

3. Wrap a length of old chain around the countershaft sprocket and clamp the ends of the chain in a vise. The countershaft nut has a left-hand thread; unscrew and remove it.

4. Remove the countershaft washer and sprocket. Tap the countershaft with a mallet from the outside of the case to remove it.

5. Pry the oil seal off of the countershaft with a screwdriver.

CRANKSHAFT ASSEMBLY

REMOVAL

1. Heat the primary side engine case, from the flywheel side, on a hot-plate or with a torch. If you use a hot-plate, heat the case for about ten minutes. If you use a torch, keep it moving around the crankshaft boss, and heat it for only about 45 seconds. Do not heat the case from the other side or you may damage the seal.

2. Using a cloth for heat insulation, pull the crankshaft assembly out of the case. The primary side main bearing will remain on the shaft.

3. To remove the primary side main bearing, clamp the crankshaft in a vise, protecting it with blocks of wood and

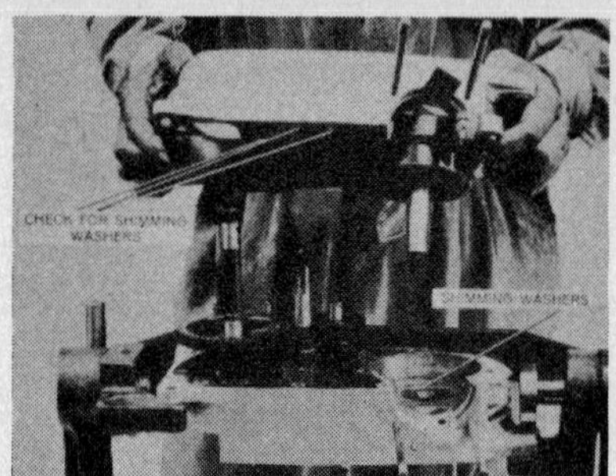

Splitting the cases

Kickstart shaft and shifter components

carefully pry the bearing off with screwdrivers. (This bearing is marked with the inscription "C3" on its face; the magneto side main bearing is not marked.)

4. If any washers were fitted between the bearing and flywheel, tag and save them.

4. Pry the crankshaft seals out with a screwdriver.

INSTALLATION

1. To install a new crankshaft seal, first warm the crankcase around the crankshaft boss. Then install the seal, open side facing in, and drive it into position.

2. To install a new main bearing in the magneto side engine case, first warm the case around the crankshaft boss (from the inside, to prevent damaging the seal). Turn the case over and tap it gently against the bench, at which point the old bearing should fall out. Drop a new bearing (which has no marking on its narrow face) into its mount before the case cools.

3. To install a new primary side main bearing on the crankshaft, first install the washers on the primary side of the shaft. Drive the new bearing (marked "C3" on its narrow face) into position using a suitably sized pipe that bears against the inner race.

CAUTION: *Take special care not to intermix the primary side and magneto side crankshaft washers; piston sideload is determined by the number and thickness of the washers on each end of the crankshaft.*

4. To install the crankshaft, heat the primary side case around the crankshaft boss, taking care not to damage the seal. Fit the washers to the primary side of the crankshaft and press the crankshaft assembly into the case by hand. Be very careful not to damage the seal lip.

Assembling The Transmission

1. If you had removed the countershaft from the magneto side engine case, reinstall it now. From the inside of the case, press or tap the countershaft into is ball bearing. Install the countershaft spacer, the sprocket, washer, and nut from the outside of the case. Wrap a length of old drive chain around the sprocket and clamp its ends in a vise. Tighten the countershaft nut securely.

NOTE: *The countershaft nut has a left hand thread.*

Bend up the locktab against two flats of the nut.

CAUTION: *Do not intermix the washers that were installed on the gearbox shafts; these washers must be installed in their original positions to maintain correct end-play.*

2. Install the detent plunger, with its nylon washer, in the engine case. Do not tighten it.

3. Examine the illustration showing the dimples in the shift drum into which the detent can fit. Install the shift drum, with its washers, into its boss so that the detent is in the neutral dimple. If the drum is in neutral, you should be able to draw an imaginary line through the middle of the peg farthest to the left, the shift drum shaft, and the selector shaft mounting boss, as shown.

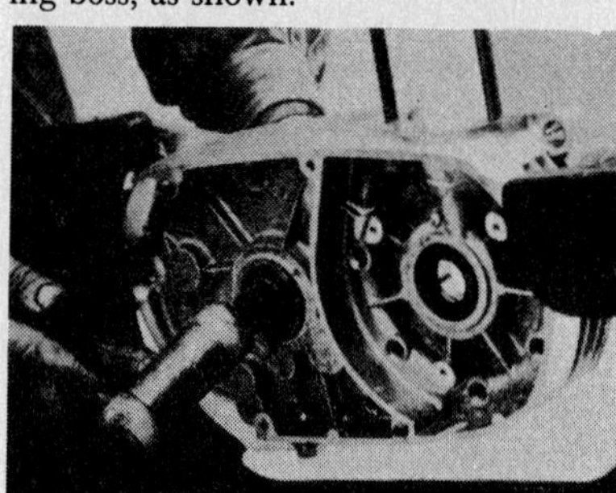

Removing the countershaft from the crankcase

4. Fit the selector shaft, with its washer, to the mounting boss. Clip the legs of the hairpin spring to the anchor pin. Gently turn the shaft; it if moves freely, then both legs of the spring are not parallel. Remove the shaft and bend one of the legs to make both legs parallel when the spring is fitted to the anchor pin. Install the shaft and check to make sure that it does not have any free-play.

5. The first peg on the shift drum will lie between the fingers of the selector. The peg should be midway between the two fingers. Rotate the shift drum to the 3rd gear position; there should be equal clearance between two of the pegs and the fingers. If there is not, remove the selector shaft and bend both legs of the spring in the opposite direction from which you wish to rotate the selector fingers. Make sure that the legs of the spring are still parallel, so that the selector shaft has no free-play. Remove the selector shaft, shift drum and detent from the engine case.

6. Place the two needle bearings into the countershaft. Fit the mainshaft bushing on top of the needle bearings with the chamfered side of the bushing facing up.

Removing the crankshaft

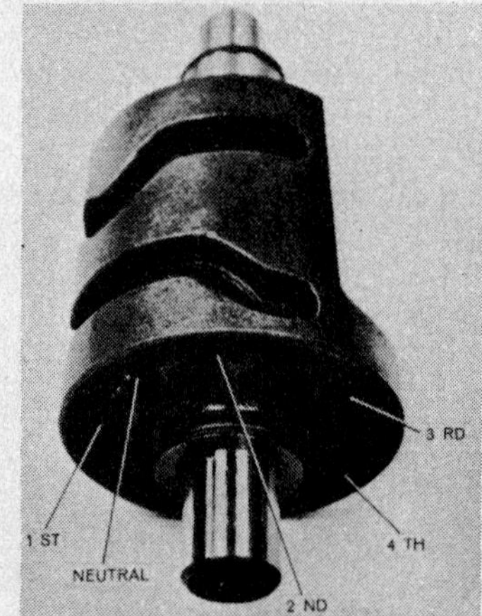

Shift drum

Shift drum installed

7. Insert the mainshaft with its washers, spiral-grooved end first, into the countershaft.

8. Install the layshaft, with washers, into its mounting boss in the case. Mesh the layshaft and mainshaft gears.

9. Insert the shift fork assembly into its boss in the engine case. The fork with the longer body should be uppermost on the shaft. Work the forks into their grooves in the mainshaft gears. It will be necessary to lift the mainshaft and layshaft to insert the forks.

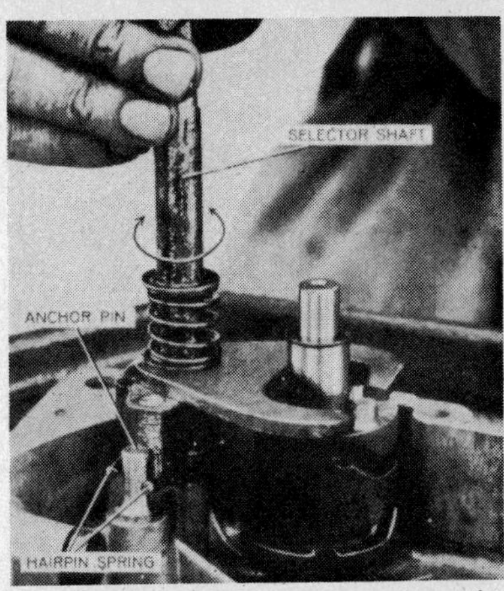

Installing the selector shaft; checking the hairpin spring

Shift drum properly positioned between the fingers of the selector

10. Fit the shift drum, with its washers, to its boss in the engine case. Move it to the Neutral position; move the two dog gears up and down until they are in Neutral. Lift the mainshaft, layshaft, and fork assembly, and engage the follower pegs of the forks in the cam grooves in the drum.

11. Install the selector shaft assembly into its mounting boss.

12. Mount the kickstart shaft assembly into its boss so that the ramp will clear the large screw in the engine case. Rotate the shaft counterclockwise against its stop.

13. Fit the slotted breather tube to the boss at the top of the case. Make sure that the slot faces up or the oil will escape when the engine is running.

14. Mount the detent assembly, with the large nylon washer, from the outside of the case. Screw the threaded part of the assembly halfway into the case.

Assembling The Engine Cases

1. Coat both sides of a new center case gasket with grease and fit it to the magneto side case. Do not use gasket cement.

2. Oil the gearbox components with SAE 90 HP gear oil.

3. Place the magneto side crankshaft shim washers on the main bearing in the magneto side case. Install the primary side engine case (with the crankshaft assembly) over the magento side case. Hold the kickstart shaft so that it is centered in its hole in the primary side engine case and tap the case at both ends with a rawhide mallet to mate it with the magneto side case.

4. Using a drift, seat the three locating dowels in the front and rear case bosses. Do not turn the engine over yet, as the cases can still easily be separated.

5. Insert the front case bolt into its bosses and install the washers and nut. Run the nut down finger-tight and then tighten it ½ turn with a wrench.

6. Turn the engine over so that the magneto side case faces up and mount the eleven case screws. The two screws at the rear of the engine are shorter than the rest, and the flat-head screw goes at the bottom of the case.

7. Using a socket-mounted screwdriver bit on a torque wrench, torque each screw, beginning in the center of the case and working out, to 12 ft. lbs. Torque the front engine case bolt to 12 ft. lbs. Tighten the detent screw.

Installing the countershaft needle bearings

Installing the mainshaft

Assembling The Primary Side Components

1. Turn the engine over so that the primary case faces up and place one of the washers on the kickstart shaft.

2. Fit the kickstart spring on its shaft with the looped end of the spring facing left. Work the end of the spring into its mounting hole in the shaft.

3. Fit a drift into the looped end of the spring and tighten the spring 1 ½ turns. The drift should now be positioned above the spring retaining boss; work the looped end of the spring off the drift and into its retaining boss. Press the spring down flat against the washer beneath it.

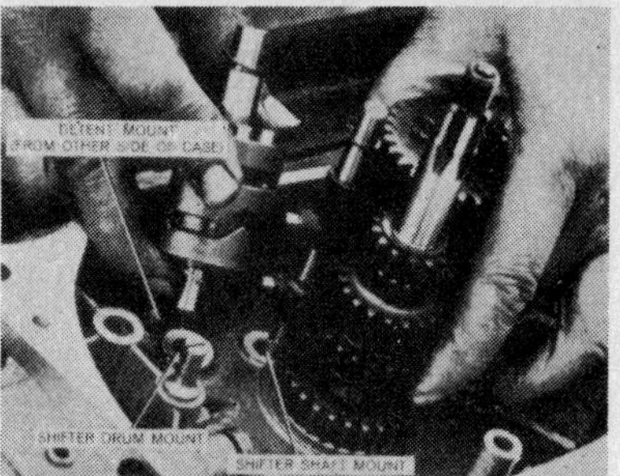

Installing the shift drum

Installing the selector shaft

Installing the kickstart shaft

4. Place the other large washer on the kickstart shaft.

5. Install the snap ring in its groove on the kickstart shaft just above the top washer.

6. Fit the kickstart lever onto the shaft and test to make sure that the kickstart shaft operates correctly. Remove the lever.

7. Place the flat spacer on the ball bearing assembly on the mainshaft.

8. Place the clutch bushing on the mainshaft and bottom the bushing against the flat spacer.

9. Thoroughly clean all oil and grease from the primary side crankshaft and the inside of the cush drive shaft. Put the cush drive shaft on the crankshaft and tap it with a rubber mallet.

10. Fit the primary drive chain to the engine sprocket and the outer clutch hub, with the master link clip facing the

clutch hub. Fit the primary drive assembly, as a unit, onto the mainshaft and cush drive shaft.

11. Install the short spacer on the mainshaft and bottom it against the clutch needle bearing. Put the inner clutch hub on the mainshaft. Align the splines of the inner hub with the splines of the mainshaft and work the hub down against the short spacer tube.

Fitting the breather tube

Fitting the kickstart return spring

12. Install the lockwasher and nut on the mainshaft and tighten finger-tight.

13. Install the cush drive coupling on the shaft and fit the spring and spring stop, with the flanged end of the stop facing up.

14. Screw the allen bolt into the threads of the crankshaft.

15. Fit the clutch holding tool to the hub and tighten the allen bolt securely using a length of pipe on the allen wrench for extra leverage.

16. With the holding tool still in position, torque the clutch nut to 60 ft. lbs.

17. Spin the inner clutch hub to make sure that it can rotate while the outer hub remains still.

18. Install the inner clutch plate, which has plain faces and is thicker than the other plates, into the hub. Oil the plate.

19. Fit an idling plate, with cork inserts, and oil it.

20. Check all the driving plates on a flat surface such as a plate of glass to make sure they are flat. Replace any plates that are bent or warped. Install a drive plate in the clutch.

21. Install an idling plate, then a drive plate, and continue to alternate the two types. The last one installed with be a drive plate.

22. Fit the outer clutch plate and install the spring cups, springs, and nuts to

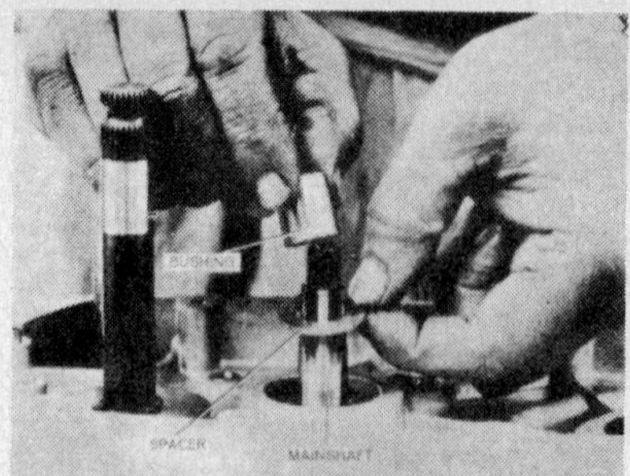

Installing the mainshaft bushing

the five studs. Tighten each nut until the bottom of its groove is level with the bottom of the cotter pin hole drilled in the stud.

23. Rotate the clutch and check to see if the outer plate wobbles. If so, mark the highest point on the outer plate and tighten the nut(s) nearest the high point. Back off the other nuts slightly and recheck. When the plate runs true, install the cotter pins.

24. Place the flat washer and spring washer on the selector shaft.

25. Grease both sides of a new primary case gasket and fit the gasket to the primary case.

26. Insert the two locating dowels into their mounts in the case and install the case carefully on the engine case. Tap the case with a rubber mallet to seat it.

27. Install and tighten the 10 primary case screws. Fit the short screws in the holes shown in the illustration.

28. Trim any protruding portion of the primary case gasket with a knife.

29. Install the shift lever on the selector shaft and work it to check the action of the shaft. Remove the lever.

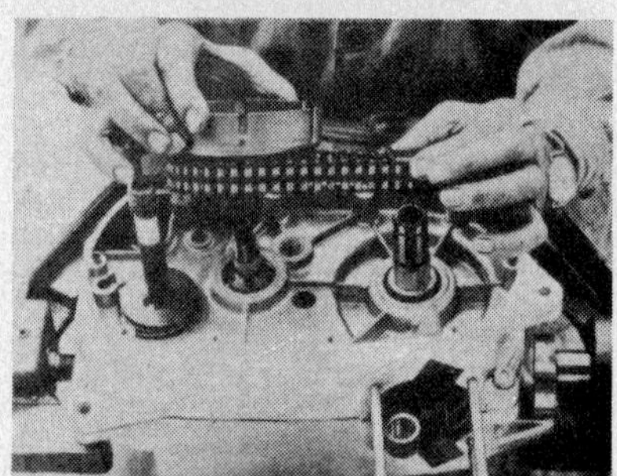

Fitting the primary drive train

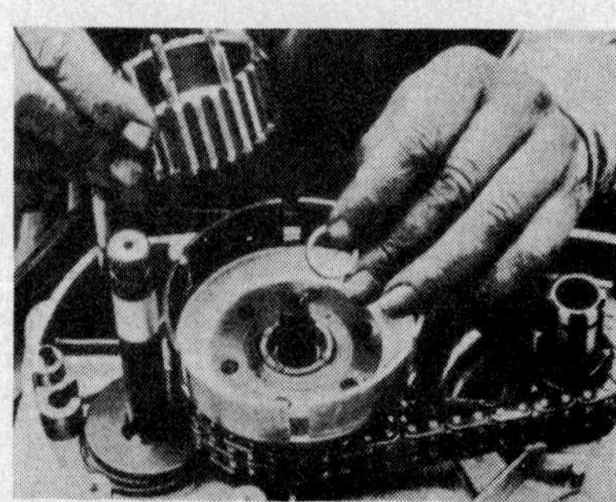

Installing the clutch hub spacer

PISTON CLEARANCE INFORMATION

1. Wash the cylinder in hot, soapy water and rinse it thoroughly. Dry it and allow the piston and cylinder to stand for two hours at room temperature.

2. Measure the cylinder bore from front to rear an inch or two down from the top.

3. Measure the outside diameter of the piston near the bottom of the skirt, at right angles to the wrist pin hole.

4. Subtract the diameter of the piston from the diameter of the cylinder to find the clearnace.

5. In the 230 cc street and trail models, the clearance should not be less than 0.-02-0.03 mm, or more than 0.06 mm. In the 230 cc scrambler, the piston clearance should not be less than 0.05-0.06 mm or more than 0.10-0.12 mm.

6. Another way to measure the clear-

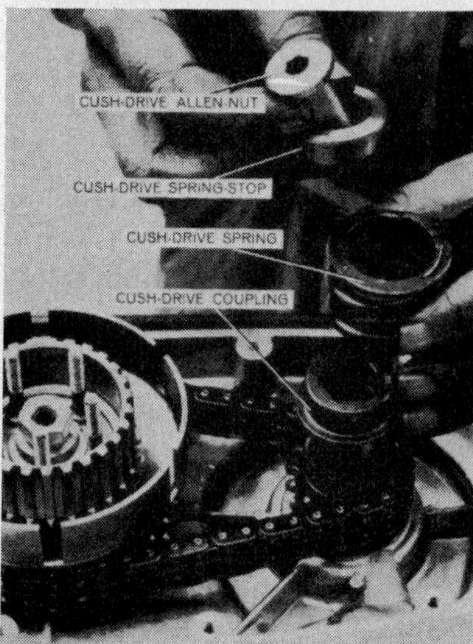

Installing the cush drive components

ance is to place the piston inside the cylinder, upside down, so that the skirt is one or two inches below the top of the liner. Insert a feeler gauge between the skirt and the cylinder to determine the amount of clearance.

7. If the piston is worn beyond the tolerance, replace it.

8. If the cylinder is worn so much that the clearance will still be to great with a new piston, you will have to install an

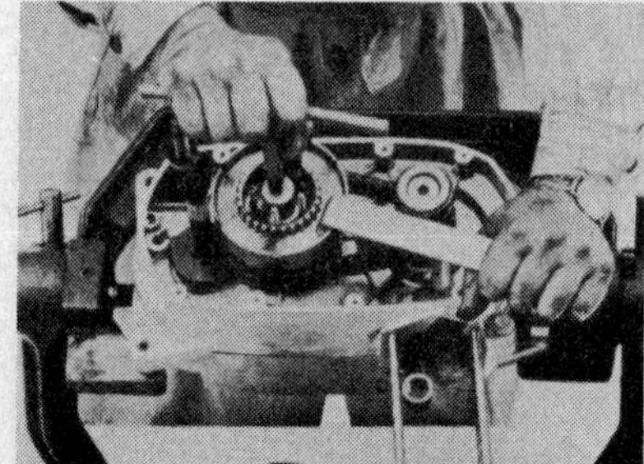

Tightening the clutch hub nut

oversize piston. Pistons are available in 0.2 and 0.4 mm oversizes. It will be necessary to bore and hone the cylinder to obtain the correct clearance. After honing, allow the cylinder to cool before measuring it again.

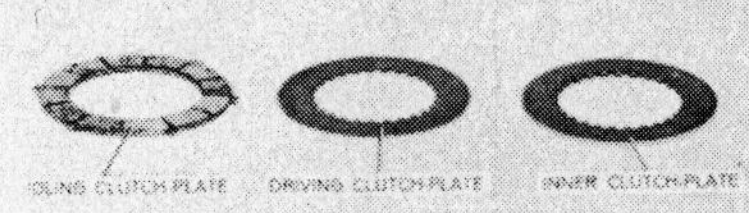

Three types of clutch plates

Clutch components assembled

Installing a New Cylinder Liner

1. Put the new liner in a refrigerator and allow it to become as cold as possible.

2. Place the cylinder in an oven and support it in such a way that the old liner is free to fall out after reaching a temperature of 450-550° F. Do not heat the cylinder to a temperature greater than 750° F.

3. Insert the new liner into the cylinder before it has a chance to cool off. Align the ports in the liner with those in the liner.

4. Support the cylinder, in its normal position, so that the bottom of the liner is not touching the bench. Place a weight on the liner flange to keep it in position as the cylinder cools

Assembling The Top End

1. Removing any protruding portion of the case gasket at the cylinder bosses with a knife. Squirt some oil into the two holes drilled into the cylinder bosses.

2. Position the connecting rod at top dead center (TDC).

3. Start the wrist pin into the piston. Install the wrist pin needle bearing in the rod and position the piston on the rod with the short skirt facing the rear of the engine.

4. Using a soft drift that is slightly smaller than the diameter of the wrist pin, press the pin into the piston while supporting it so that there is no side-load on the connecting rod. If the pin will not go in, heat the piston with an electric iron or with rags soaked in hot water.

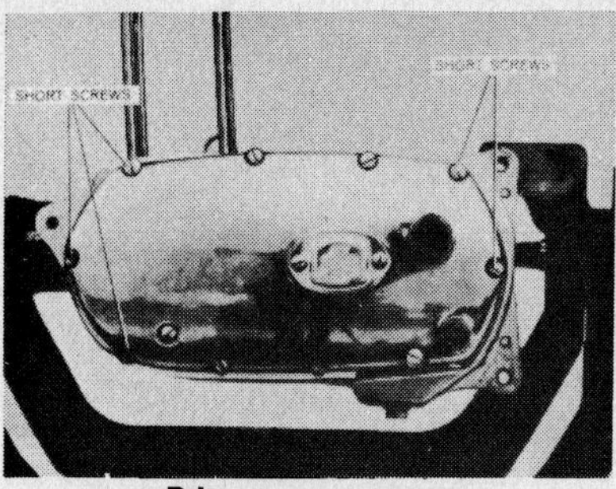

Primary case screws

5. Install the wrist pin snap rings into their grooves using needle nose pliers. If a snap-ring can be rotated easily in its groove, remove and spread it, then reinstall it.

6. Grease the cylinder base gasket on both sides and install it over the studs.

7. Clean the ring grooves and the rings, then install the rings so that the peg in the grooves is between the ring ends. Make sure that the rings do not bind in their grooves.

8. Install a ring compressor over the rings, taking care not to allow either ring to ride up over its peg. Install the cylinder onto the studs and carefully work it down over the piston until the rings are inside the liner. Remove the compressor and seat the cylinder against the cases.

9. Check to see that the mating surfaces of the head and cylinder are smooth and clean. Install the head gasket and head on the cylinder. The higher ends of the cooling fins face the front of the engine.

10. Install the head washers and nuts; run the nuts down finger-tight. Tighten the head nuts in 3 ft. lb. increments, until

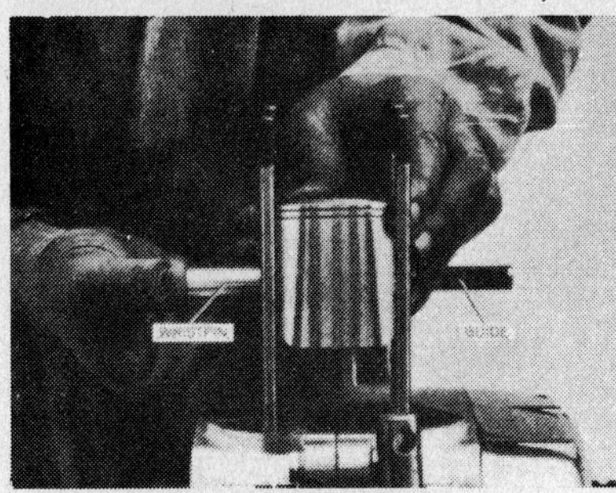

Installing the wrist pin

you reach 12 ft. lbs., in the following sequence: 10 o'clock, 4 o'clock, 8 o'clock, and 2 o'clock.

CAUTION: *Use a small, accurate torque wrench or you will run the risk of warping the head or seizing the piston.*

Assembling the Magneto Side Components

1. Peen one of the curved edges of the crankshaft woodruff key so that it will fit tightly, then install it in the keyway.

2. Remove the backing plate from the flywheel and position it on the case, aligning the marks you made during disassembly. Install and tighten the three mounting screws.

3. Install the rubber grommet in the slot in the bottom of the case and run the electrical wires through the grommet.

4. Align the slot in the flywheel with the crankshaft key and press it onto the end of the crankshaft with your hands.

5. Set the ignition timing as directed in the "Tune-Up and Maintenance" section.

6. Remove the small oil seal from the end of the countershaft with a screwdriver. Coat one of the pushrods with a heavy layer of grease, and insert it into the countershaft. Seat it with the other pushrod. Remove the second pushrod, install the bearing into the countershaft and insert the pushrod so that the bear ing is positioned between the two rods. Install the oil seal on the end of the second pushrod and press it into position in the countershaft.

ENGINE INSTALLATION

1. Install and tighten the drain plug with its washer.

2. Pour 1,000 cc of SAE 90 racing transmission oil into the inspection hole in the primary case, using a funnel.

3. Fit the engine into the frame, inserting it with the front mounting lugs positioned above their brackets and the rear lugs positioned beneath their brackets. Work the rear of the engine up so that the rear lugs are aligned in their brackets, then position the front lugs in their brackets.

4. Install the four engine mounting bolts and torque them to 14 ft. lbs.

5. Mount the high tension coil on the top frame tube with two bolts.

6. Fit the electrical harness into the clamps on the rear frame downtube. The two wires with spade clips go to the high tension coil, they are color coded with the coil terminals.

7. The remaining wires go to the electrical junction block near the top of the rear downtube. The wires are color coded with the terminals on the block. After connecting the wires, tape them to the rear downtube in two places with electrical tape.

8. Install the drive chain over the sprockets and fit the master link. The closed end of the master link clip must always be installed with its closed end facing the direction of forward chain rotation. Lubricate and adjust the chain.

9. While a helper holds the rear brake on, torque the flywheel magneto nut to 60 ft. lbs.

10. Coat the clutch arm plunger inside the magneto case with grease to keep it in position. Check to see that the two locating dowels are in position, then install the magneto case (which has no gasket) onto the engine case. The two longer mounting screws are installed at the front of the case, the two shorter screws at the rear.

11. Move the clutch arm on top of the magneto case; it should have at least 1/3 in. movement. If it does not, remove the inspection cover from the primary case and loosen the locknut on the adjusting screw that protrudes from the outer clutch plate. Turn the screw counterclockwise to increase play in the clutch arm, then tighten the locknut.

12. Using pliers or a box-end wrench for leverage, rotate the clutch arm clockwise and fit the clutch cable end into the arm.

13. Install the carburetor on the intake manifold and tighten the two nuts until they are compressing the O-ring. Plug the carburetor mouth with a cloth.

14. Install the gas tank and seat on the frame.

15. Install the rear fender and connect the wire to the taillight. Install the taillight lens.

16. Install the plastic side panel on each side of the bike.

17. Fit the carburetor slide down into the carburetor barrel with the slide cutaway facing to the rear. Install the carburetor top and secure it with the two screws. Work the throttle a few times to be sure that the slide does not bind.

18. Install the air filter on the carburetor.

19. Fit a new gasket in the exhaust pipe flange in the cylinder head. Position the exhaust system on the motorcycle and screw the exhaust pipe collar onto the flange finger-tight.

20. Install the muffler mounting nuts and bolts finger-tight, then fully tighten the pipe collar. Finally, tighten the muffler bolts.

FUEL SYSTEMS

The Ossa uses an IRZ model DG carburetor. Refer to the Bultaco section for details on carburetor tuning and overhaul.

Checking the high voltage coil

ELECTRICAL SYSTEMS

Ossa motorcycles are equipped with a magneto ignition system. Instead of using a mechanical contact breaker points system, however, Ossa uses an electrically triggered signal generator on the magneto backing plate.

TESTING THE IGNITION SYSTEM COMPONENTS

High Voltage Coil

1. Remove the gas tank.

2. Disconnect the black and blue wires from the coil. Using an ohmeter set on R × 1, connect the test leads to the two clips on the coil and check the reading. Reverse the test leads on the coil clips and take another reading. You should get 25-35 ohms in both tests.

3. Set the ohmeter on R × 100 or R × 1,000. Connect the test leads to the clip inside the spark plug cable and to ground. You should get a reading of about 7,000 ohms.

4. If you did not obtain the specified readings in either step 3 or 4, the high voltage coil is not working properly and must be replaced. Make sure that the mounting lug is grounded properly on the frame.

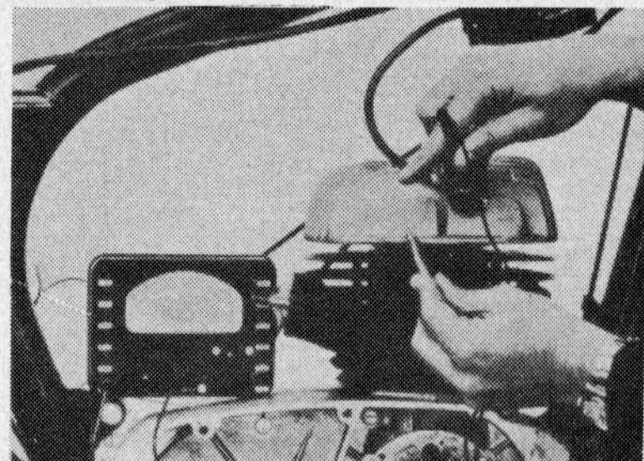

Testing the high voltage coil

Magneto Backing Plate Components

1. Remove the plastic side panels and disconnect all wires from the engine to the electrical junction box. Remove the flywheel.

2. Check the resistance across the low voltage coil (which is larger in diameter than the other coils). You should get a reading of 160-185 ohms.

3. Connect the ohmeter to the small diode on the backing plate near the low voltage coil. (This is the half-wave rectifier.) You should get a reading of 800-1,200 ohms with the meter connected one way, and an infinity reading with the leads reversed. (The diode should only pass current in one direction.)

Checking the magneto components

4. If the above tests give the specified results, check the two yellow wires at the signal generator. You should get a reading of 18 ohms across this small coil. If any of the tests at the magneto backing plate give the wrong results, replace the backing plate assembly.

CHASSIS

FRONT END SERVICE

Front Forks

DISASSEMBLY

1. Prop up the bike so that the front wheel is off the ground. Loosen the speedometer drive cap nut and disconnect the cable from the drive.

2. Push the cap nut up the speedometer cable and remove the small snap-ring from the cable. Pull the cable out of the guide on the fork tube.

3. Turn the knurled nut so that the outer brake cable moves into the handlebar lever mount. Move the front brake arm on the front wheel clockwise and remove the brake cable from the outer cable stop on the front wheel. Disconnect the brake cable from the arm.

4. Unscrew the bolt that mounts the brake anchor plate to the left slider leg.

5. Unscrew and remove the front axle nut and its washer.

6. Loosen the axle clamp bolt in each slider leg. Remove the front axle to the right, supporting the front wheel as the axle is withdrawn. A thin spacer will fall out from between the left leg and the wheel, and the speedometer drive and dust cover will fall from between the right leg and the wheel. Remove the wheel.

7. Unscrew and remove the drain plug just above the axle mount. Pull the slider leg down off of the damper tube and remove the slider leg.

8. To remove the oil seal, first loosen the dust cover clamp screw and pull the

clamp and cover off the slider leg. Remove the snap-ring from the mouth of the slider leg and pry out the seal, taking care not to scrape the inside of the leg.

9. To remove the damper tube from the fork leg, first loosen the fork tube clamp bolt on the fork crown. Unscrew the fork plug at the top of the tube and lift out the fork spring.

10. Using a pair of needle nose pliers in the slots, unscrew the plug at the bottom of the fork tube. Pull the damper tube down out of the fork tube. Remove the plug and spring from the damper tube.

11. Disassemble the other fork leg in the same manner.

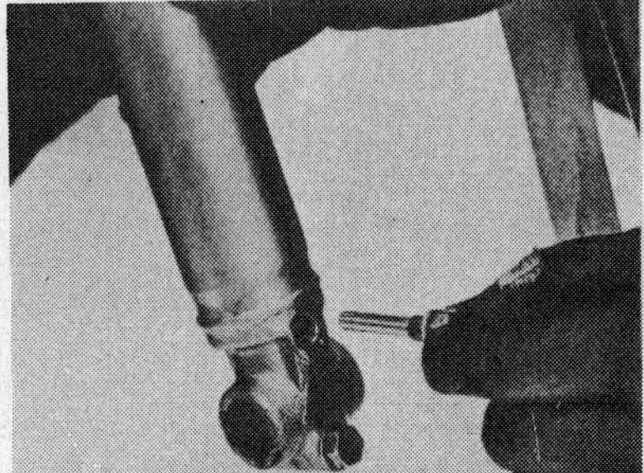

Removing the fork drain plug

Steering Head

DISASSEMBLY

1. Unscrew the two nuts and bolts that mount the headlight brackets to the fork tubes.

2. Loosen the pinchbolt on the fork crown that clamps one of the fork tubes. Loosen the other pinchbolt on the steering unit that clamps the same fork tube. Steady the headlight bracket and pull the fork tube down and out of the steering head assembly. Rotate the tube as you withdraw it.

3. Remove the other fork tube in the same manner.

4. Unscrew the four fender mounting bolts from the bottom of the steering head and remove the fender.

5. Unscrew the four U-bolt nuts and remove the handlebar assembly.

6. If a steering damper is fitted on top of the steering crown, remove it. If not, remove the rubber stopper from the top of the steering assembly tube.

7. Unscrew and remove the top fork crown nut.

8. Loosen the pinchbolt on the crown that secures the steering tube and remove the fork crown.

9. Unscrew the flat steering tube nut with a pin wrench, as shown. Lift off the top bearing dust cover.

10. Pull the steering assembly out of the steering head. The inner race of the lower bearing will stay on the steering tube, and the upper bearing will remain in the steering head. Lift the upper bearing out of the head.

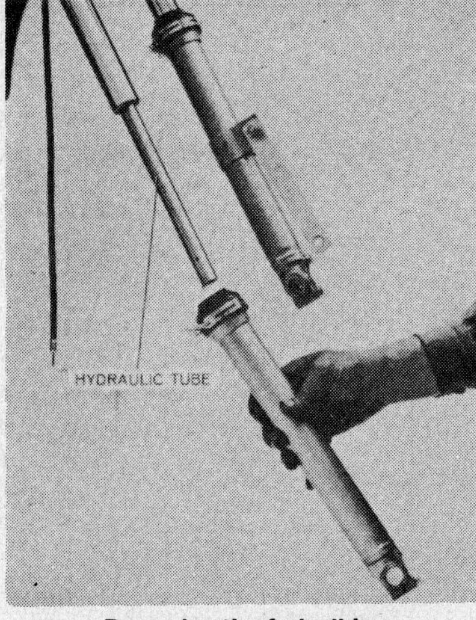

Removing the fork slider

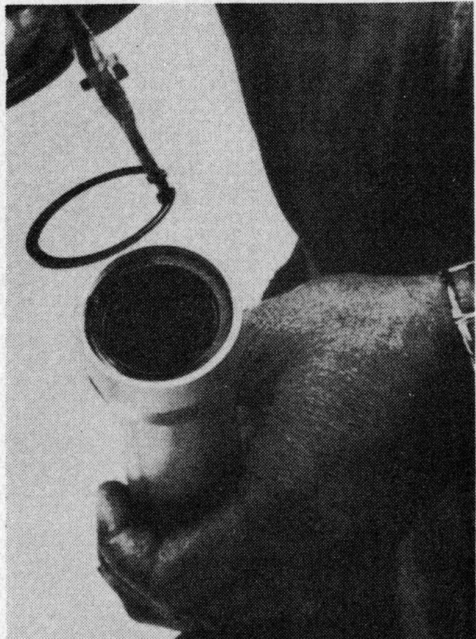

Removing the circlip

ASSEMBLY

1. Clean the steering head bearings carefully and then grease them.

2. Mount the inner race and dust cover of the lower bearing on the bottom of the steering tube, then insert the steering tube into the steering head from below.

3. Install the inner race of the upper bearing, with the small end facing down, in the top of the steering head. Install the upper bearing dust cover with the felt facing down.

4. Install the flat steering tube nut and tighten it until the bottom of the steering unit becomes difficult to rotate. Loosen the nut until you can see the smallest amount of play when the bottom of the steering unit is pulled back and forth. At this point, when the steering unit is centered, it will probably not fall to one side or the other of its own weight when released.

5. Install the fork crown onto the steering head, chamfered side first. Screw the top fork crown nut down finger-tight.

6. Insert the top of a fork tube into the steering brackets. Work the tube up until the top edge is level with the top of the fork crown. Tighten the fork tube pinchbolt on the bottom bracket. Install the other fork tube in the same manner.

7. Loosen the fork top crown nut slightly and tighten the flat steering unit nut very slightly until there is no play when you try to move the fork tube back and forth (toward the frame). Tighten the fork crown nut. There should be no play in the steering, and the forks should fall to either side of their own weight when centered and released.

8. Securely tighten the steering tube pinchbolt on the fork crown (top bracket).

9. Install both fork plugs and then tighten the fork tube pinchbolts on the fork crown.

NOTE: *Whenever any of the fork pinchbolts have been loosened, tighten them in the above sequence to avoid straining the forks. Never tighten them with the fork plugs removed.*

10. Install the front fender with the four mounting bolts.

11. Position the handlebar assembly on the fork crown and mount it with the U-bolts and nuts.

12. Install the headlight brackets on the fork legs.

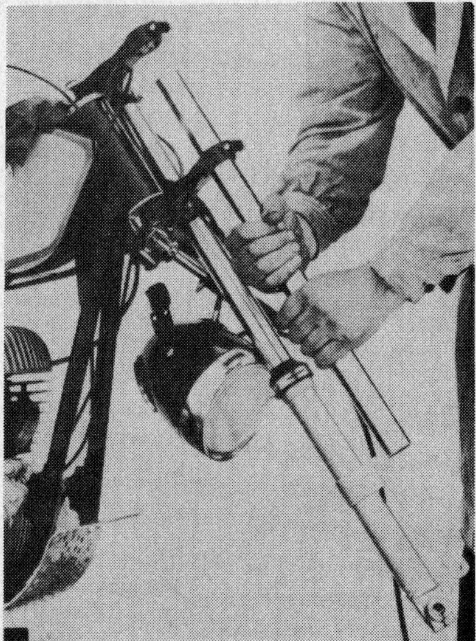

Removing the fork tube from the triple clamp

Front Forks

ASSEMBLY

1. If the damper piston shows any wear, replace the damper assembly.

2. Install the buffer spring on the plain end of the damper tube (hydraulic tube).

3. Install the threaded plug onto the plain end of the damper tube with the slots facing away from the tube.

4. Insert the damper tube into the bottom of the fork tube, piston end first.

Removing the fork crown nut

Screw the plug into the bottom of the fork tube and tighten it securely with pliers. Insert the other damper tube into the other fork tube in the same manner.

5. Lubricate a new oil seal and drive it into the mouth of the slider leg until it bottoms on its flange. Use a length of pipe that is slightly smaller than the diameter of the seal as a drift. Install the snap-ring in its groove above the seal.

6. Fit the dust cover to the bottom of the fork tube and fit the clamp to the slider leg.

7. Rotate the damper tube so that the mounting holes in the bottom of the tube align with the hole in the slider leg (just above the axle clamp). Fit the slider leg onto the fork tube.

8. Install the fork drain plug into the slider leg and damper tube, with its steel and aluminum washers.

9. Pull the dust cover down so that the bottom is over the slider leg, then secure it with the clamp.

10. Mount the other slider leg in the same manner.

11. Loosen the fork tube pinchbolts on the fork crown and then remove the plugs from the top of the fork tubes.

12. After adding the fork oil, insert the fork springs and install and tighten the top plugs. Tighten the pinchbolts on the fork crown.

13. Position the wheel in front of the forks with the brake drum to the left. Install the backing plate on the front wheel and rotate it so that the anchor plate is aligned with the mounting hole in the left slider leg.

14. Thoroughly clean the front axle and coat it lightly with grease.

15. Install the felt pad and tab plate on the speedometer drive and fit them to the right side of the front hub. Make sure that the tabs in the plate stay in the slots in the hub as the front wheel is installed.

16. Fit the wheel between the forks and insert the axle, from the right side, through the speedometer drive and wheel.

17. Fit the spacer (which is slightly thicker than the washer) between the backing plate and the left fork leg. Push the axle all the way through and fit the washer and nut. Do not fully tighten the nut.

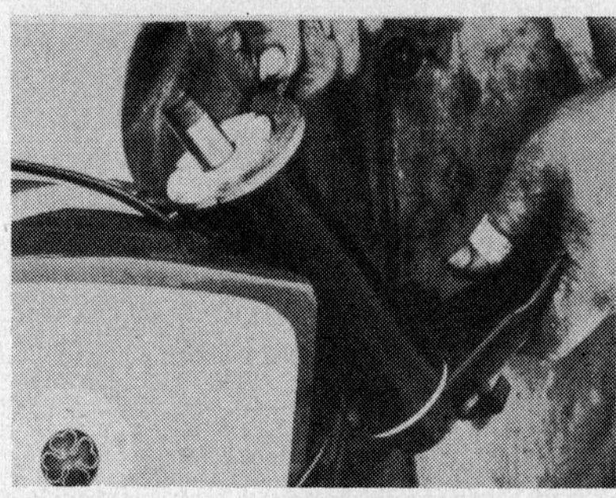
Removing the steering tube nut

18. Install the nut and bolt that secures the anchor plate to the slider leg and tighten finger-tight.

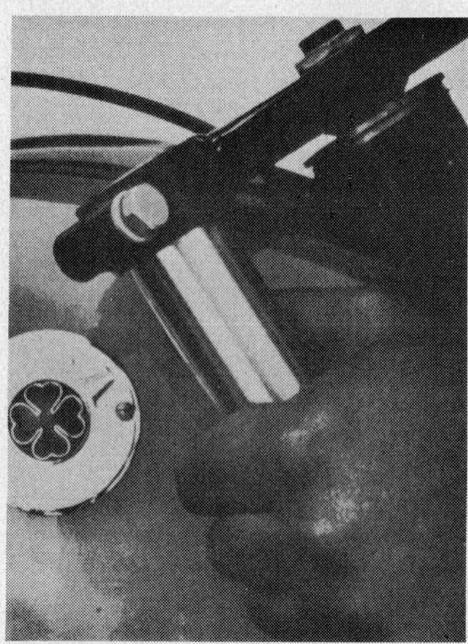
Fork tube installed flush with the top of the triple clamp

19. Tighten the front axle nut securely at this point.

20. Remove the prop and place the front wheel on the ground. Work the forks up and down a few times and then tighten the axle clamp bolts.

21. Tighten the anchor plate mounting bolt.

22. Press the brake arm up and fit the cable end into it. Adjust the front brake lever free-play with the knurled knob at the lever. If all the adjustment is taken up and there is still too much free-play, reposition the brake arm on its splined shaft.

23. Install the cap nut on the speedometer drive cable and fit the snap-ring in the cable. Tighten the cap nut on the drive unit with pliers.

INDEX
SUZUKI

MODEL IDENTIFICATION

M-31—55cc single; this is a very familiar step-through model.

M-12, M-15, M-15D—50cc sports bikes with 4-speed transmission. M-12 differs only in its upswept pipe, balde fenders, and larger lights.

A-50, AS-50, AC-50—small displacement street scramblers; all are 50cc singles with upswept pipes and 5-speed transmissions.

K-10, K-10P—79cc single; 4-speed transmission; 6.7:1 compression ratio.
K-11, K-11P—same as the K-10s only with an upswept exhaust pipe.

K-15, K-15P—79cc single; basically the same specifications as the other "K" series models but trail-ready with knobby tires, high pipe, and raised front fender.
B-105—118cc single with a two ratio transmission; this is another trail bike.
KT-120—similar in appearance to the above but this model has a 3-speed, two ratio transmission.

TC-90, TS-90—similar in appearance, the two models differ in transmissions; the TC-90 has a 4-speed with dual ratios, the TS-90 has a 5-speed.

A-100, AC-100, AS-100—98 cc singles; the engines are the same, the only differences are external. The AS and AC models feature an upswept exhaust pipe.

T-125—124cc twin cylinder sports roadster which features almost horizontal cylinders, 5-speed transmission, 1.8 gallon gas tank, and 7.3:1 compression.

TC-120—an updated version of the B-105P, this single has the same 118cc engine and a 3-speed dual ratio gearbox.

TC-125, TS-125—a pair of off-road singles featuring the newest designs and knobby tires; the TS has a 5-speed and the TC has a 4-speed, dual ratio unit.

T-20—250cc twin cylinder road bike with 6-speed transmission. TC-20—same as the T-20 only with upswept pipes: a street scrambler.

T-250 II, TC-250 II—these are updated versions of the T-20 and TC-20 respectively; modernistic paint styles, turn signal indicators, separate speedometer and tach, Ceriani-type forks, and an abundance of chrome make it easy to tell the difference.

T-305—essentially a bored-out T-250, with slightly lower (6.68:1) compression and a 6-speed transmission.

TS-250 II—a 246cc single cylinder off-road bike with the usual trail equipment: raised front fender, upswept exhaust, and Ceriani-type front forks.

T-350—road-going twin displacing 315cc; it has modern styling, chrome fenders, turn signals, and a 6-speed transmission.

GT380—three cylinder, modern two stroke with 6-speed transmission. Easily recognized by exhaust system and "Ram-Air" scoop over cylinder heads.
GT550—similar in appearance to the GT380. Latest models have disc brake and 5-speed transmission.

GT750—water-cooled triple; it features a hard-to-miss radiator and a polished water jacket instead of cooling fins on the cylinders. Also with disc brake up front.

GENERAL SPECIFICATIONS

Year	Model Designation	Displace. (cc)	Bore x Stroke (mm)	Horsepower (@ rpm)	Torque (ft lbs @ rpm)	Compress. Ratio	Transmission Type	Overall Length (in.)	Overall Height (in.)	Ground Clear. (in.)	Wheelbase (in.)	Dry Weight (lbs)	Tire Size (in.) Front	Tire Size (in.) Rear	Top Speed (mph)
1963-64	M-12 Cavalier	50	41 x 38	4.2 @ 8000	2.74 @ 7000	6.7 : 1	4-Spd.	71.5	33.5	N/A	45.7	133	2.25 x 17	2.25 x 17	53
	M-15 Collegian	50	41 x 38	4.2 @ 8000	2.74 @ 7000	6.7 : 1	4-Spd.	59.4	35.0	4.7	45.7	128	2.25 x 17	2.25 x 17	50
	M-15D Collegian	50	41 x 38	4.2 @ 8000	2.74 @ 7000	6.7 : 1	4-Spd.	59.4	35.0	4.7	45.7	133	2.25 x 17	2.25 x 17	50
	K-10 Corsair	79	45 x 50	6.5 @ 6000	5.84 @ 4000	6.7 : 1	4-Spd.	70.3	36.8	5.1	45.7	154	2.50 x 17	2.50 x 17	53
	K-11 Challenger	79	45 x 50	7.3 @ 7000	5.41 @ 6000	6.7 : 1	4-Spd.	72.1	33.6	5.3	45.7	154	2.50 x 17	2.50 x 17	60
	T-10 Crusader	246★	52 x 58	21 @ 8000	15 @ 7000	6.3 : 1	4-Spd.	81.4	41.4	5.3	53.2	308	3.00 x 17	3.00 x 17	88
1965	M-12 Cavalier	50	41 x 38	4.2 @ 8000	2.74 @ 7000	6.7 : 1	4-Spd.	71.5	33.5	N/A	45.7	133	2.25 x 17	2.25 x 17	53
	M-15 Collegian	50	41 x 38	4.2 @ 8000	2.74 @ 7000	6.7 : 1	4-Spd.	59.4	35.0	4.7	45.7	128	2.25 x 17	2.25 x 17	50
	M-15D Collegian	50	41 x 38	4.2 @ 8000	2.74 @ 7000	6.7 : 1	4-Spd.	59.4	35.0	4.7	45.7	133	2.25 x 17	2.25 x 17	50
	M-31 Suzi	55	43 x 38	5.0 @ 7000	4.65 @ 5000	6.3 : 1	3-Spd.	70.3	36.6	5.1	44.5	123	2.25 x 17	2.25 x 17	45
	K-10 Corsair	79	45 x 50	6.5 @ 6000	5.84 @ 4000	6.7 : 1	4-Spd.	70.3	36.8	5.1	45.7	154	2.50 x 17	2.50 x 17	53
	K-11 Challenger	79	45 x 50	7.3 @ 7000	5.41 @ 6000	6.7 : 1	4-Spd.	72.1	33.6	5.3	45.7	154	2.50 x 17	2.50 x 17	60
	K-15 Hillbilly	79	45 x 50	7.3 @ 7000	5.41 @ 6000	6.7 : 1	4-Spd.	72.1	33.6	N/A	45.7	N/A	2.75 x 17	2.75 x 17	60
							2 Ratio								38
	T-10 Crusader	246★	52 x 58	21 @ 8000	15 @ 7000	6.3 : 1	4-Spd.	81.4	41.4	5.3	53.2	308	3.00 x 17	3.00 x 17	88
	T-20 X-6 Hustler	247★	54 x 54	29 @ 7500	20.3 @ 7000	7.3 : 1	6-Spd.	76.8	40.6	6.5	50.4	297	2.75 x 18	3.00 x 18	100
1966	M-12 Cavalier	50	41 x 38	4.2 @ 8000	2.74 @ 7000	6.7 : 1	4-Spd.	71.5	33.5	N/A	45.7	133	2.25 x 17	2.25 x 17	53
	M-15 Collegian	50	41 x 38	4.2 @ 8000	2.74 @ 7000	6.7 : 1	4-Spd.	59.4	35.0	4.7	45.7	128	2.25 x 17	2.25 x 17	50
	M-15D Collegian	50	41 x 38	4.2 @ 8000	2.74 @ 7000	6.7 : 1	4-Spd.	59.4	35.0	4.7	45.7	133	2.25 x 17	2.25 x 17	50
	M-31 Suzi	55	43 x 38	5.0 @ 7000	4.65 @ 5000	6.3 : 1	3-Spd.	70.3	36.6	5.1	44.5	123	2.25 x 17	2.25 x 17	45
	K-10 Corsair	79	45 x 50	6.5 @ 6000	5.84 @ 4000	6.7 : 1	4-Spd.	70.3	36.8	5.1	45.7	154	2.50 x 17	2.50 x 17	53
	K-11 Challenger	79	45 x 50	7.3 @ 7000	5.41 @ 6000	6.7 : 1	4-Spd.	72.1	33.6	5.3	45.7	154	2.50 x 17	2.50 x 17	60
	K-15 Hillbilly	79	45 x 50	7.3 @ 7000	5.41 @ 6000	6.7 : 1	4-Spd.	72.1	33.6	N/A	N/A	N/A	2.75 x 17	2.75 x 17	60
							2 Ratio								38
	B-105 Bearcat	118	52 x 56	11 @ 7500	N/A	7.2 : 1	4-Spd.	74.9	37.9	N/A	48.0	194	2.75 x 17	2.75 x 17	N/A
							2 Ratio								
	B-100 Magnum	118	52 x 56	11 @ 7500	N/A	7.2 : 1	4-Spd.	74.9	37.9	5.9	48.0	N/A	N/A	N/A	N/A
	S-32-2 Olympian	149★	46 x 45	16 @ 8000	10.5 @ 7000	7.4 : 1	4-Spd.	74.8	39.4	5.1	49.6	253	2.75 x 17	2.75 x 17	80
	T-10 Crusader	246★	52 x 58	21 @ 8000	15 @ 7000	6.3 : 1	4-Spd.	81.4	41.4	5.3	53.2	308	3.00 x 17	3.00 x 17	88
	T-20 X-6 Hustler	247★	54 x 54	29 @ 7500	20.3 @ 7000	7.3 : 1	6-Spd.	76.8	40.6	6.5	50.4	297	2.75 x 18	3.00 x 18	100
1967	M-31 Suzi	55	43 x 38	5.0 @ 7000	4.65 @ 5000	6.3 : 1	3-Spd.	70.3	36.6	5.1	44.5	123	2.25 x 17	2.25 x 17	45
	M-15 Collegian	50	41 x 38	4.2 @ 8000	2.74 @ 7000	6.7 : 1	4-Spd.	59.4	35.0	4.7	45.7	128	2.25 x 17	2.25 x 17	50
	M-12 Cavalier	50	41 x 38	4.2 @ 8000	2.74 @ 7000	6.7 : 1	4-Spd.	71.5	33.5	N/A	45.7	133	2.25 x 17	2.25 x 17	53
	K-10P Corsair	79	45 x 50	7.5 @ 6500	6.4 @ 5000	6.7 : 1	4-Spd.	70.5	38.0	5.3	45.7	167	2.50 x 17	2.50 x 17	56
	K-11P Challenger	79	45 x 50	8.0 @ 7500	6.1 @ 6000	6.7 : 1	4-Spd.	71.6	38.0	5.3	45.7	167	2.50 x 17	2.50 x 17	60
	K-15P Hillbilly	79	45 x 50	8.0 @ 7500	6.1 @ 6000	6.7 : 1	4-Spd.	N/A	N/A	N/A	N/A	N/A	2.75 x 17	2.75 x 17	60
							2 Ratio								38
	A-100 Charger	98	50 x 50	9.5 @ 7500	6.9 @ 6500	6.5 : 1	4-Spd.	71.6	37.8	5.3	45.6	176	2.50 x 17	2.50 x 17	69
	AS-100 Sierra	98	50 x 50	9.5 @ 7500	6.9 @ 6500	6.5 : 1	4-Spd.	71.6	37.8	5.3	45.6	176	2.50 x 17	2.50 x 17	69
	B-100P Magnum	118	52 x 56	10 @ 7000	7.95 @ 5000	7.2 : 1	4-Spd.	74.9	37.9	5.9	48.0	190	2.50 x 17	2.75 x 17	68
	B-105P Bearcat	118	52 x 56	11 @ 7500	N/A	7.2 : 1	4-Spd.	74.9	37.9	N/A	48.0	194	2.75 x 17	2.75 x 17	N/A
							2 Ratio								
	S-32 Olympian	149★	46 x 45	16 @ 8000	10.5 @ 7000	7.4 : 1	4-Spd.	74.8	39.4	5.1	49.6	253	2.75 x 17	2.75 x 17	80

GENERAL SPECIFICATIONS

Year	Model Designation	Displace. (cc)	Bore x Stroke (mm)	Horsepower (@ rpm)	Torque (ft lbs @ rpm)	Compress. Ratio	Transmission Type	Overall Length (in.)	Overall Height (in.)	Ground Clear. (in.)	Wheelbase (in.)	Dry Weight (lbs)	Tire Size (in.) Front	Tire Size (in.) Rear	Top Speed (mph)
1967	X-5 Invader	196★	50 x 50	23 @ 7500	16.6 @ 7000	7.0 : 1	5-Spd.	75.8	40.6	5.7	49.4	269	2.75 x 18	2.75 x 18	87
	X-5 Stingray	196★	50 x 50	23 @ 7500	16.6 @ 7000	7.0 : 1	5-Spd.	75.8	40.6	N/A	49.4	259	3.00 x 18	3.25 x 18	N/A
	X-6 Hustler	247★	54 x 54	29 @ 7500	20.3 @ 7000	7.3 : 1	6-Spd.	76.8	40.6	6.5	50.4	297	2.75 x 18	3.00 x 18	100
	X-6 Scrambler	247★	54 x 54	29 @ 7500	20.3 @ 7000	7.3 : 1	6-Spd.	76.8	40.6	N/A	50.4	289	3.00 x 18	3.25 x 18	N/A
	500/Five Titan	492★	70 x 64	47 @ 7000	37.5 @ 6000	6.6 : 1	5-Spd.	85.5	44.3	6.3	57.0	408	3.25 x 19	4.00 x 18	120
1968	M-12 II Cavalier	50	41 x 38	4.2 @ 8000	2.74 @ 7000	6.7 : 1	4-Spd.	71.5	33.5	N/A	45.7	133	2.25 x 17	2.25 x 17	53
	AS-50 Colt	49	41 x 37.8	4.9 @ 8500	3.11 @ 8000	6.7 : 1	5-Spd.	70.3	35.3	5.9	45.7	160	2.25 x 17	2.25 x 17	60
	K-10P Corsair	79	45 x 50	7.5 @ 6500	6.4 @ 5000	6.7 : 1	4-Spd.	70.5	38.0	5.3	45.7	167	2.50 x 17	2.50 x 17	56
	K-11P Challenger	79	45 x 50	8.0 @ 7500	6.1 @ 6000	6.7 : 1	4-Spd.	71.6	38.0	5.3	45.7	167	2.50 x 17	2.50 x 17	60
	A-100 Charger	98	50 x 50	9.5 @ 7500	6.9 @ 6500	6.5 : 1	4-Spd.	71.6	37.8	5.3	45.6	176	2.50 x 17	2.50 x 17	69
	AS-100 Sierra	98	50 x 50	9.5 @ 7500	6.9 @ 6500	6.5 : 1	4-Spd.	71.6	37.8	5.3	45.6	176	2.50 x 17	2.50 x 17	69
	B-100P Magnum	118	52 x 56	10 @ 7000	7.95 @ 5000	7.2 : 1	4-Spd.	74.9	37.9	5.9	48.0	190	2.50 x 17	2.75 x 17	68
	KT-120 Trail	118	52 x 56	9.5 @ 6500	8.9 @ 5000	7.2 : 1	3-Spd. 2 Ratio	75.7	39.6	6.5	48.0	201	2.75 x 17	3.00 x 17	N/A
	X-5 Invader (T-200)	196★	50 x 50	23 @ 7500	16.6 @ 7000	7.0 : 1	5-Spd.	75.8	40.6	5.7	49.4	269	2.75 x 18	2.75 x 18	87
	X-5 Stingray (TC-200)	196★	50 x 50	23 @ 7500	16.6 @ 7000	7.0 : 1	5-Spd.	75.8	40.6	N/A	49.4	259	3.00 x 18	3.25 x 18	N/A
	X-6 Hustler (T-250)	247★	54 x 54	29 @ 7500	20.3 @ 7000	7.3 : 1	6-Spd.	76.8	40.6	6.5	50.4	297	2.75 x 18	3.00 x 18	100
	X-6 Scrambler (TC-250)	247★	54 x 54	29 @ 7500	20.3 @ 7000	7.3 : 1	6-Spd.	76.8	40.6	N/A	50.4	289	3.00 x 18	3.50 x 18	N/A
	T-305 Raider	305★	60 x 54	37 @ 7500	25.9 @ 7000	6.68 : 1	6-Spd.	77.8	41.9	6.3	50.8	317	3.00 x 18	3.25 x 18	110
	TC-305 Laredo	305★	60 x 54	37 @ 7500	25.9 @ 7000	6.68 : 1	6-Spd.	77.8	41.9	N/A	50.8	310	3.25 x 18	3.50 x 18	N/A
	T-500 Titan	492★	70 x 64	47 @ 7000	37.5 @ 6000	6.6 : 1	5-Spd.	85.5	44.3	6.3	57.0	408	3.25 x 19	4.00 x 18	120
1969	AS-50 Maverick	49	41 x 37.8	4.9 @ 8500	3.11 @ 8000	6.7 : 1	5-Spd.	71.5	39.0	5.9	46.7	165	2.25 x 17	2.50 x 17	65
	AC-100 Wolf	98	50 x 50	9.5 @ 7500	6.9 @ 6500	6.5 : 1	4-Spd.	71.6	37.8	5.3	45.6	176	2.50 x 17	2.50 x 17	69
	TC-120 Cat	118	52 x 56	12 @ 7500	9.5 @ 5000	6.9 : 1	3-Spd. 2 Ratio	73.4	40.7	7.9	47.0	205	2.75 x 18	3.00 x 18	60/65
	T-125 Stinger	124★	43 x 43	15.1 @ 8500	9.9 @ 7000	7.3 : 1	5-Spd.	72.2	42.5	6.7	46.9	227	2.50 x 18	2.75 x 18	75
	T-200 Invader	196★	50 x 50	23 @ 7500	16.6 @ 7000	7.0 : 1	5-Spd.	75.8	40.6	5.7	49.4	269	2.75 x 18	2.75 x 18	87
	TS-250 Savage	246	70 x 64	23 @ 6500	19.6 @ 5000	6.62 : 1	5-Spd.	83.3	44.3	9.5	53.9	280	3.25 x 19	4.00 x 18	80
	T-250 Hustler	247★	54 x 54	32 @ 8000	21.6 @ 7000	7.5 : 1	6-Spd.	77.8	42.5	6.1	50.8	283	2.75 x 18	3.00 x 18	105
	TC-250 Scrambler	247★	54 x 54	32 @ 8000	21.6 @ 7000	7.5 : 1	6-Spd.	76.8	40.6	N/A	50.4	285	3.00 x 18	3.50 x 18	N/A
	T-350 Rebel	315★	61 x 54	39 @ 7500	28.8 @ 6500	6.94 : 1	6-Spd.	77.8	42.5	6.3	50.8	285	3.00 x 18	3.25 x 18	110
	T-500 II Titan	492★	70 x 64	47 @ 7000	37.5 @ 6000	6.6 : 1	5-Spd.	85.5	44.3	6.3	57.2	412	3.25 x 19	4.00 x 18	120
1970				4.5 @ 6000	4.2 @ 5000	6.7 : 1	3-Spd.	71.5	40.5	5.5	46.5	154	2.25 x 17	2.25 x 17	44
	F-50 Cutlass	49	41 x 37.8	4.9 @ 8500	3.1 @ 8000	6.7 : 1	5-Spd.	71.5	39.0	5.9	46.7	165	2.25 x 17	2.50 x 17	65
	AC-50 Maverick	49	41 x 37.8	11 @ 7500	7.82 @ 7000	6.8 : 1	5-Spd.	73.8	42.5	6.8	47.0	197	2.75 x 18	2.75 x 18	70
	TS-90 Honcho	89	47 x 51.8	11 @ 7500	7.82 @ 7000	6.8 : 1	4-Spd.	73.8	42.5	8.7	47.0	199	2.75 x 18	3.00 x 18	60/
	TC-90 Blazer	89	47 x 51.8				2 Ratio								65
				12 @ 7500	9.5 @ 5000	6.9 : 1	3-Spd.	73.4	40.7	7.9	47.0	205	2.75 x 18	3.00 x 18	60/
	TC-120 II Cat	118	52 x 56				2 Ratio								65
	T-125 II Stinger	124★	43 x 43	15.1 @ 8500	9.9 @ 7000	7.3 : 1	5-Spd.	72.2	39.8	6.7	46.9	207	2.50 x 18	2.75 x 18	75
	TS-250 II Savage	246	70 x 64	23 @ 6500	17.2 @ 5000	6.6 : 1	5-Spd.	83.3	44.9	9.4	53.9	266	3.25 x 19	4.00 x 18	80
	T-250 II Hustler	247★	54 x 54	33 @ 8000	22 @ 7000	7.4 : 1	6-Spd.	77.8	41.9	6.3	50.8	315	2.75 x 18	3.00 x 18	105
	T-350 II Rebel	315★	61 x 54	40 @ 7500	29 @ 6500	6.9 : 1	6-Spd.	78.0	41.9	6.3	50.8	326	3.00 x 18	3.25 x 18	110
	T-500 III Titan	492★	70 x 64	47 @ 7000	37.5 @ 6000	6.6 : 1	5-Spd.	86.4	43.5	6.3	57.3	408	3.25 x 19	4.00 x 18	120
1971	MT-50R Trailhop.	49	41 x 37.8	3.0 @ 6000	2.75 @ 5000	6.9 : 1	3-Spd.	51.5	34.6	5.1	37.0	132	3.50 x 8	3.50 x 8	35
	F-50R Cutlass	49	41 x 37.8	4.5 @ 6000	4.2 @ 5000	6.7 : 1	3-Spd.	71.5	40.5	5.5	46.5	154	2.25 x 17	2.25 x 17	45
	TS-50R Gaucho	49	41 x 37.8	4.9 @ 8500	3.1 @ 8000	6.7 : 1	5-Spd.	71.5	39.0	5.9	46.7	165	2.25 x 17	2.50 x 17	60
	TS-90R Honcho	89	47 x 51.8	11 @ 7500	7.82 @ 7000	6.8 : 1	5-Spd.	73.8	42.5	6.8	47.0	197	2.75 x 18	2.75 x 18	70
	TC-90R Blazer	89	47 x 51.8	11 @ 7500	7.82 @ 7000	6.8 : 1	4-Spd. 2 Ratio	73.8	42.5	8.7	47.0	199	2.75 x 18	3.00 x 18	60/65
	TC-120R Cat	118	52 x 56	12 @ 7500	9.5 @ 5000	6.9 : 1	3-Spd. 2 Ratio	73.4	40.7	7.9	47.0	205	2.75 x 18	3.00 x 18	60/65
	TS-125R Duster	123	56 x 50	13 @ 7000	9.8 @ 6500	6.7 : 1	5-Spd.	80.7	43.3	9.25	51.6	231	2.75 x 19	3.25 x 18	70
	TC-125R Prospect.	123	56 x 50	13 @ 7000	9.8 @ 6500	6.7 : 1	4-Spd. 2 Ratio	79.7	43.3	9.3	51.6	209	2.75 x 19	3.25 x 18	65/70
	T-125R Stinger	124★	43 x 43	15.1 @ 8500	9.9 @ 7000	7.3 : 1	5-Spd.	72.2	39.8	6.7	46.9	207	2.50 x 18	2.75 x 18	75
	TS-185R Sierra	183	64 x 57	17.5 @ 7000	13.5 @ 6000	6.2 : 1	5-Spd.	79.5	44.7	9.4	52.8	217	3.00 x 19	3.50 x 18	75
	TS-250R Savage	246	70 x 64	23 @ 6500	19.4 @ 5500	6.7 : 1	5-Spd.	86.0	43.3	9.8	55.7	260	3.25 x 19	4.00 x 18	80
	T-250R Hustler	247★	54 x 54	33 @ 8000	22 @ 7000	7.4 : 1	6-Spd.	77.8	41.9	6.3	50.8	315	3.00 x 18	3.25 x 18	105
	T-350R Rebel	315★	61 x 54	40 @ 7500	29 @ 6500	6.9 : 1	6-Spd.	78.0	41.9	6.3	50.8	326	3.00 x 18	3.50 x 18	110
	TM-400R Cyclone	396	82 x 75	40 @ 6500	32.8 @ 6000	7.3 : 1	5-Spd.	85.0	44.7	8.7	55.5	236	3.00 x 21	4.00 x 18	80
	T-500R Titan	492★	70 x 64	47 @ 7000	38.5 @ 6000	6.6 : 1	5-Spd.	86.4	43.5	6.3	57.3	408	3.25 x 19	4.00 x 18	120

GENERAL SPECIFICATIONS

1972

Year Model Designation	Displace. (cc)	Bore x Stroke (mm)	Horsepower (@ rpm)	Torque (ft lbs @ rpm)	Com-press. Ratio	Trans-mission Type	Overall Length (in.)	Overall Height (in.)	Ground Clear. (in.)	Wheel-base (in.)	Dry Weight (lbs)	Tire Size (in.) Front	Tire Size (in.) Rear	Top Speed (mph)
MT-50J Trailhop.	49	41 x 37.8	3.0 @ 6000	2.75 @ 5000	6.9 : 1	3-Spd.	51.5	34.6	5.1	37.0	132	3.50 x 8	3.50 x 8	35
F-50J Cutlass	49	41 x 37.8	4.5 @ 6000	4.2 @ 5000	6.7 : 1	3-Spd.	71.5	40.5	5.5	46.5	154	2.25 x 17	2.25 x 17	45
TS-50J Gaucho	49	41 x 37.8	4.9 @ 8000	3.1 @ 8000	6.7 : 1	5-Spd.	71.5	39.0	5.9	46.7	165	2.25 x 17	2.50 x 17	60
TS-90J Honcho	89	47 x 51.8	11 @ 7500	7.82 @ 7000	6.8 : 1	5-Spd.	73.8	42.5	6.8	47.0	197	2.75 x 18	3.00 x 18	65
TC-90J Blazer	89	47 x 51.8	11 @ 7500	7.82 @ 7000	6.8 : 1	4-Spd. 2 Ratio	73.8	42.5	8.7	47.0	199	2.75 x 18	3.00 x 18	60/65
RV-90 Rover	88	50 x 45	8.0 @ 6000	7.23 @ 4000	6.2 : 1	4-Spd.	71.1	39.0	7.7	46.5	185	6.70 x 10	6.70 x 10	50
T-125J Stinger	124★	43 x 43	15.1 @ 8500	9.9 @ 7000	7.3 : 1	5-Spd.	72.2	39.8	6.7	46.9	207	2.50 x 18	2.75 x 18	75
TS-125J Duster	123	56 x 50	13 @ 7000	9.8 @ 6500	6.7 : 1	5-Spd.	80.7	43.3	9.25	51.6	231	2.75 x 19	3.25 x 18	70
TC-125J Prospect.	123	56 x 50	13 @ 7000	9.8 @ 6500	6.7 : 1	4-Spd. 2 Ratio	79.7	43.3	9.3	51.6	209	2.75 x 19	3.25 x 18	65/70
TS-185J Sierra	183	64 x 57	17.5 @ 7000	13.5 @ 6000	6.2 : 1	5-Spd.	79.5	44.7	10.0	52.8	217	3.00 x 19	3.50 x 18	75
TS-250J Savage	246	70 x 64	23 @ 6500	19.4 @ 5500	6.7 : 1	5-Spd.	86.0	43.3	9.8	55.7	260	3.25 x 19	4.00 x 18	80
T-250J Hustler	247★	54 x 54	33 @ 8000	22 @ 7000	7.4 : 1	6-Spd.	77.8	41.9	6.3	50.8	315	3.00 x 18	3.25 x 18	105
T-350J Rebel	315★	61 x 54	40 @ 7500	29 @ 6500	6.9 : 1	6-Spd.	78.0	41.9	6.3	50.8	326	3.00 x 18	3.50 x 18	110
TM-400J Cyclone	396	82 x 75	40 @ 6500	32.8 @ 6000	7.3 : 1	5-Spd.	85.0	44.7	8.7	55.5	236	3.00 x 21	4.00 x 18	80
T-500J Titan	492★	70 x 64	47 @ 7000	38 @ 6000	6.6 : 1	5-Spd.	86.4	43.5	6.3	57.3	412	3.25 x 19	4.00 x 18	120
TS-400J Apache	396	82 x 75	34 @ 6000	30 @ 5500	N/A	5-Spd.	N/A	N/A	N/A	N/A	N/A	N/A	N/A	N/A
GT380●	371	54 x 54	38 @ 7500	28.4 @ 6000	6.7 : 1	6-Spd.	82.9	43.3	6.1	53.4	377	3.00 x 19	3.50 x 18	110
GT550●	544	61 x 62	50 @ 6500	44.1 @ 5000	6.8 : 1	5-Spd.	85.0	43.3	5.9	55.3	412	3.25 x 19	4.00 x 18	115
GT750●	738	70 x 64	67 @ 6500	55.7 @ 5500	6.7 : 1	5-Spd.	87.2	44.3	5.5	57.8	482	3.25 x 19	4.00 x 18	120

★—twin cylinder models.
cc—cubic centimeters.
mm—millimeters.
rpm—revolutions per minute.
ft lbs—foot pounds torque.
in.—inches.
lbs—pounds.
mph—miles per hour.
●—3 cylinder models.

TUNE-UP AND MAINTENANCE

TUNE-UP OPERATIONS

Setting and Replacing Ignition Contact Points

SINGLES (EXCEPT TS-185R&J AND TS-250R&J)

1. Remove the flywheel cover on the left crankcase. Observe the two oblong holes in the flywheel through which the points can be seen.

2. To set the points, rotate the flywheel with a wrench until they are fully open. Check this by rocking the flywheel back and forth until the maximum gap is attained.

3. Insert a feeler gauge of the proper thickness.

4. If the gap must be adjusted, loosen the point securing screw with a long, thinbladed screwdriver and, inserting the screwdriver into the little slot in the point base, rotate the points one way or the other until the proper gap is achieved.

5. Check the condition of the points carefully before replacing them.

6. If replacement is necessary, remove the left crankcase cover after taking off the kickstarter and shift lever.

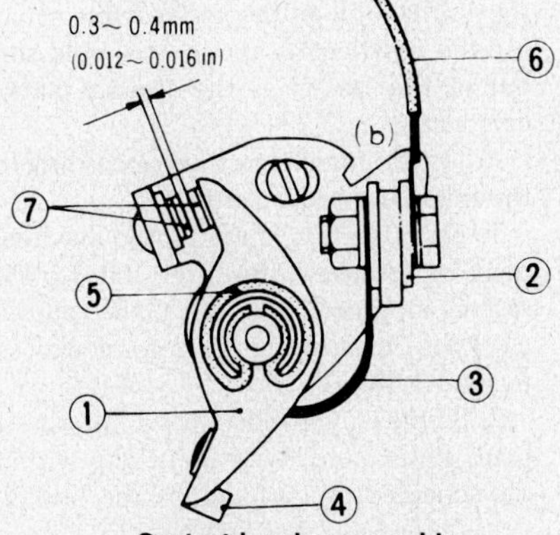

Contact breaker assembly.

1. Contact break arm
2. Insulator
3. Spring
4. Cam follower
5. Circlip
6. Wire from primary coil
7. Contact breaker points

7. Remove the nut which secures the flywheel to the crankshaft.

8. Remove the flywheel using the special puller. This tool is absolutely necessary for this job.

9. Remove the screws which secure the condenser and points, disconnect them from the stator plate, and install the new components.

10. Smear some high-melting point grease on the cam and a drop of light engine oil on the points pivot shaft.

11. Reinstall the flywheel, making sure the keyway lines up with the key in the crankshaft.

12. Tighten the securing nut to the proper torque (25–35 ft lbs).

13. Reset the point gap as described above.

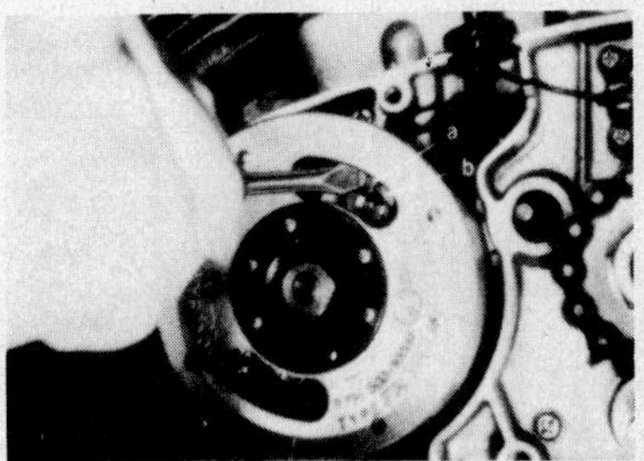

Loosening contact adjustment screw (a).

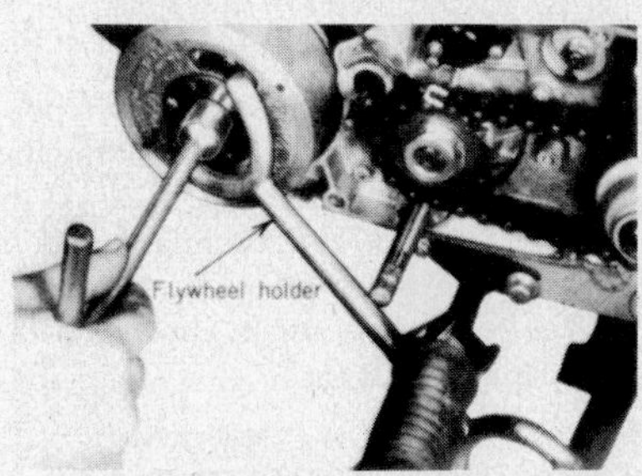

Removing the flywheel rotor nut.

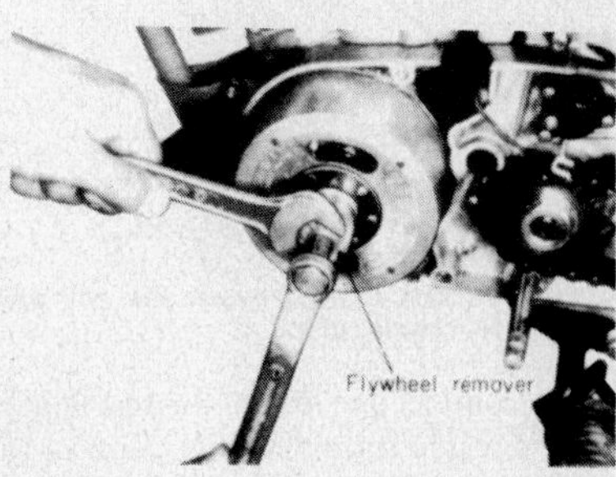

Removing the rotor with a special puller.

ALL TWINS

The points are attached to a movable stator plate which is in turn fitted to a housing over the flywheel.

1. To set the points, remove the front portion of the left crankcase cover or the round plate which covers the points.

2. Each cylinder has its own points set. These are adjusted in the same manner as described for Singles. The exception is the T–10 which has a pair of eccentric screws to change the point gap. Recheck the gap after tightening the adjusting screws.

3. Lubricate the cam with high-melting point grease and apply a drop of light oil to the points pivot shaft. If the machine has two felt lubricating pads (T–250, T–350, T–500), remove the lower one and discard it.

ALL TRIPLES

These machines have three sets of points, located on the left (750) or right (380, 550) side of the engine. Adjust or replace as described above for Twin cylinder models. Firing order is left, center, right.

Adjusting Ignition Timing

Ignition timing specifications are given in both flywheel (crankshaft) degrees before the top dead center and piston millimeters BTDC.

SINGLES (EXCEPT TS–185R&J AND TS–250R&J)

1. To check the timing with a strobe light, first remove the flywheel cover plate.

2. Hook up the strobe light as necessary (this may vary according to type).

3. Start the engine and check the timing by seeing whether the marks on the flywheel and the corresponding mark on the crankcase line up at idle speed.

The timing may also be checked with a test light as follows:

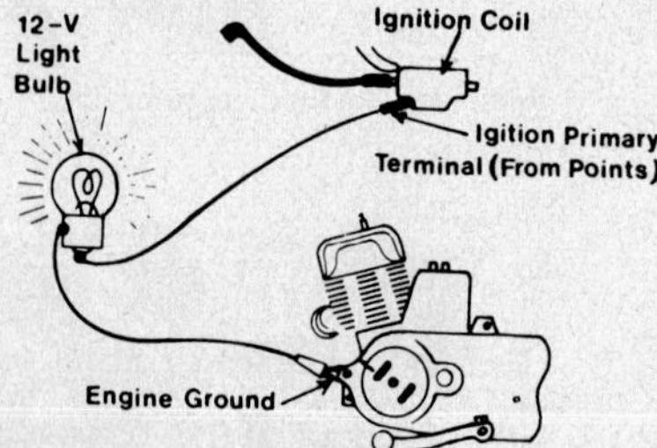

Connect a test light between the coil and ground to check timing.

1. Connect one lead of the test light to the movable spring contact point of the point set, and the other lead to the engine case (ground).

2. Turn on the ignition and slowly rotate the flywheel clockwise with a wrench while watching the light bulb.

3. The marks on the flywheel and crankcase should line up at the moment the test light goes out.

If the rotor mark (B) is below the crankcase mark (A), the ignition timing is retarded. If (B) is above (A), the timing is advanced. The flywheel rotates counterclockwise.

An easier method is to use a thin piece of paper (ie. cellophane) placed between the points. Pull on the paper while rotating the flywheel as above. It should slip out of the points as the timing marks coincide.

Adjust timing if necessary according to the following procedures:

1. On 50 to 80cc engines, the flywheel must be removed, the three stator plate screws loosened, and the plate rotated clockwise to advance, counterclockwise to retard timing.

2. Singles over 80cc have no stator plate adjustment. Vary point gap within the specified range to adjust the timing.

Loosening the stator screws to rotate the stator plate. This changes the ignition timing on 50 to 80cc engines.

ALL TWINS (EXCEPT T–10)

Each set of points must be checked separately as above. The left set of points controls the left cylinder.

1. Using the test light method, check each set of points in turn. Hook one lead to the movable point arm and the other lead to ground.

2. Rotate the flywheel, with the ignition switch on, until the test light goes out at which point the scribed timing marks should be aligned. There are two scribed marks on the rotor, 180° apart. The black mark is for the right cylinder, the red mark is for the left.

3. To adjust the timing, loosen the points base screws and adjust each set of points so that their respective rotor timing marks coincide with the stator marks. The engine rotates counterclockwise as seen from the flywheel side; therefore, moving the left point set upward will advance the timing for the left cylinder, and moving the right point set downward will advance the timing for the right cylinder.

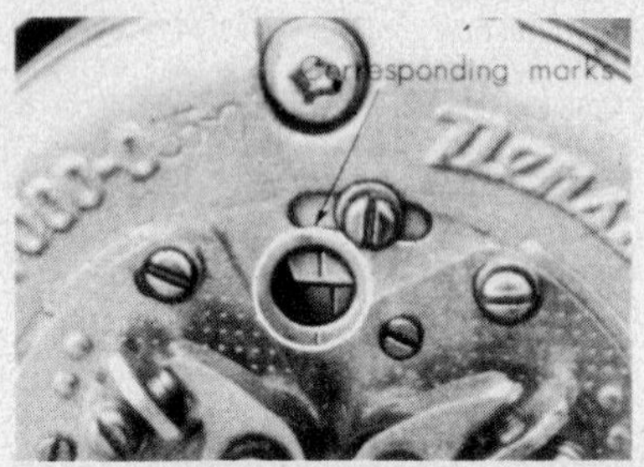

Rotor timing marks on most twins are visible through a hole in the stator plate.

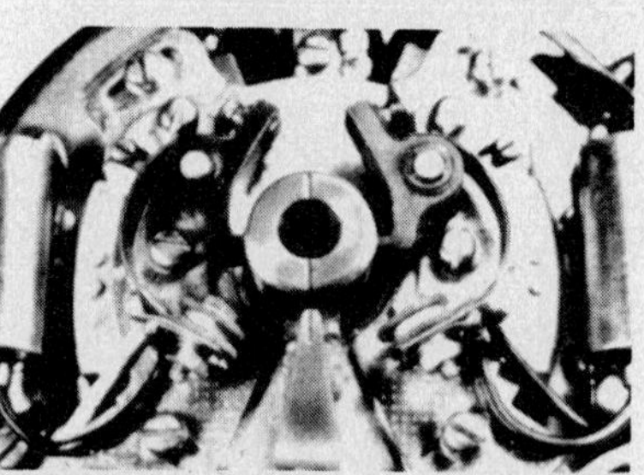

On the S-32 model, the red and blue timing marks are scribed on the distributor cam shaft and are aligned with the stator timing pointer.

T–10

Both sets of points and the timing advance mechanism are under the cover on the left side of the crankcase.

The left contact set serves the left cylinder.

1. Adjust the contact gap of both sets of points to 0.012–0.016 in., loosen the screws that hold the left point set and move the point base so that the points are

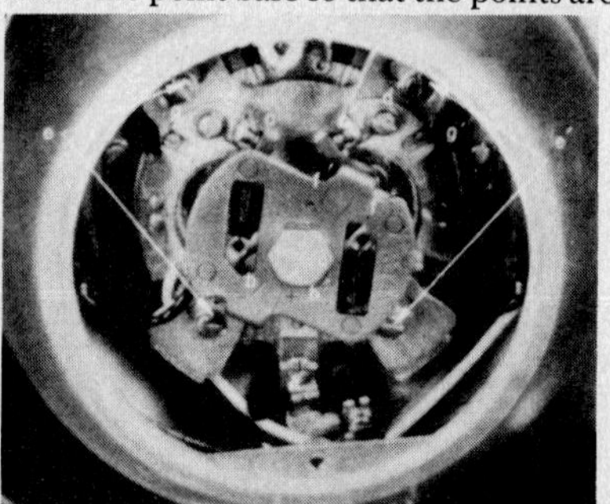

The T-10 model has the timing marks scribed on the the centrifugal advance mechanism.

just opening (check with test light) with the stator notch (a) in line with the red mark on the centrifugal advance mechanism (refer to the illustration).

2. Tighten the two base screws, then check the left points with the advance mechanism fully advanced. At this point, the notch on the stator (a) should be in line with the red notch that has a "plus" ± mark.

2. Rotate the crankshaft 180 degrees, then check the right point set in the same manner as the left, using the blue marks on the centrifugal advance mechanism.

SETTING UP THE PEI IGNITION SYSTEM ON TS-185R&J AND TS-250R&J

The Pointless Electronic Ignition system (PEI) installed on 1971–72, TS-185s and TS-250s is a capacitor discharge unit. It is therefore impossible to check in the event of a malfunction except with highly specialized equipment.

1. To check ignition timing, a strobe light is needed. Connect the light in the usual manner (i.e. to the battery terminals and the spark plug cable).

2. Remove the left crankcase cover and start the engine.

3. The line stamped on the flywheel rotor (the center line of three) aligns with the marks on the crankcase or core of the pulser coil at the specified rpm.

Adjusting PEI timing.

4. To adjust the timing, loosen the three stator mounting screws and move the stator base so that the stamped line on the stator, and the centerline scribed in the top stator mounting screw hole, line up. Tighten the mounting screws and recheck the timing at the specified rpm. Moving the stator plate clockwise advances the timing.

5. Note that the position of the scribe mark in the top screw hole may vary. It may be off center. Regardless of this, lining up the mounting screw center with the mark should insure correct ignition timing.

If the marks are aligned and the readings at the specified rpm cannot be obtained, the system may be malfunctioning.

PEI TROUBLESHOOTING

Wiring Harness

The most common place where a problem might occur is in the wiring harness. An inspection should be made at the time of initial set up and at periodic intervals thereafter to see that all couplers are properly connected and are not shorting against each other or grounding against the engine or frame. If the motorcycle is to be used for competition, the lead wires should be taped to the frame to minimize movement which might lead to loose or disconnected connectors. CDI systems are susceptible to loss of electrical current if the connectors are dirty or corroded. Take care to keep all electrical connections clean and wherever possible keep the spark plug lead away from the frame.

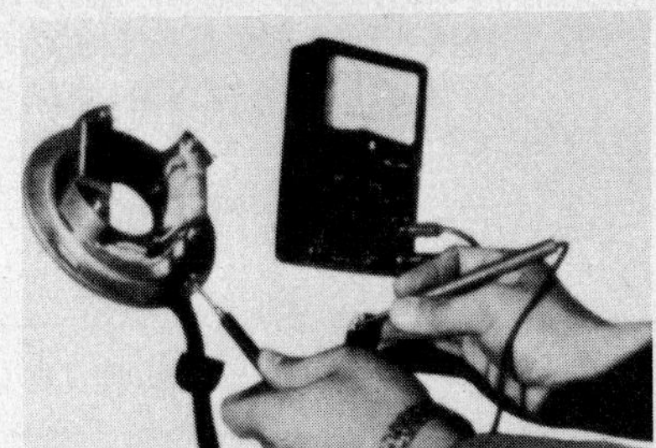

Measuring the resistance of the PEI pulsar coil.

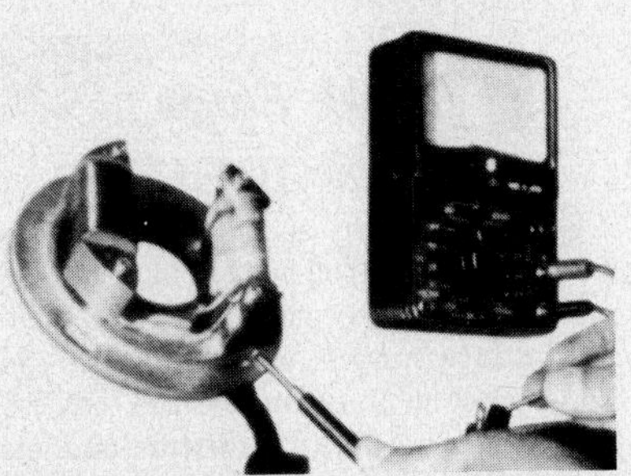

Measuring the resistance of the PEI exciter coil.

Moisture

Care should be taken to protect the PEI system from moisture since water (particularly salt water) can cause corrosion at the connectors, leading to short circuits in the system. The connectors may be taped during competition to keep out moisture.

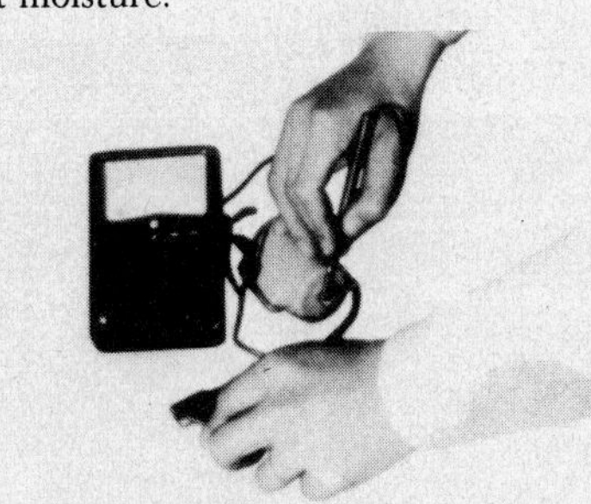

Measuring the resistance of the PEI ignition coil.

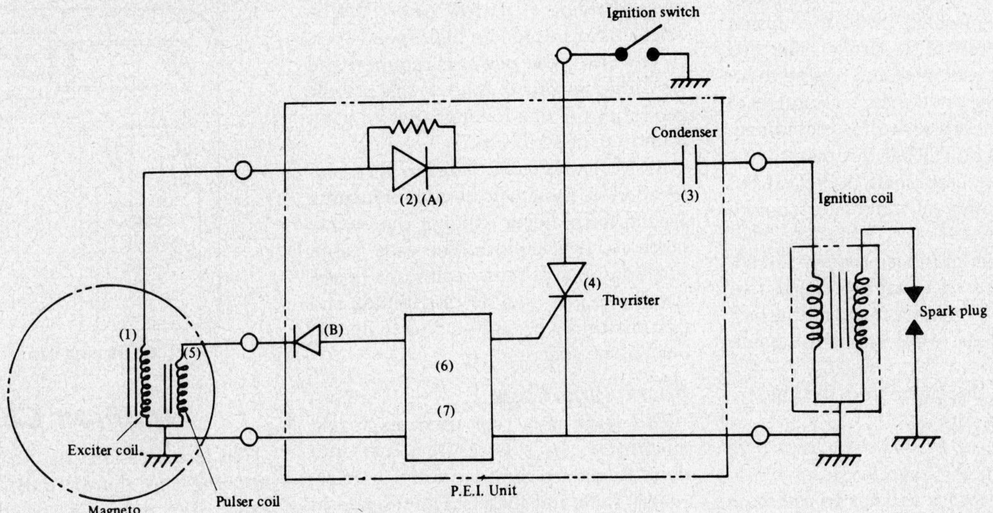

PEI circuit diagram.

TESTING BLACK BOX CONNECTIONS WITH AN OHMMETER

Red (+) terminal to:	Black (−) terminal to:	Reading (ohms) (± 10 percent)
Black/Red	Black/Yellow	No reading
Black/Yellow	Black/Red	5000
Red/White	Black/White	1700
Black/White	Red/White	No reading
Black/Yellow	White/Blue	Needle deflects
White/Blue	Black/Yellow	and returns
Black/White	Black/Yellow	No reading
Black/Yellow	Black/White	1500

TESTING COILS WITH AN OHMMETER

Test	Red to:	Black to:	Reading (ohms)	
Exciter coil	Black/Red	Coil plate	TS185, 250R	220
			TM400R	315
Pulser coil	Red/White	Coil plate	TS185, 250R	75
			TM400R	80
Ignition coil (primary)	White/Blue	Ground	TS185, 250R	0.7
			TM400R	1.5
Ignition coil (secondary)	Black	Ground	TS185, 250R	12K
			TM400R	20K

ALL TRIPLES

Ignition timing for the three cylinder machines can be set as previously described for the twin models with the obvious addition of an extra set of points. It is preferred, however, that a dial indicator be used to more accurately set the position of the piston at the proper number of degrees before top dead center; due to the engine design, triples are more sensitive to accurate timing on each cylinder.

1. Remove the spark plug of the cylinder to be timed and install the dial gauge in its place.

Dial indicator in position to find piston TDC.

2. Remove the other spark plugs and turn the crankshaft until the piston reaches the top of its stroke. The dial gauge needle will peak and begine to reverse. Turn the crankshaft back and forth until the highest dial reading is obtained. The piston is at TDC at this point.

3. Turn the crankshaft backward the specified number of millimeters before TDC.

4. When the piston is properly set, adjust the point set for that cylinder so that they are just beginning to open. It is best to use a test light to determine this point.

5. Repeat the procedure for the remaining cylinders.

NOTE: *Due to the different spark plug locations in the cylinder head, piston position readings will not be the same for all three cylinders on the 750.*

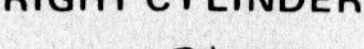

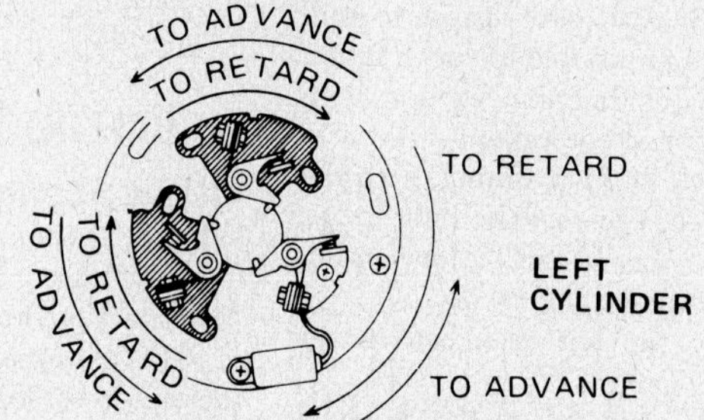

Spark Plugs

ALL MODELS

Spark plug gap specifications range from 0.018 in. to 0.024 in. On later Suzuki models, a narrower gap is specified than for the early models, mainly because the Posi-Force oil injection system has resulted in a leaner oil/gas mixture and less plug fouling.

The spark plug gap can be varied, however, to improve performance for certain types of riding. A narrow gap of 0.018–0.020 in. can be used for high-speed operation where peak power is required and very little lugging is done. If this narrow gap results in plug fouling anyway, open it up to 0.022–0.024 in.

A wide gap of 0.022–0.024 in. is recommended for those who do a lot of lugging around town, never winding the engine much above 5,000 rpm. The wide gap in situations such as these is almost a necessity due to poor fuel/air distribution and rich mixtures which cause plug fouling at low engine speeds.

Spark Plug Caps

The spark plug caps used on Suzuki motorcycles have a resistor built into them to reduce ignition noise interference in radio and TV sets. The resistors in these units are like any other resistor, in that heat and vibration can change their value to the point where the voltage required to break through to the plug is in excess to that supplied by the coil. A bad resistor can cause a no-start condition, misfiring, or other elusive ignition malfunctions.

These units can be tested with an ohmmeter, if one is available, or a new unit can be substituted. Normal resistance is 10–20 K ohms.

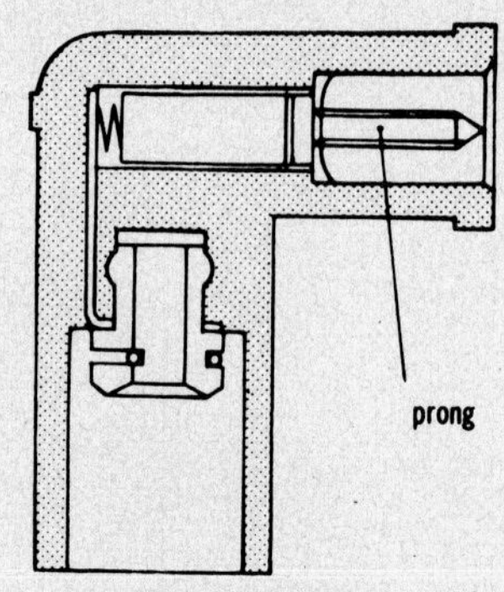

Spark plug cap.

Ignition Coil

On rare occasions, the heat and vibration the coil absorbs during operation causes the insulation on the internal windings to break down and the coil output gradually becomes less and less. The insulation also can break down intermittently, causing a misfiring condition.

The coil can be checked best, if it is suspect, by replacing it with a new unit. Coil condition can be checked in a crude way by operating the engine for a short time, then feeling the coil for excessive heat. With twins, both coils should be the same temperature. It should be noted that, on twins, the left coil fires the right cylinder and the right coil the left cylinder. Visually check the coil for melted insulation or arcing. If the primary wires are pinched between the coil body and the bracket, they can short out from wear, so it is a good idea to look for this. Also, check the nylon plug that connects the coil to the main wiring harness. Corrosion inside this connector can lead to misfiring or lack of spark from one coil.

Carburetor Adjustment

The two adjustments included in the tune-up procedure are idle speed and pilot air jet adjustment. Carburetor overhaul and specifications are to be found under "Fuel Systems."

Adjusting Idle Speed

ALL SINGLES

1. Before adjusting the idle speed, the throttle cable free-play must be set to specification as found in "Maintenance Items."

2. Start the engine and allow it to warm up for a few minutes.

Location of throttle slide and air screws on rotary and reed valve engines.

3. Turn the throttle slide adjusting screw until the slowest possible idle is obtained. (On models with the carburetor enclosed inside the right crankcase, the adjusting screw is found protruding from the rubber cable gasket. On other models, it is easily seen on top of the carburetor: spring-loaded, knurled head.)

4. Turn in the pilot air screw until it is lightly seated. On some models with the carburetor in the crankcase, this can be reached by removing a plug in the front of the right crankcase and on others by removing the carburetor cover plate.

5. Slowly back out the pilot air screw until the engine idles smoothly, the readjust the throttle slide adjuster to obtain an idle of approximately 1200 rpm.

6. The standard setting for the pilot air screw varies between 1 and 2 turns out from its seated position.

1 turn out	M-31, KT-120
1¼ turns out	F-50, MT-50, K-11, TC-90, RV-90, TC-125, TS-125, TS-250
1½ turns out	A-50, K-10, TS-90, A-100, AS-100, TC-120, B-100P, B-105P, TS-185, MT-50R, TS-50R
1¾ turns out	M-12, M-15, M-15D, K-15, K-10P, K-11P, TS-250R, TS-250J
2 turns out	AS-50, AC-50

ALL TWINS

Adjusting Idle Speed

1. Set the throttle cable free-play and check the synchronization of the cables. These procedures are described under "Maintenance Items."

2. Start the engine and allow it to warm up for a few minutes. Shut it off and remove the cap from one plug.

3. Screw in the pilot air screw on the other cylinder's carburetor until it is lightly seated, then back it out the number of turns specified in the following chart:

1¼ turns out	All 500 cc
1½ turns out	All 125, 200, 250, 305, 350 cc twins and T-10 up to engine 11825
1¾ turns out	S-32, T-20(X-6) and T-10 from engine 11826 to 16816
2 turns out	T-10 after engine 16817

4. Start the engine and allow it to run on one cylinder. Adjust the throttle slide screw to obtain the lowest possible idle speed, then turn the pilot air screw in or out (no more than one-quarter turn in either direction from the specified setting) to attain the smoothest idle speed at the lowest rpm.

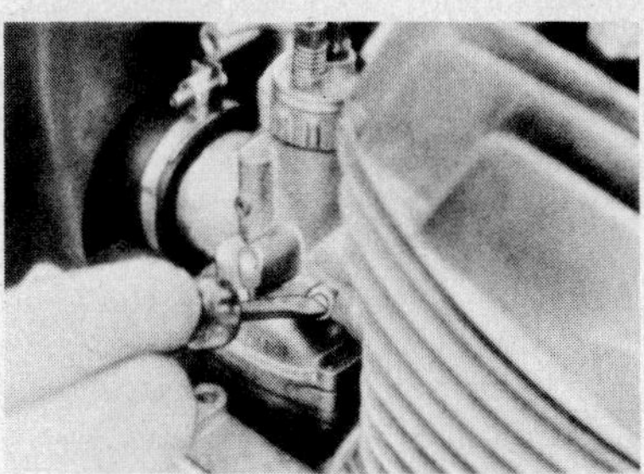

Pilot air screw adjustment (twins).

5. Readjust the throttle slide adjusting screw to obtain approximately 1000 rpm, then shut off engine.

6. Place the cap back on the plug and remove the other plug cap. Adjust the other carburetor in the manner just described.

7. Start the engine on both cylinders and allow it to stabilize. Turn down both throttle slide adjusters in small, equal increments until the idle speed is 1200–1500 rpm.

All Triples

1. Set the throttle cable free-play as described in "Maintenance Items."

2. Turn all three pilot air screws in until lightly seated, then turn them out 1 ¼ turns for the GT380 and GT550; 1 ½ turns for the GT750.

3. Start the engine and allow it to warm up for a few moments, then shut it off and disconnect two of the spark plug cables. Turn the throttle slide adjusting screw on the remaining cylinder so the engine will be able to idle.

4. Restart the engine and turn the throttle slide adjuster until the engine is running at 1000 rpm, then adjust the pilot air screw up to ¼ turn in either direction so that the cylinder is running smoothly at the lowest rpm. Readjust the throttle slide adjusting screw to 1000 rpm.

5. Turn off the engine, remove the spark plug cable, and connect another, then perform the same procedure for that cylinder. Repeat again for the last cylinder.

6. Connect all three leads and start the

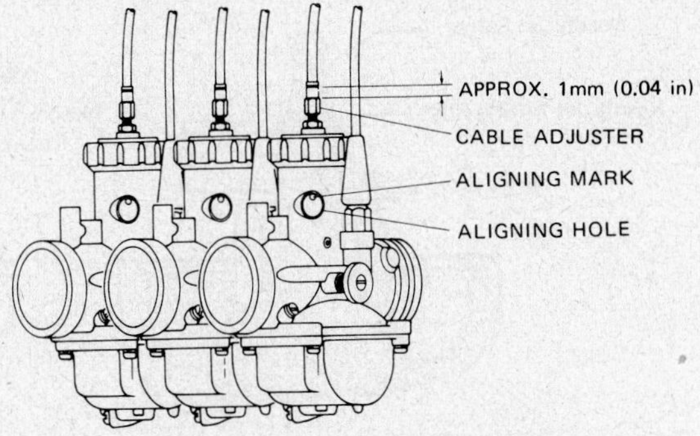

Throttle slide alignment (triples).

engine; adjust the idle by turning down the throttle slide adjusting screws in samll, equal increments until the engine runs smoothly at 1000–1200 rpm.

7. The throttle slides must now be synchronized. Remove the slide aligning hole plugs from each carburetor. Turn the twistgrip halfway through its travel while observing the slides through the holes. The punch mark on the side of each slide should be at the top of the aligning hole.

If not, adjust the throttle cables so that each slide is correctly positioned.

8. Release the twistgrip and make sure that there is still about 2 mm of cable free-play with the slides fully closed.

If not, adjust to obtain this, and recheck alignment as before.

FLOAT LEVEL ADJUSTMENT

ALL MODELS EXCEPT TS–125&R, TS–185&R, TS–250R, T–10, S–32–2

1. Remove the carburetor float bowl and float.

2. Refit the float, hold the carburetor upside down, and lower the float gradually until the float tongue just touches the upper end of the float needle.

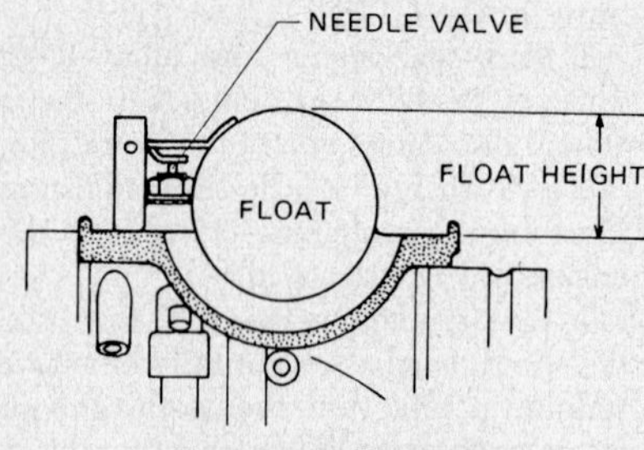

Float level adjustment.

3. Measure the distance between the float bowl gasket surface (with the gasket removed) and the bottom of the float. (See illustration)

4. Adjust if necessary by bending the float tongue according to the following specifications:

FLOAT LEVEL SETTINGS

14.00 mm (0.552 in.)	T-250R
17.33 mm (0.681 in.)	T-250II
19.00 mm (0.741 in.)	T-125 all
20.50 mm (0.810 in.)	A-50, AS-50, AC-50
22.50 mm (0.886 in.)	M-31, RV-90
23.00 mm (0.906 in.)	F-50 and F-50R, MT-50, AS-100, A-100, TS-250, TS-50R
24.50 mm (0.969 in.)	F-50 (1970)
25.00 mm (0.984 in.)	K-10, K-11, K-10P, K-11P, B100P, KT-120, T-20, T-200, TS-90R, TC-90R, TC-120R
25.10 mm (0.988 in.)	TC-90, TS-90
25.70 mm (1.010 in.)	T-250
27.00 mm (1.062 in.)	T-350R, T-500 all, GT-750
27.33 mm (1.070 in.)	T-350II
27.50 mm (1.100 in.)	T-350 all
28.30 mm (1.112 in.)	TS-250II
29.20 mm (1.150 in.)	T-350 all
24.25 mm (0.955 in.)	GT380, GT550
26-28 mm (1.02-1.10 in.)	GT750

TS–125&R, TS–185&R, TS–250R

Measure the distance between the float arm and the needle jet fitting boss with the carburetor turned upside down. The distance should be as follows:

6.8 mm (0.268 in.)	TS-125&R, TS-185
15.0 mm(0.590 in.)	TS-250R
7.0 mm (0.275 in.)	TS-185R

T–10, S–32–2

To check the T–10 float level, first remove the float bowl from one carburetor, with the fuel line still attached. Scratch a line inside the float bowl 5 mm down from the gasket surface for the T–10, 7 mm for the S–32–2. Holding the float bowl level, open the fuel tap and observe the mark you just scribed—fuel should stop coming in when it reaches this mark. If not, bend the float arm, and make sure both floats are exactly the same height afterward.

MAINTENANCE ITEMS

Cooling System (GT750)

Periodically check the cooling system for weak, damaged, or leaky hoses, damage to the radiator, reservoir tank, or any of the associated plumbing. Check the cooling solution level and top it off with distilled water if necessary. The level should not be allowed to drop beneath the level plate inside the inlet pipe when cool.

The cooling solution should be changed every 2,000 miles or two years, whichever comes first, or any time the solution becomes diluted with oil or gasoline. The solution will deteriorate with age and exposure to extreme temperature.

Refill the cooling system with 50 per cent distilled water and 50 per cent Golden Cruiser 1200 Antifreeze and Summer Coolant, or a similar ethylene-glycol solution. During storage or in very cold climates, boost the amount of coolant and antifreeze to 60 per cent.

Drain the cooling system by loosening the water drain plug at the front, center of the engine (See illustration)

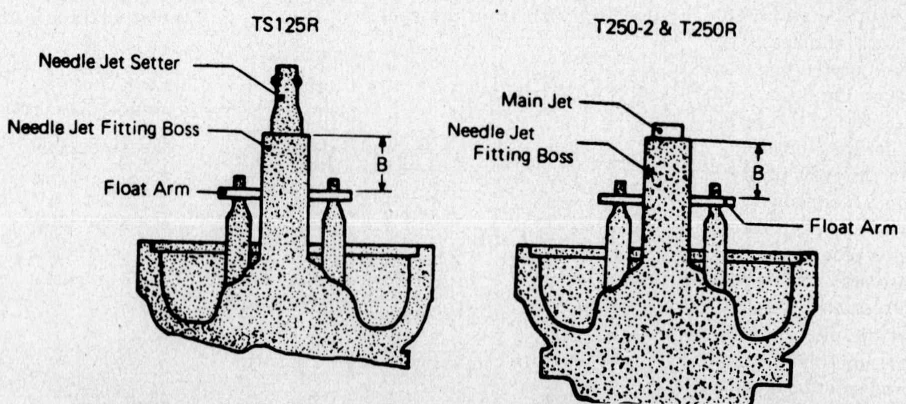

Measure the distance between the float arm and the needle jet fitting boss on these models.

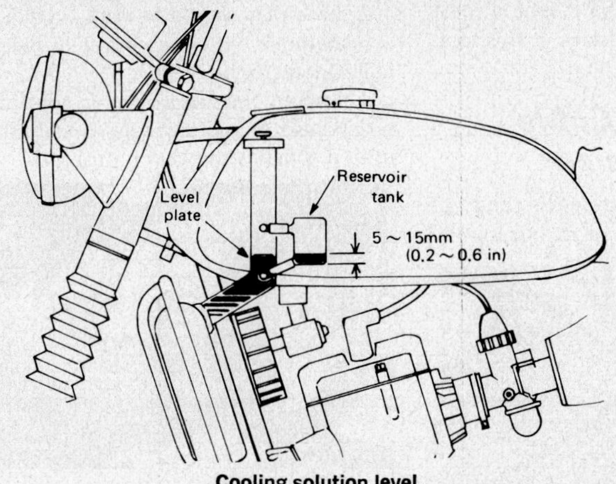

Cooling solution level.

Water drain plug.

TUNE-UP SPECIFICATIONS

Model	Std Spark Plug NGK	Spark Plug Gap (in.)	Point Gap (in.)	Static Ignition Timing Piston (mm BTDC)	Static Ignition Timing Crankshaft (deg BTDC)
AS-50, AC-50, A-50, TS-50R	B-77HC	0.020-0.024	0.014	2.00	24
F-50, R, J	BP-4H	0.020-0.024	0.012-0.016	1.56	20
MT-50R, J	BP-4H	0.020-0.024	0.012-0.016	1.40	20
M-12, M-15	B-4	0.020-0.024	0.012-0.016	2.53	27
M-31	B-6	0.020-0.024	0.012-0.016	1.41	20
K-10, K-11, K-15	B-6	0.020-0.028	0.012-0.016	3.34	27
K-10P, K-11P, K-15P	B-7	0.020-0.024	0.012-0.016	1.86	20
TC/TS-90, R, J	B-77HC	0.019	0.012-0.016	1.96	20
RV-90	BP-6HS	0.020-0.024	0.012-0.016	2.04	22
A-100, AS-100, AC-100	B-77HC	0.020-0.024	0.012-0.016	1.86	20
B-100P	B-7	0.024-0.028	0.012-0.016	3.00	24
B-105P, KT-120, TC-120R	B-77C	0.024-0.028	0.012-0.016	3.00	24
T-125, II	BP-7H	0.020-0.024	0.012-0.016	2.20	24
T-125R, J	BP-7HS	0.020-0.024	0.012-0.016	2.28	24
TC/TS-125, R, J	B-77HC	0.020-0.028	0.012-0.016	2.20-2.62	21-23
S-32-2	B-77C	0.024-0.028	0.012-0.016	2.10	25
TS-185R, J	B-77HC	0.020-0.024	PEI①	16° @ 1000①	24° @ 6000①
T-200(X-5), TC-200	B-77HC	0.020-0.024	0.014	3.62	27
T-10	B-7	0.020-0.028	0.012-0.016	3.88	7 (not adv) 30 (full adv)
T-20(X-6), TC-250	B-77HC	0.020-0.024	0.014	3.62	27
TS-250, II	B-7E	0.020-0.024	0.012-0.016	2.70	21
TS-250R, J	B-7ES	0.020-0.024	PEI①	16° @ 1000①	24° @ 6000①
T-250, R, J, T-305, 350, TC-305 all	B-77HC	0.020-0.024	0.012-0.014	2.88	24
TM-400R, J	B-8ES	——	PEI①	8° @ 1000①	24° @ 6000①
500/5, T-500, II, III, R, J	B-77HC	0.020-0.024	0.012-0.016	3.40	24
GT380	B-7ES	0.020-0.024	0.012-0.016	3.00	24
GT550	B-7ES	0.020-0.024	0.012-0.016	3.37	24
GT750	B-7ES	0.020-0.024	0.012-0.016	②	24

① PEI (Pointless Electronic) ignition: Timing is set when mark on stator plate is centered at top mounting screw. The figures in this table are used to check the "black box" circuitry. See "Tune-up Operations" for procedure.
② Right and left cylinders: 3,63; center cylinder: 3.42.
in.—inches.
mm—millimeters.
deg—degrees.
BTDC—before top dead center.

Chain Adjustment

All Models

1. Allowable chain slack for all models is 0.6–0.8 in. measured at the middle of the chain run with the motorcycle on the center stand.

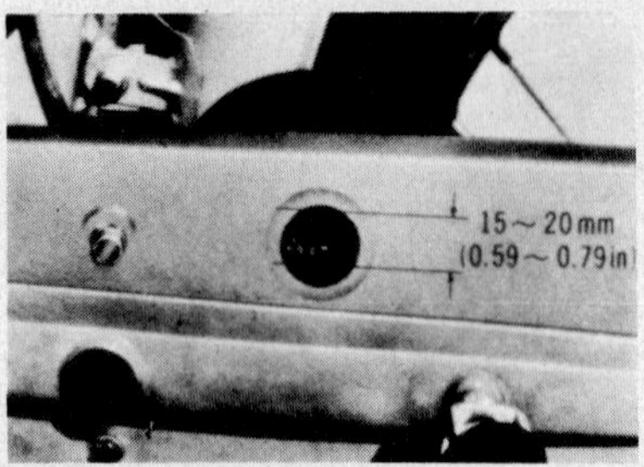

Chain slack is checked through the inspection hole on models with fully enclosed chains.

2. To adjust, loosen the rear axle nuts and the chain adjuster locknuts. Turn the chain adjusters equally to obtain proper free-play in the chain.

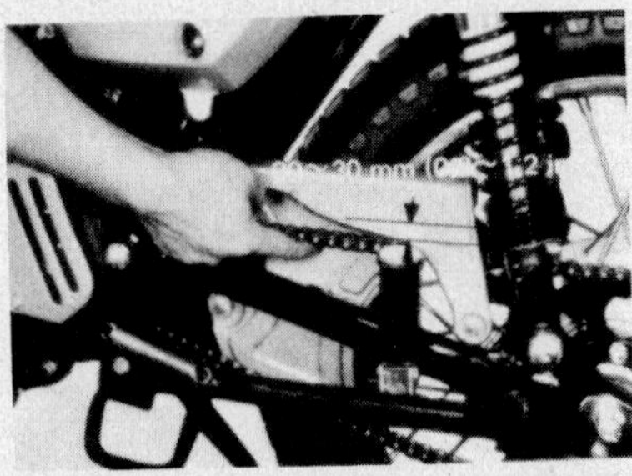

Chain slack is measured in the middle of the chain's upper run.

3. Check wheel alignment against the scribed marks on the swing arm.

4. Recheck chain slack as before.

5. Check chain slack with the machine off the center stand and with a person sitting on it as in operation to assure that the chain is not tight.

The axle nut (B) is loosened only if the axle is to be pulled. Normally, loosening locknut (A) is sufficient to allow for chain adjustment.

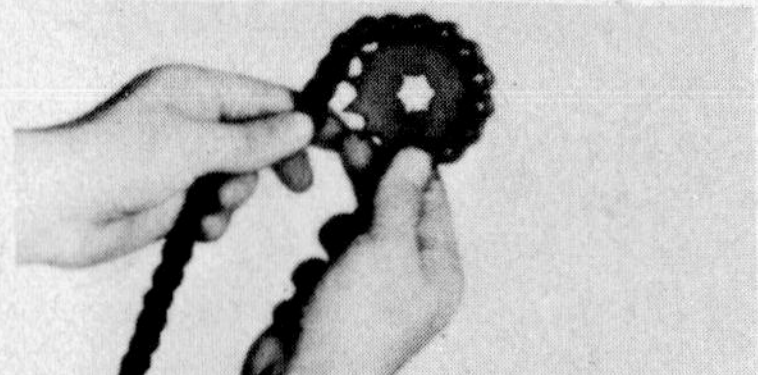

Check the play between the chain and the sprockets.

6. If the chain has a tight spot, it must be adjusted for normal slack at this spot, or replaced if possible.

Throttle Cable Adjustment

1. Loosen the locknut on the cable adjuster at the twist grip or carburetor.

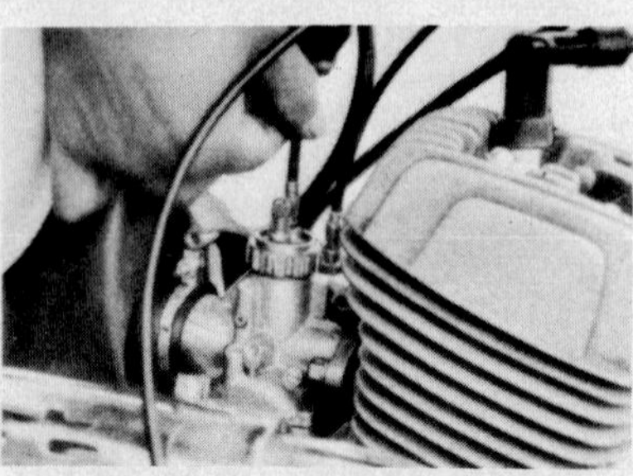

Pull up on throttle cable to check play.

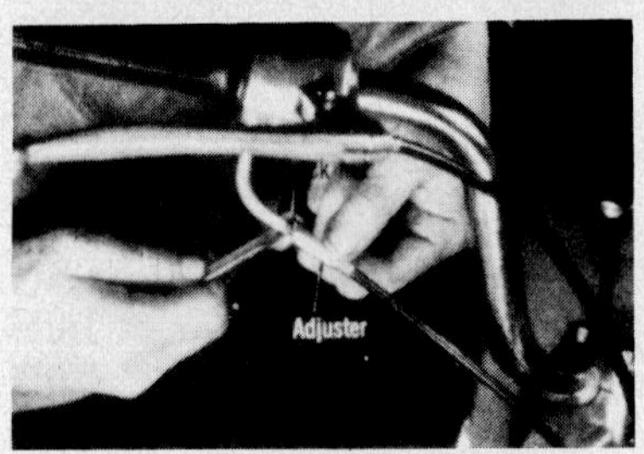

Adjusting the throttle cable at the twist grip.

2. Turn the adjuster until the cable has 0.020–0.040 in. free-play.

3. Tighten the locknut and recheck the free-play.

4. On multi-cylinder models, the cables must have equal free-play.

Adjusting the Clutch

1. Free-play is measured at the base of the clutch lever. (See illustration)

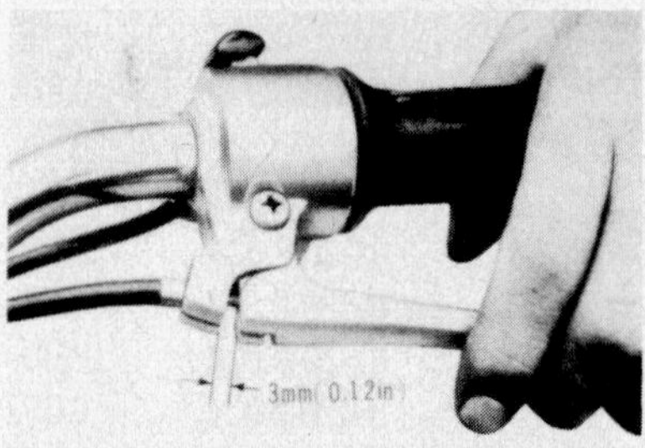

Measure clutch cable play at the base of the lever.

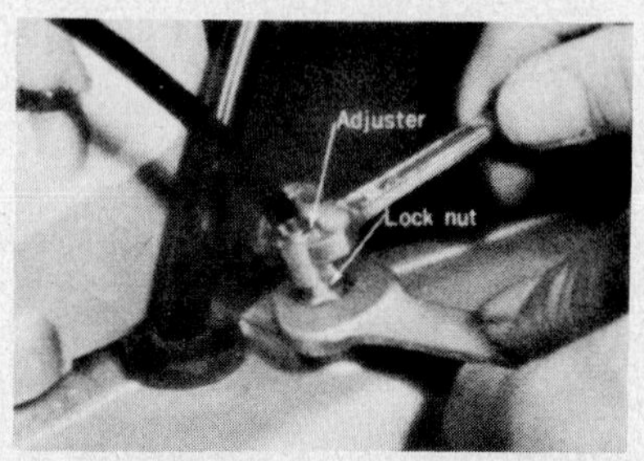

Clutch cable adjuster is at the top of the crankcase, often covered by a rubber boot.

2. Free-play should be 0.12–0.16 in.

3. Remove the clutch cover or clutch adjustment rubber cap.

4. Loosen the release lever adjusting screw locknut and screw in the adjuster until it touches the clutch pushrod.

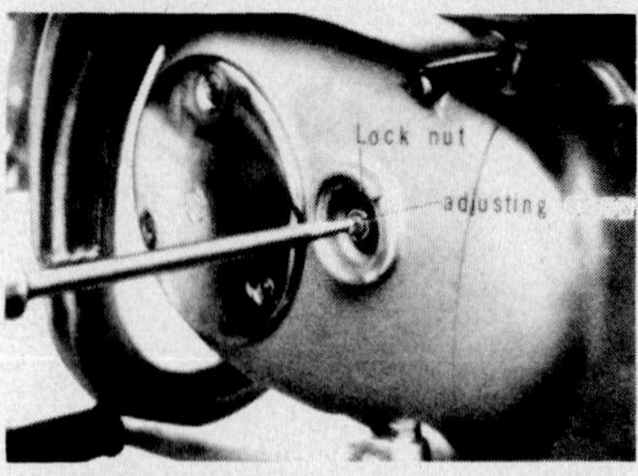

Clutch adjusting screw is located inside the left crankcase cover.

5. Back out the adjusting screw one-half turn; retighten the locknut.

6. Reset cable free-play if necessary.

Adjusting the Brakes

FRONT BRAKE

1. Turn the adjustment nut at the front wheel until there is 0.8–1.2 in. of free-play at the brake lever before the brakes contact the drum.

2. For twin leading shoe front brake connecting rod adjustment, remove the cable adjustment nut.

Twin-leading shoe brake adjusters.

3. Remove the front axle and hub.

4. Loosen the connecting rod locknut and rotate the rod until the brake cams lie flat against the ends of the brake shoes, then tighten the locknut and reassemble the front end.

REAR BRAKE

1. Adjust the nut at the rear brake to give 0.8–1.2 in. of pedal travel before engagement.

2. On models such as MT-50, with a lever actuated rear brake, adjust as with the front brake.

BRAKE LIGHT SWITCH

1. Adjust to allow 0.25 in. of lever or pedal movement before the switch is activated.

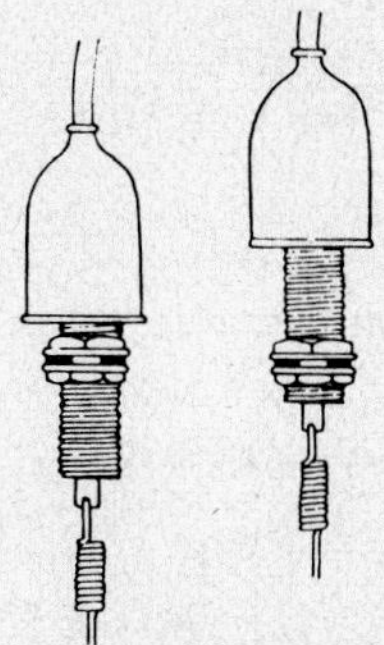

Brake light switch is adjusted so that it turns on after about 1/4 in. of movement.

Oil Pump Control Cable

K-10P, K-11P, B-100P, K-15, K-15P, KT-120, T-20

1. Remove the right crankcase cover plate to expose the oil pump and control cable.

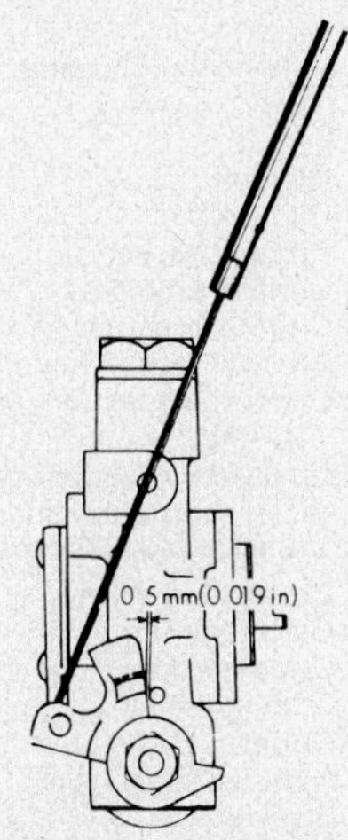

Control lever gap (T-20).

Adjusting pump cable (T-20).

2. Adjust the throttle cable(s) as previously described.

3. Loosen the oil pump cable adjusting screw locknut and turn the adjuster so that the gap between the oil pump control lever and its stop is 0.019 in. for the T-20, and 0.040 in. for others with the throttle held fully open.

Control lever gap (K-10P).

T-250, T-305, T-350, T-500

1. The oil pump is located on top of the engine just behind the right-hand carburetor.

2. If there is no inspection hole, remove the grey plastic cover.

3. Adjust the throttle cables as previously described, then hold the throttle fully open.

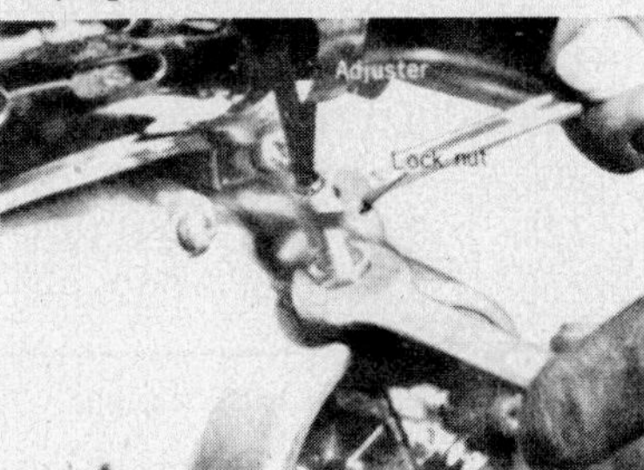

Adjusting pump cable—K-10P.

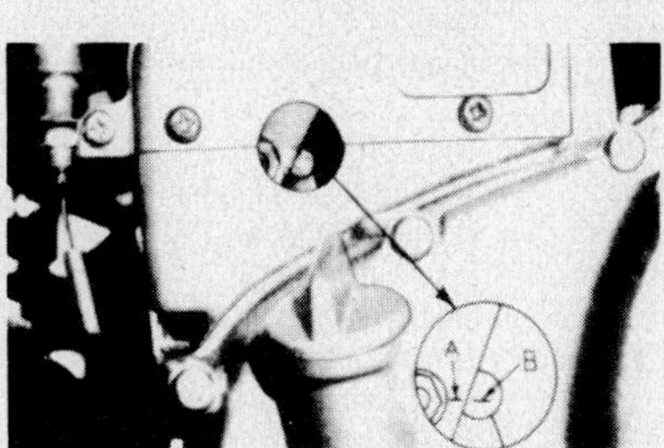

Oil pump cable inspection hole—T-350.

4. Adjust cable length with the adjuster so that the scribe marks on the oil pump and the control lever coincide.

ALL OTHER MODELS (EXCEPT TRIPLES)

1. Remove the engine sprocket cover and oil pump cover plate. This is the flat plate immediately to the rear of the drive sprocket.

2. Adjust the throttle cable(s).

3. Loosen the oil pump control cable locknut on the adjuster.

Control cable adjusting marks—other models.

4. Adjust the control cable so that the scribed marks on the control lever and the oil pump body coincide with the throttle fully open.

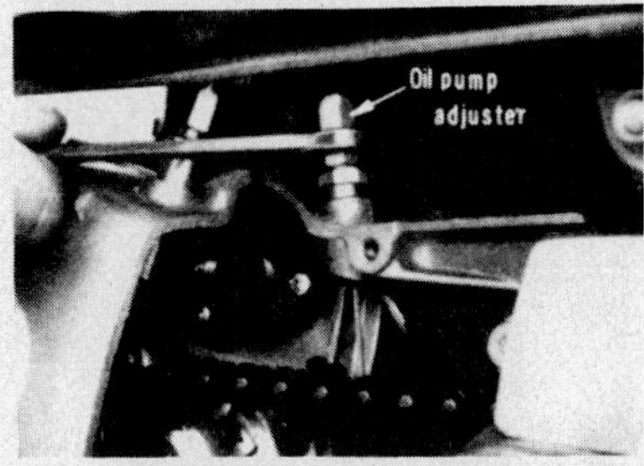

Adjusting pump cable—other models.

5. Tighten the locknut carefully, making sure the marks are still in alignment.

ALL TRIPLES

1. Adjust as for the above models EXCEPT that the throttle is to be half open when the scribe marks align.

2. Remove the throttle slide alignment hole plugs and turn the twistgrip until the punch marks on the slides are at the tope of the inspection holes.

3. Adjust the cable, if necessary, as described above.

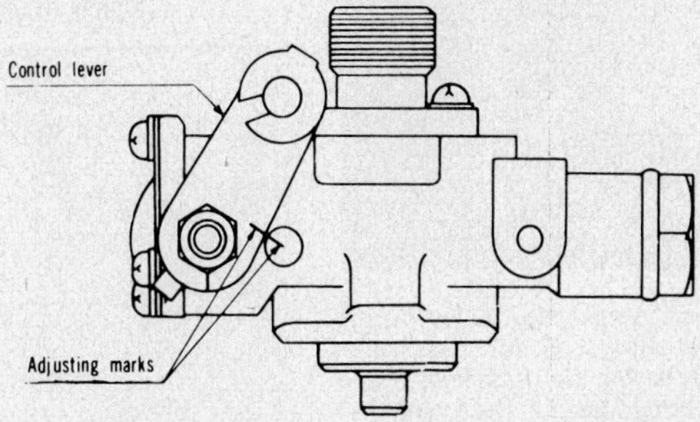

Close-up of oil pump cable adjusting marks—T-350.

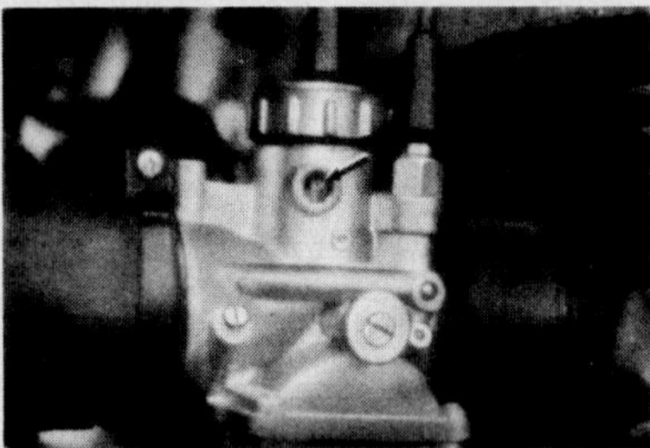

Throttle slide dent mark.

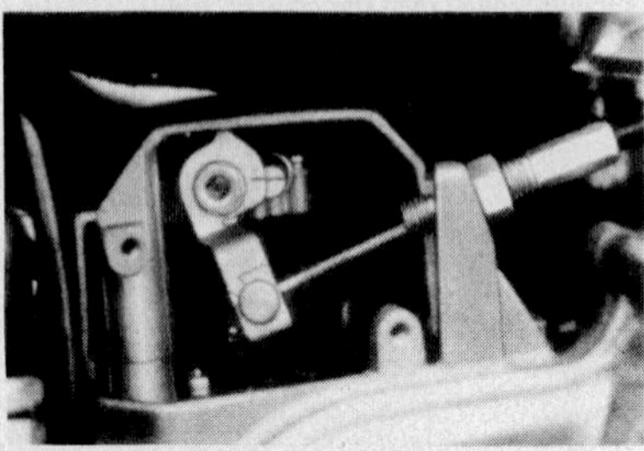

Pump lever aligning mark.

Changing the Transmission Oil

1. Consult "Capacities" chart for data.
2. Remove the drain plug(s) located on the underside of the crankcase.
3. Refill with the correct amount and grade of oil through the filler cap.
4. Check the level by removing the oil level plug.

Oil drain plug—singles.

Twins have three plugs: No. 1 is for the clutch chamber; No. 2 is for the transmission; No. 3 is for the crankcase and center main bearing. Gas in the crankcase can be drained off from plug No. 3.

FUEL MIXING RATIO CHART FOR "OIL-MIX" ENGINES

(Liter, cc)

Quantity of Gas (liter)	Quantity of Oil 15 : 1 liter (cc)	Quantity of Oil 20 : 1 liter (cc)
1	0.067 (60)	0.05 (50)
2	0.134 (134)	0.10 (100)
3	0.200 (200)	0.15 (150)
4	0.267 (267)	0.20 (200)
5	0.334 (334)	0.25 (250)
6	0.400 (400)	0.30 (300)
7	0.467 (467)	0.35 (350)
8	0.534 (534)	0.40 (400)
9	0.600 (600)	0.45 (450)
10	0.667 (667)	0.50 (500)

(US and Imperial gallon, pint)

Quantity of Gas (gal)	Quantity of Oil 15 : 1 gal (pt)	Quantity of Oil 20 : 1 gal (pt)
0.25	0.017 (0.13)	0.013 (0.1)
0.50	0.034 (0.27)	0.025 (0.2)
0.75	0.050 (0.40)	0.038 (0.3)
1.00	0.067 (0.54)	0.050 (0.4)
1.25	0.084 (0.67)	0.063 (0.5)
1.50	0.100 (0.80)	0.075 (0.6)
1.75	0.117 (0.94)	0.088 (0.7)
2.00	0.134 (1.07)	0.100 (0.8)
2.25	0.150 (1.20)	0.113 (0.9)
2.50	0.167 (1.34)	0.125 (1.0)

Factory Approved Two-Stroke Oils for All Models

Below 50° F	Shell Super Two-Stroke Oil Mobil Super Motor Oil Shell 2T Two-Stroke Oil Super Shell Motor Oil
Above 50° F	Shell 2T Two-Stroke Oil Shell Outboard Engine Oil Mobil Super Motor Oil Esso Outboard Oil Standard Outboard Oil Texaco Outboard Oil Shell Super Two-Stroke Oil Super Shell Motor Oil Mobil Outboard Oil Esso 2T Motor Oil Caltex 2T Plus Motor Oil Union 76 Outboard Oil

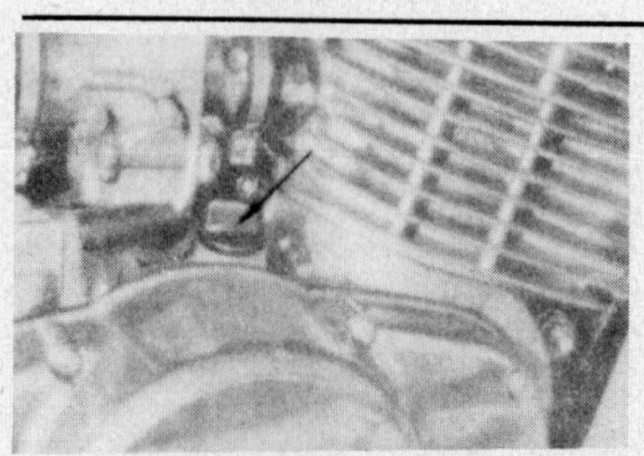

Oil filler plug—twins.

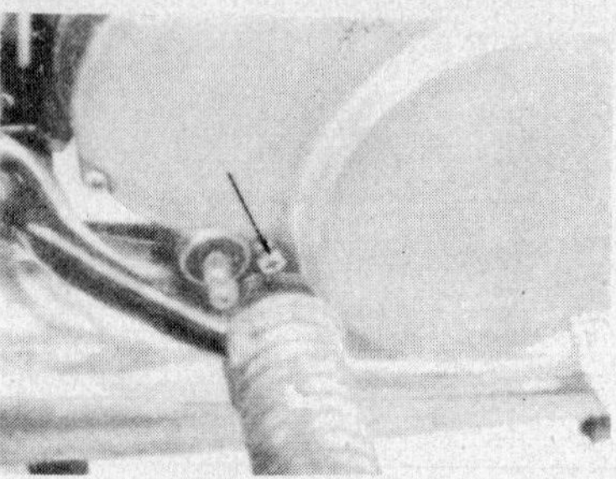

Oil level plug—twins.

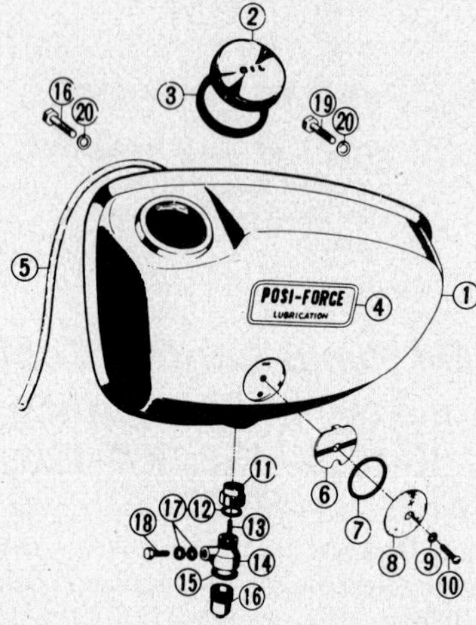

Oil tank components showing oil screen magnet.

1. Oil tank
2. Oil tank cap
3. Oil tank gasket
4. Oil tank emblem
5. Oil tank breather line
6. Oil level inspection plate
7. Oil level inspection lens O-ring
8. Oil level inspection lens
9. Oil level inspection lens gasket
10. Cross head screw
11. Outlet joint nut
12. Outlet gasket
13. Strainer net
14. Outlet
15. Strainer cup gasket
16. Strainer
17. Union bolt gasket
18. Union bolt
19. Oil tank fitting bolt
20. Lockwasher

Oil filler and oil level plugs—singles.

Decarbonizing the Exhaust System

1. Remove the screw which holds the muffler baffle into the exhaust pipe and pull out the baffle.

2. Heat the baffle with a propane torch, tapping it against a wooden block or suitable substitute to knock the carbon particles loose.

3. The rest of the exhaust pipe should be reamed out with a stiff wire (such as a coat hanger) or suitable substitute.

ENGINE AND TRANSMISSION

ENGINE REMOVAL AND INSTALLATION

M–31

1. Remove the screws that secure the leg shield and remove the shield.

2. Unbolt the carburetor from the engine and remove it.

3. Remove the shift lever and left crankcase cover.

4. Disconnect and remove drive chain and left frame cover, and disconnect the magneto and spark plug wires.

5. Remove the exhaust system.

6. Remove the engine mounting bolts and carefully lower the engine from the frame.

7. Installation is in reverse order of removal.

CAPACITIES

Model	Fuel Tank liter/gal	Oil Tank liter/pt	Gearbox cc/pt	Fork Oil cc per leg	Model	Fuel Tank liter/gal	Oil Tank liter/pt	Gearbox cc/pt	Fork Oil cc per leg
A-50, AS-50	6.5/1.7①	1.6/3.4	550/1.2	130	TC-120 all	7.0/1.8	1.4/3.0	800/1.7	175
AC-50	6.4/1.5	1.2/2.5	550/1.2	N/A	T-125 all	7.0/1.8①	1.4/2.9	850/1.8	130
TS-50R	6.5/1.7	1.6/3.4	700/1.5	123	TC-125	7.0/1.8	1.1/2.4	550/1.2	185
F-50 all	3.2/0.9②	0.8/1.7	450/1.0	—	TS-125	7.0/1.8	1.1/2.4	550/1.2	185
MT-50 all	2.5/0.7	0.8/1.7	550/1.2	—	S-32-2	10.0/2.6⑤	—	1200/2.6	180
M-12, II	6.0/1.6	1.2/2.6	550/1.2	N/A	TS-185	7.0/1.8	1.1/2.4	550/1.2	190
M-15, M-15D	6.0/1.6③	—	550/1.2	—	T-200 (X-5)	12.0/3.2	1.7/3.6	1000/2.2	180
M-31 all	3.5/0.9④	—	670/1.4	—	T-10	10.0/2.6⑤	—	500/1.1	230
K-10, K-11	7.0/1.8①	—	650/1.4	130	T-20 (X-6)	14.0/3.7	2.2/4.6	1000/2.2	220
K-10P, K-11P	6.0/1.6①	1.3/2.8	650/1.4	125	TC-250	10.0/2.6	2.2/4.6	1000/2.2	220
K-15	7.0/1.8①	1.3/2.8	650/1.4	N/A	TS-250, II	8.9/2.4	1.5/3.2	1100/2.4	250
K-15P	6.0/1.6①	1.3/2.8	650/1.4	N/A	TS-250R, J	9.0/2.4	1.1/2.4	700/1.5	255
TS/TC-90	6.0/1.6⑤	1.2/2.6	800/1.7	185	T-250	12.0/3.2⑤	1.8/3.8	1200/2.6	220
RV-90 all	3.3/0.9	0.8/1.7	700/1.5	—	T-305	14.0/3.7	1.8/3.8	1200/2.6	220
A-100, AC-100					T-350	12.0/3.2⑤	1.8/3.8	1200/2.6	220
AS-100	7.0/1.8	1.2/2.6	750/1.6	N/A	T-500	14.0/3.7⑤	1.8/3.8	1200/2.6	220
B-100, P					GT380	15.0/4.0	1.5/3.2	1400/3.0	210
B-105, P	8.0/2.1①	1.3/2.8	800/1.7	N/A	GT550	15.0/4.0	1.5/3.2	1500/3.2	235
KT-120	8.0/2.1③	1.3/2.8	800/1.7	N/A	GT750*	17.0/4.5	1.8/3.8	2400/4.7	N/A

* Cooling system capacity: 17 liters/4.5 gal.
① Including 1.0 liter reserve.
② Including 0.45 liter reserve.
③ Including 1.5 liter reserve.
④ Including 0.5 liter reserve.
⑤ Including 2.0 liter reserve.
N/A—Not available.

PERIODIC MAINTENANCE MOTORCYCLES MANUFACTURED FROM 1963 TO 1967

Service	Mileage Interval	Procedure
Oil Pump	Every 1000 mi.	check operation, adjust control lever
Gearbox Oil	Every 4000 mi.	change
Cylinder Head and Cylinder	Every 4000 mi.	decarbonize head and ports
Muffler baffle and exhaust pipe	Every 4000 mi.	decarbonize
Oil Outlet	Every 2000 mi.	clean outlet strainer cup

MOTORCYCLES MANUFACTURED FROM 1968 TO 1972

Service	Mileage Interval	Procedure
Oil Pump	Every 2000 mi.	check operation, check control lever
Gearbox Oil	Every 2000 mi.	change
Cylinder Head and Cylinder	Every 4000 mi.	decarbonize head and ports
Muffler baffle and exhaust pipe	Every 4000 mi.	decarbonize
Oil Outlet	Every 4000 mi.	clean outlet union filter

M–15 AND M–15D

1. Turn off the fuel tap, disconnect the fuel line, and unscrew the choke plunger and throttle slide caps from the carburetor.
2. Disconnect the air cleaner from the carburetor and drain the transmission oil.
3. Remove the shift lever and left crankcase cover, then disconnect and remove the drive chain.
4. Remove the tool box and disconnect the wires from the D, F, and M terminals of the regulator. Disconnect the neutral light and magneto wires.
5. Remove the kick-start lever and exhaust system.
6. Remove the battery cover, battery and battery holder.
7. Remove the right crankcase cover.
8. Remove the three engine mounting bolts and carefully lower the engine from the frame.
9. Installation is in reverse order of removal.

F–50

1. Remove the ignition switch ring and switch from the fairing by pushing it back behind.
2. Remove the fairing screws, disconnect the turn signal wires and remove the fairing.
3. Unscrew the knob that holds the left frame cover, then remove the cover.
4. Remove the battery holder, disconnect the battery wires and remove the battery.
5. Disconnect the magneto wires at their connector, then unsnap the oil tank strap and push the tank forward to disengage it. Remove the oil line clamp and line.
6. Unscrew the air cleaner nut and remove the air cleaner.
7. Remove the shift lever, engine sprocket cover, and left crankcase cover.
8. Separate the drive chain at the master link.
9. Unscrew and remove the oil pump cover plate and disengage the oil pump cable.
10. Disconnect the kick-start lever and the fuel and vacuum lines.
11. Remove the right cover plate on the crankcase to expose the carburetor. Remove the rubber cap screws and slide the rubber cap up the cables it encloses, then loosen the carburetor clip bolt and remove the throttle slide and choke plunger caps from the carburetor. Swing the carburetor out of its recess and remove it.
12. Remove the exhaust system, drain the transmission oil and remove the engine mounting bolts to allow the engine to be lowered from the frame.
13. Installation is in the reverse order of removal.

A–50 AND AS–50

1. Turn off the fuel tap, disconnect the fuel line, disconnect the spark plug wire and remove the toolbox cover.
2. Remove the battery hold-down strap and battery.
3. Disconnect the magneto wires and remove the shift lever.
4. Remove the exhaust system.
5. Remove the engine sprocket cover and left crankcase cover.
6. Disconnect the drive chain at the master link.
7. Remove the oil pump cover plate and disconnect the cable.
8. Disconnect the oil line from the tank and drain the oil into a container.
9. Remove the right cover plate from the crankcase to expose the carburetor. Disconnect the carburetor as for the F–50.

10, Drain the transmission oil, remove the air cleaner and remove the engine mounting bolts. The engine now can be lowered from the frame.

11. Installation is in the reverse order of the removal procedure.

MT–50

1. Unscrew the seat knob and remove the seat.
2. Loosen the frame cover screws, remove the fuel tank cap and the inlet pipe shroud.
3. Remove the frame cover and muffler shield, then disconnect the oil line from the CCI tank and drain the tank.
4. Disconnect the wiring connectors coming out of the crankcase, remove the air cleaner and the sprocket cover.
5. Disconnect the drive chain at the master link.
6. Remove the oil pump cover plate and disconnect the pump cable.
7. Remove the carburetor, as for the F–50.
8. Remove the exhaust system and drain the transmission oil.
9. Remove the three engine mounting bolts and lower the engine from the frame.
10. Installation is in the reverse order of the removal procedure.

K–10P, K–11P, B–100P, B–105P, KT–120, TC–120, AND TC–125

1.Turn off the fuel tap and remove the spark plug wire.
2. Remove the toolbox cover and disconnect the magneto wires.
3. Remove the shift lever and the reduction box cover on the KT–120, TC–120, and TC–125. Disconnect the reduction linkage on those models so equipped.
4. Remove the left crankcase cover.
5. Disconnect the drive chain at the master link.
6. Remove the carburetor covers and carburetor.
7. Remove the exhaust pipe on K–10P and B–100P; the entire exhaust system on the others.
8. Disconnect the oil line from the Posi-Force tank and drain the oil.
9. Remove the oil pump cover from the right crankcase half and disconnect the pump cable.
10. Disconnect the clutch cable at the hand lever and remove the skid plate on models so equipped.
11. Remove the engine mounting bolts and lower the engine.
12. Installation is the reverse of the removal procedure.

K–10 AND K–11

1. Remove the leg shield bolts and turn off the fuel tap.
2. Remove the left carburetor cover and disconnect the fuel line, choke cable, throttle cable, and vacuum line.

3. Remove the shift lever and left crankcase cover.

4. Disconnect the drive chain at the master link.

5.Remove the exhaust pipe and muffler.

6. Drain the transmission oil and remove the kick-start lever and air cleaner.

7. Disconnect the magneto wires and remove the engine mounting bolts.

8. Remove the two front downtube bolts, swing the downtube out of the way and lower the engine from the frame.

9. Installation is the reverse of the removal procedure.

TC–90, TS–90, A–100, AND AS–100

1. Turn off the fuel tap and disconnect the fuel line.

2. Disconnect the spark plug wire and remove the oil tank cover, oil tank strap and oil line, draining the oil into a container.

3. Disconnect and remove the carburetor as for the F–50.

4. Remove the exhaust system.

5. Disconnect the magneto wires, remove the shift lever and remove the left crankcase cover.

6. Disconnect the drive chain at the master link.

7. Remove the oil pump cover plate and disconnect the cable.

8. Remove the air cleaner and the engine mounting bolts, then lower the engine from the frame.

9. Installation is the reversal of the removal procedure.

RV–90

1. Drain the transmission oil, disconnect the magneto wires, and remove the air cleaner and muffler.

2. Disconnect the fuel line and oil line and drain the oil tank.

3. Remove the carburetor as for the F–50.

4. Remove the shift lever and left crankcase cover.

5. Disconnect the drive chain at the master link.

6. Remove the oil pump cover plate and disconnect the cable.

7. Remove the spark plug wire and the engine mounting bolts, then lower the engine away from the frame.

8. Installation is the reverse of the removal procedure.

TS–125, TS–185, AND TS–250

1. Swing up the seat and disconnect the battery wires.

2. Drain the transmission oil and disconnect the tach cable at the engine.

3. Remove the kick-start lever and disconnect the air cleaner.

4. Disconnect the spark plug wire and remove the left frame cover. Unsnap the oil tank strap and disconnect the oil line, draining the oil into a container.

5. Remove the oil tank and the carburetor, then disconnect the magneto wires and remove the shift lever.

6. Remove the left crankcase cover and disconnect the drive chain at the master link.

7. Remove the oil pump cover and disconnect the cable.

8. Remove the engine skid plate and disconnect the exhaust pipe spring.

9. Remove the exhaust system and the engine mounting bolts, then lower the engine from the frame.

10. Installation is the reverse of the removal procedure.

T–125

1. Turn off the fuel tap and remove the fuel lines and vacuum line.

2. Lift the seat, remove the tank bolt and disconnect the generator wires.

3. Remove the exhaust pipes and the battery.

4. Remove the shift lever and the left crankcase cover.

5. Disconnect the clutch cable at the hand lever.

6. Remove the drive chain and engine sprocket.

7. Disconnect the tach cable and oil pump cable.

8. Disconnect the oil line from the oil tank and drain the oil from the tank.

9. Disconnect the plug wires and remove the throttle slides from the carburetors. Drain the transmission.

10. Disconnect the air cleaner hoses from the carburetors.

11. Remove the engine mounting bolts and lower the engine from the frame.

12. Installation is the reverse of the removal procedure.

ALL OTHER TWINS

1. Disconnect the spark plug wires, remove the left frame cover (toolbox) and disconnect the generator wires

2. Remove the front footpegs.

3. Disconnect the exhaust pipes from the engine, then remove the left and right mufflers.

4. Remove the kick-start and gearshift levers.

5. Remove the engine sprocket cover, and disconnect the drive chain at the master link.

6. Disconnect and remove the brake light switch.

7. Remove the oil pump cover and disconnect the pump cable and tach cable.

8. Disconnect the CCI tank oil line and drain the tank.

9. Drain the transmission oil.

10. Disconnect the carburetor air cleaners and throttle slide caps, pulling the caps up and away from the carbs.

11. Disconnect any engine support bolts and the S-32 front support.

12. Loosen the rear swinging arm pivot bolt and remove the engine mounting bolts, then lift the engine sideways out of the frame.

13. Installation is the reverse of the removal sequence.

GT380

1. Shut off the fuel petcocks and disconnect the lines at the petcock.

2. Remove the gas tank; disconnect the spark plug leads.

3. Disconnect the leads for the alternator and for the ignition contact breakers.

4. Disconnect the oil line at the tank.

5. Remove the left side carburetor, the air cleaner assembly, and then the right and center carburetors.

6. Remove the oil pump cover and disconnect the oil pump control cable at the pump.

7. Remove the tachometer cable and the brake light switch assembly.

8. Remove the right front footpeg, rear brake pedal, exhaust pipe clamps, passenger footpegs, and right and left exhaust pipes.

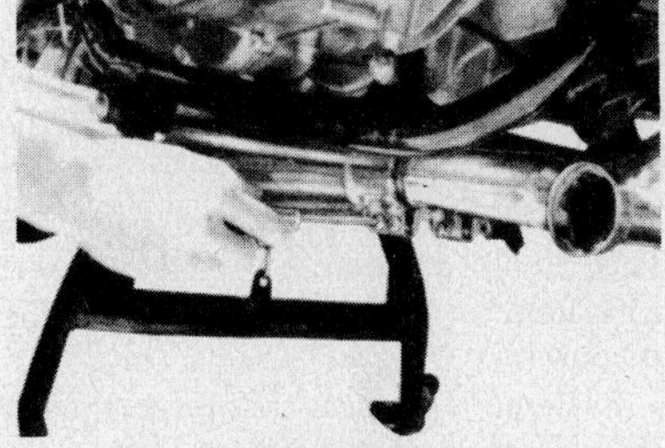

Disconnecting muffler clamp.

9. Loosen the clamps which hold the two center mufflers to the center exhaust pipe and then remove the mufflers, and the center exhaust pipe.

10. Remove the left front footpeg, shift lever, and engine sprocket outer and inner covers.

11. Remove the engine sprocket and chain assembly.

12. Remove the Ram-Air cover; remove the engine mounting bolts and plate; then take the engine out through the right side of the frame.

Engine mounting bolts.

13. Installation is the reverse of the removal procedure. The engine may be temporarily suspended on the frame by inserting a steel bar or screwdriver through the mounting points. Torque the mounting bolts to specifications.

The joints between the exhaust pipes should be sealed with some heat-resistant material such as Silicon Seal.

GT550

1. Shut off the fuel taps and disconnect the fuel lines at the tap.
2. Remove the gas tank.

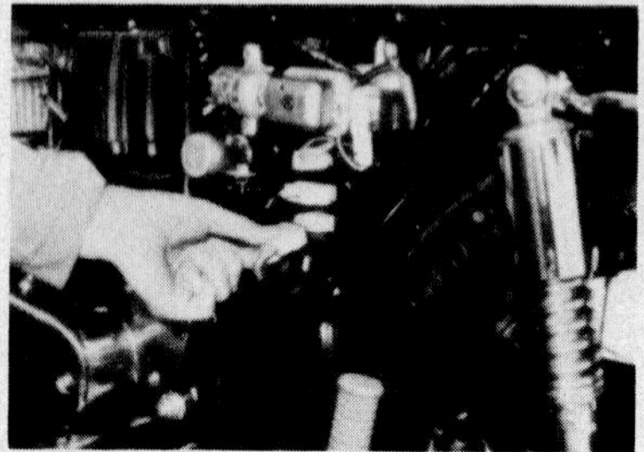

Disconnecting alternator leads.

3. Disconnect the battery ground cable, the spark plug leads from the plugs, and the lead wire from the contact breaker points; disconnect the brake light switch.
4. Disconnect the tachometer and oil pump cables, the starter motor, and the alternator leads.
5. Disconnect the oil line from the tank. Remove the brake pedal.
6. Remove the air cleaner, then the carburetors.
7. Remove the gear shift lever, the left front footpeg, the clutch release mechanism cover, and the countershaft sprocket cover.
8. Remove the sprocket fitting plate by removing the three bolts, turning the plate half the pitch of the splines, and taking off the shaft.
9. Pull the sprocket off of the shaft. It is not necessary to disconnect the master link. Place the sprocket and chain out of the way.
10. Remove the Ram-Air cover.
11. Remove the left and right passenger footpegs.
12. Remove the right and left mufflers, then loosen the clamps on the center mufflers and remove them. Remove the center exhaust pipe.
13. Remove the engine mounting bolts, and the engine mounting plate, and take the engine from the frame on the right side.
14. Installation is in the reverse order of removal. Torque the mounting bolts as per specification.

The joints between the exhaust pipes should be sealed with some heat-resistant material such as Silicon Seal.

GT750

1. Drain the cooling system by loosening the water drain plug at the front, center of the engine.
2. Disconnect the starter motor lead from the battery terminal.
3. Shut off the fuel taps, disconnect the gas lines at the taps, and remove the gas tank by disconnecting it from the setting band and sliding it backward off its mounts.

Removing the fan assembly.

4. Disconnect the radiator inlet hose and remove the fan assembly.
5. Remove the exhaust pipe clamps, rear footpegs, mufflers, and the exhaust pipe coupler tubes.
6. Remove the left side cover which will expose the electrical connections. Disconnect the alternator and contact breaker leads (1 and 2), the starter motor lead (3), and the engine ground wire from the frame.

Electrical connections.

7. Remove the air cleaner assembly by removing the two set bolts located on the frame at the rear of the gas tank, and remove the carburetor clamps.
8. Remove the left side footpeg, shift lever, and engine sprocket cover, then the engine sprocket with the drive chain on it. It is not necessary to disconnect the chain.
9. Disconnect the clutch, oil pump, carburetor, and tachometer cables.
10. Remove the right side footpeg and brake pedal assemblies.
11. Remove the engine mounting bolts and plates, then remove the engine from the frame.
12. Installation is in the reverse order of removal. Torque the mounting bolts to specifications.

The joints between the exhaust pipes should be sealed with some heat-resistant material such as Silicon Seal.

UPPER END SERVICE

The cylinder heads, barrels, and pistons can be removed on all models without removing the engine from the frame. Procedures are generally the same for all singles and twins.

Cylinder Head

ALL SINGLES AND TWINS

REMOVAL

1. Loosen the head nuts in a criss-cross pattern, then remove them. On twins, do one head at a time. They are separate units.
2. Tap the head with a rubber mallet to break it free, if necessary, and pull it up and off the studs.

INSPECTION AND INSTALLATION

1. Scrape any carbon deposits from the head and piston crown.
2. Check the spark plug threads to be sure that they are free of carbon particles after cleaning the head.

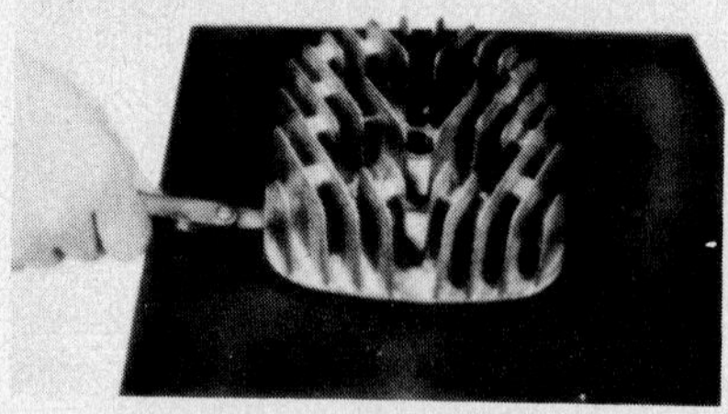

Checking cylinder head warpage with a feeler gauge.

3. Check the head for warpage by placing it on a flat surface. To lap, if necessary, coat a piece of glass or another flat, smooth surface with valve lapping compound or cover it with a piece of 400 grit wet and dry sandpaper and grind the head against it. Maximum permissible warpage is 0.0015 in.
4. Clean the head-barrel mating surface thoroughly and refit a new head gasket; refit the head and torque it to the proper value.

Cylinder and Piston

ALL SINGLES AND TWINS

REMOVAL

1. Remove the head or heads as described in the previous section.
2. Turn the piston(s) to bottom dead center.

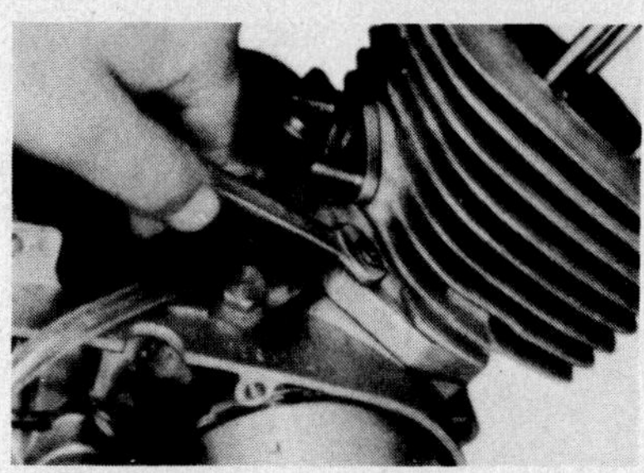

Some models have the cylinder bolted separately to the crankcase.

3. Remove the cylinder hold-down nuts, if present, and lift the cylinder straight up.

4. Remove the piston if desired by removing the piston pin circlips. Heat the piston crown gently, and push out the wrist pin.

INSPECTION

1. Measure the cylinder bore at three places in the bore: ¼ in. from the top of the barrels; ¼ in. from the top of the exhaust port; and 3/16 in. from the bottom of the intake port; all measurements should be in the same plane of reference.

Maximum accepatable bore taper is 0.002 in. If the cylinder is bored or honed, the edges of the ports must be chamfered.

Chamfering the edges of the ports can be accomplished with either a file or hand grinder and should conform to the specifications given in the accompanying illustration.

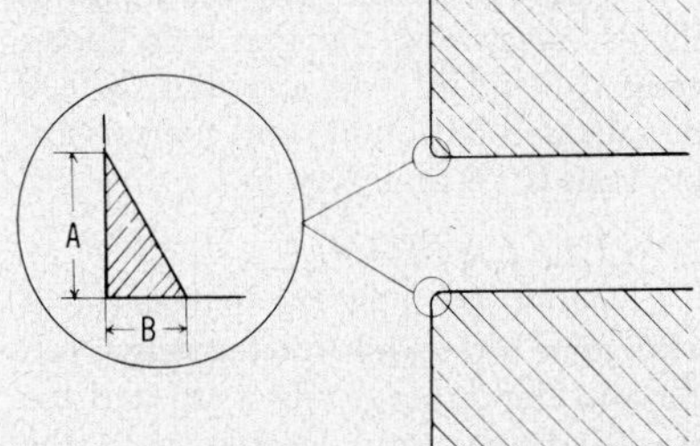

Port chamfering dimensions. A: 0.039-0.095 in. (1.0-1.5 mm); B: 0.012-0.016 in. (0.3-0.4 mm).

2. Remove any glaze on the cylinder walls with 400 grit emery paper or crocus cloth. Wash out thoroughly with kerosene or gasoline.

3. Remove all carbon deposits from the exhaust port.

4. Check the piston for scoring or signs of wear, especially around the piston pin.

5. Remove the rings and clean out the ring grooves.

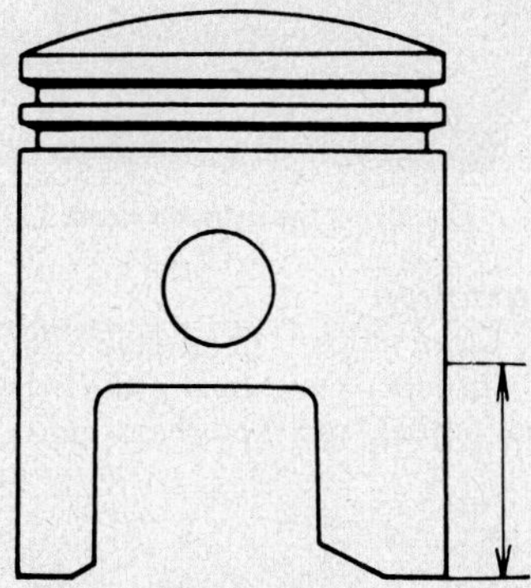

Measure piston diameter at the specified distance above the bottom edge of the skirt. See the specifications chart at the end of this chapter.

6. Referring to the accompanying illustration, measure the piston diameter at the location shown, comparing this value to the acceptable clearances shown at the end of this chapter.

7. Before refitting the rings, whether new or used, check the end-gap by inserting them in the cylinder (using the piston to align the ring properly as shown) and using a feeler gauge. If the gap is larger than the standard value (see specifications chart), replace them. If the end-gap value is smaller than standard, the ring ends should be filed.

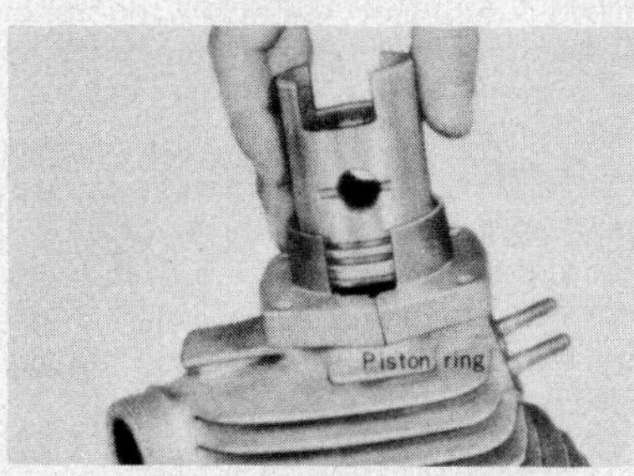

Pushing the ring into the cylinder with an inverted piston to check ring end gap.

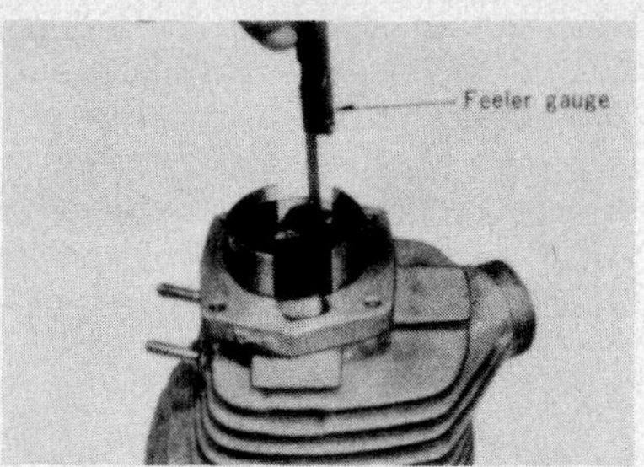

Measuring ring end gap.

INSTALLATION

1. Install the piston rings on the piston, assuring that they are of the correct size and type. Note that the piston has a ring locating pin in the ring groove. The ring must not be placed over the pin. "Keystone" type rings must be installed as shown in the illustration.

Piston ring locating pin.

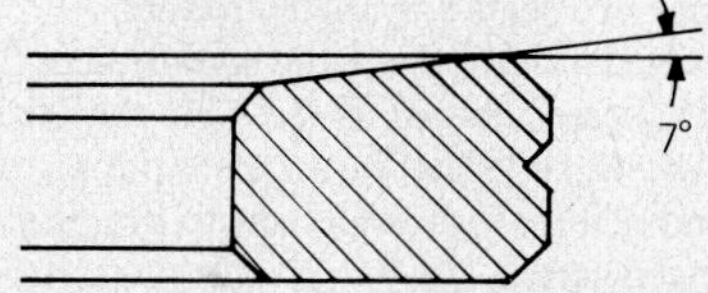

Correct installation of keystone type ring.

Letters "R," "NR," or "T," indicate the to of the ring. Some rings are marked "STD" indicating that they are standard in size.

Oversized rings are marked "50" for the first oversize (0.5 mm), "100" for the second oversize (1.0 mm), and "150" (1.5 mm) for the third oversize. Some models use expanders on the bottom ring.

2. Before refitting the piston, check the connecting rod small end bearing. The needle cage type should slip out of the rod. Bushing type bearings must be pressed out with a hand vise and sockets.

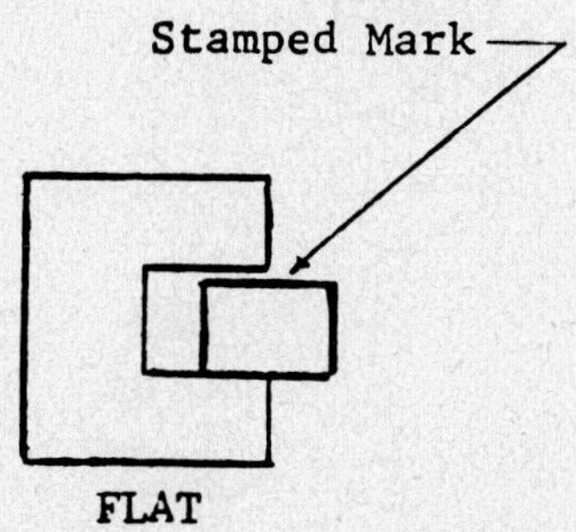

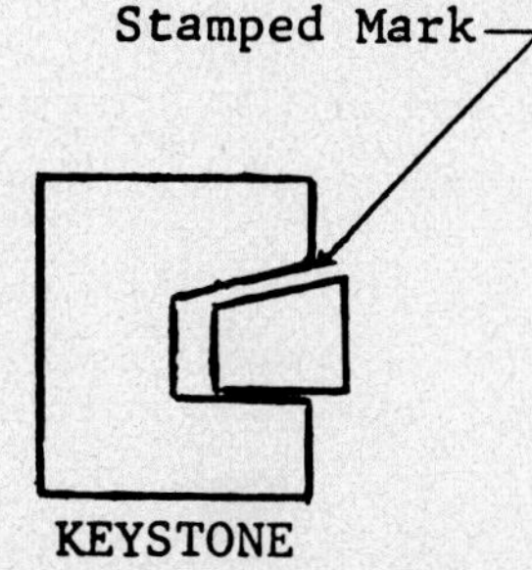

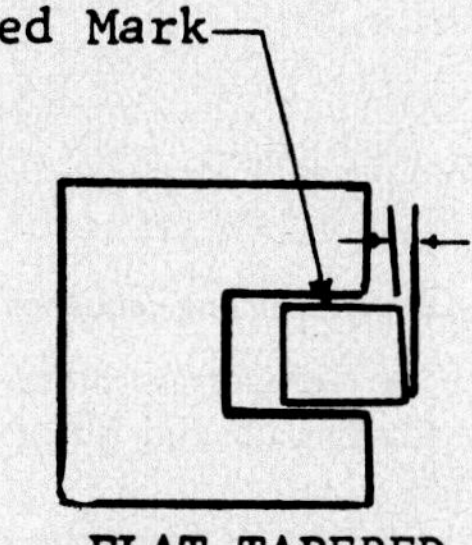

The three types of rings used on Suzuki models.

Place the piston pin into the bearing. There should be no more than about 0.-0015 in. play.

3. Check the crankshaft big end by shaking the connecting rod from side to side. Maximum allowable side play is 0.-118 in. (3.0 mm) measured at the small end of the rod.

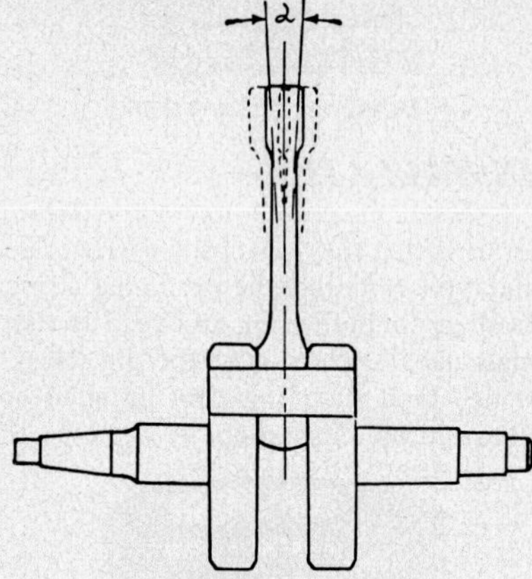

Connecting rod side-play is an indication of big end bearing condition.

4. Install the piston with the arrow on the crown pointing toward the exhaust port. Some TM–250 pistons have no arrow; install these with the notch in the wrist pin hole facing the rear of the engine. Install new circlips and assure that they are seated in their grooves.

5. Carefully check the condition of the crankcase mating surface. Fit new base gaskets, slide the barrel over the piston, and seat it. Torque all bolts to the proper specification.

Cylinder Head And Barrels

GT380, GT550

REMOVAL

1. Loosen the head nuts, in the order shown in the accompanying illustration, and remove the head.

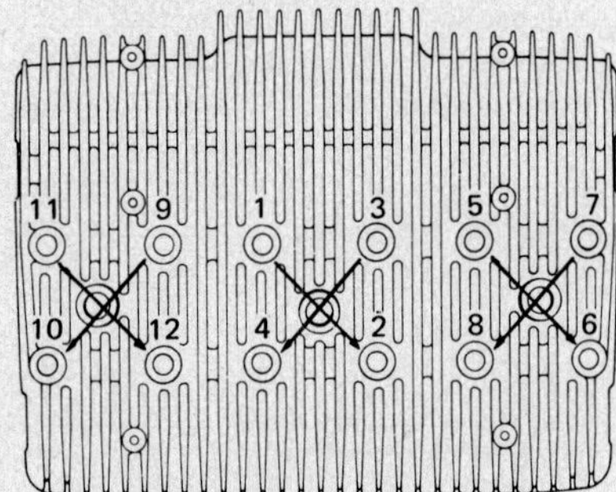

Cylinder head nut loosening sequence.

2. Remove the cylinder assemblies by lifting them straight up and off of the mounting studs.

3. Remove the pistons from the connecting rods by taking off the circlips and pressing out the piston pins.

Removing the cylinder head.

Inspection

1. Clean all parts in a suitable solvent and dry them. Decarbonize the cylinder head, pistons, and the exhaust ports.

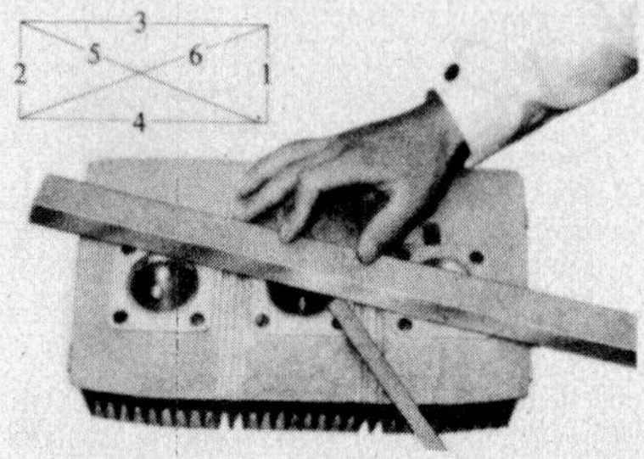

Checking cylinder head for warpage.

2. Check the cylinder head for warpage using the method outlined in the "Singles and Twins" section. Maximum allowable warp on any individual head is 0.03 mm, no more than 0.1 mm warp relative to the other heads, and no more than 0.15 mm level difference of the whole unit. Check for discrepancies along the axes depicted in the accompanying illustration.

3. Measure the cylinder bores at three places: 6 mm (0.24 in.) below the upper surface of the cylinders, 5 mm (0.20 in.) below the inlet port, and 5 mm (0.20 in.) above the exhaust port, in the same plane. Then take the same measurements in a plane 90° from the first.

If there is 0.1 mm (0.004 in.) difference between the largest and smallest measurements, the cylinder should be rebored.

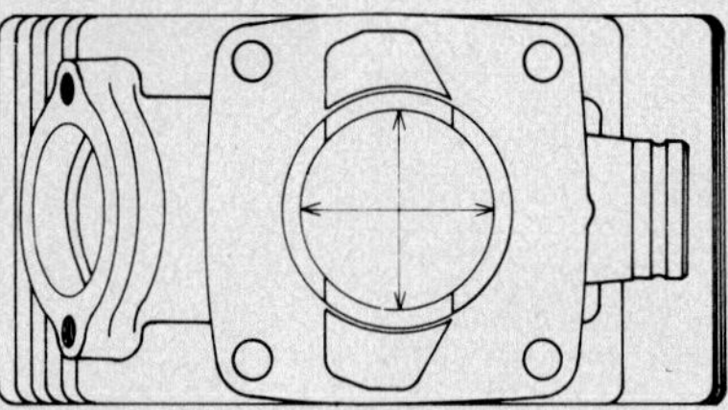

Cylinder bore measurement planes.

All cylinders must be taken out to the same dimensions.

After boring or honing, chamfer the edge of each port.

Oversized pistons and rings are available in 0.5 and 1.0 mm.

4. Inspect the piston pin for wear.

5. Inspect the piston for score marks. Diameter is measured at a point 20 mm (0.79 in.) below the crown, and 26 mm (1.02 in.) from the base of the skirt, perpendicular to the piston pin.

Clearance between the piston and the cylinder wall should not exceed 0.045 mm (0.0018 in.).

Measuring piston ring end gap.

6. Measure piston ring end-gap as shown, measuring the gap with feeler gauges. Standard end gap is 0.15–0.35 mm (0.0059–0.0138 in.) and the serviceable limit is 1.0 mm (0.04 in.).

INSTALLATION

1. Mount the rings. The bottom ring is a keystone type, while the top ring is flat. Be sure the lettered side is up and the ring ends correctly located with the locating pin in the groove.

2. Replace all circlips and gaskets.

3. Install the pistons on the rods so that

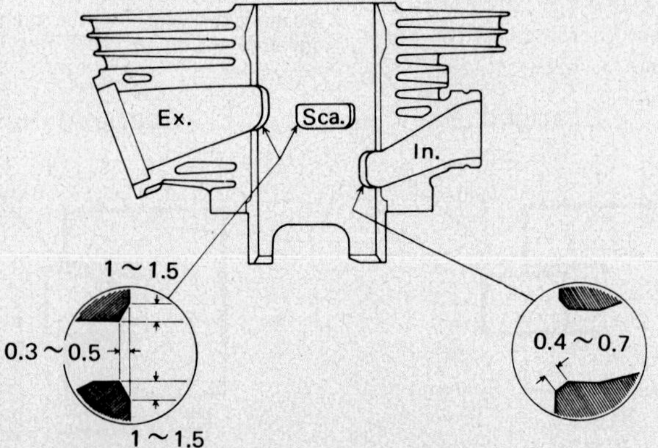

Port chamfering dimensions (mm).

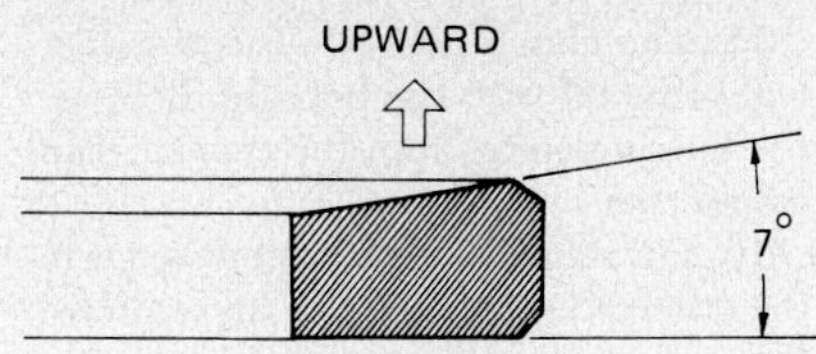

Proper position of wedge-type piston ring.

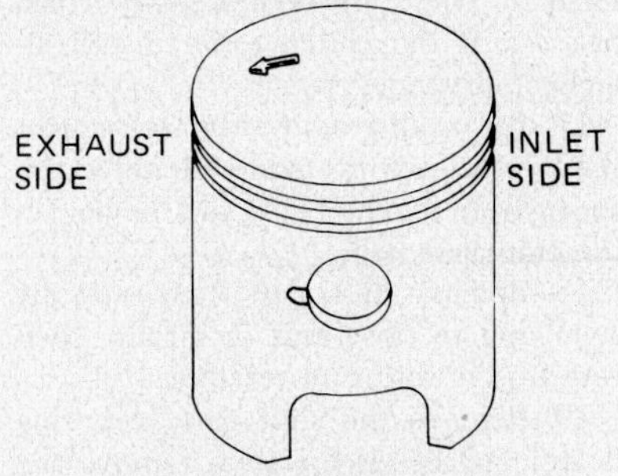

Piston position when installed.

the arrow stamped on the piston crown points toward the exhaust pipe.

4. Use ring compressors if necessary, and slide the cylinders down over the pistons.

5. Torque the head to 18–29 ft lbs in the order shown in the accompanying illustration.

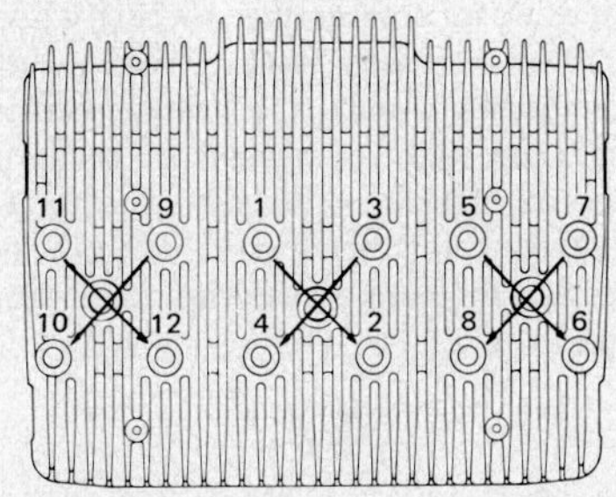

Cylinder head nut tightening sequence.

6. When installing the carburetor inlet pipes on the cylinder, be sure the notch "C" aligns with the cylinder rib "D" so that points "A" and "B" will engage correctly.

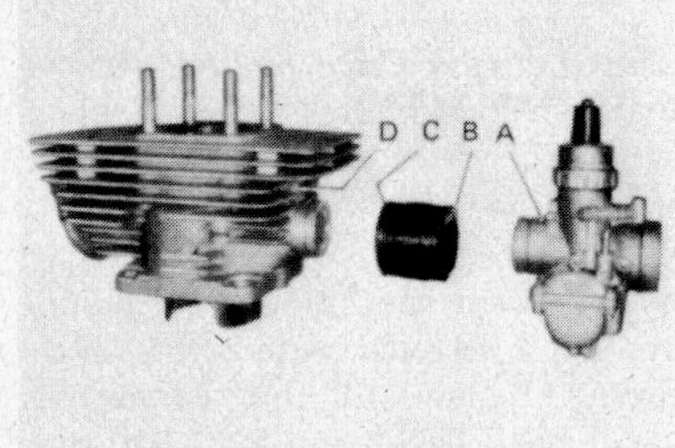

Installation of carburetor and intake pipe.

7. The remainder of assembly is the reverse of the disassembly procedure. When installing the exhaust pipes, allow 1–2 mm (0.04–0.08 in.) clearance between the cylinder and the exhaust pipe clamp.

GT750

DISASSEMBLY

1. Drain the cooling system by loosening the water drain plug, then disconnect the fuel line, remove the gas tank, and disconnect the radiator inlet hose and the water by-pass hose.

Radiator inlet hose.

2. Loosen the cylinder head mounting bolts evenly in the order shown, then remove the cylinder head.

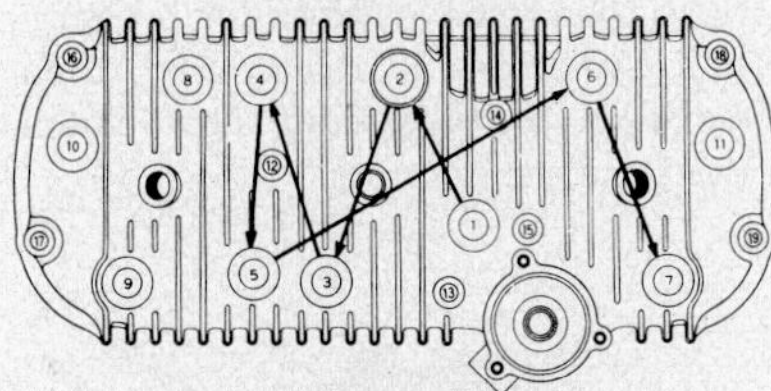
Head bolt loosening order.

3. Loosen the exhaust pipe clamps; take off the air cleaner and loosen the carburetor fitting clamps, then remove the carburetors.

4. Remove the SRIS lines from the cylinder, remove the cylinder set nut, and lift the cylinder block free.

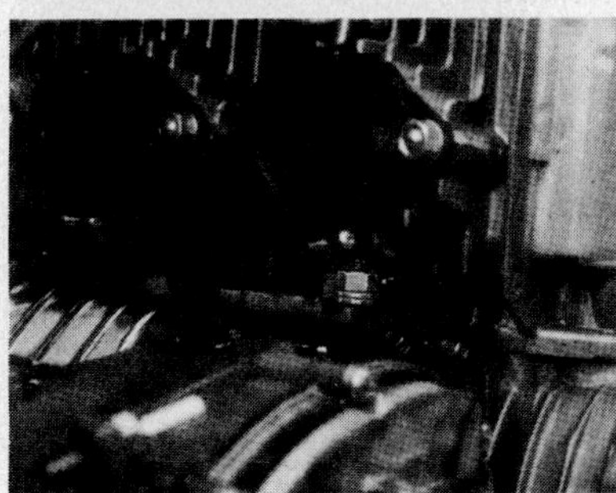
Cylinder set nut.

5. Take out the piston circlips, push out the piston pins, and remove the pistons.

INSPECTION

1. See inspection procedures for the GT380 and GT550.

2. Measure the cylinder block for warpage. If warped more than 0.05 mm (0.002 in.) it must be repaired or replaced.

3. Rebore the cylinders if any of them exceed the 70.00–70.015 mm (2.7559–2.7565 in.) standard by 0.07 mm (0.0018 in.) or more.

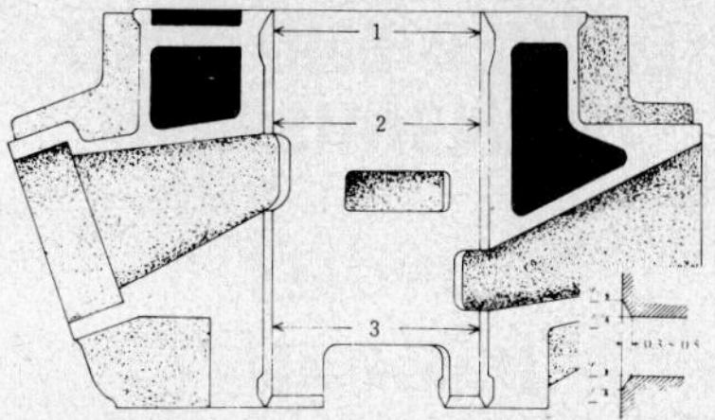

Cylinder measuring points and port chamfer dimensions.

4. Measure the pistons at the following point: 32 mm (1.26 in.) from the base of the skirt, perpendicular to the piston pin. The servicable limit of wear is 0.045–0.055 mm (0.0018–0.0022 in.) from the standard value.

5. Measure the piston/cylinder wall clearance. It should not exceed 0.070 mm (0.0018 in.).

6. Measure the piston ring end-gap and replace the ring if it is worn past the servicable limit of 0.7 mm (0.0027 in.).

7. Measure the side clearance of the ring in its groove and replace the piston if this measurement exceeds 0.095 mm (0.004 in.).

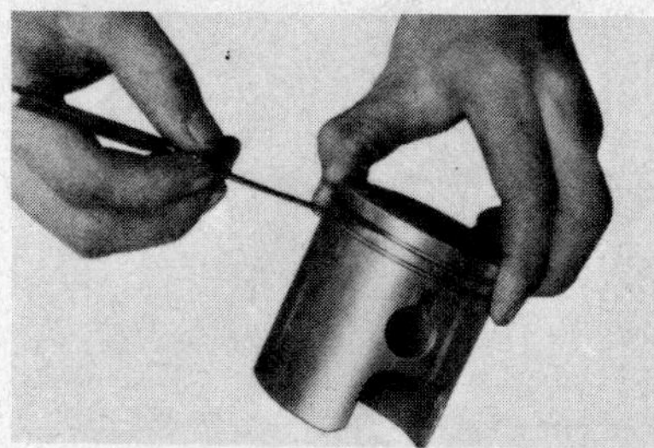
Measuring piston ring side clearance.

INSTALLATION

1. Installation is the reverse of the disassembly procedure.

2. Make sure the piston with the "R" mark is fitted on the right side, and the "L" marked piston on the left side.

3. Remember to secure the cylinder set nut.

4. Torque the 8 mm bolts and nuts to 13.0–15.9 ft lbs; and 10 mm bolts to 21.7–29.0 ft lbs.

5. Attach the SRIS pipes to their check valves on the crankcase and on the cylinder block.

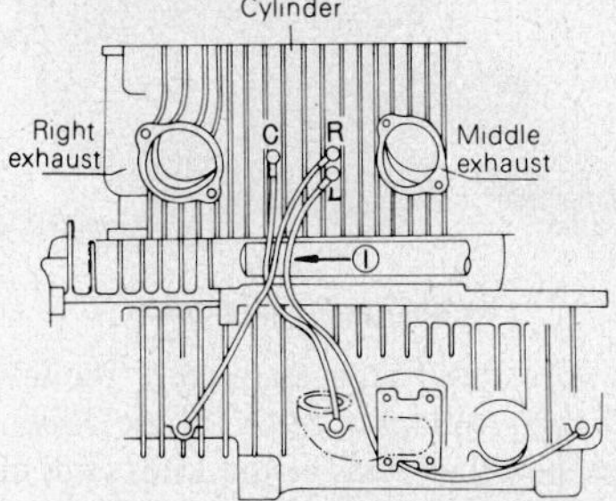

Location of SRIS pipes—GT750.

6. There should be a gap of 1 mm (0.04 in.) between the exhaust pipe clamps and the cylinder.

LOWER END AND TRANSMISSION

SINGLES

Disassembly

1. Remove the engine from the frame referring to "Engine Removal."

2.Remove the cylinder head and barrels and disconnect the piston from the connecting rod.

3. While holding the crankshaft, remove the flywheel rotor nut and rotor, using the proper puller.

4. Remove the neutral indicator switch terminal screw, then disconnnect the switch wire and remove the terminal lug.

5. Remove the stator from the left crankcase, then remove the neutral switch screws and the switch.

Stator mounting screws.

6. Bend back the lock tab on the engine sprocket and remove the sprocket nut.

7. Remove the sprocket, sprocket circlip (if fitted), and the shift lever shaft circlip. Remove the washer and the engine sprocket spacer.

8. On Posi-Force equipped models, remove the two oil pump screws, pull out the pump, and disconnect the inlet and outlet lines at the banjo fittings.

Removing the oil pump.

9. On Posi-Force equipped models, note the positions of the oil lines. Disconnect the other ends of the lines and, on models having a 14 mm check valve, remove the valve from the right crankcase half. Remove the grommet screws and grommets, if fitted, and pull out the oil lines.

10. Remove the kick starter lever after removing the 10 mm bolt.

11. Remove the right crankcase cover plate and its gasket, then the entire right cover.

Removing the right crankcase cover.

12. The clutch is now exposed for service. Using a hook made from a small diameter welding rod, or a suitable substitute, reach in and pull out the clutch release springs. Using needle-nosed pliers, pull out the clutch pins under the springs, then remove the clutch pressure plate. Withdraw the release rod, then remove all the fiber and steel clutch plates from the housing.

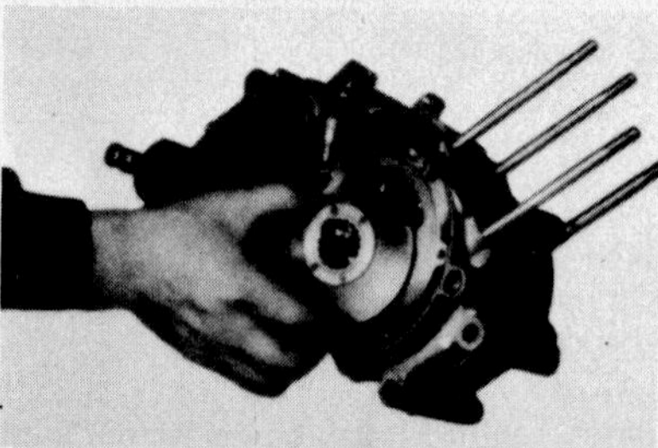

Removing the clutch spring pins.

13. Automatic clutch models have their clutch held in place by the clutch sleeve hub nut and a large snap-ring. Bend back the locktab, remove the nut, then remove the snap-ring from the inner groove in the clutch housing. The clutch plates can now be pulled out and the reaction springs removed with long nose pliers.

14. On standard clutch models, remove the clutch sleeve hub nut lock tab, then the nut. Remove the clutch housing from both automatic and standard clutch models at this time.

Removing the clutch sleeve hub nut.

15. The clutch sleeve hub and spacer will come off with the housing. Remove the housing collar from the transmission countershaft.

16. On standard clutch models, go to the other side of the engine and remove the release screw mechanism and withdraw the pushrods from the hollow countershaft. These are separated by a ball bearing. If the clutch cable is still attached, disconnect it.

17. Pry up and remove the kick-starter shaft return spring guide. Remove the spring from the shaft hole and the hole in the crankcase half.

18. Remove the shift cam stop by removing te pivot nut or circlip, then remove the shift cam retainer.

19. Remove the shift cam stop ring holder bolt or circlip, then remove the shift cam guide.

20. Pull up on the shaft, while pressing down on the shift pawl, then remove the shift stop plate and cam pin.

21. Bend back the primary pinion locktab, then remove the primary pinion nut and pinion.

22. Remove the woodruff keys from the crankshaft, then remove the rotary valve (if fitted), outer valve seat, and O-ring using an automotive steering wheel puller or by gently tapping with a soft-faced mallet. Usually, the primary pinion spacer and right crankshaft oil seal will come off with the valve seat. The rotary valve and valve spring guide can now be removed by hand, as can the guide positioner.

Removing the rotary valve.

23. On rotary valve models, remove the 16 mm (long) phillips screws that hold the inner valve seat, then remove the inner seat from the crankcase.

24. Using a phillips blade in an impact driver, loosen the crankcase joining screws in a diagonal pattern to prevent warping. Remove all the screws only after they all have been loosened, then place the engine with the right case downward and carefully remove the left crankcase half. This is usually done using a rather complicated puller, but tapping all around the cases with a fiber hammer should do the job. As a last resort, alcohol applied liberally to the joining surfaces will loosen and dissolve the stock Suzuki sealing compound. Non-stock sealers

often can be dissolved using carburetor cleaner.

25. The transmission and crankshaft are now exposed for service. The crank can be removed as a unit by tapping on its end with a fiber or plastic hammer. The reed valve also can be removed from the right case half using a screwdriver.

26. The oil seals in the crankcase halves should be replaced if possible. Using the method illustrated will ensure that the seal surfaces in the aluminum cases will not be damaged.

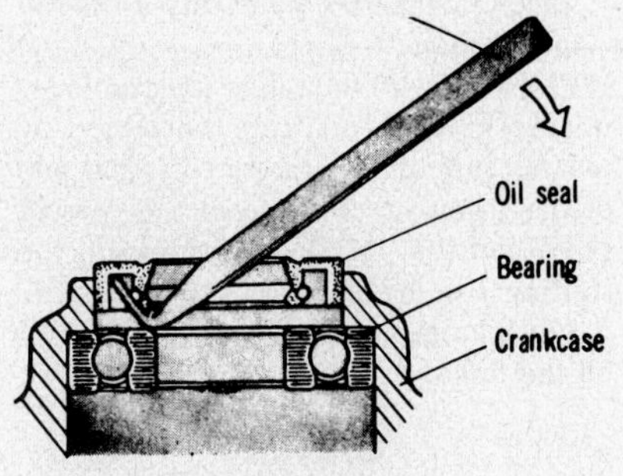

Removing the oil seals.

27. Bearings are a shrink fit in the case halves. To remove any bearing, heat the case around the bearing with a propane torch. The bearing then can be tapped out of its recess.

28. If you're going to replace any transmission parts, remove the snaprings that hold the gears and thrust washers, then remove the countershaft, drive shaft and shift drum. Lay these parts out on a clean surface in the order removed.

INSPECTION

1. The connecting rod side play with the rod moved to the top dead center position can be checked accurately, using a dial indicator preferably. Measured at the small bearing end, maximum side-to-side play is about 3 mm (0.118 in.). Check the up-and-down play of the big end bearing. It should be very small, 0.005–0.022 mm (0.0002–0.0009 in.). If these specifications are exceeded, or if the large end bearing feels rough when spinning the rod, a new bearing and perhaps crankpin is in order.

2. After the crankshaft has been taken care of, liberally lubricate it and its large end bearing with 20W-40 motor oil and set it aside for the moment. A stronger crank and rod assembly is available for the TC/TS-90 and should be installed if possible.

3. Check the left and right crankshaft roller bearings for roughness. When replacing these bearings, heat the cases with a propane torch in the same manner as was done to remove them. The bearings should drop right into place without having to be forced. The right bearing is inserted with its stop ring inside the crankcase and butted tightly against it. The left bearing may have a simple oil ring or be of two piece construction. The oil ring goes on the outside of the case, while two piece jobs are installed with the outer bearing first, then the spacer with its notches facing inward, then the inner bearing with its oil groove inside the case.

4. The driveshaft bushing, if removed, is installed with its holes facing upward into the case notch.

5. Grease the lips of all the oil seals and

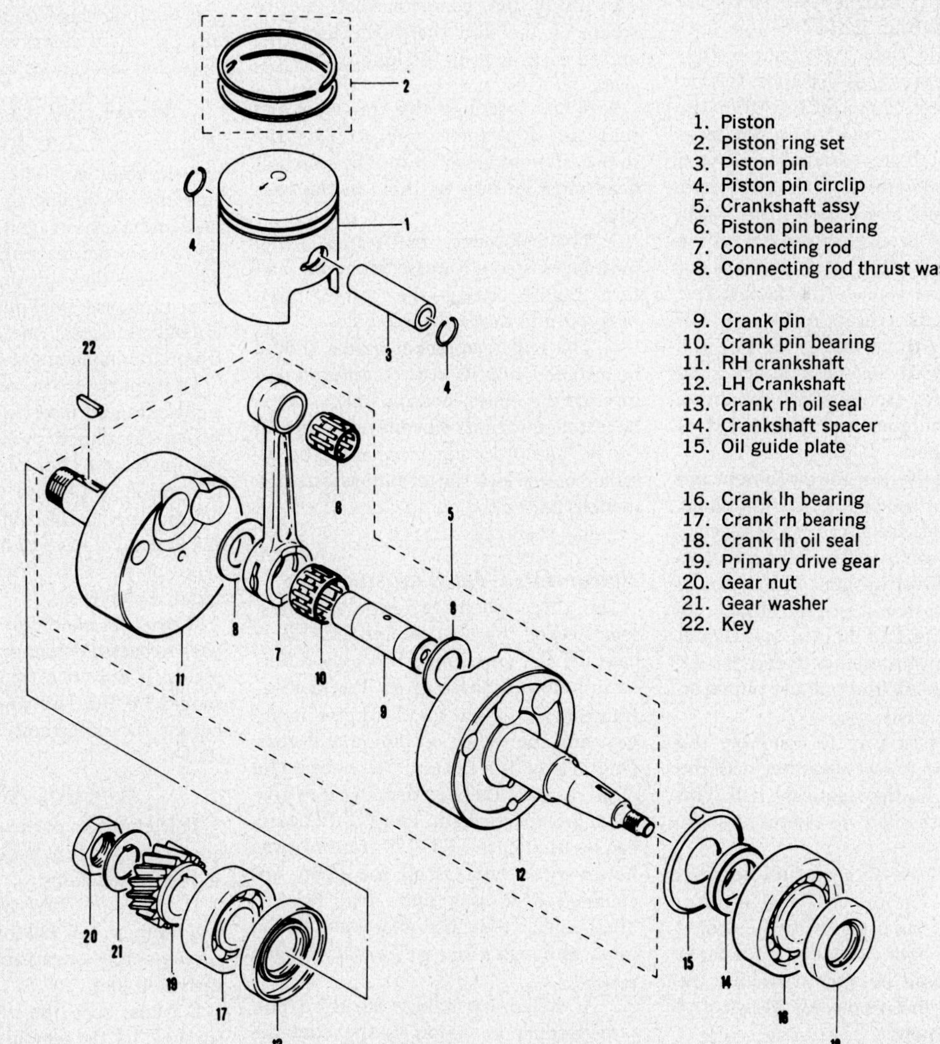

TC/TS-90 crankshaft components.

carefully drive them into place using sockets of the correct diameter as drivers to ensure that they seat correctly.

6. Inspect the transmission parts for wear or damage. The grooves in the shift drum are especially prone to burring, which can be cleaned up with an oilstone if not too bad. Transmission gears missing teeth, or chipped, obviously must be replaced. Replace the snap-rings if possible.

ASSEMBLY

1. Now, using the assembly sequence diagrams in this book as guides, install the rest of the transmission and crankshaft components into the right crankcase half. Observe the following cautions when assembling:

A. Replace all the transmission snap-rings with new ones.

B. Install the top pinion (fourth gear) snap-ring so that its open ends are away from the groove, otherwise the positioning pieces will fall out.

C. Note the thickn\u00e8ss of each thrust washer and install the washers in their proper positions.

D. Before joining the crankcase halves, (ass the Posi-Force oil lines through the right case half, if they were there originally of course. It is virtually impossible to do this after the halves are assembled. For the same reason, install any carburetor air vent lines in the grommets in the crankcase.

E. The kick-starter gear thrust washers must be properly arranged on the shaft, otherwise the case halves will not mate. If you replace the kick-starter shaft for some reason, make sure it is the same part number as the one you had. There are several modified kick-starter shafts, each of which requires a different number and placement of thrust washers.

F. Similarly, note the placement and thickness of the countershaft washers. Some models use a torrington bearing, which is sandwiched between two standard thrust washers. The rollers of this bearing should face the clutch side of the engine, and there always should be a flat thrust washer between its back side and the integral primary pinion on the countershaft.

G. The best way to assemble the transmission gears is together with the shift drum on the right case half. This will ease the job of assembling the cases.

H. Lubricate all gears and bearings with 20W–40 motor oil, then apply a thin coat of gasket shellac to the sealing surfaces of both cases, even if a paper gasket is used on your particular engine, after first removing all traces of the old cement.

2. when the sealer is tacky, join the two case halves. A helper will greatly ease this operation. Tap the crankcase with a fiber hammer to seat it, then install the screws and tighten them in a criss-cross pattern to prevent case warpage. There are no torque specifications for these screws. Spin the shafts to make sure nothing is binding.

3. Check all the oil seals and make sure the lips are facing outward. Running a piece of wire around the seal lip will sometimes pull it out.

4. On rotary valve engines, install the valve inner seat and the rotary valve. The inner valve seat screws should have their entire 16 mm length coated with Loc-Tite or a similar sealer and the excess wiped off when the screws are seated. The valve itself is installed with its timing mark outward and aligned with the guide pin on the crankshaft. Install the valve guide, pinion spacer and outer valve seat. Make sure the O-ring is properly seated. If the pinion spacer is installed after the valve plate, the oil seal lips will be pushed inward and a good gas seal will be impossible. Don't forget the other O-rings that seal the valve.

5. Install the gearshift shaft return spring on the shift shaft. The less bent end faces away from the long part of the shaft.

6. When installing the stop bolt and shift cam stop, don't forget to place the stop washer under the stop. The stop bolt head must go into the hole in the cam stop.

7. The kick-starter shaft return spring must be twisted clockwise about one-half turn before fitting the guide, then plugged into the shaft hole.

8. The engine sprocket spacer should be installed with its least chamfered end inward; the clutch housing spacer must be installed with its oil vent hole inward; the oil pump driving piece must be installed on the kick starter pinion (on some models) before the pump is installed; and the shift shaft clip.

Reduction Gear Transmission

The three-speed, two-ratio transmission used on the KT–120 and TC–120 is basically the same unit. The only difference between these two "Posi-Select" transmissions lies in the third pinion and gear and the reduction pinion and gear. On the later TC–120 unit, the helix angle of these gears has been decreased to give them greater strength. The TC–120 parts can be used in the KT–120 transmission, however, so long as all the gears are changed over as a unit. The TC–125 "Posi-Select" reduction gear is almost the same, although a four-speed transmission is used.

A. When assembling the third pinion/reduction pinion to the countershaft, make sure that the gap in the circlip is centered between the ears of the snap-ring. If this isn't done, the ears can slip out through the gap.

B. When assembling the first/second gear to the driveshaft, make sure the side stamped with a "1" faces the first gear. If the gear is installed the other way, you will have only one gear—first.

C. It's a good idea to cement the selector rod bushing into its driveshaft recess using Loc-Tite. This will correct and prevent any problem of shifting into high range. Make sure to work the selector a lot after doing this or the rod might stick.

Problems with the range selector lever not working often can be corrected by making sure all the washers on each side of the throwout arm are in the correct place and that the detent ramps on the shifting arm are smooth. Also, check the detent plunger for sufficient tension and oil the linkage.

Clutch

Clutch and transmission problems are often very closely related. For this reason, the following trouble-shooting charts are provided, along with a few service notes for the various models.

M–31 AUTOMATIC CLUTCH

A problem which has cropped up with this unit is slipping under load in high gear or during engagement. This unit has no cable or adjustment; therefore clutch adjustment depends on the thickness of the clutch pack steel plates. If there is not enough thickness, the clutch will suffer from late engagement and will slip.

To inspect for this condition, pull the right case and insert a feeler gauge between the clutch steel inner plate and the innermost fiber plate. The standard dimension is 1.4 mm (0.055 in.). If the figure exceeds 1.8 mm (0.071 in.), the thickness will have to be increased. Two types of plates are used for this adjustment, as follows:

If two thin plates are used, place them back to back between any two of the fiber plates. If only one thin plate is used, it should be the last steel plate installed before the outermost fiber plate is installed.

A–100, AS–100

This clutch is particularly sensitive to abuse, and if it slips badly can be saved by the following steps:

1. Use only 20W-40 or straight 30 weight motor oil. Oil that is too thick will prevent full engagement due to the heavy oil film.

2. Make sure the clutch springs are screwed all the way into the clutch hub and are flush with the back side of the hub.

Part Number	Description	Quantity/Unit	Thickness (mm)	O.D. (mm)
21451-02000	Clutch Steel Plate (Standard)	4-6	1.6	100
21451-02701	Clutch Steel Plate (Adjusting)	0-3 (As Required)	1.2	100

If Clearance Is: (mm)	Take Out:	Install:	Reduction (mm)	Clearance Will Be: (mm)
1.8-2.2	2 Standard Plates	3 Adjusting Plates	0.4	1.4-1.8
2.2-2.6	1 Standard Plate	2 Adjusting Plates	0.8	1.4-1.8
2.6-3.0	None	1 Adjusting Plate	1.2	1.4-1.8
More Than 3.0		Replace All Cork Plates		

3. If slipping is still a problem, install S–32 springs. These springs, Part No. 09443–12002, are 0.080 in. shorter than stock and will give more tension.

4. Stake the hub around the springs to prevent them from twisting out; also use Loc-Tite here.

ALL TWINS—CLUTCH RATTLING

With the clutch lever released and the transmission in neutral, a rattling noise will issue from the right crankcase half. Pulling in the clutch will make this noise disappear. If this is your problem, it could be caused by the clutch housing's walking on the transmission countershaft. Wear on the thrust side of the clutch hub causes this situation.

Remove the clutch and disassemble it. Remove the spacer and check its length. Measure the thickness of the clutch housing and subtract from it the spacer length —the difference is the axial play of the housing on the shaft.

Model	Maximum play (in.)	Minimum play (in.)
T-500	0.007	0.002
T-10	0.006	0.004
S-32	0.008	0.004
Others	0.007	0.003

To solve this problem, oilstone the spacer end to bring the figures into the proper relationship. Don't grind this, or the clutch will undoubtedly not release because you overdid it.

Try to pull the primary gear away from the housing. If the rubber dampers allow it to move more than 1/32 in., this could be the problem. The solution is replacement of the housing. Check the oil level and the tightness of the primary pinion nut and clutch hub nut. On the X–6 derived engines, except the T–500, of course, the kick-starter drive gear is on the rear of the clutch housing. The oil grooves in the gear must match the slots in the clutch bearing sleeve, otherwise the thrust face of the housing will wear due to a lack of oil. Check to see that similar oil starvation has not already occurred at the clutch housing bearing. If this seizes on the transmission driveshaft, it will spin in the housing and rattle.

GENERAL CLUTCH INSPECTION

Remove the clutch plates from the housing, as described earlier in this chapter under "Engine Service." The axial play of the clutch housing can be measured as described in the last section. Standard axial play for singles is 0.0039–0.0098 in., the maximum allowable being 0.0118 in.

Check the backlash between the primary pinion and the primary gear fastened to the clutch housing with the housing installed. Use a dial indicator or run a small piece of solder through the gears by rotating them with a wrench, then measure the thickness of the squashed piece of solder. Backlash for all models is 0.0006–0.0027 in., with 0.006 in. being the maximum allowable. To correct for excessive backlash, it will be necessary to replace either the primary pinoin or clutch housing, or both.

Check the thickness and warpage of both the fiber and steel plates—maximum warpage is 0.004 in. for steel plates, 0.016 in. for fiber plates. It's best to replace all the plates at one time if a few are bad.

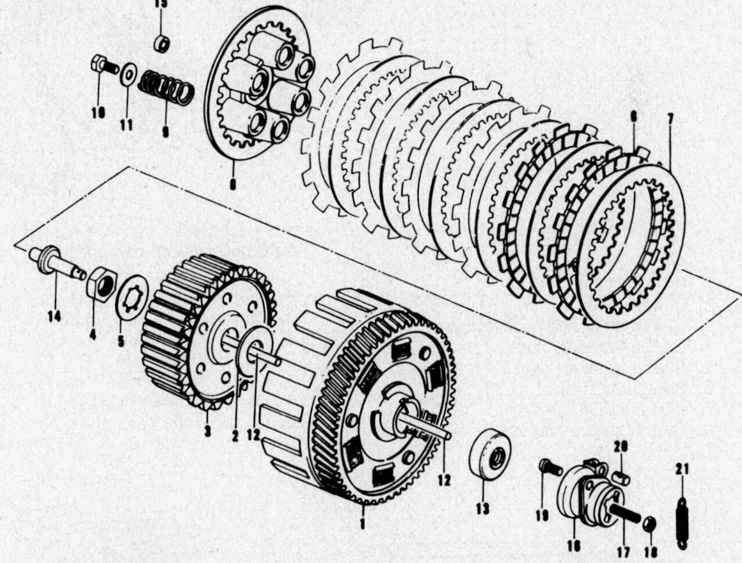

Manual clutch components.

1. Primary driven gear assy
2. Thrust washer
3. Clutch sleeve hub
4. Nut
5. Washer
6. Clutch drive plate
7. Clutch driven plate
8. Clutch pressure disk
9. Spring
10. Bolt
11. Washer
12. Clutch push rod
13. Oil seal
14. Clutch push piece
15. Oil seal
16. Clutch release screw assy
17. Screw
18. Nut
19. Screw
20. Release arm end piece
21. Spring

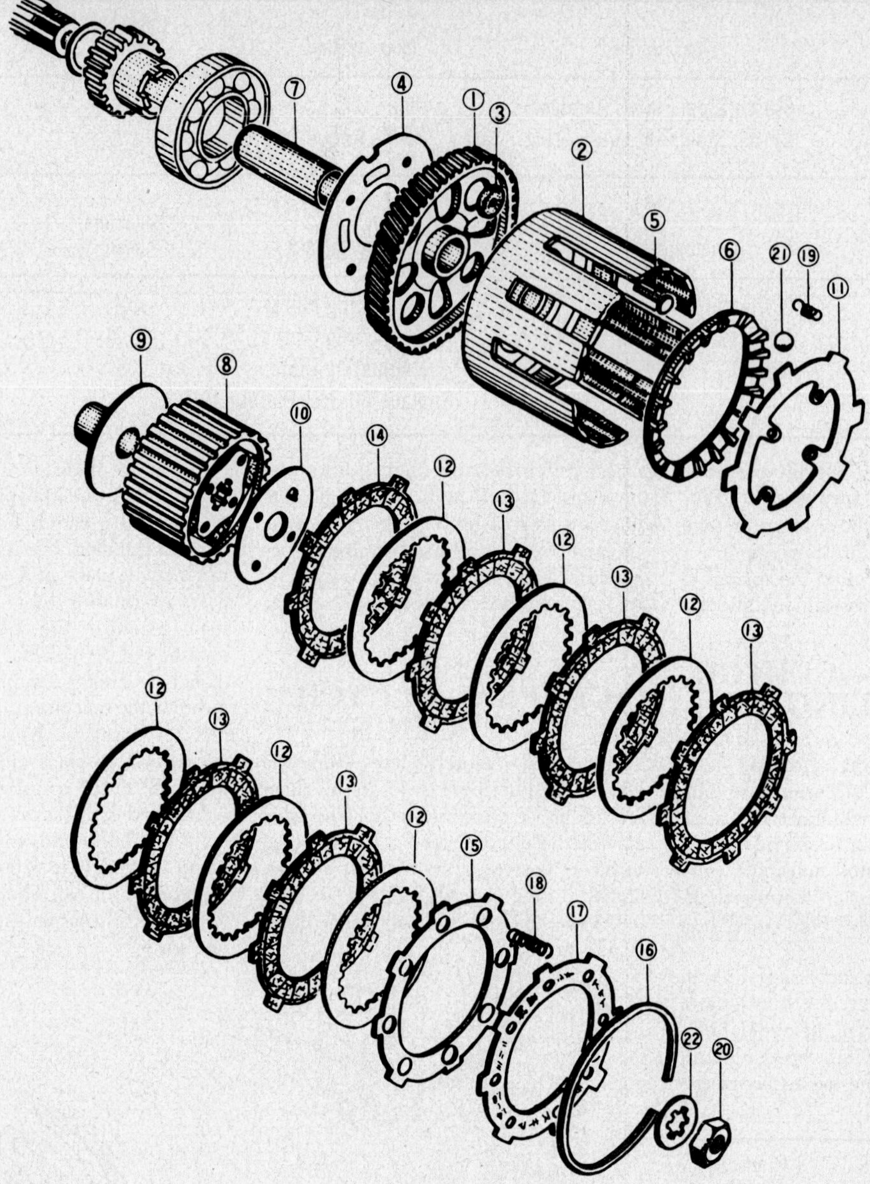

Automatic clutch components.

1. Primary gear
2. Clutch housing
3. Clutch housing shock damper
4. Clutch housing plate
5. Clutch housing rivet
6. Ball guide ring
7. Clutch housing spacer
8. Clutch sleeve hub assy
9. Clutch sleeve hub spacer
10. Clutch sleeve hub retainer
11. Clutch inner plate
12. Clutch steel plate
13. Clutch cork plate
14. Clutch inner cork plate
15. Clutch outer cork plate
16. Clutch outer plate circlip
17. Clutch outer plate
18. Clutch spring
19. Clutch inner plate return spring
20. Clutch sleeve hub nut
21. Steel ball ($1\frac{7}{32}$ in.)
22. Washer

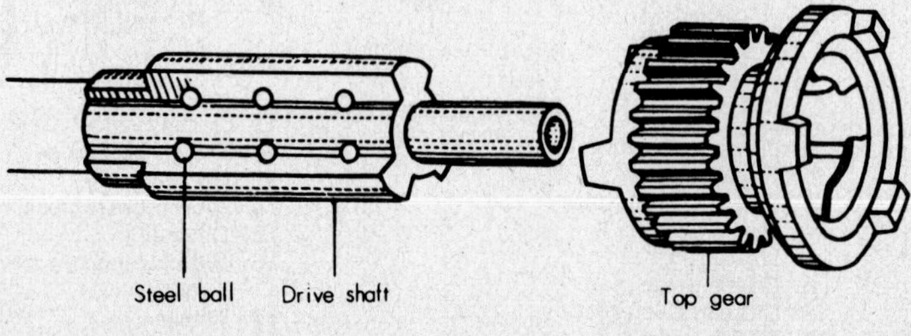

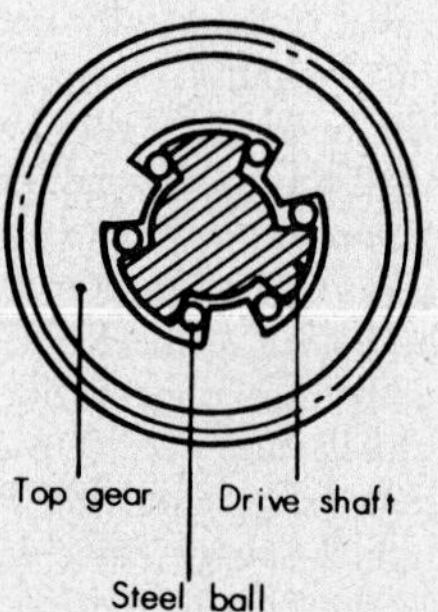

Fitting high gear (automatic clutch models).

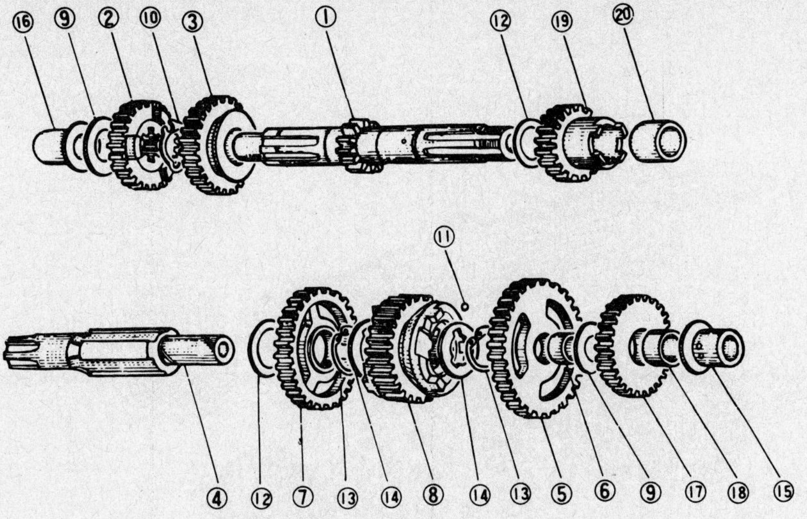

1. Countershaft
2. Second pinion
3. Top pinion
4. Drive shaft
5. Low gear
6. Low gear bushing
7. Second gear
8. Top gear
9. Thrust washer
10. Second pinion circlip
11. Steel ball (5/32 in.)
12. Countershaft thrust washer
13. Top gear washer circlip
14. Top gear washer
15. Drive shaft bushing
16. Countershaft bushing
17. Kick-starter idle gear
18. Kick-starter idle gear bushing
19. Kick-starter gear
20. Kick-starter gear bushing

M-31 transmission components.

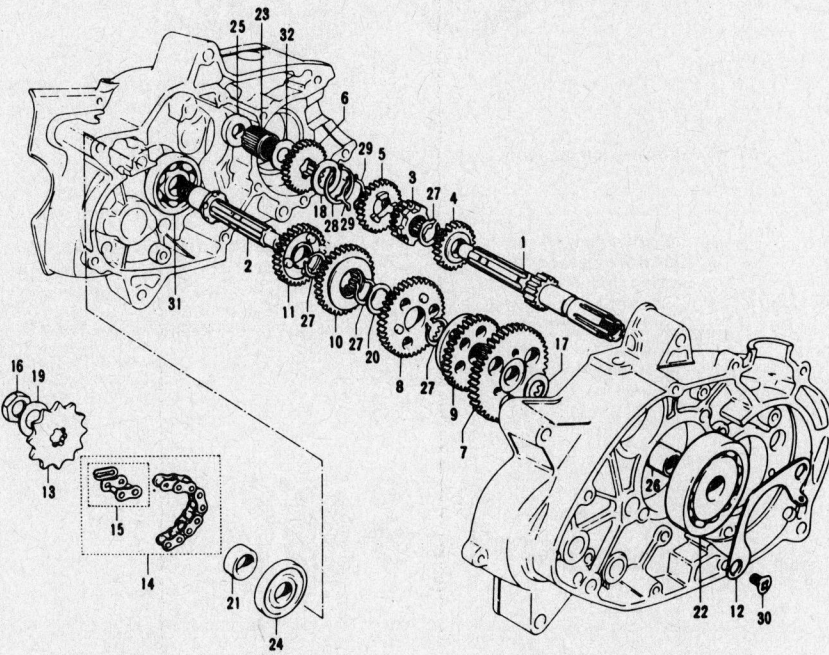

1. Countershaft
2. Drive shaft
3. Second pinion
4. Third pinion
5. Fourth pinion
6. Top pinion
7. Low gear
8. Second gear
9. Third gear
10. Fourth gear
11. Top gear
12. Counter shaft bearing retainer
13. Engine sprocket
14. Drive chain assy
15. Drive chain assy
16. Engine sprocket nut
17. Thrust washer
18. Thrust washer
19. Engine sprocket washer
20. Thrust washer
21. Engine sprocket spacer
22. Counter shaft right bearing
23. Counter shaft left bearing
24. Drive shaft oil seal
25. Push rod oil seal
26. Drive shaft bushing
27. Circlip
28. Circlip
29. Knock ring
30. Cross head screw
31. Ball bearing
32. Thrust washer

A/AS-50 transmission components.

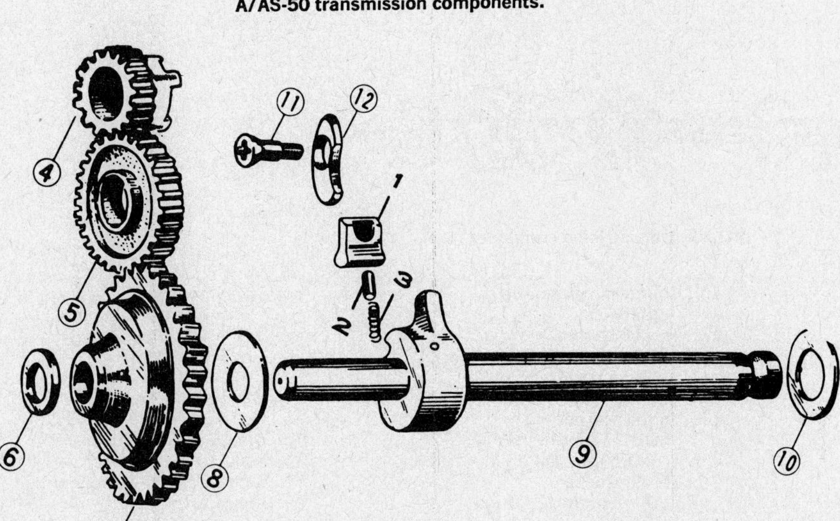

1. Kick-starter pawl
2. Kick-starter pawl roller
3. Kick-starter pawl spring
4. Kick-starter gear
5. Kick-starter idle gear
6. Kick-starter pinion spacer
7. Kick-starter pinion
8. Thrust washer
   OD-30 mm (1.18 in.),
   ID-12 mm (0.47 in.),
   T-1.5 mm (0.05 in.)
9. Kick-starter shaft
10. Thrust washer
    OD-30.5 mm (1.20 in.),
    ID-16 mm (0.62 in.),
    T-1.0 mm (0.04 in.)
11. Kick-starter stopper screw
12. Kick-starter stopper

B-100P kick starter.

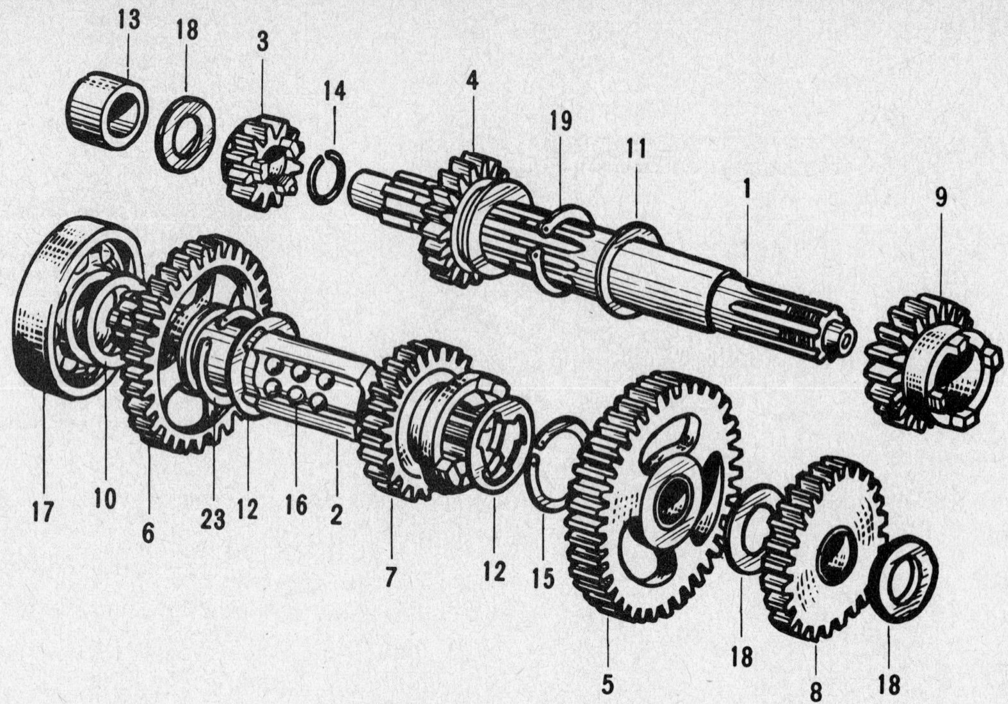

MT-50 transmission components.

1. Countershaft
2. Drive shaft
3. Second drive gear
4. Top drive gear
5. First driven gear
6. Second driven gear
7. Top driven gear
8. Kick idler gear comp
9. Kick driven gear comp
10. Second driven gear thrust washer
11. Countershaft thrust washer
12. Ball washer
13. Transmission shaft bush
14. Second drive gear circlip
15. Ball set ring
16. Steel ball
17. Ball bearing
18. Thrust washer
19. Circlip

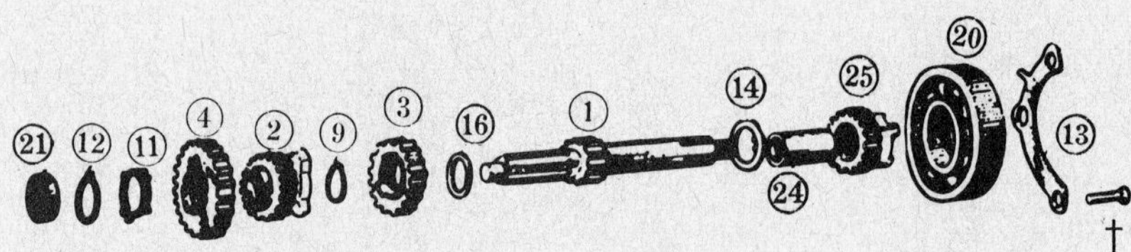

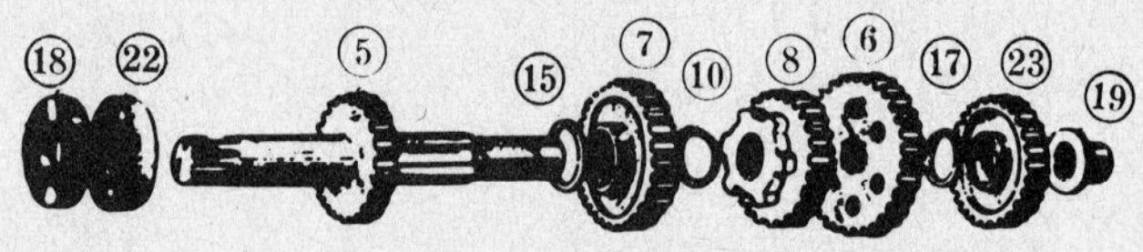

B-100P transmission components.

1. Countershaft
2. Second pinion
3. Third pinion
4. Top pinion
5. Drive shaft
6. Low gear
7. Second gear
8. Third gear
9. Third pinion circlip
10. Second gear circlip
11. Top pinion positioning pieces
12. Top pinion circlip
13. Countershaft bearing plate
14. Thrust washer OD-29 mm (1.14 in.), ID-17 mm (0.67 in.), T-1.0 mm (0.04 in.)
15. Thrust washer OD-27 mm (1.16 in.), T-0.2 mm (0.008 in.)
16. Thrust washer OD-23 mm (0.91 in.), T-1.0 mm (0.04 in.)
17. Thrust washer OD-24 mm (0.95 in.), T-1.0 mm (0.04 in.)
18. Drive shaft oil seal
19. Drive shaft bushing
20. Ball bearing (K10-2483)
21. Ball bearing (JK6001C3)
22. Ball bearing (JK6204C3)
23. Kick-starter idle gear
24. Kick-starter gear bushing
25. Kick-starter gear

† Cross head screw

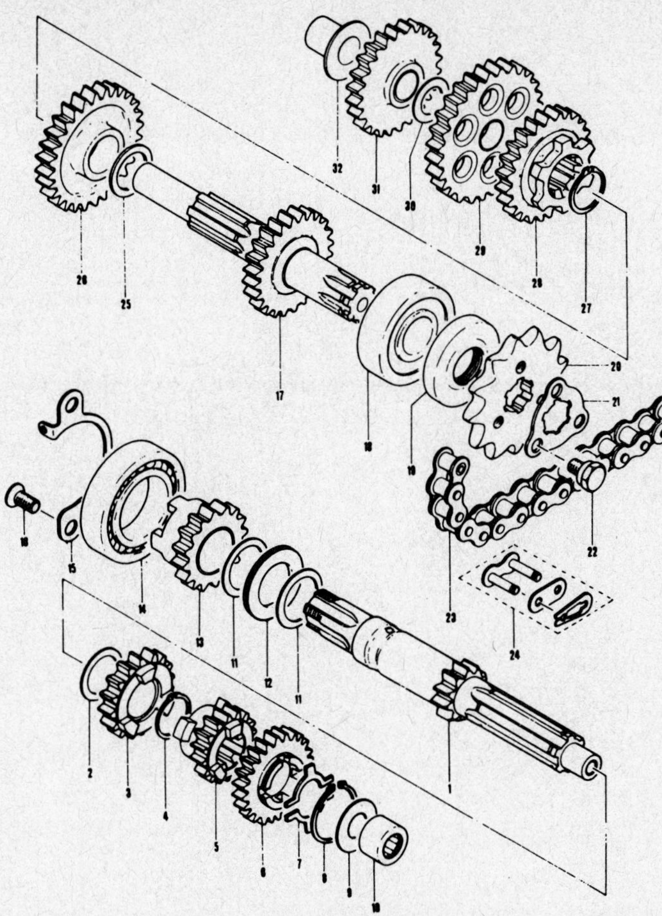

RV-90 transmission components.

1. Countershaft
2. Thrust washer
3. 3rd drive gear
4. Circlip
5. 2nd drive gear
6. 4th drive gear
7. Knock ring
8. Circlip
9. Thrust washer
10. Bearing
11. Thrust washer
12. Bearing
13. Kick-starter driven gear
14. Bearing
15. Countershaft bearing retainer
16. Screw
17. Driveshaft
18. Bearing
19. Oil seal
20. Engine sprocket
21. Engine sprocket plate
22. Engine sprocket bolt
23. Drive chain
24. Drive chain joint
25. Thrust washer
26. 2nd driven gear
27. Circlip
28. 3rd driven gear
29. 1st driven gear
30. Thrust washer
31. Kick-starter idle gear
32. Bushing

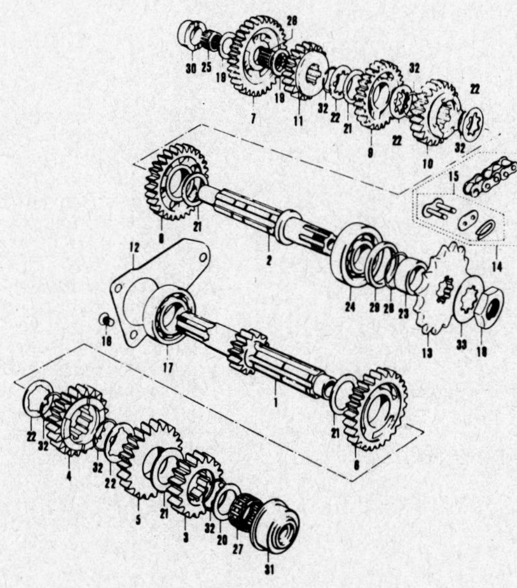

TS-25OR transmission components.

1. Countershaft
2. Drive shaft
3. 2nd drive gear
4. 3rd drive gear
5. 4th drive gear
6. 5th drive gear
7. 1st driven gear
8. 2nd driven gear
9. 3rd driven gear
10. 4th driven gear
11. 5th driven gear
12. Countershaft bearing plate
13. Engine sprocket
14. Drive chain assy
15. Drive chain joint assy
16. Cross head screw
17. Ball bearing
18. Engine sprocket nut
19. 1st driven gear thrust washer
20. Countershaft thrust washer
21. 4th drive gear thrust washer
22. 4th drive gear washer
23. Engine sprocket spacer
24. Drive shaft left bearing
25. Drive shaft right bearing
26. Ist driven gear bearing
27. Countershaft left bearing
28. Drive shaft O-ring
29. Drive shaft oil seal
30. Drive shaft bushing
31. Countershaft bushing
32. 2nd drive gear circlip
33. Engine sprocket washer

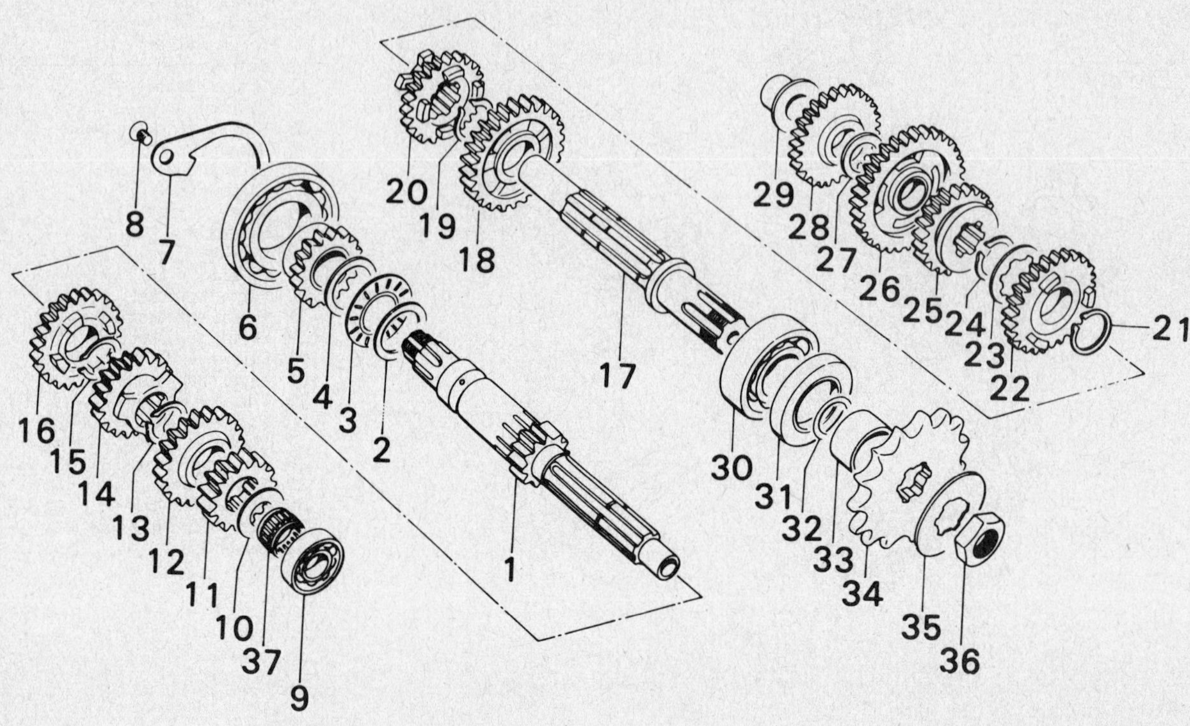

TS-90 transmission components.

1. Countershaft
   L=182.5, N.T.=11
2. Kick-starter drive gear bearing washer O.D.=3, I.D=21, T=0.8
3. Kick-starter drive gear bearing
4. Kick-starter drive gear bearing washer O.D.=30, I.D=21, T=0.8
5. Kick-starter driver gear
   N.T=16
6. Countershaft right bearing
   O.D.=62, I.D.=30, T=1.0
7. Countershaft right bearing fitting plate
8. Countershaft right bearing fitting plate screw
9. Countershaft left bearing
   O.D.=28, I.D=12, T=8
10. Countershaft left bearing wash
    O.D.=20, I.D.=12, T=2.0
11. Second drive gear
    N.T=15
12. Fourth drive gear
    N.T.=20
13. Circlip
14. Third drive gear
    N.T.=18
15. Circlip
16. Top drive gear
    N.T.=23
17. Drive shaft
    L=155
18. Second driven gear
    N.T=28
19. Circlip
20. Fourth driven gear
    N.T.=22
21. Circlip
22. Third driven gear
    N.T=25
23. Third driven gear washer
    T=1.0
24. Circlip
25. Top driven gear
    N.T=20
26. First driven gear
    N.T=31
27. First driven gear washer
    O.D.=24, I.D=15, T=1.0
28. Kick-starter idle gear
    N.T=26
29. Drive shaft bushing
30. Drive shaft bearing
    O.D.=47, I.D=20, T=14
31. Drive shaft oil seal
    O.D=40, I.D.=24.7, T=7
32. Drive shaft bearing O-ring
33. Engine sprocket spacer
    O.D.=25, I.D=20, W=13.5
34. Engine sprocket
    S.T.D, N.T=14
35. Engine sprocket washer
36. Engine sprocket nut
37. Needle bearing

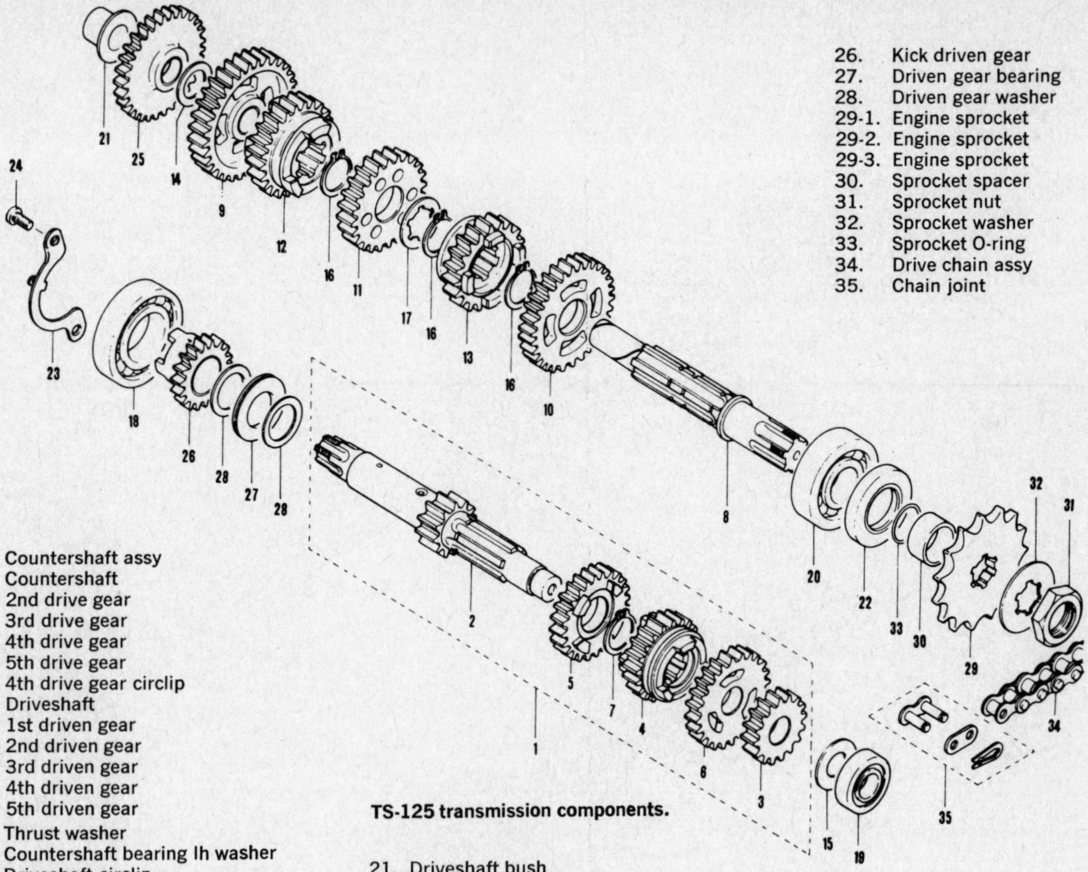

1. Countershaft assy
2. Countershaft
3. 2nd drive gear
4. 3rd drive gear
5. 4th drive gear
6. 5th drive gear
7. 4th drive gear circlip
8. Driveshaft
9. 1st driven gear
10. 2nd driven gear
11. 3rd driven gear
12. 4th driven gear
13. 5th driven gear
14. Thrust washer
15. Countershaft bearing lh washer
16. Driveshaft circlip
17. 3rd driven gear washer
18. Ball bearing
19. Ball bearing
20. Ball bearing
21. Driveshaft bush
22. Driveshaft oil seal
23. Countershaft bearing retainer
24. Screw
25. Kick idle gear
26. Kick driven gear
27. Driven gear bearing
28. Driven gear washer

29-1. Engine sprocket

29-2. Engine sprocket

29-3. Engine sprocket

30. Sprocket spacer
31. Sprocket nut
32. Sprocket washer
33. Sprocket O-ring
34. Drive chain assy
35. Chain joint

TS-125 transmission components.

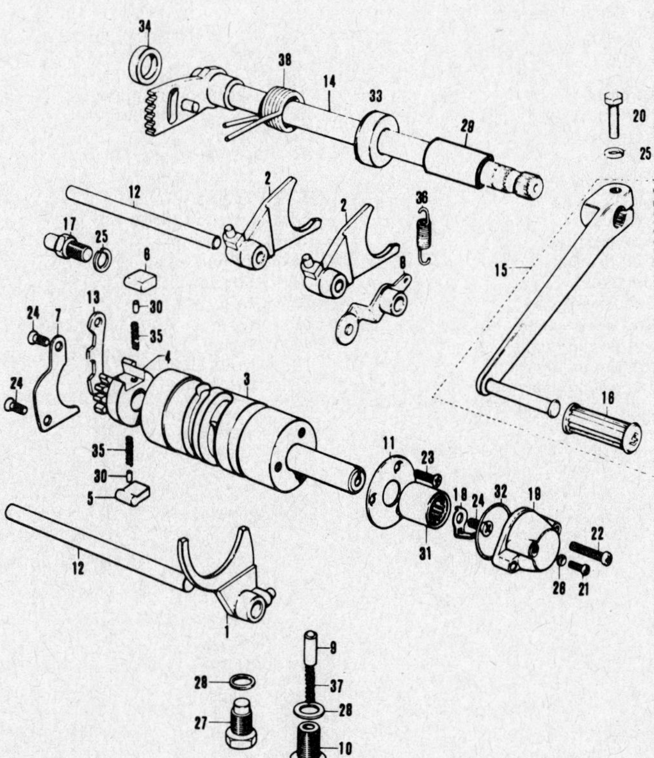

1. 3rd drive gear shifting fork
2. 4th driven gear shifting fork
3. Gear shifting cam
4. Gear shifting cam driven gear
5. Gear shifting pawl no. 1
6. Gear shifting pawl no. 2
7. Gear shifting pawl lifter
8. Gear shifting cam stopper no. 1
9. Gear shifting cam stopper no. 2
10. Gear shifting cam stopper housing
11. Gear shifting cam stopper plate
12. Gear shifting fork shaft
13. Gear shifting cam guide
14. Gear shifting shaft
15. Gear shifting lever assy
16. Gear shifting lever rubber
17. Gear shifting arm stopper
18. Neutral indicator switch contact point
19. Neutral indicator switch
20. Small hexagon bolt
21. Cross head screw
22. Cross head screw
23. Cross head screw
24. Cross head screw
25. Lock washer
26. Small flat washer
27. Gear shifting cam guide bolt
28. Gear shifting cam stopper gasket
29. Gear shifting shaft chain cushion
30. Gear shifting pawl pin
31. Gear shifting cam needle bearing
32. Neutral indicator switch O-ring
33. Gear shifting shaft oil seal
34. Gear shifting shaft spacer
35. Gear shifting pawl return spring
36. Gear shifting cam stopper spring
37. Gear shifting cam stopper spring
38. Gear shifting shaft spring

TS-250 shifting mechanism.

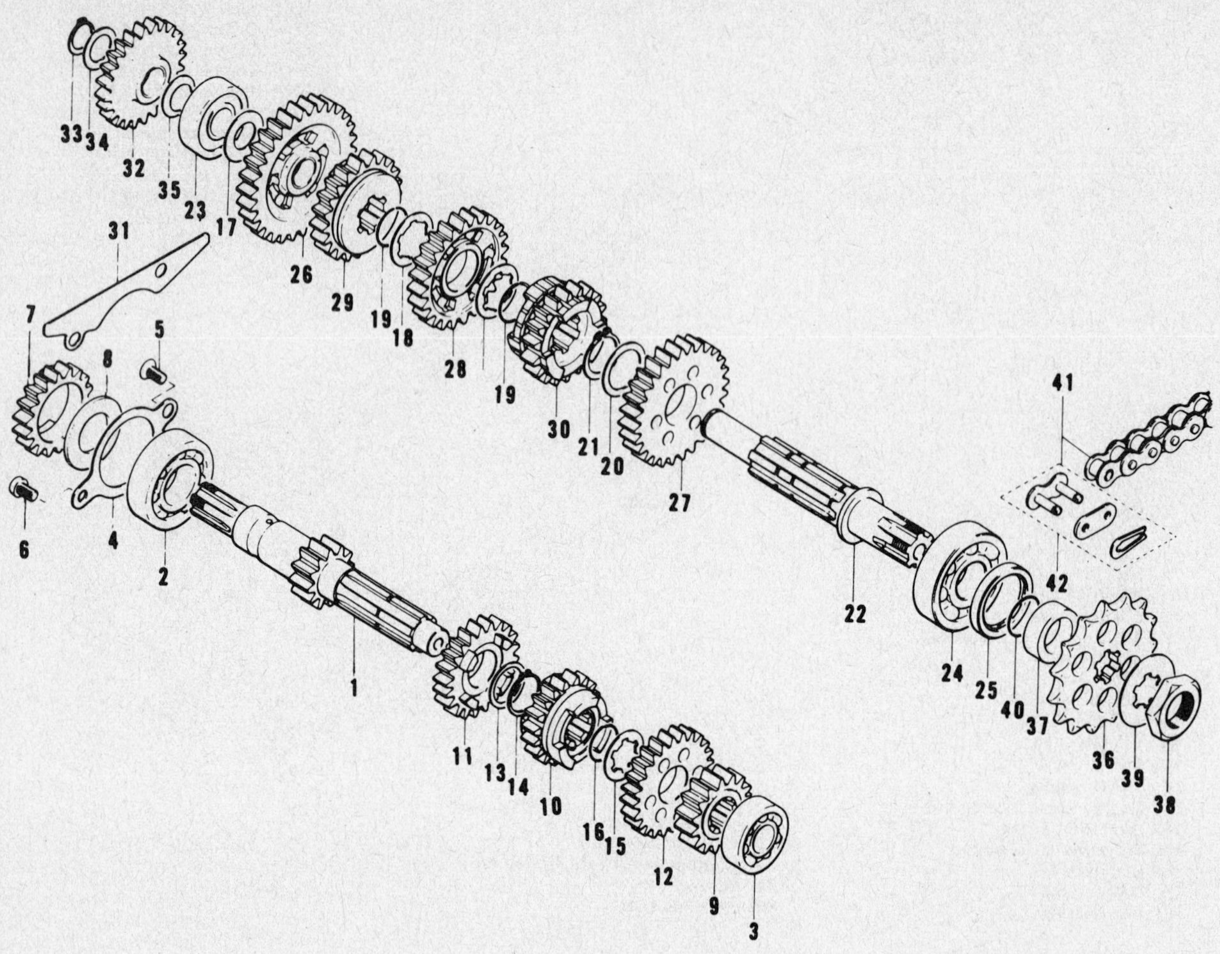

TS-250 transmission components.

1. Countershaft
2. Ball bearing
3. Ball bearing
4. Bearing holder
5. Screw
6. Screw
7. Kick-starter driven gear
8. Washer
9. 2nd drive gear
10. 3rd drive gear
11. 4th drive gear
12. 5th drive gear
13. Thrust washer
14. Circlip
15. Washer
16. Circlip
17. Thrust washer
18. Washer
19. Circlip
20. Thrust washer
21. Circlip
22. Drive shaft
23. Ball bearing
24. Ball bearing
25. Oil seal
26. 1st driven gear
27. 2nd driven gear
28. 3rd driven gear
29. 4th driven gear
30. 5th driven gear
31. Oil reservoir plate
32. Kick-starter idle gear
33. Circlip
34. Thrust washer
35. Wave washer

36-1. Engine sprocket
36-2. Engine sprocket
36-3. Engine sprocket
36-4. Engine sprocket

37. Spacer
38. Nut
39. Washer
40. O-ring
41. Drive chain assy
42. Drive chain joint

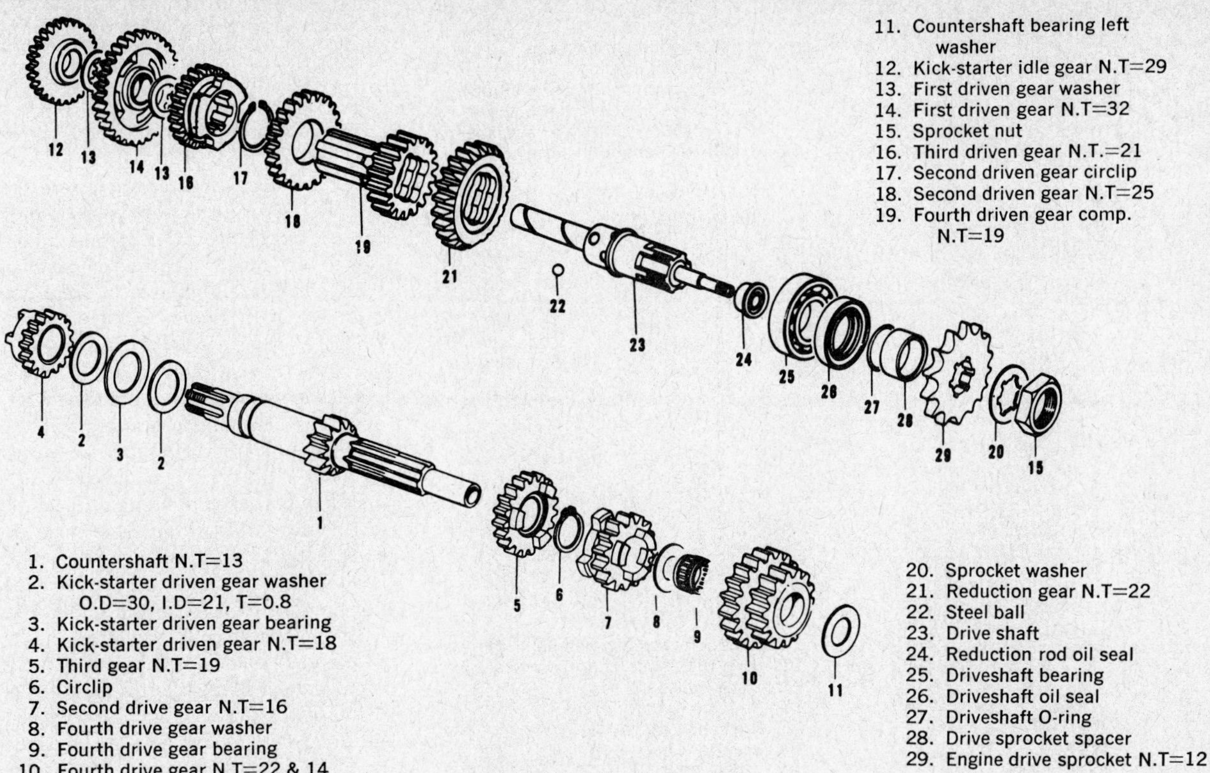

1. Countershaft N.T=13
2. Kick-starter driven gear washer O.D=30, I.D=21, T=0.8
3. Kick-starter driven gear bearing
4. Kick-starter driven gear N.T=18
5. Third gear N.T=19
6. Circlip
7. Second drive gear N.T=16
8. Fourth drive gear washer
9. Fourth drive gear bearing
10. Fourth drive gear N.T=22 & 14
11. Countershaft bearing left washer
12. Kick-starter idle gear N.T=29
13. First driven gear washer
14. First driven gear N.T=32
15. Sprocket nut
16. Third driven gear N.T.=21
17. Second driven gear circlip
18. Second driven gear N.T=25
19. Fourth driven gear comp. N.T=19
20. Sprocket washer
21. Reduction gear N.T=22
22. Steel ball
23. Drive shaft
24. Reduction rod oil seal
25. Driveshaft bearing
26. Driveshaft oil seal
27. Driveshaft O-ring
28. Drive sprocket spacer
29. Engine drive sprocket N.T=12

TC-125 transmission components.

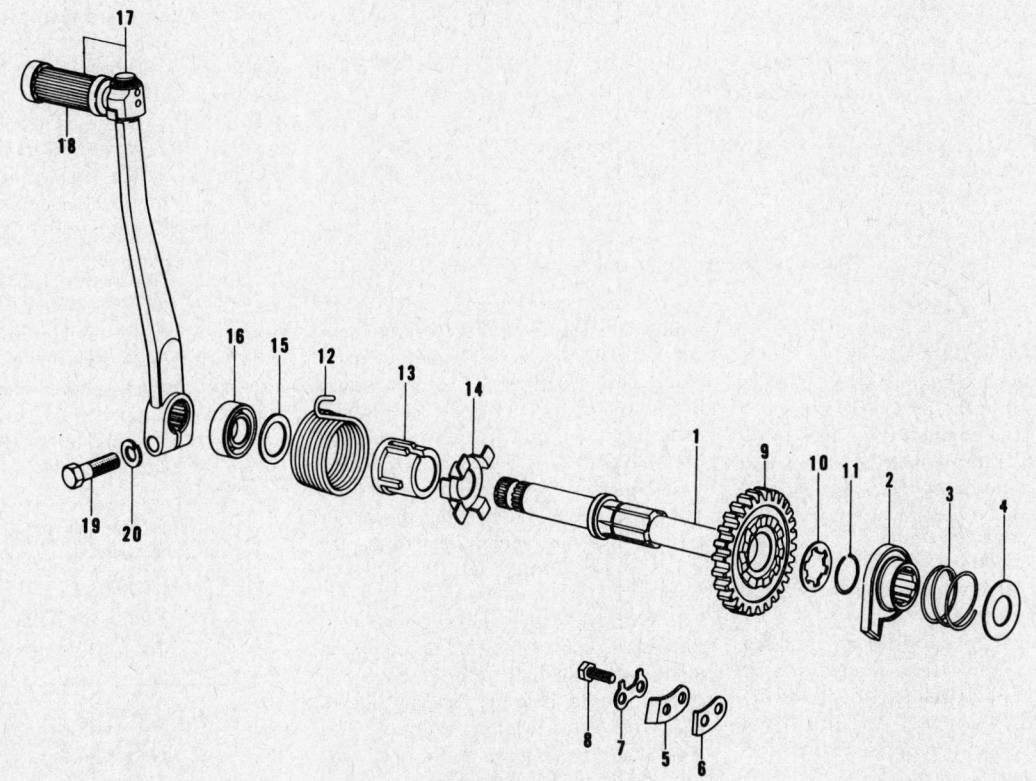

TS-250 kick starter.

1. Kick-starter shaft
2. Ratchet wheel
3. Ratchet wheel spring
4. Thrust washer
5. Ratchet wheel guide
6. Ratchet wheel stopper
7. Lock washer
8. Bolts
9. Kick drive gear
10. Washer
11. Circlip
12. Kick spring
13. Spring guide
14. Spring holder
15. Washer
16. Oil seal
17. Kick-starter lever assy
18. Kick-starter lever rubber
19. Bolt
20. Lock washer

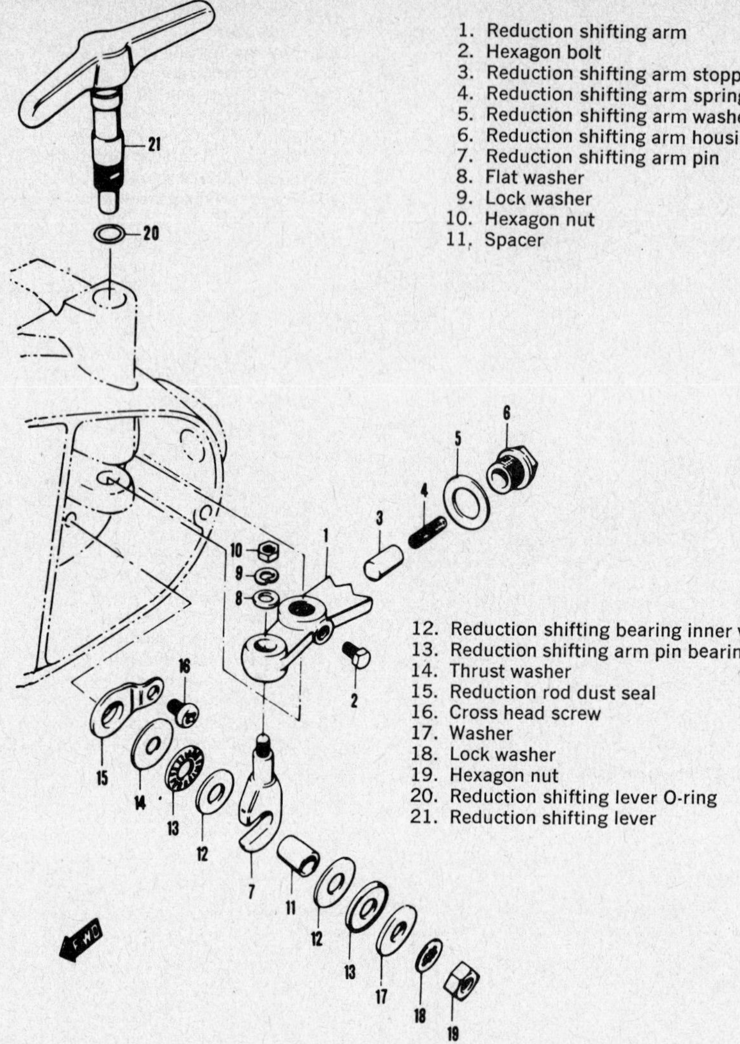

Reduction shifting mechanism.

Twins

Disassembly

1. Remove the engine from the frame as described in the previous section.

2. With the engine sitting upright on the bench, remove the left crankcase cover plate to expose the points and stator. Unhook the neutral switch wire and the wires from the stator.

3. Remove the stator and the point cam bolt, then, using the proper puller, remove the rotor.

4. Remove the woodruff key from the end of the crank, then remove the oil pump fitting bolts (clutch side of the engine) and disconnect the oil lines. Remove the right crankcase cover to expose the clutch.

5. Remove the clutch release bearing, then bend back the lock tabs on both the crankshaft pinion nut and clutch sleeve hub nut. Remove both these nuts, using an air wrench if possible. It will first be necessary to remove the clutch pressure plate on some models. On the S–32, T–200, and T–125, the pressure plate is held by release spring pins, which are removed with pliers after pulling them out with a hooked wire. The other models use either phillips (X–6) or hex screws to hold the plate. Back these screws off a few turns at a time to avoid warping the pressure plate.

6. Check out the clutch if it is suspect. The procedures for checking the plates and springs, and pinion backlash, are found under "Clutch and Transmission Service."

7. With the clutch hub nut removed, the entire clutch assembly can be pulled off the countershaft. Also remove the clutch needle bearing, bearing sleeve and any thrust washers present. The crankshaft pinion gear and spacer now can be removed if desired.

8. Remove the drive gear by bending back the locktab and unscrewing the nut. If desirable, the oil seal and spacer can be removed at this time.

9. Remove the kick-starter gear and stop, on models having this gear exposed (X–6 derived engines).

10. Remove the cylinder heads and cylinders, as previously described in this chapter.

11. Remove the pistons from the rods, as previously described.

12. Remove the con rod needle bearings (upper end).

13. The crankcases are now ready to be split. Other items, such as the clutch release mechanism, can remain in the case or be removed if desired at this time.

14. There are a number of crankcase bolts, on both upper and lower case halves. Note that there is a number cast next to each bolt. This indicates the sequence in which the bolts are to be tightened when assembling. Starting with the highest numbered bolt, gradually loosen the bolts in the lower crankcase half, reversing the order of tightening. Turn the engine over after all the lower bolts are completely loose and loosen the upper bolts in reverse sequence. Remove the upper bolts, then strike the upper case with a soft faced mallet to loosen it. On S–32 and T–10 models, the *lower* case is removed and all the internal parts rest in the upper case. The upper case on all but S–32 and T–10 models now can be pulled up and off the lower case, exposing the transmission and crankshaft for service. Starting from the front of the engine, you'll see the crankshaft, countershaft and gears, drive shaft and gears and finally the kick-starter shaft and spring assembly.

15. The kick-starter stop bolt and plate now can be removed on models having internal kick-start gears, and the shift forks and drum can also be removed now. The transmission shafts and gears can be checked in place and lifted out as units for service, as can the crankshaft. Note that there are dowel pins holding the bearings (to keep them from spinning). When assembling, the dowels must pop into their respective holes (indicated by a mark on the opposite side of the dowel hole in each bearing), otherwise the case halves will not go together.

Crankcase Bolt Torque	
6 mm	7 ft lbs
8 mm	14 ft lbs
10 mm	25 ft lbs

INSPECTION AND ASSEMBLY

1. Inspect all parts for wear or damage as described in the previous section.

2. Reassembly is the reversal of the disassembly procedure.

GT380, GT550

Disassembly

1. Drain the transmission oil.

2. Remove the engine from the frame as described previously.

3. Remove the cylinder head and barrels as described in the previous section.

4. Remove the kickstarter lever and the nine crankcase cover screws (right side). Remove the ignition points cover and remove the breaker plate to gain access to the two screws behind it.

5. Remove the right side cover. The ignition points assembly will come away with the cover.

6. Remove the alternator cover, disconnect the neutral light lead wire at the switch, and remove the stator after loosening the three screws.

7. Remove the alternator rotor by securing the left side con rod (so that the crankshaft will not move) and remove the rotor bolt; screw in the special rotor remover and torque to 6.6–10 ft lbs.

8. Remove the oil pump cover, unscrew the bolts, and remove the oil pump as well.

9. Remove the clutch spring bolts, then take away the pressure plate, pushrod, and clutch plates.

10. Bend back the locking tab of the clutch sleeve hub washer, secure the clutch sleeve hub with the special holder (Part No. 09920–51510) or a suitable substitute, and remove the clutch sleeve hub nut.

Loosening the clutch sleeve hub nut.

11. Remove the clutch hub sleeve, starter clutch (GT550), and the clutch housing.

12. Pull out the gear shifter shaft from the right side of the engine and remove the oil guide plate.

13. Remove the starter motor cover (GT550), then the starter motor.

Removing the clutch housing and starter clutch.

14. Loosen all crankcase bolts in the reverse of the order stamped on the crankcase. Tap around the crankcase mating surface with a rubber mallet, then separate the cases.

INSPECTION

Clutch

1. Clean all parts other than the friction plates in a suitable solvent and allow them to dry.

2. Inspect all parts for wear or damage and replace if necessary. The clutch release screw must not be loose or damaged and should be replaced as a complete assembly if necessary.

3. Inspect the friction plates for warpage or scoring. Measure the plates with a vernier caliper and replace if worn more than 0.3 mm (0.012 in.) past their standard thickness of 3.5 mm (0.138 in.). Warpage should not exceed 0.4 mm (0.-016 in.).

4. Inspect the clutch springs for damage or a collapsed condition. The springs should not be more than 1.5 mm (0.06 in.) shorter than their standard free length of 38.4 mm (1.15 in.) and must be replaced as a complete set.

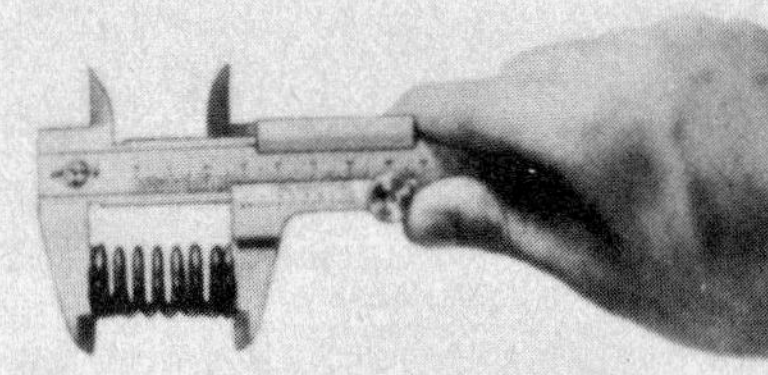

Checking the clutch spring free length.

Transmission

1. Inspect all gears for wear, chipped teeth, or foreign matter and replace as necessary.

2. Check the condition of the shifter forks, assuring they are not bent, worn on their shafts, or cracked.

3. Check the gear bearings for score marks.

Crankshaft

1. The crankshaft is a pressed together unit and must be replaced in toto if necessary machine work cannot be accomplished.

2. Check the condition of all bearings.

3. Check for a bent connecting rod by installing a piston (without the piston rings) on the rod, and installing the crankshaft in the crankcase. Replace the cylinder. Push the piston crown left and right when the piston is at top dead center. The piston should return to the center position when pressure is released. If it does not and stays positioned to one side of the cylinder, the rod is bent.

ASSEMBLY

1. Assembly is basically a reversal of the disassembly procedure. Note the following points:

2. Generously bathe the crankshaft assembly, especially the bearings, in clean Suzuki CCI oil or a suitable substitute.

3. Align the pin positions of each bearing so the pin sits in its slot on the crankcase.

4. Position each crankshaft oil seal close to the bearing side.

5. When installing the gear clusters,

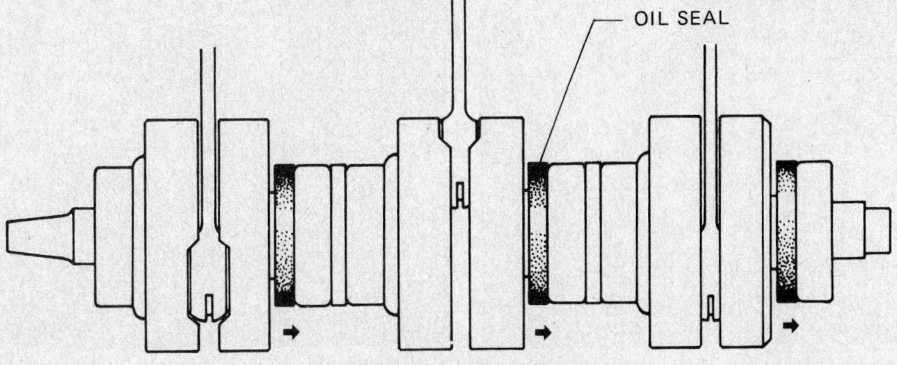

Crankshaft oil seals positions.

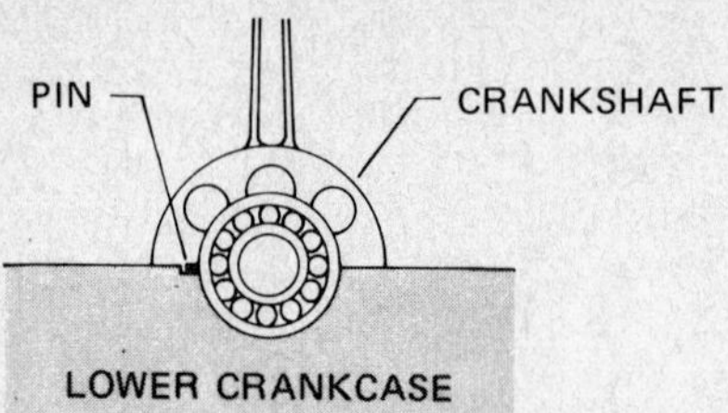

Bearing pin position.

make sure that the bearings are matched with their dowel pins.

6. Check for smooth operation of all the gears and shifters.

7. Fit the boss of the countershaft oil reservoir (GT550) in the groove in the case to properly position the oil passage.

Countershaft oil reservoir.

8. Make sure that the drive and countershafts can be rotated smoothly by hand.

9. Align the kickstarter shaft and ratchet wheel punch marks.

Position of ratchet wheel on kickstarter shaft.

Crankcase bolt tightening order.

10. Position the starter spring so that its end is seated in its proper position. Pre-load the spring by turning the shaft ¾ turn counterclockwise until the boss of the ratchet wheel is caught in the stopper plate.

11. When refitting the crankcase halves, make sure all mating surfaces are clean. Apply a light coat of a liquid gasket material to the upper case mating surface; allow it to set for five minutes, then refit.

12. Tighten all of the crankcase bolts finger-tight, then torque in the order shown: 6 mm bolts to 9.4 ft lbs and 8 mm bolts to 14.5 ft lbs.

13. Torque the starter motor bolts to 2.9–5.1 ft lbs and the cover to 1.5–2.9 ft lbs.

GT750

Disassembly

1. Remove the engine from the frame as previously described.

2. Remove the cylinder heads and cylinder block as described in a previous section.

3. Remove the starter clutch cover, then the water pump drive gear, and the starter clutch idler gear.

4. Remove the starter clutch assembly using the special starter clutch remover (Part No. 09920-53110) and the starter clutch holder (Part No. 09920-40111).

5. Remove the alternator cover, then the brush assembly and the stator assembly. The rotor can be removed with the special tool (Part No. 09930-33110) or a suitable substitute.

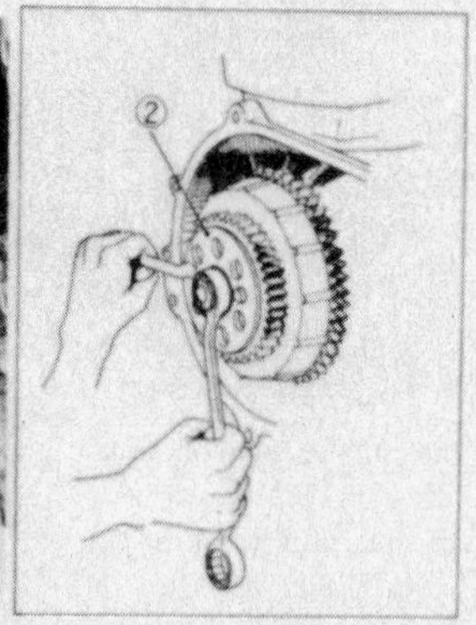

Removing the starter clutch with special remover (1) and holder (2).

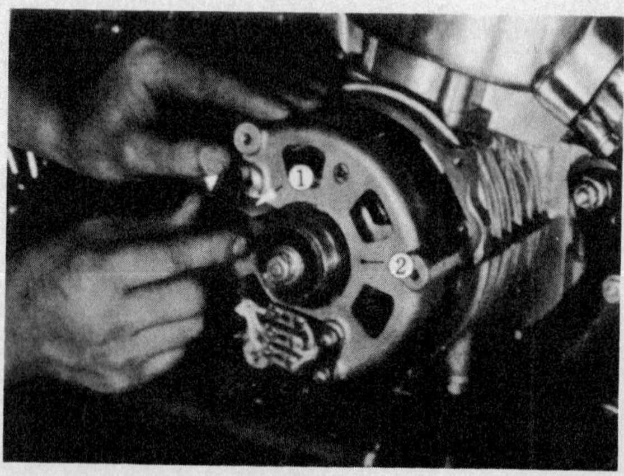

Removing the alternator brush.

Removing the alternator rotor.

6. Remove the clutch inspection cover, then the clutch release mechanism shaft nuts and the clutch release lever.

7. Remove the clutch cover, the pressure plate, and the release shaft, then remove the clutch plates. The clutch sleeve hub can be removed with the aid of the clutch sleeve hub holder special tool (Part No. 09920-53110) or a suitable substitute to keep the clutch from turning. The primary driven gear and spacer can be removed by drawing off the bushing with two suitable bolts. Remove the oil reservoir plate.

8. Once the cylinder block and the bypass hose and hose union have been removed, the starter motor cover and the starter motor itself can be removed.

Removing the gear shifter switch (1) and driveshaft oil seal retainer (2).

9. Remove the gear shifter switch and the driveshaft oil seal retainer.

10. Remove the kickstarter guide, the spring, and the spring holder.

11. Remove the crankcase securing bolts in the reverse of the order given on the crankcase, then tap around the case halves with a rubber mallet to separate the halves.

12. Lift both ends of the countershaft and driveshaft assemblies and remove them from the lower crankshaft half.

13. Disassemble the shifter mechanism in the following manner:

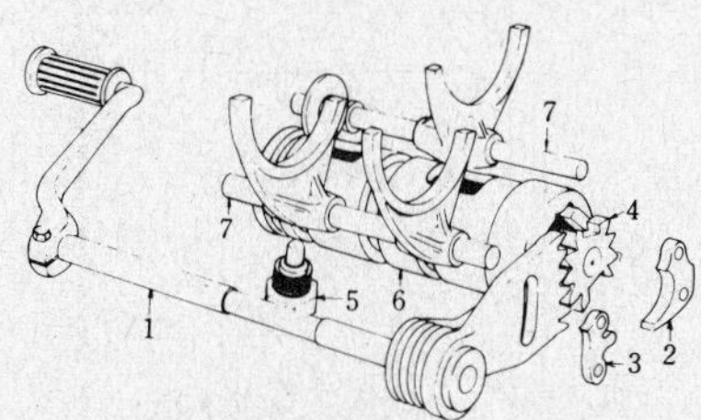

Gear shifting mechanism.

A. Remove the shifter shaft from the lower crankcase half.

B. Remove the shifting pawl lifter and cam guide.

C. Remove the shifting cam driven gear.

D. Remove the neutral stopper spring holder.

E. Remove the shifter cam and the shifting fork shafts.

14. Disassemble the driveshaft by removing the circlip.

INSPECTION

Clutch

1. Clean all parts other than the friction plates in a suitable solvent.

2. Measure the thickness of the friction plates. They should all be replaced if worn more than 0.2 mm (0.008 in.) past their standard thickness of 2.9–3.1 mm (0.114–0.122 in.).

3. Inspect the metal plates for scoring, discoloration due to excessive heat, or other damage.

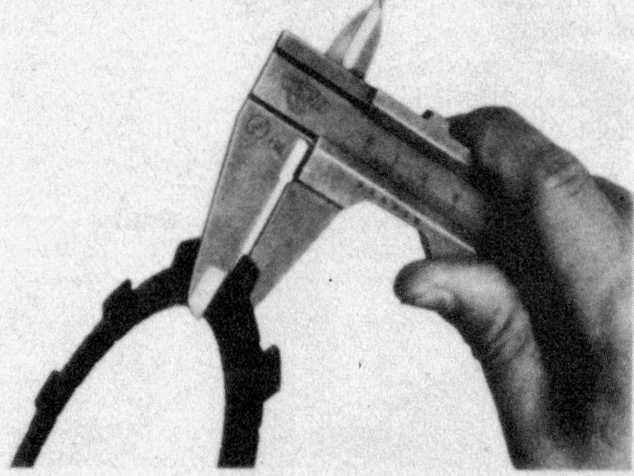

Checking clutch plate thickness.

Measuring gear backlash.

4. Check the plates for warpage and replace if warped more than 0.3 mm (0.-012 in.).

5. Measure the clutch spring free length and replace as a set if free length is shorter than 1.4 mm (0.055 in.) from the standard value of 40.4 mm (1.59 in.).

6. Inspect the bearings located in the clutch pressure plate for wear or damage and replace if necessary. The bearings must be able to turn smoothly and freely.

7. Examine the inner and outer ball guide of the clutch release mechanism for cracks, wear, or other damage and replace them as necessary.

Transmission

1. Inspect all gears for chipped teeth, worn spots, minute cracks at the base of the teeth, or foreign matter.

2. The countershaft second gear must be removed from the shaft with an arbor press. After it has been removed twice, the entire assembly must be replaced. Gears are color-coded to the crankcases. The color-code chart and directions are given at the end of the chapter.

3. Check all gears for excessive backlash by locking the shaft in position and then moving the gear against a dial indicator. The average backlash for first, second, third, and the kickstart gears is 0–0.05 mm ((0–0.002 in.), and for all other gears is 0.05–0.1 mm (0.002–0.004 in.).

4. Inspect the shifting fork and shafts for excessive clearance and replace them as necessary. The standard clearance is 0.05–0.1 mm (0.002–0.004 in.).

5. Measure the fingers of the shifting fork and replace the fork if they measure less than 4.95 mm (0.195 in.).

6. Measure the diameter of the shifter drum and replace it if less than 44.70 mm (1.7598 in.).

7. Inspect all bearings for wear or damage and replace if necessary.

Crankshaft

1. The crankshaft is a pressed together unit and requires highly specialized equipment to work on the assembly.

2. Inspect the connecting rods for a bent or twisted condition by following the procedure given for the GT380, GT550.

3. Check the rod small end for wear or

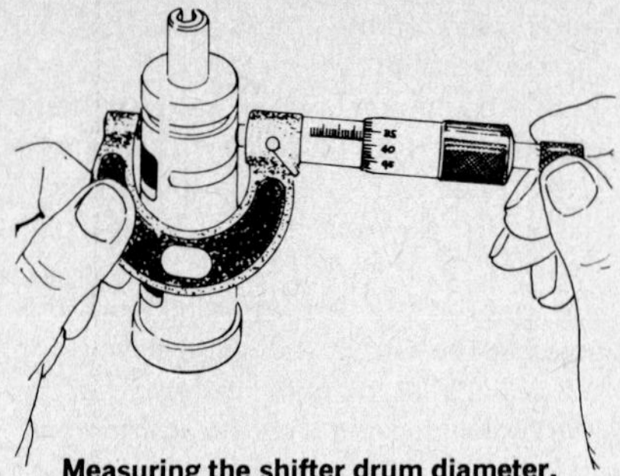
Measuring the shifter drum diameter.

excessive clearance between the bearing and the piston pin which should not exceed 0.05 mm (0.002 in.).

4. Check for play at the rod big end. This should not exceed 3 mm (0.018 in.). If play exceeds this value, the rod must be replaced. The standard play at the top of the rod is 0.5–0.8 mm (0.02–0.03 in.) and the standard thrust as measured at the big end is 0.2–0.6 mm (0.008–0.23 in.). Inspect the big end thrust washer for excessive wear or for a burned or damaged condition.

5. Check for wear, damage, or creep at the big end bearing by turning the bearing's outer race and checking for rough motion or a clicking noise. Check each bearing for excessive axial play.

6. If a V-block is available, or if you can devise some means of turning the crankshaft on a steady plane, check the assembly for excessive run-out. If the run-out is measured at the crank web or at a bearing with a dial indicator, divide the result by two, and this will give the amount of bend in the crankshaft. If greater than 0.08 mm (0.003 in.) of bend are present, the assembly will have to be straightened.

7. Inspect the oil seals, especially around the lips, for a damaged condition which might cause leakage. Seals must be replaced as a full set.

ASSEMBLY

1. The assembly procedure is essentially the reverse of the disassembly sequence.

2. Thoroughly clean all parts and lubricate with fresh oil before installation.

3. Insert the crankshaft into the crankcase so that the bearing punch marks align with the mating surface. The punch mark of the bearing should be facing the back of the crankshaft on the outermost right side bearing and the others should be facing forward.

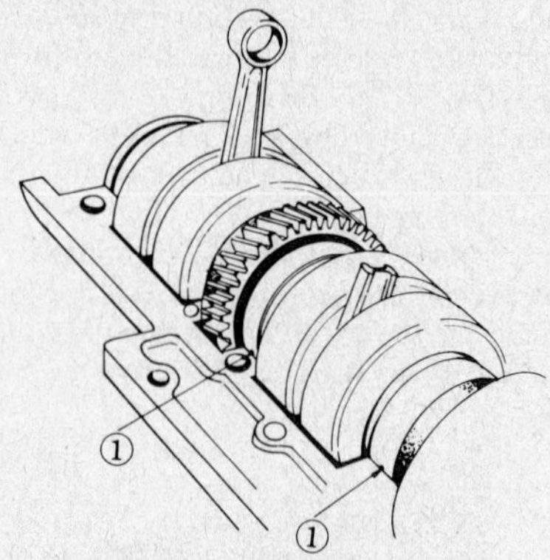

Crankshaft bearing aligning marks (1).

4. Position the oil seals firmly against each bearing, except for the one situated between the primary gear and the right crank throw.

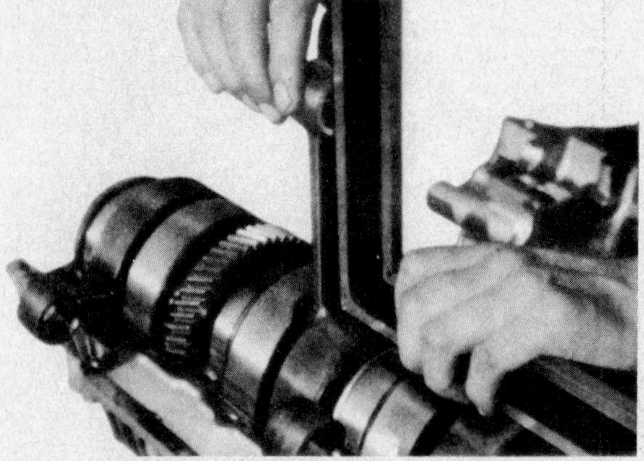
Checking connecting rod big end wear.

Checking crankshaft run-out.

<table>
<tr><th>CRANKCASE COLOUR</th><th>1ST DRIVEN GEAR</th><th>2ND DRIVEN GEAR</th><th>KICK START DRIVE GEAR</th></tr>
<tr><td>BROWN</td><td rowspan="4">YELLOW</td><td rowspan="4">YELLOW</td><td rowspan="4">BROWN</td></tr>
<tr><td>BLACK</td></tr>
<tr><td>RED</td></tr>
<tr><td>YELLOW</td></tr>
<tr><td>BLUE</td><td rowspan="3">WHITE</td><td rowspan="3">WHITE</td><td rowspan="3">YELLOW</td></tr>
<tr><td>GREEN</td></tr>
<tr><td>WHITE</td></tr>
<tr><td>PAINTED COLOUR</td><td>PAINTED COLOUR</td><td>PAINTED COLOUR</td><td>PAINTED COLOUR</td></tr>
</table>

5. Install the transmission, shifter mechanism, and the kickstarter gear assemblies in the crankcase. If gear replacement is necessary, follow these instructions:

A. If you are replacing the crankcase assembly (Part No. 11304-31802), install the color-coded gears which are supplied with the cases.

B. When you purchase replacements for the first and/or second gear, you'll get two gears in the package. One is marked with a dab of white paint, the other with yellow paint. The crankcase is also color-coded, so check the chart and use the appropriate gear. If, for example, the cases are coded brown, the yellow gear will be used, but if they are coded green, the white gear must be installed.

C. When replacing the kickstarter gear, the same procedure applies except that the gears are coded yellow and brown.

6. Insert the kickstarter into the kickstarter shaft so that the punch marks and splines on the flank of the starter shaft and the kickstarter are in alignment. The oil hole on the shaft should face upward when the kickstarter contacts the kick starter guide.

7. Install the kickstarter mechanism into the lower case half, then secure the starter guide with the two set screws. The threads of the screws should be coated with thread locking compound.

8. Assemble the crankcase halves after thoroughly cleaning and smoothing (if necessary) the mating surfaces, then apply a coat of a liquid gasket compound and allow it to dry for five to ten minutes before fitting the halves together.

9. Attach the alternator and contact breaker lead clamps to the bolts numbered 8, 10, and 14. Use a copper washer on the bolt numbered 13. Attach the engine ground wire to the bolt numbered 22. Attach the remaining clamps for the alternator and contact breaker lead clamps to the bolt numbered 6. Tighten the bolts in the order illustrated.

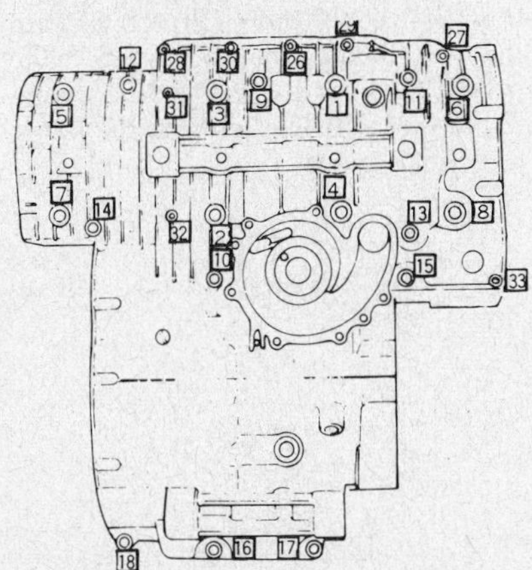

Lower crankcase bolts tightening order.

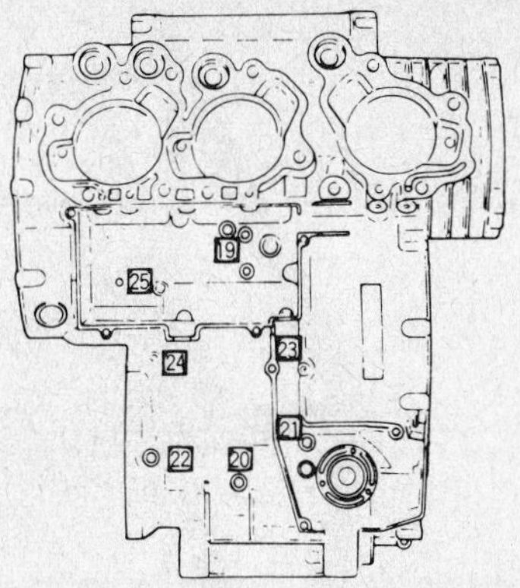

Upper crankcase bolts tightening order.

10. Torque the 6 mm bolts to 4.34–7.23 ft lbs the 8 mm bolts to 9.38–16.65 ft lbs and the 10 mm bolts to 18.08–28.90 ft lbs.

11. Be sure to fill the transmission with the correct amount of oil: 2,500 cc. This is the usual amount (2,200 cc) plus the 300 cc which is usually left in the engine during a normal oil change.

Cooling System

The cooling system is very similar to that used in usual automobile practice. The assembly consists of a radiator, thermostat, reservoir tank, cylinder block water jacket, fan, and water pump. The thermostat controls the fan in temperatures of extreme heat. The water pump is driven off the starter clutch gear and is a centrifugal-type unit.

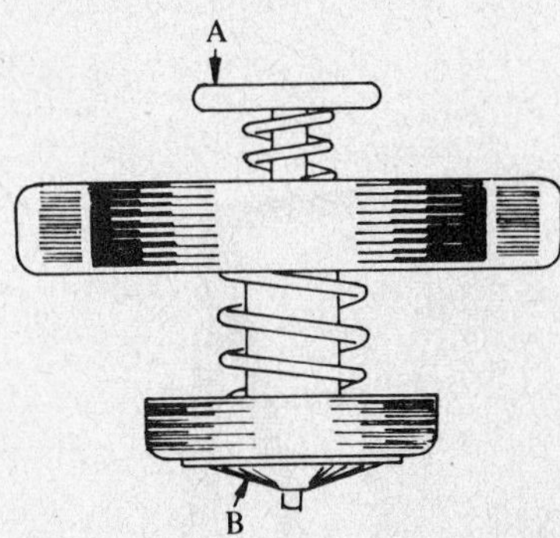

Radiator cap with release valve (A) and reverse valve (B).

The radiator cap is a self-regulating unit which is equipped with a reverse valve (B) to relieve excess pressure when it builds up over the set limit of 27.0 psi.

RADIATOR

Removal

1. Drain out the cooling solution.

2. Remove the fuel tank, the radiator inlet and outlet hoses, the coolant inlet pipe, the reservoir tank and its hosing, and the fan and its shroud.

3. Remove the radiator bumper and radiator assembly.

Inspection and Repair

1. Inspect the radiator for damage, signs of leakage, mud coated or dirty cooling fins, or bent fins. Slight leakage can be remedied with a radiator additive as in automobiles. Internal damage such as that caused by freezing of the cooling solution cannot be repaired, and the unit must be replaced.

If more than 20% of the total radiator core area is incapacitated by body damage or irremovable deposits, the unit must be replaced.

Checking radiator cap with pressure gauge.

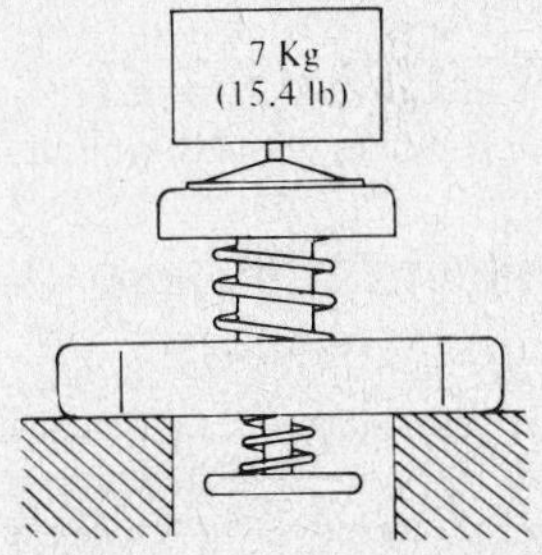

Checking radiator cap with weights.

2. Inspect the radiator cap for condition. The cap can be checked either with a pressure gauge, or by placing a 15.4 lb. weight on the cap to observe whether or not the valve opens. The proper test pressure which the cap should be able to handle is 12.78 psi.

Installation

1. Installation is the reverse of the removal procedure.

2. There are three different sizes of washers used to mount the radiator and these are color coded. They must be mounted correctly. The following information concerns the proper placement of the washers:

A. Washer (A) is 2.0 mm (0.079 in.) thick
Washer (B) is 1.6 mm (0.063 in.) thick
Washer (C) is 0.8 mm (0.031 in.) thick.

B. When the radiator is marked by white circles on the mounting plates, install the washers as illustrated.

C. When the radiator is not marked, mount it only with (B) washers.

D. In instances when only the top or bottom is marked, use (B) washers on

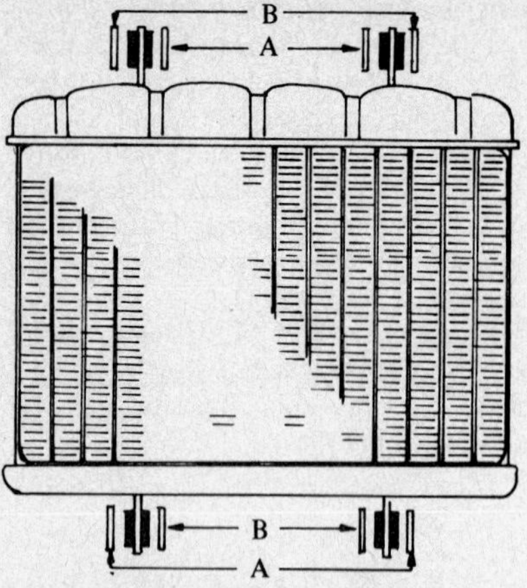

Radiator mounting washers.

Removing the driven shaft

the unmarked mounting plate and the combination of (A) and (B) washers for the marked mounting plate as illustrated.

E. If, after installing the correct number of washers in their prescribed positions, there is still a gap, use (C) washers as filler until a flush mount is attained.

THERMOSTAT

For information, see "Electrical Systems."

WATER PUMP

Removal

1. Drain the coolant.
2. Remove the central muffler.
3. Carefully remove the water pump taking care not to damage its mating surface.

5. Remove the water pump seal and the oil seal only if replacement is obviously necessary.

Inspection and Repair

1. Clean all parts.
2. Inspect the bearing for wear or damage. If the bearing action is rough or noisy, it must be replaced.
3. Inspect the pump driven shaft for a worn or damaged condition. If the shaft becomes rusted or scaled, it can be cleaned with an emery cloth.
4. Inspect the impeller blades for deflection or other damage. This must be replaced if damaged; it cannot be repaired.
5. Inspect the oil and water seals. Replace in the following manner:

A. Get a replacement set of seals which come with a replacement pump holder and install all of the parts.

Removing the impeller circlip.

4. Remove the impeller circlip and impeller, then remove the pump holder circlip using snap-ring pliers. Withdraw the water pump driven shaft by wrapping the shaft in cloth or rubber to protect it, then drawing it out with a pair of pliers. The shaft and bearing can be easily removed in the direction opposite the impeller if heated to 167–185°F. If the shaft surface is damaged, it must be replaced.

B. Install the pump holder, pump seal, and sealing seat.

C. Install the oil seal, then the two O-rings outside the pump holder.

6. Inspect the pump drive gear bearings for wear, damage, or rough motion and replace them if necessary.
7. Measure the clearance between the impeller and the crankcase using a set of feeler gauges. The gap should be no less than 0.5–1.5 mm (0.02–0.59 in.).

Assembly

1. Assembly is in the reverse order of disassembly.
2. Lubricate the holder with fresh oil during installation and align the port in the holder with the crankcase port. The notch on the holder top will align with the setting bolt of the crankcase.
3. Secure the impeller and pump driven shaft with the impeller circlip. Make sure there is a gap of 1.5 mm (0.59 in.) between the impeller and the crankshaft.
4. Apply a liquid gasket material to both sides of the waterpump case gasket before mounting the pump case.

LUBRICATION SYSTEMS

The oil pump on all Suzuki models should not be disassembled for any reason. If the unit is found to be defective, it must be replaced. Maintenance is confined to adjusting the pump cable as described in the "Tune-Up" section.

Removing and replacing the pump is described in "Engine and Transmission."

The following procedure applies to most models, including three-cylinder models.

1. Check the inlet oil pipe for air trapped inside. If there are air bubbles in the inlet oil pipe (from the oil tank to the pump), they can be removed by loosening the air expelling screw at the upper part of the pump.

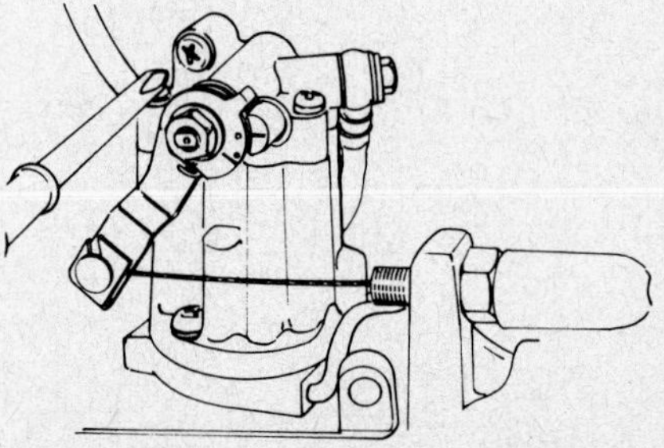
Loosening the oil pump air expeller screw (GT750).

COOLING SYSTEM SPECIFICATIONS

WATER PUMP	
Type	Six(6)-blade impeller centrifugal type
Delivery capacity	60 liters (15.8/13.2 gal US/Imp) per minute at 6,000 rpm at 20°C (68°F)
Revolution ratio with crankshaft	1.57 : 1
Water seal	Mechanical seal
RADIATOR	
Type	Pressure sealed cooling corrugated fin and tube type
Radiation capacity	200 Kcal/min
Opening pressure radiator cap valve	0.9 kg/mc^2 (12.78 lb/in^2) ± 10%
Coolant capacity	about 1.4 liters (1.47/1.23 Qt. US/Imp)
Radiation area	664 cm^2 (102.92 in^2)
Core dimension	Height, 240 mm (9.45 in.) Width, 430 mm (17.0 in.) Thickness, 59 mm (2.32 in.)

PISTON CLEARANCE SPECIFICATIONS

				Piston Clearance		Ring End-Gap		
Model	Displacement (cc)	Nominal Cylinder Bore (mm in.)	Measure @ *(mm)	Fit To (in.)	Replace At (in.)	In Cylinder (in.)	Replace At (in.)	Free (in.)
AS-50, AC-50, TS-50R	49	41/1.62	23	0.0026-0.0029	0.005	0.004-0.012	0.020	0.200
F-50R, MT-50R	49	41/1.62	23	0.0028-0.0031	0.009	0.006-0.014	0.040	0.200
TS/TC-90R	89	47/1.85	20	0.0022-0.0026	0.010	0.006-0.014	0.016	0.200
A-100, AS-100	98	50/1.98	21	0.0020-0.0024	0.004	0.006-0.014	0.016	0.200
AC-100	98	50/1.98	21	0.0018-0.0022	0.004	0.006-0.014	0.016	0.200
A-100 R-T Kit	98	50/1.98	21	0.0025-0.0032	0.005	0.006-0.014	0.016	0.200
B-100, 105, KT-120	118	52/2.05	24	0.0014-0.0018	0.005	0.004-0.012	0.040	0.240
TC-120, TC-120R	118	52/2.05	24	0.0018-0.0022	0.005	0.004-0.012	0.040	0.240
TS-125R	123	56/2.20	23	0.0024-0.0028	0.009	0.006-0.014	0.040	0.200
TS-185R	183	64/2.52	23	0.0024-0.0028	0.009	0.006-0.014	0.040	0.200
K-10, K-11	79	45/1.77	16	0.0032-0.0038	0.008	0.004-0.012	0.040	0.200
K-15	79	45/1.77	16	0.0035-0.0040	0.008	0.004-0.012	0.040	0.200
K-10, 11P, 15P	79	45/1.77	16	0.0014-0.0016	0.004	0.004-0.012	0.040	0.200
M-31	55	43/1.69	23	0.0035-0.0038	0.010	0.004-0.010	0.035	0.160
M-12, M-15, M-15D,	50	41/1.61	23	0.0020-0.0025	0.006	0.004-0.010	0.028	0.200
M-12-2, M-15-2								
S-32-2	149	46/1.81	23	0.0022-0.0026	0.005	0.004-0.012	0.060	0.180
T-125, T-125R	124	43/1.69	20	0.0035-0.0040	0.010	0.012-0.014	0.046	
T-200, TC-200	196	50/1.98	21	0.0016-0.0020	0.003	0.004-0.012	0.040	0.197
T-20, TC-250	247	54/2.13	26	0.0020-0.0024	0.005	0.004-0.010	0.040	0.177
T-10	246	52/2.05	20	0.0049-0.0050	0.008	0.006-0.014	0.040	0.236
T-250, T-250R	247	54/2.13	26	0.0022-0.0026	0.005	0.006-0.014	0.040	0.236
T-350, T-350R	315	61/2.40	26	0.0022-0.0026	0.005	0.006-0.014	0.040	0.236
T-305, TC-305	305	60/2.36	26	0.0022-0.0026	0.005	0.006-0.014	0.040	0.236
T-500	492	70/2.75	54	0.0070-0.0074	0.012	0.008-0.014	0.040	0.260

PISTON CLEARANCE SPECIFICATIONS

Model	Displacement (cc)	Nominal Cylinder Bore (mm in.)	Measure @ *(mm)	Piston Clearance Fit To (in.)	Piston Clearance Replace At (in.)	Ring End-Gap In Cylinder (in.)	Ring End-Gap Replace At (in.)	Ring End-Gap Free (in.)
T-500-II, T-500R	492	70/2.75	32	0.0026-0.0030	0.010	0.008-0.014	0.040	0.260
TS-250-II	246	70/2.75	52	0.0070-0.0074	0.012	0.006-0.014	0.040	0.260
TS-250R	246	70/2.76	26	0.0024-0.0028	0.009	0.006-0.014	0.040	0.200
TM-250	246	66/2.64	77	0.0120-0.0130	0.015	0.008-0.015	0.040	0.300
TM-400R	396	82/3.23	45	0.0041-0.0046	N/S	0.008-0.016	0.040	0.200
GT380	371	54/2.13	26	0.0018-0.0020	N/S	0.006-0.014	0.040	N/S
GT550	544	61/2.40	26	0.0018-0.0022	0.004	0.006-0.014	0.028	N/S
GT750	738	70/2.76	32	0.0018-0.0022	0.0028	0.006-0.014	0.028	N/S

*—mm up from bottom of skirt.
N/S—Not Specified.

PISTON RING TYPE AND PART NUMBER

Model	Piston Ring Data: Top Ring Type and Finish	Piston Ring Data: Bottom Ring Type and Finish	Interchange?	Piston Ring Set For One Engine Part Number: Standard	1st O/S (0.5mm)	2nd O/S (1.0mm)	3rd O/S (1.5mm)
F-50, MT-50R	Keystone Chrome	Flat Chrome	No	12140-05828	-05829	-05839	
AS, AC-50, TS-50R	Keystone Chrome	Flat Chrome	No	12140-05110	-05750	-05760	
TS, TC-90R	Flat Chrome	Flat Chrome	Yes	12140-25010	-25710	-25720	
TC-120, TC-120II, R	Keystone Chrome	Flat Chrome	No	12140-20211	-20721	-20731	
TS-125R	Keystone Chrome	Keystone Chrome	Yes	12140-28010	-28710	-28720	
T-125R	Keystone Chrome	Flat Chrome	No	12140-14010	-14700	-14720	
TS-185R	Keystone Chrome	Keystone Chrome	Yes	12140-29010	-29710	-29720	
T-250, R	Keystone Chrome	Keystone Chrome	Yes	12140-18410	-18720	-18730	
TS-250, II	Keystone Chrome	Keystone Chrome	Yes	12140-15011	-15700	-15710	
TS-250R	Keystone Chrome	Keystone Chrome	Yes	12140-30010	-30710	-30720	
T-350	Keystone Chrome	Flat Chrome	No	12140-18330	-18740		
T-350II, R	Keystone Chrome	Keystone Chrome	Yes	12140-18510	-18750		
TM-400R	Keystone Chrome	Keystone Chrome	Yes	12140-16510	-16700		
T-500, II, III, R	Keystone Chrome	Keystone Chrome	Yes	12140-15011	-15700	-15710	
A-100, AS-100, AC-100	Keystone Black	Keystone Chrome	No	12140-12818	-12819	-12820	
B-100P, 105P, KT-120	Keystone Chrome	Keystone Chrome	Yes	12140-07602	-07722	-07732	
K-10, K-11, K-15	Flat Chrome	Flat Black	No	12140-03010	-03970	-03980	
K-10P, K-11P, K-15P	Keystone Chrome	Keystone Black	No	12140-03111	-03701	-03711	
M-31	Flat Chrome	Flat Black	No	12140-02110	-02700		
M-12	Flat Chrome	Flat Black	No	12140-01010	-01760	-09289	
M-12-2, M-15-2	Keystone Chrome	Flat Black	No	12140-01600	-01760	-01770	
S-32-2/to E#14076	Flat tpd. Chrome	Flat Black	No	00037-14145	-45146		
S-32-2	Keystone Chrome	Keystone Chrome	Yes	12140-09809	-09810	-09811	
TM-250	Flat Chrome	Flat Chrome	Yes	12141-16200	-16210		
T-10	Flat Chrome	Flat Black	Yes	00031-01120	-01125	-01130	-01135
T-20, TC-250	Keystone Chrome	Keystone Chrome	Yes	12140-11012	-11702	-11712	
T-200, TC-200	Keystone Chrome	Keystone Chrome	Yes	12140-10010	-10730	-10740	-10750
T-305, TC-305	Keystone Chrome	Flat Chrome	No	12140-18030	-18700	-18710	

TRANSMISSION TORQUE SPECIFICATIONS

Model	Primary Pinion (ft lbs)	Clutch Hub Nut (ft lbs)	Sprocket Nut (ft lbs)	Trans Drain Plug (ft lbs)	Shift Cam Detent (ft lbs)	Shift Cam Guide (ft lbs)
F-50, MT-50R	31	18	5			
AS-50, TS-50R	31	18	28	10		
M-12, M-15, M-15D, M-12-2, M-15-2, M-31	25	18	22	10		
K-10, K-11, K-15, K-10P, K-11P, K-15P	33	18	25	10		
TS/TC-90, TS/TC-90R	31	18	36	10		
A-100, AS-100, AC-100	31	18	36	10		
B-100P, B-105P, KT-120, TC-120R	31	36	36	10		
T-125, T-125R	31	18		10		
TS-125R	31	36	36	10		
S-32-2, T-10	31	31	29	10		10
TS-185R	31	18		10		
T-200, TC-200	31	35	36	10		
T-20, TC-250	31	35	36	10	12	
T-305, TC-305, T-250, T-250R, T-350, T-350R	31	35	36	10	12	
TS-250, TS-250R	35	35	36	10		
TM-400R	35	35		10		
T-500, T-500R	36	36	29	10	12	12

ENGINE TORQUE SPECIFICATIONS

Model	Cylinder Head ft lbs	Magneto Rotor Nut ft lbs
F-50, AS-50, AC-50, TS-50R, MT-50R	8	25
M-12, M-15, M-15D, M-12-2, M-15-2, M-31	8	29*
K-10, K-11, K-15	14.5	29
K-10P, K-11P, K-15P	8	29
TS/TC-90, TS/TC-90R	14.5	29
A-100, AS-100, AC-100	14.5	25
B-100P, B-105P, KT-120	14.5	29
TC-120R	18	29
T-125, T-125R	8	7
TS-125R	18	29
S-32-2, T-10	12	7
TS-185R	18	29
T-200, TC-200	14.5	7
T-20, TC-250	14.5	7
T-305, TC-305, T-250, T-250R, T-350, T-350R	14.5	7
TS-250, TS-250R	14.5	7
TM-400R	14.5	7
T-500, T-500R	8mm-14 10mm-25	7

* 7 for M-15D

2. Check the oil outlet pipe which carries oil from the pump to the engine. If air is present here, the procedure is as follows:

A. For a small amount of air, allow the engine to idle, and set the oil pump lever to "full open" position; continue at this position until the air is completely removed.

B. For a larger amount of air, remove the oil pump and, using an oil can, force clean oil into the outlet pipes.

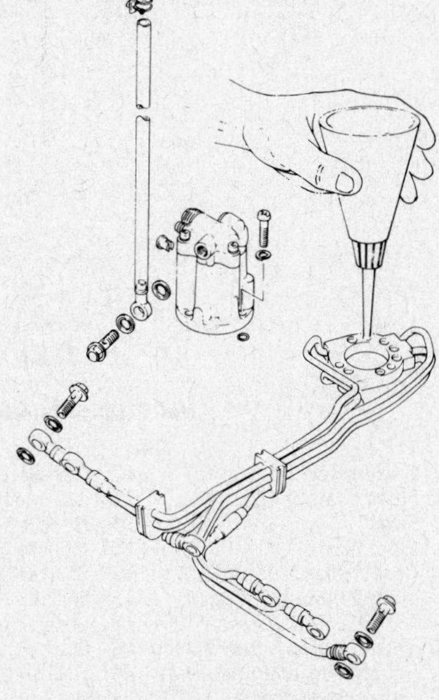

Filling oil pipes (GT750).

3. Check the oil pump itself for any air trapped inside, by loosening then tightening after confirming that oil is discharged.

4. If abnormal oil consumption is noted, and assuming that the pump cable is properly adjusted, the oil pump should be replaced. If this does not cure the problem, there may be leakage somewhere in the pump unit, or the check valve is defective.

5. If not enough oil is being fed to the engine, check the oil tank filler cap for blockage in its breather hole.

6. If the pump has been removed, it is important, upon reassembly, to fill it and all of the oil pipes with oil to expel all air in the system. Readjust the pump as described in "Tune-Up."

Check Valves

These are contained in the oil pipes to prevent oil from being returned to the oil pump due to crankcase pressure. The valve consists of a steel ball bearing loaded by a small coil spring. Service is by replacement.

SRIS

The Suzuki Recycle Injection System is fitted to three cylinder models to prevent the accumulation of unburned oil in the crankcase during periods of slow running and their inevitable discharge when the machine accelerates.

REMOVAL

1. Remove the oil pipe guide plate from the lower crankcase.
2. Disconnect the SRIS pipes at the crankcase lower side by removing the clips with a screw driver.
3. The check valves will be either press-fit into position (as on earlier models) or threaded in.

INSPECTION AND REPAIR

1. Check the oil lines for cracks and bent or pinched lines.
2. Check the operation of the check valves with a syringe as shown. Clean the valve if foreign matter has accumulated. Latest models have a nylon mesh filter fitted.

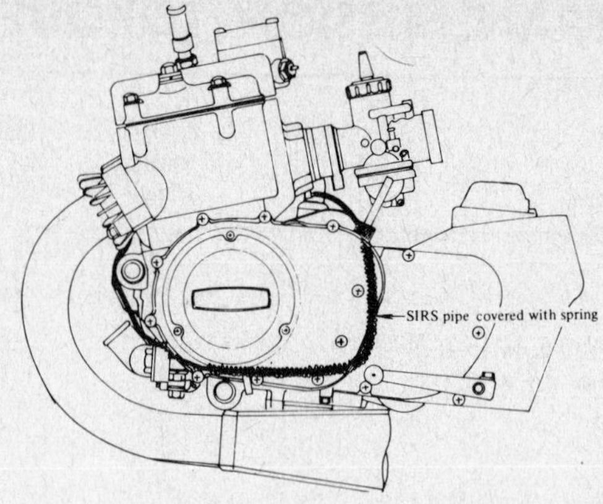

SRIS pipes (later model GT750).

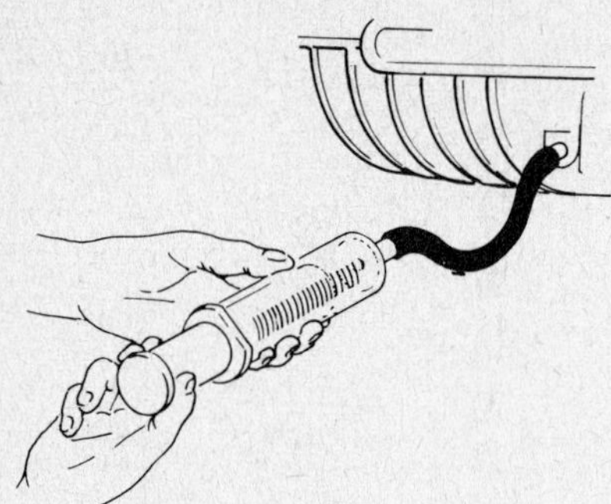

Checking check-valve operation.

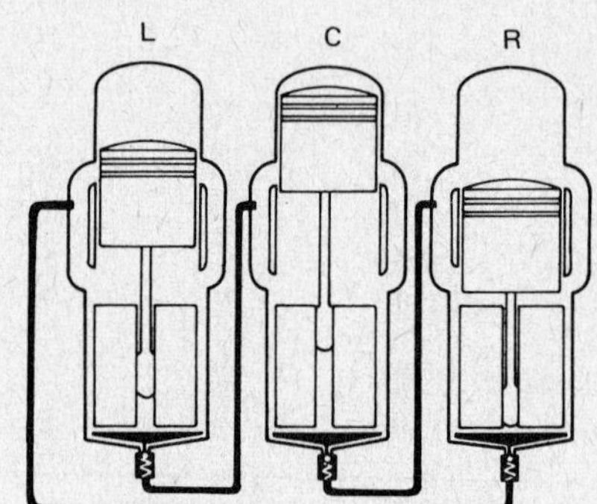

SRIS pipes (GT380 and GT550).

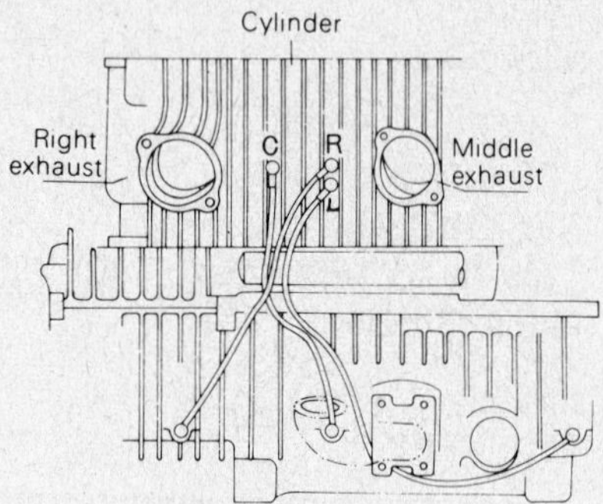

SRIS pipes (GT750).

ASSEMBLY

1. Arrangement of the pipes is as shown. Connect each end of the pipes to its union on the front of the crankcase where "R," "C," and "L" are marked

LUBRICATION SYSTEM TORQUE SPECIFICATIONS (ALL MODELS)

Check valve	3.0 ft lbs	35 in. lbs
Oil pump mounting screw	3.0 ft lbs	35 in. lbs
Oil line union bolts	—	22 in. lbs
Oil tank lens screw	—	16 in. lbs

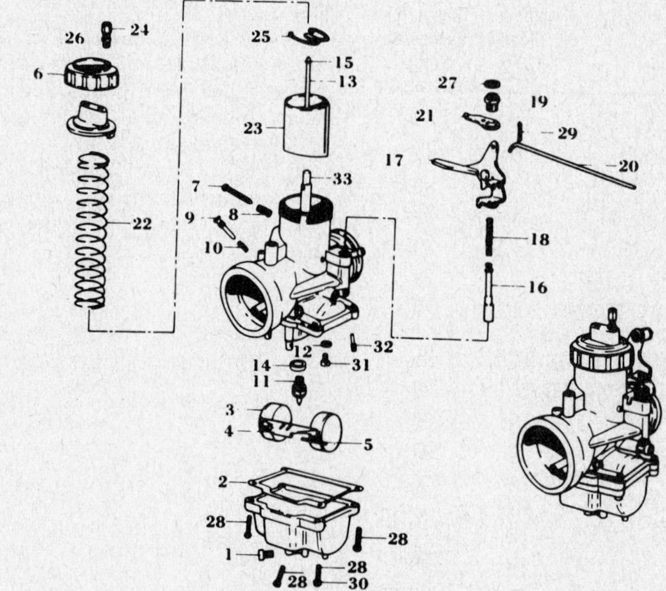

VM-32SC carburetor components.

1. Carburetor drain plug
2. Float chamber gasket
3. Float
4. Float arm
5. Carburetor arm pin
6. Mixing chamber cap
7. Throttle stop screw
8. Throttle stop screw spring
9. Pilot air adjusting screw
10. Pilot screw spring
11. Needle valve
12. Needle jet stop washer
13. Jet needle
14. Needle valve seat gasket
15. Needle clip
16. Starter plunger
17. Starter lever
18. Starter plunger spring
19. Starter plunger cap
20. Starter rod
21. Starter lever spring
22. Throttle valve spring
23. Throttle valve
24. Cable adjuster
25. Throttle valve spring seat
26. Cable adjusting nut
27. Starter rubber cap
28. Cross head screw
29. Cotter pin
30. Lock washer
31. Main jet
32. Pilot jet
33. Needle jet

FUEL SYSTEMS

All models use Mikuni carburetors. Refer to the accompanying chart for specifications. For disassembly and inspection procedures, refer to the Kawasaki, "Fuel Systems Section." Kawasaki's are also equipped with Mikuni units.

Note that float level settings for Suzuki models are given in the "Tune-Up" chapter of this section.

CARBURETOR SPECIFICATIONS

Model	Carb Type	Main Jet Std.	Needle Jet Std.	Jet Needle Std. *	Throttle Cutout (mm)	Pilot Jet	Pilot Outlet (mm)	Needle Seat (mm)	Starter Jet
A-50	VM-16SC	67.5	E-2	3G1-2	2.0	20.0	0.9	1.2	40
AS-50	VM-16SC	70.0	E-2	3G1-2	2.0	20.0	0.9	1.2	40
TS-50R	VM-16SC	75.0	E-2	3E3-3	2.0	17.5	0.9	1.2	40
F-50	VM-14SC	102.5	E-0	3F3-3	2.5	17.5	0.9	1.2	40
MT-50	VM-14SC	105.0	E-0	3G9-3	2.5	17.5	0.9	1.2	40
M-15, D	VM-15SC	80.0	E-0	14F3-2	2.0	20.0	0.9	1.2	40
M-31	VM-15SC	120.0	E-0	15F1-3	3.0	17.5	0.9	1.2	30
K-10	VM-17SC	65.0	0-0	4J5-2	2.0	20.0	1.2	1.5	40
K-11	VM-17SC	75.0	N-6	4J5-3	1.0	17.5	1.2	1.5	40
K-10P	VM-20SH	110.0	N-6	4DH5-4	2.0	25.0	1.4	N/A	30
K-11P	VM-20SH	95.0	N-6	4DH5-3	2.0	25.0	1.4	N/A	30
TS/TC-90	VM-19SC①	180.0	E-1	5F12-3	2.5	17.5	0.6	2.0	80
RV-90	VM-17SC	250.0	E-6	4I1-2	3.0	17.5	1.0	1.2	40
A/AS-100	VM-20SC	80.0	E-0	5ES-2	2.5	45.0	0.5	1.5	60
B-100P	VM-20SH	95.0	N-2	4F9-4	2.0	25.0	1.4	1.5	40
KT-120	VM-20SH	100.0	0-0	4F10-3	2.5	25.0	1.4	N/A	30
TC-120	VM-20SH	110.0	0-0	4D8-3	2.5	25.0	N/A	N/A	40
T-125	MD-18SC	72.5	2.0	4F13-4	2.5	20.0	0.9	1.5	30
TS/TC-125	VM-24SH	125.0	0-4	4DH5-2	3.0	25.0	0.7	2.0	80
S-32	VM-20SH	80.0	0-4	4D4-2	2.0	25.0	0.6	1.5	30
TS-185	VM-24SH	130.0	0-6	5DH4-2②	2.5	25.0	0.7	2.0	80
T-200 (X-5)	VM-22SH	140.0	N-8	4DG6-3	2.5	25.0	0.6	1.5	30
T-10	VM-20	70.0	N-6	24A-4③	2.5④	30.0⑤	0.6	2.5	N/A
T-20 (X-6)	VM-24SH	95.0	N-6	4DH5-3	2.5	35.0	1.2	2.0	50
TS-250	VM-28SC	115.0	P-2	5EP6-3	2.0	25.0	0.8	3.3	130
TS-250R, J	VM-28SH	180.0	0-4	5DN3-2	2.5	25.0	0.9	2.5	80
T-250	VM-24SH	87.5	N-6	4DH5-3	2.5	30.0	0.6	2.0	50
T-250R, J	VM-26SH	110.0	0-2	5CN3-3	2.5	25.0	N/A	N/A	N/A
T-305, 350	VM-32SH	170.0	Q-0	5DP2-3	2.5	30.0	0.6	2.5	60
T-350R, J	VM-32SH	112.5	P-6	5DL13-4	2.5	35.0	N/A	N/A	N/A
T-500	VM-32SC	150.0	P-4⑥	5FP8-3	2.5	30.0	0.6	2.5	70
GT380	VM-24SC	80.0	0-5	4DH7-2	3.0	22.5	—	—	60
GT550	VM-28SC	⑦	0-5	5DH21-3	2.5	27.5	0.5	2.0	60
GT750	VM-32SC	⑧	⑨	5F16-3	2.5	30.0	0.6	2.5	50

* The last number is the clipped groove.
① Double air jet type:

	TS-90	TC-90
no. 1 jet	—0.7	0.9
no. 2 jet	—1.0	0.5

② TS-185R, J: 5DH4-3.
③ After engine no. 16816: 24A-2.
④ After engine no. 16816: 3.0.
⑤ After engine no. 16816: 40.0.
⑥ T-500R, J: LP-4.
⑦ Left and right carburetors—95.0; center carburetor—92.5.
⑧ Left and right carburetors—102.5; center carburetor—100.0.
⑨ Left and right carburetors—P-4; center carburetor—P-3.

ELECTRICAL SYSTEMS

IGNITION SYSTEM COMPONENT TESTS

1. The condenser for the ignition points can be checked by noticing any sparking or arcing at the points during operation. If an ohmeter is connected between the positive lead of the condenser and ground, it would ideally read an infinite resistance, or at least 5MΩ (5 million ohms). If the reading is 1MΩ or less, the unit must be replaced.

2. The coil, on battery and coil ignition models, is best checked by replaceent. The resistance of the coil primary wind-

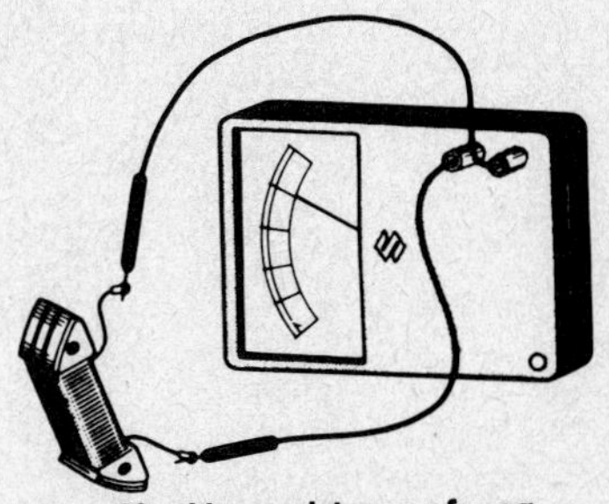
Checking resistance of magneto primary coil.

ing can be checked by connecting an ohmeter across the low tension terminals. The reading should be 3-5Ω.

Magneto ignition (primary) coils can be examined in the same way and should yield a value of 1-3Ω.

Magneto coils (see illustration) are reached after removing the flywheel. Models up to 90 cc have two coils in the magneto (one for ignition, one for lighting), while models over 90 cc have two lighting coils.

Magneto primary coil (left) and lamp coil (right) on single lamp coil models (less than 80cc).

Disconnect the primary coil lead from the points, and check the resistance. This should be 1-3Ω as mentioned above.

Check the clearance between the ends of the coils and the flywheel. There should be about 0.015–0.020 in. clearance.

The inside surface of the rotor and the laminated cores of the coils should not touch; inspect these surfaces for scuff marks.

CHARGING SYSTEM

Testing The Magneto

1. The magneto lamp coil can be tested with a continuity tester in the same way as the magneto primary coil is tested. Between the yellow/green and red/green wires, resistance should at 1.9 Ω; between the yellow/green and green/white, 0.45Ω. No reading should be attainable between the wires and stator housing.

2. The best way to test the lamp coil output is using the voltmeter and ammeter (or milliammeter). First, check out the battery voltage using the voltmeter, hooked up as per the magneto test schematic. It is important that the battery be fully charged before testing output, otherwise the results will not be accurate.

3. If the battery is fully charged, hook up the milliammeter, or better yet 0-5 DC ammeter if your tester has this range, as illustrated.

4. Start the bike and allow it to idle. No current will be shown at idle as a rule.

5. Speed the engine up to 2,000 rpm. At this speed, the output should be about 0.15 amperes, or 150 milliamperes, DC. If you don't have a 0-5 scale, you will have to stop here, otherwise the sensitive milliammeter will be damaged.

6. If you have this scale, speed up the engine to maximum rpm (about 8,000 rpm). The output should be 2.5–3.5 amperes DC.

7. Now, turn on the headlight high beam, or place the ignition switch in the headlight or night position. If all is well, output should be 100 milliamperes at about 2,500 rpm.

8. To check the light coil output, connect up an AC voltmeter as illustrated. Place the electrical system in the night mode, with all lights on. At 2,000 rpm, output should be at least 6.0 volts, and at 8,000 rpm should be not more than 9.0 volts. If these figures are not attainable, check the wiring, connectors, rectifier, and coils in that order. Sometimes the ignition switch itself is corroded or not making proper contact.

Testing The Alternator

1. Connect a 0-5 ammeter between the positive battery terminal and the wire removed from that terminal.

2. With the lights off, start the engine and gradually run it up to 2,000 rpm while watching the meter. The meter should begin to show a slight charge at this speed.

3. Run the engine up to 5,000 rpm and observe the meter. Charging current should be 1–2 amperes.

4. Turn on the lights and again observe the meter at 2,000 rpm and 5,000 rpm.

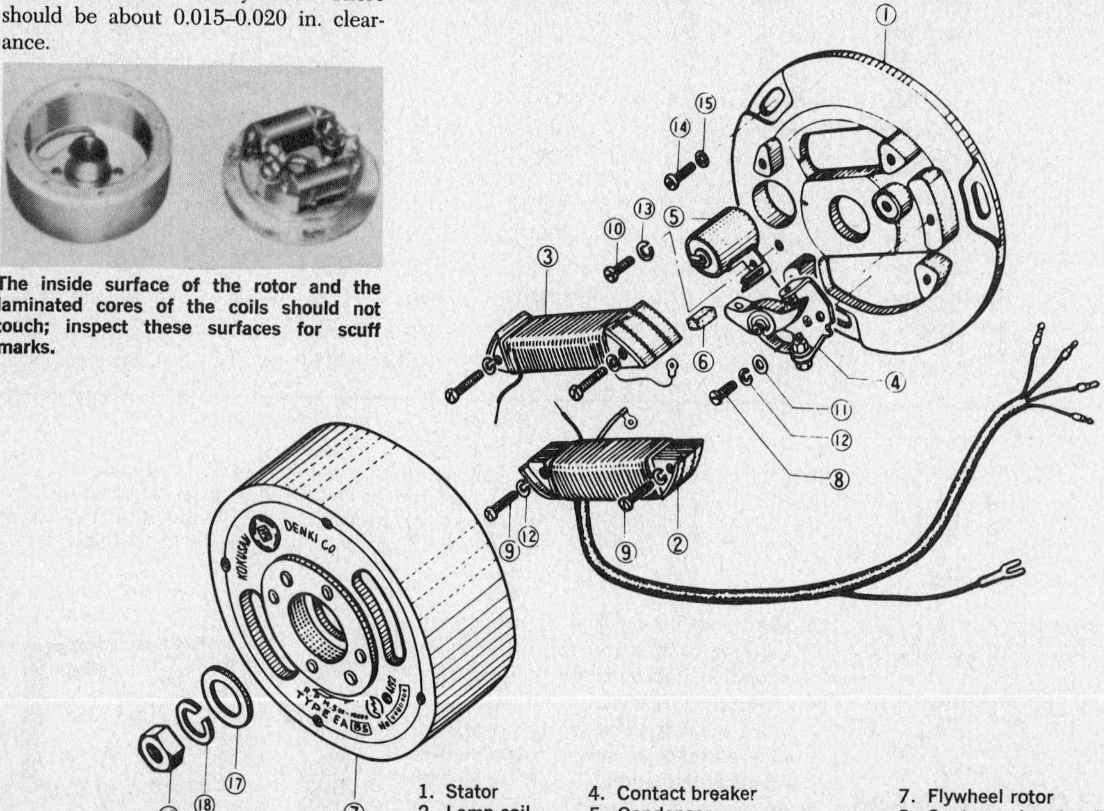

1. Stator
2. Lamp coil
3. Primary coil
4. Contact breaker
5. Condenser
6. Contact breaker cam oil felt
7. Flywheel rotor
8. Contacter breaker fitting screw
9. Coil fitting screw

Typical magneto components.

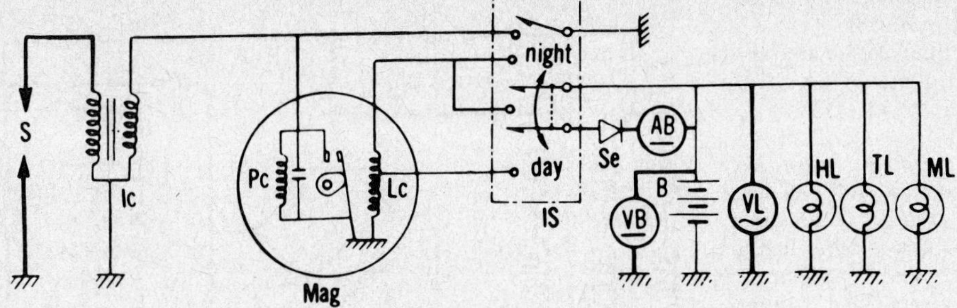

Magneto test circuit—single lamp coil system.

Mag	Flywheel magneto	AB	D.C. ammeter (charging current inspection)
LC	Lamp coil	VL	A.C. voltmeter (lighting voltage inspection)
SE	Selenium rectifier	VB	D.C. voltmeter (battery voltage inspection)
B	Battery	S	Three prong gap tester
HL	Head lamp	PC	Primary coil
TL	Tail lamp	LC	Lamp coil
ML	Lamps in speedometer	IS	Ignition switch

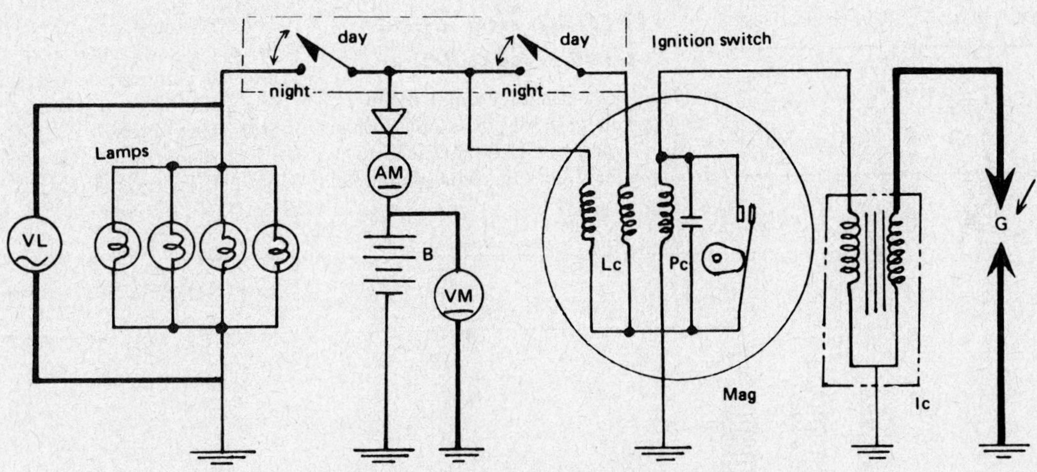

Magneto test circuit—double lamp coil system.

Mag	:	Flywheel magneto	B	:	Battery
Ic	:	Ignition coil	VL	:	A.C. Volt meter
Lc	:	Lamp coil	AM	:	D.C. Ammeter
Pc	:	Primary coil	VM	:	D.C. Voltmeter
Lamps	:	Head lamp, tail lamp and lamps in speedometer and tachometer	G	:	Three prong gap tester

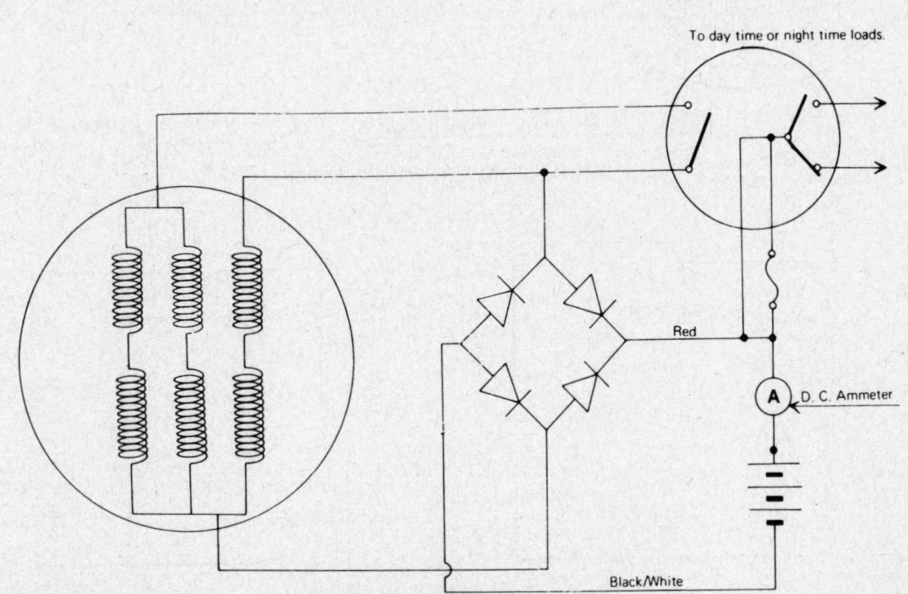

Checking alternator charging current.

Readings should be 100 milliamperes and 1.5–2.5 amperes respectively.

5. If the charging current is not to specifications, check the battery, rectifiers, and no-load voltage.

6. To measure no-load voltage, disconnect the wires from the alternator green/white, red/green and yellow/-green wires. Connect an AC voltmeter of at least 0–100 volts between the alternator red/green and yellow/green wires.

7. Start the engine and check the output. With the rectifier out of the circuit, some idea of its condition can be ascertained.

These figures may vary for different bikes, but the ratio between them should be approximately the same or the alternator could be defective.

Engine rpm	Normal	Minimum	Maximum
2,000	23	17	33
5,000	49	40	60
8,000	82	70	95

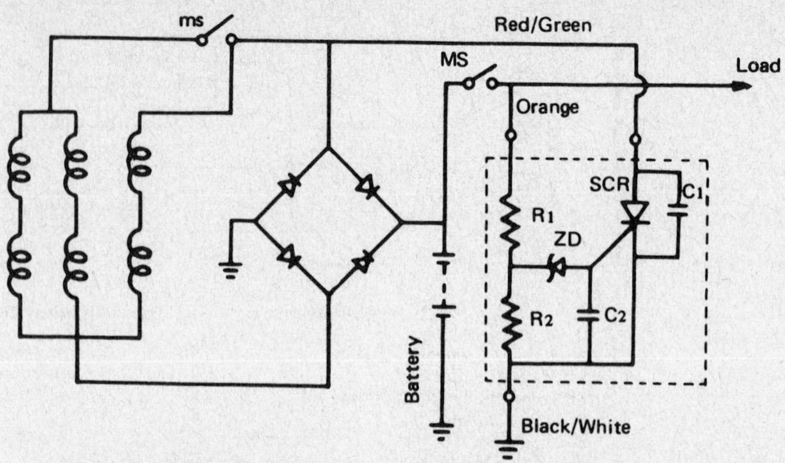

T-500 charging system uses a zener diode voltage regulator.

Testing The Zener Diode Regulator

The Titan utilizes a zener diode voltage regulator that maintains battery charge voltage at 15.8–16.6, even when running for long distances at high speeds.

The regulator is a small box hidden under the seat and attached to the frame. The internal components are shown in the schematic diagram, along with the path of current through the regulator. The zener diode, which has the capacity of prohibiting reverse current flow until a

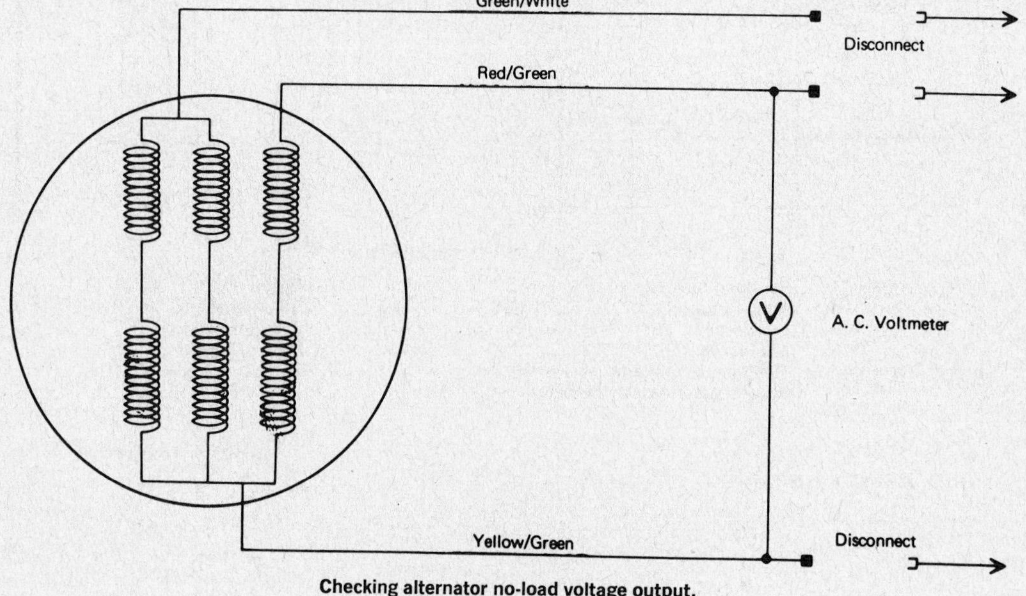

Checking alternator no-load voltage output.

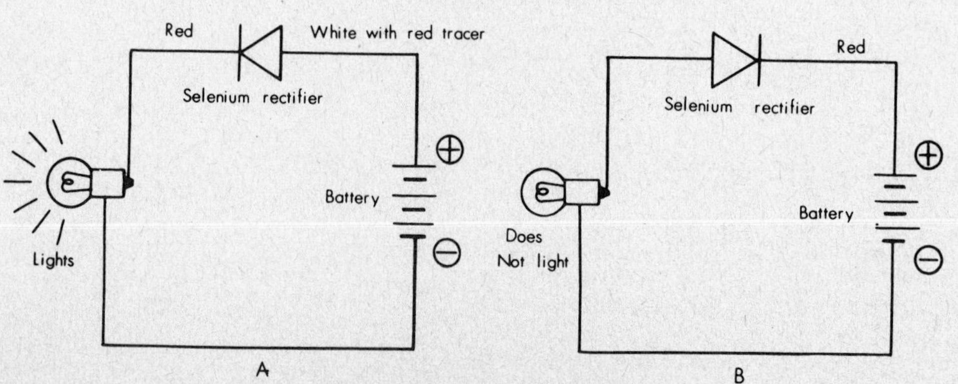

Testing rectifier with a continuity tester.

predetermined value is reached, is used as the actual regulating agent in this circuit. Current from the battery terminal flows into the zener diode (ZD) through a resistor (R1), thence to the silicon rectifier (SCR) gate through to the SCR cathode to the battery negative terminal (ground). The SCR is energized when the terminal voltage on its gate exceeds 16 V (approximately), and shorts the alternator output to lower the battery voltage. In this case, the silicon rectifier acts as a very sensitive switch that "shuts off" the alternator when it "senses" that battery voltage is too high.

1. Before disconnecting the regulator, make note of where the wires go. To hook this unit up incorrectly will result in its immediate destruction. The orange wire goes to the positive battery terminal, the green/red wire to the input side of the rectifier, and the black/white wire to the battery negative terminal. First check to make sure that all connections are tight, with the key off. Wiggling wires with the key on can damage the zener diode and silicon rectifier.

2. Check the resistance between the orange and the black/white wires: it should be 1.1KΩ.

3. Check continuity between the red/-green and black/white wires. There should be no current flow in either direction, determined by switching the test prods from one wire to the other. Make sure you use only a low-voltage continuity tester or ohmmeter, otherwise the SCR will be ruined.

For those of you who might be interested, here are a few more specifications on the regulator:

ZD zener voltage	13.0± 12 percent
C1 value	0.01 microfarad
C2 value	10.0 microfarad
R1 value	80-130 ohms
R2 value	1,000 ohms

Testing The Rectifier

As was previously mentioned, two types of rectifiers are used on Suzuki cycles: silicon-diode and selenium. Both these types will pass current in one direction only, therefore they can be tested by using a low-voltage continuity tester or ohmmeter.

No current, indicated by no ohmmeter reading or an unlit bulb, will be shown when the test prods are connected between the rectifier terminals in one direction, but switching the prods should result in current flow. Compound rectifier units, having more than one rectifier inside, can be tested as per the illustration.

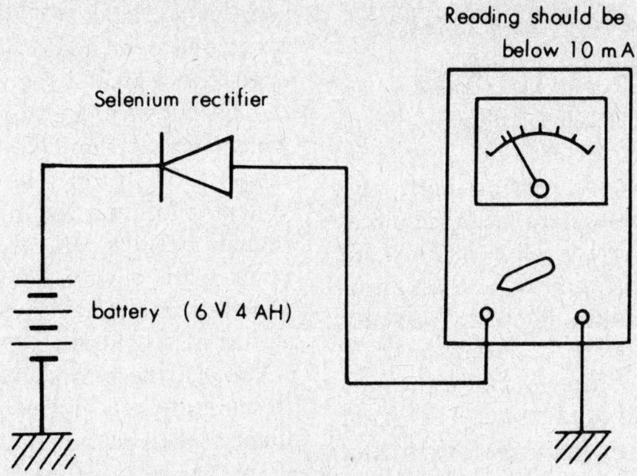

Testing rectifier with a milliameter.

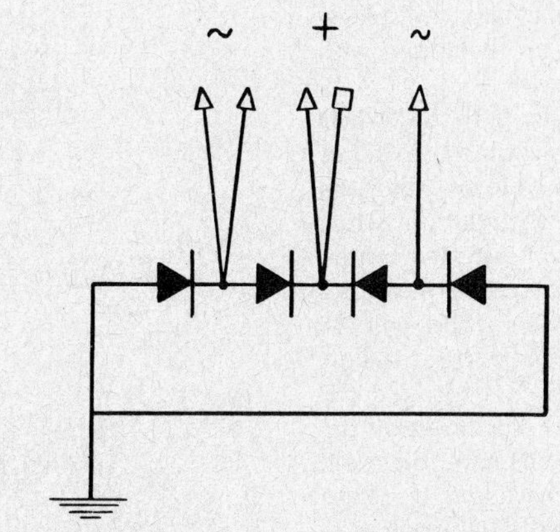

Testing multi-unit rectifier assembly.

DC starter dynamo unit.

DC Starter Dynamo

M-15D, T-10, S-32

The three models listed above utilize a combination starter and DC generator, the same armature serving both purposes. This type system, also known as "Dynastart," consists of a fixed stator mounted to the crankcase and an armature that rotates with the shaft. The stator serves as a holder for the carbon brushes, as well as the mounting point for the ignition points and condensers. The stator contains either six field coils (M-15D) or eight field coils, which do double duty as the field coils for both the generator and starter motor. Two brushes are used on the M-15D, while the larger displacement T-10 and S-32 are equipped with four brushes.

The starter circuits for both the M-15D and S-32 are identical, while the 250 cc T-10 is wired differently. In operation, on the M-15D and S-32, the ignition switch (S) is turned on and the starter button (SB) pressed, causing current to flow from the battery to the switch relay coil (3). The relay closes, causing current to flow from the battery to the starter field coil (FS) and armature, as illustrated by the solid arrows in the schematic diagram. The armature is then caused to rotate with considerable force, it being wired in this situation as an electric motor, to start the engine. At the same time, excitation current flows to the generator field coil (FD) and the voltage regulator. When the engine starts and the starter button is released, the starter switch relay opens and the generator field coil (FD) ceases to be supplied with battery current, instead of getting current from the armature, as illustrated by the dotted arrows in the schematic. The dynamo then works as a generator while the engine is running, supplying current to the lights and accessories, and to the battery through cutout relay coil (2). The charging voltage is regulated by the voltage regulator coil (1) and the resistance (6). When the generator begins to put out too much, the coil (1) opens the regulator relay points to shunt the output through the resistance (6), which causes the field current to decrease to the proper level. If generator voltage continues to rise, even with the regulator points open, the movable relay point shorts out the generator field coil, which drops the field current to zero and results in no output.

Usually, the only service required for this unit is brush replacement and adjustment of the voltage regulator and cutout relay. The field coil can be tested with a continuity tester, as illustrated, but if this unit is defective it must be replaced.

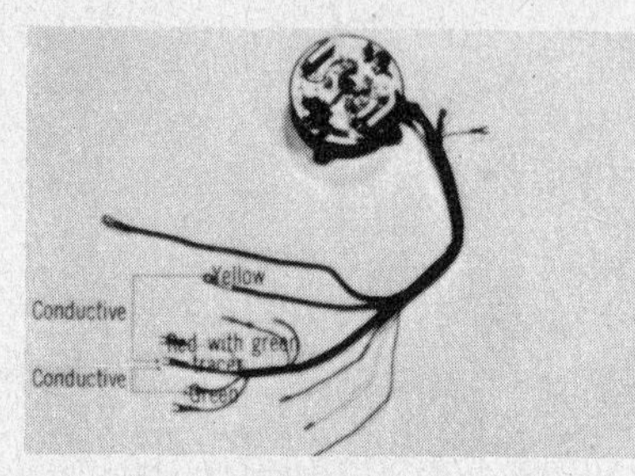

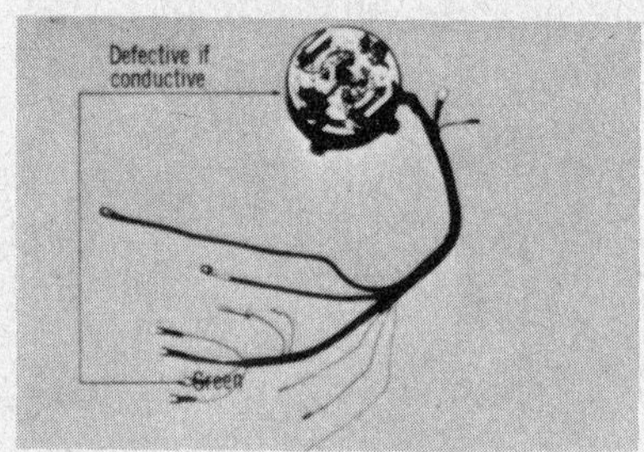

Testing field coils.

Starter Troubleshooting

1. If the starter doesn't work with the key on and button pressed, first check all the connections, the fuse, and the battery state of charge.
2. The starter button and starter switch (relay) can be checked by bypassing them. Connect a jumper wire between the positive battery terminal and the voltage regulator M terminal.
3. If the starter spins, either the starter relay or button is at fault and should be repaired or replaced.
4. The next thing to check is the brushes. If they are worn down, or if the commutator is dirty or oily, the starter will not spin. If everything is in order at this point. you'll have to disassemble the starter and check the field coils and armature, as illustrated.

Generator Troubleshooting

Check the wiring for loose connections and short circuits. The biggest cause of problems in this area is worn-through insulation where the wires contact the frame. Check the voltage regulator of the M-15D and S-32 as follows:

1. Disconnect the wires from the regulator B terminal. These are the ones that go to the positive battery terminal.
2. Connect a DC voltmeter of at least 0–25 V between this regulator terminal and ground, observing correct polarity.
3. Start the engine by momentarily touching the wires that were removed from the B terminal to the regulator M terminal, then remove these wires and hang them out of the way.
4. At 2,000–4,000 rpm, the voltage shown should be 15.1–16.3 for the M-15D; 14.5–15.5 for the S-32.

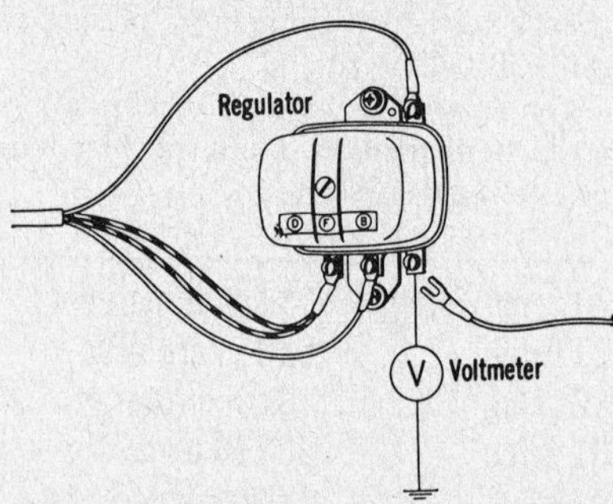

Checking voltage regulator charging voltage.

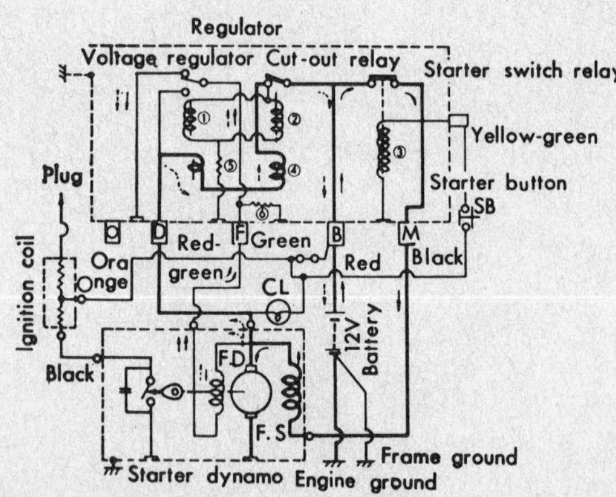

Starter circuit (M-15D and S-32).

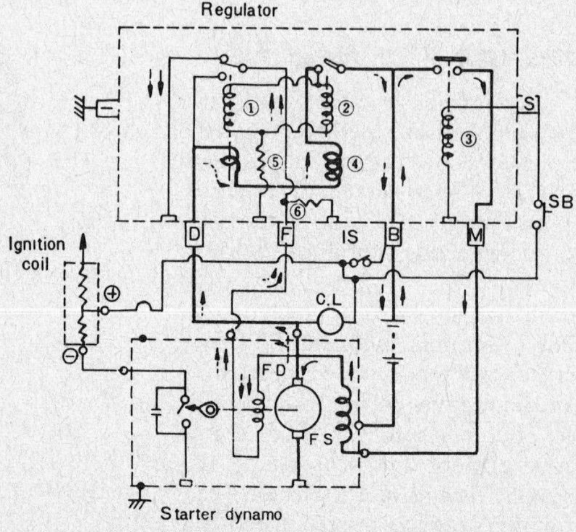

Starter circuit (T-10).

5. To find out whether it is the regulator or generator that is at fault if the voltage is not to specifications, disconnect the wire from the regulator F terminal.

6. Running the engine at 3,000 rpm, momentarily ground this wire while observing the voltmeter. If the regulator is bad, the voltage will rise to over 25 volts; if the generator is bad, there will be no change. Don't ground this wire for more than half a second at a time, or the generator will be damaged.

7. To check the regulator on the T-10, the battery's charging circuit wire must be disconnected to prevent the battery from influencing the test. Remove the regulator B terminal wire and connect a voltmeter (0–25) between the regulator D terminal and ground, observing correct polarity.

8. Start the engine and check the voltage at 2,000–4,000 rpm: it should be 14.-4–15.6 V.

Adjusting The Voltage Regulator

The voltage regulator can be adjusted by following the instructions on the diagram. Bending the adjusting arm upward increases voltage, while bending it downward decreases voltage. Check the voltage regulator points for wear or oily surfaces. The points can be filed with an emery board and adjusted by bending the highspeed contact point arm. The proper gap is 0.008–0.016 in.

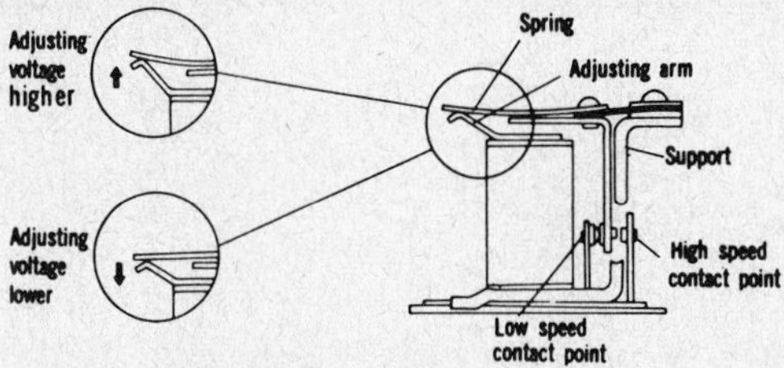

Adjusting the voltage regulator.

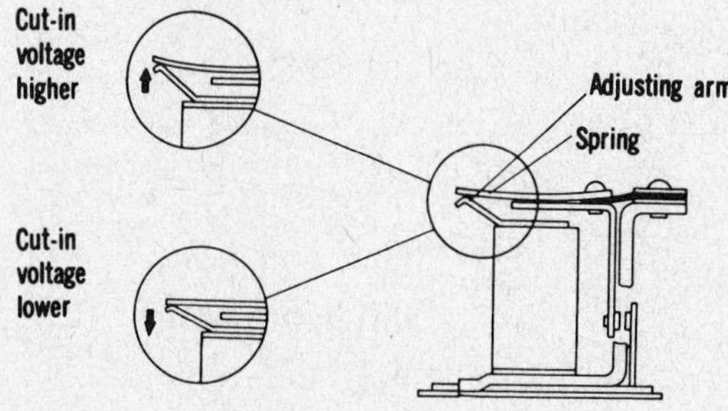

Adjusting cutout relay.

Checking And Adjusting The Cutout Relay

To check the cutout relay, disconnect the wire from the regulator B terminal and connect a voltmeter (0–25) between this regulator terminal and ground, observing correct polarity. With the engine running, gradually increase the speed until the meter needle shudders and stops. At this point, the reading should be 12.-0–13.5 volts. If not, the voltage can be adjusted by bending the adjusting arm on the cutout relay, as illustrated. Bending the arm upward increases the voltage, while bending it downward decreases voltage. As with the regulator points, the cutout relay points can be filed if necessary and adjusted to the proper specification, which in this case is 0.016–0.032 in.

Starter Motor

GT550, GT750

ARMATURE

1. Check the condition of the mica undercut and measure its depth. Using the accompanying illustration for reference, make sure that the undercut is not less the 0.3 mm.

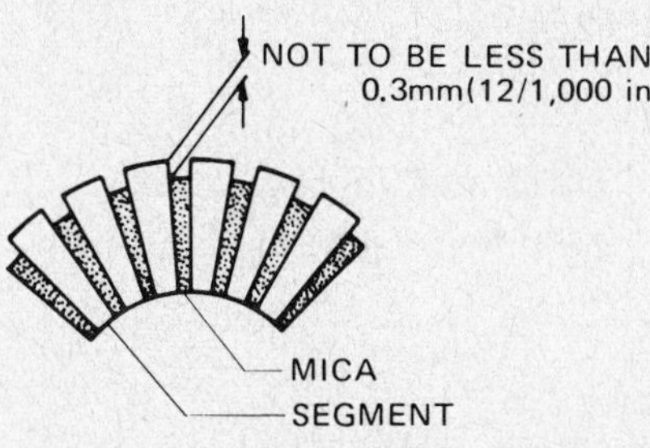

Armature undercut.

2. Clean out of the grooves any dust which may have accumulated from brush wear.

3. Check for continuity between the commutator and the opposite end of the armature (see illustration). There should not be any.

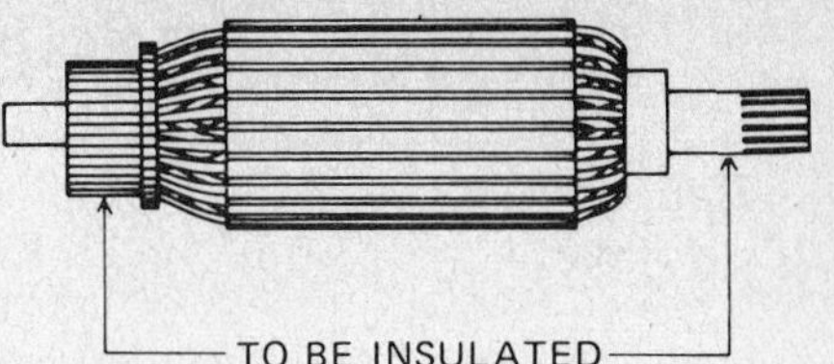

Checking armature for continuity.

FIELD COILS

Refering to the accompanying illustration for reference, check the series and shunt coils for continuity. When performing this check, disconnect the carbon brushes from the armature.

CARBON BRUSHES

Check the brushes for wear and replace them when worn to the limits shown.

Starter Motor Troubleshooting

Starter does not function

A. Weak or dead battery

B. Poor contact at the starter relay terminal

C. Poor contact at the starter switch points

D. Poor battery terminal connections

E. Poor contact at the starter brushes

F. Burned communtator

G. Shorted starter armature

H. Shorted starter field coils

I. Weak brush springs

J. Defective starter relay

2. Starter turns, but crankshaft does not

A. Slipping starter clutch

B. Defective reduction gears

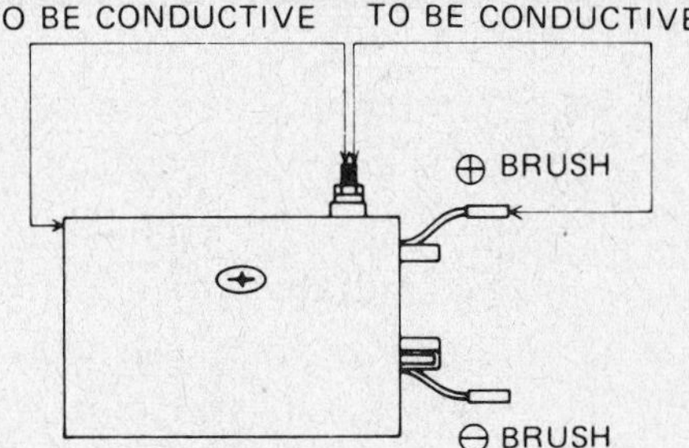

Series and shunt coil continuity tests.

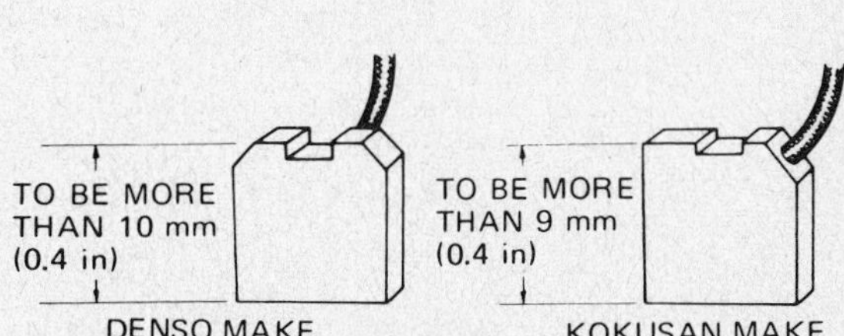

Replace the brushes when the limit shown is reached.

STARTER MOTOR SPECIFICATIONS

STARTING MOTOR	
Voltage	12 Volt
Output	0.5 KW
Actuating time	30 seconds
Direction of rotation	Counterclockwise as seen from pinion side
Number of pinion teeth	10 teeth
No-load characteristic	
Voltage	At 11 volts
Amperage	Less than 50 amperage
Revolution	More than 4,500 rpm
Load characteristic	
Voltage	At 8.5 volts
Amperage	Less than 150 amperage
Torque	More than 0.2 kg-m (1.45 ft-lb)
Revolution	More than 1,800 rpm
Lock characteristic	
Voltage	At 5.5 volts
Amperage	Less than 280 amperage
Torque	More than 0.35 kg-m (2.52 ft-lb)
Weight	2.4 kg (5.32 lb)
Battery	14 AH
Reduction ratios	
Primary	4.78 : 1 (starter motor to idle gear 9 : 43)
Secondary	2.50 : 1 (idle gear to crankshaft 22 : 55)
Total	11.95 : 1
STARTER RELAY	
Rated voltage	12 volts
Actuating voltage	More than 8 volts

Thermostat (GT750)

A thermostat is used to control the flow of the cooling solution. When the temperature of the collant reaches 180°F, the thermostat opens and allows the coolant to circulate through the radiator, as in standard automobile practice.

The thermostat is a wax pellet type and the valve is designed to open and close with the expansion and contraction of the pellet.

1. Make sure that the pellet is not cracked or damaged in any way.
2. Immerse the thermostat in water and heat the water noting the operation of the thermostat and its various operating ranges.

At 180°F, the valve should begin to open; at 203°F, it should be completely open. The operating stroke in this position should be 8.0 mm (0.3 in.).

If the thermostat does not meet these specifications, it should be replaced.

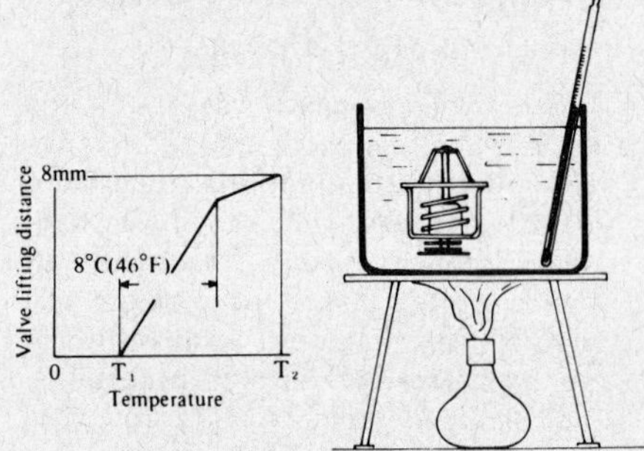

Testing thermostat operation.

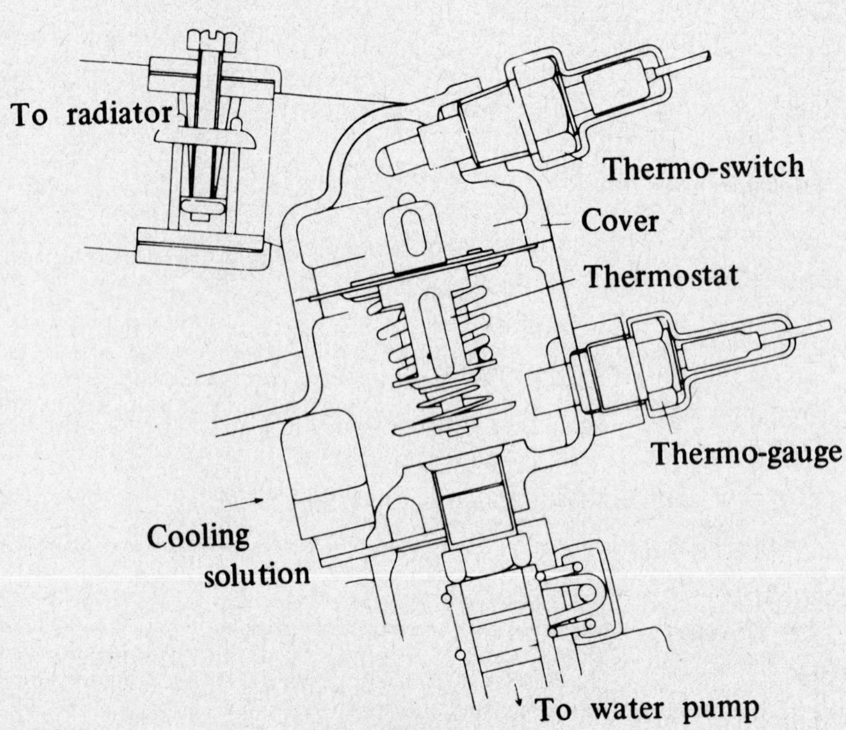

Thermostat location.

WIRING DIAGRAMS

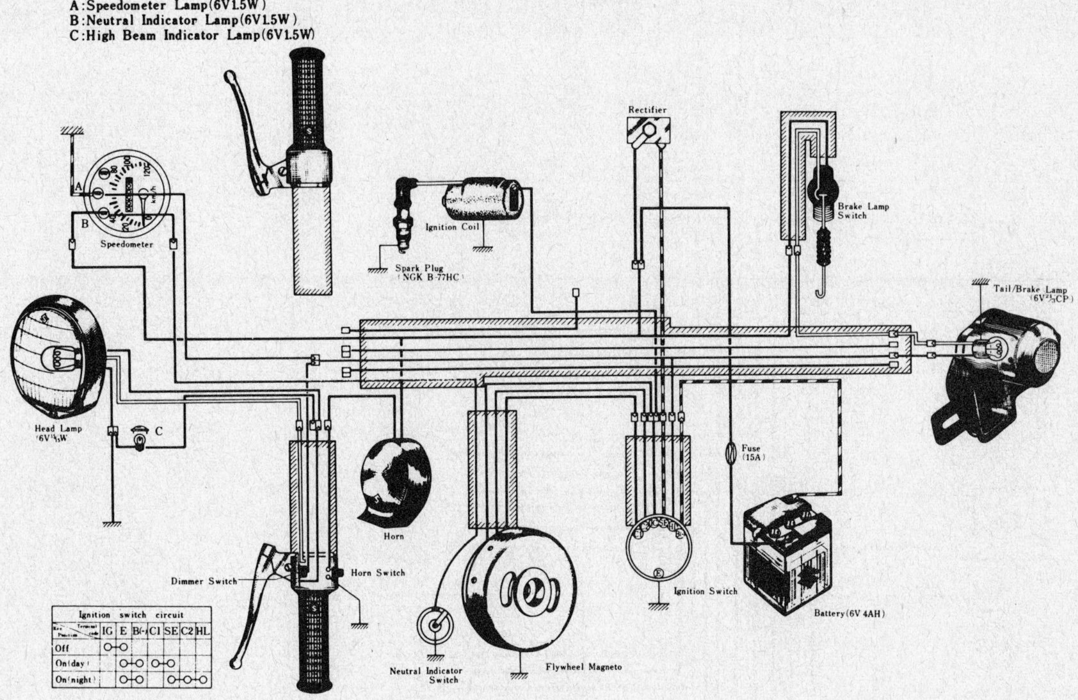

Key Position \ Terminal code	IG	E	B(-)	C1	SE	C2	HL
Off	○	○					
On(day)		○	○	○	○		
On(night)		○	○		○	○	○

A-50, AS-50.

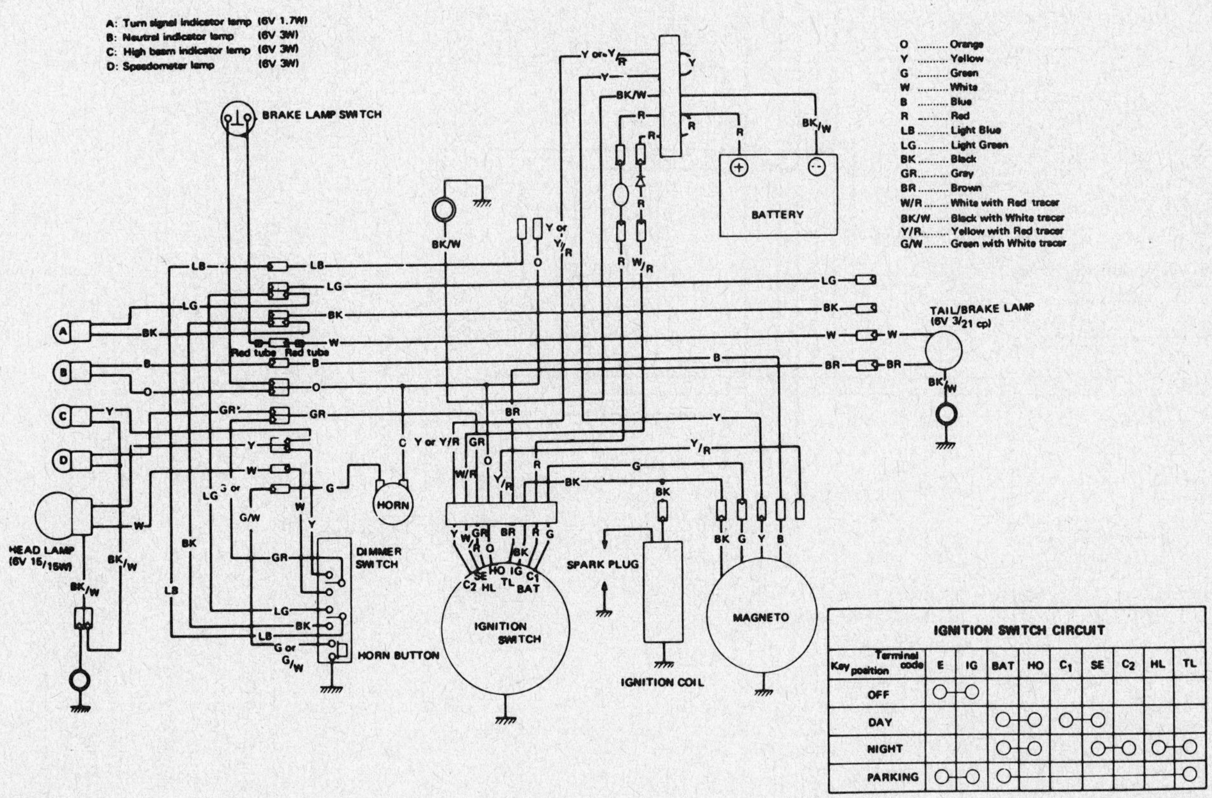

Key position \ Terminal code	E	IG	BAT	HO	C_1	SE	C_2	HL	TL
OFF	○	○							
DAY			○	○	○	○			
NIGHT			○	○		○	○	○	○
PARKING	○	○	○						○

MT-50.

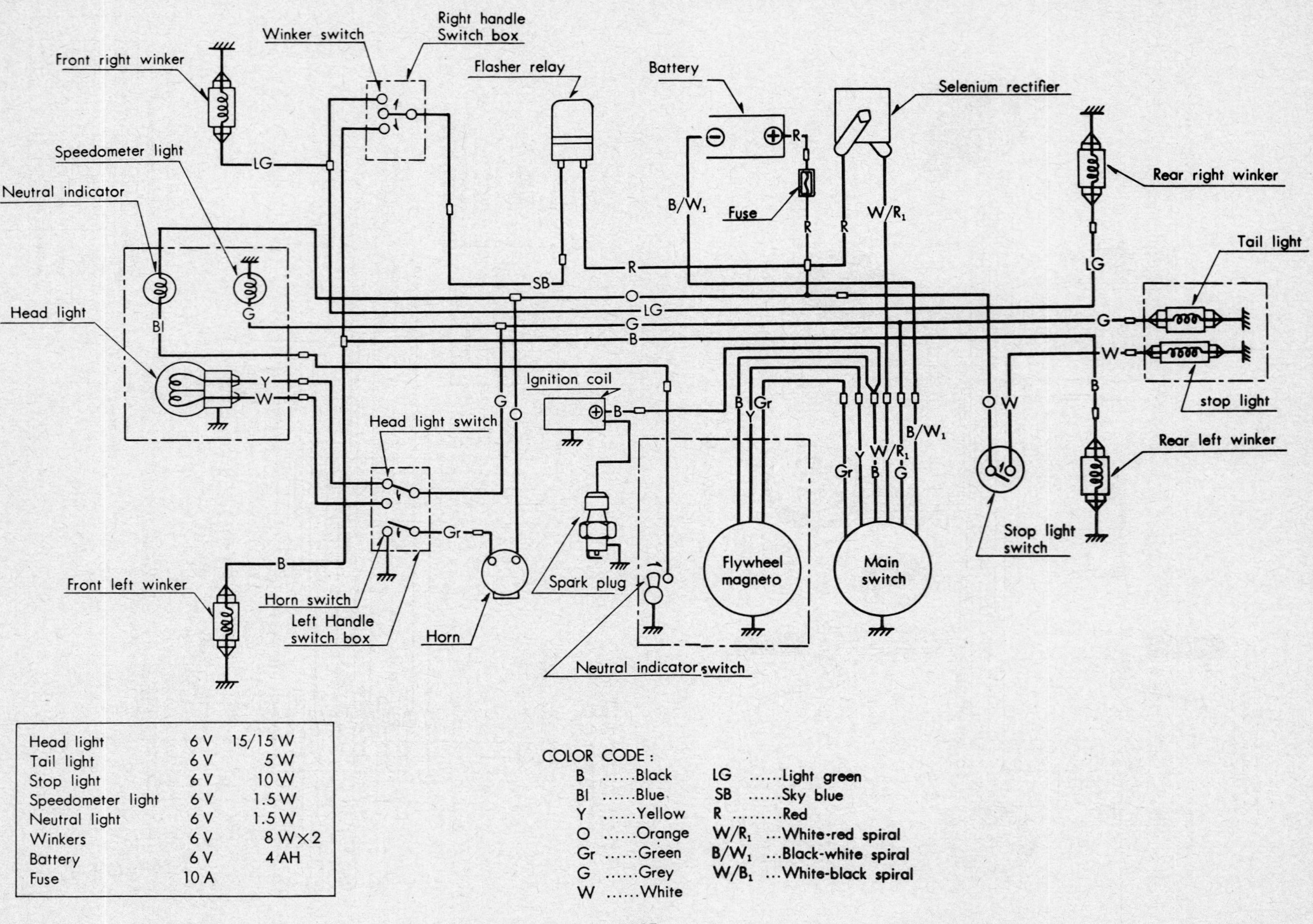

Head light	6 V	15/15 W
Tail light	6 V	5 W
Stop light	6 V	10 W
Speedometer light	6 V	1.5 W
Neutral light	6 V	1.5 W
Winkers	6 V	8 W×2
Battery	6 V	4 AH
Fuse	10 A	

COLOR CODE :

B	......Black	LG	......Light green
Bl	......Blue	SB	......Sky blue
Y	......Yellow	R	.........Red
O	......Orange	W/R_1	...White-red spiral
Gr	......Green	B/W_1	...Black-white spiral
G	......Grey	W/B_1	...White-black spiral
W	......White		

M-15.

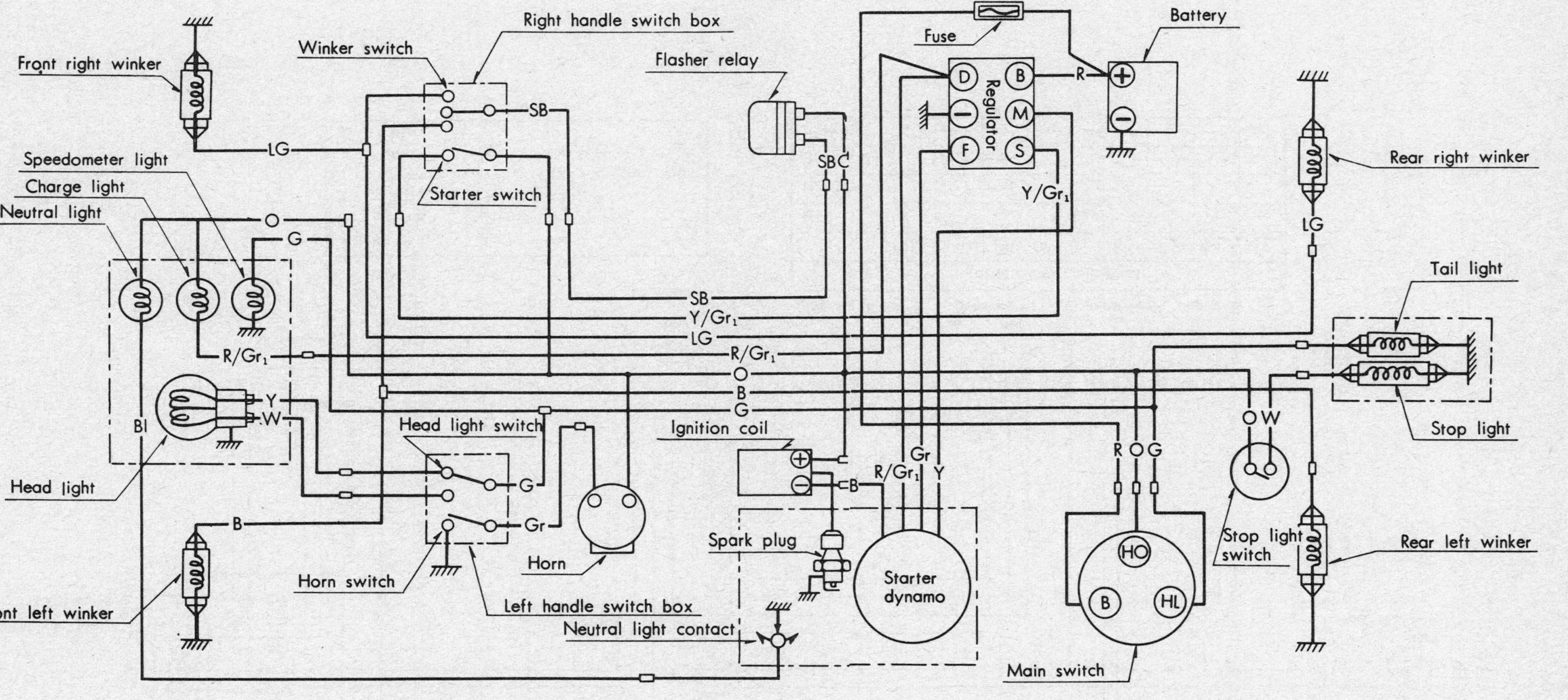

Head light	12 V	25/25 W
Tail light	12 V	5 W
Stop light	12 V	10 W
Speedometer light	12 V	2 W
Neutral light	12 V	2 W
Charge light	12 V	2 W
Winkers	12 V	10 W×2
Battery	12 V	7 AH
Fuse	10 A	

COLOR CODE:

B.........Black
Bl ......Blue
Y ......Yellow
O ......Orange
G ......Grey
W ......White
LG ......Light green
SB.........Sky blue
R ....Red
R/Gr₁ ...Red-green spiral
Y/Gr₁ ...Yellow-green spiral
Gr ......Green

M-15D.

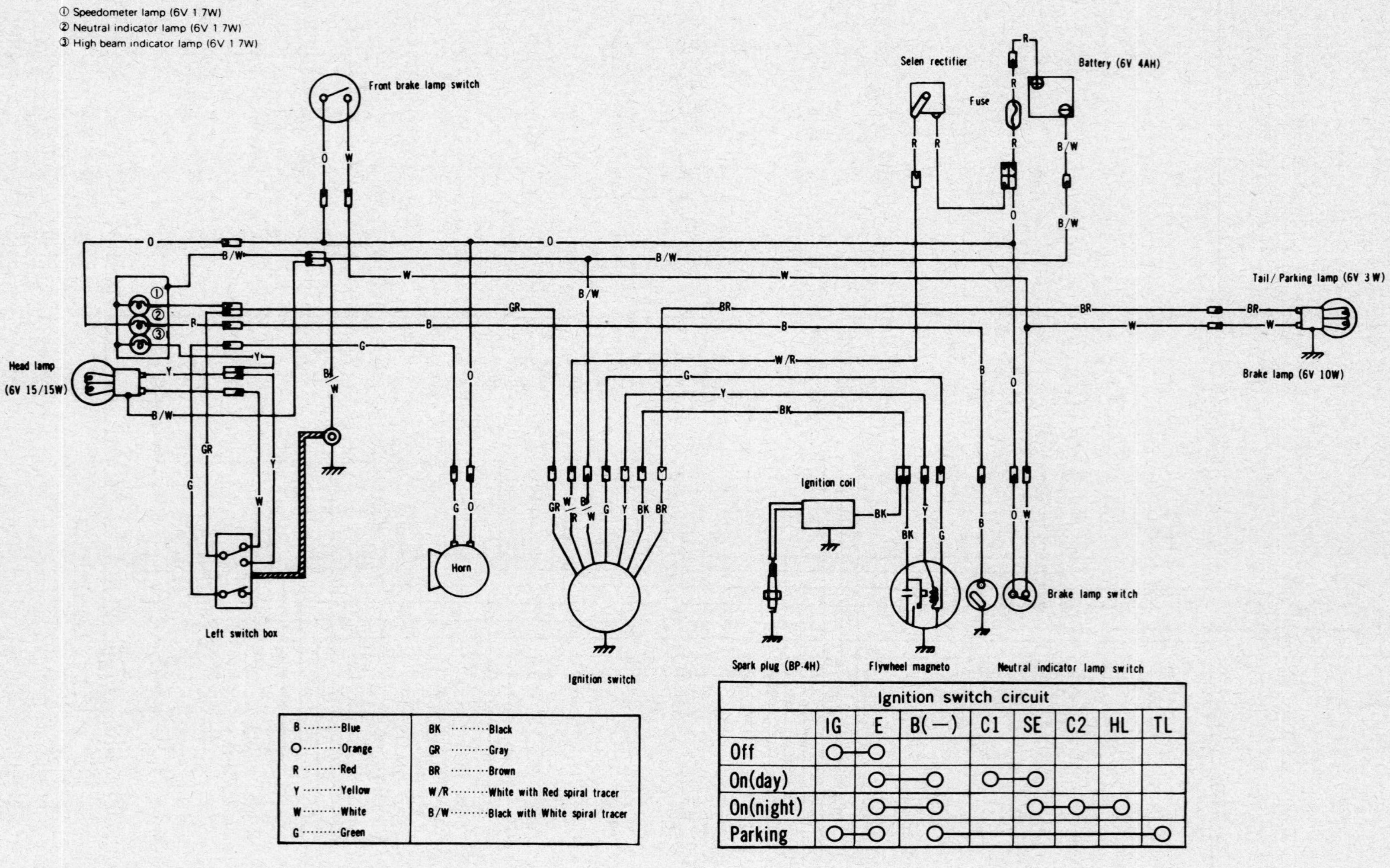
① Speedometer lamp (6V 1.7W)
② Neutral indicator lamp (6V 1.7W)
③ High beam indicator lamp (6V 1.7W)
Front brake lamp switch
Selen rectifier
Fuse
Battery (6V 4AH)
Tail/ Parking lamp (6V 3W)
Brake lamp (6V 10W)
Head lamp
(6V 15/15W)
Horn
Left switch box
Ignition switch
Ignition coil
Spark plug (BP-4H)
Flywheel magneto
Brake lamp switch
Neutral indicator lamp switch
B ......Blue
O ......Orange
R ......Red
Y ......Yellow
W ......White
G ......Green
BK ......Black
GR ......Gray
BR ......Brown
W/R ......White with Red spiral tracer
B/W ......Black with White spiral tracer
Ignition switch circuit
IG E B(−) C1 SE C2 HL TL
Off
On(day)
On(night)
Parking

F-50.

Selenium rectifier
Battery (6V2AH)
Fuse
(15A)
High beam indicator lamp
(6V1.5W)
Neutral indicator lamp
(6V1.5W)
Speedometer lamp
(6V1.5W)
Tail/brake lamp (6V 3/21 CP)
Ignition coil
Head lamp
(6V 15/15W)
Dimmer switch
Brake lamp switch
Horn switch
Spark plug
(NGK B-6)
Neutral indicator switch
Magneto
Ignition
switch
Horn

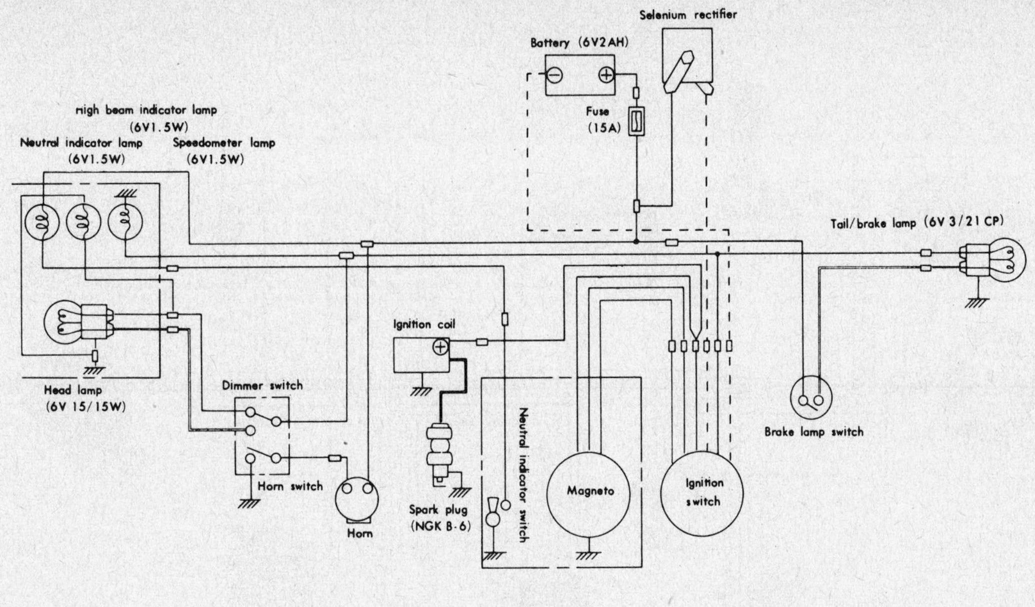

M-31.

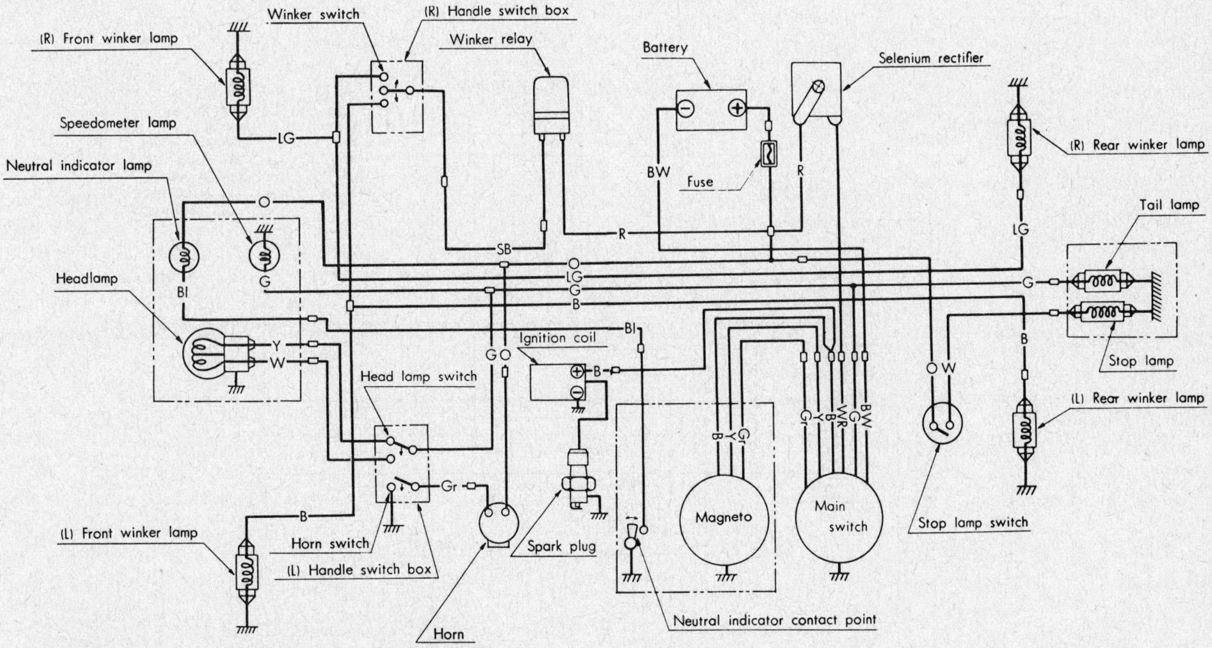

Winker switch
(R) Handle switch box
(R) Front winker lamp
Winker relay
Battery
Selenium rectifier
Speedometer lamp
Neutral indicator lamp
Fuse
BW
R
(R) Rear winker lamp
LG
O
Tail lamp
SB
Headlamp
Bl
G
B
Y
W
Ignition coil
Stop lamp
Head lamp switch
Gr
(L) Rear winker lamp
Magneto
Main
switch
Stop lamp switch
(L) Front winker lamp
Horn switch
(L) Handle switch box
Spark plug
Neutral indicator contact point
Horn

Headlamp	6 V	15/15 W
Tail lamp	6 V	5 W
Stop lamp	6 V	10 W
Speedometer lamp	6 V	1.5 W
Neutral indicator lamp	6 V	1.5 W
Winker lamp	6 V	8 W×2×2
Battery	6 V	4 Ah
Fuse	15 A	

COLOR CODE

B.........Black
Bl ......Blue
B/W ...Black with white tracer
G ......Grey
Gr ......Green
LG ......Light green
O ......Orange
R.........Red
SB ......Sky blue
W ......White
W/R ...White with red tracer
Y.........Yellow

K-10, K-11.

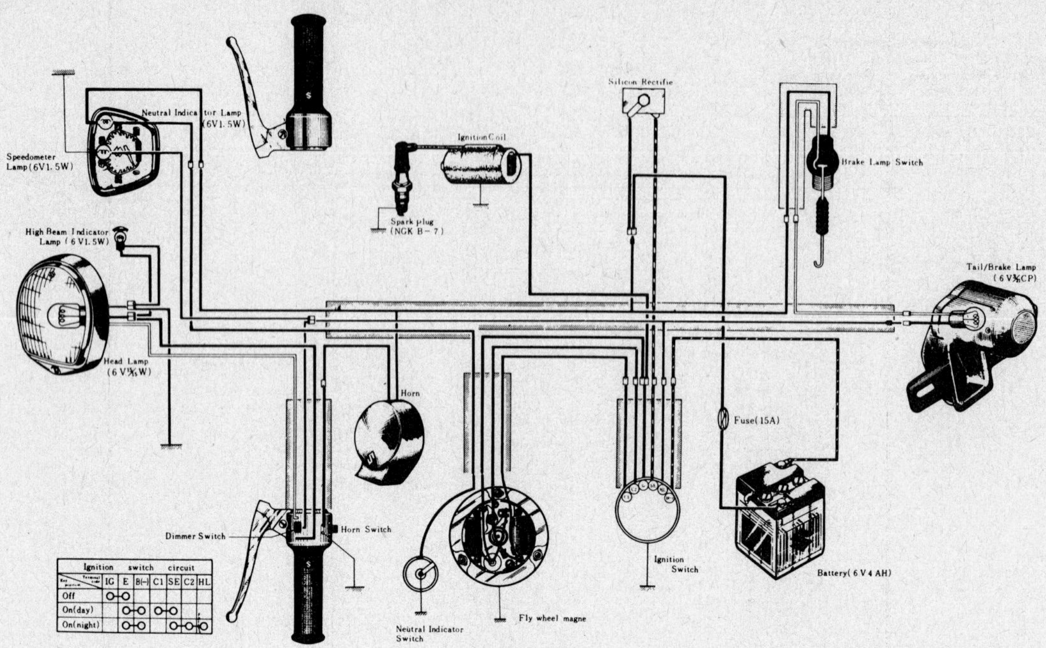
Neutral Indicator Lamp (6V1.5W)
Speedometer Lamp (6V1.5W)
Ignition Coil
Spark plug (NGK B-7)
Silicon Rectifie
Brake Lamp Switch
High Beam Indicator Lamp (6V1.5W)
Head Lamp
Tail/Brake Lamp
Horn
Fuse (15A)
Dimmer Switch
Horn Switch
Ignition Switch
Battery (6V4AH)
Fly wheel magne
Neutral Indicator Switch
Ignition switch circuit
Off
On (day)
On (night)

K-10P, K-11P.

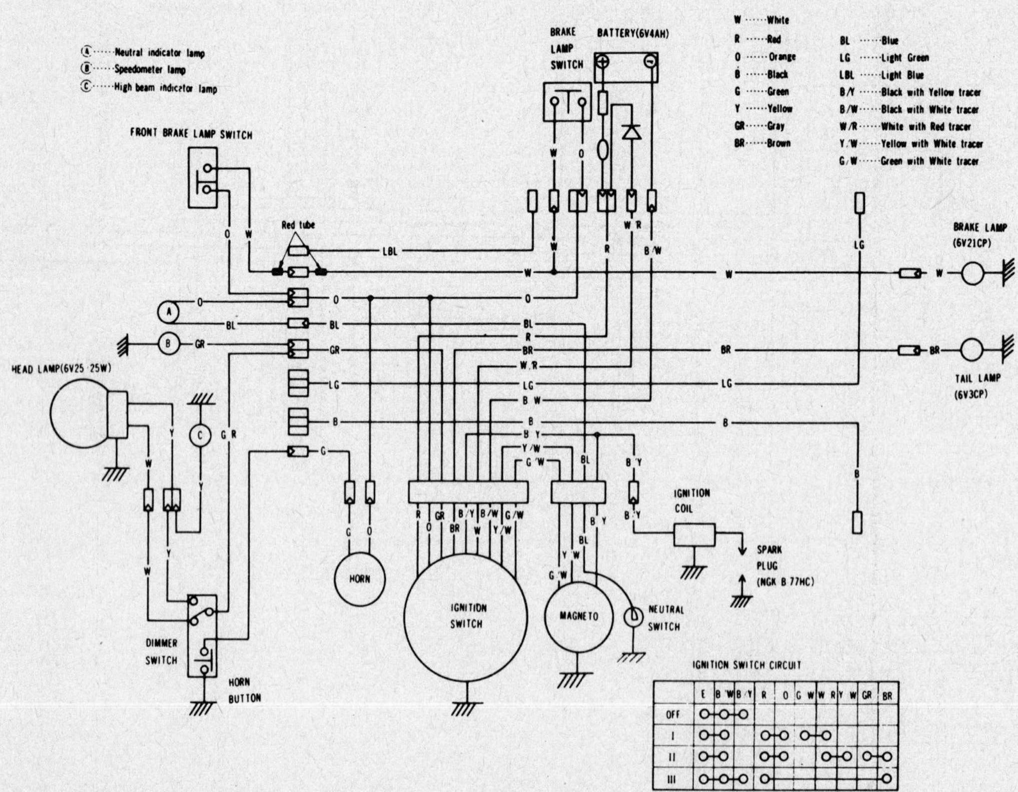
Ⓐ······Neutral indicator lamp
Ⓑ······Speedometer lamp
Ⓒ······High beam indicator lamp
FRONT BRAKE LAMP SWITCH
BRAKE LAMP SWITCH
BATTERY (6V4AH)
W······White
R······Red
O······Orange
B······Black
G······Green
Y······Yellow
GR······Gray
BR······Brown
BL······Blue
LG······Light Green
LBL······Light Blue
B/Y······Black with Yellow tracer
B/W······Black with White tracer
W/R······White with Red tracer
Y/W······Yellow with White tracer
G/W······Green with White tracer
Red tube
BRAKE LAMP (6V21CP)
TAIL LAMP (6V3CP)
HEAD LAMP (6V25/25W)
HORN
IGNITION SWITCH
MAGNETO
NEUTRAL SWITCH
IGNITION COIL
SPARK PLUG (NGK B-77HC)
DIMMER SWITCH
HORN BUTTON
IGNITION SWITCH CIRCUIT

TC-90, TS-90.

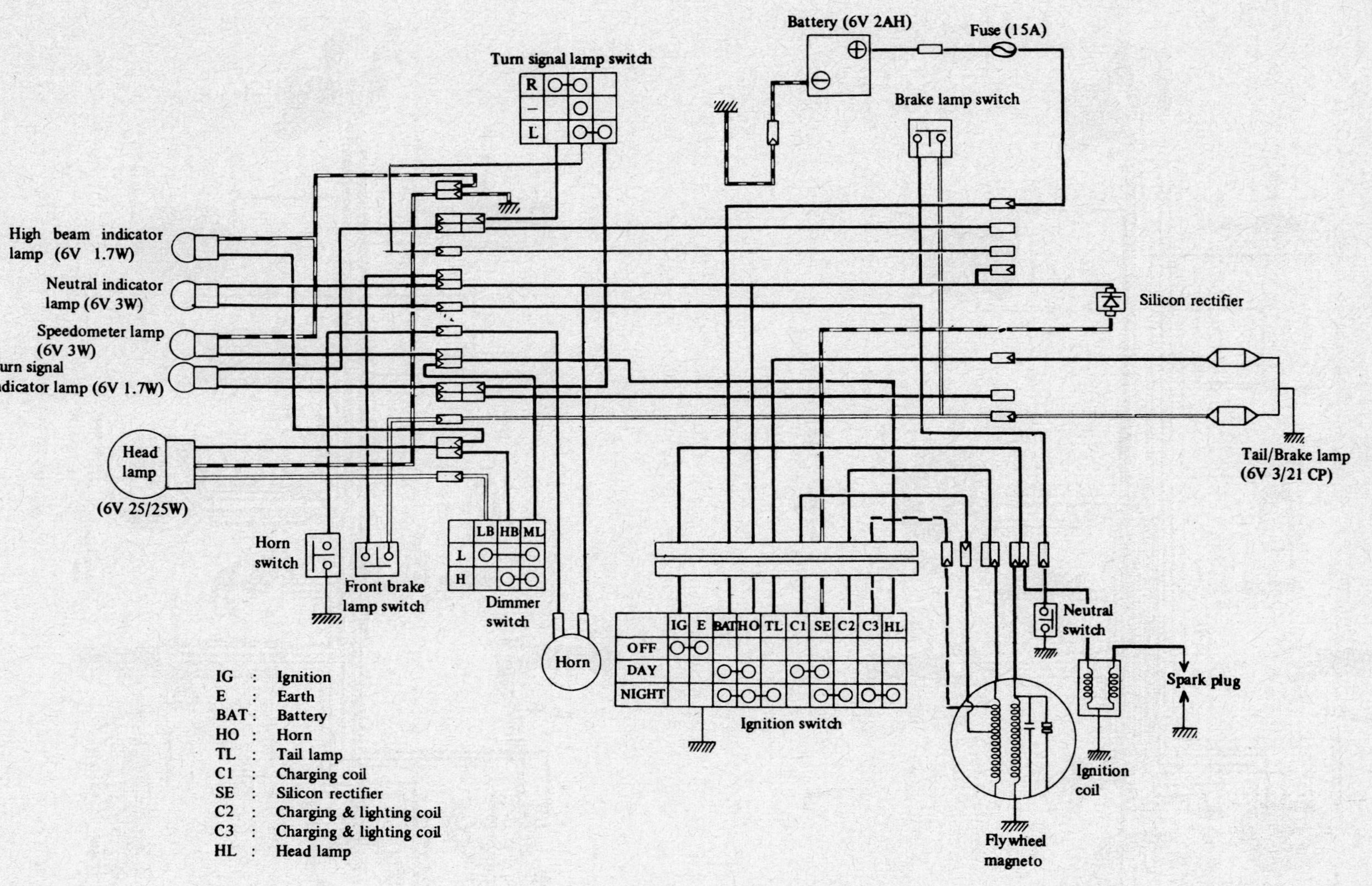

IG : Ignition
E : Earth
BAT : Battery
HO : Horn
TL : Tail lamp
C1 : Charging coil
SE : Silicon rectifier
C2 : Charging & lighting coil
C3 : Charging & lighting coil
HL : Head lamp

RV-90.

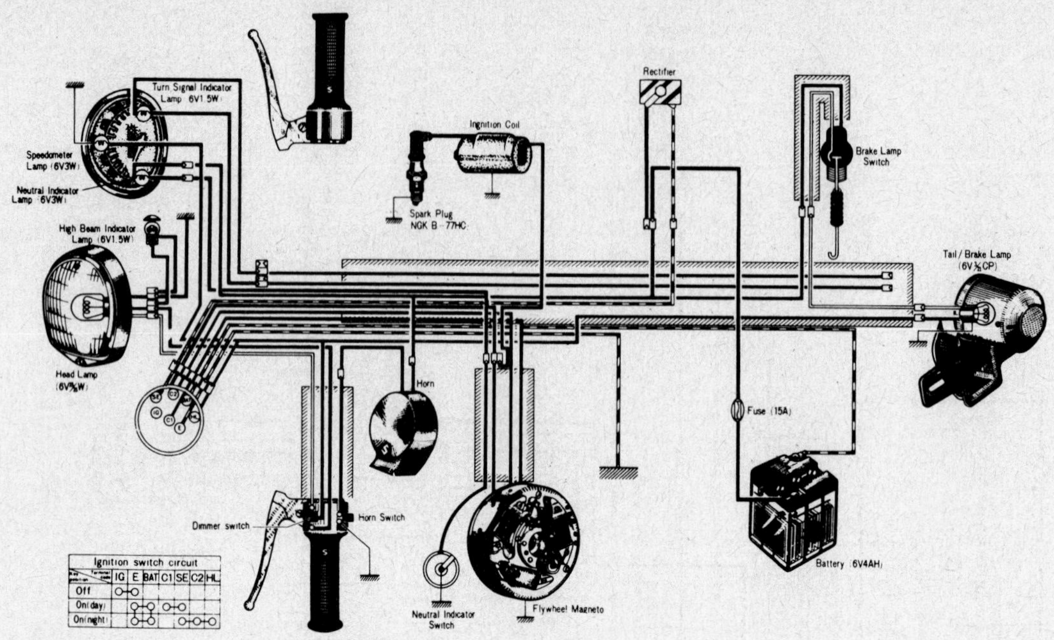
Turn Signal Indicator Lamp 6V1.5W
Speedometer Lamp (6V3W)
Neutral Indicator Lamp 6V3W
High Beam Indicator Lamp (6V1.5W)
Head Lamp (6V⅞W)
Ignition Coil
Spark Plug NGK B-77HC
Rectifier
Brake Lamp Switch
Tail/Brake Lamp (6V ⅜CP)
Horn
Fuse (15A)
Battery (6V4AH)
Dimmer switch
Horn Switch
Neutral Indicator Switch
Flywheel Magneto
Ignition switch circuit
IG E BAT C1 SE C2 HL
Off
On(day)
On(night)

A-100, AS-100.

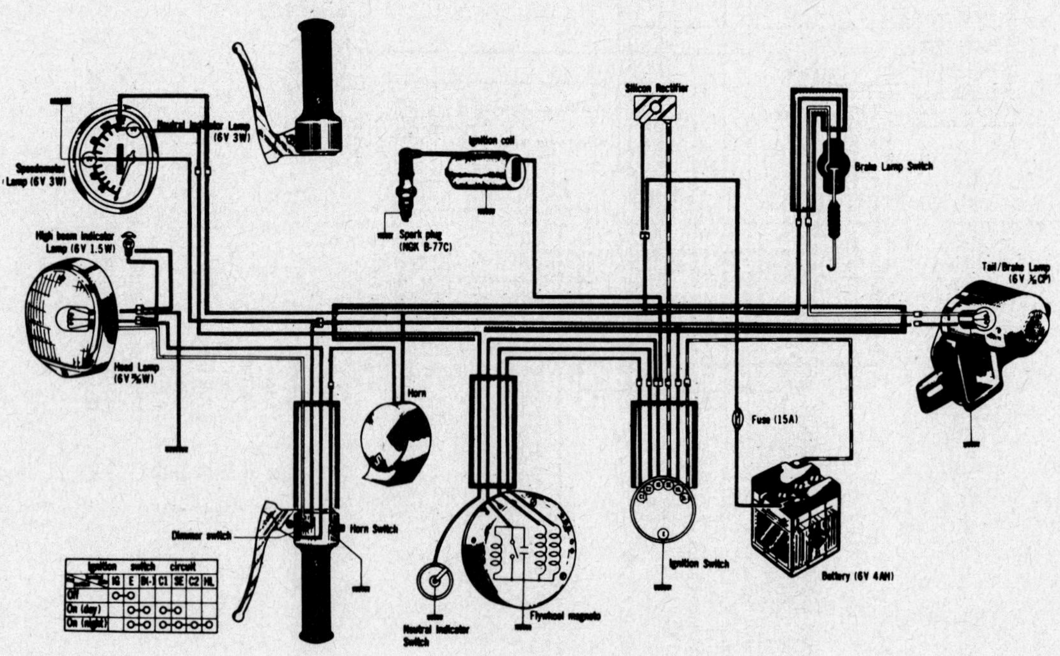
Neutral Indicator Lamp (6V 3W)
Speedometer Lamp (6V 3W)
High beam indicator Lamp (6V 1.5W)
Head Lamp (6V⅞W)
Ignition coil
Spark plug (NGK B-77C)
Silicon Rectifier
Brake Lamp Switch
Tail/Brake Lamp (6V ⅜CP)
Horn
Fuse (15A)
Dimmer switch
Horn Switch
Neutral Indicator Switch
Flywheel magneto
Ignition Switch
Battery (6V 4AH)
Ignition switch circuit
IG E BK-1 C1 SE C2 HL
Off
On (day)
On (night)

KT-120.

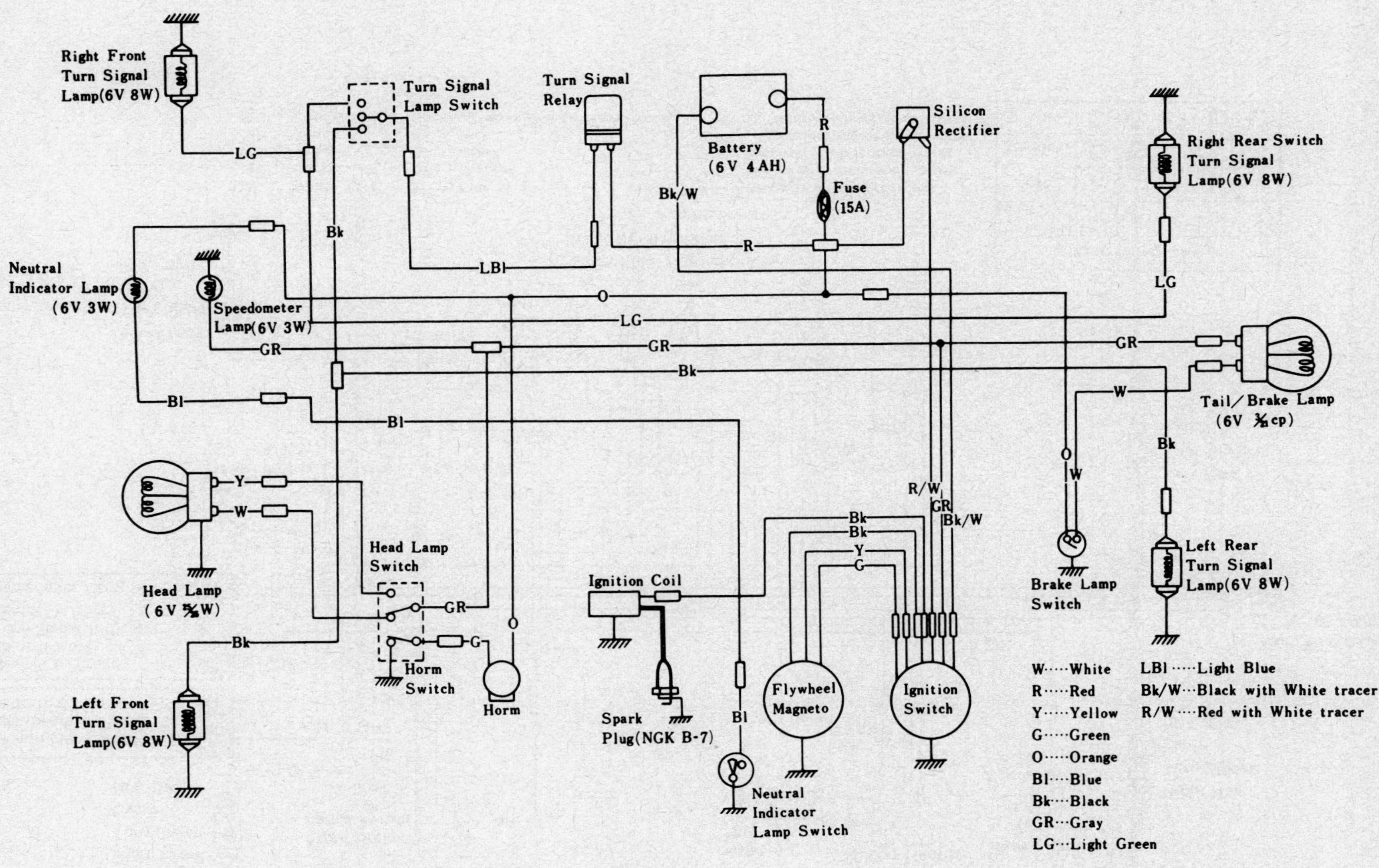
Right Front
Turn Signal
Lamp(6V 8W)
Turn Signal
Lamp Switch
Turn Signal
Relay
Battery
(6V 4AH)
Fuse
(15A)
Silicon
Rectifier
Right Rear Switch
Turn Signal
Lamp(6V 8W)
Neutral
Indicator Lamp
(6V 3W)
Speedometer
Lamp(6V 3W)
Tail/Brake Lamp
(6V 3/32cp)
Head Lamp
(6V 15/15W)
Head Lamp
Switch
Horn
Switch
Horn
Ignition Coil
Spark
Plug(NGK B-7)
Neutral
Indicator
Lamp Switch
Flywheel
Magneto
Ignition
Switch
Brake Lamp
Switch
Left Rear
Turn Signal
Lamp(6V 8W)
Left Front
Turn Signal
Lamp(6V 8W)
W·····White
R·····Red
Y·····Yellow
G·····Green
O·····Orange
Bl····Blue
Bk····Black
GR···Gray
LG···Light Green
LBl·····Light Blue
Bk/W···Black wjth White tracer
R/W····Red with White tracer
B-100, B-100P.

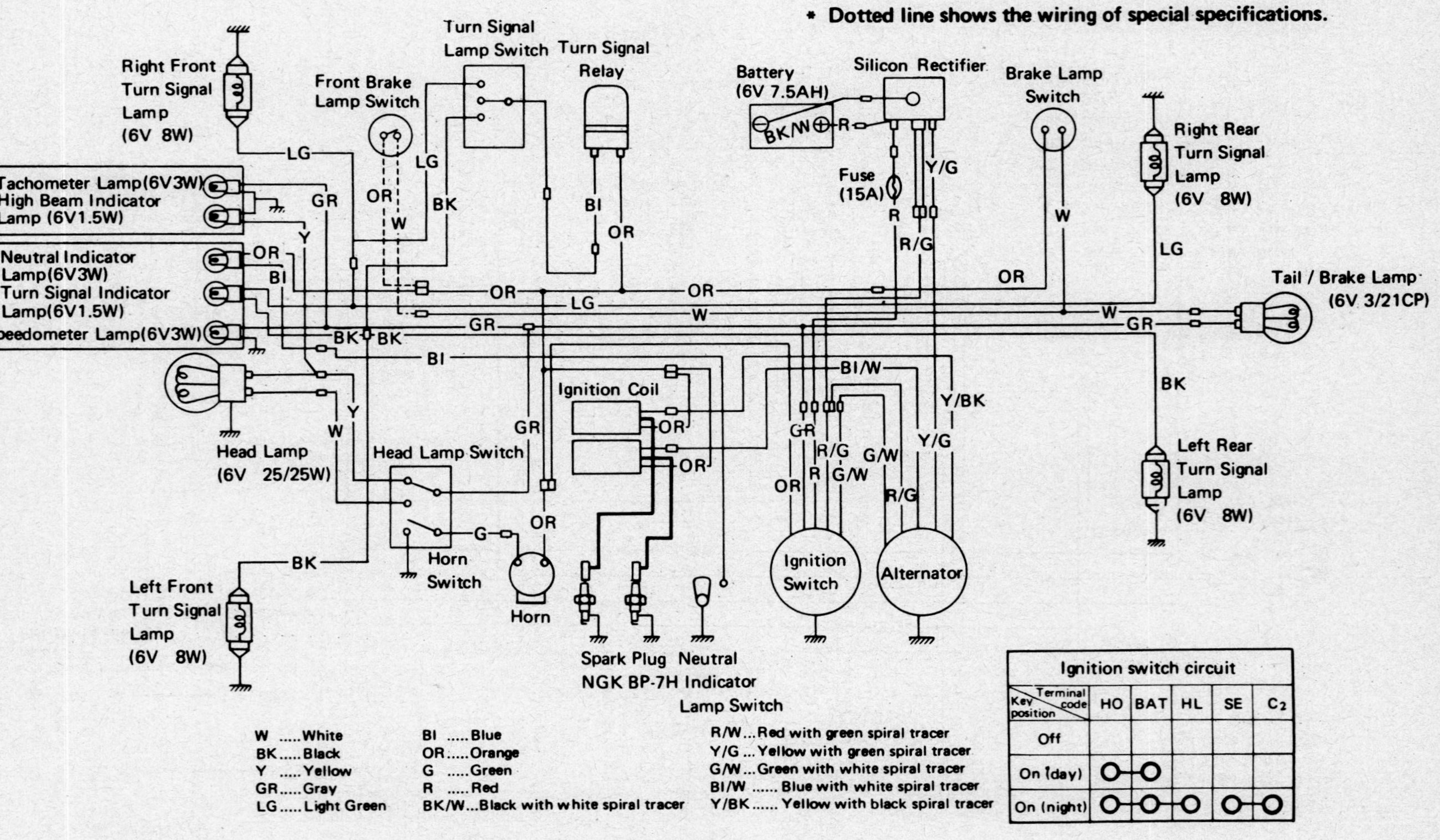
* Dotted line shows the wiring of special specifications.
Right Front Turn Signal Lamp (6V 8W)
Front Brake Lamp Switch
Turn Signal Lamp Switch
Turn Signal Relay
Battery (6V 7.5AH)
Silicon Rectifier
Brake Lamp Switch
Right Rear Turn Signal Lamp (6V 8W)
Tachometer Lamp(6V3W)
High Beam Indicator Lamp (6V1.5W)
Neutral Indicator Lamp(6V3W)
Turn Signal Indicator Lamp(6V1.5W)
Speedometer Lamp(6V3W)
Fuse (15A)
Tail / Brake Lamp (6V 3/21CP)
Head Lamp (6V 25/25W)
Head Lamp Switch
Ignition Coil
Left Rear Turn Signal Lamp (6V 8W)
Horn Switch
Horn
Ignition Switch
Alternator
Left Front Turn Signal Lamp (6V 8W)
Spark Plug NGK BP-7H
Neutral Indicator Lamp Switch
LG
GR
OR
W
BK
BI
Y
R
Y/G
R/G
BI/W
Y/BK
G/W
G
BK/W
Ignition switch circuit
Key position
Terminal code
HO
BAT
HL
SE
C2
Off
On (day)
On (night)
W .....White
BK .....Black
Y .....Yellow
GR .....Gray
LG .....Light Green
BI .....Blue
OR .....Orange
G .....Green
R .....Red
BK/W...Black with white spiral tracer
R/W...Red with green spiral tracer
Y/G ...Yellow with green spiral tracer
G/W...Green with white spiral tracer
BI/W ...... Blue with white spiral tracer
Y/BK ...... Yellow with black spiral tracer

T-125.

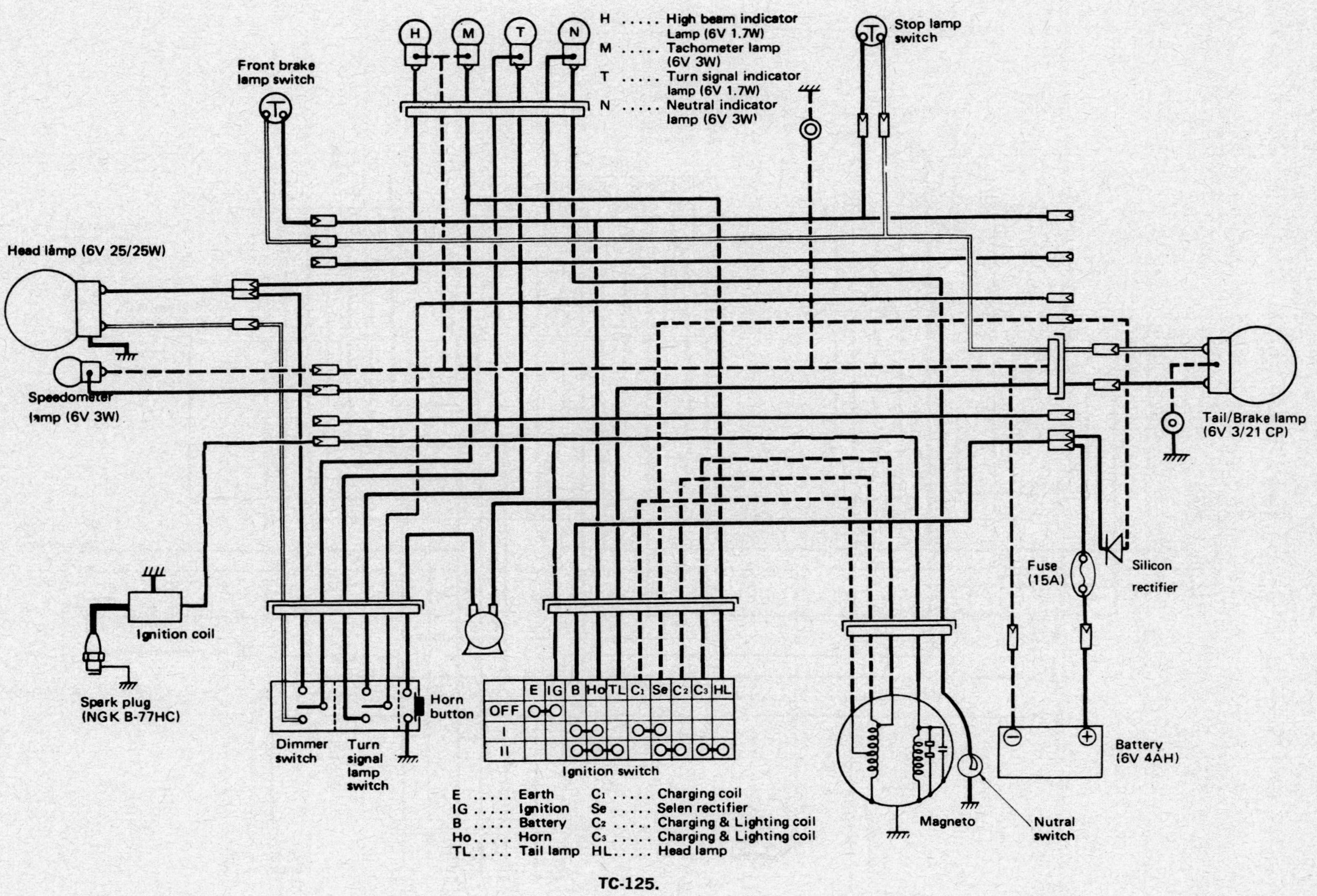
H ..... High beam indicator Lamp (6V 1.7W)
M ..... Tachometer lamp (6V 3W)
T ..... Turn signal indicator lamp (6V 1.7W)
N ..... Neutral indicator lamp (6V 3W)
H
M
T
N
Stop lamp switch
Front brake lamp switch
Head lamp (6V 25/25W)
Speedometer lamp (6V 3W)
Tail/Brake lamp (6V 3/21 CP)
Fuse (15A)
Silicon rectifier
Ignition coil
Spark plug (NGK B-77HC)
Horn button
Dimmer switch
Turn signal lamp switch
E
IG
B
Ho
TL
C1
Se
C2
C3
HL
OFF
I
II
Ignition switch
E ..... Earth
IG ..... Ignition
B ..... Battery
Ho..... Horn
TL..... Tail lamp
C1 ..... Charging coil
Se ..... Selen rectifier
C2 ..... Charging & Lighting coil
C3 ..... Charging & Lighting coil
HL..... Head lamp
Magneto
Nutral switch
Battery (6V 4AH)

TC-125.

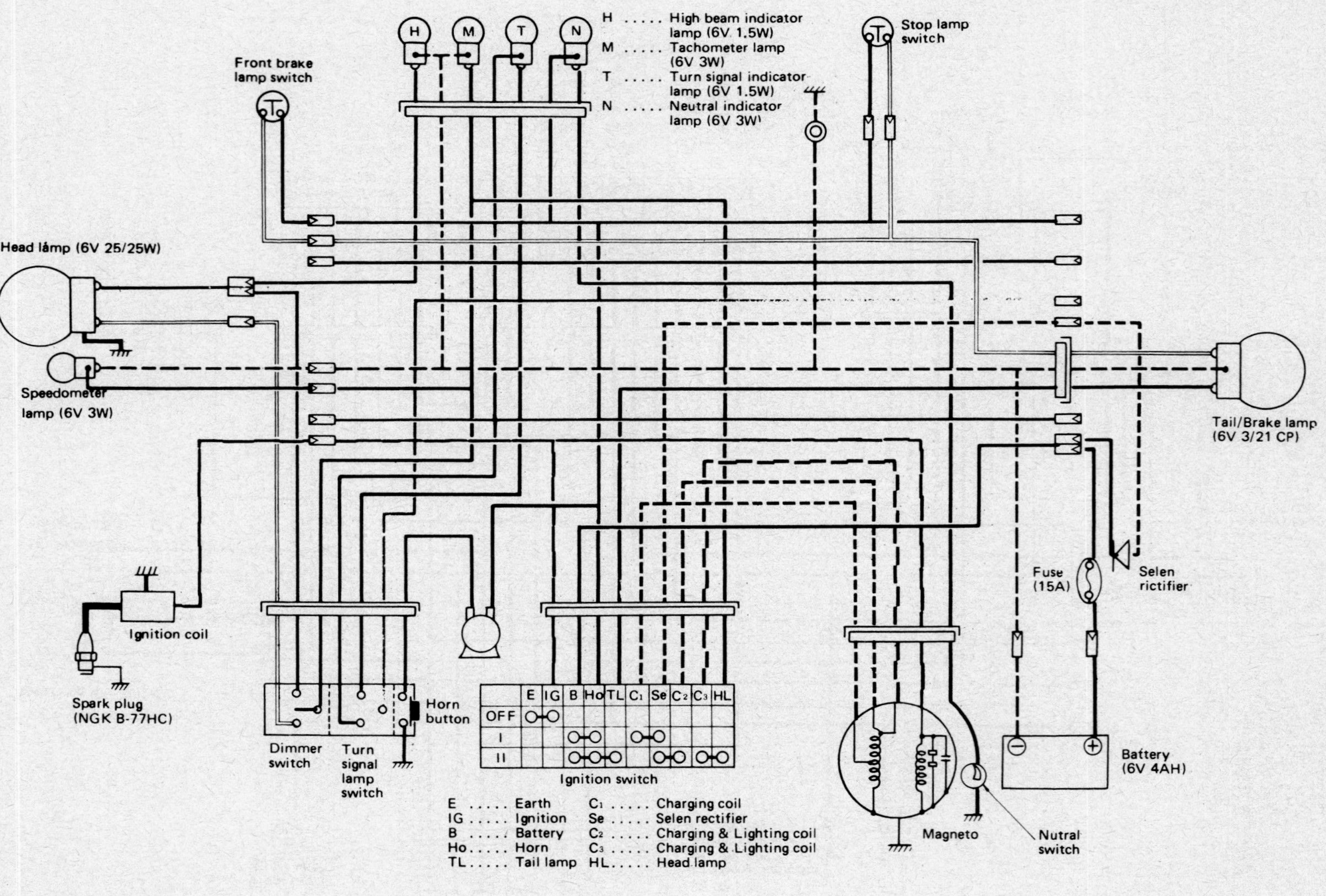
H ..... High beam indicator lamp (6V 1.5W)
M ..... Tachometer lamp (6V 3W)
T ..... Turn signal indicator lamp (6V 1.5W)
N ..... Neutral indicator lamp (6V 3W)
Stop lamp switch
Front brake lamp switch
Head lamp (6V 25/25W)
Speedometer lamp (6V 3W)
Tail/Brake lamp (6V 3/21 CP)
Fuse (15A)
Selen rictifier
Ignition coil
Spark plug (NGK B-77HC)
Horn button
Dimmer switch
Turn signal lamp switch
E IG B Ho TL C1 Se C2 C3 HL
OFF
I
II
Ignition switch
E ..... Earth
IG ..... Ignition
B ..... Battery
Ho ..... Horn
TL ..... Tail lamp
C1 ..... Charging coil
Se ..... Selen rectifier
C2 ..... Charging & Lighting coil
C3 ..... Charging & Lighting coil
HL ..... Head lamp
Magneto
Nutral switch
Battery (6V 4AH)

TS-125.

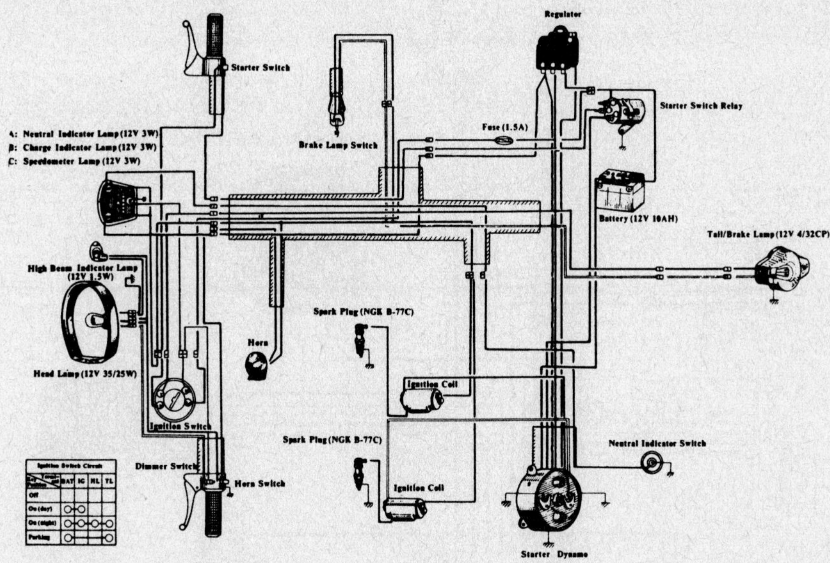
Regulator
Starter Switch
Starter Switch Relay
Brake Lamp Switch
Fuse (1.5A)
Battery (12V 10AH)
Tail/Brake Lamp (12V 4/32CP)
High Beam Indicator Lamp (12V 1.5W)
Head Lamp (12V 35/25W)
Horn
Spark Plug (NGK B-77C)
Ignition Coil
Ignition Switch
Dimmer Switch
Horn Switch
Neutral Indicator Switch
Starter Dynamo

S-32.

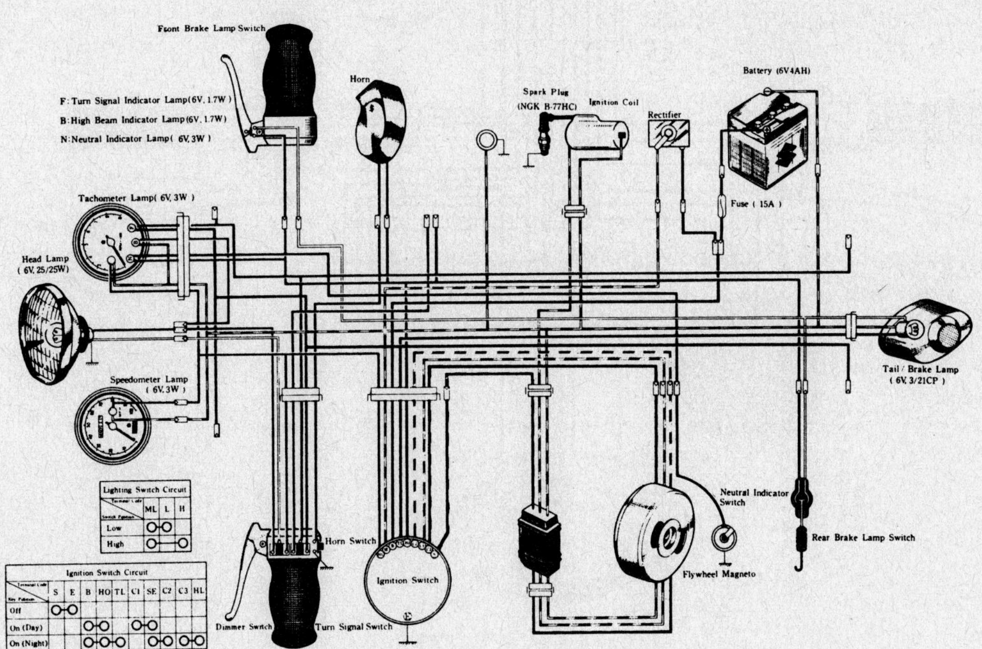
Front Brake Lamp Switch
F: Turn Signal Indicator Lamp (6V, 1.7W)
B: High Beam Indicator Lamp (6V, 1.7W)
N: Neutral Indicator Lamp (6V, 3W)
Horn
Spark Plug (NGK B-77HC)
Ignition Coil
Rectifier
Battery (6V4AH)
Fuse (15A)
Tachometer Lamp (6V, 3W)
Head Lamp (6V, 25/25W)
Speedometer Lamp (6V, 3W)
Tail / Brake Lamp (6V, 3/21CP)
Lighting Switch Circuit
ML
L
H
Low
High
Ignition Switch Circuit
S
E
B
HO
TL
C1
SE
C2
C3
HL
Off
On (Day)
On (Night)
Horn Switch
Ignition Switch
Dimmer Switch
Turn Signal Switch
Neutral Indicator Switch
Flywheel Magneto
Rear Brake Lamp Switch

TS-185.

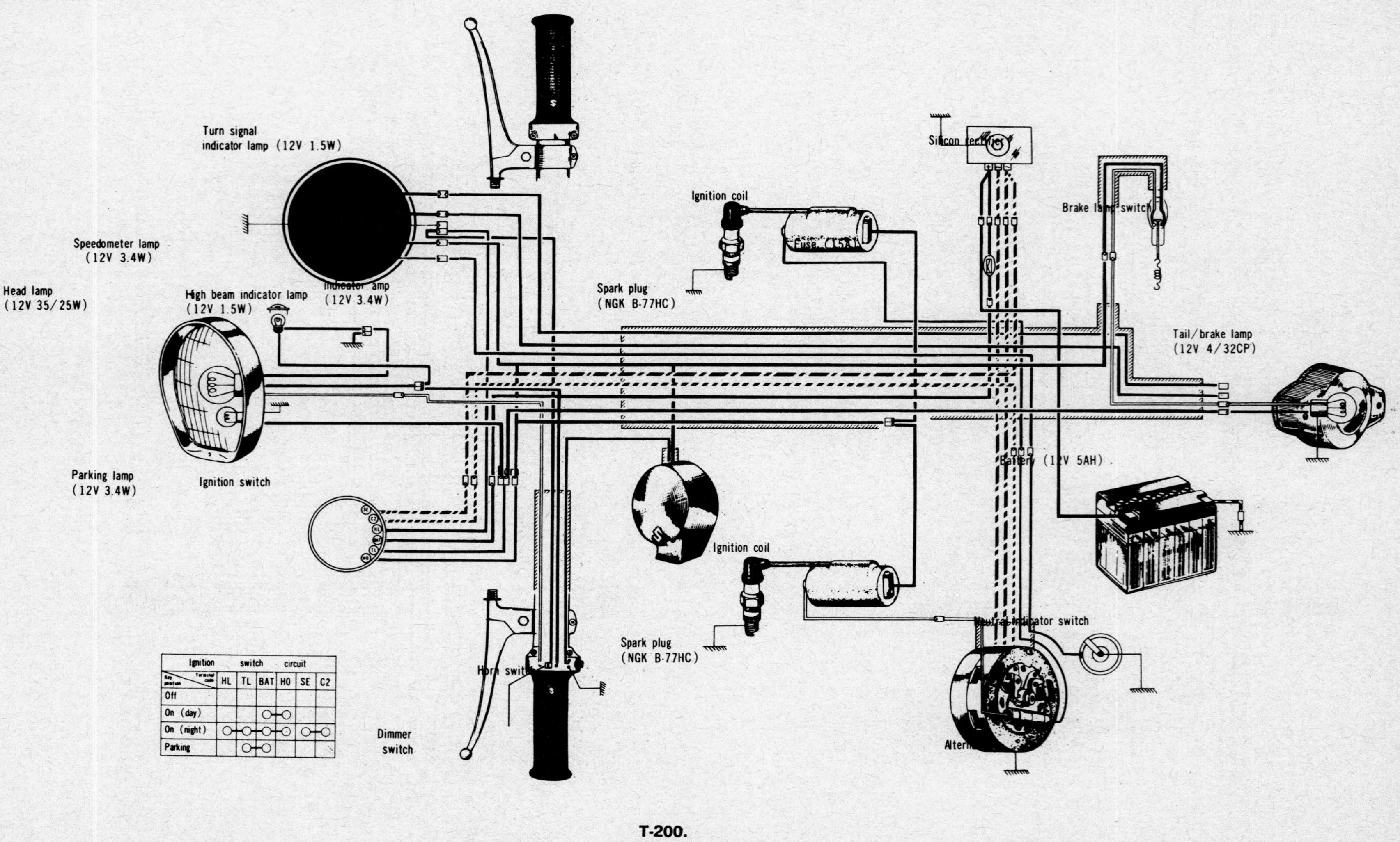

Ignition switch circuit	HL	TL	BAT	HO	SE	C2
Off						
On (day)			O	O		
On (night)	O	O	O	O	O	O
Parking		O	O			

T-200.

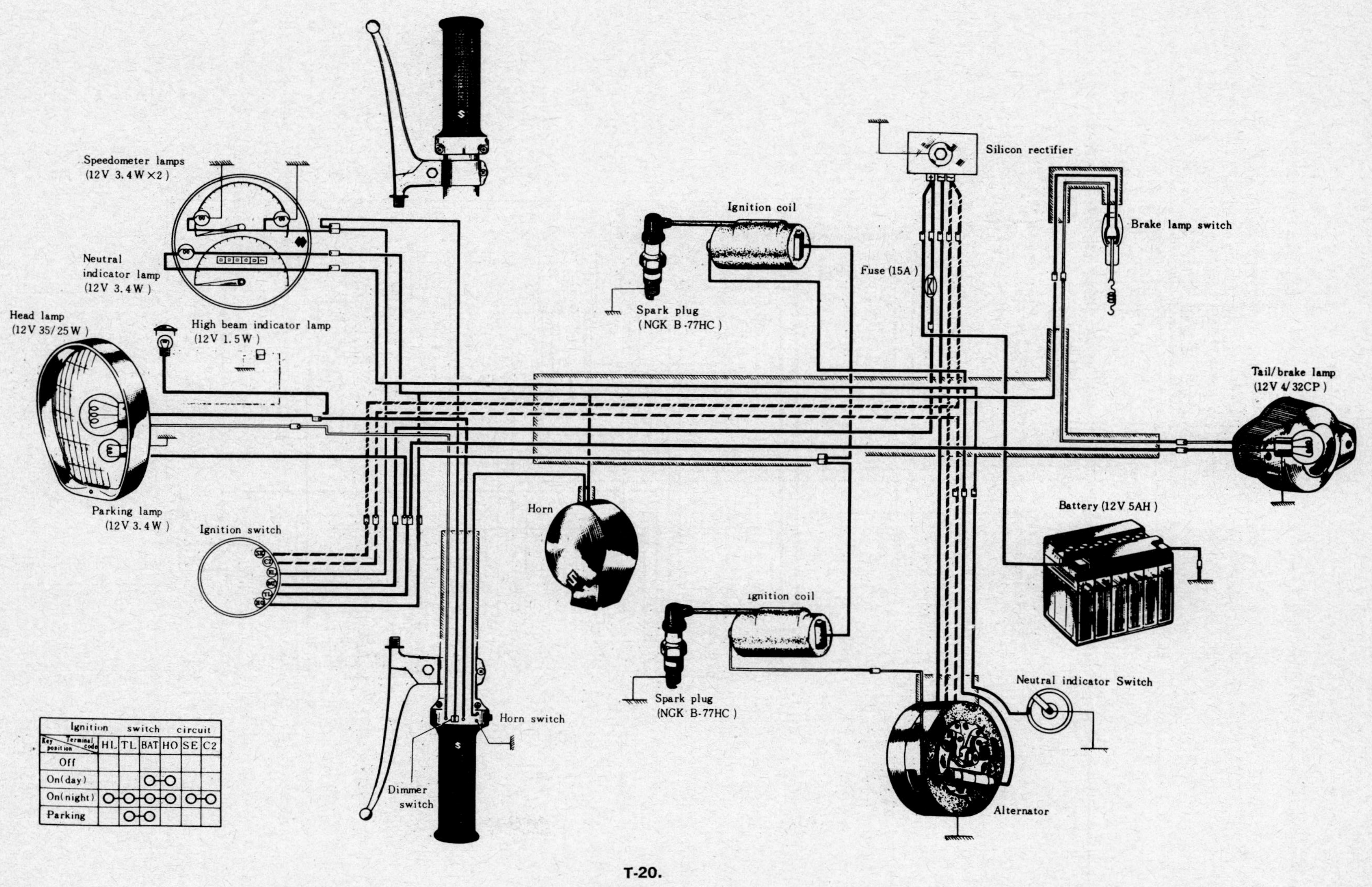
Speedometer lamps
(12V 3.4W×2)
Neutral
indicator lamp
(12V 3.4W)
Head lamp
(12V 35/25W)
High beam indicator lamp
(12V 1.5W)
Parking lamp
(12V 3.4W)
Ignition switch
Ignition coil
Spark plug
(NGK B-77HC)
Fuse (15A)
Silicon rectifier
Brake lamp switch
Tail/brake lamp
(12V 4/32CP)
Horn
Battery (12V 5AH)
Ignition coil
Spark plug
(NGK B-77HC)
Neutral indicator Switch
Horn switch
Dimmer
switch
Alternator
Ignition switch circuit
Key position / Terminal code
HL
TL
BAT
HO
SE
C2
Off
On(day)
On(night)
Parking

T-20.

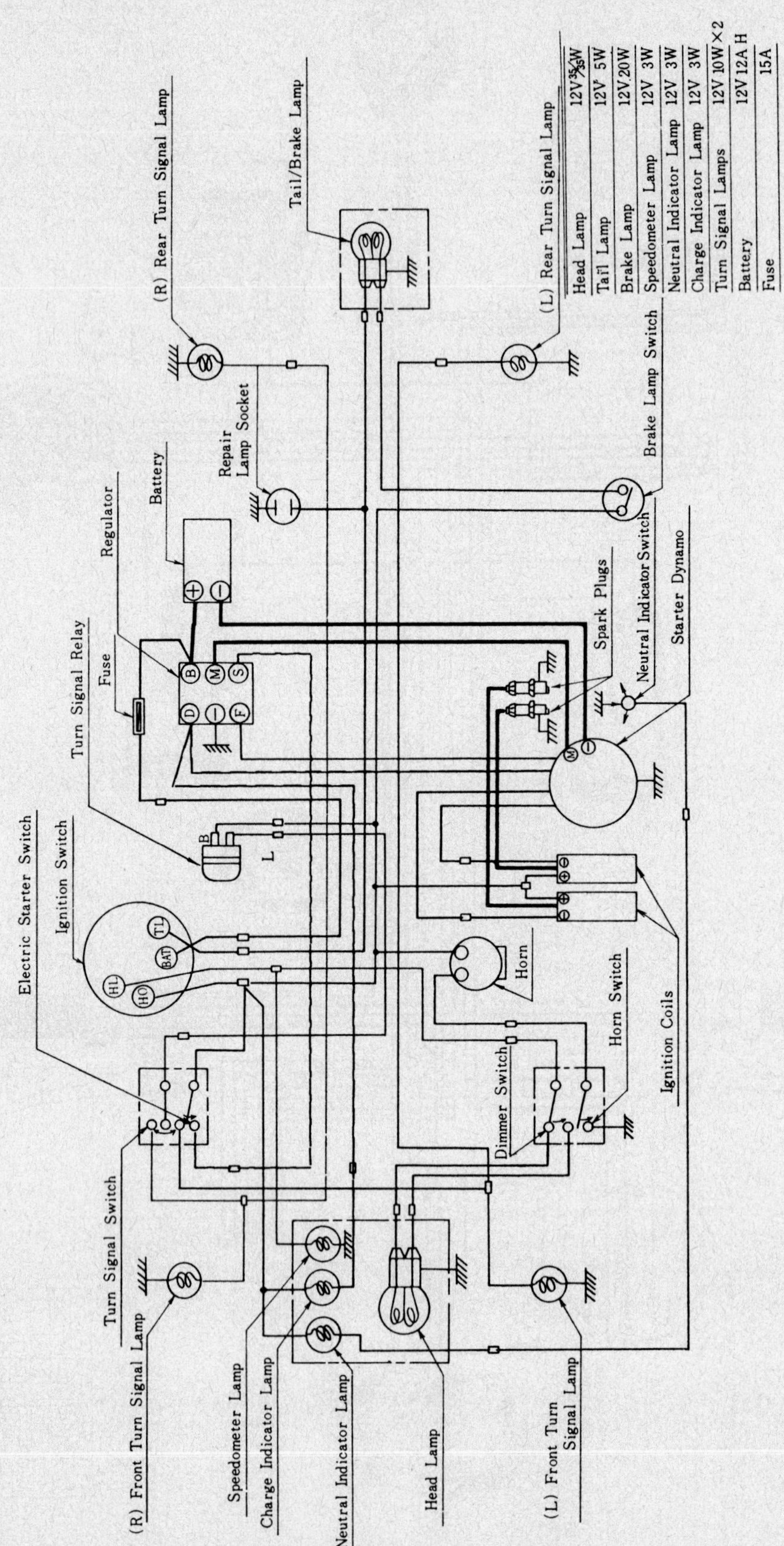
(R) Rear Turn Signal Lamp
Tail/Brake Lamp
(L) Rear Turn Signal Lamp
Head Lamp 12V 35/25W
Tail Lamp 12V 5W
Brake Lamp 12V 20W
Speedometer Lamp 12V 3W
Neutral Indicator Lamp 12V 3W
Charge Indicator Lamp 12V 3W
Turn Signal Lamps 12V 10W×2
Battery 12V 12A H
Fuse 15A
Repair Lamp Socket
Battery
Regulator
Brake Lamp Switch
Fuse
Turn Signal Relay
Spark Plugs
Neutral Indicator Switch
Starter Dynamo
Electric Starter Switch
Ignition Switch
B
L
HL
HO
BAT
TL
Horn
Horn Switch
Dimmer Switch
Ignition Coils
Turn Signal Switch
(R) Front Turn Signal Lamp
Speedometer Lamp
Charge Indicator Lamp
Neutral Indicator Lamp
Head Lamp
(L) Front Turn Signal Lamp
T-10.

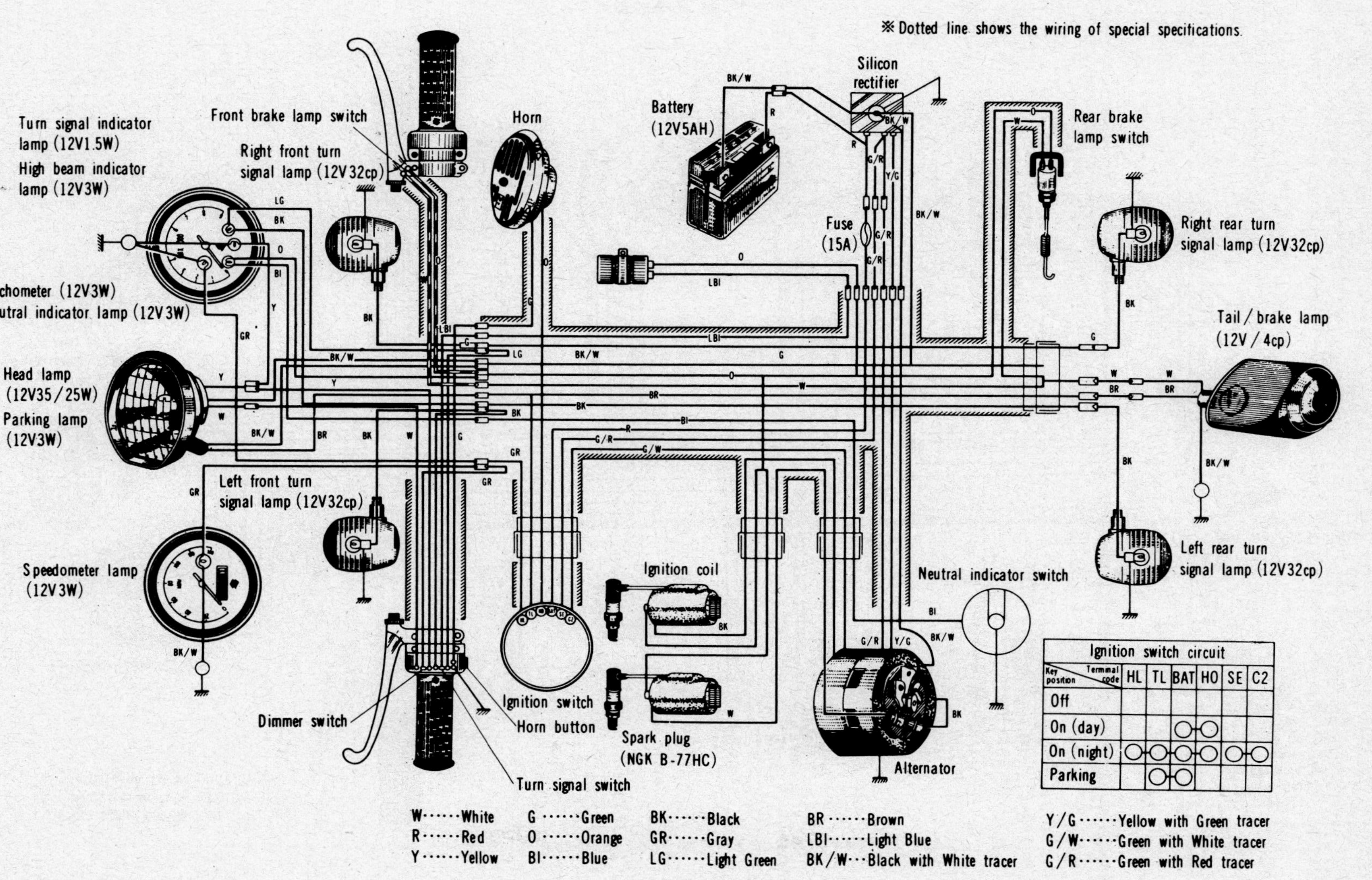
※ Dotted line shows the wiring of special specifications.
Turn signal indicator lamp (12V1.5W)
High beam indicator lamp (12V3W)
Front brake lamp switch
Right front turn signal lamp (12V32cp)
Horn
Battery (12V5AH)
Silicon rectifier
Rear brake lamp switch
Fuse (15A)
Right rear turn signal lamp (12V32cp)
Tachometer (12V3W)
Neutral indicator lamp (12V3W)
Tail / brake lamp (12V / 4cp)
Head lamp (12V35/25W)
Parking lamp (12V3W)
Left front turn signal lamp (12V32cp)
Speedometer lamp (12V3W)
Ignition coil
Neutral indicator switch
Left rear turn signal lamp (12V32cp)
Ignition switch
Horn button
Dimmer switch
Spark plug (NGK B-77HC)
Alternator
Turn signal switch
Ignition switch circuit
Key position / Terminal code: HL, TL, BAT, HO, SE, C2
Off
On (day)
On (night)
Parking
W······White
R······Red
Y······Yellow
G······Green
O······Orange
Bl······Blue
BK······Black
GR······Gray
LG······Light Green
BR······Brown
LBl······Light Blue
BK/W···Black with White tracer
Y/G······Yellow with Green tracer
G/W······Green with White tracer
G/R······Green with Red tracer
T-250, T-350.

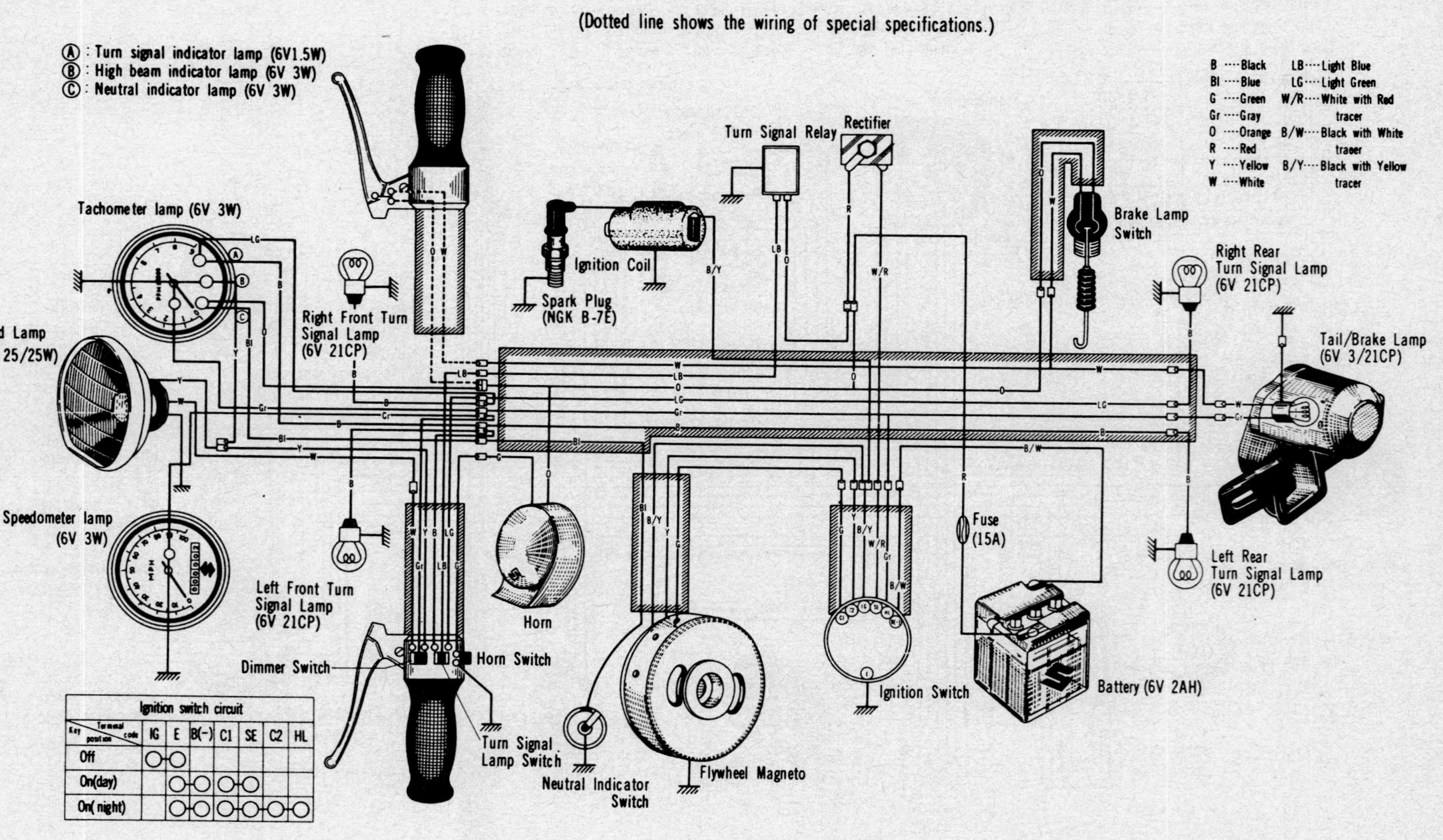

Ignition switch circuit

Key position \ Terminal code	IG	E	B(−)	C1	SE	C2	HL
Off	O	O					
On(day)		O	O	O	O		
On(night)		O	O	O	O	O	O

TS-250.

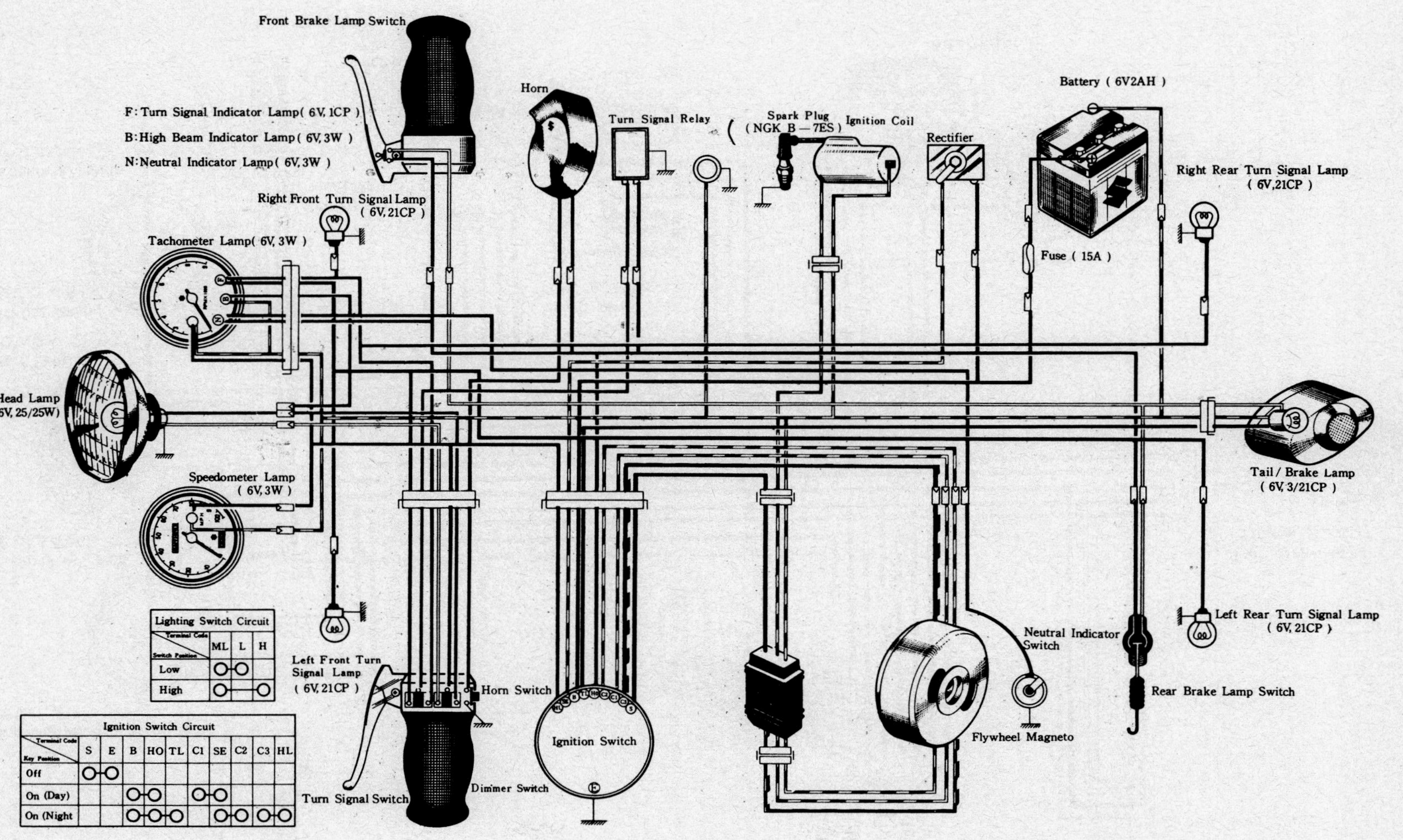

Lighting Switch Circuit

Switch Position \ Terminal Code	ML	L	H
Low	O	O	
High	O		O

Ignition Switch Circuit

Key Position \ Terminal Code	S	E	B	HO	TL	C1	SE	C2	C3	HL
Off	O	O								
On (Day)			O	O		O	O			
On (Night			O	O	O		O	O	O	O

TS-250R.

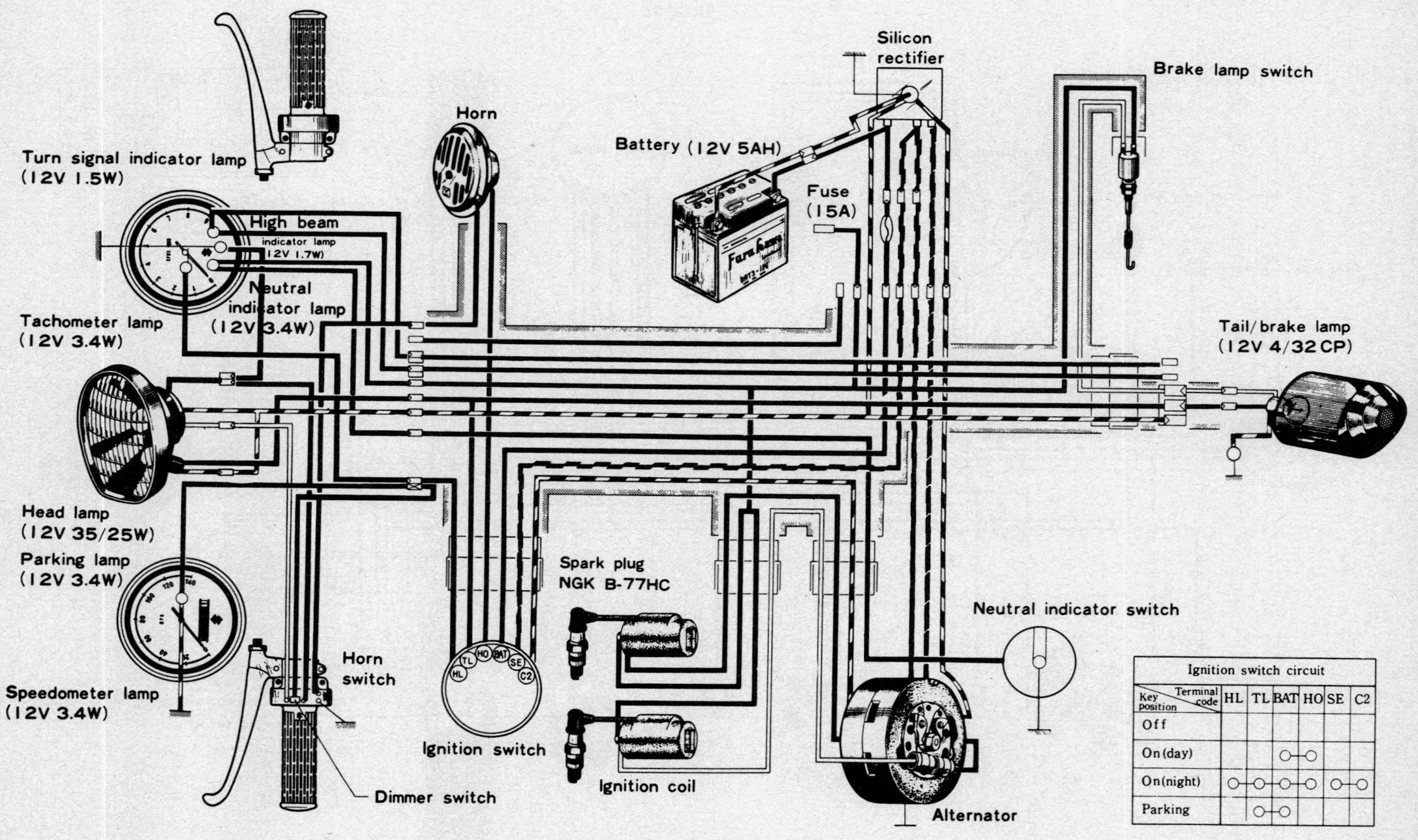

Ignition switch circuit

Key position \ Terminal code	HL	TL	BAT	HO	SE	C2
Off						
On(day)			○—	—○		
On(night)	○—	—○—	—○—	—○	○—	—○
Parking		○—	—○			

T-305, TC-305.

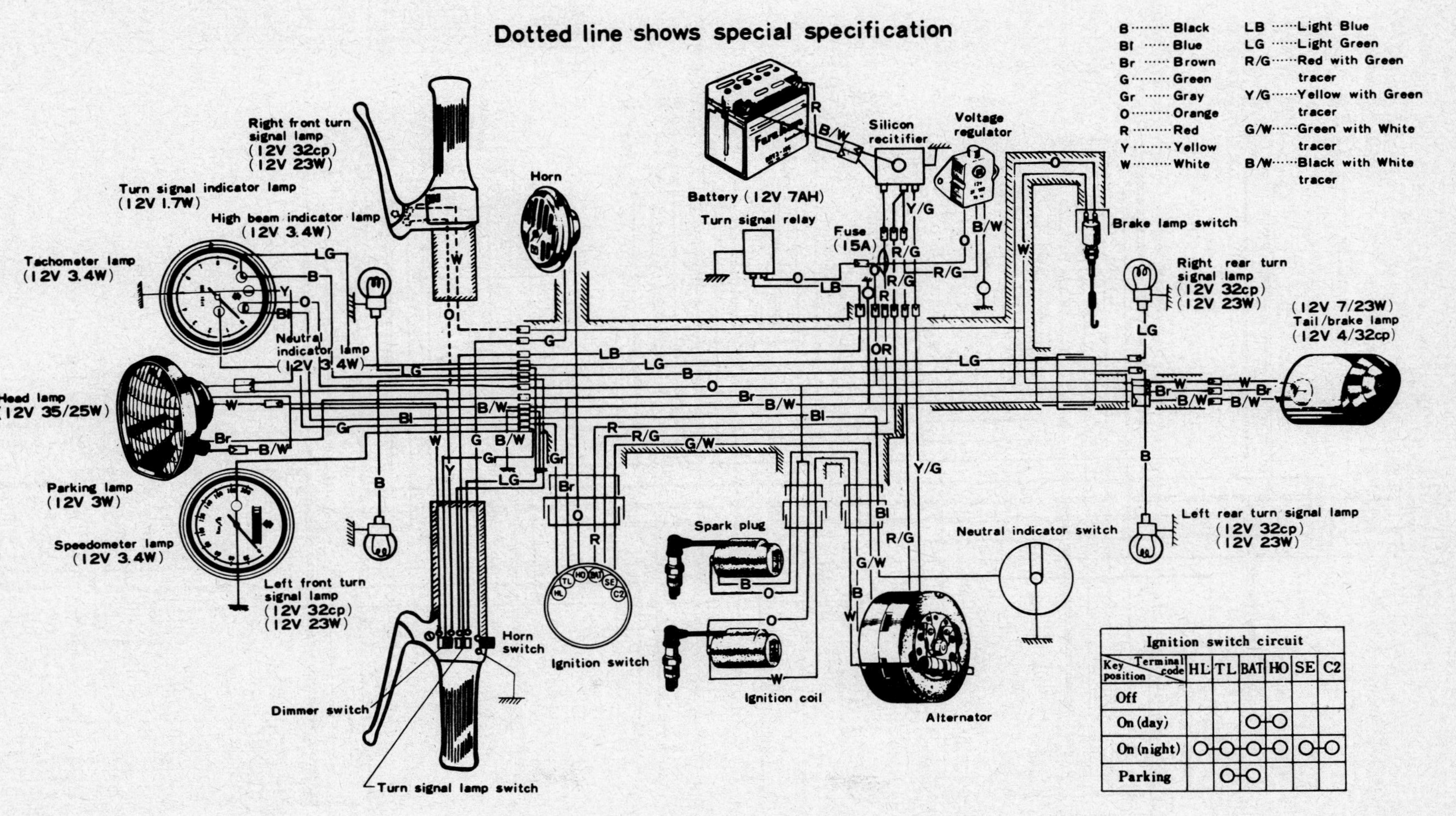

Ignition switch circuit

Key position \ Terminal code	HL	TL	BAT	HO	SE	C2
Off						
On (day)			O	O		
On (night)	O	O	O	O	O	O
Parking		O	O			

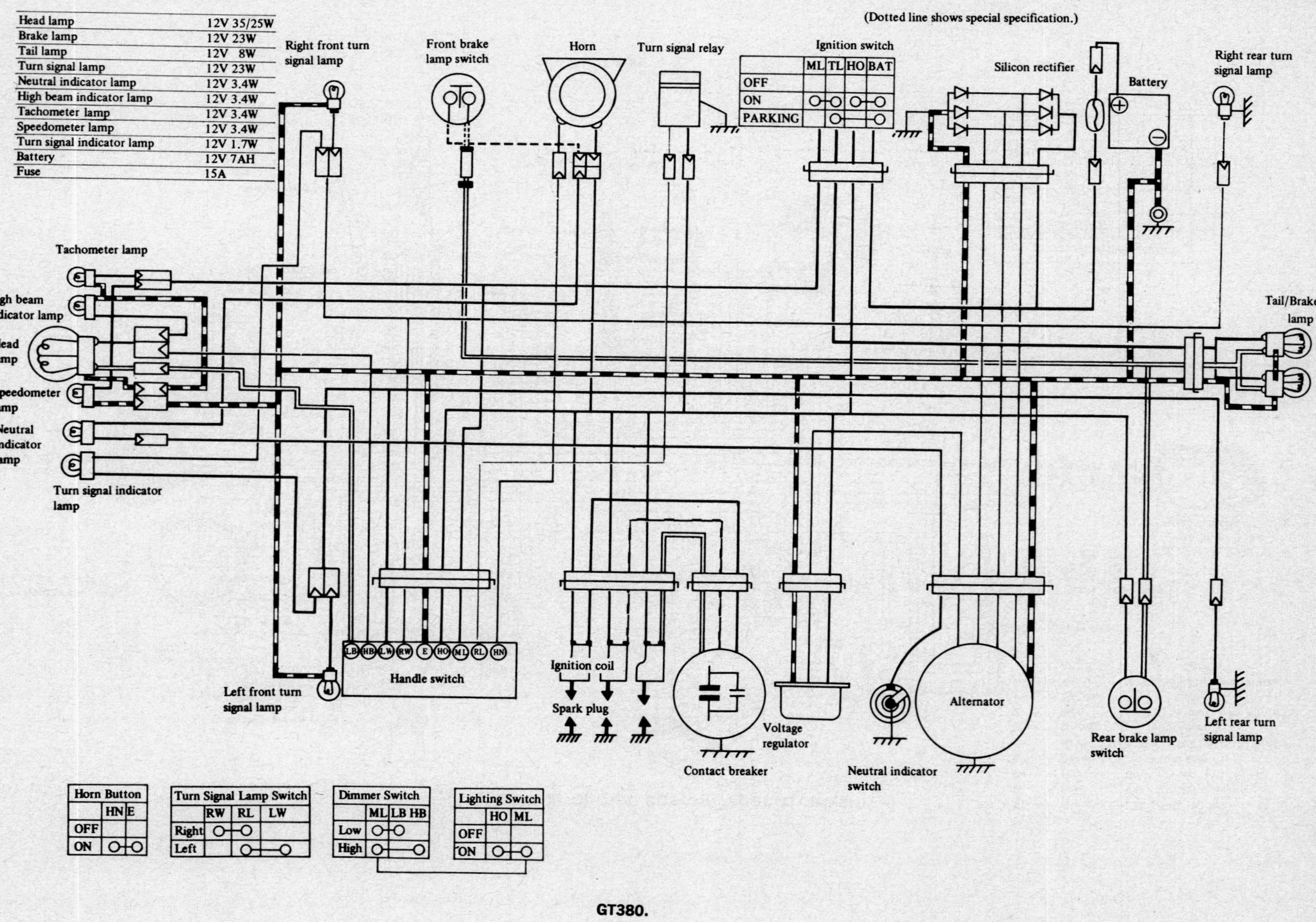
Head lamp 12V 35/25W
Brake lamp 12V 23W
Tail lamp 12V 8W
Turn signal lamp 12V 23W
Neutral indicator lamp 12V 3.4W
High beam indicator lamp 12V 3.4W
Tachometer lamp 12V 3.4W
Speedometer lamp 12V 3.4W
Turn signal indicator lamp 12V 1.7W
Battery 12V 7AH
Fuse 15A
Right front turn signal lamp
Front brake lamp switch
Horn
Turn signal relay
Ignition switch
ML TL HO BAT
OFF
ON
PARKING
(Dotted line shows special specification.)
Silicon rectifier
Battery
Right rear turn signal lamp
Tachometer lamp
High beam indicator lamp
Head lamp
Speedometer lamp
Neutral indicator lamp
Turn signal indicator lamp
Tail/Brake lamp
LB HB LW RW E HO ML RL HN
Handle switch
Left front turn signal lamp
Ignition coil
Spark plug
Contact breaker
Voltage regulator
Neutral indicator switch
Alternator
Rear brake lamp switch
Left rear turn signal lamp
Horn Button
HN E
OFF
ON
Turn Signal Lamp Switch
RW RL LW
Right
Left
Dimmer Switch
ML LB HB
Low
High
Lighting Switch
HO ML
OFF
ON

GT380.

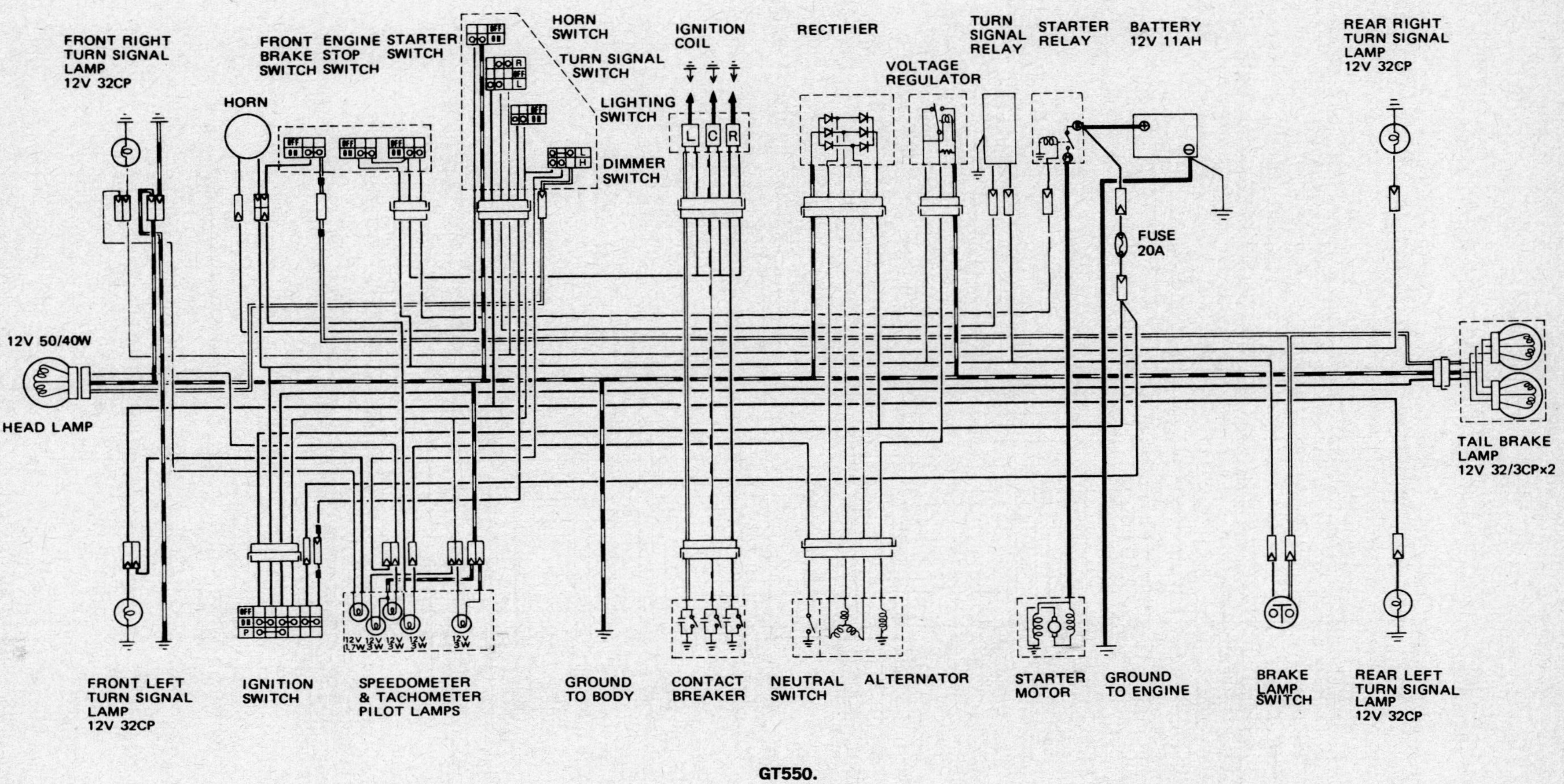
FRONT RIGHT TURN SIGNAL LAMP 12V 32CP
FRONT BRAKE SWITCH
ENGINE STOP SWITCH
STARTER SWITCH
HORN SWITCH
TURN SIGNAL SWITCH
LIGHTING SWITCH
DIMMER SWITCH
IGNITION COIL
RECTIFIER
VOLTAGE REGULATOR
TURN SIGNAL RELAY
STARTER RELAY
BATTERY 12V 11AH
FUSE 20A
REAR RIGHT TURN SIGNAL LAMP 12V 32CP
HORN
12V 50/40W
HEAD LAMP
TAIL BRAKE LAMP 12V 32/3CPx2
FRONT LEFT TURN SIGNAL LAMP 12V 32CP
IGNITION SWITCH
SPEEDOMETER & TACHOMETER PILOT LAMPS
GROUND TO BODY
CONTACT BREAKER
NEUTRAL SWITCH
ALTERNATOR
STARTER MOTOR
GROUND TO ENGINE
BRAKE LAMP SWITCH
REAR LEFT TURN SIGNAL LAMP 12V 32CP

GT550.

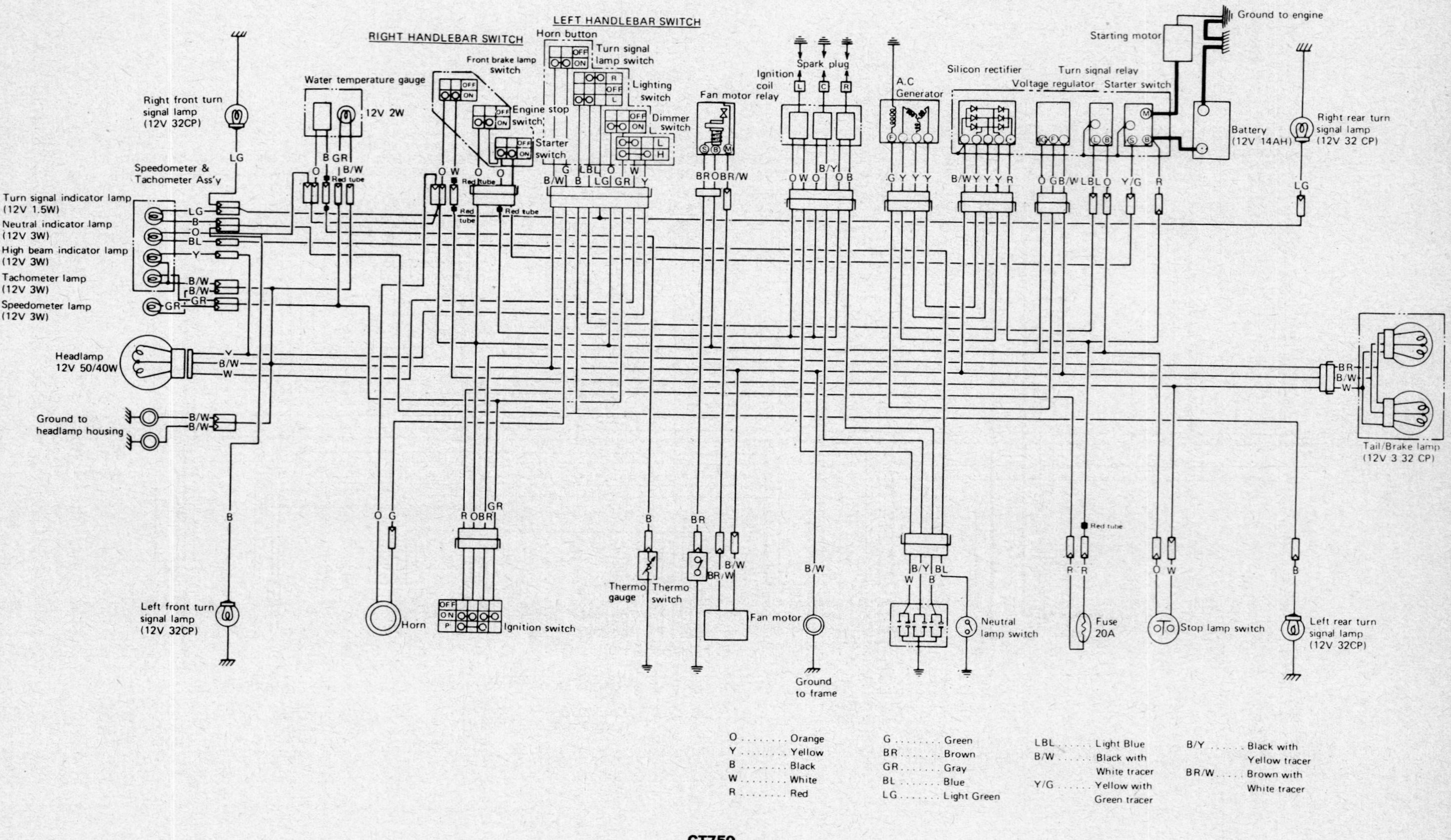

RIGHT HANDLEBAR SWITCH
LEFT HANDLEBAR SWITCH
Horn button
Turn signal lamp switch
Lighting switch
Dimmer switch
Front brake lamp switch
Engine stop switch
Starter switch
Water temperature gauge
12V 2W
Right front turn signal lamp (12V 32CP)
Speedometer & Tachometer Ass'y
Turn signal indicator lamp (12V 1.5W)
Neutral indicator lamp (12V 3W)
High beam indicator lamp (12V 3W)
Tachometer lamp (12V 3W)
Speedometer lamp (12V 3W)
Headlamp 12V 50/40W
Ground to headlamp housing
Left front turn signal lamp (12V 32CP)
Horn
Ignition switch
Thermo gauge
Thermo switch
Fan motor relay
Fan motor
Ignition coil
Spark plug
Ground to frame
A.C Generator
Silicon rectifier
Voltage regulator
Turn signal relay
Starter switch
Starting motor
Ground to engine
Battery (12V 14AH)
Right rear turn signal lamp (12V 32 CP)
Tail/Brake lamp (12V 3 32 CP)
Neutral lamp switch
Red tube
Fuse 20A
Stop lamp switch
Left rear turn signal lamp (12V 32CP)
O .... Orange
Y .... Yellow
B .... Black
W .... White
R .... Red
G .... Green
BR .... Brown
GR .... Gray
BL .... Blue
LG .... Light Green
LBL .... Light Blue
B/W .... Black with White tracer
Y/G .... Yellow with Green tracer
B/Y .... Black with Yellow tracer
BR/W .... Brown with White tracer
GT750.

CHASSIS

WHEELS

Front Wheel

REMOVAL

1. Disconnect the front brake and speedometer cables.
2. Bend back the locking tab on the nut which secures the brake anchor and disconnect the brake anchor.
3. Remove the cotter pin which secures the axle nut (if fitted); remove the nut, loosen the axle pinch bolt, and pull out the axle.

If the motorcycle is equipped with axle cups instead, loosen the axle nut, remove the two nuts on each cup, and take out the wheel.

INSPECTION

1. Inspect the brake linings for score marks, wear, or imbedded grease or oil. Clean or replace them as necessary.
2. Check the brake drum for scoring. Concentricity may be restored to the drum, if it is warped, by turning it on a lathe.
3. Check the condition of the brake springs, being especially attentive to rust or corrosion built up on the spring.
4. On twin leading shoe brakes, be sure that both brake cams lie flat against the brake shoe pad. If this is not the case, correct by positioning the rod which connects the brake arms.
5. On most models, the brake shoes are held in position by the brake springs only; they can then be removed by grasping both of them and lifting them up and in toward the center of the drum.

INSTALLATION

Installation is the reverse of the removal sequence. Be certain that the speedometer drive tabs are correctly engaged. Refit the dust seal and axle spacer (if fitted).

Rear Wheel

REMOVAL

1. Disconnect the rear brake cable (or rod). Disconnect the brake anchor.

NOTE: *There is usually a clip which must be taken off before the anchor nut can be removed.*

2. Remove the cotter pin from the axle nut, take off the nut, and pull out the axle.
3. Remove the spacer, pull the wheel over to disengage it from the driving studs, and remove it from the frame.

INSPECTION

Inspect the condition of the brake linings, drum, etc., refering to the procedures given for the front wheel if necessary. Also check the condition of the rubber shock absorbers in the hub and replace them if necessary.

INSTALLATION

Installation is the reverse of the removal procedure.

REAR SPROCKET

The rear sprocket is easily removed after the wheel is taken off by first removing the chainguard, then disconnecting the chain, removing the sprocket nut, and removing the sprocket.

1. Check the sprocket for worn teeth and for warpage.
2. Check the sprocket bearing. It may be removed by driving it out from the right side.
3. When replacing the sprocket on the hub, the nuts securing the sprocket should be tightened firmly, using a diagonal tightening pattern, and then peened over the bolts.

WHEEL BEARINGS

1. Wheel bearings should be inspected in place by checking for free rotation, wear, or play.
2. Remove the bearings by removing the oil seals on each side of the hub. These can be pried out.
3. With a rod, or suitable screwdriver, drive the bearings out from the inside of the hub.

Installing wheel bearings with the special drift.

4. Install new bearings after packing them with grease. The bearings should be drifted in as shown.
5. Fit new oil seals to both sides of the hub.

FRONT FORKS

REMOVAL

1. Support the front end of the machine well off the ground.
2. Remove the front wheel and fender.
3. Drain the oil from each fork leg.
4. Remove the headlight and shell after disconnecting the wiring.
5. Unbolt the handlebars from the upper triple clamp and lay them to one side. On some models it is necessary to disconnect the cables before moving the handlebars.
6. Disconnect the speedometer and tachometer cables.

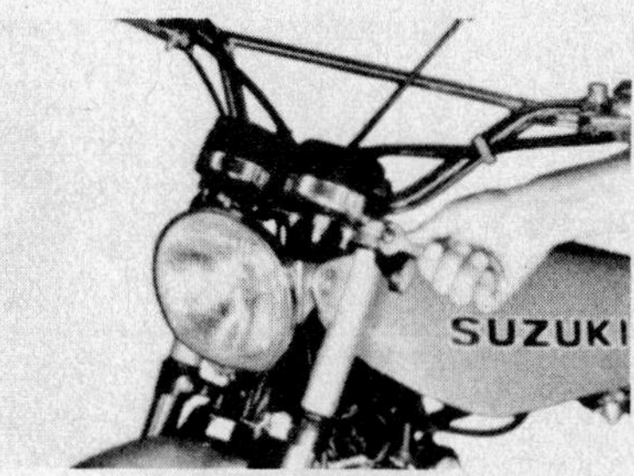

Loosening the upper triple clamp bolt.

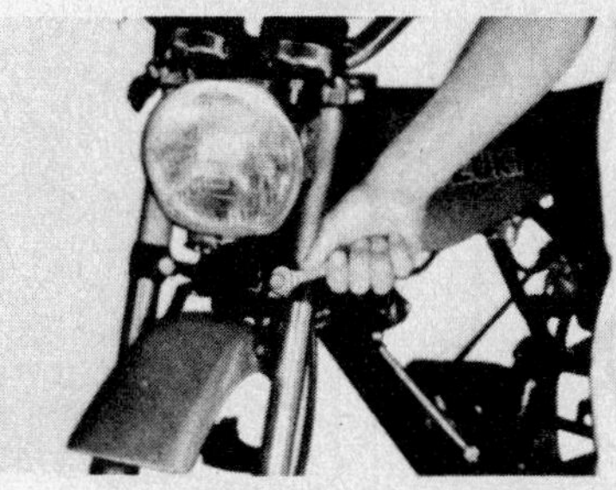
Loosening the lower triple clamp bolt.

7. Remove the top bolts of each fork tube. Loosen the upper and lower triple clamp nuts.

NOTE: *On some models it is necessary to remove the top triple clamp itself.*

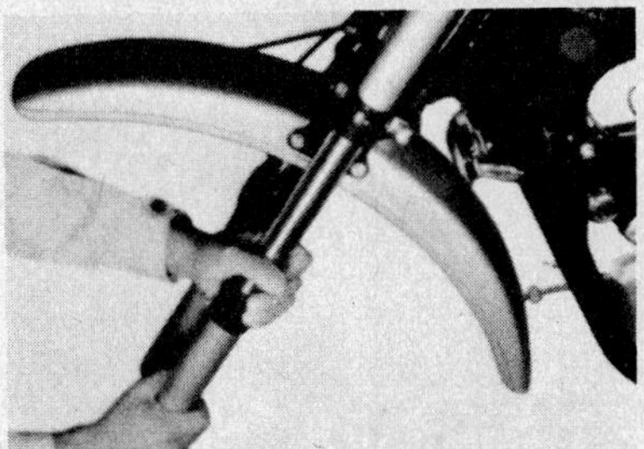
Removing the fork leg from the triple clamp.

8. Grasp the bottom of each fork leg and pull downward to remove it.

NOTE: *Steps 4–6 are not necessary for K10P, K11P, TS90, TC90, TS125, TC125, GT series, TS400, TM400.*

DISASSEMBLY

1. Remove the top fork bolt, if this has not already been done. Remove the fork spring guide.
2. Take out the inner fork spring. Some models have only an exterior spring which is easily removed.
3. Spread the fork leg as far as possible by grasping the inner tube and pulling down on the slider.

The forks are disassembled in one of three ways depending on model.

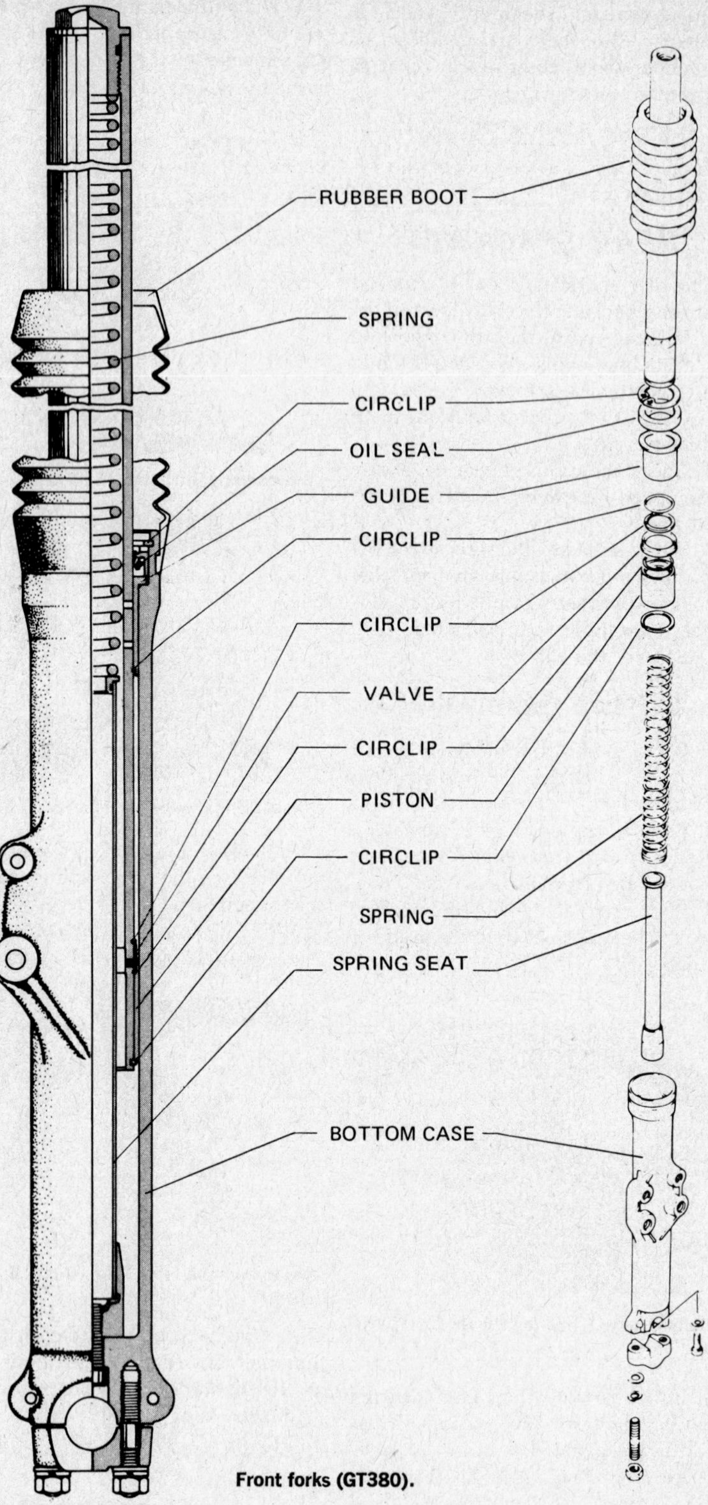

RUBBER BOOT
SPRING
CIRCLIP
OIL SEAL
GUIDE
CIRCLIP
CIRCLIP
VALVE
CIRCLIP
PISTON
CIRCLIP
SPRING
SPRING SEAT
BOTTOM CASE

Front forks (GT380).

GT Series, TM400

Remove the bolt at the very bottom of the fork tube, remove the circlip at the top of the slider, then pull off the slider.

S32-2, T-10

Protect the inner fork tube to avoid damage, then clamp it in a soft-faced vise. Use a suitable bar in the axle hole to turn the slider and remove it from the inner tube.

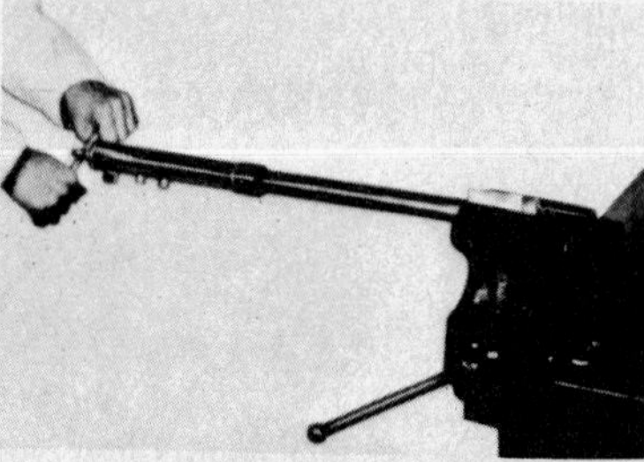

Unscrewing the fork slider (S-32).

Other Models

The inner tube and the slider are secured by a ring nut. Clamp the slider in a soft-faced vise and unscrew the ring nut with the Suzuki special tool or with a strap wrench.

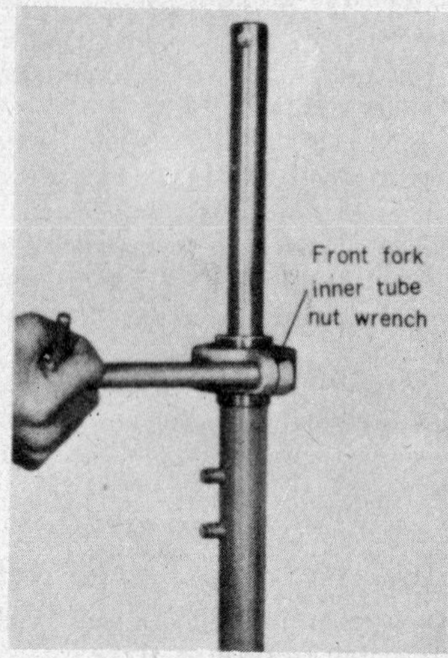

Removing the fork slider by unscrewing the inner tube nut.

4. The oil seal is removed by driving it out with a hammer and punch after first removing the 0-ring (if fitted).
5. To install the seal, drive it in with the special tool as shown.

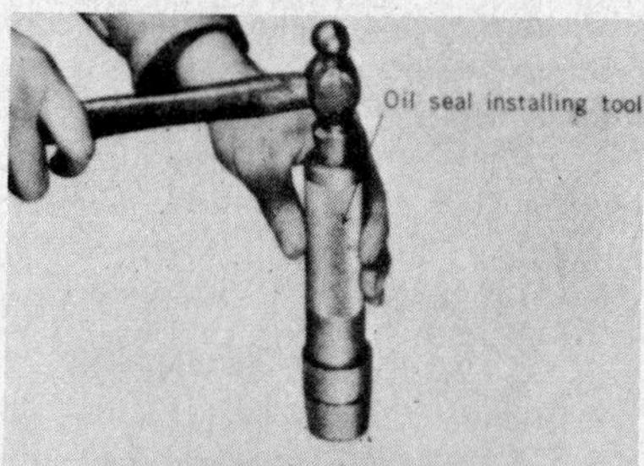

Installing the front fork oil seal with a special drift.

INSPECTION

1. Check the inner tubes for straight alignment. They should also be free of rust or corrosion on both outer and inner surfaces.
2. Check the condition of the fork springs.
3. The holes in the damper tube must be clear of any obstruction.
4. The oil seals and 0-rings should be replaced if they have been removed.

ASSEMBLY

Assemble the forks in the reverse order of the above. Lightly oil all components before refitting.

STEERING STEM

1. The adjustment of the steering head bearings should first be checked by supporting the front wheel off the ground, grasping the fork legs, and attempting to move them toward and away from the machine. There should be no play in the forks. They should still be able to move from lock to lock without binding or excessively loose spots. If adjustment is necessary, remove the upper triple clamp and loosen or tighten the steering stem nut with the special tool or with a hammer and screwdriver. To remove the steering stem, remove the nut and carefully lower the assembly downward being careful of the bearings in the lower race.

2. Check the condition of the bearing races and the bearings themselves. If the bearings are worn or pitted, they must be replaced. The bearing races should be smooth and free from pitting, cracks, etc.

3. Bearing races are driven out of the steering lug with a hammer and punch.

4. The ball cup on the steering stem is pried off with a chisel.

5. Install the bearing races in the steering lug with the appropriate drift. Grease the races and imbed the ball bearings into the grease.

Installing the steering lug bearing races.

6. Refit the steering stem and adjust the bearings as previously described.

CHASSIS TORQUE SPECIFICATIONS

(ft lbs)

Model	Engine Mounts	Handle-bar Clamp Bolts	Steering Stem Bolt	Bearing Locknut	Fork Pinch Bolts	Fork Tube Bolts	Front Axle	Rear Axle	Swing-Arm Pivot	Rear Shock Absorber	Rear Sprocket
F-50, F-50R, J	14	9	N/A	N/A	N/A	N/A	31	22	17	17	14
AS-50, AC-50, TS-50R, J	14	5	17	22	17	16	31	22	17	17	14
MT-50R, J	14	N/A	N/A	N/A	N/A	N/A	31	31	17	17	14
TS/TC-90, TS/TC-90R, J	14	10	32	N/A	17	17	29	29	17	17	33
A-100, AS-100, AC-100	14	5	17	22	17	16	29	22	17	17	33
B-100P, B-105P, KT-120, TC-120R	14	5	17	22	17	16	29	22	19	17	30
M-12, M-15, M-15D, M-12-2, M-15-2, M-31	14	5	17	22	17	16	29	22	17	17	14
K-10, K-11, K-15, K-10P, K-11P, K-15P	14	5	17	22	17	16	29	22	17	17	14
TS-125R, J	14	10	17	22	17	16	32	32	27	17	30
T-125, T-125R, J	14	11	36	22	17	17	28	28	28	17	20
S-32-2, T-10	13/9	6	17	24	20	17	40	40	28	18	20
TS-185R	14	10	17	22	17	17	32	32	40	18	30
TS-250, TS-250II	16	10	45	22	17	17	45	45	45	17	20
TS-250R, J	16	10	35	22	17	17	45	45	45	17	20
T-20, TC-20, T-200, TC-200	16	6	18	24	14	18	45	45	28	18	23
T-250, T-350, T-305, TC-305	16	9	18	24	14	18	45	45	28	18	23
TM-400R	24	15	15	55	15	18	28	45	45	18	25
T-500, T-500R, J	43	9	18	24	14	18	47	47	47	18	25

N/A—Not applicable.

INDEX

TRIUMPH

MODEL IDENTIFICATION

TR25W: 250cc Bore x Stroke 67 x 70mm compression 10:1 carburetor AMAL928

T100C "Trophy Trail": 490cc; Bore x Stroke 69 x 65.5 mm compression ratio 9.0:1

T100R "Daytona": 490cc Twin Bore x Stroke 69 x 65.5

T120R "Bonneville": 649cc Bore x Stroke 71 x 82mm compression ratio 9:1 Dual Carbs.

Tiger 750 (TR7V) and Bonneville 750 (T140V): bored and stroked 650 engine, 5-speed, disc brake, oil reservoir is the rear frame tube.

T150 "Trident": 750cc, Triple; Bore x Stroke 67c 70 mm

GENERAL SPECIFICATIONS

	TR25W	T100C	T100R	TR6R*	TR6C*
DIMENSIONS					
Net Weight (lbs)	320.0	337.0	341.0	365.0	365.0
Overall Height (in.)	43.25	38.0	38.0	38.0	38.0
Overall Width (in.)	28.0	26.5	26.5	27.5	27.5
Overall Length (in.)	83.0	83.25	83.25	84.0	84.0
Wheelbase (in.)	53.0	53.5	53.5	55.0	55.0
Seat Height (in.)	32.0	—	—	—	—
Ground Clearance (in.)	8.5	7.5	7.5	6.0	6.0
ENGINE					
Displacement (cc)	250	490	490	649	649
Bore x Stroke (mm)	67 x 70	69 x 65.5 (2)	69 x 65.5 (2)	71 x 82 (2)	71 x 82 (2)
Compression Ratio	10:1	9.0:1	9.1:1	9.0:1	9.0:1
Carburetor Type and Model	Amal 928/1	②	③	Amal R930/23	Amal R930/23
Horsepower @ rpm	22 @ 8250	34 @ 7000	39 @ 7400	43 @ 6500	43 @ 6500
Torque @ rpm	15.8 @ 7000	28.2 @ 6500	30.2 @ 6750	36.5 @ 6250	36.5 @ 6250
TRANSMISSION					
Clutch Type	wet, multi-plate	wet, multi-plate	wet, multi-plate	wet, multi-plate	wet, multi-plate
Internal Gear Ratios					
1st	2.65	2.47	2.47	2.44	2.44
2nd	1.65	1.61	1.61	1.69	1.69
3rd	1.24	1.22	1.22	1.24	1.24
4th	1.00	1.00	1.00	1.00	1.00
5th	—	—	—	—	—
Sprockets (no. of teeth)					
Engine	23	26	26	29	29
Clutch	52	58	58	58	58
Gearbox	15	18	18	18	18
Rear Wheel	①	46	46	46	46
CHASSIS					
Front Suspension	rod damper or shuttle valve-type telescopic			shuttle valve-type telescopic	
Rear Suspension	swing arm with hydraulically dampened shocks				
Tire Size: front	3.25 x 18	3.25 x 19	3.25 x 19	3.25 x 19	3.25 x 19
rear	4.00 x 18	4.00 x 18	4.00 x 18	4.00 x 18	4.00 x 18
ELECTRICAL					
System Voltage	12	12	12	12	12
Generator Type	alternator				

* Optional 5-speed gearbox available. Ratios: 1st—2.585; 2nd—1.837; 3rd—1.400; 4th—1.192; 5th—1.000.

① 52 tooth standard; 49 tooth optional.

② Amal 376/273 prior to serial no. H.57083; Amal 628/8 after serial no. H.57083.

③ Amal 376/324 and 325 before serial no. H.5708; Amal 626/9 and 10 after serial no. H.5708.

GENERAL SPECIFICATIONS

	T120R*	T150	TR7V	T140V	T150V
DIMENSIONS					
Net Weight (lbs)	365.0	470.0	402	408	460
Overall Height (in.)	38.0	43.5	38.0	38.0	43.5
Overall Width (in.)	27.5	32.5	33.0	33.0	32.5
Overall Length (in.)	84.0	86.0	87.5	87.5	86.0
Wheelbase (in.)	55.0	56.25	55.0	55.0	56.3
Seat Height (in.)	—	32.0	31.5	31.5	32.0
Ground Clearance (in.)	5.0	6.5	6.0	6.0	6.5
ENGINE					
Displacement (cc)	649	741	747	747	741
Bore x Stroke (mm)	71 x 82 (2)	67 x 70 (3)	76 x 82 (2)	76 x 82 (2)	67 x 70 (3)
Compression Ratio	9.0:1	9.0:1	8.6:1	8.6:1	9.5:1
Carburetor Type and Model	Amal R930/9 & L930/10	Amal 626	Amal R930/89	Amal L930/92 & R930/89	Amal 626
Horsepower @ rpm	47 @ 6700	58 @ 7500	NA	NA	NA
Torque @ rpm	38.5 @ 6000	45 @ 6900	NA	NA	NA
TRANSMISSION					
Clutch Type	wet, multi-plate	wet, single- plate	wet, multi-plate	wet, multi-plate	wet, single-plate
Internal Gear Ratios					
1st	2.44	2.44	2.59	2.59	2.59
2nd	1.69	1.69	1.84	1.84	1.84
3rd	1.24	1.19	1.40	1.40	1.40
4th	1.00	1.00	1.19	1.19	1.19
5th	—	—	1.00	1.00	1.00
Sprockets (no. of teeth)					
Engine	29	28	29	29	28
Clutch	58	50	58	58	50
Gearbox	18	18	20	20	18
Rear Wheel	46	52	47	47	53
CHASSIS					
Front Suspension	telescopic, hydraulically dampened				
Rear Suspension	swing arm with hydraulically dampened shocks				
Tire Size: front	3.25 x 19	3.50 x 19	3.25 x 19	3.25 x 19	4.10 x 19
rear	4.00 x 18	4.10 x 18	4.00 x 18	4.00 x 18	4.10 x 19
ELECTRICAL					
System Voltage	12	12	12	12	12
Generator Type	alternator				

TUNE-UP AND MAINTENANCE

TUNE-UP OPERATIONS

Valve Tappet Adjustment

NOTE: *Set valve clearances with the engine cold, preferably after it has been left sitting overnight.*

TR25W

1. Remove the spark plug, rocker inspection caps, and rocker spindle plate. Also, put the transmission in gear so that the engine can be easily rotated by turning the rear wheel.

2. Rotate the engine in the normal running direction until the intake valve has just completely closed.

NOTE: *This point can be accurately located by feeling the pushrod. When the valve is completely closed, the pushrod will be free to rotate.*

3. The engine is now correctly positioned for checking the exhaust valve clearance. Slide the appropriate feeler gauge between the valve stem and the tappet, and check for a snug slip-fit.

4. If an adjustment is necessary, loosen the rocker spindle locknuts opposite the spindle cover plate. Turn the slotted exhaust valve spindle in a clockwise direction until the rocker arm just touches the valve stem, then turn it back again until the correct clearance is obtained. Tighten up the locknut and recheck the adjustment.

5. Rotate the engine forward again until the exhaust valve is just about to open. This is the correct position for checking the intake valve tappet clearance.

6. Check the clearance with the proper feeler gauge and, if necessary, readjust it to meet specifications. The procedure for adjusting the intake valve clearance is the same as that outlined for the exhaust valve except that the rocker spindle should first be turned counterclockwise, rather than clockwise.

T100C, T100R, TR6R, TR6C, TR7V, T120R, AND T140V

1. Remove the spark plugs and rocker box inspection caps.

2. Loosen the tappet adjuster locknuts.

3. Slowly turn the engine over until the left exhaust valve is fully open. This is the correct position for setting the right exhaust valve tappet clearance.

4. Insert the appropriate feeler gauge between the tappet and the valve stem, then if necessary, turn the square-headed

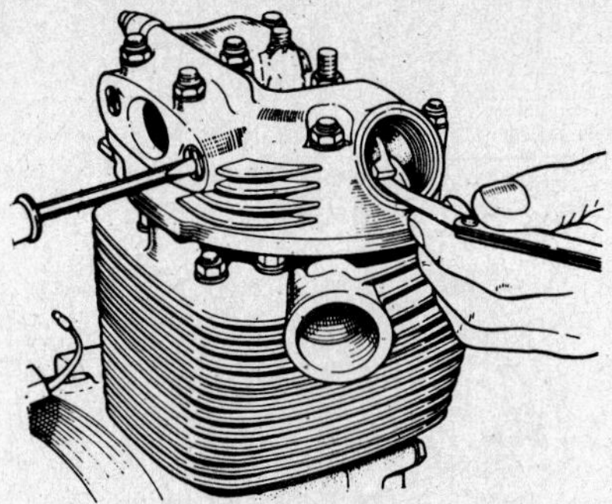

Valve tappet adjustment (250)

adjuster until a snug slip-fit is obtained.

5. Tighten the adjuster locknut and recheck the clearance.

6. Repeat the above for the left exhaust valve and then the intake valves.

NOTE: *In a situation where a feeler gauge is not available, you can set tappet clearances approximately by turning the adjuster in until it is finger-tight, then turning it back out ¼ turn per 0.010 in.*

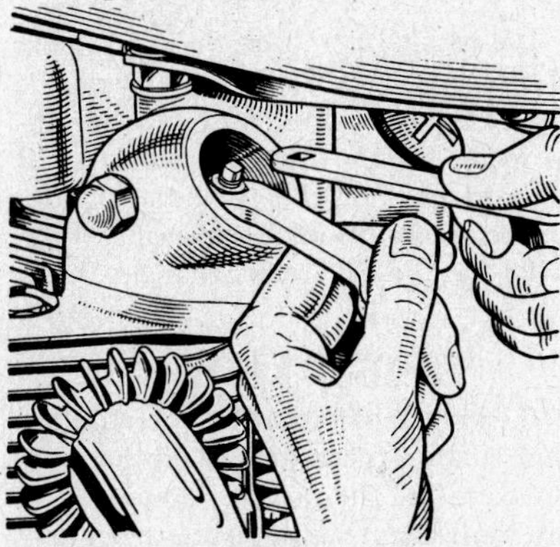

Valve tappet adjustment (500 models)

T150, T150V

1. Remove the spark plugs and rocker box inspection caps.

2. Beginning with the intake cam, rotate the engine until two valves are opened by the same amount (approximately 1/16 in.). At this point, with one of the valves just opening and the other just closing, the third valve is correctly positioned for adjustment.

3. Insert the appropriate feeler gauge and, if necessary, loosen the adjuster lock-nut and turn the adjuster until a snug slip-fit is obtained. Tighten the locknut and recheck the clearance.

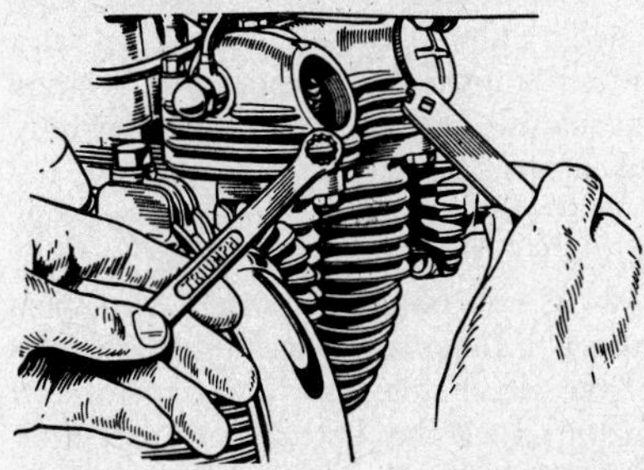

Valve tappet adjustment (650 models)

4. Continue rotating the engine until the conditions outlined in step 2 are met for another intake valve. Repeat the procedure on the remaining intake and exhaust valves.

5. Install the spark plugs and rocker box inspection caps.

Contact Breaker Points

TR25W

The contact breaker point assembly is located behind the circular cover on the right side of the engine.

Removal

1. Remove the breaker point cover.

2. Remove the securing nut, nylon sleeve, and contact breaker lead.

3. Remove the screw that fastens the fixed point of the contact breaker, then lift the unit out.

Installation

Installation is a reversal of the removal procedure. Do not forget to install the fiber washer that fits between the moving point spring and the fixed point backing plate. Reset ignition timing.

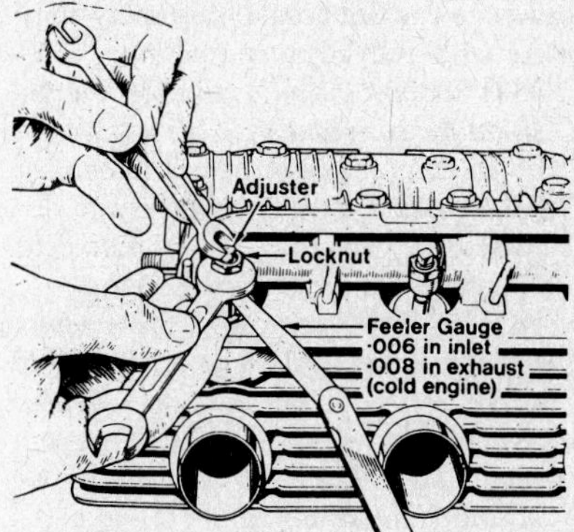

Valve tappet adjustment (Trident)

Gap Adjustment

1. Put the transmission in gear and rotate the engine by turning the rear wheel until the nylon heel of the contact breaker is aligned with the scribed mark on the breaker cam.

2. Loosen the contact adjusting screw and turn the eccentric screw until a snug slip-fit is obtained with the appropriate feeler gauge.

3. Tighten the adjusting screw and recheck the gap.

T100C AND T100R (PRIOR TO SERIAL NO. H57083)

The contact breaker point assembly is located behind a circular cover plate on the right side of the engine and is driven by the exhaust camshaft.

Removal

1. Remove the contact breaker cover and gasket.

2. Disconnect the battery.

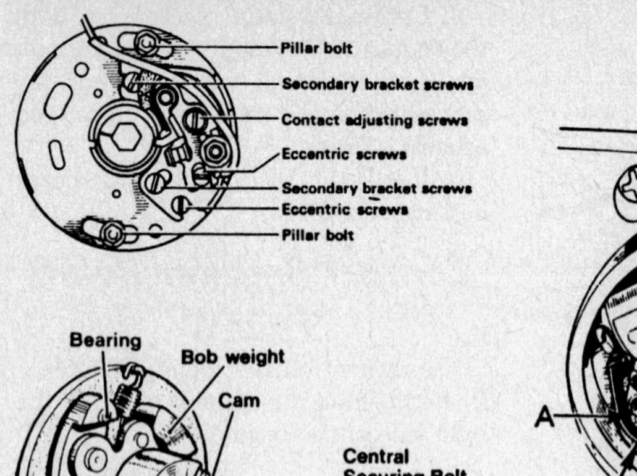

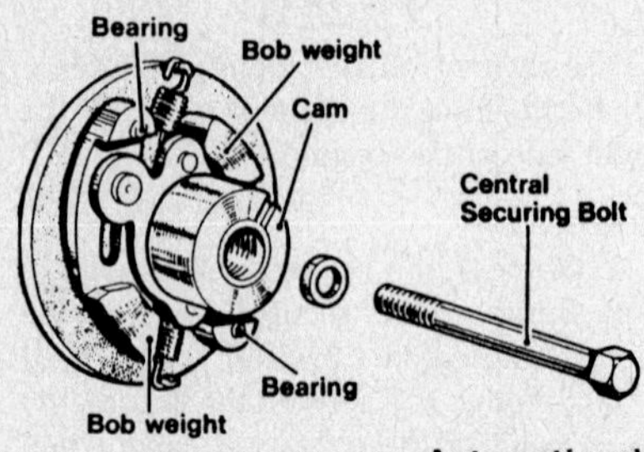

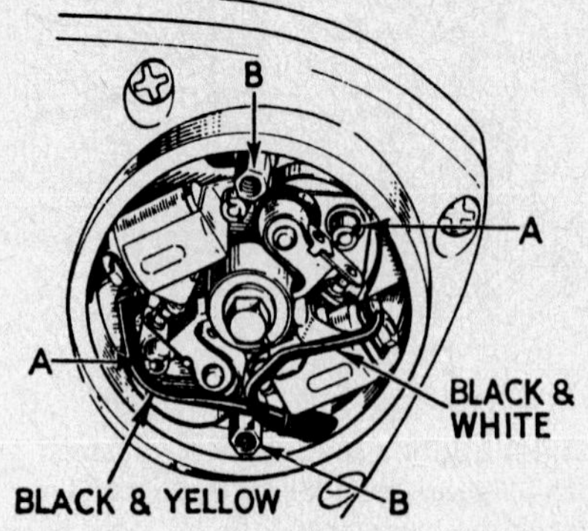

Automatic advance unit (250)

3. Remove the center bolt with the plain washer and the two hexagonal pillar-bolts and washers.

4. Install special extractor tool no. D484 and tighten it until the taper is released from the camshaft.

5. Unscrew the special tool and withdraw the contact breaker assembly complete with auto-advance unit.

NOTE: *Mark the auto advance unit position for reassembly.*

6. To completely remove the contact breaker assembly, it is necessary to disconnect the leads from the ignition coils and unfasten them from the frame.

NOTE: *When removing the contact breaker assembly, it is advisable to make note of the advance degree figures stamped on the back of the cam unit. This information is necessary for accurate static timing.*

Installation

Installation is a reversal of the removal procedure, but before installing the cam unit, add a drop of oil to the pivot pins. Make sure the cam unit slot correctly engages the peg on the camshaft.

Gap Adjustment

1. Remove the spark plugs.

2. Rotate the engine until the nylon heel of one set of points aligns with the mark scribed on the breaker cam.

3. Insert the appropriate feeler gauge and, if necessary, loosen sleeve nuts "A" (see illustration) and shift the breaker point plate until a snug slip-fit is achieved.

4. Repeat the above for the other set of points.

5. Check to make sure the breaker plate is correctly positioned. The set of points with the black/yellow lead should be situated toward the rear. Also make certain that the pillar bolts are in the center of their adjustment slots.

T100C, T100R, TR6R, TR63, T120R (After Serial No. H57083), TR7V, T140V

The breaker points on these machines are set up basically the same as on the earlier models. However, the condensers are located on the frame near the front of the gas tank and, when withdrawing the breaker point assembly, special tool no. D782 must be used rather than no. D484.

T150, T150V

The breaker point assembly on the Trident is also similar to that on the early 500 cc twins. The main difference being that the Trident has three sets of points—one for each cylinder. Other differences in procedure are outlined below:

1. Use Triumph tool no. D782 to removed the assembly center bolt.

2. Disconnect the breaker point leads at the snap connectors behind the gearbox.

3. When installing the assembly, make certain the point set with the red/black lead is in the rearmost position.

Ignition Timing

TR25W

Initial Procedure

Before actually setting static timing, the piston must be located at the specified number of degrees before top dead center and the automatic spark advance mechanism must be locked in the fully advanced position.

1. Remove the small inspection cover at the front of the primary chaincase.

2. As can be seen through the aperture, a timing mark is scribed on the face of the alternator rotor and a pointer is mounted at the bottom of inspection hole.

3. Rotate the engine until it is on its compression stroke (i.e., both valves closed), then align the rotor mark and pointer. The piston is now located 37° before top dead center.

4. An alternate method of locating the piston, only possible on later machines, is by using Triumph special plunger and body (no. 61–2915 and 61–D572). Locate the piston on its compression stroke, then rotate the engine gently backward while applying slight pressure to the plunger. The plunger will drop into position, locking the piston at 37° before top dead center.

5. Now that the piston is correctly located, the automatic advance unit must be locked in the fully advanced position. This is necessary because, due to manufacturing tolerances, slight variation in spark timing will occur at one end of the advance curve or the other. In general, it

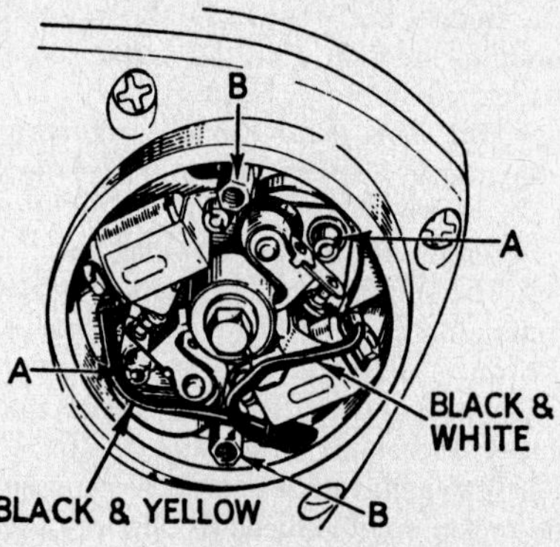

Contact breaker assembly (500 models before serial no. H57083)

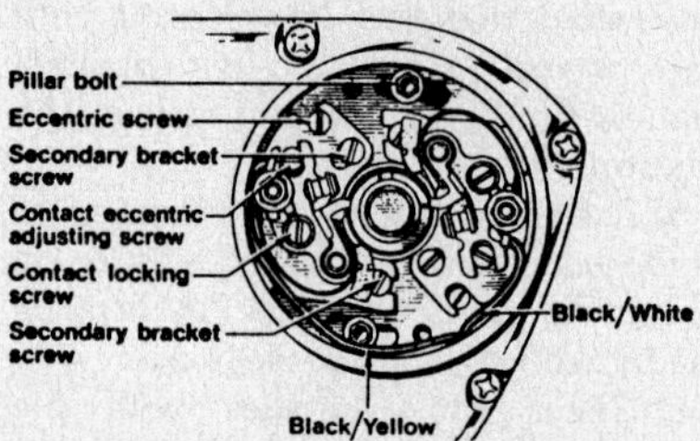

Contact breaker assembly (500 models after serial no. H57083)

is preferred that this variation does not affect high speed performance; therefore the mechanism should be set at the fully advanced position so that any fluctuations will occur only at idle speeds.

6. Carefully remove the cam central bolt and fit an extra washer on the bolt. This washer should have a hole just large enough to clear the cam inner bearing (see illustration).

7. Reinstall the bolt, but before tightening it, rotate the cam counterclockwise until the advance weights are fully extended. Hold the weights in this position and tighten the central bolt.

8. After setting the final ignition timing, don't forget to remove the extra washer on the central bolt.

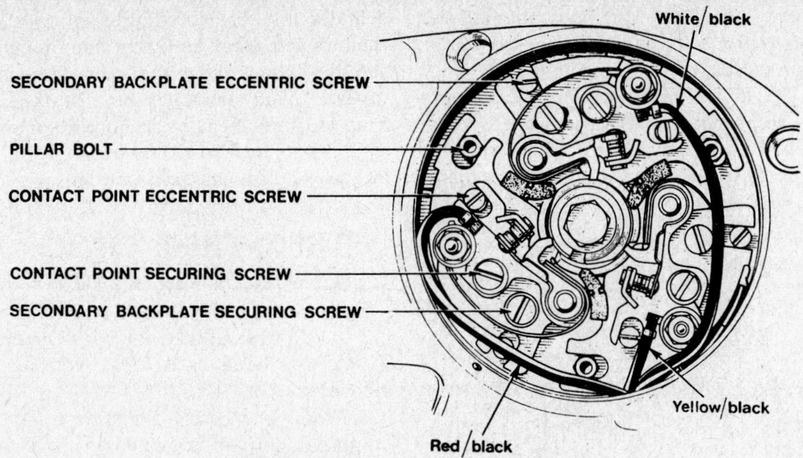

Contact breaker assembly (Trident)

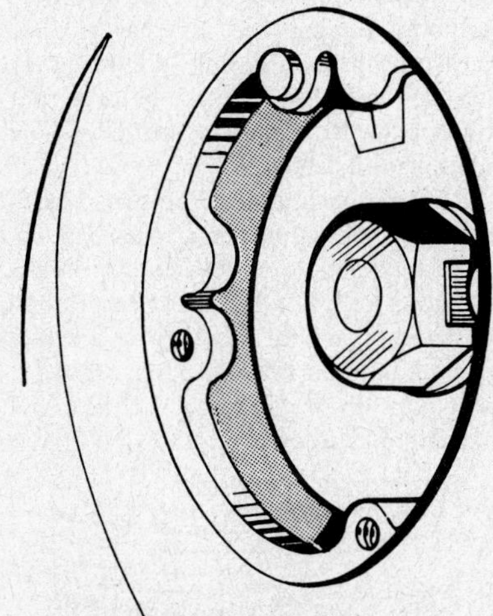
Rotor and stator marks (250)

Static Timing

1. With the piston correctly located and the advance mechanism locked in the fully advanced position, ignition timing can now be set.
2. Connect a battery and bulb or a timing light as shown in the illustration.
3. Loosen the contact-breaker plate pillar bolts and turn the plate in either direction until the points are just opening. At this point the timing light will go out.
4. Hold the plate in this position and tighten the pillar bolts.

Strobe Timing

Remove the inspection cover at the front of the primary chaincase. Connect the strobe as instructed by the manufacturer and start the engine. Shine the light on the rotor mark and pointer; at engine speeds above 3000 rpm, they should be in perfect alignment. If an adjustment is necessary, shift the breaker point plate position as described in "Static Timing."

T100C AND T100R (Prior To Serial No. H57083)

Initial Procedure

Before setting ignition timing, the piston must first be positioned at top dead center.

1. Remove the spark plugs and rocker box inspection caps.
2. Put the transmission in gear so that the engine can be rotated by turning the rear wheel.

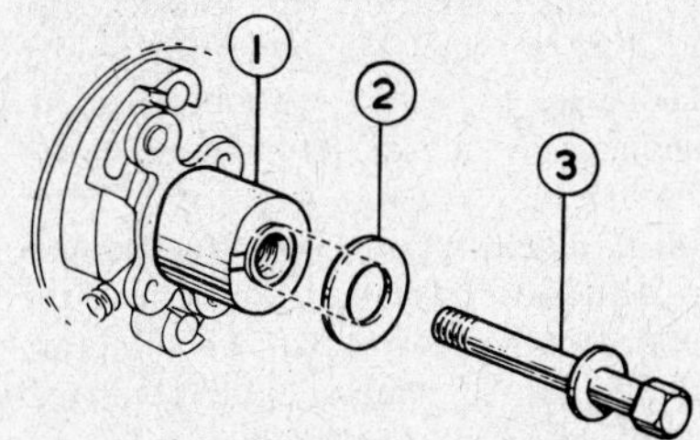

Locking the ignition advance unit (250)

3. Locate the piston at top dead center, using a dial indicator, Triumph timing plunger and body no. D571/2, or, if necessary, a stick positioned in the spark plug hole.

Static Timing

1. Remove the automatic advance unit and check the degree range stamped on the back. Make a note for future reference and reinstall the unit.
2. Double the auto-advance range and subtract it from the fully advanced degree figure (38°). This is the correct static setting for the engine. Example:

AUTO-ADVANCE
DEGREE RANGE = 12°
FULLY ADVANCED
DEGREE SETTING = 38°
2X12° = 24°
38°–24° = STATIC
TIMING

3. If a stick is used to locate top dead center, convert the degree figure into inches or millimeters by using the chart at the end of this chapter, then scribe a corresponding mark on the stick.
4. Fit a degree wheel to the auto advance unit and fasten a pointer to a convenient case cover screw.
5. If a dial indicator or timing plunger was used to locate top dead center, position the degree wheel and/or pointer to read TDC. Then remove the timing plunger (the dial indicator can remain) and carefully rotate the engine until it is at 38° before top dead center (on its compression stroke), as indicated by the degree wheel and pointer.
6. Connect a battery and bulb or a timing light (as illustrated in "TR25W Static Timing") to the right cylinder points. Rotate the engine backward to a point below the static timing position. Slowly approach the prescribed setting and, if necessary, adjust the breaker plate so that the points are just opening (light goes out) when the setting is reached.

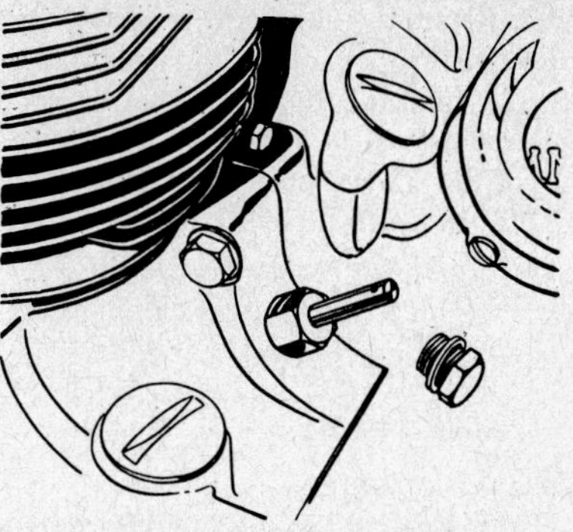
Timing plunger in position (500 models)

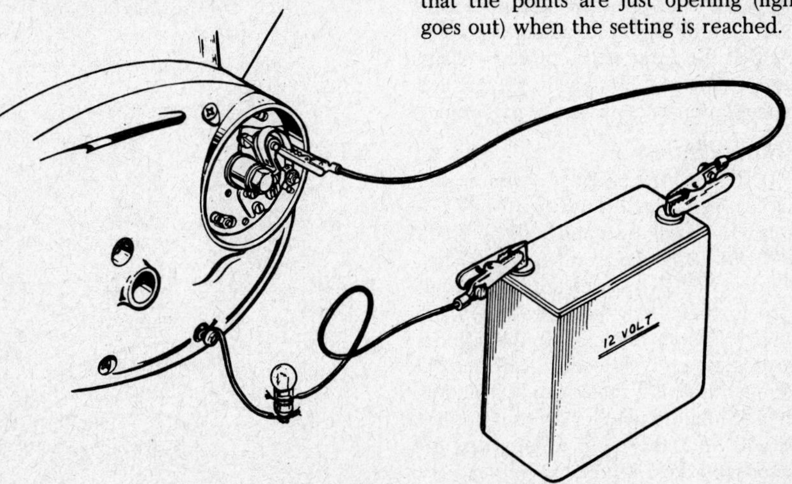

Battery and bulb ignition timing arrangement

7. Rotate the engine forward 360° and repeat the procedure on the second set of points, noting that the main breaker plate must not be disturbed.

NOTE: *To fine-tune the ignition timing, it is permissible to vary the breaker point gap slightly so that both cylinders are timed exactly the same. To advance the spark, open the points approximately 0.001 in. per crankshaft rotation degree.*

Strobe Timing

After locating top dead center and installing a timing disc as previously described, connect the strobe light on the right cylinder points as instructed by the manufacturer. If a 6 or 12-volt external power supply is needed, *do not* use the motorcycle battery. AC current pulses in the bike's low tension wiring can trigger the strobe light and lead to incorrect readings.

Aim the strobe light at the timing disc and rev the engine until the auto advance mechanism is actuated (2000 rpm). The pointer and 38° BTDC on the disc should be exactly in line. If they are not, loosen the contact breaker-plate pillar bolts and make the necessary adjustment. Repeat the procedure for the other cylinder. Remember that the main breaker plate must not be disturbed.

T100C AND T100R (After Serial No. H57083)

Initial Procedure

Late model 500 twins are all equipped with alternator rotor markings and timing plunger stops at top dead center and 38° before top dead center. This makes the timing procedure much easier to carry out. The initial procedure for this engine involves making sure that the auto-advance unit is correctly positioned on its camshaft locating peg and locked in the fully advanced position (see "TR25W Initial Procedure"), and that the engine is otherwise prepared for ignition timing. Preparation, as previously outlined, consists of removing the small inspection plate at the front of the primary chaincase, removing the spark plugs and rocker box inspection caps (static timing).

Static Timing

1. Remove the plug from behind, and in between, the cylinders. Install Triumph timing plunger and body no. D653 and D654, then rotate the engine backward very slowly, applying slight pressure to the timing plunger. When the plunger locks the crankshaft, the piston is located at top dead center. Lift out the plunger and turn the engine a little further. When the plunger drops in for the second time, the position is located 38° before top dead center.

2. An alternate and quicker method of positioning the piston is by aligning the alternator rotor mark with the pointer at the bottom of the inspection hole.

NOTE: *Late machines have the pointer built in, but some earlier models require the use of Triumph adapter no. D2014. This adapter has two markings on the pointer, "B" and "C." Only the line marked "C" should be used.*

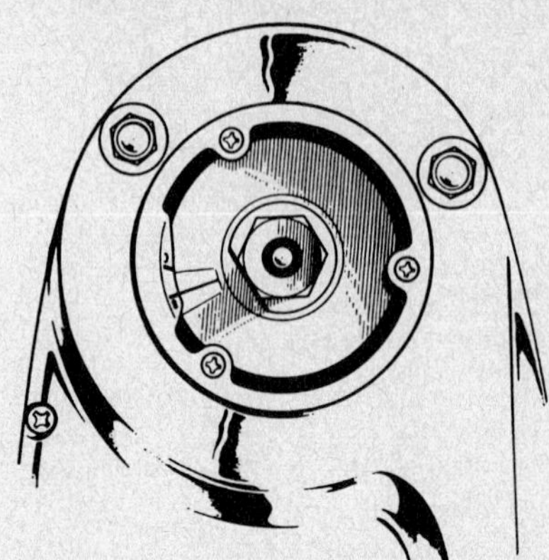

Adapter D2014 installed (500 models)

3. Connect a battery and bulb or a timing light to the right cylinder points. Make sure the right cylinder is on its compression stroke (i.e., both valves closed).

4. If necessary, loosen the contact breaker-plate pillar bolts and adjust the position of the plate so that the points are just opening. The timing light or bulb will go out when the points separate.

5. Remove the timing plunger and rotate the engine forward through 360°. Reinstall the plunger and time the second set of points. The main breaker plate must not be disturbed.

Strobe Timing

Late model 500 twins can be timed with a strobe light in the same manner as the TR25W; that is, by aiming the strobe at the alternator rotor mark and pointer. The marks should be perfectly in line anywhere over 2000 rpm. Time the right cylinder first (black/yellow point wire), then the left. Keep in mind when timing the left cylinder that the main contact breaker plate must not be disturbed. Fine adjustment can be accomplished by slightly varying the breaker point gap (0.001 in. = 1° of crankshaft rotation).

TR6C, TR6R, TR7V, T120R, AND T140V

Follow the initial and static strobe timing procedures outlined for T100C and T100R after serial no. H57083. Note the following:

1. When positioning the piston, Triumph plunger and body no. D2195 and D572 must be used. This plunger locks the piston 38° BTDC. The alternate method, aligning the alternator rotor mark and inspection hole pointer, may also be used. If the machine is not equipped with a pointer, install special adaptor no. D2014.

2. If the machine is to be timed statically, lock the automatic advance mechanism in the fully advanced position as described in "TR25W Initial Procedure."

3. If the machine is to be timed with a strobe light, and if adapter no. D2014 is used, aline the rotor mark with the "B" marking on the pointer.

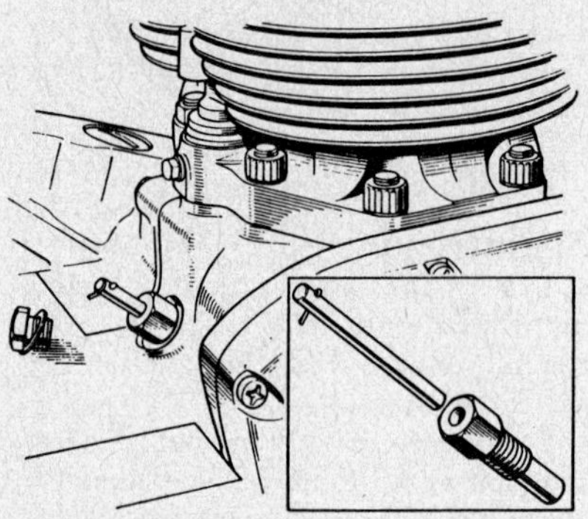

Timing plunger D2195 and body D572 (650 models)

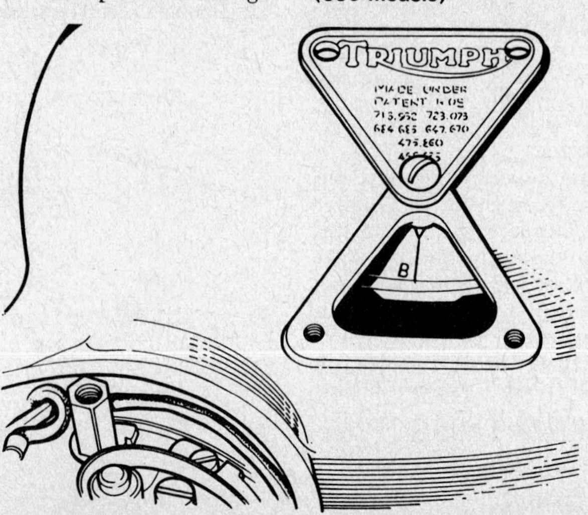

Trident timing marks (from engine No. PG01603).

T150, T150V

The Trident is equipped with one set of points for each cylinder. The firing order is one-three-two. The right (no. one) cylinder point lead is white/black; the center (no. two) red/black, and the left (no. three) yellow/black.

Static Timing

NOTE: *Early model Tridents have three timing marks scribed onto the rotor, 120° apart, each one for a different cylinder. Late models have two sets of timing marks which are distinguished by "A" or "B."*

When timing engines before Serial No. PG 01603, use the "A" timing marks. For engines after PG 01603, line up the "B" timing marks. Refer to the accompanying illustration.

1. Remove the spark plugs and rocker box inspection caps. Put the transmission in gear so that the engine can be rotated by turning the rear wheel.
2. Locate approximate top dead center by rotating the engine until no. 1 piston is at the top of its compression stroke (i.e., both valves closed with clearance at the tappets).
3. Install Triumph timing plunger and body no. D1858, then slowly rotate the engine backward until the plunger locks the crankshaft at 38° BTDC.

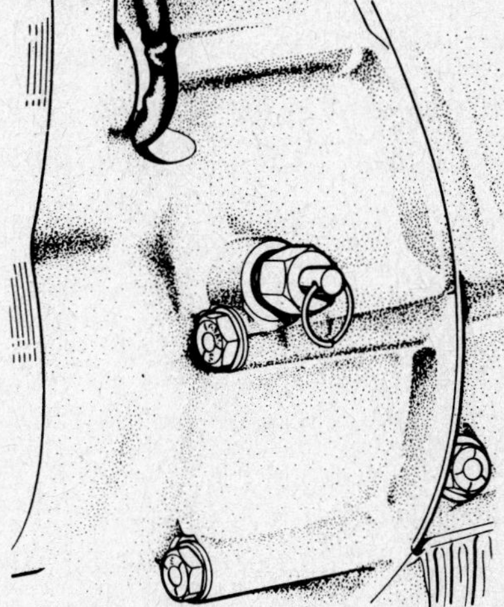

Timing plunger installed (Trident)

4. If the automatic advance unit is not installed, assemble it loosely with an extra washer on the central bolt to lock the cam in the fully advanced position. If it is installed, remove the central bolt and add the extra washer. The washer should have a hole just a little larger than the cam bearing.
5. When the auto-advance unit is fully advanced, the no. 1 cylinder points should just be opening. If this is not the case, loosen the secondary breaker plate screws and shift the plate until the points begin to open. Recheck the point gap.
6. Remove the timing plunger and locate the approximate top dead center piston position in no. 3 cylinder. Repeat the procedure outlined above on the no. 3 cylinder points, then again on no. 2 cylinder points.
7. Remove the extra washer on the central bolt.

Strobe Timing

1. Remove the two top screws of the Triumph patent plate on the primary chaincase. Just loosen the bottom screw, as it will serve as a pointer.
2. Remove the ignition inspection plate located at the front of the primary chaincase.
3. Connect the strobe light to the right cylinder as instructed by the strobe manufacturer. If the unit requires an external power source, *do not* use the motorcycle battery. AC pulses in the machine's low tension wiring can trigger the strobe light and lead to incorrect readings.

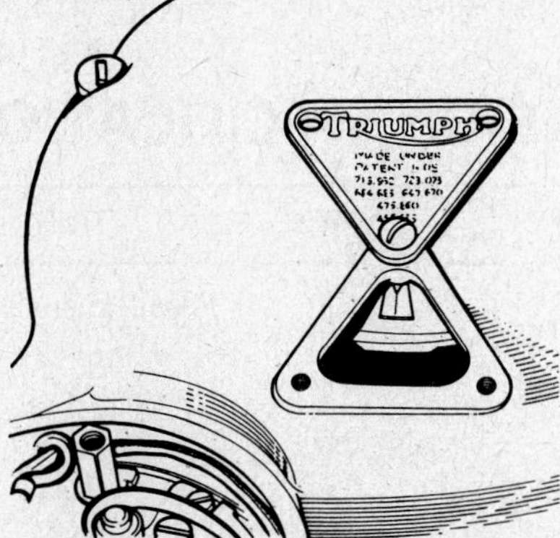

Rotor and stator marks (Trident)

4. Situate the machine in an open area and start the engine. At engine speeds above 2000 rpm, one of the three marks on the alternator rotor (exposed by the Triumph patent plate) should line up directly with the bottom plate screw. If adjustment is necessary, loosen the no. 1 point set secondary bracket and shift the plate until the marks are aligned. Tighten the plate securing screws.
5. Repeat the above procedure on no. 2 cylinder (center), then no. 3 cylinder (left).
6. Reinstall the patent and inspection plates.

Carburetor Adjustments

Idle speed and mixture are controlled by two screws located on the right side of the right carburetor and the left side of the left carburetor on twin arrangements; the right side of the carburetor on single units, and the top and right side of the right and center carburetors and the top and left side of the left carburetor on the Trident. The screws are provided with either spring washers (Monobloc carburetors) or rubber O-rings (Concentric carburetors) to secure them in position after the desired setting has been made.

IDLE SPEED AND MIXTURE

1. Turn the idle mixture (air pilot) screw in until it is lightly seated.
2. Back out the idle mixture (air pilot) screw 2½ turns. Later you can readjust it to an exact setting.
3. Start and warm up the engine; then with the throttle grip completely closed, turn the idle speed (throttle stop) screw in or out until the engine idles smoothly at between 500 and 750 rpm.

NOTE: *On twin carburetor models, you can check idle speed synchronization by holding one hand behind each muffler and noting the exhaust pulse frequency. Reset the idle speed (throttle stop) screws until both cylinders are firing alternately and at the same rate. If one side is backfiring or its pulses are erratic, stop the engine; turn both idle speed screws in until lightly seated, then back them out* equally *a couple of turns (enough to prevent stalling). Start the engine and turn either carburetor's idle speed screw in, then out, and note any increase or decrease in engine rpm. At the position where ½ to 1 turn does not cause a variation in engine speed, the cylinders should be firing smoothly and at the same rate. The idle rpm may be higher than specified, but by backing out both idle mixture screws* equally *it can be lowered to normal.*

500 TWIN CRANKSHAFT DEGREE CONVERSION CHART

Crankshaft position (BTDC) Degrees	Piston position (BTDC) in.	mm
7	0.010	0.25
8	0.015	0.38
9	0.020	0.51
10	0.025	0.64
11	0.030	0.76
12	0.035	0.89
13	0.040	1.02
14	0.048	1.22
15	0.055	1.40
16	0.060	1.52
17	0.070	1.78
18	0.080	2.03
19	0.090	2.29
20	0.100	2.54
21	0.110	2.79

MULTIPLE CARBURETOR SYNCRONIZATION

After setting ignition timing, points, plugs, idle speed, and mixture, you must also synchronize the throttle slides. This is to ensure that all cylinders are being fed the same amount of fuel at any given throttle opening.

1. Remove the air cleaner assemblies.
2. Twist the throttle grip fully open to lift up the slides.
3. Position a mirror behind the carburetors or reach into the carburetor bores with the fingers of your free hand.
4. Slowly close the throttle grip and watch, or feel, the slides as they are being lowered; they should enter their respective bores simultaneously.
5. If the slide positions are unequal, raise or lower one to match the other(s) by turning the adjuster at the top of the carburetor.

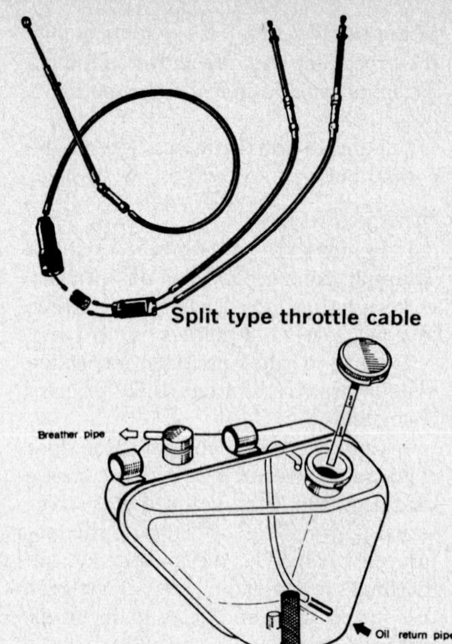

Split type throttle cable

250 oil tank

MAINTENANCE ITEMS

Oil Changes And Lubrication

ENGINE SUMP AND OIL TANK

TR25W

1. Remove the right side-panel.
2. Using a suitable container and funnel to catch the oil, remove the oil tank filter located in the lower right corner of the tank. Clean the filter in solvent or kerosine.
3. Allow the tank to drain for about ten minutes, then lean the machine toward the right side to make sure that all the oil has been removed.
4. Remove the four attaching nuts and the oil sump filter located at the bottom

TUNE-UP SPECIFICATIONS

	TR25W	T100C	T100R	TR6R	TR6C
CARBURETION			(See text procedures)		
VALVES					
Tappet Clearance (cold)					
Intake (in.)	0.008	0.002	0.002	0.002	0.002
(mm)	0.203	0.050	0.050	0.050	0.050
Exhaust (in.)	0.010	0.004	0.004	0.004	0.004
(mm)	0.254	0.100	0.100	0.100	0.100
Valve Timing					
Intake Opens					
(BTDC)	51°	34°	40°	34°	34°
Intake Closes					
(ABDC)	68°	55°	52°	55°	55°
Exhaust Opens					
(BBDC)	78°	48°	61°	55°	55°
Exhaust Closes					
(ATDC)	37°	27°	31°	34°	34°
IGNITION					
Spark Plug (standard)					
(Champion)	N3	N4	N4	N3	N3
Spark Plug Gap					
(in.)	0.020-0.025	0.020	0.020	0.025	0.025
(mm)	0.508-0.635	0.508	0.508	0.635	0.635
Contact Breaker Gap					
(in.)	0.015	0.015	0.015	0.014-0.016	0.014-0.016
(mm)	0.381	0.381	0.381	0.350-0.400	0.350-0.400
Ignition Timing					
Crankshaft Position					
(advanced)	37°	38°	38°	38°	38°
Piston Position (BTDC)					
(in.)	0.342	0.330	0.330	0.415	0.415
(mm)	8.687	8.380	8.380	10.4	10.4

TUNE-UP SPECIFICATIONS

	T120R	T150	TR7V	T140V	T150V
CARBURETION			(See text procedures)		
VALVES					
Tappet Clearance (cold)					
Intake (in.)	0.002	0.006	0.008	0.008	0.006
(mm)	0.050	0.1524	0.203	0.203	0.152
Exhaust (in.)	0.004	0.008	0.006	0.006	0.008
(mm)	0.100	0.2032	0.15	0.15	0.15
Valve Timing					
Intake Opens					
(BTDC)	34°	50°	NA	NA	50°
Intake Closes					
(ABDC)	34°	64°	NA	NA	64°
Exhaust Opens					
(BBDC)	55°	67°	NA	NA	67°
Exhaust Closes					
(ATDC)	34°	47°	NA	NA	47°
IGNITION					
Spark Plug (standard)					
(Champion)	N3	N3	N3	N3	N3
Spark Plug Gap					
(in.)	0.025	0.020	0.025	0.025	0.020
(mm)	0.635	0.500	0.635	0.635	0.500
Contact Breaker Gap					
(in.)	0.014-0.016	0.014-0.016	0.014-0.016	0.014-0.016	0.015-0.016
(mm)	0.350-0.400	0.350-0.400	0.35-0.40	0.35-0.40	0.35-0.40
Ignition Timing					
Crankshaft Position					
(advanced)	38°	38°	38°	38°	38°
Piston Position (GTDC)					
(in.)	0.415	0.357	0.415	0.415	0.357
(mm)	10.4	9.07	10.4	10.4	9.07

of the crankcase. Also, disconnect the supply and scavenge lines at the crankcase union nut.

5. Wash the sump filter in solvent or kerosine, then allow it to air dry or blow it dry with compressed air.

6. Reinstall the sump filter with a new gasket, connect the supply and scavenge lines, and reinstall the oil tank filter.

7. Add the recommended oil to the tank until it reaches the correct level mark on the dipstick. Do not overfill it, as excessive venting will result.

T100-C T100R, TR6R, TR6C, and T120R

1. Remove the sump drain plug and filter.

2. Thoroughly clean the filter in solvent or kerosine.

3. Allow the oil to drain for approximately ten minutes, then reinstall the filter (with new gaskets) and the sump drain plug.

4. Remove the oil tank filler cap.

5. Position a container under the oil tank, then remove the tank drain plug or disconnect the oil feed line.

6. Remove the oil tank filter and clean it thoroughly in solvent or kerosine.

7. If possible, clean the oil tank with flushing oil. If it is not available, use kerosine, but make sure all traces are removed before filling the tank with oil.

8. Fill the tank with the recommended lubricant. The correct level is 1½ in. below the filler cap. Do not exceed this level, as excessive venting will result.

TR7V, T140V

Note that the oil for these models is carried in the frame backbone. A filter is also fitted at the bottom of the frame oil reservoir.

1. When the engine is warm, remove the hex-head sump drain plug from beneath the engine. This plug houses the sump filter as well.

2. Allow the oil to drain from the sump for at least ten minutes. Clean the sump plug filter in a suitable solvent, check the condition of the gasket, then replace the filter and the drain plug.

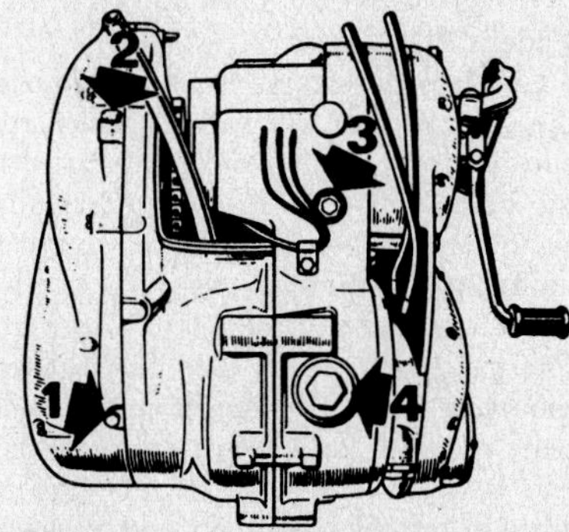

Location of oil drain and filler caps (500 models)

1. Primary chaincase level plug
2. Primary chaincase drain plug and chain tensioner adjustment
3. Gearbox drain and level plug
4. Sump drain and filter plug

3. Remove the oil reservoir filler cap. Remove the drain plug from the center

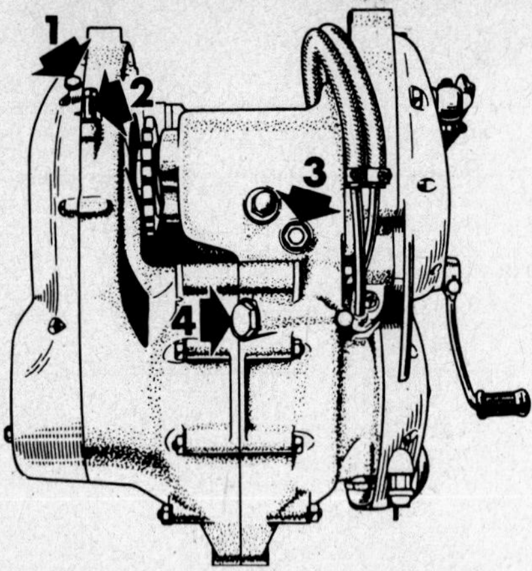

Location of oil drain and filler caps (650 models)

1. Primary chaincase level plug
2. Primary chaincase drain plug and chain tensioner adjustment
3. Gearbox drain and level plug
4. Sump drain and filter plug

of the base plate at the very bottom of the frame oil reservoir. Allow to drain for at least ten minutes.

4. Remove the four nuts which secure the cover plate at the bottom of the reservoir, and remove the plate from the studs. Noting the location of the two gaskets (one above the filter base flange, and the other below), clean the filter in a suitable solvent.

5. Flushing the reservoir with kerosene is recommended.

6. The filter gaskets should be replaced. Refit the filter, cover plate, cover plate nuts, and drain plug. Fill the reservoir with the correct amount and recommended grade of oil. Check the oil level after the engine has been run for several minutes.

T150, T150V

The procedure for changing oil in the Trident is as follows:

1. When the engine is warm, remove the six nuts and lockwashers which secure the crankcase sump filter plate to the bottom of the crankcase. Carefully remove the plate. Allow the oil to drain for about ten minutes.

2. Clean the sump filter in a solvent. The gaskets on either side of the filter should be replaced upon reassembly. Replace the filter, noting that the pocketed end is towards the rear of the engine. Tighten the nuts gradually and evenly.

3. Remove the oil tank filler cap, and the right side-panel. Drain the oil from the oil tank, then remove the tank oil filter, and wash it in a solvent.

4. Flushing out the oil tank with kerosene or a suitable solvent is recommended.

5. Remove the cartridge-type main feed oil filter. This is located beneath the large cap nut just below the forward end of the gearbox outer cover. Note that the

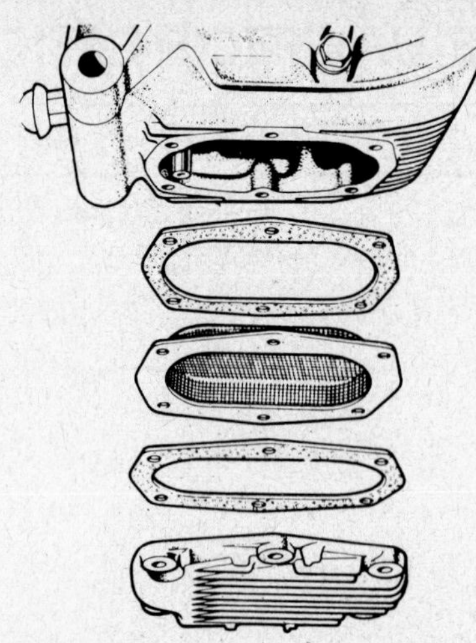

Crankcase sump filter (Trident)

filter is pulled out with a pair of needle-nosed pliers. There is a spring immediately beneath the cap nut, and an o-ring on the end of the filter. The filter should be replaced every time the oil is changed.

6. When replacing the filter, be sure that the o-ring and the fiber washer are in good condition.

CAUTION: *When the filter is refitted, be sure that the hole in the filter faces inward.*

Refill the oil tank with the correct quantity and recommended grade of oil. Check the level with the dipstick after the engine has run for several minutes.

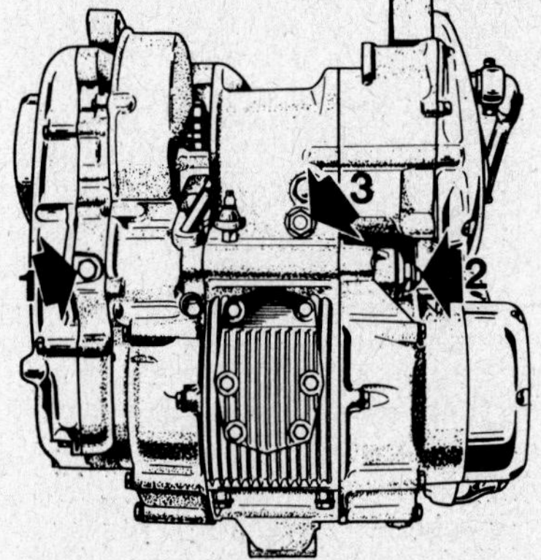

Location of oil drain and filler caps (Trident)

1. Primary chaincase drain plug
2. Oil filter housing cap
3. Gearbox drain and level plug

GEARBOX

All gearbox components, including the shifter and kick-start mechanisms, are lubricated by oil splash. The oil should be changed at 500 miles in new or reconditioned engines, and at every recommended service interval thereafter.

TR25W

1. Remove the nylon filler plug and the dipstick from the top of the gearbox.

2. Remove the plug on the bottom of the gearbox and drain the oil into a suitable container.

3. After draining, reinstall the plug, making sure that the sealing O-ring is in good condition.

4. Fill the gearbox with the recommended lubricant to the line marked on the dipstick.

500, 650, 750 Twins, 750-3

1. Remove the transmission drain plug located at the bottom of the gearbox. Drain the oil when the engine is warm.

2. After letting the oil drain for about ten minutes, reinstall the drain plug, but without the level plug that normally screws into it.

3. Remove the gearbox oil filler plug on the case cover and add fresh oil until it flows out the level plug hole.

4. Reinstall the level plug.

PRIMARY CHAINCASE

Like the gearbox, the primary chaincase is lubricated by oil bath. On all models except the T150, the primary oil supply is contained within the case, where a collection chamber and a feed pipe provide direct lubrication to the primary chain and sprockets. On the T150, an initial oil supply of one-half pint must be poured into the case, but after that, the engine lubrication system maintains the correct level by breathing through the right-side crankshaft main bearing.

TR25W

1. On early machines, two of the chaincase securing screws serve as drain and level plugs (see illustration). On later bikes, a vertical drain plug is provided at the bottom of the case and one of the case securing screws serves as a level plug.

2. Remove the chain inspection cap on top of the chaincase.

3. Position a suitable container under the chaincase, then remove the drain plug or screw and level screw.

4. Let the oil drain for about ten minutes, then reinstall the drain plug or screw.

5. Pour the specified amount of the recommended lubricant into the chaincase through the chain inspection cap until it flows out the level screw hole.

6. Reinstall the level screw and chain inspection cap.

NOTE: *Oil containing molybdenum disulfide or graphite must not be used in the primary chaincase.*

500, 650, 750 Twins

1. Remove the oil drain plug from the bottom of the chaincase.

2. Allow the oil to drain for approximately ten minutes, then reinstall the drain plug and remove the level plug at the rear underside of the case.

3. Next, remove the filler cap at the top of the case and add oil until it drips out the level plug hole.

4. Reinstall the level plug and filler cap.

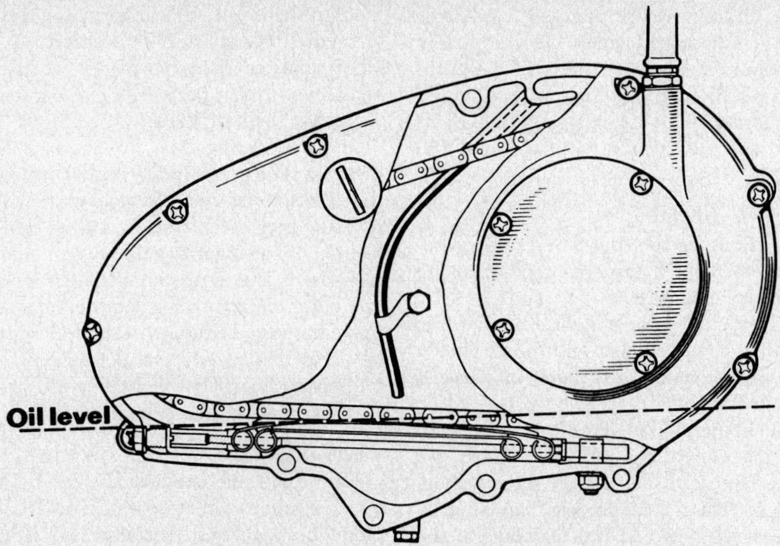

Primary chaincase oil level (Trident)

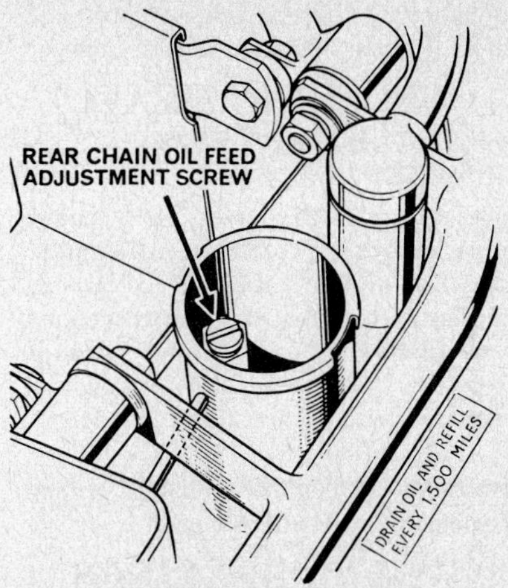

Chain oiler adjustment screw (500, 650 and 750 models)

T150

The Trident primary chaincase can be drained in the same manner as previously outlined for the 500 and 650 twins. When refilling the case, however, you must add no more than one-half pint. There is no level indicator hole.

FINAL DRIVE CHAIN

TR25W

Lubrication of the final drive chain is totally dependent on the oil level in the primary chaincase. As the primary chain spins, it throws off the oil fed by the primary case collection chamber. This oil is collected by a small well at the back of the primary case and is then drip-fed to the final drive chain.

500, 650, 750-3

The drive chain on these models is lubricated by means of an overflow tube from the neck of the oil tank. The flow is adjusted by means of a screw with a tapered tip threaded into the oil junction block in the neck of the tank. The screw is accessible after removing the tank filler cap. To increase oil flow to the chain, turn the screw counterclockwise. To decrease flow, turn the screw clockwise.

750 Twins

The chain should be lubricated by hand every 1,000 miles, or sooner, depending on conditions.

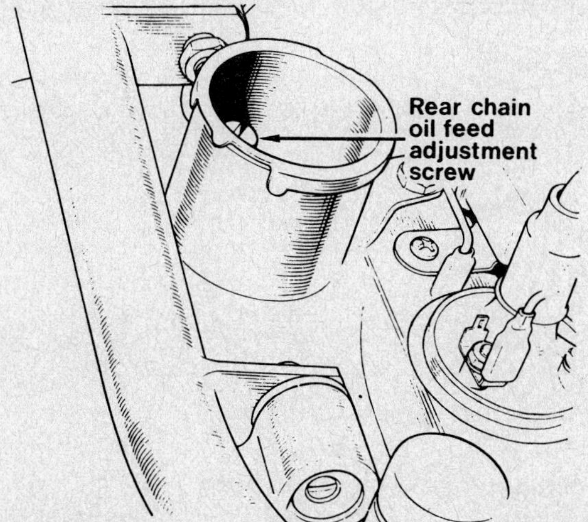

Drive chain oiler adjusting screw location (750 Twins)

GREASE NIPPLES

Both the front and rear brake cams, and the swinging arm pivot are fitted with grease nipples. The brake cams should be given only one stroke of a hand grease gun; the swinging arm pivot should be greased until the lubricant spurts out the pivot O-rings.

BRAKE PEDAL SPINDLE

The brake pedal spindle is located on the left, rear, engine mounting plate. Since the operating shaft is exposed to the air, it should be coated with grease to prevent dirt penetration and corrosion.

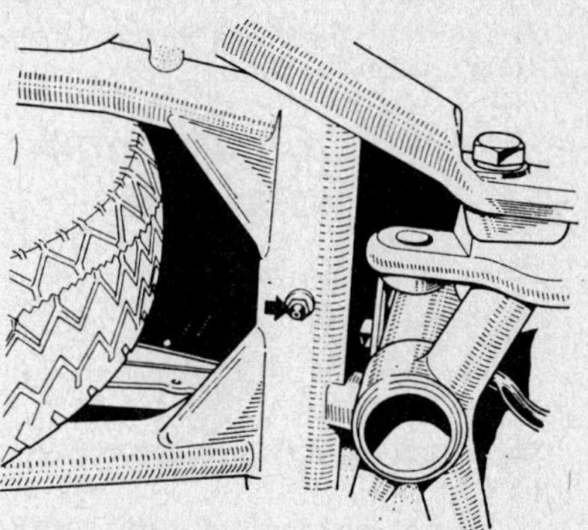

Rear swing arm grease nipple (650 models)

1. Back off the rear brake rod adjustment until there is plenty of play.
2. Remove the pedal retaining nut and pedal.
3. Clean up the operating shaft and bore of the pedal with fine emery cloth.
4. Apply the recommended grease to the shaft and reinstall the pedal. Make sure you don't forget the spring and washer that accompany the retaining nut.

FRONT FORK

The oil in the front fork should be changed at 6000 mile/6 month intervals.

NOTE: *On the more recent shuttle valve fork, use only SAE 20 viscosity oil.*

1. Remove the small, hexagonal drain plugs at the bottom of each fork leg.
2. Hold the front brake and pump the forks several times to expel all the oil.
3. Remove the fork caps at the top of each leg.

NOTE: *On machines equipped with resiliently mounted handlebars, the handlebars will have to be removed to facilitate access to the fork caps.*

4. Add the specified amount of the recommended oil, then reinstall the fork caps. If heavier or lighter dampening

qualities are desired, choose an appropriately heavier or lighter viscosity oil.

STEERING HEAD BEARINGS

The steering head bearings are packed with grease at the factory, but require repacking every 10,000 or 12,000 miles.

1. Remove the steering head ball bearings as described in the chassis section.
2. Clean the bearings, cups, cones in kerosine, then inspect them for signs of excessive wear, cracking, or pitting.
3. Reassemble the bearings, using the grease specified at the end of this section to hold the balls in the cups.

WHEEL BEARINGS

The wheel bearings are also packed with grease at the factory. They should be removed, cleaned and repacked every 10,000 or 12,000 miles.

Service Checks and Adjustments

CLUTCH

TR25W

1. Remove the primary chaincase inspection cover.
2. Loosen the pushrod adjusting screw locknut.
3. Turn in the adjusting screw until the pressure plate begins to lift. This point can be detected by a sudden increase in turning resistance.
4. Back the screw out one full turn, then secure it in position with the locknut.
5. Adjust the clutch cable at the hand lever so that there is ⅛ in. (3mm) freeplay.

500, 650, 750 Twins

The clutch adjustment procedure for these models is basically the same as for the TR25W, except that the hand-lever cable adjustment must be completely loosened before adjustment of the pushrod can be achieved. The pushrod should be backed out one-half turn on 500 twins and one full turn on 650 twins and 750 twins.

T150, T150V

1. Remove the four screws which secure the clutch inspection plate to the primary chaincase.
2. Run down the clutch cable adjusters both at the handlebar and the chaincase cover so that there is plenty of slack in the clutch cable.
3. Loosen the small locknut on the end of the clutch pull-rod. Then turn the large nut until the proper setting is obtained. This will be not less than 0.005 in. measured between the rear face of the large adjuster nut and the ball bearing in the actuating plate. Be sure that the clutch pull-rod does not turn, and retighten the small locknut. Recheck the setting.
4. Adjust the cable so that there is just a very small amount of freeplay at the handlebar lever.

BRAKES

The brakes should be checked periodically and adjusted if necessary. Brake lining wear is indicated by the angular position of the brake operating lever when the brake has been fully applied. Should the angle between the operating lever and actuating cable or rod be more than 90°, the linings should be replaced. This applies to both front and rear brakes.

Front Adjustment

On single-leading shoe brakes, the adjuster is located on the bottom fork leg. Turning the adjuster shortens or lengthens the effective length of the cable, thereby adjusting the position of the shoes in the drum. A locknut is provided to secure the adjuster in position. Another adjuster is also provided at the hand lever so that cable free-play can be set to suit the individual.

On twin-leading shoe brakes, adjustment is made at the hand-lever. Turning the knurled nut counterclockwise will take up excess cable slack. Cable freeplay should be maintained between 1/16 in. (1.5mm) and ⅛ in. (3mm). There is no operating rod adjustment on this type of brake because the length of the rod must be preset in order to seat both shoes simultaneously when the brakes are applied. The shoes are self-centering.

Rear Adjustment

The rear brake is adjustable for both pedal position and operating rod freeplay. The pedal has a serrated cam hole which enables it to be removed and repositioned for rider comfort. This position should be determined before adjusting the operating rod free-play.

Rod free-play is set by turning the self-locking sleeve at the rear end of the rod until there is approximately ½ in. (12mm) pedal play before the shoes make contact in the drum.

On all but the 500cc twins, the rear brake shoes are self-centering. To centralize the shoes on the 500 models, loosen the left, rear-wheel axle nut and, while applying the rear brake, retighten it. This will correctly position the shoes.

Disc Brake

For all disc brake checks and service, refer to the "chassis" section.

FINAL DRIVE CHAIN

If the up and down movement is greater than 1⅛ in. or less than ¾ in., the chain must be adjusted by moving the rear wheel either forward to loosen the chain or backward to tighten it.

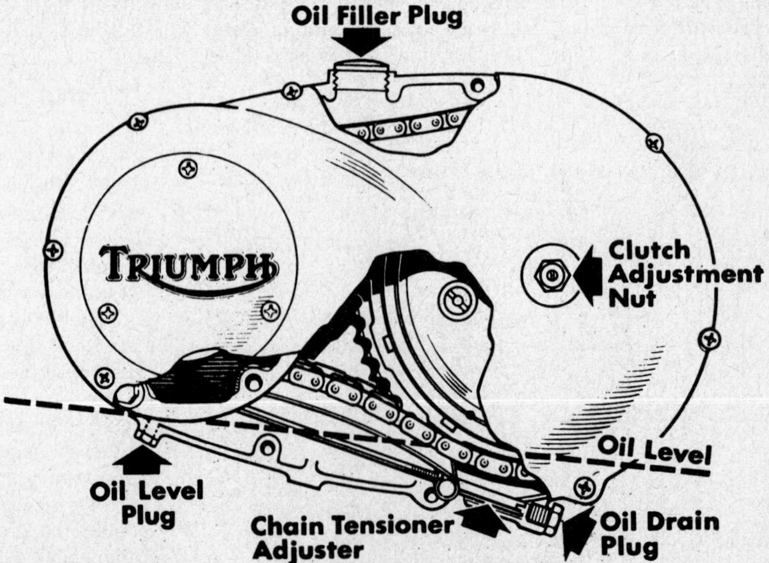

Primary chaincase view showing clutch pushrod adjustor (500 and 650 models)

PERIODIC MAINTENANCE INTERVALS

EVERY 250 MILES
- Check oil tank level (all models)
- Grease brake pedal pivot (TR25W)
- Oil exposed cables and control rod joints (TR25W)
- Check chain oiler adjustment (650 twins)
- Check oil level in primary chaincase (650 twins)

EVERY 500 MILES
- Check oil level in primary chaincase (TR25W)

EVERY 1000 MILES
- Lubricate control cables (all models except TR25W)
- Grease swing arm pivot (all models except TR25W)
- Remove and clean final drive chain (all models)
- Check oil level in primary chaincase (all models)

EVERY 1500 MILES
- Change engine oil (650 twins)

EVERY 2000 MILES
- Lubricate contact breaker (650 twins)
- Drain and refill oil tank (TR25W)
- Check oil level in gearbox (TR25W)
- Clean oil filters (TR25W)
- Lubricate side stand (TR25W)
- Lubricate brake cam spindles (TR25W)
- Lubricate final drive chain (TR25W)

EVERY 3000 MILES
- Check gearbox oil level (all models except TR25W)
- Check front forks for oil leakage (all models)
- Grease brake pedal spindle (all models except TR25W)

EVERY 4000 MILES
- Change oil in engine and primary chaincase (500 twins and T150)
- Change disposable filter element (500 twins and T150)

EVERY 5000 MILES
- Grease speedometer drive cable (TR25W)
- Lubricate contact breaker (TR25W)
- Lubricate auto-advance mechanism (TR25W)
- Change gearbox oil (TR25W)
- Change primary chaincase oil (TR25W)

EVERY 6000 MILES
- Change gearbox oil (all models except TR25W)
- Change front fork oil (all models except TR25W)

EVERY 10,000 MILES
- Change front fork oil (TR25W)
- Grease wheel bearings (TR25W)
- Grease steering head bearings (TR25W)

EVERY 12,000 MILES
- Grease wheel bearings (all models except TR25W)
- Grease steering head bearings (all models except TR25W)

MAINTENANCE DATA

	TR25W	T100C	T100R	TR6R	TR6C	T120R	T150	TR7V	T140V	T150V
FUEL TANK										
(gallon)	3.916	3.60	3.60	4.117	2.912	2.912	5.12	2.5	2.5	4.2
(liter)	14.774	13.5	13.5	15.52	10.97	10.97	19.3	—	—	15.94
OIL TANK										
(pint)	4.8	7.2	7.2	7.5	7.5	7.5	6.0	4.8	4.8	7.2
(liter)	2.273	3.5	3.5	3.0	3.0	3.0	3.41	2.27	2.27	3.8
GEARBOX										
(pint)	0.6	0.67	0.67	0.875	0.875	0.875	1.25	0.875	0.875	1.5
(cc)	264	375	375	500	500	500	710	500	500	750
PRIMARY CHAINCASE										
(pint)	0.3	0.5	0.5	0.625	0.625	0.625	0.75	0.625	0.625	0.75
(cc)	142	300	300	350	350	350	426	350	350	426
FRONT FORK LEGS										
(pint)	0.33	0.33	0.33	0.33	0.33	0.33	0.33	0.33	0.33	—
(cc)	190	190	190	190	190	190	190	190	190	230
TIRE PRESSURE										
front (psi)	16	24	24	24	24	24	24	24	24	26
rear (psi)	16	24	24	24	24	24	28	24	24	28

MAINTENANCE DATA

CHAIN ADJUSTMENT										
(in.)	1.0	1.0	1.0	1.0	1.0	1.0	1.0	0.75①	0.75①	0.75①
(mm)	25.4	25.4	25.4	25.4	25.4	25.4	25.4	19.0	19.0	19.0

①—Measurement of total up and down movement with the machine OFF the kickstand and measured at the tightest point on chain. Correct slack with the machine ON the stand (and measured at the chain's most slack point) is 1.75 in.

RECOMMENDED LUBRICANTS

Trophy 250 (TR25W)

Brand	Engine Oils Summer	Engine Oils Winter	Gearbox Oils Summer	Gearbox Oils Winter	Oil Front Forks and Primary Chain	Grease
Mobiloil	BB	A	Mobilube GX.90	Mobilube GX.80	Arctic	Mobilgrease MP
Shell	x100-40	x100-30	Spirax 90.EP	Spirax 80.EP	x100-20W	Retinax A
Castrol	XL	XL	Hypoy 90.EP	Hypoy 80.EP	Castrolite	Castrolease LM
Esso	Esso Motor Oil 40/50	Esso Motor Oil 20W/30	Gear Oil EP.90	Gear Oil EP.80	Esso Motor Oil 20/30W	Esso Multipurpose Grease H
B.P.	S.A.E. 40	S.A.E. 30	B.P. Gear Oil 90.EP	B.P. Gear Oil 80.EP	S.A.E. 20W	Energrease L2
Texaco	Havoline S.A.E. 40	Havoline S.A.E. 30	Multigrade Lubricant 90.EP	Multigrade Lubricant 80.EP	Havoline S.A.E. 20W	Marfak Multi-purpose 2

RECOMMENDED LUBRICANTS

500 Twins

Unit	Mobil	B.P.	Castrol	Esso	Shell	Caltex
Engine				Esso Extra		
Above 90°F.	Mobiloil AF	Energol SAE 40	Castrol XXL	Motor Oil	Shell X-100 40	Caltex SAE 40
32°-90°F.	Mobiloil A	Energol SAE 30	Castrol XL	20W/40	Shell X-100 30	Caltex SAE 30
Below 32°F.	Mobiloil Arctic	Energol SAE 20W	Castrolite	10W/30	Shell X-100 20W	Caltex SAE 20W
Gearbox	Mobiloil D	Energol SAE 50	Castrol Grand Prix	Esso Extra Motor Oil 50	Shell X-100 50	Caltex SAE 50
Primary Chaincase	Mobiloil Arctic	Energol SAE 20W	Castrolite	Esso Extra Motor Oil 20W/40	Shell X-100 20W	Caltex SAE 20W

RECOMMENDED LUBRICANTS

500 Twins

Unit	Mobil	B.P.	Castrol	Esso	Shell	Caltex
Telescopic Fork Above 90°F.	Mobiloil D	Energol SAE 50	Castrol Grand Prix	Esso Extra	Shell X-100 50	Caltex SAE 50
60°-90°F.	Mobiloil A	Energol SAE 30	Castrol XL	Motor Oil	Shell X-100 30	Caltex SAE 30
Below 60°F.	Mobiloil Arctic	Energol SAE 20W	Castrolite	20W/40	Shell X-100 20W	Caltex SAE 20W
*After H57083 Telesopic Fork	Mobiloil Arctic	Energol SAE 20W	Castrolite	Esso Extra Motor Oil 20W/40	Shell X-100 20W	Caltex SAE 20W
Wheel Bearings, Swinging Fork, Steering Races	Mobilgrease M.P.	Energrease L.2.	Castrolease L.M.	Esso Multi-purpose Grease H	Shell Retinax A	Marfak Multi-purpose 2
Easing Rusted Parts	Mobil Spring Oil	Energol Penetrating Oil	Castrol Penetrating Oil	Esso Penetrating Oil	Shell Donax P	Caltex Penetrating Oil

* Note: Machines after H57083 are fitted with shuttle front fork dampers. It is most important that no oil heavier than SAE 20 is used in forks.

RECOMMENDED LUBRICANTS

650 Twins

Unit	Mobil	B.P.	Castrol	Esso	Shell	Texaco
Engine Above 90°F.	Mobiloil AF	Energol SAE 40	Castrol XXL	Esso Extra	Shell X-100 40	Havoline 40
32°-90°F.	Mobiloil A	Energol SAE 30	Castrol XL	Motor Oil	Shell X-100 30	Havoline 30
Below 32°F.	Mobiloil Arctic	Energol SAE 20W	Castrolite	20W/40 10W/30	Shell X-100 20W	Havoline 20-20W
Gearbox	Mobilube GX90	BP Gear Oil 90EP	Castrol Hypoy 90EP	Esso Gear Oil GP90/140	Shell Spirax 90EP	Multigear EP90
Primary Chaincase	Mobiloil Arctic	Energol SAE 20W	Castrolite	Esso Extra Motor Oil 20W/40	Shell X-100 20W	Havoline 20-20W
Telescopic Fork	Mobiloil Arctic	Energol SAE 20W	Castrolite	Esso Extra Motor Oil 20W/40	Shell X-100 20W	Havoline 30 Havoline 20-20W
Wheel Bearings, Swinging Fork, Steering Races	Mobilgrease M.P.	Energrease L2	Castrolease L.M.	Esso Multi-purpose Grease H	Shell Retinax A	Marfak All Purpose
Easing Rusted Parts	Mobil Spring Oil	Energol Penetrating Oil	Castrol Penetrating Oil	Esso Penetrating Oil	Shell Donax P	Graphited Penetrating Oil

RECOMMENDED LUBRICANTS

750 Twins

Unit	Mobil	Castrol	B.P.	Esso	Shell	Texaco
Engine and Primary Chaincase	Mobiloil Super	Castrol GTX or Castrol XL 20/50	B.P. Super Visco-Static	Uniflo	Shell Super Motor Oil	Havoline Motor Oil 20W/50
Gearbox	Mobilube GX 90	Castrol Hypoy	B.P. Gear Oil SAE 90 EP	Esso Gear Oil GX 90/140	Shell Spirax 90 EP	Multigear Lubricant EP 90
Telescopic Fork	Mobil ATF 210	Castrol T.Q.F.	B.P. Autron 'B'	Esso Glide	Shell Donax T.7	Texomatic 'F'
Wheel Bearings, Swinging Fork and Steering Races	Mobilgrease MP or Mobilgrease Super	Castrol L.M. Grease	B.P. Energrease L2	Esso Multi-purpose Grease H	Shell Retinax A	Marfak All Purpose
Easing Rusted Parts	Mobil Handy Oil	Castrol Penetrating Oil		Esso Penetrating Oil	Shell Easing Oil	Graphited Penetrating Oil

The above lubricants are recommended for all operating temperatures above —18°C. (0°F.).
Approval is given to lubricants marketed by companies other than those listed above provided that they have similar multigrade characteristics and meet the A.P.I. Service M.S. Performance Level.

RECOMMENDED LUBRICANTS

750 Trident

Unit	Mobil	B.P.	Castrol	Esso	Shell	Texaco
Recommended Engine: Summer Winter	Mobiloil Super 10W/50	Super Visco-Static 20W/50 or 10W/40	Castrol XLR Castrolite	Uniflo	Shell Super 100 or Shell Super 101	Havoline 20W/50 or Havoline 20W/20
Approved Engine: Summer Winter	Mobiloil Special 10W/30		Castrol XL Castrolite	Esso Extra Motor Oil 20W/40		URSA Oil Extra Duty 20W/40
Gearbox	Mobilube GX90	B.P. Gear Oil 90.EP	Castrol Hypoy 90.EP	Esso Gear Oil GX90	Shell Spirax 90.EP	Multigear Lubricant EP.90
Primary Chaincase	USE SAME LUBRICANT AS ENGINE DUE TO ENGINE BREATHING SYSTEM					
Telescopic Forks	Mobiloil Super	Super Visco-Static 20W/50 10W/40	Castrolite	Uniflo or Esso Extra Motor Oil 20W/40	Shell Super 100 or Shell Super 101	Havoline 20/20W
Wheel Bearings and Swinging Fork	Mobilgrease M.P. or Mobilgrease Special	Energrease L2	Castrol M.P. Grease	Multipurpose Grease H	Shell Retinax A	Marfak All Purpose
Easing Rusted Parts	Mobil Handy Oil	Energol Penetrating Oil	Castrol Penetrating Oil	Esso Penetrating Oil	Shell Donax P	Graphited Penetrating Oil

ENGINE AND TRANSMISSION

TR25W

Removal and Installation

1. Remove the fuel tank.
2. Remove the exhaust system by disconnecting the exhaust pipe clamp at the head, and removing the two, muffler mounting bolts.
3. Remove the right side-cover and unbolt the skid plate from frame tubes. Drain the oil.
4. Disconnect the valve rocker oil line from the metal T-connection and disconnect the flexible scavenge line from the crankcase line at the rear.
5. Disconnect the alternator, oil pressure switch (if applicable), and contact breaker point leads from their snap connec'ors at the electrical box. Disconnect the spark plug wire.
6. Remove the carburetor flange nuts and tie the carburetor out of the way. Leave the rubber connecting hose attached to the air filter housing.
7. Disconnect the top engine mount (at the rocker cover).
8. Remove the chainguard front extension and remove the master link from the chain.
9. Disconnect the clutch cable using a suitable box wrench as a lever on the operating arm.
10. Loosen the footpeg mounting bolt and swing the footpeg down.
11. Remove the remaining engine mount bolts. Note that spacers are installed between the engine and frame at the right side of the front and bottom bolts.
12. Remove the rear, engine mounting plate and lift the engine unit out of the frame from the right side.

Installation is in reverse order of removal. Be sure to replace the two spacers correctly. Double-check all hardware and electrical connections when completed.

Top End Overhaul

CYLINDER HEAD AND BARREL REMOVAL

On the TR25W, the cylinder head and barrel may be removed with the engine in the frame. The procedure is as follows:

1. Remove the fuel tank.
2. Unbolt the engine mount at the cylinder head and push the bracket up out of the way.
3. Remove the carburetor from the head, leaving it suspended by the throttle cable.
4. Remove the exhaust system by disconnecting the exhaust pipe clamp at the head and removing the two, muffler mounting bolts.
5. Remove the spark plug and disconnect the rocker oil feed line.
6. Rotate the engine until the piston is at top dead center of the compression stroke (both valves closed, clearance at the rocker arms).
7. Remove the six cylinder head nuts; if the head will not move, free it with a rubber mallet.
8. Lift the head, rotate it around the pushrods to clear the frame, and remove it from the engine.
9. To remove the barrel, first rotate the engine until the piston is at the bottom of the stroke and then gently lift the barrel off. Steady the piston as the barrel is withdrawn so that it will not be damaged.

CYLINDER HEAD SERVICE

Valve Train Inspection

Remove the rocker box. Examine the ends of the rocker arms for excessive wear and damage. Check the fit of the rocker arms on the shafts; excessive clearance will make it hard to maintain proper valve adjustment. Rocker arms that are damaged or worn in any way must be replaced. If the rocker assemblies are disassembled be sure to replace any washers or seals that are worn. Check the pushrod end cups for wear and make sure that the pushrods are not bent by rolling them on a flat surface. Replace if faulty in any way.

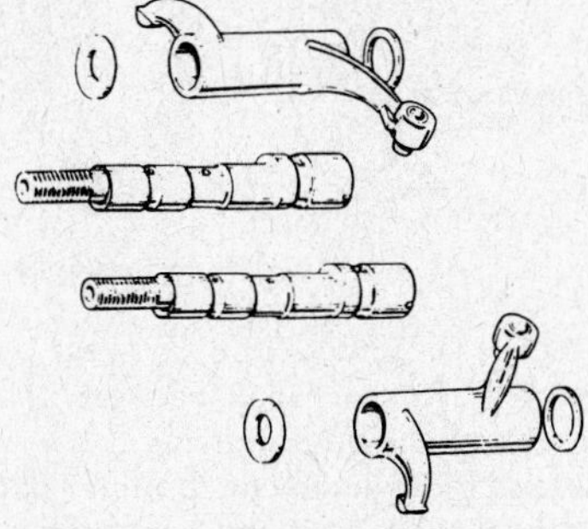

Valve train (250)

Valves

Compress the valve springs and remove the split collar. Release tension on the spring and remove the top spring retainer, the spring, and the bottom retainer. Valve springs should be replaced as a matter of course at this time. However, if the springs have not settled (spring heights are given in the specifications section) and are not cracked, they may be reused.

Check the valves in their guides for excessive side-play. If excessive clearance exists, or if the valve stems are scored or have a carbon buildup on them, the valves and guides should be replaced. valve guides can be driven out after the cylinder head has been heated in an oven or immersed in hot water. Install the new guides while the head is still warm. Note that the exhaust valve guide is counterbored at its lower end.

Replace valves that are pitted or burnt. Valve seats can be recut, if necessary, using a 45° cutter.

Remove the carbon from the combustion chamber using an aluminum or lead scraper, or a small hand-held grinder.

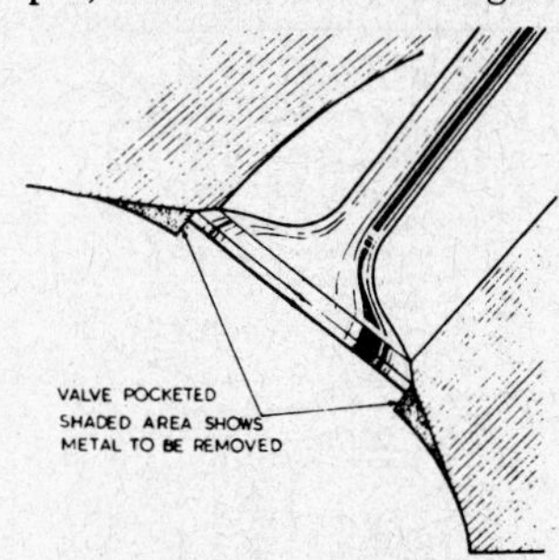

Pocketed valve face (250)

CYLINDER BARREL AND PISTON SERVICE

Measure the cylinder bore for wear and scoring. If wear is excessive the cylinder may be bored to accept the 0.020 in. or 0.040 in. oversize pistons that are available. Whether or not the cylinder is to be bored, it should be honed so that the new rings will seat properly.

To remove the piston, it will be necessary to heat it slightly to facilitate removal of the wrist pin. First remove the wrist pin circlips and then use an electric iron against the piston crown. After the piston is warm, the wrist pin should slide out fairly easily. Mark the front of the piston inside the skirt to facilitate reassembly. Thoroughly but carefully, remove all traces of carbon from the piston crown. Remove the old rings, taking care not to scratch the piston.

Break one of the old rings and use the end of it to clean the carbon out of the piston ring grooves. Check the end gaps of the new rings by placing each one into the cylinder bore and measuring with a feeler gauge. End gap should not be less than 0.009 in. Carefully install the rings onto the piston. Note that the second ring is marked TOP and must be positioned accordingly. Side clearance of the rings (up and down free movement) should not exceed 0.003 in.

See the T100C, T100R engine section for piston pin bushing replacement.

Warm the piston and install it, in correct position, on the connecting rod. Insert the piston pin before the piston has a chance to cool. Install *new* circlips and make sure that they are seated properly. Install a new cylinder base gasket and

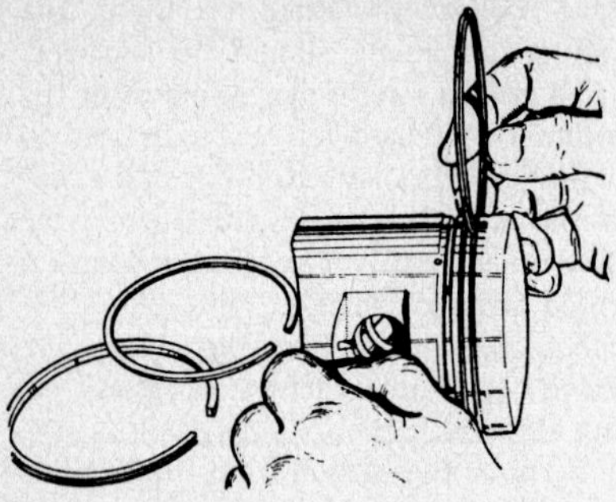

Cleaning out the piston ring grooves (250)

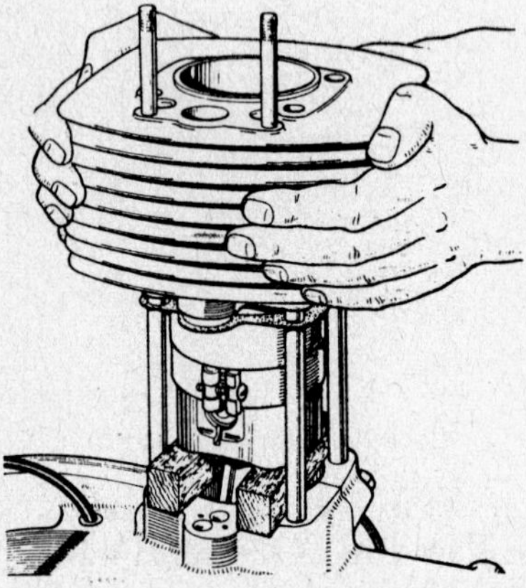

Installing the cylinder barrel (250)

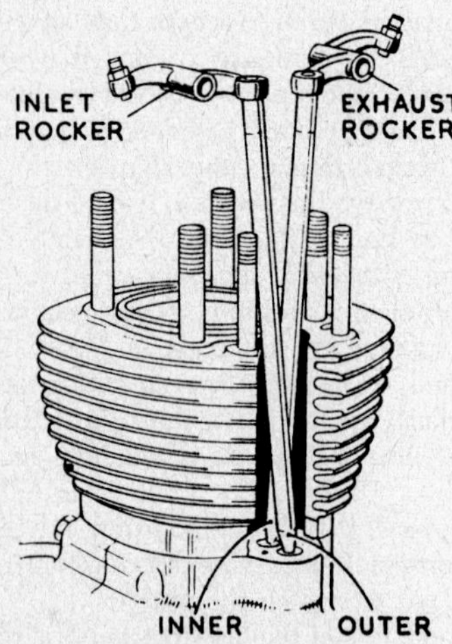

Installing the pushrods (250)

support the piston with two pieces of wood approximately ½ in. square by 6 in. long, as shown. Stagger the ring gaps 120 degrees apart, liberally oil the rings, and install a ring compressor. If a ring compressor is unavailable, it is possible to compress the rings by hand, one at a time, as the barrel is slipped over the piston. Be careful. Slide the barrel over the piston and remove the compressor and wood blocks.

Install the two pushrods, noting that the outer one operates the intake valve. The top of the exhaust valve pushrod is painted red for identification, as it is slightly shorter than the intake pushrod. *The pushrods must be positioned correctly.*

Install the rocker box on the cylinder head using a new gasket, then torque the nuts to 7 ft lbs. Install a new head gasket and fit the heat onto the barrel. Place the pushrod ends into the rocker arm ends, making absolutely sure that they are positioned correctly, as illustrated. Keep a light, downward pressure on the head and rotate the engine until the piston is at top dead center of the compression stroke. In this position both valves will be fully closed (clearance at both rocker arms). Tighten the cylinder head nuts, gradually to the figures given in specifications at the end of the section.

If the engine was removed for service, reinstall it in the frame. Check and adjust valve clearances, ignition timing, carburetor, etc.

Clutch and Primary Drive

CLUTCH SERVICE

Disassembly

1. If the engine is mounted in the frame, remove the left-side footpeg and brake pedal.
2. Drain the oil from the primary chaincase remove the screws, and take off the primary drive cover. It may be necessary to tap the cover with a rubber mallet to break it free.
3. Remove the four, clutch-spring retaining nuts and withdraw the pressure plate, springs, and cups.
4. Withdraw the clutch plates.

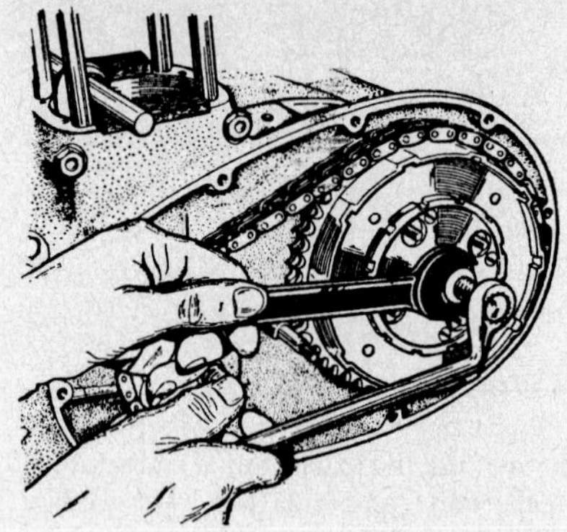

Removing the clutch center nut (250)

10. Use a gear puller to pull the clutch and sprocket off the transmission mainshaft, while at the same time pulling the front sprocket off the engine crankshaft.

Inspection

1. The clutch discs should appear to be in good condition. If the thickness of the discs measures less than 0.137 in., they should be replaced.
2. Check that the tabs at the outer edge of the discs are not worn or rounded and that the sprocket slots are not damaged. If there are burrs on the tabs, the discs must be replaced.
3. Place the clutch plates on a flat surface such as a plate of glass. If they can be rocked from side to side or there is evidence of any buckling, they should be replaced. Also replace the plates if they are scored in any way.
4. To examine the dampers located in

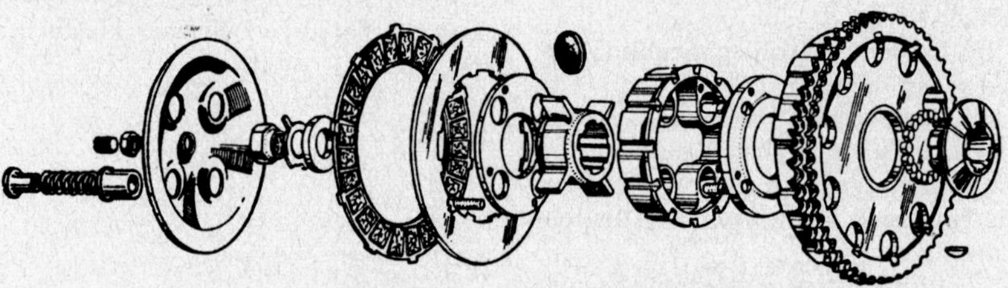

Exploded view of clutch assembly (250)

5. Keep the clutch from turning by wedging a piece of wood between the sprocket and chain or applying the rear brake, and remove the clutch center nut (after the locktab has been bent back).
6. Remove the locktab and spacer, and withdraw the clutch pushrod.
7. To remove the clutch completely, it is necessary to remove the alternator. To remove the stator (enclosing the rotor), take off the three mounting nuts, pull the alternator lead through the grommet, and pull the stator off the studs. The rotor can be taken off after the crankshaft nut has been removed.
8. Remove the primary chain tensioner, noting that a spacer is installed on the rear stud.
9. Bend back the locktab and unscrew the nut. Remove the rotor, wipe it clean, and store it in a clean place.

the clutch center, remove the four screws adjacent to the clutch spring housings and pry off the retaining plate. The dampers need not be replaced unless they are visibly damaged or worn. It may be necessary to lubricate them when reinstalling; it is recommended that a liquid detergent be used. *Do not use petroleum-based oil or grease.*

5. The clutch center slots should be smooth and undamaged or jerky clutch engagement will result. Check clutch spring free length, and if less than 1.65 in., replace the springs.

Assembly

If the sprockets or clutch hub have been replaced it will be necessary to realign the sprockets to avoid excessive primary chain wear. Refer to "Primary Drive Service." To reinstall the clutch:

1. If the clutch sleeve has been removed, smear it with grease and place the twenty-five bearing rollers in position. Slide the sprocket over the rollers and install the clutch center over the splines of the sleeve.

2. Place the primary chain over the sprockets and position the sprockets on the shafts. Make sure that the transmission mainshaft key is correctly located.

3. Install the clutch center spacer. Make sure that the mainshaft and clutch retaining nut threads are clean and dry. Install a new locktab and apply a small amount of thread-locking compound to the mainshaft threads before installing the retaining nut. Torque the nut to 60–65 ft lb.

4. Install the alternator rotor on the crankshaft with the marks facing out, making sure that the key is located correctly. Install a new locktab, apply a drop of thread-locking compound to the threads, then tighten the retaining nut to 60 ft lbs.

5. Pass the stator lead through the grommet at the front of the crankcase. Fit the stator over the studs and partially tighten the nuts. Check that there is an equal air gap between the rotor and stator at all points using an 0.008 in. feeler gauge. Variations can be corrected by repositioning the stator.

6. To adjust primary chain tension, loosen the rear stator retaining nut and adjust the tensioner to provide ¼ in. free-play on the top run of the chain midway between the sprockets. Retighten the stator nut.

7. Install the clutch discs and plates, alternately, into the clutch housing, beginning with a disc. Insert the clutch pushrod into the mainshaft.

8. Install the pressure plate complete with springs and cups. Make sure the spring cup location pips are seated in the slots in the pressure plate.

Installing the primary drive (250)

9. Install and tighten the four spring nuts until the first coil of each spring is just outside of its cup. Improper spring tension will cause excessive pressure at the handlebar lever or clutch slip. Check to see if the springs are tightened evenly by pulling the clutch lever in and kicking the engine over. If any wobble is noticeable at the pressure plate as it turns, tighten or loosen the springs as necessary until it runs true.

10. Adjust the clutch by means of the screw and locknut at the center of the pressure plate so that the clutch operating lever is angled approximately 30° away from the crankcase/side-cover joint.

11. Clean the crankcase and primary cover mating surfaces, apply a thin coat of gasket cement, and mount the cover using a new gasket. If it is possible to use a torque wrench, tighten the screws to 3.5–4.5 ft lbs.

12. Fill the primary chaincase with oil and adjust the clutch lever free-play if necessary.

PRIMARY DRIVE SERVICE

After the clutch assembly has been removed, the primary drive chain, sprockets, and sprocket hub bearing are free. Sprockets should be replaced if the teeth are rounded or hooked, or if the teeth are worn on the side. When replacing worn sprockets the chain should be replaced also, or the new sprockets may be ruined in a short time. The rear sprocket roller bearing is allowed a slight amount of free-play, but, if excessive, the roller should be replaced.

TRANSMISSION COUNTERSHAFT SPROCKET AND OIL SEAL

To examine or remove the countershaft final drive sprocket, first remove the six screws that retain the plate surrounding the shaft. Pry the plate loose and remove it with its oil seal, taking note of the felt washer that protects the seal from dirt and grit. Check for oil leakage at the back of the plate and replace the plate oil seal if necessary. Install the seal with the lip facing the countershaft sprocket.

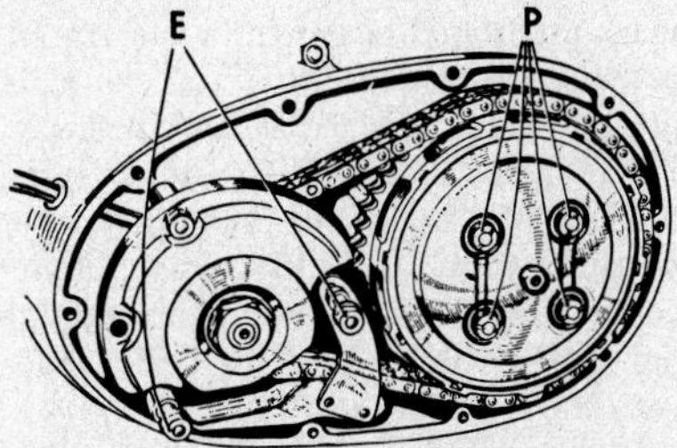

Primary chain (E) and clutch pressure plate (P) adjustment points (250)

If the sprocket teeth are hooked or if the sprocket is damaged, it should be replaced (along with the drive chain and rear wheel sprocket if it too is worn). To remove the sprocket bend back the locktab, apply the rear brake, then unscrew the retaining nut. Disconnect the drive chain and pull the sprocket off the shaft. Examine the countershaft oil seal at this time. If it shows signs of leakage, remove the circlip, pry out the seal, and replace it with a new one. Coat the new seal with oil to facilitate installation. Examine the sprocket boss for wear, which may have been causing the seal to leak. Lightly oil the boss when installing the sprocket to avoid damaging the seal. Torque the sprocket retaining nut to 100 ft lbs. When installing the round plate, make sure the gasket is in good condition or use a new one. A new felt washer should be used behind the oil seal. Make sure that the small boss cast into the rear of the plate is installed in the four o'clock position, or else it will contact the drive chain.

PRIMARY DRIVE SPROCKET ALIGNMENT

Assemble and install the clutch unit—without the primary chain—on the transmission shaft. Install the crankshaft sprocket. (The sprocket spacer must be installed with the chamfered end against the sprocket.). Place a straightedge against the sprockets as illustrated. If the sprockets are aligned properly, the straightedge will make contact at three points. Shims of different thicknesses are available for installation behind the crankshaft sprocket to correct misalignment.

Transmission and Shifter Mechanism

SERVICE

Disassembly

1. If the top end has not been disassembled, position the piston at top dead center of the compression stroke to avoid distorting the inner camshaft bushing (due to valve spring pressure) as the inner crankcase cover is removed. Drain the transmission oil at this time.

2. Disassemble the primary drive and clutch assembly including the countershaft sprocket, described previously. This is necessary to permit the transmission mainshaft to be withdrawn along with the inner crankcase cover at the right (timing) side of the engine.

3. To remove the right-side outer cover, first take off the kick-start and shift levers. Remove the cover retaining screws, noting that the screws are of different lengths and must be replaced in their original positions.

4. Unscrew the kick-start return spring anchor and remove the spring.

5. Remove the ignition advance unit from the inner cover.

6. Take out the remaining inner cover mounting screws and tap the cover with a rubber mallet to break the joint seal.

Withdraw the cover complete with transmission gear cluster. As the cover is removed, exert a slight inward pressure on the end of the camshaft to avoid disturbing the valve timing.

7. Depress the two plungers in the shift linkage quadrant and withdraw the quadrant and spring.

8. Remove the camplate pivot cotter pin from the outside of the cover. Screw one of the small inner cover screws into the pivot and pull the pivot out with a pair of pliers.

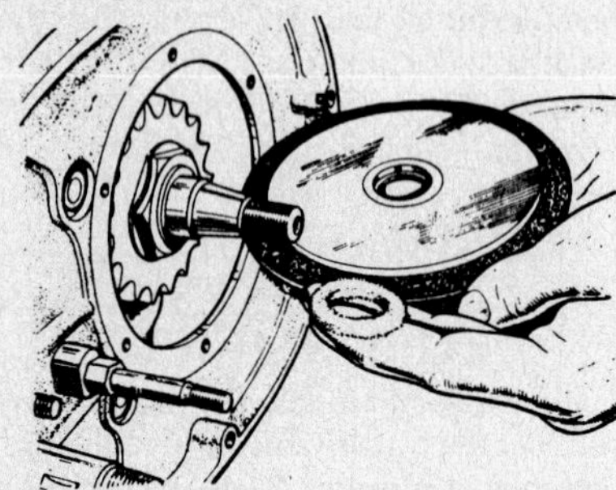

Removing the gearbox sprocket cover (250)

9. Remove the camplate, shift forks, and fork shaft.

10. Withdraw the countershaft, complete with gear assembly and mainshaft sliding gear. To remove the mainshaft assembly from the cover, unscrew the kick-start ratchet retaining nut and remove the ratchet components from the shaft.

NOTE: *When removing the countershaft gears, note that second gear is retained by a circlip.*

11. The two gears remaining on the mainshaft are an interference fit. Remove by clamping the gears in a vise (protected from the jaws with pieces of wood or cloth) and driving the shaft out using a soft metal drift.

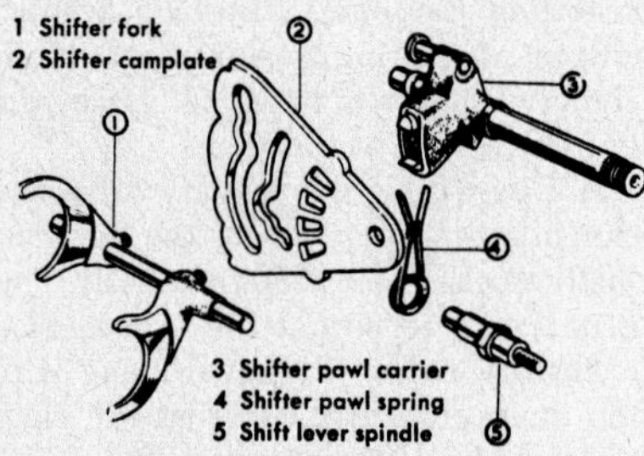

Shifter mechanism (250)

1. Shifter fork
2. Shifter camplate
3. Shifter pawl carrier
4. Shifter pawl spring
5. Shift lever spindle

12. If it is desired to remove the left-side transmission bearing from the case, drive the pinion out of the bearing and remove the oil seal. The crankcase should be heated with a propane torch before the bearing is driven out to avoid damage to both the bearing and case.

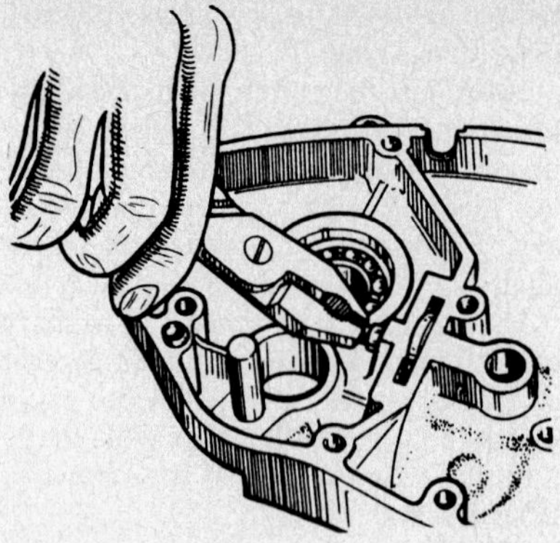

Removing the camplate pivot pin (250)

Inspection

Examine all components for wear and damage. Look for worn camplate tracks, weak springs, loose bearings, and worn bushings. Inspect gear teeth for pitting on the thrust faces and check the dogs for rounding off and breakage. Replace any parts that do not appear to be in perfect condition.

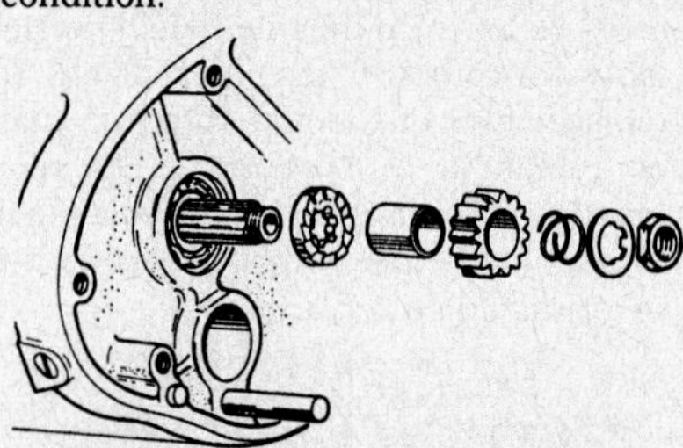

Kickstarter ratchet assembly (250)

Assembly

1. To reinstall the left-side bearing (if removed), heat the crankcase very gently around the area of the bearing housing, moving the torch slowly and evenly to prevent distortion. Install the bearing and fit a new oil seal.

2. If necessary, install a new inner cover bearing, having first heated the cover in an oven. Use new oil seals in the cover.

3. Install the camplate with the small mark positioned as shown in the accompanying illustration. Install the camplate pivot and lock in place with a cotter pin.

4. Replace the mainshaft gears on the shaft, fit the shaft into the inner cover bearing, install the kick-start ratchet components, and tighten the retaining nut to 50–55 ft lbs. Lock the nut in place with the locktab.

5. Install the kick-start half-gear into the inner cover. Place the cover, with the outside surface down, close to the edge on your workbench so that the half-gear shaft is over the edge but the gear is retained in the cover. Place the countershaft first gear shim over the bearing in the half-gear shaft. Use a small amount of grease to hold it in position.

6. Engage the mainshaft and countershaft first gears and fit the shift fork into

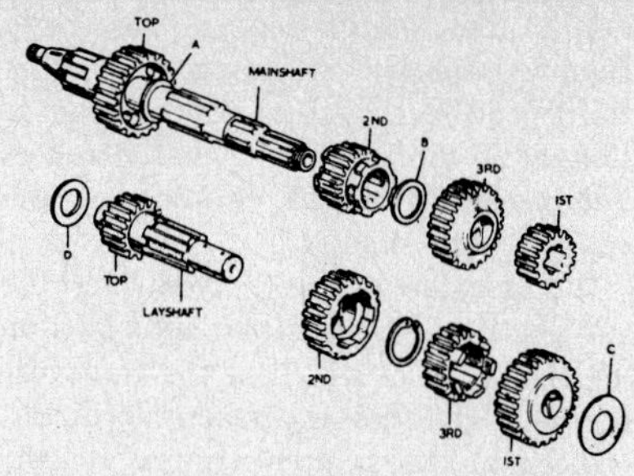

Exploded view of gear cluster (250)

the countershaft third gear with the machined (flat) side of the fork up. Engage the roller (button) of the fork in the lower camplate track.

7. Fit the mainshaft second gear with its shift fork (machined side of the fork down) and engage the fork roller in the upper track of the camplate.

8. Insert the shift fork shaft through the forks and into the inner cover. Position the countershaft second gear on the shaft and install the countershaft in the inner cover.

9. Place the mainshaft fourth gear thrust washer over the shaft, retaining it with a dab of grease. Install the countershaft thrust washer, making sure that the side with the radius faces the gear.

10. Lubricate all components with motor oil and rotate the shafts to confirm that they are free of binding.

11. If the shift return spring has been removed, it must be reinstalled so that the marked (painted) side of the coil faces the shift quadrant body. If the spring is unmarked, install it in the position in which it appears in the accompanying illustration (in line with the two pins) by trial and error.

12. Install the shift quadrant assembly into the inner cover, using a flat blade to keep the plungers depressed so they can slide over the camplate, as shown.

13. If the inner case, mainshaft, countershaft, or any gears have been replaced, it will be necessary to check end-float of the shafts and adjust if necessary. To accomplish this, mount the inner cover on the crankcase and tighten the screws. Remove the kick-start ratchet assembly and half-gear and the ends of the mainshaft and countershaft will be accessible. Thrust washers of different thicknesses are available to adjust end-float to specification.

14. When all components have been assembled on the inner cover and it is ready to be installed, clean the crankcase and inner cover mating surfaces thoroughly, and apply a thin coat of gasket cement to one of the surfaces. Lubricate the crankshaft oil seal and camshaft end, and mount the cover on the crankcase. Tighten the screws to 3.5–4.5 ft lbs. Check operation of the gears.

15. Install the outer cover, cleaning

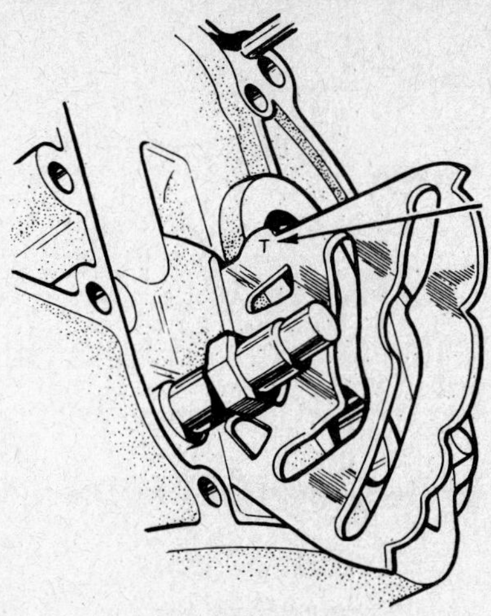

Installing the camplate (250)

the mating surfaces and applying gasket cement as above. Install the kick-start and shift levers.

NOTE: *Before the cover is installed, the position of the shift linkage quadrant can be adjusted for smoother gear selection (late models only). Loosen the adjuster locknut and select each gear in turn. If the gears do not engage positively, turn the adjuster screw a little at a time until gear selection is satisfactory. Do not turn the screw more than ¼ turn from vertical in either direction. Tighten the locknut when adjustment is complete.*

16. Install the primary drive and clutch assembly and refill the transmission and primary case with oil. Check and adjust, if necessary, the ignition timing before running the engine.

Bottom End Overhaul

DISASSEMBLY

1. Drain the oil from the engine, transmission, and primary case. Remove the engine.
2. Remove the cylinder head, piston, and barrel.
3. Remove the primary drive and clutch assembly.

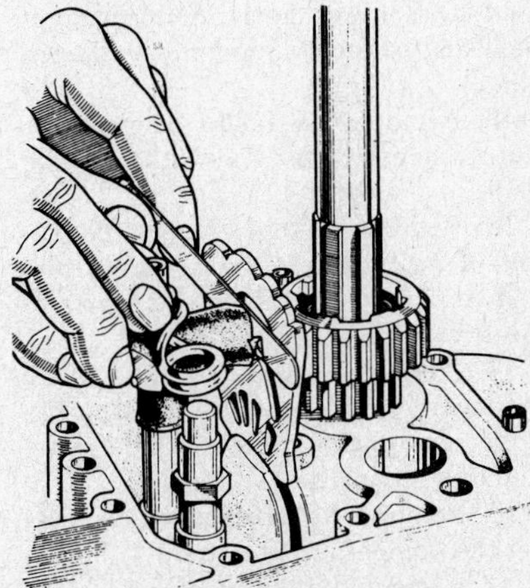
Installing the shifter mechanism and return spring (250)

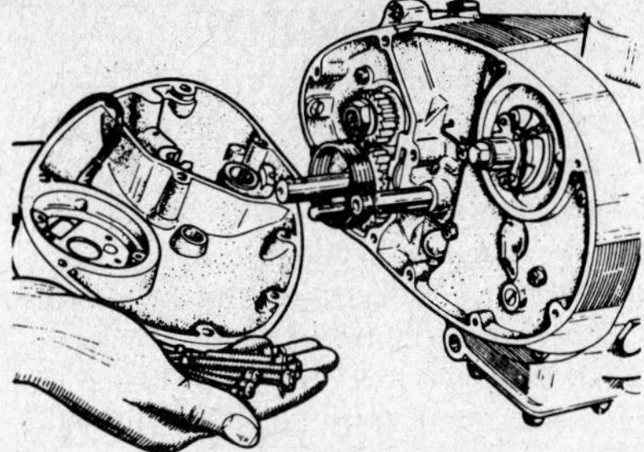
Removing the outer timing cover (250)

4. Remove the right-side outer cover and then take off the inner cover, complete with transmission gearset, as described in the preceding section.
5. Note the alignment of the marks on the timing gears and withdraw the upper gear and camshaft, allowing the tappets to fall clear.
6. Insert a bar through the connecting rod small-end, place blocks of wood under the bar to protect the crankcase, and unscrew the nut at the end of the crankshaft. The bar will keep the engine from turning over as the nut is broken free.

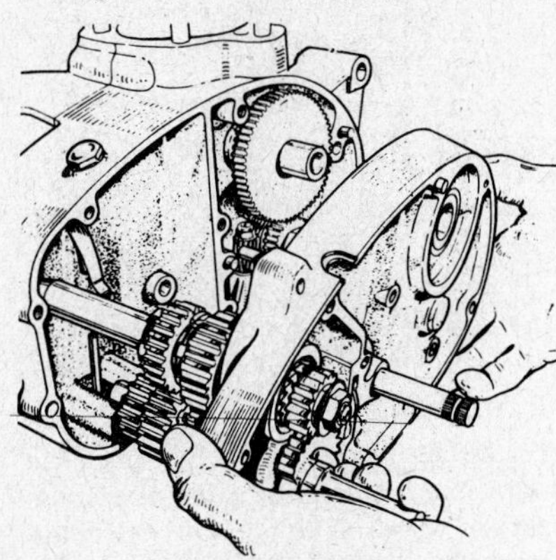
Removing the inner timing cover (250)

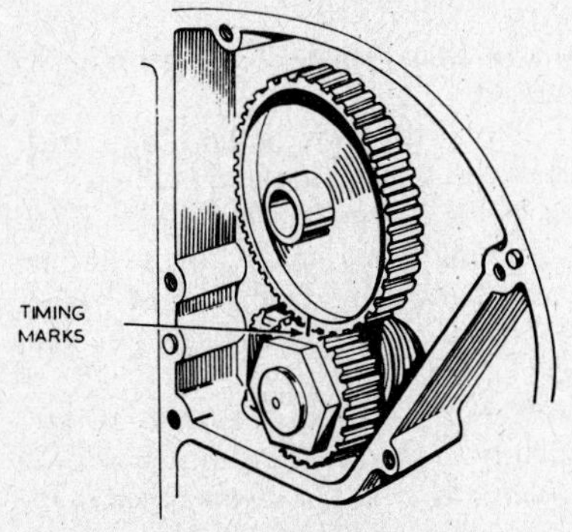

Timing gear marks (250)

7. Remove the small timing gear with a suitable gear puller.
8. Take off the nut and remove the oil pump drive-gear.
9. From the left side of the crankcase, remove the three bolts at the lower front of the case, the two stud nuts at the center of the case, and the remaining two stud nuts at the cylinder base.
10. Remove the woodruff keys from the crankshaft ends and separate the crankcase halves by tapping with a rubber mallet.
11. Lift away the right crankcase, as shown, and remove the crankshaft assembly. Note the number of shims used, if any, between the right-side flywheel and main bearing.

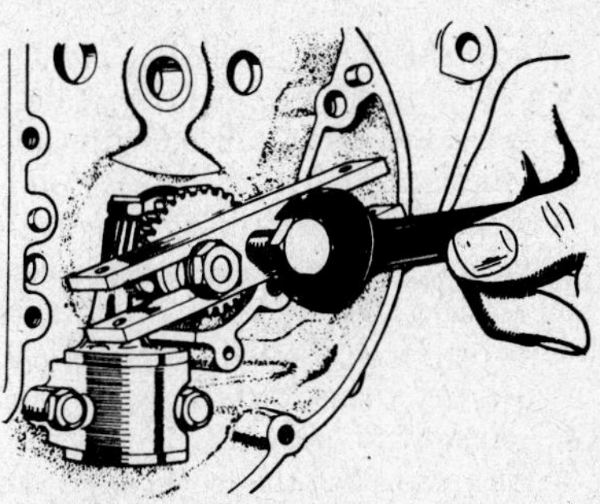
Removing the crankshaft pinion (250)

MAIN BEARINGS

The inner and outer races of the left-side roller bearing are separated as the crankcase halves are split. The outer race can be driven out after the case has been heated in an oven. The inner race, remaining on the crankshaft, can be pulled off using a suitable gear puller. The right-side (timing side) ball bearing assembly can be driven out after heating the case.

New bearings can be installed in the cases in the same manner, after the cases have been heated.

CONNECTING ROD BEARINGS AND CRANKSHAFT ASSEMBLY

The connecting rod can be removed by simply unbolting the bearing cap. Loosen the nuts alternately, a turn at a time, to prevent distortion. To facilitate reassembly, the connecting rod and cap have been marked with a center punch. Note the direction in which the marks face.

Examine the bearing shells and crankpin carefully for signs of wear, scoring, and other damage. If it is necessary to

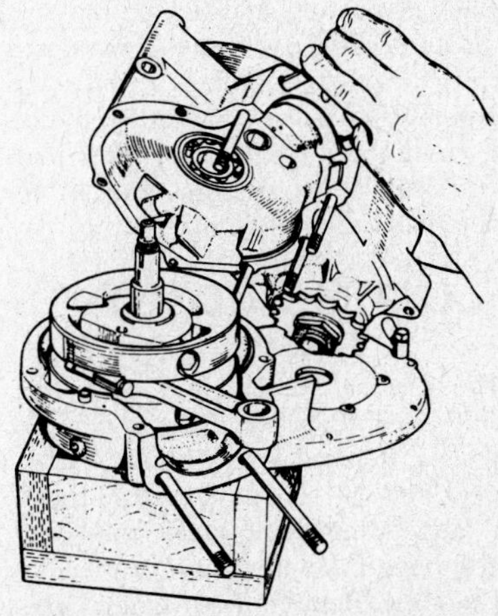
Separating the crankcase halves (250)

regrind the crankshaft, bearings are available in 0.010, 0.020, and 0.030 in. undersizes. It is very important that the radius at either end of the crankpin is machined to 0.070–0.080 in. when regrinding. Do not attempt to refinish the bearing shells or file the bearing cap mating surfaces to reduce bearing clearances.

If the crankshaft is to be reground, the flywheels must be removed. Loosen the four, short, flywheel retaining bolts (closest to the crankpin) first to avoid distortion. Remove the remaining four bolts and separate the flywheels. It would be a good idea at this time to clean the oil sludge trap, located in the right flywheel. Unscrew the plug and clean the passage with solvent and compressed air.

When reinstalling the flywheels, make sure that the flywheel incorporating the sludge trap is fitted on the *right* side. Apply a drop of thread-locking compound to the threads of each flywheel retaining bolt and tighten evenly to 50 ft lbs.

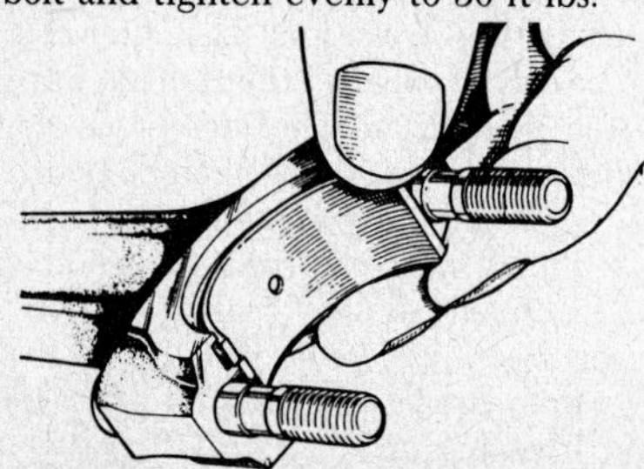

Installing new connecting rod bearing shells (250)

When installing the connecting rod on the crankshaft, make sure that the rod bearing shells are properly located in the connecting rod and cap. The oil hole should face the drive (left) side flywheel. Lubricate the bearing surfaces with fresh engine oil and install the bearing cap, taking note of the position of the punch marks to ensure that the cap is installed in its original position. It is recommended that new connecting rod bolts and nuts be used as a precaution against breakage. Clean the threads, apply a drop of thread-locking compound, and tighten the nuts to 22 ft lbs. Using a pressure oil can, force oil into the passage at the right end of the crankshaft until it is coming out around the connecting rod bearing. This indicates that the oil passages are not restricted and are full of oil.

CAMSHAFT AND TAPPETS

The camshaft lobes and tappet feet should be carefully examined for damage and wear. Replace any part that does not appear to be in perfect condition. Insert the tappets into their guide bores and check to see if they are free to move without binding. Replace if movement is restricted. Oil the tappets before installing.

ASSEMBLY

1. On the TR25W, the crankshaft end-float must be checked. Proceed with step 2, below, omitting the gasket cement. Check crankshaft end-float, disassemble the cases again and add or remove thrust washers as necessary between the flywheel and right-side main bearing to adjust end-float to within 0.002–0.005 in. Then start with step 2 again and follow the remainder of the assembly procedure.
2. Place the crankshaft assembly into the drive-side crankcase. Clean the crankcase mating surfaces and apply a thin coat of gasket cement to the mating surface of one of the cases. Fit the crankcase halves together and install the three bolts and four nuts. Tighten evenly to 16–18 ft lbs.
3. Rotate the crankshaft to make sure that it turns freely. If it does not, the cause of the trouble must be determined and rectified. Look for incorrect main bearing alignment or insufficient crankshaft endplay.

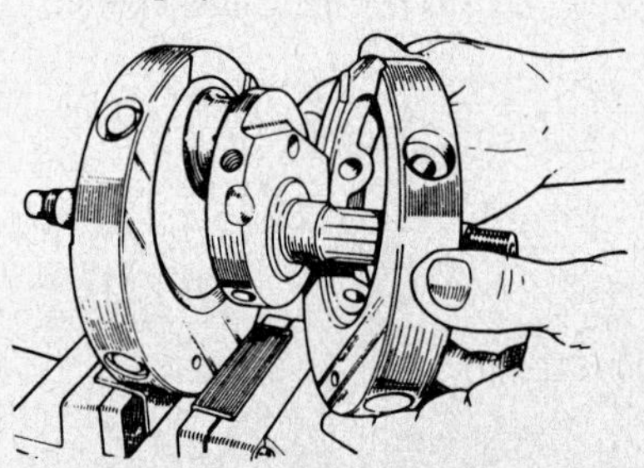

Removing a flywheel (250)

4. Install the small timing gear on the end of the crankshaft, taking care to locate the woodruff key properly. Tighten the retaining nut to 50–55 ft lbs.
5. Install the oil pump drive-gear on the pump shaft using the special locknut (or a suitable replacement) as originally installed.
6. Place the two tappets into their bores with the thinner end of the tappet foot facing forward. Install the camshaft and timing gear unit, with the timing marks aligned, and fit the thrust washer on the end of the camshaft (late models only).

NOTE: *On early engines there are two marks on the camshaft timing gear—a dash and a V. On these engines the dash must be ignored and the marks aligned as illustrated. On later engines that do not have the V mark, simply align the dash marks.*

7. Install the right-side inner cover complete with transmission gearset as described earlier in the chapter, and install the outer cover.
8. Install the primary drive and clutch assembly.
9. Install the cylinder head, piston, and barrel. Refer to "Top End Overhaul."

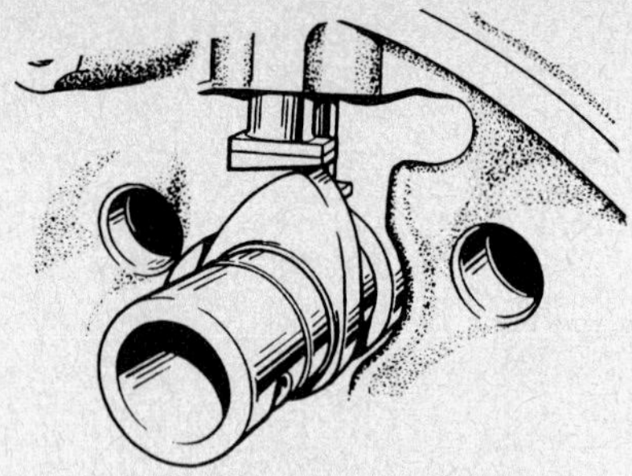

Correct tappet installation (250)

T100C AND T100R

Removal and Installation

1. Remove the gas tank and disconnect the spark plug leads.
2. Disconnect the battery terminals and the connectors at the two ignition coils.
3. Remove the ignition coils, taking care not to damage the outer casings.
4. Disconnect the snap connectors between the contact breaker assembly and the condensers.
5. Remove the two cylinder-head torque stays.
6. Disconnect the tachometer drive cable.
7. Remove the carburetor(s) complete with air cleaners.
8. Disconnect the rocker oil feed line, taking care not to bend it.
9. Drain the oil tank and disconnect the delivery lines to the engine.
10. Drain the engine sump, primary chaincase, and transmission.
11. Loosen the clutch adjustment at the handlebar, then disconnect and remove the clutch cable.
12. Remove the exhaust header pipes and mufflers.
13. Remove the final, drive-chain master link and withdraw the chain. This is a good time to give the chain a thorough cleaning and oil soak.
14. Disconnect the alternator leads at their snap connectors underneath the engine.
15. Remove the bolts securing the front engines plates and withdraw the plates.
16. Remove the stud securing the bottom of the engine to the frame and the bolt securing the rear engine plates to the transmission case.
17. Have a helper support the engine, then remove the two nuts securing the right rear engine plate to the frame. Remove the plate.
18. Remove the left front stud securing the engine torque stay.
19. Remove the right footrest.
20. With the helper, lift the engine out the right side of the machine.

21. Installation is basically a reversal of the removal procedure. Note the following:

a. when the engine is in position in the frame, install the bottom frame bolt first, then install the right rear engine plate and tighten the bolts finger-tight only.

b. Install the front, engine mounting plate, then tighten all mounting bolts snugly.

Top End Overhaul

CYLINDER HEAD AND BARREL REMOVAL

The cylinder head and barrel can be removed without taking out the engine.

1. Disconnect the leads from the battery terminals and remove the fuel tank.
2. Disconnect the high tension cables and wiring harness from the ignition coils, then remove the coils. Take care not to damage the coil outer casings.
3. Remove the cylinder head torque stays.
4. Remove the rocker oil feed line.
5. Remove the two nuts from the studs at the bottom of the exhaust rocker box.

Arrows indicate rocker box stud nuts and bolt (500 models)

6. Remove the two phillips screws from the top of each rocker box, loosen all eight cylinder head bolts and remove the central head bolts.
7. Remove the exhaust rocker box, then remove the intake rocker box in the same manner. Take care not to lose the six plain washers (one under each bottom securing nut).
8. Remove the pushrods and mark them for reassembly position.
9. Remove the exhaust header pipes.
10. Disconnect the fuel lines and plug the ends. Disconnect the throttle linkage at the carburetor(s).
11. Remove the remaining four cylinder head nuts by turning each one a little at a time in an X pattern.
12. Remove the cylinder head complete with intake manifold(s) and carburetor(s). If the cylinder head is being serviced, rather than being removed to gain access to another part of the engine, remove the intake manifolds and carburetor(s).
13. Remove the pushrod tubes, remembering to replace the rubber seals during assembly.
14. Remove the cylinder head gasket.
15. Wedge a piece of rubber between the intake and exhaust tappets to prevent them from falling into the case when the barrel is removed.
16. Rotate the engine until the pistons are both at TDC, then remove the eight cylinder base nuts and washers.
17. Raise the barrel high enough to stuff some clean, no-lint rags into the case openings. It is also a good idea to fit some kind of rubber protectors over the cylinder studs to prevent damage to the connecting rods when the barrel is removed.
18. Lift off the barrel carefully, supporting the pistons when they are free.
19. Remove and mark the tappets for reassembly.

Rocker Boxes

The rocker spindles can be removed by driving them out with a suitable drift. Once out, the spindles will release the rocker arms and washers. Clean the parts in kerosine or a cleaning solvent, then blow them dry with compressed air. Also blow out the spindle oil drillings with compressed air. Upon reassembly, the spindle oil seals should be replaced.

If the rocker ball pins require replacement, drive them out with a suitable drift and press the new ones in with the drilled flat toward the rocker spindles.

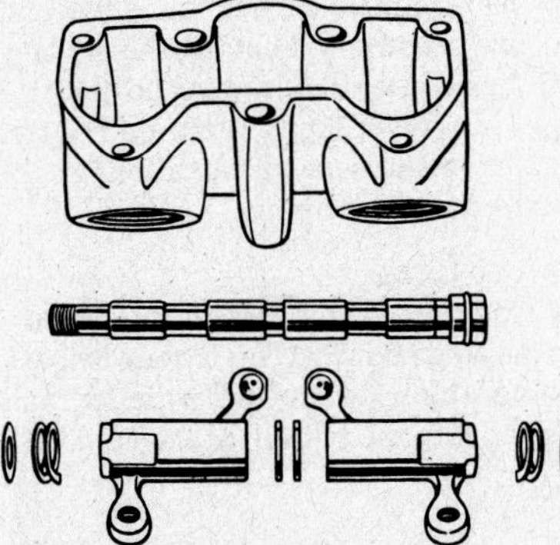

Rocker box assembly (500 models)

The rocker boxes can be reassembled using a 7/16 in. x 6 in. bar, ground to a taper at one end. This bar serves as an alignment tool for the spindles. Before beginning assembly, note that two of the washers removed from the spindles have a smaller diameter than the other washers. These are thrust washers and they must be assembled last—against the right inner face of the rocker box.

Grease two plain washers and position them on either side of the center bearing boss. Position the left rocker arm, bringing it into line with the alignment bar, and locate the plain washer, spring washer, and thrust washer as shown in the accompanying illustration. Repeat this for the right rocker arm, then oil the spindle and slide it as far into the rocker box as possible. Tap it in the remaining distance with a soft-faced hammer.

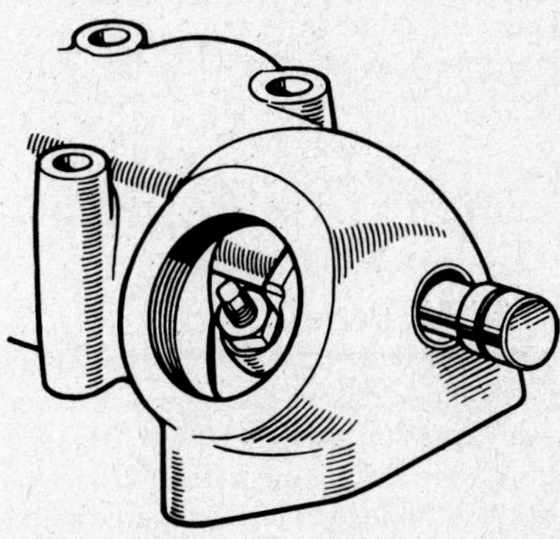

Installing the rocker box spindle (500 models)

Valves

The valves can be removed from the cylinder head with the use of a G-type clamp. When the valve spring is compressed, remove the split collars and withdraw the spring and valve. Mark the valves to locate them for reassembly. If new or reground valves are to be installed, it will be necessary to grind them in with a fine grade carborundum paste. It will not require recutting the valve seat, however, unless new valve guides have also been installed. After grinding in the valve, make sure all remnants of the grinding in process have been removed.

Compare the valve spring free-length with that given in specifications. If necessary, replace them.

Installation of the valves is accomplished in the reverse of the removal procedure. Lubricate the valve stems with graphite before positioning them in the cylinder head.

Valve Guides

The valve guides are an interference fit in the cylinder head. They can be either pressed out or driven out with special tool no. Z16 or a suitable drift. They can be installed in the same manner, although pressing is preferred. Lubricate the outside of the guide to aid installation.

New valve guides require that the valve seat be recut. This is an exacting operation and should be referred to a qualified shop. If you have the knowledge and tools, however, valve seat specifications are given at the end of this chapter.

Tappets and Guide Blocks

The only wear likely to be apparent on the tappets is at their tips which are plated with Stellite. Over a long period of time, an indentation will be worn in the center of the tip. If the width of this indentation exceeds 3/32 in., replace the tappet.

It is not necessary to remove the pressfit tappet guide blocks to check their condition. Simply insert the tappet and rock it back and forth in the block. There should be little or no lateral play. See specifications for allowable clearances.

Tappet guide block and pushrod assembly (500 models)

PISTON AND CYLINDER BARREL SERVICE

Cylinder Barrel

Most wear occurs at the upper part of the cylinder due to piston and cylinder heat expansion characteristics. Although this is partially compensated for by having the cylinder and piston tapered at the top when cold, the scraping action of the rings causes the wear to be greater at the top than at the bottom. The cylinder, therefore, is never perfectly cylindrical.

In order to accurately measure cylinder wear, several measurements should be made at different heights in the barrel, both parallel and perpendicular to the piston pin. If there is a difference of 0.13 mm (0.005 in.) between any of these measurements, the cylinder should be rebored and/or honed.

Use an inside micrometer to make the measurements.

Pistons, Rings, and Piston Pins—Removal

1. Remove the rocker boxes, cylinder head, and cylinder block as previously described.
2. Make sure the crankcase opening edges are covered with lint-free rags to protect the aluminum alloy connecting rod from being damaged.
3. Remove the inner and outer piston pin retaining circlips, then attach a piston pin removal tool and press out the pin.
4. Lay out and mark the pistons, piston pins, and retaining circlips for reassembly.
5. Remove the piston rings one at a time by lifting an end of the ring out of its groove and holding a thin piece of metal between it and the piston. Slide the piece of metal around the circumference of the piston while at the same time gently lifting the raised part of the ring upwards.

Piston Inspection

Inspect the piston skirt for any signs of scoring or seizure. These will show up as burnt or rough areas between the rings and the bottom of the piston, and are usually cause for piston replacement. If the rough spot or burned area is small or minor, however, it can be cleaned up with a fine grade emery cloth.

This is also a good time to remove the carbon buildup from the piston crown and ring grooves, so clean them up as described in cylinder head decarbonization, then check carefully for pitting and hairline cracks.

Replacement pistons are available in three oversizes. These sizes and the corresponding recommended cylinder bore sizes are given in a chart at the end of this section.

Piston Pin and Small End Bushing

Inspect the piston pin for center "step wear," scoring or burring, then slide it into the small end connecting rod bushing, and make certain that there is no lateral freeplay. If there is, replace the bushing in the following manner:

1. Obtain a threaded bolt approximately 4 in. in length and a piece of tubing 1¼ in. long with an inside diameter of ⅞ in.
2. Place a suitable washer and the new bushing on the bolt, then insert the end of the bolt through the old bushing.
3. Place the piece of tubing over the end of the bolt and screw the nut on finger-tight.
4. Centralize the new bushing and align the oil drillway with that in the old bushing.
5. Now tighten the nut on the bolt and the new bushing will extract the old one.
6. Ream the new bushing to the size given in specifications at the end of this chapter. Make sure all metal filings are removed after reaming.

Piston Rings

Piston ring wear is checked by measuring the ring end gap. This is done by positioning the ring in the cylinder and pushing it to the bottom of the bore with a piston, then measuring the end gap with a feeler gauge. Check this figure with specifications at the end of this section and determine if the ring requires replacement.

Before assembling an engine with new rings, the cylinder bore should be lightly honed in a cross-hatch pattern. Use plenty of oil for lubrication. This can also be accomplished with no. 300 grade emery cloth.

Installation

1. Install the piston rings one at a time over the top of the piston. Note that the two compression rings are marked TOP to ensure correct assembly position.
2. Position the piston on the connecting rod.
3. Install one new retaining circlip as a stop, then press the piston pin into position and install another new circlip on the other side.

NOTE: *If there is no alternative and the piston pin must be driven into its bore, it is advisable to heat the piston to 100° C prior to assembly.*

TOP END ASSEMBLY

1. Position new guide block O-ring seals at the base of the cylinder block.
2. If it was removed, lightly grease the outside surface of the exhaust guide block, then carefully align the guide block and cylinder locating holes and drive the block into position with Triumph special tool no. Z23 or a suitable drift.
3. Repeat the above step for the intake guide block, then install the locking bolts.
4. After installing the guide blocks, make sure that the exhaust guide block oil drillways are free from obstruction.
5. Install the tappets in the guide

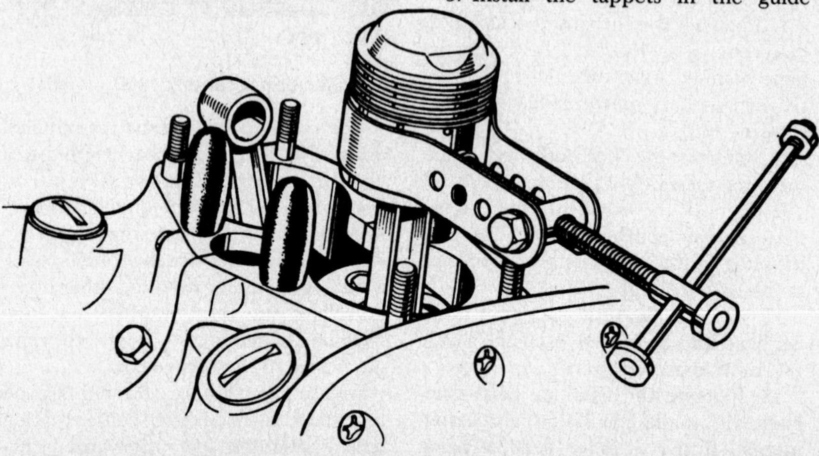

Removing the piston pin (500 models)

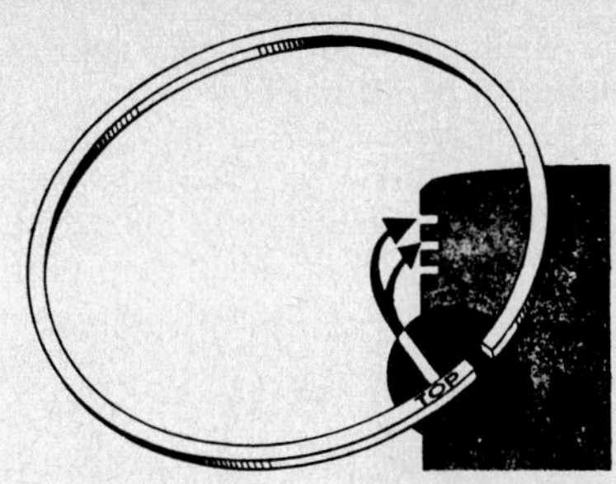

Correct piston ring installation (500 models)

blocks after thoroughly lubricating them with oil. Wedge them in position.

6. Install the cylinder base gasket, making certain that the gasket does not obscure the oil feed drillway in the crankcase.

7. Fit ring compressors over the piston rings, then carefully slide the cylinder down over the pistons. Remove the ring compressors as soon as the rings are positioned within the cylinder. Continue lowering the cylinder block and then remove the rags in the crankcase openings as late as possible.

8. Install the cylinder base attaching nuts.

9. Replace or anneal the cylinder head gasket.

10. Clean the mating cylinder head and cylinder surfaces, then grease the gasket and position it on the cylinder.

11. Coat the tappet guide blocks with grease and position the pushrod cover tubes with new O-ring seals.

12. Position the cylinder head and install the four outer and one central head bolt finger-tight.

13. Place a small amount of grease in the bottom cup of each pushrod, then locate the intake pushrods in their respective bores. This will have to be done by "feel."

14. When the pushrods are properly positioned, remove the spark plugs and turn the engine over until both intake pushrods are level and at the bottom of their travel.

15. Install the intake rocker box.

16. Repeat the above procedure for

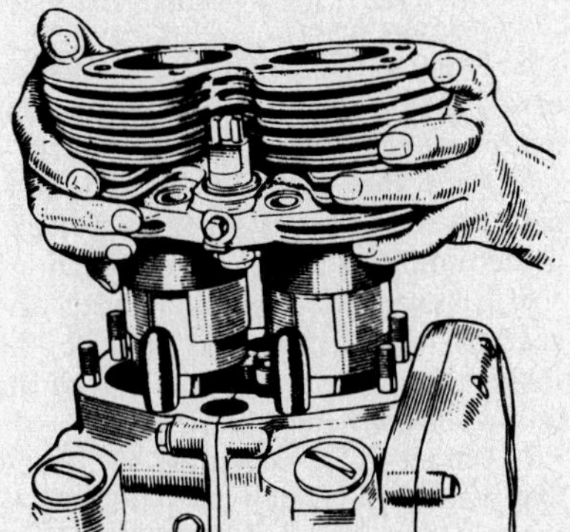

Installing the cylinder barrel (500 models)

the exhaust rocker box, noting that the central cylinder head bolts should be tightened to torque specifications before tightening the underside securing nuts.

17. Turn the engine over several times to make sure the valves are operating properly, then reinstall the torque stays and secondary ignition coils.

18. Connect the rocker oil feed line, using either new copper washers or annealed, used ones.

19. The remainder of the assembly procedure is a reversal of the disassembly instructions. Adjust valve tappet clearances.

Clutch And Primary Drive

CLUTCH SERVICE

Disassembly

1. Remove the left exhaust header pipe.

2. Loosen the rear brake adjustment until the pedal drops clear of the primary cover.

3. Remove the left footrest.

4. Drain the oil from the chaincase, then remove the chain tension adjuster.

5. Remove the ten, recessed cover-securing screws and withdraw the cover and paper gasket.

6. Remove the chain tensioner assembly.

7. The clutch pressure plate is held in place by three, slotted adjuster nuts. To remove these nuts, slide a knife or screwdriver blade under the nut and loosen it with Triumph tool no. D364 (supplied with tool kit) or a suitable substitute.

8. Remove the clutch springs, cups, and pressure plate assembly.

9. The clutch plates can be removed with the use of two, narrow, hooked tools made of 1/32 in. wire.

Inspection

1. The clutch plates should appear to be in good condition. If the thickness of the discs is 0.030 in. (0.75 mm), or more, less than specified, they should be replaced.

2. Check that the tabs at the outer edge of the discs are not worn or rounded and that the clutch sprocket slots are not damaged. If there are burrs on the tabs, the discs must be replaced.

3. Place the clutch plates on a flat surface, such as a piece of glass. If they can be rocked from side to side or if there is any evidence of buckling, they should be replaced. Also replace the plates if they are scored in any way.

4. Check the fit of the plate on the shock absorber unit. There should be little radial clearance.

5. Measure the clutch spring length and compare with specifications. If a

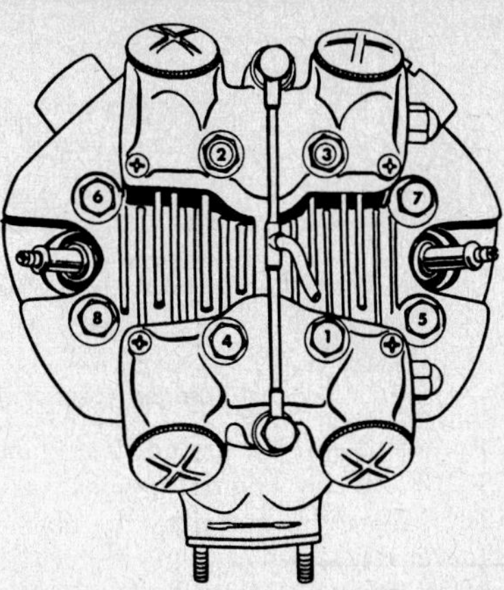

Cylinder head bolt tightening sequence (500 models)

spring has shortened by 0.10 in. (2.5 mm) or more, replace the whole set.

Assembly

1. Install the clutch plates and discs, keeping in mind that the innermost position must be occupied by a bonded plate.

2. Install the cups, pressure plate, springs, and slotted adjuster nuts.

3. True the clutch pressure plate by first tightening the pressure-plate, slotted adjuster nuts until they are even with the clutch pins, and then by kicking the engine over and observing the rotation of the plate, and then making any necessary adjustment until the plate turns evenly. If the plate wobbles even slightly, it must be corrected.

PRIMARY DRIVE AND CLUTCH HUB SERVICE

Disassembly

1. Remove the primary cover as previously described.

2. Remove the clutch assembly as previously described.

3. Disconnect the alternator stator leads at their snap connectors under the engine.

4. Remove the three stator securing nuts and withdraw the stator from over its mounting studs. Unscrew the sleeve nut and then the lead can easily be removed.

5. To remove the rotor, bend back the tab washer, put the transmission in fourth gear, hold the rear brake, and then remove the mainshaft locknut.

6. Remove the rotor key and distance piece.

7. Remove the clutch hub securing nut and cup.

NOTE: *Machines prior to serial no. H49833 have a tab washer and a different cup washer, rather than the self-locking securing nut.*

8. Screw the body of extractor no. Z13 into the clutch hub until it bottoms, then tighten the center bolt until the hub is released.

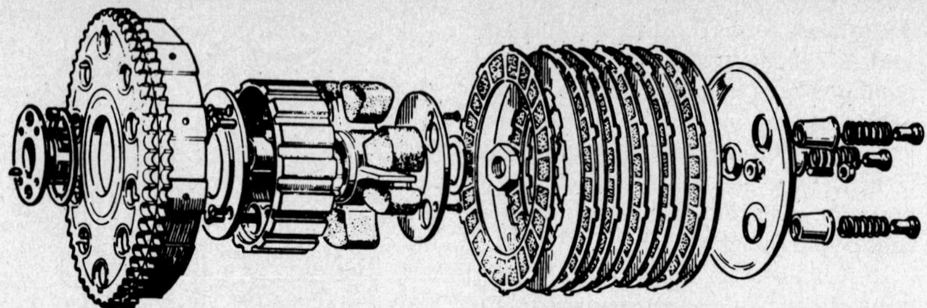

Exploded view of clutch assembly (500 models)

9. Assemble extractor no. Z151 and D662/3 on the engine sprocket and tighten its center bolt until the engine sprocket is released.

10. Withdraw the engine sprocket, clutch hub, and primary chain together.

11. Remove the transmission mainshaft key and check the oil seal for leakage.

Adjusting the clutch pressure plate (500 models)

Removing the engine sprocket center bolt (500 models)

Inspection

1. Inspect the clutch shock absorber for worn rubbers or punctures. They can be removed by prying them out, small rubbers first. Replace as necessary. When reassembling, apply thread-locking compound to the cover plate securing screws.

2. First thoroughly clean the primary chain then check it for wear by scribing two marks on a flat surface 12 in. apart, and centering two pivot pins at the scribe marks. Fully compressed, the chain link pivot should line up with the marks; fully stretched, it should not extend more than ¼ in. beyond the marks.

3. Check the chain sprockets for rounded or hooked teeth, and replace *both* if necessary. If the sprockets are replaced, also install a new chain. This will prevent the old chain from prematurely wearing out the new sprockets.

4. Check the fit between the shock absorber spider and the clutch hub splines. The spider should be a push fit on the clutch hub, with no radial movement.

5. Check the fit of the engine sprocket on the crankshaft in the same manner. There should be no radial movement.

6. Check the clutch hub bearing diameter, rollers, and clutch sprocket bearing. Replace any bearing rollers that are pitted or worn. See specifications.

7. Check the clutch operating rod for straightness by rolling it on a known flat surface, such as a piece of plate glass.

8. Make sure the shock absorber spider is a good fit in the inner and outer retaining plates, and that the arms have not excessively scored the inner surface of the retaining plates.

Assembly

1. Grease the clutch hub and install the thrust washer and twenty of the correct rollers. Do not use ¼ in. x ¼ in. rollers!

2. Position the hub and press the shock absorber, complete with the three threaded pins, on the hub.

3. Install a new tapered distance collar behind the engine sprocket, with the taper toward the crankshaft main bearing and oil seal.

4. Install the transmission mainshaft key and tap the clutch hub onto its taper.

5. Lubricate the primary chain and lay it over the clutch sprocket.

6. Wrap the chain around the engine sprocket, then position the sprocket on the crankshaft.

7. Place clutch locking tool Z13 in the clutch plate housing, then install the cup washer and self-locking nut. Torque the nut to specifications.

NOTE: *On machines before serial no. H49833, install the tab washer with the long tab in the hole in the shock absorber spider, install the securing nut and bend a tab to lock the nut.*

8. Install the alternator rotor, making sure that the key or locating peg is correctly positioned.

9. Install the alternator stator. Put a 0.-008 in. (0.2 mm) feeler gauge between each stator pole and the rotor. Turn over the engine to make sure that the rotor and stator do not touch.

10. The remainder of the assembly procedure is a reversal of the disassembly instructions. Remember to fill the primary case with oil and adjust the primary chain tension for ½ in. free-play.

Removing the engine sprocket with tool no. Z151 (500 models)

TRANSMISSION COUNTERSHAFT SPROCKET

Removal And Installation

1. Disassemble the clutch and primary drive as previously described. Remove the sprocket cover.

2. Bend back the tab washer and, while holding the rear brake, remove the sprocket securing nut.

3. Slide off the final drive chain and remove the countershaft sprocket.

4. Make sure the oil seal is in good condition, then lubricate the ground boss of the new sprocket and position it on the transmission mainshaft.

5. Replace the tab washer, screw on the securing nut finger-tight, then, with the chain in place, tighten the nut to torque specifications.

6. Oil the bushing that protrudes from the mainshaft high gear and install the sprocket cover with a new paper gasket.

7. The remainder of installation is a reversal of the removal procedure.

Clutch And Shifter Operating Mechanisms

DISASSEMBLY

1. Remove the right exhaust header pipe and footrest.

2. Drain the gearbox oil.

3. Disconnect the clutch cable from the actuating lever.

4. Remove the two nuts and four recessed screws that secure the gearbox outer cover. Remove the kick-starter.

5. Hold the gearshift lever in one hand, then tap the cover with a soft-faced mallet until it is free to be removed.

6. Unscrew the two nuts inside the gearbox outer cover and remove the shifter return springs complete with the thurust buttons and distance pieces.

7. Unscrew the countersunk screw that secures the clutch operating mechanism and withdraw the assembly.

8. Remove the shifter lever pinch bolt, remove the lever, and then withdraw the shaft from the cover.

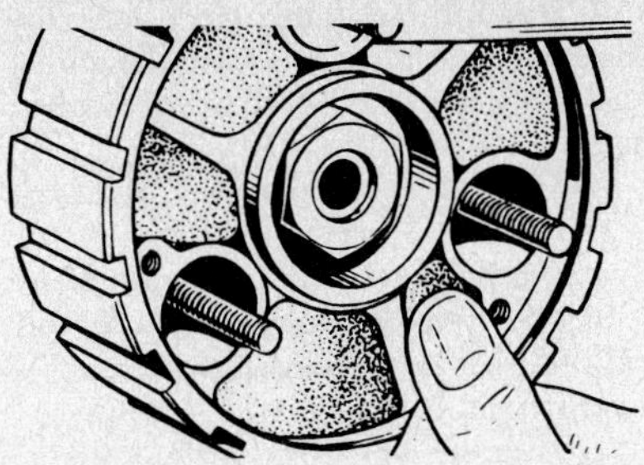

Prying out the clutch hub shock absorber rubbers (500 models)

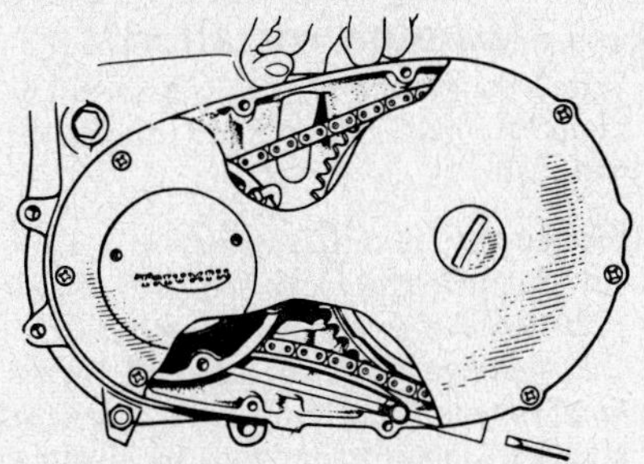

Checking primary chain tension (500 models)

9. Remove the cotter pin from the clutch operating shaft. This will release the clutch operating balls.

10. Remove the two cotter pins and disconnect the plungers and springs from the shifter quadrant.

INSPECTION

1. Inspect the shifter plungers for wear and make sure they have the correct fit in the quadrant. Check the plunger springs for fatigue by measuring their lengths and comparing with specifications.

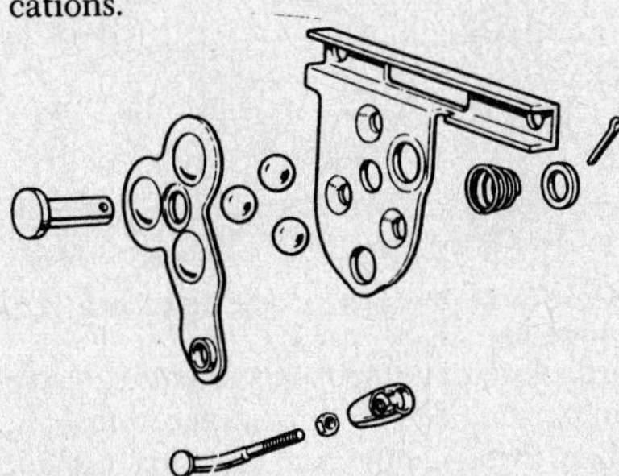

Clutch operating mechanism (500 models)

2. Inspect the shifter lever return springs for fatigue and corrosion. Replace if they are in less than excellent condition.

3. Insert the shifter quadrant in its bushing and check free-play. Replace if necessary.

4. Inspect the plungers and cutaways in the camplate for excessive wear.

5. If the shifter spindle bushing requires replacement, heat the outer cover to 100° C and drive it out with a suitable, shouldered drift. Drive in the new bushing before the cover has a chance to cool.

NOTE: *A drift for removing and installing the shifter spindle bushing can be made from a piece of ¾ in. diameter bar. Machine the bar to a diameter of ⅝ in. and cut a length of ¾ in.*

ASSEMBLY

1. Install the shifter quadrant springs, plungers, and securing cotter pins, then install a new O-ring on the spindle.

2. Lubricate the spindle and O-ring with oil, then insert the spindle in the cover.

3. Assemble the clutch-operating mechanism balls in their recesses and install the shaft and clutch lever in the order shown in the accompanying illustration. Don't forget to install the spring and washer before replacing the cotter pin.

4. Install the distance collar on the end of the shifter quadrant shaft, then install the clutch operating mechanism in the cover and secure it in place with the countersunk screw.

5. Install the distance pieces over the studs, then connect the shifter return springs and thrust buttons. Install the return spring cover plate and tighten the securing nuts.

6. Install the gearbox outer cover with sealant, tighten the securing screws, and install the kick-start lever.

7. Refill the transmission with oil.

Gearbox And Kick-Starter Mechanism

DISASSEMBLY

1. Disassemble the primary drive and clutch as previously described. Remove the transmission mainshaft nut and key.

2. Remove the gearbox outer cover, noting that the gearbox should first be positioned in fourth gear.

3. Remove the two inner gearbox cover retaining screws, then remove the entire gearbox assembly by tapping the clutch end of the mainshaft with a mallet.

4. Remove the camplate cotter pin, then withdraw the camplate spindle.

5. Pry off the kick-starter return spring and remove the distance piece. Withdraw the kick-starter spindle.

6. Remove the camplate index plunger and place it aside.

7. Remove the selector fork spindle and disengage the selector forks from the camplate.

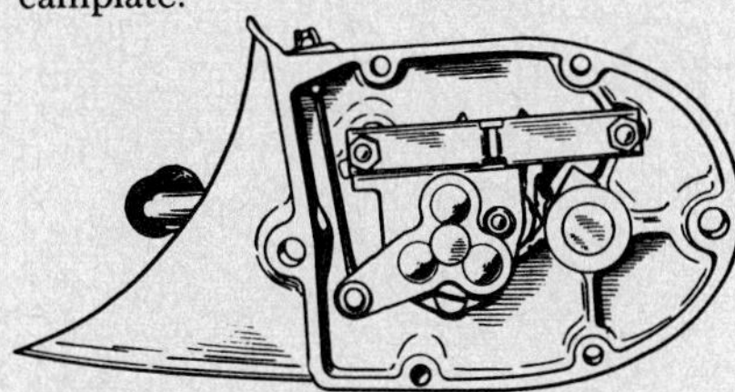

Clutch operating mechanism installed (500 models)

8. Remove the layshaft and kick-starter pawl, plunger, and spring.

9. Drive the mainshaft assembly out of the bearing with a soft-faced mallet.

10. Remove the countershaft sprocket as previously described, then drive the mainshaft high gear into the gearbox with a soft metal drift and hammer.

11. To remove the mainshaft right bearing, heat the cover to 100° C and drive it out with a suitable, shouldered drift. Install the new bearing while the cover is still hot. Replace the securing circlip.

12. To remove the high gear bearing on the left side of the machine, pry out the oil seal and remove the retaining circlip. Heat the case around the bearing to 100° C, then drive it out with a suitable, shouldered drift. Install the new bearing while the case is still hot. Replace the oil seal with the lip and spring toward the bearing, then replace the retaining circlip.

13. If it is necessary to replace the mainshaft high gear bushing, press it out with a drift measuring 5.0 X ⅞ in., having ¾ in. of one end machined to 13/16 in. diameter. Install the new bushing with the same drift, making certain the bushing oil groove is at the gear teeth end. The bushing should then be reamed to the size given in specifications.

14. The layshaft right needle roller bearing can be removed by heating the kick-starter spindle to 100° C and tapping it off with a block of wood.

15. The layshaft left needle roller bearing is of the closed-end type and can be removed through the countershaft sprocket cover plate aperture. Heat the case to 100° C and drive the bearing into the gearbox with a suitable drift. Install the new bearing while the case is still hot. A special drift, for which dimensions are given in the accompanying illustration, must be used to install the new bearing.

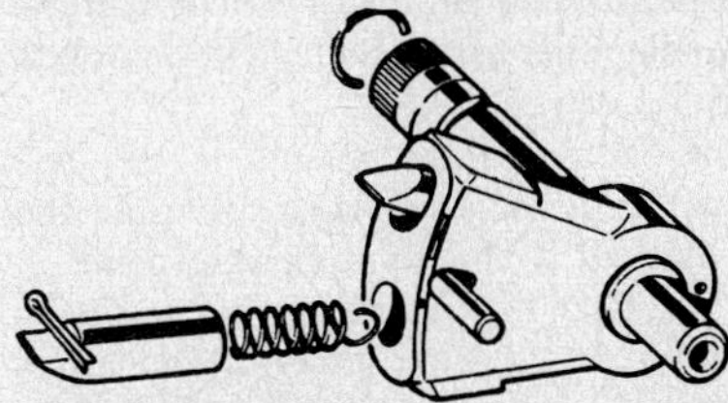

Shifter mechanism (500 models)

INSPECTION

1. Inspect the gearbox case and cover for any signs of cracking or metal fatigue. Examine the joining faces for any damage.

2. Inspect the mainshaft and layshaft for badly worn splines, cracks, etc., and compare their dimensions with those given in specifications. Also look for any signs of seizure, indicated by a local discoloration of the shaft.

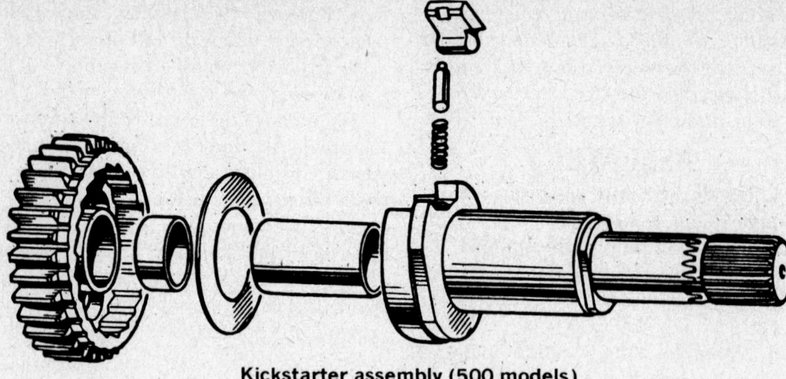
Kickstarter assembly (500 models)

3. Examine all bearings for pitting and excessive wear. Replace as described in the section on gearbox disassembly.

4. Inspect the gears for chipped, fractured or worn teeth. Also check the internal splines and bushings. Check bushing dimensions with those given in specifications.

5. Make sure the selector fork rod is not grooved or excessively worn. Inspect the selector fork faces for wear and scoring.

6. Inspect the selector camplate for wear in the roller tracks. Check the fit of the camplate spindle in its housing.

7. Inspect the camplate plunger and housing for corrosion, and check the measured length of the spring against specifications.

8. Make sure the kick-starter pawl and the layshaft low gear dogs are not excessively worn or chipped.

9. Examine the mainshaft high gear bushing for wear by inserting the mainshaft and noting the amount of free-play allowed. Make micrometer readings for true accuracy.

ASSEMBLY

1. If all replacement bearings have been installed with new seals and circlips, install the layshaft thrust washer over the needle roller cage, and hold it in position with a dab of grease.

2. Lubricate the mainshaft and layshaft captive gears, then assemble the mainshaft in the inner gearbox cover.

3. Install the plunger, spring, and pawl on the kick-starter spindle, then insert the assembly in the inner gearbox cover and slide the layshaft assembly into the kick-starter bearing. Remember to install the mainshaft distance piece between the mainshaft assembly and the main bearing in the inner cover.

4. Position the selector forks on the shafts as shown in the accompanying illustration and insert the selector fork spindle to hold them in position.

5. Assemble the camplate in the outer cover and locate the selector fork rollers in their camplate tracks.

6. Install the camplate spindle and secure it with a new cotter pin. Install the camplate index plunger and spring.

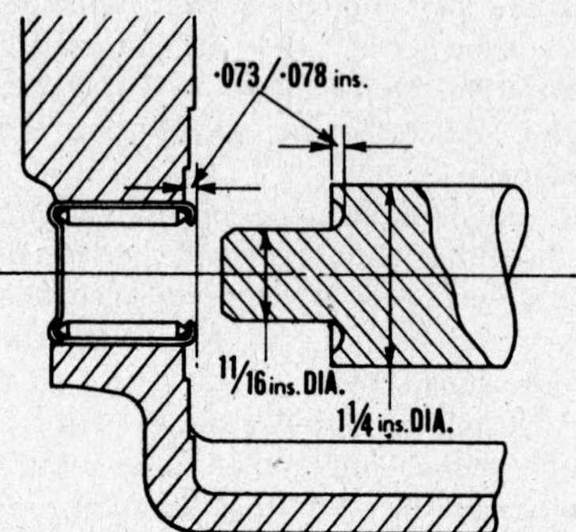

Drift for removing the layshaft left bearing (500 models)

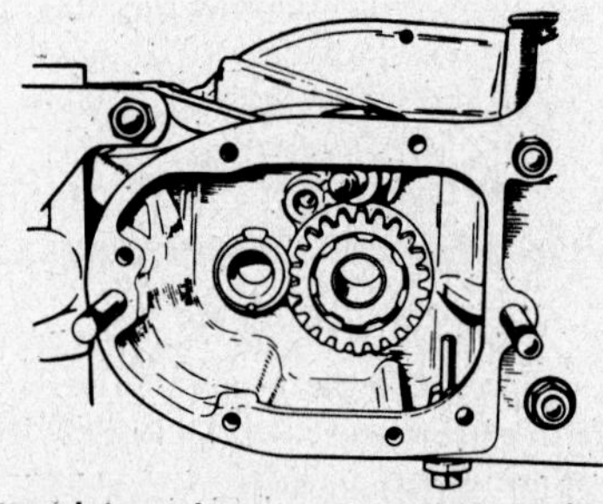
Camplate plunger, layshaft bushing and high gear installed (500 models)

7. Operate the selector forks manually to make sure that each selector fork is on its appropriate shaft. When the camplate is moved to its full extent, both selector rollers should move to the full extent of the camplate grooves in both directions. If not, the selector forks will have to be disengaged and reversed.

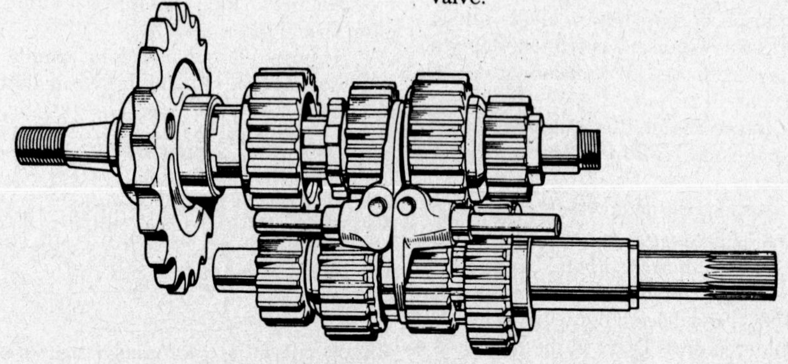
Gearbox cluster assembled (500 models)

8. Install the distance piece over the kick-starter shaft, then secure the end of the return spring with its retaining screw.

NOTE: *Use a screwdriver to tension the return spring before connecting it and installing the return spring plate.*

9. The remainder of the assembly procedure is a reversal of the disassembly instructions.

Bottom End Overhaul

CAMSHAFT SERVICE (Engine Installed)

It is not necessary to separate the crankcase halves in order to replace the camshafts.

Removal And Installation

1. Remove the rocker boxes.

2. Remove the timing cover.

3. Remove the oil pump (see "Lubrication Systems"), and temporarily block the crankcase holes to prevent oil spillage. Make sure you remember to open these holes before reinstalling the oil pump.

4. Extract the intake and exhaust camwheels. The camshaft retaining plates can now be seen.

5. Carefully pull the camshafts out the right side of the machine. Make sure the breather disc and spring, located behind the intake cam, do not fall into the crankcase. Also, lean the machine to the left when removing the cams so that the cam followers do not fall into the crankcase.

Kickstarter return spring installed (500 models)

6. Assemble the rotary breather valve and spring to the new intake camshaft, then install both cams, making certain that the slot in the end of the intake cam fully engages the dog on the breather valve.

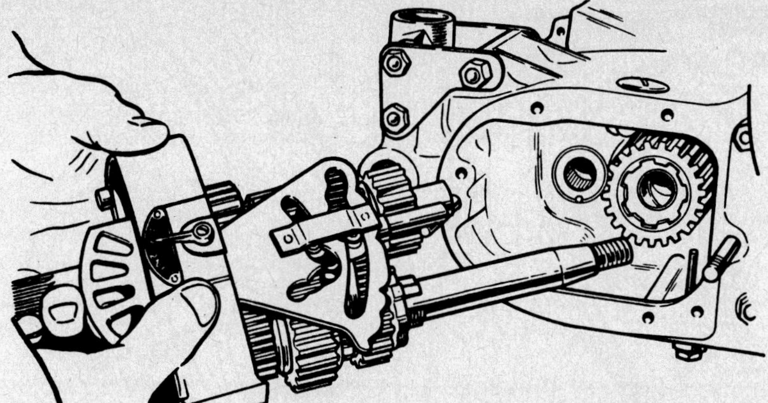
Assembling the gearbox inner cover and case (500 models)

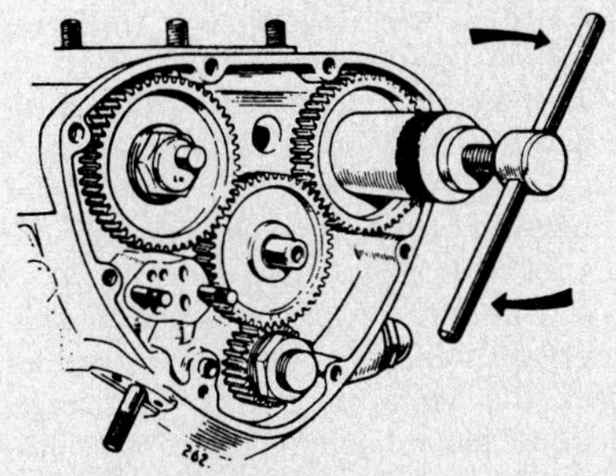
Removing the camwheels with tool no. Z89 (500 models)

7. Reinstall the camshaft retainer plates and secure them in place with new screws.

8. The remainder of the assembly procedure is a reversal of the removal instructions.

CRANKCASE SERVICE

Disassembly

1. Remove the primary chaincase cover and disconnect the alternator leads under the engine.

2. Remove the three screws that secure the alternator stator, and pull the stator off its mounting studs. Do not disconnect the leads at this time.

3. Disassemble the clutch and primary drive as previously described. Remove the stator sleeve and withdraw the stator leads.

4. Remove the gearbox outer cover and dismantle the gearbox.

5. Remove the rocker boxes, cylinder head, cylinder barrel, and pistons.

6. Disconnect the clutch cable and remove the carburetor(s).

7. Remove the contact breaker cover and the oil pump, then remove the crankshaft pinion. The camshaft pinions can also be removed at this time.

8. Remove what's left of the engine from the frame.

9. Clamp the crankcase firmly in a vise at the bottom mounting lug and remove the bolt and two screws shown in the accompanying illustration.

10. Remove the stud at the front of the engine and the two nuts next to the gearbox housing.

11. Attach Triumph extractor no. Z151 and separate the cases.

12. After the cases are apart, remove the crankshaft assembly and put it on a bench where it won't be harmed. Remove the breather valve from within the intake camshaft bushing in the left case.

Crankshaft And Connecting Rods Disassembly

1. Clamp the crankshaft assembly in a soft-jawed vise and place a rag over any sharp edges to protect the connecting rods.

2. Unscrew the cap retainer nuts a little at a time to avoid distortion, then remove the caps and connecting rods.

NOTE: *The connecting rods, caps and nut are center-punched to facilitate reassembly.*

3. Using a large impact driver, unscrew the oil tube retainer plug from the right end of the big-end journal. If necessary, drill a hole ⅛ in. deep and ⅛ in. in diameter to eliminate the locking effect of the plug center punch.

4. Remove the flywheel bolt next to the big-end journal, then pull out the oil tube with a hooked piece of stiff wire through the flywheel bolt location hole.

5. Thoroughly clean all parts in kerosine or a cleaning solvent, then blow them dry with compressed air. Make sure the oil drillways are blown clear.

6. To remove the flywheel, unscrew the two remaining bolts and press the crankshaft out of the right side plain bearing with a five ton press.

NOTE: *Before removing the flywheel, make certain it is marked for reassembly.*

Inspection

Inspect the big-end journals for any signs of scoring, etc., and measure the journal diameter. Compare with specifications. Light score marks can be removed with fine grade emery cloth, but make sure all metal filings are removed before reassembly. If the scoring is light, new connecting rod shell bearings should be installed; if the scoring is extensive, the journals should be reground to an appropriate undersize.

NOTE: *The replaceable big-end bearing shells are pre-sized to give the correct dimensions. Under no circumstances should they be scraped, or the connecting rod and cap filed to alter the bearing dimensions.*

Assembly

1. Position the oil tube in the crankshaft, aligning the flywheel bolt holes with those in the crankshaft. Temporarily install one of the flywheel bolts to secure it in position.

2. Apply thread-locking sealant to the oil tube plug and install it in the crank-

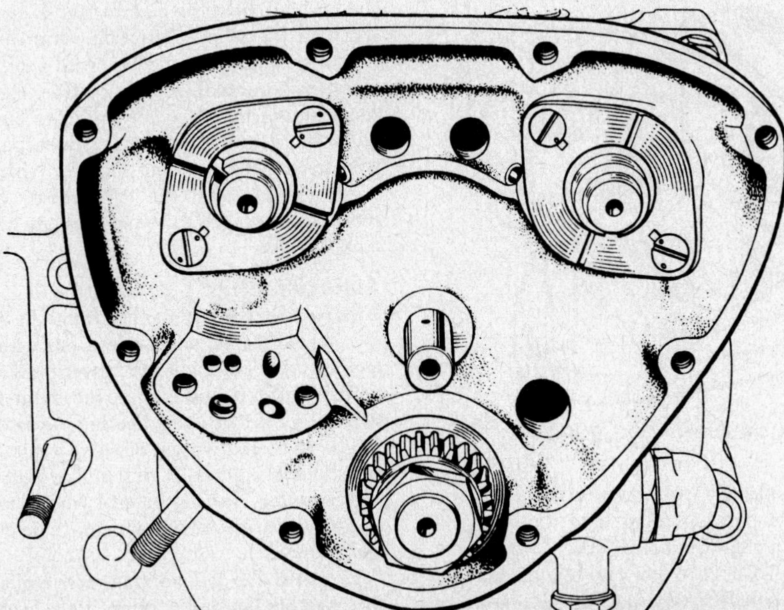
Camwheels removed, showing camshaft retaining plates (500 models)

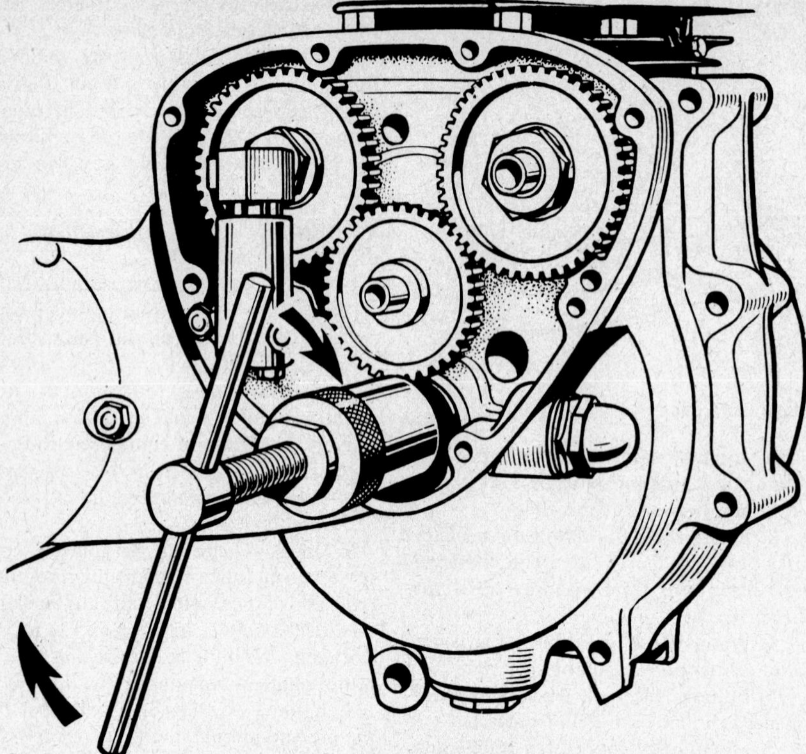

Removing the crankshaft pinion (500 models)

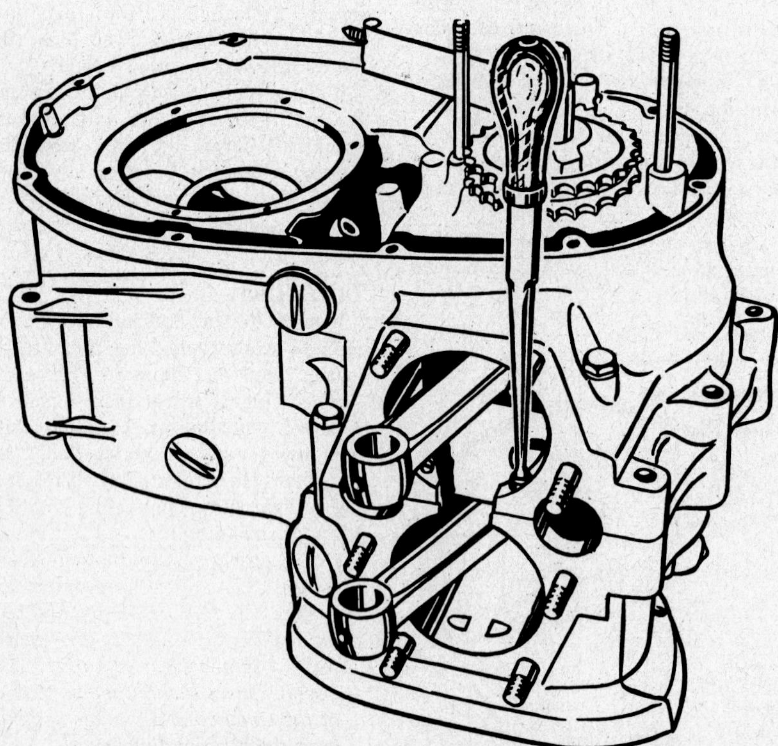

Removing the crankcase retaining screws (500 models)

shaft. Center-punch the crankshaft opposite the slot to lock the plug in position.

3. Heat the flywheel to 100° C, then position it over the crankshaft with the center punch mark to the right. Turn the flywheel through 180° to get it over the crankshaft web, then turn it to the correct position relative to the crankshaft and align the bolt holes.

4. Coat the flywheel bolt threads with a thread-locking sealant, then install and torque them to specifications.

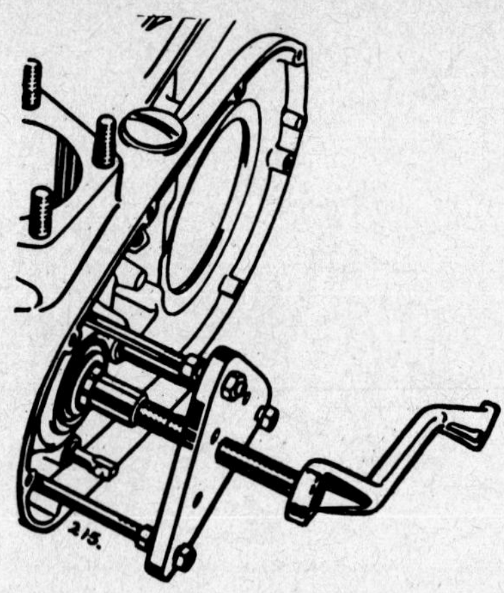

Separating the case halves with tool no. Z151 (500 models)

5. If a new or reground crankshaft, or a new flywheel was installed, the assembly should be rebalanced. This operation is best left to a qualified shop that has the appropriate special tools.

6. Check to make sure all the oil drillways are free from obstruction, then install the connecting rods and caps. Torque the retaining nuts to specifications, or better yet, the bolt extension figure given in the accompanying illustration.

7. Last, force oil through the crankshaft, right main-bearing journal drillway until it is expelled at both big-end bearings. This will provide assurance that the drillway is free from obstruction.

Camshaft Bushings

The intake and exhaust camshafts run in bronze bushings in the left case and are butted directly into the right case. To remove the bushings in the left case, a tap will be necessary. The ideal size is ⅞ in. diameter x 9 whitworth.

When a good thread has been cut in the bushing, heat the case to 100° C and screw in the appropriate bolt. Grip the bolt in a vise and tap the case with a soft-faced mallet until the bushing is free. The replacement bushings are pre-sized but will require a light reaming to meet specifications. After reaming the new bushings, make sure the crankcase is thoroughly cleaned to remove any metal filings.

Main Bearings

To remove the left main bearings, heat the case to 100° C and drive it out with tool no. Z14. The right main bearing is a bronze bushing, and is removed by first removing the lock plate, heating the case to 100° C, then driving it out with a suitable, shouldered drift. It is advisable to replace the left bearing oil seal while the engine is apart, even if it appears to be in good condition.

To install the left bearing, first make sure that its housing is clean, then heat the case to 100° C and drive the bearing

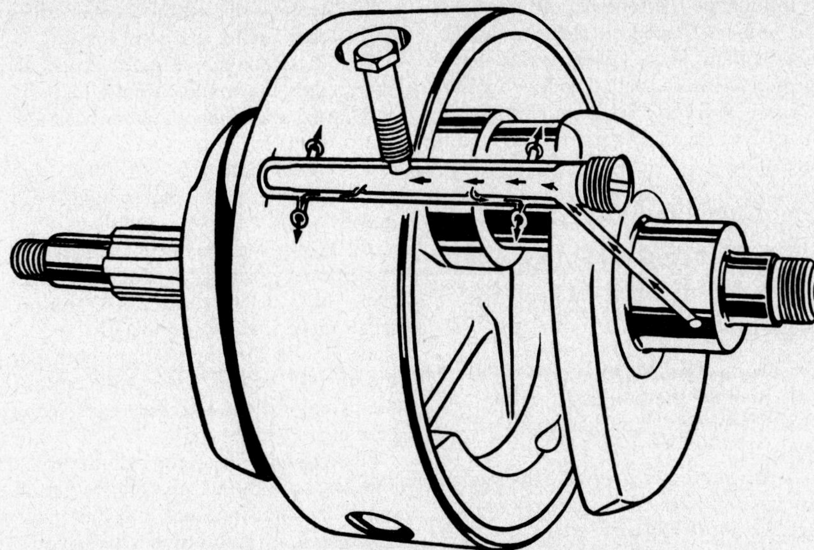

Sectional view of crankshaft assembly (500 models)

into position with a tubular drift the same size as the bearing outer race. A suitable size would be 2¾ in. diameter x 6 in. long.

To install the right bronze bushing, heat the case to 100° C and then press the bushing into position. Let the case cool, then line-ream the bushing to specifications. Tool no. Z134 is available for this purpose. To use it, the case halves must be assembled and the reamer inserted through the right main bearing, with the pilot end located in the left main bearing. Reamer Z134 is also available in 0.010, 0.020, and 0.030 undersizes.

After both bearings have been installed, press the oil seal into the left case.

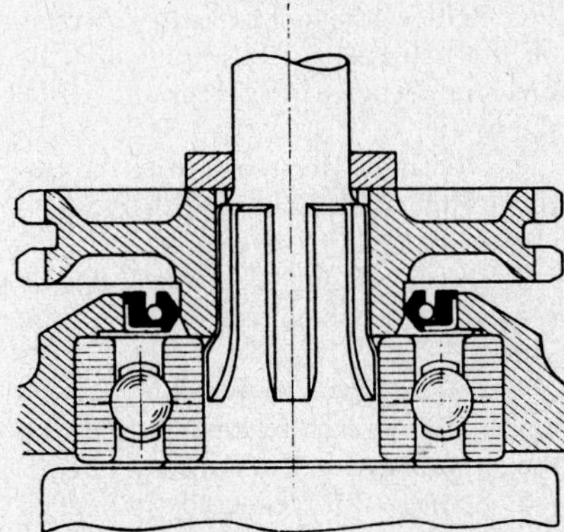

Left case oil seal and main bearing (500 models)

CRANKCASE ASSEMBLY

1. Thoroughly clean the mating crankcase halves, giving special attention to the locating dowels.
2. Position the left case on two wooden blocks, lubricate the main bearing and camshaft bushings and then install the breather valve and spring in the intake cam bushing. Assemble both camshafts, making sure the intake cam slot engages the breather valve dog.
3. Carefully install the crankshaft assembly, making sure the fit in the bearing is good.
4. Apply fresh joining compound to the mating surfaces, then position the connecting rods in the center and lower the right case over the crankshaft. When the halves are mated, check to make sure the crankshaft and camshafts are not binding. The crankshaft should rotate freely, while the camshafts should offer only slight resistance.
5. The remainder of the assembly procedure is a reversal of the disassembly instructions. Make sure all timing pinions are correctly located.

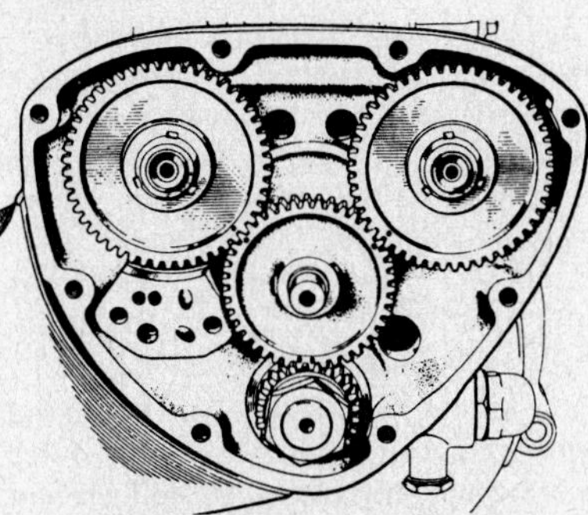

Timing gear marks (T100C)

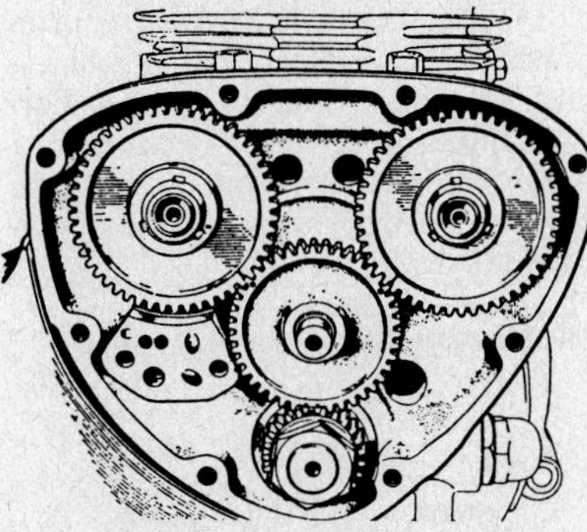

Timing gear marks (T100R)

650 AND 750 TWINS

Engine Removal and Installation

TR6R, TR6C, AND T120R

1. Turn off the fuel petcock, then disconnect and plug the fuel lines.
2. Remove the three securing bolts and the fuel tank.
3. Remove the main fuse from its holder, then disconnect the right and left ignition coil leads.
4. Remove the securing bolts and the two ignition coils. Disconnect the oil pressure switch on the timing cover.
5. Remove the attaching nuts and bolts, then remove the front and rear torque stays from the cylinder head.
6. Disconnect the tachometer drive cable from the right-angle gearbox at the front of the engine.
7. Disconnect the throttle cable at the carburetor(s).
8. On single carburetor engines, remove the air cleaner.
9. Remove the carburetor(s).
10. Disconnect the rocker oil feed line, taking care not to bend it excessively.
11. Drain the engine sump, oil tank, and transmission.
12. Disconnect all lines from the oil tank.
13. Back off the clutch adjustment at the handlebar until there is plenty of slack, then disconnect the cable at the operating arm on the right side of the engine.
14. Remove the exhaust headers and mufflers.
15. Disconnect the final drive-chain master link and remove the chain.
16. Disconnect the two generator leads at the bottom of the engine.
17. Remove the front chainguard securing bolt and loosen the rear mounting bolt. Pull the chainguard back several inches to get it out of the way.
18. Remove the four bolts and one nut securing the left and right rear engine-mounting plates. Remove the plates.
19. Remove the nuts and washers from one side of the front upper and lower mounting plates.
20. Remove both right-side rocker boxes.
21. Remove the left lower bolts securing the rear frame to the front frame.
22. Pull out the front upper and lower mounting studs, then lift the engine out the left side of the frame. A helper at this point will greatly reduce the possibility of dropping the engine.

Installation is basically a reversal of the removal procedure. To make sure the wiring harness is properly connected, refer to the appropriate wiring diagram.

TR7V, T140V

1. Shut off the fuel taps, and disconnect the fuel lines. Remove the rubber cap from the top, center, of the gas tank, and remove the sleeve nut below. Take the tank off the frame.
2. Detach the torque stay from the engine by removing the two nuts securing the stay to the cylinder head and removing the bolt and nut from the frame.
3. Disconnect the tachometer cable at the engine.
4. Remove the header pipes and mufflers.
5. Disconnect the oil pressure switch at the timing cover, the clutch cable at the engine, the contact breaker, coil, and alternator leads.
6. Remove the carburetor(s) from the manifold(s) and pull away from the air cleaner.
7. Drain the oil from the frame backbone oil reservoir by means of the drain plug at the very bottom of the reservoir.
8. Disconnect the oil feed line from the bottom of the reservoir, and the oil return line at the top. Disconnect the rocker feed line at the top of the reservoir.
9. Drain the oil from the gearbox and the primary chaincase. Drain the crankcase sump.
10. Disconnect the crankcase breather hoses at the left, rear of the crankcase by loosening the hose clamp screws.
11. Remove the chainguard by removing the securing bolt and loosening the left side bottom shock absorber bolt. Pull the chainguard out of the back of the bike.
12. Remove the drive chain masterlink and disengage the chain from the gearbox sprocket.
13. Remove both footpegs.
14. Remove the two rear engine mounting plates each of which are secured by five nuts and bolts. Remove the bottom and front engine mounting studs. Note the location of the spacers. For both studs, the wide spacer is installed on the right side of the motorcycle.
15. Remove the engine from the left side of the frame.

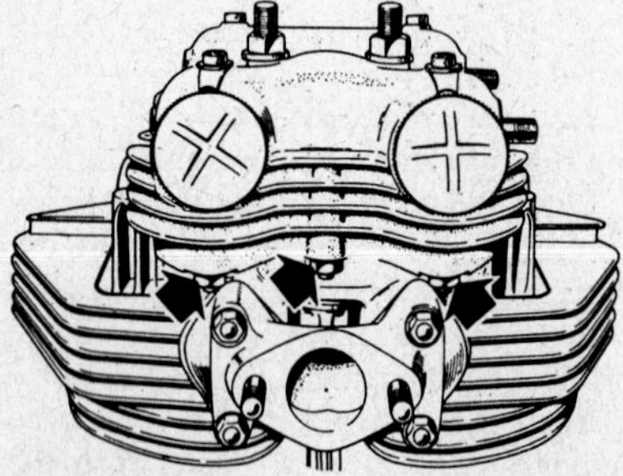

Exhaust rocker box securing nuts (650 models)

Installation is essentially the reverse of the removal procedure. Refer to the wiring diagrams in the "Electrical Systems" section to insure that all connections are correct. Refer to "Tune-Up and Maintenance" for the proper grades and quantities of oil.

Top End Overhaul

CYLINDER HEAD AND BARREL

650 Twins

REMOVAL

1. Remove the fuel tank.
2. Disconnect the battery terminal leads.
3. Disconnect and remove the secondary ignition coils, taking care not to damage the alloy cases.
4. Remove the front and rear torque stays.
5. Disconnect the rocker oil feed line, taking care not to bend it excessively.
6. Remove the rocker inspection caps.
7. Remove the three nuts from the securing studs on the underside of the exhaust rocker box.
8. Remove the exhaust rocker box outer securing bolts and the central cylinder-head bolts.
9. Remove the intake rocker box in the same manner, noting that the outer securing bolts may have to be loosened only a little at a time because of clearance difficulties.
10. Make sure to collect the six plain washers that fit underneath the securing nuts. They often stick to the cylinder-head flanges.
11. Withdraw and lay out the pushrods so that they can be installed in their original position.

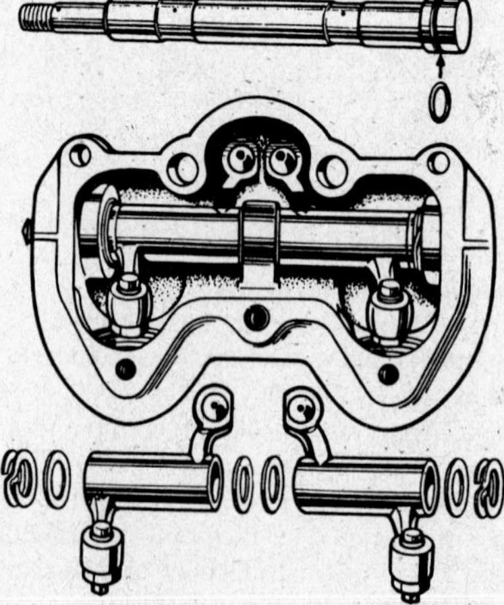

Rocker box assembly (650 models)

12. Remove the carburetor(s) and the intake manifold.
13. Remove the exhaust header pipes.
14. Loosen the cylinder head nuts, a little at a time, in a cross pattern. Lift off the cylinder head.
15. Remove the pushrod cover tubes and rubber O-ring seals.
16. Check the tappet guide blocks for sharp edges that could cut into the pushrod O-ring seals. Smooth out any of these sharp edges or rough areas with a fine grade emery cloth.
17. Remove the copper cylinder-head gasket.
18. Wedge a piece of rubber between the intake and exhaust tappets to prevent them from falling into the crankcase when the cylinder is removed.
19. Rotate the engine until both pistons are at top dead center, then remove the cylinder block attaching nuts at the base of the block.
20. Carefully lift up the cylinder block and, as soon as there is enough room, stuff some clean lint-free rags into the crankcase openings. At this time it is also advisable to fit rubber protectors (or a suitable substitute) over the cylinder base studs.
21. Remove the cylinder base gasket and make sure the two locating dowels are in position on the crankcase.
22. Remove the tappets from the cylinder block and mark them for reassembly.
23. Invert the cylinder head on a bench, remove the locking bolts, then drive out the tappet guide blocks with a suitable drift. Make sure the intake and exhaust guide blocks are marked for reassembly, as the exhaust block has drilled oilways and the intake block does not.

TR7V, T140V

REMOVAL

1. Remove the fuel tank after shutting off the petcocks and disconnecting the fuel lines. Remove the carburetor(s) from the head.
2. Disconnect the wires from the battery terminals. Remove the exhaust pipes and mufflers.
3. Disconnect the rocker feed line by removing the domed nut on each rocker spindle.
4. Remove the torque stay by removing the nut at each rocker box. Remove the torque stay bolt and nut on the frame.
5. Remove the rocker box inspection covers. Also remove the three nuts from the studs beneath each rocker box. Account for the washer on each of the studs.
6. Remove the securing bolts on the opposite side of each rocker box, and finally the two larger securing nuts on top. Remove the rocker boxes from the head.
7. Remove the pushrods and place them in a safe place.
8. There are ten cylinder head nuts and bolts. Loosen each one a single turn at a time until they can be turned easily, then remove them. Lift off the cylinder head.

9. New o-rings must be used on the ends of the pushrod cover tubes. New rocker box gaskets should also be used. Be sure that the rocker box mating surfaces are in good condition before refitting.

ROCKER BOXES

Disassembly And Inspection

1. Carefully drive out the rocker spindle, using a soft metal drift.
2. Remove the rocker arms and washers.
3. Remove the rocker oil seals.
4. If the rocker ball pins require replacement, drive them out with a suitable drift, then press in the new ones with the drilled flat toward the rocker spindle.
5. Thoroughly clean all metal parts in kerosine, then inspect them for signs of excessive wear. Roll the pushrods on a perfectly flat surface (such as a piece of plate glass) to make sure they are straight.

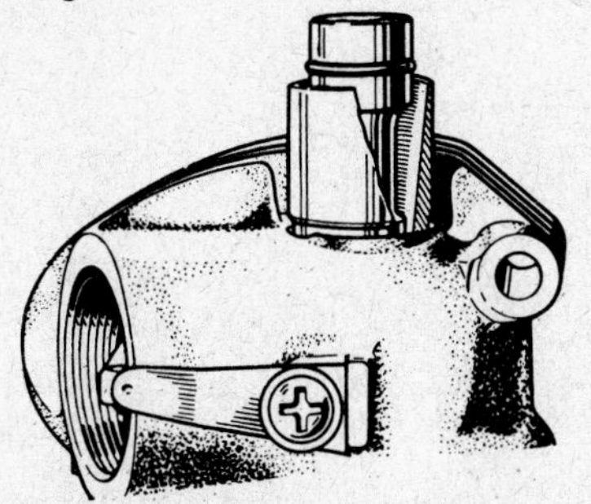

Installing the rocker box spindle (650 models)

Assembly

1. Assemble the rocker boxes using Triumph seal compressor D2221 and a 7/16 x 6 in. bolt with one end ground to a taper.
2. Apply grease to two of the plain washers and position them on either side of the center spindle bearing boss.
3. Position the left rocker arm and insert the alignment bolt, then install the outer plain and spring washers.
4. Position the right rocker arm in the same manner.
5. Install a new oil seal on the spindle, then coat the whole spindle with oil.
6. Slide the spindle into seal compressor no. D2221 (or a suitable replacement) and through the rocker box, pushing the alignment bolt out the other end. The final positioning of the spindle may require a few taps with a hammer and soft metal drift.

VALVES AND VALVE SPRINGS

Removal And Inspection

NOTE: *This operation requires the use of a "G" clamp-type, valve spring compressor.*

1. Compress the valve springs with the spring compressor and remove the split retainers with a narrow, straight-slot screwdriver.
2. Remove each valve and spring, making certain they are marked and matched for reassembly.

NOTE: *The intake and exhaust valves are marked "IN" and "EX," respectively.*

3. Thoroughly clean all parts in kerosine or cleaning solvent and allow them to dry completely.
4. Inspect the valves for pitting, broken edges, etc., and measure valve spring strength with a spring tester. The acceptable tolerances are given at the end of this chapter.
5. The installation of a new or reground valve necessitates grinding of the valve seat, but does not require recutting the cylinder head valve seat unless new valve guides have been installed.

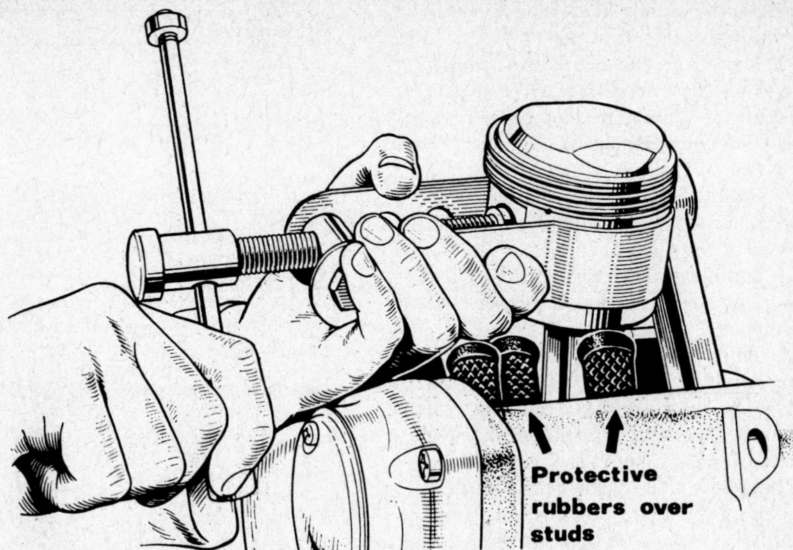

Removing the piston pin (650 models)

Installation

1. Assemble the inner and outer springs with the top and bottom cups over the valve guide.
2. Lubricate the valve stem with a little graphite oil, then slide the valve into position.
3. Compress the spring and install the two retainer halves in the exposed groove of the valve stem.

VALVE GUIDES

Triumph engines are equipped with replaceable bronze valve guides. To remove an old guide, use Triumph special tool 61–6013 or fabricate one to the dimensions given. This is a mild steel bar about 5 in. long and 0.5 in. diameter with a 1 in. section at one end machined to 5/16 in. When installing the new guide, first lightly grease the guide then press or drive it into place, using the special tool. When new valve guides have been installed, it will be necessary to recut the valve seats and grind in the valves.

NOTE: *The intake and exhaust valve guides are almost identical in appearance, except in length. The shorter guides are for the intake valves and the longer guides are for the exhaust valves.*

Valve Reseating

If the valve guides have been replaced, or the valve seats are in poor condition, it is advisabelt to recut the cylinder head seat and grind in the valve with a fine-grade grinding paste.

PISTON AND CYLINDER BARREL SERVICE

Tappets And Guide Blocks

The only noticeable tappet wear is in the center of the Stellite tip. An indentation greater than 3/32 in. indicates that the tappet should be replaced.

It is not necessary to remove the guide blocks to check wear. Simply rock the tappets in their respective guide block bores and note the amount of lateral freeplay; there should be little or no movement.

Cylinder Barrel

In order to accurately measure cylinder wear, several measurements should be made at different heights in the barrel, both parallel and perpendicular to the piston pin. If there is a difference of 0.13 mm (0.005 in.) between any of these measurements, the cylinder should be rebored and/or honed.

Use an inside micrometer to make the measurements. Although there are alternative methods, none of them approach the micrometer's accuracy.

Pistons, Rings, And Piston Pins Removal

1. Remove the rocker boxes, cylinder

head, and cylinder block as previously described.

2. Make sure the crankcase opening edges are covered with lint-free rags to protect the aluminum alloy connecting rod from being damaged.

3. Remove the inner and outer piston pin retaining circlips, then attach a piston pin removal tool (see illustration) and press out the pin.

4. Lay out and mark the piston(s), piston pin(s), and retaining circlips for reassembly.

5. Remove the piston rings one at a time by lifting an end of the ring out of its groove and holding a thin piece of metal between it and the piston. Slide the piece of metal around the circumference of the piston while at the same time gently lifting the raised part of the ring upwards.

Piston Inspection

Inspect the piston skirt for any signs of scoring or seizure. These will show up as burnt or rough areas between the rings and the bottom of the piston, and are usually cause for piston replacement. If the rough spot or burned area is small or minor, however, it can often be cleaned up with a fine-grade emery cloth.

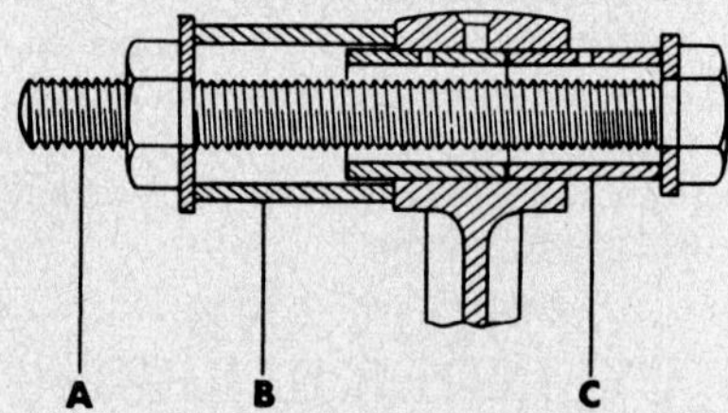

Piston pin bushing replacement. A—bolt, B—tubing collar and C—new bushing

Replacement pistons are available in three or four oversizes. These sizes and the corresponding recommended cylinder bore sizes are given in a chart at the end of this section.

TR7V and T140V pistons are available in four oversizes in increments of 0.010 in. Also note that the cylinders and pistons for these models are paired up according to a three-step grading system when the engine is assembled at the factory. There are three sizes "L" (Low), "M" (Medium), and "H" (High).

Refer to the accompanying illustrations for cylinder bore and piston skirt measurement points. Then refer to the "Suitable Re-bore Sizes" chart at the end of this section.

Piston Pin And Small End Bushing

Inspect the piston pin for center "step wear," scoring, or burring, then slide it into the small-end connecting rod bushing, and make certain that there is no lateral free-play. If there is, replace the bushing in the following manner:

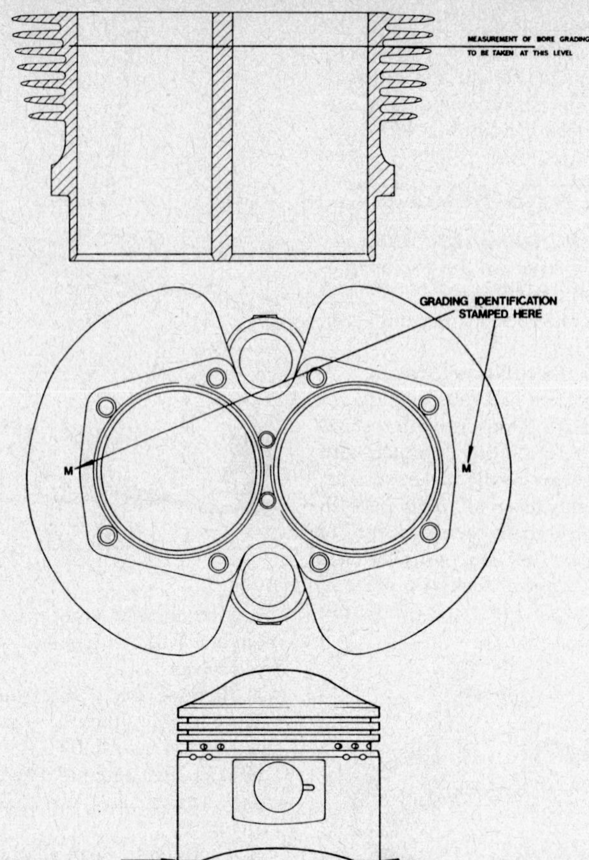

750 Twin piston and cylinder information. Arrows at piston skirt bottom indicate the piston diameter measurement point.

1. Find a threaded bolt approximately 4 in. in length and a piece of tubing 1¼ in. long with an inside diameter of ⅞ in.

2. Place a suitable washer and the new bushing on the bolt, then insert the end of the bolt through the old bushing.

3. Place the piece of tubing over the end of the bolt and screw the nut on finger-tight

4. Centralize the new bushing and align the oil drillway with that in the old bushing.

5. Now tighten the nut on the bolt and the new bushing will extract the old one.

6. Ream the new bushing to the size given in specifications at the end of this chapter. Make sure all metal filings are removed.

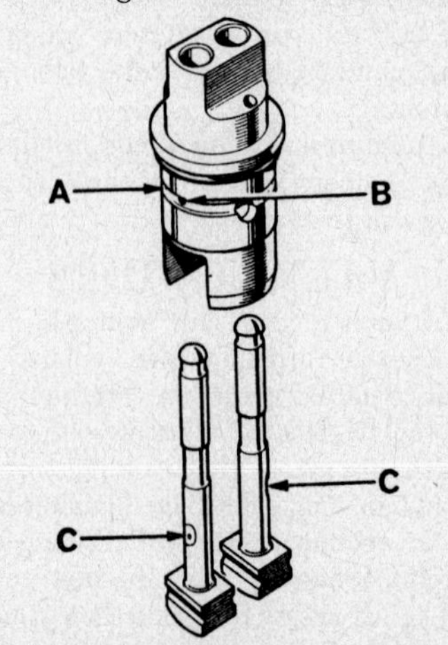

Correct tappet and guide block assembly (650 models)

Piston Rings

Piston ring wear is checked by measuring the ring end gap. This is done by positioning the ring in the cylinder and pushing it to the bottom of the bore with a piston, then measuring the end gap with a feeler gauge. Check this figure with specifications at the end of this section and determine if the ring requires replacement.

Before assembling an engine with new rings, the cylinder bore should be lightly honed in a cross-hatch pattern. This can also be accomplished with no. 300 grade emery cloth.

Installation

1. Install the piston rings one at a time over the top of the piston. Note that the two compression rings are marked "TOP" to ensure correct assembly position.

2. Position the piston on the connecting rod.

3. Install one new retaining circlip as a stop, then press the piston pin into position and install another new circlip on the other side.

NOTE: *If there is no alternative and the piston pin must be driven into its bore, it is advisable to heat the piston to 100° C prior to assembly.*

TOP END ASSEMBLY

1. Position new guide block O-ring seals at the base of the cylinder block.

2. Lightly grease the outside surface of the exhaust guide block, then carefully align the guide block and cylinder locating holes and drive the block into position with Triumph special tool no. 61–6008 or a suitable drift.

3. Repeat the above step for the intake guide block, then install the locking bolts.

4. After installing the guide blocks, make sure that the exhaust guide block oil drillways are free from obstruction.

5. Install the tappets in the guide blocks as shown in the accompanying illustration, after thoroughly lubricating them with oil. Wedge them into position.

6. Install the cylinder base gasket, making certain that the gasket does not obscure the oil feed drillway in the crankcase.

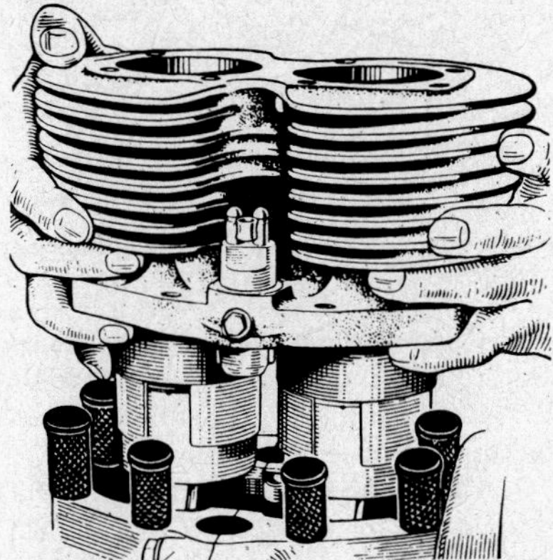

Installing the cylinder barrel (650 models)

7. Fit ring compressors over the pistons, then carefully slide the cylinder down over the pistons. Remove the ring compressors as soon as the rings are positioned within the cylinder. Continue lowering the cylinder block and then remove the rags in the crankcase openings as late as possible.

8. Install the cylinder base attaching nuts.

9. Replace or anneal the cylinder head gasket.

10. Clean the mating cylinder head and cylinder surfaces, then grease the gasket and position it on the cylinder.

11. Coat the tappet guide blocks with grease and position the pushrod cover tubes with new O-ring seals.

12. Position the cylinder head and install the head nuts and bolts finger-tight.

13. Place a small amount of grease in the bottom cup of each pushrod, then locate the intake pushrods in their respective bores. This will have to be done by "feel."

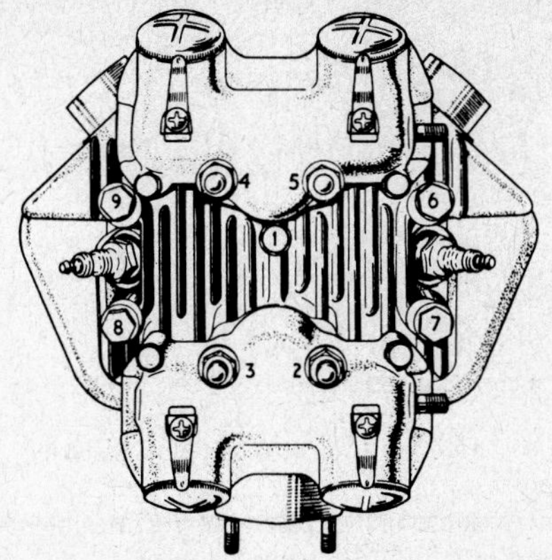

Cylinder head bolt tightening sequence (650 models)

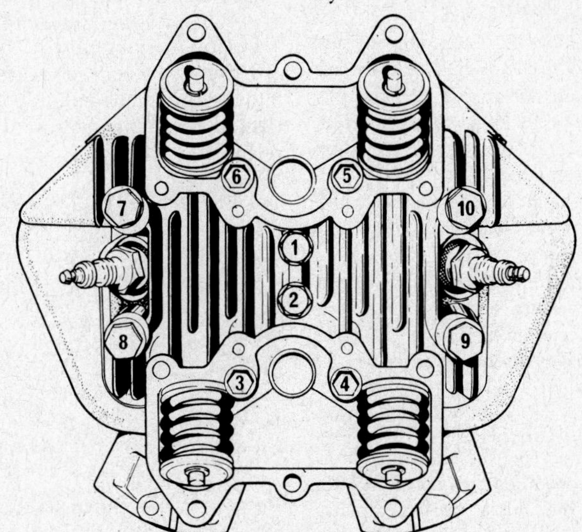

Cylinder head bolt tightening order (750 Twins).

14. When the pushrods are properly positioned, remove the spark plugs and turn the engine over until both intake pushrods are level and at the bottom of their travel.

15. Install the intake rocker box.

16. Repeat the above procedure for the exhaust rocker box, noting that the central cylinder-head bolts should be tightened to torque specifications before tightening the underside securing nuts.

17. Turn the engine over several times to make sure the valves are operating properly, then reinstall the torque stays and secondary ignition coils.

18. Connect the rocker oil feed line, using either new copper washers or annealed, used ones.

19. The remainder of the assembly procedure is a reversal of the disassembly instructions. Adjust valve tappet clearances.

Clutch And Primary Drive

CLUTCH SERVICE

Service procedures are basically the same for the 650 and 750cc twins, except that the larger models have a triplex primary drive chain in place of the duplex chain found on the 650.

Disassembly

1. Remove the left exhaust header pipe.

2. Loosen the rear brake adjustment until the pedal drops clear of the primary cover.

3. Remove the left footrest.

4. Drain the oil from the chaincase, then remove the chain tension adjuster.

5. Remove the ten, recessed, cover-securing screws and withdraw the cover and paper gasket.

6. Remove the chain tensioner assembly.

7. The clutch pressure plate is held in place by three, slotted adjuster nuts. To remove these nuts, slide a knife or screwdriver blade under the nut and loosen it with Triumph tool no. D364 (supplied with tool kit) or a suitable substitute.

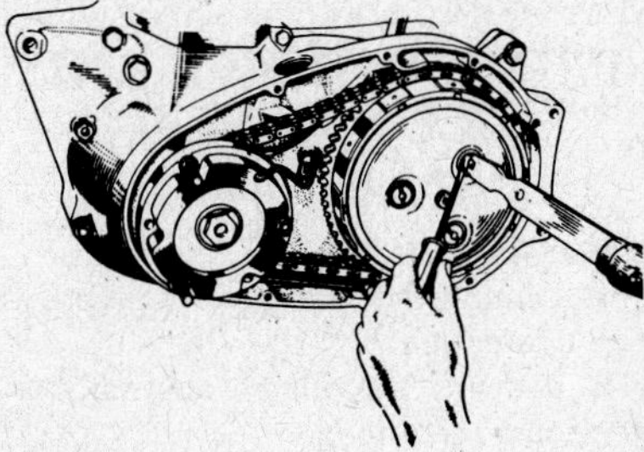

Removing the clutch pressure plate (650 models)

8. Remove the clutch springs, cups, and pressure plate assembly.

9. The clutch plates can be removed with the use of two, narrow, hooked tools made of 1/32 in. wire.

Inspection

1. The clutch plates should appear to be in good condition. If the thickness of the discs is 0.030 in. (0.75 mm), or more,

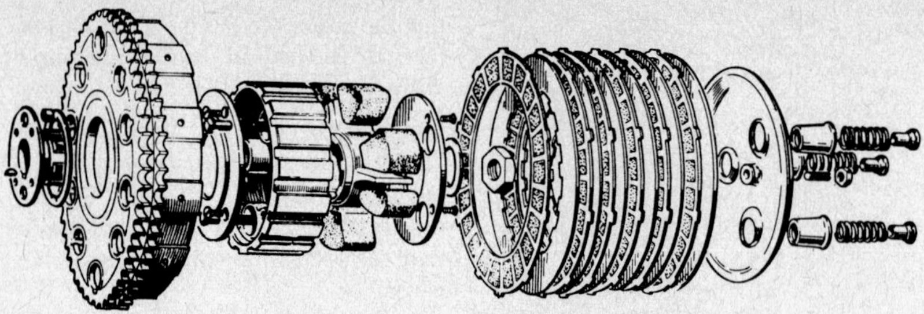
Exploded view of clutch assembly (650 models)

less than specified, they should be replaced.

2. Check that the tabs at the outer edge of the discs are not worn or rounded and that the clutch sprocket slots are not damaged. If there are burrs on the tabs, the discs must be replaced.

3. Place the clutch plates on a flat surface, such as a piece of glass. If they can be rocked from side to side or if there is any evidence of buckling, they should be replaced. Also replace the plates if they are scored in any way.

4. Check the fit of the plate on the shock absorber unit. There should be little radial clearance.

5. Measure the clutch spring length and compare with specifications. If a spring has shortened by 0.10 in. (2.5 mm) or more, replace the whole set.

Assembly

1. Install the clutch plates and discs, keeping in mind that the innermost position must be occupied by a bonded plate.

2. Install the cups, pressure plate, springs, and slotted adjuster nuts.

3. True the clutch pressure plate by first tightening the pressure-plate, slotted adjuster nuts until they are even with the clutch pins, and then by kicking with engine over and observing the rotation of the plate, and then making any necessary adjustment until the plate turns evenly. If the plate wobbles even slightly, it must be corrected.

PRIMARY DRIVE AND CLUTCH HUB SERVICE

Disassembly

1. Remove the primary cover as previously described.

2. Remove the clutch assembly as previously described.

3. Disconnect the alternator stator leads at their snap connectors under the engine.

4. Remove the three, stator securing nuts and withdraw the stator from over its mounting studs. Unscrew the sleeve nut and then the lead can easily be removed.

5. To remove the rotor, bend back the tab washer, put the transmission in fourth gear, hold the rear brake, and then remove the mainshaft locknut.

6. Remove the rotor key and distance piece.

7. Remove the clutch hub securing nut and cup.

NOTE: *Machines prior to serial no. H49833 have a tab washer and a different cup washer, rather than the self-locking securing nut.*

8. Screw the body of extractor no. Z13 into the clutch hub until it bottoms, then tighten the center bolt until the hub is released.

Removing the clutch center bolt with tool no. Z13 (650 models)

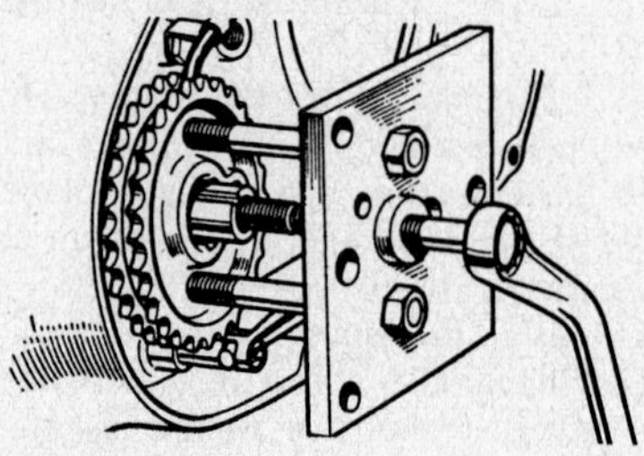
Removing the engine sprocket (650 models)

9. Assemble extractor no. Z151 and D662/3 on the engine sprocket and tighten its center bolt until the engine sprocket is released.

10. Withdraw the engine sprocket, clutch hub, and primary chain together.

11. Remove the transmission mainshaft key and check the oil seal for leakage.

Inspection

1. Inspect the clutch shock absorber for worn rubbers or punctures. They can be removed by prying them out, small rubbers first. Replace as necessary. When reassembling, apply thread-locking compound to the cover-plate securing screws.

2. First thoroughly clean the primary chain then check it for wear by scribing two marks on a flat surface 12 in. apart, and centering two pivot pins at the scribe marks. Fully compressed, the chain link pivot should line up with the marks; fully stretched, it should not extend more than ¼ in. beyond the marks.

3. Check the chain sprockets for rounded or hooked teeth, and replace *both* if necessary. If the sprockets are replaced, also install a new chain. This will prevent the old chain from prematurely wearing out the new sprockets.

4. Check the fit between the shock absorber spider and the clutch hub splines. The spider should be a push fit on the clutch hub, with no radial movement.

5. Check the fit of the engine sprocket on the crankshaft in the same manner. There should be no radial movement.

Removing the clutch hub shock absorber rubbers (650 models)

6. Check the clutch hub bearing diameter, rollers, and clutch sprocket bearing. Replace any bearing rollers that are pitted or worn. See specifications.

7. Check the clutch operating rod for straightness by rolling it on a known flat surface, such as a piece of plate glass.

8. Make sure the shock absorber spider is a good fit in the inner and outer retaining plates, and that the arms have not excessively scored the inner surface of the retaining plates.

Assembly

1. Grease the clutch hub and install the thrust washer and twenty of the correct rollers. Do not use ¼ in. x ¼ in. rollers!

2. Position the hub and press the shock absorber, complete with the three threaded pins, on the hub.

3. Install a new tapered distance collar behind the engine sprocket, with the taper toward the crankshaft main bearing and oil seal.

4. Install the transmission mainshaft key and tap the clutch hub onto its taper.

5. Lubricate the primary chain and lay it over the clutch sprocket.

6. Wrap the chain around the engine sprocket, then position the sprocket on the crankshaft.

7. Place clutch-locking tool Z13 in the clutch plate housing, then install the cup

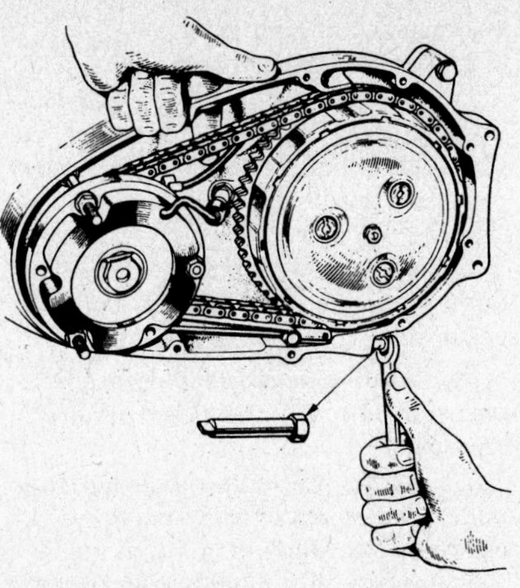

Adjusting primary chain tension (650 models)

washer and self-locking nut. Torque the nut to specifications.

NOTE: *On machines before serial no. H49833, install the tab washer with the long tab in the hole in the shock absorber spider, install the securing nut and bend a tab to lock the nut.*

8. Install the alternator rotor, making sure that the key or locating peg is correctly positioned.

9. Install the alternator stator. Put a 0.-008 in. (0.2 mm) feeler gauge between each stator pole and the rotor. Turn over the engine to make sure that the rotor and stator do not touch.

10. The remainder of the assembly procedure is a reversal of the disassembly instructions. Remember to fill the primary case with oil and adjust the primary chain tension for ½ in. free-play.

TRANSMISSION COUNTERSHAFT SPROCKET

Removal And Installation

1. Disassemble the clutch and primary drive as previously described. Remove the sprocket cover.

2. Bend back the tab washer and, while holding the rear brake, remove the sprocket securing nut.

3. Slide off the final drive chain and remove the countershaft sprocket.

4. Make sure the oil seal is in good condition, then lubricate the ground boss of the new sprocket and position it on the transmission mainshaft.

5. Replace the tab washer, screw on the securing nut finger-tight, then, with the chain in place, tighten the nut to torque specifications.

6. Oil the bushing that protrudes from the mainshaft high gear and install the sprocket cover with a new paper gasket.

7. The remainder of installation is a reversal of the removal procedure.

Shifter, Kick-Starter, And Clutch Operating Mechanisms

DISASSEMBLY

1. Remove the right exhaust header pipe.

2. Remove the right footrest.

3. Loosen the clutch cable adjustment at the handlebar lever, then disconnect the cable end from the operating lever in the gearbox outer cover.

4. Drain the gearbox oil into a suitable container.

5. Put the transmission in high gear.

6. Remove the top and bottom nuts and recessed screws that secure the gearbox outer cover. Depress the kick-start lever slightly and tap the cover lightly until it is free.

7. Loosen the kick-starter cotter pin nut a few turns, then drive out the cotter pin.

8. Slide the lever off the shaft and remove the kick-starter quadrant and spring assembly.

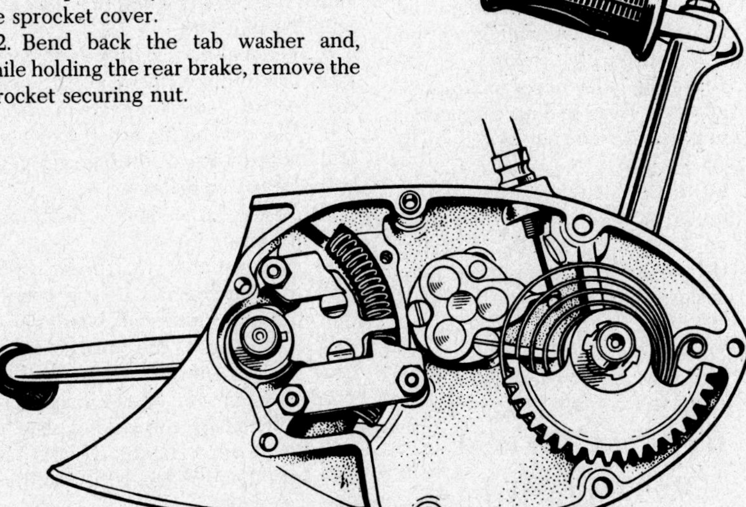

Gearbox outer cover assembled (650 models)

9. Apply the rear brake, bend back the tab washer, and remove the kick-starter ratchet pinion securing nut.

10. Remove the pinion, ratchet, spring, and sleeve.

11. If the kick-starter quadrant is to be replaced, drive out the spindle with a suitable drift and hammer. Install the new spindle so that the kick-starter lever location flat is correctly positioned with respect to the quadrant.

12. Remove the shifter foot pedal from the shaft.

13. Remove the guide plate, plunger quadrant, and curved return springs.

14. Remove the two screws that secure the clutch operating mechanism. Remove the securing cotter pin and disassemble the mechanism.

INSPECTION AND SERVICE

Kick-Starter

Examine the kick-starter quadrant for chipped or broken teeth. Make sure the spindle is not loose and check the return spring for stress cracks or metal fatigue, especially where it engages the spindle splines. Examine the spindle bushing for wear and, if possible, measure the inside diameter and compare with specifications. If a measuring device is not available, install the spindle and note the amount of free-play it has within the bushing.

Inspect the ratchet teeth for burrs, chips, or rounded edges. Make sure the ratchet spring is in good condition and that the thin-walled steel bushing is a clearance fit in the kick-start pinoin. Examine the kick-starter stop peg to make certain it is firmly pressed into the inner cover and is not distorted in any way.

If it is necessary to replace the kick-start spindle bushing, heat the cover to 100° C, then drive out the bushing with a suitable, shouldered drift. Drive in the new bushing while the cover is still hot.

Shifter

Examine the shifter mechanism plungers for wear and make sure they operate smoothly in the quadrant. Compare plunger spring free-length with specifications. Also check the plunger guide plate for wear and grooving on the taper guide surfaces. Replace the plate if grooves have been formed.

Inspect the shifter pedal return springs for fatigue and corrosion, and examine the shifter quadrant bushing for wear by installing the quadrant and noting any freeplay. Also check the tips of the plungers and camplate operating quadrant for chipping and excessive wear.

If the shifter spindle bushing requires replacement (outer cover), heat the cover surrounding the bushing to 100° C

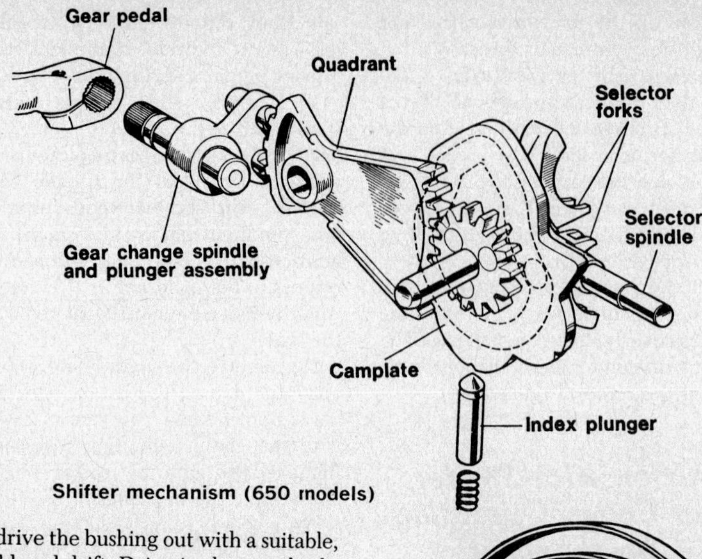

Shifter mechanism (650 models)

and drive the bushing out with a suitable, shouldered drift. Drive in the new bushing before the cover has a chance to cool.

The inner cover spindle bushing will probably never need replacement, since it suffers an insignificant amount of wear. If it does require replacement, however, it will be necessary to tap the bushing, heat the cover, install an appropriate bolt and then drive it out.

Clutch Operating Mechanism

The clutch operating mechanism is constantly immersed in oil, so wear should be negligible. Inspect the balls for pitting, etc., and make sure they operate smoothly in the plates.

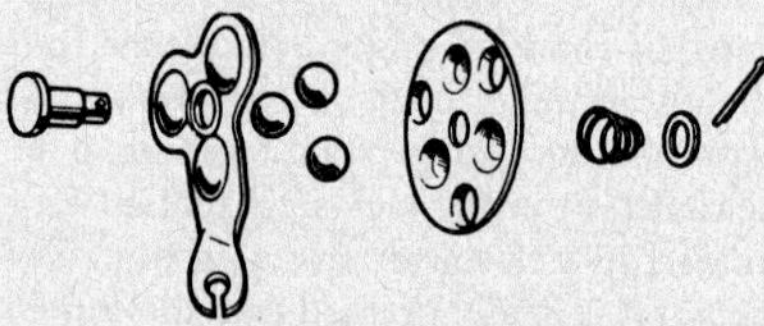
Clutch operating mechanism (650 models)

1. Assemble and install the clutch operating mechanism, using the accompanying illustration for reference.
2. Install a new rubber O-ring on the shifter spindle and install the spindle in the outer cover bushing, using a few drops of oil to aid installation.
3. Install the two quadrant-return springs, making certain they are correctly located over the step in the cover.

NOTE: *To facilitate connecting of the springs, first install the shifter pedal and clamp it in place, thereby allowing the quadrant to turn and the springs to be* compressed.

4. Install the retainer plate with its four securing nuts and lock washers.
5. Install the plungers and springs, taking care that they don't go springing off somewhere during assembly.
6. Install the kick-starter thin-walled steel sleeve, spring pinion, and ratchet.
7. Install the tab washer and the retaining nut, then torque the nut to specifications and lock it by bending up the washer tab. Do not overtorque the nut as it may cause the thin sleeve to collapse.

Kickstarter return spring installed (650 models)

8. Connect the return spring to the kick-starter quadrant as shown in the accompanying illustration.
9. Install the spindle in the kick-starter bushing and connect the return spring to the anchor peg at the rear of the cover.
10. Install the oil seal over the spindle and assemble the kick-starter lever and securing cotter pin.
11. Clean the outer cover joining surface and apply fresh sealing compound. Make sure the two locating dowels are in position.
12. Move the kick-starter lever halfway through its stroke, then fit the outer cover on the gearbox.
13. Before installing the remaining parts, make sure the kick-start lever is fully operational and returns to its upright position.
14. The rest of the assembly is a reverse of the disassembly procedure.

Gearbox Service

DISASSEMBLY

1. Remove the gearbox outer cover as previously described, leaving the gearbox engaged in high gear.
2. Remove the right rear engine plate.
3. Bend back the tabs on the lockwasher, apply the rear brake, and unscrew the kick-starter pinion ratchet retaining nut from the gearbox mainshaft.
4. Remove the clutch and primary drive as previously described. Don't forget to remove the mainshaft key.

Refer to the appropriate procedures, below, for 4-speed or 5-speed service.

4-Speed:

5. Remove the large dome nut from under the gearbox and withdraw the camplate indexing plunger and spring.
6. Remove the allen screw, phillips screw, and bolt that secure the inner gearbox cover. Tap the cover with a mallet until it is free.
7. Remove the selector fork spindle and then withdraw the mainshaft assembly.
8. Remove the layshaft and remaining gears.
9. Remove the camplate and spindle assembly and then remove the two bronze thrust washers located over the needle roller bearings.
10. Remove the circular countershaft sprocket cover from the primary inner cover. Remove the sprocket securing nut.
11. Drive the mainshaft high gear through into the gearbox with a suitable drift. Replace the oil seal.

5-Speed:

5. Remove the allen bolt, phillips screw and bolt indicated by arrows in the illustration, and remove the gearbox inner cover, tapping it outward with a soft-faced mallet if necessary.
6. Remove the engaging dog pinion from the countershaft. Remove the circlip from the countershaft.
7. Pull out the shift fork rod, then remove the countershaft first gear along with the shift fork.
8. Remove the countershaft second gear, then remove the mainshaft with its first, second, and third gears in position.
9. Take out the mainshaft fourth gear and the countershaft third gear together with the two shift forks.
10. Remove the countershaft fourth and fifth gears.
11. Remove the two thrust washers over the countershaft needle bearings: one on each countershaft bearing.
12. To remove the mainshaft high gear, remove the plate from the inside primary chaincase at the back of the clutch. Bend back the locking plate, and unscrew the sprocket nut. Drive the high gear into the gear box with a soft-faced mallet or drift.
13. Remove the camplate plunger nut at the bottom of the transmission case,

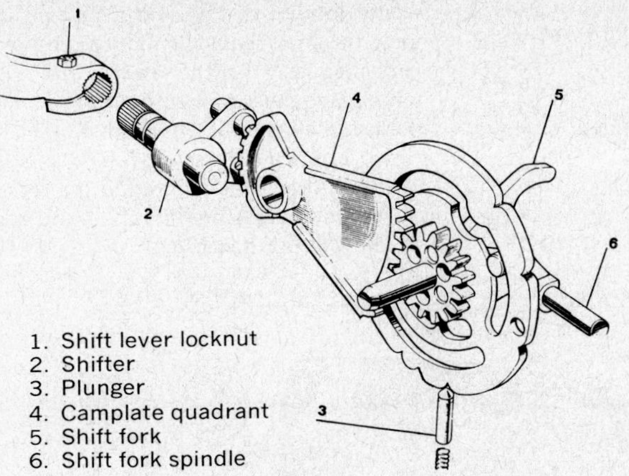

Gear shifter components (5-speed)

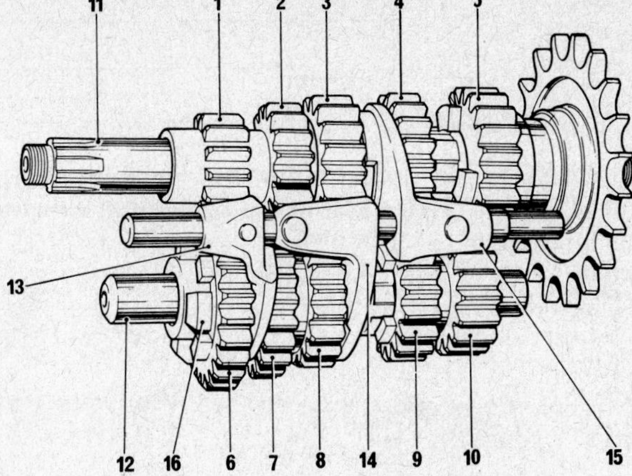

Gear cluster (5-speed)

1. 1st gear (Mainshaft)
2. 2nd gear
3. 3rd gear
4. 4th gear
5. 5th gear
6. 1st gear (Countershaft)
7. 2nd gear
8. 3rd gear
9. 4th gear
10. 5th gear
11. Mainshaft
12. Countershaft
13. 1st gear countershaft shift fork
14. 3rd gear countershaft shift fork
15. Mainshaft shift fork
16. Countershaft engaging dog pinion

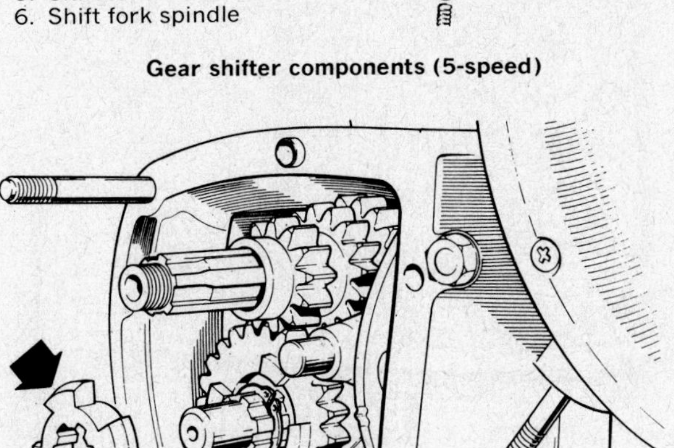
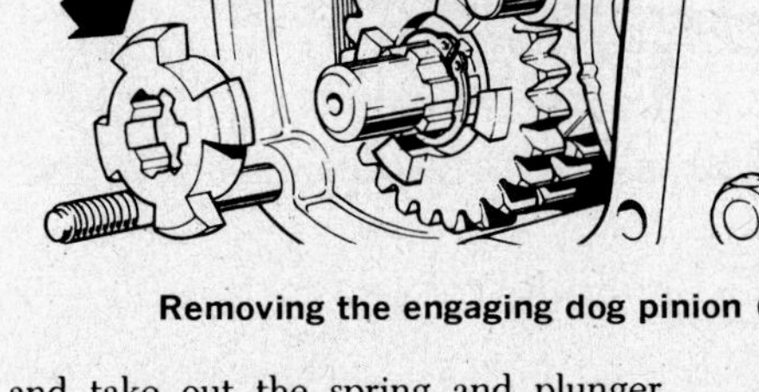

Removing the engaging dog pinion (5-speed).

and take out the spring and plunger. Remove the camplate from the gearbox.

14. Carefully inspect the condition of the mainshaft oil seal after removing the gearbox sprocket.

Mainshaft Bearings

The mainshaft bearings are press-fit into their housings and are retained by spring circlips to prevent sideways motion due to end thrust. To remove the right bearing, remove the circlip, heat the cover to 100° C, and drive the bearing out with a suitable, shouldered drift. Install the new bearing while the cover is still hot. Reinstall the circlip.

To remove the high gear bearing on the left side, pry out the large oil seal, then remove the retaining circlip. Heat the case around the bearing to 100° C, then drive the bearing out with tool no. Z15 or a suitable, shouldered drift. Install the new bearing while the base is still hot. Install the circlip and press in a new seal.

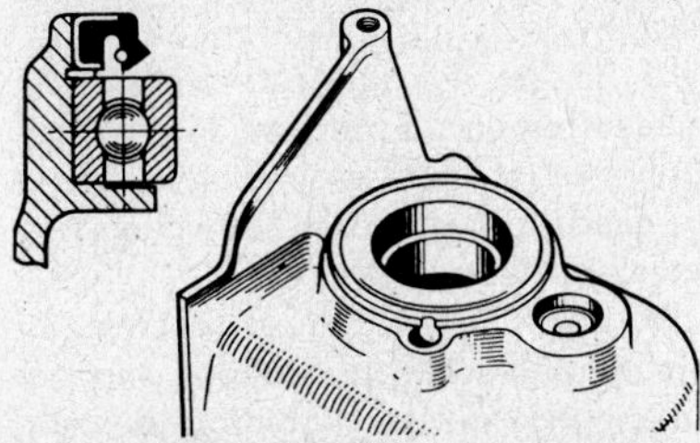

Mainshaft oil seal (650 models)

To replace the high gear bushing, (4-speed transmission) press it out with a suitable, shouldered drift. This drift can be fabricated by machining ¾ in. on one end of a ⅞ in. x 5 in. bar to 13/16 in. diamter. The bushing must be pressed out from the tooth side of the gear. Install the new bushing in the same manner, making sure the oil groove in the bushing is on the tooth side of the gear. Ream the bushing to the size given in specifications and make sure any filings are removed from the case before reassembly.

Layshaft Bearings

Remove the right bearing by heating the cover to 100° C and pressing or driving it out with a drift similar to the one

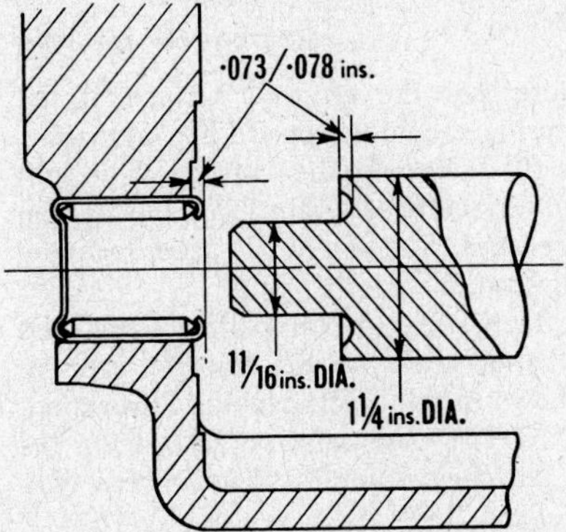

Layshaft bearing installation (650 models)

shown in the accompanying illustration. Press in the new bearing, while the cover is still hot, from the inside of the cover until 0.073–0.078 in. of the bearing protrudes, as shown in the accompanying illustraton.

Remove the left bearing by heating the cover housing to 100° C and driving it through into the gearbox with a suitable drift inserted through the countershaft sprocket aperture. Press the new bearing into place while the cover is hot. It must protrude 0.073–0.078 in. inside the gearbox.

Mainshaft High Gear Bearings (5 speed)

The mainshaft high gear is fitted with two caged needle bearings (one in each end). Press them out and in together with a drift of the dimensions shown in the illustration.

INSPECTION

1. Inspect the gearbox case and cover for any signs of cracking or metal fatigue. Examine the joining faces for any damage.
2. Inspect the mainshaft and layshaft for badly worn splines, cracks, etc., and compare their dimensions with those given in the specifications. Also look for any signs of seizure, indicated by a local discoloration of the shaft.
3. Examine all bearings for pitting and excessive wear. Replace as described in the section on gearbox disassembly.
4. Inspect the gears for chipped, fractured, or worn teeth. Also check the internal splines and bushings. Check bushing dimensions with those given in specifications.

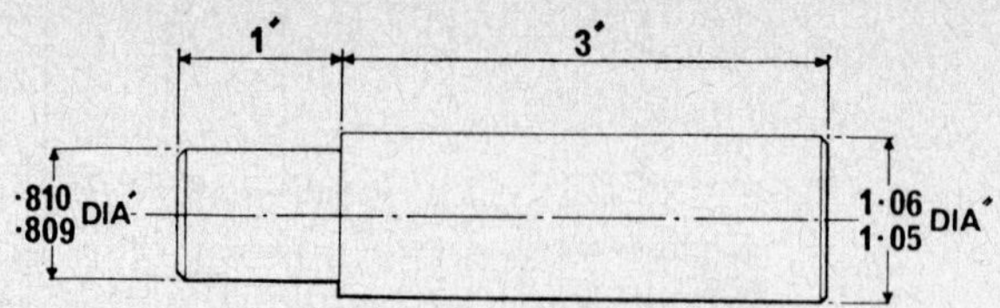

High gear needle bearing drift dimensions

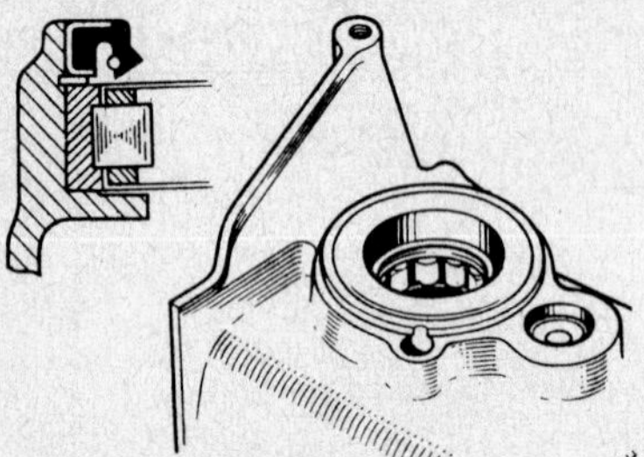

Gearbox mainshaft oil seal and roller bearing (5-speed)

5. Make sure the selector fork rod is not grooved or excessively worn. Inspect the selector fork faces for wear and scoring.

6. Inspect the selector camplate for wear in the roller tracks. Check the fit of the camplate spindle in its housing.

7. Inspect the camplate plunger and housing for corrosion, and check the measured length of the spring against specifications.

8. Make sure the kick-starter pawl and the layshaft low gear's dogs are not excessively worn or chipped.

9. Examine the mainshaft high gear bushing for wear by inserting the mainshaft and noting the amount of free-play allowed.

ASSEMBLY

4-Speed

1. Drive a new oil seal up to the main bearing with the lip and spring toward the bearing.

2. Press the high gear into the bearing.

3. Lubricate the ground taper of the countershaft sprocket with oil and slide it on to the high gear. Screw on the securing nut finger-tight.

4. Connect the final drive chain over the sprocket, then tighten the securing nut to specifications with tool no. Z63 or a suitable substitute.

5. Lubricate the extended nose of the high gear with oil, then reinstall the sprocket cover with a new paper gasket.

6. Lubricate the camplate spindle and install it in its housing within the gearbox.

7. Assemble the camplate plunger and spring in the domed retaining nut and screw it into position under the gearbox. Don't forget the fiber washer.

8. Locate the camplate plunger in the notch between second and third gear.

9. Position the thrust washer over the inner needle roller bearing. Coat the washer with grease to hold it in place and note that the grooved surface of the washer should be toward the layshaft.

10. Lubricate the captive mainshaft and layshaft gears, then assemble them in a cluster as shown in the accompanying illustration.

11. Grease the camplate rollers, then position them on the selector forks as shown in the accompanying illustration.

NOTE: *The selector fork with the smaller radius is for the mainshaft cluster.*

12. Install the mainshaft and layshaft cluster in the gearbox. As the shafts are being located in their respective bearings, the gears should be slid into position and aligned so that the selector fork rollers engage the camplate and the selector forks are approximately aligned.

13. Lubricate the selector fork spindle with oil, then slide it through the forks, shoulder end first, until it is fully situated in the gearbox housing.

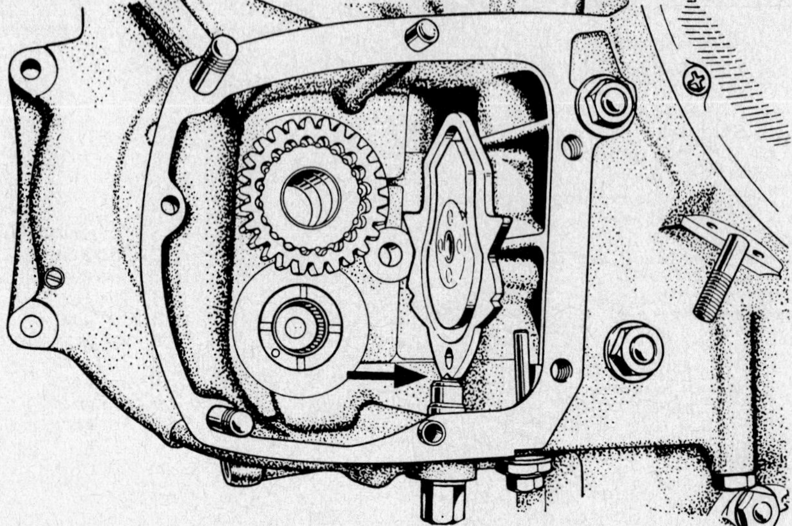

Gearbox assembly showing camplate notch between second and third gear (650 models)

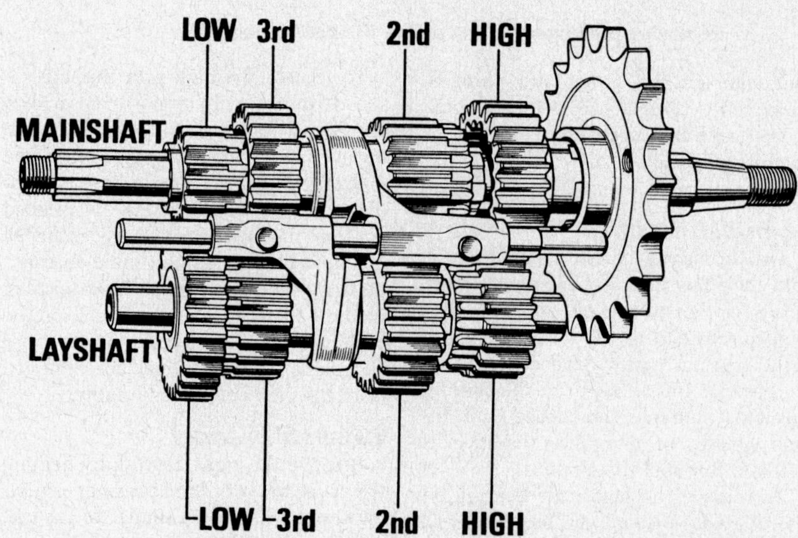

Gearbox cluster assembled (650 models)

14. Make sure the camplate quadrant is moving freely in the inner cover, then position the layshaft thrust washer over the bearing in the inner cover. Hold it in place by smearing it with grease.

15. Thoroughly lubricate all parts in the gearbox with a pressure oil can, then apply fresh sealer to the joining surface of the gearbox. Make sure the two locating dowels are in position.

16. Begin to install the inner cover assembly, and when the joining surfaces are about ¼ in. apart, position the camplate quadrant in the middle point of its

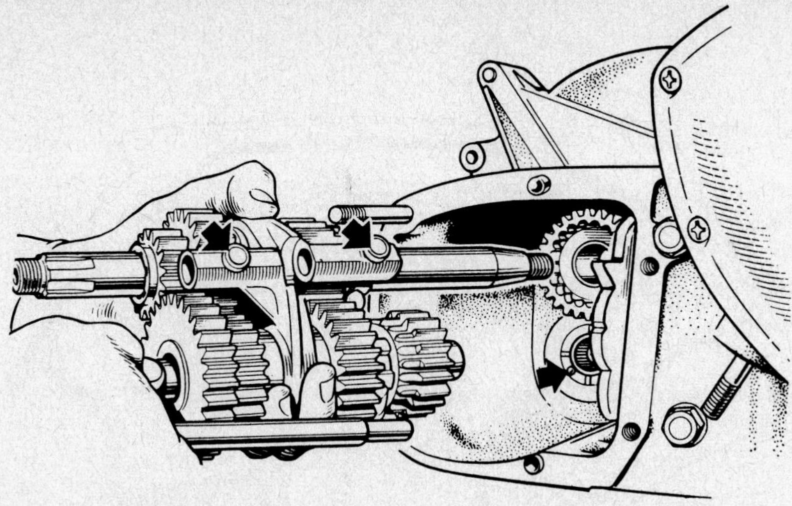
Installing the gearbox cluster. Arrows indicate camplate rollers and thrust washers correctly positioned (650 models)

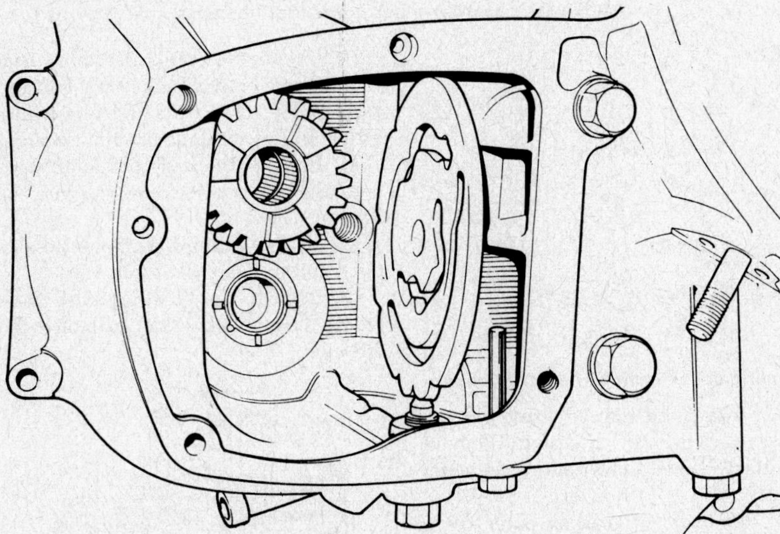
Camplate installed; gearbox in neutral (5-speed).

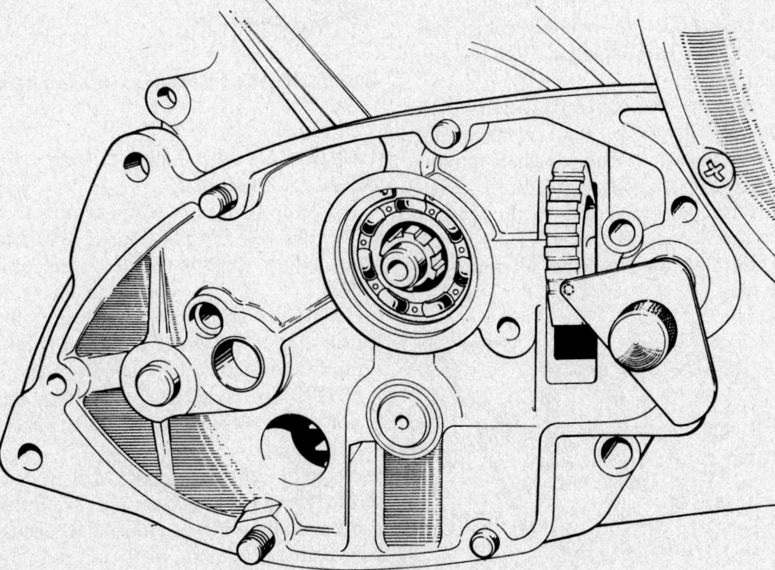
Replacing the inner gearbox cover (5-speed).

travel, and quickly complete the installation. This will align the camplate middle tooth with the mainshaft centerline.

17. Install the gearbox securing screws and nut, then temporarily install the gearbox outer cover assembly and check out the gearbox operation. If there is a problem, chances are the quadrant teeth are not correctly engaged with the camplate pinion.

18. The remainder of the assembly procedure is a reversal of the disassembly instructions.

5-Speed

1. Replace the camplate after lubricating the camplate spindle with some gearbox oil.
2. Refit the mainshaft oil bearing noting that the lip and seal face the mainshaft bearing. A new oil seal must always be used.
3. Push the mainshaft high gear into the bearing. Put some transmission oil on the tapered boss of the gearbox sprocket and place it on its shaft, in place, then replace the sprocket nut, tightening it by hand for the time being.
4. Run the drive chain over the gearbox sprocket. Apply the rear brake and tighten the sprocket nut as tight as possible.
5. Lubricate the end of the high gear which protrudes into the primary chaincase, and refit the cover plate. A new paper gasket should be used.
6. Replace the thrust washer over the inner needle bearing. The grooved surface of the thrust washer must face the countershaft. The washer may be held in place by smearing the rear surface with a bit of grease.
7. Refer to the accompanying illustration, and set the camplate in the "neutral" position, and refit the cam plunger, spring, and bolt on the bottom of the gearbox.
8. With gearbox oil, lubricate the needle bearing in the high gear and the countershaft bearing. Refer to the illustration of the 5-speed gear cluster, and place the mainshaft high gear onto the mainshaft. Also refit the shift fork to the mainshaft. Note that the three shift forks are all different, and this one has a large engaging pin and no cutaway on the housing.
9. Insert the mainshaft assembly into the high gear, engaging the pin on the shift fork with the camplate groove. Use chassis grease to hold the fork in place.
10. Replace the countershaft with its two highest gears into the gearbox, engaging these gears with their mainshaft counterparts. Note that none of the sliding gear dogs will be engaged if the transmission is set at neutral.
11. Refit the countershaft third gear and its shift fork. This shift fork has a

large engaging pin and a cutaway on the housing. Refit the mainshaft third gear and engage it with the corresponding countershaft gear.

12. Lubricate the countershaft second gear bushing and replace the gear on the countershaft.

13. Replace the first and second gears onto the mainshaft. Refit the countershaft first gear with its shift fork. Note that this shift fork has the smaller engaging pin.

14. Insert the shift fork rod. Replace the circlip on the end of the countershaft, and replace the engaging dog pinion against the circlip.

15. Turn the camplate counterclockwise (relative to a rider on the machine), which will place the transmission in first gear. Note that the engaging dog pinion on the countershaft will mesh with the dogs on the countershaft first gear, groove facing the countershaft.

16. Insure that the camplate quadrant operates freely. Replace the thrust washer over the needle bearing for the countershaft in the gearbox cover.

17. Lubricate all moving parts in the gearbox with transmission oil. Apply some gasket compound to the gearbox mating surfaces. Begin refitting the inner cover. When the inner cover is about ¼ in. away from the mating surfaces, position the camplate quadrant as shown using the special tool (60–6128). If not available, line up the top edge of the second tooth on the quadrant with an imaginary horizontal line through the center of the gearshift spindle housing. This housing is at the extreme forward part of the inner cover, and is shown occupied by the special tool in the illustration of the inner cover.

18. Refit the inner cover securing bolt and screws tightening them lightly. Assemble the outer cover and gearshift lever and check that the shifter operates properly. If not, it is probable that the quadrant teeth are not properly engaged with the camplate gear.

19. Assuming that the shifting is working properly, tighten the inner cover securing bolt and screws, and refit the kickstarter assembly, the outer cover, and refill the gearbox and primary chaincase with the correct amounts and grades of oil.

Bottom End Overhaul

CRANKCASE SERVICE

Disassembly

1. Remove the primary chaincase cover and disconnect the alternator leads under the engine.

2. Remove the three screws that secure the alternator stator, and pull the stator off its mounting studs. Do not disconnect the leads at this time.

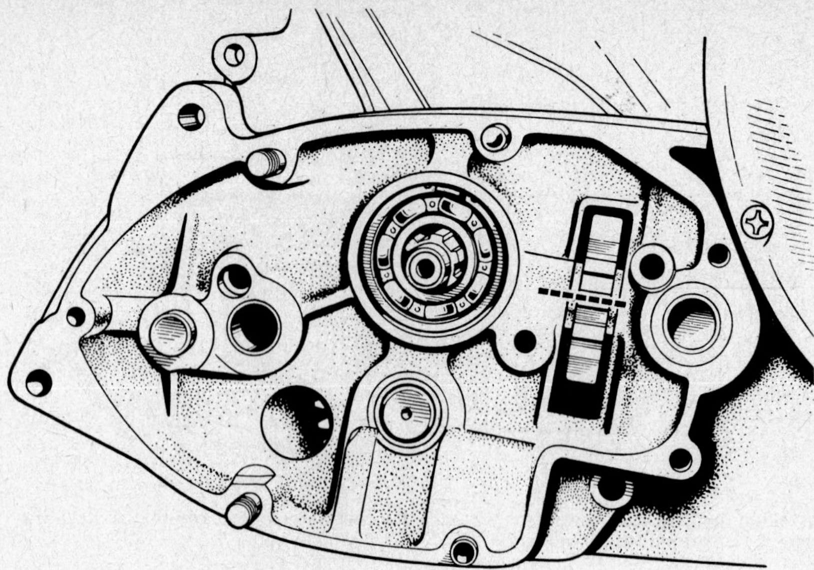

Installing the gearbox inner cover (650 models)

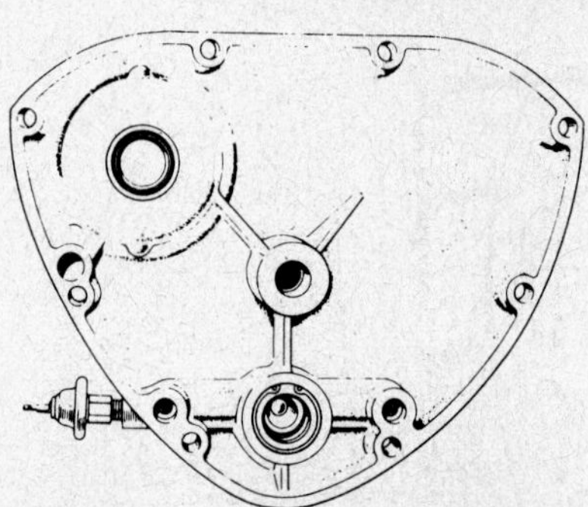

Timing cover removed (650 models)

3. Disassemble the clutch and primary drive as previously described. Remove the stator sleeve and withdraw the stator leads.

4. Remove the gearbox outer cover and dismantle the gearbox.

5. Remove the rocker boxes, cylinder head, cylinder barrel, and pistons.

6. Disconnect the clutch cable and remove the carburetor(s). Remove the timing cover.

7. Remove the contact breaker cover and the oil pump, then remove the crankshaft pinion. The camshaft pinions can also be removed at this time.

8. Remove what's left of the engine from the frame.

9. Remove the crankcase filter and oilway plug.

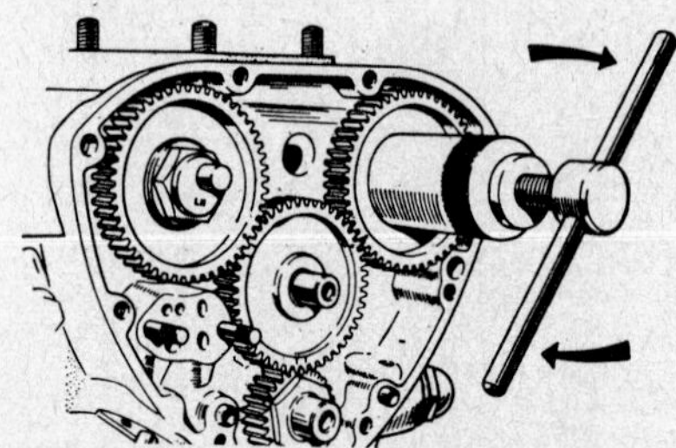

Removing the camshaft pinions with tool no. D2213 (650 models)

10. Clamp the crankcase firmly in a vise at the bottom mounting lug and remove the three bolts and two screws shown in the accompanying illustration.

11. Remove the four remaining studs and the two nuts next to the gearbox housing.

12. Attach Triumph extractor no. 61–6064 and separate the cases.

13. Remove the breather valve from within the intake camshaft bushing in the left case.

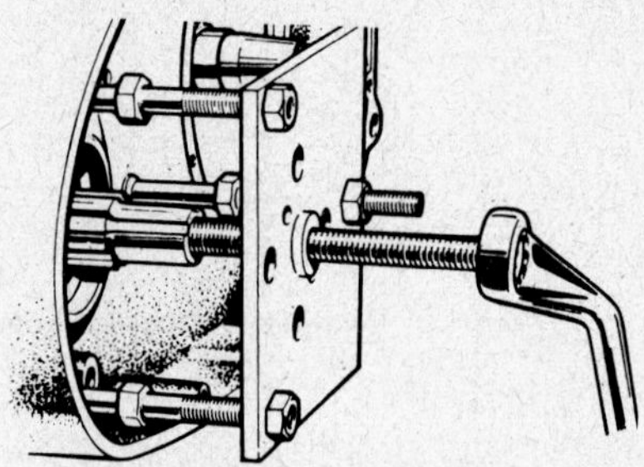

Separating the case halves (650 models)

Crankshaft and Connecting Rods Disassembly

1. Clamp the crankshaft assembly in a soft-jawed vise and place a rag over any sharp edges to protect the connecting rods.

2. Unscrew the cap retainer nuts a little at a time to avoid distortion, then remove the caps and connecting rods.

NOTE: *The connecting rods, caps, and nut are center-punched to facilitate reassembly.*

3. Using a large impact driver, unscrew the oil tube retainer plug from the right end of the big-end journal. If necessary, drill a hole ⅛ in. deep and ⅛ in. in diameter to eliminate the locking effect of the plug center punch.

4. Remove the flywheel bolt next to

the big-end journal, then pull out the oil tube with a hooked piece of stiff wire through the flywheel bolt location hole.

5. Thoroughly clean all parts in kerosine or a cleaning solvent, then blow them dry with compressed air. Make sure the oil drillways are blown clear.

6. To remove the flywheel, unscrew the two remaining bolts and press the crankshaft out of the right side bearing with a five ton press.

NOTE: *Before removing the flywheel, make certain it is marked for reassembly.*

Inspection

Inspect the big-end journals for any signs of scoring, etc., and measure the journal diamter. Compare with specifications. Light score marks can be removed with fine-grade emery cloth, but make sure all metal filings are removed before reassembly. If the scoring is light, new connecting rod shell bearings should be installed; if the scoring is extensive, the journals should be reground to an appropriate undersize.

NOTE: *The replaceable big-end bearing shells are pre-sized to give the correct dimensions. Under no circumstances should they be scraped, or the connecting rod and cap filed to alter the bearing dimensions.*

Assembly

1. Position the oil tube in the crankshaft, aligning the flywheel bolt holes with those in the crankshaft. Temporarily install one of the flywheel bolts to secure it in position.

2. Apply thread-locking sealant to the oil tube plug and install it in the crankshaft. Center-punch the crankshaft opposite the slot to lock the plug in position.

3. Heat the flywheel to 100° C, then position it over the crankshaft with the center punch mark to the right. Turn the flywheel through 180° to get it over the crankshaft web, then turn it to the correct position relative to the crankshaft and align the bolt holes.

4. Coat the flywheel bolt threads with a thread-locking sealant, then install and torque them to specifications.

5. If a new or reground crankshaft, or a new flywheel was installed, the assembly should be rebalanced. This operation is best left to a qualified shop that has the appropriate special tools.

6. Check to make sure all the oil drillways are free from obstruction, then install the connecting rods and caps. Torque the retaining nuts to specifications, or better yet, the bolt extension figure given in the accompanying illustration.

7. Last, force oil through the crankshaft, right main-bearing journal drillway until it is expelled at both big-end bear-

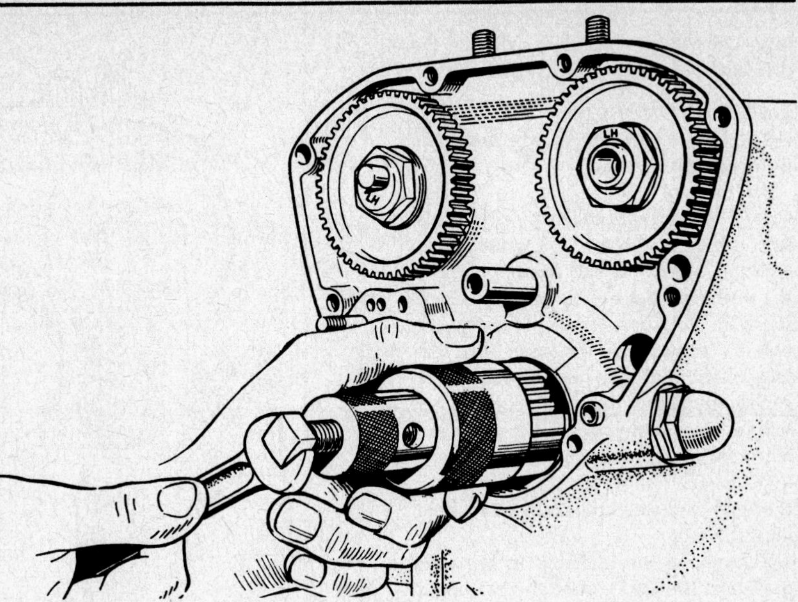

Removing the crankshaft pinion with tool no. 61-6019 (650 models)

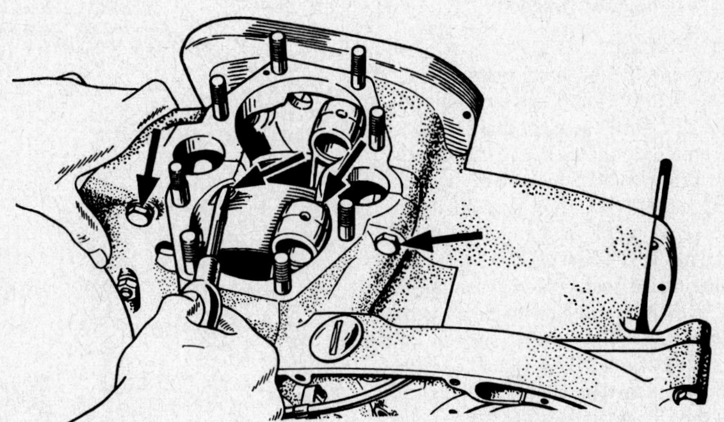

Crankcase securing screws and bolts (650 models)

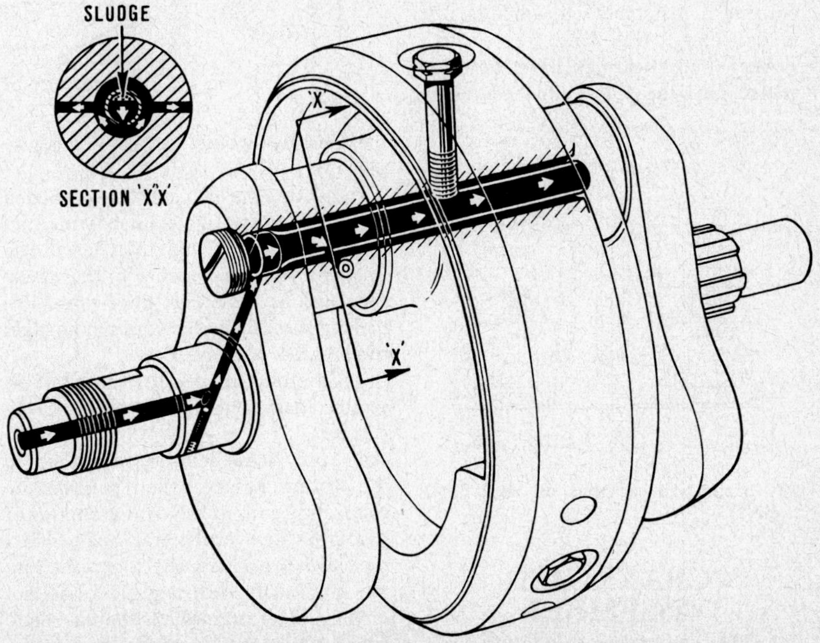

Sectional view of crankshaft assembly (650 models)

ings. This will provide assurance that the drillway is free from obstruction.

Camshaft Bushings

The intake and exhaust camshafts run in bronze bushings.

To remove the bushings in the left case, a tap will be necessary. The ideal size is ⅞ in. diameter × 9 whitworth.

When a good thread has been cut in the bushing, heat the case to 100° C and screw in the appropriate bolt. Grip the bolt in a vise and tap the case with a soft-faced mallet until the bushing is free. The replacement bushings are pre-sized but will require a light reaming to meet specifications. After reaming the new bushings, make sure the crankcase is thoroughly cleaned to remove any metal filings.

To remove the bushings in the right case, heat the area around the bushing to 100° C, then drive it out with a suitable, shouldered drift. Install the new bushing while the case is still hot, making sure the oil drillway holes are aligned.

Main Bearings

To remove the left main bearing, heat the case to 100° C and drive it out with tool no. Z14. Only the right main bearing spool remains in the case, and is removed by first removing the lock plate, heating the case to 100° C, then driving it out with tool no. Z162 or a suitable, shouldered drift. It is advisable to replace the left bearing oil seal while the engine is apart, even if it appears to be in good condition.

To install the left and right bearings, first make sure that their housings are clean, then heat the cases to 100° C and drive the bearings into position with a tubular drift the same size as the bearing outer race. A suitable size would be 2 ¾ in. diameter × 6 in. long.

After both bearings have been installed, press the oil seal into the left case.

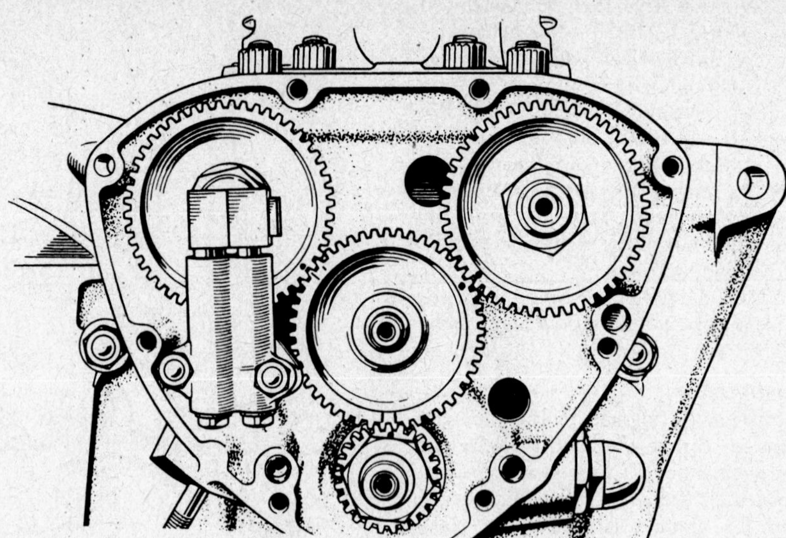

Timing gear marks (650 models)

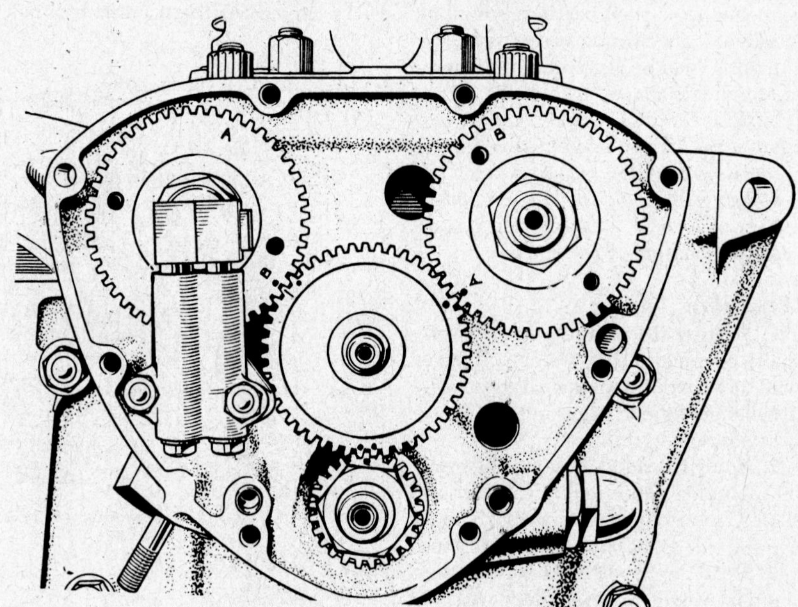

Timing gear marks (750 Twins)

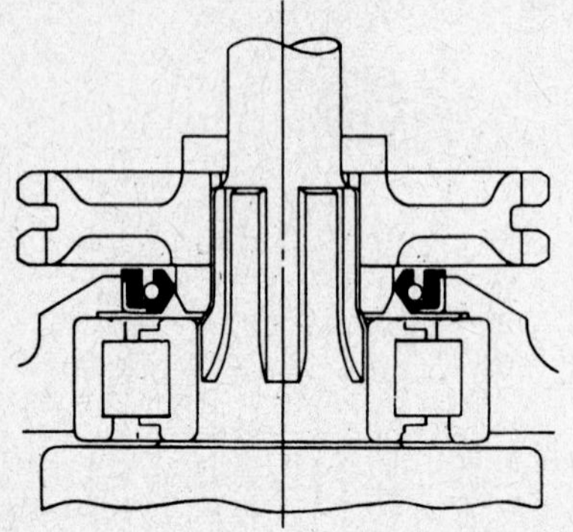

Left main bearing and oil seal (650 models)

CRANKCASE ASSEMBLY

1. Thoroughly clean the mating crankcase halves, giving special attention to the locating dowels. Install the oilway plug.

2. Position the left case on two wooden blocks, lubricate the main bearing and camshaft bushings and then install the breather valve and spring in the intake cam bushing. Assemble both camshafts, making sure the intake cam slot engages the breather valve dog.

3. Carefully install the crankshaft assembly, making sure the fit in the bearing is good.

4. Apply fresh joining compound to the mating surfaces, then position the connecting rods in the center and lower the right case over the crankshaft. When the halves are mated, check to make sure the crankshaft and camshafts are not binding. The crankshaft should rotate freely, while the camshafts should offer only slight resistance.

5. The remainder of the assembly procedure is a reversal of the disassembly instructions. Torque all bolts and nuts to specifications.

T150

Removal And Installation

1. Remove the fuel tank.

2. Drain the oil tank and crankcase. Remove the oil cooler.

3. Disconnect the rocker box oil lines, then disconnect the oil supply lines from underneath the rear of the crankcase.

4. Remove the carburetors and exhaust header pipes.

5. Unbolt and remove the right-side footpeg.

6. Unscrew the retaining bolt at the

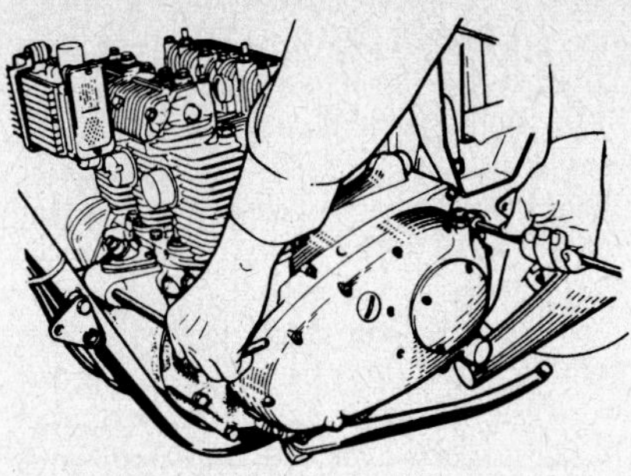

Removing the engine unit with the aid of lifting bars (Trident)

front of the chainguard, remove the lower left-side shock absorber mounting nut, and remove the chainguard.

7. Remove the masterlink and pull the drive chain off the countershaft sprocket.

8. Disconnect the alternator and contact breaker point leads at their connectors. Remove the spark plugs.

9. Turn the cable adjuster at the clutch lever all the way in until the cable is completely slack. Take out the four, clutch, inspection-cover retaining screws and disconnect the clutch cable from the release lever.

10. Disconnect the tachometer cable from the tachometer drive at the front of the crankcase.

11. Pull the engine breather tube off at the rear of the inner primary chaincase.

12. Unscrew the pinch-bolt and pull the brake pedal off its shaft.

13. Unscrew the nut from the kick-start lever shaft and drive out the locating pin by tapping on the end of the threads with a small hammer. Remove the kick-start lever.

14. Unscrew the five bolts and nuts from the right-side rear engine mount plate. Unscrew the swing arm shaft nut and remove the plate. It is not necessary to remove the left mount plate.

15. Unscrew the nut from the long engine mount bolt underneath the crankcase and drive the bolt out. Note the position of the spacer between the crankcase and frame lug before removing the bolt.

16. Support the engine and remove the engine mount bolt at the front frame down-tube. Raise the engine slightly and remove it from the left side of the frame.

Installation is in reverse order of removal. The following points should be noted:

1. Be sure to reinstall the engine mount spacers and washers in their original positions.

2. When connecting the oil lines underneath the crankcase, the smaller (delivery) oil line is attached to the small, straight, junction pipe, and the larger (scavenge) line is attached to the stepped-down junction pipe.

3. Adjust the clutch cable free-play at the handlebar lever after the cable has been reconnected.

4. Adjust the rear brake after the pedal has been installed.

NOTE: *Before starting the engine, ½ pt of oil should be poured into the crankcase. The oil can be added through the timing plug aperture in the right case.*

Top End Overhaul

CYLINDER HEAD AND BARREL REMOVAL

The cylinder head and barrel on the Trident can be removed with the engine in the frame. The procedure is as follows:

1. Turn off the fuel taps and disconnect the lines. Remove the metal strip running down the center of the fuel tank (early models) or the rubber plug at the top of the tank (later models). Unscrew the retaining nut and remove the tank.

2. Loosen the oil line clamps at the oil cooler and pull the lines off their connector pipes. Mark the lines and pipes to facilitate correct reassembly. *Do not unscrew the large hexagonal connectors from the cooler.* Unbolt the oil cooler bracket from the frame and remove the cooler. Note that the bracket is insulated from the frame with rubber bushings to protect the cooler from vibration.

3. Disconnect the throttle cable from the linkage at the carburetors and disconnect the choke cable at the handlebar lever. Loosen the carburetor-to-intake manifold clamps and remove the carburetors as a unit.

4. Unscrew the exhaust header pipe nuts at the cylinder head. Disconnect the mufflers from the pipes and remove the header pipe assembly.

5. Unbolt and remove the top engine mount (cylinder head stay).

6. Unscrew the two acorn nuts that secure the rocker oil feed lines to the rocker shafts and tie the pipes out of the way. Remove the access covers and completely loosen the valve adjusters to relieve the head studs of valve spring pressure.

7. Remove the two, small end bolts and three nuts (at the underside of the cylinder head) that secure the rocker boxes to the head. Loosen the head bolts and nuts gradually, in the sequence shown, and then lift off the rocker boxes.

8. Remove the spark plugs, unscrew the remaining cylinder head bolts, and lift the head carefully off the studs. Remove the pushrod tubes and pushrods.

9. To prevent the tappets from falling into the crankcase when removing the barrel, wrap electrical tape around the top of each tappet.

10. Loosen the cylinder-barrel retaining nuts gradually, in the sequence shown, to prevent distortion. Lift the barrel carefully off the crankcase, taking care to support the pistons as they are exposed by the cylinders so that they won't be damaged on the crankcase flange. Mark the tappets so they can be replaced in their original positions. *This is very important.*

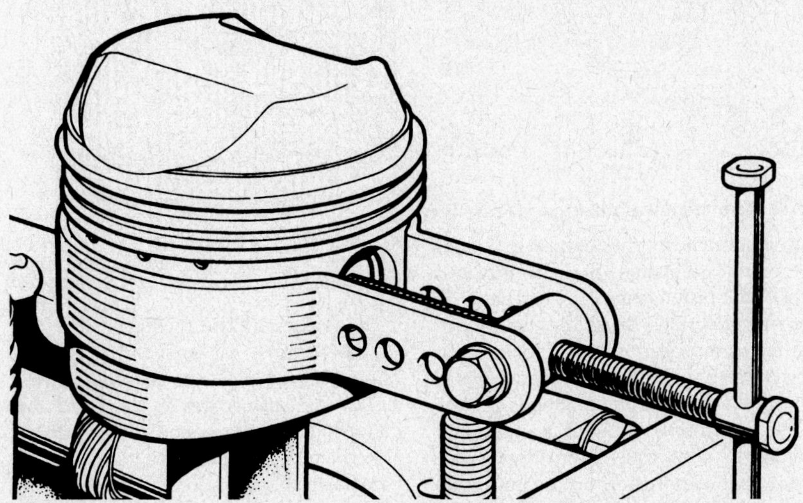

Removing the piston pin (Trident)

CYLINDER HEAD SERVICE

Valve Train Inspection

The rocker mechanism will not require disassembly unless defective. Examine the ends of the rocker arms for wear and damage. Check the fit of the rocker arms on the shafts; excessive clearance will make it hard to maintain proper valve adjustment. Rocker arms that are damaged or worn in any way must be replaced. Check the pushrod end cups for wear and make sure the pushrods ar not bent by rolling them on a flat surface. Replace if faulty. To disassemble the rocker mechanism, tap the rocker shafts out from the threaded end. Be sure to install the thrust washers and springs in their correct positions when replacing the shafts. Refer to the accompanying illustration.

Valves

Using a suitable valve spring compressor, compress each spring and remove the split collar. Release the compressor and remove the springs and retainers. Mark the valves so they can be replaced in their original positions.

Check the valves in their guides for excessive side-play. Examine the valve stems for carbon buildup or scoring. Replace the valve and guide as a set if any of these conditions exist. Valve guides can be driven out after the cylinder head has been heated in an oven or immersed in hot water. Install new guides while the head is still warm.

Valve sets can be recut if the seat is worn or if the seat area has become pocketed. Grind away the metal around the seat before recutting the seat if it has become pocketed. In any case, if valve guides have been replaced, the seats should be recut. Valve seat angle is 45°.

Remove carbon from the combustion chamber using a scraper or small, hand-held grinder. Be careful not to mar the soft metal of the cylinder head. Clean the head in solvent after the carbon has been removed.

CAUTION: *Do not use a caustic soda solution to clean aluminum parts.*

Whether the original or new valves are to be used, they should be lapped into their seats. It would be wise to replace the valve springs with new ones at this time as a matter of course; however, if the spring free-length measures within 1/16 in. of the original specification (given at the end of the section), the springs may be reused. Assemble the springs and retainers as removed. When replacing the split collars you will find that a small amount of grease will hold them in position as the spring compressor is removed. Make sure the collar is correctly seated by tapping the valve stem with a small, soft hammer.

CYLINDER BARREL AND PISTON SERVICE

1. Examine the cylinder bores for scoring, and measure the diameter in several places to determine wear. If wear exceeds 0.005 in. the cylinders should be rebored. Pistons are available in 0.01, 0.02, 0.03, and 0.04 in. oversizes.

NOTE: *The cylinder liners should protrude from the cylinders 0.002–0.007 in.*

2. Whether or not wear exceeds 0.005 in., the cylinder should be honed so that the new rings will seat properly.

3. The tappet guide blocks, pressed into the base flange of the cylinder, should not normally need replacement. If it does become necessary to replace them, the dowels must be drilled out and the cylinder must be heated before the guides can be pressed out. New dowels will have to be used along with the new guides.

4. Remove the wrist pin circlips and drive the wrist pins out of the pistons. In some cases it may be necessary to heat the pistons before the pin can be removed. Mark the piston, inside the skirt, so it can be replaced in its original position. Carefully remove all traces of carbon from the piston crown.

5. Break one of the old rings and use the end of it to clean the carbon out of the piston ring grooves. Check the end gaps of the new rings by placing each one into its bore and measuring with a feeler gauge. The ring gap should not be less than 0.009 in., nor greater than 0.013 in. Carefully install the rings on the pistons. Note that the compression rings are tapered, and the work "top" must be installed facing up.

6. Be sure to coat each moving part with fresh engine oil or assembly lube during installation.

7. Warm the pistons and install them, in their original positions on the connecting rods. Insert the wrist pins before the pistons have a chance to cool. Install *new* circlips and make sure that they are properly seated.

8. Install the tappets in their original positions. Wrap a piece of tape around the top of each tappet stem to prevent it from falling into the crankcase as the cylinder is installed. Make sure that the oil holes in the tappet stems line up with the oil holes in the guide blocks, as shown.

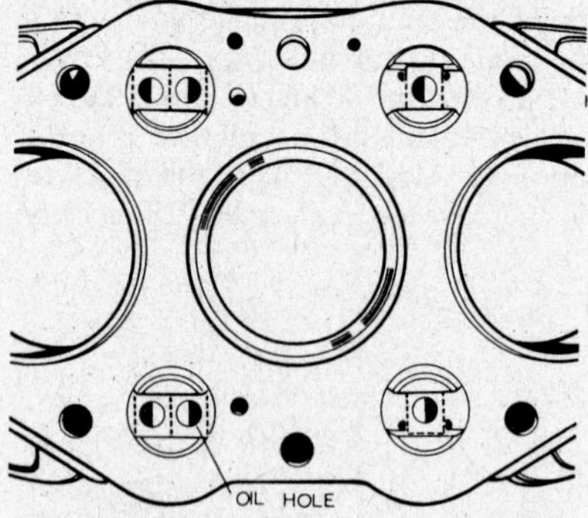

Correct cam follower positions (Trident)

9. Install a new cylinder base gasket on the crankcase flange. Stagger the end gaps of the piston rings 120° apart and oil the rings liberally. Bring the center piston up to top dead center and install a ring compressor. Slide the cylinder down over the piston. Raise the outside pistons as far as possible without accidentally pulling the center piston out of its base. Install ring compressors on the outer pistons and seat the cylinder against the crankcase. Tighten the cylinder retaining nuts gradually, in the proper sequence, to 20–22 ft lbs.

10. Remove the tape from the tappets and fit the pushrod tubes over the tappet guides. Make sure that the rubber seals at either end of the tubes are in good condition.

11. Install a new head gasket on the cylinder with the ribs facing down (toward the cylinder). Install the cylinder head carefully over the studs and onto the cylinder. Fit the four outer head bolts loosely. Insert the pushrods onto their tubes. Make sure that the pushrods line up evenly. *This is very important.*

12. Install the rocker boxes on the head using new gaskets. Coat only one side of the gaskets with cement. Make sure that the pushrods are properly seated in the rocker arms.

13. Install the remaining eight, cylinder head bolts and tighten all twelve nuts and bolts evenly, in the sequence shown, to 18 ft lbs. Refit the remaining rocker box mounting bolts and nuts.

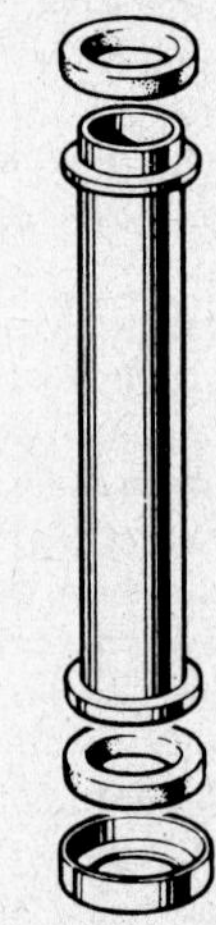

Pushrod tube assembly (Trident)

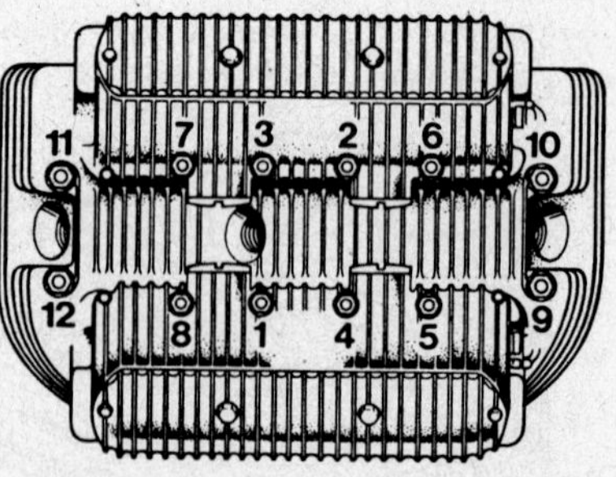

Cylinder head bolt tightening sequence (Trident)

14. Reconnect the rocker oil lines using new copper washers. Install the top engine mount and exhaust headerpipes. Install the carburetors on the head and connect the throttle and choke cables. Bolt the oil cooler onto the frame, taking care to install the rubber bushings correctly, and connect the oil lines. Install the fuel tank.

Clutch and Primary Drive

CLUTCH SERVICE

Disassembly

1. Drain the oil from the primary chaincase.
2. Take out the four screws and remove the clutch inspection cover. Unscrew the large locknut and the adjuster nut from the end of the clutch release rod.
3. Back off the primary chain adjuster, remove the fourteen screws, and pull off the primary cover. Note that the screws are of different lengths; they must be replaced in their original positions.
4. Bend back the locktab, install oil seal protector 61–6051, and unscrew the engine sprocket retaining nut, Remove the transmission sprocket (clutch hub) retaining nut and pull both sprockets off together using Triumph tools D1860 and 61–6046—or suitable gear pullers.
5. To remove the inner crankcase (clutch) cover, first take out the screws and bolts that secure the cover, noting their positions to facilitate reassembly. Pull off the inner cover, taking care not to damage or lose the oil pump O-rings.
6. Take off the spacer and pull the clutch unit off the shaft.
7. Mark the relative positions of the clutch cover, drive plate, and pressure plate. Bend back the locktabs on the twelve cover bolts and loosen the bolts gradually, a turn at a time, to prevent distortion of the cover.
8. Separate the clutch components, taking care not to lose the three dowel pins in the cover.

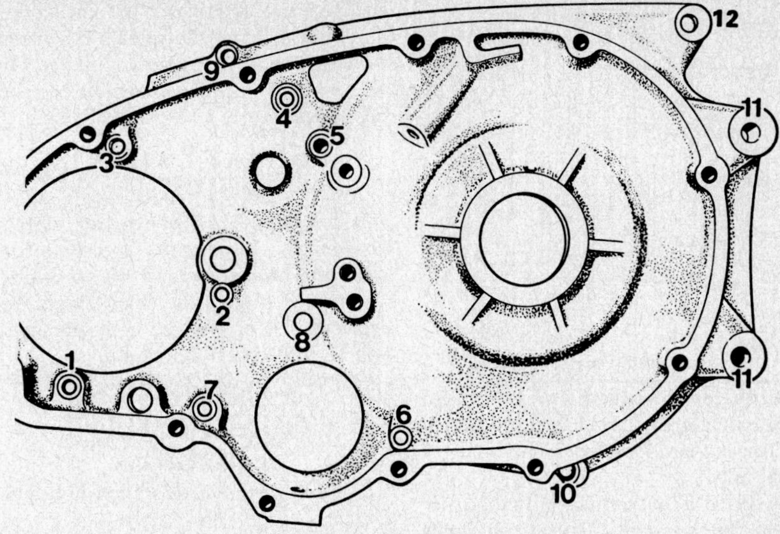

Inner primary cover securing screws and bolts (Trident)

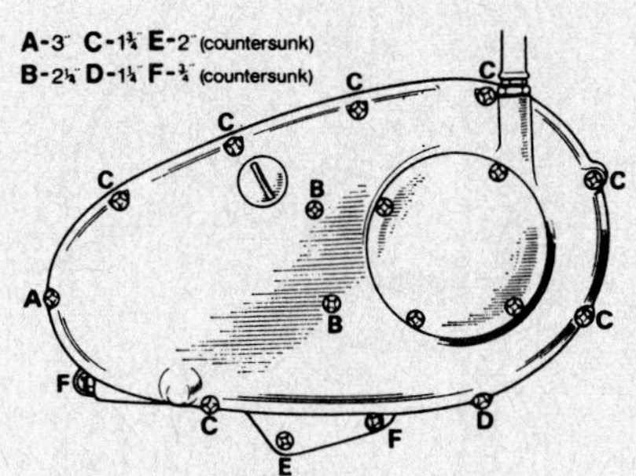

Primary chaincase securing screws (Trident)

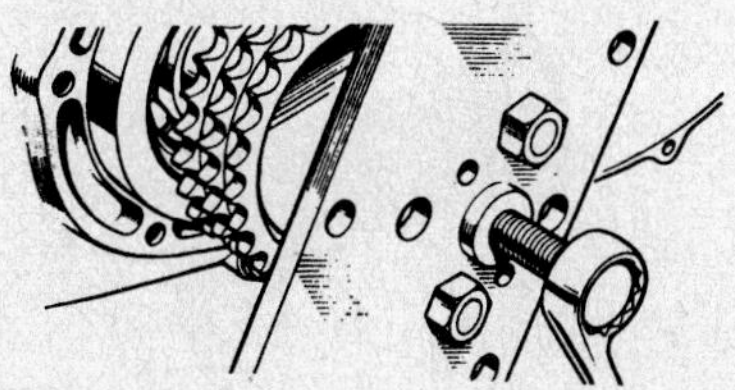

Removing the engine sprocket (Trident)

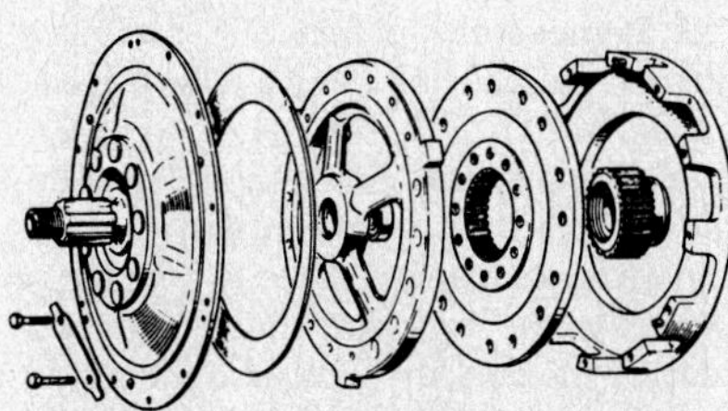

Exploded view of clutch assembly (Trident)

Inspection

The clutch unit is extremely simple in operation and construction. The disc is the only component that should require replacement. Examine the drive plate and pressure plate for cracks, scoring, and overheating (extreme blue discoloration). Check to see that the drive plate slots and pressure plate tabs are not broken or excessively worn. The diaphram spring may be reused unless it shows signs of being overheated, in which case it may have been weakened. If the bearing is worn and/or the oil seal damaged, replace both components.

Assembly

1. Apply a small amount of high temperature grease to the sides of the three pressure plate tabs and assemble the pressure plate, disc, and drive plate (aligning the positioning marks).
2. Apply a small amount of grease to the machined ridge on the pressure plate and install the diaphram on the ridge with the outer edge of the spring upward.
3. Lightly grease the ridge inside the cover and install the cover (in alignment

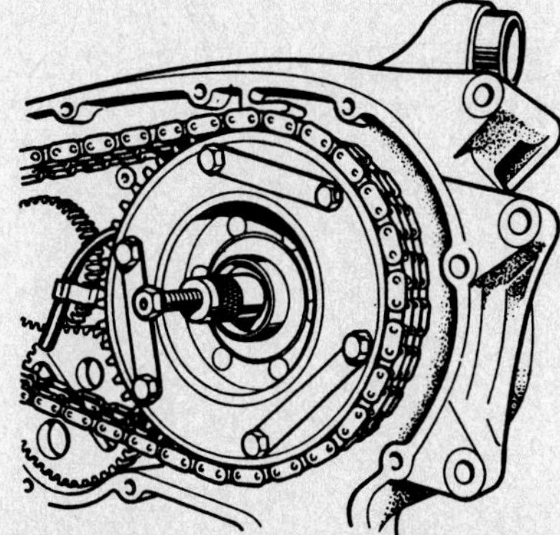

Removing the clutch hub sprocket (Trident)

Early type shock absorber rubbers (Trident)

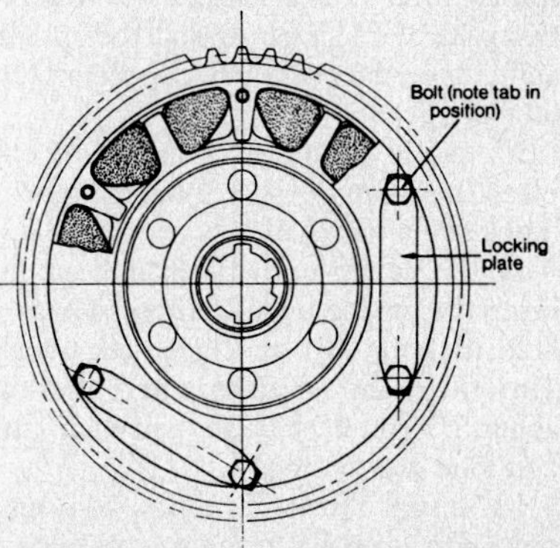

Late type shock absorber rubbers (Trident)

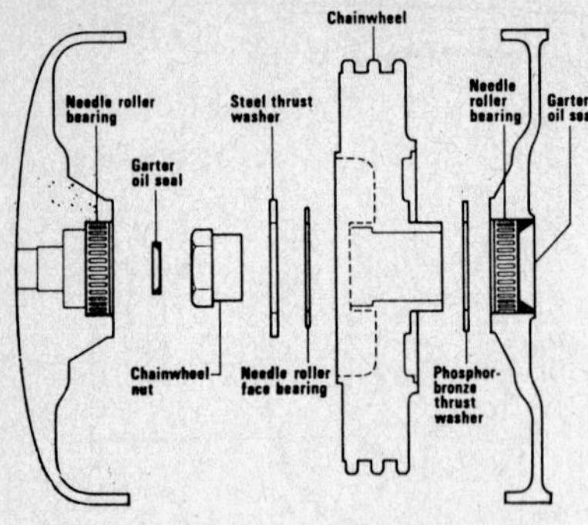

Clutch assembly order (Trident)

with the drive plate and pressure plate positioning marks) and install the twelve bolts using new locktabs. Tighten finger-tight only.

4. Install a centering tool from the rear of the clutch and tighten the twelve bolts one-half turn at a time, working around the cover, until the cover meets the drive plate. Fully tighten the bolts and lock them with the loctabs.

5. Remove the centering tool, install the release rod, lightly grease the disc splines, and install the clutch on the engine.

6. Install the oil pump O-rings and check the clutch hub needle bearing for excessive play. Check the oil seal and replace if worn or deformed.

7. Apply gasket-sealing compound to the crankcase and inner cover mating surfaces. Install the cover on the crankcase using a new gasket, and tighten the screws evenly.

8. Install the twelve damper rubbers and then the outer plate. Apply thread-lock compound to the six plate-retaining screws.

NOTE: *Later models use six bolts with locktabs and a modified plate. If the screws on earlier models were found to be in need of replacement, replace the screws and plate with the later components.*

9. Install the thrust washer on the back of the damper hub, fit the primary chain over the sprockets, and install the sprockets, on the shafts. Tighten the crankshaft sprocket nut to 60 ft lbs and lock in position with the locktab. Install the spacer and tighten the mainshaft sprocket nut to 60 ft lbs.

10. Install the thrust bearing and replace the primary cover using gasket cement and a new gasket.

11. To adjust primary chain tension, bring the engine up on compression and hold it there with the kick-start pedal. Turn the chain tensioner in until there is about 3/16 in. slack on the top chain run and lock it in position.

12. Install the large clutch adjusting nut, taking care not to damage the oil seal on the release rod threads. Insert an 0.-005 in. feeler gauge between the bearing and large nut, and tighten the small locknut while holding the release rod from turning. Refill the primary chaincase with oil and check the clutch for correct operation.

PRIMARY DRIVE SERVICE

Follow steps 1–4, above, for clutch disassembly. Inspect the sprockets for worn and broken teeth. If the sprockets are to be replaced, the chain should be replaced also or else the new sprockets will be ruined in a short time.

TRANSMISSION COUNTERSHAFT SPROCKET

1. Remove the small clutch hub and clutch housing.

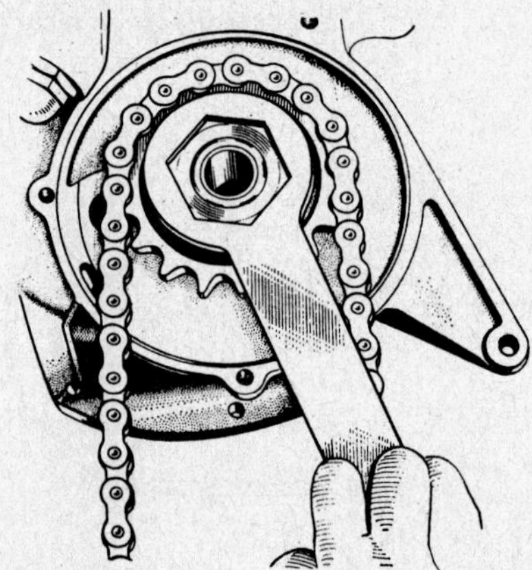

Removing the countershaft sprocket (Trident)

2. Remove the clutch hub retaining nut and pull the hub using a suitable gear puller.

.3. Remove the clutch housing from the crankcase. Check the oil seal for wear and distortion, and replace if necessary. Unscrew the sprocket nut and then remove the final, drive-chain master link. Pull the sprocket off the shaft.

4. To replace the sprocket, install it on the shaft using hardening gasket cement on the sleeve gear splines to prevent oil from leaking between the sprocket and sleeve gear.

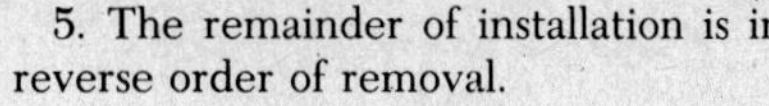

5. The remainder of installation is in reverse order of removal.

Gearbox, Shifter, And Kick-Starter Mechanisms

4-SPEED

Disassembly

1. Drain the primary chaincase and transmission.

2. Remove the clutch.

3. Take out the five screws and the acorn nut, and remove the transmission outer cover complete with kick-start assembly and shifter mechanism. The kick-start half-gear is a press fit onto the shaft. If the return spring is to be replaced, load it 1 ¼ turns before slipping the hook over the dowel pin. The kick-start seal is accessible after the kick-start lever is removed.

4. To remove the kick-start ratchet and gear, bend back the locktab and unscrew the transmission mainshaft nut. If a new gear is to be installed, use a new spring also. The ratchet need not be removed for removal of the transmission gears.

5. Take out the two screws and bolts and remove the transmission inner cover, complete with selector quadrant and mainshaft assembly. Note the countershaft thrust washer located on the inner face of the cover by a small peg.

6. Unscrew the plug from the base of the transmission case that retains camplate plunger and spring.

7. Pull out the shift fork shaft and remove the countershaft first gear. Remove the sliding gears and selector forks from the case.

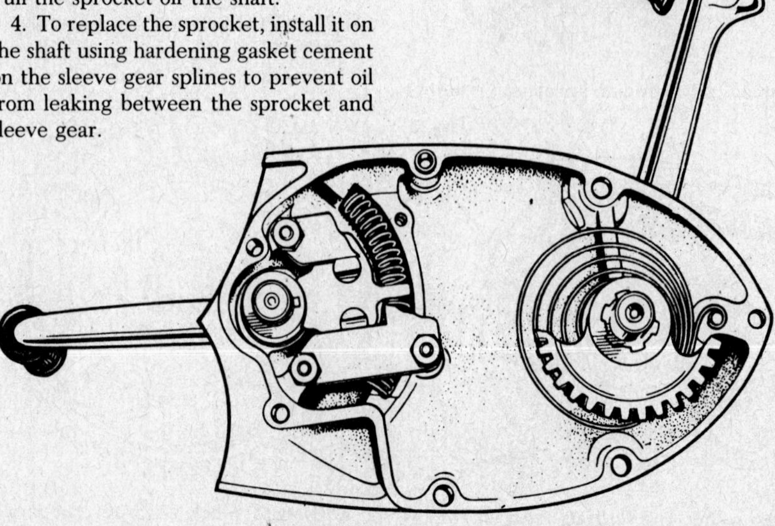

Gearbox outer cover assembled (Trident)

8. Pull the countershaft assembly out of the case and then remove the shift camplate. The countershaft top gear or sleeve pinion is attached to the final drive sprocket by a large nut.

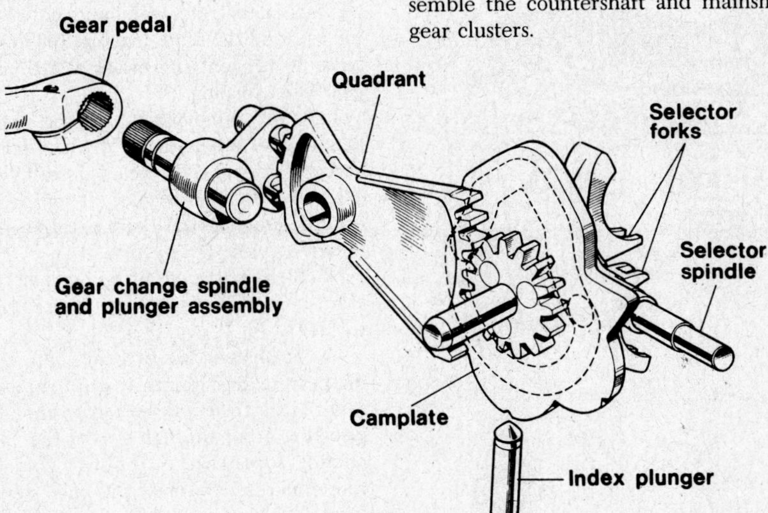

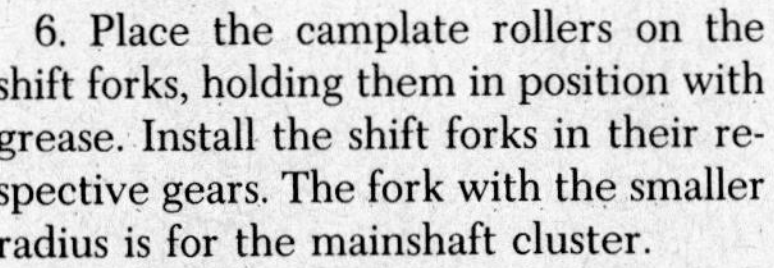

Shifter mechanism (Trident)

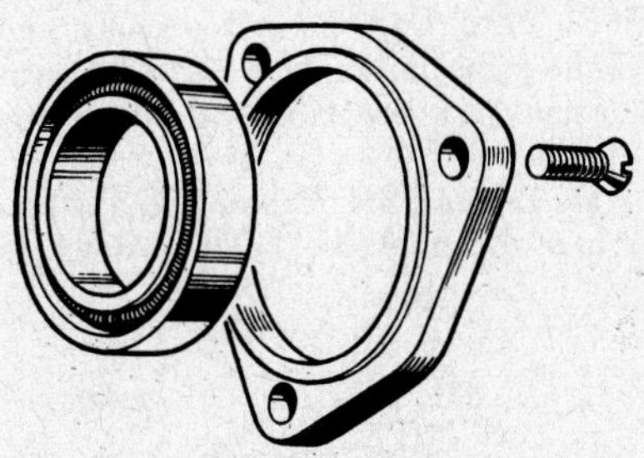

High gear bearing oil seal and housing (Trident)

Inspection

Check the gears for cracked, chipped, or worn teeth. The stationary gears can be removed from the shafts, if necessary, using a press. Look for worn camplate tracks, weak springs, sloppy bearings, and worn bushings. Examine the camplate gear for excessive wear, which can cause difficult gear selection. Check for smooth operation of the camplate plunger. Spring length should not be less than 2.65 in. Check mainshaft top gear bushing wear by measuring the diameter of the shaft and the inside diameter of the bushing. Calculated clearance should not exceed 0.005 in.

Assembly

1. Install the high gear into the bearing and then the final drive sprocket into the case.

2.Lubricate and install the camplate shaft into the case.

3. Install the camplate plunger and spring, with retaining plug, under the transmission case, and the fiber washer.

4. Set the camplate with the plunger located in the high gear notch. Install the thrust washer over the inner needle bearing. The grooved surface of the washer should face the countershaft. The washer can be held in place with grease.

5. Lubricate the components and assemble the countershaft and mainshaft gear clusters.

6. Place the camplate rollers on the shift forks, holding them in position with grease. Install the shift forks in their respective gears. The fork with the smaller radius is for the mainshaft cluster.

7. Install the mainshaft and countershaft gears, align the gears so that the shift fork rollers are located in the camplate tracks, and align the shift fork bores as closely as possible.

8. Lubricate the fork shaft and install it through the forks, shouldered end first, until it is fully engaged in the case. (The mainshaft shift fork should be at the innermost position).

9. Make sure the camplate quadrant is able to move freely in the inner cover. Position the countershaft thrust washer over the needle bearing in the inner cover, holding it with grease.

10. Lubricate all the transmission components. Apply gasket cement to the inner cover and transmission mating surfaces, make sure that the two dowel pins are in position, and install the inner cover.

11. Temporarily install the outer cover and check to see that the shift sequence is correct by operating the shift lever while turning the final drive sprocket. If the shift sequence is not correct, remove the inner cover and make sure the quadrant teeth are accurately engaged with the camplate gear. When reinstalling the inner cover, sure the top of the first tooth is on the centerline of the mainshaft.

Kickstarter return spring installation (Trident)

12. Reassemble the kick-shaft ratchet and gear as shown, tightening the nut 40–45 ft lbs. To facilitate this, install the final drive chain, put the transmission in gear, and apply the rear brake.

13. Install the outer cover using gasket cement on both mating surfaces.

14. Install the clutch.

15. Fill the primary chaincase and transmission with oil.

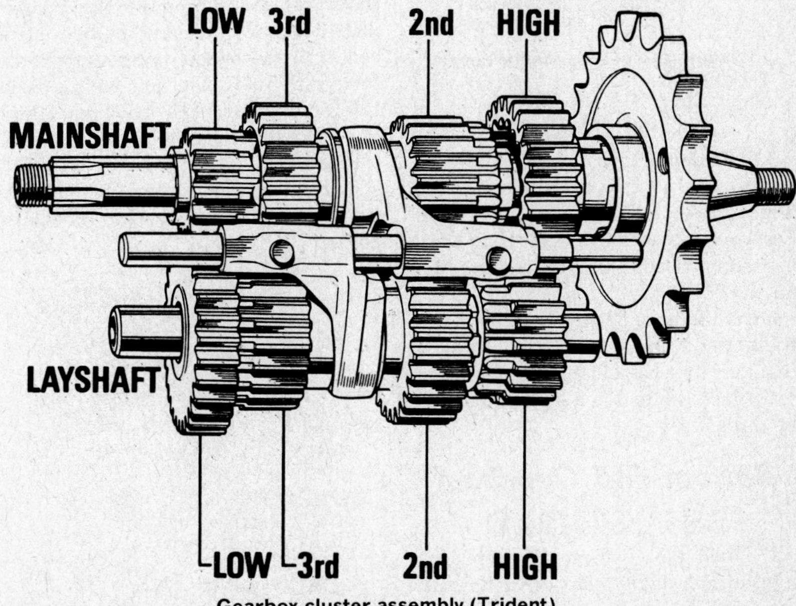

Gearbox cluster assembly (Trident)

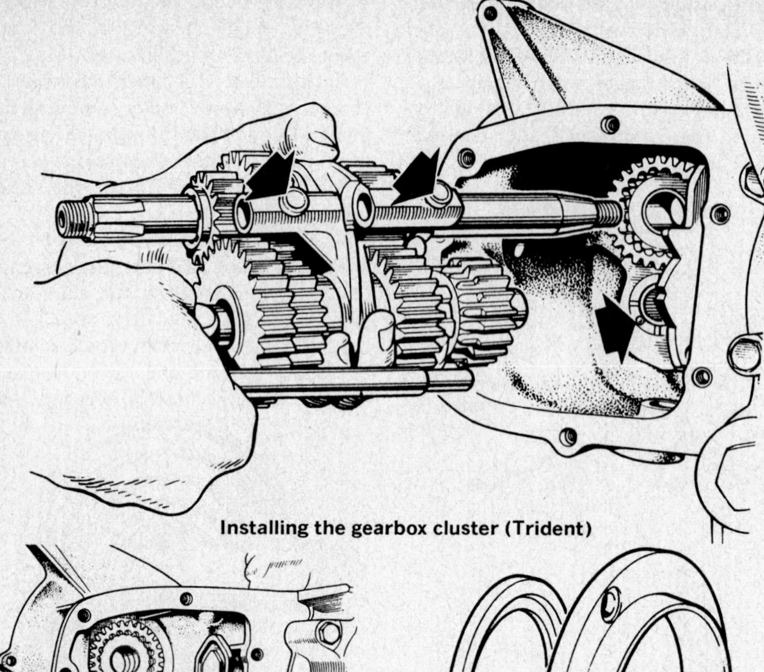
Installing the gearbox cluster (Trident)

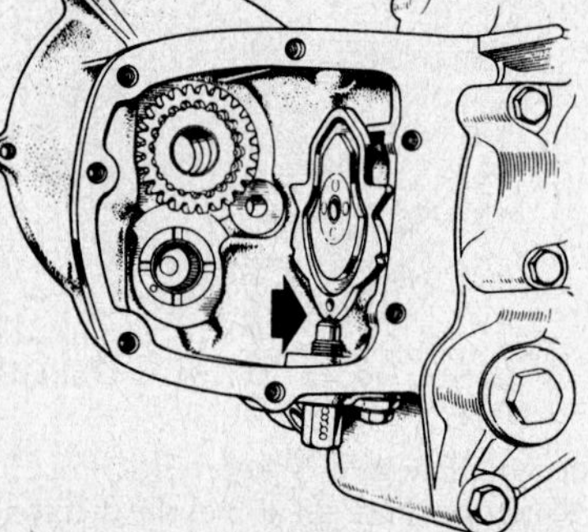
Engage the camplate in fourth gear position (Trident)

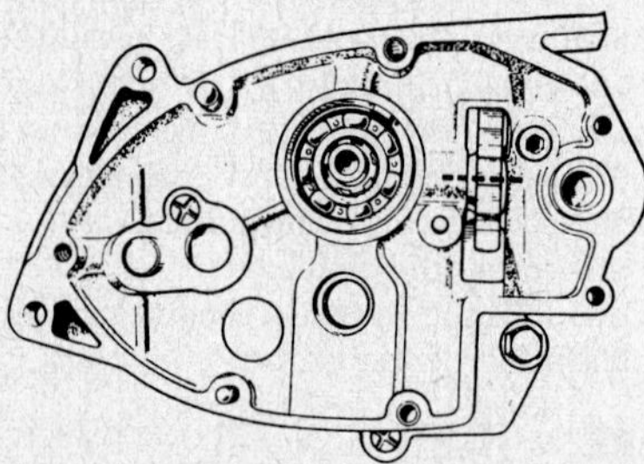
Installing the gearbox inner cover (Trident)

5-SPEED

The Trident T150V (5-speed) utilizes a transmission which is quite similar to the 5-speed found in the TR7V and T140V. For service procedures, refer to the earlier section dealing with the transmission for the 750 Twins.

One difference between the 750 Twin transmission and that for the T150V is that the latter has a high gear bearing oil seal which is found in a housing secured by three screws.

Bottom End Overhaul

DISASSEMBLY

1. Drain the oil from the crankcase, transmission, and primary drive. Remove the engine.

Mainshaft high gear oil seal and housing (Trident 5-speed).

2. Remove the cylinder head, barrel, and pistons.
3. Remove the primary drive and clutch assembly.
4. Remove the transmission gear cluster.
5. Remove the ignition points cover. Scribe a line on the breaker plate housing to facilitate reassembly, take out the three bolts, and remove the breaker plate assembly. Unscrew the bolt in the center of the breaker cam and remove the ignition advance unit with tool no. D782, or by screwing in a bolt that fits the threads in the cam until the advance unit is broken loose.
6. Take out the screws and remove the timing gear cover (right crankcase cover).

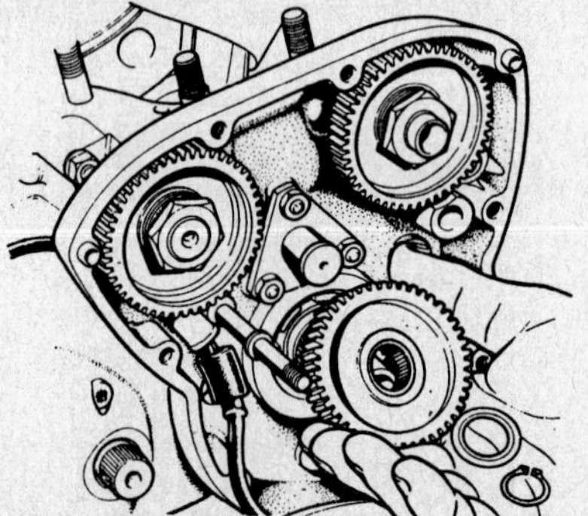
Removing the idler timing gear (Trident)

7. Unscrew the three nuts and pull the alternator stator off the studs. Unscrew the cable sleeve nut (covered by a rubber grommet) and pull the cable through.
8. Bend back the locktab and unscrew the alternator rotor retaining nut. Pull the rotor off the shaft, leaving the key in place to prevent the crankshaft timing gear from turning.
9. Before removing the timing gears, take note of the marks on the gear teeth that will line up if the gears are installed correctly. Pull the crankshaft pinion off using tool no. 61–6019 or a suitable gear puller.
10. Remove the circlip and pull off the idler (center) timing gear and its thrust washer.
11. To unscrew the two, camshaft, timing-gear retaining nuts, it will be necessary to lock the crankshaft in position by inserting a bar through two of the connecting rods. Take care not to damage the crankcase. Unscrew the nuts, *which have left-hand threads,* and pull off the camshaft timing gears using tool no. D2213 or a suitable gear puller. Remove the woodruff keys.
12. Take out the three bolts and remove the tachometer drive which is located just above the front engine mount.
13. Remove the oil filter from the bottom of the crankcase, held in place by a large brass plug.

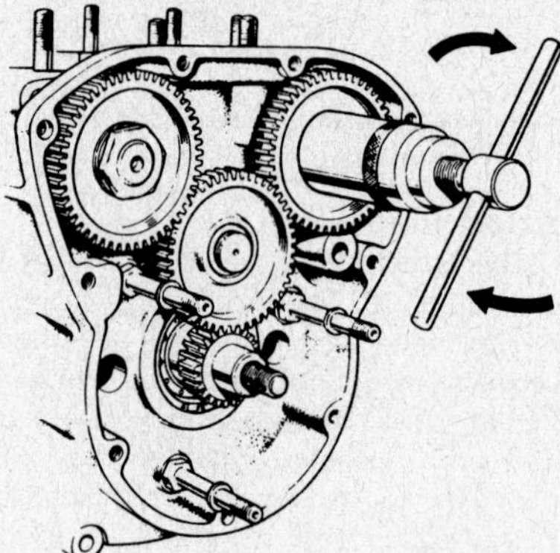
Removing the camshaft pinions (Trident)

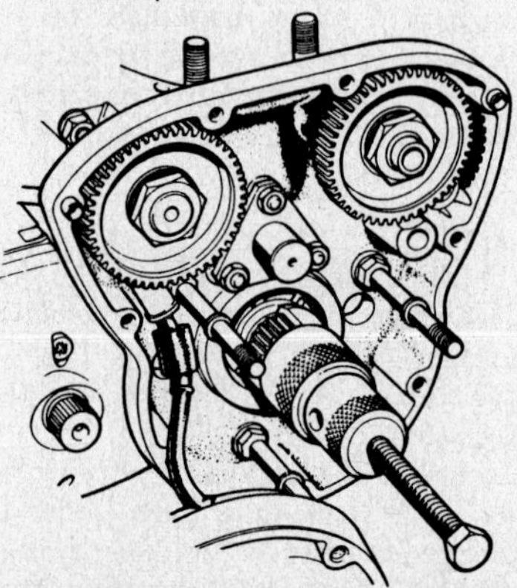
Removing the crankshaft pinion (Trident)

14. To separate the crankcases, first take out the hex bolts, allen bolt, and the six nuts from the timing side crankcase as shown in the illustration.

15. Next, remove the hex-head bolts from the drive-side crankcase. Tap off the drive-side crankcase using a soft metal drift. Place the drift against the lug at the rear of the case, as shown.

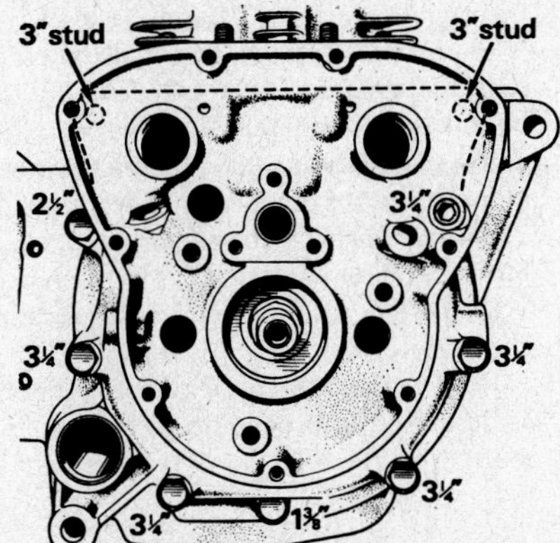

Right case securing bolts (Trident)

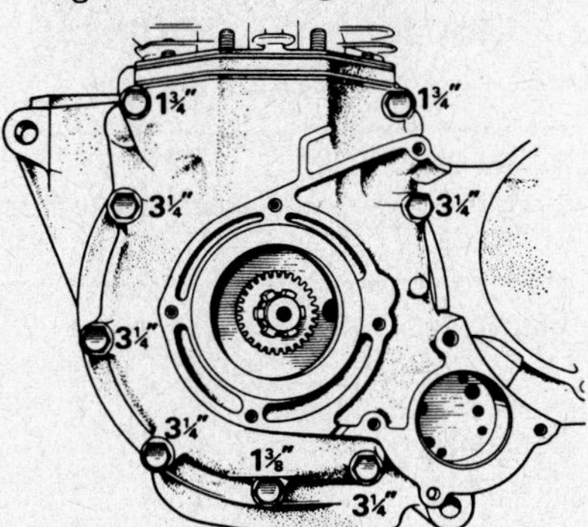

Left case securing bolts (Trident)

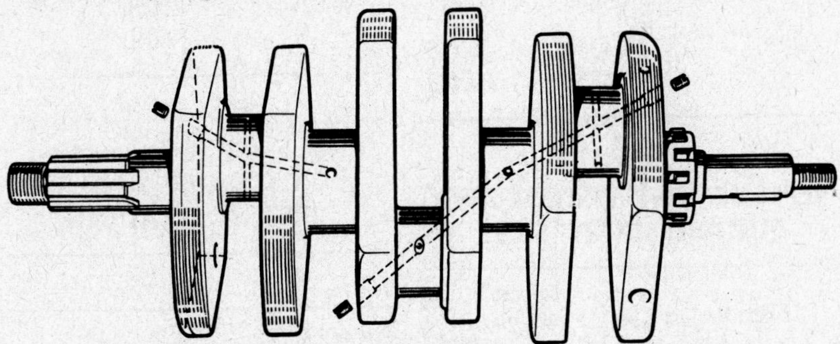

Sectional view of crankshaft assembly (Trident)

CAMSHAFTS

Withdraw the camshafts from the timing side crankcase and examine the lobes for wear and damage. Examine the tachometer drive gear on the exhaust camshaft for broken or worn teeth. Replace the camshafts if they do not appear to be in perfect condition.

CRANKSHAFT REMOVAL

1. Remove the retaining screws from the two small oil lines on top of the main bearing journal caps, pull the lines up, turn them away from the caps, and push them down and out of the crankcase.

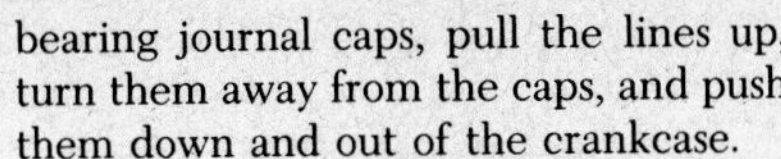

2. Remove the locknuts from the main bearing caps. To remove the caps, screw the oil line screws, with washers, back into them and pry the caps off the studs with levers.

3. The crankshaft assembly can now be removed.

CENTER MAIN BEARINGS AND CONNECTING ROD BEARINGS

The crankpins and the two center crankshaft journals run on replaceable, plain bearing inserts. Be sure to mark the rods and caps before removal so that they may be replaced in their original positions. It will be necessary to regrind the crankshaft if journal or crankpin wear exceeds 0.002 in. or if their surfaces are damaged. Bearings are available in 0.010, 0.020, 0.030, and 0.040 in. undersizes. The crankshaft assembly will *not* require rebalancing if components are replaced or if the crankshaft is reground.

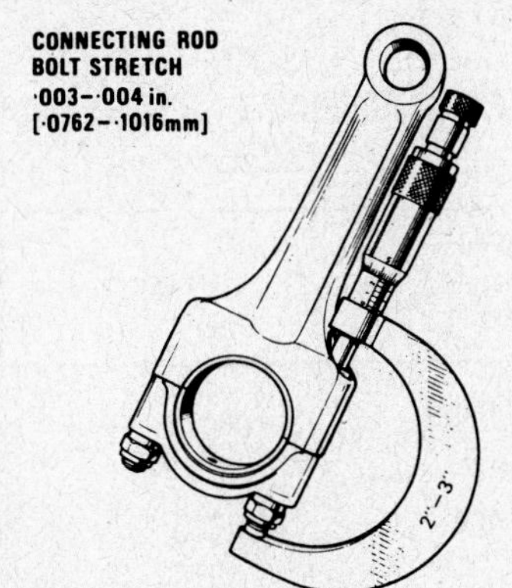

Checking connecting rod bolt stretch (Trident)

OUTER MAIN BEARING

The timing side roller and drive side ball bearing should not normally require replacemnt. If they are to be removed, it will be necessary to remove the circlips on either side of the bearing.

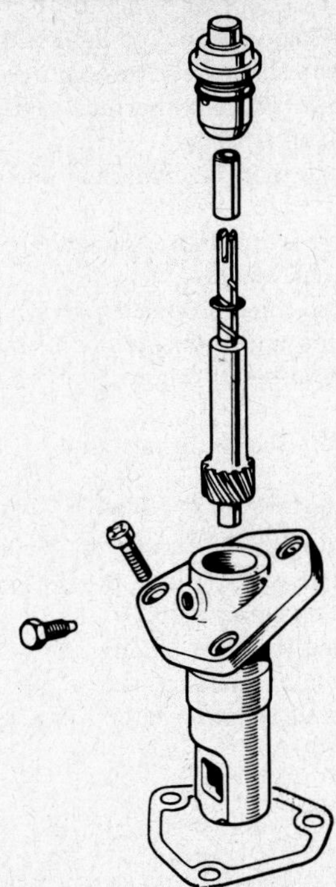

Tachometer drive assembly (Trident)

NOTE: *The center of the timing side roller bearing will remain with the crankshaft as the crankshaft is removed.*

Oil seals should be replaced at this time to avoid future trouble. Take care not to damage seals during installation. The flat side of the seal always faces outside.

ASSEMBLY

1. Fit the rod and main bearing inserts into their seats and lubricate them with fresh engine oil. Install the connecting rods and caps in their original positions and tighten the nuts to 18 ft lbs. Use new nuts if possible. Make sure that all components are completely clean and well lubricated during assembly.

2. Place the crankshaft in position in the crankcase, with the splined end on the drive side. Install the main bearing caps, making sure that the marks on the caps and lower bearing seats correspond. Install the washers and nuts (new nuts should be used) and tighten to 18 ft lbs. Check to see that the crankshaft is free to rotate easily. If it will not, switch the main bearing inserts around, make sure they are seated properly and re-oil them. Too tight a fit will require turning down the crankshaft journals slightly.

3. Install new rubber seals for the tappet oil lines (connecting at the main bearing caps) and install the lines as removed, taking care not to damage the seals.

4. Replace the oil filter O-rings in the center crankcase.

5. Apply a thin coat of gasket cement to the crankcase mating surfaces and install the crankcases (with the camshafts installed in the turning side case) in reverse order of removal. Take care to

avoid damaging tappet oil lines with the exhaust camshaft as the turning side case is installed. Tighten the nuts and bolts evenly to 15 ft lbs.

6. Check that the crankshaft and camshafts are free to rotate freely. If not, alignment is incorrect somewhere and must be corrected.

7. Install the crankshaft spacer on the timing side and then install the special key and crankshaft timing gear (with the mark facing out).

8. Install the camshaft timing gears with the no. 1 keyway (in line with the timing mark) located on the key in the shaft, and with the timing marks facing out. Install and tighten the left-hand-threaded retaining nuts.

9. Install the idler timing gear, aligning the timing marks as shown.

10. Install the alternator rotor, tightening the nut to 50 ft lbs. Install the stator and tighten the nuts to 8 ft lbs.

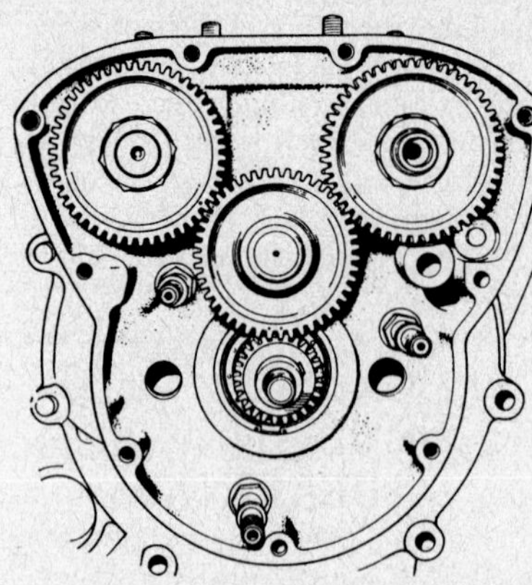

Timing gear marks (Trident)

11. Loosely install the ignition advance unit and then install the breaker plate assembly, aligning the marks. Coat the crankcase and cover mating surfaces with gasket cement and install the timing side crankcase cover, using a new gasket.

12. Install the oil filter in the bottom of the engine.

13. Install the tachometer drive unit, coating the gasket with gasket cement on both sides. Tachometer drive components generally do not require replacement unless an obvious fault is visible.

14. Install the transmission gear cluster as detailed earlier.

15. Install the primary drive and clutch.

16. Assemble the top end components as described in preceding sections.

250 CRANKSHAFT JOURNAL SIZES

Shell Bearing Marking	Suitable Crankshaft Journal Size (in.)	(mm)
Standard	1.4375	36.5125
	1.4380	36.5252
−0.010 in.	1.4275	36.2585
	1.4280	36.2712
−0.020 in.	1.4175	36.0045
	1.4180	36.0172
−0.030 in.	1.4075	35.7505
	1.4080	35.7632

500 CRANKSHAFT JOURNAL SIZES

Shell Bearing Marking	Journal Size (in.)	(mm)
Standard	1.4375	36.512
	1.4380	36.525
−0.010	1.4365	36.258
	1.4370	36.271
−0.020	1.4355	36.004
	1.4360	36.017
−0.030	1.4345	35.750
	1.4350	35.763

650, 750-2 CRANKSHAFT JOURNAL SIZES

Shell Bearing Marking	Suitable Bore Sizes (in.)	(mm)
Standard	1.6235	41.237
	1.6240	41.250
Undersize		
−0.010	1.6135	40.983
	1.6140	40.996
−0.020	1.6035	40.729
	1.6040	40.742

500 REPLACEMENT PISTON AND SUITABLE BORE SIZES

Piston Marking in. (mm)	Bore (in.)	(mm)
Standard	2.716	60.000
+0.010 (0.254)	2.726	69.254
+0.020 (0.508)	2.736	69.508
+0.040 (1.016)	2.756	70.000

650 REPLACEMENT PISTON AND SUITABLE BORE SIZES

Piston Marking in. (mm)	Suitable Bore Sizes (in.)	(mm)
Standard	2.7948	70.993
	2.7953	71.006
Oversizes		
+0.010 (0.254)	2.8048	71.247
	2.8053	71.260
+0.020 (0.508)	2.8148	71.501
	2.8153	71.514
+0.040 (1.016)	2.8348	72.009
	2.8353	72.022

750-2 CYLINDER AND PISTON GRADING

	"L"	"M"	"H"
Piston Diameter			
in.	2.9871-2.9874	2.9875-2.9878	2.9879-2.9882
mm	75.872-75.880	75.883-75.890	75.893-75.900
Cylinder Bore			
in.	2.9911-2.9913	2.9914-2.9917	2.9918-2.9921
mm	75.973-75.980	75.983-75.990	75.993-76.000

750-2 REPLACEMENT PISTON AND SUITABLE BORE SIZES

Piston Marking in. (mm)	Suitable Bore Sizes (in.)	(mm)
Standard (L, M, H)	see "Cylinder and Piston Grading"	
+0.010 (0.254)	3.0010-3.0021	76.2254-76.2533
+0.020 (0.508)	3.0110-3.0121	76.4794-76.5073
+0.030 (0.726)	3.0210-3.0221	76.7334-76.7613
+0.040 (1.016)	3.0310-3.0321	76.9514-76.9793

750—3 CRANKSHAFT JOURNAL SIZES

Shell Bearing Marking	Suitable Crankshaft Size (in.)	(mm)
Standard	1.6235	41.237
	1.6240	41.250
Undersize −0.010	1.6135	40.983
	1.6140	40.996
−0.020	1.6035	40.729
	1.6040	40.742
−0.030	1.5935	40.475
	1.5940	40.488
−0.040	1.5835	40.221
	1.5840	40.234

750—3 CENTER BEARING SIZES

Shell Bearing Marking	Suitable Crankshaft Size (in.)	(mm)
Standard	1.9170	48.692
	1.9175	48.705
Undersize −0.010	1.9070	48.438
	1.9075	48.451
−0.020	1.8970	48.184
	1.8975	48.197
−0.030	1.8870	47.930
	1.8875	47.943
−0.040	1.8770	47.676
	1.8775	47.689

750—3 REPLACEMENT PISTON AND SUITABLE BORE SIZES

Piston Size in. (mm)	Bore (in.)	Size (mm)
Standard	2.6368	66.975
	2.6363	66.962
+0.010 (0.254)	2.6468	67.229
	2.6463	67.215
+0.020 (0.508)	2.6568	67.483
	2.6563	67.470
+0.040 (1.016)	2.6768	67.990
	2.6763	67.980

ENGINE AND TRANSMISSION SPECIFICATIONS—TR25W

PISTON	
Material	"Lo-Ex" aluminum
Compression ratio	10 : 1
Clearance (bottom of skirt)	0.0023-0.0028 in. (0.05842-0.07112 mm)
Clearance (top of skirt) (measured on major axis)	0.0042-0.0053 in. (0.10668-0.13462 mm)
PISTON RINGS	
Material—compression (top)	Brico BSS 0.5004 cast iron
Material—compression (center)	Brico 8 cast iron
Material—scraper	Brico BSS 0.5004 cast iron
Width—compression (top and center)	0.0625 in. (1.5875 mm) (0.0615-0.0625 in.)
Width—scraper	0.125 in. (3.175 mm) (0.124-0.125 in.)
CRANKSHAFT	
End float	0.002-0.005 in. (0.0508-0.127 mm)
VALVES	
Seat angle (inclusive)	90°
Head diameter (inlet)	1.450-1.455 in. (36.830-36.957 mm)
Head diameter (exhaust)	1.312-1.317 in. (33.3248-33.4518 mm)
Stem diameter (inlet)	0.3095-0.3100 in. (7.861-7.874 mm)
Stem diameter (exhaust)	0.3090-0.3095 in. (7.848-7.861 mm)
VALVE GUIDES	
Material	Hidural 5
Bore diameter	0.3120-0.3130 in. (7.9248-7.950 mm)

ENGINE AND TRANSMISSION SPECIFICATIONS—TR25W

Depth—compression (top and center)	0.108-0.114 in. (2.7432-2.8956 mm)
Depth—scraper	0.094-0.100 in. (2.3876-2.540 mm)
Clearance in groove	0.001-0.003 in. (0.0254-0.0762 mm)
Fitted gap—(maximum)	0.013 in. (0.3302 mm)
Fitted gap—(minimum)	0.009 in. (0.2283 mm)
Connecting rod (length between centers)	5.312 in. (134.92 mm)
Internal die of small end	0.6892 in. (17.51 mm)
CYLINDER BARREL	
Material	Aluminum alloy with austenitic iron liner
Bore size (standard)	67 mm
Stroke	70 mm
Oversizes	1/2 mm and 1 mm
CYLINDER HEAD	
Material	Aluminum alloy
Inlet port size	1.125 in. (28.575 mm)
Exhaust port size	1.25 in. (31.75 mm)
CAMSHAFT	
Journal diameter (right- and left-hand)	0.7480-0.7485 in. (18.9992-19.0119 mm)
Cam lift (inlet)	0.345 in. (8.763 mm)
Cam lift (exhaust)	0.336 in. (8.534 mm)
Base circle radius	0.906 in. (23.0124 mm)
CAMSHAFT BUSHINGS	
Bore diameter (fitted)	0.7492-0.7497 in. (19.0297-19.04238 mm)
Outside diameter	0.908-0.909 in. (23.0632-23.0886 mm)
Camshaft clearance	0.0007-0.0017 in. (0.01778-0.04318 mm)
Crankcase bearing (timing-side)	25 x 62 x 17 mm
Crankcase diameter (drive-side and timing side)	0.9841-0.9844 in. (24.9961-22.0038 mm)
Gearbox layshaft bearings (drive-side and timing side)	0.5 x 0.625 x 0.8125 in. (12.7 x 15.875 x 20.6375 mm)
Gearbox layshaft diameter (drive-side and timing side)	0.6245-0.625 in. (15.8623-15.8750 mm)
Gearbox mainshaft bearing (drive-side)	30 x 62 x 16 mm
Gearbox mainshaft bearing (timing-side)	0.625 x 1.5625 x 0.4375 in. (15.875 x 39.2875 x 11.1125 mm)
Gearbox mainshaft diameter (drive-side)	0.7485-0.749 in. (19.0119-19.0246 mm)
Gearbox mainshaft diameter (timing-side)	0.6245-0.625 in. (15.8623-15.8750 mm)
Outside diameter	0.5005-0.5010 in. (12.7127-12.7254 mm)
Length	1.844 in. (46.8376 mm)
Cylinder head interference fit	0.0015-0.0025 in. (0.0381-0.0635 mm)
VALVE SPRINGS	
Free length (inner)	1.400 in. (35.56 mm)
Free length (outer)	1.750 in. (44.45 mm)
Fitted length (inner)	1.262 in. (32.0548 mm)
Fitted length (outer)	370 in. (34-798 mm)
VALVE TIMING	
Tappets set to 0.015 in. (0.381 mm) for checking purposes only:	
Inlet opens BTDC	51°
Inlet closed ABDC	68°
Exhaust opens BBDC	78°
Exhaust closes ATDC	37°
BEARING DIMENSIONS	
Clutch roller (25)	0.1875 x 0.1875 in. (4.7025 x 4.7025 mm)
Con-rod big-end bearing—running clearance	0.0005-0.0015 in. (0.0127-0.0381 mm)
Con-rod big-end—crank diameter	1.4375-1.4380 in. (36.5125-36.5252 mm)
Crank undersizes	0.010, 0.020, and 0.030 in (0.254, 0.508, and 0.762 mm)
Con-rod small-end bush (bore)	0.6890-0.6894 in. (17.5006-17.6108 mm)
Crankcase bearing (drive-side)	25 x 62 x 17 mm
Gearbox sleeve pinion (internal diameter)	0.752-0.753 in. (19.1008-19.1262 mm)
Gearbox sleeve pinion (external diameter)	1.179-1.180 in. (29.9466-29.9720 mm)
Piston pin diameter	0.6882-0.6885 in. (17.4803-17.4879 mm)
CLUTCH	
Type	Multi-plate with integral cush drive
Number of plates:	
Driving (bonded segments)	4
Driven (plain)	5
Overall thickness of driving plate and segments	0.167 in. (4.242 mm)
Clutch springs	4
Free length of springs	1.65685 in. (42.0687 mm)
Clutch pushrod (length)	9.0 in. (228.6 mm)
Clutch pushrod (diameter)	0.1875 in. (4.7025 mm)

ENGINE SPECIFICATIONS—T100C AND T100R

PISTONS

Material	Aluminum alloy die cast.	
Clearance:	**From H.49833 (in.)**	**Before H.49833 (in.)**
Top of skirt	0.0050-0.0072	0.0075-0.0085
Bottom of skirt	0.0030-0.0045	0.002-0.003
Piston pin hole diam.	0.6882-0.6886	0.6882-0.6886

PISTON RINGS

Material	Cast iron
Compression rings (taper faced)	
Width	0.0615-0.0625 in.
Thickness	0.092-0.100 in.
Fitted gap	0.010-0.014 in.
Clearance in groove	0.001-0.003 in.
Oil control ring	
Width	0.124-0.125 in.
Thickness	0.092-0.100 in.
Fitted gap	0.010-0.014 in.
Clearance in groove	0.0005-0.0025 in.

VALVES

Seat angle (included)	90°
Head diameter:	
Inlet	$1\frac{17}{32}$ in.
Inlet (Before H.49833)	$1\frac{7}{16}$ in.
Exhaust	$1\frac{5}{16}$ in.
Stem diameter	
Inlet	0.3095-0.3100 in.
Exhaust	0.3090-0.3095 in.

VALVE GUIDES

Material	Hidural
Bore diameter (Inlet and exhaust)	0.312-0.313 in.
Outside diameter (Inlet and exhaust)	0.5005-0.5010 in.
Length	
Inlet	$1\frac{3}{4}$ in.
Exhaust	$1\frac{3}{4}$ in.

CAMSHAFTS

Journal diameter: Left	0.8100-0.8105 in.
Diametrical clearance: Left	0.0010-0.0025 in.
End float	0.005-0.008 in.
Cam lift: Inlet	0.314 in.
Exhaust	0.296 in. (T100C) 0.314 in. (T100R)
Base circle diameter Inlet and exhaust	0.812 in.

CAMSHAFT BEARING BUSHES

Material	Steel-backed bronze
Bore diameter (fitted): Left	0.8125-0.8135 in.

VALVE SPRINGS (Inner—Yellow, Outer—L/Blue Spot)

Free length	Out. $1\frac{1}{2}$ in.	In. $1\frac{19}{32}$ in.
Total number of coils	Out. 6	In. $8\frac{1}{4}$
Total fitted load:		
Valve open	136 lbs	
Valve closed	63 lbs	

VALVE TIMING

Set all tappet clearances at 0.020 in. (0.5 mm) for checking	
Inlet opens	34° before top center
Inlet closes	55° after bottom center
Exhaust opens	48° before bottom center
Exhaust closes	27° after top center

ROCKERS

Material	High tensile steel forging
Bore diameter	0.4375-0.4380 in.
Rocker spindle diameter	0.4355-0.4360 in.
Tappet clearance (cold):	
Inlet	0.002 in. (0.05 mm)
Exhaust	0.004 in. (0.10 mm)

TAPPETS

Material	High tensile steel forging —Stellite Tip
Tip radius	$\frac{3}{4}$ in. (T100C) $1\frac{1}{8}$ in. (T100R)
Tappet diameter	0.3110-0.3115 in.
Clearance in guide block	0.0005-0.0015 in.

TAPPET GUIDE BLOCK

Diameter of bores	0.3120-0.3125 in.
Outside diameter	1.000-0.9995 in.
Interference fit in cylinder block	0.0005-0.0015 in.

CYLINDER HEAD

Material	DTD 424 Aluminum Alloy
Inlet port size	1 in. diam. (T100C) $1\frac{1}{16}$ in. diam. (T100R)
Exhaust port size	$1\frac{1}{4}$ in. diam.
Valve seatings: Type	Cast-in
Material	Cast iron

CRANKSHAFT

Type	Forged two-throw crank with bolt-on flywheel
Left main bearing size and type	72 x 30 x 19 mm. Ball Journal

ENGINE SPECIFICATIONS— (con't.)

Outside diameter: Left	0.906-0.907 in.
Length: Left inlet	1.114-1.094 in.
Left exhaust	0.922-0.942 in.
Interference fit in crankcase Left	0.002-0.003 in.
TIMING GEARS	
Inlet & exhaust camshaft pinions	
Number of teeth	50
Interference fit on camshaft	0.000-0.001
Intermediate timing gear	
Number of teeth	42
Bore diameter	0.5618-0.5625
Intermediate timing gear bush	
Material	Phosphor bronze
Outside diameter	0.5635-0.5640 in.
Bore diameter	0.4990-0.4995 in.
Length	0.6775-0.6825 in.
Working clearance on spindle	0.0005-0.0015 in.
Intermediate wheel spindle	
Diameter	0.4980-0.4985 in.
Interference fit in crankcase	0.0005-0.0015 in.
Crankcase pinion:	
Number of teeth	25
Fit on crankcase	+0.0003 in. −0.0005 in.
CYLINDERS	
Material	Cast iron
Bore size	2.7160-2.7165 in.
Maximum oversize	2.7360-2.7365 in.
Tappet guide block housing diameter	0.9985-0.9990 in.
Right crankshaft main-bearing journal diameter	1.4375-1.4380 in.
Right main-bearing bore, size, and type	1.4390-1.4385 in. Steel-backed copper lead-lined bush. Under sizes available: −0.010 in., −0.020 in., −0.030 in.
Left main bearing housing diameter	2.8321-2.8336 in.
Right main bearing housing diameter	1.8135-1.8140 in.
Big-end journal diameter	1.4375-1.4380 in.
Min. regrind diameter	1.4075-1.4080 in.
Crankshaft end float	0.008-0.017 in.
CONNECTING RODS	
Material	Alloy 'H' Section RR.56
Length (Centers)	5.311-5.313 in.
Big-end bearings type	Steel-backed white metal
Bearing side clearance	0.013-0.017 in.
Bearing diametrical clearance	0.005-0.0020 in. min.
PISTON PIN	
Material	High tensile steel
Fit in small end bush	0.0005-0.0012 in.
Diameter	0.6882-0.6885 in.
Length	2.151-2.156 in.
SMALL-END BUSHING	
Material	Phosphor Bronze
Outer diameter	0.782-0.783 in.
Length	0.890-0.910 in.
Finished bore diameter	0.6905-0.6910 in.

CLUTCH AND TRANSMISSION SPECIFICATIONS— T100C AND T100R

CLUTCH	
Type	Multiplate with integral shock absorber
Number of plates	
Driving (bonded)	6
Driven (plain)	6
Pressure Springs	
Number	3
Free-length	$1\frac{31}{32}$ in.
Number of working coils	$9\frac{1}{2}$
Spring rate	$58\frac{1}{2}$ lbs/in.
Approximate fitted load	42 lbs
Bearing rollers	
GEARS	
Mainshaft high gear	
Bore diameter (Bush fitted)	0.7520-0.7530 in.
Working clearance on shaft	0.0020-0.0035 in.
Bush length	$2\frac{19}{32}$ in.
Bush protrusion length	$\frac{3}{8}$ in. (nil after H.57083)
GEARS	
Layshaft low gear	
Bore diameter (bush fitted)	0.689-0.690 in.
Working clearance on shaft	0.0015-0.003 in.
GEARBOX SHAFTS	
Mainshaft	

CLUTCH AND TRANSMISSION SPECIFICATIONS—T100C AND T100R

Number	20
Diameter	0.2495-0.2500 in.
Length	0.231-0.236 in.
Clutch hub bearing diameter	1.37-1.3743 in.
Clutch sprocket bore diameter	1.0745-1.0755 in.
Thrust washer thickness	0.052-0.054 in.
Engine sprocket teeth	26
Clutch sprocket teeth	58
Chain details	Duplex endless— 3/8 in. pitch x 78 links
CLUTCH OPERATING MECHANISM	
Conical spring	
Number of working coils	2
Free length	13/32 in.
Diameter of balls	3/8 in.
Clutch operating rod	
Diameter of rod	3/16 in.
Length of rod	9.562-9.567 in.
RATIOS	
Internal ratios (Std): 4th (Top)	1.00:1
3rd	1.22:1
2nd	1.61:1
1st (Bot.)	2.47:1
Overall ratios: 4th (Top)	5.70
3rd	6.95
2nd	9.18
1st (Bottom)	14.09
Engine rpm @ 10 mph in 4th (Top) gear	763
Gearbox sprocket teeth	18
Left end diameter	0.7495-0.7500 in.
Right end diameter	0.6685-0.6689 in.
Length	9 1/64 in.
Length (before H.49833)	8 51/64 in.
Layshaft	
Left-end diameter	0.6845-0.6850 in.
Right-end diameter	0.6870-0.6875 in.
Length	5 3/8 in.
Camplate plunger spring	
Free-length	2 1/2
Number of working coils	22
Spring rate	5-6 lbs/in.
BEARINGS	
High gear bearing	30 x 62 x 16 mm Ball Jour.
Mainshaft bearing	17 x 47 x 14 mm Ball Jour.
Layshaft bearing (left)	1 1/16 x 7/8 x 3/4 in. Needle roller
Layshaft bearing (right)	5/8 x 13/16 x 3/4 in. Needle roller
KICK-START OPERAT. MECH.	
Ratchet spring free-length	1/2 in.
GEARCHANGE MECHANISM	
Plungers	
Outer diameter	0.3402-0.3412 in.
Working clearance in bore	0.0015-0.0035 in.
Plunger springs	
Number of working coils	16
Free-length	1 1/16 in.
Outer bush bore diameter	0.623-0.624 in.
Clearance on shaft	0.001-0.003 in.
Quadrant return springs:	
Number of working coils	18
Free-length	1 7/8 in.

ENGINE SPECIFICATIONS—TR6R, TR6C, AND T120R

PISTONS	
Material	Aluminum alloy die cast.
Clearance	
Top of skirt	0.0106-0.0085 in.
Bottom of skirt	0.0061-0.0046 in.
Piston pin hole diameter	0.6882-0.6886 in.
PISTON RINGS	
Material	Cast iron
Compression rings (tapered)	
Width	0.0615-0.0625 in.
Thickness	0.092-0.100 in.
Fitted gap	0.010-0.014 in.
Clearance in groove	0.001-0.003 in.
TAPPETS	
Material	High tensile steel body— Stellite tip
Tip radius	0.75 in. (In.); 1.125 in. (Ex.)
Tappet diameter	0.3110-0.3115 in.
Clearance in guide block	0.0005-0.0015 in.
TAPPET GUIDE BLOCK	
Diameter of bores	0.3120-0.3125 in.
Outside diameter	1.000-0.9995 in.
Interference fit in cyl. block	0.0005-0.0015 in.
CAMSHAFT BEARING BUSHES	
Material	High density sintered bronze

ENGINE SPECIFICATIONS—TR6R, TR6C, AND T120R

Oil control ring	
Width	0.092-0.100 in.
Thickness	0.124-0.125 in.
Fitted gap	0.010-0.014 in.
Clearance in groove	0.0005-0.0025 in.
VALVES	
Stem diameter: Intake	0.3095-0.3100 in.
Exhaust	0.3090-0.3095 in.
Head diameter: Intake	1.592-1.596 in.
Exhaust	1.434-1.440 in.
Exhaust valve material	21-4NS
VALVE GUIDES	
Material	Aluminum-bronze
Bore diam. (Inlet & exhaust)	0.3127-0.3137 in.
Outside diameter (Inlet and exhaust)	0.5005-0.5010 in.
Length: Inlet	$1^{31}/_{32}$ in.
Exhaust	$2^{11}/_{64}$ in.
VALVE SPRINGS (Red spot inner, Green spot outer)	
Free-length	Out. $1^1/_2$ in. In. $1^{17}/_{32}$ in.
Number of coils	Out. $5^1/_2$ In. $7^1/_4$
Total fitted load	
Valve open	Int. 143 lbs Exh. 155 lbs
Valve closed	Int. 75 lbs Exh. 87 lbs
Fitted length (valve closed)	
Inner	$1^3/_{16}$ in. $1^1/_8$ in.
Outer	$1^7/_{32}$ in. $1^5/_{32}$ in.
ROCKERS	
Material	High tensile steel forging
Bore diameter	0.5002-0.5012 in.
Rocker spindle diameter	0.4990-0.4995 in.
Tappet clear. (cold): Inlet	0.002 in. (0.05 mm)
Exhaust	0.004 in. (0.10 mm)
CAMSHAFTS	
Journal diam.: Left	0.8100-0.8105 in.
Right	0.8730-0.8735 in.
Diametrical clear.: Left	0.0010-0.0025 in.
Right	0.0005-0.0020 in.
End float	0.013-0.020 in.
Cam lift: Inlet and exhaust	0.314 in.
Base circle diameter	0.812 in.
CRANKSHAFT	
Crankshaft type	Forged two-throw crank with bolt-on flywheel located by the timing side main bearing
Main bearing (drive-side) size and type	$2^{13}/_{16}$ x $1^1/_8$ x $^{13}/_{16}$ in. Ball Journal

Bore diam. (fitted): Left	0.8125-0.8135 in.
Right	0.874-0.875 in.
Outside diameter: Left	1.0010-1.0015 in.
Right	1.126-1.127 in.
Length: Left inlet	1.104-1.114 in.
CAMSHAFT BEARING BUSHES	
Left exhaust	0.932-0.942 in.
Right inlet and exhaust	1.010-1.020 in.
Interference fit in crankcase	
Left	0.001-0.002 in.
Right	0.0010-0.0025 in.
TIMING GEARS	
Inlet & exh. camshaft pinions	
Number of teeth	50
Interference ft on camshaft	0.000-0.001 in.
Intermediate timing gear	
Number of teeth	47
Bore diameter	0.5618-0.5625 in.
Intermediate timing gear bush	
Material	Phosphor bronze
Outside diameter	0.5635-0.5640 in.
Bore diameter	0.4990-0.4995 in.
Length	0.6775-0.6825 in.
Working clear. on spindle	0.0005-0.0015 in.
Intermediate wheel spindle	
Diameter	0.4980-0.4985 in.
Interference fit in crank.	0.0005-0.0015 in.
Crankshaft pinion	
Number of teeth	25
Fit on crankshaft	+0.0003/−0.0005 in.
CYLINDER BLOCK	
Material	Cast iron
Bore size	2.7984-2.7953 in.
Maximum oversize	2.8348-2.8353 in.
Tappet guide block housing diameter	0.9990-0.9985 in.
CYLINDER HEAD	
Material	D.T.D. 424 Aluminum
Inlet port size	$1^3/_{16}$ in. diam. tapering to $1^1/_8$ in.
Exhaust port size	$1^3/_8$ in. diam.
Valve seatings	
Type	Cast-in
Material	Cast iron
CONNECTING RODS	
Length (centers)	6.499-6.501 in.
Big-end bearings—type	Steel-backed white metal
Bearing side clearance	0.012-0.016 in.
Bearing diametrical clearance	0.0005-0.0020 in.
PISTON PIN	
Material	High tensile steel

ENGINE SPECIFICATIONS—TR6R, TR6C, AND T120R

Main Bearing (timing side) size and type	$2\frac{13}{16}$ x $1\frac{1}{8}$ x $\frac{13}{16}$ in. Ball Journal
Main bearing journal diam.	1.1247-1.1250 in.
Main bearing housing diam.	2.8095-2.8110 in.
Big-end journal diameter	1.6235-1.6240 in.
Minimum regrind diameter	1.6035-1.6040 in.
Crankshaft end float	0.003-0.017 in.
Balance factor	85 per cent (using 689 gramme weights)
Fit in small-end bush	0.0005-0.0012 in. clear.
Diameter	0.6882-0.6885 in.
Length	2.151-2.156 in.
SMALL END BUSHING	
Material	Phosphor bronze
Outer diameter	0.8140-0.8145 in.
Length	1.030-1.031 in.
Finished bore diameter	0.6890-0.6894 in.

CLUTCH AND TRANSMISSION SPECIFICATIONS—TR6R, TR6C, AND T120R

CLUTCH	
Type	Multiplate with integral shock absorber
Number of plates	
Driving (bonded)	6
Driven (plain)	6
Pressure springs	
Number	3
Free-length	$1\frac{13}{16}$ in.
Number of working coils	$9\frac{1}{2}$
Spring rate	113 lbs/in.
Approximate fitted load	62 lbs
Bearing rollers	
Number	20
Diameter	0.2495-0.2500 in.
Length	0.231-0.236 in.
Clutch hub bearing diameter	1.3733-1.3743 in.
Clutch sprocket bore diameter	1.8745-1.8755 in.
Thrust washer thickness	0.052-0.054 in.
Engine sprocket teeth	29
Clutch sprocket teeth	58
Chain details	Duplex endless— $\frac{3}{8}$ in. pitch x 84 links
CLUTCH OPERATING MECH.	
Conical spring	
Number of working coils	2
Free-length	$\frac{13}{32}$ in.
Diameter of balls	$\frac{3}{8}$ in.
Clutch operating rod	
Diameter of rod	$\frac{7}{32}$ in.
Length of rod	11.822-11.812 in.
GEARS	
Mainshaft high gear	
Bore diameter (bush fitted)	0.8135-0.8145 in.
Working clearance on shaft	0.0032-0.0047 in.
Bush length	$2\frac{19}{32}$ in.
Layshaft low gear	
Bore diameter (bush fitted)	0.8135-0.8145 in.
Working clearance on shaft	0.0025-0.0045 in.
GEARBOX SHAFTS	
Mainshaft	
Left end diameter	0.8098-0.8103 in.
Right end diameter	0.7494-0.7498 in.
Length	$11\frac{19}{64}$ in.
Layshaft	
Left end diameter	0.6845-0.6850 in.
Right end diameter	0.6845-0.6850 in.
Length	$6\frac{31}{64}$ in.
Camplate plunger spring	
Free-length	$2\frac{1}{2}$ in.
Number of working coils	22
Spring rate	5-6 lb/in.
BEARINGS	
High gear bearing	$1\frac{1}{4}$ x $2\frac{1}{2}$ x $\frac{5}{8}$ in. Ball Journal
Mainshaft bearing	$\frac{3}{4}$ x $1\frac{7}{8}$ x $\frac{9}{16}$ in. Ball Journal
Layshaft bearing (r. & l.)	$\frac{11}{16}$ x $\frac{7}{8}$ x $\frac{3}{4}$ in. Needle Roller
KICK START OPERAT. MECH.	
Bush bore diameter	0.751-0.752 in.
Spindle working clear. in bush	0.003-0.005 in.
Ratchet spring free-length	$\frac{1}{2}$ in.
GEARCHANGE MECHANISM	
Plungers	
Outer diameter	0.4315-0.4320 in.
Working clearance in bore	0.0005-0.0015 in.
GEARCHANGE MECHANISM	
Plunger springs	
Number of working coils	12
Free-length	$1\frac{1}{4}$ in.
Inner bush bore diameter	0.6245-0.6255 in.
Clearance on shaft	0.0007-0.0032 in.
Outer bush bore diameter	0.7495-0.7505 in.
Clearance on shaft	0.0005-0.0025 in.
Quadrant return springs	
Number of working coils	$9\frac{1}{2}$
Free-length	$1\frac{3}{4}$ in.

ENGINE SPECIFICATIONS—TR7V, T140V

PISTONS	
Material	Aluminum alloy die cast
Clearance	see piston grading chart
Top of skirt	——
Bottom of skirt	——
Piston pin hole diameter	0.7502-0.7504 in.
PISTON RINGS	
Material	cast iron
Compression rings (tapered)	
Width	0.113-0.121 in.
Thickness	0.0615-0.0625 in.
Fitted gap	0.008-0.013 in.
Clearance in groove	0.0015-0.0025 in.
Oil control ring	
Width	0.121 in.
Thickness	0.125 in.
Fitted gap	0.010-0.040 in.
Clearance in groove	0.0015-0.0025 in.
VALVES	
Stem diameter: Intake	0.3095-0.3100 in.
Exhaust	0.3090-0.3095 in.
Head diameter: Intake	1.592-1.596 in.
Exhaust	1.434-1.440 in.
Exhaust valve material	21/4NS
VALVE GUIDES	
Material	Aluminum-bronze
Bore diam. (Inlet & exhaust)	0.3127-0.3137 in.
Outside diameter (Inlet and exhaust)	0.5005-0.5010 in.
Length: Inlet	$1^{31}/_{32}$
Exhaust	$2^{11}/_{64}$
VALVE SPRINGS (Red spot inner, Green spot outer)	
Free-length	Out. $1^1/_2$ in. In. $1^{17}/_{32}$ in.
Number of coils	Out. $5^1/_2$ In. $7^1/_4$
Total fitted load	
Valve open	Int. 143 lbs. Ex. 155 lbs.
Valve closed	Int. 75 lbs. Ex. 87 lbs.
Fitted length (valve closed)	
Inner	$1^3/_{16}$ in. $1^1/_8$ in.
Outer	$1^7/_{32}$ in. $1^5/_{32}$ in.
ROCKERS	
Material	High tensile steel forging
Bore diameter	0.5002-0.5012 in.
Rocker spindle diameter	0.4990-0.4995 in.
Tappet clear. (cold): Inlet	0.008 in. (0.203 mm)
Exhaust	0.006 in. (0.15 mm)

TAPPETS	
Material	High tensile steel body—Stellite tip
Tip radius	0.75 in. (In.); 1.125 in. (Ex.)
Tappet diameter	0.3110-0.3115 in.
Clearance in guide block	0.0005-0.0015 in.
TAPPET GUIDE BLOCK	
Diameter of bores	0.3120-0.3125 in.
Outside diameter	1.000-0.9995 in.
Interference fit in cyl. block	0.0005-0.0015 in.
CAMSHAFT BEARING BUSHES	
Material	High density sintered bronze
Bore diam. (fitted): Left	0.8125-0.8135 in.
Right	0.874-0.875 in.
Outside diameter: Left	1.0010-1.0015 in.
Right	1.126-1.127 in.
Length: Left inlet	1.104-1.114 in.
CAMSHAFT BEARING BUSHES	
Left exhaust	0.932-0.942 in.
Right inlet and exhaust	1.010-1.020 in.
Interference fit in crankcase	
Left	0.001-0.002 in.
Right	0.0010-0.0025 in.
TIMING GEARS	
Inlet & exh. camshaft pinions	
Number of teeth	50
Interference ft on camshaft	0.000-0.001 in.
Intermediate timing gear	
Number of teeth	47
Bore diameter	0.5618-0.5625 in.
Intermediate timing gear bush	
Material	Phosphor bronze
Outside diameter	0.5635-0.5640 in.
Bore diameter	0.4990-0.4995 in.
Length	0.6775-0.6825 in.
Working clear. on spindle	0.0005-0.0015 in.
Intermediate wheel spindle	
Diameter	0.4980-0.4985 in.
Interference fit in crank.	0.0005-0.0015 in.
Crankshaft pinion	
Number of teeth	25
Fit on crankshaft	+0.0003/−0.0005 in.
CYLINDER BLOCK	
Material	Cast iron
Bore size	2.9911-2.9921 in.
Maximum oversize	+0.040 in.
Tappet guide block housing diameter	0.9990-0.9985 in.

ENGINE SPECIFICATIONS—TR7V, T140V

CAMSHAFTS	
Journal diam.: Left	0.8100-0.8105 in.
Right	0.8730-0.8735 in.
Diametrical clear.: Left	0.0010-0.0025 in.
Right	0.0005-0.0020 in.
End float	0.013-0.020 in.
Cam lift: Inlet and exhaust	0.347 and 0.305 in.
Base circle diameter	0.812 in.
CRANKSHAFT	
Crankshaft type	Forged two-throw crank with bolt-on flywheel located by the timing side main bearing
Main bearing (drive side) size and type	$2\frac{13}{16} \times 1\frac{1}{8} \times \frac{13}{16}$ in. roller bearing
Main bearing (timing side) size and type	72 x 30 x 19mm ball race
Main bearing journal diameter (timing side)	1.1808-1.1812 in.
Main bearing journal diameter (drive side)	1.1247-1.250 in.
Main bearing housing diameter	2.8095-2.8110 in.
Big end journal diameter	1.6235-1.6240 in.
Minimum regrind diameter	1.6035-1.6040 in.
Crankshaft end float	0.003-0.017 in.

CYLINDER HEAD	
Material	D.T.D. 424 Aluminum
Inlet port size	1.12 in.
Exhaust port size	$1\frac{3}{8}$ in. diam.
Valve seatings	
Type	Cast-in
Material	Cast iron
CONNECTING RODS	
Length (centers)	5.999-6.001 in.
Big-end bearings—type	Steel backed with white metal
Bearing side clearance	0.012-0.016 in.
Bearing diametrical clearance	0.005-0.0020 in.
PISTON PIN	
Material	High tensile steel
Fit in small-end bush	0.0005-0.0012 in. clear.
Diameter	0.6882-0.6885 in.
Length	2.151-2.156 in.
SMALL END BUSHING	
Material	Phosphor bronze
Outer diameter	0.8140-0.8145 in.
Length	1.030-1.031 in.
Finished bore diameter	0.6890-0.6894 in.

CLUTCH AND TRANSMISSION SPECIFICATIONS—TR7V, T140V

CLUTCH	
Type	Multiplate with integral shock absorber
Number of plates	
Driving (bonded)	6
Driven (plain)	6
Pressure springs	
Number	3
Free length	1.75 in.
No. working coils	$7\frac{1}{2}$
Spring rate	169 lbs.
Approximate fitted load	83 lbs.
Bearing rollers	
Number	20
Diameter	0.2495-0.2500 in.
Length	0.231-0.236 in.
Clutch hub bearing diameter	1.3733-1.3743 in.
Clutch sprocket bore diameter	1.8745-1.8755 in.
Thrust washer thickness	0.052-0.054 in.
Engine sprocket teeth	29
Clutch sprocket teeth	58
Chain	Triplex endless—$\frac{3}{8}$ in. pitch x 84 links

GEARBOX BEARINGS	
Mainshaft bearing (left)	$1\frac{1}{2} \times 2\frac{1}{2} \times \frac{5}{8}$ in. Roller bearing
Mainshaft bearing (right)	$\frac{3}{4} \times 1\frac{7}{8} \times \frac{9}{16}$ in. Ball Journal
Layshaft bearing (left)	$\frac{11}{16} \times \frac{7}{8} \times \frac{3}{4}$ in. Needle roller
Layshaft bearing (right)	$\frac{11}{16} \times \frac{7}{8} \times \frac{3}{4}$ in. Needle roller
Layshaft 1st gear bush	
Bore diameter	0.795-0.800 in.
Shaft diameter	0.8070-0.8075 in.
Layshaft 2nd gear bush	
Bore diameter	0.795-0.800 in.
Shaft diameter	0.8070-0.8075 in.
KICK START OPERAT. MECH.	
Bush bore diameter	0.751-0.752 in.
Spindle working clear. in bush	0.003-0.005 in.
Ratchet spring free-length	$\frac{1}{2}$ in.
GEARCHANGE MECHANISM	
Plungers	
Outer diameter	0.4315-0.4320 in.
Working clearance in bore	0.0005-0.0015 in.

CLUTCH AND TRANSMISSION SPECIFICATIONS—TR7V, T140V

CLUTCH OPERATING MECH.	
Conical spring	
Number of working coils	2
Free length	13/32 in.
Diameter of balls	3/8 in.
Clutch operating rod	
Diameter	7/32 in.
Length	11.812-11.822 in.
GEARS	
Mainshaft, high gear	
Bearing type	Needle roller (Torrington B1314)
Bearing length	0.865-0.875 in.
Spigot diameter (high gear)	1.5072-1.5077 in.
GEARBOX SHAFTS	
Mainshaft	
Left end diameter	0.8089-0.8103 in.
Right end diameter	0.7494-0.7498 in.
Length	11.23 in.
Layshaft	
Left end diameter	0.6870-0.6875 in.
Righ end diameter	0.6870-0.6875 in.
Length	6.47 in.

GEARCHANGE MECHANISM	
Plunger springs	
Number of working coils	12
Free-length	1 1/4 in.
Inner bush bore diameter	0.6245-0.6255 in.
Clearance on shaft	0.0007-0.0032 in.
Outer bush bore diameter	0.7495-0.7505 in.
Clearance on shaft	0.0005-0.0025 in.
Quadrant return springs	
Number of working coils	9 1/2
Free-length	1 3/4 in.

ENGINE SPECIFICATIONS—T150

PISTONS	
Material	Aluminum Alloy-die cast.
Clearance: Top of skirt	0.0056-0.0035 in. (0.42-0.089 mm)
Bottom of skirt	0.0033-0.0018 in. (0.084-0.0457 mm)
Piston pin hole diam.	0.6885-0.6883 in. (17.9879-17.4828 mm)
PISTON RINGS	
Material	Cast iron HG10
Compression rings (tapered)	
Width	2.729-2.577 in.
Thickness	0.0625-0.0615 in. (1.5875-1.5621 mm)
Fitted gap	0.009-0.013 in. (0.2286-0.3302 mm)
Clearance in groove	0.0035-0.0015 in. (0.89-0.038 mm)
Oil control ring	
Width	2.729-2.577 mm
Thickness	0.125-0.124 in. (3.175-3.1496 mm)
Fitted gap	0.010-0.040 in. (0.254-1.016 mm)
Clearance in groove	0.0105-0.0065 in. (0.266-0.165 mm)

VALVE GUIDES	
Material	Hidural 5
Bore diameter (Inlet and exhaust)	0.3115-0.3110 in. (7.9121-7.8994 mm)
Outside diameter (Inlet and exhaust)	0.5005-0.5010 in. (12.7127-12.7254 mm)
Length: Intake	1.875 in. (47.625 mm)
Exhaust	1.875 in. (47.625 mm)
VALVE SPRINGS (Red and White)	
Free-length: Inner	1.468 in. (37.2872 mm)
Outer	1.600 in. (40.64 mm)
Total number of coils: Inner	6
Outer	5 1/2
Total fitted load	
Valve open: Inner	82 lbs (37.228 kgm)
Outer	115 lbs (51.31 kgm)
Valve closed: Inner	37-40 lbs (16.798-18.144 kgm)
Outer	43-53 lbs (21.792-24.062 kgm)
VALVE LIFT	Valve lift
Set all tappet clearances @ nil for checking	In. 0.152 in. (3.86 mm)
Measure valve lift at TBC with cold engine	Ex. 0.146 in. (3.71 mm)

ENGINE SPECIFICATIONS—T150

CYLINDER	
Material	Austenitic steel liner Aluminum Alloy
Bore size	2.6368-2.6363 in. (66.9747-66.062 mm)
Maximum oversize	0.040 in. (1.016 mm)
Tappet guide block housing diameter	1.1562-1.1557 in. (29.3675-29.3548 mm)
CYLINDER HEAD	
Material	Aluminum alloy die cast.
Inlet port size	1 in. diam. (25.4 mm)
Exhaust: Valve seatings	$1\frac{1}{4}$ in. diam. (31.75 mm)
Type	Cast-in
Material	Cast iron
VALVES	
Stem diameter: Intake	0.3100-0.3095 in. (7.8740-7.8613 mm)
Exhaust	0.3095-0.3090 in. (7.8613-7.8495 mm)
Head diameter: Intake	1.534-1.528 in. (38.9636-38.812 mm)
Exhaust	1.315-1.309 in. (33.401-33.2486 mm
Exhaust valve material	21-4 'N' heat treated
TAPPET GUIDE BLOCK	
Diameter of bores	0.3125-0.3120 in. (7.9375-7.9248 mm)
Outside diameter	1.153-1.148 in. (29.2862-29.1592 mm)
Interference fit in cyl. block	0.0027-0.0082 in. (0.06858-0.20828 mm)
ROCKER SPINDLE BUSHINGS	
Bush D/S: Bore diameter	0.497-0.498 in. (12.624-12.649 mm)
Outside diameter	0.6260-0.6265 in. (15.9004-15.913 mm)
Bush T/S: Bore diameter	0.375-0.374 in. (9.525-9.4996 mm)
Outside diameter	0.501-0.502 in. (12.725-12.751 mm)
TIMING GEARS	
Inlet and exhaust camshaft pinions	
Number of teeth	50
Interference fit on camshaft	0.000-0.001 in. (0.000-0.0254 mm)
Number of teeth	42
Bore diameter	0.5618-0.5625 in. (14.2697-14.2875 mm)

ROCKERS	
Material	NI. CH. Steel stamping (EN33)
Bore diameter	0.5002-0.5012 in. (12.7051-12.7305 mm)
Rocker spindle diameter	0.4990-0.4995 in. (12.6746-12.6873 mm)
Tappet clear. (cold): Inlet	0.006 in. (0.1524 mm)
Exhaust	0.008 in. (0.2032 mm)
CAMSHAFTS	
Journal diameter	1.0615-1.0605 in. (26.9621-26.9367 mm)
Diametrical clearance	0.0005-0.0020 in. (0.0127-0.0508 mm)
End float	0.007-0.014 in. (0.178-0.356 mm)
Cam lift: Inlet and exhaust	0.3045 in. (7.7343 mm)
Base circle diameter	0.812 in. diam. (20.6248 mm)
TAPPETS	
Material	EN32B (Stellite tip)
Tip radius	1.125 in. (28.575 mm)
Tappet diameter	0.3115-0.3110 in. (7.9121-7.8994 mm)
Clearance in guide block	0.0005-0.0015 in. (0.0127-0.0381 mm)
Main bearing (drive side) size and type	$1\frac{1}{8} \times 2\frac{13}{16} \times \frac{13}{16}$ in. (caged ball) (28.58 x 71.43 x 20.63 mm)
Main bearing (center) running clearance	0.0005-0.0022 in. (0.0127-0.05588 mm)
Main bearing (timing side) size and type	$1\frac{1}{8} \times 2\frac{13}{16} \times \frac{13}{16}$ in. (roller) (28.58 x 71.43 x 20.62 mm)
Right main bearing housing diameter	2.8110-2.8095 in. (71.3994-71.3613 mm)
Right main bearing journal diameter	1.1248-1.1245 in. (28.5699-28.5623 mm)
Center main bearing housing diameter	2.0630-2.0625 in. (52.4002-52.3875 mm)
Center main bearing journal diameter	1.9170-19175 in. (48.6918-48.7045 mm)
Left main bearing housing diameter	2.0447-2.0457 in. (51.9344-51.9608 mm)
Left main bearing journal diameter	0.9843-0.9840 in. (25.0012-24.9936 mm)
Big-end journal diameter	1.6240-1.6235 in. (41.2496-41.2369 mm)
Min. regrind diameter	1.6200-1.6185 in. (41.148-41.1099 mm)
Crankshaft end float	0.0015-0.0145 in.

ENGINE SPECIFICATIONS—T150

Intermediate timing gear needle roller	$\frac{11}{16}$ x $\frac{7}{8}$ x $\frac{5}{8}$ in. (17.46 x 22.225 x 15.87 mm)
Intermediate wheel spindle	
Diameter	0.6888-0.6885 in. (17.4955-17.4879 mm)
Crankcase pinion	
Number of teeth	25
Fit on crankcase	−0.00003 in. (−0.00762 mm) −0.0005 in. (−0.0127 mm)
CRANKSHAFT	
Crankshaft type	EN16B hardened and tempered stamping—one piece
	(0.038-0.368 mm)
CONNECTING RODS	
Material	Alloy 'H' Section RR.56
Length (centers)	5.751-5.749 in. (14.6075-14.6024 mm)
Big-end bearings type	Steel-backed white metal
Con rod side clearance	0.013-0.019 in. (0.3302-0.4826 mm)
Bearing diametrical clearance	0.0005-0.0020 in. min. (0.0127-0.0508 mm)
PISTON PIN	
Material	High tensile steel
Fit in small-end	0.0005-0.0011 in. (0.0127-0.0279 mm)
Diameter	0.6883-0.6885 in. (17.4828-17.4880 mm)
Length	2.250-2.235 in. (57.150-56.769 mm)

CLUTCH AND TRANSMISSION SPECIFICATIONS—T150

CLUTCH DETAILS	
Single diaphragm spring-clutch spring rate	1,000 lb (approx) (453.6 kgm)
Minimum travel to disengage	0.035 in. (0.889 mm)
Minimum wear to friction plate	0.06 in. (1.524 mm)
Bearing-Outer thrust plate—Size and type	$\frac{1}{2}$ x $1\frac{1}{8}$ x $\frac{1}{4}$ in. (12.7 x 28.575 x 6.35 mm)
Needle race—Size and type	(2 off) $1\frac{3}{8}$ x $1\frac{5}{8}$ x $\frac{1}{2}$ in. (34.93 x 41.28 x 12.7 mm)
Thrust race—Size and type	$1\frac{3}{8}$ x $2\frac{1}{16}$ x $\frac{5}{64}$ in. (34.93 x 52.39 x 1.984 mm)
GEARS	
Mainshaft high gear	
Bore diameter (bush fitted)	0.8135-0.8145 in. (20.6629-20.6883 mm)
Working clearance on shaft	0.0032-0.0047 in. (0.08128-0.1194 mm)
Bush length	$2\frac{1}{4}$ in. (57.15 mm)
Layshaft low gear	
Bore diameter	0.8135-0.8145 in. (20.6629-20.6883 mm)
Working clearance	0.0025-0.0045 in. (0.0635-0.127 mm)
GEARBOX SHAFTS	
Mainshaft: Left end diameter	0.8098-0.8103 in.
BEARINGS	
High gear bearing	$1\frac{1}{4}$ x $2\frac{1}{2}$ x $\frac{5}{8}$ in. Ball Journal (31.75 x 63.5 x 15.875 mm)
Mainshaft bearing	$\frac{3}{4}$ x $1\frac{7}{8}$ x $\frac{9}{16}$ in. Ball Journal (19.05 x 47.625 x 14.282 mm)
Layshaft bearing (left)	$\frac{11}{16}$ x $\frac{7}{8}$ x $\frac{3}{4}$ in. Needle Roller (17.463 x 22.227 x 19.05 mm)
(right)	$\frac{11}{16}$ x $\frac{7}{8}$ x $\frac{3}{4}$ in. Needle Roller (17.463 x 22.227 x 19.05 mm)
KICK-START OPERAT. MECH.	
Bush bore diameter	0.751-0.752 in. (19.0754-19.1008 mm)
Spindle working clear. in bush	0.003-0.005 in. (0.0762-0.127 mm)
Ratchet spring free-length	$\frac{1}{2}$ in. (12.7 mm)
GEARCHANGE MECHANISM	
Plungers	
Outer diameters	0.4315-0.4320 in. (10.9601-10.9728 mm)

CLUTCH AND TRANSMISSION SPECIFICATIONS—T150

	(20.5689-20.5816 mm)
Right end diam.	0.7494-0.7498 in.
	(19.0348-19.044 mm)
Length	$10\frac{12}{64}$ in. (262.3337 mm)
Layshaft: Left end diameter	0.6845-0.6850 in.
	(17.4063-17.419 mm)
	0.6845-0.6850 in.
	(17.4063-17.419 mm)
Length	$6\frac{41}{64}$ in. (168.6941 mm)
Camplate plunger spring	
Free-length	$2\frac{21}{32}$ in. (67.4675 mm)
Number of working coils	27
Spring rate	9 lbs/in. (0.633 kg/sq cm)
Working range	7.5 to 11.5 lbs
	(3.405 kgm-5.220 kgm)

Working clearance in bore	0.0005-0.005 in.
	(0.0127-0.127 mm)
Plunger springs	
Number of working coils	12
Free-length	$1\frac{1}{4}$ in. (31.75 mm)
Inner bush bore diameter	0.6245-0.6255 in.
	(15.7423-15.8877 mm)
Clearance on shaft	0.0007-0.0032 in.
	(0.01778-0.08128 mm)
Outer bush bore diameter	0.7495-0.7505 in.
	(19.0373-19.0627 mm)
Clearance on shaft	0.0005-0.0025 in.
	(0.0127-0.0635 mm)
Quadrant return springs	
Number of working coils	$9\frac{1}{2}$
Free-length	$1\frac{3}{4}$ in. (44.45 mm)

ENGINE SPECIFICATIONS—T150V

MAIN BEARINGS	
Right main bearing size	25 x 52 x 15mm
Right main bearing journal diameter	2.0447-2.0457 in. (51.934-51.961 mm)
Left main bearing journal diameter	2.8095-2.8110 in. (71.3613-71.3994 mm)
Left main bearing journal diameter	1.1245-1.1248 in. (28.563-28.5699 mm)
Minimum regrind diameter	1.5833-1.5840 in. (40.221-40.234 mm)

CONNECTING RODS	
Big end bearing material	Lead-bronze
CYLINDER HEAD	
Intake port size	$1\frac{1}{16}$ in. (27 mm)
CAMSHAFTS	
Cam lift (In. and Ex.)	0.329 in. (8.356 mm)

①—With the exception of the specifications on this chart, T150V information may be obtained from the T150 Engine Specifications chart.

CLUTCH AND TRANSMISSION SPECIFICATIONS—T150V

CLUTCH DETAILS	
Single diaphragm spring-clutch spring rate	1,000 lb (approx) (453.6 kgm)
Minimum travel to disengage	0.035 in. (0.889 mm)
Minimum wear to friction plate	0.06 in. (1.524 mm)
Bearing-Outer thrust plate—Size and type	$\frac{1}{2}$ x $1\frac{1}{8}$ x $\frac{1}{4}$ in. (12.7 x 28.575 x 6.35 mm)
Needle race—Size and type	(2 off) $1\frac{3}{8}$ x $1\frac{5}{8}$ x $\frac{1}{2}$ in. (34.93 x 41.28 x 12.7 mm)
Thrust race—Size and type	$1\frac{3}{8}$ x $2\frac{1}{16}$ x $\frac{5}{64}$ in. (34.93 x 52.39 x 1.984 mm)

GEARBOX BEARINGS	
Mainshaft bearing (left)	$1\frac{1}{2}$ x $2\frac{1}{2}$ x $\frac{5}{8}$ in. Roller bearing
Mainshaft bearing (right)	$\frac{3}{4}$ x $1\frac{7}{8}$ x $\frac{9}{16}$ in. Ball journal
Layshaft bearing (left)	$\frac{11}{16}$ x $\frac{7}{8}$ x $\frac{3}{4}$ in. Needle roller
Layshaft bearing (right)	$\frac{11}{16}$ x $\frac{7}{8}$ x $\frac{3}{4}$ in. Needle roller
Layshaft 1st gear bush	
Bore diameter	0.795-0.800 in.
Shaft diameter	0.8070-0.8075 in.
Layshaft 2nd gear bush	
Bore diameter	0.795-0.800 in.
Shaft diameter	0.8070-0.8075 in.

CLUTCH AND TRANSMISSION SPECIFICATIONS—T150V

GEARS	
Mainshaft, high gear	
Bearing type	Needle roller (Torrington B1314)
Bearing length	0.865-0.875 in.
Spigot diameter (high gear)	1.5072-1.5077 in.
GEARBOX SHAFTS	
Mainshaft	
Left end diameter	0.8089-0.8103 in.
Right end diameter	0.7494-0.7498 in.
Length	10.33 in.
Layshaft	
Left end diameter	0.6870-0.6875 in.
Right end diameter	0.6870-0.6875 in.
Length	6.47 in.

KICK START OPERAT. MECH.	
Bush bore diameter	0.751-0.752 in.
Spindle working clear. in bush	0.003-0.005 in.
Ratchet spring free-length	1/2 in.
GEARCHANGE MECHANISM	
Plungers	
Outer diameter	0.4315-0.4320 in.
Working clearance in bore	0.0005-0.0015 in.
GEARCHANGE MECHANISM	
Plunger springs	
Number of working coils	12
Free-length	1 1/4 in.
Inner bush bore diameter	0.6245-0.6255 in.
Clearance on shaft	0.0007-0.0032 in.
Outer bush bore diameter	0.7495-0.7505 in.
Clearance on shaft	0.0005-0.0025 in.
Quadrant return springs	
Number of working coils	9 1/2
Free-length	1 3/4 in.
Camplate plunger spring:	
Free length	2.28 in.
Number of working coils	21
Spring rate	8.80 lbs./in.

LUBRICATION SYSTEMS

TR25W

Scavenge Non-Return Valve

The scavenge non-return valve is located within the oil return pipe in the engine sump. It's a good idea to check its operation whenever the sump strainer screen is removed.

Poke a piece of wire into the pipe and force the check ball out of its seat. Allow it to drop back down of its own weight. If the ball does not seat itself properly, this indicates a sludge buildup in and around the valve. If necessary, immerse the return pipe in gasoline and let it sit until the check ball operates freely.

Feed Non-Return Valve

The oil feed non-return valve is located in the inner timing cover of the engine. Check its operation as described above and, if necessary, clean it with gasoline.

If you have a problem with the engine sump filling with oil whenever the bike is left to sit, chances are that a malfunction of this valve is the cause.

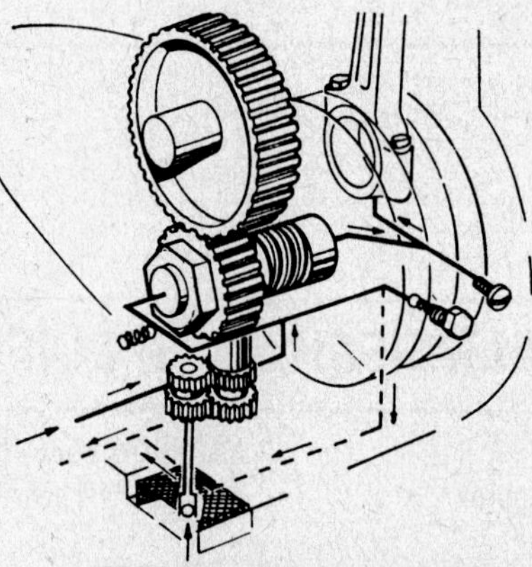

250 lubrication system

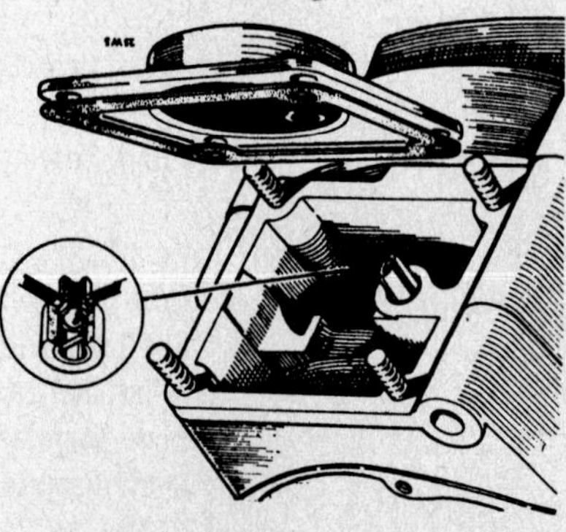

Scavenge non-return valve (250)

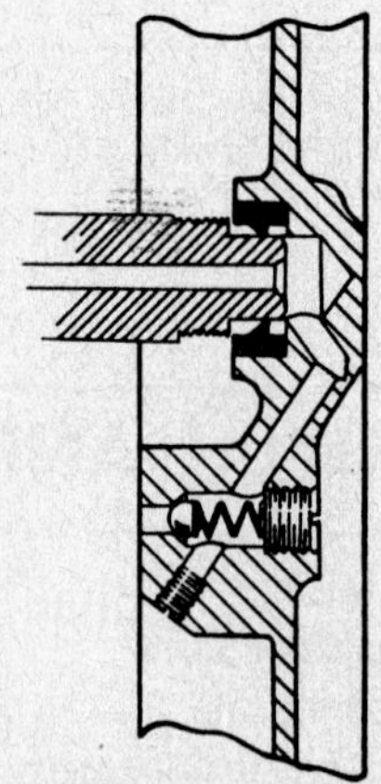

Feed non-return valve (250)

Crankcase Oil Line Union

The oil line union is secured to the crankcase with one nut. If a leak has developed at this junction, disconnect the oil lines and inspect the union sealing O-rings. Replace if necessary.

When reinstalling the union, note that the oil lines are correctly connected when they are crossed (i.e., outer line from the oil tank to the inner connection of the union).

Oil Pressure Relief Valve

The oil pressure relief valve is located at the front right side of the crankcase. Should oil pressure exceed a pre-set limit, the valve routes the excess oil directly back into the sump.

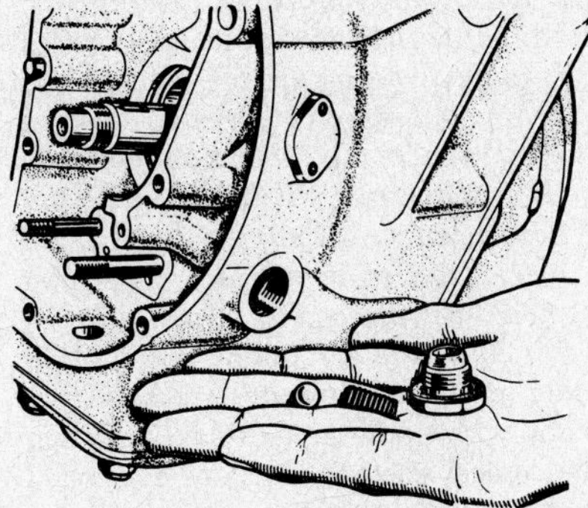

Oil pressure relief valve (250)

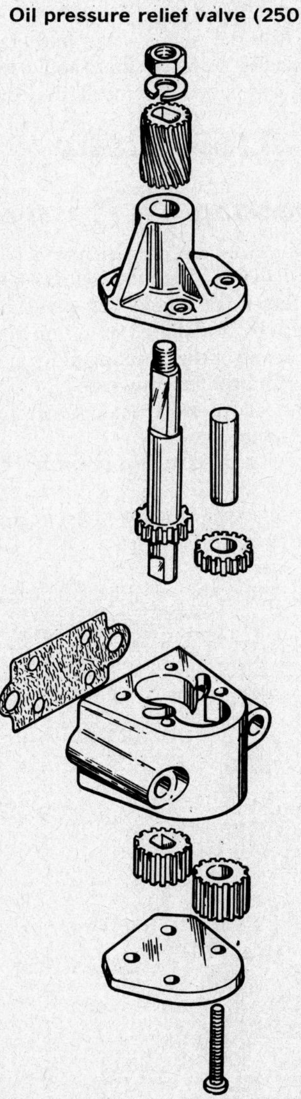

Exploded view of oil pump (250)

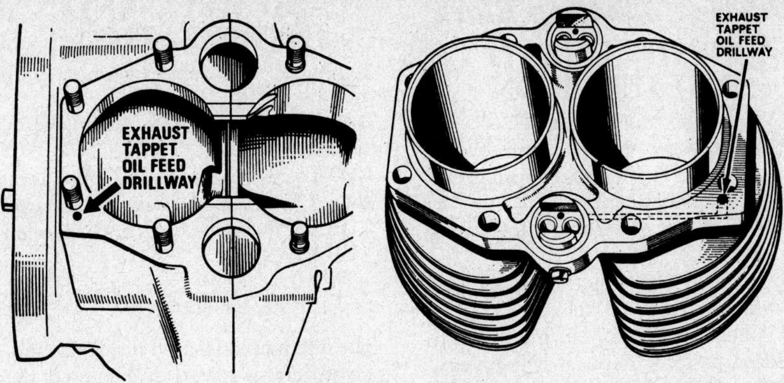

650 tappet oil feed drillways

To remove the valve, unscrew the hexagonal plug and withdraw the ball and spring. Inspect them for corrosion etc., and replace them if necessary. The spring will, in time, lose its strength, so it is advisable to replace it if the machine has accumulated high mileage. Also replace the fiber washer if it is in less than perfect condition.

Oil Pump

The oil pump is located at the front right side of the engine inside the case cover.

DISASSEMBLY

1. Remove the four screws at the base of the pump and remove the baseplate and top cover.
2. Mark the worm gear for reassembly, then remove the nut and washer that secure the gear and driving spindle to the top cover.
3. Clean all parts thoroughly in kerosine or a cleaning solvent and blow them dry with compressed air.

INSPECTION

Examine the oil pump parts for excessive scoring and foreign object damage. If oil changes have been neglected, it will be evident by the damage done to the pump gear teeth and pump body. Small scratches can be ignored, but any more substantial wear calls for parts replacement.

Inspect the pump gears for worn or broken teeth. If formerly sharp edges have become rounded off, the gear should be replaced.

ASSEMBLY

1. Make sure all parts are absolutely clean and bathed in engine oil or assembly lube.
2. Insert the driving spindle into the pump top cover.
3. Install the worm drive gear and secure it with the nut and spring washer.
4. Install the driven spindle and gear in the top cover.
5. Install the lower pump gears and baseplate.
6. Rotate the spindle and gears to make certain there is no binding, then tighten the four securing screws.
7. Check the joining surfaces of the oil pump to make sure they are all parallel. If not, the pump may not be free to operate when installed in the engine.
8. Also check the crankcase breather located near the clutch cable abutment in the timing case. This breather *must* be free from obstruction.

500, 650, 750 TWINS

Checking Oil Pressure

Normal oil pressure at idle is about 20 to 25 psi, but may rise as high as 80 psi when the engine is cold. Normal running pressure is 65 to 80 psi.

Oil pressure can be checked by connecting a gauge and adaptor in place of the relief valve.

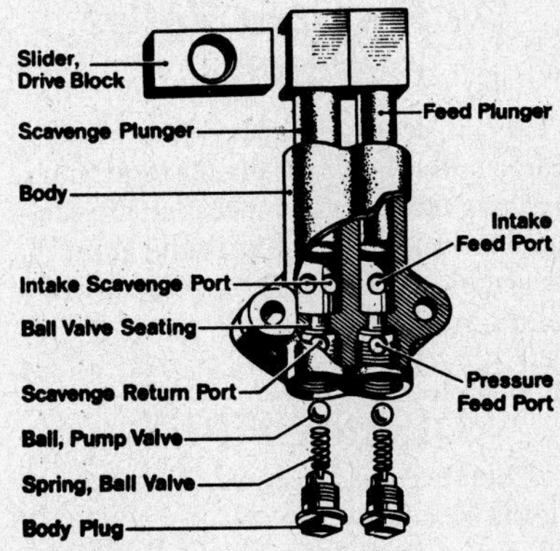

Exploded view of oil pump (500 and 650 models)

Oil pressure relief valve (500 and 650 models)

Oil Line Junction Block

REMOVAL AND INSTALLATION

1. Drain the transmission oil.
2. Remove the gearbox outer cover as described in "Engine and Transmission."
3. Drain the oil tank.
4. Disconnect the rubber lines from the oil tank.
5. Remove the junction block and clean it thoroughly in kerosine.
6. Check all lines for chafing and signs of decomposition. Replace as necessary.
7. Installation is basically a reversal of the removal procedure. Use a new gasket between the junction block and crankcase, and reconnect the oil lines carefully.

Rocker Oil Feed Line

REMOVAL AND INSTALLATION

1. Remove the two domed nuts securing the feed line to the rocker spindle.
2. Disconnect the feed line at the oil tank.
3. Remove the clips securing the feed line to the frame.

NOTE: *Take care not to bend the feed line when removing it from the frame because it may cause a future rupture.*

4. Thoroughly clean the oil feed line with kerosine, then blow it out with compressed air.
5. Check the line for proper sealing by holding your thumb over the banjo fitting at one end of the line and blowing through the other.
6. To install the rocker oil feed-line, reverse the removal procedure and replace the banjo fitting washers.

Oil Pressure Relief Valve

The oil pressure relief valve is very simple and reliable. It should require no servicing other than an occasional cleaning. The valve is located at the front of the engine on the right side, adjacent to the timing cover.

REMOVAL AND DISASSEMBLY

1. Remove the valve body by unscrewing the hexagonal cap.
2. Separate the cap from the valve body and withdraw the piston and spring.
3. Thoroughly clean all parts in kerosine, then inspect the piston and spring for signs of wear. Also check to make sure the valve filter is free from obstruction.
4. If the bike has accumulated high mileage it is advisable to check spring pressure with the standard figure given in specifications.

ASSEMBLY AND INSTALLATION

1. Replace both fiber washers with new ones.
2. Assemble the valve body, piston, and spring.

NOTE: *The open end of the piston should face toward the spring and cap.*

3. Install the valve body and screw on the hexagonal cap.

Oil Pump

The oil pump is located inside the timing cover and is driven off the end of the intake camshaft. Since the pump itself is totally immersed in oil, wear on internal parts should be negligible. The oil pump drive block slider is not as well lubricated, however, and therefore should be replaced when the machine has accumulated high mileage.

REMOVAL AND DISASSEMBLY

1. Remove the timing cover.
2. Remove the two oil pump securing nuts.
3. Lift the oil pump off the mounting studs.
4. Remove the scavenge and feed plungers.
5. Unscrew the two square end caps and remove the two springs and balls.
6. Clean all parts in kerosine, then inspect them for scoring, pitting, and excessive wear. Measure plunger diameters and spring compressed strength. Standard values are given in specifications at the end of this chapter.

ASSEMBLY AND INSTALLATION

1. Lubricate all parts generously with engine oil.
2. Assemble the plungers, balls, springs, and end caps.
3. Add approximately 1cc of oil in each plunger bore, then press the plungers until the oil is forced through both outlet ports.

NOTE: The outlet ports are the two holes nearest the square end caps.

4. Hold your thumb over the intake ports (nearest the plunger tops) and pull the plungers out slightly. If the oil level drops in either outlet port, the ball and spring in that port are not seated properly, and the end cap should be removed and the cleaning process repeated.

NOTE: *On machines equipped with a brass body oil pump, the balls can be lightly, but sharply, tapped to ensure a good seal. On machines equipped with the cast iron pump body, however, this should not be attempted since a bad seal indicates a warped body that should be replaced.*

5. Check the oil pump drive block slider for excessive wear, then install the pump with a new gasket. Make sure that the conical securing nuts are positioned so that they fit into the countersunk holes in the pump body.
6. Clean the timing cover and crankcase mating surfaces, then apply fresh sealing compound and install the cover.

T150, T150V

Checking Oil Pressure

Normal running oil pressure at 3000 rpm is 75–90 psi, but may rise above that when the engine is cold. Pressure can be checked by installing an oil pressure gauge in one of the blanking plugs at the front of the center crankcase.

If the oil pressure is unsatisfactory, check the following:

1. Faulty or dirty oil pressure relief valve.
2. Insufficient amount of lubricant in the oil tank.

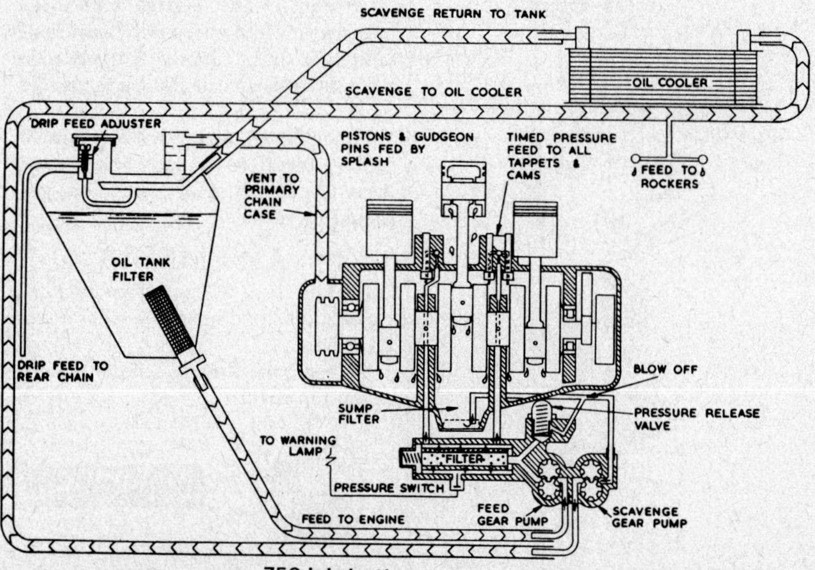

750 lubrication system

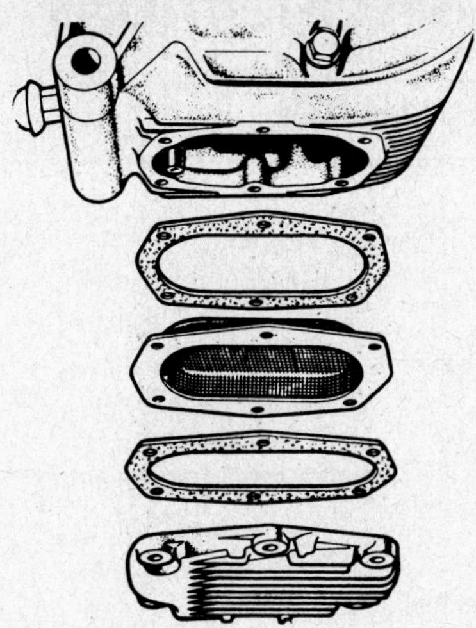

Sump oil filter (Trident)

3. Dirty or incorrectly installed oil filters.
4. Faulty oil pump.
5. Obstructed crankcase drillings.
6. Excessively worn main or connecting rod bearings.
7. Leaking crankcase union O-rings.

Oil Pressure Relief Valve

The oil pressure relief valve is located in the primary chaincase. Triumph special tool no. D2135 can be used to remove the valve with only the the primary cover removed, but if this tool is not available, the chaincase must be disassembled to gain access.

Disassemble and inspect the valve as described for the 500, 650 and 750 cc machines.

Rocker Oil Feed Line

Service the rocker oil feed line as described for the twins.

Oil Cooler

The Trident is equipped with an oil cooler mounted below the gas tank on two support brackets. Great care should be taken when handling this component.

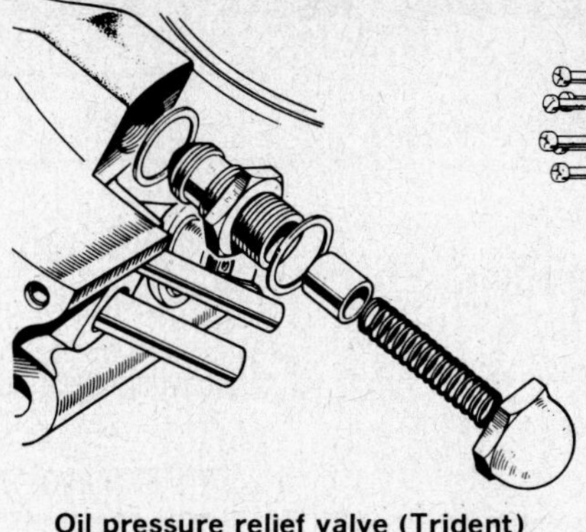

Oil pressure relief valve (Trident)

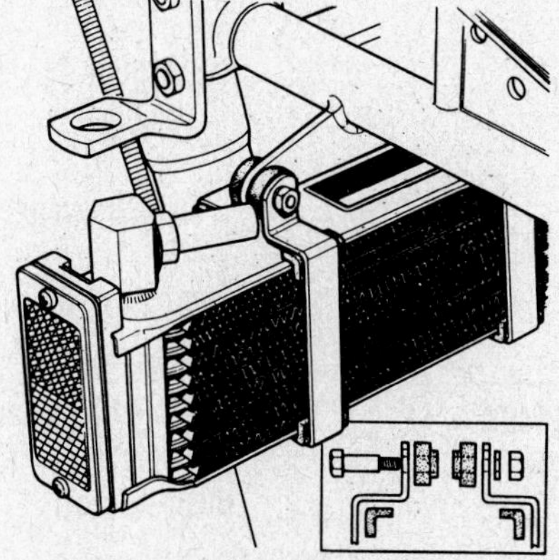

Oil cooler mounting (Trident)

REMOVAL

1. Remove the gas tank.
2. Mark both oil lines for reassembly, then disconnect the clips. Take care not to tilt the cooler as it still contains approximately one-half pint of oil.
3. Loosen the top support bracket bolts and remove the bracket corner packings.
4. Hold the cooler upright and remove the bracket bolts, nuts, and washers.
5. Lift out the cooler, then drain the remaining oil by inverting the cooler over a suitable container.
6. Clean the outside of the cooler with kerosine and a soft-bristled brush. It is not necessary to flush the cooler.

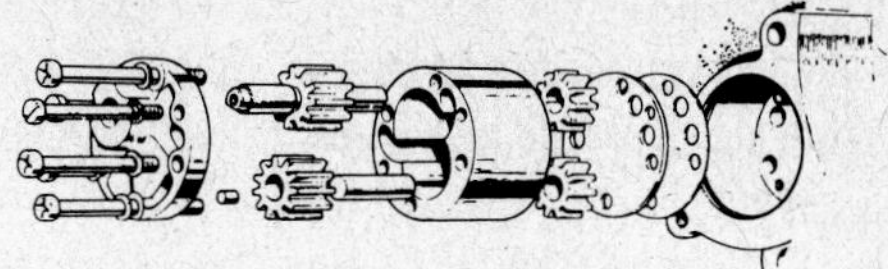

Exploded view of oil pump (Trident)

INSTALLATION

Installation is a reversal of the removal procedure. Note the following:

1. The large oil line fittings at the top of the cooler should face rearward when the cooler is installed.
2. When the cooler is properly installed, the left oil line fitting should be connected to the scavenge line and the right fitting to the oil tank return line.

Oil Pump

The oil pump is the double-gear type and is mounted in the primary side crankcase. Drive is provided by the crankshaft via reduction gears. Since the pump is immersed in oil, wear should be negligible on all but the feed and scavenge drive gears.

REMOVAL

1. Remove the outer and inner primary chaincases (See "Engine and Transmission").
2. Remove the four attaching screws and lift out the oil pump assembly.
3. Remove the two remaining screws and separate the pump parts.
4. Drive out the gear spindles with a thin, soft alloy drift.
5. Wash all parts thoroughly in cleaning solvent or kerosine, then blow them dry with compressed air.

OIL PUMP AND PRESSURE RELIEF VALVE SPECIFICATIONS

TR25W	
OIL PUMP	
Pump body material	Zinc base alloy
Type	Double gear
Drive ratio	1 : 4
Non-return valve spring (free-length)	0.625 in. (15-875 mm)
Non-return valve spring ball (diameter)	0.25 in. (6.35 mm)
Oil pressure relief valve spring (free-length)	0.6094 in. (15.4781 mm)
Oil pressure relief valve ball (diameter)	0.3125 in. (7.9375 mm)

T100C and T100R	
OIL PUMP	
Body material	Brass
Bore diameter	
Feed	0.3748/0.3753 in.
Scavenge	0.4372/0.4377 in.
Scavenge (Bef. H.49833)	0.4877/0.4872 in.
Plunger diameter:	
Feed	0.3744/0.3747 in.
Scavenge	0.4369/0.4372 in.
Scavenge (Bef. H.49833)	0.4872/0.4869 in.
Valve spring length	1/2 in.
Ball diameter	7/32 in.

OIL PUMP AND PRESSURE RELIEF VALVE SPECIFICATIONS

Aluminum cross-head width	0.497/0.498 in.
Working clearance in plunger heads	0.0015/0.0045 in.
OIL PRESSURE RELIEF VALVE	
Piston diameter	0.5605/0.5610 in.
Working clearance	0.001/0.002 in.
Pressure relief operates	60 lb/sq in. (4.22 kg/sq cm)
Spring length (Free)	1$^3/_8$ in.
Load at 1$^3/_{16}$ in.	8 lbs
Rate	42.3 lbs
OIL PRESSURE	
Normal running	60 lb/sq in.
Idling	20/25 lb/sq in.

TR6R, TR6C, T120R, TR7V, and T140V

OIL PUMP	
Body material	Brass
Bore diameter: Feed	0.40675/0.40625 in.
Scavenge	0.4877/0.4872 in.
Plunger diameter	
Feed	0.40615/0.40585 in.
Scavenge	0.4872/0.4869 in.
Valve spring length	$^1/_2$ in.
Ball diameter	$^7/_{32}$ in.
Aluminum cross-head width	0.497/0.498 in.
Working clearance in plunger heads	0.0015/0.0045 in.
OIL PRESSURE RELIEF VALVE	
Piston diameter	0.5605/0.5610 in.
Working clearance	0.001/0.002 in.
Pressure relief operates	60 lb/sq in. (4.22 kg/sq cm)
Spring length	1$^{17}/_{32}$ in.
Load at 1$^3/_{16}$ in.	12/12$^1/_2$ lbs
Rate	37 lb/in.
OIL PRESSURE	
Normal running	68/80 lb/sq in.
Idling	20/25 lb/sq in.
OIL PRESSURE SWITCH	
Operating pressure	7/11 lb/sq in.

T150 and T150V

OIL PUMP	
Body material	Cast iron
Bore diameters	0.3438/0.3433 in. (8.7325/8.7198 mm)
Scavenge gear-bore diameter	0.3438/0.3448 in. (8.7325/8.7579 mm)
Feed gear-bore diameter	0.3438/0.3448 in. (8.7325/8.7579 mm)
Spindle diameter	0.3433/0.3428 in. (8.7198/8.70712 mm)
Cover plate bore diameters	
Spindle	0.3433/0.3438 in. (8.7198/8.7325 mm)
Drive scavenge gear	0.4375/0.4370 in. (11.1125/11.0998 mm)
Pump drive ratio	1.9 : 1 (engine to pump)
OIL PUMP DRIVE	
Intermediate gear—bore diameter	0.5625/0.5620 in. (14.287/14.2748 mm)
Bush—bore	0.4387/0.4382 in. (11.143/11.1302 mm)
—length	0.755/0.745 in. (19.177/18.923 mm)
Spindle diameter	0.4360/0.4355 in. (11.0744/11.0617 mm)
OIL PRESSURE RELIEF VALVE	
Piston diameter	0.5605/0.5610 in. (14.2367/14.2494 mm)
Working clearance	1.001/0.002 in. (0.0254/0.0508 mm)
Pressure relief operates	90 lb/sq in. (6.328 kg/sq cm)
Spring length (Free)	1$^3/_8$ in. (34-925 mm)
Load at 1$^3/_{16}$ sq in.	8 lbs (3.632 kgm)
Rate	42.3 lbs (19-2042 kgm)
OIL PRESSURE	
Normal running	75-85 lb/sq in. (5.273-5.624 kg/sq cm)
Idling	20-25 lb/sq in. (1.406-1.758 kg/sq cm)
Oil pressure switch Working range	7-11 lbs (3.178/4.994 kgm)

INSPECTION

Examine the gear teeth for scoring or rounded out edges. Check the spindles and spindle bores in the gears and pump body. Replace any parts that are excessively worn.

INSTALLATION

Installation is a reversal of the removal procedure. Note the following:

1. Replace the gasket that fits between the pump and crankcase.
2. Make certain that the two screws holding the pump body together are sufficiently tightened.
3. Make sure the pump is correctly located over the dowel in the crankcase recess.
4. Replace the O-ring that fits around the pump body in the inner primary chaincase.
5. When installing the oil pump drive gear, apply a thread-locking compound to the securing screw.

FUEL SYSTEMS

All Triumph motorcycles are equipped with Amal carburetors: Monoblocs on pre-1967 models, and Concentrics on 1967 and later models. Disassembly and repair procedures for Amal carburetors are given under "BSA Fuel Systems."

Carburetor specifications for Triumph motorcycles are given below.

CARBURETOR SPECIFICATIONS

TR25W	
Amal Type	928/1 Concentric
Main Jet Size	160
Needle Jet Size	0.106 in. (2.69 mm)
Needle Position	1
Throttle Valve Cutaway	3
Venturi Size	28 mm
Throttle Slide Spring (free-length)	2.5 in. (63.5 mm)

T100C (Prior to serial no. H57083)	
Amal Type	376/273
Main Jet Size	190
Pilot Jet Size	25
Needle Jet Size	0.106 in. (2.69 mm)
Needle Type	C
Needle Position	3
Throttle Valve Cutaway	3.5
Venturi Size	1 in. (25.4 mm)

T100C (After serial no. H57083)	
Amal Type	628/8 Concentric
Main Jet Size	180
Needle Jet Size	0.106 in. (2.69 mm)
Needle Position	2
Throttle Valve Cutaway	4
Venturi Size	26 mm

T100R (Prior to serial no. H57083)	
Amal Type	376/324 and 325
Main Jet Size	200
Pilot Jet Size	25
Needle Jet Size	0.106 in. (2.69 mm)
Needle Type	C
Needle Position	3
Throttle Valve Cutaway	3.5
Venturi Size	1 1/16 in.

CARBURETOR SPECIFICATIONS

T100R (After serial no. H57083)	
Amal Type	626/9 and 10 Concentric
Main Jet Size	140
Needle Jet Size	0.106 in. (2.69 mm)
Needle Position	2
Throttle Valve Cutaway	3
Venturi Size	26 mm

TR6R and TR6C	
Amal Type	R930/23 Concentric
Main Jet Size	230
Needle Jet Size	0.106 in. (2.69 mm)
Needle Type	STD
Needle Position	2
Throttle Valve Cutaway	3
Throttle Slide Spring (free-length)	2.5 in. (63.5 mm)
Venturi Size	30 mm

T120R	
Amal Type	R930/9 and 10 Concentric
Main Jet Size	220
Needle Jet Size	0.106 in. (2.69 mm)
Needle Type	STD
Needle Position	2
Throttle Valve Cutaway	2.5
Throttle Slide Spring (free-length)	2.5 in. (63.5 mm)
Venturi Size	30 mm

T150	
Amal Type	626 Concentric
Main Jet Size	150
Needle Jet Size	0.106 in. (2.69 mm)
Needle Type	STD
Needle Position	2
Throttle Valve Cutaway	2.5
Venturi Size	27 mm

TR7V	
Amal Type	R930/89
Main Jet Size	280
Needle Jet Size	0.106
Needle Type	STD
Needle Position	2
Throttle Slide Cutaway	3.5
Venturi Size	30 mm

T140V	
Amal Type	L930/93
Main Jet Size	190
Needle Jet Size	0.106
Needle Type	STD
Needle Position	1
Throttle Slide Cutaway	3
Venturi Size	30 mm

T150V	
Amal Type	626 Concentric
Main Jet Size	150
Needle Jet Size	0.106
Needle Type	STD
Needle Position	2
Throttle Slide Cutaway	3.5
Venturi Size	27 mm

ELECTRICAL SYSTEMS

IGNITION SYSTEM

Troubleshooting

TR25W

1. Make sure the contact breaker is clean and correctly gapped. Also make certain the battery terminals are tight and in good condition.

2. Check the main wiring harness fuse.

3. Turn the ignition switch on and slowly turn the engine over while watching the ammeter needle. As the contact breaker opens and closes, the needle should flick between zero and a slight discharge. If it does not, there is a fault somewhere in the low tension circuit.

4. Recheck the condition of the points to make sure you aren't getting a false indication due to dirt, oil, or an incorrect adjustment.

500 AND 650 TWINS

1. Check the condition and gap of the contact breaker points and the tightness of the battery terminals.

2. Remove the gas tank.

3. Disconnect the white lead that connects the "SW" terminals of both ignition coils.

4. Connect the white lead to the left coil "SW" terminal, then turn on the ignition switch and slowly turn over the engine while observing the ammeter needle. As the contact breaker opens and closes, the needle should flick between zero and a slight discharge.

5. Disconnect the white lead from the left coil and connect the "SW" terminal of the right coil. Turn the ignition switch on and observe the ammeter needle as described above.

6. If the ammeter needle does not flick in the described manner for both the right and left ignition coils, a fault exists in the low tension circuit.

T150

1. Lift up the seat and disconnect the white lead that connects the "SW" terminal of all three ignition coils.

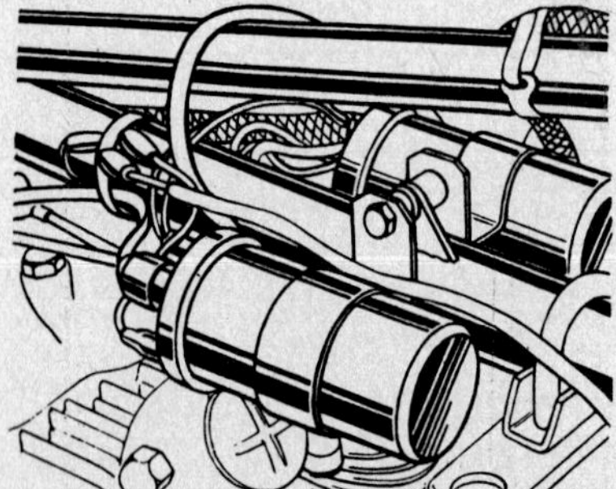

Ignition coils installed (650 models)

Ignition coils installed (500 models)

NOTE: *Lucas coils are marked "SW" and "CB." SIBA coils are marked "1" instead of "SW" and "15" instead of "CB."*

2. Connect the white lead to one coil at a time and check ammeter needle deflection as previously described for the other models.

750 TWINS, T150V

Procedures are essentially as described above, except that the coil wires are white/yellow.

Low Tension Circuit Tests

If the above tests showed that the fault exists somewhere in the low tension circuit, isolate the problem source in the following manner:

NOTE: *On 12 volt machines, disconnect the zener diode center terminal.*

1. Place a piece of non-conducting material, such as rubber, between the contact breaker points. Turn the ignition switch on.

2. Using a 0–15 volt DC voltmeter (0–10 volts for 6 volt machines) and the appropriate wiring diagram for reference, make point-to-point checks as described below.

3. Check the battery by connecting the voltmeter between the negative terminal of the battery and ground (frame). No reading indicates a blown main, or a faulty red, battery lead; a low reading indicates a poor ground.

4. Connect the voltmeter between the ignition coil negative terminal (SW or 1) and ground (one at a time on twins and triples). No reading indicates a faulty lead between the battery and coil terminal, or a faulty switch or ammeter connection.

5. Connect the voltmeter between ground and one ammeter terminal at a time. No reading at the "load" terminal indicates either a faulty ammeter or a break in the blue/brown lead from the battery; no reading on the battery side indicates a faulty ammeter.

6. Connect the voltmeter between the ignition switch "feed" terminal and ground. No reading indicates a break or faulty terminal along the brown/white lead. Check for voltage readings between ground and the brown/white lead terminals at the rectifier, ammeter and lighting switch (on singles and twins.)

7. Connect the voltmeter between the ignition switch "load" terminal and ground. No reading indicates a faulty switch. A positive reading at this point, but not in step 4, indicates a break or faulty connection along the white lead.

8. Disconnect the ignition coil lead from the positive (CB or 15) terminal and connect one voltmeter lead in its place (one coil at a time on twins and triples). Connect the other voltmeter lead to ground. No reading indicates a faulty primary coil winding.

9. Reconnect the ignition coil lead(s) and connect the voltmeter across the contact breaker points one set at a time. Leave the rubber insulator in place. No reading indicates a faulty connection, faulty insulation, or a faulty condenser.

10. On 12 volt machines, reconnect the zener diode center terminal and connect the voltmeter to this terminal and ground. The meter should read battery output voltage.

High Tension Circuit Tests

If the preliminary ignition system checks showed that the problem lay in the high tension circuit, check the following:

1. Test the ignition coil(s) as described in component tests. If the coils are in satisfactory condition, either the high tension cables or spark plug cap(s) are at fault.

2. Remove the spark plug cap(s) from the cable(s) and turn the ignition switch on. Hold the cable about ⅛ in. away from the cylinder cooling fins and kick the engine over. A bright blue spark should jump across the gap; if not, the cable is defective. If the spark does appear, the spark plug cap is faulty.

Component Tests

IGNITION COIL

1. Check the coil in the machine by removing the spark plug cap and holding the high tension cable end about ⅛ in. away from the cylinder cooling fins. Turn

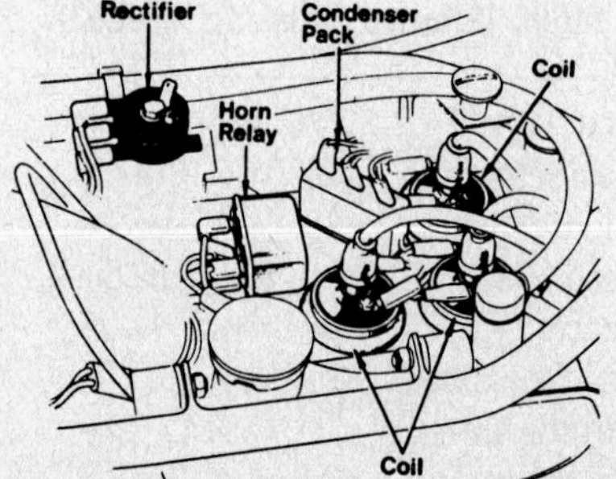

Ignition components installed (Trident)

the ignition on and kick the engine over. Observe the caution given in the "High Tension Circuit Tests."

2. Check primary winding resistance by removing the coil and connecting an ohmeter to the low tension terminals. The readings obtained should be:

TR25W

3.0 ohms minimum
3.4 ohms maximum

T100C, T100R, TR6C,TR6R, and T120R

MA6 type

1.8 ohms minimum
2.4 ohms maximum

MA12 type

3.0 ohms minimum
3.4 ohms maximum

T150, T150V

3.3 ohms minimum
3.8 ohms maximum

TR7V, T140V

3.0 ohms minimum
3.4 ohms maximum

3. Inspect the high tension cables for any signs of insulator deterioration. This is often caused by what is known as Corona discharge: a chemical reaction catalyzed by electricity.

CONTACT BREAKER CONDENSERS

A faulty condenser is usually indicated by burning or arcing of the points. On the TR25W, the condenser is located under the ignition plate in the primary chaincase; on twins and triples, they are located under the gas tank.

To check the condenser(s), first turn the ignition switch on, then take readings across the contact breaker(s) (open position) with a voltmeter. No reading indicates that the condenser insulation has broken down, and the unit should be replaced.

CHARGING SYSTEM

The charging system consists of an alternator and a full-wave bridge rectifier that converts the AC pulses in DC for recharging the battery and powering the lights. 12 volt machines are also equipped with a zener diode to absorb any excess charge.

Alternator Output Test

TR25W

1. Disconnect the two or three alternator output leads.

NOTE: *Earlier machines have three leads; later machines have two.*

2. Start and run the engine at 3000 rpm.

3. Connect a 0–15 volt AC voltmeter with a 1 ohm load resistor in parallel with each of the alternator leads as described below.

4. Three-lead-type stator:

a. White/green and green/black leads—minimum voltmeter reading 4.0 volts.

b. White/green and green/yellow leads—minimum voltmeter reading 6.5 volts.

c. White/green and green/black with green/yellow leads—minimum voltmeter reading 8.5 volts.

5. Two-lead-type stator:

a. White/green and green/yellow leads—minimum voltmeter reading 8.5 volts, for all except 47205 stator (9.0V).

6. If low or no readings are obtained, inspect the leads for damage and make sure they have tight connections. Check the alternator output again, and if the same results are obtained the difficulty lies in the alternator itself and it must be replaced.

7. To check for grounded coils within the stator, connect the voltmeter to each terminal and ground. If a reading is obtained, the coil connected to the lead being tested is grounded.

T100C, T100R, TR6R, TR6C, AND T120R

Test the alternator output as described for the TR25W. Correct output readings are given in the following chart.

RM20 STATOR
47209 (12 VOLT)

Alternator Output Minimum AC Volts @ 3,000 rpm		
green/white and green/black connected	green/white and green/yellow connected	green/white green/black and green/yellow connected
5.0	8.0	10.0

Stator Number	System Voltage	DC Input to Battery amp @ 3,000 rpm: Off	Pilot	Head	Alternator Output Minimum AC Volts @ 3,000 rpm: A	B	C	Stator Coil Details: No. of Coils	Turns per coil	S.W.G.	
47162	6V	2.75	2.0	2.0	4.0	6.5	8.5	6	140	22	
	12V	2.0*	2.1*	1.5*							
		4.8†	3.8†	1.8†							
47164	6V	2.7	0.9	1.6	4.5	7.0	9.5	6	122	21	
47167	6V	6.6‡	6.6‡	13.6‡	7.7	11.6	13.2	6	74	19	
47188	6V	Not applicable			5.0	1.5	3.5	2	250	25	IGN
								2	98	20	IGN
								1	98	20	LIGHT
								1	98	21	LIGHT
47204	12V						8.5	as 47162			
47205	12V						9.0				

Coil Ignition Machines
A—Green/White and Green/Black
B—Green/White and Green/Yellow
C—Green/White and {Green/Black, Green/Yellow} connected

* Zener in Circuit
† Zener disconnected
‡ With Boost Switch in Circuit

Note: On machines fitted with two-lead-stator, only test C is applicable as leads are colored green/white and green/yellow.

T150

Check alternator output for the Trident in the same manner as described for the three-lead TR25W stator. Correct output readings are given below.

TR7V, T140V, T150V

These models use a 47205 stator. Procedures are same as for TR25W. Minimum voltmeter reading is 9.0 volts.

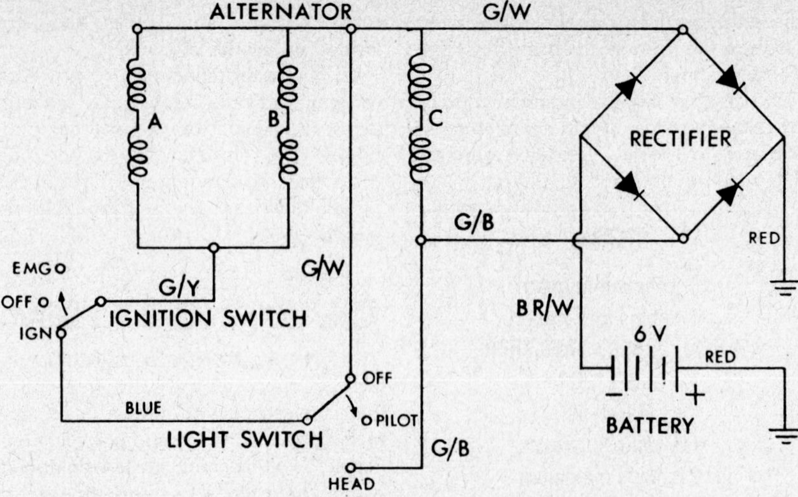

6 volt charging circuit

Rectifier Test

Two precautions should be taken whenever handling the rectifier for testing or for any other purpose.

1. When removing or installing the rectifier, prevent any possibility of twisting the rectifier plates, which could result in broken internal wiring.
2. *Never* disturb the nuts that hold the rectifier plates together.

To test the rectifier in the machine:

1. Disconnect the brown/white lead from the center terminal and wrap the end in tape to prevent a short-circuit to ground.
2. Connect a DC voltmeter in parallel with a 1 ohm load resistor between the center rectifier terminal and ground.
3. On twins, disconnect the alternator green/yellow lead and connect it to the rectifier green/black lead by using the appropriate jumper cable. Make sure this connection is insulated to prevent a short-circuit.
4. Start and run the machine at 3000 rpm and observe the voltmeter reading. It must be 7.5 volts minimum
5. If the reading is higher than specified, check the rectifier ground. If the ground is OK, replace the rectifier. If the reading was zero or less than specified, the problem lies in the rectifier or charging system wiring. First check the rectifier on a bench.

RECTIFIER BENCH TEST

1. Disconnect and remove the rectifier. Observe the note on handling the unit.
2. Connect the rectifier to a 12 volt battery and a 1 ohm load resistor.
3. Connect a DC voltmeter in the V_1 position as shown in the accompanying illustration. The meter should read 12 volts.
4. Disconnect the voltmeter and, using the accompanying illustrations for guidance, test each of the diodes with the voltmeter leads. Keep the testing time as short as possible so that the rectifier does not overheat. No reading should be greater than 2.5 volts in Test 1, and no reading should be more than 1.5 volts less than the battery voltage in Test 2 (i.e., 10.5 volts minimum).
5. If the rectifier does not meet specifications, it should be replaced.

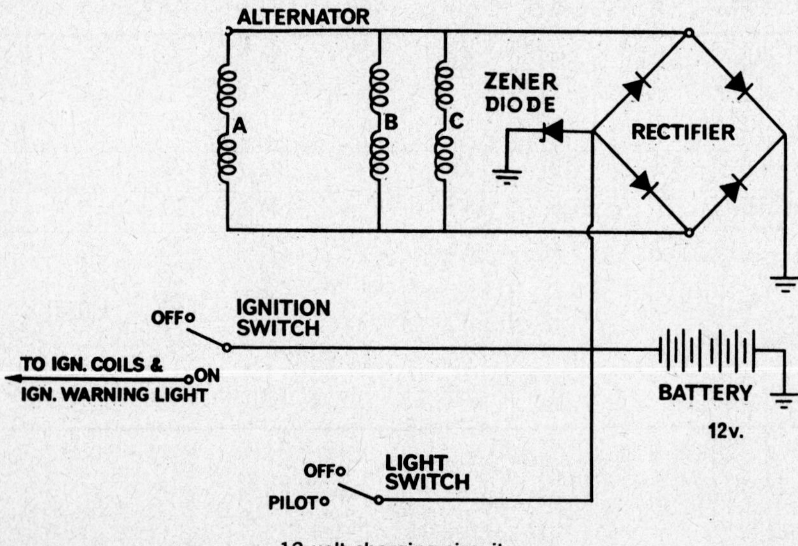

12 volt charging circuit

Charging Circuit Continuity Test

If the rectifier tests did not pinpoint the problem, it must be located somewhere within the charging circuit wiring. For checking continuity, the battery must be in a good state of charge and the alternator leads must be disconnected at their snap connectors.

TR25W

1. Make sure there is power at the rectifier by connecting a DC voltmeter, with a 1 ohm load resistor in parallel, between the center rectifier terminal and ground. The meter should read battery voltage.
2. If there is no voltage at the rectifier, repeat steps 3, 5, and 6 under "Low Tension Circuit Tests" to isolate the problem in the wiring.

500 AND 650 TWINS

6 Volt Machines

1. Repeat steps 1 and 2 given for the TR25W.
2. Connect the green/yellow lead from the main wiring harness (under the engine) to the rectifier center terminal with a jumper cable. Turn the ignition switch on.
3. Connect a DC voltmeter, with a 1 ohm resistor in parallel, between the green/white lead at the rectifier and ground. With the light switch in the "off" position, the meter should read battery voltage. If not, the leads to the ignition switch terminals 16 and 18, and the leads to light switch terminals 4 and 5, should be checked.
4. Connect the green/yellow lead from the main wiring harness to the rectifier center terminal with a jumper cable. Turn the ignition switch to to the IGN position and the headlight switch to the HEAD position.

5. Connect a DC voltmeter, with a 1 ohm resistor in parallel, to the green/-black lead at the rectifier and ground. The meter should read battery voltage. If not, the leads to ignition switch terminals 16 and 17, and the leads to light switch terminals 5 and 7, should be checked. With the light switch in the PILOT position, there should be no voltage reading between ground and the rectifier green/-black or green/white leads.

12 Volt Machines

1. Check the battery to make sure the fuse is intact and that the battery is correctly connected to ground (positive).

2. Check to see that there is voltage at the rectifier center terminal as previously described. If there is not, disconnect the alternator leads at their snap connectors under the engine.

3. Wire a jumper lead between the center and green/yellow rectifier terminals and check the voltage between the snap connector and ground. If there is no reading, the alternator harness lead is faulty.

4. Repeat the above for the rectifier green/white lead.

5. If there is voltage at the center rectifier terminal, check the ammeter terminal. If its is satisfactory here, the brown/white lead to the rectifier center connector is faulty.

6. If there is no voltage at either the rectifier or the ammeter, the blue/brown wire from the battery is faulty.

T150

Perform the charging circuit continuity test for the Trident in the same manner as described for the 500 and 650 twins.

TR7V, T140V, T150V

The test is similar to that for the 500 and 650 Twins as described above except that the wire color codes have changed. The rectifier center terminal for these models is fitted with a brown/blue wire instead of the brown/white wire for the earlier models.

Load Resistor

A 1 ohm load resistor has been referred to in several steps of the charging system test procedures. This resistor is easily obtainable from a local electrical supply outlet, or can be constructed as follows:

1. Materials:

4 yards of 18, S.W.G. (0.048 in.) Nichrome wire

1 foot of flexible, heavy gauge wire

1 alligator clip

1 piece of asbestos approximately 2 in. in diameter

2. Instructions:

Fold the thin wire double and connect the heavy wire to the folded end. Connect the other end of the heavy wire to the positive terminal of a 6 volt battery. Connect a 0–10 volt DC voltmeter between the battery terminals and an ammeter between the negative terminal of the battery and the free ends of the thin wire. Make this last connection with the alligator clip. Move the clip along the two thin wires until the ammeter reading is numerically equal to the voltmeter reading. Cut the thin wires at this point and wrap them around the piece of asbestos, making sure the wires do not touch each other.

Zener Diode Test

The zener diode serves the function of a voltage regulator, tapping off excess alternator current output and rerouting it to a heat sink. It is very important that the diode be kept clean and free from obstruction in the cooling airstream at all times. Other than this, if you make sure that the base of the diode and heat sink have firm metal-to-metal contact, the diode is a maintenance free item.

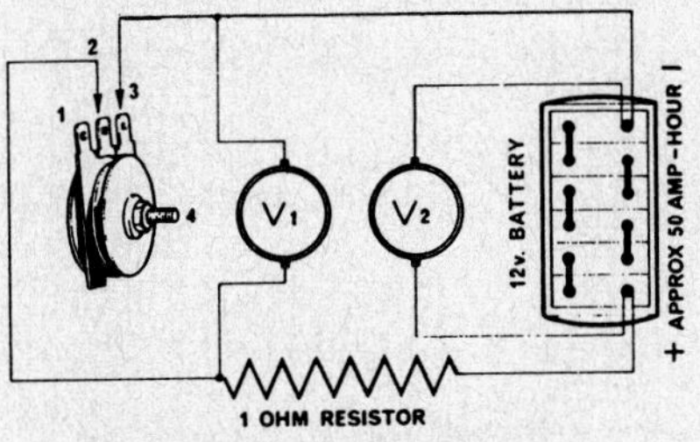

Rectifier bench test set-up

NOTE: *Before making any of the following tests, make sure the battery is in a full state of charge*

1. Disconnect the zener diode cable and connect a 0–5 amp (minimum) ammeter in series between the diode connector and the disconnected cable. The ammeter positive lead must be connected to the diode terminal.

2. Connect a DC voltmeter between the zener diode and the heat sink. The red or positive lead of the voltmeter must be connected to the heat sink, which is grounded to the frame.

3. Make sure all lights are off, then start the engine and slowly increase its speed while observing both meters.

4. Until the voltmeter reaches 12.75 volts, the ammeter should read zero.

5. Continue increasing the engine speed until the ammeter reads 2.0 amps, at which time the voltmeter should be reading 13.5 to 15.3 volts.

6. If the ammeter registers before the voltmeter reaches 12.75 volts in step 4, or if the voltage is higher than stated in step 5 when the ammeter reads 2.0 amps, the zener diode should be replaced.

CAPACITOR IGNITION SYSTEM

A capacitor ignition system kit is available to make it possible to run the machine without a battery. The kit consists only of a mounting spring and the capacitor unit itself. The system uses the same equipment as the coil ignition/battery type, with the exception of the battery.

In operation, the capacitor stores the current from the alternator and releases it at the moment of contact breaker opeing. This produces an adequate spark for starting, although not as healthy a spark as is produced by a battery. When running, the capacitor also helps to reduce DC voltage ripple. The lighting system will also operate normally, except that the parking light will not function when the engine is not running.

In addition to the obvious advantage of not requiring a battery, this system has several other points in its favor: alternator timing is not nearly as critical as on battery-powered machines; cold weather does not affect the capacitor, and the system requires less maintenance. Many owners operate the bike with the battery, but have a capacitor mounted so that it can be connected in an emergency starting situation.

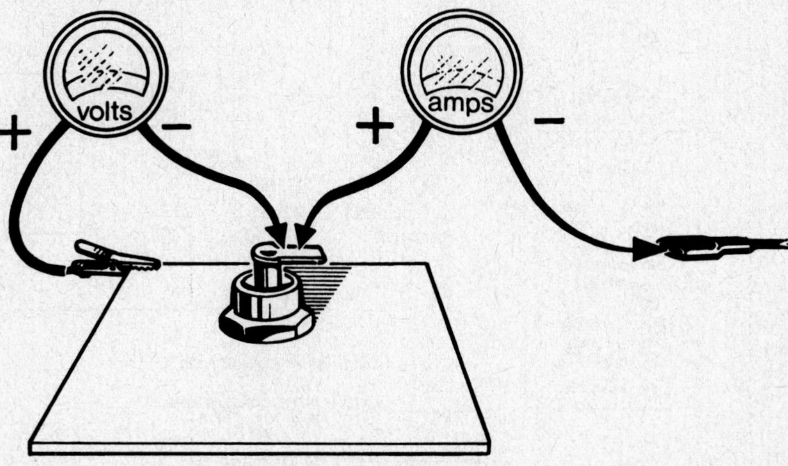

Diode test set-up

Installation

1. The capacitor terminals can be identified as follows:

Single terminal—positive (ground) marked with a red dot on the mounting rivet. Double terminal—negative

2. Install the capacitor in its spring with the terminals facing down. Push the unit into the spring until the last coils fit into the capacitor body groove.

3. Connect the capacitor negative terminal *and* zener diode to the center (brown/white lead) connector of the rectifier.

4. Connect the positive terminal of the capacitor to the rectifier center ground bolt terminal.

5. Mount the capacitor spring in any convenient spot near the battery carrier.

Before putting the machine into operation, a few precautions should be taken to avoid any damage to the capacitor or wiring system.

1. If the battery is to remain in the machine, it is essential that the negative lead be very carefully insulated to prevent it from shorting to the frame. This can be done by either wrapping the lead in electrical tape or, better yet, by replacing the battery fuse with a wooden dowel of similar dimensions.

2. If the capacitor is being used as a back-up system in case of battery failure, take the time to check it occasionally to ensure that it's still operational.

3. Do not run the engine with the zener diode disconnected as the capacitor will be destroyed due to excessive voltage.

Capacitor Ignition Test

The capacitor has a limited storage life of approximately 18 months at 68° F, or 9 to 12 months at 86° F. Therefore, it would be wise to check its condition regularly if it is not in use.

1. Connect the capacitor to a 12 volt battery for approximately 5 seconds. Make sure the terminal polarity is correct or the capacitor will be ruined.

2. Let the capacitor stand for at least 5 minutes, then connect a DC voltmeter to the terminals. Note the instantaneous reading of the meter. A good capacitor will register at least 9 volts.

CHASSIS

WHEELS, HUBS AND BRAKES

TR25W

FRONT

Removal and Disassembly

1. Support the bottom of the engine with a wooden box or wire milk basket,

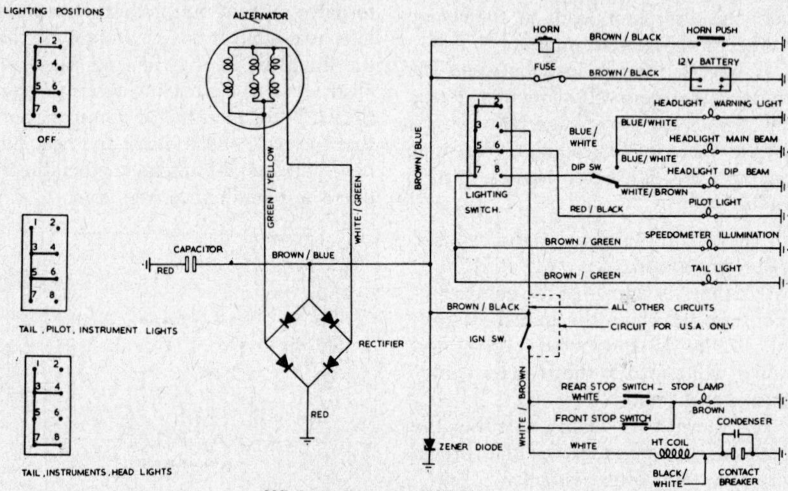

Wiring diagram (250)

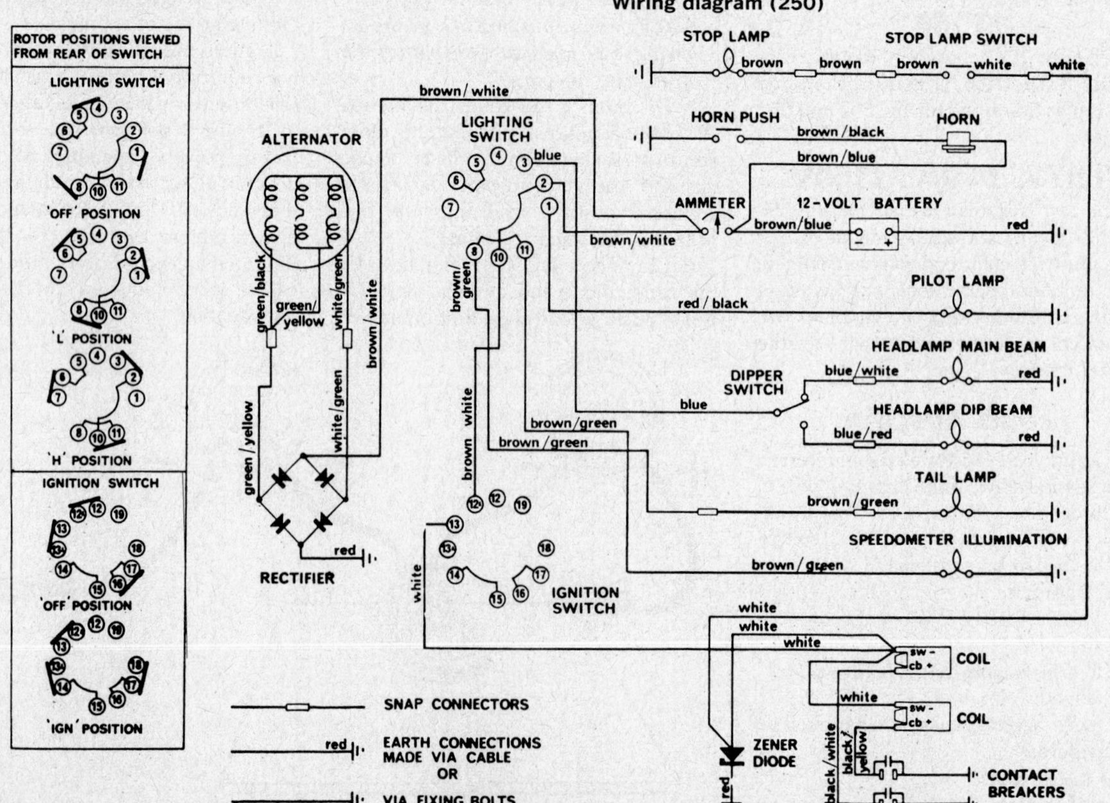

Wiring diagram (500 models, 12 volt coil ignition with nacelle up to serial no. H49832)

positioning the bike so that the front wheel is about 6 in. off the ground.

2. Loosen the front brake cable at the handlebar adjuster, then disconnect it at the brake backing plate.

3. Remove the two axle securing nuts, slide the axle through the hub, then remove the front wheel assembly.

4. Separate the front anchor plate from the wheel and remove the right retainer with Triumph special tool no 61-3694 or a suitable substitute.

NOTE: *The retainer ring has left-hand threads.*

5. Remove the right wheel bearing by driving it out from the left side with the axle used as a drift.

6. Remove the backing ring and the inner retainer disc.

NOTE: *On machines equiped with double leading shoe brakes, the backing ring and retainer disc are replaced by a single part.*

7. Remove the left wheel bearing circlip and drive the bearing (with retaining plates) out from the right side with the axle.

8. Remove the brake backing plate center nut and withdraw the brake shoe assembly.

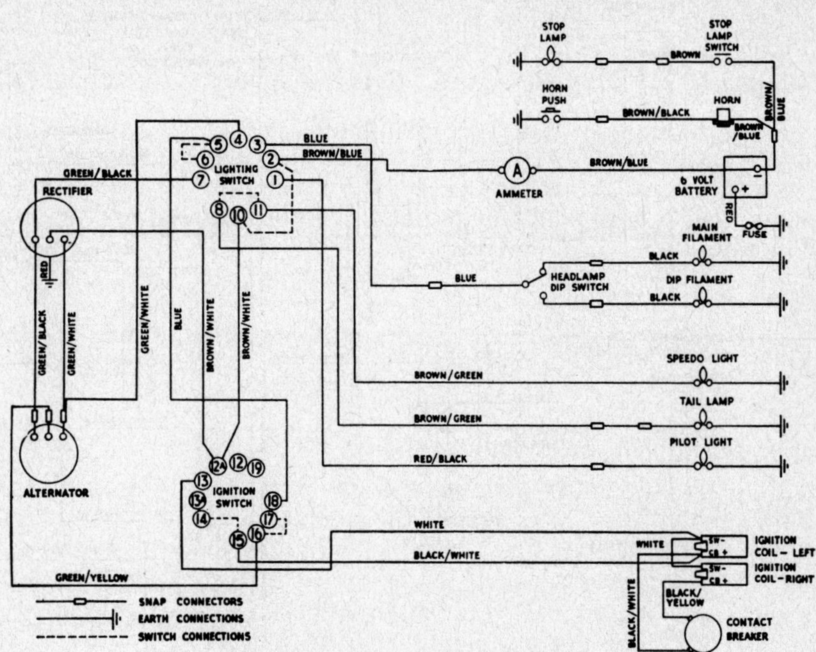

Wiring diagram (500 models with 6 volt coil ignition)

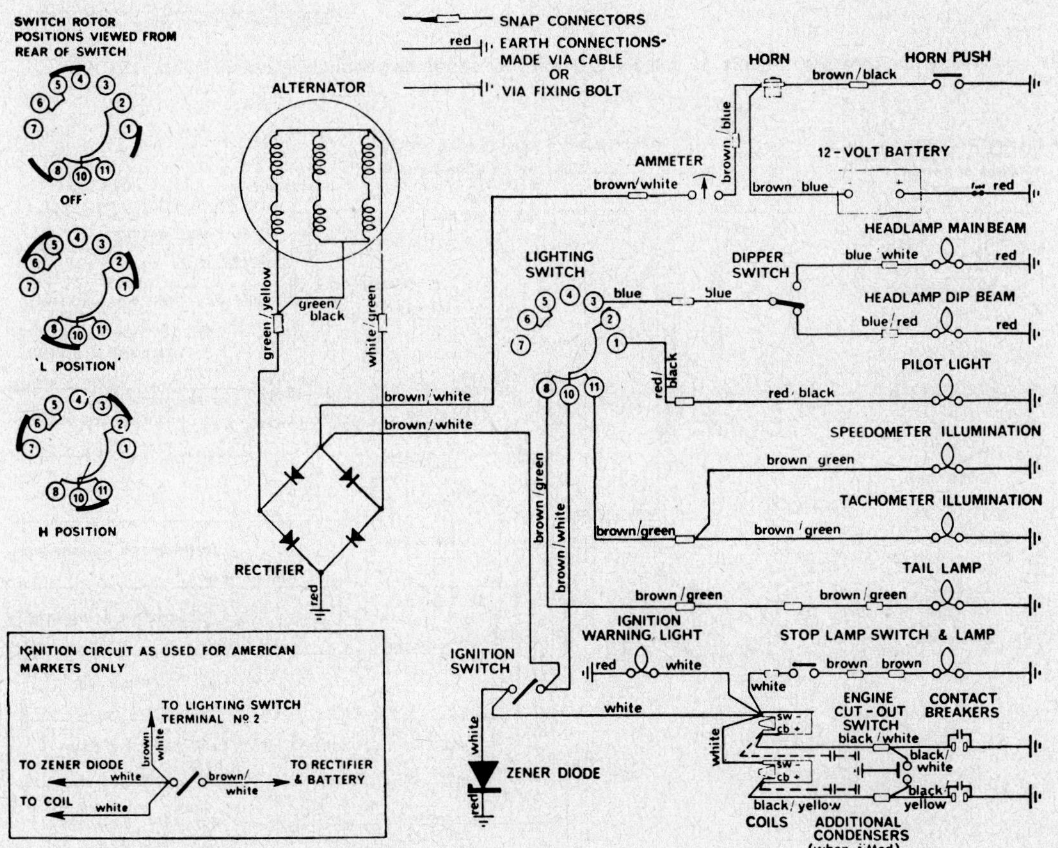

Wiring diagram (500 models, 12 volt coil ignition without nacelle up to serial no. H49832)

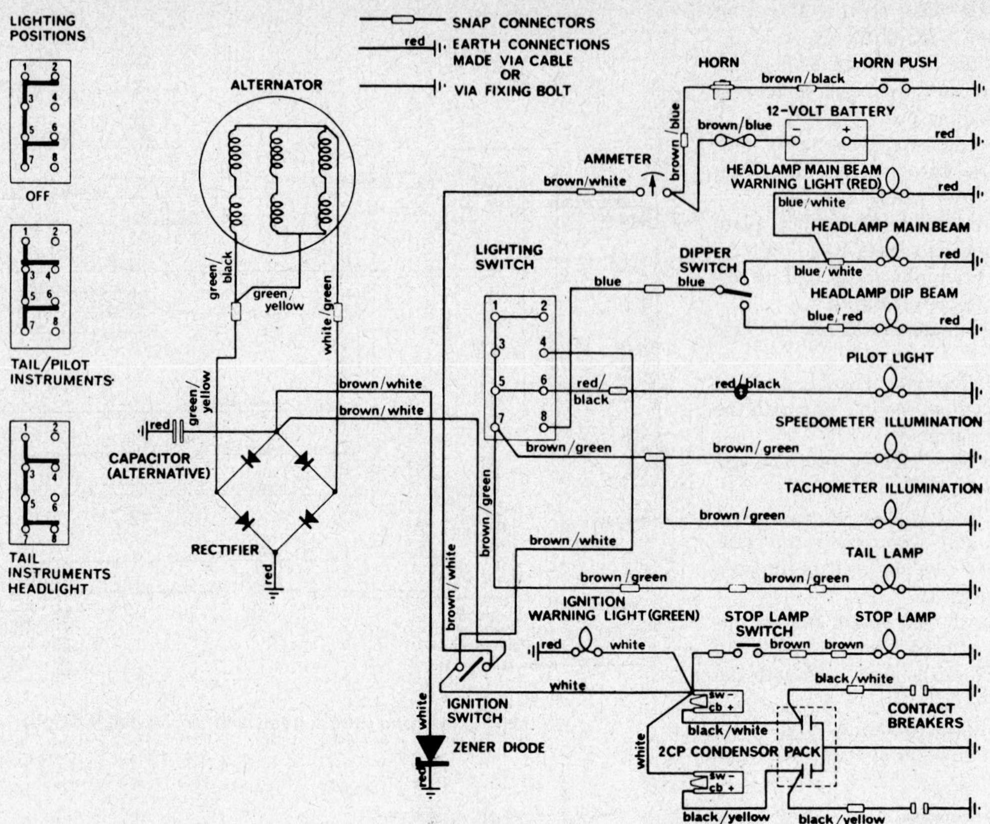

Wiring diagram (500 models, 12 volt coil ignition with separate headlight after serial no. H57083)

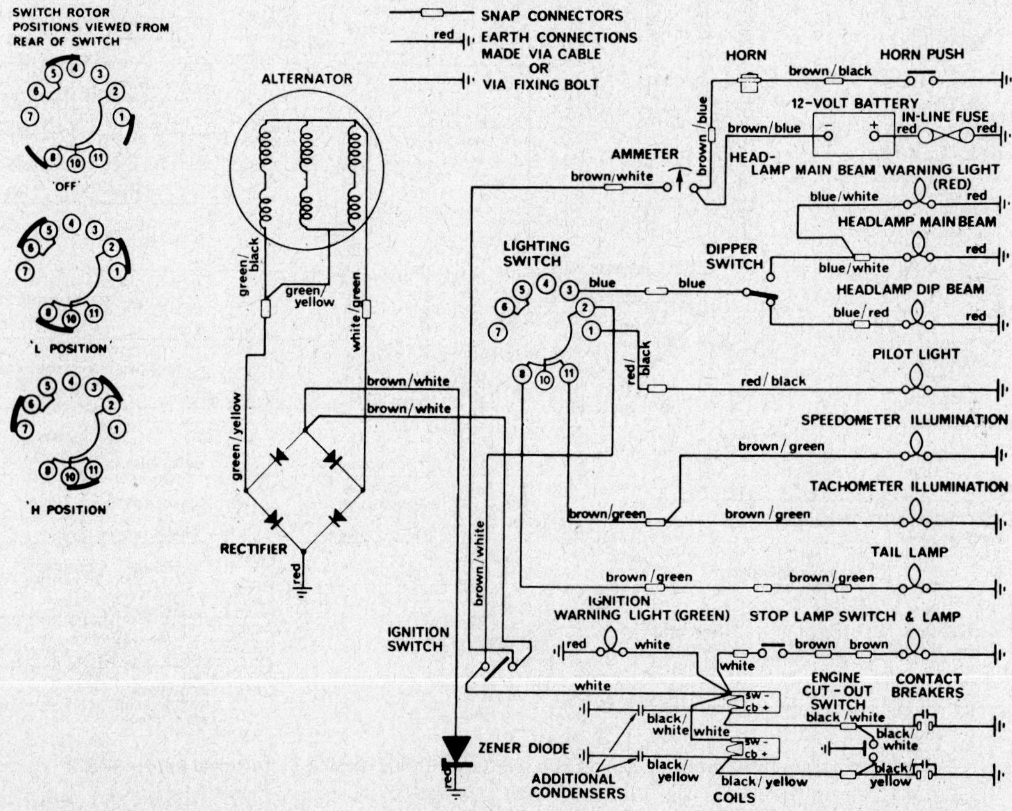

Wiring diagram (500 models, 12 volt coil ignition with separate headlight between serial nos. H49832 and H57083)

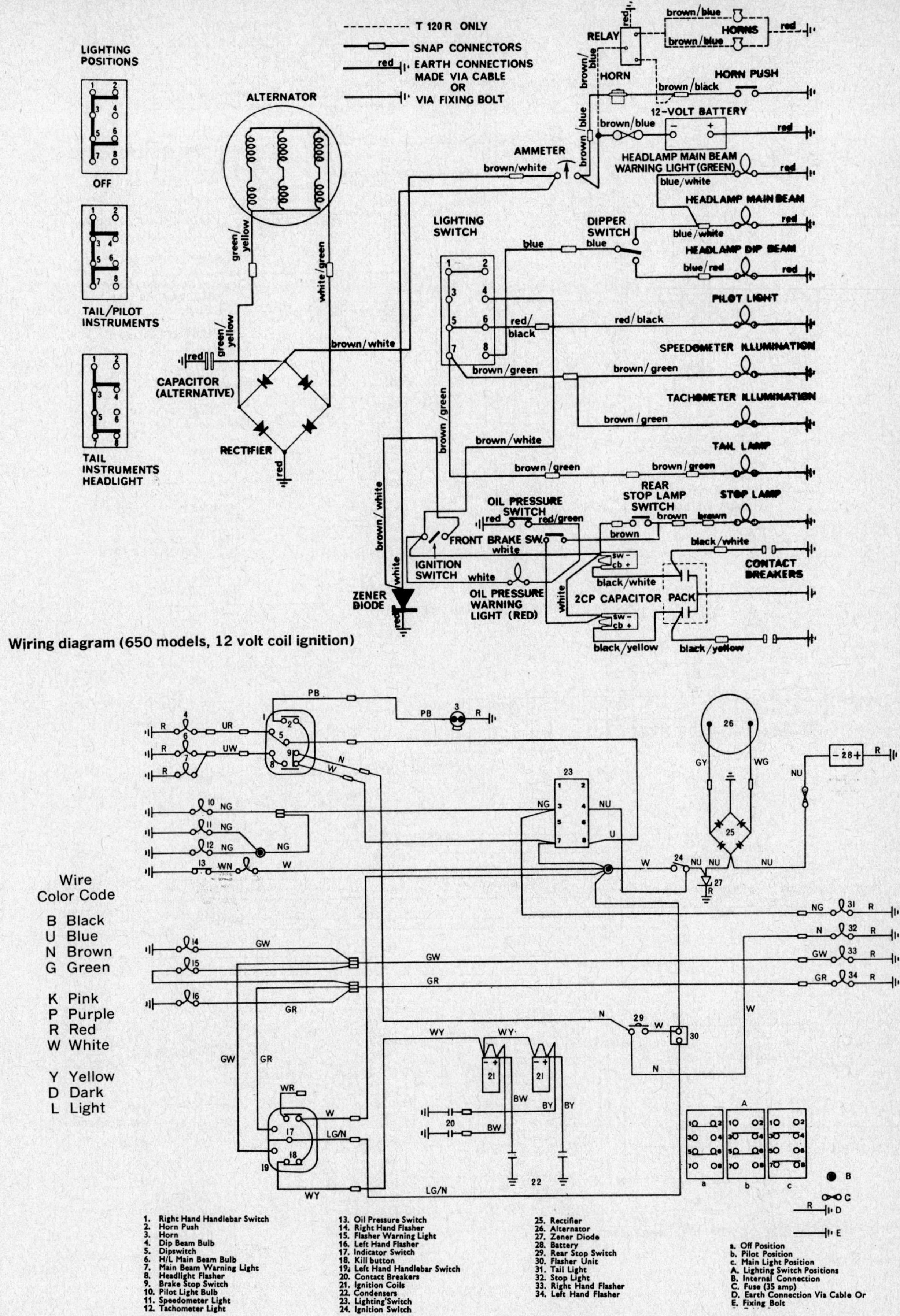
T 120 R ONLY
SNAP CONNECTORS
EARTH CONNECTIONS MADE VIA CABLE OR VIA FIXING BOLT
LIGHTING POSITIONS
OFF
TAIL/PILOT INSTRUMENTS
TAIL INSTRUMENTS HEADLIGHT
ALTERNATOR
green/yellow
white/green
brown/white
CAPACITOR (ALTERNATIVE)
RECTIFIER
red
RELAY
HORNS
HORN
HORN PUSH
brown/blue
brown/black
12-VOLT BATTERY
AMMETER
HEADLAMP MAIN BEAM WARNING LIGHT (GREEN)
blue/white
HEADLAMP MAIN BEAM
LIGHTING SWITCH
DIPPER SWITCH
blue
HEADLAMP DIP BEAM
blue/red
PILOT LIGHT
red/black
SPEEDOMETER ILLUMINATION
brown/green
TACHOMETER ILLUMINATION
TAIL LAMP
REAR STOP LAMP SWITCH
STOP LAMP
brown
OIL PRESSURE SWITCH
red/green
FRONT BRAKE SW.
IGNITION SWITCH
white
OIL PRESSURE WARNING LIGHT (RED)
black/white
CONTACT BREAKERS
2CP CAPACITOR PACK
black/yellow
ZENER DIODE
Wire Color Code
B Black
U Blue
N Brown
G Green
K Pink
P Purple
R Red
W White
Y Yellow
D Dark
L Light
1. Right Hand Handlebar Switch
2. Horn Push
3. Horn
4. Dip Beam Bulb
5. Dipswitch
6. H/L Main Beam Bulb
7. Main Beam Warning Light
8. Headlight Flasher
9. Brake Stop Switch
10. Pilot Light Bulb
11. Speedometer Light
12. Tachometer Light
13. Oil Pressure Switch
14. Right Hand Flasher
15. Flasher Warning Light
16. Left Hand Flasher
17. Indicator Switch
18. Kill button
19. Left Hand Handlebar Switch
20. Contact Breakers
21. Ignition Coils
22. Condensers
23. Lighting Switch
24. Ignition Switch
25. Rectifier
26. Alternator
27. Zener Diode
28. Battery
29. Rear Stop Switch
30. Flasher Unit
31. Tail Light
32. Stop Light
33. Right Hand Flasher
34. Left Hand Flasher
a. Off Position
b. Pilot Position
c. Main Light Position
A. Lighting Switch Positions
B. Internal Connection
C. Fuse (35 amp)
D. Earth Connection Via Cable Or
E. Fixing Bolt
Wiring diagram (650 models, 12 volt coil ignition)

TR7V, T140V

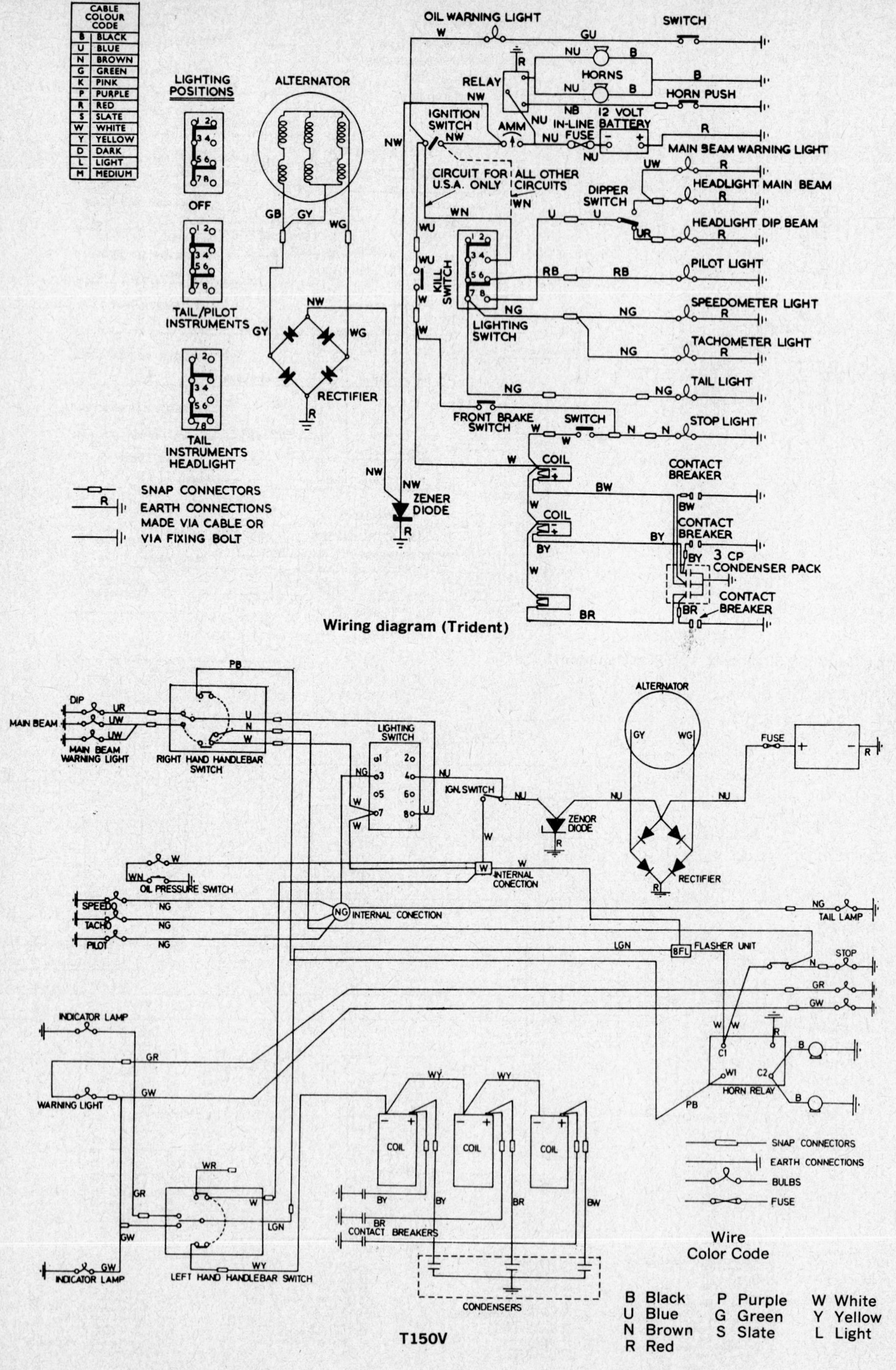

Wiring diagram (Trident)

T150V

9. On machines equipped with double leading shoes, lift up the edge of one shoe until it is free of the backing plate. Disconnect one end of each brake return spring and then remove the second shoe. Remove the pivot pin cotter key at each end of the lever adjustment rod and lift out the pivot pin. Remove the brake cam securing nuts and washers and disconnect the return spring from the front cam. Pry off the levers one at a time and remove the brake cams.

10. On machines equipped with single leading shoes, turn the brake operating lever to relieve the pressure of the shoes against the drum, then pull out the brake and backing plate assembly. Slowly release the operating lever until the return springs can be removed, then remove the springs and the brakes shoes as shown in the accompanying illustration. Remove the operating lever securing nut and washers, then remove the lever and cam spindle.

11. Thoroughly clean all parts (except brake shoes) in kerosine or a cleaning solvent and blow them dry with compressed air.

Inspection

Examine the ball bearings for any signs of pitting or excessive wear. Replace them both if there is any doubt as to their condition.

Inspect the anchor plate for any cracks or signs of distortion, particularly in the area of the brake cam housing. Check the return springs for general condition and signs of fatigue. Measure the drum diameter in several places and check for scoring, etc. If drum diameter is 0.010 in. greater than specified, replacement is in order.

Check the condition of the brake shoes. If oil-soaked, cracked, badly scored, or if the lining is worn down to the rivets, replace the shoes.

If possible check wheel rim runout on a wheel stand. Tighten any loose spokes.

Assembly And Installation

1. On machines with single leading shoes, install the operating lever, cam spindle, and pivot pin. Fasten the return springs to their respective hooks on the brake shoes, then position the shoes over the cam and pivot pin. Snap the shoes in place by pressing on the outer edges of the shoes. Position the operating lever in a counterclockwise location then connect the return spring.

2. On machines with double leading shoes, first lubricate the spindles lightly, then install both cams—wedge shape out. Install the outside return spring on the front cam, then reinstall both brake cam levers and secure them with washers and nuts. Install the abutment plates on the anchor plate with the tag side toward the anchor plate. Position the shoes with the radiused end toward the pivot pin and connect the return springs. This is most easily accomplished by installing one shoe, connecting the springs, and snapping the other shoe into place.

3. Coat the wheel bearings and retainers liberally with the recommended grease, then install the left inner retainer, bearing, and outer dust cap. Install the retaining circlip and then drive the bearing up against the circlip, using the shouldered end of the axle as a drift.

4. Install the right retainer disc and backing ring (one piece on machines with double leading brakes).

ELECTRICAL SPECIFICATIONS

TR25W

Battery	Lucas PUZ5A
Coil	Lucas MA.12
Contact breaker unit	Lucas 6CA
Generator	Lucas RM.19
Generator output	115 watt
Horn	Lucas 6H
Rectifier	Lucas 2DS.506
Zener diode	Lucas ZD.715
Bulbs: headlamp (main)	40/27 watt
headlamp (pilot)	6 watt
main beam indicator	2 watt
stop and tail lamp	6/21 watt

T100C and T100R

Battery	1 Lucas 12 volt battery PUZ5A or earlier 2 Lucas batteries connected in series (MKZ9E)	
Rectifier type	Lucas 2DS506	
Alternator type	Lucas RM19	
Horn	27899 12 volt	
Bulbs:	No.	Type
Headlight	Lucas 414	50/40 watts
Parking light	Lucas 989	6 watts MCC
Stop and tail light	Lucas 380	6/21 watts offset pins
Speedometer light	Lucas 987	2 watts MES
Ignition warning light	Lucas 281	2 watts (BA7S)
Main beam indicator light (where fitted)	Lucas 281	2 watts (BA7S)
Zener diode type	ZD 715	
Coil type	Lucas MA12 (12v) 2 off	
Contact breaker type	Lucas 4CA (12° range) After H.57083 Lucas 6CA (12° range)	
Fuse rating	35 amp	

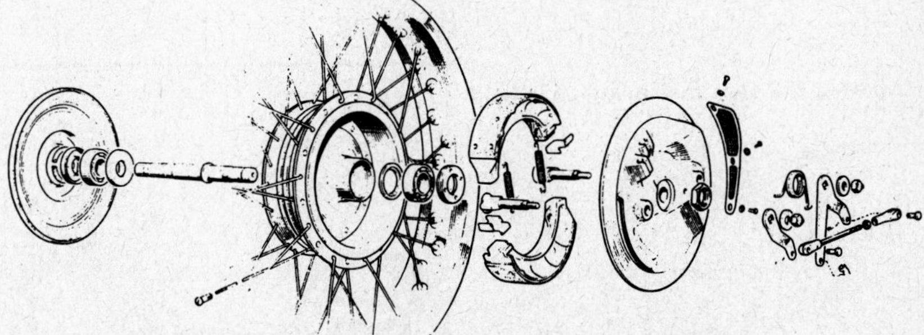

250 front wheel assembly (double leading shoe brake)

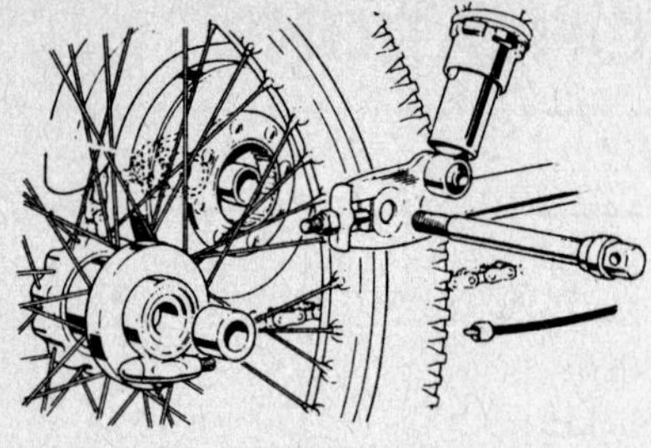

Rear wheel assembly (250)

5. Using the shouldered end of the axle as a drift, drive the right bearing into place, then install the left-hand thread retainer ring.

6. The remainder of the assembly and installation procedure is a reversal of the removal and disassembly instructions.

7. Adjust the front brake.

REAR

Removal and Disassembly

1. Disconnect the speedometer drive cable, then remove the securing nut and the rear axle.

2. The distance collar that fits between the hub and the swing arm should drop out when the axle is removed, thereby facilitating wheel removal.

3. Remove the speedometer drive unit and unscrew the end cover.

4. Withdraw the wheel, leaving the brake hub assembly fastened to the swing arm.

5. Remove the left side bearing retainer.

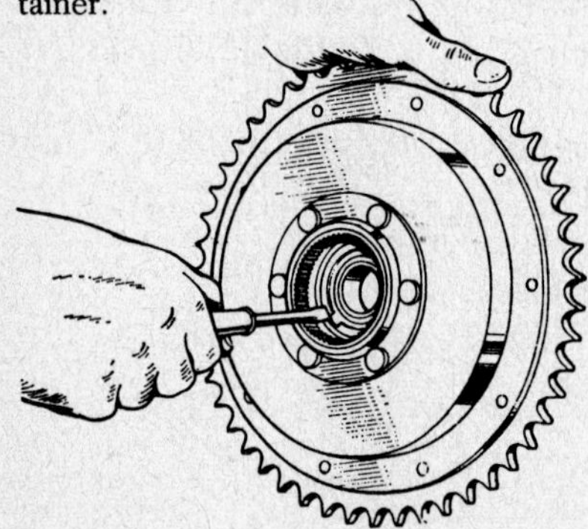

Removing the rear hub bearing circlip (250)

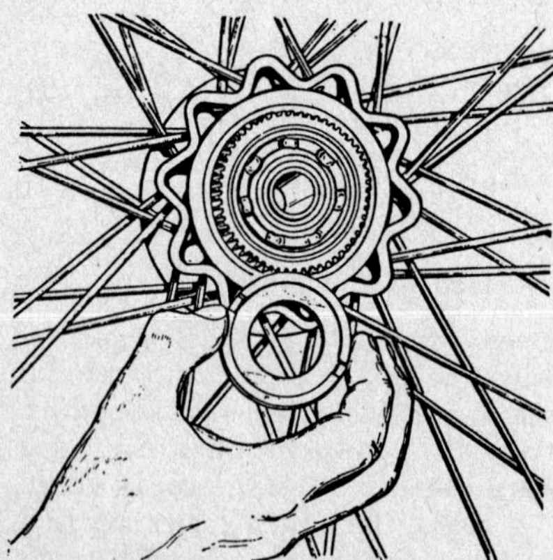

Rear wheel bearing retainer (250)

ELECTRICAL SPECIFICATIONS

TR6C, TR6R, and T120R

Battery (12v)	PUZ5A	
Rectifier type	2DS 506	
Alternator type	RM.19	
Horn type (12v)	6H	
Cutout switch	151SA	
Bulbs	No.	Type
Headlight (L/H dip)	464	40/27 watts vert-dip pre-focus
Parking light	989	6 watts—MCC
Stop and tail light	380	L679 21/6 watts—offset pin
Speedometer light	989	6 watts—MCC
Ignition warning light	281	2 watts (BA7S)
High beam indicator light	281	2 watts (BA7S)
Zener diode type	ZD 715	
Coil type (2 off)	Siba 3200/1 2 off or later, 17M12 (12v) 2 off	
Contact breaker type	6CA	
Fuse rating	35 amp	

T150

Battery type (12v)	PUZ5A	
Rectifier type	54048008 (Lucas)	
Alternator type	RM20	
Horn type (12v): R-H	P201	
L-H	P101	
Bulbs	No.	Type
Headlight (L/H dip)	446	50/40 watts—pre-focus
Parking light	989	6 watts—MCC
Stop and tail light	380	6/21 watts—offset pin
Speedometer light	987	2.2 watts—MES
Ignition warning light	281	2 watts (BA7S)
High beam indicator light	283	2 watts (BA7S)
Zener diode type	ZD 71S	
Coil type (3)	Siba 32000 3 off	
Contact breaker type	Lucas 7CA (12°)	
Oil warning light	281 2 watts (BA7S)	
Fuse rating	35 amps	

250 front wheel assembly (single leading shoe brake)

NOTE: *This bearing retainer has left-hand threads.*

6. Using a drift slightly under ¾ in. diameter, drive out the hollow hub spindle. This will release the right bearing, inner collar, and washers.

7. Drive out the left bearing and thrust washer from the right side. Do not disturb the bearing oil seal unless it must be replaced

8. To remove the brake hub assembly from the swing arm, disconnect the final drive chain and unscrew the brake adjusting rod sleeve. Remove the spindle (axle) nut and disconnect the torque arm at the hub. Lift out the brake assembly.

9. The brake assembly can now be disassembled and inspected as previously described for the front brakes.

10. To remove the brake hub bearing, first drive out the hollow spindle from the left side and remove the bearing circlip. The bearing can then be driven out with a suitable drift.

11. Do not disturb the chain sprocket unless it must be replaced. To remove it, bend back the locking tabs and remove the six securing bolts.

12. Thoroughly clean all parts (except brake shoes) in kerosine or cleaning solvent and blow them dry with compressed air. *Do not spin the bearings until they have been completely dried and lubricated.*

Inspection

Examine all parts as previously described for the front wheel and hub. Replace the chain sprocket if the teeth points have become hooked or rounded.

T150V

Battery type (12v)	PUZ5A	
Rectifier type	Lucas 2DS.506	
Alternator	RM 20/21	
Horn	Clearhooter HF 80 High/low	
Bulbs	No.	Type
Headlight	370	45/40 watts
Parking light	989	6 watts
Stop and tail light	380	21/6 watts
Instrument lights	643	2.2 watts
Zener diode	ZD.715	
Coils (3)	17M12	
Contact breakers	7CA	
Fuse rating	35 amps	

TR7V, T140V

Battery type (12v)	PUZ5A	
Rectifier	2DS 506	
Alternator	RM21	
Horn	Lucas 6H	
Zener diode	2D715	
Coils (2)	17M12	
Bulbs	No.	Type
Headlight	370	45/35 watts
Parking light	989	6 watts
Stop and tail light	380	5/21 watts
Warning lights	281	2 watts
Instrument lights	987	3 watts

Double leading shoe front wheel (500 and 650 models)

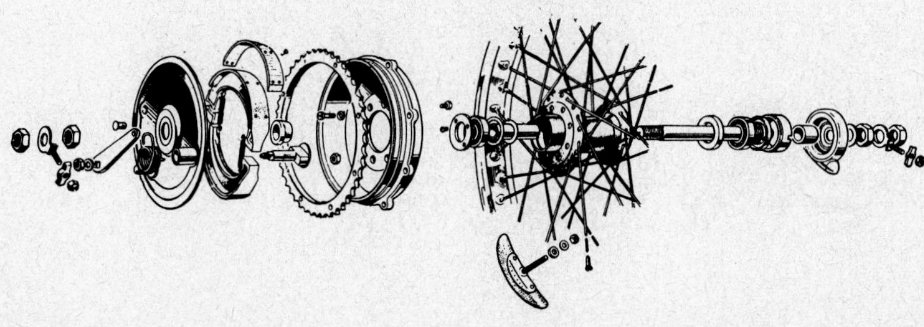

Standard rear wheel assembly (500 and 650 models)

Assembly And Installation

1. Assemble the brake hub in reverse order of disassembly. Liberally grease the bearings. Be sure to install the steel washer that fits between the bearing and circlip, otherwise the bearing will not seat properly.

2. Install the hub assembly, complete with brake shoes, etc., on the swing arm. Readjust the final drive chain.

3. Assemble the wheel hub in reverse order of disassembly. Liberally grease the bearings. Note that the bearings should be driven in place by applying pressure to the outer race only. Install the hollow spindle with the short end on the left-hand side, and install the bearing seals facing outward.

4. Isntall the wheel and hub assembly in the reverse of the removal procedure. Do not forget the distance collar between the swing arm and hub. If the brake hub assembly was not removed, it will not be necessary to readjust the chain.

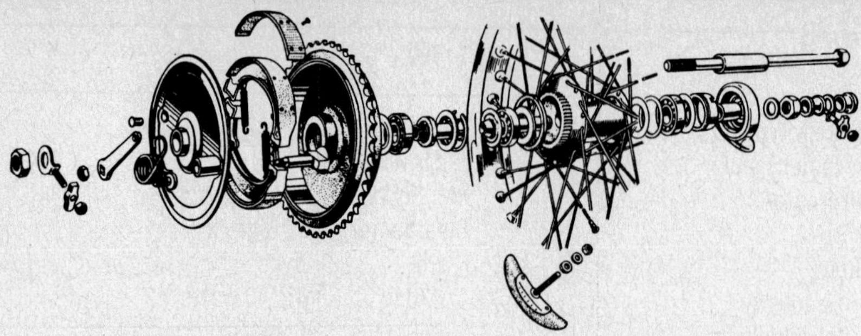

Quickly detachable rear wheel assembly (500 and 650 models)

T100C, T100R, TR6R, TR6C, and T120R

FRONT

The front wheel assembly on the 500 and 650 cc models is basically the same as the arrangement used on the TR25W. It can be serviced in the same manner, except that on 500s, Triumph special tool no. Z76 must be used to remove the left bearing retainer ring, rather than tool no. 61–3694.

Use the accompanying illustrations for reference.

REAR

NOTE: *The 500 and 650 cc models are equipped with either standard or quickly detachable rear wheels.*

Removal and Disassembly (Standard)

1. Disconnect the rear brake adjuster and the final drive chain.
2. Loosen the front securing bolt and swing the chainguard up out of the way.
3. Disconnect the torque arm at the hub.
4. Disconnect the speedometer cable.
5. Loosen the axle nuts and slide off the wheel assembly.
6. Unscrew the backing plate retaining nut and withdraw the brake assembly. Service the brake assembly as described in the TR25W section.
7. Remove the wheel spindle, complete with speedometer drive, out of the right side.
8. Remove the slotted screw that locks the left bearing retainer ring in place.
9. Remove the retainer ring with tool no. 276 or a suitable substitute. The ring has left-hand threads.
10. To gain access to remove the left bearing, drive the central distance piece from the left side (see illustration) until the grease retainer collapses. The bearing can now be driven out from the right side, using a suitable, soft drift.
11. Remove the backing ring, collapsed grease retainer and central distance piece.
12. Drive out the right bearing and dust cap with a drift approximately 1 ⅝ in. in diameter.
13. Thoroughly clean all parts (except brake shoes) in kerosine or cleaning solvent and blow them dry with compressed air.

Inspection

Examine all parts carefully as described in the TR25W section.

Assembly and Installation

1. Liberally grease the bearings and retainers.
2. Drive in the right grease retainer (new or straightened) and bearing. Install the dust cap after making sure that the bearing and the cavities on either side of the bearing are filled with grease.
3. Install the distance piece, right grease retainer and right bearing. Make sure everything is well packed in grease.
4. Bring the distance piece in line with the axle, then install the threaded (left-hand) retainer ring.
5. Install the retainer locking screw.
6. The remainder of the assembly and installation procedure is a reversal of the removal and disassembly instructions. Don't forget to readjust the rear brake and final drive chain.

Removal and Disassembly (Quickly Detachable)

1. Disconnect the speedometer cable.
2. Unscrew the axle from the right side of the machine and pull out the distance collar.
3. Pull the wheel clear of the engaging splines and remove it out the back of the machine.
4. Remove the locknut on the right side of the axle sleeve and lift off the speedometer drive unit.
5. Disassemble the wheel hub and bearings as previously described for the standard rear wheel.
6. Disconnect the final drive chain, brake operating rod and torque arm, and then remove the axle sleeve nut.
7. Disassemble the brake components as previously described in the TR25W section.
8. Press out the axle sleeve, then remove the bearing circlip located in the brake drum.
9. Pry out the retainer and felt washer, then drive out the bearing with a suitable drift.
10. Thoroughly clean all metal parts in kerosine or cleaning solvent, then blow them dry with compressed air. *Do not spin the bearings until they have been completely dried and lubricated.*

Inspection

Examine all parts as previously described and make any necessary replacements.

Assembly and Installation

Assembly and installation is a reversal of the removal and disassembly instructions. If brake work was performed and

Front wheel assembly (Trident)

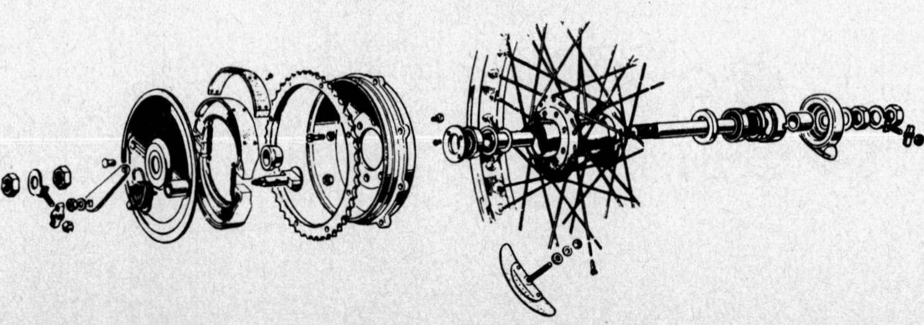

Rear wheel assembly (Trident)

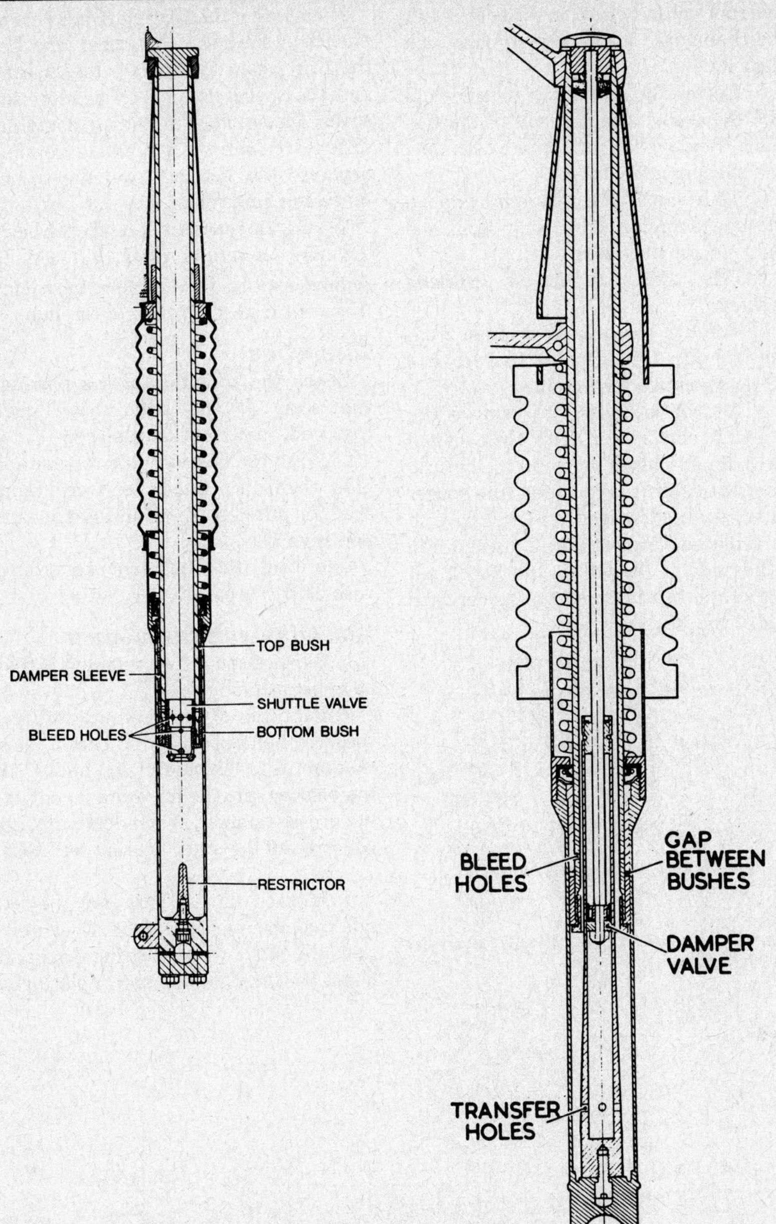

Front fork leg construction (rod damper type)

When refitting the wheel with this type of fork, place the front wheel assembly into the forks while engaging the brake anchor stud in the slot in the right fork slider. Refit the axle caps and replace all of the cap nuts, tightening them evenly until they are just a bit more than hand tight. Slacken all of them ½ turn.

Pull the wheel to the right side of the machine until the brake anchor plate facing boss touches the mating lug on the fork leg. Holding the wheel in this position, tighten the axle cap nuts *evenly* to 15 ft lbs. Check that no gap exists between the facing boss and the fork slider. Retighten the anchor stud nut.

TR7V, T140V, T150V
FRONT

Removal and Disassembly

These models are equipped with a front disc brake and the latest type of front fork. This fork is easily distinguished from earlier units in that it is *not* fitted with either external fork springs or fork gaitors. The fork tubes are chromed, and the top of each slider is fitted with a small dust seal.

1. Support the machine so that the front wheel is off of the ground.
2. Remove the four axle cap nuts at the bottom of each fork leg, remove the caps, and take away the front wheel assembly. Do not apply the front (disc) brake with the wheel removed.
3. Remove the axle nut on the left side, then unscrew the bearing retainer ring with the Triumph tool 61–3694 or a suitable substitute. The retainer has a standard right-hand thread.
4. Remove the left side wheel bearing by driving the axle through the wheel from the right side. Remove the grease seal beneath the bearing.
5. Take off the circlip on the right hand side of the wheel, and insert the

the hub was removed from the swing arm, it will be necessary to adjust the rear brake and the final drive chain. Make sure the bearings and retainers are thoroughly packed with grease and remember to soak the felt washer in oil before reassembly.

T150

Early models use a front hub not dissimilar to that described above for the TR25W. These models also used a rear hub like that of the 650 Twins (standard hub). Refer to the section above.

Note that some later model Tridents are equipped with the newer type forks (without external fork springs or fork gaitors), and these forks have four nuts on each axle cap which must be removed to remove the front wheel.

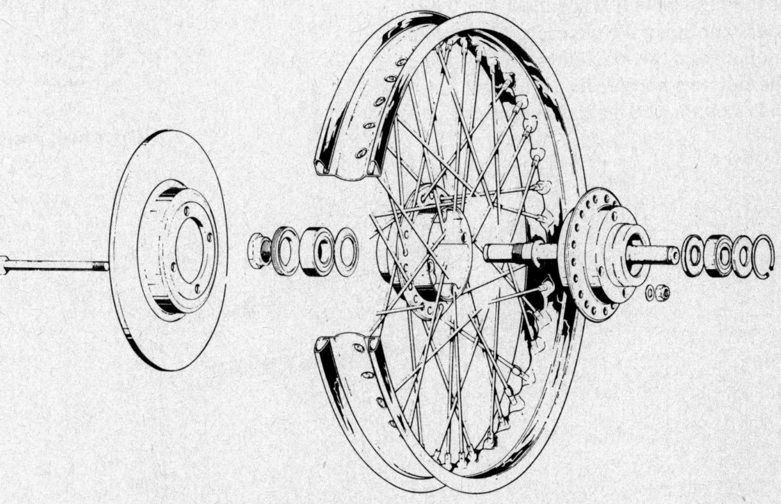
Front wheel assembly (disc brake models)

axle into the left hand side, driving out the right hand bearing along with its two grease seals (one on each side of the bearing).

Inspection

1. Clean all parts thoroughly in a solvent and blow them dry.

2. Check the bearings for wear, pitting, play in the bearing races, and rough or uneven rotation. Replace as necessary.

Assembly and Installation

1. Refit the inner grease seal for the right side wheel bearing. Lubricate the bearing thoroughly and refit it and the outer grease seal.

2. Replace the circlip for the right side bearing. Insert the shouldered end of the axle into the left side of the wheel, and use it to drift the bearing assembly up against the circlip.

3. Take out the axle, and then reinsert it into the wheel from the left in its normal position.

4. Replace the left-hand bearing grease seal, the lubricated bearing, and the retainer. Screw in the retainer until tight. Tap the axle from the right until the axle shoulder contacts the left side bearing. Replace the axle nut and tighten securely.

5. Engage the brake disc into the caliper and replace the fork caps. Tighten the four nuts on the left fork slider *first*, then tighten the nuts on the right slider. In both cases, tighten the nuts evenly and in an "X" pattern. Torque the cap nuts to 25 ft lbs.

REAR

Removal and Disassembly

1. Support the machine so that the front wheel is about 12 in. off the ground.

2. Disconnect the rear chain and disengage it from the rear wheel sprocket.

3. Disconnect the speedometer cable at the rear wheel. Disconnect the brake anchor at the brake plate and remove the anchor from the machine after removing the nut and bolt at the other end.

4. Loosen the bolt securing the left side shock absorber to the swing arm. Lift the chainguard so that the sprocket will clear it.

5. Loosen the axle nut (right side) and pull the wheel assembly out of the machine. Remove the axle, brake assembly, and speedometer drive.

6. To remove the bearings, remove the speedometer drive ring from the right side of the wheel.

NOTE: *This ring has a left-hand thread.*

7. Remove the bearing retainer from the left side. Use Triumph tool No. 61-3694 to remove this retainer.

8. A drift is needed to remove the bearings and spacer. This drift should have dimensions as shown in the illustration. If this drift is not used, the spacer tube may be damaged, and will have to be replaced. Using the drift, insert it into either side of the wheel and knock out one of the bearings and the spacer tube out of the wheel.

Removing the rear wheel bearings (1973 models).

9. Note that the bearing is an interference fit on the end of the spacer tube. Use the drift again to separate the bearing and the spacer tube, then reinsert the spacer tube in the hub, and use it and the drift to remove the remaining bearing. Separate this bearing from the spacer tube after removal.

10. Grease retainers behind each bearing may be left in place, but can be removed with a drift if desired by driving them out from the inside of the hub.

Inspection

Check the condition of the bearings and seals. If the latter have been removed, they must be replaced.

2. Wash the bearings in a solvent and blow them dry. Check for worn, damaged, or pitted balls, rough rotation, and excessive play.

Lubricate the bearings generously with chassis grease.

Assembly and Installation

1. Replace the grease retainers if they have been removed.

2. Refit one of the bearings onto the spacer tube, and place the bearing and tube into the left side of the hub. Drift the bearing into the hub until it contacts the grease retainer. When doing this, apply force to the outer bearing race only.

3. Replace the washers and the left side retainer ring and tighten it securely. Refit the other wheel bearing driving it home as with the first, and replace and tighten the speedometer drive ring (left-hand thread).

4. The remainder of the procedure is a reversal of the removal instructions.

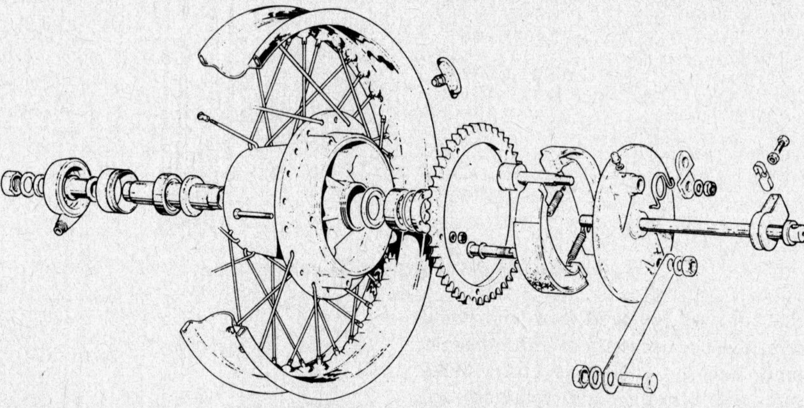

Rear wheel assembly (1973 models).

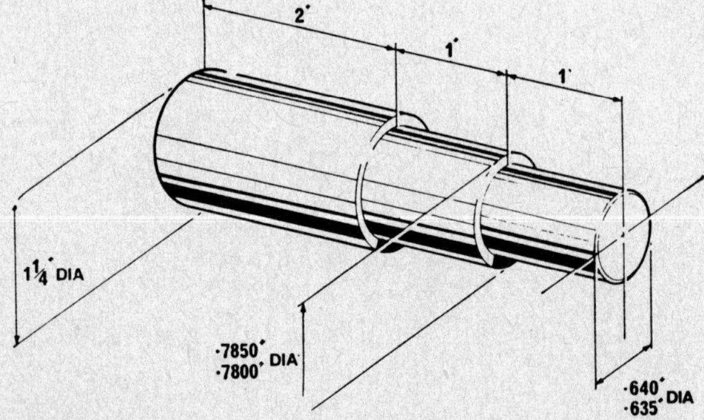

Drift for removing the rear wheel bearings (1973 models).

FRONT FORK

Late models (including the TR7V, T140V, and T150V) are equipped with a telescopic fork of the Ceriani pattern easily noticeable because of its chromed fork tubes and the absence of external springs and fork gaitors.

Other models have either rod damper

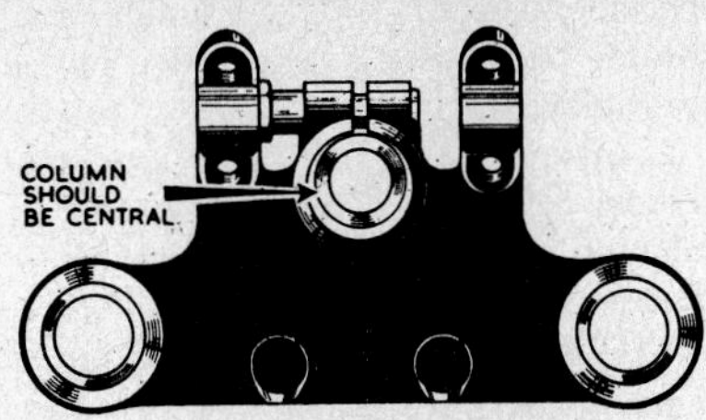

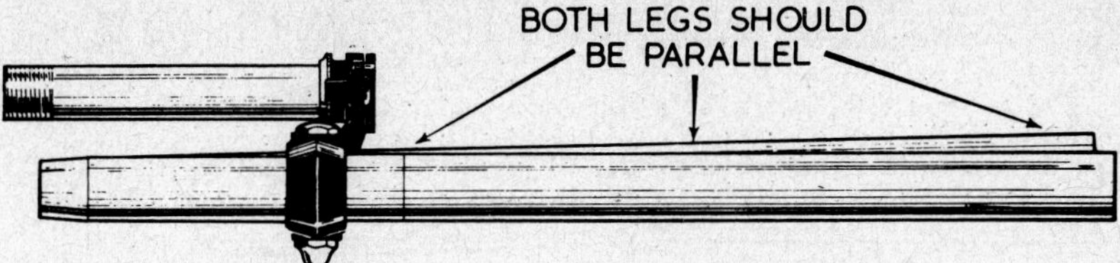

or shuttle valve-type forks. In general, the shuttle valve types can be identified by its longer and narrower spring, and by its overall slimmer appearance.

TR25W (Shuttle Valve Type)

REMOVAL

1. Drain the fork oil.
2. Remove the front wheel and fender.
3. Slide the boots clear of the top fork shrouds.
4. Remove the fork leg caps along with cable brackets.
5. Loosen the bottom yoke, fork pinch-bolts and screw Triumph special tool no. 61–3824 or a suitable substitute into the top of the fork stanchion.
6. Hit the tool sharply with a mallet and the stanchion taper will be freed of the top yoke.
7. The fork legs can now be removed.
8. After removing the fork legs, lift off the boots and main springs.

DISASSEMBLY

1. Wrap a piece of rubber around the fork leg and clamp the leg in a soft-jawed vise.
2. Remove the oil seal holder, using Triumph special tool no. 61–6017 or a suitable substitute. Turn the tool counter-clockwise.
3. Firmly grasp the stanchion tube and move it back and forth against the top bushing until the bushing is driven out of the lower fork leg. At this time, the stanchion, complete with bushings and shuttle valve, can be removed.
4. To free the shuttle valve, remove the bottom retaining circlip, and let the valve slide out the top end of the stanchion.
5. Do not disturb the bottom bushing unless it is to be replaced. If it is, then remove the bottom bearing retaining nut and drive the bushing out with a hammer and chisel. Take care not to slip and damage the stanchion tube.
6. If it is necessary to remove the re-stricter at the bottom of the leg, unscrew the bolt in the spindle cutaway.
7. To remove the oil seals from their holders, take out the loose backing washer from the threaded end of the holder, and drive the seal out through the exposed slot. Note the O-ring in the threaded end of the seal holder.

INSPECTION

Check the stanchion tubes for straightness by rolling them along a known flat surface. Any bow greater than 5/32 in. requires that the stanchion be replaced. If less than 5/32 in., the stanchion may be straightened.

Examine the top fork yoke for cracks and then insert the fork legs (if true) and tighten them down with the top caps. Take several measurements to ensure that the legs are parallel to each other and perpendicular to the top yoke. Check the bottom yoke in the same manner, but make sure at least 6 ½ in. of the fork legs protrude above the yoke. The bottom yoke is made of malleable metal and, therefore, can be quite easily straightened if need be.

Examine the bottom fork legs for any damage. Insert the stanchion tubes (with new bottom bushing) and note the amount of free-play of the bushing within the bores of the bottom legs. If excessive, or any restriction of movement is noted, the bottom legs should be replaced.

Check bottom fork leg and front axle alignment by installing the axle and measuring their inclusive angle with a square. Check one leg at a time, then both simultaneously.

Inspect the condition of the top and bottom bushings, and measure their inside or outside diameters (see specifications). Excessive wear, or too great a clearance between the busing and its mating surface, indicates that the bushings should be replaced.

Check the main springs for any stress cracks etc., and measure its freestanding height. Both springs must be within ¼ in. of their original dimension.

ASSEMBLY

Assembly is basically a reversal of the disassembly procedure. Note the following:

1. Make sure the new bottom bushing is correctly seated before installing the retaining nut.
2. Note that the large end of the shuttle valve fits into the stanchion.
3. Thoroughly lubricate all parts in the fork before reassembly.
4. Replace the oil seals and apply locking compound to the holder threads.

INSTALLATION

1. Slide the fork leg boots over the oil seal holders and install the main springs.
2. Insert one leg through the bottom and top yoke bores and install Triumph special tool no. 61–3824 on the top of the stanchion. Install the collar and nut, and tighten the nut until the stanchion is firmly locked in its taper.
3. Tighten the bottom yoke pinch bolts and then remove the special tool
4. Slide the top of the fork boot over the shroud and secure it in place.
5. Repeat the previous steps for the remaining fork leg.
6. Install the front wheel and fender.

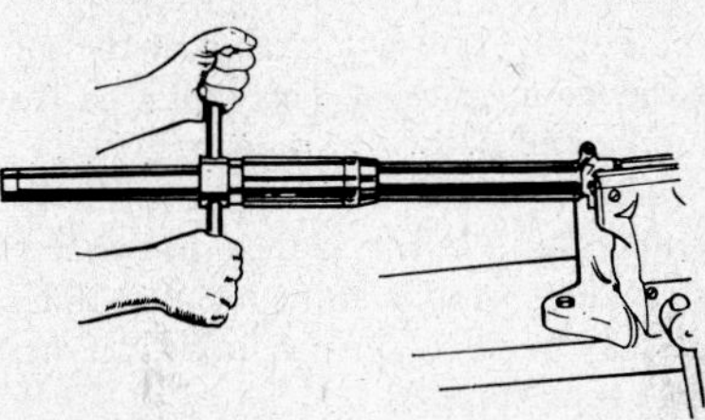

Removing the oil seal holder (rod damper type)

TR25W (Rod Damper Type)

REMOVAL

1. Drain the fork oil.
2. Remove the front wheel and fender.
3. Slide the fork boots off the top shrouds and loosen the bottom yoke pinch bolts.
4. Unscrew the fork leg caps and raise them high enough to loosen the damper rod locknut.
5. Remove the fork leg caps from the top of the rod damper.
6. Install Triumph special tool no. 61–3350 or a suitable substitute into the top of one fork leg.
7. Hold the bottom of the fork leg firmly, then strike the special tool sharply with a mallet. This will free the fork leg from its taper in the top yoke.
8. Remove the other fork leg in the same manner.
9. Remove the fork boots and main springs.

DISASSEMBLY

1. Clamp the fork leg in a soft-jawed vise at the axle lug.
2. Slide Triumph special tool no. 61–3005 over the main tube and engage the dogs at the bottom of the oil seal holder.
3. While applying pressure to the end of the tool, turn it counterclockwise and free the seal holder.
4. Remove the special tool and slide the seal holder to the end of the tube. Do

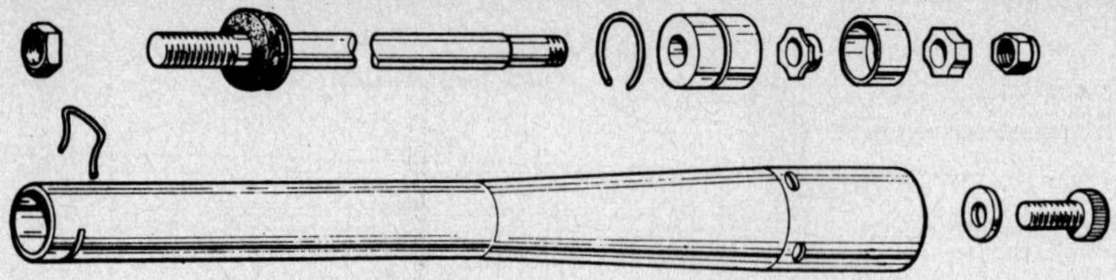

Rod and damper assembly

not attempt to entirely remove the seal holder as damage may result.

5. The main tube assembly and lower sliding leg can now be separated.

6. Clamp the un-machined portion of the tube in a soft-jawed vise and remove the large nut at the base of the shaft. Remove the bushings, spacer, and oil seal assembly.

7. Remove the allen screw that secures the damper tube to the lower portion of the fork leg.

8. Remove the two circlips at the top of the damper tube. This will free the damper rod with valve and bushing.

9. Remove the nut that secures the damper valve to the rod. Do not disturb the sealing washer and special retainer located just below the nut unless they require replacement.

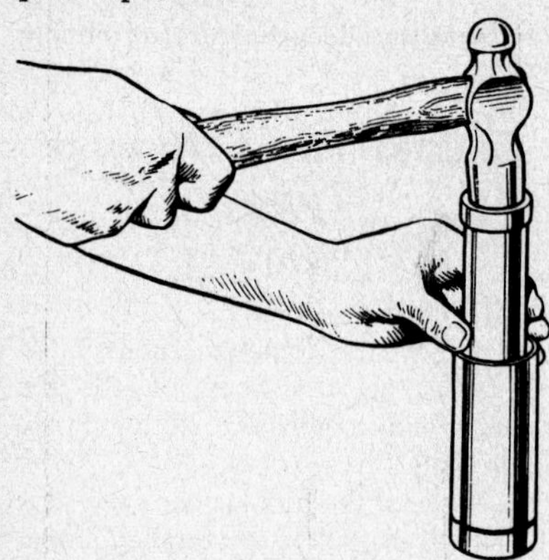

Removing the oil seal (rod damper type)

10. If an oil seal requires replacement, position the holder with the bottom edge on a wooden block and drive out the seal with Triumph special tool no. 61–3007 or a subitable substitute.

INSPECTION

Examine all parts as generally described for the shuttle-valve-type fork. Compare measurements with those given in specifications at the end of this section and make any necessary replacements.

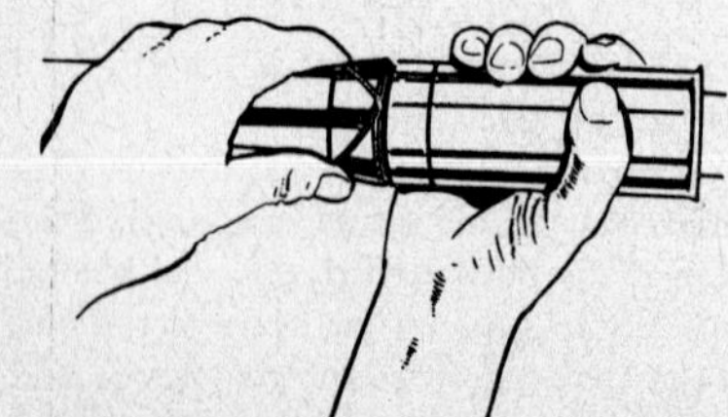

Installing twine for added protection (rod damper type)

ASSEMBLY AND INSTALLATION

1. Coat the outside of the oil replacement seals with gasket sealer and drive them into their holders with Triumph special tool no. 61–3007 or a suitable substitute. Grease the feather edge of the seal before further assembly.

2. Make certain all parts are completely clean, then reassemble the remaining parts in reverse order of disassembly.

NOTE: *When tightening down the oil seal holders, it's a good idea to wrap a piece of no. 5 twine around one of the last threads. This will provide additional protection for the seals.*

3. Triumph special tool no. 61–3350 must be used to set the fork leg in its taper, and special tool no. 61–3765 must

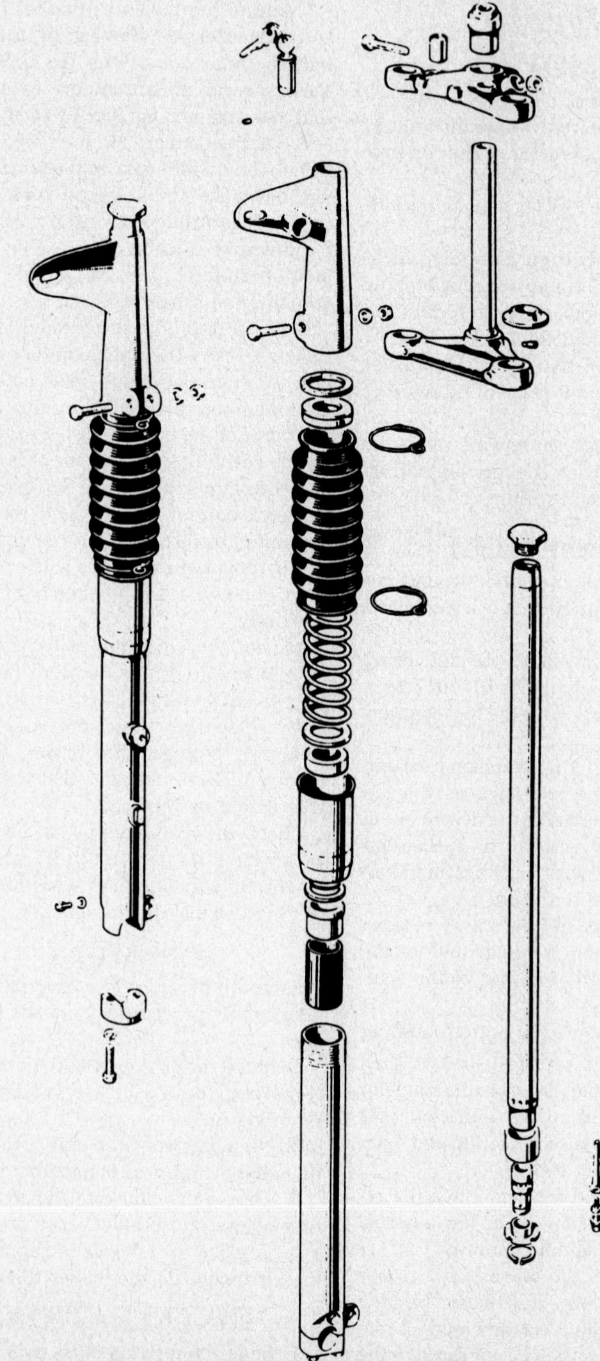

Front fork assembly (500 and 650 models)

be used to raise the damper high enough in the tube to screw on the fork leg cap.

T100C, T100R, TR6R, T120R, and T150

These machines are equipped with fork assemblies nearly, if not exactly, identical to those used on the TR25W. Disassembly, inspection, and assembly procedures remain the same, but the removal and installation instructions vary slightly to suit various instrument arrangements and the use of a steering damper.

NOTE: *Some late models 650 Twins and Tridents may use the "Ceriani-type" forks. See below.*

REMOVAL AND INSTALLATION

1. Drain the fork oil.
2. Remove the front wheel and fender.
3. Remove the headlight assembly.
4. Disconnect throttle, choke, and front brake cables.
5. Disconnect any instrument and/or diode wiring.
6. Remove the steering damper knob and loosen the top yoke pinch bolt. Unscrew the sleeve nuts.
7. On 500 models, also remove the steering damper anchor plate at the bottom of the frame head.
8. Remove the handlebar mounting bolts and swing the handlebar out of the way. It may or may not be necessary to disconnect all controls.
9. Hold on to the fork and then give the underside of the top yoke a good swat with a mallet. This should free the fork legs for further disassembly.
10. Installation is a reversal of the removal procedure. Special tool no Z161 must be used to seat the fork leg in its top yoke taper on 500 cc models; tool no. 61–3824 on 650 and 750 cc models.

TR7V, T140V, T150V

This type of fork may also be found on some 4-speed Tridents and 650 Twins.

REMOVAL AND DISASSEMBLY

1. Before beginning work on the forks, it is advisable to have two fork slider oil seals, two damper valve oil seals as well as Triumph tool 61–6113. This tool is quite necessary to the disassembly procedure.
2. Drain the forks, remove the front wheel as previously described, remove the front fender.
3. Remove the handlebars by unscrewing the two self-locking nuts which secure the handlebar clamps to the fork crown.
4. Remove the fork tube cap nuts. Disconnect the instrument cables and lights, and put them in a safe place.
5. Disconnect the hydraulic brake line at the lower triple clamp and at the fork slider.
6. Remove the caliper and put it in a safe place.
7. Loosen the pinch bolts (allen head) at the back of each fork tube fitting in the fork crown.
8. With an allen wrench, remove the cap screws from each fork tube, and lift out the fork springs.
9. Use special tool No. 61–6113 inserted down into the fork tube to hold the damper valve assembly in place while the allen bolt is removed from the bottom of the slider.
10. Remove the slider from the fork tube. Remove the fork tubes from the triple clamps by first loosening the pinch bolts on the lower triple clamp and yanking down on the tubes until free.
11. Lift the rubber dust cover off of the top of the slider. Remove the nut at the bottom of the damper assembly.
12. Take out the damper assembly. The damper assembly should not be

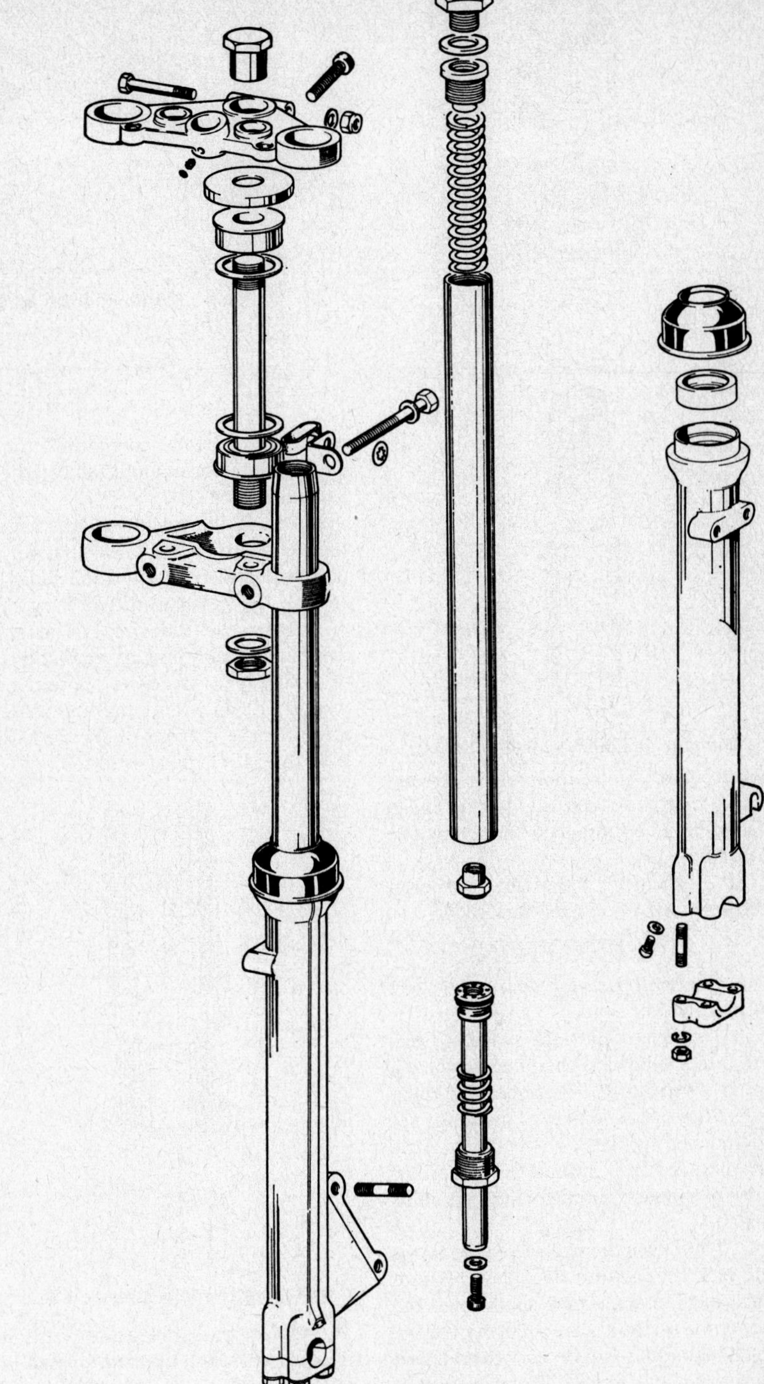

"Ceriani-type" front fork.

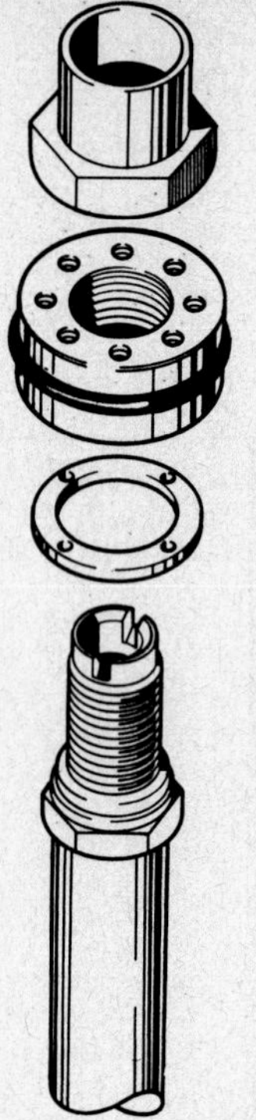
Damper assembly (1973 models).

taken apart unless absolutely necessary. The o-ring oil seal on the damper bleed valve should be removed and a new one fitted by hand.

13. Account for the sealing washer at the very bottom of each fork slider.

INSPECTION

1. Check all parts for wear or damage. Replace as necessary.

2. To replace the fork slider oil seal, use a tool similar to the one shown or a suitable substitute. The important thing is that the soft aluminum of the slider not be touched by the tool when removing the oil seal. Pry all around the circumference of the seal, gradually lifting it off its seat.

3. To replace the seal, cover the top of the fork tube with a thin plastic "sandwich bag" or something similar. Oil the lips of the seal, and slide it down over the top of the fork tube. Be very careful that the seal is not forced in any way. It is extremely easy to damage the seal.

Place the fork slider in position at the bottom of the fork tube, and bring the seal down to meet it.

A drift is needed to properly seat the oil seal in the slider. It is important that the seal fit perfectly in the slider or it will leak. After installation, remove the slider from the fork tube.

4. Clean all components thoroughly before reassembly.

ASSEMBLY AND INSTALLATION

1. Refit the damper valve assembly into the bottom of the fork leg. Use a bit

Removing the oil seal.

of thread locking compound on the damper retainer nut and tighten the nut to 25 ft lbs.

2. Locate the small sealing washer in the very bottom of the fork slider. Replace the dust cover atop the slider, and replace the slider on the fork leg.

3. Bring the slider up to meet the damper assembly and insure that the end of the damper rests on top of the sealing washer. Replace and tighten the allen screw in the bottom of the fork slider with the aid of the special tool.

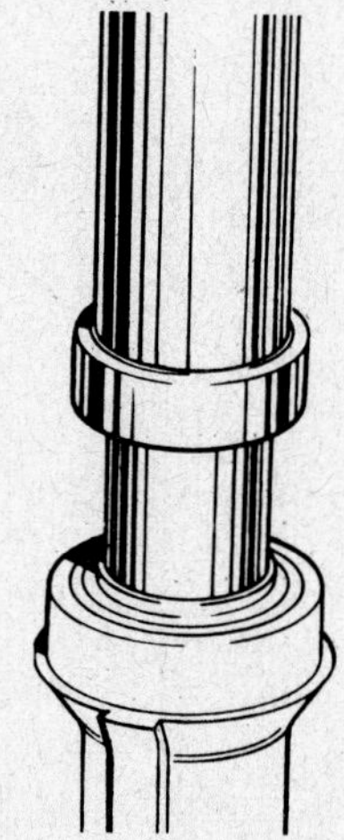
Installing the fork slider oil seal.

4. Replace the fork leg assembly in the triple clamps. Push upward until the top of the fork tube is exactly flush with the top of the fork crown. Tighten the pinch bolts on the lower triple clamp and the fork crown to 20 ft lbs.

5. Replace the fork springs. Refill each leg with the correct grade and quantity of oil (see "Maintenance Items").

6. Smear the threads of the cap screws with a gasket compound, and tighten the screws to 40 ft lbs. Replace the instruments and the fork cap nuts. Tighten them to 40 ft lbs as well.

7. The remainder of the assembly procedure is the reverse of disassembly. Refer to "Front Wheel Installation" if necessary. Remember that the axle cap nuts on the left slider are tightened first.

ALIGNMENT

In the event that the fork alignment is not correct, loosen the axle cap nuts on the left slider, and tighten those on the right. Loosen the pinch bolts on the lower triple and the fork crown, including the pinch bolt just behind the fork crown center nut.

Pump the forks up and down several times and then retighten the axle cap nuts, the lower triple clamp pinch bolts, the fork crown pinch bolts at the fork tubes, and finally the fork crown pinch bolt behind the center nut. The nuts and bolts must be tightened in that order.

STEERING HEAD

TR25W

DISASSEMBLY

1. Remove the headlight assembly and speedometer head.

2. Disconnect the front brake cable and remove the zener diode and heat sink.

3. Protect the gas tank with a piece of cloth, then remove the handlebar mounting bolts and lay the handlebar on the tank.

4. Loosen the steering head clamp bolt and top yoke pinch bolt.

5. Remove the steering head adjusting nut.

6. Unscrew the fork leg caps and disconnect them from the damper rod (if so equipped).

7. Strike the underside of the top yoke smartly with a mallet. This should free the fork legs from their tapers in the top yoke.

8. Locate the top yoke somewhere out of the way, then pull steering stem down and out of the head. Take care not to lose the bottom ball bearings as the stem is withdrawn.

9. Drive out the top cone with a long narrow drift and mallet.

10. Pry out the bottom cone by forcing it up with two levers.

11. Remove the cups by installing special tool no. 61–306, and driving them out as shown in the accompanying illustration.

INSPECTION

Examine the bearing balls for pitting, scoring, or flat spots and, if necessary, replace the bearings, cups, and cones.

Clean out the steering head bore and remove any burrs, etc., with a fine file or emery cloth. Also clean up and inspect the stem itself.

ASSEMBLY

1. Install the bearing cups by driving them into position with a homemade drift. The dimensions for this tool are given in the accompanying illustration.

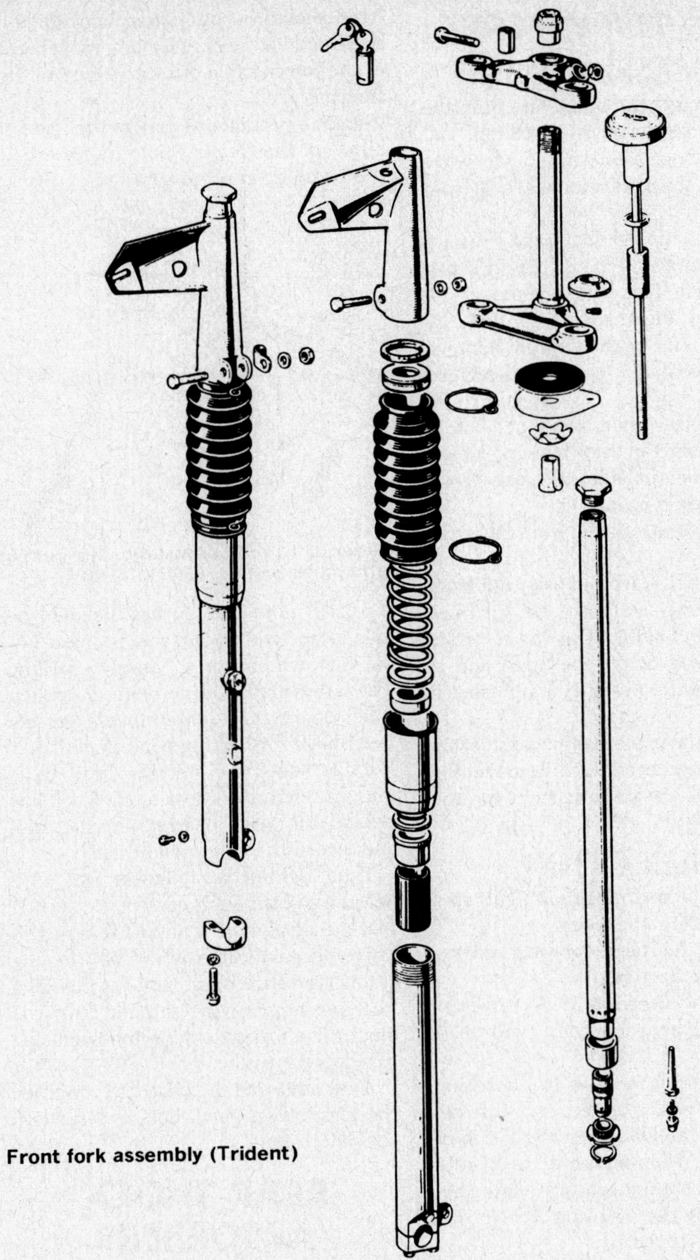

Front fork assembly (Trident)

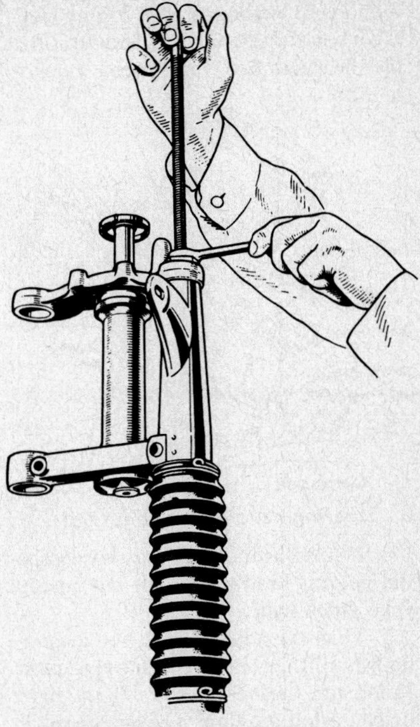

Installing the fork leg with tool no. Z161 (500 models)

Driving out the top bearing cone (250)

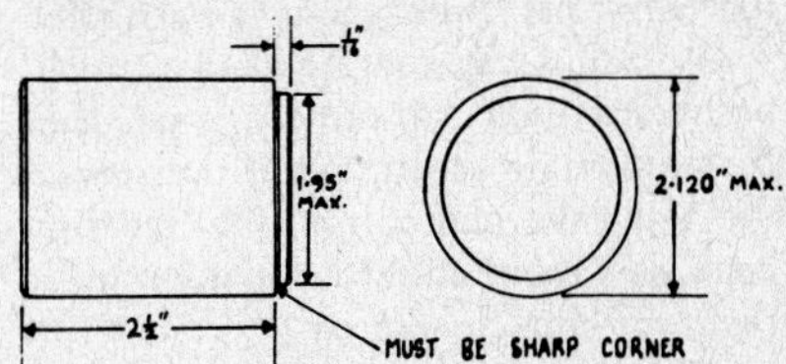

Suitable drift for cup removal (250)

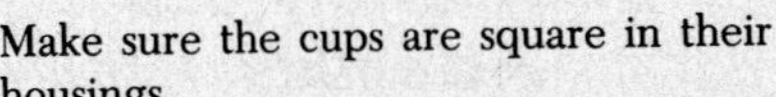

Make sure the cups are square in their housings.

2. Drive the bottom cone into position with a piece of pipe 1 ¼ in. in diameter and long enough to clear the column. Make sure it is squarely seated.

3. Liberally grease the bearing cups with the recommended lubricant and install the bearing balls.

NOTE: *There should be forty bearing balls all together; twenty for each race.*

4. Slide the stem back into the head and assemble the top cone and dust cover.

5. Install the top yoke and screw on the adjuster cap.

6. The remainder of assembly is a reversal of the removal procedure.

7. Adjust the steering head as described below.

Removing the fork leg stanchion (Trident)

ADJUSTMENT

1. Place a strong support under the engine so that the front wheel is about 6 in. off the ground.

2. Standing in front of the bike, attempt to rock the front fork back and forth. If there is any play, an adjustment will be necessary.

NOTE: *It is very difficult to distinguish between steering head play and front fork bushing wear, so a more accurate method of determining whether an adjustment is necessary is by having a helper hold the fingers of one hand on the top head bearing race while the fork is being rocked. Any play will be easily detected by the helper.*

3. Turn the fork from steering lock to steering lock. The movement should be

free of any binding, etc. A "lumpy" feeling when turning the fork indicates that the bearings and races need replacement.

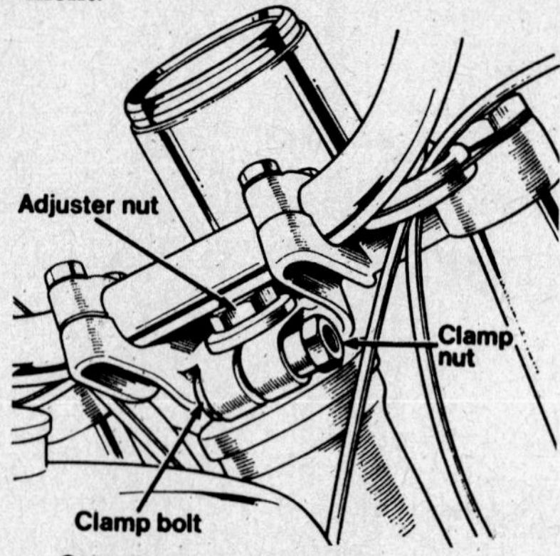

Steering head adjustment (250)

4. If an adjustment is necessary, loosen the steering head clamp bolt and the top yoke pinch bolt.

5. Turn the adjuster bolt (see illustration) until there is no rocking free-play. Make sure the bearings aren't *too* tight by centering the front fork and giving it a slight push to one side. The fork should fall freely until it reaches the steering lock.

T100C and T100R

Follow the disassembly and assembly instructions given for the TR25W, with the following exceptions:

1. When driving the bearing cones into position, use Triumph special tool no Z24 or a piece of tubing 9 in. long with a diameter of 1 1/16 in.

2. Note that there are forty-eight bearing balls total; twenty-four in each race.

Also adjust the steering head as previously described. Adjustment is achieved by loosening a pinch bolt at the rear of the top yoke and turning the steering head sleeve nut until the bearings are at their working clearances

TR6R, TR6C, and T120R

Follow the disassembly and assembly instructions given for the TR25W, with the following exception:

1. When installing the bearing cones, use Triumph special tool no. 61–6009 or a piece of tubing 9 in. long with a diameter of 1 1/16 in.

Adjust the steering head as described above for the T100C and T100R

T150

Follow the disassembly and assembly instructions given for the TR25W, with the following exception:

1. When driving the bearing cones into position use Triumph special tool no. D2218 or a piece of tubing 9 in. long with a diameter of 1 1/16 in.

Adjust the steering head as described above for the T100C and T100R

TR7V, T140V, T150V

DISASSEMBLY

1. Disconnect the brake line from the fork crown and lower triple clamp.

2. Disconnect the zener diode wires and remove the diode and heat sink from the machine.

3. Remove the headlight and the handlebar assembly. Remove the fork cap nuts. Place the instruments aside.

4. Support the machine so that the front wheel is far off the ground. Remove the front wheel and fender as described above.

5. Loosen the fork crown pinch bolt in back of the large adjuster nut, and loosen all of the pinch bolts on the fork crown and lower triple clamp.

6. Remove the fork legs from the triple clamps.

7. Remove the large adjuster nut from the fork crown and take off the fork crown while holding the lower triple clamp in place. Strike the underside of the crown with a soft-faced mallet if necessary.

8. Lower the triple clamp and steering stem from the head lug. Remove the bearings from the steering stem and the head lug.

INSPECTION

1. Clean the bearings thoroughly in a solvent and blow them dry.

2. Inspect the rollers for wear, pitting or scoring, or fractures.

3. After the bearings are completely dry, lubricate them generously with chassis grease.

4. The bearing races in the head lug can be removed, if necessary, with the aid of a drift wielded from the inside of the head lug. When replacing them, note that bearing abutment rings are fitted behind the races. Use Triumph tool No. 61–6121 to refit the races.

ASSEMBLY

Assembly is the reverse of the disassembly procedure. Note that the fork tubes must be installed flush with the surface of the fork crown. The fork spring retainer nuts will stand above the fork crown.

ADJUSTMENT

Adjustment of the steering head bearings does not necessitate the removal of any components.

1. Support the front wheel off of the ground.

2. Grasp the fork sliders, and attempt to move them forward and back, noting any movement as you do so.

3. Another method, which is also recommended, is to grasp the tip of the front fender and attempt to move the fork assembly up and down. Your other hand should be positioned beneath the steering head feeling for any movement of the lower triple clamp relative to the steering head.

4. The presence of play in the forks in either of these tests would indicate that the bearings must be adjusted.

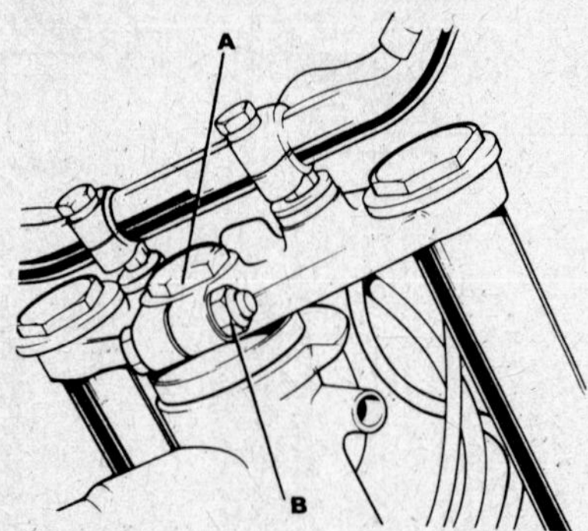

Steering head bearing adjusting nut (A) and pinch bolt (B) (TR7V, T140V).

5. Also note that the forks should be able to be turned from side to side without any binding or a "lumpy" feeling. The latter may indicate worn or broken roller bearings or dented races. See section above for bearing replacement.

6. To adjust the steering head bearings, loosen the fork crown pinch bolt just behind the large bearing adjuster nut, and loosen the adjuster nut itself.

Then tighten the adjuster nut until bearing adjustment is correct. Be certain that the adjustment is not made too tight. This will be noticable by a wobbly feeling at low road speeds, the same as though a steering damper was tightened down too much. The forks should swing from side to side very easily.

After adjusting the bearings, retighten the fork crown pinch bolt, and recheck the adjustment.

REAR SHOCK ABSORBERS

Disassembly and Assembly

The shock absorber consists of a sealed hydraulic damper unit, coil spring, dust covers, and rubber end bushings.

1. Position the cam ring or adjusting ring in its lowest (light load) setting.

2. Clamp the bottom lug of the shock in a soft-jawed vise, then compress the spring by hand and have a helper remove the spring retaining collars.

3. If the rubber end bushings require replacement, drive them out with a suitable drift.

4. Inspect the damper unit for any signs of oil leakage, bending of the plunger rod, etc. Replace it if necessary. Examine the coil spring for any stress cracks, then measure its freestanding height and compare with specifications.

5. Assembly is a reversal of the disassembly procedure. If installing new end bushings, smear them with soapy water to aid assembly.

SWING ARM

The swing arm is mounted to the rear of the frame by a spindle supported in plain bushings. In conjunction with the rear shock absorbers, it serves as the rear wheel suspension system.

TR25W

REMOVAL AND DISASSEMBLY

1. Remove the rear wheel, chainguard, shock absorbers, and rear brake pedal.
2. Disconnect the brake light switch connectors and remove the switch with its bracket.
3. Remove the large spindle nut and washer on the right side of the machine.
4. Drive the spindle out of the swing arm bore with a suitable drift and mallet.
5. Tap the left side of the swing arm down and the right side up, using a mallet. This will free the swing arm from the frame plates.
6. Each swing arm bushing consists of two steel sleeves bonded together with rubber. The inner sleeves are slightly longer than half the width of the swing arm and are locked together, thereby putting the rubber under tension when the arm swings through its arc.

If it is necessary to replace the bushings, the rubber must first be burned out to facilitate removal. This can be done with a thin rod or strip of metal heated until cherry red.

7. When enough rubber has been removed, drive out the inner sleeves and then the outer sleeves.

ASSEMBLY AND INSTALLATION

Assembly and installation is a reversal of the removal and disassembly procedure. Do not tighten the swing arm spindle nut until after the shock absorbers have been installed.

T100C and T100R (Before Serial No. H49832)

REMOVAL AND DISASSEMBLY

1. Remove the front chainguard bolt, disconnect the stoplight switch wiring and remove the switch operating clip from the brake rod.
2. Disconnect the shock absorbers from the swing arm.

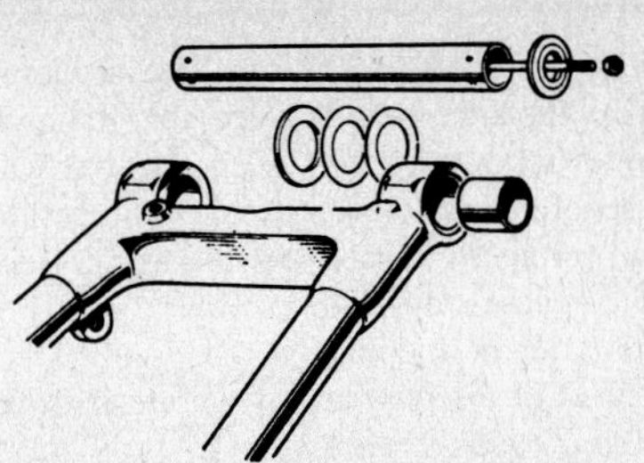

Rear swing arm construction (500 models before serial no. H49832)

3. Remove the swing arm spindle retaining rod and caps.
4. Using a threaded extractor (see illustration), draw the spindle out the right side of the machine.
5. Disconnect the chain and rear brake torque arm.
6. Disconnect the brake operating rod.
7. Remove the rear chainguard bolt and swing the chainguard out of the way.

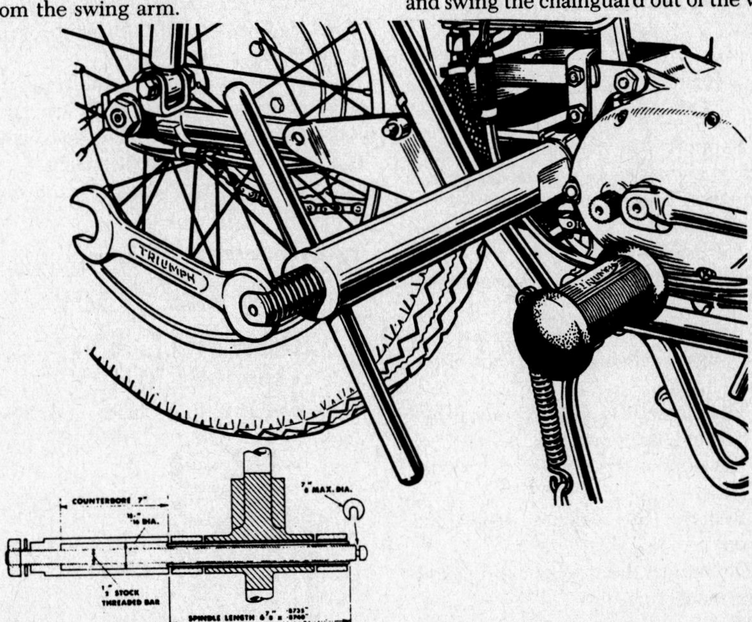

Removing the swing arm spring with extractor tool (500 models before serial no. H49832)

Disconnect the speedometer cable, loosen the rear axle nuts and remove the rear wheel.

8. Remove the swing arm from the frame lugs. Take care to mark and separate the spacers.
9. Remove the swing arm bushings by driving them out with a suitable drift and mallet.

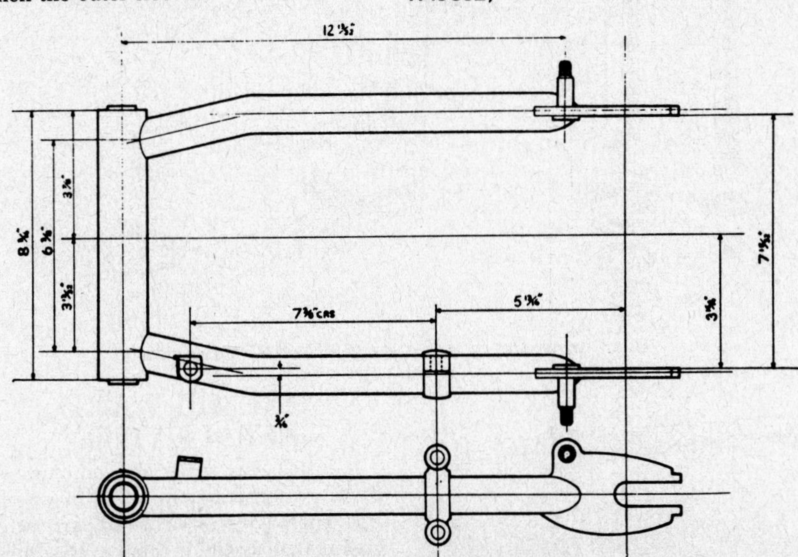

Rear swing arm construction (250)

ASSEMBLY AND INSTALLATION

1. Press or dirve in the new swing arm bushings. A drift can be fabricated out of 31/32 in. bar stock by machining 1 in. of one end to ⅞ in. diameter.
2. Line-ream the busings to the bore size given in specifications, using Triumph special tool no. Z126 or a suitable substitute.
3. Assemble the swing arm to the frame lugs, using the same spacers that

were removed. Lift the arm up and let it drop: the arm should just be able to move under its own weight. If movement was restricted, remove a spacer on each side and try again; if movement was too free, add spacers until the correct working clearance is obtained.

NOTE: *Spacers are available in 0.003 and 0.005 in. sizes.*

4. When the correct clearance has been obtained, grease the bushings and spindle, then press the spindle into position with the extractor tool used for removal.

5. Lubricate the swing arm grease nipple with the recommended lubricant, then assemble the remaining parts in reverse order of disassembly.

T100C And T100R (After Serial No. H49832)

REMOVAL AND DISASSEMBLY

1. Support the machine on its side stand or a wooden box, then disconnect the center stand spring.

2. Disconnect the chain and remove the rear brake adjuster.

3. Disconnect the brake torque arm from the hub.

4. Remove the rear chainguard bolt and swing the chainguard up out of the way.

5. Disconnect the speedometer cable, then remove the rear wheel.

6. Disconnect the rubber chain oiler tube.

7. Remove the exhaust pipes and mufflers.

8. Disconnect the stoplight spring and wiring connectors.

9. Remove the shock absorbers and rear brake pedal, complete with operating rod.

10. Remove both rider's footpegs.

11. Remove the small, front chainguard and front, lower switch panel.

12. Remove the oil tank lower mounting nuts and tap the studs back through the mounting lug. Note the position of the distance washer that fits between the oil tank bottom bracket and frame mounting lug.

13. Remove the rear fender, front, bottom mounting bolt. Loosen the top and remove the bottom nuts and bolts that secure the front and rear part of the frame.

14. Straighten the tab lockwashers and remove both swing arm spindle end bolts.

15. Pivot the rear frame upward and support it in this position.

16. Remove both swing arm spindle distance pieces noting that the thicker one fits on the chain side.

17. Remove the swing arm spindle by tapping it out with a suitable, shouldered drift. The chain side of the spindle has an extra hole that will accept a C-wrench, should it become needed on reassembly.

18. Drive out the swing arm bushings with a suitable drift.

ASSEMBLY AND INSTALLATION

1. Install new bushings as described for the "T100C and T100R before serial no. H49832."

2. The remainder of assembly and installation is a reversal of the removal and disassembly procedure. Note that when installing the swing arm distance pieces, the ribbed sides must face the rear frame side plates.

TR6C, TR6R, T120R and T150 and T150V

REMOVAL AND DISASSEMBLY

1. Disconnect the chain and rear brake torque arm, then remove the brake rod adjuster.

2. Loosen the rear axle nuts and remove the rear wheel.

3. Remove the two long and two short bolts that secure each of the rear engine mounting plates.

4. Loosen the rear chainguard bolt and remove the front chainguard bolt.

5. Disconnect the stoplight wiring connectors and remove the chainguard.

6. Remove the bottom shock absorber mounting bolts.

7. Disconnect the oil scavenge line from the oil tank for clearance, then remove the swing arm spindle locknut.

8. Unscrew the spindle until it is free to be withdrawn.

9. Remove the swing arm assembly and separate it from the end plates, outer sleeves and distance pieces.

10. Drive out the swing arm bushings with a suitable, shouldered drift.

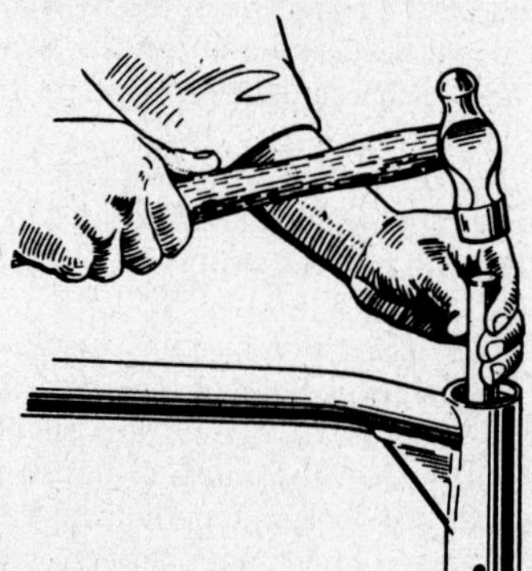

Removing a swing arm bushing (650 and 750 models)

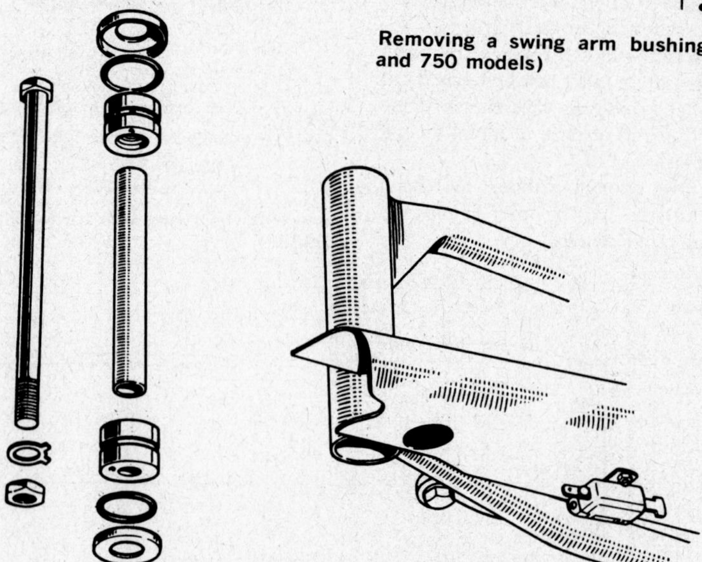

Rear swing arm construction (650 and 750 models)

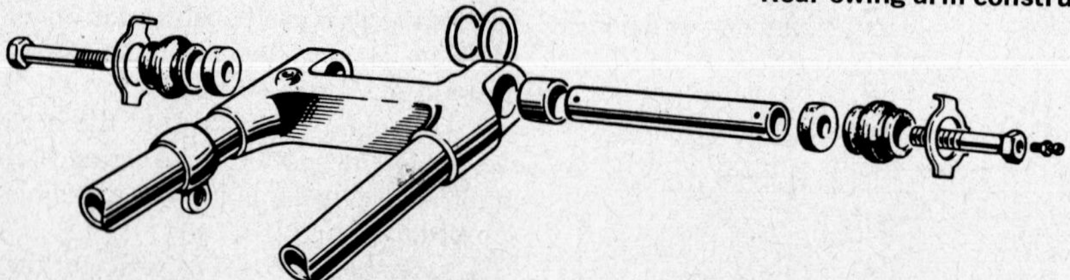

Rear swing arm construction (500 models after serial no. H49832)

ASSEMBLY AND INSTALLATION

1. Install new swing arm bushings as previously described for other models.

2. Thoroughly lubricate all parts with grease, then assemble them in the order shown in the accompanying illustration. Tighten the spindle bolt until the swing

arm will just move under its own weight.

NOTE: *If the swing arm spindle is replaced, make sure the new one has the same thread pitch as the original.*

3. To remove any spindle side-play, it is necessary only to remove the distance sleeve and file one end to shorten the length.

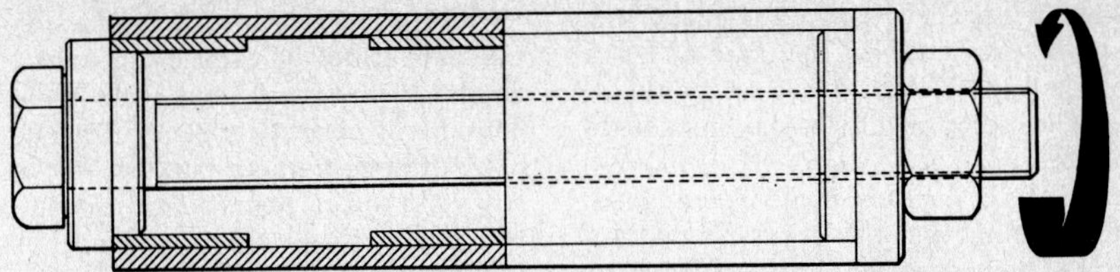

Removing the swing arm bushes with the special tool (TR7V, T140V)

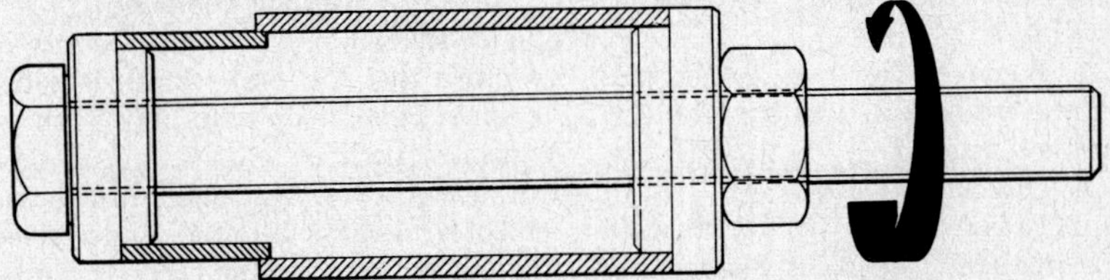

Installing the swing arm bushes (TR7V, T140V)

TR7V, T140V

REMOVAL AND DISASSEMBLY

1. Remove the rear wheel and the chainguard. Remove the shock absorbers.
2. Remove the swing arm spindle nut on the right side and pull out the spindle.
3. Take the swing arm out of the frame.
4. Remove the four dust covers (one on each side of the swing arm bush housings).
5. Note the location of the thrust washers (the thicker of the two is fitted to the right side of the swing arm); remove the spacers.

INSPECTION

1. Clean all parts thoroughly.
2. Check the bushes for wear or damage.
3. Check the dimensions of the bushes and spacer tubes against the standard values given at the end of this section. Replace any worn parts as is necessary.
4. A special tool (No. 61–6117) is used to remove and install the bushes in their housings. Note its operation in the accompanying illustrations. A drift can also be used, provided that it has a narrow section 1 in. in diameter and a 1⅛ in. shoulder.

Use some grease on the bushings to facilitate reassembly. Note that new bushes are pre-sized and need not be reamed to fit correctly.

ASSEMBLY

Assembly is the reverse of the disassembly procedure. Refer to the exploded diagram for the correct placement of the parts. Replace the dust covers in their proper positions, then place the swing arm in the frame. Fit the thrust washers (they are of different thickness: the thicker is fitted to the right side of the swing arm). Replace the spindle and the spindle nut.

Replace the chainguard and rear wheel.

DISC BRAKE SERVICE

Maintenance

1. The hydraulic brake fluid level should be set at about ¼ in. from the top of the reservoir after the system has been

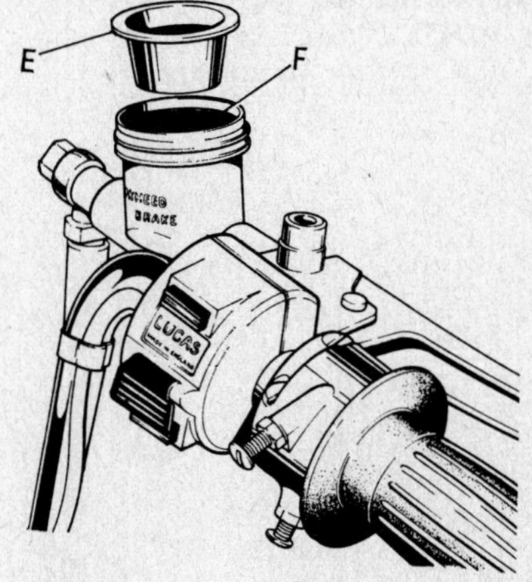

Oil reservoir diaphragm (E) and fluid level (F)

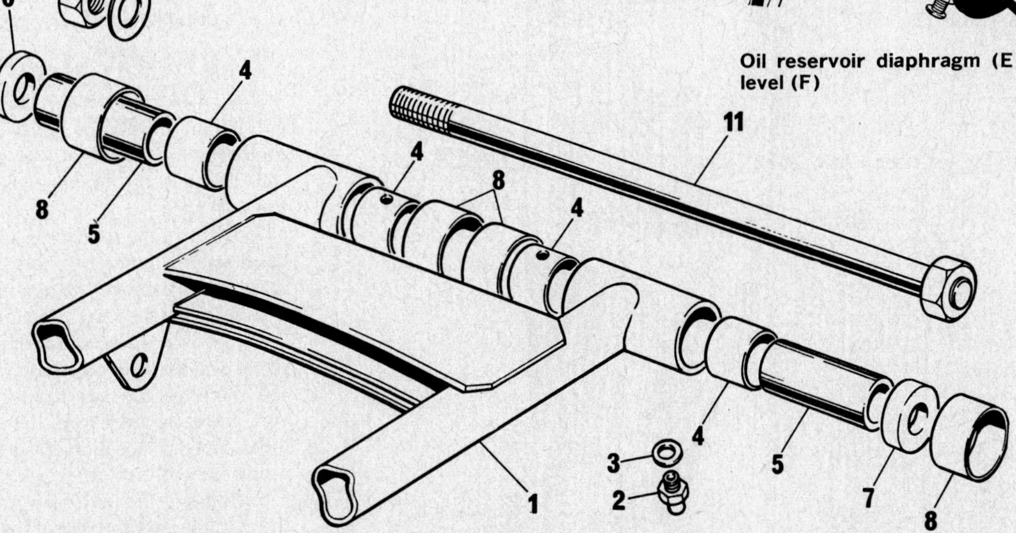

Swing arm bushing assembly (TR7V, T140V).

1. Swinging arm
2. Grease nipple
3. Sealing washer
4. Bush
5. Spacer tube
6. Thrust washer (Thin)
7. Thrust washer (Thick)
8. Dust cover
9. Nut
10. Washer
11. Spindle

bled. It is not necessary to add fluid to the system provided that there are no leaks in the lines. The fluid level in the reservoir will drop slightly as the brake pads wear.

2. The brake pads should be examined for wear at regular intervals. To do this, it will be necessary to remove the pads.

a. Remove the caliper's aluminum cover by removing the two phillips head screws.

b. Remove the two cotter pins. (These are indicated by the letter "B" in the illustration).

c. Pull out both pads.

d. Pads are bonded to the brake lining material. They must be replaced when the lining thickness is 1/16 in. (1.6mm) or less.

e. It is recommended that new cotter pins be used upon reassembly.

Bleeding

Any time any part of the brake system has been removed or the line is disconnected, it will be necessary to "bleed" the system, that is, to remove air pockets and bubbles from the system.

NOTE: *Before beginning the operation, read the following points:*

a. Brake fluid drained from the system should not be used again unless absolutely necessary, and even then only if it is perfectly clean, relatively new, and free from air bubbles. Allow it to sit for several hours before use. But new fluid is always recommended.

b. Insure that the master cylinder reservoir is kept at least half full during the entire bleeding operation.

c. Take all precautions necessary to insure that the brake fluid does not come in contact with any type of painted surface.

1. Refer to the illustration. Attach one end of a rubber hose to the caliper bleed nipple and immerse the other end in at least ½ in. of brake fluid contained in a jar. Note that the hose swings upward after leaving the bleed nipple. This is important.

2. Remove the fluid reservoir cap and take out the rubber diaphragm.

3. Loosen the bleed nipple from ½ to ¾ of a turn.

4. Insuring that the master cylinder reservoir is full of fluid, pull the brake lever all the way to the twist grip, holding it there for several seconds.

Note that the action of pulling the lever will force fluid and air bubbles through the hose and into the jar.

5. Release the brake lever and repeat the operation, always maintaining sufficient amount of fluid in the master cylinder, until air bubbles no longer issue from the end of the hose.

6. At this point, hold the brake lever *on,* and retighten the bleed nipple. Refill the reservoir to the proper level.

NOTE: *The correct fluid level, given as ¼ in. from the top of the master cylinder reservoir, should be maintained. It is important to remember, however, that if the brake pads in the caliper are not new when the system is bled, the fluid level will rise in the reservoir when new pads are installed. Therefore, it may be necessary to remove some fluid from the reservoir when this is done.*

7. Refer to the illustrations, and fold the diaphragm, as shown, before replacing it in the master cylinder reservoir. Install the paper washer in the cap, and screw on and tighten the cap securely.

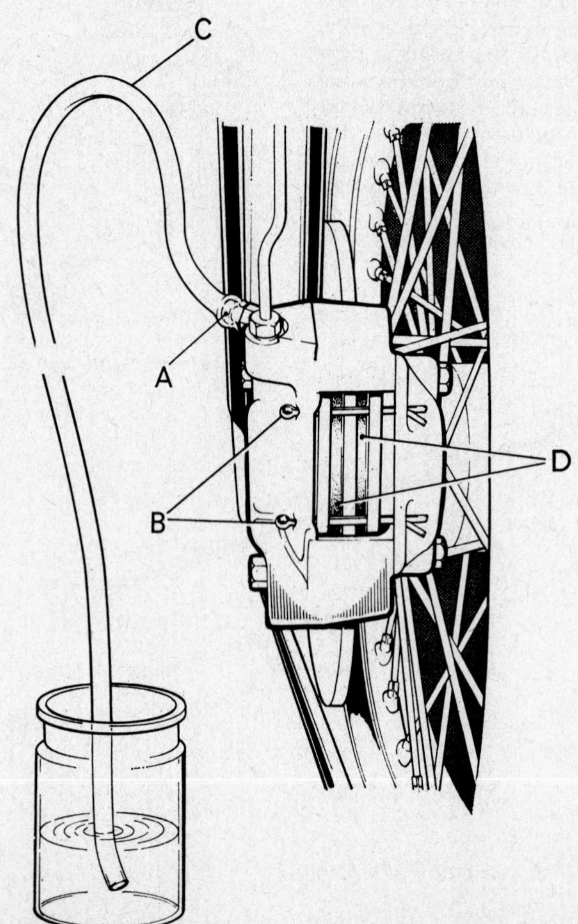

Bleeding the brake system. Note bleed nipple (A), brake pad cotter pins (B), bleed hose (C), and brake pads (D).

Flushing

Every three years, or if the system has accumulated any foreign matter, it should be flushed out as directed below:

1. Connect a hose to the bleed nipple, running the other end into a container, and squeeze the brake lever until all of the fluid in the system has been pumped out.

2. Fill the master cylinder reservoir with denatured alcohol and pump it out through the system in the same manner.

3. After all of the alcohol has been removed, fill the master cylinder with brake fluid, and bleed the system as described above.

Master Cylinder

REMOVAL AND DISASSEMBLY

1. Drain the brake fluid. Disconnect the brake line at the master cylinder.

2. Remove the brake lever and then the pushrod.

3. Remove the four screws which hold the master cylinder assembly on the handlebar, and remove the assembly.

4. Remove the reservoir cap, if this has not already been accomplished, and the paper washer and diaphragm.

5. Remove the nut inside the reservoir, and separate it from the master cylinder. Note the location of the spacer and o-ring beneath the reservoir.

6. Remove the set screw which locks the cylinder into the rest of the assembly, and unscrew the cylinder.

7. Remove the dust cover from the end of the cylinder. Use the pushrod, inserting it into the master cylinder, to push down the piston and remove the circlip.

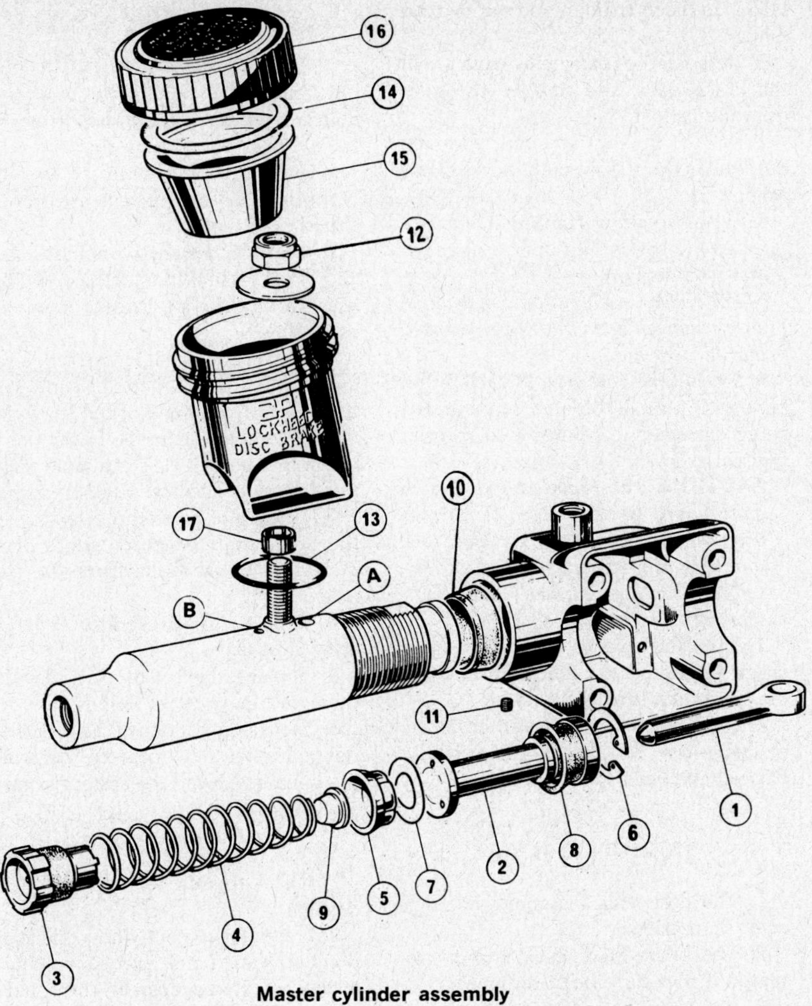

Master cylinder assembly

1. Pushrod
2. Piston
3. Check valve
4. Return spring
5. Primary seal
6. Circlip
7. Piston washer
8. Secondary seal
9. Spring retainer
10. Dust cover
11. Set screw
12. Reservoir securing nut
13. O-ring
14. Paper washer
15. Diaphragm
16. Cap
17. Spacer

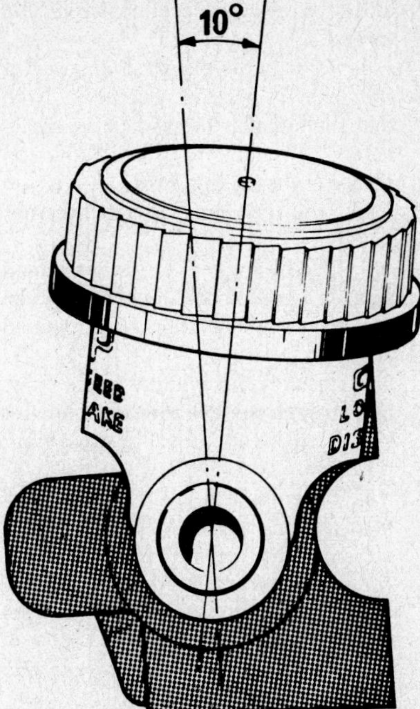

Brake fluid reservoir installation angle.

assembly into the cylinder, check valve first.

3. Fit the primary seal into the cylinder, inserting the lip end of the seal first. Do not force the seal, and make sure that the lip is not folded back upon installation.

4. Install the piston washer, convex side *outward* (towards the piston), and then the piston (drilled end first). Depress the piston with the pushrod as on removal, and replace the circlip. Be sure the circlip is properly seated.

5. Fit the dust cover boot over the end of the cylinder.

6. Install the reservoir o-ring, spacer, and the reservoir.

7. Fill the reservoir with brake fluid, insert the pushrod into its place, and push

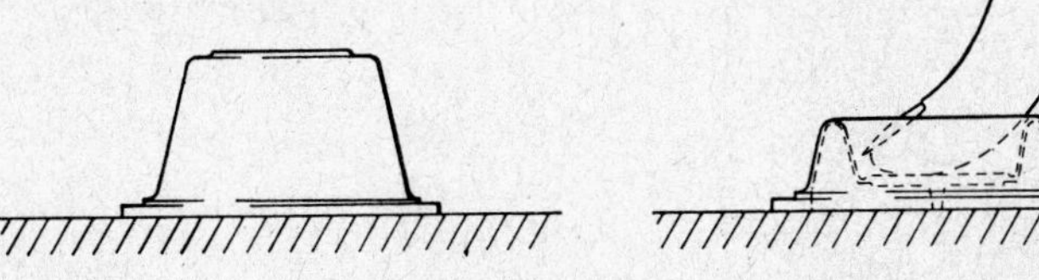

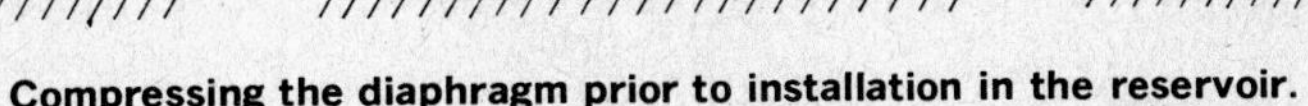

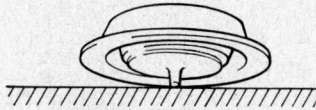

Compressing the diaphragm prior to installation in the reservoir.

8. Remove the secondary seal and piston, the piston washer, primary seal, return spring retainer, spring, and check valve. If the primary seal will not come out of the piston, try blowing into the brake line end of the piston.

9. Remove the secondary seal from the piston by stretching it over the piston flange.

INSPECTION

1. All seals and o-rings must be replaced.

2. Check the inside of the cylinder for scoring. Replace if necessary.

3. Clean all parts thoroughly in *brake fluid only.*

CAUTION: *Do not clean the parts in any sort of solvent such as gasoline.*

ASSEMBLY AND INSTALLATION

1. Fit the new secondary seal onto the piston noting that the seal lip faces the drilled end of the piston. Work the seal around the groove in the piston until it is properly seated.

2. Fit the check valve onto the large end of the return spring, and the spring retainer onto the other end. Insert the inwards on the piston. The pushrod should be pushed in several times and then brake fluid should begin to flow out of the brake line connection at the end of the cylinder.

8. Drain the fluid.

9. The master cylinder must be properly located in the housing. Proceed as follows:

a. Remove the reservoir from the cylinder.

b. Insert the pushrod in place and install the brake lever and bolt.

c. Screw the cylinder into the housing while holding the brake lever *on* until the cylinder can no longer be turned.

d. Refer to the exploded diagram of the master cylinder assembly. Note that the cylinder has two ports, designated "A" and "B" which flank the reservoir mounting stud. "A" is the main feed port, and "B" the breather port.

e. Place a finger over the main feed port "A" and blow through the brake line end of the cylinder. No air should escape.

f. Unscrew the cylinder while blowing through the cylinder until air just begins to excape from the breather port "B."

g. Unscrew the cylinder one full turn, and set the reservoir stud at about 10° from the vertical. This will allow the flat section on the threaded end of the cylinder to line up with the set screw.

h. Thread in the set screw and tighten it.

i. Refit the reservoir spacer, o-ring, and reservoir.

10. Install the master cylinder assembly on the handlebar and bleed the system as previously described.

Brake Caliper

REMOVAL AND DISASSEMBLY

1. Remove the caliper cover (2 screws), drain the brake fluid; disconnect the brake line from the caliper.

2. Remove the nuts which secure the caliper to the fork slider, and remove the caliper.

3. Remove the cotter pins which hold the brake pads, and remove the pads from the caliper.

4. Pry out the dust seal and the metal dust seal housing from both halves of the caliper.

5. With the aid of compressed air applied to the brake fluid inlet, eject each piston from its bore.

NOTE: *Mark each piston for location after removal. Each must be reinserted into its own bore.*

6. Pry out the fluid seals in each piston bore with a small, blunted screwdriver, being extremely careful not to damage the seal grooves.

CAUTION: *The brake caliper halves must never be separated. If this has been done, the fluid passage seal should be renewed if damaged, and the caliper mating surface and bolts thoroughly cleaned.*

Tighten the bolts to 35–40 ft lbs, and check the caliper for fluid tightness under maximum braking pressure.

The caliper should be returned to the manufacturer for an overhaul if the halves have been split.

INSPECTION

1. The dust seals and metal housings *must* be replaced.

2. The brake fluid seals must be replaced if they have been removed.

3. Inspect the pistons and piston bores for scoring or signs of seizure.

4. Clean all parts thoroughly.

ASSEMBLY AND INSTALLATION

1. Smear the fluid seals with brake fluid and replace them in their grooves in the cylinder bores. Note that the larger side faces outward, toward the open end of the bore. Be sure the seals are properly seated.

2. Coat the pistons with brake fluid, and insert each of them, closed end first, squarely into its bore. Press them in as far as possible.

3. Coat one of the dust seals with brake fluid and fit it into a metal housing. Place this assembly into one of the bores with the dust seal on the inside (facing the piston in that bore). Place a suitable shaped plate over the dust seal assembly, and use a "C" clamp to press the assembly into the bore until the outer edges of the metal housing are flush with the bore surface.

4. Repeat this procedure with the other dust seal.

5. Replace the brake pads, securing them with new cotter pins.

6. Secure the caliper to the fork slider, tightening the nuts securely. Reconnect the lines, and bleed the system as previously described.

Brake Disc

1. Check the disc for scoring or other damage.

2. Check for run-out with a dial gauge. Run-out should not exceed 0.0035 in. (0.089mm). Run-out can be corrected for somewhat by loosening the four disc nuts and repositioning the disc. Retighten the nuts in an "X" pattern to 20 ft lbs.

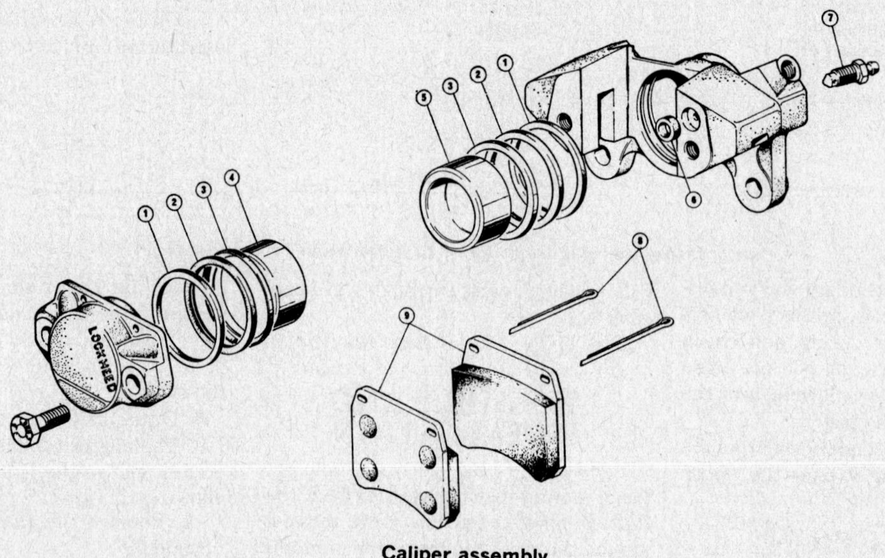

Caliper assembly

CHASSIS SPECIFICATIONS

TR25W

WHEELS	
Rim size and type (front)	WM2-18
Rim size and type (rear)	WM3-18
Spoke sizes	
Front (long) 20	10 s.w.g. x 6 in. (3.251 x 152.4 mm)
Front (medium) 10	10 s.w.g. x $5^7/_{32}$ in. (3.251 x 132.55 mm)
Front (short) 10	10 s.w.g. x $5^3/_{16}$ in. (3.251 x 131.76 mm)
Rear (long) 20	10 s.w.g. x 7.4375 in. (3.251 x 188.9125 mm)
Rear (short) 20	10 s.w.g. x 7.375 in. (3.251 x 187.325 mm)
WHEEL BEARINGS	
Front (left- and right-hand)	20 x 47 x 14 mm Ball Jour.
Rear (left- and right-hand)	20 x 47 x 14 mm Ball Jour.
Rear brake drum	20 x 47 x 14 mm Ball Jour.
Spindle diam. (front)	0.8740-0.8745 in. (22.199-22.212 mm)
Spindle diam. (rear, left-hand)	0.8745-0.8750 in. (22.212-22.225 mm)
Spindle diam. (rear, right-hand)	0.685-0.686 in. (17.399-17.424 mm)
BRAKES	
Front (diam.) twin leading shoe	—
Front (diam.) single leading shoe	7 in. (177.8 mm)
Front (width) twin leading shoe	1.557 in. (39.6875 mm)
Front (width) single leading shoe	1.125 in. (28.575 mm)
Rear (diameter)	7 in. (177.8 mm)
Rear (width)	1.125 in. (28.575 mm)
Lining thickness (front and rear)	0.146-0.166 in. (3.96 mm)
FRONT FORK	
Type	Coil-spring (hydraulically damped)
Springs: free length	10.75-10.875 in. (273.05-276.225 mm)
spring rate	34 in. lbs
number of coils	$22^1/_2$
color identification	Red-green
Bushings—Rod Damper Type	
Outer diameter (top)	1.4750-1.4755 in. (37.465-37.477 mm)
Outer diameter (bottom)	1.473-1.474 in. (37.414-37.439 mm)
Inner diameter (top)	1.250-1.251 in. (31.750-31.755 mm)
Inner diameter (bottom)	1.2485-1.2495 in. (31.711-31.737 mm)
Working clearance (top)	0.0005 in. (0.0127 mm)
Working clearance (bottom)	0.002-0.003 in. (0.0508-0.0762 mm)
Length (top)	2.125 in. (53.975 mm)
Length (bottom)	1.25 in. (31-75 mm)
Shaft diameter	1.248-1.249 in. (31.699-31.7246 mm)
Sliding tube bore diameter	1.475-1.477 in. (31.699-31.7246 mm)
Damper tube bush (outer diam.)	0.6165-0.6185 in. (15.6591-15.7099 mm)
Damper tube bush (inner diam.)	0.399-0.340 in. (8.6106-8.636 mm)
Damper tube bush (length)	0.53125 in. (13.4937 mm)
Shuttle valve outer diam. (large)	—
Shuttle valve outer diam. (small)	—
Bushings—Shuttle Valve Type	
Outer diameter (top)	1.498-1.499 in. (3.805-3.808 mm)
Outer diameter (bottom)	1.4935-1.4945 in. (3.792-3.799 mm)
Inner diameter (top)	1.3065-1.3075 in. (3.318-3.32 mm)
Inner diameter (bottom)	1.2485-1.2495 in. (3.168-3.172 mm)
Working clearance (top)	0.0035-0.0050 in. (0.0889-0.127 mm)
Working clearance (bottom)	1.0035-0.0065 in. (0.0889-0.165 mm)
Length (top)	1 in. (25.4 mm)
Length (bottom)	0.870-0.875 in. (2.221 mm)
Shaft diameter	1.3025-1.3030 in. (3.309-3.312 mm)
Sliding tube bore diameter	1.498-1.500 in. (3.802-3.81 mm)
Damper tube bush (outer diam.)	—
Damper tube bush (inner diam.)	—
Damper tube bush (length)	—
Shuttle valve outer diam. (large)	1.018-1.016 in. (2.583-2.58 mm)
Shuttle valve outer diam. (small)	0.875-0.874 in. (2.221-2.22 mm)

TR25W

REAR SUSPENSION

Type	Coil-spring (hydraulically damped)
Springs: free length	8.40 in. (213.36 mm)
spring rate	100 in. lbs
color identification	Green-pink (applies both to chrome or black springs)

SWING ARM

Bush type	Bonded rubber
Bush diameter	1.250-1.253 in. (31.75-31.8262 mm)
Housing diameter	1.247-1.248 in. (31.673-31.699 mm)
Interference fit	0.002-0.006 in. (0.0508-0.1524 mm)
Spindle diameter	0.810-0.811 in. (20.570-20.595 mm)

T100, T100R

WHEELS

Rim size: Front and rear	WM2-18
Type: Front	Spoke—single cr. lacing
Rear	Spoke—double cr. lacing
Spoke details	
Front	40 off 8-10 SWG butted $5\frac{17}{32}$ in. U.H. straight
Rear: left-side	20 off 8-10 SWG butted $7\frac{9}{16}$ in. U.H. 90°
right-side	20 off 8-10 SWG butted $7\frac{7}{8}$ in. U.H. 90°

WHEEL BEARINGS

Front and rear, dimensions and type	20 x 47-14 mm Ball Jour.
Front spindle diameter (at bearing journals)	0.7868-0.7873 in
Rear spindle diameter (at bearing journals)	0.7862-0.7867 in.

BRAKES

Type	Internal Expanding
Drum diameter: Front	8 in. } ±0.002 in.
Rear	7 in. } ±0.002 in.
Lining thickness: Front & Rear	0.183/0.197 in.
Lining area: Front & rear	23.4/14.6

FRONT FORK

Type	Telescopic with oil damping Shuttle valve after H.57083	
Spring details		
Free length	$9\frac{3}{4}$ in.	
No. of working coils	$12\frac{1}{2}$	
Spring rate	$26\frac{1}{2}$ in. lbs	
Color code	Yellow-blue	
Bushing: Material	Top bush.	Bottom bush.
Length	1 in.	0.870-0.875 in.
Outer diameter	1.498-1.499 in.	1.4935-1.4945 in.
Inner diameter	1.3065-1.3075 in.	1.2485-1.2495 in.
Stanchion diameter	1.3025-1.3030 in.	
Working clear. in top bush	0.0035-0.0050 in.	
Fork leg bore diameter	1.498-1.500 in.	
Working clear. of bot. bush	0.0035-0.0065 in.	
Shuttle valve		
outer diameter (large)	1.018-1.106 in.	
outer diameter (small)	0.875-0.874 in.	

REAR SUSPENSION

Type	Swinging fork controlled by combined spring-hydraulic damper units (Bolted up after H.49833).

SPRING DETAILS

Fitted length	8 in.
Free length	$8\frac{3}{16}$ in.
Mean coil diameter	$1\frac{3}{4}$ dia
Spring rate	145 in. lbs
Color code	Blue-Yellow
Load at fitted length	38 lbs

SWING ARM

Bush type	Phosphor bronze strip
Bush bore diameter	0.8745-0.8750 in.
Spindle diameter	0.8735-0.8740 in.
Distance between fork ends	$7\frac{7}{16}$ in.

TR6R, TR6C, T120R

WHEELS

Rim size: Front and rear	WM12-19 front WM3-18 rear
Type: Front	Spoke-single cross lacing
Rear	Spoke-double cross lacing
Spoke details:	
Front: left-side	20 off 8/10 SWG butted $5\frac{5}{8}$ in. U.H. straight
right-side	10 off 8/10 SWG butted $4\frac{25}{32}$ in. U.H. 78° head
right-side	10 off 8/10 SWG butted $4\frac{7}{8}$ in. U.H. 100° head
Rear: left-side	20 off 8/10 SWG butted $7\frac{9}{16}$ in. U.H. 90° head
right-side	20 off 8/10 SWG butted $7\frac{7}{8}$ in. U.H. 90° head

WHEEL BEARINGS

Front and rear, dimen. & type	20 x 47 x 14 mm.— Ball Jour.
Front and rea, spindle diam. (at bearing journals)	0.7862-0.7867 in.

Q.D. REAR WHEELS

Bearing type	$\frac{3}{4}$ x $1\frac{7}{8}$ x $\frac{9}{16}$ in. Ball Jour.
Bearing sleeve: Journal diam.	0.7500-0.7495 in.
Brake drum bearing	$\frac{7}{8}$ x 2 x $\frac{9}{16}$ in. Ball Jour.
Bearing sleeve: journal diam.	0.8745-0.8740 in.
Bearing housing: inter. diam.	1.9890-1.9980 in.

BRAKES

Type	Internal expanding twin leading shoes
Drum Diameter: Front	8 in ± 0.002 in.
Rear	7 in. ± 0.002 in.
Lining thickness: Front	0.183-0.193 in.
Rear	0.177-0.187 in.
Lining area: Front	24.4 sq in.
Rear	14.6 sq in.
Pre-set length of adjustable cam lever rod	$6\frac{1}{2}$ in. between centers

FRONT FORK

Type	Telescopic-Shuttle valve damping

Spring details:	Solo	Sidecar
Free length	$9\frac{3}{4}$ in.	$9\frac{3}{4}$ in.
No. working coils	$12\frac{1}{2}$	$15\frac{1}{2}$
Spring rate	$26\frac{1}{2}$ lb in.	$32\frac{1}{2}$ lb in.
Gauge	6 SWG	5 SWG
Color code	Yellow/blue	Yellow/green

FRONT FORK

Damper sleeve	
Length	$2\frac{1}{8}$ in.
Internal diameter	1.387-1.393 in.
Material	Black polypropylene

Bush details	Top bush	Bottom bush
Length	1 in.	0.870-0.875 in.
Outer diameter	1.498-1.499 in.	1.4935-1.4945 in.
Inner diameter	1.3065-1.3075 in.	1.2485-1.2495 in.

Stanchion diameter	1.3025-1.3030 in.
Working clear. in top bush	0.0035-0.0050 in.
Bleed holes	8 holes $\frac{3}{16}$ in. diam.
Fork leg bore diameter	1.498-1.500 in.
Working clear. of bot. bush	0.0035-0.0065 in.
Shuttle valve:	
Outer diameter (large)	1.018-1.016 in.
Outer diameter (small)	0.875-0.874 in.

REAR SUSPENSION

Type	Swinging fork controlled by combined coil spring/hydraulic damper units
Spring details	
Fitted length	$8\frac{3}{8}$ in.
Free-length	$8\frac{5}{8}$ in.
Mean coil diameter	$1\frac{3}{4}$ in.
Spring rate	100 lb/in.
Color code	Green/green
Load at fitted length	28 lb

SWING ARM

Bush type	Pre-sized, steel-backed—Phosphor bronze
Bush bore diameter	1.4460-1.4470 in.
Sleeve diameter	1.4445-1.4450 in.
Distance between fork ends	$7\frac{1}{2}$ in.

T150

WHEELS	
Rim size: Front and rear	WM2-19 front WM3-19 rear
Type: Front	Spoke-single cr. lacing
Rear	Spoke-double cr. lacing
Spoke details	
Front: left-side	20 off 8-10 SWG butted 5⅝ in. U.H. straight (219.075 mm)
right-side	10 off 8-10 SWG butted 4$^{11}/_{16}$ in U.H. 95° head (118.0625 mm)
right-side	10 off 8-10 SWG butted 4$^{11}/_{16}$ in. U.H. 80° head (118.0625 mm)
Rear: left-side	20 off 8-10 SWG butted 8 in. U.H. 90° head (203.2 mm)
right-side	20 off 8-10 SWG butted 8⅜ in. U.H. 90° head (212-725 mm)
WHEEL BEARINGS	
Front & rear, dimen. & type	20 x 47 x 14mm— Ball Journal
Front & rear (spindle diam. (at bearing journals)	0.7862-0.7867 in. (19.9695 x 19.9822 mm)
BRAKES	
Type	Internal expanding 2 leading shoe
Drum diameter: Front	8 in. ± 0.002 in. (203.2 mm ± 0.0508 mm)
Rear	7 in. ± 0.002 in. (177.8 mm ± 0.0508 mm)
Lining thickness: Front	0.181-0.188 in.
Rear	0.165-0.175 in.
BRAKES	
Lining area: Front	23.4 sq in. (150.967 sq cm)
Rear	14.6 sq in. (94-193 sq cm)
FRONT FORK	
Type	Telescopic-Oil damping
Spring details: Free-length	9.688-9.812 in. (246.075-249.225 mm)
Number working coils	15½
Spring rate	32½ in. lbs (4.485 kg mm)
Gauge	5 swg
Color code	Yellow-green
Damper sleeve	
Length	2⅓ in. (53.975 mm)
Internal diameter	1.387-1.393 in. (35.2298-35.3822 mm)
Bush details: Material	Sintered bronze

	Top bush	Bottom bush
Length	1 in. (25.4 mm)	0.870-0.875 in. (22.098-22.225 mm)
Out. diam.	1.498-1.499 in. (38.0492-38.0746 mm)	1.4935-1.4945 in. (37.945-37.960 mm)
In. diam.	1.3065-1.3075 in. (33.185-33.2105 mm)	1.2485-1.2495 in. (31.712-31.7373 mm)

STANCHION DIAMETER	1.3025-1.3030 in. (33.0889-0.127 mm)
Working clearance in top bush	0.0035-0.0050 in. (10889-0.127 mm)
FORK LEG BORE DIAMETER	1.498-1.500 in. (38.049-38.1 mm)
Working clear. of bot. bush	0.0035-0.0065 in. (0.0889-0.165 mm)
REAR SUSPENSION	
Type	Swinging fork controlled by combined coil spring-hydraulic damper units
Color code	Black
Extended dist. bet. center	12.875 in. (32.66 mm)
Compressed dist. bet. center	10.375 in. (23.36 mm)
SWING ARM	
Bush type	Pre-sized steel-backed-phosphor bronze
Bush bore diameter	1.4460-1.4470 in. (36.7284-36.7538 mm)
Sleeve diameter	1.445-1.4450 in. (36.6903-36.702 mm)
Distance between fork ends	7½ in. (190.5 mm)

TR7V, T140V

WHEELS	
Rim size: Front	WM2-19
Rear	WM3-18
Spoke details:	
Front	
Spoke (inner) R.H. & L.H.	20 off 10 SWG 7.75 in., 96° head
Spoke (outer) R.H. & L.H.	20 off 10 SWG 7.85 in., 80° head
Rear	
Left side (outer)	10 off 10 SWG 5.8 in., 10° head
Left side (inner)	10 off 10 SWG 5.7 in., 102° head
Right side	20 off 10 SWG 7.2 in., 135° head
WHEEL BEARINGS	
Front and rear, dimen. & type	20 x 47 x 14 mm.—Ball Jour.
Front and rear, spindle diam. (at bearing journals)	0.7862-7.7867 in.
BRAKES	
Front, type	Hydraulic disc
Disc diameter	10 in.
Friction pads, type	Mintex M64
Lining thickness	0.25 in.
Rear, type	Internal expanding, single leading shoe
Lining thickness	0.187-0.197 in.
Drum diameter	7.0 in.

FRONT FORK	
Type	Telescopic, hydraulic damped
Spring:	
Free length	19.1 in.
Compressed length	11.4 in.
Fitted length	18.5 in.
Max. load	194 lbs.
Color code	Orange
Stanchion diameter (top)	1.350-1.355 in.
(bottom)	1.3605-1.3610 in.
Outer member bore diameter	1.363-1.365 in.
REAR SUSPENSION	
Type	Swing arm/hydraulically damped springs
Fitted length	8.0 in. (mid position)
Free length	9.5 in.
Spring rate	88 lbs./in.
Mean coil diameter	1.98 in.
SWING ARM	
Bush type	phosphor bronze
Bush bore diameter	1.0 in.
Sleeve diameter	0.9972-0.9984 in.
Distance between fork ends	8.018 in.

T150V

WHEELS	
Rim size: Front	WM2-19
Rear	WM3-19
Spoke details:	
Front	
Spoke (inner) R.H. & L.H.	20 off 10 SWG 7.75 in., 96° head
Spoke (outer) R.H. & L.H.	20 off 10 SWG 7.85 in., 80° head
Rear	
Left side (outer)	10 off SWG 6.3 in., 90° head
Left side (inner)	10 off 10 SWG 6.1 in., 101° head
Right side	20 off 10 SWG 7.5 in., 134° head

FRONT FORK	
Type	Telescopic, oil damping
Spring:	
Free length	19.50 in.
No. working coils	63
Spring rate	32.5 lbs/in.
Color code	Orange
Fork leg diameter: top	1.350-1.355 in.
bottom	1.3605-1.3610 in.
Outer member bore diameter	1.363-1.365 in.
REAR SUSPENSION	
Type	Swing arm/hydraulically damped springs
Fitted length	8.0 in.
Free length	8.810 in.
Spring rate	110 lbs/in.

WHEEL BEARINGS

Front & rear, dimen. & type	20 x 47 x 14 mm—Ball Journal
Front & rear (spindle diam. at bearing journals)	0.7862-0.7867 in. (19.9695 x 19.9822 mm)

BRAKES

Front, type	Hydraulic disc
Disc diameter	10 in.
Friction pads, type	Mintex M64
Lining thickness	0.25 in.
Rear, type	Internal expanding
Lining thickness	0.187-0.197 in.
Drum diameter	7.0 in.

Mean coil diameter	1.98 in.

SWING ARM

Bush type	Steel backed phosphor-bronze
Bush bore diameter	1.4460-1.4470 in.
Sleeve diameter	1.4445-1.4450 in.
Distance between fork ends	7.5 in.

TORQUE SPECIFICATIONS

TR25W

Carburetor flange nuts	10 ft lbs (1.383 kg/m)
Clutch center nut	60-65 ft lbs (8.295-8.987 kg/m)
Con. rod end cap nuts	25-27 ft lbs (3.456-3.733 kg/m)
Crankshaft pinion nut	35-40 ft lbs (4.839-5.530 kg/m)
Cylinder barrel nuts	26-28 ft lbs (3.595-3.871 kg/m)
Cylinder head stud nuts	18-20 ft lbs (2.489-2.765 kg/m)
Fork leg cap nuts	50-55 ft lbs (6.913-7.604 kg/m)
Fork leg pinch bolts	18-20 ft lbs (2.489-2.765 kg/m)
Kick-start ratchet nut	50-55 ft lbs (6.913-7.604 kg/m)
Oil pump stud nuts	5-7 ft lbs (691-968 kg/m)
Rotor fixing nut	60 ft lbs (8.295 kg/m)
Valve cover nuts (large)	10 ft lbs (1.383 kg/m)
Valve cover nuts (small)	5-7 ft lbs (691-968 kg/m)

T100C, T100R

Flywheel bolts	33 ft lbs
Con. rod bolts	27 ft lbs
Crankcase junction bolts	15 ft lbs
Crankcase junction studs	20 ft lbs
Cylinder block nuts	35 ft lbs
Cylinder head bolts (3/8 in. dia.)	18 ft lbs
Rocker box nuts	5 ft lbs
Rocker box bolts	5 ft lbs
Rocker spindle-domed nuts	25 ft lbs
Oil pump nuts	6 ft lbs
Kickstart ratchet pinion nut	40 ft lbs
Clutch center nut	50 ft lbs
Rotor fixing nut	30 ft lbs
Stator fixing nuts	20 ft lbs
Headlamp pivot bolts	10 ft lbs
Headrace sleeve nut pinch bolt	15 ft lbs
Stanchion pinch bolts	25 ft lbs
Front wheel axle cap bolts	25 ft lbs
Brake cam spindle nuts	20 ft lbs
Zener diode fixing nut	1 1/2 ft lbs
Twin carburetor manifold socket screws	10 ft lbs

TR6R, TR6C, T120R

Flywheel bolts	33 ft lbs (4.6 kg/m)
Con. rod bolts	28 ft lbs (3.9 kg/m)
Crankcase junction bolts	13 ft lbs (1.8 kg/m)
Crankcase junction studs	20 ft lbs (2.8 kg/m)
Cylinder block nuts	35 ft lbs (4.8 kg/m)
Cylinder head bolts (3/8 in. dia.)	18 ft lbs (2.49 kg/m)
Cylinder head bolt (5/16 in. dia.)	15 ft lbs (2.1 kg/m)
Rocker box nuts	5 ft lbs. (0.7 kg/m)
Rocker box bolts	5 ft lbs (0.7 kg/m)
Rocker spindle-domed nuts	22 ft lbs (3.0 kg/m)
Oil pump nuts	5 ft lbs (0.7 kg/m)
Kick-start ratchet pinion nut	45 ft lbs (6.3 kg/m)
Clutch center nut	50 ft lbs (7 kg/m)
Rotor fixing nut	30 ft lbs (4.1 kg/m)
Stator fixing nuts	20 ft lbs (2.8 kg/m)
Primary cover domed nuts	10 ft lbs (1.4 kg/m)
Headlamp pivot bolts	10 ft lbs (1.4 kg/m)
Headrace sleeve nut pinch bolt	15 ft lbs (2.1 kg/m)
Stanchion pinch bolts	25 ft lbs (3.5 kg/m)
Front wheel axle cap bolts	25 ft lbs (3.5 kg/m)
Rear brake drum to hub bolts	15 ft lbs (2.1 kg/m)
Brake cam spindle nuts	20 ft lbs (2.8 kg/m)
Zener diode fixing nut	1.5 ft lbs (0.21 kg/m)
Fork cap nut	80 ft lbs (11.1 kg/m)

T150, T150V

Con. rod bolts	18 ft lbs (2.489 kg/m)
Crankcase junction bolts	12 ft lbs (1.659 kg/m)
Crankcase junction studs	15 ft lbs (2.074 kg/m)
Cylinder block nuts	20-22 ft lbs (2.765-3.042 kg/m)
Cylinder head bolts	18 ft lbs (2.489 kg/m)
Rocker box nuts	6 ft lbs (0.691 kg/m)
Rocker box bolts	6 ft lbs (0.691 kg/m)
Rocker spindle-domed nuts	22 ft lbs (3.042 kg/m)
Kick-start ratchet pinion nut	40-45 ft lbs (5.530-6.221 kg/m)
Rotor fixing nut	50 ft lbs (6.913 kg/m)
Stator fixing nuts	8 ft lbs (1.106 kg/m)
Headlamp pivot bolts	10 ft lbs (1.383 kg/m)
Headrace sleeve nut pinch bolt	15 ft lbs (2.074 kg/m)
Stanchion pinch bolts	25 ft lbs (3.456 kg/m)
Front wheel axle cap bolts	25 ft lbs (3.456 kg/m)
Brake cam spindle nuts	20 ft lbs (2.756 kg/m)
Zener diode fixing nut	2-2.3 ft lbs (0.277-0.3174 kg/m)
Fork cap nut	80 ft lbs (11.06 kg/m)
Clutch center nut	60 ft lbs (8.295 kg/m)
Gearbox sprocket —Lock nut	58 ft lbs (8.019 kg/m)
Shock absorber nut	75-80 ft lbs (10.369-11.06 kg/m)
Center bearing nuts	18 ft lbs (2.489 kg/m)

TR7V, T140V

Flywheel bolts	33 ft lbs (4.6 kg/m)
Con. rod bolts	22 ft lbs (3.9 kg/m)
Crankcase junction bolts	13 ft lbs (1.8 kg/m)
Crankcase junction studs	20 ft lbs (2.8 kg/m)
Rocker box bolts —inner (5/16 in. dia.)	10 ft lbs (1.38 kg/m)
Cylinder head bolts—outer (3/8 in. dia.)	18 ft lbs (2.49 kg/m)
Cylinder head bolt—center (5/16 in dia.)	16 ft lbs (2.07 kg/m)
Cylinder head bolt—inner (3/8 in. dia.)	18 ft lbs (2.49 kg/m)
Rocker box nuts	5 ft lbs (7 kg/m)
Rocker box bolts (1/4 in. dia.)	5 ft lbs (7 kg/m)
Rocker spindle domed nuts	22 ft lbs (3.0 kg/m)
Oil pump nuts	5 ft lbs (7 kg/m)
Kick-start ratchet pinion nut	45 ft lbs (6.3 kg/m)
Clutch center nut	70 ft lbs (7 kg/m)
Rotor fixing nut	40 ft lbs (4.1 kg/m)
Stator fixing nuts	20 ft lbs (2.8 kg/m)
Primary cover domed nuts	10 ft lbs (1.4 kg/m)
Headlamp pivot bolts	10 ft lbs (1.4 kg/m)
Steering head bearing adjuster nut pinch bolt	15 ft lbs (2.1 kg/m)
Fork leg pinch bolts	25 ft lbs (3.4 kg/m)
Front wheel axle cap bolts	25 ft lbs (3.5 kg/m)
Rear brake drum to hub bolts	15 ft lbs (2.1 kg/m)
Brake cam spindle nuts	20 ft lbs (2.8 kg/m)
Zener diode fixing nut	1.5 ft lbs (21 kg/m)
Fork cap nut	80 ft lbs (11.1 kg/m)
Brake disc retaining bolts	20 ft lbs (2.8 kg/m)

INDEX

YAMAHA TWO-STROKES

MODEL IDENTIFICATION

U5 Newport 50

YJ2 Campus 60

YGS1 Sport 80

YGS1t Trail 80

YL1 Twin Jet 100

YL2 Rotary Jet 100

YL2C Trailmaster 100

YA6 Santa Barbara 125

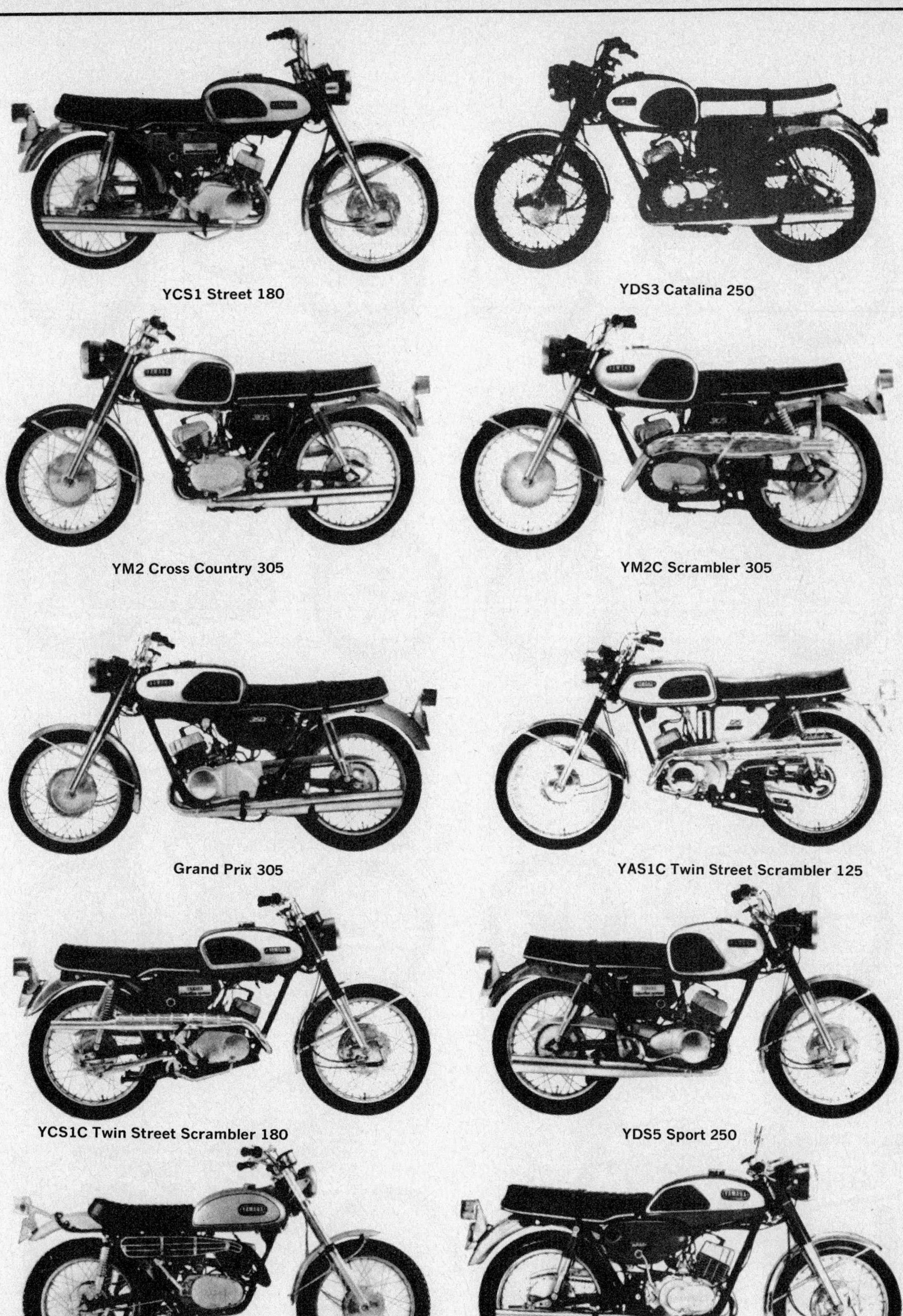

YCS1 Street 180

YDS3 Catalina 250

YM2 Cross Country 305

YM2C Scrambler 305

Grand Prix 305

YAS1C Twin Street Scrambler 125

YCS1C Twin Street Scrambler 180

YDS5 Sport 250

DT1 Enduro 250

YR2 Grand Prix 350

AT1 Enduro 125

CT1 Enduro 175

DS6 Street 250

R3 Grand Prix 350

HT1 Enduro 90

HS1 Twin Street 90

YG5T Trailmaster 80

L5TA Trail 100

CS3C Street Scrambler 200

R5 Street 350

RT1 Enduro 360

MAJOR IMPROVEMENTS AND MODEL CHANGES

1964, '65, '66

Introduction of the YL1 (98cc twin), YM1 (305cc twin) and the Autolube oil injection on all models. With the new lubrication system and other improvements, the YJ1 (55cc rotary-valve single) became the YJ2 (58cc rotary-valve single), the YG1K (73cc rotary-valve single) became the YG1K (same) and YGS1/T, the YDS2 (246cc twin) became the YDS3/C and, with the addition of electric starting, the U5 (50cc rotary-valve single) and YA5 (123cc rotary-valve single) evolved into the U5E and YA6.

1967

Introduction of the YL2/C (97cc rotary-valve single), YCS1 (180cc twin), YR1 (348cc twin) and primary kickstarting on some models. With the addition of electric starting, the YL1 became the YL1E and the YDS3/C became the DS5. The new YL2/C and YCS1 were also equipped with electric starters.

1968

Introduction of the YAS1/C (124cc twin), DT1 Enduro (246cc single), and a new five-port cylinder design. The new cylinder was used on the DT1, YAS1/C, and the YR2/C (evolved from YR1). With the addition of electric starting and other changes, the YG1K and YGS1/T became the YG5T and the YCS1 became the YCS1C.

1969

Introduction of the AT1 Enduro (123cc single with electric starting), CT1 Enduro (171cc single), and L5T (97cc rotary-valve single with electric starting and a two-range, three-speed transmission). The YAS1/C became the AS2C and the YG5T became the G5S (without electric starting). The DS5 of 1967 evolved into the DS6/C (without electric starting), the YR2/C into the newly styled R3 and the DT1 into the DT1B. The five-port cylinder was now used on all but the rotary-valve models.

1970

Introduction of the HS1 (89cc twin), HT1 Enduro (89cc single), RT1 Enduro (351cc single), and Keystone-type piston rings. The YCS1/C and R3 were completely revamped to produce the CS3C (195cc twin) and R5 (347cc twin). With new styling and internal improvements, the G5S, AT1, L5T, CT1, DT1B, and DS6/C became the G6S, AT1B, L5TA, CT1B, DT1C, and DS6B. The five-port cylinder was also used on the new HS1, HT1, and RT1.

1971

Introduction of the JT1 Mini-Enduro (58cc rotary-valve single). All 1971 models carried a last letter designation change from their 1970 versions. For example, the HT1 of 1970 became the HT1B in 1971, even though very few changes were made. The most significant improvements of the year were in the DT1E and RT1B: they were both equipped with identical frames and redesigned gearboxes, and the RT1B was fitted with a compression release.

1972

Introduction of reed valve induction on the AT2, CT2, DT2, RT2, and the new LT2 (100cc Enduro) and U7E (70cc Moped). The HS1 was enlarged to 97cc, restyled and designated LS2. The DS6 was completely revamped and designated DS7, and the JT1 Mini Enduro was made available in either street trim (JT2L) or purely off-road trim (JT2M).

GENERAL SPECIFICATIONS

U5/U5L, U5E, U7E, MJ2/MJ2T, YJ1, Early YJ2, Late YJ2

	U5/U5L	U5E	U7E	MJ2/MJ2T	YJ1	Early YJ2	Late YJ2
DIMENSIONS							
Net Weight	190	190	170	190	190	190	190
Overall Length (in.)	77.7	71.1	—	67.5	72.4	71.3	71.3
Overall Width (in.)	24.8	24.8	—	25.2	25.4	25.4	25.4
Overall Height (in.)	37.2	37.2	—	37.5	38.4	38.4	88.4
Ground Clearance (in.)	5.1	5.1	—	4.9	5.5	5.5	5.5
Wheelbase (in.)	44.9	44.9	—	44.9	45.8	45.1	45.1
Tire Size (in.)							
front	2.25 x 17	2.25 x 17	2.25 x 17	2.25 x 16	2.25 x 17	2.25 x 17	2.25 x 17
rear	2.25 x 17	2.25 x 17	2.50 x 17	2.25 x 16	2.25 x 17	2.25 x 17	2.25 x 17
ENGINE							
Displacement (cc)	50	50	72	55	58	58	58
No. of Cylinders	1	1	1	1	1	1	1
Bore x Stroke (mm)	40 x 40	40 x 40	47 x 42	42 x 40	42 x 40	42 x 42	42 x 42
Compression Ratio (:1)	6.8	6.8	6.8	7.4	7.1	6.6	7.5
Horsepower @ RPM	4.5 @ 6500	4.5 @ 6500	4.9 @ 6500	4.7 @ 6500	4.7 @ 6500	4.7 @ 6500	5.0 @ 7000
Torque @ RPM (ft lbs)	3.76 @ 5000	3.76 @ 5000	4.7 @ 4500	3.9 @ 6000	3.9 @ 6000	3.9 @ 6000	3.98 @ 6000
Fuel Induct. (RV, PP)①	RV	RV	*	RV	RV	RV	RV
Carburetion (Mikuni)	VM14	VM14	VM15SC	VM14SC	VM14SC	VM14SC	VM16
Lubrication (PM, OI)②	OI	OI	OI	PM	PM	OI	OI
TRANSMISSION							
Clutch	Auto	Auto	Auto	Auto/Manual	Manual	Manual	Manual
Reduction (pri/sec)	3.895/2.715	3.895/2.715	3.578/2.571	3.895/2.715	3.895/2.786	3.895/2.600	3.895/2.533
Transmission Ratio							
1st	3.083	3.083	3.250	3.083	3.083	3.083	3.083
2nd	1.722	1.722	1.833	1.824	1.882	1.882	1.882
3rd	1.174	1.174	1.200	1.227	1.333	1.338	1.333
4th	—	—	—	—	1.000	1.000	1.000
5th	—	—	—	—	—	—	—
ELECTRICS							
Ignition	Magneto	Generator	Generator	Generator	Magneto	Magneto	Magneto
Starting	Kick	Electric	Electric	Kick	Kick	Kick	Kick
PERFORMANCE							
Climbing Ability (deg)	20	20	—	14	15	18	18
Turning Radius (in.)	69.0	69.0	—	68.9	71.2	71.2	71.2
Braking Dist. (ft @ mph)	9.8 @ 15	9.8 @ 18	—	22.8 @ 22	9.8 @ 15	9.8 @ 15	9.8 @ 15
Fuel Consump. (mpg @ mph)	200 @ 18	200 @ 18	—	220 @ 18	220 @ 18	220 @ 18	220 @ 18

① RV—rotary valve; PP—piston port.
② PM—premix; OI—oil injection.
* Reed valve.

JT1/JT2, MG1T, YG1/YG1K, YG1T/YG1TK, YGS1, YGS1T, YG5T

	JT1/JT2	MG1T	YG1/YG1K	YG1T/YG1K	YGS1/YGS1T	YG5T
DIMENSIONS						
Net Weight	121	190	190	190	190	175
Overall Length (in.)	62.0	62.0	71.5	71.7	71.7	70.9
Overall Width (in.)	27.6	29.7	24.6	29.8	24.6/30.5	31.7
Overall Height (in.)	36.6	38.6	37.8	39.4	37.8/38.8	40.0
Ground Clearance (in.)	6.3	5.5	5.9	5.9	5.9	6.3
Wheelbase (in.)	45.1	45.1	45.1	45.1	45.1	46.3
Tire Size (in.): front	2.50 x 15	2.50 x 16	2.50 x 17	2.50 x 17	2.50 x 17	2.50 x 17
rear	2.50 x 15	2.50 x 16	2.50 x 17	2.50 x 17	2.50 x 17	3.00 x 17
ENGINE						
Displacement (cc)	58	73	73	73	73	73
No. of Cylinders	1	1	1	1	1	1
Bore x Stroke (mm)	42 x 42	47 x 42	47 x 42	47 x 42	47 x 42	47 x 42
Compression Ratio (:1)	6.4	6.8	6.8	6.8	6.8	6.8
Horsepower @ RPM	4.5 @ 7500	7.7 @ 7500	7.7 @ 7500	7.7 @ 7500	8.0 @ 7500	6.6 @ 7000
Torque @ RPM (ft lbs)	3.62 @ 5500	5.06 @ 6500	5.06 @ 6500	5.06 @ 6500	5.78 @ 6500	5.2 @ 6000
Fuel Induct. (RV, PP)①	RV	RV	RV	RV	RV	RV
Carburetion (Mikuni)	Y16P(Teikei)	VM15SC-1	VM15SC-1	VM15SC-1	VM15SC-1	VM16SC
Lubrication (PM, OI)②	OI	PM	PM/OI	PM/OI	OI	OI
TRANSMISSION						
Clutch	Manual	Manual	Manual	Manual	Manual	Manual
Reduction (pri/sec)	3.895/3.154	3.895/2.467	3.895/2.467	3.895/2.467	3.895/2.467	3.895/2.740
Transmission Ratio: 1st	3.077	3.083	3.083	3.083	3.083	3.077
2nd	1.889	1.882	1.882	1.882	1.882	1.889
3rd	1.304	1.333	1.333	1.333	1.333	1.304
4th	1.038	1.000	1.000	1.000	1.000	0.963
5th	—	—	—	—	—	—
ELECTRICS						
Ignition	Magneto	Magneto	Magneto	Magneto	Magneto	Generator
Starting	Kick	Kick	Kick	Kick	Kick	Electric
PERFORMANCE						
Climbing Ability (deg)	22	20	20	20	20	30
Turning Radius (in.)	59.1	59.9	70.1	71.2	70.1	70.9
Braking Dist. (ft @ mph)	24.6 @ 22	23 @ 22	23 @ 22	23 @ 22	23 @ 22	20 @ 22
Fuel Consump. (mpg @ mph)	176 @ 19	188 @ 19	188 @ 19	188 @ 19	131 @ 14	140 @ 25

① RV—rotary valve; PP—piston port.
② PM—premix; OI—oil injection.

G5S, G6S/G6SB/G7S, HT1/HT1B, HS1/HS1B, YL2, YL2C

	G5S	G6S/G6SB/G7S	HT1/HT1B	HS1/HS1B	YL2	YL2C
DIMENSIONS						
Net Weight	170	170	190	199	200	200
Overall Length (in.)	71.3	71.3	73.8	70.9	75.4	73.2
Overall Width (in.)	31.1	31.1	35.4	30.3	28.1	28.1
Overall Height (in.)	39.2	39.2	40.7	39.6	41.7	42.5
Ground Clearance (in.)	5.3	5.3	8.9	6.1	5.5	7.9
Wheelbase (in.)	45.9	45.9	48.0	47.0	46.9	48.5
Tire Size (in.): front	2.50 x 17	2.50 x 17	2.75 x 18	2.50 x 18	2.50 x 18	3.00 x 18
rear	2.50 x 17	2.50 x 17	3.00 x 18	2.50 x 18	2.50 x 18	3.00 x 18
ENGINE						
Displacement (cc)	73	73	89	89	97	97
No. of Cylinders	1	1	1	2	1	1
Bore x Stroke (mm)	47 x 42	47 x 42	50 x 45.6	36.5 x 43	52 x 45.6	52 x 45.6
Compression Ratio (:1)	6.8	6.8	6.8	7.5	7.0	7.0
Horsepower @ RPM	4.9 @ 7500	4.9 @ 7500	8.5 @ 7500	4.9 @ 8000	9.5 @ 7500	9.5 @ 7500
Torque @ RPM (ft lbs)	4.1 @ 5500	4.1 @ 5500	6.5 @ 6500	3.1 @ 5500	6.8 @ 5500	7.24 @ 6000
Fuel Induct. (RV, PP)①	RV	RV	PP	PP	RV	RV
Carburetion (Mikuni)	VM16SC	VM16SC	VM20SC	VM16SC(2)	VM17SC	VM17SC
Lubrication (PM, OI)②	OI	OI	OI	OI	OI	OI
TRANSMISSION						
Clutch	Manual	Manual	Manual	Manual	Manual	Manual
Reduction (pri/sec)	3.895/2.643	3.895/2.643	3.895/3.590	3.895/3.077	3.895/2.335	3.895/2.335
Transmission Ratio: 1st	3.077	3.077	3.181	3.182	3.077	3.077
2nd	1.889	1.889	2.000	1.813	1.889	1.889
3rd	1.304	1.304	1.368	1.300	1.304	1.304
4th	0.963	0.963	1.000	1.045	0.963	0.963
5th	—	—	0.800	0.840	—	—
ELECTRICS						
Ignition	Magneto	Magneto	Magneto	Alternator	Generator	Generator
Starting	Kick	Kick	Kick	Kick	Kick	Electric
PERFORMANCE						
Climbing Ability (deg)	20	20	25	20	22	22
Turning Radius (in.)	70.9	70.9	68.9	70.9	73.5	73.5
Braking Dist. (ft @ mph)	21 @ 22	23 @ 22	23 @ 22	21 @ 22	22.6 @ 21.8	22.6 @ 21.8
Fuel Consump. (mpg @ mph)	190 @ 25	190 @ 25	153 @ 25	153 @ 25	140 @ 25	140 @ 25

① RV—rotary valve; PP—piston port.
② PM—premix; OI—oil injection.

YL2CM, L5T/L5TA, LT2, LS2, YL1/YL1E, YA5, YA6, AT1/AT1B/AT1C/AT2

	YL2CM③	L5T/L5TA	LT2	LS2	YL1/YL1E	YA5	YA6	AT1/AT1B/ AT1C/AT2
DIMENSIONS								
Net Weight	200	198	187	209	180	245	245	218
Overall Length (in.)	732	70.9	—	—	71.6	74.2	75.6	77.2
Overall Width (in.)	28.1	31.7	—	—	24.8	26.8	28.5	35.8
Overall Height (in.)	42.5	40.2	—	—	37.3	37.6	41.1	42.9
Ground Clearance (in.)	6.9	6.3	—	—	5.1	4.9	5.3	8.9
Wheelbase (in.)	48.5	46.3	—	—	45.1	49.2	49.0	50.6
Tire Size (in.): front	3.00 x 18	2.75 x 17	2.75 x 18	2.50 x 18	2.50 x 17	3.00 x 16	3.00 x 16	3.00 x 18
rear	3.00 x 18	3.00 x 17	3.00 x 18	2.50 x 18	2.50 x 17	3.00 x 16	3.00 x 16	3.25 x 18
ENGINE								
Displacement (cc)	97	97	97	97	98	123	123	123
No. of Cylinders	1	1	1	2	2	1	1	1
Bore x Stroke (mm)	52 x 45.6	52 x 45.6	52 x 45.6	38 x 40	38 x 43	56 x 50	56 x 50	56 x 50
Compression Ratio (:1)	6.6	6.8	6.9	7.0	7.1	6.75	6.8	7.1
Horsepower @ RPM	9.7 @ 7000	8.0 @ 6000	10 @ 7500	10.5 @ 8000	9.5 @ 8500	11 @ 6700	11 @ 6700	11.5 @ 7500⑧
Torque @ RPM (ft lbs)	7.24 @ 6000	6.9 @ 5000	7.0 @ 7000	6.95 @ 7500	6.0 @ 8000	9 @ 5000	9 @ 5000	8.5 @ 7000⑨
Fuel Induct. (RV, PP)①	RV	RV	*	PP	PP	RV	RV	PP⑩
Carburetion (Mikuni)	VM20SC	VM20SC	VM20SH	VM17SC	VM16SC(2)	M21SI	VM22SC	VM24SH
Lubrication (PM, OI)②	OI	OI	OI	OI	OI	PM	OI	OI
TRANSMISSION								
Clutch	Manual	Manual	Manual	Manual	Manual	Manual	Manual	Manual
Reduction (pri/sec)	3.895/ 2.334	3.895/ 2.310	3.895/ 3.590	3.894/ 3.000	3.895/ 2.335	2.785/ 2.730	3.833/ 2.600	3.895/ 3.214⑪
Transmission Ratio: 1st	3.077	2.833(h) 4.647(l)	3.181	3.181	3.077	2.965	2.533	3.182
2nd	1.889	1.647(h) 2.702(l)	2.000	1.812	1.889	1.794	1.524	2.000
3rd	1.304	1.000(h) 1.640(l)	1.386	1.300	1.304	1.291	1.120	1.368
4th	0.963	—	1.000	1.045	0.963	1.000	0.828	1.000
5th	—	—	0.800	0.840	—	—	—	0.800
ELECTRICS								
Ignition	Generator	Generator	Alternator	Alternator	Generator	Generator	Generator	Generator
Starting	Electric	Electric	Kick	Kick	Kick/ Electric	Electric	Electric	Electric
PERFORMANCE								
Climbing Ability (deg)	22	35	—	—	20	33	20	30
Turning Radius (in.)	73.5	70.9	—	—	70.1	74.8	72.0	75.1
Braking Dist. (ft @ mph)	22.6 @ 21.8	27.9 @ 22	—	—	23 @ 22	40 @ 32	23 @ 22	58.3 @ 31
Fuel Con. (mpg @ mph)	140 @ 25	165 @ 19	—	—	153 @ 19	180 @ 20.4	183 @ 19	141 @ 25

① RV—rotary valve; PP—piston port.
② PM—premix; OI—oil injection.
③ YL2C after ser #550101.

* Reed valve.
⑧ AT1—11.5 @ 7500; AT2—13 @ 7000
⑨ AT1—8.5 @ 7000; AT2—10 @ 6000

⑩ AT1—Piston port; AT2—Reed valve.
⑪ AT1—3.214; AT2—3.000

YAS1/YAS1C/AS2C, CT1/CT1B/CT1C/CT2, YCS1C, YCS1, CS3C, CS3B/CS5

	YAS1/YAS1C AS2C	CT1/CT1B/ CT1C/CT2	YCS1C	YCS1	CS3C	CS3B/CS5
DIMENSIONS						
Net Weight	220	211	260	260	262	258
Overall Length (in.)	73.0	77.4	75.6	75.6	76.0	76.0
Overall Width (in.)	31.9	35.8	30.1	30.1	32.1	32.1
Overall Height (in.)	39.6	43.1	39.2	39.2	40.2	40.2
Ground Clearance (in.)	5.9	9.1	6.1	6.1	6.9	6.9
Wheelbase (in.)	47.2	50.6	49.0	49.0	49.0	49.0
Tire Size (in.): front	2.75 x 18	3.25 x 18	2.75 x 18	3.00 x 18	2.75 x 18	2.75 x 18
rear	3.00 x 18	3.50 x 18	3.00 x 18	3.00 x 18	3.00 x 18	3.00 x 18
ENGINE						
Displacement (cc)	124	171	180	180	195	195
No. of Cylinders	2	1	2	2	2	2
Bore x Stroke (mm)	43 x 43	66 x 50	50 x 46	50 x 46	52 x 46	52 x 46
Compression Ratio (:1)	7.0	6.8	7.0	6.8	6.2	7.1
Horsepower @ RPM	15.2 @ 8500	⑫	21 @ 7500	21 @ 8000	22 @ 7500	22 @ 7500
Torque @ RPM (ft lbs)	9.4 @ 7500	⑬	14.6 @ 7000	14.6 @ 7000	15.7 @ 7000	15.7 @ 7000
Fuel Induction (RV, PP)①	PP	⑭	PP	PP	PP	PP
Carburetion (Mikuni)	VM17SC(2)	VM24SH	VM20SC(2)	VM18SC(2)	VM20SC(2)	VM20SC(2)
Lubrication (PM, OI)②	OI	OI	OI	OI	OI	OI
TRANSMISSION						
Clutch	Manual	Manual	Manual	Manual	Manual	Manual
Reduction (pri/sec)	3.895/2.600	3.895/2.812	3.313/2.667	3.313/2.466	3.313/2.857	3.313/2.857
Transmission Ratio: 1st	3.182	3.182	2.833	2.833	2.833	2.833
2nd	1.875	2.000	1.875	1.875	1.875	1.875
3rd	1.300	1.368	1.421	1.421	1.421	1.421
4th	1.045	1.000	1.045	1.045	1.045	1.045
5th	0.840	0.800	0.840	0.840	0.840	0.840
ELECTRICS						
Ignition	Alternator	Magneto	Generator	Generator	Generator	Generator
Starting	Kick	Kick	Electric	Electric	Electric	Electric
PERFORMANCE						
Climbing Ability (deg)	23.5	32	23	23	25	25
Turning Radius (in.)	69.0	74.8	80.8	80.8	80.7	80.7
Braking Dist. (ft @ mph)	38 @ 30	58.3 @ 31	39 @ 31	39 @ 31	36 @ 31	36 @ 31
Fuel Consump. (mpg @ mph)	150 @ 25	129 @ 25	130 @ 25	130 @ 25	118 @ 25	118 @ 25

① RV—rotary valve; PP—piston port.
② PM—premix; OI—oil injection.
⑫ CTI—15.6 @ 7000; CT2—16 @ 7500
⑬ CTI—11.9 @ 6500; CT2—11.9 @ 6000
⑭ CTI—Piston port; CT2—Reed valve

DT1, DT1B/DT1S, DT1C, DT1E/DT2, YD3, YDT1

	DT1	DT1B/DT1S	DT1C	DT1E/DT2	YD3	YDT1④
DIMENSIONS						
Net Weight (lbs)	232	232	232	⑮	337	345
Overall Length (in.)	78.3	81.1	81.1	78.3	73.0	78.3
Overall Width (in.)	28.9	28.9	28.9	28.9	28.7	28.9
Overall Height (in.)	42.5	42.5	42.5	43.5	38.2	42.5
Ground Clearance (in.)	9.6	9.6	9.6	10.0	5.3	5.1
Wheelbase (in.)	50.8	53.6	53.6	54.7	49.4	50.8
Tire Size (in.): front	3.25 x 19	3.25 x 19	3.25 x 19	3.25 x 19	3.25 x 16	2.75 x 18
rear	4.00 x 18	4.00 x 18	4.00 x 18	4.00 x 18	3.25 x 16	3.00 x 18
ENGINE						
Displacement (cc)	246	246	246	246	247	247
No. of Cylinders	1	1	1	1	2	2
Bore x Stroke (mm)	70 x 64	70 x 64	70 x 64	70 x 64	54 x 54	54 x 54
Compression Ratio (:1)	6.8	6.8	6.4	6.4	7.0	7.0
Horsepower @ RPM	21 @ 6000	21 @ 6000	23 @ 7000	⑯	17 @ 6000	17 @ 6000
Torque @ RPM (ft lbs)	16.8 @ 5000	16.8 @ 5000	17.5 @ 6500	⑰	17.8 @ 4500	17.8 @ 4500
Fuel Induct. (RV, PP)①	PP	PP	PP	⑱	PP	PP
Carburetion (Mikuni)	VM26SH	VM26SH	VM26SH	VM26SH	VM20SC(2)	VM20SC(2)
Lubrication (PM, OI)②	OI	OI	OI	OI	PM	PM
TRANSMISSION						
Clutch	Manual	Manual	Manual	Manual	Manual	Manual
Reduction (pri/sec)	3.095/2.933	3.095/2.933	3.095/3.143	3.095/3.143	3.250/2.060	3.250/2.060
Transmission Ratio: 1st	2.231	2.231	2.533	2.533	2.500	2.500
2nd	1.624	1.624	1.789	1.789	1.530	1.530
3rd	1.211	1.211	1.304	1.304	1.227	1.227
4th	1.000	1.000	1.000	1.000	0.960	0.960
5th	0.826	0.826	0.767	0.767	—	—
ELECTRICS						
Ignition	Magneto	Magneto	Magneto	Magneto	Generator	Generator
Starting	Kick	Kick	Kick	Kick	Electric	Electric
PERFORMANCE						
Climbing Ability (deg)	35	35	35	35	N.A.	N.A.
Turning Radius (in.)	82.6	82.6	82.6	78.2	N.A.	N.A.
Braking Dist. (ft @ mph)	40 @ 30	40 @ 30	40 @ 30	49 @ 30	N.A.	N.A.
Fuel Consump. (mpg @ mph)	94 @ 25	94 @ 25	94 @ 25	94 @ 31	N.A.	N.A.

① RV—rotary valve; PP—piston port.
② PM—premix; OI—oil injection.
④ Not to be confused with the DT1 Enduro. YDT1 is a YD3 engine in a YDS2 frame.
⑮ DT1E—245; DT2—258
⑯ DT1E—23 @ 7000; DT2—24 @ 7000
⑰ DT1E—17.5 @ 6500; DT2—18.3 @ 6000
⑱ DT1E—Piston port; DT2—Reed valve
N.A.—Not available.

YDS1, YDS2, Early YDS3, Early YDS3C, Late YDS3, Late YDS3C

	YDS1	YDS2	Early YDS3	Early YDS3C	Late YDS3	Late YDS3C
DIMENSIONS						
Net Weight (lbs)	310	310	320	320	320	320
Overall Length (in.)	78.3	78.3	79.0	79.0	79.0	79.0
Overall Width (in.)	24.2	24.2	31.2	31.2	31.2	31.2
Overall Height (in.)	36.6	36.6	42.0	42.0	42.0	42.0
Ground Clearance (in.)	5.1	5.1	5.8	5.8	5.8	5.8
Wheelbase (in.)	50.8	50.8	51.9	51.9	51.9	51.9
Tire Size (in.): front	3.00 x 18	2.75 x 18	3.00 x 18	3.00 x 18	3.00 x 18	3.00 x 18
rear	3.00 x 18	2.75 x 18	3.25 x 18	3.50 x 18	3.25 x 18	3.50 x 18
ENGINE						
Displacement (cc)	246	246	246	246	246	246
No. of Cylinders	2	2	2	2	2	2
Bore x Stroke (mm)	56 x 50	56 x 50	56 x 50	56 x 50	56 x 50	56 x 50
Compression Ratio (:1)	6.8	7.5	7.5	7.8	7.5	7.5
Horsepower @ RPM	N.A.	25 @ 7500	27 @ 8000	27 @ 7500	28 @ 8000	28 @ 8000
Torque @ RPM (ft lbs)	N.A.	17.8 @ 7000	17.6 @ 6500	17.6 @ 6500	18.1 @ 7500	18.1 @ 7500
Fuel Induct. (RV, PP)①	PP	PP	PP	PP	PP	PP
Carburetion (Mikuni)	VM20SC(2)	VM20SH(2)	VM24SC(2)	VM24SC(2)	VM24SC(2)	VM24SC(2)
Lubrication (PM, OI)②	PM	PM	OI	OI	OI	OI
TRANSMISSION						
Clutch	Manual	Manual	Manual	Manual	Manual	Manual
Reduction (pri/sec)	2.500/3.358	3.250/2.438	3.250/2.600	3.250/2.733	3.250/2.600	3.250/2.733
Transmission Ratio: 1st	2.500	2.500	2.500	2.500	2.545	2.545
2nd	1.667	1.667	1.667	1.667	1.533	1.533
3rd	1.227	1.227	1.227	1.227	1.167	1.167
4th	0.960	0.960	0.960	1.042	0.950	0.950
5th	0.750	0.750	0.750	0.923	0.773	0.773
ELECTRICS						
Ignition	Generator	Generator	Generator	Generator	Generator	Generator
Starting	Kick	Kick	Kick	Kick	Kick	Kick
PERFORMANCE						
Climbing Ability (deg)	N.A.	23	23	27	23	27
Turning Radius (in.)	N.A.	86.2	88.0	88.0	88	88.0
Braking Dist. (ft @ mph)	N.A.	31 @ 30	47 @ 32	47 @ 32	47 @ 32	47 @ 32
Fuel Consump. (mpg @ mph)	N.A.	100 @ 27	100 @ 25	100 @ 25	100 @ 25	100 @ 25

① RV—rotary valve; PP—piston port.
② PM—premix; OI—oil injection.
N.A.—Not available.

YDS5, DS6B, DS7, YM1, YM2C, YR1

	YDS5	DS6C	DS6B	DS7	YM1	YM2C	YR1
DIMENSIONS							
Net Weight	325.6	309	304	304	340	326	348
Overall Length (in.)	78.4	78.3	78.3	—	78.9	73.3	81.2
Overall Width (in.)	80.3	32.9	32.9	—	31.2	31.2	28.9
Overall Height (in.)	41.4	41.9	41.9	—	42.0	38.1	39.4
Ground Clearance (in.)	6.1	5.9	6.1	—	5.9	6.1	5.7
Wheelbase (in.)	50.8	50.8	50.8	—	50.7	51.0	52.6
Tire Size (in.): front	3.00 x 18	3.00 x 18	3.00 x 18	3.00 x 18	3.00 x 18	3.00 x 18	3.00 x 18
rear	3.25 x 18	3.50 x 18	3.25 x 18	3.25 x 18	3.25 x 18	3.25 x 18	3.50 x 18
ENGINE							
Displacement (cc)	246	246	246	247	305	305	348
No. of Cylinders	2	2	2	2	2	2	2
Bore x Stroke (mm)	56 x 50	56 x 50	56 x 50	54 x 54	60 x 54	60 x 54	61 x 59.6
Compression Ratio (:1)	7.5	7.3	7.3	7.1	6.7	7.5	6.9
Horsepower @ RPM	29.5 @ 8000	30 @ 7500	30 @ 7500	30 @ 7500	29 @ 7000	31 @ 7000	36 @ 7500
Torque @ RPM (ft lbs)	19.7 @ 7500	21.1 @ 7000	21.1 @ 7000	21.1 @ 7000	19.9 @ 6000	23.4 @ 6500	27.8 @ 6500
Fuel Induct. (RV, PP)①	PP	PP	PP	PP	PP	PP	PP
Carburetion (Mikuni)	VM26SC(2)	VM26SC(2)	VM26SC(2)	VM26SC(2)	VM24SC(2)	VM26SC(2)	VM28SC(2)
Lubrication (PM, OI)②	OI	OI	OI	OI	OI	OI	OI
TRANSMISSION							
Clutch	Manual	Manual	Manual	Manual	Manual	Manual	Manual
Reduction (pri/sec)	3.250/2.733	3.250/2.929	3.250/2.733	3.238/2.666	3.250/2.353	3.250/2.500	2.870/2.563
Transmission Ratio							
1st	2.545	2.545	2.545	2.562	2.545	2.545	2.545
2nd	1.533	1.533	1.533	1.590	1.533	1.533	1.600
3rd	1.167	1.167	1.167	1.192	1.167	1.167	1.167
4th	0.950	0.950	0.950	0.965	0.950	0.950	0.950
5th	0.733	0.773	0.773	0.806	0.773	0.773	0.773
ELECTRICS							
Ignition	Generator	Generator	Generator	Alternator	Generator	Generator	Generator
Starting	Electric	Kick	Kick	Kick	Kick	Kick	Kick
PERFORMANCE							
Climbing Ability (deg)	23.5	25	24	—	23	23.5	26
Turning Radius (in.)	90.7	86.6	86.6	—	88.0	90.6	90.6
Braking Dist. (ft @ mph)	42.5 @ 31	38 @ 31	38 @ 31	—	40 @ 32	42.5 @ 31	43 @ 31
Fuel Consump. (mpg @ mph)	114 @ 35	94 @ 25	94 @ 25	—	82 @ 25	114 @ 35	95 @ 25

① RV—rotary valve; PP—piston port.
② PM—premix; OI—oil injection.

YR2/YR2C, R3C, R5/R5B/R5C, RT1/RT1B/RT2

	YR2/YR2C	R3C	R5/R5B/R5C	RT1/RT1B/RT2
DIMENSIONS				
Net Weight (lbs)	348	340	308	258
Overall Length (in.)	81.2	80.3	80.3	82.7
Overall Width (in.)	28.9	35.2	32.9	35.0
Overall Height (in.)	39.4	42.7	42.7	45.7
Ground Clearance (in.)	5.7	5.9	6.1	10.0
Wheelbase (in.)	52.6	52.8	52.0	54.7
Tire Size (in.): front	3.00 x 18	3.00 x 18	3.00 x 18	3.25 x 19
rear	3.50 x 18	3.50 x 18	3.50 x 18	4.00 x 18
ENGINE				
Displacement (cc)	348	348	347	351
No. of Cylinders	2	2	2	1
Bore x Stroke (mm)	61 x 59.6	61 x 59.6	64 x 54	80 x 70
Compression Ratio (:1)	6.9	7.5	6.9	6.6
Horsepower @ RPM	36 @ 7000	36 @ 7000	36 @ 7000	㉒
Torque @ RPM (ft lbs)	27.8 @ 6000	28 @ 6000	28 @ 6500	㉓
Fuel Induct. (RV, PP)①	PP	PP	PP	㉔
Carburetion (Mikuni)	VM28SC(2)	VM28SC(2)	VM28SC(2)	VM32SH
Lubrication (PM, OI)②	OI	OI	OI	OI
TRANSMISSION				
Clutch	Manual	Manual	Manual	Manual
Reduction (pri/sec)	2.870/2.563⑤	2.870/2.730	2.869/2.666	3.095/2.600
Transmission Ration: 1st	2.545	2.545	2.562	2.533
2nd	1.600	1.600	1.590	1.789
3rd	1.167	1.167	1.192	1.304
4th	0.950	0.950	0.965	1.000
5th	0.773	0.773	0.806	0.767
ELECTRICS				
Ignition	Generator	Generator	Alternator	Magneto
Starting	Kick	Kick	Kick	Kick
PERFORMANCE				
Climbing Ability (deg)	26	26.5	28	35
Turning Radius (in.)	90.6	90.6	90.6	78.7
Braking Dist. (ft @ mph)	43 @ 31	43 @ 31	46 @ 31	49 @ 31
Fuel Consump. (mpg @ mph)	95 @ 25	95 @ 25	82.5 @ 37	82.5 @ 37

① RV—rotary valve; PP—piston port.
② PM—premix; OI—oil injection.
⑤ YR2C—2.870/2.730.
⑥ One exhaust, one intake valve per cylinder.
㉒ RT1—30 @ 6000; RT2—32 @ 6000
㉓ RT1—26 @ 5500; RT2—27.7 @ 5500
㉔ RT1—Piston port; RT2—Reed valve

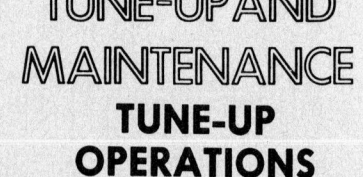

TUNE-UP AND MAINTENANCE

TUNE-UP OPERATIONS

IGNITION POINTS AND TIMING

1. Remove the ignition access cover, then separate the points and check their condition.

2. Clean up a used set of points by running a point file or piece of sand paper between them. Remove any deposits and smooth out the pitted surfaces, then apply lacquer thinner or point cleaner.

NOTE: *Apply thinner or cleaner to a new set of points as well, since many of them are coated with a protective film.*

3. Snap the points shut on a white business card (or piece of heavy paper) to remove the filings and cleaning fluid. Re-

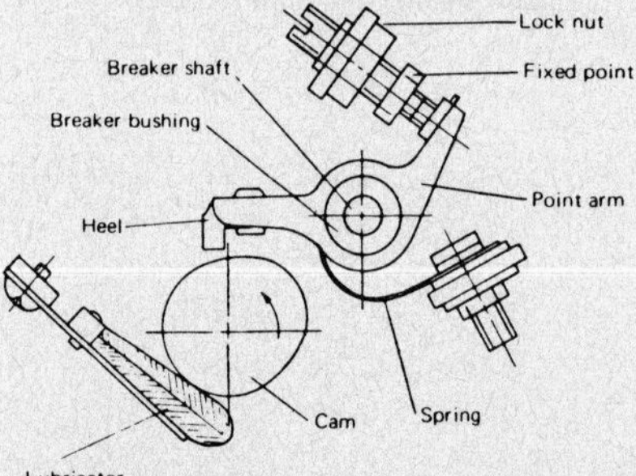

Typical breaker point arrangement on magneto models

peat this step until the points leave a clean imprint.

4. Remove the spark plug and rotate the engine until the points are at their widest gap.

5. Insert the proper size feeler gauge, loosen the point lockscrew and adjust the gap until a snug slip fit is obtained. Tighten the lockscrew and recheck the gap.

6. Apply a small amount of grease to the point cam or, if equipped with a felt lubricator, a few drops of lightweight oil to the pad.

7. Before setting the ignition timing, note the following:

a. On models equipped with a governor or electric starter, wedge the centrifugal counterweights in the OPEN position. Wooden matchsticks or a piece of wheel spoke (bent into a U-shaped spring) will do the job.

b. On magneto equipped models, ignition timing is determined by the point gap. After the gap has been set, connect the dial indicator and timing light as described below, then readjust the points so that they open at EXACTLY the correct mark. On models equipped with an alternator or generator, point gap and ignition timing are set independently.

c. On twins, each point set is gapped and timed separately. Follow the procedure for each cylinder.

8. Install a dial indicator gauge and adapter in the spark plug opening.

NOTE: *DT1 and RT1 cylinder heads must be removed to facilitate the installation of the dial gauge and a special adapter (see illustration).*

9. Rotate the crankshaft until the piston reaches top dead center (where the indicator needle stops before reversing direction). Set the dial gauge at zero.

10. Connect a low resistance (100 ohms or less) ignition test lamp or Yamaha Point Checker as follows:

(+)) RED lead—to connector on insulated side of point set.

(−) BLACK lead—to ground (engine case or frame).

NOTE: *On twins, the right cylinder points can be identified by the I_1 terminal (grey wire) and the left cylinder points by the I_2 terminal (orange wire).*

11. Loosen the breaker plate lockscrew just enough to allow SLIGHT movement (this is a precaution against any change in plate position when the lockscrew is retightened).

12. Turn the crankshaft in the direction OPPOSITE of normal rotation to a point somewhere below the timing mark, then reverse direction and slowly approach the specified number of degrees before TDC. Adjust the breaker plate so that the points just begin to open (as indicated by the test lamp) at this mark.

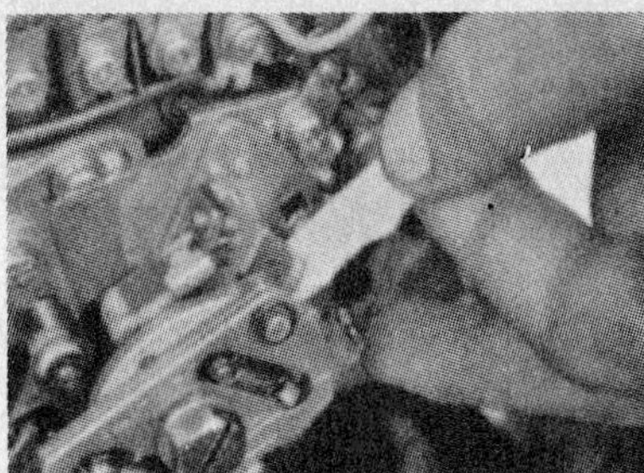

Removing the breaker point cleaner fluid

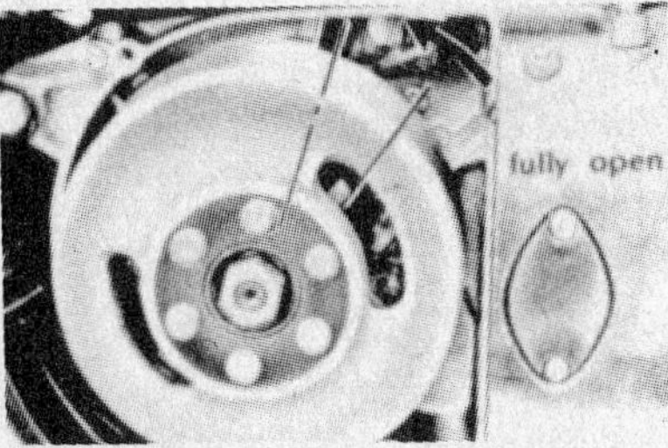

RT1 governor wedged fully open

Dial indicator installation on all models except DT1 and RT1

Dial indicator and special adapter installation on the DT1 and RT1

Adjusting ignition timing

NOTE: *Turning the breaker plate in the direction of normal engine rotation retards timing; turning opposite to normal rotation advances timing.*

13. Tighten the breaker plate lockscrew and recheck the timing. Readjust if necessary.

In a situation where only a feeler gauge is available, you can make a rough adjustment that is reasonably accurate. On magneto systems, simply adjust the points to the specified gap (this will closely approximate the correct timing); on alternator or dc generator systems, adjust the points, hold a piece of thin cellophane between them, then turn the engine in the direction of normal rotation while tugging lightly at the cellophane—the points should release the cellophane just as the timing marks on the flywheel and breaker plate match.

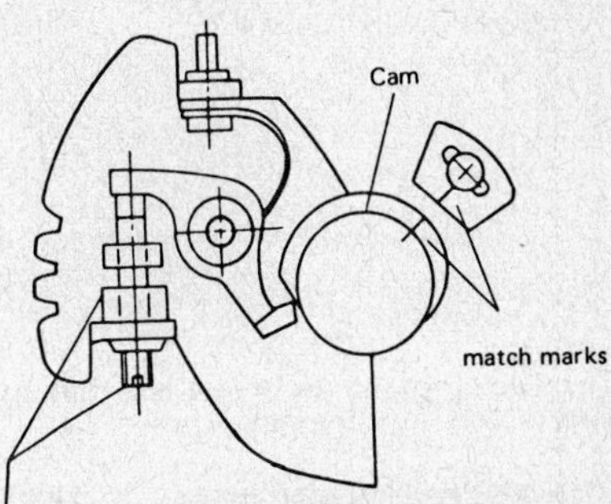

Emergency point gap and timing adjustment on magneto-equipped models

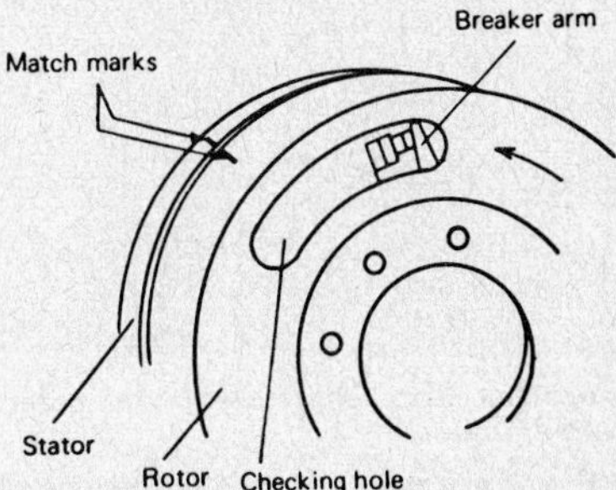

Adjustment should be made with this nut and screw when the heel is on the cam lobe

CARBURETOR IDLE SPEED AND MIXTURE

1. Turn the idle mixture (air) screw IN until it seats lightly.

CAUTION: *Too much pressure when turning in the adjustment screw will damage the seat.*

2. Back out the idle mixture (air) screw the recommended number of turns.

3. Start and warm up the engine; then, with the throttle grip completely closed, turn the idle speed (throttle stop) screw in or out until the engine idles at the specified rpm.

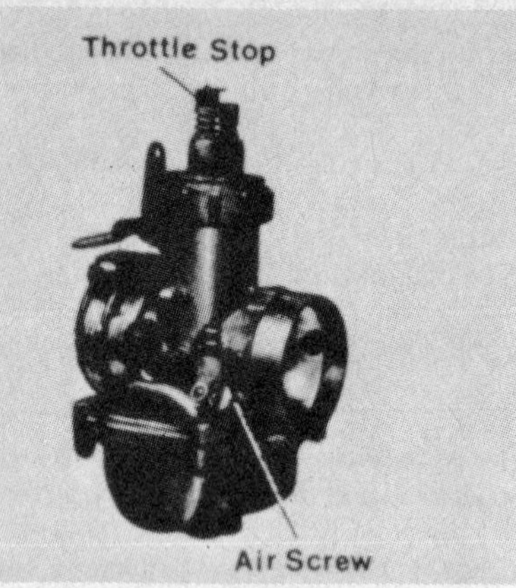

Throttle stop screw and air location on early piston port engines

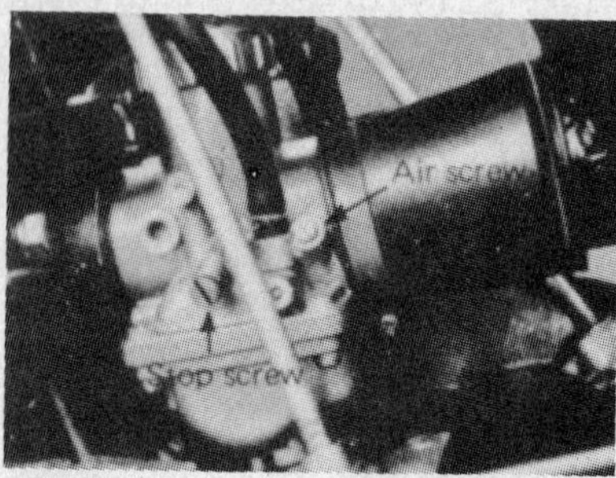

Throttle stop and air screw location on late piston port engines

Throttle stop adjustment on rotary-valve engines

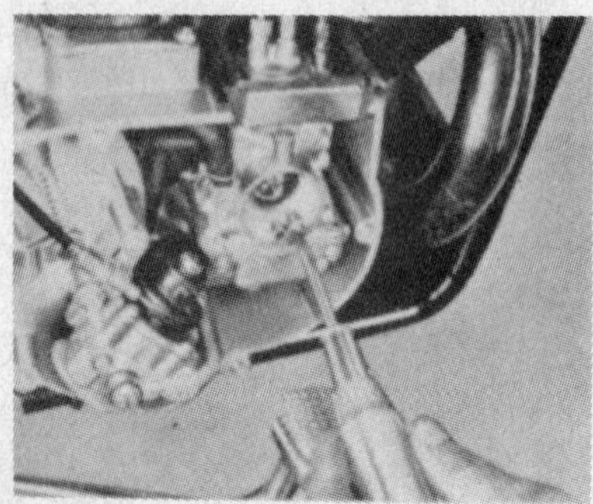

Air screw adjustment on rotary-valve engines

THROTTLE CABLE ADJUSTMENT

Set throttle cable slack at 0.5–1.0 mm at the twistgrip. Be sure the slides are synchronized. Use the cable adjustors above each carb, screwing in or out so that both carbs begin to rise at the same time.

OIL PUMP CABLE ADJUSTMENT

NOTE: *Before making this critical adjustment, the throttle cables MUST be set correctly.*

1. Remove the oil pump access cover.
2. Slowly turn the twist grip to the specified throttle slide opening. "Idle" position is where all cable freeplay is removed, but before the throttle slide begins to lift. "½" position is where the mark on the throttle slide is at the top of the slide bore.

NOTE: *Some early models don't have the "½" throttle slide mark. On these machines, use the special pump setting tool (see illustration).*

3. Loosen the oil pump cable adjuster locknut.
4. Turn the cable adjuster until the mark on the cable pulley matches the pump guide pin.
5. Tighten the cable locknut.

MINIMUM OIL PUMP STROKE

1. With the engine stopped, fully close the throttle twist grip.
2. Turn the oil pump starter plate in the direction of the arrow marked on the plate until the plunger is at the end of its stroke.
3. Using a feeler gauge, measure the clearance between the adjusting pulley and adjusting plate.
4. If the clearance is not within specifications, remove the adjusting plate and add or subtract 0.1 mm shims as necessary.

CYLINDER COMPRESSION CHECK

1. Remove the spark plug and screw a compression gauge into the hole (hold the automotive type firmly in the hole).
2. Hold the throttle grip WIDE OPEN and kick the engine over several times. Note the gauge indications.

In general, 50cc and 60cc two-stroke engines should read about 100 psi; 80cc to 125cc about 115–125 psi; 180cc to 200cc about 120–135 psi; large two-strokes 140–150 psi.

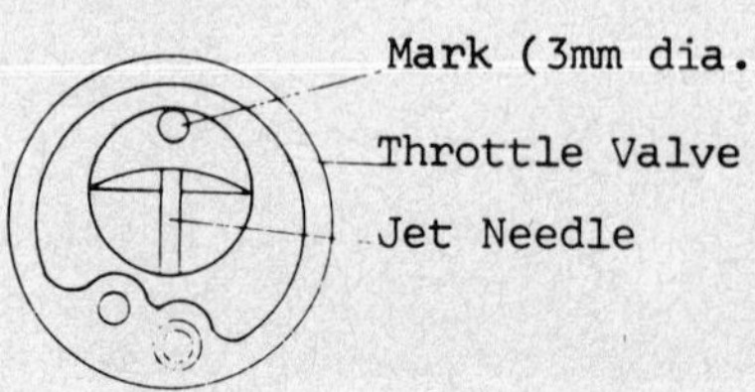

Half-open throttle slide position

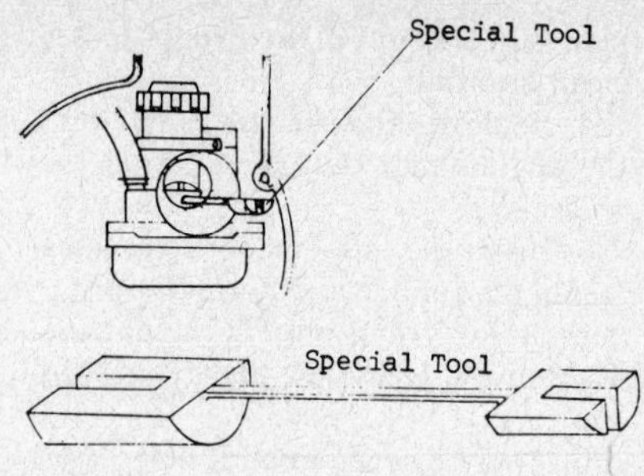

Special throttle slide tool used on early rotary-valve models

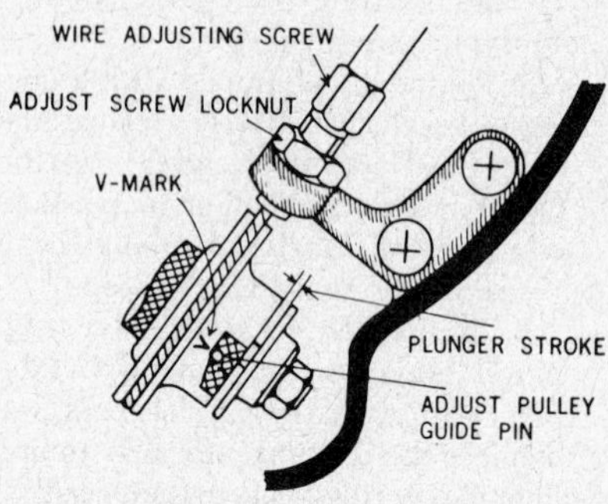

Single-cylinder engine oil pump adjustment marks

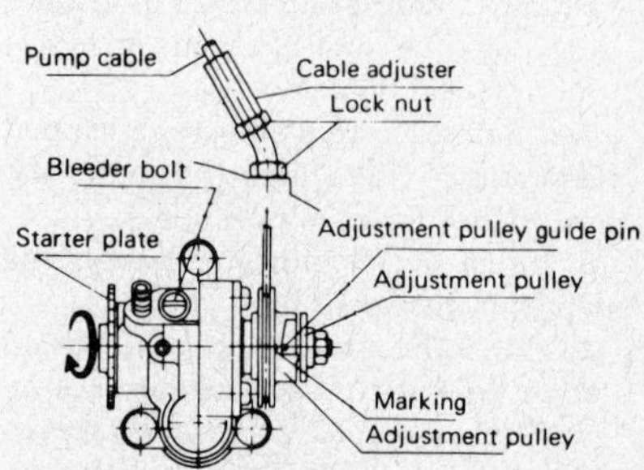

Twin-cylinder engine oil pump alignment marks

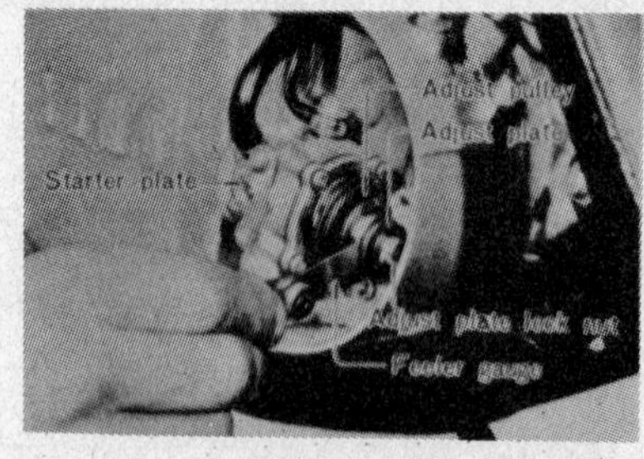

Oil pump minimum stroke adjustment

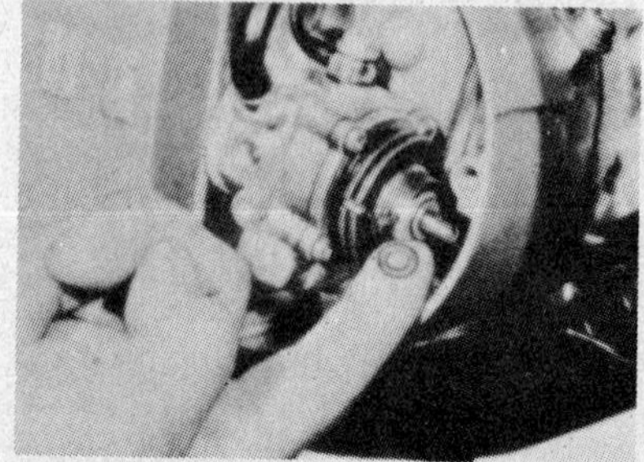

Add as many shims as necessary to achieve correct minimum stroke

TUNE-UP SPECIFICATIONS

	Breaker Point Gap (mm)	Ignition ① BTDC Adv.	Spark Plug (NGK)	Spark Plug Gap (mm)	Spark Plug Tight. Torque (ft lbs)	Carb. ② Air Screw (turns)	Idle Speed (rpm)	Throttle ③ Cable Clear. 'A'/'B' (mm)	Oil Pump Adjust-ment Position	Minimum Oil Pump Stroke (mm)
U5, U5L	0.20-0.40	1.7-1.9	B7HZ	0.6-0.7	18	1¼	1200-1400	0.0/1.5	Half Open	0.22-0.26
U5E	0.20-0.40	1.7-1.9	B7HZ	0.6-0.7	18	1¼	1200-1400	0.0/1.5	Half Open	0.22-0.26
U7E	0.30-0.40	1.7-1.9	B6HS	0.5-0.6	18	1¾	1200-1400	——	Idle	0.25-0.29
MJ2, MJ2T	0.30-0.35	2.1-2.3	B7HZ	0.6-0.7	18	1¾	1200-1400	0.0/1.5	——	——
YJ1	0.20-0.40	2.0-2.2	B7HZ	0.6-0.7	18	1½	1200-1400	0.0/1.5	——	——
Early YJ2	0.20-0.40	1.7-1.9	B7HZ	0.6-0.7	18	1½	1200-1400	0.0/1.5	Half Open	0.22-0.26
Late YJ2	0.20-0.40	1.7-1.9	B8HC	0.6-0.7	18	1¾	1200-1400	0.0/1.5	Half Open	0.22-0.26
JT1	0.30-0.40	1.7-1.9	B7HS	0.5-0.6	18	1½	1200-1400	.75/1.5	Idle	0.20-0.25
JT2	0.30-0.40	1.7-1.9	B7HS	0.5-0.6	18	1¾	1200-1400	——	Half Open	0.30-0.35
MG1T	0.20-0.40	2.0-2.2	B7HZ	0.6-0.7	18	1½	1200-1400	0.0/1.5	——	——
YG1, YG1T	0.20-0.40	2.0-2.2	B7HZ	0.6-0.7	18	1½	1200-1400	0.0/1.5	——	——
YG1K, YG1KT	0.20-0.40	2.0-2.2	B7HZ	0.6-0.7	18	1¾	1200-1400	0.0/1.5	Half Open	0.22-0.26
YG5T	0.30-0.35	1.7-1.9	B7HZ	0.6-0.7	18	1½	1200-1400	0.0/1.5	Half Open	0.20-0.25
G5S	0.30-0.35	1.7-1.9	B7HZ	0.5-0.6	18	1¾	1200-1400	.75/1.5	Half Open	0.20-0.25
G6S	0.30-0.35	1.7-1.9	B7HZ	0.5-0.6	18	1¾	1200-1400	.75/1.5	Half Open	0.20-0.25
G6SB	0.30-0.40	1.7-1.9	B7HS	0.5-0.6	18	1¾	1200-1400	.75/1.5	Half Open	0.20-0.25
HT1	0.30-0.40	1.7-1.9	B8HC	0.5-0.6	18	1¾	1300-1500	.75/1.5	Idle	0.20-0.25
HT1B	0.30-0.40	1.7-1.9	B8ES	0.5-0.6	18	1¾	1300-1500	.75/1.5	Idle	0.20-0.25
HS1	0.30-0.35	1.7-1.9	B7HZ	0.5-0.6	18	1½	1100-1200	.75/0.0	Idle	0.20-0.25
HS1B	0.30-0.40	1.7-1.9	B9HC	0.5-0.6	18	1½	1100-1200	.75/0.0	Idle	0.20-0.25
LS2	0.30-0.40	1.7-1.9	B7HS	0.5-0.6	18	1¾	1200-1400	——	Idle	0.20-0.25
YL2, YL2C	0.30-0.35	1.7-1.9	B7HZ	0.5-0.6	18	1½	1300-1500	0.0/1.5	Half Open	0.20-0.25
YL2CM	0.30-0.35	1.7-1.9	B8HC	0.5-0.6	18	1¾	1300-1500	0.0/1.5	Half Open	0.20-0.25
L5T, L5TA	0.30-0.35	1.7-1.9	B8HC	0.5-0.6	18	1¾	1300-1500	0.0/1.5	Half Open	0.20-0.25
LT2	0.30-0.40	1.7-1.9	B8HS	0.5-0.6	18	1¾	1100-1200	——	Idle	0.20-0.25
YL1, YL1E	0.30-0.35	1.7-1.9	B7HZ	0.5-0.6	18	2½	1200-1500	0.0/1.5	Idle	0.20-0.25
YA5	0.30-0.35	2.3-2.8	B7H	0.6-0.7	18	1¾	1300-1500	0.0/1.5	——	——
YA6	0.30-0.35	2.5-2.6	B7HZ	0.6-0.7	18	1¼	1300-1500	0.0/1.5	Half Open	0.22-0.26
AT1	0.30-0.35	1.7-1.9	B8E	0.5-0.6	18	1½	1400-1500	.75/1.5	Idle	0.20-0.25
AT1B	0.30-0.35	1.7-1.9	B8E	0.5-0.6	18	1½	1400-1500	.75/1.5	Idle	0.20-0.25
AT1C, AT2	0.30-0.40	1.7-1.9	B8ES	0.5-0.6	18	⑤	1400-1500	.75/1.5	Idle	0.20-0.25
YAS1(c)	0.30-0.35	1.7-1.9	B9HC	0.5-0.6	18	1¾	1200-1400	.75/0.0	Idle	0.20-0.25
AS2C	0.30-0.35	1.7-1.9	B9HC	0.5-0.6	18	1¾	1200-1400	.75/0.0	Idle	0.20-0.25
CT1	0.30-0.35	1.7-1.9	B8E	0.5-0.6	18	1½	1400-1500	.75/1.5	Idle	0.20-0.25
CT1B	0.30-0.35	1.7-1.9	B8E	0.5-0.6	18	1½	1400-1500	.75/1.5	Idle	0.20-0.25
CT1C, CT2	0.30-0.40	1.7-1.9	B8ES	0.5-0.6	18	⑥	1400-1500	.75/1.5	Idle	0.20-0.25
YCS1	0.30-0.35	1.7-1.9	B8HC	0.6-0.7	18	2	1100-1200	.75/0.0	Idle	0.20-0.25
YCS1C	0.30-0.35	1.7-1.9	B8HC	0.5-0.7	18	2¼	1100-1200	.75/0.0	Idle	0.20-0.25
CS3C	0.30-0.35	1.7-1.9	B9HC	0.5-0.6	18	2¼	1100-1200	.75/0.0	Idle	0.20-0.25
CS3B, CS5	0.30-0.40	1.7-1.9	⑦	0.5-0.6	18	2	1100-1200	.75/0.0	Idle	0.20-0.25
DT1	0.30-0.35	3.1-3.3	B7E	0.5-0.6	18	1½	1400-1500	.75/0.0	Idle	0.20-0.25
DT1S	0.30-0.35	3.1-3.3	B7E(N)	0.5-0.6	18	1½	1400-1500	.75/0.0	Idle	0.20-0.25
DT1B	0.30-0.35	3.1-3.3	B7E(N)	0.5-0.6	18	1½	1400-1500	.75/0.0	Idle	0.20-0.25
DT1C	0.30-0.35	3.1-3.3	B7E	0.5-0.6	18	1½	1400-1500	.75/0.0	Idle	0.20-0.25
DT1E, DT2	0.30-0.40	3.1-3.3	B8ES	0.5-0.6	18	1½	1400-1500	.75/0.0	Idle	0.20-0.25
YD3	0.30-0.35	2.1-2.3	B7HZ	0.6-0.7	18	1¼	1100-1200	0.0/1.5	——	——
YDT1	0.30-0.35	2.1-2.3	B7HZ	0.6-0.7	18	1¼	1100-1200	0.0/1.5	——	——
YDS1	0.30-0.35	2.5-3.0	B6H	0.6-0.7	18	1½	1100-1200	0.0/1.5	——	——
YDS2	0.30-0.35	1.7-1.8	B7HZ	0.6-0.7	18	1½	1100-1200	0.0/1.5	——	——
YDS3	0.30-0.35	1.8-1.9	B77HC	0.6-0.7	18	1½	1100-1200	.75/1.5	Idle	0.22-0.26
YDS3C	0.30-0.35	1.7-1.9	B8HC	0.6-0.7	18	1½	1100-1200	.75/1.5	Idle	0.22-0.26
YDS5	0.30-0.35	1.9-1.9	B8HC	0.6-0.7	18	1½	1000-1200	.75/0.0	Idle	0.20-0.25
DS6/DS6C	0.30-0.35	1.7-1.9	B7HZ	0.5-0.6	18	1½	1100-1200	.75/0.0	Idle	0.20-0.25
DS6B	0.30-0.35	1.7-1.9	B9HC	0.5-0.6	18	1½	1100-1200	.75/0.0	Idle	0.20-0.25
DS7	0.30-0.40	1.9-2.1	B8HS	0.5-0.6	18	1½	1100-1200	——	Idle	0.20-0.25

	Breaker Point Gap (mm)	Ignition ① BTDC Adv.	Spark Plug (NGK)	Spark Plug Gap (mm)	Spark Plug Tight. Torque (ft lbs)	Carb. ② Air Screw (turns)	Idle Speed (rpm)	Throttle ③ Cable Clear. 'A'/'B' (mm)	Oil Pump Adjust-ment Position	Minimum Oil Pump Stroke (mm)
YM1	0.30-0.35	1.9-2.0	B8HC	0.6-0.7	18	1½	1100-1200	.75/0.0	Idle	0.20-0.25
YM2C	0.30-0.35	2.0-2.2	B8HC	0.6-0.7	18	1½	1100-1200	.75/0.0	Idle	0.20-0.25
YR1	0.30-0.35	2.0-2.2	B8HC	0.6-0.7	18	2¼	1000-1200	.75/0.0	Idle	0.20-0.25
YR2, YR2C	0.30-0.35	2.0-2.2	B9HC	0.5-0.6	18	1½	1200-1400	.75/0.0	Idle	0.20-0.25
R3C	0.30-0.35	2.0-2.2	B9HC	0.5-0.6	18	1½	1200-1400	.75/0.0	Idle	0.20-0.25
R5/R5B/R5C	0.30-0.40	1.9-2.1	⑧	0.5-0.6	18	⑨	1300-1400	.75/0.0	Idle	0.20-0.25
RT1	0.30-0.35	3.3-3.5	B7E	0.5-0.6	18	1¼	1400-1500	.75/0.0	Idle	0.20-0.25
RT1B/RT2	0.30-0.40	2.8-3.0	B9ES	0.5-0.6	18	⑩	1400-1500	.75/0.0	Idle	0.20-0.25

① Given in mm except where indicated in degrees.
② May vary according to atmospheric conditions.
③ Cable 'A' at throttle grip; cable 'B' at carburetor top.
④ Cold.
⑤ AT1—1½; AT2—1¾
⑥ CT1—1½; CT2—2
⑦ CS3—B9HC; CS5—B9HS
⑧ R5/R5B—B9HC; R5C—B9HS
⑨ R5/R5B—1¾; R5C—1¼
⑩ RT1—1¾; RT2—1½

MAINTENANCE ITEMS

Oil Changes and Lubrication

AUTOLUBE

Keep a daily check on the Autolube reservoir and refill it as necessary. If two-stroke oil isn't available, use one of the following:

American Permalube SAE 30W
Atlantic Atlantic Aviation SAE 30W
Castrol Heavy Duty SAE 30W
Gulf Gulfpride SAE 30W
Humble ESSO, ENCO, Humble SAE 30W
Kendall Dual Action, Super Duty SAE 30W
Mobil Mobil A SAE 30W
Phillips Sixty-Six SAE 30W
Pure Super Duty Purelube SAE 30W
Richfield Richlube Premium SAE 30W
Shell Shell X-100 SAE 30W
Texaco Havoline SAE 30W

These are all good down to 18° F or less. Below 18° F, use a premium grade SAE 10W/30.

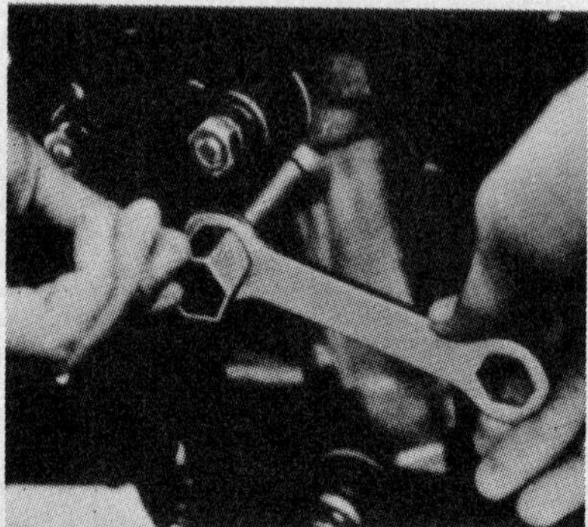

Draining the two-stroke transmission. On earlier twins the drain plug is located at the side of the crankcase, beneath the case cover

TRANSMISSION

Drain the oil into a clean container while the engine is hot, then slowly pour it out of the container and look for foreign matter. When you fill the transmission back up again, use a container graduated in cc's or ounces and remember to compensate for oil that's still clinging to the gears. Use a premium grade SAE 10W/30.

FRONT FORKS

Change the front fork oil at service intervals or when you want to change the fork's damping qualities.

1. Remove the drain screw at the bottom of each fork leg.
2. Drain the oil, then pump the forks a few times to make sure the tubes are clear.
3. Reinstall the screws and remove the fork cap at the top of each leg.
4. Add the proper amount of oil to the inner tube, then reinstall the fork caps and tighten them up snugly.

Under normal conditions, the two-stroke street models should use 10W/30 oil, the trail bikes 10W/30, and the XS1/XS2 30W or 20W (if temperatures are below 40°F). If want stiffer or softer damping, select an appropriately heavier or lighter viscosity oil.

NOTE: *The racing-type forks on the Enduro models are also equipped with an air valve to help adjust damping qualities.*

General Maintenance and Adjustments

AIR CLEANER

Wash the air cleaner at least once every two thousand miles (foam type), or blow it out with compressed air every 3000 miles (paper type); more often if you ride dusty roads or trails.

If you have the foam rubber Filtron-

Front fork oil drain screw

Front fork cap removal

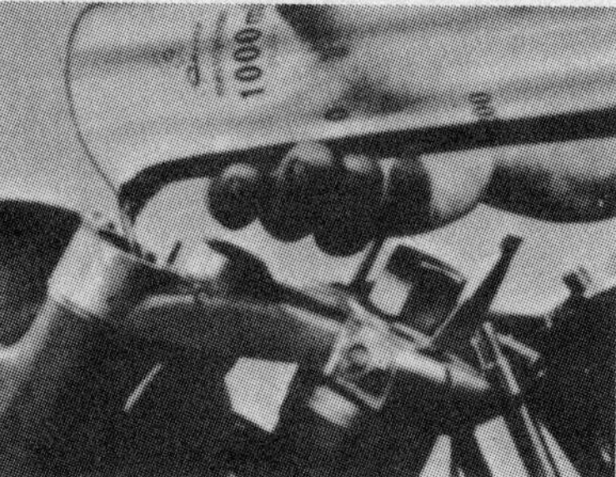

Use a graduated container when refilling the front fork legs

type cleaner element, wash it in gasoline or kerosene, then in hot soapy water. Wring out the element and let it dry completely, then place it in a container full of oil. After it is saturated, squeeze out as much oil as possible and then reinstall. This oil/foam air cleaner is the most effective available, IF it is kept clean.

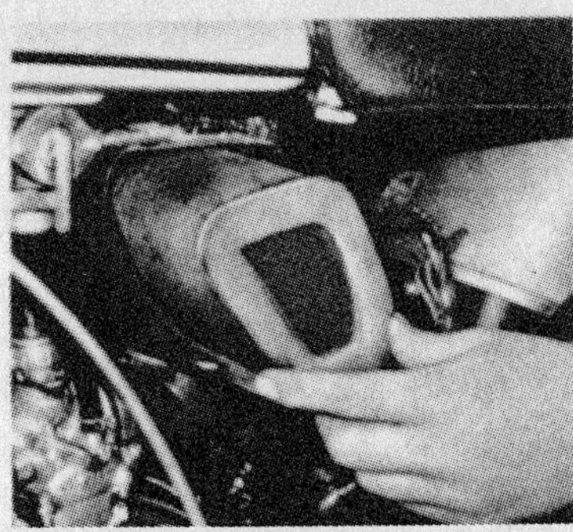

Filtron-type air cleaner element removal. On some models, access to the air cleaner is under the seat

Paper air cleaner element removal. The air cleaner is mounted either behind the side cover or directly to the carburetor(s)

GENERATOR BRUSHES

Begin regular inspection after 4000 miles. Dust from the generator brushes tends to collect on the mica undercut, so if necessary, polish up the commutator surface with emery cloth and remove any collected dust with a knife or screwdriver blade.

Polishing the generator commutator

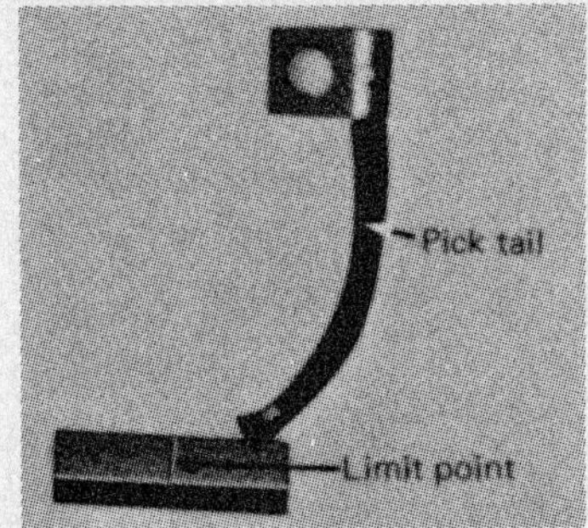

Brush wear limits are usually indicated by a line drawn on the brush. See the "Electrical Systems" section for wear limits

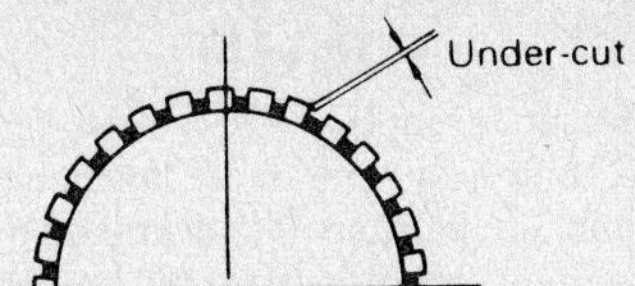

The arrows indicate the mica undercut. See the "Electrical Systems" section for wear limits

Removing brush dust from the mica undercut

DRUM BRAKE ADJUSTMENT

If the lever feels soft or spongy, chances are that both shoes aren't making contact at the same time. To correct this condition or after installing new shoes:

1. Disconnect the brake cable at the hand lever.
2. Loosen the locknut on the rod between the cam operating arms (see illustration).
3. Turn the rod so that the operating arms spread apart enough to take up all slack, but no more.
4. Tighten the locknut.
5. Connect the cable back to the lever, then spin the wheel and turn the cable adjuster. Listen at the drum and you should hear both shoes make contact at the same time. If they don't, readjust the rod and check again.
6. When the shoes are set correctly, backoff the adjuster until you have ¼ in. of slack in the cable.
7. Make the final adjustment at the hand lever to suit the rider, but keep the lever-to-bracket gap at around ⅛ in.

Adjust the rear brake at the rod (or cable) end to obtain approximately 1 in. pedal freeplay. Make this adjustment at regular intervals with the front brake and anytime the rear wheel is removed or the chain adjusted.

Arrow indicates the front brake cam operating rod locknut

NOTE: *Don't set brake clearances too close when cold; linings may drag and become glazed when warm.*

CLUTCH

Check the clutch adjustment periodically or whenever the clutch slips or grabs. There are two points of adjustment and they should be set in proper order:

1. Clutch pushrod

a. Remove the access plug on the clutch housing.

NOTE: *On some models, the right-hand case cover must be removed.*

b. Loosen the pushrod setscrew locknut.

c. Turn the setscrew IN until it bottoms against the pushrod, then back it OUT one-quarter turn.

d. Tighten the locknut and reinstall the access plug or case cover.

2. Clutch cable

Set the lever-to-bracket clearance at ⅛ in. by loosening the locknut, turning the adjuster wheel for the correct gap, then retightening the locknut.

NOTE: *On some models, the clutch cable adjustment is made at the other end of the cable, where it enters the crankcase or case cover.*

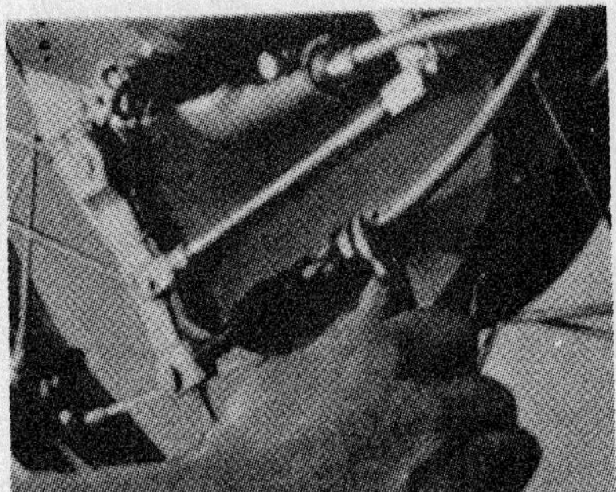

Backing off the front brake cable adjuster

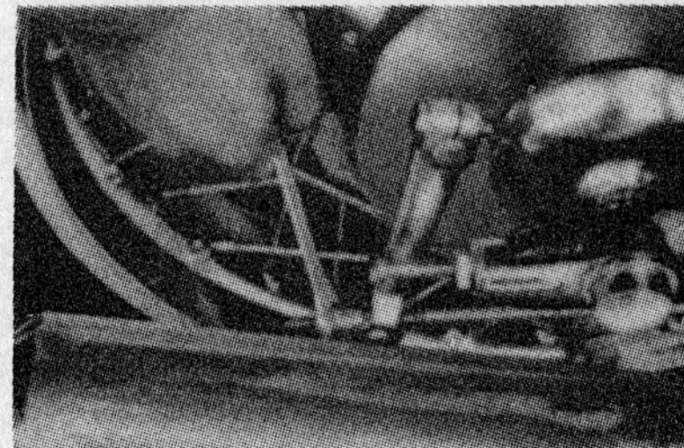

Rear brake adjustment

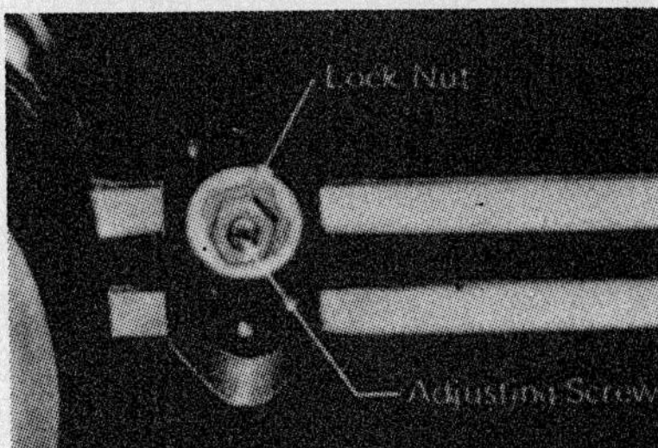

Clutch pushrod adjustment through case cover access hole

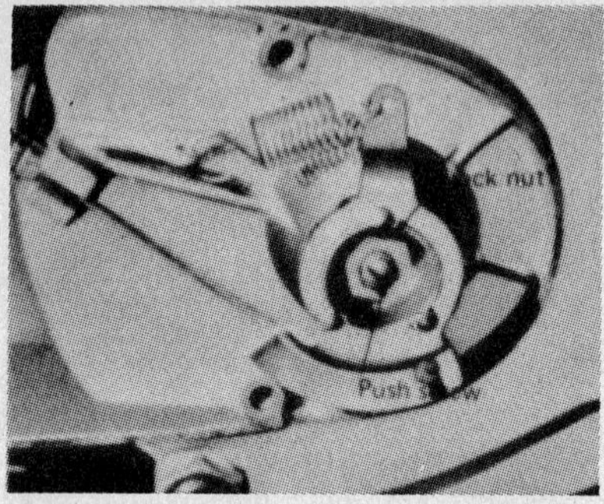

Clutch pushrod adjustment with case cover removed

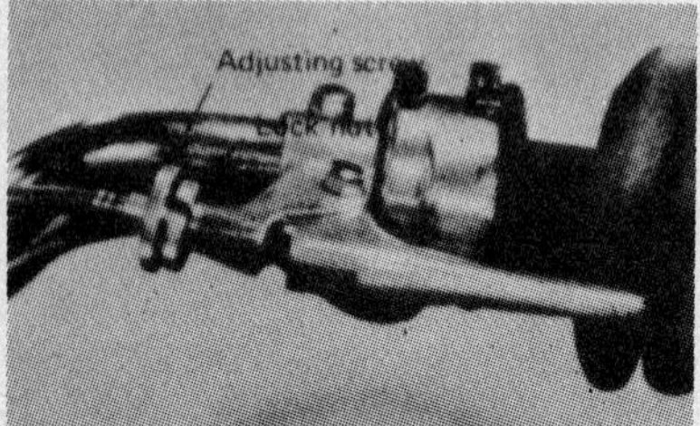

Clutch cable adjustment at the hand lever

CHAIN

Measure freeplay with a rider on the bike, but only one foot touching the ground for balance. Total up-and-down movement of the chain should be approximately ½–¾ in.; more if you ride two-up often:

To adjust the chain:

1. Remove the cotter pin and loosen the rear axle nut.
2. Loosen the chain adjuster locknut on each side.
3. Turn both adjuster bolts an EQUAL amount to achieve correct freeplay. Make certain the alignment marks on the swing arm ends are the same to ensure correct rear wheel positioning.

NOTE: *Both wheels must be on the ground, and someone should be on the seat at the time of adjustment to compensate for swingarm movement.*

4. Tighten the adjuster bolt locknuts, secure the rear axle nut and install a new cotter pin.

Clutch cable adjustment at the case

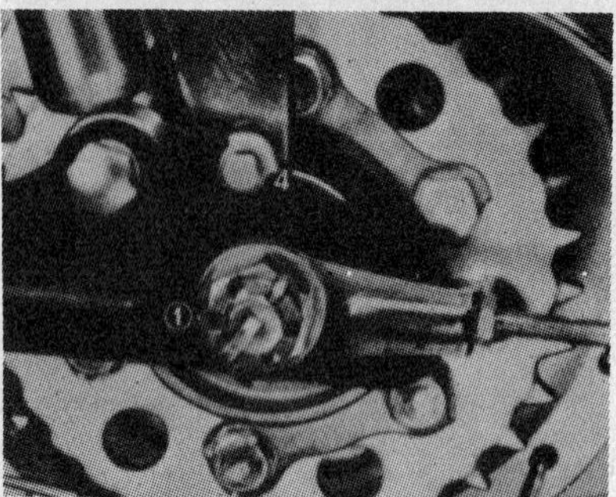

Chain adjustment points: Rear axle nut (1), adjuster locknut (2), adjuster bolt (3), alignment marks (4)

PERIODIC MAINTENANCE (After First 3000 Miles)

These are normal service intervals. In cases of hard use, maintenance should be performed more often.

Daily (*before each riding*)
Check Autolube reservoir
Check tire pressures
Check chain freeplay
Check cables
Check brake operation
Check clutch operation

Weekly (*in hot weather*)
Check battery fluid level

Monthly (*in normal weather*)
Check battery fluid level

Bi-Monthly
Charge stored battery

Every 200 miles
Lubricate chain

Every 2000 miles
Change gearbox oil (two-strokes)
Lubricate grease fittings
Lubricate cables
Soak chain in solvent
Adjust brakes
Adjust clutch
Tighten nuts and bolts
Wash Filtron air cleaner
Perform complete tune-up

Every 3000 miles
Replace paper air cleaner

Every 4000 miles
Change front fork oil
De-carbonize
Check generator brushes
Check brake linings
Clean carburetors

MAINTENANCE DATA

	Fuel Tank Capacity (Gal)	Autolube Oil Capacity (Qt)	Gearbox Oil Capacity (Qt)	Front Fork① Oil Capacity (oz/cc)	Chain Freeplay (in.)	Tire Pressure Front/Rear (psi)
U5, U5L, U5E	0.90	1.60	0.50	—	1/2-5/8	22/28
U7E	1.20	1.50	0.65	—	25/32	20/28
MJ2, MJ2T	0.90	—	0.50	130/4.4	1/2-5/8	22/28
YJ1	1.38	—	0.50	—	1/2-5/8	22/28
YJ2	1.38	1.16	0.50	130/4.4	1/2-5/8	22/28
JT1, JT2L, JT2M	1.10	1.10	0.64	②	25/32	20/28
MG1, MG1T	0.90	—	0.50	130/4.4	1/2-5/8	22/28
YG1, YG1T	1.72	—	0.50	130/4.4	1/2-5/8	22/28
YG1K, YG1TK, YGS1, YGS1T	1.72	1.15	0.50	130/4.4	1/2-5/8	22/28
YG5T	1.60	1.48	0.65	140/4.7	1/2-5/8	25/27
G5S	1.60	1.50	0.65	③	25/32	26/28
G6S	1.60	1.50	0.65	130/4.4	25/32	26/28
G6SB, GTS	1.60	1.50	0.65	③	25/32	20/28
HT1, HT1B	1.70	1.30	0.75	140/4.7	25/32	14/17
HS1, HS1B, LS2	2.00	④	0.85	147/5.0	25/32	20/28

	Fuel Tank Capacity (Gal)	Autolube Oil Capacity (Qt)	Gearbox Oil Capacity (Qt)	Front Fork① Oil Capacity (oz/cc)	Chain Freeplay (in.)	Tire Pressure Front/Rear (psi)
YL2, YL2C, YL2CM	2.20	1.70	0.75	145/4.9	1/2-5/8	25/27
L5T, L5TA	1.80	1.50	0.65	140/4.7	25/32	26/28
LT2	1.60	1.30	0.75	136/4.6	25/32	14/17
YL1, YL1E	1.95	1.16	0.75	130/4.4	1/2-5/8	25/27
YA5	2.27	——	1.05	180/6.1	5/8-3/4	22/28
YA6	2.38	1.90	1.40	170/5.8	5/8-3/4	22/28
AT1, AT1B, AT1C, AT2	1.89	1.27	0.78	⑤	25/32	14/17
YAS1, YAS1C	2.50	1.59	0.85	160/5.4	1/2-5/8	25/27
AS2C	2.00	1.59	0.85	160/5.4	25/32	26/28
CT1, CT1B, CT1C, CT2	1.89	1.27	0.78	⑤	25/32	14/17
YCS1	3.4	2.1	0.85	170/5.8	25/32	26/28
YCS1C	3.0	2.0	0.85	170/5.8	25/32	26/28
CS3C, CS3B, CS5	2.4	2.0	0.85	⑤	25/32	26/28
DT1, DT1B, DT1C	2.5	1.7	1.06	210/7.1	25/32	14/17
DT1E	2.5	1.7	1.06	175/5.9	25/32	13/16
YD3	3.2	——	1.25	200/6.7	5/8-3/4	22/28
YDT1	4.13	——	1.25	200/6.7	5/8-3/4	22/28
YDS1, YDS2	4.13	——	1.50	200/6.7	5/8-3/4	22/28
Early YDS3, YDS3C	3.70	1.70	1.50	200/6.7	5/8-3/4	22/28
Late YDS3, YDS3C	3.70	1.70	1.75	200/6.7	5/8-3/4	22/28
YDS5	4.00	2.50	1.75	200/6.7	5/8-3/4	22/28
DS6, DS6C, DS6B	2.90	1.60	1.75	200/6.7	25/32	26/28
YM1	3.70	1.70	1.75	200/6.7	5/8-3/4	22/28
YM2C	4.00	2.50	1.75	200/6.7	5/8-3/4	22/28
YR1	4.50	3.25	1.27	240/8.1	5/8-3/4	22/28
YR2, YR2C	3.80	3.40	1.27	240/8.1	5/8-3/4	22/28
R3C	4.00	3.40	1.27	240/8.1	25/32	23/28
R5, RSB, R5C, DS7	3.20	2.10	1.60	145/4.9	25/32	22/28
RT1	2.50	1.70	1.06	210/7.1	25/32	20/24
RT1B, RT2	2.50	1.70	1.06	175/5.9	25/32	13/16

① Each leg
② Right leg—97cc (3.3 oz), left leg—120cc (4.1 oz)
③ Right leg—154cc (5.2 oz), left leg—136cc (4.6 oz)
④ HS1—1.6; LS2—1.5
⑤ AT1/CT1—150cc (5.1 oz); AT2/CT2—120cc (4.1 oz)

ENGINE AND TRANSMISSION

Engine Removal

All Models With Rotary-Valve Engines Except YG5T, L5T And The JT1/JT2 Mini Enduro

1. Warm up the engine for a few minutes, then drain the gearbox oil. Reinstall the drain plug(s).

2. Remove the exhaust pipe ring nut, using the special wrench.

Removing the exhaust pipe ring nut

3. If the exhaust pipe and muffler are connected by a flange ring nut, loosen the nut and swing the exhaust pipe out of the way. If the exhaust pipe and muffler are one unit, remove all muffler mounting bolts and lift off the entire assembly.

5. Remove the left crankcase cover.

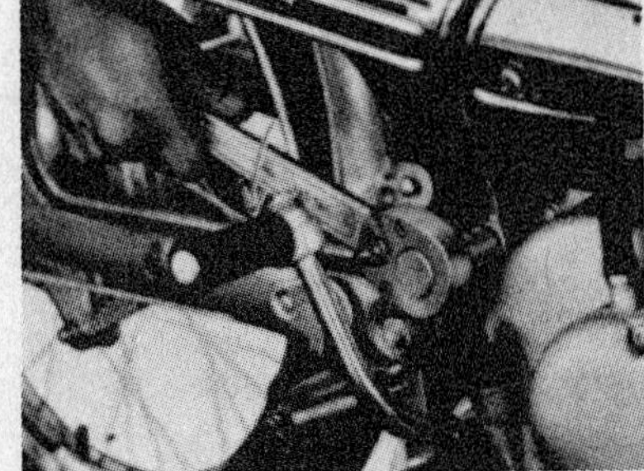

Removing the exhaust pipe and muffler as an assembly

6. If equipped with a magneto:

a. Disconnect the wiring harness at its center connector (behind side cover or under seat).

b. Remove the magneto flywheel, using the special puller tool.

Removing the gearshift pedal

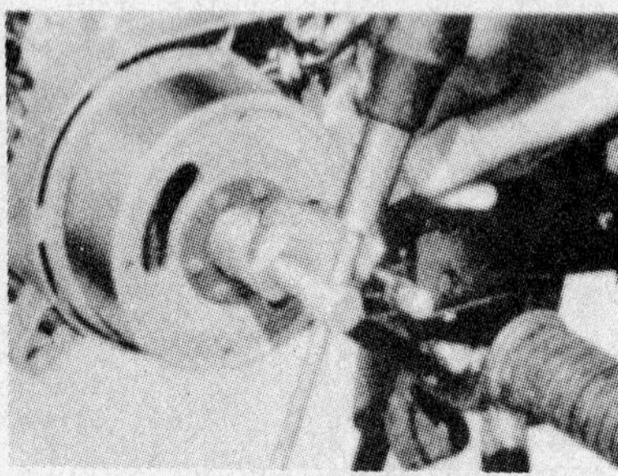
Removing the flywheel magneto

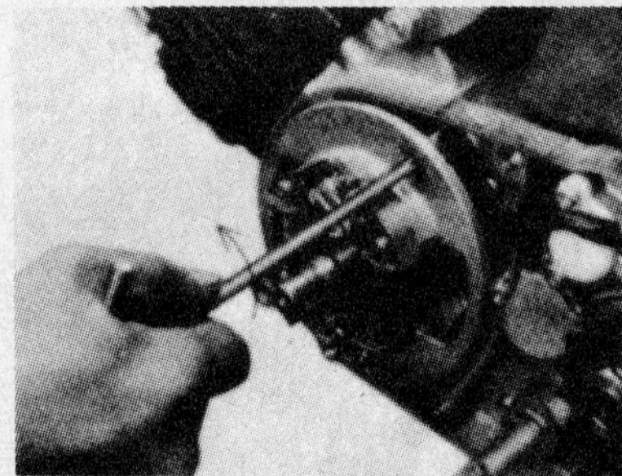
Removing the magneto base plate

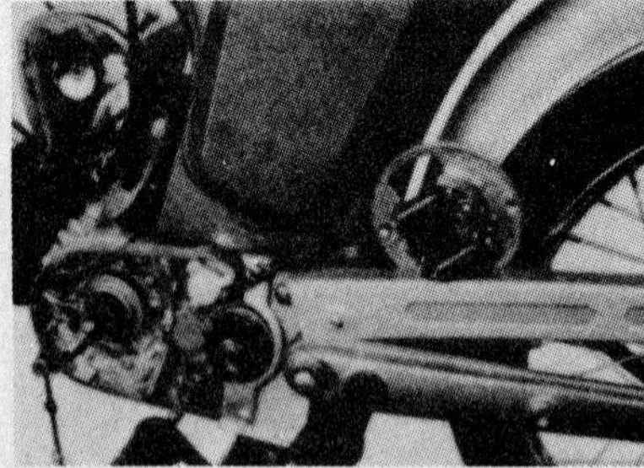
Keep the magneto base plate out of the way for the remaining steps of engine removal

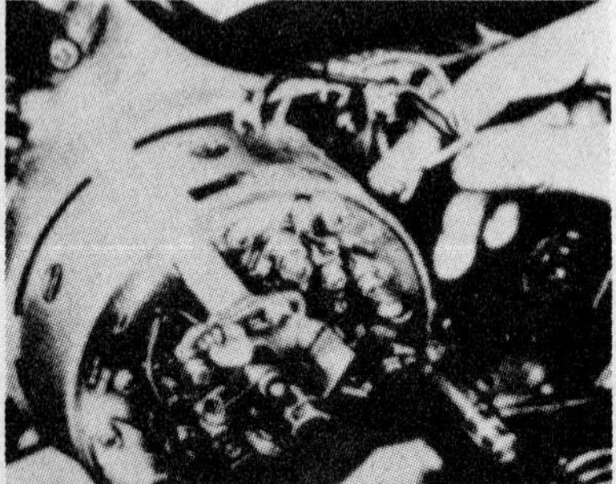
Disconnecting the DC generator wiring harness

c. Remove the phillips-head mounting screws and the magneto base plate.

d. Tie the magneto base plate to the frame, somewhere out of the way.

7. If equipped with a generator:

a. Disconnect the wiring harness terminals at the generator.

NOTE: *On some early models, the wiring harness must be disconnected in the battery compartment because the generator terminals are soldered.*

b. On models equipped with a governor, remove the mounting bolt and the governor assembly.

c. Remove the attaching screws and the generator yoke assembly.

d. Remove the armature bolt and breaker can.

e. Remove the generator armature, using the special puller bolt.

8. Pry out the crankshaft Woodruff key, using a narrow straight-slot screwdriver.

9. If the machine is equipped with a fully enclosed chain, remove the lower half of the cover.

10. Disconnect the master link and remove the drive chain. This is a good time to give the chain a solvent soak.

11. Remove the carburetor/oil pump cover.

12. Make sure the fuel petcock is shut off, then disconnect and plug the fuel line at the carburetor.

13. Remove the attaching screw at the front of the crankcase, then lift out the carburetor. To separate the throttle cable from the carburetor, remove the knurled cap and pull out the throttle slide.

NOTE: *If no carburetor repairs are needed, leave the fuel line and throttle cable connected, and tie the assembly out of the way.*

14. Disconnect the oil supply line at the Autolube tank and cover the fitting with a short piece of plugged hose.

15. Turn the oil pump pulley against its spring and disconnect the cable, then remove the adjusting bracket screws and tie the cable and bracket out of the way.

16. On models with a manual clutch, remove the clutch adjusting screw, if necessary, then the clutch arm and spring. Disconnect the cable from the arm and spring, then unscrew the cable adjustment nut on the crankcase cover and pull the cable end through. Tie it out of the way.

17. Remove the air cleaner element and housing, if necessary, or disconnect the rubber elbow at the housing or case cover.

18. Disconnect the spark plug lead.

19. Remove the two upper engine mounting bolts and loosen the footrest mounting bolt.

20. Hold the engine tilted slightly

Removing the DC generator armature bolt and breaker cam

Removing the crankshaft woodruff key

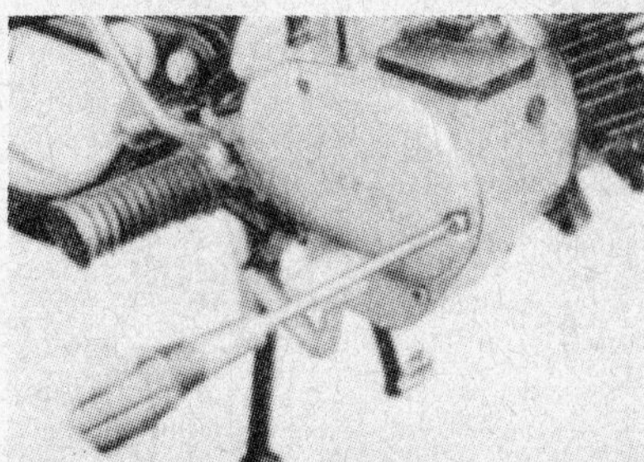
Removing the carburetor/oil pump cover

Removing the carburetor securing screw

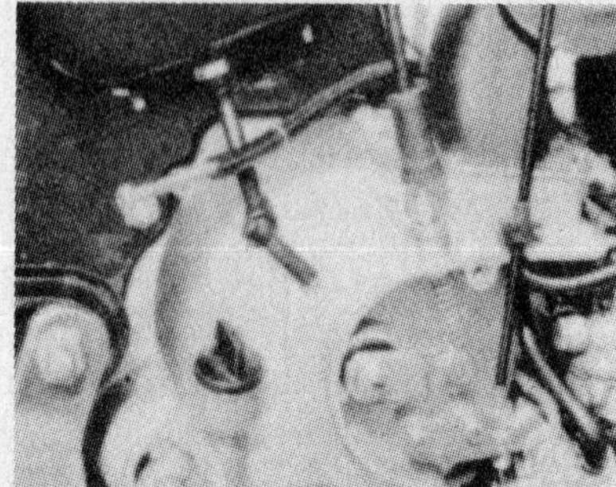
An extra piece of oil line tied in a knot will serve to plug the Autolube tank

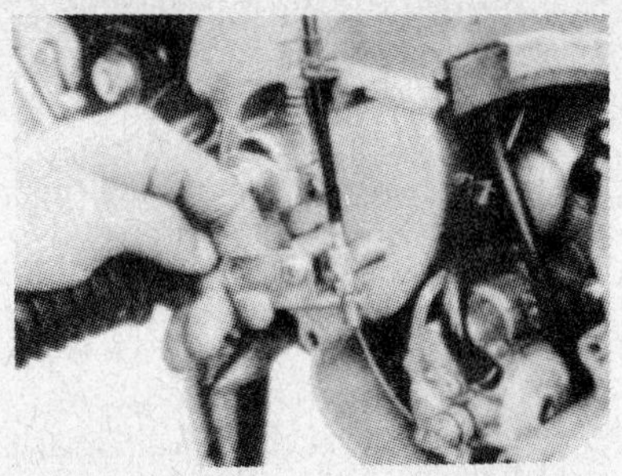

Disconnect the oil pump cable and adjuster bracket as an assembly

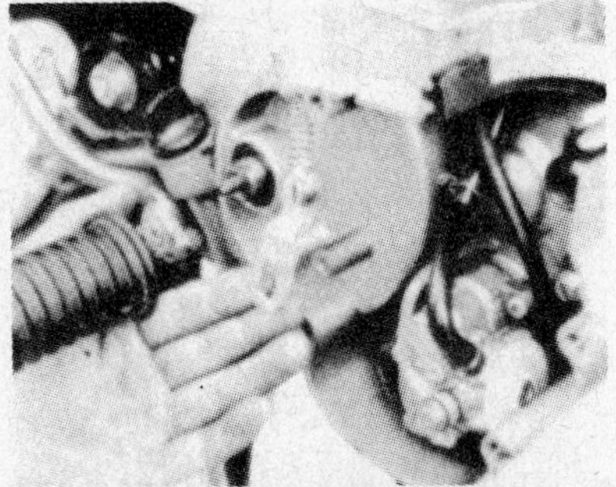

Disconnecting the clutch arm and spring

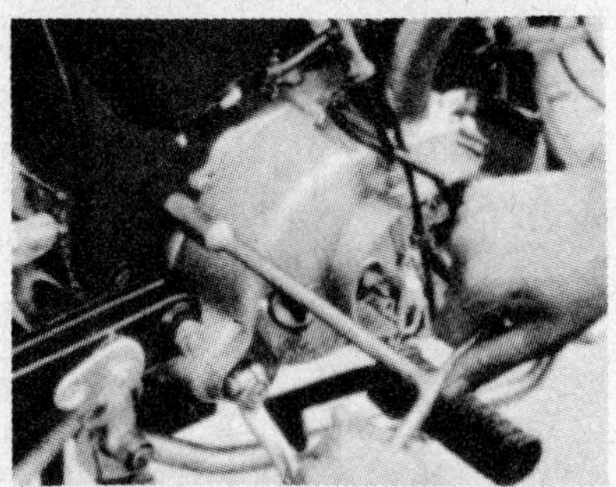

Removing one of the upper mounting bolts

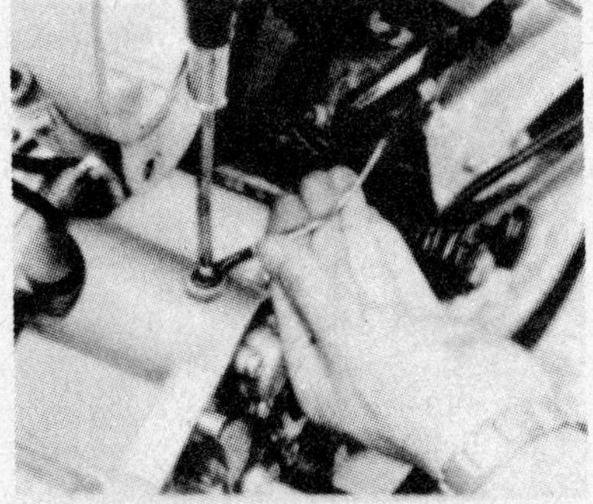

Disconnecting the neutral switch wire

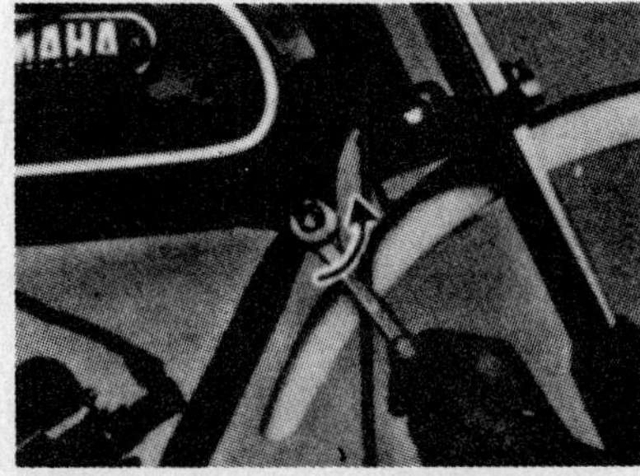

JT1 gas tank front mounting bolt

downward and disconnect the neutral switch wire. This is a good time to make certain nothing remains connected or is hanging in the way.

21. Support the bottom of the engine and remove the footrest mounting bolt. Lift the unit out of the frame.

YG5T And L5T Models

This removal procedure is basically the same as the preceding, but first the downtube support and engine protector (bash plate) must be removed.

JT1/JT2 Mini Enduro

The JT1 engine is mounted in a double-loop cradle frame (same as full sized Enduros). The removal procedure is basically the same as for the other rotary-valve singles, with the exception of the following points:

1. Before removing the muffler assembly, the seat mounting pin must be removed and the seat pulled back and off.
2. Also remove the gas tank front mounting bolt and lift off the tank. Remember to plug the fuel line.
3. Disconnect the magneto wiring underneath the gas tank.
4. Disconnect the neutral switch wiring before removing the engine mounting bolts.

Full Size Enduro Models

1. Warm up the engine, then drain the gearbox oil and reinstall the drain plug(s).
2. Remove the attaching ring nut, bolts, retaining springs, and the muffler/exhaust pipe assembly.
3. Remove the gearshift pedal.
4. Remove the lefthand case cover(s). Disconnect the clutch cable and tie it aside.
5. Disconnect the master link and remove the chain.
6. If equipped with a generator, disconnect the wiring harness terminals at the generator stator. If equipped with a magneto, disconnect the wiring harness at its center connector.
7. Remove the generator yoke assembly and armature, or the magneto flywheel as described in rotary-valve engine removal.
8. Disconnect the neutral switch wire.
9. Disconnect the spark plug lead and tie it out of the way.

NOTE: *On the RT1B, also disconnect the compression release cable.*

10. Remove the oil pump cover on the other side of the engine. Turn the pump pulley against its spring, then slip off the cable end.
11. Disconnect the oil pump supply line at the Autolube tank and cover the fitting with a short piece of plugged hose.

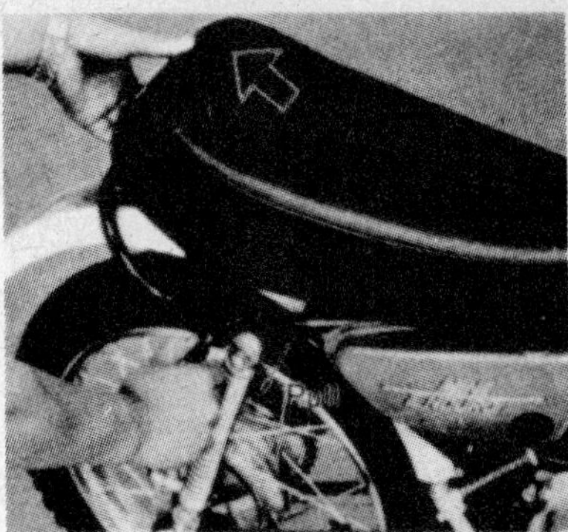

Removing the JT1 seat

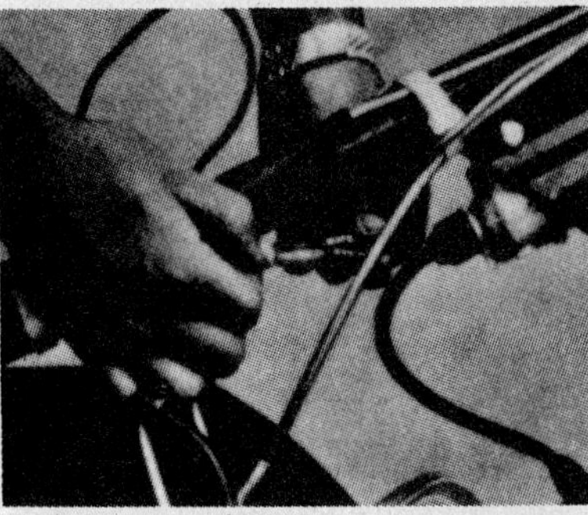

Disconnecting the JT1 magneto wiring

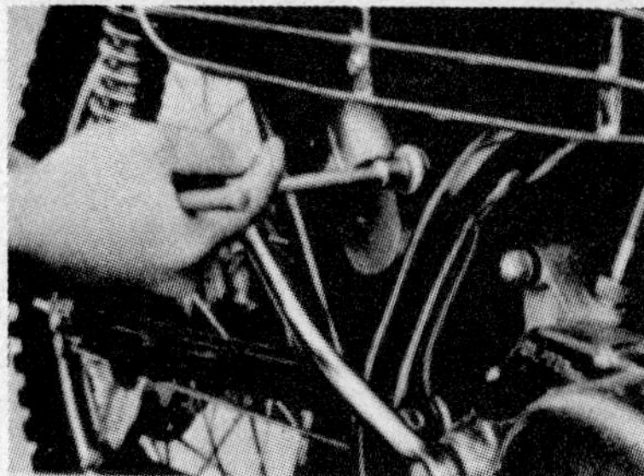

Muffler mounting bolt

Removing the front engine mounting bolt

12. Disconnect the tachometer drive cable.
13. Disconnect and plug the fuel line at the carburetor.
14. Remove the air cleaner rubber elbow.

NOTE: *On the HT1, remove the air cleaner assembly.*

15. Twist off the knurled carburetor cap after pulling back the rubber dust cover.
16. Pull out the carburetor throttle slide, then tie it and the throttle cable to the frame.

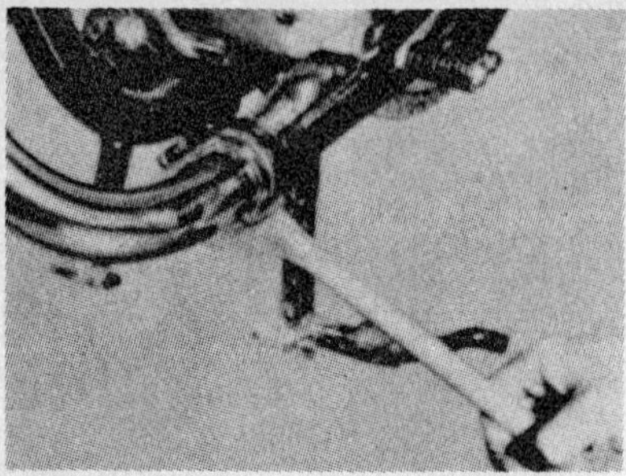

Unscrewing the exhaust pipe/muffler flange ring nut

On the R5, the clutch cable can remain attached to the case cover

17. Remove the attaching nuts or clamp screws and the carburetor.

18. Remove the engine mounting bolts and lift out the powerplant.

Twin Cylinder Engines

1. Warm up the engine and drain the gearbox oil, then reinstall the drain plug(s).

2. Remove the toolbox side cover.

3. Remove the exhaust pipe ring nut or stud nuts. If the exhaust pipe and muffler are connected by a flange ring nut, unscrew the nut and swing the exhaust pipes out of the way; if they cannot be separated, remove all attaching bolts and the entire exhaust assembly.

4. Remove the left footrest and the gearshift pedal.

NOTE: *On some models, both right and left footrests must be removed as an assembly; on others (such as the R5), there is sufficient clearance without removing either footrest.*

5. Remove all case covers.

6. Disconnect the clutch cable and tie it aside.

7. Disconnect the wiring harness at the generator terminals or the alternator center connector, and at the neutral switch.

8. Remove the yoke mounting screws and the yoke assembly.

9. Remove the armature bolt, governor, and breaker cam.

10. Remove the generator or alternator armature, using the special puller bolt.

11. Remove the crankshaft Woodruff key with a harrow slot-head screwdriver.

12. Disconnect the tachometer drive cable.

13. Disconnect the master link and remove the chain.

14. Turn the oil pump pulley against its spring, then slip out the end of the cable.

15. Unscrew the oil pump cable adjuster and pull the cable through the hole.

NOTE: *Some models have the oil pump cable situated between the crankcase and the case cover. On these machines, simply pull out the rubber grommet and remove the adjuster bracket screws. Then tie the cable and bracket assembly out of the way.*

16. Disconnect and plug the fuel lines at the carburetors.

17. Remove the attaching clamp screws and disconnect the air cleaner rubber elbows from the carburetors.

NOTE: *Remove the air cleaner assemblies on the HS1, YAS1, AS2 and early YDS models.*

18. Pull back the rubber dust covers and unscrew the knurled carburetor caps. Pull out the throttle slide assemblies and tie them out of the way (leave the cables attached).

19. Remove the attaching clamps or bolts and disconnect the starter jet linkage, then remove the carburetors. This is not really necessary, but if the engine is being torn down beyond the cylinder head, they will have to come off sooner or later.

20. Disconnect the spark plug leads.

21. On 250, 305, and 350cc models, remove the engine in the following manner:

a. Remove the four engine mounting bolts.

NOTE: *On the R5, also remove the upper rear mounting plate.*

b. Straddle the bike and hold the engine by the cylinder cooling fins on one side and by the kickstarter on the other.

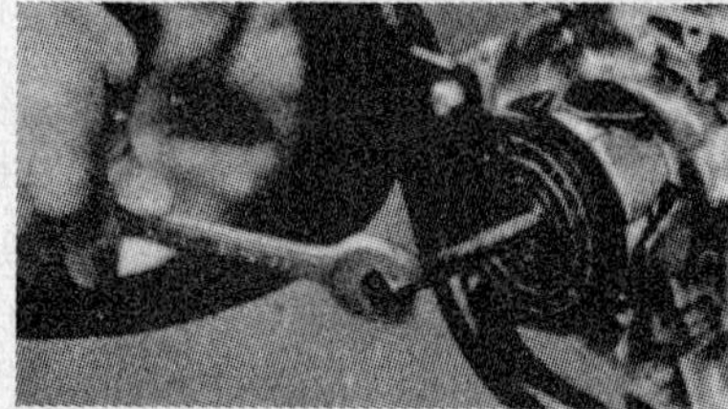

Removing the yoke assembly

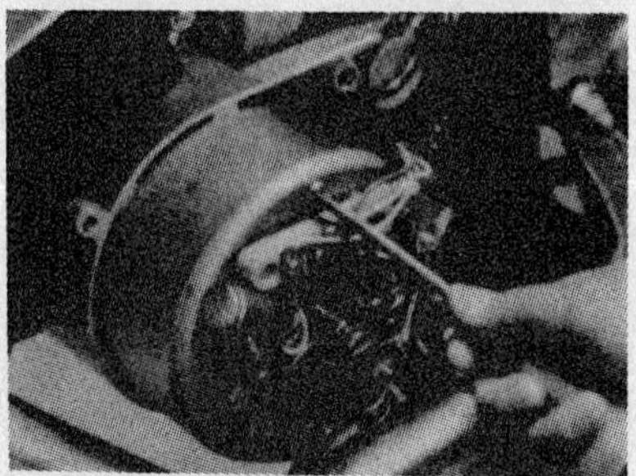

Removing the alternator armature

c. Pull the engine back slightly, then lift it out the left side of the frame.

22. On the 90, 125, 180, and 200cc models:

a. Support the bottom of the engine on a box or have a helper hold it up.

b. Remove all mounting bolts, then lift the engine up and out the left side of the frame.

23. On the 100cc YL1 models:

a. Loosen all engine mounting bolts.

b. Remove all but the lower downtube and the lower rear mounting bolts.

c. Hold up the front of the engine and remove the downtube mounting bolt, then swing the front support out of the way.

d. Let the engine tilt downward onto a box, then remove the lower rear mounting bolt.

ENGINE INSTALLATION

All Models

Installation is basically a reversal of the removal procedures, but the following points should be noted:

1. Apply a small amount of grease to the crankshaft before installing the magneto flywheel, alternator or generator armature; this will prevent them from freezing on the shaft.

2. When installing the carburetors, make certain that the manifold flange and carburetor slots (if so equipped) do NOT align.

3. Replace any worn exhaust pipe and muffler ring nut gaskets.

4. Make certain that the fuel and oil line circlips are properly seated.

5. Make certain that the engine mounting bolts are tightened down securely. If possible, use a torque wrench (see Torque Specifications at the end of this section).

6. After bleeding the oil pump and refilling the gearbox, check all points of adjustment—cables, chain, rear brake, ignition timing, carburetor synchronization, oil pump plunger stroke, etc.

Cylinder Head

ALL MODELS

Remove the spark plug and back off the nuts slowly in an X pattern, then lift off the head and gasket. Remove the carbon build-up with a blunt blade as described in Maintenance. Inspect the head for any cracks or signs of damage.

When installing the cylinder head, replace the gasket if it is old or damaged. Tighten the nuts up to torque specifications a little at a time in an X pattern.

Cylinder

ALL MODELS

Removal

Disconnect the oil line banjo fitting at the base of the cylinder, then tap the bottom cooling fins with a rubber mallet. Separate the cylinder from the crankcase and, as soon as there is enough room, stuff some CLEAN rags into the case opening. Lift off the cylinder and base gasket, being careful to hold the piston when it falls free of the cylinder.

Inspection

Scrape carbon accumulation out of the exhaust and transfer port area with a blunt blade. Also remove the carbon ridge at the top of the cylinder. If necessary, use #400 sandpaper in a crosshatch pattern.

Arrow indicates the oil line banjo fitting

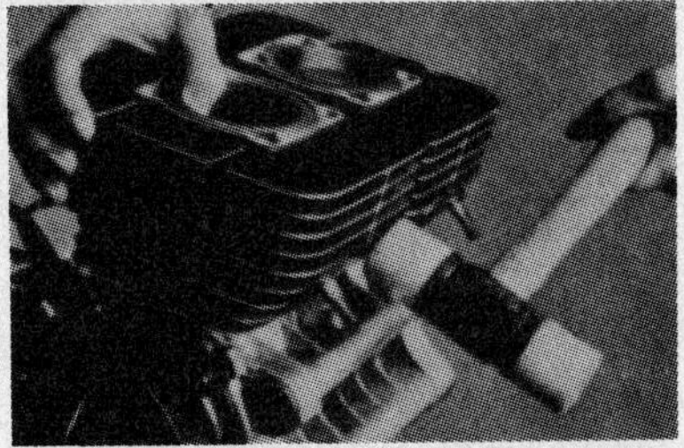

Tap lightly with a rubber mallet to remove the cylinder

Look closely for any cracks or seizure spots, then measure the cylinder with an inside-diameter micrometer or cylinder gauge.

Most wear occurs at the upper part of the cylinder due to piston side thrust and heat expansion characteristics. Therefore, the cylinder won't be perfectly cylindrical. Make eight measurements at the points indicated in the illustration, and, if the difference between the minimum and maximum diameters exceeds 0.05 mm (0.0019 in.), the cylinder should be rebored and honed.

Boring and Honing

The cylinder should be bored and then honed in a crosshatch pattern so that its minimum inside diameter will be equal to the replacement piston's maximum diameter PLUS the minimum piston-to-

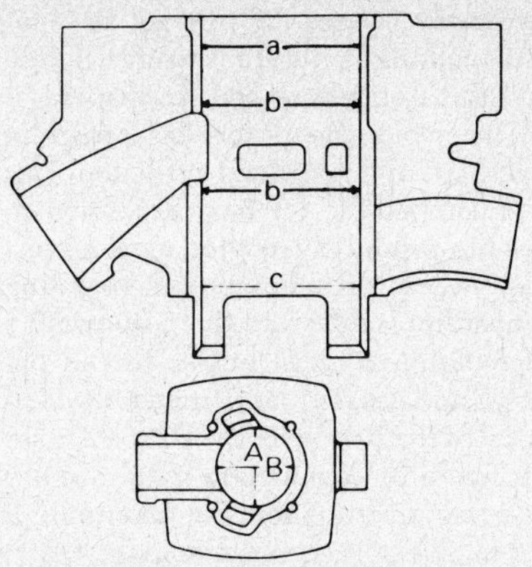

Cylinder diameter measuring points

cylinder wall clearance (see Specifications).

NOTE: *Replacement pistons are available in 0.25 mm (0.010 in.) and 0.50 mm (0.020 in.) oversizes for all models, and several additional sizes up to 1.00 mm (0.040 in.) can be obtained for the YDS series. These sizes vary slightly from piston to piston, however, so if you want to do a real careful job, get the replacement piston FIRST, then bore and hone the cylinder to match it.*

After boring and honing, recheck the diameter measurements and make certain that the difference between minimum and maximum cylinder diameters does not exceed 0.01 mm (0.0004 in.). And finally, chamfer the intake, exhaust, and transfer ports so that there are no rough edges.

Installation

Install a new base gasket, then slide the cylinder down over the studs to a point above the piston. Position the end gaps of the piston rings at their respective knock (locating) pins and squeeze them into their grooves with a ring compressor or, if necessary, your fingers. Insert the top of the piston, then CAREFULLY slide the cylinder down over the rings and piston skirt. Remove the rags and slide the cylinder down to the crankcase, then reconnect the oil line banjo fitting.

NOTE: *An automotive radiator hose clamp makes a very inexpensive and efficient ring compressor. Select a clamp approximately the same size as the piston and slip it around the rings. Tighten the clamp enough to compress and hold the rings, in their grooves, but loose enough to be pushed off. When the cylinder is lowered over the rings, it will push the clamp down around the piston skirt where you can then loosen and remove it.*

Piston

ALL MODELS

Removal and Disassembly

Once again, make sure that the crankcase opening is covered by some clean rags, then, if the factory stamp is obscured, mark the piston crown for reassembly. Remove the piston pin circlips with a pair of needle-nose pliers and push the pin out through the piston with your finger or a straight-slot screwdriver.

NOTE: *It may be necessary to heat the piston slightly to remove the pin. Soak a rag in boiling water, wring it out and apply it to the piston; if that fails, use a torch set on a very low flame.*

Place the piston away from the engine, then CAREFULLY spread the top piston ring apart with your thumbs and slide it off the piston. Remove the other ring in the same manner.

Inspection

PISTON PIN—push the pin into the piston bore: the fit should be snug, but loose enough to move with your fingers (with some effort). If the fit is too loose, replace the pin and/or the piston.

Check the center of the pin for step wear by inserting it into the connecting rod small-end bearing. If there is any up-and-down freeplay, replace the pin AND the bearing.

PISTON RINGS—Remove any carbon accumulation and note their general condition, then push one of the rings into the cylinder with the piston, keeping it parallel to the bottom of the bore.

Using a white piece of paper as a reflector, make a visual check for any spaces between the ring and the cylinder wall, then measure the ring end gap with a feeler gauge. If there are any spaces between the ring and cylinder, or the end gap is not within specifications, replace the ring. Check the other ring in the same manner.

On earlier models not equipped with keystone rings, also measure the clearance between the rings and ring lands (see illustration).

Checking piston pin fit

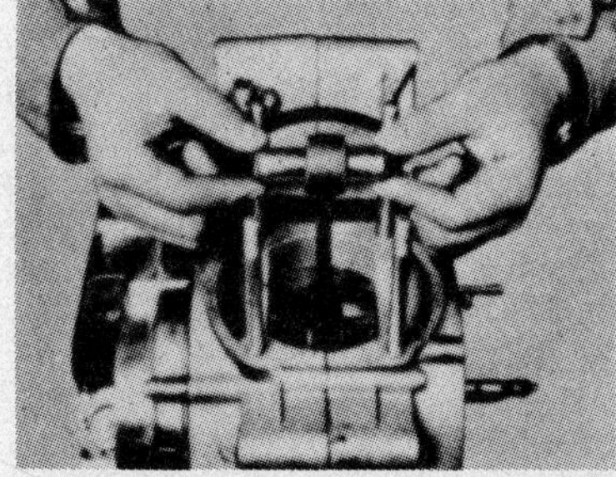

Checking the piston pin for step wear

Measuring ring end gap

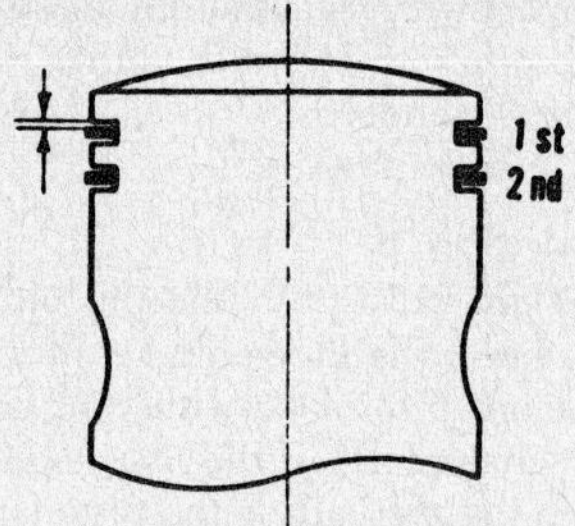

Ring land clearance

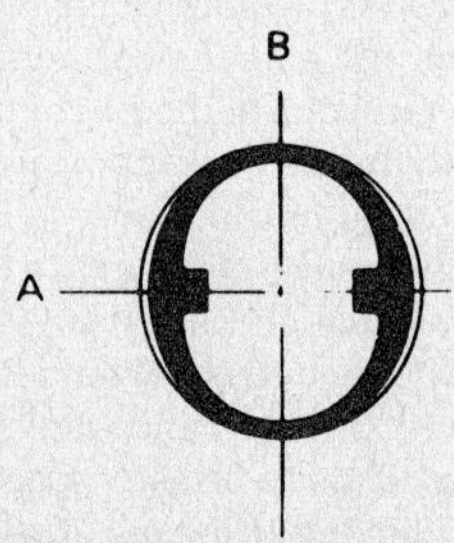

Measure piston diameter at "A" and "B"

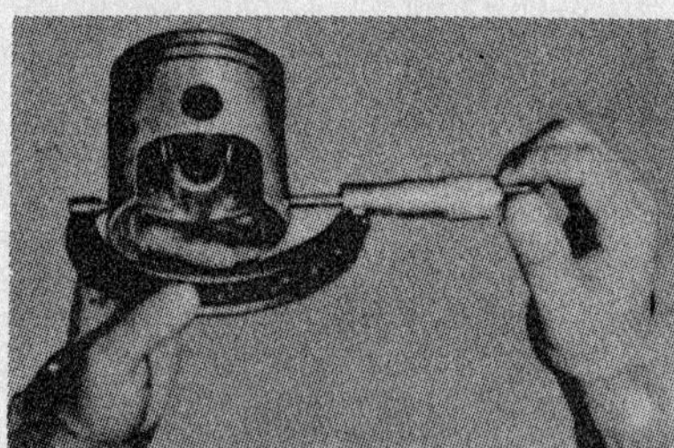
Using a micrometer to measure piston diameter

PISTON—Remove carbon deposits from the piston crown with a blunt blade and clean out the ring grooves with a narrow piece of metal.

NOTE: *Do not use a broken ring to clean the grooves of a piston with the letter K stamped after the size number (located on the piston crown). These pistons are the keystone-type; an old ring will not fit into the groove and may cause damage if forced.*

Inspect the piston for any hairline cracks or wear spots on the skirt. These spots usually indicate that the piston has seized to one degree or another (not necessarily frozen). To prevent the spot from causing a future seizure, lightly sand the area with #400 sandpaper.

When cold, the piston has a slightly oval shape and is tapered at the top. This is to compensate for heat expansion so that the piston will assume a cylindrical shape when it reaches normal operating temperatures. Measure the piston with a micrometer at right angles to the pin bosses and 10 mm (approximately 7/16 in.) from the bottom of the skirt, then use this figure in conjunction with cylinder diameter measurements to determine if cylinder reboring is necessary. If it is, an oversize replacement piston will also be required.

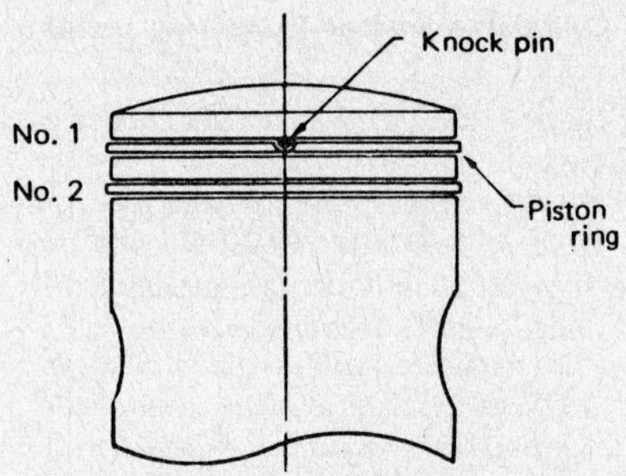

Piston ring locating pin

Piston installation

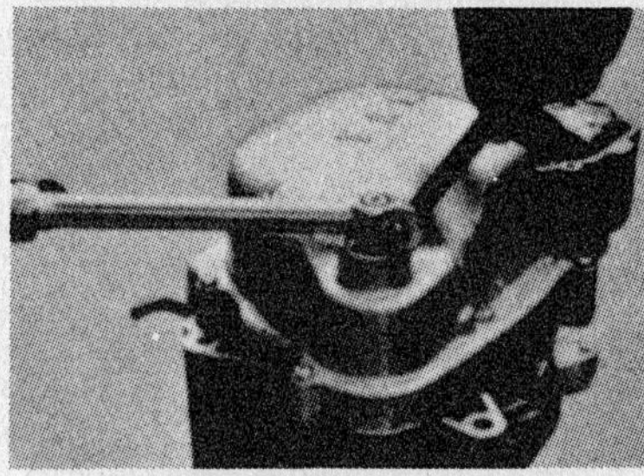
Removing the kickstart lever

Removing the right case cover

Assembly and Installation

Hold the bottom piston ring with the markings facing up and spread it apart slightly, then slide it over the top of the piston and into its groove. Do the same with the top ring, then align both ring end gaps with their respective knock (locating) pins.

NOTE: *Keystone rings are marked #1 (top) and #2 (bottom). They are NOT interchangeable with the conventional-type rings, nor are keystone pistons interchangable with conventional pistons.*

Position the piston over the connecting rod with the arrow (stamped on the crown) facing toward the front of the engine, then push the piston pin through the piston and connecting rod bearing. Make sure the crankcase opening is covered, then install the piston pin circlips.

Right Crankcase Cover

ALL MODELS

1. Remove the kickstarter lever.
2. On rotary valve engines, disconnect the oil line banjo bolt at the delivery pipe.
3. Remove the attaching screws and lift off the case cover with oil pump in place.

NOTE: *It may be necessary to tap the cover with a rubber mallet to aid removal.*

4. Remove the case cover gasket.

Installation

Installation is a reversal of the removal procedure with the addition of the following:

1. Apply Yamaha bond #5 to mating case and case-cover surfaces.
2. Replace the case-cover gasket.

Clutch

MANUAL

Removal and Disassembly

1. Remove the clutch spring retaining screws and pressure plate.
2. Pull out the clutch springs and pushrod.
3. Hold the clutch boss with the special holding tool, bend back the lockwasher tab, and remove the boss locknut.
4. Remove the clutch boss, cushion rings, and friction plates.

Inspection

CLUTCH SPRINGS—Measure the free length of the clutch springs. If 1.0 mm (or more) shorter than specified, replace the spring(s).

FRICTION PLATES—Measure the thickness of the friction plates. If 0.3 mm (or more) thinner than specified, replace the plate(s).

PUSHROD—Roll the pushrod on a flat surface to make sure it isn't bent.

SPACER—Check the inside and outside spacer surfaces for any nicks, scratches or burrs. Smooth out any rough surfaces with #400 sandpaper, then install the spacer in the primary driven gear. If there is more than 0.048 mm clearance between the spacer and driven gear, replace the spacer and/or driven gear.

Install the spacer on the transmission shaft and measure the radial clearance between the spacer and shaft. If it exceeds 0.062 mm, replace the spacer.

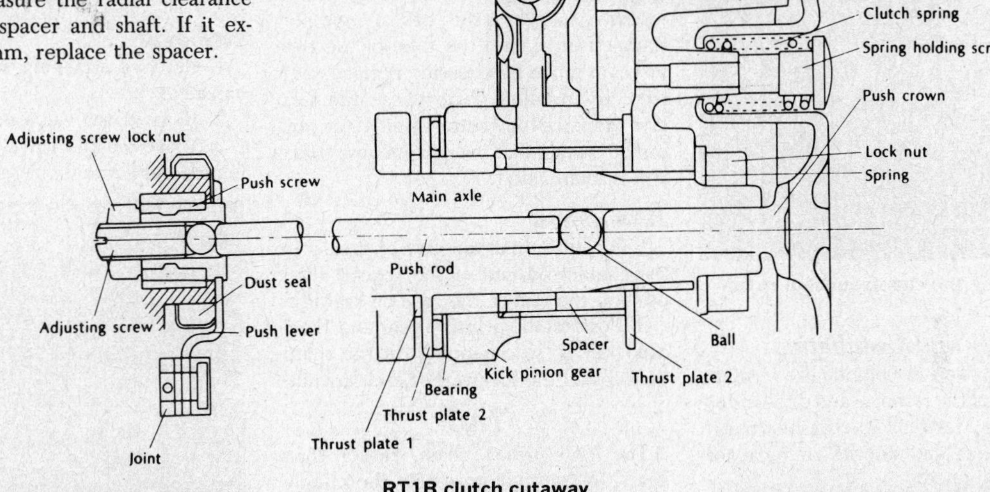

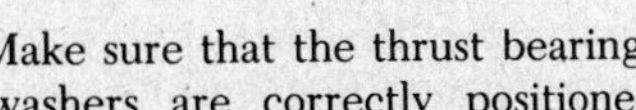
RT1B clutch cutaway

Removing the clutch spring retaining screws

Removing the clutch pushrod

Assembly and Installation

Reverse the removal and disassembly procedure and note the following:

1. When assembling the cushion rings, make certain that they are not twisted or out of position.

2. Make sure that the thrust bearings and washers are correctly positioned BEFORE installing the clutch boss.

NOTE: *The thrust bearings can best be held in place by applying grease to the bearing surfaces and retaining collar.*

CENTRIFUGAL CLUTCH

Removal and Disassembly

1. Bend in the stopper ring and lift out the ring, clutch, and friction plates.

2. Bend back the boss locknut washer tab.

3. Install the special holding tool and remove the boss locknut and clutch assembly.

Inspection

CLUTCH PLATE—With the assembly mounted on the shaft, measure the clearance between the stopper ring and clutch plate. Adjust the clearance to 1.-0–1.2 mm (0.040–0.047 in.) by installing replacement clutch plates of an appropriate thickness.

NOTE: *Clutch plates are available in 1.2 mm (0.047 in.),, 1.4 mm (0.055 in), and 1.6 mm (0.063 in)* thicknesses.

SPACER—Install the spacer in the primary driven gear and check it for radial play. If any play is present, replace the spacer because it will cause premature clutch wear and excessive noise.

Removing the clutch boss locknut

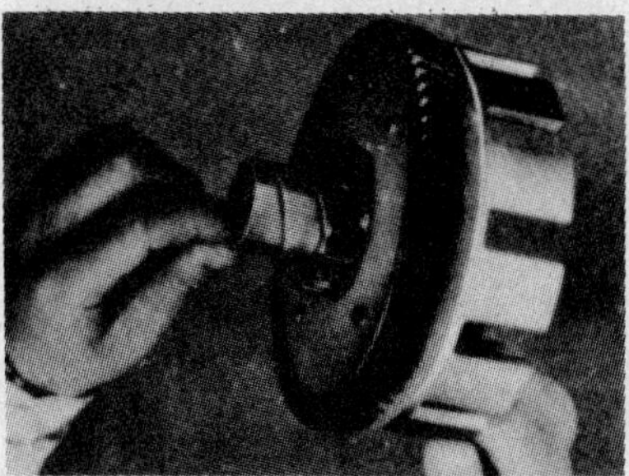
Checking spacer clearance in the primary driven gear (clutch housing)

ROLLERS AND RETAINER—Check the rollers and retainer for scratches, burrs, or rough spots. Place the rollers in the retainer grooves and roll them back and forth to make sure their movement is smooth.

Checking spacer clearance on the transmission mainshaft

Installing the clutch cushion rings

Assembly and Installation

Assembly and installation are basically a reversal of the removal and disassembly procedure. Make sure the washer, clutch plates, spacer and stopper ring are correctly positioned.

Primary Drive Gear

ALL MODELS EXCEPT YA5

Removal

1. Bend back the lockwasher tab.
2. Feed a rag between the primary drive and driven gears, then loosen and remove the locknut.
3. Lift or pry off the primary gear and spacer.

NOTE: *Some models also have a Woodruff key, which must be removed with the gear.*

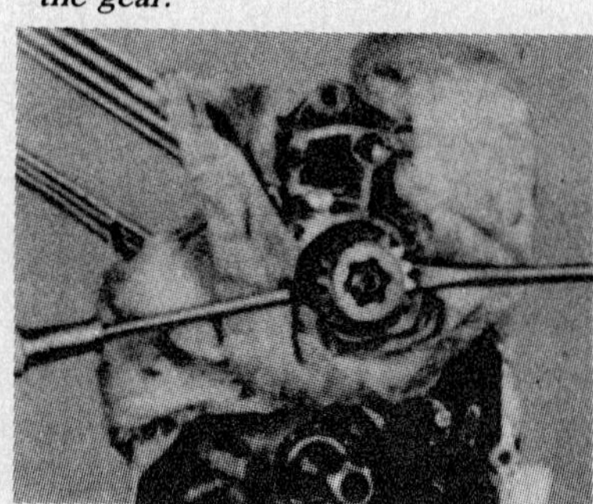

Removing the primary drive gear locknut

Inspection

Inspect the gear teeth for signs of wear. If the primary drive gear needs replacement, the driven gear (integral with clutch housing) should also be replaced. These gears are selected in matched pairs

Removing the primary drive gear

so that gear backlash is sufficient, but not excessive. Each gear has a number stamped on it, and the total of the two serves as guide for choosing replacement parts. By installing gears whose numbers give the same total as the original set, you can be certain that the correct gear backlash is maintained.

Installation

1. Apply a small amount of grease to the chamfered end of the spacer, then position the end in the case oil seal lip.
2. Position the primary gear and Woodruff key (if so equipped) on the shaft, then install the lockwasher and locknut.

YA5

The YA5 uses a chain, rather than gears, to transmit power to the clutch. Separate one link with a chain breaker, then inspect the chain and sprockets for excessive wear. Reinstall in the reverse of removal.

Kickstarter Mechanism

1. Remove the circlip on the kickstarter idle gear.

Disconnecting the kickstart return spring

Removing the kickstart idle gear circlip

2. Disconnect the kickstarter return spring.
3. Lift out the kickstarter assembly and return spring and remove the idle gear and washers.
4. Install by reversing the removal procedure.

NOTE: *Make certain the marks on the kickstarter axle and ratchet wheel are correctly aligned.*

Rotary Valve

MODELS SO EQUIPPED

Removal

1. Remove attaching screws and the valve cover.
2. Remove the valve disc.
3. Drive out the valve knock pin, being careful not to damage the crankcase.

When removing the rotary-valve cover, note the position of #1 and #2 screws

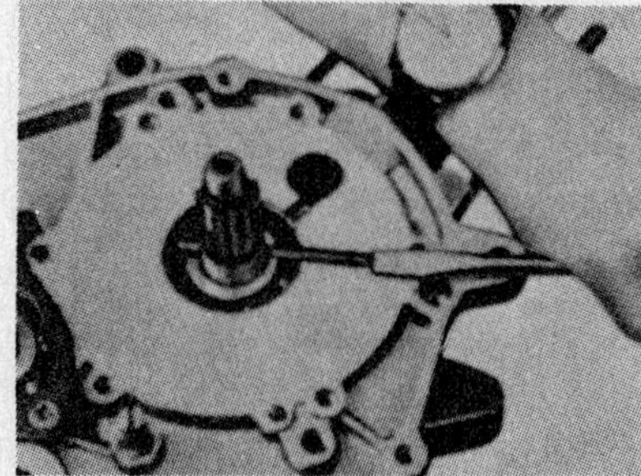

Driving out the valve knock pin

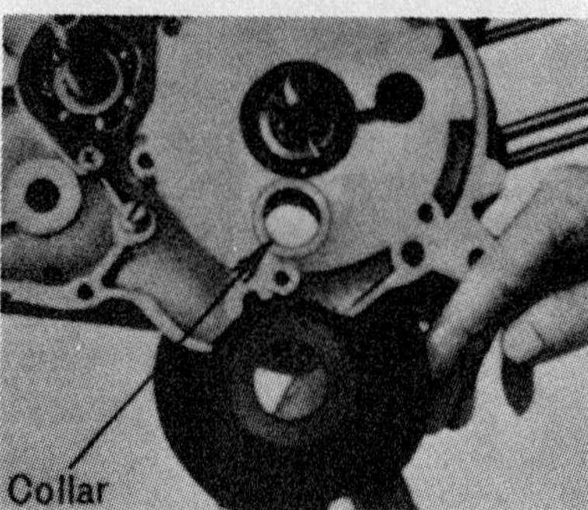

Rotary-valve unit collar

Inspection

1. Fit the valve disc over the unit collar and check for any play or collar step wear.
2. Check the valve cover O-ring by placing it in its groove: if the O-ring has

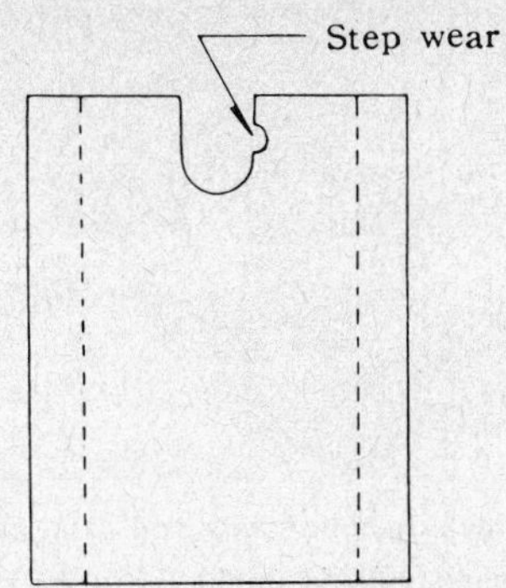

Checking rotary-valve unit collar wear

Crankshaft oil seal

stretched and is larger than the groove, replace it.

3. Check the crankshaft O-ring and valve disc seals for stretching or any signs of damage.

Installation

When installing the rotary-valve, take care not to stretch any of the O-rings. Apply a small amount of greast to each O-ring to hold it in place, then reverse the grease procedure.

Countershaft Sprocket

ALL MODELS

To remove the countershaft sprocket, bend back the lockwasher tab, hold the sprocket with the magneto holding tool or put the transmission in gear, then remove the locknut and sprocket. Check sprocket wear as described in Maintenance.

Crankcase, Shifter and Transmission

NOTE: *The following procedures may vary slightly from machine to machine, depending upon model, year, etc. The basic steps are the same, however, and by carefully examining the specific engine, you can detect any differences in construction.*

ROTARY-VALVE SINGLES

Disassembly

1. Remove the circlip and washer from the shifter change axle.

Apply grease to the rotary-valve cover seals

Removing the countershaft sprocket with the magneto holding tool

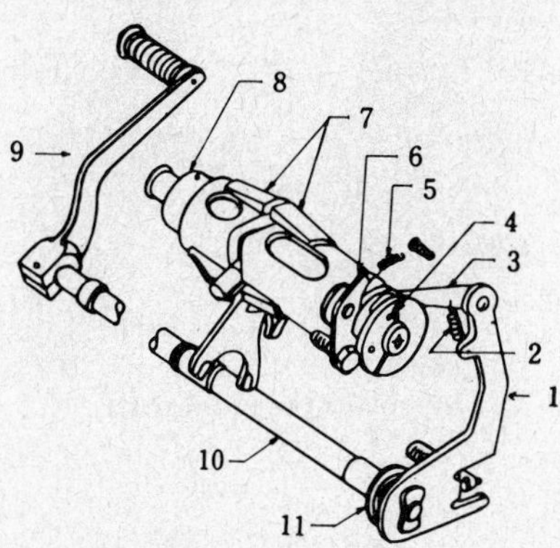

G6S shifter assembly. Other models are similar

1. Gear shift arm B
2. Gear shift arm spring
3. Gear shift arm A
4. Gear shift drum pin
5. Shift drum stopper spring
6. Shift drum stopper lever
7. Shift fork
8. Gear shift drum
9. Change pedal
10. Change axle ass'y
11. Gear shift spring

Removing the change axle circlip

2. Turn the engine over on the other side, then pull out the change axle and shifter arm assembly.
3. Remove the neutral stopper.
4. Remove the shift drum stopper lever and spring.
5. Remove all the attaching pan head screws from the left crankcase.
6. Position the connecting rod at top dead center.
7. Install the special crankcase divider tool.
8. Tighten up the divider tool bolts, making sure the tool remains parallel to the case.
9. While tightening the divider tool, alternately tap the transmission mainshaft and right half of the crankcase until it completely separates from the left half.
10. Remove the shift drum circlip, cover, and oil seal from the left crankcase.
11. Using a rubber mallet, tap out the transmission and shift drum as an assembly. Disassemble the transmission gears and shafts only if necessary.
12. Remove the crankshaft assembly with the case divider tool (see illustration).

Pulling out the shifter shaft and arm

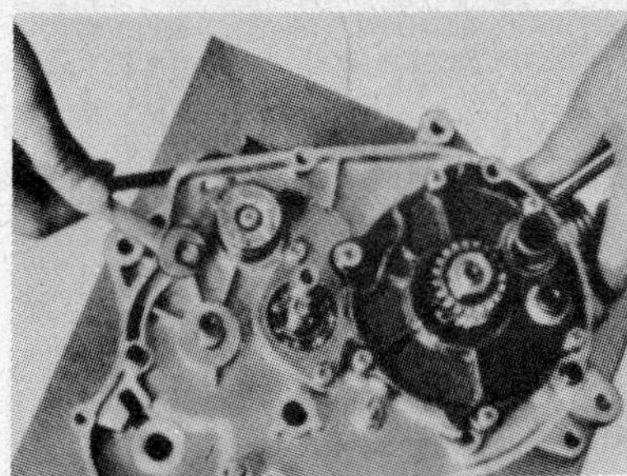

Removing the shift drum stopper

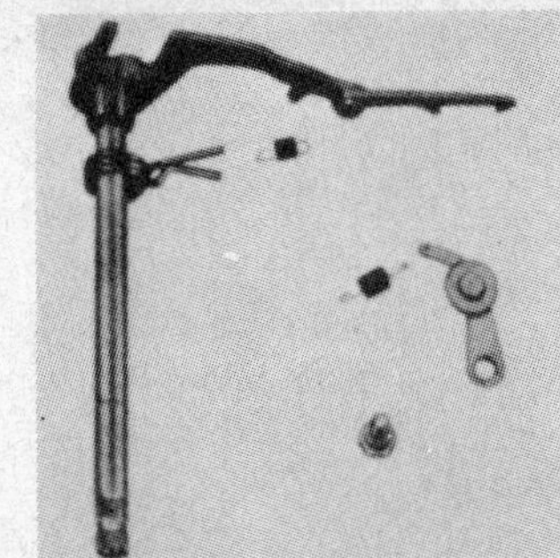

G6S shifter shaft and related parts

Removing the case half securing screws

Installing the special case divider tool

Tapping the transmission mainshaft

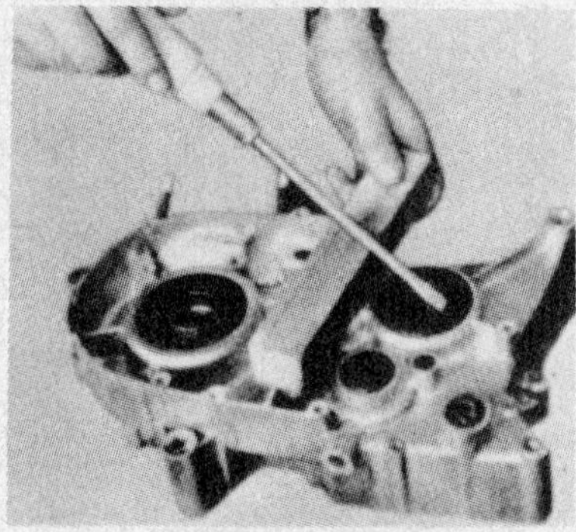
Removing the case seals

13. CAREFULLY pry out all the case seals with a straight slot screwdriver.

14. Drive out the main bearings with the special bearing tool.

Inspection

CONNECTING ROD—Check the connecting rod large end bearing and crankpin axial clearance by wiggling the small end and measuring its back-and-forth freeplay. Maximum is 2.0 mm; standard is 0.8–1.0 mm.

Hold the connecting rod to one side and check the large end bearing side play with a feeler gauge. The maximum limit is 0.1–0.3 mm.

TRANSMISSION GEARS—Check the transmission gears for any burrs, broken teeth, etc., and replace any excessively worn parts.

BEARINGS—Check the transmission and main bearings as you would any other bearings. During an engine overhaul it is wise to replace the crankshaft supporting (main) bearings, as they carry most of the load and suffer the greatest wear.

Assembly

1. Install new oil seals with the manufacturer's mark facing outward.
2. Pack all bearings with a light weight grease and install them with the special bearing tool.
3. If the transmission cluster was dissassembled, make certain each gear has between 0.003 in. and 0.005 in. side play, and that the engagement dogs have AT LEAST 50% penetration into their slots. Adjustment can be achieved by adding or subtracting gear and/or drive axle shims. Use the accompanying illustrations to ensure proper shim and circlip positioning.

Checking connecting rod axial play

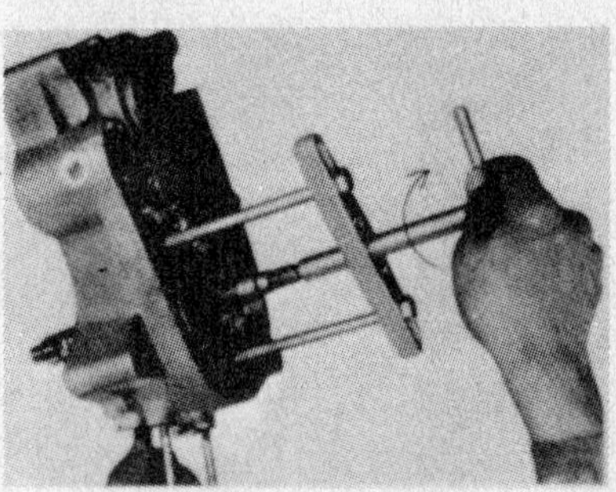
Removing the crankshaft

4. Install the crankshaft with shims, using the special crankshaft installation tool.
5. Install the transmission and shift drum assembly as one unit.
6. Clean the mating surfaces of the crankcase halves, then apply Yamaha Bond #5.
7. Make sure the transmission is NOT in first gear, then assemble the case halves.

NOTE: *If the crankcase halves are assembled with the transmission in first gear, the shift forks may be bent.*

90, 100, 125 180, AND 200CC TWINS

Disassembly

1. Remove the shifter arm circlip and washer.

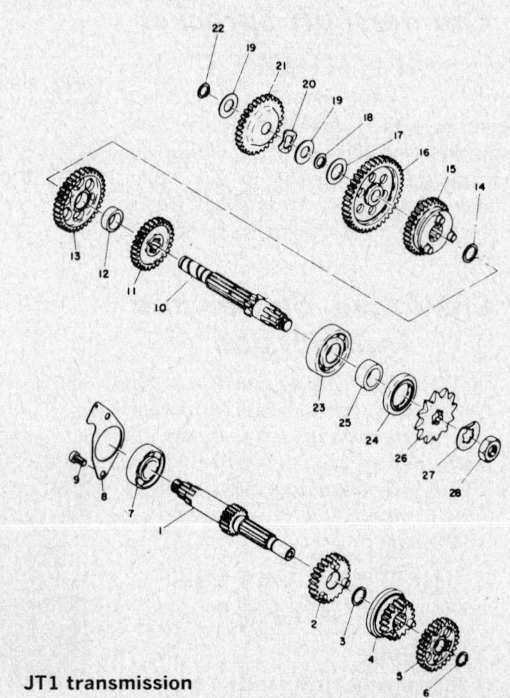

1. Main axle
2. 3rd pinion gear
3. Circlip
4. 2nd pinion gear
5. 1st pinion gear
6. Circlip
7. Bearing
8. Bearing cover plate
9. Bolt
10. Drive axle
11. 4th gear
12. Distance collar
13. 2nd gear
14. Circlip
15. 3rd gear
16. 1st gear
17. Shim
18. Circlip
19. Thrust washer
20. Wave washer
21. Kick idler gear
22. Circlip
23. Bearing
24. Oil seal
25. Distance collar
26. Drive sprocket
27. Lock washer
28. Nut

JT1 transmission

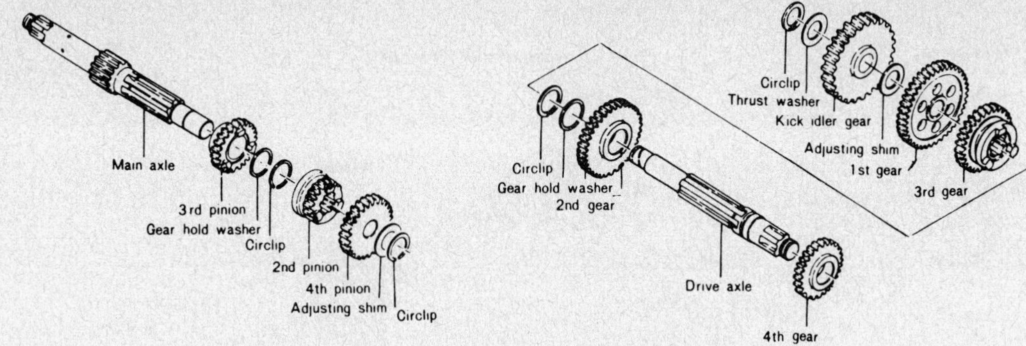

G5S and G6S transmission

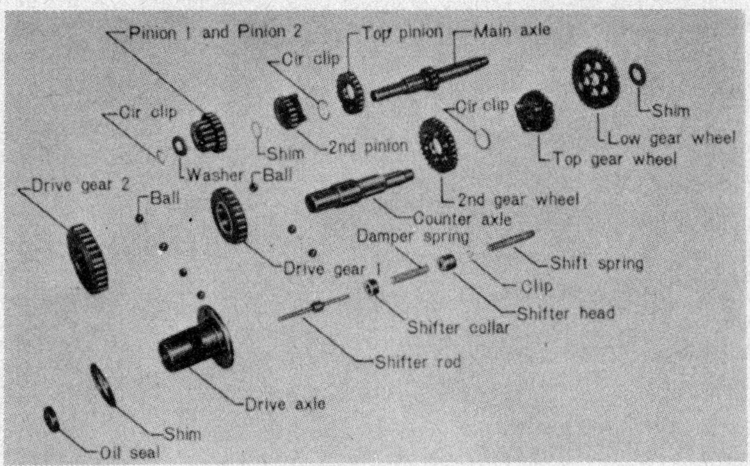

L5T transmission

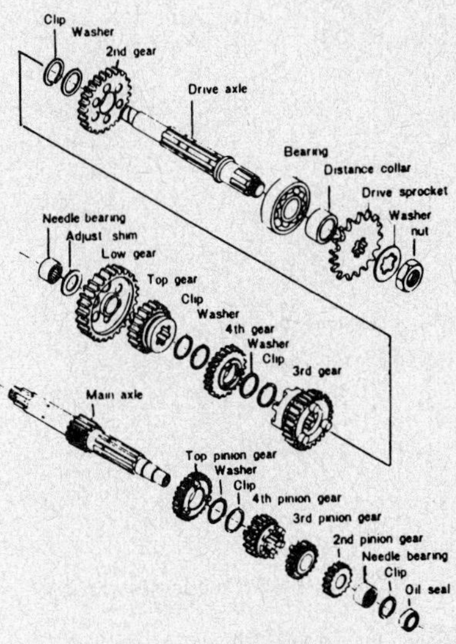

YCS1 transmission

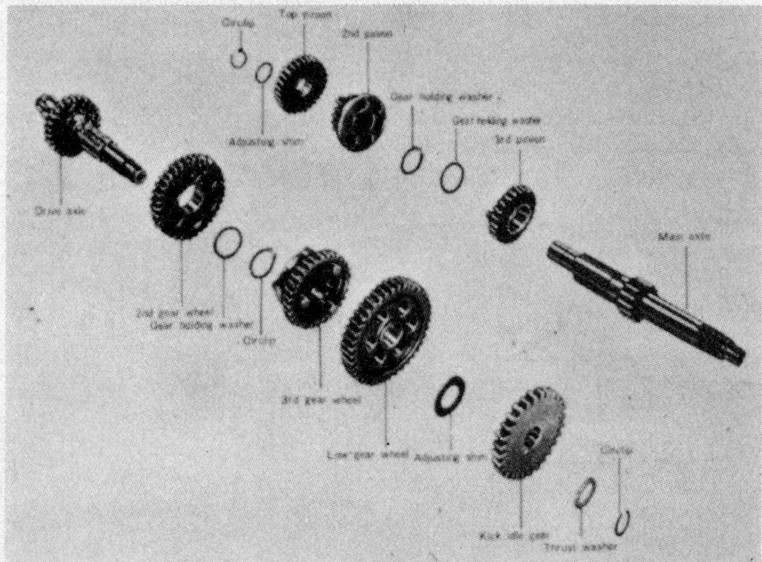

YG5T transmission

2. turn the engine over and lift out the shifter shaft and arm assembly.

3. Remove the pan head screws on the left case half.

4. Install the crankcase dividing tool and separate the case halves as described in rotary-valve case disassembly.

5. Remove the circlip, holder and washer from the shifter drum on the left case.

6. Remove the neutral stopper mechanism.

7. Tap out the transmission and shifter as one unit.

8. Remove the crankshaft, oil seals, and main bearings as described in rotary-valve case disassembly.

Inspection and Assembly

Inspect and assemble the crankcase, transmission, and shifter as described in rotary-valve case assembly.

250, 305, AND 350CC TWINS WITH VERTICALLY SPLIT CRANKCASE

Disassembly

1. Remove the shifter cover.
2. Disconnect the change link and change lever.
3. Remove the shifter cam assembly.
4. Remove the shifter shaft circlip and pull out the shaft.

NOTE: *Remove the external circlip first, then push the shaft inward and remove the internal circlip.*

5. Remove the shift fork.
6. Remove the pan head screws on the right case half.
7. Split the case halves as previously described.

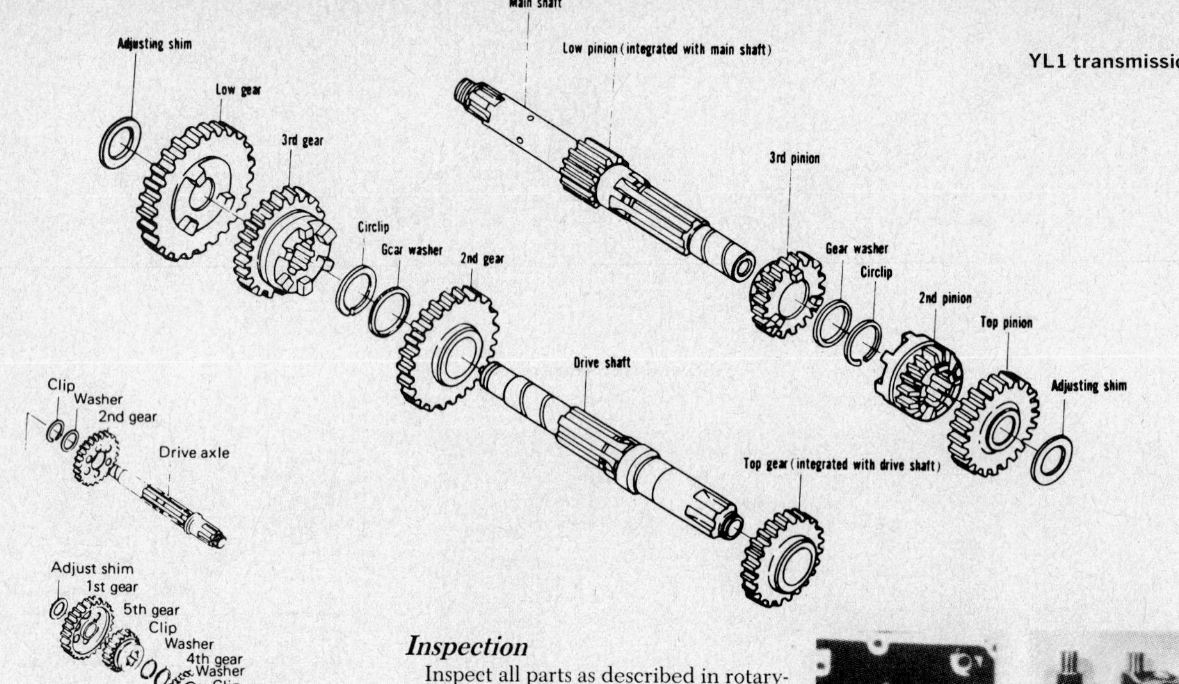

YL1 transmission

CS3 and HS1 transmission

Remove the tachometer drive housing before splitting the cases

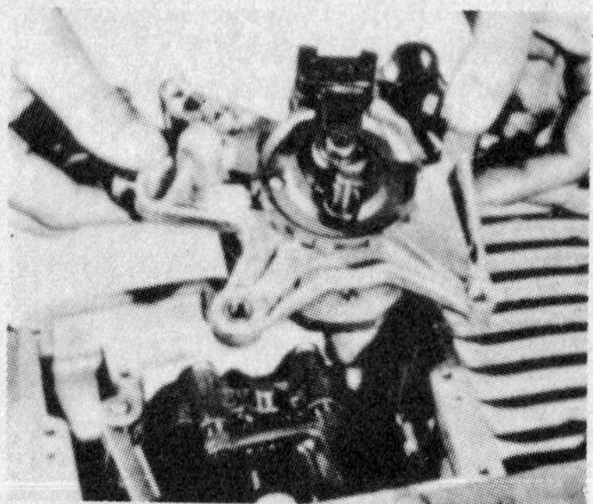

Removing the shifter mechanism

8. Remove the transmission assembly by alternately tapping drive and main axles with a rubber mallet.

9. Remove the crankshaft, oil seals, and main bearings as previously described.

Inspection

Inspect all parts as described in rotary-valve engine disassembly.

Assembly

1. Engage the kick pinion with the kick gear.
2. Install the main axle assembly.
3. Install the drive axle assembly, meshing the gears with the main axle assembly.
4. Tap both axles into position with a rubber mallet.
5. Apply Yamaha Bond #5 to the mating surfaces of the crankcase halves, then carefully tap them together with a rubber mallet.
6. Install the pan head screws and tighten them alternately a little at a time.
7. Install the shift forks on their respective gears, then insert the shifter shaft.
8. Set the transmission in neutral position.
9. Install the shifter cam assembly.
10. Install the change link and check the shifter operation.
11. Apply Yamaha Bond #5 to the mating surfaces, then install the shifter cover and packing.

PISTON PORT SINGLES

1. Remove the tachometer drive gear circlip and gear.
2. Remove the change axle rubber boot.
3. Turn the engine over and pull out the shifter shaft assembly.
4. Remove the change lever circlip and lever.
5. Remove the neutral stopper.
6. Remove the change lever guide.
7. Remove the case pan head screws.
8. Separate the crankcase halves as previously described.

Shifter forks and guide bar

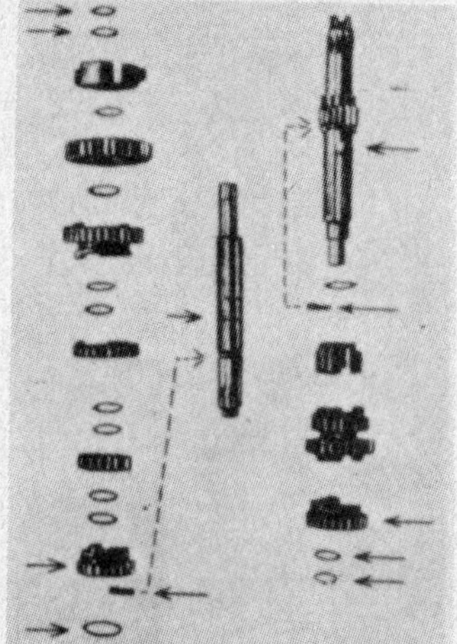

YDS3 and YM1 transmission

9. Remove the crankshaft, transmission/shifter assembly, oil seals, and bearings as previously described.

Inspection

Inspect all parts as described in rotary-valve engine disassembly.

Assembly

Assemble the crankcase as previously described and make certain that the

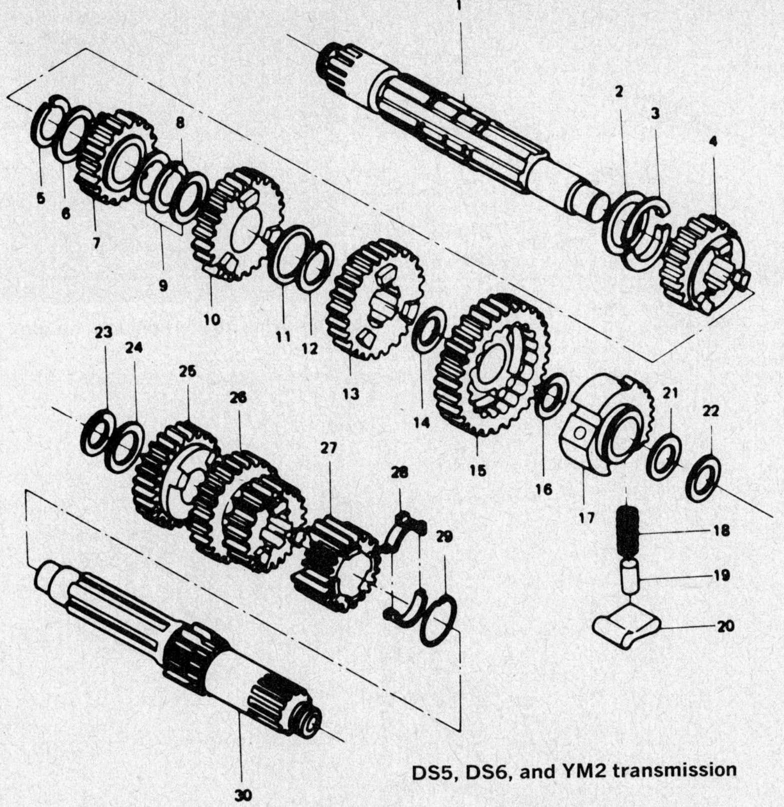

DS5, DS6, and YM2 transmission

1. Drive axle
2. 4th gear shim
3. Drive axle setting plate
4. 4th gear
5. Drive axle spline circlip A
6. Gear holding washer A
7. 5th gear
8. Drive axle spline circlip
9. Gear holding washer B
10. 3rd gear
11. Gear holding washer A
12. Drive axle spline circlip
13. 2nd gear
14. 1st gear spacer
15. Kick gear
16. Thrust washer A
17. Kick pinion gear
18. Pawl spring
19. Kick pawl pin
20. Kick pawl
21. Drive axle adjust shim
22. Drive axle adjust shim
23. Main axle circlip
24. Main axle washer
25. 4th pinion gear
26. 3rd and 5th pinion gear
27. 2nd pinion gear
28. 2nd pinion setting plate
29. 2nd pinion holding clip
30. Main axle

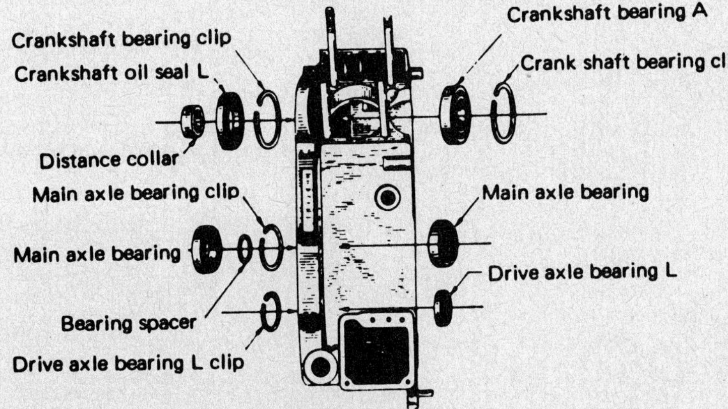

Crankcase L.H.

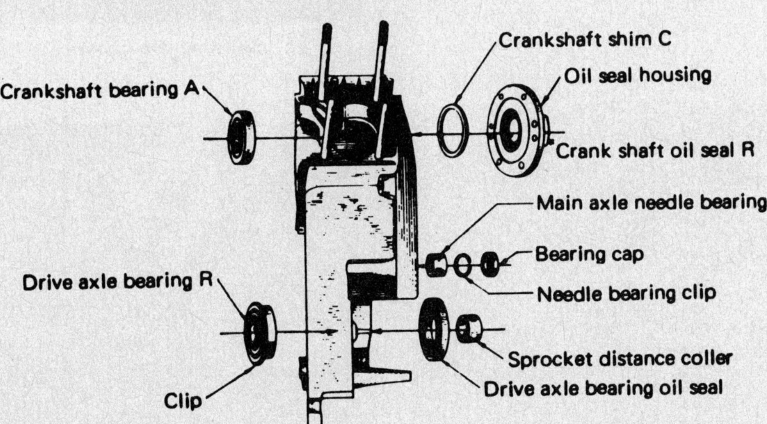

Crankcase R.H.

DS5 and DS6 bearings and oil seals. The other vertically split twins have a similar layout

crankshaft bearing circlip end gap is aligned with the arrows marked on both case halves.

TWINS WITH HORIZONTALLY SPLIT CRANKCASE

Disassembly

1. Remove the shifter shaft sealing boot.
2. Remove the shifter shaft circlip and shim.
3. Turn the engine over and pull out the shifter shaft assembly.
4. Remove the shift lever circlip and lever assembly.
5. Invert the engine and remove the crankcase holding bolts.

NOTE: *Each holding bolt is numbered. Remove them in descending order, beginning with the highest one.*

6. Using a rubber mallet, lightly tap the case halves until they separate.
7. Remove the crankshaft by lightly tapping it with a rubber mallet.
8. Remove the transmission assembly.
9. Remove the shifter lever guide retaining screws and guide.
10. Remove the attaching screws and the stopper plate.
11. Pull out the guide bars, then remove the shift fork.
12. Remove the change cam stopper.
13. Remove the stopper plate circlip, then slide out the shift cam.
14. Remove the neutral switch.
15. Remove the tachometer drive gear assembly.

YR1 and YR2 transmission

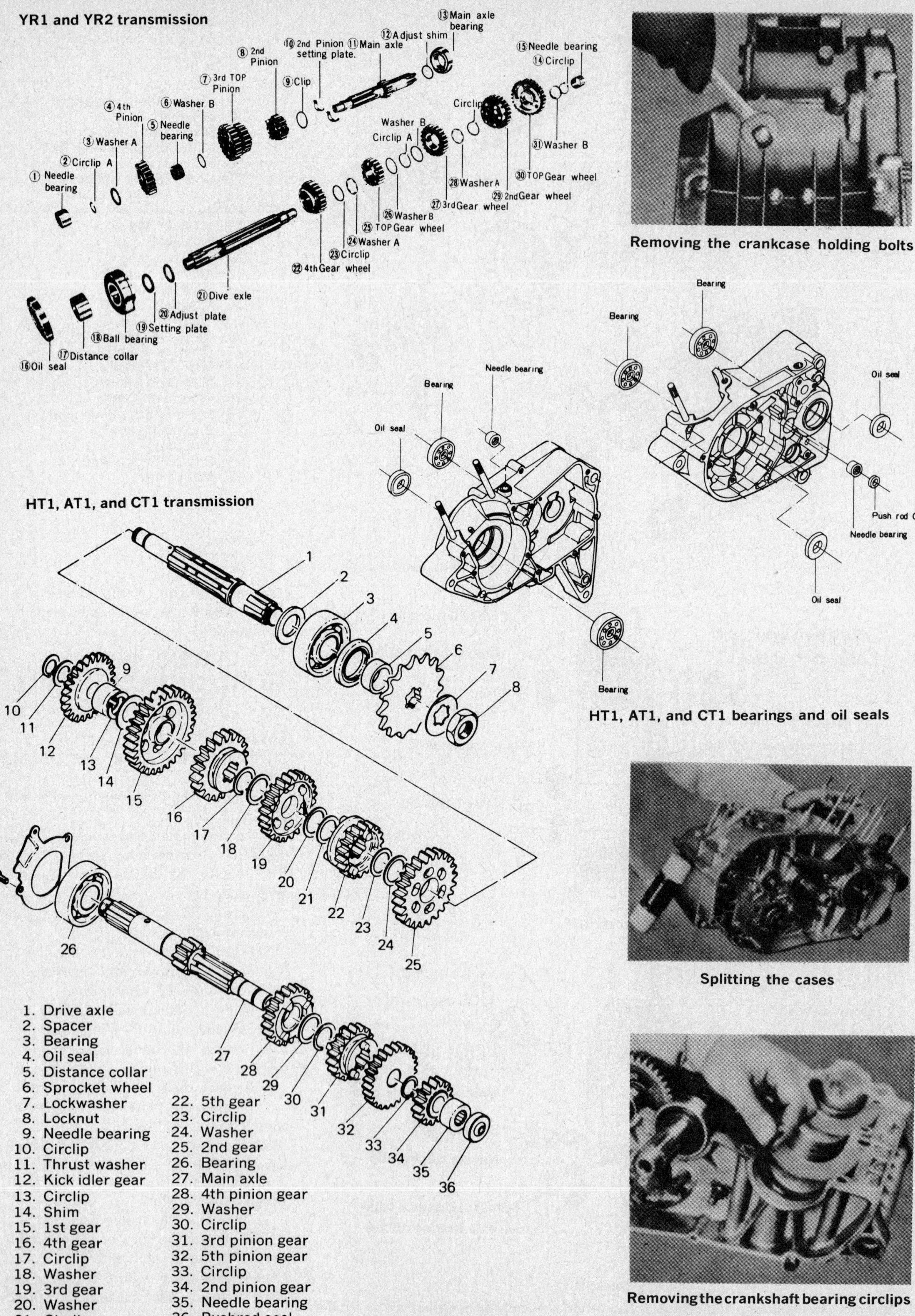

Removing the crankcase holding bolts

HT1, AT1, and CT1 transmission

1. Drive axle
2. Spacer
3. Bearing
4. Oil seal
5. Distance collar
6. Sprocket wheel
7. Lockwasher
8. Locknut
9. Needle bearing
10. Circlip
11. Thrust washer
12. Kick idler gear
13. Circlip
14. Shim
15. 1st gear
16. 4th gear
17. Circlip
18. Washer
19. 3rd gear
20. Washer
21. Circlip
22. 5th gear
23. Circlip
24. Washer
25. 2nd gear
26. Bearing
27. Main axle
28. 4th pinion gear
29. Washer
30. Circlip
31. 3rd pinion gear
32. 5th pinion gear
33. Circlip
34. 2nd pinion gear
35. Needle bearing
36. Pushrod seal

HT1, AT1, and CT1 bearings and oil seals

Splitting the cases

Removing the crankshaft bearing circlips

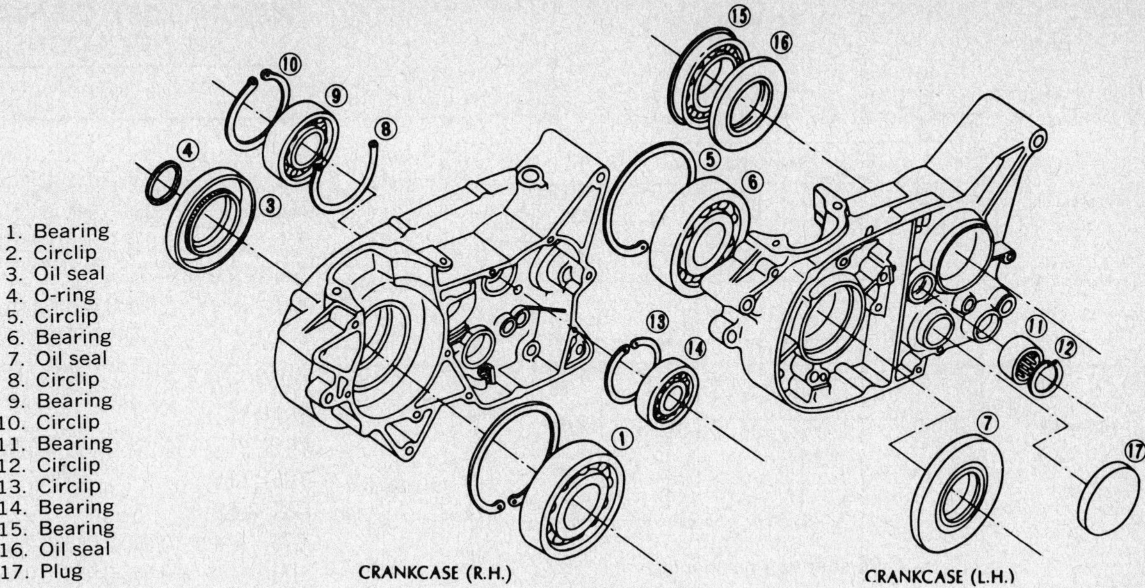

DT1 and RT1 bearings and oil seals

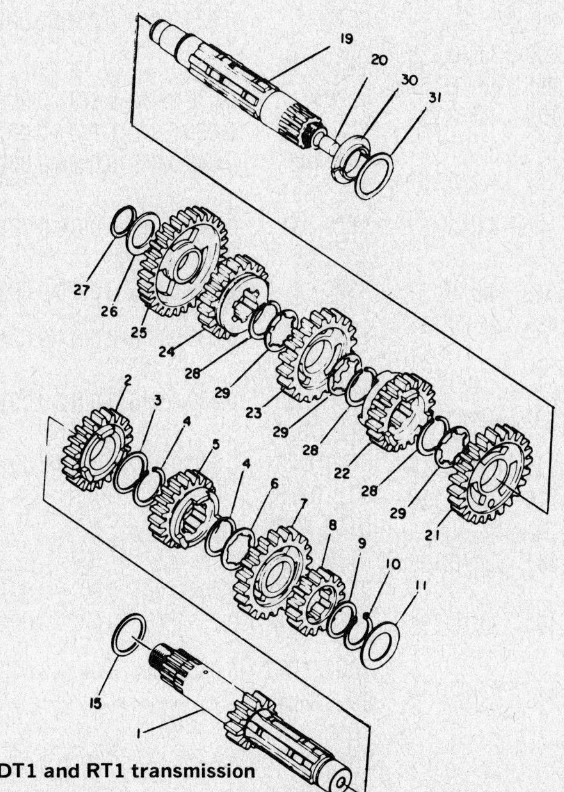

DT1 and RT1 transmission

1. Axle, main
2. Gear, 4th pinion
3. Washer, gear holding
4. Circlip
5. Gear, 3rd pinion
6. Washer, gear holding
7. Gear, 3rd
8. Gear, 2nd pinion
9. Washer, gear holding
10. Circlip
11. Shim
12. Bearing
13. Circlip
14. Oil seal
15. Shim, main axle
16. Bearing
17. Circlip
18. Gear, kick pinion
19. Axle, drive
20. Plug, blind
21. Gear, 2nd wheel
22. Gear, 3rd pinion
23. Gear, 3rd wheel
24. Gear, 4th wheel
25. Gear, 1st wheel
26. Washer, gear holding
27. Circlip
28. Circlip
29. Washer, gear holding
30. Spacer, drive axle
31. Shim, drive axle

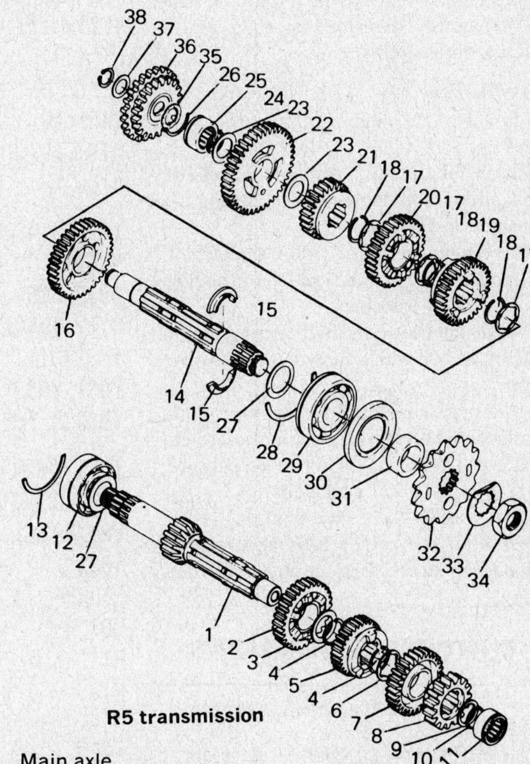

R5 transmission

1. Main axle
2. 5th pinion gear
3. Gear hold (2) washer
4. Circlip
5. 3rd pinion gear
6. Gear hold washer
7. 4th pinion gear
8. 2nd pinion gear
9. Gear hold washer
10. Circlip
11. Bearing
12. Bearing
13. Circlip
14. Drive axle
15. Drive axle spacer
16. 2nd wheel gear
17. Gear hold gear
18. Circlip
19. 4th wheel gear
20. 5th pinion gear
21. 5th wheel gear
22. 1st wheel gear
23. Gear hold washer
24. Circlip
25. Bearing
26. Circlip
27. Drive axle shim
28. Circlip
29. Bearing
30. Oil seal
31. Distance collar
32. Drive sprocket
33. Lock washer
34. Lock nut
35. Wave washer
36. Idle gear ass'y
37. Main axle shim
38. Circlip

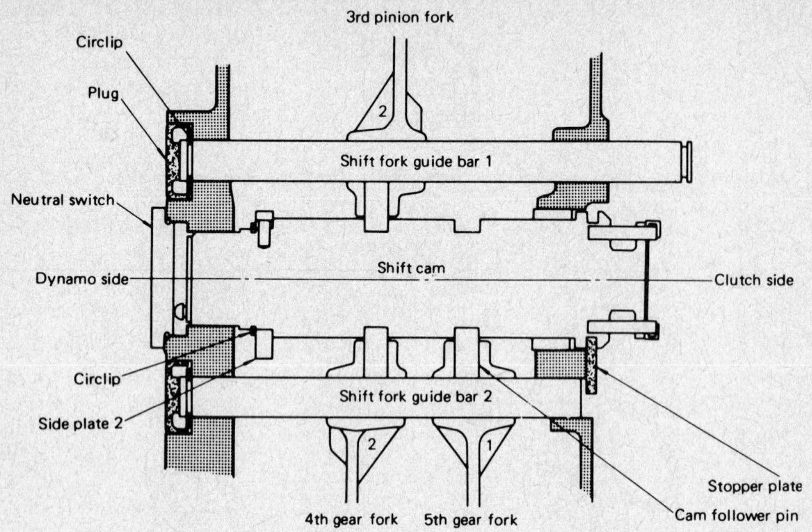

R5 shift fork positioning

Inspection

Inspect all bearings, gears, and oil seals as previously described in rotary-valve engine disassembly.

Assembly

Reverse the disassembly procedure and note the following:

1. Install the transmission main axle oil seal and circlip halves before joining upper and lower cases.
2. When installing the crankshaft, align the bearing knock pin with the hole in the lower case half.
3. Install the crankshaft bearing circlip halves and oil seal as shown in the illustrations.
4. Apply Yamaha Bond #5 to mating crankcase halves and torque the attaching bolts to the following specifications:
   6 mm bolts—90 inch pounds
   8 mm bolts—180 inch pounds

Tighten the bolts a little at a time in ascending order, beginning with Number 1.

CLUTCH SPECIFICATIONS

	Clutch Spring Standard Length (mm/in.)	Friction Disc Standard Thickness (mm/in.)
YJ1	34.0/1.340	3.5/0.138
YJ2	34.0/1.340	3.5/0.138
JT1, JT2	34.0/1.340	3.5/0.138
YG1, YGS1, YG5T, G5S, G6S, G6SB, G7S	27.0/1.060	3.5/0.138
HT1, HT1B, LT2	34.0/1.340	4.0/0.157
HS1, HS1B, LS2	31.5/1.229	4.0/0.157
YL2, YL2C, YL2CM, L5T, L5TA	28.2/1.302	3.5/0.138
YL1, YL1E	25.5/0.995	4.0/0.157
YA5, YA6	31.5/1.229	4.0/0.157
AT1, CT1 (all), AT2, CT2	31.5/1.229	4.0/0.157
YAS1(C), AS2C	34.0/1.340	4.0/0.157
YCS1(C), CS3C, CS3B, CS5	34.0/1.340	4.0/0.157
DT1 (all), DT2	36.4/1.433	3.0/0.118
YD3, YDT1, YDS1, YDS2 YDS3(C), YM1	25.5/0.995	4.3/0.168
YDS5, YM2(C)	25.5/0.995	3.0/0.118
DS6C, DS6B	44.0/1.716	3.0/0.118
YR1, YR2(C) R3(C)	36.4/1.433	3.0/0.118
R5, R5B, DS7, R5C	36.0/1.404	3.0/0.118
RT1, RT1B, RT2	36.4/1.433	3.0/0.118

TORQUE SPECIFICATIONS

size (mm)	kg/m	ft lbs	in lbs
6	1.0	7	80
7	1.5	11	135
8	2.0	15	180
10	3.5-4.0	26-29	300-500
12	4.0-4.5	29-33	350-400
14	4.5-5.0	33-37	400-450
17	5.8-7.0	40-50	500-600

PISTON SKIRT CLEARANCE SPECIFICATIONS

	(mm)	(in.)
U5, U5E, U5L, U7E	0.030-0.035	0.0012-0.0014
MJ2, MJ2T	0.038-0.040	0.0015-0.0016
YJ1	0.038-0.040	0.0015-0.0016
Early & Late YJ2	0.035-0.040	0.0014-0.0016
JT1, JT2	0.040-0.045	0.0016-0.0018
MG1T, YG1, YG1T, YG1K, YGS1, YGS1T	0.038-0.040	0.0015-0.0016
YG5T, G5S, G6S, G6SB, G75	0.040-0.045	0.0016-0.0018
HT1	0.040-0.050	0.0016-0.0020
HT1B, LT2	0.040-0.045	0.0016-0.0018
HS1, HS1B, LS2	0.035-0.040	0.0014-0.0016
YL2, YL2C, YL2CM	0.035-0.040	0.0014-0.0016
YL1, YL1E	0.035-0.040	0.0014-0.0016
YA5, YA6	0.040-0.045	0.0016-0.0018
AT1, AT1B, AT1C, AT2	0.040-0.045	0.0016-0.0018
YAS1(C), AS2C	0.050-0.055	0.0020-0.0022
YCS1	0.035-0.040	0.0014-0.0016
YCS1C, CS3C, CS3B, CS5	0.030-0.035	0.0012-0.0014
CT1, CT1B, CT1C, CT2	0.040-0.045	0.0016-0.0018
DT1, DT1B, DT1S, DT1C, DT1E, DS7, DT2	0.040-0.045	0.0016-0.0018
YD3, YDT1	0.050-0.055	0.0020-0.0022
YDS1, YDS2	0.055-0.060	0.0022-0.0024
Early & Late YDS3, YDS3C*	0.050-0.055	0.0020-0.0022
YDS5, DS6C, DS6B	0.035-0.040	0.0014-0.0016
YM1	0.053-0.057	0.0021-0.0023
YM2C	0.035-0.040	0.0014-0.0016
YR1	0.035-0.040	0.0014-0.0016
YR2, YR2C, R3(C)	0.030-0.035	0.0012-0.0014
R5, R5B, R5C	0.030-0.038	0.0012-0.0015
RT1, RT1B, RT2	①	0.0022-0.0024

① RT1—0.055-0.060; RT2—0.045-0.050

LUBRICATION SYSTEMS

Pump Repair

The factory advises against attempting to disassemble and repair the oil pump. The internal parts are machined to very exacting tolerances and it is highly unlikely that the pump could be reassembled to factory specifications. In addition to this, Autolube pump failure is VERY seldom due to internal malfunction.

PUMP ADJUSTMENT

Refer to the "Tune-Up and Maintenance" section.

PUMP BLEEDING

The oil pump must be bled of all air whenever any supply or delivery lines are disconnected or the oil tank has run dry.

1. Remove the bleeder bolt.
2. Turn the starter plate in the direction indicated by the arrow on the plate.
3. Keep turning the plate until the bleeder hole spurts oil only (i.e. no air bubbles).

NOTE: *This operation will be much easier if you hold the throttle wide open while turning the starter plate.*

4. Reinstall the bleeder bolt.
5. If the pump is being bled as part of engine reassembly after major repairs, keep in mind that the crankcase is probably stone dry. When you start the engine, let it idle for awhile and hold the oil pump cable full open for a few seconds. This will provide the moving parts with extra lubrication until the normal oil film is built up.

Location of the Autolube unit

PUMP OUTPUT CHECK

(1969, '70, and '71 Models Only)

The delivery output of the oil pump should be measured when the pump is suspected as the cause of a problem and after the more common sources have been checked.

Needed for this operation are: a laboratory tube graduated in cubic centimeters, an extra oil pump delivery line, and strong fingers.

NOTE: *This check can be performed with the pump mounted in the bike or on the bench.*

1. Cut off one end of the extra delivery line and slide it over the end of the graduated tube (see illustration).
2. Disconnect the oil pump delivery line banjo bolt and connect the measuring tube assembly in its place.

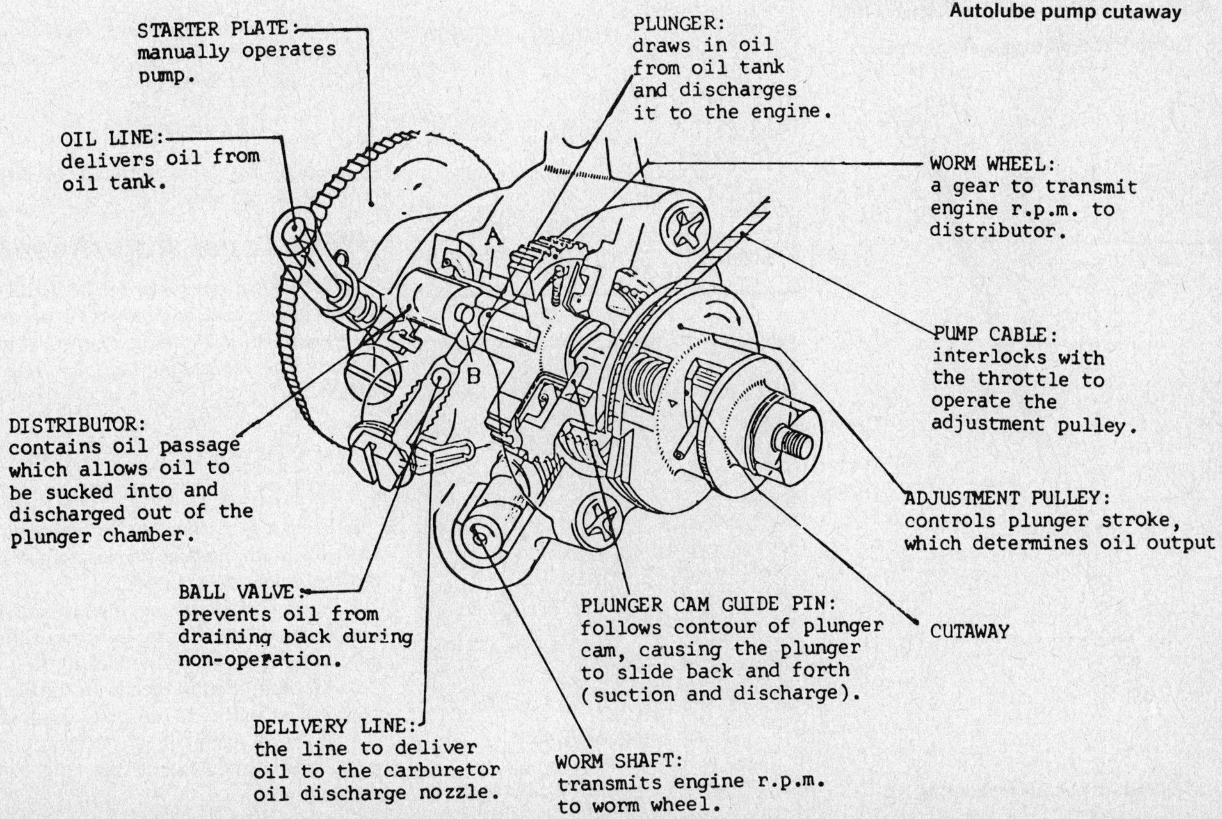
STARTER PLATE: manually operates pump.
PLUNGER: draws in oil from oil tank and discharges it to the engine.
OIL LINE: delivers oil from oil tank.
WORM WHEEL: a gear to transmit engine r.p.m. to distributor.
A
B
PUMP CABLE: interlocks with the throttle to operate the adjustment pulley.
DISTRIBUTOR: contains oil passage which allows oil to be sucked into and discharged out of the plunger chamber.
ADJUSTMENT PULLEY: controls plunger stroke, which determines oil output
BALL VALVE: prevents oil from draining back during non-operation.
PLUNGER CAM GUIDE PIN: follows contour of plunger cam, causing the plunger to slide back and forth (suction and discharge).
CUTAWAY
DELIVERY LINE: the line to deliver oil to the carburetor oil discharge nozzle.
WORM SHAFT: transmits engine r.p.m. to worm wheel.

Autolube pump cutaway

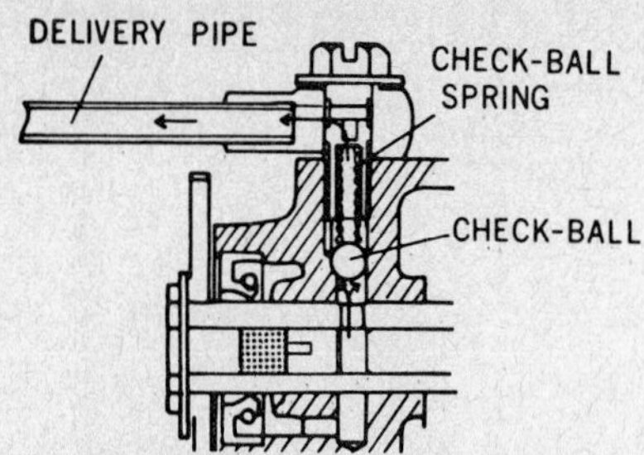

Oil pump check valve

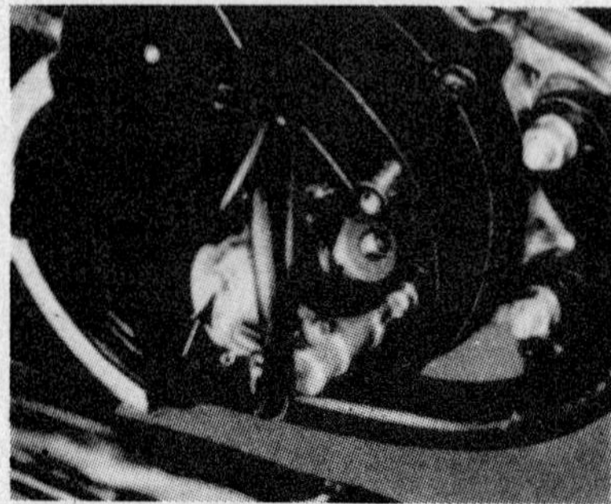
Arrow indicates the bleeder bolt

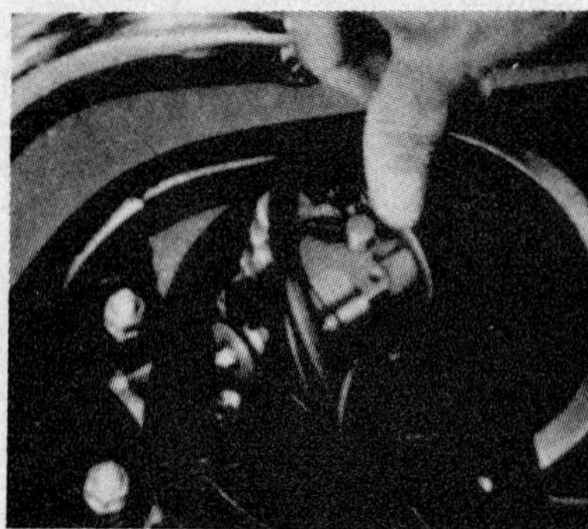
Turning the oil pump starter plate

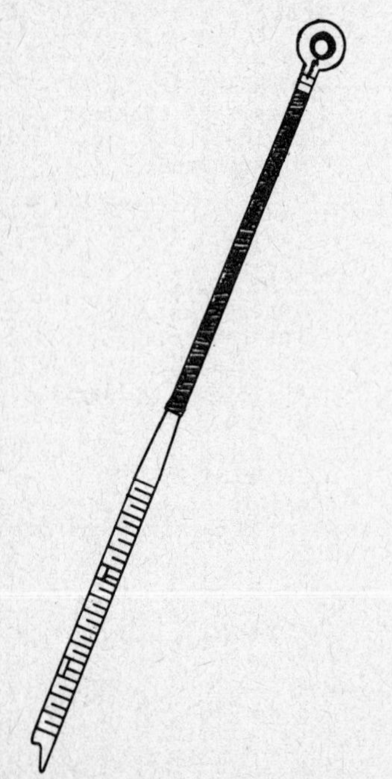
Oil pump output measuring rig

NOTE: *On twins, you can measure only one output at a time.*

3. Make sure there is some oil in the reservoir, then set the pump at minimum or maximum plunger stroke.

NOTE: *When checking maximum output, turn the pump pulley so that the ramp moves along the guide pin to the maximum position. DO NOT PUSH the pulley straight into position because the plunger stroke may then be longer than when actuated by the cable.*

4. Turn the starter pulley 200 revolutions and note the amount of oil in the graduated tube, Check this figure with the specified output.

5. If there is still some doubt, reset the pump at the maximum or minimum output position (whichever was not used the first time) and repeat the operation.

AUTOLUBE PUMP OUTPUT

	Min. Stroke (cc @ 200 rev)	Max. Stroke (cc @ 200 rev)
JT1, G5S, G6S, G6SB, HT1, HT1B, L5T, L5TA	0.50-0.63	4.65-5.15
HS1, HS1B, YL1/E, AS2C	0.50-0.63	4.20-4.80
CS1C, CS3B, CS3C, DS6B, DS6C, R2/C, R3, R5, R5B	0.50-0.63	5.15-5.70
AT1, AT1B, AT1C, CT1, CT1B, CT1C	0.50-0.63	8.80-9.76
DT1B, DT1C, DT1E, RT1 (late), RT1B	0.95-1.19	8.80-9.76
RT1 (early)	1.19-1.44	9.10-10.05

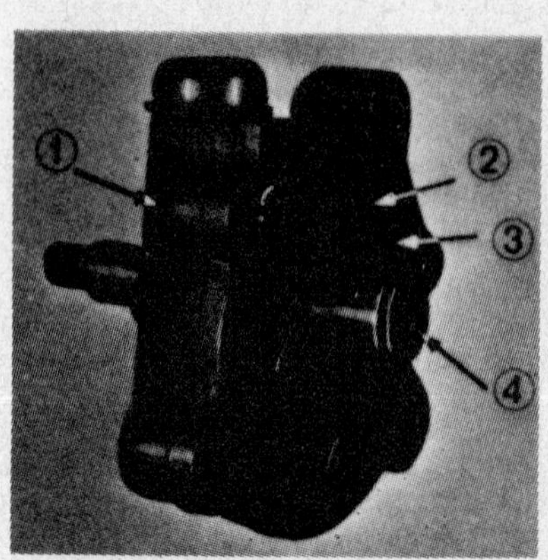

Oil pump assembly
1. Pump housing
2. Outer rotor
3. Inner rotor
4. Drive shaft

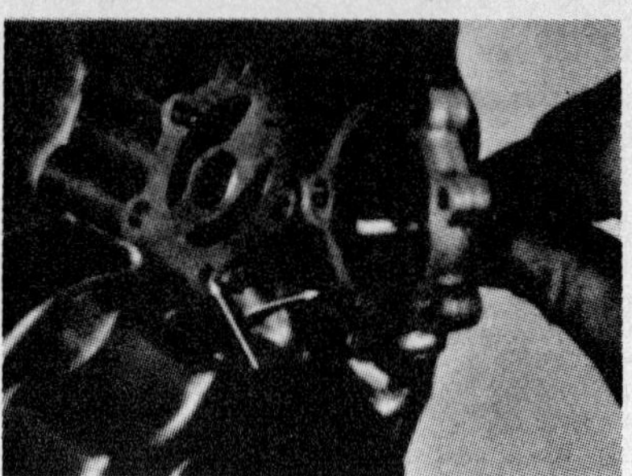
Oil pump locating pin and hole

FUEL SYSTEMS

Carburetor

Disassembly

1. Remove the four bottom float bowl screws.
2. Remove the float bowl.
3. Push out the float pin and remove the float, noting its position.
4. Remove the starter jet mechanism.
5. Remove the fuel needle and unscrew the fuel needle seat.
6. Remove the main jet.
7. Remove the needle jet.

NOTE: *Mikuni carburetors have two types of needle jets—one screws into position, the other is held in place by a small clip.*

8. Remove the pilot jet with a small flat head screwdriver.

Cleaning

Clean all parts in solvent, then blow dry with compressed air. Make sure all the jets are free from obstruction.

Assembly

Assemble the carburetor in the reverse order of disassembly.

Float Level Adjustment

NOTE: *Float level is preset at the factory. An adjustment should be necessary only after installing a new float or when the adjustable tang has been bent.*

INTERCONNECTED FLOAT TYPE (SC)

1. Turn the carburetor upside-down and tilt it until the float pivots up against the fuel inlet passage needle.
2. Make certain the fuel inlet needle is seated, then let it spring back until the adjustable tang is lightly touching it.
3. Measure the distance from the float bowl gasket surface to the top of the float.
4. If an adjustment is necessary to meet specifications, bend the tang, not the float arm.

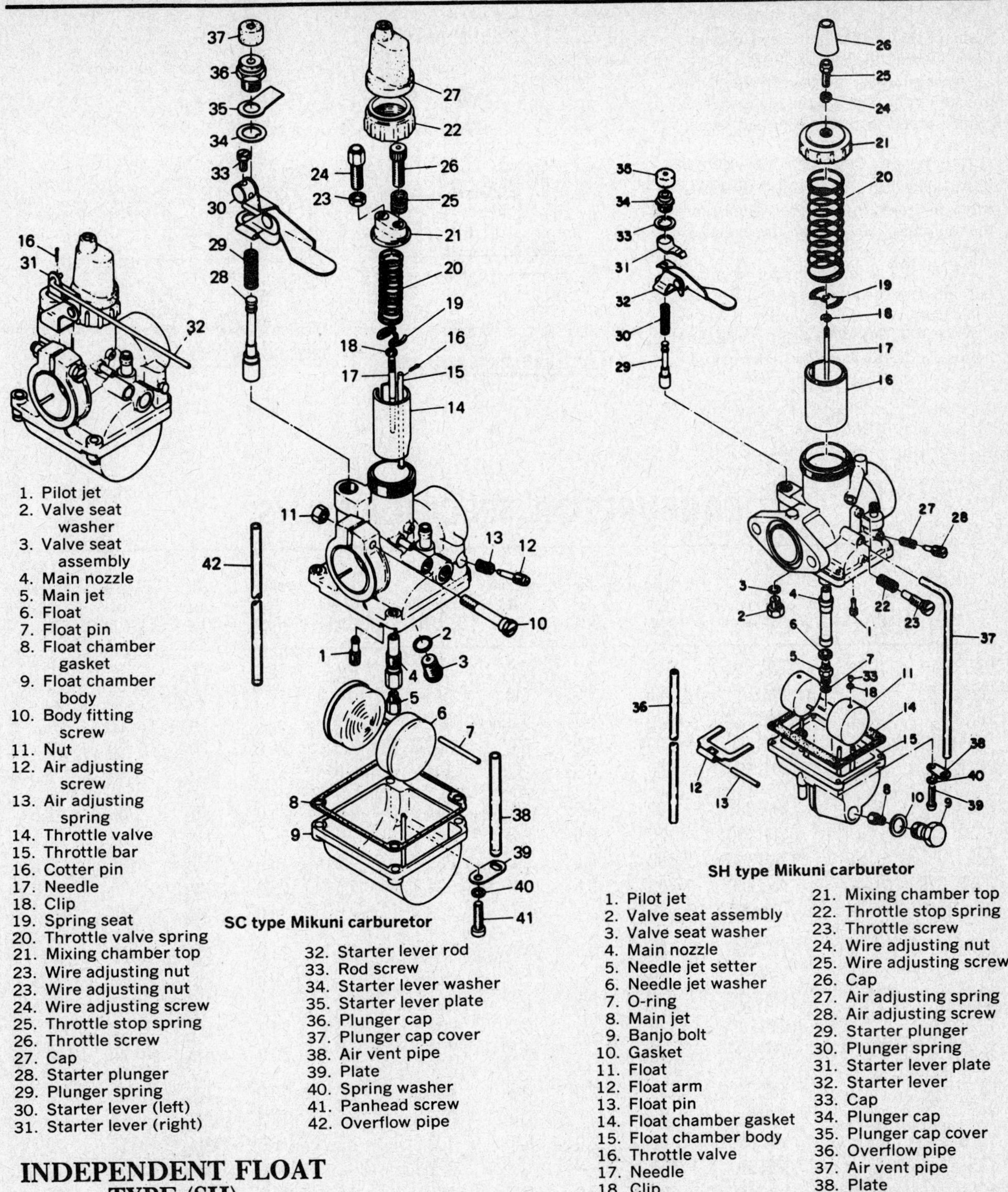

SC type Mikuni carburetor

SH type Mikuni carburetor

INDEPENDENT FLOAT TYPE (SH)

1. Remove the float bowl and turn the carburetor upside-down.

2. Measure the distance from the needle jet housing surface to each of the float arms.

3. If necessary, bend the adjustable tang to achieve the proper clearance.

Specifications and Designations

Carburetor parts are given letter and /or number designations according to their size, taper, etc. Explanations for these designations as applied to Mikuni carburetors are given below.

MAIN JET (M.J.)—Main jet size on Mikuni carburetors indicates the amount of fuel flow in cubic centimeters during one minute. For example, a size 100 indicates a fuel flow of 100 cc/minute.

NEEDLE JET (N.J.)—The needle jet inner diameter is given as a coded letter and number. A-0, for example, indicates an inside diameter of 1.9 mm. The letter determines the size in increments of 0.-050 mm; the number gives inbetween sizes in steps of 0.005 mm. Therefore, A-2 has an inside diameter of 1.910 mm, B-0 has an inside diameter of 1.950, etc.

JET NEEDLE (J.N.)—The first number indicates the overall length of the needle. 3 is 30–40 mm, 4 is 40–50 mm, etc.

The letter indicates the needle taper. A is 0° 15′, B is 0° 30′, and so on, in increments of 15′. The next letter and/or number(s) identify the manufacturer.

The last number indicates the standard groove for the clip: 1 is the top groove, 2 is the second from the top, and so on, through 5.

THROTTLE VALVE CUTAWAY (C.A.)—The degree of throttle valve cuatway is indicated by a number. The larger the number, the greater the cutaway size.

PILOT JET (P.J.)—The pilot jet number indicates the amount of fuel flow (in cubic centimeters) per minute.

STARTER JET (S.J.)—The starter jet number indicates fuel flow in cc/minute.

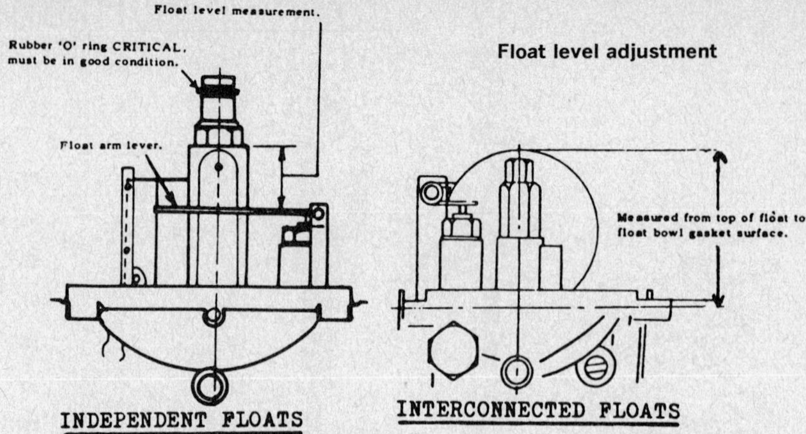

Float level adjustment

CARBURETOR SPECIFICATIONS

	Type (Mikuni)	Main Jet (M.J.)	Air Jet (A.J.)	Needle Jet (N.J.)	Jet Needle (J.N.)	Cut Away (C.A.)	Pilot Jet (P.J.)	Air Screw (A.S.)	Starter Jet (S.J.)	Flat Level (F.L.) ②
U7E	VM15SC	100	2.4	E-8	3G9-3	2.5	12.5	1¾	25	22.5
Late YJ2	VM16	60	—	E-0	3D1-3	1.5	17.5	1½	15	23
JT1, JT2	Y16P	86	0.7	2.085	032-2	1.5	38.0	1½	50	—
YG1, YG1T, MG1T	VM15SC-1	100	0.5	E-0	3G1-3	1.5	20.0	1½	20	23
YG1K, YGS1, YGS1T	VM15SC-1	100	0.5	E-2	3G1-2	1.5	17.5	1¾	40	23
G5S	VM16SC	100	0.5	E-2	3G9-3	2.5	25.0	1¾	30	20.5
YG5T	VM16SC	120	0.5	E-2	3G9-4	2.5	25.0	1½	30	20.5
G6S	VM16SC	100	0.5	E-2	3G9-3	2.5	25.0	1¾	30	20.5
G6SB, G7S	VM16SC	120	0.5	E-2	3G9-3	2.5	25.0	1¾	30	22.5
HT1, HT1B	VM20SC	85	—	N-6	4D3-3	2.0	30.0	1¾	40	21
LT2	VM20SH	120	0.5	N-6	4J13-2	1.5	25.0	1¾	30	21
HS1, HS1B	VM16SC	70	—	E-0	3G9-4	1.5	20.0	1½	30	22.5
LS2	VM17SC	70	0.8	0-0	3D12-3	2.0	15.0	1¾	40	22.5
YL2, YL2C	VM17SC	120	2.0	D-0	3D3-3	2.0	20.0	1½	40	22
YL2CM	VM20SC	95	—	N-8	4D2-3	2.0	30.0	1¾	40	22
L5T, L5TA	VM20SC	180	2.0	0-8	4D2-3	2.0	20.0	1¾	40	22
YL1	VM16	60	—	E-0	3D3-3	1.5	17.5	2½	15	23
YL1E	VM16SC	60	2.0	E-0	3D3-3	1.5	17.5	2½	15	23
YA5	M21S1	120	—	—	22M3-3	—	30.0	1¾	—	—
YA6	VM22SC	190	2.0	0-0	4J6-3	2.5	30.0	1¾	110	25
AT1, AT1B, AT1C	VM24SH	150	—	N-8	4D3-3	2.0	30.0	1½	40	25.5
AT2	VM24SH	230	—	0-6	4F10-3	1.5	25.0	1¾	40	21
YAS1(c), AS2C	VM17SC	95	0.8	0-0	4D9-4	2.0	17.5	1¾	30	22
CT1, CT1B, CT1C	VM24SH	150	—	N-8	4D3-3	2.0	40.0	1½	40	25.5
CT2	VM24SH	200	—	0-6	4L6-3	2.0	25.0	2	40	21
YCS1	VM18SC	65	0.5	0-0	4D2-3	3.0	20.0	2	40	21
YCS1C, CS3C	VM20SC	65	—	N-6	4D10-3	2.5	30.0	2¼	40	21
CS3B, CS5	VM20SC	65	—	N-6	4D10-3	2.5	30.0	2	40	21.7
DT1	VM26SH	150	0.5	0-2	5D1-3	2.5	35.0	1½	60	14.1
DT1B, DT1S, DT1C	VM26SH	160	0.8	0-2	5D1-3	2.5	35.0	1½	60	14.1

	Type (Mikuni)	Main Jet (M.J.)	Air Jet (A.J.)	Needle Jet (N.J.)	Jet Needle (J.N.)	Cut Away (C.A.)	Pilot Jet (P.J.)	Air Screw (A.S.)	Starter Jet (S.J.)	Flat Level (F.L.) ②
DT1E	VM26SH	160	—	0-2	5D1-3	2.5	35.0	1½	60	15.1
DS7	VM26SC	100	—	0-0	5DP7-4	2.0	40.0	1½	100	15.1
YDS2	VM20SH	80	—	N-6	24A1-3	2.0	25.0	1½	40	25
Early YDS3	VM24SC	120	0.5	0-0	4D4-2	2.0	20.0	1½	40	25
Early YDS3C	VM24SC	120	0.5	0-0	4D4-3	2.0	20.0	1½	40	25
Late YDS3, YDS3C	VM24	130	0.5	0-0	4D4-2	2.0	20.0	1½	40	25
YDS5	VM26SC	120	0.5	0-5	4D3-2	2.5	30.0	1½	40	25.5
DS6C	VM26SC	100	0.5	N-8	4D3-3	2.0	30.0	1½	40	25.5
DS6B	VM26SC	110	—	N-8	4D3-3	2.0	30.0	1½	40	25.5
DT2	VM26SH	160	—	N-8	5DP7-3	1.5	30.0	1¼	60	15.1
YM1	VM24	130	0.5	0-0	4D4-2	2.0	20.0	1½	40	25.1
YM2C	VM26SC	110	0.5	0-5	4D3-2	2.5	30.0	1½	40	25.5
YR1	VM28SC	190	0.5	0-2	5D1-2	1.5	30.0	2¼	40	25.5
YR2, YR2C, R3(C)	VM28SC	170	0.5	0-2	5D1-3	2.0	30.0	1½	40	25.5
R5, R5B	VM28SC	110	—	0-0	5DP7-4	2.0	40.0	1¾	100①	15
R5C	VM28SC	120	—	0-4	5DP7-4	2.0	30.0	1¼	100	15
RT1	VM32SH	240	—	0-4	6DP1-3	1.5	30.0	1¼	60	14.1
RT1B	VM32SH	240	—	0-4	6CF1-2	1.5	30.0	1¾	60	8.5
RT2	VM32SH	230	2.0	P-0	6DH3-3	3.0	45.0	1½	60	8.5

① Left carburetor only. ② Measured in mm.

ELECTRICAL SYSTEMS

COMPONENT TESTS

Use the following procedures in conjunction with the electrical specifications at the end of this section to determine faulty components.

DC Generator Voltage Output

1. Disconnect the generator wiring from the other components.
2. Connect a voltmeter to the armature terminal "A" (red) and ground field terminal "F" (black).
3. Run the engine up to about 2500 rpm and check the voltmeter reading. If within reasonable bounds of the necessary output (6 or 12 volts), the generator is not likely to be the source of your problem. If the output is nil or minimal, isolate the cause by checking the carbon brushes and field winding insulation.

a. Check all brush wire connections.

b. Measure brush length and spring tension.

c. Make sure the positive carbon brush is properly insulated.

NOTE: *Disconnect the negative brush before checking for a positive brush short.*

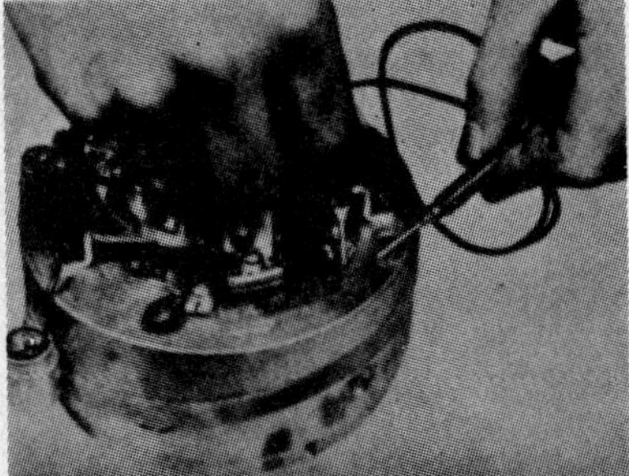

Checking positive brush insulation

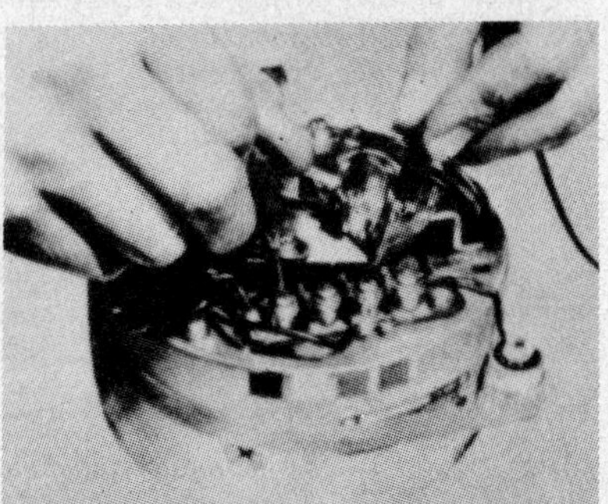

Checking continuity between the armature and field windings

d. Check for any dirt, oil, etc. that may be shorting out part of the yoke assembly.

e. Check for proper continuity between the armature and field windings (terminals "A" and "F").

NOTE: *Lift the carbon brushes off the commutator before checking field winding resistance.*

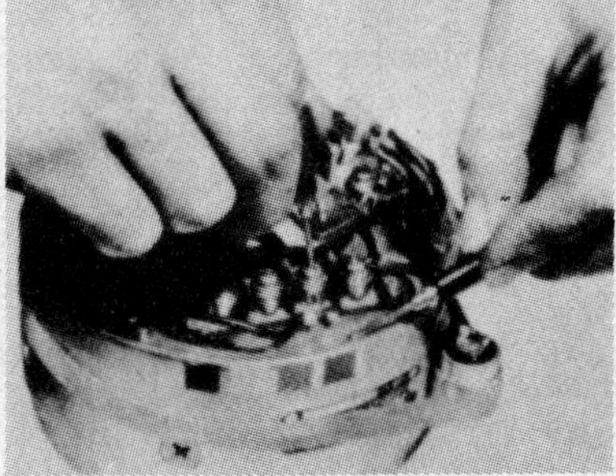

Checking field winding insulation

f. Check field winding insulation with an ohmmeter set at the highest scale. Readings between the yoke housing and terminal "A" and the yoke housing and terminal "F" should be infinite (3 megohms or more).

4. If the preceding tests didn't reveal the problem, perform the following checks on the armature:

a. Make sure the mica gaps are free from any carbon dust that could short out the individual bars.

b. Make sure the commutator surface is clean. If necessary, clean it up with a piece of fine emery cloth. Remember to remove the dust!

c. Check for continuity between the commutator segments and armature core. The readings should be infinite.

Cleaning the commutator

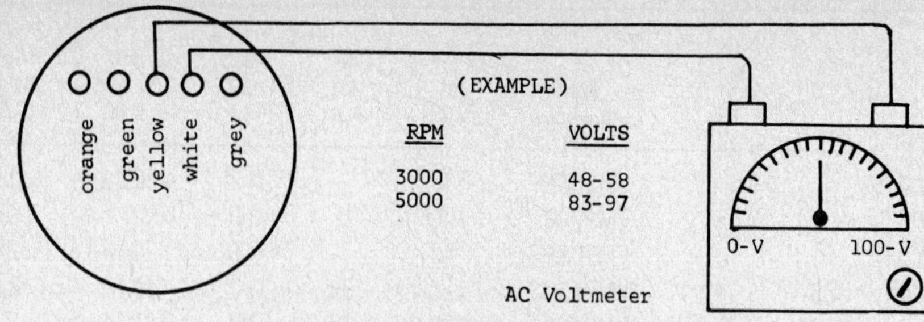

Checking alternator output to the nighttime circuit

Checking the commutator segments

There must be a completely open circuit!

d. Make sure continuity exists between all the commutator segments.

Starter Generator Brushes and Coil

1. Disconnect the negative starter brush and check the positive brush for insulation.

2. Disconnect the voltage regulator wiring and lift the positive brushes off the commutator. Make sure there is continuity between terminals "A" and "M". No resistance indicates a broken starter winding.

3. Disconnect the heavy motor winding wire from the positive brush and make sure the windings are insulated.

NOTE: *On early models, the fields and motor windings are internally connected. The readings on these machines must be exactly as specified.*

4. With the heavy motor winding wire still disconnected from the positive brush, make sure there is an open circuit between the "M" terminal and ground (at least 3 megohms).

Magneto Assembly

1. Make sure all connections are tight.

2. Check all parts for any oil or water spots.

3. The flywheel magnets eventually weaken. If the points and condenser are good, but lighting and spark are weak, replace the flywheel or have the magnets recharged.

4. Check the ignition and lighting coils for any signs of having burnt out.

5. Make sure the lighting coil wires all have continuity with each other.

6. Make sure there is no continuity between the ignition coil leads and core.

Alternator No Load Voltage Check

CAUTION: *Never disconnect the battery from an ac generating system during operational tests.*

1. Disconnect the yellow, green, and white wires from the stator.

2. Connect an ac voltmeter to the green and white wire leads, then start the engine. The voltage reading shows the output to the ignition system, battery, brake light, and horn.

3. Switch the ac voltmeter lead from the green wire to the yellow wire lead. This reading indicates output to the above mentioned components and also the lighting system.

Alternator Average Amperage Check

1. Disconnect the rectifier red wire.

2. Connect a dc ammeter positive lead to the red wire and connect the ammeter negative lead to the red wire connector.

3. Output at 3000 rpm should be 2.8 ± 0.5A—day position, 6.7 ± 0.5A—night position; at 5000 rpm, 3.2 ± 0.5A—day position and 7.1 ± 0.5A—night position.

Voltage Regulator Relay

NOTE: *If isolating a problem source, first check the generator as previously described, then check this relay.*

1. Check for any loose connections, broken solder, dirty points, etc.

2. Connect the correct voltage battery to the regulator coil as shown in the illustration, then insert a flat piece of steel into the electromagnetic field. If the steel is attracted by the field, the coil is OK.

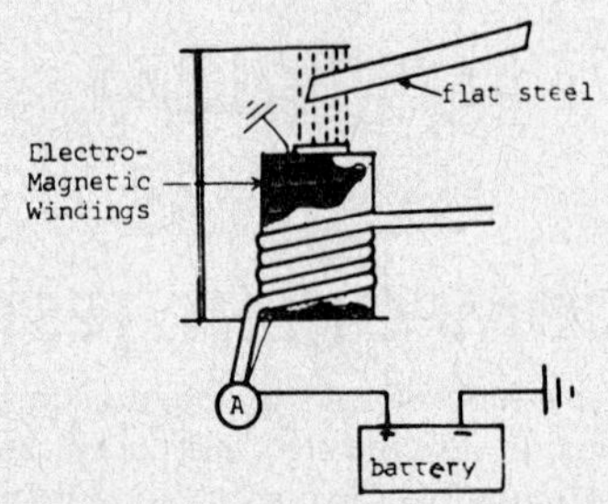

Checking the voltage regulator relay coil

3. Check the shunt resistors by connecting an ohmmeter positive lead to the "A" terminal and the negative lead to the "F" terminal. Manually operate the relay —each of the shunt positions should show a different resistance. If any of the positions indicate infinite resistance, one of the shunts is open.

4. Check the yoke, core, and point gap with specifications. Adjust if necessary.

5. Check the regulator no-load voltage by starting the engine, disconnecting the wire at regulator terminal "B", connecting the positive lead of a voltmeter to the terminal and the negative lead to ground. Increase engine speed to the specified rpm and check the reading against specifications. The voltage can be adjusted by bending the spring hook or turning the adjusting screw so that the point pressure is increased or decreased.

NOTE: *Increasing the pressure raises the voltage.*

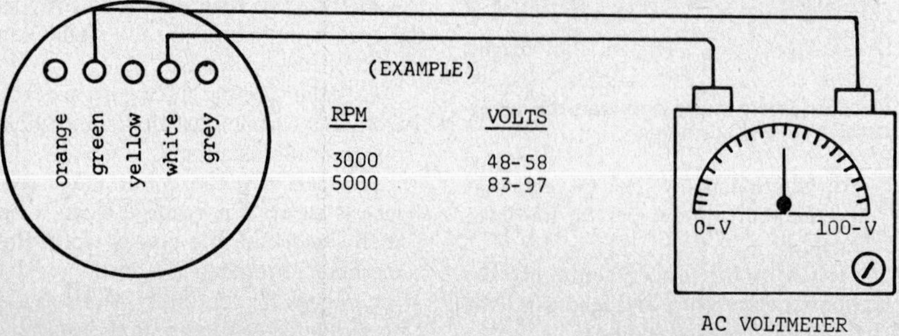

Checking alternator output to the daytime circuit

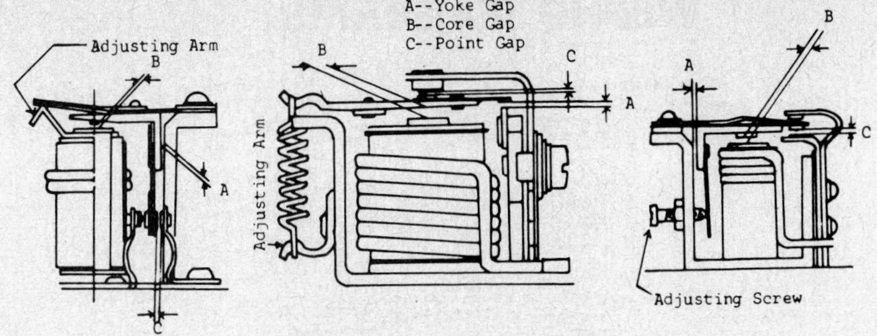

Voltage regulator relay adjustments

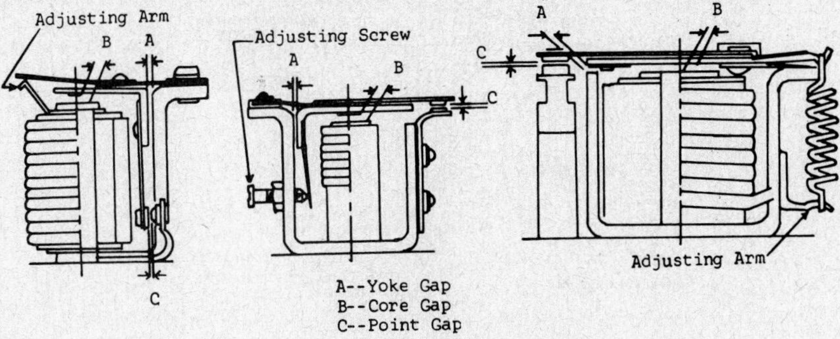

Cut-out relay adjustments

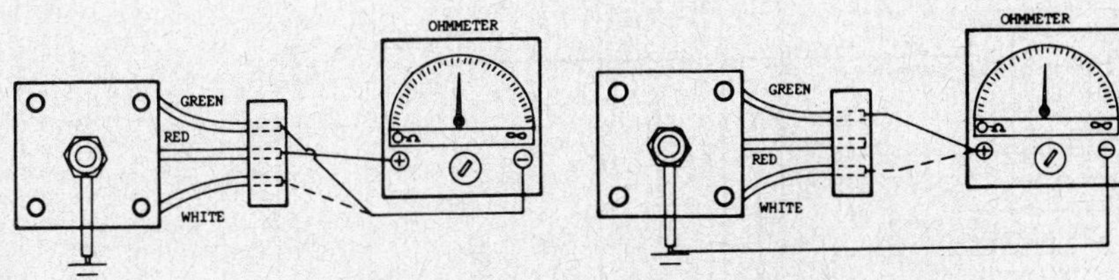

Schematic for checking silicon diode rectifiers

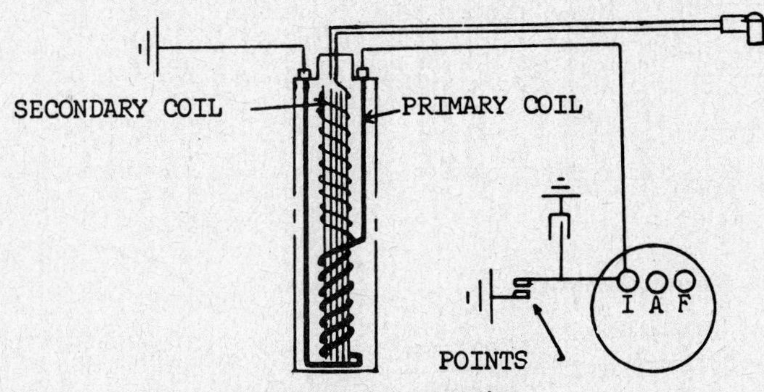

Ignition coil construction

Voltage Cut-Out Relay

NOTE: *Check the cut-out relay if the generator and voltage regulator relay are in good condition.*

1. Check the relay magnetic field as previously described.
2. Check and adjust yoke, core, and point gap as previously described.
3. Check the relay cut-out voltage in the same manner as the regulator relay no-load voltage. If necessary, bend the point spring hook so that the cut-out voltage meets specifications.

Silicon Diode Rectifier (3-Wire) Continuity Check

1. Connect the positive lead of an ohmmeter to the red rectifier lead. Connect the negative lead to the green and then the white rectifier leads. The ohmmeter should show continuity. Reverse the meter leads and there should be no continuity.
2. Repeat the above with the ohmmeter connected to ground and the green, then the white rectifier leads.

ELECTRICAL WIRING COLOR CODES

CHASSIS
- Red—battery
- Brown—current source wire
- Dark Blue—lighting, switches
- Green (in headlight shell)—low beam
- Yellow (in headlight shell)—high beam
- Pink—horn
- Light Blue—neutral light
- Yellow—stoplight switch
- Green/Yellow—front stoplight switch
- Blue/White—starter solenoid
- Brown/White—turn signal switch
- Dark Brown—left turn signal
- Green—right turn signal

MAGNETO
- Black—ignition (not ground)
- Yellow—lighting
- Green—daytime charging
- Green/Red—nighttime charging
- White—ignition switch to rectifier
- White (from magneto)—no connection

STARTER/GENERATOR
- Orange—ignition
- Gray—ignition (twins)
- Black—ground
- Dark Green—fields
- White—armature and charging light
- Light Green—starter motor

ALTERNATOR
- White (3)—AC output
- Black—ground brush
- Green—positive brush
- Orange—ignition
- Gray—ignition (twins)

Selenium Rectifier (2-Wire) Continuity Check

Connect an ohmmeter to the rectifier red and white leads, then reverse the meter leads. There should be continuity one way, but not the other.

Electric Starter Relay

If the starter motor does not function check the following:

1. Check for proper continuity in the starter relay core windings.
2. Check relay points for cleanliness.
3. When the points are closed, make sure there is continuity between the battery and motor windings.

NOTE: *The starter relay is located either on the frame, as a separate unit, or within the voltage regulator housing.*

Ignition Coil

NOTE: *Check the ignition coil if you are having spark plug firing problems and the battery, points, and condenser checked out OK.*

1. Check resistance between the positive and negative primary terminals.
2. Check continuity between one primary terminal and the high-tension secondary terminal. (should be around 6000 ohms).
3. Scrape some paint off the coil housing and check continuity between the primary winding and the coil housing. Resistance should read infinity.
4. Remove the plug cap and position the bare high-tension wire about ¼ in. from the cylinder head. Kick the engine over and check for a strong bright spark.

WIRING DIAGRAMS

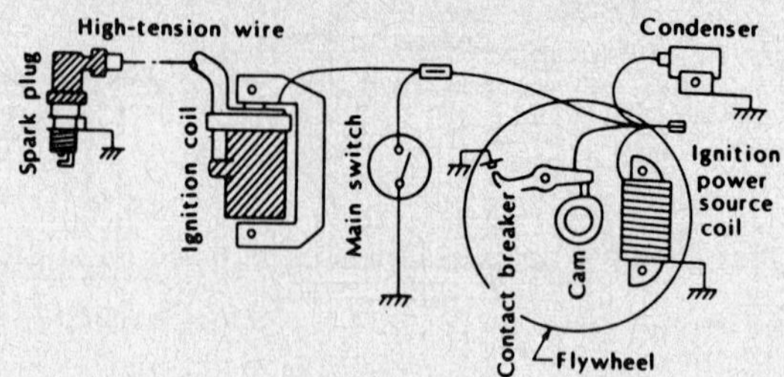

Magneto ignition circuit

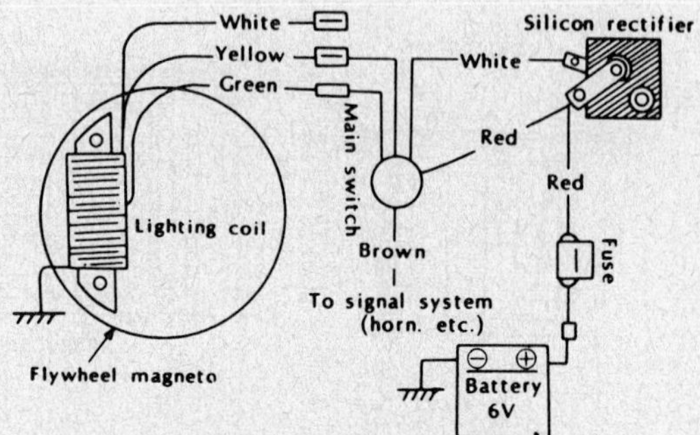

Magneto lighting circuit

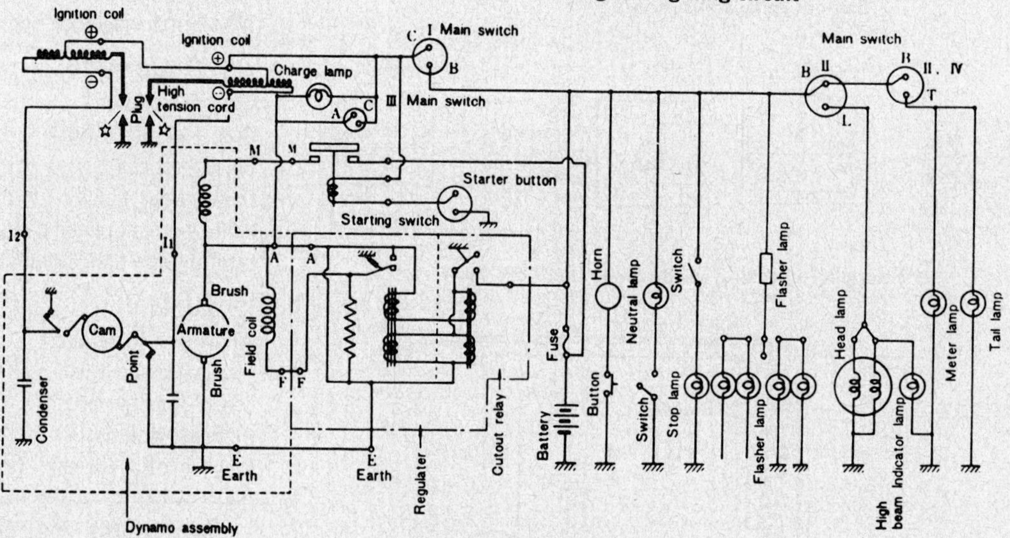

DC generator schematic

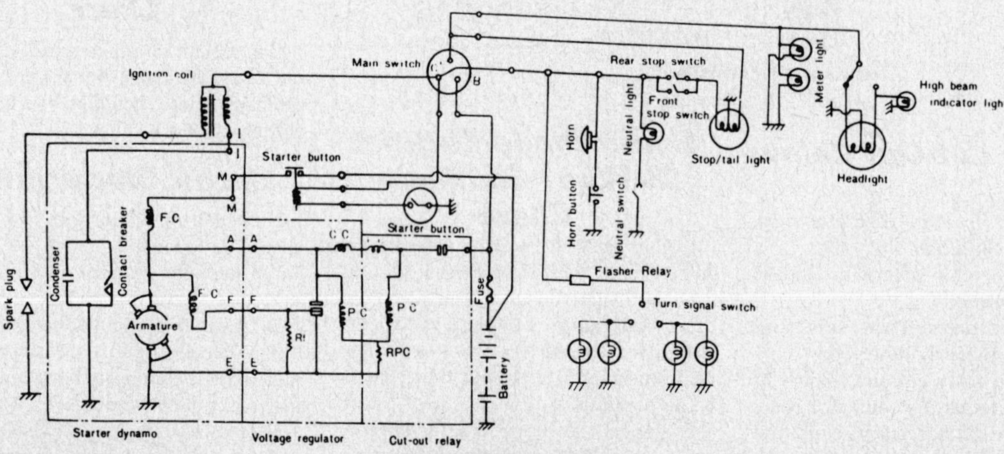

Starter generator schematic

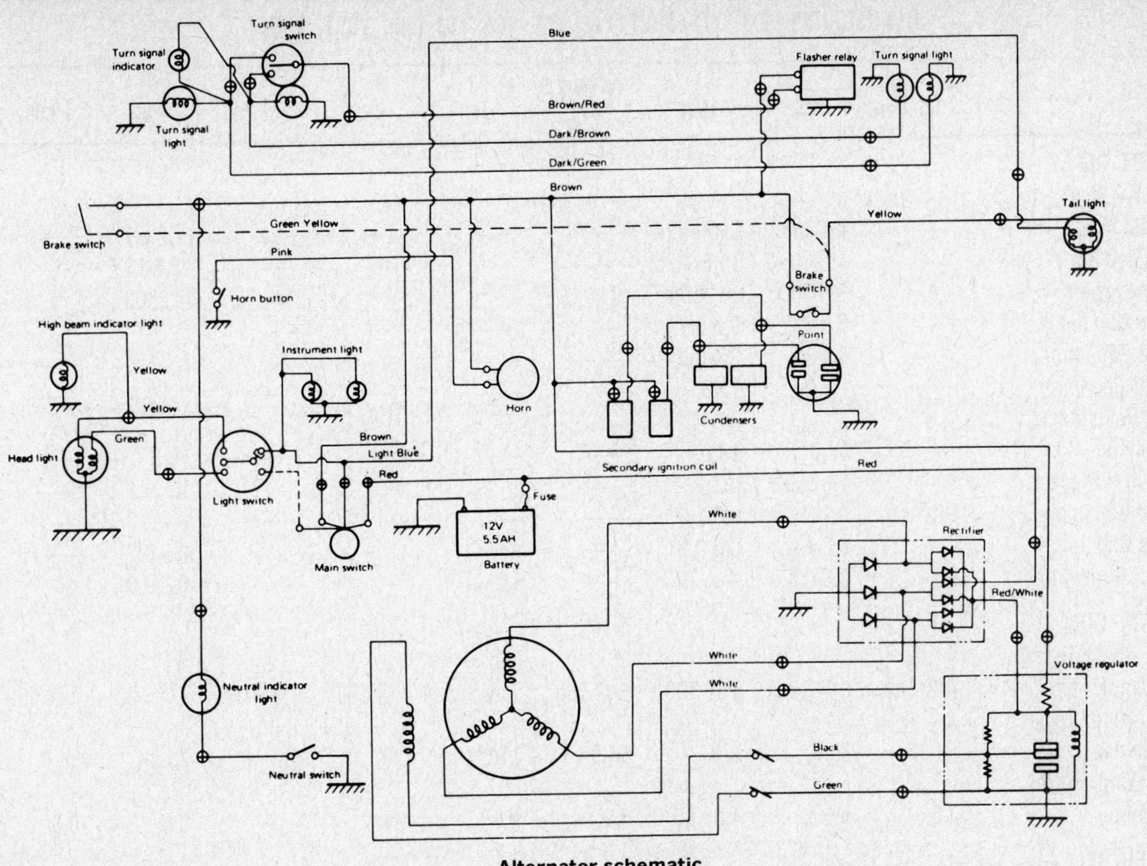

Alternator schematic

ELECTRICAL SPECIFICATIONS

U5/U5L, U5E, YJ1/MJ2T/YJ2, JT1, YG1 (all), YG5T, G5S

	U5/U5L	U5E	YJ1/MJ2T/YJ2	JT1	YG1 (all)	YG5T	G5S
DYNAMO AND MAGNETO							
Type	Magneto	Starter Dyn.	Magneto	Magneto	Magneto	Starter Dyn.	Magneto
Contact Press. (kg)	0.82 ± 10%	0.5-0.7	0.83 ± 10%	0.60-0.80	0.7-0.9	0.70 ± 10%	0.70 ± 10%
Condenser Cap. (μf)	0.3 ± 10%	0.22 ± 10%	0.3 ± 10%	0.22 ± 10%	0.27 ± 10%	0.22 ± 10%	0.22 ± 10%
Stand. Brush Dimen. (mm)	—	5 x 8 x 20	—	—	—	4.5 x 8 x 20	—
Min. Brush Length (mm)	—	11.8	—	—	—	12.0	—
Brush Spring Strength (Kg)	—	0.40-0.56	—	—	—	0.6 ± 15%	—
Commutator Dia. (mm)	—	37.5	—	—	—	40.0	—
Commutator Wear Limit (mm)	—	2.0	—	—	—	2.0	—
Stand. Mica Undercut (mm)	—	0.5-1.0	—	—	—	0.5-1.0	—
Min. Mica Undercut (mm)	—	0.2	—	—	—	0.2	—
Field Coil Resist. (ohms)	—	5.0	—	—	—	6.1	—

U5/U5L, U5E, U7E, YJ1/MJ2T/YJ2, JT1, JT2, YG1 (all), YG5T, G55

	U5/U5L	U5E	U7E	YJ1/MJ2T/ YJ2	JT1	JT2	YG1 (all)	YG5T	G5S
CUT-OUT RELAY REGULATOR									
Model No.	—	T10-6-52	T106-52A	—	—	—	—	RC2332W	—
No Load Adj. (v @ rpm)	—	15.8-16.5 @ 2500	15.8-16.5 @ 2500	—	—	—	—	15.8-16.5 @ 2500	—
Yoke Gap (mm)	—	0.6-0.7	0.6-0.7	—	—	—	—	—	—
Core Gap (mm)	—	0.4-0.7	0.4-0.5	—	—	—	—	1.1-1.2	—
Point Gap (mm)	—	0.4-0.5	11.8	—	—	—	—	0.3-0.4	—
Coil Resistance (ohms)	—	17.0	13.0	—	—	—	—	18.5	—
Cut-In Voltage	—	13 ± 0.5	0.2	—	—	—	—	13 ± 0.5	—
Yoke Gap (mm)	—	0.2	0.8-1.0	—	—	—	—	—	—
Core Gap (mm)	—	0.8-1.0	0.6-0.8	—	—	—	—	0.5-0.7	—
Point Gap (mm)	—	0.6-0.8	—	—	—	—	—	0.6-0.8	—
IGNITION COIL									
Min. Spark Test (mm @ rpm)	6 @ 500	6 @ 100	8 @ 300	6 @ 500	7 @ 500	7 @ 500	6 @ 500	7 @ 500	7 @ 500
Sec. Wind. Resist. (ohms)	8K-9K	8K-9K	11K	8K-9K	11K	11K	4K	7K-8K	5K
Pri. Wind. Resist. (ohms)	4.5	4.5	4.0	4.9	4.9	4.9	—	0.6	0.6
STARTER RELAY									
Core Gap (mm)	—	1.4-1.5	1.3-1.4	—	—	—	—	1.2-1.4	—
Point Gap (mm)	—	1.3-1.4	1.4-1.5	—	—	—	—	1.3-1.5	—
Wind. Resist. (ohms)	—	4.6	—	—	—	—	—	11.2	—
Activating Volt. (min)	—	10	12	—	—	—	—	8	—
BATTERY									
Capacity	6V-7AH	12V-5.5AH	12V-7AH	6V-4AH	—	6V-2AH	6V-4AH	6V-4AH	6V-4AH

G6S/G6SB/G7S, HT1/HT1B, LT2, HS1/HS1B, LS2, YL2, YL2C(m)/L5T(A), YL1

	G6S/G6SB/ GS7	HT1/HT1B	LT2	HS1/HS1B	LS2	YL2	YL2C(m)/ L5T(A)	YL1
DYNAMO AND MAGNETO								
Type	Magneto	Magneto	Magneto	Alternator	Magneto	Generator	Starter Dyn.	Generator
Contact Pressure (kg)	0.65-0.85	0.65-0.85	0.65-0.85	0.60-0.80	0.5-0.7	0.7 ± 10%	0.7 ± 10%	0.5-0.7
Condenser Capacity (μf)	0.22	0.25	0.30	0.22	0.22	0.22 ± 10%	0.22 ± 10%	0.22 ± 10%
Stand. Brush Dim. (mm)	—	—	—	—	—	4.5 x 8 x 20	4.5 x 8 x 20	4.5 x 8 x 20
Min. Brush Length (mm)	—	—	—	—	—	12.0	12.0	12.0
Brush Spring Strength (Kg)	—	—	—	—	—	0.6 ± 15%	0.6 ± 15%	0.6 ± 10%
Commutator Dia. (mm)	—	—	—	—	—	40.0	40.0	40.0
Com. Wear Limit (mm)	—	—	—	—	—	2.0	2.5	2.0

G6S/G6SB/G7S, HT1/HT1B, LT2, HS1/HS1B, LS2, YL2, YL2C(m)/L5T(A), YL1

	G6S/G6SB/GS7	HT1/HT1B	LT2	HS1/HS1B	LS2	YL2	YL2C(m)/L5T(A)	YL1
Stand. Mica Undercut (mm)	—	—	—	—	—	0.5-1.0	0.5-1.0	0.5-0.8
Min. Mica Undercut (mm)	—	—	—	—	—	0.2	0.2	0.2
Field Coil Resistance (ohms)	—	—	—	—	—	5.2	5.2	5.2
REGULATOR								
Model No.	—	—	—	—	—	RN226J2	RC2332W	T106-01
No. Load Adj. (v @ rpm)	—	—	—	—	—	15.6-16.3 @ 2500	15.8-16.5 @ 2500	15.6-16.3 @ 2500
Yoke Gap (mm)	—	—	—	—	—	0.3	0.3	0.6-0.7
Core Gap (mm)	—	—	—	—	—	1.0-1.2	1.0-1.2	0.4-0.7
Point Gap (mm)	—	—	—	—	—	0.3-0.4	0.3-0.4	0.4-0.5
Coil Resistance (ohms)	—	—	—	—	—	18.5	18.5	17.0
CUT-OUT RELAY								
Cut-in Voltage	—	—	—	—	—	1.3 ± 0.5	1.3 ± 0.5	1.3 ± 0.5
Yoke Gap (mm)	—	—	—	—	—	0.3	0.3	0.2
Core Gap (mm)	—	—	—	—	—	0.5-0.7	0.5-0.7	0.8-1.0
Point Gap (mm)	—	—	—	—	—	0.6-0.8	0.6-0.8	0.6-0.8
IGNITION COIL								
Min. Spark Test (mm @ rpm)	7 @ 500	7 @ 500	7 @ 500	7 @ 500	8 @ 300	6 @ 100	6 @ 100	6 @ 100
Sec. Wind. Resist. (ohms)	5.8K ± 10%	11K	6.6K	5K-8K	11K	7K-8K	7K-8K	5K-6K
Prim. Wind. Resist. (ohms)	0.6 ± 10%	4.9 ± 10%	1.6	4.2-5.2	4.0	4.8	4.8	4.7
STARTER RELAY								
Core Gap (mm)	—	—	—	—	—	—	1.2-1.4	—
Point Gap (mm)	—	—	—	—	—	—	1.3-1.5	—
Wind. Resistance (ohms)	—	—	—	—	—	—	11	—
Activating Voltage (min)	—	—	—	—	—	—	8	—
BATTERY								
Capacity	6V-4AH	6V-2AH	6V-4AH	12V-5.5AH	12V-5.5AH	12V-5.5AH	12V-7AH	12V-5.5AH

YL1E, YA5, YA6, AT1/AT1B/AT1C/AT2, YAS1(C)/AS2C, CT1/CT1B, CT1C, CT2

	YL1E	YA5	YA6	AT1/AT1B/AT1C/AT2	YAS1(c)/AS2C	CT1, CT1B, CT1C	CT2
DYNAMO AND MAGNETO							
Type	Starter Dyn.	Starter Dyn.	Starter Dyn.	Starter Dyn.	Alternator	Magneto	Magneto
Contact Pressure (kg)	0.5-0.7	0.5-0.7	0.5-0.7	0.5-0.7	0.6 ± 10%	0.6-0.8 ± 10%	0.65-0.85
Condenser Capacity (μf)	0.22 ± 10%	0.22 ± 10%	0.22 ± 10%	0.22 ± 10%	0.22 ± 10%	0.22 ± 10%	0.30

YL1E, YA5, YA6, AT1/AT1B/AT1C/AT2, YAS1(C)/AS2C, CT1/CT1B, CT1C, CT2

	YL1E	YA5	YA6	AT1/AT1B/ AT1C/AT2	YAS1(c)/ AS2C	CT1, CT1B, CT1C	CT2
Stand. Brush Dimen. (mm)	5 x 8 x 20	4.5 x 8 x 19.5	4.5 x 8 x 19.5	4.5 x 9 x 20.5	—	—	—
Min. Brush Length (mm)	11.5	8.0	11.5	9.0	—	—	—
Brush Spring Strength (kg)	0.40-0.56	0.40-0.56	0.40-0.50	0.40-0.56	—	—	—
Commutator Dia. (mm)	37.5	37.5	37.5	38.5	—	—	—
Comttr. Wear Limit (mm)	2.0	2.0	2.0	2.0	—	—	—
Stand. Mica Undercut (mm)	0.5-1.0	0.5-0.8	0.5-0.8	0.5-0.8	—	—	—
Min. Mica Undercut (mm)	0.2	0.2	0.2	0.2	—	—	—
Field Coil Resistance (ohms)	5.2	6.8	6.8	4.8	—	—	—
REGULATOR							
Model No.	T106-53	T107-11 (13)	T167-52	T107-17	—	—	—
No Load Adj. (V @ rpm)	15.8-16.5 @ 3000	15.4-16.5 @ 3000	15.8-16.2 @ 3000	15.8-16.5 @ 2500	—	—	—
Yoke Gap (mm)	0.6-0.7	0.9-1.0	0.6-0.7	0.6-0.7	—	—	—
Core Gap (mm)	0.4-0.7	0.6-0.7	0.4-0.5	0.4-0.7	—	—	—
Point Gap (mm)	0.4-0.5	0.4-0.5	0.4-0.5	0.4-0.5	—	—	—
Coil Resistance (ohms)	17.0	9.85	14.4	11.2	—	—	—
CUT-OUT RELAY							
Cut-In Voltage	13 ± 0.5	13 ± 0.5	13 ± 0.5	13 ± 0.5	—	—	—
Yoke Gap (mm)	0.2	0.9-1.0	0.6-0.7	0.2	—	—	—
Core Gap (mm)	0.8-1.0	0.6-0.7	—	0.8-1.0	—	—	—
Point Gap (mm)	0.6-0.8	0.7-0.8	0.6-0.7	0.6-0.8	—	—	—
IGNITION COIL							
Min. Spark Test (mm @ rpm)	6 @ 100	6 @ 100	6 @ 100	6 @ 100	7 @ 500	7 @ 500	7 @ 500
Sec. Wind. Resist. (ohms)	5K-6K	5K-6K	5.5K	11K ± 20%	6K-7K	11K ± 20%	6.6K
Pri. Wind. Resist. (ohms)	4.7	4.9	4.9	4.0 ± 10%	4.7	4.9	1.6
STARTER RELAY							
Core Gap (mm)	1.4-1.5	—	1.4-1.5	1.3-1.4	—	—	—
Point Gap (mm)	1.3-1.4	2.0	1.3-1.4	1.5	—	—	—
Wind. Resistance (ohms)	4.6	4.94	11.3	4.5 ± 15%	—	—	—
Activating Voltage (min.)	10	8	8	10	—	—	—
BATTERY							
Capacity	12V-5.5AH	12V-10AH	12V-10AH	12V-7AH	12V-5.5AH	6V-2AH	6V-4AH

YCS1(C), C53C/C53B, CS5, D17 (all), DT2, YD3/YDT1, YDS1, YDS2

	YCS1(C)	C53C/C53B	CS5	D17 (all)	DT2	YD3/YDT1	YDS1	YDS2
DYNAMO AND MAGNETO								
Type	Starter Dyn.	Starter Dyn.	Starter Dyn.	Magneto	Magneto	Starter Dyn.	Generator	Generator
Contact Pressure (kg)	0.7 ± 10%	0.7 ± 10%	0.7 ± 10%	0.6 ± 10%	0.7 ± 10%	0.7-0.85	0.5-0.6	0.5-0.6
Condenser Capacity (μf)	0.22 ± 10%	0.22 ± 10%	0.22	0.25 ± 10%	0.25	0.22 ± 10%	0.22 ± 10%	0.22 ± 10%
Stand. Brush Dimen. (mm)	4.5 x 8 x 20	4.5 x 8 x 20	4.5 x 8 x 20	—	—	4.5 x 8 x 19.5	18 (length only)	18 (length only)
Min. Brush Length (mm)	12.0	12.0	8.0	—	—	8.0	12.0	12.0
Brush Spring Strength (kg)	0.6 ± 15%	0.6 ± 15%	0.6 ± 15%	—	—	0.40-0.56	0.5-0.7	0.5-0.7
Commutator Dia. (mm)	40.0	40.0	40.0	—	—	37.5	35.0	35.0
Comttr. Wear Limit (mm)	2.0	2.0	2.0	—	—	2.0	1.0	1.0
Stand. Mica Undercut (mm)	0.5-1.0	0.5-1.0	0.5	—	—	0.5-0.8	0.5-0.8	0.5-0.8
Min. Mica Undercut (mm)	0.2	0.2	0.2	—	—	0.2	0.2	0.2
Field Coil Resistance (ohms)	5.0	4.9	4.9	—	—	9.04	4.06	4.06
REGULATOR								
Model No.	RC2333V	T107-S5	RC2333V	—	—	T107-03	RHG	RHG
No Load Adj. (v @ rpm)	15.6-16.3 @ 2500	15.6-16.3 @ 2500	15.6-17.2 @ 4000	—	—	15.3-16.4 @ 3000	7.6-8.0 @ 3000	7.1-7.7 @ 3000
Yoke Gap (mm)	0.3	0.3	1.0-1.2	—	—	0.9-1.0	0.30-0.45	0.30-0.45
Core Gap (mm)	1.0-1.2	1.0-1.2	—	—	—	0.6-0.7	0.9-1.1	0.9-1.1
Point Gap (mm)	0.3-0.4	0.3-0.4	0.3-0.4	—	—	0.4-0.5	—	—
Coil Resistance (ohms)	18.5	8.1 @ 20°C	8.1 @ 20°C	—	—	10.1	—	—
CUT-OUT RELAY								
Cut-In Voltage	13 ± 0.5	13 ± 0.5	14.0	—	—	13 ± 1.5	6.5-7.0	6.5-7.0
Yoke Gap (mm)	0.3	0.3	0.3-0.5	—	—	0.9-1.0	0.25 ± 0.15	0.25 ± 0.15
Core Gap (mm)	0.3-0.5	0.3-0.5	—	—	—	0.6-0.7	0.4 ± 0.1	0.4 ± 0.1
Point Gap (mm)	0.7-0.9	0.7-0.9	0.7-0.9	—	—	0.7-0.8	0.4-0.6	0.4-0.6
IGNITION COIL								
Min. Spark Test (mm @ rpm)	6 @ 100	7 @ 500	7 @ 1500	6 @ 500	7 @ 500	6 @ 100	6 @ 800	6 @ 500
Sec. Wind. Resist. (ohms)	7K-8K	7.2K	11K	5K-6K	6.5K	5.5K	5.5K	5.5K
Pri. Wind. Resist. (ohms)	4.8	4.8	4.0	0.6	0.9	4.9	1.7	1.7
STARTER RELAY								
Core Gap (mm)	1.2-1.4	1.2-1.4	1.3-1.5	—	—	—	—	—
Point Gap (mm)	1.3-1.5	1.3-1.5	1.2-1.4	—	—	2.0	—	—
Wind. Resistance (ohms)	11.2	11.2	11.2	—	—	4.94	—	—
Activating Voltage (min)	8	8	12	—	—	8	—	—
BATTERY								
Capacity	12V-9AH	12V-9AH	12V-9AH	6V-7AH	6V-4AH	N.A.	N.A.	N.A.

YDS3(C)/YM1, DS5, DS6C, DS6B, DS7, YM2(C), YR1/YR2(C)/R3(C)

	YDS3(C)/ YM1	DS5	DS6C	DS6B	DS7	YM2(C)	YR1/YR2(C)/ R3(C)
DYNAMO AND MAGNETO							
Type	Generator	Starter Dyn.	Generator	Generator	Alternator	Generator	Generator
Contact Pressure (kg)	0.7 ± 10%	0.7 ± 10%	0.7 ± 10%	0.7 ± 10%	0.7 ± 10%	0.7 ± 10%	0.7 ± 10%
Condenser Capacity (μf)	0.22 ± 10%	0.22 ± 10%	0.22 ± 10%	0.22 ± 10%	0.22	0.22 ± 10%	0.22 ± 10%
Stand. Brush Dimen. (mm)	5 x 9 x 17	4.5 x 8 x 20	4.5 x 8 x 20	4.5 x 8 x 20	6 x 7 x 11	4.5 x 8 x 20	4.5 x 8 x 20
Min. Brush Length (mm)	11.0	12.0	8.0	12.0	6.0	12.0	12.0
Brush Spring Strength (kg)	0.6 ± 15%	0.6 ± 15%	0.6	0.6	0.62	0.6	0.6
Commutator Dia. (mm)	35.0	40.0	40.0	40.0	—	40.0	40.0
Cmttr. Wear Limit (mm)	1.0	2.0	2.0	2.0	—	2.0	2.0
Stand. Mica Undercut (mm)	0.5-1.0	0.5-1.0	0.5-1.0	0.5-1.0	—	0.5-1.0	0.5-1.0
Min. Mica Undercut (mm)	0.2	0.2	0.2	0.2	—	0.2	0.2
Field Coil Resist. (ohms)	4.2	5.0	5.57	5.6	4.2	5.6	5.6
REGULATOR							
Model No.	RN6225K	RN2225M	RN2226J	RN2226J	RL215	RN2226J	RN2226J①
No. Load Adj. (v @ rpm)	7.7-8.1 @ 2500	15.6-16.3 @ 2500	15.6-16.3 @ 2500	15.6-16.3 @ 2500	14.0-15.5 @ 4000	15.6-16.3 @ 2500	15.6-16.3 @ 2500
Yoke Gap (mm)	0.3	—	—	—	0.7-1.2	—	—
Core Gap (mm)	1.1-1.4	1.0-1.2	1.0-1.2	1.0-1.2	0.8-1.1	1.0-1.2	1.0-1.2
Point Gap (mm)	0.3-0.4	0.3-0.4	0.3-0.4	0.3-0.4	0.3-0.4	0.3-0.4	0.3-0.4
Coil Resistance (ohms)	5.6	18.5	18.5	18.5	10.8	18.5	18.5
CUT-OUT RELAY							
Cut-in Voltage	6.5-7.0	13 ± 0.5	13 ± 0.5	13 ± 0.5	—	13 ± 0.5	13 ± 0.5
Yoke Gap (mm)	0.3	—	—	—	—	—	—
Core Gap (mm)	0.3-0.5	0.3-0.5	0.3-0.5	0.3-0.5	—	0.3-0.5	0.3-0.5
Point Gap (mm)	0.7-0.9	0.7-0.9	0.7-0.9	0.7-0.9	—	0.7-0.9	0.7-0.9
IGNITION COIL							
Min. Sprk. Test (mm @ rpm)	6 @ 100	6 @ 100	7 @ 100	7 @ 700	7 @ 500	6 @ 100	6 @ 100
Sec. Wind. Resist. (ohms)	5K-6K	7K-8K	8.2K	8.2K	11K	7K-8K	7K-8K
Pri. Wind. Resist. ohms)	1.6	4.8	4.6	4.6	4.0	4.8	4.8
STARTER RELAY							
Core Gap (mm)	—	1.1-1.3	—	—	—	—	—
Point Gap (mm)	—	2.05-2.35	—	—	—	—	—
Wind. Resistance (ohms)	—	4.3	—	—	—	—	—
Activating Voltage (min)	—	8	—	—	—	—	—
BATTERY							
Capacity	6V-7AH	12V-11AH	12V-5AH	12V-5AH	12V-5.5AH	12V-5.5AH	12V-5.5AH

① R3—R2220J

R5/R5B, R5C, RT1/RT1B, RT2

	R5/R5B	R5C	RT1/RT1B	RT2
DYNAMO AND MAGNETO				
Type	Alternator	Alternator	Magneto	Magneto
Contact Pressure (kg)	0.6-0.8	0.65-0.75	0.6 ± 10%	0.6-0.8
Condenser Capacity (μf)	0.22	0.22	0.25 ± 10%	0.25
Stand. Brush Dimen. (mm)	11.5 x 7 x 6	—	—	6 x 7 x 11
Min. Brush Length (mm)	6.0	—	—	6.0
Brush Spring Strength (kg)	—	—	—	0.62
Field Coil Resistance (ohms)	—	—	—	4.2-4.3
REGULATOR				
Model No.	—	—	—	RL2150X
No Load Adj. (v @ rpm)	15.5-16.5 @	—	—	14.0-15.5 @ 4000
Yoke Gap (mm)	—	—	—	0.7-1.2
Core Gap (mm)	—	—	—	0.8-1.1
Point Gap (mm)	—	—	—	0.3-0.4
Coil Resistance (ohms)	—	—	—	10.8
IGNITION COIL				
Min. Spark Test (mm @ rpm)	8 @ 500	7 @ 500	6 @ 500	7 @ 500
Sec. Wind. Resist. (ohms)	11K	6.5K	5K-6K	11K
Pri. Wind. Resist. (ohms)	5.0	0.9	0.6	4.0
BATTERY				
Capacity	12V-5.5AH	6V-4AH	6V-2AH	12V-5.5AH

FRONT WHEEL

Removal

1. Disconnect the brake cable, first from the handle bar, then from the wheel hub.
2. Disconnect the speedometer drive cable from the wheel hub.
3. Remove the securing cotter pin, then the axle nut.
4. Loosen the axle locknuts or bolts.
5. Block up the bike under the engine, then pull out the axle and remove the wheel assembly.

Hub Disassembly

1. Push out the sprocket shaft.
2. Remove the sprocket shaft collar.
3. Remove the clutch hub bearing oil seal and retaining circlip.
4. Push out the clutch hub bearing.
5. Using the bent end of the special tool and a hammer, drive out the wheel bearing spacer.
6. Remove the wheel bearing.

Inspection and Assembly

1. Anchor the wheel assembly and measure wheel rim runout. The maximum deviation is 2.0 mm (0.07 in.).
2. Make sure all the spokes are tight. If possible, tighten each nipple to 15 kg/cm (13 in. lbs).
3. Check the brake shoes for excessive wear and replace them if necessary. If the linings are glazed, rough them up with sandpaper; if they are oil soaked, replace them.

Removing the front axle nut

Removing the front axle securing bolts

Removing the front axle

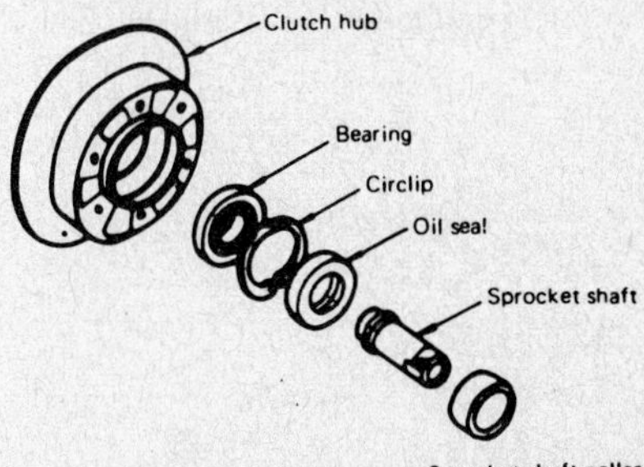

Front hub assembly

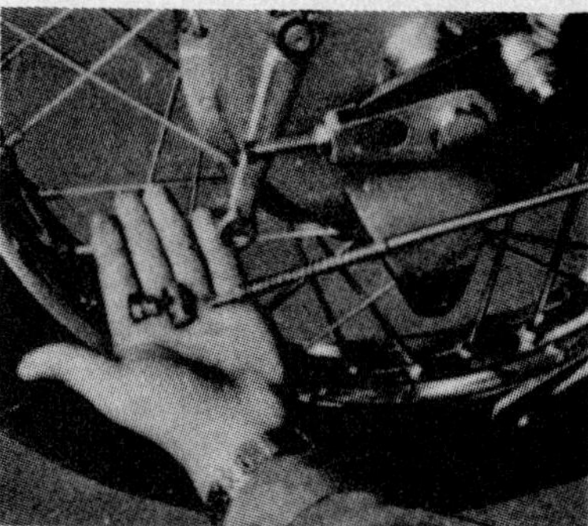
Disconnecting the rear brake rod

Disconnecting the rear brake torque arm

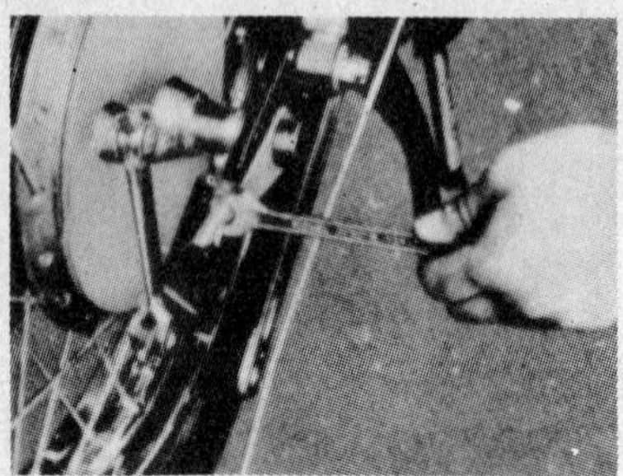

Loosening the chain adjusters

Tapping out the rear axle

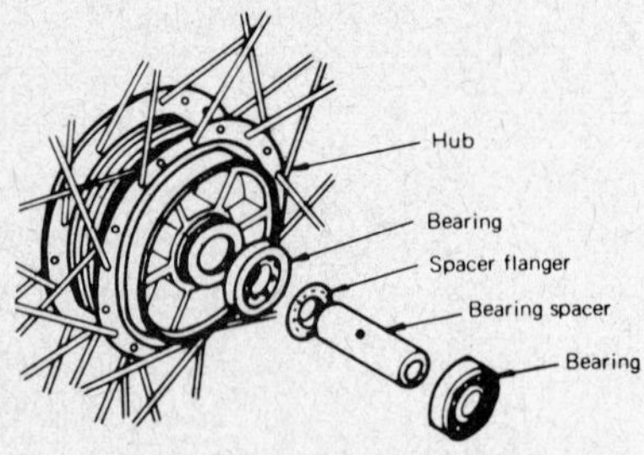

Rear wheel hub assembly

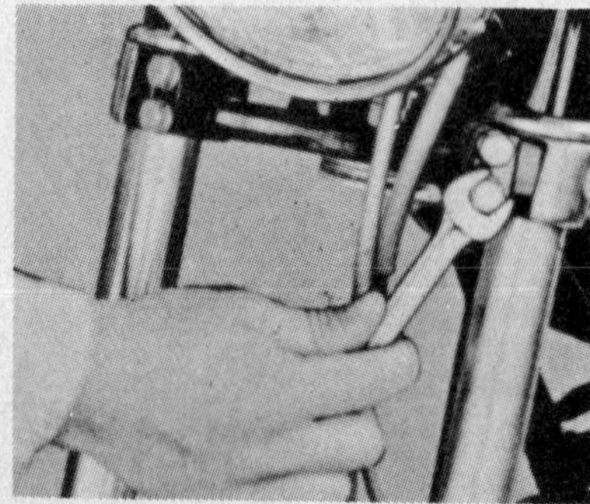

Loosening the steering head pinch bolts

4. Check the axle for straightness and replace it if necessary.
5. Inspect the speedometer drive gear for burrs, etc., and replace it if excessively worn.
6. Check the bearings for scoring, pitting, or looseness in their races.
7. Pack the bearings in grease, then reassemble the wheel with new oil seals.
8. Install the wheel in the reverse of removal, using a new axle nut cotter pin.

REAR WHEEL

Removal

1. Disconnect the rear brake rod or cable.
2. Disconnect the brake plate torque arm.
3. Loosen the chain adjusters on both sides.
4. Remove the retaining cotter pin, then remove the axle nut.
6. Remove the right chain adjuster and distance collar.
7. Slip the chain off the rear sprocket.
8. Remove the brake backing plate and roll out the wheel assembly.

Disassembly and Assembly

1. If the sprocket and hub remain on the bike, remove the sprocket shaft nut, axle, and sprocket assembly.
2. Bend back the locking tabs and remove the sprocket holding bolts.
3. Inspect bearings, etc., as described for the front wheel and measure the rim for runout.
4. Reverse the disassembly and removal procedures for assembly and installation.

FRONT FORK (Enduro Type)

Removal and Disassembly

1. Remove the front wheel.
2. Remove the front fender.
3. Remove the fork leg caps.

NOTE: *It may be necessary to loosen and pivot the handlebars for clearance.*

4. Loosen the steering head bracket bolts.
5. Pull out the fork legs.
6. Remove the fork springs and drain the inner tubes.
7. Remove the Allen bolt at the bottom of each leg, then separate the inner and outer tubes.

Assembly and Installation

1. Replace the inner tube oil seal.

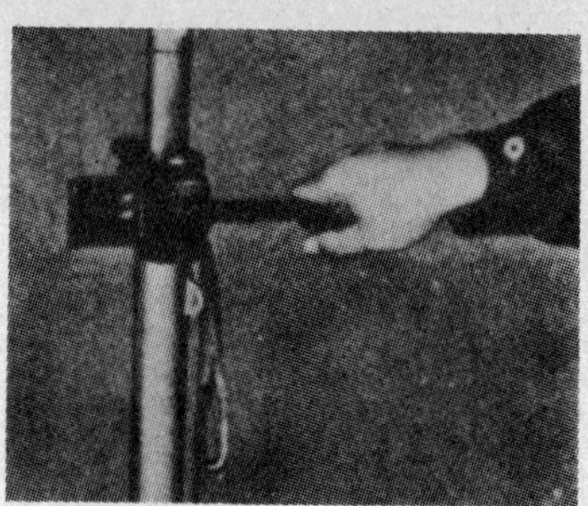

Separating the inner and outer tubes with a strap wrench

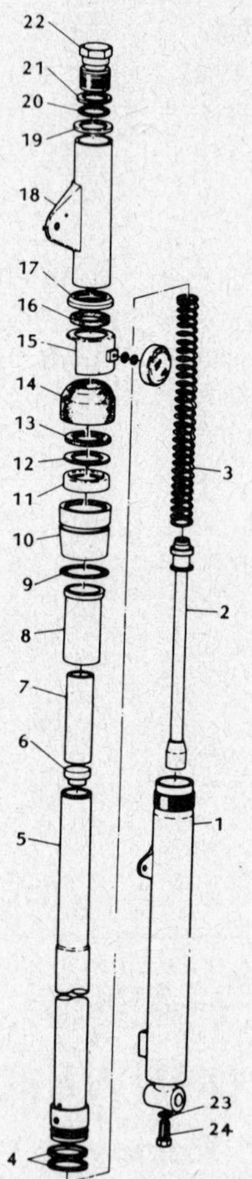

Typical Enduro fork leg construction

1. Outer tube
2. Cylinder complete
3. Fork spring
4. Piston ring
5. Inner tube
6. Spring upper seat
7. Spacer
8. Slide metal
9. O-ring
10. Outer nut
11. Oil seal
12. Oil seal washer
13. Oil seal clip
14. Dust seal
15. Outer cover
16. Packing (lamp stay)
17. Cover under guide
18. Upper cover
19. Cover upper guide
20. Packing (O-ring)
21. Cap washer
22. Cap bolt
23. Packing
24. Bolt

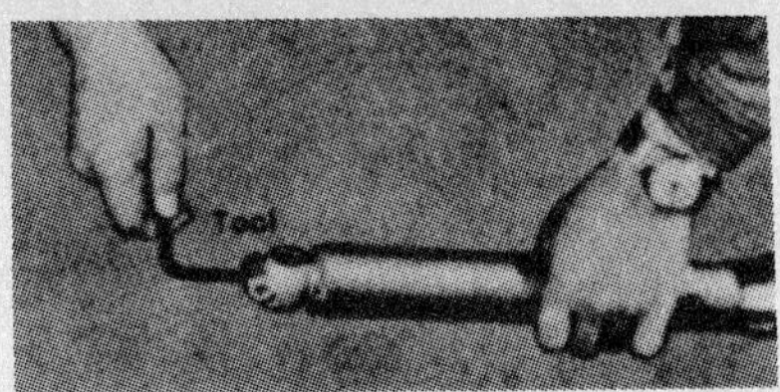

Removing the inner/outer leg securing allen bolt

2. Assemble each leg in the reverse order of disassembly.

3. Pull each fork leg through the steering head and hold it in the uppermost position with the special holding tool, then tighten the steering head bracket bolts.

4. Fill the inner tubes with the proper amount of oil, then reinstall the fork caps.

FRONT FORK (Standard Telescopic Type)

Removal and Disassembly

1. Remove the front wheel and fender.
2. Remove the fork leg caps.
3. Loosen the underbracket bolts.
4. Pull out the inner tubes and drain the oil.
5. Protect the outer tube nut with a piece of rubber, then clamp it in a vise.
6. Using the front axle as a lever, twist the inner tube counterclockwise and separate it from the outer tube.
7. Replace the oil seals, check the inner tube for straightness, then assemble in the reverse of the removal procedure and install as described for the Enduro type fork.

REAR SWING ARM

Before removing the swing arm, check it for excessive wear. Do this by moving it back and forth laterally: if there is evidence of play, either the swing arm bushing or shaft must be replaced.

To remove the swing arm:

1. Remove the chain guard.
2. Remove the swing arm shaft nut.
3. Pull out the shaft and lift off the arm.
4. Reverse the above for installation.

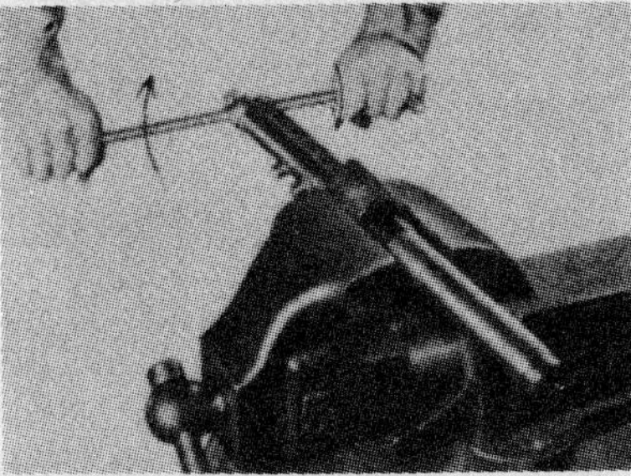

Separating standard fork inner and outer tubes

Installing the front fork legs with the special holding tool

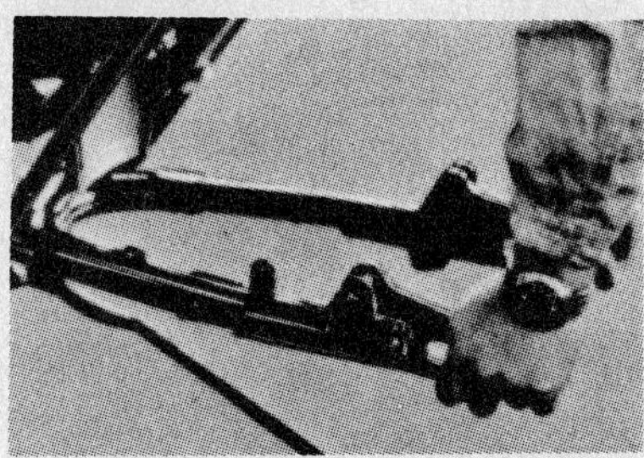

Checking rear swing arm lateral free-play

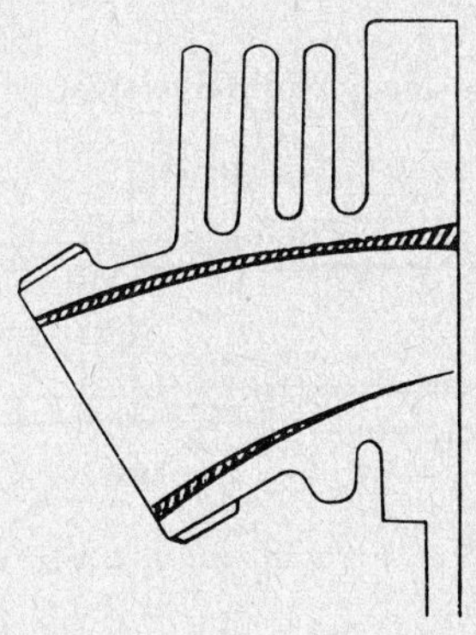

Modified YJ1 exhaust port

RACING MODIFICATIONS

Specific modification procedures are given below for those Yamahas that have proven the most suitable and popular for racing.

Use Yamaha GYT parts whenever possible. Kits containing all the necessary components are available for many recent machines, but are hard to find for older models. If you are forced to use modified stock components, bear in mind that they are not designed to withstand the additional stress of racing and are more likely to fail than their GYT counterparts.

Before making any replacements or modifications, the entire engine should be completely disassembled and all the parts measured for proper clearances, wear limits and general condition. When reassembling the engine, replace all the seals and gaskets, install the GYT or modified parts, and remember to tighten every nut and bolt to the specified torque.

YJ1 (For Off-Road Racing)

Cylinder Head

Use the GYT cylinder head or perform the following modifications on the stock head:

1. Machine 2.4 mm off the bottom of the head.
2. Remove approximately 1.5 mm along the bottom edge of the cooling fins.
3. Taper the bottom edge of the combustion chamber approximately 20°.

Cylinder

Use the GYT cylinder or perform the following modifications on the stock cylinder:

1. Remove 2.5 mm from the top of the transfer ports.
2. Remove 2.0 mm from the top of the exhaust port.
3. Bevel the reshaped ports to eliminate any rough edges.
4. Reshape the exhaust port passage as shown in the illustration.

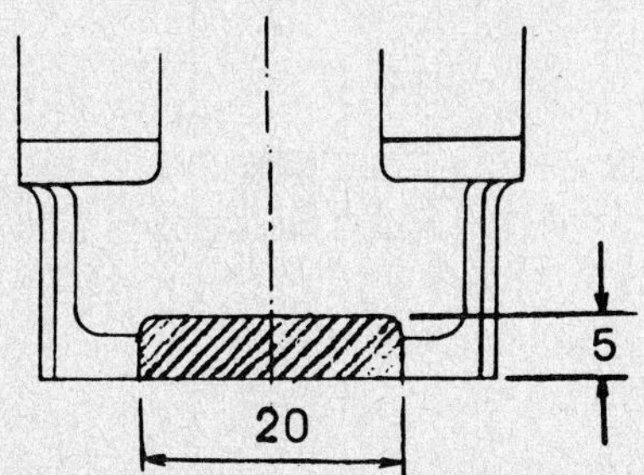

Modified YJ1 piston

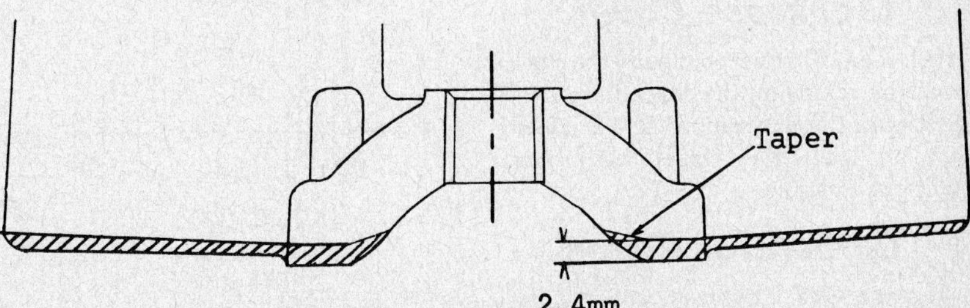

Modified YJ1 cylinder head

Piston and Rings

Use the GYT piston or modify the stock piston by cutting a 5.0 mm × 20.0 mm notch in the piston skirt directly opposite the exhaust port (facing the transfer port).

If the piston is to be installed in the GYT cylinder, use two standard lower rings; in a modified cylinder, use both standard upper and lower rings.

NOTE: *The stock upper ring and GYT cylinder cannot be used together because they are both chrome-plated and will not seat properly.*

Piston Fit

Piston-to-cylinder wall clearance should be 0.040–0.050 mm with the GYT cylinder and 0.050–0.060 mm with the modified stock cylinder.

Carburetor

Replace the stock Mikuni VM14SC with the larger VM188SC (standard on the YCS1).

Rotary Valve

Use the GYT rotary valve or modify the stock valve by increasing the cutaway to 157° 30′ (see illustration).

Rotary-Valve Cover

Use the GYT valve cover or perform the following modifications on the stock cover:

1. Enlarge the cover opening by removing the shaded area indicated in the illustration.
2. Make a cylindrical sleeve 14 mm wide with an inside diameter of approximately 20.0 mm, then sand the inside surface until it fits snugly over the end of the cover.

Crankcase Intake Port

Enlarge the intake port as shown in the illustration and taper the bottom edge 7°. Mount the GYT or modified rotary valve, valve cover, and carburetor on the crankcase. Then check the alignment of the entire intake passage. All mating seams should be free of any steps or rough edges.

Crankcase Cover

Use the GYT cover to modify the stock cover by removing the shaded areas indicated in the illustration. This is necessary to give the larger carburetor sufficient clearance.

Carburetor Cover

Use the GYT carburetor cover if the GYT crankcase cover is used. If a modified stock crankcase cover is used, remove 7.0 mm from the carburetor air horn and install the stock carburetor cover.

NOTE: *The YJ1 uses the same GYT carburetor cover as the YG1.*

Carburetor Cap

If GYT crankcase and carburetor cov-

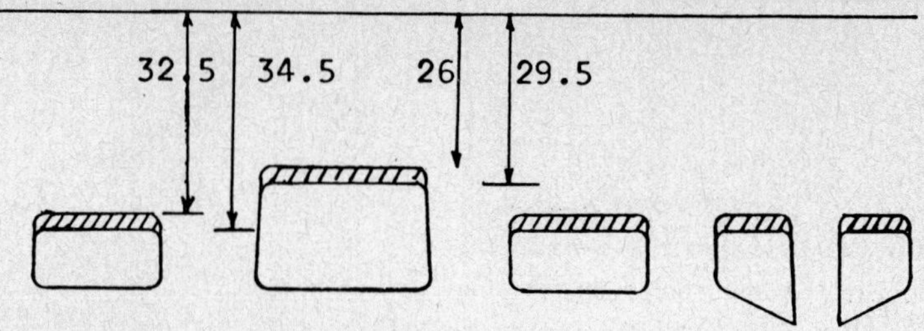

Modified YJ1 cylinder

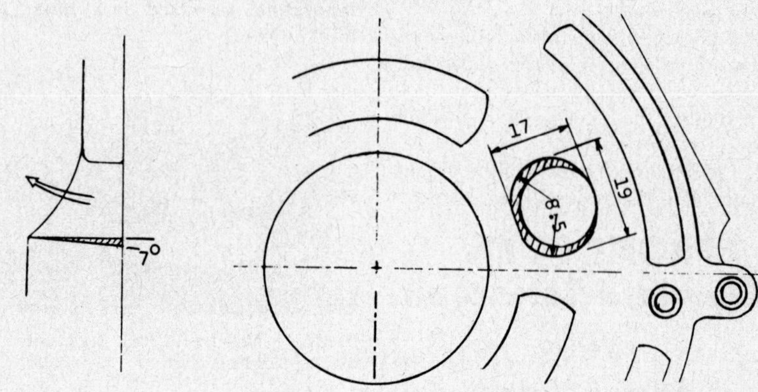

Modified YJ1 intake port

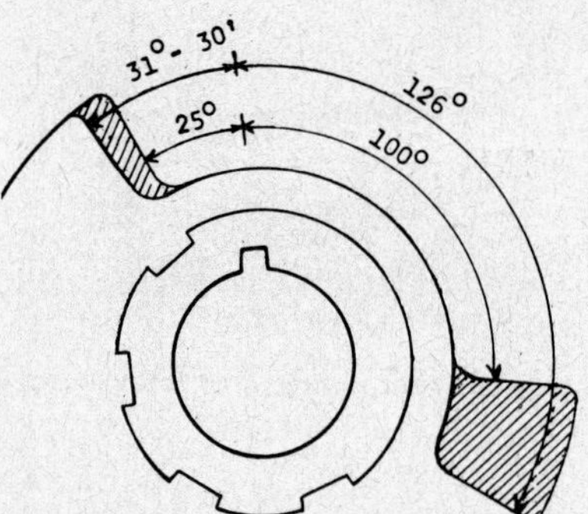

Modified rotary-valve

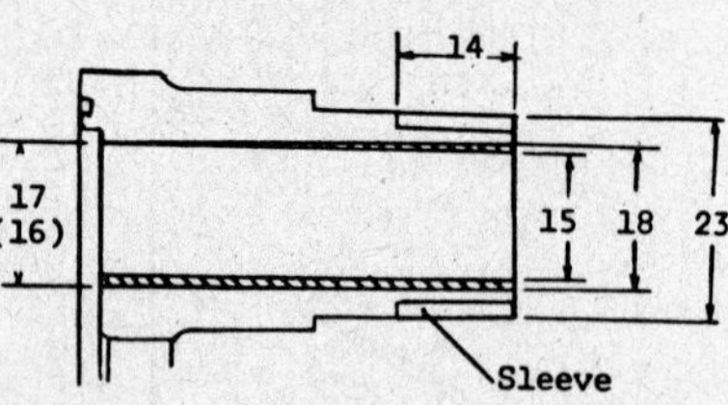

Modified YJ1 rotary-valve cover with sleeve

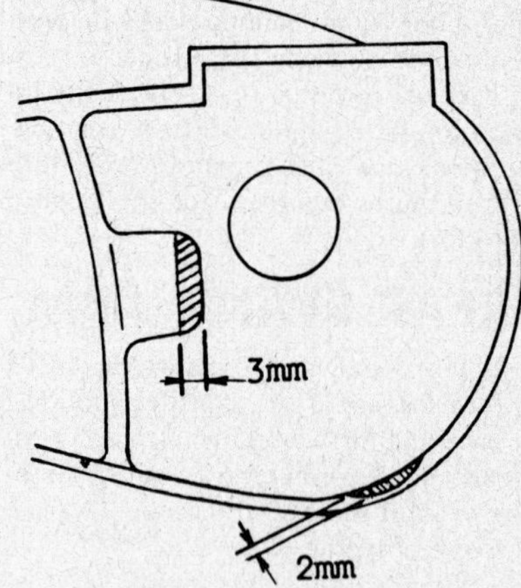

Modified YJ1 crankcase cover

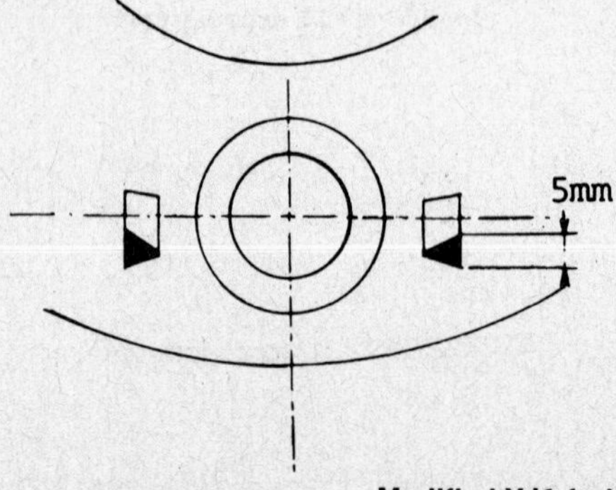

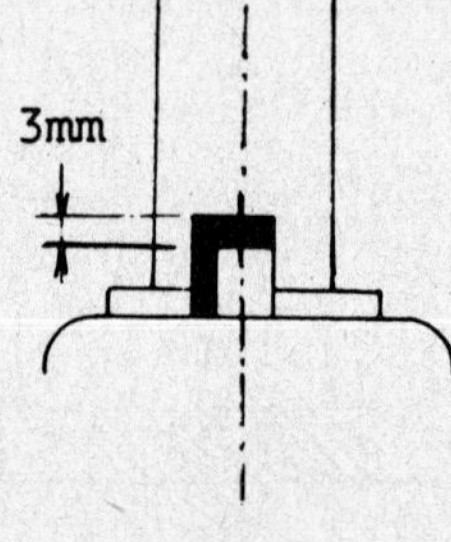

Modified YJ1 fork stops

ers are used, the GYT carburetor cap and cap plate must be installed. If modified stock covers are used, the stock cap can be used.

Exhaust System

Use the GYT expansion chamber assembly or have one made to the same dimensions. An expansion chamber MUST be used: it is the most critical single factor in two-stroke speed tuning.

Electrical System

Use the stock magneto, but remove the lighting coil and all unnecessary accessories, lights, and wiring;

Suspension

Use the front fork and brake backing plate from a YG1. Increase the spring rate by installing YG1, GYT, or YG1T springs and increase the damping by filling the fork legs with 30 to 50W oil. Also modify the fork stops as shown in the illustration.

Use the GYT rear shock absorbers or stiffer units from a larger model. If necessary for rear sprocket clearance, modify the shock mounting points as shown in the illustration.

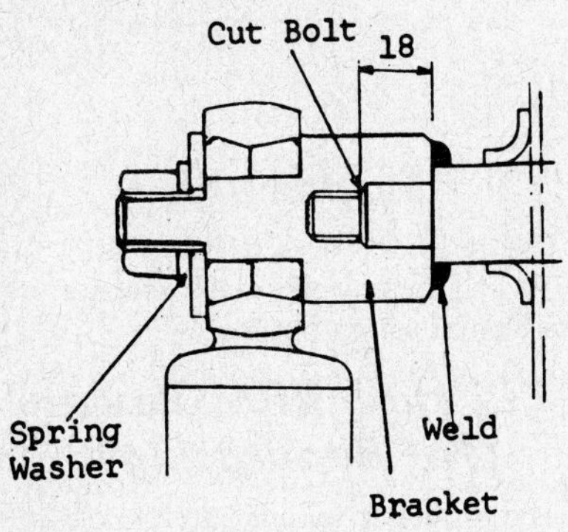

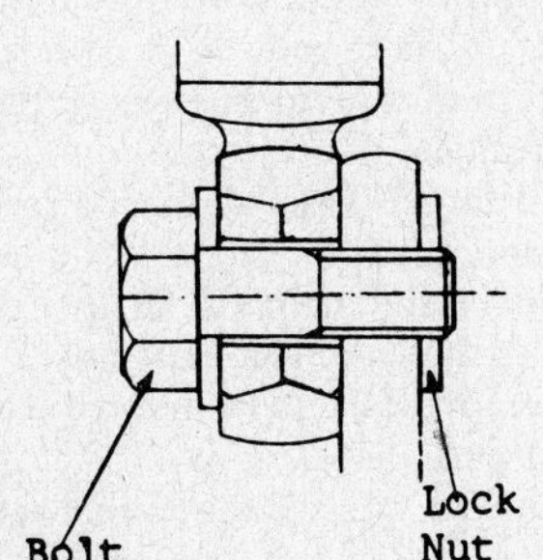

Modified YJ1 rear shock mount

Tuning Specifications

Ignition and fuel mixture settings vary greatly with atmospheric conditions, air temperature, and the type of racing to be done. The following is intended as a guide only and should be modified as necessary according to spark plug readings.

Ignition Timing	2.0 mm BTDC
Spark Plug	B8E or B9E*
Carburetor	
Main Jet	#110
Jet Needle	4J4—3 stage
Slide Cutaway	2.0
Fuel/Oil Ratio	15:1

* B8HC or B9HC if stock cylinder head is used.

YG1 (For Off-Road Racing)

Cylinder Head

Use the GYT cylinder head or perform the following modifications on the stock head:

1. Machine 3.5 mm off the bottom of the head.
2. Remove approximately 2.0 mm from the bottom edge of the cooling fins.
3. Taper the bottom edge of the combustion chamber approximately 20°.

Cylinder

Use the chrome-plated GYT cylinder or perform the following modifications on the stock cylinder:

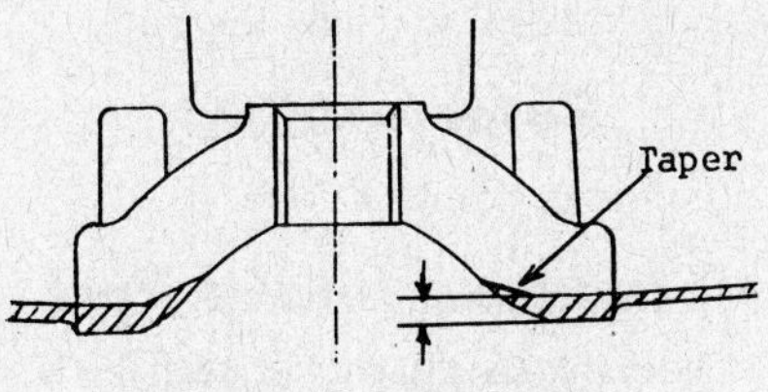

Modified YG1 cylinder head

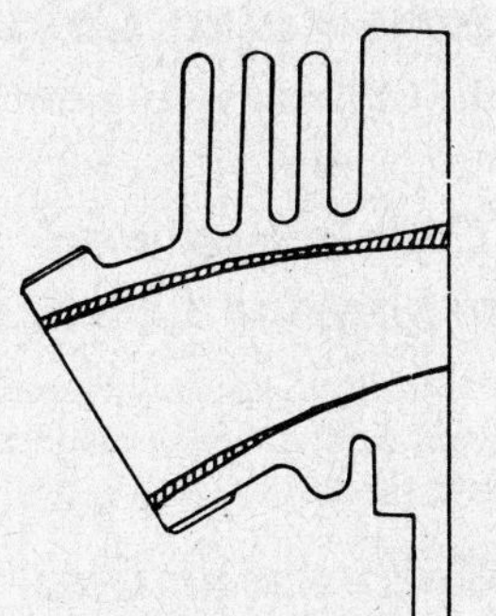

Modified YG1 exhaust port

1. Remove 2.0 mm from the top of the transfer ports.
2. Remove 3.5 mm from the top of the exhaust port.
3. Enlarge the exhaust port passage as shown in the illustration.
4. Bevel the reshaped ports to eliminate any rough edges.

Piston and Rings

Use the GYT piston or modify the stock piston by cutting a 5.0 mm × 26.0 mm notch in the piston skirt directly opposite the exhaust port (facing the transfer port).

Use standard rings in a modified stock cylinder and cast-iron rings in the GYT cylinder.

NOTE: *Ring groove width is 1.5 mm.*

Piston Fit

The piston-to-cylinder wall clearance should be 0.04–0.05 mm in the GYT cylinder and 0.05–0.06 mm in the stock cast-iron cylinder.

Carburetor

Replace the stock VM158C carburetor with a Mikuni VM22SC (standard on the YA6).

Rotary-Valve

Use the GYT valve or modify the stock valve by increasing the intake duration to 147° and widening the cutaway as shown in the illustration.

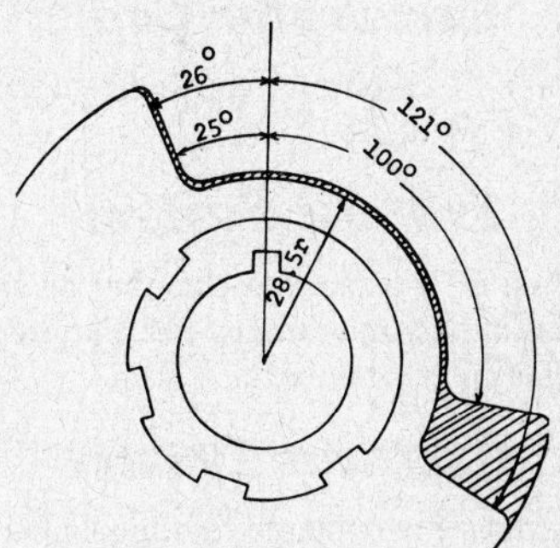

Modified YG1 rotary valve

Rotary-Valve Cover

Use the GYT valve cover and an O-ring from a standard YA6 cover. The stock cover cannot be modified to accommodate the larger carburetor.

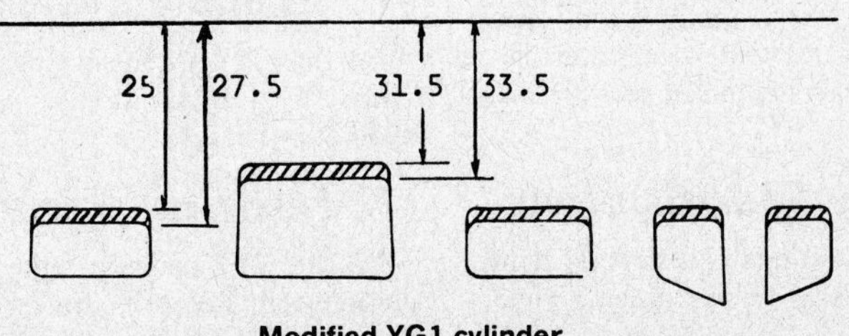

Modified YG1 cylinder

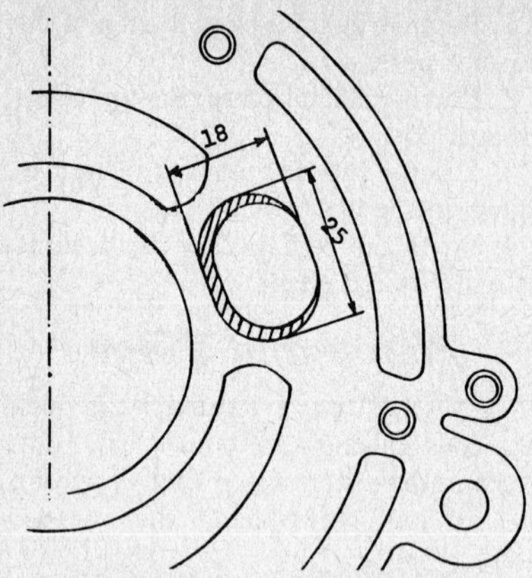

Modified YG1 intake port

Crankcase Intake Port

Enlarge the intake port as shown in the illustration and taper the bottom edge 7°. Mount the GYT or modified rotary valve, valve cover, and carburetor on the crankcase. Then check the alignment of the entire intake passage. There should be no steps or rough areas at the joining seams.

Crankcase Cover

Only the GYT crankcase cover can be used. The stock cover cannot be modified to fit the larger carburetor.

Carburetor Cover

The GYT cover must be used in conjunction with the GYT valve and crankcase covers.

Carburetor Cap

The GYT carburetor cap and cap plate must be used.

Exhaust System

Use a GYT expansion chamber or one made to the same dimensions. The stock muffler cannot be used.

Electrical System

Remove the magneto lighting coil and all unnecessary accessories, lights, and wiring.

Suspension

Use the stock front fork with GYT or YG1T springs. Increase the fork's damping effect by filling the fork legs with 30 to 50W oil.

Use GYT or YG1T rear shock absorbers. If necessary, modify the shock mounting points to accommodate a larger rear wheel sprocket (see YJ1 illustration)

Tuning Specifications

Use these settings as a starting point, then tailor them to suit varying conditions.

Ignition Timing	2.3 mm BTDC
Spark Plug	B8E or B9E*
Carburetor	
Main Jet	#260
Jet Needle	#22 M3—3 stage
Slide Cutaway	2.5
Fuel/Oil Ratio	15:1

* B8HC or B9HC with modified stock cylinder head.

YL2/C (For Off-Road Racing)

Cylinder Head

Use the stock cylinder head.

Cylinder

Use the stock cylinder.

Piston and Rings

Use the stock piston and rings.

Piston Fit

Piston-to-cylinder wall clearance should be 0.05–0.06 mm.

Carburetor

Replace the standard VM17SC with a Mikuni VM22SC (stock on the YA6).

Rotary-Valve

Use the stock rotary valve.

Crankcase Intake Port

The crankcase intake port need not be modified.

Rotary-Valve Cover

Only the GYT rotary valve cover can be used.

Crankcase and Carburetor Covers

Only the GYT covers can be used. The stock covers cannot be modified to accommodate the larger carburetor.

Carburetor Cap

Use only the GYT carburetor cap.

Exhaust system

Use the GYT expansion chamber assembly. The stock muffler cannot be modified.

Electrical System

Use the GYT magneto and the stock ignition coil. Remove any unnecessary accessories, lights, and wiring.

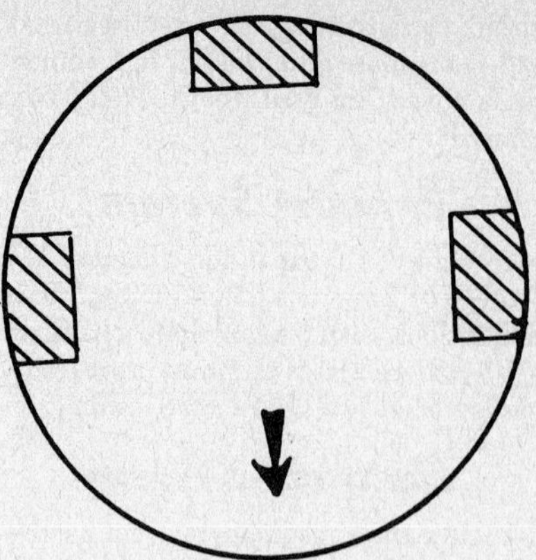
YL2 notched piston

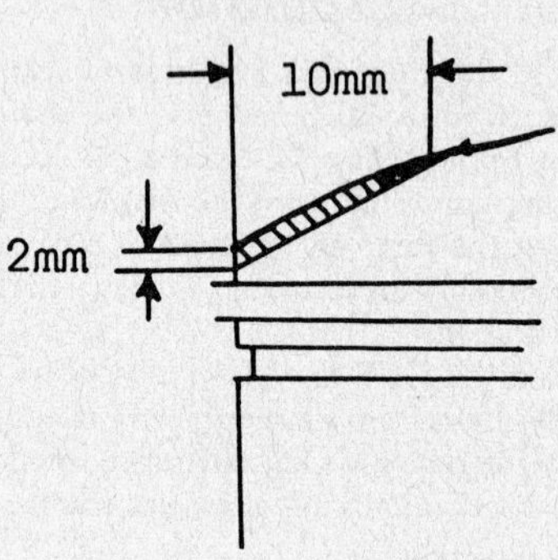

YL2 piston notch dimensions

Suspension

Use the stock forks with heavy oil (30 to 50W) and the rear shock absorbers set at the highest spring tension.

YL2 High RPM Power (For Roadracing)

The previous modifications increase power mostly in the lower-and mid-rpm ranges. If more power is needed at higher rpm, perform the following modifications:

1. Remove 7.0 mm all the way around the piston skirt.
2. Cut three notches in the piston crown as shown in the illustration.
3. Remove 2.0 mm from the top of the exhaust port.
4. Cut 9.0 mm off the carburetor air horn.

Ignition Timing	2.0 mm BTDC
Spark Plug	B9HN
Carburetor	
Main Jet	#170*
Jet Needle	4J6—2 stage
Slide Cutaway	2.5

* 160 w/cylinder modification

YL1 (For Roadracing)

Cylinder Heads

Use the GYT cylinder heads or modify the stock heads by performing the following:

1. Remove 1.5 mm from the bottom of the heads.
2. Taper the bottom of the combustion chambers 20°.

Cylinders

Use the GYT cylinders or modify the stock cylinders to the specifications shown in the illustration.

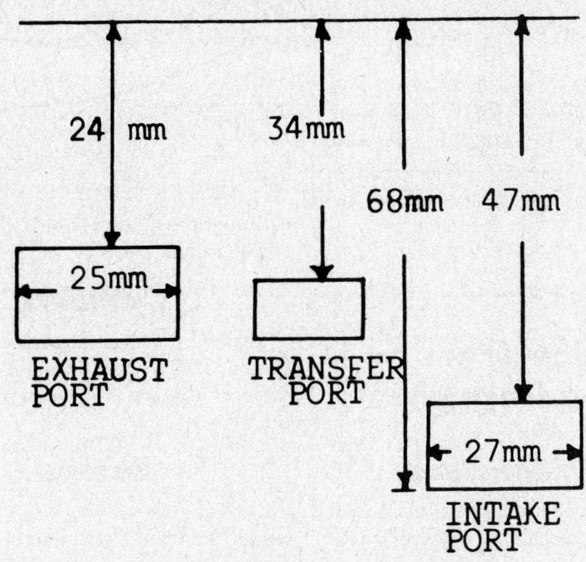

Modified YL1 cylinder

Piston and Rings

Use the GYT pistons and ring set if the GYT cylinders are used. If the stock cylinders are used, remove 5.0 mm from the piston skirt and use the standard top ring only.

Oil Pump

Remove the oil pump and install the GYT cover plate. Plug the delivery line fittings at the base of the cylinders (if stock cylinders are used).

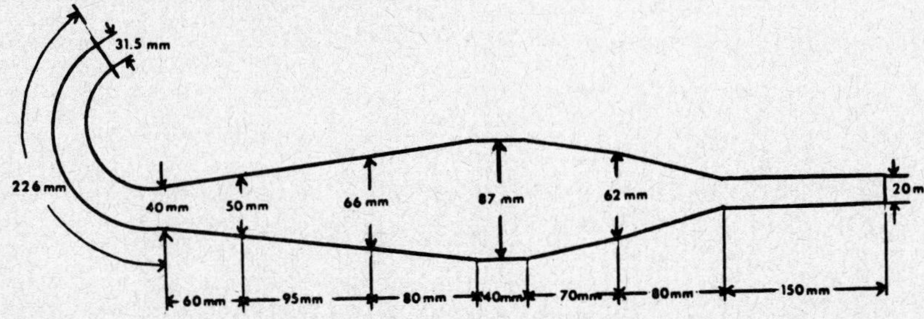

YL1 expansion chamber dimensions

Carburetors

Replace the stock VM16SC carburetors with VM18 Mikunis.

Clutch

Install the GYT clutch parts or use the entire YA6 clutch assembly.

Large End Connecting Rod Bearing

If GYT components are being used throughout, install the GYT bearing. It is considerably stronger than the stock bearing and will increase the engine's high rpm capabilities.

Exhaust System

Install the GYT expansion chambers if GYT parts are being used throughout. If modified stock parts (connecting rod bearing, cylinder, etc.) are being used, have expansion chambers made to the specifications shown in the illustration.

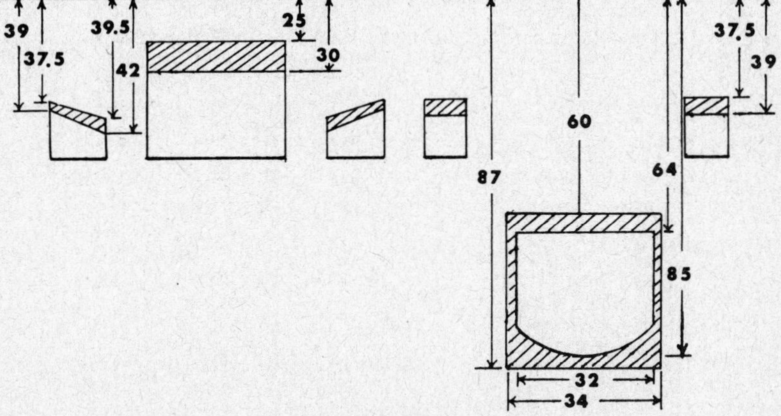

Modified DS6 cylinder

Electrical System

Install the GYT magneto assembly or perform the following on the stock unit and run a "total loss" ignition system:

1. Remove the field windings from the generator case.
2. Turn the generator armature on a lathe and machine it down to the bare shaft.
3. Disconnect the armature and field wires.

NOTE: *This total loss ignition system uses only the battery, points, and ignition coil. There is no charging circuit.*

Suspension

Use the stock front fork with YG1T springs and increase the damping by filling the fork legs with 30 to 50W oil. Use the stock rear shock absorbers set at the highest spring tension position.

Tuning Specifications

Use the following as a starting point, then modify the settings as necessary.

Ignition Timing	2.0 mm BTDC
Spark Plug	B10E*
Carburetor	
Main Jet	NA
Needle Jet	NA
Slide Cutaway	NA
Fuel/Oil Ratio	15:1

* B10H, if the modified stock cylinder head is used.

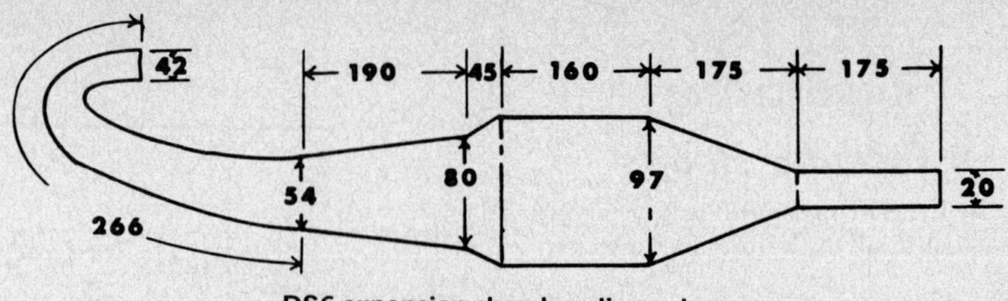

DS6 expansion chamber dimensions

DS6 (For Roadracing)

Cylinder Head

Machine the bottom of the head until the combustion chamber capacity is 11.3 cc. Taper the bottom edge to the original configuration.

Cylinders

Remove the shaded areas in the illustration. This porting arrangement is the same as that on the factory TD2 roadracer.

Pistons

Use TD2 pistons which are 54 mm in length. Standard piston length is 63 mm.

Oil Pump

Remove the oil pump and run a 15:1 fuel/oil mixture.

Carburetors

Install the 30 mm TD2 carburetors.

Exhaust System

Use the TD2 expansion chambers or have a pair made to the dimensions given in the illustration.

YAMAHA FOUR-STROKES

INDEX

MODEL IDENTIFICATION

TX500: Twin cylinder, dohc, 4 valves per cylinder. Single shaft omni-phase balancer. 9.0:1 compression; wet sump lubrication; 5-speed transmission. (Courtesy Yamaha Int. Corp.)

TX650: Updated and refined version of the XS1, XS1B, XS2 models. Twin cylinder, sohc; 653cc; wet sump lubrication; 5-speed; early models fitted with tls front brake, others with disc. (Courtesy Yamaha Int. Corp.)

TX750: Twin cylinder, sohc. 743cc; 8.8:1 compression; dry-sump lubrication; twin shaft omni-phase balancer. (Courtesy Yamaha Int. Corp.)

GENERAL SPECIFICATIONS

	500	650	750
Engine			
Type	4-s, dohc twin	4-s, sohc twin	4-s, sohc twin
Displacement (cc)	498	653	743
Bore x stroke (in.)	2.87 x 2.35	2.95 x 2.91	3.15 x 2.91
Compression ratio	9.0:1	8.4:1	8.8:1
Lubrication	wet sump	wet sump	dry sump
Ignition	battery and coil	battery and coil	battery and coil
Gearbox	5-speed	5-speed	5-speed
Dimensions			
Wheelbase (in.)	55.1	56.5	57.3
Ground clearance (in.)	6.1	5.5	6.3
Overall length (in.)	84.6	85.8	86.8
Overall width (in.)	32.9	35.4	35.8
Overall height (in.)	44.5	45.7	45.9
Tires			
Front	3.25-19	3.50 H 19	3.50 H 19
Rear	4.00-18	4.00 H 18	4.00 H 18

TUNE-UP AND MAINTENANCE

TUNE-UP OPERATIONS

Cam Chain Tensioner

500

1. Remove the spark plugs.
2. Remove the ignition points cover.
3. With a suitable sized allen wrench, remove the plug at the extreme left of the breaker points case. The plug is fitted with a copper washer which *must* be in good condition when the plug is refitted. If it is not, replace the washer with a new part.
4. Insert a 10mm allen wrench into the hole uncovered by removing the plug and engage it with the crankshaft-mounted drive gear.
5. Turn the gear clockwise so that the

Removing the breaker point cover. (500) (Courtesy Yamaha Int. Corp.)

Removing the crankshaft gear access plug (500) (Courtesy Yamaha Int. Corp.)

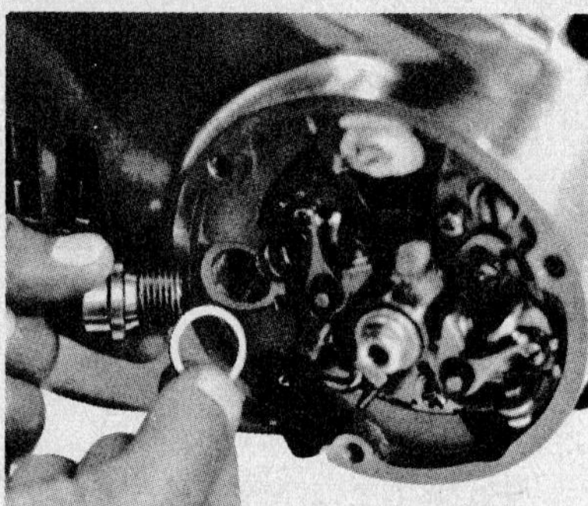
Access plug and washer (500) (Courtesy Yamaha Int. Corp.)

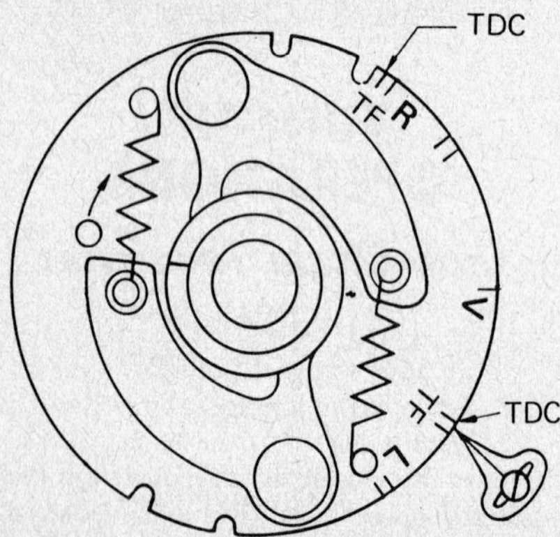

Breaker point base plate timing marks (500) (Courtesy Yamaha Int. Corp.)

"T" mark for the right cylinder is aligned with the mark on the timing plate.

NOTE: *The base plate which forms a part of the breaker cam is inscribed with a couple sets of lines and letter. "T" indicates piston top dead center and "F" the cylinder firing point with the timing unadvanced (engine static). There are, in addition, two lines which indicate cylinder firing point with the timing fully advanced.*

Notice that there are two sets of these marks designated "R" and "L" for the right and left cylinders respectively.

6. When the "T" mark for the *right* cylinder is lined up with the timing plate mark, loosen the cam chain tensioner nut (located beneath the right exhaust port), and then retighten the nut. Cam chain tension is automatically set after the nut is loosened, and the adjustment is maintained by tightening the nut.

Replace and tighten the plug in the breaker points case to the proper torque: 22.5-26.2 ft lbs.

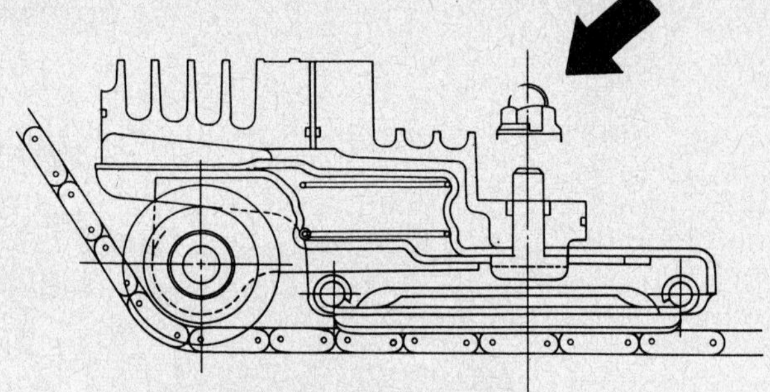
Cam chain tensioner location (500) (Courtesy Yamaha Int. Corp.)

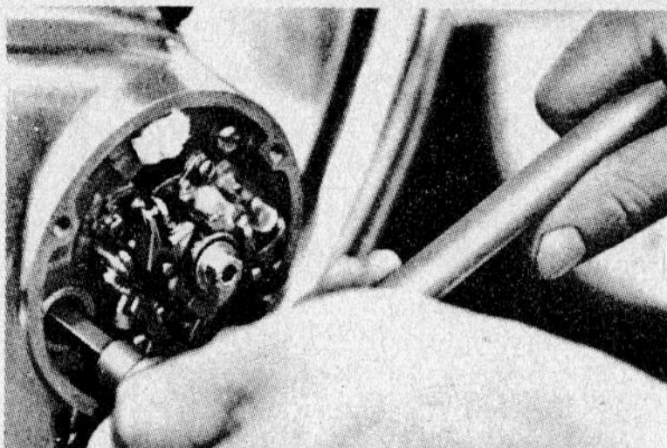
Rotating the crankshaft with the allen wrench in the crank gear (500) (Courtesy Yamaha Int. Corp.)

Adjusting the cam chain tension (500) (Courtesy Yamaha Int. Corp.)

650, 750

1. The cam chain tensioner is located at the rear of the cylinders, between and below the intake ports.
2. Rotate the engine clockwise, relative to a person looking at the engine's left side.
3. Remove the tensioner cover as illustrated. Loosen the tensioner locknut, then turn the adjuster in until the end of the tensioner pushrod is flush with the end of the adjuster.

Removing the tensioner cover (650, 750) (Courtesy Yamaha Int. Corp.)

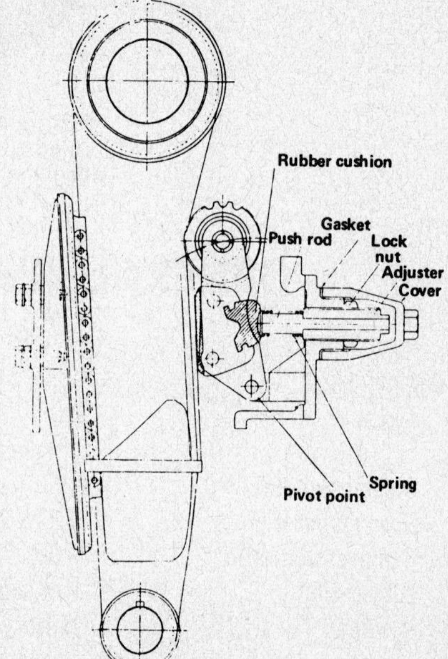

Cam chain tensioner components (650, 750) (Courtesy Yamaha Int. Corp.

4. On 650cc models, tighten the locknut.

On 750cc machines, back the adjuster off ¾ turn, then tighten the locknut.

5. Reinstall the tensioner cover.

Valve Adjustment

500

NOTE: *For proper valve clearances,*

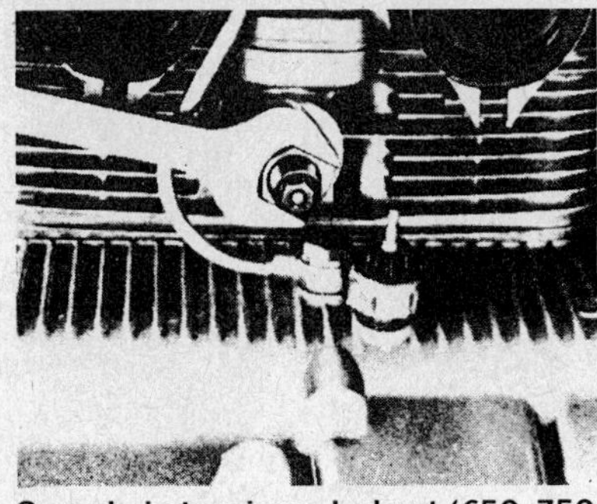

Cam chain tensioner locknut (650, 750) (Courtesy Yamaha Int. Corp.)

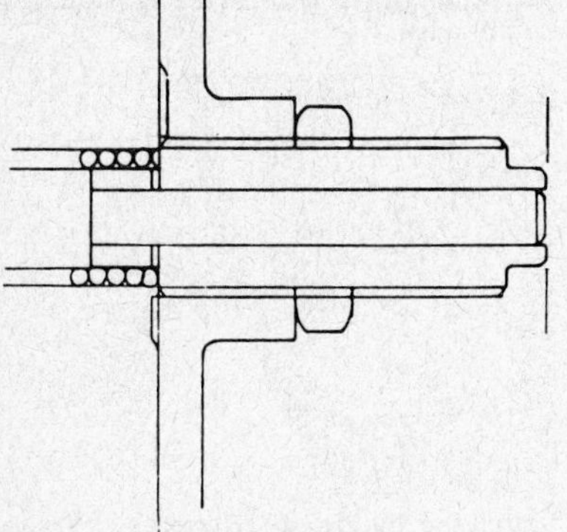

Tensioner correct

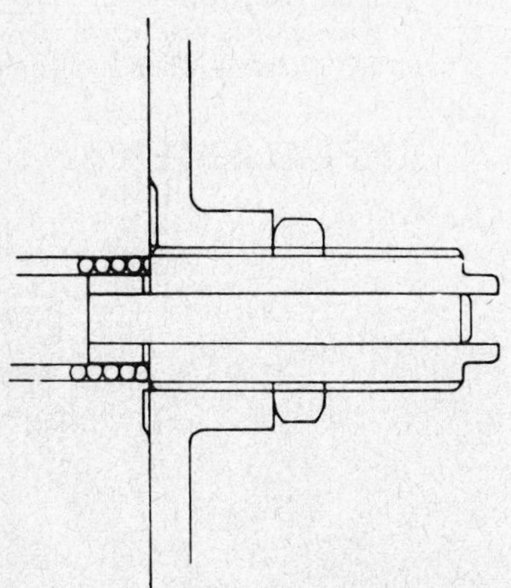

Tensioner needs adjustment

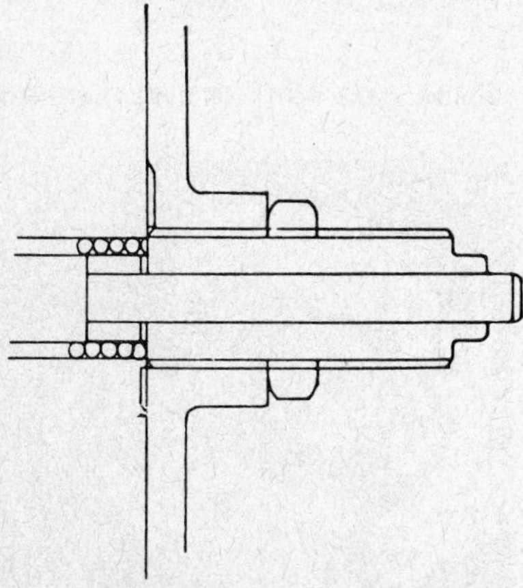

Tensioner needs adjustment

Tensioner pushrod adjustment (650) (Courtesy Yamaha Int. Corp.)

refer to the "Tune-Up Specifications" chart at the end of this section.

1. Valves must be adjusted when the engine is cold.

2. Remove the contact breaker cover. Remove the spark plugs. Loosen the 18 allen bolts which secure the camshaft case cover gradually and evenly, then remove the bolts and the cover.

3. Remove the plug at the extreme left of the breaker points case which gives access to the crankshaft-mounted drive gear.

NOTE: *The plug is fitted with a copper washer which must be in good condition. Otherwise, fit a new washer when refitting the plug.*

4. Insert a 10mm allen wrench into the plug's hole, and engage the crankshaft gear. Turn the crankshaft clockwise to position the camshafts as described below.

5. Choosing any set of rocker arms to begin adjusting, turn the crankshaft (clockwise) with the allen wrench until the heel of the cam lobe faces the pad atop the rocker arm. Refer to the illustration. For each adjustment, the respective cam lobe must be positioned as shown.

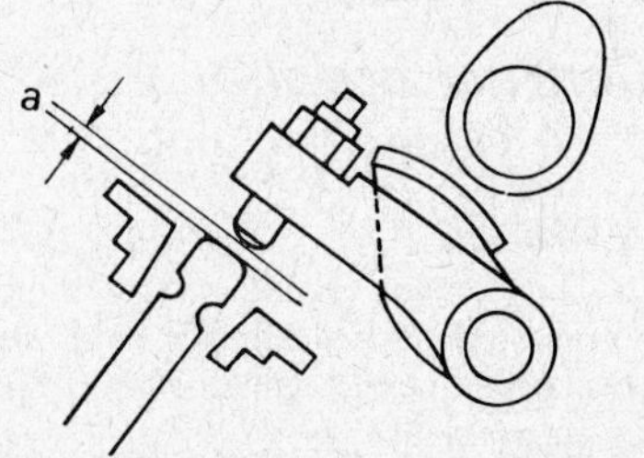

Valve clearance "a" (500) (Courtesy Yamaha Int. Corp.)

Setting the valve clearance (500) (Courtesy Yamaha Int. Corp.)

6. With the appropriate feeler gauges, check the clearance between the end of the valve stem and the adjuster on the rocker arm. This is the value "a" in the illustration. If adjustment is necessary, loosen the locknut on the rocker arm and turn the (allen head) adjuster in or out as needed, then retighten the locknut to 9.-2-11.6 ft lbs while holding the adjuster in position. Recheck the clearance.

7. Valves are paired (two valves per rocker arm) so be sure that both valves in each pair are adjusted.

8. After adjusting any pair of valves, check the other pair for that cylinder. If the piston is at or near top dead center on the compression stroke, the cam lobe for the corresponding valves should be correctly positioned. If it is not, turn the crankshaft to position the heel of the cam lobe facing the pad atop the rocker arm and repeat the procedure. Continue for the other cylinder until all valves are adjusted.

9. When replacing the cam case cover, use a new gasket, and tighten the allen bolts gradually and in a criss-cross pattern to 5.8-7.5 ft lbs.

10. Replace the plug in the breaker point case and tighten it to the proper torque (22.5-26.2 ft lbs). Refit and torque the cover bolts to 5-6.7 ft lbs.

650

1. Remove valve tappet and alternator covers.

2. Position one cylinder at TDC by aligning the rotor reference mark with the first stator mark. The cylinder at TDC can be identified by slack at both valve adjusters.

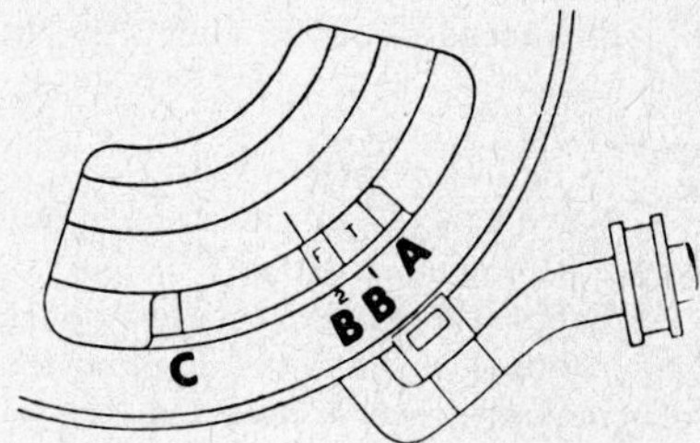

A-Top Dead Center
B[1] & B[2]—Ignition Fire Marks
C-Mark for "Fully Advanced" Ignition Timing

Rotor and stator timing marks (650) (Courtesy Yamaha Int. Corp.)

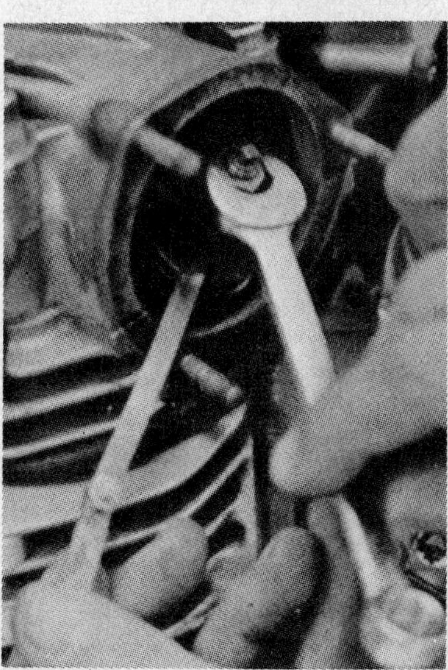

Setting valve clearance (650) (Courtesy Yamaha Int. Corp.)

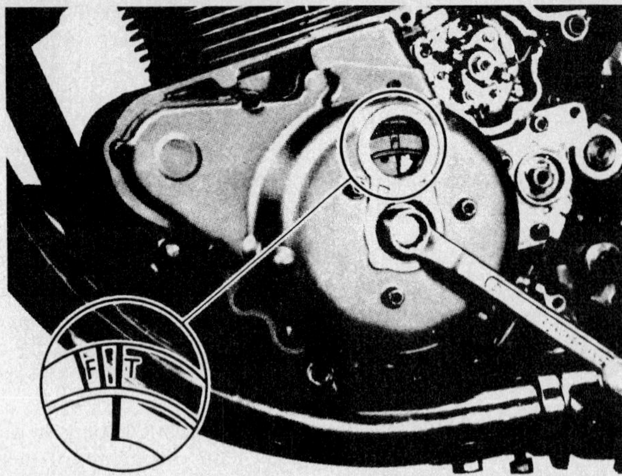

Roto and stator timing marks (750) (Courtesy Yamaha Int. Corp.)

3. Insert the specified size feeler gauge between the valve stem and tappet.

4. If adjustment is necessary to achieve a slip fit, loosen the adjuster locknut and turn the adjuster in or out until the correct clearance is obtained.

5. Hold the adjuster securely and tighten the locknut.

6. Rotate the crankshaft 360° and realign the rotor and stator marks, then repeat the procedure on the other cylinder.

750

1. Valve adjustment must be made when the engine is cold.

2. Drop the left footpeg down. Remove the gearshift lever. Remove the left crankcase cover screws and take off the cover. Remove the plugs in the inner crankcase cover which expose the alternator rotor nut and the timing marks on the rotor.

3. Remove the rocker arm access plugs.

4. Removing the spark plugs will make the procedure a bit easier.

Use a wrench on the alternator rotor nut and turn it so that the "T" (top dead center) mark on the rotor is aligned with the timing mark on the stator.

5. One of the pistons will now be at top dead center on the compression stoke. This piston will have clearance at both valves. Check the clearance at this cylinder's valves, and adjust if necessary, by loosening the adjuster locknut and turning the adjuster in or out. Retighten the locknut to 19-21 ft lbs while holding the adjuster in place. Then recheck the clearance.

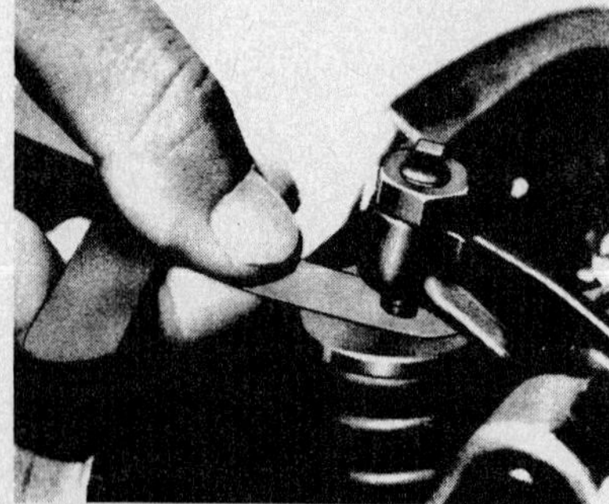

Adjusting valve clearance (750) (Courtesy Yamaha Int. Corp.)

6. Turn the engine one complete revolution until the "T" mark aligns once more, then check or adjust the other set of valves in the same manner.

Contact Breaker Points

INSPECTION

All Models

1. The contact breaker points should be inspected periodically for condition. The breaker points will display a light grey color usually.

2. The contact surface of the points must be free of pitting, unevenness, or surface irregularities. Minor imperfections may be remedied with a small file. Run the file through the points, but be careful not to remove too much metal.

3. After the points have been filed, clean them thoroughly. This may be accomplished in a variety of ways. The points can be sprayed with solvent or laquer thinner. Then run a business card or similar object through the points until they are very clean. Note that sparking at the points which may appear after filing may be due to particles of foreign matter on the points.

4. After filing or cleaning the points, check and reset the gap as described below.

5. Check the heel of the points cam follower for wear. After many miles, the heel may become so worn that the timing will be retarded. If adjusting the point gap will not bring the timing back to the proper value, the points will have to be replaced.

6. Breaker spring tension may be checked if the proper equipment is available. It will usually be 650-850 grams.

7. Note that the points must mate

Disconnecting the point leads (Courtesy Yamaha Int. Corp.)

Removing the points (Courtesy Yamaha Int. Corp.)

squarely. There will be a small amount of play in the mountings which will allow this to be accomplished when the gap is adjusted.

REPLACEMENT

All Models

1. The contact breaker points are similar for all models. To remove the points,

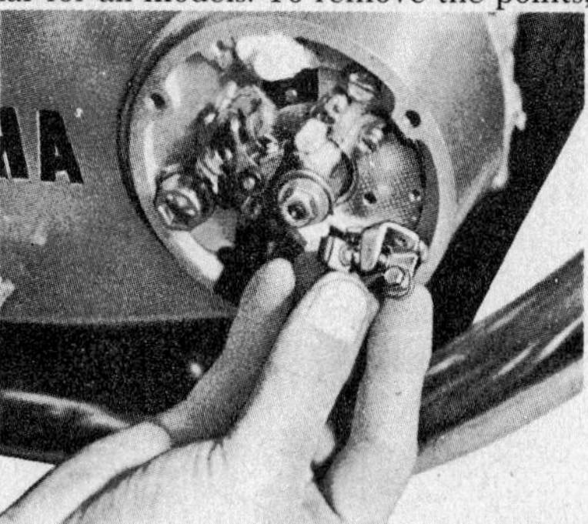

Replacing the points (Courtesy Yamaha Int. Corp.)

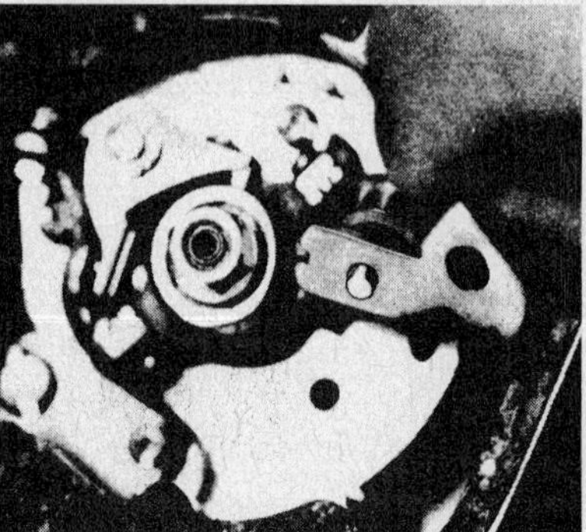

Breaker point locating pin (Courtesy Yamaha Int. Corp.)

remove the ignition points cover. On the 750, the left crankcase outer cover will have to be removed.

2. Unscrew the small nut which secures the wire to each breaker set.

3. Remove the mounting screw for each breaker set and remove the points.

4. Clean the mating surfaces of new points with a solvent and dry thoroughly.

5. Replace each new contact breaker set on the mounting plate noting that the stud on the points should engage a hole in the mounting plate.

6. Replace the mounting screws, connect the wires, and set the point gap.

GAP ADJUSTMENT

1. Rotate the engine until one of the point sets is fully open.

2. Check the gap with the proper size feeler gauge (refer to "Tune-Up Specifications" at the end of this section). The blade should be a snug slip fit if clearance is correct.

3. To adjust, loosen the points securing screw and use a small screwdriver in the adjusting slots on the points to increase or decrease the gap.

Setting the point gap (Courtesy Yamaha Int. Corp.)

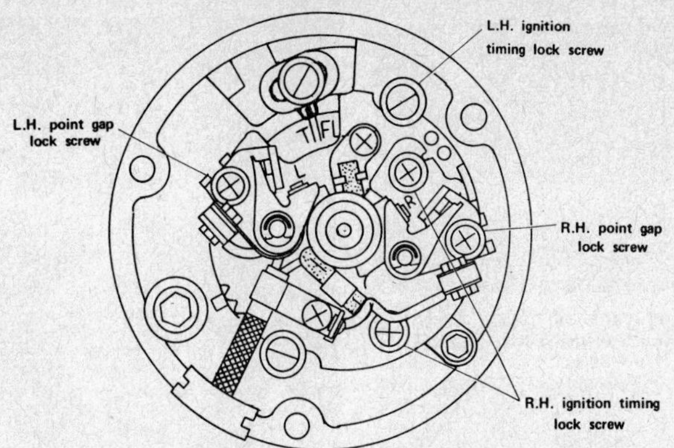

Breaker point assembly (500) (Courtesy Yamaha Int. Corp.)

4. After retightening the securing screw, recheck the gap. Repeat for the other set of points.

NOTE: *If the points are not new, they must be filed and cleaned before gapping.*

Ignition Timing

500

Ignition timing may be accomplished by either the static or the dynamic methods. The former requires the use of a "point checker" or ohmmeter to determine the exact time that the points open. The latter utilizes a strobe light.

Whichever method is used, the points should be cleaned and gapped before timing.

Inspect the contact breaker assembly and note that the points are designated by either an "L" or "R" stamped on the base plate. The "L" points fire the left cylinder.

Also note that the left cylinder points are mounted directly to the base plate. The right cylinder points are secured to a mounting plate which, in turn, is held on the base plate by two screws.

When the timing is adjusted, the right cylinder points are moved relative to the base plate, but when the left cylinder is timed, the entire base plate is moved. *Therefore, the left cylinder MUST be timed first.*

It can be seen that moving the right cylinder points will affect the timing for that cylinder only, but moving the left cylinder points (and therefore the base plate) will affect the timing of both cylinders.

Static Timing

1. Static timing the engine will result in the timing being checked *unadvanced* (5° BTDC).

2. Note the marks on the timing advance base plate. There is a set of marks for each cylinder designated "L" and "R". For static timing, the "F" mark on the timing advance base plate should

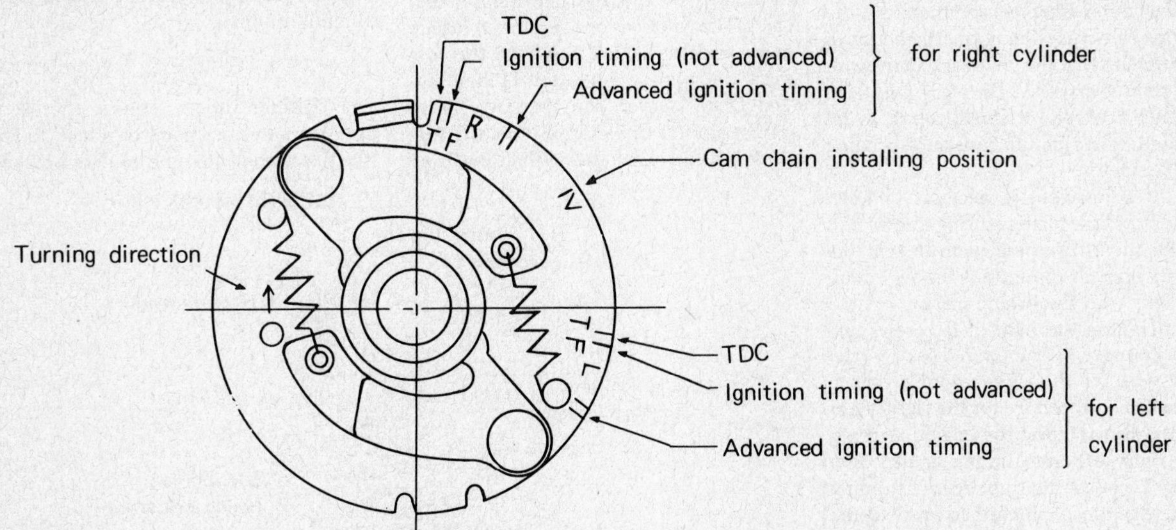

Timing marks (500) (Courtesy Yamaha Int. Corp.)

Determining instant of point opening (500) (Courtesy Yamaha Int. Corp.)

Breaker point assembly (500) (Courtesy Yamaha Int. Corp.)

align with the mark on the pointer at the very instant that the points open.

3. Remove the plug at the left of the points case which allows access to the crankshaft-mounted drive gear. Engage the 10mm allen wrench with the gear and turn the crankshaft so that the "F" mark for the *left* cylinder aligns with the timing mark.

4. Using an ohmmeter, connect the negative lead to ground and the positive lead to the orange wire where it is connected to the left set of points.

5. Turn the engine (with the allen wrench) several degrees counterclockwise so that the points are completely closed (zero resistance) and then turn the engine clockwise (the normal direction of rotation) so that the "F" mark aligns with the timing mark. At this very point the contact breaker set should open as indicated by an infinite resistance reading on the meter.

6. If adjustment is necessary, loosen the points base plate securing screws, and rotate the entire base plate so that the points open at the instant the "F" mark is aligns with the timing mark.

7. Tighten the base plate screws and then connect the meter red lead to the grey wire for the right cylinder points. Repeat the procedure for the right set of points after rotating the engine to bring the right cylinder timing marks into view. To adjust the right cylinder timing note that the points are secured to the base plate by two screws. These screws are loosened to adjust the timing. The base plate is not moved.

8. When refitting the plug in the points case, be sure the copper washer is

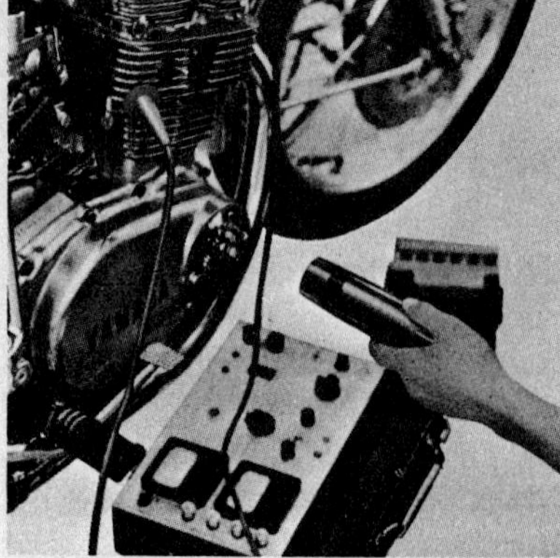

Dynamic timing (500) (Courtesy Yamaha Int. Corp.)

in good condition, or replace it. Tighten the plug to the proper torque:

M6 5-6.7 ft lbs
M10 22.5-26.2 ft lbs

Dynamic Timing

1. Clean and adjust the point gap as previously described.

2. Attach the strobe light as the manufacturer of the light directs. Time the left cylinder first.

3. Start the engine and run it at 2000 rpm. At this point the timing will be fully advanced and the timing mark should align with the two closely set slash marks which indicate fully advanced timing.

4. If necessary, move the base plate to align the marks. Refer to "Static Timing," above for more information. Repeat the procedure with the other set of points.

650

1. Remove the alternator inspection plate, ignition points cover, and centrifugal advance unit cover.

2. Inspect, clean and gap the points.

3. Ignition timing is set by matching the marks on the alternator stator and rotor. The rotor has one reference timing mark and the stator has four: the first mark (to right of the letter T) identifies Top Dead Center, the next two marks (either side of the letter F) identify idle timing (fully retarded) and the remaining mark identifies high speed timing (fully advanced).

4. Secure the centrifugal advance counterweights in the fully retarded idle position (held inward).

5. Connect an ignition timing light or Yamaha Point Checker as follows:

(+)RED lead—to grey point wire connector

(−)BLACK lead—to ground (frame or engine case)

Right and left cylinder point sets are marked R (grey wire) and L (orange wire).

NOTE: *The right cylinder timing MUST be set first. The right cylinder points are mounted directly to the base plate, the left cylinder points are mounted on a separate plate; therefore, setting the left side first would cause a position shift when timing the right.*

6. Turn the crankshaft in the direction of normal rotation until the right cylinder points begin to open (as indicated by the timing light on Yamaha Point Checker).

7. Make the necessary plate adjustment so that the points begin to open when the rotor mark is aligned with the letter F.

NOTE: *On engines with serial numbers below 11764, align the rotor with the mark to the left of the letter F.*

8. Switch the (+) RED lead to the orange point wire connector and repeat the procedure for the left cylinder.

9. After idle timing has been set on both cylinders, secure the centrifugal advance counterweights in the fully advanced (held outward) position: the points should open at the high speed stator mark or just after the mark on engines with serial numbers below 11764. Make any necessary adjustments and recheck the idle timing.

750

1. Ignition timing requires the use of an ohmmeter or "point checker" to find the exact point that the contact breakers

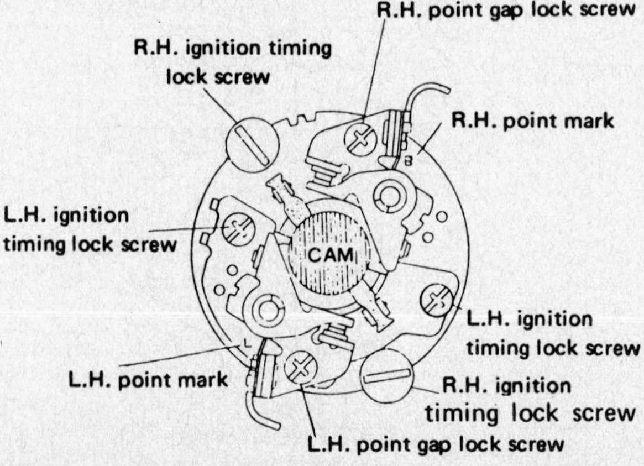

Breaker point assembly (650, 750) (Courtesy Yamaha Int. Corp.)

open. Clean and gap both sets of points before setting timing.

2. Remove the plug over the alternator rotor nut and the plug just above it which will uncover the timing marks on the rotor.

3. The rotor is inscribed with four marks. "T" indicates the piston top dead center position; "F" indicates ignition advance with the engine static. Further along to the left is the fully advanced timing mark.

4. Note that the breaker points are marked "L" and "R" with letters stamped on the base plate. The "L" point set fires the left cylinder.

Also note that the points are mounted differently. The right cylinder is mounted directly on the base plate. The left cylinder points are secured to a mounting plate which, in turn, is held on the base plate by two screws.

When the timing is adjusted, the left cylinder points are moved relative to the base plate after loosening the screws, but when the right cylinder is timed, the entire base plate is moved. *Therefore, the right cylinder must be timed first.*

It can be seen that moving the left cylinder points will affect the timing for that cylinder only, but moving the right cylinder points (and therefore the base plate) will affect the timing of both cylinders.

5. Connect the ohmmeter or points checker black (negative) lead to ground, and the red lead to the grey wire at the right cylinder contact points.

6. With a wrench on the alternator rotor nut, rotate the crankshaft in its normal direction of rotation (counterclockwise when viewed from the left).

7. Watch the rotor marks. At the instant that the rotor is positioned as shown in the illustration (i.e. with the timing plate mark between the two "F" marks), the points should open as indicated by a reading of infinite resistance on the meter.

8. If the timing must be adjusted, loosen the two base plate screws, and rotate the plate so that the right cylinder points open as soon as the rotor marks are properly positioned.

9. After tightening the base plate screws, connect the red lead of the meter to the orange wire of the left cylinder points and check the timing as previously described.

10. If the left cylinder timing must be adjusted, loosen the two screws which secure the left cylinder points to the base plate and move the points as necessary. Note that the base plate itself if not moved.

Spark Plugs

Refer to the "Tune-Up Specifications" chart at the end of this section for the proper plug heat range and gap for each machine.

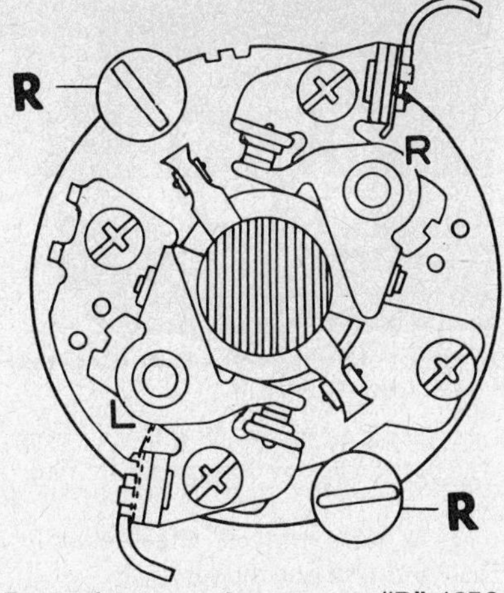

Base plate securing screws "R" (650, 750) (Courtesy Yamaha Int. Corp.)

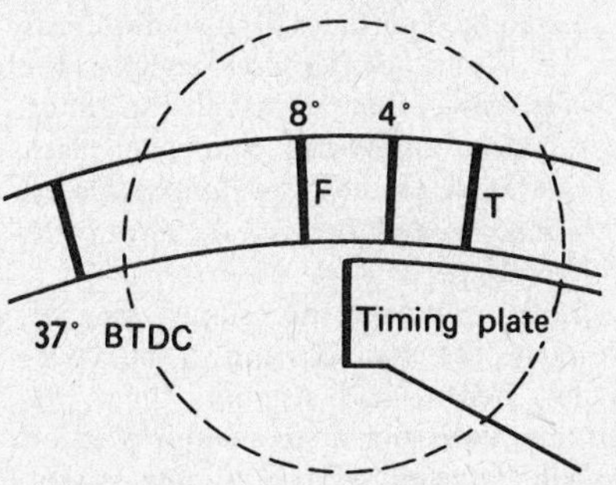

Rotor timing marks (750) (Courtesy Yamaha Int. Corp.)

Carburetor Idle Speed and Mixture

ALL MODELS

1. Set idle speed and mixture when the engine is at operating temperature.

2. Screw both idle mixture (pilot air) screws in until they are lightly seated, then back each out the proper number of turns:

500 1 turn
650 ½ - 1 turn
750 ¾ - 1½

3. Set both idle speed screws so that the engine turns at a fast idle.

4. Disconnect one spark plug lead and back out the idle speed screw for the running cylinder until the engine just dies. Repeat the procedure for the other carburetor.

5. Connect both plug leads and check engine idle. Normal idle speed is 900-1000 rpm.

6. Adjust, if necessary, by turning the idle speed screws in or out equal amounts.

7. After idle speed is set, synchronize the butterflies so that both begin to open at the same time.

TUNE-UP SPECIFICATIONS

	500	650	750
Valve Clearance			
Intake (in.)	0.006 (0.15 mm)	0.003 (0.08 mm)	0.002 (0.05 mm)
Exhaust (in.)	0.008 (0.20 mm)	0.006 (0.15 mm)	0.002 (0.05 mm)
Breaker Point Gap			
in.	0.012-0.016	0.012-0.016	0.012-0.016
mm	0.3-0.4	0.3-0.4	0.3-0.4
Spark Plug			
Type (NGK standard)	D-8ES	B-8ES	B-8ES
Plug Gap	0.027 in. (0.7 mm)	0.024 in. (0.6 mm)	0.024 in. (0.6 mm)

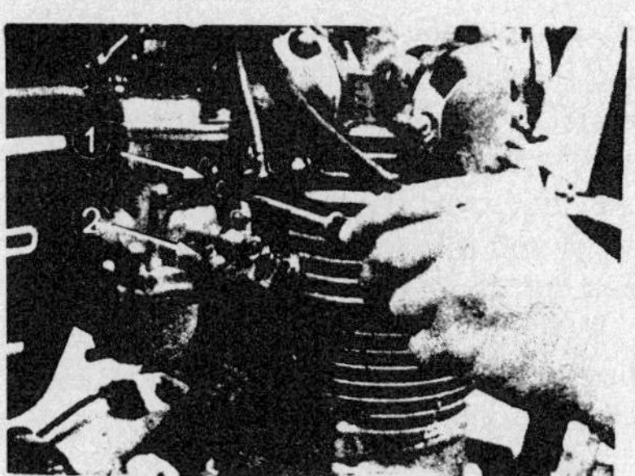

Idle mixture (1) and throttle stop screw (2) (650, 750) (Courtesy Yamaha Int. Corp.)

Maintenance Items

ENGINE OIL

500

1. Change the oil when the engine is warm.

2. Remove the drain plugs beneath the crankcase and drain off the oil.

3. Remove the left side rear crankcase cover and remove the oil filter. Replace the filter with a new element. The o-ring must be replaced as well. Smear the o-ring with a bit of grease before refitting.

Crankcase drain plugs (500) (Courtesy Yamaha Int. Corp.)

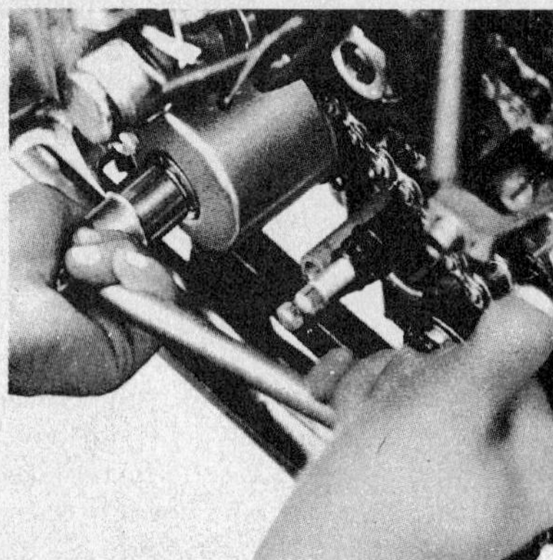
Removing the oil filter (500) (Courtesy Yamaha Int. Corp.)

Crankcase drain plugs (650) (Courtesy Yamaha Int. Corp.)

4. Tighten the filter cartridge to 15-16.5 ft lbs.

5. Pour 3.2 qts. of SAE 20W-40 "SE" rated motor oil into the crankcase.

6. Start the engine and let it run for 3-5 minutes. Check the oil level and add if necessary. Check for leaks at the filter, then replace the left rear crankcase cover.

650

1. Change the oil when the engine is warm.

2. Remove the crankcase drainplugs one at a time and drain off the old oil.

3. Clean the plugs thoroughly and wipe dry. They are magnetic.

4. To remove the oil filter:

a. Remove the attaching Allen screws and the filter cover plate.

Oil filter retaining bolt (650) (Courtesy Yamaha Int. Corp.)

b. Separate the sealing O-ring from the cover plate and inspect it for damage.

c. Remove the oil filter retaining bolt and pull out the filter.

d. Clean the filter with solvent and compressed air. Check for damage or any lodged particles in the outer mesh.

e. Clean out the filter cavity in the crankcase, then reinstall the filter, securing bolt, O-ring, and cover plate.

NOTE: *Do not overtighten the remaining bolt because the filter could collapse.*

5. To remove the sump strainer, remove the six securing bolts, cover plate, gasket, and strainer. Clean the strainer with solvent and compressed air. When reinstalling, use a new gasket. Tighten the securing bolts evenly in a criss-cross pattern.

Sump strainer retaining bolts (650) (Courtesy Yamaha Int. Corp.)

6. Fill the crankcase with 5.8 pints of SAE 20W-40 rated "SE."

7. Start the engine and let it run for several minutes, then check the oil level and top up if necessary.

750

The 750 utilizes a dry-sump lubrication system.

1. Warm the engine before draining the oil. Remove the drain plug at the oil tank, and then the crankcase sump drain plug. When the oil has drained for several minutes, replace the plugs.

2. Remove the left side crankcase cover and remove the oil filter mounting bolt and the oil filter.

3. When replacing the filter, new o-rings must be used. Tighten the oil filter mounting bolt to 21-22.4 ft lbs.

4. Fill the oil tank with two quarts of oil. Start the engine and run it for 2-3 minutes, then check the oil level in the tank. Top up if necessary.

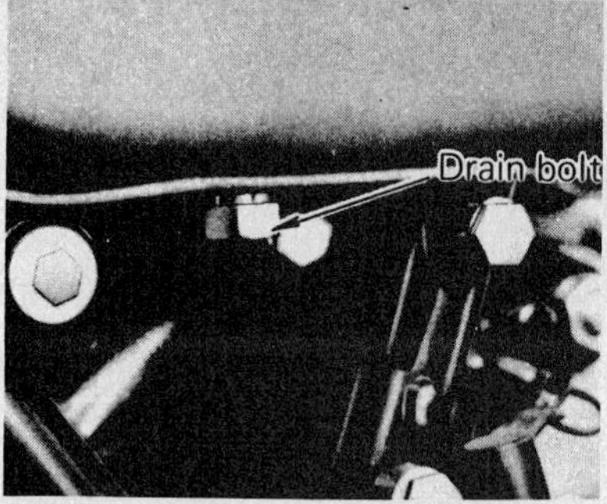

Oil tank drain plug (750) (Courtesy Yamaha Int. Corp.)

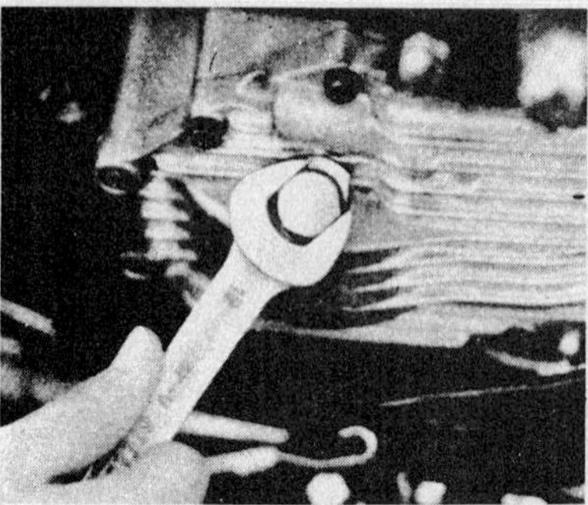
Crankcase sump drain plug (750) (Courtesy Yamaha Int. Corp.)

FRONT FORKS

All Models

1. Drain off the oil from each fork leg by removing the drain screw at the bottom of each fork slider.

2. Pump the forks up and down several times to expel all of the oil.

3. Refit the drain screws, remove the fork tube caps and add the proper quantity and grade of oil. Refer to the "Capacities" chart at the end of this section.

CHASSIS

Lubrication of the wheel bearings and steering head bearings should be accomplished every 4000 miles using a good grade of chassis grease.

Procedures for servicing these components are given in the "Chassis" section.

The swing arm pivot spindle is fitted with a grease fitting and should be lubricated every 2000 miles.

CABLES

The speedometer and tachometer cables should be removed from their housings and greased. Leave about four inches at the upper end of the cable free of grease to prevent any getting into the instruments.

Throttle and clutch cables can be lubricated with motor oil or commercial graphite or molybdenum lubricant. The throttle drum (twist grip) should be greased with chassis grease.

AIR FILTER

A paper filtering element is used.

Remove and apply an air blast from the inside to clean. The filter element must be kept dry.

Service Checks and Adjustments

CLUTCH

All Models

There are two adjustments to be made to the clutch when needed: the clutch pushrod and the clutch cable.

1. The clutch pushrod must be adjusted first. Run the cable adjuster at the handlebar down all the way so that there is plenty of slack in the cable.

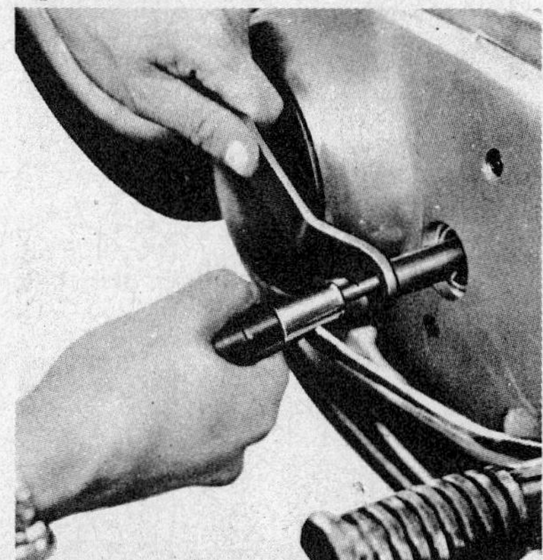

Adjusting the clutch (500) (Courtesy Yamaha Int. Corp.)

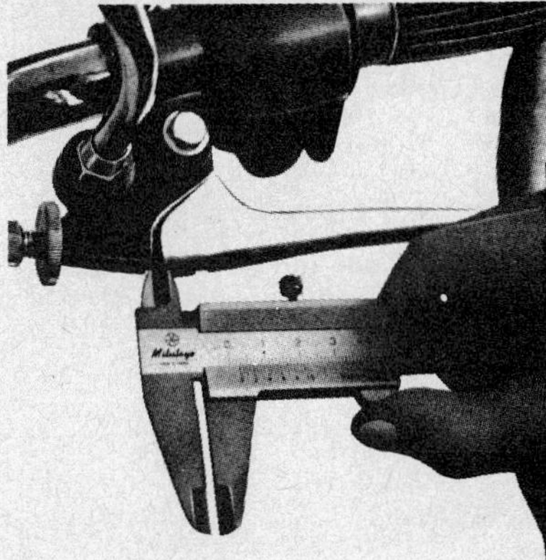

Measuring clutch cable freeplay (Courtesy Yamaha Int. Corp.)

2. Remove the plug on the left side of the engine to gain access to the clutch pushrod adjuster. On the 750, the left crankcase cover must be removed.
3. Loosen the locknut and turn the pushrod adjustment screw *in* until lightly seated, then back it off ¼ turn and tighten the locknut.
4. Adjust the cable using the adjuster on the handlebar so that there is between 1/16-⅛ in. of lever freeplay.

THROTTLE CABLES

The opening of the butterflies must be synchronized first. Then set throttle cables so that there is a minimum of freeplay at the twist grip before the butterflies begin to open. About 1mm of cable freeplay is sufficient. Swing the handlebars from side to side with the engine running. Any variation in idle speed indicates insufficient cable slack or that the throttle cable(s) are incorrectly routed.

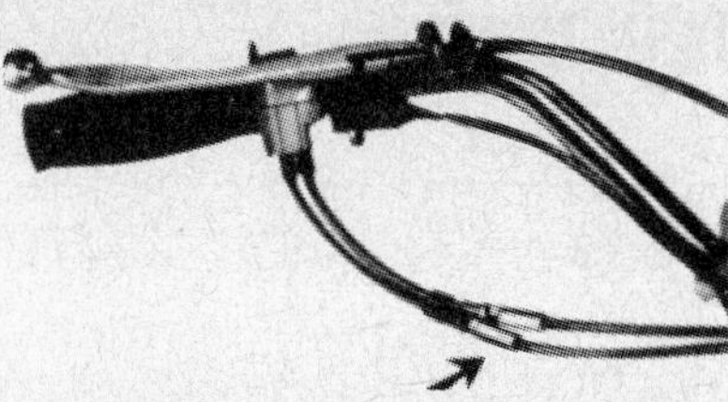

Throttle cable adjusters (650) (Courtesy Yamaha Int. Corp.)

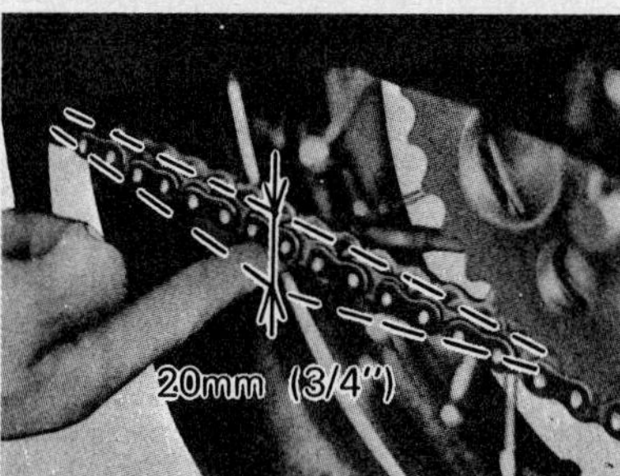

Checking drive chain slack (Courtesy Yamaha Int. Corp.)

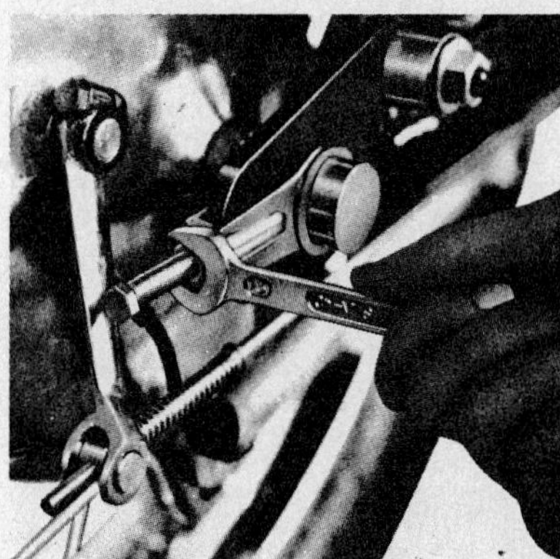

Tightening the drive chain adjuster locknut (Courtesy Yamaha Int. Corp.)

BRAKES

Cable operated drum brakes may be adjusted as desired with the cable adjusters as long as the brakes do not drag.

Rod operated rear brakes must be adjusted with the machine off the stand and with a rider sitting on the machine.

Adjust so that the movement of the swing arm will not cause the shoes to contact the drum. Adjust the rear brake light switch if necessary after adjusting the rear brake.

The front disc brake lever is adjusted by means of an adjusting screw on the handlebar. There should be ½-1 in. of lever freeplay before it contacts the piston.

FINAL DRIVE CHAIN

1. Chain slack should be about ¾ in. of total up and down movement measured in the middle of the bottom chain run.
2. Chain slack must be measured with the machine off the stand and with a rider sitting on the machine.
3. To adjust the chain, remove the cotter pin and loosen the rear axle nut.
4. Loosen the chain adjuster locknut on each side of the swing arm.
5. Turn the adjuster bolts in an equal amount to move the rear wheel back. Check that the alignment marks on each side of the swing arm to insure that the wheel is correctly aligned, then retighten the adjuster locknuts.
6. Apply the rear brake and tighten the axle nut. Fit a new cotter pin.
7. Check the rear brake adjustment.

PERIODIC MAINTENANCE INTERVALS

Daily
Tire pressure
Chain slack
Cable adjustments
Brake adjustment

Weekly
Battery fluid level

Every 250 miles
Lubricate chain

Every 1000 miles
Check oil level
Clean, gap or replace spark plugs
Check disc brake fluid reservoir
Adjust drive chain

Every 2000 miles
Check brake system
Check and adjust clutch
Clean or replace air cleaner
Clean fuel petcocks
Check ignition timing
Clean and adjust or replace breaker points
Check carburetor operation
Adjust cam chain tensioner
Adjust valve clearance
Grease frame and chassis parts
Lubricate cables and twist grip
Change engine oil

Every 4000 miles
Replace oil filter
Overhaul carburetors
Lubricate wheel bearings and steering head bearings
Lubricate breaker point pads
Chain front fork oil
Grease instrument cables

Every 8000 miles
Decarbonize engine
Flush and clean entire lubrication system
Flush and renew disc brake fluid

MAINTENANCE DATA

	500	650	750
Gas tank (gal)	3.3	3.3	3.7
Crankcase (qts)	3.2	3.2	—
Oil tank (qts)	—	—	3.2
Forks			
each leg	5.8 oz. (173 cc)	①	5.8 oz. (173 cc)
Tire pressure (psi)			
Front	23	23	23
Rear	29	28	29

① XS1: 8.1 oz. (240 cc)
XS2: 4.6 oz. (135 cc)

RECOMMENDED LUBRICANTS

	500	650	750
Engine	10W-40	10W-40	10W-40
Forks	10W-30	20W or 30W	10W-40
Control Cables	10W-30 motor oil or graphite-based lubricant		
Tach, speedo cables	Light duty Lithium grease		
Wheel bearings	Waterproof medium weight chassis grease		
Steering head bearings	Waterproof medium weight chassis grease		
Swing arm pivot	90W lubricating grease		

ENGINE AND TRANSMISSION

500

Engine Removal

1. Drain the engine oil.
2. Remove the seat. Shut off the fuel taps, disconnect the lines, and remove the gas tank.
3. Remove the left and right side covers. Disconnect the battery and remove it from the frame.

NOTE: *The negative lead should be disconnected first.*

4. Loosen the carburetor clamps at the manifold and the air cleaner. Remove the cam chain case cover breather pipe.
5. Remove the air cleaner mounting bolts and remove the air cleaner. Remove the carburetors.

NOTE: *Remove the carburetors carefully. They are taken out as a pair. It is recommended that the carb adjusting holder be pulled forward, as shown, when removing the carburetors so that it does not contact any components. This may cause the holder to be bumped out of adjustment.*

Loosening carburetor clamp (Courtesy Yamaha Int. Corp.)

Removing the carburetors. Note holder pulled back as a precaution to protect adjustment (Courtesy Yamaha Int. Corp.)

In this event, the carburetor synchronization will be thrown off. Check synchronization with a vacuum gauge after installation if in doubt.

6. Disconnect the throttle cables from the carbs.
7. Disconnect the tach cable at the engine. Take off the spark plug caps.

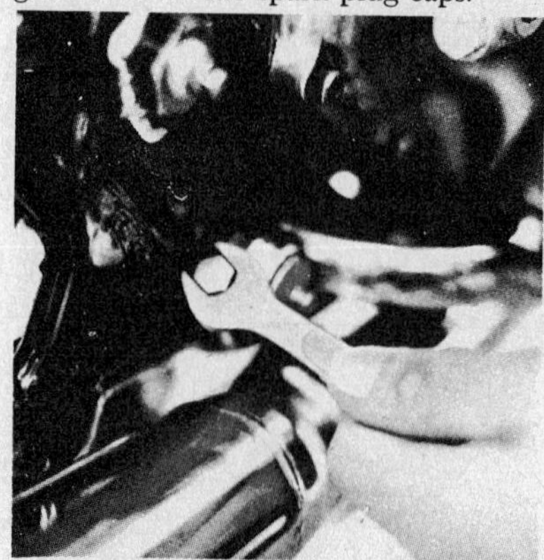

Removing the brake pedal pinch bolt (Courtesy Yamaha Int. Corp.)

Removing the footpegs (Courtesy Yamaha Int. Corp.)

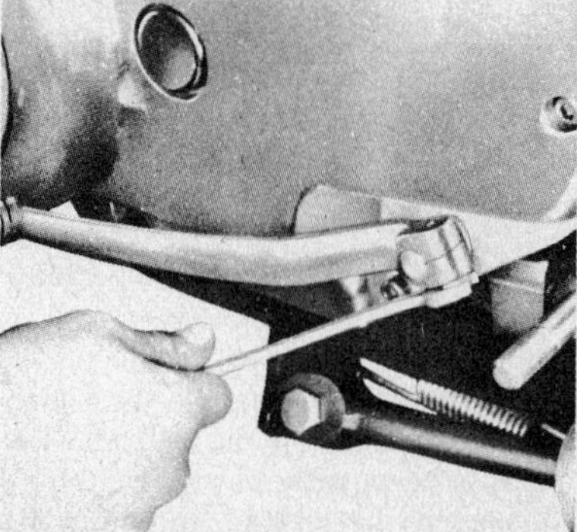

Removing the gearshift lever (Courtesy Yamaha Int. Corp.)

8. Unbolt and remove the exhaust system.
9. Remove the left rear crankcase cover. Remove the air scoop from the cam case cover.
11. Disconnect the clutch cable at the handlebar, then at the clutch pushrod.
12. Remove the drive chain.

NOTE: *The masterlink plate is a press fit on the masterlink and should be*

Driving direction

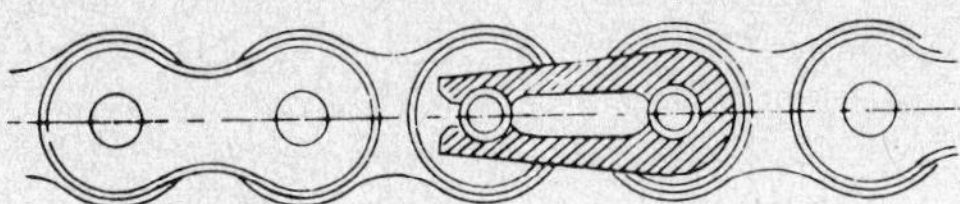

Masterlink spring clip properly fitted (Courtesy Yamaha Int. Corp.)

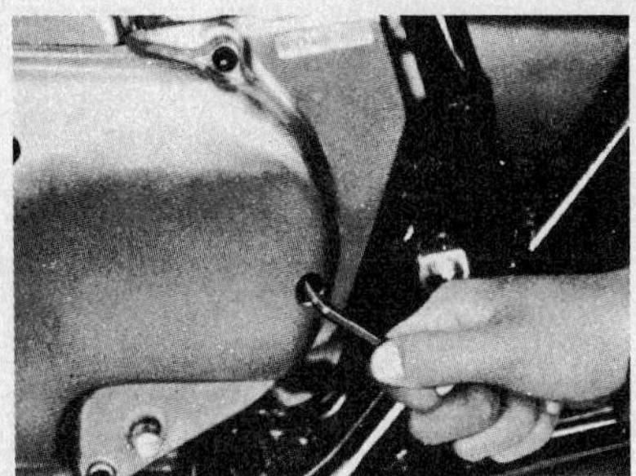

Removing the left rear crankcase cover (Courtesy Yamaha Int. Corp.)

"Breaking" the drive chain (Courtesy Yamaha Int. Corp.)

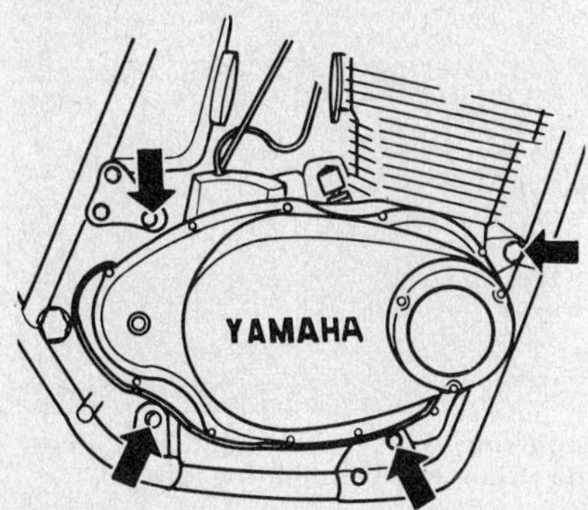

Engine mounting bolts (Courtesy Yamaha Int. Corp.)

Removing the engine from the frame (Courtesy Yamaha Int. Corp.)

removed and installed with the special tool.

13. Disconnect the starter motor cable at the starter switch. Disconnect all of the wires coming from the alternator at the plastic couplers, and the neutral switch, breaker point wires and oil pressure switch wires at the couplers.

14. Remove all of the engine mounting bolts, nuts, and mounting plates.

15. Grasping the engine's left exhaust port and kickstarter, lift the engine out of the right side of the motorcycle.

Installation

1. Installation is in the reverse of the disassembly procedure. Note the following points.

2. Engine mounting bolts are torqued as follows:

Mounting Bolt Torque

Bolt Size	*Torque (ft lbs)*
M8	11-17
M10	20-26
M12	37-52

3. When connecting wiring, insure that all wires are properly arranged.

4. Install the masterlink plate with the special tool. Fit the spring clip so that the closed side faces the direction of chain motion.

5. Be certain that the wires from the alternator are properly installed in the rubber grommet when the left rear crankcase cover is replaced.

6. Torque the footpeg bolt to 38-52 ft lbs.

7. when installing the rear brake pedal, align the punch mark on the pedal with the mark on the splined shaft.

8. When installing the carburetors, the black cable opens the throttles and the silver cable closes them.

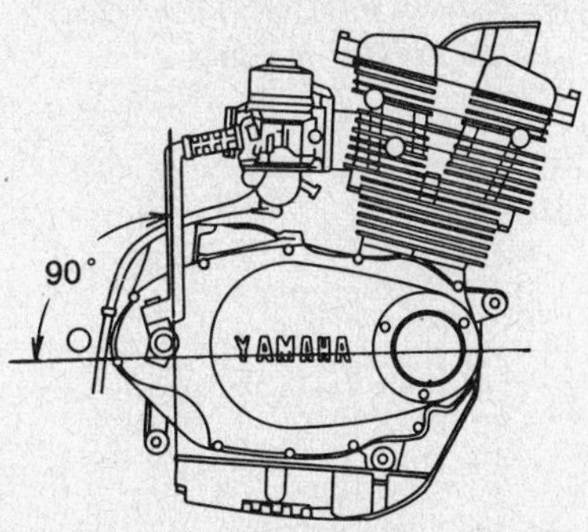

Kickstarter lever location (Courtesy Yamaha Int. Corp.)

9. The battery negative wire is grounded by the right side air cleaner mounting bolt. Remember to reconnect the wire.

10. Connect the battery overflow tube after installing the battery.

11. When replacing the drain plugs in the crankcase, torque them to 26-30 ft lbs.

Cylinder Head and Cylinder

REMOVAL

1. Remove the spark plugs and the 18 allen bolts which secure the camshaft case cover to the case.

2. Remove the three allen head screws which secure the breaker point cover to the right crankcase cover.

3. Remove the plug at the left of the breaker point case with the 10mm allen wrench.

Camshaft case cover securing bolts (Courtesy Yamaha Int. Corp.)

Cleaning the cover mating surface (Courtesy Yamaha Int. Corp.)

4. Insert the special 10mm allen wrench into the plug hole and engage it with the crankshaft mounted gear. Turn the crankshaft so that the line which is designated "V" on the timing advance base plate is aligned with the line on the stationary timing plate.

CAUTION: *The crankshaft must be in this position when the camshafts are removed.*

5. Remove the cylinder head oil delivery line at the rear, center, of the cylin-

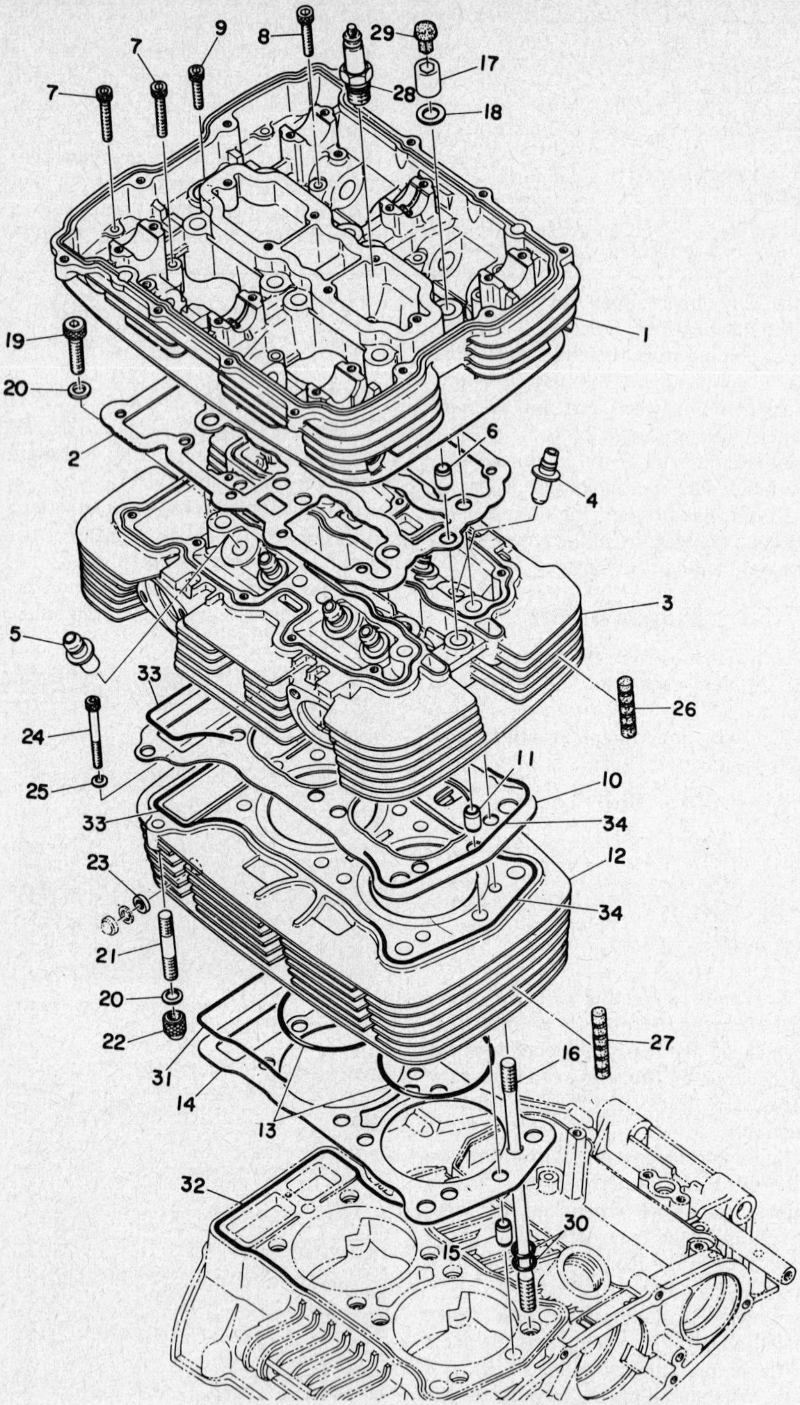

Top end assembly (Courtesy Yamaha Int. Corp.)

1. Case, camshaft
2. Gasket, head cover 2
3. Head, cylinder
4. Bushing, valve guide intake
5. Bushing, valve guide exhaust
6. Pin, dowel (6.4-10-14)
7. Bolt
8. Bolt
9. Bolt
10. Gasket; cylinder head
11. Pin, dowel (6.4-10-14)
12. Cylinder
13. O-ring (1.9-78.5)
14. Gasket, cylinder
15. Pin, dowel (6.4-10-14)
16. Bolt, cylinder holding
17. Nut, holding
18. Washer, holding
19. Bolt
20. Washer, plate
21. Stud
22. Nut
23. Oil, seal (SO-8-12-3)
24. Bolt
25. Washer, plate
26. Absorber 1
27. Absorber 2
28. Plug, spark (D-8ES)
29. Plug, blind
30. O-Ring (3.5-6.4)
31. Seal, cylinder 1
32. Seal, cylinder 2
33. Seal, cylinder 3
34. Seal, cylinder 4

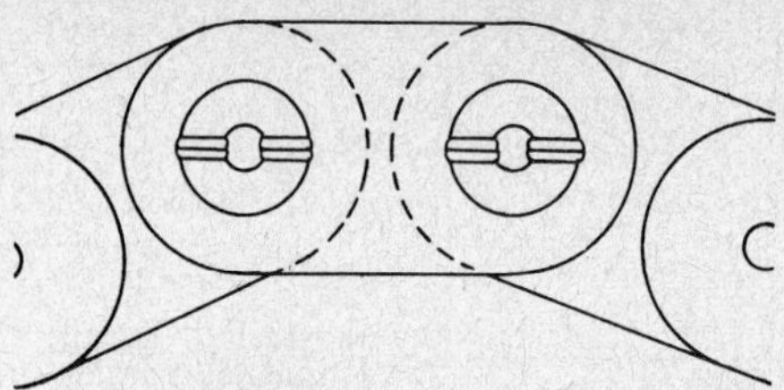

The cam chain link to be broken has these marks (Courtesy Yamaha Int. Corp.)

der. Remove both banjo bolts and remove the oil line.

6. The cam chain is a duplex endless chain. The chain should only be "broken" at the single link which has punch marks and slots across the rivet heads. And this should only be accomplished with the special tool. Stuff a clean rag between the camshaft sprockets when removing the link to catch any bits of metal.

7. Attach a length of mechanic's wire to the chain at both ends of the chain link which is to be removed.

8. Press out the chain link marked with the scribed rivets, take away the link, and then drape each end of the cam chain over the sides of the camshaft case, and secure them out of the way with the mechanic's wire.

9. Lift out the chain guide. Using a screwdriver, pry out the plug which is under the guide, and, with a 5mm allen wrench, remove the bolt beneath the plug.

Removing the cylinder head oil deliver line (Courtesy Yamaha Int. Corp.)

Breaking the cam chain (Courtesy Yamaha Int. Corp.)

Cam chain ends secured out of the way for cam case removal (Courtesy Yamaha Int. Corp.)

Removing the chain guide (Courtesy Yamaha Int. Corp.)

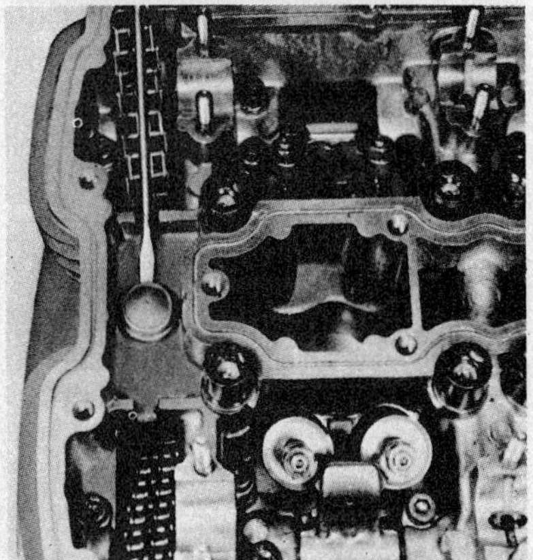

Removing the plug (Courtesy Yamaha Int. Corp.)

Removing the camshaft (Courtesy Yamaha Int. Corp.)

Removing the camshaft caps (Courtesy Yamaha Int. Corp.)

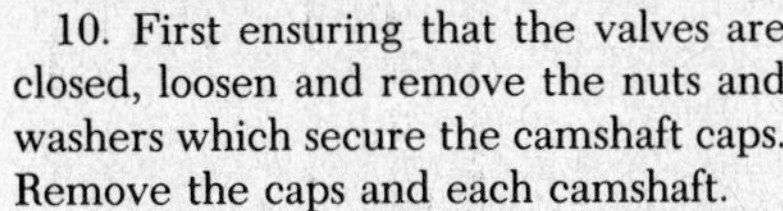

10. First ensuring that the valves are closed, loosen and remove the nuts and washers which secure the camshaft caps. Remove the caps and each camshaft.

11. Remove the 10 allen bolts which hold the cam case to the head, and then the eight allen nuts which are threaded onto studs which run through the upper end to the crankcase.

12. Remove the camshaft case.

13. The rocker arms may be removed, if desired by first removing the rocker arm shaft securing bolts. Remove the plugs covering the ends of the shafts, and use the special tool to pull out the rocker arm shafts. The special tool is actually a small "slide hammer," which threads into the end of the rocker arm shaft. The shaft is then pulled out by the action of the large weight hitting the hex head of the puller.

14. Inspection procedures for cam case components are given below.

15. Remove the bolt and two nuts which hold the cylinder head to the cylinder. These are located on the right side of the cylinder head. Lift the cylinder head straight up and off the cylinder.

16. To remove the valves, compress the springs using the proper "C" clamp tool, take out the valve keepers, the spring retainer, the two valve springs and the spring seat. Mark each spring set and valve so that it may be installed in its correct place.

17. To remove the cylinder, remove the bolt in the cam chain cutout, then tap the cylinder upwards with a soft-faced mallet.

18. To remove the pistons, remove the circlips; push out wrist pins gently. Mark the position (left or right) on each piston.

INSPECTION

Camshaft Case Components

1. The camshafts ride on plain bearings. Camshaft journal to bearing clearance should not exceed 0.003 in. The clearance may be checked with plastigauge. The bearing caps must be torqued to 5.8-7.5 ft lbs when making this measurement.

Removing the cam case to head allen bolts (Courtesy Yamaha Int. Corp.)

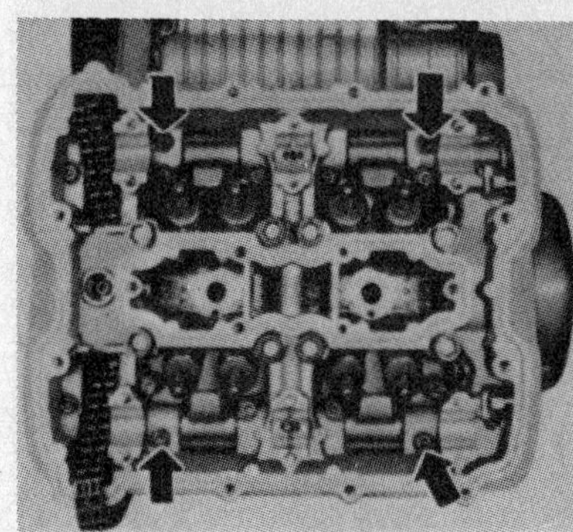

Rocker arm securing bolts (Courtesy Yamaha Int. Corp.)

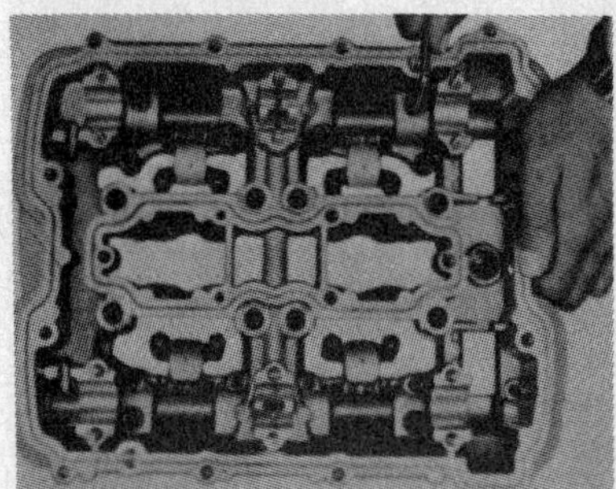

Removing the rocker arm securing bolts (Courtesy Yamaha Int. Corp.)

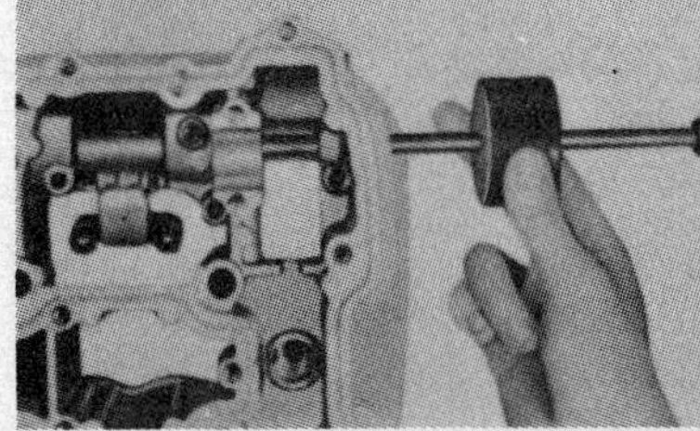

Removing the rocker arm shafts with the slide hammer (Courtesy Yamaha Int. Corp.)

Removing the cylinder head bolt (Courtesy Yamaha Int. Corp.)

Removing the cylinder head (Courtesy Yamaha Int. Corp.)

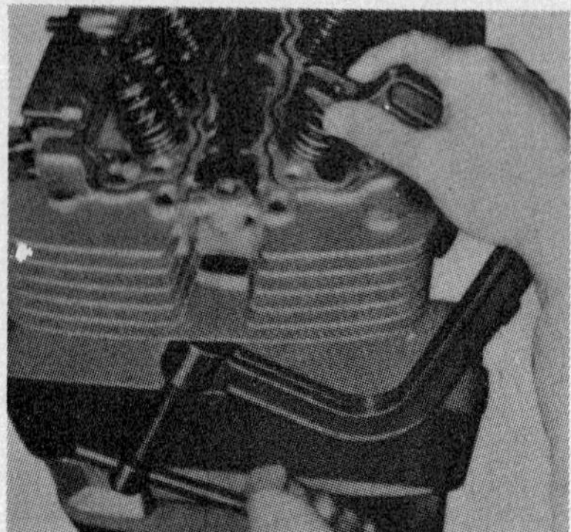

Removing the valve assemblies (Courtesy Yamaha Int. Corp.)

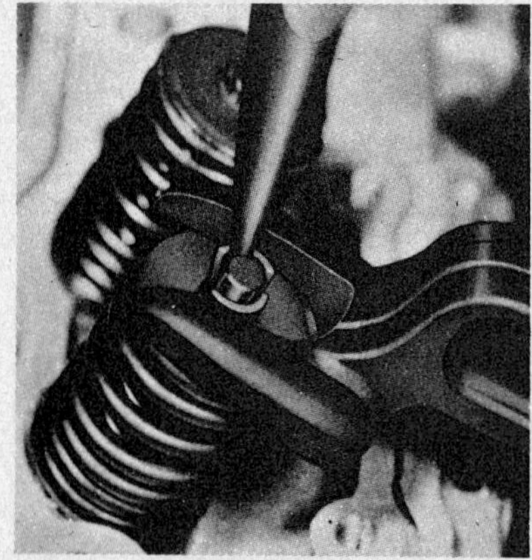

Taking out the valve keepers (Courtesy Yamaha Int. Corp.)

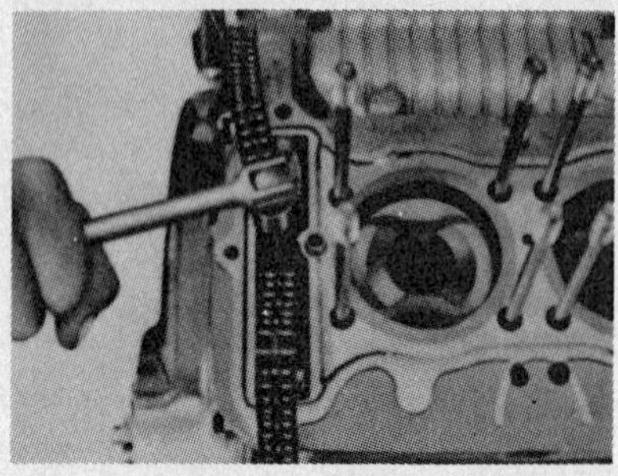

Removing the bolt in the cam chain cutout (Courtesy Yamaha Int. Corp.)

2. Assuming that the cam journals are free of scoring or other obvious signs of wear, measure the diameter of the journal. The camshaft must be replaced if the journal diameter is 0.8653 in. (21.97mm) or less.

Note that the camshaft caps should be replaced at the same time.

3. If available, an inside micrometer can be used to measure the camshaft bearings. With the caps in place on the bearings, and the cap nuts properly torqued, bearing diameter should not exceed 0.86731 in. (22.05mm).

If any of the bearings is worn more than this amount, or if any is scored or damaged, the cam case and caps should be replaced as an assembly.

4. With the camshaft installed, measure the end play between the left end of the camshaft and the cam case with a feeler gauge. Push the cam toward the cam chain side of the case and hold it there while making this measurement. Maximum allowable end play is 0.016 in. (0.4mm).

5. Check the camshaft lobes for any score marks. The lobe dimensions are given at the end of this section, and may be checked with a micrometer. The cam lift "C" is obtained by subtracting the base circle diameter "B" from the maximum lobe length, "A."

6. Each camshaft may be checked for a bent condition by supporting the cam at the outer bearing journals in a pair of V-blocks. Measure run-out at the center journal with a dial gauge. Maximum allowable run-out is 0.0039 in. (0.1mm).

7. A cam chain damper is located between the two sprockets on each camshaft. Inspect the damper for signs of wear or deterioration and replaced as necessary. The old damper may be cut off. The new damper should be greased before installation and carefully installed.

8. Check the surface of the cam chain guide for wear or damage and replace as necessary. An excessively worn chain guide may indicate a loose cam chain or too much end play in the camshafts.

9. Inspect the rocker arm and rocker arm shafts for condition. The pad on the rocker arm which contacts the cam lobe must be free of any signs of wear or damage. If this surface is not in good condition, do not attempt to remedy the surface imperfections with a stone or emery cloth. Rather, the rocker arm should be replaced. Removing material from the pad will affect valve timing.

Note any blueing or discoloration of both the rocker arm and the shaft. If present, replace the damaged part. This is indicative of overheating or lack of oil. Check the lubrication system and passages.

The rocker arm shaft bore and the shaft itself should be checked for wear. Place the shaft in the rocker arm and attempt to move it up and down. Excessive play here is usually due to wear of the rocker arm bore, since the shaft is hardened. The bore diameter (standard) is 12.00-12.018mm. Shaft diameter (standard) is 11.983-11.994mm.

Removing the cylinders (Courtesy Yamaha Int. Corp.)

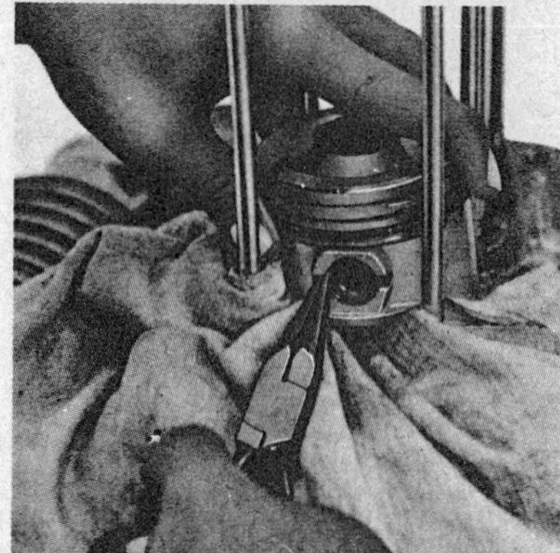

Removing the wrist pin circlips (Courtesy Yamaha Int. Corp.)

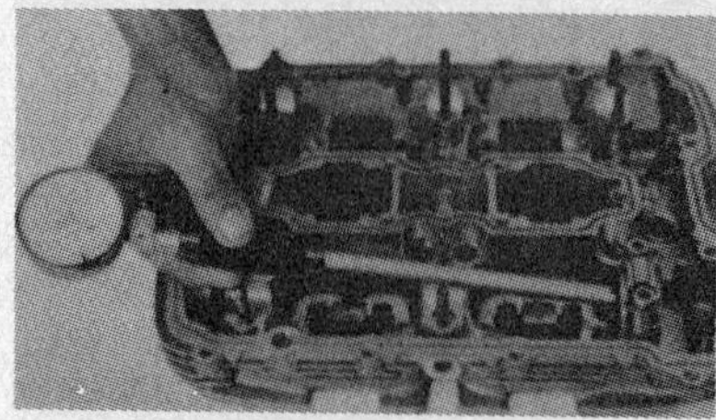

Measuring cam bearing wear (Courtesy Yamaha Int. Corp.)

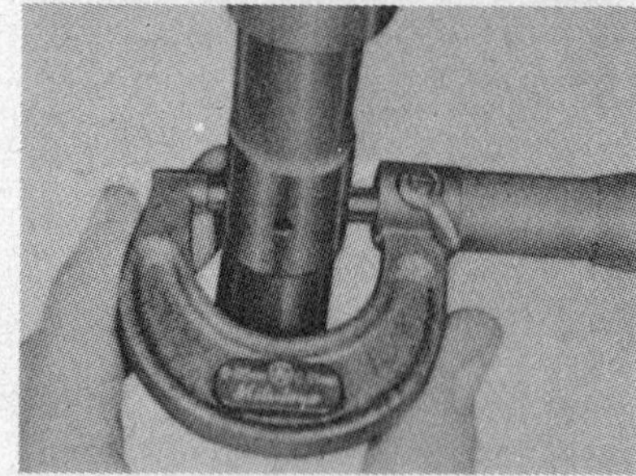

Measuring cam journal wear (Courtesy Yamaha Int. Corp.)

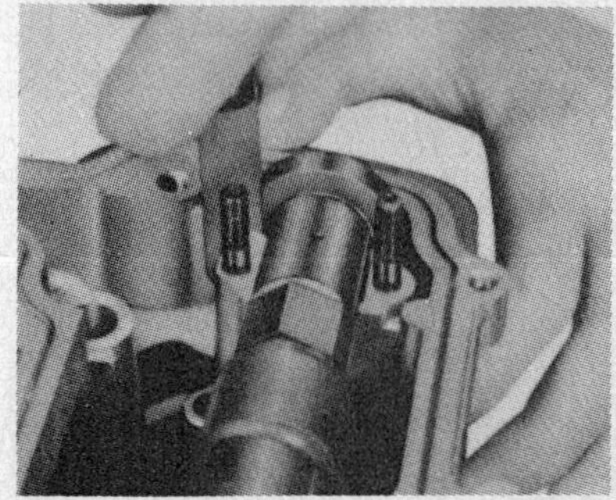

Measuring camshaft end play (Courtesy Yamaha Int. Corp.)

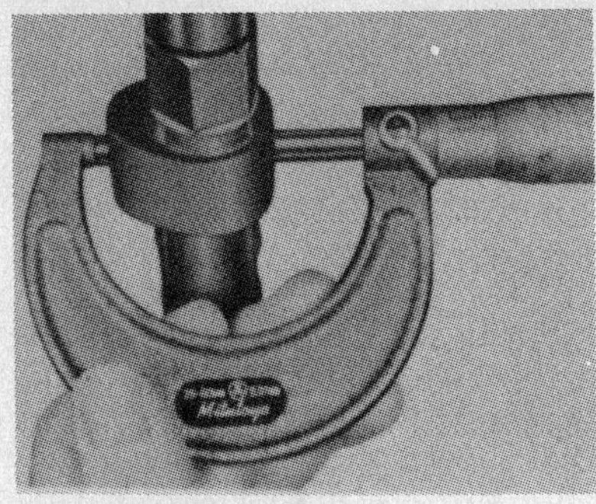

Obtaining the cam lobe dimensions (Courtesy Yamaha Int. Corp.)

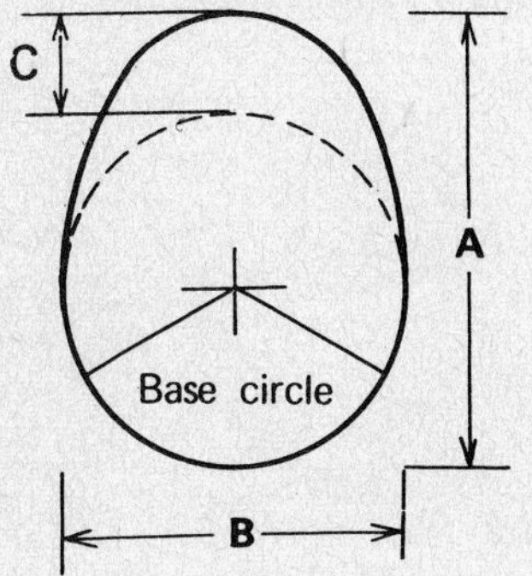

Value "A" is maximum lobe length; "B" is the base circle diameter; "C" is cam lift (Courtesy Yamaha Int. Corp.)

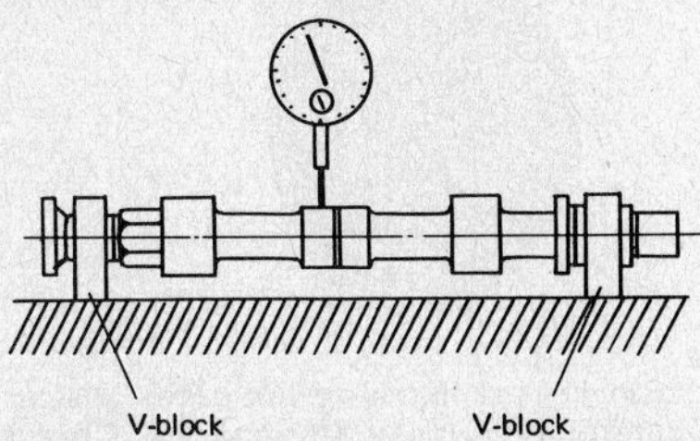

Checking camshaft for bending (Courtesy Yamaha Int. Corp.)

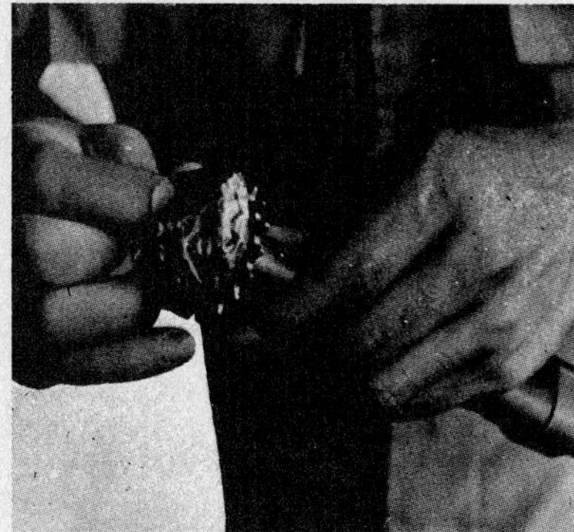

Fitting the cam chain damper (Courtesy Yamaha Int. Corp.)

Cam chain guide; check the condition of the ribbed surface (Courtesy Yamaha Int. Corp.)

Nominal clearance between the rocker arm and the shaft is 0.006mm. Maximum allowable clearance is 0.035mm.

Cylinder Head

1. After removing the valves, clean all carbon deposits out of the combustion chamber. Use a blunt knife to scrape deposits from the valve stems and faces, and finish the process with a wire wheel.

2. Valve stem-to-valve guide clearance must not equal or exceed 0.0031 in. (0.08mm) for the *intake* valves or 0.0040 in. (0.1mm) for the *exhaust* valves; both the guide and the valve must be replaced if it does.

To check valve-to-stem clearance, use a dial gauge set up as illustrated. Insert the valve into its guide. Lift the valve head up about 1.2 in. off of its seat, and position the end of the dial gauge on the valve stem. Move the valve back and forth comparing the dial gauge readings with the acceptable values.

3. Check the diameter of the valve stems measuring at three places along the stem. If the intake valves measure 5.495mm or less or if the exhaust valves measure 5.480mm or less, the worn valve should be replaced.

4. The valve may be checked for a bent condition by holding the stem between the fingers and turning it rapidly. A more accurate method, however, is to put the valve in a V-block and measure the run-out of the head with a dial gauge. If run-out equals or exceeds 0.02mm, the valve must be replaced.

5. If a gauge to measure the inside diameter of the valve guides is available, take readings at the ends and middle of the guide. Refer to the chart at the end of this section for specifications.

6. Inspect the guides for cracks or fractures at the lower end, especially if a bent valve has been found.

7. To remove the guides, heat the head in an oven if possible to 200-400°F., and drive out the guides from the combustion chamber side with a suitable drift. Drive in the new guide(s) while the head is still hot.

Coat the new guide and the valve with an anti-seize compound before installing the valve.

After installing a new guide, check that the valve is properly seated on its seat.

8. Standard valve seat width is 1.0±0.1mm. To measure the width of the valve seat, apply a small amount of valve grinding compound around the seat. Coat the valve face with a blueing dye. Place the valve in the guide and rotate it rapidly back and forth against the seat. Remove the valve, clean it off, and measure the seat width, also noting the position of the seat on the valve face. Refer to the accompanying illustrations.

Figure A indicates that the valve seat is too wide, but is properly centered on the valve face. Use a 15° seat cutter on the seat to reduce seat width to the proper value.

Figure B shows the seat in its proper

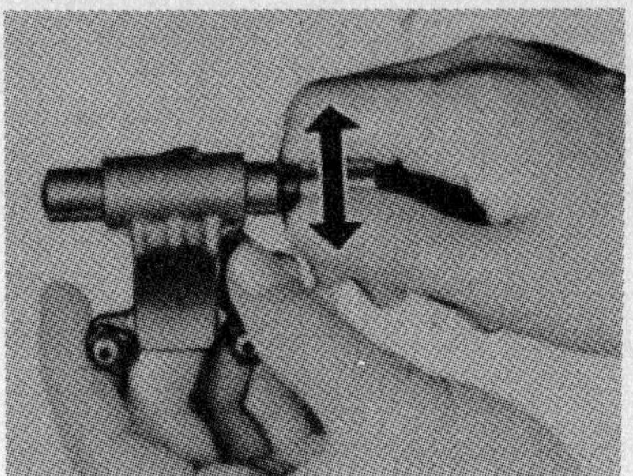

Checking for excessive rocker arm or shaft wear (Courtesy Yamaha Int. Corp.)

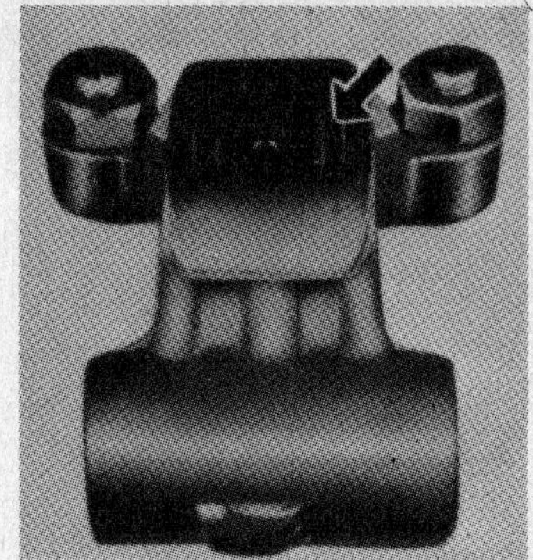

Scored rocker arm pads necessitate replacement of the rocker arm. (Courtesy Yamaha Int. Corp.)

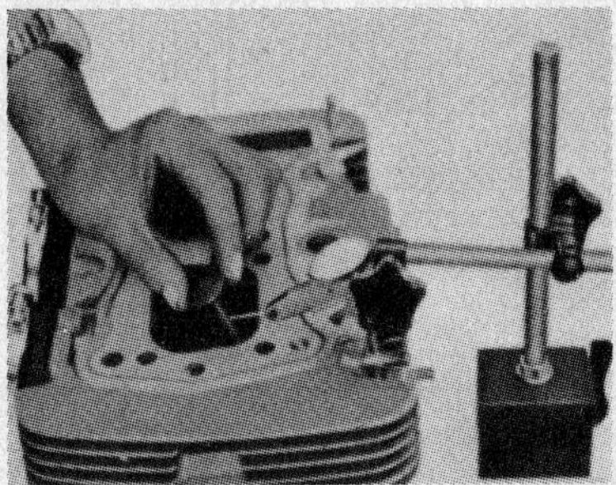

Checking valve-to-guide clearance (Courtesy Yamaha Int. Corp.)

Drifting out a valve guide (Courtesy Yamaha Int. Corp.)

Replacing a valve guide (Courtesy Yamaha Int. Corp.)

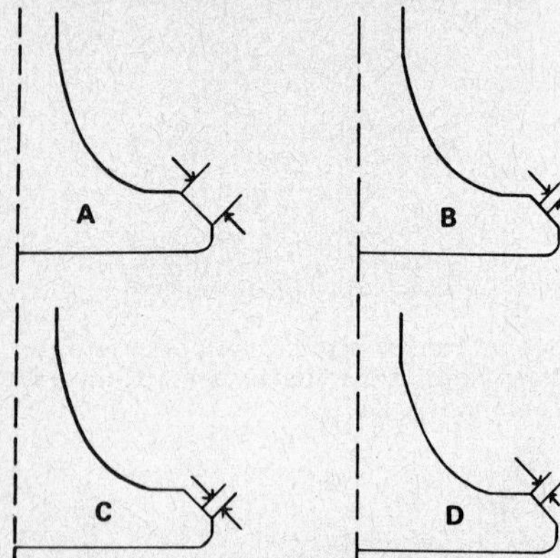

Valve seat width and location checks. Refer to text for remedies (Courtesy Yamaha Int. Corp.)

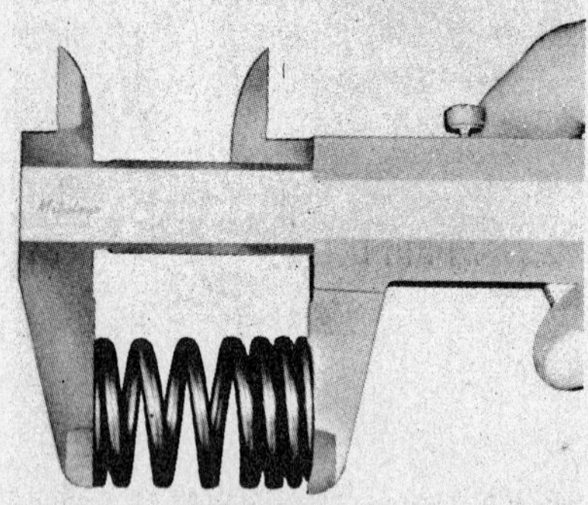

Checking valve spring length (Courtesy Yamaha Int. Corp.)

Cylinder size stamped numbers (Courtesy Yamaha Int. Corp.)

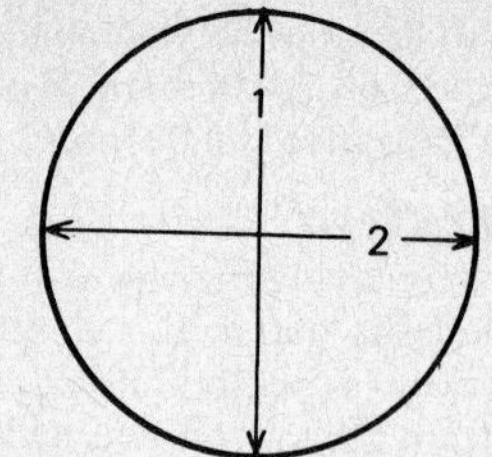

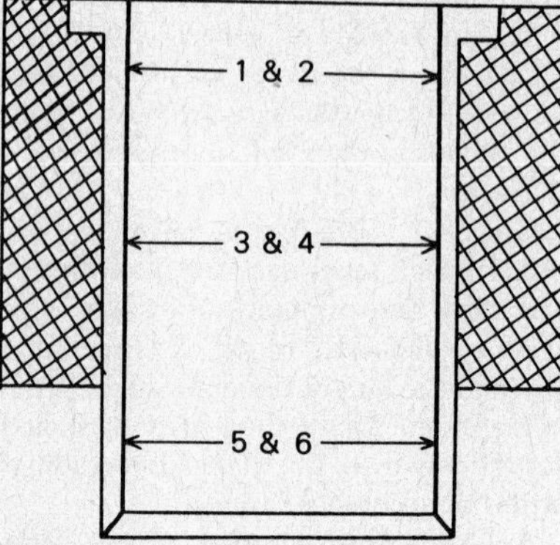

Measuring bore diameter (Courtesy Yamaha Int. Corp.)

position, but it is too narrow. Use a 45° cutter to increase width.

Figure C indicates that the seat is not only too narrow, but too near the valve edge. Use a 45° and then the flat to get the proper position and width.

Figure D shows that the valve seat is too narrow and too near the top of the valve head. Use a 15° cutter, then the 45° cutter to reposition the seat and increase its width.

The valve seat should also be cut with the 45° cutter if it is pitted or if the width varies.

9. If any cutting of the valve seat has been accomplished, the valves must be lapped into their seats.

Lapping should also be done if either new valves or guides have been fitted, or if the engine has covered considerable mileage.

10. For valve spring specifications, refer to the chart at the end of this section. Measure the valve spring free length. If any has compressed 0.080 in. (2mm) or more, it must be replaced. Inner and out springs should be replaced together.

Pistons and Cylinder

1. With an inside micrometer or dial indicator, measure the diameter of each cylinder bore at the top, middle, and bottom of the bore. Take three more bore measurements at the same points but on a plane 90° from the first.

2. Compare the readings obtained. If any of the measurements is greater than 73.1 mm (assuming the cylinder has not been bored), oversized pistons will be needed, and the cylinders will have to be bored to the proper clearance (see below).

Cylinder bore measurement points (Courtesy Yamaha Int. Corp.)

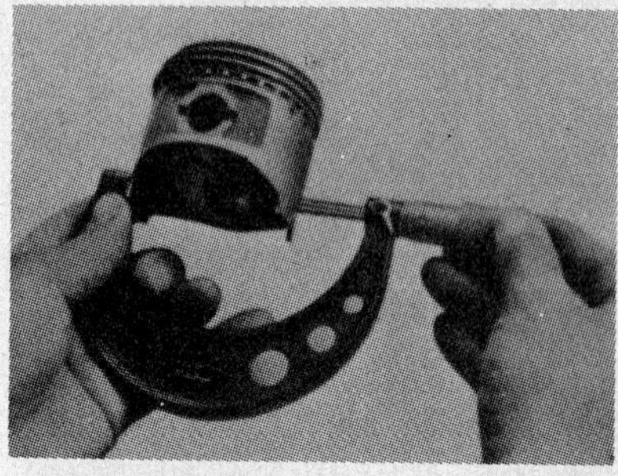

Measuring piston diameter (Courtesy Yamaha Int. Corp.)

Piston crown marking indicates piston diameter (Courtesy Yamaha Int. Corp.)

If the difference between the largest and smallest of three readings taken in a single plane equals or exceeds 0.05mm, the cylinders must be bored.

If the difference between any reading and a reading taken 90° to it at the same point on the bore equals or exceeds 0.05mm, the cylinder is out-of-round and must be bored.

3. Nominal cylinder bore is 73.0mm. Real bore diameter is obtained by adding the numbers found at the very bottom the cylinders to this amount. Example: .007 marked on the cylinder equals a bore of 73.007mm. Refer to the explanation of piston markings, below.

4. Although nominal piston diameter is 73mm, the actual piston size is obtained by adding 72mm to the number stamped on the piston crown. Therefore, if the piston is stamped .956, piston diameter equals 72.956mm.

5. Inspect the general condition of the piston noting any obvious damage such as cracks in the crown, at the wrist pin area, and on the skirt.

6. Scuffing due to insufficient lubrication may sometimes be removed from

the skirt with emery cloth. If scuffing is severe, however, the pistons should be replaced.

7. Measure the piston diameter at the bottom of the skirt, perpendicular to the piston pin.

8. Compare this value with the *smallest* of the cylinder bore measurements. Standard piston-to-cylinder clearance is 0.050-0.055mm. If clearance exceeds or equals 0.15mm, two things may be done.

A standard size piston larger than the piston fitted may bring the clearance to within tolerance.

If this is possible, it is only necessary to hone the cylinder.

If this is not possible, an oversize piston must be fitted. The cylinder will have to be bored, taking into consideration the diameter of the oversized piston, to obtain the proper clearance. After boring, the cylinder must be honed to give a cross-hatched pattern.

9. Piston rings must be checked for end-gap (installed in the bore) and side-clearance (installed on the piston). After removing the rings, clean out any carbon deposits which may have accumulated in the ring grooves.

10. Both compression rings and the oil ring rails should undergo the same tests. Insert each ring into the bottom of the cylinder bore from which it was taken. Use a piston to square the ring in the bore. Check that the ring contacts the cylinder wall at all points.

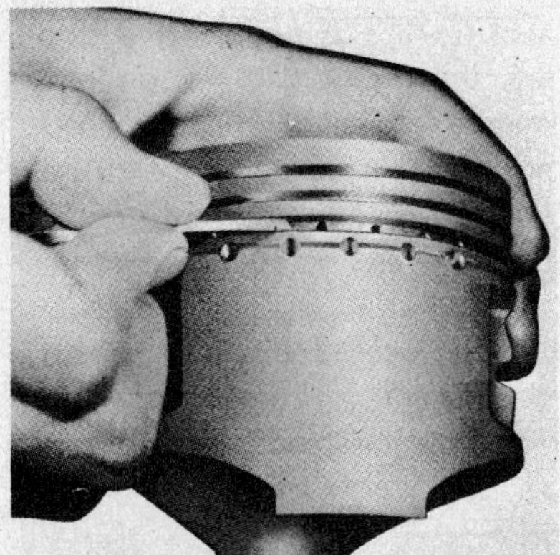

Decarbonizing the ring grooves (Courtesy Yamaha Int. Corp.)

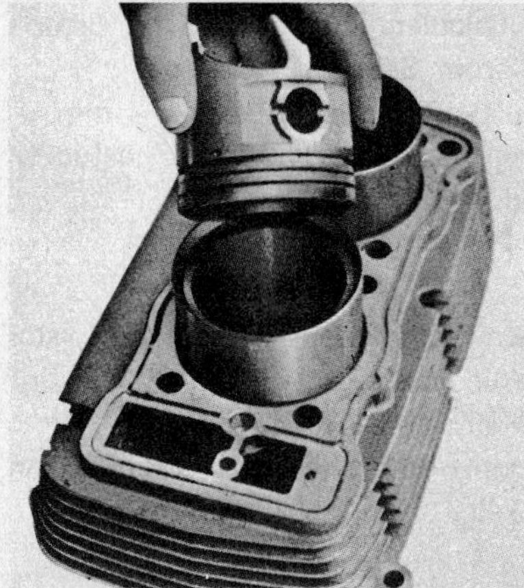

Squaring a ring in the bore to check ring end gap (Courtesy Yamaha Int. Corp.)

Measuring piston ring end gap (Courtesy Yamaha Int. Corp.)

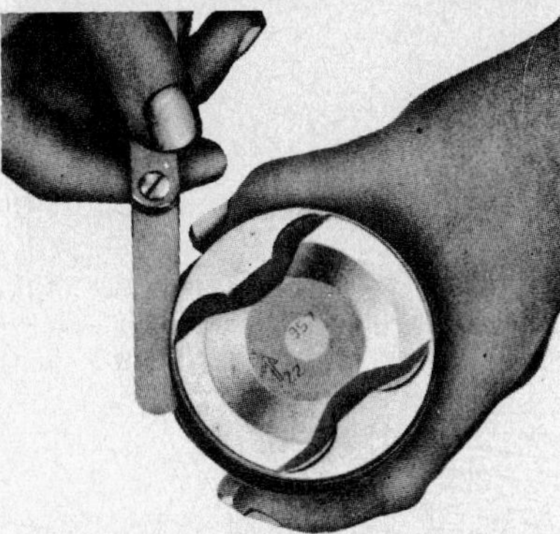

Measuring piston ring side clearance (Courtesy Yamaha Int. Corp.)

With a suitable feeler gauge, check the end-gap for each ring. Standard gap for the compression rings is 0.2-0.4mm and maximum acceptable gap is 0.8mm.

Standard oil ring end gap is 0.2-0.9mm, and maximum acceptable is 1.3mm.

If any ring or rail is worn beyond tolerance, both sets of rings must be replaced, and the cylinder honed.

11. Check the ring side play with the rings installed in their proper places on the piston. Note that both rings and grooves must be very clean to give an accurate reading.

The oil ring rails, when installed on the expander should not have any side clearance at all. If any is present, the ring set must be replaced.

The compression rings have a standard side clearance of 0.04-0.08mm (0.0016-0.0032 in.). Any value 0.15mm (0.006 in.) or greater indicates that the ring set must be replaced. Have the cylinders honed before installing new rings.

12. New rings must also be checked for end gap. If the gap is insufficient, it may be increased by filing the ends of the ring. Close the ring ends over a small file so that an equal amount of material is removed from each end.

13. Oversized compression rings have the oversize number stamped on the top of the ring.

Oversized oil rings are color-coded: both rails and the expander are painted 180° from the end gap. Blue indicates the first oversize (0.25mm) and is indicated by two marks. Red, the second oversize (0.50mm) shows one mark.

14. Inspect the piston wrist pin for wear or discoloration. If discoloration is present, the pin should be replaced and the lubrication system checked.

The pin may have a dull finish at the very center (where the connecting rod rides). This is normal.

15. Check the can chain tensioner sprockets for smooth rotation and for wear, damage, or a hooked sprocket tooth condition. Check the cam chain guides for wear. Check the tensioner spring for fatigue.

Replace parts as necessary.

Ring markings. This is the first oversize (Courtesy Yamaha Int. Corp.)

NO Good

Cam chain sprocket inspection (Courtesy Yamaha Int. Corp.)

ASSEMBLY

1. Place the cam chain tensioner in its slot in the cylinder and the chain guides as well. Tighten the mounting nuts temporarily; push the sprockets down to compress the spring. Then tighten the tensioner nut.

2. To install the piston rings, fit the oil ring first. Slip either oil ring rail down over the piston until it is just below the oil ring groove. Fit the oil ring expander into its groove. Then move the rail which is on the piston up and into the bottom of the groove. Fit the other oil ring rail into the top of the groove. Position the three end gaps 120° apart.

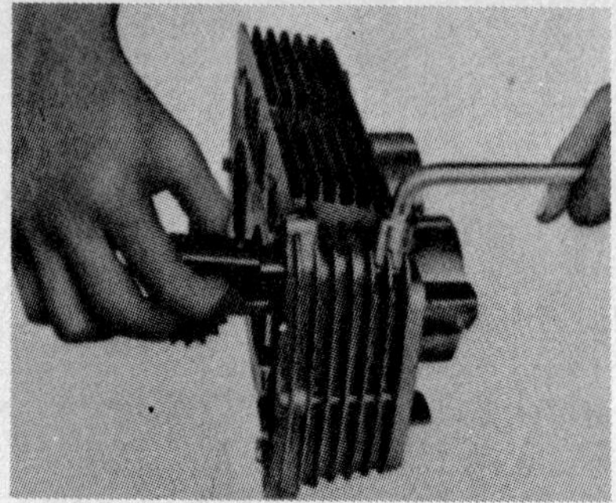
Installing the tensioner assembly (Courtesty Yamaha Int. Corp.)

Compression rings must have the "R" mark facing up when installed (Courtesy Yamaha Int. Corp.)

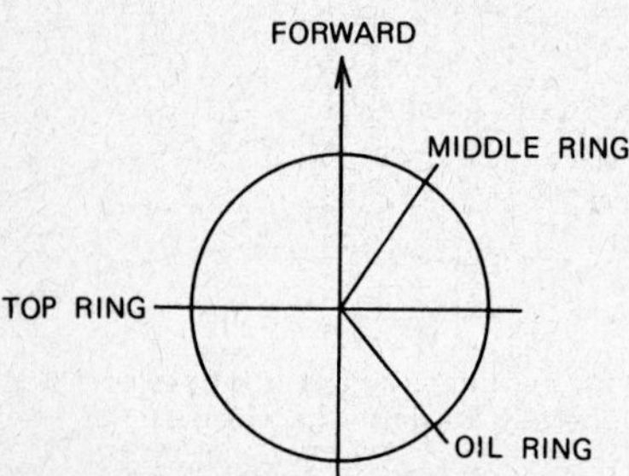

Stagger the ring end gaps as shown (Courtesy Yamaha Int. Corp.)

3. Install the lower compression ring with the "R" stamped on the ring facing up.

4. Install the top compression ring with the "R" stamped on the ring facing up.

5. The top rail of the oil ring and the two compression rings should have their end gaps spaced 120° apart.

6. Lubricate the con rod small end with engine oil. Oil the wrist pin and install the piston on the con rod. Be sure that both circlips are seated in their grooves.

7. Clean off the crankcase mating surface and install a new cylinder base gasket. Lubricate the pistons and cylinders walls with engine oil, and install the cylinder.

8. Reassemble the valve and spring assemblies in the cylinder head. Note that the valve springs have a smaller pitch on one end. This end *must* be installed *downward* (i.e. closest to the head).

9. Use a new cylinder head gasket, refit the head, threading the cam chain through the cutout. Tighten the nuts and bolt securing the cylinder head to the cylinder. Tighten these to the proper torque (15-17.5 ft lbs) *after* the camshaft case has been installed and torqued down.

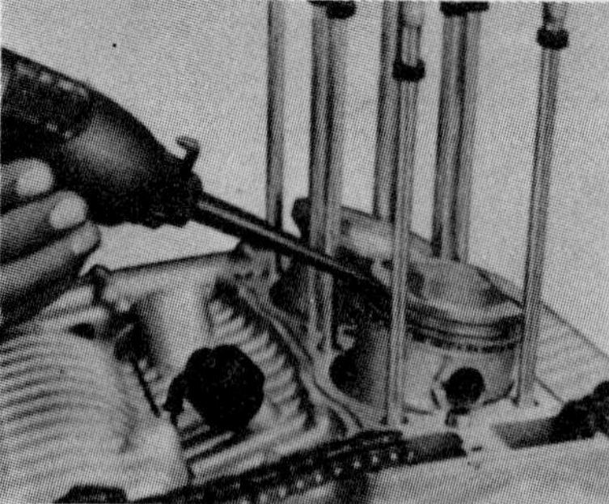
Lubing the piston rings (Courtesy Yamaha Int. Corp.)

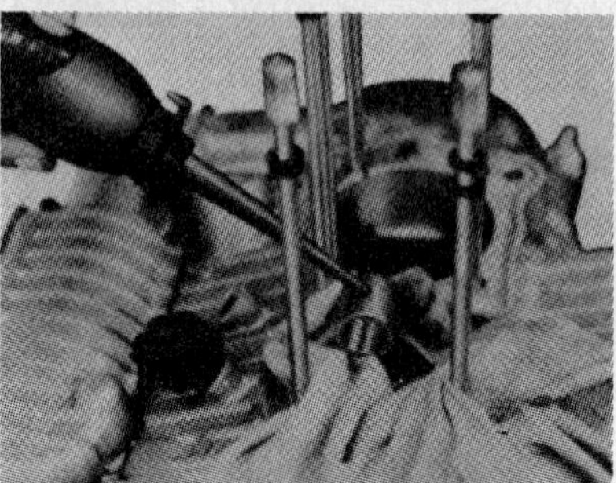
Lubricating the small end before assembly (Courtesy Yamaha Int. Corp.)

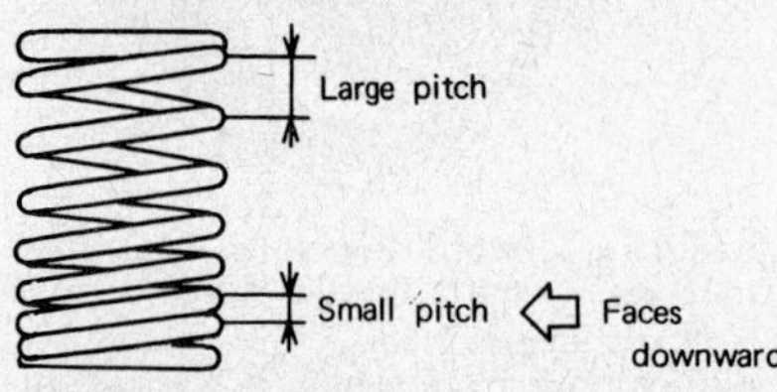

Proper valve spring installation position (Courtesy Yamaha Int. Corp.)

Installing the cylinders (Courtesy Yamaha Int. Corp.)

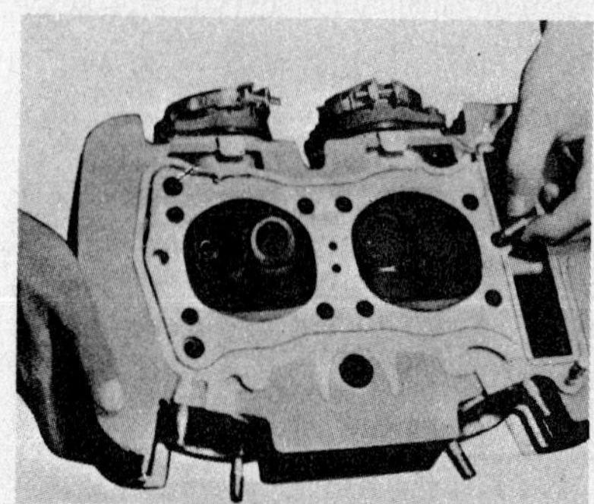
Replacing the cylinder head location pin. (Courtesy Yamaha Int. Corp.)

Fitting a cam case gasket (Courtesy Yamaha Int. Corp.)

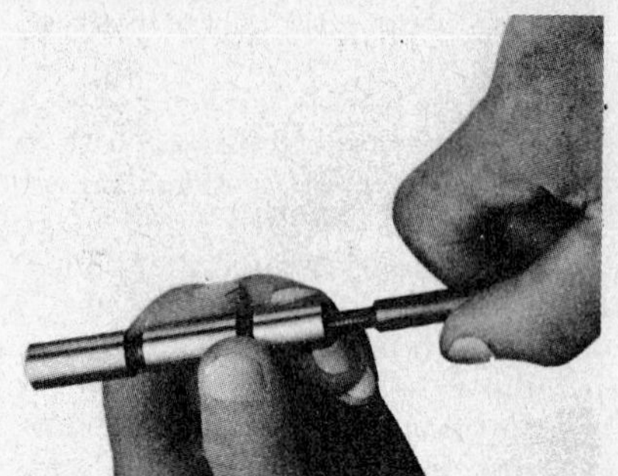
Fitting the rocker arm shaft to the special tool (Courtesy Yamaha Int. Corp.)

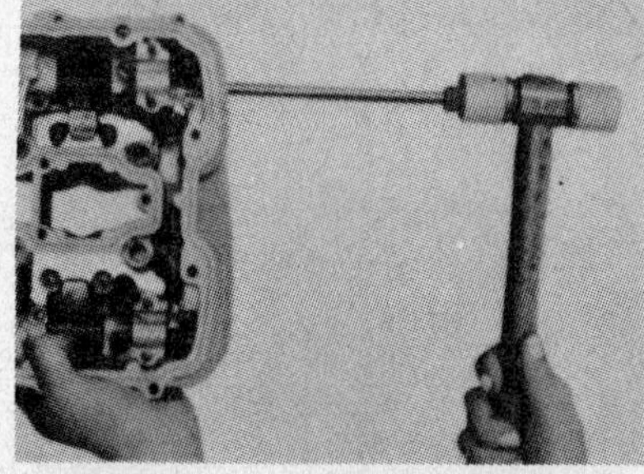
Installing the rocker arm shaft (Courtesy Yamaha Int. Corp.)

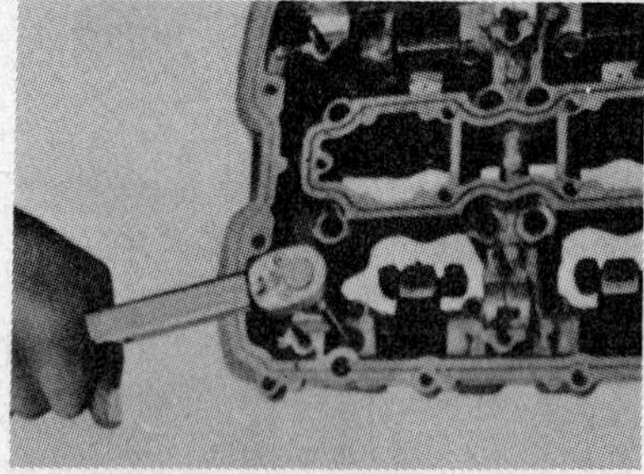
Tightening the rocker arm securing bolts (Courtesy Yamaha Int. Corp.)

10. Assemble the cam case components. The rocker arms are installed by pushing them into place, preferably with the special tool. The groove cut around the circumference of each shaft must align with the shaft securing bolt hole.

Install and tighten the rocker arm shaft securing bolts to 7.5-9.2 ft lbs. Replace the shaft end plugs using new O-rings.

11. Use a new cam case gasket, pass the cam chain through the case, and fit the case on the cylinder head.

12. Install and tighten all of the nuts

and bolts. These should be tightened gradually and evenly to the proper torque:

Cam Case Bolt Torque

Bolt Size	Torque (ft lbs)
M10	28-30
M6	7.5-9.2
M8	15-17.5

13. Loosen all of the valve adjuster locknuts. Take up the camshafts, and place a finger over one of the two oil holes in the center cam journal, injecting engine oil into the other hole. Continue until oil spills out of the oil holes on both sides of the cam. Lightly lubricate the cam case bearings with engine oil.

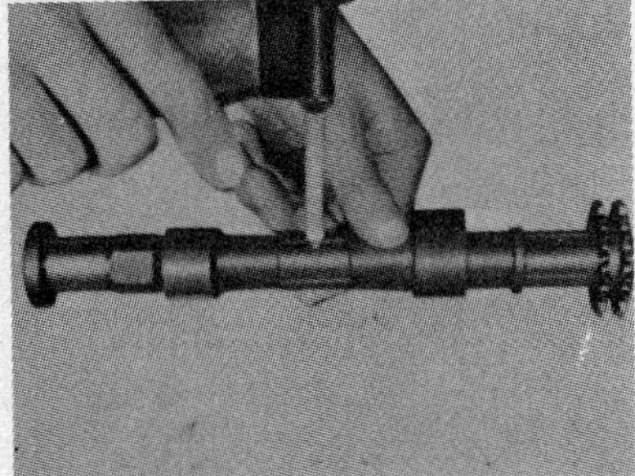

Lubricating the cam prior to installation. Note finger over the oil hole (Courtesy Yamaha Int. Corp.)

Installing the cam caps (Courtesy Yamaha Int. Corp.)

14. Locate each camshaft in its proper place. The cams are marked "EX" and "IN" for exhaust and intake.

15. Install the camshaft caps, install and tighten the lockwashers and nuts. Using new lockwashers is recommended. Torque the nuts to 5.8-7.5 ft lbs.

15. Note that the breather plates on the ends of the cams should be installed so that the gap between the plate and the camshaft cap will be as small as possible.

Positioning the breather plate for installation (Courtesy Yamaha Int. Corp.)

Checking camshaft rotation (Courtesy Yamaha Int. Corp.)

Cam and cam cap marks must be aligned (Courtesy Yamaha Int. Corp.)

Running the cam chain over the cam sprocket for installation (Courtesy Yamaha Int. Corp.)

NOTE: *If new cam cap studs have been installed, these should be secured in the cam case with a thread locking compound. Tighten the stud to 5.8-7.5 ft lbs.*

16. After the cam cap nuts have been tightened, check that the cams can be rotated by hand.

17. Assuming that all of the nuts and bolts have been torqued, replace the plug under the chain guide, and install the guide.

18. Turn the crankshaft so that the "V" mark on the timing advance base plate aligns with the mark on the stationary timing plate.

19. Turn each camshaft so that the dot mark stamped on the cam aligns with the arrow on the cam cap. Pull the cam chain which runs over the intake cam tightly while keeping the tensioner sprocket forced down.

20. Using the special tool, install a new joining link and rivet it in place.

NOTE: *A new link of the proper size must always be used.*

Installing the masterlink (Courtesy Yamaha Int. Corp.)

21. The remainder of the assembly procedure is the reverse of disassembly. When installing the cylinder head oil line, use new copper washers and torque the banjo bolts to 15-16.5 ft lbs. Adjust the cam chain tensioner. All nuts and bolts which are accessible should be retorqued after the engine has been run. The tappet clearance should be readjusted after the engine has been run and completely cooled.

Crankcase Cover Components

RIGHT COVER ASSEMBLY

Removal

1. Remove the kickstarter lever.
2. Remove the three allen bolts securing the points cover to the crankcase and remove the cover.

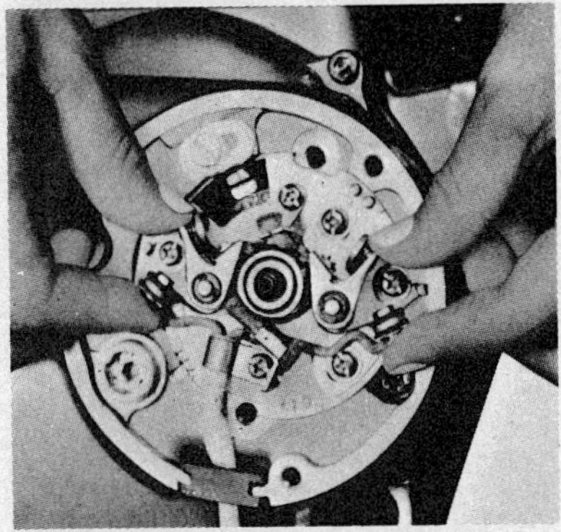

Removing the breaker point assembly (Courtesy Yamaha Int. Corp.)

3. Remove the breaker points assembly complete, after removing the screws securing the base plate.
4. Remove the nut, lockwasher, and plain washer and pull the breaker cam assembly off of the shaft.
5. Remove the 12 crankcase cover screws and remove the cover.
6. Remove the six screws on the clutch pressure plate and take away the plate.
7. Take out the clutch pushrod crown,

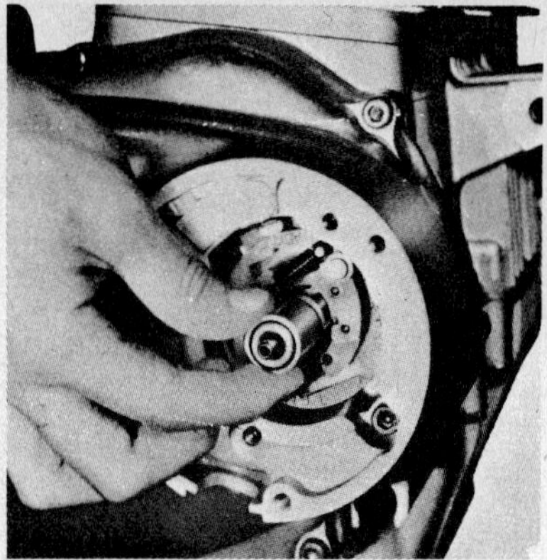

Taking out the breaker cam assembly (Courtesy Yamaha Int. Corp.)

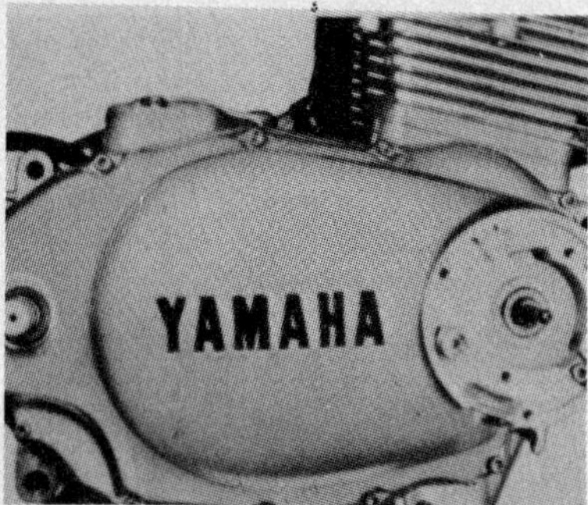

Right case cover prior to removal (Courtesy Yamaha Int. Corp.)

Removing the clutch spring screws (Courtesy Yamaha Int. Corp.)

Loosening the crankshaft drive gear allen bolt (Courtesy Yamaha Int. Corp.)

and the pushrod ball behind it; the pushrod is most easily removed from the other side of the mainshaft.

8. Hold the clutch with the special puller or with a suitable substitute.

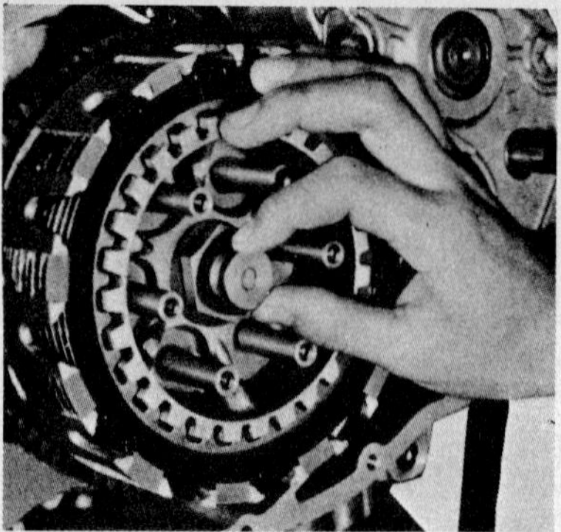

Taking out the clutch pushrod crown (Courtesy Yamaha Int. Corp.)

Removing the clutch hub nut (Courtesy Yamaha Int. Corp.)

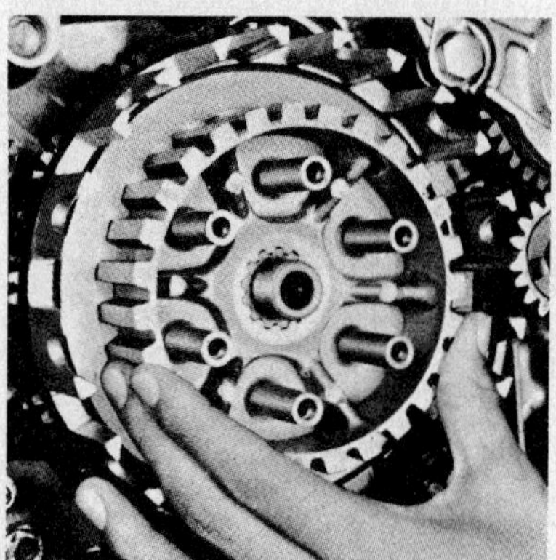

Removing the clutch hub (Courtesy Yamaha Int. Corp.)

Removing the clutch bushing spacer (Courtesy Yamaha Int. Corp.)

If only the clutch is to be removed, loosen and remove the clutch hub bolt. The clutch assembly may be taken off at this point. See below.

The top end assembly must be removed to completely remove the cam chain drive train.

If the gears in the case are to be removed, use the tool to hold the clutch, bend down the lockwasher on the crankshaft-mounted drive gear, and remove the drive gear mounting bolt with the 10mm allen wrench. *Then* remove the clutch hub nut.

9. Proceed with the clutch disassembly by pulling off the clutch boss. Remove the thrust washers and thrust bearings.

10. Take off the clutch housing and plates. Remove the clutch bushing spacer, the pump idle gear (secured by a circlip), and the clutch shaft thrust plate.

11. Remove the kickstarter return spring cover and unhook the spring from the crankcase. Pull out the kickstarter shaft assembly.

Removing the kickstarter shaft assembly cover (Courtesy Yamaha Int. Corp.)

Disengaging the return spring (Courtesy Yamaha Int. Corp.)

Removing the kickstarter assembly (Courtesy Yamaha Int. Corp.)

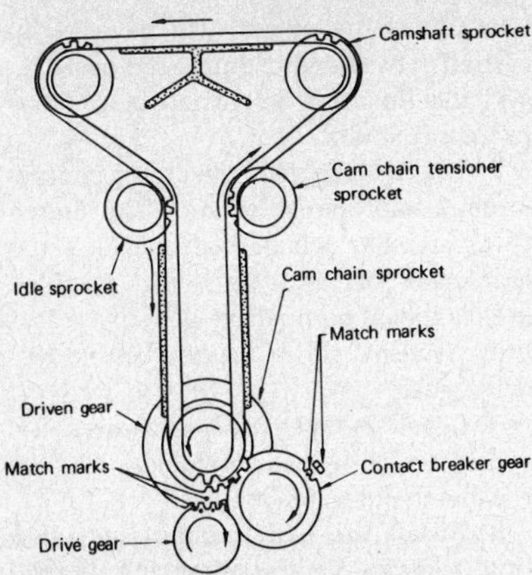

Cam chain and gear assembly (Courtesy Yamaha Int. Corp.)

Removing the contact breaker shaft bracket (Courtesy Yamaha Int. Corp.)

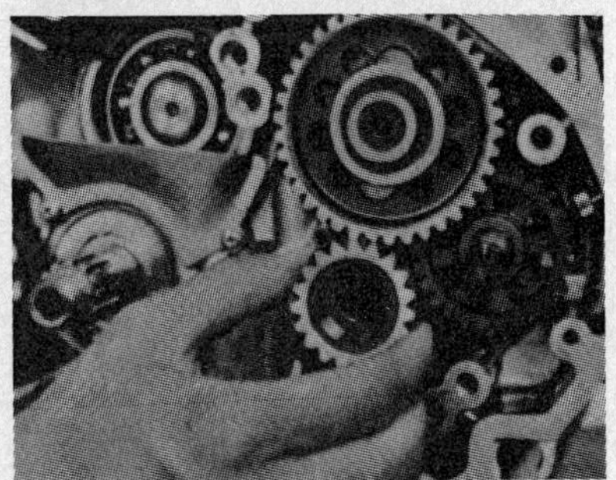

Removing the crankshaft drive gear (Courtesy Yamaha Int. Corp.)

Removing the cam chain sprocket assembly (Courtesy Yamaha Int. Corp.)

12. Remove the three bolts which secure the contact breaker shaft bracket and pull off the bracket.

13. The crankshaft drive gear bolt should have been loosened before the clutch hub was removed. Remove the bolt, lockwasher, the claw washer, and the gear. Take off the camchain sprocket assembly gear. Take the camchain out of the case.

14. Remove the contact breaker shaft assembly.

15. Pull off the crankshaft primary gear. Remove the key at the same time. Use a puller on the gear if necessary.

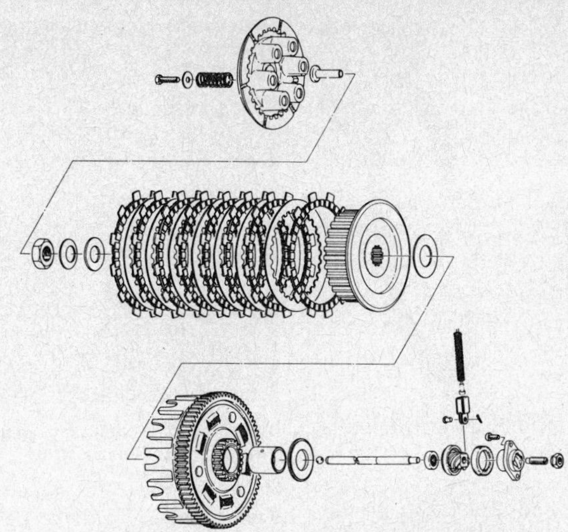

Exploded diagram of the clutch assembly (Courtesy Yamaha Int. Corp.)

Inspection

1. Inspect all parts for wear or damage.

2. Clutch spring free length is 1.68 in. (42.8mm). If any of the springs has been compressed 0.04 in. (1mm) or more, replace the springs.

Removing the breaker cam gear (Courtesy Yamaha Int. Corp.)

Removing the primary gear (Courtesy Yamaha Int. Corp.)

Removing the cam chain (Courtesy Yamaha Int. Corp.)

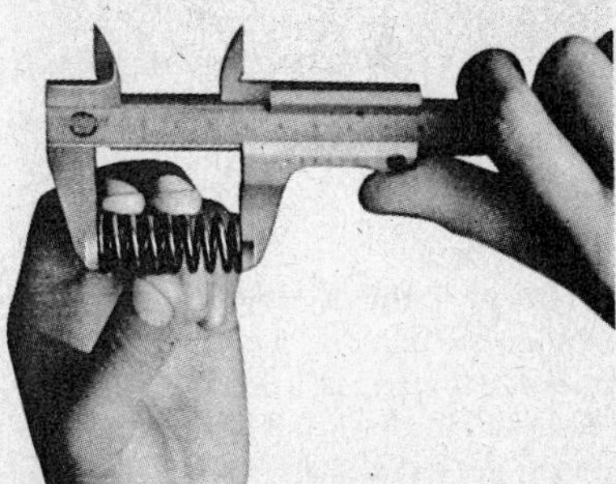

Measuring clutch spring length (Courtesy Yamaha Int. Corp.)

3. Check the clutch friction plates for scoring. Check the friction plate thickness. Standard thickness is 0.118 in. (3.0mm). The plate should be replaced if thickness measures 0.112 in. (2.8mm) or less.

4. Check all of the plates for warpage by placing each on a flat surface and probing around the circumference with a feeler gauge. Any plate which will allow a 0.008 in. (0.2mm) gauge to be slipped beneath it, must be replaced.

5. Check the clutch pushrod for bending or wear. Pushrod must not be bent more than 0.008 in. (0.2mm) or replacement is necessary.

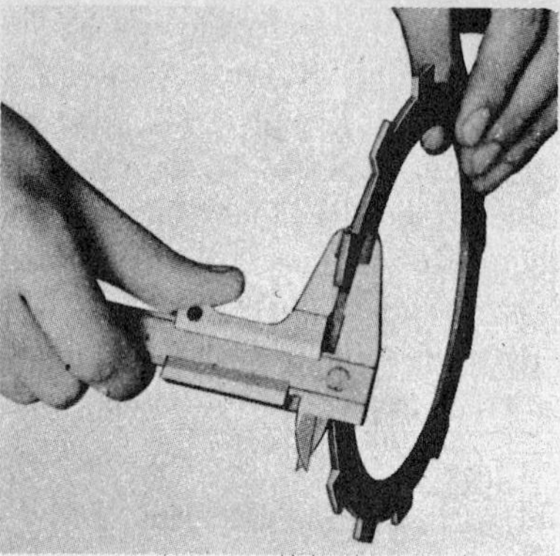

Measuring friction plate thickness (Courtesy Yamaha Int. Corp.)

Checking the steel plates for warpage (Courtesy Yamaha Int. Corp.)

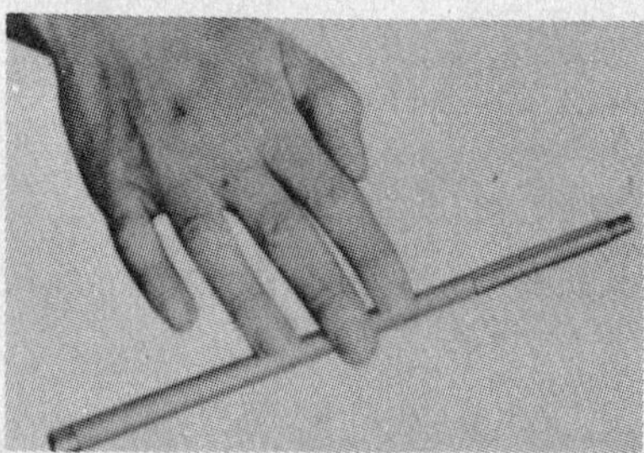

Checking the pushrod for bends (Courtesy Yamaha Int. Corp.)

Installation

1. Remove the left crankcase cover and align the mark on the balancer drive sprocket with the mark on the crankcase.
2. Install the woodruff key on the right side of the crankshaft, and install the crankshaft primary gear.
3. Fit the cam chain through the cut out in the top of the crankcase. Fit one washer on each side of the cam chain sprocket. Install the cam chain sprocket, aligning the mark on the sprocket with the marks on the crankshaft gear. Install the contact breaker gear aligning the mark on the gear with the mark on the crankcase.

Installing the primary gear (Courtesy Yamaha Int. Corp.)

4. Refit the crankshaft drive gear, claw washer, lockwasher, and allen bolt onto the crankshaft. The bolt must be torqued down after the clutch assembly is installed.
5. Install the contact breaker shaft bracket assuring that the special washers are correctly installed. Tighten the bracket bolts to 11-18 ft lbs.
6. Install the clutch components in the reverse of the removal procedure. Note that the clutch pushrod must be inserted from the left crankcase cover side. The pushrod should be greased before installation. Also, the pushrod oil seal on the left side of the engine will have its lip turned in by the insertion of the pushrod, and the lip must be turned back to its proper position.
7. Be sure that all of the clutch components are properly located. The clutch thrust washer which bears against the crankcase oil seal must be installed before the oil pump drive gear. Note that there is also a thrust washer behind this drive gear.
8. Install the clutch boss, washers, and spring washer (concave side out). Tighten the clutch nut to 58-66 ft lbs.
9. Install the clutch plates one at a time refer to the accompanying illustrations. Note that each of the steel plates has a portion of its outer edge cut away. The center of this cutaway must be aligned as shown. Install the first friction plate, then a steel plate so that the center of the cutaway is vertical. Install another friction plate. The cutaway of the second steel plate must be installed about 50° from the vertical. This is four clutch boss notches from the first steel plate. Continue the installation, locating each steel plate so that the cutaway of each is about 50° (four notches) from the plate which precedes it. This is intended to reduce clutch chatter.
10. The remainder of the procedure is the reverse of disassembly.

LEFT CRANKCASE ASSEMBLY

Removal

1. Remove the left crankcase cover complete with the starter coil assembly

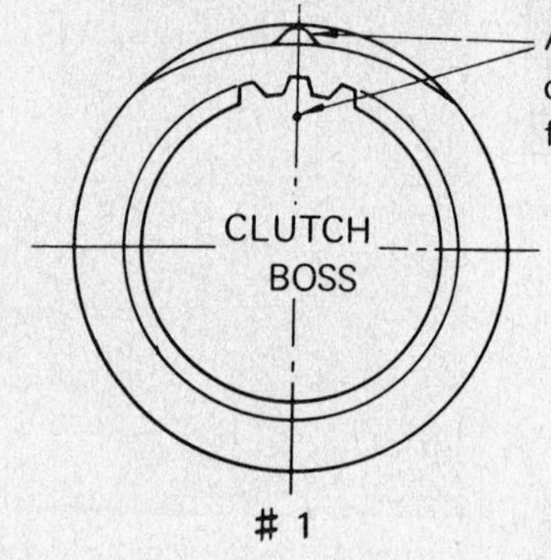
Align the projection with the center of cut-away of the first clutch plate.
CLUTCH
BOSS
1

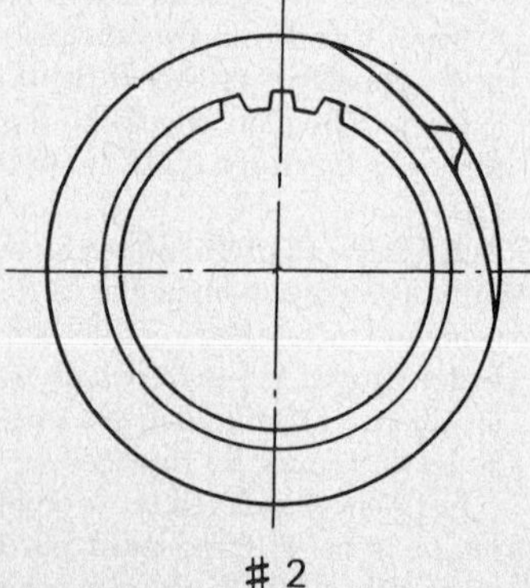
2
The centers of cut-aways of other clutch plates must be off-set approximately 50° from one another.

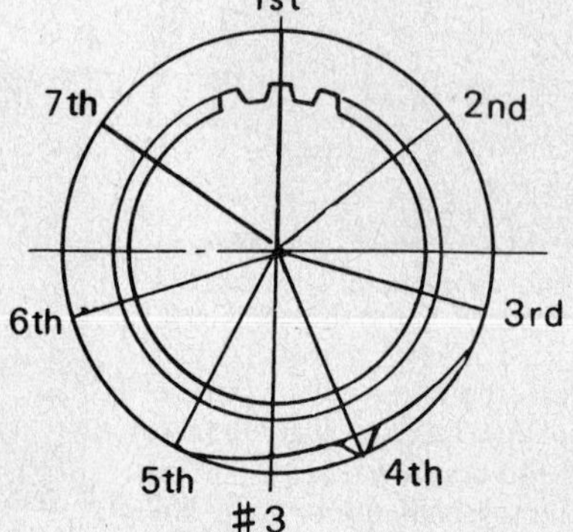
1st
2nd
3rd
4th
5th
6th
7th
3

Correct clutch plate installation (Courtesy Yamaha Int. Corp.)

and alternator stator. Note that the neutral switch wire and starter assembly lead wires must be disconnected.

2. Remove the alternator rotor mounting bolt. Then use the puller bolt to take off the rotor and starter clutch assembly. The rotor should be held by hand only while removing it.

3. Take off the electric starter sprocket, the idler sprocket and the large crankshaft sprocket and their chain at the same time. Remove the starter motor shaft.

Removing the alternator cover (Courtesy Yamaha Int. Corp.)

Removing the rotor (Courtesy Yamaha Int. Corp.)

Removing the electric starter chain and sprockets (Courtesy Yamaha Int. Corp.)

4. Unbolt and remove the starter motor cover. Unbolt the starter motor and remove it from the upper crankcase.

Inspection

Check all parts for wear or damage. Be certain that all sprocket bearing surfaces are free of scratches or foreign matter.

Assembly

1. Install the starter motor, starter motor cover; grease the starter shaft and install it on the starter motor.

2. Fit the crankshaft woodruff key.

3. Thoroughly coat all sprocket bearing surfaces and the starter chain with molybdenum disulfide or suitable substitute.

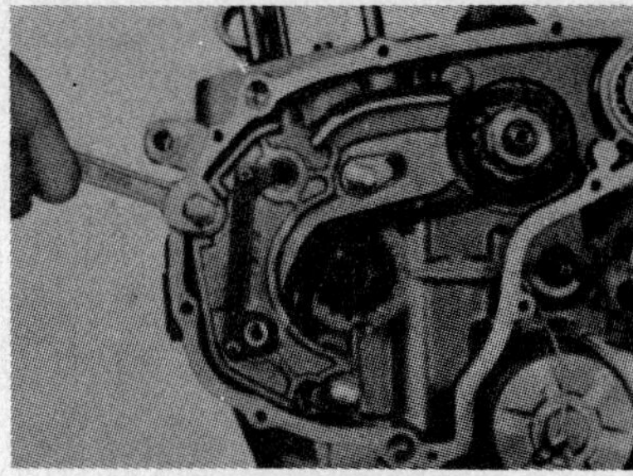

Removing the idle shaft bracket (Courtesy Yamaha Int. Corp.)

4. Place the chain around the starter motor sprocket and the crankshaft sprocket and slide them onto their respective shafts. Install the idler sprocket.

5. The rest of the assembly procedure is the reverse of disassembly.

OMNI-PHASE BALANCER

Removal and installation of the omni-phase balancer requires the use of an hydraulic press with a capacity of at least 0.5 tons.

Removal

1. Remove the right crankcase cover and all of the components therein as described above.

2. Remove the left crankcase cover, the rotor, and starter chain and sprockets.

3. Remove the idle shaft plate from the idle shaft bracket in the left crankcase, and then remove the bracket itself (3 bolts).

4. The omni-phase balancer chain runs around four sprockets. The sprocket nearest the center of the crankcase is the crankshaft mounted drive sprocket. The sprocket to the right upper portion of the case is the balancer shaft sprocket. The

Removing the idler sprocket (Courtesy Yamaha Int. Corp.)

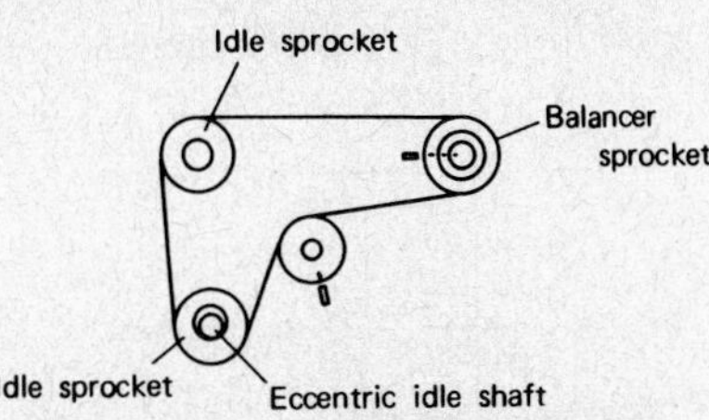

Balancer chain route. Note alignment of punch marks for installation and removal (Courtesy Yamaha Int. Corp.)

other two are idler sprockets. Note that the omni-phase shaft rotates in a direction opposite to that of the crankshaft.

5. Align the mark on the balancer shaft sprocket with the mark on the crankcase.

6. Pull out the shaft of the uppermost idler sprocket, and remove the sprocket. Remove the lower idler sprocket and shaft as well. Remove the drive chain. Bend the lockwasher tab down on the balancer shaft sprocket and remove the nut.

7. Remove the spacer, balancer shaft sprocket and buffer boss assembly from the balancer shaft.

8. Go to the right side of the crankcase, and remove the two phillips head screws which secure the sheet metal balancer shaft cover.

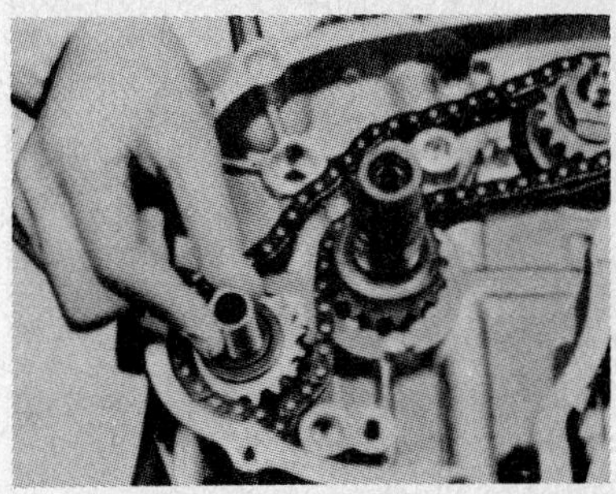

Removing the eccentric shaft idler sprocket (Courtesy Yamaha Int. Corp.)

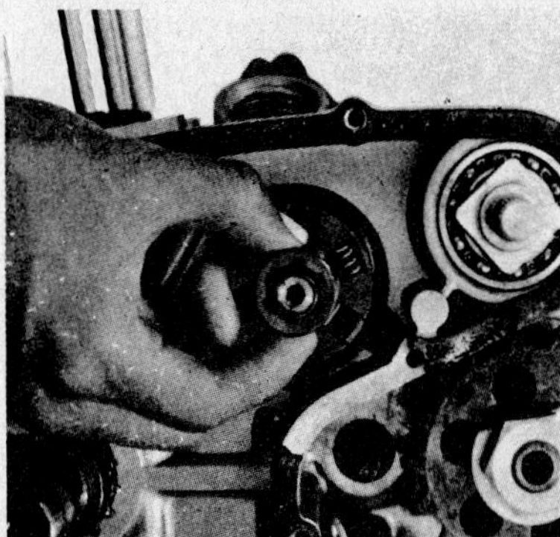

Removing the buffer boss assembly (Courtesy Yamaha Int. Corp.)

NOTE: *A thread locking compound is used on these screws. Therefore, an impact driver should be used.*

9. Remove the circlip on the right side of the crankcase which is fitted on the balancer shaft bearing.

10. Turn the crankcase assembly so that the left side faces up, and use an hydraulic press to bear on the left side of the balancer shaft and press it out of the crankcase.

11. The bearing may be removed from the balancer shaft, if desired, with a suitably sized bearing puller.

12. The left side balancer shaft bearing is secured by a circlip inside the balancer weight housing.

Inspection

Check the bearings for wear or exces-

Removing the balancer shaft cover (Courtesy Yamaha Int. Corp.)

Removing the balancer shaft bearing circlip (Courtesy Yamaha Int. Corp.)

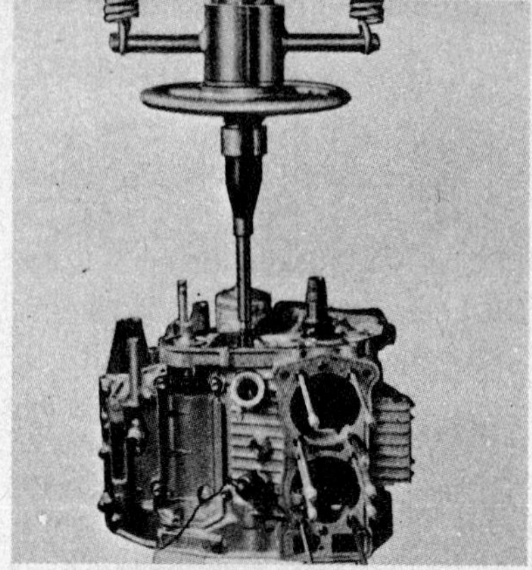
Pressing out the balancer shaft (Courtesy Yamaha Int. Corp.)

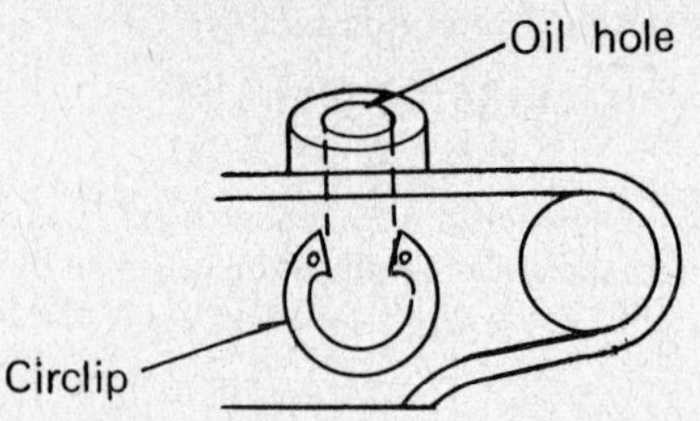

Oil hole and circlip alignment (Courtesy Yamaha Int. Corp.)

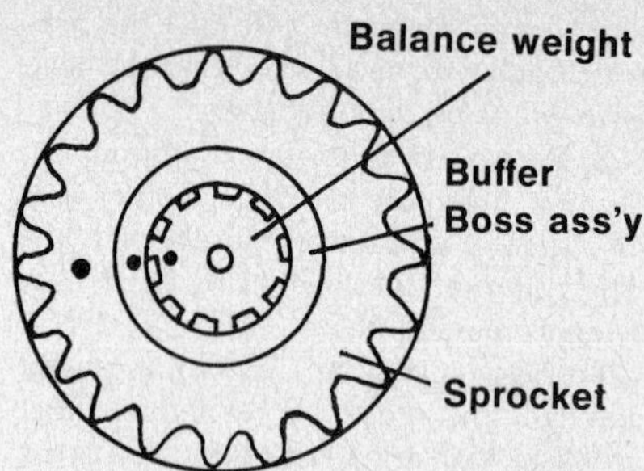

Buffer boss, balancer weight and sprocket alignment for installation (Courtesy Yamaha Int. Corp.)

Refitting the balancer chain (Courtesy Yamaha Int. Corp.)

sive play and replace if necessary. Thoroughly lubricate the bearing to balancer shaft contact surfaces, and the bearing to crankcase contact surfaces.

Installation

1. When refitting the left side bearing, note that the end gap of the circlip must be positioned over the oil hole.

2. The outer race of the right hand bearing is secured by a pin in the crankcase and must be properly installed.

3. Press load when installing the shaft is 0.5 tons.

4. Install the circlip for the right side shaft bearing. Replace the bearing cover on the right side of the crankcase and secure the two screws with a thread locking compound.

5. Install the buffer boss assembly on the left side of the shaft, being sure that the mark on the buffer boss is aligned with the mark on the balancer shaft. Install the sprocket, aligning the mark on the sprocket with both of the other marks.

6. Replace the spacer, lockwasher, and sprocket nut, tightening the nut to 26-30 ft lbs.

7. Align the mark on the balancer shaft sprocket with the mark on the crankcase. Align the mark on the crankshaft mounted drive sprocket with the mark on the crankcase. Loop the chain around the balancer shaft sprocket and over the drive sprocket as shown.

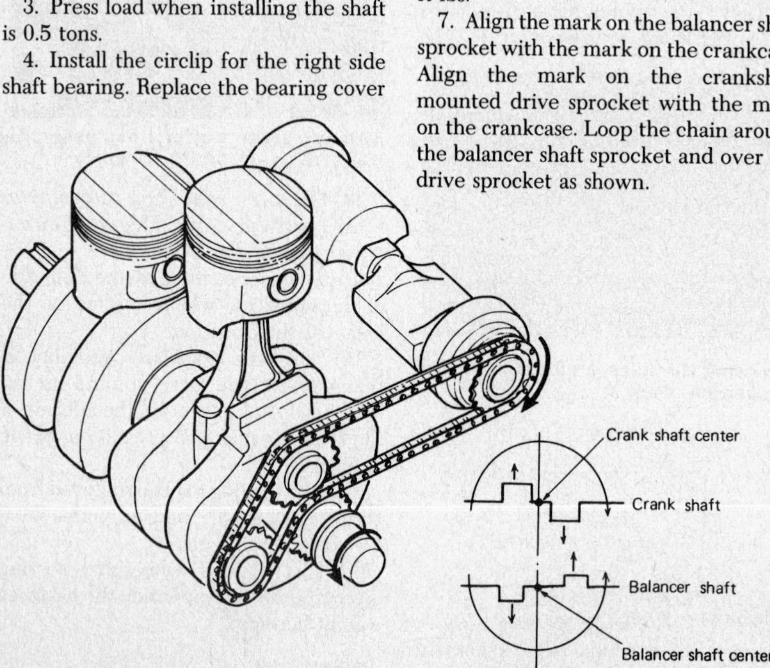

Omni-phase balancer assembly (Courtesy Yamaha Int. Corp.)

8. Engage the two idler sprockets with the chain and position them so that their shafts may be installed.

NOTE: *The sprockets are of different sizes. The larger goes in the lower position.*

9. Install the idler gear shafts. Note that the shaft for the lower idler gear is eccentric.

10. Refit the idler shaft bracket and plate. Chain slack, measured at a point midway between the drive gear and the balancer shaft gear should be 5-10mm.

The remainder of the procedure is the reverse of the removal procedure.

Splitting the Crankcases

Removal of the left and right crankcase cover components is necessary to split the cases. It is not necessary to remove the balancer unit.

1. Remove the seven 10mm bolts from the top crankcase half.

2. Remove the seven 10mm bolts from the lower case half.

3. In a criss-cross pattern, and no more than ¼ turn at a time, loosen the six nuts (17mm) on the lower case.

Separating the crankcase halves (Courtesy Yamaha Int. Corp.)

4. When all of the nuts and bolts are removed, tap upwards on the front of the upper case with a soft-faced mallet and separate the cases.

5. When reassembling the cases, note that the nuts and bolts must be tightened gradually to the proper torque.

Tighten the nuts to 7.2 ft lbs, and the bolts to 3.7 ft lbs in a cross pattern.

Then tighten the nuts to 14.4 ft lbs and the bolts to 7.2 ft lbs.

Finally, torque the nuts to 25.2 ft lbs.

Lower End Service

The crankshaft, which can be lifted out of the lower case after the upper case is removed, is a one-piece forging which rides on three plain bearings.

The connecting rods are two-piece units, also fitted with plain bearings.

1. The crankshaft main bearing inserts should be removed from the crankcase halves by hand. The inserts should be perfectly free of scratches, scoring or other signs of wear. Also, the insert surface which faces the crankcase must be free of burned-on oil deposits.

Removing the crankshaft (Courtesy Yamaha Int. Corp.)

2. Main bearing inserts are pre-sized. If the inserts must be replaced, note the numbers stamped on the crankcase (4, 5, or 6). A corresponding number (1, 2, or 3) is stamped on each crankweb. To determine the proper bearing insert to use, subtract the crankshaft number from the crankcase number. Inserts marked 1 through 5 are available and this number is stamped on the crankcase seat side on each insert.

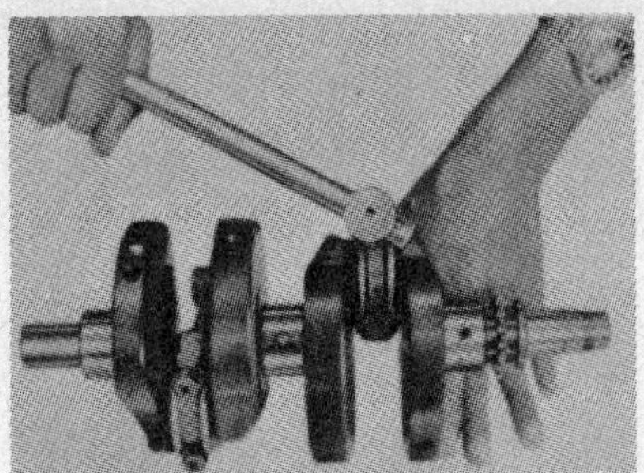

Removing a con rod (Courtesy Yamaha Int. Corp.)

3. Connecting rod bearings are numbered in the same way. Numbers 4, 5, or 6 are stamped on the connecting rod bearing housing, while numbers 1, 2, or 3 are found on the crankweb. To choose the proper bearing insert size, subtract the crankweb number from the housing number. Bearing inserts are numbered 1 through 5.

Measuring the crank journal diameter (Courtesy Yamaha Int. Corp.)

Removing the crank bearings from the case. (Courtesy Yamaha Int. Corp.)

4. Refer to the chart for correct bearing clearances which may be checked with plastigauge. Note that the connecting rod-to-crankpin clearance is taken with the con rod bolts torqued to 28-30 ft lbs.

5. Blow the oil passages in the crankshaft clear with compressed air.

6. When replacing the connecting

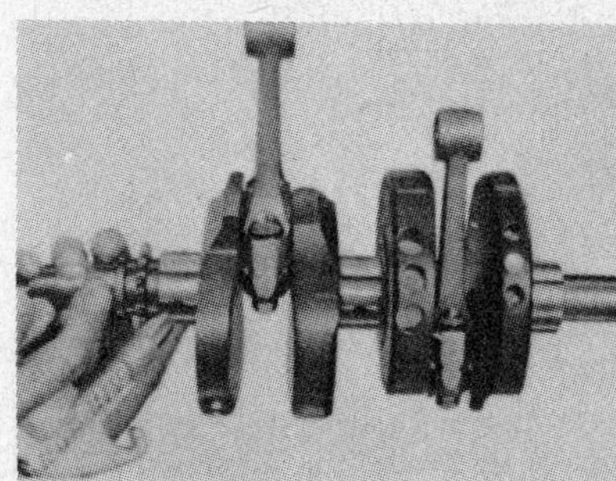

Lubricating the crankshaft prior to assembly (Courtesy Yamaha Int. Corp.)

Fitting a con rod bearing insert (Courtesy Yamaha Int. Corp.)

Bearing Clearance

Bearing	Nominal Clearance (mm)	Limit Wear (mm)
Crankshaft to Crankcase	0.036-0.059	0.08
Con Rod to Crankpin	0.034-0.057	0.08

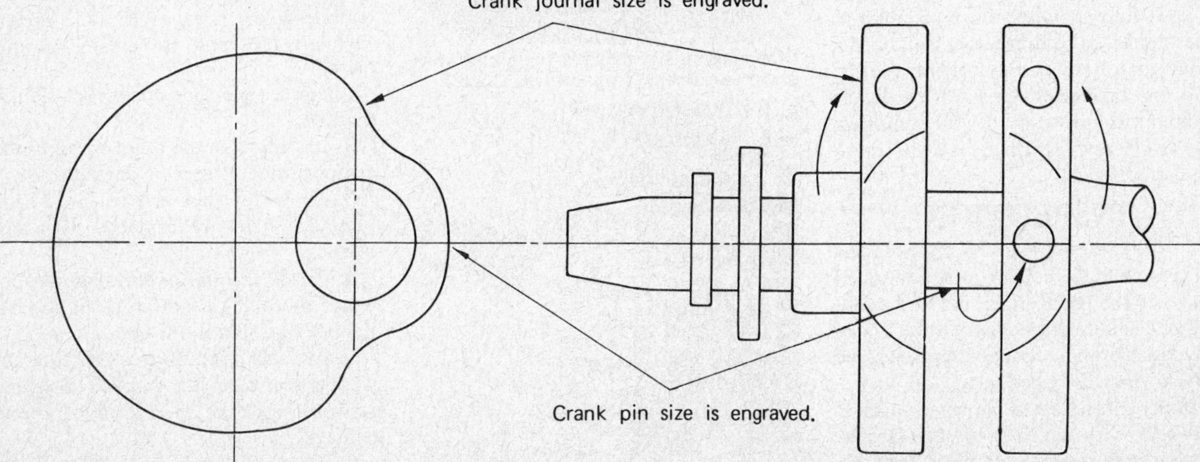
Crank journal size is engraved.
Crank pin size is engraved.

Crankshaft bearing and journal size mark locations (Courtesy Yamaha Int. Corp.)

rods on the crankshaft, note that the claw hooks on the bearing inserts (which hold the inserts in position) *must* face the *front* of the engine.

7. Oil all parts thoroughly.

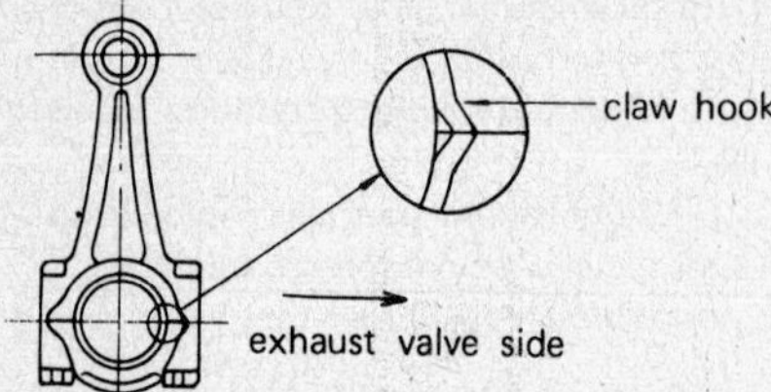

Con rod installation position (Courtesy Yamaha Int. Corp.)

Transmission

DISASSEMBLY

1. After splitting the cases, the gear clusters may be taken out of the lower case.
2. Remove the circlip which secures the gearshift shaft assembly on the left side of the crankcase, and take off the assembly from the right side.
3. Remove the circlip from the shifter ratchet then press down the shift lever to disengage it from the shifter drum and pull out the ratchet assembly.
4. Tap out the first shift fork spindle (one shift fork) from the right side of the crankcase using a soft-faced mallet. Mark the shift fork so that it can be installed in its proper location.
5. Remove the circlip on the *inside* of the crankcase which is clipped to the second shift fork spindle (two shift forks), and tap out the spindle from the right side of the case.

NOTE: *Mark the shift forks so that they can be correctly installed. They are not* interchangeable.

6. Remove the cotter pin at the bottom of the crankcase, and remove the pin.
7. Remove the shift drum by first pulling the drum out of the right side of the case about half way, removing the stopper plate circlip, and the stopper plate.
8. To fully complete the disassembly of the crankcase, remove the tachometer drive gear. Remove the locknut, the circlip, and take off the gear with a puller. Take out the drive shaft after removing the two screws which secure the drive shaft stopper.

INSPECTION

1. The gears should be checked for wear or chipped teeth. Note any rounded edges on the engagement dogs. The sliding gear shift fork grooves must be free of any discoloration. If necessary, replace any worn or damaged gears.

If any given gear is damaged, inspect the gear with which it meshes closely. Fitting one new gear to mesh with another which is worn or which has covered

Removing the gear clusters (Courtesy Yamaha Int. Corp.)

Gear cluster installed (Courtesy Yamaha Int. Corp.)

Removing shifter ratchet assembly (Courtesy Yamaha Int. Corp.)

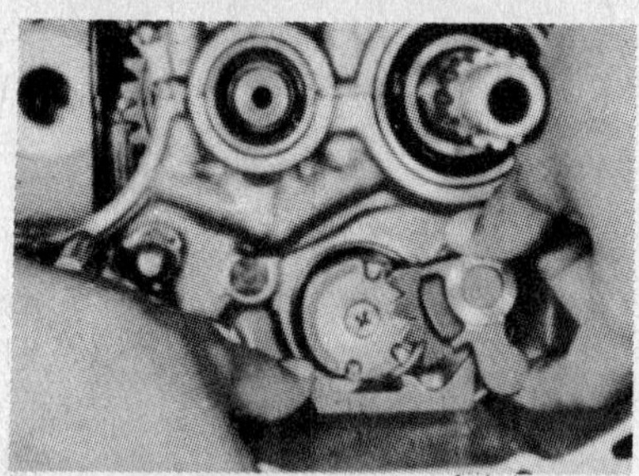

Disengaging the ratchet from the shift drum (Courtesy Yamaha Int. Corp.)

Removing the shift fork spindle (Courtesy Yamaha Int. Corp.)

Removing the circlip (Courtesy Yamaha Int. Corp.)

Removing the cotter pin (Courtesy Yamaha Int. Corp.)

Removing the shift drum stopper plate circlip (Courtesy Yamaha Int. Corp.)

considerable mileage is not recommended. It is best to replace gears in pairs.

Check the gears for smooth rotation on their shafts.

2. Inspect all of the other transmission components for wear or damage.
3. All cotter pins which have been removed should be replaced with new ones.
4. Check the shifter fork spindles for bends by rolling them on a flat surface. Replace the spindles if bent.
5. Inspect the shifter forks noting any wear or scoring of the spindle bores, bent or worn fork ends, or any other obvious damage.
6. Check the shift drum grooves for wear or scoring.

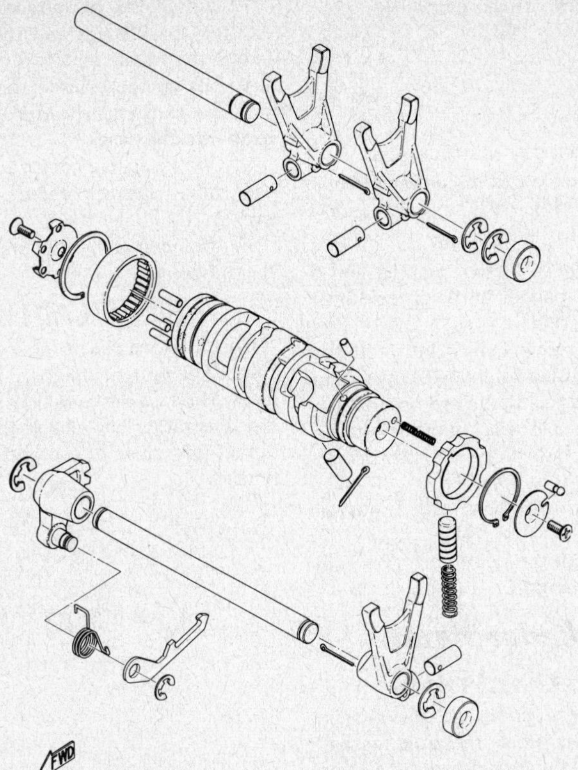

Shift drum assembly (Courtesy Yamaha Int. Corp.)

ASSEMBLY

1. Assembly is the reverse of the disassembly procedure.
2. Position the shift drum to the neutral position before installing the gear clusters.
3. After the gear clusters are installed, check the shifting action and check that the gears engage completely.

650

Engine Removal

1. Warm up the engine and drain the oil.
2. Turn off both fuel petcocks and disconnect the fuel crossover tube.
3. Lift the seat, then remove the attaching bolts and the gas tank.
4. Remove both side covers.
5. Disconnect the alternator wiring harness at the center connector.
6. Disconnect both throttle cables.
7. Disconnect the air cleaner mounting bolts.
8. Disconnect the fuel balance tube and remove the carburetors.
9. Disconnect the engine breather tube.
10. Disconnect the neutral switch wire.
11. Disconnect the spark plug leads.
12. Disconnect the tachometer drive cable.
13. Disconnect ignition point and ignition switch wires.

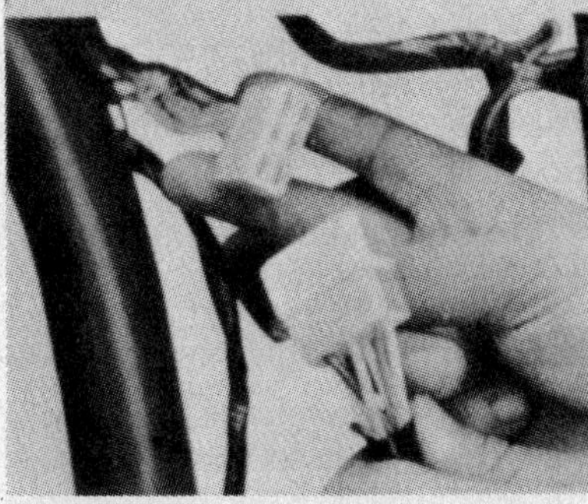

Disconnecting the alternator leads (Courtesy Yamaha Int. Corp.)

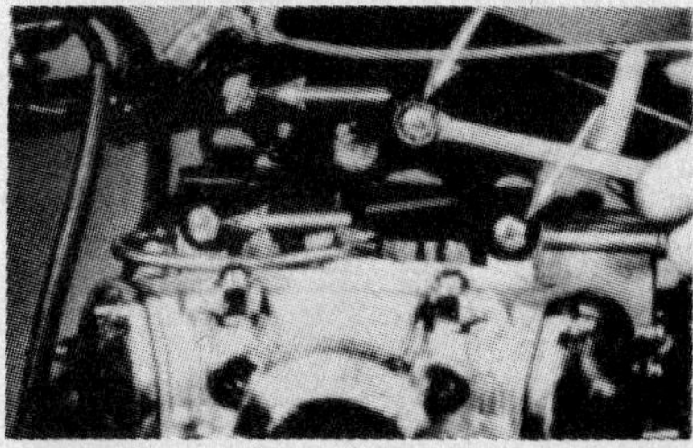

Removing the head steady nuts and bolts (Courtesy Yamaha Int. Corp.)

14. Remove the horn and mounting bracket.
15. Remove the left case cover.
16. Disconnect the master link and remove the final drive chain.
17. Remove the left footrest.
18. Remove both exhaust header pipes.
19. Remove the engine top center mounting brackets.

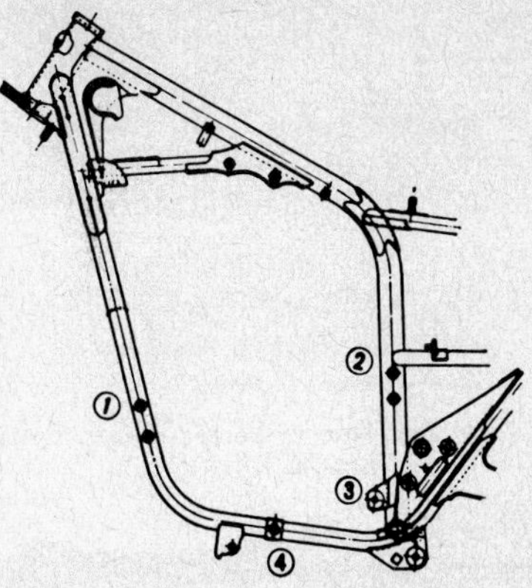

Engine mounting bolt locations and removal sequence (Courtesy Yamaha Int. Corp.)

20. Remove the brake pedal.
21. Remove the engine mounting bolts in the order shown in the illustration, then lift the engine out the left side of the frame.

Engine Installation

Reverse the removal procedure and torque the mounting bolts to the following specifications:

10 mm bolts—26 foot pounds
8 mm bolts—15 foot pounds

Cylinder Head Cover

DISASSEMBLY

1. Remove the oil delivery line.
2. Remove the points, base plate, and point housing.
3. Remove the governor locknut and plate.

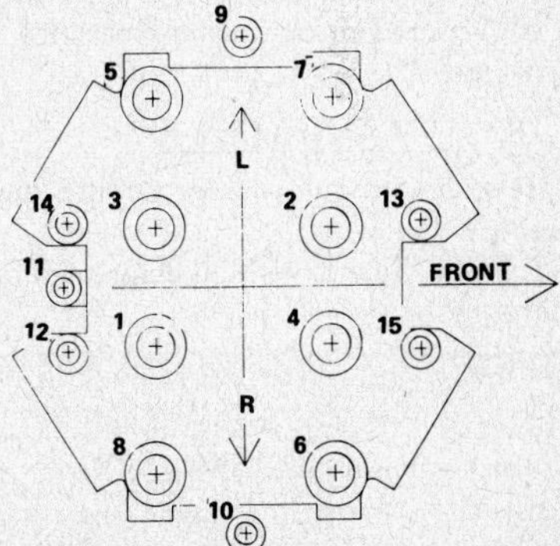

Cylinder head cover nut and bolt removal sequence (Courtesy Yamaha Int. Corp.)

4. Pull the advance rod out the left (point) side.
5. Tap loose the governor unit ring nut, then slide out the unit. Also, remove the governor locating pin.
6. Remove the three attaching screws and the governor housing.
7. Remove the four tappet covers.
8. Remove the eight retainer nuts, four retainer bolts, and the head cover. Make certain to remove the nuts and bolts in the sequence shown in the illustration.

Removing the cylinder head cover (Courtesy Yamaha Int. Corp.)

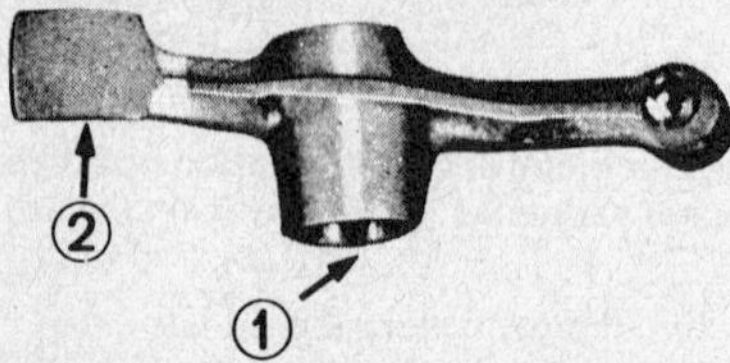

Rocker arm wear points (Courtesy Yamaha Int. Corp.)

9. Remove the rocker shaft covers, sleeves, and O-rings.

10. Remove the rocker arm shafts and arms using a 6 mm extracting screw. Keep each assembly separate!

INSPECTION

Check the rocker arm for excessive wear at the two points indicated in the illustration. Look for any grooves, scratches, discoloration, or flaking of the hardened surfaces.

Measure the rocker shaft hole with an inside micrometer. Standard size is 15.03 mm. Also measure the rocker shaft diameter and check for step wear or discoloration. Standard diameter is 14.98 mm.

Normal shaft-to-rocker arm clearance is 0.05 mm. The maximum clearance is 0.10 mm.

ASSEMBLY

Reverse the removal procedure and note the following:

1. Coat all parts with oil before assembling.

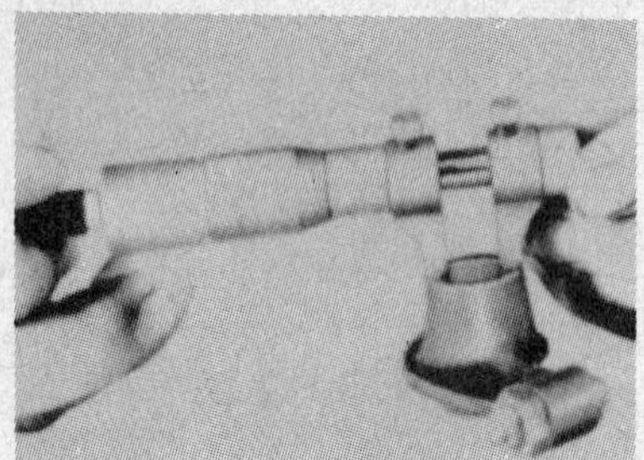

Measuring rocker arm spindle bore diameter (Courtesy Yamaha Int. Corp.)

2. Make sure the rocker arms are installed with the tapped end pointed outward.

3. Coat mating head and cover surfaces with Yamaha Bond #4.

4. Make sure to coat the mounting studs with SAE 30W before installing the cover.

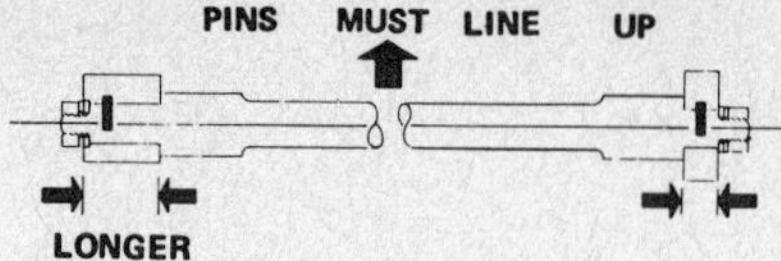

Ignition advance rod installation (Courtesy Yamaha Int. Corp.)

5. Torque 10 mm studs to 25 foot pounds, 8 mm to 14 foot pounds, and 6 mm to 7 foot pounds in the order shown in the illustration.

6. Install a new O-ring between the governor housing and head cover, and grease the oil seal lip before positioning.

7. Ignition point and governor housing are identical, but can be installed in only one position.

8. Make sure no oil has leaked onto the points.

9. Make sure the point wire grommet is in good condition.

Cylinder Head

DISASSEMBLY

1. Stuff a rag under the cam chain sprocket, then break the link marked with slots and punch holes, using a chain breaker.

NOTE: *Before breaking the chain, fasten wire to the links on either side of the marked link, so that the chain won't drop into the case.*

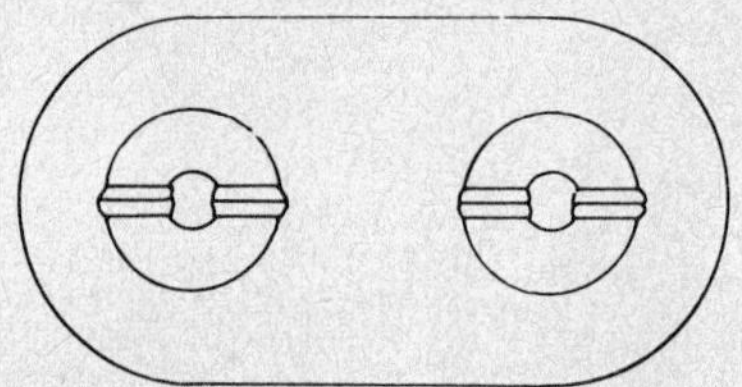

Break the chain at this link to remove the top end assembly (Courtesy Yamaha Int. Corp.)

2. Remove the chain, feeding the attaching wire into the case in its place.

3. Remove the camshaft.

4. Remove the camshaft bearings.

5. Remove the carburetor manifolds.

6. Disconnect the manifold equalizer tube.

Removing the valve springs (Courtesy Yamaha Int. Corp.)

7. Remove the two attaching bolts under the spark plugs and the screw between the intake manifold openings.

8. Lift off the cylinder head, making sure the cam chain leader wire doesn't drop into the case.

9. Using a spring compressor, remove the valve spring keepers and valve spring.

10. Remove the valve stem seal and the valve.

INSPECTION

Check the camshaft lobes for any discoloration, pitted areas, or flaking surfaces. Measure the cam lobes as shown in the illustration and check the specified dimensions given at the end of this section.

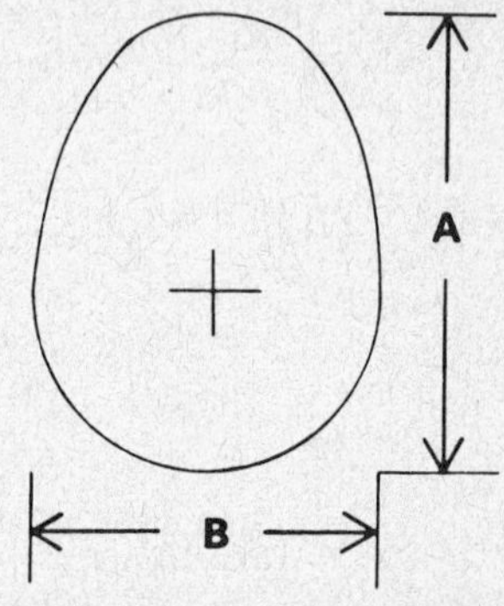

Cam lobe measurement points. "A" is the lobe length; "B" is the base circle diameter; "A" minus "B" equals cam lift (Courtesy Yamaha Int. Corp.)

Inspect the camshaft bearings for pits, rust, or chatter marks.

Check the valve stem tip for a worn spot caused by the valve adjuster. If the identation is more than 0.4–0.5 mm, grind the tip flat.

Measure the valve stem diameter and the valve guide inside diameter. Also check the valve stem for straightness by rolling it along a perfectly flat surface.

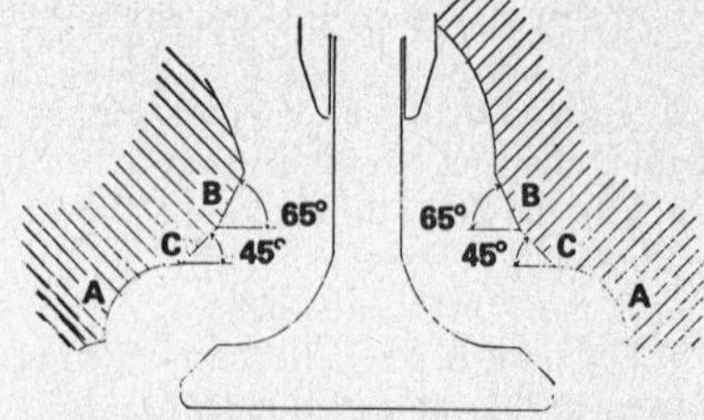

If cutting section "A" of the intake valve seat, use radiused cutter. If cutting section "A" of the exhaust valve seat, use radiused cutter.

If cutting section "B", use the 65° cutter.

If cutting section "C", use the 45° cutter.

Check the valve head for pits, warpage, excessive carbon build-up, etc. Using the accompanying illustrations for reference, lap or regrind the valve as necessary.

Check the valve seat angle and measure the seat width. Correct irregularities with the necessary valve seat cutters.

After all repair work has been completed on the valve seat, install the valve

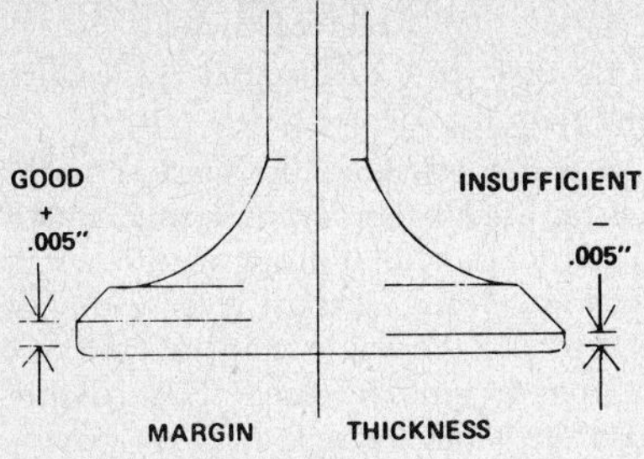

Valve margin thickness (Courtesy Yamaha Int. Corp.)

and pour solvent into the intake ports. Note any signs of leakage.

Measure the valve spring free-length and check the spring pressure with a compression rate gauge.

ASSEMBLY

1. Slide all the cam bearings in toward the center, then position the camshaft on the head.

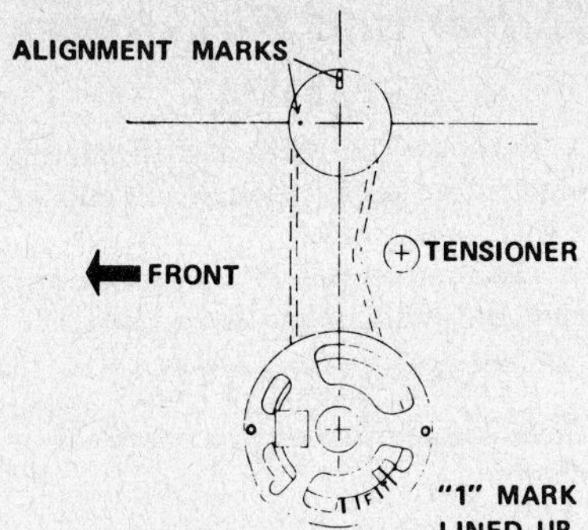

Cam chain alignment marks (Courtesy Yamaha Int. Corp.)

6. Adjust the cam chain tensioner to remove the excess chain slack.

7. Adjust the valves to the correct clearances.

8. Mount a degree wheel to the ignition rotor lockbolt.

9. Insert a wooden dowel pin in a spark plug hole and position the degree wheel to read zero with the piston at top dead center on the compression stroke.

10. Mount a dial indicator over an intake valve adjuster.

11. Rotate the crankshaft counterclockwise and watch when the valve begins to open. The degree wheel should indicate 47° BTDC. If necessary, reposition the cam chain so that the valve opens at the correct point.

NOTE: *Each chain link equals approximately 10° of crankshaft rotation.*

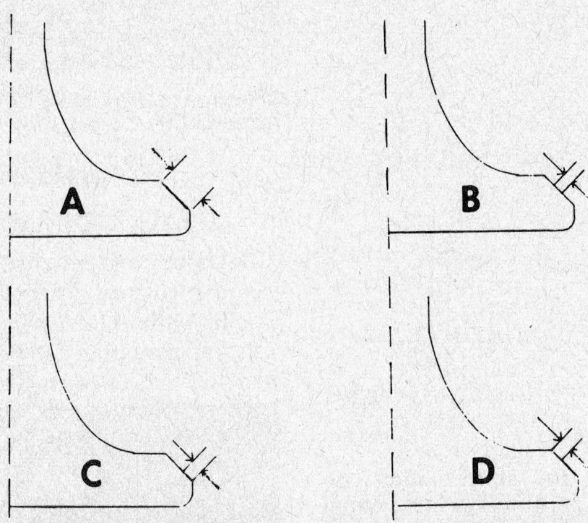

A If the valve face shows that the valve seat is centered on the valve face, but too wide; lightly use both the "R" and the 65° cutters to reduce the seat width to 1.3 mm.
B If the seat is in the middle of the valve face, but too narrow, use the 45° cutter until the width equals 1.3 mm.
C If the seat is too narrow, and right up near the valve margin; first use the "R" cutter and then the 45° cutter to get the correct seat width.
D If the seat is too narrow and down near the bottom edge of the valve face; first use the 65° cutter and then the 45° cutter.

Valve seat widths and locations (Courtesy Yamaha Int. Corp.)

2. Align the camshaft chain sprocket with the crankshaft sprocket by sliding the shaft back and forth.

3. Install a new cylinder head gasket, pull the cam chain lead wires through the cylinder head and slide the head over the studs. Install and tighten the retaining bolts and screw.

4. Position a piston at top dead center during its compression stroke.

5. Align the camshaft sprocket as shown in the illustration, then draw around and reconnect the cam chain with a new link. Use a chain riveter to secure the new link.

Dial gauge installation for valve timing (Courtesy Yamaha Int. Corp.)

Cam Chain Tensioner and Vibration Damper

REMOVAL

1. Remove the four attaching screws and the vibration damper (see illustration).

NOTE: *Note the position of the two slotted screws.*

2. Remove the attaching bolts and the tensioner housing.

3. Pull out the tensioner unit.

INSTALLATION

Installation is a reversal of the removal procedure. Replace the tensioner housing gasket and apply Yamaha Bond #4 to the mating surfaces.

Cylinders and Pistons

REMOVAL INSPECTION, AND INSTALLATION

1. Remove the oil line fitting at the cylinder base.

2. Slowly lift off the cylinders and stuff some CLEAN rags into the case opening.

3. Disassemble the pistons (and related parts) and inspect the cylinders and pis-

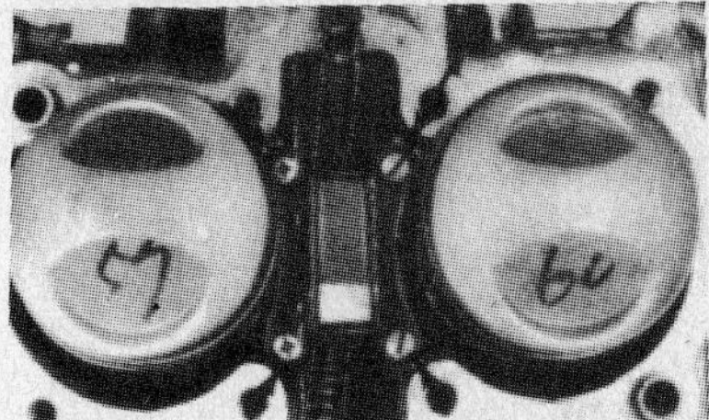

Vibration damper mounting screws (Courtesy Yamaha Int. Corp.)

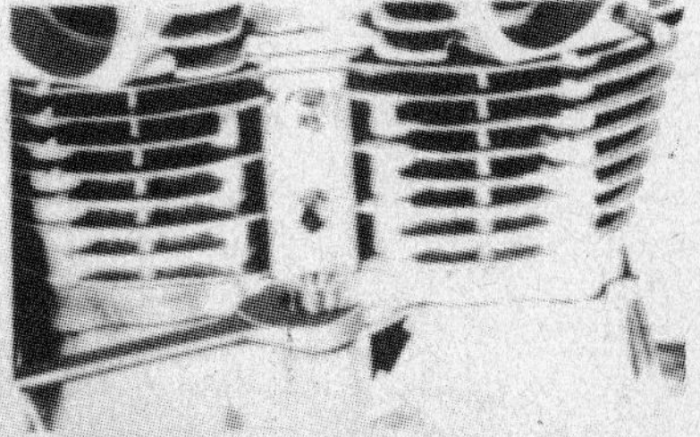

Removing the oil line fitting (Courtesy Yamaha Int. Corp.)

tons as described in the TX500 section. Ring and piston positioning data are given in the illustrations. Oversizes are found at the end of this section.

Primary Case

DISASSEMBLY

1. Remove the attaching Allen screws and the primary case cover.
2. Unscrew the tachometer shaft locknut.
3. Drive out the tachometer housing with a hammer and drift.
4. Lift out the tachometer gear.
5. Remove the oil pump (see Lubrication Systems).
6. Remove the oil filter.

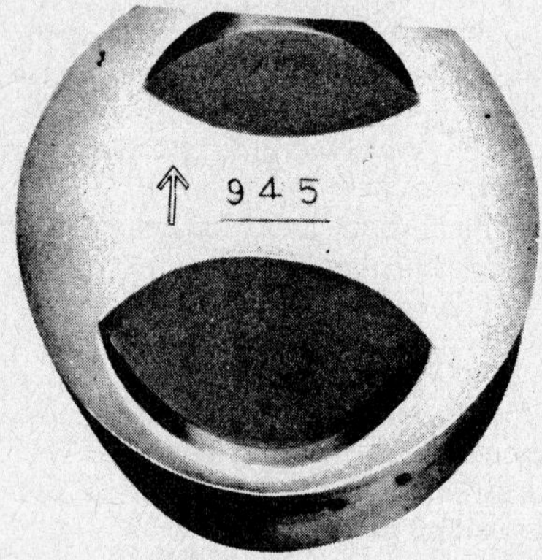

Piston crown markings. Arrow indicates exhaust port direction upon installation. Diameter of this piston is 74.945 mm. (Courtesy Yamaha Int. Corp.)

INSTALLATION

Reverse the removal procedure.

Clutch and Primary Drive Gear

Remove, disassemble, and inspect the clutch and primary drive gear as described for the two-stroke models. Standard clutch spring free length is 38.1 mm; standard disc thickness is 3.5 mm.

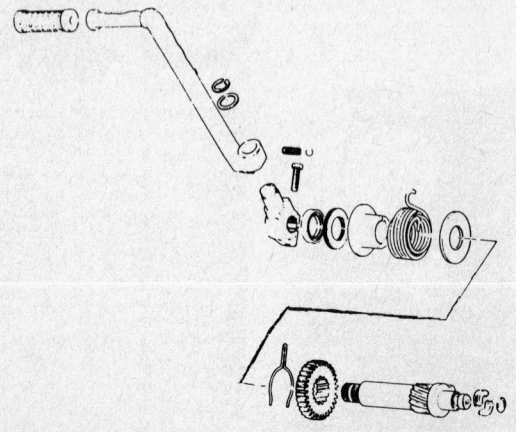

Shifter and Kickstarter

REMOVAL

1. Remove the shifter shaft circlip, then turn the engine around and pull out the shaft and arm.
2. Disconnect the kickstarter return spring and pull out the assembly.

INSTALLATION

Reverse the removal procedure for installation.

Left Case Cover

DISASSEMBLY

1. Remove the attaching Allen screws and the case cover.
2. Remove the two attaching screws and the alternator stator assembly.
3. Remove the alternator rotor locknut and washer.

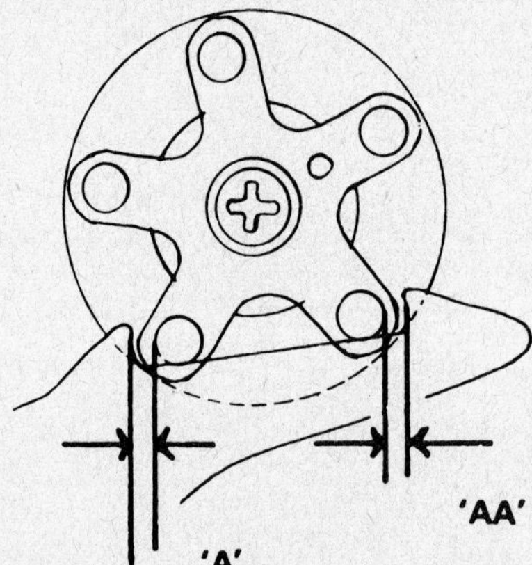

When installing the shifter shaft, be sure distances "A" and "AA" are equal (Courtesy Yamaha Int. Corp.)

4. Remove the rotor with the special rotor extractor tool.
5. Remove the crankshaft Woodruff key.
6. Flatten the countershaft sprocket lockwasher, then put the transmission in gear, or attach a magneto holding tool, and remove the locknut and countershaft sprocket.

Kickstarter assembly (Courtesy Yamaha Int. Corp.)

ASSEMBLY

Reverse the disassembly procedure and note the following:

1. When installing the kickstart mechanism, attach the return spring; rotate the kick clip until it drops into its recess, then attach the kickstart lever and push it ½ to ¾ of the way around until the kick stopper falls into its recess. This will preload the return spring.
2. When installing the shifter mechanism, make sure dimensions "A" and "AA" are equal (see illustration).

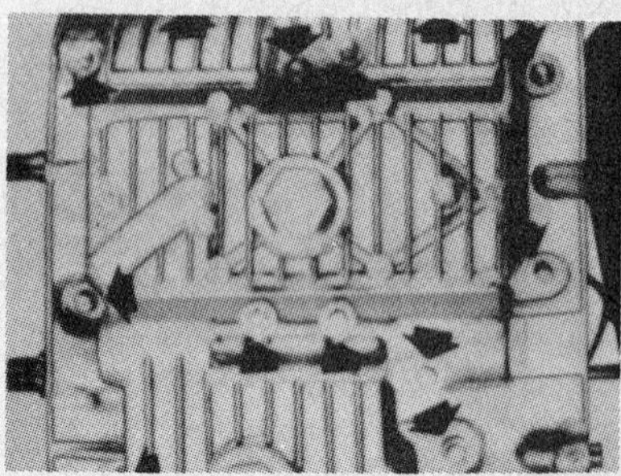

Crankcase securing bolts (Courtesy Yamaha Int. Corp.)

Crankcase

DISASSEMBLY

1. Loosen and remove the numbered securing bolts in descending order, beginning with #18.
2. Tap the upper and lower case halves apart with a rubber mallet.

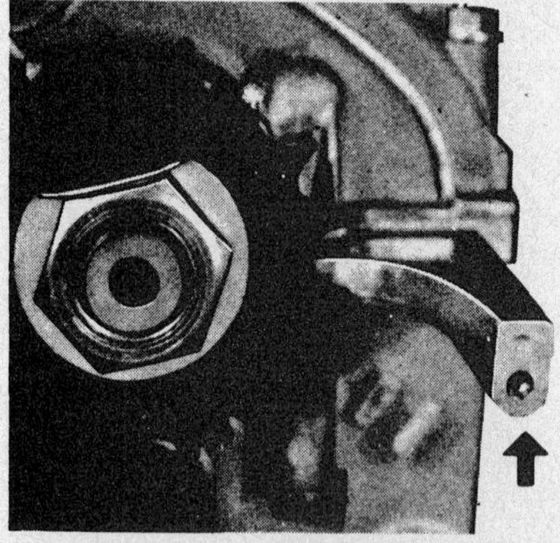

Be caution of striking the cases in this area (Courtesy Yamaha Int. Corp.)

Removing the shift drum (Courtesy Yamaha Int. Corp.)

CAUTION: *Do not tap the case cover mounting flange.*

3. Tap the transmission assembly out of the top case half with a rubber mallet.
4. Remove the neutral stopper.
5. Remove the shift drum stopper plate, then pull out the fork guide bar.
6. Remove the shift fork cam follower pin cotter keys and pins.
7. Pull out the shifter drum and remove the shift forks. Catch the cam follower rollers.
8. Tap the crankshaft out with a rubber mallet.

INSPECTION

Inspect all parts as described for the TX500.

ASSEMBLY

Reverse the removal procedure and note the following:

1. Cylinder mounting studs are replaceable. Use a stud extractor for removal and install the new stud with the rounded end facing up.
2. Line up crankshaft bearing locating pins and install the shaft by hand. Do not use a hammer!
3. Install the left crankshaft seal with the teflon lip facing out.
4. Lubricate all parts thoroughly before installation.
5. Replace all gaskets, seals, and cotter keys.
6. After installing the shift drum, check for proper actuation and engagement of dogs and slots.
7. Install the transmission assembly and crankshaft, then coat the case gasket with Yamaha Bond #4.
8. Torque all case securing bolts to 14 foot pounds in ascending order, beginning with bolt #1.

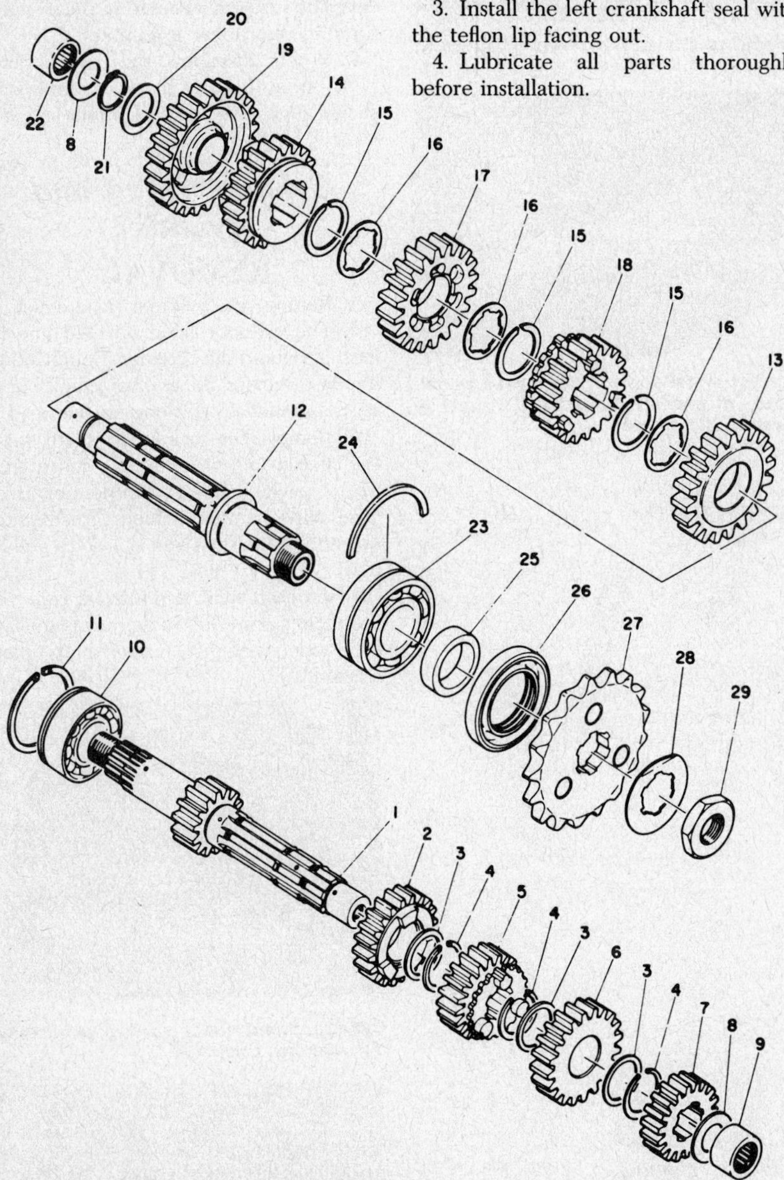

Gear clusters (XS1, XS2) (Courtesy Yamaha Int. Corp.)

1. Main axle
2. 4th gear pinion
3. Gear holding (5) washer
4. Circlip
5. 3rd gear pinion
6. 5th gear pinion
7. 2nd gear pinion
8. Drive axle shim
9. Bearing
10. Bearing
11. Circlip
12. Drive axle
13. 2nd gear
14. 4th gear
15. Circlip
16. Gear holding (3) washer
17. 3rd gear
18. 5th gear
19. 1st gear
20. Gear holding washer
21. Circlip
22. Bearing
23. Bearing
24. Circlip
25. Distance collar
26. Oil Seal
27. Drive sprocket
28. Lock washer
29. Lock nut

750

Engine Removal

1. Drain the oil from the engine and from the oil tank.
2. Remove the exhaust system and the exhaust balance pipe from the machine.

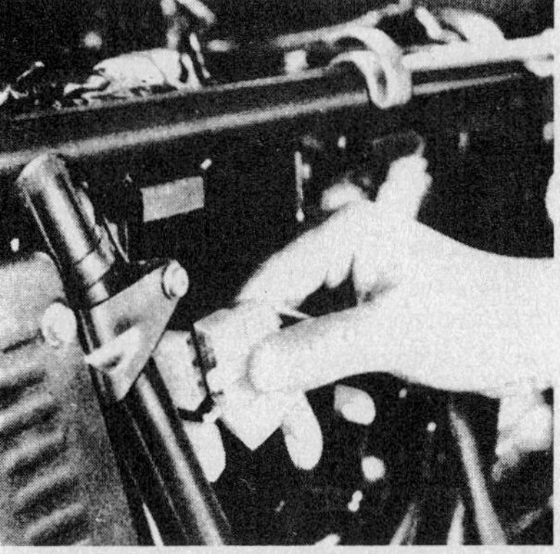

Disconnecting the alternator wires (Courtesy Yamaha Int. Corp.)

3. Disconnect the rear brake light switch from the brake pedal, then remove the brake pedal pinch bolt and pull the pedal off of the splined shaft.
4. Remove both rider footpegs. Take off the left side cover. Turn the fuel petcocks off; disconnect the fuel lines at the petcocks and take off the gas tank.
5. Loosen the clamps which secure the carburetors to the manifold and air cleaner. Disconnect the throttle cables from the carbs.
6. Remove the air cleaner screws and pull the air cleaner out of the left side of the machine.
7. Remove the carburetors.

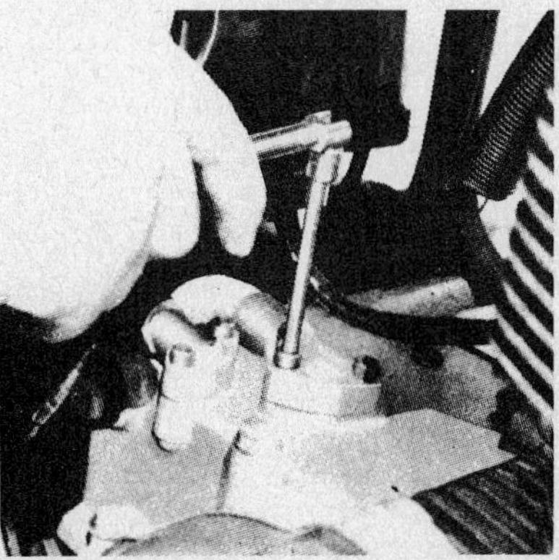

Removing the oil lines at the crankcase (Courtesy Yamaha Int. Corp.)

8. Disconnect the oil lines from the tank at the top rear of the crankcase. Arrange the lines so that they cannot be damaged when the engine is removed.

9. Disconnect the neutral indicator, oil pressure switch, and alternator wires at the plastic couplers.

Removing the engine from the frame (Courtesy Yamaha Int. Corp.)

10. Remove the gear shift lever.

11. Remove the left crankcase cover.

12. Disconnect the drive chain. Note that the masterlink cover plate is pressed on. The chain must be "broken" at the masterlink using the special tool.

13. Disconnect the battery leads and remove the battery from the machine. Disconnect the electric starter wires at the starter switch.

14. Disconnect the tach cable from the engine. Disconnect the clutch cable at the engine.

15. Remove all of the engine mounting bolts and brackets, then take the engine out of the right side of the machine.

Breaking the drive chain (Courtesy Yamaha Int. Corp.)

Correct installation of the brake pedal. Note alignment marks (Courtesy Yamaha Int. Corp.)

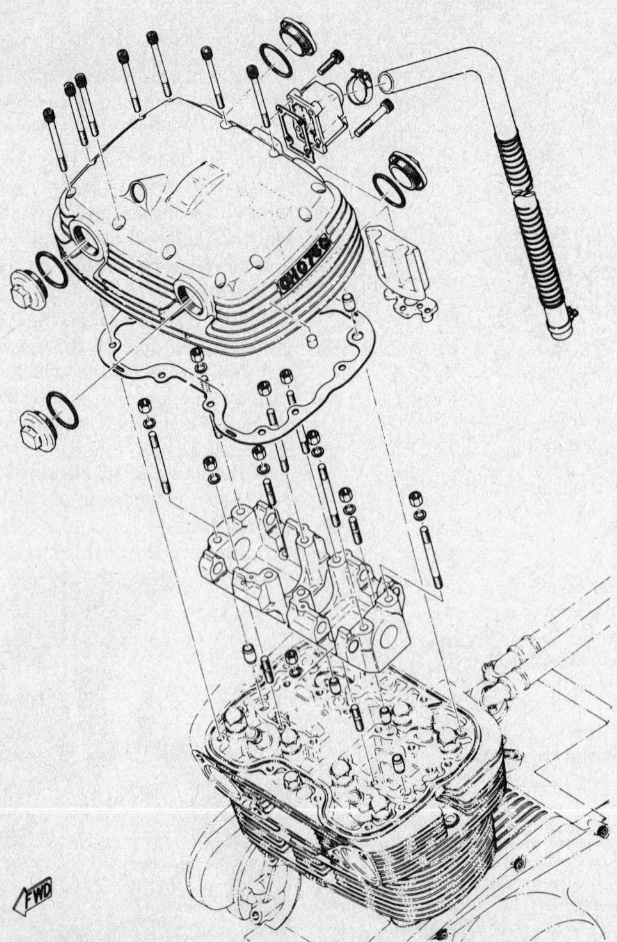

Cylinder head cover and cam case assembly (Courtesy Yamaha Int. Corp.)

Installation

1. Installation is the reverse of the above. Note that the drive chain masterlink cover plate must be pressed on with the special tool when reconnecting the chain.

2. When replacing the left crankcase cover be sure that the wiring is correctly fitted in the rubber grommet.

3. When installing the rear brake pedal, note that the mark on the pedal should align with the mark on the splined shaft.

Cylinder Head and Cylinder

REMOVAL

1. Remove the cylinder head cover.

2. The cylinder head oil feed line is located behind the cylinder. Remove the line by removing the two banjo bolts: one on the crankcase and one on the head.

3. Remove the rocker arm shafts with the special tool or a suitable substitute. The "special tool" recommended is a small slide hammer which threads into one end of the shaft and is used to pull it out.

When each shaft is removed, remove the rocker arm. The rocker arms should be installed with their proper shafts upon reassembly.

Cylinder head cover screws (Courtesy Yamaha Int. Corp.)

Removing the cylinder head oil line (Courtesy Yamaha Int. Corp.)

Removing the rocker arm spindle (Courtesy Yamaha Int. Corp.)

4. The cam chain is of the endless variety, and a special tool is required to break the chain. Turn the engine over until the cam chain link with the punch marks and slots across the rivets is accessible. Attach pieces of wire to the cam chain on either side of this link. Stuff a rag around the cam sprocket to keep any pieces of metal chipped off by the chain breaker from falling into the crankcase.

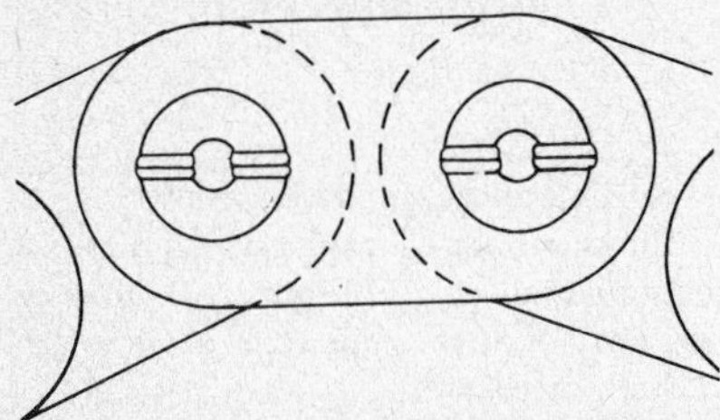
Break the cam chain at this link to remove the top end (Courtesy Yamaha Int. Corp.)

Breaking the cam chain (Courtesy Yamaha Int. Corp.)

5. With the special tool, break the cam chain, then, using the wire, tie the two chain ends out of the way.

6. The camshaft and camshaft brackets are removed together. Remove the nuts and washers which secure the cam brackets, and lift out the assembly. Take the brackets off gently, being careful that the cam lobes are not damaged.

7. The cylinder head is removed by removing the two allen head screws near the spark plug holes and the nuts and bolts located in the cam case. The nuts and bolts should be loosened gradually and evenly at first to avoid warping the head.

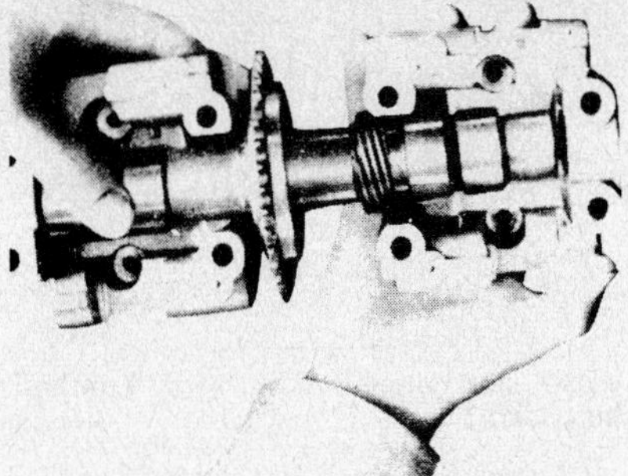
Cam and cam brackets removed (Courtesy Yamaha Int. Corp.)

Cylinder head securing (Courtesy Yamaha Int. Corp.)

8. To remove the cylinders, remove the cam chain adjuster assembly at the rear of the cylinders, then tap upwards on the cylinders with a soft-faced mallet and lift them free.

9. The pistons must be marked before removal so that they can be installed in the proper cylinder.

Remove the circlips, push out the wrist pin (heating the piston crown very gently if necessary), and set the pistons aside.

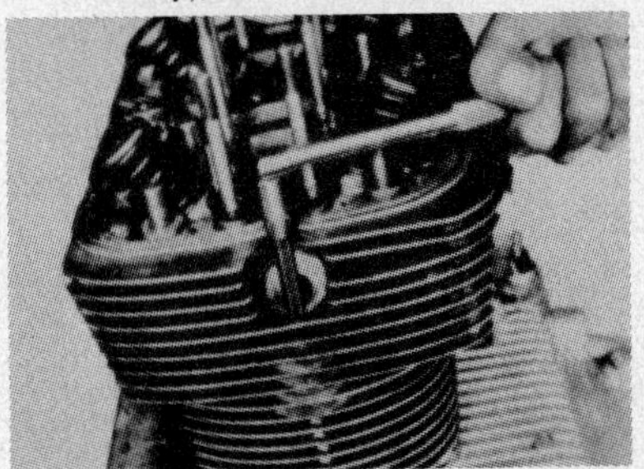
Cylinder head securing allen bolts (Courtesy Yamaha Int. Corp.)

INSPECTION

Camshaft and Rocker Arms

1. The rocker arms should be inspected for signs of wear, scoring, or other damage at the cam lobe contacting surface and the rocker arm shaft bore. Also check for signs of discoloration.

Damage to the cam lobe contacting surface cannot be remedied and the rocker arm should be replaced. Attempting to remove imperfections with emery cloth and the like may change the valve timing.

2. Clean the rocker arm shafts thoroughly and check it for damage or discoloration.

Rocker arm wear points (Courtesy Yamaha Int. Corp.)

3. The shaft is a light press fit in the rocker arm. The rocker arm shaft bore has a diameter of 12.0mm when new. This is the nominal diameter of the shaft as well. Clearance between the rocker arm and shaft is 0.03mm. If clearance exceeds 0.10mm, the arm or shaft should be replaced.

NOTE: *The shafts are hardened metal. Wear is most likely to occur on the rocker arm bores.*

4. Check the camshaft bearing journals for score marks and the camshaft bracket bores for signs of scoring or wear.

5. Check the condition of the cam sprocket teeth.

6. With a micrometer, measure the dimensions of the cam lobes and compare the results with the figures in the chart at the end of this section.

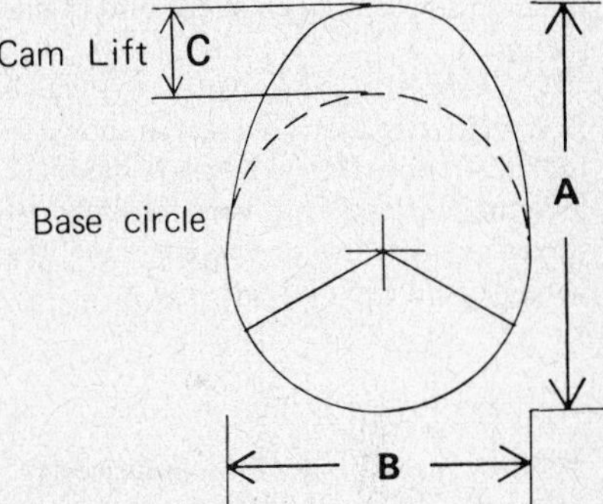

Cam lobe dimensions: "A" is the maximum lobe length; "B" is the base circle diameter; subtract "B" from "A" to obtain cam lift, "C" (Courtesy Yamaha Int. Corp.)

7. Note any scoring, chipping, or pitting of the cam lobes, or discoloration due to insufficient lubrication. Replace the cam if any of the above are present.

8. Be certain that the oil holes in the cam journals are clear. Inject oil into them before reassembly.

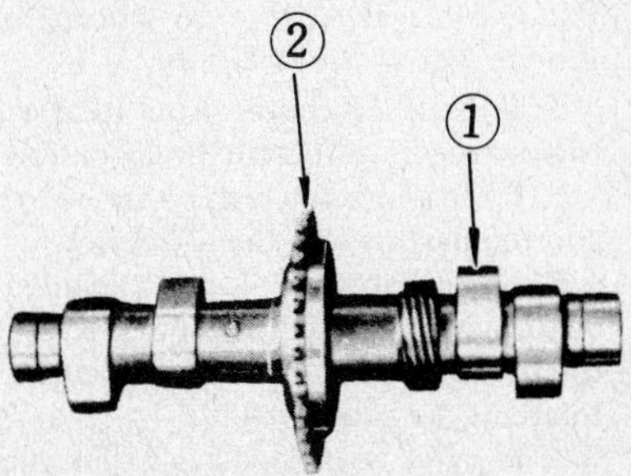

Cam lobe (1), and sprocket (2). Check for wear at these points (Courtesy Yamaha Int. Corp.)

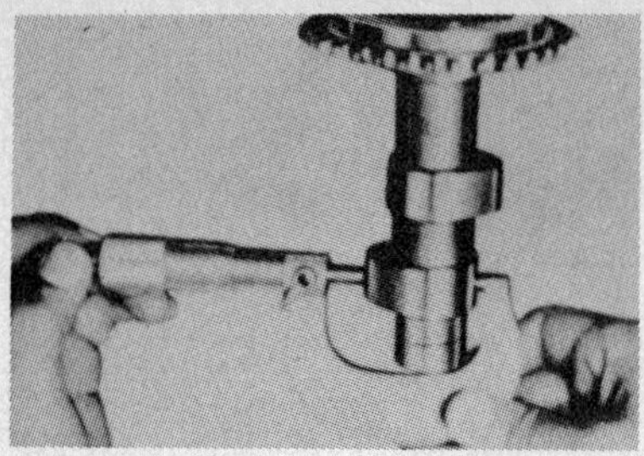

Measuring the lobe length (Courtesy Yamaha Int. Corp.)

Cylinder Head

1. With a valve spring compressor, remove the valve and spring assemblies.

2. The valve stems are stellite tipped. Note any indentation on the stems caused by the rocker arm adjuster. If 0.-015–0.020 in. (0.4–0.5mm) or more, grind the tip flat, removing no more metal than absolutely necessary.

3. Remove all carbon deposits from the combustion chamber and from the valve faces and stems.

4. Refering to the "Cylinder Head and Cylinder" section for the TX500 for procedures if necessary, and check the valve-to-guide clearance, valve condition, and the valve seat condition. TX750 specifications are given at the end of this section.

5. Check the thickness of the valve face relative to the valve seat as shown in the illustration. If thickness is 0.005 in. or less, the thickness has been reduced by excessive grinding or lapping, and the valve should be replaced.

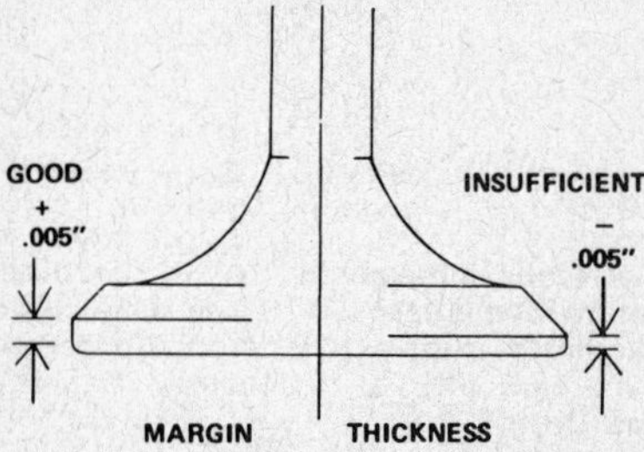

Valve seat margin thickness (Courtesy Yamaha Int. Corp.)

6. Check the width and location of the valve seat as directed in the TX500 "Cylinder Head and Cylinder" section, and note the following:

a. If the seat is centered on the valve but is too wide, use a 65° cutter to reduce seat width to 1.3mm.

b. If the seat is centered but too narrow, increase width with the 45° cutter.

c. If the seat is too high on the valve and too narrow, use the 45° cutter.

d. If the seat is too close to the edge of the valve and too narrow, first use the 65° cutter, and then the 45° cutter to attain the proper width.

7. The valve seat should also be cut with the 45° cutter if it is pitted, or if the seat width varies. If the valve is badly pitted, it should be replaced.

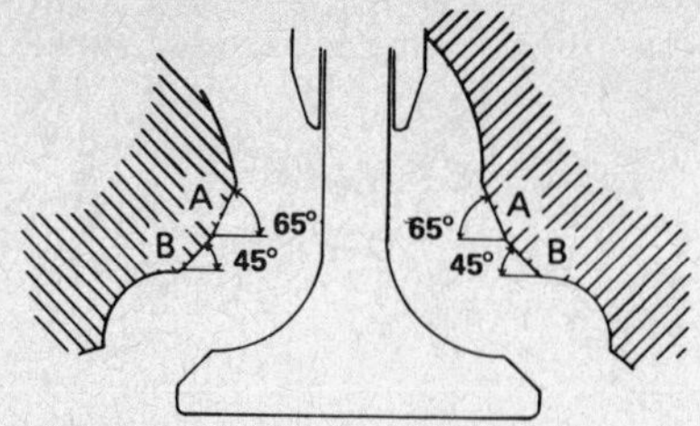

Valve seat angles (Courtesy Yamaha Int. Corp.)

Valve Seat Width

Seat Width	
Standard Width	Wear Limit
1.3 mm (0.051 in.)	2.0 mm (0.078 in.)

8. If any cutting of the valve seat has been accomplished, the valves must be lapped into their seats.

Lapping should also be done if either new valves or guides have been fitted, or if the engine has covered considerable mileage.

9. Check the general condition of the valve guides. Pay careful attention to the lower end of the guide, especially if a bent valve has been detected. The guide is liable to be broken.

If replacement is needed due to damage or normal wear, drive the guides out after heating the cylinder head to 200°–400°F.

Guides are an interference fit in the head of about 0.0015in. (0.04mm). Drive the new guides in with a suitable drift while the head is still hot.

10. Check the cylinder head mating surface for warpage. The head may be lapped if necessary.

11. Check the valve springs against the specifications at the end of this section.

Pistons and Cylinder

Refer to the "Pistons and Cylinder" section for the TX500, above. Procedures for inspection and service are the same. Specifications, however, differ, and are given below. Note the following points:

1. Standard cylinder bore is 80.0mm. If the cylinder is worn to 80.1mm or greater, it must be bored and the correct oversize pistons fitted.

2. If the cylinder taper is 0.05mm or greater, the cylinder must be bored to bring the taper within tolerance.

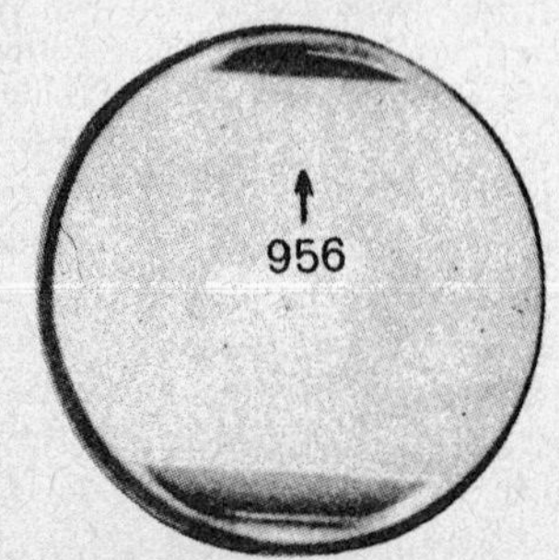

Piston crown markings (Courtesy Yamaha Int. Corp.)

3. Piston diameter is obtained by adding the number stamped on the piston crown to 79.0mm. Therefore, a piston stamped with a "956" on the crown will have a diameter, when new, of 79.956mm.

4. Cylinder bore is obtained by adding the number stamped at the very bottom of the cylinders to 80.0mm. A cylinder stamped 0.007 has a diameter, when new, of 80.007mm.

5. Piston diameters are measured at the bottom of the skirt, perpendicular to the wrist pin. Standard piston-to-cylinder clearance is 0.0020–0.0022 in. (0.050–0.055mm).

Clearance of 0.0060 in. (0.15mm) or more is not acceptable. Either bore the cylinder to fit oversized pistons, or fit standard pistons of a larger diameter if this will bring the clearance within tolerance.

Ring End Gap

Compression rings	0.2-0.4 mm
Oil ring rails	0.3-0.9 mm

6. Ring end gaps are as follows:

Rings should be replaced, as a set, if compression ring end gap is 0.8mm or greater, or if oil ring rails have a gap 1.3mm or greater.

7. Ring side clearances are as follows:

Ring Side Clearance

Compression rings	0.0016-0.0032 in. (0.04-0.08 mm)
Oil ring rails	0.0

8. Note the difference between the top and bottom compression rings. Rings must be installed with the "R" stamp facing up.

Upper compression ring profile (Courtesy Yamaha Int. Corp.)

Lower compression ring profile (Courtesy Yamaha Int. Corp.)

9. Be sure to stagger the ring end gaps upon installation.

10. Oversized rings are coded as described in the TX500 "Pistons and Cylinder" section.

INSTALLATION

1. Installation is the reverse of the disassembly procedure.

2. Note that the smaller of the valve cutaways face the front of the engine when the pistons are installed.

3. New cylinder base and head gaskets must be used.

Pistons properly installed. Note cutout locations (Courtesy Yamaha Int. Corp.)

4. The head nuts and bolts must be torqued to the correct values. Tighten the nuts and bolts evenly and in a cross pattern.

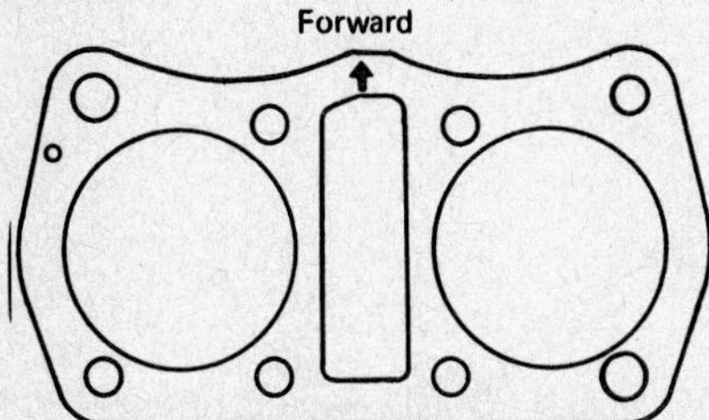

Cylinder head gasket installation direction (Courtesy Yamaha Int. Corp.)

Head Bolt Torque

Bolt Size	*Torque (ft lbs)*
8 mm bolts	15-17
10 mm nuts	28-29

5. The valve guide oil seals must be replaced with new ones. When installing new seals, wrap a thin piece of paper around the end of the valve stem, grease the seal lip well, and install the seal on the stem. Then remove the paper.

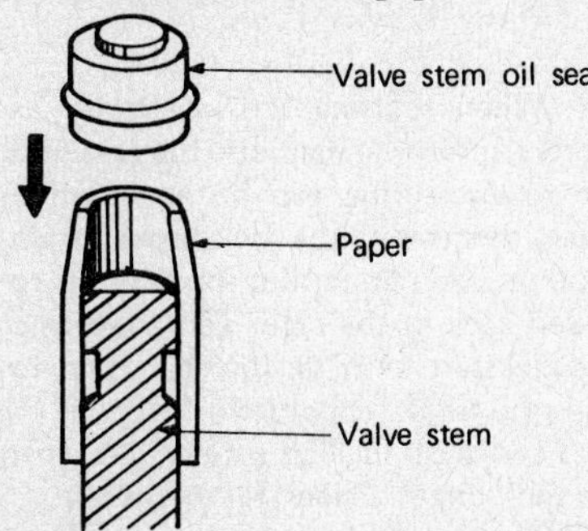

Installing a valve seal (Courtesy Yamaha Int. Corp.)

6. When installing the cam and rocker arms, be certain all parts are thoroughly lubricated. Install the camshaft so that the tachometer drive machined into the cam is positioned on the right side of the engine (when viewed from the rear).

7. Be certain the right and left cam brackets are installed on their respective sides. Torque the nuts to the proper values:

Cam Bracket Nut Torque

Nut Size	*Torque (ft lbs)*
6 mm	6-7.5
8 mm	15-17.2

Camshaft and brackets properly installed (Courtesy Yamaha Int. Corp.)

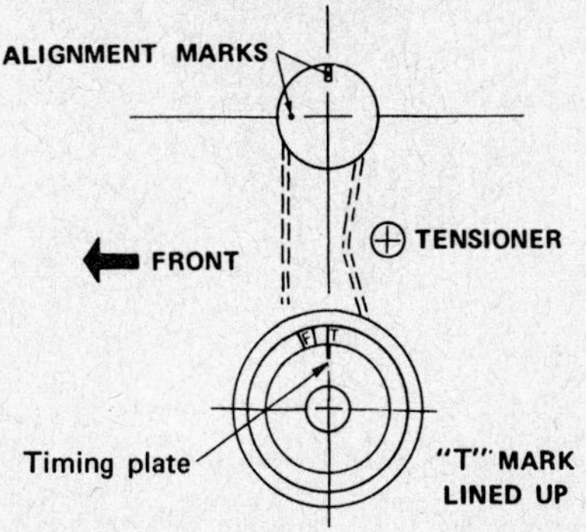

Cam chain alignment marks (Courtesy Yamaha Int. Corp.)

8. Be sure that the cam turn freely after tightening the nuts.

9. Rotate the pistons to TDC (line up the "T" mark on the rotor with the mark on the timing plate.

10. Align the camshaft. The groove on the left side of the cam sprocket must be set in the vertical position. Note that the punch mark on the sprocket will be parallel with the cylinder head cover mating surface.

11. Reconnect the cam chain, using the proper special tool to refit a new masterlink. When installing the chain, be sure that there is no slack left in the front run of the chain.

12. When installing the rocker arms shafts, engage the slot in the end of the shafts with the locating pin.

Installing the rocker arm shaft (Courtesy Yamaha Int. Corp.)

13. Cylinder head oil line banjo bolts are tightened to 15–17.2 ft lbs.

14. Cylinder head cover bolts are tightened to 6–7.5 ft lbs. Check the tachometer drive gears are properly meshed.

Crankcase Cover Components

RIGHT COVER ASSEMBLY

Removal

1. Remove the kickstarter pinch bolts, and pull the kickstarter off of the splined shaft.

2. Remove all of the allen bolts securing the right crankcase cover. Take off the cover, tapping gently around its circumference to free it if necessary. Take off the gasket, cleaning both mating surfaces thoroughly.

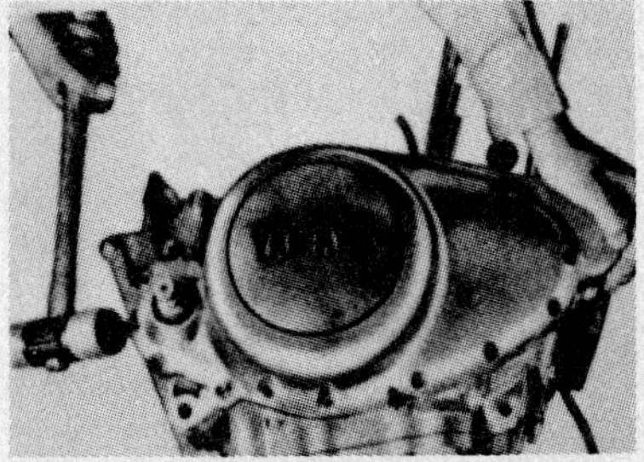

Removing the right crankcase (Courtesy Yamaha Int. Corp.)

Removing the clutch spring screws. (Courtesy Yamaha Int. Corp.)

Removing the clutch push crown (Courtesy Yamaha Int. Corp.)

Removing the clutch hub nut (Courtesy Yamaha Int. Corp.)

3. Remove the clutch spring screws and take off the clutch pressure plate. Loosen the screws gradually in a cross pattern.

4. Take out the push crown, and the ball beneath the crown. The clutch rod is behind the ball, but is most easily removed from the left side.

5. Holding the clutch hub either with the special tool or with a suitable substitute, loosen and remove the clutch boss locknut.

6. Take off the lockwasher, flat washer, and pull off the clutch boss and the plates.

7. Take off the clutch housing, the bushing spacer, and the washers behind it.

8. Remove the oil pump drive gear, and take the woodruff key from the shaft.

9. Remove the bolt and lockwasher which secure the primary drive gear to the crankshaft. Remove the gear, using a puller if needed, and remove the woodruff key from the crankshaft.

10. To remove the kickstarter, detach the end of the return spring from the crankcase, and pull out the assembly.

11. The gearshift mechanism in the right case can only be removed after removing the circlip on the *left* side of the case. See below.

Inspection

1. Standard clutch spring length is 34.6mm. If any of the springs has been collapsed 1mm (0.04 in.), the set should be replaced.

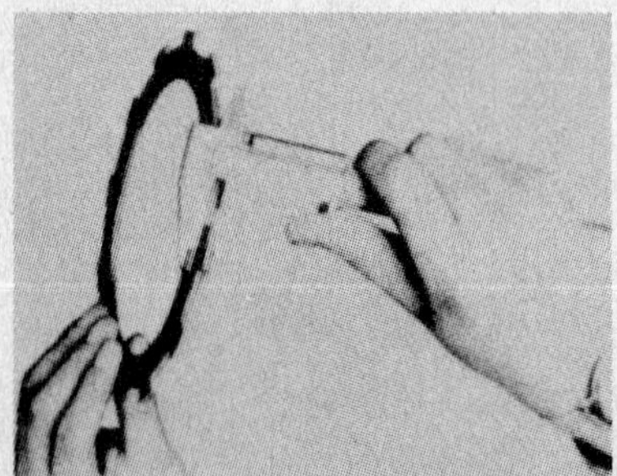

Measuring friction disc thickness (Courtesy Yamaha Int. Corp.)

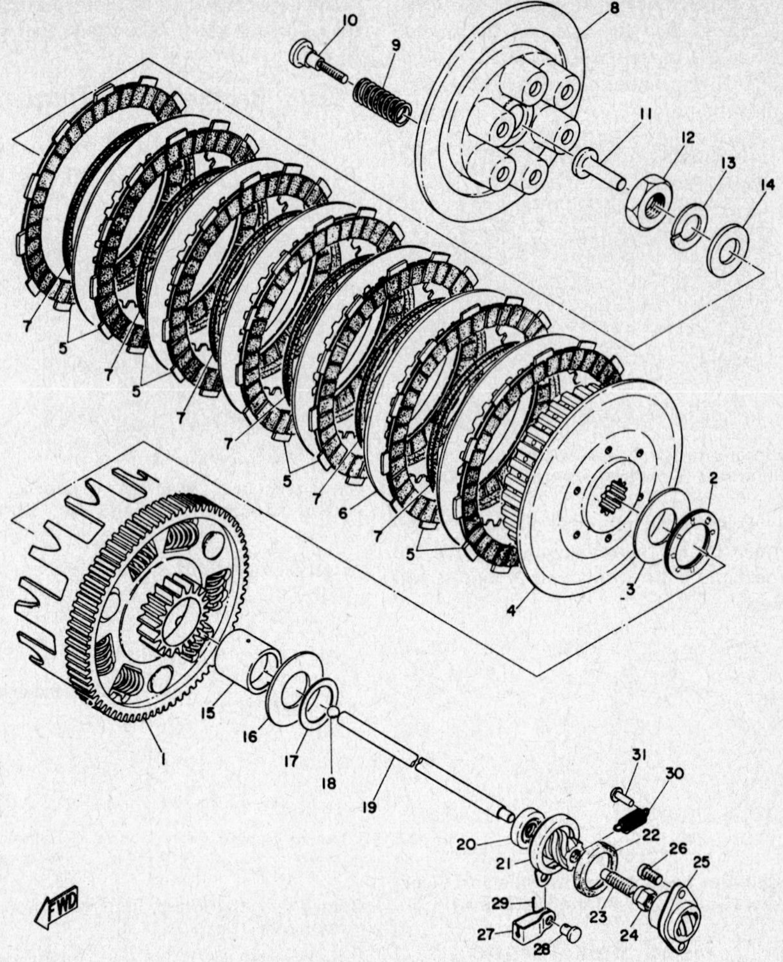

Clutch assembly (Courtesy Yamaha Int. Corp.)

1. Primary driven gear comp.
2. Bearing
3. Thrust plate 2 (25-50-2)
4. Clutch boss
5. Friction plate 1
6. Clutch plate
7. Cushion ring
8. Pressure plate
9. Clutch spring
10. Spring screw
11. Push rod 1
12. Lock nut
13. Spring washer
14. Plain washer
15. Spacer 1
16. Thrust plate 2 (25-50-2)
17. Washer (25.2-36-1.0)
18. Ball (5/16 inch)
19. Push rod
20. Oil seal (SD-8-25-6)
21. Push lever ass'y
22. Dust seal
23. Adjusting screw
24. Adjusting nut
25. Push screw housing
26. Panhead screw
27. Joint
28. Pin
29. Cotter pin
30. Return spring
31. Spring hook

2. Clutch friction plates, when new, have a thickness of 2.8mm (0.112 in.). If worn to 2.6mm (0.104 in.) or less, replace the friction plates.

3. Check all of the plates for warpage by placing them on a flat surface and attempting to slip a feeler gauge between the surface and the clutch plates. Warpage of 0.2mm (0.008 in.) or more necessitates replacement of the plates.

4. Check the general condition of the plates, noting any scoring, damage to the friction material, or heat discoloration.

5. Check all of the gear teeth for wear or damage.

Installation

Installation is the reverse of the disassembly procedure. Note the following points.

1. When refitting the kickstarter assembly, insert the shaft into the case until the return spring can be anchored in place, then rotate the kickstarter's wishbone shaped clip until it slips into its recessed area in the case. Temporarily fit the kickstart lever on the shaft, and rotate the shaft counterclockwise ½–¾ turn and push in. This serves to preload the kickstarter. Check for operation.

2. The clutch housing, oil pump driven gear, and primary drive gear must be properly aligned.

3. Insert an 8mm diameter rod through the hole in the pump driven gear and into the pump cover to hold the gear in position, and secure it.

4. Refit the primary drive gear woodruff key and then the gear itself, tightening the bolt to 85 ft lbs.

Pump driven gear locked in place (Courtesy Yamaha Int. Corp.)

Removing the rotor cover (Courtesy Yamaha Int. Corp.)

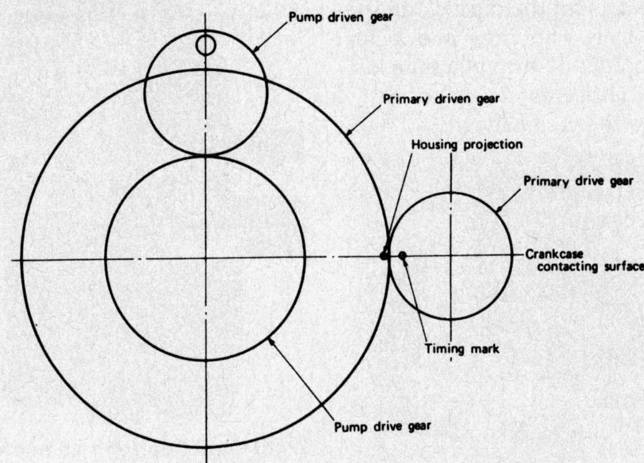

Align the gear marks as shown (Courtesy Yamaha Int. Corp.)

5. Turn the primary drive gear so that the mark on the gear is lined up with the crankcase halves mating surface (the mark should be to the left of the crankshaft).

6. Install the clutch housing so that the housing projection is in line with the mark on the primary drive gear.

7. When installing the clutch plates, note that a *fiber-backed friction plate* is fitted first.

Then fit the plates in the following order:

a. steel plate
b. fiber backed friction plate
c. steel plate
d. aluminum backed friction plate
e. steel plate
f. aluminum backed friction plate
g. steel plate
h. fiber backed friction plate
i. steel plate
j. fiber backed friction plate
k. steel plate
l. friction plate

8. Tighten the spring screws evenly and continue until they bottom out.

LEFT COVER ASSEMBLY

Removal

1. Remove the gearshift lever, the left side crankcase cover, and the alternator cover.

2. Remove the rotor with the special tool, starter clutch, woodruff key, and the starter sprockets along with the chain.

Inspection

1. Check the sprocket teeth for wear or deformity.

2. Check the surface where the starter clutch rollers contact the large sprocket. Replace both the sprocket and the rollers if surface is scored or worn.

Installation

To install, reverse the disassembly procedure. Tighten the rotor bolt to about 28 ft lbs.

Removing the rotor (Courtesy Yamaha Int. Corp.)

Shifter Adjustment

1. The shifter shaft assembly is found on the right side of the crankcase, but is removed after removing the circlip which secures it on the left side of the case. Pull the shifter shaft assembly out of the case.

To install, simply push in the shifter shaft and replace the circlip.

2. Shifter adjustment is checked by comparing the distances ("A" and "AA" in the illustration) between the two prongs of the shifter lever and the corresponding fingers of the star-shaped shift drum stopper. Refer to the illustration.

3. Shifter adjustment is made by means of an adjusting screw secured by a locknut. The screw is flanked by the ends

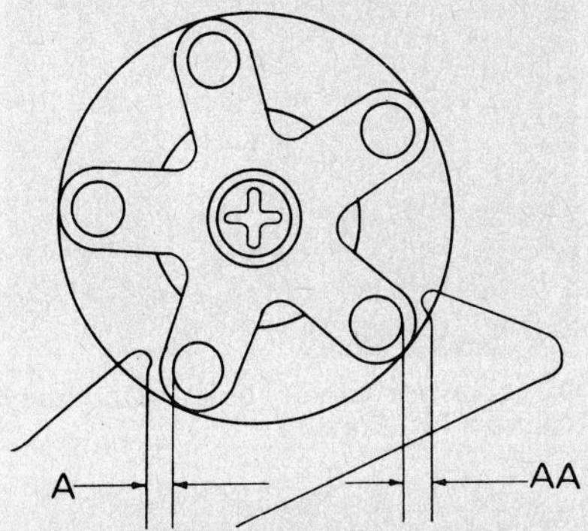

For proper shift adjustment, "A" must equal "AA" (Courtesy Yamaha Int. Corp.)

Shifter assembly installation (Courtesy Yamaha Int. Corp.)

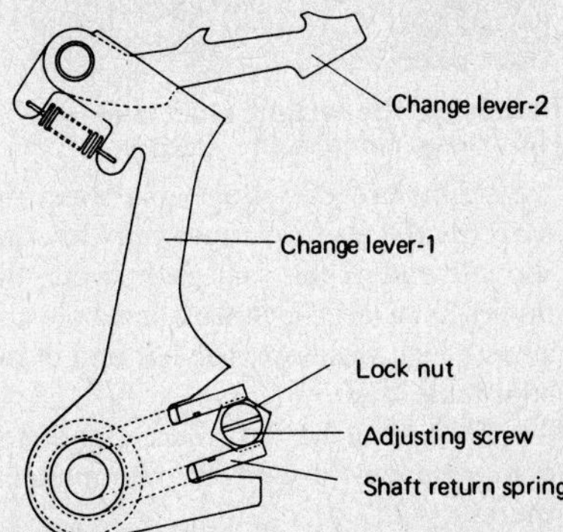

Shifter assembly (Courtesy Yamaha Int. Corp.)

of the shifter assembly pawl spring. Adjust so that distances "A" and "AA" are equal. Bend up the locktab after tightening the locknut.

Splitting the Crankcases

NOTE: *The TX750 omni-phase balancer was changed soon after introduction. Early units had both balancer weights mounted on needle-bearing mounted shafts. The rearmost shaft was then replaced with an "adjustable" unit which is threaded into the crankcase on one side. Allowances must be made for each type of balancer system when removing and installing.*

Oil strainer cover bolts (Courtesy Yahama Int. Corp.)

Loosening the balancer weight pinch bolt (Courtesy Yamaha Int. Corp.)

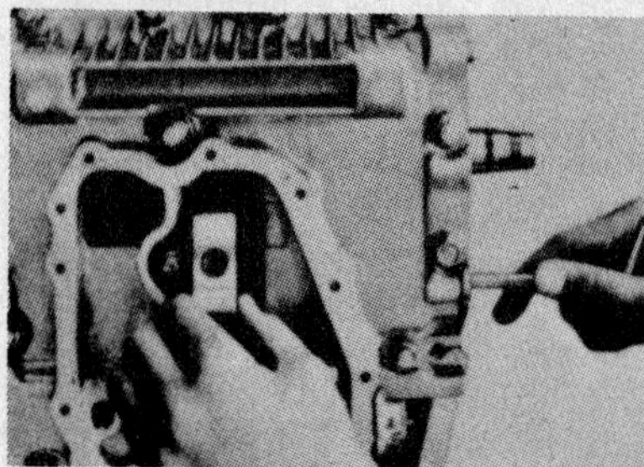

Removing the weight shaft and weight (Courtesy Yamaha Int. Corp.)

Systems are distinguishable since the early model had a simple cap covering the left end of the rear shaft, while the newer has a large lockplate, lockbolt, and a large lockwasher on the left end of the adjustable shaft.

1. Remove the left and right side crankcase covers and the components therein.
2. Remove the oil strainer cover on the lower crankcase half.
3. Remove the pinch bolt(s) on each omni-phase balancer weight.
4. Remove the plug(s) on the left side of the crankcase which cover the ends of the balancer shafts. On newer units, remove the locking bolt, plate, and locknut on the end of the balancer shaft.
5. Remove the crankcase bolt adjacent to the adjustable balancer shaft. Remove the balancer shafts using the special tool. Note that the adjustable shaft unscrews from the crankcase.
6. Remove all of the crankcase nuts and bolts on the lower crankcase half, and the bolts around the dipstick on the upper case half. The nuts and bolds should be loosened ¼ turn at a time in a cross pattern until free of tension.
7. Separate the case halves.

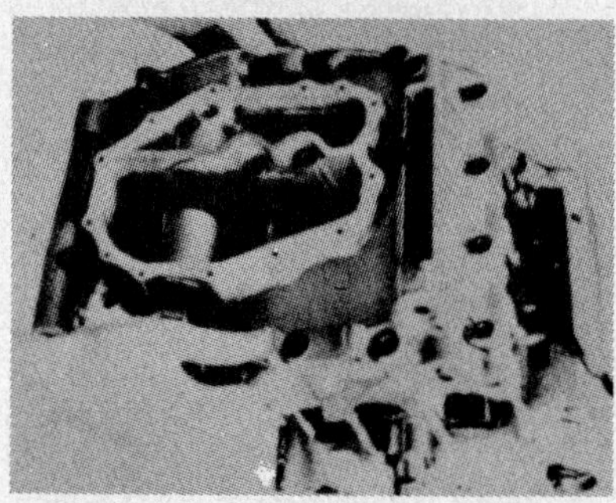

Splitting the crankcases (Courtesy Yamaha Int. Corp.)

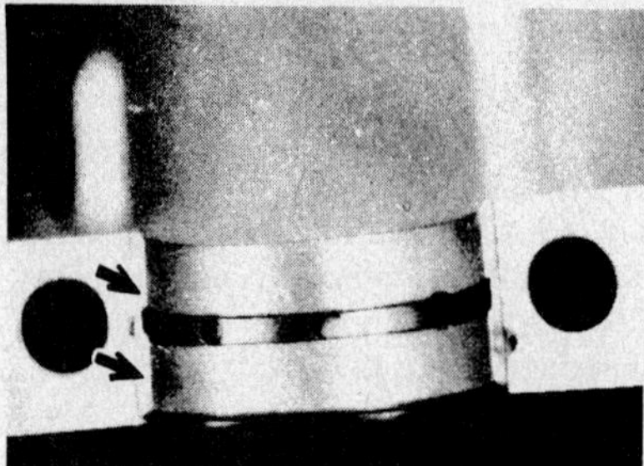

Crankshaft bearing insert (Courtesy Yamaha Int. Corp.)

Lower End Service

The crankshaft, which can be lifted out of the upper case after the lower case is removed, is a one-piece forging which rides on three plain bearings.

The connecting rods are two-piece units, also fitted with plain bearings.

1. The crankshaft main bearing inserts should be removed from the crankcase halves by hand. The inserts should be perfectly free of scratches, scoring or other signs of wear. Also, the insert surface which faces the crankcase must be free of burned-on oil deposits.
2. Main bearing inserts are pre-sized. If the inserts must be replaced, note the numbers stamped on the crankcase (4, 5, or 6). A corresponding number (1, 2, or 3) is stamped on each crankweb. To determine the proper bearing insert to use, subtract the crankshaft number from the

Crankcase bearing size marks (Courtesy Yamaha Int. Corp.)

Crankshaft bearing size marks 1: Crank bearing; 2: Con rod bearing (Courtesy Yamaha Int. Corp.)

crankcase number. Inserts marked 1 through 5 are available and this number is stamped on the crankcase seat side on each insert.

3. Connecting rod bearings are numbered in the same way. Numbers 4, 5, or 6 are stamped on the connecting rod bearing housing, while numbers 1, 2, or 3 are found on the crankweb. To choose the proper bearing insert size, subtract the crankweb number from the housing number. Bearing inserts are numbered 1 through 5.
4. Refer to the chart for correct bearing clearances which may be checked with plastigauge. Note that the connecting rod-to-crankpin clearance is taken with the con rod bolts torqued to 28–32 ft lbs.
5. Blow the oil passages in the crankshaft clear with compressed air.
6. When refitting the con rods to the crankshaft, note that the oil outlet on the

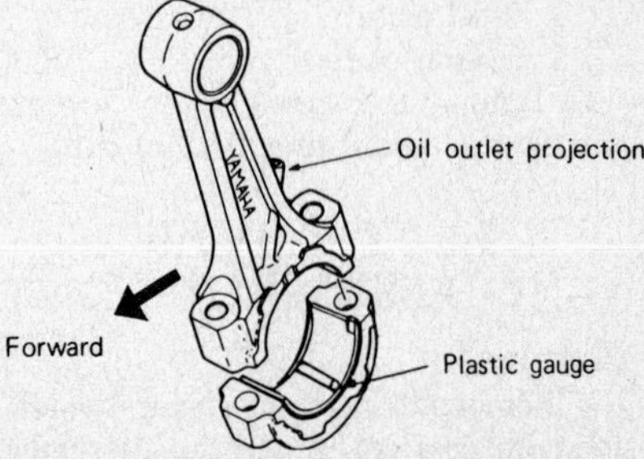

Con rod installation (Courtesy Yamaha Int. Corp.)

rods must face towards the *rear* of the engine.

7. Check the condition of the crankshaft sprockets.

8. Oil all parts thoroughly before installation.

Transmission

REMOVAL

1. Tap up lightly on the transmission shafts and remove the gear clusters.

2. Detach the shift drum stopper spring, remove the stopper bolt, and take off the stopper unit.

3. Bend down the tabs securing the locating plate bolts and remove the plate.

4. Pull out the shifter fork spindle.

5. Remove the large bolt from the top of the upper case half, and take out the spring and plunger.

Removing the gear cluster (Courtesy Yamaha Int. Corp.)

6. Note that each shifter fork is different. They should be marked for position before removal.

7. Remove the cotter pin on each shifter fork and pull out the cam follower pin and roller.

8. Pull out the shift drum, and remove the three shifter forks.

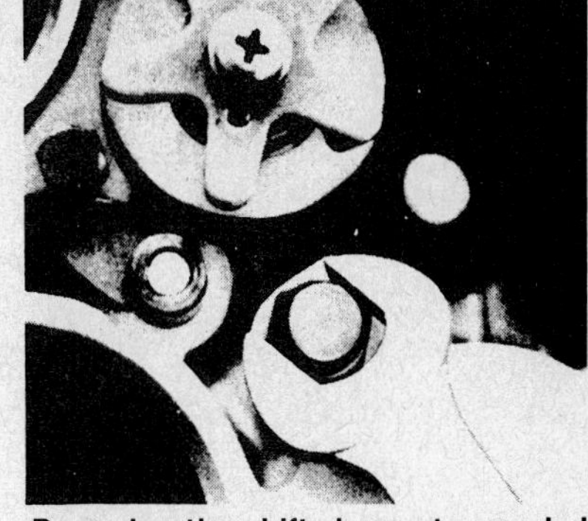

Removing the shift drum stopper bolt (Courtesy Yamaha Int. Corp.)

INSPECTION

1. The gears should be checked for wear or chipped teeth. Note any rounded edges on the engagement dogs. The sliding gear shift fork grooves must be free of any discoloration. If necessary, replace any worn or damaged gears.

If any given gear is damaged, inspect the gear with which it meshes closely. Fitting one new gear to mesh with another which is worn or which has covered considerable mileage is not recommended. It is best to replace gears in pairs.

Bending down the locating plate bolt tab (Courtesy Yamaha Int. Corp.)

Check the gears for smooth rotation on their shafts.

2. Inspect all of the other transmission components for wear or damage.

3. All cotter pins which have been removed should be replaced with new ones.

4. Check the shifter fork spindles for bends by rolling them on a flat surface. Replace the spindles if bent.

Removing the shift fork spindle (Courtesy Yamaha Int. Corp.)

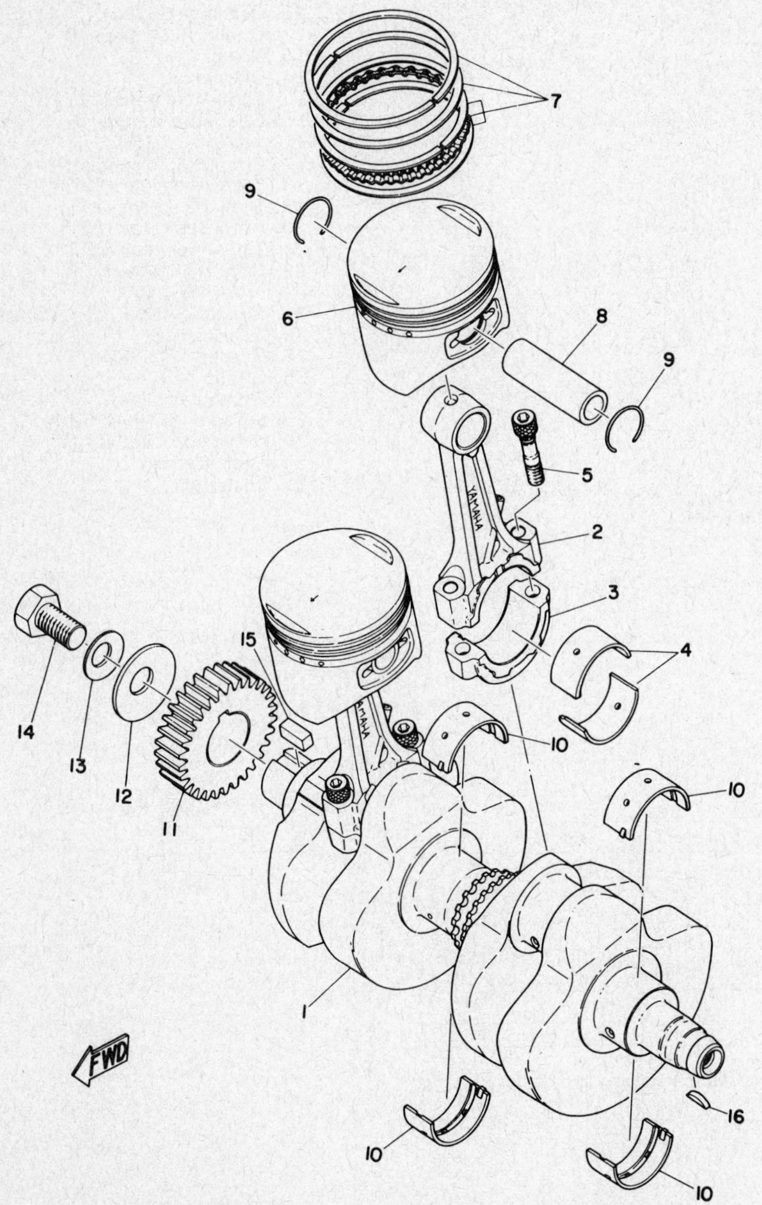

Crankshaft assembly (Courtesy Yamaha Int. Corp.)

5. Inspect the shifter forks noting any wear or scoring of the spindle bores, bent or worn fork ends, or any other obvious damage.

6. Check the shift drum grooves for wear or scoring.

ASSEMBLY

1. Assembly is the reverse of the disassembly procedure.

2. Position the shift drum to the neutral position before installing the gear clusters.

3. After the gear clusters are installed, check the shifting action and check that the gears engage completely.

Crankcase and Balancer Assembly

1. After refitting the crankshaft and transmission, apply some gasket compound to the crankcase halve's mating surfaces.

2. Position the lower case half over the upper half, and pull the omni-phase ba-

1. Main axle (13T)
2. 4th pinion gear (21T)
3. Gear hold washer 5 (25.2-30-1.0)
4. Circlip (25 ϕ special)
5. 3rd pinion gear (20T)
6. 5th pinion gear (23T)
7. Circlip (S-25)
8. 2nd pinion gear (17T)
9. Drive axle shim (20.2-23-1.0)
10. Bearing
11. Bearing (B5205)
12. Circlip (52 ϕ special)
13. Collar
14. Drive axle
15. 2nd wheel gear (27T)
16. Gear hold washer 3 (26.2-34-1.0)
17. Circlip (30 ϕ special)
18. 5th wheel gear (22T)
19. 3rd wheel gear (26T)
20. 4th wheel gear (23T)
21. 1st wheel gear (32T)
22. Gear hold washer (20-25-1.0)
23. Circlip (S-20)
24. Bearing
25. Bearing (B5206)
26. Circlip
27. Distance collar
28. Oil seal (SDO-40-62-9)
29. Drive sprocket (17T)
30. Lock washer
31. Lock nut

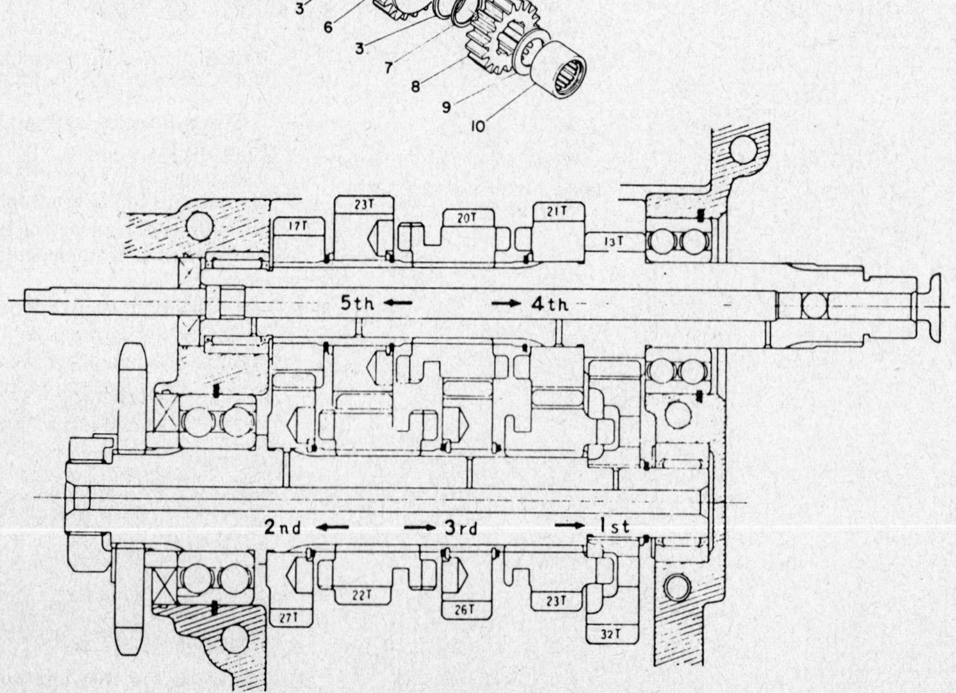

Transmission (TX750) (Courtesy Yamaha Int. Corp.)

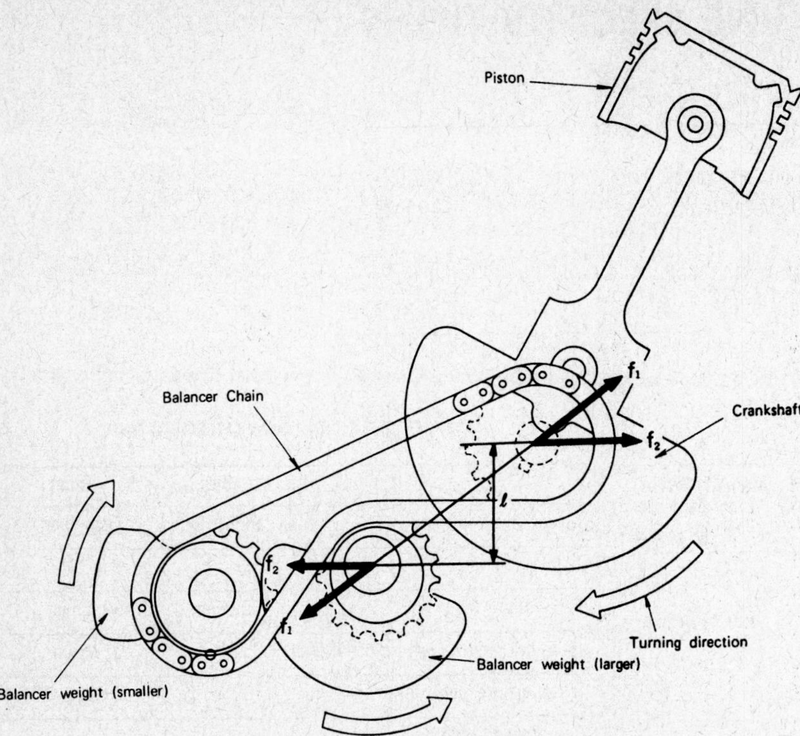

Omni-phase balancer (Courtesy Yamaha Int. Corp.)

Installing the balancer weight (Courtesy Yamaha Int. Corp.)

lancer chain through the cutout in the lower case. Mate the two halves, making sure that the chain is accessible. Tie the chain to the lower case with a piece of wire.

3. Refit all of the crankcase nuts and bolts with the exception on the bolt adjacent to the adjustable balancer shaft.

4. Tighten the crankcase nuts and bolts gradually and evenly in a cross pattern. Correct torque is:

Crankcase Nut Torque

Bolt Size	*Torque (ft lbs)*
M8	15-16.5
M10	27.5-30

5. Note the balancer sprocket alignment marks on the crankcase.

6. Place the pistons at top dead center. Take up the smaller of the balancer weights, and engage the weight's sprocket with the balancer chain. The sprocket should be engaged with the chain so that the mark on the sprocket aligns with the mark on the crankcase and, at the same time, the upper run of the balancer chain is taut.

7. Fit the washers on either side of the weight, and hold it in position.

8. Insert the adjustable balancer shaft into its hole and through the weight. Screw in the shaft until it is lightly bottomed.

9. Making sure that the pistons are still at TDC and that the first weight is properly lined up with the mark on the crankcase, install the larger weight and sprocket making sure that the thrust

Crankcase alignment marks (Courtesy Yamaha Int. Corp.)

washers are properly placed. Line up the marks on the sprocket and crankcase.

10. Install the balancer shaft. Replace the weight pinch bolt, make sure it is seated in the drilling on the shaft, and tighten the bolt 27–30 ft lbs.

NOTE: *The pinch bolt should be secured with a thread locking compound.*

11. Replace the large plug and the rubber-covered plug to complete the assembly of the front shaft.

Turn the engine over at least four times to assure that the weights do not contact each other or anything else.

12. Turn the adjustable shaft just enough (counterclockwise) to allow the installation of the crankcase bolt. Tighten the bolt to 15 ft lbs.

13. Replace the large locknut on the adjustable shaft. Do not tighten the nut. Apply RTV or Yamabond No. 4 to the small rubber plug and insert it in the oil hole near the crankcase vertical bolt.

14. Clamp a dial gauge to the crankcase (assure that the pistons are at TDC) and position the gauge so that it can measure the freeplay of the rear balancer weight. This is essentially chain freeplay.

15. Turn the crankshaft 90° before TDC and check the freeplay of the front weight.

16. Turn the crankshaft 90° after TDC and again check the freeplay.

17. Choose the crankshaft location where the balancer chain is the tightest, and turn the adjustable shaft so that chain tension is 0.3–0.4mm by turning the shaft clockwise to increase the freeplay and counterclockwise to decrease it. Tighten the locknut, install the plate and bolt.

ENGINE SPECIFICATIONS

500

Rocker arms	
Bore diameter (mm)	12.00-12.02
Shaft diameter (mm)	11.983-11.994
Valve seat	
Standard width (mm)	1.0 mm
Wear limit (mm)	1.5 mm

Valves and Guides

		Standard Clearance (mm)	Replacement Clearance (mm)
Intake			
Valve Guide ID	5.5 mm + 0.040 + 0.030	0.020-0.045	0.100
Valve Stem OD	5.5 mm + 0.010 − 0.005		
Exhaust			
Valve Guide ID	5.5 mm + 0.040 + 0.030	0.035-0.060	0.120
Valve Stem OD	5.5 mm − 0.005 − 0.020		

Valve Spring Specifications

	Outer	Inner
Direction of winding	Right Hand	Left Hand
Total windings	5.5	9.0
Free length (mm)	39.0 mm	38.2 mm
Installed length (valve closed) (mm)	35.0 mm	31.0 mm
Installed pressure (lb)	16.3 ± 2	8.03 ± 0.5
*Compressed length (valve closed (mm)	27.5 mm	23.5 mm
Compressed pressure (lb)	67.5 ± 5	19.6 ± 1.5

* Measured with collar. All measurements ± three percent

Cam Lobe Dimensions*

	"A" diameter (mm)		"B" diameter (mm)		Cam Lift "C" (mm)
	Standard	Wear Limit	Standard	Wear Limit	
Intake	34.07 ± 0.05	33.92	28.24 ± 0.05	28.09	6.07
Exhaust	34.11 ± 0.05	33.96	28.29 ± 0.05	28.14	6.11

* See illustration in text for measurement points

Piston and Cylinder Specifications

	Standard	Wear Limit
Cylinder bore (mm)	73.0	73.1
Cylinder taper (mm)	0.008	0.05
Ring end gap (mm)		
top compression	0.2-0.4	0.8
lower compression	0.2-0.4	0.8
oil rails	0.2-0.9	1.3
Ring side clearance (mm)		
compression rings	0.04-0.08	0.15
oil rails	0.0	—
Piston to cylinder clearance (mm)	0.005-0.055	0.15

Ring Identification

Oversize	Mark	Color
1st (0.25 mm)	25	Blue (2 marks)
2nd (0.50 mm)	50	Red (1 mark)

650
Valve Specifications

Seat

Standard Width	Wear Limit
1.3 mm (.051 in.)	2.0 mm (.078 in.)

Guide

	(mm)	Original Clear. (mm)	Replace. Clear. (mm)
Intake			
Guide ID	8.010-8.019		
Stem OD	7.975-7.790	.020-.044	.100
Exhaust			
Guide ID	8.010-8.019		
Stem OD	7.960-7.975	.035-.059	.120

Spring

	Outer	Inner
Diameter of Wire	4.5 mm	2.9 mm
Direction of Winding	Right Hand	Left Hand
Total Windings	6.0	7.25
Free Length	41.8 mm	41.0 mm
Installed Length (Valve Closed)	37 mm	35 mm
Installed Pressure	20.1kg (44 lbs)	9.7 kg (20 lbs)
Compressed Length (Valve Open) Measured without collar	27.8 mm	25.8 mm
Compressed Pressure	60.0 kg (132 lbs)	25 kg (55 lbs)

All measurements ± three percent

CAM LOBE SPECIFICATIONS

	Cam Lift (A) Stand. Value*	Cam Lift (A) Wear Limit	Base Circle Diameter (B) Stand. Value*	Base Circle Diameter (B) Wear Limit
Intake	39.63	39.39	32.19	32.12
Exhaust	39.36	39.39	32.24	32.17

* See illustration in text for measurement points
** ± 0.05

Piston Ring Specifications

Top and Middle Rings

Size (mm)	Mark
Standard	None
Oversize 1st	25
2nd	50
3rd	75
4th	100

Bottom Ring Rails

	Size	Color
Standard		Blue (1 mark)
Oversize 1st	25 (0.25 mm)	Blue (2 marks)
2nd	50 (0.50 mm)	Red (1 mark)
3rd	75 (0.75 mm)	Red (2 marks)
4th	100 (1.0 mm)	Yellow (1 mark)

Ring Gap

	Standard Gap (mm)	Wear Limit
Compression Ring	.2-.4	.8
Wiper Ring	.2-.4	.8
Oil Control (Rails)	.3-.6	1.0

750

Rocker arms	
Bore diameter (mm)	12.00-12.02
Shaft diameter (mm)	11.983-11.994
Valve seat	
Standard width (mm)	1.3
Wear limit (mm)	2.0

Valves and Guides

		Standard Clearance (mm)	Replacement Clearance (mm)
Intake			
Valve Guide ID	8 mm + 0.019 + 0.010	0.020-0.044	0.100
Valve Stem OD	8 mm − 0.010 − 0.025		
Exhaust			
Valve Guide ID	8 mm + 0.019 + 0.010	0.035-0.059	0.120
Valve Stem OD	8 mm − 0.25 − 0.040		

Valve Spring Specifications

	Outer	Inner
Diameter of wire	4.3 mm	2.9 mm
Direction of winding	Right Hand	Left Hand
Total windings	5.25	7.25
Free length	44.0 mm	46.0 mm
Installed length (valve closed)	40.0 mm	38.0 mm
Installed pressure	18 ± 1 kg (40 lbs)	13 kg (26.7 lbs)
*Compressed length (valve open)	30.0 mm	28.0 mm
Compressed pressure	64 ± 3 kg (140 lbs)	29 kg (64 lbs)

* Measured without collar. All measurements ± three percent

Cam Lobe Dimensions*

"A" diameter (mm)		"B" diameter (mm)		Cam Lift (c) (mm)
Standard Value	Wear Limit	Standard Value	Wear Limit	
Intake				
39.31 ± 0.05	39.16	32.23 ± 0.05	32.08	7.31
Exhaust				
39.34 ± 0.05	39.19	32.28 ± 0.05	32.13	7.34

* See illustration in text for measurement points

Piston and Cylinder Specifications

	Standard	Wear Limit
Cylinder bore (mm)	80.0	80.1
Cylinder taper (mm)	0.008	0.05
Ring end gap (mm)		
top compression	0.2-0.4	0.8
lower compression	0.2-0.4	0.8
oil rails	0.3-0.9	1.3
Ring side clearance (mm)		
compression rings	0.04-0.08	0.15
oil rails	0.0	—
Piston to cylinder clearance (mm)	0.005-0.055	0.15

Ring Identification

Oversize	Mark	Color
1st (0.25 mm)	25	Blue (2 marks)
2nd (0.50 mm)	50	Red (1 mark

TORQUE SPECIFICATIONS

500

Part	Torque (ft lbs)	Part	Torque (ft lbs)
Valve adjuster locknut	8.7-10.5	Kickstarter 8 mm bolt	10.8-18.0
Camshaft cap nuts and stud bolts	5.8-7.2	Alternator rotor 10 mm bolt	21.7-25.3
Cylinder head 10 mm nut	22.0-24.5	Alternator stator coil 6 mm allen bolt	5.1-6.5
Cylinder head 6 mm bolt	7.2-8.7	Alternator field coil 6 mm allen bolt	5.8-7.2
Cylinder head 8 mm bolt	15.2-18.0	Clutch spring screw	5.8-7.2
Cylinder head 10 mm stud bolt	10.0-14.5	Clutch boss 18 mm locknut	54.2-57.6
Con rod nut	25.2-29.0	Shifter stopper screw	8.7-14.5
Crankshaft oil hole 1/8 in. taper plug	26.7-29.0	Shifter adjuster screw	5.8-7.2
Oil warning switch 1/8 in. taper	14.5-16.6	Neutral switch 5 mm flat-head screw	1.8-3.2
Oil filter 22 mm oil cleaner ass'y	14.5-16.6	Gear shift lever 6 mm bolt	5.8-8.7
Strainer housing 6 mm pan-head screw	5.8-7.2	Drive sprocket 18 mm lock nut	18.0-32.5
Delivery line 10 mm banjo bolt	14.5-15.8	Crankcase 10 mm stud bolt	25.3
Drain plug 30 mm	25.4-29.0	Crankcase 6 mm bolt	7.2
Drain plug 14 mm	25.4-29.0	Primary drive gear 10 mm bolt	25.4-29.0
Pump cover 6 mm allen bolt	5.1-6.5	Spark plug	10.0-14.5
Strainer cover 6 mm allen bolt	5.1-6.5	Primary gear 6 mm nut	5.8-7.2

650

Stud Size (mm)	Torque (ft lbs)
6	7.5
7	11.5
8	15.0
10	25-29.2
12	29.2-33.3
14	33.3-37.5
17	41.6-50

750

Part	Torque (ft lbs)
Cylinder head bolts	15-17
Cylinder head nuts	28-29
Cam bracket nuts	
6 mm	6-7.5
8 mm	15-17.2
Cylinder head oil line banjo bolt	15-17.2
Cylinder head cover bolts	6-7.5
Alternator rotor bolt	28
Con rod cap bolts	28-32
Crankcase nuts and bolts	
M8	15-16.5
M10	27.5-30

LUBRICATION SYSTEMS

500

This model utilizes a wet-sump lubrication system. The oil pump gears are housed in the crankcase behind the transmission. The oil strainer cover at the bottom of the crankcase contains the oil pressure relief valve, a bypass valve (which allows oil to bypass the filter), and two oil strainers.

Strainer Assembly

REMOVAL

1. Remove the eleven allen bolts (5mm) which secure the strainer cover to the crankcase bottom and remove the

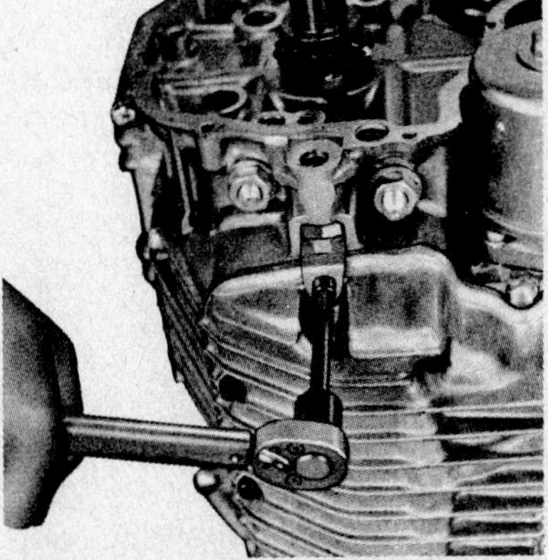

Removing the strainer cover (Courtesy Yamaha Int. Corp.)

cover. Be sure to remove the engine mounting nut holders and the mounting nuts.

2. Take off the cover gasket. It must be replaced with a new one.

Removing the strainer housing (Courtesy Yamaha Int. Corp.)

3. Remove the magnet. Then remove the four phillips head screws which secure the strainer housing to the crankcase, and remove the housing.

4. Remove the shift drum stopper and spring.

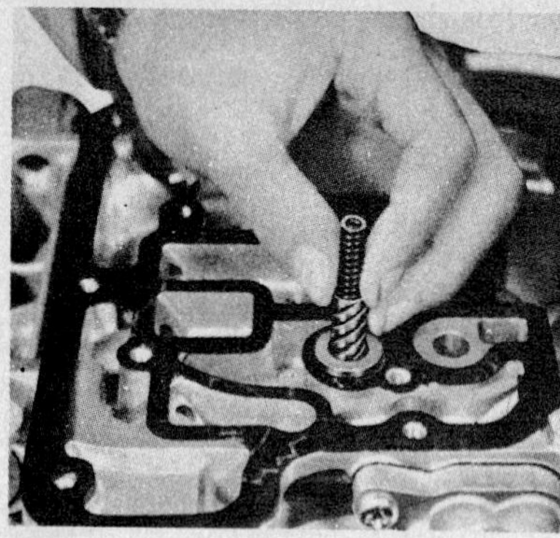

Removing the shift drum stopper and pin (Courtesy Yamaha Int. Corp.)

Fitting a new gasket (Courtesy Yamaha Int. Corp.)

INSPECTION

1. Clean both strainers thoroughly in a solvent and blow dry.

2. Check both the pressure relief valve and the bypass valve for smooth action. Clean the strainer housing assembly thoroughly, and lubricate it well. If either valve is stuck, or if action is stiff or uneven, it must be replaced.

Valve opening pressures are as follows:

Valve Opening Pressure

Relief valve	56 psi
Bypass valve	9.1 psi

3. To remove the relief valve, push it on the retainer with a screwdriver so that it is disengaged from its slot in the strainer housing, then turn the retainer 180° and take out the valve. Oil well before installation. To install, reverse the removal procedure. Check the operation of the valve.

4. The bypass valve guide pin is a press fit in the strainer housing. It is therefore impossible to remove the bypass valve, and, if it is faulty, the strainer housing must be replaced.

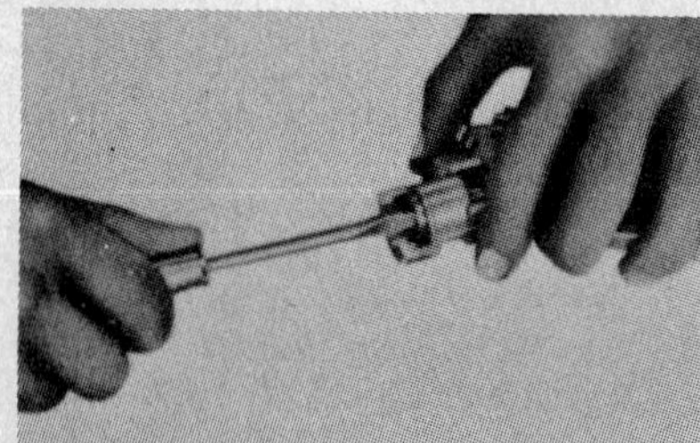

Removing the relief valve (Courtesy Yamaha Int. Corp.)

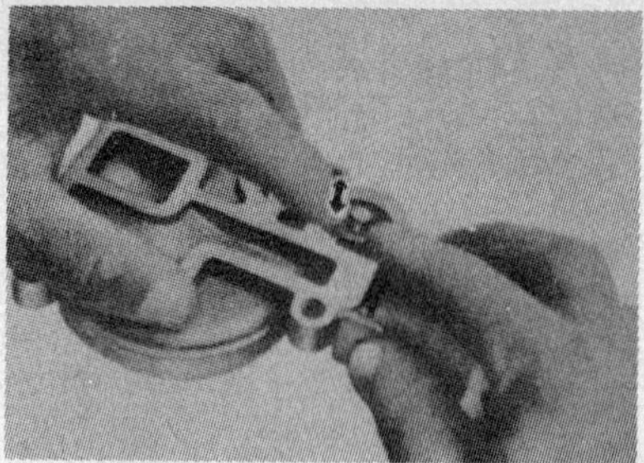

Checking bypass valve operation (Courtesy Yamaha Int. Corp.)

INSTALLATION

1. Refit a new gasket to the crankcase.

2. Refit the shift drum stopper and spring.

3. Install the strainer housing assembly. Tighten the screws to 5.8–7.5 ft lbs.

4. Install the magnet. Refit the small strainer.

5. Replace the strainer in the strainer cover.

6. Install the two engine mounting nuts and nut retainers in the hole in the crankcase, then refit the strainer cover, and tighten the bolts to 5–6.6 ft lbs.

Oil Pump

REMOVAL

1. To remove the oil pump gears, the crankcases must be split. Refer to the "Engine and Transmission" section.

2. Remove the three 5mm allen bolts which secure the pump cover, and lift out the pump shaft.

3. Remove the dowel pin from the pump shaft and separate the pump cover, shaft, and scavanger pump. Remove the feed pump assembly.

INSPECTION

1. Clean all parts thoroughly.

2. Check for damage or wear.

3. Oil all components thoroughly before reassembly.

INSTALLATION

Reverse the removal procedure. Be especially careful that the dowel pin does not drop into the oil passage.

650

Oil Pump

REMOVAL

1. Remove the tachometer shaft locknut, then drive out the tachometer housing with a punch.

2. Remove the tachometer gear, washer, and O-ring.

3. Remove the oil pump gear and woodruff key.

4. Remove the pump housing retaining screws and, while tapping the housing with a soft-faced mallet, lift out the pump.

INSPECTION

1. Check for wear or damage.

2. Oil all parts thoroughly before installation.

INSTALLATION

1. Installation is the reverse of removal. Note the following points:

2. Make sure that the notches in the inner rotor and drive shaft are correctly aligned.

3. Install the pump as a unit, using the locating pin provided for alignment.

4. Replace the tachometer gear O-ring.

750

This model uses a dry-sump lubrication system. The oil pump shaft also drives the contact breaker cam.

Oil Pump

REMOVAL

1. Remove the left crankcase cover.

2. Remove the contact breaker assembly.

3. Remove the nut which secures the breaker cam to the pump shaft. If the shaft turns, lock it in place by inserting an 8mm diameter rod through the timing hole of the oil pump driven gear (on the right side).

4. Take off the timing advance weights. Remove the nut which secures the oil pump driven gear to the shaft. Note that it is necessary to lock the gear in place with a rod through the timing hole.

Removing the oil pump driven gear nut (Courtesy Yamaha Int. Corp.)

5. Removing the gear will expose the oil pump cover. Remove the cover, washer and circlip.

6. Remove the two oil pump rotors (suction and scavenging), and then the dowel pin.

CAUTION: *Do not allow the dowel pin to fall into the oil passage.*

7. Remove the circlip on the right side of the engine. Remove the side plate and rotor filter cover by threading in the two screws and pulling out.

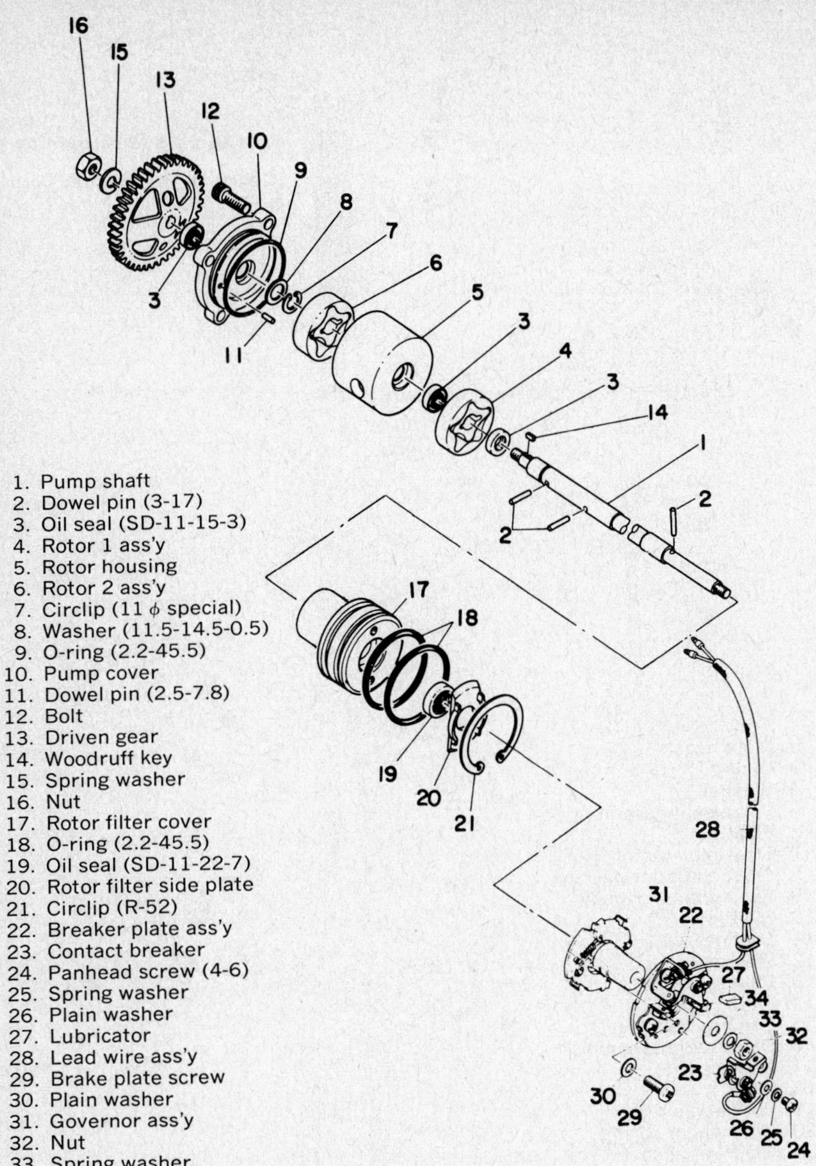

Oil pump assembly (Courtesy Yamaha Int. Corp.)

Removing the oil pump cover (Courtesy Yamaha Int. Corp.)

Removing the oil pump rotor (Courtesy Yamaha Int. Corp.)

8. Remove the pump shaft from the left side.

INSPECTION

1. Inspect all parts for wear or damage.
2. Replace all O-rings and oil seals with new ones.

ASSEMBLY

1. Assembly is the reverse of the disassembly procedure.
2. Oil all parts thoroughly before assembly.
3. When installing the pump mounting dowel pin, be sure that the pin does not drop into the oil passage.
4. Grease the rotor filter cover O-rings.
5. A special tool (which is a tapered shaft) is needed to install the rotor filter cover in order to prevent damage to the oil seal in the cover. Refer to the illustration.

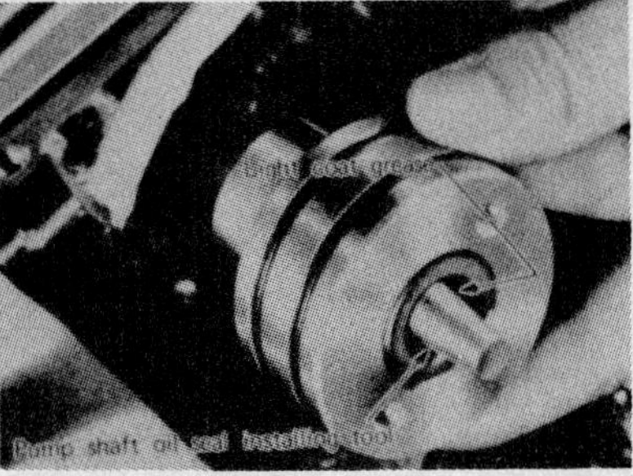

Fitting the rotor filter cover with the special tool to protect the oil seal (Courtesy Yamaha Int. Corp.)

NOTE: *This is an extremely important seal, since it is supposed to keep oil out of the breaker points compartment, so be sure installation is done properly.*

FUEL SYSTEMS

All models use constant vacuum carburetors.

CARBURETOR

500

DISASSEMBLY

1. Remove the two screws which secure the vacuum chamber top, and remove the top.
2. Pull out the spring, then the throttle slide.
3. Remove the jet needle from the throttle slide with a thin screwdriver. The needle is held in the slide by a single screw.
4. Remove the phillips head screw in the vacuum chamber which secures the

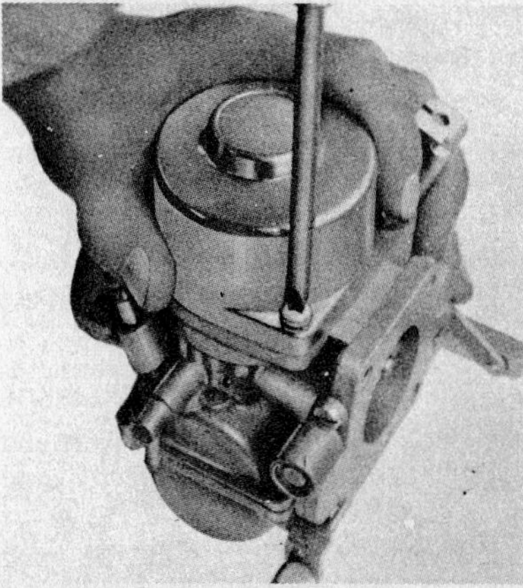

Removing the vacuum chamber top (Courtesy Yamaha Int. Corp.)

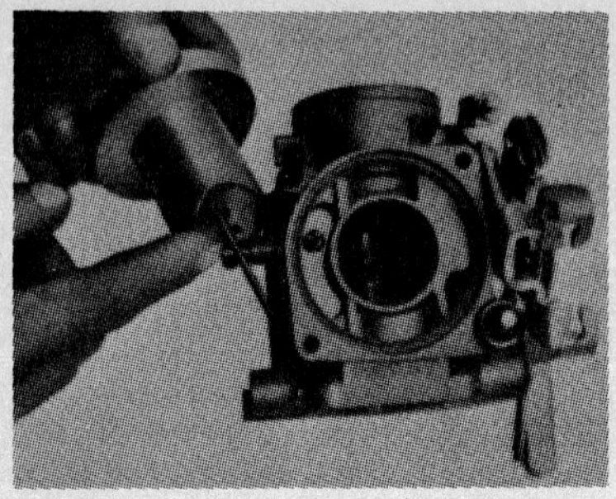

Throttle slide and jet needle (Courtesy Yamaha Int. Corp.)

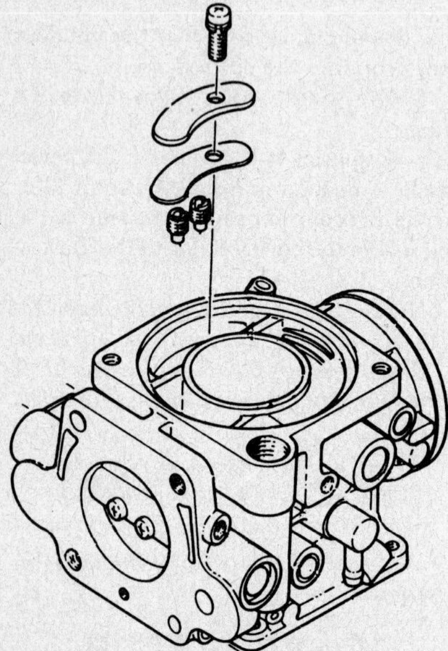

Jet location (Courtesy Yamaha Int. Corp.)

cover plate over the slow air jet and main air jet. After removing the steel and fiber cover plates, unscrew and remove the two jets. Note their location for reassembly.

5. Remove the four screws which secure the float bowl and remove the float bowl. Remove the clip plate which secures the main and needle jets.

6. Pull out the two jets.

7. Remove the float pin, and then remove the float and float needle.

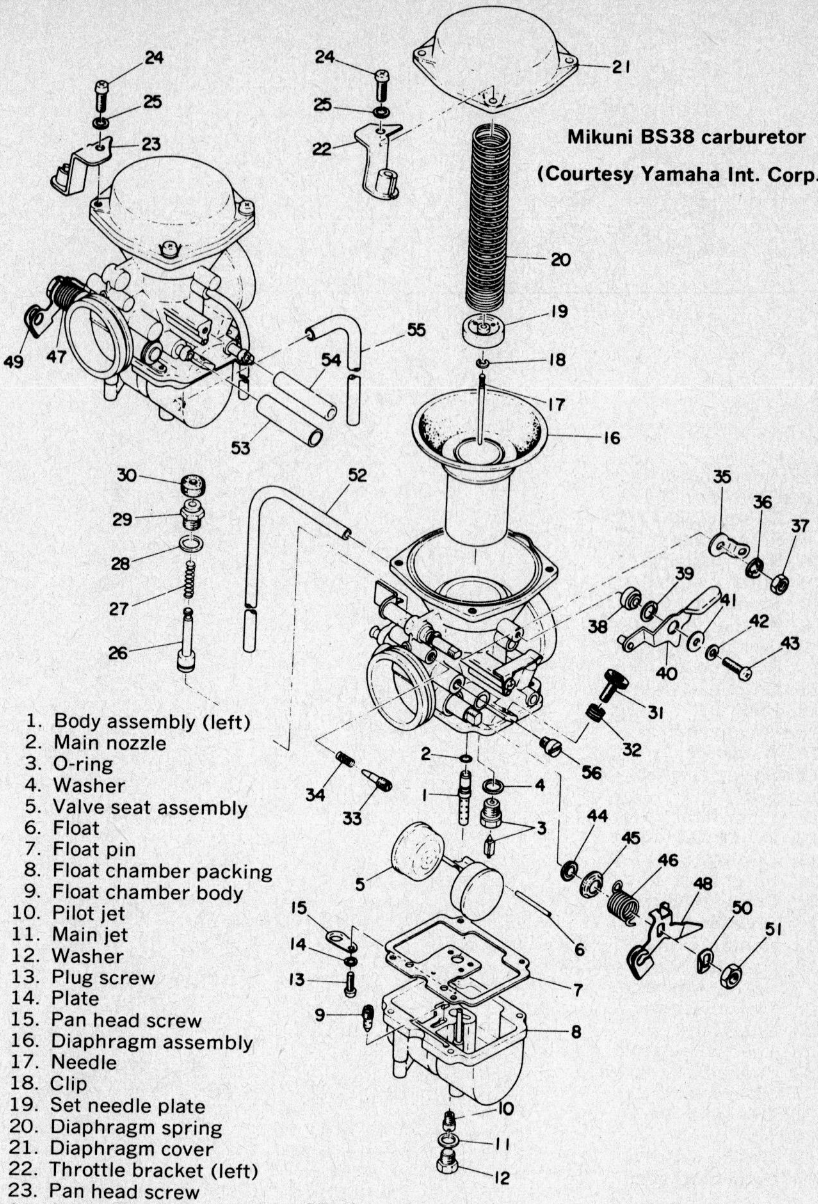

Mikuni BS38 carburetor (Courtesy Yamaha Int. Corp.)

1. Body assembly (left)
2. Main nozzle
3. O-ring
4. Washer
5. Valve seat assembly
6. Float
7. Float pin
8. Float chamber packing
9. Float chamber body
10. Pilot jet
11. Main jet
12. Washer
13. Plug screw
14. Plate
15. Pan head screw
16. Diaphragm assembly
17. Needle
18. Clip
19. Set needle plate
20. Diaphragm spring
21. Diaphragm cover
22. Throttle bracket (left)
23. Pan head screw
24. Starter body assembly
25. Starter plunger
26. Plunger spring
27. Set lever starter spring
28. Washer
29. Plunger cap
30. Plunger cap cover
31. Throttle stop spring
32. Throttle stop screw
33. Starter packing
34. Flat head screw
35. Pilot screw spring
36. Pilot screw
37. Cap
38. Throttle assembly shaft
39. Throttle spring
40. Throttle lever
41. Washer
42. Nut
43. Throttle valve
44. Oval head screw
45. Starter shaft
46. Clip
47. Seal
48. Cap
49. Starter lever
50. Washer
51. Nut
52. Connector lever
53. Spring washer
54. Spring washer
55. Ring
56. Lever assembly
57. Pan head screw
58. Spring washer
59. Overflow pipe
60. Fuel pipe
61. Spring
62. Pipe clip

INSPECTION

1. Clean the carburetor body and the jets in a solvent and blow dry. Be sure that all air and fuel passages are clear.

2. Check the float for leaks.

3. Check the float needle for wear. Be sure that the needle and needle seat are clean and free of corrosion.

4. Check the throttle slide for wear or scoring, and the carburetor bore as well.

5. Inspect the jet needle for wear and for nicks, especially along the tapered portion of the needle.

6. If considerable mileage has been covered, the needle and needle jet should be replaced. Wear of these components will be noticeable as a rich mid-range condition.

7. Check the float height adjustment.

FLOAT HEIGHT ADJUSTMENT

"Float height" as measured is the distance between the mating surface of the float bowl and the top of the float with the float tang just lightly contacting the float needle.

Be sure to remove the gasket before measuring.

Check this adjustment with a vernier caliper as shown. Float height should be 22.0mm. Check both floats. Difference between the two should be 0.5mm or less.

To adjust, gently bend the tang until the correct height is attained.

ASSEMBLY

Assembly is the reverse of disassembly. New O-rings and gaskets should be fitted.

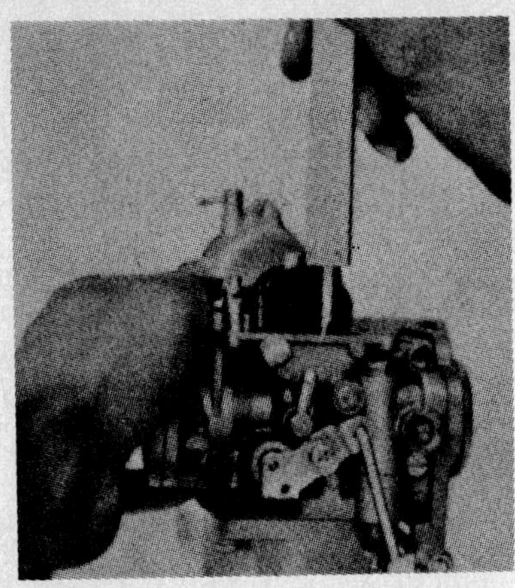

Measuring float height (Courtesy Yamaha Int. Corp.)

Vacuum chamber top securing screws (Courtesy Yamaha Int. Corp.)

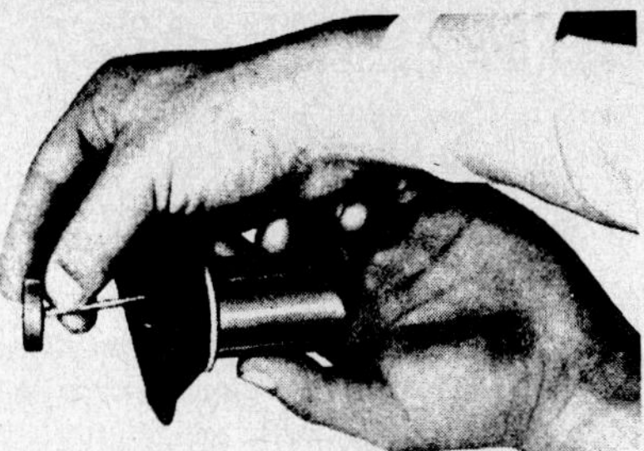

Removing the jet needle (Courtesy Yamaha Int. Corp.)

650 and 750

DISASSEMBLY

1. Remove the four screws which secure the vacuum chamber cover; take off the cover, lift out the spring.
2. Carefully disengage the diaphragm from the carburetor body, and pull out the slide assembly.
3. Remove the needle retainer and the needle.
4. Remove the float bowl screws, and take off the float bowl.
5. Remove the float pin, take away the float assembly, and the float needle.
6. Pull out the needle jet.
7. Remove the pilot jet which is threaded into the inside of the float bowl. Remove the main jet after removing the plug on the outside of the float bowl.

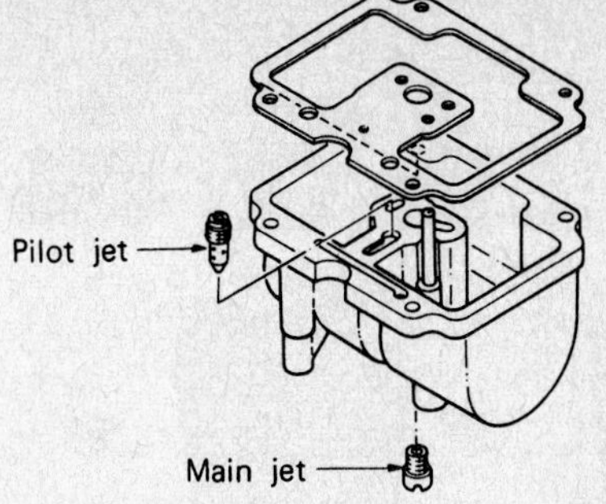

Float bowl and jets (Courtesy Yamaha Int. Corp.)

INSPECTION

Inspect and clean all components as directed in the TX500 "Inspection" section, above.

Also check the diaphragm for rips.

FLOAT HEIGHT ADJUSTMENT

Adjust as directed for the TX500, above. Standard measurement is 25mm.

ASSEMBLY

Assembly is the reverse of disassembly. Use new O-rings and gaskets.

When fitting the throttle slide, be sure that the small tab on the edge of the diaphragm is properly installed in the cutout on the carb body.

CARBURETOR SPECIFICATIONS

500

Venturi size	32.0 mm (effective)
Main jet	#140
Main air jet	#60
Jet needle	302001
Needle jet	
Vacuum piston cut-away	11° 00′
Pilot jet	#50
Slow jet	#50
Slow air jet	#110
Pilot screw (turn out)	1.0 ± ¼
Float valve seat	2.0 mm
Starter air jet	1.0 mm
Starter jet	#45
Float level (H)	22.0 mm

650

Type (BS38 Mikuni)*	W1 ①	E2 ②	E3 ③	E4 ④
Main jet (M.J.)	130	130	130	130
Pilot jet (P.J.)	45	45	42.6	42.5
Pilot outlet (P.O.)	0.8	0.8	0.7	—
Pilot Bypass #1 (P.B.1)	1.0	1.0	0.8	—
Pilot Bypass #2 (P.B.2)	0.6	0.6	1.0	—
Air jet (A.J.)	1.0	1.0	1.2	—
Needle jet (N.J.)		Z-6		
Jet needle (J.N.)		4JN19-4		4J
Air screw (A.S.)	½	1	1	¾
Starter jet (S.J.)	0.6	0.6	0.6	0.7
Float level (F.L.) (mm)	25	25	25	25
Air vent (A.V.)	2.5	3.0	4.0	—

① Engine nos. 00101 02514.
② Engine nos. 02515 03628.
③ Engine nos. 03629 100101.
* Types W1 and E2 are interchangeable; E3 carburetors must be used as a set.
④ Engine nos. 100101

750

Venturi size (38 mm measured)	32.0 mm (effective)
Main jet	#130
Jet needle	4N8-4
Needle jet	Z-4
Pilot jet	#45
Butterfly (throttle) valve	#115
Starter jet	0.7
Float level	24 ± 2.5 mm
Pilot screw (turns out)	¾
Fuel valve seat	2.0

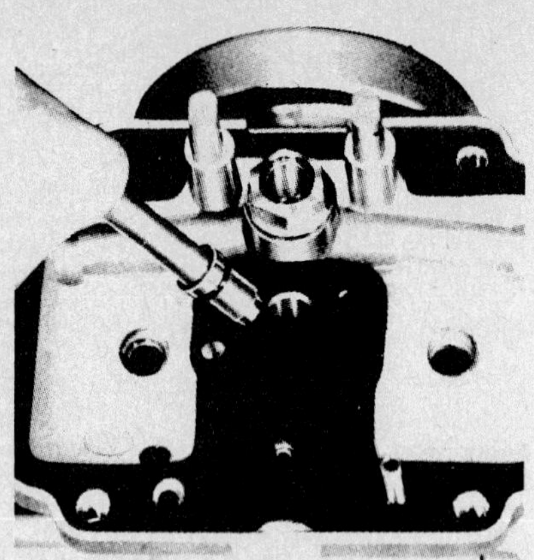
Removing the needle jet (Courtesy Yamaha Int. Corp.)

FUEL PETCOCK

Petcocks may be removed from the gas tank after removing the two securing screws. Sealing ability of the petcock is dependent upon a rubber O-ring. Replace this O-ring if damaged or if seepage occurs.

The petcock sediment bowl can be drained by removing the screw at the bottom.

The sediment bowl can be cleaned after removing the two screws securing the plate on the other side of the petcock lever.

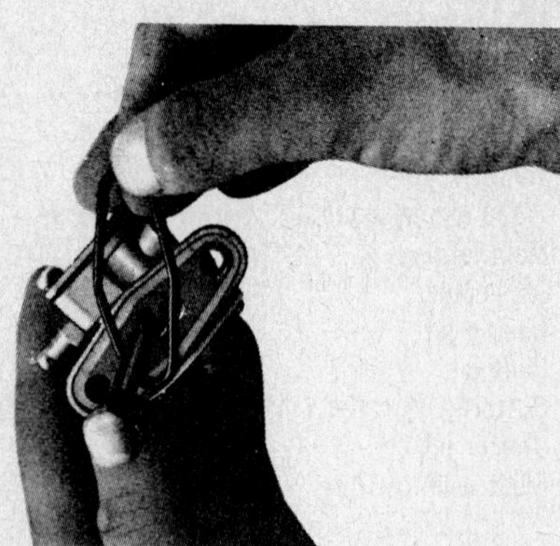
Fuel petcock o-ring (Courtesy Yamaha Int. Corp.)

ELECTRICAL SYSTEMS

500

NOTE: *The following precautions should be taken when carrying out electrical system tests:*

1. Be positive that the battery connections are not reversed. This will burn out the rectifier almost immediately.
2. Be certain all electrical connections are noted before disconnecting them so that they can be reconnected properly.
3. Do not run the engine on high rpm with the "P" terminal circuit of the rectifier disconnected.
4. When quick-charging the battery, always disconnect the rectifier at the "P" terminal.
5. Never disconnect the battery while the engine is running.
6. When testing the regulator, be sure to keep the battery connected.
7. When testing the rectifier, be sure that the battery has a full charge.

Ignition Circuit

The ignition circuit consists of two ignition coils, two condensers, and two contact breaker points.

The coils are mounted on the frame beneath the gas tank. The condensers are mounted on the battery box.

NOTE: *The Yamaha "Electro-Tester" is recommended for all ignition circuit component tests. This unit contains all of the instruments needed for testing including AC and DC voltmeters, ohmmeter, capacitance tester, and so on. Although standard electrical test equipment can be substituted, test procedures may vary according to the type of equipment used.*

In the event of ignition trouble, first check the spark plugs. Clean or replace and set the gap to 0.7mm (0.027 in.).

If trouble persists, file, clean, and gap the breaker points, and set the ignition timing as described under "Tune-Up Operations."

Check the ignition circuit wiring, making sure that all connections are clean and tight, and that continuity exists between all components.

Test the coils and condensers as described below.

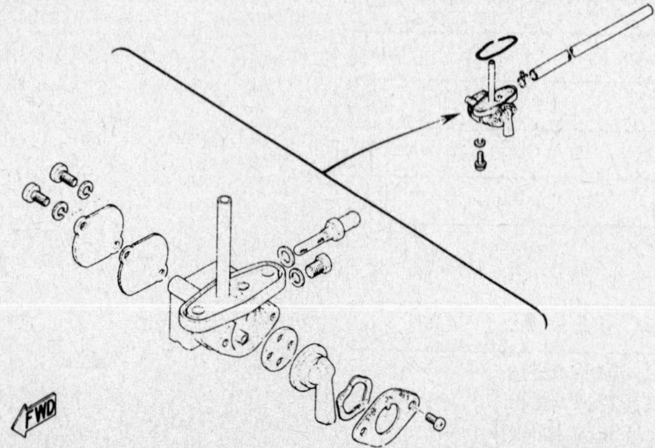

Fuel petcock exploded view (Courtesy Yamaha Int. Corp.)

IGNITION COIL

1. Very rough tests can be made which might indicate a faulty ignition coil. If, after a long period of operation, either coil becomes very warm to the touch, or if one is noticable hotter than the other, suspect the coil.
2. Remove the spark plug cap, and insert a nail (or other suitable conductive object) into the spark plug cap, and hold the end of the object about ¼ in. away from the cylinder head while kicking the engine over briskly. The spark should be able to jump this air gap with great regularity, and the spark should appear to be fat and blue in color.

Check both coils, noting any difference in the sparks or sparking characteristics.

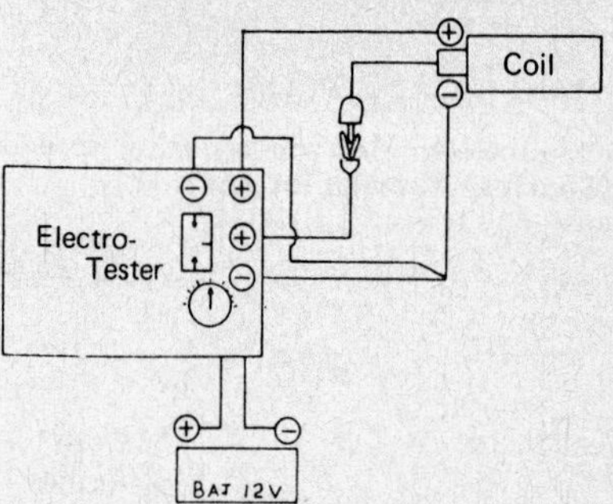

Testing the coil with the Electro-tester (Courtesy Yamaha Int. Corp.)

3. If an electro-tester is available, connect it as shown.

Place a thick piece of paper between the points. Leave the ignition key OFF.

The electro-tester has a built-in point gap. The coil should be able to spark across a 7mm gap.

4. This test may also be accomplished with the engine running. With the point gap on the tester reading "zero," start and run the engine between 2–3,000 rpm. Gradually open the point gap until the engine begins to misfire, then begin to close the gap until it runs smoothly. The point gap should be at least 7mm at this point.

If the coil fails this test, it must be replaced.

CONDENSER

1. The condensers are mounted in a single assembly and both must be replaced if either is found defective.
2. The easiest test for condensers is to note any arcing or sparking between the points. Severe sparking will quickly cause

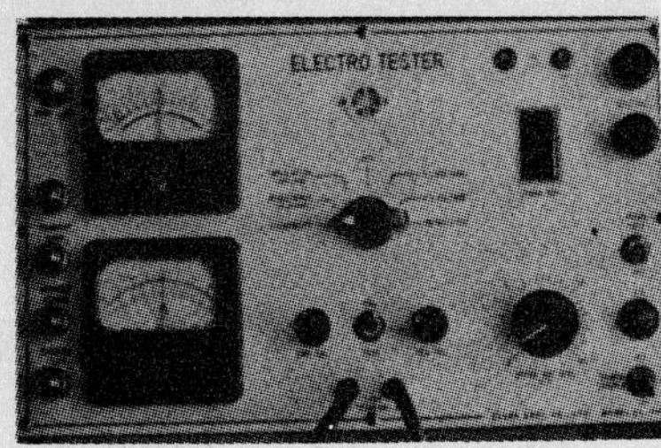

Yamaha Electro-tester (Courtesy Yamaha Int. Corp.)

pitted and burned points. If the points appear to be in this condition, replace them and the condensers.

3. Condensers can be checked with an ohmmeter. Disconnect the condensers at the connector plug. Then connect the negative ohmmeter lead to the condenser case, and the positive lead to the wire running out of the center of the condenser. Place the meter scale on the highest range.

After a moment, resistance should exceed 5 million ohms.

4. If an electro-tester is available, hook it up as for the ohmmeter above; Turn the main function switch to "C. Capacity." Turn the calibration switch to "CAL." Then turn the "CAP CAL" knob until the meter reads 0.22 MFD on the red meter scale for "Capacitance."

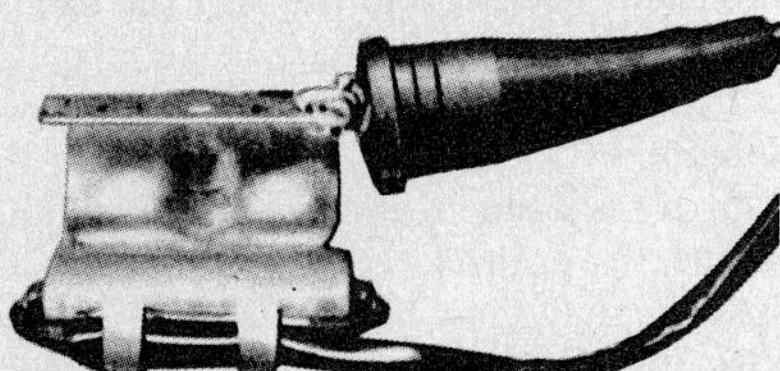

Testing a condenser (Courtesy Yamaha Int. Corp.)

Measuring resistance between field coil lead and core (Courtesy Yamaha Int. Corp.)

Switch the calibration switch to "TEST." The needle should stay in approximately the same position.

If it moves into the red area, replace the condenser assembly.

Charging Circuit

An AC generator (alternator) is used in conjunction with a six-diode full-wave rectifier. An IC voltage regulator controls battery charging.

ALTERNATOR

1. The field coil can be checked with an ohmmeter.

2. Measure the resistance between the two field coil leads. It should be about 4.04 ohms. If this value is obtained, the field coil is probably in good condition.

If infinite resistance is obtained, the field coil has a broken wire in the winding. The coil must then be replaced.

Measuring the resistance between the field coil leads (Courtesy Yamaha Int. Corp.)

3. Measure the resistance between either lead and the core. Resistance should be infinite. If continuity exists, the core is grounded. Check for damaged insulation. Be sure that the leads are not making contact with the backing plate. Replace the field coil if the ground cannot be found.

4. Check the alternator stator with an ohmmeter.

5. Check the resistance between each of the three white lead wires coming from the alternator and the bare metal of the stator coil assembly core. There should be infinite resistance between each alternator lead and the core.

If continuity exists, replace the coil assembly.

6. The stator coil windings must be checked for continuity. If each wire lead is lettered "A," "B," or "C," check the resistance between all of them: A-B, A-C, and B-C. In each case, resistance between the leads should be about 0.7 ohms.

If a higher or infinite resistance is obtained, one of the coils has a broken wire and the assembly must be replaced.

RECTIFIER

Use either a continuity (test) light or a *low-voltage* ohmmeter to test the rectifier.

1. Disconnect the rectifier from the alternator, and the red and black rectifier wires from their connectors.

2. Attach the ohmmeter or continuity light to the black and the red leads of the rectifier. Note the resistance reading or whether or not the test light goes on. Then reverse the meter or light leads. Note the meter reading or the action of the test light.

3. If current flows in both directions (resistance: zero; test light ON), replace the rectifier.

4. If current flows in neither direction (resistance: infinite; test light OFF), replace the rectifier.

5. The ohmmeter must read zero resistance or the test light must go on in only one of the two connection positions.

VOLTAGE REGULATOR

1. The voltage regulator may be checked while installed on the machine using a voltmeter.

2. The battery *must* be fully charged if valid results are to be obtained.

3. The battery must remain connected throughout the test.

4. Start the engine and increase speed until tach exceeds 2000 rpm. Measure the battery voltage across the terminals.

If 14.5v is obtained, the voltage regulator is in good condition.

If reading is below 13.5v, the regulator must be replaced.

If reading is 13.5–15.0v, the regulator should be removed and a substitute fitted. If the voltage then reads 14.5v, the original regulator was defective.

Testing questionable regulators requires the use of special equipment. Substitution is the easiest method.

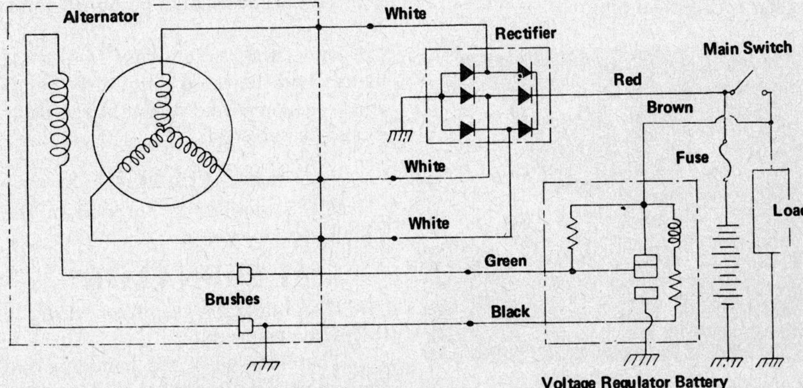

650 charging circuit (Courtesy Yamaha Int. Corp.)

650

Ignition Circuit

Refer to the "Ignition Circuit" section for the TX500, preceding; the 650 condensers are on the left side of the top engine mounting bracket. Otherwise, procedures and specifications are the same as for the TX500.

IGNITION COIL

Refer to the "Ignition Coil" section for the TX500, above. Procedures are the same, only the coil should be able to produce a spark across an 8mm gap.

CONDENSER

Refer to the "Condenser" section for the TX500, above. Turn the "CAP CAL" knob until the meter needle is mid-range on the red meter scale for "Capacitance." When switched to "TEST," the needle should not move very far into the red area, or the condenser is defective.

Charging Circuit

CHARGING VOLTAGE OUTPUT

1. Start the engine.
2. Disconnect the red wire at the fuse box. Attach a voltmeter lead the red wire (regulator side of the fuse box) and the other meter lead to ground.
3. Start the engine and run it up to 2500 rpm. The voltmeter should read 14.5–15v.
4. If voltage is lower than this value, regulator, rectifier, and alternator should be checked.

VOLTAGE REGULATOR

The voltage regulator is reached by removing the right side cover.

1. Disconnect the red wire at the fuse box (as above), start the engine, and hook up a voltmeter from the fuse box to ground. Voltage reading should be 14.5–15v. If voltage is either too low or too high, procede as described below.
2. Remove the regulator housing. Note the adjusting screw which bears on a flat spring steel plate.

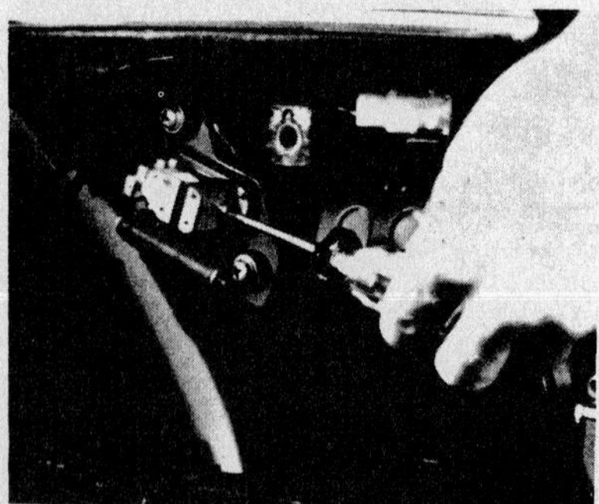

Adjusting the voltage regulator (Courtesy Yamaha Int. Corp.)

3. Turn the screw in or out to adjust the voltage to the proper value. Turning the screw IN raises the charging voltage, while turning the screw OUT decreases the charging voltage.
4. If this does not bring the charging voltage to within specification, make a visual inspection of the regulator. Note any pitting of the contact points. Be sure the points are not stuck together. Replace the regulator if necessary.
5. For further tests, make sure the engine and electrical system are off. Disconnect the regulator wires at the plastic connector junction.

Testing the voltage regulator (Courtesy Yamaha Int. Corp.)

6. Attach an ohmmeter to the black regulator wire and to the regulator base (ground). It should read zero resistance.
7. Attach the ohmmeter leads to the brown and green regulator leads. Remove the regulator housing if this has not already been done.
8. Move the central contact point as indicated below and note the readings. When the central contact point is held against the top point, resistance should be zero.

When the central contact point is midway between the top and bottom points, resistance should be 9–10 ohms.

When the central point is held against the bottom point, resistance should be 7–8 ohms.

9. Connect the ohmmeter leads across the black and the brown regulator wires. Hold the central point against the top point. Resistance should be 36–38 ohms.

If any of the reading vary from these figures, and the cause is not dirty points and broken or frayed wires, the regulator should be replaced.

RECTIFIER

Test the rectifier as outlined in the TX500 section, above.

ALTERNATOR

1. Disconnect the alternator wiring at the plastic connector.
2. There are six wires joined at the connector. Note the following tests.
3. Connect ohmmeter leads across the white wires. Do two wires at a time. If the wires were lettered "A" "B," and "C," reading would be taken across A-B, A-C, and B-C. In all cases, resistance should be 0.8–1.0 ohms.

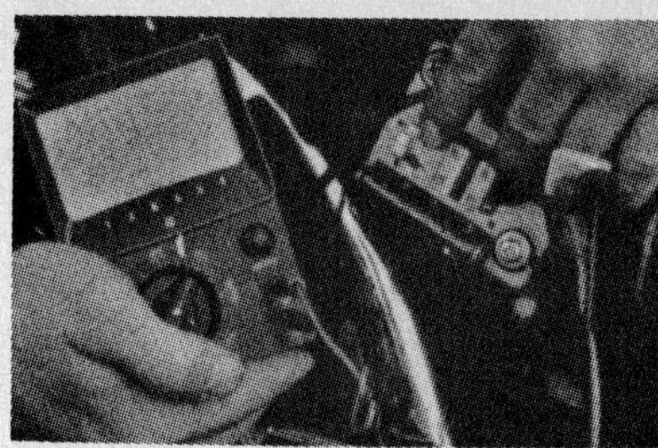

Testing the voltage regulator (Courtesy Yamaha Int. Corp.)

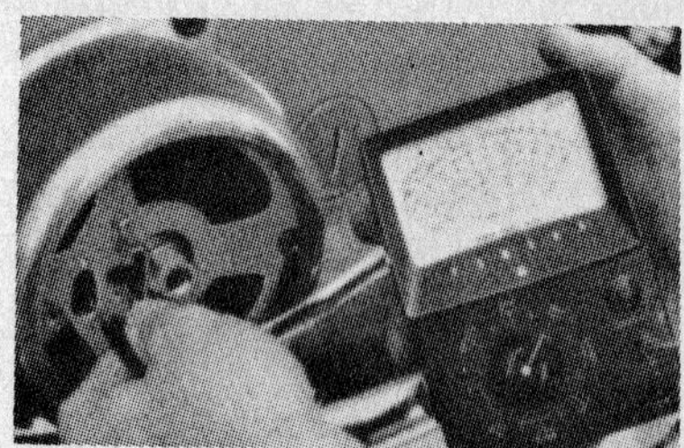

Checking slip ring resistance (Courtesy Yamaha Int. Corp.)

4. Adjusting the ohmmeter scale to the highest range, attach one meter lead to the stator housing and the other to each white wire, one at a time.

In each case, the resistance should be infinite.

5. If resistance readings vary from the above, the entire alternator stator winding assembly must be replaced.
6. Visually inspect the condition of the carbon brushes for wear or flaking. Brush length (new) is 14.5mm (0.57 in.). Replace the brushes if they are shorter than 7.0mm (0.28 in.).
7. The carbon brushes are connected to the black and green alternator wires. After disconnecting the alternator wires plastic junction, check the resistance between the green wire and the carbon brush and then the black wire and its carbon brush. In both cases resistance should equal zero ohms, or the wire(s) will have to be replaced.
8. Check the resistance between the slip rings as shown. Resistance should be

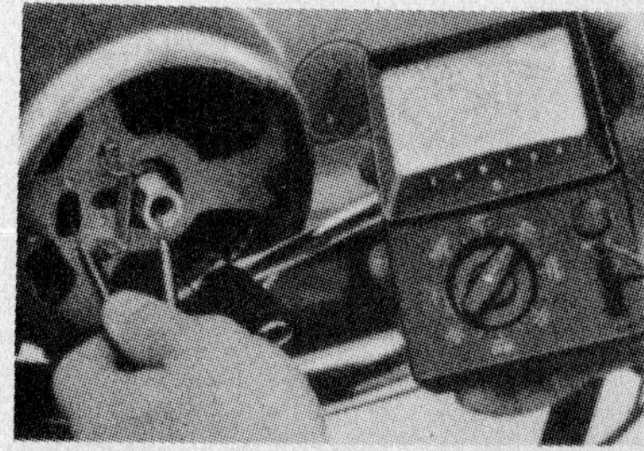

Checking the slip rings for grounds (slip ring to rotor core) (Courtesy Yamaha Int. Corp.)

5–7 ohms. Note that both slip rings must be clean for an accurate reading.

9. Using the ohmmeter's highest scale, measure the resistance between each slip ring and the rotor core. Resistance must be infinite.

10. If readings vary from those above, the field coil winding should be replaced.

750

Ignition Circuit

Refer to "Ignition Circuit" section for the TX500, above. The condensers are mounted beneath the front of the seat under the fuel tank.

IGNITION COIL

Refer to the "Ignition Coil" section for the TX500, above. Procedures and specifications are the same for the TX750.

CONDENSER

Refer to the "Condenser" section for the TX500, above. Procedures and specifications are the same for the TX750.

Charging Circuit

ALTERNATOR

When measuring the resistance across the two alternator leads, a reading of 4.9 ohms should be obtained. Other than this, alternator test procedures and specifications for the TX750 are the same as those for the TX500. Refer to "Charging Circuit-Alternator," above.

RECTIFIER

Refer to the "Rectifier" section of the TX500, above.

VOLTAGE REGULATOR

The voltage regulator found on the TX750 is similar to that of the 650cc machines in that it is adjustable by means of a screw.

To adjust the TX750 regulator, first adjust the core gap and point gap.

Core gap: 0.6–1.0mm
Point gap: 0.3–0.4mm

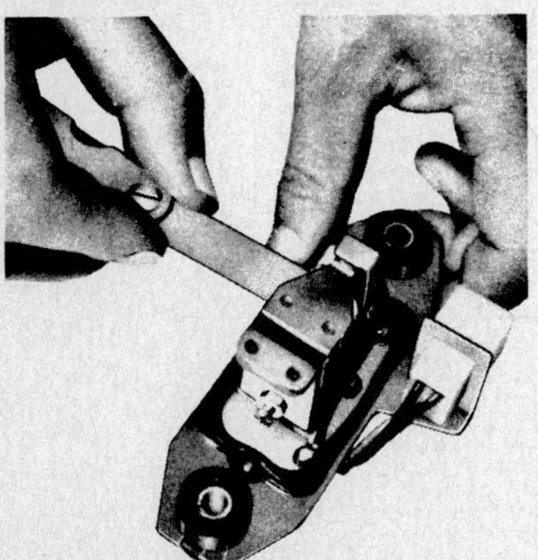

Checking the regulator point gap (Courtesy Yamaha Int. Corp.)

Cleaning the electric starter armature commutator (Courtesy Yamaha Int. Corp.)

Measuring commutator diameter (Courtesy Yamaha Int. Corp.)

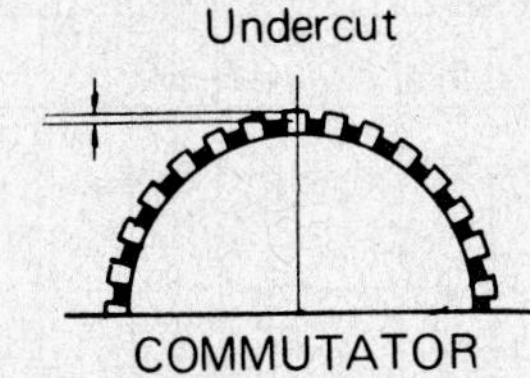

Checking commutator undercut (Courtesy Yamaha Int. Corp.)

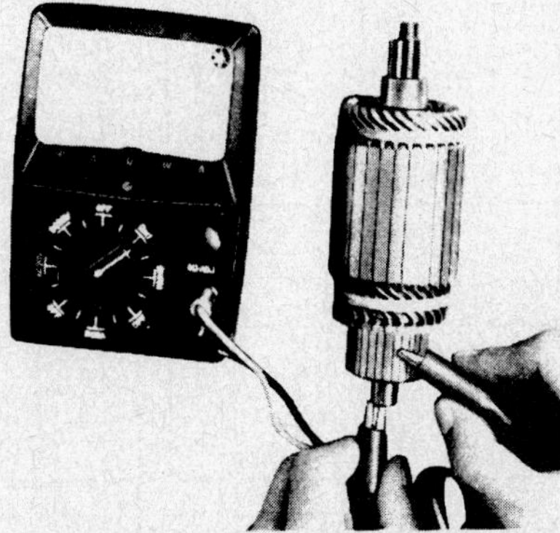

Checking the commutator segments for grounds to the core (Courtesy Yamaha Int. Corp.)

Make sure the point connections are clean and free of pitting.

Adjust as described under 650 "Voltage Regulator" so that the charging voltage is 14.5–15v at 2500 rpm.

Starter Motors

Two types of starter motors are used: Mitsubishi MAD01-D (TX500) and Hitachi S108-37(TX650,750). Procedures are similar. For specifications, refer to the charts at the end of the "Electrical Systems" section.

1. After removing the starter motor, take off the end cover, and pull out the armature.

2. Clean off the commutator surface with #600 grit sandpaper. After cleaning, wash thoroughly with electrical contact cleaner and blow dry.

3. The mica insulation between the commutator segments 0.5–0.8mm (0.-002–0.003 in.) (Hitachi) or 0.7–1.0mm (0.-003–0.004 in.) (Mitsubishi) below the commutator segments. Use a hacksaw blade to achieve the correct undercut if necessary.

4. With an ohmmeter, check the resistance between each of the commutator segments and the others. There should be zero resistance.

5. Check the resistance between each commutator segment and the armature core. If resistance is less than 3 million ohms, replace the armature.

6. Check the commutator surface for scoring or wear. The commutator may be turned down on a lathe if necessary. Refer to the specifications chart for minimum allowable diameter.

7. Check the armature for scoring. In most cases, score marks will have been caused by the armature grounding out against the field coils in the case. This is often indicated by a "dead spot" in the motor during operation. In this case, check the armature bearings, since they are probably in need of replacement.

8. Check the carbon brushes for wear. Minimum allowable length is 4.5mm (0.18 in.).

9. Clean the brush area and the starter motor housing with a solvent, then blow out with compressed air.

10. Check the resistance of each field coil and the resistance of each coil to ground against the chart specifications.

11. Check the oil seals and replace if cracked, worn, or hardened. Smear the lips of the seals with lithium soap base grease when reassembling.

12. Inspect the armature bearings for wear. Replace as necessary. Apply a light coat of 20W or 30W oil to each of the non-sealed bearings before assembly.

Turn Signals

1. If the turn signals fail to work, check for a broken wire or a short in the turn signal switch.

2. If the signals blink too quickly or too slowly, check for a burned out bulb. Check that all bulbs are the correct wattage.

3. If the turn signals blink too slowly and all the bulbs are good, replace the turn signal condenser.

WIRING DIAGRAMS

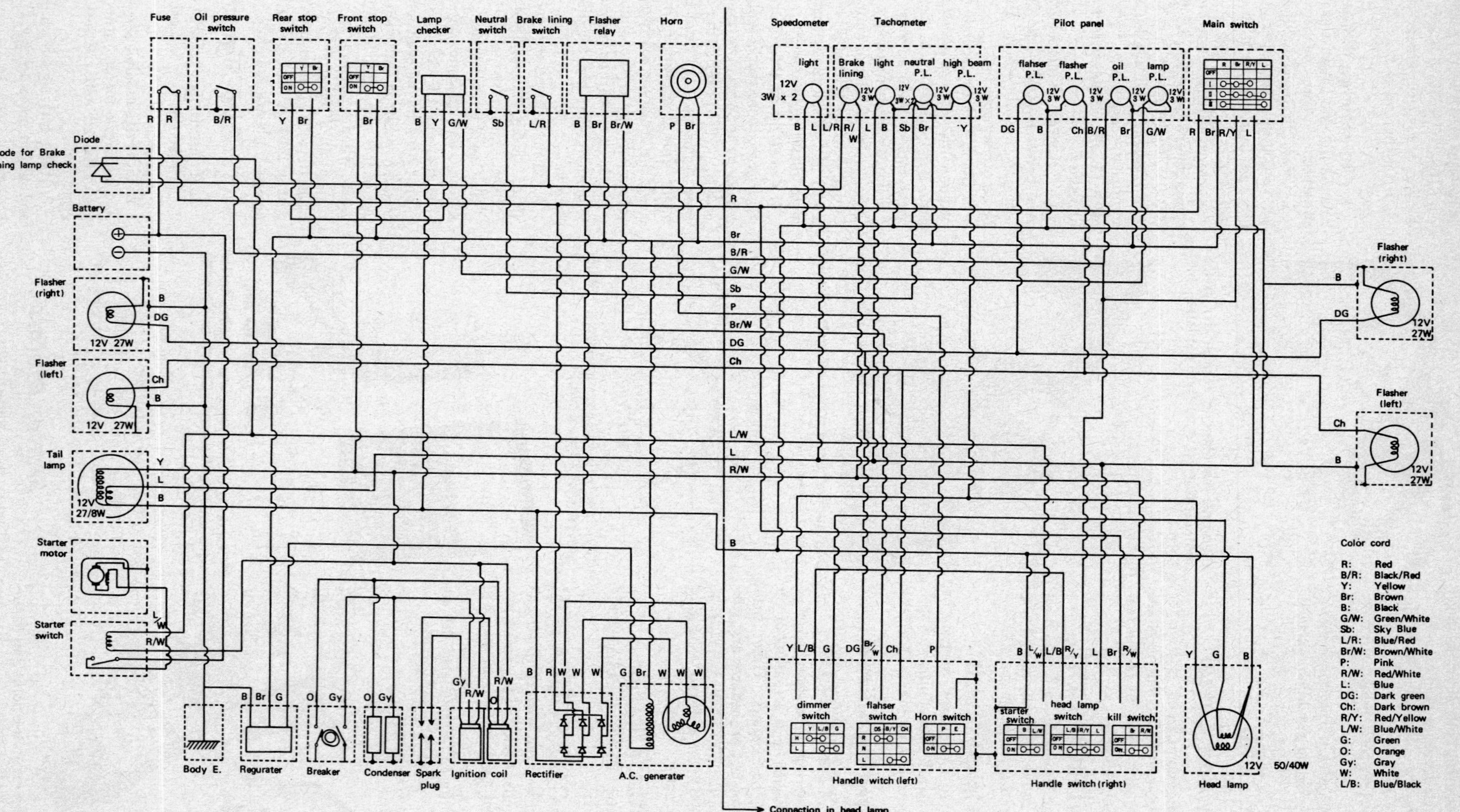

TX500 (Courtesy Yamaha Int. Corp.)

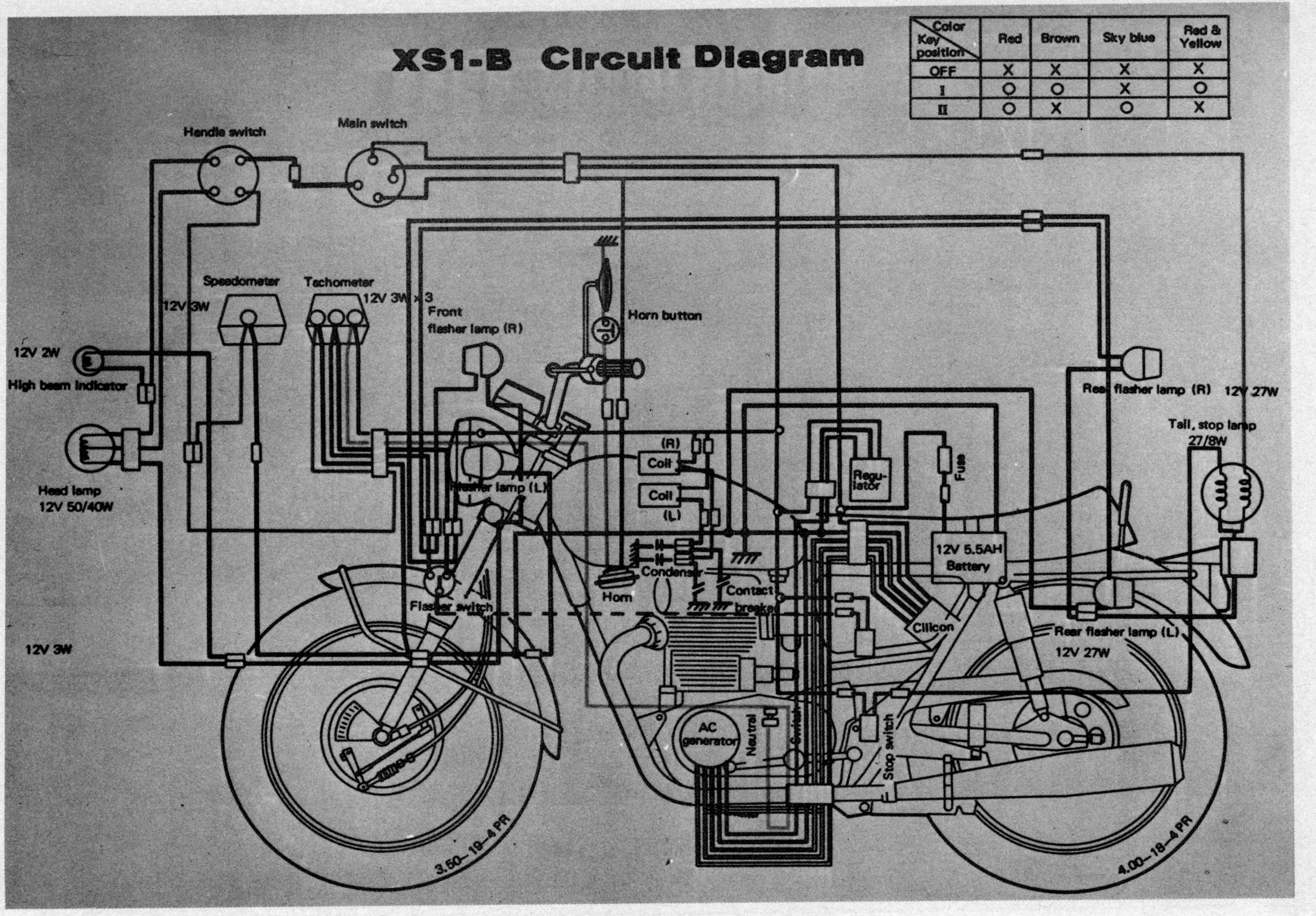

XS1B (Courtesy Yamaha Int. Corp.)

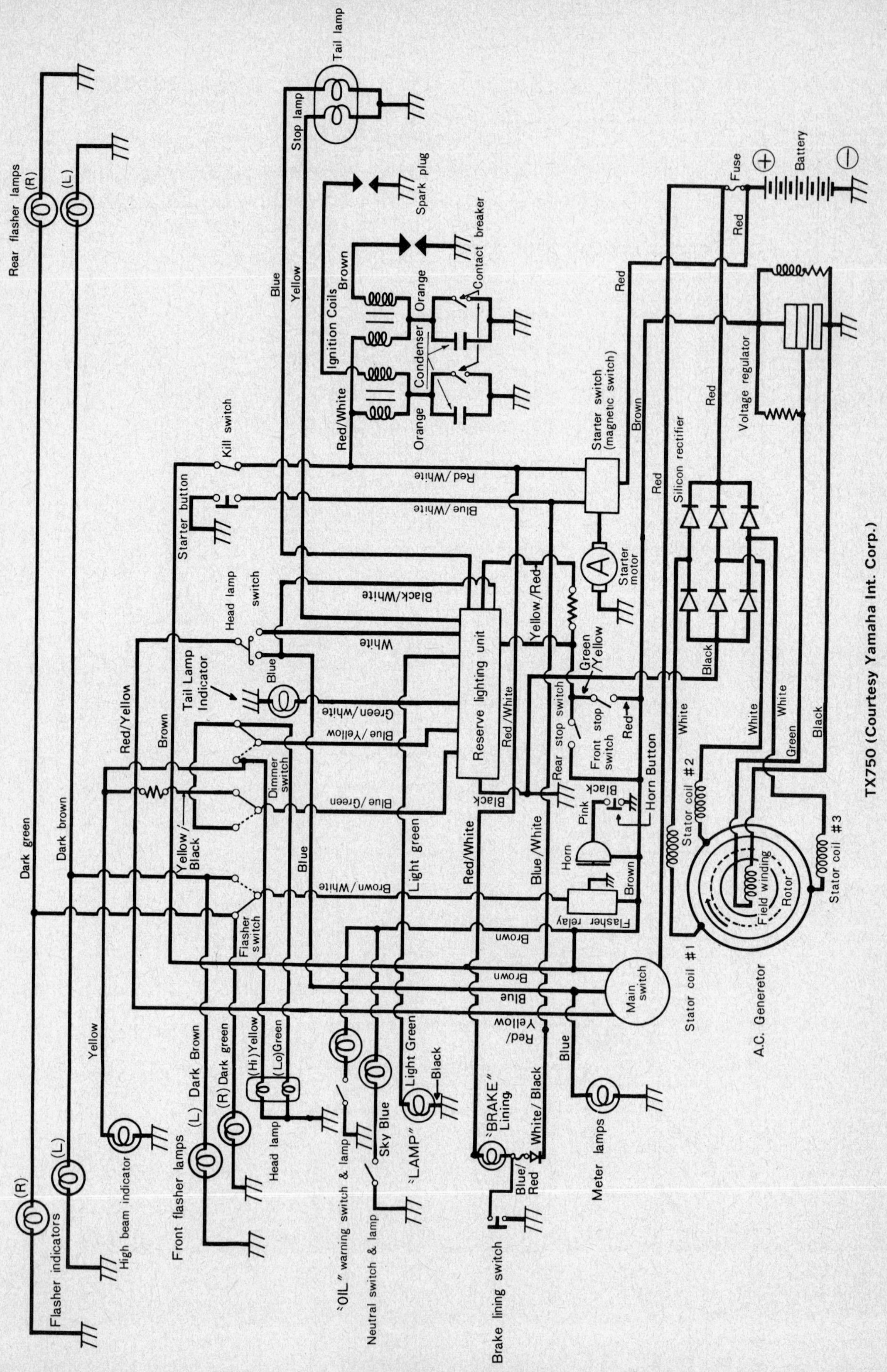

TX750 (Courtesy Yamaha Int. Corp.)

ELECTRICAL SPECIFICATIONS

Battery

500, 750	12v, 16 a-h
650	12v, 5.5 a-h

Bulb Specifications

Headlight	12v, 50/40W	Charging light	12v, 3W
Taillight-Stoplight	12v, 8/27W	Turn signal pilot	12v, 3W
Turn signal bulbs	12v, 27W	Instrument lights	12v, 3W
Parking light, front	12v, 5W	Oil warning light	12v, 3W
Parking light, rear	12v, 8W	Taillight warning light	12v, 3W
Neutral indicator	12v, 3W	Brake lining warning light	12v, 3W
Hight beam indicator	12v, 3W	Stoplight warning light	12v, 3W

STARTER MOTOR SPECIFICATIONS

Mitsubishi MAD01-D (TX500)

Field Coils	
Resistance (standard) (ohms)	0.01
Resistance (acceptable range) (ohms)	0.005-0.015
Brushes	
Dimensions (mm)	6 x 14 x 12.5
Length limit (mm)	4.5
Commutator	
Diameter (mm)	28.0
Wear limit (mm)	26.0
Mica undercut (mm)	0.7-0.1
Undercut limit (mm)	0.2
Max allowable runout (mm)	0.15
Brush Spring	
Standard pressure (gr)	650
Solenoid	
Point gap (mm)	1.5
Winding resistance (ohms)	3.1
Cut-in voltage (v)	8.0
Cut-out voltage (v)	3.0
Starter Motor Operation	
Max Draw (no load) (amps)	42
Load (580 rpm)	8.7v; 100A
Constraint (max)	4v; 300A

Hitachi S108-37 (TX 650, 750)

Field Coils	
Resistance (standard) (ohms)	0.05
Resistance (acceptable range) (ohms)	0.045-0.055
Brushes	
Dimensions (mm)	16 x 7 x 11
Length limit (mm)	4.5
Commutator	
Diameter (mm)	33
Wear limit (mm)	32
Mica undercut (mm)	0.5-0.8
Undercut limit (mm)	0.2
Max allowable runout (mm)	0.15
Brush Spring	
Standard pressure (gr)	800
Solenoid	
Core gap (mm)	1.55-1.88
Point gap (mm)	0.88-1.11
Winding resistance (ohms)	3.5
Cut-in voltage (v)	6.5
Cut-out voltage (v)	4.0
Coil circuit draw (amps)	4.0
Starter Motor Operation	
Max Draw (no load) (amps)	42
Load (580 rpm)	8.7v; 100A

WHEELS

Front

REMOVAL AND INSTALLATION

500 and 750

1. Remove the front axle nut cotter pin. Remove the axle nut.
2. Loosen the two axle cap nuts at the bottom of each fork leg.
3. Slide out the axle. Pull out the front wheel assembly, take off the speedometer drive, and place the wheel aside.
4. When installing, grease the speedometer drive with chassis grease, then install it on the forks, as shown, then replace the front wheel.

Front Wheel Torque Specifications

Location	*Torque (ft lbs)*
axle nut	50-72
axle cap nuts	5.3-9

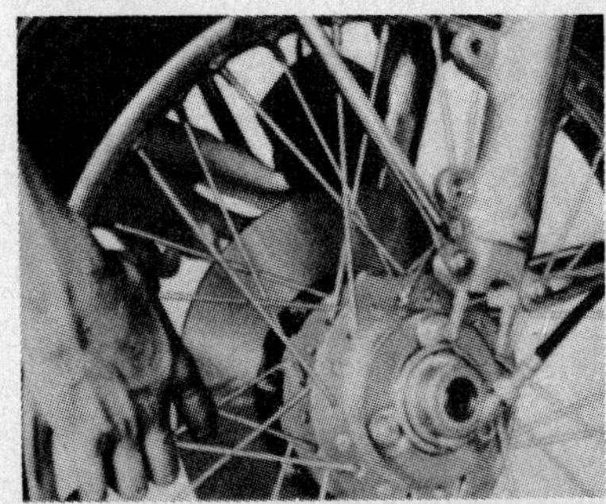

Removing the front wheel (Courtesy Yamaha Int. Corp.)

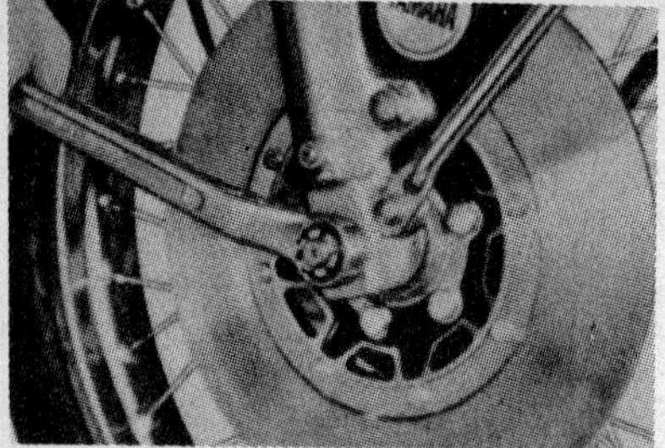

Removing the front axle nut (Courtesy Yamaha Int. Corp.)

Removing the axle cap nuts (Courtesy Yamaha Int. Corp.)

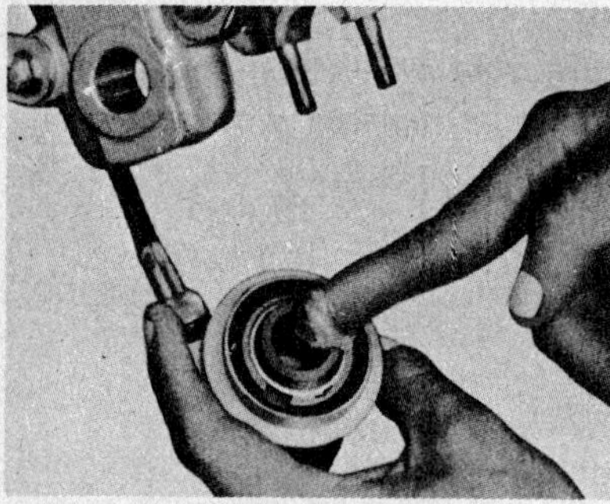

Greasing the speedometer drive (Courtesy Yamaha Int. Corp.)

Speedometer drive installed properly (Courtesy Yamaha Int. Corp.)

650

1. Remove the axle nut.
2. Disconnect the speedometer cable at the hub. On drum brake models, disconnect the brake cable.
3. Loosen the axle pinch bolt on the right fork slider, and pull out the axle. Remove the front wheel.
4. When installing the wheel, be sure that the brake hub is engaged with the anchor on the slider (drum brake).

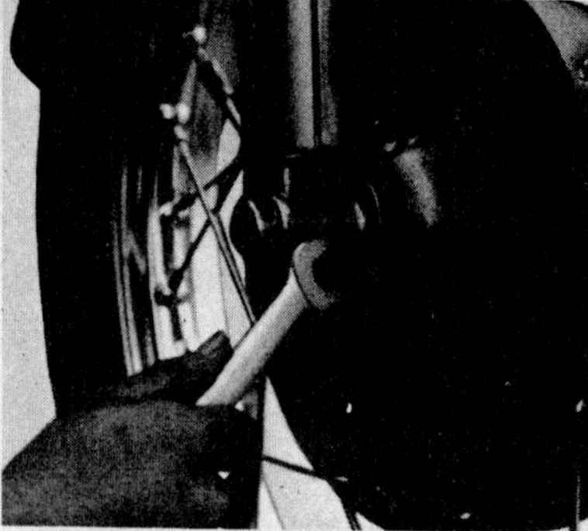

Loosening the fork slider pinch bolt (Courtesy Yamaha Int. Corp.)

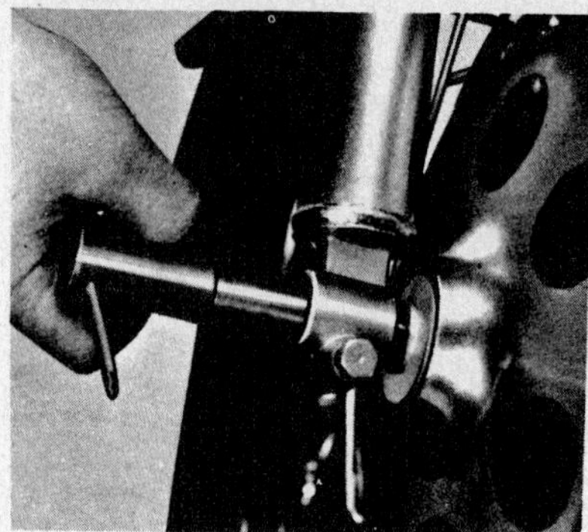

Removing the axle (Courtesy Yamaha Int. Corp.)

Rear

REMOVAL AND INSTALLATION

500 and 750

1. Remove the mufflers.
2. "Break" the drive chain with the special tool (the masterlink cover plate is pressed on).
3. Remove the brake anchor nut at the rear hub. Note that the lockwasher and cotter pin must be installed when the wheel is refitted. Disconnect the brake warning light lead, if fitted.
4. Disconnect the brake anchor from the hub. Disconnect the brake rod from the lever on the hub.
5. Loosen the chain adjuster locknuts.
6. Remove the axle nut cotter pin. Remove the axle nut; loosen the axle pinch bolts on either side of the swing arm.
7. Remove the wheel by leaning the machine to the left and pulling the wheel back.
8. Upon installation, note the following torque specifications:

Rear Wheel Torque Specifications

Location	*Torque (ft lbs)*
axle nut	150
pinch bolts	15
brake anchor nut	10-15

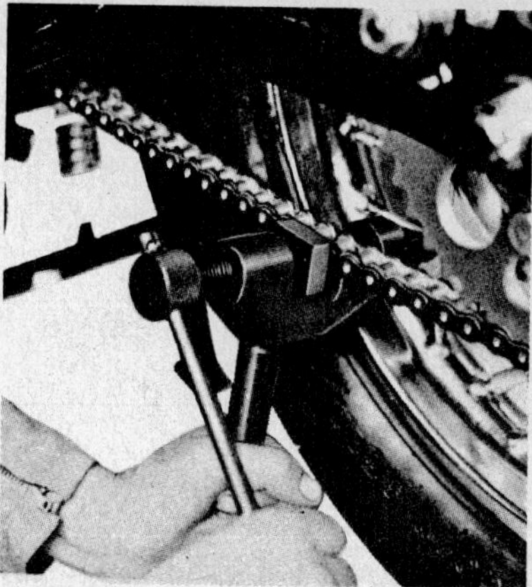

Breaking the drive chain with the special tool (Courtesy Yamaha Int. Corp.)

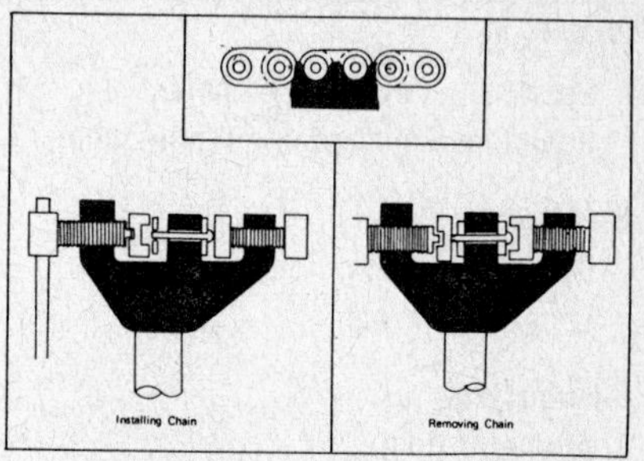

How the chain breaker works (Courtesy Yamaha Int. Corp.)

Removing the rear axle nut cotter pin (Courtesy Yamaha Int. Corp.)

Removing the rear axle nut (Courtesy Yamaha Int. Corp.)

NOTE: *It may be possible to push the rear wheel all the way forward in the swing arm, and then slip the chain off the sprocket without "breaking" it. This will be easier with a worn chain than a new one.*

650

1. Disconnect the rear drive chain.

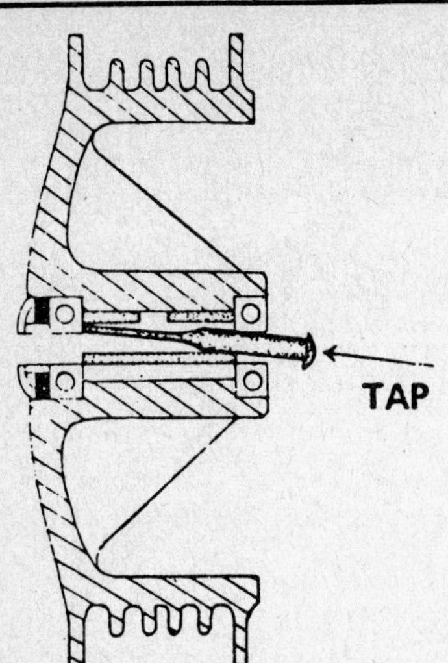

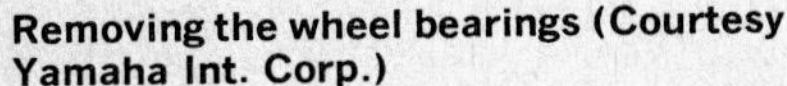

Removing the wheel bearings (Courtesy Yamaha Int. Corp.)

2. Pull out the clip which secures the brake anchor to the brake drum, and disengage the anchor from the stud.
3. Disconnect the rear brake rod.
4. Remove the cotter pin from the axle nut, then remove the axle nut.
5. Loosen the chain adjuster bolts, and remove the adjusters from the swing arm.
6. Pull out the axle. Remove the spacer on the right side.
7. Take out the brake drum, and lean the machine to the left while pulling the rear wheel assembly back and out of the frame.
8. Assembly is the reverse of the above. Tighten the axle nut to 50 ft lbs.

Wheel Bearings

Wheels are fitted with grease seals on either side of the bearings.

To remove the bearings, the seals must be pried out, and new units must be installed when the wheel is reassembled.

To remove the wheel bearings, pry out the grease seals. Move the bearing spacer off to one side, and reach through the hub with a drift to tap out the bearing. Tap out the remaining bearing in the same manner.

Remove the spacer from the hub and clean it in a solvent. Clean out the old grease in the hub cavity as well.

Clean the bearings thoroughly and

1. Hub, rear
2. Spoke set
3. Tire, rear (4.00-18-4PR)
4. Tube (4.00-18)
5. Rim (2.15B-18)
6. Band, rim (4.00-18)
7. Spacer, bearing
8. Flange, spacer
9. Bearing (B6304Z)
10. Oil seal (SO-27-52-5)
11. Brake shoe comp.
12. Spring, return
13. Plate, brake shoe
14. Camshaft
15. Shim, cam shaft
16. Seal, cam shaft
17. Lever, cam shaft
18. Bolt
19. Collar
20. Bearing (B6305Z)
21. Damper, clutch
22. Clutch, hub
23. O-ring (3.0-76.0)
24. Gear, sprocket wheel (43T)
25. Bolt, fitting
26. Washer, lock
27. Chain (DK530HDS 105L)
28. Joint, chain
29. Retainer, bearing
30. Nut, lock
31. Oil seal (SD-30-52-8)
32. Collar, shaft
33. Cover, dust
34. Puller, chain
35. Bolt, chain puller
36. Nut
37. Nut, shaft
38. Pin, cotter
39. Collar, wheel shaft
40. Shaft, wheel
41. Bar, tension
42. Bolt, tension bar 2
43. Bolt, tension bar
44. Washer, plain
45. Washer, spring
46. Nut
47. Nut
48. Pin, cotter
49. Balancer, wheel

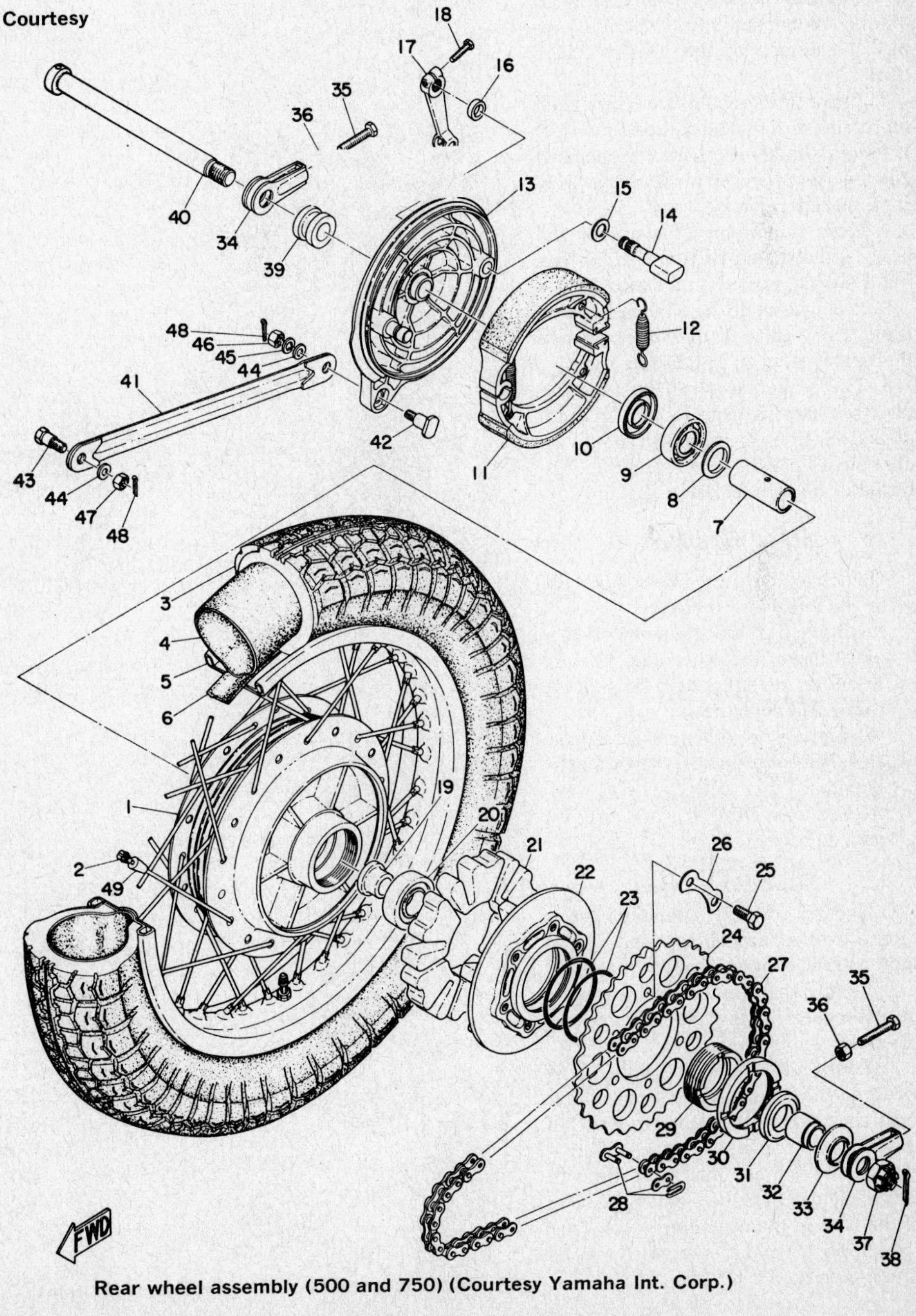

Rear wheel assembly (500 and 750) (Courtesy Yamaha Int. Corp.)

check for wear or damage, smooth rotation, or discoloration.

Pack the bearings with a good grade of chassis grease, and add a quantity to the hub cavity.

To install the bearings, use a drift which will allow the bearings to be inserted straight into the hub.

Be sure to use new grease seals.

BRAKE SERVICE

Drum Brakes

1. All rear drum brakes are single leading shoe units, while the drum fitted to the front of early 650cc models is a twin leading shoe unit.
2. Brake shoes should be inspected for wear. Lining thickness, when new, is 4mm (0.16 in.), and brakes should be replaced if lining is less than 2mm (0.08 in.) thick.
3. Brake shoes should also be checked for scoring or for an oil-soaked condition. If scored, the linings should be replaced and the drum checked for scoring as well. If oil soaked, replace.
4. Even minor imperfections of the brake drum should be removed by having the drum turned on a lathe.
5. Linings should be sandpapered to remove any glaze or dirt, then cleaned thoroughly prior to installation.
6. The brake shoes can be removed from the backing plate by pulling them up and off, after disengaging from the anchor pin. Check the brake springs for distortion, corrosion, or other damage.

Disc Brakes

When handling disc brake fluid, observe the following cautions:

a. Brake fluid absorbs moisture very quickly, and then becomes useless. Therefore, never use fluid from an old or unsealed container.

b. Brake fluid will quickly damage paint. Place a protective cover on the gas tank.

c. Use only DOT #3 or DOT #4 brake fluid.

BLEEDING

1. Needed for this operation are a torque wrench, a small cup, and a vinyl tube with an inside diameter of 4mm.
2. Be sure that the reservoir is topped up. After checking the reservoir level, replace the diaphragm.
3. Connect the vinyl tube to the bleed screw on the caliper, making sure that it is a tight fit; then insert the other end of the tube into a small container with several inches of brake fluid in it. Be sure that the end of the tube is below the level of the fluid in the container.
4. Apply the brake lever *slowly* several times, then hold it ON.

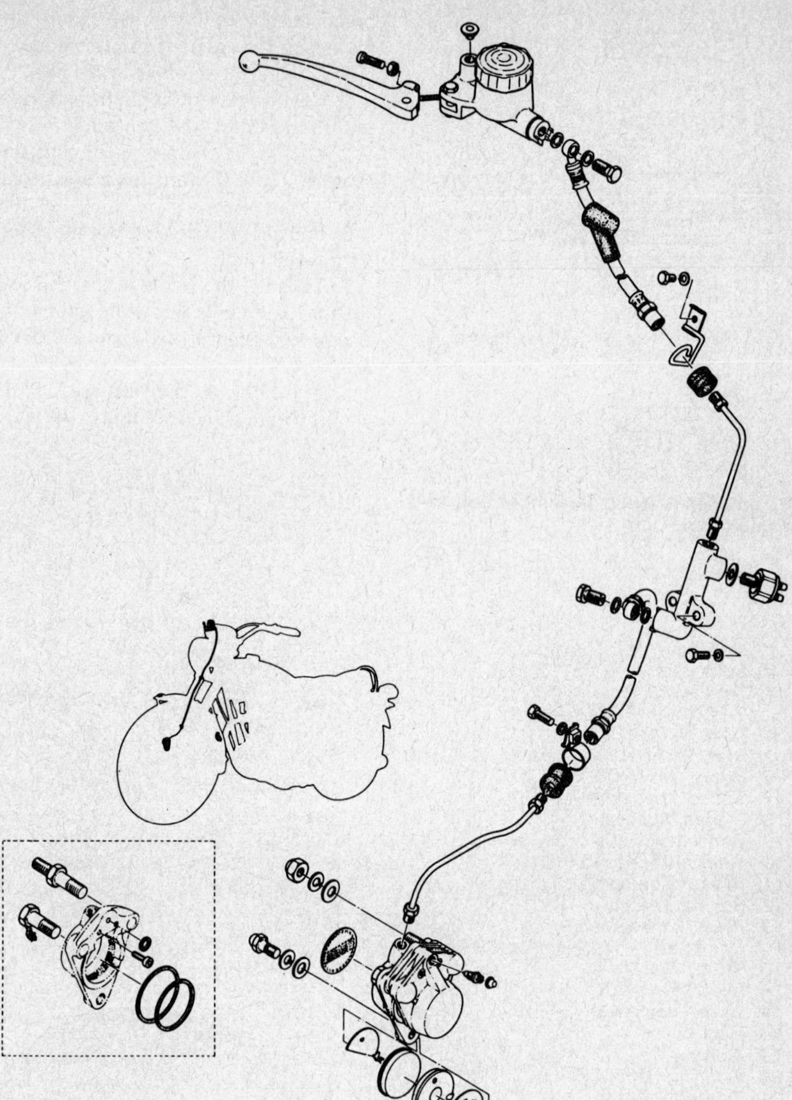

Disc brake system (Courtesy Yamaha Int. Corp.)

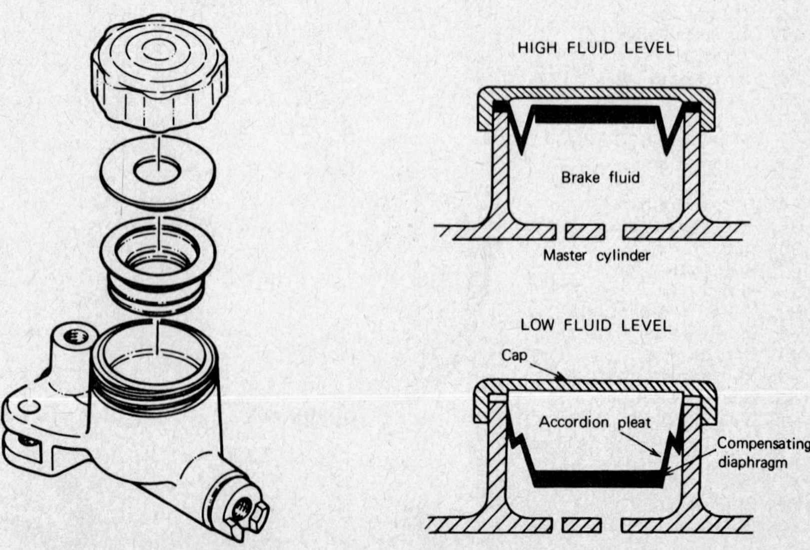

Brake fluid reservior and diaphragm positions (Courtesy Yamaha Int. Corp.)

Bleeding the front brake (Courtesy Yamaha Int. Corp.)

Loosening the bleed screw (Courtesy Yamaha Int. Corp.)

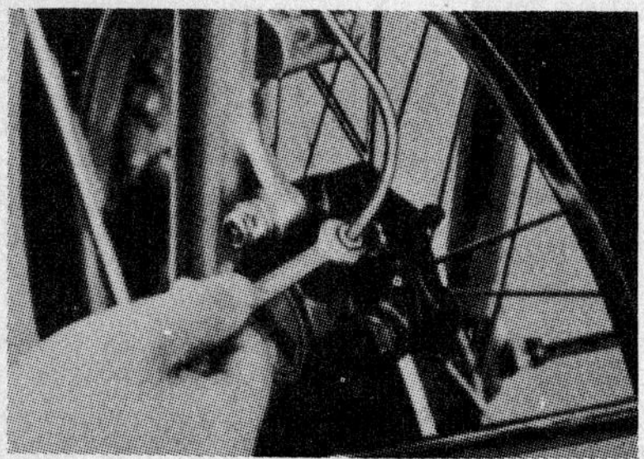

Loosening the brake line fitting (Courtesy Yamaha Int. Corp.)

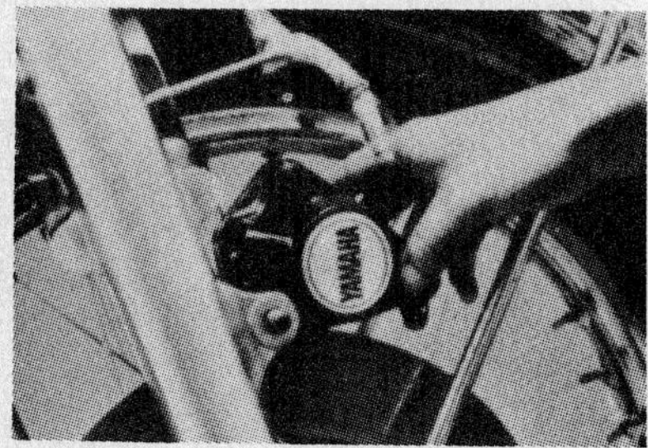

Removing the caliper (Courtesy Yamaha Int. Corp.)

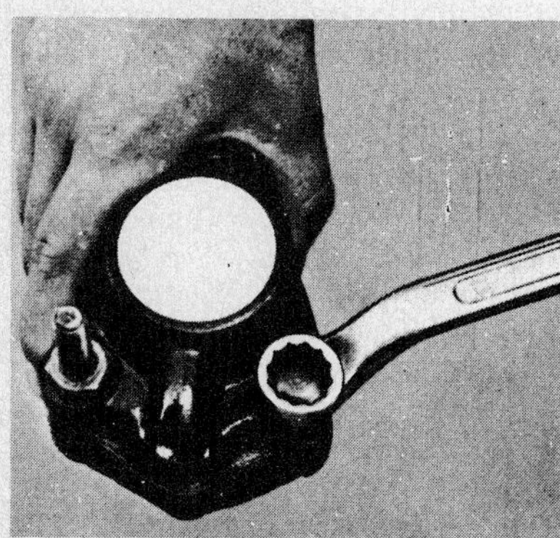

Removing the pads (Courtesy Yamaha Int. Corp.)

5. While holding the brake lever on, loosen the bleed screw. The brake lever will be pulled toward the handgrip. Close the bleed screw BEFORE the lever bottoms out on the handgrip.

6. Repeat the procedure until the fluid issuing from the lower end of the tube is completely free of air bubbles.

NOTE: *During the operation, keep a check on the reservoir fluid level, maintaining it near its normal position.*

7. Tighten the bleed screw to 4.5–6.7 ft lbs.

8. Top up the reservoir to the level line.

PADS

Brake pads are easily removed and replaced after removing the front wheel and taking the pads out of the caliper. Note that fitting new pads in place of a pair that were considerably worn will result in a rise in the reservoir fluid level. Drain off excess fluid via the bleed screw on the caliper. Minimum allowable pad thickness is 0.5mm (0.0196 in.)

CALIPER

Removal and Disassembly

NOTE: *A compressed air supply will be necessary to remove the pistons from the caliper.*

1. Use a length of tape to hold the brake lever in the "on" position.

2. Disconnect the brake line from the caliper. Cover the end of the line with a small plastic bag.

3. Unbolt the caliper, lift it up, and remove it.

4. Remove the pads. Remove the two bridge bolts and the hex-head caliper bolts, and separate the caliper halves.

5. Remove the seal from the fluid passage.

6. Apply compressed air to the fluid passage in each caliper half to force out the pistons.

NOTE: *This the only recommended method of removing the pistons.*

7. Remove the piston seal and the dust seal from each caliper half.

Inspection

NOTE: *Caliper components should be kept free of any solvent. Parts should be cleaned only in brake fluid.*

1. Check the pads for wear or scoring. Minimum allowable pad thickness is 0.5mm (0.0196 in.).

2. Inspect the pistons for scoring or other signs of wear. Replace as necessary.

3. Replace any damaged seal in the unit. All seals should be replaced every two years regardless of appearance.

4. The two bridge bolts *must* be replaced each time they are removed.

Assembly and Installation

1. Clean all parts in new brake fluid.

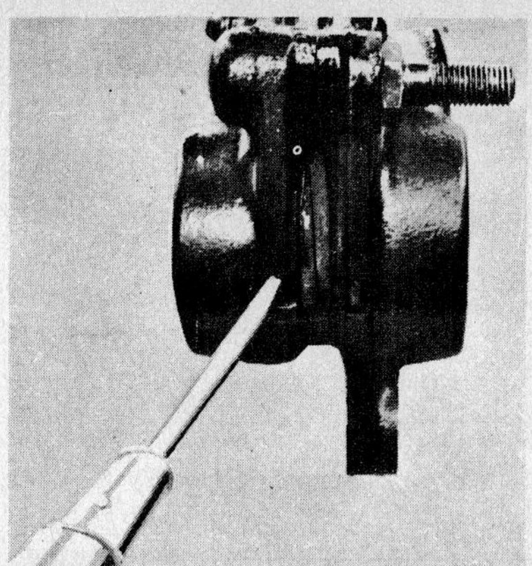

Separating the caliper halves (Courtesy Yamaha Int. Corp.)

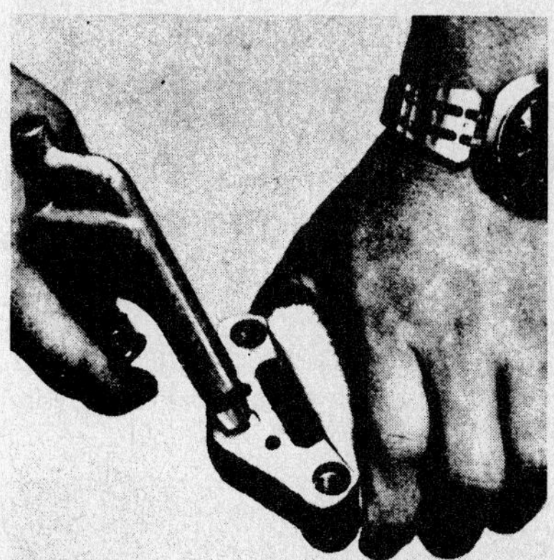

Removing the pistons (Courtesy Yamaha Int. Corp.)

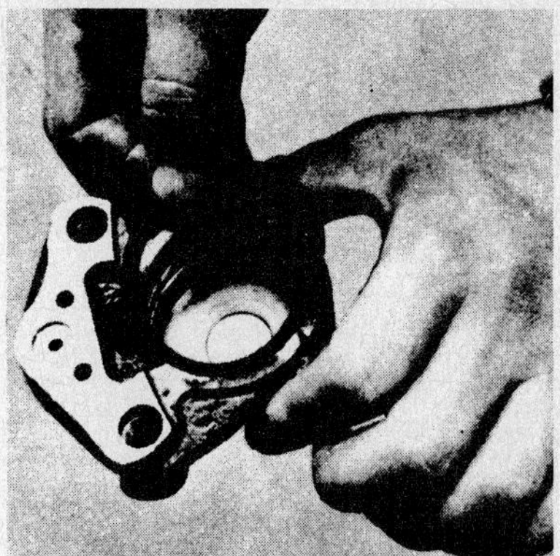

Removing the piston and dust seals (Courtesy Yamaha Int. Corp.)

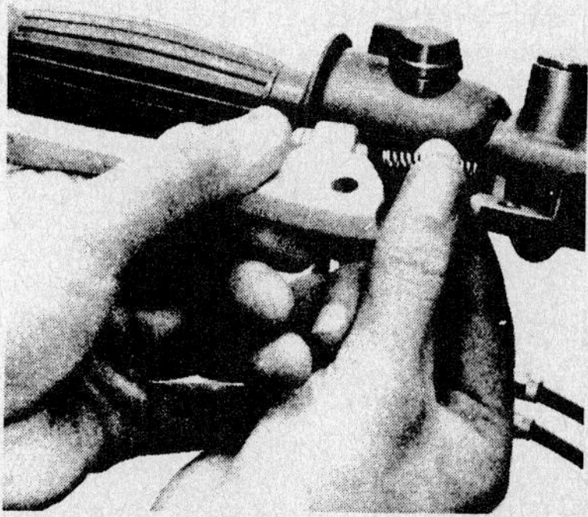

Removing the brake lever (Courtesy Yamaha Int. Corp.)

Removing the boot (Courtesy Yamaha Int. Corp.)

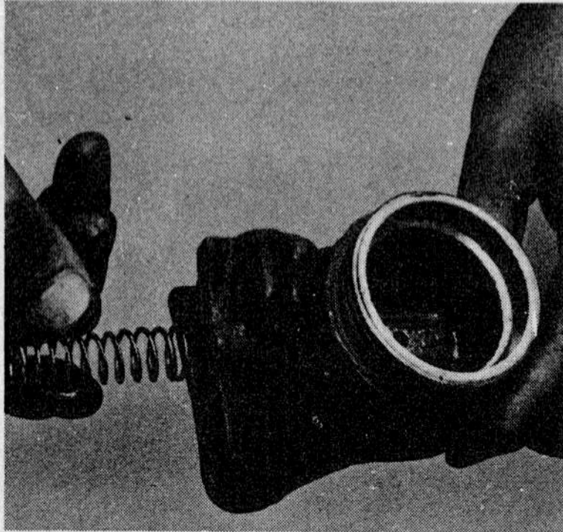

Removing the conical spring (Courtesy Yamaha Int. Corp.)

Removing the piston assembly (Courtesy Yamaha Int. Corp.)

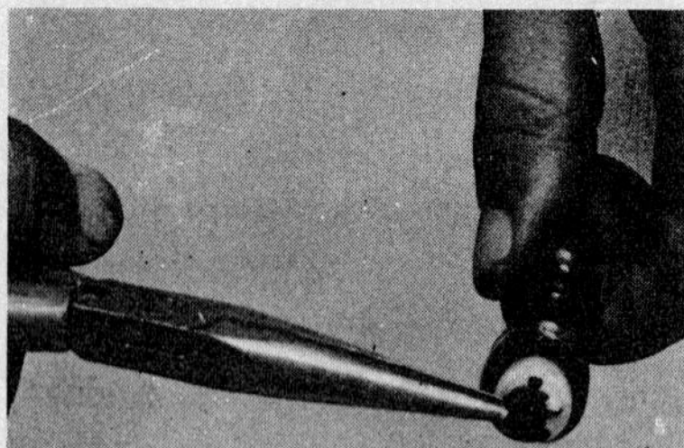

Removing the piston circlip (Courtesy Yamaha Int. Corp.)

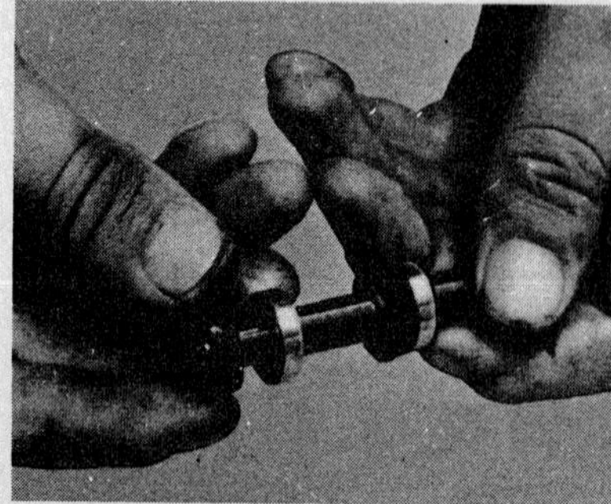

Removing the cylinder cup (Courtesy Yamaha Int. Corp.

2. Install the dust seal and piston seal in the caliper halves.

3. Coat the caliper cylinder walls and the pistons with new brake fluid, and then carefully insert each piston into its own caliper half.

Be sure that the piston goes in smoothly.

4. Install the caliper seals.

5. Fit the two caliper halves together, and replace the two hex-head bolts and tighten them to 16–23 ft. lbs.

6. Install new bridge bolts and tighten them to 56–71 ft lbs.

7. Install the pads. It will be necessary to push the pistons back by hand when installing the pads.

8. Replace the caliper on the fork slider, tightening the bolts to 30–37.2 ft lbs.

9. Refit the brake line to the caliper and tighten it to 10–13.4 ft lbs.

BRAKE DISC

1. Check the disc for runout by securing a dial gauge to the fork slider. If runout is 0.15mm or more, remove the disc and check it. If the disc is not warped, suspect the wheel bearings.

2. Measure the thickness of the disc. Minimum allowable thickness is 6.5mm.

MASTER CYLINDER

Removal and Disassembly

1. Remove the brakelight switch at the master cylinder, and remove the brake lever, watching for the return spring.

2. Disconnect the brake hose at the master cylinder.

3. Remove the master cylinder mounting bolts, and remove the assembly from the handlebar.

4. Remove the reservoir cap, take out the diaphragm, and drain off the fluid.

5. Remove the boot.

6. Remove the snap ring with a pair of snap ring pliers.

7. Take out the piston. Take out the spring behind the piston.

8. remove the circlip from the piston assembly, and take off the cylinder cup retainer, then the cylinder cup.

Inspection

1. Wash all parts in new brake fluid only.

2. Check the master cylinder port for clogging due to foreign matter.

3. Be sure that the reservoir is clean.

4. Check the walls of the master cylinder for grooves or score marks.

5. Check the outlet end for dents or other damage.

In the event of any permanent damage, replace the master cylinder body.

6. Check the piston for wear or rust and replace as necessary.

7. Check the condition of the cylinder cup noting any evidence of grooved wear on the contact surface. Replace if any is evident.

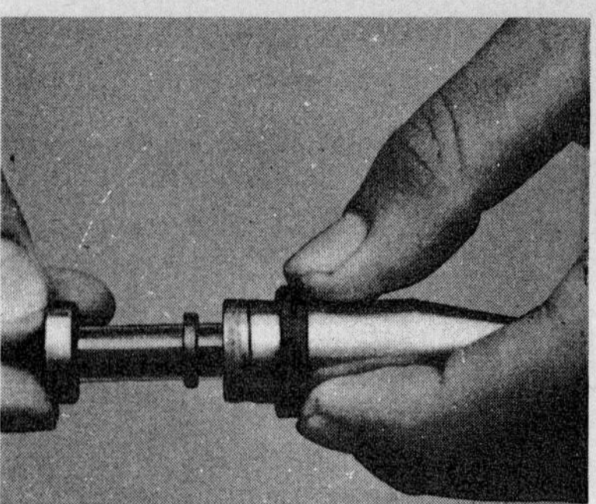

Installing the cup on the piston (Courtesy Yamaha Int. Corp.)

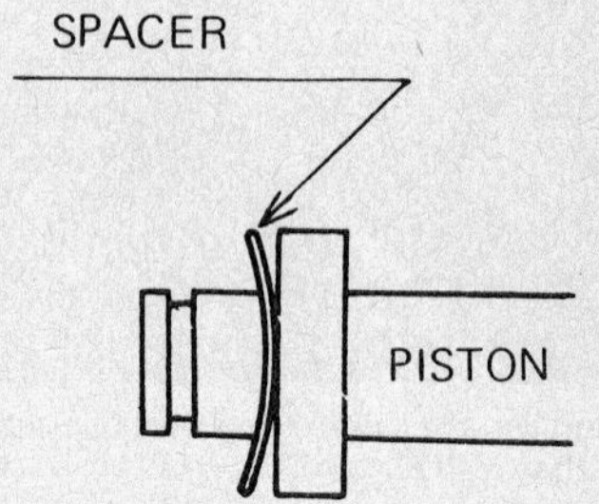

Spacer correctly installed (Courtesy Yamaha Int. Corp.)

8. Check all rubber parts for wear or damage or swelling. Replace if necessary. Note that all rubber parts should be replaced every two years regardless of appearance.

9. Check the reservoir diaphragm for cracks or damage to the edges and the accordian pleats. Check the diaphragm and the boot for swelling.

These components should be replaced if damaged or worn, and replaced every two years regardless of appearance.

10. The master cylinder spring minimum length is 60.4mm. Replace it if it is shorter than this or if it shows signs of damage.

11. Check the brake hose and line for cracks or seepage. The brake hose should be replaced every four years regardless of condition.

12. When installing the hose and line, note that they should not contact the forks or frame at any point except where attachment clips are fitted.

Assembly and Installation

1. Dip the cylinder cup in new brake fluid, and, using the special guide, install the cup on the piston.

2. Install the spacer. Note the correct position. Fit the cup retainer and circlip.

3. Fit the conical spring into the master cylinder body. Then carefully insert the piston assembly into the cylinder. Do not force the piston in.

4. Install the snap ring. Refit the boot, being sure that it is correctly installed in the cylinder and piston grooves.

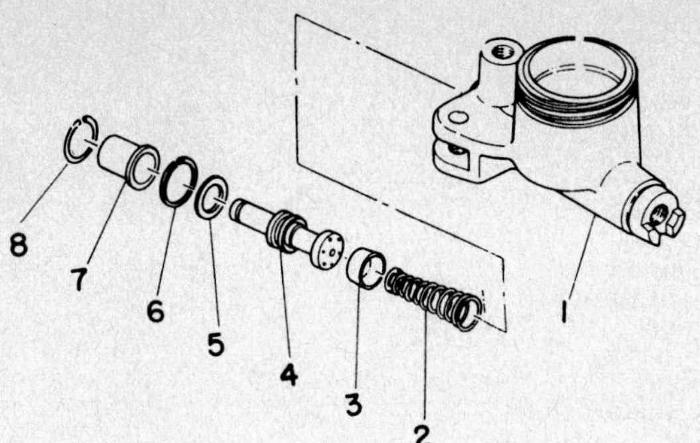

1. Master cylinder body
2. Conical spring
3. Cylinder cup
4. Piston ass'y
5. Spacer
6. Circlip
7. Master cylinder boot
8. Boot stopper

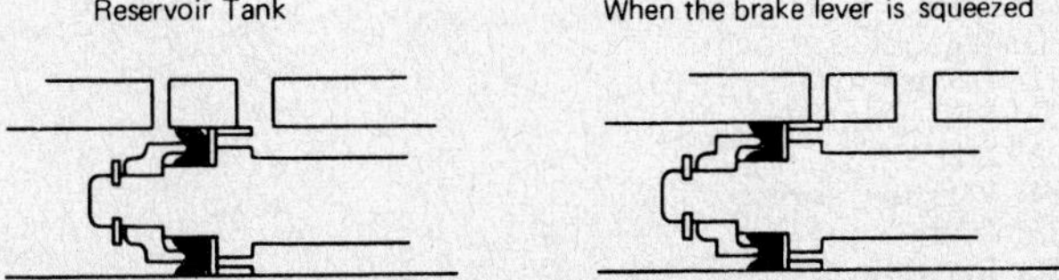

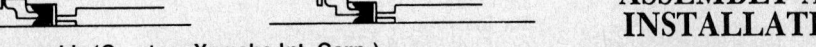

Fluid reservoir assembly (Courtesy Yamaha Int. Corp.)

5. Install the master cylinder on the handlebar. Adjust the clearance between the piston and pushrod. Make sure the adjusting screw locknut is firmly tightened.

6. Reconnect the brake hose. Put about 30cc of brake fluid into the reservoir.

7. Bleed the system as described above.

FORKS

500 and 750

REMOVAL AND DISASSEMBLY

1. Remove the front wheel and fender. Remove the caliper from the right fork slider. Remove the fork cap bolts.

2. Loosen the upper and lower triple clamp pinch bolts for one of the fork legs. Then pull down on the fork leg and remove it from the machine. Drain the oil out of the top of the fork tube.

3. Remove the dust cover from the top of the fork slider. Remove the bolt at the bottom of the slider.

4. Separate the fork slider from the tube assembly.

5. Remove the slider oil seal circlip, the washer, and then pry out the seal. New seals must always be used upon reassembly.

INSPECTION

1. Check that the fork tubes are perfectly true. If bent, they may be straightened with a press. If the tubes are kinked, or the metal creased, the tube must be replaced.

Check the outer surface of the fork tubes along the oil seal contact area. Any nicks or grooves in the tube must be removed or the seals will leak.

Removing the front wheel (Courtesy Yamaha Int. Corp.)

2. Check the fork spring for general condition, noting any closed coils or fatigue wear.

3. Check the piston for wear or damage.

ASSEMBLY AND INSTALLATION

1. Clean all parts thoroughly.

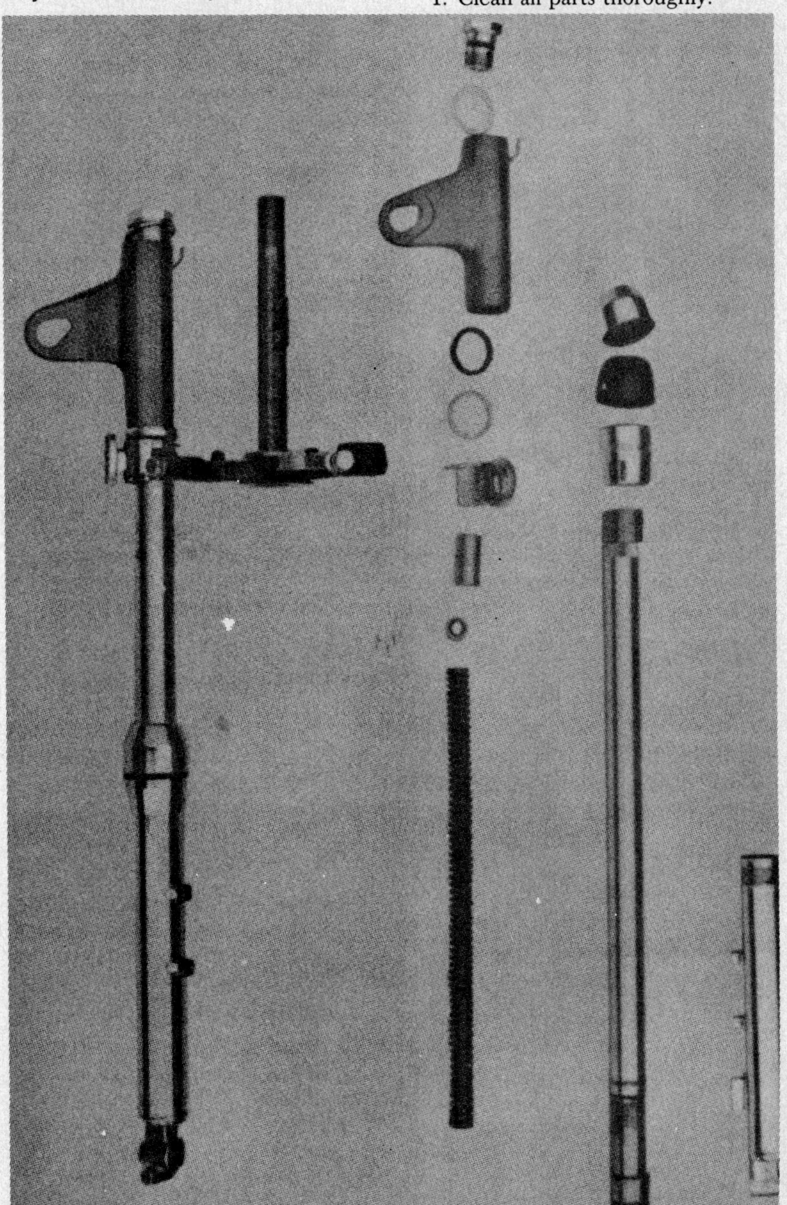

650 front forks disassembled (Courtesy Yamaha Int. Corp.)

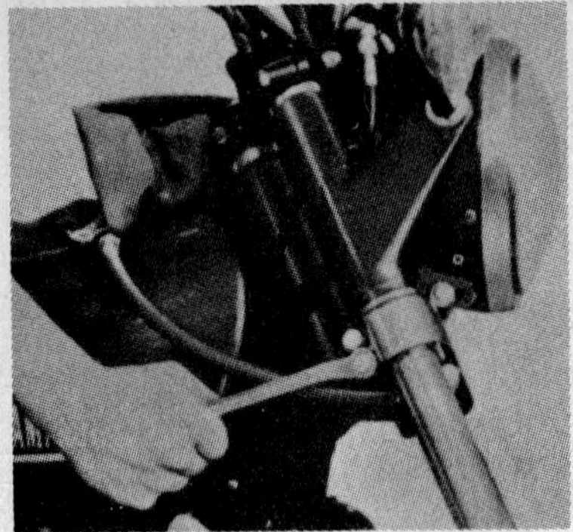

Loosening the lower triple clamp pinch bolts (Courtesy Yamaha Int. Corp.)

1. Slider, left
2. Slider, right
3. Oil seal
4. Washer, oil seal
5. Clip, oil seal
6. Circlip (R-28)
7. Piston
8. Cylinder comp.
9. Spring
10. Tube, inner
11. Seat, spring upper
12. Seal, dust
13. Cover, outer
14. Packing
15. Cover guide, under
16. Packing
17. Bolt, cap
18. Under bracket comp.
19. Bolt
20. Washer, spring
21. Holder axle
22. Bolt, stud
23. Nut
24. Washer, spring
25. Bolt
26. Packing
27. Plug, drain
28. Packing
29. Cap
30. Cover, upper left
31. Cover, upper right
32. Guide, cover upper

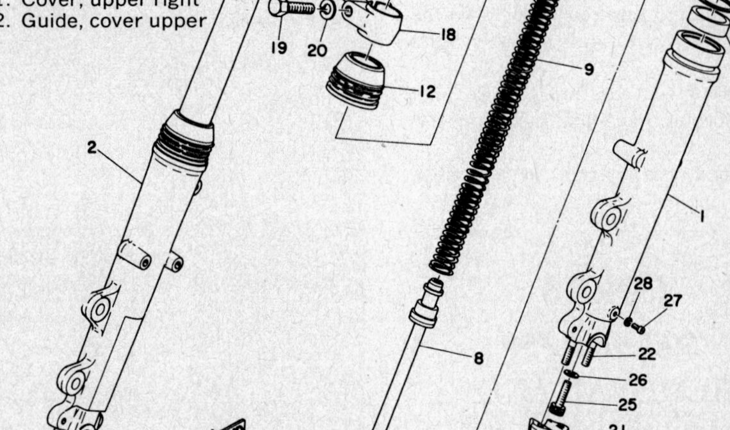

500 and 750 front forks (Courtesy Yamaha Int. Corp.)

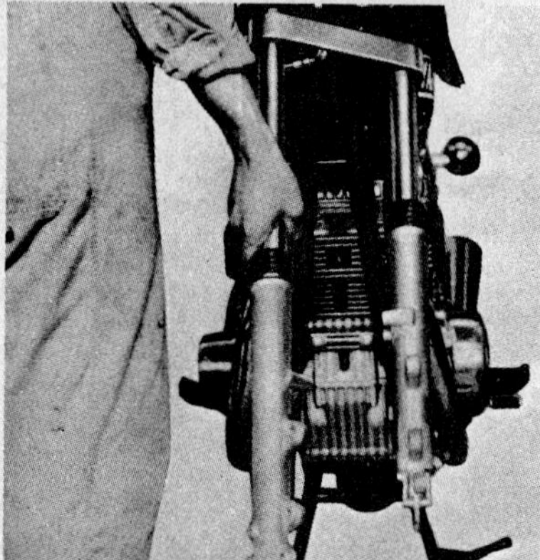

Removing the fork leg (Courtesy Yamaha Int. Corp.)

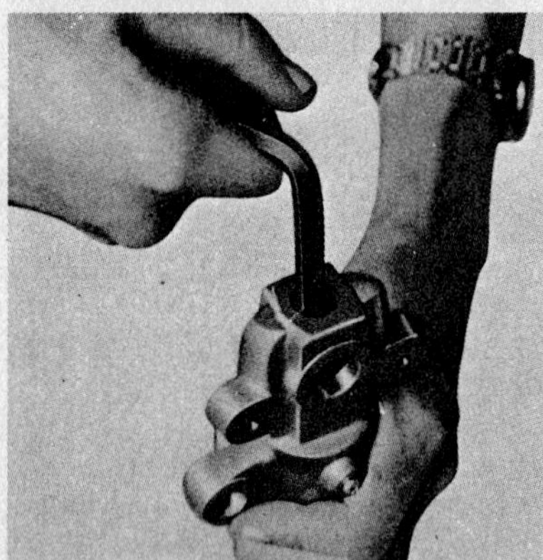

Removing the fork slider allen bolt (Courtesy Yamaha Int. Corp.)

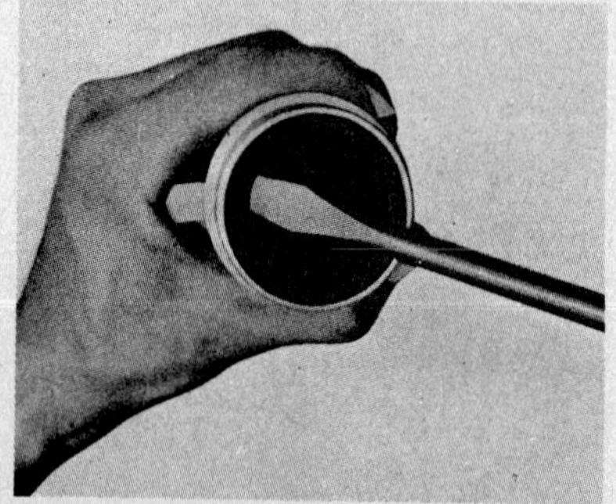

Removing the slider oil seal (Courtesy Yamaha Int. Corp.)

2. New fork seals must be used.

3. Drive in the new seal, refit the slider onto the tube assembly. Replace and tighten the allen bolt in the fork slider bottom.

4. Put the dust cover into position over the top of the slider.

5. Install the assembled fork leg up through the triple clamps. Tighten the pinch bolts to 5.6–9 ft lbs.

6. Add the correct amount and grade of fork oil (see "Maintenance Items"), and install the fork cap bolts.

650

Two different styles of fork are fitted. Early model forks have an external fork spring covered by a rubber boot.

Later model forks have an internal spring, chrome fork tubes, and a dust cover over the top of the fork slider.

In the following procedures, make allowances for the differences in each type.

REMOVAL AND DISASSEMBLY

1. Remove the front wheel and fender. On disc brake models, remove the caliper from the fork slider.

2. Lift up the dust cover from the top of the slider, or move the boot out of the way, and use a strap wrench to unscrew the outer nut from the slider. Use the axle, inserted through the sliders, to keep them from turning while the nut is unscrewed.

The chrome may be protected with a piece of rubber before fitting the strap wrench.

3. Pull the slider down and free of the fork tube. Drain out the fork oil.

4. Take out the springs if internal type.

5. To remove the fork tube, remove the handlebars, the fork crown bolts, and loosen the lower triple pinch bolt. Pull the tube down and free of the triple clamps.

6. Remove the external fork spring and boot if fitted. Remove the dust cover and dust seal if fitted.

7. Remove the outer nut, O-ring, sliding bushing, spacer, and spring seat.

INSPECTION

1. The fork oil seals are pressed into the top of the outer nuts. Seals should be replaced with new ones every time the fork is disassembled.

Grease the lips of new seals before installation.

2. Check the straightness of the fork tubes. Slightly bent tubes may be straightened with a press, but if the tubes are kinked or the metal buckled, replacement is the only solution.

3. Check the oil seal contact area on the outside of each tube and make sure it is free of dents, scoring, or other surface irregularities which would make oil sealing impossible.

4. Check the fit of the sliding bushing on the fork tube. When new, the bushing should have a clearance of 0.2mm (0.008 in.). If clearance exceeds 0.5mm (0.020 in.), replace the sliding bush.

5. Note any scoring on the inner surface of the sliding bushing or score marks on the surface of the fork tube where the bushing contacts it.

6. Check the condition of each fork spring, noting any collapsed coils, fatigue cracks, or other damage. Replace as necessary.

7. Check the condition of the slider and fork crown bolt O-rings and replace if necessary.

ASSEMBLY AND INSTALLATION

1. Wash all metal parts thoroughly in a solvent.

2. Refit the sliding bushing, O-ring, outer nut with oil seal installed, and dust seal and cover or external fork spring and rubber boot depending on fork type over the top of the fork tube.

3. Slide the fork tube through the triple clamps, replace the internal spring, spring seat, and spacer; refit the fork cap bolt and tighten it.

4. Tighten the lower triple clamp pinch bolt.

NOTE: *The fork cap bolts must be tightened* before *the lower triple clamp bolts.*

5. Replace the slider, then screw the outer nut into the slider and tighten it.

6. Refit the fender, disc brake caliper, and wheel.

STEERING STEM

All Models

Note the procedural differences for each model.

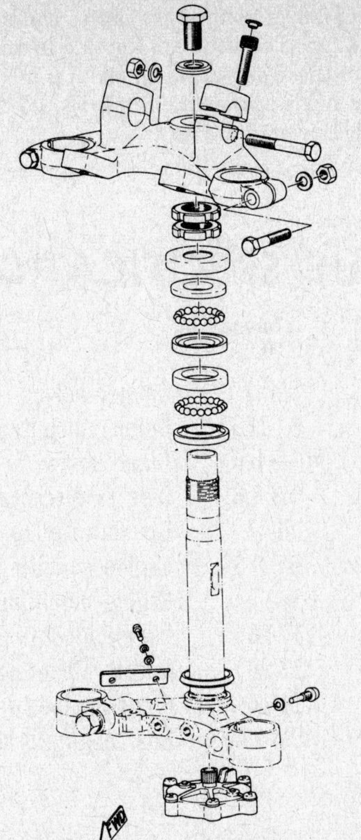

Steering stem (Courtesy Yamaha Int. Corp.)

REMOVAL

1. The steering stem may be removed with the forks intact provided the machine is supported well off the ground.

2. 500 & 750: Remove the handlebars after removing the allen bolts on the clamps. 650: Remove the handlebars after removing the nuts beneath the upper triple clamp which secure the assembly in its rubber mounts.

3. 650: Remove the steering damper knob and rod.

4. Loosen the lower triple clamp pinch bolts, and the upper triple clamp pinch bolts where fitted.

5. Loosen the upper triple clamp pinch bolt behind the steering stem nut.

6. Remove the steering stem nut and both fork crown bolts. Then remove the upper triple clamp.

7. 500 & 750: Remove the meter panel mounting bolts. Disconnect the wiring inside the headlight, remove the disc brake fluid hose joint nut, and the headlight clamp bolt.

8. Loosen the ring nut on the steering stem (650); or remove the top ring nut (500 & 750) and then loosen the lower one.

9. As the ring nut is loosened, the steering stem will begin to drop away from the frame. Remove the nut, and take away the assembly.

INSPECTION

1. Check all of the bearing balls after

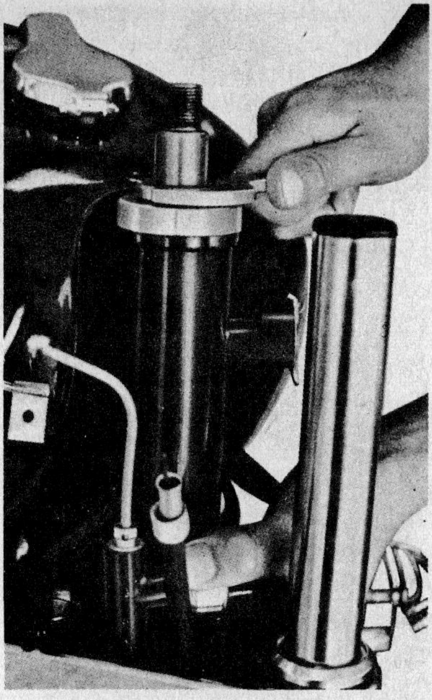

Removing the ring nut (Courtesy Yamaha Int. Corp.)

washing thoroughly in a solvent.

2. The balls should be replaced if rusted, pitted, dented, or scored.

3. Inspect the condition of the ball races checking for pitting, a rippled surface, or dents.

4. Replace all of the balls if any wear or damage is noted, and the races as well.

ASSEMBLY

1. Grease the lower race on the steering stem with a good grade of chassis grease, then arrange the balls on the lower race.

2. Arrange the balls into the race on the frame. Insert the steering stem, and replace the ring nut(s).

3. Continue to tighten the ring nut until all steering stem play has been eliminated but assure that the steering stem still pivots freely. With the front wheel off the ground, the forks should be able to swing to either side of their own weight.

SWING ARM

All Models

The swing arm can be removed after removing the rear wheel assembly, and unbolting the shock absorbers from the

Installing lubricated bearings (Courtesy Yamaha Int. Corp.)

swing arm mounts. Bend down the tab on the swing arm spindle nut. Remove the nut and pull out the spindle. Remove the swing arm from the frame.

The swing arm is fitted with bushings which are driven out and in with a drift.

Generally, the bushings can be considered in good condition of the side-to-side play of the swing arm (installed) is nil.

The swing arm grease fitting should be greased every 2000 miles.

SHOCK ABSORBERS

These units are not servicable. If damaged, or if leakage develops, they must be replaced.

TORQUE SPECIFICATIONS

Part	Torque (ft lbs)	Part	Torque (ft lbs)
Front axle nut	50-72	Caliper halves	54-68
Rear axle nut	87-113	Caliper mounting bolts	29-36
Front axle cap nuts	5.8-8.6	Bleed screw	4.3-6.5
Steering stem nut pinch bolt	5.8-8.6	Disc to disc bracket	5.8-7.2
Steering stem nut	30-47	Disc bracket to hub	12-16
Upper triple clamp fork tube pinch bolts	5.8-8.6	Engine mounting, front upper	19-24.5
Swing arm spindle nut	36-57	Engine mounting, front lower	19-24.5
Shock absorber, top	17-26	Engine mounting, rear upper	19-24.5
Shock absorber, bottom	17-26	Engine mounting, rear lower	36-51
Master cylinder to brake hose	11-14.4	Front engine bracket to frame	10-16
Brake hose and pipe junctions	9.4-13	Rear engine bracket to frame	10-16

The perfect companion to Chilton's motorcycle repair manual

CHILTON'S MOTORCYCLE

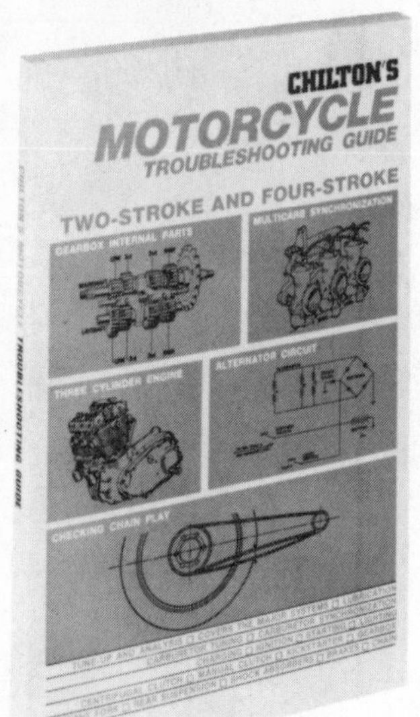

This book tells the bike owner or mechanic how to find a motorcycle problem quickly and accurately and how to go about solving it. Beginning with an introductory chapter on troubleshooting theory, necessary tools, and types of engines, the book goes on to detailed chapters on troubleshooting the 2-stroke engine, the 4-stroke engine, the fuel system, the electrical system, the clutch and transmission, and the chassis. Step-by-step troubleshooting and testing procedures, helpful tune-up hints, and ways of curing the idiosyncracies of certain models are all packed into this book. In addition, there are hundreds of photographs, drawings, exploded diagrams, testing patterns, and diagnostic flow charts that list common and not-so-common problems along with their causes and remedies. An appendix provides metric conversion charts and a degree wheel for valve timing.

The perfect gift book for every

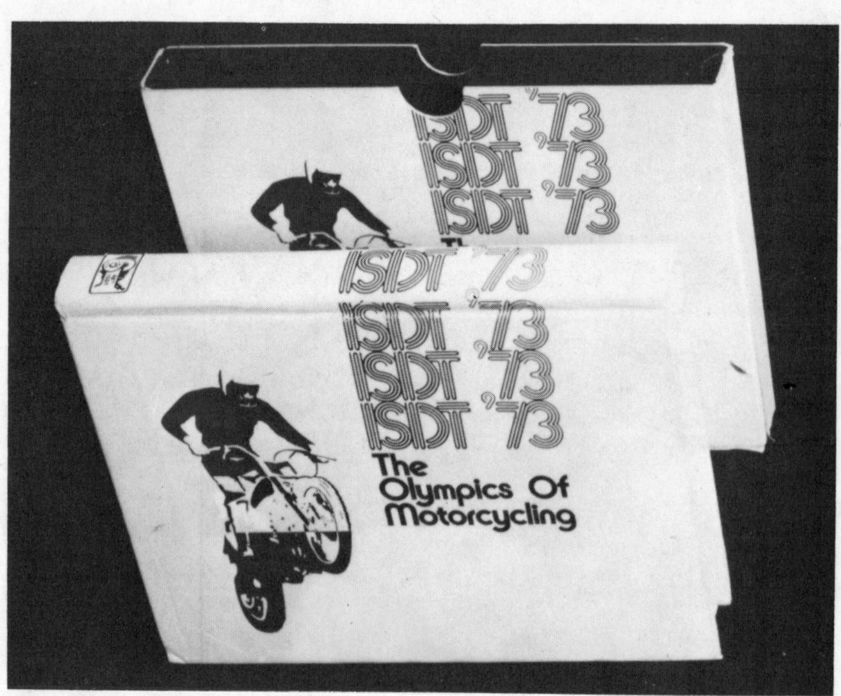

Both these